CONGRESSIONAL QUARTERLY

Almanac

102nd CONGRESS
1st SESSION . . 1991

VOLUME XLVII

Congressional Quarterly Inc.

1414 22nd Street N.W.
Washington, D.C. 20037

Congressional Quarterly Inc.

Congressional Quarterly Inc. is a publishing and information services company and a recognized leader in political journalism. For almost half a century, CQ has served clients in the fields of news, education, business and government with timely, complete, unbiased and accurate information on Congress, politics and national issues.

At the heart of CQ is its acclaimed publication, the Weekly Report, a weekly magazine offering news and analyses on Congress and legislation. The CQ Researcher (formerly Editorial Research Reports), with its focus on current issues, provides weekly balanced summaries on topics of widespread interest.

Congressional Quarterly Inc. publishes the Congressional Monitor, a daily report on Congress and current and future activities of congressional committees, and several newsletters, including Congressional Insight, a weekly analysis of congressional action, and American Caucus, a biweekly journal that looks forward to events in Congress and politics.

Congressional Quarterly Inc. also publishes a variety of books including political science textbooks under the CQ Press imprint and public affairs paperbacks to keep journalists, scholars and the public abreast of developing issues and events. CQ Books publishes highly regarded information directories and reference books on the federal government, national elections and politics, including the Guide to the Presidency, the Guide to Congress, the Guide to the U.S. Supreme Court, the Guide to U.S. Elections, Politics in America, the Federal Regulatory Directory and Washington Information Directory. The CQ Almanac, a compendium of legislation for one session of Congress, is published each year. Congress and the Nation, a record of government for a presidential term, is published every four years.

Washington Alert, Congressional Quarterly's online congressional and regulatory tracking service, provides immediate access to both proprietary and public databases of legislative action, votes, schedules, profiles and analyses.

Printed in the United States of America

Library of Congress Catalog Number 47-41081
ISBN: 0-87187-743-0 ISSN: 0095-6007

"By providing a link between the local newspaper and Capitol Hill we hope Congressional Quarterly can help to make public opinion the only effective pressure group in the country. Since many citizens other than editors are also interested in Congress, we hope that they too will find Congressional Quarterly an aid to a better understanding of their government.

"Congressional Quarterly presents the facts in as complete, concise and unbiased form as we know how. The editorial comment on the acts and votes of Congress, we leave to our subscribers."

Foreword, Congressional Quarterly, Vol. I, 1945
Henrietta Poynter, 1901-1968
Nelson Poynter, 1903-1978

SUMMARY TABLE OF CONTENTS

APPENDIXES

TABLE OF CONTENTS

Chapter 1 — 102nd Congress

Chapter 2 — Economics & Finance

Chapter 3 — Government/Commerce

Chapter 4 — Energy/Environment/Science

Chapter 5 — Law & Judiciary

Chapter 6 — Labor/Veterans/Housing

Chapter 7 — Health & Human Services/Education

Chapter 8 — Defense

Chapter 9 — Foreign Policy

Chapter 10 — Appropriations

Appendixes

Political Report

Vote Studies

Public Laws

Congress and Its Members

Text

Roll-Call Votes

Indexes

CQ

Chapter 1

102nd CONGRESS

Focus Shifted From Gulf to Home

The transition from foreign to domestic affairs defined the first year of the 102nd Congress

The year had hardly begun when its signal event arrived on Capitol Hill: After three days of somber but passionate debate, Congress on Jan. 12 gave President Bush authorization to go to war against Iraq. The debate reminded all that Congress retained the capacity to consider issues thoughtfully and expeditiously. The vote reinstated a congressional role in going to war, missing in action since Dec. 8, 1941.

Less than two months later, a triumphant Bush ascended the dais in the House of Representatives to tell the assembled Congress and the nation, "Aggression is defeated; the war is over."

But the end of the shooting war abroad marked the start of a shouting war at home — a transition from foreign to domestic affairs whose evolution chronicled the first year of the 102nd Congress.

"The war did cause attention to be focused away from the problems of the economy for a period of time," Senate Majority Leader George J. Mitchell, D-Maine, said after the session ended. But, he added, "I said all along the attention would fade and turn to domestic economic concerns."

It did. The lightning-quick victory in the Persian Gulf made the shift of focus possible. A sick economy made it urgent. But the budget deal fashioned in 1990, combined with 1991 partisan politics, made significant progress on domestic issues nearly impossible. The Republican president used his veto, real and threatened, to stall Democratic measures he did not like, such as civil rights and extended unemployment benefits. Compromises were forged only after Bush's standing in the polls began falling.

By Thanksgiving, Congress had sent the president only one major bill to create jobs, the six-year, $151 billion transportation measure. And salve for the jobless — $5.8 billion worth of new unemployment benefits — came only after months of partisan bickering.

The session ended after one last quarrel on taxes. Bush called on the House to pass tax cuts Nov. 26, and Speaker Thomas S. Foley, D-Wash., offered to bring Congress back in December to do just that.

INSIDE

Bush declined, preferring that Congress leave town and leave him alone to consider how to jump-start his poll ratings and perhaps even the economy. To cover themselves in case Bush started bashing Democrats in their absence, congressional leaders did not formally adjourn the first session when they completed legislative business on Nov. 27. Instead, they left open the possibility of a quick return by setting formal adjournment for Jan. 3, immediately before the next session started. But they did not return in the interim.

"I've been here 17 years, and I've never seen so much posturing so early" in the election cycle, said Rep. William J. Hughes, D-N.J.

"The whole session seemed to be steeped pretty bad in politics," agreed the House Republican leader, Robert H. Michel of Illinois.

But partisanship wasn't the only roadblock to accomplishment. Attempts to restructure the ailing banking industry slammed headlong into lawmakers' fear of missteps and competing pressure from the banking, insurance and securities industries. Congress did the minimum — authorizing $30 billion in new credit to cover losses of failed banks — and punted on increasing banks' powers to expand.

To those who contended that Congress' accomplishments had been modest in the first session, Mitchell rejoined: "Just as no baseball game has ever been decided in the fourth inning or any football game at halftime, no full, fair and final evaluation of the Congress can be made until the end of the Congress itself."

War Declared and Eclipsed

The Jan. 12 vote authorizing the president to go to war against Iraq was the first time since World War II that Congress had directly confronted the issue of sending troops into combat before the fact.

It did not resolve the question of whether the president had the authority to wage war without legislative action, a controversial issue since Vietnam. But the president's decision to seek the war resolution and its subsequent passage reclaimed a lost partnership.

Speaker Foley called it "the most constitutionally important Congress since World War II ... because of the action on the gulf resolution. This is the first time since World War II that Congress and the president have carried out their constitutional responsibilities on the war-making powers, to the great credit of both.

"Now it's sort of ho-hum that it happened. But it didn't happen in Vietnam. It didn't happen in Korea. And it didn't happen in any of the other military engagements that have taken place since the end of World War II. It restored Congress to its constitutional primacy and responsibility in the war-making powers."

Operation Desert Storm receded from pre-eminence on the national agenda with startling speed. The victory tasted sweet but brought no tonic for a sour economy. By late July, the celebrations were over and Congress was locked with Bush in a bitter dispute over extending unemployment benefits.

By late August, in a far more momentous development, the Soviet Union was falling apart. Saddam Hussein was still in power, but Iraq was no longer the most important concern overseas.

Many saw the collapse of the Soviet empire as an invitation to raid the Pentagon budget for domestic spending. But that would have required junking the 1990 budget deal, and there was little taste for doing that so late in the fiscal 1992 appropriations process.

In fact, Congress made no significant reduction in the $291 billion for defense spending that Bush had requested in February. But the pressure was clearly building for a major realignment in 1992.

102nd Congress Leaders

SENATE

President Pro Tempore — Robert C. Byrd, D-W.Va.
Majority Leader — George J. Mitchell, D-Maine
Majority Whip — Wendell H. Ford, D-Ky.
Secretary of the Democratic Conference — David Pryor, D-Ark.

Minority Leader — Bob Dole, R-Kan.
Assistant Minority Leader — Alan K. Simpson, R-Wyo.
Chairman of the Republican Conference — Thad Cochran, R-Miss.
Secretary of the Republican Conference — Bob Kasten, R-Wis.

HOUSE

Speaker — Thomas S. Foley, D-Wash.
Majority Leader — Richard A. Gephardt, D-Mo.
Majority Whip — William H. Gray III, D-Pa. (to Sept. 11); David E. Bonior, D-Mich..
Chairman of the Democratic Caucus — Steny H. Hoyer, D-Md.

Minority Leader — Robert H. Michel, R-Ill.
Minority Whip — Newt Gingrich, R-Ga.
Chairman of the Republican Conference — Jerry Lewis, R-Calif.
Chairman of the Republican Policy Committee — Mickey Edwards, R-Okla.

Image Problems

While the war debate was Congress' finest hour of 1991, there was considerable competition for its low point. The leading contenders included the confirmation hearings of Clarence Thomas to the Supreme Court and the revelation that House members routinely wrote checks on the House bank without funds to cover them.

The Thomas hearings turned into a national soap opera in October after law school Professor Anita F. Hill went public with allegations that Thomas had sexually harassed her, and lurid details poured out of the second round of hearings.

Thomas was confirmed, but the Senate's handling of the situation left women outraged and led even members to call it flawed.

The check-writing imbroglio stemmed from the members-only bank's practice of covering members' checks whether or not the writer had sufficient funds in his or her account. The disclosure played into the hands of those who were already criticizing Congress for members-only special privileges, and it furnished late-night comedians with staple material.

A House ethics committee inquiry was set in motion, virtually ensuring that the issue would remain fresh enough to figure into some 1992 elections.

The two-year-old Keating Five investigation also came to a conclusion in 1991. The Senate Ethics Committee issued a harsh rebuke to Alan Cranston, D-Calif., a week before the session ended, nine months after the chamber had reprimanded in milder terms the four other senators (Dennis DeConcini, D-Ariz.; John Glenn, D-Ohio; John McCain, R-Ariz.; and Donald W. Riegle Jr., D-Mich.) for their actions in behalf of Charles H. Keating Jr., owner of a saving and loan that went bankrupt at a $2 billion cost to federal taxpayers.

LEADERSHIP

After the turmoil of replacing most of their leaders in the previous Congress, members kept leadership relatively stable in the 102nd Congress. The only major changes came in the majority whip positions, where Senate Democrats installed Wendell H. Ford, D-Ky., at the beginning of the session, and House Democrats elected David E. Bonior, D-Mich., to fill a vacancy in September.

Senators chose their hierarchy in November 1990. Neither party faced a challenge at the top: Democrats gave Mitchell a second term as majority leader; Republicans continued with Bob Dole of Kansas as minority leader and Alan K. Simpson of Wyoming as assistant minority leader. Ford stepped up to the Democrats' whip job without opposition; he succeeded Alan Cranston, D-Calif., who was weakened by health troubles and ethics woes and announced Nov. 8 that he would relinquish the job. Ford retained his post as chairman of the Rules Committee. *(1990 Almanac, p. 8)*

The Senate Republican Conference took the unusual step of ousting an incumbent leader when it voted Nov. 13 to replace its politically moderate chairman, John H. Chafee of Rhode Island, with the more conservative Thad Cochran of Mississippi, by a vote of 22-21. The last time Republican senators had bounced a leader was in 1982, when they voted in favor of Richard G. Lugar of Indiana over Bob Packwood of Oregon for chairman of the National Republican Senatorial Committee (NRSC). *(1983 Almanac, p. 3)*

The conservative tilt of the conference was continued as Bob Kasten of Wisconsin beat Christopher S. Bond of Missouri for conference secretary and Don Nickles of Oklahoma won over Pete V. Domenici of New Mexico for policy chairman. Phil Gramm of Texas beat Mitch McConnell of Kentucky for chairman of the NRSC.

Democrats named Charles S. Robb of Virginia to head their campaign committee. Other Democrats elected without opposition were David Pryor of Arkansas (conference secretary), Alan J. Dixon of Illinois (chief deputy whip); Tom Daschle of South Dakota (co-chairman, with Mitchell, of the Policy Committee); Daniel K. Inouye of Hawaii (chairman of the Steering Committee).

The House caucuses met the week of Dec. 3 to choose their leaders. Republicans stuck with their incumbent team: Michel as minority leader; Newt Gingrich of Georgia minority whip; Jerry Lewis of California as conference chairman; Guy Vander Jagt of Michigan as chairman of the National Republican Congressional Committee. Lewis and Vander Jagt had to turn back challenges from colleagues Carl D. Pursell of Michigan and Don Sundquist of Tennessee, respectively.

House Democrats also left their team intact: Foley as Speaker; Richard A. Gephardt of Missouri as majority leader; William H. Gray III of Pennsylvania majority whip; and Steny H. Hoyer of Maryland as chairman of the Democratic Caucus.

On July 11, Democrats voted to replace Gray with Bonior in the fall. The move was necessitated by Gray's surprise announcement on June 20 that he would leave the House in September to become president of the United Negro College Fund.

Bonior defeated Hoyer by a 160-109 vote of the Democratic Caucus. Hoyer kept his caucus chairmanship. In a move to expand the leadership outside a core of white liberal men, Foley on Aug. 2 named a Southerner (Butler Derrick, D-S.C.), a woman (Barbara B. Kennelly, D-Conn.) and a black (John Lewis, D-Ga.) to replace Bonior as chief deputy whip. Foley also appointed another white liberal male (Marty Russo, D-Ill.) to the newly created post of floor whip.

A potential shake-up was avoided on July 17 when Gephardt announced that he would not seek the 1992 presidential nomination, as he had in 1988.

"My greatest contribution to that cause will be made, not as a presidential candidate but as majority leader, helping to shape, define and advance the Democratic message," Gephardt wrote in a letter to candidates.

Some members had already been positioning themselves to run for Gephardt's job.

One of them, George Miller, D-Calif., greeted Gephardt's announcement with a pointed attack on his party's leadership. "It is not a question of whether I am running for a leadership post," he said in a July 17 statement. "It is a question of whether there will be leadership."

Committee Shifts

No House standing committee chairmen or ranking members were ousted by the voters in the 1990 elections. In December, however, before the 102nd Congress convened, the Democratic Caucus did what the voters did not — it ousted two aging committee chairmen whose leadership had been deemed ineffective. Charlie Rose, N.C., toppled Frank Annunzio, Ill., for the chairmanship of the House Administration Committee; Public Works Chairman Glenn M. Anderson, Calif., was replaced by Robert A. Roe, N.J. To take the job, Roe gave up his chairmanship of Science, Space and Technology; he was replaced by George E. Brown Jr., Calif. *(1990 Almanac, p. 11)*

Among major House committees, retirement opened the most influential slot — on Education and Labor, where William D. Ford, Mich., succeeded Augustus F. Hawkins of California. Ford was replaced as chairman of Post Office and Civil Service by William L. Clay, Mo.

On other House panels, limits on the number of terms a member could serve created vacancies heading the Committee on Standards of Official Conduct, where Louis Stokes of Ohio took the sensitive job of keeping an eye on members' ethics, and on Select Intelligence, where Dave McCurdy of Oklahoma took the gavel.

Public Laws

A total of 243 bills cleared Congress in 1991 and became public laws. Following is a list of the number of public laws enacted since 1972:

Year	Public Laws
1991	243
1990	410
1989	240
1988	471
1987	242
1986	424
1985	240
1984	408
1983	215
1982	328
1981	145
1980	426
1979	187
1978	410
1977	223
1976	383
1975	205
1974	402
1973	247
1972	383

Those panels also got new Republican leaders: James V. Hansen of Utah on ethics and Bud Shuster of Pennsylvania on Intelligence.

The top Republican opening came on Rules, where James H. Quillen, Tenn., relinquished his leadership while staying on the panel; he was replaced by Gerald B. H. Solomon, N.Y.

There was even less turnover in the Senate. Only one incumbent (Rudy Boschwitz, R-Minn.) was defeated, and three senators retired. As a result of these changes, Malcolm Wallop of Wyoming took over to lead Republicans on Energy and Natural Resources, replacing James A. McClure of Idaho, who retired. Bob Kasten, Wis., replaced Boschwitz as ranking Republican on Small Business. Because of service limits on Select Intelligence, Frank H. Murkowski, Alaska, took the ranking Republican spot. Murkowski was replaced as lead Republican on Veterans' Affairs by Arlen Specter, Pa.

Membership Changes, 102nd Congress, 1st Session

SENATE

Member	Party	Died	Resigned	Successor	Party	Appointed	Sworn In
Pete Wilson, Calif. [1]	R		1/7/91	John Seymour	R	1/7/91	1/10/91
John Heinz, Pa. [2]	R	4/4/91		Harris L. Wofford Jr.	D	5/8/91	5/9/91

HOUSE

Member	Party	Died	Resigned	Successor	Party	Elected	Sworn In
Silvio O. Conte, Mass. [3]	R	2/8/91		John Olver	D	6/4/91	6/18/91
Edward Madigan, Ill. [4]	R		3/8/91	Thomas W. Ewing	R	7/2/91	7/10/91
Steve Bartlett, Texas [5]	R		3/11/91	Sam Johnson	R	5/18/91	5/22/91
Morris K. Udall, Ariz. [6]	D		5/4/91	Ed Pastor	D	9/24/91	10/3/91
William H. Gray III, Pa. [7]	D		9/11/91	Lucien E. Blackwell	D	11/5/91	11/13/91
D. French Slaughter Jr., Va. [8]	R		11/5/91	George F. Allen	R	11/5/91	11/12/91

[1] *Wilson resigned his seat to be sworn is as governor of Califorinia on Jan. 7, 1991. He subsequently appointed Seymour to fill the seat he vacated.*

[2] *Heinz died in a plane crash on April 4. After Wofford was appointed by Pennsylvania governor Robert P. Casey to fill Heinz's seat, he won a special election on Nov. 5, 1991, to continue filling the seat for the remainder of the term.*

[3] *Conte died after surgery to remove a blood clot.*

[4] *Madigan resigned to become secretary of Agriculture.*

[5] *Bartlett resigned to run for mayor of Dallas.*

[6] *Udall resigned for health reasons.*

[7] *Gray resigned to become president of the United Negro College Fund.*

[8] *Slaughter resigned for health reasons.*

The 1990 elections enabled Democrats to increase their representation on several committees. Democrats picked up eight additional seats in the House and one in the Senate.

On House Appropriations and Budget, Democrats added two seats without increasing GOP representation; on Energy and Commerce, Foreign Affairs and Post Office and Civil Service, Republicans lost seats; on several other panels, both parties gained seats.

In the Senate, Democrats increased their margins on Agriculture, Energy, Foreign Relations and Labor.

In House committee rosters, the biggest change was on Budget. Because the panel had a six-year term limit, about one-third of its members left. The Republicans selected Bill Gradison of Ohio to replace Minnesota's Bill Frenzel, who retired and ended his term as ranking member.

1991 Changes

Early in the 102nd Congress, several unexpected membership changes created additional movement.

The death Feb. 8 of Silvio O. Conte, R-Mass., the ranking member of the House Appropriations Committee, elevated Joseph M. McDade, Pa., to the GOP's top position on the funding panel. Jim Ross Lightfoot, Iowa, won the vacancy left by Conte's death. Andy Ireland, Fla., replaced McDade as top Republican on the Small Business Committee.

Edward Madigan's departure on March 8 to become Agriculture secretary opened the ranking Republican slot on the Agriculture Committee for Tom Coleman, Mo., and created a vacancy on the Energy and Commerce Committee. Fred Upton, Mich., lobbied successfully to win that seat.

On the subcommittee level, Madigan's resignation brought conservative William E. Dannemeyer, Calif., to the top GOP spot on Energy and Commerce's Health panel.

With the May 4 retirement of Morris K. Udall of Arizona, California's George Miller became the permanent chairman of the House Interior Committee. Miller had resigned the chairmanship of the Select Committee on Children, Youth and Families at the beginning of the 102nd Congress to serve as acting Interior chairman.

Patricia Schroeder, Colo., took the top job at Select Children.

The April 4 death of Sen. John Heinz, Pa., opened the ranking GOP slot on Special Aging for William S. Cohen of Maine. The Pennsylvania Senate seat was filled with the appointment of Democrat Harris L. Wofford Jr., who won a surprising November victory over former Attorney General Dick Thornburgh to keep it.

Several committees underwent internal reorganizations.

Frustrated by the continuing weakness of the Senate Foreign Relations Committee, the panel's Democrats persuaded Chairman Claiborne Pell, R.I., to cede some legislative authority to its subcommittees.

At the panel's opening session Jan. 29, Pell announced that, because of a "heavier than usual" workload, he would make greater use of the subcommittees. Under the plan, they were staffed independently with power to mark up bills — a function that in the past had been the exclusive province of the full committee.

On the House Judiciary Committee, Democrats reorganized to create a crime subcommittee for a chairman who wanted to seize the political initiative for Democrats. Charles E. Schumer, D-N.Y., was chosen to lead a merged Crime and Criminal Justice Subcommittee. In the shuffle of subcommittees, Judiciary Committee Chairman Jack Brooks, D-Texas, shifted jurisdiction for death row inmate appeals, known as petitions for habeas corpus, to the Subcommittee on Civil and Constitutional Rights, led by Don Edwards, D-Calif. That ensured that the administration's proposals to restrict inmate appeals would be handled by

Senate Cloture Votes in 1991

The Senate invoked cloture nine times in 1991, out of the 20 times it voted on such debate-limiting motions. Cloture motions require a three-fifths majority of the Senate, or 60 yea votes for all such motions in 1991.

The 20 cloture votes brought to 317 the number taken since 1917, when the Senate's filibuster rule was adopted; the nine successful votes brought to 112 the number of successful votes.

Following is a list of all 1991 votes. Successful votes are indicated in **boldface** type.

Bill	Date	Vote	Story
Vertical Price Fixing (S 429) [1]	**May 7**	**61-37**	**p. 291**
Vertical Price Fixing (S 429)	**May 8**	**63-35**	
Crime Bill (S 1241)	June 28	41-58	p. 262
Crime Bill (S 1241)	July 10	56-43	
Crime Bill (S 1241)	**July 10**	**71-27**	
National Motor-Voter Registration (S 250)	July 18	57-41	p. 48
Fiscal 1992 VA-HUD Appropriations (HR 2519) [2]	July 18	57-40	p. 516
National Motor-Voter Registration (S 250)	July 18	59-40	
Foreign Aid Authorization (S 1435)	**July 24**	**87-10**	**p. 470**
Foreign Aid Authorization (S 1435) [3]	July 25	52-44	
Foreign Aid Authorization (S 1435) [4]	**July 25**	**63-33**	
Extended Unemployment Benefits (S 1554)	**July 29**	**96- 1**	**p. 301**
Fiscal 1992 Defense Authorization (S 1507) [5]	Aug. 2	58-40	p. 393
Fiscal 1992 Interior Appropriations (HR 2686) [6]	Sept. 19	55-41	p. 555
Federal Facility Compliance Act (S 596)	**Oct. 17**	**85-14**	**p. 222**
Civil Rights Act (S 1745)	**Oct. 22**	**93- 4**	**p. 251**
National Energy Policy (S 1220)	Nov. 1	50-44	p. 195
Banking Reform (S 543)	**Nov. 13**	**76-19**	**p. 75**
Iranian Hostage Release Investigation (S Res 198)	Nov. 22	51-43	p. 490
Crime Conference Report (HR 3371)	Nov. 27	49-38	p. 262

[1] *First successful vote occurred on the motion to proceed to the bill.*
[2] *Vote occurred on an amendment to require the public disclosure of 1988 Resolution Trust Corporation deals.*
[3] *Vote occurred on an amendment to limit military aid to El Salvador.*
[4] *Vote occurred on an amendment to authorize funds for the United Nation Population Fund.*
[5] *Vote occurred on an amendment to allow abortions at overseas military medical facilities.*
[6] *Vote occurred on an amendment to provide for a settlement between the Tennessee Valley Authority and Swain County, N.C.*

one of the most vigorous defenders of defendants' rights. Schumer replaced William J. Hughes, D-N.J., who after 10 years on the Crime panel sought a new chairmanship. The Nov. 6 election defeat of Robert W. Kastenmeier, D-Wis., opened up a courts and intellectual property post and paved the way for Brooks to merge the crime panels. Hughes shifted to Kastenmeier's old panel, renamed the Intellectual Property and Judicial Administration Subcommittee. Its focus on copyrights, patents and high technology brought its members attention and contributions from big business (rare for a Judiciary subcommittee). Brooks shifted jurisdiction for the controversial Racketeer Influenced and Corrupt Organizations Act (RICO) from the Crime Subcommittee to Hughes' new post. Romano L. Mazzoli, D-Ky., was elected to lead the Immigration Subcommittee, regaining the post he had been stripped of two years before. He succeeded Democrat Bruce A. Morrison, who resigned to run, unsuccessfully, for Connecticut governor. That panel was renamed International Law, Immigration and Refugees.

While the House was dropping a subcommittee, the Senate Judiciary Committee was adding a new panel, Juvenile Justice, for Herb Kohl, D-Wis.

In the Senate, a Budget Committee move took a seat away from Charles S. Robb of Virginia, who was chairman of the Democratic Senatorial Campaign Committee. Robb protested the change, accusing the committee's chairman, Jim Sasser of Tennessee, of trying to punish him for his fiscally conservative views.

The Democratic Steering Committee, which made committee assignments, on March 6 voted to reduce Budget from 23 members to 21, despite a personal appeal by Robb to keep his seat.

RELATIONS WITH PRESIDENT

While the Persian Gulf War faded quickly from legislative relevance, it reverberated in the memories of members as a signal event in their careers in Washington.

Security around the Capitol was high as Bush's Jan. 15 deadline for Iraq's withdrawal from Kuwait approached. Tension was even higher.

After word reached Washington on Jan. 16 that the first bombs had been dropped, the mood on Capitol Hill shifted with the ebb and flow of military progress reports.

People with offices on the ground floor of the Capitol

Continued on p. 10

Members of the 102nd Congress, First Session . . .

(As of Nov. 27, 1991)

Representatives

D 268; R 166; I 1

A

Abercrombie, Neil, D-Hawaii (1)
Ackerman, Gary L., D-N.Y. (7)
Alexander, Bill, D-Ark. (1)
Allard, Wayne, R-Colo. (4)
Allen, George F., R-Va. (7)
Anderson, Glenn M., D-Calif. (32)
Andrews, Michael A., D-Texas (25)
Andrews, Robert E., D-N.J. (1)
Andrews, Thomas H., D-Maine (1)
Annunzio, Frank, D-Ill. (11)
Anthony, Beryl Jr., D-Ark. (4)
Applegate, Douglas, D-Ohio (18)
Archer, Bill, R-Texas (7)
Armey, Dick, R-Texas (26)
Aspin, Les, D-Wis. (1)
Atkins, Chester G., D-Mass. (5)
AuCoin, Les, D-Ore. (1)

B

Bacchus, Jim, D-Fla. (11)
Baker, Richard H., R-La. (6)
Ballenger, Cass, R-N.C. (10)
Barnard, Doug Jr., D-Ga. (10)
Barrett, Bill, R-Neb. (3)
Barton, Joe L., R-Texas (6)
Bateman, Herbert H., R-Va. (1)
Beilenson, Anthony C., D-Calif. (23)
Bennett, Charles E., D-Fla. (3)
Bentley, Helen Delich, R-Md. (2)
Bereuter, Doug, R-Neb. (1)
Berman, Howard L., D-Calif. (26)
Bevill, Tom, D-Ala. (4)
Bilbray, James, D-Nev. (1)
Bilirakis, Michael, R-Fla. (9)
Blackwell, Lucien E., D-Pa. (2)
Bliley, Thomas J. Jr., R-Va. (3)
Boehlert, Sherwood, R-N.Y. (25)
Boehner, John A., R-Ohio (8)
Bonior, David E., D-Mich. (12)
Borski, Robert A., D-Pa. (3)
Boucher, Rick, D-Va. (9)
Boxer, Barbara, D-Calif. (6)
Brewster, Bill, D-Okla. (3)
Brooks, Jack, D-Texas (9)
Broomfield, William S., R-Mich. (18)
Browder, Glen, D-Ala. (3)
Brown, George E. Jr., D-Calif. (36)
Bruce, Terry L., D-Ill. (19)
Bryant, John, D-Texas (5)
Bunning, Jim, R-Ky. (4)
Burton, Dan, R-Ind. (6)
Bustamante, Albert G., D-Texas (23)
Byron, Beverly B., D-Md. (6)

C

Callahan, Sonny, R-Ala. (1)
Camp, Dave, R-Mich. (10)
Campbell, Ben Nighthorse, D-Colo. (3)
Campbell, Tom, R-Calif. (12)
Cardin, Benjamin L., D-Md. (3)
Carper, Thomas R., D-Del. (AL)
Carr, Bob, D-Mich. (6)
Chandler, Rod, R-Wash. (8)
Chapman, Jim, D-Texas (1)
Clay, William L., D-Mo. (1)
Clement, Bob, D-Tenn (5)
Clinger, William F., R-Pa. (23)
Coble, Howard, R-N.C. (6)
Coleman, Ronald D., D-Texas (16)
Coleman, Tom, R-Mo. (6)
Collins, Barbara-Rose, D-Mich. (13)
Collins, Cardiss, D-Ill. (7)
Combest, Larry, R-Texas (19)
Condit, Gary, D-Calif (15)
Conyers, John Jr., D-Mich. (1)
Cooper, Jim, D-Tenn. (4)
Costello, Jerry F. D-Ill. (21)
Coughlin, Lawrence, R-Pa. (13)
Cox, C. Christopher, R-Calif. (40)
Cox, John W. Jr., D-Ill. (16)
Coyne, William J., D-Pa. (14)
Cramer, Bud, D-Ala. (5)
Crane, Philip M., R-Ill. (12)
Cunningham, Randy "Duke," R-Calif. (44)

D

Dannemeyer, William E., R-Calif. (39)
Darden, George "Buddy," D-Ga. (7)
Davis, Robert W., R-Mich. (11)
DeFazio, Peter A., D-Ore. (4)
de la Garza, E. "Kika," D-Texas (15)
DeLauro, Rosa, D-Conn. (3)
DeLay, Tom, R-Texas (22)
Dellums, Ronald V., D-Calif. (8)
Derrick, Butler, D-S.C. (3)
Dickinson, Bill, R-Ala. (2)
Dicks, Norm, D-Wash. (6)
Dingell, John D., D-Mich. (16)
Dixon, Julian C., D-Calif. (28)
Donnelly, Brian, D-Mass. (11)
Dooley, Calvin, D-Calif. (17)
Doolittle, John T., R-Calif. (14)
Dorgan, Byron L., D-N.D. (AL)
Dornan, Robert K., R-Calif. (38)
Downey, Thomas J., D-N.Y. (2)
Dreier, David, R-Calif. (33)
Duncan, John J. "Jimmy" Jr., R-Tenn. (2)
Durbin, Richard J., D-Ill. (20)
Dwyer, Bernard J., D-N.J. (6)
Dymally, Mervyn M., D-Calif. (31)

E

Early, Joseph D., D-Mass. (3)
Eckart, Dennis E., D-Ohio (11)
Edwards, Chet, D-Texas (11)
Edwards, Don, D-Calif. (10)
Edwards, Mickey, R-Okla. (5)
Emerson, Bill, R-Mo. (8)
Engel, Eliot L., D-N.Y. (19)
English, Glenn, D-Okla. (6)
Erdreich, Ben, D-Ala. (6)
Espy, Mike, D-Miss. (2)
Evans, Lane, D-Ill. (17)
Ewing, Thomas W. R-Ill. (15)

F

Fascell, Dante B., D-Fla. (19)
Fawell, Harris W., R-Ill. (13)
Fazio, Vic, D-Calif. (4)
Feighan, Edward F., D-Ohio (19)
Fields, Jack, R-Texas (8)
Fish, Hamilton Jr., R-N.Y. (21)
Flake, Floyd H., D-N.Y. (6)
Foglietta, Thomas M., D-Pa. (1)
Foley, Thomas S., D-Wash. (5)
Ford, Harold E., D-Tenn. (9)
Ford, William D., D-Mich. (15)
Frank, Barney, D-Mass. (4)
Franks, Gary, R-Conn. (5)
Frost, Martin, D-Texas (24)

G

Gallegly, Elton, R-Calif. (21)
Gallo, Dean A., R-N.J. (11)
Gaydos, Joseph M., D-Pa. (20)
Gejdenson, Sam, D-Conn. (2)
Gekas, George W., R-Pa. (17)
Gephardt, Richard A., D-Mo. (3)
Geren, Pete, D-Texas (12)
Gibbons, Sam M., D-Fla. (7)
Gilchrest, Wayne T., R-Md. (1)
Gillmor, Paul E., R-Ohio (5)
Gilman, Benjamin A., R-N.Y. (22)
Gingrich, Newt, R-Ga. (6)
Glickman, Dan, D-Kan. (4)
Gonzalez, Henry B., D-Texas (20)
Goodling, Bill, R-Pa. (19)
Gordon, Bart, D-Tenn. (6)
Goss, Porter J., R-Fla. (13)
Gradison, Bill, R-Ohio (2)
Grandy, Fred, R-Iowa (6)
Green, Bill, R-N.Y. (15)
Guarini, Frank J., D-N.J. (14)
Gunderson, Steve, R-Wis. (3)

H

Hall, Ralph M., D-Texas (4)
Hall, Tony P., D-Ohio (3)
Hamilton, Lee H., D-Ind. (9)
Hammerschmidt, John Paul, R-Ark. (3)
Hancock, Mel, R-Mo. (7)
Hansen, James V., R-Utah (1)
Harris, Claude, D-Ala. (7)
Hastert, Dennis, R-Ill. (14)
Hatcher, Charles, D-Ga. (2)
Hayes, Charles A., D-Ill. (1)
Hayes, Jimmy, D-La. (7)
Hefley, Joel, R-Colo. (5)
Hefner, W. G. "Bill," D-N.C. (8)
Henry, Paul B., R-Mich. (5)
Herger, Wally, R-Calif. (2)
Hertel, Dennis M., D-Mich. (14)
Hoagland, Peter, D-Neb. (2)
Hobson, David L., R-Ohio (7)
Hochbrueckner, George J., D-N.Y. (1)
Holloway, Clyde C., R-La. (8)
Hopkins, Larry J., R-Ky. (6)
Horn, Joan Kelly, D-Mo. (2)
Horton, Frank, R-N.Y. (29)
Houghton, Amo, R-N.Y. (34)
Hoyer, Steny H., D-Md. (5)
Hubbard, Carroll Jr., D-Ky. (1)
Huckaby, Jerry, D-La. (5)
Hughes, William J., D-N.J. (2)
Hunter, Duncan, R-Calif. (45)
Hutto, Earl, D-Fla. (1)
Hyde, Henry J., R-Ill. (6)

I

Inhofe, James M., R-Okla. (1)
Ireland, Andy, R-Fla. (10)

J

Jacobs, Andrew Jr., D-Ind. (10)
James, Craig T., R-Fla. (4)
Jefferson, William J., D-La. (2)
Jenkins, Ed, D-Ga. (9)
Johnson, Nancy L., R-Conn. (6)
Johnson, Sam, R-Texas (3)
Johnson, Tim, D-S.D. (AL)
Johnston, Harry A., D-Fla., (14)
Jones, Ben, D-Ga. (4)
Jones, Walter B., D-N.C. (1)
Jontz, Jim, D-Ind. (5)

K

Kanjorski, Paul E., D-Pa. (11)
Kaptur, Marcy, D-Ohio (9)
Kasich, John R., R-Ohio (12)
Kennedy, Joseph P. II, D-Mass. (8)
Kennelly, Barbara B., D-Conn. (1)
Kildee, Dale E., D-Mich. (7)
Kleczka, Gerald D., D-Wis. (4)
Klug, Scott L. R-Wis. (2)
Kolbe, Jim, R-Ariz. (5)
Kolter, Joe, D-Pa. (4)
Kopetski, Mike, D-Ore. (5)
Kostmayer, Peter H., D-Pa. (8)
Kyl, Jon, R-Ariz. (4)

L

LaFalce, John J., D-N.Y. (32)
Lagomarsino, Robert J., R-Calif. (19)
Lancaster, H. Martin, D-N.C. (3)
Lantos, Tom, D-Calif. (11)
LaRocco, Larry, D-Idaho (1)
Laughlin, Greg, D-Texas (14)
Leach, Jim, R-Iowa (1)
Lehman, Richard H., D-Calif. (18)
Lehman, William, D-Fla. (17)
Lent, Norman F., R-N.Y. (4)
Levin, Sander M., D-Mich. (17)
Levine, Mel, D-Calif. (27)
Lewis, Jerry, R-Calif. (35)
Lewis, John, D-Ga. (5)
Lewis, Tom, R-Fla. (12)
Lightfoot, Jim Ross, R-Iowa (5)
Lipinski, William O., D-Ill. (5)
Livingston, Robert L., R-La. (1)
Lloyd, Marilyn, D-Tenn. (3)
Long, Jill L., D-Ind. (4)
Lowery, Bill, R-Calif. (41)
Lowey, Nita M., D-N.Y. (20)
Luken, Charles, D-Ohio (1)

M

Machtley, Ronald K., R-R.I. (1)
Manton, Thomas J., D-N.Y. (9)
Markey, Edward J., D-Mass. (7)
Marlenee, Ron, R-Mont. (2)
Martin, David O'B., R-N.Y. (26)
Martinez, Matthew G., D-Calif. (30)
Matsui, Robert T., D-Calif. (3)
Mavroules, Nicholas, D-Mass. (6)
Mazzoli, Romano L., D-Ky. (3)
McCandless, Al, R-Calif. (37)
McCloskey, Frank, D-Ind. (8)
McCollum, Bill, R-Fla. (5)
McCrery, Jim, R-La. (4)
McCurdy, Dave, D-Okla. (4)
McDade, Joseph M., R-Pa. (10)
McDermott, Jim, D-Wash. (7)
McEwen, Bob, R-Ohio (6)
McGrath, Raymond J., R-N.Y. (5)
McHugh, Matthew F., D-N.Y. (28)
McMillan, Alex, R-N.C. (9)
McMillen, Tom, D-Md. (4)
McNulty, Michael R., D-N.Y. (23)
Meyers, Jan, R-Kan. (3)
Mfume, Kweisi, D-Md. (7)
Michel, Robert H., R-Ill. (18)
Miller, Clarence E., R-Ohio (10)
Miller, George, D-Calif. (7)
Miller, John, R-Wash. (1)
Mineta, Norman Y., D-Calif. (13)
Mink, Patsy T., D-Hawaii (2)
Moakley, Joe, D-Mass. (9)
Molinari, Susan, R-N.Y. (14)
Mollohan, Alan B., D-W.Va. (1)
Montgomery, G. V. "Sonny," D-Miss. (3)
Moody, Jim, D-Wis. (5)
Moorhead, Carlos J., R-Calif. (22)
Moran, James P. Jr., D-Va. (8)
Morella, Constance A., R-Md. (8)
Morrison, Sid, R-Wash. (4)
Mrazek, Robert J., D-N.Y. (3)
Murphy, Austin J., D-Pa. (22)
Murtha, John P., D-Pa. (12)
Myers, John T., R-Ind. (7)

N

Nagle, Dave, D-Iowa (3)
Natcher, William H., D-Ky. (2)
Neal, Richard E., D-Mass. (2)
Neal, Stephen L., D-N.C. (5)
Nichols, Dick, R-Kan. (5)
Nowak, Henry J., D-N.Y. (33)
Nussle, Jim, R-Iowa (2)

O

Oakar, Mary Rose, D-Ohio (20)
Oberstar, James L., D-Minn. (8)
Obey, David R., D-Wis. (7)
Olin, Jim, D-Va. (6)
Olver, John, D-Mass. (1)
Ortiz, Solomon P., D-Texas (27)
Orton, Bill, D-Utah (3)
Owens, Major R., D-N.Y. (12)
Owens, Wayne, D-Utah (2)
Oxley, Michael G., R-Ohio (4)

P

Packard, Ron, R-Calif. (43)
Pallone, Frank Jr., D-N.J. (3)
Panetta, Leon E., D-Calif. (16)
Parker, Mike, D-Miss. (4)
Pastor, Ed, D-Ariz. (2)
Patterson, Liz J., D-S.C. (4)
Paxon, Bill, R-N.Y. (31)
Payne, Donald M., D-N.J. (10)
Payne, Lewis F. Jr., D-Va. (5)
Pease, Don J., D-Ohio (13)
Pelosi, Nancy, D-Calif. (5)
Penny, Timothy J., D-Minn. (1)
Perkins, Carl C., D-Ky. (7)
Peterson, Collin C., D-Minn. (7)
Peterson, Pete, D-Fla. (2)
Petri, Tom, R-Wis. (6)
Pickett, Owen B., D-Va. (2)
Pickle, J. J., D-Texas (10)
Porter, John, R-Ill. (10)
Poshard, Glenn, D-Ill. (22)

. . . Governors, Supreme Court, Cabinet-Rank Officers

Price, David, D-N.C. (4)
Pursell, Carl D., R-Mich. (2)

Q, R

Quillen, James H., R-Tenn. (1)
Rahall, Nick J. II, D-W.Va. (4)
Ramstad, Jim, R-Minn. (3)
Rangel, Charles B., D-N.Y. (16)
Ravenel, Arthur Jr., R-S.C. (1)
Ray, Richard, D-Ga. (3)
Reed, John F., D-R.I. (2)
Regula, Ralph, R-Ohio (16)
Rhodes, John J. III, R-Ariz. (1)
Richardson, Bill, D-N.M. (3)
Ridge, Tom, R-Pa. (21)
Riggs, Frank, R-Calif. (1)
Rinaldo, Matthew J., R-N.J. (7)
Ritter, Don, R-Pa. (15)
Roberts, Pat, R-Kan. (1)
Roe, Robert A., D-N.J. (8)
Roemer, Tim, D-Ind. (3)
Rogers, Harold, R-Ky. (5)
Rohrabacher, Dana, R-Calif. (42)
Ros-Lehtinen, Ileana, R-Fla. (18)
Rose, Charlie, D-N.C. (7)
Rostenkowski, Dan, D-Ill. (8)
Roth, Toby, R-Wis. (8)
Roukema, Marge, R-N.J. (5)
Rowland, J. Roy, D-Ga. (8)
Roybal, Edward R., D-Calif. (25)
Russo, Marty, D-Ill. (3)

S

Sabo, Martin Olav, D-Minn. (5)
Sanders, Bernard, I-Vt. (AL)
Sangmeister, George E., D-Ill. (4)
Santorum, Rick, R-Pa. (18)
Sarpalius, Bill, D-Texas (13)
Savage, Gus, D-Ill. (2)
Sawyer, Tom, D-Ohio (14)
Saxton, H. James, R-N.J. (13)
Schaefer, Dan, R-Colo. (6)
Scheuer, James H., D-N.Y. (8)
Schiff, Steven H., R-N.M. (1)
Schroeder, Patricia, D-Colo. (1)
Schulze, Dick, R-Pa. (5)
Schumer, Charles E., D-N.Y. (10)
Sensenbrenner, F. James Jr., R-Wis. (9)
Serrano, Jose E., D-N.Y. (18)
Sharp, Philip R., D-Ind. (2)
Shaw, E. Clay Jr., R-Fla. (15)
Shays, Christopher, R-Conn. (4)
Shuster, Bud, R-Pa. (9)
Sikorski, Gerry, D-Minn. (6)
Sisisky, Norman, D-Va. (4)
Skaggs, David E., D-Colo. (2)
Skeen, Joe, R-N.M. (2)
Skelton, Ike, D-Mo. (4)
Slattery, Jim, D-Kan. (2)
Slaughter, Louise M., D-N.Y. (30)
Smith, Bob, R-Ore. (2)
Smith, Christopher H., R-N.J. (4)
Smith, Lamar, R-Texas (21)
Smith, Lawrence J., D-Fla. (16)
Smith, Neal, D-Iowa (4)
Snowe, Olympia J., R-Maine (2)
Solarz, Stephen J., D-N.Y. (13)
Solomon, Gerald B. H., R-N.Y. (24)
Spence, Floyd D., R-S.C. (2)
Spratt, John M. Jr., D-S.C. (5)
Staggers, Harley O. Jr., D-W.Va. (2)
Stallings, Richard, D-Idaho (2)
Stark, Pete, D-Calif. (9)
Stearns, Cliff, R-Fla. (6)
Stenholm, Charles W., D-Texas (17)
Stokes, Louis, D-Ohio (21)
Studds, Gerry E., D-Mass. (10)
Stump, Bob, R-Ariz. (3)
Sundquist, Don, R-Tenn. (7)
Swett, Dick, D-N.H. (2)
Swift, Al, D-Wash. (2)
Synar, Mike, D-Okla. (2)

T

Tallon, Robin, D-S.C. (6)
Tanner, John, D-Tenn. (8)
Tauzin, W. J. "Billy," D-La. (3)
Taylor, Charles H., R-N.C. (11)
Taylor, Gene, D-Miss. (5)
Thomas, Bill, R-Calif. (20)
Thomas, Craig, R-Wyo. (AL)
Thomas, Lindsay, D-Ga. (1)
Thornton, Ray, D-Ark. (2)
Torres, Esteban E., D-Calif. (34)
Torricelli, Robert G., D-N.J. (9)
Towns, Edolphus, D-N.Y. (11)
Traficant, James A. Jr., D-Ohio (17)
Traxler, Bob, D-Mich. (8)

U, V

Unsoeld, Jolene, D-Wash. (3)
Upton, Fred, R-Mich. (4)
Valentine, Tim, D-N.C. (2)
Vander Jagt, Guy, R-Mich. (9)
Vento, Bruce F., D-Minn. (4)
Visclosky, Peter J., D-Ind. (1)
Volkmer, Harold L., D-Mo. (9)
Vucanovich, Barbara F., R-Nev. (2)

W

Walker, Robert S., R-Pa. (16)
Walsh, James T., R-N.Y. (27)
Washington, Craig, D-Texas (18)
Waters, Maxine, D-Calif. (29)
Waxman, Henry A., D-Calif. (24)
Weber, Vin, R-Minn. (2)
Weiss, Ted, D-N.Y. (17)
Weldon, Curt, R-Pa. (7)
Wheat, Alan, D-Mo. (5)
Whitten, Jamie L., D-Miss. (1)
Williams, Pat, D-Mont. (1)
Wilson, Charles, D-Texas (2)
Wise, Bob, D-W.Va. (3)
Wolf, Frank R., R-Va. (10)
Wolpe, Howard, D-Mich. (3)
Wyden, Ron, D-Ore. (3)
Wylie, Chalmers P., R-Ohio (15)

X, Y, Z

Yates, Sidney R., D-Ill. (9)
Yatron, Gus, D-Pa. (6)
Young, C. W. Bill, R-Fla. (8)
Young, Don, R-Alaska (AL)
Zeliff, Bill, R-N.H. (1)
Zimmer, Dick, R-N.J. (12)

Delegates

Blaz, Ben, R-Guam
de Lugo, Ron, D-Virgin Islands
Faleomavaega, Eni F.H., D-Am. Samoa
Norton, Eleanor Holmes, D-D.C.

Resident Commissioner

Fuster, Jaime B., Pop. Dem.-Puerto Rico

Senators

D 57; R 43

Adams, Brock, D-Wash.
Akaka, Daniel K., D-Hawaii
Baucus, Max, D-Mont.
Bentsen, Lloyd, D-Texas
Biden, Joseph R. Jr., D-Del.
Bingaman, Jeff, D-N.M.
Bond, Christopher S., R-Mo.
Boren, David L., D-Okla.
Bradley, Bill, D-N.J.
Breaux, John B., D-La.
Brown, Hank, R-Colo.
Bryan, Richard H., D-Nev.
Bumpers, Dale, D-Ark.
Burdick, Quentin N., D-N.D.
Burns, Conrad, R-Mont.
Byrd, Robert C., D-W.Va.
Chafee, John H., R-R.I.
Coats, Daniel R., R-Ind.
Cochran, Thad, R-Miss.
Cohen, William S., R-Maine
Conrad, Kent, D-N.D.
Craig, Larry E., R-Idaho
Cranston, Alan, D-Calif.
D'Amato, Alfonse M., R-N.Y.
Danforth, John C., R-Mo.
Daschle, Tom, D-S.D.
DeConcini, Dennis, D-Ariz.
Dixon, Alan J., D-Ill.
Dodd, Christopher J., D-Conn.
Dole, Bob, R-Kan.
Domenici, Pete V., R-N.M.
Durenberger, Dave, R-Minn.
Exon, Jim, D-Neb.
Ford, Wendell H., D-Ky.
Fowler, Wyche Jr., D-Ga.
Garn, Jake, R-Utah
Glenn, John, D-Ohio
Gore, Al, D-Tenn.
Gorton, Slade, R-Wash.
Graham, Bob, D-Fla.
Gramm, Phil, R-Texas
Grassley, Charles E., R-Iowa
Harkin, Tom, D-Iowa
Hatch, Orrin G., R-Utah
Hatfield, Mark O., R-Ore.
Heflin, Howell, D-Ala.
Helms, Jesse, R-N.C.
Hollings, Ernest F., D-S.C.
Inouye, Daniel K., D-Hawaii
Jeffords, James M., R-Vt.
Johnston, J. Bennett, D-La.
Kassebaum, Nancy Landon, R-Kan.
Kasten, Bob, R-Wis.
Kennedy, Edward M., D-Mass.
Kerrey, Bob, D-Neb.
Kerry, John, D-Mass.
Kohl, Herb, D-Wis.
Lautenberg, Frank R., D-N.J.
Leahy, Patrick J., D-Vt.
Levin, Carl, D-Mich.
Lieberman, Joseph I., D-Conn.
Lott, Trent, R-Miss.
Lugar, Richard G., R-Ind.
Mack, Connie, R-Fla.
McCain, John, R-Ariz.
McConnell, Mitch, R-Ky.
Metzenbaum, Howard M., D-Ohio
Mikulski, Barbara A., D-Md.
Mitchell, George J., D-Maine
Moynihan, Daniel Patrick, D-N.Y.
Murkowski, Frank H., R-Alaska
Nickles, Don, R-Okla.
Nunn, Sam, D-Ga.
Packwood, Bob, R-Ore.
Pell, Claiborne, D-R.I.
Pressler, Larry, R-S.D.
Pryor, David, D-Ark.
Reid, Harry, D-Nev.
Riegle, Donald W. Jr., D-Mich.
Robb, Charles S., D-Va.
Rockefeller, John D. IV, D-W.Va.
Roth, William V. Jr., R-Del.
Rudman, Warren B., R-N.H.
Sanford, Terry, D-N.C.
Sarbanes, Paul S., D-Md.
Sasser, Jim, D-Tenn.
Seymour, John, R-Calif.
Shelby, Richard C., D-Ala.
Simon, Paul, D-Ill.
Simpson, Alan K., R-Wyo.
Smith, Robert C., R-N.H.
Specter, Arlen, R-Pa.
Stevens, Ted, R-Alaska
Symms, Steve, R-Idaho
Thurmond, Strom, R-S.C.
Wallop, Malcolm, R-Wyo.
Warner, John W., R-Va.
Wellstone, Paul, D-Minn.
Wirth, Tim, D-Colo.
Wofford, Harris L. Jr., D-Pa.

Governors

D 28; R 20; I 2

Ala.—Guy Hunt, R
Alaska—Walter J. Hickel, I
Ariz.—Fife Symington, R
Ark.—Bill Clinton, D
Calif.—Pete Wilson, R
Colo.—Roy Romer, D
Conn.—Lowell P. Weicker Jr., I
Del.—Michael N. Castle, R
Fla.—Lawton Chiles, D
Ga.—Zell Miller, D
Hawaii—John Waihee III, D
Idaho—Cecil D. Andrus, D
Ill.—Jim Edgar, R
Ind.—Evan Bayh, D
Iowa—Terry E. Branstad, R
Kan.—Joan Finney, D
Ky.—Wallace G. Wilkinson, D
La.—Buddy Roemer, D
Maine—John R. McKernan Jr., R
Md.—William Donald Schaefer, D
Mass.—William F. Weld, R
Mich.—John Engler, R
Minn.—Arne Carlson, R
Miss.—Ray Mabus, D
Mo.—John Ashcroft, R
Mont.—Stan Stephens, R
Neb.—Ben Nelson, D
Nev.—Bob Miller, D
N.H.—Judd Gregg, R
N.J.—James J. Florio, D
N.M.—Bruce King, D
N.Y.—Mario M. Cuomo, D
N.C.—James G. Martin, R
N.D.—George Sinner, D
Ohio—George V. Voinovich, R
Okla.—David Walters, D
Ore.—Barbara Roberts, D
Pa.—Robert P. Casey, D
R.I.—Bruce Sundlun, D
S.C.—Carroll A. Campbell Jr., R
S.D.—George S. Mickelson, R
Tenn.—Ned McWherter, D
Texas—Ann W. Richards, D
Utah—Norman H. Bangerter, R
Vt.—Richard A. Snelling, R
Va.—L. Douglas Wilder, D
Wash.—Booth Gardner, D
W.Va.—Gaston Caperton, D
Wis.—Tommy G. Thompson, R
Wyo.—Mike Sullivan, D

Supreme Court

Rehnquist, William H.—Va., Chief Justice
Blackmun, Harry A.—Minn.
Kennedy, Anthony M.—Calif.
O'Connor, Sandra Day—Ariz.
Scalia, Antonin—Va.
Souter, David H.—N.H.
Stevens, John Paul—Ill.
Thomas, Clarence—Ga.
White, Byron R.—Colo.

Cabinet

Alexander, Lamar—Education
Baker, James A. III—State
Barr, William P.—Attorney General
Brady, Nicholas F.—Treasury
Cheney, Dick—Defense
Derwinski, Edward J.—Veterans Affairs
Kemp, Jack F.—HUD
Lujan, Manuel Jr.—Interior
Madigan, Edward—Agriculture
Martin, Lynn—Labor
Mosbacher, Robert A.—Commerce
Skinner, Samuel K.—Transportation
Sullivan, Louis W.—HHS
Watkins, James D.—Energy

Other Executive Branch Officers

Darman, Richard G.—OMB Director
Hills, Carla A.—U.S. Trade Representative
Martinez, Bob—Director, Drug Policy
Quayle, Dan—Vice President
Sununu, John H.—Chief of Staff

Vetoes Cast by President Bush

President Bush rejected four public bills in 1991: two by direct vetoes and two by pocket vetoes that were in a legal gray area. Congress tried to override the two direct vetoes. Both attempts were unsuccessful, preserving Bush's string of not having been overridden. *(Previous vetoes, 1990 Almanac, p. 17; 1989 Almanac, p. 6)*

The White House listed 25 vetoes in Bush's three years, but that included several pocket vetoes that were not recognized by Congress. The Constitution gives the president 10 days (Sundays excepted) after receiving a bill to sign it into law or return it with his objections — at which point Congress can override by a two-thirds vote of each chamber. If the president does neither within 10 days, the bill "shall be a law ... unless the Congress by their adjournment prevent its return, in which case it shall not be a law." The latter case constitutes a pocket veto.

In 1991, Bush rejected the District of Columbia appropriations bill during the August recess and declared it a pocket veto. But he issued a memorandum of disapproval and returned the bill to Congress, the procedure used for a routine veto; Congress treated it as such. While Congress was in its end-of-the-year recess, Bush refused to sign a bill authorizing money for environmental education programs and said it was a pocket veto; this time he did not return the bill to Congress. In early 1992 Congress enacted a new bill meeting Bush's objections; it repealed the earlier measure, on grounds that it had become law.

Bill	Veto Date	Outcome	Story
Fiscal 1992 District of Columbia Appropriations (HR 2699)	Aug. 17	No override attempt [1]	p. 616
Unemployment Benefits Extension (S1722)	Oct. 11	Senate sustained 65-35, Oct. 16 [2]	p. 301
Fiscal 1992 Labor, HHS, and Education Appropriations (HR 2707)	Nov. 19	House sustained 276-156, Nov. 19 [2]	p. 501
Udall Scholarship and Excellence in National Environmental Policy (S 1176)	Dec. 20	Disputed pocket veto [3]	p. 235

[1] *President declared poket veto on this date but returned bill to Congress*

[2] *Veto overrides required a two-thirds majority vote of both chambers*

[3] *President declared pocket veto on this date; did not return bill to Congress*

Continued from p. 7

were told to keep their shutters closed. Armed police officers were stationed atop congressional buildings. Lawmakers were warned of the danger of driving cars with official congressional license plates.

After the assault on Iraq began, the state of alert was ratcheted up a notch. Police deployed vans full of bomb-sniffing dogs. Armed officers guarded congressional leaders even at their homes.

While the Bush administration notified congressional leaders late Jan. 16, shortly before the initial attack, most members got word of the war the same way their constituents did: on television. Many tuned into the live coverage provided by Cable News Network (CNN) of the initial attack on Baghdad.

State of the Union

Less than two weeks later, security was especially high when Bush gave his State of the Union address. Laying out the rationale for military action in the Middle East and his view of the U.S. role in world affairs, Bush told a joint session of Congress on Jan. 29 that Americans had a "unique responsibility to do the hard work of freedom." *(Text, p. 6-E)*

Despite wide public support for U.S. policy in the gulf, Bush went into the speech facing criticism that he had not effectively conveyed to the public the rationale and aim of U.S. involvement. While his speech offered no clear vision of the postwar Middle East, he devoted considerable time to explaining in moral terms the effort to force Iraq from Kuwait.

"What is at stake is more than one small country; it is a big idea: a new world order," he said. "Our cause is just. Our cause is moral. Our cause is right."

He drew the speech's longest, most emotional standing ovation when he praised the men and women serving in the Persian Gulf: "There is no one more devoted, more committed to the hard work of freedom."

Bush gave his speech at a time when the war had given him stratospheric public approval ratings. His public approval ratings had fallen along with his no-new-taxes pledge from 76 percent in early September of 1990 to 53 percent in mid-October. But a Jan. 27 Washington Post/ABC News poll found that 79 percent of those surveyed approved of Bush's handling of his job — the highest rating since he took office. (Bush's approval ratings were much lower — 45 percent — for his handling of the economy alone.)

By the time Bush gave a triumphant speech to Congress on March 6 to hail the end of the war, Bush's rating had soared to an unheard of level: 89 percent in the Gallup Poll — even higher than the 87 percent support given Harry S Truman as World War II ended.

Bush's strength in Congress rested principally with his veto power. He kept intact his string of never having been overridden on 25 vetoes. In the first session, he vetoed three bills (plus another that he claimed was pocket-vetoed at the end of the session — a move that congressional leaders said was invalid because Congress had not adjourned sine die. *(Veto box, above; pocket veto, 1990 Almanac, p. 21)*

On contested issues as diverse as abortion counseling, civil rights, labor laws and China's trade status, Democratic leaders learned to routinely take account of the need to find support from two-thirds of the House and Senate — the number needed to override a veto — rather than the simple majority needed to pass a bill.

In the previous 30 years, only Gerald R. Ford vetoed more bills by a comparable time in his presidency. Faced with a heavily Democratic Congress in the wake of Watergate, Ford vetoed 66 bills in three years and was overridden 12 times.

As impressive as Bush's success was in turning back override attempts, he had set no records. Dwight D. Eisenhower, for one, was well into his second term before he lost a veto fight. Eisenhower's final record: Congress overrode only two of his 181 vetoes.

Bush proved adept at shifting his position enough to win the support he needed to prevail.

In a campaign early in 1991 to defeat a resolution to curb his power to negotiate a free-trade agreement with Mexico, Bush blunted much of his opposition by issuing a plan for responding to labor and environmental concerns about the Mexico pact. When the recession deepened enough to make a second veto of extended unemployment benefits unwise, he negotiated a compromise. After threatening for years to veto a civil rights bill, he cut a deal that Democrats said was purely cosmetic so that he could sign the legislation.

Overall, Bush's success with Congress on votes on which he took a position showed only a modest improvement, from 47 percent in 1990 to 54 percent in 1991. In all three years of his term, he scored below all his predecessors at similar points since Congressional Quarterly began studying presidential votes in 1953. *(Vote study, p. 3-B)*

Skinner Replaces Sununu

In the most significant personnel shakeup of his term, Bush traded the administration's least-liked conservative for its most-liked moderate when he replaced John H. Sununu as chief of staff with Transportation Secretary Samuel K. Skinner.

Sununu told the president in a letter Dec. 3 that he feared becoming "a drag on your success" and quit as of Dec. 15. Bush praised him for intercepting "many of the arrows aimed my way" and accepted his resignation, assigning him the role of "counselor to the president with Cabinet rank" until March 1, 1992.

Sununu's overbearing style had produced few smiles on Capitol Hill, and when a series of scandals and missteps threatened his position beginning in 1990, he had very little good will in reserve.

Many Bush allies carped privately — and in the case of Rep. Dick Armey, R-Texas, publicly — that his brash chief of staff had become a liability.

A 1990 flap over Sununu's traveling habits died down, but Sununu never fully recovered and was finished after failing to do what he had always done best: catch flak for the president.

Instead of accepting the blame for a Bush remark calling for lower credit card interest rates — which indirectly sent the stock market into a dive — Sununu announced that the president had ad-libbed the line.

While Skinner was a proven compromiser, he was also a former federal prosecutor in Illinois who had shown official Washington that he could play partisan hardball.

Skinner ran Bush's successful Illinois general election campaign in 1988. Long interested in politics, he had worked on conservative Barry Goldwater's failed bid against President Lyndon B. Johnson, but he eventually became identified with Republican moderates. His longtime mentor, former Illinois Gov. James R. Thompson, also a GOP moderate, chose Skinner in 1984 to head the Chicago-area transit system, the nation's second-largest.

When he became Transportation secretary, he was far from a familiar face, but he quickly became the most visible Cabinet member. His first task was to investigate the Pan Am Flight 103 bombing over Lockerbie, Scotland. Soon afterward, Bush chose him to play a lead role in investigating the 1989 *Exxon Valdez* oil spill. To the dis-

The First Session at a Glance

Although both chambers completed their legislative business Nov. 27, the House at 7:03 p.m. EST and the Senate at 7:05 p.m. EST, the first session of the 102nd Congress did not formally end until 11:55 a.m. Jan. 3, 1992, when Congress reconvened to officially adjourn the first session and open the second session five minutes later.

The November adjournment resolution had left open the possibility that the majority and minority leadership could reconvene Congress if necessary.

Convened on Jan. 3, 1991, the first session lasted 365 days — 86 days longer than the second session of the 101st Congress. Two other sessions — the first session of the 77th and the second session of the 81st — lasted 365 days. Only the third session of the 76th Congress was longer: From Jan. 3, 1940, to Jan. 3, 1941, it lasted 366 days because of a leap year.

There were 7,758 bills and resolutions introduced during the session, compared with 6,963 in 1990 and 7,390 in 1989. A total of 243 bills cleared by Congress in 1991 became public law.

President Bush vetoed four bills for a total of 25 during his three years in office; none were overridden, although the procedure he used for some was questioned.

The Senate met for 158 days, and the House for 154. Each chamber met for 138 days in 1990.

During 1991, the House took 444 recorded votes and quorum calls, 92 less than the previous year. The Senate took 280 recorded votes, 46 less than in 1990.*

Year	House	Senate	Total
1991	444	280	724
1990	536	326	862
1989	379	312	691
1988	465	379	844
1987	511	420	931
1986	488	359	847
1985	482	381	863
1984	463	292	755
1983	533	381	914
1982	488	469	957
1981	371	497	868
1980	681	546	1,227
1979	758	509	1,267
1978	942	520	1,462

** Figures are for recorded votes and quorum calls in each chamber. In previous Almanacs (through 1987), tabulations were for recorded votes only.*

Whitten Honored for 50 Years' Service

The House on Nov. 5. took time out to recognize Rep. Jamie L. Whitten, D-Miss., for a remarkable achievement: 50 years of service. Whitten, 81, was sworn in as a House member on Nov. 4, 1941.

His tenure had spanned 10 presidents, starting with Franklin D. Roosevelt and seven House Speakers.

While voters in some states were itching to limit the terms of their lawmakers, Whitten showed no signs of retiring.

Only two others had served in Congress longer, and in January 1992, Whitten broke the record for longest service in the House. Rep. Carl Vinson, D-Ga., served 50 years, 2 months and 13 days. The champion for congressional service was Carl Hayden, D-Ariz., who served a total in the House and Senate of 56 years, 10 months and 28 days, starting in 1912.

Nothing counted in the House like seniority. Whitten had served as chairman of the House Appropriations Committee since 1978, and as head of its Agriculture Subcommittee nearly continuously for more than four decades. The latter post had earned him the title of "permanent secretary of Agriculture," and the former had made him one of the most powerful men in Washington.

"When you handle money, you're in the strongest position you can be in Congress," he observed.

Among his colleagues, Whitten had no rival. The second-longest serving House member was Charles E. Bennett, D-Fla., who was more than seven years behind. And Whitten had a 15-year jump on Strom Thurmond, R-S.C., who had served in the Senate the longest.

The power that came with his seniority helped ensure his position. That pre-eminent spot often scared aware challengers in his home state. Whitten never received less than 63 percent of the vote, and ran unopposed in 14 of 26 elections.

may of some pro-business conservatives, Skinner criticized Exxon and called for more federal oversight of cleanup and prevention efforts.

On policy, Skinner sought to shape a new national transportation strategy that would recast federal aviation, highway and mass transit programs. He successfully shepherded much of his agenda through Congress in 1990-91, aided by members who shared his views. His mission was to shift more decision-making powers — and the fiscal burden — to states. He wanted private companies not only to build but also to manage toll roads and airports. Federal efforts would be focused on repairs and congestion relief.

Congress passed part of Skinner's plan — reshaping highway policy — on Nov. 26, approving a $151 billion, six-year authorization bill for highway and mass transit programs.

Skinner displayed a knack for exchanging political favors with key members of Congress.

He visited Kentucky early in 1991 to break ground on an airport renovation with home-state Democratic Sen. Wendell H. Ford and handed over a huge check representing one of the biggest federal commitments to an airport project.

Ford, chairman of the Commerce Aviation Subcommittee, just months earlier had inserted much of Skinner's nearly dead aviation plan into a must-pass deficit-cutting bill days before the end of the 101st Congress. Ford had bitterly opposed Skinner's plan to charge passengers fees for airport improvements but went along when Skinner agreed to swallow Ford's plan for restricting noisy planes.

Sununu, the former New Hampshire governor, had become legend for his penchant for alienating members of Congress. During budget talks, he irreverently put his feet up on the table, insulting the dean of the Senate, Robert C. Byrd, D-W.Va. The former chief of staff angered House Republicans when he threatened to have Bush withhold campaign support from those who opposed an unpopular budget-and-tax deal. While successfully fighting a controversial amendment to the 1990 clean air bill, he persuaded two senators to vote against the proposal by telling one that it was certain veto-bait and telling the other the opposite.

The Republican Party's right wing considered Sununu their watchdog in Bush's otherwise comparatively moderate administration.

"I think the conservative wing of the Republican Party, at least on Capitol Hill, has lost a very important link to the White House," said Rep. Henry J. Hyde, R-Ill.

Pro-life advocates, long suspicious of Bush's anti-abortion stand, credited Sununu with acting as an effective goalie, blocking every move to soften the government's stance against supporting abortion in any way.

"We greatly regret his departure," said Douglas Johnson, the National Right to Life Committee's top lobbyist. ■

Two Campaign Finance Bills Passed

Both chambers passed Democratic campaign finance bills over Republican objections in 1991, positioning Democrats to iron out House-Senate differences in 1992 and send President Bush the first overhaul of campaign finance legislation since the 1974 post-Watergate reforms.

Bush, however, held the Republicans' trump card: a veto to use against any bill that he felt favored Democrats over the GOP. He promised to veto any bill that: 1) imposed an artificial ceiling on spending; 2) gave public funds to candidates; or 3) created separate systems for House and Senate candidates.

The congressional Democrats' trajectory pointed toward a bill that did all three. Both bills (S 3, HR 3750) sought to set an optional limit on campaign spending and offer public financing and other benefits to candidates who adhered to it.

The difficulty of coming up with one system that would apply fairly to both Senate and House campaigns made leaders talk of letting each chamber write rules for its own races when it came time for a conference committee to reconcile differences in the 1992 session.

The partisan stakes were clear, as they had been throughout a decade of sporadic efforts to rewrite the rules under which political campaigns were financed. Democrats sought to squeeze the Republicans' advantage with wealthy donors and direct-mail campaigns; the GOP pressed for ways to nullify Democrats' ties to labor and their attraction to political action committees (PACs) seeking favor with incumbents of the party that controlled Congress.

In the 101st Congress, Democrats were able to force legislation through the floors, but they made no attempt to settle differences between the House and Senate. The 1991 Senate bill was almost a carbon copy of the previous year's; the House bill differed from that chamber's 1990 version by offering some support for public financing — although, in order to keep Southern Democrats on board, it shied away from the controversial question of how to pay for it. *(1990 Almanac, p. 59)*

Outside groups cited congressional ethics problems and low ratings for Congress in public opinion polls to bolster the case for reform.

Common Cause, the public interest lobbying group, had for several years made campaign finance a centerpiece of its appeals to members. The Ralph Nader-affiliated group Public Citizen and the labor-affiliated group Citizen Action also pushed for an overhaul of the laws so that tax dollars would replace PAC dollars. Reformers were encouraged when the 33 million-member American Association of Retired Persons joined a coalition in favor of the legislation in 1990 and pushed the issue with its members in 1991.

Common Cause hoped that the Keating Five savings and loan investigation of 1990-91 would provide the impetus for a breakthrough, calling the Keating scandal "the smoking gun" that proved the corruption of the election finance system.

The televised Keating Five hearings of 1990-91 focused national attention on the influence of money on politics. The hearings showed how Charles H. Keating Jr., the powerful owner of a thrift and real estate empire, used his fundraising skills to assemble clout in Washington.

The testimony left no doubt of the urgency Senate offices attached to raising money. *(Keating hearings, p. 26)*

The Senate Ethic Committee's special counsel, Robert S. Bennett, in November 1990 flagged the relationship between favor-seeking contributors and money-chasing incumbents as inherently dangerous. He issued "a booming warning that unless these trends are recognized and dealt with . . . the reputation of this body and its members will be utterly in ruin."

BOXSCORE

➡ **Campaign Finance Overhaul (S 3, HR 3750).** Democratic-written bills to set voluntary spending limits on how much a candidate could spend on congressional elections and provide public funding and other benefits to those who complied. President Bush vowed to veto either bill, on grounds that both would unfairly disadvantage Republican candidates.

Reports: S Rept 102-102-37; H Rept 102-340.

KEY ACTION

March 20 — S 3 approved by **Senate** Rules and Administration Committee on a 7-2 vote.

May 23 — **Senate** passed S 3 by 56-42 vote.

Nov. 12 — Democratic task force unveils **House** proposal.

Nov. 14 — HR 3750 approved by **House** Administration Committee 14-9.

Nov. 25 — **House** passed HR 3750 by vote of 273-156.

Differences Between Parties

The stalemate between the parties on campaign finance had been revisited periodically since 1986 but with little change in position. Republicans and Democrats not only disagreed on how to fix the system, they could not even agree on what was wrong. Their differences were both philosophical and practical. The positions broke down like this:

- Democrats contended that the campaign finance system operated like an arms race, with candidates engaged in a never-ending quest for a financial edge. Hence, Democrats insisted that any new law had to limit campaign spending. Money they would take away from candidates, by limiting or banning PACs, they would replace with public subsidies.
- Republicans asserted that the problem lay with tainted sources of money. Instead of capping spending, they proposed curbing specific sources, such as PACs and large out-of-state contributions. Indeed, they would encourage political parties to spend even more in behalf of their candidates. What Republicans feared most was that locking in spending levels would help lock in a Democratic majority.

Most of the rhetoric on the floor in 1991 focused on public financing.

The House exhibited its history of skittishness toward public financing of its campaigns. Members rejected it in 1974, and the issue did not return to the floor for 16 years. In August 1990, House members voted down an amendment that would have subsidized campaigns with Treasury funds, although they approved indirect public financing in the form of postage discounts. In 1991, a House task force prepared legislation that would offer up to $200,000 in public funds to candidates who agreed to a $600,000 spending cap on House campaigns.

But by the time the bill hit the floor, Democratic leaders had stripped it of any meaningful way to pay for the funding, for fear that Republicans could peel off enough Southern Democrats to rewrite or defeat the bill.

The Senate-passed bill offered candidates public funds up to 20 percent of the spending limit for a state (varying from state to state), plus postage discounts, a 50 percent discount on broadcasting and further public funds to counter an opponent who broke the limit.

Republicans concentrated their fire on any proposal that smacked of giving tax money to politicians. "It takes an incredible amount of gall — when we don't have enough money for education, we don't have enough money for nutrition, we don't have enough money for the homeless — to say to the taxpayer, 'Aha, we have one new entitlement program, and it's for us,' " said Sen. Bob Packwood, R-Ore.

Differences Between Chambers

While not as deep as the chasm separating the parties, there was a clear gap between senators' visions of reform and the ideas of House members, even of the same party — and there was no legal or constitutional need to write one set of rules for House and Senate elections. Driven by the distinct campaign techniques, fundraising needs and political pressures facing their members, the two chambers were on separate courses that could produce a bewildering set of federal campaign laws — one for presidential contests, one for the Senate and another for the House.

There were some broad similarities in the way the Democrats writing the bill in each chamber viewed reform. Most important, both groups would limit spending and subsidize campaigns with public dollars. Nonetheless, significant differences dominated nearly every detail, from the role played by PACs to the cost of television ads. Some major differences between the two bills would be difficult to compromise on in a conference. *(Comparison of bills, at right)*

• **PACs.** The Senate bill would severely limit the role of PACs and bar them from contributing to candidates; the House bill would set a $200,000 limit on the PAC money candidates could accept.

Senators, with their statewide bases and national profiles, were generally less dependent on PAC money than on other sources of funding. Conversely, PACs had become financial pump houses for House incumbents. The average incumbent representative raised 49 percent of his or her money from PACs in the 1990 campaign, according to Common Cause. By contrast, PACs accounted for only 23 percent, about $33 million, of the money Senate incumbents raised. Just as important to the House was what PACs failed to give challengers. Overall, PACs contributed more than $88 million to House incumbents in 1990, nearly 13 times more money than they gave to challengers.

House members were skeptical of the depth of the Senate's commitment to gutting PACS. Several House members said they suspected senators were hoping the House would preserve PACs, or that the Supreme Court would strike down a legislative ban.

• **Financing.** The House bill was estimated to cost as much as $115 million every two years, according to the Congressional Budget Office. The Senate bill could cost as much as $91 million every two years, according to the White House Office of Management and Budget. The House bill required Congress to offset the costs before launching a new campaign finance system, and it was generally assumed that this meant raising new revenue. Several methods were discussed, such as curbing the tax break given to lobbying expenses, but neither bill addressed this issue squarely. Conferees would have to decide whether to leave the legislation as an empty vessel or finance it.

• **Soft money.** The bills took radically different approaches to the issue of party soft money — money spent by state parties on activities such as voter registration, get-out-the-vote drives and generic advertising that benefited state and federal candidates.

Under existing law, national party committees and presidential campaigns could raise soft money in excess of federal contribution limits, and it was subject only to state law, even though it primarily was spent to benefit federal candidates. The Senate bill sought to close the loophole; the House bill would codify existing practices. Democratic National Committee operatives lodged strenuous objections to the Senate bill, and they were expected to fight hard to keep soft money flowing.

SENATE ACTION

The Senate moved quickly on campaign finance. The positions of most senators were clear from the outset because they had voted so often on the issue in the past: In 1987 and 1988, the chamber had struggled with bills that were foiled by Republican filibusters on the floor. The Senate passed a bill in 1990, although it expired in a House-Senate conference that never met.

The bill (S 3) that emerged from the Senate May 23 was almost identical to the 1990 measure.

It contained one provision, a 50 percent discount for political advertising, that was markedly stronger than the previous version and inspired heated opposition from the National Association of Broadcasters.

Democrats weakened another provision, cutting from 50 percent to 20 percent the amount of the state-by-state spending limits that would be provided by taxpayers to purchase broadcast time.

In many ways, the Senate debate was a replay of 1990. Democrats spent most of their time arguing for spending limits as the only way to hold down the rising cost of campaigns and to reduce the amount of time senators spent raising money.

And they held out spending limits and public financing as a way to level the playing field for candidates challenging incumbents. "There can be no meaningful reform without spending limits," intoned Majority Leader George J. Mitchell of Maine, repeating the Democratic mantra that was anathema to many in the GOP.

The Republican whip, Alan K. Simpson of Wyoming, ridiculed the bill as the "same beat-up and tired old words and music that the majority Democratic Party has been crooning to us for years.... They call this tune the reformer's march. It should be called the incumbent-protection shuffle."

Senate Committee Action

The Senate Rules and Administration Committee on March 20 set the stage for a floor showdown by approving the Democrats' S 3 on a 7-2 vote.

The markup, which took only a few minutes, was scripted to leave the fighting for the floor. The committee also sent a Republican-sponsored measure (S 6) to the floor, but without the favorable recommendation given the Democratic bill.

S 3, sponsored by David L. Boren of Oklahoma, the Democrats' point man on the issue, would set voluntary

Continued on p. 19

Campaign Finance Bills Compared

Even though House and Senate bills passed in 1991 were ripe for conference, Democratic leaders put campaign finance legislation on the back burner, behind economic recovery legislation, in the first months of the 1992 session.

Each chamber's bill set optional spending limits and established a system of rewards and punishments to get candidates to abide by the limits. But the measures differed greatly on critical details in which members and party leaders had a vested interest.

The House bill (HR 3750) passed Nov. 25, was crafted by a House Administration Committee task force led by Sam Gejdenson, D-Conn. It restricted contributions from political action committees (PACs) but still preserved this key source of funds for House incumbents. It also provided matching funds for small donations raised by candidates.

The Senate bill (S 3) passed May 23, was modeled on similar bills passed in previous years, with some new twists, such as a ban on PAC contributions to candidates. It slashed the cost of television advertising for Senate candidates and provided public funds to assist in purchasing those ads.

While congressional leaders said one possibility was writing different sets of rules for each chamber, one issue that had to be resolved was that of so-called party soft money, money spent to influence federal elections that was not raised under federal rules. Because this primarily involved spending by party committees to benefit the entire ticket, there was no way to write separate House and Senate laws.

A comparison of the two bills follows:

Spending Limits

HOUSE PROVISIONS

• **Limit.** The optional spending limit would be $600,000 for House candidates in each two-year election cycle. Candidates would state whether they intended to obey the limit and other restrictions. Those who comply would become "eligible" candidates and would be entitled to benefits including public funds. Eligible candidates could exceed the spending limit and still get these benefits under certain circumstances designed to punish opposing candidates who do not agree to the limit.

• **Primary election.** There would be no separate spending limit for the primary. The spending limit would increase by $100,000 in case of a runoff primary.

• **General election.** No more than $500,000 could be spent during the general election period, which would begin immediately after the primary.

• **Personal funds limited.** Eligible candidates could spend no more than $60,000 of their own money. Any personal funds a candidate contributed to the campaign would count against the $200,000 limit placed on donations of more than $200. (See contribution limits below.)

The $60,000 limit on personal funds would not apply if: 1) an eligible candidate had an opponent who did not agree to the spending limit; and 2) this opponent raised or spent $250,000.

• **Exceptions.** The limit would rise in these cases:

Free-spending opponent. If an eligible candidate had an opponent who did not agree to the spending limit, and this opponent raised or spent more than $250,000 — that is, 50 percent of the general election limit — then the spending limit would be removed.

Independent expenditures. The spending limit would rise, dollar for dollar, after an independent campaign spent $60,000 against an eligible candidate or for his opponent.

Compliance fund. A campaign's legal and accounting costs would be exempt from the limits.

Fundraising/overhead. A campaign committee's spending for fundraising or overhead would be exempt from the limit, up to an amount equal to 5 percent of the limit.

Close primaries. Candidates who win their primaries by a margin of 10 percent or less could spend an extra $150,000 for the general election. This allowance was added to assuage fears that a costly primary fight could leave a candidate vulnerable in the general election.

• **Inflation.** Spending limits would be indexed every election cycle for inflation.

SENATE PROVISIONS

• **Limit.** Optional spending limits for Senate candidates would vary from state to state and would rise in part with a candidate's ability to raise money from residents of his or her state. Candidates would state whether they intended to obey the limit and other restrictions. Those who comply would become "eligible" candidates and would get certain benefits, including government vouchers to purchase television advertising. Eligible candidates could exceed the spending limit and still get these benefits under certain circumstances designed to punish opposing candidates who do not agree to the limit.

• **Primary election.** The spending limit for primaries would be 67 percent of the general election limit or $2.75 million, whichever is less. Only California candidates would run up against the $2.75 million cap. The limit for a runoff election would be 20 percent of the general election limit.

• **General election.** The general election limit would be set by the following formula: $400,000, plus 30 cents multiplied by the state's voting-age population up to 4 million, plus 25 cents multiplied by the voting-age population beyond 4 million. The limit would not fall below $950,000 or exceed $5.5 million.

• **Personal funds limited.** Eligible candidates could spend no more than $25,000 of their own or their family's money.

• **Exceptions.** The limit would rise in these cases:

Free-spending opponent. If an eligible candidate had an opponent who did not agree to the spending limit, and this opponent exceeded the general election limit, then the spending limit on the eligible candidate would rise by two-thirds. If this opponent spent more than 133.33 percent of the general election limit, the spending limit on the eligible candidate would be removed.

Independent expenditures. The spending limit would rise, dollar for dollar, to match independent expenditures after an independent campaign spent $10,000 against an eligible candidate or for his opponent.

Compliance/incidental fund. Candidates could spend an amount equal to 15 percent of the spending limit, in excess of the limit, for their campaign committee's legal and accounting costs.

Encouragement for in-state contributions. A candidate could exceed the general election spending limit by as much as 25 percent — but only with money raised in contributions of $100 or less from residents of the state.

Televison. In states with no more than one VHF television station, such as New Jersey, the spending limit would be set by the following formula: $400,000, plus 80 cents multiplied by the voting-age population up to 4 million, plus 70 cents multiplied by the voting-age population beyond 4 million.

• **Inflation.** Spending limits would be indexed annually for inflation.

Benefits

HOUSE PROVISIONS

• **Eligibility.** To qualify for benefits, candidates would have to win their primary, agree to the spending limit and raise $60,000 in contributions of $200 or less. The first $200 of any larger contribution would also count.

The benefits include:

• **Public funds/matching.** A candidate would receive matching public funds for the first $200 of any contribution, with an aggregate cap of $200,000 on the match.

• **Postage.** In every election cycle candidates could send up to three pieces of mail per eligible voter in the district at a discounted third-class rate.

• **Contingency money.** An eligible candidate with an opponent who did not agree to the spending limit would qualify for extra matching funds once his opponent raised or spent more than 50 percent of the limit. The eligible candidate also would receive matching funds for $200-or-less contributions without regard to the $200,000 cap.

Eligible candidates would qualify for triple matching funds if their opponents contributed an amount of money equal to 50 percent of the spending limit to their own campaign.

Eligible candidates would receive money to match any independent-expenditure campaign against them or for their opponent that exceeded $10,000.

• **Funding.** An account called the Make Democracy Work Fund would be created to make matching and other payments to eligible candidates. The bill would not authorize any spending until certain conditions are met. These would be the enactment of statutes that: 1) give individuals incentives to make contributions (the bill does not specify what incentives, but this could mean a tax credit or deduction); 2) permit individuals or organizations to make contributions to the Make Democracy Work Fund; 3) offset the cost of the law elsewhere in the budget. If the conditions are not met, then the spending and contribution limits would not take effect.

• **Penalties.** Eligible candidates who break the spending limit, but by less than 5 percent, would pay an equal amount to the Make Democracy Work Fund. If the overspending is between 5 and 10 percent, the payment would be an amount equal to triple the overspending. If the overspending exceeds 10 percent, matching funds would be repaid as well as the triple fine. Violators would also face a civil penalty.

SENATE PROVISIONS

• **Eligibility.** To qualify for benefits, candidates would have to agree to the spending limit, win their primary and raise $250,000 or 10 percent of the general election limit, whichever is less, in contributions of $250 or less and at least half from in-state donors.

The benefits include:

• **Public funds/vouchers.** Eligible candidates would receive a government voucher equal to 20 percent of the spending limit to be used to purchase television time in one- to five-minute chunks.

• **Postage.** Candidates could send first-class mail at one-fourth the normal rate and third-class mail at 2 cents less than the normal charge, up to an amount equal to 5 percent of the general election limit.

• **Contingency money.** Eligible candidates would receive public funds to match excess spending by their opponents. Once an opponent broke the limit, an eligible candidate would get an amount equal to two-thirds of the general election spending limit. Once an opponent spent 133.33 percent of the limit, the eligible candidate would get another third.

Eligible candidates also would receive public money to match an independent expenditure campaign mounted against them or for their opponent, once the independent campaign exceeded $10,000.

• **Discount broadcasting rates.** Television and radio broadcasters would be required to sell ads to candidates at a 50 percent discount from the most favorable terms offered any other advertiser for a comparable ad. The rates would apply throughout the general election campaign and for the last 45 days of a primary.

• **Funding.** The bill authorized no funds to pay for the benefits. It said the sense of the Senate was that the money should come from removing the tax break extended to corporations for lobbying activities and for operating a PAC.

• **Penalties.** Eligible candidates who violated the spending limit or accepted excess benefits could face up to five years' imprisonment and a $25,000 fine.

Contributions/PACs

HOUSE PROVISIONS

• **PAC contributions to candidates.** House candidates could accept no more than $200,000, in aggregate, from PACs. This limit would rise by $50,000 in the event of a "close primary" (when the margin of victory was 10 percent or less) and $50,000 in case of a primary runoff.

• **PAC contributions to party committees.** A PAC could contribute $20,000, up from $15,000 in current law, to a national party committee.

• **Large individual contributions.** Candidates could accept no more than $200,000, in aggregate, in contributions of more than $200 from individuals. This limit would rise by $50,000 in the event of a "close primary" and $50,000 in case of a primary runoff.

• **State party contributions.** A candidate could receive no more than $20,000, in aggregate, from the state and local committees of a political party. This measure was aimed at stopping state party committees from all over the country from pouring money into a tight contest, a practice that had become more frequent of late.

• **Personal funds.** The $60,000 limit on personal funds would not apply if: 1) an eligible candidate had an opponent who did not agree to the spending limit; and 2) the ineligible opponent raised or spent $250,000.

SENATE PROVISIONS

In general, the bill sought to prevent PACs from influencing federal elections but it also included provisions in case such a ban were declared unconstitutional, as many experts predict it would be.

• **PAC contributions to candidates banned.** PACs could no longer spend money to influence a federal election. This would repeal current law that allows individuals connected by ideology or other reasons to form a political committee and corporations, unions and trade associations to establish separate, segregated funds to contribute money to federal candidates.

• **Contributions to party committees.** PACs could continue to give money to party committees. A congressional campaign committee could accept PAC contributions up to an amount equal to 30 percent of what it would be allowed to spend on coordinated expenditures for its party's candidates. Coordinated expenditures were funds spent to purchase goods or services for candidates. A national party committee could accept no more than 2 cents multiplied by the voting-age population of the United States.

PACs could contribute $15,000 to a state party committee's federal account, up from $5,000.

• **Standby provision.** Because of concerns that both the PAC ban and the ban on collective giving by individuals (see bundling provision below) might be declared unconstitutional, the bill included two contingency provisions if the Supreme Court so ruled. 1) It would reduce PAC contributions to $1,000 (down from $5,000 in current law) and 2) It would set an aggregate limit on the amount of PAC contributions a candidate may accept.

The aggregate limit for a candidate would be either $825,000, or $375,000 plus 20 percent of the combined primary and general

HOUSE PROVISIONS

SENATE PROVISIONS

Contributions/ PACs (cont'd)

election limit, whichever is less.

• **Equal treatment.** The bill said it was the sense of the Senate that the same rules on PAC contributions would apply to Senate and House campaign committees.

• **Individual contributions to party committees.** Individuals would be permitted to contribute $20,000 to state party committees, up from $5,000.

Contributions to the federal account of a state party committee up to $5,000 would not count against the $25,000 aggregate limit on contributions to all candidates and committees.

Independent Expenditures

House:

The bill would define independent expenditures as spending for an advertisement or other communication that, taken as a whole, expresses support or opposition for a candidate and is made without the participation or cooperation of a candidate or campaign.

The measure would prohibit independent expenditure campaigns by: 1) party committees; 2) any political committee affiliated with an organization or person registered as a lobbyist, such as the American Medical Association or the National Rifle Association; and 3) a person who has communicated with a campaign or a representative of that campaign, such as a party committee, about any activity that influences the election.

The bill would require the reporting of independent expenditures of $1,000 or more in the last 20 days of an election to the Federal Election Commission (FEC) within 24 hours; and the reporting of any independent expenditure of $5,000 or more made before the last 20 days of an election. The FEC would in turn notify the candidates. In addition, any person who intended to spend more than $5,000 on independent expenditures in the last 20 days of the campaign would have to notify the FEC of the intent and name the candidates involved.

Senate:

The bill would define independent expenditures to preclude virtually all contact between a candidate and an organization or individuals running an independent expenditure campaign for or against the candidate's campaign.

The independent campaigner could not maintain a relationship with any political consultant who had a relationship with any of the candidates the independent campaigner is supporting or opposing.

An independent campaigner would have to inform a broadcaster of an intent to purchase broadcast time. The station in turn would have to inform the other candidates, who would be sold time to respond immediately afterward.

Political committees operated by organizations that lobby Congress would be barred from making independent expenditures. This provision is aimed at groups such as the National Association of Realtors and the American Medical Association.

A television ad run in an independent campaign would have to carry a notification of the sponsor of the ad, and the city and state of its headquarters. This notice would have to cover at least 25 percent of the viewing area of a television screen and run for the entire duration of the ad. Similar notices would have to be aired on radio or printed in newspaper ads.

'Bundling'

House:

When an organization or individual raised money for a candidate, usually from associates, members of an organization or employees, and then forwards the checks in a bundle to a candidate, it was known as "bundling." The individual or organization was known legally as a conduit or intermediary, and under current law had to disclose these activities only under limited circumstances. Bundling was a practice widely used by S&L operator Charles H. Keating Jr. to raise money for the Keating Five senators from his family and employees.

The bill would prohibit the following from serving as a conduit or intermediary: PACs connected to organizations, such as those associated with unions, corporations, trade assocations; party committees; a business, union, trade association or national bank. It provides for the following exceptions: a representative designated by the candidate; a professional fundraiser; volunteers hosting events in their homes. PACs without connected organizations could continue to function as conduits.

Senate:

When an organization or individual raised money for a candidate, generally from associates, members or employees, and then forwarded the checks in a bundle to the campaign it was known as "bundling." The individual or organization was known legally as a conduit or intermediary, and under current law had to disclose the activities only under limited circumstances. Bundling was a practice widely used by S&L operator Charles H. Keating Jr. to raise money for the Keating Five senators from his family and employees.

Contributions by an individual, if made through or arranged by an intermediary or conduit, would count against the intermediary's contribution limit if the intermediary was a political committee, an official of a political committee, a registered lobbyist, or an officer of a union, corporation or trade association acting in behalf of the organization. This was designed to prevent the bundling of contributions to a candidate or officeholder by interests that could benefit from legislation or other favors.

Executives of the same company or any other employer would be limited to aggregate contributions of $5,000 to a candidate and $20,000 to a party committee. This provision was aimed at blocking companies from replacing PACs with multiple individual contributions, but the bill does not say how it would be enforced.

Party Soft Money

House:

Soft money was the term used to describe money raised under state laws and then spent to influence federal elections. For instance, when a state party committee ran a phone bank or a get-out-the vote drive on Election Day, such "combined activities" assisted candidates for state and federal office. Because federal campaign finance laws were generally stricter than state laws, it was easier to raise large donations from wealthy interests under the state law. This often was done at the behest of federal candidates. In recent years, presidential campaigns in particular raised soft money to circumvent the restrictions on presidential campaign spending.

Senate:

Soft money was the term used to describe money raised under state laws and then spent to influence federal elections. For instance, when a state party committee ran a phone bank or a get-out-the vote drive on Election Day, such "combined activities" assisted candidates for state and federal office. Because federal campaign finance laws were generally stricter than state laws, it was easier to raise large donations from wealthy interests under the state law. This often was done at the behest of federal candidates. In recent years, presidential campaigns in particular raised soft money to circumvent the restrictions on presidential campaign spending.

Party Soft Money (Cont'd)

HOUSE PROVISIONS

In general, the bill would set overall limits on how much money could be spent on combined activities and then set a formula for how much of it must be raised under the federal system. Combined activities would include anything "in connection" with a federal and non-federal election, including but not limited to slate cards, sample ballots, voter registration, identification and Election Day turnout drives and fundraisers that benefit federal and state candidates.

• **Limits.** Parties could spend no more than $500,000 or 50 cents multiplied by the voting-age population, whichever is greater, on combined activities. (This would set limits of $500,000, in smaller states, to nearly $11 million in California.)

• **Allocation.** The bill loosely tracks an allocation system based on FEC rules developed after the 1988 elections. The allocation is as follows:

National party committees. In presidential years at least 65 percent of the cost of voter drives and administrative expenses would be paid from a federal account. In other years, the minimum would be 60 percent.

State and local party committees. In presidential years at least 50 percent of the cost of voter drives and administrative expenses would be paid from a federal account. In other years, the allocation would be determined by the number of federal and state candidates on the ballot, with a minimum of one-third to be paid from a federal account. The cost of slate cards, sample ballots and other communications with voters would be allocated according to the time or space given federal candidates, with a minimum of one-third to be paid from a federal account.

For all committees, fundraising costs would be allocated according to how much federal money is raised.

• **Mailings.** Campaign materials mailed by state and local parties tied to volunteer activities, slate cards or sample ballots, previously exempt from federal regulation, would lose this exemption.

• **Disclosure.** National party committees would have to disclose all of their fundraising and spending, regardless of whether it was for a federal election. Other political committees would have to disclose money raised or spent in connection with a federal election if they do not already.

SENATE PROVISIONS

In general, the bill would limit spending by state and federal party committees for electioneering during certain periods in years when federal candidates are on the ballot. Further, all of this money would be subject to federal law for spending, contributions and reporting.

• **Limits.** A state party's spending to elect the presidential ticket, including get-out-the-vote and voter registration activities, would be limited to 4 cents multiplied by the voting-age population of the state.

Any money raised or spent for get-out-the-vote or voter registration activity, beginning 60 days before the first federal primary, would be brought under federal limits and reporting rules.

Campaign activities conducted by federal or state party committees — even those that did not mention federal candidates specifically — would be subject to a maximum spending limit of 30 cents multiplied by the voting-age population.

A national committee could not solicit contributions that were not subject to the limits and reporting requirements of federal law in behalf of state parties.

• **Disclosure.** Money contributed for a party's building fund — i.e., for mortgage, equipment and other capital expenses — would not be subject to limits, only to disclosure.

Miscellaneous

HOUSE PROVISIONS

• **Leadership PACs.** Candidates would be barred from controlling any political committee other than their campaign committee, party committee or a joint fundraising committee.

• **Candidate fundraising.** A federal candidate would be barred from raising money for a tax-exempt organization if a significant portion of its mission was voter registration or get-out-the-vote campaigns.

• **Foreign nationals.** Foreign nationals would be prohibited from participating in or directing the election-related activities of others, such as telling them where they should give money or how to run a PAC. This was aimed at preventing foreign nationals from participating in U.S. elections in general and specifically through PACs affiliated with foreign-owned companies.

• **Candidate names.** Candidates would have to include their name in their campaign committee. Only authorized committees could use a candidate's name. Unauthorized committees would be barred from using a candidate's name in any fundraising context that would suggest that the committee was authorized.

• **Excess funds.** Candidates could not transfer more than $600,000 from one election cycle to another. When the new law took effect, any money in excess of $600,000 would be set aside in a separate account and could not be used for the candidate's own election activities.

• **Advertising disclosure.** Candidates would have to state clearly their responsibility for their campaign ads. The bill would set minimum standards for doing so in print ads, on radio and on television. For example, the candidate's image would have to appear on the television screen for four seconds.

• **Broadcast rates.** Broadcasters would have to sell advertising

SENATE PROVISIONS

• **Leadership PACs.** Candidates and officeholders would be barred from controlling any political committee other than their campaign committee or a party committee.

• **Candidate fundraising.** A federal candidate would be prohibited from raising money for a tax-exempt organization if a significant portion of its mission was voter registration or get-out-the-vote campaigns. A federal candidate or officeholder also would be prohibited from raising funds for other candidates or party committees, state or federal, unless the money was in amounts and from sources permitted by federal law. This was designed to prevent candidates from helping themselves by raising money for another committee that could in turn spend it in a fashion beneficial to the candidate.

• **Foreign nationals.** PACs would have to certify to the FEC that foreign nationals did not participate in their operations. This was aimed at preventing foreign nationals from participating in U.S. elections through PACs foreign-owned companies operated.

• **Transfers.** Party committees could no longer make unlimited transfers among each other for federal elections. Certain transfers would be subject to contribution limits.

• **Reporting requirements.** Individuals making contributions in excess of $10,000 would have to report that they had reached that figure and thereafter report every additional $5,000 increment.

Expenditures reported by candidates to political consultants would have to include the names and amounts paid to subcontractors.

• **Broadcast disclosures.** Candidates would have to state their approval of an ad, through an appearance on television, an audio

HOUSE PROVISIONS

Miscellaneous (Cont'd)

to candidates based on the lowest charge of the station for the same amount of time on the same date for any other advertiser. These lowest-unit rates would apply 45 days before the general election and 30 days before the primary.

- **Constitutional amendment.** The bill said it was the sense of Congress that an amendment to allow mandatory campaign spending limits be considered.
- **Ballot initiatives.** Committees that spend more than $1,000 for state initiatives that affect interstate commerce, federal elections, federal taxation or constitutional rights would have to register and report to the FEC. (This was primarily a response to term-limit ballot initiatives being funded by out-of-state interests.)
- **Government aircraft.** Candidates could not fly on government aircraft in connection with a federal election. This would bar the president from using Air Force One on campaign trips.

SENATE PROVISIONS

statement on radio or a written statement in print. Candidates who did not comply with the spending limit would have to say so in their ads.

- **Broadcast rates.** Broadcasters would have to sell advertising to candidates based on the lowest charge of the station for the same amount of time for the same period for any other advertiser. These lowest-unit rates would apply 45 days before the general election and 30 days before the primary. Eligible candidates would receive an additional 50 percent discount.
- **Broadcast access.** Broadcasters would have to sell time to every candidate in a race if they sold time to any candidate in the race.
- **Personal loans.** A candidate could not use contributions collected after an election to retire personal loans made to his campaign committee.
- **Franking.** Officeholders could not use their franking privilege to pay for mass mailings in an election year.
- **Debates.** Candidates for president and vice president whose campaigns take federal funds would have to debate before the general election.
- **Expedited review.** An appeal of any court ruling addressing the constitutionality of the act could be taken directly to the Supreme Court, which was directed to expedite its review.

Continued from p. 14

state-by-state spending limits for primary and general elections, with the general election limit ranging from $950,000 to $5.5 million, depending on a state's population. A candidate could break the limit by 25 percent, to the extent this extra money was raised from in-state residents in amounts of $100 or less.

As an incentive to agree to the limits, a candidate who made it to the general election would get public funds equal to 50 percent of a state's spending limit to buy broadcast time.

Other benefits would include postage discounts, a discount on broadcast advertising and public money to counter an opponent who broke the limit. Complying candidates would get additional public funds if their opponents broke the limit or if groups mounted independent campaigns to influence the election.

The central issue in the early rounds was how much the Democrats' approach would cost U.S. taxpayers. The TV and mail benefits alone could cost $64 million to $76 million every two years if every candidate participated. The cost would rise considerably if some candidates broke the limit because complying candidates would get an extra dose of public money to counter free-spending opponents. And those estimates did not include the cost of extending similar benefits to House candidates, which could exceed $200 million.

The bill did not specify how to raise the money, but its authors suggested a voluntary tax checkoff system similar to that used to finance presidential elections. Republicans pointed out that the presidential system seemed to be going broke, with only one in five taxpayers participating and its $1 checkoff generating only slightly more than $32 million a year in revenue.

The one amendment offered to the Boren bill in committee, by Mitch McConnell, R-Ky., sought to strip the measure's taxpayer financing. It failed on a 7-7 vote.

In three hearings before the vote, Republicans had focused attention on two cost questions — how much and who pays — that provided a preview of how they planned to attack the bill on the floor.

Democrats generally shied away from the cost issue, but when it arose they contended that the price paled beside the cost of doing business under a financial system that produced the Keating Five scandal.

"Every one of us can be subject to these kinds of charges so long as we depend on raising large sums of money from high-dollar [sources] and political action committees," John Kerry, D-Mass., told the committee. "The best way of moving this institution beyond these kinds of problems is to create a system of voluntary public funding."

The Democrats also noted that the tax system was used to subsidize congressional campaigns from 1972 to 1986, when tax credits and deductions were used to encourage small donations. The last such incentive — a 50 percent credit for donations of $50 or less — was killed by the 1986 tax code revision.

The credit cost the Treasury $214 million in 1985, according to the Internal Revenue Service. Bill Bradley, D-N.J., said the price of public financing would "be a more troubling question if the cost weren't so low compared with the more than $200 million that we used to spend" annually for the tax credit.

Senate Floor Action

After seven days on the floor and more than two dozen amendments, many of them Republican land mines, Senate Democrats pushed their vision of campaign finance reform to passage May 23 on a 56-42 vote on S 3. *(Vote 85, p. 12-S)*

But the bill's obstacles were reinforced May 22, when Bush reiterated previous promises to veto any legislation that limited campaign spending or resorted to taxpayer financing of congressional elections, the two tenets of the Democratic bill. Bush also said he would oppose separate rules for House and Senate campaigns.

Senators added to the bill a ban on their keeping honoraria payments by a 72-24 vote, but two months later that issue migrated to the legislative branch appropriations bill, where it was settled as part of a pay hike for senators. *(Senate pay, p. 22)*

Five members of each party crossed over to the other side. Democrats voting against the bill were Quentin N. Burdick of North Dakota and four Southern Democrats: John B. Breaux of Louisiana, J. Bennett Johnston of Louisiana, Ernest F. Hollings of South Carolina and Richard C. Shelby of Alabama. Republicans voting for the bill were John McCain of Arizona, Dave Durenberger of Minnesota, William S. Cohen of Maine, James M. Jeffords of Vermont and Larry Pressler of South Dakota.

On the floor, Republicans sought to undercut spending limits, calling them a device that would hamstring challengers who needed to outspend an incumbent to win. Moreover, they argued that the bill's benefits were a hammer held over the heads of candidates to coerce them into giving up the right to spend freely in campaigns.

But with Democrats solid on the need for spending limits, the Republicans zeroed in on the more vulnerable target of public financing. They belittled it as "food stamps for politicians" and questioned the willingness of taxpayers to expand the program.

"If we extend that to 535 additional races, every crackpot who got up in the morning and looked in the mirror and said, 'Gee, I think I see a congressman' is going to be able to reach into the federal cookie jar and get some of those tax dollars," said McConnell, the GOP floor leader for the bill.

Going into the floor debate, the Democrats had displayed some weakness on the issue by reducing the amount of public financing to be offered candidates to purchase television time.

The Republicans set up an obstacle course of amendments to test the Democrats' mettle on public financing.

In early action, Republicans plumbed the public financing issue with several ploys. McConnell tried to add a disclaimer to television advertisements purchased with public funds that would read: "The preceding political advertisement was paid for with taxpayer funds." The amendment was killed by a 54-44 vote to table it. *(Vote 70, p. 10-S)*

Republican Hank Brown of Colorado sought to limit any winning Senate candidate who accepted public financing to two terms in office. This prompted Mitchell to invite Brown to take the two-term pledge on the Senate floor, citing such public subsidies as the franking privilege that accrued to an incumbent's benefit. Brown declined, although he offered to make the pledge if Mitchell would accept the amendment. He did not, and the amendment was killed by a 68-30 tabling vote. *(Vote 69, p. 10-S)*

The first key vote was an amendment offered by McConnell to strip the bill of public financing and spending limits.

Both parties made it a test of loyalty, and the amendment failed 42-56 on a straight party-line vote that set the tone for the remainder of the action. *(Vote 68, p. 10-S)*

Republicans met with similar outcomes on attempts to kill public financing but leave the spending limits intact; to strip party presidential nominating conventions of public financing; and to strip presidential campaigns of public financing. The latter amendment, which failed on a 60-38 vote, came in response to Democratic counterpunching on the public financing issue. *(Vote 73, p. 11-S)*

Democrats noted that Republican presidential candidates continually accepted taxpayer financing, to the tune of $250 million since 1976, and the GOP had taken $32.2 million to run its nominating conventions, according to Federal Election Commission figures cited by Bradley. Bush checked off the box on his tax return to designate $1 for the presidential campaign fund and accepted more than $60 million in tax funds for his 1980 and 1988 presidential campaigns.

Democrats who disliked the public financing for broadcast advertising kept leaders in the dark for days about whether they would offer an amendment to strip it.

In the end, they settled for an amendment by Jim Exon, D-Neb., added to the bill May 23, that said broadcasting benefits would be paid for by voluntary tax checkoffs or by eliminating tax breaks that corporations could get for lobbying.

Democrats who favored more public financing fared no better than Republicans who opposed any. An amendment offered by Kerry to extend public financing to cover the cost of 90 percent of a general election campaign went down on a 39-58 vote. *(Vote 74, p. 11-S)*

The Senate also:

- Accepted, by voice vote, an amendment by Paul Wellstone, D-Minn., to prohibit a candidate who agreed to spending limits from spending more than $25,000 of his own money.
- Agreed 57-40 to table and thus kill a Dole amendment to let parties give $250,000 in seed money to candidates who challenged Senate incumbents. *(Vote 80, p. 11-S)*
- Agreed to table and thus kill, by a 54-44 vote, an amendment by Don Nickles, R-Okla., to eliminate the 50 percent discount on advertising rates that participating candidates would receive. *(Vote 78, p. 11-S)*
- Accepted, by voice vote, a McConnell amendment providing for a direct appeal to the Supreme Court of cases challenging the constitutionality of the act.
- Agreed to table and thus kill, by a 79-19 vote, an amendment by William V. Roth Jr., R-Del., to strike the spending limits and public financing from the bill and offer candidates free television time during the last 45 days of the campaign. *(Vote 77, p. 11-S)*

HOUSE ACTION

The House bill was written by a task force of the House Administration Committee chaired by Sam Gejdenson, D-Conn. He took over as House Democrats' point man on the issue for Al Swift, D-Wash. Swift had led the effort for several years as chairman of the Subcommittee on Elections but stepped back from the issue, although not the subcommittee post, in the 102nd Congress to take the chairmanship of an important Energy and Commerce panel, the Subcommittee on Transportation and Hazardous Materials.

Three Republicans were named to the task force, but they were outvoted by the five loyal Democrats, who included Majority Whip William H. Gray III, Budget Committee Chairman Leon E. Panetta of California, and Rules Committee member Martin Frost of Texas.

The task force discussed the bill widely with Democrats before introducing it, and gave a full preview at a Democratic Caucus meeting Oct. 9.

That meeting renewed reluctance among Democrats to support public financing, and led to efforts to change the bill before it went to the floor.

The provision in question would give up to $200,000 in public financing to match the first $200 of each individual contribution. The bill's sponsors estimated that this would cost $75 million every two years, a figure that would rise with inflation.

"I'm very skeptical we can get the votes for public financing," said task force member Frost. "A lot of us are concerned that because of the criticism Congress is getting for perks, passing legislation that would entitle all of us to $200,000 of federal funds would fuel the criticism."

Looming ominously over the bill's prospects was the 1990 vote in which the House rejected an amendment to provide candidates with up to $100,000 in public financing. Democrats from Southern and border states had voted 64-12 against the amendment.

A group of 46 Democrats led by Glen Browder, D-Ala., under the aegis of the Conservative Democratic Forum, asked the House Administration Committee to kill public financing and instead offer 100 percent tax credits for contributions of $50 or less. Browder acknowledged that tax credits were another form of public financing, but he contended that they were more politically palatable than public matching funds as a way to encourage small contributions.

While public financing was the most controversial feature, there were also objections to the proposed $200,000 limit on PAC contributions. Democratic incumbents from rural and inner-city districts that lacked wealthy Democratic donors said they feared the loss of PACs.

Some prominent House Democrats — including David R. Obey of Wisconsin and Swift of Washington — argued that the image of PACs should be less that of favor-seeking special interests than something resembling the political equivalent of the United Way: thousands of small donors giving part of each paycheck to match the clout of the fat cats.

Democratic leaders formally unveiled the task force's handiwork on Nov. 12.

Majority Leader Richard A. Gephardt, D-Mo., framed the legislation as a strike against special interests and the skyrocketing cost of campaigns.

"We declare ourselves strongly in favor of change and strongly in favor of opening campaigns and elections — not just to special interests but to everyone," Gephardt said.

To provide political cover for members anxious about public financing, Gejdenson adopted the same approach the Senate used: the bill did not actually raise the money, leaving that to a separate tax bill.

Instead, it merely suggested that the money should be raised by limiting the tax deduction organizations took for lobbying, an effort to make special interests bear the cost.

The bill received lukewarm but politically essential endorsements from outside lobbies pressing for change, including Common Cause, Public Citizen and the League of Women Voters.

Party-Line Committee Vote

The House Administration Committee approved HR 3750 on Nov. 14 on a 14-9 party-line vote.

The committee defeated a series of Republican amendments on party-line votes. One by Bill Thomas of California, the committee's ranking Republican, would have:

- Required that a majority of individual contributions come from residents of the congressional district;
- Cut the amount a single PAC could give candidates from $5,000 to $1,000, the same amount individuals were permitted to give; and
- Required that any money spent to influence a federal election be raised under federal law, eliminating so-called soft money.

House Floor Action

After nearly five hours of sharply partisan debate, the House passed the bill 273-156 on Nov. 25, with 21 Republicans voting yes and 12 Democrats voting no. *(Vote 427, p. 104-H)*

Democratic leaders won passage of the bill only after further backpedaling on the public financing issue to appease Southern conservatives.

In the days before the measure came to the floor, both Charlie Rose, D-N.C., the chairman of the House Administration Committee, and Gejdenson acknowledged that the opposition to using tax revenues for matching funds was costing Democrats the votes they needed to ensure passage of the bill. The duo cut a deal Nov. 22 with conservatives led by Browder, Charles W. Stenholm, D-Texas, and Liz J. Patterson, D-S.C., who feared that voters would be even more outraged at a bill with taxpayer financing of campaigns than at no bill at all.

Although the measure approved by the House Administration Committee left it to a future tax bill to actually raise the money, the legislation had at least suggested a course of action. Democratic leaders changed the bill to dodge the issue of where the money would come from. The version that went to the floor provided only for voluntary contributions to an account called the Make Democracy Work Fund.

No one held out the hope that the public would rush forward with the hundreds of millions of dollars required for both House and Senate campaigns.

Conservatives also fought for, and won, language in the bill requiring "incentives for individuals to make voluntary contributions to the candidate of their choice" — code wording for tax credits.

The rewrite allowed a parade of Southerners to come to the floor and state, as W. J. "Billy" Tauzin, D-La., did, "There is no taxpayer financing in the bill anymore."

The concession made it easier for Southerners to vote yes. Democrats from Southern and border states supported the bill 75-8. The changes didn't deter Republicans from attacking Democrats. "Who are you kidding?" asked Thomas, the Republican floor manager for the bill. "You are now gumming a political lollipop."

The Republican substitute for the Democratic bill, offered by Thomas and Robert H. Michel of Illinois, the minority leader, was rejected 165-265. It would have required candidates to raise at least half of all their campaign money from people living in their districts. It also would have cut the amount a single PAC could give a candidate from $5,000 per election to $1,000. *(Vote 425, p. 104-H)*

Claiming Victory

Comments after the floor action reflected the positions the parties would take to conference in 1992. Speaker Thomas S. Foley, D-Wash., called passage of the bill "one of the great achievements" of the House in the first session. The Republican administration's Office of Management and Budget issued a statement saying the Democratic bill "would result in nothing more than a taxpayer-financed incumbent protection plan."

Ardent backers of public financing, such as Public Citizen, said the change of language only hid the obvious; they praised the House for its first vote ever in favor of putting public funds to work in House campaigns.

"Some in Congress, shrinking from their vote, say this isn't a public financing bill," Public Citizen President Joan Claybrook said. "This was a vote for public financing, plain and simple."

Fred Wertheimer, president of Common Cause, said, "This is a big breakthrough, recognizing that there are key fights ahead." He called the matching funds a "system that would be especially helpful to challengers, who are currently starved for resources."

At the end of the session, Democratic leaders talked of putting the bill on the president's desk early in the new year, when Bush would be receiving public funding for his presidential campaign. But that strategy faded as economic proposals to combat the recession took center stage. ■

Senate Ended Honoraria, Voted 23% Raise

The Senate gave itself a 23 percent pay raise and stopped its members from keeping speaking fees and honoraria as it brought its pay in line with the House and its limits on outside income in line with the rest of the federal government.

The Senate action marked the end of a 15-year drive to stop lawmakers from pocketing speaking fees from special interest groups, a practice that had become increasingly controversial. The House in 1989 had prohibited its members from keeping honoraria, effective at the start of 1991. *(1989 Almanac, p. 51)*

The pay and honoraria provisions became law as part of the legislative appropriations bill (HR 2506 — PL 102-90). So did changes in rules governing members' acceptance of gifts that eliminated differences between the two chambers — and eased the rules in significant respects. The pay provisions took effect upon enactment; President Bush signed the bill Aug. 14. *(Appropriations, p. 544)*

There was no widespread public furor, as had greeted two 1989 attempts to raise senators' pay, largely because Senate leaders struck quickly. The key move came July 17, when with no advance public notice, Senate Appropriations Committee Chairman Robert C. Byrd, D-W.Va., offered the pay-honoraria proposal as an amendment to the legislative appropriations bill. With relatively little debate, the Senate voted 53-45 to approve it. *(Vote 133, p. 18-S)*

The Senate took no further recorded votes on the bill; final passage on July 17 and clearance of the conference report on Aug. 2 occurred by voice votes.

House leaders ushered the bill to the floor in a well-orchestrated move designed to prevent a roll-call vote. A few back-bench Republicans tried to force a vote, but the leaders thwarted them by having the chamber — usually almost vacant during debates — packed with 225 loyalists. When Republican freshman Rick Santorum, Pa., requested a recorded vote, only three colleagues supported his request — far less than the required 44.

Pay Raise History

Effective date	Salary	Percent Change
March 1789	$ 1,500*	
March 1817	2,000*	33
December 1855	3,000	50
December 1865	5,000	67
March 1871	7,500	50
January 1874	5,000	−33
March 1907	7,500	50
March 1925	10,000	33
July 1932	9,000	−10
April 1933	8,500	−6
February 1934	9,000	6
July 1934	9,500	6
April 1935	10,000	5
January 1947	12,500	25
March 1955	22,500	80
January 1965	30,000	33
March 1969	42,500	42
October 1975	44,600	5
March 1977	57,500	29
October 1979	60,663	6
December 1982		
Senate	60,663	
House	69,800	15
July 1983		
Senate	69,800	15
House	69,800	
January 1984	72,600	4
January 1985	75,100	4
January 1987	77,400	3
March 1987	89,500	16
February 1990		
Senate	98,400	10
House	96,600	8
January 1991		
Senate	101,900	3.6
House	125,100	29.5
August 1991		
Senate	125,100	22.8
House	125,100	—

* *Per diem rates converted to annual rates, based on full attendance at a 250-day session.*

SOURCES: Congressional Research Service; House Sergeant-at-Arms; Senate Disbursing Office

A Political Liability

Throughout Congress' history, efforts to raise members' salaries usually touched a raw nerve with the American public. Congress' first pay raise, in 1816, had to be repealed after many members were driven from office by public outcry. *(History of pay raises, 1989 Almanac, p. 58)*

For years, members of Congress without independent wealth had two principal sources of income: salaries from the taxpayers and speaking fees from private interests. Both forms of income were chronic sources of political headaches for incumbents.

The widespread practice of making speeches for honoraria was assailed as, at best, a source of distraction from the business of government and, at worst, as a form of legalized bribery. Reformers argued against honoraria on the grounds that public servants should be paid only with public dollars.

In 1975, a new campaign finance law for the first time limited the amount of honoraria income members could collect in one appearance and keep annually.

A spate of congressional scandals in the late 1980s — including the ethics investigations of House Speaker Jim Wright of Texas and the so-called Keating Five in the Senate — gave new impetus to proposals to curb outside income. Even though honoraria were not central to those scandals, abolition of the payments seemed a relatively simple way for Congress to do something to clean its own house.

History showed that backsliding on these matters was not out of the question: Senators repealed the cap on annual honoraria earnings in 1981 — after only six years in place — although it was restored in 1983. *(1981 Almanac p. 286; 1983 Almanac, p. 514)*

But in the wake of their 1991 action, senators expressed confidence that honoraria were gone for good. "We're never going to go back to that," said Assistant Minority Leader Alan K. Simpson, R-Wyo.

The cost of living increases, pegged to annual inflation figures, were to take effect unless Congress voted to block them. Senators expressed hope that their salaries in the future would stay out of the spotlight.

"In my 17 years in Congress, we've had a big struggle every two or three years over the pay thing," said Larry Pressler, R-S.D., one of the Senate's most persistent critics of congressional pay raises. "Now, I think the issue will subside."

However, it remained possible — as it had previously — for members to spotlight the issue by pushing amendments to block future increases. Some members were skeptical that their colleagues would resist that political temptation for long.

Said Sen. Wendell H. Ford, D-Ky., "I don't think you can change 200 years of history."

But Rep. Vic Fazio, a California Democrat who championed pay raises in the past, remained hopeful. "I would like to think this could be the last chapter of a book, maybe even the epilogue."

Guarding against voter backlash, all but eight of the 34 senators expected to run for re-election in 1992 voted against the pay raise.

Charles S. Robb of Virginia, chairman of the Democratic Senatorial Campaign Committee, voted for the plan and said he would not encourage Democratic challengers to use the pay raise issue against Republican incumbents. Nonetheless, he said, "Plenty of people are going to use it."

Senate Strategy

Senators gave most of the credit for the swift pay raise to Byrd, who often seemed even more powerful since he stepped down as majority leader three years before and began overseeing the federal budget as chairman of the Appropriations Committee.

A year and a half after a presidential endorsement and the best efforts of the Senate's Democratic and Republican leaders failed to produce the votes needed to approve a big raise for the Senate, Byrd almost single-handedly delivered the necessary votes and did so in a month's time.

He had powerful forces on his side.

The Republicans had their share of the votes lined up in 1989, and they just about had them in hand again in mid-June when Byrd first started working the issue. Pressure was mounting to end senators' unsavory-looking practice of collecting hefty speaking fees from interest groups seeking to influence them. Rank-and-file senators were growing more indignant by the day over House members' higher salaries — $23,200 more than senators' $101,900 since Jan. 1.

And then there was the supreme embarrassment: a list published July 1 in Capitol Hill's twice-weekly newspaper, Roll Call, of 81 House aides — some rather obscure — who earned more than senators.

"That wore away the rest of the opposition," said Simpson.

1989: Senators Bail Out

The stage was set much earlier for the July 17 vote. After a yearlong struggle, the House had crafted and approved on Nov. 17, 1989, a pay-and-ethics-reform package that included a 25 percent raise and a ban on keeping honoraria for both chambers.

Senate Democrats were unable to uphold their end of a bargain: Leaders of both parties had agreed that each would produce a majority for the package so neither could be blamed alone. Republican leader Bob Dole of Kansas had his majority, but Majority Leader George J. Mitchell of Maine fell short by perhaps a half dozen votes.

With a total of only about 46 votes between the two sides, the leaders retreated. The Senate voted 56-43 to exempt itself from the House plan and to approve a more modest 10 percent raise for itself with a multi-year phase-out of honoraria. (Both chambers approved automatic annual cost of living raises of up to 5 percent.)

The pay issue was largely dormant in 1990, but it resurfaced Jan. 1, 1991, when the 1989 law produced salary discrepancies: $125,100 for House members, $101,900 for senators. While the two chambers in the past had disparities in salary, this was by far the largest.

Senators were eligible to keep $23,068 in speaking fees in 1991 (although at least 40 had publicly given up doing so), putting their potential Senate-related income only $132 below House members. But criticism of the honoraria system never abated.

Sen. Christopher J. Dodd, D-Conn., twice successfully sponsored amendments to bar senators from keeping speech fees. In 1990, the Senate approved one 77-23, and a similar amendment was approved May 21, 1991, by 72-24, but both were attached to campaign finance bills that were unlikely to become law. After the first 1991 vote, editorial writers and Common Cause, a citizens' lobbying organization, urged the Senate to get more serious about the issue.

The legislative branch spending bill provided an obvious vehicle for such a move. Senators quickly realized that a ban on honoraria would force them to confront the pay issue because more than half of them supplemented their pay with speaking fees, and they were not likely to accept quietly what in effect would be an 18 percent pay cut.

Dole said publicly that Republicans could produce their share of the votes and wanted a vote before the August recess. Word leaked that Democratic Whip Ford of Kentucky was counting noses for Mitchell.

A little-noticed side effect of the 1989 law sealed the issue's fate when it became widely known.

Because top aides' pay was pegged somewhat below members' in both chambers, the Jan. 1 House pay raise allowed the salaries of scores of its staff members to zoom past the salaries of most senators. For instance, the staff director of the House District of Columbia Committee began making $115,092, according to Roll Call's July 1 list.

Worried that Senate staff would flee to the House, Byrd and Ted Stevens, R-Alaska, attached a rider to the legislative appropriations bill authorizing raises for top Senate aides and barring them from pocketing honoraria.

Though Byrd insists he had no ulterior motive, the effect was immediate: Senators realized some of their own employees soon would make more than their bosses, and senators would be virtually the only federal employees still allowed to keep speaking fees.

Byrd Stalks the Votes

After Byrd's committee approved the spending bill June 12, things moved quickly.

The next week, Byrd got word that plans were afoot to offer the honoraria ban to the legislative branch bill when it hit the floor. Dodd was undecided, but Patrick J. Leahy, D-Vt., said if nobody else did, he probably would. Byrd said in an interview that he decided about June 20 to take the lead.

Byrd told Mitchell that he would gather votes for a simultaneous pay-raise/honoraria-ban amendment and asked him to hold up the legislative appropriations bill until he either got the votes or was sure he could not do it.

Ford, who opposed the pay raise, handed his whip count of Democrats over to Byrd. According to Byrd, the tally was 22-31 against — 16 yes, six leaning yes, 29 no and two leaning no, with four unknown. That left Byrd about where Mitchell was in 1989 — about a half-dozen votes shy of a majority of Democrats.

Byrd set two goals for himself: a majority of Democrats voting yes and an overall margin of victory of more than one. He said he did not want a pro-raise senator to have to deal with an opponent saying, "If you hadn't voted for it, it wouldn't have passed."

Stevens took the lead on shoring up Republican votes, and Byrd worked that side of the aisle, too. He said he spoke with nearly 90 members, some of them two or three times, just to make sure.

A key challenge for Byrd was convincing the Senate's wealthier members. In 1989, Mitchell failed to persuade many of the millionaires to back the bigger raise, but Byrd's job was somewhat easier on this score. Several wealthy members — John D. Rockefeller IV, D-W.Va.; John W. Warner, R-Va.; and Claiborne Pell, D-R.I. — were especially skittish in 1990 because they were up for re-election.

"I urged them to vote for this so I wouldn't have to count on senators that would have to run next year," Byrd said. Though Byrd approached many of the 34 members expected to run for re-election in 1992, they all got a pass without too much pressure. In the end, only eight agreed to vote for the raise.

The two Virginia senators and Rockefeller told Byrd a day or two before the vote that they were on board. John C. Danforth, R-Mo., another wealthy member, and Pell reversed themselves to support the raise.

Not all wealthy members were persuaded. Harry Reid, D-Nev.; Herb Kohl, D-Wis.; Dennis DeConcini, D-Ariz; and Frank R. Lautenberg, D-N.J., all voted no.

Countdown to Action

Byrd's count reached 52 on July 17. He told Mitchell he was ready to go. The spending bill for veterans, housing and science programs was already on the floor. Mitchell abruptly pulled the VA-HUD bill shortly after 7 p.m. and called up the legislative bill.

For an hour, there was no official acknowledgment that a pay-raise vote was imminent — thereby assuring that the matter would not make the evening network news.

Few reporters were left in the Capitol when Reid, who chaired the Appropriations subcommittee in charge of the legislative branch bill, began a 50-minute, in-depth description of his $2.3 billion bill.

Byrd rose on the floor at 8:15 p.m. and announced that he was offering an amendment to raise Senate salaries, ban honoraria and limit members' outside earned income (as opposed to investment income) to 15 percent of their salary.

For 35 minutes, Byrd spoke in favor of his proposal, telling his colleagues that it was needed to protect the image of a great institution.

Stevens spoke next, defending honoraria but conceding that the practice's day had come and gone. Four other members spoke in favor of Byrd's proposal.

The opponents stayed mostly silent. Three spoke: Paul Wellstone, D-Minn.; Charles E. Grassley, R-Iowa; and Reid, who quickly came to the point: "I have learned that when I do not have the votes, the best thing to do is sit down and shut up," he said. "And so that is what I will do."

He did, and then the vote began, at 9:30 p.m.

The final tally was produced by a one-vote margin of Democrats (28-27) and a wider margin of Republicans (25-18). David Pryor, D-Ark., a past pay-raise opponent who was recovering from a heart attack, in effect gave Byrd half a vote by allowing himself to be "paired" with Ford, whose no vote was therefore not counted.

Gift Rules

The proposal to revise the gift rules arose late in the House-Senate conference on the legislative appropriations bill, and it received little notice or comment on the floor.

The new rules allowed senators, representatives and their employees to accept from anyone more-expensive gifts (worth up to $250) than existing rules, and an unlimited number of lesser gifts (worth $100 or less). The rules also eliminated almost all of the requirements for publicly disclosing gifts. And the limits on the value of allowable gifts and those that had to be disclosed would be pegged to inflation so that in later years they would increase automatically.

The new rules brought protests from officials at Common Cause, which successfully lobbied in 1989 for tightened gift rules. "To start weakening and walking away from ethics reforms 18 months later is an act of bad faith and totally unjustified and just plain wrong," said Fred Wertheimer, president of Common Cause. "There is absolutely no justification for the kind of ripping off that's going on here."

Members of both chambers had complained that the rules for accepting gifts and reporting them on annual financial disclosure forms were confusing, particularly because the rules were different for each chamber.

The rules were toughened in 1989 as part of the same ethics law that boosted House members' pay and banned them from pocketing honoraria. Efforts then to make the rules uniform failed when the Senate refused to go along with a House proposal because senators considered it too strict.

In 1989, the House barred its members from accepting gifts totaling more than $200 a year from anyone but relatives. That was an increase from $100, but the previous cap only applied to givers with a "direct interest in legislation," a vaguely defined term under House rules. House members also moved to raise the $200 limit automatically every three years to account for inflation. Senators considered the House threshold too low and set the total for the Senate at $300 annually. But they retained an existing rule barring members from accepting gifts worth more than $100 from anyone with a direct interest in legislation — a term defined more narrowly in Senate rules to generally include only people and organizations with ties to registered lobbyists or political action committees. Both chambers decided that gifts worth less than $75 did not have to be counted toward those limits, up from $50 in the House and $35 in the Senate. And both retained governmentwide financial-disclosure requirements with some changes: Members and other officials were required to report who gave them $100 or more in gifts worth over $75 each. The reporting threshold for travel and entertainment-related gifts was higher: $250.

All that changed under the last-minute deal engineered by Fazio, chairman of the Appropriations subcommittee in charge of the spending bill, and Reid, his Senate counterpart.

The new rules allowed members to accept up to $250 worth of gifts annually from anyone (up from $200 in the House and up from $100 under the Senate's provision on gifts from people with legislative interests). Members would not have to count gifts worth $100 or less (up from $75).

And all federal officials would only have to disclose who gave them more than $250 in gifts (up from $100) worth over $100 each (up from $75). The separate category for reporting travel and entertainment-related gifts was eliminated.

All of the new thresholds were set to rise automatically

every three years to account for inflation.

The disclosure changes meant that members of Congress and their employees were required to report only gifts they were not allowed to accept or gifts for which they had received waivers.

"If you got a gift that's legal, you don't have to report it," said Fazio.

Reporters regularly perused members' disclosure forms and publicized gifts, an embarrassing annual event for some members.

"A lot of things that used to titillate people will no longer be reported," Fazio told reporters. "We saw it as a cumbersome and unnecessary requirement.... There's no question it is somewhat looser, but it's not big enough to drive a truck through."

Common Cause disagreed.

"You can accept $100 a day from a person or $100 a week — there's no limit," said Wertheimer, referring to the provision that gifts of $100 or less would not count toward the $250 limit. Wertheimer conceded that such behavior would run afoul of the rules if the member were found to be merely evading the limits. But he asked, "Who's going to enforce it, based on what information, since there's no disclosure?"

The new rules for Congress conflicted with the approach taken by the Office of Government Ethics. Relying on the 1989 ethics law, the agency July 23 proposed much stricter limits, which were still pending at the end of the year.

They would prohibit all executive branch employees (except the president and vice president) from accepting anything but the smallest gifts from almost anyone with any interest in the work of the employee's agency. Generally, gifts worth less than $25 would be allowed, but only if one source did not give more than $100 worth a year, with even the smallest gifts counting toward the total.

And even this exemption was limited, the agency said, because "the acceptance of gifts on a recurring or frequent basis, whether from the same or different sources, gives rise to an appearance of use of public office for private gain."

The 1991 Windfall

The law allowed many senators a one-time income windfall of up to about $9,000 for 1991, in addition to the raise.

In the House-Senate conference committee, negotiators decided it would be unfair to require senators to forfeit speaking fees accepted before the bill was signed. So they agreed to let senators keep the full $23,068 allowed by law for the year.

Because the bill was signed Aug. 14, senators' government pay totaled about $111,000 for the year. Members who kept the maximum amount of honoraria took home about $134,000 — roughly $9,000 more than House members made in 1991. Judging from the previous year's financial disclosure reports, a significant number of senators could take advantage of the loophole. By Aug. 1, 1990, 29 senators had collected more than $23,068 and another seven were within two $2,000 speeches of that figure.

The Senate had to pay a price for House approval of its pay raise — acceptance of a provision barring senators from accepting stipends for regular radio shows beginning in 1992.

Two pairs of senators participated in regular staged radio debates: Simpson vs. Edward M. Kennedy, D-Mass., which aired five days a week; and Richard G. Lugar, R-Ind., vs. Tom Daschle, D-S.D., which aired 65 times a year, according to an Associated Press story about the practice. All but Kennedy, who declined compensation, were paid about $100 a show, the story said.

"We want a level playing field," said Fazio.

The House Committee on Standards of Official Conduct ruled earlier in 1991 that such stipends were prohibited under the House speaking-fee ban. But the Senate Ethics Committee in 1988 had decided that stipends were not honoraria and therefore were not covered by limits on speaking fees.

An effort by Senate Majority Leader Mitchell to raise the pay for the majority and minority leaders in both chambers and for the Senate president pro tempore was abandoned. All five members' salaries were set at $138,900; Mitchell wanted something closer to the House Speaker's $160,600 but reportedly gave up on the idea after House leaders refused to agree.

House members successfully insisted that the Senate bar its members from deriving any tax benefits from honoraria donated to charity. The tax code already blocked such benefits for House members.

Senate GOP leader Dole tried at the last minute in the conference to eliminate a $2,000-a-speech limit on honoraria that members can have donated to charity in their names, but he relented in the rush to recess.

Dole said he thought Senate rules should allow members to charge interest groups more than $2,000 for a speech, so long as it was donated to charity.

Dole's office said he had given $700,000 in honoraria to charities over the years. In 1990, he reported directing $47,700 to charities, churches and colleges, most in Kansas.

House conferees refused to go along with Dole's proposal. ■

Cranston Reprimanded by Senate Ethics

One of the most divisive ethics cases in the history of the Senate came to a novel close Nov. 20 after two years of dispute. The Senate Ethics Committee invented a new punishment to reprove Alan Cranston, D-Calif., for his conduct in the Keating Five case. Almost nine months earlier, the committee issued milder rebukes to the other four senators — Democrats John Glenn of Ohio, Donald W. Riegle Jr. of Michigan and Dennis DeConcini of Arizona, and Republican John McCain of Arizona.

The committee in effect left judgment on the highly publicized Keating affair up to the voters — except in the case of Cranston, who announced shortly before the hearings began in late 1990 that he would retire at the end of his term in 1992 because of health problems. McCain's and Glenn's terms expired in 1992; Riegle and DeConcini were scheduled to face the voters in 1994. *(1990 Almanac, p. 78)*

The Ethics Committee opened hearings into the case in November 1990; the senators and their attorneys presented their rebuttals in January 1992. The committee issued its preliminary conclusions on Feb. 27, when it chastened McCain, Glenn, Riegle and DeConcini for poor judgment in their dealings with thrift operator Charles H. Keating Jr. Riegle and DeConcini were also criticized for creating the appearance of acting improperly, and the panel chided DeConcini for being inappropriately aggressive with banking regulators. But it instituted formal proceedings only against Cranston, finding "substantial credible evidence" that he had broken Senate rules.

After months of acrimonious and often partisan internal debate, the committee concluded that Cranston had gone too far, branding the senator's conduct "improper and repugnant." But although the committee in February had signaled that it would urge the full Senate to sanction Cranston, it backed away from traditional procedures. In order to break an internal stalemate, the panel created a new form of punishment halfway between a committee rebuke and a full-Senate censure. While taking the matter to the floor, there was no vote or formal action by the full body; instead, Ethics leaders told the assembled Senate that the panel itself was reprimanding Cranston for "an impermissible pattern of conduct in which fundraising and official activities were substantially linked." *(Sanction, p. 29)*

The 95 senators who somberly gathered to watch Cranston get scolded ended up getting scolded themselves by the defendant. Cranston apologized for making the Senate look bad and then implied that some of his colleagues looked worse. He expressed sorrow that some people thought he acted improperly but said he had not. He accepted the Ethics Committee's reprimand but rejected its basis.

"My behavior did not violate established norms," he told his colleagues. "Here, but for the grace of God, stand you."

But when Cranston was done, Ethics Committee Vice Chairman Warren B. Rudman, R-N.H., rose to address the chamber in a visible rage. "After accepting this committee's recommendation, what I have heard is a statement I can only describe as arrogant, unrepentant and a smear on this institution. Everybody does not do it."

"I stand by my remarks," Cranston replied. "I have not violated the norms of this body."

Members looking for retribution were left unsatisfied because the Ethics Committee had entered into an unprecedented plea bargain with the ailing 77-year-old liberal stalwart: In return for not facing formal Senate action — and a likely divisive floor vote — Cranston would formally accept the reprimand. But that left Cranston free to defend himself in strong terms.

"The committee whitewashed him, and he tarred us," complained Malcolm Wallop, R-Wyo., after the proceedings.

A handful of similarly minded Republicans considered trying to force a vote by the full Senate to censure Cranston, though they were somewhat appeased by Rudman's blistering rebuttal of Cranston's defense, and nothing came of the talk in the remaining week of the first session.

Members looking for lessons likely also were unsatisfied because, in the end, the Senate's ethics watchdogs announced that they could not define improper conduct, but, as with pornography, they knew it when they saw it.

"Not all standards offer the opportunity to arrive at easy judgments through the mechanical application of a fixed formula," said Ethics Chairman Howell Heflin, D-Ala., who told members that Supreme Court Justice Potter Stewart's oft-borrowed pornography standard applied to their behavior.

That troubled many senators because the case raised a fundamental question: When does the relationship between members' two most time-consuming tasks — helping constituents and raising money — become improper and unethical?

As for the rest of the Senate, the committee only offered somewhat more expansive guidance than it had in the past. Its advice came down to this: Be careful out there.

"The resolution we bring before the Senate today," said Rudman, "is not a perfect solution; it is, however, for this institution an acceptable result, and it certainly is better than no resolution at all."

BACKGROUND

The Keating Five case dated back to 1985, when Keating's California-based thrift, Lincoln Savings and Loan Association, began a bitter feud with federal regulators. The officials charged that the thrift's rapid, high-risk growth had violated federal regulations. Keating fought back, charging that he was the victim of a "vendetta." (When the S&L collapsed in 1989, it cost taxpayers an estimated $2 billion.)

Keating successfully lined up well-placed politicians to help him in his fight as things heated up in late 1986 and early 1987. Among them were the five senators: Cranston, Glenn, Riegle, DeConcini and McCain.

Most of the senators' work in behalf of Keating involved contacting thrift regulators to talk about his case, though some did other favors, large and small, for him. Usually they urged the regulators to quickly make decisions about matters that Keating felt had dragged on for too long. Cranston and DeConcini were the most persistent.

The main events in the affair were two meetings in April 1987 when the senators met with top regulators to ask about their lengthy examination of Keating's thrift. (Riegle did not attend the first meeting.) The regulators later said they felt pressured and in some cases intimidated.

Over the years, Keating raised a total of $1.5 million for the senators' campaigns or political causes, with his support going back to 1982 in the case of the two Arizona senators. Two-thirds of the money went to Cranston's causes, mostly nonprofit voter groups.

The key issue in the case was whether there was any connection, real or perceived, between Keating's fundraising and their official actions in his behalf. In numerous instances — especially in the cases of Cranston, Riegle and DeConcini — Keating's donations coincided in time with official actions by the senators in his behalf.

Ethics Committee Investigation

Calls for an ethics inquiry began in 1989 as news stories raised questions about the senators' ties to Keating.

Numerous complaints, all based on newspaper reports, were filed with the panel. The chairman of the Ohio Republican Party filed the first official complaint that was made public, against Glenn alone, on Sept. 25, 1989. Common Cause, the public interest lobby, followed suit Oct. 13, 1989, with a complaint against the five senators. Several days later, interest in the case soared when the House Banking Committee started six days of hearings on Lincoln's collapse. *(1989 Almanac, p. 133)*

The Ethics Committee the following month hired a special counsel, Robert S. Bennett, to investigate, and it opened a formal inquiry that December. Bennett presented a report to the panel in September 1990.

Between Nov. 15, 1990, and Jan. 16, 1991, the committee held 26 days of hearings, filling 5,000 pages of transcripts with testimony from 27 witnesses, not counting 853 exhibits accepted into evidence.

The committee heard the case-in-chief over 18 days of public testimony, plus at least seven private sessions, in 1990. It heard Bennett's detailed overview of the case, presentations from the five senators (including Cranston's only appearance, shortly before he underwent cancer treatment at Stanford University in California), and testimony from congressional aides, banking regulators and Keating's former lobbyist, James J. Grogan.

But the panel could not accomplish its goal of completing the hearings in 1990, so it suspended proceedings from Dec. 15 to Jan. 2, when it began hearing from minor players and the defendants.

HEARINGS CONTINUED IN JANUARY

On Jan. 2, 1991, the Ethics Committee heard testimony from one former federal regulator that countered that of other ex-colleagues who testified that the actions of the five senators contributed to a delay in closing Lincoln.

According to Rosemary Stewart, former head of enforcement at the Federal Home Loan Bank Board and its successor agency, the Office of Thrift Supervision, none of the senators brought political pressure that altered her or the bank board's approach to the regulation of Lincoln.

Federal regulators based in San Francisco had recommended in May 1987 that the thrift be seized. Those recommendations were rejected by Washington-based regulators, among them Stewart, who decided a year later to remove the San Francisco regulators from their role in supervising Lincoln. Stewart said she believed that the San Francisco regulators had a vendetta against the thrift, as Lincoln was charging at the time. And, she said, the San Francisco regulators had not made their case.

"It would have been unprecedented" to have taken control of an institution that had not yet failed, as the San Francisco regulators were urging, Stewart testified. She said that she, like the five senators, had been impressed by reports from Lincoln's outside accountant, Jack D. Atchison of the Big Eight firm of Arthur Young, that Lincoln was strong financially. (It was Atchison's representations to the senators in early 1987, they said, that led them to meet twice with federal regulators in behalf of Keating.)

Stewart was called as a witness by Cranston's attorney, William W. Taylor III; her testimony was a strong counterpoint to that of the San Francisco regulators. Rudman, a former New Hampshire attorney general, challenged Stewart vigorously on her argument that federal regulators could not have moved more expeditiously against Lincoln.

McCain, Glenn Testified

During a day of mostly low-key testimony Jan. 4, the committee heard Glenn and McCain argue that they did nothing inappropriate by attending the two April 1987 meetings with federal regulators. Those two senators faced the easiest task in distancing themselves from the others. There had been almost no testimony to challenge their assertion, and Bennett had asserted previously that they did nothing wrong.

McCain's biggest potential problem in the case was his personal relationship with Keating, especially his repeated vacations at Keating's home in the Bahamas and trips to and from those vacations for McCain and family members paid for by American Continental.

Heflin took McCain through exhaustive questions about the long period of time in which he failed to either pay for the trips or to claim them as gifts. Heflin also questioned whether the amount McCain ultimately reimbursed American Continental for some of the trips was sufficient.

McCain, who became somewhat defensive during the questioning, insisted that he would have paid for them if American Continental had told him sooner that the payments had not been made. "If you have information that I didn't pay enough . . . I'll give you the check," he told Heflin. "Obviously, I didn't have a proper procedure. Otherwise, we would not be discussing this."

The trips occurred between 1983 and 1986, while McCain was still a member of the House, and he reimbursed American Continental for some of the flights at the time they were taken. In 1989, however, American Continental accountants informed McCain that about $13,400 in flight costs had not been reimbursed. In May and June of that year, McCain paid the company. At the time, both the House and Senate ethics committees said that McCain — having reimbursed the company — needed to take no further action.

McCain had filed financial disclosure forms with the House that did not claim that the trips were gifts. In letters to the Ethics Committee in late 1990, former American Continental accountant David Stevens said he believed that McCain never intended to pay the company back for trips taken by his family members.

The letter appeared to be an embarrassment to McCain. But in testimony before the committee in December, Stevens backed off that assertion.

In a Dec. 31 letter to the committee, Stevens said he wished he had not asserted that McCain had no intention of paying for family members but said there was nothing in his files to suggest that McCain did intend to do so.

McCain testified that he broke off his friendship with Keating just before the April meetings, when Keating asked him to negotiate. "I told him that he was trying to do something that was inappropriate," he said. "I would not do it."

At the conclusion of McCain's testimony, committee member Trent Lott, R-Miss., said, "I am compelled to say that you have shown repeatedly that you did nothing improper."

Glenn and McCain ended virtually all contacts with Keating after the second April 1987 meeting, at which regulators informed the senators that criminal charges might be filed against Lincoln and that the thrift was refusing to cooperate with regulators.

"I came to the conclusion that Lincoln was in deep trouble," Glenn said.

Glenn's only action after that time was to set up a lunch meeting in January 1988 between Keating and then-House Speaker Jim Wright, D-Texas. In the summer of 1987, Glenn testified, he turned down Keating's offer to raise campaign contributions because of Keating's battles with the regulators.

Skepticism Toward Riegle

Riegle testified on Jan. 7-8. He spent much of his time fielding tough questions from Bennett, attorneys for the other senators and members of the committee.

Much of the attention focused on a trip to Phoenix in March 1987, during which Riegle met with Keating, toured American Continental Corp., and — according to other testimony — discussed Keating's problems with federal regulators and proposed a meeting with the senators and then-Federal Home Loan Bank Board Chairman Edwin J. Gray.

Riegle took pains to say that more than $10,000 collected for his campaign from American Continental employees days before the trip was unrelated to his discussions with Keating. In fact, Riegle testified, the money was intended to be given as part of a Keating-sponsored fundraiser scheduled for Riegle in Detroit a few weeks later. And Riegle insisted that he had not discussed fundraising during the trip.

Rudman zeroed in on Riegle, who was repeatedly unable to recall events and conversations during testimony. Rudman said he found Riegle's testimony "remarkably inconsistent."

In particular, he seemed incredulous at Riegle's description of his trip. Rudman said he was confused about why Riegle had visited American Continental, yet told his aides not to deal with issues involving Lincoln. Riegle said he kept his aides out of the issue because the California-based thrift was not a direct constituent. But he said he visited American Continental because the firm was investing in Detroit.

Committee member Jesse Helms, R-N.C., all but demanded that Riegle admit that at least in hindsight he would have acted differently.

"If I'm disturbed about one thing — and I'm disturbed about many things — it's that not once have I heard anything remotely resembling a mea culpa about this," Helms said.

Helms referred to the senators as "Keystone Cops" and to Keating as "Daddy Warbucks." He told Riegle: "I don't believe you would have gone out to Phoenix — I don't believe anybody would have been involved with Mr. Keating, if he didn't have the ability to give away other people's money," Helms said.

Tough Questioning for DeConcini

DeConcini appeared before the committee on Jan. 9-10. Bennett questioned him closely on why he had resumed his actions in behalf of Keating after the April 9, 1987, meeting at which the senators learned of serious problems with the thrift. DeConcini ceased intervening until early 1989, when Keating was attempting to win regulator support for selling the thrift before it was seized. Such a sale would have preserved all or part of Keating's investment — and, as DeConcini pointed out, could have saved jobs at American Continental, which eventually went bankrupt.

Bennett honed in on DeConcini's calls to the superior of a California thrift regulator who had no say in a decision about the sale but was objecting to it. DeConcini denied that he had tried to keep the California regulator quiet.

DeConcini and his attorney, James Hamilton, became upset with Bennett several times over his line of questioning and his repeated raising of certain points, such as the timing of campaign contributions or whether DeConcini was aware of fundraising being done by Keating.

DeConcini protested since the hearings opened that Bennett was acting like a prosecutor rather than impartially questioning him.

Lott said he was unclear about why DeConcini again acted in Lincoln's behalf when he knew that Keating had misled him about his role with regulators. DeConcini should have seen "red flags saying this guy could be trouble," Lott said.

No More Cranston Testimony

The committee on Jan. 8 excused Cranston from further testimony, acting at the behest of Cranston's lawyer, who said the senator's treatment for prostate cancer would prevent him from returning to work until late February.

Cranston underwent five weeks of radiation therapy in late 1990 and was still recovering from side effects that included reduced stamina, Taylor told the committee. Another surgical procedure was scheduled for late January that would require several weeks of additional rest.

Cranston had delivered a lengthy opening statement Nov. 16, 1990, and testified in private on three separate occasions.

"I believe in Sen. Cranston's case the record is sufficiently complete that this committee can make a correct, informed judgment in this matter," Bennett said.

Concluding Arguments

The last two days of the hearings were given over to final arguments. Over 2½ hours on Jan. 15-16, Bennett presented his view of the facts and the standards senators should use to judge their colleagues. And the senators and their attorneys also made closing presentations.

Bennett distinguished carefully among the five senators, and without actually making recommendations, in essence urged the committee to find that Cranston, DeConcini and Riegle had acted improperly. Bennett again called upon the committee to find that Glenn and McCain had acted properly at all times. He distinguished them from the others by arguing that their acceptance of contributions was far removed in time from their actions, eliminating any taint from their fundraising.

"The ultimate disservice to some of your colleagues who

A New Sanction

By reprimanding Alan Cranston on the Senate floor on Nov. 20, the Ethics Committee established a new form of in-house punishment — one that the Senate on earlier occasions had refused to create because it smacked of leniency.

Since the first disciplinary matter arose in 1796, both chambers had relied on an accumulation of precedents to develop standards for members and sanctions for those who violate them. The Constitution allows expulsion, but other punishments evolved on a case-by-case basis.

The House recognized two lesser sanctions: censure and reprimand, which was first used in its modern sense in 1976 to reprove Robert L. F. Sikes, D-Fla., for failing to disclose financial holdings.

The Senate had only censure. Although sometimes it would substitute other words ("condemn" or "denounce"), any disciplinary resolution that went to the floor and was voted upon was considered by historians to be a censure. In either chamber, anything else — such as a chiding letter or public report — was an action taken by its Ethics Committee.

Rejecting 'Reprimand'

The Senate first considered using the word "reprimand" in 1902. In the midst of a hot debate over the Philippines, Benjamin R. Tillman got into a fistfight on the floor with his fellow South Carolina Democrat, John L. McLaurin. The Senate voted 61-0 to declare them "in contempt" and to refer the matter to a committee for further action. The panel considered a reprimand but concluded that "a reprimand would be too slight a punishment. . . . It is not sufficiently severe." The panel recommended censure, which the Senate approved 54-12.

In 1967, when the Senate was debating a resolution to censure Thomas J. Dodd, D-Conn., for financial misconduct, Texas Republican John Tower introduced an amendment to substitute the word reprimand. The chairman of the Ethics Committee, John C. Stennis, D-Miss., told the Senate that his panel had done extensive research on the term and rejected it.

"I will put it in this way, as to what we found as to the meaning of 'reprimand' in legislative parlance," said Stennis. "It just does not mean anything. It means what you might call a slap on the wrist. It does not carry any weight."

Jack Maskell, a lawyer with the Congressional Research Service who found those examples for a 1990 review of Senate discipline, said the Cranston action was unprecedented. "A committee reprimand seems to be something new," he said. "It's certainly not a censure. Historians will treat it as discipline by the committee, and it will be a new form of sanction."

Maskell noted that a House reprimand was not parallel to the Senate action. In the House, a reprimand required a floor vote, although the offender need not be present; for a censure, the member had to stand in the well of the House to listen to a formal rebuke by the Speaker.

The reprimand of Cranston was imposed by the Ethics Committee "on behalf of and in the name of the U.S. Senate." It was presented on the floor by committee leaders and rebutted by Cranston, but there was no formal action by the Senate.

---

sit in this room would be to allow them to be condemned by the failure of this committee to make tough judgments and tough calls and make decisions and separations," he argued.

Bennett was tough on the others. He argued that DeConcini had gone beyond the bounds of proper behavior to negotiate for Keating with the regulators in 1987, and he noted that DeConcini weighed in with them again in 1989 on the pending sale of Lincoln, despite knowledge that the regulators had referred evidence of possible criminal conduct at Lincoln to the Justice Department.

Bennett argued that the senators' meetings with and repeated phone calls to federal regulators were not just "status inquiries," as they contended: "If I'm sitting on a park bench, and an 800-pound gorilla comes along and says, 'Excuse me, I'm just making a status inquiry if there are any seats available,' you say, 'You're damn right, there's a seat available.' And there's a lot of 800-pound gorillas around this place."

DeConcini argued in his own defense that a senator could not be punished for the appearance of improper conduct, unless there was improper conduct. And his attorney James Hamilton argued that DeConcini had not tried to negotiate for Keating, and even if he had, there would be nothing wrong with it.

Bennett argued that Cranston's case provided the closest connections between money and action. He cited four separate occasions in which Cranston took actions for Keating after soliciting or receiving large amounts of cash for his own campaign or for voter registration groups with which he was affiliated.

But Taylor, Cranston's attorney, said senators had a duty to act in behalf of constituents — whether or not they are big contributors. "This duty may create an appearance of mutual dependence," Taylor said. However, "there is nothing improper, nor is there an appearance that there is anything improper, about that mutuality."

Regarding Riegle, Bennett also drew a connection between fundraising and action, all of which occurred in a three-month period in 1987. And he made a damning accusation that Riegle had misled the committee, perhaps intentionally, about his role in the Keating affair.

Riegle attorney Thomas C. Green blamed "whimsical circumstances" for the close scheduling between a March 23, 1987, Keating-sponsored fundraiser that netted $78,250 and the controversial April 9 meeting that Riegle attended. And he denied that Riegle had had any intention of misleading the committee. Information not provided was not considered relevant, he said.

Attorneys for McCain and Glenn were brief in their closing arguments.

"You owe John McCain something," argued his attorney, John M. Dowd. "You owe him a straight, crisp, clear finding, based on the overwhelming, undisputed evidence in the record that his actions, at all times, were honest and ethical."

Glenn attorney Charles F. C. Ruff weighed into the standards debate, urging the committee to "judge him by the sternest ethical standard that you can apply to the conduct of all of your colleagues in the Senate."

Bennett's Conduct an Issue

At the hearings' conclusion, committee members David Pryor, D-Ark., and Terry Sanford, D-N.C., complained that much of what Bennett presented was irrelevant. And Bennett was lambasted by some of those under inquiry — chiefly DeConcini — for unfairness and a one-sided presentation of the facts.

On the next to last day of the hearings, James Hamilton, DeConcini's attorney, stung Bennett with affadavits from two former U.S. attorneys accusing him of unfairness.

"Mr. Bennett's conduct is going to be an issue," Hamilton said, if the DeConcini case were to go to the Senate floor for action.

Bennett fired back: "Sen. DeConcini and his counsel would like me to be a flower girl distributing the flowers at a wedding in equal shares to each senator without regard to the evidence. I will not do that. . . . I think the not-so-subtle threat to this committee is an outrage and you should be offended by it."

The committee voted not to admit the affidavits as evidence; only Heflin voted to consider them.

Bennett had previously handled investigations for the committee of Harrison A. Williams Jr., D-N.J., in 1981 and Dave Durenberger, R-Minn., in 1989-90.

In his closing comments, Pryor acknowledged that there were major differences among the three Democrats and three Republicans on the panel. "I would dare say . . . that there are six visions — six visions — of this case and what it means or what it doesn't mean, what is relevant, what is not relevant, sitting here today," Pryor said.

The cable television public affairs network C-SPAN televised every day of the hearings, and it reported that as many as 25 million viewers had tuned in.

Inside the Jury Room

The committee struggled over the five men's fates for a month during 33 hours of secret deliberations.

The panel went behind closed doors in a small room in the Ethics Committee's suite in the Hart Senate Office Building on Jan. 30, two weeks after its public hearings into the matter ended. Members sat on well-padded upholstered chairs around two rectangular tables pushed together to make a square. Evidence and hearing transcripts were available nearby. Aides were only occasionally invited in to answer specific questions or bring in fresh pencils.

Even Bennett was consulted only occasionally. At times he could be seen pacing nervously outside this inner sanctum.

According to accounts of the deliberations that emerged afterward, opinions among committee members initially seemed to form a continuum, with Helms favoring the harshest treatment, advocating that as many as three members (Cranston, DeConcini and Riegle) faced full-Senate censure. At the other end was Sanford, who favored little or no official action by the Senate.

Lott seemed to be most closely allied with Helms. Based on his questions and comments during the public hearings, Pryor seemed closer to the Sanford camp. Heflin said little, according to one official, while Rudman was all too willing to discuss matters at length.

Even after members had worked out a basic framework — considering censure for Cranston and merely chiding the other four — the precise wording was of critical concern. "We're into minutiae here," said Lott on Feb. 20. Lott described the debate this way: "If the language has the words 'poor judgment' and 'insensitivity' and 'appearance of impropriety' — if all those words are in there, maybe that's good enough. But if one of those words is missing — is it good enough? Or if it's 'overly aggressive' — is that good enough? But if it's just 'aggressive,' is that not enough?" He added, "The words have been pounded until they're pulverized."

Cranston sent a letter to the Ethics Committee Feb. 18, expressing "roaring outrage" at news reports based on sources inside the committee room because their "main purpose seems to be to attempt to blacken my reputation no matter what the committee decides."

Referring to reports that he alone would face further action, Cranston wrote: "Is this latest leak somebody's trial balloon, to see if the public will be appeased sufficiently if only one of us is thrown into the lion's den? Am I the logical scapeboat because I am ill and because I am the only one who will not seek re-election?"

In the letter, Cranston argued that his behavior, if judged improper, was no worse than the others'. "I do not see how I can be singled out for harsher treatment," he said.

Common Cause also attempted to influence the proceedings. In a Feb. 19 letter, Fred Wertheimer, president of Common Cause, said: "The Senate Ethics Committee would do a grave disservice to both the Senate and the country by attempting to downplay the seriousness of the case involving Sen. DeConcini and Sen. Riegle. This is far too important a matter to be handled by a Senate Ethics Committee letter."

PRELIMINARY DECISION

On Feb. 27, the panel found a continuum of fault in the case: It rebuked McCain, Glenn, DeConcini and Riegle for poor judgment. DeConcini and Riegle were also criticized for creating improper appearances, and DeConcini's conduct with the regulators was found to be inappropriately aggressive. But it decided that existing Senate rules did not warrant punishment for any of the four. As far as the panel was concerned, that closed the case against them.

The panel announced its findings at a news conference attended by all six members; it issued a 12-page summary that had few details to back the distinctions it drew between the senators. Its decisions were unanimous — achieving a goal that had made the deliberations protracted. *(Text, p. 31)*

In effect, the committee indicted Cranston, finding "substantial credible evidence . . . that Sen. Cranston engaged in an impermissible pattern of conduct in which fundraising and official activities were substantially linked." It did not accuse him of breaking a specific rule, charging instead that he violated the Senate's catchall admonition that members shall not engage in "improper conduct which may reflect upon the Senate."

Committee members said they had not yet decided to recommend that the full Senate punish Cranston. But they left little doubt that they would probably do so. Cranston complained bitterly that he was made a scapegoat and

Continued on p. 34

Cranston Received Strongest Criticism

On Feb. 27, the Senate Ethics Committee released the following text of its conclusions after hearings on the Keating Five senators:

INTRODUCTION

The United States Senate Select Committee on Ethics initiated Preliminary Inquiries into allegations of misconduct by Senator Alan Cranston [D-Calif.], Senator Dennis DeConcini [D-Ariz.], Senator John Glenn [D-Ohio], Senator John McCain [R-Ariz.], and Senator Donald [W.] Riegle [Jr., D-Mich.], in connection with their actions on behalf of Charles H. Keating Jr. and Lincoln Savings and Loan Association. In the course of its Preliminary Inquiries, the Committee held hearings over a two month period which began November 15, 1990. These hearings were conducted for the purpose of determining whether there is sufficient credible evidence of possible violations by any of the five Senators involved in the Preliminary Inquiries. Because this process was investigatory in nature, a wide net was cast and evidence was admitted with few limitations.

The Committee has met on more than a dozen occasions to consider the evidence produced at the hearings and the written arguments of Special Counsel and counsel for each of the Respondent Senators. The task of the Committee has been to sort through this exhaustive record to ascertain the relevant facts, and to identify any evidence of wrongdoing and any exculpatory evidence.

FINDINGS AND RECOMMENDATIONS

Having deliberated at length upon the issues presented, the Committee has weighed the relevant evidence and makes the following findings and recommendations:

Intervention in the Administrative Process

It is a necessary function of a Senator's office to intervene with officials of the executive branch and independent regulatory agencies on behalf of individuals when the facts warrant, and it is a Senator's duty to make decisions on whether to intervene without regard to whether they have contributed to the Senator's campaigns or causes. Ample evidence was received during the hearings showing that Senators should and do provide essential constituent services. In this case, each of the Senators under inquiry had information that reasonably caused concern about the fairness of the Federal Home Loan Bank's examination of Lincoln Savings and Loan Association (Lincoln), and which was sufficient to justify the Senator's contacting Bank Board personnel.

The degree of intervention with the regulators varied as to each Senator. The evidence clearly shows that their contacts with federal regulators regarding Lincoln did not cause the eventual failure of Lincoln or the thrift industry in general.

Prior to April 1987, four of the Senators (Cranston, DeConcini, Glenn, and McCain) had officially expressed opposition to or raised questions about the adoption of a "Direct Investment Rule," promulgated by the Federal Home Loan Bank Board (FHLBB). This Rule was opposed by many Members of Congress and a large number of thrift organizations. The Committee has concluded that, when considered without regard to any contribution or other benefit, the opposition expressed or the questions raised about the Direct Investment Rule did not violate any law or Senate rule.

There were two meetings between Federal Home Loan Bank personnel and groups of Senators. The first, on April 2, 1987, between Federal Home Loan Bank Board Chairman Edwin [J.] Gray and four Senators (Cranston, DeConcini, Glenn, and McCain), ended when Chairman Gray advised the Senators that he had no knowledge about the Lincoln examination being conducted by the San Francisco Federal Home Loan Bank (FHLB), and indicated that he would arrange a meeting with, and suggested that they could obtain the information they sought from, the San Francisco FHLB personnel. When considered without regard to any contribution or other benefit, no Senator violated any law or Senate rule by merely attending the meeting.

One week later, on April 9, 1987, there was a second meeting in Washington between four representatives of the San Francisco Federal Home Loan Bank and five Senators (DeConcini, Glenn, McCain, Riegle; and Cranston making a one-minute appearance). One of the FHLB personnel wrote an account of the meeting in reasonable detail, which was amplified by testimony. The Committee finds that, when considered without regard to any contributions or other benefit, no Senator, merely by virtue of his attendance at this meeting, violated any law or Senate rule. At this second meeting, the FHLB representatives advised the Senators that a "criminal referral" was going to be filed relative to the conduct of certain unnamed officials of Lincoln.

Following the two meetings, neither Senator McCain nor Senator Riegle took any action on behalf of Lincoln.

Ten months after the April meetings, Senator Glenn was host at a luncheon meeting he arranged for Mr. Charles Keating to meet House Speaker Jim Wright. There is disputed evidence as to whether Lincoln's problems with the FHLBB were discussed at this meeting. The weight of the evidence indicates that Senator Glenn's participation did not go beyond serving as host, and there is no evidence that Senator Glenn was asked to or did take any action on behalf of Lincoln.

Between February and mid-April 1989, Senator DeConcini made several telephone calls to FHLBB members and other regulatory officials urging prompt consideration of applications for the sale of Lincoln.

In 1987 following the April meetings, and in 1988, Senator Cranston set up a meting between FHLBB Chairman M. Danny Wall and Mr. Keating, and made several telephone inquiries to Chairman Wall on behalf of Lincoln. Additionally, in 1989, Senator Cranston made calls to FHLB Board members and other regulatory officials urging consideration of applications for the sale of Lincoln.

The Committee finds that, when considered without regard to any contribution or other benefit, none of the activities of Senator Cranston, Senator DeConcini, or Senator Glenn concerning Mr. Keating or Lincoln, following the April 1987 meetings, violated any law or Senate rule.

Official Actions and Campaign Contributions

While the Committee has concluded that none of the Senators' actions described above, when considered without regard to any contribution or other benefit, violated any law or Senate rule, each act must also be examined against more general ethical standards to determine if there was any impropriety because of any relation between those actions and campaign contributions or other benefits provided by Mr. Keating and his associates.

It is a fact of life that candidates for the Senate must solicit and receive assistance in their campaigns, including the raising of campaign funds. Such fundraising is authorized and regulated by law, and contributions and expenditures under the Federal Election Campaign Act are required to be publicly disclosed. Additionally, contributions under the Federal Election Campaign Act are not personal gifts to candidates.

Mr. Keating, his associates and his friends contributed $49,000 for Senator Cranston's 1984 Presidential Campaign and his 1986 Senatorial Campaign. Mr. Keating also gave corporate funds at the behest of Senator Cranston: $85,000 to the California Democratic Party 1986 get-out-the-vote campaign; $850,000 in 1987 and 1988 to several voter registration organizations with which Senator Cranston was affiliated; and $10,000 to a PAC [political action committee] affiliated with Senator Cranston in January 1989. Mr. Keating's Lincoln Savings and Loan also made a $300,000 line of credit available to Senator Cranston's campaign in the fall of 1986 on an expedited basis, although the loan was not used.

Mr. Keating, his associates and his friends contributed $31,000 to Senator DeConcini's 1982 Senatorial Campaign and $54,000 to his 1988 Senatorial Campaign.

Mr. Keating contributed a total of $200,000 in corporate funds to the non-federal account of Senator Glenn's multi-candidate

PAC in 1985 and 1986. Mr. Keating, his associates, and his friends contributed $24,000 for Senator Glenn's Senatorial Campaign, and $18,200 for his Presidential Campaign. Senator Glenn received no contribution from or through Mr. Keating after February 1986.

Mr. Keating, his associates, and his friends contributed $56,000 for Senator McCain's two House races in 1982 and 1984, and $54,000 for his 1986 Senate race. Mr. Keating also provided his corporate plan and/or arranged for payment for the use of commercial or private aircraft on several occasions for travel by Senator McCain and his family, for which Senator McCain ultimately provided reimbursement when called upon to do so. Mr. Keating also extended personal hospitality to Senator McCain for vacations at a location in the Bahamas in each of the calendar years 1983 through 1986.

Mr. Keating organized and hosted a Riegle re-election campaign fundraising event in March 1987 in Detroit at his company's Pontchartrain Hotel. As a result of Mr. Keating's efforts, approximately $78,250 was raised from Keating associates and friends for Senator Riegle's 1988 campaign.

Based on all the available evidence, the Committee has concluded that in the case of each of the five Senators, all campaign contributions from Mr. Keating and his associates under the Federal Election Campaign Act were within the established legal limits, and were properly reported. Similarly, from the available evidence the Committee concludes that the Senators' solicitation or acceptance of all contributions made in these cases to state party organizations, political action committees, and voter registration organizations were, standing alone, not illegal or improper; nor did any such contribution constitute a personal gift to any Senator.

With respect to each Senator, there remains the question of whether any actions taken by the Senator, standing alone or in combination with contributions or other benefits, constitutes improper conduct or an appearance of impropriety. The Committee has examined the specific conduct of each Senator and has determined that under the totality of the circumstances: The conduct of each of the five Senators reflected poor judgment; the conduct of some of the Senators constituted at least an appearance of improper conduct; and the conduct of one Senator may have been improper.

The Committee believes that every Senator must always endeavor to avoid the appearance that he, the Senate, or the governmental process may be influenced by campaign contributions or other benefits provided by those with significant legislative or governmental interests. Nonetheless, if an individual or organization which contributed to a Senator's campaigns or causes has a case which the Senator reasonably believes he is obliged to press because it is in the public interest or the cause of justice or equity to do so, then the Senator's obligation is to pursue that case. In such instances, the Senator must be mindful of the appearance that may be created and take special care to try to prevent harm to the public's trust in him and the Senate.

The Committee believes that appearances of impropriety are particularly likely to arise where a Senator takes action on behalf of a contributor. Such appearances are even more difficult to avoid when large sums are being raised from individuals or corporations for unregulated "soft money" accounts and for independent expenditures by third parties. Over 80 percent of the funds raised by Mr. Keating for or on behalf of the five Senators was "soft money."

A full report respecting the Committee's decisions will be issued at the earliest possible date. The Final Report will also contain at least two recommendations (summarized below) for further Senate action.

SPECIFIC FINDINGS

The Committee finds that there is substantial credible evidence that provides substantial cause for the Committee to conclude that Senator Cranston may have engaged in improper conduct reflecting upon the Senate and, therefore, has voted to proceed to an Investigation (see attached). The Investigation will proceed as expeditiously as possible.

The Committee's conclusions in the cases concerning the other four Senators are also set forth in attachments.

Recommendations to the Senate

Section 2(a)(3) of Senate Resolution 338 (88th Congress) places a duty upon the Committee to recommend additional rules or regulations to the Senate, where the Committee has determined that such rules or regulations are necessary or desirable to ensure proper standards of conduct by Members, officers, and employees in the performance of their official duties.

In fulfilling its duty under this section, the Committee will make the following recommendations to the Senate in its Final Report on the Preliminary Inquiries.

Recommendation for a Bipartisan Task Force on Constituent Service

As noted in the course of the Committee's hearings, the Senate has no specific written standards embodied in the Senate rules respecting contact or intervention with federal executive or independent regulatory agency officials. While unknown to many Senators, there are general guidelines. These are best expressed in House Advisory Opinion No. 1 and the writings of Senator Paul Douglas.

The Committee believes that the Senate should adopt written standards in this area. A specific proposal should be developed either by the Senate Rules Committee or by a bipartisan Senate Task Force created for this purpose. The Rules Committee or Task Force will, of course, need to address the special ethical problems which may arise when such contact or intervention is sought by individuals who have contributed to the Senator's campaigns or causes.

Such standards could be similar to House Advisory Opinion No. 1 or could be more specific. Until such time as such Committee or Task Force has finished its work and the Senate has adopted specific standards respecting contact or intervention with executive or independent regulatory agencies, all Senators are encouraged to use House Advisory Opinion No. 1 as a source of guidance for their actions.

The Committee hopes that the adoption of specific standards governing contact or intervention by Senators with executive or independent regulatory agencies will minimize the potential for appearances of impropriety. Members of the Committee are especially mindful that the success of any democratic government, designed to execute the will of a free people, is ultimately dependent on the public's confidence in the integrity of the governmental process and those who govern.

Recommendation for Bipartisan Campaign Reform

The inquiries in these five cases have shown the obvious ethical dilemmas inherent in the current system by which political activities are financed. The Committee notes that over 80 percent of the funds at issue were not disclosed funds raised by candidates for Senate or House campaigns under the Federal Election Campaign Act. Rather, such funds were undisclosed, unregulated funds raised for independent expenditures, political party "soft money," and a non-federal political action committee. Any campaign finance reform measure will have to address these mechanisms for political activities, as well as campaign fund raising and expenditures directly by candidates, in order to deal meaningfully and effectively with the issues presented in these cases.

The Committee urges the leadership and Members of both the Senate and the House to work together in a bipartisan manner to address the urgent need for comprehensive campaign finance reform. The reputation and honor of our institutions demand it.

RESOLUTION FOR INVESTIGATION

Whereas, the Select Committee on Ethics on December 21, 1989, initiated a Preliminary Inquiry into allegations of misconduct by Senator Alan Cranston, and notified senator Cranston of such action; and

Whereas, the Committee retained Special Counsel Robert S. Bennett to assist the Committee in conducting the Preliminary Inquiry into the allegations, and received and considered a report related thereto; and

Whereas, in the course of its Preliminary Inquiry the Committee held hearings from November 15, 1990, through January 16,

1991, and heard evidence relating to the allegations; and Whereas, the Committee received and considered post-hearing memoranda from Special Counsel and counsel for Respondent Senators;

It is therefore RESOLVED:

(a) That the Committee finds that there is substantial credible evidence that provides substantial cause for the Committee to conclude that, in connection with his conduct relating to Charles H. Keating Jr. and Lincoln Savings and Loan Association, Senator Cranston may have engaged in improper conduct that may reflect upon the Senate, as contemplated in Section 2(a)(1) of S. Res. 338, 88th Congress, as amended. To wit, there is substantial credible evidence that provides substantial cause for the Committee to conclude, based upon the totality of the circumstances, including but not limited to the following conduct or activities, that Senator Cranston engaged in an impermissible pattern of conduct in which fundraising and official activities were substantially linked:

(1) From April 1987 through April 1989, Senator Cranston personally, or through Senate staff, contacted the Federal Home Loan Bank Board on behalf of Lincoln, during a period when Senator Cranston was soliciting and accepting substantial contributions from Mr. Keating. On at least four occasions, these contacts were made in close connection with the solicitation or receipt of contributions. These four occasions are as follows:

(i) As a result of a solicitation from Senator Cranston in early 1987, Mr. Keating, on March 3, 1987, contributed $100,000 to America Votes, a voter registration organization. This contribution was made during the period leading to Senator Cranston's participation in the April 2 and April 9 meetings with Federal Home Loan Bank Board Chairman Edwin J. Gray and the San Francisco regulators.

(ii) In the fall of 1987, Senator Cranston solicited from Mr. Keating a $250,000 contribution, which was delivered to the Senator personally by Mr. Keating's employee James J. Grogan on November 6, 1987. When the contribution was delivered, Mr. Grogan and Senator Cranston called Mr. Keating, who asked if the Senator would contact new Federal Home Loan Bank Board Chairman M. Danny Wall about Lincoln. Senator Cranston agreed to do so, and made the call six days later.

(iii) In January 1988, Mr. Keating offered to make an additional contribution and also asked Senator Cranston to set up a meeting for him with Chairman Wall. Senator Cranston did so on January 20, 1988, and Chairman Wall and Mr. Keating met eight days later. On February 10, 1988, Senator Cranston personally collected checks totaling $500,000 for voter registration groups.

(iv) In early 1989, at the time that Senator Cranston was contacting Bank Board officials about the sale of Lincoln, he personally or through Joy Jacobson, his chief fundraiser, solicited another contribution. (This contribution was never made. American Continental Corporation declared bankruptcy on April 13, 1989.)

(2) Senator Cranston's Senate office practices further evidenced an impermissible pattern of conduct in which fundraising and official activities were substantially linked. For example, Joy Jacobson (who was not a member of his Senate staff and who had no official Senate duties or substantive expertise) engaged in the following activities with Senator Cranston's knowledge, permission, at his direction, or under his supervision:

(i) Senator Cranston's fundraiser repeatedly scheduled and attended meetings between Senator Cranston and contributors in which legislative or regulatory issues were discussed.

(ii) Senator Cranston's fundraiser often served as the intermediary for Mr. Keating or Mr. Grogan when they could not reach the Senator or Carolyn Jordan, the Senator's banking aide.

(iii) Senator Cranston received several memoranda from Ms. Jacobson which evidenced her understanding that contributors were entitled to special attention and special access to official services. Senator Cranston never told her that her understanding was incorrect, nor did he inform her that such a connection between contributions and official actions was improper.

(b) That the Committee, pursuant to Committee Supplementary Procedural Rules 3(d)(5) and 4(f)(4), shall proceed to an Investigation under Committee Supplementary Procedural Rule 5; and

(c) That Senator Cranston shall be given timely written notice of this resolution and the evidence supporting it, and informed of respondent's rights pursuant to the Rules of the Committee.

DECISION OF THE COMMITTEE CONCERNING SENATOR MCCAIN

Based on the evidence available to it, the Committee has given consideration to Senator McCain's actions on behalf of Lincoln Savings & Loan Association. The Committee concludes that Senator McCain exercised poor judgment in intervening with the regulators. The Committee concludes that Senator McCain's actions were not improper nor attended with gross negligence and did not reach the level of requiring institutional action against him. The Committee finds that Senator McCain took no further action after the April 9, 1987, meeting when he learned of the criminal referral.

The Committee reaffirms its prior decision that it does not have jurisdiction to determine the issues of disclosure or reimbursement pertaining to flights provided by American Continental Corporation while Senator McCain was a Member of the House of Representatives. The Committee did consider the effect of such on his state of mind and judgment in taking steps to assist Lincoln Savings & Loan Association.

Senator McCain has violated no law of the United States or specific Rule of the United States Senate; therefore, the Committee concludes that no further action is warranted with respect to Senator McCain on the matters investigated during the preliminary inquiry.

DECISION OF THE COMMITTEE CONCERNING SENATOR GLENN

Based on the evidence to it, the Committee has given consideration to Senator Glenn's actions on behalf of Lincoln Savings & Loan Association. The Committee concludes that Senator Glenn, although believing that the Lincoln matter was in the process of resolution, exercised poor judgment in arranging a luncheon meeting between Mr. Keating and Speaker Wright in January, 1988, some eight months after Senator Glenn learned of the criminal referral. There is disputed evidence as to whether Lincoln's problems with the Federal Home Loan Bank Board (FHLBB) were discussed at that meeting. The evidence indicates that Senator Glenn's participation did not go beyond serving as host. The Committee further concludes that Senator Glenn's actions were not improper or attended with gross negligence and did not reach the level requiring institutional action against him.

Senator Glenn has violated no law of the United States or specific Rule of the United States Senate; therefore, the Committee concludes that no further action is warranted with respect to Senator Glenn on the matters investigated during the preliminary inquiry.

DECISION OF THE COMMITTEE CONCERNING SENATOR RIEGLE

Based on evidence available to it, the Committee has given consideration to Senator Riegle's actions on behalf of Lincoln Savings & Loan Association. The Committee finds that Senator Riegle took steps to assist Lincoln Savings & Loan Association with its regulatory problems at a time that Charles Keating was raising substantial campaign funds for Senator Riegle. During the course of the hearings, possible conflicts arose concerning actions on the part of Senator Riegle that caused the Committee concern, but the Committee finds that the evidence indicates no deliberate intent to deceive. The evidence shows that Senator Riegle took no further action after the April 9, 1987, meeting where he learned of the criminal referral.

While the Committee concludes that Senator Riegle has violated no law of the United States or specific Rule of the United States Senate, it emphasizes that it does not condone his conduct. The Committee has concluded that the totality of the evidence shows that Senator Riegle's conduct gave the appearance of being improper and was certainly attended with insensitivity and poor judgment. However, the Committee finds that his conduct did not reach a level requiring institutional action.

The Committee concludes that no further action is warranted with respect to Senator Riegle on the matters investigated during the preliminary inquiry.

DECISION OF THE COMMITTEE CONCERNING SENATOR DECONCINI

Based on the evidence available to it, the Committee has given consideration to Senator DeConcini's actions on behalf of Lincoln Savings & Loan Association.

While aggressive conduct by Senators in dealing with regulatory agencies is sometimes appropriate and necessary, the Committee concludes that Senator DeConcini's aggressive conduct with the regulators was inappropriate. The Committee further concludes that the actions of Senator DeConcini after the April 9, 1987, meeting where he learned of the criminal referral, were not improper in and of themselves.

While the Committee concludes that Senator DeConcini has violated no law of the United States or specific Rule of the United States Senate, it emphasizes that it does not condone his conduct. The Committee has concluded that the totality of the evidence shows that Senator DeConcini's conduct gave the appearance of being improper and was certainly attended with insensitivity and poor judgment. However, the Committee finds that his conduct did not reach a level requiring institutional action.

The Committee therefore concludes that no further action is warranted with respect to Senator DeConcini on the matters investigated during the preliminary inquiry. ■

Continued from p. 30
had previously vowed to fight a negative judgment.

The committee also recommended that two bipartisan task forces be created. One would write rules clarifying how far senators can go in helping constituents; the other would recommend campaign finance reforms.

"Good government" advocacy groups generally decried the committee's decision. Wertheimer called it a "sophisticated whitewash."

House Republican Whip Newt Gingrich of Georgia denounced the committee for a "purely partisan decision to have DeConcini and Riegle not be sanctioned more intensely."

Public reaction was muted by war news: Bush announced an end to hostilities in the Persian Gulf just hours after the Ethics Committee released its decision. *(Gulf war, p. 437)*

But despite the story being pushed off the front pages, the committee was rewarded with scathing editorials almost immediately. The Washington Post headlined its March 1 critique of the decision: "The Keating Dive." The San Francisco Examiner said: "As to Cranston, the committee did not do enough." His actions, it said, "stink to high heaven." The Arizona Republic, while defending its two home-state senators, criticized the committee's written statement as "mostly mush."

Committee members and other senators rejected the notion that they had been lenient, particularly with the four senators who would not face further proceedings.

"Their careers have been put in jeopardy, their integrity questioned — what is so light about that?" asked Daniel K. Inouye, D-Hawaii, who had testified in defense of the Keating Five during the hearings in December.

"What do they want? Do they want to hang [Cranston]? Is that when Common Cause will be satisfied?" he asked.

Rudman called the committee's rebukes "very strong language." But he and others refused to characterize them further. "The words speak for themselves," Rudman said.

And Helms, whom committee sources said was the most adamant in favor of punishing DeConcini and Riegle, denied that the committee ducked its responsibility. "I don't think you would think that you had been dealt with lightly if your peers had judged you as these men have been judged," Helms said.

Details of Decision

In its statement explaining its findings, the committee found nothing intrinsically wrong with the intervention by the five senators with federal regulators in behalf of Keating. It stated explicitly that the senators' actions had nothing to do with Lincoln's collapse. And, it said, each had ample information to justify contacting regulators about the fairness of the regulatory treatment Lincoln was receiving.

But because of the size and frequency of Keating's contributions to Cranston, and the proximity of the contribution to actions he took in Keating's behalf, the committee found the possibility of wrongdoing on Cranston's part.

With DeConcini and Riegle, the panel found an appearance of improper conduct that it chose to rebuke but not to punish because the rules on such appearances of impropriety are unclear. To take further action against the two would have amounted to "setting standards after the fact," according to Lott. In the cases of Glenn and McCain, even this appearance of impropriety was lacking, the committee said.

The idea that the Senate can punish members for the mere appearance of impropriety was central to Bennett's arguments that DeConcini and Riegle might have gone too far. Heflin and Rudman said they neither accepted nor rejected Bennett's appearance standard.

The committee was, if anything, tougher on McCain and Glenn than Bennett proposed.

In McCain's case, the committee chose to disregard what may have been his biggest liability — his repeated vacations and airplane flights paid for by Keating's companies in the early 1980s. *(McCain, p. 37-E)*

The panel's criticism amounted to a simple admonishment that he "exercised poor judgment in intervening with regulators."

In a brief statement to reporters, McCain claimed full exoneration. "To quote the committee, 'no improper conduct,' " he said.

Glenn also proclaimed that he had been vindicated, and he took issue with the fact that the committee questioned his judgment in setting up the lunch meeting between Keating and Speaker Wright. *(Glenn, p. 37-E)*

"I was just the host," he said.

Riegle Contrite; DeConcini Defiant

Riegle and DeConcini both expressed relief when the committee chose not to recommend formal punishment.

The panel called attention to the fact that Keating had raised more than $78,000 for Riegle at the same time that Riegle was acting to aid Lincoln. In his early representations to the committee, Riegle did not mention all contacts he had with Keating and the regulators. And during the hearings, he repeatedly could not recall actions that others said he had taken. *(Riegle, p. 37-E)*

The committee noted that during the hearings, "conflicts arose" between Riegle's testimony and that of others about his actions. Nevertheless, the panel found that "the evidence indicates no deliberate intent to deceive" on Riegle's part.

Riegle said he was gratified to be cleared of wrongdoing. But unlike the other senators, he chose to accept the committee's criticism, calling it "fair and constructive," adding that he had seen the possible appearance of impropriety in 1988, and at that time returned Keating's contributions.

"I certainly regret and accept responsibility for this appearance problem," Riegle said.

While Riegle was contrite, DeConcini was defiant.

Bennett had made much of DeConcini's role in the two April 1987 meetings with regulators, at which he appeared to be offering a deal that Lincoln would change practices that regulators were criticizing, if they would back off. The committee found that DeConcini's "aggressive conduct with the regulators was inappropriate." *(DeConcini, p. 37-E)*

DeConcini chose to read the committee's judgment as an exoneration, however. "I realize that my aggressiveness has been questioned by the committee," DeConcini said. "Aggressiveness is my hallmark."

As for the panel's criticism, he said, "I accept it; I don't have any recourse."

Cranston Faced Discipline

Although the committee seemed to disregard Bennett's recommendations on both DeConcini and Riegle, that was not the case for Cranston.

The panel adopted a resolution citing chapter and verse of the case developed by Bennett about Cranston's dealings with and in behalf of Keating. The panel cited four instances in which Cranston solicited or accepted money from Keating or acted in his behalf. It said Cranston's office practices "further evidenced an impermissible pattern of conduct in which fundraising and official activities were substantially linked."

Cranston, who remained in California recuperating from medical treatment, responded with a one-sentence statement: "It is clear that I have been unfairly singled out, despite the evidence in all five cases."

Officially, the panel's action on Cranston was a merely a preliminary finding, holding that the committee had found "substantial credible evidence that provides substantial cause" for the committee to take further action against him. In most Senate disciplinary cases, that would have been the start of a lengthy investigation and a possible public hearing. But the committee members made it clear that they thought they had heard all the evidence they needed. "The investigation, as far as we're concerned, is concluded," Rudman said.

Cranston had three options: he could request another hearing, submit a written defense to the committee or wait to fight on the Senate floor. A week after issuing its findings, the committee told Cranton to decide by March 18 how he wanted to proceed. But he got extensions.

CRANSTON DELIBERATIONS

In the aftermath of the Feb. 27 announcement, it seemed clear that the Ethics Committee would ask the full Senate to censure Cranston. "That's already been decided," said Helms. The major decision seemed to be the wording of the resolution.

Ethics members were clearly worn out by the case. Helms quit Feb. 28 and was replaced by Slade Gorton, R-Wash., although Helms remained on for the duration of the Cranston case. Pryor said March 7 that he would leave once the Cranston matter was settled. Heflin said he, too, wanted to depart, and on May 22 Senate Majority Leader George J. Mitchell, D-Maine, announced that he would be allowed to do so — with Sanford taking over as chairman — although Heflin would remain to wrap up the Cranston case.

But any hopes panel members had that they could put the Cranston matter behind them were shattered. Cranston took two months drafting a response and deciding not to demand another hearing on the case. Pryor had a heart attack April 16 and soon after resigned from the committee. His replacement — Jeff Bingaman, D-N.M. — was not named until May 22. He took several weeks learning details of the case and on June 18 joined the panel's deliberations for the first time.

Deliberations intensified in July, but then Bingaman suddenly recused himself after declaring that he had a conflict: His wife's law firm was owed money for representing some of Cranston's principal associates in the case, and Cranston had promised to make sure the bills were paid. He said he had learned of the potential conflict of interest on July 23, and he immediately disqualified himself.

Anne Bingaman was one of scores of partners in the firm of Powell Goldstein Frazer & Murphy.

During the Keating inquiry, another partner, Robert D. Luskin, represented four figures in the case: Cranston fundraiser Joy Jacobson; his banking issues aide, Carolyn Jordon; his administrative assistant, Roy F. Greenaway; and Kim Cranston, his son. Luskin also represented the Center for Participation in Democracy, a voter registration group tied to the Cranstons that got $400,000 of the $994,000 Keating raised for the senator's campaigns and causes.

Mrs. Bingaman likely knew that the firm had represented some Keating-case principals, Luskin said, but she did not know that Cranston had decided to help pay their bills. She learned by accident when the matter came up during a firm meeting July 23. She told her husband that night.

Luskin estimated the outstanding fees at between $50,000 and $100,000. He said he never thought to warn Mrs. Bingaman of the potential conflict because he was no longer actively involved in the case.

"I think it's a fairly classic definition of a conflict," Bingaman said.

Bingaman was not obligated to disqualify himself; committee rules left such judgments to members' discretion. The panel unanimously concurred in his decision. "He has a financial interest — that's the issue," said Rudman.

The delays dragged on long enough for Pryor to recover from his heart attack and be renamed to the panel on Aug. 21.

Helms Report

Frustrated at the delays, Ethics Committee member Helms dropped a bomb the weekend of Aug. 3, just after the Senate broke for its summer recess. He released his own scathing report on the case demanding that the full Senate censure Cranston for "reprehensible" conduct that "was clearly and unequivocally unethical."

The 247-page, 936-footnote report was based on a secret document submitted to the committee in late June by its special counsel. Bennett had proposed that his draft be used as a basis for action by the full Senate to sanction Cranston and to justify the panel's Feb. 27 decision to close the cases against the other four Keating senators.

Such a unilateral action was an unprecedented public break with the Ethics Committee's penchant for secrecy.

Ethics Committee leaders fired back at Helms, suggesting in a terse statement Aug. 5 that he violated committee confidentiality rules by releasing what it called Bennett's draft report. "We have asked the committee staff to investigate," said Sanford and Rudman. "It is regrettable that this document has been released or reported," they said. "This is simply a draft working document." The committee had "specifically rejected portions of the draft," they said.

The leaders noted that committee rules barred the unauthorized release of secret material, called "committee sensitive" documents and information.

"I did not release any information that had been designated as 'committee sensitive,'" Helms said in an Aug. 6 statement. "I properly used the special counsel's generally excellent draft report as a basis for preparing my own report bearing my own name and signature."

Murray S. Flander, Cranston's spokesman, said Helms' report confirmed what Cranston knew all along: "Once again, Sen. Helms is acting like a political enemy, not a fair-minded juror."

Report Details

Helms had signaled his frustration to the committee leaders in a letter July 15. He told Rudman and Heflin that he saw "no adequate resolution of the case in sight." He also criticized unnamed senators "who at the outset declared that there should be no penalty at all, that 'none of the so-called Keating Five did anything wrong.'"

Especially disturbing to Helms was the prospect that the committee might issue only a brief report or no report at all. "I cannot and will not be a party to that," Helms said in his letter.

Helms said he adopted Bennett's report with only minor changes in part to scuttle a proposal by some panel members to issue what he called "a truncated report — or no report at all."

In the introduction to his report, Helms said that he wanted "to preserve the historical record" and "demonstrate the thoroughness and fairness with which the committee investigated this matter."

Helms said the report "fairly, fully and accurately reflects my conclusions." After the committee got the report in late June or early July, Bennett and his staff helped make some changes for Helms, and Helms' top aide, Darryl Nirenberg, did some final editing, officials said. But the changes were minor, Helms' office said.

The report was similar in tone to Bennett's 1990 report on Sen. Durenberger's ethics woes. In fact, the sanction resolution proposed by Helms for Cranston was virtually identical in many respects to the resolution on Durenberger. The key difference: Helms advocated censuring Cranston; Durenberger was "denounced." There was no legal difference, but censure was generally viewed as more severe. *(1990 Almanac, p. 98)*

The report said: "On each of four separate occasions, Cranston solicited or accepted contributions knowing that Keating had requested or received his assistance in behalf of Lincoln. At least by the fourth occasion, Cranston knew or should have known that Keating was attempting to influence him with the contributions."

Helms said Cranston "engaged in inherently improper conduct" by allowing a political aide, Joy Jacobson, "to function as a fundraiser who viewed contributors as deserving of special consideration and who acted on that belief."

In perhaps his harshest criticism, Helms suggested that Cranston had "violated the spirit and purpose" of a criminal law: "Cranston acted in a manner that implicated the very dangers to our democratic process that the conflict of interest statute was designed to prevent."

The report also dredged up details about the other four senators. It told, for instance, how DeConcini supported Keating and an associate for presidential appointments after doing little to check their credentials, and it recalled that despite Riegle's denials, most testimony pointed to him as the first senator to suggest that several senators meet with a top thrift regulator to discuss Keating's complaints. It recounted how McCain was concerned that such a meeting might smack of "undue pressure" but went anyway.

The report included a strong endorsement of Bennett's guidelines for senators trying to decide whether helping a particular fundraiser is proper:

" . . . A member who has any doubt about whether to proceed in a particular matter [should] consider the following:

- Does the senator have reason to believe that the constituent's case has merit and did he or she attempt to verify the legitimacy of the constituent's complaint?
- If the constituent's claim initially appeared to have merit, has the senator acted despite facts or circumstances that later undermine the merits of that claim?
- Has the senator acted on behalf of a single constituent or on behalf of broader interests and do these interests conflict with the public good?
- Does the senator hold positions that enable him or her to exercise particular influence over a constituent's needs?
- To what extent does the action or pattern of action deviate from the norm of senatorial conduct?
- Is the agency performing in a quasi-judicial, adjudicative or enforcement function?
- Did the senator know or should he or she have known of the contribution?
- How close in time is the senator's action to his or her knowledge of or receipt of the contribution(s)?
- Could action by the member appear to be influenced by the contribution based on the amount of the contribution and the history of donations? Do these factors suggest that the contributor is attempting to influence the member with the contribution?"

Continuing Deadlock

The committee met several times after Congress returned in September, but Helms' bombshell had not changed the impasse. Frustrated with the delays, panel member Lott openly floated a proposal in late September to declare a deadlock and abandon the case. But more delays followed.

Its two leaders were sidetracked for weeks: Heflin by the Judiciary Committee's work on Clarence Thomas' nomination to the Supreme Court and Rudman by the Intelligence Committee's work on Robert M. Gates' nomination as director of central intelligence. *(Thomas confirmation, p. 274; Gates appointment, p. 486)*

The uproar over the Senate's handling of the Thomas nomination — and the pummeling its reputation took as a result — prompted Lott to drop his proposal. At a meeting Oct. 17, the committee renewed its effort.

A compromise finally began to take shape after Lott suggested a middle ground: a committee rebuke that the Senate would vote to accept — sort of an indirect censure.

The panel's Democrats balked at that, wanting to avoid a painful floor fight. Harry Reid, D-Nev., who had been secretly acting as Cranston's liaison to the committee for months, told the panel that Cranston would not accept a vote.

A final concession by the Republicans sealed the deal: no floor vote, but the committee reprimand would contain harsh language, and would be delivered in person in full view of Cranston's colleagues.

"We elevated everything to a level just below a Senate censure," said Lott.

Helms refused to sign on, but he was persuaded not to fight the deal. He abstained, and the rest of the Ethics Committee approved the compromise by 5-0 on Nov. 19 and presented it to the Senate the next day — two years, one month, three weeks and five days after the first public complaint on the case was received.

FORMAL FLOOR REBUKE

The Ethics Committee's report said the panel was acting "on behalf of and in the name of the United States Senate" in reprimanding Cranston "strongly and severely."

Senate lawyers had informed the members that the committee could not censure a member, so they settled for what the resolution called "the fullest, strongest and most severe sanction which the committee has the authority to impose."

The committee said Cranston's conduct breached "established norms of behavior in the Senate and was improper conduct which reflects upon the Senate" in violation of the chamber's longstanding catchall admonition that members must do more than just obey laws and specific rules.

The resolution included several clauses to soften the blow, including one that made clear that Cranston had "violated no law or specific Senate rule; acted without corrupt intent; and did not receive nor intend to receive personal financial benefit from any of the funds raised through Mr. Keating."

Aiding Cranston's cause was his illness — he was still suffering side effects from his treatments for prostate cancer — and his decision to retire after 1992. The resolution called those facts "extenuating circumstances." "The thing that finally got the votes was his horrible physical condition," Rudman said in an interview.

Cranston's Involvement

The Ethics Committee released a 79-page report, along with a copy of Helms' previous 247-page report as a harsh dissent. Cranston issued a 66-page response to the committee's resolution that argued in detail against almost all of the committee's conclusions. *(Text, p. 38-E)*

After reviewing the voluminous evidence presented at the hearings, the committee found no evidence of a corrupt bargain — an illegal exchange of contributions for official action. The committee, however, decided that Cranston's conduct veered too close to a quid pro quo, finding "an impermissible pattern of conduct in which fundraising and official activities were substantially linked."

In summary, the evidence seemed to show that it was not just that Cranston solicited and accepted much more money than the other four senators — $100,000 and more at a clip — and repeatedly did so at times when Keating was successfully seeking his assistance. No one episode sealed Cranston's fate; rather, Heflin said, it was "the totality of the circumstances."

According to the evidence, donations and official actions shared space in several memos to Cranston from his top fundraiser, Joy Jacobson. One listed contributors, including Keating, seeking Cranston's official help and said they "rightfully expect some kind of resolution" of their requests. Another informed Cranston of a news clipping about a new top banking regulator's views, saying they "obviously are good news to Keating. You should ask Keating for $250,000." Cranston did. Some meetings between Cranston and Keating included discussions of both Keating's donations and his problems with the regulators.

Keating's fundraising for Cranston went back to 1984 and totaled $994,000. The early help was of comparatively little significance. In 1984-86, he raised a total of $134,000 for Cranston's presidential and Senate campaigns and for the California Democratic Party at Cranston's request. In addition, Keating arranged a $300,000 line of credit from Lincoln for Cranston's campaign committee, although the senator never used it.

It was later donations to voter groups associated with Cranston that were most troubling to the Ethics Committee. Keating gave the groups a total of $850,000 in 1987-88 and discussed giving another $100,000 in 1989. The committee found that during that same period Cranston talked to regulators or took other actions in Keating's behalf more than a dozen times.

The panel focused on four episodes. According to its findings:

- In March 1987 — weeks before the meetings between the senators and regulators — Keating had Lincoln contribute $100,000 to one group at Cranston's request.
- In November 1987, Keating had Lincoln's parent company, American Continental Corp., contribute $250,000 to two other groups, again at Cranston's request. When a Keating aide delivered the contributions, Cranston called Keating, who asked the senator to call a top banking official for him. Cranston called the official six days later.
- In February 1988, Keating gave $500,000 from his American Continental Corp. to Cranston-affiliated voter groups. At the time, Keating was lobbying Cranston to set up a meeting for him with a top banking official.
- Another $100,000 donation was discussed by Keating and Cranston or his staff in early 1989, when Cranston was pressing regulators to make a decision on Keating's attempt to sell Lincoln. That donation was never made. American Continental declared bankruptcy on April 13, 1989; the government seized Lincoln the next day.

The committee's report offered a little new guidance to senators on how to avoid "linkage." The "cardinal principle," the report said, was to make decisions "without regard to whether the individual has contributed or promised to contribute."

It cautioned members to consider the following: the merits of the constituent's request; how much money the constituent had contributed; whether the type of official action to be taken in behalf of the constituent deviated from the senator's usual conduct; and, finally, "the proximity of money and action."

But the report did not say how to evaluate these considerations.

Floor Scene

Key to the final compromise was the desire by all concerned to avoid a full-scale floor fight. For that, the committee needed Cranston to accept its decision. Cranston made his bottom line clear on the floor: "If the committee had called for any action by the full Senate against me, I would have fought it tooth and nail."

Up until the morning of Nov. 20, when the Senate assembled to consider the Cranston report, the question of whether there would be a floor vote was a tightly held secret. There was speculation that somebody might try to force a vote, but President Pro Tempore Robert C. Byrd, D-W.Va., quashed that notion when he took the presiding officer's chair shortly after 2 p.m. and said: "The order does not provide for the taking of any votes by the Senate."

As members filed in, Senate pages dropped the committee's report on their desks, along with a copy of Helms' dissent.

The only members absent for the occasion were four Democrats — Bill Bradley, N.J.; Kent Conrad, N.D.; Bob Kerrey, Neb.; and Tom Harkin, Iowa.

Cranston briefly chatted with Heflin while members filled the chamber. Twenty-six aides and lawyers were granted floor privileges, but Byrd sternly warned them: "Only senators will be given the privilege to speak." Byrd's warning seemed aimed at Alan M. Dershowitz, the outspoken criminal defense lawyer (his recently published book was called "Chutzpah") whom Cranston persuaded to represent him for free.

Heflin read the panel's resolution and a lengthy statement slowly and deliberately. He took 35 minutes.

"The path to judgment is easy when a specific law or rule has been violated," he said. "But for those of us who believe in the rule of law, violations of unwritten ethical standards are far more difficult to resolve."

Rudman was next, reading his own lengthy statement much faster. While Heflin's statement had focused on standards, Rudman gave a more detailed accounting of Cranston's conduct. Among the most disturbing incidents, he said, was when Cranston greeted Keating once in 1988 by patting him on the back and saying, "Ah, the mutual aid society." (Cranston said he did not recall the comment.)

"If this were an isolated incident, we would not be here today," he said after telling colleagues about a $100,000 contribution followed by Cranston's participation in two key meetings with regulators about Keating's problems. "But the pattern of linkage continued," Rudman continued. "The pattern is clear, and, unfortunately, repetitive."

Cranston, frail but resolute, began on a contrite note as his colleagues turned their chairs to face him:

"I rise with deep remorse in my heart to accept the reprimand of the committee. I deeply regret the pain all this has caused my family, my friends and my supporters," he said. He choked once as he spoke of how proud he was of his work during the past 23 years in the Senate, 14 as whip.

"I am not proud of this moment," he said. His intentions were proper, "but in retrospect, I grant that I should not have solicited and received — even though it was on behalf of others — charitable donations close in time to official actions. That conduct came, in time, to reflect upon me and hence upon the Senate, this body that I love and revere, and for that I apologize."

Then came the defense: He rejected many of the committee's findings in a 126-page submission for the record. He attempted to reinterpret the panel's reasoning, saying he was being reprimanded only because "there appeared to be a proximity in time" between donations and actions.

"That is what we're talking about — appearances," he said. "I now realize that what I did looked improper. But I differ, and I differ very, very deeply, with the committee's statement in the resolution that my conduct 'violated established norms of behavior in the Senate.'"

He compared the Ethics Committee to a "tyrant king" for deciding ex post facto that any such norms existed. He said he could and had been prepared to produce "example after example of comparable" conduct to show "that my behavior did not violate any established norms." He spoke of contributions as large as $750,000. "More than a few of these contributors have benefited from actions taken by the senator involved, sometimes close in time to a contribution," he said.

"You are in jeopardy," he told his colleagues.

During his speech, many members (especially on the Republican side) appeared to grow tense. Some grumbled to each other. Steve Symms, R-Idaho, said he remarked to Wallop, "I heard the same speech 20 years ago when [Vice President] Spiro [T.] Agnew resigned."

Rudman's angry outburst followed. He called Cranston's statement "poppycock," later telling reporters, "I wanted to call it something else that begins with 'B.'"

Cranston's defense became more defiant at a later news conference dominated by Dershowitz. The lawyer told reporters that a review of public records by him and Cranston turned up many senators who "engaged in comparable linkage but covered their tracks better" and some whose linkage was "far more suspicious, far more direct."

"Neither the senator nor I are claiming that any other senator has engaged in wrongdoing," he said. "Those senators violated no rules, and neither did Sen. Cranston.... We are saying those who are without sin cast the first stone."

After the floor session, a few Republicans quickly began talking about forcing the issue to a vote. Some censure language was circulated, but it was not offered. Said Nancy Landon Kassebaum, R-Kan.: "Rudman took care of it pretty effectively. Maybe it's best to let sleeping dogs lie."

Dixon Exonerated; Keating Convicted

That was not quite the end of the protracted case. The Ethics Committee on Feb. 26, 1992, revealed that it had secretly reopened its inquiry to see if a sixth senator was involved, but concluded after three months of investigation that there was no basis to think so.

The inquiry centered on a 2-year-old memo delivered to the panel on Nov. 20, 1991. The memo, from Keating's secretary to him, suggested that someone named "Dickson" — perhaps Sen. Alan J. Dixon, D-Ill. — had taken steps to help Keating, and that Riegle had been helping Keating long after the time he had said he quit doing so.

The committee said it had tried to get Keating and his secretary to talk about the memo, but they had invoked the Fifth Amendment and refused. The committee took testimony from the senators named in the memo, key Keating underlings and federal regulators. All the senators, including Dixon, denied knowing anything about the circumstances described in the memo.

The committee concluded the memo was "incorrect and inaccurate," and declined to proceed further.

After the Keating Five case wound down in Congress, Keating's legal troubles continued. He was convicted in Los Angeles on Dec. 4 of 17 counts of securities fraud, and acquitted on one count. Later in December, Keating was indicted in Los Angeles on additional federal fraud and racketeering charges, and in January he was indicted on more federal charges in Phoenix. ■

Scandals Plague Members in First Session

The year ended on a defensive note as members saw long-simmering public suspicion of incumbents hit the boiling point over a string of unflattering reports about members' exploitation of their perquisites. The impact was strongest in the House, where mini-scandals forced leaders to close an informal bank that went back to the early 19th century, to trim members' credit at their restaurant and to stop helping members fix their traffic tickets.

The House opened an ethics investigation to determine whether some members had abused their banking privileges by repeatedly writing checks they could not cover — taking advantage of the House bank's longstanding practice of covering overdrafts without charging interest or penalties.

The inquiry spilled over into 1992, raising the prospect of some members being denounced as fast-buck artists just as the election season got into full gear.

With Congress' reputation already battered by the seamy hearings over charges of sexual harassment against Supreme Court nominee Clarence Thomas, the protracted Keating Five scandal and the Senate's move to give itself a 23 percent pay raise, public opinion polls plummeted. *(Thomas confirmation, p. 274; Keating hearings, p. 26; Senate pay, p. 22)*

The uproar further damaged Congress' reputation with the public, according to an Oct. 5-7 New York Times/CBS News poll. About three out of five respondents said they considered half or most members of Congress "financially corrupt," up from two in five in an August 1990 poll. Congress' general approval rating in the poll was 27 percent, down from 49 percent right after the debate over going to war with Iraq in January but higher than the 23 percent registered during the 1990 budget fight. Nevertheless, 56 percent approved of their own House member.

There was one immediate political casualty. Republican Rep. Larry J. Hopkins' gubernatorial campaign in Kentucky collapsed after he admitted floating checks at the House bank. *(Political report, p. 3-A)*

The political atmosphere was symbolized Oct. 1 when Iowa Republican Rep. Jim Nussle, a freshman, gave a short speech on the House floor wearing a paper bag over his head in mock embarrassment.

HOUSE BANK

The House bank was an unusual institution in which only members were allowed to have accounts. Its roots could be traced to the early 1790s, when one of the first Speakers made an unofficial agreement with the Treasury that money for members' pay would be advanced to him so he could pay them himself. Since the early years of the 20th century, the bank was run by the Office of the Sergeant at Arms as a part of the members' payroll system. It operated out of an office off the House floor and was used as a convenient check-cashing service for members and for employees and journalists working in the Capitol (although non-members could not have accounts). For decades it had honored personal checks written on members' no-interest accounts even if they did not have funds to cover them. Regular banks would have bounced such checks; by making them good and collecting from the members later, the House bank was in effect giving members interest-free loans.

The check-floating brouhaha began Sept. 18 when the General Accounting Office (GAO) reported that during the 12-month period ending June 30, 1990, 8,331 bad checks had been written against members' House bank accounts.

The bank, run by House Sergeant at Arms Jack Russ, made the checks good without penalty or interest by using other members' funds on deposit, the GAO said. During the second six-month period covered by the report, 581 of the bad checks from 134 members' accounts were for $1,000 or more.

Check-floating was a problem at the bank as far back as 1831, although it had never received much public attention. Auditors at the GAO had pressed House bank officials to tighten their check procedures in August 1988 because there were no rules in writing. Rules were drafted but not implemented, the GAO declared in 1990. An audit released that year focused mostly on bad checks written on outside, private bank accounts that were cashed by the House bank and bounced back to it.

Among 24 people who bounced checks, according to the GAO, were the sergeant at arms himself, an unidentified former House bank teller and an unidentified House member. The 1990 report noted that checks written on members' accounts with insufficient funds were being made good, but it included few details.

In response to the criticisms, Russ had promised in December 1989 to stop using the bank himself, and he limited check-cashing privileges to House members, former members and employees. Non-members' check-cashing privileges (such as those for journalists) were to be limited to $75 and cut off the second time a check bounced within a year.

But, the GAO found in its 1991 audit, the member-account problem got worse because no members were penalized. In the six months before the new rules were issued (July to December 1989), 4,006 bad checks were written on members' accounts and made good. In the six months after the rules were issued (January to June 1990), the number increased to 4,325. (The total number of member-accounts for all 8,331 checks was not disclosed.) It took some members weeks to reimburse the bank.

First reported in the Capitol Hill newspaper Roll Call, the story was quickly picked up by other media. Columnists and talk-show hosts weighed in, and the affair took on the dimensions of a scandal. Freshman Republicans, among the most vulnerable to re-election pressure, paraded to the floor calling for forceful moves.

In an attempt to stem the furor, Speaker Thomas S. Foley, D-Wash., and Minority Leader Robert H. Michel, R-Ill., took to the floor Sept. 25 to scold members and announce that the bank would no longer honor their bad checks. They resisted calls to release the names of the members responsible for the episode, which Michel called "a blot on the whole House."

Foley said he had instructed officials six months previously to stop allowing members to float checks without paying interest. "I must tell you I am distressed to learn that communications problems apparently developed and that message was not clearly understood by those who are operating the House bank," a visibly angry Speaker told the House. "The perception that members have a special privilege which is not accorded to the general public is one that I do not believe should be countenanced by the House in either appearance or substance," he said.

"This practice has ended," he said with emphasis. "Members will henceforth be treated without exception as they would be in a private depository institution."

And, the Speaker said as forcefully as he could, "This is now a matter that is over and done with."

The Heat Built

But it was not over. Several freshman Republicans, including John A. Boehner of Ohio, Rick Santorum of Pennsylvania and Scott L. Klug of Wisconsin, made daily speeches and statements to the media calling for a public airing of the names of those who abused check-writing privileges.

It appeared over the weekend that the issue might blow over, but William Safire wrote a scathing column in The New York Times on Monday, Sept. 30, that, one member said, gave resolve to the freshman Republicans.

Safire suggested fraud, tax evasion and other crimes were involved in the scandal: "At large are officials who willfully and frequently abused their privilege. All should be exposed; some should be made to pay substantial taxes with penalties; a few deserve censure."

By Tuesday, Oct. 1, members were flooding the sergeant at arms office with requests for letters declaring them clean, and more than 100 were issued, Foley said.

Several news organizations began polling members to determine who floated checks. Few admitted doing so.

Among those admitting to what came to be called "problem checks" were Foley, who had initially denied having any; Majority Leader Richard A. Gephardt, D-Mo.; Minority Whip Newt Gingrich, R-Ga.; and Klug, the freshman Republican who led the charge for a full accounting.

"Sure it's embarrassing," Klug said, adding that he only wanted to target the worst abusers.

A conservative publication, Human Events, printed a story saying the bank records of Peter H. Kostmayer, D-Pa., showed a $23,000 check written to his father in 1984 that appeared to leave his account $32,000 overdrawn. Kostmayer said no float was involved because a $29,000 deposit was made two days after the check was written, and the check to his father was not processed until five days later. But he admitted to writing 19 bad checks over a one-year period. "It's totally unjustifiable; there is no excuse," he told The Wall Street Journal.

Only one member admitted knowingly taking advantage of the float: Charles Hatcher, D-Ga. "It was not infrequent, but it wasn't everyday," Hatcher told The Associated Press. "You could write the check, and they paid it."

Headline writers had a field day. "Congress' Name Is Mud in the Midwest," declared the Chicago Tribune. "Too Many Perks," said the St. Paul Pioneer Press. "A Washington Solution — If Your Checks Keep Bouncing, Just Vote Yourself a Raise," said The Houston Post."At This Bank, Bad Checks Are on the House," said the Greensboro News & Record.

Foley suggested politics was behind the uproar and said that "some of the press reports ... do not represent the finest hour of journalistic coverage."

House Bank Closed

Any hopes the leadership had that the scandal would subside were dashed the morning of Oct. 3, when front-page stories focused on unpaid bills at House restaurants, where members could get relatively inexpensive food and sign a chit to be billed later.

Foley repeatedly delayed his usual morning news conference as he conferred with House leaders from both parties. At 3:45 p.m., Foley told reporters that the bank would be closed and that the ethics panel would be asked to investigate.

"I want to emphasize again that it is not, in my judgment, a violation of ethical standards for members to have had an overdraft or delayed check," Foley told reporters. "The question here is whether significant, substantial repeated abuses of the privileges of the bank are disclosed."

Shortly thereafter, a resolution closing the bank and ordering the ethics inquiry by the Comittee on Standards of Official Conduct (H Res 236) was offered by Gephardt and Michel with Foley presiding.

"It is an issue that has humbled us, and I hope made us wiser," Gephardt said. Said Michel: "It is unmistakably clear that the American people look at this as an intolerable exercise in arrogance or worse."

The resolution passed 390-8, with a few of the dissenters saying it did not go far enough, and others saying it went too far. It called for the bank to close by Dec. 31. It ordered the GAO to turn over its working papers for the past two House bank audits (going back to mid-1988) to the ethics committee. *(Vote 294, p. 72-H)*

The panel was instructed to review the audits and the operation of the bank to determine whether there was any "potential violation of the rules of the House or any other applicable standards of conduct." It told the committee to consider whether members or employees "abused the banking privileges by routinely and repeatedly writing checks for which their accounts did not have, by a substantial amount, sufficient funds on deposit to cover."

According to the rules of the House, a member had to "conduct himself at all times in a manner which shall reflect creditably on the House," according to the Code of Conduct. But the only member who was immediately considered to have broken the rules was Nussle, who put the bag on his head Oct. 1. He was gently rebuked by the Speaker pro tempore, G. V. "Sonny" Montgomery, D-Miss., who told Nussle that it was against the rules to subject the House to ridicule.

Stokes Stepped Aside

Fallout continued Oct. 8, when the chairman of the ethics committee had to back out of the investigation because he had floated checks himself. Louis Stokes, D-Ohio, recused himself from the first serious case confronting him since taking over the Committee on Standards of Official Conduct earlier in the year.

"I have admitted that on occasions ... my account was overdrawn," Stokes wrote Foley. "While I have done nothing violative of House rules or ethics and I feel that I could be fair and impartial, in order to avert any appearance of impropriety, I deem it in the best interests of the committee and the House that I not participate in this investigation."

Matthew F. McHugh, D-N.Y., was named acting chairman of a subcommittee named Oct. 11 to handle the job. McHugh said, "The committee clearly would like to pursue the initial phase of the investigation anonymously, that is, without knowing the names, because it will reassure people, including members of the committee itself, that this is being done without reference to personalities."

The panel leaders said they saw no need to hire a

Alexander Inquiry Suspended

The House ethics committee looked into business ties between Rep. Bill Alexander, D-Ark., and the managers of a foundation that got federal appropriations with his help. But the inquiry ended when Alexander severed his connection with the two managers.

The Arkansas Democrat acted June 28, one day after the Committee on Standards of Official Conduct declined to declare that Alexander had not broken House rules. The committee said that it could not rule unless he disclosed more information about his financial dealings.

Alexander had asked the panel June 17 whether his Appropriations Committee work in behalf of a Key Largo, Fla., ocean education foundation was a conflict of interest with his business investments with its two managers. He did so three days after The Wall Street Journal reported that Alexander had helped direct up to $400,000 a year since fiscal 1988 to the nonprofit Marine Resources Development Foundation, based in Key Largo, Fla., which specialized in teaching educators about marine life. The 1991 earmark prompted an unsuccessful Republican floor attack on the Commerce Department's spending appropriations bill (HR 2608). *(Appropriations, p. 531)*

In 1986, Alexander invested $20,000 in a venture by the two directors of the foundation, Neil Monney and Ian Koblick, to build a small underwater "hotel" and related facilities in the same lagoon as the foundation's educational programs. To sever their ties, Alexander's wife, Debra, who had assumed her husband's stock in the venture's two companies, returned the stock for free.

Alexander also ended a separate business relationship with Monney. Alexander said Monney — "as a personal favor" — served for free as president of a Key Largo company set up in 1990 to handle what Alexander called a "sizable debt" from a "bad investment" in a Colorado condominium project.

special counsel. McHugh, however, disappointed members hoping for a quick resolution when shortly before the first session of the 102nd Congress ended he told members that the inquiry would extend into the 1992 election year, principally because of the difficulty of obtaining comprehensive information from the bank's records.

Pressure for Names

Pressure kept growing for the ethics investigation to reveal the names of members who abused the system, even if there was no formal disciplinary action.

"They're going to have to — otherwise it's going to appear to be a whitewash," said GOP leader Michel.

Hansen, the panel's top Republican, said his "gut reaction" was that some individual members would find themselves in hot water.

In his speech to members, McHugh outlined four gradations of check-floating habits. Those members who found themselves in the first two categories seemed to have less to worry about: Those members wrote checks that were short by amounts that did not exceed their next paycheck. In many of these cases, the bank did not even notify the members of a problem, knowing that the shortage would be covered when their pay was automatically deposited.

The third category involved overdrafts that exceeded members' next month's pay — posing "a more serious problem because there was no assurance that they would be covered by the next scheduled salary deposit," McHugh said. These members were told to make up the shortfall, but some did not, prompting the bank in some cases to bounce their checks. McHugh said a fourth, "very limited" category involved members who attempted to cover their House bank overdrafts with bad checks written on their accounts at commercial banks. This sometimes prompted the House bank to suspend a member's privileges.

McHugh revealed in his speech that the practice of allowing members to float checks was so longstanding that old GAO audits regularly reported overdraft totals in the thousands — 12,309 overdrafts in fiscal 1972. "The reports for these years note, rather matter-of-factly, that the sergeant at arms considered the overdrafts to be an advance on salary," McHugh said.

Leaders of the House Administration Committee circulated a draft report that seemed to downplay the scandal in an apparent attempt to influence the ethics inquiry.

The report laid much of the blame on the employees in the office who ran the bank. It said members had "no implied legal responsibilities" to protect the bank's assets, which the report said was more like a no-interest "trust fund" made up of members' personal funds.

RESTAURANT BILLS

The story about the House restaurant bills hit front pages the morning of Thursday, Oct. 3: revelations that members had not paid a quarter of a million dollars in overdue bills.

The problem was longstanding, but it took on a new life once members received word of a new policy instituted by Chairman Charlie Rose, D-N.C., and the House Administration Committee: as of Oct. 1, no free credit — only cash or credit cards.

The leaders of the subcommittee that oversaw the restaurants — Mary Rose Oakar, D-Ohio, and Pat Roberts, R-Kan. — pushed the story into the news on Oct. 2 by announcing that hundreds of thousands of dollars in overdue bills were outstanding.

"There's no free lunch," said a news release by Roberts, who freely admitted that he was capitalizing on the House bank scandal to embarrass members into paying up. "Members of Congress should pay their bills or face the consequences."

According to figures released by Roberts, about 250 members owed a total of $255,000 to Service America Corp., the company that had run the restaurants from 1987 until August. Fifty members and several committees owed $47,000 to the House for bills from before Service America took over. Some of the money was owed by former and deceased members.

The numbers had been much higher, approaching $1 million at one point in 1989, with most of the debt more than 30 days old, according to a GAO audit.

Officials familiar with the problem said much of the debt involved events sponsored by members for outside groups. Under the rules, the member who sponsored the event was liable for the bill.

A similar problem existed in the Senate, where the

architect of the Capitol oversaw the dining spots, officials said. GAO audits for Senate restaurants regularly showed tens of thousands of dollars in debts more than 30 days old. In each of the fiscal years 1988-90, more than $50,000 in debt was more than 90 days old.

"I believe most of the problems stem from third parties," said William F. Raines Jr., an aide to the architect of the Capitol. "I'm not aware of any senators who are deadbeats."

In addition to the credit-tightening steps by the House Administration Committee, Foley announced Oct. 3 that outside groups no longer would be allowed to hold functions on Capitol Hill without paying in advance.

TRAFFIC TICKETS

In the midst of the furor over the House bank and restaurant, news media began focusing on the House's longstanding system for fixing members' District of Columbia parking tickets.

Under a 60-year-old District law, members on official business were allowed to park in most illegal spots. They were issued special tags to alert police, but sometimes their cars were ticketed anyway. When issued a ticket, members would hand it over to Sergeant at Arms Russ, who would initiate the process of having it voided by District officials. News reports said Russ helped fix up to about 240 tickets a year.

"We will not intermediate those cases anymore," Foley told reporters Oct. 8. "Individual members will have to make any application that is to be made to the District of Columbia and on their own behalf, if they feel their car has been improperly ticketed while on official business."

Foley said the Senate had earlier "taken similar action, and I thought it was appropriate that the House and the Senate follow the same practice." ■

D'Amato's Conduct Found 'Improper, Inappropriate'

Closing a two-year-old case, the Senate Ethics Committee rebuked New York Republican Alfonse M. D'Amato on Aug. 2 for running his office in an "improper and inappropriate manner" but declared that there was not enough evidence to charge him with breaking any rules.

D'Amato, who had been accused of improperly using his position to help campaign contributors, friends and family, declared himself exonerated.

"I am certainly chastened by it and I have learned," he said of the panel's criticism. But he added, "I'm pleased with the thoroughness of the committee and their exoneration of me."

He called the charges initially filed against him on July 17, 1989, by a defeated political opponent (New York City official Mark Green) "scurrilous" and part of a "smear campaign." *(1989 Almanac, p. 48)*

The Ethics Committee investigated 16 charges, most of them involving allegations that the senator was improperly influenced by campaign contributions and favor-seeking family members.

The committee found "no evidence" of rules violations in two cases, "no credible evidence" in 12 and "insufficient credible evidence" in two. One of the cases prompted the committee's rebuke, but the panel decided that a formal sanction by the full Senate was not warranted.

In that case, the senator's brother, Armand D'Amato, a Mineola, N.Y., attorney, represented a defense contractor seeking the senator's help in its business with the Defense Department. His brother sought help from D'Amato's office, which twice sent letters to Defense over the senator's signature, but Sen. D'Amato said his staff acted without telling him about the matter, and he denied even knowing that his brother worked for the company, Unisys Corp.

The Ethics Committee termed the office's help for Unisys "ordinary and routine." Members declined to say whether they believed D'Amato's denial of knowledge of his brother's work.

However, the panel concluded, "the committee notes that it is the duty of every United States senator to conduct his or her office in a manner that precludes its systematic misuse by members of his or her family for personal gain. The activities of Sen. D'Amato's brother on behalf of Unisys constituted such a misuse. Sen. D'Amato conducted the business of his office in an improper and inappropriate manner. Based on the evidence available to it, the committee finds that Sen. D'Amato was negligent in failing to establish appropriate standards for the operation of his office."

Ethics Vice Chairman Warren B. Rudman, R-N.H., said the rebuke was punishment enough: "That's a fairly strong statement."

Witnesses Took the Fifth

D'Amato was critical of his brother and to a lesser degree of his staff for their role in the matter: "What my brother did was wrong, absolutely wrong. . . . I should have been informed."

But the senator said: "I should have known about it; certainly that is a lesson. In the final analysis, I'm the boss. . . . I'm responsible."

He said he had taken steps to see that a similar incident would not occur. Of his brother, he said, "He has been told he is to bring absolutely no business into my office."

In one of the other cases — involving help provided by D'Amato to campaign contributors in Puerto Rico seeking grants from the Department of Housing and Urban Development — the committee said its inquiry was hampered because "essential witnesses" invoked the Fifth Amendment to avoid testifying. Though some witnesses were compelled to testify under grants of immunity, the committee did not give immunity to the main Puerto Rico witnesses because that would have "put contemplated prosecutions at grave risk." The panel declared the Puerto Rico case closed but said it could be reopened later.

A former top worker on Green's campaign, Michael Waldman, director of consumer advocate Ralph Nader's Congress Watch group, called the panel's decision a whitewash and evidence of a "corrupt buddy system." He said the Ethics Committee should be abolished.

Rudman and the Ethics Committee's new chairman, Terry Sanford, D-N.C., suggested that in the future the committee would be more hesitant to open formal inquiries into matters when, as in the D'Amato case, only press clippings were used to support the charges.

The committee released details of the investigation by special counsel Henry F. Schuelke III, who was hired in November 1989 to look into the case, to explain what took so long.

In all, the panel said Schuelke reviewed about 1 million documents. He also reviewed evidence and testimony before two grand juries. Also reviewed were law enforcement agency wiretaps of "individuals other than Sen. D'Amato." Sixty-eight witnesses were interviewed and 56 were formally deposed, though 25 invoked the Fifth. Ten others told the committee through lawyers that they would invoke the Fifth if called. Seven were forced to testify.

Rudman said the case cost taxpayers $686,379. ■

Hatfield Subject of Ethics, FBI Investigations

The Senate Ethics Committee began looking into reports that Mark O. Hatfield, R-Ore., had on numerous occasions over the years accepted gifts, favorable loans and other favors from friends with an interest in the work of the Senate.

In addition to the ethics probe, the FBI began reviewing Hatfield's annual financial disclosure statements. Three times in 1991, Hatfield filed amendments to past financial disclosure statements, bringing to six the number of corrections he had made since 1986. Hatfield had twice (1977 and 1984) been investigated and cleared by the Ethics Committee. *(1985 Almanac, p. 34)*

Hatfield announced Sept. 25 that he failed to disclose more than $55,000 in past gifts as required by government ethics laws. Most came from a former congressman who once lobbied Hatfield, and another big chunk came from the wife of a prominent California banker. In other years, Hatfield had borrowed more than $300,000 from the two men, and they forgave $134,000 of his debts as gifts, which Hatfield had disclosed previously.

"Sen. Hatfield has previously acknowledged that he devoted insufficient attention to reporting procedures in the past and pledged that he would take prompt and full remedial steps in the future," the senator's office said in a statement. The new disclosures, it said, were "part of that process. Sen. Hatfield is confident . . . that procedures are now in place to assure careful reporting in the future."

Gifts From University President

Both the Ethics Committee and the Justice Department began inquiries in the spring after the University of South Carolina released records showing that its free-spending president during the 1980s, James Holderman, gave Hatfield speech fees, travel expenses and more than $9,000 worth of gifts. Hatfield initially failed to disclose the gifts on forms required by the Ethics in Government Act.

Holderman, an aggressive promoter of his school, at the time was lobbying Congress for grants. In 1986, Congress earmarked $16.3 million for the university in a spending bill that Hatfield helped oversee as chairman of the Appropriations Committee.

Hatfield's son attended the University of South Carolina on a $15,000 scholarship given by Holderman's office. Senate rules at the time did not require disclosure of scholarships for dependent children.

After the Holderman matter surfaced, news stories, including a detailed account in Congressional Quarterly Weekly Report, cited numerous other examples of Hatfield's accepting favors from friends who could benefit from legislative actions. Over the years, developers, oil men, college officials and businessmen had given Hatfield favorable real estate deals, trips, expensive artworks and more than $700,000 in personal loans, some with low interest rates. Some of the loans had been forgiven or extended. Most of the lenders said they were motivated by religious convictions they shared with Hatfield. Their money helped finance extensive real estate dealings overseen by his wife, Antoinette, a property broker.

In March the Portland Oregonian had reported that the president of the Oregon Health Sciences University had arranged a special admissions policy that allowed Hatfield's daughter to attend the medical school in 1989. Two of the nine members of the admissions committee resigned in protest against the policy, which was not public and which the president directed be applied to Hatfield's daughter and three other applicants. The policy gave special treatment to experienced health-care professionals; Hatfield's daughter was a nurse. The paper reported that Hatfield had helped the school get about $91 million in federal grants over the previous decade. Hatfield said he had told the university not to give his daughter any special treatment.

More Gifts From Friends

The September disclosures involved gifts from Holderman and two other wealthy individuals with a long history of helping Hatfield.

Hatfield's statement said former Rep. John R. Dellenback, R-Ore., head of a group of Christian colleges during the 1980s, gave Hatfield breaks on rent and debt that the senator estimated to be worth about $40,000.

According to lobbyists and officials who were present, Dellenback in 1987 or 1988 successfully lobbied Hatfield personally to sponsor a floor amendment on behalf of the colleges. Dellenback also was part of a group that lobbied Congress to create the U.S. Institute of Peace — a goal Hatfield made a reality with a successful floor amendment. Hatfield also said that he once backed Dellenback for an appointment to the institute's board.

More than $7,500 of the newly disclosed gift was forgiven interest payments on a previously disclosed $250,000-plus loan, of which $75,499 already had been forgiven.

The rest of the gift came from an unusual real estate deal. The statement said Dellenback leased Hatfield a farm in Tigard, Ore., in 1985. In lieu of rent through 1989, Dellenback allowed Hatfield to pay all "taxes, insurance, repairs and maintenance," the statement said.

The two "did not consider the rental arrangement to be a gift at the time," the statement said, but their lawyers advised Hatfield to report it as a gift "in the form of 'below market rental' for each year in which the Hatfields occupied the farm."

Hatfield's previous financial disclosures listed several loans with interest rates that could be considered below market, including one with no interest at all for a while. Hatfield's attorney, John W. Nields Jr., said: "I don't think there were any gifts involved in the interest rates."

The statement said Dellenback repaid Hatfield $35,000 for improvements to the farm by allowing him to apply the money to his debt to Dellenback when the farm was sold in 1990.

Hatfield also declared for the first time a $17,000 gift from Dorothy Cook, the wife of the late Charles E. Cook, a California business-and-bank tycoon. "Mrs. Cook generously financed the remodeling of a bedroom at the Hatfield's Oregon residence," the statement said.

The Hatfields and others have described their close

relationship with the Cooks in familylike terms. The Cooks lent more than $73,000 to the Hatfields over the years and forgave $58,010 of the debt. The centerpiece of Cook's holdings, the Community Bank of Pasadena, was active in the California Bankers Association, which sponsored a political action committee and lobbied Congress. A former top official with the bank said that nobody from the company ever lobbied Hatfield.

Altogether, Hatfield's disclosure forms showed loans of at least $688,000 from individuals from 1977 through 1984. Financial disclosure forms listed values only in broad ranges; the figures were based on the bottom of the range. ■

Flake Case Dismissed

Federal prosecutors took Rep. Floyd H. Flake, D-N.Y., to trial on criminal charges of embezzlement and tax evasion, but the case fell apart and charges were dismissed before the prosecution finished its initial presentation.

In August 1990, Flake was charged with 17 counts of evading taxes and diverting $141,000, including federal housing funds, from his church, one of New York City's oldest with one of its largest black congregations. His wife, Margarett, faced similar charges. *(1990 Almanac, p. 106)*

The trial opened March 11 in U.S. District Court in Brooklyn, N.Y. Prosecutors said a church fund had been used in funneling income to the Flakes to subsidize a lavish lifestyle. The case fell apart after testimony from 20 witnesses failed to convince U.S. Judge Eugene H. Nickerson that the fund was anything but an official church account. Charges against both Flakes were dismissed April 3.

Prosecutors asked that the charges be dropped after the judge barred them from presenting certain evidence in the case. "The court precluded the government from presenting to the jury for its consideration the heart of the government's case," U.S. Attorney Andrew J. Maloney said in a statement.

But jurors told reporters that they considered the government's case weak. Much of it was based on confusing financial records and testimony from church members sympathetic to the defendants.

The Flakes said everything they bought using the fund was church-related, even if personal in nature. The church's business manager said Flake was required by the church to "look well, dress well and drive well."

Though the Flakes denied evading taxes, their lawyers repeatedly emphasized that the couple would discuss their returns with the Internal Revenue Service and, as Flake put it, "resolve the matter."

Flake said the outcome "reaffirms my faith in God and in the criminal justice system." He said the case "probably had something to do with politics. There also could be some racism in it." Prosecutors denied such charges. ■

New Organization of Ethics Committees

Both chambers' ethics committees underwent major membership changes, and the House Committee on Standards of Official Conduct reorganized under new procedures adopted in 1989 ethics legislation.

Each panel faced politically sensitive inquiries into members' conduct, and the impact was felt in its own organization. In the House, the panel's new chairman, Louis Stokes, D-Ohio, recused himself from the first big investigation of his tenure, into misuse of the House bank, after admitting he had floated checks himself. In the Senate, the two-year investigation of the "Keating Five" senators inspired the panel's chairman, Howell Heflin, D-Ala., to step down after 12 years as chairman or vice chairman of the committee; he was replaced as chairman by Terry Sanford, D-N.C., who was already a member of the committee. Two other members of the six-person panel resigned as well: Jesse Helms, R-N.C., and David Pryor, D-Ark. The vacancies were filled by Richard H. Bryan, D-Nev.; Slade Gorton, R-Wash.; and Jeff Bingaman, D-N.M. *(Keating hearings, p. 26; Scandals, p. 39)*

Stokes Takes Over House Committee

Most of the House's ethics committee resigned after the scandal-plagued 101st Congress. They were replaced largely by institutional loyalists in line with the panel's historically cautious approach.

House Speaker Thomas S. Foley, D-Wash., tapped as chairman Stokes, a veteran troubleshooter for the House leadership with a long record of tackling unpopular tasks. A former defense attorney, Stokes was the panel's chairman from 1981 to 1985. A 10-year veteran of the panel, James V. Hansen of Utah, was named as ranking Republican. The full House approved them Feb. 6.

The other Democrats were Matthew F. McHugh, N.Y.; George "Buddy" Darden, Ga.; Benjamin L. Cardin, Md.; Nancy Pelosi, Calif.; Jim McDermott, Wash.; and Gary L. Ackerman, N.Y. The Republicans were Fred Grandy, Iowa, the only other member already serving; Nancy L. Johnson, Conn; Jim Bunning, Ky.; Jon Kyl, Ariz.; Porter J. Goss, Fla.; and David L. Hobson, Ohio.

The 1989 legislation expanded the committee, beginning in the 102nd Congress, from 12 to 14 members.

Stokes, 65, served on the House Committee on Un-American Activities, a panel he worked to abolish. He took over a troubled committee that in the late 1970s investigated the assassinations of John F. Kennedy and the Rev. Dr. Martin Luther King Jr. He was chairman of the Intelligence Committee in the 100th Congress and won praise from many Democrats for his work on the Iran-contra inquiry.

Stokes helped draft the overhaul of the House's ethics code in 1989 (PL 101-194). Foley said he picked the former chairman to give the panel continuity and expertise. "I did not think all of them should be going on for the first time," the Speaker said.

During his 22 years in the House, Stokes had advocated the milder alternative in about 10 ethics cases in which sanctions were disputed, sometimes putting himself on the losing side of lopsided votes.

"My whole career has been one of fighting for the underdog. I'm sure that's reflected in my votes," Stokes said. "But I think that even more than that, my record for

How the House Ethics Committee Worked

Following are revised procedures for investigations by the House Committee on Standards of Official Conduct, required by 1989 legislation:

Complaints

Complaints could be filed by members on their own behalf or for others, or by any member of the public if three members had refused, in writing, to transmit the complaint.

The committee could open an investigation without a complaint; an inquiry was automatic if a member was convicted of a felony.

The committee would not accept any complaint filed 60 days before an election, but it could open an investigation on its own at any time. The committee would not investigate a complaint based on conduct more than three Congresses old, unless older violations related to more recent ones.

Preliminary Inquiry

After an accused member had a chance to respond to a complaint and committee staff had a chance to obtain further information, the committee could dismiss the complaint, open a preliminary inquiry or, if the matter was being investigated by law enforcement authorities, defer action.

An "investigative subcommittee" of four or six of the 14 members of the committee, equally divided between parties, would be appointed by the committee's leaders to conduct a preliminary inquiry. The subcommittee's proceedings would be conducted in private.

If it determined that there was "reason to believe that a violation has occurred," the subcommittee would adopt a "statement of alleged violation" containing specific charges. If it dismissed the complaint, it would send a report to the House.

Disciplinary Hearing

An "adjudicatory subcommittee" (composed of the remaining members of the committee) would hold hearings to determine whether the charges had been proved based on "clear and convincing evidence." The committee rules called for such hearings to be public, though House rules could be used to force them to close.

Sanctions

The full committee would determine what punishment, if any, to recommend. It could send a letter of reproval on its own, or recommend to the House expulsion, censure, reprimand, fines or other sanctions, and had to submit a report to the House.

being fair is what makes people respect me."

When Stokes was chairman from 1981 to 1985, the ethics committee was twice criticized for going too easy on members. When it recommended reprimands for two Democrats for having sex with pages, the House upgraded the sanctions to censure. When it declined to launch a full-blown investigation of Geraldine A. Ferraro, D-N.Y., the Democrats' 1984 vice presidential candidate, Republicans groused.

No Pre-Election Complaints

In May, the House committee decided to block anyone from filing official complaints of improper conduct against members during the 60 days before each primary and general election.

The prohibition was approved May 29 as part of the reconstituted panel's revised rules, adopted to reflect the 1989 law. It was meant to curb what ethics members said was an increasingly popular tactic among challengers — filing a complaint and then trumpeting the fact that serious charges were being investigated by the ethics committee.

Participants in the panel's closed-door discussions said some members of the panel worried about how the regulation would be perceived at a time when the public seemed suspicious of incumbency. But after rejecting several less restrictive alternatives, the 14-member panel unanimously adopted the 60-day prohibition. The committee retained the right to open an inquiry on its own.

"We don't feel this committee ought to be utilized for strictly specious, frivolous and politically motivated complaints just prior to elections," said Stokes. He said the panel would "welcome" and fully consider any complaint submitted before or after the blackout period.

Under the new procedures, the panel was to split on a case-by-case basis into two subcommittees — one investigative and one adjudicatory — if a report of misconduct was deemed worthy of inquiry. If any allegations brought by the investigative subcommittee were found to be proven by the adjudicatory subcommittee, the full committee would recommend sanctions to the House.

In addition, the committee opened a separate Office of Advice and Education to help members and employees understand ethics rules by fielding questions and organizing seminars. Under the new rules, members were shielded from punishment if they followed the committee's written advice — a protection modeled after a Senate rule.

Senate Panel Headed by Sanford

Sanford, 73, was an FBI agent in the agency's gangster-busting days of the early 1940s. In 1951, he drafted a campaign conduct code for North Carolina's Young Democratic Clubs. As governor in the 1960s, he urged state legislatures across the country to establish ethics codes backed by powerful ethics committees. He also pressed hard for prosecutions in a low-level bid-fixing scandal over protests that the matter was too petty to worry about. He was one of the South's first progressive governors on civil rights, though in his 1960 campaign he felt obliged to insist, "I am opposed to racial integration." He pushed through an unpopular food-tax hike that put his political career on hold for years.

While president of Duke University (1969-85), he persuaded students to write an honor code. He fought hard and unsuccessfully to acquire the Nixon presidential library for Duke University's campus against the protests of liberal students and faculty members.

Sanford was a partner for years in a North Carolina law firm that became one of the state's most influential lobby ing operations. From his seat on ITT Corp.'s board of directors in the late 1970s and early '80s, he oversaw a two-year internal inquiry into bribery allegations that got some people fired.

Throughout his career, Sanford remained a man slow to question people's motives and reluctant to judge them harshly. He voted in 1989 against removing from office two impeached federal judges, Alcee L. Hastings and Walter L. Nixon Jr., who were ousted by roll calls of 69-26 and 89-8, respectively.

Both times, Sanford protested what he called unfair Justice Department tactics against the jurists.

During the Ethics Committee's Keating Five inquiry, Sanford was the most sympathetic questioner.

Sanford said one of his top priorities for the Ethics Committee was to see that matters were wrapped up quickly.

"I don't think we ought to drag out these investigations over months and years," he said. "I think that's totally unfair to the people involved."

Cleared in Ethics Inquiry

The Ethics Committee in 1988 investigated Sanford and an aide for a transaction that looked like an attempt to use the promise of a government rental contract to close a real estate deal. The committee cleared Sanford.

"Fortunately, I was in Africa; I had an ironclad excuse," he said.

The case centered on Paul A. Vick, a longtime associate of Sanford, who became his top aide after Sanford came to the Senate. Sanford had for years allowed Vick to help oversee his finances, with the authority to write checks for him and make promising property investments; in return, Vick got some of the profits, Sanford said.

On Jan. 15, 1988, Vick sold a Chapel Hill, N.C., office condominium that he and Sanford owned for $110,000 — $27,000 more than the 1983 purchase price. The next day, Sanford's name was signed to a lease obligating the Senate to pay the new owners $18,200 a year to rent it for Sanford's staff.

The deal was uncovered by the Raleigh News and Observer three months later. Sanford said he knew nothing about the deal. Vick said the lease proposal was not mentioned to the new owners until after they had agreed to buy the property.

Moving quickly to quash the controversy, Sanford bought the condominium back, canceled the lease, repaid the government $7,500 in rent, put new restrictions on the use of his signature pen and asked the Ethics Committee to investigate.

"It was not illegal, and it was not in violation of Senate rules," he said at the time. "It looked bad, however. Because it looked bad, it was bad." ■

Senate Launches Probe Into News Leaks

The Senate authorized an investigation into internal news leaks that plagued the nomination of Clarence Thomas to the Supreme Court and the Senate Ethics Committee's investigation of the Keating Five. A special counsel began looking into the case at the beginning of 1992.

The leaks from the Thomas confirmation concerned college Professor Anita F. Hill's allegations that Thomas had sexually harassed her when she worked for him at the Department of Education and the Equal Employment Opportunity Commission. The Keating Five leaks consisted of letters, memoranda and reports about several senators' ties to thrift executive Charles H. Keating Jr. *(Thomas confirmation, p. 274; Keating hearings, p. 26)*

The design of the investigation was the subject of partisan bickering. Republicans wanted to keep the focus solely on the Hill leak, but two days of negotiations between the parties did not produce a compromise. The Senate on Oct. 24 passed, 86-12, a Democratic-sponsored measure (S Res 202) that included the Keating Five leaks in the scope of the inquiry. The resolution gave the Republican and Democratic leaders power to appoint a special counsel, who would have subpoena power and assistance from FBI and General Accounting Office (GAO) investigators and would have 120 days to report back. *(Vote 228, p. 30-S)*

Republicans had pressed for a stepped-up investigation focused only on the Thomas leaks.

The issue came to a head Oct. 22, a week after Thomas was confirmed, when the Senate faced an amendment to unrelated legislation (S 596 — Federal Facility Compliance Act) proposed by John Seymour, R-Calif. He sought a 30-day inquiry by the FBI into the Thomas leaks. Senate Majority Leader George J. Mitchell, D-Maine, insisted on a broader investigation using a special counsel. Mitchell said the GOP saw "a short-term political gain in this one leak." The Seymour amendment failed on a 45-33 party-line vote after Mitchell made it clear he would push his own proposal. Mitchell's resolution calling for a dual investigation passed with bipartisan support. *(Vote 229, p. 30-S)*

Mitchell and Republican leader Bob Dole of Kansas on Dec. 6 named Peter E. Fleming Jr., a New York lawyer, as special counsel to investigate the leaks. Fleming was a partner in the firm Curtis, Mallet-Prevost, Colt & Mosle. A former federal prosecutor, he served as special counsel to the House's Select Committee on Crime in June 1970.

The investigation began Jan. 1, 1992. In early February, at Fleming's request, the Senate subpoenaed several journalists to appear before Fleming to answer questions or produce documents in connection with their stories, setting up a possible clash over First Amendment rights.

Reporter Timothy Phelps of Newsday, reporter Nina Totenberg of National Public Radio (NPR) and Bill Buzenberg, vice president of news and information at NPR, were subpoenaed with regard to their stories about Hill's allegations. Paul M. Rodriguez of The Washington Times was subpoenaed in connection with stories he wrote about the Keating Five investigation.

The reporters maintained that they would not reveal their sources on First Amendment grounds. Failure to answer questions could lead to a charge of contempt, but that could only be imposed by the full Senate after action by the Rules Committee.

Recriminations Over Leaks

Thomas was cruising along toward an easy confirmation when, three days before the scheduled vote, stories surfaced that a former employee had accused the nominee of sexual harassment — and that the Senate Judiciary Committee had not aggressively investigated the allegations. The furor forced the Senate to postpone the vote and call an unusual round of televised hearings on the matter.

Reports in the Long Island, N.Y., newspaper Newsday and on NPR quoted Senate sources who had read the FBI report but made it clear that the reporters did not have the report. Only senators and fewer than five staffers had access to the report, according to a committee aide. The NPR report also quoted from a copy of a statement Hill sent the committee Sept. 23.

The GAO had looked into disclosures of confidential information in October 1990 from the Ethics Committee's Keating Five investigation, but it could not identify the leaker. In August 1991, an easier leak to investigate came when North Carolina Republican Sen. Jesse Helms released a lightly edited version of a secret report by the Senate Ethics Committee's special counsel.

Sen. John C. Danforth, R-Mo., Thomas' chief backer, and others focused suspicions for the Thomas leaks on Sen. Howard M. Metzenbaum, D-Ohio, a leading Thomas opponent, and his staff. Metzenbaum's aides initiated the talks with Hill that eventually led to an FBI inquiry and subsequent leaks to reporters.

As he delivered a fiery floor speech at the height of the Hill-Thomas controversy, Danforth turned toward Metzenbaum aides who sat watching, staring them down as he explained that members and employees who leak secret information risk expulsion or dismissal, respectively. "That is how serious leaking an FBI file is," he boomed, glaring at them across the floor.

Metzenbaum denied the suggestion that he had been responsible for the leaks: "That is wrong. That is untrue. Let me say emphatically again, nothing could be further from the truth."

Past Leak Investigations

In Washington, anonymous leaks have often begotten calls for investigations of unknown leakers. The results: usually more leaks and little else.

Two senators were disciplined by the Senate for breaking secrecy rules, both in the 19th century. The first case was not even an anonymous leak. Federalist Timothy Pickering, Mass., was censured in 1811 for reading aloud on the floor from secret documents related to the Louisiana Purchase. Benjamin Tappan, D-Ohio, was censured in 1844 for giving the press confidential papers related to the annexation of Texas. He confessed and apologized once an official inquiry was begun.

In recent years, several members of Congress — including former House Speaker Jim Wright, D-Texas, Sens. Dave Durenberger, R-Minn., and Jesse Helms, R-N.C. — have gotten in hot water for releasing allegedly secret information, but all did so publicly.

In 1987, Sen. Patrick J. Leahy, D-Vt., quietly resigned from the Intelligence Committee after NBC broke a story based on his copy of a then-secret committee report on the Iran-contra affair. Several months later Leahy went public — because, he said, CBS had been tipped to the story.

In the House, the Committee on Standards of Official Conduct never determined who in December 1984 leaked an early copy of its then-secret report on financial disclosure violations by New York Democrat Geraldine A. Ferraro, a vice presidential candidate. Nor could it figure out in 1976 who leaked a controversial Intelligence Committee report on CIA abuses.

In 1975 the committee dismissed a complaint that Michael J. Harrington, D-Mass., had discussed with reporters confidential CIA testimony after finding that the hearing in question was technically not secret.

In 1989, then-Attorney General Dick Thornburgh ordered an investigation to find out if anyone in his office had leaked word of an FBI probe having to do with then-Rep. William H. Gray III, D-Pa., who was running for whip at the time. (It turned out that Gray was not the target of the inquiry.)

Months later, Thornburgh closed the investigation because he could not determine the leaker "with certainty." The New York Times reported, based on interviews with unidentified "administration officials," that the inquiry had concluded that one of Thornburgh's top aides played a role in the original Gray story.

In a 1990 case similar to the Thomas incident, an admission of occasional past drug abuse to FBI background-checkers by T. Timothy Ryan — President Bush's nominee to head the Office of Thrift Supervision — was leaked. Ryan was confirmed with little attention to the matter. *(1990 Almanac, p. 180)* ■

'Motor Voter' Legislation Blocked in Senate

Legislation to ease the voter registration process stalled out for the year in the Senate when Republicans opposed to the so-called motor-voter bill blocked its consideration on the floor.

While support among Democrats for S 250 was strong, Republicans banded together in opposition to the bill, warning that it would dump heavy administrative costs and bureaucratic burdens on the states and lead to increased voter fraud. The final vote to invoke cloture on July 18 was 59-40, one short of the 60 needed to limit debate.

Principal sponsors of S 250, Senate Majority Whip Wendell H. Ford, D-Ky., and Mark O. Hatfield, R-Ore., were prepared to try again to break off debate on the bill late in the session but decided to put off work on the measure until the second session.

The legislation established uniform, nationwide registration procedures and allow U.S. citizens of voting age to register at most federal and state government offices, such as public libraries and unemployment compensation offices, as well as by mail.

Backers, including some black lawmakers, characterized the legislation as an effort not only to increase the size of the electorate but also to increase the voting power of inner-city minorities, comparing it to the Voting Rights Act of 1965.

State efforts to implement motor-voter techniques began in the 1970s in Michigan and were expanded to 17 states and the District of Columbia by 1991.

Techniques varied from having forms available in the offices to handling registration through computers that had been programmed for driving exams.

The House did not act on a motor-voter bill in 1991. House members easily passed, 289-132, similar legislation in the 101st Congress on Feb. 6, 1990, only to see it die later that year on the Senate calendar. *(1990 Almanac, p. 71)*

House supporters, such as Al Swift, D-Wash., chairman of the House Administration Subcommittee on Elections, said they preferred to wait until the Senate acted before taking up a motor-voter bill again.

The bill was under the constant threat of a veto from President Bush, who said it would inject new costs into many state budgets and might lead to new forms of voter fraud.

A less visible element of opposition included the fear among some in the GOP that motor-voter might lead to higher registration and Election Day turnout of Democrats. But the exact opposite prediction was given by some in Democratic circles, who said motor-voter might lead to higher registration of affluent youngsters who tended to vote Republican.

BOXSCORE

➡ **National voter registration (S 250).** The legislation allowed citizens to register to vote while applying for a driver's license or other public certificates.

The bill also allowed citizens to register through the mail and in person at many federal and state offices. To combat voting abuses, the bill required state officials to periodically update their voter logs and verify voters' home addresses.

Report: S Rept 102-60.

KEY ACTION

April 24 — The **Senate** Rules and Administration Committee approved the bill, 7-4.

July 18 — The **Senate** failed on two attempts to limit debate on a motion to proceed to S 250. The first attempt to invoke cloture failed, 57-41. A second attempt on the same day also failed, 59-40.

Senate Committee Action

The Senate Rules and Administration Committee approved S 250, 7-4, on April 24, after holding a series of hearings at which testimony was generally supportive.

Unlike similar bills in the past, the 1991 legislation was cosponsored by a Republican. Hatfield said he agreed to sponsor the bill when Ford agreed to insert tougher anti-fraud language than was found in prior legislation.

Committee Chairman Ford echoed the thoughts of many who wanted to enlarge the size of the electorate and make Congress more reflective of the changing nation. "Such low voter turnout is truly an embarrassment to our form of representative government," he said.

Federal Election Commission research indicated that even as the voting-age population had increased since World War II, the percentage turnout of voters for presidential elections had been generally the same.

For example, in 1948 approximately 48 million people voted in the presidential election, representing about half of the voting population. In 1988, about 91 million people voted, also half of those eligible.

The most vocal opponent on the committee was Mitch McConnell, R-Ky., who said there was no evidence to suggest that a motor-voter system would lead to higher turnout at the polls.

McConnell cited a motor-voter analysis completed in February 1990 by the Congressional Research Service (CRS) that supported his claim.

CRS studied turnouts in states that had already adopted motor-voter and found that voter turnout after adoption was generally the same or less than turnout before. But critics charged that the results of the CRS report were inaccurate because researchers included data from states with less sophisticated types of motor-voter registrations.

McConnell also argued that motor-voter would have the effect of diluting the quality of the national electorate by including in it citizens who did not care enough about politics or the issues that frame national debate.

As approved by committee, the motor-voter bill:

- Allowed citizens to register to vote in person at state motor vehicle departments and other government offices, such as libraries, schools, fishing and hunting license bureaus and unemployment compensation offices.
- Required states to develop procedures to register voters through the mail. Under penalty of perjury, mail applicants had to sign an application form stating that they met all conditions of citizenship. In addition, a first-time voter who registered through the mail were required to vote in person, not by absentee ballot.
- Ordered state officials to regularly update voting logs and "make all reasonable efforts" to remove from rolls

deceased persons or people who have changed their address. The bill required states to periodically verify addresses of voters.

- Raised voting fraud to a federal offense.
- Allowed state and local election officials to receive reduced postal rates for mailings related to registration programs.
- Prohibited states from requiring registered voters to re-register before a general election.

The bill did not apply to North Dakota, which lacked a registration requirement, or to Maine and Minnesota, which provided for statewide Election Day registration in all federal elections.

Senate Floor Action

Suffering from a split committee vote and sent to the Senate floor under the threat of a veto, the future of S 250 was unclear when it was placed on the calendar for possible action.

Ford called for a vote on July 18 to invoke cloture on the motion to proceed to the bill, which was objected to by Republicans.

The first attempt to break off debate failed to get the 60 votes required. The vote was 57-41. *(Vote 134, p. 18-S)*

A second vote later that day inched closer to the 60-level mark, but it also failed, 59-40. *(Vote 140, p. 19-S)*

Two Democrats who joined the Senate in 1991, Paul Wellstone of Minnesota and Harris Wofford of Pennsylvania, supported the bill, reversing the position of their Republican predecessors who opposed a similar bill they year before.

Also, two members — James M. Jeffords, R-Vt., and Howell Heflin, D-Ala. — reversed their position from the failed 55-42 cloture vote that effectively killed the 1990 bill.

The absence of one senator, David Pryor, D-Ark., might have been crucial to the outcome of the second cloture vote, Ford acknowledged later.

Pryor, a strong supporter of motor-voter, had been recuperating from a heart attack and did not return to the Senate until later in the year.

During debate on the motion to proceed, Alan K. Simpson, R-Wyo., said the bill would further imperil many troubled state budgets because no money had been included.

"If you will talk with election officials in each state, you will find they are appalled by [motor-voter], unless we give them money," he said.

And Ted Stevens, R-Alaska, warned that voting abuse would run wild under S 250. "We would all like more good-faith efforts to register more voters," Stevens said. "But to make it so easy to register that fraud runs rampant is absolutely wrong."

Stevens and Minority Leader Bob Dole, R-Kan., had planned to offer substitute language to the bill if it had been brought up. The substitute, they said, would have put more teeth into the anti-fraud sections of the bill and would allow states to test motor-voter techniques at lower cost.

The Dole-Stevens alternative bill (S 921) would have made motor-voter voluntary among the states and would have authorized a $25 million block grant program to assist states that wanted to institute motor-voter. It also would have allowed more leeway for federal courts to prosecute voter-fraud cases.

Ford said he was ready to try for cloture once again in late October when Pryor had returned, but a heavy floor schedule of must-pass authorization and appropriations bills took precedence. ■

Closed-Captioned TV Coverage Initiated

The House and Senate both initiated closed-captioned television coverage of their floor proceedings in 1991.

The House of Representatives started providing the service, which allowed televisions adapted with decoders to display the printed text of words as they were spoken, on Feb. 19 and the Senate followed suit on Nov. 18.

Senate Majority Leader George J. Mitchell, D-Maine, said the service would provide important access to the deaf, those with slightly impaired hearing and those for whom English was a second language.

"It is important in any democracy that all citizens, regardless of their abilities, have access to the workings of their government. For too long those with hearing impairments have been denied access to Senate sessions," Mitchell said. "The ability to see and comprehend important debates should be a basic right available to all Americans," he added.

In providing the service, both chambers were complying with the 1990 Americans with Disabilities Act, which required that those with disabilities have equal access to government proceedings no later than January 1992. ■

Michigan's Bonior Succeeded Gray as Whip

David E. Bonior, D-Mich., chief deputy whip since 1987, defeated Steny H. Hoyer of Maryland by a decisive 160-109 vote of the Democratic Caucus on July 11, in a relatively intense competition to succeed William H. Gray III of Pennsylvania in the No. 3 leadership job.

Bonior did not assume the whip's job until Sept. 11, when Gray left Congress to become president of the United Negro College Fund. Bonior was succeeded as chief deputy whip by a triumvirate appointed by Speaker Thomas S. Foley, D-Wash.

Members attributed Bonior's victory to his work in the lower echelons, his easygoing personality and his foresight in campaigning for whip long before anyone knew the job would be available.

The vote ended weeks of frenzied campaigning by the two candidates. Bonior predicted he had support from more than the 134 Democrats needed to win; the night before the election, he claimed 160 sure supporters. But Hoyer's camp insisted that the race remained neck and neck at about 127 each, with the outcome to be determined by a handful of uncommitted members.

Bonior's appeal clearly outweighed any opposition by conservatives who thought him too liberal or by supporters of Israel troubled by his views on the Middle East. His victory margin mocked what had seemed the most potent threat: that abortion rights advocates, who dominated the Democratic Caucus, would desert him because of his opposition to abortion.

Hoyer and other members said Bonior's victory was so decisive, in part, because he began campaigning early and had a strong base built in a past drive for the whip's office. Gray beat Bonior in 1989 on a 134-97 vote. *(1989 Almanac, p. 3)*

Foley did not attempt to play a role in the race.

A Team Player

Bonior had won praise from liberals for his commitment to their issues and from a wide array of Democrats for his low-key diligence and keen appreciation of the value of teamwork.

His 1987 ascent to a formal leadership position certified the progress he had made since his early House years, when he was a restless Vietnam-era veteran searching for a role.

Bonior was chosen chief deputy whip by Speaker Jim Wright of Texas in 1987, as a bridge to liberals and Midwesterners.

Bonior had a personal following strong enough to make him a contender for a promotion in the leadership scramble that followed the spring 1989 resignations of Wright and Majority Whip Tony Coelho of California. After finishing second to Gray in the balloting for whip, he retained his appointed position as chief deputy whip.

As a member of the Rules Committee, which he joined in 1981, Bonior remained a voice for House liberals, often floor-managing high-profile legislation, such as the major oil spill bill Congress passed in 1990.

Bonior, who was first elected in 1976, broke with party leaders on occasion; he was an opponent of abortion, and he voted against the 1990 budget summit agreement. But usually, Bonior was there when his party needed him: He voted with a majority of Democrats 95 percent of the time in 1990. He took the lead in the fight against constitutional amendments to ban flag burning and backed the controversial pay raise package enacted in late 1989. He was in the nucleus of opposition to authorizing use of force in the Persian Gulf.

Although the whip's job had for decades been filled by appointment of the Speaker, the No. 3 leader had been elected by the caucus beginning with Coelho's selection in 1986.

Bonior's election set off a scramble to succeed him as chief deputy whip — a position still filled by appointment of the Speaker. On Aug. 2, Foley appointed three chief deputy whips: Butler Derrick of South Carolina, Barbara B. Kennelly of Connecticut and John Lewis of Georgia. The appointment of a Southerner, a woman and a black came in response to complaints that the House Democratic leadership was dominated by white liberal men.

Foley also appointed another liberal male, Marty Russo of Illinois, to the newly created post of floor whip. ■

Gray Resignation

Majority Whip William H. Gray III, D-Pa., resigned from the House Sept. 11, causing the third reshuffling of the Democrats' top tier in less than five years.

Gray publicized his departure plans June 20, only two years after the House Democratic leadership underwent a wholesale shake-up due to the resignations of Speaker Jim Wright of Texas and Majority Whip Tony Coelho of California in the face of allegations of financial improprieties. *(1989 Almanac, p. 36)*

Gray, Congress' highest-ranking black member, was succeeded in the House's No. 3 leadership job by David E. Bonior, D-Mich., who had been chief deputy whip since 1987.

Gray's departure surprised many members, who could not understand why someone would give up a position that put him in line to run for House Speaker one day. It also deprived blacks of their high-level voice in the House.

Gray had not sought to articulate or enact a specific black agenda in Congress, instead reaching out to moderate-to-conservative Democrats. When he chaired the Budget Committee, there were complaints that his deal-making too often left black concerns in the cold.

On domestic issues, Gray had been in the thick of work on the civil rights bill and voter registration legislation. In foreign affairs, Gray was considered an ardent advocate of sanctions against the South African government and of increased aid for African democracies.

Gray left to take charge of 200 employees at the United Negro College Fund, whose mission was to raise money for 41 colleges and universities, all private, historically black institutions.

Gray's move away from the spotlight also spared him recurring questions about legal difficulties. Starting in May 1989, when it became known that the Justice Department had asked Gray about allegations of payroll padding on his staff, Gray had periodically had to douse rumors that he was the target of an investigation.

Helicopter Crash Claimed Pennsylvania's Heinz

Sen. John Heinz, an advocate of the elderly and a defender of Pennsylvanian economic interests, died April 4 when his charter plane collided with a helicopter and crashed in a suburban Philadelphia schoolyard. He was 52.

He was succeeded by a virtual unknown in state politics, Harris Wofford, a former college president and adviser to President John F. Kennedy. The liberal Democrat, who initially filled the seat by appointment, ran a strong enough campaign on populist themes to defeat former Attorney General Dick Thornburgh in a special election Nov. 5.

Heinz, a Republican, was heir to the H. J. Heinz family fortune and among the wealthiest men in the Senate. Forbes magazine had estimated his worth in 1990 at $500 million.

Heinz, who was first elected to the Senate in 1976 after three terms in the House, was one of a shrinking number of Republican moderates in Congress.

He was killed en route from Williamsport, in central Pennsylvania, to Philadelphia. He had been scheduled to attend a town meeting in the area that evening and to hold a hearing on Medicare the next day.

Pennsylvania's Democratic governor, Robert P. Casey, conducted a lengthy search to find an interim senator. Chrysler Corp. Chairman Lee A. Iacocca, an Allentown native who had lived nearly all of his adult life in Michigan, was offered the appointment but turned it down.

Casey finally turned May 8 to longtime ally Wofford, the state's secretary of Labor and Industry. When he was sworn in May 9, the Democratic advantage in the Senate increased to 57-43, its biggest since 1980.

Wofford was then elected to serve the final three years of the term Heinz won in 1988.

Wide-Ranging Interests

Born Oct. 23, 1938, Heinz was educated at Phillips Exeter Academy and Yale University, and received an M.B.A. from Harvard Business School.

Heinz was not among the Senate's legislative giants, but his interests and influence ranged over a wide field of complex subjects, including trade, tax, health and pension policy.

One of his last major initiatives in the Senate was an unsuccessful effort to require the Pentagon to ensure that no single parents or couples with children be deployed to the Persian Gulf during the conflict with Iraq.

In 1990, he played an active role in legislation to impose stricter regulation on the securities industry. In the 100th Congress, he had a hand in fashioning trade legislation, pressing for more assertive policy on imported steel and other basic manufactures competing with the products of his state.

Heinz had been part of the Finance Committee's efforts to shore up the Social Security system in 1983, after having served as a member of the National Commission on Social Security Reform.

In health policy, he played a leading role in a 1987 rewrite of federal nursing home rules and the ill-fated 1988 law to provide Medicare beneficiaries financial protections against catastrophic illnesses. That law was later repealed.

In 1990, he participated in the successful effort to beef up federal regulation of health insurance for the elderly.

Heinz's interest in health care for the elderly also found an outlet on the Aging Committee, which he helped establish in the 1970s. He was chairman in 1981-86, when the GOP controlled the Senate.

Conte Died After Surgery

The death of Silvio O. Conte of Massachusetts on Feb. 8 shifted the Republican leadership of the House Appropriations Committee. His No. 1 GOP slot on that committee was filled by the more conservative Joseph M. McDade of Pennsylvania.

Conte's death greatly weakened the small liberal bloc in the House GOP. None of his colleagues could match either his clout within the House or his renowned wit, which he used to lambaste wasteful spending with sarcasm, laughter and verse.

Conte, 69, died in Washington, D.C., two days after surgery to remove a blood clot from his brain.

He had had a series of bouts with ill health. In 1987, Conte had surgery for prostate cancer, and he later had a knee replaced.

Conte had been the ranking Republican on the Appropriations Committee since 1979. That position was especially important within the GOP leadership because Appropriations' tradition of bipartisan cooperation gave Republicans far more influence than they have on most committees.

Conte used his influence to champion the social programs and projects important to his Frost Belt district. He also took aim at what he saw as boondoggles, including federal aid to beekeepers and staffing excesses in Capitol elevators and parking lots.

Conte kept a tight hold on the considerable powers he enjoyed as ranking minority member: He made subcommittee assignments for other committee Republicans and controlled the minority staff.

The differing policy priorities of Conte and McDade reflected their positions, not just their politics: McDade had specialized in Pentagon matters as ranking Republican on the Defense Subcommittee; Conte focused on social programs as ranking Republican on the Labor, Health and Human Services, and Education Subcommittee.

Carl D. Pursell, R-Mich., succeeded Conte in the subcommittee post.

On key defense issues, McDade supported funding for the stealth bomber and President Ronald Reagan's Strategic Defense Initiative, while Conte opposed both. McDade supported the early 1991 resolution authorizing the war in the Persian Gulf, while Conte was one of three Republicans to oppose it.

On domestic issues, Conte was a leading advocate of programs to help low-income people pay their fuel bills. In 1990's far-reaching budget agreement, hardly anything mattered more to Conte than getting an exemption for home heating oil from proposed new energy taxes.

On environmental matters, Conte was a prominent proponent of stricter acid rain controls in the 1990 clean air bill.

McDade came from coal country, a region that had long resisted stricter pollution controls. He was a key backer of the Clean Coal Technology Reserve Fund, adopted by some as an alternative to acid rain legislation. ■

Chapter 2

ECONOMICS & FINANCE

'92 Budget Moves With Relative Ease

Previous year's battle resulted in spending caps for fiscal 1992, eliminating potential for debate

The hard-won budget deal of 1990 paid off for Congress in 1991, allowing members to move with relative ease through the year's budget process.

Lawmakers passed all but one of the 13 regular appropriations bills with little delay (the appropriations bill for foreign operations was held up for reasons unrelated to the budget). And they escaped the traditional last-minute ordeal of struggling to shave the deficit with a budget-reconciliation bill.

But the budget deal also set strict spending limits that tied Congress' hands, and it did virtually nothing to reduce the deficit, which was expected by year's end to soar to $360 billion or more in fiscal 1992. With that record, and mounting pressure to cut taxes and shift defense spending to home-front programs, the rules were certain to change in 1992. *(Appropriations, p. 499; New budget rules, p. 73)*

The five-year budget deal, codified in the 1990 reconciliation bill (PL 101-508), established strict caps for discretionary spending in three categories — domestic, international and defense programs — which did away with much of the time-consuming infighting that had often slowed the budget process in previous years. Congress was also required to pay for any increases that it made in entitlement programs — such as farm subsidies, education grants and Medicare — by increasing taxes or cutting other entitlement spending. Failure meant automatic spending cuts, a process known as a sequester, in the category where the offense was committed.

As long as Congress lived within these limits, it was spared the paralyzing job of trying to cut the deficit. The new rules set a deficit target but explicitly held Congress harmless for anything deemed to be beyond its control — including the costs of the savings and loan bailout and of Operation Desert Storm, and the revenue losses and spending increases caused by the recession.

With these budget outlines already in place, the role of the Budget committees seemed less relevant than in previous years. Still, Budget Committee members insisted on the importance of passing a budget resolution, a set of fiscal guidelines for the Congress.

If the new rules kept the budget process on track, they also caused considerable pain: With little extra money to dole out, in most cases spending for one program could increase only at the cost of cuts in another. And members, particularly Democrats with social spending priorities, struggled through the year in search of money to move their ideas from news releases into actual programs.

FISCAL 1992 BUDGET

Bush Budget Reordered Priorities

President Bush got the annual ritual started when he sent his $1.45 trillion budget to the Hill on Feb. 4. By the standards of the past decade, it was unusual, almost radical: There was no attempt to hide the enormous $281 billion deficit projected for 1992; no glossing over the grim short-term economic outlook; and for the first time in more than 20 years, a request for a cut in defense spending authority.

With little room to maneuver, Bush concentrated on reordering priorities, starving some programs to feed others while staying within the limits set in the budget accord. Overall, he sought to increase 250 domestic programs, cut 109 and eliminate 238.

Among the biggest winners were research and development, space exploration, education programs, highway construction and initiatives aimed at children.

Paradoxically, some of the winners were losers, too. Education programs were hit by crosscutting offsets and increases that failed to keep pace with inflation, leading to some cutbacks in real terms.

Other targets for cuts included the Community Services Block Grant, the Community Development Block Grant program, urban mass transit and various housing programs.

In line with the 1990 budget deal, Bush showed defense spending on a downward path designed to strip about $180 billion out of the cumulative Pentagon budget by 1995. Bush called for $290.8 billion in defense spending authority for 1992, a cut from the 1991 figure of about $300 billion, which included $14 billion in net authority for Operation Desert Storm.

Targeting Mandatory Programs

Bush also proposed a dramatic revamping of mandatory spending programs, which automatically provided benefits to anyone who met preset eligibility requirements. Insisting that spending for programs such as Medicaid and food stamps was badly out of control, he proposed to scale it back, target it more closely to the truly needy and force middle- and upper-income beneficiaries to pay more for their benefits.

The changes would have generated $6.3 billion in savings in fiscal 1992. That was less than 1 percent of the budget's $707.5 billion in mandatory spending, but the proposed cuts touched everything from Medicare premi-

Balanced Budget Amendment

The Senate Judiciary Committee voted 11-3 on May 23 to approve a resolution (S J Res 18) amending the Constitution to require a balanced federal budget.

The resolution, sponsored by Paul Simon, D-Ill., would have allowed Congress to waive the amendment by a three-fifths vote of both chambers. It could also be waived when a declaration of war was in effect or when the United States was engaged in a "military conflict" that threatened national security.

The panel rejected, 6-8, a competing resolution (S J Res 5) by Arlen Specter, R-Pa., that would also have called for a balanced budget amendment but would have required a three-fifths vote in both houses for a tax increase.

The Subcommittee on the Constitution had approved both resolutions by a 4-2 vote on March 8.

The House fell seven votes short of passing a balanced budget amendment in 1990, the third time in eight years that such an amendment had been defeated on the floor of one chamber. The Senate Judiciary Committee approved an amendment in 1990, but it was not taken up on the Senate floor.

If approved by both chambers, an amendment would have to be ratified by legislatures of three-fourths of the states within seven years. *(1990 Almanac, p. 174)*

ums to school lunch subsidies, making many of them politically volatile far out of proportion to their financial value.

In his introduction to the budget and in congressional testimony, budget director Richard G. Darman made a strong pitch for the entitlement changes. "You cannot be serious about addressing the federal budgeting problem and fail to address this piece," he said, noting that mandatory spending had grown from 28 percent of the budget during the Kennedy administration to a staggering 52 percent.

Among Bush's proposals were initiatives to more carefully target school lunch subsidies and college grants to the needy; to deny farm subsidies to persons with annual non-farm incomes of more than $125,000; and to triple the monthly Medicare premium for single beneficiaries with $125,000 in yearly income or couples whose income is $150,000 or more.

Bush also proposed further cuts in Medicare, prompting criticism from Democrats who said budget negotiators had done about all they could to that politically sensitive program during the previous year's budget summit.

Block Grant Proposal

In a move that was greeted with considerable skepticism on Capitol Hill, Bush proposed turning over to the states $15 billion worth of federally funded programs in a single block grant, along with the authority to tailor the spending to state needs. He offered a $20 billion list of programs from which states and Congress might choose. The National Governors' Association, which was meeting in Washington, provided a receptive if cautious audience ready to listen to a proposal that would cut red tape. But on the Hill, even Republicans wanted a guarantee that the plan was not a subterfuge to cut back or eliminate the programs. In 1981, Congress had consolidated 57 education, health and community services programs into seven block grants and turned them over to the states. Then it cut funding about 25 percent below that provided originally for the individual programs. *(1981 Almanac, p. 463)*

Less Rosy Forecast

If Bush's budget was unusual by previous standards, the economic forecast on which it was built was startling: Though it seemed optimistic, it generally reflected a consensus among most economists that the nation's economy was undergoing a relatively mild and short recession and that it would begin to grow rapidly out of the downturn by spring. Beyond 1992, there were no foreseeable bumps in the road to stable economic growth.

The newfound realism was a sharp contrast with earlier years, when forecasts under Bush and his predecessor, Ronald Reagan, were dismissed as rosy scenarios, deliberately out of touch with real economic trends. A White House forecast of robust economic growth had made the projected deficit look smaller, allowing the president's budget to meet the deficit limits set in the Gramm-Rudman budget law.

The Congressional Budget Office (CBO) typically offered a gloomier forecast and predicted a much larger deficit. While Democrats in Congress complained about the White House projections, they usually ended up adopting them as their own: To work from the CBO totals would have required Congress to take responsibility for much deeper spending cuts than the president had said were necessary.

Under the new rules, Congress was no longer held responsible for deficit increases caused by outside factors such as the economy.

Office of Management and Budget (OMB) Director Darman acknowledged that this had reduced the incentive for the administration to base its budget on optimistic economic assumptions. "We're not always credible on this, and I'm aware of that," he told the Senate Budget Committee. But the new budget procedure "takes the emphasis away from gaming with the estimates. . . . We are no longer the rosy forecasters. . . . For the first time in a long time, we're about in the dead middle of economic thinking."

OMB forecast an end to the recession by midyear, with minimal growth in the gross national product thereafter, until the economy rebounded in 1992 and afterward. Critics disputed the later-year projections as overly optimistic, but the budget office's short-term recession prediction agreed with many economic forecasts.

The budget projected a 1991 deficit of $318.1 billion — easily eclipsing the record 1986 deficit of $221.2 billion — and a 1992 deficit of $280.9 billion.

Darman told members that the deficit should diminish sharply after the recession, the war with Iraq and the ongoing savings and loan bailout had played out. The administration's forecast showed a deficit of $2.9 billion in 1995 and a surplus of $19.9 billion in 1996. If that happened, it would have been the first time since 1969 that the federal government had generated a surplus.

An important side benefit to downgrading the importance of the deficit was an end to the pressure to find new tax revenues to close the spending gap. The Bush budget contained very little in the way of new revenue initiatives. Treasury Secretary Nicholas F. Brady said the intent was a "still pond, no more movement; let's let people work with the tax code as it is."

Bush's top tax priority was a familiar one: a cut in the rate for capital gains (profits from the sales of stocks, real estate and other assets). Bush had made the tax cut a

Continued on p. 61

Budget Authority, Outlays By Agency

(Fiscal years; in millions of dollars †)

AGENCY	BUDGET AUTHORITY 1990 actual	1991 estimate	1992 estimate	OUTLAYS 1990 actual	1991 estimate	1992 estimate
Legislative Branch	$ 2,243	$ 2,499	$ 3,010	$ 2,230	$ 2,548	$ 2,994
The Judiciary	1,745	2,062	2,571	1,641	2,056	2,341
Executive Office of the President	292	272	247	157	258	254
Funds Appropriated to the President	12,410	13,042	25,413	10,087	11,254	12,044
Agriculture	55,327	64,398	62,136	46,012	55,432	55,691
Commerce	3,684	2,642	2,563	3,734	2,796	2,756
Defense — Military	292,999	272,953	278,282	289,755	287,451	283,045
Defense — Civil	37,258	38,944	40,468	24,975	26,415	28,231
Education	24,686	27,097	29,620	23,109	24,839	27,494
Energy	13,984	16,067	16,130	12,014	13,539	14,897
Health and Human Services, except Social Security	195,897	225,178	242,757	193,678	222,435	242,543
Health and Human Services, Social Security	303,214	324,320	345,262	244,998	263,837	282,785
Housing and Urban Development	17,315	26,979	25,581	20,167	23,473	24,297
Interior	6,690	6,735	6,455	5,796	6,386	6,475
Justice	8,596	8,884	10,181	6,507	8,689	10,042
Labor	26,608	32,322	33,235	25,316	34,503	34,759
State	4,380	4,675	5,673	3,979	4,306	4,509
Transportation	30,153	30,670	33,468	28,637	30,768	31,862
Treasury	259,118	278,427	300,011	255,266	277,047	298,581
Veterans Affairs	30,461	32,086	33,245	28,998	31,338	32,815
Environmental Protection Agency	5,380	5,949	5,983	5,108	5,776	5,896
General Services Administration	2,191	1,907	276	−123	756	719
National Aeronautics and Space Administration	12,324	13,977	15,723	12,429	13,499	14,721
Office of Personnel Management	55,947	59,185	61,163	31,949	35,161	37,046
Small Business Administration	928	464	792	692	529	318
Other Agencies	63,698	123,676	115,458	73,617	125,708	102,108
Allowances		14,000	97		8,200	4,708
Undistributed offsetting receipts	−99,025	−109,436	−118,029	−99,025	−109,436	−118,029
(On budget)	(−77,467)	(−83,445)	(−88,065)	(−77,467)	(−83,445)	(−88,065)
(Off budget)	(−21,558)	(−25,991)	(−29,964)	(−21,558)	(−25,991)	(−29,964)
TOTAL	1,368,500	1,519,972	1,577,773	1,251,703	1,409,563	1,445,902
(On budget)	(1,083,762)	(1,218,921)	(1,260,671)	(1,026,638)	(1,171,658)	(1,194,205)
(Off budget)	(284,738)	(301,051)	(317,102)	(225,065)	(237,905)	(251,697)

† Figures may not add to totals due to rounding.

SOURCE: Fiscal 1992 Budget

Fiscal 1992 Budget by Function

(Figures for 1991 and 1992 are estimates; in millions of dollars †)

	BUDGET AUTHORITY			OUTLAYS		
	1990	1991	1992	1990	1991	1992
NATIONAL DEFENSE						
Military Defense	$ 292,999	$ 272,953	$ 278,282	$ 289,755	$ 287,451	$ 283,045
Atomic Energy Defense Activities	9,656	11,578	11,780	8,988	10,513	11,443
Defense-Related Activities	609	1,053	757	587	947	756
TOTAL	303,263	285,584	290,820	299,331	298,910	295,245
INTERNATIONAL AFFAIRS						
International Security Assistance	8,393	7,756	7,395	8,652	8,458	7,759
International Development/Humanitarian Assistance	5,696	6,617	7,456	5,498	5,442	5,838
Conduct of Foreign Affairs	2,933	3,164	4,121	3,050	3,394	3,532
Foreign Information and Exchange Activities	1,317	1,240	1,303	1,103	1,352	1,398
International Financial Programs	473	1,016	15,405	−4,539	−1,692	−713
TOTAL	18,811	19,793	35,679	13,764	16,953	17,814
GENERAL SCIENCE, SPACE AND TECHNOLOGY						
General Science and Basic Research	3,184	3,483	4,292	2,835	3,259	3,779
Space Application and Technology	11,460	12,995	14,642	11,609	12,522	13,674
TOTAL	14,644	16,479	18,934	14,444	15,781	17,452
ENERGY						
Energy Supply	3,394	3,923	3,167	992	1,662	2,846
Energy Conservation	366	465	296	365	394	406
Emergency Energy Preparedness	571	439	390	442	219	236
Energy Information, Policy and Regulation	595	353	276	559	343	223
TOTAL	4,926	5,180	4,129	2,358	2,617	3,710
NATURAL RESOURCES AND ENVIRONMENT						
Pollution Control and Abatement	5,545	6,098	6,145	5,156	5,869	6,051
Water Resources	4,332	4,350	4,497	4,401	4,488	4,439
Conservation and Land Management	3,783	3,560	4,179	3,553	3,999	4,112
Recreational Resources	2,395	2,488	2,424	1,876	2,202	2,478
Other Natural Resources	2,077	2,298	2,463	2,080	2,263	2,464
TOTAL	18,132	18,795	19,708	17,067	18,821	19,545
AGRICULTURE						
Farm Income Stabilization	12,313	18,179	17,638	9,761	13,453	12,790
Agricultural Research and Services	2,229	2,506	2,581	2,197	2,404	2,470
TOTAL	14,542	20,684	20,219	11,958	15,857	15,261
COMMERCE AND HOUSING CREDIT						
Mortgage Credit	9,847	9,829	5,171	3,845	5,263	3,652
Postal Service Subsidy (on budget)	490	511	223	490	511	223
Postal Service (off budget)	3,083	2,722	1,804	1,626	59	−1,124
Deposit Insurance	45,624	106,920	96,496	58,081	111,491	88,073
Other Advancement of Commerce	3,299	2,119	2,086	3,105	2,182	1,963
TOTAL	62,342	122,100	105,780	67,147	119,506	92,788
(On budget)	(59,259)	(119,378)	(103,976)	(65,522)	(119,447)	(93,912)
(Off budget)	(3,083)	(2,722)	(1,804)	(1,626)	(59)	(−1,124)
TRANSPORTATION						
Ground Transportation	19,369	19,037	20,197	18,954	19,622	19,746
Air Transportation	8,260	8,944	10,385	7,234	8,424	9,050
Water Transportation	3,168	2,927	3,474	3,151	3,171	3,736
Other Transportation	143	251	256	146	252	175
TOTAL	30,940	31,160	34,312	29,485	31,469	32,707
COMMUNITY AND REGIONAL DEVELOPMENT						
Community Development	4,060	3,391	3,387	3,530	3,856	3,853
Area and Regional Development	4,033	4,047	1,924	2,868	2,838	2,369
Disaster Relief and Insurance	1,728	24	457	2,100	1,016	236
TOTAL	9,820	7,462	5,768	8,498	7,710	6,457
EDUCATION, TRAINING, EMPLOYMENT, SOCIAL SERVICES						
Elementary, Secondary and Vocational Education	11,293	13,132	13,729	9,918	11,596	12,756
Higher Education	11,311	11,971	13,639	11,107	11,107	12,522
Research and General Education Aids	1,633	1,896	2,002	1,577	1,820	1,959
Training and Employment	5,563	5,767	5,531	5,361	5,532	5,693
Other Labor Services	817	864	980	810	846	946
Social Services	9,727	11,652	11,062	9,723	11,899	11,652
TOTAL	40,344	45,282	46,943	38,497	42,800	45,530

Fiscal 1992 Budget by Function

(Figures for 1991 and 1992 are estimates; in millions of dollars †)

	BUDGET AUTHORITY			OUTLAYS		
	1990	1991	1992	1990	1991	1992
HEALTH						
Health Care Services	$ 50,420	$ 62,010	$ 69,478	$ 47,637	$ 60,332	$ 69,951
Health Research	8,324	9,186	9,670	8,027	8,538	9,109
Education, Training of Health Care Work Force	670	725	616	589	709	687
Consumer and Occupational Health and Safety	1,503	1,646	1,535	1,462	1,609	1,512
TOTAL	60,917	73,566	81,300	57,716	71,188	81,260
MEDICARE	98,796	104,501	113,811	98,102	104,433	113,720
INCOME SECURITY						
General Retirement and Disability Insurance	5,815	6,114	6,055	5,148	4,993	5,617
Federal Employee Retirement and Disability	87,125	92,356	96,801	51,981	56,327	59,338
Unemployment Compensation	18,960	24,028	25,400	18,889	27,133	27,237
Housing Assistance	11,135	19,973	21,488	15,891	17,753	19,933
Food and Nutrition Assistance	25,054	28,134	30,318	23,964	28,215	30,247
Other Income Security	31,679	40,483	42,628	31,404	38,769	42,467
TOTAL	179,768	211,089	222,691	147,277	173,189	184,839
SOCIAL SECURITY	306,980	329,451	351,109	248,623	268,965	288,632
(On budget)	(3,766)	(5,131)	(5,847)	(3,625)	(5,127)	(5,847)
(Off budget)	(303,214)	(324,320)	(345,262)	(244,998)	(263,837)	(282,785)
VETERANS' BENEFITS AND SERVICES						
Income Security	16,660	17,071	17,431	15,241	17,046	17,273
Education, Training and Rehabilitation	279	341	419	278	406	485
Housing	548	718	777	517	398	876
Hospital and Medical Care	12,168	13,051	13,754	12,134	12,597	13,397
Other Benefits and Services	940	1,048	999	943	1,036	970
TOTAL	30,595	32,229	33,380	29,112	31,483	33,001
ADMINISTRATION OF JUSTICE						
Federal Law Enforcement Activities	5,200	5,734	6,566	4,648	5,714	6,211
Federal Litigative and Judicial Activities	3,829	4,505	5,314	3,579	4,523	5,042
Federal Correctional Activities	2,578	1,728	2,195	1,291	1,571	2,557
Criminal Justice Assistance	774	821	767	477	759	677
TOTAL	12,381	12,789	14,842	9,995	12,567	14,486
GENERAL GOVERNMENT						
Legislative Functions	1,800	2,021	2,468	1,752	2,085	2,466
Executive Direction and Management	296	270	243	160	259	248
Central Fiscal Operations	6,215	5,032	6,687	6,004	4,951	6,497
General Property and Records Management	2,313	2,042	426	31	995	971
Central Personnel Management	156	164	173	176	160	164
General Purpose Fiscal Assistance	2,033	2,128	2,087	2,161	2,133	2,083
Other General Government	750	1,433	1,330	800	1,367	1,479
Deductions for Offsetting Receipts	−361	−780	−725	−361	−780	−725
TOTAL	13,202	12,310	12,688	10,724	11,169	13,183
NET INTEREST						
Interest on the Public Debt	264,820	286,290	303,978	264,820	286,290	303,978
Interest Received by On-Budget Trust Funds	−46,416	−50,179	−53,516	−46,416	−50,179	−53,516
Interest Received by Off-Budget Trust Funds	−15,991	−20,164	−23,733	−15,991	−20,164	−23,733
Other Interest	−17,701	−19,335	−20,386	−18,191	−18,909	−20,386
TOTAL	184,711	196,612	206,343	184,221	197,038	206,343
(On budget)	(200,702)	(216,776)	(230,076)	(200,212)	(217,202)	(230,076)
(Off budget)	(−15,991)	(−20,164)	(−23,733)	(−15,991)	(−20,164)	(−23,733)
ALLOWANCES	—	14,000	97	—	8,200	4,708
UNDISTRIBUTED OFFSETTING RECEIPTS	−36,615	−39,093	−40,780	−36,615	−39,093	−40,780
(On budget)	(−31,048)	(−33,266)	(−34,549)	(−31,048)	(−33,266)	(−34,549)
(Off budget)	(−5,567)	(−5,827)	(−6,231)	(−5,567)	(−5,827)	(−6,231)
TOTAL	1,368,500	1,519,972	1,577,773	1,251,703	1,409,563	1,445,902
(On budget)	(1,083,762)	(1,218,921)	(1,260,671)	(1,026,638)	(1,171,658)	(1,194,205)
(Off budget)	(284,738)	(301,051)	(317,102)	(225,065)	(237,905)	(251,697)

† Figures may not add due to rounding.

SOURCE: Fiscal 1992 Budget

Administration Economic Assumptions

(Calendar years; dollar amounts in billions)

	Actual 1989	FORECAST 1990 *	1991	1992	ASSUMPTIONS 1993	1994	1995	1996
MAJOR ECONOMIC INDICATORS								
Gross national product (percent change, fourth quarter over fourth quarter):								
Current dollars	5.6	4.5	5.3	7.5	7.1	6.8	6.5	6.4
Constant (1982) dollars	1.8	0	0.9	3.6	3.4	3.2	3.0	3.0
GNP deflator (percent change, fourth quarter over fourth quarter)	3.7	4.5	4.3	3.8	3.6	3.5	3.4	3.3
Consumer Price Index (percent change, fourth quarter over fourth quarter) [1]	4.5	6.3	4.3	3.9	3.6	3.5	3.4	3.3
Unemployment rate (percent, fourth quarter) [2]	5.3	5.8	6.6	6.5	6.0	5.7	5.2	5.1
ANNUAL ECONOMIC ASSUMPTIONS								
Gross national product:								
Current dollars:								
Amount	$ 5,201	$ 5,465	$ 5,689	$ 6,095	$ 6,536	$ 6,990	$ 7,451	$ 7,931
Percent change, year over year	6.7	5.1	4.1	7.1	7.2	7.0	6.6	6.4
Constant (1982) dollars:								
Amount	$ 4,118	$ 4,152	$ 4,140	$ 4,267	$ 4,415	$ 4,560	$ 4,699	$ 4,840
Percent change, year over year	2.5	0.8	−0.3	3.1	3.5	3.3	3.1	3.0
Incomes:								
Personal income	$ 4,384	$ 4,644	$ 4,856	$ 5,182	$ 5,524	$ 5,887	$ 6,259	$ 6,655
Wages and salaries	$ 2,573	$ 2,700	$ 2,802	$ 3,006	$ 3,235	$ 3,467	$ 3,703	$ 3,950
Corporate profits before tax	$ 308	$ 300	$ 294	$ 335	$ 379	$ 419	$ 447	$ 484
Price level:								
GNP deflator:								
Level (1982 = 100), annual average	126.3	131.6	137.4	142.8	148.0	153.3	158.6	163.8
Percent change, year over year	4.1	4.2	4.4	3.9	3.6	3.5	3.4	3.3
Consumer Price Index: [1]								
Level (1982-84 = 100), annual average	122.6	129.1	135.8	141.2	146.4	151.6	156.8	162.0
Percent change, year over year	4.8	5.3	5.2	4.0	3.7	3.5	3.4	3.3
Unemployment rates:								
Total, annual average [2]	5.2	5.4	6.7	6.6	6.2	5.8	5.4	5.1
Federal pay raise, January (percent)	4.1	3.6	4.1	4.2	4.7	4.3	4.1	4.0
Interest rate, 91-day Treasury bills (percent) [3]	8.1	7.5	6.4	6.0	5.8	5.6	5.4	5.3
Interest rate, 10-year Treasury notes (percent)	8.5	8.5	7.5	7.2	6.8	6.6	6.4	6.3

* *Based on data available as of December 1990.*

[1] *CPI for urban wage earners and clerical workers. Two versions of the CPI are now published. The index shown here is that currently used, as required by law, in calculating automatic cost of living increases for indexed federal programs. The manner in which this index measures housing costs changed significantly in January 1985.*

[2] *Percent of total labor force, including armed forces residing in the United States.*

[3] *Average rate on new issues within period, on a bank discount basis. These projections assume, by convention, that interest rates decline with the rate of inflation.*

SOURCE: Fiscal 1992 Budget

Continued from p. 56
personal cause in 1989 and 1990 but was unable to get it enacted.

This time, he gave it only half-hearted backing, immediately consigning it to a study commission. His chief problem, in addition to the bitter partisan controversy unleashed by the proposal, was the fact that the Joint Committee on Taxation judged it as a serious revenue loser. So Bush called for a study overseen by Federal Reserve Chairman Alan Greenspan to resolve "technical differences." *(1990 Almanac, p. 168)*

Overall, Bush called for a net total of $2.3 billion in taxes and user fees in 1992 and $12 billion over five years. His two big revenue gainers were unlikely to see action, however. The capital gains rate cut was projected to yield $3 billion in revenue in 1992 and $9.1 billion over five years. The Joint Tax Committee subsequently estimated that the plan would lose $10.6 billion from 1991-1996.

And an extension of Medicare hospital coverage to state and local employees not already covered — a proposal that had been repeatedly quashed in Congress — was credited with bringing in $1.1 billion in 1992 and $7.1 billion over five years.

Bush's revenue raisers were partially offset by revenue-losing items, including a proposal to make permanent the tax credit for research and development expenses at a loss of $6.2 billion over five years.

The president also asked for a one-year extension of several other expiring tax provisions: allocation rules for companies with research expenses in more than one country, a 25 percent deduction for health insurance costs borne by self-employed individuals, a low-income housing credit and a tax credit for businesses that hired hard-to-place workers. Tax incentives to promote business creation in depressed urban and rural areas would have lost $1.8 billion over five years. *(Tax extenders, p. 107)*

Bush also resurrected two revenue-losing ideas from his fiscal 1990 budget designed to increase savings and promote home ownership. Families who deposited up to $5,000 a year in a family savings account would have earned tax-free interest if they left it untouched for at least seven years. The cost: $6.5 billion over five years.

Taxpayers with Individual Retirement Accounts would have been allowed to withdraw up to $10,000 without penalty for a down payment on a first home. The cost: $400 million over five years.

Deficit Projections

(Fiscal years; dollar amounts in billions †)

The following shows the final deficit for 1990, the Office of Management and Budget estimate for 1991, and OMB projections for 1992-96 assuming enactment of President Bush's budget.

	1990	1991	1992	1993	1994	1995	1996
Budget authority	$1,368.5	$1,520.0	$1,577.8	$1,533.7	$1,605.8	$1,677.5	$1,759.6
Outlays	1,251.7	1,409.6	1,445.9	1,454.2	1,427.1	1,470.3	1,540.8
Revenues	1,031.3	1,091.4	1,165.0	1,252.7	1,365.3	1,467.3	1,560.7
Surplus or deficit	−220.4	−318.1	−280.9	−201.5	−61.8	−2.9	19.9

† Totals include Social Security, which is off budget; totals may not add due to rounding.

SOURCE: 1992 Budget

Democrats Focus on Recession, War

Though Democrats praised some of Bush's proposed increases for social programs, they were sharply critical of the broad thrust of his domestic spending priorities. This will be "the biggest fight in Congress: ... How do you target funds [within] the discretionary cap?" said House Budget Committee Chairman Leon E. Panetta, D-Calif., adding that Bush has "emphasized the wrong priorities, and we're going to try to reorder that."

In particular, Democrats criticized the White House for offering little to deal with the recession or the true costs of the Persian Gulf War.

During about eight hours of patient salesmanship before the House and Senate Budget committees Feb. 5 and 6, Darman asked detractors to remain calm and trust administration forecasts that the recession would be short and mild, leading to an upturn by midyear. He repeated advice that members had already heard from Greenspan and Congressional Budget Office Director Robert D. Reischauer: If most economists' forecasts proved correct, the recession would be over before Congress could do anything about it. Anti-recession legislation would not take effect until the recovery was under way and would only add to inflationary pressures.

But Darman could not make the issue go away, and his advice did not allay increasing fear that the recession might prove to be longer and deeper than forecasters thought.

While disagreeing over Bush's specific choices, Democrats could hardly attack his overall request for domestic spending, which was based on caps that they had participated in setting. That left Democrats, in effect, fighting the shadow of Reagan, whose success at cutting taxes and increasing defense spending in the 1980s helped drive up the deficits and foreclose most budget options in the 1990s.

"I'm not arguing that we could do better by spending money that we simply don't have," said Senate Budget Chairman Jim Sasser, D-Tenn. The legacy of the 1980s, he said, is that "at the very time we need to act, we find ourselves fiscally paralyzed.... We're simply reduced to cannibalizing the budget ... abandoning one very needed investment so that we can afford to finance another one."

Darman had better luck defusing partisan complaints about Bush's treatment of the costs of Operation Desert Shield/Storm. The budget, which went to the printer before war broke out Jan. 16, contained only a "placeholder" worth $14 billion in net spending authority for the war for fiscal 1991, an amount some Democrats said grossly understated the true cost.

But Darman said contributions or pledges from Saudi Arabia, Kuwait, Germany, Japan and other allies already had accounted for more than 80 percent of the $11.1 billion cost of Operation Desert Shield through the end of calendar 1990. Further, he said, the United States had received allied pledges of $41.8 billion to help defray the cost of calendar 1991 operations. ■

Function-by-Function Highlights

President Bush's $1.45 trillion budget for fiscal 1992 contained few surprises, largely because the outlines were set in the 1990 budget agreement, which imposed spending caps for domestic, international and defense programs. However, Bush had set priorities within those caps, with new or increased funding for some programs coming at the expense of others. Congress, too, had to make tradeoffs, and that was the heart of the debate on the fiscal 1992 budget.

The budget was presented in terms of budget authority, which was the money that could be obligated in 1992; it was also translated into outlays, or the money that was expected to be spent for a program during the fiscal year using previous and new appropriations.

Here are the highlights:

DEFENSE

Three weeks into the largest U.S. military operation since the Vietnam War, the Bush administration unveiled a defense budget for fiscal 1992 that officially ignored the war in the Persian Gulf. It was a budget driven by domestic constraints and by a revised U.S. strategy that had been reshaped to take account of the Soviet military decline.

The budget, which requested $290.8 billion in new budget authority and $295.2 billion in outlays, cut active-duty military manpower by nearly 200,000 from the existing level and stopped production of 81 weapons programs, a few of them major but many of them relatively minor.

After decades of gearing up to blunt a short-notice Soviet thrust into Western Europe, the reshaped U.S. force was to be oriented more toward rapid deployment of forces to distant trouble spots where no U.S. ground forces were stationed — such as the Persian Gulf.

But the 1992 budget also included ambitious funding requests for two weapons programs that were highly controversial even before the Soviet threat receded: $4.6 billion in budget authority for the B-2 stealth bomber and $4.6 billion for the strategic defense initiative (SDI) anti-missile research program. (The SDI total did not include $603 million for a separate program of research on defenses against short-range missiles such as Iraq's Soviet-developed Scuds).

The administration insisted that the effectiveness in the gulf war of the F-117 stealth fighter-bomber demonstrated the potential value of the B-2 against non-Soviet opponents and that the success of the Patriot anti-missile missile proved the same point for SDI.

But congressional critics bitterly contested the allocation of such large amounts to the two programs. They tried to shift funds from those strategic arms to conventional weapons programs, including some with particularly strong political support.

Paying for War

As stipulated in the 1990 budget-summit agreement, the budget request excluded the cost of conducting Operation Desert Storm. The gulf war's cost was covered by a fiscal 1991 supplemental request.

One element of the fiscal 1992 proposal revised by the supplemental was the active-duty personnel cutback: Congress mandated a reduction of at least 80,000 in fiscal 1991, but that target was not met because of the demands of Operation Desert Storm. The fiscal 1992 personnel ceiling was higher than initially proposed.

The supplemental request included replacements for missiles, such as the ship-launched Tomahawk cruise missiles, which were being used up in the gulf war but were slated in the fiscal 1992 budget for a production slowdown.

The gulf war aside, the defense request for fiscal 1992-93 would continue a step-by-step retrenchment that would give the Pentagon a budget in fiscal 1995 that had about the same purchasing power as it had in fiscal 1980, before President Ronald Reagan's massive defense buildup.

By fiscal 1997, under President Bush's plan, defense outlays would account for 3.6 percent of gross national product, the lowest level since before World War II. That long-range plan would slice by one-fourth — to 1.5 million — the number of service members on active duty in fiscal 1995. Paralleling the manpower and funding cuts would be a reduction in the number of combat units and a sharp cutback in weapons production funding.

For fiscal 1992, the budget earmarked $278.3 billion in new budget authority for the Defense Department and $11.8 billion for defense-related programs of the Energy Department, the latter mostly associated with testing and building nuclear weapons and warship power plants. An additional $757 million was requested for other defense-related activities, including the Selective Service System.

The Pentagon's share of the request included $1.2 billion for drug interdiction, $1.3 billion to clean up toxic waste on existing and former military bases, and $1.2 billion for compliance with existing environmental standards.

Included in the Energy Department's share of the request was $3.7 billion for waste management and environmental restoration, of which $1.1 billion was for cleaning up toxic and radioactive contamination caused by past weapons production practices.

Compared with the fiscal 1991 budget, the overall defense request marked a decline in real (inflation-adjusted) purchasing power of 0.9 percent, by the administration's calculation. That assumed that Congress would approve a request to rescind about $3 billion of the $288.3 billion appropriated for fiscal 1991 but left unspent by the administration. If Congress rejected the rescission, the fiscal 1992 request would see a correspondingly larger reduction.

In 1990, the administration proposed a large rescission package aimed mostly at canceling projects added by Congress to the prior year's defense bills. But this time, Pentagon officials insisted, the proposed rescissions merely reflected decisions to cancel production of some weapons either because of budget limits or because of imminent cutbacks in the size of the U.S. force.

Strategic Forces

Aside from the amounts requested for anti-missile programs ($5.2 billion) and the radar-evading B-2 bomber ($2.9 billion for four planes and $1.6 billion to continue development), the budget projected an austere future for strategic arms programs.

The administration finally abandoned a controversial effort to deploy a rail-mobile launcher for the 10-warhead MX intercontinental ballistic missile (ICBM). The budget requested $260 million in fiscal 1992 and $100 million in fiscal 1993 to continue development through the first launch of a missile from a railcar, after which the technology would be shelved.

The parallel effort to develop a small, single-warhead ICBM (nicknamed Midgetman) to be carried by a mobile launcher would get $202 million in fiscal 1992 and $549 million in fiscal 1993.

The Navy had decided in 1990 that the huge Trident missile-launching submarine included in the fiscal 1991 budget — the 18th of the class — would be the last one. The fiscal 1992 budget would buy only 28 of the Trident II missiles carried by the big subs ($1.2 billion), compared with 52 missiles in fiscal 1991.

The budget would accelerate production of a long-range, bomber-launched cruise missile ($502 million for 120 missiles).

Conventional Forces

One major new procurement program that the budget would continue to accelerate was the C-17 long-range, wide-body cargo plane. The budget requested $2 billion for six of the planes.

With the number of active-duty Army divisions scheduled to drop from 18 to 12 by 1995, the Army scaled back production plans for several of its major weapons, requesting no funds in fiscal 1992 for the Bradley armored troop carrier, the Patriot anti-aircraft missile or the MLRS artillery rocket.

On the other hand, the budget called for continued development of a new LH scout helicopter ($550 million), a new weapons system called Longbow for the Apache anti-tank helicopter ($239 million) and a new generation of armored combat vehicles, including a new tank ($444 million).

For the Navy, the budget requested five Aegis destroyers ($4.3 billion) and one *Seawolf*-class attack submarine.

As part of a long-term reduction in the amphibious landing fleet intended to put Marine Corps units ashore on enemy beaches, the fiscal 1993 budget did not include a planned LHD-class helicopter carrier.

But the budget did include $898 million for components that would be used in a $3 billion aircraft carrier, scheduled for inclusion in the fiscal 1995 budget.

The budget included $2.3 billion to continue development of the Air Force's advanced tactical fighter plane (ATF), scheduled to enter service in the late 1990s.

But for other tactical combat aircraft programs, the outlook was bleak. Fiscal 1991 was the last year of funding for Air Force F-15Es. Because the number of aircraft carriers would be cut to 12 by 1995, the budget dropped plans to upgrade existing F-14 fighters to the F-14D model, with new engines and radars.

The budget request started to phase out production of the Air Force's F-16 ($1.2 billion for 48 planes) and the Navy's F/A-18 ($1.9 billion for 36 planes). But it included $435 million to begin developing an improved F/A-18 with longer range.

AGRICULTURE

President Bush's $15.3 billion estimate for fiscal 1992 outlays in agriculture represented a modest decline in spending for federal farm programs, with most of the decrease coming from a continuing shift in farm-credit programs away from direct government loans and toward federal guarantees of private loans.

On the other hand, outlays for farm price- and income-support programs — by far the largest component of the agriculture budget — grew once again. Net outlays by the Commodity Credit Corporation, the Agriculture Department entity that funneled crop payments to farmers, rose from $6.5 billion in fiscal 1990 to $10.8 billion in fiscal 1991. They were expected to increase by nearly $240 million in fiscal 1992, to $11.04 billion.

Administration officials said the large increase in fiscal 1991 reflected the costs of the final stages of the 1985 farm bill. The 1990 farm bill (PL 101-624), passed by Congress and signed by Bush in late 1990 with related deficit-reduction legislation (PL 101-508), would cut farmer subsidies by limiting the percentage of acreage that qualified for benefits. Without those projected cuts, the administration said, farm program spending in fiscal 1992 would have cost as much as $2 billion more. *(1990 Weekly Report, p. 4037)*

For fiscal 1992 Bush sought another, more modest cut in farm subsidies ($36 million) with a proposal to scale back benefits for individuals with high non-farm earnings. A similar effort to "target" payments only to needy farmers was defeated in both the House and the Senate in 1990. *(1990 Weekly Report, p. 2393)*

In another potentially controversial proposal, Bush sought a slightly more substantial cut ($77 million) in federal crop-insurance subsidies, asking Congress to lower the maximum subsidy from 30 percent to 15 percent. The administration also said it could save another $50 million a year by charging higher user fees for meat and poultry inspections conducted by the Agriculture Department: It wanted the industry to share 50 percent of the costs for daily inspection provided beyond one eight-hour shift.

Bush sought a large increase in spending for the Export Enhancement Program (EEP). Under the program, the government used surplus grain to subsidize exports to countries where U.S. farmers competed the most with Europeans, who were also heavily subsidized by their governments.

The administration wanted to provide up to $900 million in EEP subsidies in fiscal 1991 and $1.2 billion in fiscal 1992 — a move that administration officials said would enhance U.S. bargaining power with the European Community in international trade negotiations on the General Agreement on Tariffs and Trade.

However, Congress would first have to remove a $425 million cap placed on EEP subsidies in 1990's agriculture appropriations bill. *(1990 Weekly Report, p. 4141)*

The administration said removing the cap would not result in increased costs to taxpayers because the new export sales would help boost overall farm prices and reduce the demand for government crop subsidies.

COMMERCE/COMMUNITY DEVELOPMENT

In each of the past several years, actual spending for the promotion and regulation of domestic and international commerce, plus housing and community development, had far outstripped budget expectations.

Bush projected $99.2 billion in outlays for this broad category in fiscal 1992. That was 22 percent less than was expected to be spent in fiscal 1991, a year when spending exploded because of the thrift crisis. In 1991's budget, Bush had projected a need for only $25 billion.

Many activities covered under this broad category involved small amounts of money and would have changed little under the president's proposal.

The big money involved the nation's deposit insurance system, particularly the cost of the savings and loan salvage operation, which had blown spending for this category out of sight.

Financial Institutions

Net outlays for the thrift bailout would be about $79 billion for fiscal 1992 (down from about $96 billion in 1991). Another $10 billion in net spending would result from closing down failing banks. Under existing proposals, none of the bank money would come from taxpayers, however; all costs would be paid from insurance premiums assessed on banks. Much of the thrift spending amounted to losses imposed on taxpayers, but a major portion was to be borrowed short-term to provide working capital and would be repaid.

The budget showed spending for both bank failures and the thrift bailout declining through 1993. And in 1994, the budget anticipated major sales of assets seized from failed thrifts and a large net return to the Treasury.

The level of spending on thrifts depended on Congress' supplying authority to the Resolution Trust Corporation (RTC), which was charged with salvaging failed thrifts but which was constrained by limits on losses it could incur and on the amount it could borrow for short-term working capital. Congress had been reluctant to raise the RTC's spending authority.

SEC

The administration requested for a 20 percent increase in outlays for the Securities and Exchange Commission (SEC) to $218.6 million. The increase would be partially offset by an increase in fees charged for the registration of new securities offerings.

Housing Credit

Reflecting 1990's budget-reconciliation legislation (PL 101-508), the Bush administration projected how much money it would set aside to support mortgage-backed securities, which indirectly provided money to home buyers.

The Government National Mortgage Association (GNMA) guaranteed payment of principal and interest on certain privately issued securities that were backed by pools of Federal Housing Administration and Veterans Affairs mortgages. The GNMA guarantee promoted lenders' access to capital markets for funds to originate loans. Bush proposed issuing securities commitments of $74.8 billion in fiscal 1992, compared with $69.9 billion in fiscal 1991.

Community Development

Bush requested $2.9 billion in budget authority for fiscal 1992 for the popular Community Development Block Grants, which went directly to state and local governments for economic development. Congress appropriated $3.2 billion for the program in fiscal 1991.

Postal Service

Bush again wanted to change the program that offered reduced postal rates to charities, which Congress had consistently protected. He would continue to provide postage subsidies but would require nonprofit groups to pay about 60 percent of the overhead costs, saving the government $265 million.

EDUCATION/TRAINING

The Bush budget projected $45.5 billion in fiscal 1992 outlays for education and training programs covered by the Departments of Education and Labor, up 6.4 percent from fiscal 1991.

Shifting funds to boost his empowerment theme, President Bush requested $29.6 billion in new budget authority for education in fiscal 1992, a 9.3 percent increase over fiscal 1991 spending of $27.1 billion.

However, a major portion of the increase had to go to pay the long-term cost of guaranteed student loans, as required by 1990's budget law.

Thus it appeared that there was a greater increase in spending in education than would actually occur, education groups maintained. They said there was really about $800 million in new money, barely enough to keep up with inflation.

Education Department officials stressed choice in schools, seeking $340 million in budget authority in fiscal 1992 for incentive grants to local school districts running magnet schools and other programs designed to increase parental choice in their children's education.

Money for choice programs was part of a proposed Educational Excellence Act, a replay of legislative proposals from Bush's first year in office. That legislation, changed substantially in Congress, was blocked by Senate Republicans on the last day of the 101st Congress. *(1990 Weekly Report, p. 3752)*

Altogether, the Bush administration sought $690 million in budget authority for the proposed legislation in fiscal 1992.

It also rewarded schools that raised student achievement and increased the endowments of historically black colleges.

The budget raised spending for elementary and secondary education, while slightly reducing funding for vocational education.

Higher education aid programs underwent an extensive restructuring under the president's proposal, with more money available for fewer students.

Elementary and secondary education would rise to $9.1 billion in fiscal 1992 budget authority, an 8.3 percent increase over 1991.

Chapter 1, which provided money to local school districts for compensatory education for disadvantaged children, increased to $6.2 billion, from $6.1 billion in fiscal 1991.

As Congress geared up to reauthorize the Higher Education Act, which provided grants and loans to students in colleges and trade schools, the Bush budget contained a number of proposals to refocus those programs, targeting aid to those in the lowest income levels.

Overall, the administration's fiscal 1992 request for student aid totaled $12.6 billion in budget authority, a $1.6 billion increase over the 1991 level. But the number of students served would fall by 300,000, to 5.7 million in fiscal 1992, the Bush team said.

The administration proposed increasing the size of Pell grants from $2,400 to $3,700 per student. But the grants would be limited to students whose parents earned $10,000 a year or less. The budget proposed spending more for the total Pell grant program — $5.8 billion in budget authority for fiscal 1992, compared with $5.4 billion the year before. But the total number of students receiving the grants would drop from 3.4 million in fiscal 1991 to 3 million in fiscal 1992.

Pell grant recipients who scored high on standardized tests or who ranked in the upper 10 percent of their high school or top 20 percent of their college would qualify for an additional $500 under proposed Presidential Achievement Scholarships. Bush requested $170 million in budget authority for the scholarships in fiscal 1992.

The guaranteed student loan program, made up of Stafford loans, PLUS loans and Supplemental Loans for Students, received $5.9 billion in budget authority for fiscal 1992, $1.7 billion more than in fiscal 1991. The number of students served would also increase by about 100,000, to 4.1 million in fiscal 1992.

To help students who would lost access to Pell grants, the administration proposed increasing the annual limits for Stafford loans from $2,625 to $3,500 for first- and second-year undergraduates, and from $4,000 to $5,000 for other undergraduates. Supplemental Loans were also increased — from $4,000 to $6,000 for second-, third- and fourth-year undergraduates and from $4,000 to $10,000 for graduate students.

For Labor's employment and training programs, Bush asked for $5.5 billion in budget authority in fiscal 1992, a reduction of about $300 million from the year before due to proposed changes to the programs.

The bulk of that money would go to Job Training Partnership Act (JTPA) programs, slated for $4.1 billion in budget authority for fiscal 1992, about the same as in fiscal 1991. Similar to 1990's failed bill, new legislation proposed by Bush would have replaced the Block Grant and Summer Youth Employment and Training programs with separate year-round programs for adults and youth. The legislation would have targeted more services to economically disadvantaged people. Bush also proposed a new $25 million Youth Opportunities Unlimited (YOU) program for young people living in high-poverty areas.

Under JTPA, the fiscal 1992 budget proposed $1.3 billion in budget authority for youth job training grants; $1.1 billion for adult job training grants; $867.5 million for the Job Corps; and $527 million for Economic Dislocation and Worker Adjustment Assistance.

Bush also repeated his call for killing the Trade Adjustment Assistance program, created in 1988 to train workers who lost their jobs due to foreign competition. The cut would save $164 million, Labor officials said.

ENERGY

The fiscal 1992 budget offered a peek at one big item in the administration's long-awaited, soon-to-be-released "national energy strategy" — its research component.

Overall, President Bush projected spending $3.7 billion in fiscal 1992 on the energy function, a 41.8 percent increase. The big jump mainly reflected long-term spending consequences of previous actions by Congress, which typically appropriated much more for this function than the administration requested.

However, new budget authority — the amount Bush wanted Congress to appropriate (but not necessarily spend) in fiscal 1992 — would decrease substantially under Bush's proposal, from $5.2 billion to $4.1 billion. If Bush's plan were accepted, future increases in outlays — how much money was actually expended in a given year — would soon taper off.

Some of the reduction reflected a change in the way the government accounted for Rural Electrification Administration loans. But Bush also wanted to significantly cut energy conservation grants, electricity subsidies and other programs popular in Congress.

A major focus of the national energy strategy would be increased federally supported research, much of it aimed at making the country more energy efficient, regenerating interest in nuclear power and developing alternatives. Energy Secretary James D. Watkins said the budget included $494.3 million in new budget authority for conservation and renewable energy research and development, a 17 percent increase.

The budget identified nearly 20 programs slated for increases under the energy strategy, some of them not part of the energy function. Spending on the programs, most in the Energy Department, would total $903 million, up 34 percent from fiscal 1991. Included were big increases for research into electric cars, computerized highway traffic-flow systems, alternative fuels, advanced oil drilling, solar energy, nuclear power and superconductivity.

But to make room for the increases in a tight budget year, the administration again proposed a sharp cutback in state and local conservation grants, from $276.5 million to $48.3 million. Congress had rejected that idea in the past.

Also taking big hits would be the department's clean-coal technology program and fossil-energy research. Together they would be cut from $847.9 million to $540 million.

To cut electric subsidies, Bush wanted to hike the interest rates paid by the five Power Marketing Administrations, which sold electricity from federal hydropower projects and use the revenues to pay off the plants' subsidized construction loans.

Another part of the energy strategy that made its way into the budget was a long-stalled proposal to allow oil drilling in Alaska's Arctic National Wildlife Refuge. Lease sales would generate no

Elder Statesman Udall Resigned Due to Ill Health

Rep. Morris K. Udall's resigned May 4 from the House, putting a poignant end to a 30-year political career that transformed the Arizona Democrat from an upstart young reformer into a beloved elder statesman. But throughout Udall's career, bad timing and health problems conspired to rob him of a broader role in history.

The combination of Parkinson's disease and injuries suffered from an accident early in 1991 dealt the final setback to Udall's congressional career. Udall was 68 when his resignation was announced in an April 19 letter from his wife to House Speaker Thomas S. Foley, D-Wash. After consultations among Udall, his doctors, his family and his staff, she said, "our reluctant conclusion is that any improvement in his condition will be insufficient to allow him to resume his duties and responsibilities."

Udall had previously announced in May 1990 that he would retire after the 102nd Congress ended in 1992.

He had long before forsaken national leadership ambitions, after his failed 1976 presidential campaign and two unsuccessful attempts to move into the House leadership. Udall shifted his focus after those defeats and became one of the House's most prolific legislators in the latter half of his career, known as a liberal activist, influential chairman of the Interior Committee and raconteur with an unmatched sense of humor.

His graceful recovery from disappointment reflected an outlook Udall expressed in a Will Rogers quote he long kept next to his desk: "We are here for just a spell and then pass on. So get a few laughs and do the best you can. Live your life so that whenever you lose you are ahead."

Critic of the Seniority System

A lawyer by vocation, Udall ran for Congress in a 1961 special election after his brother Stewart, who had represented Arizona in the House from 1955-61, resigned to become President John F. Kennedy's Interior secretary.

In 1969, Udall took up the cause of young members chafing under the seniority system and ran against John W. McCormack for Speaker. No one thought a fifth-term member would win that long-shot challenge to an incumbent leader, and Udall did not.

A bigger disappointment came two years later, when he lost a race for majority leader against Hale Boggs of Louisiana. Udall's allies had expected the popular liberal to win the No. 2 leadership post over Boggs, who had just recovered from the effects of a 1969 breakdown.

But Boggs had the advantage of already being the whip and was seen as less of a threat to the traditional power structure than was Udall, a critic of the seniority system. Although Udall supporters were claiming a big lead before the vote, Boggs won on the second ballot, 140-88.

Udall carried the reform banner more successfully in legislation, when he was sponsor of the 1971 bill that made the first real rules for campaign finance. But his proposals for public financing of congressional campaigns were still languishing on the drawing board when he resigned.

Udall made a run at his party's presidential nomination in 1976 and got remarkably far for a House member who started as a virtual unknown. He often told the story of strolling into a barbershop while campaigning in New Hampshire and declaring, "I'm Mo Udall from Arizona, and I'm running for president." The barber replied, "Yeah, I know. We were just laughing about that this morning."

Udall placed second to Jimmy Carter in seven primaries. In Wisconsin, the results were so close that Udall was prematurely declared the winner by two networks. But Udall never made up for the loss of momentum to Carter when the little-known Georgian won the early Iowa caucus.

Interior Committee Chairman

After his presidential disappointment, Udall immediately found a new outlet for his energy in the House. In 1977, he became chairman of the Interior Committee and began racking up an impressive legislative record on the environment and related areas.

Among his major achievements were a 1984 wilderness act, a 1982 nuclear waste law and the 1980 Alaska lands act. A landmark 1977 strip-mining law he pushed through prompted a revolt in the then-strong copper industry in Arizona. When home-state critics printed bumper stickers that said "No Mo Mo," Udall cheerfully slapped one on his own briefcase.

Those bills marked Udall as a reliable friend of environmentalists, but he clashed with them over some issues. He used his clout throughout his career to push the Central Arizona Project, a massive water system that was opposed by environmentalists but was a boon for the state's farmers, developers and cattlemen.

Those clashes never undercut Udall's environmentalist credentials, but as his health deteriorated he played less of a role on major environmental bills, such as the 1990 Clean Air Act.

Udall's political setbacks were compounded by personal tragedies. His first marriage ended in divorce; his second wife, Ella, died in 1988, an apparent suicide. The next year, he married Norma Gilbert, a former Interior Committee aide.

Diagnosed with Parkinson's disease more than 10 years earlier, Udall's physical condition had steadily deteriorated. By 1984, it had taken enough of a toll that he passed up another run for the Democratic presidential nomination. When House Speaker Thomas P. O'Neill Jr., D-Mass., retired in 1986, Udall might have been one of the few credible rivals to Jim Wright's ascension to Speaker, but Parkinson's made his candidacy impossible.

Parkinson's did not impair Udall's powers of concentration, but he was in obvious discomfort most of the time. As his illness progressed, Udall increasingly delegated authority for major bills to his heir apparent on Interior, ranking Democrat George Miller of California.

In 1988 and 1990, Udall ran for re-election despite advice and pleas from family members that he retire.

revenues until 1993, when the budget predicted a $1.9 billion windfall.

ENVIRONMENT

The Bush budget projected a modest 3.8 percent increase to $19.5 billion for natural resources and environmental programs for fiscal 1992.

Calling improvement of the nation's air quality "a top priority," the administration requested $516.5 million in new budget authority — a 35 percent increase in clean air funding — to carry out the ambitious requirements and deadlines in the new Clean Air Act.

The Environmental Protection Agency (EPA), which accounted for the bulk of the environmental work, was bringing on 600 new employees over the following two years to work on clean air programs, according to EPA Administrator William K. Reilly.

Under President Bush's request, the EPA's operating budget would rise to $2.5 billion in fiscal 1992 — a 7 percent increase in budget authority.

The EPA budget also called for $1.75 billion in new budget authority — an 8 percent increase over existing appropriations — to fund the "superfund" toxic-waste cleanup program. But its $1.9 billion request for grants for construction of sewage treatment plants was down from fiscal 1991's $2.1 billion because, under existing law, states were supposed to assume more responsibility for funding plant construction. What's more, $400 million of sewer construction money was earmarked for high-priority cleanups in six cities.

The budget proposed a 24 percent increase to $1.2 billion for research into global climate change.

The budget would have sharply boosted funding for the administration's "America the Beautiful" initiative, begun in 1990. The budget requested $925 billion in budget authority for the program, a 40 percent increase. Much of the increase — about $90 million — would go toward developing recreational facilities within national forests. The initiative also included tree-planting, land acquisition and recreational programs.

To meet the administration's goal of "no net loss" of wetlands, Bush requested $710 million for wetlands research, protection and enhancement.

FOREIGN AFFAIRS

The administration did not seek a significant infusion of assistance for its Middle East allies, despite their help in the Persian Gulf War.

Aid for Israel and Egypt — whose economies had been negatively affected by the war — would be largely unchanged from fiscal 1991 levels. But the two countries would continue to be the largest recipients of foreign aid: Bush asked for $3 billion in security and economic aid for Israel, and $2.2 billion for Egypt.

Among countries in the region, only Turkey, a key U.S. ally against Iraq, was likely to receive a substantial expansion of aid. The administration was reportedly requesting an increase in military aid for Turkey, which received $500 million in fiscal 1991.

Bush sought total budget authority for international affairs programs of $35.7 billion — including $12.2 billion for an expansion of the U.S. quota in the International Monetary Fund (IMF). Aside from the increased support for IMF lending, the request in budget authority was $23.5 billion, $3.7 billion more than was authorized in fiscal 1991.

Outlays in the international affairs budget would amount to $17.8 billion, according to the president's budget. But the figure was misleading because of technicalities of the budget process.

Instead, the State Department calculated the proposed international affairs outlays as effectively totaling $19.6 billion, an increase of $874 million, or 4.6 percent, over the fiscal 1991 level. The requested quota increase for the IMF, which the administration said was needed only once or twice a decade, did not involve new outlays.

The administration was so engaged in war planning that it had not determined aid allotments for most individual countries by Feb. 4, the day the budget was released.

Robert Bauerlein, an aide to Deputy Secretary of State Lawrence S. Eagleburger, said senior officials had been focusing on the war. "Suffice it to say that getting their attention on some of these things has been tough recently," he said.

The State Department asked for $15.9 billion in budget authority for foreign aid, an increase of $894 million over fiscal 1991. The budget also included $4.1 billion for State Department operations, compared with $3.2 billion in fiscal 1991.

While the department requested $853 million more in budget authority for development and humanitarian assistance, the budget for what was termed security assistance showed only a slight increase of $41 million over fiscal 1991.

The broad category of security assistance included various forms of foreign military financing, military training and direct economic aid.

As in past years, countries in the Middle East would draw a disproportionate share of U.S. security assistance. Nearly three-fourths of the $8 billion in budget authority requested for this category would benefit just six countries: Israel, Egypt, Turkey, Morocco, Oman and Jordan.

The State Department said it was reviewing aid to Jordan in light of King Hussein's increasingly vocal opposition to the U. S. position in the gulf war. Security aid for Jordan in fiscal 1991 totaled $57.2 million.

Elsewhere, Bush was expected to seek more than $100 million in security assistance for Pakistan, although the country remained barred from receiving U.S. aid. The aid program for Pakistan been suspended since October 1990, when Bush failed to certify that Pakistan did not possess nuclear weapons.

While Bush was not expected to make that certification soon, Bauerlein said, "It is still the intention and the policy of the administration to have an assistance program with Pakistan."

The White House also would request more military assistance for El Salvador, according to Bauerlein. In the 1990 bill (PL 101-513), Congress withheld half the $85 million in aid. But in December 1990 the administration said it would release the aid on the grounds that El Salvador's anti-government rebels had not met conditions of the law.

A new program for Latin America, Enterprise for the Americas, was the highlight of the administration's budget for development and humanitarian aid. Bush sought $410 million in new budget authority for the initiative, which was designed to promote market-oriented policies.

Bush requested $400 million in assistance for Central and Eastern European countries, an increase of $30 million over fiscal 1991. In addition, he wanted $70 million for a contribution to the European Bank for Reconstruction and Development, the same figure requested for fiscal 1991.

Bush did not seek aid for the Soviet Union, although the budget for the United States Information Agency included initial costs "for establishing a new Moscow cultural center," according to a State Department budget document.

The budget also proposed funding increases for other international affairs programs:

State Department Operations

The department asked Congress for $342 million in new budget authority to replace U.S. diplomatic facilities overseas. Bauerlein said that $130 million would go toward rebuilding the new U.S. Embassy in Moscow. Construction of the embassy was halted in 1985, when U.S. officials discovered that it was riddled with Soviet listening devices.

Counternarcotics

The budget proposed $611 million for international counternarcotics programs, an increase of 34 percent ($155 million) over fiscal 1991.

A total of $425 million in security assistance would be provided to the Andean nations. But the new president of Peru , Alberto Fujimori, had not yet agreed to accept such aid.

HEALTH/MEDICARE

For health and Medicare combined, Bush's fiscal 1992 budget assumed outlays of $195 billion, up $20 billion from the fiscal 1991 estimate of $175.6 billion.

But more significant was what that number did not reveal —

specifically, proposed outlay cuts of $2.8 billion for Medicare for fiscal 1992.

Even if Congress were to accept the cuts — which included payment reductions for health-care providers and fee increases for beneficiaries — Medicare benefits for the elderly and the disabled would remain one of the fastest-growing programs in the federal budget. The administration estimated that fiscal 1992 outlays for Medicare's 35 million beneficiaries would total $113.8 billion, up from the previous year's $104.4 billion.

However, initial reaction indicated that the chances of Congress going along with most of the proposed changes were slim to none.

In fact, with the ink barely dry on the five-year budget agreement that cut Medicare costs by an estimated $44.2 billion, many lawmakers voiced outrage over Bush's willingness to revisit one of the most divisive issues in the 1990 negotiations. *(Medicare deal, 1990 Weekly Report, p. 3718)*

"We're not about to ask senior citizens and Medicare providers to bear the brunt of deficit-reduction responsibility. Those issues supposedly were settled in last year's budget agreement," said House Ways and Means Committee Chairman Dan Rostenkowski, D-Ill.

His Senate counterpart, Finance Committee Chairman Lloyd Bentsen, D-Texas, said, "The proposal to cut Medicare by an additional $25 billion [over five years] on top of the $45 billion in cuts included in last year's budget deal is simply unacceptable."

But at a briefing Feb. 4, Health and Human Services (HHS) Secretary Louis W. Sullivan insisted that the proposals did not violate the spirit of the budget agreement. "There was nothing in the budget deal last year that said we should not look for prudent ways to contain health-care costs," he said.

Lawmakers also complained that the administration was revisiting proposals Congresshad rejected repeatedly in the past.

For example, the largest single proposed cut — estimated at $1 billion in fiscal 1992 — would reduce Medicare payments to teaching hospitals for "indirect" medical-education costs, such as additional tests ordered by interns and residents.

The General Accounting Office and other analysts had found that the formula by which the payment was calculated was faulty and that correcting it would make the payments more precise. Thus, the Reagan and Bush administrations repeatedly had recommended reducing the payment.

Yet in practice, large teaching hospitals were among those most financially strapped as a result of Medicare's per-diagnosis hospital payment system. Congress had shown little inclination to take money away, even in the name of accounting precision.

In Medicare's Part B — the voluntary portion of the program that funded 80 percent of physician and other outpatient costs after payment of an annual deductible — the biggest cost-saver was one rejected by Congress in 1990. The proposal, to have beneficiaries pay 20 percent coinsurance on laboratory tests, would save about $450 million in fiscal 1992. No lab coinsurance currently was required.

The coinsurance plan was part of the original budget-summit proposal, rejected by the House in October 1990. Realizing that they had to reduce the hit on Medicare to produce a budget plan that could pass, congressional leaders jettisoned the coinsurance plan.

By far the most provocative proposal in Bush's budget was a variation on another of the Medicare policies eliminated from 1190's original budget-summit agreement.

The new "income-relating" plan would triple the premiums paid by Part B beneficiaries with annual earnings higher than $125,000 for individuals and $150,000 for couples. (The 1991 premium was $29.90 per month, and the amount generally was deducted from beneficiaries' Social Security checks.)

Under existing law, as codified by the 1990 budget-reconciliation bill, beneficiary premiums made up 25 percent of Part B costs, in effect giving beneficiaries a 75 percent subsidy.

The failed budget-summit agreement would have trimmed that subsidy to 70 percent, requiring beneficiary premiums to account for 30 percent of program costs. Opponents said the projected premium increase — $4.90 per month instead of the $1.30 projected under the 25 percent rule — would have hit middle-income beneficiaries too hard.

The new proposal defused that criticism by going after only those with relatively high incomes: For them, the federal subsidy would be reduced from 75 percent to 25 percent.

"Given the rapid increase in the size of Part B, 13 percent in the coming year, I believe that it is fair to make wealthier individuals shoulder more of the burden," Sullivan said.

Though lawmakers did not reject the plan outright, they cautioned that it needed more study. Some of that wariness likely could be traced to the last such experiment, in the 1988 Medicare Catastrophic Coverage Act. Affluent beneficiaries were so outraged at having to pay more for the new benefits than their less well-off brethren that Congress repealed most of the program. *(1989 Almanac, p. 149)*

The budget plan also included non-Medicare proposals rejected by Congress in the past, including eliminating most federal aid for training of health professionals and charging user fees for services provided by the Food and Drug Administration.

HHS officials said Congress might be more amenable to some of the proposals because the budget deal required them to find savings if they wanted to boost spending for other domestic programs. "The budget agreement has predetermined the size of this ship. All [Congress] can do is rearrange the deck chairs," said Kevin E. Moley, assistant secretary for management and budget.

Other elements of the health budget called for increased spending for prevention initiatives, among them a $171 million plan to reduce infant mortality by improving access to health care and other social services for high-risk pregnant women in targeted cities. The U.S. infant mortality rate exceeded those of 23 other countries, a number Sullivan described as "shockingly high."

INCOME/SOCIAL SECURITY

Income security programs, which included food and nutrition, housing and low-income energy aid, received an increase under the Bush budget, resulting in outlays of $473.5 billion in fiscal 1992 compared with $442 billion in fiscal 1991.

Social Security would increase slightly. The administration estimated that fiscal 1992 benefits for the elderly and disabled would cost $288.6 billion, up $19.7 billion from estimated fiscal 1991 outlays of $269 million. The increase included an estimated 5.2 percent January 1992 cost of living adjustment.

Housing

President Bush's housing budget was tied to his theme of providing choice and opportunity to low-income citizens. Besides requesting $25.6 billion in fiscal 1992, he proposed a fiscal 1991 supplemental of $942.8 million to fund two key programs within 1990's National Affordable Housing Act (PL 101-625). *(1990 Weekly Report, p. 4091)*

The supplemental included $165 million for the administration's Homeownership and Opportunity for People Everywhere (HOPE) program to help low-income families buy homes and $500 million for the HOME Investment Partnerships, congressional Democrats' program to provide matching funds for state and local communities to build or renovate affordable housing. The remainder would include new money for Shelter Plus Care to combine social services with housing for the homeless, and for renewal of expiring rental assistance contracts.

The supplemental would be offset by cuts in programs. Bush proposed slashing public housing construction by $500 million. Cuts would also come from programs eliminated by the housing act.

Overall, Bush's fiscal 1992 housing budget request was smaller than the $27 billion approved in fiscal 1991. But that was because the credit reform provisions in 1990's budget-reconciliation bill (PL 101-508) changed the way the government scored costs associated with mandatory credit programs. By factoring out these mandatory programs, as well as expiring rental assistance contracts, the housing budget would increase by 15 percent over fiscal 1991.

Subsidized housing, including rental assistance and public housing, would increase in fiscal 1992 by 91,423 units, compared with an 101,157 increase in 1991. Housing construction fund cuts likely would decrease the 1991 figure.

The fiscal 1992 proposal also included budget authority of

$865.4 million for HOPE grants, the full amount allowed by PL 101-625, and $1 billion for the HOME program, half as much as allowed. No money was allocated for the National Homeownership Trust, designed by House Banking Chairman Henry B. Gonzalez, D-Texas. The program, authorized for $522 million in fiscal 1992, would provide interest-rate subsidies and down-payment assistance to first-time home buyers.

New in Bush's budget package was a proposal for $947 million in budget authority in fiscal 1992 to create a Low-Income Resident Empowerment Program. The goal was to aid private, multifamily housing that was in financial or physical trouble. Landlords who greed to provide an equity interest in their buildings to tenants would receive money to cover cash-flow problems or to make repairs. The Department of Housing and Urban Development planned to send legislation to Capitol Hill to create the program.

The budget also proposed budget authority of $718 million in fiscal 1992 to offer to landlords incentives not to pay off federally subsidized mortgages or to stop renting to poor tenants.

LIHEAP

Bush sought a controversial cut in the popular Low Income Home Energy Assistance Program. LIHEAP provided grants to states, Indian tribes and U.S. territories for household heating, cooling and weatherization costs. He would have provided $991 million, considerably less than the fiscal 1991 level of $1.7 billion. Bush also requested $100 million for a contingency fund if heating oil prices did not decline. Funding would be based on fuel oil consumption by individual states, a formula that favored the Northeast.

Bush had tried to cut LIHEAP funds by $293 million in fiscal 1991, but Congress raised them instead.

According to the Washington-based Center on Budget and Policy Priorities, the budget would result in a 39 percent cut in funding after inflation. About 5.7 million low-income families received help in 1989, the center said.

Nutrition

Bush again sought to shift money within nutrition accounts. For programs such as food stamps and child nutrition, the budget would provide $30 billion in outlays, up from $28 billion in 1991. About $19.6 billion would go to food stamps, compared with $18.3 billion in 1991.

Bush requested $2.6 billion for the Special Supplemental Program for Women, Infants and Children, a $223 million increase over 1991 spending. But program supporters argued that a greater increase was needed.

The president proposed $4.3 billion for school lunches — the level required by law — an increase of $244 million over 1991 spending. But Bush repeated his request that the government shift spending to poorer students by decreasing subsidies for children from higher-income families. The request got nowhere in 1990. Program supporters argued that unless subsidies were available for all children, poor children would be hurt because school districts would not find it cost-effective to participate.

The fiscal 1992 budget would retain some of the subsidies for students from higher-income families to advance "the cause of redistribution."

Federal Employees

The budget provided a pay increase mandated by the federal pay reform provisions in the fiscal 1991 appropriations bill for the Treasury Department and U.S. Postal Service. Under the legislation, Bush could have withheld the pay increase because of war or recession.

"Today marks a turning point in the relationship between federal employees and the Bush administration," said John N. Sturdivant, president of the American Federation of Government Employees.

Unemployment

The administration estimated unemployment compensation benefits and administrative costs of the state-run unemployment program at $25.5 billion in budget authority for fiscal 1992, compared with $24 billion in 1991. The 1992 budget authority request for administrative payments to states was $2.3 billion, up $278.4 million over 1991. With states' unemployment insurance workloads up, the administration would propose a fiscal 1991 supplemental appropriation of $100 million.

LAW

In step with the administration's emphasis on increased law enforcement and drug fighting, Bush proposed $14.5 billion in outlays for the administration of justice in fiscal 1992. That was an increase of $1.9 billion, or 15.3 percent, over the 1991 estimated level.

The bulk of the funds — $10 billion in outlays — would go to the Justice Department.

Department officials said that if the increase were approved, the agency's budget would have grown by nearly 60 percent during the Bush administration's first three years.

As had been the case in previous years, most of the new funds were earmarked for the war on drugs. The budget would boost the department's drug-related resources to $4.4 billion, up 16 percent from fiscal 1991.

The total budget proposed $800 million, a 12 percent increase, for all drug law enforcement activities, including international interdiction.

The federal prison system would get $1.7 billion in outlays, an increase over the $1.3 billion in fiscal 1991. The plan, which followed the lead of a major multi-year construction program begun in 1990, would open five prisons and expand 10 others, for 5,900 new beds.

An estimated 60,000 inmates were in prison facilities, which were near 160 percent capacity. Justice Department officials said they were trying to reduce overcrowding to 130 percent capacity.

While the budget called for increases in most federal crime-fighting programs, it cut the outlays for the Office of Justice Programs, which gave assistance to state and local police.

Bush requested $483 million, compared with $601 million in 1991.

SCIENCE/TECHNOLOGY

Funding for science and technology programs would continue to grow at a steady pace under the Bush budget.

The biggest increases would go to the National Science Foundation (NSF), which funded so-called little science projects, and to the Energy Department's superconducting super collider, one of the largest of the "big science" projects.

Research and development (R&D) was one of the few areas in the fiscal 1992 budget slated for increases higher than the level of inflation.

"We must continue to make the investments needed to ensure this country's leadership, economic strength and security into the 21st century," the budget said.

"These are long-term investments for the next American century," said D. Allan Bromley, Bush's science adviser.

Overall, Bush's proposal would increase science and technology funding 10.6 percent to $17.5 billion. The programs and projects that would be funded were run by NASA, NSF and the Energy Department. Space flight, slated to increase to nearly $8.3 billion in fiscal 1992, still accounted for nearly half of the science and technology outlays.

Most of the programs and projects cited for increases were already in place, but the budget proposes two new programs: $149 million to develop hardware and software for supercomputers and $50 million to provide universities with state-of-the-art research equipment and facilities.

Overall R&D spending — which cut across a number of civilian and defense agencies — would increase 8 percent to $71.3 billion in fiscal 1992.

The biggest chunk of R&D spending, 56 percent, was for defense research, much of which was done through the Defense Department's Defense Advanced Research Projects Agency.

• NASA, which was plagued in 1990 by projects with cost overruns and construction flaws, would receive a 13 percent increase, bringing its budget authority to $15.7 billion.

The agency's biggest-ticket item, the space shuttle, which represented nearly one-third of its budget request, $5.1 billion, would receive a 9 percent increase over 1991's funding level.

Bush's budget anticipated nine space shuttle missions each in 1992 and 1993, and 10 missions each year thereafter — a sharp drop from the 20-plus annual missions originally planned.

Developing new launch vehicles to supplement the troubled space shuttle was also cited as a priority.

• The global change initiative, which bound together scores of projects scattered across nine agencies, would receive a 24 percent boost, bringing its budget to $1.2 billion. The initiative included a hefty increase for NASA's Earth-observing system — a centerpiece of the agency's Mission to Planet Earth — which would be funded at $336 million, a 76 percent increase over 1991. The system was a series of space platforms and remote sensors for monitoring the Earth's processes from space.

• Mission from Planet Earth, including Bush's ambitious plan to launch manned space vehicles to the moon and Mars, would cost $2.5 billion.

Included in the space-exploration plan was research for the space station *Freedom*. No total construction cost was estimated because the entire project was being redesigned by NASA.

Congress shot down Bush's moon-Mars proposal in 1990, saying such an expensive project could not be justified. But Bush was pushing it again.

• NSF would receive one of the largest increases in its history — 17.5 percent — bringing its budget to $2.72 billion. Nearly three-quarters of the increase, $284 million, was for scientific research. NSF historically had funded an array of projects across the sciences, from climate change to neurotransmitters.

• The superconducting super collider's budget would increase 120 percent to $534 million because construction was scheduled to begin in 1991 on the controversial project in Ellis County, Texas.

• The Human Genome Project, a 15-year effort to map the human gene by the National Institutes of Health and the Energy Department, would receive $169 million, a 26 percent increase over 1991's funding level.

While Bush's budget called for increased spending for research, it raiseed a red flag about the way Congress was distributing the research dollars. According to a study by the Office of Science and Technology Policy, Congress was using the research budget to fund hundreds of costly regional projects targeted at specific institutions or even specific researchers. Such "earmarking," the budget said, was eroding the merit-based approach for awarding R&D grants and contracts.

TRANSPORTATION

Bush's transportation budget was touted as the first in seven years to have across-the-board increases in highway, mass transit, rail and aviation funding.

While many of the increases were illusory shifts from one account to another, there were true firsts in Bush's proposal.

It was the first time since fiscal 1985 that an administration budget had proposed funding subsidies for Amtrak rail service, and the first Republican administration to support the 14-year-old rural Essential Air Service.

Bush's budget assumed $32.7 billion in fiscal 1992 outlays for transportation programs, 3.9 percent above the fiscal 1991 level of $31.5 billion.

Most of the spending was within the Transportation Department, with proposed outlays of $31.9 billion.

Of that, $31 billion fell under the domestic discretionary category, compared with $29.8 billion in fiscal 1991. To realize such an increase, transportation would have to take money away from other domestic programs because total domestic appropriations were capped by 1990's budget deal.

Bush proposed a five-year reauthorization bill for surface transportation programs, with the spending ceiling from the Highway Trust Fund account raised to $15.7 billion, up from $14.5 billion in fiscal 1991.

But trust fund spending not subject to that ceiling was decreased by about $1.2 billion, making total trust fund spending roughly the same as in fiscal 1991.

Among the most contentious highway funding formula changes Bush wanted was a plan to reduce the federal share of funds from 75 percent to 60 percent for many so-called second-tier urban and rural roads.

Bush also proposed more reliance on motor fuel taxes, rather than on general revenues, to pay for mass transit and highway safety programs.

He would cut general revenue budget authority for mass transit from $1.9 billion to $80 million. To compensate, he would open trust fund spending by $1.9 billion to $3.2 billion. In past years, the Reagan administration had proposed zero funding from general revenues, with no compensation from the trust fund.

Outlays for mass transit general revenue programs would be cut by $948 million to $2 billion — but trust fund outlays would not make up for the decrease, increasing by only $419 million to $1.6 billion.

Bush again proposed eliminating operating subsidies for the 147 transit systems in urbanized areas with populations over 1 million.

Other Requests

Other requests for transportation programs included:

• Aviation budget authority would get an 18 percent boost to $9.3 billion in fiscal 1992. Federal Aviation Administration (FAA) trust fund outlays would rise from $5.3 billion to $5.7 billion, while general revenue outlays would go up from $2.1 billion to $2.3 billion.

FAA operations outlays would be $4.5 billion, up 7 percent over fiscal 1991 outlays of $4.2 billion. The increase would pay for 450 new air-traffic controller positions, 100 new safety inspectors and 178 new security personnel.

• The biggest surprise in railroad spending came in the administration's decision to fund Amtrak subsidies. Bush assumed $410 million in outlays for the train service.

The request gave the administration more strength with Congress to argue how Amtrak money was spent. "There is a whole list of productivity improvements that we feel could be implemented" to reduce Amtrak's operating deficit, said Deputy Transportation Secretary Elaine L. Chao.

• In another switch from the past, the administration also would provide $38.6 million in outlays for the Essential Air Service program, which subsidized airlines that operated in rural areas with few passengers. Congress had routinely rescued the program from Reagan and Bush attempts to eliminate funding.

"Clearly, we are taking a much more conciliatory point of view, I think to Congress as well," Chao said. "There are communities which do need the service. To zero it out completely, I think, would create certain battles up on the Hill that have not proven very productive in the past."

VETERANS

Veterans programs would receive an increase of more than $1 billion under President Bush's budget proposal, with the bulk of the money directed toward health care.

Bush's budget would increase Department of Veterans Affairs (VA) funding to $33 billion in outlays for fiscal 1992, up from $31.3 billion in fiscal 1991.

However, according to a statement from the House Veterans' Affairs Committee, the budget proposal did not take into account the "possible budgetary impact of Operation Desert Storm on VA resources," such as medical care and claims adjudication.

About $13 billion in outlays would be used for VA medical programs.

Included in Bush's request was a pay boost for physicians and dentists at VA hospitals, which would cost $41.5 million. Congress was seeking a similar increase that would cost about $63 million. The Bush administration had described that proposed increase as "excessive."

About $100 million would be used to hire additional staff so that VA hospitals could begin to comply with nationwide standards restricting residents' work hours.

About $12.3 billion would fund compensation payments for 2.2 million disabled veterans.

The proposal also included $303 million for a 5.4 percent cost of living adjustment for disabled veterans and survivors of veterans who died of service-related injuries.

Congress passed a bill to authorize the COLA in January. Bush signed the legislation Feb. 6.

Congressional, Bush Budgets: Virtual Twins

Hemmed in by new budget rules and unwilling to reopen the previous year's battles over big items like taxes and defense spending, the Democratic-controlled Congress approved a budget blueprint for fiscal 1992 that was virtually indistinguishable from President Bush's. The conference report on the budget was adopted with relative ease by both chambers on May 22 — the second earliest date that had happened since 1982. The House approved it 239-181; the Senate did so 57-41. *(House vote 112, p. 28-H; Senate vote 75, p. 11-S)*

The budget resolution determined how much budget authority was available to the Appropriations committees; in practical terms, however, that number had already been set for fiscal 1992 in the budget rules. The budget resolution also included detailed recommendations on how appropriators should divide up the pot, but these were advisory only.

By the time the $1.45 trillion budget resolution was in place, House appropriators had already begun making the real spending decisions. That fueled criticism that the budget resolution, setting Congress' tax and spending guidelines for the year, was largely irrelevant.

Moreover, with the room for maneuver constrained by tight discretionary spending caps and pay-as-you-go limits on entitlements and taxes, the Democratic majority was confined to recommending that money be moved from one set of programs to another in the $212 billion domestic discretionary spending category — which accounted for only about one-seventh of the budget. *(New budget rules, p. 73)*

That gave Democrats a chance to tout spending increases for education, health and job training, while Republicans said the Democrats were only tinkering at the margins of Bush's budget. Republicans also criticized the Democrats for including $1.8 billion in unspecified spending reductions that allowed them to provide extra money for their favored programs without spelling out how to make the necessary spending cuts to get there.

Spending for defense and for international programs was largely the same as in Bush's budget. The Budget committees ignored Bush's proposals to reform spending for entitlement programs such as Medicare and farm price supports.

In some years, the Budget committees' main influence had come from issuing reconciliation instructions, which directed the authorizing committees to make changes in tax and entitlement law to meet deficit targets. But the lack of deficit targets beyond the spending caps and pay-as-you-go rules in the new budget agreement eliminated the need for a reconciliation bill, and the Budget committees declined to volunteer reconciliation instructions on their own.

The only real strife came over a Senate GOP proposal to bar the use of tax increases to pay for new or expanded entitlement spending under the pay-as-you-go rules. Conferees deleted the tax prohibition, and the full Senate subsequently approved. Some analysts suggested that the budget resolution's chief value was as tangible proof that Congress intended to stick by the 1990 summit agreement.

HOUSE BUDGET COMMITTEE

The House Budget Committee marked up and approved a budget resolution (H Con Res 121) on April 9, working from a Democratic draft presented by Chairman Leon E. Panetta, D-Calif.

Among the biggest changes from Bush's budget was a $2 billion increase over fiscal 1991 spending for education. Bush had requested a $728 million increase for fiscal 1992; a $937 million increase was needed to keep up with inflation.

The panel also recommended a deep cut in the 13 percent boost that Bush had proposed for NASA, slashing it to a 4.2 percent, inflation-only increase. The difference was critical for big-ticket items such as the proposed space station.

Among other changes, the Democrats recommended: $866 million above Bush's request for a variety of energy programs, including the Strategic Petroleum Reserve, energy research and a subsidy for the purchase of more than 25,000 alternative-fuel vehicles; $649 million above Bush's request for the Low Income Home Energy Assistance Program; and $380 million more for Community Development Block Grants.

Offsetting cuts were sprinkled throughout discretionary programs. They included a 1 percent across-the-board reduction in certain "non-priority" areas and trims in operational expenses in various agencies, such as the Small Business Administration, the Department of Housing and Urban Development, and the Department of Agriculture.

Democrats insisted that the changes, though minor compared with the entire budget, were critical. "I would like you to ask a child whether it makes a difference whether we put $2 billion in education or $700 million," said Panetta.

The committee avoided making any substantive changes in defense and international spending — decisions driven in part by the fact that the new budget rules made the savings useless to members who wanted to increase spending elsewhere.

Unlike previous years, when cuts in defense or foreign aid could be used to beef up domestic spending, members were prohibited from transferring money from one category — defense, international, domestic — to another. That meant cuts would simply reduce the deficit, and few members were eager to fight for a few billion dollars in cuts when the deficit was projected to be close to $300 billion.

Moreover, budget negotiators had suffered considerable political pain in 1990 reaching the numbers and policies that went into the budget agreement. Defense spending, for instance, was targeted for substantial cuts throughout the five-year agreement. There was little appetite for reopening that fight to cut defense further — especially with many Democrats politically wounded by their vote against using force against Iraq.

Members were equally reluctant to follow Bush's proposal for restructuring entitlement programs.

Panetta said budget negotiators had already been through the mill in 1990 enacting $100 million worth of entitlement changes. Ranking Republican Bill Gradison of Ohio offered an amendment incorporating Bush's proposed income tests for Medicare premiums and agriculture subsidies. The committee compromised on language that endorsed the concept of relating entitlements to income but deferred action to other committees.

In other action, the committee adopted what Panetta described as "very innocuous language" asking the Ways and Means Committee to examine the equity of the Social Security payroll tax. Frank J. Guarini, D-N.J., and Dick Armey, R-Texas, had proposed specifically endorsing cut-

Fiscal 1992 Budget Resolution

(In billions of dollars; totals may not add due to rounding)

	Bush's Budget	House Passed	Senate Passed	Final
National Defense				
Budget Authority	$ 290.8	$ 290.8	$ 290.8	$ 290.8
Outlays	295.3	295.3	295.3	295.3
International Affairs				
Budget Authority	21.9	21.9	22.3	21.9
Outlays	17.8	17.9	17.9	17.9
Science and Space				
Budget Authority	18.9	17.7	16.5	17.1
Outlays	17.5	16.8	16.2	16.5
Energy				
Budget Authority	4.9	6.2	5.4	6.2
Outlays	4.3	4.5	4.5	4.5
Natural Resources				
Budget Authority	19.8	19.4	19.5	19.5
Outlays	20.0	19.4	19.7	19.4
Agriculture				
Budget Authority	22.1	22.3	22.6	22.4
Outlays	16.9	17.0	17.1	17.0
Commerce and Housing				
Budget Authority	107.2	107.5	107.7	107.7
Outlays	103.4	104.3	104.6	104.5
Transportation				
Budget Authority	34.3	34.6	33.8	34.6
Outlays	33.4	33.7	33.5	33.7
Community Development				
Budget Authority	5.6	6.1	5.9	6.1
Outlays	6.7	6.7	6.7	6.7
Education and Social Services				
Budget Authority	46.8	51.0	54.2	53.1
Outlays	45.0	47.4	48.2	47.9
Health				
Budget Authority	81.8	83.1	82.9	83.1
Outlays	82.7	83.4	83.3	83.3
Medicare				
Budget Authority	117.4	120.1	120.0	120.1
Outlays	114.1	116.9	116.8	116.9
Income Security				
Budget Authority	220.2	221.9	222.2	222.2
Outlays	179.8	180.1	180.9	180.3
Social Security				
Budget Authority	356.4	356.6	356.6	356.6
Outlays	287.1	286.9	286.7	286.9
Veterans' Benefits				
Budget Authority	32.9	34.4	34.3	34.3
Outlays	32.6	34.0	34.1	34.0
Justice				
Budget Authority	14.8	14.2	13.2	13.7
Outlays	14.8	14.2	13.5	13.6
General Government				
Budget Authority	12.5	11.6	12.7	11.6
Outlays	13.1	12.2	12.6	12.2
Net Interest				
Budget Authority	210.2	209.9	209.9	209.9
Outlays	210.2	209.9	209.9	209.9
Allowances				
Budget Authority	−0.2	−0.2	−1.4	−0.2
Outlays	−13.5	−13.5	−14.5	−13.2
Offsetting Receipts				
Budget Authority	−39.0	−39.1	−38.8	−40.6
Outlays	−39.0	−39.1	−38.8	−39.3
TOTALS				
Budget Authority	$ 1,579.3	$ 1,590.0	$ 1,590.2	$ 1,590.1
Outlays	1,442.2	1,448.0	1,448.0	1,448.0
Revenues	1,172.2	1,169.2	1,169.2	1,169.2
Deficit	270.0	278.8	278.8	278.8

NOTE: Numbers in this table reflect House Budget Committee adjustments. Totals in the House and Senate resolutions and the president's budget proposal have been readjusted to be comparable to the estimating assumptions used in the conference report. This makes it possible to view policy differences, rather than mechanical or estimating differences, between the various budgets. Totals for the Senate budget resolution and the conference agreement display total budget figures, instead of on-budget figures only.

SOURCES: Congressional Budget Office, House and Senate Budget committees

ting the tax. But Ways and Means Chairman Dan Rostenkowski, D-Ill., a foe of the cut, was consulted prior to the vote and demanded that the language be watered down.

The committee rejected three Republican substitute budgets, two of which would have cut discretionary spending. A substitute by John R. Kasich, R-Ohio, would have saved $8.8 billion in fiscal 1992 and about $87 billion over five years; it was defeated, 6-16, by a show of hands. Another, by William E. Dannemeyer, R-Calif., that would have cut even more deeply to save $28 billion in fiscal 1992 was turned down, 3-18, on a show of hands.

Gradison offered the Bush budget as a final GOP substitute, but that was defeated on a voice vote, with at least one Republican, Christopher Shays, Conn., indicating that he would vote against it and for the Democratic version because the latter was friendlier to urban areas.

The committee adopted the Democratic budget on a voice vote April 9.

HOUSE FLOOR ACTION

The House debated the budget resolution April 16 and 17, and approved it April 17 by a largely party-line vote of 261-163, after rejecting the president's budget by a vote of 89-335. *(Votes 71, 70, p. 18-H)*

The two-day House debate amplified arguments rehearsed in the Budget Committee. Democrats said that the roughly $13 billion in additions and deletions they made to the Bush domestic spending agenda produced a document that was fairer to working Americans.

But Republicans argued, in Gradison's words, that "the Democrats have merely rearranged a few of the deck chairs," while claiming "that they have steered the entire ship of state on a new course."

The only change approved on the floor was an amendment by William D. Ford, D-Mich., to add $400 million in budget authority and $200 million in outlays for education. That was on top of the $2 billion increase approved by the House committee. The floor change, adopted 261-158, brought the House measure closer to the Senate version on education. *(Vote 67, p. 18-H)*

The $400 million was to be shifted from programs in the categories of natural resources and the environment, transportation, justice and general government.

Votes on three GOP amendments revealed that House Republicans, who had split badly over budget policy the previous year, remained sharply divided.

Dannemeyer and Kasich offered substitutes designed to appeal to Republican sentiment that spending was still too high. Both amendments were variations on a freeze aimed at cutting spending below levels in both the Democratic budget and the Bush proposal, with Dannemeyer's cutting most deeply. Democrats opposed them for slashing what they regarded as vital areas of social spending.

Both amendments lost heavily, Dannemeyer's by 79-332 and Kasich's by 114-303. Republicans divided 78-83 over Dannemeyer and 105-56 over Kasich. *(Votes 68, 69, p. 18-H)*

The president's budget, offered as an amendment by Gradison, fared almost as poorly as Dannemeyer's and worse than Kasich's: Republicans supported it, 89-74; it lost in the full House, 89-335. Gradison said afterward that GOP discontent over high spending levels hurt the president's budget.

SENATE BUDGET COMMITTEE

The Senate Budget Committee began marking up a similar version of the budget resolution on April 11, and finished just as the House completed floor action on its version of the measure.

Unlike the House committee, which began with a Democratic draft, the Senate panel started with a "policy-neutral" resolution that Chairman Jim Sasser, D-Tenn., said represented a budget authority freeze plus a neutral, prorata allocation of additional spending permitted under the budget agreement's discretionary caps.

On April 11, the committee rejected two efforts to freeze 1992 spending at 1991 levels. One, by Charles E. Grassley, R-Iowa, would have saved $14.4 billion in fiscal 1992 spending authority and $32.4 billion over five years; it failed 10-11. The other, by Kent Conrad, D-N.D., would have cut even more deeply while protecting spending for agriculture, education, health care and veterans; it also failed 10-11.

Instead, the committee voted 15-6 to adopt a sprawling Democratic package, dubbed a Homefront Budget Initiative, that added $4.4 billion to spending in areas such as education, health and children's programs, among others. The amendment boosted spending for education to $3.1 billion and included a $1 billion increase for student aid, which backers said would boost the maximum Pell grant for the neediest students from $2,400 to $2,800. Sponsor Tim Wirth, D-Colo., said he would fund the increase by imposing a 4 percent across-the-board cut in other domestic discretionary spending.

Like its House counterpart, the Senate committee was clearly unwilling to tamper with the cap on discretionary defense appropriations. Paul Simon, D-Ill., won only his own vote for a proposal to cut defense spending by 10 percent. An alternative amendment to cut spending by 1 percent drew seven of his colleagues, but the proposal failed, 8-13, on April 11.

Over GOP objections, Democrats April 17 added procedural language to smooth the way for the Senate to consider changes in entitlement spending and taxes later in the year. Without the so-called reserve fund language, requested unanimously by the Finance Committee, bills to increase entitlement spending would have been subject to a point of order. The change explicitly made room for action on five initiatives: health and nutrition for children, general health care, economic recovery, surface transportation and the Head Start program.

Democrats said the reserve fund provision simply made it possible to make deficit-neutral changes in entitlements and taxes under pay-as-you-go budget rules, but Republicans charged that it would open the door to tax increases.

The committee rejected, 10-11, an amendment by Phil Gramm, R-Texas, to strip the reserve fund language altogether.

But the panel approved, 11-10, a controversial amendment by Hank Brown, R-Colo., and ranking Republican Pete V. Domenici, N.M., to institute a 60-vote point of order in the Senate against using taxes to pay for any of the programs protected by the reserve fund provision. By barring tax increases, the amendment aimed to force Congress to pay for any entitlement increases or tax cuts by cutting spending in other entitlement programs.

Brown got the amendment through the committee with the help of two Democrats: fellow Coloradan Wirth and South Carolina's Ernest F. Hollings. Sasser and the rest of the committee's Democrats opposed the amendment on the grounds that it would cut programs such as Medicare and cripple vital expansions in some social programs.

In other significant action, Domenici failed to win support for restoring a 60-vote fire wall against any attempts to cut the Social Security payroll tax or spend down the program's trust funds — and against any budget resolution paving the way for such a change. The 1990 budget agreement had established such a requirement, but language added by Sasser limited the scope of the restriction to bills reported to the floor. Social Security language added on the floor only required a majority vote. With members looking ahead to a vote on a proposal by Daniel Patrick Moynihan, D-N.Y., to cut the payroll tax, the committee rejected the Domenici amendment, 8-13. *(Social Security tax, p. 108)*

Domenici earlier had said that he viewed the Social Security procedural issue as the most important element of the budget resolution, and he declined to support the measure after his amendment failed.

The committee then approved the budget resolution on an almost strict party-line vote, 11-10. Conrad was the sole Democrat to join the committee's Republicans in opposing the measure.

SENATE FLOOR ACTION

After a low-key, three-day debate, the Senate approved the budget resolution by voice vote on April 25.

The emotional high point in the floor action came when Moynihan attempted, as promised, to win approval for a procedural amendment that would have opened the way for a vote later in the year on cutting the Social Security payroll tax. Passage of Moynihan's amendment would have allowed the Senate to bypass budget rules that required at least 60 votes on the floor to change Social Security, a forbidding prospect.

The Senate voted 60-38 on April 24 to table (kill) Moynihan's amendment, effectively closing the door to a later vote. Senators were clearly worried that constituents would accuse them of tampering with the Social Security system and that cutting the tax would aggravate the deficit and threaten the solvency of the retirement program.

Sasser agonized over the issue but finally came down against Moynihan, saying he agreed with the reasons for the tax cut but feared it would raise federal borrowing needs and worsen the deficit.

After the vote, Domenici managed to restore the 60-vote fire wall in the budget resolution against proposals to alter the Social Security trust funds. Sasser joined Domenici in offering the amendment, ending a feud between the two over whether Moynihan should have a chance to cut the Social Security tax on a simple majority vote. The amendment passed on a voice vote.

No effort was made to strip out the Brown amendment.

In considering floor amendments, the Senate turned down every opportunity to save more money than required under the 1990 budget deal, rejecting a spending freeze, proposals to cut defense spending and even a measure that would have eliminated a subsidy for beekeepers. In most cases, leaders warned that tampering with spending levels would violate the budget deal or unravel the fragile consensus that made the 1990 deficit-reduction package possible.

On key amendments, the Senate:

- **Spending freeze.** Voted 60-37 to table (kill) an amendment by Grassley that would have frozen fiscal 1992 discretionary spending at 1991 levels. *(Vote 47, p. 7-S)*

Grassley said the proposal was a small but necessary step toward reducing the budget deficit. He argued that it was not a spending cut but a restraint on spending increases.

Appropriations Committee Chairman Robert C. Byrd, D-W.Va., said the freeze would effectively cut spending in a multitude of critical programs because it did not allow for inflation. He said it would be particularly devastating to programs to rebuild the nation's infrastructure.

- **Campaign finance.** Rejected, 0-95, a move by Mitch McConnell, R-Ky., to table his own amendment, which would have terminated the presidential election campaign checkoff fund and transferred the money to child-nutrition programs. *(Vote 48, p. 7-S)*

- **Shifting money from defense.** Rejected, 22-73, a motion by Bill Bradley, D-N.J., to waive the Budget Act to permit a vote on an amendment that would have cut defense spending by 2 percent and split the proceeds between deficit reduction and domestic spending for education, health care and environmental cleanup. *(Vote 49, p. 8-S)*

Sasser challenged Bradley's amendment on the grounds that it violated the 1990 budget agreement, which specifically prohibited moving money from one discretionary spending category to another. Sasser's point of order prevailed, and Bradley's amendment failed.

- **Cutting defense spending.** Rejected, 25-70 and 30-64, amendments by Simon to cut defense spending authority by 2 percent and 1 percent, respectively. Because the proceeds would have gone to deficit reduction, the amendment did not violate the Budget Act. Simon argued that the declining threat from the Soviet Union and the Warsaw Pact made it unnecessary to continue spending as much for defense. *(Votes 50, 51, p. 8-S)*

Opponents argued that political instability in the Soviet Union required the United States to keep up its guard. Domenici opposed the Simon cuts on the grounds that defense spending had already taken big cuts in the previous year's budget negotiations — $177 billion over five years, or about 40 percent of the deficit reduction achieved by the budget agreement.

- **Honey program.** Voted, 57-38, to table an amendment by Brown to terminate a price support program for honey. Brown said he had chosen the honey program because it wasted money and was "one of the silliest programs ever thought up in this nation or any nation in the history of the world." Defenders said the program was cost-effective. *(Vote 52, p. 8-S)*

- **Housing programs.** Approved by voice vote an amendment by Donald W. Riegle Jr., D-Mich., and Christopher S. Bond, R-Mo., to provide $900 million in spending authority to bring the Senate's proposed level of funding up to that in Bush's budget and closer to that in the House budget resolution. Riegle said the expense would be offset primarily by cutting $643 million from a general government account that received $1.6 billion the previous year for the construction of 20 federal buildings.

- **Veterans' benefits.** Approved by voice vote an amendment by Jim Exon, D-Neb., and Alan Cranston, D-Calif., to provide $900 million to bring veterans spending up to the baseline level — the fiscal 1991 level plus an adjustment for inflation. The extra money for veterans was to be offset by unspecified cuts.

- **Highways and mass transit.** Gave voice-vote approval to two amendments by Arlen Specter, R-Pa. One urged future legislation to prohibit using the surpluses in the mass transit and highway accounts of the Transportation Trust Fund in calculating the federal deficit. The other added spending for highways and mass transit — $1.3 billion for highways and $300 million for mass transit in fiscal 1992.

CONFERENCE, FINAL ACTION

Working from similar budget resolutions, House and Senate conferees in most cases made only minor changes, reaching a compromise late in the week of May 13. The most controversial item — the GOP-backed Senate proposal to bar any tax increases in fiscal 1992 to pay for expanding entitlements — was killed in conference. *(Bills comparison, p. 70)*

House Republicans had staged a knock-down, drag-out debate on the Brown amendment May 9, trying and ultimately failing to instruct House conferees to support the provision in conference. Trading potshots that recalled some of the nastier moments of the previous year's protracted debate over taxes, Republicans accused Democrats of lusting after tax increases on working Americans, while Democrats accused the GOP of shielding wealthy fat cats and raiding benefit programs for cash. The motion to instruct the conferees failed 132-284. *(Vote 85, p. 22-H)*

Meanwhile, Brown had joined with Budget colleagues to warn that Republicans would strongly oppose the budget if it arrived on the Senate floor with the no-taxes amendment stripped out.

The prospect of trouble on the Senate floor so concerned Sasser that he put the conference on hold to conduct a whip count among Senate Democrats, sources said. Only when he was satisfied that he would probably prevail in a floor vote did he agree to move ahead, strip out the Brown amendment and wind up the conference.

When the conference report reached the Senate, the dispute fizzled.

Senate Finance Committee Chairman Lloyd Bentsen, D-Texas, outlined his sharp objections to the Brown amendment, charging that the restriction would hamstring his committee in trying to fashion critical new spending for health care, unemployment and other programs.

Brown declined to speak for his provision, leaving it to Domenici and Gramm to argue that Democrats were looking for ways to raise taxes.

In the end, it appeared that Bentsen's fury and mixed signals from Minority Leader Bob Dole, R-Kan., took the fight out of the GOP.

"You're going up against the chairman of the Finance Committee," explained one key Senate aide. "He doesn't forget these things." ■

Budget Rules Survive; Deficit Still Soars

The budget rules put in place as part of the 1990 budget-summit agreement did almost exactly what they were supposed to do in 1991: They set strict limits on new spending and tied Congress' hands to an unprecedented degree. At the same time, the rules did virtually nothing to reduce the deficit, which was expected to soar further in fiscal 1992.

With that record — and the mounting pressure to cut taxes and shift defense spending to home-front programs — the rules were almost certain to bend, and possibly break, in 1992.

"I hope [the agreement] won't break next year," said Bill Gradison of Ohio, ranking Republican on the House Budget Committee, "but the pressures to 'do something' about the economy may be so great that the budget deal passes by the wayside."

Cleared for President Bush less than two weeks before Election Day 1990 by a Congress desperate to leave town to campaign, the budget deal was so complicated that most members learned how it would affect them only gradually. For many, there turned out to be little to like and much to loathe. *(Budget summit, 1990 Almanac, p. 129; 1990 Almanac, p. 173)*

Democrats, especially liberal Democrats, chafed throughout the year at the fact that the rules locked away defense spending, making it unavailable for redirection to needy domestic programs, even after the collapse of the Soviet Union.

As the recession deepened, members were frustrated to realize that traditional job-creation programs and tax cuts were forbidden unless they were deficit neutral or mutually agreed to by the Democratic Congress and Republican president, alternatives that turned out to be almost equally unusable.

Moreover, the administration's Office of Management and Budget (OMB) had new power to punish the smallest violations of the spending categories, once even stepping in to penalize a domestic surplus with a tiny, $2.4 million spending cut that enraged appropriators. *(Sequester, p. 74)*

The deal "basically took away all their options," said Stanley Collender, director of federal budget policy for the accounting firm Price Waterhouse. "It eliminated Congress' ability to move in any direction.... Their ability to respond to any new problem [is] virtually non-existent."

But House Budget Committee Chairman Leon E. Panetta, D-Calif., an architect of the deal and one of its most passionate defenders, argued that even though the pact tied Democrats' hands it was "one of the most important disciplines we've put in place in the history of the budget process."

Many Republicans, particularly conservatives, hated the budget agreement's higher taxes and back-loaded spending cuts, which put more emphasis on slashing appropriations in the last two of the deal's five years, 1994 and 1995. Most analysts expected the deal to be renegotiated by that time.

Soaring Deficit

If members expected a lower deficit in exchange for all the discomfort, they got a rude shock. Driven by factors such as the recession, the savings and loan bailout and unexpectedly large increases in spending for Medicare, Medicaid, food stamps and other benefit programs, the deficit skyrocketed.

The $268.7 billion fiscal 1991 deficit easily eclipsed the previous record, a $221.2 billion gap in 1986. The fiscal 1992 deficit was projected to be far worse: Official predictions from the Congressional Budget Office (CBO) put the 1992 deficit at $362 billion, but some experts expected the figure to top $400 billion.

In the era that preceded the budget deal, deficits that big would have terrorized Congress, because they would have forced legislators to wrestle with the prospect of enormous spending cuts ("sequesters") to trim the shortfall. Such automatic cuts had been required under the Gramm-Rudman anti-deficit law. *(Gramm-Rudman, 1974 Almanac, p. 145)*

But the new budget deal radically altered the goal of congressional budgeting, from deficit reduction to spending control, on the theory that if Congress concentrated on what it could control — spending — and forgot about the things it could not — fluctuations in the economy, for example — the deficit would eventually take care of itself.

Obeying the Rules

In judging the first full year of the 1990 budget agreement a reasonable success, members of Congress, staff and outside analysts rated compliance with the rules fairly high. The following are specific examples:

- **Discretionary spending caps.** Despite widespread complaints that they had much less money than they needed, appropriators stuck close to ceilings on fiscal 1992 appropriations for defense, domestic and international programs.

Although appropriators generally obeyed the budget caps, they fiddled with the rules in a way that critics said would haunt them the following year.

In order to stay within their spending limits, the Labor-HHS Appropriations subcommittees delayed obligating $3.1 billion in spending authority, in most cases until the very last day of fiscal 1992. The effect was to kick $850 million in outlays into fiscal 1993, worsening the already tight outlay caps for that year. Five other subcommittees contributed another $1 billion or so in delayed obligations, kicking another $600 million in outlays into fiscal 1993.

Analysts disagreed over whether appropriators strayed over the line by classifying some funds as emergency spending. Under the budget rules, spending that was considered emergency by both Congress and the White House did not count against the budget caps. The two sides clashed often over the issue during the year on a series of supplemental spending bills, with the White House frequently insisting that it would not agree to suspend the caps. *(1992 supplemental, p. 661)*

- **Pay-as-you-go limits on entitlements and tax cuts.** The pay-as-you-go rule was intended to ensure that tax cuts, new entitlement programs and expansion of existing entitlement programs would not add to the deficit. (Entitlement programs automatically provided benefits for people who met eligibility requirements, such as income level for food stamps or age for Medicare.) The rule succeeded, so much so that only one major proposal to expand an entitlement program — a measure that provided extended unemployment benefits — passed during the year,

Darman's Mini-Sequester

The Office of Management and Budget (OMB) ordered a tiny across-the-board spending cut on April 25 to correct overspending by Congress in a supplemental spending bill (HR 1281 — PL 102-27) cleared in March. The cut was triggered by an $8 million provision — hardly a ripple in the $5.4 billion ocean of spending in the supplemental.

At stake was a move by Rep. Dan Rostenkowski, D-Ill., to do a favor for his alma mater, Loyola University of Chicago. Rostenkowski switched the source of $8 million in previously appropriated federal funding for the school.

The money was to have come from a Defense Department account, but Loyola officials reportedly worried that that might require the school to do defense-related research. Rostenkowski managed to have the funding shifted to the Department of Education.

But the new budget rules split appropriations spending into three categories in fiscal 1991-93: defense, domestic and international. Each had a strict cap, and the domestic account was already close to its ceiling for fiscal 1991. When the $8 million suddenly moved from defense to domestic, it busted the domestic cap by $2.4 million.

The amount had slipped by administration lobbyists who staked out the late-night House-Senate conference, and the administration initially had given the supplemental a clean bill of fiscal health. But when Office of Management and Budget (OMB) Director Richard G. Darman got a look at the fine print, he fired off a letter to Congress warning that the money would trigger an automatic, offsetting spending cut, known as a sequester, if Congress didn't fix it.

Darman suggested either doing away with the Rostenkowski transfer or rescinding offsetting appropriations from other domestic accounts. The letter was a call to arms for Rostenkowski and House Appropriations Committee Chairman Jamie L. Whitten, D-Miss., who refused to back down.

But under the rules, Darman's was the only opinion that counted, and OMB ordered a 0.0013 percent "mini-sequester" of fiscal 1991 domestic spending — $13 for every $1 million in appropriations.

and that only after an extended fight between Congress and the White House over whether it should be paid for. *(Unemployment benefits, p. 301)*

An attempt to transform discretionary spending for highways into an entitlement program to take advantage of potential new funding through an increase in the gasoline tax collapsed when the House balked at raising the tax. *(Transportation reauthorization, p. 137)*

Despite the apparent success of the pay-as-you-go regime, most analysts judged this rule as a major flaw, since it did nothing to put a lid on existing entitlement programs, such as Medicaid, which increased dramatically during the year.

• **Maximum deficit amounts.** Under the pre-summit version of the Gramm-Rudman anti-deficit rules, the maximum deficit amounts were the single most feared number in all budgeting. Should Congress fail to meet this annual deficit target, OMB was required to unleash an across-the-board spending cut shortly after the beginning of the fiscal year to trim the excess.

Much of the urgency that drove the summit negotiators in 1990 derived from the fact that, without a new budget deal, the cuts under Gramm-Rudman would have been enormous: With a deficit target of $64 billion and a projected fiscal 1991 deficit of nearly $170 billion, the potential Gramm-Rudman sequester was an unthinkably huge $106 billion — a cut that would have devastated the federal government.

As part of their deal, summit negotiators changed the budget rules to do away with a single, big year-end sequester, at least until fiscal 1994.

That made for a year of peaceful budgeting since Congress was spared the annual, panicky rush to find enough spending cuts and tax and fee increases to close the deficit gap. (As a result, members also did not have the usual year-end budget-reconciliation bill to serve as a vehicle for turning controversial health-care and other provisions into law.)

• **Sequesters.** The rules shifted from the old Gramm-Rudman anti-deficit law's single, year-end sequester to a series of "mini-sequesters" that more carefully targeted spending violations in the three discretionary spending categories (defense, domestic and international). That gave OMB substantial new power to involve itself early in the legislative process to head off proposals the administration did not like.

Budget analysts compared the change to switching from a nuclear bomb that budget enforcers could only threaten to use, to a baseball bat that OMB enforcers could — and frequently did — use to whack congressional committees.

The new power was most apparent in OMB's ability to force even small programs out of supplemental appropriations bills by threatening to score them as surplus spending that would violate the budget caps and cause a sequester in that particular spending category.

• **Suspending the budget rules.** If lawmakers really did not like the budget deal, they had ample opportunity all year to do something about it. An escape-hatch clause in the agreement provided for an automatic Senate vote on suspending the process whenever the projected growth of the gross national product (GNP) was below zero or actual growth was below 1 percent for two consecutive quarters. A House vote was optional.

The idea was to prevent the deal from being an impediment to necessary anti-recession activity, such as job-creating public works programs or stimulative tax cuts. The faltering economy triggered three automatic votes in the Senate, and three times senators turned down the opportunity to shelve the rules, not just decisively but overwhelmingly: Senators turned down suspension resolutions by 2-97 on Jan. 31, 5-92 on May 9 and 8-88 on Sept. 19. *(Votes 10, 55, 198, pp. 3-S, 8-S, 26-S)*

The House never exercised the option to hold a vote.

In the end, senators were apparently swayed by several arguments against doing away with the rules. Among them: Reneging on the budget deal so soon after it was concocted would have been unseemly; without budget rules, Congress would have quickly descended into fiscal chaos; and without the budget deal, Congress would have had nothing with which to defend itself from charges that it had done nothing significant about the deficit. ■

Congress Clears Slimmed-Down Banking Bill

Faced with a rising tide of bank failures and their natural consequence — bankruptcy for the federal fund that protected bank depositors — Congress moved expeditiously in 1991 to overhaul the nation's deposit insurance system and to pump needed cash into the insurance fund.

With just hours to spare, House and Senate conferees reached agreement on a comprehensive deposit insurance bill (S 543) on Nov. 27, following an all-night session that concluded at dawn on the last day of the session. Congressional aides rushed to prepare legislative language for the 437-page bill, and as soon as they were finished, the House adopted the conference report by voice vote. As almost the last act of the session, the Senate did likewise by a vote of 68-15, clearing the bill for the president. *(Vote 279, p. 36-S)*

As enacted, S 543 (PL 102-242), gave the Federal Deposit Insurance Corporation (FDIC) authority to borrow up to $30 billion to cover depositor losses in failed banks. An additional amount (roughly $45 billion) could be borrowed to acquire assets from failed banks that would be sold later. All the borrowing costs (including interest) were to be covered by insurance premiums levied on banks and by the proceeds from asset sales. In addition, the FDIC and other bank regulators were given broad new powers to prevent banks from taking risks that would expose them to failure, and to close weak banks before their capital was completely exhausted and their failure caused a loss to the insurance fund. *(Major provisions, p. 79)*

What Congress was unable to do in 1991 was to repeal or otherwise radically revise a half-century's worth of laws restricting the activities of the nation's banks. President Bush had asked for such a revision, in addition to the deposit-insurance overhaul, to make banks more profitable and less subject to the failures that had plagued the nation's financial system.

Congress came close to agreeing with the president — much closer than in 1988, when a more limited banking law overhaul bill never even reached the House floor. *(1988 Almanac, p. 230)*

The administration's proposal survived markup in the House Banking Committee, and in many respects it also survived in the Senate Banking Committee markup. But key elements never faced floor votes in either chamber. Deal-making intended to expedite passage caused many controversial changes to be dropped without votes.

In the end, the broader administration effort succumbed to institutional doubts, to a serious lack of consensus among lawmakers who wanted some change but could not agree on how much, and most importantly to pressure from assorted interest groups that opposed wholesale change. Ironically, it was Democrats who helped lead the administration's charge; Republicans provided key opposition.

The House voted on three separate banking bills in 1991, each progressively narrower than the first. The first two — HR 6 and HR 2094 — were rejected by the full House. The third — HR 3768 — was passed and provided the basis for the conference agreement that eventually cleared.

The Senate moved significantly more slowly than the House, deferring markup on its bill (S 543) until a month after the House Banking Committee approved HR 6, it's first effort. Senate floor action on S 543 did not begin until after the House voted to kill HR 6, but it concluded within hours of the House having passed HR 3768, that chamber's third banking bill of the year. *(Comparison of House, Senate bills, p. 88)*

BOXSCORE

➡ **Banking Overhaul (S 543, HR 3768; two House bills rejected: HR 6, HR 2094).** The bill provided $30 billion in borrowing authority for the Federal Deposit Insurance Corporation to cover depositor losses in failed banks. It also made numerous changes in the federal deposit insurance system to reduce the chance for losses in the future.

Reports: S Rept 102-167, H Rept 102-330, H Rept 102-407; H Rept 102-157, Parts I-VI; H Rept 102-293.

KEY ACTION

June 28 — **House** Banking Committee approved HR 6, a broad overhaul bill, by a vote of 31-20.

Aug. 2 — **Senate** Banking Committee approved S 543, a broad overhaul bill, by a vote of 12-9.

Sept. 25 — **House** Agriculture, Energy and Commerce, and Ways and Means committees approved amendments to HR 6.

Oct. 3 — **House** Judiciary Committee approved amendments to HR 6.

Nov. 4 — **House** killed HR 6 by a vote of 89-324.

Nov. 6 — **House** Banking Committee approved a new, narrower bank overhaul bill, HR 2094, by a vote of 37-15.

Nov. 14 — **House** killed HR 2094 by a vote of 191-227.

Nov. 19 — **House** Banking Committee approved its third bill, HR 3768, by a vote of 44-7.

Nov. 21 — **House** passed HR 3768 by a vote of 344-84. **Senate** passed S 543 by voice vote.

Nov. 23 — **House** passed S 543, after substituting text of HR 3768, and asked for a conference.

Nov. 27 — **House-Senate conferees** approved a slimmed-down version of S 543. **House** adopted the conference report by voice vote. **Senate** adopted the conference report by a vote of 68-15, clearing the bill for the president.

Dec. 19 — President Bush signed S 543 — PL 102-242.

THE ADMINISTRATION'S PLAN

The Bush administration on Feb. 5 unveiled a long-awaited plan to overhaul the nation's financial system. The proposal was an outgrowth of the savings and loan crisis, and was ordained by the 1989 thrift salvage law (PL 101-73), which required the Treasury Department to study the nation's deposit insurance system. Treasury used the opportunity to propose sweeping changes in banking laws to complement deposit insurance reforms. *(1989 Almanac, p. 117)*

"Our banking system is under stress," said Treasury Secretary Nicholas F. Brady in releasing the plan. "Technology is changing the way financial institutions do business, but our banks are hampered by out-of-date laws."

Treasury proposed to sweep clean an array of laws that prevented banks from being owned by large commercial conglomerates, from opening offices across state lines and from expanding into securities, insurance and other arenas. At the same time, it proposed putting stiff new limits on deposit insurance coverage and streamlining federal bank regulation. *(Administration plan, p. 92)*

There were few surprises in the 700-page administration report, "Modernizing the Financial System," except that Treasury officials at first brushed aside concerns that the FDIC's Bank Insurance Fund was desperately in need of cash. The administration's initial legislative proposal ignored the FDIC's immediate problem, and only weeks later did officials submit a plan for replenishing the fund.

Many members of Congress knew, however, that the money issue would drive the debate; it would be the engine that could pull along a bill making other changes in the banking system.

Reserves in the Bank Insurance Fund had been declining steadily under pressure from more than 1,000 bank failures since 1985. Every report from the FDIC, the General Accounting Office (GAO), the Congressional Budget Office (CBO) and outside experts was more depressing than the one before: The insurance fund would be technically insolvent by the end of 1991. A month before the administration released its plan to reform the industry, the problem had made national headlines, with the Jan. 6 failure of the Bank of New England. That failure, expected to cost the FDIC $2.3 billion, brought the problem home to taxpayers who were still reeling from the cost of salvaging the savings and loan industry.

No one wanted to talk about a taxpayer bailout of the banks, and none of the proposals on the table in 1991 called for infusion of taxpayer money. All costs were to be borne by the industry itself. But that was a difficult point to get across, and in the face of the thrift crisis, it carried a hollow ring.

Larger banks immediately praised the administration proposal as a way to consolidate and strengthen the banking industry. At the same time smaller banks and insurance agents, who stood to lose out to big financial conglomerates, opposed the proposal. Consumer groups also complained, worrying about the costs and dangers associated with banking consolidation.

The securities industry, long opposed to sharing its business with banks, called the Treasury plan "innovative," though in need of changes. That stance reflected the industry's weakened state, after years of riding a Wall Street roller coaster.

But it also grew from a split in the industry's position. Despite the 1933 Glass-Steagall Act, which was supposed to keep banks out of the securities business, bank regulators and the courts in recent years had allowed banks to make inroads into both securities dealing and underwriting. Some securities firms continued to oppose repealing Glass-Steagall, at least unless stiff new rules were imposed on actions between banks and their affiliated securities companies. Others, however, saw an opportunity to benefit from affiliations with banks and were willing to permit the change — but only in the context of full-blown commercial affiliations with banks, since many securities houses had non-financial subsidiaries.

Before the year was out, however, the split in the securities industry was papered over, thanks to the efforts of John D. Dingell, D-Mich., chairman of the House Energy and Commerce Committee. The most outspoken and powerful opponent of the administration's plan for change, Dingell erected the roadblocks that derailed the broader bill. And, as he did in 1988, Dingell proved to be the most important force preventing change in the banking industry.

On the other side, there was no such central player. Except for the incipient crisis in the bank deposit insurance fund, there was no apparent urgency driving the overhaul proposal. Members believed that they had more to lose than to gain if they granted banks broad new powers and found that a taxpayer bailout of the insurance fund was required somewhere down the road.

Many said at the outset that it would take a strong hands-on effort by Brady and Bush to move the plan. But such a push did not materialize. Brady — who had a long career on Wall Street before coming to the Treasury — did take a personal interest in the banking proposals. He briefed a roomful of reporters for an hour about the plan Feb. 5 and later that day did the same for a small group of key trade association leaders. Later, several said they were impressed with Brady's command of the subject — if not his ideas on how to reshape their industries. *(Brady's views, p. 94)*

But Bush never really engaged on the subject. And Brady's own views seemed confused at times. During the early markup sessions in the House, the administration refused to compromise — and it won those initial battles. But later, it seemed that the administration was too willing to compromise and to permit unrelated issues to be linked in the debate. One such linkage connected a proposal to allow banks to freely open branch offices across state lines with efforts by insurance agents to roll back bank inroads into their business.

Branching was far more important to Brady and most administration officials than any other single piece of the bill, but the linkage proved a killer. Banks that wanted branching found themselves pitted against those that wanted to preserve their insurance sales ability; the result was that branching powers were rejected, and the insurance agents did not win their rollback. Many proponents of the administration bill argued that had the issues not been linked, both the branching proponents and the insurance agents could have won separate showdowns on the floor.

HOUSE ACTION ON HR 6

The House spent much of the year preparing for, debating and finally rejecting the broad administration proposal.

House Banking Chairman Henry B. Gonzalez, D-Texas, and the panel's ranking Republican, Chalmers P. Wylie of Ohio, each introduced deposit insurance bills on the opening day of the 102nd Congress (HR 6, HR 15). Both were "narrow" by the standard set a month later; neither addressed the broader issues of banking law that the administration said were so crucial. Along with Senate Banking Committee Chairman Donald W. Riegle Jr., D-Mich., both Gonzalez and Wylie said they thought it was crucial to overhaul the deposit insurance system before making other changes.

Two key congressional advisers shared their view: Congressional Budget Office Director Robert D. Reischauer and Comptroller General Charles A. Bowsher, who headed the GAO. Reischauer told the Senate Banking Committee

FDIC's Seidman Resigns; Taylor Takes His Place

In the midst of debate over how to proceed on the banking overhaul bill, a leading proponent of change and the most respected banking regulator in Washington left his job. L. William Seidman — chairman of the Federal Deposit Insurance Corporation (FDIC) since 1985, and by virtue of that job, also head of the Resolution Trust Corporation (RTC) created in 1989 to salvage the failing thrift industry — stepped down Oct. 16.

He headed the FDIC for six years, and departed with the savings and loan bailout roughly half complete, with the administration's request for $80 billion more from taxpayers to close failing thrifts still on the table, and with a potentially serious banking crisis still in the formative stages. *(Thrift bailout, p. 98; banking overhaul, p. 75)*

The House and Senate Banking Committee chairmen, Rep. Henry B. Gonzalez, D-Texas, and Sen. Donald W. Riegle Jr., D-Mich., both praised Seidman, following his announcement Aug. 6 that he would step down when his term ended.

"This is a great loss for the government.... I have the highest regard for him, and he will be very difficult to replace," Riegle said. Gonzalez said: "He has been a strong voice, willing to lay out the hard facts about the industry's problems. He maintained great credibility on Capitol Hill during the most difficult period in the history of the Federal Deposit Insurance Corporation."

Smaller community banks, whose continued survival Seidman championed in the face of a growing trend toward bank consolidation, also were sad to see him retire at age 70.

That was not true of many members of the Bush administration, even though they relied on his credibility on Capitol Hill. When Seidman publicly disagreed with other administration officials in early 1990 over the cost of the thrift bailout, saying that their estimates were too low, White House Chief of Staff John H. Sununu tried to get the FDIC chief to step down early. Seidman refused, playing a cat and mouse game over the timing of his retirement and eventually serving out his term.

Taylor Named Successor

Seidman was replaced as FDIC chairman by William Taylor, 52, who had been top banking regulator with the Federal Reserve System, where he had spent most of his professional career. The Senate Banking Committee recommended Taylor's confirmation by a 21-0 vote on Oct. 18; he was confirmed by the full Senate by voice vote on Oct. 22. His term was to expire Feb. 28, 1993.

President Bush had indicated at the time of the Sununu-Seidman flap in 1990 that he intended to appoint Taylor to the FDIC post. As soon as his troubles with Sununu flared up, Seidman publicly recommended Taylor for the job. For the first days after Seidman announced he would leave in October 1991, however, the president was quiet and allowed speculation that Taylor would not get the nod.

As top regulator at the Fed, Taylor came in for questioning in 1991 about an international scandal involving the Bank of Credit and Commerce International (BCCI). Three congressional committees looked into the scandal — which involved allegations of fraud, money laundering, loss of perhaps $10 billion by BCCI depositors worldwide and the secret, decade-long, illegal ownership of several large U.S. banks. Among those was First American Bankshares, one of the largest in Washington, D.C., which was headed by longtime Democratic Party activist Clark Clifford.

Taylor was questioned closely about what the Fed knew, and when. He and other Fed officials maintained that they were misled about BCCI's ownership of those banks. The Fed's failure to catch BCCI's illegal activities ultimately did not taint Taylor's nomination.

Seidman's other job, that of running the RTC, was not handed over to Taylor. In the thrift financing bill enacted at the end of the session (HR 3435), Congress separated the FDIC from the RTC and created the new position of RTC chief executive officer, who was to be nominated by the president and confirmed by the Senate.

March 5 that he generally supported the Treasury proposal, but he criticized many of its details. He, too, urged that deposit insurance reform be in place before banks were allowed new powers, although he conceded that such changes might provide greater long-term stability to the financial system.

That question — whether to pass a narrow deposit insurance bill first — was to dominate the banking debate all year.

Another major issue was how to provide the necessary cash for the Bank Insurance Fund. Disagreement on that point was one reason why the administration failed to include a financing plan in its initial reform proposal.

On Feb. 12, a week after that plan was released, a collection of banking industry groups wrote to the FDIC, suggesting a "contingency plan" for raising the money, should the FDIC need it, without appearing to put taxpayers at risk. The banks' plan was that the FDIC would raise up to $10 billion by selling bonds that would not be explicitly guaranteed by the federal government (but certainly would carry an implicit guarantee). Banks would be assessed a special premium to repay the bonds.

The proposal was deemed unsatisfactory on several grounds. It was not expected to raise enough money; the lack of an explicit federal guarantee for the bonds would mean that they would have to pay higher interest than government bonds with similar maturities; and the plan would have required a cap on regular bank deposit insurance premiums, which at the time could be increased as needed by the FDIC.

FDIC Chairman L. William Seidman offered his own financing plan on Feb. 28, rejecting much of the banks' proposal in the process. Seidman wanted to use existing FDIC authority to borrow $10 billion to be repaid through a premium increase. And he suggested the agency get a second $20 billion line of credit with the Treasury or the Federal Reserve, that would be secured by another, dedicated premium increase. *(Seidman departure, above)*

The administration finally released the text of its banking bill March 20, complete with its FDIC replenishment plan. The Treasury plan called for the FDIC to borrow up to $25 billion from the Fed. But Fed Chairman Alan Greenspan rejected that idea on April 23 in testimony to the Senate Banking Committee. He said the move would send the wrong signal to world markets about the Fed's role and its independence. He added that there was no economic benefit to borrowing from the Fed rather than from the Treasury. To provide the cash, the Fed would have to sell part of its stock of U.S. government securities to the public, which was exactly how the Treasury would raise the money.

Some members, such as Frank Annunzio, D-Ill., who chaired the House Banking Subcommittee on Financial Institutions, had their own plans. Annunzio wanted banks to transfer 1 percent of their deposits to the FDIC. That would have provided quick cash to the agency and was the method used in the mid-1980s to shore up the deposit insurance fund for credit unions. But it was not seen as a permanent solution, and it might have helped push over the edge those banks with very slim profit or capital margins.

The trial balloons over how to finance a replenishment eventually burst, leaving only the idea of a loan from the Treasury. By May, that was the informally agreed upon plan, and the only issue on the table not to be debated again all year.

Developing a Markup Strategy

Gonzalez and Wylie agreed April 11 to work together on a narrow banking bill that would replenish the insurance fund and make a few changes in the deposit-insurance system in an effort to protect taxpayers and restore public confidence. They said they would shelve for the time being the broader administration package — especially proposals to give banks wide new investment powers and allow commercial enterprises to own banks — although Gonzalez said he expected the committee to continue debating the proposals. Both said the urgency of providing more money for the Bank Insurance Fund and the contentiousness of the administration's proposals made it necessary to separate the two issues.

Wylie was never particularly enamored of the broad Treasury plan, but under pressure from Brady, he backed off his agreement with Gonzalez within two weeks.

Key Democratic supporters of the overhaul bill, and most House Banking Committee Republicans, feared that Gonzalez and Wylie were trying to scuttle the bigger bill altogether.

Two senior committee Democrats, Doug Barnard Jr. of Georgia and Charles E. Schumer of New York, wrote to Bush on April 18, complaining that the sweeping reform bill "has been largely abandoned" by the White House.

Then, on April 24, Brady met with committee Republicans, in a successful attempt to keep them on board. Wylie announced that he was not prepared to keep the bill as narrow as Gonzalez wanted. "We got off track as to where the chairman and I started out," Wylie said.

But the same week, Gonzalez and Annunzio introduced a new, narrow FDIC replenishment and deposit insurance overhaul bill (HR 2094), and Annunzio said his subcommittee would begin work on it the first week of May. Gonzalez said he wanted to stick by his narrow-bill strategy. In particular, he wanted to finish work on a banking bill before Congress had to turn to another contentious issue — a new infusion of cash into the savings and loan salvage operation. Gonzalez said he did not want the two issues entangled. *(Thrift bailout, p. 98)*

However, Schumer, Barnard and nine other Democrats signed a letter from Stephen L. Neal, D-N.C., to Annunzio, urging that the early May markup be expanded to consider "some of the more important structural and regulatory changes recommended by the administration." Banking Committee Democrats — 31 of the panel's 52 members — met May 1 and agreed not to pursue Gonzalez's single, narrow bill plan. Instead, they embraced a two-bill strategy: They decided to support marking up a narrow bill (HR 2094) that would be held in reserve and sent to the floor only if the committee failed to approve a broader bill by the end of June.

The scheduling agreement appeared to satisfy all sides — those who wanted to press for an early solution to the insurance fund's problems and those who feared that enactment of a narrow bill would take the wind out of the sails of the broad measure. Wylie praised it and said it also pleased Brady.

Banking Subcommittee Action

Action on both the broad and narrow banking bills got under way May 7 in Annunzio's Financial Institutions Subcommittee, where HR 2094 — the narrow measure — was approved by a 34-1 vote. (The text of HR 2094 was later to become the first title of the broader bill — HR 6).

The narrow bill, which contained a $30 billion line of credit for the FDIC with the Treasury (actually an increase from an existing-law $5 billion line of credit), also would have made numerous changes in the deposit-insurance system; most but not all of them were not controversial.

In addition to providing money to the FDIC, the bill, as approved in subcommittee, would have required closer supervision of banks and quicker regulatory action against those headed for insolvency. Most significantly, it would have altered dramatically the method used most often by the FDIC to close the books on failed banks and cover their insured deposits. The intent was to save money by ending the practice of granting de facto 100 percent insurance coverage in nearly every case.

The issue of de facto 100 percent insurance was part of a bigger fight over the FDIC's so-called too-big-to-fail policy, under which some banks were deemed to be so critical to the nation's financial system that the FDIC stepped in and covered all deposits, and often all creditors, when the bank failed. The subcommittee did not directly address that issue in marking up HR 2094. It did strike language from the bill that would have restricted lending by the Fed to weak banks to no more than five days in a three-month period. Opponents of too-big-to-fail argued that Fed lending to weak banks was an integral part of that policy. But Fed Chairman Greenspan vigorously opposed limits on the Fed's role as "lender of last resort" to the financial system.

The tough deposit insurance issues — rolling back coverage and ending too-big-to-fail — were all set aside for the following week, when the subcommittee began work on the broader bill.

The subcommittee approved the broad bill (still in draft form) on May 23, by a vote of 36-0. It was an overwhelming victory for the administration, which lost only one significant battle during five long days of work on the measure. Banking industry lobbyists said they were amazed. Treasury officials beamed. And members of the subcommittee gave Annunzio a standing ovation.

Continued on p. 83

Deposit Insurance Overhaul Bill Provisions

As signed by President Bush on Dec. 19, 1992, the major provisions of HR 543 — PL 102-242:

BANK INSURANCE FUND REPLENISHMENT

Borrowing Authority

• **Treasury line of credit.** Allowed the Federal Deposit Insurance Corporation (FDIC) to borrow up to $30 billion unsecured from the federal Treasury to cover losses in failed banks — principally to pay off insured depositors. Previously, the FDIC had a $5 billion line of credit with the Treasury, which it never tapped.

• **Working capital.** Altered the statutory limit on other FDIC borrowing, chiefly used to provide temporary working capital for the purchase of assets from failed banks. Such borrowing was to be repaid from the proceeds of the assets when they were sold to another bank or to the general public. The law allowed the FDIC to borrow from multiple sources (principally the Federal Financing Bank, an arm of the Treasury) an amount equal to 90 percent of the fair market value of the assets the agency took from failed banks. Prior law allowed the FDIC to borrow up to nine times its net worth for working capital needs. But as the insurance fund neared insolvency, that limit became meaningless.

• **Borrowing from banks.** Gave the FDIC the option of borrowing from banks instead of the Treasury to cover insurance fund losses. The borrowing was subject to the $30 billion cap on money borrowed to cover losses; it was subject to the public debt limit that governed general Treasury borrowing; and the bonds had to be priced identically to comparable Treasury issues, to hold down interest rates.

Repayment by Banks

• **Repayment schedule.** Required the Treasury and the FDIC to agree to a schedule of deposit insurance premium payments by banks to repay any money borrowed to cover FDIC losses plus interest. The FDIC and the Treasury were required to consult with the House and Senate Banking committees on repayment schedules, and the FDIC had to demonstrate that insurance premiums paid by banks were sufficient to meet the schedule. The FDIC was also authorized to adjust premiums at any time during the year and to set them at any level. Under prior law, premiums could only be raised at two specific times each year.

• **Emergency special assessments.** Allowed the FDIC to impose special premium assessments on bank deposits in addition to regular assessments in order to repay loans from the Treasury or from banks.

• **GAO audit.** Required the General Accounting Office (GAO) to report quarterly to Congress on the repayment of money borrowed by the FDIC from the Treasury and on the FDIC's success at estimating the market value of assets that it purchased with borrowed working capital.

• **Recapitalization schedule.** Required the FDIC to devise a schedule of deposit insurance premiums to increase the Bank Insurance Fund's reserves to 1.25 percent of insured deposits within 15 years of enactment. The FDIC could adjust the recapitalization schedule but not in ways that would extend the deadline for meeting the required reserve ratio.

Deposit Insurance System Overhaul

Early Intervention

• **Minimum capital requirements.** Required all federal banking regulators to review their minimum capital requirements for banks and thrifts every other year to ensure that they were sufficient to minimize losses to the deposit insurance funds. At least two standards were required — a leverage standard of total capital as measured against total assets and a risk-based standard of total capital as measured against assets that had been weighted for their relative riskiness. Similar standards existed previously for banks and thrifts. Regulators were permitted to impose additional standards employing other measures. Within 18 months, banking regulators would have to adjust their risk-based standards to account for the risks associated with fluctuations in interest rates, concentrations of loans and non-traditional activities. The Federal Reserve Board was required to discuss with foreign bank regulators similar changes to international risk-based capital standards.

• **Capital levels.** Established five levels for measuring the capital of banks and thrifts. Supervision and enforcement actions were specified for an institution based on its capital level.

"Well-capitalized" institutions carried amounts of capital measured in several ways that significantly exceeded mandatory minimums. "Adequately capitalized" institutions met the minimum requirements. "Undercapitalized" institutions did not meet all minimums. "Significantly undercapitalized" institutions fell considerably short of minimums. And "critically undercapitalized" institutions failed to meet a "critical capital level."

Regulators were allowed to establish numerical minimums for each category, but the law set the critical capital level at no less than 2 percent equity capital (excluding some items frequently included in calculations of total capital) as measured against total assets, and at no more than 65 percent of the minimum standard. The critical capital level was to be used to trigger specific regulatory actions leading to closure of banks or thrifts. *(See prompt action, below)*

• **Non-capital performance standards.** Allowed regulators to downgrade the rating of a bank or thrift that was found to be operating in an unsafe and unsound manner. The new rating would have to be one level lower than that for which the bank or thrift would qualify based solely on its capital.

Regulators could also downgrade an institution if it were found to have less than satisfactory assets, management, earnings or liquidity — factors that were used along with capital in routine ratings.

• **Enhanced supervision.** Required the FDIC and other banking regulators to devise standards to measure the operations and management of banks and thrifts, as well as the appropriate proportion of bad loans to total assets and the amount of earnings needed to offset loan losses.

As a part of these standards, federal regulators were required to determine at what point salaries and benefits to officers, employees, directors or stockholders constituted excessive compensation or could cause a material loss to an institution.

Banks and thrifts that failed to meet these standards were required to submit plans to overcome the shortfall. If they failed to do so, regulators could impose restrictions, including limiting the growth of assets, limiting interest rates paid on deposits and requiring an increase in capital.

In addition, unless a bank or thrift received explicit permission from federal regulators, it could not pay dividends to stockholders if doing so would cause the institution's capital to fall below minimum standards. Also, institutions could not pay management fees if doing so would cause them to become undercapitalized.

• **Prompt corrective action.** Required any undercapitalized (or worse) bank or thrift to submit a capital restoration plan showing how it would meet minimum standards without increasing its risk of failure, and prohibited any such institution from paying dividends until it met all minimum capital requirements.

Bank regulators could not approve a capital restoration plan unless any company having control over the bank or thrift (a bank or thrift holding company) guaranteed the bank's or thrift's compliance with the plan. The holding company would be liable for an amount up to 5 percent of the value of the bank or thrift, or the amount that would have been required to recapitalize the institution at the time it was found not to be in compliance, if that amount were less.

Regulators had to sharply limit the growth of undercapitalized banks, making exceptions only where asset growth was consistent with an approved capital restoration plan and equity capital was increasing according to schedule. Acquisitions and branching were permitted only where consistent with the plan, or where the FDIC chose to waive that requirement.

For significantly undercapitalized institutions (or those that failed to submit and act on capital restoration plans), the payment of salary increases and bonuses to officers was prohibited, and regulators were required to take other actions, such as requiring the sale of additional stock, prohibiting the acceptance of deposits from other banks and capping the interest paid on deposits. Additional actions could be ordered, including further restrictions on growth or a reduction in the bank's size; replacement of officers, directors or outside auditors; and sale of the bank or any affiliate that the regulators believed threatened the bank's health.

In addition, critically undercapitalized banks generally could not make interest or principal payments on subordinated debt (a class of bond that was not payable until all other creditors were satisfied and that often counted as capital) issued after July 15, 1991. And the FDIC was generally required to prohibit such institutions from making material changes in their business.

- **Prompt closure.** Required federal banking regulators to take control of (by appointing a conservator) or seize and close (by appointing a receiver) any bank or thrift that failed to maintain capital in excess of the "critical capital level," unless an alternative action was more likely to protect the deposit insurance fund.

Notwithstanding contrary state laws, regulators were required to take action within 90 days after an institution's capital fell below the critical level. Regulators could choose to take less drastic action than closure for 90-day periods if they determined that such action would better protect the deposit insurance fund.

If the institution's capital remained below the critical level for one year, regulators would have to appoint a receiver and close the institution in most cases. Regulators could allow an institution to stay open if they certified it to be viable and if the institution had a positive net worth, was in substantial compliance with its capital restoration plan, had sustained improvement in earnings and was reducing its proportion of non-performing loans. Undercapitalized thrifts that prior to enactment had agreed to capital restoration plans under the 1989 thrift salvage law (PL 101-73) were not subject to the law's prompt closure provisions until after July 1, 1994.

- **Inspector general reports.** Required the FDIC inspector general to report to the agency and to the GAO whenever the insurance fund suffered a material loss because it provided unreimbursed assistance to a failing bank or thrift or because it closed a bank or thrift whose assets were worth less than the cost of closing the institution. This provision was to take effect July 1, 1993, and was to be triggered only when the FDIC incurred a loss greater than $25 million or 2 percent of the value of the bank or thrift. Inspector general reports were to be made public upon request.
- **Effective date.** Required federal regulators to put final regulations for these provisions into effect one year after enactment.

Too-Big-to-Fail Banks

- **Least-cost resolution.** Required the FDIC to use the least-costly method of protecting insured depositors when it closed institutions and sold them in whole or in part. The purpose was to greatly limit the circumstances under which uninsured deposits were fully protected by preventing the FDIC from incurring a loss when it protected them. When uninsured depositors were not protected, they had to wait along with unsecured creditors (including the FDIC) for the bank's assets to be sold. Uninsured depositors and other creditors then shared in the proceeds, generally a large fraction of what they were owed.

Under prior practice, most failed banks and many failed thrifts were sold virtually intact through so-called purchase and assumption transactions. The FDIC believed that such deals, which usually provided full protection to insured and uninsured depositors alike, were easier to manage and cost less. The law specifically permitted the FDIC to continue its practice of selling (and thereby protecting) the uninsured deposits of a failed bank or thrift. But to do so, it had to show that it did not incur a greater loss than it would have had it not sold them.

When making least-cost calculations, the FDIC was required to evaluate the long-term costs of various methods of case resolution. The FDIC had to discount all costs and receipts from sales of assets to "present value," subtracting for the long-term effects of inflation. The cost of forgone tax revenues resulting from the transaction had to be included as if they were revenues forgone by the FDIC. And the FDIC could not consider broad economic effects or the effects of a particular method on overall financial industry stability, unless specific consequences for the insurance fund could be identified.

- **Open-bank assistance.** Allowed the FDIC to continue to provide financial assistance to weak banks that were in danger of failing, rather than take control of or close them. However, the FDIC could provide such assistance only if doing so would cost less than closing the bank.
- **'Systemic risk.'** Permitted the government, under very narrow circumstances, to waive the general rule created by the law that the FDIC could take no action to protect uninsured depositors that would cause a loss to the insurance fund.

In those cases where a large bank failure posed a "systemic risk" to the nation's financial system, the FDIC could sustain a loss by protecting all deposits and non-deposit liabilities in a failing bank or thrift. Such action had to be approved in advance by a two-thirds vote of the FDIC board of directors, by a two-thirds vote of the Federal Reserve Board of Governors and by the Treasury secretary in consultation with the president. The Treasury secretary had to notify the House and Senate Banking committees of any systemic risk determination and the justification for it.

Any loss to the insurance fund from a systemic risk determination had to be recovered expeditiously through a special premium assessment levied against the total assets held by banks, minus their capital. By specifying total assets, that formula had the effect of requiring that insured banks pay premiums on deposits held in their overseas branches. Such foreign deposits were nominally not insured, even under prior law, but were almost always protected when big banks failed. (Banks always paid insurance premiums on the total amount of their domestic deposits, even those that were in excess of the insured amount.)

The effect of the provision was to severely restrict the regulator-devised policy under prior law of fully protecting so-called too-big-to-fail banks. Under prior law, the FDIC could protect fully all bank depositors and creditors, regardless of cost, if the bank was deemed essential to its community.

- **GAO audit.** Required the GAO to report annually to Congress on the FDIC's compliance with the least-cost provisions and to report on each instance where the government protected all depositors because of a finding of systemic risk.
- **Federal Reserve assistance.** Prevented the Fed from making loans to banks that failed to meet all capital standards for more than 60 days of a 120-day period, unless a banking regulator (which could be the Fed) certified that the bank had capital above the critical capital level and was not expected to be closed.

The Fed was permitted to make loans to critically undercapitalized institutions (or other undercapitalized institutions that were not certified as viable) for more than five days, but not without risk. If the FDIC was later forced to close the bank, and the cost of resolution was greater than it would have been to liquidate the bank at the time of the loan, the Fed was liable to the FDIC for the excess loss. The Fed would have to pay an amount equal either to the interest it earned on the loan or to the loss the Fed would have taken had its loan to the failed bank been unsecured, whichever was smaller. Losses by the Fed would reduce the central bank's earnings and thereby cut its annual payments to the Treasury. The Fed was required to report to Congress on any loss it incurred under this provision.

Limiting Fed lending to weak banks was an essential element of the law's effort to constrict the too-big-to-fail policy. The concern was that unrestrained Fed lending to a failing bank gave uninsured depositors time to withdraw their money, imposing a higher cost on the FDIC when the bank eventually failed.

- **Final settlement procedure.** Authorized the FDIC at the time it closed an insolvent bank or thrift to make payments to uninsured depositors and unsecured creditors at a rate equal to the FDIC's historic cost of closing failed institutions. Such payments would end all depositor and creditor claims on the bank's assets. In previous years, the FDIC had recovered about 85 percent of the book value of bank assets when they were sold.

• **Effective date.** Required the FDIC to produce final regulations by Jan. 1, 1994, that would put the least-cost resolution provisions into effect as of Jan. 1, 1995. The restraints on Fed loans were to take effect two years after enactment.

State Bank Powers

• **Restrictions on activities.** Prohibited, with exceptions, insured state-chartered banks from engaging in activities not permitted for federally chartered banks. As a general rule, national banks could not engage in non-banking activities or take an ownership (equity) interest in a non-banking activity. This provision paralleled restrictions imposed on state-chartered thrifts in the 1989 thrift-industry salvage law (PL 101-73).

The prohibitions on state banks applied to direct activities of state-chartered banks and to activities of the subsidiaries of state banks (which generally could not engage in activities that were not permitted to subsidiaries of national banks). State banks were given five years after enactment to sell any prohibited equity investment.

A bank or bank subsidiary that met all minimum capital standards would be exempt from the general limits on permissible activities if the FDIC did not object and found that the activity posed no significant risk to the insurance fund, except that the FDIC could not waive the general ban on equity investments of state banks.

• **Stock ownership exceptions.** Permitted state banks to hold equity stakes in subsidiaries that they controlled. And state banks could invest as limited partners in projects to build, acquire or rehabilitate low-income housing. State banks that were permitted to own publicly traded stocks on Sept. 30, 1991, and were doing so before Nov. 26, 1991, could continue to do so, provided the aggregate investment by a bank did not exceed its capital. Excess investments had to be divested over three years after enactment. State banks were also permitted to own up to 15 percent of a "bankers' bank" that serviced its investor banks.

• **Insurance activities.** Prohibited state banks and their subsidiaries from underwriting most insurance, as long as such activities were prohibited for national banks. The law permitted well-capitalized state banks that existed as of Nov. 21, 1991, to continue underwriting insurance, and it permitted state banks that were required before June 1, 1991, by their charter to underwrite title insurance to continue to do so.

The law also grandfathered the life insurance underwriting activities of New England savings banks but required the FDIC to study that issue within a year of enactment to determine if it posed a risk to the insurance fund. If the FDIC found a risk to exist, it could require a grandfathered bank to modify or terminate its insurance activities.

The law did not affect the ability of states to allow the sale of insurance by banks chartered in those states and by the subsidiaries of such banks.

• **Effective date.** Put the general bar on state-bank activities into effect one year after enactment.

Deposit Insurance Coverage Limits

• **Individual accounts.** Made no change in existing law on the amount of deposit insurance coverage provided. Individuals could still have multiple accounts at a single institution, each insured to the maximum amount of $100,000.

• **Brokered deposits.** Prohibited banks and thrifts that did not exceed minimum capital requirements from soliciting deposits by paying significantly higher interest rates than did other institutions in the same market.

On a case-by-case basis, the FDIC could allow well-capitalized institutions (and certain institutions under conservatorship) to accept brokered deposits, which typically were placed through securities dealers seeking the highest rates of interest nationwide. Rates paid on brokered deposits could not significantly exceed rates paid on deposits of similar maturity either in the local market area of the bank or nationwide.

Securities brokers who solicited such deposits had to register with and report periodically to the FDIC.

Undercapitalized institutions not only could not accept brokered deposits but could not advertise interest rates significantly above those in their local market area.

Regulations to enforce this provision were to take effect 180 days after enactment.

• **Pass-through insurance.** Required the FDIC to insure very large deposits placed in well-capitalized banks by pension funds as if each beneficiary of the affected pension plan received coverage totaling $100,000. The same restrictions that applied to accepting brokered deposits limited the types of banks that could accept deposits carrying so-called pass-through insurance coverage.

The law expressly prohibited pass-through coverage for certain types of negotiated certificates of deposit — called bank investment contracts — for which banks agreed to permit periodic withdrawals without penalty for the purpose of paying benefits.

The law continued pass-through coverage for bundled real estate escrow accounts and similar trust accounts for which the depositor was acting as agent for a large number of individuals and the total deposit exceeded the $100,000 limit.

The bar on pass-through coverage for banks that were not well-capitalized was to take effect one year after enactment.

• **Foreign deposits.** Except as allowed under provisions permitting the FDIC to cover foreign deposits under least-cost calculations or findings of systemic risk, the law prohibited the insurance fund from protecting foreign deposits.

• **Deposit insurance study.** Required the FDIC to study, in conjunction with the Fed, the feasibility and cost of tracking insured and uninsured deposits, which would be necessary in any effort to establish a systemwide limit on individual deposit insurance. The FDIC was required to report to Congress on this issue, along with recommendations, within 18 months of enactment.

Accounting and Examination Changes

• **Annual exams.** Required the FDIC and other applicable federal banking regulators (the Federal Reserve System, Office of Comptroller of the Currency or Office of Thrift Supervision) to conduct annual on-site examinations of most banks and thrifts. Regulators could allow 18 months between examinations for those banks with assets of less than $100 million that were well-capitalized, well-managed, received the highest of five regulatory ratings and had not been purchased within the previous year. Examination reports from state banking regulators could be substituted for federal exams in alternate years.

The requirement for annual examinations was to take effect a year after enactment. However, until Dec. 31, 1993, exams were required only every 18 months, except for institutions that were found in their most recent exam to be in less than satisfactory condition, or those that had been purchased.

The law also required federal banking regulators to devise coordinated examination improvement programs to increase the quality and objectivity of exams.

• **Charges and penalties.** Permitted the FDIC to assess charges against banks and their affiliates for annual exams in amounts necessary to cover the cost of the exams. The FDIC could impose a $5,000-per-day civil penalty on any bank or thrift that refused to allow an on-site exam or refused to provide any information required for such an exam.

• **Annual independent audits.** Required larger banks and thrifts to undergo annual independent audits of their financial statements after 1992. Such audits had to include the auditor's assessment of a bank's compliance with certain laws and regulations designated by the FDIC. Banks with less than $150 million in assets were exempt from this requirement. Only independent auditors that agreed to provide working papers and received a peer review acceptable to the FDIC were to be permitted to perform audits. The FDIC could bar an accounting firm from such work for good cause.

• **Accounting standards.** Required federal banking regulators to adopt uniform accounting standards for banks and thrifts that were consistent with, and no less stringent than, generally accepted accounting principles. Differences in accounting treatment among regulators had to be explained to the House and Senate Banking committees.

The law also required that, within one year of enactment, banks and thrifts disclose so-called off-balance-sheet assets and liabilities in their financial statements and quarterly reports of condition to federal regulators.

And within a year of enactment, federal regulators were required to devise a means of reporting, to the extent feasible, the market value (in addition to the book value) of the assets and liabilities of banks and thrifts.

• **Real estate loans.** Required federal bank regulators to adopt, within nine months of enactment, uniform standards for making loans for real estate acquisition, development or construction. Regulations to enforce this provision were to take effect not more than 15 months after enactment.

Other Changes

• **Risk-based premiums.** Required the FDIC to impose a system of deposit insurance premium assessments for banks and thrifts that varied based on the relative risk that each bank and thrift posed to its insurance fund. Risk-based assessments could be derived from all risks posed by a bank's capital levels, the activities in which it engaged, its mix of assets, its holding of foreign deposits and the balance of rates and maturities between assets and deposits.

Banks and thrifts were to be treated separately, and the FDIC could devise separate assessments for large and small institutions.

Proposed regulations for a risk-based premium system would have to be issued by Dec. 31, 1992, and final regulations would have to be issued by July 1, 1993. Risk-based assessments for banks were to take effect no later than Jan. 1, 1994. For thrifts, the risk-based assessment system were not to take effect until Jan. 1, 1998.

• **Uninsured state-chartered institutions.** Required all state-chartered banks, thrifts and credit unions that did not carry federal deposit insurance to prominently disclose that fact to existing and prospective customers, along with the fact that depositors were not guaranteed return of their money if the institution failed. The provision also applied to any other institution that might be mistaken for a bank. (Federally chartered banks were insured as a matter of course, but the law required them to apply formally to the FDIC for insurance, which could be denied.)

• **FDIC backup authority.** Authorized the FDIC to recommend that other federal bank regulators take enforcement action against banks or thrifts that posed a significant risk to the insurance funds. The FDIC could itself take action if the other regulators failed to act within 60 days. And the FDIC could adopt rules for taking expedited action without regard to the 60-day period.

• **Insider abuse.** Limited and in some cases prohibited preferential treatment in the granting of loans or other services to officers, directors or principal shareholders of banks. Generally, under the law, loans to insiders had to be made on terms used for outside applicants.

• **Limits on interbank liabilities.** Required the Fed to devise limits on the amounts that banks could lend to or place on deposit with other banks. The purpose was to reduce the threat of systemic risk to the nation's financial industry posed by large bank failures.

• **Appraisal standards.** Deferred from July 1, 1991, to Dec. 31, 1992, the effective date for mandatory state standards for licensed real estate appraisers. This provision was also included in a bill providing additional money for the savings and loan salvage operation (HR 3545) that Congress cleared before adjourning.

OTHER REGULATORY ISSUES

Foreign-Owned Banks

• **Deposit-taking.** Prohibited foreign banks from accepting deposits in amounts less than $100,000 except through subsidiary banks that were chartered and regulated in the United States and insured by the FDIC. Branch offices of foreign banks that were insured by the FDIC and accepted such deposits on the date of enactment could continue to accept such deposits.

• **New operations.** Required Fed approval before any foreign bank could open a branch office or buy a bank, thrift or commercial lending company in the United States. Existing law rarely gave the Fed jurisdiction in these areas, although it and other federal banking regulators had some control over foreign bank operations.

The Fed was not allowed to approve an application from a foreign company that was not engaged in banking abroad and was not subject to comprehensive supervision in its home country. In addition, the Fed had to consider whether the foreign bank's U.S. operations were approved by foreign regulators, whether its financial and managerial resources were sufficient, whether the foreign bank had violated U.S. laws and whether the foreign bank had agreed to supply information to U.S. regulators.

The law allowed the Fed to close a state-chartered bank or branch owned by a foreign bank for safety and soundness reasons if the bank or any affiliate had violated U.S. law or if the foreign bank was not subject to comprehensive regulation in its home country. The Fed could recommend such action to the Comptroller of the Currency for federally chartered banks or branches owned by foreign banks.

In addition, purchase of shares in a U.S. bank with the use of loans from a foreign bank that were secured by such shares had to be disclosed to the Fed.

The Fed was allowed to guarantee confidentiality for information provided about foreign banks by their overseas regulators.

After one year, state-chartered banks or offices owned by a foreign bank were required to phase out any activity that was not permitted for national banks or offices, unless the Fed found that the activity was consistent with sound banking and, in the case of an insured branch, the FDIC also approved.

• **State offices of foreign banks.** Gave the Fed authority to regulate certain non-banking offices of foreign banks, which were generally subject only to state regulation under existing law.

• **Capital standards.** Required the Fed and the Treasury to study the capital standards applicable to foreign banks operating in the United States and determine if such standards were equivalent to those applied to domestic banks. The Fed and the Treasury were required to report their findings to the House and Senate Banking committees no later than 180 days after enactment, and revise their report annually thereafter.

• **Consumer statutes.** Gave federal regulators explicit authority to apply federal consumer protection laws to foreign banks in the United States.

• **Penalties.** Permitted civil penalties against foreign banks for violations similar to those prohibited under the Bank Holding Company Act for U.S. companies that owned banks.

The law increased from $1,000 to $10,000 a day the penalty for failure to comply with a Fed or FDIC subpoena. And it created a criminal penalty for intentionally violating the International Banking Act (which governed most foreign bank activities in the United States) with the intent to deceive or cause financial gain or loss to any person. The penalty was up to five years imprisonment and a fine of up to $1 million a day, or both.

Consumer Issues

• **Incentives for services in distressed communities.** Reduced deposit insurance premiums for banks offering certain services to low-income people or in economically distressed neighborhoods.

Banks that offered special, low-cost checking accounts to poor people were to pay half the usual insurance premium for deposits in such accounts.

Banks that increased their deposits or housing-related loans in specially designated distressed communities would receive a 5 percent credit against their deposit insurance premium payments. Banks that established special Community Development Corporations in distressed neighborhoods would receive a 15 percent credit against their insurance premiums.

• **Low-income housing preferences.** Created within the FDIC a program to give preference to low-income persons and to state and local housing agencies in disposing of low- and moderate-income single-family and multifamily housing. The program, which paralleled one created under the Resolution Trust Corporation for the disposal of houses acquired from failed thrifts, was to take effect six months after enactment and run for three years. Low-income individuals would get a right of first refusal for six months on qualified single-family properties. Housing agencies would get preferences for acquisition of multifamily buildings. The FDIC was authorized to finance purchases at or below market rates. The program was subject to annual appropriations to cover losses due to disposal of properties at less than market rates.

• **Truth-in-savings.** Required banks, thrifts and credit unions to disclose clearly the terms and conditions on savings accounts. They were required to calculate the interest paid on such accounts based on the full account balance, but the law did not specify a particular method of calculation or whether or how interest would be compounded. The law imposed civil fines on institutions that violated these provisions. The savings account disclosure rules were to take effect within 15 months of enactment.

• **Branch-closing notification.** Required banks and thrifts to notify their customers and federal regulators 90 days before the scheduled closing of a branch office. Banks would have to establish specific policies for internal review of branch-closure decisions.

• **Small-business loan reporting.** Required banks to provide federal bank regulators annually with details of their loans to small businesses and small farms. In an effort to assess credit availability, regulators could require specific data for aggregate dollar amounts of commercial and mortgage loans to small businesses, charge-offs of bad loans and interest income from such loans. The requirement was to take effect six months after enactment.

• **Deposits in automatic teller machines.** Permitted banks to hold for up to four days deposits made at automatic teller machines not owned by the bank.

• **Whistleblower protections.** Prohibited banks and federal bank regulatory agencies from firing, punishing or discriminating against an employee for providing information to bank regulators or the Justice Department regarding possible violations of law or regulations by the bank, the agency or any official of the bank or agency.

• **Regulatory burden.** Required the Treasury secretary and federal banking regulators to report to Congress a year after enactment on laws and regulations that unduly limited the profitability of banks and on the need for changes in or repeal of those laws. The report was to consider the degree to which changes might harm the safety and soundness of banks or adversely affect consumer protections.

Miscellaneous, Studies

• **Savings and loan associations.** Permitted thrifts that converted to federal bank charters to continue being treated as savings associations, therefore subject to somewhat different regulation than other banks. They had to meet certain conditions, including the so-called qualified thrift lender test, which was designed to concentrate a thrift's loans and other assets in home mortgages and related loans. The law revised the test to reduce the total percentage of qualifying loans from 70 percent over two years to 65 percent for nine out of every 12 months. The changes also permitted a larger amount of non-housing loans and other assets to count toward the test and permitted federally chartered thrifts to hold a larger share of consumer loans.

The law also made it easier for banks to acquire thrifts or thrift branches and allowed so-called non-bank banks to acquire thrifts without regard to a statutory cap on annual growth by non-bank banks. The effect of the latter provision was to permit commercial companies that acquired insured banks under a pre-1987 loophole in the Bank Holding Company Act to greatly increase the size of their non-bank banks through thrift acquisitions.

• **Private deposit insurance.** Required the FDIC to study and conduct a demonstration project, in which the agency would seek to have private companies provide "reinsurance" of up to 10 percent of the liabilities at several banks. Within 18 months of enactment, the FDIC was required to report its analysis of the project and its recommendations on the feasibility of instituting a permanent private program to absorb some of the deposit insurance risk borne by the FDIC.

• **Uninsured deposit-taking.** Required the FDIC to study and report to Congress within six months of enactment on the feasibility and risk associated with allowing banks to accept both insured and uninsured deposits.

• **Payment of imputed interest on reserves study.** Required the Fed, the FDIC and other federal banking regulators to study the effects of paying interest on reserves that depository institutions were required to keep in Federal Reserve banks. The study was to look at the consequences for the Federal Reserve System, the deposit insurance system and depository institutions. It was due to Congress six months after enactment.

• **Federal Reserve lending to securities firms.** Clarified that, in extraordinary circumstances, the Fed could lend from its discount window to anyone, including securities firms, not just to banks. The law also made it somewhat easier for the Fed to make such loans but retained an existing requirement that borrowers show that they needed the Fed's cash to remain in business, could not borrow elsewhere and had secure collateral to back up the loans.

• **Rhode Island credit unions.** Required the Treasury secretary to guarantee repayment of up to $180 million borrowed by the state of Rhode Island to cover deposits in banks and credit unions that were not covered by federal deposit insurance, provided certain conditions were met. To qualify, the loans had to be fully secured by a dedicated sales tax or assets held by the state's deposit insurance corporation. The Treasury could assess a guarantee fee equal to one-half of 1 percent of the outstanding guaranteed principal amount, computed daily.

• **Payments system protections.** Clarified that a failed bank could not claim money due it through the federal system of interbank payments and at the same time decline to make payments that it owed. Payments to a failed bank through the system were limited to the net amount due in excess of payments that the failed bank owed.

• **Freedom National Bank.** Required the FDIC to fully protect deposits placed in the defunct Freedom National Bank by charitable and religious organizations. Freedom National, based in Harlem, New York City, held millions of dollars in deposits from organizations such as the United Negro College Fund. When the bank failed in November 1990, the FDIC could not find a buyer and was forced to liquidate it. As a result, deposits in excess of $100,000 were not fully protected; the FDIC paid about 50 cents on the dollar for uninsured deposits.

• **Securities law statute of limitations.** Reinstated securities fraud claims that had been dismissed under the terms of a June 1991 Supreme Court decision in *Lampf v. Gilbertson.* The court established a uniform nationwide statute of limitations for certain securities fraud cases, and in so doing foreclosed some pending cases. The law did not alter the statute of limitations for cases not filed before the decision.

• **Secrecy ban.** Prohibited the FDIC from agreeing not to disclose the terms of settlement of an action brought by the FDIC in its capacity as conservator or receiver of a failed bank or thrift. ■

Continued from p. 78

As approved by the subcommittee, the bill would have torn away an imperfect statutory barrier to banks engaging in securities activities. It would have opened the door to indirect ownership of banks by non-bank businesses, an even more radical idea that included allowing banks to affiliate indirectly with real estate and insurance companies. It would have allowed banks to operate nearly unfettered across state lines. And it would have preserved existing deposit insurance rules for individuals, effectively allowing multiple accounts at a single institution, each insured up to $100,000.

The latter provision was the only major instance where the subcommittee parted with the administration.

The administration wanted to roll back coverage to $100,000 per individual per bank and ultimately to restrict it to $100,000 nationwide.

Markup began May 14 on the draft bill, modeled after the administration bill (which had been introduced March 20 as HR 1505). Left out were all the provisions involving replenishment of the Bank Insurance Fund and other deposit insurance changes that were included in HR 2094, and that later became the first of six titles in the broader bill.

In the initial two days of markup on May 14 and 16, the Treasury lost its effort to roll back deposit insurance coverage, and the subcommittee also refused to force credit unions to write off the 1 percent of deposits they had paid into their deposit insurance fund.

The Treasury, however, defeated an attempt to preserve "pass-through" coverage, which allowed deposits from huge pension funds to be fully insured. And it effectively won a battle over the right of states to allow banks to engage in certain activities that the Treasury did not regard as risky.

During the remainder of the markup, the Treasury did even better. So did bigger banks, which won nearly every issue they contested. They postponed a fight on affiliations between banks and commercial businesses, beat back one effort to severely curtail their future ability to branch across state lines and preserved the bill's new securities powers for banks with only minor changes.

Smaller banks had a mixed experience, preventing the rollback of individual deposit insurance coverage, which they said would spark deposit flows into bigger banks, but losing on interstate branching, which they feared could have a similar effect.

But the interstate issue was far from settled. The subcommittee soundly defeated, 12-24, an amendment by Bruce F. Vento, D-Minn., that would have preserved states' rights to decide whether to allow banks to branch. But members and lobbyists said the May 22 vote was hardly the last word.

Meanwhile, consumer advocates were stunned by a series of defeats in a panel that had long been supportive of their efforts. Not only did they fail to win big gains in consumer protections imposed on bankers, they saw existing laws rolled back. And there seemed to be little they could do to stop the juggernaut.

Consumer advocates singled out for criticism a pair of amendments by Paul E. Kanjorski, D-Pa., that they said would have had the effect of exempting 92 percent of all banks from the central federal "anti-redlining" law, the 1977 Community Reinvestment Act that required bank regulators to rate institutions on their willingness to lend in their communities. Banks that received low grades could be prohibited from opening branches or acquiring other banks.

Also, an amendment by Joseph P. Kennedy II, D-Mass., to require banks to cash government checks and provide certain low-cost bank services to consumers was defeated by an overwhelming 9-27 vote May 23. A similar amendment had been approved by the Banking Committee in 1988.

Despite numerous changes made by the subcommittee, the bill as approved preserved most key elements of the administration's proposal. But not every battle was joined.

Foremost among the issues left untouched was that of allowing affiliation between banks and commercial firms. At Brady's request, Jim Leach, R-Iowa, withheld an amendment to delete that section of the bill. Brady met with subcommittee Republicans on May 20 and asked that Leach refrain so as not to stifle the momentum that was building.

Banking Committee Action

Action in the full Banking Committee got under way slowly June 19 and 20. But the following week the committee picked up steam. On June 28, after six days of markup during which 160 amendments were considered, the panel agreed to a broad banking overhaul bill that was little changed from the subcommittee version.

Most issues that were left untouched in subcommittee were addressed by the full panel, and there were some close votes. But the administration bill survived largely intact. The committee agreed to send HR 6 to the House floor by a 31-20 vote, after amending Gonzalez's original narrow bill (HR 6) with the much broader language that won acceptance in committee.

The strength of the vote reflected the feeling among many members that it was time to eliminate laws that banks believed gave a competitive edge to securities firms and insurance companies. But many critics of the bill warned that the margin of support was not large enough to overcome opposition from Dingell's Energy and Commerce Committee and from other quarters.

The committee made no significant changes to the portion of the bill replenishing the Bank Insurance Fund. In addition to giving the nearly insolvent fund more cash to close failing banks, the bill would have required regulators to move quickly to close weakened banks before their net worth, or stockholders' equity, was completely exhausted.

And it would have required the FDIC to use the least costly method of closing failed banks. This provision was intended to sharply limit — if not end — the FDIC's discretion to cover uninsured depositors by selling all deposits of a failed bank to new owners. After 1994, the bill would have ended the FDIC's ability to declare a bank too big to fail and to protect all of its depositors despite other restrictions on the cost of resolving bank failures.

The committee showed no hesitation about the need to restructure the financial services industry. Only three years before, the House had failed to act on a comparatively minor effort to repeal restrictions on bank activities. But in 1991, wholesale change was the order of the day in the Banking Committee.

The committee bill would have for the first time allowed banks near-unfettered opportunities to open branch offices nationwide. It would have repealed the 58-year-old Glass-Steagall Act. And it would have for the first time in 35 years removed federal bans on bank ownership by nonbanking companies, throwing open the door for companies such as General Motors Corp. or IBM to operate a bank.

Treasury Department lobbyists, who fought off repeated assaults on the bill, prevailed at almost every turn. For instance, Leach's amendment to strike the section permitting commercial ownership of banks failed June 26 on a 20-32 vote.

The issue of rolling back deposit insurance rose again, only to be knocked down by united bank opposition. Carroll Hubbard Jr., D-Ky., again led the banks' charge. And by a vote of 13-37, the committee on June 27 rejected a Gonzalez amendment to limit individuals to \$100,000 of deposit insurance coverage across the banking system, plus an additional \$100,000 for pensions.

The FDIC viewed the idea as impractical to administer and a nightmare to explain. The Treasury preferred to limit insurance to \$100,000 per person per institution (plus a pension account). A Gonzalez amendment to implement the Treasury limit was defeated 16-33 on June 28. And an amendment by Thomas R. Carper, D-Del., to phase in such a plan over five years failed the same day on a 20-29 vote.

Bankers fought the idea hard, and they were joined by some consumer advocates. The American Association of Retired Persons had supported retaining existing law, but AARP lobbyists were angered when Hubbard refused to support amendments requiring banks to provide low-cost checking accounts and to cash government checks. They stopped working in Hubbard's behalf, but their action had no noticeable effect on the outcome.

Gonzalez had one major victory, despite his inability to restrict insurance coverage. He extracted a compromise from the Fed, which was added to the bill, that the Fed would not have free rein in the future to pump cash into

Credit Card Interest Cap Flares and Dies

Like a fleeting comet, the idea of Congress voting to mandate a nationwide cap on credit card interest rates flared brightly for a week in mid-November and quickly disappeared.

Just days after the Senate voted in favor of such a cap — and House Democratic leaders rushed to sign on — House Speaker Thomas S. Foley, D-Wash., went before television cameras on Nov. 18 to urge restraint. "I suggest that the Banking Committee consider any action on credit card rates very, very carefully," Foley said. He added that a study of competition in rates "would be useful" and suggested that Congress might vote for one. But that did not happen.

The furor was set off by a last-minute insertion in a Nov. 11 campaign fundraising speech, in which President Bush called for lower credit card rates. Foley appeared to let Bush off the hook, saying, "I don't know that he anticipated what would happen in the Senate."

The Senate voted 74-19 for a rate cap Nov. 13, adopting an amendment by Alfonse M. D'Amato, R-N.Y., to a broader bank overhaul bill (S 543). Foley and other Democratic leaders immediately predicted that the House would join the Senate's action. *(Vote 251, p. 33-S)*

But in the days that followed, banks threatened to pull back credit cards from perhaps half of those who had them, bank stocks tumbled, the obscure but huge market in securities backed by credit card debt was rocked, and the Dow Jones industrial average plunged 120 points. The Nov. 15 drop was the fifth-largest numerical decline in the Dow's history; however it could hardly be attributed solely to the credit card rate cap proposal; analysts said weakness in bank stocks was a factor.

Treasury Secretary Nicholas F. Brady appeared on the NBC News program "Meet the Press" on Nov. 17, calling D'Amato's amendment, "wacky, senseless legislation."

By the end of the week of Nov. 18, a House Banking subcommittee had scheduled, and then postponed indefinitely, a credit card bill markup. Several members went to work to craft a bill calling for a study of rate caps that would produce results — and not upset financial markets.

Reps. Esteban E. Torres, D-Calif., chairman of the Consumer Affairs Subcommittee, and Charles E. Schumer, D-N.Y., developed a bill (HR 3860) requiring the General Accounting Office (GAO) to study interest-rate competitiveness among credit card issuers and whether the interest rates were set artificially high to boost bank profits. The GAO would have had to report in nine months.

If it were to find that the industry was not competitive, the president could within a nine-month period impose a rate cap tied to the average price of six-month Treasury securities. The Torres-Schumer bill would have produced a cap of 15.5 percent at the time it was drafted. The D'Amato cap, which was tied to the interest charged by the Internal Revenue Service on overdue tax payments, would have produced a 14 percent rate cap at the time the amendment was being considered.

No committee action on the Torres-Schumer bill was ever scheduled, and it did not surface as an option to D'Amato's amendment when House and Senate conferees met on the banking bill. The D'Amato amendment was quietly dropped in conference, without ever being discussed publicly.

weak banks. The Fed would be able to do so but only at the risk of incurring a loss that would be passed along to taxpayers. That was intended to give the Fed second thoughts. The change was a key element in Gonzalez's hope to put an end to the doctrine that some banks were too big to fail.

Consumer groups that had been battered in subcommittee won a victory of sorts by reversing several subcommittee decisions that would have substantially weakened federal anti-redlining law.

Bus loads of community activists traveled from New York, Chicago, St. Louis and other cities to Washington to sit in during the full committee markup. Committee members received telephone calls from some mayors and others worried that banks would use their broader powers to siphon deposit money out of communities and to make loans across the country or overseas.

But the consumer activists still faced a wall of Republicans and a sufficient number of Democrats (including several freshmen) to ensure their defeat. So, led by Maxine Waters, D-Calif., they began brokering a deal to strike all subcommittee-approved amendments to the anti-redlining law — those sponsored by Kanjorski and one that consumer groups favored. The latter, sponsored by Kennedy, would have set new standards for banks with interstate branches. Working in the consumer advocates' favor was a threat from the House Democratic leadership that the bill would be in jeopardy if it contained any rollback of the law.

Ultimately, Wylie joined with Gonzalez in proposing to strike the Kennedy and Kanjorski amendments. The motion to strike was adopted June 20 on a 40-12 vote. The turn of events caught Kanjorski and some consumer advocates — who thought they might win an up-or-down vote against him — by surprise.

The committee also abandoned an effort to restructure the maze of federal bank and thrift regulatory agencies. The Treasury had halfheartedly backed one reorganization plan, but the subcommittee knocked it out of the bill and substituted nothing in its place. Turf fights and an inability to cut the Gordian knot led the full committee also to abandon the effort.

Several committee members backed a further radical change in banking law beyond those already in the bill. Schumer and Jim Slattery, D-Kan., cosponsored an amendment that would have limited deposit insurance to so-called core banks — which would be restricted in the amount of interest they could pay on deposits and in the size of loans they could make. Presumably such core banks could affiliate with uninsured banks that could engage in all manner of theretofore prohibited activities.

For many Democrats, the core bank idea provided the best hope of restricting deposit insurance coverage sufficiently to make the other banking regulation changes in the bill palatable. But the committee rejected core banks June 26 on a 23-28 vote. Schumer, however, said the vote was far stronger than he had hoped only weeks earlier, and he said he would try to win passage for the proposal on the House floor.

Lobbying Against HR 6

The Banking Committee formally reported HR 6 to the House on July 12, two weeks after it voted to approve the bill. House Speaker Thomas S. Foley, D-Wash., then struggled to balance demands from four other committees that wanted a crack at amending the bill with his promise to Treasury Secretary Brady that Congress would move the bill expeditiously to limit risk to the teetering insurance fund.

On July 23, Foley announced that the Agriculture, Energy and Commerce, Judiciary, and Ways and Means committees would each have until Sept. 27 to act on the bill, ensuring that there would be a rush to complete action before adjournment, then set for mid-October. The deadline for the committees to report was later extended a week until Oct. 4.

The multiple referrals were directly related to a developing opposition strategy by insurance agents, securities firms, small banks and consumer groups, all of which were unhappy with the Banking Committee bill.

For example, the Independent Bankers Association of America, a small-bank lobbying group, pursued a wide-ranging strategy to try to force Congress to enact a very narrow bill. It allied with consumer groups that were worried about financial concentration and with state government officials who did not want to lose control over institutions that operated nationwide and others.

The self-styled Main Street Coalition hoped in the House to get Energy and Commerce to roll back significantly provisions allowing banks to affiliate broadly with commercial businesses, and especially to engage in securities and insurance activities.

The same coalition appealed to Agriculture and Judiciary in an effort to restrain the Banking Committee bill's provisions allowing full interstate branching.

To win support for their views in the Senate, the Independent Bankers even threw their support behind a consumer provision in a draft bill circulated by Senate Banking Chairman Riegle that would have required banks to give low-income customers some basic banking services, such as government check-cashing or inexpensive checking accounts.

Energy and Commerce Action

For years, Energy and Commerce Chairman Dingell had made it clear that he opposed allowing banks to affiliate freely with securities firms, insurance companies and non-financial businesses. Banks hoped that he might have moderated his views in 1991 — or at least be willing to compromise. On July 10, however, Dingell gave a clear signal that his views had changed little since he thwarted House passage of a banking overhaul bill in 1988.

"Should the federal government loosen regulatory controls on banks and allow them to enter into other financial fields . . . and allow the officers and owners to have entangled, conflicting fiduciary duties?" Dingell asked during a committee hearing on HR 6. "The best and simplest answer is no."

Dingell also issued a sharp challenge to the Banking Committee, asking the GAO to review HR 6 to assess the degree to which it contained special-interest provisions that contradicted its public policy aims.

It was an odd request — and patently political — since most observers marveled that the measure seemed unusually free of special-interest items. Gonzalez fired back, urging Dingell to withdraw the request. "You are the first to unsheathe the two-edged sword," he wrote. The GAO review was never done.

Edward J. Markey, D-Mass., whose Energy and Commerce Subcommittee on Finance was the first of two subcommittee stops for HR 6, held a series of hearings before Congress took its monthlong August recess to allow his members to sharply question Brady and then to allow witnesses to attack the bill.

Markey called consumer advocate Ralph Nader, an ardent foe of many elements of HR 6, to testify along with Edwin J. Gray, the nation's top savings and loan regulator in the mid-1980s. As a regulator, Gray had attempted — largely unsuccessfully — to rein in some practices that critics alleged helped wreck the thrift industry. He also fingered the so-called Keating Five senators, accusing them of improperly trying to block federal investigations into the Lincoln Savings and Loan Association in Irvine, Calif. The failure of Lincoln was projected to cost taxpayers in excess of $2 billion. Gray testified that HR 6 would lead the nation's banks down the same disastrous path taken by the thrifts. *(Keating hearings, p. 26)*

After the August recess, Markey's Finance Subcommittee and the companion Subcommittee on Commerce, Consumer Protection and Competitiveness each met Sept. 16 and rejected major portions of the reform agenda put forth by the administration and bigger banks.

Without adopting a single controversial amendment, the Finance Subcommittee approved draft language put forward by Markey and Dingell, focusing chiefly on securities issues. The subcommittee bill would have allowed banks and securities firms to join forces, but only under the most restricted of ways.

The only controversial amendment involved a section of the Markey-Dingell draft that would have prevented banks from affiliating with non-banking companies — by retaining existing law that severely restricted bank ownership.

Matthew J. Rinaldo, R-N.J., objected that the ban on affiliations between banks and commercial companies was no longer necessary. He proposed that non-banking businesses be allowed at least to buy failing banks — to bring new capital to the banking industry and save the deposit insurance fund from paying to close some failed banks.

Markey said the amendment would be "more than the camel's nose under the tent," and Dingell said no commercial business would buy a bank under those circumstances "except for the most corrupt motives." The amendment was defeated on an 11-15 party-line vote, with only one Democrat, Rick Boucher of Virginia, voting for it.

The Competitiveness Subcommittee approved language drafted by Chairman Cardiss Collins, D-Ill., that was mostly intended to limit banks' ability to get into the insurance business, in the process rolling back opportunities for banks that were permitted by existing law.

Both subcommittees approved their versions of HR 6 by voice vote.

The full Energy and Commerce Committee met Sept. 25 and on a 29-12 vote ratified nearly all the actions of the two subcommittees.

Particularly galling to bankers were the high fire walls

that Energy and Commerce wanted to erect to restrict financial connections between a bank and its securities affiliate.

But Energy and Commerce members agreed to mute a key fire wall provision approved in subcommittee that would have virtually ensured that a securities firm affiliated with a bank would get little business from companies that were customers of the bank. The change agreed to by the full committee would have preserved opportunities for a bank to lend to a commercial customer while the bank's securities affiliate underwrote stock or bond offerings for the same company.

For some bankers, that was the whole point: They wanted to be able to satisfy their customers' demands for non-bank financial services but not lose any existing business.

An amendment, offered by James H. Scheuer, D-N.Y., and approved by voice vote, would have permitted a bank to lend to an established customer that was also a client of its securities affiliate for a period of 60 days before, or 90 days after, the securities firm underwrote a stock or bond offering for the client. The subcommittee bill would have banned such loans. The provision had been the subject of more than a week of negotiations between several big banks and securities firms, and final language was not agreed upon until a few hours before the markup.

Committee Republicans made a final attempt to win permission for non-banking companies to own banks. Rinaldo offered an amendment similar to one defeated a week earlier in subcommittee that would have allowed any company to buy a failing bank. It was defeated on a party-line, 15-26 vote.

Supporters of Rinaldo's amendment argued that the wall between banking and commerce had already been breached in three places. Commercial companies could buy savings and loans. Some commercial giants owned so-called non-bank banks, which had deposit insurance but were not subject to laws restricting affiliations between banks and other businesses. These affiliations had slipped through a loophole in the Bank Holding Company Act that was closed in August 1987. And existing law permitted foreign commercial companies that owned banks abroad to own U.S. banks, although the Energy and Commerce bill would have changed that.

In fact, the Dingell-Markey version of the bill retained House Banking Committee language that would have permitted further exploitation of the non-bank bank loophole: It would have allowed existing non-bank banks to buy thrifts and avoid an existing-law cap on their growth. And the bill would only apply its new stringent fire walls to banks, not to non-banks or thrifts.

Markey said he focused primarily on curtailing provisions in the Banking Committee bill, not rolling back existing law. "That's where we put our political capital," he said, insisting that he was trying to prevent a bigger breach in the wall between banking and commerce. He denied administration charges that his bill catered to special interests by permitting existing loopholes to remain. "We tried not to let the perfect be the enemy of the good," Markey said.

Agriculture Action

The Agriculture Committee also met Sept. 25, in the process handing smaller banks and consumer groups a victory by taking a swipe at the interstate branching provisions of HR 6.

The Agriculture Committee had sought referral of the bill on the basis of narrow but serious concerns about a series of provisions relating to failed banks and their role in the settlement of contracts for future delivery of commodities, according to a July 23 letter to Foley from Chairman E. "Kika" de la Garza, D-Texas.

But by the time the panel met, concerns about branching had attracted the attention of committee members, who expressed fears that nationwide branching by large banks might reduce competition in rural areas and shrink the amount of credit available to farmers. The committee adopted an amendment to HR 6 that would have forced federal regulators to review the lending operations of interstate branches under certain conditions, to ensure that deposits were not being siphoned out of rural areas. Approval of the amendment was by an 11-10 show-of-hands vote, with de la Garza providing the deciding vote, following several hours of debate. De la Garza had worried that the amendment trod on Banking Committee jurisdiction.

Sponsored by Glenn English, D-Okla., the amendment would have allowed bank regulators to close a rural branch of an out-of-state bank if it were shown that the branch was not meeting the credit needs of the region it served. A review of lending activities would be triggered if the loan total as a percentage of deposits was less than half the statewide average.

The committee also adopted by voice vote two relatively non-controversial amendments. One was to a portion of the bill aimed at ensuring that a failing bank would not escape obligations to cover losses at the same time it collected on gains from such trades. The other would have provided so-called pass-through deposit insurance coverage to futures contract brokers who deposited their clients' money in a bank during settlement procedures. The deposits, though nominally in the name of the broker, were to carry deposit insurance of up to $100,000 for each client.

Judiciary Action

Despite pressure from small banks and consumer groups to wade into the branching issue, the Judiciary Committee agreed when it met Oct. 3 to approve two relatively narrow amendments to HR 6.

By voice vote the committee approved an amendment that was described as an effort to navigate between the Banking and Energy and Commerce panels on the question of preventing banks from "tying" their services to those provided by non-banking affiliates.

The panel also voted 27-5 to adopt an amendment striking Banking Committee language that would have subjected individuals who owned banks to the same conditions on ownership of non-banking companies that applied to corporate owners of banks. That amendment was strongly opposed by smaller banks. Despite their opposition to big banking conglomerates, many small-bank owners also owned small-town real estate, insurance or other businesses.

Big-bank critics hoped that Judiciary Chairman Jack Brooks, D-Texas, would use his panel's jurisdiction over antitrust matters to restrain interstate branching. But Brooks did not seem interested.

Small banks and consumer advocates, in raising the specter of massive consolidation of the banking industry, complained that after NCNB Corp. of North Carolina bought the failed First RepublicBank system in Texas in 1988, NCNB had siphoned money out of the state. Brooks, who owned a major interest in several smaller Texas banks,

House, Senate Banking Bills Compared

Following is a comparison of the way key issues were treated in three versions of the bank overhaul bill: the House Banking Committee bill (HR 6 — H Rept 102-157, Part 1) approved June 28, amendments to HR 6 approved by the House Energy and Commerce Committee Sept. 25, and a bill (S 543) approved by the Senate Banking Committee on Aug. 2:

	House Banking	House Energy & Commerce	Senate Banking
Bank Ownership	Would permit any company to own a bank, ending legal restrictions that effectively prohibited affiliations between commercial businesses (including insurance and diversified financial companies) and banks.	Would retain existing law.	Would retain existing law.
Glass-Steagall Repeal	Would effectively repeal the 1933 Glass-Steagall Act, which barred most affiliations between banks and securities firms.	Essentially the same as House Banking.	Essentially the same as House Banking but would bar mergers between the largest banks and securities houses.
Fire Walls	Would severely limit financial links between banks and their securities affiliates. Banks generally could not finance the purchase of securities underwritten by an affiliated securities firm or lend money that would be used to pay principal, interest or dividends, for instance.	Similar to House Banking, but tougher. If a bank's securities affiliate issued stocks or bonds for a company, the bank could not lend to that company for any purpose for three months afterward. Regulators would have some leeway to relax fire walls, however.	Similar to House Banking. The Federal Reserve could relax fire walls beginning three years after enactment.
Insurance	Would roll back regulatory and judicial interpretations of current law — in some cases still under legal challenge — that allow banks or their affiliates some insurance sales and underwriting powers. Existing law provisions that allowed only federally chartered banks located in towns of less than 5,000 people to sell insurance would be tightened so that a bank could only sell to people in that town or in similar small towns in the same state. Also, only those state banks or their affiliates currently in the business of selling insurance out of state would be permitted to continue doing so; this would permit a Delaware bank owned by Citicorp to market insurance nationwide.	Would go further than House Banking in rolling back existing law by closing the Delaware insurance sales loophole. Also, consumer protections would be imposed on bank insurance activities, such as limits on disclosure of customer information and a ban on soliciting borrowers for insurance until loan applications had been approved.	Would go further than House Banking in rolling back existing law. The town-of-5,000 loophole would be more tightly curtailed, permitting sales only in the town and not in adjacent rural areas or in similar small towns in the same state. The Delaware insurance sales loophole also would be closed.
Interstate Branching	Would permit a bank to open branches in any state where it could own another separately chartered and capitalized bank. Existing state laws limiting or barring interstate bank ownership would be overridden after three years.	Would not affect interstate branching provisions of HR 6.	Would permit interstate ownership of existing banks after one year and creation of new banks across state lines after two years. Nationwide branching would be allowed after three years, but states could vote to "opt out" of branching.

said that he was not personally aware of problems with NCNB in Texas and that such matters were the province of the Banking Committee, not his.

Ways and Means Action

Ways and Means was the only committee to adopt amendments that would not change the banking regulatory core of the bill. The committee's interest was chiefly in a provision of HR 6 that would have allowed the FDIC to raise cash by selling bonds to banks — instead of by borrowing from the Treasury.

Ways and Means met Sept. 25 and adopted two amendments to HR 6, both by voice vote.

One would have required that bonds sold to commercial banks as a means to recapitalize the deposit insurance fund would have to pay interest at Treasury bond rates and be subject to statutory caps on borrowing by the FDIC and the government as a whole. The other was intended to ensure that changes in bank ownership and activities contemplated by the bill would not affect existing tax treatment of banks and the companies that owned them. Without the change, Ways and Means was concerned that somewhat more-generous tax provisions that applied to banks but not other corporations could result in a slight revenue loss to the Treasury.

Seeking a Compromise

As other committees weighed in and pressure mounted against the Banking Committee version of HR 6, Gonzalez repeatedly lashed out at the wide scope of his panel's bill and at the delay that had effectively halted action since his committee acted at the end of June. Gonzalez also complained that Brady had backed away from the pressure he had put on Congress earlier in the year to act to replenish the insurance fund.

"It is my responsibility to say . . . that the majority [of the committee], the industry and its spokesmen, and the secretary of the Treasury, in particular, are playing craps with the safety and soundness of the system," Gonzalez said July 24. "The fund is broke, and I don't see why anyone wants to kid themselves."

After Energy and Commerce had taken steps to thwart the Banking Committee's intent, members of that panel met to decide whether to go forward or to retreat to the narrow-bill approach long advocated by Gonzalez. Banking Committee Democrats informally agreed at a two-hour closed-door caucus Oct. 3, to press forward with HR 6. Some Democrats on the committee joined Gonzalez in opposition to its broad sweep; others said they would have preferred a narrow bill to avoid a bloody showdown on the floor and to expedite action on replenishing the insurance fund. But most wanted to press ahead. The action allied a majority of the panel's Democrats with a nearly united phalanx of House Republicans and with the administration in preparation for the upcoming floor fight.

Wylie, ranking Republican on the Banking Committee, said Bush had strongly urged support for HR 6 at a private White House meeting Sept. 24. At a House GOP caucus Oct. 2, said Wylie, no one objected to his suggestion that they press for passage of the bill. He said he had dropped his personal opposition to allowing commercial companies to own banks because Bush had argued in favor of retaining that provision.

The jockeying for position between supporters and opponents of HR 6 continued well into October, but the die was cast the week of Oct. 21, when Gonzalez struck a deal with Dingell that undermined the position of his committee colleagues. In essence, Gonzalez agreed to a substitute for the key title of the bill governing bank affiliations with securities, insurance and commercial companies.

Aside from issues of substance that had arisen in disputes between the Banking panel and Energy and Commerce, there were also concerns about turf. Banking members were upset that Energy and Commerce had to be given such broad jurisdiction over bank matters, and they were worried that Energy and Commerce would expand that jurisdictional grab as time passed.

The deal between Gonzalez and Dingell appeared to give the Energy and Commerce Committee a victory on substance but not on jurisdiction.

The compromise would not have permitted commercial companies to own banks; it would have imposed higher and thicker fire walls than those in the Banking Committee version of HR 6; and in most instances, the insurance sales activities of banks would have been more severely limited than they were in the Banking Committee version or existing law. At the same time, Dingell dropped demands for new regulation of banks by the Securities and Exchange Commission that would have enhanced his panel's jurisdiction over the banking industry, and he signed a memorandum of understanding to the effect that his committee would not gain jurisdiction.

For obvious reasons, the Gonzalez-Dingell deal angered big banks and left them wondering what strategy to pursue as the bill moved forward. It pleased smaller banks and the insurance industry. Brady said the compromise "turns back the clock" on bank powers. But his strong opposition to the deal did not stop behind-the-scenes negotiations aimed at getting a bill passed.

The deal did not directly affect language in the bill permitting banks to open branch offices across state lines. However, administration officials began quietly agreeing to accept restrictions on interstate branching because they feared the whole bill was sinking. Some big banks and their congressional allies began promoting a strategy to knock the bank affiliations title out of the bill altogether. They hoped to preserve interstate branching and at the same time to continue wearing away at legal restrictions on securities and insurance activities through regulatory changes and court decisions. The strategies pursued by big banks and by the administration eventually collided — when interstate branching became inextricably linked to securities and insurance powers.

HR 6 Floor Defeat

Concern had been building for weeks that with a pre-Thanksgiving adjournment target looming and no Senate floor action yet on a banking bill, Congress might quit for the year without shoring up the insurance fund. The Gonzalez-Dingell compromise cleared the way for House floor action beginning Oct. 30 — even if it did not please all parties.

In the end, the deal did not come close to helping pass the bill. During four days on the floor, HR 6 barely survived two procedural votes that would have killed it. Then it was overwhelmingly rejected on Nov. 4 by a vote of 89-324. *(Vote 375, p. 92-H)*

The Rules Committee began meeting on the bill Oct. 29, the same day Bush issued a veto threat because of the changes in the Gonzalez-Dingell deal. The House Democratic leadership was split on the issue: Foley had promised Brady to move the bill to the floor, though he had not guaranteed what would happen there; Majority Leader Richard A. Gephardt, D-Mo., and others plainly preferred Dingell's vision of banking reform to that in the Banking Committee version of HR 6.

Both parties held caucuses the morning of Oct. 30, but neither meeting seemed to clear the air or instill a sense of confidence in what the House was about to do. Members of both parties became increasingly uneasy — and were vocal in their lack of confidence in the bill.

The Democratic gathering was sparsely attended, and members who were present said most of the participants were from the Banking and Energy and Commerce committees and were well-versed in the issues. There was no effort to get the caucus to express a point of view on any of the issues raised by the bill, members said. Republicans met with Brady, who made a strong pitch for the bill as approved by the Banking Committee. Brady got "a cordial and sympathetic reception," said Dick Armey, R-Texas, who had voted against the bill during Banking Committee deliberations. Another Banking Committee member, Marge Roukema, R-N.J., said, "I don't know if they don't want to talk about it, or if it's too complicated."

The Rules Committee then had difficulty deciding how to structure debate on the bill. Two rules were crafted. The first allowed the House to begin debate Oct. 30 but gave no instructions about what amendments would be allowed. After a day of closed-door maneuverings, Rules agreed late in the evening of Oct. 30 to a second rule that permitted the House to consider only 24 of 78 amendments that members wanted to offer.

Rules took one action that particularly offended many members: It dropped the Banking Committee's version of the bank affiliations title — and substituted the Gonzalez-Dingell compromise. Further compounding the anger directed at Rules, the committee refused to let the full House even consider the Banking Committee's original language. Though many of its proponents conceded that the original version could not have prevailed on the floor, it became a matter of principle that they should have had their shot.

Rules also disregarded the interstate branching amendment adopted in the Agriculture Committee; the Ways and Means amendments were incorporated into the bill, as were the futures trading amendments adopted by Agriculture. The anti-tying language adopted by Judiciary was subsumed in the Gonzalez-Dingell compromise.

When the House took up the second rule on Oct. 31, an angry phalanx of 153 Republicans, joined by 54 pro- and anti-bank Democrats and independent Bernard Sanders of Vermont, nearly defeated it. That would have sidetracked the measure at least temporarily — and some suspected permanently. Several members switched at the end; at one point after time for the vote had run out, the electronic vote-tally board in the House chamber showed the rule losing 208-209. The final vote was 210-208. *(Vote 358, p. 88-H)*

Eight Republicans joined 202 Democrats to support the rule. But it took Foley to corral the necessary votes. He personally worked the floor, persuading Barnard and Minority Leader Robert H. Michel, R-Ill., to vote yes, despite their opposition. (Both the administration and Barnard had been given permission to offer every amendment they sought.)

Barnard's support was tempered by a blistering floor speech in which he attacked the Democratic leadership for trampling over the Banking Committee's work. "I hate to say this about my leadership, but this is dastardly," Barnard said.

House GOP Whip Newt Gingrich of Georgia decided late Oct. 30 to try to defeat the rule, after sensing growing opposition to the Gonzalez-Dingell compromise. But, although the administration had issued a veto threat over the compromise, the White House declined to support his effort. Had it done so, Gingrich almost certainly would have prevailed. A Treasury official refused to discuss the matter. But all along the administration had made compromises in order to retain as much as possible of what it had originally sought.

The crucial vote on Oct. 31 came on Barnard's amendment to strike the Gonzalez-Dingell bank-powers language from the bill.

For years, Barnard had been the leading House supporter of allowing new investment and affiliation powers for banking companies. However, the restrictions contained in the compromise persuaded him that the best course would be to have nothing in the bill on that subject.

But Barnard could not overcome Dingell, who warned that without the sorts of safeguards contained in his version of the bill, "rapacious scoundrels" — a favored term for greedy financiers — will engage in "rascality" that will threaten the financial system and taxpayers. The amendment to strike the Gonzalez-Dingell compromise was defeated 200-216, with 28 Republicans joining Dingell, and 70 Democrats joining Barnard. *(Vote 362, p. 88-H)*

That outcome led directly to a Nov. 1 vote to abort the bill. Republicans tried a rare tactic of amending the bill to strike its enacting clause — in effect neutering it. At best the move would have sent the bill back to committee, and it might have killed it. But Democratic leaders enforced party discipline on the vote, and only Barnard and Carper — out of scores of sympathetic Democrats — voted with the Republicans. The motion failed 158-243. *(Vote 364, p. 88-H)*

Shortly after that vote, which came on a Friday, the bill was shelved until Monday, Nov. 4.

For a time, the House leadership urged members to vote for passage to keep the legislative process moving, with a near certainty that the bill would be changed in conference. Noting that a sizable majority of Democrats had voted to retain the controversial Gonzalez-Dingell compromise and that there would be few Republican votes for final passage, leadership aides tried to make the vote an issue of party loyalty — as they had on the Friday motion to strike the enacting clause.

It didn't work this time, and by midafternoon Nov. 4, it was hard to find a member who planned to back the bill on final passage. The effort to whip up support fizzled, and HR 6 was defeated overwhelmingly that evening, 89-324. Almost all the support came from Democrats — much of it from committee chairmen, members of the leadership and members of Banking and Energy and Commerce. Even then, only 12 of 31 Banking Committee Democrats and 17 of 27 Energy and Commerce Democrats voted for the bill.

During debate on the bill, the House approved one key amendment that had failed to win committee approval and rejected several others:

- By a vote of 366-4, the House agreed to a Vento interstate branching amendment to give state legislatures three years in which to vote to "opt out" of allowing out-of-state banks to open branch offices within their borders. At the same time, the House rejected, 142-250, a much more tightly drawn "opt-in" amendment and refused by 20-374 to strike the entire interstate branching section from the bill. A similar Vento amendment had been rejected in a Banking subcommittee, but the floor amendment was incorporated into HR 2094, a subsequent banking bill that was sent to the House just after the defeat of HR 6. *(Votes 367, 368, 369, p. 90-H)*

- By a vote of 153-264, the House rejected Wylie's amendment to roll back deposit-insurance coverage to $100,000 per person, per bank (with provision for a second $100,000 insured account for a pension plan). Similar amendments had been rejected in committee. *(Vote 372, p. 90-H)*
- By a vote of 106-312, the House rejected Schumer's core bank proposal that had failed in committee. *(Vote 361, p. 88-H)*
- By a vote of 137-272, the House rejected Rinaldo's amendment to permit commercial companies to buy failing banks, which had failed in committee. *(Vote 363, p. 88-H)*
- By a vote of 152-241, the House rejected a Kennedy amendment that would have imposed stiff new "fair lending" restrictions on banks, requiring them to develop plans to lend to minorities where data showed a disparity in their lending habits. The amendment had been given a boost by an Oct. 21 Federal Reserve report showing that poor whites were more likely to be granted mortgages than well-to-do blacks. But, opposed by most banks and the administration, and possibly tarred by the fights over unrelated issues in the bill, the amendment failed. *(Vote 366, p. 88-H)*

SUBSEQUENT HOUSE ACTION

Following the defeat of HR 6, supporters of broad changes in banking law began scrambling to preserve as much of the bill as possible. In the weeks leading up to the floor vote on HR 6, the administration had given up much of its overhaul plan.

Following the overwhelming vote on HR 6, Treasury Secretary Brady conceded that Congress would not agree in 1991 to allow commercial companies to own banks or to allow banks to affiliate with securities firms. (The Senate bill never included the former provision and the latter was dropped unceremoniously from the Senate bill after the House vote on HR 6.)

Interstate branching was the last remaining major piece of the package. It was still in the Senate bill — and Brady was not yet of a mind to give that up, even though most of the banking industry had. The fight in the House then became one over how to preserve interstate branching.

As a result, the House walked the plank on a second banking bill (HR 2094) that was amended on the floor to permit interstate branching. That bill was defeated Nov. 14, by a vote of 191-227. *(Vote 399, p. 96-H)*

Finally, a very narrow bill (HR 3768) aimed solely at overhauling the deposit-insurance system and replenishing the insurance fund passed overwhelmingly — 344-84. *(Vote 415, p. 100-H)*

Committee Action on HR 2094

Two days after HR 6 was rejected, the House Banking Committee quickly met to send HR 2094 to the floor. The bill had been held in abeyance since it was marked up in subcommittee the first week of May.

The committee voted somewhat reluctantly to discard almost all that was in the first bill, retaining only those provisions designed to keep the deposit-insurance system afloat. An amended version of HR 2094 contained the first of six titles in HR 6. But in that form, the bill was plainly too narrow for anyone's taste and stood no chance of passage.

The committee met Nov. 6 and, at the insistence of Gonzalez, kept the bill very narrow. As approved by the committee, the bill would have provided the FDIC with a $30 billion line of credit with the Treasury; it would have permitted regulators to close failing banks before they were completely insolvent; and it would have largely closed the too-big-to-fail loophole that resulted in protection for uninsured depositors when very large banks failed.

Wylie supported Gonzalez's request to fight off all other amendments to HR 2094 but said he would fight hard to permit interstate branching when the bill reached the floor.

Their agreement effectively prevented a revolt that could have loaded the bill down so that it was not very different from HR 6. But many Democrats objected that the result was the loss of other, mostly non-controversial changes in banking law — beyond the broad questions of powers and branching — that had been included in HR 6.

"I have serious reservations," said Peter Hoagland, D-Neb. "We're emasculating our jurisdiction. What's the point of sitting on this committee if we're not going to make decisions in this room?"

Al McCandless, R-Calif., then moved to pre-empt further amendments by ordering an up-or-down vote on the bill. His motion carried narrowly, 28-24. The committee then approved the narrow bill, 37-15. In both cases, there were large blocks of Republicans and Democrats voting on each side.

Floor Action on HR 2094

Following the committee action, it was plain that the interstate branching issue was not dead. So House leaders held lengthy negotiations among members, interest groups and administration officials over how to structure floor amendments to win support for the measure.

Gonzalez, who had wanted the narrowest possible banking bill all year long, washed his hands of the process. "It's out of our control — out of mine," he told his Banking colleagues Nov. 6. "It's what the leadership wants to do."

Vote-counting, not careful consideration of public policy, drove the backroom discussions, particularly since it was widely believed that at least 100 — and maybe many more — of the 267 Democrats in the House would vote against anything related to a banking bill. Evidence of that was clear in the 16 roll call votes taken during floor action on HR 6. With the sole exception of a vote to curtail banks' ability to open branch offices across state lines and one procedural vote that Foley personally lobbied, huge numbers of Democrats consistently voted no. That included votes on amendments promoting bread-and-butter party issues such as prohibiting discrimination in bank lending and other consumer protections.

Moreover, it was difficult to find the right mixture of policy choices that could hold a majority of those who were not automatic no votes. That was especially important if the bill was to get any Republican support. Many members wanted to help banks expand their businesses. They were in conflict with those defending the securities and insurance industries from encroachment by banks. And they were opposed by members who feared concentration of the financial services industry and increased risk to the deposit insurance system from increased bank powers.

As Schumer put it: "You can do a narrow bill, but Republicans won't vote for it without interstate branching. If you do interstate, people want insurance restrictions. If you do insurance, the securities industry wants a moratorium [on new powers]. People fall off with every addition.

Administration Bill Highlights

Following is a summary of the key points in the administration's banking industry bill. Most changes were to take effect one to two years after enactment; some were to take effect in three years.

Deposit Insurance Reform

Insurance limits. Individual depositors would be protected to a maximum of $100,000 per institution, plus an additional $100,000 coverage per institution for retirement savings. "Pass-through" coverage — such as multimillion-dollar pension accounts previously insured to $100,000 per beneficiary — would be eliminated in most cases. So would coverage for brokered deposits. The Federal Deposit Insurance Corporation (FDIC) would study the feasibility of capping insurance at $100,000 per person systemwide.

Too big to fail. The FDIC would be explicitly prohibited from covering uninsured deposits in a failed bank unless that would cost less than simply paying off insured deposits. The FDIC could not consider losses that might be incurred at other institutions as a result of a bank's failure. But the Federal Reserve Board and the Treasury could authorize the FDIC to protect all depositors if a bank failure would pose a "systemic risk."

Risk-based premiums. The FDIC would have to assess insurance premiums based on a bank's relative riskiness, determined principally by a bank's capitalization.

State-chartered banks. For the most part, state-chartered banks would be prohibited from making investments or engaging in activities prohibited to federally chartered banks. The prohibition would extend to subsidiaries of state-chartered banks. The FDIC could grant exceptions to this rule for well-capitalized banks.

Tighter supervision. New rules for bank examinations would be imposed, based on capital levels and an institution's size. Poorly capitalized banks would be subject to prompt takeover by the FDIC.

Private insurance. The FDIC would have to conduct a pilot program to examine the opportunities for private deposit "co-insurance" that would run in tandem with FDIC coverage.

Bank Insurance Fund Recapitalization

New borrowing authority. The FDIC would be permitted to borrow up to $25 billion from the Federal Reserve System, to be repaid at Treasury security rates and secured by dedicated increases in bank insurance premiums. The borrowed money could be used to cover losses due to failed banks or to assist troubled banks. The FDIC could use its existing authority to borrow from Treasury to leverage other loans.

Premium limits. Bank insurance premiums would be capped at 30 cents per $100 in the aggregate; risk-based premiums for individual institutions could exceed the cap.

Regulatory Restructuring

Regulators combined. Federal supervision of banks and savings and loan associations, now split among four agencies, would be combined. Federally chartered banks, their holding companies and subsidiaries, and all savings and loans would be supervised by a new Treasury Department agency, the Office of Depository Institutions Supervision. State-chartered banks, their holding companies and subsidiaries would be supervised by the Federal Reserve.

FDIC role. The FDIC would retain its authority to examine insured banks.

Credit unions. Credit unions would remain separately regulated and insured. They would have to write off over 12 years the 1 percent of deposits they maintain as reserves in the National Credit Union Share Insurance Fund.

New Bank Powers

Holding companies. Two new kinds of companies would be created to own banks. Financial services holding companies could directly own banks, insurance companies and securities houses. Banks themselves could not be holding companies. Only financial services holding companies whose banks were well-capitalized could engage in non-banking financial activities. Diversified holding companies could affiliate with any commercial enterprise and could own well-capitalized banks but only indirectly, through financial services holding companies. All holding companies would have to maintain their banks' capital requirements or divest.

Fire walls. Stiff limits would be put on loans from banks to their financial services affiliates to prevent unfair competitive advantages and risk to the deposit-insurance system. Loans to affiliated commercial businesses would be prohibited. Distinctions between insured and uninsured products of banks and their affiliates would have to be made clear to consumers.

Insurance. Federally chartered banks could sell insurance directly, as opposed to through an affiliate, only where state-chartered banks were permitted to do so. But states could not prevent banks from affiliating with insurance companies.

Securities. Some securities activities now permitted to banks themselves would have to be transferred to affiliates.

Real estate. Real estate development and brokerage activities would not qualify as financial services, so banks could affiliate with real estate firms only indirectly through diversified holding companies. State-chartered banks could continue existing real estate brokerage activities.

Interstate banking. Financial services holding companies would be permitted to buy banks in any state. Moreover, nationally and state-chartered banks could open initial branches in states other than where they are based. States would continue to regulate additional authority to open branches.

It's one big mess."

Administration officials said Nov. 7 that they would insist that any bill allow banks to operate freely across state lines, but they signaled a willingness to accept some restraints that might be imposed by the states. They also said they would not accept a moratorium that would prevent federal regulators from granting new powers to banks. Such a moratorium was put in place for one year in 1987; since it was lifted in 1988, the Federal Reserve Board and other regulators had expanded the authority of banks to affiliate in limited ways with securities firms.

But the administration negotiated with some bankers and with insurance agents to craft a compromise that would put restrictions on the existing ability of some banks to sell insurance across state lines.

The negotiations eventually yielded two substantive floor amendments, which were made in order by the Rules Committee. House leaders and administration officials crossed their fingers that when the bill came to the floor Nov. 14, their careful vote-counting would pay off.

One amendment, which was non-controversial and was approved by voice vote, restored a variety of banking law reforms that the committee had thrown overboard in its effort to craft the narrowest possible bill.

The other, offered by Wylie, allowed interstate branching but rolled back some existing bank powers to sell insurance and sealed forever a closed window for banks to operate real estate brokerages. Although insurance and real estate agents often appeared invincible on Capitol Hill, they were able to muster only the barest majority for the amendment. It was adopted 210-208, after Dennis Hastert, R-Ill., switched to vote yes. *(Vote 398, p. 96-H)*

An odd coalition then formed to kill the measure. Virtually the entire banking industry opposed the bill, joined by many of the banks' sharpest critics, including consumer groups and securities firms that did not want banks invading their turf. Insurance and real estate agents, together with a few regional banks and administration allies, did not have enough muscle to win passage. Foley and the House Democratic leadership put on a mild effort to whip up support for the bill, but less than a third of House Democrats voted yes. At the same time, nearly a third of House Republicans voted no, despite a personal appeal by President Bush. The bill failed 191-227. *(Vote 399, p. 96-H)*

Committee and Floor Action on HR 3768

With the defeat of a second major banking bill in little more than a week, it was clear to House leaders that only a narrow bill could win support on the floor. Administration officials reluctantly conceded the point.

The Banking Committee met Nov. 19 and approved HR 3768 by a vote of 44-7. The bill as introduced was virtually identical to the version of HR 2094 that was rejected — including the non-controversial floor amendment on banking regulation but not including the Wylie interstate branching amendment. The markup did not go as swiftly as hoped, however, and Gonzalez, in league with Wylie, fought off several amendments.

The Rules Committee met the following day and agreed to allow no amendments on the floor.

Floor debate Nov. 21 was largely desultory and almost entirely in support of the bill — though little of it was enthusiastic. Gephardt drew polite applause with a defense of the bill and the deposit-insurance system generally, but there was none of the usual self-congratulation that accompanied passage of a major bill. Gerald B. H. Solomon, R-N.Y., an ally of the insurance agents, was the only member to forcefully oppose the bill. Solomon, a member of the Rules Committee, was denied the chance to offer a floor amendment rolling back bank insurance powers.

Before the final vote, the House rejected 74-355 a procedural motion offered by Armey that would have had the effect of adding a frequently rejected amendment to pare back deposit-insurance coverage to a single $100,000 account per person per bank. The House then passed the bill 344-84. *(Votes 414, 415, p. 100-H)*

SENATE ACTION

For much of the year, action in the Senate was confined to closed-door negotiations intended to satisfy a majority of the 21 members of the Banking Committee — and the banking, securities, insurance, consumer and administration interests that they represented.

Many of the same battles that were waged publicly in the House were also fought in the Senate — only in private. Formal action in the Senate lagged the House all year long, and as the House moved progressively toward a narrower bill, Senate deliberations did likewise.

Riegle was the leading advocate in the Senate of moving slowly: first replenishing the insurance fund, then overhauling the deposit-insurance system generally, and only later lifting limits on banking in a significant way. He had introduced a deposit-insurance bill (S 3103) in late 1990 that served as an early model for elements of both the administration's bill and HR 6. Riegle's 1990 bill was revised and reintroduced in 1991 as S 543.

However, Riegle abandoned his narrow-bill approach under pressure from members of both parties who wanted to broaden the measure, in particular to permit interstate branching and to repeal Glass-Steagall. Thus he spent much of the spring and early summer in consultation with his committee members, trying to find a combination of provisions that would appeal to a majority in committee and on the floor.

By mid-July, the consultations had gone as far as they could without submitting some contentious issues to votes in committee. Riegle had hoped to gain the support of a majority of the panel, and especially that of the ranking Republican on the panel, Jake Garn of Utah. But just days before Riegle finally unveiled a draft bill for markup, it was clear that he had failed in his quest for consensus.

"There are still some issues here that need to be ventilated," said Richard C. Shelby, D-Ala., one of several committee members pressing for as broad a measure as possible.

Riegle released his draft bill July 16 without Garn's endorsement. It was far less bold than the administration or House Banking versions in key areas, and it clearly reflected the pressures that were being placed on the House bill — which was by then awaiting action in the House Energy and Commerce Committee.

Riegle's bill would not have permitted commercial companies to affiliate with banks, leaving in place existing statutory restrictions on bank ownership. However, it would have allowed strong banks the right to affiliate with securities firms. And it would have put stricter limits on banks seeking to branch nationwide.

On some points, the measure was similar to HR 6. Riegle's approach to requiring banking regulators to move quickly to shut down failing banks was little changed from his 1990 bill. While there were differences in detail on that point with HR 6, the provisions were very compatible in broad terms. Riegle's bill also would have provided the FDIC with a $30 billion line of credit with the Treasury, but with a number of refinements, including a swifter payback schedule and a controversial means of assessing banks for the cost.

Riegle's bill also contained a host of provisions not a part of any companion House measure, many of them controversial. Some would have created new consumer responsibilities for banks; others would have granted so-called lender liability protection to banks stuck with foreclosed real estate that turned out to contain toxic waste sites.

Riegle said his bill was as near to a consensus draft as could be prepared. But the measure drew immediate and antagonistic response from the interests that won biggest in the House Banking Committee, and support from those who had lost. "We disagree, but agreeably," Garn said after ticking off a list of a half-dozen issues over which he and the chairman parted company.

Administration officials were privately said to be deeply upset over parts of Riegle's bill, though publicly they were restrained. "We think it's good that it's as comprehensive as it is," Treasury Under Secretary Robert R. Glauber said

Brady's Concern

Treasury Secretary Nicholas F. Brady, in presenting the administration's plan to overhaul the financial services industry on Feb. 5, talked about the need to relieve banks' stress and to put more money in the hands of consumers and businesses by making banks more profitable.

But what Brady really had his eye on was the fact that U.S. banks were no longer the biggest in the world.

Top Banks in 1969

1. Bank of America
2. Chase Manhattan Bank
3. First National City Bank

Top Banks in 1989

1. Dai-Ichi Kangyo Bank
2. Sumitomo Bank
3. Mitsubishi Bank

"What we're trying to do is something here that strengthens the American banking system, provides more services to the consumer and makes sure that we do something about this situation here where the top bank in the United States is 27th in the world."

Not once but three times Brady pointed to a big chart showing the world's top 30 banks in 1969 and 1989. It showed U.S. banks in the top three spots a generation ago, but none there today. Citibank, the largest in the United States, was the 27th largest in the world at the end of 1990.

It was clear that rankled Brady. "You know," he said, "if there's one chart that's stuck in my mind since the very beginning of this study, that's it."

the day Riegle released his bill. "Obviously, there are elements we would like to see changed." But Riegle insisted that while changes at the margins might be acceptable, he would not support big revisions. "This bill has the items that I, for one, think have to be there," he said.

Opposition to the draft developed immediately within the committee. Aides to as many as 15 committee members — representing some key Democrats as well as most Republicans — met July 17 to discuss their objections and identify proposed changes around which members hoped to form majorities.

Garn, for example, strongly objected to tapping the deposits held in overseas branches of some of the nation's biggest banks as a source of revenue to replenish the insurance fund. Foreign deposits were nominally not insured, but banks would have paid special premiums on them under the Riegle bill in order to raise the cash to pay back any money borrowed from the Treasury.

Terry Sanford, D-N.C., worked hard to relax restraints on interstate branching that were included by Riegle. Shelby and Connie Mack, R-Fla., wanted to strike the block of consumer-oriented provisions, which were hated by banks. And Alan J. Dixon, D-Ill., wanted to give the Federal Reserve Board more discretion to relax fire walls that the bill would have erected to limit financial dealings between banks and their securities affiliates.

Each of these cut to the heart of what Riegle said he wanted to accomplish in the bill.

Despite the brewing objections, Riegle decided at the last minute before Congress left town for its August recess to mark up the bill. He was afraid that delay would be dangerous to the deposit-insurance fund. But he also was concerned that advocates of more dramatic changes in banking than those he favored might win the upper hand if he put off the markup until September.

The decision to go forward turned up the heat on the private negotiations — and led to the resolution of some, but not all, disputes. Democratic and Republican committee aides met throughout the week of July 22, often late into the night; Riegle met several times with Garn, and the two settled a pair of key issues. In return for Garn's assurance that he would not press for broad bank ownership, Riegle agreed to relax fire walls between banks and securities firms.

Banking Committee Action

Many accommodations and some tough votes were required as the committee struggled through three long days of markup July 31-Aug. 2. The course was slow and painful at times; the committee made virtually no decisions through the first day and a half. But for most of the final day the committee moved through controversial amendments at breakneck speed.

In the last hours of markup a contentious dispute over a series of amendments that would have tightened existing restraints on insurance activities by banks threatened to derail the process. Several were adopted, and Garn threatened at one point to walk out and stop the markup if yet another amendment to curtail insurance activities were offered.

In the end, the committee approved S 543 by a fairly narrow 12-9 vote. Riegle's bill suffered some bruises but remained remarkably intact, However, the final vote reflected the feeling of liberals that the measure went too far toward allowing banks into unchartered waters, and of conservatives that it did not go far enough.

Several Democrats — led by Paul S. Sarbanes of Maryland — not only voted against the bill but denounced it as a mistake. "This bill is the seeds of our destruction," Sarbanes exclaimed. "It is an assault on safety and soundness . . . that will come back to haunt us in the years ahead."

Pete V. Domenici, R-N.M., expressed the majority's feeling that the bill was an acceptable compromise. "I did not believe three days ago we would report out a bill," he said. "I think there is far more good than bad, and I don't think we ought to defeat it."

In major action, the committee made the following changes to Riegle's draft bill:

- **Interstate branching.** As in the House, branching was one of the most important fights in the markup. And in what may have been the first key compromise reached, members agreed to allow banking companies to begin in 1993 to cross state lines, both to buy banks and to consolidate their multibank systems into single banks with a network of branch offices. States, however, would have been permitted to opt-out of interstate branching by voting to do so within three years of enactment.
- **Bank Insurance Fund replenishment.** The committee adopted some changes in Riegle's original proposal for letting the FDIC borrow $30 billion from the Treasury. Surviving banks would have been forced to pay special premiums over a period of 15 years to pay off the first $10 billion borrowed to cover losses in failed banks. The committee struck a Riegle-backed plan to assess that special premium not only against all domestic deposits — even those above $100,000, which were nominally not covered by

insurance — but also against deposits in overseas branches of U.S. banks, which also did not carry deposit insurance. The compromise was to assess only domestic deposits.

The change was a victory for bigger banks with large amounts of foreign deposits, but smaller banks got a piece of the deal: In the future, if the FDIC should cover foreign deposits in a failure, the cost to the fund would be charged explicitly against those banks that held foreign deposits.

• **Deposit insurance overhaul.** These provisions in the Riegle draft generally survived. They would have created new procedures for closing failing banks before they were completely broke and virtually ended the practice of protecting big banks as too big to fail. The committee refused to cut back on existing law that guaranteed deposit insurance of $100,000 per account. Bob Graham, D-Fla., tried to substitute a limit of $100,000 per account per institution, but that was defeated.

The committee agreed to let the FDIC cover uninsured deposits when to do so would cost less than any other method of closing a failed bank. But the panel also agreed to let the FDIC impose a 10 percent "haircut," or loss, on those uninsured depositors. However, the committee rejected on a 9-12 vote an amendment by Phil Gramm, R-Texas, to strike language that would have prevented the Federal Reserve from making secured loans to weak banks. The bill was similar to the House measure in that it would have required the Fed to take a loss if it lent to a weak bank that failed, and that loss would have been passed along to taxpayers.

The committee also agreed to allow well-capitalized, well-managed banks to accept insured deposits placed by securities brokers, provided the interest rates paid were not substantially above market norms.

• **Securities affiliations.** By a 10-11 vote, the committee rejected an amendment sponsored by Richard H. Bryan, D-Nev., that would have stiffened the fire walls the bill would have erected between banks and their securities affiliates. Riegle, who negotiated a fire wall compromise with Garn, opposed Bryan and a majority of the panel's Democrats. In return for Riegle's support on fire walls, Garn never pressed amendments that would have opened the door to bank affiliations with commercial companies.

• **Bank regulatory agencies.** The committee dropped a Riegle-drafted provision, adamantly opposed by the administration, that would have created a new bank regulatory agency independent of the Treasury Department, in which most federal banking regulation had been lodged since the Civil War. The issue was too contentious for the Senate committee (as it had been in the House). And though some senators wanted to renew the fight on the floor, it never resurfaced.

Senate Floor

Nearly two months after the committee voted, a draft report to the Senate was still circulating among committee members. With the administration eager for progress, Riegle blamed committee Republicans for the delay.

After the committee report was filed on Oct. 1, the delay continued. As November approached, there was hope that the Senate could act roughly in tandem with the House; those hopes hinged on the Gonzalez-Dingell compromise on securities and insurance activities of banks. Members in both chambers believed that if the House were to accept the Gonzalez-Dingell compromise, the two bills would move close enough to each other that a House-Senate conference could quickly reconcile differences, increasing the likelihood that a broad banking bill could be enacted before Congress adjourned.

With the House defeat of HR 6 on Nov. 4, those plans were dashed, and the Senate's plans to act on S 543 were abandoned. "I want to study the aftermath," Riegle said.

Nine days later, on Nov. 13, as the House prepared to take up the second of its three banking bills, S 543 finally came to the floor. The Senate made progress Nov. 13-14, disposing of several issues before the bill was sidetracked for the balance of that week by a protracted debate over extending unemployment benefits, and by the failure of the second bill in the House. *(Unemployment benefits, p. 301)*

The Senate returned to the bill the following week and slogged through nearly two dozen amendments, adopting 17. Riegle worked hard to push his committee's comprehensive bill through, cutting dozens of deals in the process. Many of those deals were accommodated in a 165-page "managers' amendment" adopted without debate by voice vote an hour before the bill finally passed. Lobbyists said the next day that they were still trying to find out exactly what the amendment did. "We accommodated everybody who wanted to be accommodated," Riegle said.

On the evening of Nov. 21, in a sudden and surprising voice vote with fewer than 10 senators in the chamber, the Senate passed S 543. The action came within two hours of the House having passed HR 3768; the confluence of events appeared to be more than happenstance.

That passage came on a voice vote was also hardly a coincidence. "A lot of people don't want to have to vote ... to refinance the bank insurance fund," Riegle told reporters afterward. Senate aides also said there was a concern that the overwhelming House vote for a narrow bill might also stall momentum on the broader Senate measure, so they wanted to act quickly.

Moments before, Dale Bumpers, D-Ark., a strong opponent of interstate branching, asked for a roll-call vote, but none of the few other senators present would second his request. Riegle talked Bumpers into backing off, and the bill passed, leaving lobbyists outside the chamber still working on potential amendments.

An hour later, Paul Wellstone, D-Minn., took to the floor in protest: "I guess I would not have believed that we would have voted on a bill, tens of billions of dollars, on a voice vote.... I think it reflects poorly on the Senate."

During the first two days of floor action, however, the Senate agreed to several changes that were seen by the bill's advocates as enhancing its chances of passage, and one that threatened to blow up in its face.

Alfonse M. D'Amato, R-N.Y., caught nearly everyone by surprise with an amendment to cap credit card interest rates. The amendment was adopted 74-19 on Nov. 13. With credit card rates averaging nearly 19 percent, many senators found the amendment difficult to oppose. And there was a brief flurry of support for the idea in the House. The amendment was seen as certain veto bait, however. And Garn correctly predicted soon after the amendment was adopted that it would be dropped in negotiations with the House. *(Credit cards, p. 85; vote 251, p. 33-S)*

Behind-the-scenes negotiations the first two days also resulted in the adoption Nov. 14 by voice vote of three amendments to critical parts of the bill:

• **Securities powers.** Provisions that would have partially repealed the Glass-Steagall Act were the first to be dropped. Similar language had already been stripped from the House bill, and senators did not want to fight over how strictly to limit financial and other ties between banks and affiliated securities firms. This action angered Dixon, who denounced the outcome as "junk" and complained that real opportunities for banks to improve their profitability and competitiveness were gone. Dixon blamed the Bush administration for giving up too easily on the Glass-Steagall repeal, arguing that it was worth taking the issue to a joint House-Senate conference. "The administration will accept anything so they can say they got a bill, declare victory and go home," Dixon said.

- **Insurance powers.** Language in the committee version was modified to allow national banks to sell insurance in those states that allowed state-chartered banks to do so. But it would have preserved provisions in the bill that would have closed loopholes that permitted a few banks to sell insurance nationwide. This change eased the unhappiness of Garn and Gramm, who were strongly opposed to the severe insurance restrictions in the committee version. But it also upset insurance agents, who opposed letting banks into their business at all costs.
- **Interstate branching.** The committee version would have permitted banks to open branch offices across state lines unless a state voted to prohibit branching. It was altered by an amendment by Wendell H. Ford, D-Ky. As approved on the floor, banks would have been permitted to branch only by buying an existing bank — unless a state specifically voted to allow the creation of new branches. The Senate action also would have delayed for three years the ability of banking companies that owned banks in multiple states to consolidate those institutions into a single branch network. The committee bill would have allowed consolidation in about 18 months.

Before adopting the Ford amendment, the Senate rejected an amendment by Bumpers that would have permitted interstate branching only in states that explicitly voted to allow it. The Bumpers amendment was killed, 55-39, on a tabling motion. *(Vote 252, p. 33-S)*

Several amendments that could have been bill killers were defeated during the week of Nov. 18. One rejected amendment would have struck an entire title devoted to consumer protection, and another would have greatly restricted the FDIC's access to the money it needed to close failed banks. The Senate refused, 34-62, to table an amendment by Thad Cochran, R-Miss., to strike one consumer section that would have required banks to provide low-income consumers with basic banking or government check-cashing services at modest cost. His amendment was then adopted Nov. 19 by voice vote. *(Vote 257, p. 34-S)*

Senators also adopted a negotiated amendment that was certain to cause trouble with the House. Bryan wanted to reverse a June 1991 Supreme Court decision that closed the door on numerous securities fraud lawsuits seeking monetary damages from such notables as former "junk" bond king Michael R. Milken and former thrift owner Charles H. Keating Jr.

Determined to thwart Bryan, Domenici argued that a small number of law firms and professional plaintiffs were lying in wait to exploit securities laws to force unwarranted legal settlements that would harm stockholders and damage corporate competitiveness. The two agreed to preserve lawsuits that were pending at the time of the court decision and would have been halted by it, but they agreed to prevent future cases.

The Senate also adopted a host of non-banking amendments involving such disparate issues as repeal of an excise tax on yachts, a ban on imports of goods made by Chinese prison labor, U.S. policy toward Yugoslavia, the production of chemical and biological weapons, and the pension rights of Trans World Airlines employees. The Senate-passed bill also retained a provision to require the minting of a newly designed $1 circulating coin.

CONFERENCE, FINAL ACTION

A two-day House-Senate conference that ended in a marathon overnight session Nov. 26-27, produced a compromise bill that did what all sides conceded was the bare minimum — and largely avoided controversy.

The conference concluded at 4:57 a.m., and the House adopted the conference agreement by voice vote six hours later, acting just as soon as congressional staff had finished putting together the legislative language. The Senate adopted the conference agreement later in the afternoon, by a vote of 68-15, clearing the measure for the president. *(Vote 279, p. 36-S)*

The action fulfilled the pressing need to replenish the nearly depleted Bank Insurance Fund by granting the FDIC a $30 billion line of credit with the Treasury to cover losses in failed banks. The $30 billion plus interest was to be repaid over 15 years from higher insurance premiums charged to banks, and at the time of enactment was not expected to result in a direct or indirect cost to taxpayers.

The FDIC was also allowed to borrow additional money on a short-term basis, secured by assets that the agency seized from failed banks. As those assets were sold, the so-called working capital was to be repaid from the proceeds.

In addition, the bill made key changes in the deposit-insurance system in an effort to further reduce losses to the fund. But members resigned themselves to having done only half the job that they had been asked to do by the Bush administration, and that many believed was necessary to prevent major bank failures in the future.

"As far as fixing the problem for the long term, we don't do it," said North Carolina's Stephen Neal, during House floor debate on the final bill Nov. 27. "We do provide some important regulatory reform, several hundred pages of it. . . . We knew how to do much more, and we should have done much more and we didn't."

Wylie conceded that "no one was completely satisfied with the product we came out with." He and other members talked of resuming the fight in 1992, but few members of the House or Senate Banking committees had the stomach for reopening the battle wounds they received during 1991.

In the days immediately after the House and Senate passed HR 3768 and S 543, it was not clear that there would be a conference — or that differences between the bills could be reconciled before adjournment. The narrow House bill was still 339 pages long. And the Senate bill, which contained a wealth of provisions with no counterpart in the House measure, was 829 pages.

Staff and members of the House and Senate Banking committees met over the weekend of Nov. 23-24 to see how far they could get in working out differences informally. Aides worried that as many as nine House committees would have to get involved, so sweeping was the Senate measure. That could have required a huge formal conference committee and delicate negotiations to ensure that all jurisdictional concerns were accommodated.

The biggest question, of course, was interstate branching. The House had twice rejected bills that would have allowed interstate branching, raising doubts that such a provision could survive in conference. Nevertheless, Brady and Riegle decided to try to fight to preserve the provision in a final bill.

Riegle's position was out of character, because he had been reluctant to address issues beyond overhauling the deposit-insurance system since the first of the year. And, ironically, Garn, who favored sweeping changes in bank regulation, seemed to give up on branching. "We're going to end up with a narrow bill," he predicted well before the conference convened.

Congressional leaders met with rank-and-file members and Treasury Department officials over the Nov. 23-24 weekend in repeated efforts to overcome the House's reluctance to accepting interstate branching. But those meetings did not yield a compromise, in large part because insurance and securities lobbyists had succeeded in linking their issues to branching. A compromise that would give insurance agents and the securities industry what they wanted, in return for branching, was not seen as a bargain by the banks. That was particularly true since not all bankers wanted branching, and some who did not could have been harmed by the changes sought by insurance and securities interests.

On Nov. 25, however, the House finally asked for a conference on S 543, after amending it with the text of the much narrower HR 3768.

Riegle tried to pressure his colleagues to act by calling an eleventh-hour hearing on Nov. 25 with the new chairman of the FDIC, William Taylor. Riegle apparently hoped that Taylor would embrace the need for broader banking reform. Instead, while Taylor agreed that some broader change in banking law would be helpful over the long term, his short-term need for money far outweighed those considerations. "We need the money, and we need all of it," Taylor said. Other changes could wait, he said.

In a letter the same day to Riegle, Brady complained that "the narrow bill that we understand is the basis for House/Senate negotiations provides critically needed funding but is otherwise inadequate to the task at hand." But Treasury was clearly resigned to cutting deals that would at least get a narrow bill out of conference and did not insist on a broader measure.

In the end, Riegle criticized administration officials for failing to push hard for a broader bill. "There just wasn't enough appetite for it in the administration," he said at the conclusion of the conference negotiations. "The Treasury had to pursue more aggressively, and they didn't do that."

Although all sides referred to what was passed as a narrow bill, it was hardly anorexic. The final bill weighed in at 437 pages and was still credited as a sweeping measure.

Supporters stressed that the bill contained substantial reforms, particularly language requiring the FDIC to close failed banks in the least costly way possible and to step in to close banks before they went completely broke. The latter provision was tied to a series of tighter rules aimed at forcing banks to maintain a capital cushion against failure and requirements that regulators conduct annual, on-site examinations of the books of all mid-size and large banks.

The least-cost provision was intended to eliminate findings by the regulators that banks were too big to fail, except in the most dire circumstances. Only when the Treasury secretary, the president, the Federal Reserve Board and the FDIC board agreed that a "systemic risk" existed could the FDIC protect all deposits in a failing bank — including those that exceeded the $100,000 limit or were not insured for other reasons.

Supporters noted that the bill placed tighter restrictions on the operations of foreign banks in the United States. Those provisions were drafted largely by the Federal Reserve Board to respond to the worldwide scandal involving the Bank of Credit and Commerce International and its illegal ownership of several large U.S. banks, among them the Washington, D.C.-based First American Bankshares.

The bill also included the Truth-in-Savings Act, a measure that required banks to give their customers more complete and understandable information about the interest earned on deposits. Both the House and Senate had passed versions of the measure numerous times but never in concert with each other. *(1988 Almanac, p. 248)*

There was never much doubt that the conference agreement would drop language permitting interstate branching and that it would not contain any of the other changes sought by the administration and some banking interests to improve the industry's profitability. Not only had the House failed to pass bills that contained such provisions, but the chamber cast an overwhelming 398-3 vote on Nov. 25 insisting that conferees stick with the narrow House-passed bill. *(Vote 423, p. 102-H)*

It was also virtually assured that the conference would drop the Senate's credit card rate-cap amendment.

In fact, most of what was contained solely in the Senate measure fell on the floor, including provisions that would have restricted the ability of banks to sell insurance, given banks some immunity from the costs of cleaning up toxic waste sites that they inherited through foreclosures, and pressed other countries to grant U.S. banks and securities firms treatment similar to that given to their own firms (the so-called Fair Trade in Financial Services Act, which was also incorporated in other measures). *(Defense production act, p. 109)*

Ultimately — although it took time to work through the complex bills and to settle differences that seemed more a matter of style than substance — there were few real fights in conference and very few cases in which conferees actually had to vote to resolve matters.

The House forced the Senate to accept language marginally increasing supervision of credit unions, creating new FDIC programs to promote the disposition of low-income housing, giving incentives to banks that made loans in low-income neighborhoods and including the Truth-in-Savings Act.

The Senate forced the House to drop language requiring state-chartered banks, thrifts and credit unions to obtain federal deposit insurance. ■

Thrift Bailout Fund Replenished Twice

On both sides of Capitol Hill, revulsion against the rising cost of salvaging failed savings and loan associations delayed efforts in 1991 to keep the bailout operation moving — and threatened at one point to derail it.

Twice during the year, Congress passed bills that included provisions to spend more taxpayers' money for the thrift bailout: S 419 in March that provided $30 billion, and HR 3435 in November that provided $25 billion more.

Both times it seemed as if institutional intransigence would prevent action on the bills, and it was only the pressure of strong leadership, particularly in the House, that permitted passage.

Congress was forced to vote early and often on the issue for several reasons. Members refused to consider the administration's request for a permanent appropriation for the Resolution Trust Corporation (RTC), the bailout agency created in August 1989. Such an action would have given the RTC whatever money it needed to cover depositor losses that were guaranteed by the government. And it would have avoided periodic trips to the congressional well. But members argued that such a move would have removed their oversight control. House Speaker Thomas S. Foley, D-Wash., who constantly worried that the House was tying itself in knots over the RTC, was the only member to vocally support a permanent appropriation.

Another reason Congress had to act in early 1991 was that it had refused in late 1990 to act on an administration request for $30 billion for the RTC. That request was left hanging when the 101st Congress adjourned in 1990, and was waiting on the doorstep when the 102nd Congress convened in January 1991. *(1990 Almanac, p. 179)*

The final reason for the repeated votes was that the cost of the bailout continued to climb. When the RTC was created, Congress gave it $50 billion to close failed and failing thrifts. By mid-1990, the administration had conceded that the $50 billion would not come close to completing the job.

Through Dec. 31, 1990, the RTC had closed 531 thrifts and sold two-thirds of those, leaving 179 still under its control. Administration officials estimated that as many as 500 more thrifts could require government action.

Treasury Secretary Nicholas F. Brady had said in mid-1990 that $90 billion to $130 billion would be needed over the RTC's life. In mid-1991 — after Congress had given the RTC $30 billion on top of the original $50 billion — Brady asked for $80 billion more, upping the total estimate of losses in failed thrifts to $160 billion. (The higher number corresponded to the $130 billion estimate of the previous year, adjusted for inflation, he said.) *(1989 Almanac, p. 117)*

As its final act before adjourning in 1991, Congress passed HR 3435, giving the RTC whatever money it needed to stay in business through April 1, 1992, up to a maximum of $25 billion. That was far below the $80 billion requested, and it ensured that Congress would visit the issue at least one more time in early 1992.

Tied to that bill was a series of management reforms.

Opposition to the bailout came from many corners. And an unusual alliance of liberal and conservative groups, ranging from the populist Financial Democracy Campaign to the National Taxpayers Union, found itself opposing the administration's requests for more money. They wanted both a reduction in taxpayer-financed spending and better

BOXSCORE

➡ **Savings and Loan Bailout Financing — Round 1 (S 419: HR 1103, HR 1221, HR 1315).** The bill provided $30 billion to the Resolution Trust Corporation (RTC) to cover depositor losses in failed savings and loan associations, and made minor management changes in the thrift bailout.

Reports: S Rept 102-13; H Rept 102-27.

KEY ACTION

Feb. 5 — S 419 approved by the **Senate** Banking Committee by voice vote.

Feb. 26 — HR 1103 considered by the **House** Banking Committee and rejected on a 19-31 vote.

March 7 — S 419 passed by the **Senate** by 69-30 vote. **House** Banking Committee approved two separate RTC bills, HR 1221, HR 1315.

March 12 — The **House** defeated HR 1315 and three alternatives, one of which was similar to HR 1221.

March 13 — The **House** called up S 419 and amended it with a substitute similar to one of the alternatives rejected the day before. The **House** passed amended S 419 by a vote of 192-181.

March 19 — **House-Senate** conferees merged differing versions in quick session. The **Senate** adopted conference report by voice vote.

March 21 — The **House** cleared S 419 for the president by a vote of 225-188.

March 23 — President Bush signed S 419 — PL 102-18.

➡ **Savings and Loan Bailout Financing — Round 2 (HR 3435).** The bill provided such sums as needed by the Resolution Trust Corporation to cover losses in failed thrifts through April 1, 1992, to a maximum of $25 billion. It also overhauled the management structure of the RTC to eliminate its dual boards of directors and create a strong chief executive officer, and made other management changes in the bailout.

Reports: H Rept 102-358, Parts I and II.

KEY ACTION

Nov. 20 — The **House** Banking Committee approved the bill by a vote of 27-25.

Nov. 27 — The **House** adopted a comprehensive substitute to the committee bill by voice vote, then passed it on a 112-63 standing vote; the **Senate** cleared it, 44-33.

Dec. 12 — President Bush signed HR 3435 — PL 102-233.

management of the hundreds of billions of dollars in loans, real estate and other assets the RTC had acquired from failed thrifts. The opponents did not succeed in forcing a wholesale change in the bailout's financing, or win all the management changes they sought.

The administration signaled on Feb. 28 that it would not accept changes in the salvage operation attached to the financing bill that Congress considered at the beginning of the year. That, in turn, angered House Banking Committee Chairman Henry B. Gonzalez, D-Texas, who denounced the administration's "all-or-nothing intransigence." By year's end, the administration had been to the well so often that it could neither get all the money it wanted nor fend off management changes to the bailout that it opposed.

ROUND 1: $30 BILLION

Treasury Secretary Brady appealed to the Senate Banking Committee on Jan. 23, warning that a delay in giving the RTC more money would require it to shut down after Feb. 28, greatly adding to the bailout's cost.

There were no new issues raised in early 1991 that had not been debated continually since the bailout got under way in 1989. But despite the seeming urgency, it still took two months — until March 21 — for Congress to approve the $30 billion.

Both chambers had difficulty acting, but the House, in particular, went through agony, rejecting multiple bills in committee and on the floor before finally settling on a package that was acceptable to a majority of the membership.

Senate Committee

The Senate Banking Committee met Feb. 5 and by voice vote approved S 419 to provide the RTC with the $30 billion requested by the administration.

Senators were clearly unhappy with the circumstances, reflected in their willingness to send such a significant measure to the floor without a roll-call vote. But they had a relatively easy time at their markup session on the bill, especially in light of what was to happen on the Senate floor and in the House.

Lawmakers such as John Kerry, D-Mass., and Bob Graham, D-Fla., said they found it difficult to give the RTC more money without requiring greater management accountability. And some wanted the RTC to sell assets it had bought from failed thrifts to finance its activities. "It is hard to justify appropriating $30 billion to an institution that has over $140 billion in assets, two-thirds of which are liquid," Graham argued.

But committee Chairman Donald W. Riegle Jr., D-Mich., convinced skeptical lawmakers that the need was too urgent to permit delays. And, although the RTC had assets it could sell, the proceeds were earmarked to repay so-called working capital borrowed by the agency to acquire the assets in the first place.

By voice vote, the committee agreed to an amendment by Jake Garn, R-Utah, to exempt RTC officials from securities laws regulating the packaging of thrift assets into blocks of securities for sale to the public. Federal Deposit Insurance Corporation (FDIC) Chairman L. William Seidman, who also headed the bailout, had expressed concern that RTC officials could be the subject of lawsuits stemming from the sale of the asset-backed securities.

Seidman wanted a blanket liability exemption for the RTC, arguing that the legal question had effectively blocked sales of some assets, slowing down the bailout.

Senate Floor

The Senate began floor debate on S 419 on Feb. 26. But the measure was pulled from consideration two days later after Howard M. Metzenbaum, D-Ohio, an arduous RTC critic, threatened "extended debate" on the measure — a euphemism for a filibuster. The bill was also threatened by a flock of amendments to reduce the amount of money or alter the way the salvage operation was managed.

On March 5, the Senate returned to S 419, passing the bill by a 69-30 vote late March 7. But sponsors had to fend off a half-dozen RTC management accountability amendments that they said would jeopardize enactment. *(Vote 25, p. 5-S)*

Banking Chairman Riegle scheduled a hearing for April 11 on RTC management problems to deflect most amendments. "Let us provide enough money to carry them . . . through the end of September and give us time to see how the machinery itself might be re-engineered," Riegle urged his colleagues on the floor.

The Senate floor debate was neither illuminating nor particularly energetic. Although the chamber had the bill under consideration for the better part of six days, much of the time was spent in quorum calls, a peculiar form of parliamentary limbo endemic to the Senate.

Metzenbaum's filibuster threats disappeared a day or two after he met Feb. 27 with Seidman. In the end, Metzenbaum offered one of only two amendments accepted, clarifying language already in the law requiring the RTC to find ways to reduce the cost of nearly 200 thrifts closed in 1988 with financial guarantees backed by the government. Metzenbaum had made a cause of these pre-bailout 1988 deals and repeatedly but unsuccessfully called for the government to repudiate them.

The Senate also accepted an administration-drafted amendment to language previously adopted in committee to clarify that the officers and directors of the RTC could not be held personally liable for the agency's actions to package and sell mortgages and securities that were taken from failed thrifts.

In three lopsided, roll call votes March 6, the Senate rejected the following amendments:

- By Tom Harkin, D-Iowa, to cut the RTC's financing to $15 billion and stipulate that future requests for money would have to be accompanied by proposals to raise taxes in a progressive manner to cover the additional spending. The amendment was defeated on a tabling motion, 71-28. *(Vote 21, p. 4-S)*
- By Bob Kerrey, D-Neb., to eliminate the dual management structure of the RTC, replacing the agency's oversight board and its board of directors with a single board of directors. The amendment was defeated on a tabling motion, 63-37. *(Vote 22, p. 4-S)*
- By Graham to limit the RTC's additional financing to $15 billion but provide an additional $15 billion on a dollar-for-dollar basis with the net proceeds from the sale of assets held by the RTC. The amendment was defeated on a tabling motion, 80-19. *(Vote 23, p. 4-S)*

House Banking Committee

On Feb. 26, as the Senate was being frustrated in its efforts to act on an RTC financing bill, the House Banking Committee addressed the issue for the first time in early 1991.

The panel spent 10 hours debating a bill (HR 1103) to

RTC Refinancing, Restructuring Provisions

As signed by President Bush on Dec. 12, 1991, the major provisions of HR 3435 — PL 102-233:

Bailout Financing

• **Depositor loss coverage.** Provided "such sums" from the Treasury as needed by the Resolution Trust Corporation (RTC) to cover depositor losses in failed thrifts that were liquidated, sold or otherwise closed.

This open-ended appropriation was capped at $25 billion and could be drawn upon only through April 1, 1992, although money transferred to the RTC would not have to be used by that date.

The RTC previously had been granted $80 billion to cover thrift losses (about $49 billion from taxpayers and $31 billion from the thrift industry). Almost all of that money was spent or earmarked for case resolutions by the time Congress cleared HR 3435.

• **Working capital.** Made no statutory change in the limit on RTC short-term borrowing. The agency borrowed so-called working capital from the public through the Federal Financing Bank (an arm of the Treasury) to cover its cash needs. Those loans were repaid from the sale of assets taken onto the RTC's books from failed thrifts.

A complex formula in existing law limited working capital borrowing in large part to 85 percent of the value of assets held by the RTC. In 1991, the RTC had determined the cap to be $125 billion; the administration sought a statutory increase to $160 billion.

Under the formula, the increase in loss money provided in the law could be used to increase the working capital borrowing cap, but the RTC had no plans to do so, calculating that the existing $125 billion cap would not hinder the agency's operations before April 1, 1992.

• **Extension of RTC life.** Required the RTC to resolve thrifts that failed before Oct. 1, 1993. Previously, the RTC was responsible only for thrifts that failed before Aug. 9, 1992. Those that failed after Oct. 1, 1993, would be the obligation of the Federal Deposit Insurance Corporation (FDIC), unless the RTC previously had been appointed as conservator to manage a weakened institution. Thrifts that were under RTC control and failed after Oct. 1, 1993, would be resolved by the RTC.

The law did not change the Dec. 31, 1996, termination date for the RTC, after which the agency's assets and liabilities were to be transferred to the FSLIC Resolution Fund. That fund was administered by the FDIC to manage the assets and liabilities of thrifts that had failed before the RTC was established and were being managed by the now-defunct Federal Savings and Loan Insurance Corporation (FSLIC).

• **Use of proceeds.** Clarified that after the RTC is terminated on Dec. 31, 1996, proceeds from the sale of assets are first to be used to pay off working capital debt, before being diverted to pay off the $30 billion borrowed by the thrift industry through the Resolution Funding Corporation during the first year of the bailout.

• **Reports.** Required the RTC to report quarterly on details of assets held by and disposed of by the RTC, including: specifics on their book and market value, the amount of the RTC's net recovery from asset sales, specifics about auctions of RTC-held assets, details of working capital loans taken from the Treasury and repaid, updates of the annual budgets for the RTC and its oversight board, plans to phase down the agency's operations after the first quarter of 1994, and details about the number and duties of employees and others hired by the RTC and its oversight board.

The law also required a semiannual, unaudited financial statement in addition to the annual audited financial statement due after the end of each fiscal year.

The requirement for detailed reporting followed complaints from some lawmakers that it was difficult to obtain timely and complete information about RTC financing and activities.

Management Restructuring

• **Chief executive.** Created the position of chief executive officer to manage the RTC and removed the FDIC as exclusive manager of the agency. The chief executive was to be appointed by the president and confirmed by the Senate. The RTC oversight board previously had created a chief executive position, appointed by the RTC's operating board of directors (which was the same as the FDIC board of directors).

• **Operating board of directors.** Repealed existing law designating the FDIC board of directors as the RTC's operating board, leaving daily management in the hands of the newly created chief executive and further insulating the RTC from the FDIC. This and related changes were made effective Feb. 1, 1992.

• **Oversight board.** Expanded the RTC oversight board from five to seven members, adding the RTC chief executive, the director of the Office of Thrift Supervision, and the chairman of the FDIC to its membership and removing the secretary of Housing and Urban Development.

The board was also renamed the Thrift Depositor Protection Oversight Board. The Treasury secretary remained as chairman of the oversight board, and the chairman of the Federal Reserve Board of Governors and two private citizen members remained on the board.

• **Limits on oversight board authority.** Restricted the oversight board's authority by removing its ability to set policies for the RTC. That authority was given to the RTC chief executive. The board was left with the responsibility of reviewing overall strategies, policies and goals.

The law also eliminated previous statutory requirements that the oversight board be accountable for the RTC's operations; its role instead was to monitor the agency's operations.

• **National Housing Advisory Board.** Created a board, chaired by the secretary of Housing and Urban Development, to advise the oversight board on issues related to the availability of affordable housing.

This board, required to meet at least four times a year, complemented a previously created national board to advise the oversight board on issues related to the sale of real estate.

Minorities, Women and Small Businesses

• **Preferences in contracting.** Required the RTC to give companies owned by blacks, Hispanics, Native Americans, Asians and women additional points for technical merit and cost preference when reviewing bids for contracts with the agency.

Joint ventures, in which businesses owned by minorities or women had at least a 25 percent share, were made eligible for contract preferences.

• **Rent-free leasing of branch offices.** Permitted the RTC to lease branch offices of failed or failing thrifts in minority neighborhoods rent-free to banks or thrifts owned by blacks, Hispanics, Native Americans, Asians and women. If the RTC chose to lease branches under these terms, the rent-free period could not be less than five years; the leasing institution would be responsible solely for insurance, taxes and utilities; and the lease could include an option to buy.

In addition, a bank or thrift that sold a branch office in a minority neighborhood on favorable terms to an institution owned by minorities or women, or leased a branch on a rent-free basis, would receive credit for any loss connected with the transaction toward meeting its community lending obligations under the Community Reinvestment Act of 1977.

• **Acquisitions by minority-owned institutions.** Permitted and in some cases required the RTC to grant assistance to minority investors, including minority-owned banks and thrifts, who were seeking to buy a failed or failing thrift that was not minority-owned. An existing program, devised by the RTC, that granted low-interest financing to minority acquirers of a non-minority thrift was made part of the law.

The RTC would have to provide such assistance if a minority-owned acquirer submitted a bid asking for assistance and no other acceptable bid to buy the failed or failing thrift had been received. Such financing would have to be granted with a minimum two-year payback rate, and the interest rate charged could not exceed the average cost of borrowing for the RTC at the time of the loan.

In addition, the RTC was allowed to grant other assistance, including the transfer of assets from other thrifts under the RTC's control that were not part of the purchase proposal.

• **Small businesses.** Required the RTC to set an annual goal for contracting with small businesses, including those owned by socially or economically disadvantaged people.

Affordable Housing

• **Credit enhancement.** Granted the RTC broad authority to make loans, share in the risk and provide other credit enhancements for the purpose of selling housing units for low- and moderate-income people. The RTC was permitted to extend credit enhancements for tax-exempt bonds that were sold by nonprofit organizations in order to buy low- and moderate-income housing.

• **Property eligible for preferential treatment.** Broadened an existing RTC affordable housing program (created by the original thrift bailout law — PL 101-73) to include single-family and multifamily housing held by thrifts that were open and operating under an RTC conservatorship. The program made certain property available on a right-of-first-refusal basis to eligible low- and moderate-income people, and state and local housing authorities.

Previously, only property seized by the RTC from failed thrifts was eligible; the law extended the program to property held by thrifts still in business. Because this change was expected to result in a greater loss to the RTC, the provision regarding multifamily housing was only allowed to take effect to the extent that Congress appropriated money to cover the cost.

• **Time limit for sale.** Extended from 90 days (under previous law) to 180 days the right-of-first-refusal period during which single-family residences would be marketed under the affordable housing program. The period for housing agencies to submit qualified bids for multifamily housing was also extended.

• **Veterans preference.** Clarified that households with members who are veterans were eligible to purchase single-family residences under the affordable housing program.

• **Anti-speculation requirements.** Required purchasers of low- and moderate-income housing to certify their intent to occupy the property as a principal residence for one year after the purchase. As a further deterrent to speculation in RTC-held affordable housing, the RTC was required to recapture 75 percent of the profits from the resale of a unit within the first year.

• **Protection for tenants.** Permitted the RTC to sell single-family residences that fell within the affordable housing program to existing tenants who did not meet income criteria, provided that doing so would prevent unnecessary displacement of those tenants and that they agreed to occupy the residence for one year.

• **Sales price.** Removed a previous law requirement that the RTC sell single-family properties at the minimum sales price set by the agency, unless a lower price was deemed necessary to expedite the sale. The change would permit below-minimum sales at any time.

Miscellaneous

• **Appraisal standards.** Deferred from July 1, 1991, to Dec. 31, 1992, the effective date for mandatory state standards for licensed real estate appraisers. This provision was also included in the big banking bill (S 543) that Congress cleared before adjourning.

• **Capital leniency for housing loans.** Required that mortgage loans for the purchase of single-family and multifamily housing be weighted at 50 percent of their value for computation of minimum capital-to-asset ratios for banks and thrifts. The effect was to cut in half the amount of capital required as a cushion for such loans. Immediately after clearing HR 3435, the Senate passed a second bill (S 2131) to repeal the section on capital leniency.

The House did not act on S 2131, but during Senate floor debate, it was asserted that the House would agree to repeal the provision and that the administration would not put it into effect until the House had an opportunity to act. ■

provide $30 billion to the RTC before killing it on a 19-31 vote. All the Republicans and a third of the Democrats voted against sending the measure to the House floor.

The final vote came only after the committee had adopted a raft of controversial amendments, including one to require that future infusions of cash for the bailout be financed either by increased taxes or offsetting spending cuts.

Amendment authors Joseph P. Kennedy II, D-Mass., and Jim Slattery, D-Kan., said it was intended to force Congress to find a way to pay for the salvage operation up front, rather than through borrowing tens of billions of dollars and paying hundreds of billions more in interest costs over the next 30 years. But the amendment was opposed strongly by Republicans and by Speaker Foley and was seen by some as the killer amendment on the bill.

Another adopted amendment seen as a key roadblock to passage would have required states with large numbers of failed thrifts to pay part of the cleanup cost if they wanted their state-chartered institutions to remain eligible for deposit insurance.

Similar amendments were defeated during consideration of the original thrift salvage bill in 1989.

The aborted markup renewed questions about Gonzalez's ability to manage the committee. He had survived a challenge in December 1990 to his re-election as chairman that was based in large part on his relationships with committee members and on the sometimes chaotic way the committee operated.

But the day after the bill was killed, Gonzalez said the committee had merely been working its will. And he insisted that any new money would have to be accompanied by provisions making the RTC more accountable.

Gonzalez met with Foley on the afternoon of Feb. 27 and again on Feb. 28 to see if there was a way to get the refinancing bill back on track. But there was no consensus on how to proceed. Gonzalez pointedly warned of a "bloodletting" on the House floor if the leadership tried to bypass the committee and call up a financing bill devoid of the amendments.

The committee met again two weeks later, on March 7, the same day the Senate was finally able to pass its RTC bill. Compared with the panel's prior contentious and ultimately unsuccessful effort, the second markup session was a cakewalk.

In a March 1 letter to his Democratic colleagues, Gonzalez telegraphed the message he had been given in several meetings with Foley. "The leadership strongly recommends that we produce a bill Republicans can support," he wrote. And when the committee convened, it was immediately clear that Gonzalez had cut a deal with ranking Republican Chalmers P. Wylie of Ohio to keep the markup from breaking down again.

The committee ultimately approved not one but two bills on March 7:

• HR 1221, sponsored by Gonzalez, a slimmed-down measure providing $30 billion and containing some of the controversial provisions embraced a week earlier by the panel's Democratic majority.

• HR 1315, sponsored by Wylie, a "clean" bill containing only the requested $30 billion.

The committee first approved HR 1315, on a 36-13 vote, after Gonzalez and Wylie cooperated to keep it free of amendments.

The committee then approved HR 1221, on a 38-13 vote. That bill included provisions to require the RTC to use the "least cost" method of closing failed thrifts, increasing the amount of housing held by the RTC that was eligible for a special program aimed at low-income buyers and nonprofit housing agencies, and calling for the RTC to set aside 25 percent of its contracts for companies headed by minorities and women.

This last provision was criticized as a quota by Republicans. But HR 1221 was kept free of all but one technical amendment intended to deflect complaints that the measure violated congressional budget rules.

The agreement to allow both bills out of committee was obvious: Of the committee's 31 Democrats, 21 voted in favor of Wylie's bill; in return, 12 of 20 committee Republicans supported Gonzalez's bill.

House Rules Committee

The Rules Committee heard the afternoon of March 7 from many of the committee members whose amendments had been adopted the week before but were either rejected or not allowed to be offered at the second markup. The Rules panel then politely decided to keep most of the amendments off the floor.

The committee then crafted a complicated floor procedure designed to give members an opportunity to vote as many as four times for the extra $30 billion for the RTC. Each vote was tied to a different scheme to make the bailout agency more accountable or to finance it directly rather than through long-term borrowing. At the base was Wylie's bill (HR 1315), which would have simply provided the RTC with $30 billion. Under this "king of the hill" procedure, the last version passed was to be the one approved — regardless of the vote totals.

House Floor

Like the Banking Committee, the full House had to try twice in early 1991 before it succeeded in passing a bill replenishing the RTC's coffers. One effort failed March 12, but with the House leadership in control the next day, a second effort finally succeeded.

When the House convened March 12 to debate the RTC question, it had all four alternatives before it — amounting to two Republican and two Democratic options.

After about seven hours of debate, all four options were defeated. They were:

- A proposal sponsored by Slattery and Kennedy that was similar to the amendment they offered in committee to require tax increases or spending cuts to pay for future RTC financing beyond the $30 billion. The Slattery-Kennedy alternative was defeated, 186-237, but was the only option to win the support of a majority of Democrats. It got only six GOP votes, however. *(Vote 39, p. 10-H)*
- A proposal by Wylie that would have required the RTC to report on efforts at improving its management and contracting with businesses headed by minorities and women. Wylie's substitute was expected to draw some moderate Democratic support, but it wound up with only 39 votes from that side of the aisle. It was defeated 190-235. However, the bill that came back to the House floor the next day — and that passed — was modeled closely on this alternative. *(Vote 40, p. 10-H)*
- A proposal by Gonzalez that would have expanded the RTC's role in increasing the nation's stock of affordable housing, granted new tenant-rights protections to renters in RTC-owned apartments, given nonprofit groups a shot at acquiring environmentally sensitive lands held by the RTC, and set a goal that 25 percent of the RTC's contracts for asset management and disposition be earmarked for businesses headed by minorities and women. The contracting provision was a key sticking point. Republicans denounced it as a quota, but many liberal Democrats insisted on it. In the end, fewer than half the Democrats voted yes, and the option was defeated, 121-303. *(Vote 41, p. 10-H)*
- Wylie's clean bill. It was defeated 201-220, with three-fourths of the Republicans but less than a third of the Democrats in favor. *(Vote 42, p. 10-H)*

A breakdown in Democratic leadership strategy contributed to the failure of all four options. Foley, who had wanted the RTC financing issue disposed of quickly and quietly, had previously signaled his support for the clean bill. He had spoken against the Slattery-Kennedy alternative. And the Rules Committee — an arm of the leadership — had concocted a procedure for floor debate that seemed to give an edge to the Republican alternatives.

But at some point between the Rules Committee meeting March 7 and the floor vote March 12, Democratic leaders decided that they would work for adoption of Gonzalez's alternative, even though Republicans were united against it. When the Democratic whips met the morning of March 12, it was apparent that all four options would be defeated, according to members who attended. But Democrats stuck with their plan.

When the Gonzalez substitute failed and the House moved quickly to vote on final passage of Wylie's bill, there was no effort to persuade members to vote yes and get on with other business. Members stood in the aisles and well of the House watching the electronic vote boards as the measure slowly went down to defeat. Most committee chairmen voted no. So did a majority of Banking Committee members, including Gonzalez and most of the panel's senior Democrats, though they more than others knew the money had been promised to depositors and had to be provided sooner or later.

The eventual passage of a bill took intervention at the highest levels.

After the defeats on March 12, both sides dug in their heels. On the morning of March 13, President Bush called Foley, urging him to find a way to give more money to the RTC. The compromise that finally attracted a majority of the House — but importantly, not a majority of Democrats — was hammered out early that afternoon in Foley's office by the Speaker, Republican leader Robert H. Michel of Illinois and Brady. Gonzalez and Wylie were present, as were RTC officials and aides.

The compromise essentially was to take the rejected Wylie alternative and add a portion of Gonzalez's language on affordable housing.

The easiest way to proceed was to call up S 419, the Senate-passed bill, and amend it. So in a hurry-up meeting late March 13, the Rules Committee agreed to that approach.

There was some doubt that the House would agree to the procedure. It bypassed a rule requiring that measures lay over before they are considered, and thus a two-thirds majority had to agree to debate the bill. But opponents chose not to band together to defeat the procedural motion. After two more hours of debate, the House first voted 213-197 to amend the Senate measure with the compromise language. It then passed the amended bill by a 192-181 vote. The compromise got roughly the same amount of Republican support as Wylie's bill had the previous night;

it just picked up enough extra Democrats to pass. *(Votes 50, 51, pp. 12-H, 14-H)*

Passage did not come without a last moment of drama. With the running electronic tally at 144-145, Foley stepped down from the Speaker's rostrum, picked up a green card — signifying a yes vote — and handed it to the clerk. As a matter of tradition, Speakers rarely vote. At the moment Foley acted, the vote changed, and the bill was soon passed.

Final Action

House and Senate conferees had little difficulty agreeing March 19 on a compromise bill joining the two versions of S 419. That was due primarily to the fact that the Senate version had little language beyond that providing the money, and the House version had been negotiated at the highest levels — by Foley, Michel and Brady.

Conferees met for about 15 minutes and agreed to marry the two versions of the bill almost intact. They made only minor changes in Senate language — sought by the administration — to clear up concerns that RTC employees might be subject to civil suits under securities law for actions taken in trying to sell off assets, particularly securities. The RTC had a $6 billion junk bond portfolio and millions of dollars in mortgages. It planned to offer securities to private investors that were backed by these junk bonds and mortgages in order to get a better price.

The Senate called up the bill later the same day and adopted the conference report by voice vote. Two days later, on March 21, the House cleared the bill with a minimum of debate.

The House adopted the conference report by a vote of 225-188 — the biggest margin mustered in a series of contentious votes over the previous two weeks. A majority of Democrats still opposed the measure, however. *(Vote 56, p. 14-H)*

Major Provisions

As cleared, the major provisions of S 419:

- **Additional financing.** Provided the RTC with $30 billion from the Treasury to cover losses in failed thrifts.
- **Reporting requirements.** Required the RTC to submit detailed, quarterly financing plans for the bailout. The first such plan was due 30 days after enactment. The bill also required annual General Accounting Office audits of the RTC. Those audits had to be sent to Congress within six months of the end of the fiscal year.
- **Management reforms.** Directed the RTC to improve its information systems and management of conservatorships, speed its sale of assets and otherwise address complaints about its efficiency and performance.
- **Employee immunity.** Clarified that RTC officers and employees were not subject to civil securities-fraud suits resulting from the sale of securities backed by mortgages, junk bonds or other assets. The provision did not expand protections for government employees; they were still subject to a suit if there was criminal action.
- **Affordable housing.** Expanded the scope of provisions in the original salvage bill involving sales of low-income housing to individuals and public and nonprofit housing agencies. The program was extended to properties held by thrifts being run by the RTC under conservatorship — not just houses and apartments that had been in the inventories of thrifts closed by the RTC. And the bill removed a requirement that the RTC get a minimum sales price for the property, freeing the RTC to sell for nominal amounts.
- **Minority contracting.** Required the RTC to report twice a year on its efforts to contract with companies headed by minorities or women.

ROUND 2: $25 BILLION MORE

The effort to infuse the bailout with additional money in late 1991 was even more problematic.

Seidman, who as chairman of the FDIC also ran the RTC, told the Senate Banking Committee on June 21 that $80 billion would be needed to finish the job.

He also testified that the time had come to wean the RTC's salvage operation from the FDIC and give it a new board of directors and management team accountable to the administration and Congress. That recommendation paralleled an increasingly strong view on Capitol Hill that the RTC's complex management scheme was too unwieldy and contributed to the sense that the agency was out of control. *(Seidman resignation, p. 77)*

Treasury Secretary Brady and others in the administration who had previously objected to overhauling the RTC's management reluctantly accepted that argument by year's end.

In part because the RTC issue was so fractious, and in part because the House and Senate Banking committees were enmeshed in a difficult fight over how to overhaul the nation's banking laws, nothing happened for months. *(Banking overhaul, p. 75)*

In fact, the Senate Banking Committee never acted on the second RTC bill of the year, and the Senate eventually accepted a House-passed bill (HR 3435) without amendment. Final passage of HR 3435 was Congress' last act before adjourning for the year. As cleared, the bill gave the RTC only a fraction of the money it wanted, and imposed a long series of management changes on the agency. *(Major provisions, p. 79)*

House Financial Institutions Subcommittee

The House Banking Committee's work on Round 2 of the year's bailout battle picked up where Round 1 left off.

The Financial Institution's Subcommittee voted Oct. 2 to force Congress and the president to pay for the balance of the savings and loan bailout — at least $60 billion worth — through spending cuts and tax increases, not by increasing the federal deficit through additional borrowing.

The subcommittee spent three days on the bailout financing bill (HR 3435), disposing of more than 50 amendments concerning the financing and management of the bailout, real estate sales by the RTC, plus issues involving the RTC's dealings with small businesses and those owned by women and minorities.

Just before finishing on Oct. 8, the subcommittee voted a second time in favor of financing the bailout with new taxes or spending cuts, despite strong opposition from senior House Democrats and a united bloc of Republicans. A last-minute GOP effort to strike the "pay as you go" provision failed on a near party-line 16-18 vote. The subcommittee then approved the bill 20-16, with most Republicans in opposition.

The bill authorized $20 billion more for the RTC to cover losses in failed thrift institutions and required the president and congressional leaders to come up with a plan to find another $60 billion without borrowing it. The plan was crafted by Kennedy, who had unsuccessfully offered a somewhat different pay-as-you-go proposal to the RTC bill earlier in the year.

In the eyes of the administration, most Republicans and some senior Democrats, the provision created at least two problems: It could have postponed an infusion of new cash for the bailout, and it could have spurred a nasty partisan debate over the source of the money.

Deputy Treasury Secretary John E. Robson called the subcommittee-approved bill "flawed and inadequate" and said he would strongly recommend a veto if the measure cleared Congress in the subcommittee-approved current form.

Wylie cautioned: "I'm afraid that the Kennedy amendment would kill the bill."

Although the financing language caused the most heartburn for the administration, it was not the only provision in the subcommittee bill that drew fire.

The most far-reaching of these would have required the RTC to auction off real estate that it took over from failed thrifts and held in its possession for an extended period. Members on both sides of the aisle complained repeatedly about the RTC's asset sales practices, particularly about the agency's unwillingness or inability to unload land and other property. Much of the RTC's asset inventory was financed with borrowed money. The sooner the assets were unloaded, the less taxpayers had to pay to carry the debt. An amendment by Frank Annunzio, D-Ill., would have required the RTC to auction any property held more than nine months. It was adopted on an 18-12 bipartisan vote.

The subcommittee also adopted by voice vote an amendment by Bruce F. Vento, D-Minn., that would have given state and local governments and nonprofit conservation groups a right of first refusal to buy historically, environmentally or scientifically sensitive property held by the RTC. By a 22-14, mostly party-line vote, the subcommittee agreed to an amendment by Peter Hoagland, D-Neb., that would have required the RTC to maintain such properties in the condition they were in when the agency took them over.

House Banking Committee

The full Banking Committee waited nearly two months before acting on HR 3435. In the midst of its difficulties on the broader banking overhaul bill, the committee met Nov. 19-20 and narrowly approved the RTC measure.

By a 27-25 vote, with most junior Republicans and key senior Democrats opposed, the committee approved the bill, after voting to alter the financing plan that had been approved in subcommittee. The revised bill would have given the RTC $20 billion and required that any additional money for the agency come from spending cuts elsewhere in the federal budget. Thus, the already controversial pay-as-you-go plan was changed to a "cut as you go" plan that did not specifically allow for tax increases to finance the bailout.

The committee spent two long days marking up the bill and disposed of more than 75 amendments, including two comprehensive substitutes for the bill that contained alternative financing mechanisms.

As soon as the committee acted, it was clear than HR 3435 would not be enacted in that form. But just what might happen remained in doubt until Congress was almost ready to adjourn. In the end, much of the Banking Committee bill, including its financing plan, was discarded. Many of its management changes were kept in a revised form.

Other than the pay-as-you-go change, the bill approved by the Banking Committee differed little from the subcommittee version. In addition to continuing to pay for the bailout, the bill would have restructured the RTC and its Treasury-dominated Oversight Board. It would have created a new chief executive officer for the agency and required that the CEO be appointed by the president and confirmed by the Senate. The FDIC would have been stripped of its day-to-day RTC management responsibilities. And the RTC would have been given the task of closing failed thrifts until Oct. 1, 1993, a year longer than envisioned in the 1989 bailout law that created the RTC.

The bill would have imposed new requirements on the RTC's hiring of lawyers and other outside contractors, capped RTC employee salaries and permitted background checks of employees. It would have set conditions on seller financing of RTC-owned real estate and revised a special low-income housing program created when the thrift bailout began.

The full committee dropped a subcommittee-approved RTC hiring freeze and a requirement that the agency auction off real estate held for more than six months.

House Floor, Final Action

With work on the bank overhaul bill done and adjournment only hours away, the House finally passed HR 3435 on Nov. 27 — but it was not the version of the bill approved in committee.

The House passed the bill on a 112-63 division vote, a seldom-used procedure requiring members to stand and be counted. GOP efforts to force a roll-call vote failed. And approval came only after conservative Republicans tried unsuccessfully to get a rule allowing them to offer an "economic growth" tax-cut package as an amendment to the RTC bill.

"I, for one, will not be voting for one more nickel to go down the RTC rat hole" until action is taken on the economic stimulus plan, said Vin Weber, R-Minn. But other Republican leaders warned that the RTC bill was necessary to help the thousands of middle-income taxpayers who have their savings in troubled thrifts. "This is not a pleasant task, but we have, quite frankly, no alternative," Michel said.

The House vote came on a proposal that had been crafted by Democratic and Republican leaders in consultation with the Senate and the administration, once it was clear that the House Banking Committee version was unacceptable.

The plan, put together by Wylie and Doug Barnard Jr., D-Ga., dropped some of the Banking Committee's management provisions and revised others, and it provided for "such sums as may be necessary until April 1, 1992, not to exceed $25 billion." It also included language from a draft Senate bill on restructuring the RTC to consolidate its two boards of directors into one and to appoint a chief executive officer who would also serve on the board. The Barnard-Wylie substitute was adopted by voice vote before the House passed the bill.

The Senate, meanwhile, had taken no formal action on the bill. But after the House passed HR 3435, the Senate cleared it for the president by a vote of 44-33. It was the last significant act the Senate took before adjourning. *(Vote 280, p. 36-S)*

A last-minute flap over House changes in capital standards for certain real estate loans threatened to hold up the bill in the Senate, but negotiations with the House and the administration led to an agreement to repeal that provision retroactively in 1992. ■

Money Laundering Bill Still a Non-Starter

After an unsuccessful endeavor to move a money laundering initiative as stand-alone legislation in 1990, Senate sponsors attached the measure to a broad bank powers bill (S 543) in 1991, but that plan also failed.

Increasing reports about the money laundering operations of drug traffickers prompted the House and Senate to pass legislation with broad bipartisan support, but the end-of-session crush killed plans to clear the measure.

The goal was to stop what had grown into a $100 billion-a-year money laundering operation in the United States. The bill was intended to catch the attention of both unscrupulous bank operators who had cooperated in laundering schemes and banks that had shown negligence by not complying with currency transaction laws.

Under the bill, regulators could appoint a conservator or terminate the deposit insurance of banks convicted of money laundering. Individuals found guilty of laundering offenses could be banned from the banking business forever.

House Banking Committee sponsors moved a bill (HR 26) through the House early in the session, while Senate sponsor John Kerry, D-Mass., chose to add it to a measure that replenished the Bank Insurance Fund and provided banks with broad new business opportunities. Money laundering provisions were in the version of S 543 passed by the Senate, but were stripped out during a conference with the House.

Financial Institutions Subcommittee Chairman Frank Annunzio, D-Ill., had begun moving a bill in 1990 mostly out of anger at what he considered light treatment by the Justice Department of the Bank of Credit and Commerce International, a worldwide banking empire that closed after regulators in several countries accused its executives of widespread bank fraud and money laundering. In early 1990, the Luxembourg-based institution agreed to plead guilty and pay a $14.8 million fine for laundering money in the United States through Florida branches — a slap on the wrist, complained Annunzio.

After hearing from law enforcement officials, Annunzio and Kerry, the chief Senate sponsor, became convinced that denying a drug trafficker's financial lifeline could be a successful tactic in the war on drugs. The Treasury Department estimated that international drug profits amounted to about $300 billion annually.

Agents from the Federal Bureau of Investigation testified that drug dealers had found banks, thrifts and credit unions to be the most reliable means to launder profits because many institutions seldom asked questions about the source of the money.

House Action

The House Banking Committee approved HR 26 by voice vote on March 7. The Financial Institutions Subcommittee had approved it on Feb. 27.

Under the bill, banks, thrifts and credit unions faced the financial equivalent of the death penalty — revocation of their charters or deposit insurance coverage — if convicted of money laundering offenses. Bank officers would face a lifetime ban from working in a financial institution if found guilty of involvement in laundering schemes.

Although the bill provided new tools to regulators to punish banks engaged in laundering schemes, it did not require that they be used. Regulators would have to hold a disciplinary hearing for a convicted bank before deciding on a penalty. They would have to consider the extent to which top bank officials were involved in the crime, whether the institution had policies in place to prevent money laundering, and the degree of cooperation regulators received from senior management after an offense was uncovered.

The bill also required the Treasury Department to study the feasibility of withdrawing $50 and $100 bills from circulation. Traffickers operated with such a high cash volume that they needed large-denomination bills.

The language in HR 26 had been refined somewhat since the 1990 debate. The Bush administration successfully argued for a few changes.

The maximum civil penalty against a financial institution for engaging in a pattern of violating currency-reporting requirements was increased from $5,000 to $50,000.

Also at the request of the administration, a provision was removed that would have required banks to annually renew customer exemptions from currency-reporting requirements. The administration said the requirement would impose an excessive cost burden on banks.

The Banking Committee also approved, by voice vote, an amendment by Chalmers P. Wylie, Ohio, the panel's ranking Republican, to repeal a 1988 law requiring the administration to negotiate anti-money-laundering agreements with other countries. The law mandated sanctions on countries that did not respond to the negotiations. Wylie's amendment contained less explicit language directing Treasury to enter into discussions with other countries. Wylie argued that existing law offended foreign countries and impeded the conclusion of treaties.

But the negotiating requirements were reinserted when another committee with jurisdiction, the Foreign Affairs panel, considered the bill on May 21. A revised version of the negotiating provision gave the administration discretion over when to impose sanctions. But it also required Treasury to expand the scope of negotiations to include agreements on reporting suspicious transactions.

The version passed by the House by a 406-0 vote on June 11 included the Foreign Affairs Committee language after Annunzio gave his assent. *(Vote 147, p. 36-H)*

Senate, Final Action

Due to a conflict over unrelated issues, Senate Banking Committee Chairman Donald W. Riegle Jr., D-Mich., attached money laundering provisions to S 543, a comprehensive banking bill that dominated the attention of the panel in 1991. Riegle was engaged in a dispute with Jake Garn, Utah, ranking Republican on the panel, over legislation to protect lenders from liability under the "superfund" law when they foreclosed on property that needed hazardous waste cleanup. In an attempt to limit the number of bills Garn could attach the proposal to, Riegle decided to combine a number of banking-related measures with S 543.

With no debate on the provisions to crack down on money laundering, the Banking panel approved the bill, 12-9, on Aug. 2. With the session nearing a close, the Senate approved the measure on Nov. 21 by voice vote.

Senators then took the banking bill to conference to reconcile it with a much slimmer House version. Both sides agreed that only a scaled-down bill stood a chance of being cleared before adjournment. One of the extraneous provisions stripped was the money laundering language. ■

House Approved Coin, War Medal Bill

At the end of the 1991 legislative session, the House approved by voice vote legislation (HR 3337) combining several commemorative coin measures and a bill honoring Persian Gulf veterans with a medal.

As approved by the House, HR 3337 authorized the minting of commemorative coins for the 200th anniversary of the laying of the cornerstone for the White House, the soccer World Cup Games to be held in the United States in 1994 and the quincentennial of Christopher Columbus' discovery of America. It also authorized silver medals for the veterans of the Persian Gulf War.

Although the Senate approved HR 3337 by voice vote, senators attached two amendments that prevented the bill from clearing in 1991.

When the House-passed version of HR 3337 went to the Senate on Nov. 27, the last day of the session, Sen. Alan Cranston, D-Calif., amended the bill with a proposal to redesign the backs of existing coins. Cranston had tried since 1987 to get Congress to require the U.S. Mint to redesign the tail sides of the half dollar, quarter, dime, nickel and cent. In 1990, Cranston attached his proposal to a number of other measures only to see the provision stripped off at the last minute. *(1990 Almanac, p. 196)*

In 1991, when the amended version of HR 3337 returned to the House, Pennsylvania Republican Curt Weldon objected to it because along with the Cranston amendment, the Senate also attached language requiring the minting of a 1993 coin commemorating James Madison and the bicentennial of the Bill of Rights.

Weldon wanted a coin minted in 1993 that would honor Benjamin Franklin as the father of the American fire service, with the sales going to support firefighter programs around the country. But the U.S. Mint said, and House Banking Consumer Affairs and Coinage Subcommittee Chairman Esteban E. Torres, D-Calif., agreed, that Congress was authorizing too many commemoratives. The Mint wanted to produce only one commemorative coin a year.

Coin Redesign

Under Cranston's proposal, the first redesigned coin would commemorate the 200th anniversary of the ratification of the Bill of Rights. After two years, the bicentennial coin would then have its design changed again. The secretary of the Treasury would select the design after consultation with the U.S. Mint and the U.S. Commission of Fine Arts, which was authorized to oversee the redesign of the nation's coins.

The push behind coin redesign came from a former member of the U.S. Commission of Fine Arts, Diane Wolf, a prominent Upper East Side New York socialite, who called the old designs "ordinary and boring" and said the public would be happy to see them replaced.

In testimony Nov. 6 before the House Banking Consumer Affairs and Coinage Subcommittee, Eugene H. Essner, acting director of the U.S. Mint, argued that "there is no indication, other than some in the coin collecting community, that there is public dissatisfaction with our current coin designs."

COLUMBUS, COINS, MEDAL

The House on July 31 passed bills authorized the minting of two coin sets: a 1992 set celebrating the 500th anniversary of Columbus' discovery of America and a 1994 set commemorating the first-ever U.S. hosting of the World Cup Games. Another measure authorized a commemorative medal for veterans of Operation Desert Storm.

By voice vote, the House approved a bill (HR 2801) to mint 750,000 gold $5 coins, 5 million silver $1 coins and 5 million half-dollar pieces to underwrite the cost of staging the hugely popular soccer games. All would be sold to collectors at a surcharge, with proceeds going to the organizing committee for the games.

A second bill sought to resolve the dispute about who really discovered America. "The only difference is this: When Columbus discovered America, it stayed discovered," said Rep. Frank Annunzio, D-Ill. The House on July 31 voted 408-2 on Annunzio's bill (HR 500) to mint 10.5 million coins commemorating the discovery. *(Vote 243, p. 60-H)*

Proceeds from sales of the coins would endow an educational foundation to offer fellowships to scholars "to encourage new discoveries in all fields of endeavor for the benefit of mankind."

The House voted 381-37 for a bill (HR 1107) to honor Desert Storm veterans with a congressional silver medal. *(Vote 242, p. 60-H)*

Pentagon officials said Desert Storm veterans had been honored enough and that the medal might suggest lesser appreciation for the veterans of other conflicts.

The House Banking Committee had not acted on the gulf war medal measure or the commemorative coin bills, simply sending the measures directly to the House floor after the subcommittee approved them.

The Subcommittee on Consumer Affairs and Coinage on July 25 gave voice vote approval to HR 1107, HR 500 and HR 2801. Under HR 1107, about 640,000 members of the military would be eligible for the medal, which would not be worn on a uniform.

Opponents said the troops had been honored enough. The Pentagon presented two medals as well as a variety of ribbons and badges to selected Desert Storm veterans.

The majority of the bill's cosponsors had voted in January against authorizing the president to go to war with Iraq, leading the panel's ranking Republican, Al McCandless, Calif., to hint that some members supported the measure to hedge a possible backlash in the November elections.

"This is not a referendum on support for Desert Storm," McCandless said. "Our votes on the floor speak for that. The question is whether another multimillion-dollar medal is appropriate."

Officials at the U.S. Mint estimated that it would have cost roughly $6.4 million to produce the medal, although Larry LaRocco, D-Idaho, said that with less-expensive packaging it could be produced for considerably less. LaRocco included an amendment directing the Mint to defray some of the costs by marketing a bronze replica and by using stockpiled silver. And the Treasury Department would have had to certify that the Mint had garnered enough funds to cover the costs before beginning production of the medal.

When the subcommittee acted on HR 500, the Christopher Columbus coin, and HR 2801, the 1994 World Cup coin, members rejected a McCandless amendment to both bills directing that 50 percent of the surcharge on the sale of the coins go toward reducing the national debt. ■

Tax 'Extenders' Clear at Session's End

A dozen popular tax breaks won a six-month reprieve in legislation cleared in the final day of the first session of the 102nd Congress.

Earlier, Congress approved several other targeted tax changes, mostly to pay for specific programs. But lawmakers did not pass any major tax legislation in 1991, and even the so-called extenders were presumed dormant until the final days of the session. House Ways and Means Chairman Dan Rostenkowski, D-Ill., introduced several bills to simplify the tax code, but their future depended on the emergence of a larger tax bill. An attempt to cut the Social Security payroll tax never got off the ground. *(Social Security tax, p. 108)*

By year's end, however, the extremely sluggish economy and the impending presidential election campaign left little doubt that there would be a major battle in 1992 over tax changes to help the middle class and to stimulate the economy.

EXTENDING EXPIRING PROVISIONS

With adjournment approaching, key lawmakers in the House and Senate pledged not to attach any amendments to the legislation renewing the tax breaks — known as "extenders" because Congress traditionally renewed them a year at a time. That agreement paved the way for quick action on the bill (HR 3909 — H Rept 102-377) and prevented it from becoming bogged down with other controversial tax proposals, such as a Republican plan for lowering the tax rate on capital gains.

On Nov. 25, two days before the end of the session, Rostenkowski held a quickly scheduled Ways and Means markup where a bill to renew the expiring tax provisions was approved by voice vote. "Welcome to the season of giving," he told lobbyists, who had been working furiously to get the legislation passed.

Rostenkowski had been holding off, concerned in part that the Senate would make the bill a vehicle for other tax proposals. But by Nov. 26, John C. Danforth, R-Mo., sponsor of a companion measure in the Senate, had commitments from 98 senators to keep the bill clean.

The Senate Finance Committee approved the companion bill (S 2042), also on Nov. 25.

The House passed HR 3909 in the early hours of Nov. 27 by a vote of 420-0. Rostenkowski, who wanted to take the extenders off their one-year leash, promised that each of the tax breaks would be brought to a vote in 1992 and either made permanent or eliminated. *(Vote 439, p. 106-H)*

The Senate gave its assent a few hours later by unanimous consent, sending the bill to President Bush, who signed it on Dec. 11 (PL 102-227).

Bob Kasten, R-Wis., delayed action in the Senate in hope of offering an amendment to repeal a 10 percent luxury tax on expensive boats that had been passed as part of the White House-congressional budget agreement. But he withdrew the proposal after Majority Leader George J. Mitchell, D-Maine, insisted that any amendments would kill the bill. "It has been made unmistakably clear that if this bill is changed in any way whatsoever, it will not be accepted in the House and the expiring provisions will expire," Mitchell said.

The decision to renew the breaks for six months was a compromise, dictated in part by the difficulty in finding the money to pay for a full-year extension. Under the 1990 budget deal, tax changes that lost money had to be paid for by offsetting revenue increases or entitlement cuts.

Renewing the 12 provisions for six months was expected to cost $3.2 billion over five years. The extension was paid for by requiring corporations with taxable income exceeding $1 million to prepay more of their taxes. Instead of paying 90 percent of their estimated tax liability on their quarterly returns, the bill required them to pay 93 percent in 1992. The amount was to rise to 95 percent by 1995 and fall back to 90 percent in 1997.

A Dozen Provisions Renewed

The bill extended the following tax preferences:

- **Employer-provided assistance for education.** Employees could exclude from their taxable income up to $5,250 a year of tuition paid for them by their employers.
- **Group legal services.** Employees could exclude from their taxable income certain contributions made by their employers to a qualified group legal services plan.
- **Health insurance for self-employed individuals.** Self-employed individuals were able to take a 25 percent deduction for the cost of health premiums for themselves and their spouses.
- **Mortgage bonds and mortgage credit certificates.** State and local governments could issue tax-exempt bonds or mortgage credit certificates to help qualified individuals purchase, improve or rehabilitate single-family, owner-occupied homes.
- **Small-issue manufacturing bonds.** Interest on certain small issues of private-activity bonds continued to be tax exempt if at least 95 percent of the proceeds from the bonds were used to finance manufacturing facilities or certain land or property for first-time farmers.
- **Allocation of research expenses.** Multinational corporations could continue using existing rules governing the allocation of research and experimentation expenses to U.S. and foreign source income.
- **Research and experimentation credit.** Corporations got a 20 percent tax credit for new research expenditures and for certain payments to universities for basic research.
- **Low-income rental housing.** Individuals who invested in qualified low-income housing were eligible for a tax credit in annual installments over 10 years.
- **Targeted jobs credit.** Employers of certain hard-to-place workers were eligible for a tax credit of up to $2,400 for a first-year employee. The maximum for disadvantaged summer youth employees was $1,200.
- **Business energy credits.** Businesses were eligible for a 10 percent tax credit for investment in solar and geothermal energy.
- **Orphan drug credit.** Manufacturers were eligible for a 50 percent credit for the costs of clinically testing drugs to treat rare diseases.
- **Charitable contributions.** Charitable contributions of tangible property, such as artwork, were not treated as a minimum tax preference item.

OTHER TAX CHANGES

In other tax action in 1991:

- **Gasoline tax.** In August, House members balked at a

Proposed Social Security Tax Cut Defeated

Sen. Daniel Patrick Moynihan, D-N.Y., hoped to pursue his campaign to reduce the Social Security payroll tax as a way to prevent the government from accumulating surplus revenues in the Social Security trust funds and using them to pay for general government programs. But he was defeated in April on a procedural vote that was taken as part of action on the Senate budget resolution.

Moynihan had tried and failed in 1990 to win approval for a bill to cut the payroll tax and increase the amount of income subject to the tax. The effect would have been to stop the rate of growth of the trust fund surpluses, provide a tax cut for those at the lower end of the income scale and a tax increase for these at the upper end, and preserve a small reserve cushion in the trust funds. *(1990 Almanac, p. 170)*

Moynihan had many arguments for the tax cut, but they boiled down to: When Congress enacted a series of automatic payroll tax increases as part of the bailout of Social Security system in 1983, it assumed the federal deficit would be eliminated before the pension system began running a surplus. Because the deficit persisted — indeed, was bigger than ever — the tax increases should be repealed.

By law, the surplus had to be invested in Treasury securities. That meant that most of the surplus was effectively being deposited into the general federal revenue pot. Thus Moynihan argued, even though Congress removed Social Security from deficit calculations as part of the 1990 budget agreement, a regressive tax collected for old-age pensions was still being used to finance deficit spending by the federal government.

Moynihan's Defeat

Negotiators at the 1990 White House-Congress budget summit thought they had made it very difficult for Moynihan to succeed in cutting the payroll tax in 1991. They included procedural roadblocks requiring a 60-vote majority in the Senate to pass legislation reducing Social Security revenues.

But Moynihan found a big loophole in the so-called fire walls. A little-noticed phrase included in the budget law ensured that only a majority in the Senate would be needed to pass the tax cut.

The 60-vote requirement only applied to a budget resolution "as reported" by the Senate Budget Committee. An amendment offered on the floor to lower the assumed level of Social Security revenues would still need only a majority vote. Jim Sasser, D-Tenn., chairman of the Senate Budget Committee, had inserted the phrase into the budget agreement to give Moynihan an opening.

To Democrats and Republicans who thought they had constructed impervious fire walls to prevent tampering with Social Security taxes or benefits, the loophole came as a shock.

Moynihan took advantage of the loophole, and when the budget resolution came to the Senate floor in April, he offered an amendment to reduce the assumed level of Social Security revenues over the next five years. The amendment would have paved the way for Senate consideration late in the year of an actual bill to cut the payroll tax. Only a majority was needed for passage in both cases.

Democrats were badly divided on the issue. Majority Leader George J. Mitchell, D-Maine, agreed that "we are, in effect, funding the operations of the government with a regressive tax."

But Finance Committee Chairman Lloyd Bentsen, D-Texas, strongly opposed the tax cut, saying it would put only $2 to $3 a week in the pockets of wage earners, while costing the Social Security trust funds $216 billion over five years.

Republicans, by contrast, were mostly united behind President Bush, who opposed Moynihan. The White House warned that the Moynihan plan "would return Social Security to the same financing scheme that drove the system to the brink of insolvency in 1982."

"This is not the time to mess with Social Security," said Minority Leader Bob Dole, R-Kan., who argued that the tax cut would threaten benefits. "Try to explain that to a group of angry seniors at your next town meeting," he warned. In the end, it was precisely that nightmare that seemed to most worry senators, who voted 60-38 to table (kill) Moynihan's initiative. *(Vote 46, p. 7-S)*

Democrats split 26-29 over the issue, with three fewer voting against Moynihan than supporting him. Republicans voted overwhelmingly — 34-9 — against the tax cut.

After the vote, Domenici managed to restore the 60-vote fire wall against all proposals governed by the budget resolution to alter the Social Security trust funds. Sasser joined Domenici in offering the amendment, ending the feud between the two over whether Moynihan should have a chance to cut the Social Security tax on a simple-majority vote. The amendment passed on a voice vote.

Moynihan's defeat was seen as a setback for Mitchell, who had broken with other top-ranking Democrats to support the tax cut. It also took away Democrats' most obvious candidate for a tax "fairness" issue in 1991.

proposal to increase the gasoline tax by a nickel a gallon as a way to finance new spending on highways and mass transit. But Congress later agreed to pay for the highway bill by continuing, for four years, half of a nickel gasoline tax that had been set in 1990 and was due to expire after fiscal 1995. As a result, the tax, 14 cents a gallon in 1991, was scheduled to fall to 11.5 cents from 1996 through 1999 — rather than dropping to 9 cents as originally slated. *(Transportation reauthorization, p. 137)*

Congress also agreed to pay for a bill extending unemployment benefits in part by:

- **Estimated taxes.** Requiring people who paid quarterly estimated taxes to base their payments on what they owed in the current year, rather than on what they paid the year before. The change applied to taxpayers whose taxable income jumped by $35,000 in one year.
- **FUTA.** Keeping the federal unemployment tax at 0.08 percent in 1996, rather than letting it drop to 0.06 percent.

In separate action, after months of battling over a move to repeal the recreational boat tax, Congress cleared a Coast Guard reauthorization bill (HR 1776 — PL 102-241) that included non-binding language calling for such a repeal, but only after a way to offset the cost was found. *(Coast Guard reauthorization, p. 153)*

TAX SIMPLIFICATION

Working closely with the Senate Finance Committee, Rostenkowski introduced several bills during 1991 that were aimed at easing the often onerous burden of filling out a tax return, both for individuals and businesses. But he insisted that simplification could not be achieved at the cost of altering fundamental tax policy. That unavoidably reduced the simplification effort mostly to tinkering around the edges.

Rostenkowski introduced one bill (HR 2777) on June 26 covering a number of complex areas in the code. Finance Committee Chairman Lloyd Bentsen, D-Texas, introduced a companion measure in the Senate. Both bills had bipartisan sponsorship.

Rostenkowski also introduced HR 2775 covering tax-exempt bonds and estate and gift taxation. And there were bills from Rostenkowski and other lawmakers covering pension simplification and the tax treatment of mutual funds.

These bills had a future only as sections of a larger tax bill.

Here are some highlights of the main simplification bills, as introduced:

- **"S" corporations.** So-called S corporations, small companies with fewer than 35 stockholders and one class of stock, were taxed under existing law much like partnerships. HR 2777 made it easier for S corporations to comply with the code, for example, by making it simpler for companies to qualify for S corporation status and permitting them to hold subsidiaries.
- **Luxury tax.** HR 2777 sought to change the excise tax imposed in 1990 on passenger vehicles by creating an exemption for equipment installed to help disabled individuals. Existing law imposed a 10 percent tax on the portion of the vehicle price above $30,000. The exemption also applied to purchases of separate parts and accessories for such equipment bought within six months of the purchase of the car.
- **Partnerships.** HR 2777 sought to change rules for large partnerships (those with at least 250 partners) by easing reporting requirements for partners and creating a new, simplified audit system. The bill required large partnerships to furnish tax information to their partners earlier in the year to ease filing difficulties.
- **Individual income tax.** HR 2777 permited taxpayers to pay their tax bills by credit card and eased restrictions on rolling over capital gains on sales of a principal residence when the owners were divorced or separated. The bill also toughened requirements for paying payroll taxes for part-time housekeepers and other domestic workers. HR 2775 repealed a supplemental credit for young children that was part of the earned-income tax credit, a refundable credit for low-income households. The complicated provision had been enacted in 1990.
- **Mutual funds.** The bill repealed the so-called short-short rule that restricted earnings, for tax purposes, that mutual funds were allowed from stocks and other assets held fewer than three months. It also required prompter and more complete information to be reported to shareholders.
- **Pension plans.** The bill eased restrictions on rolling over pre-retirement pension payments into tax-deferred individual retirement accounts for employees who changed jobs. Businesses with 100 or fewer workers would be freed from restrictions aimed at discouraging more favorable treatment of top employees. ■

Defense Production Act Temporarily Extended

Congress cleared two short-term extensions of the Defense Production Act (DPA) but failed to complete work on a three-year reauthorization. The expired Korean War-era law granted the president broad authority to redirect domestic goods to military use during times of national emergency.

The Defense Production Act had expired and gone without renewal for extended periods several times in the previous three years, including on Oct. 20, 1990. Although a bill to reauthorize the law made it through conference in late 1990 and the conference agreement passed the House, the Senate failed to take up the agreement as the 101st Congress came to a close. As a result, President Bush had to rely on other laws and executive orders to maintain his emergency acquisition powers during the Persian Gulf War. *(1990 Almanac, p. 202)*

SHORT-TERM EXTENSIONS

While the three-year extension was pending, Congress on Aug. 2 cleared a bill (HR 991 — PL 102-99) that reauthorized the law retroactively from Oct. 20, 1990, through Sept. 30, 1991.

The Senate had approved the short-term extension (S 468) by voice vote Feb. 21. The Senate bill included controversial language aimed at giving federal banking regulators new powers to pressure foreign countries to open their financial markets to U.S. businesses. This so-called Fair Trade in Financial Services Act would have allowed regulators to bar a foreign bank or securities firm from expanding in the United States if the company's home country did not grant U.S. businesses the same rights it gave its domestic companies.

The House passed its version of the short-term extension (HR 991) on March 6 by a vote of 416-0. *(Vote 29, p. 8-H)*

The House bill included a provision that made permanent a section of the Defense Production Act authorizing the president to block foreign takeovers of U.S. businesses if he found that the acquisition would harm U.S. national security.

Known as the Exon-Florio amendment, the anti-takeover provision had been passed as part of the 1988 Trade Act (PL 100-418), but it had expired along with the defense production law.

The House bill did not include the fair trade language.

Quickly and quietly, just before leaving town for the August recess, Congress on Aug. 2 cleared the short-term bill. The measure was slipped through conference, and the agreement was adopted by voice vote in both chambers. The conference, which never formally convened, accepted the House version of the bill, including the language making Exon-Florio permanent.

The temporary reauthorization expired Sept. 30 without a permanent bill to take its place.

The House passed a second extension — this one lasting through March 1, 1992 — by voice vote Nov. 27. The Senate cleared the bill (HR 3919 — PL 102-193) by voice vote the same day.

LONG-TERM EXTENSION

During the year, both chambers approved bills extending the Defense Production Act for three years, through Sept. 30, 1994, and authorizing $200 million for loans and purchase guarantees to U.S. businesses that agreed to supply the government with militarily significant goods and services in an emergency. Such financing had long been a part of the law.

The bills also provided new steps to preserve the country's defense industrial base, requiring the president to identify so-called critical technology items that might not have a stable source of supply in the United States or abroad and to ensure that the military would always have access to these items.

One action the president could take would be to purchase certain goods only from domestic suppliers to keep them in business. The president would have discretion in his choice of actions but more so under the House version.

The bills set up a special fund for loans and purchase guarantees subject to appropriations and required an assessment of the U.S. defense industrial base.

Senate Action

The Senate approved a three-year DPA extension (S 347) by voice vote Feb. 21.

The bill, which included Fair Trade in Financial Services, was virtually identical to a measure that had died under a veto threat in the final moments of the 101st session of Congress.

The House had approved the conference agreement on that bill, but several GOP senators had refused to allow it to come to a vote in the Senate. The White House objected in particular to the fair trade provisions. *(1990 Almanac, p. 202)*

As passed by the Senate, the bill gave U.S. banking and securities regulators broad discretion to act when the Treasury Department found that U.S. businesses were not receiving national treatment abroad. It also gave the regulators discretion over what action to take, although Treasury would be required to enter into negotiations with the offending country.

Thomas R. Carper, D-Del., the sponsor of the House bill, said he believed the first three of those concerns could be addressed by explicitly protecting treaties, by "grandfathering" existing operations and by giving the president the ultimate authority to impose sanctions. Senate passage came despite a veto threat not only over the financial services language but also over the provisions aimed at giving an edge to domestic suppliers of certain essential military goods. The administration and other critics denounced this language as an unwarranted move toward a government industrial policy.

The Senate bill also included the language making Exon-Florio permanent.

House Committee Action

A House Banking subcommittee approved a draft three-year reauthorization bill (HR 3039) on July 16 that largely tracked the 1990 bill. Before approving the measure, the Economic Stabilization Subcommittee adopted without dissent two relatively minor amendments. One, by James P. Moran Jr., D-Va., included professional and technical services in the definition of the nation's defense industrial base.

The other, by Charles Luken, D-Ohio, expanded the definition of what should be included on the list of critical technology items.

The subcommittee-approved bill gave the president somewhat more discretion than did the Senate bill in choosing actions to ensure that the military would have access to critical technologies. It did not include the Senate-passed provision making Exon-Florio permanent.

On July 30, the full Banking Committee approved the measure by voice vote after agreeing to a handful of noncontroversial amendments.

House Passage

By a vote of 419-3, the House approved the bill Oct. 2 and agreed to go to conference with the Senate on S 347, after amending that bill to include the text of HR 3039. House passage required negotiations among members of at least four committees — Banking, which first reported the bill, Armed Services, Energy and Commerce, and Government Operations. *(Vote 288, p. 70-H)*

To ease passage and resolve committee differences, the House adopted an amendment by Carper that struck or altered several provisions that had drawn fire from the administration and from the Armed Services Committee, in particular.

Armed Services had objected that the Banking Committee invaded its turf by including provisions that would have enacted new standards for defense procurement and new federal rules limiting "offsets" — essentially requirements that U.S. companies share with their overseas competitors critical technology in return for purchases of U.S. military goods by foreign governments.

The Carper amendment struck the former and made the latter a general statement of government intent rather than part of the Defense Production Act, which would have given the Banking Committee a say over the issue in the future.

The House also adopted several amendments by James A. Traficant Jr., D-Ohio, including one that would give contracting preferences in certain cases to small businesses in areas that had high unemployment or were otherwise suffering from economic decline.

The most important difference between the House and Senate bills was the Senate provisions on Fair Trade in Financial Services. Although the administration had opposed them early in the year, there were indications that changes could be made that would satisfy the White House. The Treasury had vacillated during the year and seemed to have accepted the Senate bill. The State Department and the Office of the U.S. Trade Representative had focused on provisions that violated financial services treaties, restrained the existing U.S. operations of foreign banks, granted authority to independent banking agencies (such as the Fed) to impose sanctions on foreign businesses based on the actions of their home governments, and required Treasury to negotiate with offending countries. ■

CFTC Reauthorization Held Over

Both the House and Senate passed bills to reauthorize the Commodity Futures Trading Commission (CFTC), but a dispute over regulating so-called stock-index futures and other hybrid financial instruments that cut between the New York-based stock markets and the Chicago futures markets derailed legislative efforts for the third straight year.

The House and Senate bills (HR 707, S 207) made the agency permanent, with similar authorization levels for fiscal 1992 and 1993. Both contained provisions cracking down on fraud and other abuses in the trading pits; for example, they banned the practice of dual trading, whereby a broker traded futures contracts for his own and his clients' accounts on the same day.

But the House-passed version was silent on stock-index futures, special financial instruments that were tied to prices in the stock market. The Senate incorporated a compromise that would have left the CFTC with exclusive jurisdiction over these instruments while giving the Federal Reserve Board new authority to oversee margins.

BOXSCORE

➡ **Commodity Futures Trading Commission reauthorization (S 207, HR 707).** The bill reauthorized the Commodity Futures Trading Commission and made several changes in securities law aimed at curtailing abuses in the trading pits.

Reports: H Rept 102-6; S Rept 102-22.

KEY ACTION

Feb. 26 — HR 707 approved by the **House** Agriculture Committee by voice vote.

March 5 — HR 707 passed by **House** by 395-27 vote.

March 6 — S 207 approved by **Senate** Agriculture Committee by voice vote.

April 18 — S 207 passed by **Senate** by 90-8 vote.

The conflict stalled action on the bill until near the end of the session, when House and Senate conferees met briefly. No progress was made, and lawmakers decided to return to negotiations early in 1992.

The movement to beef up the enforcement tools of the CFTC came as the agency was trying to recover from trading scandals that were uncovered in 1989. But the focus of legislation ultimately turned to the more controversial issue of which federal agency should regulate stock-index futures. In one corner was the New York-based stock markets and their regulator, the Securities and Exchange Commission (SEC), and in the other was the Chicago-based futures markets and the CFTC.

Since the 1987 stock market crash, analysts had debated whether the relatively new market for stock-index futures was safe for investors. Of particular concern to many was margin levels, the money investors paid upfront to buy a futures contract or security. Futures margins, considered as good-faith deposits, varied but were generally below 20 percent of the purchase price. They were set by the exchanges on which the futures traded. Securities margins, which acted as down payments, were about 50 percent and were set by the Federal Reserve Board in consultation with the SEC.

House Action

The House kicked off action for the year on Feb. 19 when an Agriculture subcommittee approved, by voice vote, a bill (HR 707) to reauthorize the CFTC through fiscal 1993. The Agriculture Committee approved the bill by voice vote on Feb. 26.

Jerry Huckaby, D-La., tried but failed to add an amendment to the bill tightening the reins on stock-index futures. The amendment, rejected by voice vote, would have required that the CFTC regularly ensure that stock-index futures margins be sufficient to protect the futures markets and the public interest. Huckaby had tried but failed to add similar language in subcommittee.

The House overwhelmingly passed the reauthorization on March 5, endorsing the committee's bill with no changes by a vote of 395-27. *(Vote 27, p. 8-H)*

Senate Action

The Senate moved almost as fast on its version of the measure. The Agriculture Committee on March 6 approved a bill (S 207) after reaching a last-minute compromise allowing the Federal Reserve to set margin requirements for stock-index futures.

As part of the bargain, the bill largely preserved the exclusive jurisdiction of the CFTC over stock-index futures and related financial instruments but allowed some existing "hybrid" instruments that looked like both futures and stocks to be traded on stock exchanges.

Lawmakers and Bush administration officials hailed the deal, and on April 18, the Senate passed the measure, largely unchanged, by a 90-8 vote. *(Vote 45, p. 7-S) (Comparison of House and Senate bills, p. 112)*

Futures Dispute Stalled Bills

As in 1990, Congress was unable to clear the bill because of a lack of consensus over stock-index futures. *(1990 Almanac, p. 194)*

The House and Senate versions of the bill were similar in their requirements that futures exchanges collect more detailed information about trading activities in an effort to develop audit trails that could identify fraud and attempts to manipulate the markets.

Both versions also curbed dual trading and imposed other regulatory controls to prevent a recurrence of the 1989 trading scandals that led to over 40 arrests of Chicago futures traders.

But there was a long delay before conferees met on Nov. 6, and that one-hour meeting did little to resolve any of the differences between the two chambers, in particular over stock-index futures. House Agriculture Committee Chairman E. "Kika" de la Garza, D-Texas, said staff members would meet to resolve minor problems, then members would address larger differences.

In the end-of-the-year crush, negotiations at the staff level were slow-going and no additional conference meetings were held, leaving the issue unresolved going into 1992. ■

CFTC Reauthorization

The House and Senate both passed versions of a multi-year authorization bill (HR 707 — H Rept 102-6, S Rept 102-22) for the Commodity Futures Trading Commission (CFTC). Both incorporated major regulatory changes intended to give the CFTC additional tools to prevent and punish fraud and other abuses in the trading pits. (The Senate bill was originally numbered S 207.) At year's end, the bill awaited action in a House-Senate conference committee. The two versions took somewhat different approaches to the regulatory changes. More significant was the fact that the Senate bill attempted to settle a long-running fight between the futures and stock markets — and their regulators, the CFTC and the Securities and Exchange Commission (SEC) — over so-called cross-market issues. In particular, the Senate measure addressed the regulation of "hybrid" financial instruments, which combine elements of both stocks and futures, and the issue of setting margins or good-faith deposits on futures purchases.

The House bill was largely silent on the jurisdictional issues. It had taken more than two years to force the issue to the Senate floor because of disagreements between the Agriculture and Banking committees. In the House, similar disagreements between the Agriculture and Energy and Commerce committees prevented floor debate.

As passed, the House and Senate versions of HR 707 would have:

CFTC Authorization

HOUSE PROVISIONS

• Authorized $48.5 million in fiscal 1992 and $53 million in fiscal 1993 for CFTC operations. The agency's authorization had lapsed. The bill made the CFTC a permanent agency, with the need for periodic adjustment in its spending limits.

SENATE PROVISIONS

• Authorized $48.3 million in fiscal 1992, $56.1 million in fiscal 1993, $61.9 million in fiscal 1994, $68.2 million in fiscal 1995 and $71.9 million in fiscal 1996 for CFTC operations. The bill made the CFTC a permanent agency but with the need for periodic adjustment in its spending limits.

Enhanced Regulatory Powers

HOUSE PROVISIONS

• **Dual trading.** Banned the practice of dual trading, whereby a broker traded futures contracts for his own and his clients' accounts on the same day. The ban was only on those commodities in which more than 7,000 contracts traded in a day; the CFTC was authorized to adjust that limit based on market liquidity, price volatility and other considerations.

The CFTC was required to exempt any futures contract from the dual trading ban whenever it found that the public interest would be served by an exemption and an exchange could demonstrate that its system of tracking trades could identify violations due to dual trading. Also, a sizable number of futures contracts traded below the 7,000-a-day threshold and thus were exempt from this provision.

• **Self trading.** Prohibited affiliated brokers from trading with each other when one broker was trading for a client and another was trading for his own or the association's account. The bill also prohibited affiliated brokers from trading between themselves — whether on behalf of clients or for their own accounts — more than 25 percent of the time. Critics said trading between affiliated brokers could defeat the intent of the "open outcry" system, by which brokers shouted their deals across noisy trading pits.

• **Audit trail.** Required market surveillance techniques to show, within a year of enactment, the time and quantity of every transaction within one-minute intervals. Within three years of enactment, audit trails had to record transactions every 30 seconds. Futures exchanges were developing electronic recording systems to meet this requirement but were not certain that the 30-second interval could be achieved so soon.

• **Trader registration.** Required all floor traders who traded only for their own accounts to register with and report periodically to the CFTC; brokers who traded for clients already were required to register. The bill enhanced the CFTC's authority to deny, revoke or suspend a broker's or trader's registration if he had violated CFTC rules or had been convicted of crimes such as fraud or racketeering.

tions of futures trading laws from $500,000 for businesses and $100,000 for individuals to $1 million for businesses and $500,000 for individuals. The bill also made it easier for the CFTC to impose fines for non-criminal violations or to seek civil money penalties through the courts. It prohibited trading by anyone who had failed to make timely payments of civil fines.

• **Insider trading.** Established a new felony violation for certain instances of futures market trading that relied on material, non-public information. The bill also made disclosure of such information for the purpose of another person's trading activities a

SENATE PROVISIONS

• **Audit trail.** Required market surveillance techniques to show the time, sequence and terms of every transaction within one-minute intervals.

Within three years of enactment, audit trails had to make precise records of transactions in ways that were independent of the floor traders and at time intervals deemed practicable by the CFTC. Trading information also had to be fed continually to the exchange floor, and the audit trail had to track orders as they were received on the trading floor before they were executed, and when they were reported from the floor after being executed. Futures exchanges were developing electronic recording systems that might meet this requirement.

The CFTC was required to decide within 18 months after enactment if the exchanges were complying with this provision; if they were not, it could issue orders to make improvements.

• **Dual trading.** Required the CFTC to ban dual trading, whereby a broker traded futures contracts for his own and his clients' accounts on the same day. The ban was to take effect only if the CFTC found that 18 months after enactment the audit trail procedures at exchanges were unable to prevent abuses through dual trading.

• **Self trading.** Prohibited affiliated brokers from trading with each other when one broker was trading for a client and another was trading for his own or the association's account.

• **Trader registration.** Required all floor traders who traded only for their own accounts to register with and report periodically to the CFTC; brokers who traded for clients already were required to register.

The bill enhanced the CFTC's authority to deny, revoke or suspend a broker's or trader's registration if he had been convicted of violations of CFTC rules or of crimes such as fraud or racketeering. In addition, a floor trader indicted for a felony involving futures trading laws or his activities as a fiduciary could have his registration suspended by the CFTC.

• **Civil fines and criminal penalties.** Enhanced the authority of the CFTC to seek civil money penalties through the courts and to demand restitution for customers in administrative actions. Administrative fines for civil violations of futures trading laws, formerly $100,000, were increased to $100,000 or triple the monetary gain for individuals, and $500,000 for firms.

The bill authorized criminal sanctions for willful violations of law or CFTC regulations that would otherwise only draw civil penalties. And it prohibited trading by anyone who had failed to make timely payments of civil fines.

• **Insider trading.** Established a new felony violation for certain instances of futures market trading that relied upon material, non-

HOUSE PROVISIONS	SENATE PROVISIONS
felony. CFTC regulations already made such insider trading a civil violation. The felony was punishable by fines of up to $100,000, plus the amount of any profit from insider trading, and prison terms of up to three years.	public information. The bill made disclosure of such information for the purpose of another person's trading activities a felony. The felony was punishable by fines of up to $500,000, plus the amount of any profit from insider trading, and prison terms of up to five years.
• **Cooperation abroad.** Authorized the CFTC to cooperate with government futures regulators abroad and to assist them in investigating possible violations of regulations or laws, even if such actions did not constitute violations in the United States. The CFTC was authorized to accept payment for such assistance and to protect the confidentiality of information collected in a joint investigation. Similar authority had been granted in recent years to the SEC.	• **Cooperation abroad.** Authorized the CFTC to cooperate with government futures regulators abroad and to assist them in investigating possible violations of regulations or laws, even if such actions did not constitute violations in the United States. The CFTC was authorized to accept payment for such assistance and to protect the confidentiality of information collected in a joint investigation.

Futures/ Securities Jurisdictional Issues

HOUSE PROVISIONS	SENATE PROVISIONS
• **Stock-index futures.** Required the CFTC to monitor stock-index futures margins to determine whether they protected the integrity of the futures markets and the public interest. The bill required the CFTC to adjust margins if it determined that existing levels constituted "a clear and present danger" to the markets or the public interest. The CFTC already had margin-setting authority in the case of market emergencies.	• **Stock-index futures.** Required futures exchanges to report to the Fed all changes in stock-index futures margins. The Fed was authorized to direct exchanges to adjust margins to protect the financial integrity of futures exchanges and against "systemic risk." The Fed could delegate its margin-setting authority to the CFTC.
• **Index arbitrage.** Required the CFTC to monitor so-called index-arbitrage trades, in which investors simultaneously bought or sold stocks and took the opposite position with so-called stock-index futures contracts in order to profit from price discrepancies. The bill urged the CFTC to take action to curb index arbitrage trading if it found that it constituted "a clear and present danger" to the integrity of the futures markets or the public interest.	• **Hybrids.** Created a formula to determine whether new financial instruments that combined elements of stocks and futures should be regulated by the SEC or the CFTC. Those hybrids that derived more than 50 percent of their value from their futures elements were regulated as futures by the CFTC; those that derived more than 50 percent of their value from an underlying security were regulated as stocks by the SEC. The bill did not alter regulation of existing stock instruments or futures contracts, but it allowed several hybrids that existed before 1991 to be regulated by the SEC and traded on stock exchanges. A 1989 federal appeals court order had banned trading of two such hybrids that were approved by the SEC. The bill also specifically excluded from CFTC jurisdiction traditional bank deposits and loans, though the agency might find that they sometimes resembled futures contracts.
	• **Swaps.** Clarified that certain so-called swap contracts are not subject to CFTC regulation. Swaps constituted a $3 billion market in which banks, insurance companies, pension funds and similar institutional investors hedged their portfolios against changes in interest rates by negotiating to exchange similar financial instruments. The CFTC was authorized to exempt swaps not automatically excluded from its jurisdiction, provided that they were not traded on an open market and that the parties were large institutional investors.

Limited Partnerships Bill Stalled in Senate

A bill (HR 1885) aimed at protecting investors when their limited partnerships were reorganized passed the House on Nov. 5 by voice vote. Action in the Senate on a similar bill (S 1423) was postponed because Banking Committee members were immersed in must-pass banking legislation.

The bill was crafted in response to widespread complaints about so-called roll-ups, which occurred when limited partnerships were reorganized into publicly traded entities. The resulting stock issues often fared poorly in securities markets, and investors said that general partners, who typically oversaw the roll-ups, had widely abused their powers.

There was concern that the general partners — who had a fiduciary responsibility to protect the limited partners' interests — used roll-ups to pay themselves high management fees and boost their stake in the partnership's equity.

The bills required an independent evaluation of the fairness of a roll-up, changed existing proxy rules to make it easier for investors to fight the reorganization and required that those opposed to a roll-up get a chance to opt out and receive alternative compensation to the stock issue.

The measures went far beyond requirements proposed by the Securities and Exchange Commission (SEC) that roll-up prospectuses be made more understandable to investors.

The Bush administration opposed the bills, saying that the SEC already had acted on the problem and that the bills would interfere with the regulator's effort to revamp federal proxy laws.

Background

Limited partnerships were designed to be long-term, non-traded entities in which investors pooled their resources under the supervision of a general partner who managed the operation and had the responsibility of protecting the limited partners' money.

Investment in the real estate and oil and gas industries constituted the bulk of such partnerships. And with the slump in those sectors of the economy throughout 1991, many partnerships performed below expectations.

In a roll-up, a number of partnerships were combined into a single, publicly traded entity, with investors usually receiving a stock issue. Roll-ups were pitched to investors as a means of restructuring faltering partnerships to lower business costs, diversify assets, create new investment opportunities and provide investors with liquidity.

More than 1.2 million investors had seen almost $7 billion of their limited partnership assets rolled-up by early 1991. But critics said general partners often pushed the reorganizations to enrich themselves at the expense of limited partners as they created new management fees and increased their equity stake. The new stock given the limited partners generally plummeted from its original estimated value.

"There is a very serious problem in which investors are being skinned and in which wrongdoers are profiting," said Energy and Commerce Chairman John D. Dingell, D-Mich.

> **BOXSCORE**
>
> ➧ **Limited Partnership Roll-Ups (HR 1885, S 1423).** The bills gave investors opposing a roll-up — the reorganization of a limited partnership into a publicly traded investment — a chance to opt out and receive alternative compensation to the stock offering.
>
> **Reports:** H Rept 102-254.
>
> **KEY ACTION**
>
> July 30 — The **House** Energy and Commerce Committee approved HR 1885 by voice vote.
>
> Nov. 5 — The **House** passed HR 1885 by voice vote.

Congressional Action

The House Energy and Commerce Subcommittee on Telecommunications and Finance approved the bill on May 22 by voice vote.

The subcommittee bill required that roll-up prospectuses be written "in a clear, concise, and understandable" manner and be accompanied by a "fairness opinion" prepared by an independent expert with no stake in the proposed transaction. A prospectus also had to discuss alternatives to the roll-up, such as selling the partnership's assets and distributing the proceeds directly to the investors.

The bill eased federal proxy rules to allow investors to communicate with each other on preliminary plans to fight a roll-up without running afoul of securities laws. It also barred the practice of paying brokers to solicit only proxy votes favoring a roll-up. Critics of roll-ups said that unsophisticated investors had been misled and harassed by brokers who were paid if they delivered "yes" votes.

The bill also required that, whenever possible, investors opposed to a roll-up be given "dissenter's rights," or alternative compensation to the stock. Under existing law, partners opposed to roll-ups were forced to accept the stock.

"Small investors need our help," said Telecommunications and Finance Subcommittee Chairman Edward J. Markey, D-Mass. "All too often, unscrupulous fast-buck artists have used roll-ups to extract new fees for themselves and their affiliates." The full committee approved the measure by voice vote on July 30 after adopting a substitute amendment that made technical changes.

The committee's action came on the heels of new proposed SEC requirements that roll-up prospectuses be more understandable and that the proxy process be changed to make it easier for investors to fight a roll-up. The SEC subsequently scaled back the proposed regulations; it did not have the authority to require that those opposing a roll-up be given alternatives. Final rules were not issued in 1991.

The Senate bill, sponsored by Christopher J. Dodd, D-Conn., chairman of the Banking Securities Subcommittee, had attracted nearly 40 cosponsors by the end of the year. The Banking Committee held off action during the first session because members were immersed in the banking bill. ■

Government Securities Bill Considered

Congress began a re-examination of government securities regulation after a trading scandal involving fraudulent purchasing practices by the securities firm Salomon Brothers rocked Wall Street during the summer.

Even before the scandal became known, the Senate passed a bill (S 1247) designed to better protect investors who bought federal government securities. As passed, the measure permanently authorized the Treasury Department to regulate government securities dealers, especially in regard to their financial health and their ability to manage their own affairs. Treasury's authority expired Oct. 1.

The House Energy and Commerce Committee held several hearings on the Salomon trading scandal, but took no action on a measure (HR 3927) reauthorizing Treasury's authority through 1996 and giving the Securities and Exchange Commission (SEC) broad new authority to track trades, similar to the authority it had over private securities trading.

Salomon Sparks Interest

The federal government had only a limited role in regulating the $2 trillion-plus market in federal government securities. But Congress took steps to expand that oversight on the heels of the Salomon scandal.

Salomon was the largest so-called primary dealer in government bonds — one of about 40 banks and securities firms that dealt directly with the Treasury Department and the Federal Reserve System to provide a market for the bonds that financed federal government activities. Salomon officials admitted that the firm violated rules governing bids for such bonds.

The scandal resulted in the resignation of key brokerage officials, including longtime Salomon Chairman John H. Gutfreund. Financier Warren E. Buffett took over Salomon's board on Aug. 15 and apologized for the company's transgressions. "The nation has a right to expect its rules and laws to be obeyed, and at Salomon, certain of these were broken," he said.

Buffett released a detailed 52-page report outlining a series of violations in which Salomon's 20-person bond trading unit repeatedly issued fake bids for customers to evade a rule limiting the size of a dealer's bid for a single bond issue. Among the revelations in the report was that Salomon had gotten control of 86 percent of a Treasury issue of two-year notes sold on May 22, 1991.

Salomon then proceeded to drive up the market price of those notes, which was one of the first clues at the time to Treasury and Fed officials that something was arwy in the market.

Some lawmakers had harsh criticism for the failure of regulators to detect Salomon trading irregularities and called for a comprehensive overhaul of the 1986 Government Securities Act.

Edward J. Markey, D-Mass., who chaired the House Energy and Commerce Finance Subcommittee, said he planned to rework the law. "The rules which are on the books are clearly unacceptable — they're not working," he said.

Regulators from the Treasury, the Fed and the SEC urged a six-month delay to allow time to consider the effect on the market.

Senate Action

The Salomon scandal threw a wrench into an otherwise routine reauthorization of the Government Securities Act, the 1986 law giving the Treasury Department the authority to regulate government bond dealers.

The Senate Banking Committee on July 10 approved, by voice vote, S 1247, to permanently authorize the act while making no major changes other than giving the Treasury Department greater authority to write regulations designed to prevent "fraudulent, deceptive, or manipulative acts" by government securities dealers. The full Senate passed the bill by voice vote on July 30.

Admissions from Salomon officials about the company's illegal trading practices forced the Senate to craft a new measure (S 1699) reauthorizing the law for a year and explicitly forbidding dealers from making false or misleading statements to Treasury.

That was where progress on legislation ended for the year, in part because of a lack of consensus on how the law should be changed to address fraud as well as pressure from the administration to wait until 1992.

Although the Government Securities Act had expired Oct. 1, Treasury officials said they could continue regulatory practices under the general authority granted by the Liberty Bond Act of 1917. ■

Work Starts on GSE Oversight

Congress began work in 1991 on a series of bills to tighten restrictions on five government-sponsored enterprises (GSEs) and cleared a measure to provide more money to the Federal Agricultural Mortgage Corporation (Farmer Mac).

The five enterprises, which operated with implicit federal guarantees, performed the function of increasing capital flows to housing, education and agriculture. Together, their outstanding liabilities approached $1 trillion.

The legislation covered the Federal National Mortgage Association (Fannie Mae); the Federal Home Loan Mortgage Corp. (Freddie Mac); the Federal Home Loan Bank System; the Student Loan Marketing Association (Sallie Mae); and the Farm Credit System.

These corporations were privately owned, but they had been created by Congress and they enjoyed significant benefits, including tax advantages and exemption from some federal securities laws. While they did not carry explicit government guarantees, investors assumed that the enterprises' obligations would be covered by the federal government if they were to default. That greatly reduced the riskiness of investing in the GSEs and enabled them to borrow money in private credit markets at low rates.

None of the five corporations was in imminent danger. But in the wake of the savings and loan debacle, lawmakers wanted to make sure they would not one day be pouring billions of dollars into these GSEs. So as part of the 1990 budget-reconciliation act (PL 101-508), they had called for studies by the Treasury Department and the Congressional Budget Office (CBO) of the financial health of the GSEs. The law required House committees to report regulatory bills to the floor by Sept. 15 and stated the intent of the Senate that its committees do likewise.

Congress did clear a bill (HR 3029 — PL 102-237) making technical corrections in farm law that included provisions making it easier for Farmer Mac to borrow money.

In addition, the House passed a bill (HR 3365 — H Rept 102-224) on Nov. 23 under suspension of the rules aimed at making it harder for new GSEs to borrow money from the Treasury. The measure, sponsored by Ways and Means Committee Chairman Dan Rostenkowski, D-Ill., restricted the Treasury from making loans to newly established GSEs unless the loans had been approved in an appropriations bill.

Ways and Means had approved the measure by voice vote on Sept. 25. The Senate did not act on it.

Treasury Proposal

In June, the administration sent Congress draft bills to establish stricter government oversight of the five corporations. New regulators were to be created in the Department of Housing and Urban Development (HUD), the Agriculture Department and the Treasury Department to oversee the GSEs.

The legislative proposals resulted from the congressionally mandated Treasury study, which was released in April. The study found that the five GSEs posed no immediate risk to the government, but it concluded that the long-term liability presented a serious enough threat of default and a taxpayer bailout that regulatory changes were needed to better insulate the government.

Treasury recommended several changes in the government's regulatory oversight, including a plan proposed a year earlier to have private-market securities analysts rate the five GSEs based on the riskiness of their borrowing, without taking into account the implicit government guarantee.

The report recommended enhancing the authority of existing federal regulators for each of the enterprises and allowing them to impose capital requirements tied to the risk associated with the lending activities of each corporation. The capital requirement could be waived for an enterprise that received a Triple-A rating, the highest private-market rating.

Two of the enterprises — the Federal Home Loan

Banks and Sallie Mae — received Triple-A ratings in April from Standard & Poor's Corp. in a special assessment done for the Treasury Department. Standard & Poor's gave lower ratings to the other three: an A-plus to Freddie Mac, an A-minus to Fannie Mae and a Double-B to the Farm Credit System, reflecting its continued difficulties and the problems associated with farm lending. (Securities sold by all five carried Triple-A ratings in the marketplace because of their implicit federal guarantee.)

HOUSING CREDIT

The House approved a bill (HR 2900 — H Rept 102-206) on Sept. 25 tightening regulation of three enterprises that provided financial support to the housing industry. They included two of the nation's largest financial businesses: Fannie Mae and Freddie Mac, which bought mortgages from banks and other lenders, pumping money back into the institutions to be used to underwrite more home purchases. To finance their activities, they sold bonds and securities backed by mortgages. The bill also covered the 12 regional Federal Home Loan Banks that supplied cash to the nation's savings and loan industry and together made up the home loan bank system, requiring that the Federal Housing Finance Board ensure that the banks operated in a financially safe and sound manner.

Senate Banking Committee staff began drafting a bill, but no action was taken in that chamber.

House Subcommittee Action

The Banking Subcommittee on Housing and Community Development approved HR 2900 on July 24 by voice vote, agreeing to create a new regulator within HUD to oversee Fannie and Freddie. But the subcommittee put off two of the most contentious issues for the full Banking Committee: how much capital Fannie and Freddie should have available to cover unexpected losses and whether they should have to set aside a percentage of their profits for low-income housing.

Treasury and the two corporations were locked in a dispute over the amount of capital — assets in excess of liabilities — that Fannie and Freddie should be required to maintain. Treasury wanted high levels of capital to cover potential emergencies and to minimize the chance that the taxpayers would be called on to help the two corporations. It also wanted regulators to be free to determine what those levels ought to be, based on existing economic conditions.

Fannie and Freddie, on the other hand, said the capital levels sought by the Treasury were too high and would restrict them from carrying out the job of buying mortgages from banks and other lenders. They also feared that an unfriendly regulator with too much flexibility could push the standards even higher, so they favored writing the standards into the law.

The Housing Subcommittee spent the bulk of its time debating whether to set salary levels for top executives at the corporations. Many members were outraged that David Maxwell, former chairman of Fannie Mae, retired with a compensation package of $27 million.

But the subcommittee rejected an attempt by Joseph P. Kennedy II, D-Mass., to limit future salary levels. Instead, members voted 22-11 to adopt a substitute by Mary Rose Oakar, D-Ohio, tying compensation levels to performance and matching salaries of those at similar private businesses.

Still upset about the $27 million bonus, however, members voted 16-13 to adopt an amendment by Charles E. Schumer, D-N.Y., to prohibit Fannie and Freddie from providing any payment or valuable to a top executive who was leaving without first securing approval from the HUD secretary.

House Banking Committee Action

The full Banking Committee voted 49-1 on July 31 to send the bill on to the House floor, despite reservations among members about legislating new rules for Fannie and Freddie at a time when both were flush with profits and yielding high returns to stockholders. The committee first voted 49-1 to adopt a leadership amendment setting out capital levels and goals for financing low-income housing.

Key action included the following:

- **Capital standards.** In a deal accepted by Treasury and endorsed by Fannie and Freddie, the committee agreed to set three capital levels and create a regulator at HUD to see to it that the corporations worked to meet the highest of the three.

If Fannie or Freddie fell below the bottom, or "critical," level, the regulator could place them in mandatory conservatorship. To stay above that floor, a corporation would have to maintain capital equal to 0.25 percent of their assets for off-balance-sheet mortgage-backed securities and 1.25 percent for on-balance-sheet assets, such as mortgages owned by the corporations.

If either corporation fell below a middle "minimum" capital level, the regulator could restrict its activities and growth. At this level, 18 months after enactment, corporations would have to have 0.45 percent capital for off-balance-sheet securities and 2.5 percent for on-balance-sheet assets.

If Freddie and Fannie met the third, highest capital level, the regulator would simply monitor their activities. That level was to be defined by the regulator, who would spell out "stress tests," or worst-case scenarios requiring that Fannie and Freddie have enough capital to weather 10 years of severe economic conditions.

If it fell between the top and middle levels, a corporation would have to devise a capital-restoration plan showing how it would meet the highest standard.

Not everyone thought the compromise was in the best interests of the taxpayers. Jim Leach, R-Iowa, tried to boost the minimum capital requirements, but his amendment was rejected by voice vote.

- **Low-income housing.** The Banking Committee instructed Fannie Mae and Freddie Mac to negotiate with about 10 housing groups and report back with an agreement on what the two mortgage corporations would do to finance affordable housing for low-income families.

Originally, Esteban E. Torres, D-Calif., wanted to require the two corporations to spend 10 percent of their net income each year on programs to boost low-income housing. The two corporations staunchly opposed any such mandate. Most housing advocates and committee aides said Torres did not have the votes for such a plan.

After a weekend of negotiations July 27-28, Fannie and Freddie promised to finance $3.5 billion worth of single- and multifamily housing for low-income residents in 1992 and 1993. In 1994, the corporations would try to spend an amount equal to 1 percent of the volume of mortgages they bought the year before.

- **Redlining.** In one other roll call vote, the committee rejected, 22-22, an amendment by Maxine Waters, D-Calif., to prohibit Fannie Mae or Freddie Mac from buying mortgages from lenders that discriminated.

Ranking Republican Chalmers P. Wylie of Ohio said Waters was wrong when she said she had the support of

Fannie and Freddie for the change. It subsequently became clear that he was mistaken, however, and Waters vowed to offer the amendment again when the bill came up on the House floor.

• **Federal Home Loan Banks.** The Banking Committee also agreed by voice vote to remove a cap from the Federal Home Loan Bank System, allowing the home loan banks to lend more money to commercial banks and credit unions to originate mortgages.

House Floor Action

The House on Sept. 25 approved the bill by a vote of 412-8. *(Vote 278, 68-H)*

The floor debate turned fiery when Kennedy offered an amendment expressing the sense of the House that Fannie Mae should limit the amount of compensation paid to its top executives. The non-binding amendment was agreed to by voice vote.

The House adopted another Kennedy amendment requiring that Fannie and Freddie use family incomes, rather than the size of a loan or the value of the property, to calculate the portion of their loans that went to low- and moderate-income households.

Leach tried but failed to raise the capital standards set for Freddie and Fannie. His amendment was rejected 119-298. *(Vote 277, p. 66-H)*

And the House agreed by voice vote to Waters' amendment to establish guidelines for use by HUD in determining whether a lender discriminated against loan applicants.

FARM CREDIT

The House voted voted 221-203 on Nov. 26 in favor of a bill (HR 3298 — H Rept 102-277) to tighten regulation of the Farm Credit System, a 75-year-old GSE devoted to agricultural lending. But the bill fell short of the two-thirds majority required for passage under suspension of the rules, expedited procedures usually reserved for non-controversial measures. *(Vote 379, p. 92-H)*

The Farm Credit System, an agglomeration of nearly 300 farm lenders, was considered the weakest of the five GSEs. In 1987, Congress had stepped in to bail out and restructure the system, costing taxpayers $1.3 billion to date. *(1987 Almanac, p. 381)*

At the heart of the bill was a plan for system banks to repay the 1987 bailout. It would have required the four system banks that received federal assistance to make annual payments into a fund that would pay off the debt by 2005. The Treasury Department favored some other changes in the system, such as performance standards for system banks and the addition of risk-based insurance premiums. But the Agriculture Committee, which had jurisdiction over the measure, did not include such provisions in the bill.

Ranking Budget Committee Republican Bill Gradison, R-Ohio, objected to the bill, saying that it contained accounting loopholes that would have allowed banks to avoid payments into the fund. Gradison also said that the measure would have allowed the banks to count their contributions to the fund against their capital requirements.

While Gradison's objections added to the bill's problems, the critical factor was stiff opposition from Appropriations Committee Chairman Jamie L. Whitten, D-Miss. Whitten's complaint was the inclusion of provisions that likely would have merged a system bank in Jackson, Miss., into the system's Texas region. That language, inserted by Agriculture Committee Chairman E. "Kika" de la Garza, D-Texas, at a Sept. 12 committee markup, put the two most powerful shapers of farm policy in the House at odds.

The Whitten-de la Garza battle centered on a four-year-old problem at the Federal Intermediate Bank in Jackson. The bank, which offered intermediate and short-term credit to lenders, was supposed to merge with a sister bank in Jackson that offered longer-term credit. But the sister bank went into receivership, and, in 1989, the Farm Credit Administration (FCA) attempted to order the Jackson bank to merge with the Texas system. The Jackson bank prevailed in a lawsuit to block the merger, however. De la Garza's language would have effectively given the FCA the authority to force the merger.

The amendment had dominated consideration of the bill by the Agriculture Committee, which ended in voice vote approval on Sept. 12. The Conservation, Credit and Rural Development Subcommittee had approved the bill July 31 by unanimous consent.

FARMER MAC

At the end of the session, Congress cleared a bill (HR 3029) making technical corrections in farm law that included provisions making it easier for Farmer Mac to borrow money and putting it under the regulatory control of the FCA. The House approved HR 3029 on Nov. 26; the Senate cleared the measure the same day. The president signed it Dec. 13 — PL 102-237.

Farmer Mac, a new secondary market for agricultural loans, had had difficulty attracting investors. The new law allowed Farmer Mac to borrow money with unsecured notes in order to purchase securities, backed by pools of long-term agricultural loans. The securities were guaranteed by Farmer Mac.

Existing law did not specifically authorize the agency to issue unsecured debt. In a last-minute compromise, Farmer Mac had to agree to be regulated by the FCA, the federal agency that oversaw the Farm Credit System of agricultural banks. Farmer Mac had wanted to be autonomous of the FCA.

The issue of Farmer Mac's regulation had been the subject of a conflict earlier between the House Agriculture and Banking committees. The Agriculture Committee on Sept. 12 approved a bill (HR 3300) that would have kept Farmer Mac under the FCA. The Banking Committee substantially rewrote the measure. Arguing that the FCA could not fairly regulate both the Farm Credit System and Farmer Mac, the panel approved language to create a largely autonomous regulatory office. No further action was taken on HR 3300.

STUDENT LOANS

The House Education and Labor Committee reported legislation (HR 3083 — H Rept 102-203) July 30 by voice vote to regulate Sallie Mae. The Senate Labor and Human Resources Committee approved similar legislation by voice vote July 31.

Sallie Mae provided a secondary market for banks to sell their federally guaranteed student loans. Both bills required Sallie Mae to maintain capital equal to 2 percent of its assets to cover emergencies. Both bills called for creating a regulator at the Treasury Department to oversee the agency.

The House measure allowed the regulator to limit Sallie Mae's activities if its capital level fell below 1.5 percent. The Senate bill set that level at 1 percent.

No further action was taken on the measure. ■

'Fast Track' Trade Procedures Extended

After intense White House lobbying, the Bush administration won a two-year renewal of special "fast track" procedures governing congressional consideration of trade agreements.

President Bush argued that the renewal was necessary if the administration was to continue multilateral trade talks on the General Agreement on Tariffs and Trade (GATT) and begin talks on a U.S.-Mexico free-trade pact. Fast-track procedures gave Congress 60 days to act once a trade agreement was submitted, and required an up or down vote without amendments.

The renewal process turned into a referendum on the controversial U.S.-Mexico trade talks, as Democrats charged that removing trade and investment barriers would take jobs from U.S. workers and that businesses would head south to take advantage of inexpensive labor and lax environmental laws.

Bush and Mexico's President Carlos Salinas de Gotari had agreed in June 1990 to negotiate a free-trade agreement.

The plan was accelerated by a stalemate in global trade talks under GATT and by Salinas' decision in the spring of 1990 that more open trade with the United States was the best route to economic development for Mexico.

Bush formally notified Congress of his plans to negotiate such a pact in September 1990. After months of high-level talks, he announced in early 1991 that Canada — which already had a free-trade agreement with the United States — would join the U.S.-Mexico talks. The goal would be a North American Free Trade Agreement.

BOXSCORE

➡ **Fast-Track Disapproval (S Res 78, H Res 101).** The legislation would have barred extension of fast-track procedures to bills implementing trade agreements entered into after May 31, 1991. Under the fast-track procedures, Congress had to approve or disapprove a trade agreement without amendments. The U.S.-Mexico trade agreement and the General Agreement on Tariffs and Trade were covered under this bill.

Reports: S Rept 102-56, H Rept 102-63

KEY ACTION

May 1 — The administration submitted its "action plan" on the U.S.-Mexico free-trade pact to Congress.

May 14 — The **House** Ways and Means Committee voted 9-27 to reject the measure, H Res 101, to deny a two-year extension of fast-track authority.

May 14 — The **Senate** Finance Committee reported the measure, S Res 78, unfavorably, 15-3.

May 23 — The **House** voted 192-231 to reject H Res 101.

May 24 — The **Senate** voted 36-59 to reject S Res 78.

June 1 — The extension went into effect.

Central to the White House victory on the fast track was an "action plan" issued May 1 addressing concerns about the U.S.-Mexico pact. The administration pledged to reject any weakening of U.S. environmental laws, to provide for worker adjustment assistance and to provide some industries threatened by the free-trade pact with long transition periods.

Congress had until June 1 to block the fast track extension; after that, fast track procedures would have continued automatically for two more years.

Opponents in both the House and Senate tried but failed to win support for resolutions barring the extension.

If either chamber had voted for the resolution, the procedure would have been blocked.

The House defeated the effort 192-231 on May 23. *(Vote 115, p. 28-H)*

The Senate followed suit on May 24, 36-59 *(Vote 86, p. 12-S)*.

Three Months of Debate

Bush's request March 1 for an extension of the fast track set off three months of debate, in which a loose but vocal coalition of labor and environmental groups opposed to a U.S.-Mexico pact teamed up to fight the White House, and Democrats struggled to find a common stand on the issue.

The AFL-CIO, which strongly opposed the U.S.-Mexico talks, made defeat of the fast track a top priority for the year. Labor officials argued that the Bush administration was using free trade with Mexico as a substitute for foreign aid — and that U.S. workers would pay the price in the form of lost jobs.

Environmental groups warned that a U.S.-Mexico free-trade agreement would exacerbate pollution along the border, while creating pressure to loosen U.S. environmental laws as businesses moved south to take advantage of weak Mexican enforcement of its pollution controls.

Human rights advocates worried about working conditions in Mexico. And U.S. fruit and vegetable growers voiced concern about added competition.

But the opponents found it difficult to devise a common strategy. The fast track was key to both the U.S.-Mexico talks and the GATT negotiations. Some members, particularly those from farm and textile-producing states, wanted to kill the GATT talks. But a larger group, mainly lawmakers from the Rust Belt, wanted to focus on the Mexico talks. There was no easy way to stop one set of negotiations without bringing down the other.

The opposition also lacked leadership from the top. Rep. Richard A. Gephardt, D-Mo., came under intense pressure from organized labor and some environmental groups to lead the charge, turning a procedural issue into a major political confrontation with Bush. But, while he spoke frequently in support of their concerns, Gephardt ultimately backed the extension.

Most of the Democratic leadership cautiously supported extension of the fast track. That included Speaker Thomas S. Foley of Washington and the heads of the two committees that oversaw trade, Ways and Means Chairman Dan Rostenkowski of Illinois and Finance Chairman Lloyd Bentsen of Texas. In part, their leanings reflected a traditional free-trade position. But Democrats also feared that if they campaigned against a U.S.-Mexico free-trade pact, Bush would be able to portray them as protectionist.

"My incliniation is to be supportive" Rostenkowski said in March. "But I see the storm brewing out there."

Test of Presidential Authority

For its part, the White House saw the fast-track vote as a major test of presidential authority. "I am going to work tirelessly," Bush said April 7, after a meeting with Salinas. "The credibility of the United States as a trading partner is on the line here." By early May, U.S. Trade Representative Carla A. Hills had met individually with about 150 members of Congress, including two-thirds of the Senate, according to her office. Members of Ways and Means got the personal touch. Rufus Yerxa, a former top committee aide who was serving as Bush's chief negotiator at the GATT talks, was brought back to spend several months selling the fast track on Capitol Hill.

The administration's chief lobbyist in the House, Nicholas E. Calio, devoted almost all of his time to the issue and postponed plans to leave the administration for the private sector until after the House vote. "We've not left a lot to chance here," Calio said.

Bush met with key Democrats Rostenkowski, Bentsen and Gephardt to discuss the issue and pressed Republicans to hold firm.

The administration argued that a free-trade agreement would stimulate Mexican development, lessening pressure on workers to cross the Rio Grande in search of work in the United States. It would lock in reforms by Salinas' government that had transformed Mexico's economy from one of the world's most protected to one of the more open. And it would provide U.S. companies with a vast labor pool and a more stable investment climate.

"We as a country will become more of a world-class competitor," U.S. Trade Representative Hills said.

Hills discounted the possibility of "wholesale migration" of industries and jobs to Mexico, saying that most tariffs on trade between Mexico and the United States had decreased in recent years, and that U.S. industries already would have left if there were an advantage to doing so.

"Companies have stayed located in the United States for good reasons," Hills said, citing a well-educated work force, superior infrastructure and the availability of capital.

A study by the U.S. International Trade Commission released Feb. 7 concluded that the overall benefits to the U.S. economy of a free-trade agreement with Mexico would be small "in the near to medium term" but that liberalized trade probably would increase Mexican growth, making it better able to buy U.S. goods and services.

Action Plan on Mexico Trade Pact

The turning point came May 1, when the White House released its action plan. Bentsen and Rostenkowski had written to Bush in early March requesting such a plan to allay congressional fears about a U.S.-Mexico pact. Gephardt had made a similar request.

Throughout the 80-page document, the administration avoided making ironclad pledges and reiterated its contentions that the agreement would not threaten jobs and would help the environment. But, at virtually every step, it also conceded that the doomsayers had legitimate concerns. The highlights:

- Most Mexican and U.S. tariff and import barriers would be reduced gradually.
- The administration would seek a provision allowing a temporary restoration of duties or other barriers if imports from Mexico or Canada "are a substantial cause of serious injury to a domestic industry."
- The agreement would include rules to prevent third countries from funneling their goods through Mexico to evade U.S. tariffs. The administration said it would seek a domestic-content rule of more than 50 percent for automotive imports.
- The administration promised to work with Congress to craft a program to provide services to workers who lost their jobs as a result of the U.S.-Mexico pact.
- The Labor Department would sign an agreement with the Mexican government providing for cooperation in the areas of occupational health and safety, work conditions, child labor and labor statistics. Enforcement would also be reviewed.
- The administration vowed not to negotiate lower standards than were currently in law in the areas of pesticides, energy conservation, toxic waste, and health and safety. And it maintained the right to bar entry to products that did not meet those standards.

With the action plan, the administration succeeded in driving a wedge between organized labor and some environmental organizations. Among the groups that expressed cautious support were the National Wildlife Federation, the National Audubon Society, the Natural Resources Defense Council (NRDC) and the Environmental Defense Fund. Opposed to the fast track were the Friends of the Earth, Greenpeace and Public Citizen, a consumer group.

The administration won the most plaudits for promising to include officials of environmental organizations on panels that advised Hills. Organized labor conceded that

What 'Fast Track' Means

Congress initiated the fast track as part of the 1974 Trade Act, partly to avoid becoming mired in the nitty-gritty of negotiating trade agreements. The procedure gave lawmakers 60 days from the submission of a trade agreement to vote the measure up or down; amendments were not allowed.

In the 1988 omnibus trade act, Congress reauthorized the procedure until 1991. A two-year extension until 1993 was permitted if neither the House nor the Senate objected. The hope was that the short time frame would spur negotiators to complete the Uruguay Round of GATT talks. *(1974 Almanac, p. 553; 1988 Almanac, p. 222)*

Once a trade agreement was reached, the administration and Congress informally negotiated legislative language to implement it, after which the bill was formally introduced and the fast track kicked in.

The fast track provided that:

- Committees had 45 days to consider the bill; they could not amend it.
- Each chamber had to vote on the bill within 15 days after the committee deadline.
- A motion to proceed to the bill in either chamber had to be acted on without delay or debate.
- Debate in each chamber was limited to 20 hours, and amendments were not in order. In the House, the time was divided equally between those who favored the bill and those who opposed it. In the Senate, debate time was divided equally between the majority and minority leaders.

losing environmental support was a blow. Said AFL-CIO lobbyist William J. Cunningham, "A lot of members have expressed concern about the environment. This just provides them some cover."

The plan received quick endorsement from key Democrats. Rostenkowski held a news conference to urge support for an extension. A statement from Bentsen said Bush had made "significant concessions" that "will give some comfort" to undecided lawmakers.

Indeed, Rostenkowski, Bentsen and others helped shape Bush's plan in the weeks leading up to its release. At their insistence, for example, the administration softened its stance against promising government benefits for workers who lost their jobs as a result of a free-trade agreement.

On May 9, Gephardt announced that he would support Bush's request for a fast-track extension, although he reiterated his position that Congress could still reject the agreement outright or simply suspend the fast track and permit amendments after the pact had been negotiated.

"I am prepared to support an extension of fast-track authority for trade treaties," Gephardt said. "But I do so with this caveat: If the administration sends to this Congress a trade treaty that trades away American jobs, or tolerates pollution of the environment or abuse of workers, we can, and we will, amend it or reject it."

CONGRESSIONAL ACTION

With the fight against the fast track unraveling, the Ways and Means Committee met May 14 to consider a bill (HR 101) to revoke the procedure. Although Rostenkowski opposed the bill, he had promised sponsor Byron L. Dorgan, D-N.D., that he would get a vote in committee and a later vote on the floor. Dorgan, who sought to kill the fast track because he opposed administration efforts to reduce agriculture subsidies under GATT, had introduced the bill on March 6.

The committee rejected Dorgan's resolution 9-27 and reported it unfavorably by voice vote. Then, by voice vote, it approved a resolution (H Res 146) emphasizing that Congress could suspend the fast track if the administration did not keep its promise to include adequate protections for U.S. workers, industries and the environment in the U.S.-Mexico agreement. Rostenkowski and Gephardt sponsored the non-binding resolution to give cover to the rank and file.

"There are members on both sides of the aisle who want to vote for something satisfying, as much as they can, labor's demands," Rostenkowski said.

The House Rules Committee voted May 14 to send both the resolution of disapproval and the Rostenkowski-Gephardt measure to the floor.

In a private caucus the day after the Ways and Means vote, some Democrats criticized their leaders, especially Gephardt, for locking arms with the administration. Yet the decision reflected the calculation — partly political, partly philosophical — that it was not wise to oppose Bush's trade policy and risk being branded a protectionist.

The House on May 23 voted 192-231 to reject HR 101. The non-binding resolution passed easily, 329-85.

On the same day Ways and Means acted, the Senate Finance Committee met and voted 15-3 to report S Res 78 unfavorably to the floor. The measure disapproving the fast track had been introduced on March 6 by Ernest F. Hollings, D-S.C. Like Dorgan, Hollings wanted to block a GATT agreement; he was opposed to administration efforts to phase out textile import quotas as part of the accord.

The committee votes foreshadowed a robust margin of victory for the administration on the floor. "This was a pretty good indication of the support there is for fast track," said Tom Daschle, D-S.D., who voted against the extension along with fellow Finance Committee members Donald W. Riegle Jr., D-Mich., and Daniel Patrick Moynihan, D-N.Y.

The full Senate voted May 24, rejecting Hollings' resolution 36-59. The vote gave Bush a congressional endorsement to continue GATT negotiations and to begin talks on the proposed U.S.-Mexico free-trade agreement.

Bentsen, a crucial Bush ally in the trade fight, called the vote a "momentous occasion for the Senate," determining whether the United States chooses to "move forward or backward as a country."

Defeat for Labor

The Senate and House votes were a blow to organized labor. Labor lobbyists and their supporters were hampered by the fact that they could find no way to promote a vote on Mexico without also sinking the GATT talks. Democratic leaders, principally Bentsen and Rostenkowski, strongly opposed efforts to change the rules to permit a separate vote on Mexico.

Lobbyists for the AFL-CIO discarded efforts to promote a separate vote in the House when it became clear in the days before the vote that the leadership would not support such a move. Their vote count showed only 140 lawmakers solidly committed to voting against the fast-track extension, well short of the majority needed to pass the Dorgan resolution of disapproval.

So labor scaled back: It supported a plan by Sander M. Levin, D-Mich., which called on the Bush administration to report on the progress of the Mexico negotiations by May 1, 1992. Basically, labor sought to keep the issue on Congress' agenda, in hope of creating sufficient pressure for a vote on withdrawing the fast track for the Mexico talks sometime in 1992.

According to top House leadership aides, Gephardt, seeking to satisfy as many of labor's demands as possible, floated the idea of amending the fast-track extension to provide for such a midterm review. But the idea was quashed by Rostenkowski, who strongly backed the administration's desire for an unamended endorsement of its negotiating authority.

In a last-ditch effort, the AFL-CIO tried to persuade House lawmakers to reject the rule governing floor debate. When that failed, even opponents conceded that a House majority vote in favor of extending the fast track had become a foregone conclusion.

In the Senate, Riegle wanted to offer his own plan, which would have extended the fast track for one year, rather than two, and permitted amendments to the Mexico agreement in several areas, including labor standards, adjustment assistance and the environment. Riegle feared the Mexico talks would lead his state's automobile and auto parts manufacturers to move assembly plants south. But under Senate rules, the Hollings resolution could not be amended.

Riegle vowed to try to bring up his bill in the Senate later in the year, either as a free-standing measure or by attaching it to a must-pass bill. But such a measure would have been a target for a filibuster. And once the extension had been approved, the steam went out of efforts to block the fast track. ■

Bill To Limit China Trade Not Completed

Critics of President Bush's China policy failed to complete work during the session on a bill to set conditions on continued normal trade status with Beijing. Both the House and Senate approved bills to restrict renewal of China's most-favored-nation (MFN) trade status in 1992 — although the Senate vote was short of the two-thirds needed to override a certain presidential veto.

The House approved a conference agreement on the bill (HR 2212 — H Rept 102-392), but the Senate did not give final approval before lawmakers adjourned for the year.

With MFN, Chinese exports were able to enter the United States at the same low tariff rates as goods from most other countries.

Bush indicated on May 15 that he intended to renew China's MFN status for one year, effective July 3; on May 29, he formally notified Congress. His move was greeted by widespread, bipartisan opposition from lawmakers who were eager to punish Beijing for its 1989 crackdown on pro-democracy activists in Tiananmen Square, as well as for China's alleged export of missile technology, reported use of prison labor to produce exports and deepening trade surplus with the United States.

The president had deflected similar efforts on Capitol Hill in 1990 to force the administration to take a harder line toward China. The 101st Congress' effort died when the Senate failed to act on two House-passed bills or its own measures. *(1990 Almanac, p. 764)*

China had gained MFN status as part of a trade agreement with the United States completed in 1980 and renewed every three years thereafter. However, as a communist country, China had to meet a second test to retain its low-tariff status: Each year, the president had to waive the so-called Jackson-Vanik amendment to the 1974 Trade Act, which barred MFN to countries with non-market economies that did not allow free emigration. In technical terms, that is what Bush did on May 29 — he notified Congress that he was waiving Jackson-Vanik for China.

Legislation that began moving through both chambers in 1991 would bar the president from renewing the special trade status in 1992 unless he reported that China had accounted for and released citizens held as a result of the 1989 Tiananmen Square demonstrations. He would also have to report that China had made significant progress in three categories: human rights, trade and weapons proliferation. China would not be eligible if it transferred certain ballistic missiles, missile launchers or equipment for building nuclear weapons to Iran or Syria.

BOXSCORE

➡ **Conditional MFN for China (HR 2212).** The bill set conditions for renewing most-favored-nation (MFN) trade status with China in 1992.

President Bush had threatened to veto the measure because he wanted no congressional conditions attached to China's MFN status — which provided low tariffs for Chinese goods imported into the United States.

Reports: H Rept 102-392, S Rept 102-101.

KEY ACTION

May 29 — President Bush notified Congress that he intended to renew China's MFN status for one year.

June 26 — The **House** Ways and Means Committee approved HR 2212 by voice vote.

June 27 — The **Senate** Finance Committee approved S 1367, 11-9.

July 10 — The **House** passed HR 2212, 313-112.

July 23 — The **Senate** passed HR 2212, 55-44, after substituting it with the text of S 1367.

Nov. 26 — The **House** adopted conference report, 409-21.

The administration argued that withdrawing MFN status — which would have raised U.S. tariffs on Chinese imports from an average of 8.4 percent to 47.5 percent — was the wrong instrument to use to achieve human rights and other goals in China. Bush argued that it would hurt the most reformist elements of Chinese society — those in the private sector whose livelihoods were tied to exports.

"If we withdrew MFN or imposed conditions that would make trade impossible, we would punish South China . . . the very region where free-market reforms and the challenge to central authority are the strongest," Bush said in a speech May 27 at Yale University.

The same day, the White House announced that it was blocking sales of high-speed computers to China and barring U.S. companies from participating in Chinese satellite launches — sanctions aimed at halting Chinese proliferation of missile and nuclear weapons technology. The move seemed intended to demonstrate that the administration would take action on its own, without being required to do so by Congress.

Congressional critics argued that Bush — a former U.S. envoy to Beijing and a president often described as his own China desk officer — was too gentle on China. Congress argued they had no choice but to take the lead in asserting a tougher U.S. policy. Members cited reports that the Chinese were using prison labor to produce goods exported to the United States, that they were evading U.S. textile quotas by diverting shipments through Hong Kong, and that they were selling high-tech weapons and nuclear technology to Middle Eastern countries, despite promises to limit proliferation.

Media reports, based on U.S. intelligence sources, had indicated that China was helping Algeria develop a nuclear weapons capability and that it provided the government of Pakistan with mobile launchers used for firing medium-range missiles. There also were longstanding reports that China was seeking to sell missiles to Syria and Iran.

In addition, China's trade surplus with the United States had grown from $3.5 billion in 1988 to $10.4 billion in 1990. Exacerbated by a host of new tariffs and licensing requirements on imports, the surplus was expected to reach $15 billion in 1992, the second-largest, after Japan's.

Critics argued that Chinese leaders had not improved their behavior since Bush last renewed MFN, in 1990, and that they did not deserve further special treatment. "They're not acting in a way that I think would suggest they've been our friends," said Rep. Nancy Pelosi, D-Calif. "From that standpoint, they shouldn't have MFN."

SENATE ACTION

It was clear from the outset that the chief fight over extending MFN to China would occur in the Senate, and the White House concentrated its lobbying effort there. Majority Leader George J. Mitchell, D-Maine, weighed in early, introducing a bill May 16 that would have cut off MFN within six months of passage unless China met a series of stiff conditions.

"I believe that it is time to change our policies toward the leaders of China, to recognize that the president's policy has failed, and the answer to a failed policy is not to continue it unchanged," Mitchell said in a May 16 Senate floor speech.

Mitchell won approval for his bill, first from the Finance Committee and then from the full Senate, but only after modifying it to apply only to the following year's renewal of MFN. But the vote fell short of the two-thirds majority that senators knew would be needed to override a veto.

Finance Committee

The Senate Finance Committee took up Mitchell's bill (S 1367) on June 27, one day after the House Ways and Means Committee sent an equally tough measure to the floor, amid signs that many Republicans were beginning to consider loyalty to the president more important than punishing Beijing.

The effectiveness of the lobbying by the White House and the Republican leadership was apparent. Although several committee Republicans had previously expressed doubts about Bush's position, not one voted for the bill. Several said it would terminate U.S.-China relations, leaving the United States without influence and abandoning reformers within the country.

Mitchell, who served on the committee, did not even get the support of all the Democrats. Panel member Max Baucus, D-Mont., expressed the hope that Congress would forgo placing conditions on MFN if the administration would agree on its own to impose sanctions against China, including retaliating for unfair trading practices. Baucus joined in an 11-9 party-line vote to send Mitchell's bill to the floor, but he and other Democrats balked at giving it a favorable recommendation.

The committee also sent to the floor a bill introduced by Alan Cranston, D-Calif., to withdraw China's MFN status in 1991. It received an unfavorable recommendation.

The Mitchell bill would have allowed China to continue its MFN status in 1991 but would have withdrawn it in 1992 unless China accounted for and released prisoners arrested during the Tiananmen Square protests, stopped exporting products to the United States made by forced labor and stopped supplying arms to the Khmer Rouge guerrillas in Cambodia.

China also would have been required to make progress on ending human rights violations, reducing its trade surplus with the United States and limiting weapons proliferation. Further sales of ballistic missiles and missile launchers to the Middle East would have resulted in immediate termination of China's MFN status.

"Clearly, the Bush administration's China policy has failed. It hasn't produced improved human rights conditions in China. It hasn't improved China's trade record with the U.S. And it has not made China a more responsible world citizen with respect to weapons proliferation," Mitchell said.

Mitchell's problems attracting support became obvious two days before the markup, when he unveiled his legislation, a modified version of the bill he had introduced May 16.

The move was an implicit acknowledgment that he could not attract a majority for his earlier bill, which would have required Beijing to make more sweeping changes or see its MFN status cut off after six months.

Mitchell called his second bill "an effort to simplify, reduce in number and make more specific and attainable" the requirements that China would have to meet.

His original legislation would have required release of all political prisoners in China and an end to religious persecution, among other conditions.

The compromise won Mitchell the support of several Democrats, including Lloyd Bentsen, Texas, chairman of the Finance Committee. But he had only one Republican cosponsor — Malcolm Wallop of Wyoming — and lost another — Alfonse M. D'Amato of New York.

Republicans, who had been urged by the White House to reject Mitchell's approach, argued that the bill was tantamount to withdrawing China's MFN status because Beijing was unlikely to comply with the conditions. "My discomfort with the Mitchell position is simply that there's no possibility of it being successful," said Slade Gorton, R-Wash.

Mitchell not only needed Republicans, he had to woo back a block of Democrats, including Baucus, who had signed a letter urging Bush to take further steps against

What is MFN?

Most-favored-nation status (MFN) provided for normal, non-discriminatory trade. The United States extended MFN status to nearly every country in the world.

Who was eligible: In general, the nearly 100 members of the General Agreement on Tariffs and Trade granted MFN to their trading partners. In doing so, they agreed to accept each other's exports at the lowest tariff rates — the rates that each charged its "most favored nation." (Certain developing countries qualified for even lower tariffs under the Generalized System of Preferences.)

Communist countries an exception: Under the Jackson-Vanik amendment to the 1974 Trade Act, the president could grant MFN status to a communist country only as part of a commercial trade agreement — and only if he certified that the country permitted free emigration or if he waived the requirement because the country was improving its emigration policies. A waiver had to be renewed annually.

Congress could reject the president's waiver or certification by approving a joint resolution. The measure had to be signed by the president or enacted over his veto.

China's status: China first received MFN status from the United States through a commercial trade agreement in 1980 after President Jimmy Carter waived Jackson-Vanik. The waiver had been extended annually since. *(1980 Almanac, p. 356)*

China to try to lessen the pressure Congress felt to act.

Mitchell was cautious about predictions that he would put together the two-thirds majority needed to override a veto in the Senate. "We'll pass it with a majority. Whether we'll have 67 votes, I don't know," he said after the Finance Committee action.

Floor Action

Mitchell's drive to wrest control of China policy from Bush fell short on July 23, as his bill passed the Senate — but without the votes to override a veto. The 55-44 vote left the Maine Democrat 12 votes shy of a veto-proof margin (assuming that all senators voted on the override). *(Vote 142, p. 19-S)*

"The president has said that he will veto this bill, and he will," White House spokesman Marlin Fitzwater warned.

The White House had mounted an intensive lobbying campaign against the bill. Farm groups — fearing the loss of the China market, which accounted for more than $500 million in wheat sales in 1990 — lobbied heavily as well.

"When and how are members of the Senate going to get the backbone to stand up and say, that's enough?" asked Mitchell, closing the debate with a 10-minute speech that excoriated the Chinese government.

Echoing the administration's arguments, Republicans accused Democrats of trying to embarrass the president, while misguidedly moving to withdraw the best lever the United States had to force China toward reform.

Nor could Mitchell overcome a split within his own party that kept several Democrats whose states were heavily dependent on exports to China from voting for his bill. Seven Democrats voted against the measure — Baucus; John B. Breaux, La.; Quentin N. Burdick, N.D.; Kent Conrad, N.D.; Jim Exon, Neb.; J. Bennett Johnston, La.; and Richard C. Shelby, Ala. And six Republicans supported the bill — D'Amato; Wallop; Jake Garn, Utah; Jesse Helms, N.C.; Connie Mack, Fla.; and Robert C. Smith, N.H.

The administration's success also represented a victory for Baucus, who had taken a prominent role in opposing conditions on MFN status for China. Baucus worked closely with Minority Leader Bob Dole, R-Kan., in urging the White House to take additional punitive steps against China to deflect sentiment in Congress to act.

Bush responded by pledging in a July 19 letter to take several steps to increase pressure on Beijing. He promised, for example, to strengthen multilateral controls on future Chinese weapon sales and to toughen enforcement of U.S. laws prohibiting imports from China made with prison labor. The most significant element of the letter was a pledge to "work actively" to see that Taiwan was able to join the General Agreement on Tariffs and Trade (GATT). The United States had been unwilling to see Taiwan enter GATT in advance of China.

Almost all of the Republicans who had remained publicly uncommitted going into the debate sided with the administration in the end. They included Gorton; James M. Jeffords, Vt.; Bob Kasten, Wis.; and Arlen Specter, Pa.

For China to receive MFN in 1992, Mitchell's bill would have required the country to:

- Provide an accounting of citizens detained, accused or sentenced because of pro-democracy protests leading up to, during and after the Tiananmen Square crackdown.
- Release citizens imprisoned because of their participation in the protests.
- Cease exporting products to the United States produced by forced labor.
- Cease supplying arms and military assistance to the Khmer Rouge guerrillas in Cambodia.
- Adhere to the Joint Declaration on Hong Kong, which set out terms for transfer of the territory from Britain to China.

To qualify for MFN, China would have had to show "significant progress" in other areas, including:

- Fulfilling its commitment to engage in high-level discussions with the United States on human rights and take action to prevent violations of human rights in China and Tibet.
- Ending harassment of Chinese students in the United States.
- Granting access for humanitarian and human rights groups to prisoners, trials and places of detention.
- Providing protection of U.S. copyrights, patents and other intellectual property rights.
- Improving access for U.S. exports to China by lowering tariffs and other trade barriers.
- Adhering to limits and controls on proliferation of nuclear, chemical and biological arms.

Amendments adopted on the floor, all by voice vote, included language:

- By Bob Graham, D-Fla., requiring the president to certify that China had made significant progress in reducing assistance to Cuba.
- By Barbara A. Mikulski, D-Md., and Tim Wirth, D-Colo., requiring the president to certify that the Chinese government did not engage in coercive abortion or sterilization.
- By Bob Kerrey, D-Neb., requiring that, if the United States terminated China's MFN status, the president had to undertake efforts to ensure that members of GATT took similar action.
- By Jesse Helms, R-N.C., allowing public interest groups and individuals in businesses whose goods competed with imported products to petition the Commerce Department to determine whether goods imported into the United States were made with convict labor. If violations were found, the Treasury Department could confiscate the goods and impose penalties on the importers.
- By Joseph R. Biden Jr., D-Del., terminating China's MFN status in 1992 if the president determined after enactment of the bill that China had transferred to Syria or Iran M-9 or M-11 ballistic missiles or missile launchers, or technology related to the manufacture of nuclear weapons.

Biden's amendment modified a requirement in Mitchell's bill that would have denied MFN to China immediately if it engaged in such arms transfers.

By a vote of 55-35, the Senate adopted an amendment by Jeff Bingaman, D-N.M., stating that the United States had failed to use existing laws to respond to China's human rights violations, proliferation of dangerous military technology and unfair trade practices. *(Vote 141, p. 19-S)*

It directed the president to:

- Work "more forcefully" with U.S. allies, especially Japan and European countries, and with the World Bank, to restrict transfers of technology to China.
- Encourage members of the Missile Technology Control Regime to set up a working group on China's transfer of missiles to other countries.
- Direct the U.S. trade representative to take action under Section 301 of the 1974 trade act against unfair trade practices.

China Trade Restrictions Provisions

As reported by the conference committee, the bill set the following conditions for extending China's most-favored-nation status in 1992:

TIANANMEN SQUARE

China was required to:

- Provide an accounting of people who were detained, accused or sentenced as a result of political protest before, during and after the June 3, 1989, crackdown by the Chinese government in Tiananmen Square.
- Release people imprisoned because of their role in the protests.

The bill did not specify that all prisoners would have to be accounted for or released.

OTHER CATEGORIES

In addition, China was required to make "overall significant progress" in achieving the following objectives:

Human Rights

- Preventing human rights abuses inside the country and Tibet.
- Stopping the export of products made with prison labor and allowing U.S. officials and those from international humanitarian organizations to inspect prisons suspected of producing goods for export.
- Ending religious persecution and releasing incarcerated religious leaders.
- Lifting restrictions on the media and on broadcasts by Voice of America.
- Ending harassment of Chinese citizens inside the United States, including returning and renewing passports confiscated as retribution for pro-democracy activities.
- Ensuring access by international human rights monitoring groups to prisoners, trials and places of detention.
- Ensuring freedom from torture and from inhumane prison conditions.
- Lifting bans on peaceful assembly and demonstration imposed after June 3, 1989.
- Fulfilling its promise to hold high-level discussions on human rights issues.
- Adhering to the Joint Declaration on Hong Kong, which sets terms on transfer of the British colony to the People's Republic of China.

Trade

- Providing adequate protection for U.S. patents, copyrights and other intellectual property.
- Ensuring U.S. exporters non-discriminatory access to Chinese markets, including lowering tariffs, removing non-tariff barriers and purchasing more U.S. goods and services.
- Ending unreasonable and discriminatory unfair trade practices against the United States.

Weapons Proliferation

- Adhering to multilateral non-proliferation agreements, including the Missile Technology Control Regime, the standards set by the Nuclear Suppliers Group and standards set by the Australia Group on chemical and biological weapons proliferation.
- Giving clear and unequivocal assurances that it is not assisting and will not assist any non-nuclear state in acquiring nuclear weapons.

The bill specified that China would not be eligible for MFN status if it sold M-9 or M-11 ballistic missiles or missile launchers to Iran or Syria after Nov. 26, 1991, or if it provided material, equipment or technology that contributed significantly to their development of a nuclear device.

GENERAL PROVISIONS

- **Multilateral sanctions.** If the president decided not to grant China MFN status in 1992, he would be required within 30 days to try to persuade other nations that have signed the General Agreement on Tariffs and Trade to either withdraw their MFN treatment of China or to take similar action.
- **General policy.** Non-binding language encouraged the president to seek a U.N. investigation of human rights abuses in China, undertake retaliatory trade action against Chinese practices that restrict U.S. commerce, seek international support to prevent technology transfer to China, encourage stronger multilateral controls on Chinese missile exports and continue U.S. sanctions against China that were already in place. ■

- Encourage the Human Rights Commission of the United Nations to issue a report on human rights conditions in China.

HOUSE ACTION

The House had approved a bill by a seemingly veto-proof margin before the Senate acted. The strength of the House vote was no surprise, since the House had backed a previous effort in 1990 to set conditions on MFN for China by an even bigger margin.

Ways and Means Committee

Initially, it seemed likely that the House would pass a more moderate bill than Mitchell's, setting the stage for a compromise that some hoped Bush would be able to support. That scenario evaporated when the Ways and Means Committee took up the issue June 26, producing a bill (HR 2212) that was tougher than the Senate version in some respects and that was clearly unacceptable to the White House.

HR 2212 was a joint effort by Democrats Pelosi, Don J. Pease of Ohio and Stephen J. Solarz of New York. All three had opposed unconditional renewal of MFN but had dis agreed about how tough a stance to take.

Negotiations among them the week of June 10 led to agreement on a bill that would have withdrawn China's MFN status in 1992 unless Beijing disclosed the fate of protesters unaccounted for since the 1989 crackdown and released some of those arrested. In addition, the president would have had to certify that China had made "significant overall progress" in ending gross violations of human rights and religious persecution, removing restrictions on the media, ending harassment of Chinese students in the United States, ensuring freedom from torture and inhumane prison conditions, and granting humanitarian groups access to prisons.

Many Ways and Means Republicans argued vehemently that the panel should not force Bush to revoke MFN by imposing conditions that China was unlikely to meet. They were joined by Committee Chairman Dan Rostenkowski, D-Ill., and Trade Subcommittee Chairman Sam M. Gibbons, D-Fla.

"We'll end up with a bill that will be popular in the U.S. Congress but will harden the Chinese government's resolve," Rostenkowski warned.

Their pleas for restraint were ignored, however, as committee Democrats passed several amendments toughening the bill. Several Republican lawmakers joined in the amendment-fest.

Amendments approved by the committee specified that China could not receive MFN in 1992 unless it:

- Did not employ coerced abortion or involuntary sterilization to enforce its one-child-per-family policy. The amendment, sponsored by Jim Moody, D-Wis., was adopted by voice vote.
- Did not assist non-nuclear countries in acquiring or developing nuclear weapons. The amendment, sponsored by Thomas J. Downey, D-N.Y., and Jim Bunning, R-Ky., was adopted by a 21-13 vote. An amendment by Pete Stark, D-Calif., adding ballistic missiles to the restrictions was adopted 18-14.
- Dropped its opposition to Taiwan becoming a signatory to GATT, the multilateral accord governing most world trade. The amendment by Philip M. Crane, R-Ill., was adopted by voice vote.
- Took steps to prevent the export of goods to the United States made with forced labor and allowed human rights organizations access to Chinese prisons suspected of using forced labor. The amendment by Crane was adopted by voice vote.

The key test of the administration's clout came on an amendment sponsored by ranking committee Republican Bill Archer of Texas, who proposed giving Bush wide discretion to decide whether to continue MFN in 1992. All but two of the 13 committee Republicans voted for Archer's amendment, as did Rostenkowski and Gibbons. But it was not enough. The amendment failed by a vote of 15-17.

By voice vote, the committee sent the Pelosi measure to the floor with a favorable recommendation. Rostenkowski opposed the final product.

Also sent to the floor was a resolution sponsored by Gerald B. H. Solomon, R-N.Y., that would have revoked China's MFN status immediately upon enactment. The Solomon measure, which was viewed as a symbolic action unlikely to become law, was reported without recommendation.

Floor Action

Lawmakers from both parties ignored Bush's stiff opposition, approving the bill on July 10 by a vote of 313-112. The vote was well above the two-thirds majority needed to sustain a promised veto. *(Vote 205, p. 50-H)*

The House also passed, by a vote of 223-204, Solomon's measure requiring an immediate cutoff. *(Vote 203, p. 50-H)*

By administration officials' own admission, Bush never had a chance in the House. It was the second straight year that lawmakers had passed legislation to punish China's communist leaders for the 1989 crackdown; the 1990 bill passed 384-30 in the House.

Amendments were not allowed on the floor, although Rostenkowski staged a parliamentary maneuver to demonstrate his displeasure with the bill. All of the toughening amendments attached by Ways and Means were stripped out when the bill was brought to the floor and only restored in the last moments before passage without a recorded vote.

Defenders of the Bush administration's position, who were scarce, argued that Pelosi's bill would set too high a standard for Beijing to meet. But a motion by Archer to return the bill to committee with instructions to revise it in a way that would give Bush broad discretion over renewing China's MFN status was defeated 118-308. *(Vote 204, p. 50-H)*

Despite an impassioned plea from Minority Leader Robert H. Michel, R-Ill., Republicans defected from the president in droves.

Pelosi denied that supporting her bill was tantamount to withdrawing China's MFN status in 1992. "These are not impossible conditions but conditions that easily can be met," she said.

Even some of her supporters questioned that, however. Solarz said he was voting for the measure to express his displeasure with Beijing, but he said he thought the conditions were too onerous and were unlikely to be met. He expressed hope that, once the Senate passed its version of the bill, lawmakers "will come to their senses and clean up the bill" in a joint House-Senate conference.

FINAL ACTION

Both the House and Senate appointed conferees in late October. Without holding a public meeting the conferees produced a compromise version of the bill in late November. The House approved the report by a vote of 409-21 *(Vote 436, p. 106-H)*.

Under the compromise, the president would be barred from recommending a further waiver of Jackson-Vanik in 1992 unless China accounted for and released citizens detained as a result of the Tiananmen Square protests. In addition, China would not receive MFN if it transferred M-9 or M-11 missiles or missile launchers to Syria or Iran or assisted those countries in building nuclear weapons.

Beyond that, most of the other preconditions specified in the House and Senate bills were put in a second section, which simply required that China make "significant progress" in achieving human rights, trade and non-proliferation objectives. *(Provisions, p. 124)*

Only the House adopted the conference report before the first session ended. ■

Trade Barriers Lifted for Soviets, Others

In the aftermath of the Cold War, Congress cleared a series of trade measures to provide non-discriminatory treatment to exports from the Soviet Union, the Baltic nations and several other former communist countries.

Lawmakers approved most-favored-nation (MFN) status for the Soviet Union, Bulgaria and Mongolia. In addition, they gave the president authority to extend MFN status permanently to Hungary, Czechoslovakia and the Baltic nations. With MFN, a country was eligible for the same low tariff rates available to most other U.S. trading partners.

Under the Jackson-Vanik amendment to the 1974 Trade Act, the Soviet Union and most other communist countries could get MFN treatment from the United States only if the president certified that they allowed free emigration or if he waived the restriction. A waiver had to be renewed annually, and Congress could reject it. The country also was required to have a trade agreement, subject to congressional approval, with the United States. *(Jackson-Vanik, 1973 Almanac, p. 833; 1974 Almanac, p. 553)*

U.S.-Soviet Trade Agreement

The Senate on Nov. 25 approved a U.S.-Soviet trade agreement that included reciprocal MFN status. The Senate vote, taken by voice, cleared the measure (H J Res 346 — PL 102-197) for the president. The House had approved it on Nov. 20 by a vote of 350-78. The president signed the bill into law on Dec. 9. *(Vote 410, p. 100-H)*

President Bush and Soviet President Mikhail S. Gorbachev signed the trade agreement in June 1990 during a summit meeting in Washington. But Bush said he would hold off sending the pact to Congress for approval until the Soviet parliament passed a law guaranteeing Soviet citizens the right to emigrate freely. The Soviets adopted such a law on May 20.

Bush submitted the pact to Congress on Aug. 2, shortly after returning from a summit with Gorbachev in Moscow. The chief opposition on Capitol Hill came from members who were disturbed by Moscow's intransigence on the issue of independence for the breakaway Baltic republics — Lithuania, Latvia and Estonia. Sen. Bill Bradley, D-N.J., a critic of the trade pact, introduced legislation on July 31 that would have exempted the Baltic States from the U.S.-Soviet agreement and granted them separate MFN status by reinstating trade agreements with the republics that were suspended in 1951. However, these objections were overtaken by events.

The failed coup that rocked the Soviet Union in August accelerated the drive for independence by many Soviet republics. On Oct. 9, Bush sent Congress a revised U.S.-Soviet trade agreement crafted to exclude the Baltic nations, which by then were independent countries no longer part of the Soviet Union.

Lawmakers questioned whether granting MFN status to the Soviet Union was still relevant if the country was coming apart.

But the White House argued that the trade status would encourage reformers and that the republics had indicated they would abide by the terms of the pact even if they won independence from Moscow.

The near-term increase in two-way trade was not expected to be great. Though U.S. trade law set significantly higher tariff rates on goods from the few countries that did not have MFN status, most Soviet exports were raw materials and other goods that already had low tariffs. Moreover, the Soviets had little hard currency to buy U.S. goods and few products attractive enough to export.

In addition to granting MFN, the agreement ensured that U.S. companies could maintain business facilities in the Soviet Union, protected patents and other intellectual property, and established a trade dispute settlement mechanism. Adequate protections for intellectual property were among the last provisions agreed to before the August summit. *(Agreement highlights, 1990 Almanac, p. 205)*

As a prelude to gaining approval for the trade agreement, Bush had waived Jackson-Vanik for the Soviet Union on June 3; Congress did not attempt to reject the waiver. The waiver still had to be renewed annually.

Still on the books at year's end were laws that prevented more than $300 million in export financing by the Export-Import Bank and a separate $300 million cap on financing for the Soviet Union by other government agencies, except the Commodity Credit Corporation, which financed agricultural exports.

Hungary, Czechoslovakia

A bill that began as a simple measure to permanently exempt Hungary and Czechoslovakia from the restrictions contained in the Jackson-Vanik amendment, grew in the final days of the session into a broader bill (HR 1724 — H Rept 102-391) carried to final passage by provisions re-jiggering unemployment benefit formulas.

The must-pass unemployment changes had been agreed to as part of a deal that had allowed Congress to clear the Emergency Unemployment Compensation Act of 1991 (HR 3575 — PL 102-164) earlier in the month. *(Unemployment benefits, p. 301)*

The House Ways and Means Committee reported the Hungary-Czechoslovakia bill on Sept. 26. The measure noted that the two countries had dedicated themselves to respect for fundamental human rights, accorded their citizens the right to emigrate and travel freely, reversed over 40 years of communist dictatorship, embraced democracy and introduced far-reaching economic reforms.

The House passed the non-controversial measure under suspension of the rules on Oct. 8. The Senate took up the bill on Nov. 15 and passed it, after adding the compromise that had just been reached on jobless benefits.

Five days later, on Nov. 20, the House agreed to the unemployment language. But by then Ways and Means Chairman Dan Rostenkowski, D-Ill, was ready to move forward on several other trade bills, which were incorporated into HR 1724 on the floor. The bills repealed the prohibition on the importation of gold coins from the Soviet Union (HR 3347), provided MFN status for the Baltic nations (HR 3313), provided special benefits for Andean nations (HR 661) and imposed sanctions for the proliferation of chemical and biological weapons (HR 3409). The House approved the broader bill by a vote of 350-78. *(Vote 411, p. 100-H)*

The Senate was unhappy over one piece of the package, the trade benefits for Andean countries, and asked for a conference. The House was unwilling to give up the Andean initiative and had the upper hand since it was politically unacceptable to let the unemployment provisions die. The Senate gave in, the House approved the conference report on the bill Nov. 26, and the Senate cleared the measure the same day. President Bush signed the bill on Dec. 4 (PL 102-182).

The Baltics

The House Ways and Means Trade Subcommittee gave voice vote approval on Sept. 24 to a bill (HR 3313 — H Rept 102-339) exempting the Baltic nations of Estonia, Latvia and Lithuania from Jackson-Vanik restrictions and making them permanently eligible for MFN status. The legislation, sponsored by subcommittee Chairman Sam M. Gibbons, D-Fla., was supported by the Bush administration, which had promised the Baltics that they would be granted MFN status separately from the Soviet Union to emphasize their newly won independence.

The United States had extended MFN treatment to the three nations in the late 1920s when they were independent and had never formally recognized their incorporation into the Soviet Union. On Sept. 2, 1991, the United States established diplomatic relations with the three nations.

However, the Baltics bill was one of several trade measures that Ways and Means Chairman Dan Rostenkowski,

D-Ill., refused to schedule for full committee action until the Office of Management and Budget (OMB) told him how it planned to recoup revenue that would be lost to the Treasury because of the lower duties on imports. The revenue loss was expected to be small, but Rostenkowski said he wanted to avoid the tiny across-the-board cut in spending (a "minisequester") that would be triggered if the money were not recouped. OMB Director Richard G. Darman had angered Rostenkowski in April by ordering a tiny sequester because of a favor Rostenkowski did for his alma mater, Loyola University of Chicago. *(Sequester, p. 74)*

The full Ways and Means Committee reported the bill on Nov. 19, after Darman told Rostenkowsi that surplus revenue generated by passage of an unemployment compensation bill would cover the trade measures. The next day, the House folded the Baltics bill into another measure granting permanent MFN status to Czechoslovakia and Hungary (HR 1724 — H Rept 102-391); it then approved the bill, which had grown to include several other provisions as well, by a vote of 350-78. *(Vote 411, p. 100-H)*

The Senate asked for a conference on the bill because of objections unrelated to the Baltics provisions. But the House would not give in, and the Senate approved the conference report by voice vote on Nov. 26. The House cleared the bill by voice vote the same day.

Bulgaria, Mongolia

Congress approved bilateral trade agreements with Bulgaria and Mongolia that included the extension of most-favored-nation status to those countries. The two measures (H J Res 281 and H J Res 282) were approved by voice vote in the the House under suspension of the rules on Oct. 29. The Senate cleared them by voice vote Oct. 31. The measures were signed by President Bush on Nov. 13 (PL 102-157 and PL 102-158). ■

Andean Initiative

Legislation that extended duty-free treatment to such goods as leather handbags, luggage and vegetables exported by Bolivia, Colombia, Ecuador and Peru was cleared quickly by Congress at the end of the 1991 session.

The measure, known as the Andean initiative, was incorporated into a bill (HR 1724 — PL 102-182) along with other trade provisions and language reworking the existing formula for unemployment benefits. *(Unemployment benefits, p. 301)*

A centerpiece of the Bush administration's anti-drug efforts, the Andean initiative was intended to provide greater access to U.S. markets to encourage peasants in those countries to shift out of coca leaf production (the source of cocaine) and into legal products for export.

However, lawmakers retained duties on a number of important products to shield U.S. producers from greater compeiition. Excluded from the duty-free list were tuna, petroleum, footwear, apparel and textiles — including llama and alpaca wool, a lucrative export from the region surrounding the Andes mountains.

Ways and Means Action

The House Ways and Means Committee approved an Andean initiative bill (originally HR 661 — H Rept 102-337) on Nov. 19. The committee reversed a decision made in September by the Trade Subcommittee to grant duty-free treatment for llama and alpaca wool. The amendment to preserve tariffs on South American llama and alpaca wool products offered by Ed Jenkins, D-Ga., a strong protector of the domestic textile industry, was approved by a vote of 13-10.

Jenkins argued that duty-free treatment would give the imports a competitive advantage over products made with high-quality wool and other fibers.

The committee also adopted by voice vote another Jenkins amendment to bar duty-free treatment for rum imported from South America. Supporters said the amendment would cut into profits earned by rum exporters in the Virgin Islands and elsewhere in the Caribbean.

The Bush administration opposed both amendments.

Critics said that peasants would not shift out of coca production if Congress insisted on exempting products that the Andean countries were most capable of exporting.

"What we're doing here is to further reduce the incentives for these small countries in the Andes to make the transition from the goods we are trying to control," said Sam M. Gibbons, D-Fla., chairman of the Trade Subcommittee.

The committee also voted to count Andean imports along with imports from other countries in anti-dumping or countervailing duty cases in deciding whether imports were causing damage to U.S. industries. The amendment, adopted by a 13-7 vote, was proposed by Bill Thomas, R-Calif., although he had voted not to count Andean imports in the total when the issue was debated in subcommittee.

A Thomas amendment to withdraw duty-free treatment for processed tomatoes was rejected.

FLOOR ACTION

The House on Nov. 20 incorporated the Andean bill into a measure (HR 1724) extending most-favored-nation trade status for Hungary and Czechoslovakia. The House approved the broader bill by a vote of 407-21. *(Vote 411, p. 100-H)*

The Senate took up the bill the night of Nov. 20 but refused to give its assent to the Andean initiative. According to Senate aides, there was concern that no hearings had been held and that the trade preferences could have had adverse effects on U.S. producers of leather goods, cut flowers and vegetables.

But the House insisted on the Andean provisions. Senators, particularly Finance Committee Chairman Lloyd Bentsen, D-Texas, then dropped their opposition because they did not want to jeopardize the must-pass unemployment benefit provisions.

The House approved the conference report on the bill (H Rept 102-391) Nov. 26, and the Senate cleared the measure the same day. President Bush signed the bill on Dec. 4. ■

White House Pressure Blocks Export Bill

Despite strong support in Congress, efforts to pass a bill updating federal restrictions on sales of high-technology goods to foreign countries failed because of opposition by the Bush administration and other debilitating problems.

The nation's export control law — the Export Administration Act — had expired Sept. 30, 1990, and President Bush had invoked his basic national security authority to retain existing restrictions on high-technology sales abroad.

U.S. law was parallel to and, in some cases, more restrictive than an international system of controls enforced by the Coordinating Committee on Multilateral Export Controls (Cocom), a 17-nation group made up of NATO countries, except Iceland, plus Japan and Australia. With the end of the Cold War, Cocom had moved in 1990 to greatly relax restraints on exports to former countries of the East Bloc. There was bipartisan support on Capitol Hill for loosening U.S. controls, both to boost U.S. trade and to focus enforcement on the most sensitive high-technology exports.

Though the administration supported making it easier to export some U.S. goods, it opposed provisions passed by the House that were aimed at lifting controls on the export of telecommunications equipment to the Soviet Union. The White House also objected to language dropping controls on certain types of mass-marketed software and mandating sanctions against countries that exported equipment for making nuclear weapons.

Similar objections had blocked enactment of an export-control bill in 1990. Congress cleared a bill (HR 4653) to reauthorize the Export Administration Act, which had been used since 1979 to keep computers and other sophisticated technology with potential military applications out of the hands of the Sovet Union. But Bush pocket-vetoed the bill because of an amendment restricting foreign aid to countries that used chemical weapons or aided others in manufacturing them; the White House objected that the bill interfered with the president's right to conduct foreign policy. *(1990 Almanac, p. 198)*

BOXSCORE

➡ **Export Administration Act Reauthorization (S 320, HR 3489).** The bills reauthorized and updated laws controlling the export of militarily sensitive technology.

Reports: H Rept 102-267.

KEY ACTION

Feb. 20 — S 320 passed the **Senate** by voice vote.

Oct. 17 — The **House** Foreign Affairs Committee approved HR 3489 by voice vote.

Oct. 30 — HR 3489 approved by the **House** by voice vote.

Oct. 31 — S 320 sent back to the **Senate** as unconstitutional.

SENATE ACTION

The Senate voted early in the year to pass a bill that was virtually identical to the conference report that had been sent to Bush the year before. Despite administration objections, the new measure (S 320), approved by voice vote on Feb. 20, included a provision imposing economic sanctions against countries that used chemical and biological weapons and against companies that sold them.

The administration negotiated unsuccessfully for weeks for compromise language allowing it to waive sanctions in certain cases. In the end, all the administration got was an amendment offered by Minority Leader Bob Dole, R-Kan., and Jake Garn, R-Utah, to give the president up to nine months to negotiate with foreign governments to stem proliferation of the weapons before he would have to impose sanctions.

"It didn't provide the bottom line waiver the administration wanted.... They hated it," said a Republican Senate Banking Committee aide.

The Dole-Garn amendment was adopted by unanimous consent.

Before sending the export bill to the House, the Senate attached an amendment to impose the death penalty on terrorists.

Administration officials said they would accept S 320 if the chemical weapons language was stripped out. The chemical weapons fight overshadowed the rest of the bill. As passed by the Senate, the bill:

- Created a license-free zone that removed all controls on exports among Cocom countries by Dec. 31, 1991, although retaining possible exceptions.
- Required sanctions for exporting ballistic missile technology and permit control of U.S. exports that aided development of missile-delivery systems.
- Ratified the June 1990 Cocom agreement that relaxed East-West controls and streamlined export restrictions.
- Eased restrictions on exports of telecommunications equipment to Poland, Czechoslovakia and Hungary.
- Prohibited the export of satellites to be launched on Chinese rockets, unless the U.S. Trade Representative certified that China was adhering to the U.S.-China trade agreement on launch services.
- Allowed courts to review some export restrictions that could injure exporters.
- Endorsed the embargo on Iraq and spelled out conditions Iraq would have to meet before the United States lifted sanctions. The bill also gave the president authority to retaliate against countries that violated the Iraq embargo.
- Stiffened the Cuban trade embargo to prohibit foreign subsidiaries, as well as parent firms, from exporting to Cuba.

HOUSE COMMITTEE ACTION

The House Foreign Affairs Subcommittee on International Economic Policy approved a draft bill by voice vote on Oct. 1. The measure, reauthorizing the Export Administration Act for one year, contained several provisions that drew strong objections from the administration.

As approved by the subcommittee, the bill required the administration to propose that Cocom lift export controls on telecommunication equipment. Opposition by the United States and Britain had blocked such a move by Cocom, which operated by consensus. The House had passed the telecommunications provision as part of the 1990 export control bill, but it had been removed in conference with the Senate.

In addition, the bill required the United States to seek approval from Cocom to remove Poland, Czechoslovakia and Hungary from the list of countries subject to special export restrictions aimed at communist nations. The measure included a provision to speed removal of controls on certain militarily sensitive exports to Lithuania, Latvia and Estonia.

The supercomputer industry won a provision to automatically remove restrictions on older supercomputers as more technologically advanced machines became available.

The bill also required that the United States drop controls by the end of the year on exports to countries that were members of Cocom.

In addition to a generalized complaint about congressional micromanagement of export control activities, the administration focused its complaints on at least three problem areas:

- The proposal to allow sales of sophisticated fiber-optics telecommunications equipment to most countries, including the Soviet Union, for civilian use.

Supporters of the proposal argued that an August coup attempt in the Soviet Union failed in part because the plotters were unable to block all communications, and that allowing access to technically superior and more secure communications would further benefit political stability.

In any case, they argued, fiber optics were becoming available from sources outside the reach of Western export controls.

The administration countered that fiber-optic transmissions were far more difficult for the United States to intercept than microwave signals, creating a potential loss of intelligence if the technology were diverted to military use.

- A proposed statutory designation of Iran, Iraq, Libya and Syria as terrorist countries at a time when the State Department was involved in delicate negotiations to achieve a broad-based peace accord for the Middle East and to win freedom for Western hostages held in the region. The provision was included by subcommittee Chairman Sam Gejdenson, D-Conn.
- Provisions requiring sanctions on countries that spread nuclear facilities, equipment and technology. Opponents charged that this would undermine international negotiations and administration flexibility on this point, regardless of the merits of such sanctions.

The administration also opposed an amendment sponsored by Mel Levine, D-Calif., making it easier to export certain kinds of coded software.

Foreign Affairs Action

The House Foreign Affairs Committee resolved enough of the issues holding up the bill to approve it by voice vote on Oct. 17. But remaining roadblocks continued to raise serious doubts about the measure's chances for enactment.

Members voted to extend U.S. export controls through March 1, 1993, rather than Sept. 30, 1992, as approved by the subcommittee.

The panel adopted 11 amendments, all by voice vote, several of them aimed at allaying administration concerns. As a result, the bill was much closer to what the administration said it wanted on three issues:

- **Telecommunications.** The committee adopted a Gejdenson amendment addressing two administration objections. The subcommittee bill would have required that the United States urge Cocom to permit any country to purchase the most sophisticated fiber-optics communications equipment for civilian use.

Gejdenson's amendment applied the exemption specifically to the Soviet Union (or any successor country); it also limited the level of technology that could be sold there to what was currently sold to China for civilian use without special license.

- **Terrorist countries.** A joint amendment by Gejdenson and Doug Bereuter, R Neb., struck the mandatory designation of Iran, Iraq, Libya and Syria as terrorist countries. It also revised controls to be imposed on high-tech exports to countries that the secretary of State identified as supporting international terrorism. And it gave the administration greater flexibility in permitting dual-use exports (those with both civilian and military applications), where the intended use of the product clearly had an acceptable civilian purpose.

Because of Middle East peace negotiations and talks aimed at gaining the release of Western hostages held in the region, the administration had been outspoken in its opposition to naming Iran and Syria as terrorist countries.

Levine offered a second amendment that would have expressed the sense of Congress that the government of Syrian President Hafez al-Assad was not complying with the Universal Declaration on Human Rights in the treatment of its own citizens, with the intent that the U.S. government pressure Syria into allowing free emigration to about 4,000 Jews living there.

Levine withdrew his amendment after entreaties from Lee H. Hamilton, D-Ind., who chaired the Subcommittee on Europe and the Middle East. Hamilton argued that the amendment was not timely — for the same reasons the anti-terrorist language posed a problem. But he promised that his subcommittee would act soon on H Con Res 188, a Levine-sponsored measure from which the Syria amendment was adapted.

- **Nuclear exports.** Howard Wolpe, D-Mich., offered substitute language on nuclear-use exports that made several key changes to the subcommittee-approved bill.

It added a presidential waiver to permit the export of dual-use goods if the chances were remote that they would have serious implications for the spread of nuclear weapons. And the president could avoid imposing harsh sanctions on countries that permitted nuclear-use materials to be exported. But the amendment limited the waiver authority, requiring among other things that the president first notify Congress.

The administration strongly opposed any sanctions language. Deputy Assistant Secretary of State Peckham told the committee that many countries were beginning to come around to U.S. views on controlling nuclear technology. But, he said, "it would be counterproductive to extend the United States out in front just when other countries were starting to catch up."

Administration officials said they were still not satisfied with the Wolpe provisions and indicated that they wanted the section dropped altogether. They also said that industry groups were beginning to line up against the bill, in part because of constraints imposed on nuclear exports.

HOUSE ACTION

The House approved the bill Oct. 30 after rejecting several attempts by conservative Republicans to give the Pentagon more power to block high-technology exports.

The Bush administration threatened to veto the bill because of provisions to lift controls on sales of software and telecommunications equipment.

The White House also objected to the provisions mandating U.S. sanctions against countries that exported nuclear-related goods.

As passed by the House, the bill eliminated the need for U.S. companies to get licenses for exports to Japan, Australia and Western Europe, and it relaxed controls on exports bound for former Eastern European allies of the Soviets and, to a lesser extent, to the Soviet Union itself.

But critics contended that, by loosening restrictions on high-tech goods that could be converted to military use, the bill was inviting the next Saddam Hussein to go on a shopping spree — with U.S. exporters happy to assist.

"We better wake up to the fact that companies want to make money," said John R. Kasich, R-Ohio. "And if in the process of making money, they also arm somebody, they don't worry about it."

Conservative Republicans made repeated assaults on the bill during floor action but did not get far. They targeted provisions reducing the Pentagon's authority to block sales of high-tech goods that it feared might be put to military use. In the process, the lawmakers criticized the Commerce Department, the agency with primary responsibility for enforcing export control laws, for laxity in controlling militarily sensitive exports to Iraq before its invasion of Kuwait.

"The horror was created by American technology, and the horror was created most often by the Commerce Department," said Duncan Hunter, R-Calif.

But Gejdenson countered that it was the fault not of the Commerce Department but of the entire Bush administration, which, he said, had a policy of supporting Iraq with exports before the invasion. "Don't blame the Commerce Department for what was national policy," Gejdenson said. "The president of the United States wanted to protect Saddam Hussein's life."

The House rejected, by a vote of 189-217, an amendment by Hunter that would have allowed the Pentagon to review exports of goods to U.S. allies when it was deemed necessary to prevent diversion of technology to military uses. *(Vote 355, p. 86-H)*

Hunter also targeted a section affecting the Commerce Department's so-called dual-use list of goods that had both civilian and military uses.

The bill eliminated the list by Oct. 1, 1992, and supplanted it with a new list that sponsors hoped would contain only the most sensitive items. Hunter's amendment, which would have given the secretary of Defense veto power over changes to the list, was rejected by a vote of 135-270. *(Vote 357, p. 86-H)*

The House approved by voice vote an amendment by Nicholas Mavroules, D-Mass., an Armed Services Committee member, to restore some of the Defense secretary's authority to review high-tech exports. Mavroules said the amendment, a compromise between Armed Services and Foreign Affairs, "preserves some authority eroded by the bill."

The bill eliminated U.S. restrictions on items that were not controlled by Cocom. But the Senate agreed, 223-180, to an amendment by Jon Kyl, R-Ariz., to allow the president to retain controls if removing them would have a "detrimental effect" on U.S. interests.

As approved in committee, the bill would have allowed the president to retain controls on goods if lifting them imposed an "extraordinary" national security risk. *(Vote 356, p. 86-H)*

While loosening Cold War-era controls on most high-tech exports, the bill passed by the House set new restrictions on sales of civilian nuclear technology that could also have military uses.

The bill provided sanctions against countries that spread nuclear technology. The sponsors added language allowing the president to waive sanctions if he first notified Congress, but the change did not satisfy the White House.

By voice vote, the House adopted an amendment by Ron Wyden, D-Ore., specifying that the telecommunications equipment available to the Soviet Union should include equipment used in transmission of digital information.

The measure lifted export restrictions on mass-marketed computer software, such as WordPerfect. The administration said such software should remain controlled because it contained sensitive encryption technology.

The House adopted by voice vote an amendment by Bill Orton, D-Utah, whose district included a plant that manufactured WordPerfect, to clarify that the bill applied to the "tangible" software package itself, not just the trademark.

The White House wanted all of these provisions dropped and threatened to veto the measure unless Congress complied.

The House also took action, long opposed by the administration, to bar the export of U.S. satellites for launch on Chinese rockets.

Members agreed by voice vote to an amendment by Gerald B. H. Solomon, R-N.Y., striking a provision to allow a presidential waiver of the satellite ban. The amendment, intended to help the U.S. launch industry, contradicted the terms of a deal negotiated in 1989 between the Reagan administration and the Chinese government.

FINAL ACTION

The export-control bill did not make it to conference before the session ended. Indeed, the fate of the bill took an unexpected turn late in the year, when the Senate version was returned to that chamber stamped unconstitutional.

The culprit was the provision imposing higher tariffs on countries and companies that contributed to the spread of chemical and biological weapons and of ballistic missiles. The change would have raised revenue, and under the Constitution, revenue bills must begin in the House. As a result, House parliamentarians ruled the measure invalid.

Guarding his prerogative to initiate revenue bills, House Ways and Means Committee Chairman Dan Rostenkowski, D-Ill., returned the measure to the Senate in a procedural motion Oct. 31 on the House floor.

Majority Leader George J. Mitchell, D-Maine, responded by seeking consent to bring the Senate bill up the week of Nov. 11, after stripping out the import sanctions. But he was blocked by Republicans who had tried to enact the sanction repeatedly since the Persian Gulf War.

In the end, the chemical weapons sanctions were passed separately as part of an unrelated trade bill (HR 1724). *(Andean Initiative, p. 127)*

But time ran out before the Senate could take up the export control measure again. ■

House Urged To Extend Super 301 Provisions

Anticipating the 1992 trade debate, the House Energy and Commerce Committee approved legislation on Nov. 20 extending a law that threatened retaliation against countries that refused to open their markets to U.S. goods.

The bill (HR 787 — H Rept 102-400, Part 1), approved by voice vote, extended so-called Super 301 provisions through 1995. Super 301 derived its name from Section 301 of the 1974 trade act.

Super 301, created in the 1988 trade act (PL 100-418), required the U.S. trade representative to identify countries with egregious barriers to U.S. goods and target them for negotiations and possible retaliation. It expired in 1990 and had not been reauthorized. *(1988 Almanac, p. 209)*

In November, House Majority Leader Richard A. Gephardt, D-Mo., introduced a separate bill (HR 3702) renewing Super 301 but also eliminating the administration's discretion to avoid acting against countries that ran large trade surpluses with the United States. Critics complained that the Bush administration had taken advantage of leeway in the law to avoid targeting some of the worst offenders, such as the European Community. Japan was named in 1989 but not in 1990.

Subcommittee Action

The House Energy and Commerce Subcommittee on Commerce, Consumer Protection and Competitiveness approved HR 787 by voice vote on Oct. 23.

The subcommittee first agreed by voice vote to strike language in the bill that would have made retaliation mandatory. The Bush administration objected strongly to the provision.

Added to the bill were provisions requiring the Commerce Department to estimate the value of U.S. goods and services that could not be exported because of the trade barriers identified by the administration.

In 1989, the administration used Super 301 to spur negotiations with Japan, Brazil and India. In 1990, however, officials largely let the process lapse, citing only India; failure to target Japan drew strong objections on Capitol Hill.

Subcommittee Chairman Cardiss Collins, D-Ill., credited Super 301 with helping to decrease the U.S. trade deficit from $56 billion in 1987 to $41 billion in 1990.

Gephardt's Bill

In the fall of 1991, congressional Democrats vowed to work to toughen U.S. trade law in 1992 by requiring retaliation against countries that refused to open their markets to U.S. goods.

Attacking President Bush for a "failed" trade policy, Gephardt announced Nov. 4 that he was formally introducing a bill unveiled two months earlier. Gephardt's measure reauthorizing Super 301 was designed to force the president to take action once a country had been targeted for discriminating against U.S. exports. If he did not want to retaliate with trade sanctions, the president would be required to submit a market-opening plan to Congress for approval. If the plan did not succeed, retaliation would follow automatically.

"Our bill not only extends Super 301, it gives it teeth," said Gephardt, who introduced the measure along with Sander M. Levin, D-Mich.

Gephardt said the bill was likely to move in 1992, when Democrats hoped to score election year points against Bush by connecting the administration's record on trade with the sluggish economy. "We can no longer afford the do-nothing policies of the Reagan-Bush administrations," said Gephardt.

A country would be targeted under Gephardt's bill if it accounted for 15 percent of the U.S. trade deficit, maintained an overall trade surplus and engaged in discriminatory practices that excluded U.S. goods.

The administration would have to target sectors within the country that accounted for more than 10 percent of its trade surplus.

The bill would also give the House Ways and Means and Senate Finance committees the power to initiate action under Section 301. ■

Banking Nominations

After charging Robert L. Clarke with allowing hundreds of banks to sink into insolvency, the Senate Banking Committee effectively killed his appointment to a second five-year term as comptroller of the currency.

In back-to-back party-line votes of 9-12, the committee on Nov. 6 rejected a Republican motion to recommend Clarke's reconfirmation as top supervisor of about 4,000 federally chartered banks, and then rejected a Republican motion to send the nomination to the floor with an unfavorable recommendation.

Treasury Secretary Nicholas F. Brady called the committee action "crass politics and partisanship at its worst."

Clarke's term had expired almost a year before; however, no successor was named in 1991, and he remained in office until February 1992.

The committee outcome was not unexpected. Banking Chairman Donald W. Riegle Jr., D-Mich., pulled out all the stops to persuade his 11 Democratic colleagues to defeat Clarke.

Administration efforts to get at least two Democrats to vote to send the nomination to the floor met with stiff resistance from the chairman.

Committee Republican Phil Gramm of Texas said that Clarke probably would have been defeated on the Senate floor anyway.

Clarke had been charged by many Democrats — and at least one Republican — with responsibility for a big share of the 1,000-plus bank failures since 1985.

The upshot of those bank failures was that the federal insurance fund that protected bank depositors was nearly insolvent and was seeking a $30 billion Treasury loan to stay afloat. *(Banking overhaul, p. 75)*

Riegle argued that Clarke had brought a deregulatory philosophy to the comptroller's office that in effect said, "Industry had to regulate itself." As a consequence, he said, national banks greatly increased their investments in real estate and other risky ventures."During his tenure, national banks failed in numbers not seen since the Great Depression," Riegle said before the votes.

Riegle's assault on Clarke drew equally strong responses from committee Republicans, who said Riegle was trying to blame the ongoing banking crisis on the Reagan and Bush administrations, while the real culprits included a bad economy in the Southwest and failures by Congress.

Republicans coming to Clarke's defense argued that he was not the only bank regulator and that all others should share in the blame.

Some Republicans suggested that Riegle was trying to divert attention from his own difficulties, stemming from his connections in the mid-1980s to Charles H. Keating Jr. and the failed Lincoln Savings and Loan Association.

The Senate Ethics Committee had rebuked Riegle earlier in the year for his action in the Keating case but took no disciplinary action against him. *(Keating hearings, p. 26)*

Bank of New England Failure

Clarke, 49, had been nominated for a second term in December 1990, but his confirmation had been held up as the Banking Committee and others probed his office's performance in general and his role in the failure of the Bank of New England in particular.

In testimony before the Banking Committee on Sept. 19, General Accounting Office Controller Charles A. Bowsher said that Clarke's office had evidence of severe problems in the real estate loan portfolio of the Bank of New England as long ago as 1985 but took no action to remedy those until 1989. The bank failed in January 1991, largely as a result of real estate loan losses at a $2.5 billion cost to the FDIC.

Senate Banking Committee Democrats continued their attack on Oct. 3, but the committee's Republicans turned up the heat in their defense of the government's top regulator of national banks.

Pete V. Domenici, R-N.M., had urged Democrats not to reject Clarke.

"This chairman intends to get Comptroller Clarke because he wants a scapegoat. You don't need a scapegoat for anything.... Maybe the chairman does."

Alfonse M. D'Amato of New York was the only Republican to have joined in the criticism of Clarke. Other GOP members, including ranking committee Republican Jake Garn of Utah and Domenici, came out strongly in Clarke's defense.

FEDERAL RESERVE GOVERNORS

It was a busy year for vacancies on the Federal Reserve Board of Governors, with two seats coming vacant and Alan Greenspan being nominated for a second four-year term as chairman.

Fed Vice Chairman and Governor Manuel H. Johnson Jr. had resigned in June 1990 freeing one seat on the seven-member board, plus the vice chairmanship. And Governor Martha R. Seger announced in January that she would leave her position in March.

In January, President Bush named sitting Governor David W. Mullins Jr. to serve as vice chairman and White House aide Lawrence B. Lindsey to fill Johnson's unexpired term.

In July, Bush nominated Greenspan to another four years as chairman and to a full 14-year term on the Fed board, as the term he was filling was set to expire in January 1992.

And in September, he named former federal regulator Susan Meredith Phillips to fill Seger's unexpired term.

Mullins, Phillips, Lindsey Confirmed

The nominations of Mullins and Phillips moved quickly through the Senate Banking Committee and the full Senate, but that of Lindsey was held up over his political ideology and his state of residence. Lindsey was eventually confirmed.

The Banking Committee recommended by voice vote July 10 that the Senate confirm Mullins to a four-year term as vice chairman. D'Amato registered the only objection. The full Senate concurred the following day by voice vote.

Mullins was a former Harvard finance professor who joined the Bush administration to direct banking policy in the Treasury Department. He spearheaded administration efforts to enact the 1989 savings and loan salvage bill before being appointed to the Fed early in 1990. His Fed term was to expire in January 1996.

The same day it acted on Mullins, the committee voted 16-5 to recommend Lindsey's confirmation to fill Johnson's unexpired term. Five Democrats, led by Chairman Donald W. Riegle Jr. of Michigan, voted against Lindsey.

Lindsey was a Harvard University economics professor on leave as an assistant to White House domestic policy chief Roger P. Porter.

He was an advocate of supply-side economic theory, which argued for low tax rates to stimulate the economy, and he worked on the administration's banking overhaul proposal in 1990.

Democrats objected to Lindsey on grounds of his economic policy views and also because of the location of his home. He was a resident of Massachusetts until coming to Washington several years before his nomination. He lived in the Virginia suburbs and was nominated from the Federal Reserve district serving Virginia and several other Southern states.

Sen. Terry Sanford, D-N.C., held up a Senate floor vote on Lindsey's nomination until late in the year, chiefly because of the residency issue. The Senate finally confirmed Lindsey by voice vote on Nov. 22. His term was to expire in January 2000.

The Banking Committee recommended by voice vote Nov. 6 that the Senate confirm Phillips, and the full Senate concurred the following day by voice vote.

At the time of her nomination, she was vice president for finance at the University of Iowa. Before that, she served as chairman of the Commodity Futures Trading Commission during the Reagan administration.

In that post, she had supported limited government regulation of financial markets and the development of stock-index futures trading, which allowed investors to hedge their stock investments by betting on the direction in which that index would move.

Phillips' term as Fed governor was to expire in January 1998.

Greenspan Nomination Deferred

Bush said July 10 that he would renominate Greenspan. The announcement came days before Bush was to leave for his annual economic summit with the leaders of the six other major industrialized nations and was seen as a signal to the rest of the world that Bush continued to have confidence in the Fed's anti-inflationary tight money policy during Greenspan's first term.

There had been speculation that Greenspan would be cut loose, making him the scapegoat for the nation's first recession since 1982.

Bush said that Greenspan's future had never been in doubt.

"The respect that Alan Greenspan has around the world and in this country, particularly in financial marketplaces, is unparalleled," Bush said.

Throughout 1991, Greenspan signaled no shift in his basic view that the Fed must fight to keep inflation in check and that long-term economic growth was at least as dependent on prices remaining stable as it was on easy credit. Balancing the two had been Greenspan's concern since the economy began to slow in 1989, but Treasury Secretary Nicholas F. Brady and other critics in the administration complained that the Fed moved too slowly to relax credit to stimulate growth.

Neither the committee nor the full Senate acted on Greenspan's appointment because work on the banking overhaul bill prevented action as the session came to a close. Having been previously confirmed, Greenspan continued to serve into the new year.

The Senate committee recommended his reconfirmation on a 20-1 vote on Feb. 20, 1992. D'Amato who repeatedly expressed dismay at the Fed's monetary policy, cast the lone dissenting vote. The full Senate confirmed Greenspan by voice vote on Feb. 27. Greenspan took over the Fed Board on Aug. 11, 1987, barely two months before the October stock market crash that wiped out $1 trillion in paper wealth in one week. His second term as chairman was to run until August 1995, and his seat on the board, until January 2006. ■

Chapter 3

GOVERNMENT/ COMMERCE

Highways, Mass Transit Funded

While president, Congress fought over details, both embraced bill as 1991's only job-creating measure

After months of fighting among lawmakers over how to allocate road funds to states, President Bush on Dec. 18 signed into law a sweeping $151 billion measure authorizing highway and mass transit programs for the next six years.

While Bush and Congress fought over key components, including a failed bid to raise the gasoline tax by a nickel, the president and lawmakers embraced the legislation as the only job-creation measure of the year.

"It moves us closer to our three top domestic priorities: jobs, jobs and jobs," Bush told a gathering of state transportation officials in Dallas, where he signed the bill.

Congress cleared the measure on Nov. 27 after two weeks of an often rancorous conference involving 92 lawmakers representing nine House and Senate committees.

The new law promised dramatic changes in federal transportation policy, as the 44,328-mile Interstate Highway System neared completion. The National System of Interstate and Defense Highways, with its promise of linking the United States through a network of divided four-lane, limited-access highways, had embodied U.S. transportation policy since 1956.

The new law continued in the spirit of the Interstate system by retaining a federal role in maintaining the nation's highway networks. It set up a newly designated National Highway System composed of the Interstate network and primary arterial roads. The system was a key component of the Bush administration's transportation proposal.

Much of the rest of federal transportation policy was shifted to the states. State and local officials were able to transfer up to $65 billion, or 54 percent, of the law's highway funding authority to mass transit.

The law consolidated key federal highway programs into one large Surface Transportation Program, from which states were free to spend funds on nearly any transportation project. It also freed urban areas for the first time to spend federal funds as they pleased. And it gave metropolitan planning organizations new powers to negotiate funds with states.

BOXSCORE

➡ **Surface Transportation Reauthorization (HR 2950, formerly S 1204 and S 965).** The $151 billion bill authorized highway, safety and mass transit programs for six years beginning in fiscal 1992. Highways received $119.5 billion; mass transit received $31.5 billion.

Report: H Rept 102-404.

KEY ACTION

May 22 — The **Senate** Environment and Public Works Committee approved S 1204, 15-1.

July 25 — The **House** Public Works and Transportation Committee approved HR 2950.

June 19 — S 1204 passed the **Senate** by a vote of 91-7.

Oct. 15 — The **House** Public Works Committee approved revised HR 2950, 52-3.

Oct. 16 — The **House** Ways and Means Committee approved the financing mechanism of HR 2950.

Oct. 23 — HR 2950 passed the **House** by a vote of 343-83.

Nov. 27 — Approved by **House-Senate** conference as HR 2950: **House** approved by a vote of 372-47; **Senate** cleared it shortly afterward by a vote of 79-8.

Dec. 18 — President Bush signed HR 2950 — PL 102-240.

As the bill wound its way through Congress, the sweeping changes in transportation policy it proposed often were overshadowed by internecine fights among lawmakers over how best to divvy up billions of dollars among states.

Ultimately, lawmakers' complaints about money were resolved by tossing aside longstanding formulas for dividing highway funds. Much of the authorized funds was allocated to states in the form of lump-sum payments or through a record number of special road projects, rather than as part of any highway program.

What the Law Did

The legislation injected much-needed funds into state highway and mass transit coffers, mostly from gasoline tax revenues paid into the federal Highway Trust Fund. Highway programs were slated to receive $119.5 billion over six years; mass transit was to get $31.5 billion. Commuters and other road users were affected in the following ways:

- **Road construction and repair.** In addition to the funds allocated to states for highway and bridge work, hundreds of local road projects that were put off by state highway departments received special attention. The authorization included $6.2 billion for 539 priority road projects, most of which were specified by House lawmakers.
- **An economic boost.** Sponsors said 1.1 million jobs would be created and about a million other jobs would be preserved. The administration said the legislation would support 600,000 new and existing jobs in fiscal 1992.
- **Congestion and pollution relief.** The 1990 Clean Air Act amendments required urban areas to meet stringent goals for improving air quality. The surface transportation measure gave cities the resources to meet those goals. A new $6 billion program provided grants to states to find transportation methods that reduced congestion and pollution.

By emphasizing mass transit, metropolitan planning and toll roads, the legislation marked a significant shift away from solving traffic problems with new road construction.

• **Mass transit.** Mass transit systems received their biggest funding increases since the federal government began helping out in 1964. Funding was slated to more than double to $31.5 billion over six years. Also, nearly $5 billion would be authorized for 57 new rail and bus systems.

State transit operators were given new flexibility to spend highway funds on mass transit.

• **Local input.** With construction on the Interstate system nearly completed, lawmakers abandoned federal policies that had left residents powerless to stop freeways from being built through their neighborhoods. Urban areas got much more say over state funding decisions and received money that states could not touch.

• **Gasoline taxes.** A House effort to hike gasoline taxes by a nickel failed, but the legislation still imposed new gas taxes. The 1990 White House-congressional budget deal included a nickel increase that was set to expire after fiscal 1995. The new authorization extended half of that nickel through fiscal 1999.

That meant federal gas taxes were scheduled to drop only to 11.5 cents from 14 cents a gallon in October 1995, not to 9 cents as the budget deal had called for.

• **Safety.** Air bags were required for all passenger cars made after Sept. 1, 1995 — on the driver's side and front-seat passenger side. States received $1.3 billion in grants to improve safety on highways. *(Air bags law, p. 156)*

• **Research.** The authorization included $660 million for research on "intelligent" highways and vehicles in an effort to spur the development of devices such as computer-controlled traffic monitoring and dashboard navigation systems. An additional $700 million was authorized for a prototype "magnetic levitation" train system that would hover at high speeds above an electromagnetic rail.

THE ADMINISTRATION'S PROPOSAL

For lawmakers on Congress' transportation committees, 1991 was destined to be the year that Congress overhauled transportation policy. The Interstate Highway System was nearly completed.

For Transportation Secretary Samuel K. Skinner, 1991 brought another landmark: It was the year Congress paid attention to an administration transportation proposal.

Unlike previous highway bill reauthorization years in 1987 and 1982, Skinner's popularity with lawmakers — and a lot of policy legwork by the agency — gave the administration a chance to truly influence Congress in the most important highway and mass transit authorization bill since the Interstate was formally launched in 1956.

Bush, with Skinner at his side, on Feb. 13 unveiled the administration's ambitious five-year, $105 billion plan to build on and maintain the nation's road and mass transit systems. Federal highway and transit programs were set to expire on Sept. 30.

Despite some trimming down by the White House Office of Management and Budget, the plan looked formidible. Federal efforts would center on a 155,000-mile National Highway System that would better connect the Interstate network with new and existing feeder routes. States would be given more flexibility to spend highway funds on mass transit — in exchange for having to kick in a higher share of funds for road projects.

The administration was less generous with mass transit. The proposal called for transit to receive just $16.3 billion over five years. It also called for a higher local matching share for capital projects, from 80 percent to 60 percent, and proposed doing away with operating assistance for 147 transit systems with populations of more than 1 million.

But Skinner was in for a few surprises. In the next few months, an even more radical plan from the Senate — coupled with a gas-tax increase proposal in the House — pushed Skinner into a strategy of negotiating with lawmakers mostly through veto threats.

Only toward the end of the year, as the recession grew more severe, did the administration back off. Having won on a key point — the National Highway System — and having steered much of the structure and debate over the bill, Bush and Skinner ultimately claimed victory and embraced the legislation as a job-creation measure.

SENATE COMMITTEE ACTION

While the Bush administration grabbed headlines with its ambitious plan to redefine highway spending, New York Democrat Daniel Patrick Moynihan and other key senators kept their heads down and quietly plotted to revolutionize federal transportation policy.

Moynihan's staff on his Environment and Public Works Subcommittee on Water Resources, Transportation and Infrastructure drafted the bill more as a piece of environmental and energy legislation than as a traditional highway bill.

The 1990 overhaul of the Clean Air Act played a large role: The network of congressional staff and environmental lobbyists who worked on that bill saw an opportunity to apply the same goals to transportation policy.

Moynihan, flanked by unlikely rural ally Steve Symms, R-Idaho, and fellow East Coast Sens. John H. Chafee, R-R.I., and Frank R. Lautenberg, D-N.J., unveiled a bill on April 25 that made Bush's sweeping proposal look comparatively timid.

"This will prove to be the most important transportation bill in 35 years," Moynihan said. "We are about to enter a new era." The focus of the bill, he said, was to make the nation's transportation system more efficient by making urban and rural areas compete for federal funds.

Both the Bush plan and the Senate bill would cover five years, cost $105 billion and favor road repair over new construction, as the 44,328-mile Interstate Highway System neared completion.

But that's where similarities ended.

Where Bush sought to expand the federal role with a new, 155,000-mile National Highway System, the Senate plan would have reduced Uncle Sam to a caretaker for the Interstate system and a benefactor for states, granting them money with no strings attached.

"It is a radical restructuring," said Francis B. Francois, executive director of the American Association of State Highway and Transportation Officials, which helped draft Bush's plan. "It basically eliminates the highway-system concept that has been at the heart of the federal-aid highway program since 1921."

The Bush effort preached flexibility for states in spending federal funds. But many lawmakers said the plan fell short by forcing states to pay more and by offering little incentive to shift highway funds to mass transit. The Senate plan, on the other hand, was "flexibility run amok," said one critic from the highway industry.

That flexibility held the key to the Senate bill's widespread support: Urban Democrats such as Transportation Appropriations Subcommittee Chairman Lautenberg appeared on the same bill as highway-oriented rural lawmakers such as Symms and Environment and Public Works Chairman Quentin N. Burdick, D-N.D.

The bill (S 965, later numbered S 1204) proposed to:

- Replace current highway funding programs with a new surface transportation program, from which states could spend $45 billion from fiscal 1992 to 1996 on any surface transportation project.

The federal-state match would be 80-20 to maintain existing facilities or use them more efficiently. That match would be 75-25 for construction of facilities.

Bridges would get $13.3 billion, with similar matching ratios.

- Set aside $5 billion for a new congestion and air quality program that would help cities comply with Clean Air Act guidelines through more efficient transportation programs.
- Provide $14 billion to maintain the Interstate Highway System, with an 80-20 federal-state match. Funds could not be used to add new lanes.
- Provide $7.2 billion to complete the final segments of the Interstate system — principally in Los Angeles and Boston — by the fourth year of the bill.
- Require states to coordinate transportation improvement programs with local metropolitan planning organizations in urban areas with populations of more than 50,000 and to update the plans at least every two years. State governors would have to approve such plans.

A congestion management plan would be required for metropolitan areas with populations of more than 50,000 that did not comply with Clean Air Act requirements.

Any money obligated to the planning group would be redistributed to other states if the Transportation secretary certified that the group failed to meet its responsibilities.

- Provide $750 million for a magnetic levitation demonstration project. Private-sector firms and private-public consortia would compete to design and develop a conceptual train system.

The Senate Banking Committee, which handled the mass transit part of the bill, more or less ignored the administration's proposal. The committee proposed boosting transit spending annually by 7 percent — the same rate that the administration proposed increasing highway spending. Fiscal 1992 spending would be $3.8 billion, rising to $4.7 billion in fiscal 1996. The banking panel also proposed retaining operating assistance and having equal matching shares for highway and transit programs.

On the Fast Track

Moynihan put the legislation on a fast track, in part to trump a request by Bush to Congress after the Persian Gulf War to complete crime and transportation bills within 100 days. "The president said he wanted it in 100 days. I told [Moynihan] that I wanted it sooner than that," Majority Leader George J. Mitchell, D-Maine, said.

The bill's rapid progress gave the road-building industry, the administration and state officials limited time to mount a challenge. Moynihan dealt little with those groups in drafting the bill. Instead, he turned to the Surface Transportation Policy Project, a group that included environmentalists, neighborhood planners, transportation analysts, energy consultants and bicyclists.

The Senate measure took the highway lobby by surprise. At a press briefing held to criticize the bill, some lobbyists complained of being locked out of the process.

"I did not think they would go as far as they did. I don't think anybody did," said Thomas J. Donahue, president of the American Trucking Associations.

The Senate Environment and Public Works Committee on May 22 quickly approved the bill, 15-1, clearing the way for floor action.

The committee approved by voice vote an amendment by Lautenberg that would ban longer double- and triple-trailer trucks from operating outside states that then permitted them.

The amendment would permit tractor-trailer combinations of two or more trailers, with a gross vehicle weight of more than 40 tons, to operate only in the 20 states in which they were already allowed.

The American Trucking Associations opposed the amendment, preferring instead that Congress leave it up to states to decide whether to accept bigger trucks. But the amendment held throughout the bill's progress and ultimately became law.

The committee approved an amendment by Chafee, 12-4, that would allow states to repay owners of billboards that violated the 1965 Highway Beautification Act by amortizing the owners' costs for the billboards over time. A similar measure passed the committee by a wide margin in 1990. But the Chafee amendment to the surface transportation bill would suffer a bruising defeat when the bill went to the floor.

The committee also amended the bill before the markup to address the National Highway System issue. Moynihan agreed to allow the Department of Transportation to study the proposed system for two years and report back with a detailed map of which existing and new highways would make up the system.

The administration was not impressed. In a letter to Burdick, on the day of the markup, Skinner vowed to recommend a veto if Congress did not include the new National Highway System and higher state and local matching shares.

For Moynihan, the legislation was more than just a necessary duty as chairman of the Transportation Subcommittee.

A longtime critic of federal highway policy, with a strong belief that the Interstate system had ruined most urban areas, Moynihan finally saw his chance to shape transportation policy.

In a 1960 essay, Moynihan had called for many of the proposals that appeared in his bill, including complete flexibility for states in spending federal money, a strong role for urban regional planners and an emphasis on self-financing mechanisms such as toll roads.

And one of Moynihan's pet projects — magnetic levitation trains, which could travel at high speeds on an electromagnetic field — got top billing in the legislation.

Funds for States

Moynihan's colleagues did not challenge his radical vision for the future of highway policy. Instead, a more traditional battle occurred over formulas that allocated highway funds to states.

Through the years, some states routinely received far more money from the Highway Trust Fund than they contributed. Alaska's 32-year average was $7.80 in highway funds for every dollar contributed in gasoline taxes, according to the Federal Highway Administration. Montana received $2.57 for every dollar given during that time.

Conversely, since fiscal 1957, a dozen states routinely contributed more in gasoline tax revenues than they received in highway funds: Arkansas, California, Florida, In-

How the Transportation Funding Pie Was Sliced

Below are the 25 states that fared best in the scramble for special road and bridge projects in the six-year surface transportation reauthorization. In all, lawmakers specified a record 539 projects for a total of $6.2 billion, though many states simply received lump-sum amounts of cash for unspecified projects. Critics called the projects pork-barreling, and said they bypassed state planning priorities and favored the most powerful lawmakers. Defenders said the projects were needed to meet local road needs and most were cleared by state authorities.

Most states toward the top of the list are those of key transportation, appropriations and leadership lawmakers. Toward the middle are so-called donor states (including Texas, Virginia, Missouri, Ohio and North Carolina). Members from those states had fought for a higher return of highway funds on their states' gasoline-tax contributions.

Pennsylvania:	$934.8 million
Illinois:	$437.8 million
New York:	$356.5 million
Wisconsin:	$350.5 million
California:	$334.7 million
Arkansas:	$328.8 million
West Virginia:	$311.6 million
Texas:	$270.0 million
Minnesota:	$244.9 million
Maine:	$201.5 million
New Mexico:	$188.8 million
Virginia:	$155.4 million
Missouri:	$152.8 million
Ohio:	$151.4 million
North Carolina:	$147.9 million
Alabama:	$133.3 million
Washington:	$129.3 million
Michigan:	$122.2 million
Iowa:	$110.7 million
Indiana:	$105.2 million
Maryland:	$104.3 million
Florida:	$ 96.5 million
New Hampshire:	$ 93.3 million
Kentucky:	$ 79.4 million
Delaware:	$ 79.1 million

diana, Michigan, New Jersey, North Carolina, Ohio, Oklahoma, South Carolina, Texas and Wisconsin. They were referred to as the donor states.

Such disparity was needed to build a uniform national system that traversed larger and poorer states. Still, complaints about the allocations by lawmakers from donor states increased as the Interstate system neared completion.

Thirty-five senators, representing 19 states that gave more than they got, sent a letter to Burdick on May 13, urging the committee to either find a more equitable funding formula or raise an 85 percent minimum allocation put into law in 1982.

The apportionment method in the Senate bill would average the difference between what a state gave and what it got back over the previous five years.

The committee rejected, by a vote of 4-11, an amendment by Bob Graham, D-Fla., that would have given donor states a higher share of apportioned funds. Backing the amendment were John W. Warner, R-Va., Howard M. Metzenbaum, D-Ohio, and Dave Durenberger, R-Minn., all of whom represented donor states.

Committee members from states that benefited from the existing formula argued that some states always would need help from others to maintain the nation's highways. Montana Democrat Max Baucus said that states often were asked to pitch in to help other states on federal issues. He cited mass transit funding and the 1989 bailout of failed savings and loan institutions.

Symms added that rural Western states included vast acres of federal land and lacked the tax base to maintain federal-aid roads on their own.

"Any federal activity, by definition, is unequal in its impact," Moynihan said. "Is life fair?"

"It's going to be when we get to the floor," Warner responded.

Warner, in alliance with senators from Florida, North Carolina, Ohio and other donor states, introduced an alternative surface transportation bill (S 1121) that included a new allocation proposal. The bill's other components were similar to the Bush proposal and based on recommendations of the American Association of State Highway and Transportation Officials.

SENATE FLOOR ACTION

The fight over how much federal highway funding each state should receive kept floor debate going from June 11 through June 19, when the bill finally was passed, 91-7. *(Vote 101, p. 14-S)*.

In the end, the donor-state fight was settled with a promise to spend more money on all states. But the carefully crafted deal, while enough to get the bill through the Senate, would clash mightily in conference with the House, where key lawmakers vowed to rewrite the long-used formulas that were preserved in the Senate bill.

The Senate also overwhelmingly agreed to endorse Bush's proposal for a new National Highway System, removing a major reason for a threatened administration veto. It was a departure from the bill's theme of total flexibility for states, but sponsors managed to keep the bill's commitment to the system a nominal one.

Skinner called the bill "a step forward" but repeated the administration's complaints about the measure.

Donor State Fight

The donor state fight, led by Warner, was upstaged early in the debate by Appropriations Chairman Robert C. Byrd, D-W.Va., who proposed a different approach.

On June 11, Byrd offered an amendment that would reward states that had gasoline taxes higher than the national average. Those that also had per capita disposable income levels below the national average would fare even better. Thirty-three states and the District of Columbia would benefit.

West Virginia would gain $221 million over a four-year period. Wisconsin, Tennessee and Nebraska — and a few donor states such as Ohio and North Carolina — also would each gain at least $200 million under the plan.

To pay for the provision, Byrd said he found a "cushion" of $8.2 billion in highway funds made available in the budget resolution after the Moynihan bill was introduced.

Byrd's amendment carried immediate appeal, in part because Byrd was best positioned to follow through and appropriate the money.

Still, the Byrd plan did not directly address the concerns of the 20-odd donor states. In backroom negotiations, Majority Leader Mitchell intervened with the help of Lloyd Bentsen, D-Texas, the author of the 1982 law that guaranteed that states got an 85 percent return on their trust-fund dollar.

The result was a modified Byrd amendment that would divide the $8.2 billion in extra funds into two accounts: Half would go to the 33 states that would benefit under the Byrd formula, and half would be divided among donor states in a way that guaranteed each more money than they were getting.

The amendment would leave only seven states giving more to the Highway Trust Fund than they got back in transportation projects, Byrd claimed. But even those states would get back at least 98 percent of what they contributed in gasoline taxes.

Reaction from donor states to the Byrd-Bentsen proposal varied. Senators from Florida and Missouri wanted to hold out for wholesale changes in the funding formulas. Others, such as Warner and Bentsen, argued to accept the funding increases, reasoning that there were not enough votes to win formula changes.

Warner and Bentsen offered an amendment, approved on a voice vote, that would order the General Accounting Office to study the formula issue.

"I think the underlying formula is still bad, but the alternative is to get nothing extra if we turn it down," said Phil Gramm, R-Texas.

Still, some key senators remained troubled by the proposal. Minority Leader Bob Dole, R-Kan., called the Byrd plan "absurd and illogical" because not all states financed transportation projects solely through gasoline taxes.

Kansas, Dole said, gets revenues from sales taxes and vehicle registration fees, while dedicating only 33 percent of motor fuel tax revenues to highways. The Byrd method also would reward states that diverted gasoline taxes to non-transportation uses, Dole said.

Also, Republicans expressed doubts about whether the $8.2 billion would come from the Highway Trust Fund or from other programs such as defense when domestic budget ceilings expired at the beginning of fiscal 1994.

The Byrd amendment ultimately prevailed, 89-9, and later attempts to alter it by Dole and Graham failed. *(Votes 95, 99, pp. 13-S, 14-S)*

National Highway System

With hopes of dodging a White House veto threat, the Senate agreed to make a nominal commitment to the administration's proposal for a National Highway System, which would connect the Interstate system and 141,000 additional miles of principal feeder roads.

Such roads constituted 4 percent of all highway mileage but carried 40 percent of the nation's traffic and 75 percent of its goods.

Dave Durenberger, R-Minn., and John B. Breaux, D-La., won an amendment, by voice vote, that would in effect create an interim National Highway System until a study on the system was completed.

States would be required to spend at least 17.5 percent of their funds on Interstate roads and primary highways that connected with those roads. States, in consultation with local and regional officials, also would designate eligible National Highway System roads.

Baucus of Montana objected to an earlier proposal by Durenberger and Breaux that 30 percent of highway funds be applied to the new system. Because their states had fewer primary arterial roads than more heavily populated states in the East, Western senators said the 30 percent requirement would limit their flexibility to use road funds.

The amendment would set aside $22 billion over five years for the National Highway System, including $7.9 billion from the surface transportation account and $14.2 billion from a separate Interstate maintenance fund.

Billboard Lobby

The outdoor advertising industry scored a significant victory on June 12, when senators refused to ban construction of billboards along major federal highways or to make it easier for states to force the removal of existing illegal signs.

The Senate adopted, 60-39, an amendment by Harry Reid, D-Nev., that deleted billboard language put into the bill by Chafee. *(Vote 90, p. 13-S)*

The vote revealed the continued clout of the billboard industry. "They called in their chits," said Hal Hiemstra, policy director of the anti-billboard coalition called Scenic America. "This was a classic example of special interest politics. And it worked."

Reid had called the provisions "punitive and destructive to the outdoor advertising industry" and "a dangerous virus against private property rights."

The vote reaffirmed a decision made by Congress in 1978, when it amended the 1965 Highway Beautification Act (PL 89-285) in a way that made it much harder for states and localities to force removal of billboards along Interstate and primary highways. No longer could states "amortize" illegal billboards, by allowing property owners to keep the billboards up for a certain period before forcing their removal without other compensation.

Another amendment challenged a central tenet of Moynihan's bill. Trent Lott, R-Miss., wanted to continue to require the government to pick up 90 percent of the cost of Interstate maintenance and bridge projects. Moynihan had long complained that such a high federal share only encouraged states to blindly pour more concrete. Despite heavy lobbying by state highway officials, the amendment was narrowly defeated, 53-44. *(Vote 97, p. 14-S)*

Other amendments adopted by voice vote included those offered by:

- Slade Gorton, R-Wash., that required that all newly manufactured passenger cars have full front air bags by Sept. 1, 1995, and that all light trucks have air bags by 1997. The amendment also required drug and alcohol testing for transportation employees.
- Symms, that required the attorney general to certify that any new federal regulation did not violate private property rights. An effort to kill that amendment failed, 44-55. *(Vote 91, p. 13-S)*
- Symms, that eliminated the required distribution of funds and additional planning requirements for urban areas with populations between 50,000 and 250,000 that had exceeded levels of ozone and carbon monoxide.
- Jim Exon, D-Neb., that froze the length limits of trucks with double or triple trailers, as well as weight restrictions.
- Metzenbaum, that created a $31 million highway summer jobs program.

• Don Nickles, D-Okla., that allowed states to use the funds for Amtrak operating subsidies and to convert school buses to alternative fuels.

HOUSE COMMITTEE ACTION

The House put forth the first outlines of its plan for the highway and mass transit reauthorization on March 13, calling for a five-year, $153.5 billion measure that would include hundreds of special road projects for lawmakers.

Excepting those road projects, the bill bore more resemblance to the Bush administration proposal than the Senate bill, particularly because it wholeheartedly endorsed the concept of a National Highway System.

But the bill (HR 2950), unveiled on July 18, had a bumpy ride through the chamber. The Public Works and Transportation Committee reported it on July 25, 49-7, amid uncertain support for a proposed nickel increase in the gasoline tax. On Aug. 1, the bill was pulled from the floor calendar after it became clear the leadership lacked the votes to pass the gas-tax hike.

After summer recess, the House on Oct. 23 passed a revised measure that did not include the nickel tax hike. Instead, sponsors extended part of a 1990 gas-tax increase that was set to expire after fiscal 1995 and stretched the bill's funding over six years instead of five. It would become the framework for the final bill sent to the president.

Public Works Committee

The Public Works and Transportation Committee approved its $153.5 billion highway and mass transit blueprint with hopes that lawmakers would support what Public Works Chairman Robert A. Roe, D-N.J., had dubbed, "A Nickel for America."

Roe had reason to expect the House would go along with the gas-tax hike: The revenues would be used largely to fund 458 special road "demonstration" projects put into the bill for House lawmakers. The projects totaled $6.8 billion.

Roe had made it clear from the start he wanted to trade such special road projects for support on the tax.

If Congress approved the increase, he said in a May hearing before the Budget Committee, "We'll be able to meet these needs." If not, Roe said he would tell colleagues, "We have to cut back, and this is the impact it's going to have on your respective state."

Though less so than the Senate bill, the measure proposed more flexibility for states and regions to choose whether to spend federal funds on roads or mass transit projects.

The House bill was much kinder to the highway lobby by preserving the federal government's traditional emphasis on road building. It cleared the way for $40 billion in spending over five years on the National Highway System, which consisted of new and existing Interstate and primary arterial roads.

States also would be required to steer funds toward 16 regional highway corridors identified in the bill.

The bill authorized $32 billion for mass transit repairs and construction — double the amount sought by the Bush administration in its transportation proposal.

Special Road Projects

Most vital for the bill's support among lawmakers, however, was the raft of special road projects.

The projects were attached to the bill July 25 as part of what was described as a package of "technical corrections." They ranged from a new $4 million bridge over Mosquito Creek in Chattahoochee, Fla., for Public Works Democrat Pete Peterson, Fla., to a $100 million expansion of the road from Fort Worth to Springtown, Texas, into a four-lane divided highway for panel Democrat Pete Geren, Texas.

The number of special projects was about three times that of the last highway reauthorization in 1987, when 152 such projects were authorized at more than $1.3 billion. *(1987 Almanac, p. 331)*

Roe rejected the phrase "demonstration projects," a name first given to projects that demonstrated new road-building techniques but that grew into a euphemism for pork-barreling. Instead, he dubbed them "congressional projects of national significance."

Critics of such projects said they bypassed the traditional highway funding process, which allowed states to choose projects and prioritize how to spend federal road dollars. Lawmakers like Roe said states need not be the sole arbiters of worthy projects, and that lawmakers had a responsibility to meet vital local road needs.

In a July 23 letter to Roe detailing administration objections to the bill, Transportation Secretary Skinner complained that "a significant portion of the funding associated with the tax increase" was for unnecessary highway projects.

Skinner said many of the projects "have not had rigorous evaluation; have little merit in terms of advancing new technology or concepts; do not require significant state or other funding participation and are funded outside the federal-aid highway obligation ceiling of the bill."

While the projects were designed to cast a broad net of support for the bill, the "big four" leaders of the Public Works Committee — and the panel's powerful Illinois delegation — took special steps to ensure that their states fared well. Thirty-eight percent of the project dollars would go New Jersey, California, Pennsylvania, Arkansas and Illinois.

Donor State Complaints

As in the Senate, the biggest struggle during Public Works approval came from lawmakers whose states traditionally did not fare as well in such authorizations.

A fight for more funds was led by Tim Valentine, D-N.C., and Lewis F. Payne Jr., D-Va., in behalf of members from so-called donor states that paid more into the Highway Trust Fund in gasoline taxes than they received in federal highway dollars.

Donor states won an early victory by raising to 90 percent from 85 percent the formula that guaranteed each state a minimum return on what it contributed in yearly gasoline tax revenues.

But donor-state lawmakers complained that the $6.8 billion in special road projects authorized in the bill would be provided outside the minimum allocation formula — giving select states far more highway dollars than they paid in gas-tax revenues.

A subsequent deal struck between the donor states and committee leaders resulted in donor states being promised that the $6.8 billion in project funds also would be divvied up to guarantee each state a 90 percent return on its dollar. Montana, for instance, was slated to receive no special projects but would get $28 million from the special projects fund.

Job Quotas

Among other issues tackled by the panel was a politically charged debate over job quotas that resulted in an unusual defeat for Surface Transportation Subcommittee Chairman Norman Y. Mineta, D-Calif.

He and Gus Savage, D-Ill., offered amendments in the subcommittee July 23 and in full committee that would have split a minority set-aside program into one for women and another for minorities. The program required states to award 10 percent of their federal highway dollars to minority contractors and, since 1987, to women.

Mineta argued that the program was much more successful for female business owners, to the detriment of minorities. Mineta's amendment would have preserved the 10 percent minority program but also would have set up a program reserving an additional 5 percent of federal highway funds for women-owned businesses.

But opponents, led by Bud Shuster, R-Pa., called the amendment an attempt to further impose job quotas on state highway officials.

The amendment failed in both subcommittee and full committee, with 12 Democrats voting against Mineta during the full committee vote, 24-33.

Other provisions in the House bill proposed to:

- Replace existing federal-aid highway programs with five new programs, one of which was the $40 billion National Highway System.

The other new programs included a $13.9 billion "urban mobility" program for roads or transit, a similar $10.6 billion "rural mobility" program and a $13.9 billion "flexible" program for states. Safety programs would receive $3.2 billion over five years.

- Boost by more than 40 percent authority for highway construction spending and draw down the balance in the Highway Trust Fund to $2.3 billion in fiscal 1997 from $11.4 billion in fiscal 1992.
- Provide road, bridge and transit projects with a minimum 80 percent share. Interstate funding would remain at a 90 percent share.

Gas Tax

As the multibillion-dollar bill wended its way through the House, every member clamoring for an offramp or a road for his district knew the deal: You want your project, support the gas tax increase.

But the deal was in jeopardy. Some Democrats on the Ways and Means Committee quietly revolted against the leadership plan, though Chairman Dan Rostenkowski, D-Ill., backed it.

Some lawmakers were embarrassed by the implicit trade-off. Many complained that the bill was not generous enough to their states yet showered those of bill sponsors with the lion's share of projects. Other Democrats worried that raising the gas tax to pay for what looked like pork would give Bush a golden opportunity to veto the bill and sock them once again as inveterate tax-and-spenders.

"Why would we want to be pushing for a relatively regressive tax that the president is insisting he would veto?" asked Ways and Means member Byron L. Dorgan, D-N.D.

Opposition almost killed the gas tax in Ways and Means, but sponsors and House leaders rallied enough votes to pass the measure July 31, 19-17.

Among the converts to the increase were three Republicans, E. Clay Shaw, Jr., of Florida; Dick Schulze of Pennsylvania and Guy Vander Jagt of Michigan. All were urged by their party to vote no, but all were persuaded otherwise because of projects for their districts.

Vander Jagt was under special pressure as chairman of the National Republican Congressional Committee. He said there were three "life or death" projects for his Grand Rapids district contained in the bill. "Politicians understand when you have to vote your constituents' interests," he said.

Still, the victory was Pyrrhic. Though they approved the gas-tax proposal, Ways and Means leaders soon after got into an argument with Public Works bill sponsors over how much revenue the tax would raise.

Public Works leaders had assumed budget scorekeepers would, as in the past, count expected gasoline tax revenues as gross revenues — without taking any deductions for the general Treasury.

But because the revenues raised from the new nickel would be treated under new "pay as you go" rules spelled out in the 1990 budget agreement, Ways and Means members wanted to change a longtime practice of ignoring deductions businesses took off their gasoline-tax payments when calculating revenues into the Highway Trust Fund. The difference between the gross and net figures, Ways and Means estimated, took 1.25 cents away from the nickel increase. Rather than generating $6.6 billion a year, as Public Works had estimated, the tax would raise only $4.7 billion.

That complex accounting dispute only pushed the last nail into the coffin for Roe's Nickel for America. Opposition from rank-and-file Democrats already was strong enough to kill the bill for the summer on Aug. 1.

House Speaker Thomas S. Foley, D-Wash., who early on had supported the gas-tax hike, took some heat for the debacle.

"It's a confrontation that could have been avoided if a little quiet vote-counting had gone on a little earlier," said Timothy J. Penny, D-Minn. "This bill should never have been a last-minute proposition."

The delay made it certain that Congress could not complete action on the legislation by Sept. 30, when authority for states to let highway contracts with federal funds expired. When that date passed, states relied on a surplus of $6.8 billion available to them from the Highway Trust Fund to keep road construction projects going until a new authorization was enacted. Not all states fared well, though, because in some cases those funds could not be shifted toward ongoing road projects.

REVISED HOUSE BILL

After weeks behind closed doors, Public Works leaders emerged on Oct. 10 with a scaled-back $151 billion surface transportation bill (still HR 2950) that would stretch funding authority over six years rather than five.

Instead of the nickel gas-tax increase, the bill extended for four additional years half of a 1990 nickel gas-tax increase that was set to expire after fiscal 1995. The federal gas-tax rate of 14 cents a gallon therefore would decrease to only 11.5 cents per gallon after fiscal 1995.

The Public Works panel approved the revised bill on Oct. 15, 52-3. The Ways and Means panel on Oct. 16 approved the financing mechanism.

Sponsors achieved much of the savings by cutting funding by 30 percent for most of the special road and bridge projects in the original bill. About 20 projects of $1 million or less were the only projects to escape reduction.

Funding levels for the highway formula program were cut to $119 billion, rather than the $122.8 billion under the original bill. Spending authority for mass transit remained at $32 billion, but, as with all programs, the money would stretch over six years rather than five.

"We're not disappointed," Roe said. "But if we had more resources we'd be able to do a better job."

But the new House bill did not pave over all problems. The revised bill still faced a potential floor fight over state funding formulas, a stormy conference with the Senate and a possible veto.

Donor-state lawmakers posed the most immediate threat to the new bill. Roe said the revised bill treated the 20-odd donor states better than the previous measure, by increasing the spending pool from which donor states were promised at least a 90 percent return on every dollar paid into the fund.

Many lawmakers still complained that the formulas shortchanged their states. Ultimately, however, those from donor states such as Florida, North Carolina and Virginia, led by Rep. Charles E. Bennett, D-Fla., did not oppose the revised bill.

Skinner indicated he still would recommend a veto unless changes were made, including making states pay more than the 20 percent share of construction costs provided in the bill. The administration also opposed the raft of special road projects, which Skinner labeled "paving America with pork."

HOUSE FLOOR ACTION

On Oct. 23, the House passed the six-year revised bill, 343-83, but only after proponents muzzled opposition and deflected attacks on taxes and special road projects.

House proponents rallied a wide vote margin — far more than the two-thirds needed to override a threatened veto.

But a bruising conference with the Senate lay ahead, and the White House continued to sound its opposition to the House bill, largely to ensure that the administration remained a key player in the conference committee.

Skinner complained that Congress' delay in enacting a new highway bill already had cost 12,000 jobs and was hurting the economy.

The administration also criticized the bill's 2.5-cent gas-tax extension, high federal matching levels and authorization for 489 special highway projects.

The statement said the projects — which included $1.2 billion for 20 regional highway corridors — could cost more than $73 billion.

The bill moved past the House floor smoothly, mostly because controversial issues like the gas tax and complaints from donor states were ironed out beforehand.

But the bill's easy ride owed as much to the tight rein the Rules Committee kept on items open to floor debate as it did to working out early agreements on the bill's most volatile issues.

Despite Republican protests, the Rules Committee limited floor debate to only a dozen amendments and kept 41 others from being raised. Many of the amendments squelched by the panel dealt with potentially explosive issues that had tied up highway bills in the past. Among them were a limit on billboard construction, a repeal of the national speed limit, a weakening of motorcycle helmet laws, a strengthening of drunken-driving laws and a funding cut for some road projects.

"This rule is truly unprecedented, unjustified and unfair," said Gerald B. H. Solomon, R-N.Y., ranking member on the Rules panel. "What is this House coming to when a committee's bill is treated as almost sacrosanct, beyond the reach of members on this floor?"

Even sponsors agreed they had the parliamentary advantage. "We were helped immensely by the rule we had," Mineta conceded after the vote.

Republicans, including Rules Committee member Bob McEwen of Ohio, Robert S. Walker of Pennsylvania and Dan Burton of Indiana, opened their assault on the bill by attacking the rule.

The Rules Committee had denied Burton's attempts to cut seven special road projects slated to cost $67.1 million.

In protest, Republicans forced three procedural roll call votes. The rule ultimately was adopted, 323-102. *(Votes 331-334, pp. 80-H, 82-H)*

Tom DeLay, R-Texas, another bill antagonist, waged a one-man campaign against the mass-transit spending levels authorized in the measure. Apart from the $32 billion provided for mass transit, the bill allowed states to transfer up to $49 billion from highway spending to mass transit projects.

The Rules Committee had shot down four DeLay amendments that would have cut such transit funds.

Special Road Projects

After lawmakers adopted the rule limiting controversial amendments, the bill progressed with few major hitches — other than frequent eruptions by Walker, Burton and others over the bill's raft of special projects.

Though they accounted for only 3.5 percent of the authorized funding included in the bill, the $5.4 billion authorized for specific road projects was a focal point of floor debate and administration opposition.

"This is a Democratic bill, and it has a Democratic tax increase in it ... in order to build pork barrel projects in favored congressional districts," said Texas Republican Dick Armey.

Walker lambasted special treatment the bill gave a New Jersey highway project that was authorized in 1987 — a project in the district of Public Works Chairman Roe. The bill allowed the governor of New Jersey to waive "any and all federal requirements" as long as they were deemed in the public interest.

Under the provision, the governor could waive an environmental impact study due on the project in 1992 and "hand this project to a group of his cronies and violate all federal contracting procedures," Walker said. "This is outrageous, and we ought not to be doing it."

The appeal prompted a tongue-lashing from Roe. He branded Walker and other opponents as "princes of darkness" bent on trying to "belittle" and run down those seeking to help their districts with road projects.

"I resent any other members of this body coming and telling me about my district," Roe said. "You could not hurt me if you hit me with a baseball bat because you people are princes of darkness. Princes of darkness is what you are."

Public Works leaders scored a final parliamentary victory by thwarting a planned assault on the proposed extension of the 2.5-cents-a-gallon gas tax.

Under House rules, lawmakers had only one chance to send a bill back to committee for an overhaul. And Bill Archer, R-Texas, an opponent, was expected to offer such a motion to kill the gas-tax extension.

But ranking Republicans on the Public Works Committee foiled that attempt by offering the motion themselves. Bill cosponsor and key panel Republican Shuster offered a watered-down motion that cleared the way for quick House passage. *(Vote 338, p. 82-H)*

Walker, outfoxed by a fellow Pennsylvania Republican, complained bitterly, contending that only bill opponents were able to offer such motions. But Majority Leader Richard A. Gephardt, D-Mo., a bill supporter, was the presiding officer and ruled in Shuster's favor.

Other amendments were offered by:

- Anthony C. Beilenson, D-Calif., to allow states to require contractors to guarantee their work, lifting a federal ban on such warranties. The amendment passed, 400-26. *(Vote 336, p. 82-H)*

Despite that lopsided vote in favor, conferees dropped the provision in conference in exchange for language vowing to study the issue.

- Del. Eleanor Holmes Norton, D-D.C., to set separate contracting goals for businesses owned by minorities and those owned by women. Businesses owned by women would be eligible for at least 5 percent of highway contracts. Under existing law, both groups shared at least 10 percent of highway contracts. The amendment failed, 133-295. *(Vote 335, p. 82-H)*
- Walker, to kill a provision that would create a new "Office of Intermodalism." Walker said the office, which would help link various transportation systems, would make it federal policy to force people out of their cars.

The amendment failed, 69-348. *(Vote 337, p. 82-H)*

CONFERENCE ACTION

House and Senate negotiators began reconciling the two sweeping highway and mass transit authorization bills on Nov. 7, amid concern that action might not be completed before Congress adjourned for the year.

Both the five-year, $124 billion Senate measure and the six-year, $151 billion House bill would recast transportation policy in the wake of the nearly finished Interstate Highway System. But the differences between the bills were wide in many areas.

Complicating the task was the fact that the conference included a wider array of lawmakers than any previous highway authorization effort. Holding sway over select provisions were the chairmen and key members of the House Ways and Means, Energy and Commerce, Interior, Science, Merchant Marine and Judiciary committees. In total, there were 66 House and 26 Senate negotiators.

The involvement of members from so many House panels resulted in large part from the fact that the focus of both bills was on "intermodal" transportation — a concept that sought to better coordinate various transportation systems.

By emphasizing linking highways with seaports, rails and airports, the Public Works panel was forced to reluctantly include more committee members in the conference.

For example, the Science and Energy and Commerce panels had jurisdiction over research and rail transportation issues, respectively. The Merchant Marine panel oversaw seaports and wetlands preservation, both of which were eligible for transportation funds.

As the conference got under way, state highway officials grew restless. Already about 10 states had run out of authority to issue new highway contracts, and the number was expected to grow to a majority of states by the end of the year.

Concerns about state transportation programs came against a backdrop of continuing threats from the Bush administration to veto either bill. But it was increasingly more difficult for Bush to reject such domestic legislation in the face of public displeasure with the lingering economic recession, as was seen in the recent midterm elections. Also, both bills were passed with more than enough votes to override a veto.

On Nov. 14, negotiators agreed to the House bill's six-year, $151 billion scope and vowed to work through the weekends to send a final bill to Bush before Thanksgiving adjournment.

But negotiations proceeded at a snail's pace, as conferees traded accusations that the other side was stonewalling, failing to show up for meetings and getting bogged down in details. House Speaker Foley and Senate Majority Leader Mitchell kept the pressure on conferees to edge the bill toward completion.

Amid fears of a protracted recession, the Bush administration softened its harsh veto rhetoric and began to work closely with negotiators.

"The gas tax in and of itself is not enough to warrant a veto," Skinner said. A veto, he added, "is obviously not our first choice. Our first choice is to get a bill that everybody can live with."

By adopting the House funding levels, conferees boosted mass transit programs by $11 billion over the Senate measure — though the funding would be stretched over six years rather than five. Highways would receive $119 billion, rather than $103 billion in the Senate bill.

Conferees also accepted a House provision that guaranteed that states got back in highway projects at least 90 percent of what they paid into the Highway Trust Fund in annual gasoline taxes. States had been guaranteed a return of at least 85 percent.

Negotiators also agreed to a House provision that required the federal government to pay 80 percent of transportation project costs. Under the Senate bill, the government would pay only 75 percent of the cost of road projects that added new lane capacity for single-occupant vehicles.

In exchange, Senate sponsors Moynihan and Symms and others were poised to win on an issue crucial to senators: That states and urban areas be given much more flexibility to spend federal transportation money as they chose.

The decades-old rural, urban and primary highway "system" concept was headed for the dust bin.

The Interstate Highway System and the new 155,000-mile National Highway System to be made up of the Interstate network and primary feeder routes would be adopted to replace the old system.

To substitute for all other highway programs, House negotiators proposed a scaled-down version of the Senate proposal for a broad Surface Transportation Program that would allow states to spend federal money on any transportation program they chose.

The final bill authorized $119.5 billion for highways and $31.5 billion for mass transit through fiscal 1996. It marked a 39 percent average annual increase in highway spending over the previous five-year authorization period.

Gone was much of the federal control that had long dictated how transportation funds were spent. States and urban areas got unprecedented flexibility to spend money on roads, transit or other programs. For the first time, urban areas got freedom to spend funds without interference from state legislatures.

For the Bush administration, Congress' agreement to create the National Highway System was a key victory.

But even toward that system, the bill focused federal dollars on maintaining the nation's road networks instead of pouring more concrete, helping to improve mass transit systems and increase ridership, reducing traffic congestion and making the transportation system more efficient.

"This is the first transportation legislation of the post-Interstate era," said Moynihan. "It marks the transition from system building to system performance."

The bill also held out the promise of jobs at a time when the economy continued to falter. Sponsors said the measure would provide funds for up to 2 million new and existing jobs. The administration, eager to embrace the bill as a job creator on the eve of an election year, said 4 million jobs would result.

Highway Program Structure

Two new programs made up the core of the bill and both of them offered states wide flexibility to shift funds from roads to mass transit.

The bill expanded upon the Interstate network with the new National Highway System, which received $38 billion, including $17 billion for Interstate maintenance. States would have power over spending those funds, with cooperation from metropolitan planning groups. Half of the funds devoted to the system could be shifted to mass transit by states, and another 50 percent if the Transportation secretary approved.

In two years, Congress would have to approve a final road map for the system submitted by the Transportation Department.

A $23.9 billion Surface Transportation Program would be available for roads, mass transit, bridges, bicycle paths and other purposes. Each state would divide 62.5 percent of those funds among urban areas with populations of at least 200,000. The remainder could be spent anywhere in the state.

Those restrictions represented a compromise forged with Western senators, who wanted control left at the state level because their states had few large urban areas.

"We are going to have maximum flexibility for our state departments of transportation to put these funds where they're needed," said Symms of Idaho.

Other core programs included $7.2 billion to complete the Interstate system, $16.1 billion for the nation's bridges and a new $6 billion program that would provide grants to urban areas that were having trouble complying with federal clean-air rules.

Cash Categories

As was the case through the entire debate over the bill, lawmakers were most at odds when deciding how much cash each state should get. But beyond that battle, negotiators also had to overcome wide philosophical differences between the House and Senate over how to revise highway funding formulas for a post-Interstate era.

The House bill proposed rewriting longstanding formulas and distributing funds to states based on highway usage factors such as fuel consumption and vehicle miles traveled. This was done to ensure the political support of so-called donor states that paid more into the trust fund than they received in highway dollars.

The Senate bill took a completely different approach to distributing funds. Chief author Moynihan opposed usage-based formulas on the grounds that they would encourage fuel consumption. Instead, the bill based each state's funding levels on an average of its highway receipts over the previous five years.

In conference, negotiators blended aspects of both formula options. But lawmakers also decided that the only way to make states happy was to allocate most of the funds not as part of any highway program, but in the form of special road projects or lump-sum payments.

The no-strings-attached cash was used to address a chorus of complaints from lawmakers that their states were being treated unfairly.

The House reduced to $4 billion the price tag for the special projects included in its bill. Most programs were cut by equal amounts across the board.

Senate negotiators tacked on project funding of their own, adding about $2.2 billion, divided roughly evenly among 16 key states. States would be free to choose how to spend most of those funds. In total, 529 special projects were given funding authority by both chambers.

Also thrown into the projects category was another $1 billion in what was euphemistically called an "equity adjustment" for the home states of key lawmakers from Maine, West Virginia, Arkansas, Pennsylvania and others. When asked the purpose of the funds, Surface Transportation Chairman Mineta gestured as if he were doling out a stack of imaginary dollar bills.

It was just one of several provisions added as cash cows for states whose lawmakers complained bitterly that they had been treated unfairly in past years. Other categories authorized:

- **$5.2 billion to ensure that donor states such as Florida, Virginia and Michigan would receive a 90 percent return on their gas tax contributions.**
- **$4 billion to begin reimbursing states for building toll or other roads before the Interstate was begun in 1956, if those roads became part of the Interstate system.**

Moynihan had won a provision in the Senate bill that called for a study of a 1958 federal commission recommendation suggesting such a reimbursement. But in conference, Moynihan upped the ante and got negotiators to agree to a provision that would clear the way for payments to begin. The change would net New York $675 million over six years. Total reimbursement costs were expected to exceed $47 billion.

Other states that would benefit most from the payback program included California, Connecticut, Illinois, Indiana, Maryland, Massachusetts, Michigan, New Jersey, Ohio, Pennsylvania and Texas.

To help win support for the provision, 27 other states that had no such roads were promised at least $20 million each from this fund over six years.

- $1.9 billion for Western states for roads that traversed federal lands.
- $3 billion in "bonus" allocations for 19 donor states — a provision won by Bentsen when the Senate passed its bill. Also, nine donor states would share $415 million more.
- $1.7 billion to be divided among states that, for various reasons, were worse off from the conference agreement than they would have been under either the House or Senate bill.

Cash-and-Carry

The patchwork of cash-and-carry provisions marked a departure from the longstanding method of allocating federal highway funds based on such factors as a state's population density, fuel consumption and lane miles.

Lawmakers used the traditional funding formulas only

Continued on p. 150

Transportation Reauthorization Provisions

Following are provisions of the Surface Transportation Efficiency Act of 1991 (HR 2950 — PL 102-240) as cleared by Congress on Nov. 27 and signed into law by President Bush on Dec. 18.

SPENDING AND FINANCES

Spending Levels

• **Scope and cost**. Authorized $151 billion over six years for highway, mass transit, highway safety and other surface transportation programs. Highway and highway safety programs were authorized $119.5 billion and mass transit $31.5 billion.

• **Declaration of policy.** Established as U.S. policy the development of "a national intermodal transportation system that is economically efficient, environmentally sound, provides the foundation for the nation to compete in the global economy and will move people and goods in an energy-efficient manner."

The policy stressed the creation of a national highway system, composed of existing and new Interstate and primary arterial roads. It also emphasized public transportation as a way to improve air quality, conserve energy and improve mobility for the elderly and those with disabilities. The policy was required to be posted in all Transportation Department offices.

• **Obligation ceiling.** Recommended that spending from the Highway Trust Fund be raised from the $14.5 billion fiscal 1991 limit to $16.8 billion in fiscal 1992, $18.3 billion for fiscal 1993, $18.4 billion for fiscal 1994, $18.3 billion for fiscal 1995, $18.4 billion for fiscal 1996 and $18.3 billion for fiscal 1997. Appropriators set the actual spending limits.

• **Federal matching share.** Required a federal matching share of 80 percent for most programs. States put up 20 percent of the authorized federal cost for each road, transit or safety project. A federal share of 90 percent was provided for remaining Interstate construction projects.

Financing

• **Motor fuels tax.** Maintained a 14-cent-a-gallon gasoline tax through fiscal 1995. After that, half of the 1990 nickel increase for highways and transit that was slated to expire after fiscal 1995 would be extended through fiscal 1999. The provision would keep gasoline taxes at 11.5 cents and would not allow them to drop to 9 cents a gallon as had been planned.

Most funding for federal transportation programs came out of the Highway Trust Fund, which was fed by taxes on the sale of motor fuels. The 1990 budget-reconciliation law increased gasoline taxes by 5 cents to 14 cents a gallon until the end of fiscal 1995 but directed that only 2.5 cents of that increase go toward highways and transit. The other half was used to reduce the budget deficit.

HIGHWAYS

Highway Programs

• **National highway system**. Authorized $38 billion for a 155,000-mile national highway system, consisting of the Interstate highway network and major primary roads. The amount included $17 billion for maintenance of the Interstate system.

The Transportation secretary would select eligible segments and submit them to Congress, which would have to approve the system by Sept. 30, 1995, or lose the funds.

States could transfer 50 percent of their highway system funds to mass transit, and an additional 50 percent if the secretary certified that such a transfer was in the public interest.

• **Surface transportation program**. Consolidated all other highway programs, other than for the Interstate system, into one $23.9 billion Surface Transportation Program to provide funds for roads, mass transit and other transportation projects.

Road projects eligible for funding included construction and rehabilitation projects, earthquake-proofing and operational improvements for bridges and highways. Interstate highways and bridges on and off the federal aid system were eligible for additional funds.

Funds also could be used to cover capital costs for mass transit, passenger and high-speed rail and publicly owned bus terminals and facilities. Money also could be spent on passenger rail or magnetic levitation service provided by public or private carriers; car pool projects and related parking facilities; bicycle programs; transportation safety; research and planning programs; and transportation control measures required under the 1990 amendments to the Clean Air Act.

• **Interstate Highway System**. Authorized $7.2 billion to complete the Interstate Highway System, begun in 1956, from fiscal 1993 through fiscal 1996. States would receive funds based on their share of costs to complete the system, except for Massachusetts, which was authorized $2.55 billion over four years to complete Interstates 90 and 93 in downtown Boston. The law also authorized $17 billion to maintain the Interstate system as part of the National Highway System.

• **Bridges**. Authorized $16.1 billion to rebuild and replace obsolete and deficient bridges. Of that amount, $349.5 million was to go into a discretionary program to allow the Transportation secretary to direct funds to specific bridges. Timber bridges were guaranteed $50.5 million of the discretionary amounts.

• **Urban-rural mix of funds.** Required states to devote 20 percent of their Surface Transportation Program funds to safety and transportation enhancement programs. At least 62.5 percent of the remaining 80 percent of funds was to be divided among urban areas of at least 200,000 residents and other less populated areas in amounts equal to the proportion of their population. The remaining 37.5 percent of funds would be spent on projects regardless of population.

• **Minimum allocation.** Authorized $3 billion for the "bonus minimum allocation" program designed to ensure that each state received the highest possible return on its contributions to the Highway Trust Fund. That came atop the standard minimum allocation program, for which the law authorized $5.2 billion to ensure that each state received a 90 percent return on its gasoline tax contributions.

The law changed the calculation for the base amount of the minimum apportionment formula to give states more funds. The new base included all payments to states for Interstate construction, substitution and maintenance, bridge and surface transportation programs as well as prior years' discretionary allocations from those programs.

Future discretionary road grants and special road project funding were excluded from the minimum allocation formula.

• **Other apportionment formulas.** Combined the Senate proposal to average each state's allocation over the past five years with some new factors from the House bill, as well as lump-sum payments to states.

Longstanding formulas would no longer be used to allocate most funds. Instead, they were largely replaced by several lump-sum cash payments to states.

States would divide a total of $4 billion, authorized for fiscal 1996 and 1997, to begin reimbursing them for segments of the Interstate system that were constructed without federal assistance before the program began in 1956. States standing to benefit the most included New York, California, Connecticut, Illinois, Indiana, Maryland, Massachusetts, Michigan, New Jersey, Ohio, Pennsylvania and Texas. Even states with no such roads would get a minimum of $20 million each from this program.

Western states would receive $1.9 billion for roads that traversed federal lands. Another $1.7 billion would be divided among states that, for various reasons, were worse off from the conference agreement than they would have been under either the House or Senate bill.

• **High-priority corridors.** Authorized $2 billion for 21 high-priority corridors that were deemed regionally and nationally important. Those corridors would be part of the national highway system.

• **Special road projects.** Authorized $6.2 billion for 539 special road projects in lawmakers' districts and states. That amount included $4 billion in projects chosen by House members and $2.2 billion in Senate funding to states for unspecified projects.

Spending for most projects would be made through the trust fund, with some projects funded through general revenues. In most cases, the federal government would pay 80 percent of the costs.

The special road projects were initiated by House lawmakers, but during the conference, House proponents reduced funding for their projects to make room for the requests of senators. Most senators applied funds to their states in lump-sum form, while others chose specific projects.

House bill sponsors, including Robert A. Roe, D-N.J.; Norman Y. Mineta, D-Calif.; John Paul Hammerschmidt, R-Ark.; and Bud Shuster, R-Pa., came away with about 36 percent of all road projects specified by the House.

The states of several key senators also came out big winners during the conference committee. West Virginia, home of Democratic Appropriations Chairman Robert C. Byrd, received more than $200 million in special road projects. Maine, home of Majority Leader George J. Mitchell, D, received $134.5 million for a special bridge repair project. The Kennedy Expressway in Illinois received $175 million in special road funds.

- **Bicycles and pedestrian walkways.** Allowed federal transportation funds to be used to build bike and pedestrian paths along federal-aid highways, roads, trails or parkways.
- **Metric system signing.** Repealed the prohibition for the placement of metric signs along federal-aid highways.

Metropolitan and Statewide Planning

- **Metropolitan planning.** Required that urban areas of more than 50,000 residents establish metropolitan planning groups to coordinate various transportation modes.

Each group would work with states to develop a transportation improvement program that encompassed all federal transportation projects within a metropolitan area. The plan would have to conform with a long-range transportation plan and state efforts to comply with the Clean Air Act. The program would be updated every two years. Planning factors would include energy conservation; social, economic and environmental effects; enhancing transit services; and long-range transportation needs. Areas with populations of 200,000 or more were deemed transportation management areas and would have stricter planning requirements.

- **Statewide planning.** Required states to develop plans for an intermodal, or mixed transportation, system. Plans would include long-range outlooks and a transportation improvement program, and would be coordinated with metropolitan planners.

In developing such plans, the states would have to allow public involvement and consult with Indian tribal governments that had jurisdiction over lands within the state.

Safety

- **Highway safety grant programs.** Authorized $1.3 billion for National Highway Traffic Safety Administration grant programs from the trust fund. A House provision setting up new mandatory safety programs for drunken driving, speeding, motorcycle safety and other items was dropped, and listed only as priority items to be considered when making grants.

The Transportation secretary also would have to establish a national uniform data collection and reporting system of traffic-related deaths and injuries.

- **Impaired driving enforcement.** Set up a new program that authorized $125 million for grants to states that adopted alcohol- and drug-impaired driving enforcement programs.

A state would be eligible for a basic grant if it met the following five requirements: revoked drunken driver's licenses; set up sobriety checkpoints; set a 0.1 blood-alcohol content level standard for drunken driving, reduced to 0.08 after three years; stepped up enforcement of 21-year-old drinking age laws; and established laws preventing drugged driving. Grants would be given only to states that made it unlawful to possess open containers of alcohol in the passenger area of a motor vehicle (excepting charter buses) while on the road and that revoked license plates and registrations of repeat drunken-driving offenders. Videotaping drunken drivers also would be a supplemental grant criteria.

- **Other safety programs.** Authorized from general funds $291 million through fiscal 1995 for the traffic and motor vehicle safety program and $27.4 million for the motor vehicle information and cost-savings program.
- **Motorcycle helmet and safety belt use.** Required states that did not have motorcycle helmet and safety belt laws in effect during fiscal 1994 to spend 1.5 percent of their highway funds for highway safety programs. States that failed to enact such laws by fiscal 1995 would have to spend 3 percent of their highway funds on safety programs.

The law also authorized $100 million for incentive grants to states that adopted motorcycle helmet and safety belt laws.

- **Air bags.** Required that passenger cars made after Sept. 1, 1996, be equipped with driver and front-seat passenger air bags. Trucks, buses and multipurpose passenger vehicles would have until Sept. 1, 1997, to have driver's side air bags, and until Sept. 1, 1998, for front-seat passenger air bags.
- **Safety priorities for passenger cars.** Directed the secretary to begin writing safety standards by May 31, 1992, to improve the side-impact protection of cars and reduce head injuries; to reduce the risk of passenger cars, vans and light trucks rolling over; to improve the safety of child booster seats; and to improve safety belt designs and head-impact protection.
- **Rear-seat belts.** Directed the secretary to provide consumers, during fiscal 1993, with information about retrofitting their vehicles with rear-seat, lap-and-shoulder belts.

Tolls

- **Toll facilities.** Provided states up to 35 percent of the cost of building new public toll facilities on roads, bridges and tunnels other than on free segments of the existing Interstate system. Tolls set to expire were allowed to continue. The federal government would pay 80 percent of the cost of converting existing roads and bridges to tolls.
- **Congestion pricing.** Allowed the federal government to pay for up to three years for five unspecified "congestion-pricing" pilot programs to be undertaken locally. The program allowed states to levy tolls on vehicles traveling on congested routes during peak travel periods.

MASS TRANSIT

General Provisions

- **Agency name change.** Renamed the Urban Mass Transportation Administration the Federal Transit Administration.
- **Federal matching funds.** Increased the federal share of funding for mass transit projects from 75 percent to 80 percent for discretionary programs and retained the 80 percent match for formula grant programs. The federal government still would pay up to 50 percent of operating assistance grants.

Wheelchair ramps and other related equipment required by either the 1990 amendments to the Clean Air Act or the Americans with Disabilities Act were eligible for a 90 percent match.

- **Mix of general funds, trust funds.** Increased the proportion of mass transit funds that came out of the mass transit account of the Highway Trust Fund. Of the $31.5 billion authorized for transit programs, $18.2 billion, or 58 percent, would come from the trust fund and the rest would come from the Treasury.
- **Flexibility of highway and transit funds.** Allowed up to $65 billion, or 54 percent, of the federal highway program to be made available for mass transit at the discretion of state and local officials.

Conversely, some formula grant funds in urbanized areas of 200,000 or more would be available for roads or other transportation programs if requirements under the Americans with Disabilities Act were met. Approval of a metropolitan planning organization also would be required.

Discretionary Grants

- **New rail projects and extensions.** Authorized $6.2 billion primarily for new rail and bus projects. Among the 64 new projects designated was authority for $634 million for the New Jersey urban core system and $568.5 million for the San Francisco Bay area rail system.

• **Rail modernization.** Authorized $4.9 billion for rail and fixed-guideway modernization projects. The law restructured the way grants were awarded to reflect the growing number of aging rail systems.

• **Buses and bus facilities.** Authorized $2.3 billion for the replacement, rehabilitation and purchase of buses and related equipment and the construction of bus-related facilities.

• **Criteria for new starts.** Spelled out new factors to be used by the Transportation secretary in deciding where to spend money for new rail systems. Among them, the results of alternative analysis and preliminary engineering studies, cost effectiveness and whether a project was supported by an "acceptable degree of local financial commitment" would have to be considered before a proposed project could go forward.

The alternative analysis requirement could be waived if a small portion of total costs was sought from the federal government or if the project was needed to help a state comply with air quality plans.

The social, environmental and economic impacts of proposed projects would also be taken into consideration before they could go forward.

Formula Grants

• **Capital and operating grants.** Authorized $16.2 billion for capital grants and operating assistance and $941.7 million for rural transit programs.

• **Urban-rural funding proportion.** Increased the amount of formula funds available for rural transit systems to 5.5 percent from 2.9 percent.

The law directed that urbanized areas of less than 200,000 but more than 50,000 would be guaranteed a minimum 8.8 percent share of formula grant funds, up from 8.6 percent. Areas with more than 200,000 would receive at least 85.6 percent of formula funds, a slight decrease from 88.4 percent under previous law.

• **Operating assistance.** Retained federal operating assistance for all mass transit systems. The administration proposed doing away with operating assistance for urban areas of more than 1 million.

The amount of operating assistance available to transit systems was indexed to inflation. This was the case for all urban transit systems, not just those in areas with populations under 200,000, as was past practice.

• **Research, planning and administration.** Authorized $478.4 million for national- and state-level research, planning and training and $304.5 million for expenses of the Federal Transit Administration.

• **Programs for elderly, disabled.** Authorized $428.3 million for transit programs to aid the elderly and disabled. Funds would be available for operating expenses as well as capital expenses.

OTHER ISSUES

Research

• **Highway research.** Authorized $240 million for an applied technology program for highway, transit and mixed transportation systems to speed up and deploy advanced highway-building technologies.

• **Intelligent vehicle-highway systems.** Authorized $659 million to launch a new program to use high technology to help solve traffic congestion and safety problems along highways. The money would go toward installing high-tech devices along highway corridors selected by the Transportation secretary.

Such systems would include computer-controlled traffic monitoring and communication systems between transportation networks and vehicles. The systems would seek to make travel on existing roads, bridges and tunnels more efficient.

Half of the program funds would go to highly congested areas and those with air quality problems. The federal government would pay 80 percent of the cost of such technologies and all of the cost of especially innovative projects to be determined by the secretary.

• **High-speed ground transportation program.** Authorized $700 million to design and build magnetically levitated train systems along federal aid highways, including the Interstate system. Another $50 million would go toward grants to develop all forms of high-speed ground transportation, including steel-wheel rail. And $25 million would be authorized for broader research in the area.

A prototype magnetically levitated train system, which rode on an electromagnetic cushion, would be slated for operational testing within three years of enactment. The federal government would pay 75 percent of its cost. The project would be at least 19 miles long and contain at least one track-switching mechanism.

A national design program for magnetic levitation trains would be established, jointly managed by the assistant secretary of the Army for civil works and state and federal transportation agencies. The initial plan would be submitted to Congress by Jan. 15, 1992, and updated annually.

• **Bureau of Transportation Statistics.** Authorized $90 million to create an office to collect data on the performance of the nation's transportation network and to produce biannual estimates of the productivity and use of the systems.

Trucking Initiatives

• **Length and weight limits on trucks.** Limited the use of longer-combination vehicles on the Interstate system to states that allowed them before June 1, 1991. Such trucks were defined as having two or more trailers or semi-trailers that weighed more than 80,000 pounds. Included were triple-trailer combinations, long double combinations and so-called Rocky Mountain doubles that consisted of one long and one short trailer.

The law left it up to each state to determine which longer-combination vehicles could use its roads. But the Transportation secretary could challenge a state's assessment of its vehicle length and weight laws.

States would be allowed to further restrict the use of longer-combination vehicles above and beyond the federal limits.

• **Motor carrier safety assistance.** Authorized $479 million for grants to enforce federal and state trucking regulations, to train truck inspectors to enforce new rules governing hazardous materials, to fund state truck and bus accident data programs and to fund research, development and administrative functions.

• **"Bingo cards."** Repealed a law that allowed states to require truckers to be certified. The law had forced truckers to carry so-called bingo cards in their cabs with stamps from each state in which they were certified to travel.

Environmental and Scenic Issues

• **Congestion mitigation and air quality improvement.** Authorized $6 billion over five years for a program to reduce congestion and improve air quality.

Funds would be available to areas that failed to meet air quality levels under the 1990 amendments to the Clean Air Act. Metropolitan planners would select eligible programs, and the federal government would pay no more than 80 percent of the costs.

Eligible projects included those likely to contribute to an urban area's compliance with the standards and those approved as part of a state's implementation plan under the Clean Air Act.

Projects that expanded road capacity for single-occupancy vehicles would be specifically excluded unless they had designated lanes for high-occupancy vehicles during rush hours.

• **Controls on outdoor advertising.** Authorized states to use any federal aid highway funds to remove illegal signs and justly compensate sign owners for those signs. The provision also applied to signs located along Interstate and primary system roads designated as scenic byways by the states. Sign owners would have 90 days from enactment to remove their illegal signs. If not, the state would remove the billboards and charge the owner for removal costs.

Also, $3 million in authorized funds for the scenic byways program would be available to states for billboard removal.

• **Scenic and historic byways.** Authorized $30 million over three years for a program to establish national scenic and historic roads. The Federal Highway Administration would provide technical assistance to state agencies responsible for the roadways and would provide grants to the same agencies for planning, design and development of the scenic road program.

Ten percent of these authorized funds would be available to

states for billboard removal.

• **National Recreational Trails Fund**. Set up a trust fund with revenues from the excise tax on recreational fuels to help promote the use of recreational trails in states.

Fuel taxes paid into the Highway Trust Fund from outfitters and guides, snowmobile excursion operators, motorcross racing establishments, ski lodges and other commercial users had been refunded through tax credits. Those tax credits were repealed and the revenues instead put into the trust fund.

Half of trust fund revenues would be divided equally among states and the other half distributed based on recreational use. States with the highest demand for recreational trails would get the most revenues.

Miscellaneous

• **Speed limit sanctions repeal.** Repealed a 1987 law requiring federal monitoring of state speed-limit compliance. The requirements would be eased by mandating that states only submit data and certify that speed limits were being enforced. States that failed to meet those requirements still would be subject to the loss of federal highway funds.

The law made permanent the ability of states to raise the speed limit to 65 mph on certain non-Interstate highways built to Interstate standards and located outside of urban areas.

• **Documentary.** Authorized $2 million for a film documentary examining the health of the nation's infrastructure, with cooperation from a public television station to be chosen.

• **State compliance with driver's license suspensions.** Required a federal study of state efforts to comply with a 1991 law requiring that convicted drug offenders' driver's licenses be suspended.

• **Office of intermodalism.** Created an office, within the Office of the Transportation secretary, to coordinate all modes of transportation, as a way to achieve more efficient and productive transportation methods. The director would be required to develop an intermodal transportation data base with states and metropolitan planning organizations. The office also would oversee research on intermodal transportation. ■

Continued from p. 146

as a starting point for the computer programs of their staffs. The final chart showing how each state would fare that was adopted by negotiators was labeled "26A" — a title that greatly understated the numerous unofficial charts floating around Capitol Hill the week of Nov. 25.

"We had a saying in the committee," said Lautenberg of New Jersey. "I send a formula to the computer and ask for its immediate consideration."

Some longstanding factors used to calculate formulas would remain intact, though, including those for Interstate construction and maintenance, bridges and roads on federal lands. Spending for those programs would continue to be allocated according to factors such as a state's lane mileage, population and project completion costs.

The new highway categories allocated money using a blend of House and Senate formula proposals. The National Highway System, the Surface Transportation Program and a congestion-relief program relied on House-proposed factors such as diesel fuel consumption and vehicle miles traveled as well as the Senate option of averaging what a state received in funding over the past five years.

Other key provisions included in the final bill:

• Authorized $4.9 billion primarily for new rail projects, designating 57 new rail and bus projects. It also would authorize $4.9 billion for rail and fixed-guideway modernization programs, $2.4 million for buses and related materials, $17.4 billion for capital grants and operating aid, $918 million for rural transit programs and $717 million for research and planning.

• Required that urban areas of more than 50,000 residents establish metropolitan planning groups to coordinate various transportation modes.

Each group would work with states to develop a transportation improvement program for the metropolitan area, which would conform with clean-air guidelines and be updated every two years.

• Froze the length and weight limits for multi-trailer trucks at those allowed by states as of June 1, 1991. Such trucks had two or more trailers weighing a total of more than 80,000 pounds.

• Allowed states to spend no more than 10 percent of a $180 million scenic highways account to remove illegal billboards along such roads.

• Set up a trust fund from revenues generated by the excise tax on recreational fuels to help promote the use of recreational trails.

• Required states that did not have motorcycle helmet and safety belt laws in effect during fiscal 1994 to spend 1.5 percent of their highway funds for highway safety programs.

• Authorized $2 million for WETA-TV in Washington, D.C., to begin work on a documentary examining the health of the nation's transportation systems.

Negotiators dropped from the bill provisions that would have allowed states to require contractors to guarantee their work, begin a tree-planting program along highways and make it more difficult for the government to seize private property when building roads.

FINAL ACTION

After two weeks of an often rancorous conference, the Senate on Nov. 27 cleared the measure for Bush, 79-8, in the early morning hours before Congress adjourned for the Thanksgiving recess. *(Vote 277, p. 36-S)*

"This will touch the lives of everyone," Roe said as the House adopted the final bill, 372-47, and sent it to the Senate. "With this bill we are rebuilding America." *(Vote 440, p. 106-H)*

There was much congratulating but little floor debate in either chamber as the conference report was adopted.

Members from donor states had given up their last-minute efforts to extract more money from the bill.

"We will come back and try to get parity, eventually. But in the meantime, America needs this bill and so does Florida," said Rep. Lawrence J. Smith, D-Fla. The Florida delegation had led the charge against mostly Western states that received far more in highway construction projects than they contributed in taxes to the Highway Trust Fund.

Skinner on Nov. 26 praised the bill as "a constructive compromise" and said he would recommend that Bush sign it.

Despite earlier veto threats, the administration worked closely with lawmakers toward the end of the conference and Skinner took pains to identify himself with the process.

He emphasized that many aspects of the final bill originated from the transportation proposal he unveiled early in the year. Those included the bill's 155,000-mile National

Highway System, incentives for private-sector investment, toll roads and greater flexibility for states in spending federal road dollars.

He downplayed provisions remaining in the bill that had been vigorously opposed by the White House, including a 20 percent state share for most programs and the special road projects. The administration wanted states to pay a higher portion of project costs — as high as 40 percent — and branded the projects traditional congressional pork-barreling.

Skinner was apparently chastened by the prospect that failure to renew transportation programs could cost jobs. He conceded that states were not fiscally prepared to pay higher shares for road and transit projects and that 60 percent of the special projects added were along parts of the proposed National Highway System.

"What we have is controlled pork," Skinner said.

Bush signed the bill in Dallas on Dec. 18. Saying Skinner had achieved his goal of heralding in a new era for national transportation policy, Bush named him to replace John H. Sununu as White House chief of staff as of Dec. 16.

One last glitch put a crimp on the legislation, however. The White House Office of Management and Budget said across-the-board cuts of $1.2 billion in highway spending for fiscal 1992 would be needed to make the bill comply with domestic spending ceilings under the 1990 budget agreement.

Most of the excess spending was attributed to a provision put into the bill by Moynihan to authorize funds for renovation of a federal courthouse in the New York City borough of Brooklyn. Though the courthouse was expected to cost only $457 million in the later years of the bill, a complex budget scoring ruling by OMB counted the provision as requiring $1.2 billion in cuts from highway spending in fiscal 1992 to account for the $457 million in actual spending in future years. ■

Drug Testing Required for Transit Workers

A fatal New York City subway crash in August, believed to have been caused by a drunken motorman, prompted lawmakers to push anew for more stringent rules on random drug and alcohol testing for transportation workers.

Appropriators included a provision in the fiscal 1992 transportation spending bill (HR 2942 — PL 102-143) that required new drug and alcohol testing rules for aviation, rail, trucking, bus and mass transit employees performing safety-sensitive jobs. The Transportation Department and the Federal Aviation Administration had one year from the bill's enactment to require the tests. *(Appropriations, p. 603)*

The Senate had passed drug-testing legislation a dozen times since 1987 only to see it die in the House, where intense opposition from organized labor had kept such bills off the floor. The AFL-CIO opposed random testing, contending that it was an invasion of privacy and produced inaccurate results.

But the House, without the usual fight from key drug-testing opponents such as Energy and Commerce Chairman John D. Dingell, D-Mich., passed a non-binding motion Sept. 24 to instruct conferees on the appropriations measure to accept mass transit drug-testing language sponsored by Sen. Alfonse M. D'Amato, R-N.Y. The motion carried by an overwhelming 415-5. *(Vote 273, p. 66-H)*

Conferees, who in 1990 rejected similar D'Amato language, went a step further in 1991. They adopted a broader bill by Sen. Ernest F. Hollings, D-S.C., to mandate random drug and alcohol tests on all transportation workers in safety-sensitive positions. "It's a matter we can't compromise on any longer," D'Amato said. "And the unions understand that."

House appropriators, led by William Lehman, D-Fla., dropped their past opposition and accepted the Senate provision under an Oct. 2 conference agreement.

Since the beginning of 1990, the Bush administration had required random drug tests of about 4 million aviation, trucking and bus employees in safety-sensitive positions. The administration had been considering alcohol-testing rules.

Mass transit workers were not covered by the existing rules. A federal appeals court ruled that the Urban Mass Transportation Administration lacked regulatory authority to impose tests on such workers.

The drug-testing provision in the spending bill codified existing rules that required tests in specific instances. For example, they were required before workers were hired and after an accident, and could be administered for "reasonable cause," on a periodic basis and on a random basis.

The Hollings Measure

In the sixth such vote in five years, the Senate passed a separate drug and alcohol-testing bill (S 676) on May 20 by voice vote. Hollings then urged the House to pass a companion measure to cover aviation, rail, transit and bus workers.

Despite a 1989 Supreme Court ruling that upheld mandatory drug testing for workers with public-safety and law enforcement duties, efforts to extend such screening to others continued to meet with resistance. *(1989 Almanac, p. 325)*

The attitude changed after the Aug. 28 subway crash in New York, which killed five people and injured 171. Hollings said the accident "has jarred our senses and again tragically reminds us that legislation mandating alcohol and drug testing is needed." Police had charged train operator Robert Ray with five counts of murder and said they believed that he was drunk when the accident occurred. Authorities also found a vial with traces of cocaine inside the motorman's cab.

House Resistance

The House resisted drug testing largely because of intense labor opposition that had kept it from coming before two committees that shared jurisdiction over the issue. The Public Works and Transportation panel oversaw issues involving aviation, mass transit and bus employees. Rail workers fell under the purview of the Energy and Commerce Committee.

House lawmakers became more amenable after the subway crash. Despite its heavy workload, the Public Works Committee pushed the issue to the top of its agenda.

Labor groups also became more receptive than in past years. The Transit Workers Union in New York on the day after the accident issued a statement saying, "The transit workers of our city have no fear of drug or alcohol testing."

Peggy Taylor, associate legislative director for the AFL-CIO in Washington, said the union was not against drug testing but considered random testing ineffective and open to abuse by employers. Alcohol tests also posed problems for employers, she said. ■

Troubled Airlines Got No Help From Hill

The nation's airline industry had grown accustomed to sporadic financial turbulence since being cut free from most regulation in 1978, but it had not seen anything like the fiscal nose dive of 1991.

But Congress accomplished little during the first session to stem the industry's growing list of carrier casualties.

Republican Sens. John C. Danforth of Missouri and John McCain of Arizona, and Senate Commerce Aviation Subcommittee Chairman Wendell H. Ford, D-Ky., and House Aviation Subcommittee Chairman James L. Oberstar, D-Minn., attempted a major re-regulatory effort but were unable to do anything but air a series of proposals.

Even with the Persian Gulf War ended, fuel prices near normal and air bargains aplenty, the industry expected another $2 billion loss in the first quarter of 1991. That came atop a more than $3 billion record loss a year earlier.

Midway Airlines Inc. on March 26 joined three larger carriers seeking protection in federal bankruptcy court and went out of business in November. Trans World Airlines (TWA) was scheduled to file for reorganization under bankruptcy laws in 1992 even as it announced in December exploratory talks to merge with Continential Airlines Holding Inc.

Meanwhile, the healthiest carriers, American Airlines and United Airlines, weathered the storm and leveraged capital to buy London routes from troubled TWA and the defunct Pan American World Airways, respectively.

The Persian Gulf War and recession devastated airlines, accelerating what many analysts viewed as an inexorable industry shakeout. What already was a Darwinian trend toward consolidation became a feeding frenzy. Strong carriers snapped up lucrative international routes and airport gates from weakened airlines that were left limping off to bankruptcy court.

The central question that faced Congress and the industry was whether the shakeout had left so few carriers as to hamper competition. Competition, after all, was what the 1978 airline deregulation was all about.

The law was intended to do away with "unreasonable industry concentration, excessive market domination and monopoly power." *(1978 Almanac, p. 496)*

Administration Response

For its part, the Bush administration did not want to disrupt market forces. Transportation Secretary Samuel K. Skinner saw little danger in permitting, and even encouraging, the consolidation trend.

Rather than worry about the shrinking roster of domestic carriers, Skinner sought to steer the debate toward a global perspective. To foster a global airline market he:

- Gave British Airways new access to U.S. cities from Europe and won American and United Airlines access to routes held by TWA and Pan Am that served London's Heathrow Airport.
- Slated talks in April with Canada toward an open-skies treaty that could allow Canadian airlines to operate within the United States and U.S. carriers to operate within Canada.
- Relaxed rules on a case-by-case basis to allow foreign investors to own up to 49 percent of an airline's equity.

Congressional critics appreciated Skinner's global view, but they accused the secretary of forsaking the domestic airline industry in the process, especially when it involved hometown airlines. International flying routes had long been considered public licenses, and smaller U.S. airlines complained that Skinner had effectively sold them to the highest bidder.

Yet, while congressional watchdogs barked loudly at Skinner during oversight hearings, no legislative alternatives to cure the industry's woes came forth.

Appeals by the weaker airlines to temporarily keep funds collected from passengers under the 10 percent ticket tax imposed by the 1990 budget-reconciliation package fell largely on deaf ears, as did calls to open up the Strategic Petroleum Reserve to cut jet fuel costs. *(1990 Almanac, p. 384)*

LEGISLATIVE ACTION

As bad as things seemed, Congress was wary of tampering with deregulation and, as a result, was left with scant options to revive the industry. That sparked a growing sense of frustration among key lawmakers who nonetheless took steps to respond to concerns about airline competition and prices.

Danforth, McCain and Ford in the Senate, and Oberstar in the House, wanted Congress to help the airline industry. As a result, aviation staff in both chambers were dispatched to work on a series of proposals that, taken as a whole, amounted to the biggest re-regulatory effort imposed by Congress since 1978.

Proposals that came under consideration included:

- New procedures for ap-

Bill Called for Inspection Of Aging Aircraft

The House on April 23 passed by voice vote a bill (HR 172) that was intended to strengthen heavy-maintenance checks for aging commercial aircraft. The Senate did not take up companion legislation or mark up the House bill.

Under the legislation, sponsored by House Public Works and Transportation Committee Chairman Robert A. Roe, D-N.J., the Federal Aviation Administration (FAA) was required to set up a program to improve inspections of aircraft in service for 15 years or longer.

As passed by the House, the bill encouraged the FAA to get foreign governments to adopt similar standards.

The legislation came in response to a 1989 accident in which the roof of an Aloha Airlines jet ripped open in flight, killing an airline attendant and injuring several passengers.

Similar legislation passed the House in 1990, but no action was taken in the Senate. *(1990 Almanac, p. 390)*

The House Public Works and Transportation Committee on April 16 approved by voice vote the bill to toughen inspection requirements for aging commercial aircraft.

As passed, the measure ordered the FAA to require that planes at least 15 years old be inspected for metal fatigue and other effects of aging during their regular heavy-maintenance checks.

House Passed Bill To Limit Flight Attendants' Workday

While Congress in 1991 took no final steps to calm turbulence in the airline industry, the House on Aug. 1 passed, 228-195, a bill (HR 14) to limit the work hours of airline flight attendants.

As passed by the House, the bill directed the Transportation Department to issue rules to limit a flight attendant's workday to 14 hours with a minimum of 10 hours of rest between shifts. Bill sponsors said some attendants had been forced to work 24-hour shifts. *(Vote 250, p. 62-H)*

The Bush administration threatened to veto the bill, saying it would add numerous financial burdens to the airline industry.

Similar work limits were already in place for airline pilots, mechanics and air traffic controllers. Most GOP members opposed the bill, saying that it would impose a recordkeeping burden on the airline industry and increase air fares.

Supporters said most airlines did not fall under the bill because a majority already had contracts with employees that included clauses limiting allowable duty time.

The measure to limit the number of hours airline attendants could be required to work won voice vote approval May 21 from the House Public Works and Transportation Committee.

In the Senate, Daniel K. Inouye, D-Hawaii, introduced a companion bill (S 1010), and it was referred to the Commerce, Science and Transportation Committee, where no action was taken during the first session.

proving international route transfers.

- Revamping rules to allow foreign ownership of an airline's voting stock up to 49 percent.
- Breaking up the market stranglehold that financially robust American and United Airlines had over the computerized reservation system by requiring them to divest.
- Changing the slot leasing system at New York's LaGuardia and Kennedy, Washington's National and Chicago's O'Hare airports that allowed some airlines to buy and sell the takeoff and landing rights and thereby control airport access.

Senate Action

The proposals prepared by the Aviation panel posed potentially sweeping legislative remedies. They ranged from regulating international route transfers to fostering more competition in computerized reservations systems. But the drive, headed by Republicans Danforth and McCain — both of whom wanted to help home-state airlines — encountered considerable resistance.

The Commerce, Science and Transportation Committee took no action on the Danforth-McCain bill (S 1628). The challenge Danforth and McCain faced was to convince Congress, which passed a major aviation infrastructure package in 1990, that they were proposing "fine-tuning" steps.

Since 1978, lawmakers had routinely rejected efforts to slap new rules on the industry. If the re-regulatory goals of Danforth, McCain and others seemed quixotic, remedies suggested by the airline industry trade group had even less chance in Congress.

Even the airline industry's trade group, the Air Transport Association of America, backed away from any new round of legislation. Instead, the association wanted Congress to demonstrate its concern by rolling back some of the 1990 passenger taxes and user fees.

Congress' tax writers, or even the aviation authorizing committees, made no moves to repeal those fees. Such political realities frustrated lawmakers who feared a future of regional airline monopolies would require even harsher regulatory measures.

House Action

In the House, Public Works and Transportation Aviation Subcommittee Chairman Oberstar on April 24 introduced a legislative package that sought to nurse the ailing domestic airline industry back to fiscal health.

Industry officials rejected the medicine and labeled the package unnecessary government tampering. As written, the legislation (HR 2074) regulated the sale of international routes, gates, and takeoff and landing slots. It also allowed foreigners to hold 49 percent of the stock of a U.S. airline when domestic investment was unavailable and boosted competition in airline computer reservation systems.

The legislation failed to advance after Oberstar's subcommittee held hearings on it in May. ■

Congress Urged Repeal of Boat Users' Fee

Congress on Nov. 27 cleared for President Bush a bill reauthorizing the Coast Guard for fiscal 1992 after lawmakers defused a battle over efforts to repeal a user fee on owners of recreational boats. Bush signed the bill (HR 1776 — PL 102-241) on Dec. 19.

As enacted, the measure authorized $2.57 billion for U.S. Coast Guard operations and maintenance activities for fiscal 1992. It also allotted $466 million to acquire boats and airplanes and to build and renovate facilities. The bill authorized the Coast Guard to take the necessary steps to implement the Oil Pollution Act of 1990, including completion, within a year, of a study of oil tanker safety and the capability of owners to meet legal obligations in the event of a spill.

By far the biggest controversy over the bill was sparked by efforts to eliminate a user fee on owners of recreational boats. The final bill included a non-binding resolution urging the Bush administration to repeal the fee.

The House approved the final version of the authorization bill on Nov. 25, and the Senate cleared the bill Nov. 27.

HOUSE ACTION

Action on the measure got under way in the House on May 2, when the Merchant Marine and Fisheries Committee approved a bill to authorize funding for fiscal 1992 Coast Guard operations. The legislation (HR 1776), approved by voice vote, authorized $3.6 billion for the Coast Guard — about $37 million less than President Bush had requested.

The bill allocated funding for programs slated to be eliminated by the Bush administration. For example, the measure authorized $51.7 million to combat oil spills and $29 million for the Coast Guard to replace an aircraft used for sea operations. The committee bill was silent on the user fee for owners of recreational boat owners.

But on June 12, the Merchant Marine and Fisheries Committee weighed into the debate and renewed an effort to rescue recreational boat owners, who were required in 1991 to pay user fees for Coast Guard services.

Action came when the Merchant Marine panel approved, by voice vote, a separate bill (HR 534) to repeal user fees imposed as a revenue-raising measure in the 1990 budget agreement. The bill attracted opposition from the House Budget Committee. The fees, ranging from $25 for boats longer than 16 feet to $100 for boats 40 feet and longer, were projected to bring in $718 million over five years.

Finding ways around the fees had become a yearly exercise for the committee, whose members represent the nation's coastal and inland waterways. In past years, the committee had spared boat owners from user fees by finding other sources of revenue, ranging from escort fees for foreign ships passing through the Persian Gulf to higher tonnage fees on shippers that used U.S. harbors.

This time, the committee voted to levy computer-access charges on those who would use a new data base that tracks federal shipping tariffs. "We have become the Houdinis of the budget-reconciliation process," said Rep. Gerry E. Studds, D-Mass., congratulating the committee for finding yet another way to avoid the fee. The computer-fee proposal "ranks with the great escapes of all time."

Shippers had to file their rates — their shipping prices on U.S. waterways — with the Federal Maritime Commission. About 1 million tariff changes were filed each year on paper. The commission was slated to computerize the tariff filings starting in 1992.

The bill required the commission to charge an access fee of 35 cents for each minute the government data base was used by those who ship goods. Rep. Robert W. Davis, R-Mich., sponsor of the measure, said the fees stood to raise $750 million by fiscal 1996. The bill was referred to Ways and Means, where it saw no action in 1991.

The House on July 18 passed by voice vote the fiscal 1992 authorization for the Coast Guard after rejecting amendments that sought to take the teeth out of the recreational boat owners' fee and that called for random drug testing of civilian Coast Guard employees.

HR 1776 authorized $3.64 billion for the Coast Guard, compared with $3.4 billion in fiscal 1991. Included were $2.57 billion for operations and maintenance, $28.8 million for research and $466,000 to buy, build and maintain offshore facilities, boats and aircraft.

At the request of Davis, ranking member of the Merchant Marine and Fisheries Committee, the House attached to the bill a non-binding resolution that urged Congress to repeal the recreational boat fee. The amendment was approved, 412-6. *(Vote 214, p. 52-H)*

But lawmakers set aside on a point of order an attempt by Rep. Tom McMillen, D-Md., to delay for two months imposition of penalities levied on boat owners who failed to pay the new user fee.

Also rejected were amendments by Gerald B. H. Solomon, R-N.Y., to require the Coast Guard to conduct random drug tests on civilian employees and job applicants.

SENATE ACTION

Debate over the user fee for owners of recreational boats spilled over into the Senate, where the Senate Commerce, Science and Transportation Committee approved its bill by voice vote July 30. The committee bill (S 1297) to reauthorize the Coast Guard for fiscal 1992 and 1993 included a repeal of the user fee on owners of recreational boaters.

During committee action, John B. Breaux, D-La., sponsor of the user fee repeal, called the boat fee a "sham tax" that forced boat owners to bear an unfair burden for lowering the federal budget deficit. "None of the money will go to boat users. Zero," Breaux said.

Unheeded was a complaint by Ted Stevens, R-Alaska, that the panel should not vote to repeal the tax until lawmakers found a plan to offset the lost revenues. Under the 1990 budget pact, which set the boat fees, Congress had to make up for revenue losses with cuts in spending or tax increases.

Breaux endorsed a House plan to charge callers for a federal computer service providing information on tariff rates. But the issue was left unsettled.

The Senate bill authorized about $3.5 billion for the Coast Guard in fiscal 1992, about $100 million less than Bush requested. About $3.4 billion was appropriated for fiscal 1991.

But inclusion of the repeal was a short-lived success for those opposed to the boat fee. On the Senate floor, Ernest F. Hollings, D-S.C., chairman of the Commerce, Science and Transportation Committee, explained that the boat tax repeal earlier approved by his committee had to be removed after supporters failed to come up with a method for offsetting the cost of the repeal. In the end, the Senate on Nov. 21 passed by voice vote an amended version of the House bill. It included non-binding language calling for repeal of the recreational boat tax once a way to offset the cost was found.

The bill went back to the House, where it was made a one-year reauthorization bill for fiscal 1992 and was passed by voice vote Nov. 25. The Senate passed the amended bill by voice vote on Nov. 27, clearing it for the president. ■

Rail Strike Avoided Through Quick Action

Congress and the Bush administration stopped a day-long nationwide rail strike April 17 by mandating further mediations between labor and management. Had it lasted longer, the walkout by more than 200,000 rail employees could have cost the economy far more than the $50 million the administration estimated was lost.

Within a 24-hour period, the Senate gave voice vote approval to a resolution (H J Res 222) that the House had passed on a vote of 400-5. The five "no" votes were from liberal Democrats. President Bush signed the legislation before midnight (PL 102-29). *(Vote 72, p. 18-H)*

The strike by 10 rail unions shut down freight lines nationwide, upset commuter rail service in several cities and threatened to close factories.

In a rare display of quick, bipartisan cooperation, lawmakers began drafting legislation to end the strike the night before it began. As picket lines formed the morning of April 17, hearings began in the House Energy and Commerce Committee.

Congress was not required to get involved in railway labor disputes but had intervened 11 times since 1963 to prevent disruptions in the economy.

This round of labor talks began when rail contracts expired in 1988. After two years of failed negotiations, Bush formed an emergency board in 1990 to help mediate.

The board recommended annual wage increases averaging about 3 percent, including lump-sum payments and pay raises. It also recommended that workers pay a share of health-care benefits, that the number of miles a crew had to travel for a day's pay be increased to 130 miles from 108 miles and that the size of crews be reduced.

After the board's Jan. 15, 1991, findings were rejected by labor unions, a 30-day cooling-off period went into effect. Both sides agreed to extend the talks for 60 days because of the Persian Gulf War.

Although the Transportation Communications International Union and the Brotherhood of Railroad Signalmen reached settlements, eight other unions remained at an impasse with the railroads, forcing the strike April 17.

Members of Congress worked throughout that day, in consultation with the railroads and unions, to craft a resolution that could pass through both chambers without need for a conference committee.

The resolution provided that:

- The strike would end immediately.
- The president would "promptly" appoint a three-member special board, with one member coming from the previous review board. The remaining two members would be appointed from a list of arbitrators compiled by the National Mediation Board, a federal labor-dispute agency.
- The recommendations of the previous board would be subject to modification, but only if a challenger showed that a recommendation was "demonstrably inequitable or was based on a material error or material misunderstanding."
- The new board would have 65 days to reach its decisions, which would be binding. No judicial review would be allowed.

The biggest point of dissent came late in the afternoon, when Senate negotiators, led by Edward M. Kennedy, D-Mass., insisted that the new review board be composed of members chosen by the National Mediation Board.

Bush advisers were adamant, however, that the president have total discretion over whom to choose. The Senate position prevailed in the end, although one of the panelists would come from the previous emergency panel. ■

Railroad Safety Act

The House on Sept. 23 passed the first comprehensive railroad safety bill since 1988. But the effort floundered after language restricting the Federal Railroad Administration's (FRA) ability to write regulations was added by Energy and Commerce Committee Chairman John D. Dingell, D-Mich., sparking a veto threat from the Bush administration.

The bill (HR 2607) authorized $106 million through 1993 to carry out the 1970 Railroad Safety Act and authorized $75 million for local rail freight assistance, a formula grant program that helped maintain railroad right of ways.

In the Senate, the Commerce, Science and Transportation Committee approved Nov. 18 a similar railroad-safety bill (S 1571) that did not include the language regarding regulations. The full Senate failed to consider the bill.

One-year authorization for such programs expired at the end of September 1991. The last multiyear reauthorization of rail safety programs was in 1988. *(1988 Almanac, p. 589)*

House Action

The House Energy and Commerce Subcommittee on Transportation and Hazardous Materials quickly approved the reauthorization bill by voice vote July 11.

The measure required the FRA to issue rules when Congress instructed the agency to do so. This language, which eventually halted the bill's advance, was proposed because the FRA had claimed discretion to ignore congressional directives.

The Bush administration strongly opposed the provision and threatened a veto, insisting that the agency needed to maintain discretion in promulgating rules.

HR 2607 also:

- Called for boosting minimum fines for safety violations and required the FRA to beef up enforcement of railroad safety regulations.
- Raised minimum civil penalties for safety violations from $250 to $1,000. But Don Ritter, R-Pa., said that such fines could potentially harm the nation's small railroads, which he said had been making a comeback in recent years.
- Required railroads cited for safety problems to tell the FRA what corrective actions they planned to undertake.
- Mandated that the FRA monitor how well railroads carried out remedial actions.
- Authorized $51.5 million for FRA safety programs in fiscal 1992, rising to $55.0 million in fiscal 1993. It also authorized $75 million over fiscal 1992-94 for matching grants to smaller local freight railroads for track improvements.

The House Energy and Commerce Committee approved the bill July 30.

The full House followed suit Sept. 23, passing the rail safety bill by voice vote. But a feud between Dingell and the FRA continued to spark a veto threat.

Dingell, upset over the rail administration's refusal to write rules for some provisions of the last rail safety reauthorization in 1988, added language to the bill that limited the administration's ability to interpret the law.

The bill struck from the 1988 railroad law the phrases "as may be necessary" and replaced them with "as necessary." Dingell said the Bush administration had used the words to avoid writing rules, particularly those dealing with the safety of railroad crossings.

In a floor statement, Dingell singled out Transportation Secretary Samuel K. Skinner for refusing to answer committee queries about the impasse. "He tried to avoid the question all together," Dingell said.

Senate Action

The Senate Commerce Committee on July 30 approved S 1571, introduced by Sen. Jim Exon, D-Neb., that reauthorized the 1970 Federal Railroad Safety Act.

The Senate bill authorized $201 million through fiscal 1994 and $61 million for local rail freight aid.

But Dingell failed to persuade the Senate to adopt his position and the Senate companion bill (S 1571) did not include any mandate that required the agency to write rules. The full Senate failed to consider the bill. ■

Air Bag Mandates Moved

The $151 billion highway and mass transit bill signed into law in 1991 required extensive use of air bags in passenger cars and light trucks manufactured in the future. But separate mandates also advanced in the Senate in an effort to ensure passage of the new vehicle safety requirements that had been decades in the making.

Sen. Richard H. Bryan, D-Nev., a key proponent of boosting motor-vehicle safety, called for new vehicle air-bag madates in two bills in a strategy to give the provisions as many legislative vehicles as possible. The bills (S 591, S 1012) were passed by the Senate, but did not advance in the House.

In the end, new mandates were included in the sweeping highway and mass transit law — though less strict than those originally pushed by Bryan. *(Transportation, p. 137)*

The highway and mass transit law required passenger cars made after Sept. 1, 1996 be equipped with driver and front-seat passenger air bags. Trucks, buses and multipurpose vehicles were given until Sept. 1, 1997 to have driver's side air bags and until Sept. 1, 1998 for front-seat passenger air bags.

Efforts to force domestic automakers to install air bags had bounced between Congress, the Transportation Department and the courts since 1969, when the government first attempted to require them. *(Congress and the Nation Vol. V, p. 296)*

But Bryan had left nothing to chance.

He introduced S 591, a free-standing bill that required driver and passenger air bags be installed in all passenger cars made after Sept. 1, 1995, a year earlier than what finally became law.

Similarly, light trucks, such as family vans, were required to have driver-side air bags after Sept. 1, 1996 and passenger-side air bags after Sept. 1, 1997, again the proposed timetable being advanced by a year.

Bryan also introduced S 1012, which included the same air-bag mandates with the same timetable. The bill also reauthorized National Highway Traffic Safety Administration (NHTSA) programs, which had not been renewed since 1982 because of House opposition.

The Senate Commerce Committee approved the measures by voice vote May 14. The Senate followed suit and passed the two bills by voice vote July 9.

Absent legislation, automakers would have been allowed to choose between using air bags or automatic safety belts in passenger cars. Domestic automakers had announced plans to install air bags in many of their fleets by model year 1994.

But another vehicle-safety proponent, Ernest F. Hollings, D-S.C., chairman of the Senate Commerce, Science and Transportation Committee, explained that the committee was pushing the separate bills for good measure.

"We need to make sure that all consumers have this lifesaving technology in their cars." Hollings said.

A revised version of the air-bag requirements were added as a section of the five-year highway reauthorization bill. And it was this legislative vehicle that became law. ■

FCC Reauthorization on Hold

An administration proposal to levy user fees on holders of broadcast licenses gained voice vote approval in the House on Sept. 24 as part of a measure (HR 1674) to reauthorize activities of the Federal Communications Commission (FCC) through fiscal 1993.

A companion Senate bill (S 1132) awaited action in the Senate Commerce Committee at the end of the first session.

The House-passed bill authorized up to $297 million for the following two fiscal years. The new fees on most FCC license holders — radio and television stations, telephone companies, cable television systems and satellite operators — were expected to generate revenues of $65 million a year.

Adoption of the new fees also were assumed in the House-passed version of the fiscal 1992 spending bill (HR 2608 — PL 102-140) for the Departments of Commerce, Justice and State.

Those fees were not included in the final bill, which doubled the administration request of $67 million for the FCC to $126 million. The administration had recommended the reduced amount, anticipating that the difference would be made up in user-fee collections. *(Appropriations, p. 531)*

A spokesman for the National Association of Broadcasters called the fees a "bad idea philosophically" and said they would further burden many stations already operating at a loss.

"They are but the opening wedge to fees that certainly would grow to onerous proportions over the years," he said.

The fees on users of FCC services gained voice vote approval July 25 by the House Energy and Commerce Subcommittee on Telecommunications and Finance. The full committee sent it to the floor five days later.

Subcommittee Chairman Edward J. Markey, D-Mass., said the new user fees would contribute about $65 million of the $133 million that would be authorized for fiscal 1992.

But several members of the subcommittee expressed strong reservations about the plan, which passed by voice vote, albeit with a few "nays."

Ranking Republican Matthew J. Rinaldo, N.J., strongly objected, saying that the new fees would not accurately reflect "a true fee for services" and would impose an "undue hardship" for certain FCC users, especially smaller broadcasters.

Rinaldo subsequently offered a revised, sliding fee schedule that took into account the ability of license holders to pay.

As approved by the House, an annual $2 million fee was sought on each long-distance telephone company as well as a $2,000 fee on television stations.

The administration had proposed steeper fees that critics said disregarded ability to pay. For instance, rather than a flat $1,000 fee for cellular telephone companies, Rinaldo's compromise called for fees ranging from $500 to $1,900, depending on the size of a company's market.

Public safety entities, amateur radio operators, noncommercial broadcasters and government and nonprofit entities were exempt from fees. ■

Bush, Hill At Odds Over Airwave Access

Legislation to free up government-controlled radio frequencies for commercial use bogged down over a philosophical difference on how to dispense with the newly released spectrum space. The administration wanted to auction the airwaves to the highest bidder; while some lawmakers stressed that lotteries remained the most equitable way of managing a public resource.

Under existing rules, most radio frequencies were allocated at no charge by lottery.

The Senate awaited action at the end of the first session on a bill (S 218) to transfer 200 megahertz of government radio frequencies to the public marketplace, including new personal telephone technologies.

The House on July 9 passed by voice vote a similar bill (HR 531). But even before the House took up the bill, President Bush threatened a veto because the bill contained no proposal to auction the airwaves.

The sponsors of HR 531, Energy and Commerce Committee Chairman John D. Dingell, D-Mich., and Telecommunications and Finance Subcommittee Chairman Edward J. Markey, D-Mass., opposed using auctions to manage the radio spectrum.

Despite the administration's resistance, Markey pushed to move the spectrum bill quickly because of a pressing need to free up bandwidths for potential commercial spectrum users.

In the Senate, Commerce Committee Chairman Ernest F. Hollings, D-S.C., and Communications Subcommittee Chairman Daniel K. Inouye, D-Hawaii, also opposed auctions and moved their spectrum reallocation measure without it.

The committee passed the bill by voice vote in May.

BOXSCORE

➡ **Spectrum Allocation (S 218, HR 531).** Bills to transfer 200 megahertz of government radio spectrum to civilian commercial use.
Report: H Rept 102-113, S Rept 102-93.

KEY ACTION

May 2 — The **House** Energy Subcommittee on Telecommunications approved HR 531 by voice vote.

May 14 — The **Senate** Commerce, Science and Transportation Committee approved S 218 by voice vote.

May 21 — The **House** Energy and Commerce Committee gave voice vote approval to HR 531.

July 9 — The **House** passed HR 531 by voice vote.

The Need for Spectrum Space

Except for routine filing fees, the airwaves had always been free to those who met application standards set by the Federal Communications Commission (FCC). But the increasingly commercial nature of the crowded radio spectrum, including the $66 billion cellular telephone industry and the $34 billion radio and television broadcast industries, had led the Reagan and Bush administrations to recommend auctioning FCC licenses.

By the early 1990s, much of the radio band was committed, with the most valuable space around the center of the spectrum held by TV and radio broadcasters.

To help ease the shortage, legislation to push the FCC and the administration to improve their spectrum coordination and assignment policies was crafted in the 101st Congress.

The House passed a measure (HR 2965 — H Rept 101-634) to transfer 175 megahertz of government radio spectrum to commercial use. Responding to administration objections, the bill did not bar auctioning of the newly available spectrum. A companion measure in the Senate stalled in committee. *(1990 Almanac, p. 376)*

House Action

Members of the Subcommittee on Telecommunications and Finance put off a White House attempt to auction the radio frequencies in 1991 when HR 531 was approved on May 2.

The bill, passed by voice vote, sought to authorize the Commerce Department to shift up to 200 megahertz of government-held radio frequencies to commercial use.

Don Ritter, R-Pa., withdrew an attempt to auction off the frequencies after an agreement was struck with Chairman Markey to hold hearings on the auction issue.

On May 21, The Energy and Commerce Committee gave voice vote approval to HR 531. The full House passed it July 9, also by voice vote.

As passed by the House, the bill gave the Commerce secretary two years to choose 200 megahertz of government-held radio spectrum — the equivalent of 30 television channels — to be transferred to commercial use during the following 15 years.

The bill also required the Commerce Department and the FCC to report to Congress every two years on how best to manage the radio spectrum.

The transfer of spectrum "will create much-needed breathing room in which new technologies can make it to market and flourish," said Markey. The government reserved or had priority access to about 40 percent of the usable electromagnetic spectrum. The Defense Department and the Federal Aviation Administration held about 60 percent of those frequency assignments.

The commercial viability of the latest wireless telephone technology was threatened by the lack of available radio spectrum, Markey said.

More spectrum was needed to test new uses for radio spectrum, such as enabling people to communicate through laptop computers.

In its veto threat, issued July 8, the administration said the bill lacked necessary authority for a competitive bidding process to transfer the frequencies.

Relocating frequencies would cost billions of dollars, and auctions would help defray that cost, reduce the budget deficit and encourage efficient use of the limited spectrum, the administration argued.

Markey said he was committed to developing "a consensus solution" to the issue.

Senate Action

The Senate Commerce Committee on May 14 approved a bill that would transfer government-held radio frequencies to the private sector, but delayed a battle over auctioning those airwaves until the bill got a floor vote. Ted Stevens, R-Alaska, was expected to offer an auction amendment when the bill reached the floor. ■

Cable Industry Got Re-Regulation Delay

Congress was poised at the end of the first session of the 102nd Congress to launch a major debate on how to rein in the cable television industry and address complaints of escalating rates and shoddy service since the industry was deregulated in 1984.

The bill awaiting final Senate action sought to allow broadcasters to charge cable operators for use of their signal and prohibit cable programmers from refusing to sell their shows to competitors such as satellite programmers.

The legislation never reached the Senate floor in 1991 because of an end-of-session time crush and a series of potential Republican amendments to weaken its regulatory provisions. The delay bought time for the cable industry, which was on the defensive against charges that unregulated cable operators greedily abused their viewers.

Cable industry opponents said the delay would not hurt the bill's prospects. Rather, they said, waiting to move the measure in the 1992 election year would enhance its prospects by making it harder for President Bush to veto a bill that they said struck at middle-class anger over increasing cable television rates.

The 1990 House-passed bill was reintroduced early in the year, but because of the late-session collapse of the cable re-regulation effort in the 101st Congress, House lawmakers decided to wait for the other chamber to act first.

BOXSCORE

➡ **Cable Re-regulation** (S 12, HR 1303) Bills to tighten rate and service regulation in the cable television industry.
Report: S Rept 102-92

KEY ACTION

May 14 — The **Senate** Commerce Committee approved S 12, 16-3.

June 13 — The Federal Communications Commission issued new cable regulations.

Background

Pressure began mounting during the 101st Congress for legislation to restore some government regulation of the cable television industry. Members of Congress cited instances of rates doubling or tripling in the nearly four years since deregulation.

The 1984 Cable Communications Policy Act largely deregulated the cable industry by eliminating the authority of state and local governments to regulate rates cable operators charged to subscribers as of Dec. 29, 1986. The act capped at 5 percent of the system's gross revenue the franchise fee a local government could charge a cable operator. *(1984 Almanac, p. 286)*

The argument for deregulation espoused by cable operators and their trade association, the National Cable Television Association (NCTA), was that rate regulation, high franchise fees and other restrictions imposed in the franchising process limited the industry's ability to grow.

Following deregulation, lawmakers then argued that the unfettered cable operators were choking off competitors by keeping cable programming from other multichannel services such as satellite broadcasters, shutting out other program suppliers and disadvantaging broadcasters in their placement on cable systems.

Two major cable bills were introduced in 1989. A measure crafted by Sen. Al Gore, D-Tenn., and Rep. Rick Boucher, D-Va., would have allowed local government regulation of cable rates in areas with only one cable system. A second bill introduced by Sen. John C. Danforth, R-Mo., and Rep. Jim Cooper, D-Tenn., also sought to bar programmers with connections to cable operators from discriminating against other cable systems. *(1990 Almanac, p. 370)*

Most troubling to the cable industry was a provision in the Gore-Boucher bill that would have allowed telephone companies to offer cable services as long as the funds were not provided by telephone ratepayers. That proposal was removed from the Senate bill before it was sent to the floor.

Bills revised in 1990 largely had the cooperation of the cable industry because the NCTA tried to calm skittish cable investors by working to soften the legislation's regulatory bite.

But after a compromise bill passed the House by voice vote, the cable industry got cold feet, particularly over language assuring competitors open access to cable programming and a deal that would have forced cable operators to carry broadcast channels. The administration also weighed in late in the session to oppose the bill.

Cable advocate Tim Wirth, D-Colo., killed the Senate bill by preventing its floor consideration, with several anonymous Republicans lined up behind him prepared to do the same.

Feeling burned, the Senate sponsors vowed the 1991 bill would include even heavier regulatory language.

CONGRESSIONAL ACTION

By early 1991, the political sands had shifted considerably. The debate became more partisan and heated, with the Bush administration stridently opposing any re-regulation, and the cable industry refusing to cooperate as it did through most of 1990.

As a result, backers of re-regulation in Congress looked to build support by doing more for cable's biggest foes: broadcasters and the telephone industry.

Although the 1991 Senate bill (S 12) did come down tougher on cable, the bill and its House companion (HR 1303) largely mirrored 1990 efforts.

The Senate bill sought to require the Federal Communications Commission (FCC) to regulate basic cable rates in areas where there was no competition from another multichannel video provider.

Although the Senate Commerce Committee moved early to approve S 12, many Republican lawmakers did not want to bring the measure to the floor until the FCC issued its new regulations.

The FCC moved in June to tightened the standard that cable companies had to meet to avoid regulation. Still, only 18 percent to 34 percent of the nation's 11,000 cable systems were subject to regulation under the existing commission standards.

Since the industry was deregulated, cable had grown into a $20 billion dollar industry. It was available to 90 percent of all homes in 1991, and 61 percent of those households subscribed.

But the average monthly rate for basic service had

jumped by 43 percent since 1986, according to the General Accounting Office, and consumers often complained of poor service. The cable industry contended that the service remained a value and justified its price increases as the necessary result of local regulation that kept prices below costs prior to 1986.

Legislative Proposals

S 12, introduced by Danforth, sought to strengthen FCC regulations for basic cable service. Such service included local broadcast and government access channels. The proposal required the agency to set prices for cable operators who captured more than 30 percent of a market lacking "effective competition."

The bill defined competition as the presence of another video programming distributor, such as satellite or wireless cable. Such competitors must have served at least 15 percent of area households and be available to more than half of them.

The legislation made it hard for cable operators to escape new regulations. If too few customers bought the basic programming package, the rate regulation was to apply to the next tier of programming.

Prices for other cable channels, except for premium channels such as HBO and pay-per-view programs, were to be regulated only if the FCC found prices unreasonable.

The bill also required the FCC to establish customer and technical service standards and allow local authorities to adopt stronger standards.

HR 1303, introduced by Rep. Edward J. Markey, D-Mass., required the FCC to regulate basic rates for all cable operators no matter how competitive their markets. Other programming, as well as customer and technical service standards, was to be subject to regulations similar to those proposed in S 12.

Other bills by Joseph I. Lieberman, D-Conn., (S 211) and Rep. Christopher Shays, R-Conn. (HR 550) considered subjecting all cable programming to federal regulation. Operators could avert regulation only if their markets were deemed competitive based on a standard similar to that proposed in S 12. But the bill required competitors to have a stronger footing — their service was to be available to 80 percent of households and serve 30 percent.

A measure (S 431) by Sen. Howard M. Metzenbaum, D-Ohio, was similar to S 12 on regulating the basic rates. It included the stiffer competition standard of S 211 and posed other ways to prevent operators from charging unreasonable rates or packaging programming in ways that would have limited consumer choice.

The Administration's Role

The administration played an earlier, more active role in opposing the bills in 1991.

In a March 13 letter to Congress, the administration said more competition, not more regulation, was needed. Also mentioned was the White House's desire to remove restrictions that prohibited telephone companies from entering the cable programming industry. *(Baby Bells restrictions, p. 165)*

Republicans in Congress followed Bush's lead. Senior White House officials met the week of March 6 with some Republicans on the House Energy and Commerce Telecommunications and Finance Subcommittee to encourage them to fight the cable bill.

Most Republicans who spoke at a March 21 subcommittee hearing opposed the bill. Matthew J. Rinaldo, R-N.J., ranking member of the subcommittee, was not a cosponsor of the House bill, as he was in 1990. Taking his place as sole cosponsor was Energy and Commerce Chairman John D. Dingell, D-Mich.

Similar partisanship surfaced in the Senate. Chief sponsor Danforth was joined by only two other Republicans. In 1990, six other Republicans had joined him on the bill. Commerce Committee Chairman Ernest F. Hollings, D-S.C., and Communications Subcommittee Chairman Daniel K. Inouye, D-Hawaii, who supported the 1990 bill, became cosponsors in 1991.

Republicans also waited to see how the FCC ruled on its planned redefining of what would be considered lack of competition, thereby triggering regulation of basic rates.

Senate Action

The Senate Commerce, Science and Transportation Committee on May 14 approved, on a 16-3 vote, a measure (S 12) that sought new regulations on the cable television industry and encouraged competition.

But in response to criticism that the action was premature, proponents held off action on a Senate floor vote. They wanted to see what steps the FCC would take to toughen regulatory guidelines for cable providers.

But opposition became even more intense and a veto threat loomed over the bill. The administration wanted to permit telephone companies to compete with cable operators in delivering video programming.

Among other items, the cable industry strongly objected to a provision that would give broadcasters a choice of either forcing cable operators to carry their signals for free or negotiating terms to carry them.

"This supposed 'consumer bill' has deteriorated into a boondoggle for cable's main rivals," said James P. Mooney, president of the National Cable Television Association.

Though many of the bill's key provisions were expected to change before it went to the Senate floor for a vote, Commerce Chairman Hollings opted to report it. But not without complaints.

The bill would set its own new standard for effective competition. It would consider competition adequate when at least half of an area's households were served by other competitors such as satellite systems or cable operators having at least a 15 percent market share.

The 1991 bill included a new provision that would limit the ability of cable operators to avert regulation by shifting their most popular programming to another package.

It would also bar cable programmers from unreasonably refusing to sell programming to competitors. Cable operators would also be barred from discriminating against competitors in pricing or terms.

Other provisions added to the committee bill included: increasing local authority to regulate rates and service; encouraging localities to seek second cable franchises; and ensuring that satellite networks did not favor cable operators over distributors of home satellite dishes in prices and programming access.

While the 1990 bill attracted the initial cooperation of the cable industry, support for the 1991 measure was limited to consumer groups and the industry's competitors, including television broadcasters.

Inouye won the support of broadcasters by including a provision to allow local television stations to negotiate their own retransmission deals with cable operators.

The measure attempted to heal a rift within the broadcast industry over whether to force cable systems to carry local broadcast stations. Powerful broadcast stations wanted to sell their signals to cable operators. Smaller stations, on the other hand, feared being dropped by cable operators and wanted retransmission to be compulsory.

The Inouye measure sought to give broadcasters the choice of either forcing cable operators to carry their signals for free or forfeiting that option and asking cable operators to compensate them for their programs.

The FCC in 1965 required cable systems to carry local stations. But two federal courts rejected the rules in 1985 and 1987, saying they violated cable programmers' First Amendment rights.

Much of the concern over the bill in the Senate Commerce markup focused on the legal ramifications of the Inouye provision.

Inouye denied a request by John B. Breaux, D-La., to offer an amendment that would exclude home-shopping stations from the benefits of the must-carry provision.

Breaux singled out the Home Shopping Network, a Florida-based broadcaster that sold merchandise over its own television stations. Breaux said it should not be accorded the same status as other over-the-air stations.

Another must-carry amendment, by Wendell H. Ford, D-Ky., was approved by voice vote. It included low-power television stations that had locally generated programming under the definition of over-the-air broadcasts that cable operators would be forced to carry.

House Action

As the House awaited Senate action, members of the House Energy and Commerce Telecommunications Subcommittee on June 26 and 27 held hearings that focused on the demands of broadcasters and phone companies.

Meanwhile, subcommittee Chairman Edward J. Markey, D-Mass., introduced as a vehicle for the 1991 effort a cable re-regulation bill (HR 1303) identical to one that passed the House the previous year.

In the 1990 House bill, balance was achieved with a fragile accord between broadcasters and the cable industry that required cable operators to carry local broadcast stations.

FCC Action

Backers claimed a FCC ruling June 13 would improve, not diminish, support for new regulations.

The agency tightened the standard that cable companies must meet to avoid regulation. At the time, areas that had three or fewer over-the-air broadcast signals were subject to cable rate regulation.

The FCC increased that threshold to six signals, boosting the percentage of cable systems subject to local rate regulation from 3 percent to 60 percent. ■

Constraints Planned for 900 Numbers

Washington began prescribing the 900-number industry its first dose of regulatory medicine early in the 102nd Congress. By the end of the first session, however, only the Senate had passed legislation that would require the industry to provide an introductory message warning the caller of the costs involved in the telephone call. A similar House bill still awaited floor action.

Lawmakers watched as the Federal Communications Commission (FCC) proposed new safeguards in March and was prepared to pass legislation that would put the industry under even heavier regulation. Although those rules were adopted in September, Congress continued to push forward to put similar constraints into law.

Meanwhile, the 900-number industry tried to shake its fledgling image of charging outrageous prices for services of dubious value. Industry officials touted the potential for innovative audiotext marketing and cautioned against regulatory efforts they said would stifle 900-services' growth.

Fast-Growing Industry

Pay-per-call telephone services had been around since 1974, when New York telephone customers could dial-a-joke and hear Henny Youngman. The 900 area code was first used in 1980 as a polling device for ABC during the Reagan-Carter presidential debates.

But the pay-per-call industry really took off in 1984 with the breakup of American Telephone & Telegraph Co. As with many new entertainment media, adult-oriented services were among the first to notice the potential of 900 long-distance numbers and their local-exchange equivalents with the 976 prefix.

By 1988 the 900-number industry was worth $100 million, offering entertainment aimed at adults and children as well as fundraising, corporate promotions and technical help services at prices that typically ranged from $2 to $10 per call.

Four long-distance carriers contracted with 900-number services: AT&T, US Sprint, MCI Communications Inc. and a smaller carrier based in Illinois, Telesphere Communications Inc. The introduction of "interactive" 900 numbers in late 1988, for which callers could press different numbers for more options, gave the industry its biggest boost.

In most 900-services arrangements, local phone companies billed the callers, then took their cut and sent the money to the long-distance providers, which in turn paid the 900-service entrepreneurs.

Callers spent $690 million on 900 numbers in 1990 — up from $235 million in 1989, according to Connecticut-based industry analyst Link Resources.

In an industry where the simple act of placing a call incurred a debt to the local phone company, opportunities for consumer abuse were rampant, 900-line critics said.

And as the industry grew, so did stories about 900-number scams, ranging from a $29.95 call for a credit card application that could be gotten free from any bank to "contests" that told callers to keep calling back to win more prizes.

Pay-per-call services were considered tailor-made in early 1991 for fly-by-night operators. For a $10 phone call, a Cleveland man promised to fax a personalized message to Iraqi President Saddam Hussein during the gulf war. Part of the proceeds, he claimed, would go to help clean up the Persian Gulf oil spill and organize a parade.

Legitimate Players in the Field

But the explosive growth of the industry also meant more legitimate players were entering the field. Most 900 numbers offered valuable services for the toll.

Corporations used them to provide customer technical support. Newspapers provided stock quotes, crossword puzzle clues and sports scores. The Red Cross used 900 numbers to aid victims of Hurricane Hugo and the San Francisco earthquake. And supporters could call a 900 number to donate U.S. funds for the African National Congress during leader Nelson Mandela's U.S. visit.

Lawyers used 900-number services to provide legal advice. And political candidates had begun to use the numbers for fundraising.

Several factors, from negative perceptions to regulatory obstacles, kept 900 numbers from appearing on campaign posters and TV ads in the 1990 election cycle. As the 1992 election drew closer, some political consultants were adjusting their assessment of 900 numbers' potential.

The Federal Election Commission (FEC) ruled in 1990 that 900-service providers must keep detailed records of each contribution to ensure that calls for donations were coming from residential, not corporate, phone numbers. Election laws prohibited direct corporate contributions.

But the FEC had yet to resolve the problem of who should keep the records necessary for long-distance companies to ensure that they were independent from campaigns.

On Jan. 31, 1990, the commission was deadlocked, 2-2, over whether to treat a 900-service joint venture by American Telephone and Telegraph Co. and American Express as an agent of a fundraising committee or simply as a vendor providing a service. Despite the impasse, AT&T went ahead with its plans to set up a 900 political fundraising service.

BOXSCORE

➡ 900-Number Regulations (S 1579; HR 3490, formerly HR 2330 and HR 2829). Bills to regulate the pay-per-call telephone industry.

KEY ACTION

March 14 — The Federal Communications Commission (FCC) proposed new rules to regulate "pay-per-call" services.

May 9 — The **House** Energy and Commerce Subcommittee on Telecommunications and Finance approved HR 2330, which would regulate the pay-per-call phone services industry.

July 30 — The **Senate** Commerce, Science and Transpor tation Committee approved S 1579.

Aug. 1 — The **House** Transportation Subcommittee approved HR 2829 by voice vote.

Sept. 27 — FCC adopted "pay-per-call" services rules.

Oct. 8 — The **House** Energy and Commerce Committee approved HR 3490.

Oct. 29 — The **Senate** passed S 1579 by voice vote.

Regulatory Obstacles

Federal jurisdiction over the 900-services industry was split between the FCC, the Federal Trade Commission (FTC) and the U.S. Postal Service. That, plus a patchwork of state laws, made it difficult for long-distance, 900-service and local phone providers to keep track of the legal fault lines.

The FCC monitored the long-distance carriers and shared jurisdiction with states over billing and collection services. The FTC handled cases of interstate consumer fraud and deceptive practices. Postal Service inspectors could investigate for fraud if any part of a 900-call service involved mail delivery.

But no federal regulations directly governed the 900-services industry.

And the pay-per-call industry said self-regulation would be sufficient. The industry's two trade groups, the Information Industries Association (IIA) and the National Association for Information Services (NAIS), had drawn up voluntary industry standards.

The NAIS code said charges and the name of the provider should be clearly displayed in all promotions and that programming should not contain "false, misleading or untimely information and shall provide value proportionate to its price."

The IIA standards were more extensive and were revised in February to include references to the consumer's right to privacy and stronger standards on advertising to children, contests and fundraising.

In addition, all four long-distance carriers that served as the conduit for the 900-number providers instituted guidelines designed to protect consumers.

On March 15, updated guidelines went into effect at AT&T to require 900-service providers to cap at $4 all program charges for children under age 12. Preambles stating the cost of the call also were required for all children's programming and any other calls priced more than $5 per minute or a total of $10. Sprint had a similar preamble requirement and capped children's programming at $1.50 per minute and $3 per call.

MCI imposed a $4 per call maximum on 900 calls aimed at children and required a preamble for calls priced more than $5 per minute. Telesphere did not accept 900 programming targeted at children and required a preamble for its "group access bridging" party lines.

FCC RULES

The FCC proposed sweeping new rules March 14 in a federal effort to combat fraud and deception in the burgeoning arena of "pay-per-call" services.

The commission received about 1,900 complaints relating to 900-number services between January 1988 and December 1990. In November 1990, 167 of the 1,095 complaints filed with the FCC's Common Carrier Bureau concerned 900 services. "The 900-service complaints are fast becoming the commission's biggest issue, in the opinions of consumers," FCC Chairman Alfred C. Sikes told House Energy and Commerce Telecommunications and Finance Subcommittee Chairman Edward J. Markey, D-Mass., in a January letter.

As part of the new rules, the FCC would require a "preamble," or introductory message that would warn the caller about the costs of the easy-to-dial service.

For 900-service offerings aimed at children, the FCC proposed that the preamble tell children to first obtain permission of a parent before placing the call or to hang up.

The FCC also proposed the following regulations to:

- Require that consumers have the option of blocking all interstate 900 calls, where technically feasible.
- Prevent a subscriber's basic telephone service from being disconnected for failure to pay interstate charges for 900 services.

The preamble idea worried 900-service providers the most. The industry called a preamble a "kill message" that would hamper business and violate free-speech rights.

But consumer groups and state attorneys general said the FCC rules did not go far enough.

Rules Adopted

The FCC on Sept. 27 adopted the rules to protect consumers from abuses by unscrupulous providers of 900-number telephone services.

The rules required providers to disclose the fees and terms of the call in a preamble, allowing a caller to hang up early without charge. They also allowed consumers a one-time, free option to prevent 900-number calls from being made from their telephones. They prohibited a telephone company from disconnecting a person's telephone for refusing to pay a 900- number phone charge.

A comprehensive measure to restrict the 900-number industry was not considered by the full House in 1991. Two Energy and Commerce subcommittees drafted bills that would protect consumers by informing them of the costs involved through a preamble and would allow them to "block" initiation of such calls from their telephones. The bills were combined and approved by the full committee.

HOUSE ACTION

A House Energy and Commerce panel on May 9 approved sweeping consumer protections from 900-number telephone services.

The Telecommunications and Finance Subcommittee adopted a draft bill by voice vote that outlined restrictions on pay-per-call phone services using a long-distance 900 area code. It was based on a previous bill (HR 328) sponsored by Rep. Bart Gordon, D-Tenn.

"Consumers continue to be abused, deceived and defrauded by some in the industry," said subcommittee Chairman Markey.

The 900-services industry opposed the legislation, arguing instead that voluntary standards were enough to weed out dishonest practices.

The draft bill emphasized regulating the 900-services industry through local and long-distance phone companies, which contracted with 900-service providers. The panel wanted to protect long-distance carriers from lawsuits for canceling contracts with 900 providers that failed to meet standards set by the companies or the FCC.

The bill also sought to protect customers from having their local phone service disconnected for failure to pay for 900 services. It required that all 900-service charges had to be listed on a separate part of phone bills.

Customers also could block their phones from being able to place 900-number calls.

The draft bill also required providers of 900 services to:

- Include a preamble, or "kill message," at the beginning of each call to inform the caller of the service being provided, the call's total or per-minute cost, the option to hang up without incurring any charges and a parental consent requirement for calls made by children.

Such messages were not required for callers who paid in advance or for services of nominal cost.

- Include an "appropriate and clear" signal, at intervals established by the FCC, to alert callers to the passage of time during live programming.
- Refund money to consumers, when deemed appropriate under FCC guidelines. This provision was requested by Rep. Ron Wyden, D-Ore. The FCC was asked to devise ways to avoid charges for callers who incurred 900-number bills through error or misunderstanding.

On Aug. 1, the Transportation Subcommittee approved a separate bill (HR 2829) by voice vote that required 900-number services to provide consumers with details about costs. The bill was combined with HR 2330 at the full committee level.

Energy and Commerce Committee

After the FCC adopted rules in September, Markey wanted to put similar constraints into law and coordinate jurisdictional concerns between federal agencies.

On Oct. 8, the Energy and Commerce Committee approved a new bill sponsored by Markey that combined the measures approved earlier in the year by the two Energy and Commerce subcommittees — HR 2330 and HR 2829. The comprehensive measure (HR 3490) was similar to the FCC regulations to combat unscrupulous practices by some pay-per-call providers. It sought to strengthen the rules by codifying them into law. Markey said the legislation was necessary because "many consumers were enticed to call 900 numbers through advertising that was misleading or outright deceitful."

The committee bill required operators of 900-number services to disclose the cost of a call in a preamble and to provide callers enough time to hang up without charge. Customers also could block access to 900 numbers from their phones.

The bipartisan measure barred telephone companies from discontinuing service to customers who refused to pay 900-number charges. And companies that ran telephone sweepstakes had to disclose the odds of winning.

SENATE ACTION

John McCain, R-Ariz., had proposed 900-number legislation (S 471) that would require a preamble, call blocking and advertising disclosures. But it was a broader bill (S 1579) sponsored by Daniel K. Inouye, D-Hawaii, chairman of the Commerce Subcommittee on Communications, that moved through the Senate.

On July 30, the Commerce Committee advanced the bill to impose regulations on the pay-per-call industry. As approved by the committee, S 1579 gave the FCC authority to regulate the industry and crack down on unscrupulous services. In addition, the services had to include an introductory message that laid out the costs of the call. Callers could hang up during that time and not be charged.

The full Senate passed the bill by voice vote on Oct. 29. It required phone companies to provide the option to block access to such services.

The bill prohibited phone companies from disconnecting service for failure to pay disputed charges for interstate 900-number services. ■

Bill Prohibited Abusive Telemarketing

The only legislation in the telecommunications arena to clear Congress in 1991 was a measure (S 1462 — PL 102-243) to protect consumers from unsolicited telephone calls and "junk faxes."

As signed by President Bush Dec. 20, the bill required the Federal Communications Commission (FCC) to prohibit unsolicited calls from automatic dialing devices that played a recorded message to all private residences and police, fire and other emergency lines.

The measure also banned the automatic calls from facsimile machines that transmitted marketing materials via the telephone lines.

"This bill will target the abusive, robotic use of technology that has become so intrusive in our daily lives," said Edward J. Markey, D-Mass., chairman of the House Energy and Commerce Subcommittee on Telecommunications and Finance.

BOXSCORE

➡ **Telemarketing Protections. (S 1462, formerly HR 1304).** The bill prohibited unsolicited marketing calls from automatic dialing devices on telephones or facsimile machines.

Report: S Rept 102-178

KEY ACTION

July 30 — The **House** Energy and Commerce Committee approved HR 1304.

Oct. 8 — The **Senate** Commerce, Science and Transportation Committee approved S 1462.

Nov. 7 — The **Senate** passed S 1462 by voice vote.

Nov. 18 — The **House** passed HR 1304 by voice vote.

Nov. 26 — The **House** amended and passed S 1462 by voice vote.

Nov. 27 — The **Senate** cleared S 1462 by voice vote.

Dec. 20 — President Bush signed S 1462 — PL 102-243.

Background

A similar effort in 1990 died from Senate inaction and an administration veto threat. *(1990 Almanac, pp. 379, 402)*

The House had passed a bill (HR 2921) July 30, 1990, that would have allowed people and businesses who did not want their phone numbers used for unsolicited advertisements to get on a nationwide list. Telemarketers would have faced fines if calls or transmissions were made to any number on the list. The FCC was to compile the list and punish offenders.

A related, weaker measure (S 2494) passed by voice vote in the Senate Oct. 23, 1990, sought to strengthen the authority of the Federal Trade Commission regarding fraud committed in connection with telephone sales.

Bush had promised to veto the House measure because he felt the number of complaints were small and that there were already systems in place to deal with any problems.

The effort in 1991 was strengthened to include calls by live operators but was weakened by not explicitly creating the consumer phone number data base.

Energy and Commerce Chairman John D. Dingell, D-Mich., protested the weaker language, accusing the telemarketing industry of practices that were "abusive, degrading, unethical, improper and plainly obnoxious.... The telemarketing industry better clean up its act, because we're going to be looking at them."

HOUSE ACTION

Consumer privacy was another part of the 900 debate high on Markey's agenda for his Energy and Commerce panel. At the same time the Telecommunications and Finance Subcommittee on May 9 approved sweeping consumer protections from 900-number telephone services, it also approved a bill aimed at bothersome "junk" telemarketing calls.

HR 1304, passed by voice vote, would allow consumers to make their phone numbers off-limits to telephone marketers.

Data gleaned from consumers who called 900-service numbers could be used indiscriminately by entrepreneurs. So-called sucker lists were generated among the less savory segments of the 900 industry. And callers to 900 numbers often found themselves deluged by automatically dialed phone sales pitches, junk faxes and other telemarketing schemes.

HR 1304 was approved July 30 by the House Energy and Commerce Committee. The bill sought to allow consumers to avoid bothersome telemarketing calls at home.

The bill also required the FCC to consider ways of ensuring telephone privacy. One option considered was to set up a nationwide "don't call me list" that would allow consumers to avoid receiving some of the 18 million calls made daily to private homes by 300,000 direct marketers, said Markey.

The committee bill covered phone sales pitches made by computer-dialed recorded messages and live operators and through fax machines but exempted telemarketers with whom callers had an established business relationship. Tax-exempt and nonprofit groups were exempt from the bill's scope.

The House on Nov. 18 passed HR 1304 by voice vote. As passed, it required the FCC to find ways to ensure the privacy of residential and emergency telephone lines in an effort to end "the nightly ritual of phone calls to the home from strangers and robots," said Markey.

Transportation Panel Action

A separate bill to make it easier for federal and state agencies to sue unscrupulous companies for telemarketing fraud was approved by voice vote on Oct. 31 by another House Energy and Commerce subcommittee.

The measure (HR 3203) required the Federal Trade Commission to issue rules that barred fraudulent telemarketing practices and "coercive or abusive" calls.

Transportation and Hazardous Materials Subcommittee Chairman Al Swift, D-Wash., said that federal laws were needed to crack down on fraudulent telemarketers who jumped from state to state to avoid prosecution.

Using deceptive tactics, telemarketers cheated consumers out of billions of dollars annually, Swift said.

The panel approved, by voice vote, a substitute amendment that protected from retaliatory lawsuits consumers who called in to complain about a company. State law enforcement agencies, and in some cases individuals, were slated for new authority to sue to stop deceptive telemarketing activities.

Blocking the Blockers

Legislation to allow telephone users, on a per-call basis, to block disclosure of their phone number to the person they were calling received committee approval in both chambers during the first session.

The House Energy and Commerce panel approved HR 1305 (H Rept 102-324) on July 30; the Senate Judiciary Committee on Oct. 31 approved S 652 (S Rept 102-247), 10-1.

Caller ID, available only in the District of Columbia, Maryland, New Jersey and Virginia, revealed the number of anyone calling a phone linked to the service.

The Federal Communications Commission on Sept. 27 proposed new rules that allowed telephone customers to block Caller ID on a per-call basis.

Through this caller-identification technology, people who placed 800- or 900-number calls to homes or businesses often unknowingly revealed their phone number and potentially even their address and consumer preferences.

"We are now on the cusp of a new age in telecommunications," said Telecommunications and Finance Subcommittee Chairman Edward J. Markey, D-Mass., "where a person's phone number truly is the key to a treasure trove of information about them."

House Action

HR 1305, as approved by the House Energy and Commerce Committee July 30, allowed telephone users, on a per-call basis, to block disclosure of their numbers.

An amendment to the bill, adopted by voice vote, also allowed consumers who used Caller ID to buy a device that would "block the blocker." Callers who had blocked their numbers from appearing on Caller ID devices would have their calls automatically rejected. The provision was authored by Joe L. Barton, R-Texas.

Thomas J. Bliley Jr., R-Va., opposed the bill, arguing that states and state regulators should not be forced to order local phone companies to offer caller-ID blocking.

The House panel rejected, by voice vote, a Bliley amendment that would have exempted states, including Virginia, from that provision if they currently offered Caller ID services without the blocking option.

Also opposing the bill was William E. Dannemeyer, R-Calif., who said it would protect people making obscene phone calls from being revealed.

Senate Action

The Senate Judiciary Committee approved its measure Oct. 31 to protect the privacy of telephone customers by limiting the use of caller-identification devices.

The bill (S 652), approved 10-1, required telephone companies to let customers block the display of their numbers on a per-call-basis, free of charge. Supporters said the measure sought to protect the privacy of those with unlisted numbers, as well as abused spouses living in shelters who were trying to reach their children.

The measure also allowed receivers of obscene phone calls to immediately refer the caller's number to the police by touching two buttons. Sponsor Herb Kohl, D-Wis., said the technology needed already existed and would not result in higher costs to consumers.

There was no further action on HR 3203 in the first session.

SENATE ACTION

The Senate passed two bills by voice vote Nov. 7 that covered phone sales pitches made by computer-dialed recorded messages and live operators, as well as those sent by fax.

The Senate went further than the House with S 1462, which imposed an all-out ban on automatic telephone calls to residences, emergency phone lines or cellular phone services. Unsolicited advertisements to fax machines also were prohibited under the bill, which was sponsored by Commerce, Science and Transportation Committee Chairman Ernest F. Hollings, D-S.C.

S 1462 curbed the use of automatic telephone dialing devices. Businesses were banned from placing automatically dialed calls to either fax machines or homes. Consumers who received such calls could sue in state courts.

The Commerce Committee had approved S 1462 Oct. 8.

The Senate also passed S 1410, which was similar to the House measure. The bill, sponsored by Larry Pressler, R-S.D., had been approved July 30 in the Senate Commerce, Committee.

S 1410 directed the FCC to halt the intrusion of unsolicited marketing calls. Businesses with whom consumers had an established relationship were exempted. The bill also prohibited computer-generated calls to emergency phone lines or pagers used by doctors or health-care facilities. Calls made for purposes other than for a commercial solicitation were not to be regulated.

FINAL ACTION

Congress cleared for the president on Nov. 27 legislation aimed at protecting consumers from unsolicited telephone calls and junk faxes. The bill (S 1462, formerly HR 1304) represented a compromise worked out informally during the waning days of the session. The House passed the revised Senate measure on Nov. 26 by voice vote, and the Senate sent it to the president the following day.

The FCC was required to find ways to ensure the privacy of phone consumers and emergency phone lines. Among the options for protecting consumers from bothersome calls that were under FCC consideration were a nationwide "don't call me list," as well as a new rule that put all telemarketers under a single phone exchange. Consumers then could "block" their phones from receiving calls from that exchange.

Businesses with a pre-existing relationship with a telephone subscriber were exempted from the prohibition on solicitations, as were nonprofit organizations. Other exceptions included emergency calls and cases where there was prior consent expressed.

Another protective provision required computer-generated calls to disconnect as soon as the receiver hung up.

The FCC could carve out additional exceptions, as long as those did not affect the basic privacy rights of consumers or involve unsolicited advertisements. ■

Baby Bell Restrictions Unresolved

Congress left dangling the issue of business restrictions on the Bell operating companies, even though a pivotol federal court decision had posed a challenge to lawmakers to act quickly on new regulations for the seven regional local telephone holding companies.

Lawmakers had been pondering ways to free the Baby Bells from court-imposed manufacturing and information services restrictions, when U.S. District Judge Harold H. Greene on July 25 ruled to allow the companies to provide information services ranging from home banking and electronic yellow pages to video programming.

The court decision shifted the lobbying pressure from the Bell companies to their opponents in the newspaper and electronic information industries, who feared being trounced by the Bells' potential market power.

Before the Greene ruling, the Bells were asking Congress to save them from the court restrictions. Afterward they cautioned against any legislative action that might impede their new business activities.

Federal courts since the 1984 breakup of the American Telephone & Telegraph Co. (AT&T) had prevented the Baby Bells from entering the fast-growing information services field, as well as from providing long-distance service and manufacturing telecommunications equipment, on the grounds that the Bells' dominance over the local phone networks would lead to consumer and competitive abuses.

The phone companies scored their first major legislative victory when the Senate on June 5 approved a bill (S 173) introduced by Commerce Chairman Ernest F. Hollings, D-S.C., to allow the Bells to manufacture telecommunications equipment, while also imposing separate-subsidiary requirements and forcing the Bells to sell equipment to non-affiliated manufacturers at the same prices and terms that they sold to their own divisions.

A companion measure to S 173 was introduced in the House. But no action was taken during the first session.

Another bill (HR 3515) unveiled by Rep. Jim Cooper, D-Tenn., after the Greene ruling, sought to allow the Bells to offer information services only in areas where at least 50 percent of local phone consumers had access to competing services and 10 percent of them subscribed.

The House Energy and Commerce Subcommittee on Telecommunications and Finance was working on an unnumbered draft bill that broadly examined both the manufacturing and information services restriction issues.

Background

Judge Greene oversaw and enforced the 1982 consent decree that led to the breakup of AT&T and restricted the regional Bell companies in the areas of long distance, telecommunications equipment manufacturing and information services.

BOXSCORE

➡ **Baby Bells Business Restrictions (S 173, HR 3515).** Bills to allow the Bell operating companies into new ventures such as the manufacture of telecommunications equipment and the provision of information services, while providing some consumer and competitive safeguards.

Report: S Rept 102-41 (S 173).

KEY ACTION

March 19 — The **Senate** Commerce Committee approved S 173, 18-1.

June 5 — The **Senate** passed S 173, 71-24.

July 25 — District Judge Harold H. Greene ruled to allow the Bells to provide information services.

As the restrictions continued through the late 1980s, some lawmakers had begun to complain that one unintended result of the major antitrust case was to give a federal judge single-handed control over U.S. telecommunications policy.

The Bell companies and others who wanted to see more enterprise permitted in the growing telecommunications arena argued that the business restrictions hurt U.S. competitiveness by slowing the introduction of new technologies that were available abroad.

But consumer groups countered that the phone companies would dip into funds from phone ratepayers to pay for expensive new technologies. And companies that saw their interests threatened by efforts to unleash the phone companies — such as the politically powerful newspaper industry — said it would be difficult to keep the Baby Bells from using their monopoly over phone lines to run competitors out of business.

A controversial bill left pending in 1990 before the House Telecommunications panel sought to lift the business restrictions and give authority to regulate back to the Federal Communications Commission (FCC). *(1990 Almanac, p. 377)*

The proposal, hammered out between Democratic and Republican staff members on the committee, would have allowed the Baby Bells to offer information services, including electronic publishing, in areas outside their own regions where they did not have a monopoly over telephone lines. It would also have allowed the companies to research, design and develop telecommunications equipment.

Also in 1990, the Senate Commerce, Science and Transportation Committee approved a Hollings-sponsored bill (S 1981 — S Rept 101-355) that would have permitted the Bell companies to manufacture equipment. But the bill never reached the Senate floor.

COURT ACTION

Judge Greene clearly was not happy with his own decision on July 25 to release the Bell companies from the binds that narrowed their business opportunities.

He had upheld all three business restrictions in 1987, but in 1990, the U.S. Court of Appeals for the District of Columbia ordered that he reconsider his continued ban on information services, saying he failed to prove that letting the Bells into that industry would raise prices or stifle competition.

Despite his suspicions, Greene said he could not meet such a test and had no choice but to reverse his previous ruling. Greene held out little hope that the Bells could be adequately regulated on the federal or state level.

"As the structure of the corporation becomes more complex . . . it becomes increasingly difficult for regulation and regulators to oversee its operations and restrain anti-competitive efforts," he wrote.

The long-anticipated lobbying war between the regional Bell telephone companies and media conglomerates began in earnest Oct. 7, when the D.C. Appeals Court cleared the way for the phone monopolies to immediately offer information services.

But Greene delayed that decision and ordered that it not take effect until appeals were exhausted.

The appeals court Oct. 7 called Greene's delay "an abuse of discretion" not in the public interest.

The Supreme Court on Oct. 30 denied a petition by newspaper publishers to block the seven regional Bell telephone companies from providing news and information services. The 8-0 decision meant that regional telephone monopolies were free to own and transmit over their phone lines a range of information services through data base texts and video signals.

Bell opponents, including consumer groups and publishers that offered electronic information services, pressed for restrictions on the Bells before Congress and a federal appeals court. They argued that the Bells would use revenues from their regulated local phone services, which were guaranteed a profit, to subsidize their new ventures and create unfair competition.

The phone companies had dismissed that argument, saying regulators would not allow it.

SENATE COMMITTEE ACTION

The bill (S 173) to allow the seven regional Bell telephone companies to design and manufacture telecommunications equipment took an expected step toward the Senate floor March 19.

The 18-1 Commerce Committee approval was considered the easy step. Before committee Chairman Hollings successfully denied a Judiciary Committee request for jurisdiction over the bill, Judiciary members were considered likely to plan floor amendments to strengthen consumer safeguards — or even keep the bill from a floor vote.

In a letter to Hollings, Judiciary Chairman Joseph R. Biden Jr., D-Del., said his committee "has a deep and ongoing interest in the AT&T consent decree," which was based on antitrust statute. The decree's line-of-business restrictions "fall within the jurisdiction of the [Judiciary] Antitrust, Monopolies and Business Rights Subcommittee," the letter said.

Hollings was able to fend off the request for sequential jurisdiction.

The Hollings bill was similar to one that passed through his committee late in 1990. It sought to allow the Bells to design and manufacture equipment while requiring certain consumer safeguards that Hollings said protected against two potential abuses: using ratepayer revenues to finance the new ventures and selling equipment to their local phone monopolies at inflated prices paid by phone customers.

Hollings argued that the manufacturing restrictions shackled seven of the nation's top corporations, while global competitors moved ahead in the telecommunications equipment industry.

Opponents, led by AT&T and groups representing the 9,000-plus U.S. telecommunications equipment manufacturers, said the new industry was thriving without Bell involvement.

Consumer groups said that Hollings' protections did not go far enough to protect ratepayers from potential Bell abuses and that the FCC was ill-equipped to monitor the Bells' behavior.

The Bells wanted to make switching and network equipment for local and long-distance telephone exchanges. They also hoped to form joint ventures with the few foreign companies that made large-scale switching equipment.

The Hollings bill sought to permit the regional Bell companies to enter the manufacturing arena. To guard against ratepayer abuses, the bill required that any equipment a Bell company bought from its manufacturing affiliate be bought at the open-market price. All manufacturing also had to take place out of separate affiliates.

The 1991 bill also included an agreement struck between the Bells and the Communications Workers of America to require all manufacturing to take place in the United States using some U.S.-made parts. The administration opposed that provision but supported the bill.

Several Commerce Committee members expressed concerns about the bill, but only Larry Pressler, R-S.D., voted against it. Pressler was vexed at one of the Bell companies, U.S. West Inc., for failing to respond adequately to his inquiry about how ratepayers were affected by the company's $10 million settlement with the Justice Department for violating several terms of the AT&T breakup.

Bob Packwood, R-Ore., opposed the domestic manufacturing agreement on the grounds that it ran counter to U.S. efforts during trade talks to encourage open markets. John Kerry, D-Mass., discounted the idea that the Bells were likely to set up joint ventures with firms from countries that did not allow U.S. firms to enter their markets.

SENATE FLOOR ACTION

The Bells scored their first legislative victory June 5, when the Senate voted, 71-24, to let the regional firms design and manufacture telecommunications equipment. *(Vote 89, p. 13-S)*

The vote was a strong signal that lawmakers were willing to ease some restrictions imposed on the regional Bell companies when they were created as part of the 1984 consent decree that broke up AT&T.

It also was a major setback for AT&T and consumer groups, which had argued that lifting the ban would lead to higher phone bills and anti-competitive behavior by the Bell companies. Opponents' plans to offer amendments to erect stronger consumer and competitive safeguards largely failed to materialize.

An attempt by Phil Gramm, R-Texas, to remove the bill's requirement that the Bells manufacture within the United States and use domestic components also failed when a tabling motion was approved, 64-32. The Bush administration, which otherwise supported the bill, promised a veto unless that requirement was dropped. *(Vote 88, p. 12-S)*

Hollings cited figures that painted a picture of a domestic telecommunications industry in decline: The largest European and Japanese companies had increased research and development spending by as much as 20 percent a year. AT&T had increased its spending by about 6 percent a year. Since the divestiture of AT&T, Hollings said, 66 U.S.-based computer and telecommunications equipment companies had been bought by or had merged with foreign companies.

ment companies had been bought by or had merged with foreign companies.

The Bell companies wanted to link financially with smaller U.S. companies to gain a foothold in the world switching and transmission equipment market.

They also hoped to form joint-ventures with foreign giants such as Germany's Seimens A. G. and Canada's Northern Telecom Ltd. to produce and sell large-scale switches, which can cost more than $25 million each.

AT&T was the only U.S. company to operate in this market and said it would be harmed irreparably if the Bells were to enter the field.

Groups representing small and mid-size telecommunications manufacturers opposed the bill, though a coalition of small-business owners who supported the bill had emerged.

Daniel K. Inouye, D-Hawaii, who chaired the Commerce Subcommittee on Communications and opposed the bill, rejected Hollings' claims. He argued that thousands of manufacturers had entered the market since the AT&T breakup and that research spending by the Bells and other U.S. companies had increased.

Consumer activists believed that the Bell companies would use revenues and other resources of their local phone service monopolies to subsidize manufacturing ventures. They also contended that the Bell companies would prevent manufacturing competitors from having an equal chance to sell to their various phone companies.

The Hollings bill took steps to guard against such abuses. It required each regional Bell company to:

- Set up a separate subsidiary for the design, development and manufacture of equipment and to maintain separate accounting ledgers.
- Sell their equipment to non-affiliated manufacturers at the same prices and terms set for their own divisions.
- Give non-affiliated and affiliated manufacturers comparable opportunities to sell equipment to their telephone companies.

Joint ventures between Bell companies were to be prohibited. And Bell companies would be banned from using revenues from their regulated telephone activities to help underwrite the cost of manufacturing.

Still, most of the criticism of the bill centered on those safeguards, and opponents argued that they were not strong enough to deter abuses.

Amendments that would strengthen protections against self-dealing and cross-subsidization were planned but not offered by Howard M. Metzenbaum, D-Ohio.

The closest that opponents came to making major changes in the bill was an amendment, offered but then withdrawn, by Inouye that would have required, among other things, that the Bell companies sell at least 20 percent of their manufacturing equipment to unaffiliated customers.

The domestic manufacturing and content language was the final fight on the bill, but it also involved little debate. As expected, an effort to remove the provision by Gramm failed.

In a letter to Hollings, several Cabinet members argued that the provision could violate international trade rules and lead to "costly retaliation against U.S. exports."

A Win for Small Companies

While long-distance giant AT&T scored the bill as a loss, small rural telephone companies got most of what they wanted. An amendment offered by Pressler to protect rural phone companies passed by voice vote.

While it was thought to be a contentious issue, Pressler and Hollings reached accord behind the scenes, with Pressler agreeing to alter the amendment to meet some concerns of Bell companies.

Pressler sought to ensure that small rural companies would have access to state-of-the-art telephone equipment made by the Bell companies.

The revised Pressler amendment largely achieved his goals. It required the Bell companies to make the latest software and telecommunications equipment available to other local exchange carriers without discrimination or self preference. But it also required the Bell companies to continue to provide older equipment to the rural telephone companies, as long as making such equipment remained profitable.

The amendment also required the Bell companies to engage in joint network planning and design, and ensured that small and rural phone companies had a voice in those plans.

Other amendments adopted by voice vote included those by:

- Paul Simon, D-Ill., to require annual audits by state regulatory authorities, financed by the Bell companies, to determine whether they were complying with the bill's requirements.
- Metzenbaum, to give the FCC and state regulatory authorities access to the accounting books of the Bell companies' manufacturing affiliates during audits.
- Pressler, to increase the fine for violating the bill's accounting requirements from $6,000 to $10,000 per violation.
- Metzenbaum, to ensure that no provisions of the bill be construed as having any effect on antitrust laws.

HOUSE COMMITTEE ACTION

The House did not act on any Bell legislation in 1991. Energy and Commerce Telecommunications Subcommittee Chairman Edward J. Markey, D-Mass., opted to wait and watch the developments in the Senate and in Judge Greene's court.

Early in the year, Markey had said he hoped to treat much of his panel's communications agenda — including the Bells issues, spectrum allocation and perhaps even cable television re-regulation — as part of a sweeping, omnibus bill. But two days after the strong Senate endorsement of Hollings' manufacturing bill, Markey indicated he might move a bill that dealt broadly with the issues of Bell consumer and competitor protections.

Markey's package of telephone consumer and competitive safeguards was expected soon after Greene's decision to allow the seven regional Bell phone companies to enter the information services industry.

"The Greene decision has thrown down the gauntlet to Congress," Markey said. But while an early committee draft of the legislation was circulated, it never was formally introduced.

Along the way, there was plenty of rhetoric by Bell advocates and opponents about the wisdom of allowing the phone companies into the manufacturing and information services fields.

Jim Slattery, D-Kan., and W. J. "Billy" Tauzin, D-La., introduced a companion bill (HR 1527) to Hollings' effort March 20. That day, Michael G. Oxley, R-Ohio, also offered a measure (HR 1523) similar to Hollings' bill but without the requirement for domestic manufacturing.

On the other side of the issue, Cooper on Oct. 8 introduced a bill to allow the Bells to offer information services only in areas where at least 50 percent of local phone consumers had access to a competing service and 10 percent subscribed to them. Media companies that offered information services, including newspaper publishers, backed the idea.

On Nov. 26, Inouye introduced a similar bill in the Senate. ■

Senate Conservatives Halted PBS Funding

The House easily passed a bill (HR 2977) to reauthorize the Corporation for Public Broadcasting (CPB) for three years. But concern about a liberal bias in the network's programming snagged the effort in the Senate.

Members of Congress had traditionally supported the public broadcasting and radio network. Even detractors praised its educational, cultural and entertainment programming as the best available alternative to commercial television.

But controversy flared in 1991 when the political slant of programming on hotly debated issues such as global warming was called into question.

Complaints surfaced after the CPB refused to provide to local public television stations a documentary called "The Greenhouse Conspiracy," which challenged conventional theories about the threat of global warming. The public television network had distributed several documentaries staking out the opposite view and stressing the environmental dangers of global warming.

House Action

Absent concerns about CPB programming choices, the House Energy and Commerce Subcommittee on Telecommunications and Finance on July 25 approved by voice vote a $1.1 billion bill (HR 2977) that reauthorized the CPB for fiscal years 1994-96.

The measure by Edward J. Markey, D-Mass., was about $90 million below the corporation's request. But subcommittee member Michael G. Oxley, R-Ohio, said the funding level was more in line with expected appropriations.

The bill stood to reduce the number of CPB board members from 10 to nine to avoid voting deadlocks and staggered the terms of board members.

Public broadcasters faced criticism from Bill Richardson, D-N.M., but it was for failing to hire enough minority employees. Richardson won approval of an amendment to strengthen requirements that public broadcasters report their compliance with federal equal-opportunity laws.

A month later, on July 30, the House Energy and Commerce Committee approved the reauthorization legislation (H Rept 102-363) by voice vote. The measure also included $126 million for extending and upgrading communications facilities through the Public Telecommunications Facilities Program.

It was in the full committee that concern about bias in the public network's programming surfaced. The committee approved an amendment by Don Ritter, R-Pa., that expanded reporting requirements for the network's board. The reports were to include data on board funding for programs developed by the Independent Television Service, which was created by Congress as part of the last CPB reauthorization in 1988 to help smaller independent producers make films. *(1988 Almanac, p. 582)*

Ritter offered the amendment because he was upset that the board had denied local stations satellite access to "The Greenhouse Conspiracy," the documentary critical of global warming theories.

He noted that the public network had aired other documentaries contending that global warming posed a serious environmental threat.

The controversy spilled over on the House floor Nov. 25 before the reauthorization measure was passed by voice vote.

Ritter chastised the board for making program decisions without seeking opinions from its audience. Ritter also repeated his criticism of the public network's decision not to distribute "The Greenhouse Conspiracy." But he stopped short of calling for more oversight of program choices.

Senate Action

The bill was referred to the Senate Commerce, Science and Transportation Committee, where a companion measure (S 1504) by Daniel K. Inouye, D-Hawaii, also was under consideration. The Senate Commerce Subcommittee on Communications completed hearings on the Senate measure July 23, and the full committee marked it up Oct. 3 (S Rept 102-221).

In the final days of the session, it was thought that Alan K. Simpson, R-Wyo., had placed a hold on the bill. Simpson had bitterly clashed with Nina Totenberg of National Public Radio over leaks about sexual harassment charges against Supreme Court Justice Clarence Thomas by former aide Anita F. Hill. But Simpson took to the Senate floor Nov. 27 to deny that he had held up the bill. Nonetheless, action on the bill screeched to a halt. ■

Attempts to Limit Dairy Production Unsuccessful

In response to plummeting milk prices, farm-state lawmakers in early 1991 took steps to limit dairy production. By the end of the year, however, milk prices began climbing again, and the combined opposition of the Bush administration, cattlemen and anti-poverty groups helped kill the dairy legislation.

Legislation (HR 2837, S 1527) in the House and Senate Agriculture committees sought to place quotas on the amount of milk farmers could produce and continue to receive federal price supports.

But the idea of imposing such production controls raised concerns in the Bush administration and among agricultural economists that Congress was moving away from a recent trend toward free-market policies. Such controls also lacked incentives for farmers to adopt emerging technologies because the amount of money a farmer could earn would be limited by his quota.

Government support for dairy farmers dated back to World War II, when farmers received assistance in order to boost production during the war. Under those programs (which remained largely intact in 1991), the Agriculture Department bought all unsold milk at a price set by Congress, thereby setting a floor for milk prices nationwide. The result was that dairy farmers had a guaranteed customer for whatever amount of milk was produced.

The push to overhaul dairy programs in 1991 was driven by six months of rapidly dropping milk prices — the lowest prices in 13 years. The price for a hundred pounds of milk was $11.50 in May, compared with $14.40 during the same period a year earlier.

The legislative proposals were largely aimed at helping small farmers, particularly those from states such as Wisconsin and Vermont. Midwestern and New England dairy farms generally were smaller and lacked financial resources, and thus often could not benefit from technological innovations best suited to large operations, located in California and elsewhere in the country.

HOUSE COMMITTEE ACTION

A House Agriculture subcommittee on June 25 approved a plan to sharply increase the support prices paid to dairy farmers and to institute a quota program to control milk surpluses.

The draft bill, approved by voice vote, was largely framed by the National Milk Producers Federation. It was designed to reduce milk surpluses and bolster market prices, which were at their lowest in 13 years.

However, the bill provoked sharp opposition from the Bush administration, which was opposed to any change in current law.

As originally drafted by Charles W. Stenholm, D-Texas, chairman of the Subcommittee on Livestock, Dairy and Poultry, the bill raised the support price for milk from $10.10 per hundred pounds to $11.60. During the markup, the subcommittee voted 10-9 for an amendment by Harold L. Volkmer, D-Mo., to hike the support price even further, to $12.60 per hundredweight.

To curtail the increased cost of the milk subsidy, the bill sought to limit the amount of milk the government was forced to buy. If the Agriculture Department estimated that government purchases in the next year would exceed 7 billion pounds, then it would have to put a two-tier payment program into effect.

In addition, each farmer would be assigned a set amount of milk for which he would be paid the $12.60 price. Any milk a farmer produced in excess of his quota would qualify for only a fraction of the support price, making it a losing proposition to produce the excess milk.

Opposition to Bill

The Bush administration delivered a blow to the proposal on July 10 when Agriculture Department officials sent a letter to lawmakers opposing almost every section of the bill.

The livestock industry and consumer groups also objected to the bill. Ranchers feared that it would prompt dairy farmers to sell more cattle than usual and drive down meat prices. Consumer groups said the bill would result in higher milk prices, which, according to the Agriculture Department would also reduce the purchasing power of those on food stamps and force the government to drop 170,000 pregnant women and children from the popular Women Infants and Children (WIC) feeding program.

"A dairy bill that is going to take 170,000 needy, pregnant women and children off WIC, that's a loser," said Leon E. Panetta, D-Calif., a member of the Agriculture Committee and chairman of the Budget Committee.

Agriculture Committee Approval

On July 16, the Agriculture Committee gave voice vote approval to HR 2837.

The bill also included protections for cattle ranchers, to ensure that the bill would not force meat prices down, and for the poor, to ensure that government nutrition programs would not be forced to cut back even if milk prices rose.

However, because the bill included a boost in the government price support for milk, it was expected to result in higher consumer milk prices. That, in turn, would lead to a $460 million annual increase in the cost of food stamps, school lunch programs and other feeding programs for the poor in fiscal 1993-95, Agriculture Department officials said.

The committee rejected, 21-23, a substitute version of the bill that would have given dairy farmers a less generous income boost. The substitute was supported largely by Republicans and was given qualified support by the administration.

To avoid being tagged as taking from the poor to give to the rich, the committee approved by voice vote an amendment that ensured poor people would maintain their current level of benefits from government food programs. The increased cost of government feeding programs due to milk price hikes was to be paid for in fiscal 1992 by a reduction in the government subsidy paid to dairy farmers.

Other House Committees

HR 2837 was scheduled to be ready for House floor action by Sept. 27, but after the Agriculture Committee action, it remained tied up in the tax-writing Ways and Means Committee, which claimed jurisdiction over a provision to assess dairy farmers for the increased costs of the program.

The Education and Labor Committee also had partial jurisdiction over the bill, but that panel signed off on Sept. 24 after adding an amendment to require the Agriculture secretary to ensure that needy Americans served by government feeding programs experienced no decrease in their benefits.

Farm Bill Corrections

A year after passing the massive 1990 farm bill (PL 101-624), which reauthorized most of the government's agriculture and nutrition programs for five years, Congress returned in 1991 with a bill of so-called technical amendments. As cleared by the Senate on Nov. 26, the bill (HR 3029 — H Rept 102-175) contained hundreds of non-controversial changes in the adminstration of farm programs sought by lawmakers from Kansas to Florida.

President Bush signed the bill (PL 102-237) on Dec. 13.

The most significant provision made it easier for the Federal Agriculture Mortgage Corporation (Farmer Mac), a new secondary market for farm loans, to borrow money. It also placed Farmer Mac under the regulatory control of the Farm Credit Administration. *(Government-sponsored enterprises, p. 115)*

Among the special interest provisions was one added by the House Agriculture Committee during its consideration of the bill on July 25. The so-called Pizza Hut amendment offered by Charles W. Stenholm, D-Texas, and modified by Dan Glickman, D-Kan., in whose district the company was based, allowed the Agriculture Department to include fresh pizza with meat toppings for the federal school lunch. Existing rules allowed frozen pizza, sausage sandwiches and hot dogs to be offered for school lunches but barred fresh pizza because of fears that meat toppings would require cumbersome and costly inspections.

The final bill was scaled down sharply from the version approved by the Wheat, Soybeans and Feed Grains Subcommittee on July 10 and estimated to cost $265 million over four years. Bush administration officials objected to any bill that added costs to existing farm programs.

The full committee subsequently dropped subcommittee provisions that had costs associated with them. The House passed the bill on July 31, 417-5. *(Vote 239, p. 58-H)*

The Senate Agriculture Committee approved its version of the bill Nov. 21, with Senate passage occurring next day on a voice vote. The House passed the bill again on Nov. 26 with small changes, and the Senate cleared it later that day.

Ways and Means, however, sought and received more time to review the assessment on dairy farmers. On Oct. 16, Ways and Means stripped the tax from the bill, saying it would set a precedent of taxing small groups to pay for specific government programs.

SENATE COMMITTEE ACTION

For Patrick J. Leahy, D-Vt., chairman of the Senate Agriculture Committee, an issue that at first seemed a natural soon became a headache, if not a political liability. He introduced a bill (S 1527) to put strict caps on milk production and boost price supports, but the Bush administration vowed to veto it. Leahy postponed a scheduled July 25 markup of the bill in an effort to seek a compromise.

Yet if Leahy had compromised with the administration, he would have been giving small dairy farmers only a fraction of the help they said they needed to save their farms. Dairy farmers nationwide were facing the lowest milk prices in 13 years, and nowhere were the problems more severe than in the traditional dairy states in New England and the Great Lakes region.

But to help his farmers, Leahy could have faced equally fierce complaints from advocates for consumer and nutrition programs, which he also championed. Raising government milk support prices as Leahy proposed would have increased the consumer price for milk by about 25 cents a gallon every year that the price supports stayed in effect.

After nearly nine months of stalemate, the Senate Agriculture Committee on Oct. 23 approved a plan to overhaul the federal dairy program and increase milk prices.

The action, originally intended as an antidote to milk prices that hit a 13-year low in the spring, came at a time when prices were steadily increasing. Indeed, dairy farmers were getting nearly the same price for milk as they received a year before.

The panel approved the bill by voice vote and folded it into an unrelated House-passed measure (HR 2893) to renew disaster assistance programs. *(1992 supplemental, p. 661)*

Republicans suggested that it could run into trouble on the Senate floor.

"This bears no resemblance to any legislation that might actually be signed into law," said Richard G. Lugar, R-Ind., the committee's ranking minority member and an opponent of changing the dairy program.

Key dairy provisions in the Senate bill would have required:

- A 10 percent increase in the milk support price, boosting it from $10.10 per hundred pounds to $11.10 per hundred pounds.
- A voluntary diversion plan to pay farmers to slaughter cows to reduce milk production levels by 5 percent to 30 percent.
- An increase in the milk solids in milk to increase its protein level but not its fat content.

The committee also adopted by voice vote an amendment requiring that enrollment in the diversion program be staggered to minimize its impact on the cattle markets.

FINAL ACTION

The yearlong effort by farm-state lawmakers to bolster the income of dairy farmers ultimately fell victim to strong opposition from the Bush administration and to fears that it would increase consumer milk prices.

The final blow came Nov. 22, when the Senate rejected, 47-51, an amendment by Agriculture Committee Chairman Leahy to the fiscal 1992 supplemental spending bill (H J Res 157) that would have increased the amount of money dairy farmers were paid for milk.

The potential for failure could be seen as early as summer, when the fragile coalition of regional and national dairy groups that had united behind the bill began to collapse. Opposition from the administration, consumer groups, advocates for the poor and cattlemen, coupled with deep divisions within the dairy industry, made it all but impossible for lawmakers to push through a bill.

"You would feel kind of silly standing up on the floor of the House and saying, 'The consumers are against us, the cattlemen are against us, the administration is against us and the dairy industry is against us,'" said Stenholm. ■

Relief Sought for Drought-Stricken West

A late-breaking compromise bill to ease the effects of a drought in the West passed the Senate on the last day of the session, but did not make it to the House floor.

Both chambers had earlier passed versions of the bill (HR 355) to give the Interior Department's Bureau of Reclamation new powers to manage Western water resources to cope with the region's longstanding drought.

House and Senate negotiators had struck a deal on a measure and Sen. John Seymour, R-Calif., held up last-minute floor action in the Senate to ensure a vote on the drought bill before adjournment.

The late-session negotiations were required after Interior Committee Chairman George Miller, D-Calif., failed in an attempt to repass HR 355 by bundling it with an equally popular water subsidies bill (HR 429). Miller brought the expanded version of the bill to the floor under suspension of the rules, but it failed, 245-164, to garner the required two-thirds majority. *(Water subsidies, p. 218)*

House Action

Action on the bill kicked off in the House Interior Committee, which approved a $42 million measure by voice vote on March 13.

As approved by the committee, the bill authorized the Bureau of Reclamation to purchase additional water from willing sellers and give it the power to transfer water — both its own and that from state water projects — throughout all the Western states for one year from date of enactment. Under existing law, state and federal water projects were kept separate.

The initial version of the bill would have authorized about $30 million for construction of wells and other minor projects to speed the flow throughout the system.

To protect the environment, the bill directed the bureau to release extra water from both state and federal sources to aid fish and wildlife affected by drought conditions.

California's Shasta Dam was slated to receive the remaining $12 million in fiscal 1992 for devices to control the temperature of water released from the dam in order to protect the Trinity and Sacramento rivers' endangered salmon runs.

The bill passed the House on March 21 on a 387-23 tally. *(Vote 55, p. 14-H)*

"This bill gets help to people who are in trouble now," said Miller, Interior Committee chairman. "This bill provides the flexibility needed in a time of crisis to move the limited resources around the state to the areas of greatest need."

Senate Action

Six months after the House passed HR 355, the Senate Energy and Natural Resources Committee approved, 20-0, a similar version on Sept. 26 also aimed at easing the five-year Western drought.

As in the House bill, the Senate measure sought to lift a ban against diverting water from federal irrigation projects and to allow the government greater flexibility to use its maze of projects to move water to parched cities. The Senate bill, however, made the new powers permanent, while the House bill extended the powers for one year after enactment.

The Senate bill also allowed the Interior Department's Bureau of Reclamation to transfer water from those willing to sell excess federal water to those willing to buy it at prices sufficient to cover government costs. For example, cities or rural water districts could receive water from farmers who decided to forgo their full water allocation.

The Interior Department would receive money to drill wells and construct other temporary facilities to deliver water in the West, particularly California.

Unlike the House-passed version, the Senate bill included a federal loan program to assist in the construction of small, local projects to help mitigate the drought's effects. However, Energy and Natural Resources Committee Chairman J. Bennett Johnston, D-La., who also chaired the Energy and Water Development Appropriations Subcommittee, cautioned that "there's just not any money" for the program.

The measure authorized $90 million from fiscal 1992 to fiscal 1996 to implement the bill — about $48 million more than the House.

The bill passed the Senate by voice vote on Oct. 31.

Final Action

After Senate passage, the expanded drought relief bill was scheduled to quickly move under suspension of the rules on Nov. 18. But it screeched to a halt when Miller tacked on his bill to overhaul Western water policy (HR 429) to the drought bill. That added language sought to prohibit the Interior Department from renewing water contracts for any term longer than three years. Miller explained that despite the six-year-old California drought, the department had been renewing subsidized water contracts for farms for 40-year periods — action that, he said, made it vastly more difficult to alter the state's water system in the 20th century.

But Western farming representatives, such as Richard H. Lehman, D-Calif., were furious that such a radical change was offered at the last minute. "It would simply be impossible for farmers to do any long-term planning or financing under the provisions of the three-year moratorium," Lehman said. He demanded a recorded vote. Under the rule, the proposal needed a two-thirds majority to pass, and the final tally, 245-164, fell short. *(Vote 401, p. 98-H)*

The expanded bill would have cleared the way for completion of the billion-dollar Central Utah Project, among the nation's last large uncompleted water projects, as well as a raft of other projects.

On Nov. 20, Miller agreed to bring back the drought bill, stripped of his proposal to revamp Western water and a host of popular water projects.

Negotiations to reconcile the two versions produced a compromise bill on the last day of the session. In the compromise version, the House accepted most of the broader Senate bill but allowed some of the Bureau of Reclamation's special powers to expire after 10 years. The compromise also dropped Senate language that would have allowed financially strapped farmers to defer paying for federal water.

Seymour managed to get the compromise through the Senate, but the House was operating under an agreement that barred most last-minute bills from reaching the floor. ■

Export Enhancement Program Expanded

The administration pushed for and won a provision in a 1991 supplemental spending bill that raised the amount of subsidies it could offer U.S. exporters under the Agriculture Department's Export Enhancement Program (EEP).

Under this program, the Agriculture Department compensated exporters who agreed to discount agricultural sales abroad by giving the exporters government-owned commodities such as wheat, corn and other feed grains. The subsidies were intended to cover the difference between the world market prices and the generally higher U.S. prices.

Although President Bush's stated policy was that export subsidies should be eliminated worldwide, he wanted added authority to use the export program in the hope that it would spur the European Community (EC) to pull back on its use of subsidies.

However, by the time the Senate passed the $5.2 billion "dire emergency" supplemental appropriations bill (HR 1281) on March 20, the administration's grain export provision had been so taken over by provisions for other commodities — dairy products, in particular — that the White House was threatening to veto the entire bill. *(1991 supplemental spending bill, p. 668)*

It was that threat and the longstanding opposition of House Appropriations Committee Chairman Jamie L. Whitten, D-Miss., that forced House and Senate negotiators late in the week of March 18 to strip the Senate additions from the supplemental spending bill. The provision that remained in the bill repealed the cap of $425 million on the EEP.

The controversy surrounding the export program dated from its inception in 1985, when it was part of a deal struck by Sen. Bob Dole, R-Kan., and then-President Ronald Reagan's budget director, David A. Stockman, in order to get the votes needed to pass the president's budget. *(1985 Almanac, p. 527)*

At the time, the White House opposed export subsidies on the grounds that they violated Reagan's free-market approach to agriculture. But during the Senate negotiations on the fiscal 1986 budget resolution, the administration agreed to initiate a $2 billion subsidy program in return for several key votes, including that of Edward Zorinsky of Nebraska, the ranking Democrat on the Senate Agriculture Committee.

The Reagan administration at the time viewed the export-subsidy program as a concession to farmers — something to make them feel that Washington was trying to bolster the sagging position of American products in overseas markets.

The Bush administration first sought to remove the cap on export subsidies in 1991 through a freestanding bill, but that measure (HR 805) bogged down in the House in an arcane dispute between the White House and the House Democratic leadership over budget "scorekeeping" calculations.

BOXSCORE

➡ **Agricultural Exports (HR 805, passed as a provision in HR 1281).** HR 805 sought to raise funding for the Export Enhancement Program by $475 million in fiscal 1991 and authorize the Agriculture Department to spend up to $5 billion on the program over the next five years. HR 1281 repealed the cap of $425 million on the export program, with estimates that about $900 million would be spent in fiscal 1991 to subsidize exports of wheat and other commodities.

KEY ACTION

Feb. 26 — The **House** Agriculture Committee approved HR 805 by voice vote.

March 12 — The **House** Foreign Affairs Subcommittee on International Economic Policy and Trade, by 9-2, approved HR 805.

March 19 — The **House** Foreign Affairs Committee approved HR 805 by voice vote.

March 20 — The **Senate** included a provision to increase funding for the Export Enhancement Program in the "dire emergency" supplemental (HR 1281) and approved the measure 92-8.

March 22 — The **House** approved the conference report on the $5.4 billion dire emergency bill 340-48; the **Senate** cleared the bill by voice vote.

April 10 — President Bush signed HR 1281 — PL 102-27.

HOUSE ACTION

With some discomfort but little opposition, the House Agriculture Committee on Feb. 26 approved by voice vote the first bill of 1991 that had the potential to bust the new budget deal and trigger automatic spending cuts in domestic programs.

HR 805 proposed to raise funding for the Export Enhancement Program by $475 million in fiscal 1991 and authorize the Department of Agriculture to spend up to $5 billion on the program over the next five years.

Most Agriculture Committee members and the administration liked the export program because they believed it stimulated international sales of commodities, especially wheat, pushing up or at least stabilizing the price.

However, under the new congressional budget rules, every piece of legislation was to be "scored" to determine how much in offsetting cuts should be exacted to abide by Congress' new "pay as you go" guidelines. If the cuts were not included in the bill, its enactment would trigger across-the-board cuts in all domestic appropriations.

The House Democratic leadership, in a highly controversial move, had chosen to abide by the estimates of the Congressional Budget Office (CBO), a nonpartisan agency of Congress, instead of the estimates of the White House Office of Management and Budget (OMB).

The administration had threatened to veto any legislation that came through with a CBO estimate. "This is our first, small skirmish in pay-as-you-go government," said Rep. Charles W. Stenholm, D-Texas.

In this case, Agriculture Committee members preferred the OMB scoring. OMB had estimated that HR 805 would not cost any more than current spending because of its potential to raise market prices and reduce government price-support subsidies. *(New budget rules, p. 73)*

However, CBO estimated that the bill would increase spending by $20 million in fiscal 1991 and $125 million over the next three years, which would trigger automatic cuts.

This confusion made HR 805 a test case for the newest of the House budget rules.

Rep. Dan Glickman, D-Kan., who introduced HR 805, and others on the committee realized that between the new budget agreement and the new House rule, they were in a virtually spending-proof box. "We're being strangled by details," said Glickman.

Empty Program Coffers

The impetus for the bill was that the export program coffers were almost out of money. The EEP was the main program that the United States used to compete for grain markets with the heavily subsidized EC, and because of dropping grain prices, it was the first time in the past couple of years that the program had run out of money.

The administration looked favorably on the program because trade negotiators were in the midst of a late push to get the EC to agree to reduce farm subsidies as part of the General Agreement on Tariffs and Trade.

U.S. trade officials wanted the additional export funds as leverage to show the EC that the United States was ready to enter a subsidy trade war if it refused to lower price supports for its farmers.

The program had been sharply criticized for, among other things, putting money into the pockets of large grain-exporting companies such as Cargill Inc., rather than helping farmers, and for mainly subsidizing wheat sales.

Throughout the 1990 marketing year, 80 percent of subsidized sales were for wheat and wheat flour, according to Agriculture Department figures.

In the 1990 farm bill, the export program was authorized to spend at least $500 million; however, the Appropriations Committee put a $425 million ceiling on it. *(1990 Almanac, p. 323)*

Under the bill proposed by Glickman, the ceiling on EEP payments would be lifted, and the department could use up to $900 million in export bonuses in fiscal 1991.

Five months into fiscal 1991, 86 percent, or $364 million, of that $425 million had been used, according to Agriculture Department officials who ran the program.

The administration had recommended spending $900 million on the program in fiscal 1991 and $1.2 billion in 1992.

Potential Budget-Buster

On March 12, the House Foreign Affairs Subcommittee on International Economic Policy and Trade, on a vote of 9-2, approved HR 805.

The bill's supporters wanted to use different accounting rules to avoid the possibility that the bill would be shot down on the floor. They were concerned it would threaten to trigger automatic cuts in other mandatory domestic programs under new spending rules.

Doug Bereuter, R-Neb., who voted against the bill, said the bill would ultimately have more impact on budget policy than on export programs.

The bill would authorize an additional $400 million for fiscal 1991 (for a total of $900 million) in certificates that exporters could redeem for such government-owned commodities as wheat, corn and other feed grains.

But if exporters redeemed these certificates in fiscal 1991, it could push spending above the cap agreed on during the previous year's budget negotiations.

To get around that, members approved, by voice vote, an amendment by subcommittee Chairman Sam Gejdenson, D-Conn., that made the bill identical to the version approved by the House Agriculture Committee in February.

Gejdenson's amendment would authorize an increase in the amount of certificates allowed, but it would not allow the certificates to be redeemed until Oct. 1, 1991 — the start of fiscal 1992. This timing would keep the program from exceeding its fiscal 1991 budgetary cap.

Members rejected, by voice vote, an amendment by Bereuter that would have accelerated the time under which exporters could redeem their grain certificates at government warehouses.

On March 19, the House Foreign Affairs Committee approved HR 805 by voice vote. Lawmakers also approved by voice vote an amendment offered by Toby Roth, R-Wis., to clarify that dairy cattle would be eligible under the export program.

Lawmakers in the House were prepared on March 20 to take up HR 805.

SENATE ACTION

The Senate on March 19 considered raising subsidies for the EEP as part of the fiscal 1991 supplemental appropriations bill. The Senate bill, similar to HR 805, recommended lifting the current $425 million cap for export subsidies.

Farm lobbyists for individual commodities had thought that, when the export program was added to the supplemental late in the week of March 11, they had better take advantage of the opportunity because it might be the only farm bill of the year.

Dairy farmers wanted the provision to increase the price they were paid for their milk by as much as 30 percent, and they found a ready sponsor in Patrick J. Leahy, a Democrat from the dairy state of Vermont who was also the chairman of the Agriculture Committee.

Leahy insisted on attaching the milk-price increase to the administration's export-subsidy provision. For good measure, he added some minor changes to farm law sought by cotton, rice and corn growers.

Despite heated objections from the administration, conservative Republicans and some urban liberals, who said the milk price increase would be unfairly passed on to consumers, the legislative package proved irresistible on the Senate floor.

Leahy prevailed on a 60-40 vote. *(Vote 32, p. 5-S)*

Afterward, some of Bush's staunchest GOP allies in the Senate criticized the administration's legislative strategy.

"I would never have advocated putting the export program in the supplemental to begin with," said Richard G. Lugar, ranking Republican on Agriculture, who led the fight against Leahy's dairy amendment.

The export program had some powerful supporters, including Senate Minority Leader Dole and the multinational grain trading companies, such as Cargill, Continental Grain Co. and Louis Dreyfus Corp. But it also had many critics, both inside and outside the farm lobby.

Critics said that the subsidy program actually drove down wheat prices because it allowed exporters to sell at or below the world market price.

Some farm-state lawmakers agreed. "When you subsidize a grain sale, you have the effect of depressing the market price," said Dave Nagle, D-Iowa, a member of the House Agriculture Committee.

Either way, most farmers benefited hardly at all from the export program. Their income was protected from the vagaries of the marketplace by government subsidies. If the world market price dropped, a larger portion of their income came from the government; if the price rose, the government paid a smaller amount. The export subsidies simply determined who bought their grain: grain companies or the government.

That sentiment was the driving force behind the momentary success of Leahy's dairy amendment, which would require the Agriculture Department to raise the price that milk processors must pay dairy farmers for milk. The money raised by the price hike would go into a national pool to be distributed to all dairy farmers. It picked up support from key milk-state senators, including those from Wisconsin and New York.

Leahy won over Southern senators by adding clauses that would allow rice, cotton and feed grain farmers to get around restrictions in the 1990 farm bill that regulated what could be planted on idle acres.

To mollify opponents, who said a price hike in milk could adversely affect government nutrition programs, Leahy added a final provision:

If the amendment caused the price of milk to go up, then the government could take money from the milk pool to ensure that there was no decrease in the number of people served by the Women, Infants and Children (WIC) feeding program. *(Dairy, p. 169)*

FINAL ACTION

For two days, the proposal to bolster foreign wheat sales tied up conference action on the entire $5.2 billion supplemental appropriations bill (HR 1281), which Congress was trying to pass before leaving March 22 on its two-week Easter recess.

The administration finally won what it had wanted: a provision that would raise the amount of subsidies it could offer U.S. exporters under the export program.

The victory came only after House and Senate conferees removed a Senate amendment that would have increased milk prices and given other breaks to cotton, rice and feed grain producers.

A veto threat and pressure from House Appropriations Chairman Whitten, who was also chairman of the Agriculture Subcommittee, forced the House and Senate negotiators late in the week of March 18 to strip much of the Senate additions.

The final measure signed by the president April 10 repealed the cap of $425 million on the export program. The Agriculture Department estimated that with no cap on the EEP, it would spend about $900 million in fiscal 1991 to subsidize exports of wheat and other commodities.

House and Senate conferees said in the conference report that they expected the Agriculture Department to use the Commodity Credit Corporation and other authority to remove surplus milk products from the domestic market and donate them as a bonus (in addition to regular purchases) to various domestic feeding programs, such as the WIC nutrition program.

The conferees also strongly urged the Agriculture Department to use the EEP to export 100 million pounds of nonfat dry milk and 100 million pounds of butter during the remainder of 1991. The conferees asked that added emphasis be given to the export of oils, poultry and rice under the export program. ■

New Agricultural Credit Guarantees for Soviets

After pressure from farm-state lawmakers, President Bush in 1991 granted the Soviet Union a total of $2.75 billion in new credit guarantees for agricultural products.

The new credits had a twofold purpose: to attempt to add stability to the Soviet economy to prop up the foundering regime of President Mikhail S. Gorbachev and to boost the fortunes of American farmers. *(Soviet aid, p. 463)*

The new assistance came in two installments: $1.5 billion was announced on June 11, with an additional $1.25 billion awarded on Nov. 20, as the economic and political situation in the Soviet Union continued to deteriorate.

The first extension of loan guarantees was announced on the Senate floor Minority Leader Bob Dole, R-Kan., and came on the heels of Senate passage May 15 of a nonbinding resolution (S Res 117) that urged the president to extend the guarantees.

During Senate debate on the loan guarantees, there was considerable opposition to the credit guarantee in light of the Soviet Union's economic instability and its crackdown on independence movements in the Baltic States. Despite such concerns, the Senate passed the resolution on a 70-28 vote. *(Vote 62, p. 9-S)*

However, Bill Bradley, D-N.J., one of the Senate's strongest critics of aid to the Soviets, opposed Bush's announcement in June that he would grant agricultural credit guarantees to the Soviets. "This is a waste of taxpayers' dollars," Bradley said. "The Soviet economy is essentially in a free fall."

Under the credit guarantee program, private lenders extended credit to a foreign country after the United States, through the Agriculture Department, agreed to service the debt if the country defaulted.

The 1990 farm bill (PL 101-624) had strengthened the law's section on creditworthiness by specifying that credit could not be extended if the secretary of Agriculture determined that a country could not service the debt.

Previously the law said merely that the secretary had to "take into consideration" a country's ability to repay the debt.

Bush initially expressed concern that the Soviet Union could not meet the creditworthiness standard. He had waited for a report from a team of agricultural experts that visited the Soviet Union in late May.

Ultimately, the administration defined the issue narrowly in announcing the credit guarantee. White House spokesman Marlin Fitzwater emphasized that the Soviets "have never defaulted on an official loan involving this country."

Helping the American Farmer

The June decision on the first installment of credit guarantees, made public by Dole, had taken months of behind-the-scenes maneuvering by the White House, Agriculture Department officials and farm-state lawmakers.

Dole said the extension of credits went beyond the complex foreign policy issues at stake. He noted in a statement that the credits would lead to "increased sales of agricultural products," and he said that "will help the American farmer."

Taxpayers also stood to benefit. Dole said that additional grain sales to the Soviets would boost the price of wheat and corn and save taxpayers as much as $800 million by reducing the amount that the government would have to pay to farmers in agricultural price supports.

Farm-state Democrats also backed the subsidized sale as an opportunity to help farmers.

"Selling agricultural commodities to other countries increases demand and increases prices and income for farmers," said Democrat Tom Harkin of Iowa, one of the nation's largest corn producing states. "Improving farm income is critical to small towns and rural communities across this nation."

Indeed, rural lawmakers for more than a decade had viewed subsidized sales of farm products to the Soviets as a prime political tool. In the heartland, farmers considered a large Soviet sale as a way to stimulate overseas agricultural markets and boost prices.

For Republicans, the sales were also an opportunity to identify with U.S. farm interests and to head off Democratic charges that they were not sympathetic to agriculture.

In 1986, on the eve of an election, Dole pushed the Reagan administration to subsidize 4 million metric tons of Soviet wheat sales despite the administration's stated opposition to any subsidized exports to communist countries.

In 1991 the debate over Soviet agricultural credits unfolded against a far more complex and unpredictable foreign policy backdrop.

At issue was whether the credit assistance should have been extended to support Gorbachev at a time when he seemed to be moving away from rather than toward democratic reforms. Prominently noted throughout the Senate debate was the ongoing assault of the Soviet army on the Soviet republics, particularly Lithuania and Latvia.

Also, fresh in the minds of some lawmakers was the Bush administration's extension of similar loans to Iraq before Saddam Hussein invaded Kuwait in August 1990.

Economic troubles in the Soviet Union also raised questions about whether it was creditworthy. The Soviet government was tottering, and its economy was in disarray. ■

Senate Approved Madigan As Agriculture Secretary

The Senate on March 7 easily approved President Bush's nomination of Rep. Edward Madigan as secretary of Agriculture, culminating an unusually public campaign by the Illinois Republican to join the Cabinet after 19 years in the House.

The 99-0 vote followed accolades from Democrats and Republicans.

Madigan, the former ranking Republican on the House Agriculture Committee, had gained a reputation as a steady and thoughtful lawmaker who worked well with Democrats and Republicans alike. *(Vote 24, p. 4-S)*

"He is a tough but fair and open-minded legislator," said Patrick J. Leahy, D-Vt., chairman of the Senate Agriculture Committee.

He won confirmation after being nominated by Bush on Jan. 25 to replace Clayton Yeutter, who resigned March 1 to become chairman of the Republican National Committee.

Madigan, 55, had just been elected to his 10th term when Bush gave him the nod. He was a key negotiator at the final stages of the 1990 and 1985 farm bills and was also an influential member of the Energy and Commerce Committee.

In picking Madigan to replace Yeutter, Bush called him "an aggressive leader on all agriculture issues." Madigan appeared with Bush at a news conference and thanked him for the opportunity to seek "to carry out your desire that rural Americans have a strong voice in the councils of the government. . . . I'm going to work hard with you to ensure that their concerns are heard in these councils of government."

His ranking position on House Agriculture fell to Tom Coleman of Missouri, who once had aspirations for the Cabinet post himself. Coleman had lobbied for the job at the beginning of the Bush administration before it was given to Yeutter.

Madigan also was the ranking Republican on the House Energy Subcommittee on Health and the Environment, which oversaw the Public Health Service and Medicaid programs as well as major environmental issues. With his departure, the ranking post fell to the much more conservative William E. Dannemeyer of California.

Madigan also served for two years as chief deputy whip, but his hope of moving up was dashed in 1989 when he lost by only two votes his chance to become House minority whip to the GOP's Newt Gingrich of Georgia. Madigan was endorsed by Minority Leader Robert H. Michel of Illinois, but too many Republicans had grown impatient with his pragmatic brand of politics to move him into the No. 2 GOP leadership slot.

Madigan said at the time that he had no ambition to succeed Michel as leader, but the defeat essentially ended Madigan's future in the House leadership. *(1989 Almanac, p. 7)*

All-Out Campaign

Madigan engaged in an all-out lobbying campaign to persuade Bush and his chief of staff, John H. Sununu, to appoint him to the post.

Madigan said he sent a letter to the White House in early January seeking to replace Yeutter after Republicans told him Bush needed to build a better relationship with the agriculture community as the 1992 election drew closer. And fellow House Republicans circulated letters in his behalf, one signed by 132 members.

If Madigan's public bid for the Agriculture job was evidence of some edginess on his part, the condition did not result from his standing in public opinion.

He had not been seriously challenged since 1972, when he first ran for his eastern Illinois House seat. And in two of his previous three elections he had run without Democratic opposition.

However, Madigan did have reason to worry about the redistricting slated to precede the 1992 election. Illinois was losing two House seats, and there was concern among Republicans that the redistricting plan — to be crafted by the Democratic-controlled state legislature and sent to GOP Gov. Jim Edgar — would try to protect downstate Democratic House seats by merging parts of Madigan's 15th District with Michel's 18th.

Although there were retirement rumors about Michel, the House minority leader would have had first call if he and Madigan had been thrown together. Madigan's move was seen by many Illinois delegation watchers as a sign that Michel would run for re-election in 1992. ■

Insurance Industry Kept Exemptions

A bill to roll back some of the insurance industry's exemptions from federal antitrust laws advanced through the House Judiciary Committee too late in the session to be considered on the House floor. A companion measure was introduced in the Senate.

Insurers had been exempt for 46 years under the McCarran-Ferguson Act, but critics led by Rep. Jack Brooks, D-Texas, said the industry did not deserve special legal protection.

Brooks advanced his assault on the insurance industry Nov. 19 when the Judiciary Committee he chaired voted 19-14 to report HR 9, which would end many longstanding insurance industry exemptions from antitrust laws under the 1945 law.

The vote came just five days after the bill cleared the Economic and Commercial Law Subcommittee, which Brooks also chaired. Brooks was hopeful it would win consideration on the House floor early in 1992.

In the Senate, Howard M. Metzenbaum, D-Ohio, introduced a parallel bill (S 430) in February, but that measure did not move through committee during the first session.

Originally intended as a temporary legal umbrella, the McCarran-Ferguson Act had become a way of life for the insurance industry. Rival insurers collaborated in a range of ways, including sharing data on projected losses, developing standard policy forms and jointly underwriting some projects.

Brooks and others had been trying for years to change that, claiming insurance companies had abused their privileges to fix prices and thwart competition.

A previous measure by Brooks to restrict insurance companies from sharing price information and engaging in monopolistic practices narrowly won approval from the House Judiciary Committee on June 20, 1990. It went no further in the 101st Congress. Similar measures had been pushed unsuccessfully in the 100th and 99th Congresses. *(1990 Almanac, p. 401; 1988 Almanac, p. 574)*

The 1991 bill did not repeal McCarran-Ferguson outright and specifically retained antitrust immunity for some practices.

But it sought to end the antitrust exemption for activities that constituted price fixing, monopolization, dividing up insurance markets geographically or forcing consumers to buy a package of insurance policies to receive one type of coverage.

Noting that politicians called for free markets in other nations, Brooks said, "It is high time that we ensure that purchasers of insurance here in America enjoy the benefit of a marketplace where price fixing has no place and where skyrocketing premiums for no cause are not permitted."

But opponents warned that the bill would actually undermine competition and create chaos at a time when many insurance companies were on shaky financial ground.

"Make no mistake," said Hamilton Fish Jr., N.Y., the committee's ranking Republican, "this bill could very seriously and negatively impact the financial solvency and stability of thousands of insurers."

Although most insurance groups fiercely opposed ending the exemption, some did negotiate with Brooks' staff on a possible compromise bill.

BOXSCORE

➡ **Insurance Antitrust (HR 9, S 430).** Bills to end some of the insurance industry's exemptions from antitrust laws.

KEY ACTION

Nov. 14 — The **House** Judiciary Subcommittee on Economic and Commercial Law approved HR 9, 10-5.

Nov. 19 — The **House** Judiciary Committee approved HR 9, 19-14.

HOUSE SUBCOMMITTEE ACTION

Brooks, unwilling to let the legislative year end quietly for the insurance lobby, forged ahead with efforts to bust up the industry's longstanding legal privileges. On Nov. 14, his Economic and Commercial Law Subcommittee approved his insurance antitrust bill, 10-5.

As passed by subcommittee, insurers could be sued for antitrust activities in four areas: price fixing, colluding to divide territory, monopolization and unfairly forcing customers to buy a package of insurance policies to obtain one specific type of coverage.

That could allow challenges to longstanding insurance practices that had been allowed under state regulation. However, bill supporters said those changes would not apply in states that actively regulated insurers.

Brooks and other advocates maintained the changes would promote competition and drive down insurance prices. They were backed by consumer activists, organized labor and some small-business groups.

But insurance groups and their allies insisted the industry was unique and entitled to the special treatment McCarran-Ferguson provided.

Far from benefiting consumers, critics said, Brooks' proposal would destabilize the industry and ultimately drive up costs.

"Its first victim would be the small insurance companies and the second would be the consumers," said Henry J. Hyde, R-Ill.

Dan Glickman, D-Kan., one of three committee Democrats to vote against the bill in 1990, gave it his tentative support this time.

But Glickman said he still worried that the changes would cause a disadvantage to small insurers.

Glickman urged Brooks to include greater assurances that small insurers would retain access to loss data. Without such changes, he warned, "Every insurance agent in America will dedicate his or her efforts to fight this bill on the floor of the House."

The subcommittee's Republicans echoed that concern and added others. Fish said the bill would undermine the authority of states, which regulated insurance. Contrary to the claims of bill proponents, Fish believed the bill would pre-empt state rules even where there is active oversight.

But Fish's amendment to bolster state regulatory authority failed on a 5-10 party-line vote.

HOUSE COMMITTEE ACTION

The committee debate on Nov. 19 was largely a replay of subcommittee action. As in subcommittee, the vote split along partisan lines with virtually all Democrats supporting the bill and Republicans uniting to oppose it, 19-14.

Peter Hoagland, whose Nebraska district included the insurance center of Omaha, was the only Democrat to vote against the bill.

All 13 Republicans voted against the proposal. Fish said the Bush administration opposed the bill, although it had not taken a high-profile stance against it.

Even without Republican votes, Brooks' victory margin was slightly stronger than in 1990 when the committee approved a similar bill, 19-17.

Brooks was able to win over two Democrats who opposed the bill in 1990 — Glickman and Edward F. Feighan of Ohio — after he cooperated with Glickman's effort to add more protections for small and medium-size insurers.

Glickman's amendment allowed small and midsize companies to continue sharing statistical data to project the volume of claims — a practice called trending. Companies would qualify for the continued exemption provided they did not have net assets of more than $10 million, or assets of $100 million and did not hold more than 2.5 percent of a state's market share.

Consumer lobbyists complained that the amendment would effectively gut the bill. But Brooks successfully added language specifying that the exemption would not apply if the companies sharing information collectively controlled 20 percent of the market or more. With that restriction attached, Glickman's amendment passed by voice vote.

Members turned away a Fish amendment to bolster state regulatory authority over insurance practices.

Brooks maintained that his bill would not apply to insurers operating in states that actively regulated the industry.

But Fish disputed this interpretation, saying the bill would actually pre-empt state oversight in many areas. The amendment to ensure that state authority prevailed failed 13-20.

Fish's second amendment, also unsuccessful, would have gone beyond Glickman's proposal to keep certain smaller insurers under the McCarran-Ferguson antitrust umbrella. ■

Congress Again Attempted To Limit Product Liability

As they had for more than a decade, lawmakers tried yet again in 1991 to restrict collections for injuries caused by faulty products. Legislation advanced through one committee in the Senate, and a companion measure was introduced in the House.

It was the sixth time since 1980 that a business coalition had gotten a product liability bill out of committee only to watch it falter before coming to a floor vote.

But proponents said they had a newfound momentum in the second session for their longstanding cause. "It's clear to me the momentum is building," said lead sponsor Sen. Bob Kasten, R-Wis.

In past years, advocates usually had focused on either the House or the Senate. This time, advocates had 35 cosponsors for Kasten's bill (S 640 — S Rept 102-215). And in the House, J. Roy Rowland, D-Ga., sponsored a companion measure (HR 3030) had attracted more than 99 cosponsors.

On Oct. 3, S 640 was approved by the Senate Commerce Committee by a vote of 13-7. It was expected to go next to the lawyer-dominated Judiciary Committee, where product liability legislation had traditionally encountered more resistance than from the more business-oriented Commerce panel.

Arrayed against it were consumer activists, the politically potent trial lawyers' lobby and some state organizations that opposed the federal pre-emption of state liability laws.

Bill supporters said they had amended the proposal over the years to respond to consumer groups' concerns. They noted that in certain areas of product liability law, the bill gave plaintiffs more rights than they were accorded in some states.

But most critics were unswayed.

One of the bill's most vocal opponents — Sen. Ernest F. Hollings, D-S.C. — was chairman of the Commerce Committee and a former trial lawyer.

Hollings lambasted many of the justifications, saying there was no evidence that juries were spitting out irresponsible damage awards. "They are really trying to amend the Constitution and take away that trial by jury," he said.

Decadelong Battle

The push to change the nation's product liability laws sprang up in the early 1980s as the so-called tort reform movement. Proponents argued that runaway damage awards were driving up liability rates and making it impossible for groups to buy insurance.

In the 1990s, supporters emphasized competitiveness. They argued that product litigation was too arbitrary, time-consuming and expensive — ultimately crimping productivity and deterring development of innovative products. And supporters said the patchwork of state laws encouraged plaintiffs to "forum shop" for the most favorable state laws, adding still greater uncertainty to the outcome.

Kasten's bill was identical to one he sponsored unsuccessfully in the 101st Congress. The legislation (S 1400) got a small boost early in the year when President Bush included product liability reform in a laundry list of legislative items in his State of the Union address. Even so, the bill never reached the floor for debate after being approved by the Senate Commerce Committee on May 22. *(1990 Almanac, p. 400)*

SENATE ACTION

The Senate Commerce Committee re-enacted the first scene of a familiar drama Oct. 3, approving a bill (S 640) to create nationwide standards on how much consumers could be compensated for damage caused by faulty products.

Unlike previous bills, the new version did not place a cap on lawyers' fees or punitive damages. However, the bill generally pre-empted state liability laws with federal standards that, in many cases, made it harder for plaintiffs to recover damages.

Critics said that the bill would aggravate state-by-state disparities as each sought to reconcile federal standards with state laws.

Some of the bill's proponents had argued that uniform laws could ease liability insurance rates. During markup Hollings sought to require that, if enacted, insurance companies release information about the bill's potential impact. But bill cosponsor Sen. John D. Rockefeller IV, D-

W.Va., labeled Hollings' proposal a "killer amendment," and it was defeated, 10-10.

Some of the key provisions:

- Limited each party's liability to pay non-economic damages in cases in which there was more than one defendant.
- Set a uniform statute of limitations for product liability cases. Plaintiffs could file suit within two years of discovering that they were harmed by the product, even if that discovery came years after the injury.
- Set a national standard for awarding punitive damages that was higher than the standards in place in many states. Also, manufacturers could be exempt from liability on products that had been pre-approved by the Food and Drug Administration. ■

New Procurement Rules Passed by Senate

Legislation (S 260, S Rept 102-137) to require federal agencies to buy off-the-shelf, commercially available supplies passed the Senate on Sept. 13 by voice vote and was sent to the House Government Operations Committee.

The bill, which had been approved by the Senate Governmental Affairs Committee on a voice vote May 23, aimed to lower federal procurement costs by eliminating lengthy production start-ups and the need for costly research and development.

It was sponsored by Carl Levin, D-Mich., who said that along with the Department of Defense, other federal agencies should be encouraged to buy their equipment and supplies in the commercial market.

Supporters said that agencies often had products specially designed and built that were already available on the commercial market at a lower cost.

This measure required government purchasers to order, when possible, commercial or off-the-shelf products, known in the government as non-developmental items or NDIs. Agencies were also required to streamline their product requirements, increasing the possibility that a commercial product could meet their needs. ■

House Approved Gambling On U.S. Cruise Ships

The House on Nov. 23 approved by voice vote a bill to allow gambling on U.S.-flag cruise ships in international waters. However, the Senate did not act on the legislation during the first session.

The bill (HR 3282) was needed, sponsors said, to correct an inequity in U.S. law that allowed foreign-flag vessels but not U.S.-flag ships to offer gambling at a time when the domestic cruise ship industry was faltering.

Ships could provide gambling entertainment in international waters only if the gambling activities had not been prohibited under the laws of the state from which the ship was operated.

But the bill did not legalize the operation of ships that engaged solely in gambling.

"A dinner cruise could have gambling on board since the principal purpose of the vessel is not the operation of a gambling establishment," said Walter B. Jones, D-N.C., chairman of the House Merchant Marine and Fisheries Committee. "But it would not legalize the voyage of a vessel which is nothing more than a floating crap game."

Jones' committee had approved the bill on Nov. 20 by voice vote. The Subcommittee on the Merchant Marine had approved it Nov. 14.

Bill sponsor Gene Taylor, D-Miss., had offered a substitute version of the measure during the subcommittee markup that would have effectively given U.S. ships a monopoly in the voyages-to-nowhere market — trips that left a port, offered gambling on the open seas and returned to the same port. The amendment would also have allowed operators to offer gambling as the principal purpose of the voyage.

However, ranking subcommittee Republican Norman F. Lent, N.Y., successfully amended the measure to delete those two sections, which he said might have landed the bill in the Judiciary and Foreign Affairs committees. ■

Both House, Senate Acted To Curb Sports Gambling

At the urging of the major sports leagues, both chambers acted in 1991 to stem the spread of legalized betting on sporting events. Cash-starved states were turning to sports-based lotteries as a way of raising revenue without increasing taxes.

Legislation (S 474) that barred gambling on sporting events, except in Oregon, was approved by the Senate Judiciary Committee on Nov. 21, by voice vote. Casinos in Nevada were also allowed to continue sports betting.

The House version of the gambling bill (HR 74), which was incorporated into that chamber's omnibus crime bill (HR 3371), also exempted New Jersey from the proposed ban. *(Crime bill, p. 262)*

The sports leagues feared that other states would emulate Oregon, which in 1989 had begun a state-sponsored betting operation for pro football and pro basketball games.

The basketball lottery was scrapped after just one year due to lack of interest. The football lottery had mixed success. Its $7 million in sales the first year was below original expectations, according to lottery director Jim Davey, though it did attract customers who normally did not play the lottery.

Lottery directors argued that sports betting operations like the one in Oregon were really nothing more than glorified office pools.

They said it was hypocritical for the leagues to try to quash sports lotteries while accepting the huge sports gambling enterprise based in Nevada.

House Action

The leaders of all the major professional and college sports organizations, testifying before the Judiciary Subcommittee on Economic and Commercial Law on Sept. 12, strongly urged Congress to block the spread of legalized sports gambling, whether in casinos or state lotteries.

"Gambling and sports do not mix," said Arnold "Red"

Auerbach, president of the Boston Celtics, representing the National Basketball Association (NBA). If gambling on pro basketball games were legal, Auerbach said, every time Michael Jordan, star of the Chicago Bulls, missed a shot, "Some fans might yell, 'How much did you bet on this one, Michael?' "

Soon, fans would be more interested in whether they covered the point spread than in the game, Auerbach added.

As approved by the Judiciary subcommittee on Sept. 17, HR 74 did not affect betting on horse and dog racing, or the numbers games that were the most common type of lottery. Only betting on professional and collegiate sports such as basketball, football and baseball were prohibited.

The bill approved by the House panel permitted Oregon and Nevada to continue their policies. But Jack Brooks, D-Texas, who chaired both the subcommittee and the full Judiciary Committee, said he might seek to remove that "grandfather" clause in the future.

John Bryant, D-Texas, said that the grandfather clause was included so that Nevada and Oregon senators would not hold up the bill.

However, when the bill was folded into the House omnibus crime bill on Sept. 26, the Judiciary Committee approved, 17-16, a William J. Hughes, D-N.J., amendment to also exempt New Jersey from the ban on sports gambling. New Jersey state officials considered a referendum to permit sports gambling, and Hughes said he wanted to help his home state preserve the option.

Senate Action

A Senate Judiciary subcommittee had approved a similar bill (S 474) to the House measure on July 17. The full committee approved it Nov. 21. Chairman Joseph R. Biden Jr., D-Del., said that the spread of lotteries would endanger the vitality of pro sports and that he would prefer to bar sports betting altogether if it were politically possible.

Panel member Charles E. Grassley, R, registered several concerns, in part because his state of Iowa had been considering the introduction of a sports-based lottery of its own. ■

Time Ran Out on Measure Promoting U.S. Tourism

Congress came close to approving legislation to promote tourism within the United States. But time ran out in 1991 before a conference committee could be empaneled to hammer out a final version.

Legislation passed by the House and Senate (S 680) reauthorized the Commerce Department's U.S. Travel and Tourism Administration and mandated some reorganizational changes to respond to criticism of the agency. It also limited the amount of money to be spent on overhead and created a fund to promote tourism in rural areas.

Action began in the Senate Commerce, Science and Transportation Subcommittee on Foreign Commerce and Tourism, which approved the bill sponsored by John D. Rockefeller IV, D-W.Va., on July 10. The full Commerce Committee followed suit July 30, approving the measure by voice vote.

The bill required that the Commerce Department analyze tourism, including enticements and barriers for foreigners, and report back to Congress. The Senate panel sought to attract more tourists to rural areas in the United States.

With little debate, the Senate took up the measure, known as the Tourism Policy and Export Promotion Act of 1991, and passed it by voice vote Oct. 24. In response to Bush administration concerns, Rockefeller amended his bill on the floor to delete some of the proposed restructuring of the government's foreign offices to promote tourism.

Rep. Al Swift, D-Wash., introduced Oct. 29 a measure (HR 3645) that was similar to the Senate bill. It was quickly approved Oct. 31 by the Energy and Commerce Subcommittee on Transportation and Hazardous Materials. The full House Energy and Commerce Committee approved the bill by voice vote Nov. 7.

The House on Nov. 23 passed the Senate tourism bill. The House approved S 680 after stripping its contents and replacing them with the text of the companion House measure, HR 3645.

The action came too late in the session for negotiators to be named to iron out differences between the two measures. Supporters said conference negotiators were expected to gather in early 1992. ■

Bush Signed Law Assisting Entrepreneurial Women

Congress on Nov. 21 cleared a measure that helped women start and keep their own businesses. President Bush signed the bill Dec. 5. (HR 2629, H Rept 102-178 — PL 102-191)

The bill reauthorized two Small Business Administration programs of use to women: a small-loan program and a demonstration program that provided management training and technical assistance to businesses owned by women. The bill authorized $4 million for the programs in fiscal 1992 and $5 million for them for each of the following three years.

As initially passed by the House on Oct. 8, HR 2629 expanded the National Women's Business Council from nine to 11 members and stipulated that the additional seats be filled by an African-American and a Hispanic woman.

The administration objected to setting criteria for who might sit on the council.

At the urging of the Senate, the House agreed to drop the provision to add two seats to the National Women's Business Council, one each for an African-American and a Hispanic woman.

House and Senate negotiators agreed on the compromise version of the bill, which was passed by the Senate on Nov. 20 and cleared by the House the next day. ■

Efforts To Adjust 1990 Census Fail

Despite the apparent undercount and its bias against minorities, there was little consensus within Congress for legislation forcing an adjustment of the 1990 census. Republicans generally opposed any deviation from the traditional, Constitution-based head count. They were buttressed by Democrats from states that stood to lose a House seat if the 1990 reapportionment were adjusted for the undercount.

The Census Bureau itself favored a statistical adjustment but was overruled by its parent agency, the Commerce Department. Secretary Robert A. Mosbacher said July 15 that he would not adjust the census because the adjusted figures would not be accurate in the block-by-block detail needed for redistricting. That same week, a federal court was asked to order such an adjustment, and members of Congress vowed never to face the same dilemma again.

Eventually, Congress did mandate a study on ways to improve the nation's future decennial census. The bill, HR 3280, authorized the Commerce Department to contract with the National Academy of Sciences for a three-year study on census reform. The administration did not oppose the bill.

The study was to examine methods used in the 1990 census and recommend how they could be made more timely and accurate. Congress included $1.4 million for the study in a fiscal 1992 spending bill (HR 2608) for the Departments of Commerce, Justice, State and the judiciary. *(Appropriations, p. 531)*

Mosbacher's July 15 decision prompted protest from cities, big states, various spokesmen for minority groups and most Democrats. Seats in the House and in state and local lawmaking bodies hung in the balance, and lawmakers wanted new numbers that might save key seats before redistricting for 1992 was completed. Also at stake was the distribution of about $40 billion in federal aid under various population-based funding formulas.

After Mosbacher refused to order an adjustment, Democrats in Washington and several state capitals tried to obtain the new population figures that would have been used in an adjustment. One such lawsuit, filed under the Freedom of Information Act by California state legislators, was awaiting a hearing in a federal appeals court in San Francisco in early 1992.

BOXSCORE

➡ **Decennial Census Improvement Act (HR 3280)** The bill authorized a $1.4 million study by the National Academy of Sciences to examine methods to improve the accuracy of future censuses of the United States.

Report: H Rept 102-227.

KEY ACTION

April 18 — Data released from a follow-up survey indicated that the 1990 census missed as many as 6.3 million people.

June 13 — Census Bureau officials released new estimates of the 1990 census undercount that showed a national net undercount of 5.27 million or 2.1 percent.

July 15 — Commerce Secretary Robert A. Mosbacher said that he would not adjust the 1990 census to correct for the apparent undercount.

Aug. 22 — The General Accounting Office released a report estimating that the 1990 census contained "a minimum of 14.1 million gross errors and perhaps as many as 25.7 million errors." These numbers included an estimated 9.7 million persons uncounted altogether — far more than the 5.27 million net undercount reported by the Census Bureau.

Sept. 17 — The **House** Post Office and Civil Service Subcommittee on Census and Population approved HR 3280, 4-0.

Sept. 25 — The **House** Post Office and Civil Service Committee unanimously approved HR 3280, 22-0.

Sept. 30 — The **House** passed HR 3280 by voice vote.

Oct. 3 — The **Senate** passed HR 3280 by voice vote, with amendments.

Oct. 9 — The **House** cleared HR 3280 for the president.

Oct. 24 — President Bush signed HR 3280 — PL 102-135.

The 1990 Head Count

The U.S. Census Bureau spent much of 1990 in the throes of counting residents, household by household, for the 21st time since the founding of the Union. Preliminary 1990 figures were released on Aug. 29, 1990, and then subjected to additional months of tabulation, review and legal challenges. *(1990 Almanac, p. 415)*

The final tally, released Dec. 26, 1990, added about 4 million to the preliminary numbers. Data released April 18, 1991, indicated that the 1990 census missed as many as 6.3 million people; a subsequent estimate released June 13 showed a national undercount of 5.27 million or 2.1 percent. Two months later, the General Accounting Office (GAO) released a study saying that nearly twice that number went uncounted and many more were mislocated.

If Mosbacher had chosen adjustment, the House would have been reapportioned according to the totals released in June, rather than those announced in December or April.

The states where the undercount was apparently worst had had high immigration rates in the 1980s: California, Arizona, New Mexico and Texas.

Among the eight cities with more than 1 million people, the final estimate showed the census to have been least accurate in Los Angeles. Adjustment would have set that city's population 5.1 percent higher than the original count.

Philadelphia, however, would have found itself even worse off, proportionately, under adjustment. It was the city the survey found to have been undercounted the least (1.3 percent) among cities larger than 1 million.

Philadelphia officials had argued that about 130,000 people were missed, but the bureau estimated it missed only about 20,000 people.

The revision found that the count in Washington,

Baltimore, Dallas and Houston was off by about 5 percent; in San Diego and San Jose, Calif., by about 4 percent; in New York and Phoenix, by 3 percent; and in Chicago, by 2.6 percent.

ADMINISTRATION ACTION

The official 1990 census results released by the U.S. Census Bureau late in 1990 pegged the national population at 248,709,873 — an increase of more than 22.2 million people (9.8 percent) over the 1980 total.

The Commerce Department had said it would decide by July 15, 1991, whether to use its authority to adjust the census tally to correct for undercounting.

The Census Bureau had agreed to do a post-enumeration survey as part of a 1989 settlement of a lawsuit brought against the Commerce Department by the nation's four largest cities (New York, Los Angeles, Chicago and Houston) and by New York state and Dade County (Miami), Fla. Those plaintiffs alleged an undercount and asked for a post-census evaluative survey of 300,000 households before settling for 165,000.

The case for adjusting the 1990 census was poised on whether 165,000 constituted an adequate sample size for evaluation.

Data released April 18 from the follow-up survey indicated that the 1990 census missed as many as 6.3 million people. Bureau officials said this first-ever "post-enumeration survey" did not mean that the Commerce Department would order an adjustment to the 1990 head count.

However, the data indicated that the undercount was particularly acute among racial minorities. Three times as many blacks as non-blacks went uncounted — an estimated 2 million. As many as 1.8 million Hispanics might have been missed.

The survey also found a disparity of undercount between states and regions. The least accurate counting apparently was done in California, New Mexico, West Virginia, Virginia, the Carolinas, Georgia and Florida.

Winners and Losers

Census Bureau officials released new estimates of the 1990 census undercount on June 13, 1991. Those data showed a net national undercount of 5.27 million or 2.1 percent. If those figures were to supplant the census numbers, Pennsylvania and Wisconsin would each lose a seat that had looked safe on the basis of census results. California and Arizona, already winners in the census and in reapportionment, would each have added yet another new seat.

Peter A. Bounpane, the assistant census director, said bureau experts would make a formal recommendation regarding adjustment to Bureau Director Barbara E. Bryant, who would then advise Mosbacher. Bounpane said the next announcement would come from Mosbacher.

But there were hints of the bureau's viewpoint in the lengthy news conference Bounpane held June 13. He noted that the survey-based, computer-generated data were more accurate in the larger aggregates — nationwide or statewide. The smaller the geographical unit, he noted, the less reliable the projections.

Political observers had generally predicted that Mosbacher would stick with the 1990 count. But Democrats sought to cast the question as a conflict between good numbers and bad.

"The post-enumeration survey is telling us that the original census numbers are demonstrably wrong," said Tom Sawyer, D-Ohio, chairman of the Census and Population Subcommittee of the House Post Office and Civil Service Committee.

The numbers released June 13 represented the latest massaging of data collected in an unprecedented post-census check by the bureau itself. The new data were rife with political contradictions. The states that had gained most in the actual census — such as California, Texas, Florida and Arizona — would generally be even better off under an adjustment. Many of the states that had sued to force an adjustment — such as New York, Pennsylvania, Illinois and Michigan — would do worse if one were ordered.

Further complications developed because urban, suburban and rural jurisdictions within individual states would not fare the same under an adjustment. Generally speaking, cities would have done better under an adjustment and rural areas would have done worse.

If the census were adjusted according to the June figures, Pennsylvania would lose three House seats instead of the two it was slated to lose at the end of 1990. Wisconsin, which had expected to stand pat with nine seats on the basis of the census, stood to lose one.

The Pennsylvania seat would, in effect, go to Arizona, which was already expected to gain a seat on the basis of the census. The new seat would bring the state's total to seven. Wisconsin's ninth seat would go to California, bringing that state's gain to eight seats for a delegation total of 53.

Confronting the Wisconsin change was obviously disconcerting for the state's Democratic senator, Herb Kohl, who announced June 13 that he was "unequivocally opposed to any adjustment."

Kohl was Sawyer's Senate counterpart as chairman of the Government Information Subcommittee of the Governmental Affairs Committee.

Kohl said he knew his view "may be discounted as simply parochial" but insisted that statistical experts had convinced him "an adjusted census could very well be less accurate and less objective than the original census."

If reapportionment were based on adjusted figures, all 50 states would also be presented with new numbers on which to base the redrawing of their own congressional and legislative district boundaries. About a dozen states had already done most of the work toward adopting their new congressional or legislative lines.

Mosbacher's Decision

As expected, Commerce Secretary Mosbacher said July 15 that he would not adjust the 1990 census to correct its undercount. Although he pronounced himself "deeply troubled" by the disproportionate undercount of racial minorities, Mosbacher said sticking with the head count would be "fairest for all Americans."

Mosbacher's political task was made no easier when Census Director Bryant announced that her recommendation to him had been in favor of adjustment. That news came after it was learned that the bureau's internal panel, the Undercount Steering Committee, had voted 7-2 in favor of adjusting.

Bryant made it clear in statements all week that she saw every flaw in the post-census survey data that Mosbacher did. But she said her judgment was that the minority undercount was severe enough to require redress.

Mosbacher did not attempt to dispute the difference

Demographic Analysis of Census Undercount

Category	Census Count	Demographic Estimate	Undercount Percentage
Total	**248,709,873**	**253,394,000**	**1.8**
Male	121,239,418	124,720,000	2.8
Female	127,470,455	128,674,000	0.9
Black	**29,986,060**	**32,320,000**	**5.7**
Male	14,170,151	15,759,000	8.5
Female	15,815,909	16,561,000	3.0
Non-black	**218,723,813**	**221,074,000**	**1.3**
Male	107,069,267	108,961,000	2.0
Female	111,654,546	112,113,000	0.6

Percentage of Historical Undercounts

(As estimated by demographic analysis)

	1990	1980	1970	1960	1950	1940
Total population	1.8	1.2	2.7	3.1	4.1	5.4
Black	5.7	4.5	6.5	6.6	7.5	8.4
Non-Black	1.3	0.8	2.2	2.7	3.8	5.0

between minority and white undercounts. But he said he did not believe that adjustment was "the appropriate vehicle" for addressing that inequity.

Mosbacher's decision prompted protest from cities, big states, various spokesmen for minority groups and most Democrats.

And although Mosbacher's decision restored life to a lawsuit that had been pending in a court in New York, resolution of that suit was considered far off.

"Any adjustment now will be too late for impact on redistricting for 1992," said Jeffrey M. Wice, counsel to the Democratic State Legislative Leaders Association. "The issue of adjustment will probably not reach the Supreme Court for one or two terms."

A similar suit challenging the census of 1980 was not finally disposed of until 1987, Wice noted.

Beyond the judicial recourse, states and communities sought to increase their share of federal funds by altering the census-based formulas by which the funds were distributed. Mosbacher said the administration might support some adjustment to census figures for distributing federal dollars.

In the meantime, states and communities tried to obtain the figures Commerce would have used for an adjustment had Mosbacher ordered one. Possession of the numbers could enable states to perform their own internal census adjustment before distributing funds. Depending on their constitutions, some states could also have used adjusted numbers in their own redistricting. But the Commerce Department refused to release the figures.

In seeking those figures for his subcommittee, Sawyer gave Mosbacher a deadline of Sept. 30. On that day, Sawyer got a letter from Mosbacher reiterating the secretary's opposition to adjustment and asking why Sawyer thought the subcommittee had any use for the numbers.

"I have to ask why he does not want us to see those numbers," said Sawyer. "What is he afraid they might show?"

Mosbacher's letter said the revised numbers were only useful for redrawing district lines for congressional and legislative elections. "The department has already released the official figures intended for redistricting," Mosbacher wrote. "Release of the rejected adjusted figures would serve no useful purpose and would only confuse the public and disrupt and distort the redistricting process."

Subpoena Issued

The confrontation led Sawyer's subcommittee to issue a subpoena Nov. 19 ordering Mosbacher to release all the Census Bureau's computer tapes relating to adjustment. When Mosbacher did not comply he was ordered to appear before the subcommittee Dec. 10 and explain himself.

Mosbacher did not show up, sending a deputy who said the subcommittee's subpoena had been issued improperly. In the meantime, a court in New York had ordered a partial release of the adjustment data, and Commerce officials had offered to release half of all the data to the subcommittee if that data could be kept confidential.

On Jan. 9, Sawyer announced that he had reached an agreement with Commerce that accepted the release of half the data. Sawyer said Mosbacher had dropped his insistence on confidentiality. "With all due respect to the secretary," Sawyer said, "he was just plain wrong in trying to withhold these numbers."

COURT ACTION

A pro-adjustment lawsuit filed by New York City and 31 other plaintiffs was already pending in federal court in Brooklyn when Mosbacher refused to adjust on July 15, and fresh briefs were being filed in that case before the week was out. Suits were also filed in federal courts in Georgia and Illinois.

The New York lawsuit had begun in 1987 when the city, along with other cities, states and civil rights groups, called on the Census Bureau to plan for statistical adjustment of the 1990 census tally to account for people who were missed. The suit was suspended after the Commerce Department agreed to consider an adjustment and respond by mid-July 1991.

The federal judge in that case, Joseph M. McLaughlin, had since been elevated from the district bench to the Federal Court of Appeals for the Second Circuit (also in New York). But McLaughlin had chosen to carry the census case with him and was expected to preside over its renewal.

One of the plaintiffs' attorneys, Robert Rifkind, said: "This matter has been driving people frantic with uncertainty, so we'll be pressing the case vigorously."

Justice Department lawyers representing Mosbacher had asked McLaughlin not to hold a new trial in the New York case but to rule on the evidence and records already accumulated. Without a trial, the plaintiffs' attorneys would not be entitled to dig through the most recent Commerce and Census Bureau files and records under pretrial discovery rules.

A major focus of such digging would be to determine "how the decision not to adjust was made," said Rifkind, adding that the search would be conducted "up and down

Pennsylvania Avenue."

The governments suing along with New York to gain a correction were Chicago; Cleveland; Denver; Houston; Inglewood, Calif.; Los Angeles; New Orleans; Oakland, Calif.; Pasadena, Calif.; Philadelphia; Phoenix; San Antonio; San Francisco; Broward and Dade counties in Florida; and five states: California, Florida, New Jersey, New York and Texas. Also suing were the U.S. Conference of Mayors, the League of United Latin American Citizens, the National League of Cities, the National Association for the Advancement of Colored People and several individuals.

LEGISLATIVE ACTION

Another potential recourse for advocates for adjustment lay in legislative remedies. Among House Democrats who had proposed bills in early 1991 to force some form of undercount adjustment were Ronald D. Coleman of Texas and Mervyn M. Dymally of California.

Legislation to force retroactive adjustment of the 1990 figures was dismissed as a virtual non-starter by Speaker Thomas S. Foley, D-Wash., on Jan. 16. Foley said nothing of the sort would be signed by the president and that it was neither "a partisan issue" nor the kind of issue on which a two-thirds vote could be mustered for a veto override.

While the pro-adjustment forces were overwhelmingly Democratic, some prominent Republicans — including California Gov. Pete Wilson and House Whip Newt Gingrich of Georgia — wrote to Mosbacher to urge redress of the undercount. All the same, legislators turned instead to the problem of improving the next decennial census.

"This should never happen again," said Rep. Paul E. Kanjorski, D-Pa. "We should make adjustments so that we're closer to Ivory Soap and 99-and-44-hundredths pure."

Kanjorski was among the handful of Democrats who opposed adjustment. Most of those Democrats came from Pennsylvania or Wisconsin — the two states that would each lose a House seat (as well as substantial federal funding) if an adjustment were ordered.

"We need an independent, nonpartisan commission to advise us as to how we might get the best census at the turn of the century," said Sen. Daniel Patrick Moynihan, D-N.Y., who introduced a bill to create such a panel.

"The 1990 census proved [that] the old methods don't work," said Charles E. Schumer, D-N.Y., Moynihan's co-author in the House. "We need a blue-ribbon panel of experts."

Study Approved

Actual legislation did not move until the fall, after the House Post Office and Civil Service Subcommittee on Census and Population gave quick 4-0 approval Sept. 17 to a measure (HR 3280) to authorize an independent study of possible changes in the U.S. census.

The principal sponsor of the bill was the subcommittee's chairman, Sawyer, who said he had seen "real consensus that early planning for 2000 will improve the process."

Sawyer estimated the study would cost $1.4 million in fiscal 1992.

Ranking Republican Tom Ridge, Pa., agreed that "improvements can be made" and added that it was "time that the design of the census is reviewed." Ridge also noted that the 1992 spending bill (HR 2608) for the Commerce Department, already passed by the House and Senate, included the $1.4 million for the study.

The full committee unanimously approved, 22-0, the bill Sept. 25.

With almost no controversy, and by voice vote, the bill passed the House on Sept. 30 and the Senate on Oct. 3.

Before sending the bill to the president, however, the two chambers had to resolve a minor difference over a provision that called for improving geographic census data. The Senate wanted a more in-depth study than specified in the bill of the population, including states, areas, communities and city blocks.

The House accepted that change by voice vote on Oct. 9, paving the way for the bill to be sent to the White House.

As cleared, the bill authorized a $1.4 million study to examine whether traditional methods of census-taking — such as mailed questionnaires — were still effective and whether alternatives such as fieldworkers with hand-held computers would improve the accuracy of the population count. ■

No Progress Made on Puerto Rico Plebiscite

Congress could not untangle its own debate on a Puerto Rico's status bill in 1991 to authorize a referendum that would allow the people of that island to choose whether to remain a commonwealth, to become the 51st state or to break off as an independent country.

Although the issue was declared a priority by members of both chambers, chances for passage appeared slim from the start.

Legislation was declared dead for the year on Feb. 27 when Senate Energy Committee members voted 10-10 against an island referendum sanctioned by Congress.

BOXSCORE

➡ **Puerto Rico Plebiscite (S 244, HR 316).** The bills would have authorized an islandwide referendum to give residents the choice of statehood, commonwealth status or independence.

KEY ACTION

Feb. 27 - The **Senate** Energy Committee voted 10-10 against S 244. No further action taken.

Only a month earlier, Sen. J. Bennett Johnston, D-La., chairman of the Energy and Natural Resources Committee, had introduced a bill (S 244) Jan. 23 to allow island residents to choose their future relationship with the United States.

The House bill (HR 316) was introduced Jan. 3 by Del. Ron de Lugo, D-Virgin Islands, chairman of the House Interior Subcommittee on Insular and International Affairs, to also allow Puerto Ricans to choose their status.

The House bill broadly defined the three options, each of which would have left Congress to determine specifics after the vote, such as what the economic benefits of the chosen option would be. By contrast, the Senate version narrowly defined the three options and would have automatically put the result of the plebescite into effect.

A similar House bill was passed by voice vote on Oct. 10, 1990, but died when Johnston announced the same day that not enough time remained in the session to work out differences with the House. *(1990 Almanac, p. 424)*

House aides said it also would be difficult in 1991 to reconcile the House and the Senate bills because they were seeking to do different things. The House bill sought a referendum while the Senate bill was geared toward the implementation of a status.

Among other obstacles, congressional supporters of plebiscite legislation struggled against a ticking clock. Puerto Rico's three political parties had said a bill must be enacted by the Fourth of July recess to hold the referendum in the fall. The parties wanted to avoid a vote on status in 1992 — an islandwide election year. The issue of status was so emotional on the island that the parties feared that holding a plebiscite during a regular election would create would create a furor at the polls. The Mainland Republican Party traditionally had supported statehood for Puerto Rico. But support for the referendum faded as more Republicans realized the state of Puerto Rico would probably send a majority of Democratic members to Congress.

Senate Minority Leader Bob Dole of Kansas also had been lukewarm to the idea of statehood. Island delegatesthrew their support to Bush instead of him in the 1988 presidential campaign.

Under the Senate bill, commonwealth was described as "a unique jurisdictional status . . . like a state to the extent provided by the Tenth Amendment of the United States Constitution."

Critics said that placing Puerto Rico on the same footing constitutionally with the 50 states would effectively give the island the powers of a state while it maintained a measure of autonomy. The definition also exempted Puerto Rico from the rules governing U.S. territories that gave Congress power over them.

LEGISLATIVE ACTION

The cost of granting statehood to Puerto Rico became only one in a series of roadblocks that led to the collapse of the island status referendum bill.

Johnston pleaded with skeptical Energy and Natural Resources Committee members Feb. 20 to approve S 244.

After considerable debate , he was forced to reschedule the markup for Feb. 27 to give members a chance to resolve remaining questions about the measure.

Wendell H. Ford, D-Ky., and others expressed longstanding problems connected with the bill, including its costs, concerns about the island's lingual and cultural differences from the mainland, and the lack of an overwhelming majority of island residents who supported any one option.

Many also questioned whether Congress should become involved with the referendum at all. Leaders of the island's three political parties maintained that to make the outcome binding, Congress was required to sanction the plebiscite and agree to abide by its results.

As a compromise, Johnston had discussed offering an amendment that would release Congress from any implied "moral commitment" to act on the choice of the voters.

Under the amendment, Congress would not have to accept the outcome of a referendum. Other members of the committee and Puerto Rico's party leaders argued that such an amendment would render the bill meaningless.

Ford said he was also informed by the Senate Agriculture Committee that if Puerto Rico became a state, its nutrition aid would be doubled from $900 million to $1.8 billion.

Johnston disputed that, saying that under a funding formula in the bill, Puerto Rico would receive less nutrition assistance than other states because its per capita income was lower than that of all the 50 states.

Senate Energy Committee members voted 10-10 on Feb. 27 against S 244. The vote followed the 10-10 defeat of an amendment by Wallop that would have left it up to Puerto Rico to initiate the referendum.

Even an eleventh-hour appeal by President Bush, a longtime supporter of statehood for Puerto Rico, did not persuade Republicans on the committee to vote for the bill.

Failure of the legislation meant that a status referendum would not be held for at least two years. Members of Puerto Rico's three political parties — who had lobbied for two years for a congressional commitment for a referendum — said the plebiscite had to be held in 1991 to avoid disruption of islandwide elections in 1992.

With the Senate bill on ice, de Lugo did not attempt to push through House legislation (HR 316) that had broader definitions on the three status options. He acknowledged that the bill lacked key Republican support in the House. Puerto Rico's representative in Congress, Resident Commissioner Jaime B. Fuster, an Interior committee member who belonged to the island's Popular Democratic Party, said he believed status legislation for Puerto Rico was dead for the session.

The vote was evidence, he said, that senators would not agree on a bill this Congress. "There is such a deep split."

Surprise Vote

Despite the overwhelming objections to many of the bill's provisions — especially those dealing with the cost of statehood — some members, including Johnston, expressed surprise that the measure was defeated. Some lawmakers and staff said they expected Johnston to postpone the markup if he knew he did not have the votes needed to approve the legislation.

But Johnston said, "I didn't know I didn't have the votes."

Among the stronger supporters of the bill were Democrats Dale Bumpers of Arkansas and Bill Bradley of New Jersey. Only two Republicans, Pete V. Domenici of New Mexico and Mark O. Hatfield of Oregon, voted for the measure. Domenici said he did so with reservations. Votes against the bill included Republicans Wallop and Don Nickles of Oklahoma. Three Democrats — Richard C. Shelby of Alabama, Kent Conrad of North Dakota and Wendell H. Ford of Kentucky — voted against the bill.

According to José Berrocal, counsel to Puerto Rico Gov. Rafael Hernández Colón, who supported the commonwealth option, Johnston was assured of at least seven votes the night before the markup, and members were still being courted.

"They were doing deals this morning," Berrocal said.

Although the vote meant that the commonwealth party won another round in its ongoing battle against the competing statehood movement, Berrocal said island residents should be allowed to vote. Puerto Rico would remain a commonwealth until a plebescite was held.

"I would not call this a victory for commonwealth," he said. "I would call this a defeat of the process."

Bush, in a letter to Johnston dated Feb. 26, had urged the committee to vote for S 244 to authorize the referendum for this fall.

"If we do not act now to resolve this question," the letter said, "it will call into question whether we truly believe in self-determination for 3.6 million of our fellow citizens, many of whom have fought America's wars of this century and are fighting today." ■

Veto Threat Thwarted Hatch Act Revisions

Congress took no action on legislation (S 914, HR 20) to ease restrictions on the political activities of federal workers as Senate Democrats feared they lacked the needed votes to override a promised veto.

The measures sought to simplify the 1939 Hatch Act and make a distinction between political activities on the job and those on an employee's own time. "This legislation puts an end to the game of trivial confusion," said sponsor John Glenn, D-Ohio, chairman of the Senate Governmental Affairs Committee.

The nation's 3 million federal employees were constrained as well as confused by the jumble of rules that prohibited them from running for office, working on partisan campaigns or holding office in a political party.

Efforts to revise the law, which had become controversial because of the complicated language and outdated restrictions, had repeatedly been blocked. President Gerald R. Ford vetoed legislation to revise the Hatch Act in 1976. Revision efforts also fell short in the 100th Congress. *(1988 Almanac, p. 620)*

In the 101st Congress, the Senate had fallen two votes short of overriding President Bush's veto of a bill that would relax, but not repeal, the Hatch Act. The 65-35 Senate vote — 67 "ayes" were needed to achieve the two-thirds majority to override — came on the heels of a 327-93 vote in the House on June 20, 1990. All but three House Democrats and nearly half their GOP counterparts had voted to make the bill law over Bush's objections. *(1990 Almanac, p. 408)*

Before the Senate would take up a bill in 1991, Majority Leader George J. Mitchell, D-Maine, wanted assurances that Glenn had the 67 votes needed to override a veto. And Speaker Thomas S. Foley, D-Wash., who had the override votes in the House, said that that chamber would wait until the Senate approved a bill before he would take action.

Opponents said that relaxing the law would politicize civil servants and make them vulnerable to coercion. When Bush vetoed the 1990 bill, he said it would have destroyed the political neutrality of the federal work force.

When Sen. Carl A. Hatch, D-N.M. (1933-49), first advocated strict limits on political activity by federal employees 52 years earlier, it was after a Senate panel had found that political appointees in the Works Progress Administration had coerced workers into making political contributions to protect their jobs.

Provisions

S 914 and its House companion, HR 20, did not give government employees free political rein, but the legislative proposals did allow them to be politically active outside the workplace.

Permissible activities under the bills included holding office in political parties, working on campaigns and running for nonpartisan offices. The ban on running for a partisan office remained in effect under the legislation.

Another obstacle to an early passage of a Hatch Act revision bill in the 101st Congress was regulations in the works by the Office of Personnel Management that attempted to clarify the rules.

Those regulations were awaiting release, and Republicans were hopeful that they would sway some senators not to support the revision legislation.

The regulations drafted by the administration that circulated around Capitol Hill did not make wholesale changes in the Hatch Act. Instead, they allowed federal employees greater political freedom, as long as their activities were not part of an organized effort sponsored by a political party. Federal workers were allowed to solicit votes or endorse a candidate for political office only if the worker was acting independently of an organized political group. Hatch Act rules were also changed to allow workers to contribute to candidates running in partisan elections. The Office of Special Counsel, not individual federal agencies, would be charged with investigating and prosecuting allegations of Hatch Act violations.

Officials from federal unions, who had been fighting for years to change the law, called the regulations a political ploy by the administration to deter legislation. George B. Gould, chief lobbyist for the National Association of Letter Carriers, called them "downright silly." The rules, he contended, would allow federal workers "to become involved in the process only if they sat in their basement and drew up their own placards."

William V. Roth Jr. of Delaware, ranking Republican on the Governmental Affairs Committee and the most vocal opponent to Hatch Act revision, countered that most federal workers did not support easing the Hatch Act. He cited a survey released in March 1991 by the Federal Executive Institute Alumni Association that indicated that only 18.5 percent of more than 1,100 respondents wanted the law changed so that government employees could be more politically active.

Although the regulations were supposed to be issued for comment in mid-1991, by the end of the year they had not been released and some GOP staff aides said they might not be released at all. With the regulations in limbo, Glenn scheduled a markup of S 914 for early 1992. ■

Workers Remained Caught in Ethics Net

Legislation to change a provision in the 1989 Ethics Reform Act that banned federal workers from accepting honoraria passed the House in 1991 but got caught in a series of political battles in the Senate.

What started as a quick fix ended in obstruction and delay as members fought over a number of issues. Last-minute passage of HR 3341 in the House did not create enough momentum to bring a related version to the Senate floor, even though support for lifting the ban was widespread and bipartisan.

Background

As of Jan. 1, 1991, the effective date of the 1989 Ethics Reform Act (PL 101-194), all federal employees except senators and Senate staff members were prohibited from accepting writing and speaking fees, even on topics that are unrelated to their work and presented to audiences with no knowledge of the writers' or speakers' official duties.

Violations of the ban carried a civil penalty of up to $10,000 or the amount of the honoraria, whichever was higher.

When the 1989 law was passed, the House accepted the honoraria ban for itself and House staff in exchange for a salary increase of nearly 40 percent by 1991.

Rank-and-file federal employees, however, were saddled with the ban without the compensatory pay raise. *(1989 Almanac, p. 51)*

Members did not realize they had caught federal workers in the ethics net until outraged constituents contacted them.

"This is wacky," said Rep. Barney Frank, D-Mass. "We never realized we had picked up this honoraria ban" for the civil servant pursuing a hobby or moonlighting. "No one had alleged any pattern of abuse here."

BOXSCORE

➡ **Honoraria Ban (S 242, HR 3341, formerly HR 325).** The bills sought to amend the 1989 Ethics Reform Act (PL 101-194) by lifting the honoraria ban on most rank-and-file federal workers.

Reports: S Rept 102-29, H Rept 102-385.

KEY ACTION

Feb. 27 — S 242 approved by the **Senate** Governmental Affairs Committee by voice vote.

Feb. 27 — HR 325 approved by the **House** Judiciary Subcommittee on Administrative Law by voice vote.

Sept. 12 — A clean bill was approved by the **House** Judiciary Subcommittee on Administrative Law by voice vote for introduction in lieu of HR 325.

Nov. 25 — HR 3341 passed by the **House** by voice vote.

The ban was decidedly uneven, prohibiting fees only for certain kinds of writing and speaking.

For example, a federal employee could work as a horticulturalist and be paid for growing roses in his spare time, but he could not deliver a lecture to the local garden club for a fee.

A worker could teach a full-semester class at a college or university on his own time but could not make a single paid speech on the same campus.

An amendment to an unrelated bill (HR 2431) passed by the Senate on Oct. 26, 1990, might have eased the ban for rank-and-file workers before it became effective.

However, that effort failed when House Judiciary Chairman Jack Brooks, D-Texas, refused to clear any bill that did not also lift the ban for higher-level employees. *(1990 Almanac, p. 74)*

The New Legislation

On Jan. 3, Frank introduced legislation (HR 325) to overturn the ban for all federal employees except those requiring Senate confirmation.

A slightly different bill (S 242) was introduced Jan. 22 by Sens. John Glenn, D-Ohio, and William V. Roth Jr., R-Del., chairman and ranking member, respectively, of the Senate Governmental Affairs Committee.

It exempted all workers whose annual rate of basic pay was less than that of a GS-16 — about $60,000 to $70,000.

Both bills stipulated that federal employees could not use government time or resources for outside activities and had to meet certain conditions before honoraria would be permitted.

Both also set the maximum for any speaking or writing fee at $2,000, and made repeal of the ban retroactive to Jan. 1, 1991.

In addition, both bills prohibited employees from

speaking or writing about subjects related to their official duties.

COMMITTEE ACTION

The Senate Governmental Affairs Committee approved S 242 by voice vote on Feb. 27.

An hour later, the House Judiciary Administrative Law and Governmental Relations Subcommittee approved an amended version of HR 325 that closely resembled the Senate bill.

HR 325, as introduced by subcommittee Chairman Frank, exempted all civil servants except members of Congress and presidential appointees who required Senate confirmation.

At the markup, Frank offered an amendment to extend the ban to presidential appointees who did not require Senate confirmation (58 positions).

Frank suggested that the ethics law was primarily intended to clean up the image of Congress. "Some of our colleagues were accepting honoraria for articles they had not read, much less written," Frank said.

He termed the ban for non-elected federal officials an "unnecessary and unfair restriction" on people against whom "there has been no allegation of abuse."

Frank's almost total reversal of the ban enjoyed the support of full committee Chairman Brooks.

But the subcommittee's ranking member, George W. Gekas, R-Pa., offered an amendment to maintain the ban for senior executives and other upper-level workers, saying that the ban "should apply to the so-called decision-making cadre of federal employees" only. The Gekas proposal, like the Senate bill, allowed employees below the GS-16 level to accept honoraria. The amendment prevailed on a 5-3 vote.

But that measure was never sent on to the full committee because of Frank's opposition to the Gekas language.

Instead, with the backing of Brooks, Frank worked out a compromise with Gekas to ban honoraria for non-career employees at a salary level above $101,300.

On Sept. 12, the Subcommittee on Administrative Law and Governmental Relations by 8-0 approved a clean bill incorporating the compromise.

The measure included provisions that required federal workers above the GS-15 level to report honoraria to their agency's ethics official before accepting the payment.

Revolving Door Amendment

The subcommittee tackled another sticky problem in the ethics law in an amendment that relaxed the so-called revolving door policy — rules that prohibited former senior government officials from lobbying former co-workers for one year after they left office.

Republican National Committee Chairman Clayton Yeutter brought the issue into the spotlight when he left his job as Agriculture secretary in January to head the RNC, only to find that he could not lobby most senior White House officials, including the president.

Responding to Yeutter's plight, the administration on July 26 asked Congress to exempt former government officials (including former members of Congress and their staff) who lobbied in behalf of political candidates or parties.

Although the proposal originated with the administration, it had broad support in both parties.

House Judiciary Markup

After the second subcommittee markup, a clean bill, HR 3341, was introduced on Sept. 16 by Frank and approved by the full committee by voice vote Oct. 29.

Brooks was unhappy that close to 100 senior House staff members remained banned from accepting honoraria under the Franks-Gekas compromise, but he did not oppose or attempt to amend the bill at the markup.

The committee approved an amendment offered by Frank to change Federal Election Commission regulations requiring campaign workers who temporarily paid incidental expenses to declare such expenses as campaign contributions, even if the worker was reimbursed. For example, if a worker paid for office supplies and was later reimbursed, that payment was to be treated as a campaign contribution.

Under the amendment, such payments would not be considered contributions so long as reimbursement took place within 60 days.

HOUSE FLOOR ACTION

On Nov. 25, with only a handful of members in attendance, the House passed HR 3341 by voice vote after less than five minutes of debate. That brought an angry protest from an opponent of the bill, Paul E. Kanjorski, D-Pa., who complained that members had not been alerted that the bill would be considered.

Kanjorski opposed the measure because he wanted a cap placed on the total amount of honoraria that could be earned. He had also proposed toughening reporting requirements.

Frank responded that he had given adequate notice and that he was unaware that Kanjorski wanted to be personally notified that the bill would come to the floor.

SUBSEQUENT SENATE ACTION

In the Senate, although S 242 had been approved by the Governmental Affairs Committee on Feb. 27, Christopher J. Dodd, D-Conn., put a hold on the measure in an attempt to pressure senators into accepting a ban on honoraria for themselves and their staffs.

Dodd had introduced a bill (S 469) to bring senators within the scope of the honoraria ban and had announced his intention to attach it to S 242.

Senate Majority Leader George J. Mitchell, D-Maine, while expressing his support for a ban on Senate honoraria, said it "should be at the same time accompanied by a corresponding increase in compensation to offset the loss of income from honoraria."

The Senate finally passed an honoraria ban and a pay raise July 17 as part of the legislative spending bill (PL 102-90). President Bush signed it on Aug. 14. *(Pay raise, p. 22)*

Dodd, having won his honoraria ban for senators, removed his hold on S 242.

But the bill still faced opposition from Robert C. Byrd, D-W.Va., the powerful chairman of the Appropriations Committee.

Byrd opposed provisions in both the Senate and House measures that would have allowed all but a small number of higher-level congressional staff to accept honoraria. He did not want to relax the ban for Senate staff so soon after passage of the pay raise and new ethics rules.

As the session entered its final days, another obstacle

developed. The Senate Democratic leadership decided it might use S 242 to pressure the administration to accept new presidential campaign finance proposals that the White House opposed.

Democratic leaders knew that the administration wanted quick passage of the revolving door provisions included in the House bill, both to help Yeutter and to smooth the way for other administration officials who might shift to the Bush re-election campaign in 1992.

But the White House did not want those provisions badly enough to accept Democratic-backed legislation (HR 3750, S 3) that sought to overturn the rules by which presidential campaign matching funds collected through the $1 taxpayer checkoff were to be distributed in 1992.

Because the checkoff fund was facing a shortfall, the Treasury Department planned to set aside the funding needed for the two party conventions and the general election before allocating any money for the primaries. Only the dollar amount in the checkoff fund as of Dec. 31, 1991, would be available to match private funds raised by primary candidates.

Democrats claimed that this system favored Bush, because only he had raised enough money to qualify at the start of the year for his full matching allotment.

The fund was not large enough to meet all its potential obligations, forcing Democratic candidates to borrow against the promise of future payment. *(Campaign financing, p. 13)* ■

Government Operations Bills Considered in 1991

The committees charged with overseeing the day-to-day operations of the federal government and its 3 million workers — House Government Operations, House Post Office and Civil Service, Senate Governmental Affairs — considered numerous bills during the first session of the 102nd Congress. Those included:

GSA OVERHAUL

The groundwork was laid at the end of the first session for the consideration of sweeping legislation to give Congress more oversight of the General Services Administration (GSA) — the agency responsible in 1991 for more than $10 billion in federal purchases and construction.

The House Government Operations Committee approved Nov. 13 by voice vote a bill (HR 3161, H Rept 102-364)) that sought to overhaul the management agency. A similar measure (S 1958) was introduced in the Senate that same day.

Committee Chairman John Conyers Jr., D-Mich., sponsor of HR 3161, labeled the GSA a "stealth agency" operating virtually free from accountability.

Appropriators gave the GSA $467 million for fiscal 1992 in the Treasury-Postal spending bill (HR 2622 — PL 102-141). The agency also controlled a $4 billion building fund and an equally large procurement program. *(Appropriations, p. 591)*

As a first step in seeking greater control, the House measure put the GSA on an annual authorization cycle. The Senate version called for a reauthorization of the agency every two years. The agency had a permanent authorization.

At a House hearing Oct. 29, GSA Administrator Richard Austin questioned the wisdom of altering the status quo, claiming that permanent authorization ensured that the agency's programs retained much-needed continuity.

The House bill changed the federal procurement process to require the government to emphasize purchasing commercial products rather than items that were custom-made and generally more expensive.

HR 3161 also restricted the number of senior officials at the agency who did not have significant federal service experience. The restrictions were intended to combat the reported high incidence of what Conyers had termed "inexperienced, low-level persons" in high-level positions.

The Senate version (S 1958), introduced by John Glenn, D-Ohio, chairman of the Governmental Affairs Committee, did not include the provision to require agencies to buy more commercial products.

A separate bill (S 260) passed by the Senate on Sept. 13 encouraged but did not require federal agencies to buy more commercial products. *(Off-the-shelf supplies, p. 178)*

JOB LOSS NOTIFICATION

Faced with layoffs on military bases slated for closure, the House moved quickly to approve legislation that required that federal employees be given 60 days' advance written notice before losing their jobs. But a companion measure was still awaiting Senate floor action when Congress adjourned.

The Defense Base Closure and Realignment Commission was still reviewing the initial list of bases when House members passed, by voice vote, the employee notification measure (HR 1341, H Rept 102-124) on June 24. *(Base closings, p. 427)*

The Senate Governmental Affairs Committee approved companion legislation (S 1292, S Rept 102-110), also by voice vote, on June 27.

Supporters of the bills said workers at defense bases slated to close would be among the first beneficiaries of the bill, which applied notification requirements to government agencies similar to the plant-closing notification requirements in the private sector.

"If anything, this measure is tardy in bringing the federal government in line with the requirements Congress has placed on the private sector," said Eleanor Holmes Norton, the Democratic delegate from the District of Columbia. Under existing regulations, federal agencies were required to give employees 30 days' advance written notice before terminating their jobs.

Advocates of the measure said employees needed more time to find a new job or enroll in a job training or placement program.

As passed by the House, the measure allowed the president to shorten to no less than 30 days the notification period if he determined that circumstances requiring the reduction in an agency's work force were not reasonably foreseeable.

Also, the bill did not apply if fewer than 50 employees were to be affected by a reduction in the work force.

The administration opposed the bills, saying the Office of Personnel Management was already in the process of issuing regulations similar to ones that were ordered by the legislation.

HR 1341 had been approved, 4-1, on June 5 by the House Post Office and Civil Service Subcommittee on Human Resources.

GULF WAR COMPENSATION

Legislation (HR 3209, H Rept 102-426) to compensate federal and Postal Service employees who were in the Persian Gulf War for income lost during their service was approved, 22-0, on Nov. 13 by the House Post Office and Civil Service Committee.

The bill authorized payments to make up the difference between the workers' government salaries and their military pay. The payments were to be made from funds already appropriated for federal workers' salaries.

The measure also allowed the 17,000 federal and postal employees called to active duty to make up back contributions to the Thrift Savings Plan, a federal retirement program. HR 3209 extended life and health insurance to federal employees called to active military duty for the duration of their duty instead of for one year, as provided under existing law.

ENERGY EFFICIENCY

With the federal government spending about $13 billion on energy each year, legislation (S 1040, S Rept 102-138) promoting energy efficiency governmentwide easily won broad support in the Senate Governmental Affairs Committee on June 27.

But Congress became absorbed by a major energy initiative in 1991 and S 1040 never proceeded to the floor as a separate measure. However, some of the provisions were similar to those incorporated in the broader energy bill (S 1220). *(Energy bill, p. 195)*

Committee Chairman Glenn, who sponsored the government energy bill, had predicted that if passed, S 1040 could save the federal government about $900 million per year in energy costs.

However, the bill was estimated to cost as much as $51.5 million, with $40 million of it being directed to promote the use of alternative-fuel vehicles. The remaining $11.5 million was to finance various projects over the next four fiscal years aimed at increasing energy efficiency at the departments and agencies.

Supporters said some of the costs could be absorbed into agency budgets and offset by energy savings. They also viewed the bill as key to carrying out an executive order signed by President Bush in April requiring the government to achieve a 20 percent reduction in energy usage by the year 2000.

Of all agencies, the Department of Defense consumed more energy than any other, spending $6.6 billion, or more than 75 percent of the total spent by the government for operations in 1989. Jet fuel accounted for more than half of the department's energy expenditures.

Of the civilian agencies, the Department of Energy had the highest direct-energy cost, with its nuclear research and production programs accounting for 40 percent of the nearly half billion dollars spent by the department.

The government energy management bill tackled these high costs by directing the Office of Management and Budget to establish guidelines for monitoring energy consumption at federal facilities. In addition, the General Services Administration was required to identify and promote the use of energy-efficient products and services as well as train employees in energy and conservation planning. Federal agencies and workers were to be offered monetary incentives for significant reductions of energy use at their facilities.

FIRE ADMINISTRATION

The House on June 3 overwhelmingly passed, 326-5, a bill that authorized spending $25.6 million in fiscal 1992 for the U.S. Fire Administration, an arm of the Federal Emergency Management Agency, to combat and reduce the risk of fires. *(Vote 123, p. 30-H)*

The bill (HR 2042) reauthorized the Federal Fire Prevention and Control Act of 1974. It directed the federal agency to focus its resources on fire prevention for residential areas and for those most vulnerable: the very young, the elderly, and those living in rural areas and inner cities that were hardest hit by fire.

PERFORMANCE STANDARDS

Congress cleared legislation (HR 1316, H Rept 102-20) March 19 that modified the performance system used by the federal government to evaluate and compensate employees. It was signed by President Bush on March 28 (PL 102-22).

The bill removed the requirement that federal employees who were rated "outstanding" were to receive a bonus of at least 2 percent.

The bill also called for the director of the Office of Personnel Management to appoint a committee to advise OPM of further improvements needed in the Performance Management and Recognition System (PMRS), the criteria federal supervisors used to grade employees.

Authorization of the PMRS system expired March 31. The bill extended authorization until Sept. 30, 1993.

OPM supported the bill, and, according to the Congressional Budget Office, changes did not mean any additional costs to federal agencies over what they had appropriated for fiscal 1991.

The House Post Office and Civil Service Committee had given voice vote approval March 13 of the legislation. Both chambers passed the bill March 19, also by voice vote. ■

Congress and the District of Columbia

In its relationship with Congress, 1991 was a good year for the District of Columbia government. The new administration of Mayor Sharon Pratt Kelly gave the federal city greater credibility on Capitol Hill, which responded by generously aiding the District with its financial troubles.

During her dark horse mayoral campaign in 1990, Kelly was a harsh critic of former Mayor Marion S. Barry Jr. and was the first candidate to call for Barry's resignation. Barry's arrest Jan. 18, 1990, on cocaine charges had badly deteriorated the already strained relations between his administration and Congress. *(1990 Almanac, p. 428)*

The former mayor began serving a six-month jail term on Oct. 26.

Soon after Kelly swept into the job in January with her "clean house" style, lawmakers gave the city, after strong lobbying by the new mayor and new D.C. Del. Eleanor Holmes Norton, a Democrat, a $100 million supplemental appropriation for fiscal 1991.

Congress also approved a record $630.5 million federal payment for fiscal 1992 for the city, up from $430.5 million in fiscal 1991. The federal payment was made to the city government to compensate for the expenses associated with hosting the federal government.

And Congress agreed to authorize a federal payment formula for the District at 24 percent of local revenues, indicating for the first time that members were willing to relinquish some control over the annual process of deciding the size of the federal payment.

The House District of Columbia Committee took that confidence in the District's ability to manage its own affairs one step further and approved a bill (HR 3581) that would remove congressional oversight of the city's own locally generated funds. The House had not acted on the bill by the end of the session.

After her successful year changing the image of the city, the mayor in December made a more personal change. On Dec. 7, she married Washington businessman James R. Kelly III and changed her name from Sharon Pratt Dixon to Sharon Pratt Kelly.

SUPPLEMENTAL FUNDING INCREASE

When lawmakers on March 22 cleared a $4.1 billion dire emergency supplemental spending bill (HR 1281 — PL 102-27) for fiscal 1991, they included $100 million for the cash-strapped District of Columbia government. *(1991 supplemental, p. 668)*

The House approved the bill on March 7; the Senate followed on March 20.

D.C. Del. Norton and Mayor Kelly had steadily lobbied members of both houses for weeks before the votes, attempting to repair a tattered relationship with Congress.

Lawmakers had few kind words for the District during the administration of former Mayor Barry, who was arrested and convicted of cocaine possession in 1990.

Although Democrats, both Barry and former Del. Walter E. Fauntroy were viewed as ineffective in winning significant support for the District from members of Congress.

By contrast, Kelly, former treasurer for the Democratic National Committee (DNC), and Norton, former head of the Equal Employment Opportunity Commission, knew their way around the Capitol and were at home with the brand of political horse-trading unique to Congress.

While both women won votes in campaigns in 1990 that portrayed them correctly as outsiders in city politics, nationally, both were the Democratic Party's own.

Lawmakers said that the willingness of the District's new representatives to work with Congress signaled the beginning of a new relationship with the city.

Before approving HR 1281, Senate Appropriations Committee Chairman Robert C. Byrd, D-W.Va., commended Kelly for her efforts. "I have been very much impressed with this new mayor.... She's taken some bold action," Byrd said, referring to Kelly's proposals for cutting the city budget and deferring pay raises.

Byrd was instrumental in the appropriation of an additional $3.5 million to aid law enforcement in the District, which added responsibilities stemming from the Persian Gulf War and the threat of terrorist attacks. *(Gulf war, p. 437)*

"I think there is a new atmosphere," said Sen. Barbara A. Mikulski, D-Md., another member of the Appropriations Committee.

Mikulski noted that Norton had attended the committee meeting, creating an immediate contrast with Fauntroy, who was widely criticized for absences when District business was under consideration.

No Vote To Trade

Approval of the supplemental money indicated that Appropriations Committee members in both chambers opted to put aside the interests of their own constituents in favor of the District, a city with no vote to trade — a rare event in Congress.

Kelly and Norton said that members were compelled by their arguments and those of their powerful champions in both houses, including Byrd and Mikulski. However, the two also acknowledged that without friends among the Democratic leadership in both the House and the Senate and an understanding of the congressional process, the effort would likely have been defeated.

With the city facing a $316 million deficit and consideration of the supplemental looming, Norton said, her knowledge had to be put to use as soon as she took office.

Kelly and Norton wasted no time contacting their old friends and acquaintances, including "so many Democrats I've known for years and years," Kelly said.

In addition to handling the finances for the DNC, Kelly also raised funds for the organization and its candidates.

House District of Columbia Appropriations Subcommittee Chairman Julian C. Dixon, D-Calif., said that before the mayor took office, she visited him to discuss the city's financial problems.

Dixon said he advised her that she would have no chance of securing the money unless she could demonstrate a good-faith effort to make substantial cuts on her own.

After taking office, she developed a budget plan that called for $2 in cuts for every $1 the District would receive from Congress, including $137 million in cuts in fiscal 1991 alone.

The mayor did not limit her lobbying to Democratic friends.

Shortly after her election, she was invited to the White House for a meeting with President Bush.

On Feb. 4, Bush proposed an increase of $53.5 million in the annual federal payment to the District in lieu of taxes for the use of District land. While some said that much of the proposed increase was offset by hidden cuts elsewhere, the gesture was seen as a thaw in relations between the administration and the city government. *(Bush budget, p. 55)*

Norton Lobbies House

Norton visited House Appropriations Committee Chairman Jamie L. Whitten, D-Miss., as did subcommittee Chairman Dixon, in behalf of the District.

Julian Dixon said lawmakers also noticed that, like members of delegations from the 50 states, Norton and the mayor worked together to win dollars for the District, another contrast with Barry and Fauntroy.

"They did not work well as a team," Dixon said of the two men.

Norton and Mayor Kelly said they believed that if members of Congress had understood the city's problems, they would have been more inclined to help long before now.

"People have not always fully appreciated that 50 percent of the property was beyond our tax reach," Mayor Kelly said.

The city also received no tax dollars from the many embassies located in the city and had not been allowed to levy a commuter tax on thousands of Maryland and Virginia residents who worked in the city.

"Yet at the same time we continue to have all the responsibilities of the federal city in terms of police protection in demonstrations, police protection of embassies," Mayor Kelly said.

FUNDING FORMULA SUCCESS

Another show of congressional support for the new District of Columbia mayor came on Aug. 2, when the Senate cleared a measure (HR 2123 — PL 102-102) that established a formula for determining the annual federal payment to the city. The president signed the bill Aug. 17.

Congressional support for the measure marked a major victory for Kelly in her efforts to garner a long-term and predictable increase in federal financial support.

The legislation only authorized a larger federal contribution — it did not guarantee it. City supporters still had to persuade Congress to appropriate the funds, and with strict limits on federal spending approved by Congress in 1990, that meant shifting money from other domestic programs.

The funding formula bill was expected to help direct future appropriations battles by setting the annual federal payment to the city at 24 percent of locally generated revenue for fiscal 1993-95. HR 2123 authorized a $630 million federal payment for fiscal 1992, a $99.5 million increase over fiscal 1991 and $150 million more than President Bush had proposed.

Each year's authorization was to be calculated on revenues raised two years before. The fiscal 1993 authorization, for example, was based on local revenues for fiscal 1991. This was to reduce any temptation on the part of the District government to hike service fees and taxes for a quick fix to fiscal woes on the theory that the more the city raised in taxes, the more it would receive from the federal government.

Democrats on the House District of Columbia Committee had originally planned to ask Congress for a 30 percent formula, as had been recommended by a commission led by former Congressional Budget Office Director Alice M. Rivlin, but settled on 24 percent to ensure Republican support.

D.C. Committee Vote

The 10-2 bipartisan vote by the House District of Columbia Committee on April 30 on the funding formula demonstrated members' confidence in the new mayor's ability to make the city solvent.

"This is a historic day," said Del. Norton. "This is a day District residents have been waiting for for many years."

Thomas J. Bliley Jr., Va., the committee's ranking Republican and a cosponsor of the bill, said, "This mayor is doing a great job. She's forthright and has lived up to everything she's said she's going to do. Congress appreciates this, and I fully expect Congress to meet her more than halfway."

In 1990, a bill (HR 5760) containing a provision setting the federal payment to the city at 19.5 percent of local revenues cleared the House District of Columbia Committee but, lacking bipartisan support, was never considered by the full House.

Even those who voted against the bill, Larry Combest, R-Texas, and Dana Rohrabacher, R-Calif., said they were pleased with Kelly's performance and supported a formula-based payment.

The committee vote in 1990 on HR 5760 was 9-3, with the three opponents being Combest, Rohrabacher and former Rep. Stan Parris, Va. As former ranking Republican on the panel, Parris vociferously criticized increased federal funding for the District and was considered influential because of the proximity of his constituency to the city.

Rohrabacher, a critic of the Barry administration, said, "This new administration is light years ahead of the previous one, and I believe we should recognize this.... However, when we are facing a $350 billion [federal] deficit, we cannot give even the most beloved and deserving federal programs as much as we would like."

Before reporting the bill, the committee defeated, 2-10, an amendment by Rohrabacher that would have authorized $596 million in funds in fiscal 1992 and set the annual payment at 22 percent of locally generated revenue.

At the time, city administrators could only guess the size of the payment, appropriated by Congress annually to offset the taxing restrictions and other costs of hosting the nation's capital.

The federal government owned 42 percent of District property, which the city could not tax. More than 60 percent of jobs in the District were filled by non-residents, which meant the city could not tax their income.

The city's federal payment had not increased in the prior four years, and federal aid to the District had shrunk from 30 percent of local tax revenue when the city received home rule in 1973 to 14.5 percent in 1991.

"The fact is, in the last five or so years, the District has taken in the neighborhood of a 25 percent cut because there was no increase in the federal payment," Norton said.

House Passage

House passage June 11 of HR 2123, approved by voice vote, provided another illustration of the bipartisan congressional support for the new mayor and eagerness to help restore the battered reputation of the city government.

"This is something we've struggled for for the last 20 years," said District of Columbia Committee Chairman

Ronald V. Dellums, D-Calif.

Meanwhile, the House District of Columbia Appropriations Subcommittee voted June 13 to increase the federal payment to the city for the first time in five years.

By voice vote, the subcommittee approved $695.8 million for the District government, a $44.5 million increase over the fiscal 1991 allocation of $651.3 million. The 1991 figure included the $100 million added in the supplemental appropriations bill (HR 1281) approved by the House on March 22. *(Appropriations, p. 616)*

Members of both parties praised Kelly, who watched from the House gallery, as well as Del. Norton.

Steny H. Hoyer, D-Md., said that Norton "has a debility that we do not have. She cannot vote. That is unfortunate. That, perhaps, is clearly the next step we ought to take."

On May 29, Norton introduced legislation (HR 2482) to create the "State of New Columbia." The House District of Columbia Committee held hearings on the bill in the fall of 1991.

Although statehood remained a controversial issue, the payment formula bill was given a significant boost when both Democratic and Republican House leaders circulated letters praising Kelly and endorsing the measure.

Confusion in Senate

The Senate Governmental Affairs Committee never acted on HR 2123 and sent it directly to the Senate floor.

On Aug. 2, the final day of legislative action before Congress left for its summer recess, last-minute confusion over the administration's position on the funding formula measure nearly stalled the bill.

During the week of July 29, administration officials had expressed their opposition to the measure in conversations with Republican Senate Governmental Affairs staff members.

Consequently, William V. Roth Jr., Del., ranking Republican on the panel, put a hold on sending the measure to the floor.

Hearing that the authorization measure was bottled up in committee, Mayor Kelly called the White House. The mayor was told there was some confusion at the Office of Management and Budget and that the bill should not have been held up, according to an aide.

President Bush called Roth on Aug. 2 and asked him to allow the measure to go to the floor, where it was cleared by voice vote.

BUDGET AUTONOMY

In November, Congressional Democrats gave another strong indication that they had new confidence in the District of Columbia government's ability to manage its affairs.

The House District of Columbia Committee on Nov. 19 approved a bill (HR 3581), on a straight party-line vote of 7-4, that would give the District government more budget autonomy.

Besides removing locally raised funds from the lengthy appropriations process, HR 3581 proposed to waive the congressional review period for laws passed by the District's City Council and signed by the mayor.

Mayor Kelly told the committee that it was extremely difficult to govern efficiently under a 15-month budget process that she called "unnecessarily cumbersome."

"When you look at this process, it is clear that the District of Columbia's budget faces — on a dollar-for-dollar basis — more scrutiny than that of the Pentagon," she said.

But panel Republicans argued that Congress had a constitutional responsibility to oversee city affairs.

Virginia Republican Bliley, the committee's ranking minority member, said that Congress should wait to see whether Kelly can put the city on a sounder financial basis before providing more autonomy.

But committee Chairman Dellums called such concerns "patronizing and paternalistic."

Assault Weapons Liability

On Nov. 21, the committee again proved its support of local rule when it rejected, 4-7, a measure (HR 3712)that would have repealed a 1990 D.C. Council act to make assault-weapons manufacturers liable for injuries from the guns.

District voters on Nov. 5 had approved, by 77 percent, a referendum endorsing the 1990 council law. The law was in the process of being repealed, under pressure from federal lawmakers, when the referendum was held.

Bill sponsors Rohrabacher and Combest argued that it was unconstitutional for District residents to approve a law that would affect companies outside of the city's jurisdiction and that the law would make gun manufacturers reluctant to supply weapons to D.C. law enforcement agencies.

That argument was backed up by representatives of gun manufacturers and suppliers who told the committee that they would stop supplying guns to the D.C. Metropolitan Police and federal agencies because of the liability risk imposed by the act.

But those testifying in favor of not overturning the referendum said Congress should not go against residents' wishes.

"Those who oppose the will of the people must live where we live and experience what we experience before they choose bullets over bodies and weaponry over humanity," said the Rev. H. Beecher Hicks Jr., Metropolitan Baptist Church senior minister and a leader of the move to pass the referendum. ■

Chapter 4

ENERGY/ ENVIRONMENT/ SCIENCE

ANWR Drilling Kills Energy Bill

Fierce debate over Arctic exploration, fuel efficiency holds up J. Bennett Johnston's sweeping package

In the opening days of the 102nd Congress, the oil jitters surrounding the Persian Gulf War appeared to have created an inexorable push for new energy legislation. Many Democrats insisted that American soldiers were being sent to defend a national policy of oil gluttony and demanded strong new conservation and efficiency programs. Other lawmakers called for new assistance to domestic energy producers.

Legislators were alarmed that U.S. oil imports had climbed to account for roughly half of the nation's oil consumption, and threatened to grow larger still.

But those concerns and sensibilities receded following the rapid conclusion of the gulf war. And as they did, traditional conflicts and inertia on energy issues re-emerged to dampen the push for new legislation.

Energy bills did move in both chambers but failed to reach the floor in either.

In the Senate, Louisiana Democrat J. Bennett Johnston crafted a sweeping energy bill (S 1220, S Rept 102-72) and raced it through his Energy and Natural Resources Committee. Despite strong opposition from environmental groups, the committee approved the bill 17-3 on May 23.

But critics were able to slow the bill's progress; several junior Democrats announced plans to filibuster because of the bill's provision to open the Arctic National Wildlife Refuge to oil and gas drilling, and their opposition helped dissuade Majority Leader George J. Mitchell, D-Maine, from scheduling a floor vote on the measure until late fall.

When it did come up in the closing days of the session, senators refused to even debate it. On Nov. 1, they voted 50-44 to cut off a filibuster on the motion to take up the bill, 10 votes short of the 60 needed. *(Vote 242, p. 32-S)*

Although many senators predicted that some version of the energy bill would return early in 1992, the vote did reveal daunting divisions on energy policy and threatened the prospects for a major rewrite of federal energy policy.

A parallel House energy bill proceeded on a slower but less controversial course in 1991.

Rep. Philip R. Sharp, D-Ind., drafted a wide-ranging energy bill in his Energy and Commerce Subcommittee on Energy and Power over the summer and fall. The final version (HR 776) was approved 21-1 on Oct. 31.

BOXSCORE

➨ **National Energy Strategy. (S 1220, formerly S 341, and HR 776)** The sweeping bills included measures to increase domestic energy production and limit oil consumption. S 1220 would have opened Alaska's Arctic National Wildlife Refuge to oil and gas drilling and directed the Transportation secretary to consider raising federal gas mileage standards. Other provisions sought to streamline licensing for nuclear power plants, natural gas pipelines and hydroelectric projects, to promote non-gasoline transportation fuels and energy-efficiency technologies, and to overhaul the Depression-era law regulating electric utilities.

Reports: S Rept 102-72.

KEY ACTION

May 23 — S 1220 passed the **Senate** Energy and Natural Resources Committee, 17-3.

Nov. 1 — The **Senate** voted 50-44 to cut off debate on the motion to proceed on S 1220, 10 votes short of the 60 required to invoke cloture.

Sharp's bill included many components found in the Senate bill but generally gave greater weight to the concerns of environmental and consumer groups. His bill sidestepped the controversial issue of gas mileage standards, and was silent on the matter of drilling in the Alaska wilderness — an issue that fell to the jurisdiction of the Merchant Marine and Fisheries Committee.

At the close of 1991, Sharp's bill was on target to go to the full committee early in 1992. But there were risks that it would bog down there in election-year politics and a fight over whether to add higher gas mileage standards.

On the Crest of a Crisis

Johnston's bill marked the first time in more than a decade that Congress had undertaken the difficult business of writing serious energy policy.

Ambitious legislative proposals on energy have typically followed a crisis, such as the 1973 Arab oil embargo, that frightens lawmakers into activity, if not always into action.

It was the oil embargo and 1979 oil shortfalls that prodded Congress to adopt dramatic new energy policies proposed by President Jimmy Carter. The 1980 Energy Security Act established a massive federal synthetic fuels project to encourage production of non-gasoline fuels. *(1980 Almanac, p. 477)*

But the synfuels corporation became a huge pork barrel program that absorbed billions of dollars before being dismantled in the mid-1980s amid fierce criticisms. Lawmakers also became disillusioned with other pieces of their energy handiwork and spent much of the 1980s undoing previous regulations, such as natural gas controls.

The oil price shocks following Iraq's invasion of Kuwait triggered a new round of congressional concern, and also the customary disputes over whether to emphasize production incentives or consumption penalties.

That split affected debate not only on whether to open the Arctic refuge and coastal areas to drilling but also on issues of siting gas and oil pipelines or building hydroelectric plants. While the war strengthened the case for the pro-production arguments, many lawmakers remained skeptical that it had fundamentally altered the political strength of the pro-environment forces.

Many Democrats joined with environmentalists in blaming the administration for lacking a policy to curb oil imports. But they had trouble uniting behind a new energy proposal.

While some Democrats saw substantive merit in a conservation-based energy policy, its political benefits were less apparent. Such a bill would have come at great cost within Congress, facing a near-certain presidential veto and providing dubious political gain: Environmental groups were unlikely to throw their support to Republican candidates, whose party had produced the policies they so despised.

Nor were Democrats of one mind on energy policy. Some members from oil- and gas-producing states backed tax breaks and other incentives to boost production. And many Democrats appeared unwilling to assume the political risk of advocating major energy taxes to boost prices, a step many experts said was the essential appetite suppressant for America's oil gluttony.

For example, although U.S. gas prices remained far below those of Western Europe, members in 1990 fought bitterly over increasing the federal gas tax by 5 cents a gallon. Analysts said it would take a far larger boost to deter consumption significantly.

Nevertheless, the war did provide Congress with a powerful reminder of the geopolitical costs of U.S. oil imports. And even as that crisis receded during 1991, lawmakers fretted about the sustained drag on the nation's balance of trade from imported oil.

Ongoing concern about global warming also argued for new energy policies, giving strength to calls for greater conservation and, in some minds, for more nuclear power.

And there were institutional pressures to move: Throughout the years in which Congress did not address energy planning, members had stockpiled energy-related proposals. Many of the energy measures that blossomed early in the year had no direct relation to the gulf crisis, but represented a decade of pent-up legislative need.

ADMINISTRATION PROPOSAL

The administration made its opening gambit in the energy policy debate early in 1991. On Feb. 18, Energy Secretary James D. Watkins released a 214-page "National Energy Strategy" that had been 18 months in the making. Watkins had promised to base the strategy on extensive public input, and lawmakers and some lobbyists had initially looked forward to its release. But the plan bogged down in the final months when free-market advocates in the administration successfully stripped out some of the proposed mandates and incentives designed to cut oil consumption. When the final version was released, it drew quick and vehement criticism from many quarters.

The administration's plan acknowledged that there was no hope of ending the nation's strong reliance on oil imports. Instead, it laid out measures aimed at containing that dependency. They included proposals to boost domestic energy production, most notably by encouraging oil and gas drilling in Alaska's Arctic National Wildlife Refuge and in some portions of the outer continental shelf. Other production-related proposals included measures to streamline the construction and licensing of nuclear power plants and natural gas pipelines. To boost competition and supply in electricity generation, the administration proposed loosening the 1935 Public Utility Holding Company Act governing utilities.

The proposal also contained some measures aimed at cutting oil consumption, most notably mandating that private fleets buy increasing numbers of vehicles that ran on non-gasoline fuels such as methanol or natural gas.

But other mandatory conservation and efficiency proposals were watered down or deleted by free market advocates in the White House. The conservationists' top priority of strengthening gas mileage standards, known as Corporate Average Fuel Economy or CAFE, was weeded out early on. Other proposals, such as a tax credit for renewable energy production and a federal fund to pay for energy efficiency improvements by government agencies, were crossed out when the draft reached the Office of Management and Budget.

Bush won credit for producing a major energy initiative, and the proposal was warmly received by some producing groups. But environmental groups and their allies quickly jumped on the administration plan, branding it a "Drain America First" policy.

The administration plan drew criticism from other quarters as well. Some legislators said it did not provide enough incentives, such as tax breaks, for domestic oil and gas drilling.

CONGRESSIONAL MEDLEY

Congress had not tackled serious energy legislation since the oil shocks of the 1970s, and in another time a major administration energy package would have captured the floor on the issue.

But the oil price jump following the Iraqi invasion of Kuwait in August 1990 drew many eyes to the nation's oil import ledger, and the administration plan had to compete with a bevy of congressional proposals on energy policy. These bills varied considerably but generally indicated lawmakers' willingness to take more dramatic steps both in mandating conservation and encouraging production.

Senate Energy Committee Chairman Johnston was among the first to jump into the fray, unveiling his legislation (initially S 341, later amended and reported as S 1220) in early February as the administration was putting the finishing touches on its plan. Johnston's bill was cosponsored by Malcolm Wallop, R-Wyo., the ranking Republican on the Energy Committee. It sought to create a broad coalition for energy legislation by including the top priority of energy producers — access to potential oil and gas reserves in the Alaska wilderness refuge — along with a proposal to potentially increase federally mandated gas mileage standards, which was a key goal of conservationists. Johnston also proposed to pay for a host of energy conservation and research programs with federal revenues from the Alaska drilling.

But Johnston, like the administration, faced competition from proposals that ranked higher with environmental groups.

Sen. Richard H. Bryan, D-Nev., reintroduced his bill (S 279) to boost gas mileage mandates 40 percent by 2001. Environmentalists pledged to make his bill one of their top goals for the 102nd Congress and called it an essential component of any credible energy bill. *(Fuel standards, p. 199)*

In the House, Sharp signaled that he would play a leading role in shaping new energy proposals. He introduced five bills touching on energy issues such as natural gas and promised to do more in the Energy subcommittee he chaired.

But Sharp did not move immediately on that front, drawing gibes from House Republicans who presented a large energy bill (HR 1543) in March.

The GOP bill, similar to one the group had proposed in the fall of 1990, greatly resembled the administration and Johnston-Wallop proposals. But it also had features designed to please environmentalists, such as a tax credit for energy produced from renewable resources and minimum energy-efficiency standards for some products. On the production side, the GOP bill proposed new tax incentives for domestic oil and natural gas producers that were not in the White House plan.

In addition to these and other large energy bills, members submitted a flurry of one-shot proposals addressing isolated portions of the energy question.

SENATE COMMITTEE ACTION

Johnston put his Energy and Natural Resources Committee on a breakneck schedule to move his energy bill. The committee throughout March held back-to-back hearings on the Johnston-Wallop and administration energy proposals, then began intensive drafting sessions in mid-April, using the chairman's bill as its base.

The committee began revising the comprehensive energy bill the week of April 15, mindful of already fading attention to energy policy after the Persian Gulf War.

Johnston set the tone for the brisk markup schedule at the opening session April 16, when he asked members to eschew their traditional opening statements and get right to work.

He supplied Energy Department officials with a table at the front of the committee room where the markups took place.

Deputy Energy Secretary W. Henson Moore attended most of the sessions and was frequently called on to clarify administration policy or react to member proposals.

Johnston deftly steered the measure through potential stumbling blocks.

The bill was reported, 17-3, after a dramatic final markup session May 23, during which members voted to allow oil and natural gas drilling in the Arctic National Wildlife Refuge and rejected for the second time an effort to mandate automobile fuel economy.

Boosting Coal

To ensure a speedy start, Johnston began the markup with the bill's least controversial issues. Those included government support for renewable energy and energy research. In the opening week of markups, members agreed to measures to encourage renewable energy and so-called clean coal technologies and energy-related research and development programs.

The committee, which included several senators from coal-producing states, approved measures designed to boost the domestic coal industry.

During markup, Democrats Kent Conrad of North Dakota and Wendell H. Ford of Kentucky both won voice vote approval to add coal research and development programs and other industry boosts to the original draft bill.

As approved, the committee bill authorized several federal research and demonstration projects designed to promote coal, including efforts to burn coal with fewer acid emissions and to convert coal for use as a transportation fuel.

It also called for the creation of a council to promote the export of so-called clean coal technologies as well as a national clearinghouse on coal technologies.

Renewable Energy Sources

With little debate, members agreed to a range of measures to boost energy production from renewable sources, including authorizing millions in federal research to promote such energy sources as biofuels, geothermal energy, solar, photovoltaic and wind energy systems.

But there was considerable discussion of proposed changes in federal hydroelectric power regulation.

Members eventually agreed to streamline the licensing for hydroelectric plants, including federal environmental reviews, and generally eliminate federal licensing review in favor of state regulation for hydro plants producing 5 megawatts of power or less.

Freshman Democrat Paul Wellstone of Minnesota objected to the proposed changes, claiming that they would effectively gut the clean water act as it pertained to hydro projects.

The committee waved aside the bulk of his objections, but did make some changes to accommodate environmental concerns. At the urging of Bill Bradley, D-N.J., and Mark O. Hatfield, R-Ore., for example, the committee agreed to retain federal regulators' rights to review the potential impact of a hydropower project on fish and wildlife.

Wallop tried to amend the bill to loosen some of the spending authorization caps on existing hydropower projects, but his proposal failed, 8-12.

In the opening week of the markup, committee members also authorized tens of millions of dollars for research and demonstration programs related to cutting consumption of imported oil.

Johnston's bill included a healthy number of research projects, and several committee members succeeded in adding their pet projects to the list. Some of the projects targeted the energy potential from oil shale, tar sands and fusion energy, as well as boosting technologies for electric vehicles and high-efficiency heat engines.

Natural Gas Proposals

Proceeding at a frenetic pace, the committee in its first week also began work on natural gas measures, but the debate spilled into the second round of markups the week of April 22.

On the table were three natural gas proposals — the markup vehicle (S 341) written by Johnston and Wallop, the Bush administration's energy package, and an energy bill (S 741) written by committee member Tim Wirth, D-Colo. All three bills sought to promote natural gas and decrease the regulatory hurdles of licensing new gas pipelines. But members haggled over how far to go in accommodating industry desires in the face of possible environmental and consumer objections.

In the end, the committee agreed to create a streamlined licensing process for natural gas pipelines that would allow companies to build pipelines faster if they assumed greater financial risk.

However, Larry E. Craig, R-Idaho, questioned whether companies that built pipelines under those expedited conditions should have the right to seize property by eminent domain, as they did under existing procedures that included closer federal review.

Craig sought to eliminate the eminent domain provision for the fast-track licensing but was voted down, 6-13, after

Johnston insisted that pipeline builders needed the powers.

Another natural gas dispute, concerning competition between domestic and Canadian natural gas interests, also had to be settled on a roll call vote.

Wirth and Pete V. Domenici, R-N.M., had on April 18 won support for an amendment they said would block Canadian gas companies from unfairly undermining domestic producers. They complained that Canadian natural gas producers had been exploiting a regulatory loophole — which their amendment would eliminate — to undercut American gas producers.

But three wary committee members registered objections, while Energy Department officials worried that the amendment could violate the U.S.-Canadian Free Trade Agreement that took effect in 1989.

The committee returned to the issue in its April 24 markup when Bradley argued that their effort would protect domestic gas producers at the expense of consumers and would violate free-trade practices. But Bradley's move to delete the language was rejected, 7-13.

Also in that week's markups, committee members agreed to:

- Restructure the Energy Department's uranium-enrichment program into a government corporation aimed at processing uranium ore more efficiently and staving off foreign competition. Enriched uranium was sold to nuclear power plants.

  Ford had sponsored the same provisions in a separate bill (S 210), which members also sent directly to the floor.

- Encourage offshore drilling by giving states a greater portion of revenues from the oil and gas leases.

Nuclear Power

When the Senate returned from spring recess the week of May 6, Johnston could no longer postpone arguments over his bill's most nettlesome provisions. At sessions on May 8-9, members rehashed a debate over streamlining licensing for nuclear power plants, and clashed over how to promote cars that ran on fuels other than gasoline.

The nuclear power debate had begun the week of April 22, when the committee tentatively agreed to simplify licensing for nuclear power plants. The Johnston-Wallop bill proposed replacing the original two-phase process — whereby plant operators must first get a construction license, then an operating license — with a single, preconstruction license as proposed by the administration. It also sought a limit on the terms under which plant critics could gain a second hearing to challenge licensing.

Advocates of the revisions complained that anti-nuclear forces had exploited the two-step licensing process, endlessly tying up new plants with trivial or procedural objections. Opponents countered that continued full public participation was critical to exposing potential hazards and ensuring public confidence in nuclear power.

Johnston's bill originally did not go as far in helping nuclear power plant owners as did the administration's energy plan (S 570). However, Wallop won approval for an amendment that added some of the administration provisions.

As was often the case during the markups, committee newcomer Paul Wellstone was the loudest voice against the chairman and in support of a policy more to the liking of environmental groups.

At the May 8 session, Wellstone attempted to undo the committee's previous nuclear handiwork and strike the provisions to establish a one-step licensing process for nuclear power plants. But Wellstone's proposal to delete the one-step licensing from the energy bill failed, 6-14. He also failed, on a 4-13 vote, to win approval for bill language ensuring that states could regulate certain low-level radioactive waste.

Alternative Fuels

As originally drafted, Johnston's bill said relatively little about promoting cars that ran on non-gasoline fuels. However, the administration's energy strategy advocated forcing private fleets to phase in alternative-fuel vehicles, and other energy bills went further still.

At the May 9 markup, Republican Conrad Burns of Montana offered an alternative-fuels amendment based on a bill (S 716) sponsored by James M. Jeffords, R-Vt. Jeffords' proposal would have set a target goal for alternative-fuel use and required the private sector to supply those fuels.

The issue prompted heated debate, with members split over how deeply to involve the federal government in energy markets.

Johnston praised Jefford's intentions but pronounced his goals "arbitrary, unrealistic and unworkable." The chairman offered a substitute amendment directing the Energy secretary to assess the demand and supply of alternative fuels, urge suppliers to make up any shortfall and, if he found it necessary, mandate that they do so.

Johnston's proposal drew fire from both sides, with members attacking it as either inadequate or excessive.

Burns was one of several senators to argue that the alternative-fuels market could work well but needed a jump-start from the federal government. Kent Conrad, D-N.D., threatened to oppose the entire bill if it did not include aggressive provisions on alternative fuels.

But Oklahoma Republican Don Nickles saw in the same proposal unwarranted intrusions into the private sector, particularly in provisions to grant the Energy Department the power to order production of the fuels.

Nickles' effort to delete the mandatory-supply powers from the amendment failed 7-13, and Johnston's proposal was later approved by voice vote.

That outcome troubled Moore, of the Energy Department, who said the administration had chosen fleet-purchase requirements as the best way to stimulate alternative-fuel use and would not accept any other form of mandates.

That issue arose in a subsequent committee debate over Johnston's proposed requirements for public and privately owned vehicle fleets, offered as another amendment to his own bill.

Johnston advocated requiring federal agencies to phase alternative-fuel vehicles into their fleets, beginning with 10 percent of new vehicles purchased in 1995 and rising to 90 percent by 2000. The committee approved those federal fleet mandates, 15-5.

Under Johnston's related proposal, certain private and state-owned fleets would have to meet slightly less ambitious targets. After considerable debate, members eventually approved an amended version of those mandates, 14-6, at a subsequent markup.

Among the changes, Seymour won approval, 11-8, to make state-owned fleets comply with the more rigorous alternative-fuel requirements for federal fleets rather than those for private fleets, as Johnston had originally proposed.

Conservation Proposals

During the week's markups, Wirth had mixed luck with a series of amendments aimed at boosting conservation and

No Action on Fuel Efficiency Mandates

Just as oil companies saw the energy debate as an opportunity to open new areas for drilling, environmental groups perceived it as an opportunity to force automakers to build more fuel-efficient cars.

In an effort to cut oil consumption, Congress in 1975 mandated that automakers' fleets, on average, achieve certain minimum mileage standards known as Corporate Average Fuel Economy, or CAFE. Environmentalists and their allies in 1991 set out to raise that above the existing 27.5 miles per gallon standard, noting that transportation fuels accounted for a large portion of oil imports and the gasses believed to create global warming.

Their rallying point was a bill (S 279, S Rept 102-48), sponsored by Sen. Richard H. Bryan, D-Nev., to increase gas mileage mandates 40 percent by 2001. Bryan's bill easily cleared the Commerce, Science and Transportation Committee, 14-5, on March 19. But the bill went no further in 1991, becoming mired in the controversial politics of broader energy legislation. The Energy and Natural Resources Committee in May voted against including specific new mileage mandates in Sen. J. Bennett Johnston's omnibus energy bill (S 1220).

Bryan's proposal had originally been debated as part of the Clean Air Act reauthorization in the 101st Congress. Dropped from that legislation, it got a political second wind after the Iraqi invasion of Kuwait, as legislators focused on its impact on cutting oil consumption. The bill drew 57 votes in a Sept. 25 floor vote, three short of the 60 needed to avert a threatened filibuster. *(1990 Almanac, p. 279)*

Bryan returned with his bid to boost gas mileage standards early in the 102nd Congress.

The updated version of the bill had some new features, including indexing existing civil penalties to keep pace with inflation. The penalties had not been adjusted since 1975. It also proposed to give the Department of Transportation some leeway to reduce the mandates beginning in 1996, not 2001 as specified in the earlier version of the bill.

The bill lacked a previous fuel efficiency credit for manufacturers of small cars with air bags, an omission that Republican John C. Danforth of Missouri warned he might try to correct on the Senate floor.

During the Commerce Committee markup, Bryan agreed to an amendment offered by Republican Ted Stevens of Alaska that relaxed fuel standards for four-wheel-drive vehicles and vehicles used for car pools.

Another committee amendment permitted manufacturers to earn credit for exceeding mandates in one year, to be used to offset a shortfall in a subsequent year.

With those additions, Stevens voted for the bill, reversing his opposition of the previous year.

But the bill's momentum stalled soon thereafter, victim to a broader debate on energy policy. The administration had threatened to veto new mileage standards, and the Energy Committee twice rebuffed Johnston's efforts to add some to his energy bill.

In the House, the Energy and Commerce Subcommitte on Energy and Power held hearings on increasing gas mileage standards in connection with its work on energy policy but eventually approved a draft energy bill that did not address the issue.

As the Bryan bill languished on the Senate calendar, it nonetheless generated a furious lobbying campaign.

Campaigning in its behalf was a coalition of environmental and consumer groups that helped stall the broader energy bill. That network included the Sierra Club, the Union of Concerned Scientists, the National Wildlife Federation and the U.S. Public Interest Research Group.

Opposing any mandated increase was the Coalition for Vehicle Choice, a lobbying group that was created by the auto industry but which also included such groups as the American Farm Bureau Federation and the National Campground Owners Association. The United Auto Workers also opposed the Bryan measure.

Both sides inundated Capitol Hill with an array of brochures, studies and testimony. Each accused the other of distortions. Below are some of the chief arguments presented for and against new fuel efficiency mandates:

- **Oil imports.** An estimated 40 percent of oil was consumed by the transportation sector, making automobile fuel economy one of the prime arenas for gaining real cuts in oil consumption. Supporters of the Bryan bill estimated that it would save 2.5 million barrels of oil daily. But opponents said it was impossible to know what oil savings would result, since consumers might react by driving more frequently or longer distances.
- **Emissions.** Automobile tailpipes were a major source of the carbon dioxide emissions believed to help cause global warming. By reducing the amount of gas a car needed to burn, efficiency technologies could cut carbon dioxide emissions. But critics argued that there were trade offs as well; for example, they said some pollution control devices had added weight to new cars, which cut into fuel efficiency.
- **Safety.** Auto safety was the rallying cry of opponents of the Bryan bill and other proposed CAFE mandates. They argued that to meet Bryan's ambitious targets, manufacturers would have to build smaller, less safe cars. Advocates of the higher efficiency standards disputed these claims, saying smart engineering could yield better mileage without sacrificing safety.
- **Consumers.** Critics said new mileage mandates would force manufacturers to phase out some of their larger cars and light trucks to meet new fleetwide efficiency goals, thus depriving consumers of certain showroom choices and curtailing the best-selling portion of the U.S. fleets. Adding fuel efficiency and safety technologies would also drive up the price of new cars, they said. Consumers had been favoring less efficient cars and light trucks in recent years, but environmentalists maintained that Americans wanted more fuel efficient cars, provided they were well-designed, and were willing to pay more for them.
- **Big Three.** The failing economic health of the Detroit automakers had prompted some lawmakers to question whether automakers could afford heavy investments in efficiency technologies, especially for cars the public might not want. Both the auto manufacturers and the United Auto Workers lobbied against new mandates. But supporters said that this view was short-sighted and that prodding Detroit to build better cars would ultimately enhance its competitiveness.

energy efficiency.

Wirth won backing for measures to promote energy efficiency in buildings — Wallop's effort to strike the measure failed, 5-12 — and to set minimum efficiency standards for a range of appliances. But Wirth was unable to stop a Bumpers amendment to exempt the electric motors used inside many appliances; the amendment was approved 10-7.

Wirth backed off a controversial proposal to make specified industries report their energy consumption, and the committee instead gave the Energy secretary one year to recommend ways to boost industrial energy efficiency. And after agreeing to soften a directive to assess global warming, Wirth saw that section further weakened when the committee voted 12-8 for a Wallop amendment that, among other things, deleted its call for policy recommendations.

The committee the week of May 6 also voted to:

- Allow power plants to make certain modifications — such as adapting boilers to use a different fuel — without triggering strict environmental reviews for new pollution sources. Johnston tried unsuccessfully to include similar language in the 1990 Clean Air Act.

Advocates said the change would make it easier for plants to install pollution controls, but critics remained wary that it would become a loophole for avoiding clean air regulation.

- Abandon the bill's original demonstration program for a new nuclear reactor model but set a January 1996 deadline for the Energy secretary to choose a model design for a new nuclear reactor technology.

Gas Mileage Standards

During the week of May 13, the committee at last turned to the hot-button issue of federal gas mileage standards. The administration was dead-set against an increase, but environmental groups and many legislators insisted that higher standards must be part of any credible energy plan. Badly divided over how much to raise the standards, committee members ultimately voted not to increase them at all. They defeated two proposals to add specific mileage standards to the energy bill and voted to retain the original language of the Johnston bill, which called on the administration to address the issue but did not mandate any increase.

The existing Corporate Average Fuel Economy, or CAFE, standards, established by Congress in 1975, mandated that each manufacturer's fleet average 27.5 miles per gallon.

As originally written, Johnston's bill directed the secretary of Transportation to set new fuel efficiency standards for 1996 and again for 2001. But it did not include numerical targets, instead laying out guidelines under which the administration should determine a "maximum feasible" gas-mileage requirement. Critics said the language included too many loopholes and questioned whether an administration that had argued against new CAFE standards would voluntarily increase them.

Johnston acknowledged that specific targets would be needed to counter the political appeal of a fuel efficiency bill (S 279, S Rept 102-48) sponsored by Sen. Bryan, which set ambitious fuel-economy mandates for the coming decade. Bryan's bill had already been approved by the Commerce, Science and Transportation Committee 14-5 on March 19.

Johnston's Fuel Standard Compromise

On May 14, Johnston unveiled a compromise to set national mileage targets of 30.2 miles per gallon as of model year 1996, 34 mpg as of 2001 and 37 mpg as of 2006. As proposed, automakers would have to raise their fleet averages by the percentage needed to bring the nation's automobiles under compliance. The administration would retain considerable leeway to adjust those numbers.

By contrast, Bryan's targets required fleet averages of roughly 34.4 miles per gallon in 1996 and roughly 40 miles per gallon in 2001.

Johnston had hoped his new CAFE proposal would create a middle ground on the issue. Instead, he watched it come under fire from both camps. While some senators claimed that the auto industry was dragging its feet on efficiency and needed a regulatory prod, others insisted that new mandates could cripple an already ailing industry.

Several senators wanted to wait to set standards, but Johnston was determined to keep moving and called for votes. Members initially voted 15-5 on a tabling motion to kill the Bryan proposal. They then tabled Johnston's own amendment, 13-7.

But a motion to strike the original bill language on CAFE was defeated 8-12, and the language was preserved.

The tallies had a clear partisan cast. Republicans voted as a bloc for the bill's original language and against both the Bryan standard and Johnston's compromise.

Democrats divided their support between the two fixed mileage targets, and the split left the status quo intact.

Afterward, some Democrats questioned the bill's commitment to conservation, and even Johnston had doubts about its political viability. He postponed voting on the Alaska drilling in hopes of persuading some members to change their minds on CAFE. Some members, such as North Dakota's Conrad, had indicated that their drilling vote would depend on the bill's fuel economy provisions, and Johnston wanted to win strong majorities for both.

Complicated political bargaining hung over the final week of the markup. At times, senators openly alluded to trading showdown votes for provisions of their liking.

After lobbying members on the eve of the final markup, Johnston thought he might have changed some minds on his CAFE proposal. On the closing day, May 23, he pleaded for support from both parties and called for a second vote.

But senators were unmoved.

All nine committee Republicans voted against Johnston's proposal as they had the first time, reportedly after strong lobbying from the White House. And there was no movement on the left, where Democrats complained that Johnston's targets were too weak to produce significant fuel savings. Only five other Democrats supported his amendment, which failed, 6-14.

Alaska Drilling

With the possibility of a CAFE deal exhausted, Johnston was at last ready to vote on whether to permit drilling in the Arctic refuge.

The Energy Committee had approved the drilling before, and was widely expected to do so again. But this time the vote was intertwined with the politics of a broad energy package, and groups on both sides of the issue had redoubled their lobbying. While environmentalists conceded that they were short of the 11 votes needed to strike the drilling language, they wanted to make the vote as close as possible.

Johnston's bill authorized oil and natural gas drilling in the coastal plain of the Arctic National Wildlife Refuge. The bill specified that drilling be carried out in a way that did not harm fish and wildlife. It would levy a per-barrel fee on oil or gas extracted from the refuge to create a $50 million fund to restore the area's environment after drilling was complete.

The measure also required that government revenues from the oil and gas leases be split equally between the federal government and the state of Alaska, and that the federal share go to a fund for energy-related programs. However, that money could not actually be spent without the approval of the regular appropriating committees, greatly diminishing the odds that it would really be used for energy projects.

Senators took up several amendments to the drilling title the week of May 13.

Sen. Frank H. Murkowski, R-Alaska, challenged the bill's formula to split government revenues from the drilling activity evenly between the state and the federal treasury.

He unsuccessfully offered an amendment, 8-12, requiring that Alaska receive 90 percent of the revenues as it had for past drilling on federal land in the state.

But Murkowski was able to win, 12-8, backing for his amendment to remove the bill's so-called blackmail clause, which would have voided the 50/50 revenue split if the state challenged that formula in court.

When the committee took up the issue again May 23, Wirth made a final pitch against the drilling. He argued that oil from the Arctic preserve would barely dent U.S. oil dependency and was not worth destroying the irreplaceable beauty of the refuge.

But Wirth's motion to strike the drilling language failed, 8-11. Johnston and Richard C. Shelby, D-Ala., joined all nine Republicans in supporting the drilling.

Seymour, who had been considered a critical swing vote on the issue and who was seeking a drilling ban for the California coast, backed the Alaska drilling. Seymour explained that while Californians were strongly against coastal drilling in their state, many Alaskans were eager to begin oil and gas exploration in the Arctic refuge and reap its revenues.

Electric Utility Restructuring

Overshadowed by the final votes was the committee's May 21 decision to restructure the electric utility industry.

The committee-approved changes sought to loosen restrictions on who could enter the wholesale electricity business, freeing utilities and independent producers to compete to build wholesale power plants. Advocates said the move would increase competition, boosting supply and lowering prices. But critics said that, absent more stringent consumer protections, the changes would simply invite utilities to repeat the same abuses that inspired the law in the first place.

Although so-called PUHCA reform (named for the 1935 Public Utility Holding Company Act, which regulates electric utilities) had initially been considered one of the most controversial in the bill, members approved most of the proposed changes with little debate. During the weeks in which senators had haggled over other sections of the bill, committee staff had worked out arduous compromises on the terms for loosening utility regulation. Members eventually voted on a revised version of the bill's electricity regulation section that included some protections against potential consumer abuses.

Coastal Drilling Ban

The committee made two other significant changes at its final markup. It banned oil drilling off the California and New Jersey coasts until the year 2000 and dropped a de facto oil import fee.

Seymour successfully sought the California coastal drilling ban. President Bush had already declared much of the state's coast off-limits until 2000, but Seymour's amendment, approved 15-3, extended that protection to 87 tracts not covered by Bush's order. Bradley won voice vote approval to extend that protection to the New Jersey coast. But Wirth failed, on a 6-12 vote, to win the same moratorium for drilling off the Florida coast.

The committee also turned aside Johnston's revised proposal to make oil importers set aside 3 percent of their imports for the Strategic Petroleum Reserve. Johnston had called for a 9 percent set-aside in his original bill.

He said the set-aside would provide a way to bolster national petroleum reserves at a relatively small price.

But Ford led critics in arguing that it would act as a de facto oil import fee, raising prices for consumers and discriminating against refiners who used imported rather than domestic oil. Ford's tabling motion to kill the petroleum reserve set-aside passed, 10-8.

The Aftermath

Johnston's bill was the most ambitious energy legislation that had come through Congress in years, and the Louisianan disproved some skeptics by moving it through committee so quickly. But once out of the protected waters of Johnston's own panel, the bill was slowed by considerable lack of interest and outright opposition.

Johnston had hoped to get the bill to the floor in June, but found no commitment to do so in Majority Leader George J. Mitchell, D-Maine. Mitchell had cited energy policy as a Democratic priority, and appointed a Democratic task force on the issue. But he had opposed drilling in the Alaska refuge and was a cosponsor of Bryan's fuel efficiency bill — two positions that had prompted administration veto threats.

Some of the most positive reactions to the bill came from disparate points of the political spectrum.

As the bill neared committee passage, Energy's Moore praised the legislation as "the best we've seen in 20 years."

Some environmentalists were equally cheered, but for a different reason. They were optimistic that a bill they had never liked had become weak enough to die. "This is the bill that ate Bennett Johnston," said Daniel Becker of the Sierra Club. "I haven't been this happy in a while."

Environmental groups found something to dislike in almost every title. Some of their strongest objections came over proposals to aid coal and nuclear industries and to ease environmental regulation of some hydroelectric dams.

Although floor debate appeared distant, both sides waged strong publicity campaigns on the bill over the summer.

In late June, several senators staged an assault on the bill from the Senate television gallery. Eight Democratic senators were represented in person or by press release: Max Baucus of Montana, Tom Harkin of Iowa, Frank R. Lautenberg of New Jersey, Joseph I. Lieberman of Connecticut, and Howard M. Metzenbaum of Ohio, as well as Bradley, Bryan and Wellstone.

Baucus chaired a key panel of the Environment and Public Works Committee that held jurisdiction over several portions of the bill. He said he would oppose bringing it to the floor until that committee was granted referral — a notion Johnston had strongly resisted.

Johnston and Wallop waged their own press offensive to

promote the bill and criticize its attackers. They maintained that the bill provided ample conservation and efficiency measures sought by environmentalists, together with other critical provisions to cut U.S. dependence on imported oil.

On July 24, President Bush added some clout to their campaign. Appearing before a group of energy executives, Bush praised the Senate bill and urged that it go to the floor after the August recess.

HOUSE COMMITTEE ACTION

After letting the Senate take the lead on crafting energy policy, the House Energy and Commerce Subcommittee on Energy and Power in July began writing its own comprehensive bill. The panel held markups on and off throughout the summer and fall, and approved a draft bill (HR 776) 21-1 on Oct. 31. However, the bill was not acted on by the full Energy and Commerce Committee in 1991.

Summer Start

Subcommittee Chairman Sharp, a moderate who learned his way around energy policy when shepherding President Carter's energy proposals through Congress in the late 1970s, led the drafting process. Instead of working from a complete bill, as had Johnston, the panel approved pieces of the energy bill incrementally. Typically, Sharp would circulate a draft of one title several days before markup. At the end, the separate titles were rolled into one bill.

Panel members were constrained by House jurisdiction rules that made it harder for them to take on the gamut of energy proposals.

Perhaps the most controversial energy proposal — to open Alaska's Arctic National Wildlife Refuge to oil and gas drilling — was outside the House subcommittee's domain, as were tax incentives for energy production. While House leaders talked of moving those issues in other panels and linking all the energy-related bills on the House floor, only Sharp's panel began drafting its part.

Energy Efficiency

Sharp had been criticized for taking too long to start drafting an energy bill. But his preparations were evident in the subcommittee's quick approval of energy efficiency and natural gas provisions at opening markup sessions July 17 and 18. The panel voted 22-0 in favor of the energy efficiency section, which went far beyond the proposals in the administration's package.

Included in the efficiency package were provisions requiring states to upgrade building codes to improve energy efficiency. It also required mandatory efficiency standards for certain appliances and equipment, including some lamps, shower heads, electric motors, and heating and cooling equipment.

It prodded state utility regulators to adopt policies that emphasized the advantages of conservation and energy efficiency investments over building new power plants.

To cut the federal government's energy consumption, the bill required agencies to install efficiency improvements that would pay for themselves within 10 years. It also authorized a federal fund to help pay for such improvements.

Natural Gas Regulation

On natural gas, the subcommittee gave voice vote approval to a bill that dovetailed certain administration and Senate proposals. Members voted to let gas companies skip some regulatory steps and build pipelines more quickly if they assumed greater financial risk. The bill streamlined other aspects of the pipeline licensing process as well but did not go as far as the Senate bill in modifying environmental regulations.

However, the House panel took a different tack than the Senate Energy Committee on the issue of Canadian gas imports, which some lawmakers claimed enjoyed preferential treatment under existing regulations.

In the Senate committee, Wirth and Domenici added language, targeted at Canadian natural gas, requiring the administration to address the harmful effects that gas import rules might have on domestic producers.

But the House bill, approved by voice vote, specified that imports generally be treated the same as domestic natural gas. Members also added an amendment by Norman F. Lent, R-N.Y., and Edward J. Markey, D-Mass., that specifically sought to block the Senate bill's proposal affecting Canadian gas.

Strategic Petroleum Reserve

Over the strong objections of the Bush administration, the House panel on July 23 agreed to force oil importers and refiners to help fill the nation's rainy-day oil stockpile.

The mandatory set-aside program, approved on a party-line 14-8 vote, was aimed at amassing 1 billion barrels of oil in the Strategic Petroleum Reserve. The petroleum reserve is a government-controlled reservoir of crude oil stored in salt domes in Louisiana and Texas. Advocates said the diversion program would give the nation a stronger buffer against foreign oil shocks, while raising gas or heating oil prices only about a half cent per gallon.

However, the administration believed the program would amount to an unwise tax on oil and said there were better ways to fill the reserve. All eight Republicans on the Energy and Power Subcommittee voted against the proposal.

The subcommittee bill required all oil importers and domestic oil refiners to provide a percentage of their oil — about 1 percent — to fill the Strategic Petroleum Reserve. Under the proposal, companies would continue to own the oil and would be reimbursed if it was sold.

An amendment to that plan, offered by Rep. Mike Synar, D-Okla., and approved by voice vote, allowed the importers and refiners to choose to pay the government enough to cover their required contribution rather than shipping oil to the reserve.

However, members rejected two Republican amendments to weaken the diversion program: one to exempt stripper wells and heavy oil, and another to make the set-aside apply only to importers. Oil-state members complained that the set-aside could drive some domestic oil producers out of business.

Sharp's original proposals to fill the oil reserve would have demanded a 3 percent set-aside from importers only. But that proposal drew sharp objections, particularly from Northeastern representatives whose districts relied most heavily on imported oil and who feared it would drive up prices.

The revised proposal was more to the Northeasterners' liking because it treated domestic and imported oil equally and also specified that 12 percent of the diverted oil go toward filling a 50-million-barrel stockpile of refined oil products, to be located in the Northeast.

It also broadened the president's authority to sell oil

Continued on p. 205

Energy Bill Provisions

The Senate Energy and Natural Resources Committee approved the energy bill (S 1220 — S Rept 102-72) on May 23.

As reported by the panel, the measure:

Title I — Findings and Purposes

• **Global climate.** Created a director of climate protection within the Energy Department to serve as its representative for all administration work on global climate change.

• **Objectives.** Set energy objectives, including boosting domestic production and cutting consumption to slow the growth of U.S. dependence on foreign oil and eventually decrease it.

• **Energy strategy.** Required the Energy secretary to develop a least-cost national energy strategy that promoted energy efficiency and sought to limit the emission of carbon dioxide and other greenhouse gases.

• **Repeal.** Repealed a section — Title III — of the Energy Security Act, which required the Energy secretary to give Congress targets for energy consumption, production and imports.

Title II — Definitions

• Provided a brief definition of select terms used in the act.

Title III — Corporate Average Fuel Economy

• **Fuel efficiency.** Directed the Transportation secretary to set new fuel efficiency standards by July 1992, with separate standards for each automaker and class of vehicle, including cars, light trucks, and other trucks. Two standards would be set, one for 1996-2001 models and another for subsequent models, in an effort to reflect the highest feasible gas mileage. However, the Transportation secretary would be required to factor in other considerations, such as maintaining existing performance levels, selection options and safety standards, that would be likely to curtail attainable fuel efficiency increases.

• **Guzzler fee.** Increased the fee on manufacturers who did not meet mandated fuel economy standards. Revenues from the fee could be used to fund state programs to retire older, gas-guzzling cars and other efficiency programs. However, it would no longer be unlawful to fall short of the mandated gas mileage targets.

In 1991, automobile manufacturers had to meet a fixed standard of 27.5 miles a gallon. However, the Johnston-Wallop bill required that new standards be in the form of a percentage increase from manufacturers' existing fleet average, rather than a single mileage target for all carmakers. Automakers who equipped their small cars with air bags would be able to receive credit against their gas mileage minimum standards. And those who exceeded mandated mileage standards would earn a credit that could be traded among manufacturers and vehicle classes.

Title IV — Alternative Fuels

• **Alternative fuel fleets.** Mandated that government and private businesses with fleets of automobiles or trucks phase in vehicles that ran on non-gasoline fuels, such as methanol, ethanol and natural gas. Exceptions included emergency, law enforcement and rental vehicles.

Beginning in 1995, at least 10 percent of the new vehicles purchased for federal fleets would have to be capable of running on alternative fuels. That percentage would rise to 90 percent by the year 2000.

State-operated fleets would have to meet the same requirements, if the state operated at least 50 vehicles statewide and ran a fleet of 20 or more in a major urban area.

Municipal and private fleets of more than 50 vehicles — at least 20 of which were in a central, urban area — would have to purchase the alternative-fuel vehicles at a rate of 30 percent beginning in 1998, rising to 70 percent by 2000.

Eligible alternative fuels would include methanol, ethanol, alcohol mixtures with less than 15 percent gasoline, natural gas, liquefied petroleum gas, hydrogen, and coal-derived liquid fuel. Operators of diesel truck fleets could continue to use that fuel.

Electric cars would also qualify as alternative-fuel vehicles, and the bill authorized federal programs to promote electric vehicles and related services.

• **Alternative fuels.** Directed the Energy secretary to develop a plan to promote alternative transportation fuels, with a target goal of replacing 30 percent of projected petroleum-based motor fuel use by the year 2010. If the projected supply of alternative fuel threatened to fall short of demand, the Energy secretary would be directed to craft a mandatory supply plan requiring motor fuel suppliers to make up the shortfall and submit the plan to Congress.

• **Alternative-fuel transit.** Authorized $30 million a year in fiscal 1992-94 to work with local governments or transit authorities to promote alternative fuels for mass transit.

Title V — Renewable Energy

• **Promote renewable energy.** Expanded the duties of a federal working group to promote renewable energy and established a parallel group for energy efficiency. The Energy secretary would chair both groups. They would seek to promote exports of domestic products and technologies that advanced renewable energy sources and energy efficiency.

• **Authorization.** Authorized $3 million a year for fiscal 1992-94 to promote each of the following technologies: biofuels, high-temperature geothermal energy, low-temperature geothermal energy, solar water heating, photovoltaic and wind energy systems, biomass and fuel cells. The bill also allocated $6 million annually for the same three years to transfer renewable energy technologies to lesser-developed countries and $9 million for each of three years to promote a utility-scale project of photovoltaic technology.

• **Hydropower licensing.** Streamlined licensing for hydropower plants, including federal environmental reviews. The bill generally eliminated federal licensing review of hydroelectric projects of 5 megawatts or less in favor of state regulation.

• **Hawaii research center.** Established a facility at Keahole Point, Hawaii, as a cooperative research and development center on renewable energy and associated marine research, to be called the Spark M. Matsunaga Renewable Energy and Ocean Technology Center after the late Democratic senator from Hawaii. However, the bill's report language specified that the federal government would not be authorized to acquire those facilities, which were not federally owned.

Title VI — Energy Efficiency

• **Efficiency standards.** Required the Energy secretary to set minimum building efficiency standards and ensure that all new federal buildings and private buildings and residences receiving federal mortgages through agencies such as the Federal Housing Administration and Veterans Administration met those minimum standards. The bill also promoted voluntary efficiency standards for the private sector.

• **Industrial efficiency.** Funded federal research and development of technologies to cut industrial energy use.

• **Efficiency labels.** Authorized the federal government to help industry develop a voluntary efficiency labeling program for windows and lights and to establish its own mandatory program if the private sector failed to establish one within two years.

• **Appliance standards.** Authorized federal efficiency standards for certain lamps, commercial air conditioning and heating equipment and utility distribution transformers. The bill also established a federal cap on the water flow of shower heads manufactured after June 1992, unless the American National Standards Institute developed its own stricter standards.

• **Federal deadline.** Set a Jan. 1, 2000, deadline for federal agencies to install efficiency improvements that would pay for themselves within 10 years. The bill also established a $50 million federal fund to encourage agencies to undertake such energy-saving projects. The bill allowed the federal government to present bonuses of up to $5,000 to federal managers who successfully saved energy.

• **Utilities.** Required state utility commissions to consider decoupling regulation of utility profits from sales in order to promote investment in conservation. The bill also directed states to consider mandating that utilities evaluate increased energy efficiency and conservation steps as alternatives to building new power plants. It established a state grant program to encourage this so-called demand-side management.

• **Left turns.** Mandated that states allow drivers to turn left on a red light, after stopping, if they were turning from a one-way street onto a one-way street in order for the states to receive federal funds under a program designed to encourage state and local energy conservation planning.

Title VII — Drilling in ANWR

• **Drilling.** Authorized oil and natural gas drilling in the Arctic National Wildlife Refuge (ANWR). The bill specified that drilling be carried out in a way that did not unduly harm fish and wildlife. It also levied a per-barrel fee on oil or gas extracted from the refuge to create a $50 million fund to restore the area's environment after drilling was completed. The measure also required that government revenues from the oil and gas leases be split equally between the federal government and Alaska and that the federal share go to a fund for energy-related programs. However, that money could not actually be spent without the approval of the regular appropriating committees.

• **Drilling bans.** Prohibited oil and gas leases on the outer continental shelf off California and New Jersey before the year 2000.

Title VIII — Nuclear Power

• **Research.** Authorized a research, development and demonstration program designed to lead to the commercial use of advanced reactor technologies after 1995. The bill set 1995 as the target date for approval of a standardized design for near-term advanced technologies, such as advanced light water reactors. The bill also set a 1995 target date for researching other technologies, such as high-temperature gas-cooled reactors and liquid metal reactors, to determine whether the federal government should select one of those technologies for a demonstration project.

Title IX — Nuclear Power Licensing

• **Streamline.** Adopted the Nuclear Regulatory Commission's proposed rule, which was being debated in the courts, to issue a combined construction and operation license for nuclear power plants instead of the two-step process of granting two separate licenses. The change would cut out a second public hearing required before a plant could begin to operate, unless critics could show that the plant had failed to follow the specifications of the combined license in a way that could endanger public health or safety.

Title X — Uranium

• **Processing ore.** Restructured the Energy Department's uranium enrichment program into a government corporation aimed at processing uranium ore more efficiently and staving off foreign competition. Enriched uranium was sold to nuclear power plants.

The bill included other provisions to help the domestic uranium industry, such as establishing a 50-million-pound strategic uranium reserve. It also authorized $300 million to clean up sites used to produce uranium and thorium.

The uranium provisions were similar to those included in a bill that passed the Senate in 1989 but that drew House opposition as a bailout for the uranium industry. The Senate on June 12 also passed these provisions as a free-standing bill (S 210).

Title XI — Natural Gas

• **Pipelines.** Streamlined regulations for building natural gas pipelines, including creating a new regulatory path that would enable pipeline builders to proceed more quickly in exchange for assuming greater financial risk. The bill also consolidated federal environmental review of proposed new pipelines and enabled applicants to save time by hiring outside contractors to prepare required environmental documents.

• **Pipelines hookups.** Authorized the Federal Energy Regulatory Commission to mandate that interstate pipelines hook up smaller pipelines bringing gas from a production area so long as doing so would not require the owner of the interstate pipeline to enlarge its facilities or damage service to existing customers.

• **Oversight.** Shifted oversight of natural gas imports and exports from the Energy Department to the Federal Energy Regulatory Commission. The bill also directed the commission to consider whether those transactions would have an anti-competitive effect on U.S. gas producers. The language was targeted at Canadian importers, who some senators claimed were exploiting a regulatory loophole to undercut U.S. producers.

• **Sales.** Deregulated pipeline sales rates so long as the pipelines served a "competitive" natural gas market.

• **Open meetings.** Specified that policy discussions by members of the Federal Energy Regulatory Commission were exempt from the federal open meeting law — Sunshine Act (PL 94-409) — and need not be open to the public.

Title XII — Outer Continental Shelf

• **Offshore drilling.** Sought to encourage offshore oil drilling by giving coastal states and communities 37.5 percent of new federal revenues from leases as impact aid.

Title XIII — Research and Development

• Research. Authorized an array of research and demonstration programs related to cutting consumption of imported oil, including:

Promoting natural gas use through improved emissions control, fuel cells and efficiency.

Increasing natural gas supplies through such means as surface gasification of coal and methane recovery from biofuels.

Examining high-efficiency heat engines, though not more than $25 million a year would be made available for this for fiscal 1992-94.

Developing Eastern and Western oil shale, high temperature superconducting electric power systems and renewable energy.

Encouraging use of natural gas and electric heating and cooling systems for buildings, though not more than $15 million a year could be spent for this program during fiscal 1992-94.

Promoting fusion energy.

Boosting use of electric vehicles.

Developing advanced oil recovery techniques and studying the potential of extracting oil from so-called tar sands.

Studying the use of telecommuting, which would allow people to work at home on a computer or telephone rather than commuting to an office.

Minimizing the amount of nuclear waste produced.

Studying whether existing nuclear waste programs were equipped to handle waste that would be produced by newly licensed nuclear plants.

Providing postsecondary programs to promote math and science education for low-income and first-generation college students.

Title XIV — Coal

• **Research.** Authorized several federal research and demonstration projects to promote coal, including efforts to burn coal with fewer acid emissions and to convert coal for use as a transportation fuel. In the case of a research and development project to promote low-rank coal, accompanying report language recommended that the Energy Department continue ongoing research on low-rank coal at the University of North Dakota's Energy and Environment Research Center and target that center for future research on low-rank coal.

The bill created a council to promote the export of so-called clean coal technologies as well as a national clearinghouse on coal technologies, to be run by an unnamed university in a Western coal-producing state and one in an Eastern coal-producing state.

• **Plant modifications.** Allowed power plants to make certain modifications — such as adapting boilers to use a different fuel — without triggering new environmental reviews. The condition would hold so long as the changes would not increase overall hourly emissions from the plant above the maximum emissions allowed for the plant for the last five years of operation. J. Bennett Johnston, D-La., tried unsuccessfully to include similar language in the 1990 Clean Air Act. The issue arose in a case involving the Wisconsin Electric Power Co., and the provision had become known as the WEPCO fix.

Title XV — Public Utility Holding Companies

• **Wholesale generators.** Exempted wholesale electricity generators from the 1935 Public Utility Holding Company Act, allowing utilities to operate wholesale plants in more than one state and potentially encouraging independent producers to operate generating plants. The bill would include some protections against possible abuses stemming from the eased federal oversight, such as sham transactions in which a third party bought electricity wholesale and resold it to disguise what was basically a retail transaction.

• **State regulators.** Required state regulators to consider whether the debt level of a wholesale generator could jeopardize a steady supply of electricity. State regulators would be allowed access to the financial records of those wholesale producers.

Title XVI — Strategic Petroleum Reserve

• **Expansion.** Directed the administration to complete the existing expansion of the Strategic Petroleum Reserve to 750 million barrels, and to 1 billion barrels as soon as possible. The bill also authorized creation of a 10-million-barrel stockpile of crude oil for the Defense Department.

• **Oil purchases.** Authorized the president to procure foreign oil for the Strategic Petroleum Reserve or the Defense Petroleum Inventory without following competitive bidding procedures. ■

Continued from p. 202
from the reserve, authorizing releases to relieve big jumps in oil prices as well as to ease a physical shortage of oil.

At the markup, the subcommittee also:

• Approved draft legislation to discourage so-called octane cheating — deliberately mislabeling the octane content of gasoline. The legislation, similar to a bill passed by the House in the preceding year, bolstered states' authority to enforce accurate octane labeling and extended labeling requirements to other transportation fuels, such as reformulated gasoline, ethanol and methanol. *(1990 Almanac, p. 282)*

Clean-Coal Program

The subcommittee on July 31 voted 19-3 in favor of proposals that would direct federal dollars toward finding ways to burn coal more cleanly and to export U.S. coal technologies. The subcommittee's coal bill reauthorized the Energy Department's clean coal technology program and established new commercialization programs for certain coal-related projects. For example, the bill promoted the recovery and use of the methane gas found in coal beds, and instructed the Energy Department to help fund a program to show its commercial potential.

Synar and W. J. "Billy" Tauzin, D-La., blasted the bill as a giveaway for the coal interests. They likened its provisions to the ill-fated Synthetic Fuels Corporation, which Congress created in 1980 to promote alternative fuels but later dismantled as an inefficient, pork barrel program. Synar was especially critical of a provision that would provide money for demonstration "clean coal" plants abroad.

But Sharp defended the proposal as a relatively inexpensive effort to curb the emission of so-called greenhouse gases, which were believed to promote global warming. He stressed coal's importance as a plentiful domestic fuel source.

Nuclear Waste

After a six-week hiatus, the energy panel resumed work on Sept. 11 and voted to speed up the licensing process for a proposed high-level nuclear waste dump in Nevada. The bill authorized the Energy Department to begin dump studies at Yucca Mountain in Nevada without obtaining state environmental permits for the work. *(Yucca mountain dump site, p. 226)*

Nevada had been in the epicenter of the nuclear waste debate since 1987, when Congress singled out Yucca Mountain as the only site to be studied for a high-level waste dump. State officials called the 1987 law unconstitutional and initially refused to process environmental permits for site work at Yucca Mountain. However, the courts subsequently ordered Nevada to begin processing permits, and some had been granted by the time of the markup.

Despite that progress, Bush administration officials had pushed for legislation, saying the state could not be trusted to process the 15 additional permits that would be needed. Members of the House Energy panel repeated those concerns and said customers who received nuclear-generated electricity had already paid billions toward a waste dump.

Rep. James Bilbray, D-Nev., and several environmental lobbyists decried the bill as a political end run around state environmental safeguards, setting a dangerous precedent for other controversial projects.

Nevertheless, the Energy panel's verdict was considered a foregone conclusion.

Full committee Chairman John D. Dingell, D-Mich., was the bill's prime author and made his first extended appearance at the Energy markups for the nuclear waste debate.

While Dingell spoke publicly of the need to jump-start the dump program, many lobbyists and staff believed his private interest was finding a stick to hold over the head of Nevada's Sen. Bryan. Bryan was the lead sponsor of an automobile fuel efficiency bill fiercely opposed by Michigan automakers.

One potential subcommittee opponent was Rep. Jim Cooper, D-Tenn., whose state was a strong contender to host a planned temporary nuclear dump. Cooper disliked language in the bill that would have let the administration begin work on the temporary dump before a permanent waste repository had been licensed.

On the eve of the markup, however, Cooper and Dingell agreed on a compromise amendment. It retained existing requirements to license the permanent dump first but added instructions to locate the temporary dump "as close as possible" to the permanent site. Combined with the bill's other provisions, that language threatened to place both dumps in Nevada.

That agreement squelched a potential conflict on the measure and paved the way for easy passage. Members first approved Cooper's amendment, then the underlying bill, both on voice vote.

Delayed Actions

House lawmakers postponed a difficult fight on streamlining the licensing process for nuclear power plants.

Rep. Joe L. Barton, R-Texas, wanted to replace the two-step construction and operating licenses for nuclear plants with a single combined license. But he conceded that he might not have the votes and opted to try later in the process.

Sharp also delayed a planned Sept. 12 markup on his global warming proposal, which directed the president to follow the broad recommendations of a recent National Academy of Sciences report. Panel members had criticized that draft as alternately too stringent or too timid. And anti-abortion groups were upset about the academy's call for renewed U.S. support for international population control.

Electricity Regulation

Sharp put the energy markups on hold in mid-September as Energy and Commerce members focused on an unrelated banking bill. But the panel resumed work on the energy bill Oct. 9 and 10, approving dramatic proposals to restructure electric utility regulation and promote alternative transportation fuels. Both items had slowed progress on drafting a comprehensive energy bill, and the subcommittee approval marked a major step forward for Sharp.

On electricity regulation, the panel voted 17-5 to loosen restrictions in the Public Utility Holding Company Act, a 1935 law governing the electricity industry. The bill proposed to exempt wholesale power producers from the law in an effort to spur competition and efficiency in electricity supply.

The proposed change, known as PUHCA reform, had split the electric industry and become one of the most controversial issues of the year's energy debates. Proponents hailed the subcommittee vote as proof of growing momentum for revamping the law.

A similar provision in the Senate energy bill had been attacked both by utilities that said it could undermine stable market relationships and by consumer groups that feared it could jeopardize existing ratepayer protections.

But Sharp won over consumer activists by including more protections against potential utility abuses.

Most significant, Sharp's bill clarified that the federal government could order utilities to give independent producers access to their transmission lines. Critics of the Senate provisions had said utilities would deny transmission access to stifle competition from independent producers.

The House bill provided that federal regulators review power sales by new wholesale producers to ensure they would not hurt consumers. Another provision sought to ban utilities from building an affiliated, independent power plant and then selling the electricity to itself.

Rep. Michael G. Oxley, R-Ohio, tried to strike that ban, arguing that such transactions at times save utilities and their ratepayers money. But Sharp and others said consumer risks outweighed any potential gains, and Oxley's proposal was defeated on a voice vote.

Members also voted down, 2-8, a proposal by Texas' Barton to repeal the PUHCA law entirely.

Alternative Fuels

The subcommittee voted 21-1 to approve proposals to promote non-oil transportation fuels, known as alternative fuels. Alternative fuels included ethanol, methanol, natural gas, electricity and hydrogen.

Similar to the Senate energy bill, the panel's measure greatly expanded existing requirements for the federal government to buy alternative-fuel vehicles.

Unlike the Senate bill, however, the House version did not mandate that state, local and all private fleets phase in a fixed number of alternative-fuel vehicles. But it did include incentives for state and local governments to promote non-oil motor fuels. And the bill also required producers, transporters and marketers of alternative fuels to start purchasing only alternative-fuel vehicles for their fleets beginning in 1994.

The measure sought to displace 10 percent of oil-based motor fuels by the year 2000 and 30 percent by 2010. If the national goals were not being met, the Energy secretary could require private fleets to buy more alternative-fuel vehicles.

Uranium Enrichment Effort

The House panel on Oct. 17 gave voice vote approval to legislation aimed at reviving the flagging fortunes of the U.S. uranium enrichment effort.

The measure sought to establish a government corporation to take over the Energy Department's business of enriching uranium for use in nuclear power plants. Under the proposal, the corporation also received the exclusive rights to a new enrichment technology, called AVLIS, which was expected to be much more profitable than existing methods. The new corporation would be given a $364 million federal loan to get off the ground but was eventually intended to be totally privatized.

The Senate on June 12 passed a bill (S 210) to establish a similar corporation, which also would take over the Energy Department's three existing enrichment plants. House members said that strategy would make the corporation difficult to privatize because it would have responsibility for billions of dollars in decommissioning and decontamination costs.

Under the House measure, the corporation leased the plants and paid royalties on the federally developed AVLIS technology. If payments from the corporation to the federal government were not enough for a $500 million cleanup fund, "backup" fees on the nuclear power industry and other purchasers of enriched uranium would make up the difference.

Final Markup

The Energy and Power Subcommittee wrapped up the bill on Oct. 31 after approving proposals to encourage development of renewable energy and voluntary reductions of emissions of carbon dioxide and other gases thought to lead to global warming.

The subcommittee had been intermittently marking up the measure since July and drafted 12 titles that were bundled together and combined into one bill (HR 776), which was approved on a 21-1 vote.

Renewable Energy

The renewable energy provisions authorized a subsidy of 2.5 cents per kilowatt hour to producers who built facilities that generated electricity from solar, wind and geothermal energy. The section also authorized new joint ventures between the Energy Department and industry to commercialize renewable energy technologies such as photovoltaics and biomass.

But Sharp said he could not muster enough votes for his proposed funding mechanism for the subsidy — a user fee of one-twentieth of 1 cent per kilowatt hour, to be borne by consumers.

Sharp said the tax would have increased the average electric bill by only 32 cents per month, but in the face of monolithic Republican opposition and several Democratic defections, he dropped it from the measure.

Without the funding mechanism, the renewable energy incentives were effectively gutted, as money to pay for the title would have to come from an already strapped Appropriations Committee. Sharp thanked "all who support renewables and the handful who are willing to pay for them."

The global warming provisions reflected a panel badly divided between members who pushed for mandatory reductions of greenhouse gas emissions and those who argued that the scientific jury was still out on the severity of the global warming threat.

The global warming section required several studies of ways to curtail emissions of greenhouse gases, such as carbon dioxide. The provisions called for the establishment of a voluntary system for reducing greenhouse gas emissions and allowed utilities and industries to accumulate credits against any future emissions reductions mandated by Congress.

Post Mortem

Sharp called the bill "a very significant achievement" that would reduce American dependence on imported oil by 3 million barrels a day by 2010.

Although not as sweeping as the Senate version, the House energy bill included many similar provisions such as revamping regulations for public utilities and promoting the construction of new natural gas pipelines. And the House bill went further in some areas, such as mandating increased energy efficiency for buildings and appliances. Environmental groups praised Sharp's bill as a relatively sound foundation for energy policy.

But the subcommittee ignored the controversial issue of whether to draft stricter Corporate Average Fuel Economy (CAFE) standards. Dingell, an automobile industry ally, was expected to try to block higher fuel economy standards in full committee.

Also, the House did not address the issue of drilling in the Arctic refuge. The House Merchant Marine Committee had been set to mark up a pro-drilling bill (HR 1320) in the fall but postponed action in the face of Senate delays on the issue as well as allegations of wrongdoing by Alyeska, the consortium of oil companies that operated the trans-Alaska pipeline.

SENATE FLOOR ACTION

The Senate on Nov. 1 refused to take up Johnston's massive energy bill, dealing a severe setback to the bill's proponents and throwing the energy policy debate into turmoil.

The vote was a blow to Johnston and the Bush administration, which had proposed similar energy legislation. The Senate adjourned for the year without further action on the issue, although there was talk among the bill's proponents and opponents of trying to move some energy legislation early in 1992.

Democratic Divisions

As soon as the Energy Committee reported out the bill, a core group of junior Democratic senators denounced it as environmentally unsound and threatened to try to block floor consideration with a filibuster. Their discontent, which had been percolating over the summer and early fall, bubbled over and spread out in mid-October as Democrats began to focus on the issue in advance of an expected floor vote.

The most heated exchange came at an Oct. 17 meeting of the party's policy committee, called to discuss the energy bill. At the session, senators raised loud complaints about the package, particularly its Alaska drilling provision. Johnston's bill included many components of the administration's energy strategy, and Democrats complained that they would be advancing Bush's interests, not the party's, by moving ahead with it.

Some were particularly loath to begin an intraparty floor fight at that time, shortly after Democratic defeats on the nomination of Supreme Court Justice Clarence Thomas and Bush's successful veto of an unemployment bill.

That feuding prompted Tom Daschle, D-S.D., co-chairman of the Democratic Policy Committee, to try to negotiate an agreement to move ahead. After several rounds of shuttle diplomacy, Daschle met with Johnston and his opponents to consider separate votes on Arctic drilling and gas mileage standards, the two most controversial items in the bill.

But Johnston ultimately refused the deal, mindful that any move to accommodate Democratic critics could cost him Republican support. The administration had threatened to veto any energy bill that did not allow drilling in the Arctic refuge.

Some opponents hoped Mitchell would delay action on the bill to avoid a messy family squabble. But Mitchell let it be known that he planned to keep his promise to hold a vote on the energy bill that year.

As the promised showdown neared, both sides stepped up already superheated lobbying campaigns.

While a few Republicans, most notably William V. Roth Jr. of Delaware, indicated that they would support a filibuster, most of the opposition was centered in the Democratic Party. Bolstering them was a coalition of roughly 20 environmental and consumer groups that had been meeting regularly to oppose the bill and keep up a steady stream of public criticism.

They found some unlikely allies on the filibuster effort.

A group of electric utilities opposed the bill's provisions to restructure federal regulation of the electricity industry. Its lobbying arm, known as the Electric Reliability Coalition, backed the filibuster effort.

There was also support among some of the groups opposing an increase in federal gas mileage standards. Although the bill did not mandate an increase, lawmakers and lobbyists recognized that there would undoubtedly be efforts to do so on the Senate floor.

Atop that was displeasure among some committee chairmen who had prime jurisdiction over chunks of the bill and had tried unsuccessfully to win referral.

Johnston, meanwhile, had allies of his own. Various energy and business groups were part of a coalition, instigated by Johnston, lobbying to bring the bill up for debate.

Many Democrats considered the filibuster a Republican tactic, and even some who strongly opposed parts of the bill were reluctant to keep it from the floor.

Halloween Debate

Senators began debating the measure the morning of Oct. 31, paused to vote on an appropriations bill, then continued late into Halloween night.

Bill opponents were chastised for seeking to block debate on an energy policy after many had cried out for one during the Persian Gulf War.

"If you want to defeat national energy strategy, it's probably within your power to do so," Johnston said at the outset. "I think the country would be in a much worse position if that was done."

But some senators insisted that the bill was too skewed toward production to provide the foundation for an energy policy. The bill "suffers from the tunnel vision of chasing cheap oil," said Baucus. "It is flawed because it has no vision of the future."

The controversial Alaska drilling provision dominated much of the debate.

Wirth, who had tried to strip out the Arctic drilling provision during markup, on the Senate floor said he and other opponents had a right to use the filibuster to block its passage. And because the drilling provision was wrapped into a comprehensive energy bill, he said, they had to filibuster the entire bill.

Johnston urged Wirth to let the Senate move ahead on

the rest of the bill and save the fight on Arctic drilling until the end. But Wirth's calculations showed that he would be forced to gain 51 or more votes to strip the drilling provision from the energy bill, while only 41 votes would suffice to keep the bill from the floor.

Wirth said he supported many other parts of the energy bill and believed it could have moved through the Senate months earlier without the controversial Alaska drilling proposal. But other critics had far broader objections; Wellstone urged colleagues not to "waste good thread on rotten cloth."

The night before the vote, lobbyists backing the filibuster estimated they were close to the 40 votes they needed to block the bill. By the next morning, the scales seemed to have tipped in their favor.

Energy's Moore was outside the Senate chamber noting that some of the senators aligned with Johnston and the administration had left town for the weekend, probably dropping them short of the needed 60. Moore predicted that the filibuster coalition might prevail on the first round, but would be routed on a second vote the following week.

But when the votes were taken, after a short round of additional debate, opponents of the bill had 44 votes, four more than needed.

Environmental lobbyists were jubilant. "This is one we don't need to spin," said Alden Meyer, a lobbyist for the Union of Concerned Scientists.

The vote had a partisan cast, with Democratic votes running 2 to 1 against Johnston.

The opposition had begun as the plaint of a few freshman Democrats, but ultimately included nine committee chairmen. Ernest F. Hollings, D-S.C., whose Commerce Committee had prime jurisdiction over the controversial issue of federal gas mileage standards, became an energetic supporter of the filibuster effort in the closing week.

The margin of defeat was far greater than even Johnston's opponents had predicted, and it clearly left the Louisiana senator dismayed. "In case there is anyone who wants to know what this vote means," Johnston said on the Senate floor, "it means we lost."

Apart from the bill's prime sponsors, proponents did not match the intensity of the opposition.

Reflecting on the battle several days later, Johnston criticized the administration's effort in behalf of his bill as weak, despite loud complaints among Democrats that his bill was a clone of President Bush's energy proposal. For example, Johnston said the White House letter supporting cloture did not arrive until the vote had begun and that Bush said nothing about the issue immediately afterwards.

Johnston said he believed White House Chief of Staff John H. Sununu did not want an energy bill, in part because it was likely to include some new mandates on business.

Leaders of the filibuster were quick to paint it as a philosophical watershed, with senators repudiating past energy approaches in favor of greater conservation and environmental sensitivity.

"We have drawn a line in the tundra," said Lieberman, who fiercely opposed the bill's provision to allow oil and gas drilling in the Arctic National Wildlife Refuge.

While he and some other opponents of the Johnston bill called the vote a clear sign against Arctic drilling, they insisted that it did not mean the death of energy legislation in the 102nd Congress.

Supporters of the Johnston bill interpreted the vote differently. Wallop attributed the defeat to an array of senators opposed to pieces of the bill. Because these critics were afraid they could not win their issues on the merits, Wallop said, they united to block the overall bill from coming to the floor.

In the days immediately following the vote, Johnston seemed pessimistic about the prospects for moving ahead. But by the time Congress adjourned for the year in late November, he was speaking of pushing ahead with the bill in 1992 minus its controversial fuel economy and Alaska drilling proposals. At the same time, some of the senators who led the fight against Johnston's proposal said they had an obligation to assemble an alternative package that would take a far more conservation-oriented approach to energy policy. ■

Arctic Plain Was Legislative Battlefield

Environmentalists, oil companies and their respective legislative allies during 1991 continued a longstanding battle over whether to open the coastal plain of Alaska's Arctic National Wildlife Refuge to oil and gas drilling. During 1989, the environmentalists gained the upper hand when the *Exxon Valdez* oil spill in Prince William Sound highlighted the environmental risks of the oil business. Two years later, drilling advocates believed the oil shocks accompanying the Persian Gulf War might have tipped the political scales in their favor.

The drilling debate did generate intense attention and lobbying early in the 102nd Congress and became the most explosive component of several proposals to rework the nation's energy policies. But the controversial issue brought down a massive Senate energy bill in early November, leading even some advocates to conclude that the drilling proposal was dead for the foreseeable future.

The refuge's coastal plain, a strip 100 miles long and 30 miles wide, represented the last piece of the Arctic shoreline in the United States free of oil development. Congress had long debated the area's fate. In 1980, it prohibited oil development in most of the refuge but directed the Interior Department to study the coastal plain's oil and gas potential. Members subsequently debated proposals to open it to drilling, or place it off-limits for all time. *(1990 Almanac, p. 315; 1989 Almanac, p. 678)*

In 1991, the administration made opening the refuge a centerpiece of its new energy strategy, and Sen. J. Bennett Johnston, D-La., included a similar provision in his energy bill (S 1220).

Although there was no proof of how much oil lay under the Arctic wildlife refuge, some specialists believed its coastal plain might be the nation's last great oil field. The Interior Department estimated that the refuge could yield as much as 9.2 billion barrels of oil, about the amount contained in Prudhoe Bay, 65 miles to the east. With the United States importing almost half its oil, administration officials and other drilling advocates argued that it was absurd not to tap this domestic resource. The oil could displace imports, help control the trade deficit and provide domestic jobs. Alaska officials and the Inupiat Eskimos who owned the coastal plain wanted the economic boost that would accompany drilling and strongly supported opening the refuge.

Drilling advocates minimized the beauty and environmental significance of the refuge, and noted that the area was already home to three military radar stations and the small Eskimo village of Kaktovick.

But the drilling proposal enraged environmental groups, who made protecting the refuge their top legislative priority for 1991. These activists, as well as the local Gwich'in Indians who subsisted on carbibou that fed and calved in the refuge, were unimpressed by industry claims that they could drill without significant harm to the caribou and other wildlife.

Johnston's bill sought to protect wildlife habitat at the same time that it would open the area to oil development. It would set aside 5 cents from every barrel of oil to pay for restoring the environment. But environmentalists were skeptical of such efforts, citing a test well in the refuge that remained barren four years after it was abandoned, despite an oil firm's best efforts to reclaim the land.

For both sides, the symbolism of the Alaska drilling debate at times seemed to overpower factual considerations. Drilling proponents saw opening the refuge as a signal that lawmakers were serious about promoting the country's domestic energy supply, while opponents claimed it would send a dangerous "business as usual" message about sacrificing the environment to feed the nation's appetite for oil. These critics said that even under the most optimistic scenarios, the refuge would not yield enough oil to significantly dent imports.

Sen. Tim Wirth, D-Colo., tried unsuccessfully to strike the Arctic drilling proposal from Johnston's energy bill in the Energy and Natural Resources Committee markup. But the Environment and Public Works Committee on Oct. 17 voted 12-4 to report a bill (S 39, S Rept 102-241) placing the refuge off-limits by designating it a wilderness area, thereby setting up a direct confrontation with the energy bill's drilling provision.

When the energy bill came up for debate in late October, anti-drilling forces provided the critical blast to block it from being considered. *(National energy strategy, p. 195)*

The House had been considered even less friendly to the drilling proposal, and leaders there did not even bring the matter to a vote.

Rep. Walter B. Jones, D-N.C., had planned to bring his Arctic drilling bill (HR 1320) before the Merchant Marine and Fisheries Committee he chaired. But Jones pulled back in late fall, noting both the possibility that the Senate would not act on the matter as well as ethical allegations against Alyeska, the U.S. business consortium that operated the Alaska oil pipeline. ■

Endangered Species Act Revision Looms

With the 1973 Endangered Species Act facing reauthorization in 1992, Congress grappled the previous year with the increasingly difficult task of reconciling the toughness of that law with the needs of communities whose businesses might have hastened the extinction of various species.

Throughout the first session, lawmakers introduced and held hearings on bills to stem the decline of the northern spotted owl in the Pacific Northwest, restore several endangered species of salmon and steelhead trout that ran the Columbia River watershed and continue helping the Atlantic striped bass.

A striped bass protection bill (HR 2387 — PL 102-130) cleared Congress, and help for the salmon was included in the fiscal 1992 Interior appropriations bill (HR 2686 — PL 102-154).

Bills (HR 2082, HR 585) were also drafted to make the federal government take an ecosytems-wide approach that placed a premium on biological diversity.

A particularly bruising battle was waged over the spotted owl. The controversy produced a hodgepodge of bills (HR 1590, HR 3263, HR 2463, S 1156, among others) that attempted to deal with it.

They ranged from timber-industry-supported proposals to make end runs around the Endangered Species Act (PL 93-205) and judicial review of timber policy, to environmentalist-supported measures that would give ironclad protection to whole swaths of the owl's ancient forest habitat.

Attention to the 1973 law was heightened toward the end of the session by Interior Secretary Manuel Lujan Jr.'s plan to convene a high-level panel that could overturn decisions made in line with that act.

Known as the "God Squad," the committee was asked to consider whether to allow Oregon timber sales that were halted because of the spotted owl.

ENDANGERED SPECIES ACT

The reauthorization battle did not get under way in earnest until Nov. 27 when Rep. Gerry E. Studds, D-Mass., introduced a wide-ranging reauthorization bill (HR 4045) to force the government to take quicker steps to protect declining species and require the federal government to consider habitat preservation in protecting species.

The bill quickly attracted 30 cosponsors, including Reps. John D. Dingell, D-Mich., Energy and Commerce Committee chairman and the original sponsor of the 1973 act, and Bruce F. Vento, D-Minn., chairman of the Interior Subcommittee on National Parks and Public Lands.

Although only six pages long, HR 4045 was considered tough.

As introduced, it sought tighter deadlines for recovery plans and to make it easier in emergency cases for legal action to be taken to stop a species' decline.

Prospects for reauthorizing the act were dimmer in the Senate, where senators sensitive to Western resource users were more hostile to the bill.

The Senate had taken no action to promote biological diversity or reauthorize the species protection law by the end of 1991.

The Senate was the major roadblock during the act's last reauthorization in 1988.

In that case, Western senators objected to penalties for hunting, and Southern senators fought provisions that would have forced shrimpers to add devices to prevent them from inadvertently capturing endangered sea turtles. *(1988 Almanac, p. 156)*

THE NORTHERN SPOTTED OWL

By the end of 1991, lawmakers had not legislated their way out of the controversy that pitted timber-industry interests against protection for old-growth forests that provided breeding ground for the threatened spotted owl.

Instead, Interior Secretary Lujan announced his decision on Oct. 1 to convene the high-level Endangered Species Committee known as the God Squad. Only the committee had the power to grant exemptions to the Endangered Species Act. The panel, which was to continue to meet in 1992, was asked to weigh the economic dislocation facing the logging industry against protecting the owl.

Lujan's decision to convene the high-level committee came at the request of the Bureau of Land Management, which had targeted about 750 million board feet of timber to be cut down for sale in 1991. But in June, the Fish and Wildlife Service issued an opinion that 52 of the sales would jeopardize the spotted owl, which would violate the Endangered Species Act. The bureau modified eight of those sales to meet Forest Service objections, but the remaining 44, located on a small fraction of Oregon federal forestland, had been in limbo.

Members of Oregon's congressional delegation were pleased with Lujan's decision but cautioned that it would not be a panacea for the region's problems.

"In requesting God Squad review, the secretary of the Interior has hardly solved the Northwest timber crisis. But, he has put a lie to the contention that there is no place in the Endangered Species Act for people," said Rep. Les AuCoin, D-Ore.

Peter A. DeFazio, D-Ore., whose district encompassed some of the disputed land, said, "We're in this morass because of a series of half-baked and procedurally deficient actions by the Bush and Reagan administrations" that had exacerbated the situation.

DeFazio said that a legislative solution was still needed. Several bills, including a compromise measure (HR 3263) from the Washington, Oregon and California lawmakers, were attempting to find a way of managing timber harvests and protecting the owl — though none was approved by committee during the first session.

The God Squad

The Endangered Species Committee was created by Congress in 1978 after a Supreme Court decision enjoined the Tennessee Valley Authority from destroying the habitat of the tiny snail darter during construction of the Tellico Dam on the Little Tennessee River.

The God Squad could grant exemptions to the Endangered Species Act after a host of economic factors was considered in bids to allow the completion of federal projects. The committee was authorized in amendments to the Endangered Species Act in 1978 (PL 95-632).

It was composed of the secretaries of the Departments of the Interior, Army and Agriculture and the administrators of the Environmental Protection Agency and the National Oceanic and Atmospheric Administration. The chairman of the White House's Council of Economic Advisers and a state representative also sat on the special committee.

The panel could be convened only at the request of a federal agency, the governor of an affected state or an applicant for a permit or license who had been turned down primarily because of the Endangered Species Act.

Bureau of Land Management Director Cy Jamison, flanked by Oregon Republican Sen. Bob Packwood, announced Sept. 11 that he had formally asked Lujan to empanel the committee. The move represented the first time a federal agency had sought to convene the special panel and highlighted the increasingly incompatible efforts to save both the owl and the timber-dependent communities of the Pacific Northwest.

Jamison's action came after the June 18 decision by the bureau's sister agency, the Fish and Wildlife Service, to halt 44 timber sales on Bureau of Land Management tracts in Oregon.

Jamison said the Fish and Wildlife Service's actions had severely affected the'bureau's ability to schedule and make timber sales, which generated $195 million in 1989. He estimated that timber sales in 1992 would be down 75 percent from levels of the mid-1980s.

The Bureau of Land Management was a major producer of timber in Oregon, managing 2.4 million acres of forests.

The bulk of the forestland fell under a 1937 law that required the bureau to consider community stability in managing its timber resources in Oregon and California. To Jamison, that requirement had led the bureau to sell a steady supply of timber for mills in those states.

But bureau land also contained some of the region's fragile old-growth forests. Such forests were the prime habitat for the spotted owl, which the Fish and Wildlife Service listed as a threatened species. The designation meant the owl was considered one step from being endangered by extinction.

Legislative Action

By May, four bills had been introduced in the House offering varying solutions to the crisis. A science advisory panel had been formed to give Congress options for old-growth forest management and preservation, and a dozen experts and officials were called to Capitol Hill for two days of hearings on May 29-30.

The hearings were made urgent by a May 23 ruling of U.S. District Judge William L. Dwyer to ban logging on 66,000 acres of old-growth forests inhabited by the owl. Standing-room only hearings of the Agriculture Subcommittee on Forests were marked by sharp exchanges between lawmakers and increasingly defensive Bush administration officials.

Even pro-timber lawmakers showed impatience with an administration that consistently had not implemented spotted-owl protection policies mandated by Congress, causing disruption and uncertainty in timber harvest levels.

The subcommittee hearings, chaired by Harold L. Volkmer, D-Mo., was originally scheduled to air concerns of pro-logging lawmakers who had introduced bills to "protect" communities from the economic effects of spotted owl restrictions. Oregon Republican Bob Smith's bill (HR 1309) sought to prevent precipitous declines in logging to protect dependent communities. Louisiana Democrat Jerry Huckaby's bill (HR 2463) sought to supersede environmental protection laws to ensure continued timber sales.

But proposals from the pro-environmentalists' forces also gained panel interest, including a bill (HR 842) by Indiana Democrat Jim Jontz to protect wide swaths of the Northwest's old-growth forests. Minnesota Democrat Bruce F. Vento's Ancient Forest Protection Act (HR 1590) was the most comprehensive of the proposals. It set aside 6.3 million acres of "national forest reserve," guaranteed about 3 billion board feet of timber for sale annually and provided for economic assistance to rural timber-dependent communities.

A stumbling block to quick action was the fact that there was no consensus in the Northwest delegation. Urban, coastal legislators such as Jim McDermott, D-Wash., contended that timber harvest levels had been unsustainably high. But others, such as Smith — a rancher — said Vento's bill would only push the region further into recession.

Al Swift, D-Wash., told the committee that district residents "have gone from being able to make a living to where their economy is dead, not dying."

In a consensus-building move, Volkmer and Agriculture Committee Chairman E. "Kika" de la Garza, D-Texas, put together a blue-ribbon advisory panel to identify old-growth forest areas, prepare maps of these areas and develop management options for the committee to consider.

Lawmakers from the region professed determination to act quickly. "The spotted owl crisis has come to rest right here in the Longworth House Office [Building]," said DeFazio. "The administration is apparently paralyzed for whatever reason . . . and now it is incumbent upon us as the U.S. Congress to legislate a solution."

On Aug. 1, Sid Morrison, R-Wash., introduced a bipartisan bill (HR 3263) that attempted to balance spotted owl protection with preservation of the region's dwindling number of timber jobs.

STRIPED BASS PROTECTION

Extended protection of the striped bass — one of the East Coast's premier game fishes — cleared Congress on Oct. 2 when the Senate approved a striped bass conservation measure by voice vote. President Bush signed the bill Oct. 17 (HR 2387 — PL 102-130).

As cleared, the bill renewed for three years the 1984 Atlantic Striped Bass Conservation Act (PL 98-613), which required states along the Atlantic seaboard to follow the recommendations of the federally chartered Atlantic States Marine Fisheries Commission or face a moratorium on commercial bass fishing. *(1984 Almanac, p. 333).*

The bill's quick legislative route began June 20, when the House Merchant Marine and Fisheries Subcommittee on Fisheries and Wildlife Conservation and the Environment approved the bill by voice vote. Frank Pallone Jr., D-N.J., chose not to offer an amendment to the measure that would designate the striped bass as a sport fish and eliminate commercial harvest of the bass. His proposal, included in a separate bill (HR 393), met with resistance from some panel members who said that it would infringe on states' rights.

On June 27, the House Merchant Marine Committee also gave it voice vote approval. The House passed the measure by voice vote on July 9.

The measure, cosponsored by Studds and Don Young, R-Alaska, authorized the National Marine Fisheries Service to board and inspect ships at sea and to seize their contents if necessary. It also authorized the continuation and expansion of a long-term study by the Interior Department into the reasons for the decline of the striped bass and the compilation of a data base on their numbers and breeding rates.

Sen. Ernest F. Hollings, D-S.C., said that while scientific evidence had shown an increase in young fish stocks, sustained recovery was still far from certain in 1991 and that extended state management was needed.

The striped bass, a tasty and sought-after fish that suddenly declined during the early 1980s, was commonly called the striper in the New England reaches of its habitat and the rockfish in the mid-Atlantic region. An anadromous fish, it spawned in the fresh waters and adjacent estuaries of the Chesapeake and Hudson bays and spent its adult life in the ocean. The striped bass could be found as far north as Maine and as far south as North Carolina.

Since the passage of the 1984 law, the striped bass had enjoyed a bit of a resurgence. The law authorized a limited commercial harvest, only about 20 percent of historical levels, and set very strict limits for sports fishermen. In 1990, total commercial landings were about 823,000 pounds, according to the National Marine Fisheries Service.

Merchant Marine Committee documents indicated that the bill's cost was minimal — less than $1.5 million a year, divided between the Commerce and Interior departments.

SNAKE RIVER SALMON AND TROUT

Appropriators made saving the Northwest's Snake River salmon stocks and steelhead trout a priority in the fiscal 1992 Interior Department spending bill and allotted $10.8 million to build a dozen hatcheries in Idaho and Oregon. The Bonneville Power Administration had agreed to reimburse the government for the hatcheries at the end of fiscal 1992. *(Appropriations, p. 555)*

While the Pacific Northwest delegation had spent months piecing together a strategy for saving the region's salmon, prospects for the sockeye salmon species had remained so bleak that it officially was declared endangered on Nov. 14.

The announcement by the National Marine Fisheries Service was expected to have far-reaching effects on a regional economy dependent on cheap hydropower. A drawdown of some of the basin's reservoirs to allow the salmon to more easily complete their spawning runs could lead to an increase in electric rates and a decrease in navigability, according to regional officials.

The listing was also expected to spur already intense efforts in Congress to find a solution for other threatened species. A series of high-level regional "salmon summits" in 1990 sought to avoid the stark "jobs vs. the environment" dichotomy that had dogged efforts to save the region's northern spotted owl.

Sen. Mark O. Hatfield, R-Ore., said the action came as no surprise. "The good news is that the region has been preparing itself for this listing for nearly a year and a half, and we are way ahead of the game," he said.

Congress had poured millions of dollars into saving the salmon, including $31.7 million for screens to protect the salmon from the turbines of the region's massive dams that also acted to block the salmon in their upstream runs; more than $23 million for fish hatcheries by various agencies; $8 million for Corps of Engineers dredging of the Columbia and Snake rivers; and $5 million to upgrade the fish's natural habitat. Yet only four Snake River sockeye completed their September spawning run from the ocean to Redfish Lake in Idaho, according to the service.

BIODIVERSITY

Bills were introduced in both chambers to require the government to consider entire ecosystems in managing public lands.

The issue of biodiversity also became a source of contention during debates over the Bureau of Land Management reauthorization. An amendment attached to the House bill (HR 1096) required the bureau to consider biodiversity in managing its vast holdings. *(BLM reauthorization, p. 216)*

Biodiversity was much talked about during battles to save the habitats of the northern spotted owl and red squirrel. Supporters of habitat preservation argued that subspecies, such as the two in question, were a distinctive and important part of their ecosystems. They contended that destroying a subspecies not only eliminated a unique gene pool, but it also directly affected other species within that ecosystem by altering the food chain.

Most scientists estimated that there were between 10 million and 1 billion species of plants and animals on the Earth and only a fraction of them had been identified.

Many in the scientific community worried that the loss of biodiversity would deprive mankind of potential medical and agricultural breakthroughs.

House Action

The House Science, Space and Technology Subcommittee on the Environment on July 18 gave voice vote approval to a bill (HR 585) sponsored by James H. Scheuer, D-N.Y., that sought to strengthen protections for dwindling species by seeking to preserve entire habitats rather than taking piecemeal steps. The bill was amended in subcommittee to take into account a Bush administration suggestion that the Council on Environmental Quality be given a larger role in preparing a national biodiversity strategy.

The House Science Committee on July 30 agreed to the Scheuer legislation by a vote of 20-5.

Members, by voice vote, agreed to an amendment by ranking panel member Robert S. Walker, R-Pa., to require that spending for programs in the bill come from existing budgets at participating agencies, and not from a new authorization that would add to the deficit.

Studds introduced a similar biodiversity bill (HR 2082) to amend the National Environmental Policy Act of 1970 to require that the impact on biological diversity be considered in the preparation of environmental impact statements. As approved by the Merchant Marine and Fisheries Subcommittee on Fisheries and Wildlife Conservation on July 18, HR 2082 authorized an additional $5 million annually for the conservation of unprotected, naturally diverse ecosystems.

The House Merchant Marine and Fisheries Committee postponed its hearing of the bill so that staff members could review its provisions. Shrimpers and loggers complained that the measure would hurt their industries.

BLM Reauthorization

During the House consideration of the Bureau of Land Management reauthorization bill (HR 1096), fierce debate centered on an addition to the bill to compel the bureau to manage its lands with "biological diversity" in mind.

Opponents did not try to strike the provision. In fact, an amendment offered by Jontz strengthened the biodiversity provisions of the bill by ordering that the BLM restore its land to its "natural productive capability."

Some members, such as Young of Alaska, expressed concern that the amendment would mean an end to ranching, because cattle were animals introduced by man onto BLM land. Jontz responded that the bureau would still be required to manage the land for multiple uses, including grazing.

The amendment received voice vote approval and the reauthorization was passed by voice vote in the House on July 23.

Senate Action

Hearings were held on biodiversity legislation (S 58) introduced in the Senate by Daniel Patrick Moynihan, D-N.Y.

Scientist and author Stephen Jay Gould testified at the Environment and Public Works Subcommittee on Environmental Protection hearing on July 26. He offered an aesthetic justification for efforts aimed at preserving biologically diverse habitats: "What a bleak world it shall be if none but the hardy city dwellers remain, and we come to share our planet only with pigeons, rats, cockroaches and flies." ■

Clean Water Act, Wetlands Revision Begins

Although both chambers began work on a comprehensive reauthorization of the clean water act, no measure was acted on during the first session. The clean water debate proved an explosive mix for a busy Congress in 1991, posing the potential for high costs as well as for far-reaching environmental regulation.

The clean water act had previously been revised in 1987 with amendments to the original water pollution control law, the Federal Water Pollution Control Act of 1972 (PL 92-500). *(1987 Almanac, p. 291)*

The key challenge before lawmakers in 1991 was how to limit polluted runoff that drained over fertilized farmland directly into streams. They also faced the issue of how to stem sewer overflows that bypassed treatment plants after heavy rainfall. Such "non-point source" pollution defied broad-stroke fixes.

The Environmental Protection Agency (EPA) said such pollution accounted in 1991 for half the pollution entering the nation's lakes, streams and coasts.

Meanwhile, several proposals (HR 1330, HR 404, HR 251) floated through Congress to amend Section 404 of the original law, which prohibited the destruction of wetlands.

Congress considered a range of changes to the clean water law, including new taxes to discourage land management practices that contributed to non-point source pollution, such as cutting down trees, and outright bans on commonly used industrial and agricultural chemicals.

Facing Congress also was the question of how to deal with a byproduct of years of pollution: submerged "toxic hot spots." Such ocean and riverbed sediments were so contaminated with metals and chemicals that they threatened entire populations of fish and plants.

Amid tight budget constraints, questions also remained about how much new federal money to authorize to help state and local governments build treatment plants to keep pace with growing populations and development.

The administration sent no reauthorization draft to Congress in 1991 but declared the issue a priority, said Michael R. Deland, chairman of the president's Council on

Environmental Quality.

Administration officials were caught off guard by the House Public Works and Transportation Committee's early March hearings. Most congressional observers had expected House lawmakers to turn first to the reauthorization of the Resource Conservation and Recovery Act (RCRA) that governed solid wastes.

But Deland said the White House planned to propose economic incentives to spur businesses to resolve their own water pollution problems and to seek regional solutions to tackle water pollution threatening entire ecosystems.

The 1972 Act

The original 1972 law marked a turning point in efforts to clean up the nation's waterways. It set the first federal minimum levels of pollution for industries and municipalities and authorized federal grants to help state and local governments pay for building sewage treatment systems.

Over the ensuing years treatment plants steadily reduced conventional sources of water pollution flowing into the nation's waterways, so-called point-source pollution.

While largely considered a success, the original law's promise of meeting deadlines for eliminating pollution in the nation's lakes, streams and estuaries was unfulfilled. It had set goals of assuring fishing and swimming in all waterways by 1984 and for eliminating the discharge of water pollutants by 1985.

WETLANDS

Under Section 404 of the 1972 clean water law — the basis for wetlands regulation — landowners were required to get permits from the U.S. Army Corps of Engineers before dredging or tilling property meeting the wetland definition.

With the nation losing about 290,000 acres of wetlands a year, the federal government in 1989 tightened those rules and sharply limited development. Howls of outrage from landowners, who discovered they owned undevelopable lands, began almost immediately.

Rep. Jimmy Hayes, D-La., said "The definition is so overreaching that it has in effect denied property rights to many people, which is unconstitutional."

Congress, the Bush administration and even the EPA struggled to devise a way to loosen the rules while maintaining protections for "ecologically significant" wetlands.

Hayes introduced a bill (HR 1330) to narrow the wetlands definition, prioritize the remaining wetlands according to their ecological value and productivity, and compensate owners whose lands were "taken" under the guise of wetlands preservation. Low-value wetlands would lose much of their protection under the proposal.

The bill had 52 cosponsors, including some from relatively dry states, such as Arizona's John J. Rhodes III and Nevada's Barbara F. Vucanovich, both Republicans.

HR 1330 was joined by two others — one (HR 404) from John Paul Hammerschmidt, R-Ark., to prioritize protection of wetlands according to their ecological value, and another (HR 251) by Charles E. Bennett, D-Fla., to create a Wetlands Preservation Trust, which would give landowners tax breaks for donating their wetlands to the public.

None of those bills moved during the first session.

In the Senate, the Environment and Public Works Subcommittee on Environmental Protection considered incorporating a wetlands provision into its reauthorization bill (S 1081) to clear up the problems posed by Section 404. The version pending committee action at the end of the first session did not include such a proposal.

Amid the debate, Louisiana Democrat J. Bennett Johnston on Aug. 2 managed to get a provision attached to the fiscal 1992 energy and water appropriations bill (HR 2427 — PL 102-104) that barred the corps from enforcing its controversial 1989 wetlands rule. Under the bill language, the corps could not enforce those rules until it submitted them or a revised version to a public-approval process. *(Appropriations, p. 569)*

In late July, EPA Administrator William K. Reilly did release a revised wetlands manual that attempted to ease the wetlands regulation.

CONGRESSIONAL ACTION

The Public Works and Transportation Committee, which struggled all year with the reauthorization of the nation's surface transportation programs, kicked off hearings on clean water on March 20. In the end, the panel put no comprehensive reauthorization bill forward.

Henry J. Nowak, D-N.Y., chairman of the Water Resources Subcommittee, sketched the contours of any reauthorization, calling for flexibility for states to find cost-efficient solutions. The EPA put the potential costs to governments and businesses of battling water pollution at more than $115 billion in 1991 alone.

Environment and Public Works Committee member Max Baucus, D-Mont., and ranking Republican John H. Chafee of Rhode Island in May introduced a reauthorization bill (S 1081). The Subcommittee on Environmental Protection wrapped up hearings on the measure July 18, but no markup was held.

The bill authorized new funding for an $18 billion revolving loan account for state sewage-treatment plant construction. The measure placed emphasis on pollution prevention and called for expanded authority to develop guidelines to stem industrial wastewater pollution.

The measure was silent on wetlands. But Baucus remained open to adding a wetlands section to his bill in 1992. ■

Hill Begins Reshaping Federal Lands Policy

Congress embarked in 1991 on a review of longstanding land policy in response to pressure to increase the recreational use of public lands, predominantly in the West.

This development took shape piecemeal. But a host of initiatives, when taken together, charted the beginning of a move to revamp how the Agriculture Department's Forest Service and the Interior Department's Bureau of Land Management (BLM) handled 460.8 million acres of federal ranges, deserts, forests and mountains.

Bitter battles were fought over increasing grazing fees to strip subsidies for cattle ranchers; revamping the 1872 mining law to make it harder for speculators to lay claim to valuable land; charging Western states substantially more for oil- and gas-royalty collections; and overhauling federal water subsidies.

In the end, there was no dramatic turn away from the deference long shown to rural Westerners toward the needs of an increasingly urban and environmentally minded nation. But the battles revealed that preservation and recreation were firmly positioned in Congress as the new guiding principles of public land policy.

Factors contributing to this development included:

- A phalanx of lawmakers calling on the federal government to charge more money for the use of public lands by those who profit from them.
- An increasing demand for public lands for recreation — a trend that generated both significant federal revenues and billions of dollars in state tourism funds.
- Demographic changes. The 1990 census showed that the West was nearly as urban as the Northeast, with more than 83 percent of its residents living in cities.
- Federal court decisions that forced Congress to face up to years of conflicting mandates about public land management.
- The political makeup of the House Interior and Insular Affairs Committee, which crafts public land policy. By 1991 it had all but lost its rural Western composition — the result of an effort launched in the 1970s by the late Phillip Burton, D-Calif., a senior member of the committee. It was as second vice chairman of the Democratic Steering and Policy Committee and Democratic Caucus chairman that Burton helped alter the panel's onetime Western makeup.
- The sophistication and clout of the environmental lobby. Since the first Earth Day in 1970, membership in the major environmental groups skyrocketed.

Competition for Land

Federal land agencies, under congressional mandates, had long favored the Western rancher, miner and homesteader. Under existing rules, ranchers, hikers, miners, off-road motorists and hunters were supposed to coexist peacefully. Every patch of federal land, under "multiple use" policy, was available for competing groups to share.

Critics of multiple use argued that in practice the policy had led the Bureau of Land Management and the Forest Service to defer repeatedly to the wishes of ranchers, loggers and miners.

Such critics challenged Congress to endorse a "public use" policy, a new term in the lexicon of the modern-day public-land user. Public use policy promised not to eliminate extractive uses such as mining and grazing. Instead, it called for shifting the focus of federal policy to watershed protection, wildlife and recreation.

The Western Lawmakers

In the House, at least a dozen bills dealing with public land issues were aided as much by the increasingly urban character of the Interior Committee as by the ascent to chairman of reform-minded George Miller, D-Calif.

In the Senate there remained a bulwark of respect for traditional land-use policy. Western senators, who often depended on ranchers and miners for political support, remained particularly sensitive to changes in policy.

But legions of industry associations representing ranchers, miners and loggers remained well-organized and actively countered restrictions on their operations. They employed top Washington lobbyists, such as former Idaho Sen. James A. McClure, who represented the mining industry on public lands issues. McClure had been ranking Republican on the Energy and Natural Resources Committee and vigorously resisted changes in the management of federal lands during his 18 years in Congress before he retired in 1991.

And to drive home their point that the "little guy" would be hurt by policy changes, traditional Western land users began to team up with affected labor organizations, creating alliances such as that forged among the timber industry's American Forest Resource Alliance and the carpenters and woodworkers' unions of the AFL-CIO.

While such tactics revealed that these once-dominant user groups found themselves under attack, they still won a sympathetic hearing from Western lawmakers. Traditional land users successfully rallied Western lawmakers to their defense to defeat efforts to raise gazing fees, overhaul the mining law, alter the oil and gas royalty program and restrict water subsidies for Western farmers.

Westerners Block Hike In Grazing Fees

Faced with the environmental and fiscal cost of grazing cattle on public land, a coalition of lawmakers and environmentalists sought unsuccessfully in 1991 to force Western ranchers to pay higher grazing fees.

Western lawmakers mounted a vigorous campaign to stop the grazing fee boosts included by the House in a bill (HR 1096) to reauthorize the Bureau of Land Management (BLM) and in the fiscal 1992 Interior appropriations bill (HR 2686 — PL 102-154). In the end, higher fees fell victim to the political strength of Western senators. *(BLM Reauthorization, p. 216; Appropriations, p. 555)*

For years, select cattle ranchers grazed herds on the 268 million acres of Western rangeland operated by the BLM and the Forest Service.

Based on a complex formula, federal grazing permits allowed ranchers to graze each head of cattle for $1.97 a month, even though private pastures often charged at least four times that amount. Critics said the fee cost tens of millions of dollars in lost federal revenue each year and gave an unfair advantage to ranchers with grazing permits.

Two bills (HR 944, HR 481), introduced by Reps. Mike Synar, D-Okla., and George "Buddy" Darden, D-Ga., respectively, proposed to sharply increase the existing fee:

Synar's, by steadily raising it to $8.70 per animal unit month (AUM) — the amount of forage a cow and a calf typically consumed in that time — and Darden's, by changing the formula to reflect market values.

Synar and Darden pushed their bills. But the measures stalled before the full House Interior Committee, which remained deeply divided over the issue.

Background

Western ranchers had run their herds on unclaimed public land long before the BLM was started in 1936 out of the ashes of the General Land Office and the U.S. Grazing Service.

Rangeland was free until 1906 and cost only pennies thereafter, which led to overgrazing across the West.

The Franklin D. Roosevelt administration and the 75th Congress in 1934 tried to solve the problem of overgrazing by passing the Taylor Grazing Act, which instituted a system of grazing permits and fees.

The next overhaul, 44 years later, was in 1978, when Congress passed the Public Range Improvement Act (PL 95-514). At that time, lawmakers were pushed to come up with a grazing fee formula that brought fees close to fair-market values. Instead, the devised formula reflected a much more complex "ability to pay" standard. *(1978 Almanac, p. 716)*

Even the Interior Department opposed the new standard. And President Jimmy Carter called it an unfair subsidy. Two years later, the "ability to pay" standard was embraced by President Ronald Reagan, Interior Secretary James G. Watt and Western ranchers. That action revived attempts to increase fees in 1991.

BLM REAUTHORIZATION

A bill to reauthorize the BLM became an early battleground for efforts to increase grazing fees. A grazing fee boost was added to the reauthorization in the House, but the bill died in the Senate.

At first, Western interests helped force the withdrawal of an amendment by Darden to raise federal grazing fees to reflect market rates at a May 22 House Interior Committee markup of HR 1096.

Darden's provision lacked support among Western lawmakers of both parties. But he vowed to take it to the full House, while also eyeing the Interior spending bill as an alternative avenue for his effort.

Westerners saw their early success fade when the House on July 23 added a grazing fee boost to the BLM reauthorization. After several hours of heated debate over the future of the BLM, tempers of Western lawmakers flared anew when Synar and Darden offered an amendment to raise grazing fees to $8.70 per AUM by 1995 to make them roughly even with market rates. The amendment was approved by voice vote.

Synar said the existing $1.97 AUM fee was a fraction of what ranchers paid to graze their cows on private land, and momentum was his ally. Less than a month earlier, the House had already approved a fee hike as part of the Interior appropriations bill.

The proposal was bitterly opposed by Western conservatives, who maintained that ranchers more than made up for low grazing fees by paying for fencing and other improvements required on public land.

In an effort to forge a compromise, Ralph Regula, R-Ohio, offered another amendment to soften the Synar-Darden amendment by capping grazing-fee increases at 33 percent a year. The House approved, 254-156, Regula's amendment, which imposed a top grazing fee of $4.68 per AUM by 1995. *(Vote 218, p. 54-H)*

In the Senate, the BLM reauthorization encountered vigorous resistance and finally died of inaction.

INTERIOR SPENDING BILL

A parallel effort to increase grazing fees on the Interior spending bill continued to advance in the House. Over the objections of Western members, the House Interior Appropriations Subcommittee voted to raise grazing fees by 33 percent at a June 6 markup of its draft of the Interior spending bill.

Joe Skeen, R-N.M., who led the charge against an increase, tried to stop the boost. He said the move stood to cost ranchers $10 million annually.

Resource users, however, found no ally in Sidney R. Yates, D-Ill., the panel's chairman, who wanted to lock in grazing fee increases for five years.

Brushing aside a Skeen effort to hold the line on grazing fees, the subcommittee voted, 4-3, to raise grazing fees to $2.62 per AUM. The House Appropriations Committee followed suit June 19, endorsing the proposal to raise grazing fees by 33 percent to $2.62 a month.

Skeen had been expected to offer in the full committee an amendment to strip the provision from the bill. But he resisted after being assured by Yates that he could attempt to strip the provision on the House floor. Skeen argued that plans to increase grazing fees deserved studied attention and should not be slapped onto a spending bill.

But as Skeen relished the chance to fight the issue on the floor, Synar positioned himself to offer his plan to raise the fees if Skeen succeeded in removing the grazing boost.

Westerners Ready for House Battle

With Western lawmakers protesting every step of the way, the House on June 25 voted, 232-192, to more than quadruple grazing fees over four years as an amendment to the Interior spending bill. *(Vote 194, p. 48-H)*

The amendment by Synar proposed to raise fees to $8.70 per AUM by 1995. Synar said the fee increase allowed the government to run the grazing program "like a business."

The vote came after lawmakers stripped from the bill the more moderate fee hike approved by appropriators after Skeen raised a point of order objecting to legislation on appropriations bills.

Western lawmakers argued that the existing $1.97 per AUM fee was a fair one, even though studies from the General Accounting Office and elsewhere had determined that the average market rate for private rangeland was $9.22.

Led by Synar, Darden and Chester G. Atkins, D-Mass., critics of low fees called them unwarranted subsidies for select ranchers. Joining in were environmentalists who said fees encouraged overgrazing and the destruction of the West's fragile environment.

Western lawmakers vehemently opposed the amendment. Some, such as Skeen, said grazing fees in effect were too high, given the amount of work ranchers had to do to keep up federal rangelands as part of their grazing permit.

But others, such as Pat Williams, D-Mont., acknowledged that the low fees amounted to a worthy subsidy. Williams said the fees helped keep the economy of the West afloat and spurred small operators and attendant businesses.

Atkins attacked the idea that small ranchers depended on grazing fees. He said the bulk of the program was controlled by wealthy individuals, hobby farmers, corpora-

BLM Reauthorization Died in Senate

The House on July 23 passed by voice vote a reauthorization of the Bureau of Land Management that sought to heighten the agency's environmental consciousness. The effort stalled in the Senate.

The four-year reauthorization (HR 1096) was intended to improve the natural quality of the bureau's 270 million acres and to give more voice to public land users other than ranchers, loggers and miners.

Rep. Bruce F. Vento, D-Minn., chairman of the Interior Subcommittee on Public Lands, championed the effort. Ron Marlenee, R-Mont., led the opposition, saying the bill aborted "a balanced management policy."

Vento characterized the measure as a modest revision of the Federal Land Policy Management Act (PL 94-579), the 1976 law that first authorized the Interior Department bureau and codified its mandate to manage public lands by combining the needs of private commercial use with those of public recreational use. *(1976 Almanac, p. 182)*

Members of Congress from the West warned that the bill threatened to shatter the bureau's multiple-use mandate and transform the bureau into a conservation agency.

Interior Secretary Manuel Lujan Jr. recommended that President Bush veto the bill. Among objections, the administration opposed limitations placed on the number of political appointees at the bureau.

The bill became even more contentious when the House, over the objections of Western lawmakers, saddled it with an increase in grazing fees. *(Grazing fees, p. 214)*

A similar BLM reauthorization bill easily passed the House on July 17, 1989, but was strongly opposed by the administration and disappeared without even a hearing in the Senate. *(1989 Almanac, p. 688)*

Congressional Action

The House Interior Committee on May 22 approved the reauthorization bill by voice vote. Ire engendered among Western Republicans manifested itself at the markup in heated statements and delaying tactics. In the end, Republicans stalked out of the markup in an unsuccessful effort to jeopardize a quorum.

The full House July 23 pushed through the BLM reauthorization after hours of heated debate about the future of an agency that controlled an area the size of Texas and California combined.

Much of the controversy centered on the plan to raise grazing fees, but tempers flared over other issues too. An amendment to make the bureau manage its lands with "biological diversity" in mind drew a fierce attack from Western members.

Proponents said the long-term productivity of BLM land depended on the conservation of all plants and animals found on them. But Barbara F. Vucanovich, R-Nev., said the amendment presented "a clear and present danger for crippling, environmental lawsuits brought by non-residents of the rural West."

Opponents did not strike the provision, however. Another amendment offered by Jim Jontz, D-Ind., and approved by voice vote, strengthened the biological diversity provision by directing the BLM to manage its land to restore its "natural productive capability."

In the Senate, the reauthorization bill fell victim to vigorous resistance by Western lawmakers and died of inaction. No companion legislation was introduced.

---

tions, conglomerates and syndicates.

When the House approved the grazing fee boost, proponents had lost 19 votes from a similar vote a year earlier during House consideration of the fiscal 1991 Interior appropriations measure. *(1990 Almanac, p. 871)*

Westerners Look to the Senate

Westerners fared better in the Senate, where the Appropriations Committee on July 24 marked up an Interior spending bill that included no grazing fee increase.

By combining emotional talk of endangered cowpokes with hard-nosed threats of a filibuster, Westerners held the line on grazing fees during days of Senate debate on the Interior appropriations bill.

On the floor, Malcolm Wallop, R-Wyo., led the charge to preserve low grazing fees. But James M. Jeffords, R-Vt., and Howard M. Metzenbaum, D-Ohio, countered with calls for higher fees.

Jeffords offered an amendment to raise grazing fees to $5.13 by 1996. As co-chairman of the Northeast-Midwest Senate Coalition, Jeffords said he offered the amendment to highlight subsidies to Western states. He said the fees allowed 27,000 ranchers with grazing permits to feed cattle at a far lower cost than ranchers who used privately owned land.

Western senators fought the increase with a passion that belied its relatively small impact on the federal budget — estimated at $7 million to $8 million in its first year.

The Senate voted, 60-38, on Sept. 17 to table the Jeffords amendment, in a vote that split along ideological and regional lines. *(Vote 195, p. 26-S)*

The vote marked the Senate's first consideration of the issue since 1978, when it last voted to raise grazing fees.

'Corn for Porn'

Conference negotiators on Oct. 17 sealed victory for Western lawmakers battling an increase in grazing fees. Negotiators reached a hastily arranged deal that guaranteed a freeze in federal grazing fees for a truce on arts funding.

In agreeing to the trade-off that was quickly labeled "corn for porn," negotiators killed new restraints on federal arts funding in exchange for dropping the House-passed proposal to raise fees to $8.70 an AUM by fiscal 1995.

The deal came after days of deadlock. Rep. Les AuCoin, D-Ore., who had been siding with the ranchers, broke the impasse Oct. 16. He first offered an unsuccessful proposal that the House drop any increase in grazing fees. AuCoin then suggested the trade-off that called on House negotiators to drop the grazing fee boost in exchange for Senate abandonment of the restrictions on arts funding sought by Sen. Jesse Helms, R-N.C.

Seizing the compromise as the only viable way to complete action on the spending bill, House conferees voted, 7-2, for it over the objections of House appropriator Regula, who branded it an "unholy deal."

Senate negotiations quickly followed suit.

The Final Deal

The House on Oct. 24 narrowly rejected, 205-214, an effort to strike the corn-for-porn deal that rebuffed higher grazing fees. Lawmakers sent the conference report back to the Senate, where the arts funding issue continued to simmer. *(Vote 341, p. 82-H)*

In the Senate, a rare alliance of arts-supporting liberals and pro-rancher, Western conservatives teamed up Oct. 31 to bury the final attempt to undo the corn-for-porn deal.

Western conservatives, usually allies in Helms' battles to restrict arts funding, seemed keenly aware of what such an effort might portend — a vengeful Yates. Senate Appropriations Chairman Robert C. Byrd, D-W.Va., warned that Yates had the procedural powers of the House Rules Committee at his disposal to reconsider a grazing fee boost if the corn-for-porn deal was broken.

Yates' revenge was the last thing Western conservatives wanted after winning the bruising fight to keep the fees unchanged. So by the time Helms tried to amend the final conference report with new restrictions on federal arts funding, the Senate had grown weary of the contentious and long-running bill. Byrd moved to kill Helms' amendment, and the motion passed, 73-25. *(Vote 241, p. 32-S)*

Moratorium on Mining Claims Defeated

Members of Congress again attempted in 1991 to block the "giveaway" of federal lands under an 1872 mining law. But a one-year moratorium on the patenting of all mining claims included for the second year in a row in the House version of the fiscal 1992 appropriations bill (HR 2686) for the Interior Department and related agencies was dropped in conference after an agreement was reached to consider an overhaul of the mining law the following year.

Under the 119-year-old law, hard-rock mining claims were legally "patented," or converted into private property at prices as low as $2.50 an acre. Critics said the law was being abused by speculators able to buy up federal land at far less than fair-market rates. The law also was criticized for allowing individuals and corporations to extract hard-rock minerals without paying royalties.

Sen. Dale Bumpers, D-Ark., who had worked for years to update the law, unsuccessfully tried to attach an overhaul proposal to the fiscal 1992 Interior appropriations bill on the Senate floor. Bumpers failed to win passage of an amendment to place a one-year moratorium on the patenting of all mining claims.

Bumpers also introduced a bill (S 433) to greatly restrict the mining law, but the measure stalled in the Senate Energy and Natural Resources Committee. A related bill (HR 2614) by Rep. Peter A. DeFazio, D-Ore., died of inaction in the House Interior Committeee.

In 1990, language designed to stop the sale of federal lands claimed for oil-shale development — just a fraction of the lands covered under the mining law — was attached to a must-pass budget-reconciliation bill. It was later dropped in conference amid Senate objections. *(1990 Almanac, p. 316)*

In 1990, the House also passed a one-year moratorium on the issuance of mining patents on federal land. The moratorium, attached to the House version of the fiscal 1991 Interior Department appropriations bill, was later dropped in conference — again up against Senate resistance. *(1990 Almanac, p. 873)*

House Action

In a move to make it harder for speculators to lay claim to valuable land, the House Appropriations Committee on June 19 approved a $12.9 billion spending bill (PL 102-154) that imposed a one-year moratorium on the patenting of mineral claims under the 1872 mining law and increased fees paid by Western miners holding such claims. *(Appropriations, p. 555)*

Supporters called for the one-year moratorium in an effort to give lawmakers time to push through an overhaul of the mining law. Critics chronicled examples of the law being abused by speculators and developers.

The fee provision included by House appropriators imposed a $100 a year fee on mining patent claim holders if they wished to keep their claims active. It was intended to replace the law's $100 a year work requirement, which was branded as outmoded. Interior Appropriations Subcommittee Chairman Sidney R. Yates, D-Ill., correctly predicted the proposal was likely to face a floor challenge.

The mining law required claim holders to spend $100 a year to develop their claim. When the requirement was set in 1872, $100 represented about 20 days of work and by meeting the requirement claim holders could show a commitment to developing mining claims. But by 1991, the work requirement had become almost meaningless. The only commitment to mineral development it showed was that claim holders had spent $100 on their claim each year and usually done so within a few hours. The revision had the added attraction of generating revenues for the Treasury, while the work requirement generated no revenues.

Appropriators were critical of the $100 work requirement in the committee report (H Rept 102-116) and said it bore "no relationship to the serious intent to develop claims." Environmentalists also said claim holders needlessly scarred federal lands in order to satisfy the work requirement.

By the time the Interior spending bill reached the House floor on June 25, Western opponents had marshaled their forces and successfully got the fee provision stripped out of the bill. Nick J. Rahall II, D-W.Va., raised a technical objection to it and said the issue was slated to be considered by the Interior Subcommittee on Mining and Natural Resources, which he chaired.

The one-year moratorium on mining patent claims remained in the Interior spending bill, which the House passed, 345-76, on June 25. *(Vote 196, 48-H)*

Senate Action

Bumpers unsuccessfully sought to strengthen the hand of those pushing for an overhaul of the mining law when the Interior appropriations bill reached the full Senate. He offered an amendment imposing a one-year moratorium on the patenting of mineral claims under the law.

Westerners were able to hold the line on federal land policies as the Senate passed its version of the Interior appropriations bill. During eight days of debate on the spending measure, the Senate considered placing a moratorium on mining patents and another on oil-shale claims. But faced with the united Western front, the Senate on Sept. 19 approved only the oil-shale provision, and that for just nine months. It then passed the bill, 93-3. *(Vote 200, p. 26-S)*

Defeat of the moratorium came Sept. 13. The Senate narrowly killed, 47-46, in a tabling motion, the Bumpers amendment to freeze for one year applications for hard-rock mining claims. Western opponents successfully argued that overhauling the mining law was complicated and required full hearings. They said adding a provision to the Interior spending bill was inappropriate.

Final Action

The conference on the fiscal 1992 Interior spending bill got off to a slow start Oct. 9. After six hours of negotiations over two days the group of 27 negotiators agreed to put off difficult issues until Oct. 15. Among them was the House-passed moratorium on issuing mining patent claims.

The logjam was not broken until a day before negotiators wrapped up work and cleared the compromise $12.6 billion fiscal 1992 Interior appropriations bill (H Rept 102-256) on Oct. 17. Senate conferee Harry Reid, D-Nev., pledged that Westerners would allow the Energy and Natural Resouces Committee in 1992 to consider a legislative plan to overhaul the mining law. That vow cleared the way for Senate negotiators to unite in asking House appropriators to drop the one-year moratorium on mining patent claims.

Water Subsidies Fight Heated Up

California Democrat George Miller's ascent to the helm of the House Interior and Insular Affairs Committee in 1991 rekindled efforts to restrict federal irrigation subsidies for large farm operations in the West.

But House-passed provisions curbing irrigation subsidies and phasing them out for Western farmers who grew surplus crops died in the Senate for the second year in a row.

And a last-minute effort to win passage of the water reform measure stalled in the House on a separate track. Miller tried to win passage of the reform measure by attaching it onto a separate bill (HR 355) intended to ease the effects of a drought in the West. *(Drought relief, p. 171)*

On Nov. 18, Miller brought the expanded version of the drought bill to the House floor under suspension of the rules, but that version failed to garner the required two-thirds majority to pass.

At issue were millions of dollars in irrigation subsidies received by large Western farm operations. Urban and environment-minded lawmakers tried to tighten enforcement of acreage limitations designed to target the subsidies to small and midsize farms.

Farms of more than 960 acres had been ineligible for federally subsidized water since Congress passed the Reclamation Reform Act in 1982 (PL 97-293). But many had gotten around the limit by dividing their land into smaller tracts. For years, Miller championed efforts to close that loophole.

The House adopted by voice vote water-subsidy limits as amendments to the bill (HR 429) authorizing funding for several Bureau of Reclamation water and power projects. The bill also called for reducing salinity and water pollution problems caused by existing water projects and for protecting the Grand Canyon by requiring the Interior Department to regulate releases from the Glen Canyon Dam in northern Arizona. *(BLM reauthorization, p. 216)*

But when the bill reached the Senate it stalled in the Energy and Natural Resources Subcommittee on Water and Power, which held several days of hearings in October.

Background

Since 1902, the federal government had provided low-cost water to many farms under a law that limited the subsidized water to farms of 160 acres for an individual farmer and 320 acres for a couple. But as machinery helped expand the size of farms the limits became outmoded and some landowners devised elaborate schemes to circumvent the limits.

The law had been amended several times. Most recently, Congress yielded to calls for change in 1982 and passed the Reclamation Reform Act, which represented a compromise among environmentalists and agricultural interests in the West. The law lifted the acreage limitation to 960 acres for an individual or small corporation. Federal water could be used on leased acreage beyond the limit, but the law required farm operations to pay higher fees for such water. *(1982 Almanac, p. 353)*

The 1982 law did not dampen controversy for long. In 1985 and 1986, when the Bureau of Reclamation issued rules implementing the compromise, critics assailed them as slanted toward agricultural interests. Miller, who hailed from a water-rich, suburban part of Northern California and headed the effort to tighten the law in 1982, considered his work unfinished.

After failing to win a broad revision in 1987, Miller got attached to that year's budget-reconciliation bill curbs on the use of revocable trusts that had been used to skirt the limits and a requirement that the Bureau of Reclamation audit large farms to ensure that they qualified.

A 1989 General Accounting Office (GAO) report heightened growing concerns. It confirmed the suspicions of critics that some large landholders had used a variety of legal schemes to split their farms into smaller parcels to qualify for subsidized water. A 1990 GAO report found that a single farm, the 23,000-acre J. G. Boswell ranch, had split itself into 326 trusts to avoid $2 million a year in water payments.

Spurred by the reports, Miller again tried to tighten the law. In 1990, he won a significant victory in the House only to see the measure die in the Senate. *(1990 Almanac, p. 356)*

In 1991, Miller repeated his effort but confronted a similarly unsuccesful outcome.

Miller's Ascent

Miller had been the committee's acting chairman since January, after longtime Chairman Morris K. Udall, D-Ariz., suffered serious injuries in a fall. But because Parkinson's disease had taken its toll on Udall, Miller had been the panel's de facto leader for much longer. *(Udall resignation, p. 51)*

When he formally assumed the post after Udall announced that he was resigning effective May 4, Miller reclaimed jurisdiction over matters that had slipped from the committee as Udall's health waned. This put water-subsidy reform back on the committee's agenda.

Miller's opinion of such subsidies went to the root of his basic philosophy of the committee's work. Confronted with conflicts between private interests and the public good, Miller considered public resources "the people's resources."

House Action

What began as a simple measure to authorize funds for a Wyoming dam quickly became the focus of a heated dispute over costly water subsidies for large farms in the West.

The Interior Subcommittee on Water, Power and Offshore Energy Resources on April 24 approved by voice vote a bill (HR 429) authorizing an additional $5 million for the Buffalo Bill Dam in Wyoming and funds for more than a dozen other Western water projects.

Miller won adoption of an amendment that eliminated irrigation subsidies for large Western farms. It was the second year in a row that Miller had used a bill by Rep. Craig Thomas, R-Wyo., as a vehicle to close loopholes in the 1982 reclamation law.

In 1990, Miller's effort died, taking Thomas' bill in its wake. Thomas ended up getting funds for the dam included in the fiscal 1991 dire emergency appropriations bill (HR 1281 — PL 102-27) that cleared Congress on March 22. *(1991 supplemental, p. 668)*

But when Thomas sought an additional $5 million to complete the dam, Miller decided again to use the bill as a vehicle to limit big farms' use of subsidized water.

During the subcommittee markup, Richard H. Lehman, D-Calif., offered an amendment to kill Miller's move, saying it would pose a hardship for many small California farmers. Members barely rejected it, 11-14, and kept Miller's reforms alive. The closeness of the vote telegraphed that Miller's effort would be no cakewalk.

The subcommittee also approved an amendment by Sam Gejdenson, D-Conn., that called for phasing out water subsidies for farms that received federal subsidies for not growing surplus crops.

On May 1, the full Interior Committee approved the bill 38-2 after working out a compromise to protect family farmers.

The compromise, which was forged April 30 between Miller and Lehman, allowed families in which several members had farms that together totaled more than 960 acres to continue to get water subsidies if each of the farms was run separately.

At the full committee markup, Lehman offered the compromise as an amendment, and it was approved by voice vote. It also provided an exception for large group farms owned by fewer than 25 people, allowing them to remain eligible for subsidies for as long as nine years after enactment. It enabled groups of more than 25 to retain subsidies for six months.

But the bill retained prohibitions against large corporate farms whose land was broken into several parcels from continuing to get the subsidized water.

The panel also approved, 24-17, an amendment that allowed farmers who grew surplus crops to continue to get subsidized water as long as they received no other federal subsidies. This weakened the subcommittee draft that had called for phasing out water subsidies for all farms that grew surplus crops.

The full House strengthened the bill before overwhelmingly passing the measure June 20. The bill called for cutting off subsidized water for agribusinesses masquerading as small family farms and phasing out water subsidies for farmers who grew surplus crops.

But the bulk of the 220-page, 29-title measure, which passed 360-24, authorized additional funding to complete the Buffalo Bill Dam in Wyoming and a host of other Western water projects. *(Vote 187, p. 46-H)*

Miller said the history of the reclamation program was "filled with clever irrigators and their even more clever lawyers, who have found ways to string together parcels of land partnerships, trusts and other landholdings that were only transparently 'small' farms . . . in order to qualify for multimillion-dollar subsidies."

The bill placed the burden on Western farmers to demonstrate that they had not created legal schemes to divide up their farms only to qualify for the lucrative subsidies. It phased in over nine years for trusts with fewer than 25 members, and over six months for bigger trusts, a change added at the urging of Lehman.

But even small farmers stood to be affected by the provision that cut water subsidies to those growing surplus crops. The provision applied only to farmers enrolled in the federal acreage reduction program, which paid farmers not to grow certain surplus crops. For them, it phased out water subsidies over four years.

Miller again used the water projects bill as a vehicle for his reforms in a tactical move to help win approval in the Senate, where efforts to revamp water subsidies faced significant opposition from Western lawmakers whose states were served by the Bureau of Reclamation.

During the debate, the House rejected an amendment offered by Peter H. Kostmayer, D-Pa., to make irrigators pay a greater share of the long-term costs of water projects.

Western lawmakers such as James V. Hansen, R-Utah, argued against the amendment. They said that it stood to affect water projects in 34 states, that it would boost electricity costs in the West and that it was too far-reaching to be considered absent hearings.

Among the Western water projects authorized in the bill was $922.5 million for the Central Utah Project, a huge water system under construction for decades to capture Colorado River water for Utah residents and shunt water from mountain streams east of Salt Lake City by a system of tunnels, natural streambeds and pipes into the Colorado River's Bonneville Basin.

Completion of modifications to the 81-year-old Buffalo Bill Dam near Cody, Wyo., also stood to get a $12 million authorization under the bill. Congress had already authorized $106.7 million for the project.

Another bill provision was aimed at the Colorado River's Glen Canyon Dam in northern Arizona. Fluctuating water releases due to changing requirements of the dam's hydroelectric generators had been blamed for downstream beach erosion in the Grand Canyon.

The bill required the Interior Department to regulate releases from the dam and to launch a monitoring program to block further damage.

The House approved an amendment offered by Frank Riggs, R-Calif., to increase water supplies to California's Trinity River salmon fishery by increasing flows from the Shasta Reservoir. *(Vote 186, 46-H)*

The White House officially opposed the bill. Office of Management and Budget officials said the administration specifically objected to its price tag and a provision dealing with a $240 million Indian water rights settlement with the Ute tribe in Utah. The administration supported reclamation reform, however.

Senate Action

From the start, the bill's fate in the Senate remained uncertain. Staff aides to the Water and Power Subcommittee of the Energy and Natural Resources Committee said Chairman Bill Bradley, D-N.J., was in the process of fashioning a companion bill.

The panel held three days of hearings on the House bill beginning Oct. 22. Bradley did not introduce a companion bill in 1991 and no further action was taken on the issue in the Senate.

Reclamation critics closely watched the reaction of freshman John Seymour, R-Calif., to the closing of the 960-acre loophole. His predecessor, Pete Wilson, who became the governor of California, helped stall Miller's similar reform effort in 1990.

A staff aide said Seymour was "looking at the fine print" of the House bill, but it appeared "far less onerous than previous versions."

Final Action

Miller spotted a vehicle to revive his effort to overhaul western water practices in a separate Senate-passed bill that offered drought relief to the parched West. The drought relief bill was scheduled to quickly move in the House under suspension of the rules on Nov. 18. Miller attached his bill (HR 429) to revamp Western water subsidies onto the drought relief bill and sought to pass the expanded measure.

The added language sought to prohibit the Interior Department from renewing water contracts for any term longer than three years. But Western farming representatives, such as Lehman, were furious that such a radical change was offered at the last minute. Lehman demanded a recorded vote. Under the rule, the expanded bill needed a two-thirds majority to pass. The final tally, 245-164, fell short, driving a nail into the coffin of water reform and leaving resurrection for another year. *(Vote 401, p. 98-H)*

Royalties Collections for Oil and Gas Leasing

Congress in 1991 shifted its focus from limiting offshore oil and gas leasing to reducing the administrative costs of the onshore leasing program administered by the Interior Department's Mineral Management Service.

Appropriators sought to raise to 50 percent the states' share of the cost of collecting royalties from onshore leasing to reap the government an additional $68 million annually. But they were rebuffed in the House and Senate. *(Appropriations, p. 555)*

In the House, Nick J. Rahall II, D-W.Va., objected to the change, saying it amounted to new legislation. In the Senate, Malcolm Wallop, R-Wyo., and other Western lawmakers were able to win approval of an amendment effectively keeping the state share of costs at the existing 25 percent. In conference, negotiators left the fees unchanged.

Royalties from oil and gas companies operating on federal lands were shared by the states and the federal government. Western states depended on the royalties to fund important programs such as education and were vehemently opposed to any change. In the end, Congress directed the Mineral Management Service, in cooperation with the Bureau of Land Management and the Forest Service, to study revising the way in which royalties were collected and distributed, with an eye to giving more responsibilities to the states.

Congressional Action

The House Appropriations Committee on June 19 approved a $12.9 billion Interior spending bill (HR 2621 — PL 102-154) that called for states to pick up a larger share of the cost of the onshore royalty collection program.

When the Interior spending bill reached the House floor June 25, opponents got the fee provision stripped out of the bill after Rahall raised a point of order against it. Rahall, chairman of the Interior Mining and Natural Resources Subcommittee, objected to legislation being attached to an appropriations bill and instead called for the issue to be fully considered by his panel.

The Senate Appropriations markup July 24 of the fiscal 1992 Interior spending bill was supposed to be free of controversy. The measure came in at $91 million less than the House version and contained no controversial provisions.

But a provision to hike states' share of oil- and gas-collection costs included in the spending bill so upset Western senators that committee member Pete V. Domenici, R-N.M., darkly warned of a floor fight, and Wallop sent word that he was considering a filibuster.

The proposal threatened to cost Domenici's fiscally squeezed state nearly $21 million a year. Instead of states paying 25 percent of the leasing program's administrative costs, language in the bill increased that to 50 percent. The language proposed to remove $68.2 million from the royalty fund before it was distributed to the states.

Because mineral-rich states such as Wyoming and New Mexico traditionally got a higher percentage of the royalties, they stood to suffer a disproportionate cut. Domenici lambasted the proposal, saying paperwork costs were the same regardless of the value of fossil fuels extracted. "This is not a fee, it's a tax," Domenici said.

Domenici told Appropriations Chairman Robert C. Byrd, D-W.Va., that Westerners planned to wage a Senate floor fight over the plan. Though no amendments were offered to strip the controversial provision from the spending bill in committee, Don Nickles, R-Okla., the Interior Appropriations Subcommittee's ranking Republican, acknowledged that the proposed collection system needed modification.

On the Senate floor, Western senators slipped through a late-evening agreement to prevent an increase in the states' share of royalty collection fees. The oil- and gas-royalty deal was included in a block of otherwise uncontroversial amendments, which the Senate approved by voice vote Sept. 12. The amendment left the royalty collection costs assessed states at 25 percent. Funding for the amendment came from the unused allocation for the fiscal 1992 energy and water development spending bill that appropriators had divvied up, according to Nickles.

The deal was the result of efforts by Byrd, Nickles and Wallop to prevent stalling the Interior spending bill. The trio continued negotiations until the appropriations bill was brought up on the Senate floor late Sept. 12. In the end, Wallop agreed to drop his threat of a filibuster and Byrd agreed to roll back the planned increase in collection costs.

Wallop vowed to seek further changes in the way administrative costs for the royalty program were collected — including the possibility of allowing states to do collections themselves. On the floor, he won an assurance from Byrd that the West Virginia senator would seek changes in the way individual state administrative shares were calculated.

The agreement cleared the way for final Senate action on the Interior spending bill. "This is a big, big win for Wyoming," Wallop said. "The mineral royalty program is vital to Wyoming and a handful of other states." On Sept. 19, the Senate passed the Interior appropriations bill, 93-3. *(Vote 200, p. 26-S)*

In conference committee the deal was left intact, and states' share of royalty collection costs remained at 25 percent. ■

Cabinet Status Sought for EPA

The Environmental Protection Agency (EPA) was to join the ranks of the 14 existing Cabinet-level departments under a bill that passed the Senate on Oct. 1 with the hard-won support of the Bush administration.

Despite pleas late in the session to pass a House bill, that chamber did not act on similar legislation (HR 67).

Under the legislation the agency was to be transformed into the Department of the Environment. President Bush had indicated that if the bill became law, the agency's administrator, William K. Reilly, would be named the department's first secretary.

As a department, the agency's goals were to remain largely unchanged. It was to continue to seek to reduce pollution, clean up hazardous wastes and regulate and monitor polluters. But as a department, the agency was to take the lead role in negotiating international environmental agreements and eventually assume environmental functions being carried out by other federal agencies.

The bill (S 533) passed by voice vote. Only Jesse Helms, R-N.C., spoke against it, saying the EPA's Cabinet-level status stood to add another layer of bureaucracy and burden small businesses.

But John Glenn, D-Ohio, the bill's sponsor, said elevating the agency to Cabinet-level status signaled that the United States planned "to be a world leader in this area of environmental concern."

The House had passed a Cabinet-status bill in 1990. Efforts to clear the bill in the 101st Congress stalled over differences about how much power the new department should wield. *(1990 Almanac, p. 291)*

"I strongly support legislation to make the Environmental Protection Agency the 15th Cabinet department, and I will work to make that occur as soon as possible," said John Conyers Jr., D-Mich., chairman of the House Government Operations Committee.

BOXSCORE

➡ **Environmental Protection Agency Cabinet Status (S 553).** A bill to make the Environmental Protection Agency (EPA) the nation's 15th Cabinet department.

Report: S Rept 102-82.

KEY ACTION

May 23 — The **Senate** Governmental Affairs Committee approved S 553 by voice vote.

Oct. 1 — Bill passed the **Senate** by voice vote.

Background

President Richard M. Nixon used his executive reorganization powers to create the EPA in 1970. The new agency consolidated existing environmental programs from the Departments of Interior, Agriculture and Health, Education and Welfare; the Atomic Energy Commission; the Federal Radiation Council; and the Council on Environmental Quality.

No vote was needed on the plan unless Congress wanted to veto it. The House Government Operations Committee endorsed the creation of the EPA, and the House rejected by voice vote a resolution to disapprove the action.

Twenty years later the EPA had established itself as the lead federal agency on environmental issues. Environmentalists hoped to increase the EPA's clout and began pushing to raise it to Cabinet-level status.

Legislation to make the agency a Cabinet department seemed to be on the fast track in early 1990. President Bush endorsed the idea in principle, bills were introduced in both houses early in the session and spokesmen from the administration, Congress and environmental groups predicted a bill would soon be on the president's desk.

But the 1990 effort derailed after the House passed a bill — by a 371-55 vote — that gave the EPA and states the power to force federal agencies such as the Energy and Defense departments to clean up their facilities.

Bush also objected to language in the 1990 bill that created an independent Bureau of Environmental Statistics.

The new bureau stood to be able to release data on environmental quality without review by the executive branch, notably the Office of Management and Budget and the new Environment secretary.

Cabinet status, said supporters, promised to help the EPA get better funding over the long term and give it greater clout in international forums. Not in the least, supporters expected that a Department of Environmental Protection would have enhanced influence over the environmental activities of other federal agencies, which were increasingly entangled in internecine disputes over their hazardous wastes.

The agency's reputation suffered a setback in the early 1980s, when President Ronald Reagan's appointee, Anne Gorsuch Burford, tried to institute environmental deregulation, going so far as to propose repealing restrictions on lead in gasoline and on dumping toxic wastes into unlined landfills.

It took years for Congress and environmentalists to regain their trust in the EPA. President Bush helped matters by appointing as EPA administrator Reilly, a well-known environmentalist who had headed the World Wildlife Fund and the Conservation Foundation.

SENATE ACTION

Action on the Cabinet-status bill kicked off in the Senate Governmental Affairs Committee, which approved the measure on May 23 by voice vote. The bill was similar to a version reported by the committee in the 101st Congress.

As approved, the bill (S 533) established a Bureau of Environmental Statistics and a Commission on Improving Environmental Protection to examine and coordinate environmental law.

But the new statistical bureau, designed to serve as a clearinghouse on environmental data, was to report to the president and was not to report statistics independently. Instead, it was to rely on data collected by other governments and agencies. The new commission was to function in an advisory capacity and not have the authority to issue regulations — thus greatly reducing its policy-making power.

Bill sponsor Glenn said he hoped that the new measure would allay concerns raised in the 101st Congress about the statistics bureau and the commission.

As originally envisioned, the statistics bureau was to have been assigned to collect information about the health of the environment. But it was to have been independent of EPA, a requirement intended to insulate its findings from political tampering.

The commission was to have been charged with coordinating the government's maze of environmental regulations.

Senate Floor

Negotiations among senators, the administration and the EPA over the additional responsibilities that a new Environment Department was to assume held up floor consideration until the fall.

The Senate passed S 553 by voice vote after adopting two amendments, including an en bloc amendment by Glenn that assuaged administration concerns. The amendment attempted to guarantee that any information collected from private businesses would remain confidential. The amendment also gave the administration greater power to name department officials by removing language from the bill that would have required more than half of the department's deputy assistant secretaries be chosen from career officials, rather than by political appointment.

On the floor, Steve Symms, R-Idaho, won voice vote approval of an amendment that forced the government to pay compensation when it issued regulations stripping private property owners of the use of their land. It left up to the attorney general to determine when a regulation resulted in the "taking" of property.

Glenn said that lawmakers had been hamstrung by the lack of independent data on the environment. "This bureau should help get us the true facts on the environment," Glenn said.

A displeased Daniel Patrick Moynihan, D-N.Y., said that the meager authorization for the bureau included in the bill — $2.8 million for fiscal 1992 — paled in comparison with the $308.9 million budget for the Bureau of Labor Statistics and the $86.9 million budget for the National Agricultural Statistical Service.

The 13-member Commission on Improving Environmental Protection was to be charged with developing a plan to streamline the new department to eliminate duplication between it and other federal agencies.

The bill included an $8 million authorization to cover the costs of elevating the agency. Such costs included ordering new stationery and forms and redoing printed information with the agency's new title.

The only senator to speak against the bill was Helms. He said the bill would unnecessarily add to the federal bureaucracy. He also attacked the agency for its handling of statistics and its analysis of the risks of toxic substances.

"This new department, mark my word, will extend its tentacles across America just like an octopus and bring every small business within its grasp," Helms said.

House Waits Until 1992

Conyers adopted a wait-and-see attitude in 1991, after watching his bill die in 1990. After the Senate passed its bill, Conyers chided that body for acting "18 months later ... after much debate and compromise" to craft a bill with several provisions that he found unacceptable.

He also unfavorably compared the Senate-passed bill with the House-passed bill of 1990, which he said threatened to make the proposed Environment Department more independent from partisan interference.

Particularly objectionable to Conyers was the Senate language on "takings," which he said "would give radical new powers to the Department of Justice to block any federal agency regulation."

Conyers pledged to act on a Cabinet-status bill early in 1992. ■

Federal Facilities Cleanup

Legislation to give states and the Environmental Protection Agency (EPA) greater power to require federal agencies to obey hazardous waste laws passed both chambers in the first session. The bills (HR 2194, S 596) were not reconciled before the end of the year.

The federal government was considered one of the nation's worst polluters, with the main culprits being the Energy Department's nuclear weapons plants and the Defense Department's military installations. However, none of the federal agencies was exempt from anti-pollution laws, including the 1976 Resource Conservation and Recovery Act (RCRA), which was the nation's principal hazardous waste law.

The bills gave the EPA additional authority to force federal agencies to comply with RCRA. The legislation also clarified states' authority to force compliance with state environmental laws. Such authority had been hindered because some courts had ruled that federal agencies were immune from state regulation.

The House passed HR 2194 on June 24; the Senate followed suit on S 596 on Oct. 24.

The principal difference that remained between the two bills was Senate language that allowed agencies to put off action on wastes that were untreatable mixtures of radioactive and hazardous materials.

Similar legislation had passed the House by wide margins during the 101st Congress — as a stand-alone bill in 1989 and as an amendment to a 1990 bill to give the EPA Cabinet status. *(1989 Almanac, p. 679; 1990 Almanac, p. 308)*

House Action

Legislative action for the year kicked off in the House Energy and Commerce Subcommittee on Transportation and Hazardous Materials, which approved HR 2194 on May 8. The subcommittee approved the bill as introduced by voice vote with no amendments.

As approved by the subcommittee, the bill gave the EPA the authority to issue administrative orders — backed up by potential fines — to force compliance with RCRA.

Under existing law, the EPA could only issue compliance agreements to the agencies. But such compliance agreements were easily broken, according to environmental activists and state officials.

State governments, which had the authority to enforce RCRA, also said that they lacked adequate enforcement tools because some courts had affirmed the federal government's sovereign immunity claims. The states asked for the ability to issue administrative orders and levy fines to force compliance. As it was, they were often forced to resort to full-scale litigation.

The bill "is going to go downtown for a signature," Dennis E. Eckart, D-Ohio, said to Energy and Defense officials at a hearing that preceded the markup. "You all better figure that out and understand that."

The full committee acted quickly and approved the bill on June 4 by a 42-1 vote. Ranking committee Republican Norman F. Lent, N.Y., who cast the sole vote in opposition, was blocked from offering several amendments that reflected administration concerns about the bill.

Lent held off after Transportation and Hazardous Materials Subcommittee Chairman Al Swift, D-Wash., said that such issues would be better addressed in the context of a future reauthorization of RCRA.

A key concern was how to treat wastes that mixed hazardous and radioactive materials, for which no treatment technologies existed. The Bush administration also wanted exceptions for byproducts from nuclear weapons production.

The administration was also concerned that the bill could expose the federal government to a flood of costly lawsuits that would slow federal efforts to clean up the most polluted government facilities first.

The bill passed the House by voice vote under suspension of the rules on June 24.

"For all too long, the federal government has practiced a hypocrisy which says, 'Do as I say, not as I do,' and has allowed federal facilities to be the nation's single leading environmental polluter," said Eckart.

BOXSCORE

➡ **Federal Facilities Cleanup (HR 2194, S 596).** As passed by both chambers, the legislation gave the Environmental Protection Agency and state governments the right to fine or penalize federal facilities that violated provisions of the Resource Conservation and Recovery Act, which governed the disposal of solid wastes.

Reports: H Rept 102-111; S Rept 102-67.

KEY ACTION

May 15 — The **Senate** Environment and Public Works Committee approved S 596, 16-0.

June 4 — The **House** Energy and Commerce committee approved HR 2194, 42-1.

June 26 — The **House** passed HR 2194 by voice vote.

Oct. 24 — The **Senate** passed S 596, 94-3.

Senate Action

With the backing of Senate Majority Leader George J. Mitchell, D-Maine, sponsor of S 596, the bill gained approval from the Environment and Public Works Committee on May 15. The committee approved the bill by a 16-0 vote.

An identical bill had been reported by the committee in the waning days of the 101st Congress.

Like the House bill, S 596 stripped federal agencies of the sovereign immunity defense. The bill also required each federal agency or department to assess the release of hazardous wastes from its facilities to determine whether they were in compliance with existing environmental law. The bill required the EPA to inspect each of the facilities annually and report that information to the public.

"The issue is a very simple one," said Mitchell. "Should the federal government be subject to the same laws and enforcement provisions of those laws that it applies to others? It seems to me that the only possible answer is yes."

Concerns of the administration and Republican senators held up floor consideration until October. The Senate passed the bill on Oct. 24 by an overwhelming 94-3 tally.

Administration officials said the proposal could invite a flood of suits from state agencies that could bankrupt the government and impede the orderly cleanup of the nation's hazardous waste sites.

They also voiced concern that the bill would lead to some federal ships being classified as hazardous waste sites and that federal agencies would become liable for the cleanup and storage of mixed radioactive and solid wastes, for which no treatment was available.

It was the concern over the mixed waste that led Malcolm Wallop, R-Wyo., to threaten to filibuster the bill. He said the measure could "set agencies at war with each other" and lead to fines that would drain funds from the development of new treatment technologies.

But a compromise was struck Oct. 17 that allowed all federal agencies to store mixed wastes until the end of 1993. After that, those able to demonstrate that storage technology was unavailable would be allowed to continue to stockpile such materials until as late as July 1997. Under the agreement, government ships at sea were also exempted from classification as hazardous waste sites.

Despite the compromise, the bill snagged again over negotiations on an unrelated amendment offered by Sen. John Seymour, R-Calif., that called for the FBI to probe the disclosure of sexual harassment charges against Clarence Thomas, whose nomination to the Supreme Court had been confirmed Oct. 15.

Although Seymour's attempt was quashed, the only additional action on the bill during the first session was to choose conferees. ■

Energy Prodded Hill on Nuclear Waste Issue

Energy Department efforts to open a billion-dollar facility in New Mexico to store defense-generated nuclear waste passed the Senate and gained approval from three House committees during the first session.

Congressional action was spurred by the Energy Department's attempt to pave the way for the opening of the project — the Waste Isolation Pilot Plant (WIPP) — without congressional approval.

Frustrated by congressional inaction, the Energy Department on Oct. 3 attempted to obtain control of the site from the Interior Department through an administrative land transfer. The state of New Mexico filed suit and prevailed in a decision issued Nov. 26.

But the attempt to seize the WIPP site by executive fiat prodded Congress into moving legislation to allow the site to open. Under an administrative land withdrawal, the Energy Department stood to have broad powers to open the facility, though not permanently. A legislative solution promised to require greater environmental oversight of the facility as well as authorized financial compensation to New Mexico.

A bill (S 1671) to give the green light to begin testing WIPP passed the Senate by voice vote on Nov. 5. The Energy and Natural Resources Committee had approved the measure on Oct. 16 on a 19-0 vote.

The logistics were more complicated in the House, where three committees had jurisdiction over WIPP: Interior, Energy and Commerce, and Armed Services. Each of the three committees approved different versions of a bill (HR 2637), but efforts late in the session to get a bill to the floor proved fruitless.

BOXSCORE

➡ **Waste Isolation Pilot Plant (HR 2637, S 1671).** Bills to pave the way for the opening of the Energy Department's underground nuclear waste-storage facility, located near Carlsbad, N.M.

Reports: H Rept 102-241, Parts I, II and III; S Rept 102-196.

KEY ACTION

June 26 — The **House** Interior Committee approved HR 2637 by voice vote.

Oct. 3 — Energy Secretary James D. Watkins seized the WIPP site by administrative order.

Oct. 16 — The **Senate** Energy and Natural Resources Committee approved S 1671 by a 19-0 vote.

Nov. 5 — The **Senate** passed S 1671 by voice vote.

Nov. 20 — The **House** Energy and Commerce Committee approved HR 2637, 29-14.

Nov. 21 — The **House** Armed Services Committee approved its version of HR 2637 by voice vote.

Nov. 26 — Federal judge blocks administrative transfer of WIPP site.

Background

In 1979, Congress authorized the Department of Energy to begin construction of the WIPP project for the "express purpose of providing a research and development facility to demonstrate the safe disposal of nuclear wastes" resulting from U.S. defense activities (PL 96-164).

The facility was designed and constructed as a permanent repository for transuranic nuclear waste. Such waste was relatively low in radiation, but often contained highly toxic plutonium.

The WIPP site was located on 10,240 acres near Carlsbad, N.M. The repository for the waste was constructed 2,000 feet below ground in a salt dome. The relatively weak salt walls of the repository were designed to gradually entomb the waste.

Before WIPP could open for a series of tests to determine its suitability as a permanent repository, its site had to be transferred from the Interior Department's Bureau of Land Management to the Energy Department. Such a "land withdrawal" was to be done either administratively or legislatively, though only a legislative withdrawal would have been permanent.

Both the state of New Mexico and the Energy Department were pushing for a permanent legislative withdrawal. New Mexico wanted the environmental safeguards and federal dollars a land withdrawal bill promised to bring; the department was eager to open the site unencumbered by the litigation an administrative withdrawal would guarantee.

The Energy Department had planned to open WIPP in 1988, but in 1987 a federal court struck down the Environmental Protection Agency's (EPA) disposal standards for transuranic waste because they violated other EPA standards for drinking water. Technical differences between the Energy Department and New Mexico's Environmental Evaluation Group (an independent watchdog group authorized to monitor WIPP) in designing WIPP tests further delayed the plant's opening.

In addition, congressional investigators had doubts about the safety and stability of the facility. A key problem was rock falls within WIPP's caverns that could have endangered workers and the integrity of waste containers during the test phase.

As 1991 began, a central aspect of the WIPP debate was an increasingly strained relationship between the Energy Department and congressional Democrats. Congress thought the department was poorly managing the project and determined to open WIPP while being insufficiently concerned with meeting safety and environmental standards. Energy Department officials said that Congress was dragging its feet in failing to clear a WIPP bill.

HOUSE ACTION

Action on WIPP kicked off before the House Interior Committee, whose Energy and the Environment Subcommittee approved HR 2637 on June 12 by voice vote. The full committee followed suit on June 26, also by voice vote.

As approved by the Interior Committee, the bill required that WIPP be subject to EPA oversight during the six-year test phase. In addition, before the facility could open, the EPA had to issue its long-delayed revamp of nuclear waste disposal regulations. Also, test fills of WIPP were limited to one-half of 1 percent of the facility's capacity, or about 4,250 barrels of waste. The Energy Department had originally wanted to place up to 125,000 barrels — about 15 percent of capacity — in the plant during testing.

The committee bill contained a total authorization of $397 million for New Mexico. The money was to be used for safer roads and preparedness plans in case of WIPP-related emergencies.

But some members thought that providing funds to New Mexico seemed suspiciously like a payoff for accepting the waste, and they thought it was a bad precedent because nuclear waste was shipped through many states and it was not possible to give money to every one.

"I think we're starting down a course in which many, many congressional districts in this country can claim a right" to compensation, said Philip R. Sharp, D-Ind. Sharp indicated that New Mexico would face tougher sledding before the Energy and Commerce Subcommittee on Energy and Power, which he chaired.

The committee approved the bill after adding several amendments offered by Bill Richardson, D-N.M., that sought to strengthen the environmental criteria for opening the site.

The committee approved a Richardson amendment by voice vote requiring the Interior secretary to certify that the caverns were stable enough to outlast the storage tests.

More controversial was his amendment mandating that the Energy Department draw up an alternative storage plan for any waste that might have to be removed from the New Mexico site during the six-year test period.

However, Richardson was forced to withdraw another two-part amendment. It required federal officials to prove, before testing, that the project met Environmental Protection Agency standards and gave New Mexico officials additional powers to review environmental safeguards for the site.

Richardson did not have the votes to gain adoption of the amendment, which several in the committee believed gave New Mexico too much power to block WIPP's opening.

The bill also placed a 10-year time limit on the land transfer to the Energy Department, which required the department to get a second go-ahead from Congress if it decided to use the site as a permanent waste repository.

Interior Committee Chairman George Miller, D-Calif., said such restrictions were needed to allay public unease over the Energy Department's spotty track record at running its nuclear facilities.

The committee rejected a series of amendments offered by Joel Hefley, R-Colo., on behalf of John J. Rhodes III, R-Ariz., who was absent, aimed at easing some of the bill's conditions on operating the site.

In the end, committee Republicans supported the bill, despite the Energy Department's objections to the restrictions it placed on the department. Republicans said it was important to get the legislation moving.

Administrative Withdrawal

The Energy Department maintained that the WIPP facility was ready to open by the middle of the year. Frustrated by the lack of further congressional action, Energy Secretary James D. Watkins attempted on Oct 3. to seize control of the WIPP site.

Watkins' action, though long-anticipated, angered most of the New Mexico delegation and sent New Mexico state officials into federal court, where they filed suit to block the takeover. "They've made a permanent enemy out of me," said Richardson.

Under an administrative withdrawal, the department stood to have nearly free rein over the facility, without environmental safeguards drafted by Congress. In addition, the administrative action did not authorize new funds for New Mexico.

Watkins announced plans to begin shipping waste to WIPP, but agreed to hold off until after a Nov. 15 court hearing.

But the department's plans were thrown into turmoil on Nov. 26 when a federal judge ruled in New Mexico's favor and blocked the administrative land withdrawal.

Federal Judge John Garrett Penn ruled the administrative withdrawal invalid because the Energy Department had not demonstrated that it had adequate plans to retrieve waste from the facility if testing failed or if rock falls within the caverns made it impossible to remove the waste.

The judge said that because the department could not guarantee removal of waste shipped to WIPP, the temporary administrative withdrawal could become a de facto permanent one — thereby exceeding the department's authority. The Energy Department appealed the decision and a final ruling was expected in 1992.

Senate Action

While the administration's action did not please New Mexico's senators, Republican Pete V. Domenici and Democrat Jeff Bingaman, it appeared to prompt them to resolve most of their differences over the Senate WIPP bill (S 1671).

Both senators were members of the Energy and Natural Resources Committee, which had sole Senate jurisdiction over the project. With the Energy Department playing a central role in the negotiations, the two New Mexicans were able to draft a compromise bill that was satisfactory to the department.

The committee approved the compromise only two weeks after Watkins had attempted to seize the WIPP site. By a 19-0 vote on Oct. 16, the committee approved S 1671, giving a significant boost to efforts to open WIPP.

Watkins said he moved for the administrative transfer after negotiations between Bingaman and Domenici had stalled over how much waste could be shipped to the facility during the approximately six-year test phase.

Bingaman had insisted that testing be limited to about 4,250 barrels of waste — only one-half of 1 percent of the capacity of the facility. But Watkins wanted to retain flexibility to double that.

The compromise, written by Domenici, allowed the Energy Department to fill the facility up to 1 percent of its capacity during the test phase. But storage levels of more than 4,250 drums first required the approval of the EPA.

Bingaman's attempt to limit to 4,250 drums the amount of nuclear waste shipped to the facility during the test phase failed. Energy Committee Chairman J. Bennett Johnston, D-La., and Richard C. Shelby, D-Ala., joined with the panel's nine Republicans to defeat the amendment, 9-11. Johnston successfully argued that Bingaman risked "losing the whole ballgame." He said the Bingaman amendment would cause the Bush administration to abandon its support of the bill and press ahead with the administrative transfer.

Idaho Republican Larry E. Craig, whose state was home to the bulk of the waste slated to be buried in the facility, accused New Mexico of suffering from a "disease called NIMBY" — not in my back yard.

"NIMBY is corrected by massive doses of dollars," said Craig, referring to the bill's provisions that sought to sweeten the deal for New Mexico.

The bill authorized $20 million a year in aid to New Mexico, as well as payments to make up for forgone state and local taxes that local governments would have received if the facility were private. In addition, $43 million in previously appropriated funds would be released to New Mexico once testing began.

The bill went to the floor on Nov. 5, where it was approved by voice vote.

Further House Action

Action in the Senate and Watkins' attempted administrative withdrawal appeared to prompt further action by the two remaining House committees with jurisdiction: Energy and Commerce and Armed Services.

Action came amid intense pressure from the New Mexico delegation, which was desperate for a bill in order to stave off an administrative land withdrawal.

The Energy and Commerce Committee's version of HR 2637 was drawn from the Interior Committee's bill, except that Energy's version authorized no new impact aid for New Mexico beyond the $40 million already appropriated for 1992.

The Energy and Power Subcommittee approved the bill on Nov. 14 by a 14-8 vote. The panel's Republicans opposed the measure after members adopted several amendments that placed additional restrictions on testing of the facility.

The full committee approved the bill on Nov. 20 by a 29-14 vote.

The Armed Services Committee weighed in on Nov. 21 with another version of the measure that broadly resembled the Senate-passed WIPP bill. John M. Spratt Jr., D-S.C., who wrote the Armed Services bill, said that his bill found middle ground between the Senate version and competing House measures.

The Armed Services bill added a new twist to the issue of compensation to New Mexico. Under the Spratt bill, the state received payments pegged to the amount of waste that WIPP received. Once WIPP began full-scale operation, the state was to have received $600 per barrel of waste shipped to the facility.

With committee action complete, late-session efforts to bring a bill to the floor proved fruitless, as differences among the three committee versions were too nettlesome to overcome. ■

Yucca Mountain Dump Site Still Debated

Legislation to speed up the licensing process for a proposed high-level nuclear waste dump in Nevada moved forward in both the House and Senate in 1991.

Ever since Yucca Mountain was designated as the likely site for the repository in 1987, Nevada officials contended that the area, about 100 miles north of Las Vegas, was unsuitable. The Energy Department had repeatedly complained that Nevada officials had refused to issue permits necessary to proceed with studies to determine whether the site was suitable to permanently hold high-level radioactive waste, such as spent reactor fuel.

To get around the problem, both House and Senate bills enabled the Energy Department to study the site without the state's input. The department was allowed to begin construction of a temporary waste dump, known as a monitored retrievable storage facility, at Yucca Mountain. Under existing law, a temporary dump could not be built until a permanent facility was licensed.

The Senate Energy Committee voted 14-5 on June 12 to approve its bill (S 1138), which would let the federal government pre-empt state permit laws to allow the federal government to move ahead with the project.

As it drafted a national energy strategy bill (HR 776), the House Energy and Commerce Subcommittee on Energy and Power approved similar language on Sept 11 by voice vote.

Opposition by Nevada's senators delayed Senate floor action; full committee markup of HR 776 was slated for 1992.

Background

The 1982 Nuclear Waste Policy Act (PL 97-425) originally envisioned two nuclear dump sites, one in the East and one in the West. But political pressures led the Reagan administration to suspend its search for a site in the East in 1986, while the search for one in the West soon focused on three potential locations: Deaf Smith County, Texas; Hanford, Wash.; and Yucca Mountain, Nev. *(1982 Almanac, p. 304)*

Although the 1982 law called for the Energy Department to study all three sites before choosing one, politics and budget pressures again intervened in 1987. First the Senate voted to restrict the dump study to one site, with language tilting the selection toward Nevada. Then the House, with direction from its powerful Texas and Washington members, explicitly fingered Yucca Mountain.

The agreement was passed and became known in Nevada as the "Screw Nevada" bill. While some observers said there was scientific cause to choose the Nevada site over the Texas and Washington sites, few disputed the critical role politics played.

"We did arbitrarily reach out and pick Yucca Mountain, no question about that," Sen. Larry E. Craig, R-Idaho, said at a Senate hearing in March.

State officials called the 1987 law unconstitutional and initially refused to process environmental permits for site work at Yucca Mountain. However, the courts had since ordered Nevada to begin processing permits, and some had been granted.

Despite that progress, Bush administration officials had pushed for legislation, saying they could not trust the state to process the 15 additional permits that were needed.

Members said customers who received nuclear-generated electricity had already paid billions of dollars toward a waste dump.

But the Nevada delegation and environmentalists said legislation represented a political end run around state environmental safeguards, and threatened to set a dangerous precedent for other controversial projects.

Senate, House Committee Action

Action on the measures kicked off in the Senate Energy and Natural Resources Committee, which approved S 1138 on June 12 by a 14-5 tally. Four of the committee's more liberal Democrats voted against the measure: Daniel K. Akaka, Hawaii; Bill Bradley, N.J.; Paul Wellstone, Minn.;

and Tim Wirth, Colo. Also opposed was Republican John Seymour of California, which is close to the Yucca Mountain site.

Committee Chairman J. Bennett Johnston, D-La., did not express enthusiasm for the bill, but said it was necessary because Nevada was impeding the licensing process.

But Nevada Sen. Harry Reid, D, promised to block floor consideration of the bill and placed a procedural "hold" on it.

In the House, a key backer of the measure was Energy and Commerce Committee Chairman John D. Dingell, D-Mich., who chose the Sept. 11 markup session on the Yucca Mountain measure to make his first extended appearance at the Energy and Power Subcommittee's markups on a national energy bill.

While Dingell spoke publicly of the need to jump-start the dump program, many lobbyists and staff believed his private interest was to find a stick to hold over the head of Sen. Richard H. Bryan, D-Nev. Bryan was the lead sponsor of an automobile fuel efficiency bill (S 279) that was fiercely opposed by Michigan automakers.

One potential subcommittee opponent was Rep. Jim Cooper, D-Tenn., whose state was a strong contender to host a planned temporary nuclear dump.

Cooper disliked language in the bill that let the administration begin work on the temporary dump before a permanent waste repository was licensed.

However, Cooper and Dingell agreed on a compromise amendment that retained existing requirements to license the permanent dump first but added instructions to locate the temporary dump "as close as possible" to the permanent site. Combined with the bill's other provisions, that language threatened to place both dumps in Nevada.

That agreement set the stage for a lopsided committee vote. Members first approved Cooper's amendment, then the bill, both on voice vote.

Mike Synar, D-Okla., was the only panel member to publicly oppose the measure, saying the sponsors "seem hellbent on undoing whatever semblance of fairness or accountability remains" in the waste program. ■

Congress Moved Closer To RCRA Revision

Congress laid the groundwork in 1991 to reauthorize the nation's main solid-waste law, the Resource Conservation and Recovery Act (RCRA), governing the disposal of garbage and the storage of hazardous waste.

The United States was facing a garbage crisis, generating 180 million tons of waste each year. The number of available landfills continued to drop. Communities shunned incinerators and states increasingly refused to become dumping grounds for out-of-state trash.

Lawmakers gave top billing to controlling interstate transportation of solid wastes and increasing recycling of paper, plastic and glass.

Taking the lead was Sen. Max Baucus, D-Mont., chairman of the Environment and Public Works Environmental Protection Subcommittee.

In the House, Al Swift, D-Wash., chairman of the Energy and Commerce Subcommittee on Transportation and Hazardous Materials, shepherded the reauthorization drive.

The Bush administration unveiled its opposition to reauthorization when Environmental Protection Agency Administrator William K. Reilly told a Senate hearing in September that it was unnecessary and stood to cannibalize scarce resources needed to deal with other environmental problems.

Background

RCRA — pronounced "rick-ra" — was last amended in 1984 and expired on Sept. 30, 1988. The original law (PL 98-216) was enacted in 1976 and set up a "cradle-to-grave" regulatory scheme to track the transport, storage, treatment and disposal of hazardous wastes. *(1984 Almanac, p. 305)*

While the reauthorization of the solid-waste law lacked the broad appeal of the 1990 Clean Air Act amendments and offered none of the hefty government spending promised by the pending rewrite of the clean water act, revamping it was nonetheless a top priority for the 102nd Congress.

Similar legislation to revamp the waste disposal law had failed to advance in the 101st Congress because lawmakers were preoccupied with the task of rewriting the Clean Air Act.

In 1990, the key legislative vehicle (HR 3735) focused on changing regulations governing solid wastes and avoided proposals to alter hazardous waste rules after they drew opposition. *(1990 Almanac, p. 308)*

SENATE ACTION

Baucus introduced on April 25 a reauthorization bill (S 976) that prohibited states from banning out-of-state trash unless they had an environmentally sound waste management plan in place. Baucus headed off a measure by Daniel R. Coats, R-Ind., that allowed states to ban out-of-state garbage by pledging to complete action on his bill by April 1992.

States, unhappy with Baucus' bill, were clamoring for ways to limit out-of-state garbage because they had been blocked from doing so after the Supreme Court ruled in 1978 that such bans interfered with interstate commerce.

The bill also set a goal of recycling 50 percent of all municipal waste by the year 2000 and gave the EPA broad authority to set rules on classifying and handling hazardous wastes.

Some states and businesses pushed for a new section in the law to deal with materials that were neither hazardous nor common garbage.

Environmentalists called on Congress to control wasteful manufacturing and excessive packaging to slow the creation of garbage. They also sought bottle recycling nationwide and new standards to encourage the use of recycled materials in paper products.

The Administration's Opposition

Reilly disclosed the administration's opposition to the rewrite Sept. 17 at the last of a set of hearings held by Baucus' Environmental Protection Subcommittee in advance of marking up a bill in 1992.

In testimony, Reilly at first seemed supportive, calling the original RCRA law "pivotal." But he said the rewrite failed to target funding at the most significant environmental problems and added new layers of regulations that threatened to be "technically infeasible, inefficient or administratively unworkable."

He said states and businesses were already paying about $32 billion a year to comply with RCRA regulations. What was needed, he said, were not new federal regulations but market-based solutions.

"The potential economic impact of a major new federal legislative initiative ... could be extraordinary and would be unlikely to result in substantial benefits," Reilly stated.

Those comments angered John H. Chafee, R-R.I., ranking member on the Environmental Protection Subcommittee. Chafee said, "This isn't a major imposition of costs on this country, it's a saving."

Senators on the panel vowed to push ahead with or without the administration. But Baucus was disappointed. "I'm astounded, frankly, that the administration does not want to take advantage of this opportunity," he said.

HOUSE ACTION

Swift, who assumed the chairmanship of the Energy Committee's Transportation and Hazardous Materials panel in 1991, unveiled the first half of the RCRA rewrite dealing with municipal solid waste on Nov. 22.

In 1990, Swift's predecessor, retired Rep. Thomas A. Luken, D-Ohio, failed to generate sufficient interest in rewriting the disposal law.

Swift's legislation (HR 3865) regulated the municipal solid-waste stream, encouraged recycling and tightened regulation of municipal waste and landfills.

He put off crafting the industrial and hazardous waste sections of the reauthorization until early 1992. But he disclosed his intention to marry those key sections with HR 3865 once they were completed.

Swift labored to draft a consensus bill, crafting the legislation only after numerous informal meetings with committee members and collecting comments from interested parties.

It helped that Energy and Commerce Committee Chairman John D. Dingell, D-Mich., set his sights to complete the legislation in 1992 so his panel could turn to reauthorizing the "superfund" law in 1993. While RCRA dealt with the transportation and disposal of new hazardous wastes, the 1980 superfund law ordered polluters to pay to clean up the nation's worst existing hazardous waste sites. ■

California Desert Protection Stalled in Senate

The House passed on Nov. 26 a bill (HR 2929) to protect millions of acres of California's vast and fragile desert over Republican and Bush administration objections. But the effort stalled in the Senate.

The California desert stretched across 25 million acres, from the southernmost reaches of the Sierra Nevadas to the U.S.-Mexican border. Its lonesome stretches harbored rare species such as Desert Bighorn Sheep and the threatened desert tortoise. They also held lucrative gold and mineral deposits, more than 100,000 archaeological sites and acres of shifting sand dunes that beckoned off-road vehicle enthusiasts.

HR 2929, known as the California Desert Protection Act, sought to turn 4.1 million acres of Interior Department Bureau of Land Management land into 73 national wilderness areas to limit activities such as mining and off-road vehicle access.

The bill also sought to expand the 3.3 million-acre Death Valley and 800,000-acre Joshua Tree National Monument into similarly protected national parks and to turn 1.5 million acres of the East Mojave Desert into a national monument. The two designations essentially offered equal protections, though national parks were more diverse in character, and national monuments had a defining feature.

Interior Secretary Manuel Lujan Jr. and Defense Secretary Dick Cheney called on President Bush to veto the bill. They claimed the bill jeopardized operations at five major military installations in Southern California and threatened a possible expansion of Fort Irwin, home of a national training center where troops had prepared for the Persian Gulf War.

Manufacturers of off-road vehicle equipment were at the forefront of the bill's opponents. The Mojave area had numerous "play areas" designated for such vehicles, and was the locale of the Barstow-Vegas off-road motorcycle race, which had been sidelined because of environmental concerns.

Calls to protect the desert, however, were politically popular in California. A 1988 Field Institute poll found that three out of every four Californians wanted more protections for the desert. The bill also garnered support among the state's largest local governments.

And key California Democrats made its approval a priority. They included:

- House Interior Committee Chairman George Miller, who thought the bill important enough to create a California desert subcommittee in 1991 out of the ashes of the General Oversight and Investigations Subcommittee.
- Desert Subcommittee Chairman Richard H. Lehman, who helped fashioned a compromise that sought to accommodate environmentalists, ranchers and farmers.
- Mel Levine, the bill's sponsor, who had pushed the legislation since 1986 and saw the issue as a politically popular asset to his 1992 senatorial bid to fill a seat being vacated by Democrat Alan Cranston.

BOXSCORE

➡ **California Desert Protection (HR 2929, S 21).** Bills to grant additional park and wilderness status to California's vast desert.

Report: H Rept 102-283.

KEY ACTION

Oct 1 — The **House** Interior and Insular Affairs Subcommittee on General Oversight and California Desert Lands approved HR 2929.

Oct. 16 — The **House** Interior Committee approved HR 2929, 28-16.

Nov. 26 — The **House** passed HR 2929, 297-136.

Senate Bills Stymied

Cranston, who had been pushing protection for the desert since 1974, had his own desert protection bill (S 21). But the Senate bill had been stymied by Pete Wilson, R-Calif., who left the Senate in 1990 to become governor of California.

Wilson's successor, John Seymour, R-Calif., was left in the middle of the controversy. In June, he introduced a bill

(S 1225) that called for protecting more desertland than the administration had proposed, but less than the Democrats were pushing. The Energy and Natural Resources Subcommittee on Public Lands, National Parks and Forests held a hearing on it Oct. 17.

But in the Senate, Republicans were dealt a better hand. The Senate Energy and Natural Resources Committee remained unwilling to act on California desertland bill until Cranston and Seymour reached an agreement. The two were talking, but no compromise emerged.

Special House Subcommittee Action

The House Interior and Insular Affairs Subcommittee on General Oversight and California Desert Lands — a panel set up especially to handle the legislation — approved Oct. 1 the long-disputed bill to expand protection of 10 million acres of the California desert.

The committee approved a multifaceted amendment during the Oct. 1 markup. The amended bill placed outside protected areas tens of thousands of acres used for mining, utility and railroad rights of way. It also continued access to more than 15,000 miles of dirt roads used by recreational motorists.

The subcommittee's action marked the first time that the bill had moved beyond the hearing stage — a reflection of the controversial nature of wilderness proposals for California.

In a series of concessions, panel members agreed not to include in the bill dozens of areas that had been actively mined or used by a handful of area ranching families for grazing herds.

The bill was strongly opposed by the Bureau of Land Management, which stood to lose control of some 3 million acres to another Interior agency, the National Park Service. Bureau officials asserted that they were best-suited to manage the conflicting needs of Western land users.

Another wild card was the military. Just west of the proposed protected desert stood Edwards Air Force Base, the site of the space shuttle landings. Pilots based at Edwards used the Mojave Desert for more than 88,000 low-altitude military overflights in 1990. Also nearby was Fort Irwin and its national training center. The bill, however, did not limit overflights or training.

The administration had put forth its own proposal, HR 3066, introduced by Rep. Jerry Lewis, R-Calif. But the subcommittee did not consider the legislation.

House Interior Committee Action

The House Interior Committee on Oct. 16 approved, 28-16, the Democratic-backed HR 2929. No Republicans voted for the bill.

Republicans were steadfast in their opposition to the bill and the Senate companion measure because the bills stood to severely limit recreational and commercial activities on the land. Democrats, backed by environmentalists, pushed the bills because they said the desert was being destroyed by off-road vehicles and mining.

The House Interior Committee approved HR 2929 with no Republican involvement, either in crafting the bill or in the vote.

In an Oct. 15 letter to Miller, the Interior Department laid out 15 reasons why it opposed HR 2929, including the proposal's cost to taxpayers. The letter also said the designated lands did not possess the minimum wilderness characteristics to qualify for protection and that the acreage far exceeded the amount of wilderness and parkland necessary to protect the California desert.

It took months of negotiations among Democrats to come up with an acceptable bill. Although most of the Democratic proposal had been approved earlier by the General Oversight and California Desert Lands Subcommittee, subcommittee Chairman Lehman worked to perfect the bill.

A provision Lehman successfully offered to the full committee version struck about 18,000 acres from the protected wilderness proposal.

Republicans called the measure a wish list that stood no chance of becoming law. The panel rejected several GOP amendments that sought to decrease the number of protected acres or restrictions on activities on the land.

Lawmakers voted, 16-26, to reject an amendment by Barbara F. Vucanovich, R-Nev., that struck protections for about 3.3 million acres until they were studied for mineral resources.

By a 5-6 vote, members also narrowly rejected an amendment by James V. Hansen, R-Utah, to protect grazing rights on the protected land.

And an amendment by Ron Marlenee, R-Mont., to allow hunting and trapping on about 1.5 million acres of the land was rejected 20-23.

Panel members, protective of their jurisdiction over land bills, omitted from the measure a provision that related to military training and overflights in desert areas. The House Armed Services Committee had the opportunity to demand a referral if the language remained in the measure. Bill supporters feared that the administration stood to have more success in persuading the bipartisan Armed Services panel to revise the number of acres protected under the measure.

The removed provision exempted from the bill activities on public lands used by the military. For example, the 1.1 million-acre China Lake Naval Weapons Center and the 227,000-acre Chocolate Mountain Aerial Gunnery Range were used for training exercises and for aerial bombing and missile-firing tests.

Bruce F. Vento, D-Minn., introduced separate legislation (HR 3565) on the military use of the desert that Democrats planned to add to HR 2929 on the House floor.

House Floor Action

After taking nearly a full working day to dispose of a raft of amendments offered by property rights-oriented conservatives, the House on Nov. 26 passed, 297-136, the California desert protection bill. *(Vote 435, p. 106-H)*

Levine, the bill's sponsor, said the overwhelming vote would send a forceful message to opponents in the administration and the Senate "that the people of California want the desert protected."

But Lewis, the bill's chief opponent, predicted that Bush would veto the bill unless the Senate crafted "a strong compromise."

On the floor, bill supporters sought to allay the concerns of opponents with a variety of amendments that the House eventually adopted.

The first, offered by Lehman, took away proposed wilderness designation from 165,000 acres near Fort Irwin. The amendment left the land designated as a "wilderness study area," to be managed as wilderness. But the language did not preclude Fort Irwin's expansion.

Another amendment, successfully offered by Del. Ben Blaz, R-Guam, and Vento, specified that nothing in the bill would stop the military from conducting low-altitude aerial ducting low-altitude aerial training flights or creating new training flights or creating new flight-training routes.

The amendment provided that the China Lake Naval Weapons Center and the Chocolate Mountain Aerial Gunnery Range remain in military control for the following 15 years, and allowed the Navy to keep using the 45,000-acre El Centro range until 1994.

Protecting the rights of the private property owners attracted heated concern among Republicans. Tom DeLay, R-Texas, sponsored two unsuccessful amendments to prohibit taking privately owned land in any area covered under the bill.

The House rejected, 143-289, one amendment to mandate that the government could buy privately held land that fell within protected areas only from willing sellers and could not use condemnation procedures. *(Vote 430, 104-H)*

To partially address the issue, the bill allowed for land swaps to accommodate numerous privately owned "inholdings" that were poised to fall within newly created wilderness and park areas.

The two largest were about 270,000 acres of land owned by the California State Lands Commission to benefit the state's retired teachers, and about 410,000 acres held by the Catellus Development Corp., which owned railroad rights of way once given to the Santa Fe Pacific Corp. The California retirement system for state employees other than teachers owned a substantial stake in Catellus.

The swaps consolidated the wilderness areas and gave entities that owned land within the areas new land elsewhere that was more economically developable.

The House turned back a variety of amendments by Republican lawmakers intended to gut the bill. The strongest challenge came from Lewis when he unsuccessfully offered on Nov. 22 his substitute bill (HR 3066) calling for halving the protected acreage of the Democratic bill. The substitute also did not redesignate Joshua Tree and Death Valley as national parks and continued indefinitely current military activity in the area. It was rejected, 150-241. *(Vote 420, p. 102-H)*

The House also rejected, 110-316, another amendment by William E. Dannemeyer, R-Calif., that called on the Interior Department to study each designation to ensure that its environmental benefits outweighed its economic costs, and that required individuals and businesses be paid for losses resulting from the new protections. *(Vote 432, p. 104-H)*

One amendment that received House approval was by Marlenee to allow hunting in what would be East Mojave National Park. ■

Niobrara River Designated Wild and Scenic

The House on May 14 cleared for President Bush's signature a measure to designate parts of the Niobrara River in Nebraska as wild and scenic, ending a decadelong dispute among Nebraska lawmakers over efforts to preserve the waterway.

Bush on May 24 signed the bill into law (PL 102-50). It protected a 95-mile stretch of the Niobrara River and a 39-mile segment of the Missouri River in Nebraska and South Dakota by placing them within the federal wild and scenic river system.

There was only limited debate in the Senate, where the measure passed by voice vote April 17. On March 7, the Energy and Natural Resources Committee had reported it to the full Senate.

Debate over the measure centered in the House, where the bill (S 248) passed, 333-71, after supporters declared the Niobrara River a prime candidate for protection from increasing commercial and residential development. *(Vote 89, p. 22-H)*

Passage came despite the objections of Republican opponents who argued that the designation inadequately protected the rights of private property owners.

The House rejected, 124-283, an amendment by Don Young, R-Alaska, to require the Interior Department to get the consent of property owners before condemning private land. *(Vote 88, p. 22-H)*

An amendment by Bill Barrett, R-Neb., to require additional studies of the river was rejected, 109-293. Barrett, a freshman lawmaker through whose district the river flows, was the bill's lone opponent among Nebraska's delegation. *(Vote 87, p. 22-H)*

Two of the three members of Nebraska's House delegation supported the measure, as did Democratic Gov. Ben Nelson and Democratic Sens. Bob Kerrey and Jim Exon.

By opposing the bill, Barrett took up the fight of his predecessor, Rep. Virginia Smith, a Republican who ardently opposed the designation. Smith's ranking position on the Appropriations Subcommittee on Agriculture may have helped her block the measure. As a freshman, Barrett had no such leverage.

The longstanding dispute among the Nebraska congressional delegation over the legislation was replayed during a House Interior Committee markup April 24. But the panel approved the bill on a 28-16 vote.

Barrett had warned that hundreds of landowners would lose control over their property. But sitting in the audience during the markup, Barrett could only observe as the panel approved the bill over the objections of ranking Republican Young of Alaska. ■

Tall-Grass Prairie

The House overwhelmingly passed a bill (HR 2369) to create an 11,000-acre national park to preserve a tall-grass prairie in the Flint Hills of Kansas. But the measure failed to advance in the Senate.

Leading the effort was Dan Glickman, D-Kan., whose bill authorized the Interior Department's National Park Service to purchase the Z-Bar Ranch to create the first national monument in Kansas.

The federal park was to be known as the Flint Hills Prairie National Monument.

From the start Glickman faced significant opposition from Republicans, including Dick Nichols, R-Kan., in whose district the park was to be located. Joining the opposition were Kansas ranchers and farmers who argued that local groups were better suited to preserve the prairie than the federal government.

The House Interior Committee's National Parks and Public Lands Subcommittee on Sept. 12 approved the bill by voice vote after holding a hearing on the measure July 16. The full House Interior Committee on Sept. 25 approved the bill, 27-17, with no Republican support.

Republicans lined up against the measure on the House floor. But they were unable to stop the bill, which passed 284-121 on Oct. 15. Passage came after Nichols unsuccessfully offered an amendment intended to gut the measure. The amendment sought to delay enactment until the federal government ran a budget surplus. *(Vote 306, p. 74-H)*

Nichols argued that the $8 million authorized for the park was an unnecessary expense at a time of tight budget constraints. The House rejected his amendment, 153-249. *(Vote 305, p. 74-H)*

The bill was referred to the Senate Energy and Natural Resources Committee, where no action was taken. ■

Global Moratorium Sought On Drift Net Fishing

Responding to a growing threat to the world's marine life, both the House and Senate in 1991 approved legislation that sought a global moratorium on the practice of drift net fishing.

Japan, possessor of the world's largest drift net fishing fleet, announced on Nov. 26 that it would phase out all drift net fishing by the end of 1992.

Drift nets used by commercial fishing fleets were sometimes 30 miles long and snared not only tuna, but also dolphins, turtles, sea birds, and threatened species of fish.

The practice was initially looked upon as a problem with Japanese vessels in the North Pacific Ocean, but Rep. Gerry E. Studds, D-Mass., said that signs of the practice had been detected in the Northeast Atlantic and other areas.

Japan, Taiwan and South Korea historically had the largest commercial drift net fishing fleets.

House Action

The House Merchant Marine and Fisheries Committee on June 27 gave voice vote approval to two resolutions calling for a worldwide ban on all large-scale drift net fishing: H Con Res 113 and H Res 182.

The second measure was directed specifically at the European Community (EC).

During the committee hearing, Doug Bereuter, R-Neb., stressed the urgency of an EC ban, pointing out that some European nations were petitioning the Fishery Council of the European Communities to use 10-kilometer nets.

The House gave voice vote approval to the two measures on July 9.

A third House bill (HR 2152), introduced by Studds, won voice vote approval from the House Subcommittee on Fisheries and Wildlife on Sept. 27.

That bill allowed the president to ban imports from any nation that permitted drift net fishing and required the imposition of sanctions on any country not heeding the United Nations' call for a ban on drift nets by June 30, 1992.

It also authorized the Coast Guard to use Defense Department equipment to enforce laws banning drift net fishing in areas within U.S. jurisdiction.

HR 2152 was approved in full committee Oct. 3 and referred to the House Ways and Means Committee.

Ways and Means, however, failed to mark up the bill prior to the end of the session.

Senate Action

Bob Packwood, R-Ore., introduced a bill (S 884) to mandate sanctions on the fish products of countries that used the nets after June 1992 and gave authority to the president to impose broader sanctions in some cases. The measure was later amended to affect all countries, not just Japan, Taiwan and South Korea.

S 884 was passed by the full Senate by voice vote on Aug. 1. The Senate also approved the concurrent resolution (H Con Res 113) in support of the U.N. ban after attaching sanctions language to that measure.

On July 30, the Wellington Convention, which declared the South Pacific off-limits to drift netters, was approved by the Senate Foreign Relations Committee.

The full Senate, on Nov. 26, ratified the Wellington Convention (Treaty Doc. 102-7) by a standing vote. ■

National Monument and Wilderness Protection

Congress in 1991 worked on a number of measures to preserve federal wilderness areas and protect existing national monuments. Two of the less controversial measures easily cleared during the first session.

COLORADO WILDERNESS

The Senate in 1991 bucked the will of the House in passing a bill that sought to break a deadlock over a proposed addition to federal wilderness areas in Colorado. But the measure stalled in the House over the hotly contested issue of water rights.

The bill (S 1029) designated about 700,000 acres of federal land as protected wilderness. Years in the making, the bill by Tim Wirth, D-Colo., was snagged by language that retained jurisdiction for Colorado over water rights within wilderness areas created in the bill.

House leaders strongly opposed the Senate water-rights language because it differed from wilderness laws that gave the federal government the right to water found within wilderness areas.

Among key House lawmakers and environmentalists the bill stood to reverse existing law and played into fears that state water authorities were more likely to rule in favor of the claims of landowners or municipalities to water, possibly threatening preservation of wilderness areas dependent upon scarce water resources. In the past, the House had granted such water rights to the federal government. To address such concerns, the bill barred any future water development on wilderness lands created in the bill in an effort to protect water flows within those areas from any depletion.

Senate Action

The Senate Energy and Natural Resources Subcommittee on Public Lands, National Parks and Forests completed hearings on the Colorado wilderness bill (S 1029) on June 18.

Dale Bumpers, D-Ark., chairman of the Public Lands Subcommittee, called the water rights language "a draconian departure from what I believe in." But despite his reservations, Bumpers voted for the bill, which the full committee approved (H Rept 102-129), 18-1, on July 24.

Paul Wellstone, D-Minn., cast the only dissenting vote.

The Senate on Aug. 2 passed the bill by voice vote.

House Action

Ben Nighthorse Campbell, D-Colo., introduced a related Colorado wilderness measure (HR 762) that was silent on the water-rights issue. Campbell, whose district contained most of the designated areas, had indicated that the Senate language was acceptable to him. However, it was not acceptable to Interior Committee Chairman George Miller, D-Calif., or National Parks and Public Lands Subcommittee Chairman Bruce F. Vento, D-Minn.

The National Parks Subcommittee held a hearing on the bill May 23, but the bill was never marked up.

MONTANA WILDERNESS

The Senate Energy and Natural Resources Committee on Nov. 20 unanimously approved a controversial bill (S 1696, S Rept. 102-255) to designate 1.19 million acres of national forestland in Montana as wilderness. No House companion bill emerged.

It was not until the night before the committee met that the compromise was hammered out. Montana's two senators, Democrat Max Baucus and Republican Conrad Burns, Nov. 19 reached an agreement on the compromise affecting more than 5 million acres of publicly owned land in Montana.

The compromise bill also designated 215,000 acres of land to be studied for possible future inclusion in the wilderness system, designated 285,200 acres for special management and released more than 4 million acres of roadless land in 10 national forests for logging. The original bill, introduced Sept. 10, had more wilderness and wilderness study areas than the compromise version.

The committee passed the bill on a 20-0 vote, subject to review by the committee. The review was allowed because the final version of the bill had not been printed when the committee acted. The condition was added after Don Nickles, R-Okla., objected to voting on what he called a "monumental" bill without being able to see the final version.

BONNEVILLE SALT FLATS

The Senate on Nov. 23 passed by voice vote a bill to study the puzzling shrinkage of Utah's Bonneville Salt Flats, a popular tourist attraction and the site of automobile speed tests. A companion measure did not advance in the House.

The bill (S 1184) was to have mandated a $1.5 million study to examine why the Salt Flats had diminished during the 1980s from approximately 96,000 acres to about 25,000 acres. The study also was slated to explore whether the Salt Flats should be designated a national recreational area.

The Senate Energy and Natural Resources Subcommittee on Public Lands, National Parks and Forests completed hearings Oct. 1, and the full Energy Committee unanimously approved the bill (S Rept 102-207), 20-0, Oct. 30.

The House version (HR 1727), by James V. Hansen, R-Utah, and Wayne Owens, D-Utah, was attached in July to a bill (HR 1096) to renew Bureau of Land Management (BLM) programs. The Senate failed to act on the BLM reauthorization bill. *(BLM Authorization, p. 216)*

OLD FAITHFUL GEYSER

The House on Nov. 25 passed by voice vote a bill (HR 3359, H Rept 102-374) to give added protection to the Old Faithful Geyser — the crown jewel of Yellowstone National Park. The bill by Rep. Pat Williams, D-Mont., prohibited wells from being drilled to tap the geothermal power of Corwin Springs, which runs under the park.

The Senate failed to act on the measure.

The House Interior Mining and Natural Resources Subcommittee and its National Parks and Public Lands Subcommittee on Oct. 31 held a joint hearing on protecting the geyser, which is famous for erupting, on average, every 61 to 67 minutes. The Mining and Natural Resources Subcommittee marked up the bill Nov. 19 and the full committee followed suit the next day.

The bill was prompted by increased commercial interest in geothermal energy by the power industry. Lawmakers also wanted to avert potential damage to Old Faithful by disturbances in the complex underground plumbing of the area. This was triggered by the fact that a religious group, known as the Church Universal and Triumphant, planned to drill into a hot spring on its property in nearby Livingston, Mont.

BIGHORN BATTLEFIELD

The House on Nov. 25 cleared for President Bush a bill (HR 848) that authorized a monument to honor American Indians who fought to preserve their way of life at the Battle of the Little Bighorn. President Bush signed the bill Dec. 10 (PL 102-201).

The measure, which had passed the Senate on Nov. 22, authorized $1.5 million to build the monument to help provide visitors with an "improved understanding of the events leading up to and the consequences of the fateful battle," where Gen. George A. Custer made his last stand in 1876.

The bill also changed the name of the battlefield from the Custer Battlefield National Monument to the Little Bighorn Battlefield National Monument. According to the Park Service, battlefields are named after places, not individuals.

The Interior Subcommittee on National Parks and Public Lands approved the bill June 18 and the full Interior Committee (HR 102-126) turned around and approved it the next day. The House passed the bill by voice vote June 24.

In the Senate, the Energy Subcommittee on Public Lands, National Parks and Forests completed hearings on the bill July 25, and the full committee approved it on Sept. 26, 18-1. The Senate passed by voice vote an amended bill Nov. 22. The House cleared the final version Nov. 25.

MARK TWAIN NATIONAL FOREST

The Senate on Nov. 26 cleared for President Bush a bill (HR 3604) to authorize the U.S. Forest Service to buy 6,900 acres in Missouri, known as the Dennig Tract, to add to the Mark Twain National Forest. Bush signed it Dec. 11 (PL 102-220).

Passed on a voice vote, the bill barred mining and logging on about 2,800 acres that ran along a river protected from development under the 1968 Wild and Scenic Rivers Act. The remaining 4,100 acres were designed as a Greer Spring Special Management Area to be used for outdoor recreation.

In the House, the bill had been considered by the Agriculture and Interior committees. Agriculture approved the bill (H Rept 102-346) Nov. 6 and Interior followed suit Nov. 20. The full House passed the bill Nov. 22 by voice vote. On Nov. 26, the Senate cleared the bill by voice vote. ■

Antarctica Treaty

The United States signed a treaty to ban the exploration for oil and other minerals in Antarctica, joining with other voting members of the 26-member Antarctica Treaty.

The Oct. 4 signing came on the heels of House approval April 30 of a resolution (H Con Res 109) calling for Bush administration support. The administration had earlier opposed the treaty, but reversed itself in July.

The action also followed the enactment of a law in the 101st Congress that barred U.S. exploration or development of Antarctica (PL 101-594). *(1990 Almanac, p. 305)*

Environmental groups strongly supported a ban on mining in Antarctica, saying that the fragile ecosystem of the icy continent would be disrupted by mining activity. Mining company lobbyists pointed to possible deposits of strategic minerals as one reason to explore the continent.

The administration had earlier declined to support the pact because of a provision that would have required unanimous approval by treaty signatories to lift the mining ban after 50 years. The United States later agreed to sign a compromise version that would have required a vote of two-thirds of the treaty participants to overturn the ban. Senate approval was still required.

The resolution, which passed the House by voice vote, called for an international agreement banning commercial mineral development in Antarctica for 99 years.

"[Antarctica] should be preserved as a land of nature and science," said Rep. Wayne Owens, D-Utah. "The world is not so poor that it must exploit the Antarctic." ■

House Committee Passed Beach-Water Testing Bill

A measure aimed at developing and implementing quality criteria for coastal recreational waters was passed by the House Merchant Marine and Fisheries Committee late in the session, but did not proceed to the floor.

The bill (HR 12) required the Environmental Protection Agency (EPA) to set criteria for beach water quality and mandated that states test their coastal waters. States not meeting new minimum standards were to post signs along their beaches.

In 1990 a similar bill (HR 4333) was attached to the must-pass budget-reconciliation bill by the Merchant Marine and Fisheries Committee, but was stripped out in conference. Unlike the 1990 bill, the 1991 version did not require states to close beaches that did not meet the EPA standards. *(1990 Almanac, p. 290)*

As introduced, the bill would have authorized $3 million in federal matching grants for states to implement the new rules.

The bill, authored by William J. Hughes, D-N.J., was a high priority for the New Jersey delegation, whose state had strict beach water quality rules and had been hurt by lost tourism revenues due to beach closings.

The Merchant Marine and Fisheries Subcommittee on Oceanography approved the bill by voice on Oct. 1 with little debate.

Proponents of the testing bill beat back an amendment proposed in full committee by Merchant Marine and Fisheries Chairman Walter B. Jones, D-N.C., that would have allowed states to petition the EPA for exemption from testing requirements. The vote on the amendment was 19-24.

Jones argued that states with insignificant water quality problems, such as North Carolina, should not be forced to bear the cost of comprehensive testing. Hughes insisted that such an amendment would render the testing requirements meaningless.

The bill was approved by voice vote by the Merchant Marine and Fisheries Committee on Nov. 20. ■

Senate Sought To Reduce Indoor Air Pollution

The Senate overwhelmingly passed a bill that sought to reduce the exposure of Americans to harmful indoor air pollutants. But a companion measure never made it to the House floor.

With indoor air pollutants thought to be responsible for more than 14,000 cancer deaths a year and more than $4 billion in lost productivity, the Senate on Nov. 6 passed, 88-7, a bill to set up a separate office at the Environmental Protection Agency (EPA) to handle indoor air pollution research and regulation.

The bill (S 455), sponsored by George J. Mitchell, D-Maine, authorized $242.5 million through fiscal 1996 for programs related to indoor air pollution. The Bush administration opposed the bill. *(Vote 245, p. 32-S)*

It directed the EPA to develop a national response plan to coordinate the federal government's efforts to stem indoor air pollution. The plan was to be submitted to Congress within two years after enactment and every two years after that.

Joining Mitchell in supporting the bill were John H. Chafee, R-R.I., who was ranking member on the Environment and Public Works Committee, and Frank R. Lautenberg, D-N.J., chairman of the Environment Subcommittee on Superfund, Ocean and Water Protection.

Action on the measure got under way on May 8, when the Superfund, Ocean and Water Protection Subcommittee held a hearing.

The panel marked up the bill on July 29. The full Environment and Public Works Committee on Aug. 1 approved the measure by voice vote.

On the floor, John Seymour, R-Calif., offered an amendment to include the U.S. Capitol and its attendant buildings under the bill along with other federal facilities, and it was approved by voice vote. Mitchell then offered a companion amendment to expand the definition of the federal facilities covered under the bill to also include the White House and the vice president's residence. It also was approved by voice vote.

In the House, the measure was referred to the Energy and Commerce and the Science, Space and Technology committees, where no action was taken.

A companion measure (HR 1066) sponsored by Joseph P. Kennedy II, D-Mass., was considered by the House Science Environment Subcommittee and marked up July 18. The full Science, Space and Technology Committee approved the bill Aug. 1.

The bill also was the subject of five hearings in June and July by the House Education and Labor Subcommittee on Health and Safety. ■

Various Energy, Environmental Bills Moved

Congress advanced several other energy and environmental bills in 1991.

ENERGY DEPARTMENT RESEARCH

The House Science Committee gave voice vote approval to the Energy Technology Research and Development Act (HR 2399) on May 22, which included the authorization for energy research by the Department of Energy for fiscal 1992.

The House Science Subcommittee on Energy on April 25 had approved, by voice vote, the draft measure to authorize $2.8 billion for Energy research programs.

The Bush administration had requested $2.5 billion for the programs, which included advanced energy construction projects, geoscience research and nuclear energy research.

The measure included $471 million for fossil energy research, significantly more than the $227 million requested by President Bush in his 1992 budget plan.

The House Science Committee also approved by voice vote on May 22 the fiscal 1992 authorization for the Environmental Protection Agency's Office of Research and Development. The measure (HR 2404) authorized $446.5 million for an array of environmental research and development programs.

Neither bill advanced further during the first session.

INDIAN ELECTRIC PROJECT

The Senate on Nov. 25 cleared for President Bush a bill (HR 1476 — PL 102-231) to transfer the electric transmission and distribution systems of the San Carlos Indian Irrigation Project in Arizona from the Interior Department to a local water district and two American Indian tribes. President Bush signed the bill Dec. 12.

The bill represented the fruits of lengthy negotiations to transfer the facilities. The transmission and distribution system grew out of an irrigation project to supply water from the Gila River to the San Carlos Reservation. The power system had been run by the Bureau of Indian Affairs, which faced years of complaints of mismanagement from customers.

The House Interior Committee approved the bill (H Rept 102-360) on Nov. 20. The full House passed the measure Nov. 23 by voice vote.

The Senate followed suit Nov. 25, clearing it for the president.

OIL AND GAS PIPELINE STANDARDS

The Senate propelled legislation to establish stricter environmental standards for oil and natural gas pipelines. But the full House did not act on a similar measure during the first session.

The Senate on Oct. 7 passed a bill (S 1583 — S Rept 102-152) to reauthorize the Natural Gas Pipeline Safety Act of 1968 and the Hazardous Liquid Pipeline Safety Act of 1979, both of which expired in 1991.

The measure also expanded the pipeline oversight responsibilities of the Transportation Department to include environmental protection as well as the protection of human life and private property. The bill subjected abandoned underwater pipelines to federal safety regulation.

Other bill provisions:

- Promoted the so-called excess flow valve, a controversial new safety device that automatically shut off the flow of gas when leaks occurred. The valve was touted as a potential lifesaver, but some industry associations claimed that it would be costly to install.
- Encouraged owners to replace cast iron pipelines.
- Created civil penalties for anyone who damaged a pipeline during excavation work if that person had failed to determine if there were pipelines in the area being dug up.
- Directed the Transportation secretary to study the hazards of abandoned underwater pipelines and report to Congress on the need for federal action.

The Senate Commerce, Science and Transportation Committee approved the pipeline safety bill on July 30.

In the House, the Energy and Commerce Subcommittee on Energy and Power approved a similar bill (HR 1489) by voice vote July 10. The full Energy and Commerce Committee approved the bill (H Rept 102-247, Part 1) on July 30.

Subcommittee Chairman Philip R. Sharp, D-Ind., said the government's record of protecting the environment had "been mixed." Carlos J. Moorhead, R-Calif., said the bill closed loopholes in current law that had done little to halt pipeline leaks.

RESTRICTIONS ON LEAD USE

The Senate Environment and Public Works Committee on Aug. 1 approved legislation designed to improve the environment and protect children from lead poisoning.

The bill (S 391 — S Rept 102-179), approved by voice vote, called on the Environmental Protection Agency to restrict the use of lead in a variety of products most likely to result in lead concentrations in the environment and human food chain.

The bill mandated recycling of lead-acid batteries, which contained nearly 75 percent of all lead used in the country. But members voted, 9-7, not to ban the sale of leaded gasoline in urban areas.

Opponents of the measure argued that it could kill the domestic lead industry and cost jobs. Steve Symms, R-Idaho, argued that it threatened to put a "stranglehold on business" by restricting development and forcing industries offshore.

But the bill's chief sponsor, Harry Reid, D-Nev., argued that the bill "is not directed at wiping out the lead industry, but at saving children. Even the lead industry recognizes it as a problem."

Members approved, by voice vote, an amendment to require real estate firms and landlords to disclose the lead paint levels of houses being sold or apartments being rented.

The Senate Environment Subcommittee on Toxic Substances, Environmental Oversight, Research and Development approved the bill April 17.

In the House, two related measures were introduced (HR 3554, HR 1750) by Al Swift, D-Wash., and James H. Scheuer, D-N.Y., respectively. The bills failed to advance. ■

Bill Honoring Udall Pocket-Vetoed

A popular bill (S 1176) honoring former Rep. Morris K. Udall, D-Ariz., first cleared Congress in 1991. But President Bush pocket-vetoed it, challenging on constitutional grounds a provision that would have given Congress appointment power.

Udall retired in early 1991 after a 30-year career. *(Udall resignation, p. 51)*

The Senate declined to fight the pocket veto and instead passed a new version of the bill in 1992 without the appointment provision. That bill (S 2184) cleared the House on March 3.

The original bill, sponsored by Sen. Dennis DeConcini, another Democrat from Arizona, would have established an environmental studies foundation and scholarship fund in Udall's name. The Senate approved the measure by voice vote Nov. 21, and the House cleared the bill Nov. 25, also by voice vote.

Bush, in a memorandum of disapproval that never used the word veto, announced Dec. 20 that he would not sign the bill even though it had sailed through both chambers without objection. Bush said the bill would "violate the Constitution" because a majority of the 10-member Udall Foundation's board was to be appointed by Congress and the University of Arizona.

Nonetheless, Bush stressed his agreement in principle with the goals of the foundation and expressed willingness to work with DeConcini to fashion a reworked bill.

DeConcini blasted the president's move, blaming White House Counsel C. Boyden Gray for the administration's inflexible stance. "In vetoing this legislation for seemingly minor and technical objections from his staff, the president has once again demonstrated how hypocritical it is for him to call himself 'the environmental president,'" DeConcini said.

The bill authorized up to $40 million for a new Morris K. Udall Scholarship and Excellence in National Environmental Policy Foundation. The money was to be used for scholarships, fellowships and research into environmental studies.

Of the 10-member board of trustees, four were to be appointed by Congress and four by the president. The president of the University of Arizona was to appoint one member and serve as a non-voting trustee. Similar arrangements were in place in congressionally sponsored fellowships in the names of former Arizona Republican Sen. Barry Goldwater and Presidents Harry S Truman and James Madison, DeConcini said.

The cleared bill, nearly identical to the pocket-vetoed measure, authorized $40 million for the creation of the foundation and established a trust fund to receive private gifts. The foundation, which was to be an independent executive branch entity, was charged with raising awareness of environmental issues.

Pocket Veto Question

The president's asserted veto raised questions. Bush and other presidents had maintained that when Congress was not in session, a bill could not become law if the president let it languish for more than 10 days.

Leaders of Congress insisted that a president could not pocket-veto a bill as long as representatives — in this case the secretary of the Senate — were on the Hill available to receive a veto message.

Technically, when Congress recessed Nov. 27, it did not officially adjourn "sine die," ending the first session. Sine die adjournment occurred only briefly Jan. 3, when the 102nd Congress formally reconvened into a second session and then recessed again until Jan. 21-22. *(First session statistics, p. 11)*

Since the bill was not returned, congressional legal experts said that under normal circumstances the bill would automatically become law. But what that meant was unclear, especially as the administration took no action to publish or codify the proposal so that the law would take effect.

The Supreme Court had declined to rule on the intrasession pocket-veto question. ■

President's Letter

Following is the text of President Bush's Dec. 20 letter to Congress explaining his pocket veto of S 1176, a bill that would have established a scholarship in honor of retiring Rep. Morris K. Udall, D-Ariz.:

With great regret, I am withholding my approval of S 1176, the Morris K. Udall Scholarship and Excellence in National Environmental Policy Act. Although the bill has a worthy goal and attempts to honor a respected public servant, it would violate the Constitution.

Under this bill, determinations about eligibility for federal funds would be made by the board of trustees of a foundation created by the bill. Of the board's nine voting members, four would be appointed by the leadership of the Congress, and one would be appointed by the president of the University of Arizona. Under the Appointments Clause of the Constitution, however, the Congress may not reserve to itself the power to appoint those who execute the laws, nor may it vest such power in a person outside the federal government.

In addition, the legislative history indicates that the members of the board to be appointed by the congressional leadership might themselves be members of Congress. Such appointments would raise serious problems under the Incompatibility and Ineligibility clauses of the Constitution.

Accordingly, I have decided not to sign the bill within 10 days after presentment. Because the Congress is adjourned, this means that the bill will not become a law. I stress that I am withholding my signature for constitutional reasons alone and not because of any objection to the substantive goals of this bill or any lack of regard for Mo Udall. Rep. Udall has had a long and distinguished public career. He has brought humor, intelligence, and dedication to the discharge of his duties and earned the esteem of his colleagues on both sides of the aisle.

Since funds appropriated to the foundation will not be available until Sept. 30, 1992, sufficient time remains for the Congress to present me a bill without constitutional defects. My administration will work with the Congress to enact such a bill promptly.

I hope to sign legislation, early in the next session of the Congress, to honor Rep. Udall in a constitutionally permissible fashion. ■

NOAA Bill Got House Nod; Didn't Reach Senate Floor

The House on Nov. 20 gave voice vote approval to a bill that renewed weather and coastal research programs at the National Oceanographic and Atmospheric Administration (NOAA) for two years. However, a companion bill in the Senate did not make it to the floor during the first session.

As passed by the House, HR 2130 (HR 102-133) authorized ongoing activities and permitted spending for new programs to update weather satellites and radar systems used to predict hurricanes, tornadoes and other dangerous storms. It also authorized spending to modernize the atmospheric administration's aging fleet of 23 research ships and established a national coastal pollution monitoring program.

The House bill, which authorized $1.63 billion in fiscal 1992 and $1.7 billion in fiscal 1993, was a compromise that combined aspects of measures approved earlier by the Merchant Marine and Fisheries and the Science, Space and Technology committees.

Closing Weather Stations

During the 1980s, the bill ran into trouble in the House primarily because of the efforts of Reagan administration budget-cutters to reduce funding for the National Weather Service and close its weather stations. Moves to close the stations drew strenuous opposition from members with threatened stations in their districts.

The bill again faced opposition in 1991 after the Science and Merchant Marine committees approved their portions of it and merged them. The compromise bill was about $100 million more than the Bush administration had requested for the agency.

And many of the policy changes included in the compromise made it unacceptable to the administration, which threatened on Oct. 30 to veto it. On the same day, Republicans Robert S. Walker and Don Ritter, both of Pennsylvania, threatened to block the bill, saying it was too costly.

The House bill included many proposals that the administration had gone on record as opposing, but concerns about excessive spending were allayed because the price tag of the compromise bill was at least lower than earlier versions.

Before passing the bill, lawmakers approved with little debate 10 amendments, including a controversial plan to continue operating weather radar systems, some of which were slated to be closed.

Successfully offered by Carl C. Perkins, D-Ky., the controversial plan would have delayed any agency move to shut down existing radar systems — even when new, more modern systems were in place — until the Commerce secretary certified that the closure would not hurt weather forecasting.

The Perkins amendment was politically attractive because it offered one more guarantee that most existing weather stations would remain open. Walker opposed it, saying it would make it impossible to even test new radar systems.

Closing weather bureaus was also an issue when the Senate Commerce Committee on July 30 approved by voice vote its bill (S 1405) to reauthorize NOAA. The panel approved an amendment that blocked NOAA from closing state weather bureaus before the National Academy of Sciences had a chance to study the issue.

John Kerry, D-Mass., opposed the amendment, saying it would lead to a veto by President Bush, who said NOAA should have control over bureau closings.

Ways and Means Weighs In

The House Ways and Means Committee on July 10 weighed in on an obscure provision in HR 2130, deleting a section that panel members said could reduce the revenues collected from the shipbuilding industry.

The bill was referred to Ways and Means at the request of committee Chairman Dan Rostenkowski, D-Ill. Usually, only the Merchant Marine and the Science committees had jurisdiction over the NOAA authorization.

The section that Ways and Means members objected to would have allowed a tax-exempt fund for building certain ships to be used also for building NOAA vessels. Since shipbuilding companies paid into the fund, Ways and Means staff members argued that the addition of another eligible vessel would entice shipbuilders to put additional money into the fund, reducing the amount of their taxable income and, thus, federal revenues.

However, Rostenkowski said his main concern was to avoid sending a revenue bill to the Senate that could become a vehicle for other tax provisions. ■

Multi-Year NASA Reauthorization Signed

The NASA reauthorization bill, which the Senate cleared for President Bush on Nov. 22, restricted spending for major space projects by requiring annual estimates of the full cost of multi-year projects. But as in past years, the bill was largely symbolic because Congress already had approved the fiscal 1992 NASA spending bill.

On Dec. 9, Bush signed the bill, which authorized $15.2 billion in fiscal 1992, $15.6 billion in fiscal 1993 and $17 billion in fiscal 1994 for the National Aeronautics and Space Administration.

There had been hopes among some members that the authorizers would act on legislation well before appropriators finished work. But those hopes dissolved when the reauthorization bill bogged down in the Senate.

Even so, House passage in May raised the profile of the House Science, Space and Technology Committee and its new chairman, George E. Brown Jr., D-Calif. And when House appropriators later refused to fund the orbiting laboratory known as space station *Freedom*, the Science Committee had a strong platform from which to fight for the station. *(Space station, p. 239)*

The Science Committee had been widely viewed as virtually irrelevant because it had tended to rubber-stamp past NASA budget requests and had failed to act early enough to affect Appropriations Committee decisions. As a result, the Appropriations Committee, which had real control over spending decisions, had largely set space policy.

But in 1991, the House committee helped set the tone

for the new Congress by proposing early in the session to reduce the president's budget request by nearly $500 million — the first time in several years that lawmakers had attempted to curb the space agency's funding authority.

While the House bill largely served as a blueprint for the Senate bill, there were a few important differences.

The House fully funded an administration priority aimed at landing Americans on the moon and Mars; the Senate provided no funding for it. The conference report split the difference, funding the program at $41.5 million.

The House also included a random drug-testing program for all NASA employees, but the Senate bill did not. Negotiators compromised by calling for drug testing for a more limited group of NASA employees.

Both bills authorized full funding for the space station and required the agency to make annual estimates of the long-term costs of all major projects.

Lawmakers had been frustrated by the agency's practice of describing only the first- and second-year costs of new projects. Costs during planning stages were usually low. But once projects got off the ground, costs ballooned and Congress was left with the choice of spending much more money than planned or killing a project in progress.

BOXSCORE

➡ **NASA Reauthorization (HR 1988).** A multi-year authorization for space programs.

Reports: H Rept 102-41, S Rept 102-97.

KEY ACTION

April 24 — The **House** Science Committee approved HR 1988 by voice vote.

May 2 — The **House** passed HR 1988, 361-36.

July 2 — The **Senate** Commerce Committee approved HR 1988 by voice vote.

Sept 27 — The **Senate** amended and passed HR 1988 by voice vote.

Nov. 7 — The **House** passed the revised HR 1988 with amendments.

Nov. 22 — The **Senate** agreed to House amendments.

Dec. 9 — President Bush signed HR 1988 — PL 102-195.

Unlike in previous years, the 1991 bill authorized multi-year funding for the space agency. The two chambers had battled over the number of years to be authorized, which resulted in a deadlock on a measure in 1989 after the House approved a three-year authorization and the Senate a one-year bill. *(1989 Almanac, p. 695)*

The problem started to unfold again in 1990 when the House Science Committee, led by Chairman Robert A. Roe, D-N.J., again pushed for a multi-year authorization bill. But a one-year authorization prevailed when pitted against the Senate Commerce, Science and Transportation Committee's chairman, Ernest F. Hollings, D-S.C., who exerted additional influence as a top member of the Appropriations Committee. *(1990 Almanac, p. 434)*

The $13.9 billion authorization bill (PL 101-611) passed by Congress in 1990 faced further hurdles as a series of space mishaps tarnished lawmakers' enthusiasm for new space endeavors. Although the year opened with expectations of an exciting new start for space science and exploration, it rapidly disintegrated after the $2 billion-plus Hubble Space Telescope was discovered to have a focusing flaw in its mirror, the shuttle fleet was grounded for months by fuel leaks and the $20 billion-plus space station was troubled by serious design flaws.

The one-year authorization that finally passed in 1990 reflected not only Hollings' muscle, but Congress' skepticism of the space agency's ability to effectively administer multi-year, multibillion-dollar projects.

Waning Support

Although NASA salvaged funding for its centerpiece spacecraft, the space station, the amount of congressional opposition to continuing a massive project so far into its development marked a turning point for the space agency in its relations with Congress.

Waning congressional support was particularly evident in the making of the fiscal 1992 appropriations bill for NASA. It canceled key programs, slowed others and left the agency with a spending level that barely kept pace with the previous year. *(Appropriations, p. 516)*

Reductions in 1991 gutted at least three of NASA's proposals for new projects and reduced the growth of many ongoing space science projects by 25 percent to 35 percent.

"For many years, Congress didn't question NASA much," said Robert S. Walker, R-Pa., ranking member on the House Science Committee. "But in times of diminished resources, Congress has become more questioning."

Frustration with NASA was not limited to Congress.

Bush administration officials echoed congressional concerns. They feared that NASA had failed to face internal management problems that might have contributed to technical botches and cost overruns on such programs as the Hubble Telescope, the GOES-NEXT weather satellite and the space station.

Some NASA officials blamed the agency's woes on bad publicity from the troubled course of some of the agency's more high-profile endeavors. But lawmakers said they were less willing to defend spending when projects failed and found it even more difficult to win the agency additional funds when things were going wrong.

"One thing that fuels NASA is success," said Democratic Sen. Richard C. Shelby of Alabama, home to several NASA contractors and facilities.

Problems with the space station and the weather satellite prompted authorizers and appropriators in both chambers to consider revamping NASA's management.

Brown wanted NASA to streamline its nine space centers. He cosponsored a bill (HR 2162) with Charles E. Schumer, D-N.Y., that sought to make contractors more accountable by holding them liable for the cost of correcting technical problems, such as Hubble's flawed mirror.

Both House and Senate versions of legislation to reauthorize NASA also included mandates requiring the agency to estimate a project's costs over its lifetime.

"This is a new and needed congressional oversight," said Al Gore, D-Tenn., chairman of the Senate Commerce Space Subcommittee.

HOUSE SUBCOMMITTEE ACTION

For the first time in years, a House Science panel in charge of space programs cut the space agency's 1992 budget proposal. Members of the Space Subcommittee were usually NASA's biggest boosters.

The panel on April 11 sliced nearly half a billion dollars out of the NASA budget plan but authorized full spending for the agency's flagship project, the space station.

Among the cuts were $125 million from the proposed new launch system for the space shuttle and $75 million from a system of satellites that would be used to observe Earth for global climate change research.

Only Dick Zimmer, R-N.J., opposed the panel's action, saying members should not fund the space station at all.

Although panel members took pains to support the nation's space program in general, there was little doubt that the cuts amounted to a warning that NASA needed to put its house in order.

NASA had sought a 13 percent spending boost in fiscal 1992 at a time when many other programs had barely kept pace with inflation.

"You can't just pitch your briefcase on the table and tell Congress what you want anymore," said Ralph M. Hall, D-Texas, chairman of the Space Subcommittee.

NASA officials seemed dismayed by the panel's action. "We need the money that we have requested," said William B. Lenoir, associate administrator for NASA space flight programs. "We're cut to the bare bone as it is."

Members said they hoped that by making cuts and completing work on the NASA authorization bill early in the budget cycle they would have more of an impact on spending decisions and policy than in past years.

"Today's markup will be remembered in the history of the subcommittee as the time when the subcommittee asserted itself by identifying spending priorities," said F. James Sensenbrenner Jr., R-Wis., ranking minority member.

The panel approved funding for the space station at the same level as requested by Bush — $2.03 billion for fiscal 1992. Under the existing schedule, astronauts were to begin building the station in 1996; it would be fully manned in the year 2000.

The committee cut $485 million out of the proposed $15.8 billion NASA budget. Among the cuts were:

- $125 million from the new launch system for the space shuttle, a 71 percent cut.
- $75 million from the Earth observing system of satellites, a 22 percent cut.
- $50 million from a space instrument intended to provide information about the electromagnetic spectrum, a 24 percent cut.

HOUSE COMMITTEE ACTION

The House Science Committee on April 24 gave voice vote approval to the subcommittee's $15.3 billion authorization bill for NASA that sought to make record cuts in the president's budget request.

"We are going to apply different and more rigorous standards to NASA, and I'm sure that is going to cause some tension," Brown said. "But I think overall it will increase our ability to support NASA."

The most contentious debate of the markup was over a proposal by Zimmer to request a study on alternative ways to perform scientific work on the space station *Freedom.*

The proposal divided station supporters, some of whom saw the study as a threat to the station, which was already on somewhat shaky ground in Congress. The amendment was defeated, 23-27.

HOUSE FLOOR ACTION

The House overwhelmingly passed the fiscal 1992 NASA authorization bill on May 2 amid growing concern about the cost of the space station.

The $15.3 billion bill (HR 1988), passed on a 361-36 vote, was $488 million lower than Bush requested. Although the bill was subject to appropriations, it marked the first time in several years that Congress had reduced the NASA budget from the White House request. *(Vote 76, p. 20-H)*

The $2.03 billion slated to be spent on the space station was left intact. However, the overall reduction, coming on the heels of a highly critical General Accounting Office (GAO) report of NASA's latest cost estimates for the space station, represented increasing oversight by Congress of the space agency.

"Over the past 30 years, NASA has had many successes and also its share of setbacks," said Science Committee Chairman Brown. "We are now trying to figure out what should be the role of the space program in the 21st century."

The bill followed the key recommendations of the blue-ribbon panel, known as the Augustine Commission, whose report on the future of U.S. space policy was released in the fall of 1990. The report suggested that Congress prioritize NASA projects, saying the agency was trying to do too much with too little money. The report skirted the question of which programs to cut, and the House bill took a similar tack.

Still, the House bill included funding for almost every major program requested by the space agency, though some at lower levels. Hardest hit was research for the new launch vehicle, the advanced X-ray astrophysics observatory, and planetary probes to observe Saturn and its moon Titan and conduct a rendezvous with a comet.

Though the controversial space station program was unscathed, it did receive a blow. An amendment offered by Zimmer, and approved by voice vote, authorized a $200,000 study by the prestigious National Academy of Sciences, a nonpartisan science group, to examine alternative ways to do the research that the station was slated to conduct.

The same amendment failed when offered in committee largely because station supporters considered it a threat. Station backers feared that the academy would find that similar research could be done without a station, which would undermine the justification for building it.

Rep. Barbara Boxer, D-Calif., who chaired the Government Operations Subcommittee on Government Activities and Transportation, was the harshest critic of the station during the floor debate. Boxer held the hearing on May 1 at which the GAO cost estimates were released.

The GAO found that the station would cost $40 billion to build, $10 billion more than NASA estimated, and that the station's operating costs for its 30-year life would be close to $78 billion, $24 billion more than NASA projected.

"For $30 billion, what we would have is an empty garage in space with nothing happening in it or around it," Boxer said.

"There are astronomical differences between the NASA estimate and the GAO," Boxer said, calling for an audit by the independent National Academy of Public Accountants.

Space station supporters accused Boxer of applying unreasonable standards.

"We do not require any other project to include its operational costs for any project," said Sensenbrenner. "When we build a homeless shelter in California, we don't estimate its 10-year costs."

In other action on the bill, the House added a drug-testing amendment offered by Gerald B. H. Solomon, R-N.Y. The amendment required random drug testing of all NASA employees.

As passed by the House, the bill:

- Authorized a $2.97 billion shuttle program to pay for nine flights, $53 million less than Bush recommended.
- Authorized $2.03 billion for continued research and development of the space station, a 30-year research facility to accommodate four astronauts. About $128.9 million of the total was to be withheld until NASA submitted an engineering review of the redesigned station.
- Recommended reducing funding for a new launch vehicle to $50 million, a cut of $125 million from Bush's request, leaving $20 million for research on the new launch vehicle.
- Continued a joint effort by NASA and the Defense Department to design the National Aerospace Plane (NASP), which was expected to fly several times faster than the supersonic Concorde. NASA's share of the program was $72 million.
- Recommended withholding spending for the Earth observing system of satellites — a portion of NASA's Mission to Planet Earth project — until an engineering study was completed. The bill also increased by $10 million spending for the Earth probes portion of the project, making it $83 million.

SENATE COMMITTEE ACTION

The Senate Commerce, Transportation and Science Committee on May 14 approved a $15.3 billion NASA authorization bill including the full $2.03 billion Bush requested for the space station for fiscal 1992.

The Commerce Committee, on a voice vote, decided to cut nearly $500 million from Bush's $15.8 billion budget request but opted to spare NASA's three largest programs: the space shuttle, the station and Mission to Planet Earth.

The Senate authorization bill (HR 1988) mostly mirrored the House version.

Although the Commerce Committee left the space station intact, it dealt Bush a blow by virtually gutting the $94 million requested for research on manned travel to the moon and Mars.

The committee also approved on a voice vote an amendment offered by Richard H. Bryan, D-Nev., that eliminated all spending for research on extraterrestrial life. Bush had requested $14 million for the program.

The committee bill also:

- Authorized a $2.95 billion shuttle program to pay for nine flights.
- Authorized $780.6 million for Earth sciences, including full funding for Mission to Planet Earth, NASA's $40 billion environmental satellite program.
- Recommended killing the Comet Rendezvous Asteroid Flyby program. Bush had sought $65 million for fiscal 1992.
- Recommended $50 million in funding for a new launch system — a reduction of $125 million.

SENATE FLOOR ACTION

The Senate passed, by voice vote, a $15 billion fiscal 1992 authorization bill (HR 1988) for NASA on Sept. 27.

The bill passed just as Congress was preparing to clear a $14.3 billion appropriation for the space agency.

Prior to the measure's passage, Gore, D-Tenn., chairman of the Commerce Subcommittee on Space, touted such agency undertakings as the NASP, designed to take off like an airplane and fly into orbit. "Critical programs such as the National Aerospace Plane receive full funding," Gore said on the Senate floor.

However, only intervention by Jake Garn, R-Utah, saved the plane from being zeroed out altogether from the cleared spending bill for veterans', housing and space programs. The appropriations bill cut the fiscal 1992 NASP appropriation by 90 percent — from $67 million to $5 million.

The authorizing committees had requested in HR 1988 that NASA estimate the full cost of projects when submitting annual budget requests. This was a significant departure from the way the space agency operated and was designed to give Congress greater ability to oversee major endeavors.

Although the bill fell short of the president's request, the Senate endorsed full funding for several of the administration's high-priority programs, including $2.03 billion for space station *Freedom* and $336 million for the satellites required for the Mission to Planet Earth project. The satellites were designed to carry scientific instruments to study global climate change.

As passed, the Senate bill:

- Canceled any funding for Bush's proposal to send Americans to explore the moon and Mars. The request was for $67 million. The House provided $66.5 million.
- Cut $125 million for the proposed new launch system for putting heavier cargoes into space. The request was for $175 million. The House also cut funding.
- Prohibited spending on the search for extraterrestrial intelligence. The request was for $14.5 million. The House provided full funding.

FINAL ACTION

The House on Nov. 7 amended a three-year, $47.8 billion bill renewing the federal space agency and sent it back to the Senate.

The amended bill authorized $15.2 billion for fiscal 1992, $15.6 billion for fiscal 1993 and $17 billion for fiscal 1994 for NASA. The fiscal 1992 amount fell $594 million short of the Bush administration request.

The Senate cleared the bill by voice vote Nov. 22.

The authorization included full funding of $2.03 billion for the space station. The revised bill also represented a step toward multi-year funding of NASA. ■

Space Station at Heart of Program Controversy

The space station *Freedom* was the touchstone of controversy during the 1991 debate over the beleaguered space program. House appropriators attempted to kill the project, arguing that its ballooning budget would siphon money from smaller science projects and domestic programs. But supporters, led by the White House, successfully argued that killing the project would undermine U.S. leadership in manned space exploration.

This was the first year of such efforts to strip the $30 billion project from the fiscal 1992 spending bill for the Departments of Veterans Affairs (VA) and Housing and Urban Development (HUD), which funds the National Aeronautics and Space Administration (NASA). *(Appropriations, p. 516)*

In the end, the House and Senate voted to maintain

funding for the station but agreed to cap it at $2.03 billion in fiscal 1992 and at $2.25 billion in fiscal 1993.

The station supporters were a coalition of lawmakers who served on the House and Senate Science committees, most Republicans and White House lobbyists.

Opponents came from two camps: those who believed that Congress should be spending more money on social programs rather than on big science and military projects, and those who feared that big science projects would largely eliminate spending on smaller science programs.

Although the station was a vulnerable target of criticism from both camps, it continued to attract political appeal, especially among members with hometown companies that had a piece of the project.

The multibillion-dollar endeavor was too expensive to fund fully when it was first launched in 1984 by President Ronald Reagan, who dubbed it *Freedom* and pushed Congress to include enough money to guarantee the project's survival. The original plan called for the space station to be constructed in orbit from 1995 to 1999 and then be permanently occupied by a crew of up to eight scientists and astronauts.

President Bush kept the momentum going for the project through its early stages. But the resistance by skeptical lawmakers to such an ambitious and risky undertaking solidified in 1990 when a long-awaited study concluded that the station would require so much maintenance by spacewalking astronauts that it might not be feasible to build as designed. *(1990 Almanac, p. 436)*

Opponents also pointed out that since 1984 the government had spent $5 billion on the project, although construction had not yet begun. Originally, it was expected to cost about $8 billion and to be finished by 1992. In 1991, cost estimates topped $40 billion, and it was not slated for completion until the end of the century.

House appropriators ordered a redesign in their report on the fiscal 1991 NASA spending bill after the complaints that NASA's previous design had flaws and was too expensive. They wanted the design problems worked out before NASA got too far into the actual bending of metal.

The First Blow: Redesign Criticized

NASA released its new design, which trimmed $8.3 billion off the price, early in 1991. But the Space Studies Board of the National Research Council, a nonpartisan group of scientists, concluded the week of March 11 that NASA's redesign of the space station "does not meet the basic research requirements of the two principal scientific disciplines for which it is intended: life sciences and microgravity research and applications."

This latest attack on NASA's massive endeavor compounded a growing sense on Capitol Hill and in the scientific community that big science projects spent too much on construction and too little on reaping benefits from research.

Even the member most responsible in 1991 for shepherding the space project through the House Science, Space and Technology Committee, Chairman George E. Brown Jr. of California, said he thought the project would survive, "but I wouldn't want to bet too much money on it."

Yet the administration seemed undeterred by the searing criticism from the National Research Council.

"Science is but one reason for building a space station," wrote Vice President Dan Quayle in a letter to NASA Administrator Richard H. Truly.

"The ultimate mission of the Space Station is . . . the reaffirmation of the leadership in space of the United States of America, the world's only superpower," the Quayle letter said.

Many on Capitol Hill agreed that the manned space program had much to do with the national mythology of space as the last frontier, a part of America's manifest destiny.

Space exploration also played to some members' deeply held belief that miraculous discoveries could be made in space. "I fully and firmly believe that we're going to find some cures for the dreaded diseases, cancer and diabetes, there because we can't find them on Earth," said Rep. Ralph M. Hall, D-Texas, chairman of the Science subcommittee that controlled spending authorization for the space program.

Despite Congress' and the country's romance with space, even supporters correctly predicted that the pressures on the budget would prompt Congress for the first time to scrutinize the need for the space station and the value of its mission. "Plainly, there is a lot of competition for funds," said Bill Green, R-N.Y., the ranking minority member on the House Appropriations subcommittee that oversaw NASA.

"And it's more difficult to piece together funds for these very large postponable projects like the space station. There is no reason to get there by 2016; it will still be there by 2049," said Green.

The chairman of the House Appropriations subcommittee with NASA jurisdiction, Bob Traxler, D-Mich., said that he would like funding for the station allocated so that Congress could pay for it a "foot at a time, and if all we can afford to put up there is two feet, then that's all we'll put."

The Second Blow: Budget Elimination

Despite the warnings that NASA's flagship project had little merit as a science project, space station supporters were caught off guard on June 3 when $1.9 billion for the project was eliminated by the powerful House Appropriations Committee. The appropriators' action directly clashed with the House Science Committee, which promoted full funding for the space station.

The VA, HUD and Independent Agencies Appropriations Subcommittee on May 15 recommended the elimination of space station funding, despite earlier overwhelming House approval and White House support for the project. The House on May 2 had already passed, 361-36, a bill (HR 1988) to keep the space station going as part of NASA's reauthorization. *(NASA authorization, p. 236)*

Traxler and Green had decided that the only way to meet budget limits was to drop the space station. They insisted that there was not enough money to meet the needs of smaller science projects and social programs in addition to reaching Bush's proposed $15.8 billion budget for NASA — a 13 percent increase over fiscal 1991.

On the eve of the House floor vote, an all-out lobbying effort took place by the White House, with phone calls from Bush and Quayle to key members of Congress. NASA circulated among members a district-by-district breakdown of space station contracts, employment and dollars spent, showing what each would lose if the project were killed.

House Floor Debate

At stake for NASA throughout the eight-hour debate on the House floor over space station funding was the future of its manned space program, which had been the core of its mission since the Apollo moon program in the early 1960s. The agency had been troubled in the past year by problems and cost overruns in many of its key programs, forcing officials to more closely define program goals. The space station was designed to be the steppingstone for planetary exploration by allowing scientists to study how human beings reacted to long periods in the weightless environment of outer space.

In past years, when House members wanted to increase space program spending, they took largely from housing programs for the poor and homeless. But in 1991, space station supporters instead opted to take the majority of the funds from within the space agency and focus the debate on the merits of the space station.

Leaders of the effort to drop the space station emphasized that their complaint was with the cost, not the value, of the station.

Also underlying the space station debate was a struggle between the Science Committee, which authorized NASA spending, and the Appropriations Committee, which made the actual spending decisions. In 1991, the Science Committee's new chairman, Brown, set out to make his committee a power broker on the space station vote. With the backing of the administration, he succeeded.

Supporters were intensely passionate in their appeals over the course of the lengthy debate. "The destiny of mankind will be in the stars," said Robert S. Walker, R-Pa., ranking member on the Science Committee. VA-HUD Subcommittee member Jim Chapman, D-Texas, said medical breakthroughs were on the horizon. "The space station *Freedom* will have a first-class medical laboratory that will allow us to do research in hypertension, diabetes, osteoporosis and research into diseases like cancer and AIDS," he said.

Critics countered that under the current design the scientific capability of the space station could not live up to those promises. They pointed out that a number of science groups, including the prestigious and nonpartisan National Academy of Sciences, viewed the station's scientific capability as virtually non-existent.

Opponents also complained that NASA's existing space station plan was a far cry from its original scope, which envisioned a multitude of purposes for the station: as a space observatory, a life sciences laboratory, a manufacturing facility and a staging area for deep space missions.

"If we fund this, it's clearly not for scientific reasons, it's for the contractors who work on the project," said Rep. Richard J. Durbin, D-Ill. "This has become a WPA [Depression-era Work Projects Administration] project for the aerospace industry."

HOUSE ACTION

The House voted June 6 to continue its funding of the space station in the fiscal 1992 spending bill by freezing every other space program and cutting public housing money for the poor.

The House voted 240-173 on an amendment to restore the station's funding. *(Vote 141, p. 34-H)*

The final bill (HR 2519) passed, 363-39. *(Vote 143, p. 36-H)*

The key amendment to restore space station funding to the spending bill was drafted by the Office of Management and Budget (OMB) and offered by Reps. Chapman and Bill Lowery, R-Calif., VA-HUD Subcommittee members.

In funding the space station, the House cannibalized every other NASA program, including its environmental satellite project, Mission to Planet Earth, and its orbiting observatories.

After the vote, NASA Administrator Truly conceded that unless the final 1992 appropriation for his agency increased, it would be very difficult to run NASA's other programs.

Lowery was a longtime space buff with a passion for NASA's manned space program. Although there were no NASA facilities or jobs in Lowery's North San Diego district, California aerospace companies had some of the largest contracts to build the station.

Chapman's Texarkana district also received no direct benefits from NASA or the space station. But as a member of the cohesive Texas delegation, Chapman had taken a stand in behalf of his state, which would receive at least $3.1 billion in contracts for the space station.

Chapman, Lowery and other space station proponents argued that the project was symbolic of America's leadership in space and could lead to groundbreaking discoveries that would inspire students to go into the sciences. They also said that if the United States backed out of the station, it would damage the country's reputation as a partner in international science ventures. Japan, the European Community and Canada had already committed more than $1.5 billion to the station's development. Japan had said that if the United States withdrew from the project, it would be leery of contributing to other U.S. science projects, including the superconducting super collider. *(Super collider, p. 242)*

Lawrence J. Smith, D-Fla., however, tried to broker a compromise. He offered an amendment to leave housing dollars alone and force NASA to fund the space station entirely from its own budget. It was rejected, 122-296. *(Vote 140, p. 34-H)*

SENATE ACTION

The space station *Freedom* persevered through another round of name-calling as the Senate voted, 35-64, against killing NASA's top project.

Dale Bumpers, D-Ark., led the fight July 17 to cut $1.9 billion of the $2 billion appropriation. *(Vote 132, p. 18-S)*

The Senate gave voice vote approval July 18 to the $80.9 billion bill after two long days of interrupted debate over the space station, the savings and loan bailout and $72.8 million in pork projects.

Bumpers complained that the space station had little scientific merit and little cachet with the American people. He proposed cutting $1.9 billion from the project in fiscal 1992 and redistributing $600 million to several NASA programs, the National Science Foundation and veterans' medical care and prosthetic research. The remaining $1.3 billion would have been applied to reducing the deficit.

Bumpers was up against a former astronaut-hero, John Glenn, D-Ohio; a guest astronaut, Jake Garn, R-Utah; and many other senators with multimillion-dollar NASA contracts and space centers in their states.

Barbara A. Mikulski, D-Md., chairman of the VA, HUD and Independent Agencies Appropriations Subcommittee , said she, too, had been skeptical about the space station, too. She said she thought it was "a condo in the sky." Now, however, she said the project's design and mission had been streamlined and clarified.

Mikulski, whose state was home to the Goddard Space Flight Center, said she was a convert as well as "a true believer." And Glenn told of the scientific progress that had been made from space exploration, such as the development of lighter, stronger materials.

"Every single advance we have made has been because someone was curious about the unknown," Glenn said, urging senators to fund the project.

FINAL ACTION

Congress on Oct. 3 easily cleared the $81 billion spending bill that included the full $2.03 billion allocation for the space station. Yet conferees on HR 2519 had difficulty juggling the competing demands of the centerpiece space project, housing for the poor and environmental cleanup.

Jack F. Kemp, secretary of Housing and Urban Development, had threatened to ask Bush to veto the bill because it funded special projects at the expense of a new program to help public housing tenants buy their homes. But the full funding for the space station went a long way toward easing the bill's enactment.

The House adopted the conference report (H Rept 102-226) Oct. 2 on a 390-30 vote; the Senate gave it voice vote approval the same day, although a disagreement over standards for veterans' medical laboratories delayed final action until Oct. 3. *(Vote 286, p. 70-H)*

The president signed the bill Oct. 28 — PL 102-139. ■

Super Collider Survived Another Year

Lawmakers unsuccessfully sought for the second consecutive year to kill the $8.2 billion giant atom smasher, slated to be built in Waxahachie, Texas, that had come to symbolize the role and troubles of big science projects in Congress. The project not only survived its critics, but won a healthy $484 million appropriation to keep it going through fiscal 1992.

The Energy Department project, called the superconducting super collider, was expected by early 1991 to cost nearly twice as much as advertised when the House voted in June 1989 to break ground at a site 25 miles south of Dallas. It was conceived as a 54-mile tunnel ring that physicists intended to use to collide electrons at high speeds and, they hoped, learn more about the building blocks of matter.

Critics complained that the escalating cost of the super collider was crowding out many other less expensive, and potentially more fruitful, scientific endeavors.

Conferees on the energy and water spending bill (HR 2427 — PL 102-104) settled on the $484 million appropriation for the project as a compromise between the House and Senate amounts.

That figure was $50 million less than President Bush had sought but nearly twice its appropriation for the 1991 fiscal year. *(Appropriations, p. 569)*

Efforts to cap spending as well as eliminate funding for the super collider surfaced again in 1991. But there was not a renewed struggle to pass an authorization bill that could place any additional constraints on the project.

The year before, Energy Committee Chairman J. Bennett Johnston, D-La., an avid proponent of the project, successfully blocked efforts to move an authorization bill because he could control funding through his other chairmanship — the Appropriations Subcommittee on Energy and Water Development. *(1990 Almanac, p. 438)*

House Action

The House Appropriations Committee on May 22 sent a spending bill for energy and water development to the House floor that reopened the debate over how much the government should invest in the giant atom smasher under construction in Texas.

The committee's fiscal 1992 appropriations measure included a $434 million installment on the super collider.

Bush had requested $534 million, but Appropriations members accepted the recommendation of the Energy and Water Subcommittee to cut the request by $100 million. Even so, the super collider was one of the few growth items in the bill, jumping from its fiscal 1991 appropriations of $243 million.

On May 23, Sherwood Boehlert, R-N.Y., a member of the House Science Committee, sought permission from the House Rules Committee to offer a floor amendment to cap the U.S. investment in the project at $5 billion. He was denied that request because it involved putting legislative language on an appropriations bill.

Meanwhile, at the Appropriations markup, Sidney R. Yates, D-Ill., proposed cutting $43 million more from the super collider appropriation to start upgrading a new particle collider ring at the Fermi National Accelerator Laboratory, located outside Chicago, Yates' hometown.

Tom Bevill, D-Ala., chairman of the Energy and Water Subcommittee, said funding the new particle injector at Fermi would unravel the subcommittee's pact not to fund any new construction projects.

Yates' motion failed, 11-32, but not before drawing some sympathy from members who worried about the super collider's rising cost. "This has turned out to be one of the hungriest hogs at the federal trough," said Richard J. Durbin, D-Ill.

Super collider opponents also were unable to muster enough support to scrap the project when the House passed the spending bill for energy and water projects on May 29, its first appropriations bill of the year.

Lawmakers were split over whether to provide funding for the super collider. Some members, such as Boehlert, had supported the project in the past but said its spiraling costs led them to oppose further funding.

By a 165-251 vote, the House rejected an amendment by Jim Slattery, D-Kan., to eliminate super collider funding. *(Vote 117, p. 30-H)*

Senate Action

The Senate Appropriations Subcommittee on Energy and Water Development on June 11 approved by voice vote a fiscal 1992 spending bill that provided a little more than $508 million for the atom smasher. As approved, it restored $75 million of $100 million in cuts made by the House.

The next day, Senate Appropriations Committee members voted, 20-0, to approve the spending bill without any changes to the funding level for the super collider.

The hurdle came on July 9, when the Senate for the first time was forced to go on record supporting the controversial project. Senate appropriators readily agreed to the committee's funding proposal. But when the bill came to the floor, Dale Bumpers, D-Ark., proposed eliminating funding for it. He argued that the tight economic times overshadowed any scientific merit.

"It would be nice to know the origin of matter," Bumpers said. "It would also be nice to have a balanced budget."

But Johnston and both Texas senators sprang to the project's defense.

They argued that the United States could ill-afford to turn its back on the scientific and technical promise of the project. Phil Gramm, R-Texas, cast it as a choice between investing in future technological competitiveness and spending programs with more immediate political popularity.

Bumpers was the only senator to speak in favor of his amendment and acknowledged that he lacked the votes for passage. The Senate eventually voted 62-37 to reject the proposal, but Bumpers did win some prominent votes, including those of Majority Leader George J. Mitchell, D-Maine, and Assistant Minority Leader Alan K. Simpson, R-Wyo. *(Vote 121, p. 17-S)*

FINAL ACTION

House-Senate conferees agreed to give $484 million to the superconducting super collider, $50 million more than the House-passed bill but $24 million less than the Senate had approved for the project.

The completed $21.8 billion energy and water bill was on its way to the White House after the House adopted the conference report (H Rept 102-177) July 31, 393-32, and the Senate cleared the measure Aug. 2 by voice vote. *(Vote 245, p. 56-H).*

The president signed the bill on Aug. 17 (PL 102-104). ■

Technology Bill Snagged By GOP Opposition

For the third consecutive year, Congress failed to clear key legislation designed to increase the competitiveness of U.S. high-technology companies in world markets. Objections by the Bush administration and Senate Republicans stalled the bill, which was known as the American Technology Pre-Eminence Act.

About an hour before adjourning Nov. 27, the Senate passed HR 1989 by voice vote. But the vote on a compromise measure came too late for final House action during the first session.

Congress cleared the bill Jan. 28, 1992, after the House voted, 392-1, to agree to the Senate amendments.

President Bush supported the compromise, which authorized two years of spending — $348 million for fiscal 1992 and $359 million for fiscal 1993 — for programs run by the Commerce Department's National Institute of Standards and Technology (NIST), a top government laboratory that assisted private industry.

Included in those authorizations was $100 million to help companies doing research in cutting-edge technologies. The bill also provided $25 million annually for five regional technology centers to help small and medium-size manufacturing businesses learn how to use new technologies.

Although an earlier version of the bill had attracted support from the information and manufacturing industries and from a bipartisan group of lawmakers, it ran afoul of the Bush administration, which objected to a $10 million loan program added by the House Science Committee.

The program, inserted at the behest of Rep. Norman Y. Mineta, D-Calif., would have set aside $10 million for a loan program for high-technology companies seeking to commercialize new products.

Administration opponents called the program a form of industrial policy and argued that by selecting which companies should receive loans, the government would be interfering in the marketplace.

But the week before lawmakers adjourned, a compromise was struck that called for the controversial loan program to be dropped.

In exchange, House Republicans agreed to drop a bill provision that would have required companies whose research led to the commercialization of successful products to pay back grants.

The Senate passed the compromise version after an unidentified Republican dropped a hold on it, clearing the way for a vote on the bill.

BOXSCORE

➡ **Technology Programs (HR 1989, S 1034)** Bills to authorize manufacturing and technology programs at the Department of Commerce.

Reports: H Rept 102-134, S Rept 102-157

KEY ACTION

May 1 — The **House** Science, Space and Technology Committee approved HR 1989, 26-5.

July 16 — The **House** passed HR 1989, 296-122.

July 30 — The **Senate** Commerce, Science and Transportation Committee approved S 1034 by voice vote.

Nov. 27 - The **Senate** passed HR 1989 by voice vote after substituting it with S 1034.

Background

Both chambers passed similar legislation in 1990 (S 1191, HR 4329) but failed at the eleventh hour after Sen. Bob Kasten, R-Wis., insisted that the bill include product-liability reforms. Commerce Committee Chairman Ernest F. Hollings, D-S.C., blocked Kasten's move.

Although Hollings was a strong proponent of the advanced technology programs, he was an equally strong opponent of tampering with the product-liability law. *(1990 Almanac, p. 440)*

The legislation was aimed at encouraging companies to form joint ventures to develop new technologies, such as high-definition television and advanced manufacturing materials.

Supporters cited efforts by a semiconductor industry consortium that was successful in competing with the Japanese semiconductor industry.

The Advanced Technology Program also was popular with industry because it gave seed money to companies to explore technological processes that were needed to develop commercially viable products.

The program was first funded at $10 million in 1990; in fiscal 1991, $36 million was appropriated for it.

Appropriators increased that amount to $47 million in fiscal 1992, $11 million more than the administration's request. *(Appropriations, p. 531)*

In the first year the program was funded, it received 249 requests for grants but had money for just 11 awards. Among the grants awarded was $266,000 for a new technology to correct production flaws caused by the heating and cooling of machine tools and $823,000 for a new form of disk drives and magnetic tape.

House Action

After a partisan debate on technology loans to commercial firms, the House Science, Space and Technology Committee approved HR 1989 on May 1 by a 26-5 vote.

The committee's fiscal 1992 authorization bill for Commerce Department technology programs included $90 million for the Advanced Technology Program.

The bill also authorized approximately $340 million for National Institute of Science and Technology programs for fiscal 1992; 1991 funding was $215 million.

Before approving the measure, lawmakers disagreed over an amendment that would shift $10 million from the Advanced Technology Program, which offered technology grants, and instead use the money for loans to help companies commercialize specific emerging technologies, such as those in the electronics or computer fields.

GOP members opposed the amendment, offered by Mineta, saying it would lead to a U.S. industrial policy in which Congress would choose which products would get government loans.

The amendment was approved by a 15-13 vote but immediately faced an uncertain future. Republicans warned that it could lead to a veto. Chairman George E. Brown Jr., D-Calif., said it was not worth killing the bill over the amendment.

The controversy over the loan program for companies seeking to commercialize new high-technology products or processes continued during House floor action on July 16.

Administration officials said that the loan program was tantamount to industrial policy, which the administration opposed as unfairly tilting toward specific industries.

Robert S. Walker of Pennsylvania, the ranking Republican on the Science Committee, mounted an unsuccessful effort against the provision. His amendment to strike it from the bill failed 172-246. *(Vote 206, p. 50-H)*

"This smacks very definitely of industrial policy by beginning to have government picking winners and losers.... The government is not a very good repository of wisdom about the marketplace," Walker said.

The House also rejected, by voice vote, an attempt by Walker to attach a non-binding resolution to the bill endorsing a reduction in the capital gains tax — as sought by the Bush administration — to spur U.S. competitiveness.

As passed by the House 296-122, the bill authorized $210 million in fiscal 1992 for the Commerce Department's National Institute of Standards and Technology and $90 million for the Advanced Technology Program. *(Vote 207, p. 50-H)*

Senate Action

The Senate Commerce, Science and Transportation Committee approved S 1034 by voice vote on July 30. The Senate version authorized spending $357 million in fiscal 1992 and $436 million in fiscal 1993 for the expansion of an array of programs run by the Department of Commerce. It included a $211 million authorization for the National Institute of Standards and Technology.

The Senate committee bill omitted the controversial loan program included in the House bill. The Bush administration had threatened to veto the House version primarily because of the provision requiring that $10 million be spent on a loan program that would help companies commercialize new technologies. The administration charged that by making loans to specific companies the government would be interfering in the free market, which went against the White House's longstanding opposition to industrial policy. However, John D. Rockefeller IV, D-W.Va., threatened to add a similar provision when the bill went to the Senate floor.

Overall, the Senate committee bill authorized more generous funding levels than the House for several of the programs, including the Advanced Technology Program at a $110 million level in fiscal 1992, $20 million more than the House authorization and triple its fiscal 1991 funding level.

The committee bill also authorized $25 million for the Regional Centers for the Transfer of Manufacturing Technology. Also known as the Hollings Centers, for the Commerce Committee chairman who encouraged development, they were in Columbia, S.C.; Troy, N.Y.; Cleveland; Ann Arbor, Mich.; and Topeka, Kan. The centers helped companies with fewer than 500 employees learn how to use advanced technologies to become more competitive with foreign companies.

The centers received $11.9 million in fiscal 1991. For fiscal 1992, the administration requested $10.3 million. The House and Senate approved $15 million for fiscal 1992.

Although the House and Senate worked out a compromise measure prior to adjournment, the Senate passed it by voice vote only moments before the end of the first session. The House did not act on it before adjournment. ■

Bill Enacted To Advance High-Speed Computing

The Senate on Nov. 22 cleared for President Bush a bill (S 272 — PL 102-194) that authorized multi-year expenditures for advancing the U.S. role in high-speed computing. It was signed into law Dec. 9.

The supercomputer bill had been three years in the making and authorized $2 billion over the next five years to develop supercomputers and to design a high-speed computer network. The measure, which was cleared by voice vote, was intended to aid U.S. competitiveness in the field of information technology.

With little debate, the Senate on Sept. 11 had passed by voice vote its initial bill (S 272, S Rept 102-57) known as the High-Performance Computing Act. The bill was similar to the House measure (HR 656, Rept 102-66, Part 1) passed July 11. The differences between the two bills were largely technical. Both measures conformed to the proposals made by the White House in its fiscal 1992 budget request.

Both bills authorized a five-year program of at least $2 billion for research and development of supercomputers at eight federal agencies and the creation of a network linking them.

But action on the bill was delayed for months over a provision inserted at the request of House Majority Leader Richard A. Gephardt, D-Mo., and the House Science Committee.

The controversial provision would have required Congress to be notified of the purchase of foreign goods or services to carry out the program. The Bush administration opposed the provision.

In the end, the notification requirement was dropped from the final bill, which was passed by the House by voice vote on Nov. 20. Instead, the amended bill mandated that the government report annually to Congress on foreign services and goods purchased for the program.

The development of supercomputers — a term that connoted the fastest type of computers in operation at any given time — was thought to be essential to advancing the U.S. role in high-technology fields. A report by the General Accounting Office, the investigative arm of Congress, found that supercomputers could allow automobile manufacturers, oil producers and aerospace, chemical and pharmaceutical companies to speed up design of new products and decrease costs.

The development of supercomputers also was considered crucial to making government research data available to scientists at universities and in private industries nationwide. For example, private researchers would have access to environmental information from such big government science projects as the superconducting super collider and the space agency's Earth Observing System of satellites.

Senate Action

The nearly $1 billion federal research program to create a national network of supercomputers won unanimous approval from the Senate Commerce Committee the week of March 18.

The bill (S 272), written by Al Gore, D-Tenn., established a research program to develop supercomputer hardware and software. The technology, he hoped, would enable scientists to gain access to and analyze large amounts of information through a national network.

It authorized $338 million for the National Aeronautics and Space Administration (NASA) and $650 million for the National Science Foundation over the following five years.

The Bush administration supported the program and included funding for it in its fiscal 1992 budget proposal, after failing to do so the year before.

Gore had introduced a virtually identical bill the previous year. But the measure died of inaction in the House Science Committee, after it had easily passed the Senate on Oct. 25, 1990. High-performance computing had been identified as a "critical technology," necessary to help the United States remain competitive in the rapidly evolving field of supercomputers.

Such computers were as much as 100,000 times more powerful than a standard personal computer and were capable of making billions of mathematical calculations a second.

The bill tapped the Federal Coordinating Council for Science, Engineering and Technology, chaired by presidential science adviser D. Allan Bromley, to set goals for and assign tasks to the nine agencies to be involved in the project.

The program was intended to expand industry, government and university research in supercomputer technology and link researchers to supercomputers, computer data bases, other research facilities and libraries. The Pentagon's Defense Advanced Research Projects Agency, which ran leading edge scientific research programs, was involved in developing the network's technology.

House Action

The House on July 11 passed legislation (HR 656) authorizing $2.9 billion over the following five years to promote research on high-performance supercomputers and to establish a national network of computer "information highways" capable of transmitting billions of bits of information a second. The Science, Space and Technology Committee had reported the bill on May 15, as had the Education and Labor Committee on May 22.

The bill covered spending in six federal agencies, with the bulk of the money going to the National Science Foundation and NASA. The White House science office was responsible for coordinating the program.

The Bush administration supported the bill, which was one of a number of science initiatives that spanned several federal agencies.

Patent and Trademark Office Reauthorized

Congress on Nov. 27 cleared for President Bush a bill (HR 3531 — PL 102-204) that renewed the Commerce Department's Patent and Trademark Office and boosted user fees to make the office completely user-supported. Bush signed the bill Dec. 10.

Final action came when the Senate on Nov. 27 passed the bill by voice vote. The House on Nov. 25 had passed the measure by voice vote. It authorized fiscal 1992 appropriations for the patent office.

The office was last authorized in 1988, and that authority expired on Sept. 30. That legislation (HR 4972 — PL 100-703) authorized the commissioner of patents and trademarks to set fees for public use of the office's automated search systems. Those fees could be used to defray up to 30 percent of the costs of automation. *(1988 Almanac, p. 118)*

This measure renewed the patent office's programs for only one year in an effort to allow Congress to more closely monitor it, said William J. Hughes, D-N.J., chairman of the House Judiciary Subcommittee on Intellectual Property and Judicial Administration.

Patent and trademark fees were increased across the board, following the mandate of the 1990 budget deal to raise an estimated $95 million from user fees to offset agency costs. ■

Copyrights, Patents For Chip Producers

The House cleared a bill (S 909 — PL 102-64) by voice vote on June 25 that allowed the secretary of Commerce to continue to grant copyright and patent protection to producers of semiconductor chips. Also by voice vote, the Senate had passed the bill on June 12. President Bush signed it June 28.

The legislation extended through fiscal 1995 the authority of the 1984 Semiconductor Chip Protection Act (PL 98-620), which granted protection to U.S. companies whose semiconductor chips could not be patented because they did not meet certain criteria, namely that an invention be novel or not obvious to someone skilled in the art. Differences in semiconductor designs were too subtle to allow for such protection. *(1984 Almanac, p. 254)*

The 1984 law protected the topographies (or masks) that were used to produce the layers of integrated circuits that went into creating a semiconductor chip. The act also allowed the secretary to extend patent protection to chips from countries that offered reciprocal treatment to U.S. producers or were in the process of doing so. The secretary's authority to extend reciprocal protection had expired on July 1. It had been renewed once before in 1987.

Action on the House measure (HR 1998, H Rept 102-122) began on May 1 when the Judiciary Subcommittee on Intellectual Property approved the measure quickly by voice vote after holding a hearing on the topic.

Similar legislation (S 909, S Rept 102-78) was approved by voice vote in the Senate Judiciary Committee on May 23. That bill was sent to the House Judiciary Committee on June 13 and became the vehicle that cleared both chambers.

Industry advocates estimated that U.S. companies lost billions of dollars every year to foreign companies that pirated designs and made their own chips.

The semiconductor chip business was one of the most competitive in the world. The United States lagged behind the Japanese and other Pacific Rim countries, and, to recapture the domestic market, the government wanted to limit imports.

The Bush administration also concluded an agreement with Japan on June 11 governing trade in semiconductor chips. The agreement was designed to make it easier for the United States to sell chips to Japan and discourage the Japanese from dumping chips on the U.S. market. ■

Senate Sought To Curb Animal Rights Activists

Legislation to penalize animal activists who took violent action against scientific research facilities passed the Senate on a voice vote Oct. 16.

The bill (S 544), by Howell Heflin, D-Ala., sought to make it a federal offense to damage animal research facilities.

Similar provisions were included in a reauthorization of the National Institutes of Health (NIH) (HR 2507) that was passed by the House in July but did not advance in the Senate. *(National Institutes of Health reauthorization, p. 346)*

Lawmakers were responding to increasing attacks on research facilities in the name of animal protection and the prevention of cruelty to animals. Radical animal groups had broken into facilities that experimented on animals, kidnapped the animals, and destroyed property and records in the laboratories.

The NIH reauthorization measure made it a federal crime to steal, destroy or alter records or property or to steal or injure research animals in any federally funded health facility. Violators would face up to five years in prison.

The measure also barred protesters from physically restraining people from entering or leaving a health facility.

The bill also required the National Institute of Environmental Health Sciences to establish a program to develop ways to test products for safety that eliminated or minimized the use of animals. Animal welfare organizations had long complained that many routinely required toxicity tests conducted on laboratory animals were inaccurate or unnecessary.

Another bill (HR 2407), introduced by Charles W. Stenholm, D-Texas, extended the federal penalties to damage done to farms by animal rights activists. That bill did not advance during 1991.

Legislation to clamp down on animal groups passed the Senate in 1989 but failed to pass the House after jurisdictional delays and vociferous opposition from animal rights activists. *(1990 Almanac, p. 441)* ■

Other Science, Technology Legislation Considered

The science and technology committees acted on several bills during the first session of the 102nd Congress aimed at promoting research into new and competitive fields. Those included:

NSF REAUTHORIZATION

The House on July 11 approved language to limit the amount of overhead costs that universities could charge to the government when receiving National Science Foundation (NSF) research grants.

The provision was attached to a two-year reauthorization bill for the NSF. The Senate did not act on the measure during the first session.

As passed by the House on a voice vote, the bill (HR 2282, H Rept 102-131) authorized a total of $5.8 billion for foundation activities and research grants in fiscal 1992-1993. It funded a wide range of scientific research — from social sciences to engineering — at universities across the country.

The House Science Committee had approved HR 2282 on a voice vote May 22. The committee accepted on a voice vote an amendment by Rick Boucher, D-Va., to cap the amount that universities could charge for indirect costs.

Under existing administration regulations, universities that received federal research dollars charged the government for a portion of the costs of maintaining the university's infrastructure and research facilities. Universities charged the government an additional 20 percent to 75 percent of the federal grant to pay for these indirect costs. The Boucher amendment limited the indirect cost reimbursement to 26 percent and required that it be based on items such as salaries and wages, fringe benefits, materials and supplies, services and subcontracts.

The move to limit indirect costs came in response to a government audit showing that Stanford University overbilled the government by as much as $200 million for research-related expenses in the 1980s, using some of the money to pay for such extraneous expenses as a school yacht.

The measure also reflected congressional concern over wildly different overhead billing practices at other universities.

HIGH-TECHNOLOGY TRAINING

The House advanced two bills to encourage education, training and employment in high-technology industries to improve the competitive position of U.S. industries.

One measure (HR 2936) called for extending National

Science Foundation grants to community colleges that provided training in skills needed for high-technology jobs.

The other bill (HR 3507, H Rept 102-418, Part 1) created an apprenticeship program at the Labor Department for high school students to train in manufacturing or technology.

It also authorized the Commerce Department to set up programs linking colleges and universities with private industry to train employees.

The House Science Subcommittee on Competitiveness and Technology approved both bills by voice vote Oct. 31. The full Science, Space and Technology Committee approved HR 3507 on Nov. 22.

ELECTRIC VEHICLES

Legislation promoting electrically powered vehicles advanced in the House after winning approval from the House Science, Space and Technology Committee.

The bill (HR 1538), by Chairman George E. Brown Jr., D-Calif., established a federal research and development program for electric cars and other vehicles aimed at overcoming the barriers that had prevented their widespread use.

The measure authorized about $570 million over seven years for research, including a joint battery project with the private sector. The Science Subcommittee on the Environment approved the bill June 25 by voice vote after including an amendment by James H. Scheuer, D-N.Y. The full Science Committee followed suit July 30, approving the package by voice vote.

HIGH-SPEED RAIL

Two bills aimed at promoting transportation research and the development of high-speed train systems were advanced through House committees during the first session.

The Science, Space and Technology Committee approved a bill (HR 2941, H Rept 102-417, Part 1) on Nov. 7 authorizing $164.5 million in fiscal 1992 for research into such transportation technology as computerized automobile navigation devices; high-speed, steel-rail trains; and trains that levitated on an electromagnetic cushion. It authorized $180 million for research in fiscal 1993 and $200 million in fiscal 1994.

The committee passed the bill largely to show its support for magnetic levitation trains as negotiators hammered out a final surface transportation authorization bill (HR 2950 — PL 102-240). The broad bill authorized $700 million for a prototype train system that would hover at high speeds above an electromagnetic rail. *(Transportation, p. 137)*

The Energy and Commerce panel approved on Nov. 7 a bill (HR 1087, H Rept 102-297, Part 1) to make high-speed rail projects eligible for loan guarantees under a program for upgrading railroads. ■

Chapter 5

LAW & JUDICIARY

Compromise Civil Rights Bill Passed

Law counters nine recent Supreme Court decisions that made job-discrimination lawsuits harder to win

Congress on Nov. 7 cleared for President Bush a compromise civil rights bill that was two years in the making and had become a flash point in his relationship with black Americans.

The bill (S 1745 — PL 102-166) was Congress' first successful attempt to reverse the conservative Rehnquist Court, which in 1989 had restricted the reach and remedies of federal anti-discrimination laws. Bush vetoed a 1990 version, contending that it would induce employers to hire certain numbers of minorities and women to avoid lawsuits. His warning played to the belief of some whites that race preferences had cost them jobs, and it led to months of often bitter political wrangling. *(1989 Almanac, p. 314; 1990 Almanac, p. 462)*

Bush, who endorsed the 1991 compromise measure in a deal with Senate leaders in late October, said S 1745 would not lead to quotas. He signed the bill on Nov. 21.

The final legislation countered the effects of nine Supreme Court decisions from 1986 to 1991 that made it harder for workers to bring and win job discrimination lawsuits.

It also amended Title VII of the 1964 Civil Rights Act to allow limited money damages for victims of harassment and other intentional discrimination based on sex, religion or disability.

Racial minorities already could win unlimited money damages under a Reconstruction-era law. *(Provisions, p. 258)*

Some members wanted no limits on money damages for women, religious minorities and the disabled. But the ceiling was a key part of the compromise reached by the White House and congressional leaders.

Although Democrats gave ground on the damages question, most of the compromising was done by Bush.

The deal was reached in the wake of the divisive Senate hearings into Anita F. Hill's sexual harassment allegations against Supreme Court nominee Clarence Thomas and the strong Oct. 19 primary election showing of former Ku Klux Klansman David Duke, a Republican, in the Louisiana governor's race. *(Thomas confirmation, p. 274)*

Both events caused problems for Bush and the Republicans.

In the first, they were accused of insensitivity to sexual harassment, and in the second, aligned with a former Klansman known for his continued racist statements.

Bush clearly did not want to be caught reading from the same script as Duke on the quota issue.

Republican supporters of the bill insisted that Bush prevailed in the negotiations.

"There is absolutely no quota language in this bill," said Rep. Robert S. Walker, R-Pa., adding that Bush "won a major victory in negotiations."

But Democrats scoffed. "Where did the quotas go? They swam upstream, as red herrings often do," declared Craig Washington, D-Texas, during House floor debate. What made the difference, Washington suggested, was "David Duke took the sheet off that [quota] argument."

Key Points Left to the Courts

Still in question as the bill became law was how much help workers would actually receive under its provisions, many of which were vaguely worded to ensure passage. Only time was likely to tell who had won on the most troublesome issue, reversal of the Supreme Court's 5-4 June 1989 decision in *Wards Cove Packing Co. v. Atonio*, which made it harder for workers to prove indirect job discrimination.

Such "disparate impact" cases arose when workers challenged hiring practices, such as physical tests and academic requirements, that were ostensibly neutral but had an adverse impact on women or minorities. *Wards Cove* had shifted the burden of proof in suits alleging indirect discrimination: Instead of employers having to show that there was a legitimate business necessity for challenged practices, workers were required to prove that there was not.

In the White House-Senate deal, both sides agreed to return the burden of proof to employers and to reinstate a requirement from a 1971 court ruling, *Griggs v. Duke Power Co.*, that hiring and promotion requirements be related to job performance. But S 1745 threw to the federal courts some key issues of interpretations.

The law said that all employment practices had to be "job related for the position in question and consistent with business necessity." However, it did not define "business necessity" beyond stating that the measure's purpose was to reinstate the standard set forth in *Griggs* and subsequent rulings prior to *Wards Cove*.

The courts also were left to decide whether the new law applied to cases pending at the time of its enactment. The bill's language was not clear. Democrats said that it should cover worker-plaintiffs who were engaged in litigation at the time the law took effect. Republicans said the bill applied only to cases brought after enactment. The Equal Employment Opportunity Commission (EEOC), a federal agency that brought lawsuits in behalf of aggrieved workers, issued a statement in December saying that the law covered only cases begun after enactment.

BACKGROUND

Bush's 1990 veto of the initial version of the job rights bill marked the first defeat of a major civil rights bill in a quarter-century. The Senate fell one vote short of overriding his veto.

Members of Congress and civil rights activists who were outmaneuvered by the administration in 1990 revived their fight for the job-discrimination bill in early 1991 with a new political strategy: a sales pitch to women.

They had been stung by the administration's dismissal

of the 1990 legislation as a "quota bill" and decided they would no longer make equal opportunities for minorities the main public relations emphasis of their campaign.

By promoting the bill as a help to working women, advocates hoped to build a broader base of support and defuse charges that the job protections would lead to quotas. Nonetheless, the debate in early 1991 quickly picked up where the 1990 fight had left off.

"Republicans say this is a live issue out in the country," Sen. Richard G. Lugar, R-Ind., said. "So if Democrats want to keep pushing the same old bill, bring it on. As a matter of fact, we think we have more going for us now than we did at the time of the [1990] fight."

In November 1990, a month after Bush's veto of the first bill had been sustained, Sen. Jesse Helms, R-N.C., won a narrow re-election victory, in part by accusing his black opponent of supporting racial quotas. GOP strategists said at the time that painting Democrats as supporters of quotas might become part of the 1992 presidential campaign.

Democrats likened such assertions to Bush's successful 1988 use of murderer-rapist Willie Horton's case to suggest that Democrats were soft on crime. Rep. Don Edwards, D-Calif., said of the quotas attack, "We'll name that for what it is. Politics and racism. It's to get votes."

Lugar rejoined separately, "Strategists saw Willie Horton as a very good campaign."

BOXSCORE

➡ **Civil Rights Act of 1991 (S 1745, formerly HR 1).** The legislation countered nine Supreme Court decisions that made it harder for workers to bring and win job discrimination lawsuits. It also for the first time allowed limited money damages for victims of harassment and other intentional discrimination based on sex, religion or disability. Racial minorities already could win unlimited money damages under a post-Civil War law. The earlier version (HR 1) would have reversed more court rulings and been more generous toward workers suing their employers for bias.

Reports: H Rept 102-40, Part I (to accompany HR 1 as reported by the Education and Labor Committee); H Rept 102-40 Part II (to accompany HR 1 as reported by the Judiciary Committee). There were no Senate committee reports.

KEY ACTION

March 12 — HR 1 approved by the **House** Education and Labor Committee by voice vote.

March 19 — HR 1 approved by the **House** Judiciary Committee by 24-10.

June 5 — HR 1 passed by the **House** by 273-158.

Oct. 30 — S 1745, a compromise bill, passed by the **Senate** by 93-5. (The Senate never voted on HR 1.)

Nov. 7 — S 1745 cleared by the **House** by 381-38.

Nov. 21 — President Bush signed S 1745 — PL 102-166.

THE FIRST EFFORT: HR 1

HR 1, the main bill on the table through the first half of 1991, sought to amend two laws: Title VII of the Civil Rights Act of 1964, which barred job discrimination on the basis of race, sex, national origin or religion; and Section 1981 of Title 42 of the U.S. Code, an 1866 law prohibiting intentional race discrimination in contracts. Following were its major provisions:

- In cases in which an employee challenged an ostensibly neutral practice (such as a test or academic requirement) that had an adverse effect on women or minorities, the bill required an employer to prove that the practice was necessary for the conduct of business.

The bill defined a necessary job practice as one bearing "a significant relationship to successful performance" of the job. The bill said this would codify the meaning of "business necessity" as used in the 1971 Supreme Court case *Griggs v. Duke Power Co.* and overrule the *Wards Cove* use of business necessity as a defense.

- The bill sought to broaden Section 1981 to prohibit racial harassment on the job and other forms of race bias that occurred after a person was hired. The provision reversed *Patterson v. McLean Credit Union*, also from 1989, in which the court ruled that the law applied only to conduct when a contract was made. Section 1981 prohibited racial discrimination in "making and enforcing" private contracts. The bill included "the making, performance, modification and termination of contracts, and the enjoyment of all benefits, privileges, terms and conditions of the contractual relationship."
- To counter the 1989 ruling in *Price Waterhouse v. Hopkins*, the bill made clear that employers were prohibited from considering race, color, religion, sex or national origin as a motivating factor in employment decisions. It forbade decisions that took such factors into account even if they were made primarily for legitimate motives.
- The bill made it harder for individuals to challenge court settlements called "consent decrees," in which parties to a discrimination lawsuit agreed on a remedy. Typically, these settlements created affirmative action plans for shops that had engaged in past discrimination; white workers said such plans fostered "reverse discrimination."

Under HR 1, challenges could not be mounted if the potential challenger had been notified of a proposed deal and given an opportunity to object before the case was settled. A person also could be prevented from challenging the order if a court determined that he was adequately represented by another person who challenged the decree. This provision countered the court's 1989 ruling in *Martin v. Wilks*.

- The bill broadened the time frame for workers to bring lawsuits against discriminatory employment policies. Intended to reverse *Lorance v. AT&T Technologies*, also from 1989, this tied the deadline for lawsuits to when a worker was harmed rather than to when the policy took effect. The bill also made clear that a seniority system in a collective-bargaining agreement that was intended to discriminate on the basis of race, color, religion, sex or national origin was illegal.
- To reverse the 1989 *Independent Federation of Flight Attendants v. Zipes*, the bill stated that parties who prevailed in job discrimination cases could recover reasonable attorneys' fees if they had to defend their awards in a subsequent challenge. The bill stated that the plaintiff was entitled to recover attorneys' fees from the original defendant and/or the third party.

Addressing other Supreme Court cases since 1985, the bill also sought to:

- Amend Title VII of the 1964 Civil Rights Act to allow winning plaintiffs in bias cases against the federal government to recover interest for delays in getting relief.

• Make clear that prevailing plaintiffs could recover the reasonable costs of hiring experts to help them in their cases.

• Provide that in certain job-bias cases, plaintiffs could not be required to relinquish claims to attorneys' fees as a condition of settlement. This was intended to keep businesses from pressuring workers to forgo money for their lawyers' fees in order to get a settlement.

• Dictate that anti-bias protections under Title VII apply to U.S. citizens working overseas for U.S.-owned or controlled companies.

In a key feature not related to court cases, the bill established a new money remedy for victims of intentional job discrimination. HR 1 gave victims the right to recover compensatory and, in egregious cases, punitive damages under Title VII. If such money damages were sought, either a worker or his company could demand a jury trial.

At the time HR 1 was being considered, only injunctive relief, back pay and attorneys' fees were allowed under Title VII. So the provision was intended to make the remedies available for sex, religious and ethnic discrimination the same as the remedies already available under Section 1981 for race discrimination. The bill also extended the new remedies to victims who sued under the 1990 Americans with Disabilities Act. *(ADA, 1990 Almanac, p. 447)*

HOUSE COMMITTEE ACTION

The House Education and Labor Committee approved HR 1 on March 12 by voice vote, after first adding a "glass ceiling" proposal and other items designed to appeal to working women.

Some Republicans said the new emphasis on women was only cosmetic. But William D. Ford, D-Mich., who took over the Education and Labor chairmanship in 1991, said from the start that he wanted to pitch the bill to women, who he believed would benefit more than minorities from the legislation.

Following were the main additions adopted by the Education and Labor Committee:

• **Title change.** The title was changed to "Civil Rights and Women's Equity in Employment Act of 1991."

• **Glass ceiling commission.** The bill stipulated that "despite a dramatically growing presence in the workplace, women and minorities remain underrepresented in executive, management and senior decision-making positions in business [and] artificial barriers exist to the advancement of women and minorities in employment." The bill established a 19-member, four-year "Glass Ceiling Commission" to study the representation of women and minorities in executive, management and senior decision-making positions in business. The commission was to make recommendations to help eliminate artificial barriers to the advancement of women and minorities on the job.

• **'Pay equity' study.** The bill set up a program at the Labor Department to study disparities in the wages of men and women and whites and minorities. The idea was to disseminate information on efforts to eliminate wage disparities based on sex, race, national origin or ethnicity. The program was to provide technical assistance to employers to modify wage-setting practices or eliminate such disparities.

The above amendments were adopted by voice vote.

In other action, the committee adopted an amendment by Rep. Jose E. Serrano, D-N.Y., to authorize a new outreach and public information program at the EEOC. Serrano said there had been reports that the commission had not adequately responded to Hispanic workers. The amendment was adopted by voice vote.

Two amendments by Harris W. Fawell, R-Ill., were rejected. Both were aimed at making it easier for employers to justify practices that disproportionately affected minorities and women.

By 9-25, the Education and Labor Committee voted against inserting in the bill a presumption that an employer's academic requirements met a "business-necessity" test.

The committee also rejected, by 10-23, a move to lessen the standard for evidence an employer might use to justify a business practice that had a disparate impact on women or minorities.

The administration's bill was offered as a substitute amendment by Bill Goodling, R-Pa. After partisan debate, it was voted down by a voice vote.

House Judiciary Committee Action

On March 19, a week after the Education and Labor Committee approved HR 1, the Judiciary Committee followed suit, 24-10. The committee first defeated six Republican-sponsored amendments, including the administration's bill, which lost on a voice vote.

Three Republicans voted with the Democrats to report HR 1 favorably to the House. All three had also backed the 1990 bill: ranking Republican Hamilton Fish Jr., N.Y.; Tom Campbell, Calif.; and Steven H. Schiff, N.M., who was new to the Judiciary Committee but had voted for the bill on the floor in 1990.

Before trying to substitute the administration's proposal for HR 1, GOP members attempted to attach various parts of it to the bill. Henry J. Hyde, R-Ill., first tried to substitute the administration's test for whether a disparate-impact practice, such as an aptitude test, could be justified as necessary to business.

His amendment said that an employer could justify a practice, thereby avoiding liability for bias, by showing that the practice had "a manifest relationship to the employment" or that the employer's goals were "significantly served." HR 1 set a tougher test, saying a job requirement must "bear a significant relationship" to the employee's ability to perform the job.

William J. Hughes, D-N.J., said he was afraid HR 1 went too far in making it easier for workers to challenge indirect bias. Barney Frank, D-Mass., responded that anti-bias legislation was difficult to enforce and that it was unlikely that federal judges, mostly appointed by Ronald Reagan and Bush, would liberally construe HR 1.

Hughes and George E. Sangmeister, D-Ill., joined all Republicans but Fish in voting for administration-backed language to reverse the court's *Wards Cove* ruling. The amendment failed, 14-20.

Carlos J. Moorhead, R-Calif., tried to amend the bill so that none of the provisions would take effect until the date of enactment. As HR 1 was written, provisions were tied to the dates of the court cases they sought to reverse.

Moorhead argued that employers should not be bound by legal requirements that were not in effect when the alleged discrimination occurred. The amendment lost 15-19, with Democrats Rick Boucher, Va., and Romano L. Mazzoli, Ky., joining the Republicans.

F. James Sensenbrenner Jr., R-Wis., tried to strip out the section to allow women and religious minorities who suffered intentional discrimination to win unlimited money damages. The proposal failed on a voice vote.

An amendment by Bill McCollum, R-Fla., sought to

limit money damages to $150,000 and restrict them to cases involving harassment, rather than all intentional discrimination. The amendment lost, 10-23, with all Democrats and Fish and Schiff opposed.

The committee also rejected a move by Hyde to bar employers from adjusting hiring test scores because of race, color, religion, sex or national origin. The proposal had not been subject to any prior committee hearing or discussion and failed, 13-21.

Senate Maneuvers

While House Democratic leaders made HR 1 a priority, the Senate had no similar bill until summer. In 1990, an unlikely coalition of senators, led by Edward M. Kennedy, D-Mass., and John C. Danforth, R-Mo., had come close to a winning deal on civil rights. They steered a bill through a contentious Senate floor fight, but fell one vote short of the two-thirds necessary to override Bush's veto.

In early 1991, the senators who were at the core of negotiations a year earlier shifted alliances.

Liberal Kennedy wanted a bill similar to HR 1. Danforth, a middle-of-the-road Republican, tried to interest colleagues in a more conservative version. Southern Democrats who voted for the 1990 bill — after winning compromises just before a floor vote — talked among themselves. All parties said they wanted a bill, but their ideological differences pushed them in different directions.

David L. Boren, D-Okla., who was among the Southern Democrats seeking alternatives, said, "There are people in both parties who did not like the choices last year of either no civil rights bill or the one being offered at the time." Danforth said HR 1 would go too far and set a nearly impossible standard for employers trying to defend hiring policies. "My understanding is that the differences that were narrowed last year are back," he said, and he began to work on compromise legislation.

White House, Lobbyists

Meanwhile, the White House geared up with its own strategy shift. In its new bill (HR 1375, 611), the Bush administration retreated from the compromises it had offered Congress in 1990. John R. Dunne, assistant attorney general for civil rights, said that while the bill was not as "accommodating" as the 1990 proposals, it was a good-faith effort toward negotiations.

Following were differences between the House bill (HR 1) and the administration version in two key areas:

Disparate impact cases. Under the administration's bill, an employer could justify a challenged practice, such as a test or academic requirement, by showing that it had "a manifest relationship to the employment" or that the employer's goals were "significantly served" by the practice.

HR 1 set a higher test for a discriminatory practice, saying it had to "bear a significant relationship" to an employee's ability to succeed at the job.

The Bush bill also set a stiffer standard, compared with HR 1, for evidence to prove discrimination. It required workers to pinpoint which hiring practices caused the discrimination, and abandoned language offered in 1990 that would have allowed workers in certain situations to challenge discrimination caused by a group of practices.

Both proposals said that it should be up to the employer to prove that a practice was necessary for the business. The Supreme Court ruled in *Wards Cove* that the worker should bear the burden of proving that a test or other screening device was not necessary for the business.

Monetary damages. The Bush bill sought to allow victims of harassment to sue for money damages up to $150,000, provided they had first used an in-house grievance procedure. HR 1 covered all cases of intentional discrimination, not only harassment. It did not require a worker to first use an in-house procedure. And it set no limit on damages.

Civil rights lobbyists met with business interests from December 1990 to April 1991, trying to strike a deal. In the lead was The Business Roundtable, a consortium of chief executive officers from 200 large companies.

Working on the assumption that some bill was inevitable, business negotiators said they wanted to try to shape legislation to their liking.

The talks ended when the White House and small and mid-size businesses banded together to attack both the bill and the efforts of big corporations. They waged an all-out opposition blitz, including mass mailings to employers, to discredit any deal that might come out of the talks. Those opponents argued that the bill would increase litigation and costs to businesses, especially small ones that did not have longstanding affirmative action programs in place.

Under pressure, the lead negotiator for The Business Roundtable announced in the spring that talks were called off. Robert E. Allen, chairman of AT&T, said the Roundtable would "move to the sidelines for the time being." Allen said politics had overtaken the negotiations.

He voiced dismay at a column in The Wall Street Journal on April 19 with the headline: "Big Business Shouldn't Sleep with the Enemy."

Civil rights lobbyists accused the White House of trying to destroy the business community's fragile interest in reaching a compromise that they said would restore equality in the workplace. Small businesses and administration aides countered that the bigger companies, better equipped to handle stepped-up anti-discrimination rules, were sacrificing the interests of their smaller brethren.

Leadership Compromise

Lacking strong support for HR 1, House Democratic leaders prepared a substitute bill that set limits on proposed money damages and stiffened the standards for proving indirect bias. The move was an overture to wavering Southern Democrats and was also intended to take the air out of business opposition.

House leaders agreed on the compromise over protests from some women and liberal members who said that a $150,000 limit on damages, especially, was a sellout.

But the leadership was trying to move the bill out of second gear and it did not want to force a floor vote without being able to win close to 290 votes — the number needed for a two-thirds majority to override Bush's threatened veto.

Substantively, the Democrats' amendments were not new. The 1990 civil rights bill, passed by both chambers, included the $150,000 cap on money damages for women. And sponsors characterized the language on indirect discrimination, picked up from the suspended Business Roundtable talks, as only a clarification of legal standards.

Following were the changes incorporated into a substitute HR 1:

Limit on money damages. The substitute plan limited punitive damages for intentional discrimination to $150,000, or an amount equal to compensatory damages.

Quota prohibition. It dictated that nothing in it be construed to "require, encourage, or permit an employer to adopt hiring or promotion quotas on the basis or race, color, religion, sex or national origin, and the use of such quotas shall be deemed to be an unlawful employment practice." Voluntary or court-ordered affirmative action still was allowed.

The bill defined a quota as "a fixed number or percentage of persons of a particular race, color, religion, sex or national origin which must be attained, or which cannot be exceeded, regardless of whether such persons meet necessary qualifications to perform the job."

The Supreme Court had previously ruled that hiring by the numbers was illegal, but HR 1 sought to put that ban into statute. The move was aimed almost exclusively at giving political cover to those who wanted to vote for the job-rights bill but faced constituent complaints about "reverse discrimination."

New definition for indirect discrimination. The substitute allowed employers to justify their hiring practices by showing that they "bear a substantial and manifest relationship to the requirements for effective job performance." That language was a meeting point of sorts between HR 1 and the administration's bill.

Also under the substitute, a worker who challenged employment practices would have a tougher standard for pinpointing discriminatory practices. The standard was intended to be more acceptable to business than HR 1 but not as stiff as the Bush alternative.

Test adjustments. Under the substitute, employers, labor organizations and employment agencies could not adjust employment test scores based on the race, color, religion, sex, or national origin of individual test-takers. The measure prohibited using tests that did not validly and fairly measure an individual's ability to perform the job. This provision was added by Democrats after Hyde pressed for a broader ban on "race norming" of test scores.

Date of enactment. The substitute said provisions of the bill were to cover only lawsuits filed after the date of enactment, unless a court found that a "manifest injustice" would occur without retroactive application. The original HR 1 would have applied retroactively.

HOUSE FLOOR ACTION

In June, after months of intense lobbying and difficult tradeoffs, the civil rights bill offered by House Democratic leaders passed with no more support than it had in 1990, when a similar bill fell to a veto.

The House vote, 273-158, came June 5 after a day and a half of debate and the rejection of two alternative proposals — a White House plan and a hard-line effort from liberal Democrats. When the votes on final passage were in, nine Republicans who had backed the 1990 bill switched to oppose HR 1. *(Vote 131, p. 32-H)*

Black and female members offered a substitute bill that had no restrictions on new money damages for victims of intentional discrimination; it was defeated 152-277. *(Vote 127, p. 32-H)*

The House also rebuffed an attempt to substitute Bush's own legislation, which would have taken a more limited approach to bolstering legal redress for victims of job bias. That vote was 162-266. *(Vote 128, p. 32-H)*

On the overall bill, the 273 votes were 15 short of two-thirds of those present and voting, the number needed to override a veto. The 1990 tally of 273 on the job-rights conference report was 12 short of two-thirds voting.

Democrats said it was hard to get around Bush's politically potent quota assertion because of latent racial divisions and Americans' fears of joblessness. Majority Leader Richard A. Gephardt, D-Mo., said during debate: "Some Americans want to blame this recession on someone, and so I think the administration wants to blame quotas. They want to find a villain."

But a lead opponent, Minority Whip Newt Gingrich, R-Ga., said the failure to pick up more votes indicated "a long-term trend is against the bill."

The nine GOP members who switched from a "yes" vote in 1990 to "no" in 1991 said they had come to believe that the bill would lead to quota hiring or that substance had been overtaken by partisan politics and they wanted to side with Bush.

The Republicans switching from "aye" to "nay" were Joe L. Barton, Texas; Thomas J. Bliley Jr., Va.; Lawrence Coughlin, Pa.; Craig T. James, Fla.; Nancy L. Johnson, Conn.; Jan Meyers, Kan.; Carl D. Pursell, Mich.; Ralph Regula, Ohio; and Marge Roukema, N.J.

Only one Democrat who voted for the 1990 bill switched to oppose it in 1991: Jimmy Hayes of Louisiana. And one Democrat who had opposed it in 1990 voted for it: Bill Sarpalius of Texas.

Only one black member, freshman Gary Franks, R-Conn., voted against the bill. All but six of the female House members backed HR 1; the six were Republicans.

Before the House voted for HR 1 on June 5, it adopted the substitute version by Jack Brooks, D-Texas, and Fish by a vote of 264-166. A handful of black and women members voted against it to protest the compromises it contained, notably the damage cap and quota ban. *(Vote 130, p. 32-H)*

Although the bill on its face was about the technicalities of bias lawsuits, the emotion surrounding quotas and race discrimination steered debate.

"It is a shame and a disgrace that in 1991 we are still debating whether or not we should protect our fellow American citizens from discrimination," said John Lewis, D-Ga., who was physically beaten during civil rights struggles of the 1960s and spoke of signs posted to segregate blacks and whites. "The scars and stains of racism are still deeply embedded in the American society."

Republican Hyde countered, however, that the bill would further separate Americans. HR 1 "is about dividing people — tribalizing and balkanizing our society — and in the end . . . it will not have the support of the American people but their resentment and indignation."

Both sides bought advertising, worked key members' districts and lobbied aggressively. Bush was especially visible, driving home the quota charge in speeches before the House vote.

SENATE TALKS

The week of the House vote, Danforth introduced a compromise job-rights package in the Senate. With the House bill lacking momentum, Danforth's proposal became the focus of attention by civil rights activists.

The Missouri Republican said he was trying to disentangle the debate from politics and find a bill that would please GOP moderates and Southern Democrats. "It's important to extricate the racial question from partisan politics," he said as he and eight other GOP moderates offered their alternative June 4.

Danforth split the original legislation into three bills. The idea, he said, was to isolate the most difficult topics so that the less controversial proposals might readily pass.

Under Danforth's plan, one measure (S 1207) addressed five court rulings in provisions that were relatively non-controversial and attracted some Bush administration interest. A second bill (S 1208) reversed the hotly disputed ruling in *Wards Cove Packing Co. v. Atonio*, which involved standards for indirect bias resulting from tests and other seemingly neutral hiring practices. The third measure (S 1209) gave limited money damages to women, religious minorities and the disabled for deliberate bias.

A major difference between Danforth's offering and Democrats' proposals was that he further limited compensatory damage awards for women and non-racial minorities in intentional bias cases. He also would not have allowed women to win punitive damages.

For unintentional-bias cases, arising from the *Wards Cove* ruling, Danforth's test for employers trying to justify their hiring practices was a cross between the standard of HR 1, which tilted toward workers, and the administration's bill, which tilted toward business.

Throughout the summer, Danforth continued to revise his legislation, talking informally with administration officials and other senators and reintroducing his three-bill package. He said he was trying every avenue to win Bush's support. It was never forthcoming.

Thomas Hearings: A Breakthrough

A major breakthrough for the legislation came in the fall, on the heels of the explosive battle over confirmation of Clarence Thomas as associate justice of the Supreme Court.

The White House-Senate agreement averted a brewing confrontation that threatened to divide Senate Republicans and intensify tensions over race and gender issues. While both sides claimed victory, the administration appeared to have made the most concessions as it tried to avoid a veto fight it was not certain to win.

However, because the final agreement left one of the toughest issues, dealing with the *Wards Cove* decision, to be resolved in the federal courts, it was difficult to determine how much each side had won or lost.

Senate Majority Leader George J. Mitchell, D-Maine, said that Bush had agreed to a measure similar to the one he vetoed a year earlier. "I only wish the president had been willing to do a year and a half ago that which he is now willing to do," said Mitchell. "We would all have been spared a long and painful ordeal."

Bush disagreed. He said he won significant concessions that eliminated his main concern — that the legislation would lead to quota hiring by companies fearful of costly lawsuits. "We didn't cave," he said. "We worked out in a spirit of compromise a negotiated settlement where I can say to the American people, this is not a quota bill."

But Senate Republicans conceded that the administration was under great pressure to negotiate with moderate Republicans, led by Danforth, who had been working with Kennedy to craft a bipartisan bill.

In the week before the breakthrough, it appeared that support for Danforth's bill was about one or two votes short of the 67 needed to override a veto. Several Republicans said they warned the White House that they did not want to be put in a position of opposing their colleagues in a brutal override battle.

Their reluctance was fueled by widespread respect for Danforth, who in early October had gone to the mat for Bush in guiding the controversial Thomas nomination through the Senate.

"From our Republican standpoint, it's better to be in a position supporting a bill rather than going against Danforth trying to override a veto," said Minority Leader Bob Dole, R-Kan., who acted as a broker between the administration and Danforth to reach the settlement. But Dole insisted that the administration could have sustained a veto.

Other Republicans were less sure. John W. Warner, Va., said that he and Ted Stevens, Alaska, told Bush on Oct. 23 that they could not be counted on to support him in an override battle.

Some members on both sides of the aisle speculated that Bush was also reluctant to veto civil rights legislation after the bruising battle over Thomas and allegations that the nominee had sexually harassed an employee.

Mitchell said he thought the administration was concerned as well about racial backlash from the emergence Oct. 19 of Republican David Duke, a former Klansman, as one of two candidates in the November runoff election for governor in Louisiana.

The Final Compromise

Following were highlights of the final compromise:

- **Money damages for intentional bias.** The compromise set caps on the compensatory and punitive damages women and minorities could win: Employers with 100 or fewer workers were liable for up to $50,000; employers with 101 to 200 workers, $100,000; 201 to 500 workers, $200,000; and employers with more than 500 workers, $300,000. Employers of fewer than 15 workers were exempt from damages.

Title VII of the 1964 Civil Rights Act was amended to allow the new damages and changed to permit jury trials for victims of bias. Juries were generally thought to be more sympathetic to workers than judges.

- **'Business necessity.'** In the key *Wards Cove* section, the compromise bill returned the burden of proof to employers to defend job practices challenged as discriminatory, but basically left it to the courts to decide what constituted a "business necessity."
- **Racial harassment on the job.** To reverse *Patterson v. McLean Credit Union,* another 1989 decision, the bill barred racial harassment and other forms of bias that occurred after a person was hired. The court had ruled that Section 1981 of Title 42 of the U.S. Code, which prohibited racial discrimination in contracts, applied only to hiring decisions.
- **Consent decrees.** To reverse the 1989 *Martin v. Wilks,* the bill spelled out rules under which third parties could challenge a consent decree in an anti-discrimination case. It precluded challenges by those who had to have been notified beforehand that the agreement might hurt their interests and who had opportunity to object. They could not object if their interests had been fairly represented by a direct party to the suit. The settlements in question typically involved affirmative action plans in which employers who had engaged in past discrimination agreed to give preference for some period to minorities or women.
- **Forbidden considerations.** The bill made clear that an employer could not make an employment decision based in any way on race, color, religion, sex or national origin, regardless of whether other factors also motivated the decision. This countered the 1989 *Price Waterhouse v. Hopkins.*
- **Seniority and filing deadlines.** The bill allowed workers challenging a seniority system as discriminatory to wait until the adverse impact of the system was felt to bring a lawsuit. That reversed the court's 1989 ruling in *Lorance v. AT&T*, which tied the deadline for bringing a lawsuit to a company's adoption of the policy.
- **Other cases.** The bill also addressed two court cases

from the 1980s and two from 1991.

To overrule the Supreme Court's 1986 decision in *Library of Congress v. Shaw*, the bill amended Title VII to allow winning parties in bias cases against the federal government to recover interest to compensate for delays in obtaining payment. The filing period for actions against the government was increased from 30 to 90 days.

In response to parts of the 1987 *Crawford Fitting Co. v. J. T. Gibbons Inc.* and the 1991 *West Virginia University Hospitals v. Casey*, the bill permitted winning parties to recover the costs of hiring experts who assisted them in cases filed under the damages provisions of this bill, the 1866 racial bias statute and Title VII.

Finally, the bill allowed American workers abroad to sue their U.S.-based employers for discrimination, reversing a 1991 ruling, *Equal Employment Opportunity Commission v. Arabian American Oil Co.*

SENATE PASSAGE

The Senate approved the compromise bill (S 1745) on Oct. 30 by 93-5. *(Vote 238, p. 31-S)*

All of the opponents were Republican: Daniel R. Coats, Ind.; Jesse Helms, N.C.; Robert C. Smith, N.H.; Steve Symms, Idaho; and Malcolm Wallop, Wyo.

Opponents who spoke on the floor said that the court rulings were correct and that the bill would hurt business and spur litigation.

In the end, one of the more hotly disputed questions was whether the Senate would abide by the anti-bias rules imposed by law on private employers.

After three days of debate, the Senate voted Oct. 30 to partially apply the bill and other major anti-discrimination laws to Senate employees, allowing them redress through an internal process and a final limited right of appeal in federal court.

Senators themselves were made personally liable for damages.

Some previously exempt administration and state and local employees also were given new civil rights protections. The provision, offered by Majority Leader Mitchell and Charles E. Grassley, R-Iowa, was adopted by voice vote.

Senators from both parties noted the sweep of the bill, which reversed all or part of more court rulings than any other legislation in recent history.

Although some provisions arose because statutes were outdated, the bill's major elements stemmed from supporters' belief that the Supreme Court had read civil rights law too narrowly.

"Here is a way we can remind ourselves where we have been coming from in the last 30 years and saying we are not going to turn back," said Dale Bumpers, D-Ark.

Business groups that had fought the bill for two years pulled back after the White House deal, saying a bill was inevitable.

Other than the highlighted provisions, which were subject to negotiations for months, the bill also prohibited adjusting test scores by race and established a Glass Ceiling Commission to recommend ways to lift barriers to women and minorities seeking job advancement. At Dole's urging, the latter provision was adopted 96-0 on Oct. 29. *(Vote 232, p. 30-S)*

The Senate rejected an amendment by Mitch McConnell, R-Ky., to limit attorney contingency fees to 20 percent of the award in civil rights cases. The proposal was tabled, 68-30, after bill proponents argued that despite the increasing costs of litigation, civil rights lawyers were not reaping huge fees. *(Vote 233, p. 31-S)*

Legislative History

Somewhat obscured in the Senate's push to wrap up civil rights legislation was a skirmish over how members tried to dictate court interpretations of the new law.

Finessing the trickiest section, lawmakers had agreed Oct. 25 to put a three-paragraph memo in the Congressional Record as the bill's "exclusive legislative history." Judges commonly looked to floor statements, committee reports and other congressional materials to understand what lawmakers intended, and bill leaders hoped to prevent individual senators from making end runs around the hard-won, if vaguely worded, compromise.

Supreme Court Justice Antonin Scalia had been pushing for courts to ignore such floor statements, saying they were unreliable guides to what most lawmakers intended.

But as Danforth said, you can't "muzzle the Senate."

In floor speeches during debate over S 1745, senators tried to put their own spin on the bill, hoping to create "legislative history."

The result was dueling colloquies, a warning by Dole that the civil rights deal might be off, and, finally, an amendment directing courts to pay attention only to the short memo and to recognize that the sponsors did not agree on how to interpret a key element of the bill.

Danforth acknowledged that the Senate probably could not pass the long-controversial bill if it had "nailed down every particular word and phrase." But, he argued, "Justice Scalia was correct. Any judge who tries to make legislative history out of the free-for-all that takes place on the floor of the Senate is on very dangerous grounds.... It is a muddle."

At the heart of the dispute were standards determining the "business necessity" of challenged job practices.

The "exclusive legislative history" said: "The terms 'business necessity' and 'job related' are intended to reflect the concepts ... of *Griggs v. Duke Power Co.* [1971] and other Supreme Court decisions prior to *Wards Cove Packing Co. v. Atonio.*"

The memo also said that when a challenged practice included several interlocking components measuring the same criterion, such as height and weight requirements to assess strength, the practices could be generally challenged. In other cases, a worker would have to pinpoint the specific employment practice that led to indirect discrimination.

Democrat Kennedy and Utah Republican Orrin G. Hatch offered conflicting floor statements of how a court should read the bill and memo.

Danforth, saying he would probably disagree with both readings, tried to defuse the dispute:

"It is very common for members of the Senate to try to affect the way in which a court will interpret a statute by putting things into the Congressional Record.... Every time we have a tax bill we try to do that. I remember one night literally following one of my colleagues around the floor of the Senate for fear that he would slip something into the Congressional Record, and I would have to slip something else" in.

Dole was not reassured. He said the Bush administration believed the entire deal on the bill was off because of Kennedy's elaboration. "And now we are saying: 'Oh well, nobody knows what anything means.' "

Senators resolved their differences Oct. 29 and ap-

Continued on p. 260

1991 Civil Rights Law Provisions

The civil rights law (S 1745 — PL 102-166) cleared by Congress on Nov. 7 and signed by President Bush on Nov. 21 was the product of more than two years of negotiations.

The compromise, reached in the politically charged wake of the Clarence Thomas/Anita F. Hill hearings, came after Democrats and Republicans decided to adopt vague, open-ended language to settle the most controversial questions.

As a result, the breadth of S 1745 and some of its applications were left to federal courts interpreting the law.

For example, although the bill stated that it would take effect on the date of enactment, no agreement existed among bill sponsors about whether pending cases could be decided under the new law. Democratic sponsors said pending cases should be subject to the new law. Republican sponsors said such cases should be decided under laws in place when the cases were filed.

Similarly, the bill did not fully define standards for justifying work practices, such as achievement tests, that appeared fair but had a disproportionately adverse effect on women, blacks or other minorities.

Nonetheless, the law offered workers more protection against bias, and for those who won in court, money damages and reimbursement of costs. The impetus for the bill was the reversal of a series of Supreme Court rulings. Five of the decisions addressed were from the 1988-89 term, when the court's conservative majority began coalescing.

Unrelated to the nine court cases involved, the law also allowed, for the first time, limited money damages for victims of harassment and other intentional discrimination based on sex, religion or disability. Racial minorities already could win unlimited money damages under a Reconstruction-era law, Section 1981 of Title 42 of the U.S. Code.

As enacted, the 1991 civil rights law:

Findings. Stated that Congress found that additional remedies were needed to deter unlawful harassment and intentional discrimination in the workplace.

Singled out the Supreme Court's 1989 decision in *Wards Cove Packing Co. v. Atonio*, saying it weakened the scope and effectiveness of federal civil rights protections. That decision had shifted the burden of proof: The court held that a worker who contended that a company's practices had a "disparate impact" on women, blacks or other minorities had to disprove an employer's assertion that the practices served a legitimate business purpose. The decision also eased the standard for justifying a discriminatory practice.

Purposes. Stated that the legislation's purpose was:

- to provide appropriate remedies for discrimination;
- to codify the concepts of "business necessity" and "job related" offered by the Supreme Court in *Griggs v. Duke Power Co.* in 1971, and in related Supreme Court decisions before *Wards Cove Packing Co. v. Atonio*;
- to provide statutory guidelines for disparate-impact lawsuits under Title VII of the Civil Rights Act of 1964; and
- to respond to recent court decisions by expanding the scope of relevant civil rights statutes to provide adequate protection to victims of discrimination.

Civil Rights Remedies

Racial discrimination. Prohibited all racial discrimination in the making and enforcement of contracts by amending Section 1981 of Title 42 of the U.S. Code to add the following: "For purposes of this section, the term 'make and enforce contracts' includes the making, performance, modification and termination of contracts, and the enjoyment of all benefits, privileges, terms and conditions of the contractual relationship." Dictated that anti-discrimination rights under this section were protected for both government and private employees.

This section reversed the 1989 *Patterson v. McLean Credit Union* case, in which the court ruled that Section 1981 applied only to hiring decisions.

New money damages in cases of intentional discrimination. Allowed workers bringing cases of intentional bias under Title VII of the 1964 Civil Rights Act, the Americans with Disabilities Act (ADA) of 1990 and the 1973 Rehabilitation Act to recover compensatory and punitive damages in addition to any relief already authorized by Title VII, such as attorneys' fees and back pay.

"Malice or reckless indifference" required. Dictated that to be eligible for money damages, a worker had to demonstrate that an employer engaged in a discriminatory practice with malice or with reckless indifference to federally protected rights.

Limitations. Set limits on the total amount of punitive and compensatory damages awarded under this section. Compensatory damages would be given for future financial loss and for non-financial losses such as emotional pain, suffering, inconvenience, mental anguish and loss of enjoyment of life.

- For a business or other covered entity with more than 14 and fewer than 101 employees in each of 20 or more calendar weeks in the current or preceding calendar year, the limit on combined compensatory and punitive damages was $50,000.
- For a business with more than 100 and fewer than 201 employees, the limit was $100,000.
- For a business with more than 200 and fewer than 501 employees, the limit was $200,000.
- For a company with more than 500 employees, the limit was $300,000.

Jury trial. Allowed plaintiffs and defendants in these lawsuits to demand a trial by jury. Required that the court not tell the jury of the above limits.

Disability. Excluded from the new money remedies those cases in which a discriminatory practice involved the providing of a reasonable accommodation under the ADA or the Rehabilitation Act. The exclusion applied only if a business or other covered entity demonstrated a good-faith effort to make a reasonable accommodation.

Indirect Discrimination Cases

At issue was how employers could justify practices, such as physical tests and academic requirements, that were ostensibly neutral but had an adverse impact on a particular class of people.

Threshold. Stated that an unlawful employment practice was established only if a worker or other complaining party demonstrated that an employer used a particular practice that caused a disparate impact on the basis of race, color, religion, sex or national origin, and the employer failed to show that the challenged practice was job-related for the position in question and consistent with business necessity. The worker also could prevail if he showed an alternative practice that met the goals of the business, without a disparate impact, and the business refused to adopt it.

Specificity. Required a worker to demonstrate that each particular challenged employment practice caused a disparate impact. The law included an exception: If the worker could show that elements of a company's decision-making process could not be separated for analysis, the entire process could be analyzed as one employment practice. An example would be when several tests were used to assess one particular attribute, such as physical strength.

Drug use. Exempted from disparate-impact challenges employers' efforts to screen out drug abusers. Under the new law, workers could not challenge any hiring practices that barred the use or possession of a controlled substance that was not taken under the supervision of a licensed health-care professional or otherwise legally used.

Open-ended definitions. Dictated that no statements other than the interpretive memo appearing in the Congressional Record on Oct. 25, 1991, be considered legislative history or relied upon in construing the provisions relating to this section.

That memo said, "The terms 'business necessity' and 'job related' were intended to reflect the concepts enunciated by the Supreme Court in *Griggs v. Duke Power Co.*, 401 U.S. 424 (1971), and in other Supreme Court decisions prior to *Wards Cove Packing Co. v. Atonio*, 490 U.S. 642 (1989).

"When a decision-making process includes particular, functionally integrated practices which are components of the same criterion, standard, method of administration, or test, such as the height and weight requirements designed to measure strength in *Dothard v. Rawlinson*, 433 U.S. 321 (1977), the particular, functionally integrated practices may be analyzed as one employment practice."

Lawmakers expected judges trying to interpret the new law to look to these paragraphs of "exclusive legislative history." Because key sponsors could not agree on how to resolve standards for justifying indirect bias, the vagueness was part of the compromise. Still, Democrats and Republicans tried to put their spin on the legislation by inserting their own interpretations in the record. Republicans generally favored a narrow interpretation of the new law, while Democrats said it should be read to give workers more of an advantage when suing their bosses. Bush said he favored an interpretation providing more flexibility to employers than Republican sponsor Sen. John C. Danforth, Mo., sought and especially more than Democratic sponsor Sen. Edward M. Kennedy, Mass., said he intended.

Wards Cove cannery workers. Exempted the Wards Cove Packing Co. and workers who had sued the company from these provisions. Stated that nothing in this act "shall apply to any disparate-impact case for which a complaint was filed before March 1, 1975, and for which an initial decision was rendered after Oct. 30, 1983." Only the original *Wards Cove* case that led to the Supreme Court ruling met those criteria. This provision, included at the urging of Alaska's senators, was aimed at protecting one of the state's largest employers. The workers' lawsuit against the fish cannery had been going on for nearly 20 years.

Impermissible Hiring Considerations

Motives. Stated that an unlawful employment practice was established when a worker demonstrated that race, color, religion, sex or national origin was a motivating factor for any employment practice, even when other factors also motivated the practice.

This addressed the 1989 ruling in *Price Waterhouse v. Hopkins*, which said an employment decision motivated in part by prejudice did not violate Title VII if the employer could show that he would have made the same decision for non-discriminatory reasons.

Relief. Allowed workers who proved that they were denied a position because of an impermissible motive to win declaratory and injunctive relief (for example, a court order that the company stop the discriminatory practice), attorneys' fees and court costs. No compensatory or punitive damages would be permitted.

Consent Judgments

The court settlements involved in this provision usually called for affirmative action plans in which employers who had engaged in past discrimination agreed to give preference to minorities or women. The 1989 *Martin v. Wilks* decision concerned white firefighters who had not intervened while a consent decree settling a job bias suit was negotiated and approved in federal district court. The Supreme Court held that the firefighters could later challenge the decree in a separate lawsuit.

Bar to most challenges. Stated that an employment practice arising from a consent judgment could not be challenged by a person who had actual notice of the proposed judgment or order sufficient to apprise him that the order might adversely affect his interests. This would have the effect of preventing whites competing for those jobs from mounting challenges to court-ordered affirmative action plans. However, the would-be challengers had to have had an opportunity to object to the order while it was in the works.

Fraud exception. Allowed challenges to orders obtained through collusion or fraud, and ensured that no one was denied the due process of law required by the Constitution.

U.S. Workers Abroad

Extending protection. Required that both Title VII and the Americans with Disabilities Act apply to persons working abroad for U.S.-based companies. This provision reversed a 1991 court ruling, in *Equal Employment Opportunity Commission v. Arabian American Oil Co.*, that Title VII did not cover U.S. workers abroad.

Offered an exception to employers, labor organizations or other covered entities if compliance with the civil rights law would cause them to violate the law of the country in which the work was located.

Other Court Rulings

Challenges to discriminatory seniority systems. Revised the deadlines for challenges to discriminatory seniority systems to be timed to when the system was adopted, when an individual became subject to the seniority system or when a person was injured by the application of the seniority system. This countered *Lorance v. AT&T Technologies*, also from 1989, which held that the statute of limitations for challenging discriminatory seniority plans began to run when the plan was adopted, rather than when the plan began harming a worker subject to it. The change was designed to give workers more time and flexibility to bring a lawsuit based on a seniority plan.

Expert fees. Allowed winning parties to recover the costs of hiring experts who assisted them in their cases filed under the damages provisions of this law, Title VII of the 1964 Civil Rights Act and Section 1981 (the 1866 racial bias statute). This section responded to parts of the 1987 *Crawford Fitting Co. v. J. T. Gibbons Inc.* and the 1991 *West Virginia University Hospitals v. Casey* decisions. Critics said the court's rulings had a chilling effect on aggrieved workers who might need experts to help them in their anti-bias lawsuits.

Actions against the federal government. Amended Title VII to allow winning parties in bias cases against the federal government to recover interest to compensate for delays in obtaining payment. The filing period for actions against the government was increased from 30 to 90 days. This reversed the court's 1986 decision in *Library of Congress v. Shaw*.

Discriminatory Use of Test Scores

'Race-norming.' Barred employers from adjusting the scores of, using different cutoff scores for, or otherwise altering the results of employment-related tests on the basis of race, color, religion, sex or national origin. This provision stemmed from concern among lawmakers in both parties that "race norming" was leading to discrimination against qualified white applicants.

Glass Ceiling Commission

Findings. Stated that, despite a growing presence in the workplace:

- women and minorities remained underrepresented in management and decision-making positions;
- artificial barriers to the advancement of women and minorities existed;
- U.S. corporations were increasingly relying on women and minorities to meet employment requirements and were increasingly aware of the advantages derived from a diverse work force; and
- the "Glass Ceiling Initiative" undertaken by the Department of Labor, including the release of the report entitled "Report on the Glass Ceiling Initiative," had been instrumental in raising public awareness of the underrepresentation of women and minorities at the management and decision-making levels in the U.S. work force.

Purpose. Established a Glass Ceiling Commission to study how business filled management and decision-making positions, the developmental and skill-enhancing practices used to foster qualifications for advancement, and the pay and reward structures used in the workplace.

Commission makeup. Required 21 members:

- six individuals appointed by the president;
- six appointed jointly by the Speaker of the House and the Senate majority leader;
- one individual appointed by the House majority leader;
- one appointed by the House minority leader;
- one appointed by the Senate majority leader;
- one by the Senate minority leader;
- two House members named jointly by the House majority and

minority leaders;

- two senators appointed jointly by the Senate majority and minority leaders;
- the secretary of Labor, who was to be the commission chairman.

Report. Ordered that no later than 15 months after the date of the enactment of the legislation, the commission prepare and submit to the president and the appropriate congressional committees a written report containing findings of the study and the commission's recommendations.

An award. Established an annual award for excellence in promoting a more diverse skilled work force at the management and decision-making levels in business. Stated that the National Award for Diversity and Excellence in American Executive Management was to be accompanied by a medal bearing the inscription "Frances Perkins-Elizabeth Hanford Dole National Award for Diversity and Excellence in American Executive Management."

EEOC Technical Aid and Education

Training institute. Required the Equal Employment Opportunity Commission (EEOC) to establish a Technical Assistance Training Institute to provide technical assistance and training on the laws and regulations enforced by the commission. Authorized funds needed to set up the institute. (No amount was specified.)

Education and outreach. Ordered the commission to carry out educational and outreach activities, including the dissemination of information in languages other than English and targeted to individuals who historically had been victims of employment discrimination and had not been equitably served by the commission.

Government Employee Rights

Purpose. Stated that Congress intended to provide procedures to protect the rights of Senate and other government employees to be free of job discrimination on the basis of race, color, religion, sex, national origin, age or disability.

Fair Employment Office. Established the Office of Senate Fair Employment Practices. The director of the office was to be appointed by the Senate president pro tempore, upon the recommendation of the majority leader in consultation with the minority leader.

The director, in turn, was to adopt rules governing the procedures of the office, including the procedures of hearing boards that were to resolve complaints.

(The law left in place for House employees procedures adopted in 1988 through a Fair Employment Practices Resolution. Under that House resolution, an Office of Fair Employment Practices provided counseling and mediation of complaints, conducted hearings on unresolved complaints, and imposed remedies.)

Procedures. Required that a Senate employee alleging a job-bias violation first request counseling by the fair employment office. The office was to provide the employee with all relevant information on the employee's rights.

A request for counseling had to be made within 180 days of the alleged violation.

Mediation. Dictated that if the employee wished to pursue the complaint, he or she had to file a request for mediation with the office within 15 days after the end of the 30-day counseling period. The mediation period was set at 30 days.

Formal complaint and hearing. Required that at the end of the mediation period, if the complaint was still unresolved, the worker file a formal complaint with the office within 30 days. No complaint could be filed unless the employee had made a timely request for counseling and had completed the mediation procedures. The director of the Office of Fair Employment Practices was to then choose a hearing board, made up of three independent hearing officers who were not senators or officers or employees of the Senate.

The hearing was to be conducted in closed session, and the board was to make a decision on the case within 45 days. The hearing board could order equitable relief and compensatory damages but no punitive damages.

Ethics review. Allowed an employee or boss to request that the Select Committee on Ethics review the decision.

Court appeal. Permitted either side to petition for review in the U.S. Court of Appeals for the Federal Circuit within 90 days.

Coverage of presidential appointees and certain state employees. Similarly extended the protections of Title VII, the ADA, the 1973 Rehabilitation Act and the Age Discrimination in Employment Act of 1967 to presidential appointees. (Exempted were appointees who were subject to advice and consent by the Senate.)

Permitted a worker to file with the EEOC a complaint not later than 180 days after the alleged violation occurred.

As in the provision for Senate employees, it allowed compensatory damages but no punitive damages, and allowed review by the U.S. Court of Appeals for the Federal Circuit.

Also extended the protections of Title VII, the ADA, the 1973 Rehabilitation Act and the Age Discrimination in Employment Act of 1967, with similar remedies, to state employees who worked for elected officials.

Miscellaneous Provisions

Age-discrimination statute of limitations. Required the EEOC to notify a person who had filed an age-discrimination charge when the commission dismissed or otherwise terminated the complaint. The person could then bring a civil lawsuit within 90 days of receipt of notice.

Lawful court remedies. Dictated that nothing in the legislation be construed to affect court-ordered remedies, affirmative action or conciliation agreements that were in accordance with already existing law.

Alternative means of dispute resolution. Stated that when appropriate, the use of alternative means of resolution — including settlement negotiations, conciliation, facilitation, mediation, fact-finding, mini-trials and arbitration — was encouraged to resolve job-bias disputes. ■

Continued from p. 257

proved the amendment by voice vote. Whether courts would follow it was another matter. A judge's use of legislative history, in the words of the late appeals court Judge Harold Leventhal, was like "looking over a crowd and picking out your friends."

FINAL ACTION

The House on Nov. 7 cleared S 1745 by a 381-38 vote. Five Democrats and 33 Republicans opposed the bill. Many of those who voted against the bill said it would clog the courts with job-bias lawsuits and hurt small businesses. *(Vote 386, p. 94-H)*

Most members, however, seemed relieved that a bargain had been struck and the battle was over. "I didn't think we'd ever get it done," said House Judiciary Committee Chairman Brooks.

Lewis, who had been on the front line of the civil rights movement of the 1960s, said of the bill, "It is not perfect. It is not a panacea. But it is a step in the right direction."

No amendments were allowed because congressional leaders and the White House agreed that amendments would shatter the fragile deal.

Alaskan Cannery Workers

As a result, floor debate was anticlimactic, except for disagreements over the fate of the parties to one of the lawsuits that helped spawn the legislation. Alaska cannery workers who had sued Wards Cove Packing Co. would not benefit from the new law.

As part of a compromise with the White House and Senate Republicans, the bill specifically exempted ongoing litigation involving the Wards Cove Packing Co. from provisions making it easier to prove indirect job bias.

Many House Democrats were outraged that the estimated 2,000 Alaska cannery workers were not covered, but only two Democratic lawmakers, Neil Abercrombie and Patsy T. Mink, both from Hawaii, voted against the bill because of it. Abercrombie called the compromise "extortion," adding: "Do you think for a minute that this would be happening if it involved 2,000 Irish-Americans in Boston? Or 2,000 Jews in New York?"

He and Mink represented large constituencies of Asian and Pacific Americans who shared a heritage with the Alaskans who sued Wards Cove in the early 1970s.

But Alaska Sens. Frank H. Murkowski and Ted Stevens, both Republicans, won assurances that the law would exempt ongoing litigation affecting the cannery. Murkowski described Wards Cove as a "substantial employer" in Alaska.

Alaska's only House member, Republican Don Young, also supported the exemption, which came into public view during Senate debate and drew more attention when, through a technical gaffe, it was dropped from the bill.

Senators thought the provision had been adopted when the Senate passed the bill Oct. 30, but an unrelated amendment by Dole had inadvertently canceled out that part of the bill.

When the error was discovered, the Senate returned on Nov. 5 to debate reinserting the exemption. Brock Adams, D-Wash., opposed the move, saying it would be unjust to bar the cannery employees — primarily low-paid, seasonal workers — from the benefit of the new law. He quoted dissenting Justice John Paul Stevens, who said the company's practices "bear an unsettling resemblance to aspects of a plantation economy."

Murkowski countered that Wards Cove had won at earlier stages of the lawsuit and had spent $2 million and 20 years defending itself. The Senate subsequently restored the Wards Cove exemption, 73-22. *(Vote 244, p. 32-S)*

During House debate, Speaker Thomas S. Foley, D-Wash., urged concerned House members to support the compromise despite the exemption. He promised to move a separate bill to protect the cannery workers.

Bush Signs Bill

Bush on Nov. 21 signed the bill, but even that finale was not without controversy.

In the hours before the signing ceremony a faction in the White House revealed its smoldering opposition to affirmative action and generated a partial boycott of the signing ceremony by Democrats who had pushed for the legislation.

A draft signing statement had directed the government to end the various affirmative action programs it had carried on for decades under executive orders. The draft was prepared under the direction of Counsel to the President C. Boyden Gray.

Disclosure of the preliminary statement reignited political tensions over affirmative action and quotas and prompted Bush at the bill signing to declare that he supported affirmative action.

"This historic legislation strengthens the barriers and sanctions against employment discrimination," Bush said in a statement.

During the Rose Garden signing, he added that the compromise would bring a new "civility" to the divisive race issue.

But some congressional Democrats were not so sure. Rep. Edwards of California, who refused to attend the ceremony, said he did not believe that the administration would abandon its efforts to kill affirmative action. He said the message was: "Let's not put a damper on today's festivities. We'll lower the boom tomorrow."

Danforth, pivotal in negotiating the rights compromise, termed the draft statement "regressive." He said, however, that he was satisfied that Bush supported affirmative action. He said he thought Gray's office had been acting without guidance from Bush.

Asked about reports that he threatened not to attend the ceremony unless the statement was changed, Danforth grinned and said, "I expressed myself clearly."

Three statements in the draft particularly angered bill sponsors and civil rights activists.

Two were dropped; one, favoring a narrow interpretation of the bill by Senate Minority Leader Dole, remained in Bush's final speech.

The original remarks ordered the heads of all federal departments to review immediately their equal opportunity programs and called for elimination of the Uniform Guidelines on Employee Selection Procedures, used to meet anti-discrimination goals.

The draft remarks said: "Any regulation, rule, enforcement practice or other aspect of these programs that mandates, encourages or otherwise involves the use of quotas, preferences, set-asides or other similar devices on the basis of race, color, religion, sex or national origin is to be terminated as soon as legally feasible."

Kennedy, the only Democratic lawmaker to attend the ceremony, said he was willing to give Bush the benefit of the doubt and judge him by his actual remarks rather than "a memorandum that's been prepared by staff."

However, Kennedy as well as other lawmakers were concerned that both the draft statement and Bush's final remarks said the civil rights bill should be interpreted according to Dole's remarks on the Senate floor Oct. 30 and Nov. 5.

Dole's interpretation gave more flexibility to employers than Danforth's and Kennedy's, although the latter senators also differed over the law's effects.

While he did not agree with Bush's interpretation, Danforth said, the president was entitled to offer his own spin on the bill language.

And as for the abandoned directives: "At least we didn't go backwards." ■

Anti-Crime Bill Falls Victim to Partisanship

Picking up where they left off in 1990, the Bush administration and congressional Democrats vied throughout the year to see who could appear toughest on crime. And for the second time in a row, the quarrel ended in stalemate.

In the waning hours of the session Nov. 27, the Democratic-controlled House narrowly approved the final version of a sweeping bill (HR 3371) to apply the death penalty to more than 50 federal crimes, impose a five-day waiting period for the purchase of handguns and limit appeals by death row prisoners.

But with President Bush insisting the bill did not go far enough to restrict appeals by convicted criminals and relax evidentiary rules, Senate Republicans blocked action on it.

That suspended the political argument until the 1992 election season and left the legislation in limbo.

Nonetheless, the bill was a landmark of sorts: It marked the first time that both chambers had approved a waiting period for handgun purchases. That proposal was known as the Brady bill, after its chief advocate, former White House press secretary James S. Brady, who was permanently disabled by a handgun fired in the 1981 assassination attempt on President Ronald Reagan.

A second gun-control provision, to ban sales and possession of at least nine types of U.S.-made semiautomatic assault-style weapons, was dropped from the final bill.

The Senate had approved the ban as part of its version of the crime bill (S 1241), but the House voted 244-177 to strip it out. The administration already had banned some foreign-made semiautomatic weapons but opposed extending the prohibition to U.S.-made firearms. Bush also opposed the waiting-period provision, but said he would consider it as part of a broader crime bill that met his approval. *(Brady bill, p. 271)*

BOXSCORE

➡ **Crime Bill (HR 3371, S 1241).** The bill authorized the death penalty for more than 50 federal crimes, restricted habeas corpus petitions by convicted criminals, authorized more than $3 billion for prisons and law enforcment, and imposed a five-day waiting period for handgun purchases.

Reports: H Rept 102-242, Parts I and II; H Rept 102-405.

KEY ACTION

July 11 — The **Senate** passed S 1241 by 71-26.

Sept. 26 — The **House** Judiciary Committee approved HR 3371 by voice vote.

Oct. 22 — The **House** passed HR 3371 by 305-118.

Nov. 24 — **House-Senate** conferees reached agreement on HR 3371.

Nov. 27 — The **House** adopted conference report on HR 3371 by 205-203. Cloture vote in Senate fell 11 votes short, 49-38.

The 1990 Crime Bill

For almost a decade, anti-crime proposals had generated a lot of rhetoric but little action until the waning days of a biennial Congress, when an election was just around the corner. *(1989 Almanac, p. 259; 1988 Almanac, p. 85; 1986 Almanac, p. 92; 1984 Almanac, p. 215; 1982 Almanac, p. 419)*

In 1991, however, Bush threw down the gauntlet early in the session and challenged Congress to act on a crime bill within 100 days. Much of what he demanded had been on the legislative table in 1990, only to get swept away in House-Senate bargaining at the end of the 101st Congress.

The 1990 crime package was gutted in a conference committee on the eve of adjournment. Stripped out were an assault-weapons ban, death penalty provisions, limits on death row appeals and a proposal to allow prosecutors to use illegally obtained evidence in court if police had acted in good faith when gathering the evidence.

The two provisions that effectively killed any chance of compromise were a Senate ban on semiautomatic weapons and a House proposal that would have allowed defendants to challenge their death penalties if they could show, based on statistics, that their sentences were the result of racial bias. House conferees refused to accept gun control, and Senate conferees refused to go along with the so-called racial justice provision.

The White House had threatened a veto if the bill was cleared with the racial justice provision. Attorney General Dick Thornburgh argued that because prosecutors would have an "unrealistic burden" of disproving the statistics, the provision could result "in the invalidation of every capital sentence now in effect."

The bill that was eventually enacted (PL 101-647) included largely non-controversial items: new sanctions against thrift fraud; prison alternatives, such as house arrest; more funding for local law enforcement; and increased authorizations for federal law enforcement agencies such as the FBI. *(1990 Almanac, p. 486)*

The 1991 Proposals

The Bush administration's 1991 crime proposal (HR 1400, S 635) was introduced by House Minority Leader Robert H. Michel, R-Ill., on March 12, and Sen. Strom Thurmond, R-S.C., ranking Judiciary Committee member, on March 13.

It sought to apply the federal death penalty to about 40 crimes, most of which involved murder. It also limited the ability of death row inmates to challenge the constitutionality of their sentences through so-called habeas corpus petitions. And it stiffened penalties for firearms offenses.

It also proposed an expanded "good faith" exception to the exclusionary rule, which barred prosecutors from using illegally obtained evidence against a defendant.

Senate Democrats, led by Judiciary Committee Chairman Joseph R. Biden Jr., D-Del., countered with a bill (S 618) to authorize capital punishment for 44 federal offenses, restrict habeas corpus petitions, loosen the exclusionary rule, ban assault weapons and authorize $1 billion in aid to state and local law enforcement agencies. The measure also included racial-justice safeguards and required that death row prisoners have adequate counsel as a condition to limits on habeas corpus.

Death row inmates routinely sought writs of habeas

corpus in federal courts after their regular appeals failed, in an effort to overturn their convictions and delay execution. Often such proceedings postponed executions for years, to the frustration of state prosecutors and victims' families.

Although Congress had weighed numerous proposals for habeas corpus revision over the preceding year or two, most of the movement on the subject was taking place in the Supreme Court. As Presidents Ronald Reagan and Bush transformed the makeup of the high court, the justices took an increasingly tough line on the rights of criminal defendants. *(Supreme Court crackdown, p. 264)*

SENATE FLOOR ACTION

Because the Senate crime bill contained proposals that had been thoroughly debated the year before, Senate leaders decided to skip the usual public hearings and Judiciary Committee action and put the legislation directly on the Senate floor.

Debate began June 20 and culminated July 11, when the Senate passed the bill by 71-26. *(Vote 125, p. 17-S)*

Bush's Proposal Rejected

Bush's 100-day deadline for action on a crime bill was June 14. But when it came time for the Senate to act on the president's bill June 20, Republicans didn't want to vote on it. Thurmond said he wanted to amend the measure to win more votes.

He added more than $3 billion for state and local law enforcement, patterned after Biden's proposals, and removed two particularly controversial provisions. One would have allowed for closed deportation hearings for foreigners suspected of terrorism, and another would have allowed illegally seized firearms to be used as evidence at trial.

Civil libertarians and some editorial writers had denounced the proposals as threats to due process of law. A Washington Post editorial June 19, calling the terrorism plan "a nightmare that could allow the worst kind of injustice," particularly got the administration's attention, GOP aides said.

Thurmond said he made the changes to make S 635 as pleasing as possible. He insisted that it was still the administration's bill, even though the administration up to the day before the vote had said the extra $3 billion for law enforcement was neither necessary nor available. Appropriators had not been able to find enough money for existing law enforcement programs.

Phil Gramm, R-Texas, said the Thurmond offering was still the only way to go "if you want a tough, grab-'em-by-the-throat bill."

Democrats at first protested that Republicans were too cowardly to put up their original "draconian" bill and that by including most of Biden's language, the GOP was offering a strange hybrid neither side really wanted.

Biden ripped the cover off his bill and said Thurmond might as well staple it to the back of the GOP bill because he had taken "95 percent of it."

Even amended, the Bush bill failed to carry. The 40-56 vote split mostly along party lines, with Democrats losing Ernest F. Hollings, S.C., and Richard C. Shelby, Ala. Joining the Democratic majority were Republicans John H. Chafee, R.I.; Dave Durenberger, Minn.; James M. Jeffords, Vt.; and Warren B. Rudman, N.H. *(Vote 103, p. 14-S)*

The Racial Justice Provision

The Biden bill allowed death row prisoners to make a prima facie case that their sentence was the result of bias by producing statistical evidence that people of their race in a given jurisdiction were more likely than others to be charged with murder or sentenced to die.

A state or federal entity could rebut the showing by "clear and convincing" evidence that factors unrelated to race caused the disproportionate statistics.

Edward M. Kennedy, D-Mass., the sponsor of the provision, cited studies that showed that blacks were more likely to be sentenced to death than whites and that defendants accused of killing whites were more likely subjects for capital punishment than those accused of killing blacks.

"Race discrimination is unacceptable everywhere, and it is particularly unacceptable in capital punishment — the awesome decision by a free society of those whom government can legally kill," Kennedy said. "If that decision is to be made at all, it must be made without racial bigotry."

However, many members in both parties were uneasy about the racial justice language. Bob Graham, D-Fla., offered a motion to strike the section from the bill, asserting that it would "effectively end the ability of the states to constitutionally apply the death penalty."

Graham said prosecutors would have difficulty rebutting general statistics, which he said distorted individual situations. "The decision to execute is an individualized decision-making process . . . taking into account the character and record of the murderer and the circumstances of the offense."

Graham and other senators said the criminal justice system already had built-in safeguards to protect defendants from racial discrimination.

He prevailed; the Senate deleted the section, 55-41. *(Vote 102, p. 14-S)*

But Graham lost some ground from 1990, when the same provision was struck from the crime bill by 58-38.

Death Penalty, Quotas, Guns

Biden tried to strike a GOP plan for capital punishment for defendants convicted of operating big-time drug enterprises. His motion to substitute life imprisonment unless an intentional killing was involved was rejected, 30-68. *(Vote 106, p. 15-S)*

The Senate also rejected, 25-73, an attempt by Paul Simon, D-Ill., to substitute life in prison without parole for all death penalty provisions in the bill. *(Vote 107, p. 15-S)*

In a move that had the effect of extending capital punishment to states that did not authorize it themselves, the Senate adopted an amendment by Alfonse M. D'Amato, R-N.Y., to allow federal prosecutors to seek the death penalty for homicides if the gun involved had moved across state or national borders. The vote was 65-33. *(Vote 109, p. 15-S)*

The Senate adopted by 60-39 an amendment by Steve Symms, R-Idaho, to mandate at least a 20-year prison term and to allow the death penalty for drug-related murders in the District of Columbia, which did not have capital punishment for any offenses. *(Vote 111, p. 15-S)*

That amendment was held up for about 24 hours by a surprise move by Jesse Helms, R-N.C., to outlaw any race preferences in hiring.

Helms proposed that it be illegal for any employer to give anyone "preferential treatment" in hiring, pay or other job conditions based on race, color, religion, sex or national origin. He tried to attach the proposal to an unrelated death penalty amendment.

Civil rights activists called Helms' proposal "a full-scale assault" on affirmative action. And Senate Minority Lead-

Court Continues Crackdown On Crime . . .

While Democrats and Republicans in Congress argued throughout 1991 over who was toughest on crime, the Supreme Court was winning the title hands down.

As it had for several terms, the court continued to dismantle defendants' rights in favor of state authority to do what was necessary to catch and punish criminals.

"The court is going much further than Congress has and probably than Congress will," said Johnny Killian, a senior specialist in American law at the Library of Congress' Congressional Research Service.

The Supreme Court traditionally had been the last refuge for the accused. Under Chief Justice Earl Warren (1953-69), it strengthened defendants' protections against police abuse and overzealous prosecutors. During Warren E. Burger's tenure (1969-86), the justices showed a new deference to police, but the court remained a shield for defendants.

Under Chief Justice William H. Rehnquist, however, the court took an increasingly hard line on defendants. For example, in the 1990-91 term the court:

- Restricted the ability of death row inmates to seek federal court review of their cases.
- Ruled that coerced confessions did not automatically invalidate a conviction.
- Said that an individual could be jailed for up to 48 hours without a hearing before a magistrate to determine whether his arrest was proper.
- Ruled that police could approach passengers on buses and ask to search their luggage without suspicion that the passengers were engaged in wrongdoing.

These decisions drew sharp criticism from dissenting justices, and outside experts said the rulings were dramatic departures from criminal justice precedents.

Justice Thurgood Marshall, in one ruling involving habeas corpus petitions filed by death row inmates, wrote that the majority was serving as a "backup legislature." The court enforced a standard for death penalty appeals similar to one that was dropped from a crime bill in 1990. "Unfazed by Congress' rejection of this legislation, the majority arrogates to itself the power to repeal [an existing guideline] and replace it with a tougher standard," Marshall said in his dissent.

A Changing Court

David Robinson, a criminal law professor at George Washington University National Law Center, said the Rehnquist court was going further than the Burger court.

Appointing Burger, President Richard M. Nixon announced that he wanted a law-and-order court that would undo the Warren precedents. But, Robinson said, "the great monuments of the Warren Court were only marginally modified in the Burger years." By contrast, "Rehnquist is a more consistent conservative than Burger."

Rehnquist, appointed to the court by Nixon in 1971 and elevated to chief justice by President Ronald Reagan in 1986, had always sided with the government's interests over those of the individual. But only in the late 1980s, as Reagan-Bush justices joined the court, was he able to win majorities for broader rulings for police power.

The 1990 resignation of liberal William J. Brennan Jr. ensured Rehnquist at least five votes on most criminal law disputes, with Brennan's successor, David H. Souter, providing the crucial fifth vote.

While dissenting justices complained that defendants' rights were being steamrolled, pollsters said the public wanted tougher law enforcement. For example, polls showed increasing public support for the death penalty. In 1960, 45 percent of Americans favored the death penalty for murderers. About 43 percent said they opposed it.

In 1972, the year the Supreme Court struck down all death penalty laws as unconstitutional without certain safeguards, 50 percent supported the death penalty.

States rewrote death penalty laws, and by 1990, polls showed that 72 percent favored the death penalty. The Bush administration lauded many of the court rulings.

Attorney General Dick Thornburgh said the court-ordered restrictions on habeas corpus filings would put an end to "mocking assaults on the criminal justice system."

Sen. Orrin G. Hatch, R-Utah, added that he thought the Rehnquist court was "trying to bring the law back into balance" from the Warren era. "That is not particularly a preference for prosecutorial rights over defendants' rights. Defendants' rights will still be adequately protected."

Death Penalty, Habeas Corpus

The crime proposals in Congress covered many issues within and beyond court rulings. But in the much-disputed area of death penalty appeals, the court took the lead in tightening standards.

Prisoners' petitions for habeas corpus (sought after state appeals are exhausted) had been a longstanding concern of Rehnquist and of many members of Congress, because death row inmates often used successive petitions to delay execution. Prisoners filed the petitions on the grounds that their conviction was for some reason unconstitutional.

In *McCleskey v. Zant,* announced April 16, the court adopted a standard that limited death row inmates to one round of federal court review after state court appeals were exhausted. The ruling came on the heels of two years of decisions narrowing the opportunities for

er Bob Dole, R-Kan., cautioned that what Helms proposed could hurt "good affirmative action programs" and jeopardize any compromise on a job rights bill. *(Civil rights bill, p. 251)*

Helms, who used a taped commercial attacking minority preferences in his 1990 re-election campaign, wanted senators on record: "In the last few months, almost every member of the Senate has proclaimed that he or she looks with disfavor on quotas. This amendment will give senators an opportunity to reinforce their statements with a clear-cut vote against quotas."

The crime bill managers wanted no quota language in already contentious legislation. Late June 26, Majority Leader George J. Mitchell, D-Maine, moved to table Helms' amendment. The motion carried, 71-28. *(Vote 110, p. 15-S)*

Also on June 26, the Senate adopted an amendment to

. . . As Critics See Loss of Defendants' Rights

inmates whose convictions had become final to appeal based on a new, favorable court ruling in another case.

Writing for the majority, Justice Anthony M. Kennedy said in *McCleskey* that a prisoner could file only one habeas corpus petition in federal court unless there was good reason why an alleged constitutional error was not raised on the first round. The standard for a second petition was difficult to meet, and the prisoner also was required to show that he suffered "actual prejudice" from the error he asserted.

Under earlier decisions, second or subsequent habeas corpus petitions were dismissed out of hand only if a prisoner deliberately had failed to mention the grounds for appeal (possibly to raise the arguments in later petitions).

The court also had tried to limit habeas corpus petitions by denying requests for pauper status (which enabled a death row inmate to avoid a $300 filing fee) in cases where the filing was "frivolous or malicious."

Limits on who could be executed had also been subject to debate at the court and in Congress. In the 1989 *Penry v. Lynaugh*, the court ruled that executing a mentally retarded defendant did not violate the Eighth Amendment's ban on cruel and unusual punishment.

The Supreme Court also took a hard line on execution of young criminals. In 1989, it said it did not violate the Eighth Amendment for states to execute a person who had been 16 or 17 at the time he committed a capital crime.

Other Criminal Law Issues

In its 1990-91 term, the high court stepped away from several criminal law precedents, particularly those involving interrogations and searches and seizures. The decisions generally involved state law enforcement and would not be affected by the pending federal anticrime proposals.

Key rulings came on 5-4 or 6-3 votes, with justices in the majority not always splitting neatly along a conservative-liberal divide. Robinson said the court was "still sharply conflicted in the area of criminal law."

The constant was Rehnquist.

In *Arizona v. Fulminante*, announced March 26, the court ruled that a coerced confession did not automatically invalidate a conviction. That decision was a 180-degree turn from a 1967 ruling that it was a denial of due process to use a forced confession against a defendant, regardless of other evidence.

The Warren court in the 1967 case had held that a coerced confession could never be "harmless error" and must result in reversal of the conviction.

Rehnquist, writing for the five-justice majority in *Arizona v. Fulminante,* said if other evidence was enough to convict the defendant, a compelled confession could be viewed as "harmless error" — and thus not compel a new trial.

Justice Byron R. White, who generally sided with Rehnquist on criminal cases, dissented, saying the court had overruled a "vast body of precedent." He said, "Permitting a coerced confession to be part of the evidence . . . is inconsistent with the thesis that ours is not an inquisitorial system" of justice.

The court also modified a 1975 decision that warrantless arrests must be followed by a "prompt" judicial hearing to determine whether there was probable cause for arrest. In a 5-4 ruling May 13, the court said police could hold a person for 48 hours without a hearing. Sandra Day O'Connor, writing for the majority in *County of Riverside, Calif. v. McLaughlin,* cited burdened justice systems. She said local courts needed flexibility to combine the probable cause hearing with a bail hearing or arraignment.

Justice Antonin Scalia, who, like White, usually sided with the conservatives, dissented. He said 24 hours should be the limit: "While in recent years we have invented novel applications of the Fourth Amendment to release the unquestionably guilty, we today repudiate one of its core applications so that the presumptively innocent may be left in jail."

By 6-3 the court on June 20 upheld spot searches on buses. O'Connor said the ruling in *Florida v. Bostick* flowed from prior decisions allowing random searches in other public places. Dissenting, Marshall said the policy bore the mark of "coercion and unjustified intrusion."

Generally, police needed a court-issued warrant to search a person or his property. But the court historically had allowed great leeway in situations involving automobiles, allowing police to search if they had probable cause. In the May 30 *California v. Acevedo*, the court by 6-3 increased that leeway. It said police did not need a warrant for a thorough search of a car and all closed containers therein, even if police lacked probable cause to believe that individual containers contained contraband.

Justice Harry A. Blackmun, writing the opinion, said the ruling would end confusion from conflicting court decisions about what could be searched when police stopped a vehicle. He asserted that the warrant requirement had burdened effective law enforcement.

Dissenting, John Paul Stevens commented:

"No impartial observer could criticize this court for hindering the progress of the war on drugs. On the contrary, decisions like the one the court makes today will support the conclusion that this court has become a loyal foot soldier in the executive's fight against crime."

---

tightly restrict a prisoner's ability to challenge a conviction in federal court after exhausting direct appeals.

The proposal, by Orrin G. Hatch, R-Utah, required prisoners to file habeas corpus petitions within six months of exhausting their state appeals. It restricted the grounds for appeals and it allowed a federal judge to dismiss a petition if the judge decided the prisoner had received a "full and fair hearing" on his claims in a state court.

Hatch's amendment carried, 58-40. *(Vote 108, p. 15-S)*

Senate Democrats held the line on the exclusionary rule, which barred use at trial of illegally seized evidence. Bush and key GOP senators, led by Thurmond, had wanted to allow use of evidence seized without a warrant if the police officer acted in a "good faith" belief that the seizure was constitutional.

The Senate rejected that, retaining current case law,

which allowed use of evidence seized by an officer relying in good faith on a warrant later found to be defective. The vote was 43-54. *(Vote 104, p. 14-S)*

Late on June 28, the Senate approved a compromise Brady bill provision that required a waiting period for handgun purchases of five business days, and a plan for an immediate national background check of buyers that would take effect in two and a half years. The new language, approved 67-32, supplanted a provision for a seven-day wait with no timetable for an instantaneous check. *(Vote 115, p. 16-S)*

Other Amendments

In the days preceding final passage, the Senate disposed of several amendments.

On July 8, members tabled, 49-39, an amendment by Rudman that would have directed that most of the law enforcement funds in the bill be given to local police departments based on their numbers of officers. Rudman said, "I want to make the point that crime in America is inversely proportional to the number of police we have on the streets. The more policemen, the less crime. The less policemen, the more crime." *(Vote 116, p. 16-S)*

The vote left intact the bill's authorization of about $3.3 billion, including $1 billion in aid to state and local law enforcement agencies; $700 million for 10 regional prisons for drug offenders, and $400 million for police training and scholarships.

On July 9, Thurmond successfully amended a Jeff Bingaman, D-N.M., proposal to provide literacy training in prisons to make the program discretionary. Bingaman's amendment would have ordered states to set up literacy programs in prisons with 100 or more inmates.

Thurmond said that states had enough trouble paying for their school systems without having to pay for special education for inmates. His amendment was adopted 55-39. *(Vote 117, p. 16-S)*

Also on July 9, the Senate rejected a Thurmond bid to dilute a provision of the Biden bill that required police departments to adopt a police officers' "Bill of Rights" setting standards for internal investigations. The Thurmond amendment failed 43-55. *(Vote 118, p. 16-S)*

Senate Passage

The Senate passed S 1241 on July 11 by a vote of 71-26. *(Vote 125, p. 17-S)*

Daniel Patrick Moynihan, N.Y., one of 10 Democrats who voted against the measure, said its message was "throw the switch and watch them twitch."

But the administration, which had been blasting Democrats for inaction on crime legislation, praised the measure, even though in the past Bush had opposed the gun-control sections. "This legislation will strengthen the ability of federal, state and local law enforcement to remove drug traffickers and violent offenders from our streets — once and for all," Attorney General Thornburgh said.

The passage vote came after Senate leaders spent a day trying to dissuade Helms from pressing amendments setting criminal penalties on health-care personnel who transmit the AIDS virus and mandatory jail time for people who sell, produce or possess child pornography.

They finally got Helms to agree to have his amendments on AIDS and child pornography considered July 18 as part of Senate action on the Treasury-Postal Service appropriations bill (HR 2622) for fiscal 1992. *(Appropriations, p. 591)*

Even before Helms stalled the Senate bill, opponents of the gun provisions had temporarily delayed action. A July 10 attempt to invoke cloture, thus limiting debate and amendments, fell short of the requisite 60 votes, 56-43. *(Vote 120, p. 16-S)*

The vote came one day after the National Rifle Association (NRA) had urged senators to reject cloture, calling the Brady bill and assault-weapons ban "nothing less than an unmitigated attack on the rights of law-abiding gun owners."

Cloture was finally invoked on a second try that evening, after a handful of GOP senators won approval of amendments for pet anti-crime projects. The vote was 71-27. *(Vote 123, p. 17-S)*

HOUSE SUBCOMMITTEE ACTION

House leaders denounced many provisions of the Senate-passed crime bill.

House Judiciary Committee Chairman Jack Brooks, D-Texas, and the subcommittee chairmen who handled crime issues criticized the Senate for "loading up" the bill and said it disregarded cost, the effects of stiffened mandatory sentences on prison space and due process for defendants.

But Judiciary Committee Republicans viewed the Senate package more favorably. F. James Sensenbrenner Jr., R-Wis., ranking member of the Crime Subcommittee, said GOP members would not stand for Democratic "foot-dragging" on a tough crime package.

By 13-0, the Subcommittee on Crime and Criminal Justice on July 31 approved a bill that cost about one-third as much as the Senate bill but took the same get-tough approach.

The Subcommittee on Civil and Constitutional Rights on July 31 approved a separate bill (HR 2851) that allowed racial minorities on death row to use statistics in capital sentencing to claim that their sentences were discriminatory. The two were later combined.

The $1 billion draft bill approved by the Crime Subcommittee attempted to put more emphasis on prevention through drug-treatment programs and rehabilitation for young criminals. But it also permitted the death penalty for about 50 federal crimes.

While it allowed capital punishment for a drug kingpin who headed a large organization, as would the Senate bill, it did not permit the same penalty for smaller-scale drug crimes, manslaughter or obstruction of justice, as did the Senate bill.

Firearms Offenses

The most spirited debate during the Crime Subcommittee action came when GOP members tried to make the House bill as tough on firearms offenders as the Senate measure.

Sensenbrenner tried to amend the bill so that anyone found guilty of murder involving a firearm that had crossed state lines would be eligible for the death penalty. The provision was intended to give federal prosecutors jurisdiction over state homicides and invoke the death penalty even in states — like Sensenbrenner's — that did not provide for capital punishment.

William J. Hughes, D-N.J., said it would be the "height of arrogance" for the federal government to impose a death penalty on states that had elected not to use it.

The Sensenbrenner amendment was defeated 4-9, along party lines with the exception of Florida Republican Bill McCollum's vote against it.

Sensenbrenner also was rebuffed in an effort to set mandatory prison terms for possession of a firearm during a state crime involving drugs or violence. The amendment lost 5-8, along party lines.

HOUSE COMMITTEE ACTION

By voice vote, the House Judiciary Committee on Sept. 26 approved HR 3371, which took a less stringent approach to fighting crime than Bush and the Senate wanted.

The bill allowed prisoners to challenge their death sentences as racially motivated, prohibited use of coerced confessions at trial and extended other protections to defendants. It also banned certain types of semiautomatic assault-style weapons.

The legislation authorized the death penalty for about 50 federal crimes, mostly involving murder, and stiffened other criminal penalties. It set a one-year deadline for prisoners to file habeas corpus petitions in federal court after exhausting appeals of their state convictions, and it restricted successive petitions.

The measure authorized $1.2 billion for law enforcement and crime prevention, compared with more than $3 billion authorized by the Senate bill.

The most contentious House provision allowed defendants to challenge their death sentences as discriminatory if they could show that a disproportionate number of people of their race were condemned to die. Bush strongly opposed the provision, and the Senate rejected it 55-41.

Another key difference was the House committee's refusal to give federal prosecutors jurisdiction over any murder committed with a firearm that had crossed state lines. Federal judges said that proposal would swamp the federal courts and violate states' rights. Chief Justice William H. Rehnquist on Sept. 19 wrote to the House committee asking members not to adopt it.

Charles E. Schumer, D-N.Y., chairman of the House Judiciary Crime Subcommittee, insisted that the House committee bill was "every bit as tough as" Republican and Senate proposals. But Bush aides disagreed and said the president would veto the House bill if it cleared Congress.

During four days of deliberations, the House committee rejected GOP amendments that would have made it easier to impose the death penalty and harder for condemned prisoners to pursue habeas corpus appeals.

Republicans vowed a floor fight.

"In the last several sessions of Congress, we have prevailed on the floor on a whole array of death penalty provisions," said George W. Gekas, R-Pa., after his death penalty amendments were shot down in committee.

Republicans and some Democrats also fought provisions banning the sale of 13 types of assault-style semiautomatic weapons. The NRA sent letters to its members trying to stir up opposition to what it called "a massive attack on your gun rights."

The House bill did not include a waiting period for handgun purchases because the House had already passed the Brady bill (HR 7) in May.

Death Penalty

About half of the capital offenses in the bill already were on the books. But the old penalties had been invalidated in 1972 when the Supreme Court struck down all existing capital punishment laws.

The court later set out guidelines for imposing the death penalty constitutionally, and Congress and the states began rewriting their laws. In 1974, Congress approved capital punishment for airline hijackings that resulted in death, and in 1988, as part of an omnibus anti-drug law, it supported capital punishment for certain drug-trafficking murders.

Under the House bill, as in the Senate measure, capital punishment was authorized for only a few crimes that did not involve murder. Examples were treason, espionage and attempts on the president's life. Of the remaining offenses, all except terrorist killings and drive-by drug shootings required proof of an "intent to kill."

Also like the Senate bill, HR 3371 allowed imposition of the death penalty on leaders of enterprises trafficking in large amounts of drugs and reaping large profits. During House committee consideration, Hughes maintained that the provision was "patently unconstitutional" because it allowed the ultimate penalty for a crime that did not involve an intent to commit murder.

On Sept. 23, the committee defeated, 12-21, a McCollum move to strip out the racial justice section.

Hughes tried to cut the so-called drug kingpin provision from the bill Sept. 26 but was voted down by voice vote. Harley O. Staggers Jr., D-W.Va., sought to amend the bill so that all the capital punishment crimes in the bill would instead be punishable by life in prison without parole. His amendment, too, was defeated by voice vote.

Gekas proposed that prosecutors be able to seek capital punishment for cases in which a death resulted from rape or child abuse and in certain situations that involved "a reckless disregard for life," even if prosecutors could not prove an intent to kill. His amendment was defeated 12-22.

Related amendments by McCollum to allow the death penalty for drug killings stemming from "a reckless disregard for life" and to permit capital punishment for drug kingpins who attempted to kill to obstruct justice also were rejected by separate votes of 13-21.

Appeals, Defendants' Rights

Another issue destined to be revisited on the floor involved habeas corpus petitions, used by prisoners to challenge the constitutionality of their convictions and sentences after they exhausted their direct appeals. Death row prisoners often used repetitive filings to delay their executions.

The Bush administration proposed allowing a federal judge to dismiss a habeas corpus petition without a hearing if he determined that the inmate received a "full and fair" hearing at the state level.

The Senate approved such a provision, along with six-month deadlines for filing an allowed petition and tighter limits on any successive filings.

House Committee members on Sept. 23 rejected, 11-23, a similar proposal by Henry J. Hyde, R-Ill.

Instead, the House bill set a one-year deadline and barred successive petitions unless new facts in the case emerged or the defendant could not have reasonably included a claim in his first petition.

The bill also required states that had the death penalty to provide competent lawyers for trial, appellate and habeas corpus proceedings, overseen by a committee or other authority that would set standards and monitor the performance of court-appointed attorneys.

Further departing from the Senate and Bush proposals, the House measure also partially reversed a 1989 Supreme Court decision in *Teague v. Lane* that made it harder for inmates to use favorable court decisions, issued after their own convictions, in their habeas corpus petitions. The Senate bill left the ruling intact.

The House bill sought to overturn a 1991 Supreme Court ruling that made it easier for prosecutors to use coerced confessions against defendants. In a 5-4 ruling on March 26, the court held in *Arizona v. Fulminante* that the use of a coerced confession at trial did not automatically invalidate a conviction, provided other evidence of guilt was overwhelming.

The Judiciary Committee voted to bar use of a coerced confession under any circumstances.

Separately, the House panel, like the full Senate, rejected a Bush proposal to allow use at trial of evidence seized without a search warrant, provided the police were acting in "good faith" that their conduct was legal.

McCollum pressed the amendment, but it was superseded by one by George E. Sangmeister, D-Ill., to allow a good-faith exception only for evidence sought with a warrant that was later found to be invalid. That basically restated current case law. The vote for the Sangmeister alternative was 19-15.

Police Officers

The House committee rejected a Senate-backed provision to require states to adopt a police officers' "Bill of Rights" setting standards for departments' internal, noncriminal investigations. The amendment, offered by Rep. Tom Campbell, R-Calif., required an officer under investigation to be notified of the inquiry, ensured a full hearing on all complaints and given an avenue for appeal.

"These provisions are a minimum to guarantee fair treatment," Campbell said.

Other members asserted that the federal government should not interfere with states' ability to regulate local police, and the committee adopted a substitute amendment by Mike Synar, D-Okla., calling for an attorney general's study of procedures in police internal investigations. The vote was 24-10.

The House bill also instituted guidelines for private parties to go to court to seek injunctions to stop police brutality. At the last minute, under pressure from police, bill sponsors dropped proposed prison terms for police officers found guilty of brutality. The panel's interest in the issue was spurred earlier in the year by the Los Angeles police beating of suspect Rodney King, videotaped by a bystander and televised nationwide.

Committee members defeated a proposal that would have authorized $100 million for scholarships for aspiring police officers. Similar to a Senate bill provision, the amendment by Peter Hoagland, D-Neb., would have provided scholarship funds to college students who agreed to serve for four years in a state or local police department after graduation. The committee rejected it 14-20, citing the price tag.

Other Provisions

In other action, the committee approved, 17-16, a Hughes amendment to exempt New Jersey from a proposed ban on sports gambling. The bill already exempted Nevada and Oregon. New Jersey state officials were considering a referendum to permit sports gambling, and Hughes said he wanted to help his home state preserve the option.

The bill barred all other states from holding sports-based lotteries. It was adapted from HR 74, a separate bill approved by the Judiciary Subcommittee on Economic and Commercial Law Sept. 17.

The $1.2 billion funding authorization in the bill included $300 million for "drug emergency" areas, where the president determined that trafficking and abuse levels required federal aid to protect lives. The bill also authorized $200 million for intermediate-level prisons and boot-camp type facilities, $150 million for grants to local police, $100 million for anti-drug programs in prisons, and $100 million for anti-drug and crime education in schools.

Ways and Means Action

On Oct. 10, the Ways and Means Committee gave voice-vote approval to HR 3371 after stripping three of four provisions under its jurisdiction.

At the behest of Chairman Dan Rostenkowski, D-Ill., the panel, by voice vote, eliminated three provisions that could have cut revenues to the Treasury.

Two of the three provisions would have extended the statute of limitations for gun registration violations and eliminated a hearing requirement before firearm forfeitures. The Treasury raised money by fining violators of registration requirements and selling forfeited guns.

The third provision would have changed U.S. import quotas for opium used in medical drugs such as codeine.

India and Turkey had an 80 percent share of the market, with Australia, France, Hungary, Poland and Yugoslavia supplying the remaining 20 percent. The proposal would have given the five a total of 40 percent of the opium market by fiscal 1993. That could have affected import duties.

Rostenkowski opposed any provisions that in any way changed the existing revenue structure.

Left intact was a provision to allow the U.S. Customs Service to impose criminal penalties of up to three years in prison for pilots of planes suspected of carrying controlled substances who did not obey an order to land. At the time, only a civil fine of up to $5,000 could be imposed.

HOUSE FLOOR ACTION

The House began work on HR 3371 on Oct. 16 and passed it Oct. 22 by a vote of 305-118. *(Vote 327, p. 80-H)*

On the floor, Republicans assailed the Judiciary Committee's bill as a criminal-coddling measure. With help from some Democrats, they proceeded to broaden the number of cases that could be eligible for the death penalty and to allow prosecutors more leeway in using illegally obtained evidence.

Republicans also provided the political heft to squash the bill's ban on certain assault-style weapons and automatic loading devices. Despite emotional references to a gunman's murder of 22 people in a mass shooting in a Killeen, Texas, cafeteria the day before, members voted 247-177 on Oct. 17 to strip out the ban. *(Vote 318, p. 77-H)*

"Let's not fall into the politically expedient device of blaming an inanimate object for the behavior of human beings," said Dick Schulze, R-Pa.

But the House narrowly rejected another Republican proposal, blocking an amendment that would have greatly restricted appeals by inmates on death row.

Bush, who disliked the bill approved by the House Judiciary Committee, warned that "the American people will not accept a crime bill that is tougher on law enforcement than it is on criminals."

Assault Weapons Ban

Each camp found its own message in the Texas tragedy.

Gekas seized upon the story as proof that the House should back his amendment to make more crimes eligible for the death penalty.

Schumer argued that the shooting spree bolstered the case for an assault weapons ban. Although the Glock semiautomatic pistol used in Killeen would not have been covered by the ban, the gun clip used by the killer would have been. "Twenty-two people died. Maybe they didn't have to," Schumer said. "This House will decide today whether they died in vain."

Harold L. Volkmer, D-Mo., who sponsored the amendment to strike the provisions, urged his colleagues not to be swayed by such appeals.

Volkmer and others said that killers could always find ways to kill and that honest gun-owners should not be penalized for others' abuses.

The shooting incident did sway one vote — Democratic freshman Chet Edwards, who represented Killeen.

Edwards had planned to vote against the ban and used to cite statistics suggesting that state gun bans did little to deter crime. But he said, "I'll never see this issue quite the same again. Statistics don't mean as much to me now."

Proponents of the ban said election and redistricting concerns persuaded some members not to back gun restrictions. But members generally cited the NRA as the most powerful deterrent.

The gun lobby's powerful mystique was somewhat diminished by the House vote earlier in the year to support the so-called Brady bill, which mandated a seven-day waiting period for handgun purchases. But lobbyists and members for gun control said that vote worked against them in the assault weapons ban because some members felt they had to make amends with the NRA.

Death Penalty

Like the Senate bill, the House measure enlarged the list of federal crimes that could draw the death penalty. In one of the tighter floor battles, the House voted 213-206 to adopt language that went further still. *(Vote 313, p. 76-H)*

The amendment, offered by Gekas, allowed capital punishment of a defendant who showed a reckless disregard for human life, replacing the more stringent "intent to kill" test.

As he had in committee, Staggers sought to replace the death penalty in all cases with life imprisonment without parole. He lost, 101-322. *(Vote 311, p. 76-H)*

Republicans won another victory when the House by 247-165 adopted a McCollum amendment to adopt the broad good-faith exception to the exclusionary rule rejected by the Senate. *(Vote 320, p. 78-H)*

Habeas Corpus Petitions

Republicans fell short in their efforts to tighten the committee bill's restrictions on habeas corpus petitions.

Hyde sought to allow federal courts to dismiss a habeas corpus petition if the inmate had received a "full and fair" consideration of his claim in the state courts. "There must be an end to litigation. There must be finality," Hyde said.

But Judiciary Committee members said they had already included provisions to cut down on excessive appeals. The amendment failed 208-218. *(Vote 316, p. 76-H)*

Members adopted another Hyde amendment, 281-137, allowing states to use federal funds for prosecutors to fight death row appeals and to require that money equal to the federal funds available to help death row prisoners pursue such appeals be available for prosecutors. *(Vote 319, p. 78-H)*

Racial Justice Issue

When debate resumed Oct. 22, the most controversial amendments dealt with race and the death penalty.

One amendment, offered by McCollum and adopted 223-191, eliminated the bill's racial justice provision. *(Vote 322, p. 78-H)*

The same amendment, offered by Sensenbrenner, was rejected in 1990.

"Comparing similar cases, blacks consistently get the death penalty where whites do not," said Edwards, chairman of the Judiciary Subcommittee on Civil and Constitutional Rights. "The bill allows courts to look at that evidence."

McCollum and his allies countered that the committee's bill would effectively bar the death penalty.

"Once one case is thrown out, the statistics can never change, and capital punishment for one race in that jurisdiction will be forever outlawed," said Craig T. James, R-Fla.

"If somebody takes a .45 and puts it to my head and wants to blow my brains out and does, I do not care what color of skin that person has," Hyde said. "He ought to get the chair."

Twenty-one Democrats and six Republicans who voted to leave racial justice language in the bill in 1990 voted to delete it in 1991. Among the Democrats were Rostenkowski and William H. Natcher, Ky. Among GOP switch votes were Christopher H. Smith and H. James Saxton, both of New Jersey.

Freshman members also broke in favor of McCollum's amendment, with 29 voting for it and 18 against. Maxine Waters, D-Calif., did not vote.

Seven members, among them John D. Dingell, D-Mich., chairman of the Energy and Commerce Committee, voted in 1990 to kill racial justice language and switched in 1991.

Another Republican amendment, offered by Hyde, struck from the bill provisions crafted by Howard L. Berman, D-Calif., that would have allowed death row prisoners to use racial discrimination as grounds to challenge their sentences in habeas corpus filings. Hyde's amendment was adopted 238-180. *(Vote 324, p. 78-H)*

Also on Oct. 22, the House adopted, 369-51, an amendment to establish a Police Corps to provide a federal college scholarship of up to $10,000 a year in exchange for a four-year commitment to serve on a state or local police force. The administration opposed this provision. *(Vote 325, p. 78-H)*

Conservative Coalition

The conservative coalition — Republicans and Southern Democrats — was evident in voting on the crime bill. In 1990, the coalition appeared on 12 votes on the crime bill and was defeated only once. The coalition appeared and won on seven votes on the bill in 1991.

Schumer, chairman of the Judiciary Subcommittee on Crime and sponsor of the bill, said political pressures and risks of appearing soft on crime were too great for many members. "I think the bill came at an inauspicious time when members felt under political assault," he said. "We're close to an election year and a presidential election year."

Many members also faced redistricting. With the potential of new constituents, Schumer said, many members did not want to take chances.

CONFERENCE/FINAL

The way was paved for House and Senate conferees to begin work on HR 3371 after GOP senators on Nov. 21 dropped their objections to naming conferees.

Thurmond, the lead GOP senator on the bill, had protested the Democratic majority's plan to appoint five Democrats and three Republicans as conferees. To help avoid a repeat of 1990's conference, at which most GOP initiatives were dropped, Thurmond wanted more Republicans.

After Democrats accused Republicans of not wanting a crime bill, Thurmond accepted the 5-3 ratio.

Steve Symms, R-Idaho, also had blocked the conference, opposing Senate provisions to require a waiting period for handgun buyers and ban nine types of assault weapons.

Symms said Bush called him to the White House on Nov. 21 and told him "the bill is really important."

Meanwhile, the House voted to name conferees Nov. 21 and rejected a motion by Sensenbrenner to instruct them to accept a Senate provision to set mandatory minimum prison terms for firearm use in drug-related or violent crimes. The vote was 155-271. *(Vote 413, p. 100-H)*

The next day, the House Ways and Means Subcommittee on Trade voted 8-4 to approve a permanent ban (HR 1559) on the importation of assault-style semiautomatic weapons. Most weapons involved already were banned by a 1989 executive order.

Agreement Reached

Meeting in a rare Sunday session, the conferees reached agreement on the final version of HR 3371 on Nov. 24.

Republicans complained they were "steamrollered" on a series of party-line votes that led to the adoption of the weaker provisions of the House or Senate bills on habeas corpus, the exclusionary rule and the death penalty for state gun crimes.

"I'll take any step I can to stop this bill," said Thurmond. "It is a travesty."

The conferees dropped the ban on semiautomatic assault weapons approved earlier by the Senate but rejected on the House floor. However, they kept the Brady bill provisions calling for a five-day waiting period for the purchase of a handgun.

Final House Action

When House leaders brought the conference report to the floor shortly after dawn Nov. 27, they realized they faced a Senate filibuster and a veto from Bush, who also vehemently opposed the measure. They wanted to leave it to Republicans to be blamed for collapse of the bill.

Amid a flurry of vote switching, Democrats eked out a 205-203 passage of the bill. Members split along party lines, with 199 Democrats and six Republicans supporting it. *(Vote 443, p. 108-H)*

The legislation appeared moribund late Nov. 26, as both chambers hastened to finish work before Thanksgiving. Beginning Nov. 25, Bush's attacks on the bill and the opposition from local prosecutors had robbed the measure of expected support.

Schumer said he could count only 70 supporters when the week began. But over the next 48 hours, bill proponents gained ground. By about 9 p.m. on Nov. 26, the Democrats had 180 votes, and Schumer said it was not until after 3 a.m. Nov. 27 that he believed they had 199 Democrats ready to vote for the measure.

The morning newspapers Nov. 27 had declared the bill dead in the House. But two key factors gave Democrats their slim majority: Judiciary Committee Democrats convinced edgy colleagues that, on balance, the bill would be tougher than existing law on criminals, and the House leadership kept many wavering Democrats on board by calling for a united front against Bush.

Four conservative Texas Democrats turned out to be among the critical swing supporters, influenced by Brooks, dean of the Lone Star State's delegation. The four last-minute votes were Chet Edwards, Pete Geren, Ralph M. Hall and Charles W. Stenholm.

They said Texas Democrats Jim Chapman and Greg Laughlin, a former district attorney and assistant district attorney, respectively, also helped convince them that the bill would not interfere with prosecutors.

"I decided right there on the floor," Geren said, adding: "The bill isn't as tough as I wanted, but I feel like it is a step forward in toughening up the criminal justice system."

Asked about the pressure from Brooks, Geren laughed and said, "He did a real comprehensive job."

What did Brooks tell his colleagues? "You're in your mothers' arms. Trust me," Brooks recounted.

Speaker Thomas S. Foley, D-Wash., also worked through the night to round up "yea" votes.

In the end, 26 members did not vote, some of them deliberately.

"I filled out three voting cards," said Craig Washington, D-Texas. "Yes, no and present." He told bill sponsors, "If my vote were needed, I would vote yes."

Washington, who was on the floor, wound up not voting at all. "I should have voted present," he said. "I just panicked" in all the activity.

House Republicans who broke ranks and supported the bill were Benjamin A. Gilman, N.Y.; Bill Green, N.Y.; Paul B. Henry, Mich.; Frank Horton, N.Y.; Constance A. Morella, Md.; and Jim Ramstad, Minn.

Final Senate Action

Later on Nov. 27, the Senate failed, 49-38, to quell a Republican-led filibuster against the bill. The vote was 11 short of the 60 needed to invoke cloture and cut off debate. Only one Republican voted for cloture, and three Democrats joined the rest of the Republicans against the bill. *(Vote 278, p. 36-S)*

The lone Senate Republican to vote for cloture on the crime bill was John H. Chafee, R.I.

Senate Democrats who voted against cloture were Howell Heflin, Ala.; Richard C. Shelby, Ala.; and Paul Wellstone, Minn.

"This is the toughest crime bill that has ever come before the Senate," said Biden, "and now it's dead." He blamed extensive White House lobbying and gun enthusiasts' opposition.

But Thurmond rejoined, "What blame is there? This is a terrible bill. This bill extends the rights of criminals."

Police generally backed the bill, which called for the authorization of $1 billion in new funds for state and local law enforcement.

But Bush, other Republicans, district attorneys and attorneys general protested the inclusion of new safeguards for defendants' rights.

"The conference report does more for those convicted of crimes than it does for those victimized by them," Attorney General William P. Barr wrote in a letter to Congress.

The administration particularly objected to the decision by the Democratic-dominated conferees to discard a Bush proposal for greater restrictions on prisoners' appeals and a plan to allow evidence seized without a warrant to be used at trials.

"I would have to veto this bill because it would weaken our criminal justice system," Bush vowed. ■

Brady Bill Part of Stalled Crime Package

As violent crime continued to plague America's cities, both the House and Senate approved legislation mandating a waiting period of five business days and a police background check for the purchase of a handgun. But the proposal was rolled into an omnibus crime bill that snagged at adjournment.

The waiting-period measure was known as the Brady bill, after former White House press secretary James S. Brady, who was severely wounded and permanently disabled by a handgun fired in the March 30, 1981, assassination attempt on President Ronald Reagan. *(1981 Almanac, p. 6)*

Its progress in 1991 was the high point of a four-year lobbying effort by Brady and his wife, Sarah, chairman of Handgun Control Inc.

The Senate version of the crime bill (S 1241) also included a ban on sales and possession of semiautomatic assault-style guns, which had become the weapon of choice for many urban gangs and drug dealers. But the House stripped out that proposal, 247-177, and it was dropped from the final bill (HR 3371) in conference. *(Crime bill, p. 262)*

In 1988, the House derailed the Brady bill when it substituted, 228-182, a requirement that the Department of Justice instead study ways to conduct an instantaneous background check of would-be gun buyers. *(1988 Almanac, p. 100)*

The assault-weapons ban had been approved by the Senate in 1990, but it was dropped from that year's omnibus crime bill during a conference with the House in the waning days of the session. The House Rules Committee blocked floor consideration of the Brady bill in 1990. *(Background, 1990 Almanac, p. 500)*

BOXSCORE

➡ **Brady bill — waiting period for handgun purchases (HR 7; part of crime bill, S 1241, HR 3371).** The bill as introduced required a seven-day waiting period for handgun purchases. As incorporated into S 1241 and HR 3371, it set a waiting period of five business days and required a police background check of prospective handgun buyers. The measure was named after former White House press secretary James S. Brady, who was critically wounded in 1981 during the assassination attempt on President Ronald Reagan.

Reports: H Rept 102-47

KEY ACTION

April 23 — The **House** Judiciary Committee approved HR 7 by 23-11.

May 8 — The **House** passed HR 7 by 239-186.

June 28 — The **Senate** adopted compromise version of Brady bill as an amendment to the crime bill, S 1241, by 67-32.

July 11 — The **Senate** passed S 1241, 71-26.

Nov. 24 — **House-Senate** conferees on HR 3371 (House version of crime bill) agreed to the compromise Brady bill.

Nov. 27 — The **House** adopted conference report on HR 3371; **Senate** failed to invoke cloture, 49-38, 11 votes short.

Reagan's Endorsement

The Brady bill (originally HR 7 and S 257) received a major boost March 28, when Reagan held a Washington news conference to urge its enactment. He had not publicly endorsed it previously, despite his affection for James S. Brady.

Reagan's endorsement put the Bush administration on the spot. President Bush had consistently opposed a waiting period for handgun purchases, and he clearly did not like the 1991 proposal any better than its predecessors.

On April 9, Attorney General Dick Thornburgh, in a letter to Rep. Charles E. Schumer, D-N.Y., chairman of the House Judiciary Subcommittee on Crime, said he would recommend that Bush veto the bill unless it was part of a broad anti-crime package sought by the president.

The Justice Department supported an instantaneous background check rather than a waiting period for handgun purchases, but conceded that its own studies showed it would take years to computerize and standardize criminal records nationwide.

The Lobbying Campaign

Approval of the Brady bill, even though it did not clear, represented a major defeat for the National Rifle Association (NRA), one of the most feared lobbying organizations in the nation. The NRA's vaunted political power derived not only from the longstanding American cultural affinity toward guns but also from how quickly it could mobilize its members.

"It's a lobby that can put 15,000 letters in your district overnight and have people in your town hall meetings interrupting you," said Rep. William J. Hughes, D-N.J.

Officials from the NRA's nemesis, Handgun Control, tried to dispel the notion that the gun lobby could make or break a campaign. And they said candidates' support for gun control could actually mean victory.

Chairman Sarah Brady and other Handgun Control spokesmen pointed to the 1990 election of Rep. Thomas H. Andrews, D-Maine. A major reason for Andrews' primary victory and eventual win, according to local news reports, was his support for a waiting period for handgun purchases. Andrews' staff agreed.

Still, opposition from the NRA could cause trepidation among members. One reason was the gun lobby's formidable ability to pour money into individual contests.

In 1990, the NRA spent $916,135 on congressional campaigns, while Handgun Control spent $178,882, according to the Federal Election Commission. Both sides homed in on certain races, with mixed results.

Handgun Control's prime target was Rep. Jolene Unsoeld, D-Wash., who had been the sponsor of an amendment to the 1990 crime bill to weaken a ban on semiautomatic weapons. It spent $18,587 against her. But the NRA spent $52,892 in her behalf, and she won with 54 percent of the vote. She said the NRA played an important but not necessarily decisive role in her victory.

Other big-money races showed that neither the NRA nor Handgun Control was decisive.

The NRA spent $36,108 on Republican Rep. Tom Tauke, who challenged Sen. Tom Harkin, D-Iowa. Tauke lost. It spent $23,380 for GOP Sen. Jesse Helms against Democrat Harvey B. Gantt in North Carolina. Helms won. It spent $19,742 for Republican Sen. Rudy Boschwitz over Democrat Paul Wellstone in Minnesota, and $15,686 for GOP Rep. Bill Schuette over Democratic Sen. Carl Levin in Michigan. Both Boschwitz and Schuette lost.

Aside from its attempt to beat Unsoeld, Handgun Control spent its largest sums in favor of Sen. Paul Simon, D-Ill., $9,000; Levin, $6,000; Gantt, $5,000; and Harkin, $5,000. All but Gantt won, but those funds were a small fraction of what the candidates received overall.

If Handgun Control had less money than the NRA, it easily matched the gun lobbying in emotional intensity. In his wheelchair, with his wife at his side, Brady worked the corridors of Congress indefatigably in search of votes for the waiting-period proposal.

HOUSE SUBCOMMITTEE ACTION

The Brady bill was sponsored in the House by Edward F. Feighan, D-Ohio, a low-key but persistent lawmaker first elected to Congress in 1982. He had been pushing the gun-control measure since 1987. His interest was spurred in part by a gunman's 1984 rampage in a Cleveland public library that killed or wounded several people.

The Brady bill started on the road to passage on April 10, when the House Judiciary Subcommittee on Crime and Criminal Justice approved HR 7 by 9-4. This version of the bill called for a seven-day waiting period to allow — but not require — a police background check of the would-be buyer.

Voting for the bill was one Republican, F. James Sensenbrenner Jr., Wis., and eight Democrats: Feighan; John Bryant, Texas; George E. Sangmeister, Ill.; Mel Levine, Calif.; Craig Washington, Texas; Peter Hoagland, Neb.; Schumer; and Hughes. Opposing the bill were Republicans Bill McCollum, Fla.; Steven H. Schiff, N.M.; George W. Gekas, Pa.; and Jim Ramstad, Minn.

McCollum said that because the bill as approved did not order police to check criminal records, but merely gave them seven days in which to do so if they wished, the measure would do no good. At the same time, he said, it would hurt people who wanted to buy a handgun for a legitimate purpose.

HOUSE COMMITTEE ACTION

The full House Judiciary Committee approved the bill, 23-11, on April 23.

The measure required a handgun customer to sign a statement that he was not a felon, fugitive or drug addict and was not mentally ill. Purchasers already had to swear to such a statement, but the forms did not leave the dealer's shop.

An amendment adopted by the committee made clear that gun dealers would not have to wait longer than seven days if they had not heard back from police.

The committee rejected, 11-23, a substitute amendment by Harley O. Staggers Jr., D-W.Va., that would have required states to set up within six months an instant-check system allowing a gun dealer to find out with a telephone call whether a buyer had a criminal record.

Thornburgh acknowledged to the Senate Judiciary Committee on April 18 that such a deadline for an instant-check system was not feasible.

Feighan on May 1 released a draft report from the congressional Office of Technology Assessment finding that the point-of-purchase system Staggers proposed could not be in place for five to 10 years. Only Virginia had such a system at the time.

During the April 23 committee showdown, all but four Democrats voted for HR 7. The four were Staggers; Jack Brooks, Texas; Rick Boucher, Va.; and Mike Kopetski, Ore.

Six Republicans voted for the bill: Hamilton Fish Jr., N.Y.; Henry J. Hyde, Ill.; D. French Slaughter Jr., Va.; Craig T. James, Fla.; Tom Campbell, Calif.; and Sensenbrenner.

All but two members who backed the Brady bill voted against the Staggers amendment. The exceptions were Schiff, who voted no to both, and Slaughter, who voted yes to both.

Among Republicans voting against the Brady bill was Howard Coble, N.C., who in 1990 Judiciary Committee action had voted for it. He said he had been overwhelmed that time by an emotional appeal by Sarah Brady. This time, Coble said, he had returned to his conviction that gun control laws did not reduce crime.

RULES COMMITTEE ACTION

The days following the Judiciary Committee vote were marked by frenetic lobbying and behind-the-scenes maneuvering for procedural advantage.

Supporters and foes of the bill focused on the House Rules Committee, which controlled the rules for floor action. Competing for a procedural edge were HR 7, with its seven-day waiting period, and the Staggers alternative, requiring an immediate background check on gun buyers.

The latter, offered as a substitute amendment, could have killed the waiting-period measure if adopted.

That is exactly what the amendment by McCollum did to the Brady bill in 1988. McCollum's amendment called for a study of an instant background check.

House Speaker Thomas S. Foley, D-Wash., who opposed the Brady bill, said on May 1 that he was inclined to follow regular House order, meaning that members would vote first on the Staggers amendment.

But House Rules Committee Chairman Joe Moakley, D-Mass., said Foley wanted the process to be as fair as possible and would agree to further parliamentary procedures for a clean vote on HR 7.

"He said, 'I've been accused of a lot of things and I just want to get this bill behind us,' " Moakley recounted. Late in the 1990 session, Foley kept the bill from a floor vote, saying he did not want to force congressmen to cast a difficult vote on the emotional gun-control issue right before the election but also acknowledging his longstanding opposition to firearms restrictions.

While the rules controversy swirled, newspaper opinion pages filled with editorials and columns for and against the Brady bill. House floor speeches on gun control proliferated as well. The administration supported the Staggers amendment but left the door open for acceptance of a waiting period as part of a comprehensive crime bill.

Feighan and Schumer considered asking the Rules Committee to guarantee a vote on the Brady bill no matter what happened with the Staggers amendment. But they finally decided against that course.

HOUSE FLOOR VOTE

The weeks of lobbying ended May 8 with a thumping House vote in favor of the Brady bill. The measure passed by 53 votes, 239-186. *(Vote 83, p. 20-H)*

First, the House defeated the Staggers amendment, 193-234. *(Vote 81, p. 20-H)*

Then it rebuffed, 162-265, a last-ditch motion by McCollum to send the bill back to the Judiciary Committee. *(Vote 82, p. 20-H)*

Passage of the bill was important for three reasons.

First, it reflected a sea change in attitudes on gun control in the House, which just three years earlier had blocked the measure by 46 votes. Second, it represented a stunning defeat for the NRA, which some had thought invincible. And third, the decisive House vote made it impossible for the Senate to avoid a vote on the Brady bill.

The Bradys worked with Feighan and Schumer to line up votes. Although Speaker Foley opposed the bill, other Democratic leaders helped whip votes. And former President Reagan phoned wavering Republicans.

Polls showed resounding support for gun control, and constituent pressure was starting to boil over.

Personal appeals made a difference in several cases. For freshman Charles Luken, D-Ohio, it was a heart-to-heart talk with the Cincinnati chief of police on the morning of the vote. For New York Republican Benjamin A. Gilman, it was constituent concern about gun deaths — and a telephone call from advice columnist Ann Landers.

Compared with the 1988 vote, 36 members switched from favoring the McCollum substitute to opposing the Staggers amendment. Three members shifted to support the alternative to the Brady bill.

Members elected since the 1988 vote were a virtual wash, voting 41-44 on Staggers. But pro-Brady forces picked up about half of their new backing among Southern Democrats.

Southerners huddled with delegation colleagues during the floor vote. In some cases, when one turned against the Staggers substitute, another followed. In 1988, only one member of the Georgia delegation voted against a substitute — but six did in 1991.

Gilman, who had voted for the McCollum amendment in 1988, said he received more than 3,000 calls and letters. He ended up switching, voting against the Staggers alternative, because the Brady bill was "a reasonable stopgap measure that we can undertake until an instantaneous data system can be implemented."

Charles Wilson, D-Texas, who did not change his opposition to the Brady bill, said, "I think President Reagan was a major factor. It gave a lot of cover to moderates and conservatives of both parties."

Brady said he called about 125 House members the day before the vote. He was one of the few supporters who had voiced confidence before the vote.

The House votes left the NRA bruised, defensive and spoiling for a fight. "We're certainly not going to fold up our tent and go home," said James J. Baker, executive director of the NRA's Institute for Legislative Action.

SENATE ACTION

Senate Majority Leader George J. Mitchell, D-Maine, on June 6 unveiled a compromise proposal for a handgun waiting period coupled with a mandatory police background check. He initially had criticized the Brady bill, asserting that a waiting period for gun purchases was useless without a mandatory background check and uniform, computerized crime records.

But after the bill's dramatic House victory, Mitchell proposed his compromise. It authorized $40 million to help states update criminal records. The House-passed bill required a seven-day waiting period but did not mandate the background check or authorize local funding.

Under Mitchell's plan, states that accepted federal funds to update their criminal records would be required to run a background check of all would-be handgun buyers. They also would have to share their criminal record data with the FBI's interstate index by 1993. Mitchell said only 21 states did so in 1991.

House gun-control supporters praised the offering, as did Sarah Brady. The NRA opposed it, however.

After Mitchell announced his plan, Senate Judiciary Committee Chairman Joseph R. Biden Jr., D-Del., introduced a revised omnibus crime bill (S 1241), combining his original bill (S 618) and the Mitchell proposal.

Senate Vote

The Senate began debate on the crime bill on June 20, but it did not get to the Brady bill provision until June 28. Late that day, the Senate approved a compromise that required a waiting period of five business days for handgun purchases and a plan for a nationwide instant background check of buyers that would take effect in two and a half years.

By voice vote, the Senate rejected an amendment pushed by the gun lobby that would have allowed longer state-mandated waiting periods to be pre-empted by federal law.

The new Brady bill language, approved 67-32, supplanted a provision for a seven-day wait with no timetable for an instantaneous check. *(Vote 115, p. 16-S)*

"It's a total victory for our side," said Howard M. Metzenbaum, D-Ohio, Senate sponsor of the Brady bill, who worked with Majority Leader Mitchell and Minority Leader Bob Dole, R-Kan., on the winning language.

By a vote of 44-54 early June 28, the Senate rejected a move by Ted Stevens, R-Alaska, to replace the waiting period with an instantaneous background check. Nine Democrats — all from Southern or rural states — voted for the Stevens plan. *(Vote 113, p. 16-S)*

That vote was not decisive, yet it paved the way for the final compromise. Brady bill advocates had a 10-vote lead, but they were six short of the 60 votes needed to quash a filibuster. And while GOP opponents could filibuster the Brady bill, they would be blocking a crime bill they wanted.

GOP leader Dole said he helped craft the final compromise to speed action on the crime bill, which Bush had been seeking. Dole said that he generally did not support waiting periods but thought the plan adopted by the Senate was workable because it laid the groundwork for an instant-check system.

Athough the waiting period was to be phased out after two and a half years, it could be ended only if the attorney general certified that a national system was in place with access to the preceding five years of state criminal records and that the records were at least 80 percent current.

If a state failed to meet the attorney general's criteria within six years, it would lose half of its federal law enforcement funds. The compromise authorized $100 million in aid to states to update records, up from $40 million originally proposed by Mitchell.

The Senate passed the crime bill, 71-26, on July 11. *(Vote 125, p. 17-S)*

Conference/Final

When House-Senate conferees on the crime bill met Nov. 24, they agreed to accept the Senate-passed version of the Brady bill. The House on Nov. 27 adopted the conference report on the crime measure (HR 3371), but Republicans stalled it in the Senate, where a cloture vote failed, 49-38. *(Vote 278, p. 68-H)* ■

Clarence Thomas Wins Senate Confirmation

After months of controversy and unprecedented last-minute hearings into allegations of sexual harassment, the Senate on Oct. 15 narrowly confirmed Clarence Thomas as an associate justice of the Supreme Court.

At 43, he became the youngest justice on the Rehnquist Court and only the second black to serve on the nation's highest court. He succeeded the first, Justice Thurgood Marshall, who retired.

Confirmation came in spite of many senators' concerns over a former employee's assertion that Thomas had sexually harrassed her in the early 1980s and the frustration that Democrats felt over the nominee's refusal to say where he stood on crucial issues of the day.

The vote was 52-48, with 11 Democrats and 41 Republicans supporting Thomas and 46 Democrats and two Republicans opposing him. *(Vote 220, p. 29-S)*

That was the closest vote in favor of a Supreme Court nominee in more than a century. And the eleventh-hour hearings on the sexual harassment allegations constituted one of the wildest spectacles in modern congressional history, prompting an outpouring of public anger and scorn that rocked the Senate.

The harassment charges by Anita F. Hill, a professor of law at the University of Oklahoma, had received only a cursory behind-the-scenes examination before the Senate Judiciary Committee deadlocked 7-7 on the Thomas nomination on Sept. 27.

But the weekend before the full Senate's scheduled Tuesday, Oct. 8, vote on the nomination, word of the allegations leaked to the Long Island, N.Y., newspaper Newsday and to a National Public Radio reporter. The latter obtained an interview with Hill confirming that she had submitted an affidavit to the Judiciary Committee outlining Thomas' unwelcome sexual advances to her when she worked with him in the early 1980s at the Department of Education and the Equal Employment Opportunity Commission (EEOC).

The disclosure of the allegations — and the fact that the committee had failed to investigate them thoroughly — touched off a storm of criticism and demands for a delay. Women were particularly outraged, and they let senators know it.

On Oct. 8, the day of the scheduled vote, the Senate agreed to postpone its decision until the Judiciary Committee could take testimony from Hill, Thomas and witnesses supporting each.

THE NOMINATION

President Bush knew from the outset that Thomas would face a rougher ride than David H. Souter, the New Hampshire jurist who was Bush's first appointee to the Supreme Court. The Senate confirmed Souter by 90-9 on Oct. 2, 1990. *(Souter nomination, 1990 Almanac, p. 508)*

Unlike Souter, who was virtually unknown outside his home state, Thomas was an established — and controversial — figure in Washington. He had been confirmed by the Senate on March 6, 1990, for a seat on the U.S. Court of Appeals for the District of Columbia Circuit after serving nine years in political appointments under Presidents Ronald Reagan and Bush. When Bush nominated him for the appeals court on Oct. 30, 1989, the move was widely viewed as a preliminary to a future Supreme Court appointment. *(1990 Almanac, p. 518)*

Thomas was chosen by Bush on July 1 to succeed Marshall, who announced his retirement after 24 years on the court. Like Marshall, Thomas was black, but the resemblance ended there. *(Marshall's resignation, p. 275)*

While Marshall was a civil rights pioneer and steadfast liberal voice on the court, Thomas was a conservative who opposed affirmative action and other efforts to redress past discrimination through group preferences.

His appointment to the high court was expected to cement the shift to the right that began when Reagan made his first appointment in 1981 — that of Justice Sandra Day O'Connor. By 1991, she had become a moderate swing vote, pushed to the center by more conservative subsequent appointees. And there were only two justices left who could be considered liberals — Harry Blackmun and John Paul Stevens. *(O'Connor nomination, 1981 Almanac, p. 409; Supreme Court review, p. 286)*

Interest groups that had successfully pushed senators to reject the Supreme Court nomination of conservative jurist Robert H. Bork in 1987 were slower to criticize Thomas, but most eventually came out against him. *(Bork fight, 1987 Almanac, p. 271)*

Civil rights organizations and women's groups were especially prominent in opposing the Thomas nomination, fearing for the future of affirmative action programs and a woman's right to an abortion. Challenges to the landmark 1973 *Roe v. Wade* decision legalizing abortion nationwide were wending their way to the high court as Thomas was confirmed. *(Abortion issue, p. 339)*

Thomas had never decided an abortion case or commented directly on the correctness of *Roe v. Wade*. But in a 1987 speech he warmly praised an article by an author who said that abortion should be illegal and that *Roe v. Wade* had led to a "holocaust."

Furthermore, his writings hinted that he thought both *Roe* and *Griswold v. Connecticut*, a 1965 privacy case involving birth control from which the right to abortion eventually flowed, had been wrongly decided.

Civil rights organizations and senior citizens' groups expressed concerns about Thomas' views on civil rights and his record in the 1980s as EEOC chairman.

During Thomas' tenure, the EEOC allowed hundreds of age-discrimination complaints to lapse without acting on them, prompting Congress to extend the deadline.

Benjamin L. Hooks, executive director of the National Association for the Advancement of Colored People (NAACP), said that while it was important that another black be appointed to the court, the organization wanted someone "who embodies many of the attributes Justice Marshall so ably articulated."

The NAACP came out against Thomas in the month before the hearings began Sept. 10, as did several other major groups, including the Leadership Conference on Civil Rights and the AFL-CIO.

The U.S. Chamber of Commerce, the National Catholic Education Association and a variety of conservative organizations such as Young Americans for Freedom and the American Conservative Union endorsed the nomination.

The White House, meanwhile, systematically began lobbying senators in behalf of Thomas and encouraging out-

Thurgood Marshall, High Court's Last Liberal, Retires

Supreme Court Justice Thurgood Marshall, the first black justice in the court's history and its last consistent liberal, announced June 27 that he would retire when his replacement was confirmed.

Clarence Thomas, a conservative black judge on the U.S. Court of Appeals for the District of Columbia Circuit, was named by President Bush July 1 to succeed Marshall. However, it was not until Oct. 23 that Thomas quietly took the oath as a Supreme Court justice, following several explosive weeks of confirmation hearings.

Marshall, who turned 83 on July 2, said his "advancing age and medical condition" prevented him from continuing his service. Appointed to the court in 1967 by President Lyndon B. Johnson, he championed civil rights and individual liberties and opposed the death penalty at every turn.

He was the last justice named to the court by a Democratic president.

With the court's shifting from left to right, in his last years Marshall had become a bitter voice of dissent. This legacy haunted the Senate's Democratic majority as it considered Bush's nominee against a backdrop of partisan confrontations over civil rights and abortion. The hearings opened a second front in the war between the White House and Democrats over numerous issues, not least of which was the confirmation process itself.

Marshall's exit also enhanced the prospect that Congress increasingly would become the battleground for politically troublesome civil rights issues. Women's and civil rights organizations had turned to Congress to regain ground they said had been lost through court decisions, particularly over abortion rights and broad protections against job discrimination.

Marshall's retirement gave the president an opportunity to strengthen the court's conservative majority on abortion and other issues important to his party's right wing.

In one of his final dissents as a justice, Marshall voiced concern that the court's conservative juggernaut was about to gain momentum and overturn precedents of more liberal eras. "The majority today sends a clear signal that scores of established constitutional liberties are now ripe for reconsideration," Marshall wrote.

Ambiguous Legacy

Marshall fought passionately for the underprivileged throughout his nearly six-decade legal career — 28 years as the mastermind of the civil rights revolution and 24 years as the high court's lone black justice. But he became frustrated and bitter as the causes he championed lost favor, and he retired with an ambiguous legacy imperiled by the likelihood of a further conservative shift on the high court.

Marshall earned a place in U.S. legal history before going on the court. In 1933, a Baltimore native recently graduated from Howard University Law School, he initiated a successful suit to integrate the University of Maryland Law School. As special counsel for the National Association for the Advancement of Colored People and then chief counsel of the separate NAACP Legal Defense and Educational Fund, he engineered the litigation that abolished white-only party primaries, barred racial covenants in private housing and outlawed racial segregation in public schools.

Marshall argued 32 cases before the Supreme Court — including one of the four companion school cases in the 1954 *Brown v. Board of Education* decision — and lost only three. His work not only dismantled legally mandated racial segregation but also demonstrated the techniques later adopted by the modern public interest law movement.

As a justice, Marshall authored relatively few major opinions — and some of those had been overturned. He eschewed the type of internal court politics practiced by his liberal colleague, William J. Brennan Jr., who retired in July 1990. And some insiders had said that he did not always prepare for argument and delegated too much opinion-writing to clerks.

Marshall's most important doctrinal contribution — influential though never officially adopted — was to advocate a relaxed standard for deciding whether state or federal laws violated equal protection rights. He articulated the theory most extensively in dissenting from the 1973 decision *San Antonio Independent School District v. Rodriguez* that rejected an attack on the school financing system in Texas.

Marshall also wrote decisions expanding free speech rights for public employees, including a 1987 ruling reinstating a government worker fired for an offhand comment about shooting the president.

Other Marshall decisions had not survived, however. His 1968 opinion protecting the right to picket at private shopping centers was effectively overturned four years later. His 1969 decision establishing the right to possess obscene materials in the home had been seriously undermined. And the court's 1972 decision invalidating the death penalty — which he strenuously lobbied for — was overturned four years later.

Marshall continued to vote to overturn every death penalty reviewed by the court and dissented as the court under Chief Justices Warren E. Burger and William H. Rehnquist weakened other protections for criminal defendants. He dissented in poverty law cases, such as a 1971 ruling allowing a caseworker entry into welfare recipients' homes. And, beginning in the mid-1970s, he often found himself in dissent in civil rights cases, including the series of 1989 rulings that restricted minority set-aside programs and limited remedies in job discrimination suits.

Just before announcing his retirement, Marshall sharply dissented from a decision, *Payne v. Tennessee*, overturning two recent precedents to uphold the use of "victim impact" statements in death penalty cases. Marshall described 17 other recent 5-4 court decisions on constitutional rights as "endangered" by the court's disregard of precedent.

"Tomorrow's victims may be minorities, women or the indigent," he concluded. "Inevitably, this campaign to resurrect yesterday's 'spirited dissents' will squander the authority and legitimacy of this court as a protector of the powerless."

Clarence Thomas

Born: June 23, 1948, Savannah, Ga.

Education: Immaculate Conception Seminary, 1967-68; Holy Cross College, bachelor's degree, 1971; Yale Law School, law degree, 1974.

Family: Married, one child.

Career background: Assistant attorney general, Missouri, 1974-77; attorney, Monsanto Co., 1977-79; legislative assistant to Sen. John C. Danforth, R-Mo., 1979-81; assistant secretary of Education for civil rights, 1981-82; chairman, Equal Employment Opportunity Commission, 1982-90; U.S. Court of Appeals for the District of Columbia, March 1990 to October 1991.

side supporters to organize behind the nomination. The administration called in Kenneth Duberstein, a former White House chief of staff and onetime liaison to Congress, to gird Thomas for the hearings. Duberstein had done the same for Souter.

A Rise From Poverty

In explaining his choice of Thomas, Bush said, "He has excelled in everything that he has attempted. He is a delightful and warm, intelligent person who has great empathy and a wonderful sense of humor. He's also a fiercely independent thinker with an excellent legal mind who believes passionately in equal opportunity for all Americans."

Thomas rose above an impoverished early childhood in rural Georgia and stressed the importance of individual will rather than group empowerment.

He was raised by his grandparents in Pin Point, Ga., and during his confirmation hearings, he made much of his climb from poverty. When Bush first introduced the nominee, Thomas choked up as he thanked his grandparents and the Roman Catholic nuns who were his first teachers and who, he said, spurred him to excellence.

"As a child I could not dare dream that I would ever see the Supreme Court, not to mention be nominated to it," Thomas said.

Thomas graduated from Holy Cross College in 1971 and from Yale Law School in 1974.

He began his legal career as an assistant Missouri attorney general under John C. Danforth for three years, before Danforth's 1976 election to the Senate. He worked for Danforth a second time as a legislative assistant from 1979 to 1981.

Sen. Danforth shepherded Thomas around the Senate in the weeks before the Judiciary Committee hearings began, and defended his protégé fiercely throughout the confirmation process.

In so doing, he performed the same service for Thomas that Sen. Warren B. Rudman, R-N.H., had offered Souter, who once worked for him as an assistant attorney general.

Such strong support from respected middle-of-the-road senators was critical. Bork, who was the only Supreme Court nominee rejected since 1970, had no such guardian in the nomination process.

The ABA Rating: 'Qualified'

The American Bar Association (ABA) on Aug. 28 rated Thomas "qualified" for the Supreme Court. The rating was a step down from what most nominees in the preceding two decades had received: "well qualified" or a comparable top rating.

Also, of the 15 members of the ABA's Standing Committee on Federal Judiciary, two found Thomas "not qualified." None of the confirmed Supreme Court justices, going back at least to 1970, received any "not qualified" votes, according to the Senate Judiciary Committee and the ABA.

Several liberal anti-Thomas groups, including the Alliance for Justice, said the rating raised questions about the nominee's ability to serve on the high court.

According to the ABA, to receive a "qualified" or "well qualified" the nominee "must be at the top of the legal profession, have outstanding legal ability and wide experience and meet the highest judicial standards of integrity, professional competence and judicial temperament. The evaluation of 'well qualified' is reserved for those found to merit the committee's strongest affirmative endorsement."

A Senate Judiciary Committee report in 1987 said that before the nomination of Bork that year, the only time since 1970 that the ABA panel did not unanimously give a "well qualified" evaluation was in 1971, when William H. Rehnquist was first appointed to the court. Rehnquist, who became chief justice in 1986, received a unanimous "qualified" rating, after a majority voted "well qualified" and three voted "not opposed."

Bork, whose nomination was rejected, received 10 votes of "well qualified," four votes of "not qualified" and one "not opposed."

O'Connor, named in 1981, presented another exception. The ABA wrote the committee saying O'Connor met the highest standards for judicial temperament and integrity, but that her "professional experience was not as extensive or challenging as that of some other persons who might be available for appointment."

After the Bork rejection, conservative groups and some GOP senators accused the ABA screening committee of bias against conservative nominees.

Two organizations — one liberal and one conservative — filed lawsuits challenging the secrecy of the committee's deliberations. The Supreme Court in 1989 upheld the panel's right to conduct its business in secret. ABA leaders reached a deal with Attorney General Dick Thornburgh the same year to remove any consideration of political philosophy from the ABA's screening of judicial nominees. *(1989 Almanac, p. 321)*

THE FIRST JUDICIARY HEARINGS

The Senate Judiciary Committee opened its confirmation hearings on Sept. 10. In five days of testimony, Thomas invoked his boyhood poverty and carefully avoided taking stands on controversial issues — much to the frustration of committee Democrats. *(Text, p. 17-E)*

The conservative nominee's appearance mirrored the winning strategy of evasion used by Souter the year before. Since the bitterly divisive Bork episode, the White House had carefully controlled every nominee's performance before the panel, and senators had been hard pressed to wrest much from any of them about their judicial philosophy.

Thomas' White House advisers sat behind him during his testimony before the Judiciary Committee.

Senators complained that constitutional issues were getting short shrift when, as in Thomas' case, a nominee refused to talk even about issues he had written about in the past.

"The vanishing views of Judge Thomas have become a major issue in these hearings," said Edward M. Kennedy, D-Mass.

"Something has gone badly wrong, and I think we need to fundamentally rethink how we do this," said Walter Dellinger of Duke University. He was one of a number of law professors who had advised Judiciary Chairman Joseph R. Biden Jr., D-Del., on constitutional issues before the nationally televised hearings began.

Dellinger said one solution would be to rely solely on a candidate's record, and not have the nominee testify. That had been the general practice until the mid-1950s. "I think the hearings are distorting the process and playing too central a role in evaluating the nominee," Dellinger said.

Thomas' Republican supporters responded that Democrats who engineered Bork's defeat had caused nominees to watch what they said. "They have made the process into the process it has become," said Orrin G. Hatch, R-Utah.

But some Republicans acknowledged that the White House's desire to avoid controversy could lead to problems.

Sen. Alan K. Simpson, R-Wyo., a Thomas supporter, said Sept. 17, "We are slowly going to get to the point where we will just not know anybody at all when they get here. Some big zip will be presented to us and we will mess around trying to figure out who he or she is, and the more zip, the better chance they will have — I mean zip as in zero and not zip as in spirit."

Some outside the Senate said that without a clear message from the institution, the nominees likely would continue to be reticent. "The Senate can send signals that it doesn't like it," said Louis Fisher, a senior specialist in separation of powers at the Congressional Research Service. "But the only signal that will matter is rejection."

Fudging the Record

Thomas brought a contentious record to the hearings. The former head of the EEOC had disparaged affirmative action, faulted Congress as meddlesome and criticized a law setting up a special prosecutor to investigate executive branch wrongdoing, suggesting that it violated the constitutional separation of powers doctrine. (The Supreme Court ruled to the contrary.)

In numerous writings and speeches, Thomas had seemed to endorse looking beyond the Constitution to "natural law" to resolve cases. And he had previously hinted that he opposed abortion.

But through five days of testimony, Thomas tempered or divorced himself from those views. He said he had voiced some of his positions as an administration advocate. Since becoming a federal appeals court judge in 1990, Thomas said, he had purged himself of many opinions so that he could look at any dispute impartially.

He described his interest in natural law not as a constitutional philosophy but as an off-hours interest in political theory.

He would not talk about abortion, but he said he believed that the Due Process Clause of the 14th Amendment embodied a privacy right for married and single people on procreation. This contradicted Bork's ultraconservative beliefs and went further than Souter, who had extended the right only to married couples.

Overall, Thomas kept hidden what many senators most wanted to understand about a Supreme Court nominee: his vision of the Constitution. Instead, Thomas sounded his own themes. He referred often to his impoverished youth in Pin Point, Ga., and what he said had been his constant quest in a conservative administration to bring civil rights to the fore.

And for as much as he evaded questions, Thomas exuded enough earnestness and humor that senators were restrained in their criticism. Danforth sat immediately behind his former protégé, nodding in agreement with Thomas and showing distress when questions got particularly rough.

Dennis DeConcini, D-Ariz., a moderate, said his more liberal colleagues were "chipping away at him a little bit, but he hasn't gotten caught in anything."

DeConcini said he was inclined to support Thomas. Howell Heflin, D-Ala., another possible swing vote, described the nominee as "cool and collected" and said that despite some concern about inconsistent statements, he was initially impressed with Thomas.

But Heflin, too, asked on Sept. 13, "What is the real Clarence Thomas like? What would the real Clarence Thomas do on the Supreme Court?"

Thomas responded, "I am the real Clarence Thomas, and I have attempted to bring that person here.... And I try to do what my grandfather said, stand up for what I believe in.... I am simply different from what people painted me to be."

Groups Weigh In

The hearings concluded Sept. 20 after three days of comments from witnesses representing more than 75 groups for and against Thomas.

The panel heard from law professors, civil rights and women's groups, lawyers, labor leaders, politicians, law enforcement officials, religious figures and personal friends of Thomas.

Supporters described Thomas as a competent, caring person who would bring to the court a deep understanding of the rights of the individual. Opponents said Thomas was not in touch with his roots and that his attitudes would lead him to undermine the Constitution and reject congressional intent in ruling on statutes.

Kate Michelman, executive director of the National Abortion Rights Action League, recounted Sept. 19 the trauma of her own abortion and urged the committee to reject Thomas on the grounds that he would vote on the court to make abortion illegal. "I was raised Catholic, married young, and as a young woman I had three wonderful daughters in three years. But in 1970, my husband suddenly announced that he was leaving me and the children." She discovered she was pregnant.

Without money or a job, she said, she was forced onto welfare and decided to have an abortion. She was required to appear before a hospital board and get permission from her husband.

Michelman said of abortion rights, "No issue — none — has a greater impact on the lives and futures of American women and their families."

Hooks, executive director of the NAACP, testified against Thomas on Sept. 20: "He talks about his experiences, that his grandfather was called 'boy,' but those experiences did not leave him with the lesson" of overcoming bias.

But Edward Hayes Jr., who appeared for Thomas on behalf of the Council of 100, a national organization of black Republicans, said that Thomas' disagreement with national organizations' quest for affirmative action demonstrated independent thinking. "Judge Thomas' independence of mind has not come without a great deal of per-

Thomas Remains Silent on Abortion . . .

Over five days of questioning, Sept. 10-13 and Sept. 16, Senate Judiciary Committee members asked Clarence Thomas about his views on a wide range of topics. The most prevalent subjects were abortion and natural law, a theory that an individual is endowed with certain inherent rights that cannot be restricted by written law.

Thomas would not comment on his judicial or personal views of abortion or *Roe v. Wade*, the 1973 case that made abortion legal nationwide. He distanced himself from his previous writings on natural law and said, contrary to the impression left by some of his statements on the theory, he would not use it to adjudicate a dispute.

Regarding his reluctance to comment on controversial issues, Thomas said, "I think what I have attempted to do is, to the best of my ability, without judging or prejudging the case, to simply set out in an area that you [senators] have requested the analysis of what the court has done and where it has gone.

". . . I have indicated and I think it is important to indicate that the area of *Roe v. Wade* is a difficult, it is a controversial area. Cases are coming before the court in many different postures. . . . I think it would undermine my ability to impartially address that very difficult issue, if I am confirmed, to go further than I have gone."

While senators failed in repeated attempts to draw Thomas out on abortion rights, they had some success in eliciting his views on other topics.

Among his answers:

Natural Law

Senators wanted to know whether Thomas would use natural law to decide constitutional issues in cases and whether he would extend his idea of natural law to rights for unborn children or to protections for business against governmental regulation.

Thomas: My point has been that the framers [of the Constitution] . . . reduced to positive law in the Constitution aspects of life principles that they believed in; for example, liberty. But when it is in the Constitution, it is not a natural right; it is a constitutional right. And that is the important point.

But to understand what the framers meant and what they were trying to do, it is important to go back and attempt to understand what they believed, just as we do when we attempt to interpret a statute that is drafted by this body, to get your understanding. But in constitutional analysis and methodology, as I indicated in my confirmation to the Court of Appeals, there isn't any direct reference to natural law. . . . At no time did I feel nor do I feel now that natural law is anything more than the background to our Constitution. It is not a method of interpreting or a method of adjudicating in the constitutional law area.

"Stare decisis," or letting precedents stand

This doctrine holds that principles of law in judicial decisions should be authoritative in later cases, even when a justice might believe the original case was wrongly decided. Some senators feared Thomas would vote to roll back earlier decisions on abortion and civil rights.

Thomas: I think that the principle of stare decisis . . . is an important link in our system of deciding cases in our system of judicial jurisprudence. . . .

We have got to have continuity if there is going to be any reliance, if there is going to be any chain in our case law. I think that the first point in any revisiting of the case is that the case be wrongly decided. . . .

But more than that is necessary before one can rethink it or attempt to reconsider it. And I think that the burden is on the individual or on the judge or the justice who thinks that a precedent should be overruled to demonstrate more than its mere incorrectness. And at least one factor that would weigh against overruling a precedent would be the development of institutions as a result of a prior precedent having been in place.

Ninth Amendment

"The enumeration in the Constitution of certain rights shall not be construed to deny or disparage others retained by the people." The court has rarely mentioned the Ninth Amendment, although individual justices have used it to support Roe v. Wade *and* Griswold v. Connecticut, *a 1965 privacy case from which the right to abortion eventually flowed. Thomas had written of his "misgivings about activist judicial use" of the amendment. Senators wanted to know how much weight it should be given.*

Thomas: I think that whatever we do with open-ended provisions such as the Ninth Amendment, that we make sure as judges that those decisions are fettered to analysis or something other than our own predilections or our own views. That would be the concern, the generic concern . . . with any of the open-ended or more open-ended provisions. The court, to my knowledge, has not used the Ninth Amendment, a majority of the court, to decide a particular case. And there has been debate about what the purpose of the Ninth Amendment is. There could be a time when there could be an asserted right under the Ninth Amendment that would come before the court in which there could be found to be a basis for that right in the Ninth Amendment. I don't know. But as scholars do more work and certainly as individuals begin to assert rights and the court begins to consider those, I wouldn't foreclose that from occurring.

Church-State Separation

Among other things, the First Amendment bars government action "respecting an establishment of religion." To decide whether a practice breaches that ban, the court used a three-pronged test spelled out in the 1971 case of Lemon v. Kurtzman, *which involved state aid to parochial schools. The court said a government action is permissible if: It is intended to achieve a secular legislative purpose; its primary effect neither advances nor inhibits religion; and it does not foster*

. . . Comments on Other Important Issues

excessive government entanglement with religion. Senators wanted to know whether Thomas would make it easier for government to get involved in religion, as some senators feared individual justices were inclined.

Thomas: I am aware of the tests enunciated in *Lemon v. Kurtzman.* The court has applied the tests with some degree, I think, of difficulty over the years. I have no personal disagreement with the tests, but I say that recognizing how difficult it has been for the court to address just the kind of problem that you have pointed out when the church is on fire or when there is this closeness between the activity of the government and the activity of the church. I think the wall of separation is an appropriate metaphor. I think we all believe that we would like to keep the government out of our beliefs, and we would want to keep a separation between our religious lives and the government.

Equal Protection Clause of the Constitution

Senators wanted to know whether Thomas agreed with Supreme-Court-adopted tests for applying equal protection to laws that are based on race or gender.

Thomas: I have no reason and had no reason to question or to disagree with the three-tier approach . . . the 'rational basis' test being the least structured or least strict of the tests, the 'heightened scrutiny' test, which has been used in the area of gender and alienage and legitimacy, and the 'strict scrutiny' test, which has been used in the area of fundamental rights and race. I think that those tests attempt in our society to demonstrate the concern that we have for classifications that could infringe on fundamental rights.

Death Penalty

Retiring Justice Thurgood Marshall believed that the death penalty violates the constitutional ban on cruel and unusual punishment. Other justices had voted to uphold state death penalty laws. Congress was weighing bills to expand the federal death penalty to more crimes and to limit death row appeals.

Thomas: There is nothing that would bother me personally about upholding it in appropriate cases. My concern, of course, would always be that we provide all of the available protections and accord all of the protections available to a criminal defendant who is exposed to or sentenced to the death penalty.

Statutory Construction

This concept went to the heart of how justices construe the work of Congress, and senators wanted to know whether Thomas would tilt toward the administration's view, or a justice's own opinion, of what a law means rather than to congressional statements of legislative intent.

Thomas: I do not believe that there is room in opinions in our work of judging for the personal predilections, the personal opinions and views of judges. I think in statutory construction, the ultimate goal for us is to determine the will of the legislature, the intent of the legislature, not what we would have replaced the legislative enactment with, if we were in the legislature, and we have no role in legislating.

Affirmative Action

Thomas said that he opposed affirmative action and other government programs that gave preferences to specific groups but supported remedies for individual cases of discrimination and equal opportunity for all.

Thomas: There is a tension, and how far do you go in trying to include people who are left out, and not be unfair to other individuals, and it is one that I had hoped that we could wrestle with in a constructive way. . . . Whether or not I agree with all of them [affirmative action programs] I think is a matter of record. But the fact that I don't agree with all of them does not mean that I am not a supporter of the underlying effort. I am and have been my entire adult life.

Antitrust

A number of bills on antitrust issues were pending before Congress. Thomas was asked generally about antitrust laws and prohibitions on price fixing.

Thomas: I think that all of our efforts, including the antitrust laws, to keep a free and open economy, one in which there is competitiveness, where the smaller businesses can have an opportunity to compete and where consumers can benefit from that — those efforts, including the antitrust laws, have been beneficial to our country. . . . I believe consumers and the country benefit from strong competition. We certainly as consumers benefit when there are new products, when there is development of products, when the quality of the products is improved as a result of competition and, of course, when there is no temptation toward supra-competitive pricing; in fact, pricing is at the lower levels.

Contradictions in His Record

Some senators accused Thomas of trying to separate himself from past controversial writings in order to win Senate approval.

I think that various individuals created their own images of me, and what they see is that the real person does not fit those images. . . .

I am the same Clarence Thomas. I have been a sitting federal judge for about a year and a half, and the person that you see here is the same sitting federal judge, someone who attempts to be open-minded, who works at it, being impartial, objective; listen and to work through very difficult problems. And a final point: When I was in the executive branch . . . there were battles and there were give-and-takes. I participated in that, but I am not in the executive branch anymore, I am not a part of the tension between the two political branches.

sonal cost to him and to his family," Hayes said, referring to Thomas as well-qualified and possessing great character.

Police officers, testifying for Thomas, said he struck the right balance between defendants' rights and law enforcement's efforts to catch wrongdoers.

THE JUDICIARY COMMITTEE VOTE

The Senate Judiciary Committee's split 7-7 when it voted on the Thomas nomination Sept. 27.

All six committee Republicans voted for Thomas, as did Democrat DeConcini.

The seven committee Democrats who voted against Thomas all cited the nominee's refusal to give direct answers to questions during five days of testimony.

Most said they were not ready to settle for evasive responses, particularly on questions of individual privacy. "The costs of adding yet another right-wing member are too high," said Biden.

After the committee deadlocked on a motion to favorably recommend the nominee, the panel voted 13-1, with Paul Simon, D-Ill., dissenting, to send Thomas' name to the full Senate without recommendation.

The first signs that Judiciary Committee action would be close emerged after Thomas had finished testifying Sept. 16 and senators began voicing their uneasiness over how reluctant the nominee was to be forthcoming on constitutional matters.

When Heflin announced he was against Thomas on Sept. 26, he virtually assured the deadlocked vote. Heflin was one of two swing Democrats on the committee. (The other was DeConcini.)

The former Alabama Supreme Court chief justice said he had to vote his "conscience," after Thomas' testimony before the committee was riddled with contradictions and "outright disavowals" of his previous positions.

By the morning of the committee vote, only Biden had not announced his position.

The chairman, whose vote was needed for the deadlock, said it was a close call but that his dissatisfaction with Thomas' answers on privacy and his general judicial philosophy sealed his "no" vote.

Biden said the court was dominated by "ultraconservatives" and that "we are at a place in the country's history where the risks are simply too high" to approve a nominee whose views were unknown.

Committee Republicans, who voted together for Thomas, pointed to his triumph over poverty in Georgia, his 18 months as an appeals court judge, respect among his colleagues and the "qualified" rating from the ABA. Voting for Thomas were Republicans Strom Thurmond, S.C.; Orrin G. Hatch, Utah; Simpson; Charles E. Grassley, Iowa; Arlen Specter, Pa.; and Hank Brown, Colo.

DeConcini, the one Democrat to support Thomas, also referred to his "remarkable life story" and said he believed the 43-year-old Thomas was capable of growing into a fine jurist.

Democrats who opposed Thomas criticized Bush for trying to "pack the court" and said Thomas' performance reflected White House cynicism over the Senate confirmation process.

In addition to Biden, Heflin and Simon, the other Democratic "noes" were Kennedy; Howard M. Metzenbaum, Ohio; Patrick J. Leahy, Vt.; and Herb Kohl, Wis.

Although the tie vote of the Judiciary Committee heartened opponents of the nomination and spurred them into renewed efforts to defeat Thomas, the judge appeared to be closing in on a Senate majority.

The Calm Before the Storm

Republicans were pressing to have Thomas seated by Oct. 7, when the court's 1991-92 term was to begin. But the Senate's confirmation vote was scheduled instead for Oct. 8.

Thomas appeared to have a comfortable majority ready to back him. Danforth, Thomas' main Senate advocate, predicted the final vote for Thomas would be in the 60s. Confirmation required a simple majority: 51 votes, if all senators were present and voting.

Metzenbaum, a leading opponent of Thomas, conceded on Oct. 3 that there was only a "very slim chance" Thomas would be defeated.

By midday Oct. 4, 13 of the 57 Democrats had announced they would support Thomas. None of the 43 Republican senators had voiced opposition, and Danforth said 41 were committed to confirmation.

Thomas picked up Democratic support mostly from Southerners, who were pivotal in a confirmation battle. It was Southern Democrats who had sealed Bork's rejection in 1987.

THE SEXUAL HARASSMENT ALLEGATIONS

Just when Thomas and his supporters thought their battle had been won, Hill's allegations of sexual harassment, made public Oct. 5, totally changed the nature and tenor of the contest.

Within two days, the Senate's judicial screening process was under attack, the nominee's career and reputation were thrown in doubt and the Senate as an institution was under siege.

Senators were barraged with accusations that they were insensitive to women and out of touch with America. Angry women asked whether the male-dominated institution recognized the seriousness of Hill's charge, why the committee had not pursued it until it became public and why the full Senate had been left in the dark.

Senate leaders said Hill originally had sought confidentiality and that they had acted properly.

Even after Hill's allegations were reported, both Biden and Minority Leader George F. Mitchell, D-Maine, argued against postponing the scheduled Oct. 8 floor vote.

"I see no reason why the addition of public disclosure of the allegations — but no new information about the charges themselves — should" alter the vote schedule, said Biden in a statement on Oct. 7.

Hatch, a Judiciary Committee member, agreed: "If any of the Democrats had wanted to pursue Hill's charges further they could have put off the committee vote.... They all knew about it."

DeConcini told reporters that he had not found Hill to be very credible: "If you're sexually harassed, you ought to get mad about it and you ought to do something about it and you ought to complain instead of hanging around a long time and then all of a sudden calling up anonymously and saying, 'Oh, I want to complain.' I mean, where is the gumption?"

But as news coverage mushroomed and Hill appeared on television reiterating her charges, such sentiment was quickly stifled. With Thomas' character in question, many of the Democrats who had announced their backing for the nominee suddenly became swing votes again. These sena-

The Confirmation Process Comes Under Fire

President Bush termed the Senate's confirmation process "a messy situation." Clarence Thomas called it a "national disgrace." Senators said it was "flawed" and "perverted."

As the second round of Thomas hearings ended, following emotional discussions of alleged sexual harassment and prime-time talk of pornography, demands for reform reverberated around the capital.

Several senators called for a re-examination of the entire confirmation process, swifter investigations of sensitive charges and punishment for the person who leaked Anita F. Hill's complaint to the news media.

But the greatest attacks on the "process" came as a result of three days of nationally broadcast hearings that included explicit descriptions of alleged conversations about sex. Bush said the hearings should have been held behind closed doors: "I was troubled thinking of my little grandchildren, hearing some of the graphic sex allegations."

But given that Hill's charges had become public through a leak and the nation's newspapers were questioning whether the Senate was trying to cover up a serious charge, a closed hearing was virtually impossible.

Although senators had called for an open airing, some said closed hearings should be the rule for future sensitive allegations. Ultimately, however, it appeared unlikely that there would be any significant changes in the process. "The process is a constitutional process that was determined by our forefathers in Philadelphia in 1787. That is the process," said Sen. Robert C. Byrd, D-W.Va., dismissing complaints from both sides.

Byrd said critics should look to the person who leaked the complaint and to senators who might not have been aggressive enough in pursuing Hill's allegations.

Criticism From the Start

Dissatisfaction with the process first arose from the frustration of Democrats who were unable to pin Thomas down on his approach to constitutional issues.

But the public outcry came when the country learned from a leak to the media that the Judiciary Committee had kept from the full Senate Hill's sexual harassment complaint. The committee had not interviewed Hill in person nor had it called her to testify. The message women across the country said they got was that the complaint was not taken seriously.

Committee Chairman Joseph R. Biden Jr., D-Del., said the problem was Hill's initial request that only the committee know of her complaint.

Critics said Biden should have been more vigorous in seeking Hill's story while the first Thomas hearings were still going on, Sept. 10-20. Senate staff members were tipped to Hill's story in August by the Alliance for Justice, a liberal organization that reviewed judicial nominations. Biden said committee staff members were not told of the Hill complaint until shortly before she called the Senate on Sept. 12.

Another problem, Biden said, was the disclosure of Hill's statement to the media. Someone on the committee also verified to the media contents of an FBI investigation into the matter.

Leak Investigation

Majority Leader George J. Mitchell, D-Maine, said he would attempt to identify and punish the leaker. "I don't know what happened," he said before the Oct. 15 vote, "but I am going to try to find out."

Judiciary Committee Republicans asked acting Attorney General William P. Barr to have the FBI investigate. And conservative groups offered thousands of dollars in rewards. Sen. Hank Brown, R-Colo., urged appointment of a special counsel.

Mitchell chided Republicans for complaining about leaks only when their causes were hurt. Mitchell and other Democrats expressed outrage in 1990 when repeated leaks about the Keating Five case skewered only their party's members. "Let us deplore it and regret whenever it occurs," he said, "not just when ... it is adverse to the case that that senator is pursuing."

Senate leaders Dec. 6 named Peter E. Fleming Jr., a New York lawyer, as special counsel to investigate leaks in both the Thomas and Keating Five cases. Fleming, 62, was a former federal prosecutor who served as special counsel to the House's Select Committee on Crime in June 1970. He was to begin work Jan. 1, 1992.

Only two senators had been disciplined by the Senate for breaking secrecy rules. But both cases were a century old, and one was not even an anonymous leak. Federalist Timothy Pickering, Mass., was censured in 1811 for reading aloud on the floor from secret documents related to the Louisiana Purchase. Benjamin Tappan, D-Ohio, was censured in 1844 for giving the press confidential papers related to the annexation of Texas. He confessed and apologized once an official inquiry was begun.

In a case similar to the current flap, an admission of occasional past drug abuse to FBI background checkers by T. Timothy Ryan — Bush's ultimately successful nominee to head the Office of Thrift Supervision — was leaked in 1990. Both supporters and opponents of Ryan cried foul, but nothing happened.

The House's ethics committee twice failed to determine who leaked confidential information, once in 1984, when a secret copy of one of its own reports was released, and once in 1976, when someone disclosed a secret Intelligence Committee report.

The biggest recent Washington leak inquiry involving Congress was undertaken by the Bush administration. In 1989, Attorney General Dick Thornburgh ordered an investigation to find out who leaked word of an FBI probe having to do with then-Rep. William H. Gray III, D-Pa., who was running for whip at the time. (It turned out that Gray was not the target of the inquiry.)

Months later, Thornburgh closed the investigation because he could not determine the leaker "with certainty." The New York Times revealed the inquiry had in fact concluded that one of Thornburgh's top aides played a role in the original Gray story.

The Times story was based on interviews with unidentified administration officials.

tors said they were not ready to oppose Thomas but wanted a delay so that new hearings could be held.

"Sexual harassment is a serious offense, and it goes directly to the question of personal character, which is, for me, a vital consideration in making a decision about a Supreme Court nominee," said Joseph I. Lieberman, D-Conn.

Danforth joined with other Republicans in describing the allegations against Thomas as character assassination and last-minute mudslinging.

Danforth accused the nominee's opponents of "peddling" the new revelations in a desperate attempt to defeat the nominee. He said Oct. 8 that the leak was explosive "because it alleges sexual harassment; therefore it has an enormous emotional effect on the women of this country."

In an impassioned speech on the floor, he told his colleagues that Thomas had told him: "They have taken from me what I have worked 43 years to create ... my reputation."

The dramatic unraveling of what had seemed a locked-up nomination prompted the Senate to postpone its scheduled confirmation vote a week, to Oct. 15.

The Senate Under Attack

As the committee girded for new hearings, senators were stunned by the public response to Hill's allegations. Their offices reported dozens of calls from women wanting them to get to the bottom of the charges.

"What disturbs me as much as the allegations themselves," said Barbara A. Mikulski, D-Md., "is that the Senate appears not to take the charge of sexual harassment seriously. We have indicated that it was not serious enough to be raised as a question in the Judiciary Committee."

Although there was no single definition of sexual harassment, the EEOC's version was widely accepted: "Unwelcome sexual advances, requests for sexual favors, and other verbal or physical conduct of a sexual nature constitute sexual harassment when 1) submission to such conduct is made either explicitly or implicitly a term or condition of an individual's employment, 2) submission to or rejection of such conduct by an individual is used as the basis for employment decisions affecting such individual, or 3) such conduct has the purpose or effect of unreasonably interfering with an individual's work performance or creating an intimidating, hostile or offensive working environment."

Members of the committee went on the defensive for the handling of Hill's allegation, which had been passed on to some Democratic aides as early as August.

Biden insisted that the committee "didn't screw up." He said that Hill's request for confidentiality had led him to tell only panel members of her charge.

A group of female House members marched over to the Senate and tried to get into a Democratic senators' policy meeting to, in the words of Rep. Patricia Schroeder, D-Colo., "demand justice."

Major newspapers devoted exhaustive coverage to harassment in the workplace.

"This is an issue that will never again be treated lightly or casually by the U.S. Congress," said Rutgers University Professor Ruth Mandel, director of the Center for American Women and Politics.

The Allegations Surface

While the trail of Hill's complaint to the Judiciary Committee was not entirely clear, it appeared to have begun in August with George Kassouf, director of the Judicial Selection Project of the Alliance for Justice.

The Alliance for Justice, a liberal-leaning organization, collected information on judicial candidates and helped coordinate opposition to nominees it believed unfit for the bench. It helped spearhead opposition to Bork in 1987.

Kassouf said he had received a tip from a source about a former Thomas employee's allegations of harassment, but was told only that the woman was now at the University of Oklahoma law school. Kassouf then obtained a faculty directory and found that an Anita Hill had listed her EEOC experience in her biography.

Kassouf said he did not call Hill. In early August, he said, he turned her name and phone number over to aides of Democratic senators pursuing information on Thomas. He declined to identify them.

The public record picked up on Sept. 5, when Ricki Seidman, an aide to Kennedy, contacted Hill. Seidman worked with Kennedy on the Labor and Human Resources Committee, which he chaired, but was helping him with his Judiciary Committee work.

A Kennedy spokesman, who released a chronology of Kennedy staff involvement, said that Seidman interviewed Hill about a number of issues at the EEOC, including reports of sexual harassment. Hill, the spokesman said, indicated that she wanted more time to decide whether she would be willing to talk about sexual harassment.

In a follow-up call from Seidman on Sept. 9, Hill said she would talk about her situation. Seidman referred Hill to James J. Brudney, a Labor Committee aide to Metzenbaum. Brudney and Hill had both attended Yale University Law School.

On Sept. 10 — the day the confirmation hearings began — Brudney talked to Hill, heard of her charges, told Metzenbaum, and on the senator's direction turned the allegations over to the full Judiciary Committee staff run by Biden.

Biden said Hill contacted the committee Sept. 12 and detailed her allegations about Thomas' conduct when she worked with him at the Department of Education and EEOC.

"Professor Hill specifically states that she wanted her allegation to be kept completely confidential," Biden reported. "She did not want the nominee to know that she had stated her concerns to the committee."

Biden said it was on Sept. 19 — three days after Thomas had finished testifying and other witnesses were before the committee — that Hill contacted Biden's staff and said she wanted all members of the committee to know about her complaint.

She was told her name would not be given to other committee members unless Thomas had an opportunity to respond. Biden said an aide proposed that if Hill wanted to proceed, the FBI would be called in to investigate.

Biden said Hill did not give permission to go ahead with an investigation until Sept. 23. The FBI interviewed her late Sept. 23 and Thomas shortly after that.

With reports from accuser and accused in, Biden and the committee's ranking GOP member, Thurmond, began on Sept. 25 to tell other committee members about Hill's report. Biden said all Democratic members were briefed. Thurmond failed to notify two or three of his Republican colleagues, but none said it would have affected their votes for Thomas. Senate Majority Leader Mitchell and Minority Leader Bob Dole, R-Kan., also were told of Hill's and Thomas' account.

Sparring With Congress Over Federal Statutes

Clarence Thomas, who had a history of criticizing Congress and its procedures, steered clear of any minefields when Senate Judiciary Committee members asked how he would determine what Congress means in federal statutes.

"I think in statutory construction, the ultimate goal for us is to determine the will of the legislature . . . not what we would have replaced the legislative enactment with, if we were in the legislature," Thomas said.

During the 1980s, as a Reagan administration official, Thomas had disparaged individual members of Congress, said the institution was less than deliberative and said overzealous staff members were taking control. After he became a federal appeals court judge in 1990, he hinted that he might opt for an administration interpretation of a statute over its legislative history.

But under questioning from committee Democrats and Republicans, Thomas said he could not envision interpreting a statute at the heart of a dispute without looking to the legislative history, such as committee reports and floor statements.

The most persistent questions came from Arlen Specter, R-Pa., who in the preceding two years had voiced concerns about moves by conservative Supreme Court justices, particularly Antonin Scalia, to reject legislative history as a measure of congressional intent. Scalia's approach often caused the court to rely on an executive branch reading of a statute or the court's own interpretation, thereby shifting power from Congress.

"You have stated what you think of the Congress," Specter noted, before asking if Thomas would, nonetheless, follow the institution's will.

Thomas attributed his complaints about Congress to his experiences in the executive branch, as head of the Equal Employment Opportunity Commission in 1982-90. "There is tension between the two political branches," he said. "And certainly I have had a sufficient number of oversight hearings and a sufficient number of battles to know that that tension was alive and well."

He added that the court should not "legislate or establish policy."

Turning to specifics, Specter referred to a 1989 Supreme Court case that was at the core of bitterly contested civil rights legislation in Congress. In *Wards Cove Packing Co. v. Atonio*, the court, by 5-4, made it harder for workers to prove indirect discrimination on the job. That ruling overturned a 1971 court decision in *Griggs v. Duke Power Co.* Specter wanted to know whether Thomas would lend his voice to future efforts to overturn precedent and, in Specter's view, distort Congress' will.

"Congress was satisfied with that [1971] interpretation — left it alone," Specter said. "Then 18 years later, the Supreme Court comes up 5-4 and changes that law and does so with four Supreme Court justices who put their hands on the Bible in this room or similar rooms [during confirmation hearings and] swore to interpret the law and not to make new law."

Thomas answered that he would have been concerned about the fact that Congress had implicitly approved the 1971 ruling by leaving it alone.

"If there is a longstanding interpretation, and Congress does not act, that certainly would seem to be considerable evidence of Congress' intent," Thomas said. "And it certainly would be, at least from my way of looking at a statute, evidence that cannot be ignored in revisiting that particular statute."

Not yet satisfied, Specter asked what "cannot be ignored" meant. He wanted to know whether the length of time could determine whether a court interpretation should stand. "It seems to me that when Congress lets a unanimous Supreme Court decision stand for 18 years, that is long enough," Specter said. "Or if it is not, I would like to know what is long enough."

Thomas said he did not want to put a number on it but added, to Specter's apparent satisfaction, "that the fact that Congress did not act for 18 years is an important consideration" in deciding whether to let an interpretation stand. Thomas, hewing to the cautious approach he was taking in all his responses, concluded: "It would be a part of the calculus of legislative history."

The committee went ahead and acted on Thomas' nomination Sept. 27. The seven Democrats voting against a favorable recommendation cited reasons unrelated to the harassment charges, primarily Thomas' reluctance to give direct answers to questions. Six Republicans and Democrat DeConcini voted for Thomas.

THE SECOND ROUND OF HEARINGS

As the second round of Senate Judiciary Committee hearings opened Friday, Oct. 11, Hill and Thomas, accuser and accused, delivered some of the most extraordinary public testimony ever offered to a congressional committee.

Here were two individuals — who shared backgrounds of poverty and prejudice and had built successful and highly respected careers — blaming each other for devastating wrongs. Both spoke convincingly and with great emotion, and both told their stories to a huge national television audience that found it hard to turn away.

The drama was larger than the individuals themselves. At stake was a lifetime seat on the highest court in the country. In doubt was how the president and Senate screened candidates for the bench. And at issue were sexual harassment and how men and women treat each other on the job.

Thomas' Opening Statement

The extraordinary day began in the historic Senate Caucus Room with a moving declaration of innocence by Thomas. *(Text, p. 23-E)*

"Throughout the time that Anita Hill worked with me, I treated her as I treated my other special assistants. I tried to treat them all cordially, professionally and respectfully. And I tried to support them in their endeavors and be interested in and supportive of their success," Thomas testified.

The nominee "categorically" denied that he had ever harassed Hill, or indeed, even tried to date her.

"I have not said or done the things that Anita Hill has alleged," he insisted.

Thomas said the allegations and their leak to the public had caused him and his family "enormous pain and great harm." He lashed out at the committee and its confirmation process:

"Mr. Chairman, I am a victim of this process. My name has been harmed. My character has been harmed. My family has been harmed. My friends have been harmed. There is nothing this committee, this body or this country can do to give me my good name back. Nothing.

"I will not provide the rope for my own lynching or for further humiliation. I am not going to engage in discussions, nor will I submit to roving questions, of what goes on in the most intimate parts of my private life or the sanctity of my bedroom. These are the most intimate parts of my privacy, and they will remain just that: private."

After Thomas completed his statement, committee members fell into noisy squabbling about how to proceed. Republicans started to ask Thomas about Hill's sworn affidavit to the committee, but Biden refused to allow references to that document. Biden said Hill wanted to tell her story in person before panel members questioned Thomas regarding her allegations.

Hatch exploded, threatening to quit the committee on the spot unless members were allowed to refer to Hill's statement in their questioning.

Biden finally called a recess and, after a half hour, returned to say that Hill would testify before Thomas was recalled to answer questions.

Hill's Testimony

For the next seven hours Hill meticulously recounted her story of how Thomas had humiliated her with lewd comments and unwanted advances. *(Text, p. 23-E)*

Hill said that while Thomas was her boss at the Department of Education and the EEOC, he had repeatedly asked her out, despite her efforts to discourage such advances.

She said she believed he wanted to have sexual intercourse with her. She provided embarrassing details of what she said were Thomas' comments to her on the job: talk of women's breasts, the size of his penis, accounts of movies of group sex and bestiality.

"Because I was extremely uncomfortable talking about sex with him at all, and particularly in such a graphic way, I told him that I did not want to talk about this subject. I would also try to change the subject to education matters or to non-sexual personal matters, such as his background or his beliefs.

"My efforts to change the subject were rarely successful," she said.

Hill spoke of the anguish she had suffered since being contacted by the committee about her experiences with Thomas. "It is only after a great deal of agonizing consideration that I am able to talk of these unpleasant matters to anyone except my closest friends," she said.

"Telling the world is the most difficult experience of my life, but it is very close to having to live through the experience that occasioned this meeting," she added. "I may have used poor judgment early on in my relationship with this issue. I was aware, however, that telling at any point in my career could adversely affect my future career, and I did not want, early on, to burn all bridges to the EEOC."

Senators pressed Hill on that point, with several Republicans expressing incredulity that she could have endured the harassment she described without filing a formal complaint.

Hill replied: "Well, it was a very trying and difficult decision for me not to say anything further. I can only say that when I made the decision to just withdraw from the situation and not press a claim or charge against him, that I may have shirked a duty, a responsibility that I had.

"And to that extent, I confess that I am very sorry that I did not do something or say something. But at the time that was my best judgment. Maybe it was a poor judgment, but it wasn't a dishonest [one], and it wasn't a completely unreasonable choice that I made, given the circumstances."

Thomas' Rebuttal

After nightfall, and throughout the next day — a Saturday — an angry Thomas was back with his own accusations.

Although he said scornfully that he had not watched Hill's testimony, he once again denied "each and every single allegation against me."

And he again attacked the committee, its hearings and the confirmation process.

"This is a circus, it's a national disgrace, and from my standpoint as a black American," Thomas said, "it's a high-tech lynching for an uppity black who in any way deigns to think for himself."

Thomas said the message was "that unless you kowtow to an old order, this is what will happen to you. You will be lynched, destroyed — caricatured by a committee of the U.S. Senate rather than hung from a tree."

Republican senators used their questioning time to speculate on Hill's motives for stepping forward, suggesting she might have been victim of fantasies or a "martyr" complex that made her eager to sacrifice her own reputation for the sake of stopping Thomas' confirmation to the court.

Democrats, clearly unnerved by Thomas' injection of racism charges into the proceedings, made little effort to counterattack or defend Hill.

Hill's Corroborating Witnesses

On Oct. 13, a Sunday, the committee first heard from a panel of four witnesses who testified that Hill had told them years earlier that Thomas was sexually harassing her.

Three of the witnesses — Susan Hoerchner, a workers' compensation judge in Los Angeles; Ellen M. Wells, a project manager for the American Public Welfare Association in Washington, D.C.; and John W. Carr, a New York lawyer; were current or former friends of Hill. The fourth, Joel Paul, was an American University law professor who had tried to recruit her for his faculty in 1987.

Hoerchner, Wells and Carr — who was dating Hill in 1982-83 — all said she told them of Thomas' advances at the time they occurred, although she did not give them the graphic details she presented to the committee.

"It was clear to me at that time that she found this very painful to talk about, and I did not push her to speak of it further," Carr testified. He told the committee he had not seen or spoken to Hill since 1983, when their social relationship trailed off.

Paul, who said he was a professional acquaintance of Hill, told the committee he had talked with her about a possible job at American University in July 1987 and had asked her why she left the EEOC. "Professor Hill responded reluctantly and with obvious emotion and embarrassment that she had been sexually harassed by her supervisor at the EEOC," he recounted.

All four witnesses told the committee that they had stepped forward on their own to support Hill's story because they realized they had important corroborating testimony to offer. All four said they had believed Hill at the time she informed them of Thomas' behavior, and that they believed her still.

Wells eloquently defended Hill's decision to remain silent in the face of sexual harassment. "There are things that you have to put up with," she said. "And being a black woman, you know you have to put up with a lot. And so you grit your teeth and you do it."

Thomas' Character Witnesses

After the four corroborating witnesses had answered questions from committee members, the senators heard from a second panel of four — all women who had worked with Thomas at the EEOC and had never experienced or observed any improper behavior on his part.

J. C. Alvarez said of Hill: "I cannot believe one word of her testimony."

Another witness, Phyllis Berry, said she believed Hill "had a crush on the chairman" and was unhappy that Thomas did not reciprocate her feelings. She could not point to any evidence for that claim, however.

A third former employee, Temple University Professor Nancy Fitch, said she did not agree with Berry that Hill exhibited a romantic interest in Thomas. But neither did she believe Thomas guilty of sexual harassment, she said.

Diane Holt, Thomas' former secretary at the EEOC, said she recalled more telephone calls to him from Hill than the 11 noted in his logs over the years since Hill left his employ — calls that Republicans repeatedly cited as evidence that Hill had maintained friendly contacts with Thomas long after the alleged harassment.

Holt said she had never seen any sign that Hill was uncomfortable around Thomas. "I can't find any conceivable motivation for her saying that it did happen," she testified.

During the day Oct. 13, while the hearings continued, Hill's lawyers released the results of a polygraph examination she took that showed "no deception" in her account of Thomas' behavior toward her.

Charles Ogletree, a Harvard Law School professor, noted Hill had offered twice previously to take a polygraph test — in her first interview with the FBI and later before the committee. "It was my judgment, given the accusations that have been made over the last few days about fantasy, about grudges, about being a martyr . . . that this has just gone too far" and that Hill should try to prove she was telling the truth, he said.

The polygraph, he said, was administered by the man who ran the FBI's polygraph program from 1978-87.

Danforth and other Republicans quickly said no polygraph result should be admitted as evidence. And some Democrats, who had long opposed use of such tests, agreed. Biden said it would be "a sad day for the civil liberties" of Americans if polygraph results became the basis of important judgments.

THE SENATE VOTES

On Oct. 15, a scant two days after the hearings ended, the long battle finally came to an end.

The Senate voted 52-48 to confirm Thomas.

Two Republicans — James M. Jeffords of Vermont and Bob Packwood of Oregon — voted against the nominee, and 11 Democrats, mostly Southerners, voted for him: David L. Boren, Okla.; John B. Breaux, La.; DeConcini; Alan J. Dixon, Ill.; Jim Exon, Neb.; Wyche Fowler Jr., Ga.; Ernest F. Hollings, S.C.; J. Bennett Johnston, La.; Sam Nunn, Ga.; Charles S. Robb, Va.; and Richard C. Shelby, Ala.

In the end, most senators said Hill's charges and Thomas' defense — a categorical denial — were inconclusive. Senators fell back on their previous positions based on Thomas' judicial philosophy or his determined character and rise from poverty.

Both sides estimated that Thomas lost about 10 votes that he might have had before the Hill allegations emerged. But only three senators publicly shifted positions.

Influenced by Hill's testimony, three Democrats — Richard H. Bryan, Nev.; Lieberman; and Harry Reid, Nev. — withdrew their support for Thomas.

"I spent all day agitating about it," Lieberman said after the vote. "Earlier in the day I had even drafted a statement of support. But I just kept reading over it, and it didn't feel right."

Bryan said, "A couple of things troubled me. I thought his refusal to watch Anita Hill's testimony was part of a contrived strategy calculated to make it more difficult to examine him."

Bryan also faulted Thomas for using racism to divert attention from the sexual harassment story.

Thomas left the hearing room when it was Hill's turn to testify. When he returned, the nominee said he had not watched her testimony and blasted senators for a "high-tech lynching."

Most other senators stressed that their votes had nothing to do with the sexual harassment allegations. Supporters said Thomas would be an outstanding justice, sensitive to the disadvantaged and, now, to the accused. Opponents said that his judicial philosophy was outside the mainstream and that he would vote to remove protections for individual rights.

Robert C. Byrd, D-W.Va., who voted against Thomas, said that he had written a speech supporting him but changed his mind after seeing the testimony of Hill, "who did not flinch," and Thomas, who "astonished" him by refusing even to watch Hill's testimony.

"I had substantial doubts after this episode about the judicial temperament of Judge Thomas — doubts that I did not have prior to this weekend's hearings," Byrd said.

"He professed to want nothing more than to clear his name. And yet he could not be bothered to even hear what the allegations were from the person who is making the allegation," Byrd said.

Byrd also said he was offended by Thomas' "injection of racism" into the hearings.

"It was a diversionary tactic intended to divert both the committee's and the American public's attention away from the issue at hand, the issue being: Which one is telling the truth?"

But Shelby, a Democrat for Thomas, said, "Coming out of the Deep South, from Alabama, I think he framed an issue. I could see how, growing up in Georgia, he could see the circus over there as a high-tech lynching." Shelby, who Bush had called to request support for Thomas, noted that polls in his state showed that most people backed Thomas. ■

High Court Executes Conservative Agenda

The Supreme Court appointees of Presidents Ronald Reagan and Bush helped to form a seemingly invincible conservative majority that moved with increasing boldness in the 1990-91 term to execute a conservative political agenda.

Bolstered by David H. Souter, its newest conservative, the Rehnquist Court was writing broader opinions than it did in the 1988-89 and 1989-90 terms. In those years, the court basically said it was up to Congress and the states to do the policy-making. Unlike the more liberal Warren and Burger courts, it declined to write law that would address social dilemmas. *(1989 Almanac, p. 293)*

In the 1990-91 term, however, the court clearly had policy objectives in mind, most notably in the area of criminal law. And with Clarence Thomas, another conservative, named to replace retiring Justice Thurgood Marshall, sweeping rulings were possible in other areas such as abortion, church-state, affirmative action and free speech. *(Thomas nomination, p. 274)*

Judicial Activism?

Senate Judiciary Committee Chairman Joseph R. Biden Jr., D-Del., said the Rehnquist Court "in too many cases" was taking "a pro-active stand in changing the laws."

During Supreme Court confirmation hearings in the 1980s and 1990s, Judiciary Committee members repeatedly asked nominees if they believed in "judicial activism."

The responses were predictable and safe. Antonin Scalia said in 1986, "I assure you, I have no agenda. I am not going onto the court with a list of things that I want to do." Anthony M. Kennedy said in 1987, "Judges are not to make laws; they are to enforce the laws." Souter said in 1990 that a justice "has to constantly guard against substituting his values for the values which he is sworn to uphold."

In the same vein, when William H. Rehnquist was to be elevated to chief justice in 1986, he told senators, "I think that the chief justice can exercise a certain amount of leadership on the court, but I do not think it is apt to be in a philosophical direction."

By 1991, Democratic senators said they had been had.

"I think they've turned judicial activism on its head," said Edward M. Kennedy, D-Mass., as the court finished its 1990-91 term June 27.

"I think Scalia is an example of a judicial activist as much as any liberal was," Biden said. Scalia and Rehnquist tended to be boldest in asserting their socially conservative philosophies.

Republican senators tended to sidestep when asked whether the court was "activist" — an approach traditionally abhorred by conservatives — but they praised its rulings.

Sen. Orrin G. Hatch, R-Utah, said it was "a little too early to tell" whether this was an activist court. He defended its overruling of criminal law precedents that had favored defendants: "The court shouldn't allow bad precedents to stand."

Overturning Precedents

The court overruled five precedents during the 1990-91 term and at times reached beyond the questions directly before it to address constitutional issues that dissenting justices said did not have to be tackled. That was precisely the kind of activism conservatives used to excoriate during the reign of Chief Justices Earl Warren and Warren E. Burger.

In two key cases involving habeas corpus petitions (a form of appeal by death row inmates), the court adopted policies similar to those that Rehnquist, in vain, had been urging Congress to pass. And it did so as the Senate was considering legislation that would accomplish similar results. *(Crime bill, p. 262; Supreme Court crackdown, p. 264)*

The Rehnquist majority, in another significant case of interest to Congress, went beyond the straightforward question at issue in *Rust v. Sullivan* to decide the constitutionality of administration regulations barring abortion counseling in publicly funded clinics.

Rehnquist himself defended the court's departure from precedent in one case, saying, "*Stare decisis* [the principle of adherence to settled cases] is not an inexorable command." He said the court during the preceding 20 terms had overruled in whole or in part 33 of its earlier constitutional decisions. Statute-based decisions were rarely overruled because the court traditionally believed such reversals were best left to legislators.

Abortion 'Gag Rule'

Overall, the 1990-91 session lacked the kind of fiery issues that had drawn Congress' attention in the preceding two terms: abortion, civil rights, flag burning.

Aside from the criminal law decisions bolstering police power, the most noticed ruling was *Rust v. Sullivan.* A 5-4 majority held that 1988 administration regulations barring workers at publicly funded clinics from counseling pregnant women on abortion were constitutional. Abortion rights advocates in Congress tried but failed to win enactment of legislation that would block or lift the so-called gag rule. *(Abortion issue, p. 339)*

The opinions in *Rust* were not very revealing for those who wondered whether a court majority was ready to overrule *Roe v. Wade*, the 1973 landmark decision that made abortion legal nationwide. Court decisions since 1989 had narrowed a woman's right to abortion, and a new case testing *Roe* was expected to reach the court as early as 1992.

Declining Caseload

The high court issued 112 signed opinions in its 1990-91 term, down from the 129 opinions announced in the previous term and its lowest total in 20 years. Several factors appeared to be at work. First, decisions of the lower courts, dominated by Reagan and Bush appointees, were in step with the high court's views. Second, the court's remaining liberals voted not to hear certain cases, fearing that precedents would be overturned; and, finally, the Bush administration was asking the court to review fewer cases than Reagan's did.

It takes four justices to accept a case. Justices who wanted cases heard but could not muster the votes increasingly complained that the high court was allowing conflicts among the lower courts to stand.

Another recurring theme, particularly affecting Congress, was the court's tendency in construing a statute to defer to an executive branch interpretation rather than

Major Supreme Court Decisions of 1990-91

Following are some of the most important rulings of the Supreme Court's 1990-91 term. Dissenting justices are in parentheses.

Individual Rights

United Automobile Workers v. Johnson Controls Inc., 9-0 and 5-4, March 20. Companies may not exclude women from jobs that might harm a developing fetus. Congress intended anti-discrimination laws to forbid all job practices that were based on workers' ability to have children. (White, Rehnquist, Kennedy and Scalia)

Equal Employment Opportunity Commission v. Arabian American Oil Co., 6-3, March 26. Title VII of the 1964 Civil Rights Act, which bars discrimination in employment, does not cover U.S. workers employed in overseas offices of U.S.-based companies. (Marshall, Blackmun and Stevens)

Rust v. Sullivan, 5-4, May 23. The administration may forbid workers at publicly funded clinics to counsel pregnant women on abortion. Title X of the Public Health Service Act can be read to bar not only abortions but also abortion counseling. (Marshall, Blackmun, Stevens and O'Connor)

Masson v. The New Yorker, 7-2, June 20. Fabricated quotes may be libelous if they are published with knowledge of falsity or give a different meaning to what the speaker actually said. (White and Scalia)

Barnes v. Glen Theatre, 5-4, June 21. States may ban nude dancing even at adults-only clubs without breaching the First Amendment right of expression. (White, Marshall, Blackmun, Stevens)

Cohen v. Cowles Media Inc., 5-4, June 24. The First Amendment does not shield news media from lawsuits if they break their promises of confidentiality to their sources. (Marshall, Blackmun, O'Connor, Souter)

Criminal Law

Arizona v. Fulminante, 5-4, March 26. A coerced confession, introduced at trial, does not automatically taint a conviction. (White, Marshall, Blackmun and Stevens)

McCleskey v. Zant, 6-3, April 16. A death row prisoner may file only one habeas corpus petition in federal court unless there is good reason why any alleged constitutional error was not raised on the first round. (Marshall, Blackmun and Stevens)

Coleman v. Thompson, 6-3, June 24. A death row inmate may not file a habeas corpus petition in federal court if he failed to abide by state court procedural rules. (Marshall, Blackmun and Stevens)

Payne v. Tennessee, 6-3, June 27. Evidence of a victim's character and the impact of a crime on his family may be used against a murder defendant in a sentencing hearing. (Marshall, Blackmun and Stevens)

Harmelin v. Michigan, 5-4, June 27. A state may require life in prison without parole for a first-time drug offense without violating the constitutional ban on cruel and unusual punishment. (White, Blackmun, Marshall and Stevens)

Others

Pacific Mutual Life Insurance Co. v. Haslip, 7-1, March 4. Juries have broad discretion to decide punitive damages, even when the awards are greatly disproportionate to actual damage suffered. (O'Connor; Souter did not participate.)

McCormick v. United States, 6-3, May 23. An extortion conviction under the Hobbs Act, arising from an elected official's receipt of a campaign contribution, requires a "quid pro quo," the realization of some benefit to the contributor. (Stevens, Blackmun and O'Connor)

Chisom v. Roemer, Houston Lawyers' Association v. Attorney General of Texas, 6-3, June 20. The Voting Rights Act of 1965 applies to elections for judges. (Scalia, Rehnquist and Kennedy)

relying on legislative history. Some scholars believed that gave greater "lawmaking" power to the executive branch.

Souter's Impact

In the conservative camp were Rehnquist, Scalia, Kennedy, Souter and (most of the time) Byron R. White and Sandra Day O'Connor. All were named by Reagan or Bush except White, appointed by President John F. Kennedy, and Rehnquist, selected by President Richard M. Nixon. Reagan elevated Rehnquist to chief justice.

On the liberal side were Marshall, Harry A. Blackmun and, usually, John Paul Stevens. They were appointed by Presidents Lyndon B. Johnson, Nixon and Gerald R. Ford, respectively.

Souter's first year on the bench cast little light on his judicial temperament, except that he could be counted on in most cases to side with Chief Justice Rehnquist.

The new justice wrote eight opinions, the fewest of any justice, and the majority of those cases had been decided by unanimous votes. *(Souter's appointment, 1990 Almanac, p. 508)*

While Souter remained the mystery he was when he emerged from the Senate confirmation hearings, his vote changed the court.

In the 1989-90 term, one-third of the court's decisions were 5-4 rulings. In the 1990-91 term, only one-fifth were so narrowly decided, and many pivotal cases were settled by 6-3 votes. There is more freedom in the wording and breadth of an opinion when six justices sign on than when the author is struggling to hold together a slim five-member majority.

Souter gave Rehnquist a majority even when the more centrist conservatives, O'Connor and White, opposed the chief.

Without Souter, Rehnquist would not have been able to uphold the abortion-counseling ban in *Rust v. Sullivan.* Nor is it likely that the court would have ruled, in the 5-4 *Barnes v. Glen Theatre* decision, that states could outlaw nude dancing in adult clubs.

Souter, however, also provided a fifth vote for liberal-leaning Blackmun's decision on fetal protection policies in *United Automobile Workers v. Johnson Controls Inc.* The court ruled unanimously that companies could not exclude women from jobs that might harm a developing fetus. It divided, however, over standards in federal anti-discrimination law.

Blackmun's five-justice majority said that Congress had intended to forbid all hiring practices that were based on a worker's ability to have children. Four justices (White, Rehnquist, Kennedy and Scalia) said there could be situations in which a company, because of personal-injury liability and workplace costs, could exclude women based on hazards to unborn children.

Dissents Grow Pointed

O'Connor chided the Rehnquist majority in the *Rust* decision for violating "a fundamental rule of judicial restraint that this court will not reach constitutional questions in advance of the necessity of deciding them." She said the court could have ruled on the abortion counseling regulations by confining itself to the statute.

O'Connor, however, joined a majority opinion by Kennedy in *McCleskey v. Zant*, holding that a death row prisoner could file only one habeas corpus petition in federal court unless there was good reason why an alleged constitutional error was not raised on the first round. In *Coleman v. Thompson*, O'Connor wrote an opinion forbidding a prisoner from bringing a habeas corpus petition in federal court if he failed to meet state court procedural rules.

Both of those rulings, accomplishing what Rehnquist had urged Congress to pass, were attacked by three-justice minorities (Marshall, Blackmun and Stevens). Marshall in *McCleskey v. Zant* said the majority was serving as a "backup legislature."

Marshall reserved his fiercest criticism for the last day of the term, when the majority ruled in *Payne v. Tennessee* that evidence of a victim's character and the effect of a crime on his family could be used against a defendant at a sentencing hearing.

That ruling reversed a 1987 decision that had been reiterated in 1989.

"The implications of this radical new exception to the doctrine of *stare decisis* are staggering," Marshall said in a dissent issued just hours before he announced his retirement. "The majority today sends a clear signal that scores of established constitutional liberties are now ripe for reconsideration." ■

Bush Nominated Judges From the Ranks

President Bush, whose insider credentials carried him from Congress through a series of top government jobs to the White House, put a similar premium on job experience when choosing federal judges.

By 1991, it was clear that his administration had developed a "farm team" approach to judicial nominations, looking mainly to the lower courts for candidates to fill scores of federal appeals court and district court openings.

Even in his two appointments to the Supreme Court, Bush had turned to the federal appeals courts for David H. Souter and Clarence Thomas. *(Thomas nomination, p. 274)*

Their ascensions were only the most visible indicators of a deeper trend. Bush also was promoting federal district court judges to appeals court openings — more so than either of his immediate predecessors, Ronald Reagan and Jimmy Carter. In 1991 alone, seven of Bush's nine appeals court appointments came from district courts. During his first three years in office, 63 percent of his 27 appeals court nominations came from the district courts.

Reagan and Carter, by contrast, tapped experienced judges for about half of their appeals court appointments.

For nominees to district judgeships, the lowest rung on the federal courts ladder, Bush recruited more nominees with experience on state courts or as federal magistrates than had past presidents. Twenty-three of his 47 district court appointees in 1991 rose from judicial posts, maintaining a three-year trend in which half of his district court appointees came from the judiciary.

A Bench of Wealthy White Males

The result of turning primarily to jurists, rather than lawyers in private practice, academics, U.S. attorneys, politicians and other outside sources, was a "growing professionalism of the judiciary," said Sheldon Goldman, a political science professor at the University of Massachusetts at Amherst. Goldman had been tracking judicial appointments since the 1960s.

Bush had said he wanted conservatives "who won't legislate from the bench." He often praised a particular candidate's judicial experience but made no public statements about that being a priority.

The obvious advantage to the administration in choosing experienced judges was that a potential nominee had a track record and his positions on a range of issues could be assessed before he became embroiled in the confirmation process. Further, given the complexity of litigation in the 1990s, there was a benefit to having a more experienced judiciary.

But one consequence was that, even while Bush insisted he was trying to diversify the bench with more women and minorities, the practice of promoting from within contributed to the monolithic face of the Bush judiciary: white, male and wealthy. As of the end of 1991, about 90 percent of Bush's appointees were white; 85 percent were men; and two-thirds had a net worth of more than $500,000.

Another disadvantage to promoting from within the judiciary, Goldman noted, was that potential candidates with legislative and political experience were more likely to be excluded. As a result, career judges could end up being less flexible in deciding cases. "When lives haven't been fired in the crucible of American politics," said Goldman, "people tend to view [disputes] in black and white."

That, in turn, could lead to narrow interpretations of federal statutes because those unfamiliar with how statutes were written were less likely to heed "legislative history," the floor statements and supplementary report opinions of lawmakers that often went to the heart of a court case.

The idea that a growing number of judges might be unfamiliar with, or even disdainful of, the legislative process took on added significance in light of Supreme Court Justice Antonin Scalia's repeated efforts to recruit more adherents to his view that judges should interpret statutes based only on their actual text.

A Passive Senate

In February, Senate Judiciary Committee Chairman

Joseph R. Biden Jr., D-Del., along with committee members Paul Simon, D-Ill., Edward M. Kennedy, D-Mass., and Howard M. Metzenbaum, D-Ohio, sent a letter to the Justice Department saying that more women and minorities should be chosen for the courts.

"We encourage you to make every effort to reach out to black, Hispanic, Asian American and women's bar associations so that the administration's judicial nominees will better reflect their recent advances in the bar," they said.

Promoting from within the judiciary "sounds as if it's the right thing to do — it's meritorious on its face," said Metzenbaum, a leading Democratic critic on the Judiciary Committee. "But it provides for inbreeding, more of the same kind of people," he said.

Yet the Senate's majority Democrats helped perpetuate the lack of diversity by routinely confirming Bush's court nominees. Except for Thomas, who overcame stiff opposition to win confirmation, and Kenneth L. Ryskamp, who was rejected for the 11th U.S. Circuit Court of Appeals, every one of Bush's 58 nominees considered in 1991 was approved by the Judiciary Committee and by the full Senate on uncontested voice votes. *(Ryskamp, this page)*

Democrats said it was difficult to challenge an experienced judge, and because many of the lower court nominees had been recommended by Republican senators, the Senate was predisposed to confirm them.

"A number of members feel that unless there is something specifically wrong with a nominee, then we have to approve him," Metzenbaum said. "We have the burden of proof, and on the floor, 12 to 15 Democrats are always willing to go with the president."

When those mostly Southern, conservative Democrats joined with the Senate's 43 Republicans, the White House could count on a clear majority vote for Bush's nominees.

The Bush Appointments

Since taking office, Bush had appointed two Supreme Court justices, 27 judges to the appeals courts of general jurisdiction and 95 district court judges.

To some extent, it was unsurprising that Bush elevated more judges than either Reagan or Carter did. Bush had a huge pool of Reagan judges, eight years of appointments (51 percent of the judiciary by 1988) from which to pick.

Conversely, Reagan, who actively sought conservatives for the federal bench, was not inclined to draw on lower court judges appointed by his predecessor, a Democrat; when Carter was in office, the majority of judges had been appointed by his Republican predecessors, Gerald R. Ford and Richard M. Nixon.

Of the seven district court judges whom Bush elevated in 1991, all but one was originally appointed by Reagan. The seventh judge was appointed in 1975 by Ford.

Administration officials and Senate Republicans defended Bush's choices and rejected Democratic and liberal group assertions that he was building a bench that was isolated and out of touch with most Americans.

"We have a good mix of jurists, including those from the bench, from the private sector and from public service positions," said Paul McNulty, chief spokesman of the Justice Department, which carried out the judicial selection process in concert with the White House.

Orrin G. Hatch of Utah, a senior Republican on the Senate Judiciary Committee, said it was not easy to fashion a diverse judiciary.

"It is difficult to find moderate to conservative women lawyers who have the requisite experience and capabilities," Hatch said. "It has only been in the last 20 years that women have been coming into the law."

Charles E. Grassley, R-Iowa, another member of Senate Judiciary, also said it was natural for Bush to seek nominees who had a judicial track record.

Grassley said he did the same thing in making appointment recommendations to the White House. "I'm not a lawyer, so I can rationalize that these people have been through the process before," he said. ■

Senate Judiciary Rejected Ryskamp Nomination

President Bush was handed his first defeat of a judicial nominee on April 11 when a majority of the Senate Judiciary Committee refused to send the nomination of Kenneth L. Ryskamp to the floor.

By a party-line vote of 6-8, the committee opposed the elevation of Ryskamp, a district court judge, to the 11th U.S. Circuit Court of Appeals. The panel then failed, on a 7-7 tie, to send the nomination to the floor.

The Ryskamp defeat was not the result of a great ideological battle, as with a number of President Ronald Reagan's nominations. Senators opposing Ryskamp said he had failed to dispel criticism that he was unsympathetic to minorities, had too quickly rejected legal precedents and was given to intemperate remarks from the bench.

Each of Bush's previous 77 judicial nominees had passed through the confirmation process with little of the negative publicity that greeted many of Reagan's nominees. Indeed, the only Bush nominee rejected by the Judiciary Committee before the Ryskamp nomination was William Lucas, to be assistant attorney general in charge of civil rights. Lucas' critics said he lacked legal experience and an understanding of civil rights laws, and the committee blocked his nomination from proceeding to the Senate floor. *(1989 Almanac, p. 236)*

Ryskamp, 58, had been appointed to the Southern District of Florida by Ronald Reagan in 1986. Bush nominated him in 1990 to the 11th Circuit appellate court, which covered Florida, Georgia and Alabama and was one of the last appeals courts not dominated by appointees of Republicans Bush and Reagan.

After allegations arose regarding Ryskamp's record on civil rights and membership in a private club that reportedly had discriminated against blacks and Jews, the Judiciary Committee shelved his nomination in the 101st Congress. On Jan. 8, Bush renominated him.

People for the American Way, a civil liberties group, attacked Ryskamp over civil rights, saying that he had ruled overwhelmingly against civil rights plaintiffs.

Justice Department officials countered that the nominee had a commitment to civil rights, and a majority of an American Bar Association review panel gave Ryskamp its highest rating.

In the end, opposition from one of Ryskamp's home-state senators, Democrat Bob Graham, helped tip the balance against the nominee. Typically, senators of both parties support their home-state judicial nominees. But groups representing Cubans, women, Jews and blacks lobbied hard against the nominee, targeting Graham in the hope that if he opposed Ryskamp, so would wavering Judiciary Committee members. After hearing from Ryskamp opponents while making the rounds of dinners and meetings in Florida, Graham wrote an eleventh-hour letter to Judiciary Committee Chairman Joseph R. Biden Jr., D-Del., opposing the nomination. The letter helped seal the committee's 6-8 vote against the nomination.

Police Brutality Issue

One of the key cases Ryskamp critics cited involved a complaint by blacks — not all of whom were found guilty of a crime — who were attacked by city police dogs in West Palm Beach.

In this case, the jury found that the city of West Palm Beach, its former police chief and individual police officers had violated the plaintiffs' civil rights. Ryskamp left alone the verdict against individual police officers but threw out the verdict against the city and the former police chief. Ryskamp said of the complainants: "It might not be inappropriate to carry around a few scars to remind you of your wrongdoing in the past, assuming the person has done wrong." The 11th Circuit said Ryskamp erred in setting aside the verdict.

By the time Ryskamp appeared for his confirmation hearing before the Judiciary Committee on March 19, concerns about police brutality had been raised nationwide by the actions of Los Angeles police officers, who repeatedly beat a fleeing suspect. The incident, videotaped by an observer, inflamed fears that blacks were being brutalized by white police officers. Ryskamp called the beating "shocking and disturbing."

Ryskamp said in his opening statement that he had "always been committed to the cause of civil rights in this country."

"Discrimination is illegal and unconstitutional," he said. "I also believe that it is morally wrong, according to the most fundamental Judeo-Christian tenets. All men and women are created equal in the image of God and stand equal before Him."

Yet when Ryskamp was asked to explain his comments in the West Palm Beach police dog case, he seemed to undermine his nomination further among skeptical Democrats.

Under questioning by Chairman Biden, Ryskamp said that he was talking only about suspects who were convicted of stealing; others who were mauled by the dogs were not charged with any crimes. He said: "I was thinking for their own welfare . . . and the idea of keeping them from committing other crimes, that that painful experience might be a deterrent, whereas, the irony would be if they got a lot of money, it may be a vindication, and they would go on to commit other crimes. That is all I meant by it."

Biden said later he was "astounded" by Ryskamp's remarks on the case. Other senators who expressed dismay over Ryskamp's comments on that case and other issues were Edward M. Kennedy, D-Mass.; Howard M. Metzenbaum, D-Ohio; and Paul Simon, D-Ill.

While some GOP senators said they were generally inclined to back the nominee, two — Charles E. Grassley, Iowa, and Arlen Specter, Pennsylvania — pressed Ryskamp on his civil rights rulings.

Country Club Membership

Democratic and Republican senators also voiced concerns about Ryskamp's longtime membership in a private club that had a reputation for discriminating against blacks and Jews. The private club in question, the Riviera Country Club in Coral Gables, had a reputation in the Miami area for discrimination. In 1990 it adopted a no-discrimination clause in its bylaws, although the club manager, Donald Beaver Jr., said that had been the unwritten policy for "many years."

For more than 20 years, Ryskamp belonged to the Riviera Country Club. He resigned in mid-March 1991.

At the March 19 confirmation hearing he was asked why it had taken him so long to leave. Ryskamp replied that he had asked the club's directors about allegations of bias and had been told that the club did not discriminate. He said he resigned to avoid any appearance of impropriety.

Earlier, in August 1990, the Judiciary Committee had unanimously adopted a resolution saying that it was inappropriate for nominees or potential nominees to belong to discriminatory clubs "unless such persons are actively engaged in bona fide efforts to eliminate the discriminatory practices."

Committee Action

By the time the committee was to vote on the Ryskamp nomination in April, activists for the Alliance for Justice and People for the American Way had stepped up their pressure on Graham. Although not a member of the committee, Graham's views would be crucial in swaying undecided members of the panel, the activists said.

Graham's turning point came after weeks of conversations with people for and against the judge's appointment. On the eve of the committee's vote, the senator was near a decision, but there were two other people he wanted to consult: Howell Heflin, D-Ala., and Dennis DeConcini, D-Ariz. Seven of the eight Democrats on the Judiciary Committee would be needed to defeat the judge, and these two traditional swing votes were considered likely to back Ryskamp.

Graham wanted one or both of the senators to validate his position and to vote against Ryskamp, so he wouldn't be out there alone, according to an aide. Florida's other senator, Republican Connie Mack, was pushing for Ryskamp as a "man of the highest integrity."

Graham, while hearing no assurances, got what he wanted. Heflin, also under pressure from various groups and unimpressed by Ryskamp's testimony, independently had begun to come down against the nominee. DeConcini was still undecided.

Graham called Ryskamp and said that he was sorry but that he would not support him, then dictated his letter to Committee Chairman Biden. That night Graham released it to the media.

In his letter, Graham said he thought Ryskamp should be rejected because "serious questions have been raised about whether this nominee would be fair and unbiased."

On April 11, the committee cast its 6-8 party-line vote against Ryskamp. Voting against the nominee were Democrats Biden; Kennedy; Metzenbaum; Simon; Heflin; DeConcini; Patrick J. Leahy, Vt.; and Herb Kohl, Wis. Supporting him were Republicans Strom Thurmond, S.C.; Grassley; Specter; Orrin G. Hatch, Utah; Alan K. Simpson, Wyo.; and Hank Brown, Colo.

On the subsequent motion to send the nomination to the floor without a recommendation, members refused on a 7-7 tie vote. DeConcini, who voted "no" the first time, switched on the second motion.

White House spokesman Marlin Fitzwater expressed disappointment after the committee's action. "We don't believe that he is, in fact, insensitive to minorities, and we feel the evidence submitted to the committee supports our view." ■

Weak Support Stalls Final Price-Fixing Bill

Both the House and Senate passed legislation that sought to block manufacturers from trying to fix product prices in the retail market by cutting off supplies to outlets that sold at discounts. But the two chambers did not act on a final version in 1991.

At year's end, the House had appointed conferees on the legislation (S 429), but the Senate had not. Bill supporters planned to move to a conference early in 1992.

The vertical price-fixing bill had fairly strong Democratic support, but prospects for its enactment were guarded at best.

President Bush vowed to veto the bill if it ever made it to his desk. And while both chambers approved the legislation on voice votes, roll calls on amendments and on cloture motions clearly indicated that the legislation did not have the kind of support necessary to override a veto.

The bill's Senate sponsor, Howard M. Metzenbaum, D-Ohio, and other supporters characterized the measure as "pro-consumer" and said it would spur competition.

But opponents argued that the bill would be unfair to businesses and would effectively make manufacturers and full-price retailers guilty until proven innocent by a court. They also said the legislation would bring on a rash of expensive litigation — the cost of which would be borne by the consumer.

BOXSCORE

➡ **Vertical Price Fixing (S 429, HR 1470).** The bill sought to make it easier for discount retailers to bring and win vertical price-fixing cases against a manufacturer and a competing retailer. It made clear that vertical price fixing was automatically illegal and tightened the ban on such price-fixing deals, under which a manufacturer and a retailer worked in tandem to force a rival retailer to charge at least a certain price for goods.

Reports: S Rept 102-42; H Rept 102-237.

KEY ACTION

March 21 — S 429 rejected on merits, 6-8, by the **Senate** Judiciary Committee. But the committee voted, 10-4, to report the bill to the floor without a formal recommendation.

May 9 — S 429 passed the **Senate** by voice vote.

June 25 — HR 1470 was approved by the **House** Judiciary Committee by voice vote.

Oct. 10 — S 429 passed the **House** by voice vote after House members inserted the text of HR 1470.

Background

Congress had been trying to tighten laws against vertical price fixing for several years. *(1990 Almanac, p. 539; 1989 Almanac, p. 285; 1988 Almanac, p. 131; 1987 Almanac, p. 280).*

The practice had been considered illegal *per se,* or by its very nature, since 1911. But two Supreme Court decisions in the 1980s created ambiguities about how much and what type of evidence was needed to prosecute a vertical price-fixing complaint.

The first was the 1984 finding in *Monsanto Co. v. Spray-Rite Service Corp.* that a plaintiff must provide direct evidence — not merely a complaint about pricing practices — that a manufacturer and a competing retailer had intended to maintain retail prices in the market.

The second was the 1988 decision in *Business Electronics Corp. v. Sharp Electronics Corp.* that no *per se* violation of antitrust law could be deemed to have occurred in a vertical price-fixing case unless a manufacturer and a retailer agreed to set a specific price for a product.

A handful of large discounters had gone out of business, and bill supporters said the administration had been lax in pursuing vertical price-fixing cases. The Justice Department had not brought a vertical price-fixing suit since 1980, and supporters said this indicated the need for stronger federal laws to protect discount outlets.

Typically, the sort of case that the legislation addressed occurred when a retail outlet chose to sell a certain product at a discounted price to boost sales. Then a competing retailer — such as a department store — would step in and persuade the manufacturer to cut off supplies to the discounting store.

A key aspect of the legislation would allow discount retailers to bring a manufacturer and a competing retailer to court without detailed proof that a price-fixing arrangement had been made.

SENATE ACTION

In testimony before the Senate Judiciary Committee, a number of consumer groups and representatives of the discount industry came out in strong support of the bill. Large manufacturers and some specialized retailers were opposed to it, saying it would lead to unfounded lawsuits and result in heavy legal costs.

James F. Rill, assistant attorney general in charge of the Antitrust Division at the Justice Department, concurred. The "legislation at the very least would cause a great deal of confusion in resale price maintenance cases and would likely distort their outcome to an unknowable extent," Rill told the committee.

Committee Action

The price-fixing bill made it to the Senate floor largely as the result of a deal reached in late 1990 between its sponsor, Metzenbaum, and Sen. Strom Thurmond, R-S.C., ranking member of the Judiciary Committee.

Metzenbaum agreed to drop a filibuster threat against legislation (HR 5316 — PL 101-650) important to Thurmond that was taken up late in the 101st Congress and led to the creation of 85 new federal judgeships. *(1990 Almanac, p. 520)*

In return, Thurmond agreed not to object to consideration of price-fixing legislation early in the 102nd Congress, although he was adamantly opposed to its intent and voted against it in committee.

The committee on March 21 voted, 6-8, to reject the merits of S 429, but members agreed, 10-4, to send the bill to the full Senate without a recommendation.

Four Judiciary members — Republicans Thurmond, Arlen Specter of Pennsylvania and Charles E. Grassley of Iowa; and Democrat Dennis DeConcini of Arizona —

changed their votes in reporting out the bill.

Senate Passage

The Senate on May 9 passed S 429 by voice after enough votes were assembled to overcome a Republican filibuster.

The Bush administration opposed the bill. A May 2 administration statement warned that the legislation could create an inference of unlawful conspiracy in certain cases where none existed.

The measure cleared a critical hurdle when the Senate on May 7 voted, 61-37, to limit debate on a motion to proceed to the bill. On May 8, the Senate voted, 63-35, to again invoke cloture on the bill itself. A minimum of 60 votes is required to limit debate. *(Votes 53, 54, 8-S)*

While the cloture votes cleared the way for Senate passage of S 429, they also served as a gauge indicating that the bill lacked the two-thirds support it would need to surmount a likely veto.

The Senate by voice vote adopted an amendment by Hank Brown, R-Colo., that tightened the evidence standard plaintiffs would have to meet under the bill before being granted a jury trial. The amendment required at least some direct evidence of vertical price fixing to be obtained by a plaintiff before a case could be brought.

HOUSE ACTION

The House Judiciary Committee, like its Senate counterpart, was divided over the vertical price-fixing legislation.

The committee approved its bill (HR 1470) by voice vote on June 25, after rejecting, 12-12, an amendment by ranking Republican Hamilton Fish Jr. of New York to require plaintiffs who brought price-fixing suits to show evidence of a conspiracy and a price-fixing attempt.

Fish argued that the bill's language was too broad and that valid actions by a manufacturer and retailer could be challenged by a disgruntled discounter.

House Passage

Following sometimes prickly debate over the bill, the House passed S 429 by voice vote on Oct. 10 after inserting the language of its own bill (HR 1470).

Advocates contended that the measure would lead to price cuts of perhaps 10 percent to 20 percent on a wide variety of brand-name clothing, television and stereo equipment, computers and other consumer products.

Sounding an economic and somewhat populist theme in a year marked by recession, House Judiciary Committee Chairman Jack Brooks, D-Texas, said that if the "economy will revive quickly, it will be because people won't have to pay the Bloomingdale's price for a product."

But opponents countered that the beneficiaries of the bill would be lawyers, who would clog the courts with antitrust litigation while siphoning off cash from manufacturers struggling to stay afloat.

"These cases take years to resolve, and the million-dollar settlements will do nothing to keep prices low," said Fish, who led the opposition.

Members rejected, 196-218, a Fish amendment that would have effectively gutted the bill, according to Democratic supporters. The Fish language would have required a plaintiff to show direct proof that a conspiracy existed and further show that a rival retailer's pricing policy was the major reason that a manufacturer had cut off supplies to the discounter. *(Vote 303, p. 74-H)*

Speaking against the amendment were lawmakers who doubted that such direct evidence of vertical price fixing could ever be obtained legally by a discount retailer.

But in a move that rankled bill supporters, the House adopted, 218-195, an amendment by Rep. Tom Campbell, R-Calif., that exempted from the price-fixing ban any manufacturer "so small in the relevant market as to lack market power." *(Vote 304, p. 74-H)*

Although the amendment included no language on what constituted "market power," Campbell cited Justice Department figures that defined it as the ability to control 15 percent of a product's market.

Supporters of the bill were shaken by Campbell's success. They said the amendment greatly weakened the bill by effectively excluding large manufacturers who often could claim that their sales represented a small slice of a product's market in a particular community.

Despite the Campbell amendment, many GOP lawmakers remained opposed to the bill, saying it would only serve to line the pockets of lawyers and decrease jobs in the manufacturing sector.

"This is another one of those bills coming from the people who want to kill jobs," said Rep. Robert S. Walker, R-Pa. ■

Bill To Limit RICO Fails To Reach Floor

Efforts to scale back the civil provisions of the Racketeer Influenced and Corrupt Organizations Act (RICO) won approval from the House Judiciary committee in 1991, but the measure did not reach the floor.

Business groups had long complained that RICO provisions of the Organized Crime Control Act of 1970 (PL 91-452), intended as a tool against organized crime, had been misused against legitimate businesses, lawyers and other professionals.

These critics contended that plaintiffs were tempted by the possibility of collecting triple damages in a successful RICO civil action.

Over the last three Congresses, a number of bills were introduced to curb the use of the law in civil suits. But a coalition of powerful members and special interest groups consistently opposed these measures, fearing that an important law enforcement tool would be weakened.

In 1990, the press of other last-minute legislation left little room for negotiation and sealed the fate of RICO bills in both the House and the Senate.

The legislation's chief sponsor in the House, William J. Hughes, D-N.J., had hoped that an early start in the 102nd Congress and some compromises designed to satisfy critics would give the bill its best shot yet. *(1990 Almanac, p. 536)*

But a number of House committee chairmen — among them John D. Dingell, D-Mich., of Energy and Commerce, and John Conyers Jr., D-Mich., of Government Operations — still had reservations about the legislation. And the

Senate did not even introduce a counterpart measure.

"I want to make sure we don't weaken the law at a time when it is absolutely necessary," said Conyers, citing well-publicized thrift and bank scandals.

The pressure was on Congress not to approve legislation that could appear to spare perpetrators of financial fraud from heavy penalties.

Opponents of the bill cited in particular the scandal related to the Bank of Credit and Commerce International (BCCI), asserting that RICO as written provided needed remedies for such wrongdoing.

But Hughes defended the measure, saying that a revised RICO would still help plaintiffs who wanted to bring civil lawsuits arising from serious criminal conduct.

Hughes claimed the bill would prevent RICO from being used in insubstantial lawsuits, such as divorce and landlord-tenant disputes.

BOXSCORE

➡ **RICO Revisions (HR 1717) 578).** The bill sought to limit the use of civil RICO remedies to cases stemming from "egregious criminal conduct." Judges would act as gatekeepers, keeping out suits that failed to meet the standard.

Reports: H Rept 102-312.

KEY ACTION

May 2 — **House** Judiciary Subcommittee on Intellectual Property and Judicial Administration approved HR 1717 by voice vote.

July 30 — **House** Judiciary Committee approved HR 1717 by voice vote.

The House Proposal

The legislation was intended to reserve civil RICO remedies for cases stemming from "egregious criminal conduct." Its centerpiece was a provision making judges "gatekeepers" who could keep out suits that failed to meet the standard.

The bill required judges to dismiss civil cases unless the defendant was a key participant in wrongdoing that caused "significant injury."

The bill retained RICO's triple damages but sought to eliminate routine fraud cases from RICO treatment by tightening an existing "pattern of racketeering" requirement on which a complaint had to be based. It also required plaintiffs to show "clear and convincing" proof of injury.

When a plaintiff brought a case that was not based on conduct that had produced a criminal conviction, the judge would have to determine at the outset:

- The magnitude of the plaintiff's injury.
- That the defendant was a major participant in the injury.
- That there was a need to deter the type of conduct alleged with a triple-damages remedy.

If all those criteria were not met, the judge would be expected to dismiss the case.

COMMITTEE ACTION

The House Judiciary Subcommittee on Intellectual Property and Judicial Administration approved HR 1717 by voice vote on May 2.

No amendments were offered at subcommittee. But the measure was slightly modified when it was approved by the full committee on July 30 by voice vote.

At that markup, Conyers voiced concerns that the legislation might exempt many white-collar criminals. As the bill was originally written, only conduct related to failed savings and loans would have been presumed to meet the bill's criteria for egregious wrongdoing without a judicial determination.

Conyers contended that that provision would exclude too many serious cases. He tried to amend the bill so that all civil cases arising from wrongdoing at financial institutions, including institutions that had not failed, would not have to be screened.

Conyers' language, however, raised concerns that it would open the way for legal maneuvering that would undercut the purpose of the bill.

Committee members instead approved by voice vote a substitute offered by Rick Boucher, D-Va. It went part of the way toward addressing Conyers' concerns that victims of financial fraud would face too tough a standard to get their cases to trial. Boucher's amendment said that failed institutions that were insured by the Federal Deposit Insurance Corporation, not only failed savings and loans, would be presumed to meet civil RICO standards and not have to go through the judicial screening.

The committee also approved by voice vote an amendment by Dan Glickman, D-Kan., aimed at making sure that the RICO revision would not infringe on juries' constitutional responsibility to determine facts.

While the Boucher amendment answered some of Conyers' concerns, it did not satisfy other skeptics. The markup was the last formal action on the bill in 1991, leaving supporters of the legislation looking for a possible compromise in the next session to break the deadlock. ■

Barr Confirmed As Attorney General

No senator spoke against William P. Barr's nomination to be attorney general before the full chamber approved President Bush's choice on Nov. 20 by voice vote. Instead, they praised the nominee's public service background and his forthrightness.

Barr, 41, had been acting attorney general since Dick Thornburgh resigned in August to run for the Senate in Pennsylvania. Thornburgh lost in the upset election of Democratic Sen. Harris Wofford on Nov. 5.

Democrats hoped Barr's appointment would lead to more cooperative relations between Capitol Hill and the Justice Department. Thornburgh and Edwin Meese III, attorney general from 1985 to 1988, jousted often with the Democratic-controlled Congress over the department's operations and ideological focus.

The Senate Judiciary Committee on Nov. 15 unanimously approved the nomination. Committee Chairman Joseph R. Biden Jr., D-Del., said that although Barr held conservative views similar to those of his predecessors, "he's a throwback to the days when we had an attorney general who would actually talk to you."

Once deputy to Thornburgh, Barr had worked for the department for three years. From 1973 to 1977, he was a midlevel professional at the CIA. He also served on the White House domestic policy staff and worked in private practice.

The committee vote was delayed while Dennis DeConcini, D-Ariz., talked by telephone to Barr about whether the department's Nov. 14 indictments in the 1988 bombing of a Pan Am jumbo jet over Lockerbie, Scotland, was timed to coincide with Barr's confirmation.

Barr said the timing of charges against two Libyan intelligence officers was unrelated to the nomination. DeConcini did not attend the committee meeting but sent a proxy, making the final vote 14-0.

During hearings Nov. 12-13, Barr defended the Justice Department's role in the investigation of the Bank of Credit and Commerce International (BCCI), boldly stated his opposition to legalized abortion and said a special counsel was reviewing allegations that Justice Department officials conspired to force a computer software company into bankruptcy.

In a departure from recent judicial nominees' reticence about abortion, Barr said the Supreme Court decision legalizing abortion "was wrongly decided," and that he hoped it would be overturned so the issue could be decided by the states. ■

Bills Introduced To Stop Violence Against Women

Senate Judiciary Committee Chairman Joseph R. Biden Jr., D-Del., pushed legislation (S 15) to curb violence against women, but the measure was essentially set aside as Congress tried but failed to clear a comprehensive anti-crime bill (HR 3371).

"In the past year, 3 million women have been battered and the United States has set an all-time record for rapes," Biden said. S 15 sought to stiffen penalties for such crimes, doubling the federal penalty for rape to 10 years. It also established a commission on violent crime against women.

BOXSCORE

➧ **Violence Against Women (S 15, HR 1502).** The bills made it easier for victims of sexual assault crimes to bring civil rights suits against their attackers and increased penalties for sex crimes.

Report: S Rept 102-197.

KEY ACTION

July 18 — S 15 approved by **Senate Judiciary Committee** by voice vote.

The measure allowed victims of these crimes to bring civil rights suits against their attackers. It also increased penalties for sex crimes and mandated restitution for victims.

The bill authorized $300 million for law enforcement efforts to fight sex crimes, with $100 million earmarked for the 40 metropolitan areas most dangerous for women. Another $65 million was authorized for rape prevention and education.

Additionally, the measure required states to pay for a medical examination to determine whether a woman had been raped.

A similar measure was approved by the Judiciary panel in 1990, but time ran out in the 101st Congress before the full Senate could take up the measure. A companion bill (HR 1502) was introduced in the House by Barbara Boxer, D-Calif., but none of the five committees with jurisdiction took action on it.

Senate Committee Action

The Senate Judiciary Committee approved S 15 in July after members delayed action on the bill for two months so that it would not get entangled in debate over a broad anticrime package.

A week after the Senate passed its version of an anticrime bill (S 1241), the Judiciary Committee on July 18 approved S 15 by voice vote.

Before approving the bill, the panel adopted two amendments by Charles E. Grassley, R-Iowa. The first allowed victims to address the court after a guilty verdict, but before sentencing. The second expressed the sense of Congress that the media should not publish the names of rape victims.

The Justice Department opposed a provision that classified rape and other crimes against women as hate crimes violating federal civil rights laws. The provision allowed victims to sue their attackers on those grounds. The administration also objected to the cost of the bill, estimated at about $500 million. ■

Civil Rights Commission Extended Three Years

After working out a compromise, the House and Senate passed and President Bush signed legislation (HR 3350 — PL 102-167) extending the Civil Rights Commission for three years while ensuring that Congress maintained tight control over the organization.

The two chambers differed over the duration of the reauthorization, with the House approving a two-year bill and the Senate preferring a four-year extension. But they quickly struck a deal, and the bill was cleared in early November.

Background

Established in 1957 and restructured in 1983, the eight-person commission was responsible for examining discrimination in areas such as employment, housing and voting rights and reporting its findings to the Congress and the president. The executive and legislative branches each appointed four commissioners.

Democrats had been complaining since the early 1980s that the commission had abrogated its fact-finding responsibility. Civil rights activists claimed that these problems stemmed from the Reagan administration's efforts to destroy the organization by appointing commissioners hostile to important programs such as busing and affirmative action. *(Background, 1983 Almanac, p. 293)*

In 1989, when the commission was last authorized, members from both parties seriously considered eliminating it before deciding instead on a 22-month extension. *(1989 Almanac, p. 289)*

This time, while members praised some signs of improvement — better internal management and a reopening of some regional offices closed during the 1980s — lawmakers were still dissatisfied with the rate of progress. Don Edwards, D-Calif., chairman of the House Judiciary Subcommittee on Civil Rights, complained that the commission had produced only one report in the past two years.

On the other hand, Arthur A. Fletcher, chairman of the commission since February 1990, charged that Congress was unwilling to make the financial commitment needed to transform the commission into an effective organization. Fletcher complained that his staff of 108 people was a far cry from the 1983 level of 250.

House members "expect us to play in the Super Bowl, and they don't even give us enough players to have a practice game," he said in response to the $6 million authorization proposed in the House.

Fletcher said that the commission needed between $10.5 million and $12 million annually in order to carry out its mandate. He proposed a three-year authorization at the higher funding level. "If we haven't delivered at the end of that time," he said, "put us out of our misery."

BOXSCORE

➡ **Civil Rights Commission Reauthorization (HR 3350).** The bill reauthorized the Civil Rights Commission for three years, setting funding for fiscal 1992 at $7.16 million. Funding for the remaining two years was to be determined each successive period.

KEY ACTION

Sept. 24 — HR 3350 was approved by the **House** Judiciary Committee.

Sept. 25 — S 1754 passed the **Senate** by voice vote.

Sept. 30 — HR 3350 passed the **House** by voice vote.

Oct. 28 — HR 3350, as amended, passed the **Senate** by voice vote.

Nov. 6 — **House** agreed to the Senate amendments to HR 3350 by a vote of 420-7, clearing the bill for the president.

Nov. 26 — President Bush signed HR 3350 — PL 102-167.

House and Senate Action

In the House, HR 3350, sponsored by Edwards, was introduced on Sept. 17 and approved by the Judiciary Committee on Sept. 24.

The measure authorized the commission for two years and cut its annual budget from $7 million to $6 million. And while the bill passed the House by voice vote on Sept 30, members of both parties used the occasion to criticize the agency, though for different reasons.

"The commission seemed to be expending its energies more on divisive rhetoric," said House Judiciary Committee Committee Chairman Jack Brooks, D-Texas, during the debate on the House floor. He said the limited reauthorization was a warning to commission members to get more involved.

Republicans, on the other hand, questioned whether the commission served any useful purpose, especially at a time when the money was needed elsewhere.

Henry J. Hyde of Illinois highlighted the probationary nature of the bill when he warned that "Congress and the American people must have the confidence that [its work] is being performed in a thoughtful and focused manner."

Other GOP critics were more severe. "It's time to put this commission out of its misery," said F. James Sensenbrenner Jr., R-Wis.

Meanwhile, the Senate on Sept. 25 passed a four-year authorization bill (S 1754) introduced that same day.

This measure, which set no funding cap, left the commission with fewer restrictions than its counterpart in the House.

Both bills were a far cry from the 10-year reauthorization requested by the administration.

Final Action

A final compromise was worked out between Edwards and Sens. Paul Simon, D-Ill., and Orrin G. Hatch, R-Utah, chairman and ranking member, respectively, of the Senate Judiciary Subcommittee on the Constitution. Hatch, who favored the administration proposal, was concerned that a one- or two-year reauthorization would force the commission to devote its energies to its own survival, turning it into a "political football."

Edwards, on the other hand, wanted to use the authorization process to force the commission to make what he regarded as much-needed changes.

In crafting the compromise, a Senate Democratic staff member said, "we wanted to make sure we looked at the authorization every year, but we didn't want to leave them in limbo."

Commission officials were not pleased. "We would have liked a longer authorization and more money to accomplish the goals that Congress set out for us," a spokesman said.

As a result of the compromise, HR 3350 reauthorized the commission for three years with $7.16 million in fiscal 1992, including a one-time $1.2 million authorization to enable the commission to relocate its headquarters.

Funding for the remaining two years was to be determined each year. If no funding was approved during one of those two years, the commission was automatically reauthorized at the 1992 level.

Unlike the provisions of its last 22-month extension, which required the organization to shut down if it lacked an authorization, HR 3350 guaranteed the life of the commission for at least three years.

The Senate amended and passed the bill by voice vote on Oct. 28. On Nov. 6, the House (which had already passed HR 3350 on Sept 30) approved, by a vote of 420-7, a motion to suspend the rules and agree to the Senate amendment. The bill was signed by the president on Nov. 26. *(Vote 378, p. 92-H)* ■

Legal Services Corporation

Congress in 1991 failed to break an 11-year impasse over the reauthorization of the Legal Services Corporation (LSC), as legislation advanced no further than the Judiciary Committee in the House.

The committee on July 16 approved HR 2039 by a vote of 25-7. The measure offered a five-year reauthorization to the quasi-independent corporation, which provided federal funds for civil legal aid for the poor. No funding limits were set.

In the Senate, Warren B. Rudman, R-N.H., a longtime legal aid supporter, and Edward M. Kennedy, D-Mass., chairman of the Labor and Human Resources Committee, expressed an interest in reauthorizing the LSC, but no such measure was introduced.

BOXSCORE

➡ **Legal Services Corporation Reauthorization (HR 2039).** The bill sought to reauthorize the the Legal Services Corporation for five years, setting no funding limit.

KEY ACTION

July 16 — HR 2039 approved by the **House** Judiciary Committee by a vote of 25-7.

Background

The LSC had lacked formal authorization since 1980, as Democrats bickered with Republicans over how much freedom LSC-funded lawyers should have.

But 1991 witnessed a rapprochement between Hill Democrats and some Republicans.

"Some of the things that were controversial three years ago are not controversial anymore," said bill sponsor Barney Frank, D-Mass. He was referring to debate during President Ronald Reagan's administration over whether LSC lawyers should engage in political or social advocacy.

Debate over the LSC, created in 1974, boiled down to whether participating local attorneys should represent the poor only in specific civil cases such as divorces and landlord-tenant disputes, or should also engage in broader political and social causes, through class action lawsuits and lobbying. The Reagan administration, arguing that LSC lawyers spent too much time on political advocacy, tried to abolish the LSC.

Veto threats blocked enactment of any reauthorization bill in the 1980s. Lawmakers instead used appropriations bills to influence legal aid policy and to limit the ability of the LSC board, appointed by the administration through a series of recess appointments, to impose new restrictions on legal aid.

But with President Bush adopting a more conciliatory attitude and with a new board in place, much of the controversy over the agency faded. *(1990 Almanac, p. 531)*

The corporation received $328 million in funding for fiscal 1991 and $350 million for fiscal 1992 (PL 102-140). The House stripped the LSC appropriation from the Commerce, Justice and State (HR 2608) funding bill on June 13, in part for lack of authorization, but funding was restored in conference. *(Appropriations, p. 531)*

House Action

Recognizing that the appropriations process gave only limited direction to the LSC, House members wanted a reauthorization bill to set comprehensive rules for the LSC board and the lawyers who accepted its money.

HR 2039 included compromises aimed at making sure lawyers did not neglect needy clients in favor of high-profile causes.

One such provision was a ban on lawyers using LSC funds for federal- or state-level lobbying unless a client's legal rights or responsibilities were directly involved. Another was a prohibition on LSC lawyers' taking cases intended to revise or reapportion a congressional or state legislative district.

George W. Gekas, R-Pa., proposed a broader ban on lobbying, but the committee defeated it, 11-22.

The bill also barred any lawyer from encouraging a client to engage in any public demonstration, boycott or strike and allowed a class action lawsuit against the government only with the approval of the local legal aid group's project director and when it would primarily benefit a needy client.

Responding to complaints that LSC lawyers encouraged workers to bring frivolous complaints about wages and benefits, the measure allowed defendants to win attorneys' fees if a court ruled a plaintiff's lawsuit was "frivolous, unreasonable, or without foundation."

Additionally, it required recipients of LSC funds, when appropriate, to try to negotiate rather than sue.

To protect lawyers, the bill also precluded the LSC board from issuing other rules that would limit the types of cases lawyers took.

The bill required the corporation to study whether competitive bidding should be used to distribute LSC funds. In committee, Rep. Bill McCollum, R-Fla., pushed an amendment that would have mandated competitive bidding, saying it would ensure the most cost-efficient use of federal funds. But Judiciary Committee Chairman Jack Brooks, D-Texas, said the lowest bidder might not be the best professional.

Frank added that LSC recipients already were "the lowest paid lawyers by far who work for the federal government." The committee rejected the McCollum amendment, 10-23.

McCollum also tried to restrict cases that legal aid programs could take with non-federal funds. He said he wanted the lawyers to abide by federal restrictions, even when handling cases financed by state or private groups.

Several committee members said their state bar associations opposed that amendment, and it failed. ■

Other Legislation Moved in Judiciary Committees

The year saw the Judiciary committees in the House and Senate preoccupied with important legislation involving crime control and civil rights. But amid the headline-grabbing battles, the committees also tackled issues ranging from the upsurge in bankruptcy cases to civil suits against foreigners accused of crimes committed outside the United States. Most of the bills were still pending final action at the end of the first session.

BANKRUPTCY JUDGES

On Aug. 1, the Senate approved, by unanimous consent, a measure (S 646 — S Rept 102-156) to authorize the appointment of 32 new federal bankruptcy judges in districts that had seen a significant increase in bankruptcy filings.

The bill had won the voice vote approval of the Judiciary Committee the day before, but such quick action was confined to the Senate. In the House, the measure was passed over amid the flurry of larger issues, forcing proponents in the Senate to wait until 1992 for almost certain House passage.

Bill sponsor Dennis DeConcini, D-Ariz., claimed that in fiscal 1990 there was a 14.2 percent increase in the number of bankruptcy filings nationwide. Much of the boost resulted from a downturn in the real estate market and an increase in the number of failed financial institutions.

In 1991, there were 291 bankruptcy judges. The measure sought to create additional judgeships in Florida, Arizona, Georgia, California, Texas, New Jersey, Pennsylvania, New York, Connecticut, New Hampshire, Massachusetts and South Carolina.

CONFLICT OF INTEREST

Legislation (HR 3381) to allow the president to waive conflict of interest statutes when appointing people to temporary government posts awaited committee action at the end of the first session.

During crises, presidents sometimes appointed experts from the private sector, such as special envoys abroad. Under existing law, the same restrictions that governed permanent workers applied to those temporary employees. For example, a person who worked temporarily at an agency would not be able to lobby that agency for a year.

HR 3381 won the approval of the House Judiciary Subcommittee on Administrative Law and Governmental Relations on Oct. 23. At the behest of Chairman Barney Frank, D-Mass., the panel approved an amendment to cut down on paperwork by allowing the president to waive the conflict laws for groups of temporary appointees.

CONSOLIDATION OF LAWSUITS

Late on Nov. 25, the House passed by voice vote a measure (HR 2450 — H Rept 102-373) to allow federal district courts to consolidate 25 or more lawsuits arising in multiple state courts against the same defendant. The Senate did not act on the measure in 1991.

The House-passed bill allowed consolidation at the federal level only if: all the cases arose from the same incident, such as a plane crash; the plaintiffs each sued for more than $50,000 in damages; and the suits were pending in more than one state.

"The consequences of duplicative mass accident litigation are several," said William J. Hughes, D-N.J., chairman of the Intellectual Property Subcommittee and sponsor of the bill. "For victims, duplicative litigation can result in some accident victims recovering fully while others in the same accident recover nothing, for no better reason than that the judges, juries and lawyers were different. For defendants, duplicative litigation can result in the imposition of multiple punitive damage awards."

HR 2450 had won the voice vote approval on Nov. 6 of the House Judiciary Subcommittee on Intellectual Property and Judicial Administration. The full committee approved the bill on Nov. 19.

COPYRIGHT RENEWAL

On Nov. 25, both chambers passed by voice vote separate but similar measures (HR 2372 — H Rept 102-379, S 756 — S Rept 102-194) to eliminate the requirement for certain authors to formally seek a second term of copyright protection for their works. Each term lasted 47 years.

The measures sought to create an automatic renewal system for all works copyrighted before 1978. For works copyrighted in 1978 or later, the law already provided a copyright term of 50 years after the death of the author.

Both bills also included a provision to renew the National Film Registry at the Library of Congress to preserve significant U.S.-made movies.

In addition, S 756 included a "fair use" provision allowing libraries and archives to provide single photocopies of copyrighted materials for use by students and scholars. HR 2372 had also included this provision, but it was dropped during subcommittee markup.

S 756 had won voice vote approval by the Senate Judiciary Committee on Aug. 1.

In the House, HR 2372 won voice vote approval in the Judiciary Subcommittee on Intellectual Property and Judicial Administration on Oct. 1. The full committee approved the measure by voice vote on Nov. 19.

Both bills were left for consideration in 1992, with members in both chambers calling for the naming of conferees to resolve differences.

TORTURE SUITS

Legislation (HR 2092 — H Rept 102-367) to allow U.S. citizens to file civil lawsuits against foreigners who were residing in the United States but who had engaged in torture or execution outside the country passed the House by voice vote on Nov. 25.

A similar measure (S 313 — S Rept 102-249) won the voice vote approval of the Senate Judiciary Committee on Nov. 21, with passage by the full Senate expected in early 1992.

Both bills sought to allow such suits to be filed within 10 years of the alleged abuse. The victim was to have exhausted all legal remedies in the country where the torture took place. In addition, the defendant had to have acted under the authority of his government.

Arlen Specter, R-Pa., sponsor of S 313, claimed that the bill was needed so that the United States would not become a haven for foreigners who had engaged in torture or other human rights violations.

HR 2092 won the voice vote approval of the House Judiciary Subcommittee on International Law, Immigration and Refugees on Sept. 11. On Nov. 19, the Judiciary and Foreign Affairs committees each approved HR 2092 by voice vote. ■

Resident Status for Aliens In the Armed Forces

Congress cleared and President Bush signed legislation (S 296 — PL 102-110) that gave resident alien status to foreigners who served in the U.S. armed forces.

Those who were serving at least a second six-year tour or who had been honorably discharged after 12 or more years of duty were eligible to become resident aliens and U.S. citizens. The vast majority of the 5,000 people who were immediately eligible for resident alien status were Filipinos, with the remainder from Micronesia, Palau and the Marshall Islands.

By treaty, citizens of those nations could enlist in the U.S. armed forces but could not become officers or hold positions that required a security clearance because they were not U.S. residents. Most of these aliens served as support staff on Navy vessels.

Similar legislation was passed by the House in 1990, but never came to the Senate floor because of the press of other business. This time the Senate acted first, passing the measure by voice vote on Jan. 30.

In the House, the bill was approved by the Subcommittee on Immigration, Refugees and International Law on May 15 by a vote of 8-0.

The full committee followed suit with a voice vote approval on June 18, leading to House passage on Sept. 24., also by voice vote.

President Bush signed S 296 into law on Oct. 1. ■

Naturalization Procedures, Visa Requirements Eased

Wrapping two immigration bills together, Congress on the final day of the session cleared a measure (HR 3049 — PL 102-232) that partially restored the exclusive authority of the courts to naturalize citizens and eased temporary visa requirements for entertainers and artists.

As passed by the House on Nov. 12, HR 3049 had dealt with only the court's naturalization authority. But the Senate amended it to include the temporary visa provisions, passing the bill by voice vote on Nov. 26. The House approved the amended bill by voice vote on Nov. 27 and President Bush signed it on Dec. 12.

Until 1991, federal and state courts had exclusive jurisdiction over the process of naturalizing American citizens. While the Immigration and Naturalization Service (INS) handled all citizenship applications, making recommendations that the courts almost always heeded, the judges usually administered the oath of citizenship.

But after applicants complained about waiting years to become citizens because of court delays, Congress gave people the option to be sworn in by the INS.

This option was included in the omnibus Immigration and Naturalization Act of 1990 (PL 101-649). *(1990 Almanac, p. 474)*

That in turn brought complaints from some judges who claimed that they had lost a fundamental power.

HR 3049 gave the state and federal courts the option of naturalizing citizens. If a court did not request exclusive jurisdiction, or no swearing-in ceremony was scheduled within 45 days, resident aliens could ask the INS to naturalize them.

The bill also required the INS to expedite the applications of persons with grave illnesses or other special circumstances.

Introduced in the House on July 25, HR 3049 was approved by the Subcommittee on Immigration, Refugees and International Law on Sept. 12 and the full committee on Oct. 29 — on both occasions the bill won voice vote approval.

The measure passed the House by voice vote on Nov. 12. It won voice vote approval in the Senate on Nov. 26, where it was amended to include the provisions of HR 3048, the legislation easing visa requirements for artists and entertainers.

The House passed the newly amended bill the next day by voice vote.

New Visa Rules

As cleared, HR 3049 relaxed conditions on foreigners applying in the so-called P and O visa categories — primarily people such as artists and entertainers recognized internationally for their performance or extraordinary ability.

The legislation was prompted by provisions of the 1990 immigration law (PL 101-649) that made it more difficult for performers to gain entry into the United States. Those provisions, adopted somewhat inadvertently, had been temporarily suspended.

BOXSCORE

➡ **Restoring the Courts' Naturalization Power, New Visa Rules for Artists (HR 3049, HR 3048).** The bill partially restored the judiciary's exclusive authority to naturalize citizens and eased temporary visa requirements for artists and entertainers.

Reports: HR 3049 — H Rept 102-287; HR 3048 — H Rept 102-380).

KEY ACTION

Oct. 29 — HR 3049 was approved by the **House** Judiciary Committee by voice vote.

Nov. 12 — HR 3049 passed the **House** by voice vote.

Nov. 13 — HR 3048 was approved by voice vote by the **House** Judiciary Subcommittee on International Law, Immigration and Refugees.

Nov. 19 — HR 3048 was approved by the **House** Judiciary Committee by voice vote.

Nov. 25 — HR 3048 passed the **House** by voice vote.

Nov. 26 — The **Senate** passed HR 3049 by voice vote after amending it to include the provisions of HR 3048.

Nov. 27 — The **House** passed HR 3049, as amended, by voice vote.

Dec. 12 — President Bush signed HR 3049 — PL 102-232.

HR 3049 also allowed certain support personnel accompanying entertainers to obtain temporary visas. The measure required the attorney general to consult with labor and management organizations to determine the need for such foreign workers in the United States. In addition, the General Accounting Office was commissioned to study U.S. policy and that of other countries on the admission of athletes and entertainers. The report was due Oct. 1, 1994. ■

Chapter 6

LABOR/ VETERANS/ HOUSING

Unemployment Benefits Extended

Despite a six-month effort, it took a last-minute deal and two measures to satisfy everyone's demands

After months of haggling over a temporary extension of unemployment benefits, it took the crafting of two measures to finally satisfy the demands of both chambers and the administration. Two previous bills had been blocked by the White House.

Even the third attempt to aid the long-term jobless would have fallen apart if disgruntled senators had not struck a last-minute deal with the administration that kept one bill on the fast track and sent another to the House.

President Bush had agreed to sign a $5.3 billion bill (HR 3575) to extend unemployment benefits for either six, 13 or 20 weeks, depending on a formula devised by House leaders and the administration. Some of the senators whose states would have received only six weeks argued that they had been left out of the deal-making.

To keep the first bill on track, Bush agreed to sign a trade bill (HR 1724 — PL 102-182) with new provisions that raised the six-week states to the 13-week tier and allowed workers in all states to qualify for extra benefits if they exhausted their state unemployment benefits after March 1 and were still unemployed. HR 3575 had excluded workers in 19 states from that eligibility. *(Andean initiative, p. 127)*

As scheduled, the Senate cleared HR 3575 on Nov. 15 and immediately sent it to the presidential retreat in western Maryland, Camp David, where it was signed that night.

Congress cleared HR 1724 on Nov. 26, one day before departing for the year. The president signed the bill Dec. 4.

The two bills capped a six-month effort to get checks out to the long-term jobless as economic barometers gave off mixed signals on whether the recession was subsiding or getting worse. Bush continued to thwart the efforts of congressional Democrats to get an unemployment measure enacted by citing the more optimistic reports on the number of jobless. The president disagreed that the economic climate warranted triggering emergency spending.

Under the 1990 budget agreement between the White House and Congress, any new programs had to be paid for by cuts in other programs or by tax increases. An emergency that warranted adding to the deficit had to be declared by Congress and seconded with a signature from the president in order for the cost to be borne straight out of the Treasury.

On the first round, Bush signed a bill (HR 3201 — PL 102-107) Aug. 17 but because he refused to designate an unemployment emergency, the money could not be spent.

The second effort culminated in a bill (S 1722) that was vetoed Oct. 11. Senate Republicans narrowly quashed a major effort to override the veto.

It was only after Bush agreed in late October that a bill to extend unemployment benefits was essential in the pre-election year of 1991 that House and Senate leaders seriously began crafting a measure that he would sign. The president said he would continue to veto any measure that either broke the 1990 budget agreement or that sought to raise taxes.

Congress and Bush finally compromised on several mechanisms to cover the costs of the extended benefits. HR 3575 tightened a loophole on those paying quarterly taxes; extended a law allowing Internal Revenue Service collection of debts owed the federal government; extended the federal unemployment tax at 0.08 percent; and garnisheed the wages of those who defaulted on student loans.

Bush, by agreeing to give states either 13 or 20 weeks of extended benefits, provided far more than the Democrats had initially asked for. The changes in HR 1724 added $380 million to the original $5.3 billion unemployment measure, according to administration estimates.

But while lawmakers congratulated each other for finally reaching a compromise to get extra money to jobless workers before Thanksgiving, the hard exercise of getting an unemployment extension passed exposed weaknesses in the entire benefits system.

"This is a temporary fix in a program that is completely broken," Rep. Thomas J. Downey, D-N.Y., said. "Until there is a permanent fix in the law, we are going to find ourselves in this situation recession after recession."

Even so, the ultimate passage of the bill proved the political necessity of getting the money paid out in 1991.

Congress had not voted to extend unemployment benefits for the jobless since 1983, when legislation (PL 98-135) was approved to extend a temporary program of extra benefits through March 31, 1985.

A major argument in 1991 was over whether the bill would provide a short-term payout of supplemental benefits rather than permanently altering the system. Bush's opposition to a permanent fix pushed Congress to extend the benefits only into 1992.

FIRST ROUND: HR 3201

After intense political maneuvering over jobless benefits and how to pay for them, Congress reached a temporary bipartisan truce in time for its August recess and cleared legislation (HR 3201) to help jobless workers. The measure, approved Aug. 2, was designed to give up to 20 weeks of extra compensation to 3 million unemployed workers.

But despite Republican acquiescence and Bush's signing the bill, the Democratic-sponsored measure did not go into effect. The bill contained no offsetting revenues, and Bush declined to declare an emergency, a step necessary to pay out the estimated $5.3 billion in benefits the bill provided for.

Provisions

Sen. Lloyd Bentsen, D-Texas, was chiefly responsible for crafting the measure that prevailed in both chambers. Depending upon a state's unemployment rate, it provided

BOXSCORE

➡ **Unemployment Benefits (HR 3575, amended in HR 1724).** Unemployment compensation was originally extended for the long-term jobless for six, 13 or 20 extra weeks. Because that measure drew protests from senators whose states would get only six weeks' extra benefits, Congress and the president agreed to move a second bill, raising the six-week states to the 13-week tier and allowing all workers in all states to qualify for extra benefits if they had exhausted their state benefits after March 1 and were still without jobs. The bill tightened a loophole on those paying quarterly taxes; extended the federal unemployment tax; and garnisheed wages of those who defaulted on student loans.

Reports: H Rept 102-184; H Rept 102-185; H Rept 102-391.

KEY ACTION

Aug. 1 — S 1554 was passed by the **Senate** by voice vote.

Aug. 2 — HR 3201 was passed by the **House** by 375-45, after it accepted the text of S 1554.

Aug. 2 — HR 3201 was cleared by the **Senate** by voice vote.

Aug. 17 — President Bush signed HR 3201 — PL 102-107, but said he would not designate an unemployment emergency. Hence the money could not be spent.

Sept. 17 — The **House** passed HR 3040, 283-125.

Sept. 24 — The **Senate** passed S 1722, 69-30.

Sept. 25 — The **House** voted again on HR 3040, 294-127.

Sept. 26 — **House-Senate** conference approved compromise measure.

Oct. 1 — The **Senate** adopted conference report, 65-35; the **House** cleared it, 300-118.

Oct. 11 — President Bush vetoed S 1722.

Oct. 16 — The **Senate** voted 65-35, falling two votes short of a veto override.

Oct. 22 — **House** Ways and Means approved HR 3575, 22-14.

Nov. 13 — **House** Ways and Means approved a substitute to HR 3575, 22-14.

Nov. 14 — The **House** passed HR 3575, 396-30.

Nov. 15 — The **Senate** cleared HR 3575, 91-2; passed HR 1724 by voice vote. President Bush signed HR 3575 — PL 102-164.

Nov. 20 — The **House** amended and passed HR 1724, 407-21.

Nov. 26 — The **Senate** passed by voice vote; the **House** cleared the conference report on HR 1724 by voice vote.

Dec. 4 — President Bush signed HR 1724 — PL-102-182.

for four to 20 weeks of benefits in addition to the standard 26 weeks.

Under existing law, insured workers who had received 26 weeks of benefits and who lived in states with high unemployment rates were eligible to receive an additional 13 weeks of compensation. But only workers in Alaska, Maine, Rhode Island and Puerto Rico already qualified for those extra 13 weeks.

Bentsen's bill switched the trigger for additional benefits from an insured unemployment rate, which only counted people who qualified to receive compensation, to a total unemployment rate, which counted everyone who was out of work.

The extra benefits were to be paid out Sept. 1, 1991, through July 4, 1992. The bill covered workers who ran out of their 26 weeks of compensation April 1 or later.

Background

For three years, Downey tried to attract Democrats to the unemployment issue.

In 1990, he proposed allowing workers in metropolitan areas to qualify for 13 weeks of extended benefits even though the state did not qualify. That would have required raising the unemployment insurance taxes paid by employers — enough to add $8 billion to the coffers by fiscal 1995. *(1990 Almanac, p. 368)*

What tripped him up was getting members to vote for a tax increase. "This is just a very contentious issue," he acknowledged. "Employers don't want to pay any more taxes, ever."

With the recession worsening in 1991, Downey was looking to see whether new taxes could be deferred until after the economy improved. And he was looking at the possibility of a millionaire's surcharge tax. As acting chairman of the Ways and Means Subcommittee on Human Resources, he held a series of hearings on the unemployment compensation system.

In Downey's Long Island district, the largest single employer was Grumman Aerospace Corp., a defense contractor. There was the potential for massive unemployment if the Defense Department canceled its contract for the F-14D airplane.

Nationwide, about 40 percent of unemployed workers received benefits, compared with about 70 percent during the 1970s. Only two states, Rhode Island and Alaska, had released the federal trigger allowing them to provide 13 weeks of extended benefits on top of the standard 26 weeks.

Downey wanted to reshape the system so that it would be more uniform across the country and more easily trigger extended benefits.

His proposal, which received the blessing of organized labor, was antithetical to those of the business community, which paid the bulk of the unemployment tax.

House Subcommittee Action

Downey introduced his jobless benefits bill (HR 1367) on March 11, proposing to double the standard 26 weeks of benefits.

To pay for it, he proposed raising employer-paid taxes to bring in an additional $6 billion in fiscal 1992 — a 100 percent increase over the $5.4 billion expected under existing law. The legislation would have reduced the federal unemployment tax rate to 0.3 percent from 0.8 percent, but would have raised the taxable wage base from the existing $7,000 to $55,800 in 1992.

Downey's bill faced immediate hurdles: the reluctance of members of the full Ways and Means Committee to raise taxes and a general perception that the economy was starting to pick up.

But for the third year in a row, Downey pushed the bill through his Ways and Means panel. On a party-line voice vote June 26, the Subcommittee on Human Resources approved HR 1367, a scaled-down version of Downey's unemployment benefits proposal.

Recognizing the difficult road his bill faced, Downey offered the scaled-down substitute. His original bill would have cost about $23 billion over six years. The substitute would have cost about $9 billion over the same period.

Downey would have replaced the extended benefits program with a three-tiered system:

- If a state's unemployment rate reached 6 percent and that was 120 percent of the average unemployment rate for the past two years, workers would automatically qualify for an additional 10 weeks of benefits on top of the usual 26 weeks.
- At 7 percent, 15 weeks of benefits would kick in.
- At 8 percent, 20 more weeks of compensation would be available.

And, for fiscal 1992, if the national unemployment rate hit 6 percent, then all states would qualify for 10 more weeks of benefits for the unemployed.

An amendment by Jim McDermott, D-Wash., would have let workers collect unemployment benefits for a year if they lost their jobs because of closure of a military base or federal government efforts to protect an endangered species. Unemployment among loggers had been a big problem in McDermott's state because of efforts to save the northern spotted owl. The panel agreed to the amendment by voice vote.

Senate Democratic Action

Senate Democrats began to look early at unemployment as a potentially hot political topic for the 1992 election season.

At the behest of the Democratic Caucus, Finance Committee Chairman Bentsen proposed a $6 billion emergency plan to provide additional benefits to unemployed workers.

The administration, which insisted that the recession was ending and the economy was looking up, immediately came out against the plan.

Richard G. Darman, director of the Office of Management and Budget (OMB), said July 17 that the government already took care of unemployed workers and did not approve of extending benefits either on an emergency basis or a pay-as-you-go plan.

Unlike the House bill, Bentsen's plan would be a temporary measure that would not raise taxes. Instead, Bentsen would have Congress declare an emergency, allowing it to avoid the 1990 White-House congressional budget law requirement to raise the money to pay for any spending.

Bentsen said he was persuaded that the unemployment situation had become an emergency, too, as he saw benefits expiring in the states even though workers had not yet found jobs. In June, the national unemployment rate hit 7 percent, up from a low of 5.3 percent the previous June, according to the Bureau of Labor Statistics.

As an incentive to senators to support the plan, Bentsen proposed giving every state at least four weeks of extended benefits, paid solely by the federal government. States with a 6 percent total unemployment rate would receive 7 weeks of benefits; states with 7 percent unemployment would get 13 weeks; and states with an unemployment rate of 8 percent or more would receive 20 weeks.

Those rates would be based on a six-month average of the total unemployment rate. Payments would begin Oct. 1 but would reach back to include people who used up their benefits April 1 or later. The extended benefits would last through June 30, 1992.

The Senate legislation would also allow veterans who had just left the service — including those who were in the Persian Gulf War — to collect unemployment benefits for 26 weeks. They were only entitled to collect 13 weeks' worth of unemployment compensation. This was the only provision of the plan that would be permanent.

Bentsen said the total cost would come to $5.8 billion over five years. Of that, $5.4 billion would be spent in fiscal 1992. He also said there was already more than $8 billion in the federal unemployment trust fund from federal unemployment taxes paid by employers. But that money was not kept separate from the general Treasury fund, which covered the deficit, and administration officials said they would have to borrow that money, increasing the nation's debt.

Downey/Bentsen Bill Compromise

Until mid-July, it looked like once again that Downey was short the votes to move a measure through the full Ways and Means Committee. Even committee Chairman Dan Rostenkowski, D-Ill., was uninterested.

But when Senate Democrats decided as a group to do something, dynamics in the House shifted abruptly. House Speaker Thomas S. Foley, D-Wash., took Rostenkowski aside and told him to drum up some enthusiasm for Downey's bill.

Before Ways and Means marked up the bill July 30, Rostenkowski trimmed back Downey's $9 billion proposal to $5.6 billion. But other committee members resisted the employer tax provisions, which would have increased the amount of a worker's salary that could be taxed from $7,000 to $69,800. The committee stripped the tax increase out of the bill.

That left two key differences between the Downey and Bentsen bills. Both would have cost roughly the same amount of money and provided similar benefits. But Downey's bill was a permanent plan to change the unemployment insurance system, while Bentsen's would last just under a year.

And Downey's measure considered Bush's signature on the legislation to be a declaration of an emergency. Bentsen required Bush to sign the bill and to sign a separate document certifying the emergency situation.

Some House Democrats feared Bentsen's plan would allow Bush to sign the bill but not sign off on the emergency, letting the issue slip away. "We want him to make a decision one way or another," Downey said.

However, Downey's way could have violated the budget agreement, which required both Congress and Bush to declare an emergency.

If Bush vetoed the unemployment bill and Congress overrode that veto, then the law would be enacted without the president declaring an emergency.

That troubled not only Republicans but also Senate Democrats, who insisted that the House yield to their proposal.

Once the agreement was struck among Democrats, House Republicans said they would let the measure come to a vote.

Neither the House nor Senate bill was acceptable to Bush, according to White House spokesman Marlin Fitzwater. He said that if the legislation included budget cuts to pay for the new program, Bush might consider it. Without such cuts, Fitzwater said Bush would veto any such bill.

Senate Committee Action

The Senate Finance Committee voted 16-4 July 25 to report out the $6 billion measure (S 1554) crafted by Bentsen. Voting against the bill in committee were Republicans Bob Dole, Kan., minority leader; William V. Roth Jr., Del.; Steve Symms, Idaho; and Orrin G. Hatch, Utah.

"We think we are coming out of the recession, and now is not the time to be piling on a big spending program when indeed the recovery has the promise of creating jobs and carrying through on ending the recession," Fitzwater said July 24.

At the markup, Dole complained that Bentsen's plan to declare an emergency to pay for the bill would violate the budget agreement. He offered an amendment to limit the program. First, he proposed using the rate of jobless people who were covered by unemployment insurance, rather than the total unemployment rate. That would weed out college students and others who should not qualify, he said. For states with more than 5 percent he would give six more weeks of benefits; over 5 percent would bring on 13 more weeks.

The panel rejected Dole's amendment, 6-13.

Dole then objected to the provision that would have required all states to provide people who had just left military service with 26 weeks of compensation, rather than 13 weeks. Non-military people in most states got up to 26 weeks of unemployment compensation paid through taxes by employers.

He said it was unfair to give unemployment benefits to those who had voluntarily left the military, when civilians did not get the same benefits when they quit or retired from a job. The panel, by voice vote, rejected his amendment to modify the provision.

Dole also suggested repealing a luxury tax on boats costing more than $100,000, which some members contended cost more to collect than it brought in.

But tax bills were required by parliamentary procedure to originate in the House, not the Senate. "The reason to put it on this bill is to kill it," Bentsen said. Bentsen's motion to table the amendment was approved, 12-6.

Finally, Dole offered an amendment to delete the bill's requirement that Bush declare an emergency to pay for extra jobless benefits. The panel rejected Dole's move by voice vote.

Senate Floor Action

Dole said he would not gum up the works on the Senate floor as long as he could offer one alternative plan and if Democrats would not insist upon a roll call vote.

Dole's substitute would have cost $3.2 billion in fiscal 1992 and would have provided up to 10 weeks of benefits.

However, Dole would have adhered to the pay-as-you-go rules of the budget agreement, raising $3.4 billion from auctioning frequencies on the electromagnetic spectrum for new communications uses and keeping tax refunds that would have gone to people who had defaulted on student loans.

On Aug. 1, the Senate rejected his amendment by voice vote and adopted the Bentsen bill, also by voice vote.

House Action

On Aug. 2, the Ways and Means Committee agreed to Bentsen's version of the unemployment bill, sending it quickly to the House floor that same day.

Only moments before the House voted 375-45 for the bill, Bush reiterated his belief that the economy was recovering. He pointed to a Labor Department report released earlier in the day showing that the rate of unemployment in July had dropped 0.2 percent to 6.8 percent. While acknowledging that the rate was "still too high," Bush said unemployment was "moving in the right direction." *(Vote 253, p. 62-H)*

Administration officials said the president would sign the legislation but not the emergency designation that would release the funds.

"We're going to take a little bit of heat, but that's life," said one Bush official. "Obviously we're not anxious to have people say we don't care about the unemployed."

The Senate passed HR 3201 later that day by voice vote, clearing the measure for Bush's signature.

Rostenkowski said that Democrats let Bush off the hook by not forcing him to veto the bill. "We gave the president every way out," he said.

The original House bill (HR 3040) would have considered Bush's signature on the legislation to be a declaration of an emergency. In reconciling the two measures, Democrats gave Bush the leeway to sign the bill but not declare the costs of the bill an emergency. Without that second step, the benefits could not be triggered.

House Democratic leaders agreed to give up their version of the bill for the Senate's when they heard that Sen. Phil Gramm, R-Texas, had threatened to filibuster the House provisions.

House Democrats also argued that they had not lost what had snowballed over the course of two weeks into a huge political issue.

Presidential Action

Citing improved economic indicators, Bush announced Aug. 15 that he would not take the step necessary to implement legislation that would have given from four to 20 weeks of extra compensation to 3 million unemployed workers.

Bush said at his vacation home in Kennebunkport, Maine, that while he would sign the $5.3 billion bill (HR 3201) extending unemployment benefits, he would not "bust the budget" by agreeing with Congress that the money was emergency spending.

Foley vowed Aug. 16 that Democrats would force the president to provide extended unemployment benefits when Congress returned in September.

ROUND TWO: S 1722

Democrats found during the August recess that the unemployment issue embarrassed Republicans and played well with constituents. Foley met Sept. 11 with other top leaders of the House and Senate, and they agreed to move quickly on unemployment legislation.

The House passed a $6.3 billion measure (HR 3040) Sept. 17 that would not give Bush the wiggle room of the previous measure. He would be forced to either sign it or veto it, without the outlet of an emergency spending trigger. The bill also called for permanent changes to the unemployment system.

The key battleground became the Senate, where a less

confrontational version of the bill (S 1722) passed on Sept. 24. Even after Congress cleared a conference version Oct. 1 that conceded to the Senate on almost every substantive point but the mandatory language, the Senate still could not muster the two-thirds necessary to override a veto.

As expected, Bush on Oct. 11 vetoed the bill, complaining that it was too expensive.

On Oct. 16, Republicans stopped the Senate from overriding Bush's veto. The vote was 65-35, falling two votes short of the two-thirds necessary for an override. *(Vote 221, p. 29-S)*

Provisions

The $6.4 billion measure would have given an additional seven weeks of unemployment benefits to workers in 30 states and the District of Columbia, an additional 13 weeks to workers in 14 states and an additional 20 weeks to workers in six states where unemployment exceeded 8 percent. The bill would have expired July 4, 1992.

Background

Democratic leaders continued to approach the unemployment issue in a sharply partisan fashion, attacking Bush for his willingness to aid the people of foreign countries over his own.

Bush fought off Democratic attempts to aid unemployed workers by arguing that the economy was on the upswing. But even the House Republicans returned from the August break with tales of woe about their districts' economies.

And a study by the Center on Budget and Policy Priorities reported that in July, the largest number of workers in any month since at least 1950 exhausted their state unemployment benefits without being eligible for any additional unemployment money. Almost 350,000 people had exhausted their state benefits, but only 18,000 were receiving extended benefits.

Initially, neither the administration nor the Democrats indicated any desire to compromise. The Office of Management and Budget (OMB), in a statement of administration policy, charged that offering extra weeks of unemployment compensation would encourage workers not to work.

But Democratic leaders believed they had a winning issue — one that had grabbed headlines and allowed them to pound the president for insensitivity toward Americans in crisis. They even considered the possibilities of overturning a certain veto of S 1722.

Congress, however, had never overturned a Bush veto, failing in 11 previous attempts. And the president stood his ground on this bill as well.

House Action

Refusing to retreat after the earlier defeat in August, the House on Sept. 17 voted overwhelmingly to pass a $6.3 billion unemployment measure (HR 3040) to provide up to 20 extra weeks of compensation to jobless workers. The 283-125 vote gave Democrats 11 more ayes than necessary to exceed the two-thirds margin needed to override Bush. Forty-eight Republicans supported the bill, eight more than the Democrats had predicted. *(Vote 267, p. 64-H)*

And what were temporary provisions under the bill to provide an additional four to 20 weeks of unemployment compensation on top of the usual 26 weeks became permanent changes providing an additional five to 20 weeks of compensation.

The House resoundingly killed an amendment by Ways and Means Chairman Rostenkowski that would have paid for the bill by raising the maximum salary that could be taxed. His amendment, rejected by 65-341, would also have given Bush the option of declaring an emergency and eliminating the increased taxes. *(Vote 264, p. 64-H)*

Republicans attacked the Democrats for busting the budget agreement. Under that agreement, Congress and the president would have had to declare an emergency in order to pay for something without raising money to cover the costs. The House bill declared an emergency. But if Bush vetoed the bill and was overridden, the law would have gone into effect without the emergency declaration.

Budget Chairman Leon E. Panetta, D-Calif., argued that that did not undermine the budget agreement because "no one ever intended Congress to lose the right to override a veto."

Minority Whip Newt Gingrich, R-Ga., also accused Democrats of paying the jobless, rather than working to create jobs. The House Rules Committee refused to allow Gingrich to offer a substitute that, among other things, would have killed the existing tax on capital gains and allowed first-time home buyers to use their Individual Retirement Account funds for their down payments.

On the floor, Gingrich offered a motion to send the bill back to committee to add his amendment, but it was ruled out of order.

And Bill Archer, R-Texas, the ranking minority member of the Ways and Means Committee, tried to persuade the House to rewrite the bill to allow Bush to have until the end of 1991 to declare an emergency and release the benefits. The House rejected his motion, 129-279. *(Vote 266, p. 64-H)*

Republicans thought they could trip up the bill once it reached the Senate by refusing, 84-324, to take out a provision that raised money from states for unemployed school workers, such as custodians, crossing guards and cafeteria workers. Such a revenue-raiser could have opened the bill up to divisive tax amendments. But the Senate was not considering the House bill, making the point moot. *(Vote 265, p. 64-H)*

Although the House had voted on the bill on Sept. 17, members voted again, for procedural reasons, on Sept. 25, and the vote was 294-127. That was 13 votes more than the two-thirds present and voting that would be needed to override a veto. *(Vote 280, p. 68-H)*

Senate Action

The Senate passed a weaker bill (leaving it up to Bush to declare the emergency necessary to put it into effect) on Sept. 24 by a vote of 69-30. *(Vote 205, p. 27-S)*

The Senate had begun debate four days earlier on its $5.8 billion bill (S 1722), the same one that had been sent to Bush in August. The Senate version would require Bush to sign a separate declaration of a budget emergency in order to release the money to pay for the extra weeks of unemployment benefits.

Bentsen, primary author of the bill, indicated that he was leaning toward supporting a provision in the House bill that would definitely lead to a clash. The House would give Bush no choice — he would either have to sign the bill or veto it.

Bentsen's bill was a temporary measure, designed solely to aid those hurt by the recession. And many Republicans had said they were uncomfortable with permanently changing the system.

The House bill would have permanently changed the trigger for extra benefits to the total unemployment rate.

Workers could qualify for 10, 15 or 20 more weeks of benefits if their state unemployment rate reached 6, 7 or 8 percent. All states under 6 percent would get five extra weeks of benefits for their workers.

The Senate bill, on the other hand, temporarily would have changed the extra benefits trigger during the recessionary period. Workers could receive seven, 13 or 20 more weeks of benefits if their state jobless rate hit 6, 7 or 8 percent. Workers in all other states would get four more weeks.

Neither bill would have followed the pay-as-you-go requirement of 1990's budget agreement. Instead, each would have declared a budget emergency, thus adding to the federal deficit.

Dole again proposed to cover the cost by raising $4 billion by auctioning airwave frequencies and allowing the Internal Revenue Service to collect delinquent student loans out of tax refunds. The extra $1.5 billion would have gone toward cutting the deficit.

But Democrats continued to dismiss the Dole bill, saying it did not go far enough.

Attention was focused on the Senate, where just four switched votes would have meant victory for Bush. Dole said he had the votes to sustain a veto. And Bob Packwood, R-Ore., a cosponsor of the bill, conceded that he was worried that Bush might be able to sway three or four of the 13 Republican senators who supported the bill.

Conference Action

A House-Senate conference resolved differences between the two versions on Sept. 26, adopting the House requirement that Bush either sign or veto the bill. Unlike the House version of the bill, the conference version was temporary, designed to see people through the recession. It would expire July 4, 1992. In fact, the House conceded to the Senate on almost every substantive point but the veto language. Both chambers voted on the conference report Oct. 1, clearing the measure for the president.

The conference bill gave an additional seven weeks of unemployment benefits to workers in 30 states and the District of Columbia; an additional 13 weeks of compensation to workers in 14 states; and an additional 20 weeks of benefits to workers in six states where unemployment exceeded 8 percent.

Sen. Gramm, who helped lead the fight against the Democrats, said it would be easy to win over the votes he needed. He expected Republicans to switch their votes gracefully because the conference committee had changed the measure.

But Sen. Dave Durenberger, R-Minn., a supporter of the bill, said reversing a vote because of a slight change in the bill "would be tough to explain to voters."

Of the 13 Republican senators who voted for the bill, four had supported it from the start, beginning with the Finance Committee vote in July. They were: John H. Chafee, R.I.; Durenberger; John C. Danforth, Mo.; and cosponsor Packwood. Only Charles E. Grassley, R-Iowa, voted for the bill in committee and against it on the floor.

One other, Mark O. Hatfield, Ore., said he would not switch. "Not me. With all my loggers unemployed?"

Six of the 13 were up for re-election in 1992 and would be forced to explain their votes before the sting of the recession had faded.

Of those six, only Christopher S. Bond of Missouri faced a safe race. The other five — Bob Kasten, Wis.; Packwood; John Seymour, Calif.; Alfonse M. D'Amato, N.Y.; and Arlen Specter, Pa. — faced difficult re-election bids.

That left Conrad Burns, Mont.; James M. Jeffords, Vt.; and William S. Cohen, Maine. Unemployed workers in Montana and Vermont would qualify for an extra 13 weeks of benefits; Maine would receive the maximum 20 additional weeks.

"We have got some hurting, especially in the timber and wood industry," Burns said. But he conceded the next vote would be tough. "I'm going to have to consider the president's position."

That position was not to be taken lightly. "I never underestimate the power of the president," Packwood said.

For Democrats, more was at stake than unemployment compensation. They saw the issue as a political sledgehammer against a president with an iron lock on the White House.

"It's a huge winner," Downey said. "It's a defining issue for the party, and the party has been woefully short of issues these past few months."

In Fall River, Mass., Democrat Barney Frank represented a district hit hard by the recession. He argued that the issue resonated throughout the ranks of the employed, with storekeepers, landlords and relatives feeling the pain of the jobless, too.

"It's a pretty good marker for whether you care or don't care," Frank said. "It's the most graphic illustration of Bush's incorrect priorities."

But to conservative Republicans, the Democrats were only exposing their addiction to spending.

Gingrich predicted that the Senate would sustain Bush's veto and Democrats would be to blame for the unemployed who did not receive their benefits. It was the Democrats, he said, who refused to compromise.

Gingrich said he was prepared to vote for a less costly plan offered by Dole that Bush was willing to sign.

House Republicans never offered the Dole plan. Instead, Gingrich pushed a package of tax measures, including a reduction in the capital gains tax.

Gramm offered that same proposal in the Senate. He failed to table a point of order against his amendment, by a vote of 39-60. *(Vote 202, p. 27-S)*

Twelve of the 13 Republican senators who voted for the Democratic bill also supported Dole's plan, which would have given workers either six or 10 more weeks of benefits, depending on their state's unemployment rate. Dole proposed to finance his plan through student loan reforms and the auction of frequencies on the electromagnetic spectrum. The Senate tabled the plan, 57-42. *(Vote 201, p. 27-S)*

The Senate also rejected an amendment by John McCain, R-Ariz., that would have required three-fifths of all senators to vote in favor of any tax increases in order for them to take effect. The Senate voted 37-62 against waiving the budget act in order to consider the amendment. *(Vote 204, p. 27-S)*

Finally, the Senate refused to table an unrelated "sense of the Senate" amendment by Hank Brown, R-Colo., that urged the United States against joining any trade agreement that would increase the price of coffee for consumers. The tabling motion failed, 40-59, and the amendment was agreed to by voice vote. *(Vote 203, p. 27-S)*

The 65-35 final vote in the Senate to adopt the conference report left the White House confident that it could muster the 34 votes necessary to prevent an override and doom the Democratic bill. *(Vote 213, p. 28-S)*

With 55 Republicans voting for passage, the 300-118

Unemployment Bill Vetoed by Bush

Following is the text of President Bush's Oct. 11 message accompanying his veto of S 1722, a bill that would have extended unemployment benefits.

I am returning herewith without my approval S 1722, the Emergency Unemployment Compensation Act of 1991. I would gladly sign into law responsible legislation that does not threaten economic recovery and its associated job creation, a fact that members of my administration and I have repeatedly made clear. We have worked diligently with members of Congress to encourage them to adopt a well-crafted alternative program of extended unemployment benefits that is paid for, as required under the bipartisan budget agreement. Unfortunately, the Congress has rejected this alternative and ignored my call for passage of measures that will increase the nation's competitiveness, productivity and growth.

The administration is deeply concerned about the needs of the unemployed and their families.

It is essential that we take responsible actions to ensure that the economic recovery continues and strengthens, creating new employment opportunities.

If a bill providing unemployment benefits in a responsible manner — financed under the budget agreement — reached my desk, it would be signed immediately so we could provide real additional benefits to the unemployed.

S 1722 would effectively destroy the integrity of the bipartisan budget agreement and put into place a poorly designed, unnecessarily expensive program that would significantly increase the federal deficit. Enactment of S 1722 would signal the failure of budget discipline, which would have a negative effect on financial markets that could threaten economic recovery and lead to increased unemployment. This legislation would not well serve the unemployed or our nation's taxpayers.

S 1722 violates essential elements of last year's bipartisan budget agreement. It does not include offsets for costs that the Congress projects at $6.5 billion during for fiscal years 1992-1995. Instead, it simply adds this cost to the federal deficit by requiring that the provisions of the bill be treated as "emergency requirements" designated by the president and the Congress under the Balanced Budget and Emergency Deficit Control Act of 1985. This breaches the budget agreement by denying me the independent authority to determine when an emergency exists, thereby removing a key safeguard for enforcing budget discipline.

In addition, S 1722 is substantively flawed. It would establish a new, temporary federal program providing three tiers of extended unemployment benefits. This complex, cumbersome system could slow re-employment and would result in benefit delays, payment inaccuracies and escalating administrative costs. Moreover, the bill inappropriately abandons the measure of unemployment that has historically been used to trigger extended benefits, substituting an overly broad measure that is not based upon the target group — insured workers.

The administration will continue to support alternative legislation that effectively addresses the needs of the unemployed while also maintaining the budget discipline that is imperative to the prospects of future employment and economic growth. ■

vote in the House to clear the report gave Democrats a comfortable two-thirds margin for the coming override vote. *(Vote 285, p. 68-H)*

Prospects for Overriding a Veto

A third of House Republicans had fled their president in their Oct. 1 vote. And further evidence of the damaging fallout for the Republican Party came a day later when Bush campaigned in Pennsylvania for Dick Thornburgh, the GOP Senate candidate. Thornburgh, who less than two months before had been Bush's attorney general, said if he were a senator he would vote to override the president.

"The Democratic leaders, I think they sense a political issue they can use next year against all of us," Bush said Oct. 2. "They were determined to pass and ram down my throat a budget-busting bill."

House Majority Leader Richard A. Gephardt, D-Mo., acknowledged that the presidential campaign was driving the Democrats' legislative strategy. Interviewed Oct. 2 on "CBS This Morning," Gephardt reiterated the Democrats' theme that Bush "seems more worried about what happens in Kuwait or other countries around the world, and not paying attention to our people here at home who have real needs."

Gephardt further promised that "the Congress in the next few months is going to be putting bill after bill on his desk that will begin to define the difference between the president's approach and what a Democratic president would do."

As the week ended, Democrats were left in the ironic position of needing bad economic news, not only to strengthen their case but also to heighten the political damage Bush would suffer from a veto. They were disappointed. The Labor Department reported Oct. 4 that the unemployment rate eased in September, falling to 6.7 percent after hovering for two months at 6.8 percent.

Bush convened a White House news conference within hours after the new figure was announced. "I'll sign a bill that helps people and also protects the overall economy by keeping to the budget agreement," he said. Asked what the unemployed should do in the meantime, he said they should tell their representatives to pass the Republican measure.

The new language that would "bust the budget" by declaring it emergency spending provided political cover for the five Republicans who had voted for the earlier Democratic bill. They were: Danforth, Bond, Seymour, Burns and Durenberger.

Gramm argued that if the budget agreement was breached once, then Congress would begin drinking regularly from the well.

In floor speeches, Democrats recounted their encounters with unemployed workers whose benefits had long since run out. "Let us give them some hope; they have earned it," said House Democratic Whip David E. Bonior of Michigan.

"This is the issue that divides the Democrats from the Republicans," he said. "This is the issue that cuts at who we are and who they are."

Bonior's speech was indicative of the belief among Democrats that unemployment was a winner as a "defining issue."

The Veto

As expected, President Bush on Oct. 11 vetoed the $6.4 billion bill to provide extended unemployment benefits to jobless workers.

Bush complained that the bill (S 1722) was too expensive and would bust the 1990 budget agreement. He said he preferred a less-expensive Republican alternative crafted by Dole.

Democrats immediately attacked Bush — not only for his veto but also for his timing. Democratic Party Chairman Ronald H. Brown said the president slipped the veto through while the nation's attention was riveted on Senate Judiciary hearings on Supreme Court nominee Clarence Thomas. *(Thomas confirmation, p. 274)*

Downey, the bill's chief backer in the House, said, "By once again turning a deaf ear to the suffering of the unemployed, the president has confirmed that he is out of touch with America."

The bill had become a political rallying cry for the Democratic Party.

In the Senate, Democratic leaders held the bill for eight days before sending it to the White House in order to delay the eventual override vote. Their hope was that constituents might be able to persuade two Republican senators to change their votes during the intervening days.

On Oct. 16, Republicans stopped them from overriding Bush's veto of S 1722. The vote was 65-35, falling two votes short of the two-thirds necessary for an override. It was the 12th time that Congress failed to reverse a Bush veto. *(Vote 221, p. 29-S)*

Following the unsuccessful veto override, Majority Leader George J. Mitchell, D-Maine, refused to allow Republicans to call up two alternative unemployment bills. The Republican bills were much less costly and would have helped about 850,000 fewer people.

Eight Republican senators supported the unemployment measure and voted for the override. They were: Chafee, Cohen, D'Amato, Hatfield, Jeffords, Kasten, Packwood and Specter.

ROUND THREE: HR 3575, AMENDED IN HR 1724

House and Senate Democratic leaders were divided over what to do next, while organized labor was urging them to end the empty exercises and get the money moving to the unemployed.

The situation changed dramatically when Bush decided it was time to push for a bill that he would sign. Congressional Democrats scrambled to come up with a compromise plan after Bush signaled on Oct. 26 that he wanted to put the issue behind him.

Senate Finance Chairman Bentsen proposed paying for the measure by closing a loophole on wealthy taxpayers. He sought to require people who paid income taxes on a quarterly basis to base their payments on the total income they expected to earn during the tax year, not on the amount of taxes they paid the year before.

The Bentsen plan won the support of other Senate and House leaders and the administration. It hit a wall, however, among House Ways and Means members, who worried that the financing provision would apply not just to the wealthy but to people of more modest incomes, such as those who sold a house during the year.

After another week of negotiations, House leaders reached a new deal with the administration on a formula for paying out six, 13 and 20 weeks of additional benefits to the states. The bill modified the Bentsen plan and included additional financing mechanisms for paying for the extra benefits.

Senators whose states were slated to receive only six weeks balked at the formula in the House-passed bill.

To keep the original bill on the fast track, the administration agreed to new provisions that pushed the states in the six-week tier into the 13-week tier and offered retroactive benefits to all states.

Provisions

Under a formula in HR 3575, states would have received either six, 13 or 20 weeks of benefits at a cost of $5.3 million.

The bill was paid for by tightening a loophole on those paying quarterly taxes; extending a law allowing Internal Revenue Service collection of debts owed the federal government; extending the federal unemployment tax at 0.08 percent; and garnisheeing the wages of those who defaulted on student loans.

New provisions tagged on to HR 1724 raised the six-week states to the 13-week tier and allowed workers in all states to qualify for extra benefits if they exhausted their state unemployment benefits after March 1 and were still unemployed. HR 3575 had excluded workers in 19 states from that eligibility.

Those changes added $380 million to the $5.3 billion unemployment measure, according to administration estimates. But $285 million of that cost was offset by moving the expiration date for extended benefits from July 4, 1992, to June 13, 1992. That left the cost at $95 million, which the administration said would be covered by $123 million in excess savings from the bill that the president first signed into law.

House Committee Action

The House Ways and Means Committee took yet another stab Oct. 22 at providing benefits to the long-term unemployed. This time, a sharply divided panel approved a tax increase to pay for the $5.3 billion measure.

The committee reported out HR 3575 in a 22-14 vote.

Ways and Means Chairman Rostenkowski had long urged his colleagues to find a way to cover the cost of the bill. In July, committee Democrats joined with Republicans in stripping out tax provisions that would have paid for the bill. In September, the House rejected Rostenkowski's approach by 65-341.

But this time the committee voted 17-17 on an amendment by Jim Moody, D-Wis., to strike the increase in the taxable wage base on which employers paid federal unemployment taxes. The tie vote meant Rostenkowski's provisions would stay in the bill.

Rostenkowski would have kept the tax rate at 0.8 percent instead of allowing it to drop to 0.6 percent. He would have applied that tax to the first $7,700 of a worker's income, rather than the existing $7,000. And he would have also required the Internal Revenue Service to withhold tax refunds to people who owed money to the federal government.

The panel agreed to an amendment by Benjamin L. Cardin, D-Md., that would have ensured that the tax provisions expired after five years, in fiscal 1997.

Rostenkowski was surprised the tax proposal survived the markup. That left House Democratic leaders groping for their next move after adamantly opposing any plan to pay for the bill beyond the emergency spending statement.

There was concern that if the taxes stayed in, the measure could become a vehicle for contentious tax proposals, such as a reduction in the capital gains tax or tax relief for the middle class.

"The issue of taxes is going to be joined when we send this over to the Senate," said Downey, who supported Rostenkowski's effort to pay for the benefits.

The Ways and Means panel rejected, 13-20, an amendment by Archer to substitute the Dole amendment for HR 3575. The Dole bill would have cost $3.1 billion and provided either six or 10 extra weeks of benefits compared with the Democrats' seven or 13 extra weeks.

Bush Agreed to a Compromise

After a White House luncheon Oct. 29 with Republicans who complained about the economy, Bush called House Minority Leader Robert H. Michel, R-Ill., and told him to cut a deal with Rostenkowski.

"The gist of our conversation on unemployment was to get our heads together [with Democrats] and craft a compromise acceptable to him," Michel said.

Michel said he pointed out to Bush that the economy was not bouncing back and not just low-income people were losing jobs.

"We've got a different mix today among jobless workers — not only factory workers but a lot of middle-class, middle-income [people] who've got big house payments, big car payments, college tuitions, who are facing real, traumatic changes," he said he told Bush.

Those people, he said, were the very ones who voted Republican.

Michel's assessment of the economy was confirmed Nov. 1 when the Labor Department announced that the nation's unemployment rate had climbed one-tenth of 1 percent in October to 6.8 percent. That brought the number of jobless workers to 8.6 million. About 300,000 people a month were exhausting their state unemployment benefits without finding work.

Following Bush's phone call and conversations between Michel and Rostenkowski, top Democrats from the House and Senate got together Oct. 30. Bentsen suggested his financing concept.

Mitchell, however, wanted to continue pressing the Democrats' political advantage on the issue. He proposed freezing or cutting foreign aid to pay for the unemployment bill — something that would be unacceptable to Republicans and would break the budget agreement by shifting funds from the foreign to the domestic account.

In a speech Oct. 31, Mitchell said, "Not since President Hoover told Americans the country had turned the corner has an American president been so consistently wrong in his judgment of the economy."

But other Democrats said they had already extracted as much political flesh from Bush as possible on the unemployment issue and that it was time to get the benefits out to the people who needed them.

At a photo opportunity session Oct. 31, Bush said he had wanted an unemployment bill all along. "I want it to be one that does not bust the budget agreement," Bush said. His words angered Democrats who remembered when Bush originally said the economy was recovering and a bill was not necessary.

The Deal That Collapsed

Democrats and Republicans came to the brink of a deal to provide $5.6 billion in benefits to the long-term unemployed only to see it all fall apart once again over how to pay for it.

The new unemployment plan proposed by Bentsen would have been offered as a substitute amendment to HR 3575. But House Ways and Means Committee members objected Nov. 1 to the plan, which would have required people who paid income taxes on a quarterly basis to base their payments on the total income they expected to earn during the tax year, not on the amount of taxes they paid the year before. The stricter requirement would have applied to people whose income had jumped by at least $30,000 in one year.

After two days of talks, that idea had the backing of Foley, Rostenkowski, and eventually Mitchell.

Just prior to the Ways and Means meeting, Michel said he had no problems with Bentsen's plan. "We've got to get something signed by the president before we leave here," he said.

But the financing idea faced harsh criticism when it was presented to the committee. Rep. Sam M. Gibbons, D-Fla., said: "There is no way you can make these estimates. You can't do it; it's absolutely stupid."

Rostenkowski finally said, "It's evident there's not going to be a consensus here," and postponed further consideration of the measure until Nov. 4.

A Deal Was Nearly Forged

Congressional leaders finally settled down to write a bill the president would sign. The negotiations were conducted by Rostenkowski, Michel and Dole, with Treasury Secretary Nicholas F. Brady and OMB Director Darman.

The talks led to a refined Bentsen plan to raise money to pay for up to 20 weeks of benefits by changing the rules for upper-income people who estimated their taxes quarterly.

"They're virtually there," said a top House Democratic leadership aide Nov. 8.

The Senate, however, had taken another tack, preferring to let Bush choose one of three options for paying for an unemployment bill. One of the choices was the House-backed Bentsen proposal, making it likely that that plan would prevail.

Mitchell and Bentsen had proposed sending Bush a $5 billion-plus unemployment bill that provided seven, 13 or 20 weeks of benefits, depending on a state's unemployment rate. Bush's financing choices would be to:

- Declare an emergency, which would have eliminated the need for offsetting cuts or a tax increase. That would require deficit spending, however, and Bush had twice rejected that route. Democrats said the money could come from an $8 billion trust fund, but the administration said that money did not exist.
- Cut foreign aid growth by $3.6 billion over five years, exempting housing loans for Israel and grain sales to the Soviet Union. That would have been combined with collecting $2 billion in delinquent student loans. House Speaker Foley had not embraced the foreign aid plan since it was first floated by Mitchell.
- Require certain high-income people to estimate their quarterly tax payments on the total income they expected to earn during the tax year, not on the amount of taxes they paid the year before. The provision would have applied to people whose income jumped by $30,000 in one year, bringing in about $2.45 billion. The money would have been combined with student loan collections and an extension of the 0.08 percent federal unemployment tax paid by employers.

"We're trying very hard to be accommodating," Mitchell said of the three choices. "This is not a political effort to box anyone in."

Neither Michel, Foley nor Dole was interested in giving Bush a multiple-choice bill. The administration had indicated that the Bentsen plan was the only one Bush would be willing to accept.

Rostenkowski met with Ways and Means Democrats two days in a row behind closed doors to cultivate their support. And Michel brought committee Republicans in for a private meeting Nov. 7 to persuade them to support the Bentsen plan.

Rostenkowski said he would modify the Bentsen plan to exempt people who received income from partnerships or subchapter S corporations, which were corporations that resembled specialized limited partnerships. He would also have exempted people who received a one-time lump sum from selling a home.

In an odd reversal, some House Republicans began talking about raising taxes to pay for the unemployment bill. And in another reversal, Republicans in both chambers became vehement that an unemployment bill had to be enacted before Congress could recess.

"We can't go home without it — neither party can," said Gradison.

Although both sides predicted that they could work out a deal the week of Nov. 4, the Mitchell foreign aid proposal threw another element into the mix, slowing down talks.

A Final Deal Was Struck

The Ways and Means Committee, which had earlier rejected some of the financing provisions, voted 29-7 on Nov. 13 to approve the bill, just hours after Rostenkowski and Michel agreed to the deal.

To pay for the measure, the bill would save an estimated $2.6 billion by requiring people who estimated their taxes quarterly to pay based on what they owed the government, rather than what they owed the year before. That was to apply only to taxpayers whose income jumped by $40,000 in one year.

The second compromise in the Senate changed that to $35,000 to offset the higher cost.

That provision had prevented a deal from going through two weeks earlier, when members of House Ways and Means complained that it was too complicated. But negotiators massaged the idea and excluded income from partnerships or subchapter S corporations. Also excluded was income received from selling a home.

Besides the refined Bentsen proposal, financing was also made possible by an estimated $1.7 billion to be saved by extending a law that allowed the Internal Revenue Service to collect debts owed the federal government by taking the money out of people's tax returns. Most of these debts came from student loan defaults.

The federal unemployment tax, scheduled to drop from 0.08 percent to 0.06 percent in 1996, would remain at 0.08 percent, saving an estimated $878 million.

However, according to the Congressional Budget Office, the bill would actually lose $895 million in fiscal 1992. While that would violate congressional budget laws, OMB had ruled that it would not add to the deficit and therefore would not trigger across-the-board cuts in every other domestic program.

Once both chambers agreed that the Bentsen plan would prevail, the House easily voted 396-30 the afternoon of Nov. 14 to pass HR 3575. *(Vote 396, p. 96-H)*

The momentum slowed in the Senate by nightfall and Mitchell and Dole were forced to fend off angry senators whose states did not fare well under the deal. The battle shaped up not over the funding mechanisms, which were accepted almost without debate, but over the formula used to determine which states qualified for how many extra weeks of benefits.

The previous bills sent to the president had calculated which state got what according to the total unemployment rate.

But Darman strenuously objected to that method, preferring to calculate state need according to an insured unemployment rate, which measured the people who were eligible under state rules to receive compensation, rather than all people who were unemployed. To save money, many Southern states in particular had made it extremely difficult for workers to qualify to receive unemployment benefits.

To determine how many weeks of benefits each state would receive, negotiators agreed to a formula that calculated an "adjusted insured unemployment rate" combined with the exhaustion rate of workers using up their state benefits.

Kansas would have qualified for 13 weeks of extra benefits even though it had the fifth-lowest unemployment rate in the country.

One big loser would have been Kentucky, where jobless workers would have gotten six additional weeks of benefits under the compromise, compared with the 13 weeks they would have received under the bill Bush vetoed Oct. 11 (S 1722).

That prompted a direct challenge to Mitchell, whose request to call up the House bill Nov. 14 was rebuffed by his own majority whip, Kentucky's Wendell H. Ford.

Ford complained that Senate Democrats were not represented in the negotiations with the administration to put the unemployment deal together.

Mitchell's repeated attempts to call up the House bill were met with objections from both sides of the aisle until 11 p.m. on Nov. 14. Eventually, he promised to allow four amendments to be offered the next day, although both Mitchell and Dole insisted that all four would have to be voted down to preserve the agreement with the House and the White House.

The Senate killed, 74-21, the only amendment offered, by Robert C. Smith, R-N.H. It would have cut foreign aid to boost the benefits for five states, including New Hampshire. *(Vote 253, p. 33-S)*

The whole bill might have collapsed at the last minute if the administration had not agreed to raise all the six-week states to the 13-week tier. The administration also promised to allow all states to qualify for retroactive benefits, rather than excluding 18 states. That added $95 million to the cost of the bill, which would be partially paid for by moving the bill's expiration from July 4, 1992, to June 13, 1992.

The changes enabled the Senate on Nov. 15 to vote 91-2 to pass the bill in the same form that it had come over from the House. Sens. Brown, R-Colo., and Kent Conrad, D-N.D., voted no. *(Vote 254, p. 33-S)*

Those changes were added to a most-favored-nation trade status bill (HR 1724) for Czechoslovakia and Hungary and sent to the House.

This final deal allowed the original unemployment compromise to go to Bush on Nov. 15; he signed it that day.

"They've waited too long for the checks, and we apologize for the delay," said Rostenkowski, who negotiated the deal on behalf of Democrats. "Politics has sabotaged this measure for too many months." ■

Family Leave Bill Remained Political Pawn

After a quick start, legislation mandating unpaid leave for workers with newborn or recently adopted children or with a seriously ill family member was left unfinished at the end of the first session. Instead, lawmakers held over conference action on the bill (HR 2) until 1992 to force President Bush, who opposed the bill, to veto it in an election year.

The legislation was one of the Democrats' top priorities early in the year. But after it became clear that, for the second year in a row, Democrats could not muster the votes to override a veto, it lost its momentum.

As sent to conference, the Family and Medical Leave Act mandated that businesses give up to 12 weeks of unpaid leave to employees at the birth or adoption of children or when employees or their children, spouses or parents were seriously ill. Because the bill applied only to companies with 50 or more workers, about 95 percent of all businesses were exempt.

Protesting new federal requirements on businesses, Bush had vetoed a similar measure in June 1990. The House failed to override that veto; the 232-195 vote was 54 short of the two-thirds majority necessary. *(1990 Almanac, p. 359)*

In 1991, the House Education and Labor Committee had started the new version (HR 2) on a fast track. Pat Williams, D-Mont., chairman of the Subcommittee on Labor-Management Relations, held a hearing Feb. 28.

Early in the year, the chances for passage of the legislation seemed good. Jane O'Grady, a legislative representative of the AFL-CIO, said the American Association of Retired Persons was putting its muscle behind the bill.

In the Senate, Daniel R. Coats, R-Ind., announced that he would work with Christopher J. Dodd, D-Conn., an original sponsor, toward a parental leave bill (S 5).

And Lynn Martin, who voted for the legislation in 1990 as a Republican House member from Illinois, was Bush's new Labor secretary.

"We're hopeful," O'Grady said.

But business groups argued that the bill would be too costly, and they had an ally in the president, who remained dug in against federal mandates on businesses.

Bush threatened another veto, and proponents of the bill faced an uphill battle to get the votes to override him.

The key test of support would come in the Senate, which had passed the previous year's bill (HR 770) by voice vote and did not have a chance to vote on an override after the House killed it.

Ultimately, both chambers signaled a similar stalemate in 1991: Senators again opted to pass the bill by voice vote (after a 65-32 vote on compromise language within the measure), and the House's approval of the bill fell well short of two-thirds.

Proponents hoped to press for the legislation in 1992 — an election year — but business lobbyists countered that they did not expect the issue to move voters, as it had failed to make much of an impact during the 1990 elections.

BOXSCORE

➡ **Family and Medical Leave (S 5, HR 2).** As passed by both chambers, the legislation required businesses to give their employees up to 12 weeks of unpaid leave to care for a newborn infant or newly adopted child or to care for a seriously ill family member. The mandate applied only to companies with 50 or more employees — roughly 5 percent of the firms in the United States.

Reports: H Rept 102-135; S Rept 102-68.

KEY ACTION

March 13 — The **House** Post Office and Civil Service Committee approved HR 2.

March 20 — The **House** Education and Labor Committee approved HR 2 by voice vote.

April 24 — The **Senate** Labor and Human Resources Committee approved S 5 by voice vote.

Oct. 2 — The **Senate** passed S 5 by voice vote.

Nov. 13 — The **House** passed HR 2, 253-177. (Subsequently, the House passed S 5 after striking all after the enacting clause and inserting the language of HR 2.)

HOUSE COMMITTEE ACTION

Less than a month after the hearing, with little more than pro forma debate, Williams' Education and Labor Subcommittee on Labor-Management Relations steamrolled over GOP protests and approved the legislation.

Marge Roukema, R-N.J., joined panel Democrats in voting 16-7 on March 7 to approve HR 2 for consideration by the full Education and Labor Committee.

While Republicans said that the measure would have unfairly burdened businesses, Democrats — and Roukema — said that not providing for leave had hurt families.

"This is not about working families getting rich, it's about working families getting by," said Roukema, who helped lead the fight in 1990.

Other Republicans reiterated their complaints about the bill. "I have serious concerns about Washington dictating mandates," said Dick Armey of Texas.

Williams said that the same GOP arguments against parental leave legislation had been used by Republicans against past legislation that outlawed child labor, set minimum-wage standards, instituted a Social Security system and created the Occupational Safety and Health Administration.

Only one amendment was offered during the markup. Tom Petri, R-Wis., proposed limiting unpaid leave to six weeks for the birth or adoption of a child and two weeks for serious illness. Employers could have required workers to apply paid vacation or sick leave against the unpaid leave.

"I'm not against giving people leave," Petri said. "We do it in my office and I don't know anyone who doesn't."

But he cautioned against the federal government running ahead of the states. His amendment, based on a Wisconsin parental leave law, was rejected by voice vote.

The House Post Office and Civil Service Committee on March 13 gave its approval to the measure. The committee had jurisdiction over parts of the bill that related to federal employees.

The committee endorsed the version of the bill approved March 12 by the Subcommittee on Compensation and Employee Benefits, which agreed to grant federal workers 18 weeks of unpaid leave over a two-year period and allowed them to take up to 26 weeks of unpaid leave annually if they were ill.

The subcommittee also approved an amendment by Gary L. Ackerman, D-N.Y., that granted federal employees leave to care for an ill spouse, a provision that was inadvertently left out of the original bill.

Existing law provided that unpaid leave be granted to federal workers at the discretion of their supervisors.

The full Education and Labor Committee approved HR 2 by voice vote March 20, sending the bill to the floor.

Roukema warned her GOP colleagues: "I don't think you want to oppose such a distinguished pro-family bill."

And she told them that she did not think they would want to be perceived as telling a pregnant woman or the parent of a terminally ill child to "go find another job."

But Bill Goodling, R-Pa., the committee's ranking minority member, warned of another Bush veto. Goodling said members had underestimated the cost to business.

Although the measure was approved by voice vote, two other Republicans had announced their support. They were Scott L. Klug, Wis., and Susan Molinari, N.Y.

SENATE COMMITTEE ACTION

Action on the bill shifted to the Senate, where the Labor and Human Resources Committee — which had backed a family leave bill in 1989 — approved S 5 on April 24.

Bill sponsor Dodd expressed confidence in the fate of the new measure. "For the first time ever, we have a strong bipartisan consensus — in this committee and the Congress at large — that federal legislation is necessary to ensure job security for working parents in times of family and medical emergency."

But ranking Republican Orrin G. Hatch of Utah disagreed: "Nothing has changed. Neither the legislation nor the political landscape has changed."

Two Republicans — Coats and James M. Jeffords, Vt. — voted with all 10 Democrats in the 12-5 committee vote. Coats was opposed to the bill during the last committee vote in 1989. *(1989 Almanac, p. 348)*

As approved by the committee, S 5 guaranteed employees 12 weeks of unpaid leave to care for a newborn or newly adopted infant or to care for a seriously ill family member. Workers would be eligible for this benefit only after exhausting all other forms of leave, such as vacation or sick time.

HR 2, as passed by the House Education and Labor Committee, provided 12 weeks of leave for all workers except federal employees, who received 18 weeks for family leave and 26 weeks for medical leave. The Senate bill did not include a provision in the House measure that exempted key employees.

According to Dodd, only about 40 percent of the work force was covered by S 5.

During the Labor Committee markup, Chairman Edward M. Kennedy, D-Mass., proposed an amendment — adopted by voice vote — that applied the provisions of the measure to senators and Senate staff.

Dave Durenberger, R-Minn., proposed an amendment to lower the leave to 10 weeks and change the medical leave provisions. But he withdrew his proposal when it became clear that it would fail.

Kennedy disputed businesses' contention that the bill would be too expensive, saying April 24 that the costs were greatly exaggerated. He cited a survey commissioned by the Small Business Administration (SBA), which argued that the costs to businesses for permanently replacing a worker were significantly higher than for granting leave.

The SBA report — released March 27 — was based on interviews with 1,730 small businesses nationwide. One finding was that, although most businesses did not have formal leave policies, between 74 percent and 90 percent used existing leave programs to meet the needs of workers with sick children or other unanticipated leave needs.

The study also suggested that the costs of the bill would be less than the business community had claimed. "The net cost to employers of placing workers on leave is always substantially smaller than the cost of terminating an employee."

Bid for Compromise

Trying to pick up votes in the face of Bush's threatened veto, lawmakers on Sept. 18 unveiled a proposal that scaled back the committee bill.

Yet while the new proposal loosened some of the bill's requirements, it left unresolved the principal objection of Bush and business groups: It still mandated that businesses with more than 50 workers offer family leave.

Christopher S. Bond, R-Mo., who along with Dodd worked out the compromise version, said the changes had attracted some senators' support.

"I think we still have the basic elements needed to protect the family unit, and we have done so in a way that really minimizes the burdens on business," Bond said. Most members of the business community disagreed. They argued that Congress should not force businesses to provide benefits to workers and said that the compromise was not significantly different from S 5.

"These changes are simply marginal and underscore the myriad problems with this legislation," said Mary Tavenner, a lobbyist for the National Association of Wholesaler-Distributors. "You just can't fix it."

Like the committee-approved version, Bond's proposal required businesses to give up to 12 weeks of unpaid leave for the birth or adoption of a child or for the serious illness of the worker or an immediate family member.

S 5 restricted employee eligibility to employees who had worked 1,000 hours or 19 hours a week over the previous 12 months. The compromise raised the number of hours to 1,250 or 25 hours per week.

Members of the business community saw a more substantive change in the softening of potential penalties against businesses that violated the bill. As approved by the Labor Committee, the bill allowed employees to collect quadruple damages including wages, salary, employment benefits and other compensation, plus interest.

The new version allowed double the actual losses.

The compromise also allowed employers to deny leave to "key employees," who were defined as those who were the highest paid 10 percent of the company's work force. The provision was included in the House bill but not in the original Senate version.

Thomas A. Scully, an associate director at the White House's Office of Management and Budget (OMB), predicted that Bush would still veto the bill. "The compromise isn't much of a compromise," he said. The administration continued to encourage businesses to provide flexible family leave policies but did not want to force them to do it, he said.

SENATE FLOOR ACTION

When S 5 came to the Senate floor Oct. 2, members passed the legislation by voice vote, as they had the previous year. But senators appeared to have breathed new life into the measure when, apparently with enough votes to override a veto, they approved the Bond substitute.

While the 65-32 vote for the substitute was two short of the 67 needed to guarantee the two-thirds majority that could override a veto, supporters and opponents alike assumed that all three absent Democrats — David Pryor, Ark., and presidential candidates Tom Harkin, Iowa, and Bob Kerrey, Neb. — would have voted for the substitute. *(Vote 215, p. 28-S)*

"This is a strong message to House members and to the White House," said Rep. Roukema, one of the earliest GOP supporters of the family and medical leave concept.

The 15 Senate Republicans who voted for the Bond substitute included such longtime liberal backers as Jeffords and John H. Chafee, R.I.; moderates John C. Danforth, Mo., and Arlen Specter, Pa.; and a few conservatives, among them Coats and John McCain, Ariz.

But Bush was adamant. "Should S 5 or any other mandated leave legislation be presented to me, I will veto it," Bush wrote Dole on Oct. 1. A Sept. 30 White House statement made clear that that threat included Bond's language.

Before adopting the Bond compromise, members rejected, 32-65, a Hatch substitute that would have replaced the requirement that employers offer leave with a less stringent requirement that returning workers be given preference in rehiring and resume their seniority and benefits. *(Vote 216, p. 28-S)*

Under Hatch's plan, workers would have been entitled to take as much as six years of leave to "bond" with a new child and up to two years for medical leave.

Members also rejected, 40-57, an amendment by Durenberger that would have required that disputes over leave between employers and workers be settled by arbitration rather than in court. Opponents said the complicated arbitration process would have unfairly burdened workers who had legitimate complaints. *(Vote 214, p. 28-S)*

HOUSE FLOOR ACTION

If the Senate floor vote on the Bond compromise raised supporters' hopes of eking out enough votes to override the president on family leave, the House's Nov. 13 vote on HR 2 brought a dose of cold reality.

The House passed HR 2, its version of the legislation, by 253-177 — well short of the 290 needed to override Bush's promised veto if all members were present and voting. *(Vote 393, p. 96-H)*

The House later passed S 5 by voice vote after amending it to contain the provisions of HR 2.

Conceding they lacked the votes to enact the legislation, Democrats planned to wring political advantage out of defeat. Democrats said that they would not reconcile the House and Senate bills until 1992, giving them more months to paint Bush as unwilling to help working Americans.

For weeks before the bill was brought to the floor, the House Democratic leadership lobbied members for votes.

Pending was a substitute, sponsored by Bart Gordon, D-Tenn., and Henry J. Hyde, R-Ill., that mirrored the compromise crafted in the Senate by Dodd and Bond. It would have watered down the bill as approved by the House Education and Labor Committee.

But in search of the elusive two-thirds support, the leadership floated an alternative offered by Timothy J. Penny, D-Minn., and John J. LaFalce, D-N.Y. That version would have given 12 weeks leave for the birth or adoption of a child, but limited leave for the care of a seriously ill child, spouse or parent to six weeks.

When the Penny-LaFalce proposal failed to muster two-thirds, the leadership decided to stick with the Gordon-Hyde language. The Gordon-Hyde substitute:

- Raised to 1,250 from 1,000 the number of hours per year an employee must work in order to be eligible for up to 12 weeks of unpaid leave.
- Required workers to provide 30 days' notice for non-emergency leave.
- Lowered potential penalties against businesses that violated the bill from quadruple damages to double damages.
- Allowed companies to deny leave to "key employees," defined as those who were the highest-paid 10 percent of a company's work force.

In a statement opposing the legislation, the OMB reiterated the administration's view that government should not mandate that businesses offer leave policies. Instead, the president preferred that people negotiate for the option with their companies, the statement said.

The House passed the Gordon-Hyde substitute by an overwhelming 287-143. *(Vote 391, p. 96-H)*

By itself, the vote on the substitute would have given the House the numbers to override a veto that day. But many who voted for the compromise voted against passage of the bill. Business lobbyist Tavenner, who headed the effort against the bill, explained the discrepancy between the two votes this way: "Members wanted to be on record voting for something, but they didn't want it to become law." ■

House Acted To Protect Workers on Strike

Under lobbying pressure from business and organized labor, the House passed legislation (HR 5) to prohibit employers from hiring permanent replacements for striking workers on July 17 by a 247-182 vote. *(Vote 213, p. 52-H)*

The vote fell 39 short of the 286 needed to override a threatened veto from President Bush. Democratic leaders said that they did not care if they had the votes to supersede Bush. "We go to the floor because we're right," said Education and Labor Committee Chairman William D. Ford, D-Mich.

A companion Senate bill (S 55) was reported by the Labor and Human Resources Committee on a party-line 10-7 vote on June 19 but did not make it to the floor in 1991.

Existing law gave private-sector workers the right to strike and barred employers from firing them for doing so. But a 1938 Supreme Court decision allowed employers to hire people to temporarily or permanently replace striking workers.

The bill was a high priority of organized labor and its Democratic allies, who said that in preceding years, some businesses took advantage of the loophole by forcing union workers into a strike and then replacing them with lower-paid, non-union employees.

HOUSE ACTION

The House Education and Labor Subcommittee on Labor-Management Relations kicked off action on HR 5, approving the bill on March 13 by a 15-7 vote.

The subcommittee rejected, by voice vote, an amendment by the full committee's ranking Republican, Bill Goodling, Pa., that would have allowed companies to hire permanent replacement workers after eight weeks of a strike.

The amendment also would have required unions to conduct secret ballot votes on strike motions and would have required a two-thirds majority vote for a strike.

Subcommittee Republicans said that Democrats were trying to embarrass Bush by goading him into vetoing a popular and well-publicized bill. And they also said that the bill would tilt the balance in labor relations too far toward unions and could lead to greater unrest and precipitous striking.

But supporters of the bill said that according to a report by the General Accounting Office, employers increasingly were threatening to hire permanent replacements.

They said that such threats — and widely publicized replacements of striking workers by companies such as Eastern Airlines and Greyhound — had given employers an edge in many negotiations.

Reflecting the high priority given the bill by organized labor and Democrats and the full Education and Labor Committee, the committee approved the bill on April 18 by a party-line 25-14 vote.

Goodling tried again for his amendment, saying, "This cannot become law as it is presently written."

But committee Democrats signaled little willingness to broaden the measure's support beyond the Democratic Caucus, and the panel rejected Goodling's amendment by voice vote.

Goodling said panel Democrats did not appear willing to work out a compromise to secure the two-thirds majority vote required to override a veto.

"I don't worry about two-thirds. I worry about passing legislation," said Education and Labor Committee Chairman Ford.

The Public Works and Transportation Committee, which shared jurisdiction with the Energy and Commerce Committee over those portions of the bill affecting railroads and airlines, approved the measure April 16 by voice vote.

The Energy and Commerce Committee approved the bill on May 21, clearing the way for floor action.

Education and Labor adopted, 25-14, an amendment by Pat Williams, D-Mont., aimed at clarifying that the protections offered by HR 5 would apply only to union-represented employees.

BOXSCORE

➡ **Replacement of Striking Workers (HR 5, S 55).** The bills banned employers from permanently replacing workers who were on strike.

Reports: H Rept 102-57, Parts I-III; S Rept 102-43.

KEY ACTION

April 16 — HR 5 approved by the **House** Public Works Committee by voice vote.

April 18 — HR 5 approved by the **House** Education and Labor Committee 25-14.

May 21 — HR 5 approved by the **House** Energy and Commerce Committee by voice vote.

June 19 — S 55 approved by the **Senate** Labor and Human Resources Committee by a 10-7 vote.

July 17 — HR 5 passed by the **House** by a vote of 247-182.

The Public Works Subcommittee on Aviation had approved that amendment April 11. The two other committees approved similar language.

Republicans had earlier objected that the bill as introduced would have led to strikes at non-union companies.

But Republicans objected to Williams' amendment as well, saying the language would treat non-union employees as "second-class citizens" because they would not be entitled to the same protections under the law as union members.

Republican amendments to continue to allow hiring permanent replacements in cases of labor violence or to protect public health or safety were also rejected by the Democratic majority on the Education Committee.

Some moderate Republicans in Congress had signaled that they could support a bill that would bar hiring permanent replacements during the first parts of a strike and would require the National Labor Relations Board to speed up rulings in labor-management cases that involve permanent replacements.

But "there is simply no middle ground," said Rep. Steve Gunderson, R-Wis. "We are going to have a political issue, not a legislative solution."

House Floor

The 247-182 July 17 floor vote fell 39 short of the 286 needed to override an expected veto from Bush.

All of the 33 Democrats who voted against the bill (HR 5) were from the South, while only 16 Republicans voted in favor of the legislation.

Although business groups expected Bush to veto the legislation, some lobbyists worried that the issue could gain the same type of political resonance as the 1988 plant-closing law (PL 100-379).

That law, which required 60 days' notice of plant closings or mass layoffs, passed as a separate measure and became law without President Ronald Reagan's signature after he vetoed it as a provision on the omnibus trade bill. *(1988 Almanac, p. 213)*

Several weeks before the floor debate, Bush invited about a dozen Democrats to the White House to talk about the bill. On the morning it was brought up, Labor Secretary Lynn Martin met with the Republican conference at the Capitol.

And in a July 15 letter to Speaker of the House Thomas S. Foley, D-Wash., Martin said, "HR 5 would promote labor unrest, disrupt the flow of commerce, expose our economy to anti-competitive effects of inflationary collective bargaining agreements, and injure innocent non-striking workers, customers, suppliers and consumers."

Debate on the bill was generally lackluster, with Democrats talking about their union experiences and Republicans sharing tales of life in the business world.

Goodling tried yet again to strike a middle ground with his amendment, which would have barred permanent re—

placements during a strike for eight weeks or less. But neither side was interested, and the amendment, offered as a substitute, was rejected, 28-399. *(Vote 211, p. 52-H)*

Rep. Pete Peterson, D-Fla., then offered a substitute to the bill designed to attract moderate members who felt queasy about HR 5. The substitute required that a majority of workers vote to organize at least 30 days before a strike and be certified by the National Labor Relations Board before they could be protected from permanent replacements.

But other members complained that Peterson's provision was just another tool to be used by the unions in gathering members and preparing for a strike.

The House adopted Peterson's amendment, 252-174, before proceeding directly to pass the bill. *(Vote 212, p. 52-H)*

SENATE COMMITTEE ACTION

The Senate Labor and Human Resources Committee approved S 55 on June 19 by a party-line 10-7 vote.

The committee approved by voice vote an amendment offered by Howard M. Metzenbaum, D-Ohio, and Jeff Bingaman, D-N.M., clarifying that the legislation was intended to apply only to union workers.

Committee Chairman Edward M. Kennedy, D-Mass., said he could not understand why business lobbyists continued to oppose the legislation after complaining that it would affect non-union workers. "We changed it, and now they say it will encourage people to join unions. Which is it?" Kennedy asked.

Opponents of the bill said it would lead to more strikes and upset the balance of power between labor and management that had reigned for 50 years. "If this bill passes, one side will have the upper hand," said Orrin G. Hatch, R-Utah.

By the end of the year, the bill — which was highly unlikely to garner a veto-proof margin — had not made it to the floor.

Another key labor bill, to extend expired unemployment benefits (HR 1724), had moved higher on the labor agenda. Backers of the striker-replacement measure looked ahead to 1992. *(Unemployment bill, p. 301)* ■

House Moves To Renew Job-Training Act

Steering clear of complicated and divisive formula changes, the House passed a measure to reauthorize the federal government's major job-training program for disadvantaged youths. However, the Senate bill was not introduced until the last week of the session and not enough time remained to clear legislation.

Under the existing Job Training Partnership Act (JTPA), job-training allocations were based largely on the number of unemployed people in states and local communities. Lawmakers during the 101st Congress had tried to change the formula for the federal funding that each state received for summer youth programs, while leaving intact the formula for funding adult programs.

Legislation (HR 2039) was passed by the House on Sept. 27, 1990, 416-1. The Senate Labor and Human Resources Committee had approved its version (S 543) on July 26, 1989. However, the bill never reached the floor because some members worried that its new funding formula would cost their states money. *(1990 Almanac, p. 365)*

The effort that failed in 1990 was the first major attempt to amend the 1982 job-training law, which was coauthored by Sen. Edward M. Kennedy, D-Mass., and Vice President Dan Quayle, then a GOP senator from Indiana.

JTPA replaced a problem and abuse-plagued public-service employment program known as CETA (the Comprehensive Employment and Training Act).

In 1991, with members eager to help the jobless in a time of recession, committees did not attempt to change the formula. Instead, they focused on trying to make programs under the act more effective and efficient.

The bill (HR 3033) passed by the House on Oct. 9 mandated that in addition to being economically disadvantaged, at least 60 percent of the participants in the adult and youth programs had to have limited job skills or other barriers to employment.

Like the House bill, the Senate measure (S 2055) introduced Nov. 26 by Paul Simon, D-Ill., chairman of the Labor Subcommittee on Employment and Productivity, targeted the country's neediest and did not alter the formula that determined the amount of money each state received.

With no major differences between the House and Senate bills, the legislation was expected to clear in 1992.

BOXSCORE

➡ **Job Training Partnership Act (HR 3033, S 2055).** Legislation to reauthorize the 1982 Job Training Partnership Act and change the focus to target the nation's most needy.

Report: H Rept 102-240

KEY ACTION

Sept. 24 — The **House** Education and Labor Committee approved HR 3033 by voice vote.

Oct 9 — The **House** passed HR 3033, 420-6.

HOUSE COMMITTEE ACTION

The House Education Subcommittee on Employment Opportunity on July 31 approved, 7-0, a bill to revise the $4 billion federal job-training program. Critics of the program said it failed to serve the poorest, least-skilled individuals, while assisting many who might have gotten jobs without training.

The measure, drafted by Carl C. Perkins, D-Ky., was similar to the legislation passed by the House in 1990.

On Sept. 24, HR 3033 was approved by voice vote by the House Education and Labor Committee.

The committee measure did not call for a specific dollar amount for the programs, which had a permanent authorization, but expressed the desire of Congress that funding increase 10 percent. The fiscal 1991 appropriation for adult and youth programs under the act was $4.08 billion.

The goal of the legislation was to focus federal job-training aid on those who needed it most.

As the program existed, states and localities, in a part-

Helping Women Find Non-Traditional Jobs

Congress on Nov. 27 cleared a bill (S 367) aimed at steering more women to non-traditional jobs such as construction and technical work. President Bush signed the measure Dec. 12 — PL 102-235.

The bill concerned the placement of women under the Job Training Partnership Act (JTPA). Although the job training program was already supposed to help place women in non-traditional jobs, critics complained that women were typically directed to clerical and service jobs with lesser pay and benefits.

"Equal opportunity may be the law of the land, but occupational segregation of the sexes is a fact of life," Sen. Howard M. Metzenbaum, D-Ohio, said. For example, Metzenbaum said, women accounted for 87 percent of data entry keyers, but men made up 87 percent of data processing equipment repairers. Keyers' average pay was $290 per week; repairers averaged $515 per week.

"Non-traditional" job fields were defined as those in which less than 25 percent of the workers were women. Construction, technical jobs in construction, plumbing and electromechanics were such jobs.

Cindy Marano, executive director of Wider Opportunities for Women, a national women's employment organization, said a recent study indicated that less than 9 percent of female participants in the jobs program were placed in non-traditional jobs.

The bill enjoyed bipartisan support, sponsored in the House by Constance A. Morella, R-Md., and George Miller, D-Calif., and in the Senate by Metzenbaum and Orrin G. Hatch, R-Utah.

"This is an important step toward gaining economic security for millions of single-parent families," said Morella.

The bill required agencies receiving the job training funds to set goals for placing women in unconventional fields and to keep records on those placements. The secretary of Labor was required to report to Congress on progress in this area.

The bill also established a grant program to help states promote these placements. It designated $1.5 million a year for four years from the program's regular funds for such grants.

Congress appropriated $4.2 billion for the overall JTPA program for the year running from July 1, 1992, through June 30, 1993.

A broader bill (HR 3033) to reauthorize and revise the JTPA was passed by the House on Oct. 9. *(Job training, p. 315)*

The Senate Labor and Human Resources Committee approved S 367 (S Rept 102-65) by 17-0 on Feb. 20 with no substantive debate and no amendments.

The Senate passed a similar measure (S 975) in the 101st Congress, but it died after it was attached to a broader JTPA bill (HR 2039). *(1990 Almanac, p. 365)*

---

nership with private industry, were responsible for administering the programs. Although states and communities played the primary role, local private industry councils helped with policy-making and planning for the programs.

Reflecting the concern of some members that too much had been spent on administrative expenses, HR 3033 required that the majority of funding be used for training. Administrative costs could not exceed 20 percent of allocations, and 30 percent was to be used for support and training services.

The bill tightened procedures by requiring that program officials determine each new participant's needs and tailor training accordingly.

The measure also limited to six months the time that employers could receive training subsidies and provide on-the-job training. There was no existing cap.

The bill required the Labor Department to ensure that employers who continually failed to retain their participants no longer were eligible to receive the subsidies.

The existing program trained youths during the summer. The bill set up another program designed to provide job training for young people year-round. While the bulk of the bill's provisions were designed to help people leave welfare for employment, one component was aimed at helping them become self-employed.

Amendments

Tony P. Hall, D-Ohio, chairman of the House Select Committee on Hunger, worked through Perkins, the bill's sponsor, to get language included to clarify that states could use federal funds to help communities train poor, jobless people to start their own businesses.

But Hall failed to get a related amendment appended to a bill being marked up in the Ways and Means Subcommittee on Human Resources.

Only Ways and Means could permit welfare recipients to continue receiving benefits while they started businesses because it controlled Aid to Families with Dependent Children, the primary welfare program.

During the Education and Labor Committee markup, Pat Williams, D-Mont., successfully offered three amendments.

One went beyond the bill's purpose of finding jobs for the poorest. It was designed to help people ages 16 to 19, regardless of income, so long as they met school attendance and performance standards during the past school semester.

Under the amendment, adopted by voice vote, businesses or groups could receive federal subsidies for providing jobs for youths.

Another Williams amendment, also adopted by voice vote, established a national program for about $15 million that trained employees of the program.

A third amendment offered by Williams prompted a replay of a controversy that divided committee Democrats and Republicans in 1990. It created a program for providing employment assistance to victims of disasters.

The amendment met with strong opposition from Republicans, among them ranking member Bill Goodling of Pennsylvania and Steve Gunderson of Wisconsin.

Goodling said creation of the program would increase red tape and the time that disaster victims had to wait for assistance. "This amendment could not be included in a bipartisan bill because it changes the whole focus," from job training to disaster relief, Gunderson said.

The amendment was adopted on a party-line vote of 25-14.

Local concerns bubbled up when Jolene Unsoeld, a Democrat, proposed an amendment that would have authorized employment assistance for hard-hit timber workers in her home state of Washington.

But after lengthy debate and Republican threats to pile on amendments benefiting workers in their own states, Unsoeld withdrew her amendment.

A final amendment by Matthew G. Martinez, D-Calif., on behalf of Government Operations Committee Chairman John Conyers Jr., D-Mich., and Tom Lantos, D-Calif., received voice vote approval.

The amendment required the Labor Department to submit a report to Congress on administration and enforcement of anti-discrimination laws within the program.

During hearings earlier in the year, before the Government Operations Committee, witnesses had testified about instances of the job-training program discriminating against minorities and women.

HOUSE FLOOR ACTION

As growing unemployment lines made lawmakers eager to help the jobless, the federal job-training legislation passed the House Oct. 9, 420-6. *(Vote 298, p. 72-H)*

The bill called for no specific funding level for existing programs, which had a permanent authorization. However, the measure did express the desire of Congress that funding increase by at least 10 percent.

The measure also authorized $135 million for a number of new initiatives, including a youth program aimed at poverty-stricken communities.

The government funds were used by employers to provide on-the-job training to program participants. Under the locally administered program, the community's business people had a say in determining policies and in linking employers with those in need of skills training.

Lawmakers had complained that in order to improve success rates, program officials in some communities had provided assistance primarily to people with some skills who could have found a job without federal help.

According to a 1989 report by the General Accounting Office (GAO), high school dropouts were underserved by the program, which it said served about an equal number of skilled and unskilled people.

The bill's chief sponsor, Perkins, attempted to address this criticism.

The measure mandated that at least 60 percent of the participants in the adult and youth programs have only limited job skills or face other barriers to employment.

The same GAO report also found that some program participants worked in unskilled occupations, such as dishwashing, for months while their employers collected subsidies.

Members pointed to those findings and others and called for changes to prevent waste, fraud and abuse.

The bill aimed to make program officials, employers and job trainees more accountable by limiting to six months the time that employers could receive training subsidies and provide on-the-job training.

Also, HR 3033 required the Labor Department to ensure that employers who continually failed to retain their participants no longer be eligible to receive the subsidies.

It also attempted to expand help for youth and welfare recipients. ■

ERISA Made for Much Talk, Little Action

The 1974 law that covered pensions and other employee benefits was the subject of considerable discussion in 1991 but very little legislative action.

The Employee Retirement Income Security Act (ERISA) was under increasing attack because of its complexity and its loopholes.

The Bush administration weighed in with a proposal to make pensions more attractive for small businesses, but the plan stalled in Congress.

And bills (HR 1602, HR 2782) designed to close some of ERISA's loopholes were approved by a House Labor subcommittee but went no further in 1991.

ADMINISTRATION PLAN

The administration sought to encourage small businesses to offer pensions to their employees by easing paperwork demands and relaxing some ERISA restrictions. But small-business groups voiced reservations about the proposal, and it saw no legislative action in 1991.

Labor Secretary Lynn Martin unveiled the proposal April 30. She said it could lead to pension coverage for an additional 42 million workers, nearly 45 percent of the nation's work force.

A major feature of the proposal would have made pensions "portable" by encouraging employees who changed jobs to move their pensions to an Individual Retirement Account (IRA), and penalizing them with higher taxes if they did not.

Martin said that provisions that would lose tax revenues would be offset by others that would increase tax revenues by eliminating retirees' right to spread their tax liability over five to 10 years when they took their pensions in a lump sum.

But the Labor Department offered no figures on the tax trade-off, and opinions differed on whether the plan would cost money. An aide said that Dan Rostenkowski, D-Ill., chairman of the House Ways and Means Committee, was skeptical. "The initial response is that it costs money," the aide said. "How can they have IRAs that are budget-neutral?"

A Democratic aide to the Senate Finance Committee expressed skepticism of another kind. He said the administration and members of Congress were betting that the proposal would not end up costing any money because few people would take advantage of it.

"It doesn't cost anything," the aide said. "The reason is nobody's going to do it. If people really did this, it would cost more money than we've got."

No legislation accompanied Martin's proposal.

Instead, she said she wanted to work with members of the House Ways and Means and Senate Finance committees to draft legislation.

Despite Martin's effort to craft a proposal that would appeal to small companies, business groups found many holes in the plan. The National Federation of Independent Businesses (NFIB), which lobbied Congress on issues affecting small businesses, said proposals that would force employers to pay a minimum contribution per employee were too expensive for most small companies.

D. J. Gribben, legislative representative for NFIB, said the organization liked the concept of making the pension process simpler but predicted that it would not meet the administration's goal of increasing the participation of small businesses.

"They've priced it out of range of most small businesses, so a lot of them won't be participating," Gribben said.

The Martin plan did the following:

- Encouraged small businesses to provide tax-deferred retirement plans by exempting them from compliance with non-discrimination tests designed to safeguard lower-paid workers. Employers with 100 or fewer employees would not have been forced to comply with non-discrimination testing if they provided a base contribution of 2 percent of an employee's pay, up to $2,000 a year. A worker could save up to $8,300 a year tax-deferred, combining employer and employee contributions. Non-discrimination testing, toughened as part of the 1986 tax overhaul law, was designed to prevent top executives from sheltering vastly more income than lower-paid workers could.
- Ensured that workers covered by multi-employer pension plans gained vested interest in their benefits in five years, the same period as workers covered by single-employer plans. Under existing law, many workers covered by these plans had to wait 10 years to become vested.
- Extended tax-deferred savings plans known as 401(k) to tax-exempt organizations and state and local governments, extending coverage to about 12 million employees, 3.1 million of whom had no pensions, according to the Labor Department. Coverage for many of these workers was eliminated by the 1986 tax overhaul.
- Paved the way for employees who changed jobs to roll over lump-sum pension benefits to an IRA. Under existing law, the money went to the employee, making it easier for him or her to decide to spend the cash instead of saving it for retirement. Under Martin's plan, employers could send the payment directly to the worker's IRA.
- Removed tax incentives for lump-sum cash payments. The plan imposed a 10 percent excise tax on people younger than 59½ who cashed in their pension benefits, and it penalized retirees older than 59½ by eliminating their existing five-to-10-year income averaging for tax purposes.

PACKWOOD ALTERNATIVE

Members of Congress floated their own pension-expansion proposals in 1991. Sen. Bob Packwood, R-Ore., ranking member of the Finance Committee, introduced a pension portability bill (S 318) on Jan. 31.

Packwood's bill was preferred by business interests, including the NFIB. Gribben said the Packwood plan gave employers the option of providing pensions only to workers who requested them. Under the administration's proposal, if an employer chose to establish a pension plan, he had to provide pensions for all workers.

Packwood's bill dealt with the realities of the U.S. work force, Gribben said. Most workers placed pensions behind health plans and paid vacation on their list of priorities, he said. Given a choice, many would not choose a pension.

The Joint Tax Committee estimated that Packwood's plan would cost about $100 million over five years.

ERISA LOOPHOLES

The House Education and Labor Subcommittee on Labor-Management Relations approved two bills (HR 1602, HR 2782) that were designed to make it easier for people to collect in lawsuits against insurance companies involving health-care coverage.

ERISA prohibited states from enacting their own laws regulating any employee benefit, including health insurance. The Supreme Court ruled in 1987 that ERISA preempted state laws on remedies for unfair insurance claims practices. Because ERISA did not permit suits for punitive damages, policyholders who sued their insurers could collect only the costs of their illness. The law also limited lawyers' fees.

One measure (HR 1602) allowed policyholders to sue for damages from unfair claims practices so long as their states allowed such suits. The other bill (HR 2782) narrowed the instances in which federal law superseded state law in health benefits cases.

Both bills were approved on a party-line vote of 15-7 but went no further in 1991. ■

House Panel Advances Bill Aiding Black Lung Victims

The plight of coal miners who suffered from black lung disease received some attention from one House panel in 1991, but the legislation quickly drew administration opposition because of its costs.

The House Education and Labor Subcommittee on Labor Standards on July 24 approved the $4.3 billion bill that was aimed at helping miners and their dependents get benefits through two approaches: easing eligibility rules and lessening the burden on miners to prove that they were entitled to the money. The bill (HR 1637) was approved on a party-line vote of 5-3.

Subcommittee Chairman Austin J. Murphy, D-Pa., said black lung cases currently were weighed in favor of the employer, who could afford to supply stacks of medical evidence to support his position. Miners often could afford as a witness no more than a family physician.

Under the bill, an employer disputing a miner's claim for benefits would be allowed to present only one doctor's opinion and one X-ray to support his case. Miners would not have to face the same limits.

Further, if benefits were awarded and the case was reversed on appeal, the miner had to repay the money. Under the bill, if the miner received the benefits at least two years before final settlement of the claim, the miner would not have to return the money.

Eligibility rules for miners and dependents would be eased through new guidelines. Existing rules allowed dependents to receive benefits if the miner was getting the money when he died or if the miner was totally disabled by black lung contracted on the job.

The bill allowed benefits to survivors if the miner

worked for 25 years or more in the coal mines; if his death was due "in whole or in part" to black lung; and if the miner was receiving black lung benefits at the time of his death or had a claim pending supported by medical evidence.

The bill also allowed benefits to a miner who worked for 10 years in the mines if he produced one piece of evidence to support his claim. He would not have to prove total disability. "We believe this legislation is needed to give back to the disabled miner a fair chance," Murphy said.

Although the text of the bill included no price tag, the Congressional Budget Office estimated that the bill would cost about $4.3 billion over five years.

The cost was a chief reason for the Bush administration's strong opposition. Labor Secretary Lynn Martin wrote to the committee protesting the bill, but stopped short of a veto threat. She said the black lung trust fund was $3 billion in debt to the Treasury.

The fiscal 1992 spending bill for the Labor Department (HR 3839 — PL 102-170) earmarked $815 million for black lung benefits. Funding for the trust fund also came from an excise tax on coal and payments made by mine operators. *(Appropriations, p. 501)* ■

Martin Named To Head Labor

The Senate on Feb. 7 confirmed, 94-0, former Rep. Lynn Martin, R-Ill., as secretary of Labor after she had demonstrated her independence from key administration positions. *(Vote 11, p. 3-S)*

Martin's nomination had been approved 17-0 the day before by the Senate Labor Committee. Martin told the panel Jan. 30 that she would continue to voice her opinions about such matters as parental leave and civil rights, even though she and President Bush had disagreed. But she emphasized that she would back whatever position Bush took.

Martin had served five terms in the House until she left in 1990 for an unsuccessful run at the Senate.

She succeeded Elizabeth H. Dole, who stepped down as Labor secretary to head the American Red Cross.

Martin voted in 1990 in favor of the legislation mandating unpaid leave for workers caring for newborn children or seriously ill family members, a bill that Bush vetoed. She said she thought it was significant that Bush selected her for the Labor post even though they disagreed on the Family and Medical Leave Act. *(Family leave, bill p. 311)*

"He doesn't want yes women and yes men," she told the Senate Committee. "I assure you, I intend to give him my best advice."

Martin also differed with Bush over civil rights legislation designed to shore up guarantees against employment discrimination and on an increase in the federal minimum wage. *(Civil rights act, p. 251)*

Martin told the Senate committee that she did not believe quotas helped people meet the American dream, adding: "I couldn't serve the president if I did not share his policies of opportunity."

Committee Chairman Edward M. Kennedy, D-Mass., said Martin's past independence from Bush — and his willingness to nominate her despite those differences — spoke well of both her and the president.

Republicans Try To Halt Construction-Safety Bill

Legislation (HR 1063) to protect construction workers by setting stricter safety guidelines for construction companies won committee approval in the House despite strong Republican opposition.

The bill required contractors to produce a written safety and health plan to show how workers would be protected from accidents. Construction companies were to keep detailed safety records and tell federal authorities of serious accidents.

The strongest GOP critic was Paul B. Henry of Michigan, ranking member on the House Education and Labor Subcommittee on Health and Safety. He complained that the new reporting requirements would overburden the Occupational Safety and Health Administration (OSHA), impeding its capability to inspect construction sites and probe accidents.

The subcommittee approved HR 1063 on July 23 on a 5-3 party-line vote. During the markup, Republican members offered more than 20 amendments to highlight their many objections to the bill. Most were rejected by voice votes.

The full committee approved the measure, 24-14, on Sept. 24.

Subcommittee Chairman Joseph M. Gaydos, D-Pa., said he drafted the bill because about 2,500 construction workers were killed each year and more than 200,000 seriously injured in construction accidents. Many accidents could have been prevented, he said.

Although guidelines had been set by the industry, Gaydos said, the plans were voluntary. "But past history shows that voluntary compliance with safety guidelines does not and will not work because unsafe contractors refuse to follow them."

The bill also sought to address complaints that OSHA's method of targeting sites for inspections was unfair.

"Some safe employers are inspected regularly while other dangerous sites are never inspected because OSHA does not even know that the sites exist," Gaydos said.

Under the measure, a construction site would have to notify OSHA before work began in potentially dangerous work areas. OSHA could then target those sites for inspection.

Gaydos said the bill covered companies that dealt mainly in construction, not utilities. The measure required them to produce a written safety and health plan specific to each project. Companies would have to hire or designate a project constructor who would be responsible for the site, oversee the plan and conduct frequent inspections. Builders also would be required to hire a safety coordinator to implement the plan and investigate any serious injuries or deaths at the site.

The bill established within OSHA an Office of Construction Safety, Health and Education to be headed by a deputy assistant secretary for construction. The office would investigate deaths and injuries "where appropriate" and help develop construction rules. The office would also help educate employers and employees on accident prevention. ■

Patriotic Fervor Steers Gulf War Vets Bill

From the moment President Bush informed the country on the evening of Jan. 16 that he would be sending U.S. forces into battle against Iraq, there was an outcry of concern for the troops and their families left behind. Congress, brimming with patriotic fervor, quickly began considering a special benefits package to help alleviate the financial burdens of those fighting in the Persian Gulf.

However, congressional proponents of legislation to increase the pay and benefits of Persian Gulf military personnel and veterans had to worry about paying for the legislation without violating spending limits imposed by the 1990 budget law (HR 5835 — PL 101-508). Much of the debate centered on how the benefit package could be crafted so that it would qualify for a provision in the law that exempted spending for the gulf war from the caps.

Leaders from the House and Senate sorted through a grab bag of proposals that included raising combat pay, extending GI Bill education benefits and providing child-care services for gulf families. Some of the proposals were new, but others had been kicked around for years, and sponsors saw their chance to latch onto a surefire piece of legislation.

While enthusiasm for providing new military and veterans' benefits was widespread in Congress and at the White House, administration officials worked closely with senators to try to keep costs down and benefits restricted to those who actually had participated in the Persian Gulf War.

Through much of the debate, Democrats faced Republican complaints that their enthusiasm for expanded military benefits was largely an effort to win back favor for voting against authorizing the war.

Both the House and Senate approved generous veterans' and military benefits packages a week after the president announced the liberation of Kuwait and began pulling troops out of the Persian Gulf.

Conferees met to hash out the differences the week of March 18, and the Senate approved the final measure, reintroduced as a new bill (S 725) March 21, by voice vote; the House cleared it shortly afterward by a vote of 396-4. *(Vote 58, p. 14-H)*

As cleared, the legislation, estimated to cost $655 million, increased imminent danger, or combat, pay from $110 a month to $150 a month for those who served in the gulf war. The increase was effective from Aug. 1, the day before Iraqi troops invaded Kuwait, until 180 days after Bush declared the war ended.

The death gratuity for families of those killed in the war was doubled to $6,000, and the group life insurance benefit for service members and veterans doubled to $100,000.

A House provision was dropped that would have prevented the Pentagon from activating reservists who were mothers — or fathers with sole custody — of children under 6 months of age.

The largest increase for veterans was in GI Bill education benefits. Monthly payments were raised from $300 a month to $350 a month for those who enlisted for more than three years. Similar increases were provided for two-year enlistees, reservists and National Guard members.

The increases became effective Oct. 1, 1991, through Sept. 30, 1993, but the secretaries of Defense and Veterans Affairs had the option of continuing the increased levels. The legislation also provided authorization for $15 billion in supplemental appropriations to cover U.S. Persian Gulf costs and $340 million for defense-related nuclear waste management and environmental restoration activities. *(Desert Storm supplemental, p. 680)*

BOXSCORE

➡ Benefits for Persian Gulf Troops (S 725, formerly HR 1175, S 578). The bill increased combat pay and other benefits for military personnel and provided additional GI Bill education and other benefits for veterans. It required funding to come from foreign contributions for the war effort and authorized up to $15 billion from the U.S. Treasury to pay for the war.

Reports: H Rept 102-16, Part I; S Rept 102-18.

KEY ACTION

March 13 — HR 1175 passed the **House** by a vote of 398-25.

March 14 — The package of benefits passed the **Senate** by voice vote, followed by a 97-1 vote in favor of S 578.

March 21 — Approved by **House-Senate** conference as S 725: Senate approved by voice vote; House cleared it shortly afterward by a vote of 396-4.

April 6 — President Bush signed S 725 — PL 102-25.

SENATE COMMITTEE ACTION

A Senate task force headed by John Glenn, D-Ohio, started early in the 102nd Congress to sift through scores of bills relating to the Persian Gulf War in an effort to shape an omnibus package.

Among them was legislation (S 335) unanimously approved by the Senate Labor and Human Resources Committee on Feb. 20 to give military personnel serving in the Persian Gulf region additional time to repay student loans. Under the measure, approved 17-0, soldiers serving in Operation Desert Storm would have been given until the end of hostilities before they would have had to begin repaying their student loans. Also on Feb. 20, the Senate Small Business Committee approved, 11-2, legislation (S 360) that would have authorized the Small Business Administration to provide loans to small businesses hurt by the loss of key employees to service in the war and would have imposed a moratorium on repayments of any Small Business Administration loans held by activated members of the National Guard or reserves.

However, these items were not incorporated into the package that was finally considered on the Senate floor.

In its Jan. 30 markup, the Senate Armed Services panel approved five measures to be rolled into an omnibus bill for floor consideration.

One measure (S 237) introduced by Chairman Sam Nunn, D-Ga., would have hiked imminent-danger pay for gulf troops from $110 to $150 per month.

The panel also approved a bill (S 232) that would

have doubled — from $50,000 to $100,000 — life insurance provided for members of the military.

The other measures would have:

- Given members leaving the military the same 26 weeks of unemployment benefits available to civilians who lost their jobs (S 160).
- Allowed retired military personnel recalled to active duty to serve at the highest grade they held while on active duty (S 204).
- Authorized troops serving in the gulf to invest their pay in a Treasury savings program with an interest rate of up to 10 percent (S 221). Meanwhile, the Senate Finance Committee began sifting through numerous proposals to expand tax and pension benefits for troops serving in Desert Storm. Members also looked for ways to offset the costs.

Proposals considered by the committee included extending the combat pay tax exclusion to prisoners of war and soldiers missing in action; allowing reservists to deduct expenses associated with Desert Storm from their taxes, including uniforms, travel and meals; and extending the earned-income tax credit, a refundable income tax credit available to low-income workers, to qualified military personnel stationed overseas.

None of these tax bills were eventually approved by the Senate, in part because there was no interest in the House Ways and Means Committee in extending unemployment benefits and certain tax breaks to those serving in the Persian Gulf.

As Senate leaders worked the week of Feb. 25 to package these bills and other proposals introduced to help families and troops involved in Desert Storm, Republicans charged that Democrats were loading up the legislation with everything but the kitchen sink.

Some said the Democrats were trying to counter any political setbacks they faced because most of them voted Jan. 12 against authorizing war (H J Res 77 — PL 102-1). *(Vote 9, p. 2-H)*

Others said that the Democrats wanted to put President Bush in the embarrassing position of having to either veto or lobby to scale back what was certain to be popular, but expensive, legislation.

"The very people who didn't vote for the war are unburdening their guilt with a tremendous package of benefits," said Sen. Assistant Minority Leader Alan K. Simpson, R-Wyo. "It's an orgy."

Democrats dismissed the allegations. Leadership aides said they were trying as best they could to weed out extraneous measures and to keep the cost under control, and they noted that Republicans as well as Democrats were promoting new benefit plans.

As these various pieces of the package were fashioned, Democrats agreed that the $311 million price tag on it for fiscal 1991 should be considered a cost of Operation Desert Storm, exempting it from spending caps set under the 1990 budget agreement.

However, Office of Management and Budget Director Richard G. Darman had already warned that the administration did not consider many of those costs to be directly related to the war. In a Feb. 5 letter to a number of members, he said passage of the legislation could set off automatic spending cuts under the new budget law.

A more modest benefits package was recommended March 1 by a Republican Senate task force headed by John McCain, Ariz.

The Senate Armed Services Committee approved a number of the Democrats' recommendations March 5 as part of its authorization (S 578) of supplemental funding for the war.

Among other things, the committee agreed to authorize $20 million for the Defense secretary to provide child care for families of active-duty personnel, $30 million for education and family support services, transitional medical benefits for deactivated reservists, an increase in the death gratuity from $3,000 to $6,000 and a one-year delay in the Feb. 15 effective date for reduction in mental health benefits under the Civilian Health and Medical Programs of the Uniformed Services (CHAMPUS.)

It also incorporated four measures (S 237, S 204, S 331 and S 221) that the committee had approved earlier in the year, including a proposal to raise combat pay from $110 a month to $150 a month.

HOUSE COMMITTEE ACTION

As the House package (HR 1175) that authorized supplemental appropriations for the war took shape in several committees, it included potentially troublesome language designed to avoid tough new budget requirements that such spending be offset by tax increases or cuts in other spending.

Republicans had complained about the funding maneuver during a closed-door markup of the bill by the Armed Services Committee on March 6.

The House package tied the veterans' benefits cost to Operation Desert Storm by setting aside $1 billion over the next five years from the appropriations account that was being used to pay for the Persian Gulf War. A number of Republicans objected that such a move would require U.S. allies, whose contributions were largely funding the account, to pay for long-term benefits unrelated to the war.

"That was not negotiated with our allies," said Armed Services Republican Jon Kyl, Ariz.

In addition, the bill included language stating that enactment of the measure would signify congressional designation of the veterans spending as emergency-related, a step required to exempt it from the new budget requirement.

That provision caused concern among House budget leaders who saw it as the first step in the unraveling of the 1990 budget deal.

"It creates an incentive for every other committee to use exactly the same language," said Budget Committee Chairman Leon E. Panetta, D-Calif.

Nevertheless, the language put Bush in an uncomfortable position. If he signed the bill, but did not declare the veterans spending an emergency — as he was also required to do — across-the-board cuts would be triggered in veterans and other entitlement programs.

House opponents of the funding mechanism also found themselves in a similar predicament when it came to voting on the popular benefits package.

"When push comes to shove, I don't know how you vote no," said Armed Services Chairman Les Aspin, D-Wis.

OTHER VETERANS BILLS

Benefits for Persian Gulf Troops

Following are provisions of the Benefits for Persian Gulf Troops Act. As signed by the president on April 6 (S 725 — PL 102-25), the act:

- Authorized the Department of Defense to use funds in the so-called Defense Cooperation Account, composed of foreign contributions to help pay for the Persian Gulf War, to cover incremental defense costs associated with the war.
- Established the Persian Gulf Conflict Working Capital Account to pay war-related costs until they could be covered by the Defense Cooperation Account. The bill authorized $15 billion in appropriations for the working capital account and provided that any funds remaining after the account was terminated revert to the Treasury. The secretary of Defense was required to report to Congress regularly on operations of the accounts.
- Authorized $655 million in appropriations from the Defense Cooperation Account to pay for the benefits provided in the bill for military personnel and veterans. Of that amount, no more than $255 million could be used for veterans' benefits, and any continuation of GI Bill benefit increases after fiscal 1993 could not be funded through the Defense Cooperation Account.
- Excluded costs of the benefits from budgetary caps by providing that they be considered incremental costs associated with Operation Desert Storm.
- Required the director of the Office of Management and Budget to submit monthly reports to Congress on the costs of U.S. military operations associated with the gulf war and the status of allied pledges and contributions to the effort.
- Raised combat, or imminent danger, pay from $110 a month to $150 a month, effective from Aug. 1, 1990, until the start of the first month following 180 days after the end of the war was formally declared.
- Increased family separation pay from $60 a month to $75 a month, effective from Jan. 15 until the start of the first month following 180 days after the end of the war.
- Authorized special pay for optometrists, veterinarians and other non-physician health-care workers who were reservists called up to active duty, or those involuntarily retained on, or recalled to, active duty in the Persian Gulf. The provision was effective Nov. 5, 1990, until the start of the first month following 180 days after the end of the war.
- Authorized board certification pay for health-care providers unable to complete the certification process due to service in the war.
- Required that graduates from military language schools who were sent to the Persian Gulf before they could be certified receive foreign language proficiency pay.
- Doubled to $6,000 the death gratuity paid to survivors of those killed during the war or within 180 days after it ended.
- Exempted those missing in action from a $10,000 limit on the amount military personnel could set aside in a Department of Defense savings plan.
- Ensured payment to survivors of the unused leave of those who died in the war.
- Authorized a basic housing allowance for unmarried reservists called to active duty in the gulf war.
- Allowed retirees recalled to service to be paid at the highest grade they held satisfactorily while on previous active duty.
- Delayed from April 1 until Oct. 1 the scheduled increase in deductibles for dependents of those serving in the gulf under the Civilian Health and Medical Programs of the Uniformed Services (CHAMPUS). The bill also allowed health-care providers to waive payments for such families.
- Delayed until Oct. 1 the effective date for CHAMPUS mental-health reimbursement limits that had been set to go into effect Feb. 15.
- Provided one month of transitional health-care coverage for deactivated reservists and those involuntarily retained on active duty if they were not covered by an employer-provided plan.
- Authorized $20 million for the secretary of Defense to provide child-care services and $30 million for school-based and other support services for families of Desert Storm troops.
- Authorized filing extensions for senior military officials who had served in a combat zone and were required to submit financial disclosure forms under the Ethics in Government Act.
- Increased the maximum group life insurance coverage for servicemen and women from $50,000 to $100,000, effective upon enactment, with higher premiums. Payments to survivors of those who died after Aug. 1, 1990, and before enactment were doubled from the amount of coverage held at the time of death.
- Allowed federal workers to donate their annual leave to a pool that would be divided equally among returning Desert Storm troops who worked for the federal government.
- Allowed deferment of government student loan repayments for those serving in the war.

The bill included sense-of-Congress language that post-secondary institutions should refund tuition paid for courses that could not be completed by those who were called to active duty in the Persian Gulf War.

- Provided certain protections and waivers for those who served in the war and participated in federal farm programs. This included farm credit relief for activated reservists.
- Reduced from 180 days to 90 days the minimum active-duty service required for Persian Gulf veterans to qualify for certain dental benefits.
- Extended to Persian Gulf veterans eligibility for readjustment counseling, certain drug benefits for homebound veterans and treatment for psychosis.
- Increased Montgomery GI Bill education benefits for full-time study from $300 a month to $350 a month for those serving on active duty for three years or more, from $250 a month to $275 a month for those serving for two years, and from $140 a month to $170 a month for reservists and National Guard members. Smaller increases were provided for part-time study. The increases were effective for fiscal years 1992 and 1993. After that time, the secretaries of Veterans Affairs and Defense could continue the increased rates and adjust them for inflation.
- Required that employers make certain accommodations for disabled veterans returning to their previous jobs and make every effort to retrain returning workers.
- Extended eligibility for VA home-loan benefits to Persian Gulf veterans with service of 90 days or more.
- Defined the Persian Gulf War as the period beginning on Aug. 2, 1990, the day Iraqi troops invaded Kuwait, and ending on a date prescribed by law or presidential proclamation.
- Required the secretary of Defense to submit a preliminary report on the war to congressional defense committees by July 1, 1991, with a final report by Jan. 1, 1992.
- Expressed the sense of Congress that in awarding contracts for the reconstruction of Kuwait, preference be given to U.S. firms employing American workers, especially veterans, and to small and minority-owned firms.
- Required the secretary of Defense to study departmental policies related to reservists and active-duty personnel who have children and to report back to Congress no later than March 31, 1992. The bill included sense-of-the-House language that the Pentagon should not deploy reservists or active-duty personnel who are mothers of children under the age of 6 months.
- Allowed the military services to waive statutory limits on the number of active-duty members and the number of officers and enlisted personnel holding certain ranks because of the war.
- Authorized $283 million for operating expenses at the Rocky Flats nuclear weapons plant in Golden, Colo. The bill also directed the secretary of Energy to develop a program to relocate the Rocky Flats plant, within 10 years of enactment, to a site "where public health and safety can be assured." The secretary was directed to report to Congress on the relocation plan within 60 days of enactment.
- Authorized $340 million for defense-related nuclear waste cleanup activities. ■

The $1 billion veterans portion of HR 1175 was largely crafted by Veterans' Affairs Committee Chairman G. V. "Sonny" Montgomery, D-Miss., who was also a member of Armed Services. It sought to increase veterans education, health and housing benefits as well as retarget survivors' compensation to provide greater protection for younger families.

In addition, the legislation included numerous changes in military personnel benefits, as approved March 5 by Armed Services' Military Personnel and Compensation Subcommittee. Among other things, the package raised combat and family-separation pay, increased death gratuity payments and provided transitional medical coverage for reservists after they left active service in Operation Desert Storm.

The bill also sought to protect mothers and single fathers of children under 6 months of age from being called to active duty or reassigned.

The fiscal 1991 cost for the provisions approved by the Personnel subcommittee was estimated at $375 million.

HOUSE FLOOR ACTION

The House passed HR 1175 March 13 by an overwhelming vote of 398-25 after a bitter partisan debate over the funding mechanism. *(Vote 48, p. 12-H)*

Republicans charged that language inserted by House leaders to require a presidential emergency declaration for the benefits to go into effect was a ploy to embarrass Bush and bust the budget at the same time.

"Do you know what that means? That means that Congress is blackmailing the president," said an angry Gerald B. H. Solomon, R-N.Y. "It is a hell of a way to do business with the veterans of this nation."

Added Ohio Republican Bob McEwen: "This is a nasty, nasty thing to do. This is an effort to be able to go home and say, 'I voted to give money to the veterans and the president is holding it up.' "

But House Democrats, who had suffered scathing GOP attacks for their Jan. 12 vote against authorizing the war, were in no mood to cave in. They argued that the price was not too much to pay to show appreciation to U.S. troops.

"We are talking here about 500,000 young men and women who gave of their time and their service and sacrifice, and in many instances life and limb for their country," said David E. Bonior, D-Mich.

On March 12, Rules Committee Chairman Joe Moakley, D-Mass., had worked with his panel to craft a rule governing floor debate on the bill that would allow some amendments. The rule was approved by a largely party-line vote of 247-171. *(Vote 44, p. 12-H)*

Budget Committee leaders then made a futile attempt to amend the legislation so that the spending would be subject to the pay-as-you-go provisions in the 1990 budget law. They argued that if the language declaring the funding emergency-related was successful, it would encourage the use of similar language in other bills to avoid budget restrictions.

"The point is, if we believe that these benefits are important, let's pay for them," said Budget Committee Chairman Panetta. He argued that because the administration had already said Bush would not make the required emergency declaration, the bill would raise false expectations among veterans.

The amendment was defeated by a vote of 175-248. However, Panetta and cosponsor Bill Gradison, R-Ohio, later said they were surprised they got as much support as they did, given the popularity of veterans' benefits. *(Vote 45, p. 12-H)*

"I thought we'd get creamed," said Gradison. "I think under the circumstances, it was not a kick in the pants" to the budget process.

The House also defeated, 165-260, an amendment by Minority Leader Robert H. Michel, R-Ill., that sought to restore a budget-law requirement that the Office of Management and Budget, rather than the Congressional Budget Office, determine the cost of tax and entitlement bills. *(Vote 46, p. 12-H)*

By voice vote, members approved several proposals to encourage the use of U.S. contractors and citizens, especially veterans, in the reconstruction of Kuwait.

Also adopted was an amendment to withhold U.S. payments to foreign workers at Defense Department installations overseas if those countries failed to pay their pledges to the war effort. An amendment was also approved by voice vote to exclude U.S. military installations from a required 4 percent personnel reduction if they had experienced an equivalent increase in work due to the war.

Members rejected, 145-281, a Republican motion to send the bill back to committee with instructions to attach language expressing support for development of an anti-ballistic missile defense system as part of the Strategic Defense Initiative (SDI). *(Vote 47, p. 12-H; SDI, p. 407)*

SENATE FLOOR ACTION

The Senate package was brought to the floor March 14 as a leadership amendment to S 578, an Armed Services Committee bill that already included a number of the military personnel benefits. The package was crafted after weeks of negotiations between Democratic and Republican leaders and was based on the recommendations of Glenn's task force.

Leaders warned at the start of the debate that approval of amendments to the package could unravel bipartisan backing for the bill.

They vowed to oppose all changes, and Glenn, who chaired the Armed Services Committee's Military Manpower and Personnel Subcommittee, said there would be other chances during the year to provide additional benefits.

The first attempt to amend the package came from Dale Bumpers, D-Ark., chairman of the Small Business Committee, who complained that his panel's bill to provide assistance to gulf war veterans who owned small businesses had not made the final cut in the leadership amendment. A motion to table (kill) his amendment to provide government assistance to such small-business owners was approved 58-38. *(Vote 26, p. 5-S)*

The next attempted change was more successful. A motion to table an amendment by Jesse Helms, R-N.C., to prevent the use of any funds authorized by the bill to rebuild Iraq was defeated, 0-98. *(Vote 28, p. 5-S)*

Initially, about 40 senators, supporting leaders' attempts to block all amendments, had voted to table the Helms proposal. But when it became clear the motion would fail, all of the "yea" votes were quickly switched to "nays," lest anyone be accused of supporting the Iraqi regime of Saddam Hussein.

Subsequently, the Senate agreed, 98-0, to substitute language expressing the sense of the Senate that none of the funds in the bill be used to rebuild Iraq so long as

Saddam remained in power. *(Vote 29, p. 5-S)*

The benefits package was then approved by voice vote, followed by a 97-1 vote in favor of the entire bill. The dissenting vote was cast by Oregon Republican Mark O. Hatfield, who had been a strong opponent in January of going to war. *(Vote 30, p. 5-S)*

Earlier, John W. Warner, R-Va., agreed to withdraw an amendment to promote development of a space-based anti-missile defense system as part of the Strategic Defense Initiative.

FINAL ACTION

Representatives of the two chambers tried during the week of March 18 to work out differences between the two bills, in the hope of reaching agreement before Congress departed for its Easter recess. Differences were resolved through a series of informal meetings among members, aides and administration officials. An official conference was never held.

The biggest difference was cost. The House bill (HR 1175) carried a price tag of about $1.4 billion over the next five years. It provided a wide variety of education, pay, health, housing and other benefits, not only for veterans of the gulf war but also for other veterans and military personnel.

White House officials had warned that Bush would veto the measure because of its high cost.

The bill also included language that put the onus on Bush to declare all of the spending to be emergency-related before any of the provisions could go into effect.

By contrast, the Senate package targeted most of the benefits to veterans of the gulf war, at a five-year cost of about $500 million.

While it, too, bypassed budget caps, the legislation (S 578) was drafted with broad bipartisan input and had won White House backing. The package was to be financed largely by foreign contributions to the fund set up to cover U.S. costs of the Persian Gulf War.

Administration Targets

In the unofficial conference negotiations, which involved OMB Director Darman, the administration's prime target was the House proposal to greatly expand GI education benefits. The administration said the benefits were 10 times greater than similar proposals in the Senate bill.

However, administration lobbyists expected strong resistance from House negotiators, especially Veterans' Affairs Chairman Montgomery, prime author and proponent of the GI Bill, which provided the education benefits.

Referring to House approval a week earlier of $650 million in aid to Israel, Montgomery complained: "We're worrying more about weapons systems and people who didn't fight, like the Israelis, than we are about people who did fight."

However, opponents of the size of the package noted that most of those participating in the war volunteered for service.

Both bills defined the war as U.S. military activities conducted between Aug. 2, 1990 — the day that Iraq invaded Kuwait — and a future date set by law or presidential proclamation as the end of the war. The definition was important in determining who was eligible for many of the proposed benefits.

After a week of negotiations, House and Senate conferees reached an agreement that was acceptable to the White House. The biggest change was a substantial paring back of the new veterans education benefits that had been included in the House package.

Just before heading home for the two-week Easter recess, Congress sent Bush the package of new benefits for veterans and military personnel.

"The troops of Operations Desert Shield and Desert Storm were there when America needed them," said Senate Minority Leader Bob Dole, R-Kan. "By passing this bill, we will ensure that they and their families receive the benefits they so richly deserve."

The package was expected to cost $655 million over the next five years, far less than the $1.4 billion called for in the House bill but more than the $500 million cost of the original Senate version.

All funding authorized in the bill was appropriated in a related spending measure (HR 1281 — PL 102-27) that was cleared by Congress March 22 and signed by the president April 10. Under the agreement reached between Congress and the administration, spending for the veterans' and military benefits was excluded from the existing budget caps.

The administration refused to declare the spending emergency-related, fearing that it would set a bad precedent for exemptions from budget limits.

But costs of the gulf war were also exempt from the limits, so negotiators tried to work out a package that could justifiably be labeled a cost of the war, to be paid for by allies.

The Senate approved the final measure, introduced as a new bill (S 725) March 21 by voice vote; the House cleared it later that day by a vote of 396-4. As cleared, the legislation increased imminent danger, or combat, pay from $110 a month to $150 a month for those serving in the gulf war. The increase was effective from Aug. 1, the day before Iraqi troops invaded Kuwait, until 180 days after Bush declared the war ended.

The bill also raised family separation pay from $60 a month to $75 a month, effective Jan 15 — the day before allied bombing began — until 180 days after the war ended.

Dropped was a House provision that would have prevented the Pentagon from activating reservists who were mothers — or fathers with sole custody — of children under 6 months old.

The largest increase for veterans was in GI Bill education benefits. Monthly payments were raised from $300 a month to $350 a month for those who enlisted for more than three years.

Similar increases were provided for two-year enlistees, reservists and National Guard members.

The legislation also provided authorization for $15 billion in supplemental appropriations to cover U.S. Persian Gulf costs and $340 million for defense-related nuclear waste management and environmental restoration activities. ■

Cost of Living Increases

Congress in 1991 approved two measures that gave cost of living increases to disabled veterans and to spouses and children of veterans who died of service-related injuries.

In 1990, legislation to give the increase as of Jan. 1, 1991, stalled after some members of Congress tried to attach provisions ensuring compensation for some veterans suffering from cancer after exposure to Agent Orange. Opponents of the Agent Orange provisions questioned the link between the chemical defoliant and cancer and argued that the bill would be too costly. *(1990 Almanac, p. 418; Agent Orange, p. 326)*

It was the first time Capitol Hill had failed to pass a veterans COLA in the same year in which it granted such increases to Social Security recipients.

With national attention riveted on U.S. military forces in the Persian Gulf as Congress returned in the new year, members hastened to break the impasse. Late in January, they overwhelmingly approved a 5.4 percent cost of living increase for disabled veterans in 1991.

When Congress turned to the 1992 COLA later in the year, the measure was less controversial. The 3.7 percent increase reflected inflation as measured by the Consumer Price Index and was cleared by Congress at the end of October.

BOXSCORE

➡ **Veterans Compensation Amendments of 1991 (HR 3).** The bill provided a 5.4 percent cost of living adjustment (COLA), effective Jan. 1, 1991, for disabled veterans and for spouses and children of veterans who died of service-related injuries.

KEY ACTION

Jan. 23 - HR 3 passed in the **House**, on a vote of 421-0, under suspension of the rules.

Jan. 24 - HR 3 cleared by the **Senate** on a vote of 99-0.

Feb. 6 - President Bush signed HR 3 — PL 102-3.

➡ **Veterans Compensation Amendments of 1991 (HR 1046).** The bill provided a 3.7 percent COLA in 1992 for disabled veterans and for spouses and children of veterans who died of service-related injuries.

Reports: H Rept 102-164; S Rept. 102-139.

KEY ACTION

July 29 - HR 1046 (calling for 4.8 percent increase) passed by the **House**. Revised bill authorizing 3.7 percent increase passed by voice vote Oct. 30, clearing the measure for the president.

Oct. 28 - S 775 passed by the **Senate** by voice vote.

Nov. 12 - President Bush signed HR 1046 — PL 102-152.

1991 COLA

As they convened the 102nd Congress, members had promised irate veterans they would make the disability benefit boost a top priority. But first they had to avert a new fight over Agent Orange.

In the House, the two protagonists were Veterans' Affairs Committee Chairman G. V. "Sonny" Montgomery, D-Miss., and committee member Lane Evans, D-Ill. Evans, a Vietnam War veteran, long had tried to push Agent Orange legislation, only to be blocked in committee by Montgomery. In 1990, however, the panel did attach the Agent Orange legislation to the COLA bill, producing a House impasse.

On Jan. 3, Montgomery, reintroduced legislation (HR 3) that would provide the 5.4 percent COLA for 2.2 million veterans with service-connected disabilities and 300,000 spouses and children of veterans who died from service-connected injuries.

The same day, Evans reintroduced his competing legislation (HR 321) that would provide the COLA as well as compensate veterans for several diseases linked to Agent Orange exposure.

In the Senate, Veterans' Affairs Committee Chairman Alan Cranston, D-Calif., and Tom Daschle, D-S.D., had supported Agent Orange compensation, while Alan K. Simpson, R-Wyo., and Frank H. Murkowski, R-Alaska, had thwarted it.

Daschle and Cranston, along with Senate Majority Leader George J. Mitchell, D-Maine, introduced S 1, a version of an earlier bill (S 2100) that would have provided the COLA and Agent Orange benefits. Bob Graham, D-Fla., introduced a clean COLA measure (S 107).

However, on Jan. 17, the day after bombing began over Iraq, the two camps settled the issue. Montgomery and Evans agreed to consider the two veterans bills in a way that would speed action on both.

Under the agreement, the House would consider a COLA bill without amendments that could complicate enactment. An Agent Orange bill also would be considered without amendments.

"Quick passage of this [COLA] bill will send a clear message to veterans who have fought in previous wars and to the tens of thousands of our brave young men and women who are part of Operation Desert Storm that we stand behind them," Montgomery said.

Simpson and Murkowski also shifted to back free-standing Agent Orange legislation.

With the impasse broken, action in both chambers was swift. The House passed HR 3 by 421-0 on Jan. 23; the Senate cleared the bill 99-0 the next day. *(House vote 14, p. 4-H; Senate vote 5, p. 2-S)*

1992 COLA

The Senate Veterans' Affairs Committee opened the bidding on the COLA for 1992, approving a bill (S 775) by voice vote on June 26. The increase was estimated to cost $486 million in new budget authority, but the actual COLA boost would not be determined until the fall. COLAs for Social Security and veterans' benefits were based on the rate of inflation as measured by the Consumer Price Index, announced in October.

During the panel's markup, Simpson tried to avert future controversies by amending the bill to make the boosts automatic. He cited the Agent Orange controversy's delay of the 1991 COLA in arguing for automatic benefit adjustments.

"It means that the people do not have to depend on the political posturing of members of Congress," Simpson said. But his amendment failed on a 5-5 tie, with Graham the lone Democrat to support it.

A Graham amendment that would reinstate benefits to widows of some veterans won approval. Until 1990, a veteran's widow would lose survivor's benefits when she remarried but would regain them if her second husband died or she was divorced. The

1990 budget-reconciliation act disqualified such women from getting resumed benefits if the second husband died or if she was divorced after Oct. 31, 1990.

Graham's amendment would help women whose husbands died or who were divorced before Oct. 31, but who did not file for benefits. A committee aide said some women might have been unaware of the change in the law.

The Senate bill did contain provisions that drew opposition from the White House. Committee Chairman Cranston included language that would have revised existing law providing for compensation of veterans suffering from diseases related to exposure to radiation during military service.

House members also opposed that approach, and the version (HR 1046) marked up by the House Veterans' Affairs Committee was a "clean" COLA bill.

As approved by the panel July 23, the legislation was to provide disabled veterans and survivors of military personnel who died from service-related illnesses with a 4.8 percent benefits increase, based on an early estimate of what the Consumer Price Index would be. The COLA boost, to be effective Dec. 1, was to show up in January checks.

In writing HR 1046, the Subcommittee on Compensation, Pension and Insurance had provided for a 5.2 percent COLA. But full committee Chairman Montgomery offered a substitute amendment holding the raise to no more than 4.8 percent, to comply with the 1990 budget agreement between Congress and the White House. The panel approved the amendment by voice vote.

The Department of Veterans Affairs estimated the bill would cost $520.4 million in fiscal 1992 and $3 billion through fiscal 1996.

The House passed the bill authorizing the 4.8 percent increase on July 29.

Cranston had hoped to get Congress to enact his version that would also compensate veterans suffering from radiation exposure. But the added money remained controversial and the Department of Veterans Affairs (VA) warned Senate committee members that if the COLA was not enacted by November, the department would not be able to process it in time for money to appear in January checks.

Cranston opted to heed the VA's admonition and move for floor consideration of the House measure. But, he said, "The clean COLA we are about to pass will diminish my efforts to enact the radiation provisions."

The Senate passed HR 1046 on Oct. 28 by voice vote, after amending it to include the 3.7 percent COLA increase based on the Consumer Price Index.

Two days later, the House approved the amended HR 1046 by voice vote, clearing the measure for President Bush's signature. ■

Agent Orange Impasse Comes to an End

Strong support for U.S. forces in the Persian Gulf propelled Congress to clear legislation aimed at helping veterans of another, less popular war. Ending a long-running dispute, both chambers passed HR 556, which sought to ensure compensation for Vietnam veterans for some diseases linked to Agent Orange and set up a process for determining whether other ailments were caused by exposure to the defoliant.

A bipartisan compromise on the bill, reached in January as the gulf war got under way, marked the first time in more than a decade that leaders of the House and Senate Veterans' Affairs committees had agreed that the government should compensate veterans exposed to Agent Orange for specific illnesses.

The compromise paved the way for Congress to pass legislation to provide a cost of living adjustment for disabled veterans and for spouses and children of veterans who died of service-related injuries.

That bill (HR 3) was a top priority and had been held up by the Agent Orange dispute in 1990. *(COLA bill, p. 325; background, 1990 Almanac, p. 418)*

After clearing the COLA legislation, Congress turned to the Agent Orange bill at the end of January. Both chambers passed it with no opposition.

BOXSCORE

➡ **Agent Orange Act of 1991 (HR 556).** The bill codified the decision by the Secretary of Veterans Affairs to compensate veterans for some diseases linked to Agent Orange; it also set up a process for determining whether other ailments were caused by exposure to the defoliant.

KEY ACTION

Jan. 29 - HR 556 passed the **House** by a vote of 412-0.

Jan. 30 - HR 556 passed the **Senate** by a vote of 99-0.

Feb. 6 - President Bush signed HR 556 — PL 102-4.

Putting Vietnam to Rest

Members said they hoped the Agent Orange bill would resolve an issue that had become a symbol of a divisive war. "As war rages in the Middle East, we today take a big step in putting the Vietnam War behind us," said Rep. Lane Evans, D-Ill., a Vietnam era veteran who had pushed the Agent Orange bill for years.

MAJOR PROVISIONS

HR 556 codified two decisions by Veterans Affairs Secretary Edward J. Derwinski in 1990 to provide benefits to veterans who suffered from either of two forms of cancer, non-Hodgkins lymphoma or soft-tissue sarcoma. The bill also put into statute an earlier department decision to compensate veterans for a skin ailment, chloracne, also linked to Agent Orange.

The legislation also required the National Academy of Sciences (NAS) to analyze existing Agent Orange studies to determine whether scientific evidence linked the disease with other cancers. The NAS would then make recommendations to the secretary.

The Congressional Budget Office estimated the bill would cost $11 million in outlays in 1991 and $17 million in 1992.

The bill also extended through Dec. 31, 1993, veterans' eligibility for free medical care they already received because of Agent Orange or radiation exposure. The eligibility had expired Dec. 30, 1990.

Tom Daschle, D-S.D., a proponent of legislation in the Senate, said the bill "intended to make clear" that veterans would get the benefit of the doubt when evidence of a linkage was equal to or outweighed evidence to the contrary.

BACKGROUND

In the House Veterans' Affairs Committee, Evans had often crossed swords with Chairman G. V. "Sonny" Montgomery, D-Miss., over Agent Orange.

Montgomery had thwarted efforts to get federal medical benefits for diseases that veterans asserted were caused by the defoliant, arguing that the link between cancer and Agent Orange was inconclusive.

Over four years, Montgomery had blocked Evans' efforts to push Agent Orange legislation through the committee. In 1990, however, the panel voted 16-14 to attach Evans' amendment to the veterans' COLA bill. The bill passed the House by voice vote Oct. 15.

On the Senate side, members had passed Agent Orange legislation only to see final action thwarted by protests from Alan K. Simpson, R-Wyo., and Frank H. Murkowski, R-Alaska.

In 1990, the Senate omnibus veterans package was derailed anew because of objections to inclusion of Agent Orange provisions.

The standoff effectively killed major veterans legislation for the year and blocked the COLA boost, due in January 1991.

LEGISLATIVE ACTION

The Agent Orange issue resurfaced on the first day of the 102nd Congress.

Montgomery reintroduced legislation (HR 3) on Jan. 3 that would provide a 5.4 percent COLA for disabled veterans and for spouses and children of veterans who died from service-connected injuries. It contained no Agent Orange compensation.

The same day, Evans reintroduced his competing legislation (HR 321) that would provide the COLA as well as compensate veterans for several diseases linked to Agent Orange exposure.

The bill would have codified previous Department of Veterans Affairs decisions to compensate Vietnam veterans for some diseases presumed to have been caused by Agent Orange. The bill also called for further study of the effects of the chemical.

In the Senate, supporters of Agent Orange compensation, including Veterans' Affairs Committee Chairman Alan Cranston, D-Calif., and Daschle, also revived the matter. Along with Majority Leader George J. Mitchell, D-Maine, Cranston and Daschle reintroduced S 1, a version of a bill (S 2100) that would provide the COLA and Agent Orange benefits. Bob Graham, D-Fla., introduced a clean COLA measure (S 107).

Patriotic Sentiment

That set the stage for a repeat of a legislative struggle that could block the veterans' COLA again. But with the nation rallying behind U.S. service personnel in the Persian Gulf, a compromise was worked out among House members, including Montgomery and Evans.

Under the agreement, the House would consider the clean COLA bill (HR 3) without amendments and also consider a separate Agent Orange bill without amendments.

On Jan. 17, the day after war began in the Persian Gulf, Montgomery joined with Evans to introduce the Agent Orange bill (HR 556).

Simpson and Murkowski, like Montgomery, shifted to back the free-standing Agent Orange legislation.

The House passed HR 556 by 412-0 on Jan. 29. The Senate cleared it, 99-0, the next day. *(House vote 16, p. 4-H; Senate vote 9, p. 3-S)* ■

Veterans Affairs Doctors, Dentists Get Raises

Congress cleared legislation (HR 598) in April to give doctors and dentists at the Veterans Affairs Department raises through special rates of pay.

The bill authorized the new rates for health-care personnel in specialties in which federal salary levels were not competitive with the private sector. The special pay was to supplement a regular salary.

A priority of House and Senate Veterans' Affairs committees and veterans' groups, the measure was designed to help the VA recruit and retain physicians and dentists.

After initially objecting to some of the bill's provisions, the president signed the bill May 7.

Rep. John Paul Hammerschmidt, R-Ark., said the bill would help VA hospitals compete with the private sector for qualified dentists and doctors. "The current pay structure has perpetuated a staffing shortage . . . of immense proportion," he said.

> **BOXSCORE**
>
> ➡ **VA Doctor/Dentist Pay (HR 598).** The bill increased pay rates for physicians and dentists employed by the Department of Veterans Affairs and authorized collective bargaining for health-care workers.
>
> **KEY ACTION**
>
> Jan. 30 - The **House** passed HR 598 , 399-0, under suspension of the rules.
>
> April 17 - The **Senate** passed HR 598 by voice vote.
>
> April 23 - The **House** cleared the Senate-amended version by voice vote.
>
> May 7 - President Bush signed HR 598 — PL 102-40.

The bill was expected to help the VA save money because the shortages forced its hospitals to hire outside personnel.

In addition to increasing pay, the bill gave federal medical professionals the same collective bargaining and grievance rights that other VA workers had. "This legislation represents a major breakthrough," said John N. Sturdivant, president of the American Federation of Government Employees.

The bill also did the following:

- Allowed VA medical directors the flexibility to set special pay rates, subject to review by the VA secretary, to meet specific needs of their facilities.
- Increased the maximum rates of special pay for those with exceptional qualifications, scarce specialties and long-time service. Special pay for those with expertise in areas in

which there were "extraordinary difficulties" in recruitment and retention was set at a maximum of $40,000 a year.

- Authorized the secretary to protect special pay for personnel in non-scarce specialties by creating a new category: "retention pay." The aim was to keep the new law from penalizing those in non-scarce specialties.
- Prevented "unnecessarily high salaries" by requiring a facility director to submit to the VA secretary any agreement that would boost a doctor's total basic pay plus special pay over $134,100 for calendar 1991. The secretary would have 60 days to disapprove.

LEGISLATIVE ACTION

Congress long had tried to revise the VA pay scales for doctors and dentists. In 1990, the House passed a version of the bill (HR 4557), but it was one of several veterans measures that stalled over whether to compensate some veterans exposed to the defoliant Agent Orange. With the Persian Gulf War under way in January 1991, Congress compromised on Agent Orange compensation, freeing other veterans bills. *(Agent Orange, p. 326; background, 1990 Almanac, p. 418)*

Members tried to move the legislation on special pay quickly in the 102nd Congress.

The House version, authorizing a higher scale of special pay for medical personnel based on such considerations as length of service, geographic location, specialty and level of expertise, passed on Jan. 30 by 399-0. *(Vote 18, p. 6-H)*

But subsequent action was slowed after the Bush administration and some senators raised objections.

The Bush administration opposed a number of the bill's provisions and called the pay boosts "excessive."

The main sticking point, however, was a House provision that would have allowed health-care workers to accept honoraria for lectures and articles. The Ethics Reform Act of 1989 (PL 101-194) prohibited federal employees, except senators and their staff, from accepting honoraria other than necessary travel expenses. House members wanted to exempt full-time and part-time VA health professionals from that ban.

Some senators, among them John Glenn, D-Ohio, chairman of the Governmental Affairs Committee, argued for lifting the ban for all non-appointed federal employees rather than doing it piecemeal. *(Honoraria ban, p. 186)*

The Senate passed the House bill April 17 by voice vote but amended it to exclude the honoraria provision. That put the ball back in the House's court. Veterans' Affairs Committee Chairman G. V. "Sonny" Montgomery, D-Miss., argued that the ban would "clearly discourage from VA employment the very specialists and teachers VA hopes to recruit and retain."

But House members decided not to let the honoraria question further stall the bill and approved the Senate's version by voice vote April 23. ■

Education, Job Assistance

Reservists who served on active duty in the Persian Gulf War received a boost in educational benefits and employment assistance under legislation (S 868) cleared by Congress on Sept. 16.

Approved by the Senate Veterans' Affairs Committee on June 6, the bill restored education benefits to those who began studies but were not able to complete them because they were called to active duty or were given assignments that prevented them from finishing.

The measure also extended eligibility for employment and job-training services to reservists who served on active duty by a period of the length of their active-duty service plus four months.

Under existing law, reservists who served less than 180 days on active duty did not qualify for school benefits. The bill expanded eligibility to include reservists with less than 180 days of active duty if the person served in wartime and was honorably discharged.

Some sections of the bill were identical to those in bills already approved by the House. Provisions of the bill were also included in HR 1175 passed by the House March 13 as part of the large benefits package for Operation Desert Storm. *(Gulf veterans benefits, p. 320)*

The bill was also similar to HR 1108, approved May 15 by the House Veterans' Affairs Subcommittee on Education, Training and Employment.

The Senate passed S 868 by voice vote Aug. 2, and the House followed suit on Sept. 16.

The Department of Veterans Affairs estimated the bill would cost $3 million a year beginning in 1993.

Money for the bill, which had the support of the Bush administration, would come from other programs with a cost of $10 million or less under budget rules, according to Bob Stump of Arizona, ranking member of the House Veterans' Affairs Committee. Under the 1990 budget agreement between the White House and Capitol Hill, new spending had to be paid for by a tax increase or cuts in other programs to prevent further growth of the federal deficit.

"Failure to enact this type of remedial legislation ... due to quibbling over a minor detail would be indefensible," Stump said. ■

BOXSCORE

➡ **Veterans' Educational Assistance (S 868).** The bill provided education aid to reservists who served on active duty in the Persian War.

Report: S Rept 102-124.

KEY ACTION

Aug. 2 - The **Senate** passed S 868 on a voice vote.

Sept. 16 - The **House** cleared S 868 on a voice vote.

Oct. 10 - President Bush signed (PL 102-127).

Vets Services Improved

After compromising over cost, Congress on July 29 cleared for President Bush's signature a bill (HR 1047) that sought to improve a number of veterans services, among them pension, compensation and life insurance programs. The bill authorized $3 million in fiscal 1992.

Congress had tried to enact many of these benefits in 1990, including them in legislation (HR 5326) that would have provided a cost of living adjustment (COLA) to disabled veterans and survivors of veterans killed in military service. But that measure died after the attachment of controversial provisions to compensate some victims of exposure to the defoliant Agent Orange.

Early in 1991, Congress approved separate COLA and Agent Orange bills, and Douglas Applegate, D-Ohio, chairman of the House Veterans' Affairs Subcommittee on Compensation, Pension and Insurance, introduced HR 1047, the new pensions, compensation and life insurance bill. *(COLA bill, p. 325; Agent Orange, p. 326)*

BOXSCORE

➡ **Veterans' Benefits Programs Improvement Act (HR 1047).** The bill boosted certain veterans' services, pensions, compensation and life insurance.

KEY ACTION

April 11 — HR 1047 passed in the **House**, on a vote of 399-3, under suspension of the rules.

July 25 — HR 1047 passed in the **Senate** by voice vote.

July 29 — The Senate-amended version cleared the **House** by voice vote.

Aug. 14 — President Bush signed HR 1047 — PL 102-86.

HR 1047 contained several provisions designed to help disabled veterans collect benefits, among them:

- Extending from 30 to 40 years the time during which leukemia had to develop after radiation exposure in order to be judged service-connected. Some veterans were exposed to radiation during nuclear weapons testing and during the U.S. occupation of the bombed Japanese cities of Hiroshima and Nagasaki. Reservists who had served on active duty or training and were exposed to radiation also would be covered.
- Giving veterans more time to seek Service Disabled Life Insurance, by increasing — from one to two years — the period after veterans had been judged service-connected disabled that they could apply for coverage.
- Authorizing dental care that must be done for medical reasons before the veteran entered a hospital.
- Increasing from $500 to $1,000 the amount the Veterans Affairs Department could spend per year for outpatient dental services for each veteran.

LEGISLATIVE ACTION

As originally introduced by Applegate, HR 1047 would have authorized $5 million annually for fiscal 1992 through 1996.

The House passed the bill on April 11 on a roll call vote of 399-3. *(Vote 65, p. 16-H)*

But questions remained over where the money would be found.

Under the 1990 budget deal between Congress and the Bush administration, the new spending for the bill would have to be offset by cuts in other areas of the veterans budget.

Although Veterans Affairs' Committee Chairman G. V. "Sonny" Montgomery, D-Miss., said on the House floor that he understood that cuts would have to be made elsewhere, concern remained among some members about the spending.

The three opposing the bill were Minority Leader Robert H. Michel, R-Ill.; Bill Gradison, R-Ohio; and Jim Nussle, R-Iowa.

Before the Senate took up the legislation, both chambers' Veterans' Affairs committees agreed to a compromise that would make the bill conform to the budget agreement.

They agreed to drop a provision in Applegate's bill that would have increased coverage for the disabled under the Veterans Mortgage Life Insurance Program from $40,000 to $90,000. That provision would have cost $2 million in fiscal 1992, and its removal pared the overall cost of the bill that year to $3 million.

On July 25, the Senate adopted by voice vote the compromise in a substitute amendment and passed HR 1047 by voice vote.

On July 29, the House cleared the amended bill by voice vote. Bush signed it Aug. 14. ■

Congress Updates 1940s Reservists Protections

A holdover measure from the 101st Congress that would increase financial and civil protections for reservists called to active duty got a boost early in 1991 from Congress' desire to help U.S. troops in the Persian Gulf.

BOXSCORE

➡ **Veterans' Protections (HR 555).** The bill amended the Soldiers' and Sailors' Civil Relief Act of 1940 to protect re-employment and other rights of those called to active military service.

KEY ACTION

Jan. 29 - HR 555 passed in the **House,** on a vote of 414-0, under suspension of the rules.

Feb. 21 - HR 555 passed by the **Senate** by voice vote.

Feb. 27 - The Senate-amended version cleared by the **House** by voice vote.

March 18 - President Bush signed HR 555 — PL 102-12.

Congress cleared the Veterans Protections legislation (HR 555) on Feb. 27 as an amendment to the 1940 Soldiers' and Sailors' Civil Relief Act.

"While it is still a sound piece of legislation, its effectiveness has been grossly eroded by time and inflation," said Dennis DeConcini, D-Ariz., Senate floor manager of HR 555.

Members on both sides of the Capitol had tried in 1990 to enact substantially similar legislation (HR 5814, S 3248) to update the law. The House passed its version on Oct. 15, 1990, and the Senate Veterans' Affairs Committee reported its bill.

But the legislation died at the end of the 101st Congress, one of several veterans bills that were casualties of a dispute over whether to compensate veterans who were disabled by the defoliant Agent Orange.

One of the first actions of the 102nd Congress was to settle the Agent Orange matter, which it did just as the gulf war was getting under way, thus clearing the way for the other veterans measures to move. (Agent Orange, p. 326)

MAJOR PROVISIONS

As enacted, the Soldiers' and Sailors' relief provisions:

- Made clear that reservists called up to active duty for 90 days or more were guaranteed re-employment rights when they were demobilized. Under existing law, reservists serving longer than 90 days were not protected.
- Prohibited eviction of the families of those serving in the gulf if their rent was $1,200 per month or less. The previous rent limit — $150 per month — had been set in 1966, during the Vietnam war.
- Guaranteed service personnel the right to resume their individual and family health insurance upon return to civilian life with no interruptions or coverage exclusions.
- Permitted doctors and other health professionals called to active duty to suspend payment of their malpractice insurance premiums until they returned.
- Required courts, upon request, to suspend civil legal proceedings against those on active duty.

LEGISLATIVE ACTION

The legislation was developed by G. V. "Sonny" Montgomery, D-Miss., and Alan Cranston, D-Calif., chairmen, respectively, of the House and Senate Veterans' Affairs committees.

HR 555 was not controversial, and the House passed it under a procedure that allowed no amendments but required a two-thirds majority of those present and voting. The Jan. 29 vote was 414-0. *(Vote 17, p. 4-H)*

The Senate had a version (S 330) that was altered slightly to make technical and clerical corrections. Backers of the legislation expected that if the Senate acted quickly, the House would approve the Senate version, clearing it before Congress' scheduled mid-February recess.

Majority Leader George J. Mitchell, D-Maine, sought unanimous consent to have the Senate also consider the bill without change. But quick action was blocked Feb. 6 by John Heinz, R-Pa., who wanted to offer an amendment to ask the Pentagon to ensure that no single parents or couples with children be deployed in the gulf.

The proposal was vehemently opposed by the Department of Defense, which argued that the change would reverse longstanding policy and disrupt military operations.

Mitchell said Heinz's action had the "most regrettable result" of delaying action on the protections for gulf troops and their families.

Heinz offered his amendment on Feb. 20, when the chamber was debating a measure (S 320) to reauthorize the Export Administration Act, which imposed sanctions on countries that used chemical and biological weapons and foreign companies that helped them. (Export bill, p. 128)

Heinz's amendment would have demanded that the Pentagon offer an exemption from duty in "the imminent-danger area of Operation Desert Storm" to single parents of minor children and to one parent in families in which both the mother and father had been deployed in the Persian Gulf region.

Americans had failed "to protect the welfare of American children from being made orphans at the same time we are going to extraordinary lengths to prevent Iraqi children from being made orphans," Heinz said.

But a majority on Capitol Hill were determined not to place any obstacles in the way of the Pentagon as it conducted the gulf war. Heinz's amendment was rejected, 38-54. *(Vote 15, p. 3-S)*

Instead, the Senate adopted, 91-0, language by John Glenn, D-Ohio, commending the Pentagon for its efforts "to be sensitive to the family needs of members of the Armed Forces" and urging it to devise "uniform" family policies for the different branches of the services. *(Vote 14, p. 3-S)*

"Single military parents and military members who are married and have children know and accept the risk of military service," argued Glenn. He maintained that the Pentagon had gone to great lengths to make exceptions in hardship cases in which no relative or guardian could care for children.

Ultimately, Congress finessed the issue in its omnibus gulf war benefits legislation (S 725), passed in March. The final version required the secretary of Defense to study departmental policies related to reservists and active-duty personnel who had children and to report back to Congress no later than March 31, 1992. The bill included sense-of-the-House language that the Pentagon should not deploy reservists or active-duty personnel who are mothers of children under the age of 6 months. (Gulf veterans benefits, p. 320)

With the Heinz amendment disposed of on Feb. 20, the Senate took up the Soldiers' and Sailors' bill the next day. It passed HR 555 by voice vote, after amending it with the text of S 330.

The House agreed to the Senate amendment and cleared HR 555 on Feb. 27. ■

Job Discrimination Bills Not Completed

Spurred by concern for returning veterans of the Persian Gulf War, both chambers began work on bills to clarify the re-employment rights of military personnel, but Congress did not complete action on the legislation in 1991.

The House on May 14 passed HR 1578, which reiterated and strengthened provisions of existing law that prohibited employers from discriminating against job applicants or employees because of their military obligations.

The Senate Veterans' Affairs Committee approved S 1095 on June 26, but the bill did not reach the floor before adjournment.

Veterans had been guaranteed re-employment rights ever since World War II, but lawmakers said the relevant statute (Chapter 43 of Title 38, U.S. Code) had become a confusing and sometimes ambiguous jumble of provisions.

The executive branch had had a task force working for three years on a revision of the law, and the legislation advanced in 1991 was built largely upon that group's recommendations.

HR 1578 was introduced by Timothy J. Penny, D-Minn., and Christopher H. Smith, R-N.J. It built upon an update (HR 555 — PL 102-12) of the 1940 Soldiers' and Sailors' Civil Relief Act that was cleared by Congress on Feb. 27. (Veterans' protection, p. 329)

Among other things, HR 1578 reiterated that workers who left their jobs for military duty had an unqualified right to re-employment upon their return. It did not matter what type of service — active duty or training — was involved.

The bill extended job protection rights to federal employees and guaranteed them representation if needed to secure those rights.

The legislation specified that a worker could serve for up to five years in the military and still have civilian re-employment rights; existing law allowed an absence of only four years. Extensions were possible in time of war and under certain other circumstances.

Workers returning home after military service of 31 to 180 days were allowed two weeks to report to their old jobs; those returning after more than six months' service were given 90 days to report. Wounded veterans were assured extensions.

The bill specified that a returning veteran was to be employed in the same position he or she would have attained if continuously employed.

BOXSCORE

➡ **Uniformed Services Employment and Re-Employment Rights Act (HR 1578, S 1095).** The bills barred employment discrimination against job applicants or workers on the basis of their military obligations and clarified re-employment rights of returning veterans.

Reports: H Rept 102-56; S Rept 102-203.

KEY ACTION

April 11 - HR 1578 was approved by the **House** Veterans' Affairs Committee by 33-0.

May 14 - HR 1578 passed the **House** by voice vote.

June 26 - S 1095 was approved by the **Senate** Veterans' Affairs Committee by voice vote.

HOUSE ACTION

The House Veterans' Affairs Committee approved HR 1578 on April 11 by 33-0.

Two technical amendments offered by Penny and Smith were adopted by voice vote, along with a substantive amendment by Maxine Waters, D-Calif.

Waters' amendment allowed veterans who sued for discrimination to collect money for attorneys' fees and other legal expenses.

The amendment extended to veterans the same protection given to those who sued for discrimination under the Civil Rights Attorneys Fee Awards Act of 1976 (PL 94-559).

House Passage

HR 1578 was passed by the House on May 14 by voice vote under suspension of the rules, a procedure that precluded amendments and required a two-thirds vote for passage.

There was little debate and no opposition expressed. Penny, the bill's chief sponsor, said, "The activation of over 200,000 members of the Selected Reserve in connection with the Persian Gulf War has reminded all of us of the importance of employment and re-employment protection for members of the uniformed services. If the total force concept is to succeed, we must facilitate non-career military service by minimizing disruption to the lives and careers of those who contribute to our national defense."

Penny read into the record a letter from Labor Secretary Lynn Martin expressing strong administration support for HR 1578.

SENATE ACTION

The Senate Veterans' Affairs Committee approved S 1095 on June 26. The measure had been introduced May 16 by committee Chairman Alan Cranston, D-Calif., and ranking Republican Arlen Specter of Pennsylvania.

Like the House bill, the Senate measure sought to clarify and strengthen veterans' re-employment rights and to prohibit discrimination and acts of reprisal against reservists.

It provided for a five-year limit on the cumulative length of service-related absence. And it gave protection to workers with temporary as well as permanent positions.

S 1095 set slightly different deadlines than the House bill for a returning service member to report to his old employer: within 31 days after completing military duty of 31 to 180 days and within 90 days of completing a longer service stint.

The bill sought to ensure that employees of intelligence agencies were given, to the maximum extent possible, re-employment protection equal to those of other federal employees.

It provided for a continuation, at the worker's request and expense, of employer-sponsored health benefits for up to 18 months after the individual began duty in a uniformed service. The House bill contained a similar provision. ■

Vets Counseling Bill Derailed in Senate

The House on Nov. 25 passed legislation (HR 2280) to enhance health and counseling benefits for veterans, but the measure snagged in the Senate over a provision that curtailed the power of appropriators to funnel money to projects in their home states.

The bill authorized about $10 million for fiscal 1992 for marriage and family counseling for veterans returning from the Persian Gulf War and required the Department of Veterans Affairs (VA) to develop a plan for expanding services to veterans who suffered from post-traumatic stress disorder.

The measure also exempted the VA from calculation of drug prices for Medicaid programs. The fiscal 1991 budget-reconciliation law (PL 101-508) had required pharmaceutical manufacturers to give Medicaid the same volume discounts they offered to the VA and other groups. Instead, drug makers raised prices for everyone. *(1990 Almanac, p. 570)*

Although lawmakers concerned about Medicaid costs wanted to find a way to force prices down for everyone, the Veterans' Affairs committees in both chambers were determined to make sure that VA programs did not suffer in the meantime. They moved to exempt the VA altogether from the pricing decisions affecting Medicaid.

Congress did just that in the fiscal 1992 VA-HUD appropriations bill (PL 102-139), which contained the provision sought by the Veterans' Affairs committees. *(Appro-*

New Chief Minority Affairs Officer for Vets

The Senate on Nov. 27 cleared for the president legislation (HR 3327) to designate one of the existing assistant secretaries of the Department of Veterans Affairs (VA) as the chief minority affairs officer for the department.

The House had passed the bill two days earlier, on Nov. 25. President Bush signed it into law (PL 102-218) on Dec. 11.

The bill had long been pushed by Rep. Charles B. Rangel, D-N.Y., who, though not a member of the committee, worked with Veterans Affairs' Chairman G. V. "Sonny" Montgomery, D-Miss., to craft it.

The chief minority affairs officer was to coordinate VA efforts to aid minority veterans and ensure that their concerns were addressed. Minority veterans, Rangel said, had a more difficult time readjusting to civilian life because of unemployment and lack of access to counseling and other agency services.

Rangel originally wanted five deputy officers in addition to the assistant secretary's position, but the administration complained that that cost too much. Rangel settled for one slot.

Bias Allegation

The House committee approved the bill by voice vote Nov. 13 and formally reported it (H Rept 102-347) on Nov. 22.

Although the bill was approved without major dissent, freshman Democrat Maxine Waters of California used the occasion to rebuke Chairman Montgomery for not hiring enough blacks and other minorities as staff for the panel.

During discussion of the bill, Waters called it "unconscionable" that only one black, a midlevel aide, worked for the committee. "I can't sit here as an African-American member of Congress and tolerate this," she said.

Montgomery tried to defuse the situation, saying, "I know we have a problem." But ranking Republican Bob Stump, Ariz., took on Waters, saying: "I'll make you a deal. I won't tell you who to hire on your staff, and you don't tell me who to hire on my staff."

Montgomery later defended his hiring practices. "We thought we had done a good job on minorities," he said, adding that the panel was trying to hire more.

priations, p. 516)

Estimates of the overall cost of HR 2280 varied. The Congressional Budget Office projected about $15 million in new budget authority in fiscal 1992. The Office of Management and Budget put the cost at $10 million.

Power Struggle

While the House and Senate had to iron out a number of disagreements in their bills, the item that snagged the legislation was a requirement that the congressional Veterans' Affairs committees approve any move by appropriators or the VA secretary to fund construction of VA medical facilities.

House Veterans' Affairs Committee Chairman G. V. "Sonny" Montgomery, D-Miss., and other House members insisted on the provision, saying appropriators were spending scarce VA dollars on pork-barrel projects. The chairman of the Senate Veterans' Affairs panel, Alan Cranston, D-Calif., supported Montgomery's effort.

But Barbara A. Mikulski, D-Md., chairman of the Senate Appropriations Subcommittee for the VA and the Department of Housing and Urban Development, objected. She threatened to block the bill from coming to the Senate floor, according to an aide to Cranston.

Each year appropriators funded many VA construction projects — hospitals, nursing homes, clinics and parking lots. While the projects were needed, according to a House aide, they were not always at the top of agency priority lists. For fiscal 1992, House appropriators wanted to spend $522 million for major construction projects; the Senate side proposed spending $309.9 million. Conferees agreed on $414 million.

BOXSCORE

➡ Veterans Health Care, Counseling (HR 2280). The bill authorized marriage and family counseling for returning Persian Gulf War veterans; expanded services for veterans suffering post-traumatic stress disorder; exempted Department of Veterans Affairs (VA) drug prices from consideration in Medicaid rebate calculations; and extended and increased the authorizations for VA programs for homeless veterans.

Report: H Rept 102-130.

KEY ACTION

June 25 — HR 2280 passed the **House** by voice vote.

Nov. 20 — HR 2280 passed the **Senate** with amendments.

Nov. 25 — HR 2280 further amended by **House**, returned to Senate.

Veterans Services

The veterans health bill originally was passed by the House on June 25. The Senate passed the bill by voice vote Nov. 20 after amending it to include the text of another measure (S 869) that allowed Vietnam War veterans to receive treatment for post-traumatic stress disorder without having to prove it was war-related.

The VA already provided counseling to Vietnam veterans for stress disorder. The fiscal 1991 appropriation for stress disorder programs was about $21 million, and appropriators boosted that by $10 million for fiscal 1992.

HR 2280 ordered the VA to develop a plan to expand and improve services available for post-traumatic stress disorder and to ensure that all veterans had access to such services.

The bill also sought to ensure that veterans who served on active duty were treated in a timely fashion for stress disorder and that waiting lists were eliminated.

The amended House version of the bill also:

- Provided a three-year authorization for marriage and family counseling for spouses and children of veterans of the Persian Gulf War. The Bush administration opposed this provision as redundant; other legislation (S 725 — PL 102-25), signed April 6, included such counseling services, an administration statement said. And a separate Senate bill on the subject (S 1553) had passed that chamber as well. *(Gulf veterans benefits, p. 320)*

- Boosted services to homeless veterans and authorized additional funding. The bill authorized $50 million for fiscal 1993 to care for homeless veterans and to fund another existing program for homeless veterans who also suffered from chronic mental illness. The VA secretary was to decide how to split the money between the two programs. Congress had already authorized $33 million for fiscal 1992, to be divided equally between the two programs. ■

Various Vets Bills Remained Incomplete

The Senate passed several bills late in the year that were designed to improve health care for veterans, but the measures did not clear the House before adjournment.

The legislation included:

- S 1358, to authorize the Department of Veterans Affairs (VA) to establish a five-year hospice-care pilot program for terminally ill veterans in 15 to 30 VA medical facilities around the country. Introduced by Sen. Bob Graham, D-Fla., the bill was approved June 26 by the Veterans' Affairs Committee (S Rept 102-160) and passed by the Senate on Oct. 16.
- S 1553, to make Persian Gulf War veterans and their families eligible for marriage and family counseling. The bill, passed by the Senate on Nov. 15, sought to create a counseling program to assist enlisted and reserve personnel who had served on active duty during the war. It would have authorized funding through September 1994, with counseling to be provided by a mental health professional designated by the VA.

The bill was approved Sept. 12 by the Veterans' Affairs Committee (S Rept 102-159). The measure drew fire from Alan K. Simpson, R-Wyo., who said it set a bad precedent. "You're for the first time allowing non-veterans to receive care from the VA system," he said.

Simpson noted Congress had already authorized readjustment counseling for gulf war veterans in separate legislation (S 725 — PL 102-25). *(Gulf veterans benefits, p. 320)*

- S 775, to direct the VA to expand the list of diseases presumed to be connected to radiation exposure during service on nuclear submarines, ships and military flights over weapons test sites.

The radiation compensation provisions were initially part of a wider bill that carried a cost of living adjustment (COLA) for disabled veterans and survivors of military personnel who died from service-connected causes. But because of controversy over the radiation provisions, Congress cleared a clean 3.7 percent COLA bill (HR 1046) separately. *(COLA, p. 325)* ■

No Agreement Reached On Housing Funds

In 1991, lawmakers and the administration disagreed over how much money to give two contradictory housing programs included in the 1990 landmark housing reauthorization bill (PL 101-625). *(1990 Almanac, p. 631)*

One, called the Home Ownership and Opportunity for People Everywhere (HOPE) program, would sell off federally assisted housing to public housing tenants and other poor people. The other, the HOME Investment Partnerships program, would expand the supply of low-income housing.

Housing and Urban Development Secretary Jack F. Kemp had developed and staked his reputation on the HOPE program. Senate Democrats had devised the HOME program, a block grant to states and local governments to build and renovate affordable housing, as well as to provide rental vouchers.

Congress included funds for both programs in the fiscal 1992 appropriations bill (HR 2519 — PL 102-139) for Veterans Affairs (VA), Housing and Urban Development (HUD) and independent agencies. *(Appropriations, p. 516)*

But conferees on the VA-HUD bill reordered Kemp's housing priorities and gave $136 million for the HOPE program, while the HOME partnerships received $1.5 billion. Kemp had wanted $865 million for the HOPE program.

The House had provided $361 million for the HOPE grants. The HOME partnerships program received $500 million, compared with $1 billion requested by the White House.

The Senate doubled Bush's HOME request to $2 billion but provided only $215 million for the HOPE grants.

Because of the shortfall in funds for the HOPE program, Kemp said he would ask the president to veto the bill.

In a Sept. 25 letter to the conference chairman, Kemp charged that the House-Senate compromise was a "betrayal of low-income families" and amounted to a return "to the failed scandal-prone housing programs of the past."

But the veto never came because conferees had fully funded the president's highest priority, the space station *Freedom*. The spending bill also provided funding for the National Aeronautics and Space Administration (NASA).

Legislative Action

When the House received the VA-HUD appropriations bill, it turned around two decisions made by its own Appropriations Committee. First, the House voted June 6 to continue funding for NASA's space station *Freedom*. The committee had eliminated the $1.9 billion for the space station.

The House also went against the wishes of the appropriators and voted 216-183 to give Kemp $361 million for the HOPE program by shifting money within HUD. The committee had recommended that no money be provided to sell public housing. Many of the VA-HUD Appropriations Subcommittee members were philosophically opposed to the idea of selling public housing. *(Vote 142, p. 34-H)*

As the House prepared to vote, Kemp worked the floor. HUD officials were uncertain how the vote would go, concerned that members would not want to vote against the VA-HUD Subcommittee chairman, Bob Traxler, D-Mich., after rebuking him on the space station.

But with a coalition of Republicans, a few black Democrats and some of their party colleagues, such as Dan Rostenkowski, Ill., and Leon E. Panetta, Calif., Kemp won.

Most of the big housing groups, however, were lobbying for money for the HOME Investment Partnerships, not HOPE.

Congress created the HOME program to encourage state and local governments, along with private nonprofit groups, to build new housing and renovate old housing for the poor. It authorized the program at $2 billion.

The House bill gave it $500 million. But public housing advocates did not want more money for HOME to come at the expense of other housing programs.

The Senate passed the VA-HUD spending bill by voice vote on July 18. Senators provided $215 million for HOPE, with $175 million going to the public housing ownership component.

The Senate also recommended spending $2 billion to start the HOME program. When the House-Senate conferees considered the VA-HUD spending bill the week of Sept. 23, Joseph M. McDade of Pennsylvania, ranking Republican on the House Appropriations Committee, tried to appease Kemp with an amendment to add $25 million to the section of the HOPE program that would help public housing tenants buy their units. Conferees agreed to add $10 million but merely shifted the money from another section of the HOPE program.

Committee members expressed frustration with Kemp, a former House member, saying that he was looking a gift horse in the mouth.

"We really are treating the secretary very well," Traxler said. ■

Flood Insurance Bill Passes House

The House on May 1 passed a bill (HR 1236) to shore up the National Flood Insurance Program.

But the White House threatened to veto the measure unless the Bush administration's cost estimates were used.

Members voted 388-18 to pass HR 1236. *(Vote 75, p. 20-H)*

The Senate did not act on the measure in 1991.

Under the bill, mortgage companies could be fined up to $100,000 if they failed to require businesses or home buyers to purchase flood insurance on all mortgaged structures in areas prone to flooding.

As passed by the House, the bill also re-

BOXSCORE

➡ **Flood Insurance (HR 1236).** The bill would bolster the National Flood Insurance Program by penalizing mortgage companies if they failed to require businesses or home buyers to purchase flood insurance on mortgaged buildings. Banks could be fined up to $100,000 for repeated violations.

Report: H Rept 102-38.

KEY ACTION

May 1 — HR 1236 passed the **House** by a vote of 388-18.

quired a mortgage lender or servicer already putting money aside for insurance or taxes to establish an escrow account for flood insurance premiums.

Ben Erdreich, D-Ala., chairman of the House Banking Subcommittee on Policy Research and Insurance, said that out of 11 million households in flood hazard areas, only 1.7 million were insured with flood policies, a rate of 15 percent.

"We cannot afford to expose the Treasury or the taxpayer to this tremendous financial risk," Erdreich said.

The legislation also required a community rating system, which would allow communities to reduce their costs of flood insurance if they took steps to protect against flooding.

In addition, a flood hazard mitigation fund would be established, providing to states, communities and individuals matching grants to relocate or elevate buildings, and institute flood-proofing measures. It would be financed by a $5 per policy fee.

The bill also encouraged developers to build away from wetlands, the coasts and the Great Lakes.

According to both the Congressional Budget Office (CBO) and the Office of Management and Budget (OMB), the bill would save the program about $11 million a year. But the measure included the CBO estimate rather than OMB's.

Republicans and Democrats had been squabbling in 1991 over which agency should be the "scorekeeper" on costs of legislation.

Bill Gradison, R-Ohio, objected, saying the bill violated the 1990 budget agreement, which Republicans contended required Congress to use OMB estimates. His amendment to strike the CBO language was rejected on a party-line vote, 160-248. *(Vote 74, p. 18-H)*

The administration had threatened to veto any bill that used CBO rather than OMB estimates.

Committee Action

The House Banking Committee approved HR 1236 on April 11.

Approved by voice vote, the bill sought to expand participation in the National Flood Insurance Program by stepping up civil penalties against banks that repeatedly failed to comply with a 1986 law mandating that lenders require the purchase of flood insurance for properties secured with a federally backed mortgage.

Authorization for the program through fiscal 1995 was included in the fiscal 1991 budget-reconciliation bill. *(Budget resolution, p. 69)*

Panel members approved, by voice vote, an amendment by Erdreich to exempt the Federal National Mortgage Association and the Federal Home Loan Mortgage Corporation from new requirements that lenders establish escrow accounts for flood insurance premiums paid by property owners. Erdreich said the agencies, which operated in the secondary market for mortgages, would be duplicating the work of the original issuers of the loan. ■

Chapter 7

HEALTH & HUMAN SERVICES/ EDUCATION

Vetoes Foil Abortion Rights Gains

Despite lawmakers' increased willingness to loosen restrictions, Bush held fast against policy changes

Abortion rights advocates made modest but demonstrable gains in Congress in 1991. But while both chambers approved a variety of bills that sought to loosen or overturn existing federal restrictions, abortion rights advocates could not muster the supermajority needed to override threatened vetoes by a stalwartly anti-abortion President Bush.

The slight shift in favor of abortion rights — particularly in the House, long an anti-abortion stronghold — came in the wake of *Webster v. Reproductive Health Services of Missouri,* the 1989 Supreme Court decision that allowed states more leeway to restrict abortions. *(1989 Almanac, p. 528; 1990 Almanac, p. 296)*

Both as a result of the 1990 elections and the decision by some members to modify or actually change positions, both chambers voted to jettison five separate federal abortion-related restrictions. But two Bush vetoes and repeated veto threats on other bills prevented any policy changes.

"The president's consistent position was important," said Douglas Johnson, legislative director of the National Right to Life Committee, one of the leading anti-abortion groups. "Not only the actual vetoes, but the certitude of the vetoes helped get some language dropped," he said.

Bush in 1991 vetoed two appropriations bills — for the District of Columbia and the Departments of Labor, Health and Human Services (HHS) and Education — over abortion provisions, and his threats to veto both the fiscal 1992 defense authorization and spending bills helped get abortion provisions in those measures dropped.

The president also threatened to veto three bills that did not reach his desk in 1991: a House-passed reauthorization of the National Institutes of Health that sought to overturn a ban on research using fetal tissue obtained from abortions, and foreign aid authorization and appropriations bills that would have renewed funding for the United Nations Population Fund.

Abortion foes opposed funding for the U.N. organization, charging that it had provided money to China, which had policies that coerced abortion. *(NIH bill, p. 346; Foreign aid bill, p. 470; Appropriations, p. 646)*

The inability of abortion rights advocates to produce actual policy changes despite majority votes in both chambers left many frustrated.

"We don't have a democratic system anymore. It's ruled by two-thirds," said Rep. Patricia Schroeder, D-Colo., referring to the margin needed to override Bush — a feat that no one accomplished during the first three years of his presidency.

Indeed, said political scientist Thomas E. Mann of the Brookings Institution, "we're pretty much in a form of deadlock" on the abortion issue.

While Mann agreed that abortion rights forces had made some gains, he said that abortion hadn't "fully blossomed as an issue." And it likely would not, he predicted, until and unless the Supreme Court overturned *Roe v. Wade,* the landmark 1973 ruling that legalized abortion nationwide.

Legislative Roundup

Congress fought about abortion in a variety of legislative venues in 1991, mostly on much larger bills whose primary purposes were not abortion-related. Following are the main bills that included abortion-related controversies and the particular issue in dispute:

- **Fiscal 1992 Labor-Health and Human Services-Education Appropriations** (HR 2707) included language to bar enforcement of administration regulations prohibiting abortion counseling in federally funded family planning clinics.
- **Family Planning Reauthorization** (HR 3090) included language to overturn administration regulations prohibiting abortion counseling in federally funded family planning clinics.
- **Counseling Restrictions** (S 323) to overturn administration regulations prohibiting abortion counseling in federally funded family planning clinics.
- **National Institutes of Health Reauthorization** (HR 2507) included language to overturn administration ban on research using tissue from aborted fetuses.
- **Fiscal 1992 Department of Defense Authorization, Appropriations** (HR 2100, HR 2521) included language to permit servicewomen and military dependents to obtain abortions in Defense Department medical facilities overseas if they paid for the procedure themselves.
- **Fiscal 1992 Foreign Operations Appropriations** (HR 2621) included language to resume U.S. funding for the United Nations Population Fund. Abortion opponents fought it because the organization aided China, a country with a history of forced abortions.
- **Fiscal 1992-93 Foreign Aid Authorization** (HR 2508) included language to resume U.S. funding for the United Nations Population Fund, as well as to overturn the so-called Mexico City policy, which since 1984 had barred funding for international family planning programs that performed or "actively promoted" abortion.
- **Fiscal 1992 District of Columbia Appropriations** (HR 2699) included language that would have allowed the city to use locally raised funds to pay for abortions for poor women.

A Shift, Not a Breakthrough

After more than a decade in which anti-abortion forces successfully imposed a series of federal bans and restrictions on abortion, 1991 was supposed to be the breakthrough year for abortion rights advocates.

Ever since the issue broke onto the congressional

agenda in the mid 1970s, the Senate had on most issues been more supportive of abortion rights than the House.

But the first abortion vote of the year showed that the 1990 elections had produced a shift in the House.

During consideration in May of the annual defense authorization bill (HR 2100), members by 220-208 voted to allow servicewomen and military dependents to obtain abortions in overseas military medical facilities if they paid for the procedure themselves. In 1990, members had rejected an identical amendment by a vote of 200-216. *(Vote 109, p. 28-H; 1990 Almanac, p. 683)*

It was the newly elected members who made the difference. Freshmen in 1991 voted 29-16 in favor of the amendment, while the members they replaced voted 16-23, with six not voting.

Abortion foes conceded that on some issues, at least, the House had undergone a shift. "We went from a slight edge in our direction to a slight edge in the other direction," said Johnson of the National Right to Life Committee.

ABORTION COUNSELING

Still, when the Supreme Court on May 23 — the day after the House vote on the defense bill — upheld controversial regulations banning abortion counseling in federally funded family planning clinics, abortion rights forces thought they finally had an issue that could produce the two-thirds vote in both chambers needed to win a policy change in their favor.

It was, they pointed out, an issue that transcended abortion and addressed matters of free speech between doctors and their patients.

Strategists settled on a two-track plan. The first was to begin pushing legislation to formally overturn the rules and codify counseling and referral guidelines in effect from 1981 to 1988.

The Senate in July passed a free-standing bill addressing solely the regulations (S 323), while the House began work on a measure (HR 3090) that not only sought to overturn the rules but also reauthorized the underlying federal family planning program, Title X of the Public Health Service Act. Various abortion-related controversies, including the counseling issue, had kept the program operating on stopgap funding since 1985.

At the same time, abortion rights advocates successfully inserted into the fiscal 1992 spending bill (HR 2707) for the Department of Health and Human Services language to bar enforcement of the contested regulations for a year. Procedural rules governing spending bills precluded any attempt to overturn the regulations outright on an appropriations measure.

During the summer and fall, more and more anti-abortion members declared their opposition to the regulations, dubbed the "gag rule" by opponents.

During House Appropriations Committee consideration of the Labor-HHS appropriations bill, Jerry Lewis, R-Calif., told an emotional story of a young woman who stayed with his family, became pregnant during a vacation, and after receiving counseling at a federal family planning clinic decided to continue the pregnancy and keep the baby. Lewis, a reliable anti-abortion voter, voted to block the counseling ban.

Abortion foes, who strongly supported the regulations, fought back with the creation in July of the "Abortion Is Not Family Planning Coalition." Spearheaded by the National Right to Life Committee and National Conference of Catholic Bishops, the coalition used its $1 million budget to run a series of newspaper advertisements in support of the rules.

"We really needed to correct a campaign of disinformation" by abortion rights advocates, said Helen Alvare of the National Conference of Catholic Bishops. Despite claims to the contrary by opponents of the ban, Alvare said, allowing family planning clinics to counsel and refer for abortion undermined contraceptive efforts and resulted in more unintended pregnancies.

On Aug. 2, Christopher H. Smith, R-N.J., co-chairman of the House Pro-Life Caucus, said a survey of members "confirms that we have a comfortable margin to preserve the president's policy of separating abortion from family planning."

Few on the other side believed him, however, and as late as the day before the House attempted to override Bush's veto of the Labor-HHS bill over the abortion language, House Speaker Thomas S. Foley, D-Wash., predicted the override would succeed.

Foley was wrong; Smith was right. The 276-156 vote Nov. 19 was a dozen short of the necessary two-thirds. *(Vote 403, p. 98-H)*

Court Ruling, Senate Response

The 1991 abortion debate began in earnest May 23. That was the day the Supreme Court, in *Rust v. Sullivan*, upheld controversial regulations originally issued by the Reagan administration barring abortion counseling and referrals in federally funded family planning clinics.

Not surprisingly, abortion opponents hailed the ruling, while abortion rights proponents condemned it.

"It's truly a landmark decision that underscores that abortion is not a method of family planning," said Smith.

But abortion rights advocates, noting that even some abortion foes disagreed with the ruling on free-speech grounds, predicted that they might finally have an issue that could garner the two-thirds vote needed to override a Bush veto.

"I think this is the spark that could do it," said Ron Wyden, D-Ore., who sponsored legislation in both the 101st and 102nd Congresses to overturn the counseling ban. "This might be the one that Congress could override the president on."

The immediate effect of the ruling was to haul from legislative limbo efforts to reauthorize the federal family planning program, Title X of the Public Health Service Act. The program helped fund about 4,000 clinics that served an estimated 4 million low-income women and teenagers every year. But abortion-related controversies — including the issue of abortion counseling and referrals — had blocked efforts to reauthorize the program, leaving it operating on stopgap funding since 1985.

In the Senate, however, Edward M. Kennedy, D-Mass., chairman of the Senate Labor and Human Resources Committee, opted to take a different tack. Having had to pull a reauthorization bill that would have overturned the rules from the Senate floor in 1990, Kennedy decided to move through his committee a free-standing measure (S 323) that overturned the rules without reauthorizing the family planning program. *(1990 Almanac, p. 604)*

"We'll have a chance later this year to address other controversial aspects of Title X," Kennedy said at the June 6 markup. The year ran out, however, with no further Senate action on a reauthorization bill.

As approved by the panel on a 12-5 vote, S 323 would have codified guidelines for the family planning program in effect from 1981 through 1988. Those required that women with unintended pregnancies be given "non-directive counseling, and referral on request" on all options — prenatal care and delivery, adoption and foster care, and "pregnancy termination."

House Appropriations Bill

But even as opponents of the rules pursued a permanent overturn, they sought to append language to the fiscal 1992 appropriations bill for the Departments of Labor, Health and Human Services (HHS) and Education that would block enforcement of the rules for a year. To prevent the amendment from running afoul of the strict rules governing spending bills, sponsors led by John Porter, R-Ill., drafted it as a "funding limitation" to bar the department from spending money to enforce the regulations.

Porter's amendment was approved by the House Appropriations Committee June 20 by a vote of 35-20 during markup of the Labor-HHS bill.

But abortion opponents scored points of their own, adding to the measure a separate amendment requiring that at least one parent be notified before any facility receiving family planning funds could perform an abortion on a minor. It was approved on a 28-10 show of hands.

The author of the parental notification language, abortion foe Vin Weber, R-Minn., wanted to append the amendment to Porter's amendment. But that attempt was defeated by a vote of 24-31.

Adding the language to the Porter amendment, argued Les AuCoin, D-Ore., "will have no substantive effect, only a political effect as a poison pill" by making the Porter language subject to being struck on the floor for impermissibly legislating on an appropriation.

Indeed, the stand-alone Weber amendment was struck for that reason when the House took up the bill June 26. But members took no separate vote on the Porter language, leaving its fate unclear.

Abortion rights backers said the 353-74 vote by which the House approved the overall spending bill showed that they had more than enough support to override a veto promised by Bush in a June 4 letter to congressional leaders. *(Bush letter, p. 344)*

But supporters of the rules dismissed that assessment, saying that many members who voted for the popular Labor-HHS bill on final passage would vote to sustain a veto over the abortion counseling issue. Included among abortion foes who voted "aye" was Weber, a member of the subcommittee that drafted the measure.

Abortion foes announced the day before the House took up the measure that they would not try to strike Porter's provision. "This is a tactical decision and a tactical decision only," said Smith. "It's a matter of when we're going to engage it, not if."

But abortion rights advocates read the decision not to fight the Porter provision differently. "By not calling for a vote, they're indicating their weakness," said Vic Fazio, D-Calif.

Senate Action on S 323

The Senate likewise avoided an on-the-record vote on the counseling ban when it approved an amended version of S 323 by voice vote July 17. While there was little doubt the Senate strongly supported an overturn of the rules, no one knew whether backers could muster a veto-proof two-thirds majority.

Although the final roll call had been widely anticipated as an indicator of Senate sentiment, both sides felt the stakes were such that they should not risk a politically costly loss.

"I think it's fair to say both sides were happy to have a voice vote," said Orrin G. Hatch, R-Utah, who managed floor opposition to the measure.

Senators also engaged the sensitive issue of parental notification for abortion, adopting two contradictory proposals. One, offered by Daniel R. Coats, R-Ind., would have required that at least one parent be notified in most cases; the other, sponsored by Majority Leader George J. Mitchell, D-Maine, had numerous exceptions.

Abortion foes opposed Mitchell's plan, which was based on Maine's law. The proposal, said Hatch, "is not a parental consent amendment, but an abortionist consent amendment."

Still, the amendment was adopted by 54-45. *(Vote 130, p. 18-S)*

Then, to the surprise of those on both sides, the much more stringent Coats plan passed, too, 52-47. *(Vote 131, p. 18-S)*

That left the measure with conflicting requirements that would have to be reconciled later in a House-Senate conference.

Seven senators voted for both parental notification amendments: Democrats Robert C. Byrd, W.Va., Herb Kohl, Wis., and Richard C. Shelby, Ala.; and Republicans Nancy Landon Kassebaum, Kan., Alan K. Simpson, Wyo., Ted Stevens, Alaska, and John W. Warner, Va.

House Committee Action, HR 3090

After numerous delays, the House Energy and Commerce Subcommittee on Health and the Environment took up its Title X reauthorization, including language to overturn the counseling ban, on July 30. Subcommittee Chairman Henry A. Waxman, D-Calif., had been trying to hold the markup since June but kept delaying it in an attempt to fend off efforts by abortion opponents to add parental notification language.

Waxman used the additional time to his advantage as the subcommittee defeated an amendment that would have required parents to be notified before a minor could receive an abortion from a facility receiving federal family planning funds. Instead of taking the parental notification amendment, offered by Thomas J. Bliley Jr., R-Va., members adopted a Waxman amendment requiring recipients of family planning funds to abide by whatever law, if any, each state was enforcing on the subject.

The subcommittee also ignored a presidential veto threat from HHS Secretary Louis W. Sullivan and defeated an attempt to strike from the bill the language overturning the counseling ban. Members rejected, 8-14, an amendment by ranking Republican William E. Dannemeyer, Calif., that would have in effect written the counseling ban into law.

The story was much the same when the full committee took up a clean version of the bill (HR 3090) Aug. 1 and approved it by a vote of 27-16.

Members again rejected Dannemeyer's amendment to codify the counseling ban, 17-26.

But, to the surprise of many, the full committee also rejected the Bliley parental notification amendment, by a vote of 20-23. It marked the first time the committee with jurisdiction over family planning had voted on what had been considered abortion foes' most potent issue.

Family planning supporters tried, unsuccessfully, to focus the debate on matters other than abortion.

"This program has become the focal point for much of the debate about the legality of abortion and I think that's a mistake," said Waxman.

Even some abortion opponents praised Title X. "This is a program that has done a lot of good over two decades," said Gerry Sikorski, D-Minn., a frequent anti-abortion vote. "And regardless of where you are on abortion, it's done a lot of good to prevent a lot of abortions."

But others insisted that abortion was tainting the program. "Family planning should not be used for suggesting, advocating or tolerating abortion," said Dannemeyer.

Parental Notification

By far the most spirited debate was over Bliley's parental notification amendment. It would have required notification of one parent at least 48 hours before an abortion could be performed on a minor by an entity that received Title X funds. Although the family planning program had since its inception forbidden the use of program funds for abortion, many Title X recipients were hospitals or other facilities that also performed abortions.

Exceptions to the rule would have been allowed only for medical emergencies "that would, with reasonable medical certainty, cause the death of the minor" unless an abortion was performed. In cases in which the pregnant minor stated in writing that the pregnancy was the result of incest, or that she had been neglected or was at risk of physical or sexual abuse, notification was to be made to law enforcement authorities instead of a parent.

The amendment also did not contain a so-called judicial bypass, allowing a pregnant teenager to obtain consent from a judge rather than have her parents notified. Bliley, however, said the requirement would not have applied in states with notification laws and judicial bypasses already in place, as long as the notification law was at least as strict as his proposal.

"In poll after poll Americans have expressed strong support for a law requiring parental involvement in the decision to have an abortion," said Bliley at the subcommittee markup. Citing a March study in the American Journal of Public Health showing that teen pregnancies declined after Minnesota enacted a two-parent notification law, Bliley said his amendment "would promote responsible sexual behavior among teenagers."

But opponents, even some who said they supported parental notification laws, complained that Bliley's amendment was too strict.

"Most people in this committee think there ought to be notification generally," said Waxman. "The dispute is over the circumstances in which you should not have it."

"I'm for parental notification and parental rights," said Sikorski, who noted that Minnesota's strict two-parent notification law, upheld by the Supreme Court in 1990, would be unaffected by either the Bliley or Waxman amendments. But Sikorski called Bliley's plan "unworkable, unenforceable, and downright mean."

Another frequent abortion foe, Jim Slattery, D-Kan., complained that the measure provided no exception for girls made pregnant by a mother's boyfriend. "Notify who? The mother who has a live-in friend who has molested her?" asked Slattery. He said the amendment was "fatally flawed ... because it doesn't take into account those terrible situations we don't even like to think about."

HR 3090 did not make it to the House floor in 1991, as sponsors waited to see the outcome of the appropriations effort to block the counseling ban.

Final Appropriations Action

The Senate took one final stab at the parental notification issue during debate Sept. 12 on the Labor-HHS bill.

By a vote of 92-8, members overwhelmingly approved a compromise proposal drafted by Kassebaum, despite the fact that it was vehemently opposed by advocacy groups on both sides of the abortion issue. *(Vote 186, p. 25-S)*

The proposal would have required notification of, or consent by, at least one parent before a minor could obtain an abortion at a clinic receiving federal family planning funds. But the compromise also included a long list of exceptions to the general requirement. Among those were cases in which: a physician certified the presence of a health emergency; a judge permitted the girl to obtain the abortion; or a professional counselor with no financial interest in the abortion certified that notification could put the girl at risk of physical abuse or emotional harm.

The amendment also would not have applied in states that passed their own laws on the subject or in states, such as Oregon, where voters had voted against notification or consent laws.

Abortion rights forces fought Kassebaum's proposal because they opposed the concept of required parental notification. "We really don't feel this is an area the federal government should legislate in," said a lobbyist for Planned Parenthood Inc.

Abortion foes opposed the plan for opposite reasons. "It's got so many loopholes, it would only apply in nine states," said Susan Smith of the National Right to Life Committee.

Earlier in the debate the Senate rejected, 45-55, a much more stringent notification measure offered by Don Nickles, R-Okla. It would have required notification of at least one parent but provided exceptions if the abortion was necessary to save the girl's life, the pregnancy resulted from parental incest, or the girl had been abused or neglected, in which case law enforcement authorities would have had to be notified. *(Vote 185, p. 25-S)*

With her consent, Kassebaum's compromise amendment was dropped during the House-Senate conference on the bill. She said she would seek instead to append it in 1992 to legislation to reauthorize the family planning program.

The House overwhelmingly adopted the conference report on the Labor-HHS appropriations bill — including the language to block the counseling ban — on Nov. 6, but the 272-156 vote was well short of the two-thirds required to override. *(Vote 380, p. 92-H)*

And while the Senate voted 73-24 the next day to clear the bill, Bush on Nov. 8 reiterated his vow to veto the entire measure over the abortion language. *(Vote 246, p. 32-S)*

The House vote was complicated by a long-simmering budget dispute over $4.3 billion in appropriations that was not actually to be spent until fiscal 1993. Without the budget issue, abortion rights advocates said, they might well have produced the two-thirds margin that had been their goal.

But even without the budget issue, it was by no means clear that the measure would have received the needed two-thirds majority. Abortion opponents insisted that they would have prevailed even without the extra votes they gained for budgetary reasons.

Still, administration fears of what might become Bush's first veto defeat were evident. The night before the House vote, a memo from Bush to Sullivan was distributed on Capitol Hill. The one-page memo, which purported to "clarify the purpose and intent of these regulations," actually included little new information about the controversial rules, but it apparently provided a few swing votes.

"Nothing in these regulations is to prevent a woman from receiving complete medical information about her condition from a physician," said the memo, in part.

As far as the president was concerned, that settled the matter. "Under my directive ... patients and doctors can talk about absolutely anything they want, and they should be able to do that," Bush told reporters Nov. 8.

But opponents of the rule said the memo did not solve the underlying problem.

"This is an attempt to get rid of the problems of the gag rule without removing the gag," said Sen. John H. Chafee, R-R.I., who led that chamber's effort to overturn the counseling ban. Chafee noted that while the memo permitted physicians freedom of speech, it continued to muzzle nurse-practitioners and other health professionals who did the bulk of the counseling in family planning clinics.

Opponents also pointed out that the memo did not legally alter the regulation. The memo, said Rep. Porter, "is nothing. It is a last-minute attempt to confuse the issue."

On Nov. 19, the House finally answered the biggest abortion-related question of the year, failing by a dozen votes to override Bush's veto, issued only hours earlier. The vote was 276-156, which fell 12 short of the two-thirds needed. *(Vote 403, p. 98-H)*

Key to the president's victory were 43 Democrats who broke with their leaders to vote to sustain the veto.

Indeed, the House Democratic leadership pulled out all the stops, with Speaker Foley not only speaking in favor of the override, but also taking the rare step of casting his vote.

But abortion opponents worked the issue hard, too. And their success in framing the vote as purely an abortion test convinced two Democrats, Dale E. Kildee, Mich., and James L. Oberstar, Minn., to vote to sustain Bush's veto after they had voted for the conference report two weeks earlier.

Kildee, a self-described liberal, said the vote was particularly difficult because he had worked so hard for so many of the education funding increases in the bill. But in the end, he said, he had to vote with Bush because blocking the regulations "still could and would lead to the death of unborn babies."

FETAL RESEARCH

Although the counseling rules provoked the hottest abortion fight in 1991, the debate over the propriety of allowing research using fetal tissue ran a close second. The House passed legislation on the matter, but the Senate took no legislative action.

At issue was a funding moratorium — originally imposed by the Reagan administration in 1988 and continued by Bush appointees the next year — on research involving tissue from aborted fetuses.

In 1989, HHS Secretary Sullivan announced that he would continue the funding ban because such research might have the effect of encouraging women to have abortions.

Fetal-tissue research conducted with private funds had shown promise in treating a wide variety of maladies, including juvenile diabetes and Parkinson's disease.

Advocates of the research said Sullivan should not have rejected the recommendations of two expert advisory committees of the National Institutes of Health (NIH). The committees found that such research could be conducted ethically if precautions were taken to ensure separation of the decisions to obtain an abortion and to donate the tissue for scientific use.

Before taking over as NIH director in 1991, Dr. Bernadine Healy had served on both advisory committees and had voted to recommend that the moratorium be overturned. But at her March confirmation hearing before the Senate Labor and Human Resources Committee, Healy said she would uphold the funding ban.

House Committee Action

Waxman, an opponent of the ban and chairman of the House Energy and Commerce Subcommittee on Health and the Environment, inserted a provision overturning it into his omnibus reauthorization bill (HR 2507) for NIH. *(NIH bill, p. 352)*

Legislation including similar provisions was approved by the subcommittee and full committee in 1990, but everything controversial was stripped from the measure before it reached the House floor. *(1990 Almanac, p. 600)*

"We shouldn't accord greater reverence for dead tissue than for living people," said Waxman at the subcommittee's May 7 markup of the bill, where it was ultimately approved on a 14-7 vote.

The full Energy and Commerce committee approved HR 2507 on a straight party-line vote of 27-16 on June 4. Before approving the measure, members voted 16-27 to reject an amendment by Dannemeyer, the Health Subcommittee's ranking Republican, to strike from the bill provisions overturning the administration's ban.

House Floor Action

The House overwhelmingly approved the measure July 25, but the 274-144 vote was well short of the margin needed to override the veto promised by Bush. *(Vote 229, p. 56-H)*

"The bill would allow unwarranted and unwise intrusions into the authority of the Secretary of Health and Human Services," said a July 24 White House statement that called the measure "unacceptable."

Although the fetal research issue provoked some heated rhetoric, opponents of the provision declined to offer a separate amendment to strike the language. With Bush dug in against it, said Rep. Christopher H. Smith, R-N.J., co-chairman of the House Pro-Life Caucus, "the feeling was ... the bill is coming back vetoed," so abortion opponents opted to spare members a bruising floor fight.

Backers of fetal tissue research suggested that opponents were called off by White House officials who feared the amendment would not get enough votes to sustain a Bush veto. "We had many pro-life members tell us they just didn't see this as an abortion issue and they were with us," said Waxman. "That's why there wasn't a vote."

The lack of a separate vote did not stop members from debating the issue, with abortion opponents lined up against an array of medical groups and advocates for those suffering from diseases that fetal-tissue research showed some promise of curing.

Among those urging that the funding ban be overturned was Anne Udall, daughter of former Rep. Morris K. Udall, D-Ariz. The elder Udall resigned from Congress earlier in 1991 due to complications from Parkinson's disease. *(Udall resignation, p. 51)*

Advocates argued that it was wrong to refuse funding for such research. "I can't see how members can look people in the eye who are suffering from these diseases ... and tell them it is better to take the fetal tissue that is already dead and bury it, rather than let it be used for a transplantation that could save someone's life," said Waxman.

But Smith countered that the knowledge that fetal

President's Message

President Bush, who repeatedly had opposed congressional efforts to relax restrictions on abortion, did so again in a June 4 letter to House and Senate leaders. Following is the text:

Legislation is now being considered by several committees in both the House and Senate that would substantially change federal policy with respect to abortion. Given the importance of this issue, I am writing to make sure there is no misunderstanding of my views or convictions.

I have not reached these decisions easily or lightly. Abortion is a difficult, deeply emotional and very personal decision for all Americans. It is made even more difficult when the underlying issue is whether the government — and ultimately the American taxpayer — is asked to pay for abortions and under what circumstances. Since 1981, the federal government has determined that taxpayer funds should be used for abortion in only the most narrow of circumstances: where the life of the mother is endangered.

Current law also prohibits contributions made to international organizations that fund coercive abortion programs. The Department of Defense prohibits abortions at U.S. military facilities, unless the life of the mother is endangered. And the Department of Health and Human Services has promulgated regulations that prohibit the use of federal family planning funds for abortion-related activities.

I believe all these policies should continue. I will veto any legislation that weakens current law or existing regulations.

tissue could help someone "serves as a powerful incentive and justification for a woman to get an abortion."

Members did agree on one minor issue, adopting by voice vote an amendment by Fred Upton, R-Mich., that sought to apply to privately funded research the provisions in the bill prohibiting fetal tissue from being sold and barring pregnant women from directing that fetal tissue be given to a specific person.

Senate Does Not Act

The Senate took no legislative action on the controversy in 1991. Kennedy, chairman of the Labor and Human Resources Committee, only days before the House action introduced a companion to Waxman's NIH bill (S 1523) without any language regarding the issue. Aides said Kennedy thought the matter too controversial to make it through the Senate.

But in late October, Kennedy joined committee member Brock Adams, D-Wash., in introducing stand-alone legislation (S 1902) to overturn the ban, suggesting that the two bills might be merged when the committee took up the NIH reauthorization in 1992.

ABORTIONS AND THE MILITARY

A holdover question from 1990 was whether servicewomen and military dependents living overseas should be allowed to get abortions in military medical facilities if they paid for the procedures themselves. The Defense Department had banned such "prepaid" abortions by directive in 1988.

Members in both chambers tried unsuccessfully in 1990 to overturn the ban during consideration of the defense authorization bill: In August the Senate by a vote of 58-41 refused to invoke cloture (and cut off a threatened filibuster) on an amendment offered by Tim Wirth, D-Colo., and in September the House by 200-216 rejected a similar amendment offered by Vic Fazio, D-Calif.

In 1991 members seeking to overturn the ban had more success but still were unable to achieve their goal.

House Action

The first skirmish came May 22, when the House by 220-208 approved virtually the same amendment it had defeated the previous September. The action came during consideration of the fiscal 1992 defense authorization bill (HR 2100). *(Vote 109, p. 28-H)*

Abortion rights forces also sought to append the language to the fiscal 1992 defense appropriations bill (HR 2521).

During Appropriations Committee consideration of the measure June 4, members voted 21-18 to approve an amendment offered by AuCoin that would have lifted the abortion ban. However, the language was deleted during June 7 House floor consideration on a point of order as impermissibly legislating on an appropriation.

AuCoin complained loudly after John P. Murtha, D-Pa., chairman of the Defense Appropriations Subcommittee and an abortion foe, did not ask the Rules Committee to protect the language on the floor.

"Never in my 17 years here has the committee adopted an amendment and then the chairman not asked the Rules Committee to protect that amendment" from procedural points of order on the floor, said AuCoin.

Senate Action

The Senate wound up in the opposite situation, with language to overturn the ban included in its version of the defense spending bill but not in the authorization measure.

During floor consideration of the authorization bill Aug. 2, the Senate by a vote of 58-40 refused to cut off debate on Wirth's amendment, leaving abortion rights forces two votes short of the 60 required. *(Vote 177, p. 24-S)*

However, Frank R. Lautenberg, D-N.J., appended language overturning the ban to the Senate version of the appropriations bill during subcommittee consideration Sept. 19, and it remained in the bill unchallenged, through Senate passage Sept. 26.

Conference, Final Action

House and Senate negotiators dropped the language from the defense authorization bill on Nov. 4, after Bush reiterated his threat to veto the legislation if the disputed abortion language remained.

Conferees on the appropriations bill dropped the language as well Nov. 14, but only after what Lautenberg described as "a fairly tough debate." Ultimately, the House refused to accept the Senate's language on a tie vote of 7-7, which included the vote of House Appropriations Chairman Jamie L. Whitten, D-Miss., who while technically a member of every conference committee, rarely voted. Subsequently, Senate conferees refused to insist on their language by a vote of 10-8, and the language died.

FOREIGN AID

Although no legislation reached Bush, both the House and Senate in 1991 voted to end two policies affecting abortion and family planning overseas.

At issue in both the fiscal 1992-93 foreign aid authorization bill (HR 2508, S 1435) and the fiscal 1992 foreign operations appropriation (HR 2621) was funding for the United Nations Population Fund, known as UNFPA. Lawmakers were also divided, in debate on the authorization measures, over the "Mexico City" policy, which since 1984 had barred funding for international family planning programs that perform or "actively promote" abortion.

Funding for UNFPA had been barred since 1985 by appropriations language that prohibited funding of any organization that "supports or participates in the management of a program of coercive abortion or involuntary sterilization."

The key question was the extent to which UNFPA's aid to China bolstered that nation's strict population-control programs, which in some cases included coerced abortions. Abortion opponents said even demographic and other technical assistance facilitated the policy, while rights advocates said UNFPA's participation in China was minimal and depriving the agency of U.S. funds hurt other nations needing aid.

Opponents of the Mexico City policy, so named because it was announced at a conference in that city in 1984, argued that it amounted to an international version of the domestic abortion-counseling ban upheld by the Supreme Court in May. But abortion opponents, who supported the policy, said it was needed to prevent organizations such as the international arm of Planned Parenthood from using U.S. funds to undermine other nations' anti-abortion laws.

Authorization Bill

Members first engaged the abortion elements of the foreign aid authorization during floor debate in the House and committee consideration in the Senate.

On June 12, the Senate Foreign Relations Committee by a vote of 6-13 rejected an amendment by Jesse Helms, R-N.C., that would have stripped from that chamber's version of the bill the provision overturning the Mexico City policy. The panel subsequently approved the bill by a vote of 17-2.

Also on June 12, the House took up its bill, and immediately quashed abortion foes' attempts to remove the disputed language. By a vote of 234-188, members approved an amendment by Peter H. Kostmayer, D-Pa., that effectively blocked another amendment by Christopher H. Smith to strike the UNFPA funds. *(Vote 148, p. 36-H)*

Similarly, members adopted by a vote of 222-200 an amendment by Howard L. Berman, D-Calif., that blocked another Smith amendment that would have reinstated the Mexico City policy. *(Vote 149, p. 36-H)*

The House ultimately approved the bill by a vote of 274-138 June 20. *(Vote 185, p. 46-H)*

Abortion rights supporters got a big win during Senate consideration of its bill July 25, when members voted 63-33 to cut off debate on an amendment by Paul Simon, D-Ill., to authorize $20 million for UNFPA. Simon's amendment was subsequently adopted by voice vote. *(Vote 151, p. 20-S)*

During the House-Senate conference in September, members tried in vain to reach an accord with the White House that would have produced the first foreign aid authorization since 1985. But Bush rejected a compromise that would have left the Mexico City policy intact and tightly restricted how UNFPA could spend its $20 million in U.S. funds.

Bush never got to follow through on his veto threat, though. By a vote of 159-262 the House on Oct. 30 rejected the conference report on the measure, thus killing the bill. *(Vote 354, p. 86-H)*

Appropriations Action

Consideration of the fiscal 1992 foreign operations spending bill, which included $20 million for UNFPA, was complicated by the successful effort Foreign Operations Appropriations Subcommittee Chairman David R. Obey, D-Wis., to link the family planning funds to Bush administration efforts to obtain preferential trade status for China. Bush had been lobbying hard for Congress to extend most-favored-nation (MFN) trade status to China, but repeatedly threatened to veto any bill including funds for UNFPA because of its activities in that country. *(China trade status, p. 121)*

Obey called his amendment, approved by the full Appropriations Committee June 12 by a vote of 30-19, the "Hypocrisy Reduction Act of 1991," a thinly veiled reference to the president's desire to have it both ways on China policy. Under the amendment, UNFPA was to get the $20 million (which Bush opposed) if Congress also granted MFN to China (which Bush supported). If Congress did not grant MFN, no funds would be provided to UNFPA.

"If we're going to isolate China, we ought to isolate them across the board," argued Obey.

The matter was not contested during a brief House floor debate June 19. Before the Senate could act, the bill was put on hold until 1992 over the issue of housing loans for Israel, and the stopgap measure to fund foreign aid programs in the interim (H J Res 360) included no UNFPA funding.

DISTRICT OF COLUMBIA

The House's vote in August 1989 to allow the District of Columbia to use locally raised tax funds to pay for abortions for low-income women — the first abortion rights victory in that chamber since 1980 — heralded the new political potency of the issue in the wake of the Supreme Court's *Webster* ruling a month earlier. But despite support for the policy in both chambers, in 1991, the D.C. prohibition remained in law for the third straight year.

Bush on Aug. 17 vetoed the the District's fiscal 1992 spending bill (HR 2699 — H Rept 102-181), which would have repealed the funding resriction.

In fact, little mention was made of the abortion language in either chamber during committee or floor debate, with both sides of the abortion issue holding their fire in anticipation of a probable veto.

But when that veto came, abortion rights forces opted not to attempt an override, aware they did not have the needed two-thirds majority in the House.

From the beginning of the process, House District of Columbia Appropriations Subcommittee Chairman Julian C. Dixon, D-Calif., conceded the House could not override and said if Bush vetoed the bill he would drop the abortion language rather than subject the bill to a lengthy delay, thus depriving the financially strapped city of its record federal payment of $630.5 million. *(Appropriations, p. 616)*

With the abortion restriction restored, the House passed a new bill (HR 3291) Sept. 16 by voice vote. The Senate cleared the measure, also by voice vote, Sept. 26; and Bush signed it Oct. 1 (PL 102-111). ■

NIH Reauthorization Stalled in Senate

Legislation (HR 2507) to reauthorize the two largest of the National Institutes of Health (NIH) was passed by the House in late July but did not advance in the Senate.

Controversy centered on provisions that sought to lift an administration ban on federal funding of research using tissue from aborted fetuses. This research had shown considerable promise in treating such conditions as juvenile diabetes and Parkinson's disease, and many lawmakers were eager to lift the four-year-old funding moratorium. But President Bush threatened to veto any measure that eased the ban, saying it could encourage women to have abortions. *(Fetal tissue research, p. 343)*

The bill's primary reason for existence was to reauthorize the National Cancer Institute and the National Heart, Lung and Blood Institute. They were the biggest of NIH's 13 institutes and the only ones requiring periodic congressional reauthorization.

The bill authorized $2 billion for the cancer institute in fiscal 1992 and $1.3 billion for the heart, lung and blood institute; the administration had asked for $1.8 billion and $1.2 billion, respectively, in its fiscal 1992 budget.

Besides reauthorizing the cancer institute and the heart, lung and blood institute, HR 2507 for the first time set a funding authorization level for the National Institute on Aging: $500 million in fiscal 1992. Bush had asked for $349 million.

NIH as a whole received appropriations of more than $8.3 billion in fiscal 1991.

As introduced by House Energy and Commerce Health and the Environment Subcommittee Chairman Henry A. Waxman, D-Calif., HR 1532 — the precursor to HR 2507 — was virtually identical to the NIH reauthorization bill he sponsored in 1990. That measure was approved by the subcommittee and full committee but never came to the floor for a vote. Congress ultimately cleared a stripped-down Senate NIH bill that created a non-governmental, nonprofit foundation for biomedical research and established a National Center for Medical Rehabilitation Research within the National Institute on Child Health and Human Development. *(1990 Almanac, p. 600)*

As in years past, the 1991 reauthorization bill served as an engine to haul all manner of health-related riders. NIH bills had become major bones of contention between Congress and the executive branch. Typically, members of Congress accused presidents of politicizing scientific research while chief executives accused Congress of trying to micromanage NIH.

Although the specific sticking points were different, the Bush administration's complaints about HR 2507 were reminiscent of the arguments made by the Reagan administration in 1984 and 1985, the last time Congress and the president were at loggerheads over NIH. During that fight, President Ronald Reagan vetoed two bills at the end of 1984 and early in 1985; Congress overwhelmingly overrode the latter veto. *(1984 Almanac, p. 474; 1985 Almanac, p. 287)*

Presaging Bush's complaints about HR 2507, Reagan in 1985 said that year's reauthorization "manifests an effort to exert undue political control over decisions regarding scientific research" and was "overloaded with objectionable provisions that seriously undermine and threaten the ability of NIH to manage itself."

BOXSCORE

➡ **NIH Reauthorization (HR 2507).** A bill to reauthorize the two largest institutes of the National Institutes of Health, lift a Bush administration ban on research involving tissue from aborted fetuses, and mandate the inclusion of women and minorities in most clinical tests of new treatments or drugs.

Report: H Rept 102-136.

KEY ACTION

June 4 — HR 2507 was approved 27-16 by the full **House** Energy and Commerce Committee.

July 25 — HR 2507 was passed by the **House** by 274-144.

HOUSE COMMITTEE ACTION

The Health and the Environment Subcommittee approved a clean bill May 7 in lieu of HR 1532, Waxman's original NIH reauthorization measure. The vote was 14-7.

The measure's provision to lift the Bush administration ban on fetal tissue research was only one of a raft of controversial elements in the legislation.

Among other things, the bill ordered the creation of research centers to study infertility and contraception, required guidelines to protect whistleblowers who reported cases of alleged scientific misconduct and capped the amount of "indirect costs" grant recipients could charge to the federal government.

In an eight-page, single-spaced May 6 letter to Energy and Commerce Committee Chairman John D. Dingell, D-Mich., Health and Human Services (HHS) Secretary Louis W. Sullivan said that if the measure was not significantly altered, Bush's advisers would recommend a veto.

Among the objections cited by Sullivan was cost: The administration said the funding ceilings set by the bill for the two institutes were too high.

The White House and committee Republicans also complained that the bill represented an effort on the part of congressional Democrats to micromanage NIH.

"This bill is simply a repeat of attempts of past years to manage NIH from Capitol Hill," said Norman F. Lent, N.Y., ranking Republican of the Energy and Commerce Committee.

Lent, along with six of the panel's remaining seven Republicans, voted against the measure. The remaining Republican, Michael Bilirakis, Fla., did not vote.

As approved by the subcommittee, the bill did allay at least some of the administration's concerns, worked out in an omnibus technical amendment offered at the markup by subcommittee Chairman Waxman.

Among the changes was a rewrite of the section of the bill requiring that clinical studies of various drugs and other medical treatments include women and minorities. The administration strongly opposed the original provision.

"Such an inflexible requirement could in fact jeopardize the initiation of NIH clinical trials, including the very trials that would provide valuable data relevant to women's health," Sullivan's letter said.

The rewritten language still required that women be included in all research projects but relaxed the requirement that members of minority groups be included in every project. Instead, the new language sought to ensure that minorities were included on a more general basis.

Both the new and old language explicitly permitted women and minorities to be excluded from studies if it would be inappropriate to the purpose of the research or could put participants at risk.

As expected, fetal tissue research was the subject of the most heated debate during the subcommittee markup. About the only major new issue to come up involved indirect research costs.

A series of hearings held by the Energy and Commerce Committee's Oversight and Investigations Subcommittee had uncovered serious abuses of the mechanism used by grant recipients, particularly universities, to recoup from the federal government costs associated with federally funded research.

At the markup, William E. Dannemeyer, R-Calif., the subcommittee's ranking minority member, offered an amendment that sought to impose a cap on the administrative expenses for which grant recipients could claim indirect costs. The 26 percent cap, he said, represented a median amount.

Waxman — who usually disagreed with Dannemeyer on almost everything — supported the amendment, but other members of the panel questioned it.

The Oversight Subcommittee's hearings "really did turn up some horror stories," said Thomas J. Bliley Jr., R-Va., a member of that panel. Still, Bliley and others said they were not convinced that a cap on indirect costs was the answer.

"In some cases you may be too high, and in others you may do serious injustice to a university," he said.

The amendment ultimately was approved by voice vote, after several members said they hoped to examine the issue more closely before the bill went to the full committee for markup.

Full Committee Markup

HR 2507 was approved by the full House Energy and Commerce Committee on June 4. The Bush administration threatened to veto the bill, and HHS Secretary Sullivan, in a letter sent to committee members the day of the markup, included eight single-spaced pages of objections.

Members ordered the bill reported on a straight party-line vote of 27-16.

The administration and panel Republicans said their primary problem was that the legislation allowed Congress to micromanage the nation's premier biomedical research establishment.

The bill "will handcuff the secretary in making some of his most important decisions," said Lent.

Before sending the measure to the House floor, members approved several amendments, including one that modified language adopted by the subcommittee to limit federal payments to universities for indirect costs related to federally funded research.

By voice vote, members rejected a Dannemeyer amendment that would have limited NIH funding increases to 2.4 percent annually from fiscal 1992 through fiscal 1996.

Members adopted by voice votes the following amendments:

- By Ron Wyden, D-Ore., to expand NIH research and dissemination of information related to nutritional disorders and obesity.
- By Edward J. Markey, D-Mass., and Jack Fields, R-Texas, to require NIH to establish a comprehensive program to research trauma care.

HOUSE PASSAGE

The struggle over whether the executive or legislative branch should play the larger role in setting biomedical research priorities continued July 25 as the House approved HR 2507. The vote was 274-144, a strong showing but short of the two-thirds margin needed to override a promised veto. *(Vote 229, p. 56-H)*

"The bill would allow unwarranted and unwise intrusions into the authority of the Secretary of Health and Human Services and is too directive in its effort to expand certain research programs," said a July 24 White House statement that called the measure "unacceptable."

Women's Health Issues

The administration's objections to provisions that required NIH to devote more resources to women's health and mandated the inclusion of women and minorities in more of NIH's clinical tests infuriated many women members in the House.

When clinical studies of treatments for diseases affecting both sexes used only men, doctors "have to guess" about their effectiveness on women, said Patricia Schroeder, D-Colo., co-chair of the Congressional Caucus on Women's Issues. "Women pay half the tax dollars, and we're not getting anything out of it."

In 1990, the General Accounting Office found that NIH had not been enforcing its own 1986 policy requiring the inclusion of women in research trials. As a result, many landmark studies told nothing about the effect of treatments on women.

Louise M. Slaughter, D-N.Y., pointed to a study released in mid-July showing that exercise could reduce the risk of certain types of diabetes. The research was conducted only on white men, she said, "while women and minorities are three times more likely to get the disease."

The bill also sought to create by law an Office of Research on Women's Health that would help administer requirements regarding the inclusion of women in research and identify research on women's health that should be conducted.

Although NIH established such an office in September 1990, when Congress was first addressing the issue, the committee report said the provision remained necessary "to ensure that NIH both complies with its own requirements ... and provides adequate support for research on women's health throughout the various institutes."

Finally, the bill set aside funding for NIH to study a variety of ailments affecting women primarily or exclusively, including osteoporosis ($40 million) and breast and ovarian cancer ($50 million). And it earmarked $5 million for the development and operation of centers to study infertility and contraception.

During Rules Committee consideration of the bill July 24, Dannemeyer complained that the women's health provisions amounted to "affirmative action and quotas" and said that "to inject it into scientific experimentation is where politics doesn't belong."

But he was sharply rebuked by Slaughter. To say that research should not be required on women, she said, "is to deny the rights of the half of the population that pays the taxes that supports this research."

Indirect Research Costs

In response to revelations earlier in the year that major universities were charging unwarranted expenses as "indirect costs" of research, the bill sought to narrow the definition of such costs and cap several categories.

The committee report said, "Audits have determined that federal biomedical research funds allocated for the payment of indirect costs have been used to help finance the cost of luxury yachts, 19th-century Italian fruitwood commodes, wedding receptions, trips to the Grand Cayman Islands and executive jet service. Such expenditures are unjustified and clearly unrelated to the necessary costs of conducting federal scientific research."

The administration, however, opposed the provisions, calling them "unnecessary at this time because abuses are being addressed administratively."

Animals for Research

The bill also sought to make it a federal crime to steal, destroy or alter records or property or to steal or injure research animals in any federally funded health facility. Violators could face up to five years in prison. The measure also barred protesters from physically restraining people from entering or leaving a health facility.

The provisions were in response to incidents over the preceding several years in which radical animal rights groups had broken into facilities that experimented on animals, kidnapped the animals, and destroyed property and records in the laboratories.

At a Rules Committee hearing July 24, Waxman said the provisions were necessary to fight an "interstate terror network ... that local police are clearly unable to deal with."

The bill required the National Institute of Environmental Health Sciences to establish a program to develop ways to test products for safety that eliminated or minimized the use of animals. Animal welfare organizations had long complained that many routinely required toxicity tests conducted on laboratory animals were inaccurate or unnecessary.

Ethics Issues

The bill codified NIH's establishment of an Office of Scientific Integrity within the NIH director's office. The office was charged with both monitoring investigations undertaken by universities or other recipients of NIH funding and conducting its own inquiries into reports of scientific misconduct.

The bill defined such misconduct as fabrication, falsification, plagiarism and any other serious deviation from the scientific community's recognized standards of conduct concerning scientific research. Unintentional errors in the interpretation of data and genuine differences of opinion about an interpretation were not to be considered misconduct.

The bill also required NIH to develop a set of regulations to protect "whistleblowers" who reported or cooperated with investigations of alleged misconduct. "It is the committee's conclusion that in general, scientists who, in good faith, question the work of their colleagues continue to find themselves pariahs, literally and figuratively," said the committee report.

Similar regulations were required to specify potential conflicts of interest between researchers and companies or other entities with a financial interest in such research.

Amendments

Amendments adopted by the House included:

- By Schroeder, to require a $9 million longitudinal study on adolescent health and behavior. By 271-142. *(Vote 226, p. 56-H)*
- By Carl D. Pursell, R-Mich., to redesignate the National Center for Nursing Research as the National Institute of Nursing Research, thereby making it NIH's 14th institute. By voice vote.

Members rejected, 132-283, a Dannemeyer amendment to limit authorizations to 2.4 percent more than the amount appropriated for the preceding fiscal year. *(Vote 228, p. 56-H)* ■

Substance Abuse, Mental Health Programs

Separate — and very different — legislation was pushed in both chambers to reauthorize the big federal block grant financing treatment of substance abuse and mental illness. While a House subcommittee sought to divide the block grant in two, the Senate wanted to keep it intact but alter the formula for disbursing the money.

The $1.3 billion Alcohol, Drug Abuse and Mental Health Services Block Grant had been created 10 years earlier to help treat those who suffered from alcoholism, drug addiction and mental illness. Although members had fought for years to control the formula to benefit their constituencies, the fight heated up in 1991 because so little federal money was available and so many states were in the red.

By voice vote, the Senate on Aug. 2 passed a $1.5 billion bill (S 1306) that left the block grant intact but revised the allocation formula to satisfy members from states with large rural populations.

A bill (HR 3698) pending before the House Energy and Commerce Committee proposed splitting the block grant, establishing one grant for mental health and another for substance abuse programs. Its sponsor, Henry A. Waxman, D-Calif., chairman of the Health and the Environment Subcommittee, said states should be more accountable to Congress for how the money was spent.

Waxman's bill drew objections from Republicans and tobacco interests because of language aimed at curbing smoking by minors. The bill originally would have given the administration the power to cut off grants to states that did not enact and enforce laws to discourage smoking by minors. Although that provision was removed during subcommittee markup, Waxman intended to revive it.

Background

During 1981, his first year in the White House, President Ronald Reagan sought to replace many categorical grants with block grants. GOP lawmakers had been push-

ing block grants since the 1960s as a way of moving decision-making authority back to state and local governments. Where Presidents Richard M. Nixon and Gerald R. Ford had failed, Reagan was more successful because of growing resentment of federal regulations and paperwork.

Some lawmakers, including Waxman, continued to support categorical grants as the best means of ensuring that federal money was spent as Congress intended. But Congress cleared legislation (PL 97-35) that created a number of block grants, including one that combined 10 substance abuse and mental health programs. *(1981 Almanac, p. 463)*

To ensure that no state lost money, the grants were based on the dollars each state had received from the affected programs that year or on a formula that protected the 1981 allocations from cuts. Although allocations were frozen to protect states, the plan also ensured that funding for some states would grow more quickly than others.

The formula was changed in 1988 to channel more funds to urban areas. The House reauthorization bill carried no urban bias, while Senate legislation pushed by Edward M. Kennedy, D-Mass., had a 20 percent urban weight. After the two bills went to conference, the legislation that emerged held a 40 percent urban weight. *(1988 Almanac, p. 86)*

Members such as Sen. Ernest F. Hollings, D-S.C., who had supported the original Senate bill on the floor, felt they had been blindsided. Since then, several had pushed for a more equitable formula.

In 1991, Kennedy, chairman of the Senate Labor and Human Resources Committee, sought to change the formula to satisfy senators from predominantly rural states, who argued that abuse of drugs other than cocaine was severe in rural areas and that treatment was needed.

The existing formula was derived from studies that found higher numbers of people at risk for drug abuse in urban areas than in rural communities. Those most at risk were defined as people from age 18 to 24.

However, the formula also considered the general urban population, and that skewed the funding distribution, according to a November 1990 study by the General Accounting Office. The study said that, although urban rates of people at risk for drug abuse were about three times higher than those of rural areas, the use of the total urban population in the formula produced a funding difference of 15 to 1.

HOUSE ACTION

While senators were negotiating formula changes, Waxman moved ahead with his plan to split the block grant. On June 25, the Energy and Commerce Health Subcommittee, which he chaired, approved HR 2311, a bill to create a separate block grant for mental health programs. Waxman deferred addressing substance abuse funding until he introduced HR 3698 on Nov. 1.

HR 2311, approved by a vote of 14-8, authorized $270 million for the mental health program for fiscal 1992. The measure authorized the program for three years.

Funding was to be based on a state's population at risk for mental illness and its ability to pay for treatment.

The subcommittee rejected, 8-14, an amendment by ranking Republican William E. Dannemeyer, Calif., to restrict funding increases in fiscal 1993-94 to 2.4 percent.

The panel also rejected, 8-14, another Dannemeyer amendment to amend the law governing the advisory panel for a federal program charged with protecting the rights of the mentally ill. Included in Dannemeyer's amendment was a requirement that either the chairman of the panel or a family member had received mental health services.

HR 3698: Separate Grants

On Nov. 6, the Health Subcommittee by 6-4 approved Waxman's revised bill, HR 3698, which split the big federal block grant in two. The measure authorized $303 million for a Community Mental Health Services Block Grant and $1.1 billion for alcohol and drug abuse programs. The bill also authorized new treatment programs that pushed the bill's total above $2 billion.

Waxman's plan retained the existing funding formula for substance abuse programs, leaving the urban bias untouched. But he made changes in the formula for mental health grants, based on the number of people at risk.

During the markup, members adopted by voice vote an amendment by Edolphus Towns, D-N.Y., to allow states to phase in over three years one of the bill's funding requirements. The bill required states to spend 25 percent of substance abuse funds for pregnant women and women with dependent children. Existing rules required states to spend 10 percent on these programs.

Cigarette Debate

The panel's liveliest debate erupted over Waxman's efforts to force states to deny cigarettes to minors under 18.

The bill required states to enact laws setting the legal age for buying cigarettes at 18. Only three states, Missouri, Montana and New Mexico, had no law on minors and smoking. The bill directed the Health and Human Services (HHS) secretary to cut off grants to states that did not enact laws by 1994 and allowed him to withhold funding from those that did not enforce the laws.

Thomas J. Bliley Jr., R-Va., a former Richmond mayor and perennial foe of anti-smoking legislation, offered an amendment that gutted Waxman's provision. The amendment barred the secretary from withholding block grants from states over enforcement of smoking restrictions on minors. Bliley argued that the bill would "provide HHS the authority to dictate law enforcement to states on their own laws."

Members approved his amendment, 11-10, primarily along party lines, with Democrats Towns, Terry L. Bruce of Illinois and J. Roy Rowland of Georgia siding with Bliley.

SENATE ACTION

By voice vote, the Labor and Human Resources Committee on July 17 approved a Kennedy bill (S 1306) that set a new formula based on the population at risk for drug abuse, the state's ability to provide treatment and the cost of services. States' existing allocations were protected for two years to satisfy members with big urban populations. Later, some states would face cutbacks of 5 percent.

The legislation authorized $3.87 billion for the block grants and some new programs in fiscal 1992.

While the bill was approved by voice vote, some members, including Claiborne Pell, D-R.I., and Daniel R. Coats, R-Ind., were not satisfied. "I continue to be very concerned about the formula," Pell said. "It involves a cut for my own state of Rhode Island."

S 1306 also reorganized the Alcohol, Drug Abuse and Mental Health Administration by placing the agency's research arms under the National Institutes of Health and renaming the agency the Alcohol, Drug Abuse and Mental Health Services Administration.

Also by voice vote, the full Senate approved S 1306 on Aug. 2. ■

Health-Care Reform Held Over for 1992

Congress took no action in 1991 to overhaul the nation's $660 billion health-care system, but the call for reform grew louder and more insistent in both political parties.

Driven by a cost spiral that seemed to have no end, and by the plight of 35 million Americans who lacked any type of health insurance, members vowed to tackle the health crisis in earnest during the 1992 election year.

Voters demonstrated their growing concern over the issue in Pennsylvania's special Senate election Nov. 5, in which Democrat Harris Wofford won an upset victory over former Attorney General Dick Thornburgh after a campaign built around a demand for national health insurance.

"The American people signaled, I think particularly in the Pennsylvania election, that they want some attention to this problem," said House Speaker Thomas S. Foley, D-Wash., on Nov. 13.

"It's the one that's causing more anxiety for their economic future than any other."

But the health-care issue's rise from a "might" to a "must" on the congressional agenda entailed political risks as well as opportunities, particularly as members struggled with such controversial details as who would foot the bill.

Wofford's election, said Sen. Dave Durenberger, R-Minn., "confirmed the diagnosis we've suspected for years. The health system is sick. But what it did not do was prescribe the cure."

Proposals for reform were coming in from all corners, from the American Medical Association (AMA) to the National Association of Social Workers, from the bipartisan Pepper Commission to the conservative Heritage Foundation. Yet the competing pressures for change were so strong that they canceled out each other.

"For any one proposal, I can find you support from two or three" of the nation's leading medical, business, labor and consumer groups, said Pete Stark, D-Calif., chairman of the House Ways and Means Subcommittee on Health. "But for the same proposal I can also find you two or three of the above who will spend millions of dollars to oppose it."

During the course of the year, members of Congress introduced more than three dozen health-care reform proposals. Wofford's win hastened the process of boiling down those plans into Democratic and Republican alternatives. *(Heath-reform concepts, p. 351)*

"The race is now between the parties to flesh out some of the specifics," said Rep. Ron Wyden, D-Ore.

A Short-Term Patch?

Privately, leaders in both parties said that the most likely outcome before the 1992 elections was an incremental bill similar to legislation introduced in October by Sen. Lloyd Bentsen, D-Texas, and Rep. Dan Rostenkowski, D-Ill, the chairmen of the Senate Finance and the House Ways and Means committees, respectively.

Those bills (S 1872, HR 3626) sought to make health insurance more available and affordable for small businesses. They also proposed an increase in the tax deductions for self-employed individuals and small businesses; an expansion of preventive services under Medicare, the federal health insurance program for the elderly and disabled; and creation of a commission to advise Congress and the president on strategies for reducing health-care costs.

A comprehensive overhaul, Bentsen told reporters in October, was certain to take time "and in the meantime, a lot of people are going to suffer." He said his bill addressed "things we can do now, not things that will block more major reform later."

That was a strategy with which many Republicans agreed. Congress should "do whatever we can do without waiting for utopia and perfection" said Rep. Bill Gradison, R-Ohio, a leading health authority on the Ways and Means Committee.

The need to help small businesses obtain affordable insurance was one of the few points on which all the members of the bipartisan Pepper Commission agreed in its 1990 report.

The 15-member group, made up of members of Congress and Reagan administration appointees, was created in 1988 to make recommendations on coverage for the uninsured and on long-term care. *(Pepper Commission, 1990 Almanac, p. 607)*

Plenty of Problems

Health-care costs had grown faster than overall inflation in every year since 1980 and faster than any other segment of the economy every year since overtaking housing costs in 1981.

By 1990, spending on health care had climbed to 12.2 percent of the gross national product (GNP), up from 11.6 percent in 1989. Early projections showed it reaching about 13 percent in 1991.

Health costs were also consuming an ever-larger share of the federal budget — 15.3 percent of federal expenditures in 1990, up from 14.7 percent in 1989 and 11.7 in 1980.

After interest on the national debt, Medicare was the fastest growing portion of the federal budget, costing $123.8 billion in fiscal 1992. If unchecked, Medicare's portion was expected to exceed those of Social Security or defense, the two largest items in the federal budget, soon after the turn of the century.

Costs were skyrocketing for employers as well. According to a survey released Jan. 28 by A. Foster Higgins & Co. Inc., a New York benefits consulting firm, companies paid 21.6 percent more to provide workers with health insurance in 1990 than in 1989, and costs had risen by almost half (46.3 percent) over two years.

While costs were exploding, more and more Americans were going without needed care. An estimated 31.5 million to 37 million Americans lacked health insurance coverage, and a study published in January in the Journal of the American Medical Association found that patients who lacked insurance were up to three times as likely to die in the hospital as those with insurance and were less likely to undergo expensive medical procedures.

Simultaneously, the "graying" of America was expanding the need for expensive long-term care, either in the home or in an institution.

By the year 2030, the number of Americans over age 65 — those most likely to need long-term care — was expected to double, while the number of "old old" individuals, those over age 85, was to balloon from 2.5 million to as many as 12 million.

That meant the number of people requiring long-term

Health-Reform Concepts Explored in 1991

During the first session of the 102nd Congress, members introduced dozens of bills to overhaul the nation's health-care system, ranging from cosmetic changes to a complete restructuring. Most of the plans shared at least some general concepts:

Cost Containment

The No. 1 priority for health-system reform was slowing the rise of medical costs, which had been climbing at double-digit rates for most of the preceding decade. No one knew for sure how to accomplish that goal, so sponsors of various bills applied the cost-containment label to any provision they thought might save money.

For example, the Senate Democratic leadership's bill (S 1227), introduced by Majority Leader George J. Mitchell, D-Maine, sought to create a board similar to the Federal Reserve. It was to set national health-care spending goals and organize negotiations between those who paid for health care, such as insurance companies, and those who provided it, such as doctors and hospitals.

Rep. Marty Russo, D-Ill., and other sponsors of bills calling for a single government-financed health system said their approach would save money by eliminating duplicative administrative costs and paperwork.

And Senate Republicans said their proposal (S 1936), introduced by John H. Chafee, R.I., would cut costs by reshaping the medical malpractice system, increasing access to preventive care and broadening "managed health care."

Access for All

After containing costs, the goal of virtually all of the overhaul plans was to expand access to health care for the estimated 35 million Americans who lacked health insurance.

Most of the Democratic bills included some sort of required coverage, on the theory that that was the only way to guarantee access for all. The "play or pay" schemes included in several of the plans, most notably those of Senate Democrats, required employers to provide workers and their dependents with coverage or pay into a fund from which insurance coverage would be provided. The most sweeping mandate, in Russo's bill (HR 1300), required the government to insure everyone for health care, as Canada did.

GOP plans, by contrast, eschewed mandates as counterproductive, arguing that they would drive some employers out of business. Instead, Republicans preferred incentives to expand health insurance. Most of their plans leaned heavily toward providing tax credits and deductions for individuals and businesses to help offset insurance costs.

Malpractice Reform

Just about all the major plans, Democratic and Republican, sought to overhaul the medical liability system. The Bush administration offered its own proposal in May. Studies showed that "defensive medicine," such as unnecessary tests and lab work ordered by doctors who feared lawsuits, was driving up costs. Also, the physicians sued most often for malpractice frequently were not guilty, while many negligent doctors never got sued, studies suggested.

The administration's proposal and the Senate Republicans' bill sought to cap non-economic damages, such as those for "pain and suffering," arising from medical negligence. Both those plans, the Senate Democrats' plan, and several free-standing bills also encouraged states to test ways to settle disputes out of court.

Preventive Care

Policy-makers agreed that more and better preventive care, such as immunizations for children and prenatal examinations for pregnant women, could help hold down future health-care costs. Health and Human Services Secretary Louis W. Sullivan emphasized that persuading Americans to eat a healthy diet, exercise more, and reduce smoking and drinking could avert costly illnesses.

Most of the proposals that mandated insurance coverage included language to ensure that preventive services were part of any insurance package. The Senate Republican plan, which had no mandate, sought to increase the authorizations for two existing programs — Community Health Centers and the National Health Service Corps — that provided primary and preventive care in medically underserved areas.

Managed Care

Finally, most of the bills gave a nod to making "managed care" more available, long a goal of the Reagan and Bush administrations. These plans included health maintenance organizations, which charged a flat fee for all services, and preferred provider organizations, which required patients to choose from a fixed universe of doctors who had agreed to charge less. Managed-care plans sought to contain costs by providing patients with a single point of entry into the health-care system and restricting access to specialists and hospitals.

---

care could nearly double from 7 million to 13.8 million.

The crumbling of the health-care system posed different problems for each of the major players:

- For business, the prime woe was runaway health costs eating up profits and making U.S. products less competitive overseas.
- Conversely, labor leaders complained that employers were trying to shift more and more health-care costs onto workers, mainly by increasing the employee share of insurance premiums or by requiring higher copayments and deductibles. No issue was more contentious at the bargaining table.
- Health-care providers, particularly doctors, complained that they are drowning in what one AMA official calls "paper snow" — an overload of authorizations, receipts and "utilization reviews" required by various insurance companies before claims would be processed and paid, or even before patients could be treated.
- Insurers also were unhappy. Smaller companies said they could not compete with firms that engaged in "redlin-

National Health Insurance: A Very Old Issue

The federal government adopted its first health insurance program in 1798 for merchant marine sailors who contributed a few cents a month to pay for hospital care provided by a marine hospital.

But it was not until the early 20th century that the idea of mandating health insurance for the general public became an issue.

Doctors and lawyers argued for national health insurance. The 1915 recommendation of the American Association for Labor Legislation, a group of lawyers, academics and other professionals, prompted the first serious debate. Their proposal gained momentum in 1917, when the American Medical Association's (AMA) House of Delegates voted for a government health insurance program.

Labor leaders, among them Samuel Gompers, criticized the concept, arguing that national insurance would result in government control over the working class. But it was not labor that scuttled the idea; it was the anger of an important lobby — burial insurers, who complained that a proposed burial benefit would undercut a thriving private industry.

"It was a simple tactical error, and tactics have always mattered," said Paul Starr, a sociology professor at Princeton University.

The Roosevelt-Truman Era

The idea remained dormant until the 1930s. As the nation reeled from the Great Depression, the coalition backing national health insurance reform had reversed itself. By then, the AMA stood in opposition, labor in support.

In 1934, President Franklin D. Roosevelt's Committee on Economic Security considered compulsory health insurance. But word that the panel was studying the matter "was responsible for so many telegrams to members of Congress that the entire Social Security program seemed endangered," Edwin Witte, the committee's executive director, told a historian. Roosevelt dropped the idea.

The national health service debate was revived less than a decade later, as the country called up men to serve in World War II. Nearly one-third of those between the ages 18 and 37 were found physically or mentally unfit. In response, the first comprehensive national health insurance bill was introduced June 4, 1943, by Sens. Robert F. Wagner, D-N.Y., and James E. Murray, D-Mont., and Rep. John D. Dingell Sr., D-Mich.

"Dad's bill was crafted with the help of the [Roosevelt] administration," said Dingell's son, chairman of the House Energy and Commerce Committee, who had reintroduced the bill in every Congress since he succeeded his father in 1955. "It's still the best national health insurance approach around."

Roosevelt included in his 1944 State of the Union address an "economic bill of rights" incorporating the "right to adequate medical care and the opportunity to achieve and enjoy good health."

But it was his successor, Harry S Truman, who made health care a political priority.

"We should resolve now that the health of this nation is a national concern; that financial barriers in the way of attaining health shall be removed; that the health of all its citizens deserves the help of all the nation," said Truman on Nov. 19, 1945.

Truman rode the issue in his narrow 1948 victory, and the Wagner-Murray-Dingell bill got its first hearing in 1949. But as the Cold War became a fact of American life, the AMA's dire warnings that the proposal amounted to "socialized medicine" reverberated across the country.

After a few liberal senators campaigned on the issue and lost in 1950, Democrats dropped the idea.

Scaling Back to Medicare

The political atmosphere changed. With the AMA's power proved and the new Eisenhower administration resisting national health insurance, Democrats scaled back their ambitious health-care plans. The idea of hospital insurance for the aged began to take hold, and the first bill toward that end was introduced in 1952.

"At that time, there were no retiree health plans, and the pressure for us to act came from the middle-aged, middle class who were beginning to pay the bills for their parents," said Joseph A. Califano, a former top aide to President Lyndon B. Johnson and secretary of Health, Education and Welfare under President Jimmy Carter.

Dwight D. Eisenhower responded by launching the idea of catastrophic coverage for the low-income elderly, while Democrats continued to push broader insurance

ing," the practice of refusing to cover people likely to be major users of medical care, and "cherrypicking," or seeking out low-risk young and healthy people to insure.

Diagnosis Easier Than Cure

All of these groups wanted change, but as much as they hated the status quo, they had yet to move off their own positions. The reason was that, as with many maladies, the diagnosis was simpler than the cure.

"We just see a lack of resolve on the part of any to make moves aside from advancing the interests of their own individual constituencies," said Dr. James Todd, executive vice president of the American Medical Association.

"It's hard to get people to understand just how complex this all is," said Calvin P. Johnson, legislative representative for the AFL-CIO.

Efforts to revamp the system were further complicated by the constricted federal budget, which thwarted major new spending initiatives.

The lack of consensus created a chicken-and-egg problem on Capitol Hill. If Congress made it clear that it intended to move forward on health-system reform, it probably could have forced the key players to the negotiating table.

But even some lawmakers who supported such action were loath to move forward without a consensus, especially after having been burned badly by the quick repeal of the 1988 Medicare Catastrophic Coverage Act.

for the aged. Republicans and Democrats divided as John F. Kennedy made health insurance for the elderly an important piece of his 1960 presidential campaign.

In office, Kennedy tried to rally support with stories of people mortgaging their homes to pay for their parents' health care, and in 1962, he tried to personalize the issue for Congress.

"I talked to a member of Congress from my own state a week ago," Kennedy said, "who told me he was going to send his daughter away to school, but because his father had been sick for two years he could not do it. And congressmen are paid $22,500 a year — and that's more than most people get."

However, Kennedy struggled against formidable resistance within his own party: conservative Southerners led by Ways and Means Chairman Wilbur D. Mills of Arkansas. Congress took no action during Kennedy's administration.

In 1964, Johnson took the issue to the nation in his presidential campaign and came back with a mandate for action. Johnson agreed to rework a funding formula for coverage for the poor that had been directing the overwhelming majority of funds to large states. That done, Congress in 1965 created Medicare for the aged and Medicaid for the poor, crowning achievements of Johnson's Great Society.

A Call for Broader Coverage

Inflation in the 1970s revived calls for broader national health coverage. Presidents Richard M. Nixon and Carter supported some form of broad health insurance reform, but the idea had no real champion and faced continued animus from the AMA and business.

The issue briefly took center stage as Sen. Edward M. Kennedy, D-Mass., challenged Carter over it. But as Kennedy prepared to enter the presidential primaries in 1980, the substantive debate was lost in the political struggle between the two men. The election that year of Ronald Reagan, a longtime opponent of big government, temporarily ended talk of major changes.

The pinch on the middle class later forced Reagan to reconsider his position, however. In 1986, he called for a study on "how the private sector and government can work together to address the problems of affordable insurance for those whose life savings would otherwise be threatened when catastrophic illness strikes."

Over 18 months, Congress crafted legislation that went well beyond Reagan's aim, creating the largest expansion of Medicare coverage since its inception. Reagan was presented the bill just weeks before the 1988 presidential nominating conventions, and he not only signed it but also hailed it as a measure that would "remove a terrible threat from the lives of elderly and disabled Americans."

It wasn't long, however, before support for the program unraveled, as senior citizens discovered they were expected to pay for their new benefits through higher monthly premiums and a special income surtax on more affluent elderly. Angry seniors besieged Congress with complaints, and in 1989, the law was repealed. *(1989 Almanac, p. 149)*

Shifting Political Winds

By 1991, the climate appeared to have shifted yet again. Part of the business community — squeezed by the high cost of health insurance premiums — was on board.

And Democratic Sen. Harris Wofford of Pennsylvania proved the political saliency of the national health insurance issue in his upset special election victory Nov. 5 over former Attorney General Dick Thornburgh. Wofford repeatedly emphasized the notion that health care was a basic right of all Americans.

On the surface, the political pressures of the 1990s were similar to those that stirred Washington a generation earlier.

People talked of mortgaging homes and farms, fighting off bankruptcy or being unable to send children to college, all because of crushing medical bills.

Lawmakers, in turn, talked of plans to radically expand the government's role in guaranteeing health care for Americans.

But the political realities were very different.

In 1965, President Johnson was fresh from a landslide victory, with an expanding economy and a brute determination to pass his Great Society legislation. Even so, he had to compromise with a reluctant Congress and battle a hostile physicians' lobby to win enactment of Medicare and Medicaid. "It took all his horses," recalled Califano.

Unlike Johnson, President Bush headed into an election with his public approval rating falling. He faced a Congress controlled by the opposition party, and he had yet to spell out a plan.

"There's always been a permissive consensus on the concepts," noted Theodore Marmor, a political science professor at Yale University. "But the more details people have, the less they support any program."

After passing the largest-ever expansion of Medicare, Congress was forced to dump it a year later after a grassroots backlash against the law's requirement that senior citizens foot the bill for their new benefits through higher monthly premiums and an income surtax. *(1989 Almanac, p. 149)*

That experience spooked members of Congress, said Gradison, one of the authors of the ill-fated program. "I think it has had a major effect, especially on those closest to the development of legislation," he says.

Stark, another author of the 1988 law, agreed. "We're not about to go in and give something to someone unless we're damn sure they want it and are willing to pay for it," he said.

No Plan From Bush

Finally, a major obstacle to achieving a consensus on health issues was what Democrats and Republicans on Capitol Hill referred to as the "deafening silence" from the Bush administration.

Lawmakers and their aides said Bush could totally change the dynamic, much as he did on clean air legislation when he introduced his own comprehensive bill in 1989.

But while Bush gave health-system reform some passing references in both his 1990 and 1991 State of the Union messages, his advisers recommended that he not push for legislation until a consensus formed.

Administration officials did try to convince the public that they had a health agenda of their own, summoning reporters to the White House on May 15 to hear their proposals to overhaul the medical malpractice system, combat infant mortality and beef up the rates of childhood immunization.

All three initiatives had been included in the fiscal 1992 budget that Bush submitted to Congress in February. And Congress already had provided $25 million in startup funds for the infant mortality initiative in a fiscal 1991 supplemental appropriations bill (HR 1281 — PL 102-27) — although members blocked the administration from carrying out its original plan to pay for it by taking money from other maternal and child-health programs.

The malpractice plan, formally submitted to Congress on May 15, sought to encourage states to pass laws to help stem rising medical liability costs that were exacerbating health-cost inflation.

Malpractice costs hindered the health-care system in three ways.

First, many doctors passed on higher malpractice premiums in the form of higher prices to patients and insurers.

Other doctors abandoned the specialties that were most likely to trigger malpractice suits and that carried the highest insurance premiums. Prime among them was obstetrics, and many areas of the country could no longer find doctors willing to deliver babies.

The third element — and the one most costly to the health system — was "defensive medicine": doctors performed tests or procedures that were not medically necessary but that could be used as a defense in future lawsuits.

Bush proposed that states take a number of steps, among them capping damages for pain and suffering. States also would be required to put into effect ways to resolve disputes out of court and to improve oversight of doctors through state medical boards.

The most controversial element of the plan proposed to withhold 2 percent of administrative payments made to states under Medicaid, the federal-state health program for the poor, and 1 percent of hospital payments to Medicare. Funds would be sent back to states that passed laws meeting the federal guidelines.

Bush domestic policy adviser Roger B. Porter described the plan as "a carrot approach, by providing incentives to states to change."

But under questioning, Porter conceded that it could also be viewed as a stick.

Post-Pennsylvania

In the weeks after the Pennsylvania election jump-started the health debate, Sen. John Chafee, R-R.I., and a dozen colleagues on Nov. 7 unveiled the long-awaited Senate GOP plan. The bill (S 1936) focused largely on incentives to encourage employers to offer workers insurance. It emphasized preventive health care and sought to overhaul the handling of malpractice claims.

The National Leadership Coalition on Health Care Reform, whose members included business and labor groups as well as former Presidents Gerald R. Ford and Jimmy Carter, on Nov. 12 announced a plan that called for a "play or pay" system.

The plan called for employers to provide workers and their dependents with health insurance or else pay into a fund from which insurance would be provided. Play-or-pay was also the central concept in the Senate Democratic leadership's bill (S 1227) introduced in June by Majority Leader George J. Mitchell of Maine.

The House Democratic Caucus on Nov. 14 unanimously approved a resolution calling for "comprehensive national health insurance legislation" to guarantee insurance coverage to all Americans and contain health-care costs. The move marked the first step toward resolving a feud between House Democrats who supported the play-or-pay approach and those who preferred a "single payer" plan such as Canada's, in which the government paid all the nation's health bills.

Bush, who had never followed up on promises in his 1990 and 1991 State of the Union addresses to study the issue, began hinting that he would soon make public a plan of his own.

"I'd like to have a comprehensive health-care plan that I can vigorously take to the American people," Bush told reporters in Rome on Nov. 8.

Overhaul vs. Marginal Repairs

Democrats were stressing the need for a total health-care overhaul, emphasizing universal coverage — the guarantee that every American receive health insurance, however financed.

Republicans described the current system as a good one that required only marginal repairs.

"Our system has much to commend it," House Minority Leader Robert H. Michel, R-Ill., testified before the Ways and Means Committee in October. "We ought to seek solutions that build on what we have."

The Chafee proposal's centerpiece called for tax incentives to encourage individuals and businesses to buy insurance.

The measure also sought to make it easier and less expensive for small businesses to obtain insurance by encouraging them to form insurance-buying groups and by requiring insurance companies to make small-business policies available and limiting rate increases.

The bill emphasized preventive health care, by both providing tax credits and by increasing authorizations for existing programs.

Finally, it gave states more opportunity to experiment with health reform by making it easier to "waive" federal rules and by allowing them to establish programs to provide health coverage to low-income, uninsured individuals not otherwise eligible for Medicaid, the joint federal-state health program for the poor.

Like the Senate Democrats' plan, the GOP version did not include proposals to cover the estimated $150 billion cost over five years.

Financing "is so controversial, no one party can step forward on it," said Chafee. "It's got to be a consensus."

Play-or-Pay vs. Single Payer

House Democrats were split over whether to proceed with a play-or-pay plan similar to Mitchell's or to line up behind a government-paid plan such as one (HR 1300) introduced by Marty Russo, D-Ill.

"Sometimes I think the play-or-pay people hate the single-payer people even more than they hate the current system," said one exasperated House leadership aide.

But at year's end, lawmakers were edging toward a compromise under which Democrats would endorse play-or-pay as a first step toward a single-payer system.

"The advantage of play-or-pay is it requires fewer federal dollars up front and disrupts the health-care system less," said Rep. Henry A. Waxman, D-Calif., chairman of the House Energy and Commerce Subcommittee on Health and the Environment. ■

States Restricted on Medicaid Fundraising

As states scrambled to cope with the skyrocketing costs of Medicaid, Congress cleared legislation designed to limit the way states could raise funds to pay their share of the joint federal-state health program for the poor.

The bill (HR 3595 — PL 102-234) was cleared by Congress Nov. 27 and signed by President Bush on Dec. 12.

The federal government paid roughly 55 percent of Medicaid's total costs, with wealthier states splitting costs 50-50 and poorer ones putting up as little as 20 cents on the dollar. States paid the bills for Medicaid recipients, applying for and receiving federal matching funds based on their actual expenditures.

In September, the Bush administration issued regulations that, beginning Jan. 1, 1992, would have severely curtailed states' ability to obtain federal Medicaid matching money for funds raised by donations from or taxes levied on hospitals, nursing homes and other health-care providers.

The House on Nov. 19 passed a version of HR 3595 that would have blocked the regulations through Sept. 30, 1992.

But before the Senate could take up the bill, the Bush administration and the National Governors' Association (NGA) reached a deal: Contributions would be banned but most provider taxes would be allowed, with a temporary cap on the total amount states could raise using the technique.

The compromise "grandfathered" states already over the allowable limits and staggered effective dates of the restrictions, so state legislatures would have adequate time to retool laws to bring their systems into compliance.

A separate part of the deal addressed what the administration saw as a potential budget problem: special payments states made to hospitals that served large numbers of low-income patients.

BOXSCORE

➡ **State Funds for Medicaid (HR 3595).** As introduced, the bill suspended enforcement through Sept. 30, 1992, of Bush administration regulations severely limiting how states could raise their share of Medicaid funds. As cleared, the bill prohibited use of voluntary contributions from health-care providers to qualify for federal Medicaid matching funds but allowed states to assess special taxes on those providers, provided funds raised in that manner did not amount to more than 25 percent of a state's total Medicaid share.

Reports: H Rept 102-310; H Rept 102-409.

KEY ACTION

Oct. 13 — The **House** Energy and Commerce Subcommittee on Health and the Environment approved HR 3595 by 16-6.

Nov. 7 — The **House** Energy and Commerce Committee approved HR 3595 by 36-7.

Nov. 19 — The **House** passed HR 3595 by 348-71.

Nov. 26 — The **Senate** passed HR 3595 by voice vote.

Nov. 27 — **House-Senate** conference agreement reached, reflecting compromise with National Governors' Association, and HR 3595 cleared for the president by voice vote in both chambers.

Dec. 12 — President Bush signed HR 3595 — PL 102-234.

BACKGROUND

Medicaid was projected to cost the federal government $65 billion in fiscal 1992, up from $41 billion in 1990 and $14 billion in 1980.

An analysis by the Federal Funds Information for States found that state Medicaid costs grew 200 percent in the past decade.

Medicaid's spiraling costs were stretching state budgets beyond the breaking point, and the governors were up in arms about "mandates" from Congress requiring that coverage be extended to certain populations or specific services.

For several years running, Congress had passed laws requiring states to give Medicaid coverage to more pregnant women, infants and young children, as well as to certain elderly Medicare beneficiaries with low incomes. *(Eligibility rules, p. 356)*

Although the governors had suggested some of the changes, by 1991 they said their states could not keep up with the added costs.

"We need to get a handle on the Medicaid mandates or else some of us are going to go broke," said Arkansas Gov. Bill Clinton, D, at the winter meeting of the NGA on Feb. 3 in Washington.

Two days later, the governors without dissent approved a policy statement asking Congress to grant them a two-year reprieve from putting into effect new Medicaid mandates for children and the elderly that were included in the fiscal 1991 budget-reconciliation bill. *(1990 Almanac, p. 569)*

Statistics showed why governors were so upset.

In 1980, according to the NGA, Medicaid spending accounted for 9 percent of state budgets overall. By 1990 that had risen to 14 percent. And by 1995, state Medicaid spending was projected to more than double, rising from $31.4 billion in fiscal 1990 to $66 billion.

And most states, unlike the federal government, had to balance their budgets. New money for Medicaid had to be taken from other programs, or states had to raise taxes.

For example, Republican Gov. Michael N. Castle of Delaware said, "In a year when my budget is going up by 1 percent, Medicaid is going up by 25 percent."

The situation was made even more desperate by the recession, which was lowering revenues just as more people lost jobs and qualified for Medicaid and other income assistance.

The resolution the governors approved Feb. 5 was not the first missive in the spat between Congress and state executives over Medicaid mandates. That came in 1989, when 48 governors signed a letter calling for Congress to refrain from enacting new mandates for two years. *(1989 Almanac, p. 171)*

Congress ignored that request, adding new coverage requirements for women, children and the elderly in both

Bit by Bit, Congress Eased . . .

In the past decade, Congress had moved to bring under Medicaid's umbrella significant new populations of children, poor elderly people and pregnant women who could not get Medicaid because they did not qualify for welfare. Many of the changes were made in very small steps to lessen the effects on both federal and state budgets.

In major expansions, Congress:

1984

• **Women and children.** Required states to extend Medicaid to certain women (for pregnancy-related services only) and young children who were poor enough to qualify for Aid to Families with Dependent Children (AFDC) but who, for various reasons, did not receive welfare. Previously, states were required to provide Medicaid only to those receiving welfare.

The mandate was designed to cover:

• single women pregnant with a first child (not eligible for welfare because they had no "dependent child");

• pregnant women and children born after Sept. 30, 1983, up to age 5 living in two-parent families who did not get welfare. The bill mandated Medicaid coverage in states that did not offer welfare to these families.

Bill: *Fiscal 1984 Budget Reconciliation (DEFRA — PL 98-369); 1984 Almanac, p. 148.*

1986

• **Pregnant women.** Required states to give Medicaid coverage to pregnant women in two-parent families even if a parent worked, if their income was at or below the welfare level. Two-parent families qualified for welfare only if the principal earner was unemployed.

• **Hospice care.** Allowed states to cover hospice care for terminally ill Medicaid patients.

Bill: *Fiscal 1986 Budget Reconciliation (COBRA — PL 99-272); 1986 Almanac, p. 255.*

• **Women and children.** Allowed states to offer Medicaid to pregnant women, infants up to age 1, and, incrementally, children up to age 5 in families with incomes below the federal poverty line who did not qualify for welfare. (In most states, the income ceiling for welfare eligibility was well below the poverty line.)

• **Elderly and disabled.** Permitted states that extended Medicaid coverage to pregnant women and children also to extend it to elderly and disabled people whose incomes were below the poverty line but too high for Supplemental Security Income (SSI) benefits, the federal program for the low-income aged, blind and disabled. (Those who qualified for SSI automatically qualified for Medicaid.)

Bill: *Fiscal 1987 Budget Reconciliation (OBRA '86 — PL 99-509); 1986 Almanac, p. 564.*

1987

• **Children.** Required states to continue to cover children included in the 1984 DEFRA mandate as they turned 5 in fiscal 1989 and 6 in fiscal 1990.

• Allowed states to increase coverage of such children up to age 6 in fiscal 1989, age 7 in fiscal 1990 and age 8 in fiscal 1991.

• Allowed states to cover all children up to age 5 born after Sept. 30, 1983, in families with incomes below poverty.

• **Women, infants.** Allowed states to extend Medicaid coverage to pregnant women and infants up to age 1 in families with incomes up to 185 percent of poverty.

• **Elderly, disabled.** Included legislation to overhaul regulation of nursing homes that participated in both Medicare and Medicaid. The nursing home bill imposed staffing, training and oversight obligations on the states, to be phased in over several years.

Bill: *Fiscal 1988 and 1989 Budget Reconciliation (OBRA '87 — PL 100-203); 1987 Almanac, p. 558.*

---

the fiscal 1990 and 1991 budget-reconciliation bills.

Shifting Focus

Medicaid, which began in 1965 as a program to help the nation's poorest mothers and children, was being overwhelmed by forces that its planners never expected.

The main problem was that the program continued to become more expensive but served fewer of the people it was created to help.

Instead, a growing share of Medicaid money was paying for nursing home care for the elderly. As the payer of last resort, Medicaid in 1988 underwrote 44.4 percent of the nation's $43.1 billion nursing home bill.

Another set of escalating costs was for the mentally retarded. Although they represented a tiny portion of the caseload, people with mental retardation and other developmental disabilities were among the most expensive Medicaid clients.

In 1986, mentally retarded people made up 0.6 percent of Medicaid's total beneficiary population, yet they accounted for 12 percent of all Medicaid costs. While Medicaid spending for children in welfare families averaged $521 per capita that year, spending for each mentally retarded individual averaged $35,139.

Even though Medicaid was expanded in the late 1980s, only 51 percent of the estimated 33 million Americans officially classified as "poor" were enrolled in it in 1988, according to the Urban Institute, a Washington think tank.

Health-care providers were unhappy with the program, as well. Hospitals, contending that payments were too low to cover costs, had sued Medicaid programs in 21 states, according to an April survey by the American Hospital Association. And they were winning those lawsuits.

In its 1991 report to Congress, the advisory Physician Payment Review Commission confirmed what almost everyone knew: Medicaid in general paid doctors considerably less than private insurance or Medicare, the federal health-care program for the elderly and the disabled, and that resulted in many doctors refusing to take Medicaid patients.

Even when doctors were available, many did not want to take Medicaid patients for reasons aside from money.

"It's just a terribly complicated thing to take care of these patients," said Dr. James B. Todd, executive vice

. . . Eligibility Rules for Medicaid

1988

Although most of the year's landmark catastrophic-care expansion of Medicare was repealed in 1989, Congress preserved the Medicaid portions, which generally turned the options offered states in the fiscal 1987 reconciliation bill into mandates.

• **Elderly.** Required states to pay premiums, deductibles and coinsurance for Medicare beneficiaries with incomes below the federal poverty line who did not otherwise qualify for Medicaid. Payments were to be phased in over four years.

• Required states gradually to increase the amount of income and assets a person could keep while Medicaid paid for the nursing home care of his or her spouse. Previously, both members of a couple had to spend themselves into poverty before Medicaid would pay for nursing home care.

• **Pregnant women, infants.** Required states to provide coverage by July 1, 1989, for pregnant women and infants up to age 1 in families with incomes below 75 percent of poverty.

On July 1, 1990, states were to cover such services for pregnant women and infants in families with incomes up to the poverty line.

Bill: *1988 Medicare Catastrophic Coverage Act (PL 100-360); 1988 Almanac, p. 281; 1989 Almanac, p. 149*

• **Families and jobs.** Required states to continue Medicaid coverage for 12 months for families who left the welfare rolls for jobs.

• Required continuing Medicaid coverage as part of a mandate that every state provide welfare for two-parent families in which one parent was unemployed. Under the mandate, states could limit cash welfare payments to six months out of every 12, but Medicaid would have to be continued.

Bill: *1988 Family Support Act (PL 100-485); 1988 Almanac, p. 355.*

1989

• **Women, children.** Required states to provide Medicaid for pregnant women and for children born after Sept. 30, 1983, up to age 6 in all families with incomes below 133 percent of poverty. This provision superseded the Medicaid mandate in the catastrophic-care law.

• Set statutory requirements for Medicaid's core preventive program for children under 12, the Early and Periodic Screening, Diagnostic and Treatment Services program.

Bill: *Fiscal 1990 Budget Reconciliation (OBRA '89 — PL 101-239); 1989 Almanac, p. 100.*

1990

• **Children.** In one of the largest-ever expansions of Medicaid, required that states gradually cover all children under age 19 in families with incomes below poverty. This essentially required continuing coverage for the population of children born after Sept. 30, 1983, every year until they reached age 19 in 2002.

• **Elderly.** Speeded up by a year the catastrophic-care act's requirement for Medicaid to pay premiums, deductibles and copayments for those low-income elderly who also qualified for Medicare. Beginning Jan. 1, 1993, states were to pay the premiums only for those Medicare beneficiaries with incomes between 100 percent and 110 percent of poverty. Then, starting Jan. 1, 1995, states were to pay premiums for those up to 120 percent of poverty.

• **Elderly, disabled.** Offered two new optional programs with limited funding. One was to help provide home care to frail elderly people who might otherwise require institutional care; the other was to pay for home- and community-based services for the mentally retarded and others with developmental disabilities.

Bill: *Fiscal 1991 Budget Reconciliation (PL 101-508); 1990 Almanac, p. 569.*

president of the American Medical Association.

"Medicaid patients present doctors with difficulties far beyond those of other patients, in terms of lifestyles, exposure to violence and ignorance that's not their fault," he continued.

The Contributions, Tax Issue

The states were pressing Congress and the federal government for more flexibility in Medicaid policy.

One of the year's big fights involved whether states should be able to use "voluntary contributions" from hospitals and other health-care providers to pay the state share of Medicaid costs.

In 1990, the Bush administration wanted to disallow such contributions, arguing that letting states use revenue other than from their own treasuries would drive up the matching funds the federal government had to pay without imposing any fiscal restraints on the states.

Congress stepped into the argument in a partial way in the fiscal 1991 budget-reconciliation bill, authorizing states to levy specific taxes on health-care providers. But the bill delayed a decision on voluntary contributions, ruling that the Bush administration had to wait at least a year before outlawing such contributions by regulation.

The states in 1991 began urging that voluntary contributions be put in the same category as provider taxes.

"States must be allowed to maintain their complete authority to raise funds to match federal Medicaid dollars without restrictions from the federal government," the governors agreed at their February meeting.

On Sept. 12, the Health Care Financing Administration (HCFA) published regulations — scheduled to take effect Jan. 1, 1992 — that severely limited the ways states could raise funds.

The Sept. 12 regulations sought to ban voluntary contributions outright and to limit severely "provider tax" programs, in which the state taxed hospitals and nursing homes but not other businesses.

The state transferred the revenues to its Medicaid agency, collected the federal match, and paid the entire amount back to those providing care to Medicaid patients. "These devices are contrary to the cost-sharing partnership that has been the hallmark of Medicaid," said Health and Human Services Secretary Louis W. Sullivan on Sept. 10.

If left unchecked, HCFA Administrator Gail R. Wilensky said, the funding devices would permit Medicaid spending to rise exponentially.

"The requirement for a state share of payment has always acted as a restraint on the otherwise open-ended Medicaid program," she said.

Since HCFA first allowed voluntary donation programs in 1985, Wilensky said Oct. 16, donation and provider tax arrangements had boomed. In 1991, only six states did not operate either a donation program or a provider tax program or both.

HOUSE SUBCOMMITTEE ACTION

Contending that the new regulations broke the deal codified in the previous year's budget-reconciliation bill (PL 101-508), Congress set out to block them.

Legislation (HR 3595) to that end was approved 16-6 on Oct. 23 by the House Energy and Commerce Subcommittee on Health and the Environment.

Members acknowledged that the budget bill had allowed the administration to ban voluntary contributions as of Jan. 1, 1992. But by banning most provider taxes, the regulation "violates congressional intent as expressed in" the reconciliation bill, said an Oct. 7 letter to Sullivan signed by the chairmen of the full committees and subcommittees that oversaw Medicaid in the House and Senate, and by Senate Budget Committee Chairman Jim Sasser, D-Tenn.

The House subcommittee's bill permitted states to continue to claim federal matching funds for both voluntary donation and provider tax programs through Sept. 30, 1992. States then were given until Dec. 31, 1992, to make the transition from voluntary donation programs to taxes, although in that last quarter states could not claim more funds than they did in fiscal 1991.

The bill also permanently authorized states to claim federal matching money for payments made on behalf of Medicaid patients by state and local public health agencies.

Subcommittee Chairman Henry A. Waxman, D-Calif., acknowledged after the markup that he had agreed that voluntary donation programs could be eliminated a year earlier, but said he presumed states would convert their voluntary programs to taxes. Since the Sept. 12 rules prohibited that, too, states needed another year to make the transition, he said.

Most panel Republicans, however, said the bill would lead to an unprecedented drain on the Treasury.

"This is nothing less than voodoo economics," said Norman F. Lent, N.Y., the full committee's ranking Republican.

Lent likened Democrats' claims that barring the practices would hurt Medicaid recipients to catching a bank cashier embezzling funds to support his wife and children. "Should he be allowed to do it for another year lest we lower the standard of living for his family?" he asked.

In the end, Republicans Dennis Hastert, Ill., and Jack Fields, Texas, voted with Democrats for the bill.

HOUSE COMMITTEE ACTION

The full House Energy and Commerce Committee on Nov. 7 approved the legislation to block the administration regulations, as White House and state officials continued negotiating toward a compromise.

Members voted 36-7 to approve HR 3595. Nine of the panel's 16 Republicans joined all of the Democrats in voting for the bill.

The administration on Oct. 29 had issued a "clarification" of its September regulation. But while the new document refined some language, it did not change the underlying effect. "We are not backing off on this at all," said Wilensky.

The new document did address concerns that the September version was written so broadly it would ban all payments made on behalf of Medicaid patients by state and local public health agencies. "That was never our intent," said Wilensky.

The new language made clear that payments made by other state or local agencies would still be permitted unless funding came from donations or taxes the regulations would prohibit.

Several conservative GOP members said they supported the bill only because their states would lose too much money if the regulations took effect as planned Jan. 1.

"This is troubling legislation," said Don Ritter, R-Pa., but added he would vote for it "as a Pennsylvanian concerned about other Pennsylvanians."

Other Republicans voting for HR 3595 were Michael G. Oxley, Ohio; Fields; Sonny Callahan, Ala.; Matthew J. Rinaldo, N.J.; Joe L. Barton, Texas; Hastert; Fred Upton, Mich.; and Dan Schaefer, Colo.

As the committee was meeting, representatives from the National Governors' Association and the Bush administration were continuing discussions begun a month earlier to try to find a compromise.

HOUSE PASSAGE

In a Nov. 19 White House policy statement that included a veto threat, the administration objected that "state donation and provider-specific tax programs, if unchecked, will undermine a basic premise of the Medicaid program — that states have a stake in the costs of the program."

But that same day, the House passed HR 3595 by 348-71, ignoring the White House threat. *(Vote 407, p. 98-H)*

As passed, the measure would have blocked the administration's revised rules through Sept. 30, 1992.

Debate was a rerun of markups in the Energy and Commerce Committee.

If the regulations took effect, Waxman warned, "many states will have no choice but to cut eligibility, cut benefits and cut provider reimbursement — in some cases drastically. This would be disastrous for the elderly and disabled and mothers and children."

But Republicans called the financing mechanisms merely artful ways for states to make the federal government underwrite Medicaid.

"How dumb can we get, deliberately looking the other way while our Treasury is being looted?" said Lent.

Before approving the bill, members rejected, 156-262, an amendment offered by Bill Gradison, R-Ohio, to strike two budget-related provisions of the bill.

One required that the Congressional Budget Office, rather than the White House Office of Management and Budget, estimate the cost of the bill, while the other exempted the bill from the pay-as-you-go requirements of the 1990 budget act. *(Vote 405, p. 98-H)*

Officials of the governors' association said that their negotiations with the White House were given a significant boost by the House floor vote.

No Progress on Oregon's Medicaid Reform Plan

Oregon officials went to Capitol Hill on Sept. 16 to promote the state's Medicaid overhaul plan, but a skeptical Congress took no action on it during 1991.

Opponents, led by Rep. Henry A. Waxman, D-Calif., and Sen. Al Gore, D-Tenn., said the state's program would unfairly ration care to the poor and could set a bad precedent.

Oregon needed federal permission to start its program, which was designed to dramatically reshape the way it administered Medicaid, the joint federal-state health program for the poor.

Under existing law, all states had to provide certain "medically necessary" services to everyone covered by Medicaid. But they were relatively free to regulate who and how many people qualified for coverage.

Arguing that too many poor people were arbitrarily cut off from eligibility, Oregon wanted to turn that system around.

Under existing law, only Oregonians with incomes below 50 percent of the federal poverty line qualified, and then only if they met other specific requirements.

A plan enacted by the state legislature in 1989 and formally completed in the summer of 1991 sought to extend Medicaid to all Oregonians with incomes at or below the federal poverty line ($11,140 for a family of three).

That could have given coverage to about 120,000 low-income individuals who did not have it in 1991.

The controversy arose because of the way the state wanted to finance the broadened coverage: by denying payment for some potentially life-saving services that fell below the cutoff point on a priority list ranking 709 ailments and their treatments.

In August the state applied to the Department of Health and Human Services (HHS) for permission to start the program. HHS officials cautiously endorsed the plan but did not take formal action in 1991.

If the department granted the waiver, Congress could still block it. And some lawmakers said the department lacked authority to grant such permission, contending that for Oregon to proceed, Congress first had to pass legislation affirming the plan.

Congressional Concerns

Oregon officials said providing basic health care for many people made more sense than providing everything to a few.

Oregon's plan represented "a significant improvement over the status quo," said Oregon Senate President John A. Kitzhaber. An emergency room physician, Kitzhaber was the chief architect of the plan.

But while the plan enjoyed enthusiastic bipartisan backing from the state's congressional delegation, some key members of Congress called it ill-conceived.

"Oregon has made a tragic choice and a horrible mistake in responding to the plight of the uninsured by developing a scheme that takes from the poor and only the poor to help the poor," Gore said at the Sept. 16 hearing before the House Energy and Commerce Subcommittee on Health and the Environment.

Gore said Oregon's plan deserved special scrutiny precisely because it was new and different and could set a precedent for other states.

Of even more concern to backers of Oregon's plan was the opposition of subcommittee Chairman Waxman, who had enough clout on Medicaid issues that he could effectively block the experiment from taking place.

Waxman said he feared Oregon would be pressured into paring services to an inadequate level. In an attempt to win his support, Oregon Gov. Barbara Roberts, D, and Rep. Ron Wyden, D-Ore., a longtime Waxman ally and a member of the subcommittee, spent three days trying to reach a compromise.

But at the hearing, Waxman was non-committal. While he was "encouraged" by the discussions and called the state's efforts to broaden health-care coverage "a noble goal," Waxman said he still had serious concerns.

Chief among them, he said, was that while the state legislature voted to spend an additional $33 million over the following two years, enough to fund all services through line 587 (treatment for esophagitis) on the 709-item list, fiscal pressures could erode benefits in future years.

Roberts sought to allay Waxman's fears, promising that if during the proposed five-year experiment "our benefit package to the poor drops to a level of inadequate care, I will personally withdraw our waiver request."

Somewhat frustrated with the process was Kitzhaber, who, deferring to Roberts, did not testify but watched the hearing from the back row.

"One of the great ironies of this whole thing is that Mississippi doesn't need to ask permission to throw huge numbers of people off the rolls, but Oregon is required to beg and cajole to give services to another 100,000 low-income people," Kitzhaber told reporters. "I've never seen so much resistance to spending money on poor people."

Indeed, the administration and the governors reached a tentative compromise on Nov. 21, two days later.

SENATE ACTION

The Senate Finance Committee on Nov. 22 approved two separate measures. The first simply blocked the regulations through March 1992; the other codified the compromise agreement.

The Senate then passed HR 3595 by voice vote Nov. 26.

Under the deal, voluntary donations were banned. States could tax providers, but in most cases those taxes could not account for more than 25 percent of a state's Medicaid costs. The 25 percent cap was to expire after three years.

On another point, the deal permanently capped payments to hospitals that served a "disproportionate share" of Medicaid patients.

State Medicaid Finance Provisions

Following are provisions of the Medicaid contribution and tax law (HR 3595 — PL 102-234), which was cleared by Congress on Nov. 27 and signed by President Bush on Dec. 12.

Voluntary Donations

- Prohibited, beginning Jan. 1, 1992, federal matching payments for funds raised through donations from health-care providers. (The bill did not cover donations from organizations that did not provide health-care services.)
- Exceptions included:

States that already had donation programs in effect or that had formally planned and submitted documents to the federal government regarding such programs by Sept. 30, 1991. Those states could continue to receive donations until certain effective dates, which depended on when their fiscal years began and were noted below. Donations received in any quarter of fiscal 1993 could not exceed the amount received in the corresponding quarter of fiscal 1992 or within five days after the end of the quarter.

Funds provided by health-care providers (particularly hospitals and clinics) to maintain on-site state or local workers to determine patients' Medicaid eligibility. Beginning in fiscal 1993, however, to continue to draw federal matching funds such donations could not exceed 10 percent of the state's total administrative expenditures, including both state and federal funds.

Another provision sought to prevent hospitals and other providers from using donations as a conduit to obtain federal funds. In some states, providers had put up money, which they then received back along with federal funds. Federal officials complained that such schemes circumvented requirements that states pay a share of Medicaid costs. In deliberately imprecise language, the bill said that federal matching money would be available only to "bona fide provider-related donations." These were defined as donations that had "no direct or indirect relationship" to Medicaid payments made to that specific provider, nor to other providers in the same class (such as other hospitals or nursing homes).

Exactly what constituted bona fide donations was to be determined by the secretary of Health and Human Services (HHS), who was instructed to issue regulations.

Taxes

- Required that in order to receive federal matching payments, taxes on health-care providers had to be broad-based, meaning that they had to be applied uniformly to all providers in a particular class, such as all doctors.
- Such taxes could exclude public hospitals and other health-care providers. States could choose to tax any or all of the following classes of services. But to prevent states from specifically targeting Medicaid providers, states had to tax all services within that particular class. The classes were: inpatient hospital services, outpatient hospital services, nursing home care (other than for the mentally retarded), nursing home care for the mentally retarded, physician services, home health services, outpatient prescription drugs, services provided by health maintenance organizations and other classes that the HHS secretary could designate by regulation.
- States could apply for waivers of the above rules. Permissible exceptions included those for rural providers or providers who offered the only such services in a community.
- In imposing taxes, states could not include "hold harmless" provisions that had the effect of guaranteeing, in whole or in part, that the amount of tax paid would be returned to the specific provider. Proceeds from the tax, however, could be used to reimburse providers for Medicaid services, and such reimbursement could be the basis "to justify or explain the tax in the legislative process."
- Included a transition period during which states could continue to receive matching funds for taxes that did not meet the new requirements until the effective dates below, if the taxes were in effect or legislation or regulations imposing the tax were enacted or adopted as of Nov. 22, 1991.

States could pay such hospitals more money for serving Medicaid patients, and critics said some states were abusing the designation to collect federal funds.

The agreement, said Wilensky, "puts in a stable platform for the future" to control the potentially unlimited costs of the financing mechanisms.

But not everyone liked the deal. Governors of Alabama, Georgia, Kansas, Virginia, West Virginia and Wisconsin opposed the agreement.

Placating Specific States

The agreement nearly died several times between the time it was reached late Nov. 21 and the time it finally passed both chambers.

As the deal took shape, opposition grew. As of Friday, Nov. 22, only five states were objecting to the agreement, but when proposed legislative language was drafted over the weekend, that number expanded.

By early Nov. 25, about 10 states were expressing serious concerns about the agreement, and senators and staff members were privately predicting that the Senate would follow the House's lead and approve a simple suspension of the regulations.

But administration officials refused to give up. Over a period of several hours, in a room off the Senate floor, Thomas A. Scully, the associate director of the White House Office of Management and Budget, and Wilensky cut deals one by one to alleviate state concerns.

Many of the state officials, said Wilensky, were actually the "worried well," representing states that in fact would not have been adversely affected.

But they wanted administration assurances that their programs could continue.

Other states, however, needed actual changes in the agreement to win support. A last-minute date change, for example, protected the three states that had passed new tax programs since September — West Virginia, New Hampshire and Wisconsin.

Among the last states to be accommodated was Texas, home of Finance Committee Chairman Lloyd Bentsen, a Democrat.

Texas needed assurances that it could continue its unique program that funded hospitals using local taxes.

Some members expressed concerns about the process. Passing a bill making a major change in an important program with such little time for deliberation "is a rather shoddy way of doing business," John D. Rockefeller IV, D-W.Va., said on the Senate floor.

But Rockefeller later conceded that he had "cut a few deals myself" with Scully and Wilensky to ensure that West Virginia's tax program would be allowed. Even Majority Leader George J. Mitchell, D-Maine, joined in the parade of exception-seekers.

Recognized on the floor as "the senator from Maine" rather than as the majority leader, Mitchell at one point entered into the record a letter to him from Scully assuring

However, the combination of taxes and donations that could be matched before the new rules took effect could not exceed the higher of 25 percent of the state's Medicaid expenditures or that state's individual limit (*see below*). This was to prevent states from combining existing donations and taxes in order to circumvent the limits imposed by the bill, below.

Limit on Taxes

- Provider taxes could account for no more than 25 percent of a state's share of Medicaid costs until Sept. 30, 1995, after which the cap was eliminated.

States already over the cap in fiscal 1992 could continue at their 1992 percentage until Sept. 30, 1995.

Effective Dates

- For states with fiscal years ending June 30, 1992, or before, the effective date for the new tax and donation rules was Oct. 1, 1992.
- For states with fiscal years ending after June 30, 1992, the effective date was Jan. 1, 1993.
- States with no regular legislative session scheduled in 1992 or 1993 had until July 1, 1993.

Disproportionate Share Hospitals

- Beginning Oct. 1, 1992, limited the total amount of payments states could make to so-called disproportionate share hospitals, generally those that served a higher than average number of low-income patients. The Bush administration was concerned that states might start using their broad authority to designate "disproportionate share" hospitals to reap excess federal funds.
- States could not receive matching funds for disproportionate share payments that exceeded 12 percent of a state's total Medicaid expenditures.

To soften the blow for states already over the 12 percent threshold, the bill allowed those states to continue at their fiscal 1992 dollar amount until inflation enlarged the overall Medicaid pie to the point that the fiscal 1992 amount equaled the 12 percent cap.

- After Jan. 1, 1996, states were given a choice. They could either stay within the 12 percent cap, retaining authority to designate any hospital as a disproportionate-share hospital, or else opt for a new payment limit to be set by Congress.

States opting for the new limit, however, also had to abide by rules restricting the designation of disproportionate-share hospitals to those with above-average Medicaid or low-income caseloads or which provided at least 1 percent of a state's Medicaid hospital services.

- The HHS secretary was precluded from otherwise restricting state authority to designate which hospitals were eligible for disproportionate-share payments. But the secretary could preclude payments if the effect of the funding was to reimburse a hospital for paying a provider tax.

Disproportionate-Share Hospital Study

- Required the Prospective Payment Assessment Commission (which advised Congress on Medicare and Medicaid payment issues regarding hospitals) to study the feasibility of establishing payment minimums and maximums for hospitals designated as disproportionate-share hospitals. The study was due Jan. 1, 1994.

Intergovernmental Transfers

- Codified the ability of states to obtain federal matching funds when their Medicaid agencies received funds or services from local or other state government agencies. Such "intergovernmental transfers," without which states said Medicaid could not operate, had been previously allowed by regulation.
- Matching funds for intergovernmental transfers could be denied if the funds were originally obtained from disallowed donations or taxes.

Reporting Requirements

- Required states to submit annual reports detailing the amount of provider-related donations and taxes received by the state or local governments during the previous fiscal year.

Consultation With States

- Required the secretary of HHS to "consult with the states" before issuing regulations under the act. ■

him that Maine would receive permission to continue its program through June 30, 1992.

CONFERENCE/FINAL

In one of its last actions of the session, Congress cleared the conference report on HR 3595 on Nov. 27. The final version of the legislation codified a slightly revised version of the agreement reached between administration officials and the governors on Nov. 21.

Culmination of the deal was a major setback for Waxman, who had made a career of forcing opponents' hands at the eleventh hour.

But this time Waxman had the tables turned on him. With colleagues eager to depart for Thanksgiving, Waxman was forced to swallow the White House-governors' deal or risk implementation of the administration regulations.

As part of the final deal, the contested regulations, originally scheduled to take effect Jan. 1, were withdrawn.

"We think this is a very good deal," said Alicia Pelrine, one of the lead negotiators for the governors' association. "For states whose [legislative] sessions begin in January, they'll know what they can do and what's allowed, and that's very important."

Administration officials were pleased as well. "It's a reasonable compromise," said Scully, who led Bush's negotiating team.

Waxman, however, remained unhappy with the deal, which he called "quite a fundamental change without a whole lot of scrutiny."

Waxman said, "I think the governors made a mistake in entering into this agreement. I think they're going to regret very soon the framework of allowing the federal government to interfere so heavily in the way they run and finance their Medicaid programs."

Most upsetting to Waxman and Democratic colleagues on his Health and the Environment Subcommittee was the permanent cap on disproportionate-share payments to hospitals.

At a hearing on the deal Nov. 25, Waxman grilled Wilensky about the need for the cap.

Wilensky said no abuses of the sort associated with provider tax and donation programs had been seen yet, but she feared states could use the mechanism if others were closed off.

"That smacks of assuming states will misbehave before the fact," Waxman said. "What you have here is a solution that goes beyond the problem."

Shot back Wilensky: "Now we have a huge problem [with provider taxes and donations] with no solution. You can decide which is worse."

Conferees ultimately weakened the language slightly. After four years, states could, at their option, use an alternate method to calculate hospital payments if they wanted to get out from under the disproportionate-share payment cap. ■

Recruitment and Training Of Health Professionals

In the waning days of the session, both chambers passed legislation to reauthorize programs providing aid to recruit and train health professionals.

However, Congress adjourned before a House-Senate conference committee could resolve differences between the two versions.

The Senate passed its $3 billion version of the reauthorization measure on Nov. 26. The House had passed the bill Nov. 12.

The programs in question, outlined in Titles VII and VIII of the Public Health Service Act, provided aid to students and to institutions that trained doctors, nurses and a variety of other professional health workers.

Aid to students was provided through direct loans, loan guarantees and scholarships, while funds for institutions were awarded through grants and contracts.

Separately, Congress on Nov. 26 cleared legislation (S 2050) to reauthorize the Health Education Assistance Loan guarantee program, known as HEAL, and cap loan guarantees at $290 million for fiscal 1992.

The separate reauthorization for HEAL was needed to guarantee the availability of loans to first-time borrowers.

The administration had informed Congress that absent formal authority for the program, which expired Oct. 1, it could not make new loans.

BOXSCORE

➡ **Health Professionals Training and Recruitment (HR 3508, S 1933, S 2050).** The first two bills reauthorized programs to recruit and train health professionals; the third ensured the availability of loan insurance guarantees to those borrowing funds for a medical education.

Reports: S 2050 — no report; HR 3508 — H Rept 102-275; S 1933 — S Rept 102-227.

KEY ACTION

Oct. 8 — HR 3508 approved by the **House** Energy and Commerce Committee by voice vote.

Nov. 12 — HR 3508 passed by the **House** by voice vote.

Nov. 13 — S 1933 approved by the **Senate** Labor and Human Resources Committee by 17-0.

Nov. 26 — HR 3508, amended by text of S 1933, passed by the **Senate** by voice vote.

Nov. 25 — S 2050 passed by the **Senate** by voice vote.

Nov. 26 — S 2050 amended by the **House** and cleared by the **Senate.**

Dec. 11 — President Bush signed S 2050 — PL 102-222.

Bill Highlights

The House bill authorized appropriations of up to $2 billion through fiscal 1994 for the training programs. It also authorized government guarantees in fiscal 1992 on up to $365 million in loans to students under the HEAL program.

The Senate committee version authorized nearly $3 billion for the programs through fiscal 1996 and $400 million in student loan guarantees.

Both measures included new steps to cut down on the high default rate on these loans. One provision sought to change the way the government assessed fees on new loans.

Under existing law, the same loan origination fee was charged to all who requested loans under the HEAL program. The fees went into a pool that was supposed to cover defaults.

The House bill allowed the government to charge a loan origination fee based on the number of defaults for students in each field (podiatry vs. chiropractic, for example). The more defaults in a particular field, the higher the origination fee.

The Senate bill contained similar provisions and also prohibited any loans to institutions with default rates of 25 percent or more.

The Senate version also cut the origination fee in half for borrowers who got a creditworthy co-signer.

In addition, the Senate bill authorized $1 million in demonstration grants to experiment with direct government loans.

The program was to involve 20 schools with low default rates, and the schools were to be responsible for all loan-servicing costs.

This provision was in response to a proposal floated earlier in the year by the Bush administration to scrap the loan-guarantee system for all postsecondary students and provide loans directly to needy students. The administration later backed away from that idea, and it agreed to support the guaranteed-loan program after sponsors revised their bills to crack down on defaults. *(Higher education bill, p. 365)*

Both bills sought to add social workers and therapists to a program that trained health-care personnel to deal with AIDS patients. The House bill authorized $17 million for this program in fiscal 1992; the Senate measure authorized $21 million. ■

FDA Given Authority Over Generic-Drug Industry

The House on Oct. 31 unanimously approved legislation to give the Food and Drug Administration (FDA) significant new authority to oversee and police the generic-drug industry.

By 413-0, members approved HR 2454, which sought to give the FDA broad authority to punish those found to have defrauded or otherwise abused the abbreviated approval process for marketing generic copies of brand-name drugs. *(Vote 359, p. 88-H)*

The Senate did not act on the legislation in 1991.

Background

Sponsored by Energy and Commerce Committee Chairman John D. Dingell, D-Mich., and cosponsored by every member of the committee, the bill grew out of a 1988 investigation by the panel's Oversight Subcommittee into allegations of fraud in the generic-drug approval process.

The subcommittee's investigation, along with subsequent probes by federal officials, uncovered scores of cases in which officials of generic-drug companies abused the new process, including bribing FDA officials to gain preferential treatment and substituting samples of brand-name drugs in tests to determine if the generic copy was "equivalent" to the original drug.

In an Oct. 28 floor statement, Dingell said the investigations had resulted in 26 criminal convictions or guilty pleas and scores of products recalled or withdrawn.

The bill "has been drafted to remedy this disgraceful mess," said Dingell.

Among other things, it sought to allow the FDA to bar from the market companies or individuals found to have abused the generic-drug approval process, grant the agency authority to recall drugs whose approval was tainted and impose civil fines of up to $1 million.

More than a year of backroom bargaining led to the July 29 voice vote approval of HR 2454 by the Energy and Commerce Subcommittee on Health and the Environment.

The full Energy and Commerce Committee approved the bill Sept. 25.

Thomas J. Bliley Jr., Va., ranking Republican on the Oversight Subcommittee, said Congress had a responsibility to tighten the regulatory process because "the generic-drug industry, unique among the industries regulated by FDA, is a creature of the Congress."

Companies that manufactured low-cost copies of brand-name prescription drugs got a tremendous boost from Congress with the 1984 passage of the Drug Price Competition and Patent Term Restoration Act (PL 98-417). *(1984 Almanac, p. 451)*

That law was a compromise in which makers of brand-name drugs won longer patents to compensate for the time it took the FDA to grant drug approvals, and makers of generic drugs won the right to bring their products to market faster and less expensively once the brand-name patents expired.

The law eliminated the requirement that generic drugs be shown to be safe and effective before they could be put on the market.

Instead, makers had to demonstrate only that the copy was "bioequivalent" to the brand-name drug, meaning that it would have the same effect.

Congress, however, did not anticipate the tremendous economic advantage for the first generic to make it to market.

Because that first copy often ended up with as much as half the generic market, some manufacturers took illegal means to ensure that their drug was first. In some cases that involved bribing FDA officials to slow down competitors' applications.

In other cases, makers of generics cheated on testing, sometimes substituting copies of the brand-name drug for their copies, thus ensuring that the "generic" would test equivalent. ■

BOXSCORE

➡ Generic Drug Regulation (HR 2454). The bill sought to strengthen the authority of the Food and Drug Administration to regulate the generic drug industry.

Report: H Rept 102-272.

KEY ACTION

Sept. 25 — HR 2454 approved by the **House** Energy and Commerce Committee.

Oct. 31 — HR 2454 was passed by the **House** by 413-0.

Other Health Programs Considered in 1991

Congress considered a number of bills during the first session that expanded or reauthorized federal health programs. They included:

DISEASE PREVENTION PROGRAMS

Legislation to expand federal activities aimed at disease prevention and health promotion was approved by both chambers late in the session but did not clear before adjournment.

The Senate passed S 1944 on Nov. 27, the last day of the session. The measure sought to reauthorize through fiscal 1996 the Preventive Health and Health Services Block Grant, which funneled money to the states for health promotion and disease prevention activities.

The House had passed its version of the legislation (HR 3635) on Nov. 19.

The block grant was created in 1981 when Congress consolidated eight separate smaller programs. States could use their share of the funds for any of the specified activities, including water fluoridation, rodent control, home health services, health education, high blood pressure control, rape crisis counseling, emergency medical care or general preventive health services.

The Senate bill authorized $275 million for the block grant for fiscal 1992, considerably more than the $135 million authorized by the House bill. The House ceiling was also the amount actually appropriated for the program for fiscal 1992.

"What we really have is not a health-care system but a sick-care system," said Sen. Tom Harkin, D-Iowa, a long-time advocate of spending boosts for prevention activities. "Over half of the $700 billion we will spend this year on health care will go to treat conditions that are preventable."

The Senate bill incorporated the text of S 507, which authorized $40 million for fiscal 1992 for increased efforts to prevent and screen for lead poisoning. It authorized $120 million for fiscal 1992 to prevent and control sexually transmitted diseases.

Other provisions called for the creation of a federal Office of Adolescent Health, authorized $3 million in state grants for improving health in minority communities, authorized programs to screen for prostate cancer and an $80 million program to prevent diseases that caused infertility in women.

The bill was approved by the Labor and Human Resources Committee on Nov. 14 and reported Nov. 25 (S Rept 102-244).

The House legislation, HR 3635, not only reauthorized the preventive health programs through fiscal 1996 but also sought to create a private foundation to fund health research.

The bill was approved by the Energy and Commerce Committee on Nov. 7 and reported Nov. 15 (H Rept 102-318).

The bill authorized $135 million in fiscal 1992 for the block grant, with unspecified sums for the remaining years. The bill also reauthorized the Year 2000 health objectives planning program. Created in 1990 legislation (PL 101-582), the program channeled funds to states that met specific health goals for reducing rates of disease and injuries by the turn of the century.

Finally, the measure authorized the establishment of a private, nonprofit foundation to underwrite activities to supplement work done by the federal Centers for Disease Control. Such activities could include funding temporary staff and long-term projects.

ADVOCACY FOR MENTALLY ILL

Legislation (S 1475) to reauthorize a program to protect the legal rights of the mentally ill was cleared by the House on Nov. 19 and signed into law (PL 102-173) Nov. 27 by President Bush.

The bill authorized $19.5 million for fiscal 1992 and unspecified amounts through fiscal 1995 for state "protection and advocacy" programs that Congress first authorized in 1986 (PL 99-319). Such agencies were charged with investigating cases of abuse or neglect. *(1986 Almanac, p. 251)*

In fiscal 1990, advocates handled more than 20,000 cases for mentally ill people living in a variety of settings, including hospitals, nursing homes, community facilities and prisons.

The bill made several minor changes to the program, including providing for increased involvement by family members of mentally ill people in protection and advocacy systems, and clarifying that state agencies could represent people living in federal facilities.

The Senate Labor and Human Resources Committee approved the bill on July 17 and reported it (S Rept 102-114) on July 22. The Senate passed the bill on July 31.

The House Energy and Commerce Committee Subcommittee on Health and the Environment approved the measure Oct. 23 and the full committee followed suit on Nov. 7. The bill was reported by the House committee on Nov. 15 (H Rept 102-319)

ALZHEIMER'S DISEASE

The Senate on Nov. 26 approved legislation to reauthorize programs to aid victims of Alzheimer's disease and their families. But the bill did not see action in the House.

The measure, S 1577, authorized a little more than $90 million over five years for a series of programs first enacted as part of an omnibus health bill in 1986 (PL 99-660). The programs helped underwrite research into the disease and support services for patients and the people who cared for them.

The Senate Labor and Human Resources Committee approved S 1577 on Oct. 30 and reported it Nov. 25 (S Rept 102-242).

DISABILITY PREVENTION

Legislation to establish a disability prevention program at the federal Centers for Disease Control (CDC) was passed by the House by voice vote Oct. 28. While a companion measure (S 509) was approved March 13 by the Senate Labor and Human Resources Committee, it did not pass that chamber.

The five-year authorization bill (HR 3401) outlined funding priorities for research, public education and training of health-care professionals, demonstration projects and technical assistance.

The bill authorized $15 million for fiscal 1992, $20 million for fiscal 1993, $25 million for fiscal 1994 and such sums as necessary for fiscal 1995 and 1996. Just under $10 million was appropriated for the programs in fiscal 1991.

The bill was named for Rep. Silvio O. Conte, R-Mass., who died in February. Conte had introduced similar legislation in 1990 that would have created a prevention program at the CDC. The House passed the bill, but time ran out before the Senate could consider the measure. *(1990 Almanac, p. 589)*

Supporters of the measure noted that about 15 percent of Americans suffered from some type of disability, according to a study by the Institute of Medicine, health sciences arm of the National Academy of Sciences. The institute study also found that about $170 billion was spent each year to care for the disabled, including $82 million by the federal government.

The House Energy and Commerce Committee approved HR 3401 on Oct. 8 and reported it Oct. 24 (H Rept 102-271). ■

Education Bills Advanced in Committees

Committees in both chambers approved legislation in 1991 to overhaul the Higher Education Act of 1965, but the bills did not reach the floor before adjournment.

Both measures were designed to make student aid available to more middle-income families and to increase the grants or loans that each student could receive.

The five-year House bill (HR 3553), priced at $20 billion a year, was the more dramatic of the two; it sought to scrap the existing student loan program and to replace it with a system of direct loans disbursed by a student's college, university or trade school.

The House bill also sought to transform Pell grants, the principal stipend for low-income students, into an entitlement program. (The grants were named for Sen. Claiborne Pell, D-R.I., chairman of the Senate Labor Subcommittee on Education.)

The seven-year Senate measure (S 1150), at $17.4 billion in the first year, was more modest in scope, leaving existing aid programs intact.

Unlike the House bill, its funding levels did not break the 1990 budget law, although it proposed significant increases in some areas. And it made Pell grants an entitlement after budget law constraints came off in the late 1990s.

Both chambers were expected to take up their respective higher education bills early in the second session of the 102nd Congress.

The law had last been reauthorized in 1986. *(1986 Almanac, p. 231)*

BOXSCORE

➡ **Higher Education Act Reauthorization (HR 3553, S 1150).** The bills reauthorized and revised the principal law governing federal aid to colleges, universities, trade schools and their students. The $20 billion House version made Pell grants an entitlement and replaced the guaranteed student loan program with a direct loan system. The $17.4 billion Senate measure kept existing programs intact and gradually transformed Pell grants into an entitlement.

Report: S Rept 102-204.

KEY ACTION

Oct. 8 — The **House** Education and Labor Subcommittee on Postsecondary Education approved a draft reauthorization bill by voice vote.

Oct. 23 — HR 3553 was approved 26-14 by the **House** Education and Labor Committee.

Oct. 24 — S 1150 was approved 14-0 by the **Senate** Labor and Human Resources Subcommittee on Education.

Oct. 30 — S 1150 was approved 17-0 by the **Senate** Labor and Human Resources Committee.

BACKGROUND

A generation after Congress passed the landmark 1965 Higher Education Act, creating scholarships for students with "exceptional financial need" and guaranteeing bank loans to students from both lower- and middle-income families, members were losing faith in the student aid program.

A litany of horror stories about shaky loans and rising defaults, coupled with the collapse of the nation's largest student loan guarantee agency, forced education leaders to rethink the premises of their higher education policy.

"Our current student loan programs may be just one step ahead of disaster," said Edward M. Kennedy, D-Mass., chairman of the Senate Labor and Human Resources Committee, which oversaw education programs.

The stated goal of the 1965 law was to give every American the opportunity to go to college.

The program proved to be a boon, both to prospective students and to a variety of institutions of higher learning. In 1991, the federal government channeled $18 billion a year to nearly 6 million students in the form of grants, loans, work-study assistance and fellowships. The nation's 8,000 institutions of postsecondary education, from Harvard University to Maharishi International University to the Midwest Barber College, reaped the windfall, using the money to pay for faculty salaries, research projects, classroom and dormitory construction and, in some cases, to line the pockets of so-called deans and professors.

Federal student aid programs enabled millions of young people to pursue careers that were beyond the reach of many of their parents. But after 25 years, the programs were in trouble. Middle-income, working-class students were finding it harder to borrow money as eligibility rules tightened. And poor students, who had the most difficulty carrying debt, were receiving fewer direct grants and were being forced to take on more loans to get through.

"We have a system of financing higher education which simply isn't working and has become a nightmare for most people," said Richard F. Rosser, president of the National Association of Independent Colleges and Universities.

Rising Loan Defaults

Congress and the administration were also concerned about the growing number of student loan defaults and the commensurate increase in cost to the U.S. Treasury, which guaranteed the loans made by private banks and savings institutions.

Both the volume of loans and the amount of defaults had increased. Since fiscal 1980, the number of loans had more than doubled to 5 million a year, and the amount of money lent to students had almost tripled, to $13 billion in fiscal 1990.

During that time, the percentage of students who failed to repay their loans climbed from 12.5 percent in 1980 to 14.9 percent in 1990.

As guarantee agencies and private businesses mounted collection efforts, some of those students eventually began repaying their loans, bringing the default rate down to a constant 10 percent a year. But contacting those students could take months, if not years, saddling the federal government with even more debt.

Congress took steps in 1990 to cut off guaranteed loans to students at colleges and trade schools with high default rates, but that program had yet to show much effect. *(1990 Almanac, p. 626)*

Meanwhile, the combination of more loans and higher

default rates continued to push costs up. Taxpayers had to pony up $2.4 billion in fiscal 1990 to cover the cost of loan defaults, and Education Department officials expected that figure to rise to $2.7 billion in fiscal 1991. In 1981, the cost of defaults was only $200 million.

"The American taxpayer is not going to support that program unless we get a grip on it," Kennedy warned.

Indeed, Kennedy and other education leaders in Congress, notably William D. Ford, D-Mich., chairman of the House Education Committee, and Pell were talking about scrapping the system of student aid they had helped to create in 1965 and starting over.

Policy Questions

Among the policy questions the education leaders sought to address were the following:

- Should students continue to be forced to incur big debts to finance an education?

Over 15 years, the emphasis of federal aid had shifted from direct government grants to guaranteed private loans. In 1975, grants made up 80 percent of all federal financial assistance to students. By 1989, however, they accounted for 49 percent.

- Should bank loans, which involved a government subsidy of the interest rate, be targeted to middle-income students or just to the poor?

Increasingly stringent eligibility formulas, the result of efforts during the 1980s to cut the cost of federal education aid, were freezing out middle-income families. The Bush administration said that future government assistance should be targeted to the neediest.

- Should trade schools, which generally had higher default rates than colleges, be taken out of the student loan program? Or should they be required to meet different standards for their students to qualify for loans?

Lobbyists for some colleges and universities said trade schools, with their high loan default rates, had unduly hurt the image of student loans and should be divorced from the existing Education Department program. Trade school proponents, however, said the universities were trying to hoard scarce loan dollars at the expense of poor (and largely minority) students trying to learn a vocation.

HOUSE SUBCOMMITTEE ACTION

The House Education and Labor Subcommittee on Postsecondary Education approved a draft reauthorization bill Oct. 8 that carried a price tag of about $100 billion over five years.

The measure included a number of proposals by Democrats and Republicans to increase both loans and grants to middle-class students. That put the bill at odds with the goals of the Bush administration, which wanted to target money to the neediest students.

The reauthorization, drawn up by Education and Labor Chairman Ford, proposed a big boost in the amount of money the government could lend and give to students.

One controversial provision called for transforming the Pell grant program into an entitlement, thus guaranteeing that every student who qualified would receive a grant.

A second contentious proposal called for replacing the guaranteed student loan system with direct government loans to students, cutting 13,000 private lenders out of the process.

The administration and Republicans in Congress sharply opposed both proposals as costly and cumbersome. Ranking Republican Tom Coleman, Mo., warned that the provision guaranteeing open-ended grants for college and trade school students, at a cost of nearly $12 billion, had put the bill on a "collision course" with President Bush.

Coleman tried to strip out the entitlement provisions for Pell grants, but Democrats rebuffed him, 9-17, with Paul B. Henry, R-Mich., not voting.

Coleman decided to wait until full committee markup to take aim at the direct loan proposal.

Pell Grant Entitlement

Changing Pell grants into an entitlement was a top priority for a number of higher education groups interested in the bill.

"The entitlement is important to keep hope alive," said James B. Appleberry, president of the American Association of State Colleges and Universities.

"Without that, [students] are subject to the whims of the budgetary process," he said.

Ford conceded that the bill, as written, would break the budget agreement reached in 1990 by the White House and Congress. But he said the measure would not take effect until 1994, when members would be free to cut defense spending to boost domestic programs.

Republicans wanted to help the middle class, too, but said that the entitlement plan — coupled with relaxed income eligibility standards — was too expensive and would shatter the bipartisan comity that had marked previous reauthorizations of higher education.

Coleman said that making Pell grants an entitlement was financially irresponsible.

"It's just absolutely incredible that Congress would be willing to tie its hands when we have a budget deficit of $350 billion," Coleman said.

Despite those two areas of disagreement, Coleman said Republicans were happy with about 90 percent of the bill, which they helped draft.

"The people who pay America's bills should also enjoy some of the benefits," said Ford. "Hard-working middle-income families should not see the dream of a college education slipping beyond their grasp."

One of the more prominent provisions in the bill designed to aid the middle class sought to remove a family's home, farm or small business from the calculation of income eligibility for federal assistance. That change had bipartisan support.

Another proposal sought to raise the family income threshold for Pell grants to $50,000 per year, from $30,000.

The federal government spent about $5.4 billion annually on Pell grants to 3.4 million students, mostly from lower-income families. Of all Pell grant recipients, 71 percent came from families earning less than $15,000 a year and 24 percent from families earning between $15,000 and $30,000.

William H. Natcher, D-Ky., chairman of the Appropriations subcommittee that funded higher education, said a Pell grant entitlement would take away his ability to decide which programs should receive money.

"Generally speaking, I'm against any further entitlements at this time," Natcher said. "With the deficit like it is, we only have so many dollars."

Budget Chairman Leon E. Panetta, D-Calif., whose committee had to weigh competing domestic requests as defense spending was scaled back, said he was nervous about changing the Pell grant program without a long-range budgetary plan:

Education Bills at a Glance

Issue	House Bill (HR 3553)	Senate Bill (S 1150)
Pell Grants	Would establish grants as an entitlement, guaranteeing full funding for eligible college and trade school students. Would boost the maximum grant to $4,500 from $2,400. Would raise the income level for the average family to $50,000 from $30,000. Would exclude a family's home, farm or small business from being considered when determining how much aid a student needs for all grants and loans.	Would establish an entitlement beginning in academic year 1997-98, guaranteeing full funding for eligible college and trade school students. Would boost the maximum grant from $2,400 to $3,600 in academic year 1993-94; $3,800 in 1994-95; $4,000 in 1995-96; $4,200 in 1996-97; $4,400 in 1997-98; $4,600 in 1998-99; and $4,800 in 1999-2000. Would raise the income level for the average family to $40,000 from $30,000. Would exclude a family's home or farm from being considered when determining how much aid a student needs for all grants and loans. This only applied to families with incomes of $50,000 or less.
Student Loans	Would allow all students, regardless of family income, to obtain loans. Students from moderate- and low-income families would have all or some of the interest on their loans paid by the government while they attended school. Would eliminate the existing loan system, which was funded by private banks, and replace it with a direct-loan program, run by the federal government. Would increase annual loan limits from $2,625 per year for first- and second-year students to $6,500, from $4,000 per year for other undergraduates to $6,000 per year, and from $7,500 per year for graduate and professional students to $13,000 a year. Would set the interest rate at 8 percent. Would cut off schools from student loans when their default rate was 30 percent or above.	Would increase annual loan limits in the subsidized Stafford loan program from $2,625 per year for first- and second-year students to $3,000, from $4,000 per year for other undergraduates to $5,000, and from $7,500 per year for graduate and professional students to $9,000. Would raise the interest rates for Stafford loans to 9 percent during the first four years from the existing 8 percent; during the years thereafter, would use a variable rate, capped at 11 percent, up from 10 percent. Would cut off schools from student loans when their default rate was 25 percent or higher. Would impose a 5 percent origination fee on the Supplemental Loans for Students (SLS) and PLUS loan programs to be paid to the federal government. For example, a student who borrowed $2,500 would actually receive $2,300, with $200 going to the government. The student would still have to repay the $2,500 plus interest.
Application Forms	Would require students to apply for federal financial aid using one free, federal form. Would allow students to reapply for aid by updating the original application, rather than filling out a new one.	Would allow students to continue applying for federal financial aid using forms provided by private companies as well as the free federal form. Would allow students to reapply for financial aid by updating the original application. Would include incentives to states to use the free federal form in awarding state aid.
Total Cost	$20 billion a year, according to the House Education and Labor Committee. In fiscal 1991, federal financial aid programs, including Pell grants and guaranteed student loans, received $10 billion from appropriators.	$17.4 billion during the first year, according to the Senate Labor and Human Resources Subcommittee on Education.

"You can't do this in an ad hoc fashion."

Though Ford said he wanted to be the first in line to scoop up a chunk of the "peace dividend," Panetta said Congress first should decide how far to cut defense and then balance education against health care, housing and other priorities.

Grant Size

The bill sought to increase the maximum Pell grant to $4,500 a year, from $2,400. It also linked the grants to the Consumer Price Index to keep pace with inflation.

Under existing law, appropriators set an overall total for Pell grants and divided the money among all eligible students. Although students in theory could qualify for a maximum grant of $3,100, they did not receive the full amount if enough money was not available.

Since the program was created in 1972, Ford said, appropriators had funded the authorized maximum only three times — the last in 1979.

Appropriators were spending twice as much money overall on Pell grants as they had 10 years earlier. But the number of students receiving the grants had gone up, and college tuition had risen faster than the rate of inflation.

When Pell grants were originally envisioned by Congress, Ford said, they were supposed to be the foundation of all student aid. By the 1990s, loans were the real foundation.

In the 1976-77 academic year, Ford said, students received slightly more Pell grant money than loan money. In 1990-91, student loans accounted for more than two and a half times the amount of grants.

While Pell grants bought 50 percent of the average cost of higher education in 1980, by 1991 they covered only 25 percent, he said.

"Simply writing more authorization levels in the law will only be another exercise in making empty promises and will do nothing to redress the imbalance between loans and grants," Ford said.

Subcommittee Republicans countered that guaranteeing Pell grants would cost too much.

The Congressional Budget Office estimated that requiring full funding of Pell grants would cost $11.7 billion in

Continued on p. 370

Student Loan Program . . .

When Congress created the student loan program in 1965, it was to help young people get a college education. But the program also spawned an entire industry, one that by 1991 pumped $55 billion in new and old loans back and forth among students, schools, banks, collection agencies and Wall Street.

The financiers had as great a stake in the student loan program as its beneficiaries did. And as Congress moved to reauthorize the Higher Education Act, money questions were unavoidable.

The system's broad sweep included most of the nation's banks, thrifts and credit unions; a network of state and private guarantee agencies that insured the loans; and a highly profitable secondary market for student loans, led by the federally chartered Student Loan Marketing Association (Sallie Mae).

"It's quite a lucrative program," observed Marge Roukema, R-N.J., a member of the House Banking and the Education and Labor committees.

"You can't lose," agreed Education Chairman William D. Ford, D-Mich.

Ideas for Change

Given the program's emphasis on money, proposals for revamping student loans dealt not only with social policy questions but also with the industry that handled the flow of cash.

One recommendation, which originated in the White House but was later denounced by it, sought to cut out the banks that provided up to $12 billion a year in taxpayer-subsidized loans to students. Charles E. M. Kolb, a former under secretary of Education who was a policy adviser to President Bush, suggested that the federal government provide loans directly from the Treasury, via a student's school — saving about $1 billion to $2 billion a year that was going to banks in the form of "special allowance" interest subsidies.

Although Education Secretary Lamar Alexander later disavowed the idea, Kolb's suggestion got the attention of the House Education and Labor Committee — and of the banks, which had long complained that student loans were not that lucrative and could be more trouble to deal with than they were worth.

The direct loan proposal "caused a flutter in the hearts of all the bankers as they saw their special allowance going out the window," Ford said with a smile.

Another proposal, offered by Sen. Sam Nunn, D-Ga., after a yearlong investigation into fraud and abuse in the student loan system, cut to the bone of every financial player. Nunn questioned whether the government should continue to reimburse banks for 100 percent of loans that went into default; whether the guarantee agencies that insured those loans should remain in business; and whether Sallie Mae, a private corporation with profits of several hundred million dollars a year, should be required to kick back a portion to cover the cost of the loan program.

Associations representing the colleges were pushing for a modified version of the direct loan idea that would allow some schools to administer direct loans and others to continue with guaranteed loans. Many of the smaller colleges, ill-equipped to handle the paperwork, preferred to let the banks continue managing the loans.

Some members of Congress were hesitant to stake out positions on the financial aspects of the student loan system. Indeed, simply sorting through the competing issues and interests involved was no small order for the humanities-oriented members of House Education and Senate Labor committees.

"This isn't education policy, this is a banking program," said a Republican aide on the House Education panel.

How the Loan Program Worked

When Congress created the guaranteed student loan program, its objective was to get the banks to finance students' college education. The government offered to pay banks approximately the market interest rate for their money while a student attended school and then to supplement the student's payments after graduation.

For example, if a student borrowed $2,500, the government paid interest to the bank equal to the amount the government paid on money it borrowed for 91 days plus 3.25 percentage points in order to provide a profit for the bank. The 91-day Treasury security rate, as of May 29, was 5.4 percent, which translated to an 8.65 percent interest rate for the banks.

After graduation, the student paid the bank 8 percent interest on the loan for four years and 10 percent interest for the remaining life of the loan. The government paid the bank a special allowance — the difference between what the student paid and the Treasury rate plus 3.25 percentage points.

If the student defaulted on the loan, the government reimbursed the bank for 100 percent of the loan.

While it sounded like a sure-fire investment, banks were leery of lending to 18-year-olds with no credit history and little work experience. "We spent years getting them in," Ford said.

Sen. Paul Simon, D-Ill., said the banks' reticence about joining the program required Congress "to make it attractive enough for banks to make the loans but not too attractive so they make too much money."

Ford said the secret to bringing in the banks was to make sure that the government's guarantee meant something. In the 1970s, Congress set up the mechanism for that guarantee by creating Sallie Mae and authorizing the guarantee agencies to infuse the banks with new capital to make more loans and to ensure that banks were reimbursed for defaults.

Guarantee agencies were nonprofit organizations usually run by the states, but they lived or died by money, too. Essentially, their job was to act as the federal government's local representative, making sure that the banks followed the rules of the program. The guarantors approved the loans, certifying that students had not previously defaulted on a loan, and charged the students an insurance fee of up to 3 percent of the amount borrowed.

If a student stopped paying back a loan, the bank or secondary institution holding that loan had to spend up to six months trying to collect. If they were unsuccessful,

. . . A $55 Billion Business

they turned over the loan to the guarantee agency and the agency reimbursed the holder for 100 percent of the loan.

If the guarantee agency could not collect the loan after another 90 days, it could file a claim with the Department of Education for reimbursement. Alternatively, the guarantee agency could continue to hold the loan and try to collect it. If the agency ultimately collected from the student, it could keep 30 percent of the money and return the rest to the federal government.

In his report, Nunn criticized the guarantee agencies for playing the "arbitrage game" with student loans. The report said the agencies delayed submitting claims to the federal government from one year to the next in order to escape penalties that came with too many defaults.

For loans that did not go into default, there was still the job of processing monthly payments and keeping tabs on the students. Not all banks wanted that responsibility. Many contracted with student loan servicing companies to handle the paperwork. Others simply sold the loans to Sallie Mae or to state secondary institutions.

At the top of the secondary market was Sallie Mae, a for-profit, shareholder-owned corporation with assets of $41 billion and net income of $301 million in 1990. Essentially, Sallie Mae bought loans from lenders, pumping money back to the banks so the banks could make more loans. It made profits by collecting interest on the loans and selling bonds in financial markets.

Due to its federal charter, Sallie Mae enjoyed benefits that other secondary institutions did not have. It cost Sallie Mae less to borrow money in the private market than it did other businesses because lenders believed that the federal government would stand behind a student loan. The corporation also was exempt from taxes on state and local income and from sales and property taxes.

The Bankers' Brief

The federal government spent about $5.6 billion in fiscal 1990 on the student loan program, covering interest for $55 billion in outstanding loans. But the banks were practically pleading poverty.

Fleet/Norstar Financial Group, based in Providence, R.I., made $250 million in guaranteed student loans to more than 95,000 students each year. (It would not divulge its profits on the program.) Fleet/Norstar also owned a loan servicing company, called AFSA Data Corp., that collected payments from 2.3 million students who had borrowed about $6 billion.

Michael R. Zucchini, executive vice president, said the bank provided student loans because it satisfied a need and served the community. "We're a bank and people expect us to make loans," he said.

But because of large penalties to the banks, Zucchini said, lenders no longer had confidence in the federal guarantee of reimbursement upon default.

For example, on a $4,400 loan, Zucchini said, the bank's after-tax return amounted to $39.59 a year, about half of what the bank earned on other consumer loans.

If the student receiving that $4,400 loan moved and failed to tell the bank, Fleet/Norstar had to begin a search, according to government regulations. But if that search began one day later than the rules prescribed, the bank had to pay a penalty equal to 180 days of accrued interest on the loan.

John Dean, special counsel to the Consumer Bankers Association, whose members wrote up to 80 percent of all student loans each year, said that people who believed banks were making excessive profits were dead wrong.

"We think lenders are voting with their feet," Dean said, contending that the number of banks making student loans was declining.

The Department of Education could not confirm this assertion, a spokeswoman said, because its files were out of date.

Others said that if the number of banks participating in the program was dropping, it was the smallest banks with the fewest loans that were leaving. For those banks, it did not make sense to stay in the program and keep up with all of the rules governing such a small investment.

"They see this less and less as a profit-generator," said Rep. Tom Coleman, R-Mo., ranking minority member of the Subcommittee on Postsecondary Education, who had met with bankers and reviewed confidential information on profits. "They can't continue to do it if they lose money."

The Direct Loan Alternative

Over the years, the banks had threatened to walk away from the program whenever lawmakers tried to change it. But their reaction to the idea of scrapping the system altogether and replacing it with direct loans indicated just how important student loans had become to them. Bankers were meeting privately with members such as Coleman, opening their books to prove that they were not getting rich off the loan program.

Their greatest protection probably lay in the fact that whenever policy-makers tried to come up with an alternative to the guaranteed loan system, they encountered more problems to solve.

Within the Bush administration, many top officials did not think direct government loans were feasible. "It doesn't take too much math to figure out we're going to be putting out $150 billion in 10 years without getting any money back," said Tom Scully, associate director of the Office of Management and Budget. "It's like starting up a bank with nothing, from scratch."

Others said that the Education Department simply was not equipped to run an entirely new program on such a large scale. "You have to build a new infrastructure to push that much paper out," said Lawrence A. Hough, president of Sallie Mae.

Hough said that the government would have to hire contractors to manage and collect loans. But contractors would not have the same incentive that banks, guarantee agencies and secondary loan businesses had to maintain and collect those loans — profits.

"On every dimension that I can think of, where the present system has a problem, a direct loan program may well have the same problems," he said.

Continued from p. 367
the first year — more than twice what was being spent under existing law.

"We have a $350 billion deficit," Coleman said. "To increase that further is to say we're going to add to the debt or raise taxes."

And boosting the cost of the Pell grant program could end up costing the elementary and secondary education programs, he said.

Coleman also tried to appeal to Ford's sense of turf. Under a mandatory spending plan, Pell grants could be cut in the budget-reconciliation process, leaving their fate in the hands of other lawmakers. "We won't be the important committee anymore."

Steve Gunderson, R-Wis., argued that the plan also could be counterproductive. He said Budget Committee members had cut Medicare by $54.9 billion between 1982 and 1991 through the reconciliation process. "We run the risk of legislating with our hearts, rather than our heads, and the end result may be worse for students," Gunderson said.

Finally, the administration would never accept a bill with the Pell entitlement plan, Coleman said.

Direct Loans

Taking the lead in the direct loan debate was a committee freshman, Robert E. Andrews, D-N.J., who was a law professor at Rutgers University before winning election to Congress.

He estimated that direct lending could save $1.4 billion a year by eliminating federal interest subsidies for lenders.

The federal government would finance the loans by selling government securities. The money would be farmed out to schools to lend to students. "This will be a true test of who supports corporate welfare and who doesn't," Andrews said.

Coleman said he wished to avoid fireworks by finding a compromise with Ford and Andrews. One possibility that he suggested was a pilot program with 20 schools participating, rather than a full-scale program.

However, Marge Roukema, R-N.J., said she could see no reason to compromise.

"I am totally opposed to it," Roukema said. "It's another policy Pandora's box. They do not understand the potential for harm and cost."

Under Andrews' plan, first-year students could borrow $6,500, while other undergraduate students could borrow $8,000 a year. Graduate and professional students would be eligible to borrow $13,000 a year. The maximum amount students could borrow under existing law was $4,000 a year.

All students could borrow money under the proposed program, but only lower-income students would receive interest subsidies from the government while they attended school.

The Bush administration and an array of interest groups opposed the direct loan plan. Education Secretary Lamar Alexander sent Ford a letter Oct. 2 saying "there are far too many problems, risks and costs."

Alexander warned that the federal debt was likely to rise by more than $10 billion a year under the new system.

He also cautioned that schools would be given too much responsibility for managing federal funds and that starting up such a massive program would be expensive.

Those arguments were echoed by the groups that benefited from the guaranteed student loan program — banks, guarantee agencies and the Student Loan Marketing Association. They earned hundreds of millions of dollars from the program each year.

Among the higher education lobbying groups, opinions were split.

Officially, about a dozen of the top organizations said they supported direct loans as an additional option for schools to choose from, rather than a substitute for the guaranteed student loans.

HOUSE COMMITTEE ACTION

After two days of partisan squabbling and party-line votes, the House Education and Labor Committee approved HR 3553 by 26-14 on Oct. 23.

Coleman, the ranking Republican, once again tried but failed to strip out the measure's two most controversial components — one to provide open-ended funding for Pell grants, the other to institute an entirely new direct loan program.

Education Secretary Alexander said Bush's senior advisers would recommend that he veto the House bill, according to an Oct. 21 letter sent to Ford, the committee's chairman.

And Panetta complained to Ford in a meeting the day after the full committee's action that he did not want another mandatory spending program. The two chairmen agreed to have their staffs try to work out a compromise before the bill reached the floor.

At the markup, Coleman said the deficit was too high to contemplate another mandatory spending program. Members rejected his bid to kill the Pell provision, along with the direct loan program, by 15-26.

Coleman also offered an amendment to cut back the direct loan program to a pilot project of 100 schools. It was rejected, 12-27.

The General Accounting Office estimated that the direct loan plan could save more than $1 billion a year. The Congressional Budget Office, in a preliminary study, estimated that direct loans could save 25 cents on the dollar out of the 52 cents spent for Stafford loans, Supplemental Loans for Students (SLS) and PLUS loans for parents.

But opponents said direct loans would be difficult to administer and would add to the federal debt.

The House bill sought to allow all students, regardless of family income, to obtain student loans. It increased annual loan limits and set their interest rate at 8 percent annually. Under existing law, students who took out Stafford loans paid 8 percent interest during the first four years and 10 percent each year after.

Other Amendments

Scott L. Klug, R-Wis., offered an amendment on behalf of the administration that sought to authorize $170 million to provide $500 awards to Pell grant recipients who finished in the top 20 percent of their college class or the top 10 percent of their high school class. The name of the program was to be the Presidential Achievement Scholarship Program.

Ford said that since the administration wanted the program so badly, it should first agree to the Pell grant entitlement. The Republicans demurred.

Pat Williams, D-Mont., suggested changing the name to the Congressional Achievement Scholarship Program. Ranking Republican Bill Goodling, Pa., suggested naming the program the Bill Natcher Achievement Scholarship Program, after the House Appropriations subcommittee chairman who funded education. After more sniping about partisan politics, the committee agreed by voice vote to the Klug amendment, as named by Williams.

The committee also delved into the issue of student drug use, anticipating a floor amendment by Gerald B. H. Solomon, R-N.Y. Solomon was expected to try to cut off financial aid for any student convicted of possessing or using illegal drugs.

While Gunderson was working on a compromise, Dick Armey, R-Texas, offered Solomon's amendment. It was rejected, 3-32.

Gunderson's compromise cut off financial aid to drug users unless the student enrolled or was accepted for enrollment in a drug rehabilitation program. It was accepted, 28-13.

Craig Washington, D-Texas, urged his colleagues to resolve the questions regarding minority scholarships. He offered an amendment to allow all scholarships funded on the basis of race, color or national origin if their purpose was to promote diversity in a school's student body.

An official at the Department of Education created confusion among college officials in late 1990 when he said minority scholarships violated the Civil Rights Act of 1964. At his confirmation hearing, Alexander promised to start over and review the policy. *(Race-exclusive scholarships, p. 376)*

Ford said he believed that the scholarships were legal and the amendment would only cause more trouble. The committee rejected the amendment, 9-22.

SENATE SUBCOMMITTEE ACTION

On Oct. 24, a day after the House committee had acted, the Senate Labor and Human Resources Subcommittee on Education approved its higher education bill (S 1150) by 14-0. The measure continued all existing student aid programs at higher funding levels, but created no new ones.

Like the House bill, the legislation sought to loosen eligibility standards for grants and loans so that more middle-class students could get them. "This will mean new opportunities for millions of children from working families," said Kennedy.

However, the Senate version was slightly less generous than the House bill. For example, the House measure excluded a family's home, farm or small business from being considered when officials determined how much money a student should receive to help pay for tuition. The Senate excluded a family's home or farm — not business — and only for families with incomes of $50,000 or less.

The differences between the bills did not necessarily stem from philosophical disputes. Rather, the House committee chose to disregard the 1990 budget agreement and the Senate panel tried to obey it.

"The House assumes that political will and the importance of these programs can override the attachments members have to the budget enforcement act," said Becky H. Timmons, congressional liaison director for the American Council on Education. "The Senate always assumed they would have to live within that."

The split also reflected the different parliamentary rules that governed the two chambers. The Senate tended to be more conservative because minority members could easily block legislation. In the House, the Democratic leadership could roll over GOP opposition because a simple majority prevailed under House rules.

The controversy between the House and Senate bills centered on two key proposals. *(Bills comparison, p. 367)*

First, the House version nearly doubled the amount of money a student could get for a Pell grant and transformed the grants into an entitlement.

The Senate measure, by contrast, phased in less generous Pell grant increases and did not immediately make them an entitlement. The Senate committee wrote a seven-year reauthorization and made Pell grants an entitlement in the sixth year to avoid the budget law's pay-as-you-go rules.

The second major difference involved the House plan to replace the guaranteed student loan program with a direct loan system, cutting out thousands of private lenders. The Senate measure left the guaranteed loan system intact.

Paul Simon, D-Ill., and Dave Durenberger, R-Minn., proposed a different direct loan program but pulled back in the face of subcommittee skepticism. Kennedy agreed to hold a hearing on the idea, but Simon and Durenberger faced an uphill struggle.

The Senate bill was expected to cost $17.4 billion during the first year, compared with $20 billion for the House version. It sought to gradually phase in the Pell grant entitlement, boosting the maximum grant to $3,600 in the 1993-94 academic year and then raising it by $200 a year.

It also proposed a raise in the top family-income level for Pell grants from $30,000 to $40,000. The House bill eased the ceiling to $50,000.

Lobbyists for the United States Student Association said they were disappointed with the Senate measure. "It appears to be completely budget driven, rather than policy driven," said Selena Dong, legislative director.

Dong also said the Senate added to students' already heavy financial burden by raising interest rates for Stafford loans and requiring "origination fees" of 5 percent on SLS and PLUS loans.

The Senate measure required students who borrowed under the Stafford loan program to pay 9 percent interest during the first four years and a variable interest rate not to exceed 11 percent in the remaining years.

Although those costs for students were higher, the Senate also opened up the SLS loan program, which had been limited to financially independent students. Dependent students who could demonstrate the ability to repay could also borrow under the SLS program, regardless of their family income.

SENATE COMMITTEE ACTION

Despite a veto threat from the Bush administration, the Senate Labor and Human Resources Committee on Oct. 30 unanimously approved S 1150. However, the 17-0 vote to send the measure to the floor masked sharp partisan divisions over the provision to gradually transform Pell grants into an entitlement.

Although the panel worked in bipartisan harmony on provisions to expand eligibility to more middle-income families and to increase the maximum grant from $2,400 to $3,600 in the 1993-94 academic year, Democrats pushed through a provision to make the grants an entitlement in six years.

Republicans strongly objected to making Pell grants automatic.

"A lot of us would like to get out of the entitlements," said Utah's Orrin G. Hatch, the committee's ranking Republican. "The deficit is running out of control."

The day before the markup, Deputy Secretary of Education David Kearns told senators that Bush would veto any legislation that included a new entitlement program.

A Tale of Two Students

College students in 1991 were borrowing more to go to college, and their money was buying less.

Ohio Dominican College in Columbus offered a prime example.

The majority of its students came from working-class families, the kind that the federal loan programs were designed to help. Most were the first in their families to attend college. Their parents earned enough to cover the family's housing and other basic needs — but not college tuition, room, board and expenses.

Over the course of the 1980s, however, the financial resources available to these students changed dramatically.

Mike Irish, a student in 1978-79, came from a single-parent household, with one brother in college and another at home. His divorced mother earned $9,362 a year as a clerk for an insurance company. His father paid no alimony or child support.

Of the $5,170 Irish needed to attend college, federal grants covered 42 percent and loans covered 19 percent, leaving him to come up with about $1,300. Other aid programs from the state and college defrayed that amount by $400.

David Ridgeway, enrolled in 1991, he also came from a single-parent family, with one sibling in college and another at home. His mother worked as a florist, earning $17,495 a year, and received $3,751 in child support from Ridgeway's father.

For Ridgeway, however, the proportion of grants to loans was the reverse of what it was a dozen years earlier. Of the $11,855 Ridgeway needed for tuition, room and board, federal grants covered only 16 percent, while federal loans took care of 41 percent, leaving him to come up with about $5,000. Of the $5,000, other aid programs from the state and the college kicked in $1,500.

Ridgeway's experience was typical of the financial aid shift at Ohio Dominican in the past decade: Pell grant recipients dropped by half, while the number of students getting guaranteed loans doubled.

Ten years earlier, grants provided 36 percent of the school's financial aid funds, and loans made up 48 percent. By 1991, grants had dropped to 16 percent of all aid, and loans had jumped to 74 percent.

"For a first-generation college student, particularly those from disadvantaged families, taking on debt is a real scary thing," said Sister Mary Andrew Matesich, president of the college.

And Pell grants didn't go as far as they used to. At Ohio Dominican, the average grant covered 22 percent of tuition, compared with 33 percent a decade earlier. Tuition, on the other hand, had outstripped inflation, rising 27 percent in constant dollars during the same period.

Sister Matesich also worried about the students who no longer qualified for loans, who didn't even register on her list of statistics.

"A lot of these kids are not getting anything, and they're working 30 or 40 hours a week," Matesich said. "A whole lot of extracurricular activities have died out.... The whole campus experience has changed. You don't have college life at Ohio Dominican the way we had it 15 or 20 years ago."

Education Secretary Alexander had already written to House Education Chairman Ford to say that he would recommend a veto of the House bill, which included a Pell grant entitlement that was to take effect immediately.

Senate Democrats sought to evade the "pay as you go" rules of the 1990 budget agreement by delaying enactment of the Pell grant entitlement until the sixth and seventh years of the seven-year bill.

Nancy Landon Kassebaum of Kansas, ranking Republican on the Education Subcommittee, offered an amendment to strike the mandatory spending provision for Pell grants and restrict the bill to a five-year reauthorization.

"I am troubled by adding another entitlement," Kassebaum said. "It is automatic, and it gives up the ability to analyze and reshape [the program]."

But Kennedy, chairman of the full committee, insisted that education programs deserved entitlement status as much as agriculture, for which Congress had created automatic spending programs such as price supports and crop insurance. "It's a pretty good indicator of what the priorities are in a society," Kennedy said.

Though she came from a state dominated by wheat farming, Kassebaum faulted Kennedy's premise. "I think crop insurance as an entitlement is a mistake, too," she said.

Hatch said the Pell entitlement was impractical despite its appeal.

"We just can't afford to make entitlements out of all worthwhile programs," he said. "Everyone here feels deeply about education."

Committee Democrats and one Republican, James M. Jeffords of Vermont, voted to reject Kassebaum's amendment, 6-11.

Before approving the bill, the committee quashed the direct loan proposal put forward by Simon and Durenberger.

Simon and Durenberger urged their colleagues to stop subsidizing banks and to use that money for more grants and loans to students. They said a direct loan program could shift $2.7 billion a year from banks to students.

Their plan allowed loans to students regardless of income, with repayments based on a student's earnings after he or she left school.

The Internal Revenue Service was to collect loan payments directly from monthly paychecks.

Committee members did not even vote on the plan. Many said that the two senators were not sure of the details and could not guarantee its success.

"I don't want to be a damp blanket on this," Kennedy said. "If you roll the dice on this program ... you are going to have the most dramatic impact on the lives and education of young people in this country."

Kennedy and others said they would be willing to consider a demonstration project. But Barbara A. Mikulski, D-Md., said she would vote against that, too, calling it "typical politics as usual to cool out anyone with an idea." ■

Adult Literacy Programs Expanded

Long held hostage to other education legislation, an adult literacy bill cleared Congress and was signed by President Bush in July.

The measure (HR 751) expanded existing adult literacy programs and created new ventures in an attempt to reach the estimated 30 million functionally illiterate adults in the United States.

It created a National Institute for Literacy to coordinate federal literacy programs, plus State Literacy Resource Centers to coordinate federal, state and local literacy programs. The bill authorized new funding of $197.5 million in fiscal 1992 and $1.1 billion in adult education and literacy programs through fiscal 1995.

Senators voted 99-0 to pass similar legislation in 1990.

But that year's bill to expand literacy programs died after it was attached to legislation by Democrats who wanted to test President Bush's pledge to be the "education president."

Those Democrats included many of Bush's own education initiatives but included far more money than the administration was willing to accept. After several fits and starts, bill sponsors failed to move the omnibus measure in the waning hours of the 101st Congress. *(1990 Almanac, p. 610)*

In 1991, Democrats and Republicans again agreed on literacy provisions, but partisan politics detoured them. Democrats, seeking to counter Bush's America 2000 proposal, included the literacy bill to beef up their education legislation. *(Education bill, p. 377)*

But after Labor and Human Resources Chairman Edward M. Kennedy, D-Mass., promised to consider the administration's package in a bipartisan fashion, the literacy bill moved as a free-standing bill.

Supporters said the new bill was vital to address a problem that affected at least one in 10 Americans: the inability to read and write at a fourth-grade level.

They said existing literacy programs reached only a small portion of those in need. Of the overall 30 million functionally illiterate who had access to adult education, most did not not receive enough help to solve their reading and writing problems.

Sponsors warned that as many as 50 million workers could be functionally illiterate by the year 2000, as demand for skilled workers increased. Illiteracy already cost businesses an estimated $200 billion in 1990 in lost productivity.

HR 751 was passed, by voice vote, in the House on March 19 and in the Senate on June 16 — but with differences over whether to include a requirement for literacy programs in prisons. Those differences were resolved before the August recess when both chambers agreed on a compromise provision requiring prisons to offer literacy programs to their inmates on a discretionary basis. The Senate had adopted similar language July 9 in the omnibus crime bill (S 1241), but unrelated controversies loomed as hurdles to that legislation. *(Crime bill, p. 262)*

The House adopted the crime bill language on prison literacy and passed HR 751 by voice vote on July 11; the Senate cleared it July 15.

BOXSCORE

➡ **Adult Literacy Programs (HR 751).** The bill coordinated federal, state and local efforts to wipe out illiteracy among adults and children and authorized new funding of $197 million in fiscal 1992 and $1.1 billion in adult education and literacy programs through fiscal 1995.

Report: H Rept 102-203.

KEY ACTION

March 12 — The **House** Education Committee approved the measure, 35-1.

March 19 — The **House** passed HR 751 by voice vote.

April 17 — Literacy provisions included in a broad education bill (S 2) were approved by the **Senate** Labor Committee, 10-7.

June 26 — The **Senate** passed HR 751 by voice vote.

July 11 — The **House** adopted language on prison literacy and passed HR 751 by voice vote.

July 15 — The **Senate** cleared HR 751 by voice vote.

July 22 — President Bush signed PL 102-73 — HR 751.

HOUSE ACTION

The House Education and Labor Committee was the first panel to move on HR 751. The Subcommittee on Elementary, Secondary and Vocational Education approved the bill by voice vote on March 7. The full committee followed suit on March 12, approving the measure 35-1.

The bill called for several new adult literacy programs to be authorized through fiscal 1995, including up to $125 million in fiscal 1992.

In addition, the bill authorized $260 million for a program under the Adult Education Act that gave grants to states to teach basic skills. The administration requested $251 million in fiscal 1992 for programs under the act; $242 million was appropriated in fiscal 1991.

To improve adult education programs and make them more accessible, the bill authorized $25 million for states to establish resource centers designed to keep local governments and literacy instructors up to date on programs and information.

For example, business owners could use state resource centers to develop a literacy program for employees.

Initially, the federal government would bear almost all the burden for financing the centers. In the first two years, states were to be required to pay for only 20 percent of their costs.

But by the fifth year, states would pay for at least 40 percent of the costs of the resource centers.

The network would be overseen by a National Institute of Literacy as a central depository of information and expertise on literacy programs.

The institute would be administered through an agreement by the secretaries of Education, Labor, and Health and Human Services, who would sit on a task force to monitor its progress.

Avoiding Duplications

One of the obstacles to moving the bill was a congressional dispute with the Education Department over a national institute and an interagency education task force.

Ted Sanders, the acting secretary of Education, wrote Dale E. Kildee, D-Mich, chairman of Elementary, Secondary and Vocational Education subcommittee, that those proposals "duplicate federal activities well under way." An Institute for Literacy for Research and Practice planned to begin operating in July 1991 and Bush had established an interagency task force in 1990, he said.

Just before the bill went to the full committee, lawmakers and the administration resolved the difference over the creation of a task force to coordinate and monitor federally funded programs.

Lawmakers bowed to the Education Department's argument that the new group was unnecessary because the department had created a similar task force the previous year.

Lawmakers removed the provision, and the administration signaled its support for the measure.

New Programs

The measure was a boon to community groups, who had been fighting for the past decade to gain access to millions of dollars in federal funds earmarked for literacy programs.

The bill introduced competition into the way states awarded money for literacy programs and gave Congress a mechanism to press the states to ensure that the money was producing results.

Under existing law, states could allocate the literacy funds — authorized under the Adult Education Act — as they saw fit.

Most states doled out the money to state agencies and institutions. Other literacy groups said some of those programs did not use the latest techniques and approaches to combat illiteracy.

Under the bill, before a state could receive its share of grants, it would have to assure the Department of Education that nonprofit and community groups would have equal access to the funds.

Among the other new programs called for in fiscal 1992 were:

- $5 million for a new program to improve the skills of workers with few basic skills. Small- and medium-sized businesses would get technical assistance to develop literacy programs.
- $60 million to bring together the public and private sectors to develop long-term anti-illiteracy strategies.
- $2.5 million for a Commercial Driver Education Program to provide drivers with the necessary skills to pass tests required by the Commercial Motor Vehicle Safety Act of 1986.
- Educational programs in prisons for functionally illiterate inmates. The bill required states to establish the programs contingent upon federal funds.

The measure went to the House floor on March 19 and easily won voice-vote approval under suspension of the rules.

SENATE ACTION

Just as in 1990, Senate sponsors initially included literacy provisions in a broad education bill (S 2). The bill was approved by the Senate Labor Committee, 10-7, on April 17.

The omnibus measure's literacy provisions generally tracked the House bill. The $160 million measure called for the creation of a National Literacy 2000 Federal Interagency Council to coordinate and monitor existing programs.

At the Education Department, the assistant secretary for vocational and adult education was charged with coordinating all literacy-related programs. The measure also authorized $10 million for a National Center for Literacy. About $260 million was authorized for the Adult Education Act, with the annual authorization to go up a $100 million over the previous year's appropriation.

During the markup, Nancy Landon Kassebaum, R-Kan., offered an amendment to strip the literacy provisions from the catchall bill and make them a separate measure. Democrats and Republicans differed over the broader bill's thrust, and Kassebaum said the literacy portion should not be held hostage any longer.

But panel members rejected her amendment on a party-line 10-7 vote.

When it became clear that the broad measure would not move quickly, bill sponsor Paul Simon, D-Ill., persuaded Kennedy to allow the literacy provisions to move separately.

On June 26, the Senate took up HR 751 and passed it by voice vote.

FINAL ACTION

The Senate cleared a revised bill for Bush's signature July 15, after differences between the two chambers were resolved.

Originally, a provision by House Minority Whip Newt Gingrich, R-Ga., contained in the House version of HR 751 passed March 19 would have required all prisons to put literacy programs into place within five years if federal funds were available.

In the Senate, however, many members were concerned that the provision sounded like a mandate on the states and eliminated it when they passed the bill the first time on June 26.

Sen. Jeff Bingaman, D-N.M., brought the issue up again during debate on the crime bill the week of July 8. He offered an amendment to order states to provide literacy training in prisons with 100 or more inmates. But Strom Thurmond, R-S.C., amended the proposal to make the program discretionary. Thurmond said states have enough trouble paying for their schools without paying to educate their inmates, too.

So as to ensure that the discretionary language on prison literacy also would be attached to fast-moving legislation, the House adopted the provision before passing HR 751 again by voice vote July 11; the Senate followed suit.

PROVISIONS

Following are provisions for the literacy bill as signed by the president:

- **National Institute for Literacy.** Authorized $15 million in fiscal 1992 to start a national institute to coordinate federal literacy programs and conduct research into literacy issues and programs. The institute would operate a toll-free information hot line on literacy.
- **State Literacy Resource Centers.** Authorized $25 million in fiscal 1992 for the secretary of Education to make grants to states, to provide training and coordination of federal, state and local literacy programs.
- **National Work Force Literacy Assistance.** Authorize $5 million in fiscal 1992 for the Department of Labor

to help small- and medium-size businesses and labor groups put together literacy programs.

• **Workplace Literacy Partnerships and National Strategies.** Authorized $60 million in fiscal 1992 to expand the Workplace Literacy Partnerships program. The secretary of Education could fund programs to design national strategies for helping small- and medium-size businesses develop literacy programs. National strategies grants were authorized at $5 million when appropriations for the partnerships program reached $25 million.

• **Adult Education Act Amendments.** Required the secretary of Education and each state to develop methods of evaluating the quality of literacy programs and to judge applicants on that basis. The authorization increased from $200 million to $260 million in fiscal 1992.

• **Elementary and Secondary Amendment.** Allowed the Chapter 2 state block grant program, which provided funds to states to improve elementary and secondary education, to be used to help teachers and counselors identify students with reading difficulties.

• **Even Start Family Literacy Program.** Changed the name of the Even Start program to the Even Start Family Literacy Program. The program was designed to teach parents to read and to teach them how to encourage their children to read. The bill allowed services to begin at the birth of a child instead of at age 1, establishing a minimum grant of $75,000 and reserving 5 percent for migrant programs, U.S. territories and Indian tribes.

• **Family Literacy Public Broadcasting Program.** Authorized $2 million in fiscal 1992 for the secretary of Education to fund family literacy programming by the Corporation for Public Broadcasting.

• **Literacy for Prisoners.** Authorized grants from the Department of Justice to correctional systems to start literacy programs. Inmates who were functionally illiterate (unable to read at an eighth-grade level) would have to participate until that person achieved functional literacy, was granted parole, completed his or her sentence or was released due to a court order. The bill prohibited parole from being granted to any person who refused to participate in the program unless the state parole board waived the prohibition. It required screening and testing of all inmates for functional literacy and disabilities affecting a prisoner's ability to read or write upon arrival at the prison. The literacy requirements did not apply to prisoners serving a life sentence without possibility of parole, to prisoners who were terminally ill or to prisoners living under a death sentence. The bill authorized $10 million in fiscal 1992 for the attorney general to provide grants to state correctional agencies.

• **Volunteers for Literacy.** Authorized $2.5 million in fiscal 1992 for the director of the ACTION agency to award challenge grants to organizations establishing volunteer literacy programs. ■

Alexander Confirmed as Secretary of Education

Despite some concern over his financial dealings, the Senate confirmed former Tennessee Gov. Lamar Alexander as secretary of Education by voice vote March 14.

The Senate vote came just one day after the Labor and Human Resources Committee recommended that Alexander be confirmed. Sixteen members of the committee voted to support the nomination, with only Tom Harkin, D-Iowa, voting present.

Alexander succeeded Lauro F. Cavazos, who had headed the Department of Education since September 1988. Cavazos, appointed by President Ronald Reagan and kept on by President Bush, had been criticized as ineffectual. He resigned at the request of the White House in December 1990. *(1990 Almanac, p. 614)*

On Capitol Hill, where Bush's education proposals died at the hands of Senate Republicans during the 101st Congress, lawmakers and education aides described Cavazos as a dolphin among sharks — an ineffective spokesman and lobbyist for education.

Both Democrats and Republicans initially greeted Alexander's nomination with warm words and high expectations. But revelations that Alexander had earned large sums with little investment of his own money while governor of Tennessee, and subsequently as president of the University of Tennessee system, prompted members to take a closer look. His net worth jumped from about $321,000 in 1984 to between $2 million and $3 million in 1991, according to the Labor Committee.

The disclosure led to impromptu outbursts of concern about ethics just as the Senate had closed a chapter on its one Republican and four Democratic colleagues examined by the Ethics Committee in connection with the Keating thrift scandal. *(Keating hearings, p. 26)*

In the end, however, committee members said they felt Alexander's potential to improve the nation's education system outweighed doubts about his finances.

"My concern is, who in the heck is worrying about the kids?" asked Barbara A. Mikulski, D-Md. "Right now the Department of Education is flunking and needs a new principal."

Chairman Edward M. Kennedy, D-Mass., said Alexander "has assured us that he will be a full-time secretary of Education and will not pursue private enrichment from business activities while he is secretary."

Only Harkin, reminding his colleagues that he was chairman of the Appropriations subcommittee that handled funding for the Department of Education, said he could not vote for Alexander's nomination.

"Frankly, the whole thing sounds to me like someone paying a lot of attention to making money while in public service," said Harkin. "In my mind, the jury is still out."

That concern was reflected on the floor. Claiborne Pell, D-R.I., chairman of the Labor Subcommittee on Education, said he would vote for Alexander but added that the "poor taste in his investment practices had cast an unfortunate shadow on his nomination."

But Orrin G. Hatch, R-Utah, predicted that "he's going to make a tremendous difference in our lives."

Alexander's Background

Two years into his term as the "education president," Bush had made only slight headway in pursuing his No. 1 domestic priority. His selection of Alexander appeared to be an attempt to win some credibility as he neared the 1992 election.

"I think a lot of people have the feeling with Alexander that the cavalry is coming over the hill to the rescue," said one top Democratic education staff member in the Senate.

Alexander, unlike Cavazos, was a determined and savvy politician.

In the middle of his eight years as governor, from 1979 through 1986, he pushed a major education package through a Democratic-controlled legislature.

He also pulled the public on board, asking taxpayers to foot the bill with a 1-cent sales tax increase, in a state that regularly had ranked last in per capita spending on children from kindergarten through 12th grade.

"Remember, this is a guy who got elected governor by walking from one end of the state to another in boots and a red flannel shirt," said Chester E. Finn, Jr., professor of education and public policy at Vanderbilt University.

His focus on education extended to his work as chairman of the National Governors' Association, in which he served as a catalyst, prompting other governors to examine their states' education systems. Since January 1988, Alexander had been president of the University of Tennessee system.

A Friend in High Places

Despite his track record, Alexander's appointment might not have come about were it not for a key sponsor — White House Chief of Staff John H. Sununu.

Bush initially met with Alexander in July 1987 during the Tennessee Republican Leadership Conference in Nashville. At the time, Bush's campaign was gearing up, and he was sizing up potential running mates.

Alexander, on the other hand, had just gotten off the plane from Australia, where he had been on vacation for six months with his family after eight years in office.

By several accounts, the meeting went poorly. "Lamar was fresh back from Australia, and frankly, he looked like an Aborigine: very tan, very thin, long hair, dressing kind of funny, full of energy," said one Tennessee Republican insider, who asked not to be named.

"He sat down with George Bush, who had a governmental résumé as long as the country, and he asked Bush why he wanted to be president. I think that didn't go over real well."

While governor, however, Alexander had became close friends with Sununu, a former governor of New Hampshire.

Though sources said Alexander and Bush did not "connect" during their visit in Nashville, Bush subsequently conferred in person and by telephone with Alexander on education issues, and appointed him to his Education Policy Advisory Committee.

Minority Scholarship Issue

During courtesy calls before his Feb. 6 confirmation hearing, Alexander reassured senators that their concerns were his, without tipping his hand on specific issues.

In a meeting with Kennedy, chairman of the Labor and Human Resources Committee, Alexander promised that settling the issue of minority scholarships for college students would be his first priority.

Education Department officials had angered black leaders and caused confusion among higher education institutions in December 1990 when they first sought to ban race-based scholarships at schools receiving federal aid, then later agreed to allow such stipends if they were privately funded rather than financed by the institution.

"I would start over; I would step back," Alexander testified. "I would simply admit that sometimes you make a false step." ■

Ban on Race-Exclusive Scholarships Announced

After a politically sensitive review, Education Secretary Lamar Alexander announced Dec. 4 that he would bar colleges from handing out scholarships based solely on race but would allow schools to consider race as a factor.

Alexander had ordered the review of federal policy on March 20, six days after he was confirmed as Education secretary. *(Alexander appointment, p. 375)*

He was seeking to dampen a firestorm created in December 1990 when Michael Williams, assistant secretary for civil rights, said that minority-only scholarships violated Title VI of the Civil Rights Act. That title prohibited discrimination in any program receiving federal funds. Williams had tried to stop Fiesta Bowl officials from donating money for minority scholarships to the two schools playing in the football game.

Williams' move had angered black leaders and caused confusion among higher education institutions.

An American Council on Education study found that 4 percent of the 1.3 million minority students in four-year colleges received "race-exclusive" scholarships.

Alexander disputed Williams' interpretation of the civil rights law, saying that minority scholarships could be awarded legally in many instances. Examples included minority scholarships financed solely with private funds, minority scholarships awarded by schools operating under a court desegregation order and scholarships created by Congress solely for minorities.

Schools that provided scholarships to promote student body diversity could continue to do so, Alexander said, so long as all students were eligible and race was not the only factor considered.

Robert H. Atwell, president of the American Council on Education, an umbrella group for higher education, said he planned to tell colleges and universities to continue their existing practices. "We are simply committed to minority-targeted scholarships," he said. "We think that's compatible with the law."

House Education and Labor Committee Chairman William D. Ford, D-Mich., said in a statement: "We will carefully study the secretary's proposal from the perspective of ensuring that no student is denied an educational opportunity." He had opposed writing provisions into the Higher Education Act specifically allowing minority scholarships; he said that such scholarships already were legal.

Williams, who had touched off the furor, was standing by Alexander's side as the secretary announced the new policy.

At his confirmation hearings in March, Alexander said the administration's initial position "sent off exactly the wrong signal." The message to minority students, he said, should be, "We want you in, not we want you out."

Alexander promised that in his first days at the Department of Education, he would restore its old policy, which allowed minority scholarships, no matter what their funding source.

Alexander, a former Tennessee governor who was president of the University of Tennessee system at the time of his appointment, said he went further in discussing the minority scholarship issue than a nominee usually would because every member of the Senate Labor and Human Resources Committee had privately expressed concerns to him about the matter. ■

Hill Counters President's Education Plan

President Bush and congressional Democrats danced a minuet around primary education initiatives, but the maneuvering produced only modest legislative accomplishment.

To try to back up his "education president" pledge, Bush on April 18 unveiled a plan to overhaul the nation's troubled education system at the state and local levels, using a limited amount of federal money to fund model programs and offer incentives for change. Included in the "America 2000" proposal was voluntary national testing for fourth-, eighth- and 12th-graders and creation of non-traditional schools.

House and Senate Democrats responded by taking up a competing package establishing block grants to school districts that put education reforms into effect.

House Democrats went along with Bush's controversial proposal to give parents a choice of whether to send their children to public or private schools with federal support; Senate Democrats did not and drew a veto threat.

In the waning days of the legislative session, Majority Leader George J. Mitchell, D-Maine, tried but failed to have the Senate take up S 2, which had been approved by the Labor and Human Resources Committee.

BOXSCORE

➡ **Primary and Secondary Education Programs (S 2, HR 3320).** Bills to send out block grants to school districts to put education reforms into effect. The House bill allowed states to use money for school choice for public and private schools if the state constitution allowed it. The Senate version only allowed the funds to go for public schools.

Reports: H Rept 102-294; S Rept 102-43.

KEY ACTION

April 17 — S 2 approved by **Senate** Labor and Human Resources Committee by voice vote.

Sept. 26 — HR 3320 approved by **House** Education and Labor Subcommittee on Elementary, Secondary and Vocational Education.

Oct. 17 — HR 3320 approved by 26-12 vote by **House** Education and Labor Committee.

Nov. 13 — S 2 (modified) approved by **Senate** Labor and Human Resources Committee by voice vote.

BACKGROUND

Ever since Bush pledged in 1988 to be the education president, Democrats had said his goals, developed with the help of the nation's governors in 1989, were meaningless without more money. In the first three years of Bush's presidency, the Democrat-controlled Congress bottled up his proposals or linked them to large money increases the administration was unwilling to accept. *(Bush goals, 1989 Almanac, p. 191)*

Stung by criticism that he lacked a domestic agenda, Bush sacked Education Secretary Lauro F. Cavazos in January and replaced him with Lamar Alexander, an aggressive former governor from Tennessee. As governor, Alexander had pushed a major education package through the Tennessee state legislature and convinced taxpayers to pay for it with a 1-cent sales tax increase.

Alexander went straight to work crafting the education package. The plan he came up with would have cost $690 million in fiscal 1992; the spending was already included in the administration's budget request.

Some of the specifics included:

- **National standards and tests.** Standards would be set in five core subjects — English, mathematics, science, history and geography. Bush asked governors to adopt national tests for fourth-, eighth- and 12th-graders. The test would be optional, because the idea was controversial, with overtones of federal curricula and loss of local control.
- **Choice.** Using performance "report cards," parents could decide to move their children to another school, public or private. About $200 million in financial incentives would be given to state and local governments to develop school-choice policies. Washington would not necessarily pay for students to go to private school; it would only encourage local school districts to experiment with ideas. And the Chapter 1 program of aid to schools with disadvantaged students would allow federal dollars to follow students from school to school, assuming local policy permitted it.
- **Flexibility.** Schools could ignore federal rules governing their funding in order to cut through red tape and raise achievement levels.
- **Merit schools.** The federal government would award grants to 10,180 schools that had made progress toward national goals.
- **Governors' Academies.** Federal seed money would establish centers for principals and teachers to learn to make their schools better.
- **Merit Pay.** School districts would be urged to boost pay for those who taught well, who taught core subjects, who taught in "dangerous" settings or who were mentors for new teachers.
- **New Schools.** Bush planned to raise up to $200 million from the business community to fund research and development of non-traditional schools. An additional $550 million would have to be appropriated by Congress to create 535 "new American schools" in each congressional district by 1996.

Democrats complained that the $690 million fell far short of what was needed. The House and Senate Budget committees approved education increases for fiscal 1992 that at least tripled what Bush was proposing.

SENATE ACTION

On April 17, a day before the Bush proposal was made public, the Senate Labor and Human Resources moved to fatten up a $160 million literacy bill (S 2). The panel added $312 million in authority for programs to spur school-based management, reward excellent schools and improve math and science education. The panel's bill included a controversial provision to monitor the president's education goals.

But that was only the first step. Months later, after the literacy programs and other initiatives were enacted as separate legislation, the panel reconsidered S 2 and made several changes. *(Literacy bill, p. 373)*

The revised S 2, approved by voice vote on Nov. 13, authorized $850 million in fiscal 1992 for block grants to

National Achievement Test

A key feature of the Bush administration's package of education initiatives, a national achievement test, had already stirred vigorous debate among members of Congress and the education community.

Business leaders and lawmakers were pushing the idea, arguing that U.S. schools were not adequately teaching basic skills and that a vast decline in student competency was jeopardizing the United States' economic future and international competitiveness. A national test, they said, could chart what students should know by the time they graduated from high school and measure their progress in learning it.

But national testing was anathema to many education groups, teachers, administrators and superintendents, who saw it as the wrong solution to an urgent problem.

Educate America Inc. — a policy group chaired by Thomas H. Kean, former GOP governor of New Jersey — kicked off the debate over a national test by asking Congress to mandate that all 12th-graders take one. Kean, president of Drew University, said that the high school diploma had "become a proof of age more than any kind of achievement." He argued that a national test would provide employers, parents and schools with "reliable accountability" of student performance.

Germany, Japan, Britain and France routinely measured students' progress. The United States was one of a few industrialized nations that did not require all students to take a standardized test.

Yardsticks that were used, testing advocates said, showed a need for big improvements. In 1987, for example, American 12th-graders placed last in biology tests given to students in 13 countries. In geometry, they ranked 12th of 15; Japan ranked second and England third.

Supporters of a national test said that efforts to improve education — highlighted by goals set by Bush and the nation's governors in 1989 — were of little value without a comprehensive method of evaluating progress. "There can be no meaningful education reform without a clear sense of what the purposes of school are," said Denis Philip Doyle, a senior fellow at the Hudson Institute. "And these purposes are revealed in the standards we set for our children."

Opponents said that a national test would hurt, not help, efforts to improve the quality of schools. "National testing proposals largely are based on the false premise that measurement by itself will produce positive change," said Monty Neill, associate director of the National Center for Fair & Open Testing, a private organization supporting changes in the way students were tested. "During the 1980s, U.S. schoolchildren became probably the most overtested students in the world — but the desired educational improvements did not occur."

Teachers' unions also weighed in. American Federation of Teachers President Albert Shanker supported the idea of a national standard. Another teachers' union, the National Education Association, recommended a common set of performance standards demonstrated through "cumulative assessments," tests given over a span of years.

Some lawmakers, however, were wary of taking assessment and evaluation too far, too fast. Dale E. Kildee, D-Mich., chairman of the House Subcommittee on Elementary and Secondary Education, said that increasing assessments without giving schools more resources to help students improve their scores would be a mistake.

Educators had several complaints. "Society has pinned entirely too much of its hopes for the improvement of American education on the testing of children," said Karl V. Hertz, superintendent of Wisconsin's Mequon-Thiensville School District.

Others warned that instructors would teach and students would study only for what appeared on the test and disregard subjects not covered, similar to the way drivers studied for license-renewal exams.

Opponents also said that the tests would add to the stigma already faced by minorities and the poor. Studies showed that standardized tests had cultural and gender biases and that underprivileged students scored lower than those from higher socioeconomic groups.

A possible compromise was an idea proposed by University of Pittsburgh researcher Lauren B. Resnick; it operated much like the merit badge system used by Scout programs. Students of different backgrounds could work at different paces through performance-based examinations, portfolios and projects.

the states for education improvement plans and funding at unspecified levels for fiscal 1993-96. Congress appropriated $100 million for these kinds of programs in fiscal 1992.

In general, the Senate bill was much less specific than the Bush plan on how the states should spend the funds. In the first year, states could use the funds to create their own education reform proposals. Each state would be required to form a task force to draw up the proposals.

The state plans would then be reviewed by a newly created federal task force.

Over the following four years, the states would dole out funds to the localities after reviewing each local district's plans for education reform.

Some elements of Bush's plan, such as the creation of merit schools, were not called for under the Senate bill but would be allowed if that is what the state plan proposed.

Despite negotiations, panel Democrats and Alexander stalemated over a Bush proposal to allow parents to choose their children's school. S 2 would allow choice only among the public schools.

Alexander contended that choice for public schools did not go far enough. "If we want the benefits of educational reform and innovation to reach all of our children, we must give parents far greater choice than they now enjoy in deciding where their children will go to school," he said in the Nov. 12 letter to the committee.

Without extending choice to private schools, Alexander said, the measure was inadequate. "The president has called for fundamental reforms in our educational system, which our nation urgently needs. Unfortunately, S 2 prom-

School-Choice Plan Sparked Controversy

At the center of the debate over the direction of primary and secondary education was President Bush's proposal to allow parents to choose where to send their children to school.

The concept of choice had been debated in Congress for more than a decade, embroiling members in the constitutional issue of whether the government should subsidize parochial schools as well as the basic policy question of how best to educate children.

Indeed, top educators said school choice was like electricity — a powerful tool that must be used correctly and carefully. "It can also create a lot more problems than it solves," said Joe Nathan, director of the Center for School Change in Minnesota.

"Choice" was a nebulous word with various meanings among the school districts experimenting with it. In Minnesota, children could choose any public school in the state. In Milwaukee, the state provided $2,500 to private, non-sectarian schools to cover tuition for low-income children. In District Four in East Harlem, N.Y., no student was assigned to a particular school; each had to select the school he wanted to attend.

Under the Bush plan, grants would be awarded from a $200 million federal pot to school districts that already had started choice programs. Another $30 million would be earmarked for new demonstration projects.

Moreover, the Bush plan revised Chapter 1 — the federal government's $6 billion-plus program for educationally disadvantaged students — so that the money would follow students to whatever school they attended. Under previous law, grants went directly to the public schools to pay for such costs as teachers specializing in remedial education.

The idea, as Education Secretary Lamar Alexander described it, was to allow parents and students to send their children to either public or private schools, with federal and state governments picking up the tab. This would insert market pressures into the system, Alexander said, forcing all schools to compete for students.

But the choice idea carried a great deal of political baggage that Bush and Alexander had to overcome to sell the program to Congress and educators.

Every time the issue had come up — whether as federally subsidized vouchers that parents could use to pay for private-school tuition or as tuition tax credits — it raised the issue of separation of church and state.

"By offering public dollars to private schools, including religious schools, the administration is reopening the bitter and divisive policy and constitutional debates of the past about public aid to private schools," Sen. Edward M. Kennedy, D-Mass., told Alexander.

Yet many experts on constitutional law dismissed that question as moot. The federal government already provided Pell grants to students at private, religiously affiliated colleges, noted Michael W. McConnell, a law professor at the University of Chicago. The GI Bill even covered tuition at seminaries.

Laurence Tribe, a liberal constitutional scholar at Harvard Law School, said opponents of choice would have to look elsewhere for ammunition: "I don't think there is any chance at all that the [Supreme] Court as currently composed would find a reasonably designed school-choice plan as a violation of church and state. If there are objections, they should be debated on policy grounds and not recast as constitutional arguments."

On the merits, however, education specialists and key members of Congress had many more questions. They pointed to one school-choice program — the Milwaukee experiment — that was experiencing troubles.

That program, devised by a state legislator from the inner city, never caught on with parents, said Herbert Grover, the Wisconsin state superintendent of public instruction.

Other educators said that if lawmakers wanted to enable parents to make choices about schools, then government programs had to be fully developed and funded, lest they created more inequities.

"You're either for people having choice or for nobody having choice," said Ted Sizer, head of the Coalition for Essential Schools at Brown University and an adviser to Alexander. "If poor folks don't have choice, we ought to give them the money to have choice."

Nathan, a member of Bush's Education Policy Advisory Committee, said choice would not work without such key elements as transportation. "Otherwise you're creating choice for affluent families," he said.

However, just moving children around among existing schools was not good enough, Nathan said. Teachers and parents should be allowed to restructure schools, he said, giving students a range of options in selecting the learning environment best for them.

In Congress, the concerns crossed party lines. Lawmakers with large numbers of private schools in their districts were more likely to lean toward choice, while those with a preponderance of public schools wanted to keep federal dollars in public hands.

Members such as Rep. Jose E. Serrano, D-N.Y., who represented a poor urban district, complained that choice was irrelevant to their children when all of the nearby schools were bad.

In the Senate, Nancy Landon Kassebaum, Kan., ranking Republican on the Labor Subcommittee on Education, said she feared that transportation costs alone "could grow and grow," making choice programs infeasible.

Other lawmakers worried that choice would leave some students behind in the poorer schools. "If students have this choice and go from school A to school B because they perceive that B is a better school, what do we do for school A and for the students who remain in school A?" asked Dale E. Kildee, D-Mich., chairman of the House Education Subcommittee on Elementary, Secondary and Vocational Education.

Rep. Bill Goodling of Pennsylvania, ranking minority member of the Education and Labor Committee and a former school superintendent, shared Kildee's concerns: "If you have 500 students in a school and 250 of them are the 'thousand points of light' and decide to go to a school of choice, that leaves 250 fallen angels behind."

ises only more of the same old approach," he wrote.

But Howard M. Metzenbaum, D-Ohio, said that there would be "no yielding on the question of choice."

The measure came under fire from panel Republicans, who objected to the many levels of bureaucracy involved in developing the reform plans. It not only called for a state panel to create the plans but mandated a federal task force to review them.

This task force would consist of the Education secretary and 12 other members. Members of the task forces were supposed to be non-political, but the bill specified that the federal task force consist of six Republicans and six Democrats. Alexander strongly objected to the federal task force, arguing that it should be his responsibility to review the state plans and to ensure that they would make substantial reforms.

HOUSE ACTION

The House Education and Labor Committee took a less confrontational approach than its Senate counterpart. The $700 million measure (HR 3320) approved 26-12 by the panel on Oct. 17 included Bush's school choice proposal, which would allow parents to choose whether to send their children to public or private schools, and federal funding would be provided for either.

Opponents on the committee lined up to wage a two-day battle to limit choice to public schools. The effort, led by freshman William J. Jefferson, D-La., failed as key Democrats voted with Republicans to preserve the administration's support for the bill.

While the House bill included that key Bush provision, it differed in many other areas. It left it up to the local school district to decide what changes to make. If the district wanted to put into place a choice plan, federal funding would be provided. States could apply for five-year grants to be approved by the Education secretary. States would be required to set up panels to devise plans that included specific goals.

States could make funds available to school districts, which could use the money for a variety of activities, including non-traditional schools and choice.

The measure was crafted with direct input from the Education Department, although that did not ensure full administration support at first. In a letter Sept. 25, Education Secretary Alexander said the bill was "not an acceptable alternative" to Bush's plan.

Jefferson and his supporters, among them Marge Roukema, R-N.J., wanted choice limited to public schools. "I believe choice would undermine any attempt to revitalize neighborhood schools," Jefferson said.

The committee began marking up the bill Oct. 16 but held off debate on a Jefferson amendment on choice while members negotiated with administration officials. The next day, Goodling got a letter from John H. Sununu, the White House chief of staff, signaling support for the measure — so long as the choice provision remained.

Sununu said Bush would support the plan because it "will provide, at state and local discretion, the opportunity for the full range of choice options," not just a choice between public schools, as some members preferred. "The current framework, if not weakened, is acceptable."

Jefferson pressed ahead with his amendment, arguing that states would still have the option to institute choice programs, as some had done. "It leaves states and local districts as free as they are to implement choice plans," he said. "My amendment takes away the carrot of federal dollars."

Other members raised the issue of separation of church and state. Pat Williams, D-Mont., said religious organizations were concerned that if federal funding were provided to send children to their schools, the government could dictate school policy. "They expressed alarm at federal entanglement in their teaching, in their curriculum if they accept federal money."

Ford and a number of other members said they believed in Jefferson's amendment but, in the interest of holding onto the deal with the administration, could not support it.

"I'm willing to make a political gamble that they will keep their word," Ford said, but "I'm not comfortable with it on a philosophical basis at all."

The committee defeated Jefferson's amendment, 17-23.

Choice Stalemate

The dispute over Bush's choice proposals hampered progress on the measure. Negotiations continued throughout the fall, but members of the Labor and Human Resources Committee and the Bush administration were both unyielding on the issue.

By session's end, it became apparent that GOP objections would stop Democrats from bringing the bill to the floor in 1991. On Nov. 27, the last day of the session, Majority Leader Mitchell filed a motion for the Senate to vote first thing in 1992 whether to cut off debate on whether to consider the bill. The procedural move — called a cloture motion — requires 60 votes to pass. ■

Other Education Bills Considered in 1991

Congress acted on a handful of other education bills, including one to study proposals for establishing a longer school year and others that sought to increase skills in the labor force for jobs in high-technology fields.

LONGER SCHOOL YEAR

President Bush on June 27 signed legislation (S 64 — PL 102-62) that established a National Commission on a Longer School Year to study proposals to lengthen the school year so U.S. students could better compete with students in other countries.

The bill authorized $1 million in fiscal 1991 and such sums as necessary in fiscal 1992-94 for operations of the commission, which would report on the feasibility and value of extending both the school year and the school day.

Bill backers argued that the composition of the school year was outdated and that students tended to forget much of what they had learned over long stretches of summer vacation. A significant portion of the school year was devoted to relearning lessons from the year before, they said.

Supporters said the broken school year made more sense when the country was agrarian-based and when students were needed on the family farms during summer months.

The commission was ordered to submit its report to the president and Congress within one year after its first official meeting.

The Senate Labor and Human Resources Committee on March 13 approved the legislation (S Rept 102-26) in a 17-0 vote. The full Senate passed the measure by voice vote on April 17.

The measure went directly to the House floor, where it was amended and passed by voice vote on June 10. A June 11 conference produced an agreement (H Rept 102-110) that the House adopted on June 13, and the Senate cleared the legislation the following day — both on voice votes.

As enacted, the bill also:

- Authorized grants for the National Writing Project, a nonprofit educational network composed of numerous university and school writing programs that was established in 1973 to improve students' writing skills and the teaching of writing classes.
- Authorized the Department of Education to work with the Center for Civic Education to educate students on the history and significance of the U.S. Constitution.
- Authorized a grant program for companies agreeing to assist commercial truck drivers with reading and writing skills. The provision was included to address problems that some truckers encountered in trying to meet the requirements of the Commercial Motor Vehicle Safety Act of 1986 (PL 99-570), which required drivers to pass a federally mandated written test in order to obtain a commercial driver's license.

HIGH SCHOOL DROPOUTS

On Aug. 17, the president signed a measure (HR 2313 — PL 102-103) that reauthorized funds for programs designed to help prevent youths from dropping out of school.

The measure aided mentor programs and other methods aimed at keeping children in school. The bill also included $50 million for the Stars School program, which linked via satellite classrooms across the country with some of the nation's best teachers. The students and teachers could see and talk to each other over the satellite.

The bill also expanded program services to others, including disabled children and adults who were housebound or in hospitals.

The authorization bill included about $115 million for fiscal 1992 and such sums as necessary in fiscal 1993.

The House Education and Labor Committee reported the bill (H Rept 102-77) on May 23. The full House passed it by voice vote on June 3.

The Senate passed the measure on July 30 on a voice vote with an amendment, and the House cleared the bill by voice vote on Aug. 1.

CAMPUS SPEECH

Legislation that would make it easier for students at private colleges to sue when disciplined under restrictive speech codes was introduced on March 12 and referred to the House Judiciary Committee. While the bill (HR 1380) was the subject of much talk at the time of its introduction, there was no action taken on it.

The legislation, sponsored by Henry J. Hyde, R-Ill., and supported by the American Civil Liberties Union, sought to bar colleges receiving federal funds from disciplining students solely on the basis of speech. It allowed aggrieved students to win injunctive relief and the payment of attorneys' fees.

Public schools already were subject to suits for overly restrictive speech codes, but the law barred students from bringing constitutional challenges to private institutions.

A number of colleges had begun instituting codes of speech conduct in response to the apparent rise of racist and sexist demonstrations on campuses.

The bill included an exemption for religious schools and did not protect faculty speech. ■

Older Americans Act Stalls

Both the House and Senate approved legislation in 1991 that reauthorized the Older Americans Act of 1965 (PL 89-73) for four years. The law provided for transportation and employment programs and federal meals, including the popular Meals on Wheels program, for the elderly poor.

But the reauthorization bill (HR 2967) stalled at the end of the session because the Senate added an amendment to repeal the federal law that limited the amount of money older Americans could earn and continue to receive full Social Security benefits. *(Earnings test, p. 384)*

The so-called earnings test for Social Security was expected to be resolved when HR 2967 went to a House-Senate conference in 1992. House conferees were not yet named by the end of the 1991 session.

Both the House and Senate measures authorized nearly $2 billion for services and programs under the act. About $1.6 billion was authorized for fiscal 1991, but only $1.2 billion was appropriated.

BOXSCORE

➡ **Older Americans Act Reauthorization (HR 2967, S 243).** The legislation reauthorized for four years programs under the 1965 Older Americans Act that helped the elderly poor, including job training and the Meals on Wheels federal food program. Both the House and Senate bills authorized $2 billion for the programs.

Reports: H Rept 102-199; S Rept 102-151.

KEY ACTION

July 17 — The **Senate** Labor and Human Resources Committee approved S 243, 13-3.

July 30 — The **House** Education and Labor Committee approved HR 2967 by voice vote.

Sept. 12 — HR 2967 passed the **House** by a vote of 385-0.

Nov. 12 — HR 2967 passed the **Senate** by voice vote.

HOUSE ACTION

The House Education and Labor Committee gave voice vote approval July 30 to HR 2967.

A minor section of the bill included a provision requiring the administration to hold a National Conference on Aging in 1993.

White House aides threatened to recommend a veto of the $1.7 billion measure on grounds that the conference mandate impinged on executive branch prerogatives and improperly politicized the interests of the elderly.

In 1990, Congress appropriated $1 million for President Bush to pay for the conference, which had been held every 10 years to highlight the concerns and needs of the elderly.

The administration had no plans to put on the event in 1991. House Democrats retaliated by including the mandate in the older Americans bill.

As approved by the committee, the measure also changed the name from the White House Conference on Aging to the National Conference on Aging. Congress was to set the agenda and policies of the conference along with the administration.

House Democrats, including Matthew G. Martinez, Calif., chairman of the House Education Subcommittee on Human Resources, said the administration had not acted on a 1991 conference because it did not want to address cuts in programs and services for older Americans.

Bill Goodling of Pennsylvania, ranking Republican on the full committee, acknowledged the Democrats' complaint, saying he could find "no justification for not holding it."

Some House members doubted whether a bill to authorize funding for the elderly who were poor and sick would engender a veto. Education Committee Chairman William D. Ford, D-Mich., said that if the president vetoed the bill, funding for services to poor older people could be cut off because the bill's authorization expired in September.

"Who is going to take the blame if Meals on Wheels comes to a screeching halt?" Ford asked. But Thomas A. Scully, associate director of human resources at the White House Office of Management and Budget (OMB) said the veto threat was no bluff. "There's no question about it," he said. "We've never threatened a veto that we didn't deliver on."

Programs under the act could still be funded through appropriations. Under House rules, members could move to strike unauthorized funding on a point of order, although it would be rare for anyone to move against politically popular programs such as funding for the elderly poor.

Aside from the fight over the conference on aging, the legislation sailed through the committee with only minor changes to the version approved by the Human Resources Subcommittee on July 25.

The bill was aimed at reaching the elderly, including minorities, who were most in need of nutrition, health-care and counseling services.

The bill strengthened data-collection efforts to determine where the most disadvantaged elderly were located. Martinez said the bill also gave the commissioner of the Administration on Aging, a division of the Department of Health and Human Services, more control over the agency.

The committee approved by voice vote an amendment by Goodling to raise the authorization levels for supportive services for the elderly to fiscal 1991 levels. It increased the allotment for services such as transportation, legal counseling and adult day care from $400 million to $439 million. The fiscal 1991 appropriation for those services was $290.8 million.

Goodling's amendment also boosted the authorization for in-home services for the frail elderly from $26 million to $28.9 million. The fiscal 1991 appropriation was $6.8 million.

The panel also approved an amendment by Jolene Unsoeld, D-Wash., to authorize $15 million to provide meals for the elderly in school cafeterias.

Floor Action

After smoothing over the conference on aging dispute, the House passed HR 2967 on Sept. 12. The $2 billion bill, which passed 385-0, extended the 1965 act through fiscal 1995. *(Vote 257, p. 62-H)*

When the House Education and Labor Committee marked up the legislation, Republicans had warned that Bush might veto it over a provision that would have required the administration to hold a National Conference on

Aging in 1993.

Bush aides were also unhappy that the bill changed the name of the conference from the White House conference to the "national" conference.

Breaking the impasse, Martinez successfully offered a block of amendments on the floor that still set the 1993 date but changed the name back to the White House Conference on Aging.

The amendment, which passed by voice vote, also decreased the number of members of the policy committee for the event from 30 to 25: 13 members to be appointed by the president and 12 by Congress. Under the bill reported by the Education Committee, the policy committee for the conference would have been 30 members, half appointed by the president and half by Congress.

Provisions

As passed by the House, provisions in HR 2967 included:

- For supportive services, such as transportation, legal counseling and adult day care, the bill authorized $439 million. The fiscal 1991 appropriation for those services was $290.8 million.
- Respite for caregivers, including counseling and training, was authorized at $15 million.
- In-home services for older people who were not well enough to perform such chores as shopping for food and cleaning house received an authorization of $28.9 million. The fiscal 1991 appropriation was $6.8 million.
- Nutrition programs, including congregate meals served in senior citizens' centers, were authorized at $505 million, plus $120 million for home-delivered meals. The bill reported by the committee included $480 million for congregate meals, but Martinez included extra funding in his block of amendments.
- Job programs employing low-income people ages 55 and over were authorized at $470.5 million.

HR 2967 also created a long-term-care ombudsman to monitor nursing home care for the elderly. The ombudsman could investigate nursing homes and subpoena witnesses to testify. Bush administration officials opposed the ombudsman provisions as unnecessary and "inappropriately" having subpoena power.

Some members, including Harris W. Fawell, R-Ill., said the bill placed an added burden on the Administration on Aging, which was responsible for administering programs for the elderly. "It's highly unlikely that resources will grow to meet these demands," Fawell said.

During consideration of the bill, members took the opportunity to speak out on the controversial issue of the Social Security earnings test. Existing federal law limited the amount older people might earn and still receive Social Security benefits. But members had been reluctant to raise the amount the elderly could earn because taxes would have to be raised to cover the cost.

Members adopted, 383-0, an amendment offered by Dennis Hastert, R-Ill., expressing the sense of Congress that the 1993 White House Conference on Aging should consider the impact of the earnings limit on the elderly who worked. *(Vote 256, p. 62-H)*

SENATE ACTION

The Senate Labor and Human Resources Committee on July 17 approved a measure (S 243) that expanded federal programs for older Americans.

The four-year reauthorization of the Older Americans Act was approved on a 13-3 vote. It authorized $1.7 billion for programs in fiscal 1992, $121 million more than in fiscal 1991.

Drawing the most fire to the otherwise non-controversial measure was an amendment to provide benefits to workers whose companies had defaulted on agreements to provide pensions.

Despite a threat from Republicans that Bush was likely to veto the bill over it, the amendment offered by Howard M. Metzenbaum, D-Ohio, was adopted by a vote of 12-5.

Metzenbaum said the pension plan would cost about $50 million and funding would come from the Pension Benefit Guaranty Corporation, the federal fund that paid benefits to workers whose pension plans defaulted.

The amendment, which was supported by the American Association of Retired Persons, would have provided $75 for each year of service to the company, with the lump sum total not to exceed $1,500.

Metzenbaum said the bill would help retirees not covered by the 1973 Employment Retirement Income Security Act, which included retroactive coverage for three months before its enactment in July of that year.

About 40,000 workers were not covered when companies closed their doors or laid off workers before the rule was changed in 1973. According to a Metzenbaum aide, in the 1950s and '60s a number of companies either had no pension plans or promised to put aside pension funds for workers and did not.

Ranking member Orrin G. Hatch, R-Utah, said the bill would actually cost $500 million to pay workers and their survivors who lost benefits.

Other Republicans, including Strom Thurmond of South Carolina and Dave Durenberger of Minnesota, said the amendment was too costly and that funds should not be taken from a fund designed to help another group of disadvantaged workers.

"While I can be terribly sympathetic to the cause, I can't associate myself with the solution," Durenberger said.

The Senate committee bill authorized increases in funding levels of 5 percent annually for programs for the elderly, except elder-abuse prevention and preventive health programs. Elder-abuse prevention programs were increased from $10 million to $15 million per year and preventive health services from $10 million to $25 million. About $1.3 billion was appropriated for programs under the act in fiscal 1991.

In addition to the 5 percent increase, members also added funding for new programs and demonstration projects.

Brock Adams, D-Wash., chairman of the Subcommittee on Aging, said the measure provided more assistance to those who had to care for elderly family members at home, especially care providers who were often elderly themselves.

An amendment to the bill by Thad Cochran, R-Miss., ranking member of the Aging Subcommittee, authorized an additional $15 million for in-home services. The amendment, adopted by voice vote, included programs to help older, infirm people with house-cleaning and grocery shopping, and to provide respite care for care providers.

The bill targeted funding to the most needy senior citizens, including minorities. To better target the funding, the committee bill contained a new requirement that the commissioner on aging approve the interstate or intrastate distribution of funds.

The bill authorized $5 million favored by the Bush administration to pay for a White House Conference on Aging in 1993. Adams and Cochran were able to get $1 million for the

Earnings Test: To Repeal Or Not To Repeal

In what had become an annual ritual, Congress in 1991 again grappled with whether to revise the earnings test for Social Security — the federal limit on the amount of money Americans ages 65-69 could earn and still receive Social Security benefits. (There was no cap on the amount those over 70 could earn.) While relaxing the earnings test was a popular idea with retirees, lawmakers disagreed over how to pay for it.

Under existing law, an individual's benefits were reduced $1 for every $3 the person earned above the limit of $9,720. Repeal of the test would cost the federal government $3.9 billion in fiscal 1992 and $28 billion over five years, according to the White House Office of Management and Budget (OMB).

Under the 1990 White House-congressional budget agreement, any loss of revenue to the federal government had to be offset by an increase in taxes or cuts in other spending.

But House Ways and Means Committee aides said that repeal of the earnings test would not trigger the cuts because Social Security matters were exempt from the 1990 budget rules.

Senate Minority Leader Bob Dole, R-Kan., and other Republicans wanted to repeal the test, but many Democrats contended that the repeal would help only the wealthiest beneficiaries. Senate Finance Committee Chairman Lloyd Bentsen, D-Texas, and House Ways and Means Committee Chairman Dan Rostenkowski, D-Ill., instead favored increasing the amount retirees could earn while receiving Social Security benefits.

During the Nov. 12 Senate consideration of a measure (HR 2967) reauthorizing programs under the 1965 Older Americans Act, senators adopted an amendment by John McCain, R-Ariz., that sought to repeal the earnings test. *(Older Americans Act, p. 382)*

Two days before Congress adjourned on Nov. 27, Bentsen introduced S 2038, a free-standing bill that would have phased in increases in the amount older Americans could earn and receive full benefits. The measure would also would have made the Social Security Administration an independent agency.

The House version of the Older Americans Act reauthorization did not contain provisions repealing the earnings test. A free-standing House bill (HR 967) to repeal the limit, introduced by Dennis Hastert, R-Ill., had 268 cosponsors. However, despite bipartisan support in both the House and the Senate for the repeal, Rostenkowski opposed the outright repeal, as did OMB Director Richard G. Darman.

Rostenkowski in 1991 had introduced a measure (HR 2838) that would have phased in increases in the amount those 65 to 69 could earn and continue to receive Social Security benefits.

Rostenkowski had said earlier in the year that he would leave it up to the Ways and Means Committee members to decide which measures they would fund. His bill was not marked up by the committee in 1991.

Congressional Republicans were expected to continue to push in 1992 for an outright repeal. Bentsen and Rostenkowski had worked out a compromise between their bills to phase in increases in the earnings limit.

Rostenkowski and other Democrats hoped that President Bush would step in to dissuade Republicans from pushing the issue, Hill aides said. Yet the Senate's move confronted Bush with an awkward choice: to side with his fellow Republicans or join Democrats in heading off a large spending boost he opposed in principle.

A compromise on the provision in the Older Americans Act was expected to come early in 1992, allowing that measure to be cleared.

conference included in the appropriations bill for the Departments of Labor and Health and Human Services. *(Appropriations, p. 501)*

Floor Action

After striking the pension-benefit provision that had drawn a presidential veto threat, the Senate on Nov. 12 gave voice vote approval to HR 2967.

However, senators revived an even more prickly issue: repeal of the limit on the amount of money older Americans could earn while continuing to collect Social Security benefits.

Every year, Republicans tried to repeal the so-called earnings test, but members had not been able to come up with a tax increase or other plan to offset the cost to the Treasury. Also, many Democrats argued that repealing the test would benefit only the wealthy.

The Senate adopted by voice vote an amendment by John McCain, R-Ariz., that sought to repeal the test. OMB had estimated that the repeal would cost the government $3.9 billion in fiscal 1992 and $28 billion over the next five years.

Members did not challenge the amendment even though it appeared to violate budget rules. Realizing that Republicans would fight hard for the earnings test repeal, senators elected to move the bill and bank on the provision falling in conference with the House, an aide to McCain said.

Pension Benefit Dispute

While senators sidestepped a floor fight over Social Security, they spent the bulk of the day Nov. 12 debating the pension-benefits provision. In the end, Republicans prevailed in their efforts to strip the provision after winning over some Democrats with the argument that it would open the door to a raid on an already troubled federal fund established to safeguard pensions of workers.

The Pension Restoration Act (S 351), introduced by Metzenbaum and later included in the older Americans bill, would have authorized benefits for about 38,000 workers whose companies, during the 1960s and early '70s, defaulted on agreements to provide pensions. Among the businesses was the Studebaker car company of South Bend, Ind.

Each worker would have received an annuity of $75 for each year of service to the company. The total could not exceed $1,500 per year. Widows of workers would have received a maximum of $750 per year.

Metzenbaum said the plan would cost about $50 million

in fiscal 1992 and a total of about $340 million for the expected 20-year life span of the surviving workers.

Thad Cochran, Miss., ranking Republican on the Labor Subcommittee on Aging, offered an amendment to strike what members call the "pension losers" provision.

Republicans said the total cost would be closer to $500 million and complained that the money would come from the Pension Benefit Guaranty Corporation. That fund, which paid benefits to workers whose pension plans had defaulted, already had a $2 billion deficit, Republicans said.

A motion by Adams to table Cochran's amendment failed 46-51, a mostly party-line vote. However, 12 Democrats voted with Cochran, among them, Lloyd Bentsen, Texas; Jeff Bingaman, N.M.; and Dale Bumpers, Ark. *(Vote 248, p. 32-S)*

Cochran's amendment then was approved by voice vote. ■

Child Welfare Overhaul

A bill that sought to expand and overhaul federal programs for abused and neglected children was approved by a House Ways and Means subcommittee on Sept. 24. But it faced vehement opposition from the Bush administration and unanswered questions about how to pay its estimated $6.9 billion cost.

It was the second year in a row that child-welfare legislation stalled in the House after winning subcommittee approval. The Senate took no action on its companion measure, S 4. *(1990 Almanac, p. 556)*

Republicans contended that the legislation violated the 1990 budget agreement between Congress and the White House by dictating who should estimate its costs and by seeking to circumvent limits on domestic spending.

As approved by voice vote by the Subcommittee on Human Resources, the bill (HR 2571) sought to expand programs in the child-welfare sections of the Social Security Act that paid for efforts to keep families together. Under the system as it existed, federal funding for foster care for children who would otherwise qualify for welfare was unlimited, but funding for services that could prevent children from needing expensive foster care was restricted.

That made no sense, said supporters of the legislation, led by Thomas J. Downey, D-N.Y., acting subcommittee chairman. The emphasis on foster care, they contended, cost the federal Treasury too much and hurt children in troubled families at the same time.

The federal government spent more than $2.3 billion annually on the child-welfare programs.

During the subcommittee's markup, no member opposed the bill's thrust. Rather, members disagreed along partisan lines over how to finance the overhaul, which the Congressional Budget Office (CBO) estimated would increase federal spending by $6.9 billion between fiscal 1992 and fiscal 1996.

The Bush administration said it favored expanding services for abused and neglected children, but wanted funding for an expansion to come from amounts being spent on administrative costs for the foster-care program.

In a sharply worded letter to Downey, Health and Human Services Secretary Louis W. Sullivan raised numerous objections to the bill, "including its excessive cost and highly prescriptive provisions." In addition, he decried the bill's financing scheme as an "egregious" attempt to end run the budget agreement.

Panel Republicans agreed with Bush officials that the bill as currently approved violated the 1990 budget accord.

Certain provisions, said E. Clay Shaw Jr., Fla., the subcommittee's ranking Republican, "violate the spirit if not the letter" of the 1990 agreement.

Yet Republicans did not dissent as the panel approved the measure by voice vote.

BOXSCORE

➡ **Child Welfare Overhaul (HR 2571, S 4).** Bills to expand and revamp federal programs for abused and neglected children; and to increase support for family services so that foster care would not be needed as often.

KEY ACTION

Sept. 24 — HR 2571 approved by the **House** Ways and Means Subcommittee on Human Resources by voice vote.

Bill Highlights

The key element of the bill increased funding for the Social Security Child Welfare Services Program, which helped finance services to prevent families from breaking up. The measure sought to put that program on the same financial footing as Social Security's foster-care program.

The foster-care program was an unlimited entitlement, with the federal government paying a set share of whatever it cost to keep in foster care children who would have qualified for welfare if they had remained with their families.

The child-welfare services program, by contrast, was funded through the regular appropriations process. It had to compete for funds each year with hundreds of other health, social services and education programs. In fiscal 1991, the program received $273.9 million of its authorized level of $325 million. For fiscal 1992, the Bush administration requested, and both the House and Senate approved, keeping funding at the fiscal 1991 level.

Downey and other proponents of overhauling the system said that increasing funding for prevention services through the child-welfare services program could ultimately reduce costs for foster care, which was much more expensive.

The bill sought to make the child-welfare services program a "capped entitlement," with funding automatic up to a set ceiling, beginning at $600 million in fiscal 1993 and rising to $1.3 billion in fiscal 1996. After that, the ceiling was to be adjusted annually for inflation.

The bill also increased funding for an existing capped entitlement program that states could use for child welfare, the Social Services Block Grant. By 1996 the bill raised that program's cap from its existing $2.8 billion annually to $3.4 billion.

The Budget Issue

The Bush administration opposed both the increases and making the child-welfare program an entitlement. Sullivan's Sept. 24 letter said the "excessive new funding" was "ill advised given current budgetary constraints."

Administration officials were even more outraged by two provisions in the bill that they said violated the 1990 budget agreement, enacted in that year's budget-reconciliation bill (PL 101-508).

The first contested provision wrote into the bill the estimates provided by CBO. Under the budget agreement, estimates for changes to entitlement programs were to be made by the White House Office of Management and Budget. But in January, House Democrats pushed through a rule change giving that authority to CBO.

The second provision stipulated that although the child-welfare program was to be made an entitlement, its removal from the category of domestic discretionary programs was not to result in the lowering of that cap. The budget agreement set caps for three categories of appropriated programs — defense, domestic discretionary and foreign aid — and stipulated that funds could not be transferred among the categories.

Downey acknowledged that leaving the domestic discretionary cap unchanged would give appropriators an additional $273.9 million to spend.

"The point of keeping the cap where it is is to give the appropriators room to meet other pressing needs," Downey said.

That is exactly what Republicans opposed. "This is nothing more than a budget gimmick to free up funds for additional domestic discretionary spending," Sullivan said in his letter. Together with writing the CBO estimates into the bill, "these provisions are among the most egregious attempts to violate the [budget agreement] to date."

Nancy L. Johnson, R-Conn., who had been working on her own overhaul proposal, said, "As much as I care about foster care, I am deeply distressed about these provisions being included in the bill."

Panel Democrats ignored Republicans' complaints. By identical 4-7 party-line votes, they defeated two Shaw amendments to remove the contested provisions.

Also on a 4-7 party-line vote, members defeated an amendment offered by Fred Grandy, R-Iowa, that would have allowed welfare recipients to start their own small businesses and accumulate up to $10,000 in assets without losing eligibility for benefits.

That day the Education and Labor Committee added a related provision to legislation (HR 3033) to reauthorize the Job Training Partnership Act. *(Job training, p. 315)*

Downey, while voicing interest in the proposal, was not so accommodating: "It's an intriguing idea. But this subcommittee does not adopt intriguing ideas without hearings." ■

Other Children's Aid Bills Considered in 1991

Congress in 1991 worked on a number of measures aimed at helping the nation's children, but only two of them were sent to President Bush.

CHILDREN WITH DISABILITIES

The Senate on Sept. 16 cleared for the president legislation (S 1106 — PL 102-119) that reauthorized funding to states for early intervention services for infants and toddlers with disabilities. Bush signed it Oct. 7.

The bill reauthorized the program for three years, with $220 million in fiscal 1992. The measure was similar to legislation (HR 3053) passed by the House on Sept. 11. The provisions of HR 3053 were then inserted in S 1106, which the House passed by voice vote.

The program was created in 1986 when the 1975 Individuals with Disabilities Education Act (PL 99-457) was amended to set up guidelines for states to coordinate education of disabled infants and toddlers. Proponents said the programs were needed to smooth developmentally disabled children's transition to preschool.

Bush signed a measure in 1990 (PL 101-476) that reauthorized most of the programs under the 1975 law. But the section covering disabled infants was not included because its authorization extended through the end of fiscal 1991. *(1990 Almanac, p. 616)*

The bill targeted low-income, rural and minority communities. It authorized $15.1 million for training centers for fiscal 1992 for parents of disabled children up to age 5.

The Senate Labor and Human Resources Committee on May 22 had approved S 1106 (S Rept 102-84).

The House Education and Labor Committee had approved HR 3053 (H Rept 102-198) by voice vote July 30.

TEMPORARY CARE

The House on Sept. 11 passed by voice vote legislation (HR 3034) that would extend for three years benefits under a program to provide temporary care for children and infants with disabilities and chronic illnesses.

States had assisted private and public agencies in providing temporary non-medical care to children and infants. Introduced by William J. Jefferson, D-La., the bill authorized $20 million in fiscal 1992 for respite care for children.

Jefferson said the services provided a needed break for families of children who required constant care and supervision. Children who were abused or at risk of abuse would also have sbeen covered under the bill.

The House Education and Labor Committee approved HR 3034 by voice vote on July 30.

AID FOR ABANDONED CHILDREN

On Nov. 27, the House cleared a measure (S 1532 — PL 102-236) that reauthorized for four years programs to help find foster homes for "boarder babies" — children abandoned at hospitals by parents unwilling or unable to care for them. Bush signed the bill Dec. 12.

The legislation bolstered programs included in the 1988 Abandoned Infants Assistance Act (PL 100-505) for boarder babies, who often suffered from AIDS, prenatally developed drug addiction or other afflictions. *(1988 Almanac, p. 318)*

The measure authorized $20 million in fiscal 1992, $25 million for fiscal 1993, $30 million for 1994, and $35 million for fiscal 1995.

The bill authorized funding to 32 agencies and programs that offered early intervention services to prevent the abuse, neglect, and abandonment of these children.

The measure directed the secretary of Health and Human Services to set up demonstration projects to provide family training and assistance to help prevent abandonment.

The Senate first approved its version of the bill Oct. 29 by voice vote. The House followed suit, passing the bill on Nov. 19 with minor amendments. The bill then went back to the Senate, where the House-passed amendments were approved and an additional Senate amendment was added, by voice votes. The House then agreed by voice vote to the

Senate amendment, clearing the bill.

The Senate Labor Committee had approved the bill (S Rept 102-161) on July 31 by voice vote.

The House Education and Labor Committee on July 30 had approved, by voice vote, a companion bill, HR 2722 (H Rept 102-209, Part 1). The House Energy and Commerce Committee approved HR 2722 (Part 2) on Oct. 8.

ANTI-ABUSE EFFORTS

Programs aimed at helping abused children and victims of domestic violence would have been expanded under a $375 million bill that passed the Senate, 96-0, on Nov. 7. *(Vote 247, p. 32-S)*

The legislation (S 838), sponsored by Christopher J. Dodd, D-Conn., chairman of the Labor Subcommittee on Children, Families, Drugs and Alcoholism, reauthorized the programs for three years.

The bill focused on improvement of child protective services with up to $100 million in grants to states, subject to appropriations. Additional support would have been available to states to enhance court procedures to include civil as well as criminal cases, plus cases of child abuse and neglect, not just child sexual abuse.

Community-based child-abuse prevention programs would also have qualified for added assistance.

The bill created a $30 million grant program for state and local agencies for treating abused and neglected children outside their home environment. The aim of the program was to reunite children with their families.

Family-violence prevention provisions written by the bill's cosponsor, Daniel R. Coats, R-Ind., would have expanded grants to states for programs serving victims of domestic violence and their children. In addition, the bill directed the secretary of Health and Human Services to provide at least 10 percent of all domestic violence funds to Indian tribes.

The Senate Labor and Human Resources Committee had approved S 838 (S Rept 102-164) on July 31.

On July 9, the House passed its version of the bill (HR 2720). Introduced by Major R. Owens, D-N.Y., HR 2720 called for a one-year reauthorization of child-abuse prevention programs.

DRUG ABUSE EDUCATION

The House on Sept. 11 approved legislation (HR 3057), by voice vote, to extend federal drug-education initiatives for children. The measure, introduced by Jose E. Serrano, D-N.Y., authorized funding for the National Diffusion Network, which disseminated information about successful anti-drug abuse programs to schools.

The bill authorized $1.2 million in assistance for existing drug-education programs that served rural areas and inner cities, both underserved populations, Serrano said.

The House Education and Labor Committee approved HR 3057 by voice vote July 30.

ACCESS TO IMMUNIZATIONS

The Senate Labor and Human Resources Committee approved a bill (S 493) on July 31 increasing access to immunizations for children in poor rural and inner-city areas.

S 493, the Comprehensive Maternal and Early Childhood Health Care Act, authorized new grants for community, migrant and homeless health-care centers. In addition, it provided for programs to lower infant mortality, increase access for immunizations for preschoolers, and coordinate preventive services for pregnant women and young children.

But the bill, sponsored by committee Chairman Edward M. Kennedy, D-Mass., set no specific funding levels, leaving that decision to House and Senate appropriators. Increases for both the popular immunization and community health center programs had already been limited by the 1990 budget agreement. ■

Hill Acts on Several Bills To Help American Indians

Congress acted on a handful of bills in 1991 aimed at benefiting American Indian tribes by providing them new types of aid, reinstating their authority to prosecute criminals for crimes committed on reservation land and officially recognizing more tribes and thereby making them eligible for a host of federal benefits and services.

SELF-GOVERNING PROGRAMS

The president signed legislation (HR 3394, PL 102-184) on Dec. 4 that authorized $700,000 for the addition of 10 tribes to a demonstration project established to help tribes manage programs that were previously administered by the Bureau of Indian Affairs and the Indian Health Service.

Under the self-governing demonstration project, Native Americans in certain tribes could determine funding priorities and make other decisions that routinely were decided in Washington.

The legislation (H Rept 102-320) expanded the authorization under the Indian Self Determination and Education Assistance Act of 1988 (PL 100-472), which set up a demonstration program under which 20 Indian tribes were given the authority to carry out certain tribal services, such as medical and health programs, that otherwise would have been handled by the federal government. *(For more background on Indian self-governing projects, see 1974 Almanac, p. 672)*

The House Interior Committee approved the bill on Nov. 13, and the full House passed it on Nov. 18. The Senate cleared the legislation on Nov. 19.

Another bill (S 668 — S Rept 102-125) that sought to authorize demonstration grants to assist tribes in establishing environmental protection and cleanup programs and apply for related federal grants passed the Senate on Aug. 2 on a voice vote. The House Interior Committee approved the bill also by voice vote on Nov. 13.

MICMAC INDIANS

President Bush on Nov. 26 signed legislation (S 374, PL 102-171) that provided federal recognition to the Aroostook Band of Micmac Indians in Aroostook County, Maine, and made them eligible for federal benefits.

The bill authorized a $900,000 deposit for a land-acquisition fund for the Micmacs and also authorized them to organize as a government and establish rules for tribal membership.

During its consideration in Congress, the Bush administration had threatened to veto the measure, saying it would circumvent the federal government's tribal-recognition procedures, which were handled by the Interior Department.

But bill supporters said the legislation was necessary to correct the omission of the Micmacs from the 1980 Maine Indian Claims Settlement Act, which provided funds for 12.5 million acres of land taken by the federal government. *(1980 Almanac, p. 569)*

The House cleared the legislation (H Rept 102-136) on Nov. 12. The Senate had passed it on Sept. 19. A similar bill failed in the House in 1990. *(1990 Almanac, p. 424)*

NAVAJO-HOPI RELOCATION

Bush on Dec. 2 signed a bill (S 1720, PL 102-180) that reauthorized the Navajo-Hopi Relocation Housing Program through fiscal 1995.

The program had been established to help relocate Indian families displaced by the 1974 congressionally negotiated settlement of land disputes (PL 93-531) between the two tribes in Arizona that dated back to the 1880s when nomadic Navajo herders settled on Hopi lands.

Under the mandated settlement, a number of Navajo families were left inside Hopi territory. The program offered relocation services for such families. *(1988 Almanac, p. 637)*

The bill authorized $30 million to be spent for the relocation program for each year through fiscal 1995.

The Senate passed the bill (S Rept 102-176) by voice vote Oct. 25. The House cleared the bill (H Rept 102-321) on Nov. 18.

ALASKA NATIVE LANGUAGES

The Senate on Nov. 25 passed by voice vote legislation (S 1595, S Rept 102-213) to ensure the survival of Alaska's indigenous languages. Of the 20 original native languages that were still being spoken in Alaska, only two were being actively spoken by children, and many Alaska Native Americans said the loss of the other languages had led to a disintegration of their communities.

The program would provide grants to villages and eligible Alaska Native groups for language preservation projects, such as community-sponsored language programs, training courses for teachers and the compilation of oral histories.

The grant program would be run by the Administration for Native Americans within the Department of Health and Human Services.

The legislation was pending in the House Education and Labor Committee at the end of the session.

CRIMINAL JURISDICTION

President Bush signed legislation (HR 972, PL 102-137) on Oct. 28 that reinstated the authority of Indian tribes to exercise limited criminal jurisdiction over all Indians within a tribe's territorial limits. Jurisdiction was limited under the bill to criminal misdemeanors.

Before 1990, a tribe had jurisdiction over all criminal cases on its land involving misdemeanor charges as long as the defendant was an American Indian. But in May 1990, the Supreme Court ruled that while a tribe had such jurisdiction over its own members, it had no legal authority over Indians from other tribes.

The legislation reestablished a tribe's jurisdiction over all Indians on its reservation. Jurisdiction over non-Indians was to remain in the hands of state and federal authorities.

The Senate passed the conference report (Conf Rept 102-261) on HR 972 on Oct. 17, and the House cleared the legislation on Oct. 22.

LUMBEE TRIBE RECOGNIZED

The House on Sept. 26 passed legislation (HR 1426 — H Rept 102-215) by a 263-154 vote to recognize the Lumbee Tribe of Cheraw Indians of North Carolina, an action necessary to make the tribe eligible for social programs and protection under federal Indian laws. *(Vote 282, p. 68-H)*

The measure was designed to get around a decision by the Bush administration that the tribe was ineligible for federal recognition. Members first defeated, 159-251, a Republican-sponsored amendment that would have required the tribe to go through the Interior Department's recognition procedures. *(Vote 281, p. 68-H)*

At the end of the session, the House bill was awaiting action in the Senate. The Senate Indian Affairs Committee held hearings on a similar bill (S 1036) in August. ■

Few Developments in War on Drugs

Once a stormy issue that galvanized both Republicans and Democrats, the war on drugs had notably subsided a year before the 1992 elections. Little more happened than a quiet changing of the guard at the Office of National Drug Control Policy and a multi-year reauthorization of some of the treatment programs initially passed in a massive 1988 anti-drug bill.

Some questioned the need for new legislation as statistics showed a decline in drug use and Congress had already passed a raft of laws, including two major drug packages in five years. According to a nationwide household survey by the Department of Health and Human Services' National Institute on Drug Abuse, drug use was down 11 percent from 1988 levels.

Election-year politics had typically fueled major anti-drug legislation. In 1982, Congress passed crime legislation that included creating the drug policy office and a Cabinet-level "drug czar." President Ronald Reagan vetoed the bill over the drug czar provisions, which he viewed as unnecessary and likely to produce turf battles.

In 1984, just three weeks before the presidential election, Reagan signed into law a sweeping anti-crime package that substantially increased penalties for major drug offenses and gave federal prosecutors new authority to seize the assets and profits of drug traffickers.

As that campaign wrapped up, Republicans took credit for cracking down on drugs while painting Democrats as soft on crime.

In 1988, as the presidential campaigns heated up, the climate changed. Jesse Jackson made drugs and drug-related violence a theme of his campaign, and Republicans were on the defensive, focusing on law enforcement.

"I challenge the Democrats to stand up on this point," Vice President George Bush said. "You say this is a war — then treat it as such. Don't let these killers back on the street."

Jackson and other Democrats supported creating a drug

czar, additional funding for local law enforcement and treatment on request for drug addicts.

In 1988, Congress passed yet another anti-drug bill, a massive $2.8 billion package. Besides the drug czar, the bill included a provision that would allow the death penalty for major drug traffickers. The drug czar provisions faced little opposition in Congress this time. Also, an obstacle to GOP support, language establishing Cabinet status for the administrator of the drug policy office was removed. *(1988 Almanac, p. 85)*

In 1990, President Bush announced his anti-drug strategy. A drug summit followed in Cartagena, Colombia, with heads of South American countries under siege in the drug war. But with so much legislation already enacted, and no consensus on what to do next, Bush championed no new bill and Congress passed none. *(1990 Almanac, p. 502)*

Martinez: New Drug Czar

When former Florida Gov. Bob Martinez was sworn in March 28 as the nation's new drug czar, the fanfare that accompanied the term of former drug policy chief William J. Bennett was gone.

After Bennett's stormy 19-month term however, many in Congress said the calm was welcome.

Bennett, who left the job to head the Republican National Committee, was criticized by Democrats in Congress for his combativeness and partisanship. He later withdrew from the GOP position to write a book and do public speaking.

Martinez, confirmed by the Senate 88-12 on March 21, had moved to head off policy criticisms by vowing to boost treatment programs. *(Vote 41, p. 7-S)*

"States must have a statewide comprehensive treatment plan," Martinez said. "I think that's something we need to have Congress pass."

Martinez's approach — showing sensitivity to congressional concerns that treatment programs were underfunded — appeared to mark a shift in the White House's rhetorical strategy in the drug war.

White House officials said that the country had entered a different phase of the drug war. When Bennett was in charge, his job was to create a drug-fighting strategy and push it through Congress.

In 1991, with a strategy in place and interest in the drug problem ebbing, Martinez's goal was to keep Congress and the public committed to continuing anti-drug programs.

Edward M. Kennedy, D-Mass., opposed Martinez's nomination on the Senate floor.

"Under the Martinez administration," said Kennedy, "Florida ranked first in the nation in incarceration, but 21st in the nation in substance-abuse treatment funding and 32nd in prevention funding."

Program Reauthorization

Legislation authorizing drug abuse prevention and education programs for youth gangs and runaways for three years was cleared by the Senate Oct. 2. Bush signed the bill Oct. 18 (HR 3259 — PL 102-132).

The first section of the bill, introduced by Rep. Matthew G. Martinez, D-Calif., chairman of the Education Subcommittee on Human Resources, targeted drug education and prevention programs to youth gangs.

The bill authorized $15 million for fiscal 1992, $18 million for fiscal 1993 and $20 million for 1994 for programs under that section. The program had been funded at $14.8 million in fiscal 1991.

The second section was aimed at runaway and homeless youths and authorized the same amount for those programs.

Both sections reauthorized programs under the Anti-Drug Abuse Act of 1988 (PL 100-690).

HR 3259 was approved Sept. 24 by voice vote by the House Education and Labor Committee (H Rept 102-222). The measure was passed by the House Sept. 30 by voice vote. ■

Nutrition, Food Stamps Bills Left Pending

The Senate Agriculture Committee considered measures to expand existing nutrition and food stamp programs. Still pending at the end of the first session were:

FARMERS' MARKET NUTRITION PROGRAM

Legislation to expand a program that provided fruits and vegetables to low-income individuals and families at risk of poor nutrition was passed by voice vote in the Senate Sept. 27 but did not move in the House.

The bill (S 1742) sought to reauthorize for four years funding for the Farmers' Market Nutrition Program, which provided the needy with fruits and vegetables from local farmers. Established as a demonstration project in 1989, the program helped poor families as well as farmers, according to Charles E. Grassley, R-Iowa, who sponsored the bill with Agriculture Committee Chairman Patrick J. Leahy, D-Vt.

The program in 1991 reached Iowa and nine other states, and the bill permitted other states to participate.

Low-income people received Farmers' Market checks to be spent at authorized markets.

The measure authorized $5 million for fiscal 1992, $6.5 million for fiscal 1993, $8 million for fiscal 1994 and $9.5 million for fiscal 1995.

FOOD STAMPS

The Senate Agriculture Committee on Nov. 21 approved legislation (S 757) by 14-1 that sought to make more people eligible for food stamps.

The measure allowed applicants for foods stamps to deduct more of their housing expenses from their incomes, which could not exceed specified levels for eligibility.

Under existing law, recipients who rented could deduct up to $186 a month from their income. The measure eliminated the cap on housing expenses.

A House Agriculture Committee bill (HR 1202 — H Rept 102-396), approved Oct. 16, sought to raise the cap gradually to $335 per month by fiscal 1995. The following year, the cap was to be eliminated.

Senate Agriculture Chairman Patrick J. Leahy, D-Vt., said he would delay action on the measure until the Finance Committee came up with a plan to pay for it. Under the 1990 White House-Congress budget deal, the $1 billion-plus in annual spending authorized by the bill had to be offset by raising taxes — an option opposed by the Bush administration — or cutting entitlement spending elsewhere. ■

Chapter 8

DEFENSE

No Rush To Restructure Military

Despite gulf war and Soviet breakup, Congress moved cautiously on changes and cutbacks

Extraordinary events in the world bolstered and buffeted U.S. defense policy in 1991. In the end, however, Congress made no significant reduction in the $291 billion defense budget that President Bush had requested in February.

And members did not go much beyond the pace set by the Pentagon in restructuring U.S. forces and weaponry to reflect the end of the Cold War and the emergence of what Bush called the "new world order."

Early in the year, the quick U.S. victory in the Persian Gulf War bolstered support for the military and the reputation of its high-tech weaponry. Later in the year, the very purposes and dimensions of the military were called into question by the collapse of the Soviet empire, which had been the motivating threat behind U.S. defense policy since World War II. The defense authorization bill cleared Congress more than a month before Soviet President Mikhail S. Gorbachev resigned, making final the dissolution of the Soviet empire. But the members who shaped and approved the defense bill were well aware that they were preparing a budget for the post-Cold War era.

The conflicting tugs and pulls of the year's tumultuous international events were reflected in HR 2100 (PL 102-190), the fiscal 1992 defense authorization measure:

- Congress erected a substantial barrier to further production of the controversial B-2 stealth bomber. *(B-2 bomber, p. 403)*
- But lawmakers went on record in favor of early deployment of a limited version of the equally disputed Strategic Defense Initiative. *(SDI, p. 407)*
- Impressed by the performance of women in combat in the Persian Gulf War, Congress removed the statutory ban on women serving in combat as pilots and flight crews in the Navy and Air Force. *(Women in combat, p. 414)*
- Members accepted the administration's proposal to reduce military personnel by more than 106,000 (to 1,886,400) but balked at the plan to cut the politically popular National Guard and reserves by more than 107,000 (to 1,068,400). HR 2100 cut the Guard and reserve rolls by 38,000, but the companion appropriations bill gave the Defense secretary discretion to cut about 23,000 more personnel.
- Changes were made in the measure to reflect a package of unilateral arms reductions that Bush announced on Sept. 27 in light of the eclipse of the Soviet threat. For example, House-Senate conferees eliminated funds that the administration had requested earlier for two supersonic, air-launched missiles and for development of a rail-mobile launcher for the MX intercontinental missile. *(Bush proposals, p. 421)*
- And Congress approved separate legislation permitting up to $500 million from the defense budget to be used to demilitarize and deliver humanitarian assistance to the newly independent nations that formerly were part of the Soviet Union. *(Soviet aid, p. 463)*

At least for 1991, however, Congress stopped short of more fundamental cutbacks in defense. Defense Secretary Dick Cheney warned that the defense establishment would be damaged if Congress forced a speedier budget cutback than his program to reduce the size of the force roughly 25 percent by the end of fiscal 1995. But the more persuasive deterrent against deeper cuts seemed to have been members' fear of the political chaos that would result if Congress junked the budget law passed late in 1990.

That law limited the allowable deficit each year through fiscal 1995 and also limited annual discretionary appropriations through fiscal 1993 for defense, international affairs and domestic spending. Funds cut from defense could have gone to deficit reduction but could not have been transferred to popular domestic programs without violating the cap on domestic spending. *(1990 Almanac, p. 173)*

Nonetheless, many members made it clear during the defense debates of 1991 that they expected the budget law's walls to crumble eventually. "At some juncture, we're going to have to revisit the budget agreement," said Senate Budget Committee Chairman Jim Sasser, D-Tenn., an architect of the deficit deal. The unwinding of the Soviet Union "could have a tremendous impact [in 1992] — on strategic weapons in particular," said Senate Defense Appropriations Subcommittee member Warren B. Rudman, R-N.H.

After an era of expanding military budgets, members of Congress began to anticipate both the fiscal rewards and the political and strategic difficulties of an era of dramatic cutbacks. "In many ways," John McCain, R-Ariz., a member of the Senate Armed Services Committee told the Senate on Nov. 21, "it is easier to build up a defense establishment than it is to reduce it."

The Senate cleared HR 2100 on Nov. 22, and the president signed the defense bill on Dec. 5.

BOXSCORE

➡ **Fiscal 1992 defense authorization (HR 2100):** The bill authorized $291 billion in defense spending. It restricted production of B-2 bombers but backed deployment of a limited version of the Strategic Defense Initiative.

It removed a statutory ban on women serving on air combat crews in the Navy and Air Force.

Reports: H Rept 102-60; S Rept 102-113; H Rept 102-311.

KEY ACTION

May 22 — HR 2100 passed the **House**.

Aug. 2 — S 1507 passed the **Senate**, which then amended it into HR 2100.

Nov. 18 — The **House** approved conference report on HR 2100.
Nov. 22 — The **Senate** cleared it for the president.

Dec. 5 — President Bush signed HR 2100 (PL 102-190).

HOUSE COMMITTEE ACTION

The House Armed Services Committee's task in drafting a fiscal 1992 defense authorization measure was framed by the spending limits set by the 1990 budget deal and by the Bush administration's proposal for a six-year drawdown of defense spending that would shrink the military by one-fourth.

The budget submitted by the administration in February was the first increment of a plan to eventually allocate to the Pentagon the smallest share of the gross national product since World War II.

Bush Proposal

Funds requested for the defense-related programs of other agencies, principally the nuclear weapons development and production work conducted by the Energy Department, boosted Bush's total defense budget for fiscal 1992 to $290.8 billion in budget authority.

The slimmed-down force was to have a new focus: After four decades of planning to head off on short notice a Soviet invasion of Western Europe, Pentagon planners were to concentrate more heavily on dealing with so-called regional threats to U.S. interests. Iraq had proved to be a particularly timely, if unusually well-armed, example. *(Gulf war, p. 437)*

The force Bush proposed was not only cheaper but considerably smaller than the Cold War-oriented force that reached its apogee under President Ronald Reagan. The number of active-duty military personnel was to drop from about 2 million in fiscal 1990 to 1.65 million in fiscal 1995, and the number of combat units also was to decline: active-duty Army divisions from 18 to 12; Navy ships from 545 to 451; active-duty Air Force fighter wings from 24 to 15.

A smaller proportion of personnel would be deployed overseas, but they would be better equipped to be dispatched on short notice to distant trouble spots where no U.S. combat units were regularly stationed.

So that the forces could keep their fighting edge, training operations were to continue at a relatively high tempo. "I'm a great believer in keeping readiness levels as high as possible and letting force structure [the number of combat units] drop" to accommodate budget limits, Gen. Colin L. Powell Jr., chairman of the Joint Chiefs of Staff, told House Armed Services.

Bush's plan called for reducing by 4 percent the weapons procurement budget that Congress had slashed in fiscal 1991 by 24 percent (adjusting for inflation), canceling 81 programs large and small. But it would continue to bet heavily — though selectively — on high technology for combat leverage. "The fantastic success of American arms in the Persian Gulf today relates directly to the investment ... made over the years in technology," Cheney told House Armed Services on Feb. 7.

Although Cheney cautioned that he might recommend a halt to the U.S. military drawdown if international circumstances turned more dangerous, even the hawkish Defense secretary discounted the likelihood that the Soviet military threat to U.S. interests would revive. "The Soviet ability to project power beyond their borders will continue to decline," he said, either "as part of a broad strategy of improving relations with the West, or ... because of the simple, continued economic collapse of the Soviet Union."

Committee Bill

On May 8, a bipartisan majority of the House Armed Services Committee approved, 45-6, an authorization bill (HR 2100) that demonstrated that military prudence can produce some politically advantageous byproducts.

Insisting that the Pentagon hedge its bets on a new generation of high-tech arms, the committee added to the bill funds to keep open weapons production lines the Pentagon wanted to shut down.

"The threats we face are real, but they are not such that we must rush to produce next-generation systems," the committee said. "Cost-effectiveness and technological maturity should not be sacrificed in the post-Cold War world."

The only new weapon for which the committee made a significant cut for fiscal 1992 was the B-2 stealth bomber, for which it denied the entire $3.2 billion production request.

By contrast, the committee bill backed the billions of dollars requested to develop the F-22 fighter plane for the Air Force, the A-X bomber for the Navy, and the Comanche armed helicopter and several armored combat vehicles for the Army.

But in each case, the committee coupled its approval with an admonition: With the decline of the Soviet threat, it said, the Pentagon should pace development programs so that new weapons go into production only after they have been thoroughly tested.

The political payoff came on the other side of the committee's procurement equation: keeping in business several production lines, including those for the M-1 tank, the F-14 and F-16 fighter jets, the Army's scout helicopter, and the Patriot and Stinger anti-aircraft missiles.

Pending development of planned new weapons, the committee argued, it would be unwise to go for several years with no active production line for certain types of arms.

Moreover, in some cases — the M-1 tank, for example — the committee maintained that the Persian Gulf War had demonstrated that thousands of weapons needed extensive upgrading. Each such add-on could save jobs in the district of one or more House members, broadening the bipartisan coalition that Armed Services Chairman Les Aspin, D-Wis., was lining up behind the bill.

In only one case did the committee try to force a major new weapons program on the Pentagon: the V-22 troop-carrying aircraft, vigorously promoted by the Marine Corps and the congressional delegations from Pennsylvania and Texas, where it would be built.

Cheney had tried to kill this program since 1989 on the grounds that it was too expensive.

As had been customary for years in the House, the cost of added conventional arms was to be paid for by stripping funds out of the budget request for strategic weapons — this time, the B-2 and the Strategic Defense Initiative (SDI) anti-missile research program.

President Bush and other supporters had hoped that both programs would gain political momentum from the highly touted performance in the gulf war of two similar systems: F-117 stealth planes that bombed Iraq and Patriot missiles that were used in the effort to intercept Iraqi Scud missiles.

Against vigorous lobbying by Bush, Cheney, top Air Force commanders and the Northrop Corp., Aspin held the committee in line to reject building B-2 bombers beyond the 15 planes previously funded.

The bill included the $1.56 billion requested to continue developing the B-2 but none of the $3.2 billion that was sought to buy four planes in fiscal 1992 plus spare parts and components that would be used in the future to build aircraft.

The only test of strength came May 7, when the panel's Procurement Subcommittee voted 4-15 against a motion to build more B-2s.

For anti-missile defense research, viewed by many conservative activists as a touchstone of President Ronald Reagan's defense legacy, the committee sliced the budget request by nearly one-third. Beyond approving only $3.54 billion of the $5.17 billion requested, the panel demanded a substantial shift in the program's focus.

It knocked out the entire $1.61 billion requested for the conservatives' priority within the anti-missile program: developing by the end of the decade a so-called Phase I defense. Such a rudimentary space-based defense system would be intended to fend off a few hundred long-range missile warheads, such as might be launched at the United States by a renegade military commander.

An effort to restore the cut was rejected on a party-line vote of 18-25.

By contrast, the House panel approved the entire $883 million requested to develop defenses against shorter-range missiles, such as the Scuds fired by Iraq during the Persian Gulf War. But the committee bill put this "anti-tactical missile" program under control of the Army, rather than the SDI office created by Reagan in 1983 to develop a long-range missile defense.

Three projects absorbed most of the money Aspin cut from the B-2 and SDI. Compared with the amounts requested in the budget, the Armed Services Committee bill added:

- $1.07 billion for Guard and reserve forces. Of this amount, $650 million was to buy new equipment. The remainder was set aside to cover the cost of keeping on the rolls more Guard and reserve members than the Pentagon requested. The president's budget called for reducing Guard and reserve strength by more than 107,000 to a total of 1.07 million, but the committee approved a cut of fewer than 38,000.
- $625 million — plus $365 million of unspent funds from prior budgets — to continue development of the V-22 Osprey, the troop-carrying aircraft designed to take off like a helicopter and fly like an airplane.
- $896 million to rebuild a dozen 1970s-vintage F-14 Navy fighter planes as F-14Ds, with more powerful engines and radars. The add-on would have kept in the airplane manufacturing business the Long Island-based Grumman Corp., which supplied the Navy with combat planes since the 1930s.

The Armed Services Committee also approved by voice vote on May 8 the amendment to remove the statutory ban on female combat pilots in the Air Force and Navy.

Bipartisan Support

What was striking was the whopping, bipartisan majority that Aspin lined up for the bill, with its shift of funds from strategic to conventional weapons.

Only five of the committee's 22 Republicans voted "nay," as did liberal Democrat Ronald V. Dellums of California.

Bill Dickinson of Alabama, the panel's senior Republican, who criticized the prior year's committee bill as a Democratic porkfest, gave this year's a passing grade of "C."

"Policy and harsh fiscal realities drove most of the cuts in the bill," said Dickinson, who voted for it.

Even taking into account the enthusiastic constituency behind each program for which the committee authorized more money than the Pentagon requested, the breadth of GOP support was striking.

Aspin, with his growing mastery of the art of the committee chairman, made the cuts happen. In particular, he invested an enormous amount of personal political capital to fight the B-2.

Supporters of the plane, such as Ike Skelton, D-Mo., said some of that capital was green. "The money was spread out like butter" to fund members' favored projects, Skelton said.

And the hardball got rough a few times. Albert G. Bustamante, D-Texas, a B-2 supporter, bitterly complained that Aspin had refused to include in the bill a few small planes built in his district. "They can't understand principle," Bustamante said of Aspin and his staff, "so they're going to treat me like a little boy and take the candy away."

Bustamante strongly backed Aspin's bid for the committee chairmanship in 1985. "How I regret that vote," the Texan said.

But by several accounts, most of Aspin's leverage with committee members had a much more subtle — and much more resilient — basis. Backed by counselor Larry K. Smith and other veteran political operatives on the committee staff, Aspin appeared to have forged a genuine esprit de corps in his once fractious panel.

The committee's resources were at the disposal of a member who needed a little clout to get an access road to a military base or a disaster loan for small businesses near a base whose troops were suddenly shipped to the Persian Gulf. "It's equivalent to what members do for constituents in casework," one committee source said.

HOUSE FLOOR ACTION

Republicans had hoped that the victory over Iraq would boost President Bush's leverage in the annual congressional defense debate. But a laurel wreath does not necessarily come equipped with political clout, judging by the $291 billion defense authorization bill that the House passed May 22.

HR 2100 was approved by a vote of 268-161 despite a threatened veto over the bill's cuts in funding for the B-2 bomber and the Strategic Defense Initiative and its failure to cut the National Guard and reserves as deeply as the administration wanted. *(Vote 110, p. 28-H)*

The committee's approach would be more prudent from a military standpoint, said Aspin, complaining that Cheney's budget would strip the country of any capacity to build certain types of weapons for years, pending the development of new designs.

But Aspin's bill also locked in the support of members whose constituents would keep their jobs because the House bill kept alive the weapons they made.

The power of that ironclad political logic was demonstrated May 21, when House GOP leader Robert H. Michel, Ill., offered an amendment that would have wiped out Aspin's changes, restoring Cheney's budget request.

Michel and other Republicans invoked the popularity not only of Cheney but also of Joint Chiefs of Staff Chairman Powell and gulf war chieftain Gen. H. Norman Schwarzkopf. The Republicans cast the issue as a choice between a budget prepared by the heroic victors of Operation Desert Storm and one cobbled together by political opportunists on Capitol Hill.

"We are good critics of the strategies of others and we are expert protectors of our own interests," said Dickinson, the senior Armed Services Republican. "We are not, however, military planners."

Condemning Aspin's bill as the product of pork-barrel tradeoffs, Armed Services Republican Jon Kyl, Ariz., said, "Members are asked, 'What do you want?' It is all added up and ... [the funds] taken from programs like SDI and B-2, and then you have a bill."

But Aspin countered that Cheney's original budget had been drawn up before the gulf war and thus reflected none of that conflict's lessons. "If we go back and vote for the Cheney budget, it is as if Desert Storm never happened," he said.

Aspin also pointed out that the committee had funded several other stealth aircraft, though not the B-2, and that it supported anti-missile defense work, except for the space-based weapons that Republicans favored. Michel's amendment was rejected 127-287, with more than 20 percent of the voting Republicans bucking their leader. *(Vote 99, p. 24-H)*

The 37 Republicans who opposed the Michel amendment included:

- All six Republicans from New Jersey, which would have been hit especially hard by Cheney's planned cuts in the Guard and reserve.
- Five from New York, where Aspin's bill kept open the Long Island-based F-14 production line.
- Four from Pennsylvania, home of one of two contractors for the V-22 Osprey, which Aspin's bill saved from Cheney's ax.

Republican leaders did a little better when they tried to round up votes against final passage: Only 26 Republicans voted "yea." Although Bush's postwar popularity remained high, just 22 Democrats backed the GOP position and opposed the bill.

SDI Skirmishes

If the House bill underscored the political weakness of those who shared the administration's goals for SDI, an amendment by Ronald V. Dellums, D-Calif., highlighted the weakness of those who opposed any effort to deploy a large-scale anti-missile system.

Dellums' amendment, rejected 118-266, would have reduced from $2.7 billion to $1.1 billion the authorization for research on defenses against long-range missiles. It also would have limited such research to laboratory efforts and would have disbanded the SDI program office. *(Vote 97, p. 24-H)*

The amendment would not have affected the bill's separate authorization of $882 million to develop defenses against tactical missiles.

Dividing essentially along party lines, the House also rejected, 161-265, an amendment by SDI proponent Duncan Hunter, R-Calif., to require that the anti-tactical missile program develop only weapons that could intercept several types of modern, long-range ballistic missiles in service or under development in various Third World countries. *(Vote 105, p. 26-H)*

Hunter's opponents suspected that the amendment was intended to preserve the more ambitious goals for SDI by de-emphasizing development of defenses against short-range missiles, which are far more numerous.

Submarines and Jobs

In its most direct confrontation with the dilemmas of downsizing the defense establishment, the House voted, 235-157, to eliminate from the bill a provision to summarily award to Newport News Shipbuilding & Drydock, in Virginia, the contract to build a *Seawolf*-class nuclear submarine authorized by the bill. *(Vote 98, p. 24-H)*

The ship was planned as the third of its class. The first two such subs were being built by the Electric Boat Division of General Dynamics, in Groton, Conn., which underbid the Virginia firm for each contract.

The provision to guarantee a sub contract for Newport News was added by the Armed Services Committee at the behest of its three members from Virginia. Their rationale was that the Virginia yard would stop bidding on the subs if it lost the job, thus giving Electric Boat a monopoly on submarine construction.

The committee provision had stipulated that the Navy would pay the Virginia firm for the third sub the same amount it had paid the Connecticut firm for the second ship, plus an increase for inflation.

The floor amendment to delete the provision was offered by Sam Gejdenson, D-Conn., who represented Groton. "Common decency says let us get a bid in there," he said. "Let the Defense Department decide whether they want two shipyards or one." Under existing law, the Pentagon had discretion to award a contract to the higher of two bidders for the sake of maintaining a competitive production base.

But Herbert H. Bateman, R-Va., of Newport News denounced Gejdenson's amendment as having "an 'Alice in Wonderland' quality. ... It is touted as being pro-competition, when the underlying reality is to foreclose competition and to confer upon Electric Boat a sole-source position."

Burden-Sharing Votes

Laying the groundwork for future efforts to cut Pentagon spending, liberal Democrats offered amendments to the defense bill on May 22 to make U.S. allies pay a larger share of mutual defense costs.

In the short run, their victories were largely symbolic: The most far-reaching of the amendments adopted was purely advisory, calling for a large reduction in U.S. forces in Europe. And the House rejected by large majorities binding proposals to slice $8 billion from the fiscal 1992 defense budget and to reduce deployments in South Korea.

For more than a decade, resentment had festered on Capitol Hill over the belief that the United States shouldered far too much of the cost of collective defense, permitting economic dynamos such as Japan and Germany to pour money instead into extending their competitive edge.

Democratic burden-sharing advocates — including Patricia Schroeder, Colo.; Byron L. Dorgan, N.D.; and Charles E. Schumer, N.Y. — bet that the issue could fuel a long-term effort to pare back U.S. military spending.

"We don't mind doing our fair part," said Schroeder, "but we think that the times have changed."

These critics argued that the dominant U.S. share of total defense spending by NATO members and Japan was a relic of an earlier era, when only the United States could mount a plausible defense against a potential Soviet attack.

"Every dollar that we spend on a troop in Japan — that is not spent on educating our children, on building our infrastructure or improving the health of our citizens or improving the kind of factories that we have — is one dollar lost in our economic battle to stay No. 1," said Schumer.

But Dickinson accused the Democrats of "thinly disguised efforts to bash our allies and force a return to 'Fortress America.' " Their real aim, some Republicans argued, was not to share the burden of leadership but to shed it.

And some members rejected the premise that U.S. deployments abroad were for the sake of the host countries. "We have troops abroad, not as a favor to anybody in the world, but . . . to protect our interests as well as those of our allies," said Henry J. Hyde, R-Ill. "We have troops in Japan because we would just as soon not have Japan join the nuclear club."

The House adopted three burden-sharing amendments:

- By Schroeder, expressing the sense of Congress that no more than 100,000 U.S. military personnel should be stationed in Europe by fiscal 1995. The fiscal 1991 defense authorization bill reduced to 262,000 the statutory ceiling on U.S. troops in Europe, and Gen. John Galvin, the U.S. commander in Europe, had called for slicing at least 100,000 from that number by 1995. Adopted 260-193. *(Vote 100, p. 24-H)*
- By Dorgan, requiring the president to try to negotiate within six months of the bill's enactment a defense cost-sharing agreement with each U.S. military ally. The president would have to report to Congress every six months on his progress toward that goal. Adopted 357-58. *(Vote 102, p. 26-H)*
- By John Bryant, D-Texas, cutting by three-quarters by 1995 the 76,500 foreign nationals working at overseas U.S. bases whose salaries are paid by the United States. The amendment was intended to force the host governments to pay the salaries. Adopted by voice vote.

The House rejected two amendments:

- By Barney Frank, D-Mass., that would have reduced by $8 billion the amount that could be spent in fiscal 1992 to deploy U.S. forces in Europe, Japan or Korea. Rejected 167-255. *(Vote 101, p. 26-H)*
- By Robert J. Mrazek, D-N.Y., that would have reduced to 30,000 the number of U.S. personnel deployed in South Korea by 1995. By that date, the Bush administration planned to reduce personnel in South Korea to 36,000. Rejected 143-275. *(Vote 103, p. 26-H)*

Other Amendments

By a vote of 109-317, the House rejected an amendment by Frank to drop from the bill $549 million to develop a small intercontinental ballistic missile (ICBM), nicknamed Midgetman. *(Vote 106, p. 26-H)*

The House also rejected two amendments by Gerald B. H. Solomon, R-N.Y., that would have mandated drug testing of civilian Pentagon employees: An amendment requiring random drug testing of all Defense Department employees was rejected 157-269; one requiring tests of all prospective employees was rejected 197-231. *(Votes 107, 108, p. 26-H)*

Neither amendment would have affected military personnel, who are subject to random drug tests as a matter of Pentagon policy.

A non-binding amendment urging the president to negotiate a ban on underground nuclear test explosions was agreed to by voice vote.

Also by voice vote, the House agreed to an omnibus amendment by Aspin, which incorporated 20 non-controversial amendments offered by other members.

SENATE COMMITTEE ACTION

The Senate Armed Services Committee approved its version of the defense authorization bill (S 1507) on July 17.

The unanimous vote belied the fierce and intricate negotiations that were required to develop the committee bill's most significant feature — a long-term plan for the controversial SDI.

The committee's plan for changes in the anti-missile program amounted to a fundamental shift in U.S. policy. *(SDI, p. 407)*

By a vote of 16-4, the panel included the $4.6 billion SDI package in the bill.

It called for deployment by 1996 of an anti-missile defense that would comply with the 1972 U.S.-Soviet treaty that limited anti-ballistic missile (ABM) defenses. The treaty permitted deployment of 100 ground-based interceptor missiles at a single base.

At least as important, the committee backed an effort to liberalize the ABM treaty to allow deployment of a much more extensive anti-missile system that would be aimed at blocking "limited" attacks by a relatively small number of missiles, such as might be launched by a Third World country or a renegade military unit.

Unlike the House, the Senate committee voted to approve President Bush's request for $3.2 billion to continue production of the B-2 stealth bomber.

Several conservative Republicans surprised colleagues by supporting an effort by William S. Cohen, R-Maine, to end production of the B-2.

The conservatives were apparently attempting to signal their suspicion that the administration was not fighting hard enough for the SDI program's space-based interceptors, known as Brilliant Pebbles. Cohen's anti-B-2 motion was rejected by a vote of 8-11.

Armed Services Committee Chairman Sam Nunn, D-Ga., a vigorous B-2 proponent, warned that the plane faced an uphill battle. "We've got a 50-50 chance of saving it in the Senate if the president goes to work on the Republicans," he said.

Other Highlights

In other provisions of its bill, the Senate committee proposed a 15-member presidential commission to study the question of women in combat, sidestepping the House bill's provision to repeal laws that banned women from serving as combat pilots.

Rejecting the administration's decision to end production of the MX ICBM, the committee added to the bill $191 million for a dozen more of the 10-warhead missiles. By law, the Pentagon was permitted to deploy no more than the 50 MXs that were already in silos in Wyoming, so the additional missiles were slated for routine test launches.

The committee approved $245 million of the $260 million requested to develop a rail-mobile launcher for the MX but added a provision barring any test launch from the device.

The committee also agreed to authorize production of 49 Trident II submarine-launched missiles ($1.2 billion) instead of the 28 missiles requested ($977 million). The panel wanted to speed up the Trident II production rate to reduce the unit-cost.

The panel approved the amounts requested to develop the Midgetman single-warhead ICBM ($549 million) and an air-launched nuclear missile with a range of about 250 miles, designated SRAM-T ($34 million). The House bill called for canceling SRAM-T.

The committee approved the $401 million requested to develop tanks and armored combat vehicles for production. But it also added to the bill $225 million to modernize early production models of the Army's M-1 tank with the larger cannon and more sophisticated target-finding gear on later models.

The panel said it wanted to prevent the premature dispersal of critical engineering talent. For that reason, it increased the funding requested for several production lines, authorizing in its bill:

- $200 million for Bradley armored troop carriers;
- $165 million for launchers for the MLRS artillery rocket; and
- $200 million for 300 additional Patriot anti-aircraft missiles.

The panel's bill also authorized nearly $900 million for programs aimed at giving combat commanders readier access to tactical intelligence, a need that became clear during the Persian Gulf War.

Most of this amount ($653 million) was earmarked to buy two JSTARS radar planes, designed to track enemy columns far behind their own lines. An additional $25 million was to develop a more portable terminal with which ground commanders could receive JSTARS data. The remaining $194 million was for other projects, such as equipping Marine Corps F/A-18 jets for reconnaissance missions.

The committee dropped from the bill $1 billion requested to buy 48 F-16 fighters. But it added to the bill roughly the same amount to resume production of the F-117 stealth fighter, which played a prominent role dropping highly accurate "smart" bombs against Iraqi targets. The committee approved adding 24 F-117s to the 56 in service.

The panel also approved the $1.6 billion requested to continue developing the Air Force's new F-22 fighter.

Noting that the first prototype of the C-17 long-range cargo jet had not yet flown, the committee approved production of four of the planes ($1.52 billion) rather than the six requested ($1.98 billion).

The panel also added to the bill $550 million to modernize the ground combat equipment stored aboard so-called pre-positioning ships for use by U.S. forces in distant trouble spots.

The committee bill authorized the warships requested, with only minor funding reductions, approving a *Seawolf*-class nuclear submarine ($1.43 billion) and five *Arleigh Burke*-class destroyers ($4.11 billion).

The bill also illustrated the longstanding partnership between Nunn and John W. Warner of Virginia, the committee's ranking Republican. The bill reportedly was drafted with a provision intended to steer the submarine contract to Newport News Shipbuilding & Drydock, in Warner's state, though the Pentagon was strongly inclined to build the ships only at a General Dynamics shipyard in Connecticut.

When Edward M. Kennedy, D-Mass., moved to strike Warner's provision, the effort was defeated on a 10-10 vote: The "nays" were all nine committee Republicans and Nunn.

SENATE FLOOR ACTION

The Senate rejected challenges to deployment of a limited anti-missile defense system and to the B-2 stealth bomber as it passed the defense authorization bill for fiscal 1992 by voice vote on Aug. 2.

Both outcomes were victories for Nunn and Warner.

Senate approval of $3.2 billion to build four additional B-2s was a clear win for President Bush. And although Bush remained officially committed to his more ambitious version of SDI, administration officials indicated that they were very pleased with the modified $4.6 billion version of the anti-missile plan that was engineered by Nunn and Warner and included in the bill.

The companion bill passed by the House on May 22 (HR 2100) had included no funds for B-2 production and only $3.5 billion for a much more restricted SDI program.

The Senate Armed Services Committee leaders suffered their only dramatic defeat on July 31, the first of three days of debate on the bill, when they tried to stave off an amendment to repeal the statutory ban on assigning women in the Navy and Air Force to fly combat planes. An effort to kill the amendment was rejected 30-69. The amendment was then adopted by voice vote. *(Vote 167, p. 22-S)*

The Senate also adopted, 97-2, an amendment by Minority Leader Bob Dole, R-Kan., supporting the president if he decided to use force to eliminate Iraq's nuclear weapons-making capability. The only votes against the resolution were cast by Mark O. Hatfield, R-Ore., and Paul Wellstone, D-Minn. *(Vote 178, p. 24-S)*

And a threatened filibuster forced Tim Wirth, D-Colo., to withdraw an amendment that would have allowed female service members or military dependents stationed abroad to obtain privately funded abortions in local U.S. military hospitals. *(Abortion, p. 339)*

The Senate bill authorized $213 billion for defense-related programs, essentially the amount requested by Bush. Counting the $78 billion budget for military personnel costs, which were not covered by this bill, the Senate action provided for a defense budget in fiscal 1992 totaling $291 billion.

SDI Floor Votes

The deal on deployment of a limited SDI system was a delicate compromise, linking Democrats who favored relatively modest, ground-based defenses with Republicans who hoped this would be the first step toward a global network of orbiting anti-missile interceptor rockets.

Al Gore of Tennessee and Joseph R. Biden Jr. of Delaware were among several Democrats who tried to unhinge the committee compromise, arguing that it would shatter the ABM treaty between the United States and Soviet Union and might provoke a renewed buildup of Soviet nuclear missiles.

But the Senate rejected two amendments that challenged fundamental elements of the committee's anti-missile program. A third amendment, specifying that the bill did not authorize any ABM deployment not allowed by the treaty, was adopted 99-0, amid conflicting claims about its practical significance.

As most of the critics saw it, their best chance to undermine the Senate panel's SDI package before conference was to drive a wedge into the philosophical crevasse dividing most committee Democrats, who favored a modest change in the ABM treaty, from those Republicans who freely acknowledged their intention to use the limited deployment as an opening to deploy a global ABM system over the long run.

An amendment by Gore would have recast the committee package to emphasize deployment by the mid-1990s of ground-based defenses against short-range missiles such as the Iraqi Scuds. The amendment called for modifying the ABM treaty only as needed to clarify the distinctions between such anti-tactical missile defenses and defensive systems intended to fend off strategic missiles.

Gore's amendment was rejected 39-60. All but four Republicans and more than a third of the Democrats voted "nay." *(Vote 168, p. 22-S)*

Jeff Bingaman, D-N.M., took the second shot at diluting the SDI package engineered by Nunn. Bingaman and

Wirth, both members of the Armed Services panel, had supported the deal in the committee. But both wanted to water down the bill's implied threat to abrogate the ABM treaty if the Soviet Union refused to negotiate changes.

Bingaman's amendment would have declared that maintenance of "strategic stability" between Washington and Moscow was the overriding goal — and that deployment of a limited ABM defense would be subordinated to it. It also would have deleted all references to the treaty-compliant ABM deployment due by 1996 as an "initial" deployment.

Under Bingaman's approach, any U.S. anti-missile deployments beyond those allowed by the treaty would be subject to the Soviet government's eventually agreeing on treaty changes.

Many liberals balked at signing on even to the Bingaman amendment's acceptance of deploying anti-ballistic missiles at a single site.

Bingaman slightly modified his amendment in hopes of conciliating the liberals. A few, such as Patrick J. Leahy, D-Vt., voted against it. But Biden and most of the other liberals voted for it.

The amendment was rejected 43-56. Of 56 Democrats voting, 41 backed the amendment. Only two Republicans supported it. *(Vote 169, p. 23-S)*

Nunn's critics were counting on one more shot before the Senate approved the limited deployment scheme and sent it to conference with the House: an amendment by Carl Levin, D-Mich., declaring that nothing in the bill should be construed "to imply congressional authorization for development, testing or deployment" of a system violating the ABM treaty.

But Levin, too, had to water down his amendment in the hunt for support. Levin's floor amendment specified that any system "authorized" by the bill had to comply with the ABM treaty. Nunn reasoned that he could live with it because establishing a goal of going beyond the current treaty did not authorize anything.

Nunn and the conservatives accepted Levin's amendment, thus depriving Levin and his allies of a clear test of political strength.

The amendment was adopted 99-0. *(Vote 170, p. 23-S)*

The Senate also rejected three other SDI-related amendment:

- By Tom Harkin, D-Iowa, deleting the goal of deploying a treaty-compliant anti-missile system by 1996. Tabled (killed), 64-34. *(Vote 172, p. 23-S)*
- By Harkin, to reduce the authorization for SDI by $1.4 billion, to $3.2 billion. Tabled (killed), 60-38. *(Vote 171, p. 23-S)*
- By Dale Bumpers, D-Ark., to reduce the authorization for SDI by $1 billion, to $3.6 billion. Rejected 46-52. *(Vote 173, p. 23-S)*

B-2 Floor Action

B-2 opponents coalesced behind an amendment offered jointly by Leahy and Cohen. The amendment, which essentially matched the House position, would have deleted from the bill $3.2 billion to build four more bombers but have allowed completion of the 15 planes previously funded.

It was rejected 42-57. *(Vote 174, p. 23-S)*

Other Provisions

The Senate also acted on the following amendments to S 1507:

- By Jim Exon, D-Neb., to terminate production of the short-range, air-launched nuclear missile designated SRAM-T. The bill would authorize $92 million in fiscal 1992 to continue the $2 billion program. Tabled (killed), 51-47. *(Vote 176, p. 23-S)*
- By John B. Breaux, D-La., requiring that closed military bases be turned over to local communities that have suffered severe economic dislocation because of the closure, rather than allowing federal and state agencies priority in claiming the property. Adopted by voice vote after a motion to table was rejected, 30-67. *(Vote 175, p. 23-S; Base closings, p. 427)*
- By McCain, requiring the heads of federal agencies to disclose information concerning U.S. military personnel classified as prisoners of war (POWs) or as missing in action. Approved by voice vote.
- By Bingaman, requiring that tobacco products sold in post exchanges or military commissaries be sold at prices comparable to those at local commercial outlets. Because certain operating costs of those stores were subsidized by the Pentagon, they typically sold products at a discount. Tabled (killed), 55-43. *(Vote 179, p. 24-S)*
- By Howard M. Metzenbaum, D-Ohio, a non-binding expression of the sense of Congress that the Defense Department should begin planning to have no more than 100,000 U.S. military personnel stationed in Europe by the end of 1995. Adopted by voice vote.
- By Jim Exon, D-Neb., deleting from the bill the entire $225 million requested to conclude development of a rail-mobile launcher for the MX missile. Tabled (killed), 49-48. *(Vote 180, p. 24-S)*

FINAL ACTION

The House adopted the conference report on HR 2100, 329-82, on Nov. 18. The Senate cleared the measure, 79-15, on Nov. 22. *(House vote 400, p. 98-H; Senate vote 265, p. 35-S)*

No Cutback Instructions

The House on Sept. 16 turned back an initial effort by liberal Democrats to capitalize on the collapse of communist power in the Soviet Union.

The action came on a procedural question. By a 220-145 vote, the House closed debate on a non-binding motion to instruct conferees on the defense authorization bill to permanently extend certain benefits to Persian Gulf veterans. That prevented Massachusetts Democrat Frank from offering an instruction that conferees insist on lower House funding levels for strategic weapons programs such as the B-2 bomber.

For conventional weapons programs, Frank's amendment would have urged conferees to back the lower of the amounts authorized by the two chambers, "consistent with emerging national security needs."

The convoluted logic of the procedural vote, coupled with the low-profile lobbying by Frank and his allies, contributed to the poor showing. But one veteran arms control activist discerned a broader meaning. "There is not a huge, stomping majority to cut, cut, cut," said the lobbyist. "It's going to have to be done in an orderly fashion ... with careful arguments."

Conference Agreement

Conferees reached tentative agreement on a final version of HR 2100, the defense authorization measure, on Nov. 1.

They had spent three months ironing out more than 1,400 items in disagreement, according to Exon, who later called it the "most difficult" conference he could remember.

The conferees essentially adopted the Senate position by backing a limited deployment of SDI and authorizing $4.15 billion for it.

They reached a deal on the B-2 stealth bomber that permitted $1.6 billion for additional research and development of the B-2 bomber and $1.8 billion for parts and assembly. But their agreement barred production of any B-2s beyond the 15 previously authorized unless both chambers voted approval of an additional $1 billion to buy a single additional plane.

And the conferees agreed to drop the statutory ban on assigning women in the Navy and Air Force to fly combat aircraft.

The conferees struggled until Nov. 13 over a plan crafted by the Armed Services Committee chairmen, Rep. Aspin and Sen. Nunn, to authorize as much as $1 billion from the Pentagon budget to aid the disintegrating Soviet Union.

Eventually, Aspin and Nunn bowed to strong resistance in both parties and both chambers and removed the Soviet aid plan. A stripped-down, $500 million version was later passed as separate legislation. *(Soviet aid, p. 463)*

Once the disputed Soviet proposal was dropped from the defense bill, the conferees agreed to drop the other emotional issue that could have been an obstacle to final approval of the bill or would have prompted a veto: They eliminated a House provision to allow service personnel or their dependents stationed abroad to obtain abortions in U.S. military hospitals, provided the procedure was paid for privately.

Republican Warner told reporters, "This conference report reflects the basic goals and objectives of the president."

The conference agreement provided most of what the administration requested for major weapons programs. But it also provided funds for programs not requested by the Pentagon, including: $225 million to convert early-model M-1 tanks to the new M-1A2 model; $274 million to equip an additional 24 scout helicopters with sophisticated target-finding equipment; $625 million to move toward full-scale production of the V-22 Osprey, the hybrid airplane/helicopter that the Marine Corps wanted to use as a troop carrier; and $560 million to resume production of the F-117, a small stealth bomber.

While approving a proposed cut of 106,000 from the services' active-duty rosters, the bill approved a reduction of fewer than 38,000 from the rolls of National Guard and military reserve units. The administration had proposed a Guard and reserve cutback nearly three times that size and strongly criticized Congress' reluctance to cut deeper.

The Measure Clears

As the House and Senate voted final approval of HR 2100, members laid the rhetorical groundwork for the battles they expected in 1992 over deeper cuts in the defense budget.

"There are a lot of people lusting after this $300 billion defense budget," Armed Services Chairman Aspin said in House floor debate on Nov. 18. "There are a lot of people here who are interested in getting some money out of this defense budget in the future for U.S. domestic purposes here at home."

Rep. Bernard Sanders of Vermont, an independent socialist, made the rhetorical case to cut more from defense as he opposed the authorization measure: "On behalf of 5 million children who are hungry, on behalf of 9 million American workers who are unemployed, on behalf of 2 million homeless Americans . . . I ask that we reject this grossly inflated military budget and use the savings to reinvest in America and to protect the interests of our people."

But others warned that lawmakers were cutting the budget "too far, too fast," as Sen. Robert C. Smith, R-N.H., argued during the Senate debate. "Hopefully, future Congresses will oppose further pillaging of the defense budget."

Bush signed the bill (PL 102-190) on Dec. 5. ■

Provisions of Defense Bill

HR 2100 (PL 102-190) authorized $291 billion in defense spending for fiscal 1992. Following are the bill's major provisions, including comparisons with President Bush's budget request and with the versions of the bill passed by the House and Senate. As enacted, the legislation:

Strategic and Nuclear Arms

- Authorized $1.6 billion for additional research and development of the B-2 stealth bomber and $1.8 billion for parts and supplies. No bombers beyond the 15 previously authorized would be permitted unless the Pentagon certified that the plane's problems had been solved and both chambers of Congress voted approval of an additional $1 billion for a 16th plane.

Bush requested $4.8 billion to continue development and build four more B-2s. The Senate approved the request, but the House opposed any further production.

- Approved spending $4.15 billion on a limited version of the Strategic Defense Initiative (SDI). An initial, ground-based defense would be installed in Grand Forks, S.D., by 1996. Negotiations would be sought to amend the Anti-ballistic Missile Treaty of 1972 to permit additional deployments. The administration would be permitted to spend $390 million on research into space-based Brilliant Pebbles missile interceptors.

The administration sought $5.2 billion for SDI, including $690 million for Brilliant Pebbles. The House approved $3.5 billion, with no funds for Brilliant Pebbles and no support for short-term deployment of anti-missile defenses. The Senate forged the basic outline of the deal accepted by the conferees.

- Authorized $203 million to beef up the B-1 bomber fleet, including $116 million for safety modifications to the 97 planes, $20 million to upgrade their radar-jamming equipment and $67 million for miscellaneous support equipment.

The administration request for B-1 equipment totaled $304 million, and the House more than doubled that to $642 million. The increase included $40 million to equip the planes for conventional bombing missions and $298 million to improve the radar jammers. But the Senate, reflecting the low opinion of the B-1 held by Armed Services Committee Chairman Sam Nunn, D-Ga., approved only the $116 million requested for safety modifications.

- Acted on nuclear weapons cutbacks that Bush announced Sept. 27 by eliminating funds that had been requested earlier in the year for two supersonic, air-launched missiles: $177 million to gear up for production of the SRAM II, to be carried by bombers, and $61 million to develop a variant designated SRAM-T, to be carried by smaller planes.

• Authorized $610 million, the amount requested and approved by both chambers, to continue development and production of a stealthy, bomber-launched cruise missile with a range of nearly 2,000 miles. The funds were to buy 120 missiles in fiscal 1992 and components to be used in the 102 missiles slated for inclusion in the fiscal 1993 budget.

• Authorized $587 million to continue equipping with more powerful engines the fleet of KC-135s, 1960s-vintage midair refueling tankers that the Air Force planned to fly for another three decades. The budget request included $465 million; the House approved $630 million, and the Senate $427 million.

• Eliminated the $260 million requested to develop a rail-mobile launcher for the 10-warhead MX intercontinental ballistic missile (ICBM) because it was another of the programs marked for extinction in Bush's nuclear arms reduction announcement in September. However, the conferees added $252 million to buy five more MX missiles, which were intended for test launches during the years the Air Force expected to keep 50 of the weapons deployed in underground silos. The budget request included $195 million to shut down the MX production line.

• Challenged Bush's decision to cancel development of a road-mobile launcher for the smaller, single-warhead Midgetman missile. Both chambers had approved the $549 million requested for the program, including $115 million earmarked to continue work on the mobile launcher. The conferees appended a provision to bar use of the mobile launcher money until the Pentagon certified to Congress that future requests would include enough funds to retain the option of deploying the missiles on mobile launchers.

• Ordered the Defense secretary to report on the cost and feasibility of keeping in service beyond the year 2020 the silo-based Minuteman III missile, which the Midgetman had been slated to replace.

• Authorized $1.3 billion for 49 Trident II submarine-launched missiles. This followed the approach of the Senate rather than the administration and the House, which sought $977 million for 28 missiles.

• Authorized the $65 million requested to develop an anti-satellite missile. Both chambers had supported the request. The conferees added a provision to bar for one year tests of a large experimental laser as an anti-satellite weapon. The House had banned such laser tests for two years.

Ground Combat

• Authorized $90 million to build 60 new "A2" versions of the M-1 tank, as well as $225 million to modernize older M-1s. This was intended to keep a tank production line intact for several years.

The conference report provided that, if the Army canceled production of the A2 model, older tanks — which carry a 105mm cannon — would be upgraded to M-1A1s, carrying a 120mm gun. But if A2 production began as planned, the tanks would be converted to that model, carrying both the larger gun and more sophisticated electronic equipment for fighting at night.

Conferees also added to the budget $55 million to complete development of the A2 model.

• Agreed to $161 million of the $183 million requested for heavy-duty trucks to haul tanks long distances at high speeds. The Senate had wanted the Pentagon to fund this from the allied contributions toward U.S. costs of the Persian Gulf War, arguing that hundreds of tank haulers had been worn out in that campaign.

• Authorized the Senate-approved $110 million — $75 million less than requested — to beef up armor on the newest model of Bradley troop carriers. The House had approved the requested funds, plus $150 million to begin upgrading older-model Bradleys.

• Added $21 million to the administration's request, for an authorization of $422 million, to develop a "family" of armored combat vehicles for the next century — a tank, troop carrier and other vehicles that would use common automotive components. Of that amount, $62 million was earmarked for a new mobile artillery piece.

Because Iraq and several other countries had mobile guns with longer ranges than U.S. models, both Armed Services committees wanted a new mobile gun developed before work began on a new tank (designated Block III) that the Army had made its top priority within the family of vehicles.

• Authorized $151 million to buy 300 ATACMS bombardment rockets with a range of 60 miles. That was the amount requested and approved by both houses.

• Expanded the administration's plans for 20-mile-range MLRS rockets and launchers. The conferees authorized $196 million to buy them for the Army and an additional $95 million to outfit the Marine Corps with them. The administration had requested $181 million to buy MLRS launchers for the Army only.

• Backed accelerated production of the JSTARS radar surveillance plane, following the Senate's lead. The plane was designed to locate ground targets more than 100 miles behind enemy lines.

In addition to the $312 million approved by both chambers to continue developing the plane, the conferees wrote into the bill $125 million for components that could be used in two JSTARS to be bought in fiscal 1993. The administration requested components for only one. The conference report also added $25 million to develop a lighter-weight ground terminal to receive JSTARS data.

But the conferees turned down a Senate proposal to buy two JSTARS planes outright with allied contributions from the gulf war.

• Authorized $120 million to continue developing the Javelin, a one-man anti-tank missile (formerly designated AAWS-M). The administration requested $49 million for development and $71 million to prepare for production, but the House put all the money into development, citing difficulties in perfecting the weapon's infrared guidance system. For the same reason, the Senate approved only the $49 million requested for development.

Conferees ordered the Army to report anticipated increases in the program's cost and to declare a ceiling cost above which the program would not be worthwhile.

• Authorized the $152 million requested — and backed by both the House and Senate — to develop the LOSAT tank-hunting vehicle, armed with large, high-speed, guided rockets intended to punch through the heaviest tank armor with brute force.

• Included $233 million, which had been approved by both the House and Senate, to develop a much improved Longbow model of the Apache anti-tank helicopter, equipped with a target-finding radar and a more powerful engine.

But both chambers had objected to the Army's plan to first modify some Apaches to a modestly improved "B" model. Conferees authorized the $83 million requested to begin the "B" model modifications, including improved navigation equipment and Stinger anti-aircraft missiles. However, they added to the bill $32 million to develop a "C" model that would have all the features of the Longbow model except the radar and the new engines.

• Authorized the $550 million requested to continue to develop the Comanche (formerly LH) missile-armed scout helicopter and the $183 million requested to arm existing Kiowa scout helicopters with missiles. Both requests had been approved by both chambers.

But the conferees added $135 million to modify 24 more armed Kiowas.

• Added $20 million to the $9 million requested to develop equipment to thwart land mines.

Tactical Air Combat

• Authorized the $1.6 billion requested to develop the Air Force's F-22 fighter (formerly ATF), which had been approved by both chambers. Conferees added a House-passed provision stipulating that the Air Force should verify that the plane could easily be mass produced.

• Provided for the $1.1 billion requested to buy 48 F-16 fighters for the Air Force.

The administration had planned to close out its F-16 purchases with 24 aircraft in 1993, but the House bill called for buying 48 more planes in each of the succeeding two fiscal years. The plane was built by General Dynamics Corp. in Fort Worth, and members of the Texas House delegation lobbied strongly for the House language.

The Senate, contending that the 1,100 F-16s already funded were adequate for the Air Force's declining size, had approved only $78 million to shut down the production line.

• Authorized $560 million to buy four new Air Force F-117s, plus $83 million to modify the existing fleet. The F-117 was a small stealth fighter that won popular attention through its performance in the Persian Gulf War.

The administration had not sought to revive F-117 production, which had been shut down in 1989. The House added to the bill $83 million to begin updating the 56 existing F-117s and $140 million to develop further F-117 improvements.

But the Senate added to the bill $1 billion to resume F-117 production.

Ultimately, renewed production of the F-117 was blocked because no funds for the plane were included in the defense appropriations bill. *(Appropriations, p. 621)*

- Authorized $173 million, as requested, to shut down the production line for the Navy's F-14 carrier-based fighters.

The conferees rejected House provisions that would have added $680 million to begin converting existing F-14s to an improved "D" model. Also rejected was a separate House provision adding $50 million to adapt the F-14D to attack ground targets.

- Approved, as requested, $2.1 billion for Navy 48 F/A-18s.
- Boosted by $20 million the $452 million authorization requested to develop improvements in the F/A-18, with most of the funds earmarked for new "E" and "F" models, with longer range and larger payloads.
- Backed the start of work on developing a carrier-based bomber designated AX, earmarking $167 million authorized in prior years. Those funds initially had been provided to develop the A-12 naval bomber, which the Pentagon had canceled in January.
- Authorized buying 891 AMRAAM air-to-air missiles for Navy and Air Force fighters but only $740 million for the purchase, $120 million less than requested.
- Dropped a House initiative to continue building an air-launched version of the 60-mile-range Harpoon missile ($175 million) and to develop an improved version of that weapon ($100 million).

Naval Combat

- Cut only $55 million from the administration request, authorizing $4.2 billion to buy five *Arleigh Burke*-class destroyers equipped with the Aegis anti-aircraft system.
- Endorsed the $415 million requested to buy 525 Standard anti-aircraft missiles and the $506 million requested to buy 236 new long-range Tomahawk cruise missiles and to modernize 401 Tomahawks. Both chambers had approved those amounts.
- Authorized using $105 million appropriated in fiscal 1991 to begin overhauling the aircraft carrier *John F. Kennedy* at the Philadelphia Naval Shipyard late in 1993. The money originally was set aside for a more extensive reconstruction.

Even with the less ambitious overhaul plans, an additional $386 million was expected to be spent in later years. The carrier renovation was expected to be the last major project at the Philadelphia yard, which was earmarked for closure.

- Authorized $1.8 billion for the third *Seawolf*-class nuclear submarine in addition to $425 million to continue developing the design and $376 million for components that would be used in additional ships.

Members of both chambers had sparred over provisions intended to steer the contract for the new sub to one of two competing shipyards in Connecticut and Virginia. But the conference report was silent on the issue.

- Endorsed the request for $229 million to develop long-range submarine detection equipment. But the conferees added to the bill $20 million to develop a more portable sub detection system that could quickly be deployed to a trouble spot.
- Authorized a naval minesweeping program nearly half again as large as requested, including:

— $361 million for three *Osprey*-class minesweepers, as recommended by the Senate, one ship ($130 million) more than requested.

— $129 million for four minesweeping helicopters, the amount requested.

— $14 million to continue developing the Magic Lantern program, using a helicopter-borne laser to find submerged mines; the budget request included no funds.

— $20 million more than the $18 million requested for anti-mine research.

- Subtracted $40 million from the $540 million requested for a high-speed supply ship to replenish a carrier and its escort ships midocean.

Air and Sea Transport

- The conferees approved $1.53 billion for four C-17 wide-body cargo planes, $122 million to buy components for eight planes in fiscal 1993 and the full $377 million requested to continue a testing program. But no more than $400 million of the procurement funds could be spent until the Pentagon sent Congress a report on problems that had delayed tests of the plane.

The administration had requested $2.6 billion for the C-17, which was designed to land tanks and other heavy gear on primitive airstrips. That included $2 billion for six planes, $224 million for components to be used in 12 C-17s slated for inclusion in the fiscal 1993 budget and $377 million to continue developing the aircraft. Both chambers sought to slow the planned production rate because of the plane's problems.

- Authorized the amounts requested and voted by both chambers for the Army's two largest transport helicopter programs:

— $508 million to continue production of Blackhawk troop carriers.

— $257 million to conclude an 11-year program of modernizing 472 Chinooks, used to haul artillery pieces, ammunition and other cargo around the battlefield.

- Authorized an LSD-class amphibious landing ship ($245 million) and a dozen air-cushion landing barges ($289 million), as requested and approved by both chambers.
- Authorized $625 million in new funds, plus $365 million appropriated but not spent in prior years, to build three additional V-22 Ospreys, a hybrid airplane/helicopter designed as a troop carrier for the Marine Corps.

As in each year since 1989, Defense Secretary Dick Cheney tried to cancel development of the Osprey. But once again, the effort was thwarted by the Marines, their many congressional supporters and members of Congress from Pennsylvania and Texas, where the program's principal contractors were located. The conferees followed the House's lead in backing the Osprey.

- Authorized 20 large CH-53E helicopters, used by the Navy and Marine Corps to carry cargo and troops.

Military Personnel

- Approved the administration's proposal to reduce the ceiling on active-duty military personnel to 1.88 million members, a cut of more than 106,000. Both chambers had backed the cuts.
- Backed the 4.2 percent military pay raise recommended by the administration.
- Endorsed an increase from $110 to $150 in the monthly bonus paid to personnel stationed in places where they were deemed to be in "imminent danger."
- Backed an increase from $60 to $75 in the monthly bonus paid to married personnel assigned to posts where they could not be accompanied by their families.
- Approved two alternative severance packages intended to encourage career-minded members to leave the service in an era of declining military personnel, thereby minimizing the number who would have to be involuntarily dismissed to meet that timetable. Personnel leaving voluntarily before the 20 years of service required to qualify for a military pension could choose:

— A lump-sum payment equal to 15 percent of their basic annual pay times their number of years in service, or

— An annuity equal to 2.5 percent of their basic pay times their number of years of service, to be paid for twice the number of years served.

- The conferees agreed on a roster for the National Guard and reserves of 1.15 million, reducing manpower by 37,580 rather than by the more than 105,000 proposed. (The companion appropriations measure later gave the Defense secretary discretion to cut about 23,000 more personnel.)

Both chambers had trimmed the administration's proposed cutback in National Guard and reserve manpower.

- Approved adding $1.04 billion to the budget for equipment earmarked for Guard and reserve units.
- Established an independent commission to recommend how to

distribute missions between active-duty units and their counterparts in the Guard and reserves.

- Repealed 1948 laws that banned the assignment to combat air crews of women in the Navy and Air Force. Both chambers had adopted such language, which did not eliminate the discretion of the armed services to maintain the ban.

In addition, the conferees accepted a Senate provision to establish a presidential commission to study how the assignment of women to additional combat roles might affect combat readiness. The commission was to report to the president by Nov. 15, 1992, and he was to report his recommendations to Congress by Dec. 15.

Construction, Closings

- Made minor adjustments in the base-closing review process, which targeted installations in 1991 and was to be repeated in 1993 and 1995. The changes:

— Required the president to submit in January 1993 and 1995 a complete list of his nominees to each year's base-closing commission, who would be subject to Senate confirmation.

— Extended by one month the commissions' review of the Pentagon's list of bases recommended for closure.

— Required the commissions to hold public hearings before adding to their lists any installations not recommended by the Pentagon.

- Opposed any funds for construction at bases slated for closure on the 1991 list.
- Rejected a Senate provision that would have given local communities first crack at taking over closed bases without paying for them. Existing law gave other federal agencies the right of first refusal and allowed the Pentagon to sell the surplus property.
- Authorized $297 million, $197 million more than the administration's request, to clean up toxic and hazardous waste on bases in the 1991 list of bases to be closed. For hazardous waste cleanup at other bases, the conferees authorized $1.18 billion, $69 million less than requested.
- Backed only $225 million of the $359 million requested for the annual U.S. contribution to NATO's Infrastructure Fund, the alliance's kitty for construction projects of mutual benefit. It also included a House provision barring the use of any funds to transfer a U.S. fighter wing or associated activities to a new NATO base at Crotone, Italy.
- Authorized $100 million less than the $2.7 billion requested to pay foreign nationals employed on U.S. bases abroad.

Other Provisions

- Accepted a Senate provision to require the Pentagon to open its files on U.S. military personnel counted as prisoners of war or missing in action in the Vietnam War.
- Authorized buying 19 combat planes, 18 M-1 tanks, 300 Patriot anti-aircraft missiles, 14 helicopters and 794 trucks using funds contributed by allied countries to cover the cost of the Persian Gulf War. The purchases were intended to replace equipment lost or used up in the war. ■

B-2 Stayed Alive but On Hold

Already on shaky political ground because of its cost, the B-2 stealth bomber took another hit on Capitol Hill in 1991 because of the precipitous decline of the Soviet nuclear threat and doubts about whether the costly plane could evade radar detection as intended.

President Bush had requested $4.8 billion for fiscal 1992 that would have included funds to buy four additional B-2s. As in recent years, the House voted to end B-2 production while the Senate supported Bush's request.

Conferees on the defense authorization bill (HR 2100 — PL 102-190) forged a deal that balanced House opposition to the B-2 against continuing Senate support. The agreement, which was also included in the companion appropriations measure (HR 2521 — PL 102-172), authorized $1.6 billion for continued research and development of the B-2.

It also authorized $1.8 billion to build additional parts and components — keeping the production line intact — while barring construction of additional planes beyond the 15 previously authorized.

And it provided for an additional $1 billion that could be used for a 16th plane — but only if Congress subsequently approved it by law. *(Defense authorization, p. 393; appropriations, p. 621)*

There had been disputes for years over the cost and mission of the B-2, which was shaped and constructed of special materials as a stealth aircraft that would be nearly invisible to enemy radar. The plane's defenders had always insisted that it was needed to counter the ever-improving strategic forces of the Soviet superpower. That rationale evaporated in 1991 with the dissolution of the Soviet Union.

Instead, officials at the Pentagon and executives of the Northrop Corp., the prime contractor for the B-2, began to promote it as an awesome weapon for conventional, high-intensity warfare. As a prime selling point, they cited the success in the Persian Gulf War of the smaller F-117 stealth fighter.

But their efforts were set back when the Pentagon announced during the week of Sept. 9 that an undisclosed flaw had been found in a flight test of the bomber's crucial radar-evading capabilities. In addition to requiring a vote by Congress, the defense authorization measure barred production of a 16th B-2 unless the Defense Department certified that the plane's problems had been solved.

BACKGROUND

President Jimmy Carter's administration first made public in 1980 what had been a top-secret effort to develop the stealth bomber.

By 1991, the Pentagon had spent $31 billion to develop the B-2 and build the first 15. The Bush administration planned to buy 60 additional copies of the aircraft, which owed much of its cost to its complex, radar-evading design.

The United States' edge in aerial combat — and billions of dollars of defense spending — was riding on the stealth design as the high-tech premise for a new generation of U.S. warplanes.

Stealth was not a single design technique or piece of hardware. Making an airplane stealthy involved masking the many telltale indicators that would allow an enemy to locate and destroy it.

The B-2 bomber was the most costly and controversial of the Pentagon's stealth aircraft. Its manta ray shape and some of its other exotic features were intended to muffle its radar "signature," while its jet engines were designed and placed to mask the heat of their exhaust.

The B-2 was designed mostly of curved surfaces that were sculpted so that probing radio waves would glance off without producing a strong echo.

Its wing was thick enough that the plane's engines, bombload and fuel all could be stored inside, rather than being slung underneath on pylons that would stick out like sore thumbs on a radar screen. And its skin and skeleton were made of a synthetic material that absorbed most energy from a radar wave instead of reflecting it as metal would. A skin of wood or conventional plastic would be nearly transparent to radar waves but would expose the B-2's engines, electronic gear and other metal innards.

B-2 critics warned that history had shown other supposed technological edges to be weak reeds on which to base long-term military planning.

While the Cold War arms race was still going full force, the critics argued that a large B-2 fleet was not worth the cost because chances were too great that Soviet scientists would come up with a way to detect the plane despite its stealthy shroud.

In Congress, the B-2 had enjoyed support in the Senate, although its victory margins in floor votes had narrowed. The House had twice voted to end production of the B-2, leaving its fate to compromises crafted by House and Senate conferees on the annual defense authorization bill.

In 1990, conferees sidestepped the conflict: Their fiscal 1991 defense authorization bill (HR 4739 — PL 101-510) called for $2.3 billion for B-2 procurement. But in the accompanying report conferees were calculatedly vague about whether the funds could be spent only to pay cost overruns on the 15 bombers previously authorized (as House members asserted) or used to buy additional B-2s (as senators maintained). *(1990 Almanac, p. 687)*

Lobbying for the B-2

President Bush's $4.8 billion request for B-2s in fiscal 1992 included funds to buy four additional B-2s ($2.46 billion), components that could be used in building seven planes in fiscal 1993 ($455 million) and spare parts ($289 million), and to allow continued development of the complex aircraft ($1.56 billion).

The Pentagon began a full-court press to convince Congress that the expensive plane was still needed in the post-Cold War era. And Northrop Corp., which built the B-2, opened a campaign to drum up grass-roots support among the constituents of 100 members of Congress who were deemed potential supporters.

Supporters of the B-2 believed they had some tactical advantages in the political fight because of the Persian Gulf War. They speculated that some Democrats who had voted in January against authorizing the war would be fearful that a vote against the bomber would open them to the charge of being "anti-defense."

And the Air Force vigorously touted the performance of its much smaller F-117 stealth jets over Iraq as proof that stealth technology worked — and would work even better in the more heavily armed and longer-range B-2.

The Pentagon argued that the B-2 would be invaluable for conventional missions. But critics scoffed that the Air Force was merely seeking a new rationale for the expensive, radar-eluding airplane because the evaporating Soviet threat had made its nuclear mission less compelling.

The overall air commander of the Persian Gulf War, Lt. Gen. Charles A. Horner, led a team of Air Force officers arguing the case April 30 to the House Defense Appropriations Subcommittee.

"Would I have used a B-2 in Desert Storm? You bet I would," Horner told the panel.

He cited examples of targets that the B-2 could have attacked. Each of them was destroyed by planes that were already in service, including F-117s dropping laser-guided "smart bombs" with pinpoint accuracy. But the B-2 could carry 10 times the bombload of the F-117 (up to 20 tons) and fly more than five times the distance (in excess of 5,000 miles).

Had the larger plane been in service, Horner said, such missions could have been accomplished sooner while placing fewer planes and pilots at risk. The missions he cited included eight small armored chemical weapons bunkers that had to be pounded by more than 50 F-117 missions, according to Horner, but could have been handled by two B-2s.

Horner's theme was bolstered by two pilots home from the war, who gave rousing accounts to the Defense Subcommittee of their bombing runs over Baghdad in the stealthy F-117. They said that the anti-aircraft fire they faced from the Iraqis was wildly inaccurate.

"They felt that we were coming," one of the pilots said, "but they didn't have a clue where we were coming from."

Some B-2 opponents, such as Kevin Knobloch of the Union of Concerned Scientists, worried that the gulf war stories about the F-117 could give the larger stealth plane a significant boost: "A very potent dog-and-pony show," Knobloch said of Horner's presentation.

But B-2 opponents emphasized that Horner was able to knock out his targets without B-2s. "There appears to be no rhyme or reason to go to such a sophisticated system when the assets we had were able to achieve air superiority," said Rep. Ronald V. Dellums, D-Calif.

The argument that the B-2 would save lives in future wars was also a theme of Northrop's lobbying effort, designed by the public relations firm of Bonner & Associates.

"The idea is to generate letters to members from [constituents] who are substantial people in the community or who represent organizations," said Northrop spokesman Loye Miller.

The effort yielded more than 3,700 letters to Congress from B-2 supporters in such diverse groups as civic associations, ethnic societies, farm bureaus and the Boy Scouts.

HOUSE ACTION

On May 22, the House approved a defense authorization measure (HR 2100) that rejected any production of the B-2 bomber beyond the 15 planes previously authorized. The bill included the $1.56 billion requested to continue developing the B-2 but none of the $3.2 billion that Bush sought to buy four planes in fiscal 1992 plus spare parts and components.

The overall measure passed, 268-161, setting up another annual round of conference committee negotiations between the anti-B-2 House and the pro-B-2 Senate. *(Vote 110, p. 28-H)*

The House provisions were crafted in the Armed Services Committee and reflected the influence of committee Chairman Les Aspin, D-Wis., who had turned from supporter to opponent of the B-2 in 1990.

House Committee Action

On May 8, Aspin mustered a strong committee vote of 45-6 for the committee markup of the defense authorization bill that included the provision calling for an end to B-2 production.

The only test of strength came May 7, when the panel's Procurement Subcommittee voted 4-15 against building more B-2s.

Despite the Air Force's strong pitch for the B-2 as a conventional bomber, committee member John R. Kasich, R-Ohio, said most members still thought of the plane in its nuclear-deterrent role. "People are opting for conventional systems, not more systems to blow up the Russians," said Kasich, a leading B-2 opponent.

B-2 supporters such as John M. Spratt Jr., D-S.C., said that the committee's stand on the B-2 was intended largely to strengthen Aspin's hand when he sat down in conference with Senate Armed Services Committee Chairman Sam Nunn, D-Ga., to negotiate a compromise on the issue. "He wanted to control his bargaining position by coming in with a 15-bomber force," said Spratt. "I supported [him] only for the purpose of furthering the bargaining process."

House Floor Action

The Armed Services' version of the defense authorization bill won House passage by a vote of 268-161 on May 22 after the defeat of a Republican amendment that would have restored funds for B-2 production and other programs backed by Bush.

On May 21, the amendment by House GOP leader Robert H. Michel, Ill., was rejected 127-287, with more than 20 percent of the voting Republicans bucking their leader. *(Vote 99, p. 24-H)*

As Aspin waited for the Senate to craft its defense measure, he refused to tip his hand on a potential compromise in the long-running fight over the B-2.

"At some point, we need to get both sides together to see whether we can't figure out a number," the Armed Services chairman told reporters May 22. He insisted, "I've got no bottom line. My negotiating position is that we should build no more than 15."

Moreover, Aspin said, the time might not be ripe to end the B-2 battle in 1991. "Politically, there's a time when people are tired of fighting, and they want to cut a deal," he said. "I can't tell if that's the case yet."

The House position on the B-2 was repeated in the chamber's version of the defense appropriations measure that was approved, 273-105, on June 7. *(Vote 145, p. 36-H)*

SENATE ACTION

On Aug. 2, the Senate passed by voice vote a version of the defense authorization bill (HR 2100, formerly S 1507) that included the $3.2 billion sought by Bush to continue B-2 production.

The Senate rejected, 42-57, an amendment that would have deleted the funds to build four more bombers, essentially matching the House position. *(Vote 174, p. 42-H)*

The pro-B-2 position had been included in the defense bill approved by the Senate Armed Services Committee on July 17. An amendment to stop B-2 production was defeated in committee, 8-11.

Senate Committee Action

The considerable influence that Nunn had accumulated as the leading defense expert among Senate Democrats was in some doubt as his Armed Services Committee marked up the defense authorization bill. Unlike Aspin, Nunn had opposed the resolution authorizing force against Iraq, a position that became politically unpopular with the quick and overwhelming U.S. victory in the Persian Gulf War.

Nunn, the B-2's most important advocate in Congress, was cautious going into the year's Senate negotiations over the aircraft. "I've got to make sure we've got enough votes in the committee," he said, pointing out that nine of the panel's 20 members had voted against B-2 production on the Senate floor at least once in 1990. "That's close, in committee," he noted.

On June 19, a prominent backer of the stealth bomber warned that the program could be in serious trouble in the Senate unless Bush quickly launched a vigorous public campaign for the plane.

"We could lose this," Senate Armed Services Committee member Jim Exon, D-Neb., told top Air Force brass during a hearing by his subcommittee on strategic weapons. "The bully pulpit is something the president is going to have to use," he said.

Urging Air Force Secretary Donald B. Rice and Air Force Chief of Staff Gen. Merrill T. McPeak to carry his warning to the White House, Exon said that Bush "has to be more on board than he has been. He has to do more than say he's going to veto the bill."

As if to highlight Exon's gloomy political prognosis, conservative committee member Robert C. Smith, R-N.H., announced that he might abandon his support of the B-2 unless the administration showed as strong a commitment to saving the anti-missile Strategic Defense Initiative (SDI) as it did to the B-2. *(SDI, p. 407)*

"I've moved into a grayer area," Smith said. "The Air Force is going to have to demonstrate a very specific commitment to all aspects of strategic modernization."

As foreshadowed by Smith's remarks, the sometimes intense negotiations over SDI produced an unusual alliance against the B-2 bomber when the Senate Armed Services Committee marked up its defense authorization bill during the week of July 8.

Apparently to signal their suspicion that the administration was not fighting hard enough for the SDI program known as Brilliant Pebbles — small, space-based missile interceptors — several conservative Republican advocates of SDI supported an effort by William S. Cohen, R-Maine, to end production of the B-2 bomber. The anti-B-2 motion was rejected by a vote of 8-11.

In its report on the defense bill, the Senate committee argued for the B-2's value in conventional warfare, citing an Air Force estimate that two of the planes carrying precision-guided "smart" bombs would be as effective as a flotilla of non-stealthy attack planes carrying gravity bombs and accompanied by dozens of escort planes and midair refueling tankers. Compared with the larger force, the committee said, these B-2s would be less expensive to buy and operate, would expose fewer pilots to the risk of combat and would require no overseas bases.

While acknowledging that only a small percentage of the planned B-2 test flights had been completed, the committee contended that the plane's basic effectiveness had been demonstrated.

The General Accounting Office had recommended that only a few planes be built annually until more testing was completed. But the committee said such a go-slow approach would be counterproductive: "The guaranteed program cost increases that would be incurred by keeping B-2 production at a low rate for another year outweigh the potential repair costs to B-2s already produced [to rectify] potential defects that might be discovered during the next year's testing."

In fact, the panel urged the Air Force to consider speeding up B-2 production to 16 planes annually, rather than the planned maximum rate of 11 planes, a move it said could save $3 billion and two years over the life of the program.

But the committee set the stage for funding battles that would pit the B-2 against other programs: It ordered the Pentagon to suggest cutbacks in other weapons programs or overseas deployments that could compensate for the purchase of B-2s by saving $6 billion to $12 billion over the next 10 years.

As the defense authorization bill awaited action by the full Senate, Nunn again cautioned B-2 supporters that the plane faced an uphill battle. "We've got a 50-50 chance of saving it in the Senate if the president goes to work on the Republicans," he said.

Senate Floor Action

The Senate rejected a challenge to the B-2 as it passed the defense authorization bill for fiscal 1992 on Aug. 2.

Senate approval of $3.2 billion to build four additional B-2s was a clear win for President Bush as well as for Nunn and John W. Warner of Virginia, the Armed Forces Committee's senior Republican.

In 1990, 51 senators had voted for one or the other of two amendments to the fiscal 1991 defense bill that would have killed off production of the B-2. But because several of them voted for one and against the other, an amendment by Patrick J. Leahy, D-Vt., that would have killed production immediately drew only 43 votes, while 45 senators voted for an amendment by Cohen that would have ended production after completing the 15 B-2s already funded. *(1990 Almanac, p. 687)*

To avoid such fragmentation in 1991, B-2 opponents vowed to mass their efforts behind a single amendment, to be offered jointly by Leahy and Cohen. The amendment, which essentially matched the House position, would have deleted from the bill $3.2 billion to build four more bombers but would have allowed completion of the 15 planes previously funded. It was rejected 42-57.

With the easing of the U.S.-Soviet nuclear standoff and with several kinds of high-tech missiles entering the U.S. strategic arsenal, Cohen argued, the B-2's exotic and expensive features no longer were needed. "The enhancements we have made ... in our nuclear forces, combined with recent and ongoing changes in the world, will allow us to maintain our security even if we forgo [the B-2]," he said.

On the other hand, B-2 supporters touted the big plane's value for quick-reaction non-nuclear attacks against non-Soviet enemies: "None of us can pinpoint the source of the next major threat," said John Seymour, R-Calif. "[The B-2] can meet any of those unknown threats with swiftness, accuracy and reliability."

Shortly before the Senate voted, a letter from Air Force Secretary Rice was distributed to senators, informing them that cracks had been discovered in the skeletons of several of the B-1 bombers built in the mid-1980s. The Air Force's case for the B-2 in its nuclear role rested on the argument that the B-1 would no longer be able to penetrate Soviet air defenses by the end of the 1990s.

Cohen called the last-minute announcement "curiouser and curiouser.... They wait until the last day, just before the vote on the B-2, and say, 'By the way, folks, we do not have a plane that works.' "

Although the Senate version of the defense appropriations bill (HR 2521) contained the chamber's pro-B-2 language, the margin of support for the plane was smaller.

During debate on the appropriations bill, the Senate voted to table (kill), 51-48, an amendment to end production of the B-2. In a sign of shifting sentiment, opponents rounded up six more votes than they had mustered only seven weeks earlier in action on the authorization bill. *(Vote 206, p. 27-S)*

"As I have watched that statue of the KGB founder topple and really looked at what the B-2 is designed to do, and looked at what it is we are defending against, there is no mission for the B-2 bomber," said Sen. J. Bennett Johnston, D-La., one of those who had switched his position between August and September. "There is no need for a triad [of nuclear forces] against the Soviet Union. There is no need for a penetrating bomber."

FINAL ACTION

On Nov. 1, House and Senate conferees on the $291 billion defense authorization bill reached tentative agreement on the measure, including a compromise that erected a barrier before continued production of the B-2 bomber.

The conference report authorized $1.8 billion to keep open the B-2 production line but barred work on any planes beyond the 15 previously authorized — unless Congress approved spending $1 billion on a 16th plane.

That formulation gave the House, which had strongly opposed the B-2, an effective veto over its continued production. But it also left open to the Bush administration the opportunity to lobby aggressively to save the high-tech weapon.

The conference report was adopted by the House, 329-82, on Nov. 18. The Senate cleared the measure, 79-15, on Nov. 22. *(House vote 400, p. 98-H; Senate vote 265, 35-S)*

President Bush signed the defense bill (PL 102-190) on Dec. 5.

New Doubts About the B-2

In the weeks before conference committee action on the defense bill, two events created new doubts about the B-2's prospects for survival.

During the week of Sept. 9, the Pentagon announced that a flaw had been found in a flight test of the B-2's radar-evading capabilities. Although Defense Department officials declined to provide any information on the classified tests, they insisted that the problem was manageable. Nonetheless, the admission of a problem gave critics of the B-2 new ammunition in the debate over the costly plane.

On Sept. 27, Bush proposed a series of unilateral arms reductions to reflect the fading of the Soviet threat. Although the B-2 was spared from cutbacks by Bush, the president's move emboldened the plane's critics.

House Armed Services Committee member Patricia Schroeder, D-Colo., said, "I don't think we can pass the defense bill if it comes back with the B-2 in it. People want [a weapons program] to die."

Even some past supporters of the B-2 were rattled.

"The American people are going to ask the question, 'If there's that much less threat ... why do we need to put that much money into a bomber?' " Senate Armed Services Committee member Trent Lott, R-Miss., said Sept. 30. "I'm a guy who's voted for the B-2 every time, but ... it's getting tougher every time."

On the Senate side, Nunn conceded Oct. 1 that his bargaining leverage to protect the B-2 had been eroded by Bush's cancellation of several smaller strategic weapons programs that were authorized in the Senate bill and could have been traded for House concessions. "The larger the negotiating pot, the more negotiating flexibility you have," he said.

Warning that the Air Force's long-range plan to buy 75 B-2s was not practical, Nunn also urged the Air Force to settle for fewer of the planes, suggesting a fleet half that size. "Coming down to a more realistic number will save the B-2," he said.

Conference Agreement

House and Senate conferees reached tentative agreement Nov. 1 on a final version of the defense authorization measure. Although they bickered a while longer about provisions to aid the Soviet Union, they stood by a compromise that left the future of the B-2 in doubt.

The agreement authorized $1.6 billion for additional research and development of the bomber and $1.8 billion to keep open the B-2 production line. But it barred work on any planes beyond the 15 previously authorized — unless Congress approved an additional aircraft.

The deal did not slam the door on further production of the costly bomber as the nation set its post-Cold War defense plans. But it created a formidable obstacle by requiring House approval of additional production. The House had not taken a free-standing vote on the B-2 since 1989. But in 1990 and 1991, defense bills that denied additional production funds had been easily approved.

The B-2 compromise was so open-ended as to be a political spin-artist's dream, allowing both critics and proponents to claim victory.

Dellums, a leading B-2 opponent, told reporters the conference provision "sounds the death knell" for the B-2. Kasich, Dellums' co-leader of the B-2 opposition, contended that there was "virtually no chance" that the House would ever vote to allow additional production.

On the other hand, B-2 supporter Warner claimed victory in having defeated House efforts to deny production funding and to establish a legislative cap on the number of B-2s that could be procured. By 1992, Warner predicted, the Air Force would be able to prove that it had surmounted the difficulties that had resulted in one B-2 prototype being detected by radar more easily than expected.

Nunn said the B-2 program was "alive, but not completely healthy."

Floor Debate

The implications of the B-2 compromise were debated once again when the House and Senate approved the conference report on the defense authorization measure, HR 2100.

"On the B-2, I believe we have seen the death of the program," said Kasich, the B-2 opponent.

But Bill Dickinson of Alabama, the senior Republican on the House Armed Services Committee, countered that those who boasted of killing the B-2 had to explain why they had agreed to spend billions of dollars more "on the coffin."

Even some who wanted to kill the program agreed that the fight was not over. "The B-2 is not terminated. . . . We will have to revisit the entire issue again next year," complained John Conyers Jr., D-Mich.

In Senate debate, Patrick J. Leahy, D-Vt., called the deal requiring congressional approval for an additional plane "a Trojan horse" that ignored "some small print."

Arguing that the Pentagon could continue piecemeal construction of additional planes, Leahy said the $1.8 billion for parts would provide "kits to be used for future B-2s." Asserting that the Pentagon also had $3 billion in unobligated B-2 funds from past years, he said, "It's almost like their own Swiss bank account." ■

Global Changes Reshaped SDI Goals

Following the Senate's lead, Congress reshaped the Strategic Defense Initiative (SDI) in 1991 to place much more emphasis on the early deployment of ground-based defenses against limited attacks by both intercontinental and short-range missiles.

Equally important, Congress went on record for the first time in favor of a rapid deployment of a limited ground-based SDI system. *(SDI provisions, p. 410)*

The SDI agreement was written into the fiscal 1992 defense authorization bill (HR 2100 — PL 102-190) and was repeated in the companion defense appropriations measure (HR 2521 — PL 102-172). *(Defense authorization, p. 393; appropriations, p. 621)*

Compared with the program's initial goal in the Reagan administration of thwarting a full-fledged Soviet attack, President Bush's $5.2 billion budget request for fiscal 1992 already had reoriented SDI toward a more modest aim of fending off a small number of missiles that might be launched by a rogue military commander or a Third World country.

But Bush's plan, like earlier versions, relied in part on space-based interceptor missiles, which would violate the 1972 U.S.-Soviet treaty limiting anti-ballistic missile (ABM) systems. In the end, Congress provided $4.2 billion for SDI, including $398 million for continued research into the orbiting interceptors called Brilliant Pebbles. But it excluded Brilliant Pebbles from the initial anti-missile deployment. *(ABM treaty, Congress and the Nation, Vol. III, p. 895)*

Although the restriction on deploying space-based weaponry disappointed the most enthusiastic backers of SDI, the program's enthusiasts won a significant victory in Congress' endorsement of moving rapidly toward a ground-based system.

The agreement directed the president to deploy by 1996 a ground-based anti-missile system at a single site near Grand Forks, N.D. This initial deployment of 100 missiles was expected to cost $7 billion to $10 billion.

Such a system was consistent with the ABM treaty. But the agreement also called on the president to negotiate with the Soviet Union changes in the treaty that would allow more extensive ABM tests and deployments.

The House version of the defense authorization bill, passed 268-161 on May 22, would have authorized $3.54 billion for anti-missile defenses, not including any funds for Brilliant Pebbles. An amendment that would have reduced research on defenses against long-range missiles from $2.7 billion to $1.1 billion was rejected, 118-266.

Bush threatened to veto the defense bill if it cut back his SDI plans so severely.

The Senate version of the defense bill, passed by voice vote on Aug. 2, included the fundamentals of the SDI deal that was eventually enacted. But the Senate would have authorized slightly higher funding — $4.6 billion for SDI, including $625 million for Brilliant Pebbles. The Senate rejected a series of amendments by liberals that would have restricted SDI.

The SDI deal emerged against a backdrop of dramatic global changes.

Early in the year, backers of the anti-missile system seized on the use of U.S. Patriot missiles to intercept Scud missiles that Iraq fired at Saudi Arabia and Israel during the Persian Gulf War. Although doubts were raised later about the effectiveness of the Patriot interceptions, dramatic television tape of the Patriot at work gave new popular currency to the idea of anti-missile defenses. *(Persian Gulf War, p. 437)*

As the year went on, the disintegration of the Soviet Union undercut the case for a global strategic defense. On the other hand, uncertainty over the safety and security of Soviet nuclear weapons in a time of disarray encouraged the shift toward defenses that could fend off a limited attack. *(Soviet aid, p. 463)*

On Sept. 27, Bush offered a package of strategic arms cuts and urged in return that then-Soviet President Mikhail S. Gorbachev "join us in taking immediate, concrete steps to permit the limited deployment of non-nuclear defenses to protect against limited ballistic missile strikes — whatever their source — without undermining the credibility of existing deterrent sources." *(Bush arms cuts, p. 421)*

In responding in kind to Bush's arms cutbacks, Gorbachev on Oct. 5 appeared to temper the Soviet Union's longstanding opposition to any SDI deployment.

"We are prepared to consider proposals from the United States of America on non-nuclear anti-missile defense systems," he said, suggesting "joint systems for warning against a nuclear missile attack with elements based in space and on land." By late December, Gorbachev had resigned, and the Soviet Union no longer existed.

BACKGROUND

Eight years after President Ronald Reagan launched the Strategic Defense Initiative with the visionary goal of neutralizing the threat of nuclear missiles, Bush was presented in 1991 with an opportunity to assemble a solid, bipartisan coalition behind his own, more modest version of the fiercely disputed SDI.

To do it, however, Bush had to accept a version of the missile defense program that was more down to earth — literally — than the revisions in the program that he had already proposed.

Almost $23 billion had been spent on SDI and associated programs from fiscal 1985 through fiscal 1991. Bush's plan had anticipated spending an additional $46 billion over the long-term.

Supporters had embraced the quest for strategic defenses as a revolutionary antidote to the arms race, while opponents had ridiculed it as a destabilizing quest for "star wars."

Reagan's Vision

For four years after it was launched by Reagan in 1983, the Strategic Defense Initiative was defined by his sweeping rhetoric of rendering nuclear missiles "impotent and obsolete." The implication that the system would shield the country like an impenetrable bubble was underscored by the emphasis on "directed-energy weapons" — futuristic devices intended to zap distant missiles at the speed of light, using lasers or atomic particles.

But the type of weapon SDI would use, whether lasers or old-fashioned guided missiles, was less important to the logic of the program than the fact that the weapons would be deployed in orbiting satellites. Thus the U.S. weapons supposedly could pick off Soviet missiles in the "boost phase" — the first few minutes after launch — before they could spew out the multiple warheads and clouds of decoys that would overwhelm ground-based defenses located near the target.

The debate over anti-missile defenses turned in part on the concept of "strategic stability." In the paradoxical logic of mutual nuclear deterrence that dominated defense policy during the Cold War, this term reflected the conviction that the safety of each superpower depended on the vulnerability of both.

The premise was that, so long as each superpower was vulnerable to the other's nuclear-armed missiles and bombers, neither would attack the other for fear of devastating retaliation. By that reasoning, it would be provocative and destabilizing for either superpower to deploy a nationwide anti-missile defense.

That view was enshrined in the ABM treaty, which barred deployment of nationwide defense systems. It permitted only modest defenses that were limited to minimize the risk that either party could use them as a jumping-off point to "break out" of the treaty's limits.

During the 1980s, a growing number of conservatives condemned the acceptance of this mutual hostage relationship with the Soviet government as morally repugnant and politically enervating.

As Reagan presented it, SDI was intended to break the stalemate through anti-missile weapons deployed in orbiting satellites.

"What if free people could live secure in the knowledge that their security did not rest upon the threat of instant U.S. retaliation to deter a Soviet attack, that we could intercept and destroy strategic ballistic missiles?" Reagan asked.

But most Democrats sharply discounted the technical feasibility of such a protective umbrella against a full-bore Soviet attack. Congressional Democrats stymied Reagan's efforts to push his program irreversibly toward deployment.

When the Joint Chiefs of Staff first defined a concrete mission for SDI in 1987, the goal still was to block a full-scale Soviet missile attack. But this "Phase I" SDI system was intended only to destroy enough attacking Soviet missiles to disrupt the meticulously timed assault that would be needed to wipe out a large percentage of the U.S. retaliatory force.

Over the following three years, the design of Phase I shifted toward what the Pentagon called "distributed battle management." In successive revisions, the orbiting interceptor missiles were conceived as increasingly autonomous in picking out their targets, thus eliminating from the defensive system any central control nodes that would be vulnerable to Soviet attack.

The result was Brilliant Pebbles: interceptors small enough and supposedly inexpensive enough to be deployed by the thousands. In its final form, the Phase I plan called for putting 4,000 Brilliant Pebbles in orbit.

But Phase I faced persistent resistance from congressional Democrats.

The critics were uneasy that an effort to disrupt a

Soviet attack might be seen by Moscow as an effort to undermine its nuclear deterrent, thus kicking off a new nuclear arms race. As Cold War tensions faded, the critics also contended that SDI needed to be oriented toward threats that were more likely than a Soviet attack.

Bush's Version

Congress had generally backed research into anti-missile defenses, but it had balked at increasing the SDI budget over the $4 billion mark.

As 1991 began, Bush set out his redefined vision of SDI in his State of the Union address on Jan. 29.

"I have directed that the SDI program be refocused on providing protection from limited ballistic strikes — whatever their source," he said. "Let us pursue an SDI program that can deal with any future threat to the United States, to our forces overseas and to our friends and allies."

Bush built his new version of SDI around a program known as GPALS, an acronym for "global protection against limited strikes" It was envisioned as a combination of space-based Brilliant Pebbles interceptors and ground-based missiles. It was intended to protect U.S. territory, allies or overseas forces against relatively small attacks, such as might be launched by a Third World country with short-range (or "tactical") missiles or by a renegade military unit.

Officially, the Phase I goal of a nationwide defense remained on the books. But SDI's top priority became developing systems that could protect U.S. territory, allies and military forces anywhere in the world against as many as 200 warheads launched by three potential sources:

- Developing countries, which might not be deterred by the threat of U.S. military retaliation — a prospect highlighted by Iraq's use of Soviet-built Scud missiles during the gulf war. As of 1991, 14 developing countries had short-range ballistic missiles, according to the administration, with the number of countries expected to rise rapidly.
- Unauthorized attacks by an isolated unit of Soviet or other military forces. Although the Soviet Union existed until the end of 1991, political turmoil there raised the question of how tightly the central government controlled the thousands of nuclear-armed missiles and aircraft deployed across the vast country.
- An accidental launch of an unspecified nature.

Specifically, the GPALS plan called for 750 ground-based interceptor missiles at six U.S. sites, ground-based and space-based missile detection equipment and 1,000 of the controversial Brilliant Pebbles. Any one of those elements required modification of the ABM Treaty.

Several prominent defense-minded Democrats responded positively, if tentatively, to GPALS in the months after Bush introduced it.

"I commend you . . . for bringing the SDI program into the realm of reason," Chairman Jim Exon, D-Neb., told SDI program officials at a June 20 hearing of his Senate Armed Services Strategic Forces Subcommittee.

Senate Armed Services Committee Chairman Sam Nunn, Ga., and some other centrist Democrats had urged for years that SDI be reoriented to deal with limited missile threats.

But Brilliant Pebbles remained a bone of contention between Bush and such potential Democratic allies, who not only questioned whether the complex weapon would work but also challenged the wisdom of reopening the U.S.-Soviet ABM treaty in order to permit deployment of anti-missile weapons in space.

The 1972 treaty, which limited anti-ballistic missile (ABM) weapons, permitted deployment of only 100 ground-based interceptors at a single base and barred deployment of any ABM-related equipment in space.

Even the limited defense systems championed by Nunn and other Democrats eventually would have required revision of the pact.

For much of 1991, administration officials spurned proposals from senators to seek a compromise on GPALS.

"GPALS is the compromise," Defense Secretary Dick Cheney wrote to Senate Minority Leader Bob Dole, R-Kan., on June 20. The word "is" was underlined.

Nevertheless, the possibility of significant, long-term Democratic support for SDI gave Bush a powerful incentive to deal.

At the same time, conservative activists, infuriated that Democrats such as Nunn had professed support for SDI while slashing its budget, urged Bush to stand firm against compromise.

A First Skirmish

Defense Secretary Cheney attempted on Feb. 7 to sell the House Armed Services Committee on the administration's new rationale for the Strategic Defense Initiative. He was able to invoke what was perceived as successful interceptions of Iraqi Scud missiles by U.S.-made Patriot missiles during the gulf war.

But a first skirmish over SDI during the week of March 11 indicated that the congressional lineup had not changed overnight.

Republicans tried unsuccessfully to capitalize on enthusiasm for the Army's Patriot to boost development and deployment of space-based anti-missile defenses as part of SDI.

When the House and Senate took up legislation authorizing benefits for veterans of the Persian Gulf War (S 725 — PL 102-25, formerly HR 1175, S 578), Republicans in each house tried to attach a non-binding provision urging the president to negotiate with Moscow a revision of the ABM treaty to lift restrictions on SDI. *(Gulf veterans benefits, p. 320)*

But the effort in the House to amend HR 1175, led by Jon Kyl, R-Ariz., was rejected March 13 by a vote of 145-281, with only seven Democrats supporting the effort. *(Vote 47, p. 12-H)*

In the Senate, John W. Warner, Va., the senior Republican on the Armed Services Committee, abandoned his parallel effort to amend S 578 on March 14, when Armed Services Chairman Nunn seemed on the verge of trumping the Republican move with a substitute proposal. The alternative would have furthered the Democrats' effort to tilt SDI toward development of ground-based defenses against limited attacks. And it would have funded that effort at the expense of the more ambitious space-based ABM projects favored by Warner and other Republicans.

Nunn's amendment would have earmarked $224 million from the Army's fiscal 1991 budget to buy additional Patriot batteries for deployment with U.S. expeditionary forces. It also would have increased by $218 million funding for four SDI programs aimed at developing ground-based defenses, drawing the money from other SDI programs.

The episode was hardly conclusive evidence of the political fallout on Capitol Hill from the gulf war. Kyl and Warner had sought to attach their amendments to authorization measures that included increases in benefits for veterans of the conflict. Members did not want to be seen

The SDI Deal

The anti-missile defense package that was adopted as part of the fiscal 1992 defense authorization bill (HR 2100 — PL 102-190) approved $4.15 billion for the Strategic Defense Initiative (SDI), including funds for defense against short-range, or tactical, missiles.

This was $1 billion less than was requested by President Bush and $450 million less than was authorized by the Senate but it was $630 million more than was approved by the House. The bill:

- Declared a national goal of deploying an anti-ballistic missile (ABM) system as one way of reducing the threat posed by ballistic missile proliferation. It also endorsed other methods for dealing with that threat, including further reductions in nuclear arms and reinvigorated efforts to stem the spread of ballistic missiles and weapons of mass destruction.
- Ordered the Pentagon to develop an ABM system that would comply with the 1972 U.S.-Soviet ABM treaty, which permitted deployment of only 100 ground-based interceptor missiles at a single site. The system was to be deployed as soon as technology was available, or by 1996. This provision was left deliberately ambiguous in that some SDI proponents believed the technology already was in hand, while critics insisted it was years away.
- Stipulated that the bill did not constitute final authorization for the system that would comply with the treaty, and that Congress did not authorize development of an anti-missile system that would violate the ABM treaty.
- Authorized $390 million to develop Brilliant Pebbles space-based interceptor missiles, with the proviso that Congress did not authorize their inclusion in any ABM system being developed for deployment.
- Urged the president to begin immediate discussions with the Soviet government on the feasibility and mutual desirability of amending the ABM treaty to allow deployment of more than 100 interceptor missiles at more than one site, greater use of space-based detection and control systems and more flexibility for testing novel ABM weapons.
- Recommended that the president and Congress consider the options available under the ABM treaty in light of the progress made in the discussion of treaty amendments. The language did not specifically mention the option many Republicans had in mind, which was withdrawing from the treaty.

as doing anything to delay enactment of the politically popular benefits.

HOUSE ACTION

The House version of the fiscal 1992 defense authorization called for cutting back Bush's $5.2 billion request for anti-missile defense programs to $3.54 billion, with no money to be spent on Brilliant Pebbles space-based interceptors. The measure passed, 268-161, on May 22. *(Vote 110, p. 28-H)*

Before passing the bill, the House rejected amendments that would have restored Bush's full budget request, cut back SDI more deeply or prohibited the program from straying from its original emphasis on defenses against strategic missile attacks.

House Committee Action

The defense authorization bill was approved by the House Armed Services Committee, 45-6, on May 8. It included the language on SDI that was adopted later by the full House.

The committee sliced Bush's budget request by nearly one-third. Beyond approving only $3.54 billion of the $5.17 billion requested, the panel demanded a substantial shift in the program's focus.

It knocked out the entire $1.61 billion requested for the conservatives' priority within the anti-missile program: developing by the end of the decade a rudimentary space-based defense.

An effort to restore the cut was rejected on a party-line vote of 18-25.

By contrast, the House panel approved the entire $883 million requested to develop defenses against shorter-range missiles, such as the Scuds fired by Iraq during the Persian Gulf War. But the committee bill put this "anti-tactical missile" program under control of the Army, rather than the SDI office that was created by Reagan in 1983 to develop a long-range missile defense.

Like a judo wrestler turning an opponent's strength to his own advantage, the House Democrats used Bush's most politically resonant argument for the Strategic Defense Initiative against him.

The House Armed Services Committee endorsed the president's contention that SDI should focus on dealing with relatively small, near-term threats. But in its report on the fiscal 1992 defense authorization bill, the panel complained that Bush's SDI funding request was out of sync with his rhetoric because nearly a third of his anti-missile budget was earmarked for the space-based Brilliant Pebbles.

The Democrats rejected contentions that Brilliant Pebbles could aid in fending off a small-scale attack. "Brilliant Pebbles would have no capability against missiles that did not reach out of the atmosphere," the panel said. "[G]round-based defenses would still be needed . . . to deal with missiles with ranges less than 600-800 km," such as Iraq's modified Scuds.

Denouncing the committee's SDI provision, Vice President Dan Quayle said on May 14, "Some congressional Democrats are as determined as ever to destroy SDI." He called SDI "a crucial building block of the new world order."

House Floor Action

Before approving the defense authorization bill, the House rejected, 127-282, an amendment by House Republican leader Robert H. Michel, Ill., that would have granted Bush's full request for SDI and other major weapons. *(Vote 99, p. 24-H)*

But the House also rejected, 118-266, an amendment by liberal Democrat Ronald V. Dellums, Calif., that would have reduced the authorization for research on long-range missiles from $2.7 billion to $1.1 billion. It would have limited such research to laboratory experiments and disbanded the SDI program office. The amendment would not have affected the House bill's separate authorization of $882 million to develop defenses against tactical missiles. *(Vote 97, p. 24-H)*

"The way you defend the American people is not by some absurd illusion that we can engage in technological defense," Dellums told the House. "We defend the American people by going to the negotiating table . . . and negotiating back from the nuclear abyss."

The House also rejected, 161-265, an amendment by SDI proponent Duncan Hunter, R-Calif., to require that the anti-tactical missile program develop only weapons that could intercept several types of modern, long-range ballistic missiles in service or under development in several Third World countries. Hunter's opponents suspected the purpose of the amendment was to preserve SDI's emphasis on defenses against long-range missiles rather than the more numerous short-range ones. *(Vote 105, p. 26-H)*

SENATE ACTION

The essentials of the compromise supporting the Strategic Defense Initiative were negotiated in the Senate and embodied in that chamber's version of the defense authorization bill, which was approved by voice vote on Aug. 2.

The Senate agreement called for $4.6 billion for SDI programs in fiscal 1992 and committed support for early deployment of an initial ground-based system at a single site by 1996. It called for negotiations to permit more such systems, which were prohibited by the ABM treaty of 1972. And it deferred deployment of Brilliant Pebbles but approved $625 million to continue research on those space-based interceptors.

The Senate action on the defense bill came after SDI opponents failed to win approval of several amendments to reduce or restrict the anti-missile program.

The SDI deal was engineered by Armed Services Chairman Nunn and Warner, the committee's senior Republican. The concerted push to forge a new consensus on SDI was begun in mid-year by Warner and William S. Cohen, R-Maine.

On May 23, Warner and Cohen proposed that the controversial space-based weapon be taken out of the center of the debate through a two-year deferral of the decision to deploy it — although robust funding and testing would continue.

In return, the plan sought congressional support for an administration effort to negotiate with Moscow changes in the ABM treaty to allow:

- Deployment of 700 to 1,200 ground-based launchers for anti-missile missiles at five to seven sites.
- Space-based missile-detection satellites such as the GPALS system's "Brilliant Eyes," which not only would warn of an attack but also would guide ground-based interceptors toward their targets.
- Development and testing of all ABM technologies, including space-based interceptor missiles such as Brilliant Pebbles.

The Warner-Cohen plan recommended a two-year deadline for reaching agreement with Moscow on the treaty revision.

Warner's goal appeared in part to be getting the proverbial camel's nose under the tent of ABM restrictions on space-based deployments. At a Senate Armed Services hearing, he spoke of trying to break the treaty's ban on space-based equipment as it applied to attack warning satellites, referred to as "sensors," rather than the more controversial interceptor missiles.

"The sooner we come to grips [with the certainty] that missile defense shall incorporate some elements in space," he said at the hearing, "the better off we'll be."

Conservatives who insisted that a public referendum between SDI and the ABM pact would break their way complained that Warner's proposal maddeningly fuzzed the issue. "No one's ever forced the Senate to make a hard choice," protested Malcolm Wallop, R-Wyo., Capitol Hill's leading advocate of anti-missile defense for more than a decade.

Some liberals were equally opposed to seeking any revisions in the ABM treaty, which they viewed as a bulwark of arms control.

Defense Secretary Cheney had tersely rejected the approach on Bush's behalf — but Nunn was interested.

Senate Committee Action

The Senate Armed Services Committee marked up its annual defense authorization bill during the week of July 8. But Nunn and Warner postponed a vote to approve the bill as they attempted to assemble a majority of the committee to back a compromise that they had crafted on the administration's Strategic Defense Initiative.

Their proposal, which was based on the plan floated earlier by Warner and Cohen, called for deployment by 1996 of a ground-based anti-missile system limited to one site. And it sought to line up Congress behind an effort to liberalize the 1972 ABM treaty to permit deployment of additional anti-ballistic missile defense sites.

The compromise was opposed by some Republicans because it would defer deployment of Brilliant Pebbles. The space-based interceptors were viewed as a crucial aspect of SDI by conservatives but were opposed by many Democrats.

"I think that we have a chance of putting together some more votes next week," Nunn told reporters July 12. But he also warned that the $4.5 billion for SDI in the draft version of the bill presumed a bipartisan deal on the program's future course. "If we don't get a conceptual agreement here, the funding level is going to come down — very severely down," he said.

During closed-door negotiations on the authorization bill, Nunn and Warner were able to count only nine of the 11 votes needed to win approval for the SDI deal in the 20-member committee.

According to committee sources, some Democrats were interested in the Nunn-Warner concept but rejected the amendment as it was drafted because they believed it entailed too firm a commitment to eventually deploy ground-based defenses at more than one site.

This implied an intent to abrogate the ABM treaty unless the Soviet Union agreed to amend it.

Initially, Strom Thurmond, S.C., was the only other committee Republican to join Warner and Cohen in support of the SDI proposal.

But on July 17, a broad but fragile coalition of the Armed Services Committee agreed on a long-term plan for SDI.

By a vote of 16-4, the panel included a $4.6 billion SDI package in its version of the fiscal 1992 defense authorization bill (S 1507). The committee unanimously approved the bill.

Warner emphasized that the package would put Congress on record in favor of liberalizing the ABM treaty to allow deployment of an extensive anti-missile system aimed at fending off "limited" attacks.

"This program puts the United States on the path to actually deploying a ballistic missile defense system," declared Warner.

But the hefty, bipartisan vote in favor of the SDI deal

masked profound disagreements over how hard — and to what end — the Soviets should be pushed to amend the ABM treaty:

- Republican conservatives led by Wallop insisted that the one approved site that could be built within the treaty was only the first of many; that a revised treaty must allow full-scale testing of space-based SDI weapons, including Brilliant Pebbles interceptor rockets; and that if Moscow did not agree to U.S. demands for a less restrictive treaty, the United States should exercise its right to withdraw from the pact.
- Chairman Nunn and many other Democrats envisioned much more modest changes in the treaty in order to allow more than 100 ground-based missiles at more than one site and to allow the deployment of missile-detection satellites that would guide anti-missile interceptors.

However, these Democrats wanted to change the rules of the arms competition very carefully in order to preserve "strategic stability."

Carl Levin, D-Mich., a liberal opponent of the deal, argued it could set off a new arms race. "Why should we take a step that is likely to provoke an undesirable Soviet response?" he asked.

Many Democratic opponents of the deal feared what many of its conservative backers hoped: that it would create unstoppable political momentum for full-scale SDI deployment.

To bring in Wallop and the five other Republicans members of the Armed Services Committee who had previously resisted the deal, the proposal was revised to highlight Brilliant Pebbles' potential as a follow-on to the initial ground-based defense. Overall SDI funding also was increased by $92 million and a provision was added to require the president to report by 1994 on efforts to negotiate amendments to the ABM treaty.

However, Nunn was also intent on lining up a majority of committee Democrats. So additional changes were made to bring aboard Jeff Bingaman, N.M., who had initially opposed a deal, and to keep aboard Tim Wirth, Colo.

Wirth had supported the plan partly because Nunn wrote into the bill conditions that would have to be met before the Energy Department could reopen the controversial Rocky Flats nuclear weapons plant near Denver. But Wirth gave Bingaman his proxy to demand changes in the SDI package to place more emphasis on maintaining strategic stability.

The SDI provision also was rewritten to make it deliberately ambiguous as to whether the anti-missile site deployed in 1996 was intended as the first of many. Also dropped was a specific reference to the option of withdrawing from the ABM treaty if Moscow had not agreed to treaty amendments by 1996.

After the revised SDI package was approved, Levin tried to expose the underlying disagreements among supporters with an amendment stating that the plan's goal was a system that would comply with the ABM treaty. It was rejected, 5-15.

Senate Floor Action

After turning aside a series of amendments advanced by liberal critics of SDI, the Senate on Aug. 2 passed by voice vote the defense authorization bill that included the elaborate deal to go forward with the anti-missile defense system.

The deal — which survived the Senate as it was crafted by the Senate Armed Services Committee — was a delicate compromise. It linked Democrats who favored relatively modest changes in the ABM treaty with Republicans who hoped that this would be the first step toward a global network of orbiting anti-missile interceptor rockets.

Al Gore of Tennessee and Joseph R. Biden Jr. of Delaware were among several Democrats who tried to unhinge the committee compromise, arguing that it would shatter the ABM treaty and might provoke a renewed buildup of Soviet nuclear missiles.

But the Senate rejected two amendments that challenged fundamental elements of the committee's anti-missile program. A third amendment, specifying that the bill did not authorize any ABM deployment not allowed by the treaty, was adopted 99-0, amid conflicting claims about its practical significance.

Biden later contended that the opponents had hobbled the committee provision by forcing Nunn to avow repeatedly that it was not a commitment to unilaterally discard the ABM treaty: "He had to say an awful lot of things that underscored the fact that the goal is not as broad as it appears."

But Warner, who had set out months earlier to line up a strong bipartisan coalition behind deployment of ABM defenses, said he was "more than satisfied" with the outcome: "We laid the foundation for a bipartisan consensus. We got it. And it was not by a majority of two or three votes."

After the Armed Services Committee approved its SDI deal, intense opposition had quickly coalesced around three Democrats: Armed Services Committee members Gore and Levin and Foreign Relations Committee member Biden.

The critics contended that, even if the number of interceptor missiles deployed was sharply limited, a nationwide defense against small attacks was fundamentally hostile to the ABM treaty's purposes.

With several interceptor bases scattered across the country, Biden warned, "you very quickly move into the realm of building a base for a territorial defense." Moreover, he argued, that prospect would dissuade Moscow from agreeing to further reductions in nuclear missiles, going beyond the Strategic Arms Reduction Treaty (START) signed in Moscow by Bush and then-Soviet President Gorbachev. *(START, p. 419)*

Gore warned fellow Democrats on July 31 that conservatives would accept a ground-based system only as "the device by which the Senate opens the way to a space-based system. That's what the administration is interested in. That's what the committee Republicans are interested in."

Nunn bristled at this fear of an uncontrollable slide toward full SDI deployment. "That's a pretty low estimate of our political system . . . an estimate that the Congress is not going to use its judgment," he told the Senate.

As most of the critics saw it, their best chance to undermine the Senate panel's SDI package before conference was to drive a wedge into the philosophical crevasse that divided most Armed Services Committee Democrats, who favored a modest change in the ABM treaty, from those Republicans who freely acknowledged their intention to use the limited deployment as an opening to put an end to the "strategic stability" doctrine.

Although the SDI critics did not expect to beat the committee head on, they highlighted the issues through an amendment by Gore. It would have recast the committee package to emphasize deployment by the mid-1990s of ground-based defenses against short-range missiles such as the Iraqi Scuds. The amendment called for modifying the ABM treaty only as needed to clarify the distinctions between such anti-tactical missile defenses and defensive systems intended to fend off strategic missiles.

Biden cited official testimony that, despite domestic turmoil in the Soviet Union, the top military authorities were keeping the country's nuclear arsenal securely under control.

As for potential nuclear strikes by terrorist nations, they contended that a limited ABM would be irrelevant to the most likely methods of attack. "It's more likely to come in a suitcase than on the tip of a missile," said Biden.

In response, Nunn cited statements by high-ranking Soviet officials and reports in the Soviet media that warned of low morale and indiscipline in the Soviet military. "Perhaps *we're* not concerned about Soviet command and control [of nuclear weapons], but *they* are," he said.

Gore's amendment was rejected 39-60. All but four Republicans and more than a third of the Democrats voted "nay." *(Vote 168, p. 22-S)*

Bingaman took the second shot at diluting Nunn's package. Bingaman and Wirth had supported the deal in the committee. But both wanted to water down the bill's implied threat to abrogate the ABM treaty if the Soviet Union refused to negotiate changes.

Bingaman's amendment would have declared that maintenance of strategic stability was the overriding goal — and that deployment of a limited ABM defense would be subordinated to it. It also would have deleted all references to the treaty-compliant ABM deployment due by 1996 as an "initial" deployment.

Under Bingaman's approach, any U.S. anti-missile deployments beyond those allowed by the treaty would have been subject to the Soviet government eventually agreeing on treaty changes.

"If we take a confrontational approach," he warned, "we will hurt our security.... About the only comparative advantage the Soviet Union enjoys is in the production of ballistic missiles," which it could easily accelerate.

Nunn protested, "I do not want to tell [the Soviets] in advance of sitting down to negotiate that we are not going to do anything, ever, if they do not agree to it, because if we do that, we will not have a negotiating position."

Many liberals balked at signing on even to the Bingaman amendment's acceptance of deploying anti-ballistic missiles at a single site.

"If we get the one site, all the momentum's going to be to continue," Biden argued to anti-SDI lobbyists who were pressing him to vote with Bingaman for the sake of undermining Nunn's package.

Bingaman slightly modified his amendment in hope of conciliating the liberals. A few liberals, such as Patrick J. Leahy, D-Vt., voted against it. But Biden and most of the other liberals voted for it.

Biden said his decision on the amendment was "a close tactical call" but that his underlying judgment was unchanged: "I think it's a disaster to build anything."

The amendment was rejected, 43-56. Of 56 Democrats voting, 41 backed the amendment. Only two Republicans supported it. *(Vote 169, p. 23-S)*

Nunn's critics were counting on one more shot before the Senate approved the limited deployment scheme and sent it to conference with the House: an amendment by Levin declaring that nothing in the bill should be construed "to imply congressional authorization for development, testing or deployment" of a system violating the ABM treaty.

They hoped that Wallop and his fellow conservatives would choke at the prospect of endorsing continued compliance with the treaty they so disliked.

But Levin, too, had to water down his amendment in the hunt for support. In effect, Levin's floor amendment specified that any system "authorized" by the bill had to comply with the ABM treaty. Nunn reasoned that he could live with Levin's floor amendment because establishing a goal of going beyond the existing treaty did not authorize anything.

In the endgame, Nunn and the conservatives accepted Levin's amendment, thus depriving Levin and his allies of a clear test of political strength.

The amendment was adopted, 99-0. *(Vote 170, p. 23-S)*

The Senate also rejected three other SDI-related amendment:

- By Tom Harkin, D-Iowa, deleting the goal of deploying a treaty-compliant anti-missile system by 1996. Tabled (killed), 64-34. *(Vote 172, p. 23-S)*
- By Harkin, to reduce the authorization for SDI by $1.4 billion, to $3.2 billion. Tabled (killed), 60-38. *(Vote 171, p. 23-S)*
- By Dale Bumpers, D-Ark., to reduce the authorization for SDI by $1 billion, to $3.6 billion. Rejected 46-52. *(Vote 173, p. 23-S)*

FINAL ACTION

The House-Senate conferees who drafted the final version of the defense authorization bill incorporated most of the fundamentals of the Senate-crafted deal on SDI. The conference report was adopted by the House, 329-82, on Nov. 18 and was cleared by the Senate, 79-15, on Nov. 22.

The final version authorized $4.15 billion for the SDI anti-missile program, with $390 million earmarked for the space-based missile interceptors known as Brilliant Pebbles. But the deal put actual development and deployment of those weapons on the back burner.

It mandated deployment of 100 ground-based interceptors at a single site — as permitted by the ABM treaty — by 1996, or whenever the technology was available. And it directed the president to begin immediate discussions with the Soviet government of possible changes in the treaty to allow deployment of more extensive anti-missile defenses.

As House and Senate negotiators sought to craft a compromise version of the defense bill, the position of SDI supporters was bolstered when Gorbachev responded tenatively but positively to Bush's call to negotiate limited anti-missile defenses.

The conferees reached tentative agreement on the defense bill on Nov. 1, although action on the measure was delayed by a dispute over aid to the crumbling Soviet Union.

When the conference agreement reached the House and Senate, members rehashed their longstanding positions on strategic defenses.

Some complained that their negotiators gave away too much in reaching a deal on SDI.

Rep. Dellums, a longtime critic of the SDI program, said, "We have crossed ... the psychological and political threshold, taking SDI from research to deployment."

Sen. Jim Sasser, D-Tenn., chairman of the Budget Committee, condemned the provision as "strategically unwarranted [and] fiscally unsupportable."

But many conservatives and Republicans praised the SDI agreement as the best part of the authorization bill. "For the first time, the Republican position has been accepted that a strategic defense is a legitimate player in the overall building of a defense system," said House Armed Services Committee member John R. Kasich, R-Ohio.

Bush signed the defense authorization bill (PL 102-190) on Dec. 5. ■

Way Is Cleared for Women To Fly Combat Missions

Compared with the usual glacial pace of congressional action, the campaign to clear the way for women to fly combat aircraft rolled through Congress in a political blitzkrieg. Inspired by the role of women just behind the front lines of the Persian Gulf War, lawmakers quickly repealed the law that had prevented women in the military from flying combat missions. They did so as a part of the annual defense authorization measure (HR 2100 — PL 102-190).

The repeal of the combat-exclusion provision did not force the armed services to open up their combat positions to women. But during a hearing on the subject, both the military chiefs of the Air Force and the Navy said that if the exclusion were repealed, they would find it hard not to offer the combat positions to women. All four chiefs who headed the military branches told members of Congress that they opposed repealing the law.

The combat-exclusion law did not apply to the Army, which had its own policy prohibiting women from combat positions.

Members also created a 15-member commission to study how combat readiness might be affected by opening up combat positions to women.

Under existing law, women could fly transport and tanker planes and serve on crews of repair and supply ships — including some that operated in the Persian Gulf region during the war with Iraq. But women were not assigned to armed aircraft or combat vessels.

The combat prohibition law did not apply to the Army, but that service had a policy barring women from direct combat roles.

The 540,000 U.S. personnel stationed in the gulf region during the war included more than 35,000 women, according to the Defense Department.

Since the United States switched to an all-volunteer force in 1973, the percentage of women serving on active duty in the military had increased from 2 percent to 11 percent. Fifteen women died during the U.S. deployment to the Persian Gulf; five of those were killed by enemy fire, although none were officially in combat positions.

HOUSE ACTION

Momentum for changing the law began in the House Armed Services Committee where Rep. Patricia Schroeder, D-Colo., offered an amendment to HR 2100 on May 8 to repeal the combat-exclusion law. The panel approved the amendment by voice vote.

Schroeder initially proposed removing the combat restriction for the Air Force. She accepted an amendment by Personnel Subcommittee Chairman Beverly B. Byron, D-Md., to extend the provision to the Navy as well.

Committee support was strong. Even panel member G. V. "Sonny" Montgomery, D-Miss., who had opposed the provision, said at a news conference that he realized early on that he was going to lose. "I saw the light," he said. According to Montgomery, the Armed Services staff cheered as the committee passed the provision.

The crisis in the gulf and the invasion of Panama in 1989 also highlighted a change in the nature of the modern battlefield: The ubiquity of ground-attack planes, long-range artillery and fast-moving ground forces had eroded the distinction between a dangerous "front" and a safer "rear area," where women in non-combat jobs were once considered relatively immune from attack.

"Where is the front line?" Byron asked. "Where is combat?"

SENATE ACTION

The Senate Armed Forces Committee did not include the repeal of the combat ban for pilots in its bill, but the full Senate added it on the floor.

The committee bill did include a provision that established a 15-member presidential commission to study issues involved in assigning women to combat roles, including the effect on unit morale, the cost of required changes in equipment and quarters and whether it would render unconstitutional the draft registration law, which applied only to men.

The commission's findings and recommendations would be sent to the president by Nov. 15, 1992, and the president's recommendations would be due on Capitol Hill a month later.

The amendment offered July 31 to repeal the combat ban was cosponsored by Edward M. Kennedy, D-Mass., and William V. Roth Jr., R-Del. Some of the Senate's most conservative Republicans and nearly all of its liberal Democrats joined forces to reject, 30-69, an effort by Armed Services Committee leaders to table (kill) the amendment. The Senate then adopted the proposal by voice vote. *(Vote 167, p. 22-S)*

"They flew behind enemy lines and transported troops into enemy territory," Roth told the Senate. "We owe our victory, in part, to the superb performance of these women pilots."

Former fighter pilots John Glenn, D-Ohio, and John McCain, R-Ariz., led the effort to stave off immediate repeal of the combat-exclusion law for female pilots, contending that so sweeping a change in policy should await more thorough study. The debate was "all too driven by emotions and far too little driven by national security requirements," McCain said.

"We're proud of the role women played in the Persian Gulf War," he insisted. "But it also brought to light questions that need answering." He noted, for example, that strong opposition surfaced to the deployment of single parents who had custody of young children and to the deployment of both parents in some families.

McCain contended that — unlike pilots, who are officers — "the overwhelming majority of enlisted women in the Army and Marine Corps do not wish to be in combat."

In an effort to counter the Kennedy-Roth proposal, Glenn and McCain offered an amendment that would authorize the secretary of Defense to waive the combat-exclusion laws so that women could be assigned to some combat units on a trial basis to gather data for the commission's study.

But Kennedy disputed the need for additional study to determine whether women could handle the stress of flying jet fighters. "Women have been flying high-performance airplanes since 1975," he declared, noting their role as test pilots and flight instructors. "The performance is out there."

Defense Secretary Dick Cheney endorsed the study commission but declined to oppose Kennedy-Roth.

The Senate adopted the Glenn-McCain amendment by a 96-3 vote, immediately before rejecting the motion to kill the Kennedy-Roth proposal. *(Vote 166, p. 22-S)* ■

Arms Treaties Mitigated By Soviet Breakup

Under ordinary circumstances, 1991 would have been a year of substantial accomplishments in the arcane but momentous annals of arms control treaties.

On Nov. 25, the Senate overwhelmingly approved the treaty on Conventional Forces in Europe (CFE) that required the destruction of tens of thousands of tanks and other weapons, most of them deployed by the Soviet Union.

The same day, President Bush submitted to the Senate the Strategic Arms Reduction Treaty (START), which was intended to cut by about one-third the arsenals of U.S. and Soviet long-range, nuclear-armed missiles and bombers.

But world events moved so quickly and dramatically during the year that such traditional arms control agreements — arrived at through laborious superpower negotiations and loaded down with intricate tradeoffs and safeguards — were effectively eclipsed by the crumbling of the Soviet Union.

On Sept. 27, Bush attempted to scramble ahead of the curve of change by announcing an unprecedented decision to scrap thousands of U.S. nuclear weapons — many unilaterally and others if the Soviet Union agreed — and to ease up on the triggers of thousands more. Soviet President Mikhail S. Gorbachev responded by offering to match and exeed the U.S. cuts.

By the end of 1991, the former Soviet republics had declared their independence and the demise of the Soviet Union. On Dec. 25, Gorbachev resigned, and the Soviet flag over the Kremlin was lowered.

That left the Bush administration without the leader — and, for that matter, without the country — with which it had negotiated arms control treaties. The administration sought, and generally received, assurances from republics in the loose-knit new Commonwealth of Independent States that they would honor arms agreements, including the CFE and START treaties.

Members of the Senate indicated that their deliberations on the START agreement would turn in large part on how reliable such commitments would be in the uncertain post-Soviet era.

In the short run, U.S. efforts — including legislation authorizing the use of up to $400 million in defense funds — were devoted to guaranteeing the security of the former Soviet arsenal and helping the republics dismantle the weapons. *(Soviet aid, p. 463)*

Senate Ratified CFE Treaty Overwhelmingly

Amid unease over the Soviet Union's future, the Senate on Nov. 25 closed a chapter from the era of superpower military competition by overwhelmingly endorsing the Conventional Forces in Europe treaty.

The Senate approved, 90-4, a resolution of ratification for the CFE treaty (Treaty Doc. 102-8), which had been signed in Paris the previous November by President Bush, Soviet President Mikhail S. Gorbachev and the leaders of 20 other nations. *(Vote 273, p. 36-S; background, 1990 Almanac, p. 696)*

The treaty imposed ceilings on military equipment deployed by the NATO states and the former members of the Warsaw Pact in an area between the Atlantic Ocean and the Ural Mountains. *(Treaty effects, p. 417)*

Most senators agreed that the pact was "demonstrably and overwhelmingly favorable to the United States and its NATO allies," as Senate Armed Services Committee Chairman Sam Nunn, D-Ga., put it.

But a handful of Republicans opposed the resolution, charging that the Soviets had violated the treaty's provisions even before its ratification.

In what Nunn referred to as an "astonishingly asymmetrical outcome," the Soviet Union was required to destroy more than 20,000 pieces of military equipment while the United States was committed to scrap fewer than 3,000.

The goal of the treaty from the outset was sharp reductions in weapons that were seen as particularly useful in a blitzkrieg, which NATO had feared for 20 years from the tank-heavy forces of the Soviet Union and its Warsaw Pact allies.

By the time the agreement was signed, it essentially ratified an unraveling of Soviet military power that had greatly outstripped the arms control negotiations. Since late 1988, Gorbachev had orchestrated a dramatic military retrenchment in response to political tensions and economic collapse at home.

Meanwhile, largely peaceful revolutions in the former Soviet satellites of Eastern Europe supplanted Communist regimes with popularly elected governments less pliant to Kremlin wishes and eager to slice their own defense costs.

Even though the Warsaw Pact was moribund by the time the CFE Treaty was signed, the agreement retained its initial structure: It imposed equal ceilings on weapons that could be deployed in Europe by NATO and by the six countries that formerly made up the Warsaw Pact.

Each group of countries could deploy between the Atlantic Ocean and the Ural Mountains no more than 20,000 tanks, 30,000 armored troop carriers, 20,000 artillery pieces, 6,800 combat airplanes and 2,000 attack helicopters.

To further inhibit the concentration of forces for an attack, the treaty also set regional sublimits on the number of tanks, troop carriers and artillery.

The treaty also barred either group from deploying more than 740 mobile bridges. A separate agreement attached to the treaty — but not formally part of it — barred either group of countries from deploying more than 430 land-based naval planes.

Any weapons in excess of the treaty limits that were in the area covered by the treaty at the time it was signed had to be demolished within 40 months. But a certain number of those could be used for other purposes after they had been disarmed under specified procedures.

To verify compliance, the treaty provided for detailed exchanges of data about the organization of each country's military forces and about the number, model and location of its treaty-limited weaponry.

Disputes Resolved

On June 14, seven months after the treaty was signed, the CFE participants formally settled two disputes that had blocked the pact's implementation.

One issue was the Soviet effort to exempt thousands of weapons from the treaty even though it permitted only a few narrow exemptions.

The Kremlin insisted that more than 5,400 tanks and other items were exempt because they were assigned to ground combat units of the Soviet navy or to units defending strategic missile bases.

More than 1,100 of the disputed weapons were assigned to four long-established naval infantry regiments, corresponding to U.S. Marine Corps units. But more than 2,600 of the weapons were assigned to three Soviet army divisions stationed near the coast, which were shifted to navy control as the CFE negotiations drew to a close.

Most Western observers believed that the sudden reassignment of the army divisions as naval units was intended partly as a ploy to underscore Soviet frustration with the longstanding U.S. refusal to discuss limits on naval forces.

Though none of the other countries that were parties to the treaty supported Moscow's contention that these weapons were exempt, a compromise was struck allowing the Kremlin to keep the disputed equipment in the naval units but requiring the destruction of a corresponding number of weapons within the treaty area.

Of the additional weapons earmarked for destruction to offset the equipment assigned to the naval units, half had to be destroyed within the treaty area under costly procedures stipulated by the CFE pact.

The remainder were permitted to be moved east of the Urals and then destroyed in any way that provided "sufficient visible evidence" that they were rendered militarily useless.

The armored troop carriers assigned to protect missile bases were exempted from the treaty outright.

The compromise also stipulated that all other weapons in the treaty zone of the designated types were covered by the treaty limits unless specifically exempted, regardless of the organization to which they were assigned.

The deal was embodied in a unilateral Soviet statement attached to, but separate from, the CFE treaty and having the same binding force in international law.

The second issue settled June 14 involved about 59,000 tanks and other weapons that the Soviet government moved east of the Urals shortly before the treaty was signed, thus exempting them from coverage.

In a statement that was described as "politically binding" but not binding in international law, the Kremlim pledged that the equipment would not be used to create a strategic reserve force and would not be stored in a way that would allow its rapid redeployment into the area covered by the treaty.

The Soviet government also promised to destroy or demilitarize 14,500 of these weapons by 1995.

COMMITTEE HEARINGS

There was little dissent from members of the Senate Foreign Relations Committee when Joseph R. Biden Jr., D-Del., called the treaty that would sharply reduce the levels of conventional forces in Europe a "real good deal" for the United States and its allies.

But as the panel opened hearings on the historic treaty July 11, many members echoed former President Ronald Reagan's favorite dictum concerning arms pacts with the Soviet Union: "Trust but verify."

Senators pressed Secretary of State James A. Baker III for assurances that the Soviet Union would abide by terms of the CFE treaty. Conservative Jesse Helms, R-N.C., harshly criticized the Soviets for failing to comply with previous arms control treaties.

"To put it as politely as possible, the Soviets are cheats, liars and scoundrels," he said. "I would get angry about this [CFE] treaty if it meant anything."

Helms, who had applied his formidable parliamentary skills to toughen or defeat prior arms control agreements, depicted the CFE pact as not worth the effort of strong opposition. He said it had been overtaken by the end of the Cold War. But Helms warned that "START, unlike CFE, is a treaty that matters." That agreement "needs full scrutiny."

Other senators focused more attention on the treaty at hand. But even the liberal Biden — who presided over the CFE hearings instead of the increasingly disengaged committee Chairman Claiborne Pell, D-R.I. — indicated he would propose conditions to the pact to ensure Soviet compliance.

Biden said he intended to offer a condition to ensure that the Soviets adhered to the political commitments that Moscow had agreed to implement but that technically were not part of the treaty.

His condition "would simply formalize a United States policy of treating violations of the Soviet Union's militarily significant pledge as a possible circumvention of the treaty — of a kind proscribed by the treaty itself," Biden said.

Baker said he hoped that "we could move forward with ratification of this treaty" without conditions. But he indicated that the administration was willing to discuss the concerns of the committee.

SENATE COMMITTEE ACTION

The Senate Foreign Relations Committee took a step toward formalizing the end of the Cold War on Nov. 19 as it unanimously approved the CFE agreement.

A year to the day after the CFE pact was signed in Paris, the committee voted 18-0 to send a resolution of ratification of the treaty to the full Senate (Treaty Doc. 102-8).

But some Republicans charged that the resolution failed to adequately address the possibility that newly independent Soviet republics might not accede to the treaty's weapons ceilings.

They forced postponement of Senate consideration of the treaty, which had been expected on Nov. 22, and said they were considering possible amendments reflecting their concerns.

Biden said no previous arms control agreement had led to such deep reductions. Helms was far less enthusiastic, although he said that the treaty "codifies the former Soviet Union's military withdrawal from Eastern Europe" by reducing its major armament holdings in the area by half.

With the military threat posed by the Soviet central government sharply diminished, members of the Foreign Relations Committee focused on the potential dangers arising from the independence movement sweeping what had been the Soviet empire.

The committee attached a condition to the resolution requiring Bush to seek Senate approval for changes in the pact that might arise if any of the breakaway republics refused to abide by provisions of the treaty.

That was one of five conditions and four declarations — essentially sense of the Senate statements — that were

Conventional Forces in Europe

The treaty limiting conventional forces in Europe (CFE) called for the Soviet Union to destroy or disarm more than 20,000 of the 73,000 tanks, artillery and other heavy weapons that equipped its forces west of the Ural Mountains as of mid-1991.

But that 27 percent reduction was dwarfed by the massive decline in Soviet conventional power in Europe since CFE negotiations began early in 1989. Measured against the Soviet weapons deployed less than three years previously, the arsenal controlled by former republics of the Soviet Union was to be reduced by more than two-thirds under the treaty.

Of the more than 147,000 Soviet weapons covered by the treaty that were deployed early in 1989, nearly 60,000 had been shipped by mid-1991 to Soviet Asia, where they were exempt from CFE limits. Before the Soviet Union crumbled, its leaders assured the Bush administration that 14,500 of those weapons would be destroyed or demilitarized by 1995; the Senate conditioned its approval of the treaty on observance of that side deal.

The rest of the weapons shifted east of the Urals were to remain intact but so far from Europe as to be useless for the kind of surprise attack the CFE treaty was intended to prevent. The remaining Soviet weapons above the CFE limit of 52,975 were slated for destruction or disarmament.

For each of five types of weapons, the treaty imposed equal ceilings on NATO and what were at the time the six surviving members of the former Warsaw Pact. Each of the two groups of countries, in turn, allocated among themselves national ceilings for each class of weapon.

The following chart describes the effects of the CFE treaty that were expected at the time the Senate considered the pact. It is based on estimates provided by the Institute for Defense and Disarmament Studies.

	U.S.	Other NATO [1]	Soviet Union	Eastern Europe	Comments
Tanks					
Mid-1991	5,904	16,188	20,725	10,988	Category includes wheeled or tracked vehicles carrying a gun of 75mm or larger and weighing at least 16.5 metric tons (excluding the weight of crew, ammunition, fuel and removable armor).
Post-treaty [2]	4,006	15,136	13,150	6,850	
Armored Combat Vehicles					
Mid-1991	5,747	22,661	29,890	11,941	Of the 30,000 permitted for each group of states, no more than 18,000 could carry a gun of 20mm or larger. Of those 18,000, no more than 1,500 could weigh more than 6 metric tons or more and carry a gun of 75mm or larger.
Post-treaty [2]	5,372	24,450	20,000	10,000	
Artillery					
Mid-1991	2,601	16,003	13,938	10,818	Category includes both guns and rocket launchers firing projectiles of 100mm caliber or larger.
Post-treaty [2]	2,492	15,794	13,175 [3]	6,825 [3]	
Airplanes					
Mid-1991	626	4,690	6,611	1,757	Category includes "combat-capable" aircraft, excluding basic trainers and carrier-based planes. Each alliance would be permitted an additional 430 land-based naval aircraft.
Post-treaty [2]	784	5,878	5,150	1,650	
Helicopters					
Mid-1991	243	1,300	1,481	181	Category includes armed helicopters but not land-based naval helicopters.
Post-treaty [2]	518	1,482	1,500	500	

[1] *Excludes 10,674 weapons of former East German forces, which would be counted against NATO limits as part of the forces of unified Germany. Virtually all of them would be destroyed.*

[2] *Projected levels. Based on treaty ceilings or lower levels announced by countries.*

attached to the resolution of ratification.

The administration had originally hoped to win approval of a "clean" resolution of ratification but raised no objections to the committee's conditions.

According to Richard G. Lugar, R-Ind., the condition requiring Senate approval for changes in the treaty was largely directed at Ukraine, which he said intended to maintain a large army as an independent nation.

"This condition resolves the problem of Senate consent at a time of uncertainty in the Soviet Union," said Biden.

But William S. Cohen, R-Maine, said he would probably attempt to add language requiring the president to seek Senate "advice and consent" for other contingencies relating to the Soviet breakup.

Of the five conditions in the Senate Foreign Relations package, two were intended to ensure Soviet compliance with commitments that Moscow had agreed to but were not technically part of the treaty.

One of the deals was the Soviet promise to scrap weapons to compensate for those it had shifted to navy units exempt from the treaty.

The pledge was embodied in a unilateral Soviet statement that was described as having the same binding force in international law as the treaty. The Senate committee amendment stipulated that the United States would treat Soviet violations of that statement as equivalent to a treaty violation.

The other side agreement that the Senate committee amendment aimed to lock in was a Soviet pledge to neutralize the weapons that had been transferred east of the Ural Mountains shortly before the treaty was signed, thus escaping the pact's coverage. In another unilateral statement — this one described as "politically binding," but not binding as a matter of international law — Soviet officials promised that the equipment would not be used to create a strategic reserve force nor stored in a way that would allow its rapid redeployment to the region covered by the CFE pact.

The Senate committee's condition stipulated that Soviet adherence to that pledge was so important to U.S. vital interests that, if it were violated, the United States would consider exercising its rights to withdraw from the pact or to deviate from compliance in some way that was proportionate to the Soviet action.

Another condition in the Foreign Relations amendment dealt with the erosion of Soviet control over territory in which Soviet forces were deployed. It stipulated that the United States would count against the Soviet Union's allowance under the treaty any Soviet weapons deployed in the Baltic republics of Estonia, Latvia and Lithuania, which had declared independence from Moscow.

The final condition in the Foreign Relations amendment highlighted a remaining discrepancy in counting the number of Soviet weapons subject to disposal under the treaty. U.S. estimates exceeded the Soviet count by about 800 weapons. The condition provided that, if the higher U.S. estimate turned out to be correct, the United States had to insist that the Soviet Union destroy 800 additional weapons.

The Foreign Relations amendment also included four other provisions intended to stake out the Senate's position in long-running disputes with various adversaries, foreign and domestic.

One of these so-called declarations stipulated that Senate approval of the CFE treaty was based on the assumption that administration witnesses testifying to Senate committees had provided "authoritative" testimony about the interpretation of the pact.

This provision was rooted in the Senate's battle with Reagan over his 1985 claim that some provisions of the anti-ballistic missile (ABM) treaty did not mean what most witnesses from the executive branch had told Senate committees in 1972. According to the Reagan administration, the 1972 testimony had not been "authoritative." *(1985 Almanac, p. 132)*

In response, Democrats incorporated in the Senate's resolution approving the 1988 treaty banning intermediate-range nuclear forces (INF) a declaration that the Senate's approval was contingent on the assumption that administration testimony about that pact was authoritative. The Senate amendment to the CFE resolution stipulated that the INF provision applied to all treaties.

The other declarations:

- Urged the president to seek formal assent to the CFE treaty of any new state formed in the area covered by its limits.
- Said that future international agreements mandating a militarily significant reduction in U.S. arms should be enacted as treaties, which required approval by two-thirds of the Senate, rather than as executive agreements, which were confirmed by a joint resolution adopted by a majority vote of both the Senate and House.

Existing law permitted the president to use either type of agreement. But when Bush indicated that he might submit as an executive agreement a U.S.-Soviet pact to provide for sweeping reductions in chemical weapons, senators complained that the White House was derogating the Senate's constitutional prerogative to subject important international agreements to its power over treaties.

- Put the Soviet Union on notice that, when the Senate took up START in 1992, it would take into account the extent to which the Soviet Union had corrected violations of previous arms control agreements, including the construction of a huge radar at Krasnoyarsk.

The Senate committee, by voice vote, also approved legislation (S 1987) authorizing the president to transfer to NATO allies virtually all of the equipment scheduled to be disposed of under the CFE treaty. The House Foreign Affairs Committee approved an identical measure the same day (HR 3807).

Under the procedure, known as "cascading," the United States could transfer 2,968 tanks, combat armored vehicles and artillery pieces. The NATO allies were required to eliminate a comparable number of older weapons. Turkey was to be the leading recipient, followed by Greece and Spain.

Explaining the arms tradeoff, Terrence O'Donnell, general counsel of the Defense Department, wrote the Senate in July, "This program will, at no cost to the U.S., modernize NATO's forces."

The "cascading" measure (PL 102-228) later became the legislative vehicle to authorize up to $500 million in aid to the former Soviet republics. *(Soviet aid, p. 463)*

SENATE ACTION

In the Senate debate on the CFE treaty, Biden and Majority Leader George J. Mitchell, D-Maine, expressed hope that it would pave the way for sweeping nuclear arms reductions.

Yet even among supporters of the treaty, its benefits were overshadowed by the military dangers associated with the imminent breakup of the old Soviet empire. Al Gore, D-Tenn., who voted for the resolution, complained that "we are asked to vote on this even though there is uncertainty" on several issues. Many senators were particularly concerned about the possibility that a republic in possession of a large amount of Soviet weaponry might declare its independence and reject the treaty's limits on military equipment.

Ukraine, which held an estimated 6,500 battle tanks, was on the verge of holding a referendum on withdrawing from the Soviet Union. (The vote, on Dec. 1, overwhelmingly favored the independence that all of the Soviet republics achieved later that month.)

While officials from Ukraine indicated their new nation would abide by the treaty's terms, the Senate attempted to address members' concerns with a condition attached to the resolution of ratification. It was one of six such conditions included on the resolution either by the Foreign Relations Committee or on the Senate floor.

The committee amendment required the president to submit for the Senate's "advice and consent" significant changes in the pact that might be negotiated by the treaty signatories if a well-armed republic were to spurn the treaty's terms.

But Cohen, a member of the Armed Services Committee, said that condition did not go far enough in protecting senatorial prerogatives. He said it did not cover a situation in which a future president might decide that the United States should remain committed to the treaty — even if a military power such as Ukraine declared itself not bound by the treaty and the signatories did not agree to alter the pact.

He offered language amending the condition to require that a future president — either "President Bush, or President Harkin, or President Cuomo," he said — also seek Senate advice and consent under that scenario.

But Biden said the inclusion of such a condition would be likely to provoke a constitutional conflict with the administration. He modified the amendment to require that, under a scenario such as the one outlined by Cohen, a president needed only to seek a resolution of support. A resolution needed only a simple majority to be approved, not the two-thirds required for the Senate's advice and consent.

The president could theoretically disregard the Senate's rejection of such a resolution, Biden said, "but he will have paid a big political price for doing it."

Cohen's amendment, as modified by Biden, was approved by voice vote.

Conservative Republicans also amended the resolution in an effort to address the problem of "data discrepancy" — inaccuracies in Moscow's estimates of the level of Soviet military equipment in the area covered by the treaty at the time it was signed.

Robert C. Smith, R-N.H., and Malcolm Wallop, R-Wyo., offered an amendment that conditioned U.S. adherence to the treaty on a presidential certification that the Soviet Union "is not in violation or probable violation of the terms of the CFE treaty."

Biden charged that the condition was a "killer amendment, plain and simple," adding that the White House was strongly opposed to the amendment. He proposed a modification that required the president to report on Soviet compliance to the treaty but did not link the report to continued U.S. participation in the treaty.

Biden's amendment was approved by voice vote. But Smith and Wallop, along with Idaho Republicans Larry E. Craig, and Steve Symms voted against the resolution of ratification.

Helms did not vote.

President Submitted START Treaty to Senate

On Nov. 25, President Bush submitted the Strategic Arms Reduction Treaty (START) to the Senate in the expectation that hearings on the nuclear weapons pact would begin early in 1992.

The START negotiations that produced the complex treaty were initiated during the administration of President Ronald Reagan, who argued for a U.S.-Soviet agreement that would reduce nuclear weapons stockpiles rather than simply constrain their growth.

After years of off-and-on negotiations, Bush and Soviet President Mikhail S. Gorbachev signed the agreement in Moscow on July 31, only weeks before the botched hardliners' coup attempt of Aug. 19 that led to the unraveling of the Soviet superpower.

At the treaty-signing ceremony in the Kremlin, Bush said the U.S.-Soviet pact reflected a conviction that "stabilizing reductions in our nuclear forces reduces the risk of war." Gorbachev cautioned that "the treaty will have to be defended" against critics in both countries.

Although Senate conservatives such as Jesse Helms, R-N.C., argued that the START cuts went too far and that the Soviets still could not be trusted, some Democrats urged the administration to go further.

Joseph R. Biden Jr., D-Del., argued that START alone was insufficient because it would "bring superpower arsenals down only to the levels that existed when the talks began some 10 years ago."

Agreement on the treaty was clinched by Bush and Gorbachev at a summit of major economic powers in London on July 17.

The mood was as much one of relief as euphoria as almost a decade of negotiation had at last yielded the first treaty to reduce arsenals of strategic nuclear weapons.

In the space of a few hours, U.S. and Soviet negotiators hammered out the last nettlesome details.

The president confidently predicted that the treaty "ought to sail through the Senate."

The treaty required both sides to reduce their stockpiles of nuclear warheads. In particular, it called for an overall decrease in intercontinental ballistic missiles (ICBMs). This mandated a 50 percent cut in Moscow's arsenal of 308 SS-18s — the most potentially devastating missiles the Soviet Union possessed.

Two key members of the Senate Foreign Relations Committee, which had jurisdiction over the treaty, offered the same initial prognosis: Republican Richard G. Lugar, Ind., and Democrat Biden predicted the Senate would ratify START but much less quickly and easily than the Conventional Forces in Europe (CFE) treaty reducing conventional arms.

But some conservatives were unwilling to see START ratified without tough questions, if not outright opposition.

Helms, who said he was concerned over the treaty's compliance provisions, charged that the Soviets "have always cheated on every arms control measure."

START was the third major arms reduction agreement reached in four years to require the Soviet Union to give up far more firepower than the United States.

Under the treaty barring U.S. and Soviet intermediate-range nuclear force (INF) missiles, signed in 1987, the Soviet Union scrapped more than 1,800 missiles, compared with the 859 U.S. weapons that were eliminated.

Moreover, a third of the Soviet weapons were triple-warhead SS-20s while all the U.S. weapons carried single warheads. More than three times as many Soviet warheads as U.S. warheads were removed from service. *(1988 Almanac, p. 379)*

The CFE treaty also required such "asymmetrical" reductions. And the START pact called for substantial reductions in the ICBMs that had been the backbone of the Soviet force. By contrast, the treaty permitted much larger deployments than seemed likely for the bomber-launched weapons that accounted for a large part of the U.S. arsenal.

In considerable measure, these sharply asymmetrical treaties merely ratified the retrenchment of Soviet military power over the previous five years as Gorbachev wrestled with economic collapse and political crisis at home.

The Genesis of START

START also codified the views of one of the contending perspectives in a U.S. debate over strategic arms that had gone on for more than 20 years.

One side of that debate emphasized the thousands of strategic weapons deployed by each superpower and the enormous destruction that either could wreak on the other with only a fraction of its force.

Under those circumstances, liberals such as Paul Warnke, who had been President Jimmy Carter's arms control chief, contended that each arsenal served only to deter the other's use through the threat of retaliation. By this argument, so long as one side was not drastically stronger than the other, mutual deterrence would work regardless of marginal disparities in the number and types of nuclear weapons deployed by each side.

But START, with its strong emphasis on cutting the Soviet missile force, was largely a product of the competing view, held by many conservatives such as Richard N. Perle, the Reagan administration's most influential nuclear arms policy expert.

The big Soviet ICBMs, designated SS-18s, were particularly dangerous, according to this argument, because their warheads were sufficiently powerful and accurate to destroy U.S. missiles in their armored, underground silos in a lightning-quick strike. This capacity was unmatched in the U.S. arsenal.

The hard-liners' premise was not so much that Moscow ever would launch such a strike, but that its theoretical capability to do so would give Soviet leaders an edge in diplomatic face-offs.

From this perspective, Reagan and other Republican conservatives contended that arms control agreements reached in the 1970s during the strategic arms limitation talks (SALT) were fatally flawed even though GOP administrations played key roles in both:

- SALT I, an executive agreement signed in 1972 by President Richard M. Nixon, froze the number of U.S. and Soviet strategic missiles and bombers. This left the Soviet Union with a monopoly on heavy ICBMs and codified Moscow's numerical superiority, partly because it did not limit the Soviet Backfire bomber.
- SALT II, agreed to in principle by President Gerald R. Ford in 1974 and signed as a treaty by Carter in 1979, would have set equal numerical limits on U.S. and Soviet missiles and bombers. But conservatives argued that it still left unchecked the threat to U.S. ICBMs; that it still did not fully cover the Backfire; and that Soviet compliance with its limits could not be verified in any case.

SALT II never was ratified, partly because of conservative opposition and partly because of outrage over the Soviet invasion of Afghanistan. *(Congress and the Nation, Vol. V, p. 193)*

Reagan won the White House in 1980 warning that the United States had ceded strategic superiority to the Soviet Union. He promised a two-pronged effort to redress the U.S. disadvantage and to reduce — rather than merely freeze — the U.S. and Soviet arsenals.

First, to improve the U.S. bargaining position, he launched a far-reaching effort to expand and modernize the U.S. strategic force, including deployment of the 10-warhead MX missile, which could bust Soviet missile silos. Only 50 were actually deployed.

Then, in 1982, he unveiled his own approach to strategic arms control, demanding a treaty to reduce the number of weapons, especially the Soviet ICBM force.

Reagan's proposal was so one-sided in its impact on Soviet defenses that many critics dismissed it as a sham, intended merely to palliate the public demand for arms control efforts while ensuring that no agreement would be reached.

But five years later, Reagan and Gorbachev agreed at Reykjavik, Iceland, on the major elements of a treaty that embodied Reagan's approach.

It took nearly four more years to nail down the definitions and details, with the Bush administration particularly eager to avoid giving conservatives such as Helms ammunition with which to fight Senate approval of the pact.

For example, the last detail, reportedly settled in London, was the definition of a missile's throw-weight — the total mass of the warheads and guidance equipment it could launch. That, in turn, was a key element of the treaty's definition of a "new type" of missile, which was central to the limits on the number of missile warheads that could be deployed.

The treaty provided that each existing type of missile could be tested with no more than a specified number of warheads — fewer than 10, in most cases — but a "new type" could be tested with up to 10 warheads. The U.S. goal was to prevent the Soviets from making minor changes in an existing type, declaring it a new type, testing it with more warheads than it had carried and then quickly deploying additional warheads on the existing missiles.

Negotiators eventually agreed that, to qualify as a new type, a missile would have to differ from existing types by at least 5 percent in some dimension and by at least 21 percent in throw-weight.

With that settled, all that remained was agreement on a technical definition of how throw-weight would be calculated.

As the Senate prepared for its 1992 debate on START, the administration collected assurances from the new Soviet republics that they would honor the agreements. The Senate made it clear that its deliberations would depend in significant measure on the reliability of those assurances. ■

Bush Offered Unilateral Arms Cutbacks

On Sept. 27, President Bush went on national television to announce a bold new initiative to reduce strategic arms in recognition of the dramatic changes in the Soviet Union.

"If we and the Soviet leaders take the right steps — some on our own, some on their own, some together — we can dramatically shrink the arsenal of the world's nuclear weapons," Bush said.

The unilateral initiative was a recognition of the dizzying pace of change in the Soviet Union, which pushed the administration to make a radical break from the tradition of mutual arms control agreements crafted in months or years of negotiations.

Bush announced that the United States would scrap more than 3,000 short-range nuclear weapons, pull back 1,275 more from the front lines and remove from alert nearly 2,700 weapons on strategic bombers and missiles.

Bush canceled development of several weapons, including mobile launchers for the MX and Midgetman intercontinental ballistic missiles (ICBMs). He called on Moscow to negotiate a ban on land-based ICBMs with multiple warheads and to ease the 1972 anti-ballistic missile (ABM) treaty to permit deployment of limited anti-missile defenses. *(Key changes and effects, p. 422)*

The tactical nuclear weapons that Bush unilaterally scrapped had been a source of political controversy for years in Western Europe, where more than 6,000 such weapons were stationed in the late 1970s.

"When the Soviet Union and its Warsaw Pact allies had the edge in non-nuclear military power, we felt we needed nuclear weapons to compensate," said House Armed Services Committee Chairman Les Aspin, D-Wis.

"Now, the United States has the edge in conventional military forces, and we're concerned with such things as terrorist use of nuclear weapons and unauthorized or accidental use."

Congress' Reaction

Bush's arms cutbacks drew enthusiastic support at home and abroad.

But the political impact of the initiative threatened to tilt the congressional playing field against Bush and in favor of largely Democratic critics of two costly and controversial programs: the B-2 stealth bomber and the strategic defense initiative (SDI) anti-missile defense program.

"The American people are going to ask the question, 'If there's that much less threat ... why do we need to put that much money into a bomber?' " Senate Armed Services Committee member Trent Lott, R-Miss., said Sept. 30. "I'm a guy who's voted for the B-2 every time, but ... it's getting tougher every time."

Moreover, Bush's speech appeared to bolster Democratic demands to amend the long-term budget control act in order to shift billions of dollars from defense to domestic spending.

Responding to Bush's speech on behalf of the Democratic Party, Senate Majority Leader George J. Mitchell of Maine applauded the nuclear reduction moves as steps toward a more secure peace. But he pointedly added that they also were important because "they will enable us to concentrate our efforts and our resources on meeting urgent needs at home."

Most domestic criticism of Bush's proposal came from Democrats unhappy that he still championed the B-2 and SDI. "He conceded the obvious while defending the dubious," said Sen. Joseph R. Biden Jr., D-Del. *(SDI, p. 407)*

But some conservative members warned that the package went too far. Senate Armed Services Committee member Malcolm Wallop, R-Wyo., argued that the nuclear cutbacks were risky, in part because they would be difficult to reverse if the Soviet Union's political reforms failed.

"You're playing on the dreams and hopes and fears, not only of Americans, but of our allies," Wallop told Gen. Colin L. Powell Jr., chairman of the Joint Chiefs of Staff, at a Sept. 30 hearing. "Those are powerful political forces that we have ... been unable to resist in a lot of other ways."

Senate Armed Services Chairman Sam Nunn, D-Ga., endorsed the thrust of Bush's package but argued that development of a mobile launcher for the single-warhead Midgetman missile should have been continued as a non-threatening hedge against future dangers.

Nunn also objected to taking all U.S. bombers off alert, warning that the crews might lose their edge and that officials would become loathe to put bombers back on alert in a crisis for fear of creating a panic. He recommended that the Pentagon routinely put on alert some randomly selected bombers.

House Armed Services Committee member Patricia Schroeder, D-Colo, a Pentagon critic, said Oct. 3 that Bush's unilateral weapons cuts had made it more politically acceptable for Democrats to challenge weapons systems. "The president removed them from the sacred cow list," she said.

Gorbachev's Response

On Oct. 5, Soviet President Mikhail S. Gorbachev matched Bush's initiative with a pledge to scrap unilaterally thousands of short-range (tactical) nuclear weapons.

But Gorbachev also upped the diplomatic ante by announcing that he would retire unilaterally 1,000 long-range (strategic) Soviet weapons in addition to those that would have to be scrapped under the Strategic Arms Reduction Treaty (START), signed July 31.

"We are decisively advancing the process of disarmament," he said.

Bush called Gorbachev's announcement "good news for the whole world."

Gorbachev also renewed arms control measures that the Bush administration already had rejected, such as a one-year ban on underground nuclear testing.

Responding to Gorbachev's plea, House freshman Mike Kopetski, D-Ore., backed by Majority Leader Richard A. Gephardt, D-Mo., and 36 other Democrats, called for a moratorium on U.S. nuclear weapons tests in fiscal 1992.

Pentagon officials had long insisted that continued testing was essential to ensure the safety and effectiveness of the U.S. nuclear stockpile.

On the other hand, Gorbachev appeared to temper the Soviet Union's longstanding opposition to the Pentagon's SDI.

"We are prepared to consider proposals from the United States of America on non-nuclear anti-missile defense systems," he said, suggesting "joint systems for warning against a nuclear missile attack with elements based in space and on land."

Paralleling Bush's decision to withdraw most U.S. tacti-

President Bush's Cutbacks . . .

President Bush's nuclear arms reduction proposal scrapped about 3,050 U.S. weapons unilaterally and offered a deal to the Soviet Union to scrap 1,500 more.

Nearly 4,000 U.S. weapons were removed from readiness for immediate use, but more than 10,000 nuclear weapons in the U.S. stockpile were not affected.

Here are the key changes President Bush announced in his speech Sept. 27 and the effects, based on data provided by the Defense Department and the Arms Control Association:

Strategic Bombers: Off Alert

BUSH: *"I am directing that all U.S. strategic bombers immediately stand down from their alert posture."*

EFFECTS: Of the 280 B-1s and B-52s earmarked to carry nuclear weapons, about 40 planes at any time had been loaded with weapons and fuel, sitting near their runways, warmed up and ready to take off on a few minutes' notice.

The day after Bush's speech, this continuous alert was suspended for the first time since 1957, though it could be restarted on 24 hours' notice.

The more than 4,000 long-range cruise missiles and nuclear bombs that the bombers would carry in wartime were stored at the bomber bases.

ICBMs: Off Alert

BUSH: *"The United States will immediately stand down from alert all intercontinental ballistic missiles scheduled for deactivation under START. Rather than waiting for the treaty's reduction plan to run its full seven-year course, we will accelerate the elimination of these systems, once START is ratified."*

EFFECTS: The 450 single-warhead Minuteman II missiles earmarked for elimination under the START treaty were removed from alert status the day after Bush's speech, as were the crew members who work in underground control rooms at the missile sites.

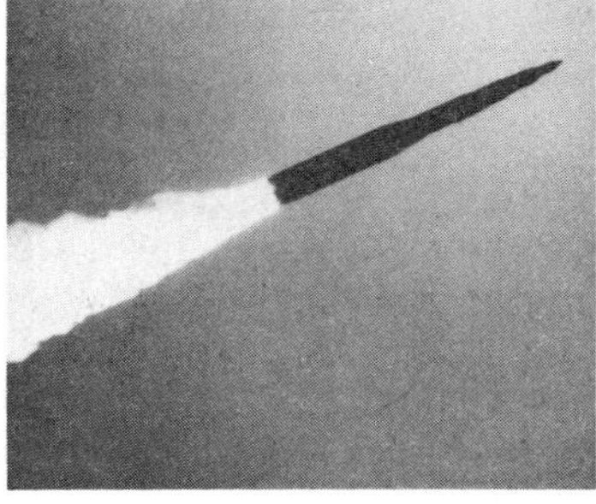

Previously, the Pentagon had accelerated its plans to retire those missiles as well as Poseidon submarine-launched missiles and older B-52 bombers, all of which would be scrapped under START.

Ground-Launched Tactical Weapons: Eliminate

BUSH: *"I am therefore directing that the United States eliminate its entire worldwide inventory of ground-launched short-range — that is, theater — nuclear weapons. We will bring home and destroy all of our nuclear artillery shells and short-range ballistic missile warheads. We will, of course, ensure that we preserve an effective air-delivered nuclear capability in Europe."*

EFFECTS: All of the approximately 1,300 artillery shells and 850 Lance missile warheads in the U.S. arsenal were to be eliminated. Because such tactical weapons must be near the front lines to reach enemy troops, congressional critics had warned that U.S. officials might feel pressure to use them quickly in a war, lest they be captured. Once Soviet troops left Eastern Europe, short-range U.S. weapons had no obvious targets. Because they were relatively portable, similar Soviet weapons were seen as vulnerable to seizure by factions in a potential Soviet civil war.

More than 1,000 tactical bombs to be carried by U.S. jets were to remain in Europe, and about 100 were to remain in South Korea.

Naval Tactical Weapons: Withdraw

BUSH: *"The United States will withdraw all tactical nuclear weapons from its surface ships and attack submarines as well as those nuclear weapons associated with our land-based naval aircraft. . . . Under normal circumstances, our ships will not carry tactical nuclear weapons."*

EFFECTS: An estimated 350 nuclear-armed versions of the Tomahawk cruise missile — about 100 of which are at sea at any time — were to be stored in a U.S. depot. More than 1,800 nuclear bombs and anti-submarine depth charges stored on aircraft carriers and at the land bases that are used by P-3 patrol planes also were to be withdrawn to depots and about half of them destroyed.

Several other types of nuclear-armed anti-aircraft and anti-submarine missiles had been scrapped over the previous few years, partly because of the political and operational limitations on their use.

. . . And the Consequences

Mobile ICBMs: Cancel

BUSH: *"I am terminating development of the mobile Peacekeeper [MX] ICBM as well as the mobile portions of the small ICBM [or "Midgetman"] program."*

EFFECTS: Both programs were intended to protect U.S. missiles from a surprise Soviet missile attack, a threat that was always a subject of vigorous debate in Congress, but which seemed, in any case, much less likely with the Soviet Union's elimination.

The Pentagon had planned to spend $6.8 billion to develop a rail-mobile launcher for the 10-warhead MX and to build 25 trains, each with two launchers. In 1991, it decided to develop and test a train but defer production. In the first vote on either mobile missile program since the collapse of communist power in Moscow, the Senate voted 67-33 on Sept. 26 to deny the $260 million requested for rail-MX development in fiscal 1992.

The projected cost of 300 mobile launchers for the single-warhead Midgetman was $11.2 billion. However, the fiscal 1992 request for $115 million was linked to a decision to develop the launcher but defer any commitment to deploy it. Bush's announcement left the Midgetman itself under development as a potential replacement for 1970s-vintage Minuteman missiles.

Air-Launched Missiles: Cancel

BUSH: *"I am canceling the current program to build a replacement for the short-range attack missile for our strategic bombers."*

EFFECTS: The $2.2 billion program to develop and build 700 supersonic SRAM II bomber-launched missiles with a range of more than 200 miles was canceled. A separate program to develop a version of that weapon that could be launched from smaller fighter jets — designated SRAM-T — also was canceled.

The administration's fiscal 1992 budget request included $177 million for SRAM II and $34 million for SRAM-T, but both the House and the Senate had denied all funds for the latter program. An earlier version of the missile — the SRAM-A — was removed from service in 1990 because its design might permit nuclear material to be scattered if a bomber crashed while taking off or landing.

Multi-Warhead ICBMs: Negotiate Elimination

BUSH: *"I propose that the U.S. and the Soviet Union seek early agreement to eliminate from their inventories all ICBMs with multiple warheads. After developing a timetable acceptable to both sides, we could rapidly move to modify or eliminate these systems under procedures already established in the START agreement."*

EFFECTS: On the U.S. side, such an agreement would require that the 50 MXs be scrapped. In addition, the 500 Minuteman III missiles that carry three warheads (or reentry vehicles) apiece would be converted to single-warhead missiles. The 480 submarine-launched Trident I and II missiles, with up to eight warheads apiece, would remain in service.

Compared with the U.S. arsenal, a much larger proportion of Soviet warheads were on such land-based "multiple independently targetable re-entry vehicle" (or MIRVed) missiles. Moreover, no Soviet sub-launched missiles matched the accuracy of the Trident II. Soviet President Mikhail S. Gorbachev questioned the exemption of sub-launched missiles from the proposed MIRV ban.

Anti-Missile Defenses: Ease ABM Restrictions

BUSH: *"I am calling on the Soviet leadership to join us in taking immediate, concrete steps to permit the limited deployment of non-nuclear defenses to protect against limited ballistic missile strikes — whatever their source — without undermining the credibility of existing deterrent forces."*

EFFECTS: This invited Moscow to reverse its previous opposition to amending the 1972 treaty that limited anti-ballistic missile (ABM) systems.

The treaty revision would permit deployment of defenses such as the so-called GPALS, which was Bush's version of the Strategic Defense Initiative. The ABM Treaty permitted deployment of no more than 100 ground-based anti-missile rockets at one site and banned anti-missile weapons in space. But GPALS would place several hundred interceptor rockets at up to six U.S. sites in addition to several hundred so-called Brilliant Pebbles interceptors in orbit.

cal nuclear weapons, Gorbachev announced that the Soviet Union would:

- Demolish all nuclear artillery shells and nuclear warheads for short-range missiles.
- Remove nuclear weapons from all warships other than submarines carrying long-range ballistic missiles. Some of the weapons would be scrapped and the rest put in storage.
- Remove all nuclear warheads from anti-aircraft missiles, scrapping some. There were no such U.S. warheads.

But Gorbachev went beyond Bush by announcing that he would withdraw from forward bases nuclear bombs for tactical aircraft. Moreover, he proposed scrapping all such weapons and all naval tactical nuclear arms.

Regarding strategic weapons, Gorbachev announced that he was canceling the alert status of the Soviet's small force of long-range bombers and of 503 intercontinental ballistic missiles (ICBMs), including 134 missiles with multiple warheads.

He said the Soviet Union would:

- Freeze at existing levels its force of large, multi-warhead ICBMs on rail-mounted mobile launchers.
- Halt development of a new, smaller mobile ICBM and a bomber-launched missile.
- Cut Soviet military manpower by 700,000 to 3 million.

Beyond announcing that the Soviet Union would deploy only 5,000 START-limited weapons instead of the 6,000 the pact allowed, Gorbachev called on Bush to negotiate an additional 50 percent reduction in strategic arms.

Bush's Nuclear Weapons Announcement

On Sept. 27, President Bush announced that he was taking steps to eliminate about 3,000 short-range nuclear weapons. Following is the transcript of his remarks:

Good evening. Tonight I'd like to speak with you about our future and the future of the generations to come. The world has changed at a fantastic pace, with each day writing a fresh page of history before yesterday's ink is even dried. And most recently, we've seen the peoples of the Soviet Union turn to democracy and freedom and discard a system of government based on oppression and fear.

Like the East Europeans before them, they face the daunting challenge of building fresh political structures based on human rights, democratic principles and market economies. Their task is far from easy and far from over. They will need our help, and they will get it.

But these dramatic changes challenge our nation as well. Our country has always stood for freedom and democracy, and when the newly elected leaders of Eastern Europe grappled with forming their new governments, they looked to the United States; they looked to American democratic principles in building their own free societies. Even the leaders of the U.S.S.R. republics are reading "The Federalist" papers, written by America's founders, to find new ideas and inspiration.

Today, America must lead again as it always has, as only it can. And we will. We must also provide the inspiration for lasting peace, and we will do that, too. We can now take steps in response to these dramatic developments, steps that can help the Soviet peoples in their quest for peace and prosperity.

More importantly, we can now take steps to make the world a less dangerous place than ever before in the nuclear age. A year ago I described a new strategy for American defenses, reflecting the world's changing security environment. That strategy shifted our focus away from the fear that preoccupied us for 40 years, the prospect of a global confrontation. Instead, it concentrated more on regional conflicts, such as the one we just faced in the Persian Gulf. I spelled out a strategic concept, guided by the need to maintain the forces required to exercise forward presence in key areas, to respond effectively in crises, to maintain a credible nuclear deterrent, and to retain the national capacity to rebuild our forces, should that be needed.

We are now moving to reshape the U.S. military to reflect that concept. The new base force will be smaller by half a million than today's military, with fewer Army divisions, Air Force wings, Navy ships and strategic nuclear forces. This new force will be versatile, able to respond around the world to challenges, old and new.

As I just mentioned, the changes that allowed us to adjust our security strategy a year ago have greatly accelerated. The prospect of a Soviet invasion into Western Europe, launched with little or no warning, is no longer a realistic threat. The Warsaw Pact has crumbled. In the Soviet Union, the advocates of democracy triumphed over a coup that would have restored the old system of repression. The reformers are now starting to fashion their own futures, moving even faster toward democracy's horizon.

New leaders in the Kremlin and the republics are now questioning the need for their huge nuclear arsenal. The Soviet nuclear stockpile now seems less an instrument of national security and more of a burden. As a result, we now have an unparalleled opportunity to change the nuclear posture of both the United States and the Soviet Union.

If we and the Soviet leaders take the right steps, some on our own, some on their own, some together, we can dramatically shrink the arsenal of the world's nuclear weapons. We can more effectively discourage the spread of nuclear weapons. We can rely more on defensive measures [and] on our strategic relationship. We can enhance stability and actually reduce the risk of nuclear war.

Now is the time to seize this opportunity. After careful study and consultations with my senior advisers, and after considering valuable counsel from [British] Prime Minister [John] Major, [French] President [François] Mitterrand, [German] Chancellor [Helmut] Kohl and other allied leaders, I am announcing today a series of sweeping initiatives affecting every aspect of our nuclear forces on land, on ships and on aircraft.

I met again today with our Joint Chiefs of Staff, and I can tell you, they wholeheartedly endorse each of these steps. I'll begin with the category in which we will make the most fundamental change in nuclear forces in over 40 years: non-strategic or theater weapons.

Last year, I canceled U.S. plans to modernize our ground-launched theater nuclear weapons. Later, our NATO allies joined us in announcing that the alliance would propose the mutual elimination of all nuclear artillery shells from Europe as soon as short-range nuclear forces negotiations began with the Soviets.

But starting these talks now would only perpetuate these systems while we engage in lengthy negotiations. Last month's events not only permit but indeed demand swifter, bolder action. I am therefore directing that the United States eliminate its entire worldwide inventory of ground-launched, short-range — that is, theater — nuclear weapons. We will bring home and destroy all of our nuclear artillery shells and short-range ballistic missile warheads.

We will of course ensure that we preserve an effective air-delivered nuclear capability in Europe. That's essential to NATO's security.

In turn, I have asked the Soviets to go down this road with us, to destroy their entire inventory of ground-launched theater nuclear weapons, not only their nuclear artillery and nuclear warheads for short-range ballistic missiles but also the theater systems the U.S. no longer has, systems like nuclear warheads for air defense missiles and nuclear land mines.

Recognizing further the major changes in the international military landscape, the United States will withdraw all tactical nuclear weapons from its surface ships and attack submarines, as well as those nuclear weapons associated with our land-based naval aircraft. This means removing all nuclear Tomahawk cruise missiles from U.S. ships and submarines, as well as nuclear bombs aboard aircraft carriers.

The bottom line is that under normal circumstances, our ships will not carry tactical nuclear weapons. Many of these land- and sea-based warheads will be dismantled and destroyed. Those remaining will be secured in central areas where they would be available if necessary in a future crisis.

Again, there is every reason for the Soviet Union to match our actions by removing all tactical nuclear weapons from its ships and attack submarines by withdrawing nuclear weapons for land-based naval aircraft and by destroying many of them and consolidating what remains at central locations.

I urge them to do so.

No category of nuclear weapons has received more attention than those in our strategic arsenals. The Strategic Arms Reduction Treaty, START, which [Soviet] President [Mikhail S.] Gorbachev and I signed last July, was the culmination of almost a decade's work. It calls for substantial stabilizing reductions and effective verification.

Prompt ratification by both parties is essential. But I also believe the time is right to use START as a springboard to achieve additional stabilizing changes. First, to further reduce tensions, I'm directing that all United States' strategic bombers immediately stand down from their alert posture. As a comparable gesture, I call upon the Soviet Union to confine its mobile missiles to their garrisons, where they will be safer and more secure.

Second, the United States will immediately stand down from alert all intercontinental ballistic missiles [ICBMs] scheduled for deactivation under START. Rather than waiting for the treaty's reduction plan to run its full seven-year course, we will accelerate elimination of these systems once START is ratified. I call upon the Soviet Union to do the same.

Third, I am terminating the development of the mobile Peacekeeper ICBM as well as the mobile portions of the small ICBM program. The small single-warhead ICBM will be our only remaining ICBM modernization program, and I call upon the Soviets to terminate any and all programs for future ICBMs with more than one warhead and to limit ICBM modernization to one type of single-warhead missile, just as we have done.

And fourth, I am canceling the current program to build a replacement for the nuclear short-range attack missile for our strategic bombers.

And fifth, as a result of the strategic nuclear weapons adjustments that I've just outlined, the United States will streamline its command and control procedures, allowing us to more effectively manage our strategic nuclear forces.

As the system works now, the Navy commands the submarine part of our strategic deterrent while the Air Force commands the bomber and land-based elements. But as we reduce our strategic forces, the operational command structure must be as direct as possible, and I therefore approve the recommendation of [Defense] Secretary [Dick] Cheney and the Joint Chiefs to consolidate operational command of these forces into a U.S. strategic command under one commander, with participation from both services.

Since the 1970s the most vulnerable and unstable part of the U.S. and Soviet nuclear forces has been intercontinental missiles with more than one warhead. Both sides have these ICBMs in fixed silos in the ground where they are more vulnerable than missiles on submarines. I propose that the U.S. and the Soviet Union seek early agreement to eliminate from their inventories all ICBMs with multiple warheads. After developing a timetable acceptable to both sides we could rapidly move to modify or eliminate these systems under procedures already established in the START agreement.

In short, such an action would take away the single most unstable part of our nuclear arsenals.

But there is more to do. The United States and the Soviet Union are not the only nations with ballistic missiles. Some 15 nations have them now and in less than a decade, that number could grow to 20.

The recent conflict in the Persian Gulf demonstrates in no uncertain terms that the time has come for strong action on this growing threat to world peace. Accordingly, I am calling on the Soviet leadership to join us in taking immediate, concrete steps to permit the limited deployment of non-nuclear defenses to protect against limited ballistic missile strikes, whatever their source, without undermining the credibility of existing deterrent forces.

And we will intensify our effort to curb nuclear and missile proliferation. These two efforts will be mutually reinforcing. To foster cooperation, the United States soon will propose additional initiatives in the area of ballistic missile early warning.

And finally, let me discuss yet another opportunity for cooperation that can make our world safer. During last month's attempted coup in Moscow, many Americans asked me if I thought Soviet nuclear weapons were under adequate control. I do not believe that America was at increased risk of nuclear attack during those tense days. But I do believe more can be done to ensure the safe handling and dismantling of Soviet nuclear weapons.

And therefore I propose that we begin discussions with the Soviet Union to explore cooperation in three areas:

First, we should explore joint technical cooperation on the safe and environmentally responsible storage, transportation, dismantling and destruction of nuclear warheads; second, we should discuss existing arrangements for the physical security and safety of nuclear weapons, and how these might be enhanced; third, we should discuss nuclear command and control arrangements, and how these might be improved to provide more protection against the unauthorized or accidental use of nuclear weapons.

My friend, French President Mitterrand, offered a similar idea a short while ago. After further consultations with the alliance, and when the leadership in the U.S.S.R. is ready, we will begin this effort.

The initiatives that I'm announcing build on the new defense strategy that I set out a year ago, one that shifted our focus away from the prospect of global confrontation. We're consulting with our allies on the implementation of many of these steps, which fit well with the new post-Cold War strategy and force posture that we've developed in NATO.

As we implement these initiatives, we will closely watch how the new Soviet leadership responds. We expect our bold initiatives to meet with equally bold steps on the Soviet side. If this happens, further cooperation is inevitable. If it does not, then a historic opportunity will have been lost.

Regardless, let no one doubt, we will still retain the necessary strength to protect our security and that of our allies and to respond as necessary.

In addition, regional instabilities, the spread of weapons of massive destruction and, as we saw during the conflict in the gulf, territorial ambitions of power-hungry tyrants still require us to maintain a strong military to protect our national interests and to honor commitments to our allies. And therefore, we must implement a coherent plan for a significantly smaller but fully capable military, one that enhances stability but is still sufficient to convince any potential adversary that the cost of aggression would exceed any possible gain.

We can safely afford to take the steps I've announced today, steps that are designed to reduce the dangers of miscalculation in a crisis. But to do so, we must also pursue vigorously those elements of our strategic modernization program that serve the same purpose. We must fully fund the B-2 and SDI [Strategic Defense Initiative] program. We can make radical changes in the nuclear postures of both sides to make them smaller, safer and more stable. But the United States must maintain modern nuclear forces, including the strategic triad, and thus ensure the credibility of our deterrent.

Some will say that these initiatives call for a budget windfall for domestic programs, but the peace dividend I see is not measured in dollars but in greater security. In the near term, some of these steps may even cost money. Given the ambitious plan I have already proposed to reduce U.S. defense spending by 25 percent, we cannot afford to make any unwise or unwarranted cuts in the defense budget that I have submitted to Congress. I am counting on congressional support to ensure we have the funds necessary to restructure our forces prudently and implement the decisions that I have outlined tonight.

Twenty years ago, when I had the opportunity to serve this country as ambassador to the United Nations, I once talked about the vision that was in the minds of the U.N.'s founders, how they dreamed of a new age when the great powers of the world would cooperate in peace as they had as allies in war.

Today, I consulted with President Gorbachev, and while he hasn't had time to absorb the details, I believe the Soviet response will clearly be positive. I also spoke with [Russian Republic] President [Boris N.] Yeltsin, and he had a similar reaction — positive, hopeful. And now the Soviet people and their leaders can shed the heavy burden of a dangerous and costly nuclear arsenal which has threatened world peace for the past five decades. They can join us in these dramatic moves toward a new world of peace and security.

Tonight, as I see the drama of democracy unfolding around the globe, perhaps we are closer to that new world than ever before. The future is ours to influence, to shape, to mold, and while we must not gamble that future, neither can we forfeit the historic opportunity now before us. It has been said, destiny is not a matter of chance. It is a matter of choice. It is not a thing to be waited for. It's a thing to be achieved.

The United States has always stood where duty required us to stand, and now let them say that we led where destiny required us to lead, to a more peaceful, hopeful future. We cannot give a more precious gift to the children of the world.

Thank you, good night, and God bless the United States of America. ■

Efforts To Block Base Closures Fail

BOXSCORE

➨ **Base Closure and Realignment Disapproval (H J Res 308, S J Res 175).** Congress rejected a joint resolution to disapprove the Defense Base Closure and Realignment Commission's 1991 list of military installations for closure or realignment. The House acted first in defeating the effort to block the base closings, rendering Senate action moot. Congress had crafted the base closure procedure to permit itself only such an all-or-nothing vote.

Reports: H Rept 102-163, S Rept 102-123.

KEY ACTION

April 15 — Defense Secretary Dick Cheney sent the 1991 list of base closings to the eight-member Defense Base Closure and Realignment Commission for review.

July 1 — The commission sent a slightly revised list of base closings to President Bush.

July 10 — Bush approved the list.

July 24 — The **House** Armed Service Committee voted 46-8 to recommend that the House reject H J Res 308.

July 25 — The **Senate** Armed Services Committee voted, 17-3, to send S J Res 175 to the Senate floor with an unfavorable recommendation.

July 30 — The **House** voted 60-364 to reject H J Res 308. This action permitted the closings to go into effect.

Congress revisited the politically painful process of closing domestic bases in 1991. After four months of deliberation and debate, lawmakers approved a proposal to close 34 military installations — 25 of them major — and realign 37 others. The closings would save an estimated $1.5 billion annually after fiscal 1998.

The roots of this action dated back to a proposal by Defense Secretary Dick Cheney in early 1990 to close a group of bases. The list he released that January set off an explosion among Democrats, who said Cheney had unfairly singled out their bases.

In the fiscal 1991 defense authorization measure (PL 101-510), Congress blocked Cheney's list and included new rules to be used in closing bases. The 1991 base-closing process was the first of three rounds of base closings created in the bill, to be followed by potential closings in both 1993 and 1995. *(1990 Almanac, p. 693)*
ney assembled a new list of bases the Defense Department wanted to close and sent them on April 15 to an eight-member independent commission for review. The Defense Base Closure and Realignment Commission then took up its assigned task of determining whether Cheney had "deviated substantially" from the published list of eight criteria that the Pentagon had used to decide which bases to close.

After months of hearings and lobbying by members, the commission, in a daylong meeting, voted to accept the vast majority of Cheney's proposals — deleting only four bases from the original list. The commission sent the revised list to President Bush July 1, and Bush approved the list July 10, passing it on to Congress. Congress had 45 working days in which to accept or reject the list.

In a procedure established by Congress to shackle its own pork-barrel proclivities, members were only able to cast an all-or-nothing vote on whether to reject the entire list. And, over the passionate objections of many members who were going to lose bases in their districts, the House voted 60-364 on July 30 against a resolution that would have blocked the base closings. *(Vote 232, p. 56-H)*

That sealed the fate of the bases on the list, which were scheduled to close between 1992 and 1997.

ADMINISTRATION ACTION

Defense Secretary Cheney proposed April 12 to close 31 major domestic military bases. His recommendations, which formally were submitted to a new commission on base closings on April 15, also called for shutting 12 smaller bases and reducing operations at 28 others.

The Defense Department estimated that phasing out the facilities would cost $5.7 billion from fiscal 1992 to fiscal 1997, outweighed by operating savings of about $6.5 billion — for a net gain of $850 million.

Beginning in fiscal 1998, the department estimated that it would save $1.7 billion a year.

"By 1995, the number of people in the U.S. military will be about one-fourth smaller than it is today," Cheney said. "Smaller forces need fewer bases. It's as simple as that."

But for the affected communities, nothing was that simple. And members of Congress from some of the hardest-hit areas vowed to work to reverse Cheney's recommendations.

"As far as we're concerned, the fight's not over," said Sen. Frank R. Lautenberg, D-N.J., whose constituents faced the recommended shutdown of Fort Dix in his state and the Philadelphia Naval Shipyard in neighboring Pennsylvania.

Although initial attention focused on the 31 major bases that Cheney sought to close, they were part of a broader plan to cut back some facilities and consolidate operations at others. While some states emerged as losers, others emerged as big potential winners.

The state hit hardest was California, scheduled to lose about 27,000 jobs from a combination of base closings and realignments. The state was to lose more than 16,000 jobs from the closing of the Army's Fort Ord alone.

Florida was to lose nearly 19,000 jobs, mostly from the recommended shutdown of the Navy's training facility in Orlando.

But the Orlando shutdown would be good news for Illinois, which stood to gain more than 14,000 jobs from the relocation of the training facility. That made Illinois far and away the top winner in the base-closing realignment process.

Some congressional Democrats charged that the new list was tilted against their districts or states.

But Cheney insisted that there was "no political spin" involved in the effort. His assessment won important support from House Armed Services Committee Chairman Les Aspin, D-Wis.

Aspin, who examined the 31 major bases plus three slightly smaller ones, said the pain of those shutdowns would hit the districts of 19 House Democrats and 14 Republicans, with one base straddling districts of different parties. At least at first glance, he said, the list "appears fair."

The Defense Department had established eight criteria to use in evaluating all U.S. domestic bases to determine which bases should be closed. These criteria were part of the procedure requested by Congress.

To determine the military value of a base, the Pentagon looked at:

- Mission requirements and operational readiness of the total force.
- Availability and condition of land, facilities and associated airspace at both the existing and potential receiving sites.
- Availability to accommodate contingency, mobilization and future total force requirements at both existing and potential receiving sites.
- Cost and manpower implications.

To determine the impact of a closing, the Pentagon considered:

- The economic impact on communities.
- The ability of the infrastructures in both the existing and potential receiving communities to support forces, missions and personnel.
- The environmental effects.

The Pentagon's final criterion was relative costs — how much it would cost to close and move the base as opposed to keeping it open.

To justify adding or subtracting a base from Cheney's list, the commission had to demonstrate that the Defense Department deviated substantially from the force structure requirements and other criteria established by the department.

The Commission Begins

On April 15, the Defense Base Closure and Realignment Commission went into business in a suite of offices on Washington's K Street. The eight-member panel was in charge of reviewing the list of base closings that was announced April 12 by Defense Secretary Cheney. The commission had the power to add or delete bases from Cheney's chosen sites — and its chairman insisted that it would not be a rubber stamp.

"We intend, obviously, to take a total fresh look at the data and the work and the process that the Pentagon went through and render our own independent, nonpartisan judgments," said commission Chairman Jim Courter.

In addition to Courter, a former Republican representative from New Jersey (1979-90), the panel consisted of: Alexander B. Trowbridge, a former secretary of Commerce and past president of the National Association of Manufacturers; Robert Douglas Stuart Jr., a former ambassador to Norway and past chief executive officer of Quaker Oats; Arthur Levitt Jr., a former chairman of the American Stock Exchange; Howard Hollis "Bo" Callaway, a Colorado Republican who represented the 3rd District of Georgia from 1965 to 1967; James C. Smith II, an executive with Brown & Root Inc., an engineering firm based in Houston; Gen. Duane H. Cassidy, a former commander in chief of the Military Airlift Command; and William L. Ball III, a former secretary of the Navy.

From the end of April through the beginning of June, the commission held five hearings on Capitol Hill. But Courter emphasized that the panel also gave local officials a chance to argue in behalf of their military installations as commission members visited affected communities across the country.

Defense Laboratories

One aspect of the base-closing plan that affected relatively few workers but which created a stir among members of Congress was Cheney's proposal to reduce employment at several of the military services' research laboratories.

Only one lab, however, was proposed to be closed outright: The Naval Electronic Systems Engineering Center in rural St. Inigoes, Md.

Several other labs were to have substantial reductions in size but would remain open.

Some state congressional delegations had promised to take their cases to the commission in the hope that it would conclude that the research labs did not belong on the list it would send to Bush.

The Pentagon's 76 defense labs, which employed 60,000 people, did much of the invention and testing of new weapons systems and technologies. Each service — Army, Navy and Air Force — operated its own labs.

The concern in Congress stemmed partly from apprehension that many of the labs' skilled employees would seek jobs in the private sector rather than accept transfers to other federal facilities, further reducing the technical expertise at the Defense Department.

Some members argued that the Pentagon was ignoring Congress' order to follow the recommendations of a lab consolidation commission, which was scheduled to complete a review of the entire defense lab system in September.

Saving Facilities

For many members of Congress, the commission was their best hope of saving a local base on Cheney's list. The lobbying of the commission began in earnest after the release of the list.

The affected lawmakers focused on proving that Cheney's calculations were flawed.

Most tried a coolheaded rebuttal to the Pentagon report, hoping that would prove more effective than an emotional appeal by a distraught community facing the loss of its local base.

Just three days after Cheney targeted the Philadelphia Naval Shipyard for closure, Rep. Thomas M. Foglietta, D-Pa., the member in whose district the huge facility lay, released a 43-page report full of facts and figures to show why the facility should not be shut down.

The report, signed by 31 members of Congress from three states near the shipyard — Pennsylvania, New Jersey and Delaware — dissected the eight criteria one by one, listing purported mistakes in the Pentagon's analysis.

"Long on facts and short on rhetoric, it tracks the Defense Department's own criteria to prove that the Navy yard fits into the naval strategy of the 1990s and beyond," Foglietta said of the report.

The General Accounting Office (GAO) also was critical of the Navy's methods for choosing which facilities to close. In the law that set up the base-closings process, lawmakers included a provision that called on the GAO to audit the Pentagon's base-closing procedures and report on its findings May 15.

"GAO considers the closure and realignment recommendations made by the Army and the Air Force to be adequately supported" said the report. But the GAO concluded that the Navy had offered "insufficient documentation to support its efforts." Courter warned the Navy on May 22 that if its representatives could not prove that their selection criteria were applied evenly, then the commission was fully prepared to draw up a fresh list of recommendations.

Commission staff and members of the Navy responsible for the closure list met several times over the following weeks. Eventually, the commission decided it was satisfied with the amount of information the Navy provided.

Members were given a rare opportunity to persuade the commission to spare their local bases when hearings were held on May 22-23. Congress designed the base-closing procedure to limit its own opportunities to interfere.

During those two days, 150 lawmakers representing 30 states stepped up to the podium in hearing rooms on Capitol Hill to ask the commission to take a second look at their endangered local installations. Their lobbying techniques ranged from solo efforts to sophisticated group presentations by entire state delegations.

Confronted with so many members seeking to plead their cases, the commission allotted only five minutes per person and enforced the limit with a red light and a bell. Although accustomed to far greater deference, most members observed the rule.

Also during the week of May 20, the commission itself came under scrutiny after press reports revealed that Courter had signed on as a lobbyist for Grumman Corp., a defense contractor. Courter denied that he faced a conflict of interest but canceled his contract with the airplane builder May 23.

Another member of the eight-person commission resigned May 17, citing conflict of interest questions. Trowbridge was on the board of directors of two firms that had substantial contracts with many military bases. He was not replaced.

COMMISSION ACTION

Despite boasts of independence, the commission hewed closely to the Pentagon's wishes in the final recommendations for base closings that it sent to Bush on July 1.

Although commissioners repeatedly pledged that "our job is to close bases and save money," the panel's final recommendations would save nearly $176 million less per year than Cheney's original recommendations.

The commission had announced May 31 that it was considering adding 35 more military facilities to Cheney's list for possible closure. The following week, the panel took more than half of the newly added bases off the list; the rest of them were dropped before a final list was developed.

The commission largely accepted the initial recommendations of Cheney after deleting four of the 31 major facilities he wanted to close and recommending cutbacks rather than closure of two others.

Sen. John B. Breaux, D-La., charged that the commission, for "all its public activity to the contrary, was simply a rubber stamp for the Pentagon."

The unanimous vote to take Whidbey Island Naval Air Station in Washington state off the list accounted for 39 percent of the lost savings. According to the commission staff's calculations, closing that facility would have saved the Pentagon $69 million annually.

Also given reprieves from closure were Fort McClellan in Anniston, Ala.; the Naval Training Center at Orlando, Fla.; and Moody Air Force Base in Valdosta, Ga.

Rep. Patricia Schroeder, D-Colo., who lost the battle to

Final List of Bases Slated for Closure or Realignment, 1992-97

CLOSURES

Army
Fort Benjamin Harrison, Ind.
Fort Devens, Mass.
Fort Ord, Calif.
Sacramento Army Depot, Calif.

Navy
Chase Field Naval Air Station, Texas
Construction Battalion Center, Rhode Island
Hunters Point Annex to Treasure Island Naval Station, Calif.
Marine Corps Air Station, Tustin, Calif.
Moffett Field Naval Air Station, Calif.
Long Beach Naval Station, Calif.
Philadelphia Naval Shipyard, Pa.
Philadelphia Naval Station, Pa.
Puget Sound Naval Station, Sand Point, Wash.

Army and Navy labs (8 facilities)

Air Force
Bergstrom Air Force Base, Texas
Carswell Air Force Base, Texas
Castle Air Force Base, Calif.
Eaker Air Force Base, Ark.
England Air Force Base, La.
Grissom Air Force Base, Ind.
Loring Air Force Base, Maine
Lowry Air Force Base, Colo.
Myrtle Beach Air Force Base, S.C.
Richards-Gebaur Air Reserve Station, Mo.
Rickenbacker Air Guard Base, Ohio
Williams Air Force Base, Ariz.
Wurtsmith Air Force Base, Mich.

REALIGNMENTS

Army
Aviation Systems Command/Troop Support Command, St. Louis
Fort Chafee, Ark.
Fort Dix, N.J.
Fort Polk, La.
Letterkenny Army Depot, Pa.
Rock Island Arsenal, Ill.
10 Army RDT&E laboratories
7 Army medical labs

Navy
Midway Island Naval Air Facility
7 Navy RDT&E Engineering and Fleet Support Activities

Air Force
Beale Air Force Base, Calif.
Goodfellow Air Force Base, Texas
MacDill Air Force Base, Fla.
March Air Force Base, Calif.
Mather Air Force Base, Calif.
Mountain Home Air Force Base, Idaho

save Lowry Air Force Base in her district, complained that the use of military staff compromised the commission's independence. The commission had created teams of analysts, each led by members of the military on loan from the Pentagon.

"How do you come over [to the commission staff] temporarily and attack your boss' numbers and go back and expect to be promoted?" she told the Denver Post on June 29.

Courter responded that "the decisions were based on the merits."

Bush quickly approved the list July 10, sending it on for congressional action.

In all, 25 major bases were slated for closure over the next five years and operations at other facilities were to be cut back, for an expected savings of $2.3 billion each fiscal year from 1992 to 1997. The savings would be partially offset by closing costs of $4.1 billion.

Many of the commissioners described the vote to close the Philadelphia Naval Shipyard as the most difficult, even though, as with many of the votes, it was unanimous. The remarks of some of the seven commission members in the days leading up to the votes had even left advocates for the Philadelphia yard upbeat about its prospects for survival.

But the commission ultimately rejected the intensive lobbying for the base by the congressional delegations from Pennsylvania, New Jersey and Delaware.

The commission estimated that closing the Philadelphia installation would save $36 million annually.

Even commission Chairman Courter, a former representative from neighboring New Jersey, voted to close the installation. He called the vote "excruciating ... the most difficult decision I've faced in a long, long time."

Commission members also agonized late into the night of June 30 about the need to close Carswell Air Force Base in Texas and Maine's Loring Air Force Base.

Some of the communities whose bases ended up on the short end of the commission's recommendations reacted with anger, others with resignation.

"With this many closings needed to pare down America's military force to post-Cold War proportions, it was only reasonable to expect Colorado to take a share of the hit," said an editorial in the Denver Post on July 2, reacting to the commission's vote to close Denver's Lowry Air Force Base.

And Rep. Leon E. Panetta, D-Calif., said June 30, "I believe the time has come now for the community to face the reality that Fort Ord will be closed and move on."

But freshman Sen. John Seymour, R-Calif., lambasted the panel's decision to close Castle Air Force Base in his state. "This decision is going to needlessly and severely compromise our nation's defense," he said. "I plan on taking this issue directly to President Bush."

Predictably, there was rejoicing in communities surrounding the four installations that were spared.

"It was an uphill battle," said Rep. Bill McCollum, R-Fla., who fought to save his Orlando facility. "But I am proud to say we still have our naval training center, despite the hopes of some at the Pentagon."

Reorganizing the Corps

The most daring action taken by the base-closing commission was its recommendation to forge ahead with a reorganization of the U.S. Army Corps of Engineers. That move severely irritated key members of Congress who used their influence to block the commission's work.

Lawmakers included in the fiscal 1992 defense authorization measure (PL 102-190) language that retroactively prohibited the commission from taking any action regarding the corps.

The reorganization plan, crafted by the corps, would have consolidated many of its administrative and advisory functions.

The corps would have been reduced from 10 divisions across the country to six. And districts within those divisions would have been cut from 50 to 29.

About 2,600 jobs would have been eliminated, a 6 percent decrease. The annual savings were projected at $112 million, with a one-year cost of $266 million to implement the changes.

The corps builds projects such as dams, ports and water control facilities. Its public works are among the most tangible benefits a member of Congress could provide for his or her district. And lawmakers were sensitive to any change that might impinge upon their ability to bring home the "pork" of public works projects.

Cheney deliberately excluded a revamping of the corps on April 12, when he recommended bases for the commission to close. While agreeing that corps facilities needed to be pared down, he offered a plan to do so as a separate piece of legislation to allow congressional committees with jurisdiction over the corps — Public Works in the House and Environment and Public Works in the Senate — an opportunity to review it.

Demonstrating less deference to the committees, the independent base-closing commission unanimously decided on June 30 to recommend that the president act on the plan to revamp the corps. Attempting to avoid offending the affected lawmakers, the commission included language in its recommendation that would give Congress a year to act on its own.

If Congress passed a plan to reorganize the corps and the president signed it by July 1, 1992, such a plan would supersede the commission's recommendations. But even those provisions did not appease lawmakers.

Acknowledging the touchiness of the issue, commission Chairman Courter said before the vote on the corps that it was the "strong feeling of many, many members of Congress" that the commission should not take up the issue. Cassidy argued that he thought it was "a little arrogant" to tell lawmakers what to do.

But commission member Smith said the only reason for not including the corps proposal was if "by doing so we would jeopardize the entire package." He was supported by Callaway, who argued that it would be a "tragic mistake if we don't save $112 million for something the corps wants to do."

The law that created the base-closing commission did not mention the Army Corps of Engineers. While the commission maintained that the omission allowed it to consider the corps' reorganization, some members, including Courter, expressed concern that Congress never intended the commission to take on the issue.

CONGRESSIONAL ACTION

A resolution that would have prevented the bases from closing (H J Res 308) garnered little support from members on the House Armed Services Committee. On July 23 the Military Installations Subcommittee voted to report the resolution to the full committee unfavorably.

The next day the full committee voted 46-8 to recommend that the House reject the resolution. The resolution was sponsored by Foglietta, who was attempting to save the Philadelphia Naval Shipyard, and Olympia J. Snowe, R-Maine, who was fighting for Loring Air Force Base.

The Armed Services panel could have defeated outright the resolution disapproving of the closures, but House leaders had promised that the entire membership would have an opportunity to vote on the issue.

Finally, on July 30, the full House crushed a resolution to keep the bases open. Only 60 members voted to kill the base-closing list; 364 voted to accept it. All the members who voted to keep the bases open were losing a base in or near their districts.

Many of the 60 votes for H J Res 308 — a resolution of disapproval that would have kept the bases open — came from the Pennsylvania and New Jersey delegations, which were fighting to save the Philadelphia Naval Shipyard, and the Massachusetts delegation, which sought to save Fort Devens.

But even those groups could not hold all of their members together. Of the 37 members from the region surrounding Philadelphia, only 15 voted to kill the list.

None of the arguments opposing the commission's report in the two-hour House debate were new, but for members with thousands of constituents on the verge of losing their jobs, there was nothing wrong with a little repetition.

Curt Weldon, R-Pa., who led the 14 Republicans supporting the resolution of disapproval, accused the commission of unquestioningly accepting the flawed work of the Pentagon and particularly of the Navy.

"It was a sham. It was a rubber-stamp process from the beginning," said Weldon, who illustrated his point by keeping a two-foot-tall rubber stamp at his side during the debate.

One side of the stamp said "rush" in response to complaints that there had not been enough time to address all issues. The other side bore the dates 1991, 1993, 1995. That was to remind members that the closings were only the first of three sets of shutdowns authorized by Congress.

"We will remember your vote today," Weldon warned colleagues whose districts escaped the first round unscathed. "We will remember it in 1993. We will remember it in 1995, so do not come back then and tell us the process is flawed."

Overseas Shutdowns

The House also registered its belief that other countries should share the pain of losing U.S. military installations, voting on a joint resolution (H J Res 313) to include overseas bases in additional rounds of closings in 1993 and 1995.

Before voting on the domestic military base closings, the House voted, 412-14, to put foreign military bases under the jurisdiction of the Defense Base Closure and Realignment Commission. *(Vote 231, p. 56-H)*

Members argued that, just as the changing world necessitated closing domestic bases, so should it result in the closure of foreign bases.

As Schroeder, chairman of the Armed Services Military Installations Subcommittee, put it: "Here we are with all these installations in West Germany protecting it from East Germany — except now it is all one Germany, and the East Germans are in West Germany shopping at the mall. Tell me that makes sense."

The Bush administration strongly opposed the resolution, arguing that it would make closing overseas bases more cumbersome rather than easier.

Shortly before the House took up the issue, Defense Department spokesman Pete Williams announced that the United States planned to close 72 overseas bases in six countries over the next four years. Of those bases, 38 were in Germany.

On July 25, the Senate Armed Services Committee also voted, 17-3, to reject a resolution (S J Res 175) that would prevent bases from closing.

That resolution never made it to the floor of the Senate because the House action (defeat of the resolution) made the Senate bill moot. ■

Cheney Killed Troubled A-12 Program

In a surprise move, Defense Secretary Dick Cheney on Jan. 7 canceled the Navy's A-12 attack plane because of production delays and cost overruns. It was considered a turning point for reform of the Pentagon, but it may ultimately have offered a windfall to aerospace companies scrambling for business.

The Pentagon chief stunned those involved in defense when he canceled the bat-winged aircraft that was to be the Navy's next carrier-based bomber. Cheney spurned the Navy's recommendation to revise contracts for the project so that the government would pick up a larger share of the contractors' escalating costs.

The Navy had planned to spend an estimated $52 billion on a fleet of 620 A-12s to replace aging A-6Es as the round-house punch of Navy carriers against surface targets. But the program was plagued with delays and cost increases.

One of the few major weapons to be dropped so far into development, the A-12 would have been considerably costlier than the $39 billion DIVAD anti-aircraft gun canceled in 1985. *(1985 Almanac, p. 154)*

"I do not believe a bailout is in the national interest," Cheney said. "If we cannot spend the taxpayers' money wisely, we will not spend it." After Cheney's decision to kill the A-12, members held hearings to look into charges that the two aerospace companies involved had misused funds.

Cheney was greeted as an unlikely hero by reformers who had long accused the Pentagon of giving contractors a blank check on weapons. "This is the best thing that's happened for defense management," said former Navy budget director Stanley Fine, a senior fellow with Business Executives for National Security.

But Cheney also launched a push for another high-performance, high-tech aircraft, the A-X.

Later in the year, Congress earmarked $167 million in funds for the development of the A-X as a replacement for the A-12. These were funds that had already been authorized for the A-12 but had not been spent. *(Defense authorization p. 393)*

Chief of Naval Operations Adm. Frank B. Kelso II told a House Armed Services subcommittee on April 10 that it would cost $10 billion over a decade just to develop the new plane. The first A-X would reach the fleet in 2003.

In the interim, the Pentagon was to buy more F-18 fighter planes and more of an improved, larger version of the F-18. Lawmakers also appropriated funds to equip many of the Navy's A6Es with new, synthetic wings so that they could be flown well into the next century. Previously, the Navy had planned to "re-wing" about half of the more than 300 planes. *(Appropriations, p. 621)*

Warning signs of the A-12's troubles had been gathering for months. In mid-December 1990, with the A-12 at least 18 months behind schedule, the Navy dismissed or reassigned two admirals and a captain involved in managing the program and charged them with failure to keep their superiors informed of the program's difficulties. A few days later, John Betti, the Pentagon's top procurement manager, resigned as the Defense Department's third-ranking official.

In canceling the A-12, Cheney said he had been given no reliable estimate of how much more money it might have taken to complete the program. Pentagon spokesman Pete Williams said that the cost of developing the plane and building eight prototypes could have gone from $4.78 billion to more than $7.5 billion.

General Dynamics Corp. and McDonnell Douglas Corp., the two firms that had been developing the A-12, denied Cheney's assertion that they were in default on the A-12's contract and blamed the Navy's insistence in 1988 that they sign a "fixed price" contract. It required them to absorb any cost overruns in a development program that was "on the cutting edge of technology," in the words of a General Dynamics spokesman.

The Pentagon subsequently abandoned such contracts for development programs that required major technical breakthroughs.

Beyond the A-6E

At a time of improved U.S.-Soviet relations, the demise of the A-12 underscored a debate over the Pentagon's commitment to a new generation of combat planes, all of which incorporated radar-evading stealth design and construction.

The A-12 was to replace the A-6, a barrel-bellied plane the size of a large corporate jet with a bulbous radar dome for a nose. It was designed in the mid-1950s by the Long Island-based Grumman Corp. to carry up to 15 tons of bombs and strike targets with pinpoint accuracy, even at night or in bad weather.

The "E" version, first flown in 1970, had an improved radar and bomb-aiming computer, supplemented since the late 1970s by a night-vision television camera and a laser for steering guided missiles.

In the 1980s, the Navy and the Marine Corps had about 300 A-6Es, more than half of them rebuilt versions of earlier models. When the wings on some A-6Es began to wear out in the mid-1980s, the Navy equipped some of them with new wings of composite material. But when the service proposed yet another full-bore upgrade of the basic A-6 design, Congress balked.

With its chunky profile and as many as 30 bombs slung beneath its wings, critics said, a new A-6 would have stood out like a sore thumb on enemy radars.

The alternative was supposed to be the A-12, designed from the outset to provide the smallest possible radar echo.

In 1990, the contractors released an artist's conception of the previously secret new plane: a flying wing with neither a tail nor any other protuberances to reflect radar beams. The plane's engines, radar antennas and bombload all would be tucked inside its smooth, non-metallic structure, which was shaped like a giant Dorito corn chip.

After a Pentagon review of six major new aircraft programs, Cheney announced on April 26, 1990, that the A-12 program would continue but with a total purchase of 620 planes rather than the 858 initially planned. An important reason for the cutback was a planned reduction of the number of aircraft carriers from 14 to 12.

Only a month later, on June 1, the contractors officially informed the Navy that the program was in significant trouble. Pentagon officials began a series of reviews that led first to the personnel changes in December and then to Cheney's cancellation decision in January of 1991.

There were problems with the new plane's engines and with efforts to build radar antennas into its skin. But according to a Navy post-mortem, the biggest problem was that the plane was 10 percent overweight.

The contractors had had little experience building large structures of the synthetic material required for "stealthiness." They made its skeleton thicker, and thus heavier, than had been planned to let the plane absorb the strains of being flung into the air by carrier catapults, flying missions with heavy bombloads, slamming back onto flight decks and being jerked to a halt.

The trouble was that the greater the plane's weight, the greater the strain of launchings and landings.

Managing the Program

The A-12 fiasco provided ammunition for critics of the Pentagon's weapons-development system:

- The discovery of cost increases by senior Pentagon officials was delayed for as long as a year by the fact that it was a "black" — classified — program. This contributed momentum to the effort of House Armed Services member John R. Kasich, R-Ohio, and others to greatly restrict the Pentagon's ability to insulate big-ticket development programs from routine administrative and congressional oversight.
- The program's perilous state was evident to Navy officials running it long before they passed along the bad news. The damning explanation provided by the Navy's trouble-shooting report was that the highly trained and experienced officer who was the Navy's A-12 program manager — and his immediate superiors — cast all the program's problems in an optimistic light, lest their superiors withdraw their support for the program.

"The fundamental problem," wrote Navy Deputy General Counsel C. Paul Beach, "is to create appropriate incentives to enable senior leaders to rely upon responsible, accountable line managers for realistic perspectives on the cost, schedule and technical status of their programs."

But House Armed Services member Dennis M. Hertel, D-Mich., and others, had long argued that such detached, critical judgment of a major weapons program was nearly impossible for a military officer whose service was depending on the program and whose career was in the hands of his seniors in that service. Hertel and his allies called for transferring the weapons procurement process from the armed services to an independent agency.

A-12 INVESTIGATION

After the plane program was killed, members of the House Armed Services Committee held hearings the week of July 22 to determine just what had gone wrong.

Lawmakers demanded in the report accompanying the fiscal 1992 defense authorization bill (HR 2100 — H Rept

102-311) that secrecy requirements be far less restrictive for the development of the next carrier-based attack plane, the A-X.

Two Pentagon analysts testified under oath before the House Armed Services Investigations Subcommittee on July 23 that they had warned superiors that the plane's development, handled jointly by McDonnell Douglas and General Dynamics, was headed for trouble.

But they said their admonitions went largely unheeded because the program's manager, Navy Capt. Lawrence Elberfeld, either ignored them or convinced superiors that the problems would be resolved.

Subcommittee Chairman Nicholas Mavroules, D-Mass., announced the following day that, as a result of the testimony, Elberfeld had applied for retirement and asked that his previously announced promotion be withdrawn. Elberfeld had been reassigned shortly before Defense Secretary Dick Cheney's decision Jan. 7 to cancel the A-12.

Debbie D'Angelo, a former Navy cost analyst, testified to Mavroules' subcommittee that she had given Elberfeld monthly cost estimates that were higher than those he passed on to superiors as early as March 1989.

Elberfeld had told the subcommittee in April that he had not received D'Angelo's estimates until September 1989, at the earliest, and probably not until two months later.

D'Angelo disagreed. "Problems were indicated from the very beginning of the contract," she said.

Tom Hafer, a former budget analyst with the Pentagon comptroller's office, testified that he reviewed D'Angelo's reports in August 1989 and determined then that "the program was in very deep trouble." He said he told D'Angelo after reading the reports that "this program is going to hell in a handbasket. I said I've never seen anything so bad in such a short period of time." The contract was awarded in January 1988.

Hafer's concerns were presented to the Pentagon's Conventional Systems Committee, which met to review the program in November 1989, but he said the warnings were offset by Elberfeld's "very spirited defense" of the program.

Hafer said such optimism was not unusual for a program manager and speculated that his own warnings about runaway costs and other problems did not have much impact because "a lot of senior decision-makers probably came to the conclusion that if it's so bad, we'll find out about it" in time.

But Mavroules said there were dozens of "warning flags that should have alerted the Navy."

Repayment Delayed

The House Government Operations Legislation and National Security Subcommittee on July 24 heard sworn testimony on the Pentagon's subsequent decision to allow McDonnell Douglas and General Dynamics to defer repayment of half of the $2.7 billion the firms had been paid for the A-12 contract.

Pentagon officials said they approved the deferral because McDonnell Douglas was experiencing financial difficulties that could lead to bankruptcy and loss of important defense contracts. In addition, the two companies had planned to appeal the Pentagon's demand that half the contract funds be returned.

"We faced the likelihood that we would not receive the money and that we would also set in motion a series of actions that would have ended up costing the taxpayers even more money," said Donald J. Yockey, under secretary of Defense for acquisition.

Assistant Comptroller Frank C. Conahan also testified that while the Pentagon had poorly documented its decision, the General Accounting Office found no evidence that it was inappropriate.

But subcommittee members said evidence of McDonnell Douglas' weakened finances was unconvincing. They criticized Pentagon officials for being reluctant to discuss publicly many of the details of the case.

"I think it's an absolute outrage that you cannot show the American people and us a document that justifies this decision," said Christopher Shays, R-Conn., who accused the Defense Department and its contractors of being "one and the same."

The subcommittee also released a Jan. 24 letter to Yockey from McDonnell Douglas requesting a $1 billion advance payment for other ongoing contracts because of the company's "very tight" cash requirements.

The Pentagon did not make the advance payments, but members said the request was further evidence of the unusually cozy relationship between the Pentagon and its contractors.

Of the $2.69 billion that had been paid under the A-12 development contract at the time it was canceled, the Pentagon asserted that the contractors were obligated to refund $1.35 billion for which the government had received no value.

On Feb. 5, however, the Navy agreed to defer collecting the refund while the contractors appealed Cheney's decision through federal courts or the Pentagon's own contract claims process.

The two companies denied that they were in default on the A-12 contract and blamed the program's difficulties on several Navy actions, including its insistence in 1988 that they sign a fixed-price development contract. That required the companies to absorb any cost overruns, an approach the Pentagon subsequently abandoned for projects such as the A-12, which required major technical breakthroughs. ■

U.S. Military Told To Leave Philippines

A series of international and domestic events — ranging from a natural disaster to the breakup of the Soviet Union — turned 1991 into a turning point for relations between the United States and the Philippines. The culmination came Dec. 27, when the government of President Corazon C. Aquino told U.S. troops to leave the country.

The decision signaled the end of the vast U.S. military presence in the area, a presence that dated back to 1898 when control of the islands was wrested from the Spanish. The Philippines gained independence from the United States in 1946, although the bases continued to play a principal role for U.S. armed forces in the Pacific theater for decades afterward.

In negotiations with the United States throughout 1991, Philippine officials insisted on $825 million in annual U.S. compensation — half in cash and half in trade and other concessions — in return for a seven-year agreement to continue operation of the military bases. U.S. negotiators said they wanted a 10-year pact tied to $360 million in annual aid.

The talks were disrupted by a volcanic eruption of Mount Pinatubo in early June that nearly destroyed Clark Air Base and damaged the Subic Bay Naval Station. But negotiators finally settled on treaty language that would have provided a 10-year lease for the Subic Bay naval base and $203 million in annual aid for the duration. The operating lease for the naval base expired in September 1991.

But lawmakers in both countries were unhappy with the agreement.

A powerful contingent of Philippine nationalists argued against the base treaty, saying that the presence of the U.S. military amounted to a colonial dominance and an intrusion on Philippine sovereignty. On Sept. 16, the 23-member Philippine Senate voted to reject the base treaty.

U.S. lawmakers, meanwhile, were frustrated by the persistent requests from the Philippines for infusions of aid, especially as a prerequisite for continued U.S. military presence there.

Members of Congress were questioning the strategic importance of the military bases, given the diminished Cold War atmosphere that was accompanying the breakup of the Soviet Union.

There was also reluctance to pay the Philippines billions of dollars to keep open bases overseas when declining defense budgets were forcing the closing of domestic bases in congressional districts across the country. *(Base closings, p. 427)*

"This has the Filipinos competing in the U.S. Congress with the Alabama National Guard," said Rep. Jim Leach, R-Iowa. "Everyone in Congress is sympathetic to the Philippines. On the other hand when the tough choices have to be made, the handwriting is on the wall."

Other lawmakers, such as House Minority Whip Newt Gingrich, R-Ga., said the Philippine rejection of the treaty could free money that could be redirected as foreign aid in places such as the former Soviet republics.

"Countries are lined up for the money that might be available," said Sen. Richard G. Lugar, R-Ind., a member of the Foreign Relations Committee.

Volcano Mired Deal

The volcanic eruption in early June of the Philippines' Mount Pinatubo, located 10 miles west of Clark Air Base and approximately 25 miles north of the Subic Bay naval base, dumped billions of tons of ash throughout the surrounding areas. The disaster forced the evacuation and subsequent closing of the Clark base and the curtailment of operations at Subic Bay.

Following the eruption, about 18,000 U.S. citizens were evacuated from the bases, which also employed more than 70,000 Filipinos. Many more islanders were uprooted from their homes as the volcano smothered large swaths of land with deep heavy ash.

Members of Congress who had been skeptical about the need to retain the bases and frustrated by Philippine resistance to the treaty were even more doubtful that the cost of repairing the bases would be worthwhile. U.S. officials in the Philippines were reported to have estimated that Clark's repair bill would have approached $300 million and possibly more.

The future of the bases had been further clouded by geological reports that indicated that the volcano might remain intermittently active for as long as 25 years, potentially disrupting any costly repair of the two remaining U.S. bases. Four other bases had been returned to Philippine control during the year.

"What's the point of spending a fortune to put it all back together, if it's all going to come apart again?" asked Rep. Patricia Schroeder, D-Colo., the chairman of the House Armed Services Subcommittee on Military Installations and Facilities, and an outspoken critic of U.S. military spending abroad.

Strategic Considerations

While the volcano sealed the fate of the Clark base, U.S. lawmakers and the Bush administration were careful to clarify that they wanted to maintain a strategic relationship with the Philippines, and especially to continue to lease the base at Subic Bay. Abandonment of the bases was not the expressed desire of the administration, either before or immediately following the eruption of Mount Pinatubo.

"All things being equal, we would very much like to stay at both Clark and Subic," Pete Williams, the spokesman for the Pentagon, had said on June 25.

But others held different views. A number of experts, including a handful in the Pentagon, had professed the view even prior to the volcano that operations performed at Clark and Subic Bay could be undertaken elsewhere, such as in Guam, Okinawa, Singapore and Hawaii, and that such a move would make sense, given the undercurrent of resentment of the U.S. presence in the Philippines.

Most agreed, however, that the massive, 60,000-acre Subic Bay facility held a unique and highly valued position with the U.S. Navy, providing it a deepwater port in a strategic location that could accommodate almost every maintenance, repair and supply need of the Pacific fleet.

According to a published report, U.S. officials tried to salvage the Subic Bay lease late in the year by proposing a three-year phased withdrawal from the Philippines, in the hope that the lease agreement might be revived and extended following election of a new Philippine government the following year. But that attempt also foundered, apparently over U.S. reluctance to agree to a firm schedule for removal of troops and equipment under Philippine direction.

Philippine President Aquino, who had strongly supported renewal of the lease agreement, also floated a proposal that a national referendum be held to save the bases. But in the face of widespread political opposition she backed away from that proposal and later expressed more interest in the U.S. plan for a phased withdrawal.

When all efforts failed, Aquino ordered U.S. troops out of the naval port by the end of 1992.

Defense Department officials had told Congress earlier that if the base were closed, the United States would not seek a new naval base in Asia.

"New bases are neither fiscally feasible nor in keeping with the security relationships we have with our friends in the region," Deputy Assistant Secretary of Defense Carl W. Ford Jr. told the House Foreign Affairs Asian and Pacific Affairs Subcommittee on Sept. 25. "Functions and missions would be dispersed among existing facilities in the region and in the U.S." ■

Chapter 9

FOREIGN POLICY

1991 Begins With War in the Mideast

As its first order of business, the 102nd Congress was asked to authorize use of force against Iraq

Deciding whether to commit troops to war was the first decision that awaited the 102nd Congress.

Despite a spate of diplomatic initiatives that followed Iraq's invasion of neighboring Kuwait on Aug. 2, 1990, the elements for a major war were in place on Jan. 1: nearly 1 million troops poised along either side of Kuwait's border with Saudi Arabia; U.N. authorization for member nations to "use any means necessary" to secure Iraq's removal from Kuwait after Jan. 15; and Iraqi leader Saddam Hussein's unwavering insistence that he would hold on to his conquest.

One of the few missing pieces was a firm and formal stand by Congress.

As the new Congress convened, its Democratic leaders spurned President Bush's renewed invitation for an open-ended vote of support. The leaders, fearful of undermining final attempts at a diplomatic solution, also urged their members to delay action on the gulf crisis. But the Senate haltingly began the long-delayed debate Jan. 4.

In an atmosphere of almost mournful solemnity, a sharply divided Congress voted Jan. 12 to authorize the president to go to war against Iraq if it did not end its occupation of Kuwait. The historic action marked the first time since World War II that Congress had directly confronted the issue of sending large numbers of American forces into combat.

The vote came just three days before the expiration of a U.N. deadline, after which member nations could force Iraq to withdraw from Kuwait. The joint resolution authorized the president "to use United States Armed Forces" to enforce the ultimatum set Nov. 29, 1991, by the U.N. Security Council.

Passage of the congressional resolution put the political and constitutional weight of the legislative branch behind Bush as he prepared the nation for battle. But the divided vote revealed deep fissures in Congress over the wisdom of going to war.

The Senate voted 52-47 for the "Authorization for Use of Military Force Against Iraq Resolution." Ten Democrats joined with virtually unanimous Republicans in support of the resolution. *(Vote 2, p. 2-S)*

Minutes later, the House approved identical legislation by a vote of 250-183. *(Vote 9, p. 2-H)*

On the evening of Jan. 16, a resolute Bush told the nation of his decision to transform the massive military deployment known as Operation Desert Shield into the war that was given the military code-name Operation Desert Storm. *(Text, p. 3-E)*

Having already authorized Bush to begin a war, members were well aware that they were reduced — politically and even constitutionally — to the role of bystanders.

PERSIAN GULF CRISIS

For further coverage, especially on events that led to the war, see 1990 Almanac, p. 717.

In the first days after waves of fighters, bombers and missiles crushed strategic targets throughout Iraq, leaders of Congress voiced support, and the Senate unanimously approved a resolution Jan. 17 backing Bush. The House passed it the next day.

Several members were also concerned about the possibility of an early confrontation between U.S. and Iraqi ground forces. But after a briefing Jan. 17 from Defense Secretary Dick Cheney and Gen. Colin L. Powell Jr., chairman of the Joint Chiefs of Staff, members expressed confidence that the early phase of the war would continue to be fought in the air.

As events rapidly progressed, members moved from cautious optimism to gloom in a matter of hours. Encouraging reports of U.S. air superiority were replaced almost immediately by news of Iraqi Scud missile attacks on Israel.

The House and the Senate weighed in on Israel's behalf, passing resolutions that commended Israel's performance during the crisis. Support for the non-binding resolutions was unanimous in both chambers.

Noted for responding swiftly and massively to any attack, Israel adopted an uncharacteristic posture of restraint — at the Bush administration's behest. The United States immediately rushed Patriot defensive missiles and their crews to Israel.

The huge numbers of U.S. casualties that many members feared from a ground war against Iraq never materialized. The United States lost fewer troops during the entire war — 89 were listed as killed and another 38 as missing in action — than it did during some weeks of the long and grim Vietnam conflict.

The first vague reports of peace were heard on Feb. 15, when a communiqué from Iraq's Revolutionary Command Council raised hopes in Washington that Saddam had agreed to an unconditional pullout of his forces from Kuwait. But the statement premised the action on an exhaustive list of demands — including an Israeli withdrawal from occupied territories — that the White House deemed unacceptable.

Following a week of intense diplomatic maneuvers by the Soviet Union and Iraq to craft a peace settlement, President Bush gave Saddam an ultimatum Feb. 22 to begin withdrawing his troops from Kuwait by noon the next day or risk the brutal combat of a ground war.

Bush's demand, which demonstrated confidence that allied forces held the upper hand in the Persian Gulf War, won broad support from Congress, despite qualms about resorting to a potentially deadly ground war.

Iraq's initial response to Bush's ultimatum was negative, with a government spokesman saying that his country

U.N. Resolution 678

Following is the text of the resolution the U.N. Security Council adopted Nov. 29, 1990:

THE SECURITY COUNCIL, RECALLING, AND REAFFIRMING its resolutions 660 (1990) of 2 August, 661 (1990) of 6 August, 662 (1990) of 9 August, 664 (1990) of 18 August, 665 (1990) of 25 August, 666 (1990) of 13 September, 667 (1990) of 16 September, 669 (1990) of 24 September, 670 (1990) of 25 September, 674 (1990) of 29 October, and 677 (1990) of 28 November,

NOTING THAT, despite all efforts by the United Nations, Iraq refuses to comply with its obligation to implement resolution 660 (1990) and the above-mentioned subsequent relevant resolutions, in flagrant contempt of the Security Council,

MINDFUL of its duties and responsibilities under the Charter of the United Nations for the maintenance and preservation of international peace and security,

DETERMINED to secure full compliance with its decisions,

ACTING under Chapter VII of the Charter,

1. DEMANDS that Iraq comply fully with resolution 660 (1990) and all subsequent relevant resolutions, and decides, while maintaining all its decisions, to allow Iraq one final opportunity, as a pause of good will, to do so;
2. AUTHORIZES Member States cooperating with the Government of Kuwait, unless Iraq on or before 15 January 1991 fully implements, as set forth in paragraph 1 above, the foregoing resolutions, to use all necessary means to uphold and implement resolution 660 (1990) and all subsequent relevant resolutions and to restore international peace and security in the area;
3. REQUESTS all States to provide appropriate support for the actions undertaken in pursuance of paragraph 2 of the present resolution;
4. REQUESTS the States concerned to keep the Security Council regularly informed on the progress of actions undertaken pursuant to paragraphs 2 and 3 of the present resolution;
5. DECIDES to remain seized of the matter. ■

would instead pursue a Soviet initiative that called for a more gradual troop withdrawal.

In the early morning hours of Feb. 24, U.S. and allied troops, backed by air assaults, launched a massive ground operation that obliterated Iraqi defenses in a 100-hour ground war.

President Bush announced a cease-fire on Feb. 27. "Kuwait is liberated," he said. "Iraq's army is defeated. Our military objectives are met." *(Cease-fire announcement, p. 449)*

DEBATE AND VOTE

By the first week in January, five months after the crisis in the Persian Gulf had begun, members had for months been demanding that President Bush recognize their authority to declare war. Yet, less than two weeks before American troops could be ordered into combat, Congress had failed to assert its views beyond the language of vague resolutions and the clamor of inconclusive committee hearings.

"To cast the vote to place other Americans in the line of fire is the most humbling, painful decision I can imagine," said Sen. Joseph I. Lieberman, D-Conn. Virtually every lawmaker, in some fashion, echoed Lieberman's concern.

The anxiety was justified. Since Iraq's invasion of Kuwait the previous Aug. 2, the Bush administration had been moving almost inexorably toward conflict with Baghdad.

As the Senate fitfully began debate Jan. 4, Iraq accepted Bush's final offer for high-level talks in the Persian Gulf crisis.

Iraqi Foreign Minister Tariq Aziz said he would go to Geneva on Jan. 9 to discuss the gulf confrontation with Secretary of State James A. Baker III.

Emerging from the White House after a meeting with Bush, congressional leaders announced that they had canceled the customary January recess to remain available to act in the gulf crisis. But they offered to delay floor debate to await the results of Baker's diplomatic effort.

Even though the full-scale debate was postponed, both chambers engaged in initial maneuvering and discussion. Within minutes after the Senate convened on Jan. 3, liberal Democrats Brock Adams of Washington and Tom Harkin of Iowa sought to introduce a resolution demanding that Bush seek "explicit authorization" from Congress before launching a military attack.

"Now is the time and here is the place to debate the constitutional prerogatives of the president of the United States," Adams said.

Majority Leader George J. Mitchell, D-Maine, surprised and visibly angered, responded, "It may be the place. I do not believe it is the time."

Minority Leader Bob Dole, R-Kan., supported Mitchell in urging delay. "When we should have been debating, we were on vacation," Dole said. "Now, when we should be quiet, we want to vote."

After hours of negotiations in caucus, Senate Democrats arranged for a day of debate on the issue on Jan. 4 — but no action.

In the House, members introduced several resolutions that marked the boundaries of the conflict.

Joseph P. Kennedy II, D-Mass., offered a resolution demanding that Bush wait one year before initiating military action against Iraq. Democrats Richard J. Durbin, Ill., and Charles E. Bennett, Fla., introduced legislation demanding a congressional role. "The decision to go to war should not be left to one man," they said in a statement.

But a group led by Elton Gallegly, R-Calif., introduced a resolution that would give Bush exactly what he would want from Congress — approval to use "all necessary means" to force Iraq from Kuwait.

The Opening Round

The Senate's opening round of debate Jan. 4 concerned Congress' right to authorize war as much as the merits of Bush's policy in the gulf.

"We can no longer shun our responsibilities," said Harkin. "Each senator, each congressman must stand up and be counted."

Ernest F. Hollings, D-S.C., asked, "Is Kuwait worth the life of a GI? Not really. . . . They haven't been our friend. They're certainly not a friend of democracy, freedom and human rights."

But Alfonse M. D'Amato, R-N.Y., said crucial American interests were threatened by Saddam. "The issue isn't the Constitution," D'Amato said. "It's vital, bottom-line, live-or-die, long-term national interests. . . . Let's stop the hand-wringing."

Many lawmakers were determined to erase the stigma of Vietnam, when Congress effectively acquiesced while two successive administrations waged a costly and bloody war in Southeast Asia. "Congress simply ducked its responsibility in Vietnam," said Patrick J. Leahy, D-Vt.

But for all of the preoccupation with the legacy of that war, congressional opinion on the gulf crisis had not divided along the stark fault lines of the Vietnam debate.

This time there were not simply "hawks" who sup-

Resolution Authorizing Use of Force

Following is the text of the Authorization for Use of Military Force Against Iraq Resolution (H J Res 77 — PL 102-1) passed by Congress on Jan. 12, 1991, and signed by President Bush on Jan. 14. The House approved the resolution by a vote of 250-183; the Senate passed the measure (originally introduced as S J Res 2) by a vote of 52-47.

To authorize the use of United States Armed Forces pursuant to United Nations Security Council resolution 678.

Whereas the Government of Iraq without provocation invaded and occupied the territory of Kuwait on August 2, 1990; and

Whereas both the House of Representatives (in H J Res 658 of the 101st Congress) and the Senate (in S Con Res 147 of the 101st Congress) have condemned Iraq's invasion of Kuwait and declared their support for international action to reverse Iraq's aggression; and

Whereas, Iraq's conventional, chemical, biological, and nuclear weapons and ballistic missile programs and its demonstrated willingness to use weapons of mass destruction pose a grave threat to world peace; and

Whereas the international community has demanded that Iraq withdraw unconditionally and immediately from Kuwait and that Kuwait's independence and legitimate government be restored; and

Whereas the U.N. Security Council repeatedly affirmed the inherent right of individual or collective self-defense in response to the armed attack by Iraq against Kuwait in accordance with Article 51 of the U.N. Charter; and

Whereas, in the absence of full compliance by Iraq with its resolutions, the U.N. Security Council in Resolution 678 has authorized member states of the United Nations to use all necessary means, after January 15, 1991, to uphold and implement all relevant Security Council resolutions and to restore international peace and security in the area; and

Whereas Iraq has persisted in its illegal occupation of, and brutal aggression against, Kuwait: Now, therefore be it

Resolved by the Senate and House of Representatives of the United States of America in Congress assembled,

Section 1. Short Title. This joint resolution may be cited as the "Authorization for Use of Military Force Against Iraq Resolution."

Section 2. Authorization for Use of United States Armed Forces

(a) AUTHORIZATION. — The President is authorized, subject to subsection (b), to use United States Armed Forces pursuant to United Nations Security Council Resolution 678 (1990) in order to achieve implementation of Security Council Resolutions 660, 661, 662, 664, 665, 666, 667, 669, 670, 674, and 677.

(b) REQUIREMENT FOR DETERMINATION THAT USE OF MILITARY FORCE IS NECESSARY. — Before exercising the authority granted in subsection (a), the President shall make available to the Speaker of the House of Representatives and the President pro tempore of the Senate his determination that —

(1) the United States has used all appropriate diplomatic and other peaceful means to obtain compliance by Iraq with the United Nations Security Council resolutions cited in subsection (a); and

(2) that those efforts have not been successful in obtaining such compliance.

(c) WAR POWERS RESOLUTION REQUIREMENTS. —

(1) SPECIFIC STATUTORY AUTHORIZATION. — Consistent with section 8(a)(1) of the War Powers Resolution, the Congress declares that this section is intended to constitute specific statutory authorization within the meaning of section 5(b) of the War Powers Resolution.

(2) APPLICABILITY OF OTHER REQUIREMENTS. — Nothing in this resolution supersedes any requirement of the War Powers Resolution.

Section 4. REPORTS TO CONGRESS.

At least once every 60 days, the President shall submit to the Congress a summary on the status of efforts to obtain compliance by Iraq with the resolutions adopted by the United Nations Security Council in response to Iraq's aggression. ■

ported U.S. intervention and "doves" who opposed it. Instead, there were nearly universal agreement on the fundamentals — that Saddam was a dangerous enemy of U.S. interests and that strong action had to be taken to counter his invasion of Kuwait.

But many Democrats argued that war should be only a last resort. They insisted that the administration and its allies should have waited for months — and perhaps for as long as a year — on the expectation that the pressure of economic sanctions could eventually force Iraq to relent and withdraw from Kuwait. It was a view that was strongly endorsed by some scholars and former Pentagon officials who had testified before congressional committees but was just as emphatically disputed by others.

Constitutional Authority

Much of the initial debate centered on whether any military offensive against Iraq required congressional approval. Senate Majority Leader Mitchell and House Speaker Thomas S. Foley of Washington tirelessly argued that only Congress had the constitutional authority to decide whether the country went to war.

Although Bush disputed that assertion, it was a widely shared view on Capitol Hill.

The dispute was only the latest installment in a long-running debate over the ambiguous mandates of the Constitution. It states that Congress has the power "to declare war." But it also states that "the executive power shall be vested in a president," and that "the president shall be commander in chief of the Army and Navy."

Sen. Edward M. Kennedy, D-Mass, said that going to war without Congress' consent would precipitate a "constitutional crisis." House Majority Leader Richard A. Gephardt, D-Mo., had said that Congress might cut off funding in an undeclared war. Rep. David R. Obey, D-Wis., went even further, raising the specter of impeachment if the president ignored Congress.

At the same time, the White House had begun to hint that it had the right to defy any congressional restrictions. In the end, some members of both parties acknowledged that the decision was likely to rest with the executive branch, regardless of what Congress did.

A letter to leaders of Congress on Jan. 8 marked the first time Bush had openly requested congressional action on the gulf crisis. It was the first such request by a president since the 1964 Gulf of Tonkin resolution that authorized the use of force in Vietnam. But Bush skirted the question of whether such an authorization was constitutionally required, stating only that it would "greatly enhance the chances for peace if Congress were now to go on record supporting the position adopted by the U.N. Security Council on 12 separate occasions." *(Letter to Congress, 1990 Almanac, p. 747)*

By the time Congress finally debated an authorization for war, months of feuding with the White House over the constitutional role of the two branches was beside the point.

Key Dates in Persian Gulf Crisis

Jan. 3 — Bush proposes talks in Geneva between Secretary of State James A. Baker III and Iraqi Foreign Minister Tariq Aziz. 102nd Congress convenes.

Jan. 4 — Senate begins debate on gulf situation. Iraq accepts offer of Baker-Aziz talks, and they are scheduled for Jan. 9.

Jan. 8 — Bush sends a letter to leaders of Congress requesting for the first time congressional approval on actions being taken in the Persian Gulf. It is the first such request by a president since the 1964 Gulf of Tonkin Resolution that authorized use of force in Vietnam.

Jan. 9 — Baker meets with Aziz in Geneva. Baker brings with him a letter from Bush to Saddam reiterating demands for Iraqi forces to leave Kuwait. After reading the letter, Aziz refuses to take it to Saddam because Bush did not use "polite language."

Jan. 12 — The Senate votes 52-47 for a resolution (S J Res 2) to authorize the use of military force if Iraq has not withdrawn from Kuwait and complied with U.N. resolutions by Jan. 15. The House votes 250-183 to approve a similar resolution (H J Res 77).

Jan. 15 — U.N. deadline for Iraqi forces to leave Kuwait.

Jan. 16 — Bush gives the go-ahead for aerial bombing to begin in the gulf and notifies certain congressional leaders about one hour before the information is released to the public. CNN correspondents broadcast eyewitness accounts of damage from the Al-Rashid Hotel in downtown Baghdad.

Jan. 17 — Israel is struck by at least seven Iraqi Scud missles. Commander in chief of the operation, U.S. Army Gen. H. Norman Schwarzkopf, reports 80 percent of allied attacking planes have reached their targets.

Jan. 18 — Attacks continue around the clock at a rate of more than 1,000 sorties a day, with 159 separate targets hit in the first wave of attacks against Iraq.

Jan. 21 — Bush states Saddam's parading of allied POW pilots on television violates the Geneva Convention governing treatment of prisoners. Two days later, House votes 418-0 for resolution (H Con Res 48) condemning Iraq for treatment of POWs. Senate votes 99-0 on companion measure (S Con Res 5) the next day.

Jan. 26 — U.S. forces bomb two Kuwaiti pipelines in an effort to cut off the flow of oil being dumped into the Persian Gulf since Jan. 19. The situation has been called an environmental catastrophe and is threatening marine life and Saudi Arabian water supplies. U.S. blames Saddam for "environmental terrorism."

Jan. 27 — The 2nd Battalion of the 7th Air Defense Artillery has destroyed 10 Iraqi Scud missiles in the last eight days.

Jan. 29 — Iraqi troops launch attacks across the Saudi border, and 11 U.S. Marines are killed, more than have died in the air war up to this point. Iraq takes over Khafji, an abandoned port city in Saudi Arabia.

Jan. 31 — Saudi forces proclaim the recapture of Khafji. Reports from the front line say that Iraqi tanks and other vehicles are moving into southern Kuwait. The Iraqi forces come under massive strikes by B-52 bombers and other allied aircraft.

Feb. 1 — The Pentagon confirms that an AC-130 gunship with 14 airmen aboard is lost over Kuwait.

Feb. 5 — During a news conference, Bush says he is "somewhat skeptical" that "air power alone [will] get the job done," and that he will not go against sound military doctrine in order to "just delay for the sake of delay, hoping that it would save lives."

Feb. 13 — U.S. bombing kills hundreds of Iraqi civilians. U.S. officials have reported the target to have been a hardened bunker used as a military command center, while Iraqi authorities claim it was an air raid shelter.

Feb. 15 — Saddam sends message by Baghdad radio announcing "Iraq's readiness to deal with Security Council Resolution No. 660 of 1990 with the aim of reaching an honorable and acceptable political solution, including withdrawal" from Kuwait. The United States rejects the proposal, saying it is filled with demands and conditions for withdrawal.

Feb. 18 — Soviets offer peace proposal assuring Saddam of his security as well as promises to deal with other Middle East issues such as the future of Palestinians in Israel's occupied territories.

Feb. 22 — Bush gives Saddam an ultimatum to

Rep. Richard J. Durbin, D-Ill., cosponsor of a concurrent resolution asserting congressional war-making powers (H Con Res 32), said the action by members on an authorization for war demonstrated that "the Constitution had prevailed."

With little controversy, Durbin's resolution, cosponsored with Rep. Charles E. Bennett, D-Fla., passed the House on Jan 12, 302-131. The Senate took no similar action. *(Vote 7, 2-H)*

Nonetheless, the broader dispute over constitutional powers lingered in a reference to the War Powers act in the resolution that passed both houses.

The legislation stated that the 1973 law granted Congress specific statutory authority for using force.

Sen. John W. Warner, R-Va., said that although Bush would sign the congressional resolution, he would reassert that he viewed the Vietnam-era resolution as unconstitutional, as had every president since it was signed into law.

In his statement on signing the resolution on Jan. 14, Bush wrote, "As I made clear to congressional leaders at the outset, my request for congressional support did not, and my signing this resolution does not, constitute any change in the long-standing positions of the executive branch on either the President's constitutional authority to use the Armed Forces to defend vital U.S. interests or the constitutionality of the War Powers Resolution. I am begin withdrawal of Iraqi troops from Kuwait by noon Feb. 23 or risk the brutal combat of a ground war. Soviets announce a revised peace proposal excluding many of the promises in the earlier proposal.

Feb. 24 — A massive ground invasion of Kuwait begins hours after Iraq rejects the ultimatum. Iraqi troops fold at first contact with allied forces and thousands of POWs are taken into captivity.

Feb. 25 — Saddam agrees to withdraw his troops from Kuwait in compliance with U.N. Security Council Resolution 660, according to a Baghdad radio announcement.

Feb. 27 — Bush announces a cease-fire and declares Kuwait free.

March 3 — Iraqi military commanders accept the cease-fire terms imposed by coalition forces.

March 6 — Bush tells a joint session of Congress, "The war is over." U.S. troops begin to return home. But Kurds in northern Iraq and Shiites in southern Iraq mount major rebellions against Saddam's troops.

March 7 — Iraq frees about 1,700 Kuwaiti prisoners.

March 10 — All 21 American POWs in Iraq return to the United States.

March 21 — U.S.-based human rights organizations charge Kuwaiti soldiers and citizens with torturing and killing hundreds of Palestinians and other residents of Kuwait suspected of collaborating with Iraq.

March 22 — The Senate clears a supplemental appropriation (HR 1282 — PL 102-28) providing $42.6 billion to cover war costs, with allies expected to underwrite most of the expenses. The Senate also clears a $5.4 billion "dire emergency" supplemental appropriation (HR 1281 — PL 102-27) that includes benefits for war veterans and aid to Israel and Turkey.

March 31 — Kurdish insurgency collapses. Kurdish insurgents and civilians flee to mountains along Iraq's borders with Turkey and Iran.

April 3 — U.N. Security Council approves resolution establishing a permanent cease-fire in the Persian Gulf War and setting conditions for a gradual lifting of international sanctions against Iraq. The vote is 12-1, with Cuba in opposition.

April 4 — Rejecting criticism that U.S. forces should have intervened in behalf of rebels in Iraq, Bush says, "We're not going to get sucked into this by sending precious American troops into battle."

April 17 — U.S. and coalition troops secure a "safe zone" and begin to build relief camps for some of the 850,000 Kurdish refugees.

April 19 — U.S. officials charge Iraq with failing to fully comply with U.N. resolutions and omitting information about its nuclear weapons capability in its report to the United Nations.

May 13 — U.S. military transfers control of Kurdish refugee camps to United Nations. Approximately 26,000 Kurds were estimated to live in the camps.

May 15 — U.N. atomic energy experts begin inspecting Iraq's nuclear installations and chemical warfare facilities after Iraq promises unrestricted access.

May 19 — Trials begin in Kuwait for those accused of collaborating with Iraqi occupation forces.

May 22 — The Senate clears a $572 million supplemental appropriation (HR 2251 — PL 102-55) devoted mostly to emergency refugee aid.

June 23-28 — Iraq obstructs U.N. inspection team from obtaining full access to facilities. Bush accuses Iraq of violating cease-fire agreement.

July 28 — Kuwait exports oil for first time since Iraq's invasion in August 1990.

Sept. 18 — U.N. Security Council authorizes Iraq to sell $1.6 billion in oil to buy food and essential supplies. But Iraq balks at tight restrictions, including compensation for victims of the invasion of Kuwait.

Sept. 24-26 — Iraq detains U.N. inspectors after U.N. team finds papers said to prove Iraq's plans to manufacture nuclear weapons. Iraqi officials contend that the United Nations seized the papers with the intent of targeting Iraqi scientists for assassination.

Nov. 6 — The last of more than 700 Kuwaiti oil wells that had been set on fire by Iraqi forces is capped. Cost is estimated to be more than $1.5 billion.

Dec. 25 — Iraqi opposition groups meet in Beirut to develop new strategies to remove Saddam from power. But Kurdish factions are divided over whether to renew military actions or accept Saddam's promise of autonomy for the Kurds.

pleased, however, that differences on these issues between the President and many in Congress have not prevented us from uniting in a common objective."

But many members came away from the debate over war in the gulf confident that Congress had asserted its authority and performed its duty.

A Divided Congress

Throughout the months of debate leading up to the war vote, opinion among the Democrats had begun to splinter when the debate turned to the crucial question of precisely when to use force against Saddam.

The most prominent, and perhaps most unexpected, voice of restraint was Sen. Sam Nunn, D-Ga., the conservative chairman of the Armed Services Committee.

Nunn's committee hearings in November 1990 on gulf policy, which featured surprisingly cautious testimony from former chairmen of the Joint Chiefs of Staff, amounted to a public plea to slow the rush toward war.

Nunn had become the party's point man in arguing for continuing tough economic sanctions against Iraq rather than resorting to a quick use of military force.

Nunn played a pivotal role because his opposition to the early use of force deprived the administration of the united support it usually received on defense issues from conservative Southern Democrats.

Meanwhile, Rep. Stephen J. Solarz, D-N.Y., had emerged as the leading proponent of the view taken by some prominent Democrats who wanted the party to move beyond the "force as last resort" stance adopted by the leadership.

House Armed Services Committee Chairman Les Aspin, D-Wis., who also presided over high-profile hearings during the congressional recess, reached a far different conclusion than did Nunn, his Senate counterpart.

"I am not very bullish on sanctions," Aspin said, adding that while economic measures inflicted pain on the Iraqi people, "that is not the same thing as pain to Saddam Hussein."

The issue divided old political friends. While Nunn called for delay, a resort to force drew more support from Charles S. Robb, D-Va., a fellow Senate conservative and a co-founder of the moderate Democratic Leadership Council.

Robb took an increasingly high-profile role in expressing what he called a "more hawkish" view than many of his colleagues. "We are now beyond the point of sanctions taking an indefinite period," he said.

Despite those divisions of opinion, there was a sense of a common purpose and a shared burden as Congress finally debated the war resolution on Jan. 12.

The grim sense that the United States could soon go to war pervaded the more than 20 hours of debate that preceded the climactic vote.

Congressional anger at Saddam only grew after Aziz rebuffed Baker at their meeting in Geneva on Jan. 9. Aziz refused to give Saddam a letter from Bush that Baker had asked him to pass on. The foreign minister complained that Bush had not used "polite language."

"He stiffed us," complained Rep. John P. Murtha, D-Pa.

Both veteran lawmakers and freshmen facing their first major vote welled with emotion as they described grappling with the enormity of the decision.

During the dignified, often moving, congressional debate, some members offered prayers for the country, the president and the nearly 400,000 U.S. troops arrayed against Iraqi forces in the Persian Gulf region.

Even though lawmakers differed significantly over U.S. gulf policy, they said they would close ranks behind the president after the debate and vote.

Gephardt said before the final vote, "Whatever our decision, we will leave this room one again and whole again."

The Senate Votes

Although approval of the resolution authorizing war was a victory for President Bush, it fell far short of unanimity.

When it became clear that Bush's position would prevail by a small margin in the Senate, Paul Simon, D-Ill., said the vote "shows a deeply divided Congress and a deeply divided American people." He added that it represented the most narrow margin backing military action since the War of 1812.

Most Democrats in both chambers backed alternative resolutions, offered by their leaders, which called for maintaining economic sanctions against Iraq while deferring the decision to use military action.

In the weeks before the vote, a contingent of Senate Democrats supporting Bush had begun to take shape. Lieberman, an early supporter of the administration's policy, cosponsored the resolution (S J Res 2).

But the process of lining up Democrats and keeping Republicans on board was difficult. Key conservative Democrats, such as Intelligence Committee Chairman David L. Boren, Okla., joined Nunn instead. And Charles E. Grassley, Iowa, became a surprise Republican defector, joining Mark O. Hatfield, R-Ore.

In the end, the administration cobbled together a group of 10 Senate Democrats — three more than needed: Lieberman; Robb; John B. Breaux, La.; Richard H. Bryan, Nev.; Al Gore, Tenn.; Bob Graham, Fla.; Howell Heflin, Ala.; J. Bennett Johnston, La.; Harry Reid, Nev.; and Richard C. Shelby, Ala.

With the exception of Hatfield, who voted against both resolutions, senators split the same way on the Mitchell-Nunn resolution demanding a continued reliance on economic sanctions. That measure (S J Res 1) was defeated Jan. 12, 46-53. *(Vote 1, p. 2-S)*

The Senate then voted 52-47 for S J Res 2, which gave Bush the authority he needed to use force against Iraq.

The House Votes

In the House, the administration had a much more comfortable margin entering the debate. The opponents of the resolution authorizing force, led by Foley, faced what both sides agreed was an uphill battle.

Nunn's counterpart on the House Armed Services Committee, Aspin, weeks before had voiced his skepticism that sanctions would ultimately be effective and predicted as the debate began that war would produce a quick U.S. victory.

Solarz, who cosponsored the winning resolution with Minority Leader Robert H. Michel, R-Ill., worked to bring together disparate Democrats to support the president.

Among the 86 Democrats who backed the House resolution authorizing force, H J Res 77, were several committee chairmen, including Dan Rostenkowski, Ill., and John D. Dingell, Mich.

Because the issue was deemed "a conscience vote" by the leadership, there were promises of no recriminations against those who voted with the administration.

But one supporter of the Solarz-Michel resolution, Howard L. Berman, D-Calif., predicted a party rift that might last for some time.

"It won't heal until the crisis is resolved," he said in an interview before the vote.

On Jan. 12, the resolution urging continued reliance on sanctions (H Con Res 33), which was cosponsored by Gephardt and Lee H. Hamilton, D-Ind., fell on a vote of 183-250.

H J Res 77 passed the House that same day on a 250-183 vote.

WAR BEGINS

"The balloon is up."

With that prearranged code, Secretary of State Baker told Jesse Helms, N.C., the ranking Republican on the Senate Foreign Relations Committee, on Jan. 16 that the United States had gone to war with Iraq.

For all the gravity of that call at 7:02 p.m., most members had already learned that the United States was at war almost half an hour earlier. Like other Americans, they had heard or seen reporters broadcasting descriptions of the fighter attacks and anti-aircraft fire that lit up the skies over Baghdad.

At 7 p.m., White House spokesman Marlin Fitzwater read a statement from Bush that said, "The liberation of Kuwait has begun." At 9 p.m., Bush addressed the nation from the Oval Office, saying, "The world could wait no longer."

The imperfect process of congressional notification was one more reminder that while Congress authorizes war, the executive branch makes it. The bombers had been in the air for 30 minutes when Bush reached Michel at 5:20 p.m. Michel was the first member of Congress to get a call.

Others rating heads-up calls were either members of the congressional leadership or the chairmen and ranking Republicans of four committees concerned primarily with national security. At the top of the list was a group known informally as the "Big Five" — House Speaker Foley, Senate Majority Leader Mitchell, Senate Minority Leader Dole, House Majority Leader Gephardt and Michel — as well as a sixth key figure, Robert C. Byrd, D-W.Va., president pro tempore of the Senate.

Complying with Congress' resolution authorizing the use of force against Iraq, Bush also wrote to Foley and Byrd that efforts to secure Iraq's peaceful compliance with the U.N. Security Council resolutions had failed. But Bush was on the phone before the paperwork reached Capitol Hill.

In the first days after waves of fighters, bombers and missiles crushed strategic targets throughout Iraq, leaders of Congress voiced support, and the Senate unanimously approved a resolution backing Bush. The House approved it the next day.

Yet lawmakers sensed that all of their resolutions and statements would make little difference in the end. Having already authorized Bush to begin a war, members were well aware that they were reduced — politically and even constitutionally — to the role of bystanders.

There was no business as usual on Capitol Hill as Congress' attention was riveted on an international crisis in the Persian Gulf spinning far beyond its control.

Home-state visits were called off. Lobbyists cut short an annual junket for members of Congress. Concern about the sagging economy took a back seat to the war.

Security around the Capitol was high. Tension was even higher.

Other issues faded into insignificance as Congress monitored the awesome consequences of its Jan. 12 vote authorizing the use of force in the gulf.

Through the tense early days of the conflict, members of Congress, like millions of other Americans, mostly stayed glued to the television and prayed for the U.S. servicemen and women at risk.

During the first day of battle, a general air of optimism appeared justified, as U.S. armed forces launched more than 1,000 air strikes and lost only one pilot and his aircraft.

Secretary of Defense Dick Cheney contributed to the upbeat mood with his early assessment of the U.S. air assault.

At a press briefing Jan. 16, Cheney said: "I will simply say that preliminary reports we have received in terms of the success of the operation — and that includes the possibility of casualties — have been very, very encouraging."

As events rapidly progressed, members moved from cautious optimism to gloom in a matter of hours. Encouraging reports of U.S. air superiority were replaced almost immediately by news of Iraqi Scud missile attacks on Israel.

The administration also attempted to dampen the early, unrealistic expectations of a quick and virtually painless victory.

"We must be realistic," Bush said at a Jan. 18 news conference. "There will be losses. There will be obstacles along the way. And war is never cheap or easy."

Support Resolutions

With the dramatic events in the Middle East dominating the attention of official Washington, Congress got down to the somewhat mundane task of drafting a resolution.

Foley and Mitchell had several aims in pressing for the resolution backing U.S. forces. The first was to signal the unity of the country during a time of crisis. "I think it's not inappropriate at this time to demonstrate that, regardless of the debate last week, that the Congress stands behind the armed services," said Foley.

The question most members faced was whether to rally around the president or the forces in the field. Although the distinction appeared academic, considering that Bush was functioning as commander in chief of those forces, it was rich in political implications.

Democrats were particularly anxious to record their support in light of the divisions that had surfaced in the prewar debate. But many in the party also wanted to stop short of lauding Bush, in part because they sharply disagreed with him on a range of domestic issues.

Privately, Democrats admitted that the 1992 presidential race was inescapably at issue as well. One senior Democrat, in explaining why he would not support a resolution that offered more open-ended backing for the president, said: "I'm not going to support Bush for re-election. I'm going to support a Democrat, obviously."

Yet Republicans showed that they, too, were not utterly above politics when it came time to craft a resolution.

Senate Republicans wanted to highlight Bush's performance as prominently as possible. An early draft asserted that "the Congress commends the president for his decisive leadership in the Persian Gulf crisis."

Democrats countered with language that understated Bush's role. Their draft would have supported the efforts of Bush "to provide to our armed forces all appropriate resources."

At one point, the two sides were so far apart that most senators believed that they would have to delay a vote on the resolution. At the last minute, Democrats grudgingly agreed to "commend" Bush for his performance in the gulf war.

The concurrent resolution (S Con Res 2) passed Jan. 17, 98-0, "commends and supports the efforts and leadership of the president as Commander in Chief in the Persian Gulf hostilities," and it "unequivocally supports the men and women of our Armed Forces." Democratic Sens. Alan Cranston, Calif., and John Glenn, Ohio, did not vote. *(Vote 3, 2-S)*

In the House on Jan. 18, there also were differences over whether to single out Bush for praise. But members approved the resolution 399-6 with six members voting "present." *(Vote 10, p. 4-H)*

Few reservations were expressed over Operation Desert Storm — and no one spoke of the U.S. military forces in the region in any but the most glowing terms.

Virtually the only cohesive opposition to the resolution came from members of the Congressional Black Caucus. Of the 12 lawmakers who voted either "present" or "no" on the resolution, 10 were members of the caucus.

Rep. Charles B. Rangel, D-N.Y., said during the floor debate on the resolution: "We can support the men and women in the military and still disagree vigorously with the president of the United States. Nobody in this country is going to browbeat me into agreeing with the president on the Persian Gulf."

ISRAEL'S ROLE

The lull ended, and the war took a dangerous turn on Jan. 18 when Iraq bombarded Tel Aviv and Haifa, two heavily populated Israeli cities, with Scud missiles.

Noted for responding swiftly and massively to any attack, Israel adopted an uncharacteristic posture of restraint — at the Bush administration's behest. The United States immediately rushed Patriot defensive missiles and their crews to Israel.

Israeli officials did not initially rule out the possibility of retaliating with a strike against Iraq, thus raising the prospect of a regionwide war.

More ominous from the U.S. perspective was the chance that Israeli participation in the war might jeopardize the Arab coalition against Iraq that the administration had carefully pieced together.

Several members of Congress, including Rep. Hamilton, chairman of the Foreign Affairs Subcommittee on Europe and the Middle East, expressed the belief that an Israeli attack would not "blow this coalition apart."

"The coalition is much firmer than that," said Hamilton.

But no one was certain. And the awareness that Israel was vulnerable to nighttime missile raids — possibly involving chemical warheads — dispirited lawmakers in Washington.

Israeli Cabinet members repeatedly asserted Israel's right to defend itself and hinted that retaliation might be forthcoming at some point. But Israel held its fire.

Admired and appreciated for enduring the terror of Iraq's Scud missiles, Israel again assumed its traditional role as the United States' "special" ally.

But praise from the Bush administration and Congress did not guarantee that Israel would get the billions of dollars in additional U.S. aid it had requested. Nor had the sudden warming of relations erased the differences that had strained U.S.-Israeli relations in the few years before the war.

Through most of its four decades, Israel had enjoyed what had often been termed a "special relationship" with the United States — an alliance that seemed to transcend the usual state-to-state relations.

For much of the previous two years, however, Israel's conservative government had been at odds with the Bush administration over the wrenchingly difficult issue of Palestinian rights. Prime Minister Yitzhak Shamir had rebuffed repeated U.S. efforts to persuade Israel to open a dialogue with Palestinian leaders.

The disagreements were pushed aside when Saddam began launching Scud missiles at Israel.

Bush remained in close telephone contact with Shamir, as did Secretary of State Baker. Deputy Secretary of State Lawrence S. Eagleburger was dispatched on an emergency mission to Israel.

Most supporters of Israel, on Capitol Hill and elsewhere, believed that the Iraqi attacks could produce long-term benefits by educating Americans to the dangers confronting the Jewish state in the Middle East.

"If nothing else, the events of the last week have been a tremendous reminder of the neighborhood in which Israel finds itself," said Rep. Howard L. Berman, D-Calif.

Rep. Lawrence J. Smith, D-Fla., was less optimistic that lasting benefits would accrue to Israel. "I don't think anybody ought to be too euphoric over short-term closeness," he said.

"There's an institutional memory in the State Department that is not going to go away because of the closeness," he said. He also worried that by accepting the Patriot missile, "Israel has left itself open for a chit that may be cashed later."

Nonetheless, the mood had changed so quickly and significantly that during Eagleburger's visit to Israel he found himself being praised by Tel Aviv residents as he inspected Scud missile damage.

Sen. Bob Kasten, R-Wis., reflecting on the suddenly changed nature of U.S.-Israel relations, asked, "When was the last time you heard of a Bush administration official cheered in the streets of Tel Aviv?"

Congressional Support Resolutions

The House and the Senate weighed in on Israel's behalf, passing resolutions that commended Israel's performance during the crisis. Support for the non-binding resolutions was unanimous in both chambers.

For Congress, the resolutions of support were a quick and easy reward for Israel's stance.

The House resolution (H Con Res 41) "condemns the unprovoked attack by Iraq on Israel" and "commends Israel for its restraint." The concurrent resolution passed the House, 416-0, on Jan. 23. *(Vote 11, p. 4-H)*

The Senate acted the next day, approving a similar resolution (S Con Res 4), 99-0. *(Vote 8, p. 2-S)*

During the debate on the resolution, several lawmakers compared Saddam to Adolf Hitler. "When he [Saddam] talks about turning Tel Aviv into a crematorium, we all know in this country and worldwide with whom he is associating himself," said Rep. Don Ritter, R-Pa.

Sen. Frank R. Lautenberg, D-N.J., a cosponsor of the Senate resolution, said Saddam "is clearly trying to traumatize the Israeli public in a sadistic manner."

Even if Israel were to launch a strike against Iraq, it probably would do little to affect its support on Capitol Hill, many lawmakers said. "If they retaliate, I think everyone here would understand," said Rep. Bill Richardson, D-N.M.

The far more complicated issue that confronted Congress was how much aid to provide for Israel, in light of its policy of restraint. Israel's finance minister floated a proposal for $13 billion in additional aid over five years. It eventually became a formal request for $10 billion loan guarantees. *(Mideast policy, p. 451)*

WAR CONTINUES

As the war in the Persian Gulf entered its second week, Congress and the country faced the harsh reality it might not be the quick, low-casualty war some hoped for in the first days of the conflict.

With security against terrorists tightened to the point that some leading members were assigned full-time bodyguards, Congress' mood was swayed during the week of Jan. 21 by events that presented a sobering contrast to the intoxicating military successes of the first days of the war.

Painfully aware that politicians of both parties had said

that the American public did not have the stomach for a protracted war, administration officials began trying to lay the political groundwork for an operation that might last months, not days or weeks.

Congress continued to play a peripheral role as the war widened. And as a symbol of its commitment to U.S. military personnel, Congress quickly approved two bills increasing veterans' benefits and easing tax requirements for forces in the gulf. *(Gulf veterans benefits, p. 320)*

To keep members abreast of developments, administration officials provided briefings on Capitol Hill every day but Sunday. Even after a week, more than 100 House members were still showing up.

But some members complained that briefers were giving little information that could not be learned from watching round-the-clock television coverage on Cable News Network (CNN) — complete with the inaccuracies of hair-trigger reporting.

At one briefing of House members, an administration official reportedly read from CNN copy to tell members that U.S. Patriot missiles in Israel had knocked out two incoming Scud missiles. The members broke into cheers, according to sources attending the meeting. But members got a very different story when they returned to their offices and learned that, in fact, one of the Scuds was not destroyed but landed in Tel Aviv, inflicting heavy casualties. The first missile to elude Israeli defenses landed on Jan. 22, increasing U.S. concern about Israeli retaliation. Iraq released videotapes of seven allied prisoners of war.

Many politicians had been saying for months that domestic political support for the war hinged largely on its not dragging on too long.

"The agony of Vietnam is still with us. People remember a protracted war," Bush had said in December. "I don't think . . . that support would last if it were a long, drawn-out conflagration."

But administration officials and some of their congressional allies had begun to warn that pressure to keep the war short could run afoul of another political and moral imperative: keeping casualties down. That was why some had been hoping to avoid a potentially disastrous ground war.

POW Treatment and Casualties

Most Americans' first glimpse of the potential for casualties was the videotape of allied POWs, who appeared bruised and dazed. They criticized the attack on Iraq in stilted tones that made their statements seem coerced.

Congress responded by approving companion unanimous resolutions (H Con Res 48, S Con Res 5) condemning Iraq's treatment of the POWs. The resolutions, passed 418-0 by the House on Jan. 23 and 99-0 by the Senate the next day, declared Iraq's actions in violation of the Geneva Conventions governing treatment of prisoners. *(House vote 12, p. 4-H; Senate vote 7, p. 2-S)*

Sen. John McCain, an Arizona Republican who was a POW in the Vietnam War, said the resolution sent a clear message to the Iraqis that they would be treated as war criminals: "We will give you the same punishment that was meted out at the Nuremberg trials after World War II."

More sparks flew when the Pentagon indicated that no media coverage would be allowed when soldiers' caskets arrived at Dover Air Force Base in Delaware.

"That's not a real war if you don't take pictures of casualties," said Rep. Don Edwards, D-Calif.

The Pentagon assuaged some of the grumbling about lack of information by holding a broad, lengthy briefing Jan. 23 by Powell and Cheney.

Two weeks into the bombing campaign, 11 U.S. Marines died Jan. 29 in the first sustained land battle of the Persian Gulf War. More Americans died in the fighting on the ground that day than had been killed in the air war up to that date.

Even so, the U.S. commanding general, H. Norman Schwarzkopf, belittled the Iraqi attacks as "no more significant than a mosquito to an elephant."

Anticipating a Ground War

The first few Marine deaths underscored a consensus within the Bush administration, the senior military command and Congress — to defer a ground attack on Iraqi forces while the coalition air forces continued trying to cripple the enemy garrisons.

But while Saddam refused to abandon his claim to Kuwait, the question of whether — and when — to accept the risk of a ground assault had to be faced.

There was also concern about how the U.S. Army and Marine Corps — flush with high-tech weapons and first-class training but untested in battle for a generation — would fare against the fourth-largest army in the world.

The 11 Marines were killed when an Iraqi unit pushed across the Saudi border between the abandoned port city of Khafji and a point about 50 miles inland, west of the Kuwaiti city of Wafra.

That attack and two others were quickly repelled with heavy Iraqi losses. But a fourth Iraqi column occupied Khafji, six miles south of the Saudi-Kuwait border, for about 36 hours before it was ejected by Saudi forces and

Persian Gulf Exemption

Congress cleared legislation (HR 4 — PL 102-2) on Jan. 24 that broadened an order by President Bush granting military personnel in the Persian Gulf an extension for filing and paying their income taxes.

Moving quickly, the House passed the bill on Jan. 23 by 415-0. The Senate passed the legislation, 99-0, the next day, clearing it for the president, who signed it Jan 30. *(House vote 13, p. 4-H; Senate vote 4, p. 2-S)*

Bush signed an executive order Jan. 21 that designated Iraq, the entire Arabian Peninsula and surrounding waters as a combat zone, meaning that troops who served in the Desert Storm operation did not have to file their 1990 tax returns or pay any balance owed until 180 days after returning from the combat zone.

The bill went beyond the president's order in several respects. First, it applied to personnel who had served in the Persian Gulf any time after Aug. 2, rather than only those on duty after Jan. 16, when combat started.

Additionally, interest on income tax refunds began accruing after April 15, even if the military taxpayers had not filed their returns by then.

Finally, the measure granted the tax relief for up to five years to soldiers who were hospitalized as a result of wounds received while serving in the gulf.

As passed, the bill was expected to cost $10 million per year. Red Cross workers and journalists accredited by the Pentagon who were serving in the combat theater also qualified for the tax extension.

Other Resolutions Related to The Persian Gulf War

Although Congress' most important action concerning the Persian Gulf War came in its approval of HJ Res 77, which authorized the use of force, members also passed a number of other resolutions related to the conflict. They included:

- S Con Res 2, which commended the president for his leadership and supported the armed forces, passed the Senate Jan 17, 98-0. In the House on Jan. 18, it was approved 399-6.

- H Con Res 41, which condemned the "unprovoked attack" by Iraq on Israel, passed the House, 416-0, on Jan. 23. S Con Res 4, with similar wording, was approved by the Senate the next day, 99-0.

- H Con Res 48, S Con Res 5 — companion unanimous resolutions that condemned Iraq's treatment of prisoners of war. The resolutions were passed 418-0 by the House on Jan. 23 and 99-0 by the Senate the next day.

- S Con Res 13, a non-binding resolution passed by the Senate on Feb. 28 that commended Bush as commander-in-chief and the armed forces for the success of Operation Desert Storm.

troops from neighboring Qatar, backed by U.S. Marines.

U.S. commanders touted the border battles as a striking victory, claiming that 40 Iraqi tanks and 37 other armored vehicles were destroyed and more than 300 Iraqi prisoners taken.

As Saudi forces proclaimed the recapture of Khafji on Jan. 31, reports began filtering back from the front lines of a large force of Iraqi tanks and other vehicles moving into southern Kuwait. The Iraqi forces came under massive strikes by B-52 bombers and other allied aircraft.

In the first two weeks of the war, allied planes had flown more than 30,000 missions, according to figures provided by the U.S. command in Saudi Arabia. Initially, the attacks concentrated heavily on strategic targets: command and communications centers, air bases, supply routes and facilities related to nuclear, chemical and biological weapons.

In addition, far more missions than had been planned were dedicated to hunting down the elusive launchers from which Iraq hurled modified Scud missiles at Israel and Saudi Arabia.

But from the outset, the targets in the air campaign included Iraqi ground units, particularly the elite Republican Guard divisions that were dug in along the northern border of Kuwait as a reserve force.

By Jan. 30, more than 300 air missions a day were being flown against the elite Republican Guard divisions, including sorties by the giant B-52s, each of which could carry up to 30 tons of bombs. On some days, the big planes hit the Guards with more than 400 tons of bombs.

As Iraqi forces near the Saudi border began moving out of their dug-in positions Jan. 29, hundreds of air strikes each day were funneled to that region. Pilots and reporters in front-line ground units reported large numbers of so-called secondary explosions in Iraqi positions, signs that bombs had ignited ammunition or fuel.

The air war was not risk-free. The Pentagon confirmed Feb. 1 that an AC-130 gunship with 14 airmen aboard was lost over Kuwait.

Despite the massive air attack, Pentagon officials remained cautious in estimating its impact, noting that it was much more difficult to estimate the damage of a bombing raid on a tank division than on a factory complex.

Iraq's troops were often described as battle-tested by their long, fierce war against Iran from 1980 to 1988. But Schwarzkopf and other U.S. officials belittled the relevance of that combat experience in light of the crude tactics and poor armament of many Iranian troops.

Nevertheless, by most accounts, one thing that Iraqi forces did very well in that war was to fight off attacks on their fortified positions.

By all accounts, the Iraqis had capitalized handsomely on those natural advantages along their front lines in Kuwait, creating a belt of fortified positions behind thick layers of ditches and tank traps, thoroughly salted with hundreds of thousands of mines.

U.S. forces had specialized equipment for breaching such defensive barriers, including armored bulldozers to cut through berms, prefabricated bridges to carry tanks over deep ditches, and daisy chains of explosives, carried by rocket across minefields and then set off to detonate the mines and clear a lane through which tanks could be driven.

Besides sending a mass of tanks and armored troop carriers around the western flank of the Iraqi line, U.S. commanders also could send Marines ashore from the large fleet of amphibious landing ships stationed in the Persian Gulf.

Also, while Schwarzkopf was building up his force with tank divisions, he held onto two Army divisions that were much less heavily armed but were equipped for aerial deployment behind enemy lines: the helicopter-borne 101st Air Assault Division and the 82nd Airborne.

The allied challenge was not only to outflank the Iraqi defenses but to place the attackers in so commanding a position that the Iraqis would have to abandon their bunkers for a counterattack, thus exposing themselves to the umbrella of allied planes above.

"It depends on how you confront them," said Senate Armed Services Committee Chairman Sam Nunn, D-Ga. "Can you maneuver, get them out of their holes, and then use air power?"

HINTS OF PEACE

The first sign of peace with Iraq proved to be no more than a hoax. A Feb. 15 communiqué from Iraq's Revolutionary Command Council raised hopes in Washington that Saddam had agreed to an unconditional pullout of his forces from Kuwait. But the statement premised the action on an exhaustive list of demands — including an Israeli withdrawal from occupied territories — that the White House deemed unacceptable.

"There is nothing new here," Bush said. "It is a hoax. There are new demands added."

Again demonstrating his firm opposition to offering any concessions to Saddam, Bush for the first time issued a direct call for Iraqis to oust their president. "There is another way for the bloodshed to stop, and that is for the Iraqi military and the Iraqi people to take matters into their own hands to force Saddam Hussein, the dictator, to step aside," Bush said.

Yet the president acknowledged that the communiqué represented the first recognition by Saddam's government that "Iraq must leave Kuwait." The Iraqi statement indicated a "readiness to deal with" U.N. Security Council Resolution No. 660 of Aug. 2, 1990, which demanded that Iraq "withdraw immediately" from Kuwait.

Although many members of Congress joined Bush in criticizing the Iraqi communiqué, some said the statement might offer at least a glimmer of hope for a diplomatic resolution of the Persian Gulf War.

"I do think there is something new here," Hamilton said in a statement. "Iraq is blinking and may be rethinking its policies."

Hamilton and others said that Iraq's seriousness in pursuing peace could well be determined by talks between Iraqi envoys and Soviet President Mikhail S. Gorbachev, scheduled to take place in Moscow on Feb. 17.

"This could be the opening bid in Saddam's move toward diplomacy," Nunn told an interviewer during an appearance in Raleigh, N.C. "In the Arab world you always have to be prepared for bargaining, and this may be the opening gambit."

Judith Kipper, an expert on Arab affairs who was affiliated with the Brookings Institution, said Saddam was "very good at devising his own face-saving," and "the Soviets gave him an opportunity."

Saddam's new offer came as U.S. forces appeared poised to begin the ground combat that was expected to bring the war to a bloody climax.

There was a widespread belief among members of Congress that the relentless air assaults on Iraq had badly undermined Iraq's military capabilities.

"It's clear that he [Saddam] must be hurting," said Frank H. Murkowski, R-Alaska, vice chairman of the Senate Intelligence Committee.

"Right now, it looks like he's down for the count," said Senate Minority Leader Dole. Dole and other Republicans were dubious that the Iraqi statement would result in any momentum toward peace. "It's going to fall like a Scud," he said.

Most Democrats also supported the president's no-concession stance. "Saddam Hussein's announcement will only assume significance if it is accompanied by the movement of soldiers from Kuwait," said House Majority Leader Richard A. Gephardt, D-Mo.

But Rep. Ronald V. Dellums, D-Calif., a consistent critic of Operation Desert Storm, said the president should respond to the Iraqi statement by ordering a temporary halt in the air campaign. "It will cost the U.S. and its allies nothing to pause, if only for 48 hours," he said, "to see if the Iraqi government is willing, as the French called for, to establish a definitive timetable for withdrawal."

For many lawmakers, the optimistic signals that Iraq might be weakening were tempered by the possibility that Saddam could be inching toward a diplomatic solution that could end the war but permit him to remain in power.

The Iraqi announcement "provides little hope that the U.S. and our allies will be able to claim decisive victory by the removal of Saddam Hussein from power," said Rep. Glenn English, D-Okla.

And while that objective was not included in the U.N. Security Council resolutions on Iraq, it was clearly the outcome sought by most Americans.

"People in Nebraska want this guy dead," said Sen. Bob Kerrey, D-Neb., in an interview before the release of the Revolutionary Command Council's communiqué.

Before the war, administration officials had feared what they termed "a nightmare scenario," in which Saddam would withdraw from Kuwait with his military arsenal intact. With the success of the allied bombing campaign — U.S. officials estimated that up to 40 percent of Iraq's armored forces had been destroyed or damaged — concerns over the survival of the Iraqi military abated somewhat.

But the administration still appreciated the value of ousting Saddam, as demonstrated by the president's suggestion that the Iraqi people "take matters into their own hands." At the same time, the White House was aware that establishing Saddam's ouster as a goal raised the stakes of Operation Desert Storm.

It also risked alienating the Soviet Union, which was increasingly cautionary in its comments on the U.S.-led operations in the Persian Gulf.

On Feb. 9, Gorbachev warned that the war was taking on "an ever more alarming and dramatic scope" and that the U.S.-led alliance was in "danger of exceeding the mandate" of U.N. Security Council resolutions, which set the goal of reversing Iraq's invasion of Kuwait.

In an apparent response, Iraq's communiqué expressed "appreciation" for recent Soviet diplomatic efforts.

Despite the Soviet criticism, many members of Congress urged the administration to continue the air war — and to delay for as long as possible a ground assault, with its likelihood of heavy U.S. casualties.

"The air campaign is having an impact on the Iraqi government's thinking," Hamilton said. "Under present circumstances, we should continue our current military strategy."

Dole adamantly insisted that Saddam be granted no relief: "No pause, no cease-fire, no timeouts, no jump balls."

But when asked whether a ground war should begin, the Senate minority leader was more tentative. There is "no hurry for that," he said. "Let's keep our casualties low."

On Feb. 11, Bush said, "The air campaign has been very, very effective and will continue for a while."

The president made his comment after being briefed by Defense Secretary Dick Cheney and Gen. Colin L. Powell Jr., chairman of the Joint Chiefs of Staff, upon their return from a visit with U.S. and allied commanders in Saudi Arabia.

Internationally, however, the level of criticism for the aerial bombardment increased dramatically in the wake of a U.S. bombing attack Feb. 13 on Baghdad that killed hundreds of civilians seeking shelter in a bunker.

The grim scene, which Iraqi officials displayed to visiting Western reporters, underscored that the U.S.-led air war was not solely the pristine exercise in high-tech destruction of bridges and missile batteries that had been portrayed by Pentagon briefers.

Iraq described the attack on the bunker as "a brutal crime" and emphasized that the "victims were children, women and elderly." But U.S. officials said that the facility was a military "command-and-control center," and they suggested that Saddam had stationed hundreds of civilians in it.

"We don't know why civilians were at this location," said White House spokesman Fitzwater. "But we do know that Saddam Hussein does not share our value in the sanctity of life.... He kills civilians intentionally and with purpose."

LAST BID FOR PEACE

The complexities of the international alliance arrayed against Iraq were underscored by the drama of Moscow's attempt during the week of Feb. 18 to broker a resolution to the conflict. Soviet President Gorbachev's peace proposals immediately set off a diplomatic scramble and caught the allies off-guard. But the week ended with Bush issuing an ultimatum on Feb. 22 that Iraq begin withdrawing from Kuwait by noon the next day or risk the brutal combat of ground war.

A Soviet proposal for peace was presented to Aziz in a meeting with Gorbachev on Feb. 18. But Bush rejected the plan, which he described as falling "well short of what would be required." Although specifics of that initial Gorbachev plan were not made public, it was widely reported to have called for Iraq's withdrawal while providing Soviet assurances that Saddam's security would be protected and that other Middle East issues — including the future of Palestinians in Israel's occupied territories — would be dealt with.

A more comprehensive proposal was crafted in a Moscow meeting late on Feb. 21 (Eastern Standard Time) between Gorbachev and Aziz.

According to the Soviets, Aziz agreed tentatively to an "unconditional" withdrawal of troops from Kuwait beginning two days after a cease-fire. But the proposal's requirement for the lifting of all U.N. resolutions against Iraq would have, among other things, relieved Iraq of paying reparations for its invasion and left the future status of Kuwait up in the air. The United States said it could not accept those conditions.

Nonetheless, the Soviet-drafted proposal omitted some conditions from earlier offers — including linkage of withdrawal to discussion of the fate of the Palestinians — that the administration had viewed as particularly objectionable.

Many lawmakers viewed the Soviet-Iraqi discussions with suspicion, fearing that they would only lead to a compromise that would allow Saddam to rebuild his military machine after the war.

"What the coalition could not stand is Iraq bringing all of its arms back over the border — sitting there, prepared to menace Kuwait and Saudi Arabia in perpetuity as we moved out," Sen. Richard G. Lugar, R-Ind., said on NBC's "Today Show." "That would be a disaster."

"The problem for us is that a muddy, ambivalent, political solution could undercut a military victory, which we all think is close," Hamilton said on CBS shortly after the Feb. 21 announcement by Soviet officials of the tentative peace proposal.

However, Hamilton added, the proposal is "a very, very serious one. I do not think we can lightly dismiss it."

Some on Capitol Hill expressed concerns about the Soviet Union's motives in trying to negotiate a Mideast settlement.

"I think that the last-minute manipulations by Gorbachev in the Persian Gulf are mischievous and are ominous," said Pennsylvania Republican Rep. Don Ritter. "There cannot be peace while Saddam Hussein remains in power, and any proposal that the Soviets make that keeps their client in power in Iraq runs counter to the cause of peace in the Middle East."

Senate Minority Leader Dole echoed similar concerns Feb. 21: "Let's remember that the Soviet Union has only been an observer in this process. They haven't contributed any materiel or any young men or young women to the gulf coalition forces."

Although the administration said it "appreciated" the Soviet efforts, it clearly preferred taking matters into its own hands.

Cutting short Gorbachev's efforts at compromise, Bush issued his ultimatum on Feb. 22. He called for Saddam's "immediate and unconditional withdrawal from Kuwait" to begin by noon on Feb. 23, and added that coalition forces would need to hear "publicly and authoritatively his acceptance of these terms."

The president accused the Iraqis of undertaking a "scorched earth" policy in Kuwait even as their foreign minister, Aziz, was in Moscow talking of peace.

"I have decided that the time has come to make public, with specificity, just exactly what is required of Iraq if a ground war is to be avoided," Bush said. Later, the White House elaborated, insisting that the withdrawal be completed within seven days and that troops leave Kuwait City within 48 hours.

Several hours after Bush's ultimatum, Kremlin officials announced that their plan had been revised to require that Iraq begin its withdrawal from Kuwait within one day after a cease-fire and complete the withdrawal within 21 days.

But the revisions made little impact in Washington, and members of Congress, who had generally deferred to Bush's authority in conducting the war, praised his unyielding stance.

"Saddam Hussein has already lost the war," said House Armed Services Committee Chairman Les Aspin, D-Wis., adding that the Iraqi army "is on the verge of collapse. This is not the time for us to lose our nerve and compromise ... to allow Saddam to 'save face.' "

Sen. John Glenn, D-Ohio, also endorsed the president's ultimatum, saying: "It was becoming increasingly obvious that Saddam Hussein was trying to delay things."

However, some lawmakers expressed reservations about immediately launching a ground war, even if Saddam failed to meet Bush's weekend deadline.

"We don't need yet to risk the infantry unless the military tells us we've done everything we can from the air," said Rep. Henry J. Hyde, R-Ill., "We're clearly getting somewhere [with the air war]."

The Liberation of Kuwait

In the end, forces of the U.S.-led coalition recaptured Kuwait and dismembered the occupying Iraqi forces in a 100-hour blitzkrieg of breathtaking scope and dizzying tempo.

Iraq's was the fourth-largest army in the world. It was widely assumed to be well-equipped, battle-hardened by eight years of war with Iran and well dug in. But the allied ground attack that started Feb. 24 — the evening of Feb. 23, Washington time — followed 38 days of aerial bombardment, which had ravaged Iraq's military infrastructure and eviscerated its navy and air force. The Iraqi ground forces were left starved for supplies, badly damaged and virtually blind to allied movements.

The last point was particularly critical to the plan engineered by Gen. Schwarzkopf. "When we knew he couldn't see us anymore," he told reporters Feb. 27, "we did a massive movement of troops all the way out to the west," bypassing Iraqi border fortifications.

President Announces Cease-Fire

Following is President Bush's announcement, on Feb 27., of a cease-fire in the Persian Gulf War:

Kuwait is liberated. Iraq's army is defeated. Our military objectives are met. Kuwait is once more in the hands of Kuwaitis in control of their own destiny. We share in their joy, a joy tempered only by our compassion for their ordeal.

Tonight, the Kuwaiti flag once again flies above the capital of a free and sovereign nation, and the American flag flies above our embassy.

Seven months ago, America and the world drew a line in the sand. We declared that the aggression against Kuwait would not stand, and tonight America and the world have kept their word.

This is not a time of euphoria, certainly not a time to gloat. But it is a time of pride: pride in our troops, pride in the friends who stood with us in the crisis, pride in our nation and the people whose strength and resolve made victory quick, decisive and just. And soon, we will open wide our arms to welcome back home to America our magnificent fighting forces.

No one country can claim this victory as its own. It was not only a victory for Kuwait but a victory for all the coalition partners. This is a victory for the United Nations, for all mankind, for the rule of law and for what is right.

After consulting with Secretary of Defense [Dick] Cheney, the chairman of the Joint Chiefs of Staff [Gen. Colin L.] Powell [Jr.] and our coalition partners, I am pleased to announce that at midnight tonight, Eastern Standard Time, exactly 100 hours since ground operations commenced and six weeks since the start of Operation Desert Storm, all United States and coalition forces will suspend offensive combat operations.

It is up to Iraq whether this suspension on the part of the coalition becomes a permanent cease-fire. Coalition political and military terms for a formal cease-fire include the following requirements:

Iraq must release immediately all coalition prisoners of war, third-country nationals and the remains of all who have fallen.

Iraq must release all Kuwaiti detainees. Iraq also must inform Kuwaiti authorities of the location and nature of all land and sea mines.

Iraq must comply fully with all relevant United Nations Security Council resolutions. This includes a rescinding of Iraq's August decision to annex Kuwait and acceptance in principle of Iraq's responsibility to pay compensation for the loss, damage and injury its aggression has caused.

The coalition calls upon the Iraqi government to designate military commanders to meet within 48 hours with their coalition counterparts, at a place in the theater of operations to be specified, to arrange for military aspects of the cease-fire.

Further, I have asked Secretary of State [James A.] Baker [III] to request that the United Nations Security Council meet to formulate the necessary arrangements for this war to be ended.

This suspension of offensive combat operations is contingent upon Iraq's not firing upon any coalition forces and not launching Scud missiles against any other country. If Iraq violates these terms, coalition forces will be free to resume military operations.

At every opportunity, I have said to the people of Iraq that our quarrel was not with them but instead with their leadership, and above all with Saddam Hussein. This remains the case. You, the people of Iraq, are not our enemy. We do not seek your destruction. We have treated your POWs with kindness. Coalition forces fought this war only as a last resort and looked forward to the day when Iraq is led by people prepared to live in peace with their neighbors.

We must now begin to look beyond victory and war. We must meet the challenge of securing the peace. In the future, as before, we will consult with our coalition partners. We've already done a good deal of thinking and planning for the postwar period.

And Secretary Baker has already begun to consult with our coalition partners on the region's challenges. There can be and will be no solely American answer to all these challenges, but we can assist and support the countries of the region and be a catalyst for peace.

In this spirit, Secretary Baker will go to the region next week to begin a new round of consultations.

This war is now behind us. Ahead of us is the difficult task of securing a potentially historic peace. Tonight, though, let us be proud of what we have accomplished. Let us give thanks to those who risked their lives.

Let us never forget those who gave their lives.

May God bless our valiant military forces and their families, and let us all remember them in our prayers. Good night, and may God bless the United States of America. ■

Even considering that the attack was launched at a crippled enemy, the coalition campaign that followed had an epic scale and deadly elegance likely to earn it a mention in future textbooks on the awful art of war.

Iraq's supposedly formidable border defenses were easily breached, and the Iraqis never used their huge stockpile of chemical weapons. For the most part, the defenders folded at the first contact with allied forces.

Fewer than 100 members of the allied force were killed in the five-day-long ground campaign, a tiny fraction of the Iraqi casualties.

President Bush went before the nation Feb. 27, announcing a cease-fire in the six-week war. His unadorned language only began to capture the historic drama of the triumph by U.S. and allied forces.

"Kuwait is liberated," he said. "Iraq's army is defeated. Our military objectives are met."

The fighting stopped later that evening. Iraq subsequently agreed to the cease-fire, and the next day Bush said that commanders from each side would meet to arrange military aspects of the truce.

The relative ease with which the United States and its coalition allies reversed Iraq's invasion of Kuwait and smashed Saddam's army stunned military analysts and elated members of Congress.

The huge numbers of U.S. casualties that many members feared from a ground war against Iraq never materialized. The United States lost fewer troops during the entire war — 89 had been listed as killed and another 38 as missing in action — than it did during some weeks of the long and grim Vietnam conflict.

Only months later would critics emphasize that a number of the allied dead were victims of errant "friendly fire" by their own forces.

"It's a proud day for America and, by god, we've kicked the Vietnam syndrome once and for all," Bush emphatically told a gathering of state legislators March 1.

Nothing succeeds like success, and the decisive allied triumph was hailed on Capitol Hill, as it was throughout the country.

"Today, victory is ours," Sen. Joseph I. Lieberman, D-Conn., said Feb. 27. "VG Day — Victory in the gulf — is here."

Almost overlooked in the afterglow of victory were the enormous losses borne by Iraqi forces. While allied commanders refused to provide numbers of Iraqi casualties, there were estimates that 50,000 of Saddam's troops were killed and perhaps even twice that.

The Defense Department resolutely refused to offer any estimate of Iraqi casualties, just as its tight controls on news coverage of the war had restricted the images of the conflict seen in the United States mostly to Pentagon-released videotape of precision "smart bombs" hitting bridges and military installations.

Democrats, most of whom had voted in January against authorizing Bush to use force against Iraq, joined Republicans in a chorus of congratulations for the president and the troops. Ebullient lawmakers proposed everything from honoring returning troops with a ticker-tape parade in Manhattan to inviting the allied commander, Gen. Schwarzkopf, to address a joint session of Congress. All of that happened, and more, to celebrate the victory.

Bush drew some of the most effusive praise.

"This man is due every bit of respect this Congress has to offer," said Rep. Bob McEwen, R-Ohio. In an interview, Sen. Patrick J. Leahy, D-Vt., said he "had never seen a president in a stronger position" during his 17 years in Congress.

Reaping Success

The Senate passed a non-binding resolution (S Con Res 13) — with 100 cosponsors — on Feb. 28 commending Bush and the armed forces for the success of Operation Desert Storm.

While basking in nearly universal acclaim, Bush cautioned against premature optimism.

"We have Saddam Hussein still there, the man that wreaked this havoc upon his neighbors," Bush told a news conference March 1. "We have our prisoners still held. We have people unaccounted for."

He also vowed, "I want to move fast" to tackle broader problems of the region, including the Palestinian question, Lebanon and bringing Iraq back "into the family of nations."

Saddam, still in control of the government in Baghdad when the shooting stopped, remained the most tangible threat to regional security.

Some lawmakers were optimistic that the Iraqi people would turn against Saddam once they realized the devastating extent of their military defeat. "Quite obviously, Bush has gotten Saddam politically cornered," said Rep. Peter H. Kostmayer, D-Pa.

Yet some members wanted to ensure that the Iraqi leader was punished, regardless of whether he stayed in power. There were several proposals to create special war crimes tribunals to place Saddam and his subordinates on trial.

Defense Secretary Cheney warned that U.S. forces would be ready to swing back into action if Iraq lagged in fulfilling United Nations resolutions or initiated new attacks against Saudi Arabia and Israel. "Probably what we would do is to open up the air campaign again," Cheney said.

Even as members of Congress praised what U.S. troops had accomplished in the desert of Kuwait and southern Iraq, some lawmakers pressured the White House to bring American forces home as quickly as possible. "We cannot afford to be the world's policeman or the Middle East riot squad," said Sen. Robert C. Byrd, D-W.Va. "I feel certain that the states of the Middle East do not wish a permanent American armed presence."

The administration agreed. According to White House Chief of Staff John H. Sununu, "We may store heavy equipment over there [in the Middle East].... There might be a set of agreements on a country-by-country basis, but the ground troops will be back home."

But the administration warned that the drawdown would take some time.

"Don't delude yourself," said White House spokesman Fitzwater. "It took seven months to get in, and it's going to take a lot of months to get out."

Rep. Susan Molinari, R-N.Y., captured the exuberance in Congress with her proposal for a ticker-tape parade down Broadway. "I believe now, after successful completion of this mission, we owe it to our troops and we owe it to ourselves to 'let go' a little," she said.

Democrats insisted that, despite their party's opposition to the war resolution, they were just as enthusiastic about the war's conduct and its outcome. "Since the first shots were fired, this war has drawn bipartisan support," Sen. John Kerry, D-Mass., said.

But there was no cease-fire when it came to scoring postwar political points. For the Republicans, the primary lesson to be learned from the war was simple: When it came to the military, they asserted, Democrats had opposed buying the weapons needed to fend off the Saddams of the world.

On Feb. 27, Cheney opened a not-so-subtle attack on the Pentagon's critics before an approving audience at a conference of the American Legion. "It's clear," he said, "that over the last 10 years the Department of Defense has spent money on something other than $600 toilet seats."

House Minority Leader Michel called for an end "to the ritualistic denigration of the American military that unfortunately has been prevalent in certain ideological quarters for the last 20 years."

And Sen. Phil Gramm of Texas, chairman of the National Republican Senatorial Committee, predicted that Democratic opposition to the war would become a political issue.

The Democratic votes against the war resolution were "in the pattern of Jimmy Carter, Walter Mondale and Michael Dukakis," Gramm told The Washington Post.

Democrats denied that they had opposed the weapons that won the war, and they emphasized that few in their party had ruled out force as the ultimate means to oust Saddam from Kuwait.

While eager to give Bush his due as commander in chief, the Democrats also issued reminders that a spate of domestic issues could still undermine Bush's unprecedented support in the polls. "When our forces do return home, they will find an America which is deep in recession, an America in which the infrastructure is badly in need of repair and upgrading," Byrd said.

But some Democrats who had supported the war resolution agreed that the party had been dealt a serious blow. "For the American people, we left the impression of being reluctant on the issue," said a House Democrat, who added that it would be difficult for the party to surmount its image of being weak on defense issues.

According to Sen. Richard C. Shelby, D-Ala., who voted for the resolution, "This is not a party vote. If it is seen as a party vote, we're in deep trouble."

Even as the parades and celebrations were being scheduled, the week of victory on the battlefield closed with Bush and members of Congress warily assessing the future shape of the Middle East.

"The war is now behind us," Bush said. "Ahead of us is the difficult task of securing a potentially historic peace." ■

Mideast Policy Still Being Shaped After War

Even before the victory parades that sent triumphant soldiers in tanks through the streets of Washington and New York, it became clear that the U.S. military success in the Persian Gulf War had created new challenges in foreign policy as well as new opportunities.

President Bush's decision to stop the allied offensive short of Baghdad meant that Iraq's President Saddam Hussein remained in power to taunt the United States. During 1991, Bush repeatedly urged the Iraqi people to oust Saddam and predicted that they would.

Saddam's survival led to an unsuccessful revolt against him by Kurdish and Shiite rebels.

U.S. forces were compelled to remain in and near Iraq to protect the Kurds from retaliation and to spearhead a massive allied relief effort. On May 22, Congress sent the president a $572 million supplemental appropriations bill for fiscal 1991 (HR 2251) that included $556 million in disaster and refugee relief aid, much of it for the Kurdish aid effort. *(Kurdish relief, p. 458)*

In the months after the gulf war, the United Nations also maintained stringent, U.S.-backed economic sanctions against Iraq, and its inspectors engaged in a long-running struggle to force Saddam to reveal and relinquish the elements of his massive effort to develop nuclear, chemical and biological weapons.

Nothing that followed subtracted from the military prowess that U.S. forces had demonstrated, although reports after the war spotlighted certain weaknesses.

Questions were also raised as to whether U.S. policy toward Iraq had been too conciliatory in the years before Saddam invaded Kuwait in August 1990, an issue dramatized when congressional committees summoned April Glaspie, who had been U.S. ambassador to Iraq at the time of the invasion. *(Prewar policy, p. 455)*

The new alignment of power in the Middle East had immediate tangible benefits. With the intercession of Syria and Iran, terrorists in Lebanon released long-held U.S. hostages. And Bush capitalized on the new power lineup to prod Israel and its Arab neighbors into peace talks that he later called "an historic first." *(Mideast talks, p. 460)*

By the end of 1991, the glow of the gulf war victory had faded as Bush was confronted with a stalled domestic economy and with Democratic criticism that he was preoccupied with foreign policy. Nonetheless, Bush and other Republicans found opportunities to chide the majority of Democrats who had voted against authorizing war against Iraq.

SADDAM'S OPPOSITION

Even before confronting the plight of Iraq's Kurdish minority, Congress vented its collective frustration that Saddam and his high command had survived the war.

On March 14, the Senate adopted, 97-0, a resolution (S Res 76), by Arlen Specter, R-Pa., urging the president to consult with other nations to establish a war crimes tribunal that would prosecute Saddam and his deputies. *(Vote 27, p. 5-S)*

But it was Saddam's postwar battle with his internal opposition that raised a vexing question for the administration and Congress: When would the war really be over?

Iraqi forces engaged on two fronts, battling Kurdish separatists in the north and Iran-backed Shiite Muslims in the south. The harsh tactics employed by Iraq's Republican Guard in quelling the uprisings slowed the U.S. withdrawal from the region.

Bush warned on March 13 that helicopter attacks against rebel forces endangered the cease-fire in the war. "[We're] warning them: Do not do this," he said.

During the U.S.-led war that drove Iraqi forces out of Kuwait, Bush had repeatedly said he would welcome the overthrow of Saddam. During the postwar insurrections, however, Bush emphasized that he had never promised to intervene in Iraq's "internal affairs."

"We're not going to get sucked into this by sending precious American lives into this battle," Bush said April 4. "We have fulfilled our obligations."

But the next day, Bush announced that U.S. cargo planes would drop food and other relief supplies to Kurdish refugees thronging the mountains along Iraq's border with Turkey. He also earmarked $11 million in relief funds for victims of the Persian Gulf War and for refugees from the failed uprisings against Saddam.

On April 11, White House spokesman Marlin Fitzwater announced that U.S. agencies had rounded up supplies to sustain 700,000 people for a month. The Bush administration said April 10 that it had warned Iraq the previous weekend to keep its military forces away from a large section of northern Iraq where relief agencies were trying to aid hundreds of thousands of Kurdish refugees.

For nearly a week before the U.S. ultimatum, congressional Democrats and some conservative Republicans had blasted Bush for standing by while Iraqi troops brutally crushed insurrections by Kurds and Shiites.

Nearly half of the 4 million Kurds in Iraq had fled toward Turkey and Iran in late March and early April.

Prominent among the critics were Democrats, such as Senate Majority Leader George J. Mitchell of Maine and Senate Armed Services Committee Chairman Sam Nunn of Georgia, who had opposed going to war with Iraq in January. They urged Bush to forbid Iraq from using armed helicopters against Kurdish refugees fleeing toward Turkey.

"I do think we encouraged an awful lot of people to believe our policy was to support the overthrow of the government," said Nunn, who added, "I worry that we are seeing something close to genocide."

The anti-Iraq coalition had prohibited any use of Iraqi combat airplanes since the informal cease-fire that ended the gulf war on Feb. 27. U.S. fighter jets patrolling Iraqi airspace had destroyed two Iraqi planes that had violated the ban. Flights by armed helicopters, however, were not barred.

Bush remarked on April 11 that those urging him to use force had been among the "severest critics" when he was preparing for war against Saddam. Vice President Dan Quayle ridiculed the "newly hatched hawks."

On April 11, the Senate approved by voice vote a resolution (S Res 99) urging "sustained humanitarian" relief for Iraq's refugees. Meanwhile, the formal cease-fire between Iraq and the U.S.-led coalition came into force April 11, after Iraq accepted under protest conditions set by the U.N. Security Council on April 3.

Under terms of that deal, Iraq's weapons of mass destruction — including ballistic missiles with a range greater than 80 miles — had to be scrapped and part of its oil revenues used for war reparations. In addition, a U.N.

peacekeeping force was to patrol a buffer zone between Iraq and Kuwait, replacing U.S. forces that then withdrew from southern Iraq.

Bringing Troops Home

Bush's refusal to consider further large-scale military intervention in Iraq reflected a political judgment that the U.S. public wanted its troops home, no matter how tragic the plight of the refugees. "I want these kids to come home," Bush declared April 11, adding that Americans did not want "to see us bogged down in a civil war."

Beyond that, the administration had geopolitical reasons to keep its distance from the Kurds. Turkey and Syria — two key U.S. allies in the gulf war — as well as Iran were wary that their own Kurdish minorities might be aroused if Iraqi Kurds achieved their long-sought independence.

Administration officials also contended that whatever fragile hopes there were for political stability in the Persian Gulf region depended on Iraq's survival as a cohesive state.

Even while complaining that Bush had moved too slowly to aid Iraq's refugees, many leading Democrats said they were no more eager than the administration to become mired in Iraq's internal affairs. "The history of that country is bloody and messy," House Foreign Affairs Committee member Lee H. Hamilton, D-Ind., said April 10. "I don't believe we have the wit and I don't believe we have the capabilities to work through the problems in Iraq."

However, some Democrats who had been among Bush's leading supporters in the decision for war in January pressed for a much more assertive U.S. role.

Stephen J. Solarz, D-N.Y., a leading sponsor of the House resolution authorizing war, urged Bush on April 10 to seek a new U.N. resolution demanding that Saddam resign and authorizing the use of military force to back up the demand.

Sending Troops Back

Bowing to the necessities of a human tragedy, Bush announced on April 16 that U.S., British and French forces would go back into Iraq to aid the Kurdish refugees. The administration said that U.S. troops, running supply operations out of Silopi, Turkey, would construct tent cities in dry, relatively low terrain and then would encourage and assist the movement to those sites of hundreds of thousands of Kurds huddled in cold, inaccessible mountain encampments near the Turkish border.

"If we cannot get adequate food, medicine, clothing and shelter to the Kurds living in the mountains," Bush said, "we must encourage the Kurds to move to areas . . . where the geography facilitates rather than frustrates such a large-scale relief effort."

The deployment of an estimated 16,000 U.S., British and French troops in the resettlement operation risked Bush's often-stated commitment to avoid interference in Iraq's internal affairs. "Some might argue that this is an intervention into the internal affairs of Iraq," Bush said April 16 in announcing the new policy, "but I think the humanitarian concern . . . is so overwhelming that there will be a lot of understanding about this."

Democrats generally backed Bush's decision to aid the Kurds despite the risk of an open-ended entanglement.

House Foreign Affairs Committee Chairman Dante B. Fascell, D-Fla., said, "There simply are moments when action must be taken and the consequences sorted out later. With more than 1,000 Kurds dying each day and hundreds of thousands starving on the frigid mountainsides, there is no question that such a moment had arrived."

Iraq denounced the U.S. plan April 18 as an interference in its internal affairs. But the same day, it agreed to a U.N. plan to organize relief efforts inside Iraq.

Criticizing Other Countries

Having authorized the use of U.S. force to free Kuwait from Iraqi conquest, some members of Congress grew increasingly critical of Kuwait's lack of democracy, its treatment of resident foreigners and its prosecution of those accused of collaborating with Iraqi occupiers. In acting on a foreign aid authorization bill in June, the House approved by voice vote an amendment criticizing Kuwait's human rights record. *(Foreign aid, p. 470)*

Although the foreign aid bill stalled short of final passage, the House also signaled anger at Jordan for siding with Iraq during the war. The House approved, 410-8, an amendment by John Miller, R-Wash., that would have cut off military aid to Jordan unless the president certified that its government demonstrated a willingness to enter into negotiations with Israel, recognized Israel's right to exist and did not provide aid to Iraq. *(Vote 170, p. 42-H)*

Members also expressed concern over the administration's improved relations with Syria, which had been branded as supporting terrorism but had joined in opposing Iraq. On June 5, the Senate adopted, 92-6, a resolution objecting to reports that the Syrian flag would fly in Washington during a parade honoring U.S. troops who fought in the gulf war. The resolution, an amendment to a telecommunications bill (S 173), opposed any place in the parade for "a country the government of which has repeatedly provided support for acts of international terrorism." *(Vote 87, p. 12-S; Baby Bells, p. 165)*

REVIEWING THE WAR

In the months after the war, those in Congress and outside did some second-guessing about the military lessons that were learned in the desert fighting.

Some experts questioned the formidable reputation that had been gained by the Patriot missile, which was used to counter Iraqi Scud missile attacks on Israel and Saudi Arabia. The Patriot interceptions, captured in television images of bursts of light in the night sky, caught the popular imagination and were promoted by the administration as an argument for the development of the anti-missile Strategic Defense Initiative. *(SDI, p. 407)*

But Theodore A. Postal, a professor associated with the Massachusetts Institute of Technology, told the House Armed Services Committee on April 16 that the Patriot's reputation was more myth than reality. "During the period of Patriot defense there were 15 fewer Scud attacks [on Israel] relative to the period when there was no defense," he said. "Yet the number of apartments reported damaged almost tripled, and the number of injuries from attacks increased by almost 50 percent."

Under questioning, Postal acknowledged that his damage estimates involved speculation. Other witnesses maintained that the Patriot performed admirably, considering that it was initially designed to shoot down aircraft in battle, not missiles over cities.

Gen. H. Norman Schwarzkopf, the commander of the allied forces in the gulf war, singled out the need to improve intelligence collection and analysis as a prime lesson learned.

In separate appearances before the Senate and House Armed Services committees June 12, Schwarzkopf complained that intelligence analyses sent to him during the war by Washington-based agencies were too cautious to be useful.

"It was unhelpful because it was so caveated," he told the Senate panel. "There were so many disclaimers that . . . no matter what happened, they would have been right."

Without specifically identifying the targets of his criticism, Schwarzkopf complained that intelligence agencies had been unduly conservative in estimating how badly Iraq's military had been damaged during six weeks of intensive aerial bombing that preceded the war's closing four-day ground blitz.

If he had waited to launch the final assault until intelligence agencies concluded that Iraq had been sufficiently weakened, "we'd still be sitting over there waiting," he said.

Although the separate armed services and their equipment had meshed well in Operation Desert Storm, Schwarzkopf said, one exception was the difficulty in transmitting large blocks of intelligence data between Air Force and Navy units because of technical differences in their communications equipment and computers.

Schwarzkopf also called for more equipment that would permit commanders in the field to collect detailed intelligence about specific targets on short notice. Army and Marine division commanders had made the same point before Senate Armed Services early in May.

Schwarzkopf also urged:

- More high-speed cargo ships designed with loading ramps so that tanks and other combat vehicles could quickly be loaded and unloaded.
- More Navy minesweepers and more minesweeping gear for the Army that could detonate high-tech mines that could not be tripped by the usual method of setting off a large explosion nearby.
- More heavy-duty trucks able to operate off highways.
- More reliable methods for U.S. aircraft to identify friendly tanks and other vehicles in the confusion of battle. Some allied casualties in the gulf war resulted from accidental attacks by U.S. aircraft on military vehicles.

Critics charged that the incidents of "friendly fire" were far too high and that the Pentagon was too slow and reluctant to inform the families of soldiers that they had died as a result of fire from their own forces rather than enemy attacks.

On July 16, the Defense Department issued its own initial assessment of the military's performance in the war. The interim report spared few accolades:

"Decisive presidential leadership set clear goals. . . . A revolutionary new generation of high-technology weapons, combined with innovative and effective doctrine, gave our forces the edge. . . . The high quality of our military, from its skilled commanders to the highly ready, well-trained, brave and disciplined men and women of the U.S. Armed Forces, made an extraordinary victory possible."

But some candid assessments of shortcomings were interspersed with the praise in the study, which was required by Congress in a bill authorizing benefits for those who fought in the Persian Gulf War (S 725 — PL 102-25). The study also underscored how ill-prepared Iraqi President Saddam Hussein was to take advantage of those shortcomings.

For example, Saddam could have exploited the U.S. reliance on satellites for communications. Because not all of the troops had the proper receiving equipment, the report said, communications using these satellites were not always encoded. It would have been relatively easy for Saddam to intercept battlefield communications. And any disruption to the satellites would have caused dramatic problems for U.S. troop commanders.

The report blamed the problem in estimating the effectiveness of allied aerial bombing on weaknesses in reconnaissance systems — the inability to take good aerial photos of enemy territory, troops and buildings, especially in bad weather. The report said that "estimating attrition in Iraqi defensive forces was often more art than science."

A faster start to combat could have found U.S. forces ill-prepared, the report said, because the Pentagon was unable to move large, heavy pieces of military equipment quickly. The Ready Reserve fleet, which was supposed to be quickly deployable in most situations, was criticized for not being able to activate rapidly.

SADDAM'S SURVIVAL

Saddam's survival — and his defiance of U.S. and world opinion — dominated the debate over the foreign policy aftereffects of the gulf war.

Doubts about the decision to end the war short of Saddam's elimination were first raised not by Bush's Democratic critics but by the popular commander of Operation Desert Storm.

On March 27, newspapers published excerpts from an interview on public television with Gen. Schwarzkopf. In a comment that echoed for months, Schwarzkopf asserted that Bush had called an end to the massive U.S.-led assault on Feb. 27 despite the general's recommendation to press on in the effort to finish off Saddam's war machine.

"Frankly, my recommendation had been, you know, continue the march," Schwarzkopf said. "I mean, we had them in a rout, and we could have continued to, you know, wreak great destruction upon them. We could have completely closed the door and made it in fact a battle of annihilation. And the president, you know, made the decision that, you know, we should stop at a given time, at a given place; that did leave some escape routes open for them to get back out."

But Schwarzkopf immediately added, "I think it was a very humane decision and a very courageous decision on his part also because it's, you know, it's one of those ones that historians are going to second-guess, you know, forever. . . . Why didn't we go for one more day vs. why did we stop when we did when we had them completely routed?"

The administration moved quickly to deny Schwarzkopf's account and to politely rebuke the general whose battlefield success and avuncular manner had taken him to the top of opinion polls.

Defense Secretary Dick Cheney issued a terse statement indicating that before Bush decided to order an end to combat, "the president and I spoke personally with Gen. Schwarzkopf that evening to congratulate him on the outstanding success of the campaign. He raised no objection to terminating hostilities."

As Saddam's defiance continued throughout 1991, members of Congress expressed growing irritation with Iraq's failure to comply with the cease-fire agreement that ended the gulf war. Members backed the administration's threats of new military action against Saddam if needed to ensure destruction of Iraq's ability to develop nuclear weapons.

"It's just exasperating . . . that we still have this barbarian in power exercising the type of discretion that he does," Rep. Mel Levine, D-Calif., told administration representatives at a hearing July 18 before two House Foreign Affairs subcommittees. "Defiance of the cease-fire cannot and will not be tolerated."

Members of Congress, distressed by reports of suffering

by the Iraqi people, urged the administration to seek ways to deliver humanitarian assistance without abandoning economic pressures on Saddam.

In testimony on July 18 before the Foreign Affairs subcommittees, U.S. ambassador to the United Nations Thomas R. Pickering and Assistant Secretary of State John R. Bolton, said the administration was discussing the options with coalition partners.

But Bolton said it would be a "very daunting task" to distribute food, medical and other aid to the neediest Iraqi people without some of it being diverted to Saddam's military forces and inner circle of supporters.

"Saddam Hussein has proven that he cannot be trusted," he said. "Any mechanism developed to provide essential supplies to the Iraqi people must include strict control and close monitoring."

Discussing Iraq's defiance of the U.N.'s efforts to track down Saddam's nuclear weapons program, Pickering said Iraq had yet to provide "an accurate accounting." He noted the revelation by U.N. investigators July 15 that they had uncovered a previously undisclosed uranium-enrichment facility north of Baghdad.

On the anniversary of Iraq's invasion of Kuwait, the Senate voted overwhelmingly to support President Bush if he decided to once again go on the attack against Saddam.

By a 97-2 vote, the Senate on Aug. 2 attached to its version of the defense authorization bill (S 1507) a non-binding amendment by Minority Leader Bob Dole, R-Kan., backing action unless the Iraqi leader fully complied with a U.N. resolution ordering him to reveal and turn over all his materials for nuclear, chemical and biological weapons. *(Vote 178, p. 24-S; Defense authorization, p. 393)*

The amendment stated that "the Congress supports the use of all necessary means to achieve the goals of [U.N.] Resolution 687." But it also urged Bush to continue consulting with U.S. allies, and it cautioned, "Should the use of force prove necessary, the president is urged to take all reasonable precautions to ensure that innocent civilian casualties are avoided or minimized."

In remarks on the Senate floor, Dole called his resolution "an anniversary present to Saddam Hussein" and said it put "Congress squarely behind the president."

Although Joseph R. Biden Jr., D-Del., criticized the resolution as vague, the only votes against it were cast by Mark O. Hatfield, R-Ore., and Paul Wellstone, D-Minn. Wellstone, who said the resolution could open the way for anything from air attacks to a ground war, asked, "Why the rush? Why not continue to tighten the screws diplomatically and economically?"

By voice vote, the Senate also approved an amendment by Foreign Relations Committee Chairman Claiborne Pell, D-R.I., expressing support for the "use of all necessary means to protect Iraq's Kurdish minority."

On Sept. 18, the U.N. Security Council eased economic sanctions slightly, authorizing Iraq to sell $1.6 billion in oil to buy food and other essential supplies. But Iraq balked at tight restrictions, including compensation for victims of the invasion of Kuwait.

From Sept. 24 to Sept. 26, Iraqi forces held 44 U.N. inspectors captive in a parking lot outside the Iraqi Atomic Energy Commission, where the U.N. team had tried to remove documents on Iraq's nuclear weapons program. The inspectors determined that Iraq's program to develop nuclear bombs was far more extensive and advanced than the Bush administration or independent experts had predicted before the gulf war.

The White House denounced Saddam's "pattern of cheat and retreat" in resisting cease-fire terms. And Senate Intelligence Committee Chairman David L. Boren, D-Okla., who had voted against authorizing the war, lamented on Sept. 26, "I think it's a shame we didn't get rid of Saddam when we had a chance."

At the end of the year, Congress and the administration continued to wrestle with the vexing question about what to do about Saddam.

"President Bush has been very clear about what he doesn't like — namely, Saddam and the way he acts — but not clear at all about what he intends to do about it," said House Armed Services Committee Chairman Les Aspin, D-Wis.

In a Dec. 12 report titled "Winning the War and Losing the Peace in Saddam Hussein's Iraq," Aspin argued that the administration needed to act far more aggressively to eliminate Iraq's ability to develop nuclear weapons.

Aspin, who was an important Democratic supporter of the decision to authorize war in January, called for the United Nations to "flood" Iraq with inspectors, providing armed escorts if necessary. He said the United States should get U.N. approval to seize an Iraqi airfield to use as a permanent inspection base.

Such calls for more aggressive U.S. action against Iraq were limited, however, by a reluctance to involve U.S. troops once again in combat and by the absence of any clear-cut alternative to the Saddam regime.

"It is not yet visible to me and to many others precisely what structure there is for an alternative government in Iraq," said Sen. Richard G. Lugar, R-Ind. "The age-old animosities and hatred endemic in that society do not instill a great deal of confidence in terms of democratic institution-building or human rights."

The difficulty in patiently waiting for the end of Saddam's era was the continued suffering of Iraqis, especially opponents such as the Kurds.

A Harvard University study team found in October that infant deaths in Iraq had increased by more than 350 percent in the first eight months of the year, compared with the same period a year earlier. The researchers also reported that at least one-third of Iraqi children under the age of 5, or almost 1 million, were malnourished, and they found a widespread collapse of the country's water and sewage treatment systems.

In a public television interview broadcast Jan. 3, 1992, Bush maintained that the United Nations' objective in ousting Iraq from Kuwait had been achieved. He rejected the persistent criticism that the war should have been extended until Saddam had been eliminated.

Bush said that a "march to Baghdad" to overthrow Saddam would have split the U.S.-led coalition and could have bogged down the United States in a lengthy conflict. "I don't want to send young men into a war where I can't see that they're going to prevail and prevail rapidly," he said.

Describing Saddam as "increasingly isolated," Bush said, "It is my understanding that the people are getting more and more discontented with this brutal dictator as each day goes by. History will show a tyrant of that nature simply cannot last forever by brutalizing his own people."

POLITICAL AFTEREFFECTS

"They are going to pay for that vote," Sen. Phil Gramm, R-Texas, said after most Democrats voted in January against authorizing what proved to be a successful and popular war against Iraq.

Rep. Dan Glickman, D-Kan., said, "There is no question that we have suffered a bit from this experience, but it's not going to be permanent." Republicans did not hesitate to depict the votes against war as yet another sign that the Democrats were weak on defense.

In November, when his popularity had slumped and Democrats were faulting him for paying too much attention to international rather than domestic problems, Bush retorted, "If I'd had to listen to advice from the United States Senate leadership, the Democrats, or from the House, the leadership over there, to do something about the Persian Gulf, we'd have still been sitting there in the United States, fat, dumb and happy, with Saddam Hussein maybe in Saudi Arabia."

The Republican attempts to capitalize on the gulf war vote included recruiting several veterans of Operation Desert Storm as candidates to run in 1992 races for the House and Senate. The National Republican Congressional Committee also used the issue in a special election in Virginia's 7th District.

In a controversial television commercial produced for Republican George F. Allen, his Democratic opponent, Kay Slaughter, was criticized for opposing the Persian Gulf War. Her photograph was superimposed on a scene of antiwar marchers holding a banner that read "Victory to Iraq." With the help of the commercial, Allen successfully defined Slaughter as a liberal in the conservative 7th. Allen won with 62 percent in the November election.

But by year's end, Republicans were no longer describing the Democratic war vote as a "silver bullet" that could in itself defeat an incumbent who had opposed going to war. "For most voters, the gulf war is ancient history," said Jim Innocenzi, a Republican consultant. "I don't think people care a whole helluva lot [anymore]." ■

Members Questioned Bush's Prewar Policy

Although Congress rallied to support President Bush during the Persian Gulf War, members raised questions afterwards concerning the administration's prewar relations with Iraq. Suspicions that the administration had appeased Iraq were crystallized by the case of April C. Glaspie, who was U.S. ambassador to Iraq when Saddam Hussein's forces invaded neighboring Kuwait.

Purported transcripts released by the Iraqis indicated that Glaspie had assured Saddam shortly before the invasion that the United States had "no opinion" about his dispute with Kuwait's ruling family. After a long silence, Glaspie testified before Senate and House committees in March that Saddam had assured her that he would not resort to violence to resolve the differences over money, oil and territory. Members appeared impressed by her performance.

In July, however, members of Congress complained that newly obtained diplomatic cables written by Glaspie before the war had cast doubt on her account. The ambassador appeared before a closed session of the Senate Foreign Relations Committee in November, but no further action was taken.

Several congressional committees also raised questions about the administration's approval of export licenses for high-technology shipments to Iraq in the years before the war. But Congress had repeatedly stopped short of passing legislation that would have blocked trade with Iraq, backing down at the urging of the administration, which did not want to have restrictions on its foreign policy options, and members, who were interested in Iraq as a market for U.S. exports.

Like Glaspie, some members were also forced to explain seemingly sympathetic comments that they had made in a visit with Saddam less than four months before he invaded Kuwait on Aug. 2, 1990.

Glaspie Speaks

After a seven-month wait, members of Congress heard from the U.S. ambassador to Iraq, and her message was simple: Saddam Hussein lied.

In back-to-back appearances March 20 and 21 before the Senate Foreign Relations Committee and a House Foreign Affairs subcommittee, Glaspie said she told the Iraqi leader in a meeting only eight days before his invasion of Kuwait that the United States wanted him to resolve disputes with his neighbor peacefully.

After he spoke with Egyptian President Hosni Mubarak on the telephone during their meeting, she said, Saddam returned to the room and said "he wanted me to inform President Bush that he would not solve his problems with Kuwait by violence. Period.

"As far as I was concerned, the only possible interpretation I could make on his remarks, which were very straightforward, was that he was not going to invade," she said.

The picture painted by the ambassador, who had been restrained by the administration from telling her side of the story since Iraq's invasion of Kuwait, was far different from the one depicted in an Iraqi government transcript of the meeting.

In that transcript, which had been widely cited as evidence of a U.S. policy of appeasement toward Iraq before the war, Glaspie was alleged to have told Saddam that the United States had "no opinion on the Arab-Arab conflicts, like your border disagreement with Kuwait."

Most members of the panels seemed impressed by Glaspie's explanation, confounding expectations that her long-awaited appearance would provide a clear opening to attack the administration's prewar policies.

Glaspie answered most questions with a forcefulness and confidence that belied the image of an obsequious diplomat portrayed in the Iraqi transcript. She said her remark about the U.S. having "no opinion" was in response to hints by Saddam that the United States should side with Iraq in the border dispute. She told Foreign Relations that she believed such border disagreements were not U.S. business, "but it was emphatically our business that they make the settlement in a non-violent way."

Glaspie said that half of the sentence in which she called for a peaceful resolution of the dispute was left out of the "so-called transcript." Also deleted, she said, were her statements that the United States would defend its vital interests in the Persian Gulf.

"This is fabrication. This is disinformation. This is not a transcript," she told Foreign Relations.

On the second day of testimony, Lee H. Hamilton, D-Ind., chairman of Foreign Affairs' Subcommittee on Europe and the Middle East, questioned Glaspie's contention that U.S. policy toward an Iraqi invasion of Kuwait had been made clear.

Hamilton cited what he said were confusing administration statements before the invasion, including one from State Department spokeswoman Margaret D. Tutwiler that the United States did not have a defense commitment to Kuwait. Hamilton also recalled that Assistant Secretary of State John Kelly told his panel only three days before the invasion that the United States would be "extremely concerned" by such aggression, but that he refused to discuss whether force would be used.

"Now this record is not a record of unambiguous clarity with respect to the American position. It is a record that confused me, confused this subcommittee, confused much of the Washington press. And it is not unreasonable for me to think that it might have confused Saddam Hussein as well," Hamilton said.

"Well, Mr. Chairman," Glaspie responded, "I'm glad to reassure you: Saddam Hussein had no question in his mind, I am quite convinced of that."

Although she acknowledged that she had never told Saddam directly that the United States would fight if he crossed the Kuwaiti border, she said, "I am absolutely sure that he knew we would fight."

However, she said, Saddam made two crucial miscalculations. He did not believe other Arab nations would join the United States in opposing him, and he thought he could win.

In his opening remarks, Foreign Relations Chairman Claiborne Pell, D-R.I., said he did not fault Glaspie for carrying out her instructions, but "rather, I question the instructions." He said that it was the administration's opposition over several years to repeated attempts by some in Congress to impose sanctions against Iraq "that sent the real signal to Saddam Hussein that his ambitions in the region were unlikely to be thwarted by the West."

But Glaspie, who had been working in obscurity in Washington since the invasion, defended overall U.S. policy in the region. She argued that sanctions would have been ineffective before Aug. 2 because Iraq could have purchased whatever it needed from other nations, which were more than willing to trade with Baghdad. She also said such a policy would have fueled Iraq's "paranoia" that the United States was trying to overthrow the regime.

Glaspie argued that the only option the United States had in dealing with Saddam was to try to show him that "constructive" international activity on his part "would bring rewards.... We were trying to educate him."

Sen. John Kerry, D-Mass., questioned why the United States would expect Saddam to react rationally to such a policy when he headed a government that, by Glaspie's own account, was isolated and ignorant of the outside world.

Glaspie countered that she thought the United States had much more influence over Iraq by keeping the lines of communication open. But she acknowledged that, in hindsight, U.S. policy had a crucial flaw: "Our mistake was, like every government in the world, we foolishly did not realize he was stupid."

Some members expressed puzzlement at why, if the Iraqi transcript of her meeting with Saddam was so inaccurate, the State Department had not corrected the record earlier on. Shortly after the Iraqis released the transcript in September 1990, Secretary of State James A. Baker III appeared to distance himself from Glaspie, and repeated attempts by congressional committees to get Glaspie to testify were rebuffed.

She responded that the administration was more concerned in the months following the invasion with conducting its war campaign than with "retrospectives."

"Now we've won. The war is over. The troops are back. And I'm here on instructions to answer your questions," she said. Nonetheless, Rep. Wayne Owens, D-Utah, told Glaspie he was one member who "believes you were hung out to dry."

Second Impressions

But the favorable impression that Glaspie created in her March testimony faded with some members as they saw reports about what she had written in her classified diplomatic cables from Baghdad to Washington.

Sniping was especially intense between members of the Senate Foreign Relations Committee and the State Department. In a July 11 letter to Baker, Pell complained that Glaspie's testimony was inconsistent with her classified report to the department on her meeting with the Iraqi leader.

Pell said the tone of the cable, which the panel did not receive until July 10, was far more conciliatory than the tough message she had assured committee members she had delivered to Saddam.

"The title 'Saddam's Message of Friendship to President Bush' is reflective of the tone of the cable," wrote Pell. "No place does she report clearly delivering the kind of warning she described in her testimony to the committee."

The following day, committee member Alan Cranston, D-Calif., accused Glaspie of "deliberately" misleading Congress.

In response, Deputy Secretary of State Lawrence S. Eagleburger requested July 12 that he and Glaspie be allowed to appear before the committee to set the record straight. However, he said Glaspie was in an "unfair" position because she would have to respond to charges about discrepancies involving a classified cable.

A hearing was tentatively scheduled for July 19, but it was postponed, according to the committee, because panel members sought more time to review Glaspie's testimony and the cables. Committee aides had also said there were concerns that it would be pointless to hold the hearing if the cable, which had been leaked to several newspapers, remained classified. Pell had asked Eagleburger to declassify the document.

The committee was also reportedly worried that a joint appearance by Eagleburger and Glaspie might blur two separate issues: the allegations that Glaspie misled the committee and the administration's prewar policy toward Iraq.

State Department spokesman Richard Boucher on July 18 called the committee's decision to prevent Glaspie and Eagleburger "from responding promptly and publicly to the committee's allegations ... censorship, pure and simple."

Glaspie appeared before Senate Foreign Relations in a closed-door session Nov. 21 to answer members' questions about discrepancies between her account of the final days before Iraq's invasion of Kuwait and statements she made in cables to the State Department.

According to a committee aide, Glaspie stood by her statements that she thought U.S. policy was made clear to Saddam and that it was not necessary for her to say it in so many words either to him or, especially, to her superiors in the State Department. Some senators reportedly expressed disbelief in her account. But the issue went no further because the hearings remained closed and the cable remained classifed.

An Awkward Visit

Like Glaspie, several senators found themselves struggling to explain a prewar visit with Saddam. The members were widely criticized for their seemingly obsequious behavior toward the Iraqi leader.

But to the five, the visit reflected one side of a debate over whether the best way to influence a recalcitrant foreign leader is with a threat or a promise.

The senators said they were seeking ties with a leader who had isolated himself from Western officials but who was also a critical wild card in ongoing efforts to craft a Middle East peace settlement. It was a gamble that events would later show they lost.

The five — Ohio Democrat Howard M. Metzenbaum and Republicans Bob Dole, Kan.; Alan K. Simpson, Wyo.; James A. McClure, Idaho; and Frank H. Murkowski, Alaska — met with Saddam on April 12, 1990, less than four months before he invaded Kuwait and set off an international tempest.

In the meeting, the senators said that the United States sought improved relations with Iraq but that they had concerns about reports that Saddam was developing biological and nuclear weapons and about his belligerence toward neighboring countries, especially Israel.

But it was the words they used, as described in a transcript released by the Iraqis after their invasion of Kuwait, that later caused an uproar.

Said Metzenbaum: "I am now aware that you are a strong and intelligent man and that you want peace."

Said Simpson: "I believe that your problems lie with the Western media and not with the U.S. government."

Said Dole: "We have not come to you with preconceived ideas or impressions."

Critics said the words and the entire tone of the visit, as characterized by the transcript, left the impression that the United States was more eager to improve ties with Saddam than it was to get tough on him for outlaw behavior.

Less than two weeks before, Saddam had threatened to burn up "half of Israel" if it attacked him first. His agents had been apprehended shortly before by U.S. and British authorities for trying to smuggle components that could be used in nuclear weapons. And his nation had a long record of human rights abuses, including the use of chemical weapons against Kurds in 1988.

Critics argued that if U.S. officials had taken a tougher line earlier, Saddam might have thought twice before invading Kuwait, a move he clearly did not expect would inspire a major U.S. assault.

"It was scandalous," David A. Korn, author of a 1990 Middle East Watch report on Iraqi human rights abuses, said of the senators' visit. "The illusion was being fostered in Washington ... that Saddam Hussein was changing, that Iraq was changing. But all you had to do was look at the internal repression, the record of the regime, the treatment of its own people, to see that this was not so."

Like Glaspie, the senators did not dispute the quotes in the Iraqi transcript as much as they argued that exchanges were left out.

A Dole spokesman, who was at the meeting but had his tape recorder confiscated by the Iraqis, said Dole repeatedly challenged Saddam about what he had meant by his threat to burn Israel, questions not included in the transcript.

The senators also emphasized later that they had handed Saddam a letter at the start of the meeting that stated their "deep concerns" about his military buildup and threats to use chemical weapons against Israel.

"It is clear to us that we can never resolve the serious differences between our nations if we ignore them or fail to take advantage of opportunities to communicate with each other clearly and candidly," said the letter, which was included in the Iraqi transcript. "For that reason, we believe it is important that you hear our very deep concerns about certain policies and activities of your government."

Indeed, on their return to the United States, several of the participants went to the Senate floor to express reservations about the direction of U.S.-Iraqi relations. At the same time, they cautioned colleagues against moving too hastily to cut off ties through sanctions or other pending legislation.

"Iraq's President Hussein's anti-Israel rhetoric was distasteful to all of us," Dole told Senate colleagues April 20. "... But at the same time it is a country that cannot be ignored."

Export Controls

During 1991, some members of Congress attempted to focus attention on what they viewed as a dangerously loose U.S. export policy toward Iraq before the war.

Doug Barnard Jr., D-Ga., chairman of the House Government Operations Committee's Subcommittee on Commerce, Consumer and Monetary Affairs, asked the Justice Department on July 10 to investigate whether Commerce Department officials violated the law by altering export licensing documents sought by his subcommittee late in 1990.

His request came in response to a report in June by Commerce's inspector general that concluded that some "unjustified and misleading" changes were made in the records before they were submitted to Capitol Hill.

While most of the changes were inconsequential, according to the inspector general, some of those made by Bureau of Export Administration personnel were not.

The most serious was the revision of the description of trucks, for which five export licenses were sought, from "vehicles designed for military use" to "commercial utility cargo trucks" or simply "vehicles."

On another license, the bureau deleted an exporter's comment that "according to our information the end user is involved in military matters."

The Government Operations Committee released a report July 14 that detailed what Barnard described as a "breakdown" in the U.S. export control system, which led to the export of equipment and technology that Saddam was able to use to strengthen his military capabilities.

The Commerce Department approved export licenses for about $1.5 billion in so-called dual-use goods to Iraq from 1985 until the invasion in August 1990.

The International Economic Policy and Trade Subcommittee of the House Foreign Affairs Committee averted a confrontation with the administration over the late delivery by the Commerce and Defense departments of similar documents subpoenaed by the panel.

The subcommittee had threatened to call Defense Secretary Dick Cheney and Commerce Secretary Robert A. Mosbacher before the panel July 17 but dropped its plans after receiving the documents it sought the week of July 8.

Congress' Role

As the administration faced accusations that it went easy on Saddam in the years before the gulf war, some members of Congress acknowledged that the legislative branch also had a record of compromise and inaction.

Despite efforts by a handful of members, Congress

mostly acquiesced in administration efforts to deal gently with the Iraqi leader throughout the 1980s.

For most of the 1980s, Iran, not Iraq, was the Persian Gulf enemy in U.S. eyes, as memories lingered of Iran's holding of U.S. hostages in 1979-80.

Legislation to punish Saddam for using chemical weapons and supporting terrorism and to prevent his access to potentially dangerous technology seldom made it to the White House — and then only if it gave the administration flexibility to waive the restrictions.

"Looking back, it never seemed terribly difficult to get House and Senate support for pursuing the relationship," recalled Richard W. Murphy, assistant secretary of State for Near Eastern and South Asian affairs during most of the Reagan administration.

Members who fought for tougher action against Iraq blamed their defeat largely on strong White House opposition. The Reagan and Bush administrations resisted having their hands tied on foreign policy and, more specifically, to having limits imposed on their efforts to moderate Saddam's behavior with carrots, not sticks.

But failure also resulted from members' desires to help constituents tap lucrative Iraqi markets for rice and wheat, computers and construction projects. Only six days before Iraq's invasion of Kuwait, for example, the House voted to gut an amendment that would have cut off $1 billion in annual U.S. farm guarantees for oil-rich Iraq. *(1990 Almanac, p. 723)*

During the 1980s, members heard little if anything from constituents about Iraq and saw little or nothing about it on television or in newspapers. As a result, most were inclined to do little or nothing about it.

"It's a very big institution and it's very hard to get everybody's attention on something which isn't on the front pages every day," said Howard L. Berman, D-Calif., who began pushing legislation to limit U.S. trade with Iraq soon after he came to the House in 1983. "There was no grass-roots campaign. The American people weren't aware of or that interested in our policy toward Iraq at that time."

After it was revealed in late 1988 that Saddam had used chemical weapons against Kurdish citizens, for example, both houses quickly passed legislation to impose sanctions against Iraq. But the measures, which later died, received little debate. *(1988 Almanac, p. 510)* ■

Aid for Kurdish Refugees Easily Approved

Responding to the plight of waves of Kurdish refugees who fled into the mountains of Iraq and Turkey to escape Iraqi forces, Congress on May 22 sent the president legislation (HR 2251) that included $556 million in disaster and refugee relief.

The conference report on the bill (H Rept 102-71) passed with little opposition. The House approved it, 387-33, then the Senate cleared the measure by voice vote. *(Vote 113, p. 28-H)*

Bush signed the bill (PL 102-55) on June 13.

Committee Action

Congress and the administration moved with near-unanimity to respond to the crisis of Iraq's Kurdish minority, which fled in massive numbers when the forces of Iraq's Saddam Hussein crushed a rebellion that followed the Persian Gulf War. *(Postwar policy, p. 451)*

On April 18, the Senate Foreign Relations Committee approved its version of a Kurdish relief bill (S 786), which authorized $50 million.

On April 23, the House Foreign Affairs Committee marked up legislation authorizing supplemental spending for Kurdish relief.

The panel approved up to $400 million in aid and also approved increased spending authority for the State Department's emergency refugee account of $25 million.

On April 25, the administration sent Congress a letter formally requesting a $150.5 million supplemental appropriation to underwrite "Operation Provide Comfort," as the administration's refugee relief effort was called.

Richard G. Darman, director of the Office of Management and Budget, proposed that the funding come from the interest on contributions that foreign governments provided in support of U.S. military activities in the Persian Gulf.

In late April, the United States broadened the scope of its relief efforts, providing direct aid for the first time for the estimated 1 million people who fled from southern Iraq into neighboring Iran.

Allied forces also greatly expanded the size of a security zone established for hundreds of thousands of Kurdish refugees. The allies, encountering no resistance from Iraqi forces, created a safe haven for the refugees that encompassed more than 1,800 square miles in northern Iraq.

During the week of April 29, Kurds began to leave their squalid encampments in mountains across the border in Turkey, some returning to their villages and others staying in the first camp constructed by allied troops, near Zakho. But the slow process was complicated by the Kurds' lingering fear that Saddam still threatened their survival.

On May 2, two House Appropriations subcommittees acted to approve a total of $556.5 million in supplemental appropriations for fiscal 1991. But members also signaled their unease at the prospect of an open-ended U.S. presence in postwar Iraq.

The Subcommittee on Foreign Operations approved $235.5 million to meet costs incurred by the State Department for refugee aid, $85 million more than the administration requested.

The extra relief was to be financed largely out of aid originally slated for Pakistan that was suspended because of that country's nuclear weapons program.

But the Subcommittee on Defense balked at the administration's request for unlimited authority to pay for the military component of the refugee relief operation from $15 billion that Congress advanced in March to underwrite the costs of the gulf war.

Instead, the panel voted in closed session to approve $321 million for the military's relief efforts.

Floor Action

Both chambers of Congress acted on May 9 to provide more than half a billion dollars to aid displaced people in and around Iraq and to help disaster victims in other parts of the world.

The legislation (HR 2251), a supplemental appropriation for fiscal 1991, passed the House, 384-25, with minimal debate. The Senate subsequently approved the measure by voice vote, adding several amendments. *(Vote 84, p. 22-H)*

Both versions of the bill provided $320.5 million to pay the U.S. military's costs in providing relief to the waves of refugees who fled Iraq.

Both chambers approved $235.5 million — $85 million more than the amount requested by the administration — to replenish the State Department refugee and disaster-assistance accounts, which had been depleted by the refugee operation and other emergencies.

But there were distinctions. The House proposed funding the $85 million increase with a reduction in foreign aid already allocated for fiscal 1991, primarily using economic support fund assistance for Pakistan that had been frozen because of evidence that it was developing nuclear weapons.

The Senate, with administration backing, chose to leave aid for Pakistan untouched. Instead, it took advantage of the administration's proposal to use the interest that was accruing on contributions made by foreign governments to the United States to defray costs of the war.

Administration officials estimated that the interest would reach $295 million by the end of May.

The administration came up with the idea, using some of the interest on foreign contributions to fund its original request of $150.5 million to restore State Department relief accounts. The Senate turned to the accumulating interest for the extra $85 million as well.

The House and Senate also approved different totals for the overall supplemental appropriation: The House bill contained $572 million; the Senate figure was $16 million lower.

The difference stemmed from a Senate amendment to strip a House-passed provision to appropriate $16 million — once again from the interest on foreign contributions — for organizations that aided families of U.S. servicemen.

The appropriations measure included $143 million for refugee aid, $67 million for international disaster assistance — urgently needed because the $40 million annual budget of the State Department's Office of Foreign Disaster Assistance had been depleted — and $25.5 million for international peacekeeping activities.

On the same day that both chambers approved the supplemental appropriation, the Senate tied up some loose ends by clearing a measure (HR 2122) to authorize emergency aid for displaced Iraqis. The House had passed the bill on April 30. In both chambers, the bill was approved by voice vote. President Bush signed the measure (PL 102-45) on Aug. 8.

The administration was scrambling to address a series of competing emergencies — from the Kurdish crisis to starvation in the Horn of Africa and a devastating storm and flooding in Bangladesh — while attempting to limit funding requests.

A last-minute effort by some House Democrats to add $15 million to the supplemental appropriation in assistance for Bangladesh was opposed by administration officials, who told lawmakers that the money would not be needed.

Privately, however, some State Department officials said the additional money would be welcome.

BOXSCORE

➡ **Kurdish Refugee Relief (HR 2251).** The $572 million supplemental appropriations bill included $556 million in disaster and refugee relief aid, much of it for Iraq's displaced Kurds. The bill provided $235.5 million for State Department activities and $320.5 million to fund the military's relief efforts.

Report: H Rept 102-71.

KEY ACTION

May 9 — HR 2251 passed the **House,** 384-25. The measure passed the **Senate** by voice vote the same day.

May 22 — The conference report on HR 2251 (H Rept 102-71) was approved by the **House,** 387-33. The measure was cleared by the **Senate** by voice vote the same day.

June 13 — President Bush signed HR 2251 — PL 102-55.

Final Action

On May 22, Congress approved the conference report for the $572 million supplemental appropriation bill (HR 2251) for fiscal 1991. It included $556 million in disaster and refugee relief aid.

The House approved the conference report, 387-33, and the Senate cleared the measure by voice vote the same day.

The House and Senate approved an $85 million increase over the administration request for State Department disaster and refugee aid accounts, which had been drawn down to respond to the Kurdish crisis as well as emergencies in Bangladesh, the Horn of Africa and elsewhere.

The spending bill included $235.5 million for State Department activities, to be derived largely from interest accumulating on foreign contributions to the U.S. war effort. The conference report stated that the contributions themselves could also be spent.

Most of that money, $210 million, went to replenish the department's disaster and refugee aid accounts, and $25.5 million went to support peacekeeping activities of international organizations such as the United Nations.

In addition, the interest on foreign donations was tapped to provide $16 million for private organizations that provided services to U.S. military personnel and their families.

The remaining $320.5 million, to fund the U.S. military's relief operations, was drawn from a separate Treasury Department account established for war costs.

Because HR 2251 was intended to defray incremental costs associated with the war — and because the funding was either previously appropriated or came from interest on foreign contributions — the measure was deemed to be exempt from federal spending limits.

In conference, House negotiators agreed to drop the provision in their version of the bill to fund the extra $85 million in State Department spending from unspent foreign aid, mostly frozen assistance for Pakistan.

House negotiators also accepted Senate language funding the State Department's activities entirely from interest on foreign contributions, but they won inclusion of a requirement that the administration notify Congress before reallocating the Pakistan aid.

The House conferees also agreed to a Senate amendment removing restrictions on the International Trade Administration's expenditures for export promotion.

And senators dropped their objection that the House provision funding $16 million for organizations that aided military personnel would trigger similar requests by other private groups. ■

Israelis, Arabs Opened Peace Talks in Spain

The Bush administration achieved a historic breakthrough on Oct. 30, when it succeeded in bringing together Israel and its Arab neighbors for the opening of peace talks in Madrid, Spain.

Congress' contribution came in what it did not do: At President Bush's insistence, members delayed into 1992 any action on Israel's request for $10 billion in U.S. loan guarantees to assist in its absorption of immigrants. Bush argued that action on the guarantees could disrupt the peace talks.

Once the Middle East adversaries sat at the same table in Madrid, they quickly lapsed into familiar denunciations of one another. Little progress was made by the end of 1991. But the convening of talks — arranged through the tireless efforts of Secretary of State James A. Baker III and with the devolving Soviet Union as cosponsor — demonstrated the changing relationships of power balances in the Middle East after the Persian Gulf War.

Members of Congress generally expressed support for the talks, although some strong supporters of Israel worried that the administration could prove an insufficiently staunch ally.

Friends, More and Less

Admired and appreciated for enduring the terror of Iraq's Scud missiles during the gulf war, Israel again assumed its traditional role as the United States' "special" ally.

But the sudden warming of relations did not erase differences that had strained U.S.-Israeli relations. Prior to the war, Israel's conservative government had been at odds with the Bush administration over the wrenchingly difficult issue of Palestinian rights. Prime Minister Yitzhak Shamir rebuffed repeated U.S. efforts to persuade Israel to open a dialogue with Palestinian leaders.

The disagreements were pushed aside when Iraqi President Saddam Hussein began launching Scud missiles at Israel.

Noted for responding swiftly and massively to any attack, Israel adopted an uncharacteristic posture of restraint at the Bush administration's behest. The United States immediately rushed Patriot defensive missiles and their crews to Israel. *(Gulf war, p. 437)*

Bush remained in close telephone contact with Shamir, as did Baker. Deputy Secretary of State Lawrence S. Eagleburger was dispatched on an emergency mission to Israel.

The House and the Senate also weighed in in Israel's behalf, passing resolutions that commended Israel's performance during the crisis. Support for the non-binding resolutions was unanimous in both chambers.

The House resolution (H Con Res 41) "condemns the unprovoked attack by Iraq on Israel," and "commends Israel for its restraint." The concurrent resolution passed the House, 416-0, on Jan. 23. *(Vote 11, p. 4-H)*

The Senate acted the next day, approving a similar resolution (S Con Res 4), 99-0. *(Vote 8, p. 2-S)*

During the debate on the resolution, several lawmakers compared Iraq's Saddam Hussein to Adolf Hitler. "When he [Saddam] talks about turning Tel Aviv into a crematorium, we all know in this country and worldwide with whom he is associating himself," said Rep. Don Ritter, R-Pa.

For Congress, the resolutions of support were a quick and easy reward for Israel's stance. But the tangible evidence of Israel's special standing always had come in unmatched levels of U.S. aid, and Israel's expectations were high.

In a trial balloon for the $10 billion in guarantees that was later requested, Israel's finance minister floated an audacious proposal for U.S. loan guarantees.

Yitzhak Modai said on Jan. 22 that he had presented Eagleburger with his list of short- and medium-term needs. Israel's costs stemming from the war — including expenditures for heightened military readiness — could reach $3 billion, he said. "We also raised a request for general economic aid tied to the absorption of immigrants from the Soviet Union," Modai said.

Because more than 1 million Soviet Jews were expected to arrive in the country by the end of 1992, he said, Israel would need $20 billion in foreign aid for housing, with perhaps $10 billion coming from the United States.

Eventually, Israel confirmed that it would request the $10 billion in loan guarantees but agreed to wait until September before seeking congressional action on the controversial proposal.

But U.S.-Israeli relations were clouded by Israel's hard-line response to Palestinian protests and by U.S. opposition to the expansion of Jewish settlements in occupied territories.

According to a State Department report to Congress released March 19, more than 200,000 settlers resided in the territories. The territories included the West Bank and Gaza Strip, occupied since the 1967 Arab-Israeli war, as well as East Jerusalem and the Golan Heights, which had been formally annexed by Israel.

While the number of new settlements had grown only slightly since 1984, "settlement activity has proceeded apace," according to the State Department. Most activity was focused on expanding existing settlements in East Jerusalem and the West Bank.

The Shamir government pledged — after considerable coaxing by the administration — that it would not provide incentives for Soviet émigrés to settle in the territories. More than 200,000 Soviet Jews arrived in Israel in 1990, with up to 1 million expected by the end of 1992.

The State Department survey was requested by the House Appropriations Committee as part of the fiscal 1991 foreign aid bill (PL 101-513).

In order to meet demand created by Soviet immigration, Housing Minister Ariel Sharon said that the government would build 13,000 new housing units on the West Bank within two years.

Prodding Toward Peace

"By now it should be plain to all parties that peacemaking in the Middle East requires compromise," Bush said March 6 in his address marking victory in the gulf war.

Echoing sentiments expressed by President Jimmy Carter 13 years earlier, Bush told a joint session of Congress that "the time has come to put an end to Arab-Israeli conflict." *(Text, p. 9-E)*

The administration sought to take advantage of the scrambled power relations in the region after the war. The Palestine Liberation Organization lost influence by backing Saddam's losing cause, and Iraq was neutralized as a major player. Jordan's King Hussein, who usually attempted to play a kingmaker's role in the region, also lost influence because of his all-but-official support for Saddam.

On the other hand, Israel had established new credibility with the administration by enduring the Scud attacks.

And Syria enjoyed improved relations by joining the anti-Saddam alliance, even though it remained on the State Department's list of nations supporting terrorism.

The administration set out to break the long stalemate in the Middle East through a two-track approach that a senior State Department official described as "parallelism." Said Bush: "We must do all that we can to close the gap between Israel and the Arab states — and between Israelis and Palestinians."

Baker began pressing for talks in an eight-nation tour of the region that began on March 11.

There were aspects of Bush's speech that made some congressional supporters of the Jewish state uncomfortable. Bush said a "comprehensive peace" must be grounded in the "principle of territory for peace.

"This principle must be elaborated to provide for Israel's security and recognition, and at the same time for legitimate Palestinian political rights," he said.

It was a principle, predicted Rep. Lawrence J. Smith, D-Fla., "that will set teeth on edge in Israel."

Conservatives such as Shamir had never embraced the notion that Israel should give up land in return for recognition from neighbors. If anything, they became more adamant after the gulf war and Iraq's repeated missile attacks.

When Baker appeared before the House and Senate Foreign Operations Appropriations subcommittees on May 22-23, members promised him a free hand to pursue Arab-Israeli peace talks but expressed frustration with the lack of progress. Baker said the United States had a "unique obligation" to continue pushing for the peace talks in the aftermath of a war that found Arabs, Israel and the United States on the same side.

However, Baker came under fire from several senators for telling the House subcommittee on May 22 that there was "no bigger obstacle to peace" than Israel's continued settlement of occupied territories in the West Bank and Gaza Strip. "Nothing has made my job of trying to find Arab and Palestinian partners for Israel more difficult than being greeted by a new settlement every time I arrive," Baker said.

New York Republican Sen. Alfonse M. D'Amato called those remarks "unfortunate" because they raised doubts about even-handedness in the negotiations and gave Arab nations an excuse not to come to the bargaining table.

Legislators also told Baker they hoped the administration would take the lead on limiting the sale of both conventional arms and weapons of mass destruction to the Middle East. Proposals to limit arms proliferation were offered at the committee level as amendments to authorization bills for foreign aid and for the State Department. *(Foreign aid, p. 470; State Department authorization, p. 493)*

"We do believe it's important that our friends in the region have the ability to maintain and enhance their ... ability to defend themselves," Baker said in response to a suggestion by House subcommittee Chairman David R. Obey, D-Wis., that the United States suspend Mideast arms sales to "set an example to the rest of the world."

Baker said he thought such unilateral action would be ineffective and possibly counterproductive: "It is much better to try and work in a multilateral context."

On May 29, Bush proposed for the Middle East a freeze on the development and sale of surface-to-surface missiles, a ban on production of nuclear weapons materials and "supplier guidelines" on exports of conventional weapons. But the administration's proposal left the door open for continued arms sales to the region by coupling the goal of curbing proliferation with the sometimes contradictory goal of "supporting the legitimate need of every state to defend itself."

Postponing a Confrontation

By fall, Baker's months of shuttle diplomacy had succeeded in extracting assent from Israel, the Palestinians and Arab states to participate in a Middle East conference that was tentatively set for October. But Israel had previously agreed to wait only until September to press Congress for action on $10 billion in loan guarantees, an issue that the administration feared could torpedo the delicate agreement on peace talks.

Israel sought the U.S. guarantees to back commercial loans of $10 billion to the government of Israel over five years. Loan guarantees were widely used in domestic programs, such as student loans and home mortgages, but granting the Israeli request would represent an exponential expansion of their use abroad.

With such U.S. guarantees, Israel could negotiate lower interest rates on 30-year loans, which it said would be used to build thousands of houses, schools and roads for Israel's increasing population.

On Sept. 5, Bush sought and received the assurance of Sen. Patrick J. Leahy, D-Vt., that he would try to postpone a confrontation on the issue by delaying consideration of the entire foreign aid appropriations bill for fiscal 1992.

Leahy said in a statement that he "strongly supported" providing the loan guarantees. "At the same time," he said, "if the president of the United States asks for a delay in the guarantees to help the chances for peace in the Middle East, I believe I should support him."

Ultimately, Congress did not pass a foreign aid appropriations bill in 1991. Instead, foreign assistance was provided through a short-term continuing resolution (H J Res 360 — PL 102-145) that skirted the Israeli loan request and other international developments by maintaining funding at past levels. The resolution expired at the end of March 1992. *(Appropriations, p. 646)*

Baker had asked Prime Minister Shamir to hold off on requesting the guarantees. But Shamir rejected Baker's plea, and on Sept. 6 Israel formally requested the guarantees.

That day, Bush put his prestige on the line, announcing that he would "ask every single member of Congress to defer for just 120 days consideration" of Israel's request.

Highlighting the importance of the issue for his administration, Bush said during a White House photo opportunity, "I know it is in the best interest of world peace to have this deferred."

Not all members shared Leahy's willingness to wait. Charging that Baker and other administration officials had "an anti-Israel bias," Rep. Eliot L. Engel, D-N.Y., said a showdown between Bush and American Jewish organizations had been inevitable "and this is as good a place to draw the line as any."

"This has more to do with the pique of the president than peace," said Rep. Charles E. Schumer, D-N.Y. "Everyone knows the president doesn't like the settlements."

Sen. Connie Mack, R-Fla., protested that any delay in granting the guarantees "would be perceived by the Arab world as a clear invitation to link U.S. humanitarian assistance to Israel to concessions in the peace process."

Meeting with reporters on Sept. 12, Bush raised the stakes by saying he would veto any congressional attempts to provide the guarantees more quickly. "Quite simply, a 120-day delay is not too much for a president to ask for with so much in the balance," he said. "We must give peace a chance. We must give peace every chance."

Israel's supporters in the United States sounded just as adamant that the loan guarantees could not wait. "Congress will not take the president's intention to bring this fight lying down," said Rep. Wayne Owens, D-Utah.

The pro-Israel lobby, which, like Bush, was accustomed to getting what it sought from Congress, turned up the heat on the issue, deploying 1,200 leaders of major American Jewish organizations to Capitol Hill on Sept. 12.

The message they brought to Congress was simple but emotional, said Shoshana S. Cardin, chairman of the Conference of Presidents of Major American Jewish Organizations. Referring to the influx of immigrants pouring into Israel, she said, "We must respond to their needs now — not 120 days from now, not six months from now."

Apparently feeling the pressure from the well-coordinated lobbying blitz, Bush tried to portray himself as the underdog in a public political struggle. "I heard today there were something like 1,000 lobbyists on the Hill working the other side of the question," he said. "We've got one lonely little guy down here doing it."

Bush offended many Jewish leaders by adding that he was "up against some powerful political forces." They saw the reference as invoking an age-old prejudice that Jews represented a conspiratorial force. Bush later sent them a letter of apology, saying that his comments "were never meant to be pejorative in any sense." But both sides recognized that the potential costs of a long and divisive battle could be steep for backers of Israel, as well as the administration.

"Most friends of Israel recognize this is a fight you lose even if you win," said Rep. Smith of Florida, a stalwart supporter of the Jewish state. He said a bitter battle could result in an erosion of future presidential backing for Israel.

As it sought support for a delay, the administration issued a statement pledging that it would seek "no further delay" at the end of the 120-day period "no matter where the peace process is at that time." And, the statement said, "if there is cost to Israel associated with deferral, the administration will agree that such cost be offset in the ultimate package." But such assurances remained vague because the administration did not offer outright support for guarantees, commit to a certain amount or indicate that it would refrain from seeking conditions on settlements.

Gradually, Israel's supporters on Capitol Hill acknowledged that they could not buck Bush's demand for a delay. Efforts to frame the terms for loan guarantees eventually supplanted the debate over postponing action on them.

An idea floated by Leahy attracted increasing attention. Under Leahy's proposal, Bush would pledge to back the loan guarantees, and Israel would agree in turn not to use any U.S. aid in the occupied territories.

To demonstrate U.S. displeasure with the settlements, the guarantees would be reduced by the amount that Israel devoted toward building settlements.

Sen. Bob Kasten, R-Wis., a leading supporter of Israel, objected to connecting the loan guarantees to limits on the expansion of settlements. The Leahy proposal "implies linkage, and I don't want linkage," he said. Kasten gathered the signatures of 70 senators on draft legislation to approve $10 billion in loan guarantees. But he acknowledged that a number of the cosponsors also backed Bush's request for a delay.

A Peace Conference Convenes

Secretary of State Baker announced in Jerusalem on Oct. 18 that a Middle East peace conference would be convened in Madrid under U.S.-Soviet sponsorship.

But Baker, whose prodigious shuttle diplomacy brought about the event, cautioned that the talks were only the beginning of a long process. He said, "Old suspicions will not disappear quickly. . . . So we have no illusions about the hard work that lies ahead."

In Washington, Rep. Lee H. Hamilton, D-Ind., chairman of the House Foreign Affairs Subcommittee on Europe and the Middle East, called the announcement a "significant procedural achievement" for the administration. "We've been trying to get these people to sit down and talk to each other for a long time," he said in an interview.

The conference was to proceed along a two-track process, Bush said, with Israel negotiating separately with its Arab neighbors and with Palestinian representatives. The basis for the negotiations, he added, was to be U.N. Security Council Resolutions 242 and 338, which called for Israel to return occupied territories to Arab nations in return for formal Arab recognition of the Jewish state.

Hours before the conference was announced, Israel and the Soviet Union renewed full diplomatic relations, which Moscow had severed after the 1967 Mideast War.

The Middle East peace conference began Oct. 30 with all sides guardedly optimistic that the old hatreds that divided Arabs and Israelis for generations eventually could be overcome. But the ceremonial opening of the conference in Madrid became a forum to rehash those ancient enmities, with only glimmers of compromise or conciliation.

On the final day of the three-day opening session around a T-shaped table in Madrid's Royal Palace, Shamir labeled Syria "one of the most oppressive tyrannical regimes in the world."

Syrian Foreign Minister Farouk al-Sharaa responded by waving a poster of Shamir from the 1940s that he said showed that the Israeli prime minister had been sought by British authorities on charges of terrorism.

In a blunt speech opening the conference that his administration had engineered, President Bush was hopeful but realistic. Merely ending belligerency in the region would not be enough, Bush said. "Rather we seek peace, real peace," he said, calling for treaties, diplomatic exchanges and "territorial compromise."

Bush previewed the "painful" process that lay ahead. "There will be disagreement and criticism, setbacks — who knows, possibly interruptions," he said.

In Washington, members of Congress reacted to the diplomatic fits and starts with a mixture of admiration for the Bush administration's achievement in bringing the historical adversaries together and apprehension that the process could fall apart.

Some lawmakers were unabashedly optimistic about the chances for peace. Rep. Owens of Utah, who rose at 4:30 a.m. to watch the opening of the conference on television, said it "will be the dawn of a new age of peace" in the Middle East. Rep. Jim Leach, R-Iowa, said he believed that there were "better prospects of something coming from this than any other single event since the creation of Israel."

Yet there also was a strong undercurrent of concern over Israel's security. While most lawmakers applauded the administration for taking the role of honest broker in the peace process, some lambasted Syria for past acts of terrorism and its restrictive emigration policy toward Jews.

D'Amato introduced a resolution (S Res 204) urging the administration to address Syria's terrorist activities as part of the peace process. Two House Foreign Affairs subcommittees approved by voice vote a resolution (H Con Res 188) offered by Mel Levine, D-Calif., which condemned Syria for not allowing Jews the right of free emigration. ■

$500 Million Approved for Soviet Aid

Like others around the world, members of Congress spent much of 1991 transfixed by the extraordinary changes that culminated at year's end in the dissolution of the Soviet Union. But the lawmakers had the added task of debating whether to spend money from the U.S. Treasury to encourage, and perhaps even subsidize, the change from communism and a command economy to democracy and capitalism.

Ultimately, Congress voted to give the president authority to spend up to $400 million in Defense Department funds to assist in the dismantling of the Soviet nuclear arsenal and up to $100 million in Pentagon funds to deliver humanitarian aid.

More ambitious proposals for direct economic assistance stalled amid doubts about the efficacy of such aid and resistance to increased spending abroad at a time of domestic economic problems.

The debate over aid unfolded against the backdrop of changes that would have seemed unimaginable a few years earlier.

After the failure of a hard-liners' coup in August, it became clear that the course of change in the Soviet Union was inexorable.

In early November, broad opposition forced sponsors to drop an initial proposal from the fiscal 1992 defense authorization bill (HR 2100). It would have permitted the Defense Department to spend up to $1 billion to aid its Cold War nemesis. *(Defense authorization, p. 393)*

But Congress dramatically reversed course on Nov. 27. Both chambers overwhelmingly cleared a $500 million plan that permitted the president to use Pentagon funds to help the Soviet people survive the winter and to dismantle some of their 27,000 nuclear weapons.

The aid was proposed in the Senate on Nov. 25 as a $700 million package that was amended into legislation (HR 3807 — PL 102-228) authorizing the transfer to NATO allies of equipment disposed of under the Conventional Forces in Europe (CFE) treaty. *(CFE, p. 415)*

But a conference committee on a supplemental appropriations measure (H J Res 157 — PL 102-229), which funded the aid, reduced the amount involved to $500 million. By voice votes on Nov. 27, the House approved HR 3807 after amending it to match the appropriations proposal, and the Senate cleared the bill.

President Bush, whose administration had ignored pleas by sponsors of the aid plan to endorse it, signed the authorizing and appropriating measures on Dec. 12, and Secretary of State James A. Baker III later announced that the administration would make use of the authority it provided for Soviet aid.

In December, most of the Soviet republics proclaimed the end of the Soviet Union and the creation of a loose Commonwealth of Independent States. On Dec. 25, Soviet President Mikhail S. Gorbachev bowed to that reality and resigned from office.

BOXSCORE

➡ **Soviet Aid (HR 3807).** The measure authorized the president to use Pentagon funds to aid the former Soviet republics, with up to $400 million to dismantle weaponry and up to $100 million to transport humanitarian assistance.

KEY ACTION

Nov. 25 — The **Senate** amended HR 3807, a bill providing for weapons transfers under the Conventional Forces in Europe Treaty, to authorize the president to transfer Pentagon funds. It voted 86-8 to permit $500 million in aid for demilitarization and to permit up to $200 million to transport humanitarian assistance.

Nov. 27 — To match action on a supplemental appropriations measure, the **House** approved by voice vote an amended version of HR 3807, with the maximum aid reduced to $400 million for demilitarization and $100 million to transport humanitarian aid. The **Senate** cleared the amended version by voice vote.

Dec. 12 — President Bush signed HR 3807 — PL 102-228.

BALTIC CRACKDOWN

Early in 1991, as Washington remained riveted by the Persian Gulf War, a crackdown in the Baltic States shook Congress' confidence in and enthusiasm for the changes promised by Gorbachev. *(Gulf war, p. 437)*

Lashing out at a swelling independence movement, Soviet forces killed 15 people in Lithuania and at least four in Latvia. The raw display of Soviet force was more reminiscent of the days of totalitarian Kremlin rule than of the promised *glasnost* (openness) and *perestroika* (restructuring) that were Gorbachev's slogans.

By voice vote on Jan. 16, the Senate approved a non-binding resolution (S Res 14) that called on the administration to review and possibly cut off economic and other aid to the Soviet Union until it withdrew troops from the Baltic States and undertook good-faith negotiations with the republics of Lithuania, Latvia and Estonia.

"It would be a travesty to concentrate so much of our nation's energy on stopping Iraqi aggression and freeing Kuwait, while ignoring Soviet aggression in the captive Baltic nations," said Robert C. Byrd, D-W.Va. "There should be no confusion in our response to this latest brutal crackdown."

Gorbachev had "to choose between the road to the future and the road to the past," said House Minority Leader Robert H. Michel, R-Ill. "He has chosen to ride a tank down the road to the past, waving his Nobel Peace Prize as he passes by."

On Jan. 23, the House passed a concurrent resolution (H Con Res 40), 417-0, condemning the violence and asking Bush to work with allies in Europe toward a "coordinated approach" to sanctions if the Soviets continued to use force to suppress the movements for independence by the Baltic States of Lithuania, Latvia and Estonia. *(Vote 15, p. 4-H)*

The Senate passed a similar resolution (S Con Res 6) on Jan. 24. *(Vote 6, p. 2-S)*

Despite the widespread outrage and disappointment over Gorbachev's turn toward traditional Soviet authoritarianism, some members appeared reluctant to cut short a new era of U.S.-Soviet cooperation.

The debate concerned whether it was in the best interest of the United States to support Gorbachev as a wayward but indispensable reformer or attempt to pressure him back toward the path of reform.

Even for the diplomatically attuned Bush administration, the situation required a delicate balancing act: maintaining good relations with the Soviet Union while signaling displeasure with the Soviet army's violent suppression of the democracy movement in the Baltic States.

The week of Jan. 28 began with the expected announcement from the White House of an indefinite postponement of a U.S.-Soviet summit, originally set to take place in Moscow Feb. 11-13. But administration officials took pains to state that the Baltics crisis had not caused the delay.

"If the [gulf] war was not going on, we'd go" to the summit, said White House spokesman Marlin Fitzwater.

The only other impediment to a summit that Fitzwater cited was the slow progress toward reaching a bilateral agreement to limit strategic arms.

During his State of the Union address Jan. 29, Bush announced that Gorbachev's government had provided "representations" that it would "move away from violence" in the Baltic States. Kremlin officials announced Jan. 30 that a tentative troop withdrawal had begun in Lithuania.

In a letter to Bush in March, Gorbachev asked for $1.5 billion in U.S. agricultural credits beyond the $1 billion that the administration had extended in December 1990. But the turmoil in the Soviet Union added to confusion on Capitol Hill. Farm-state members of Congress were anxious to see the administration approve Gorbachev's request. But concerns were raised about the Soviet Union's ability to repay the loans and about the impact such assistance might have on independence movements in the Baltic States and several Soviet republics.

Former Soviet Foreign Minister Eduard A. Shevardnadze told Bush and congressional leaders in meetings May 6 and 7 that the extension of food aid, which Gorbachev requested in a letter to Bush in March, was crucial to the "fate of reform and democracy in the Soviet Union."

But the three Baltic leaders argued in meetings with Bush and legislators May 7 and 8 that democratic movements in the Soviet Union would only be hampered by providing aid to the central government. They insisted that any credit assistance go directly to the republics or follow concrete actions by the Soviet government to grant independence to the Baltic States.

Granting Gorbachev's loan request "may be understood by the Soviet government as encouragement to continue its policies and to use violence," Lithuanian President Vytautas Landsbergis told congressional members of the Commission on Security and Cooperation in Europe, also known as the Helsinki Commission.

But the Senate approved a non-binding resolution (S Res 117) on May 15 favoring the agricultural credits. The 70-28 vote did little to demonstrate a consensus in Congress on Soviet affairs because the farm credits enjoyed strong backing from farm-state lawmakers anxious to secure commodity sales for their constituents. *(Vote 62, p. 9-S)*

The White House paved the way for the credits June 3 by waiving the Jackson-Vanik restrictions on trade with the Soviet Union. The restrictions were imposed in 1974 because of Moscow's policy of limiting Soviet emigration. On June 11, the administration announced it was granting the $1.5 billion in credits. *(Soviet credit, p. 174)*

DEBATING A 'GRAND BARGAIN'

By summer, Congress was torn over whether the Bush administration was doing too little to support historic change in the Soviet Union or too much to coddle a Soviet regime that had stopped short of fundamental economic and political change.

Some members were intrigued by the arguments of academics who urged a "grand bargain" in which massive direct aid to the Soviet Union would be granted in return for specific promises of reform from the Gorbachev government.

But others believed that substantial Western aid would only prop up the communist bureaucracy, permitting it to put off the traumatic transition to free markets and democracy.

In June, U.S.-Soviet relations began to improve as tensions over the Baltic crackdown eased.

The notion of a "grand bargain" of aid-for-reform grew out of informal talks between Soviet officials and international finance experts. It was then refined by an informal group of Soviet economists and academics from Harvard University and given a wider circulation.

A pair of top House Democrats, Majority Leader Richard A. Gephardt, Mo., and David R. Obey, Wis., floated their own, more cautiously formulated, version of the proposal.

They refrained from using the politically loaded term "grand bargain."

Both men said the administration was moving with excessive caution at a time when bold action was needed so that a historic opportunity would not be lost.

Obey, chairman of the Foreign Operations Appropriations Subcommittee, had raised the profile of the economic aid issue by including the proposal that also had Gephardt's support in the report accompanying the fiscal 1992 foreign operations appropriations bill approved May 29 by his subcommittee. *(Appropriations, p. 646)*

"While in the end these efforts may prove futile," the report said, "the committee believes that it would be negligent for the West to miss an opportunity to clearly lay out our conditions for assisting the Soviet Union," along with the "nature, timing and levels" of possible Western economic aid.

The conditions in the report were tough. Moscow would have been required to hold scheduled elections and allow each of the dissident Baltic States to "determine the future of its own association with the Soviet Union."

In the economic sphere, the Soviet Union would have had to put into place most of the elements of a free-market system, including a convertible currency and floating exchange rates.

As the conditions illustrated, there was considerable caution on Capitol Hill.

Members of both parties were wary of embarking upon what Rep. Richard J. Durbin, D-Ill., called "the fast train to Moscow."

With the Gorbachev government appearing to change its internal and external policies each month — was he a budding democrat or a throwback to a repressive era? — many in Congress were content to let the administration set the diplomatic course.

Sending Strauss

The White House seemed eager to underscore the prospects for improving U.S.-Soviet business ties by nominating veteran Democratic insider Robert S. Strauss on June 4 to be the U.S. ambassador in Moscow.

There was wide praise for the appointment of Strauss, who was nearly devoid of experience in Soviet affairs but was a skilled operator in the worlds of politics and commerce.

"He'll be in Moscow at a time when a guy with his kind of skills would be particularly useful," said Sen. Joseph R. Biden Jr., D-Del., chairman of the Foreign Relations Subcommittee on European Affairs.

Although a few members privately expressed astonishment at the unorthodox selection of Strauss, his Democratic pedigree and close friendship with Bush and Secretary of State Baker ensured Senate approval of his nomination.

Testifying before the Foreign Relations Committee on July 16, Strauss, a high-priced corporate lawyer and dealmaker, called the Soviet Union "an environment where hopefully my personal experiences as a communicator, negotiator, a problem-solver and an interpreter of politics are best-suited and best challenged."

The 72-year-old Strauss also struck a chord with the committee when he promised to continue to press the Soviets to improve their human rights record, both at home and abroad. "I may not speak Russian, but no Soviet leader will have any illusions as to how Americans react to intimidation in the Baltics or support of Castro's brutality in Cuba. Of that you can be sure," he said.

The Senate confirmed Strauss' nomination by voice vote on July 30.

Sticker Shock

Lawmakers and the administration had begun to focus on an issue of domestic economics: At a time of recession, huge federal deficits and declining foreign aid budgets, how could the United States afford to bail out the Soviet Union?

Many U.S. officials suffered sticker shock after hearing some of the aid amounts being floated by Soviet economists and U.S. academics.

Jeffrey D. Sachs, a Harvard economist who helped devise Poland's economic-reform plan and was one of the architects of the grand bargain, estimated that the "radical market reforms" to be undertaken by Moscow needed to be backed with a Western aid package "on the order of $30 billion per year for five years."

Estimates of the U.S. contribution varied, but Sachs and Gephardt indicated it could approach $3 billion a year. According to some reports, Soviet officials privately said that even more could be required from the West — perhaps $250 billion over five years.

An aid package of that size would be a "tough sell," said Rep. Lee H. Hamilton, D-Ind., the chairman of the House Foreign Affairs Subcommittee on Europe and the Middle East.

Administration officials were harsher, openly deriding what Baker called the "big-bang approach" of sending massive aid to the Soviet Union. Calling the proposal "really a non-starter," Vice President Dan Quayle said, "Don't ask the American taxpayer to subsidize an economic system that doesn't work."

Yeltsin Visits

While the Bush administration kept its relations tethered to Gorbachev, Boris N. Yeltsin, the newly elected president of Russia, was greeted warmly on Capitol Hill during the week of June 17.

The first freely elected official in Russia's 1,000-year history, Yeltsin was treated as a major world leader, and celebrity, as he was whisked from one side of the Capitol to the other for meetings, luncheons and photos with anyone who could get close.

After an hourlong meeting between Yeltsin and about 70 senators, Ernest F. Hollings, D-S.C., joked with Majority Leader George J. Mitchell, D-Maine, that Yeltsin was such a hit that Democrats should put him at the top of their 1992 presidential ticket. "We finally found one," Hollings said.

Senate Minority Leader Bob Dole, R-Kan., told Yeltsin that lawmakers "want to engage in more direct contact with the [Soviet] republics rather than with the central government. I hope you make that point clear to President Bush."

Yeltsin replied: "That's why I've come here."

In fact, Yeltsin told members almost everything they wanted to hear.

He said he "did not come here asking for money" but to let lawmakers know of Russia's commitment to reform. He said his election "demonstrated that Russia stands firmly on its way toward a market system, privatization, greater democracy."

Yeltsin's greeting at the White House was friendly but less exuberant, as the administration sought to avoid offending Gorbachev.

At a meeting on June 20, Bush told Yeltsin that he looked forward to working together with him. But, the president added, "I want to be very clear about this: The United States will continue to maintain the closest possible official relationship with the Soviet government of President Gorbachev."

Nor was Congress' enthusiasm toward Yeltsin matched by dollars in aid to the Soviet Union. As the House took up a foreign aid authorization bill in June and the Senate did the same in July, members loaded on tough conditions for any aid to Moscow. The bill stalled short of enactment, but it provided a clear measure of the lawmakers' continuing ambivalence toward the ambiguous course of change in Moscow.

Bush and Gorbachev Meet

No cash was on the table when the leaders of the Group of Seven (G-7) leading industrial nations sat down with Soviet President Gorbachev on July 17.

The world leaders shrugged off weeks of expectations that Gorbachev would come to the economic conference in London seeking a "grand bargain" of billions of dollars in aid in return for Soviet economic and political reforms.

"He really was trying to explain more what was going on inside the Soviet Union — what the pressures were, what he was up against in terms of history, if you will, and how they were coping and how determined they were to work with the republics and how much help they did need in terms of technical assistance," President Bush told reporters. "But he really stopped short of what some had predicted might be on his agenda."

"We're going through a difficult time now," Gorbachev said at a separate news conference. "We shall find our way through this, we shall extricate ourselves, whether you help us or not. That's not the point. And we're not even talking about assistance. We're talking about the new quality of cooperation when we are an organic part of this world economic space."

Instead, British Prime Minister John Major, the G-7 chairman and summit host, announced far more modest and incremental steps to help the struggling Soviet reform effort. These included a "special association" with the In-

State Department Assumed Fate of

After five years of bitter debate, Congress voted in 1991 to shift to the State Department the burden of deciding what to do with the unfinished U.S. Embassy building in Moscow, which was riddled with listening devices. At the end of the year, department officials were reportedly near agreement to build a new U.S. Embassy near the unfinished building.

Congress appropriated $100 million for embassy "reconstruction" in Moscow as a part of the appropriations bill for the Departments of Commerce, Justice and State (HR 2608 — PL 102-140), which President Bush signed Oct. 28. But the bill did not restrict how the money was to be spent; it required only that the State Department report to Congress on its decision. *(Appropriations, p. 531)*

Similar language was contained in the law that authorized the activities of the State Department for fiscal 1992-93 (HR 1415 — PL 102-138). *(State Department, p. 493)*

The unfinished building had stood unused since August 1985, when the listening devices were discovered embedded in its walls. Since then, lawmakers and the executive branch had struggled over how to fix the problem. While some wanted to tear down the building and start anew, others wanted to keep it for unclassified purposes or to add new, secure top floors.

Both the Reagan and Bush administrations advocated tearing down the building and starting over as the option most likely to produce a secure facility. That decision got the support of Ernest F. Hollings, D-S.C. — chairman of the Senate Appropriations subcommittee in charge of the embassy — the Senate Intelligence Committee and various members of the House.

But for three years, Neal Smith, D-Iowa, Hollings' counterpart in the House, and members of Smith's House Appropriations Subcommittee on Commerce, Justice, State and the Federal Judiciary successfully blocked attempts to implement the tear-down option. Smith and his allies said tearing down the building was a waste of money. Surely, they argued, some use could be found for a nearly complete building.

Congressional advocates for tearing down the facility said they would renew their efforts during the second session in 1992.

The Long Road

The year began with a proposal, contained in the president's budget request, to use $130 million to begin tearing down the bugged Moscow embassy building and constructing a new one. That plan ran into immediate problems with Smith, who had vehemently opposed tearing down the building ever since the problem was discovered. His power as chairman of the Appropriations subcommittee with jurisdiction over the embassy and his panel's bipartisan support for his position allowed him to block this proposal.

The State Department then came up with a proposal nicknamed Top Hat. That proposal, announced March 7, called for knocking down the top two floors of the eight-story building and adding four secure floors.

The administration estimated that the Top Hat option would cost about $215 million over three or four years, compared with $280 million over five years to tear down and replace the building.

In appeasing Smith, however, the State Department infuriated other members, who accused the department of not pushing hard enough to raze the bug-riddled embassy.

At a June hearing of the Senate Appropriations Subcommittee with jurisdiction over the embassy, Secretary of State James A. Baker III implored senators to make a decision — any decision — to push the embarrassing episode to a close. But Hollings, the subcommittee chairman, warned Baker that the Top Hat proposal would have been met with a chilly reception in the Senate. "You're not passing it through the Senate," he said.

The embassy situation had taken on new urgency after a fire in the old U.S. Embassy in Moscow on March 28 destroyed portions of the building. Baker, responding to arguments by Hollings that the Top Hat solution would not make for a secure embassy, said, "If we put it on security grounds, Mr. Chairman, the worst situation is to continue the status quo because we do not have ade-

ternational Monetary Fund and the World Bank to "offer expert help and advice" in economic reforms.

The meeting represented a milestone in U.S.-Soviet relations because Bush and Gorbachev announced that nine years of negotiations had yielded agreement on the Strategic Arms Reduction Treaty (START), which called for significant reductions in U.S. and Soviet arsenals of strategic nuclear weapons. At a follow-up meeting in Moscow on July 30 and 31, Bush and Gorbachev signed the treaty. *(START, p. 419)*

At the Moscow summit, the two leaders also announced joint U.S.-Soviet sponsorship of a Middle East peace conference, and Bush announced he would send to Congress a long-awaited U.S.-Soviet trade agreement. It gave the Soviet Union most-favored-nation (MFN) trade status, which was cut off at the height of the Cold War. *(Postwar policy, p. 451; Soviet trade status, p. 125)*

Bush submitted the trade pact to Congress on Aug. 2. The House approved it on Nov. 20, the Senate did so on Nov. 25, and Bush signed the trade bill (H J Res 346 — PL-102-179) into law on Dec. 9.

AFTER THE COUP

Gorbachev's halting course toward fundamental change, two steps forward and one back, proved not only disconcerting to the West but unsustainable over the long run. Communist hard-liners, whom the reformist leader had kept in key positions in his government, turned on him and his policies on Aug. 19.

They seized Gorbachev and his family at their seaside dacha in the Crimea and announced that they had taken control. Tanks surrounded the Russian Federation building in Moscow on Aug. 20, and massive bloodshed was feared. But Yeltsin led a people-power revolt in Moscow that led to the coup's rapid collapse on Aug. 21.

'Bug-Ridden' Moscow Embassy Building

quate facilities there now, both from an operational standpoint and from a security standpoint."

Congressional Action

Four congressional panels had legislative jurisdiction over the Moscow embassy question: the two appropriations subcommittees, which oversaw how the money for the State Department was allocated, and the House Foreign Affairs and the Senate Foreign Relations committees, which authorized the State Department's activities. All four acted on the question in 1991.

The House Foreign Affairs Committee approved its biennial authorization for the State Department (HR 1415) on April 30. During the committee markup, panel members approved by voice vote an amendment by Howard L. Berman, D-Calif., that incorporated the new Top Hat approach into the bill. That followed a 10-16 vote to defeat an amendment by Olympia J. Snowe, R-Maine, to require that the bugged building be torn down.

The dynamics changed when the bill came to the floor. Snowe again offered her tear-down amendment, which Berman quickly moved to amend. His amendment deleted the tear-down provision and inserted language leaving the decision to the State Department. The House approved this amendment, 223-185. *(Vote 90, p. 22-H)*

Another attempt to force the tear-down option narrowly failed. Fred Upton, R-Mich., offered an amendment to knock down the building and start over again. It failed by 11 votes, 196-207. *(Vote 91, p. 22-H)*

Members did vote overwhelmingly, 414-0, to send Moscow the bill for any reconstruction of more than $215 million on the rationale that the Soviet secret police were responsible for bugging the embassy building. *(Vote 92, p. 22-H)*

On the other side of the Capitol, the Senate Foreign Relations Committee also included language to leave the final decision to the State Department in its version of the State Department authorization. The panel approved the bill, 18-0, on June 12. The full Senate passed the measure July 29.

The House Appropriations Committee included the $130 million in its version of the funding bill (HR 2608), which it passed June 11. The bill contained no restrictions on how the money could be spent. The full House adopted the bill June 13.

The Senate version of the measure also included the $130 million but specified that the funds were to be used for the tear-down option. The Senate Appropriations Committee approved the bill July 11; the full Senate followed suit July 31.

In a surprise move, the two Appropriations panels worked out a compromise during the conference on the bill. Both Hollings and Smith agreed to a plan to build a small embassy on the compound, near the bug-riddled building. No decision was made as to what to do with the unfinished building.

But members of the House, angry that the plan for a new building was added in conference with no warning and little debate, narrowly voted Oct. 3 to delete the compromise from the final bill. Instead, they inserted language to give $100 million to the State Department but require that State report back on its plan. The Senate agreed, and the bill was sent to the president. *(Vote 293, p. 70-H)*

A postscript to the long embassy debate demonstrated how much the world had changed with the collapse of the Soviet Union and the end of the Cold War. In a speech on Dec. 13, U.S. Ambassador to Moscow Robert S. Strauss revealed that Vadim Bakatin, the latest chief of the KGB spy agency, had within the previous week given him a sheaf of plans and a suitcase of "high-tech devices."

Strauss told the National Press Club that Bakatin said, "Mr. Ambassador, these are the plans that disclose how the bugging of your embassy took place, and these are the instruments that were used. And I want to give them to you and I want them turned over to your government, no strings attached, no quid pro quo, in the hope that maybe we can repay you, save you some money, maybe you can use that building again some day."

"I don't know if we'll ever be able to use the building," Strauss said, "but this is the most amazing thing that's happened to me in my life."

A still-shaken Gorbachev returned to power. No longer an uncertain reformer, he proclaimed the Communist Party dissolved.

But his control was uncertain, his judgment in surrounding himself with men who betrayed him was doubted and Yeltsin's more assertive style of leadership was in the ascendant.

Within hours of Gorbachev's return to Moscow after the collapse of the coup, Bush moved to put U.S.-Soviet relations back on track, lifting a hold on agricultural credit and other programs that he had imposed at the outset of the crisis.

"This is a watershed event for the Soviet Union and perhaps the world," said Rep. Dave McCurdy, D-Okla., chairman of the House Intelligence Committee, as the putsch by hard-liners was ending.

McCurdy proclaimed the Gorbachev era over, and with its passing the "ushering in of the period of the Yeltsin era." He criticized the administration for being "slow to react to the legitimacy of Yeltsin in the first place."

"If this coup is foiled, it is due to the Russian republic," Sen. Bill Bradley, D-N.J., said at a news conference shortly before the coup ended. He had little regard for Gorbachev, who he said "was unduly influenced by the forces that ultimately deposed him."

In the immediate aftermath of the coup, however, the United States continued to do business directly with Moscow. Bush appeared to recognize reality, however, at his Aug. 22 news conference, mixing support for Gorbachev with newfound praise of Yeltsin.

"We are very pleased that constitutional government has been restored," Bush said.

The president said he did not think Gorbachev's stature had been weakened because "here's a man who stood by his desire for reform and democracy, and he was seized and put under house arrest."

But Bush added, "Now, if you ask me, has Boris Yeltsin's stature been enhanced? The answer is clearly yes."

DEVELOPING AN AID PACKAGE

In the weeks after the failed coup, the Soviet republics declared independence, one after another.

With the world turned on end by the political convulsions in the Soviet Union, members of Congress grappled far more urgently than before with the questions of whether, when and how to send aid to the United States' longtime adversary.

Influential Democrats called for siphoning money from the Pentagon to provide emergency food and other aid to the Soviet people — even if that would bust the budget deal painstakingly negotiated in 1990 by Congress and the White House.

"We do not want the first winter of freedom after 70 years of communism to be a disaster for the Soviet Union," said House Armed Services Committee Chairman Les Aspin, D-Wis. On Aug. 28, he proposed taking $1 billion from the defense budget to provide humanitarian aid to the Soviet Union.

But the Democrats could not even agree among themselves over post-coup policy. While the Armed Services Committee chairman wanted to send $1 billion abroad, the new House majority whip, David E. Bonior, D-Mich., said U.S. domestic needs should come first.

Bush moved slowly to grant full diplomatic recognition to the Baltic States, but other Western countries recognized their independence soon after the coup collapsed. It became apparent that the central government's hold on the Baltics would not last long.

Bush also remained cautious about massive aid to the Soviet Union or its republics and urged more study before providing emergency food and humanitarian aid for the winter.

"Let's get the facts," Bush said, ". . . not try to get out there and have an instant solution to a problem when you don't know the major parameters of the problem."

Aspin's plan called for taking $1 billion from the defense budget to establish a "Humanitarian Aid and Stabilization Fund" in fiscal 1992.

Aspin refused to say what defense programs should be trimmed to provide the Soviet aid. His plan gave the administration wide latitude to use the money as it saw fit.

Aspin's proposal came under fire from administration officials and other Republicans who said that, even if new aid was warranted, it should not come from cutting defense.

"I think it's way too premature," said Bush. "I'm not going to go out there and say we can afford to cut defense."

Defense Secretary Dick Cheney, in an Aug. 29 speech, underscored the uncertainty about the Soviet future: "Five years from now, who will control the Soviet nuclear arsenal? Will there still be a central government in charge?"

Critics also argued that Aspin's proposal would violate the 1990 budget agreement, which set limits on three categories of spending — defense, foreign and domestic — and barred transferring funds among them.

Other Democrats said that, if the budget deal was renegotiated, it should be to benefit domestic spending. "I don't think we should do anything for the Soviets until we take care of our own," said Bonior, who was elected by Democratic colleagues to take over as House majority whip in September, succeeding William H. Gray III, D-Pa., who had resigned from Congress.

But Aspin insisted his plan would not violate the budget deal or require its revamping: "This is defense by different means, but defense nevertheless, so it should come out of the Pentagon budget."

Baltic Independence

For years, Congress had routinely approved symbolic resolutions calling for the independence of the Baltic States, with little hope that those calls would ever be heeded.

In a typical example, the fiscal 1983 defense authorization bill (PL 92-252) required that maps prepared or bought by the Pentagon show the Baltics as independent.

Such gestures seemed both quaint and prophetic by the fall of 1991. On Sept. 2, a long-held hope among supporters of Baltic nationhood became a reality as Bush announced U.S. recognition of Baltic independence.

And on Sept. 6, in its first official act, the newly formed Soviet State Council voted to grant independence to Estonia, Latvia and Lithuania. The council was established, at Gorbachev's urging, to lead a new union of republics.

The euphoria among supporters of the Baltic States in Congress swept away any lingering bitterness that Bush had not moved more quickly to grant recognition.

"The delay was totally unnecessary," said Rep. Richard J. Durbin, D-Ill. "But we have to put that behind us."

At least initially, aid plans being floated for the Baltic nations fell into the million — not billion — dollar range.

"We need to provide whatever credit and loans we can, but not gifts — those people don't want gifts," said Rep. Gerald B. H. Solomon, R-N.Y., another veteran Baltics supporter.

Later in the year, Congress approved legislation that included most-favored-nation trade status for the Baltic nations. *(Soviet trade status, p. 125)*

On Sept. 27, Bush recognized the epochal change in U.S.-Soviet relations by proposing significant cutbacks — some of them unilateral — in the U.S. nuclear arsenal.

An Aid Package Failed

Mounting pressure to give domestic needs priority over foreign policy doomed Aspin's $1 billion proposal for the Pentagon to provide assistance to the Soviet Union.

Bipartisan opposition greeted the provision when House-Senate conferees sought to write it into the fiscal 1992 defense authorization bill (HR 2100).

The architects of the aid provision — House Armed Services Committee Chairman Aspin and Senate Armed Services Committee Chairman Sam Nunn, D-Ga. — touted it as a pragmatic effort to head off national security nightmares that were latent in the Soviet Union's domestic turmoil.

"What we're trying to do with this billion dollars is make sure that the reform movement in the Soviet Union sticks," an embattled Aspin said Nov. 6. "It's important because of the potential for chaos in a country with just under 30,000 nuclear weapons."

But work on the annual defense bill concluded as Washington was embroiled in a frenzied search for ways to aid the troubled domestic economy. Democrats were accusing Bush of caring more about other countries than about unemployed Americans, and Republicans were determined to show that they, too, cared most about those in this country.

"Let us look at people in our states, the laid-off defense workers. What about retraining them?" Sen. Alfonse M. D'Amato, R-N.Y., said Nov. 7. He called the Soviet aid plan "shameful."

Nunn and Aspin sought in vain to recruit admininstration support for their plan. "What we're looking for," said Aspin, "is an endorsement [by Bush] . . . to get votes for it among Republicans or at least get the Republicans to keep quiet."

The administration's response was tepid at best. Defense Secretary Cheney said the administration could accept the provision because Bush would retain full discretion over how much defense money, if any, to spend on Soviet aid.

On Nov. 13, Aspin and Nunn dropped their Soviet aid plan from the defense authorization bill after their final pleas for White House support had gone unanswered. They blamed the growing America-first sentiment.

"There was a sea change in terms of the U.S. economy," said Aspin. "It was a feeling, as much as it was statistics coming in, that the economy had stalled out."

Nunn was less philosophical in defeat, blasting the rejection of the Soviet aid provision as shortsighted. "I can't think of a better way to 'take care of your own' than by reducing the threat of [weapons] proliferation around the world," he told the Senate Nov. 13. "We are sitting back on our hands, waiting for there to be great public demand to take steps that anyone with common sense would understand should be taken now."

On Nov. 20, as the situation in the Soviet Union continued to deteriorate, Bush announced an additional $1.25 billon in agricultural credits.

AN AID PACKAGE SUCCEEDED

After pondering the breakup of the Soviet Union for most of 1991, lawmakers waited until adjournment day, Nov. 27, to clear authorizing legislation (HR 3807) and a supplemental appropriation (H J Res 157) that made available up to $500 million for Soviet assistance.

The congressional package was only a fraction of the massive direct aid that some outside experts had urged. Nonetheless, it represented a sea change of attitudes from only weeks earlier, when Nunn and Aspin were forced to abandon the $1 billion aid plan that they had attempted to write into the defense authorization bill.

The measures that succeeded where Nunn and Aspin had initially failed gave the president the authority to use up to $400 million in defense funding to help the former Soviet Union dismantle its nuclear arsenal. The president also was given authority to use up to $100 million in defense funds to provide U.S. military or commercial transport for emergency food, medical and other humanitarian aid.

Senior senators — concerned that domestic politics were playing havoc with long-term national security interests — pressed hard in the final days of the session to enact the trimmed-down plan.

They did it with minimal White House support and against a strong anti-foreign-aid tide that was sweeping Congress. In the end, they convinced colleagues that failure to act could prove devastating if instability in the Soviet Union loosened controls over that country's nuclear arsenal.

"It is not foreign aid; it is self-defense," said Nunn. "I cannot think of a better way to help the American people than reducing the potential military threat that we will have to face in the years ahead."

Nunn said that the threat could come not only from within the Soviet Union but from around the world if Soviet weapons and know-how were sold or stolen by an increasingly disorganized and desperate people.

Jim Exon, D-Neb., added: "A hungry bear who has lost control of its nuclear devices is a very dangerous bear."

Some lawmakers said they were fearful that the United States might be duped into providing the aid, only to have the Soviet Union turn around and build newer weapons.

"What worries me is that the taxpayer is being asked to foot a bill that ultimately will be directed, or could ultimately be directed, against him," said Sen. Malcolm Wallop, R-Wyo.

But sponsors noted that before the demilitarization assistance could be provided, the president would have to certify to Congress that the recipient was making a "substantial investment" of its own in dismantling weapons and was not undergoing a major military modernization program.

"This is one time when the Congress of the United States should have some faith and confidence in the president of the United States," Nunn said. He and others who worked on the plan were unable to get the administration to take a public position on the proposal, although they said they were privately encouraged to press ahead.

Republicans said the administration kept a low profile to avoid Democratic complaints that President Bush devoted too much attention to foreign affairs and not enough to pressing domestic concerns. Senate Minority Leader Dole said Bush was "getting a little tender from being beaten up for trying to be of help to people who are in need overseas, and I hope this debate and this vote may end some of that unfair criticism."

But some Democrats said Bush should have been out front on both domestic and foreign issues, instead of devoting attention to one to the exclusion of the other.

Sen. Patrick J. Leahy, D-Vt., said there should at least "be a postcard from the White House saying it is a good idea."

The demilitarization aid was proposed in the Senate on Nov. 25 as an amendment by Nunn and Richard G. Lugar, R-Ind., to legislation (HR 3807) authorizing the transfer to NATO allies of equipment to be disposed of under the CFE treaty.

The amendment, approved by a vote of 86-8, called for up to $500 million to dismantle the Soviet arsenal. *(Vote 274, p. 36-S)*

Another amendment to HR 3807 called for up to $200 million in emergency transport authority for humanitarian assistance. The provision, proposed by David L. Boren, D-Okla., and William S. Cohen, R-Maine, was approved, 87-7. *(Vote 275, p. 36-S)*

But conferees on a fiscal 1992 supplemental appropriations bill (H J Res 157), which provided the funding authority for the plan, lowered the maximum amount for demilitarization aid to $400 million and the amount for humanitarian assistance to $100 million. *(1992 supplemental, p. 661)*

The House, whose leaders had introduced a broader, $1 billion aid package on Nov. 22, approved the Senate proposal early Nov. 27 by voice vote. However, the House amended HR 3807 to lower the aid figures to those provided in the supplemental appropriations bill.

The Senate cleared the amended, $500 million bill by

voice vote late in the day.

On Dec. 8, the leaders of Russia, Ukraine and Belarus joined in a new Commonwealth of Independent States and proclaimed that the Soviet Union no longer existed. Russian President Yeltsin gathered support from other republics as Gorbachev threatened to resign.

President Bush signed HR 3807, which authorized the Soviet aid, on Dec. 12 (PL 102-228). The same day, he signed the supplemental appropriations bill (H J Res 157 — PL 102-229) that provided funds for the Soviet assistance. On Dec. 12, Secretary of State Baker announced that "the administration is prepared to draw upon" the $500 million package provided by Congress.

Baker's speech represented a tone of increased urgency toward U.S. involvement in support of change in the former Soviet Union.

"We are not the leaders of this revolution, but neither are we mere bystanders," Baker said in the speech at Princeton University. "But the time for action is short. Much as we will benefit if this revolution succeeds, we will pay if it fails.... History is giving no one a breathing space."

Baker also invited world leaders to a conference in Washington to coordinate aid, and he announced that the administration would ask for $100 million in technical assistance to support Soviet economic reform. (In January 1992, Bush expanded the request, seeking $620 million in new budget authority over two years for technical and humanitarian aid for the former Soviet republics.)

Calling Baker's speech "a qualitative step forward," House Armed Services Chairman Aspin said, "Until this announcement, the administration's response to the opportunities and dangers of the post-coup former Soviet Union has been tepid and piecemeal."

House Majority Leader Gephardt said, "These modest measures are steps in the right direction, but, given the enormity of the crisis, more explanations are needed, and more actions may be necessary."

On Dec. 25, Gorbachev resigned from office, and the Soviet flag was lowered at the Kremlin, marking the end of an empire and sealing the close of the Cold War. ■

Foreign Aid Bill Falls; Domestic Need Cited

In an America-first backlash against foreign aid that transcended partisan and ideological divisions, the House on Oct. 30 defeated the conference report for the foreign assistance authorization act.

The lawmakers rebuffed a $25 billion measure (HR 2508) that had progressed further than any such bill since 1985, the last time a foreign aid authorization bill was enacted.

Despite epochal changes in the world — from the collapse of the Soviet Union to peace talks for the Middle East — Congress ended 1991 without clearing any broad foreign assistance legislation. In addition to spurning the authorization measure, Congress deferred action until 1992 on a foreign operations appropriations bill after President Bush requested a delay in action on Israel's request for $10 billion in loan guarantees. Foreign aid programs were funded through a short-term continuing resolution. *(Appropriation, p. 646)*

The authorization bill's prospects had been fragile even before the House rejection. Bush had vowed to veto it on several grounds, including provisions that would have overturned restrictions on aid to international family planning organizations that promoted abortion as a method of family planning.

Despite the measure's ultimate failure, its progress through Congress during 1991 provided significant signposts of lawmakers' attitudes toward foreign aid in particular and toward the historic changes in the world more generally.

HOUSE COMMITTEE ACTION

Bush attempted to frame the year's debate on foreign aid by proposing to streamline the foreign aid authorization process — and to give the chief executive the maximum possible leeway in choosing where to channel funds.

Bush's proposed International Cooperation Act of 1991 would have significantly streamlined foreign aid by consolidating development assistance in a single account and removing restrictions from many aid programs. The centerpiece of the administration's plan would have been the virtual elimination of earmarks, Congress' mandating of foreign aid funds for particular countries and purposes. In a letter to congressional leaders April 12, Bush said, "The law governing foreign assistance has become so complex, splintered and restrictive that it no longer serves our national interest."

No one on Capitol Hill disputed the idea that the Foreign Assistance Act of 1961 (PL 87-195) that governed foreign aid was an unwieldy vehicle for providing aid abroad in the post-Cold War era. But when lawmakers heard pleas from the administration for greater flexibility, they assumed that it would come at the expense of congressional power. *(1961 Almanac, p. 293)*

In fact, Bush's letter pulled no punches: "The restitution of presidential authorities would extend to all aspects of the proposed legislation."

Once they received the president's plan, members largely ignored it. Lawmakers engaged in their customary practice of asserting a role in foreign policy by earmarking funds or attaching tough conditions to aid.

Aid for Turkey

In the case of Turkey, the administration wanted to reward the government of President Turgut Ozal for its key role as a strategically situated ally in the Persian Gulf War against Iraq. At a time of little growth in the foreign aid budget, the State Department requested an increase of $125 million, or 25 percent, over fiscal 1991 in military grant assistance for Turkey.

But Lee H. Hamilton, D-Ind., chairman of the House Foreign Affairs Subcommittee on Europe and the Middle East, concerned over the rapid growth in military aid for Turkey, pressed instead to provide more economic assistance to Istanbul.

In his draft bill, the subcommittee chairman substantially altered the administration request, keeping military grant aid at its prior-year level of $500 million and raising economic support fund aid from $75.4 million to $190.4 million.

Hamilton also had other motives, and they went to the heart of the president's complaint of congressional "micromanagement" of foreign aid. For several years Congress had kept military aid at a ratio of $7 to Greece for every $10 provided to Turkey. The changes proposed by Hamilton and approved by the subcommittee on April 17 were designed to keep aid for the historical adversaries in that approximate balance.

BOXSCORE

➡ **Fiscal 1992-93 foreign aid authorization (HR 2508).** The two-year authorization bill would have been the first enacted since 1985. But in a backlash against foreign aid in a time of domestic economic troubles, the House rejected final approval of the measure.

Reports: H Rept 102-96; S Rept 102-100; H Rept 102-225.

KEY ACTION

June 20 — The **House** passed HR 2508, 274-138.

July 26 — The **Senate** passed HR 2508, 74-18.

Oct. 8 — The **Senate** approved the conference report on HR 2508, 61-38.

Oct. 30 — The **House** rejected the conference report, 159-262.

Limits on Pakistan

Another subcommittee chairman, Stephen J. Solarz, D-N.Y., of the Asian and Pacific Affairs panel, rebuffed a presidential request to lift restrictions on aid to Pakistan.

The Pressler amendment to the Foreign Assistance Act of 1985 (PL 99-83), named for Sen. Larry Pressler, R-S.D., barred aid for Pakistan unless the president certified that the government did not possess nuclear weapons. Bush was unable to make the certification in 1990 because of evidence that Pakistan was continuing to develop its nuclear potential, and aid to Pakistan was suspended that October. *(1990 Almanac, p. 768)*

Although Bush's proposal to revise foreign aid would have scrapped the Pressler amendment, the president added that it would remain the "essential basis" for administration policy toward Pakistan.

The pledge had no appreciable effect on Solarz, who drafted language to apportion the $260 million in aid requested for Pakistan to other nations unless the president made the certification by the start of the next fiscal year.

Foreign Affairs Committee Chairman Dante B. Fascell, D-Fla., fearing that a fight over earmarks could stop the process before it really started, deferred consideration of the president's proposal to eliminate them..

At a committee markup on May 9, ranking Republican William S. Broomfield, Mich., tried to get the panel to split the aid package into two bills. He warned that the panel was on the verge of becoming "irrelevant in the foreign aid process."

One bill would have included what Broomfield called the core elements of aid, including economic assistance and military sales. The other would have included most of the earmarks specifying how U.S. aid should be spent.

Without substantial revisions, Broomfield said, "Our legislation has little chance of moving beyond the markup." But the amendment was rejected by voice vote after Fascell said the plan would not have the support of most House Democrats.

Family Planning Disputes

By mid-May, the full Foreign Affairs Committee had completed consideration of only two of the authorization bill's 10 titles. But it was already burdened with provisions sufficient to garner a veto.

The panel approved amendments to scrap U.S. restrictions on funding abortions overseas. Bush repeatedly had stated he would veto any bill that lifted the restrictions.

On May 9, the panel adopted an amendment by Peter H. Kostmayer, D-Pa., that called for setting aside $300 million to assist U.S. and foreign nonprofit family planning programs.

Then, the panel adopted another, potentially fatal amendment to earmark $20 million of the funds for the U.N. Population Fund (formerly the U.N. Fund for Population Activities), which gave family planning assistance to about 140 developing nations.

Abortion foes Christopher H. Smith, R-N.J., and Henry J. Hyde, R-Ill., opposed the amendment because the U.N. fund operated in China, which had been condemned for forced abortions and sterilizations. The Reagan and Bush administrations opposed any funds to the U.N. agency on that basis, and Smith warned that Bush would veto a bill that supported the U.N. fund.

Kostmayer's language prohibited the United Nations from using U.S. funds for programs in China, but Smith said any financial support would free other money to go to that country.

On May 14, the committee approved by voice vote an amendment to overturn the so-called Mexico City policy, which imposed restrictions on U.S. aid to family planning organizations abroad.

Named for the 1984 conference at which it was unveiled, the Mexico City policy "prohibits Agency for International Development [AID] funds from being given to foreign non-governmental organizations who provide or promote abortion as a method of family planning," according to Duff G. Gillespie, AID's director for population programs.

Rep. Jan Meyers, R-Kan., who offered the amendment to eliminate the restriction, said she realized that her amendment could result in the veto of the bill. "The president has to do what he has to do," said Meyers, usually a staunch supporter of the administration, "and I have to do what I have to do."

Arms Proliferation Debate

Proposals to stem the relentless flow of weapons into the Middle East proliferated in the 102nd Congress. On May 23 the Foreign Affairs Committee became the first panel to approve an arms control plan, as it passed an amendment to the authorization bill.

Several members sharply criticized the administration for moving too slowly on non-proliferation.

The Foreign Affairs Committee's proposal, similar to several bipartisan plans in both chambers, called for the administration to declare a unilateral, open-ended moratorium on arms transfers to the region. During the moratorium, the United States and other weapons exporters would have negotiated more permanent restraints.

The committee's proposal, spearheaded by Chairman Fascell, would have lifted the moratorium if the president determined that "another major arms supplier nation" had concluded an agreement to provide "major" military equipment to a country in the Middle East or Persian Gulf.

The committee also rejected an amendment by Hyde to scrap the Pressler amendment that permitted aid to Pakistan only if the president certified that Islamabad did not possess nuclear weapons.

Hyde said punishing Pakistan while aiding other potential nuclear powers represented a double standard. In one of the panel's few recorded votes, the Hyde amendment was defeated, 8-13, with members split along partisan lines. The committee then rejected, by voice vote, an amendment by Robert J. Lagomarsino, R-Calif., which would have exempted development aid from the Pressler amendment.

Turkey's Aid Cut

The full committee supported a reduction in the administration's military aid request to Turkey, as recommended by the Subcommittee on Europe and the Middle East, and approved several amendments that could have affected U.S. relations with nations in the Middle East.

Solarz again assumed center stage in the debate over aid to Turkey, supporting the administration's argument that the Ozal government earned increased military assistance by vigorously supporting the war against Iraq.

The New York Democrat offered an amendment to restore the aid levels the administration originally requested. Cutting aid to Ankara would be "a slap in the face," Solarz said.

But Solarz's amendment was rejected by voice vote, as the panel's members were far more concerned with the impact increased military assistance for Turkey could have on another U.S. ally, Greece.

Mideast Amendments

To no one's surprise, the Foreign Affairs panel continued to earmark aid for the recipients of the most U.S. assistance, Egypt and Israel. The committee approved $2.5 billion in military and economic aid for Egypt and $3 billion for Israel for fiscal 1992 — about the same as in fiscal 1991. But it did propose to raise military assistance for Israel by $200 million in fiscal 1993.

The committee also retained restrictions, added at the subcommittee level, on contacts between U.S. officials and members of the Palestine Liberation Organization. And the panel approved sense of Congress language urging the administration to persuade "Arab coalition partners" to lift their economic boycott against Israel.

Kostmayer offered a provision, which the committee approved by voice vote, to condition arms sales to Kuwait on the emirate's institution of democratic reforms in the aftermath of the Persian Gulf War.

Kostmayer said he was responding to trials of residents of Kuwait who allegedly collaborated with Iraq during the war, especially the "outrageous" case of one man who reportedly received a 15-year sentence for wearing a T-shirt with the picture of Iraqi President Saddam Hussein.

When one lawmaker said such a measure could offend the emir of Kuwait, Kostmayer fired back, "I'd like to offend him."

Other Committee Action

Despite the administration's campaign against earmarks, conservative Smith of New Jersey won passage of an amendment to earmark $265 million for international health and child-survival programs.

The administration received some unanticipated cooperation from Democrats, however. The liberal chairman of the Africa Subcommittee, Mervyn M. Dymally, D-Calif., withdrew many of the earmarks on the Africa Development Fund that his panel had added. The full committee approved Dymally's proposal to raise the amount of aid to be provided the fund from $800 million to $1 billion in fiscal 1992.

As the Foreign Affairs Committee approved the foreign aid bill by voice vote on June 4, a bipartisan agreement was emerging to defer the contentious issue of military aid to El Salvador, pending the outcome of peace talks aimed at resolving that country's long-running civil war.

The chairman of the Rules Committee, Joe Moakley, D-Mass., announced Democratic support for postponement on June 6, when his panel took up a rule for floor debate on the foreign aid authorization bill. At the same time he urged the administration to continue to forgo providing $42.5 million in fiscal 1991 assistance that had not yet been spent.

In a letter on June 5 outlining the unusual arrangement, Moakley and 98 other House members asked Bush "to join us in not rocking the boat at this delicate stage in the peace process."

SENATE COMMITTEE ACTION

Even before the Senate Foreign Relations Committee began to frame its fiscal 1992 foreign aid measure, the committee confronted its own record of failure. Under the leadership of Claiborne Pell, D-R.I., and Jesse Helms, N.C., the ranking Republican, the Foreign Relations Committee had fallen on hard times.

On Capitol Hill, the ideologically diverse panel was recognized more for its failure to gain quorums at meetings than as a force in setting foreign policy. Frustrated by the panel's continuing weakness, its Democrats persuaded Pell to cede some legislative authority to its subcommittees.

At the panel's opening session Jan. 29, Pell announced that, because of a "heavier than usual" workload, he intended to make greater use of the subcommittees. For the first time, they were to be staffed independently and to mark up bills, a function that had been the exclusive province of the full committee.

But a veteran member of the committee said that Pell, under pressure from committee Democrats, had little choice other than to go along with the change. "The Democrats are about to divide up his domain," Richard G. Lugar, R-Ind., said shortly before the committee met.

Joseph R. Biden Jr., D-Del., chairman of the Subcommittee on European Affairs, said he presented the proposal for change to Pell. Biden declined to say whether the action was taken because of the problems in moving legislation through the full committee. "After two craniotomies, I've learned that there are some questions I shouldn't answer," quipped Biden, who twice underwent surgery for a brain aneurysm in 1988.

But Lugar addressed the sensitive topic: "Claiborne has not had strong views as to what ought to occur, and Jesse has been very adept at stymieing even those views that [Pell] has."

Although Pell defended the committee and its legislative productivity, committee member Mitch McConnell, R-Ky., said, "There is a widespread feeling on both the committee and throughout the Congress that the committee doesn't have the prestige it once had even 10 or 12 years ago."

The new subcommittee arrangement withstood its first test on June 5, when its Subcommittee on International

Economic Policy, by a 9-0 vote, approved a draft bill authorizing foreign aid.

But the subcommittee deferred consideration of virtually all contentious issues to the full committee.

Like the House committee's bill, the Senate draft legislation called for reducing the Bush administration's request for $625 million in military grant aid to Turkey for fiscal 1992 by $125 million.

In addition, it proposed a ban on new U.S. arms sales to the Middle East for 60 days after enactment of the bill unless the president certified that the administration had undertaken "good-faith efforts" toward negotiating proliferation controls with other major weapons suppliers.

The Senate bill — again like the House legislation — called for overturning the administration's Mexico City policy, which prohibited aid for family planning organizations that supported abortion overseas.

Yet there were elements of the Senate draft bill that the administration clearly welcomed.

Both the chairman of the subcommittee, Paul S. Sarbanes, D-Md., and the ranking Republican, McConnell, said they had made a concerted effort to heed the administration's request to omit the numerous report requirements and earmarks that had been attached to past foreign aid bills. "I see a little more change from business as usual," McConnell said.

Even Helms praised a provision authorizing aid for Eastern Europe and the Soviet Union. In 1990, the senior senator from North Carolina almost single-handedly held up a Support for East European Democracy bill (S 2944) because it would have authorized the president to provide technical aid to the Soviet Union. *(1990 Almanac, p. 207)*

The Senate subcommittee's bill took a different approach. Although it would have authorized aid for "all nations of Europe that experienced communist rule after World War II" — which could encompass the Soviet Union — there was no specific mention of assistance for Moscow.

The legislation would have authorized $20 million for the Agency for International Development to furnish humanitarian aid "for the relief of the Estonian, Latvian and Lithuanian peoples."

The full Foreign Relations Committee approved the authorization measure on June 11 by a 17-2 vote. But the pride of accomplishment was shadowed by the realization that the measure could be doomed by the provision touching on the sensitive issue of abortion.

At the full committee markup on June 11, an amendment striking the provision requiring repeal of the Mexico City policy, offered by Helms, was defeated, 6-13.

In a letter to House and Senate leaders on June 4, Bush had put Congress on warning that he would veto "any legislation that weakens current law or existing regulations" on abortion, including the law that he said "prohibits contributions to international organizations that fund coercive abortion programs."

HOUSE FLOOR ACTION

The House approved the foreign aid bill (HR 2508), 274-138, on June 20. The measure would have authorized $12.4 billion for fiscal 1992 and $13 billion for fiscal 1993. *(Vote 185, p. 46-H)*

Floor action on the bill produced a few surprises. Barred by law from receiving U.S. assistance, the government of Pakistan won a significant symbolic victory June 13, when the House voted to slap similar economic sanctions on India, its chief rival in South Asia.

By a surprising 242-141 vote, the House approved an amendment from an unlikely alliance of lawmakers to prohibit U.S. aid for India if it attempted to increase its nuclear arsenal. By an equally lopsided vote of 151-252 on June 12, lawmakers rejected efforts to lift similar conditions that already had led to a cutoff of aid to Pakistan. *(Votes 155, 151, p. 38-H)*

The administration had requested $259.5 million for Pakistan in fiscal 1992.

For India, which reportedly detonated its first nuclear device in 1974, the cost of continuing a nuclear program would not be as steep, even if the congressional restriction were enacted. The administration requested $22 million in development aid for India in 1992; an additional $77.6 million in food aid would not have been affected.

Many House members voted for both measures out of "a sense of fairness," said Robert J. Lagomarsino, R-Calif. He cosponsored the amendment to make aid to India conditional with Charles Wilson, D-Texas, Pakistan's most tireless congressional supporter. Kostmayer added language to slightly ease the conditions.

But lawmakers had other motivations as well. Supporters of Pakistan, stung by the resounding defeat of the amendment offered by Hyde, which would have lifted restrictions on aid to Islamabad, redoubled their lobbying efforts on the India amendment.

But Solarz, a strong supporter of India, warned that the amendment could have an impact even if did not become law. The measure was likely to be "seen in India as a [U.S.] tilt toward China," Solarz said. Chinese troops attacked India in 1962.

Abortion Debate

The debate over India and Pakistan, while lively at times, had only a fraction of the intensity of the wrangling over abortion and family planning.

Smith, leading the anti-abortion forces in the House, targeted two provisions that had been approved by the Foreign Affairs Committee. He proposed stripping $20 million from the bill for the U.N. Population Fund because it had been condemned for operating in China, which had a record of forced abortions.

And he attempted to eliminate the language repealing the Mexico City policy, arguing that it had not interfered with U.S. support for family planning. "The United States remains the leading donor of population aid in the world," he said.

Opponents of the Mexico City policy attacked what they termed "an international gag rule" on abortion. Rep. John Porter, R-Ill., charged that the policy prevented organizations from using their own funds "to even tell a woman she has the option of choosing an abortion."

Kostmayer blocked Smith's effort to eliminate money for the U.N. fund by offering a substitute amendment, which carried, 234-188. Then, a substitute by Howard L. Berman, D-Calif., overturning Smith's amendment to revive the Mexico City policy, was approved, 222-200. *(Votes 148, 149, p. 36-H)*

Abortion rights activists were encouraged by the vote margins, noting that in 1990, Smith had won approval for an amendment to the foreign aid appropriations bill striking aid to the U.N. fund. *(1990 Almanac, p. 838)*

But Smith said in an interview, "What we have proven in the endgame here is that we can sustain a veto."

The House fended off an effort to remove from the bill

another provision that also triggered a veto threat: a "cargo preference" requirement.

The provision would have required that countries that received cash transfers of foreign aid spend an equivalent amount to buy U.S. services and goods; half of the goods shipped by sea would have to go on U.S. vessels.

The provision enjoyed strong backing from U.S. maritime interests and their supporters in Congress. Most Midwestern lawmakers, who feared that the provision could cut foreign grain shipments, opposed it.

The House defeated, 175-246, an amendment from Doug Bereuter, R-Neb., to strip the provision from the authorization measure. A similar provision had been put in the Senate version of the foreign aid bill by Foreign Relations Chairman Pell. *(House vote 150, p. 36-H)*

A Message to Jordan

The House also amended the foreign aid bill to punish the government of Jordan for its support of Iraq during the gulf war.

An amendment by John Miller, R-Wash., would have cut off military aid to Jordan unless the president certified that its government demonstrated a willingness to enter into negotiations with Israel, recognized Israel's right to exist and did not provide aid to Iraq. The amendment passed 410-8. *(Vote 170, p. 42-H)*

"The administration is strongly opposed to legislation that would prohibit U.S. assistance to Jordan," State Department spokesman Richard Boucher said June 20.

Boucher indicated that the kingdom probably would not meet the conditions in the measure. The administration had suspended aid to Jordan several months before the House action, but it wanted to retain the option of resuming assistance if the kingdom proved helpful to the Mideast peace process. It eventually restored the aid.

But emotions ran strong in the House concerning the tilt toward Iraq by Jordan's King Hussein during the gulf war. "We had 550,000 young Americans at risk, in harm's way, in the Middle East," said Dan Burton, R-Ind., "and King Hussein was on television giving aid and comfort to the enemy, in my opinion."

On the Republican side, Randy "Duke" Cunningham, Calif., inadvertently weakened an amendment by his colleague Burton that would have terminated all aid for Jordan. Trying to be helpful, the freshman inserted a clause allowing the president to waive the provision if he determined it to be in the national interest. But Cunningham, who favored the aid cutoff, realized belatedly that he had written a loophole into the provision. He tried unsuccessfully to withdraw his amendment, which was approved, 315-105. *(Vote 168, p. 42-H)*

Hamilton attempted to further blunt congressional calls for aid restrictions. He at first appeared to succeed as the House approved, 289-135, his version of language — added to a substitute for the Burton amendment — to give the president a national security waiver. *(Vote 169, p. 42-H)*

But Miller then offered his tougher conditions, which were opposed by only a handful of members.

At the same time, congressional backing for old allies such as Israel apparently had not eroded. An amendment by John Bryant, D-Texas, which would have withheld a portion of Israel's aid unless the president certified that its government was not expanding settlements in its occupied territories, was defeated, 44-378. *(Vote 173, p. 42-H)*

The Bryant amendment would have withheld $82.5 million of the more than $3 billion in aid Israel was due to receive for each of the following two years if the president determined that Israel was investing in "new and expanded" settlements in the West Bank. Bryant said that $82.5 million was the amount that Israel was spending annually on West Bank settlements.

Although Israel's settlement policy had been the target of considerable criticism, most members agreed with H. James Saxton, R-N.J., who charged that the amendment would undermine U.S. relations with Israel, "our only staunch ally in the Middle East."

Addressing lingering issues arising from the gulf war, the House approved by voice vote an amendment criticizing the human rights record of the Kuwaiti leadership and, by 421-1, another urging that Saddam be tried as a war criminal. *(Vote 172, p. 42-H)*

Hard Line on Moscow

Lawmakers also showed that — at least before the failed coup in August that led late in 1991 to the dissolution of the Soviet Union — they had not forgotten a generation of conflict with Moscow. In their actions on the foreign aid bill in June, they piled on amendments setting tough conditions on any potential U.S. assistance to the Soviet central government.

Jon Kyl, R-Ariz., offered an amendment placing stiff conditions on any U.S. aid to the Soviet Union. But the Kyl amendment also included a waiver of the conditions if the president determined it to be in the national interest — an escape hatch that perhaps freed lawmakers from any reluctance to add further restrictions on Soviet aid.

The original Kyl amendment would have barred any direct aid to the central Soviet government unless the president certified that it met a series of conditions, including a halt to modernizing its strategic forces and the end of support for nations "engaged in activities inimical to the national interests of the United States."

Then, Richard J. Durbin, D-Ill., attached a condition that Moscow return all buildings that Soviet forces were occupying in the Baltic States to "their lawful owners."

Hamilton complained that "those conditions simply cannot be met."

He supported an amendment by Harry A. Johnston, D-Fla., that would have substituted a sense of Congress resolution for the binding Kyl amendment. In an interview, Johnston referred to the numerous attempts to add tougher aid restrictions as a "shark frenzy."

But the House voted down Johnston's weakening substitute, 130-286, and passed the Kyl amendment, with all of its restrictions on aid, 374-41. Even liberals such as Barney Frank, D-Mass., supported the tough-on-Moscow conditions. *(Votes 175, 176, p. 44-H)*

Mandela and Communists

The House also approved an amendment targeting the African National Congress (ANC), the South African anti-apartheid organization led by Nelson Mandela, for its ties with that country's Communist Party. *(South Africa, p. 478)*

But the hastily drafted amendment was undermined by an embarrassing blunder.

The amendment offered by Mervyn M. Dymally, D-Calif., was intended to permit aid to the ANC as a "democratic" organization. Democrats flocked to vote for the measure. Then, it was discovered that the misdrafted amendment, prepared with the help of Solarz, would have done the opposite by permitting U.S. assistance only to organizations that "do not have in place democratic processes."

Democrats lined up to change their votes rather than be on record as opposing democracy, no matter how inadvertently.

Although Dymally later won approval by voice vote for a corrected version of the botched amendment, his efforts were superseded by House approval of an amendment by Republicans Robert S. Walker, Pa., and Burton barring aid to South African groups "affiliated or associated with the Communist Party."

The amendment, which passed 279-134, could have prohibited U.S. assistance for the ANC. The organization had been allied with the South African Communist Party in the struggle against apartheid, although members of Congress disagreed over whether the ANC was "affiliated" with the Communist Party. *(Vote 182, p. 44-H; vote 183, p. 46-H)*

The House also demonstrated the customary skepticism over foreign aid programs generally, approving an amendment by Toby Roth, R-Wis., to cancel the authority to use foreign aid funds that have been approved but not yet expended. The amendment passed 216-203. *(Vote 167, p. 42-H)*

The day after House approval of the foreign aid bill, the State Department's Boucher said that the bill "falls well short" of Bush's goals for foreign aid and that senior aides would "recommend a veto of the bill in its present form."

SENATE FLOOR ACTION

On July 26, the Senate managed a feat that it had not accomplished since Ronald Reagan was just starting his second term as president: passage of a foreign aid authorization bill.

Defying predictions from both lawmakers and Bush administration officials that the bill would never pass, the Senate approved, 74-18, a measure (HR 2508) that would have authorized slightly more than $14 billion in foreign aid for each of the following two fiscal years. *(Vote 153, p. 38-H)*

But the Senate bill, like the foreign aid authorization measure passed by the House in June, included several provisions that appeared nearly certain to trigger a veto.

Nonetheless, in action on their amendments to the bill, Senate Democrats mounted a strong challenge to Bush administration policies on international family planning and military aid for El Salvador. While the Democrats did not appear capable of overriding vetoes, they demonstrated solid majorities on both issues.

In a victory for abortion rights advocates, the Senate voted to close debate — eliminating the threat of a filibuster — on an amendment from Paul Simon, D-Ill., to provide $20 million in assistance for the U.N. Population Fund.

The administration had denied funding for the agency because it operated in China, which had been condemned for its policy of coerced abortions. The Senate approved the cloture motion on the Simon amendment, 63-33, on July 25. *(Vote 151, p. 20-S)*

Members then became mired in lengthy procedural wrangling over the amendment, which nearly scuttled the authorization measure.

Middle East Maneuvers

Left with no opportunity to filibuster Simon's amendment, Jesse Helms, R-N.C., offered a potentially explosive amendment expressing the Senate's opposition to linking U.S. aid for Israel to that government's policy of establishing settlements in occupied territory.

With the administration embroiled at the time in negotiations that led to the convening of a Middle East peace conference, members from both parties had fears about the amendment's timing. *(Mideast talks, p. 460)*

Joseph R. Biden Jr., D-Del., then proposed another highly controversial amendment on the Middle East. His measure would have made any future arms sales to wealthy Middle East countries contingent on their implementation of democratic reforms and contributions to the region's economic development.

Some Republicans criticized Biden's proposal, complaining that his "report card" for regional governments could also upset administration negotiating efforts.

But in a signal of congressional dissatisfaction over reports of postwar human rights abuses in Kuwait, members from both parties joined to defeat a motion to table (kill) Biden's amendment, 39-57. *(Vote 152, p. 20-S)*

With the possibility of a filibuster looming on both amendments, Biden and Helms — who insisted that he had the votes to pass his amendment — heeded the pleas of party leaders and dropped their measures. That finally cleared the way for Simon's amendment on family planning funds to be approved, by voice vote.

El Salvador Debate

Despite a strong lobbying effort from top administration officials and from El Salvador President Alfredo Cristiani, Republicans failed in a motion to kill an amendment that would have withheld half of the $85 million military aid package for El Salvador for fiscal 1992, as well as half of the military assistance that had already been approved for that country but not yet delivered.

The motion to table (kill) the amendment by Democrats Christopher J. Dodd, Conn., and Patrick J. Leahy, Vt., failed, 43-56, with the vote largely split along party lines. *(Vote 148, p. 20-S)*

Dodd and Leahy subsequently withdrew their amendment in the face of a Republican filibuster, but they claimed a symbolic victory.

The House had previously agreed to an administration request to postpone the question of military aid for El Salvador until September.

The administration initially had viewed the Senate's foreign aid authorization bill as a slight improvement over the House-passed version. According to administration officials, the legislation approved by the Foreign Relations Committee contained fewer earmarks and congressional restrictions than the House measure.

But as senators piled on policy amendments, the bill became less and less acceptable to the administration. And no proposal drew more opposition from the White House than the Dodd-Leahy amendment on El Salvador.

The provision was tougher than a similar amendment attached by the two senators to the fiscal 1991 foreign aid appropriations bill (PL 101-513), which also was devised to pressure both sides to seek peace in that country's decade-old civil war. *(1990 Almanac, p. 779)*

While that amendment withheld half of the administration's military aid request, it allowed the president to lift the restrictions if he determined that the country's anti-government guerrillas were violating the bill's conditions.

Bush did just that in January, and he announced in June that the State Department once again would begin expending the assistance. Dodd and Leahy crafted their amendment to the 1992 authorization bill to ensure that the administration would have to seek congressional assent before once again lifting conditions on the assistance.

The debate had echoes from the highly partisan battles over military aid for El Salvador during the mid-1980s. Minority Leader Bob Dole, R-Kan., said sarcastically that the Democratic proponents of the amendment were "some of the great strategists who helped us in Nicaragua and the [Persian] Gulf crisis."

But Dodd insisted that the restrictions approved in the 1991 appropriations bill had "some very real success" in spurring both sides to negotiate. Several Democrats argued that the conditions should be retained as long as El Salvador failed to make progress in prosecuting the murders of six Jesuit priests in 1989.

In the end, both sides could claim a limited victory: Through their filibuster, led by John McCain, Ariz., Republicans prevented the amendment from being adopted. A motion to invoke cloture in the debate drew 52 votes, eight short of the required 60. *(Vote 150, p. 20-S)*

But Senate Democrats demonstrated that they had majority support for tough conditions on the military aid program, even when developments in El Salvador were no longer front-page news.

Doubting Soviet Aid

Senators proved to be just as resistant in July to the notion of providing aid for the Soviet Union as their House counterparts had been in debating their version of the bill in June.

A Helms amendment to bar any U.S. assistance for the Soviet Union unless Moscow cut off its aid to Cuba was approved 98-1. Only California Democrat Alan Cranston, who planned to retire in 1992, voted against the measure. *(Vote 145, p. 20-S)*

The Senate approved by voice vote a more comprehensive measure by Larry Pressler, R-S.D., to apply broad conditions to Soviet aid. The provision was similar to the amendment to the House bill sponsored by Kyl.

Biden, who had called for the United States to support economic reform in the Soviet Union with assistance, said approval of the amendments was "meaningless." Biden scoffed that Helms devised his measure for "a 30-second [television] advertisement."

But the Delaware Democrat nonetheless voted for the amendment.

Yet senators were not skeptical solely about assistance to the Soviet Union. Republicans and Democrats lined up to propose amendments limiting assistance to foreign governments and international organizations.

Hank Brown, R-Colo., offered an amendment to eliminate an administration request for a $12 billion increase in the U.S. quota in the International Monetary Fund (IMF). The Senate rejected the amendment, 31-65. *(Vote 149, p. 20-S)*

And the Senate approved, 99-0, a "Buy American" amendment offered by David L. Boren, D-Okla., to reduce the amount of cash assistance provided to foreign governments and raise the amount of credits that would be expended on U.S. projects and equipment.

As combined with a similar proposal by Joseph I. Lieberman, D-Conn., the amendment would have also increased the amount of foreign aid for capital projects from $573 million to $1 billion by fiscal 1993. The administration had opposed the amendment on the grounds that it would restrict the president's flexibility in providing foreign aid.

Committee's New Strategy

For members of the often-criticized Foreign Relations Committee, just winning passage of a foreign aid authorization bill was far more significant than any of its provisions.

In an unusual twist, neither the committee chairman, Pell, nor the ranking Republican, Helms, managed the bill on the floor.

Sarbanes, chairman of the Subcommittee on International Economic Policy, and McConnell, the subcommittee's ranking Republican, were appointed by Pell and Helms as the floor managers.

In addition to his Middle East amendment, Helms offered a proposal to reduce all categories of aid by 10 percent, using those funds to aid state law enforcement and education programs, but that was killed on a motion to table, 87-12. *(Vote 144, p. 19-S)*

But Pell sat quietly during most of the floor debate. A committee aide said the chairman was pleased with the success of the bill, despite his own limited role in bringing it to fruition.

"He's like a friendly uncle who takes pride in the success of his two nephews," Sarbanes and McConnell, the aide said.

FINAL ACTION

The final version of HR 2508 that was crafted by House-Senate conferees (H Rept 102-225) barely took note of the dramatic changes in the world that unfolded as the measure inched through Congress. And the conferees gave only tentative approval to their handiwork on Sept. 17 because they wanted to continue difficult negotiations on compromises with the White House that would free the bill from a veto threat.

Those negotiations failed to bear fruit, and architects of the bill eventually sought final approval anyway. Some of them expressed hope that after sending Bush a bill that he would veto, Congress could quickly pass a version of the bill stripped of provisions unacceptable to the president.

On Oct. 8, the Senate approved the conference report on HR 2508, 61-38. But on Oct. 30, the House rejected the conference report, 159-262. *(Senate vote 219, p. 29-S; House vote 354, p. 86-H)*

Conference Agreement

In their version of the bill, House-Senate conferees granted the president authority to provide at least $15 million under the Support for East European Democracy (SEED) program to the newly independent Baltic States, but they did not authorize aid for other breakaway Soviet republics or the central government in Moscow.

The panel, with no debate, struck a provision in the Senate-passed foreign aid measure that would have authorized assistance for any Eastern European nation that "experienced Communist rule after World War II."

While the administration did not express reservations about the language authorizing Soviet aid, there were concerns that its inclusion could trigger opposition from conservatives.

Despite such efforts to smooth the bill's sharper edges, the prospect of a veto worried members of the Foreign Relations and Foreign Affairs committees, especially senators who had spent most of the year trying to jump-start the foreign aid authorization process. "I hope that we don't lose at the very end," said McConnell, the Republican manager of the bill.

Those concerns produced on-and-off efforts to reach a compromise on the sensitive issue of family planning funds.

Under a compromise engineered by Senate Minority Whip Alan K. Simpson, R-Wyo., the conferees at first eliminated language to repeal the Mexico City policy, which restricted U.S. funding for international family planning organizations. The provision, almost certain to trigger a veto, was in both the House and Senate versions.

The committee retained $20 million in annual assistance for the U.N. Population Fund, another provision that risked a veto.

But as part of the compromise, the conferees specified that any disbursement of U.S. money to the agency would be "subject to the approval of the permanent representative of the United States to the United Nations."

Simpson and the foreign aid conferees insisted that the tightened control would prevent U.S. money from being used for the population fund's activities in China. The administration staunchly opposed funding for the agency because it operated in China, which had a policy of forced abortions.

But conferees and the administration were unable to reach agreement on the family planning issue. The White House rejected the compromise restrictions on aid to the U.N. fund — and the conferees responded during the week of Sept. 23 by restoring the hotly disputed provision to eliminate the "Mexico City language" that restricted aid to family planning organizations.

The conference committee also weakened the amendment to the House bill that would have placed stiff new conditions on U.S. military aid to Jordan.

Conferees agreed to drop some of the restrictions and allow Bush to provide aid if he determined it to be in the national interest. They also watered down a proposal, which had won broad bipartisan backing in both chambers, to restrict new U.S. arms sales to the Middle East.

The committee took similar action with regard to India, dropping the House-passed amendment that would have conditioned aid to that country on the termination of its nuclear weapons program.

And the conference committee, which included members of the House Banking Committee, authorized U.S. contributions to several international organizations, including an increase of $12.2 billion in the U.S. quota in the IMF. The increase had been included in the Senate version of the bill but not in the House version. (The quota fund increase was left in limbo when the authorization bill later perished because Congress did not include the provision in its short-term funding bill for foreign operations appropriations.)

Administration officials said the veto threat loomed partly because the committee retained a Senate provision that, before the conference, nearly everyone was sure would be removed.

The Senate version would have eliminated authority for the administration to provide foreign military assistance in the form of both grants and loans, instead extending only the grant authority.

But administration officials and members of the committee were surprised by the strong resistance against removing the provision from Sarbanes, the Democratic manager of the legislation.

The Senate provision could have directly benefited Greece by requiring the administration to turn its $350 million military aid program, which was a mixture of grants and loans, into an all-grant program.

Sarbanes, a longtime supporter of Greece and the son of Greek immigrants, refused to bow to repeated entreaties from House conferees and administration officials to drop the provision.

In one of the few recorded votes during the conference, House members voted 5-3 to accept the Senate amendment in the final report on the legislation.

The administration also was dissatisfied by the conferees' efforts to water down a "Buy American" provision that had strong backing in both chambers. Deputy Secretary of State Lawrence S. Eagleburger had warned the committee that inclusion of the "cargo preference" provision in the bill "would result in senior advisers recommending a veto."

Both the House and Senate had approved amendments to require countries or governments that received cash transfers of foreign aid to spend an equivalent amount on U.S. goods and services. Half the goods shipped by sea would have to go on U.S. vessels.

The conferees agreed to delay the requirements from taking effect until fiscal 1993 and to phase in the provisions over four years. The committee also exempted Israel.

Senate Approval

The Senate's approval of the conference report on Oct. 8 was largely symbolic in light of Bush's vow to veto the bill for its provisions involving family planning and the insufficient support in the Senate for an override. McConnell, Republican manager of the bill in the Senate, confirmed that the bill passed by that chamber stood little chance of becoming law in the face of a threatened veto.

But in the floor debate on the measure, McConnell said he hoped "at some point we will get the objectionable features out and will have a bill that the president can sign."

House Rejection

The House's vote to reject the conference report on HR 2508 brought together members ranging from hard-line conservatives to the only independent socialist in Congress, Bernard Sanders of Vermont.

While the president's veto threat contributed to the defeat of the conference report, lawmakers clearly were not eager to support a $25 billion foreign aid bill during a domestic recession. Sanders echoed sentiments expressed by many Republicans when he urged his colleagues to "take care of some of the problems that we have at home first."

Democrats also had clear political incentives to oppose the bill. Party leaders had sought to portray Bush as more concerned with foreign policy than with the sluggish U.S. economy.

The Democrats' message would have been undermined by massive support for a foreign aid bill. In debate leading up to the vote, conservative Gerald B. H. Solomon, R-N.Y., challenged Democrats to either oppose what he called a "giveaway" measure or "knock off your criticism of President Bush."

Democrats, who customarily backed foreign aid with solid majorities, responded by supporting the conference report by only four votes, 131-127. In June, party members had backed HR 2508, which was not substantially changed in conference, 196-58.

Howard L. Berman of California, a Democrat who supported the measure, criticized many of his colleagues for taking the view that "the antidote for George Bush's mistakes is a return to isolationism."

But Durbin insisted that in spite of the veto threat, foreign aid was largely an administration initiative. "And many people realize if there's going to be no unemployment benefits for Americans, there will be no foreign aid for President Bush," he said in an interview after the vote.

Perhaps equally important, there was virtually no downside for lawmakers from both parties who heeded the calls to "come home."

Foreign aid funding for the first six months of fiscal 1992 had been ensured with passage of a continuing resolution Oct. 24. Many of the same Democrats who opposed the authorization bill had supported the stopgap appropriations measure.

While a veto had long been assured, anti-abortion Republicans still wanted to kill the bill because of its provisions to assist international family planning organizations.

Henry J. Hyde, R-Ill., said it was a "shame this good bill gets weighted down with abortion language."

Many members also were angered by the inclusion in the conference report of the Senate-passed provision authorizing a $12.2 billion increase in the U.S. quota in the IMF.

Solomon said the IMF quota increase effectively pushed funding in the bill to $37 billion. "That is $37 billion," he said. "A $37 billion monstrosity."

Midwestern lawmakers from both parties objected to the bill's "cargo preference" provision.

Many members from the Midwest said that the provision would result in a loss of U.S. commodity exports by driving up shipping costs.

Noting the strong opposition to the abortion and cargo preference provisions, Jim Leach, R-Iowa, said, "Foreign aid can pass if it has no single-issue red flags and if it's supported by the president."

But those red-flag provisions had been included in HR 2508 when it was approved by the House in June, 274-138. Republicans, who opposed that measure by only 77-80, voted against the conference report by 28-134.

What had changed since June, said many lawmakers, was the U.S. economy.

"What's the big difference? The big difference is the change in the attitude toward domestic issues," said Fascell. "It was almost a free vote."

Most of the members who spoke in behalf of the measure during the House debate cited personal and procedural factors in its favor rather than the substance of the bill.

Fascell urged his colleagues "not to leave everything up to the appropriators and the administration" in setting foreign assistance policy.

Democrats from economically hard-hit regions said they felt loyalty to the Foreign Affairs Committee but that "the committee is in a rut," as Don J. Pease of Ohio put it. Too large a percentage of U.S. foreign aid goes to just a handful of countries, Pease said.

For years, Fascell and other Foreign Affairs members had gained House approval for authorization measures only to watch them die in the Senate.

The defeat of the bill was a devastating setback not only for Fascell's committee but also for the Senate Foreign Relations Committee. Foreign Affairs members who were known for their foreign policy expertise, such as Hamilton and Solarz, were silent during the debate on the measure. Instead, the day belonged to lesser-known critics, such as Toby Roth, R-Wis.

Roth, a longtime opponent of foreign aid, quoted from a stack of letters that he said came from people outraged that Congress would vote to fund programs overseas: "A man in Columbus, Ga., asks, 'Is it better to be buddy-buddy with foreign countries at the expense of the working people in this country?' A woman in Chicago writes, 'No more loans or foreign aid! The American people have had it with our government.' A veteran in Harlingen, Texas, says, 'I am sick of our national lifeblood being squandered on international schemes.' " ■

Sanctions Against South Africa Lifted

In 1986, a nearly united Congress seized control of U.S. policy toward South Africa, imposing economic sanctions over President Ronald Reagan's veto. On July 10, 1991, President Bush lifted those sanctions. Congress was divided over the decision and did not challenge it.

Bush declared that South Africa had met all the requirements of the 1986 Comprehensive Anti-Apartheid Act (PL 99-440) and that President F. W. de Klerk had led his nation on an unalterable march toward abolishing its policies of discrimination against the black majority.

"This is a moment in history which many believed would never be attained," Bush said of South Africa's steps toward ending its policy of racial segregation, apartheid. "I really firmly believe that this progress is irreversible."

Bush's order to lift the sanctions took effect immediately. The president and his supporters predicted that his action would bolster South Africa's economic growth, thereby contributing to an atmosphere for peaceful change.

Supporters had long argued that sanctions were the international community's best method to label South Africa an outlaw state because of its institutionalized racism. But opponents of sanctions had retorted that black South Africans were hit hardest when foreign businesses pulled out.

The South African government's dramatic release of imprisoned black leader Nelson Mandela on Feb. 11, 1990, along with other efforts to dismantle its system of racial separation, had won considerable praise. But no efforts were made by the United States to lift congressionally enacted economic sanctions against the white-minority regime. *(1990 Almanac, p. 787)*

Some members of Congress insisted that 1991 was too early to ease pressure on the South African government and that Bush had acted illegally and improperly by lifting the sanctions.

Rep. John Conyers Jr., D-Mich., said that Bush had strengthened the political position of the white South African government against the wishes of most of the country's black political leaders, who had sought to sustain the sanctions as they conducted talks on political reform.

"This is great news for General Motors and everyone that was doing business" in South Africa, said Conyers. "But what we're doing is shoring up the economic basis of a system of apartheid that can have fateful consequences in the very sensitive period that is now going on."

That view reflected the attitude of African National Congress (ANC) leader Mandela, who spoke to Bush just before the announcement and said the repeal was premature.

Sen. Edward M. Kennedy, D-Mass., decried the sanctions repeal on the Senate floor but afterward said that Congress' hectic schedule would not give critics enough time to challenge Bush's action before Congress adjourned for the year.

The Sanctions

The U.S. sanctions that were lifted included bans on most new corporate investment in South Africa and loans to the Pretoria government, as well as a prohibition on trade between the two countries of products such as uranium ore, iron, steel, textiles and gold coins.

Bush's move also affected a provision that blocked corporations from writing off taxes paid to the South African government. That taxation measure, which Rep. Charles B. Rangel, D-N.Y., attached to the sanctions bill, had been considered an especially potent deterrent to corporate investment in South Africa. *(1986 Almanac p. 359)*

Bush's action solidified an international trend toward easing South Africa's isolation. The European Community in December 1990 lifted its ban on new investment in the country and had moved toward eliminating other trade sanctions. The International Olympic Committee on July 9, 1991, ended a two-decade ban on South African participation in the Olympic Games.

Administration officials emphasized that some sanctions remained, giving them leverage to push for further progress toward racial equality. The continuing sanctions included bans on arms or intelligence deals with the South African military, on most Export-Import Bank loans and on support for International Monetary Fund loans to South Africa.

But congressional critics said the sanctions contained in the 1986 law were a more powerful tool and that removing them prematurely could be a devastating signal.

"We need to understand how fragile this process is," said Howard Wolpe, D-Mich. "If anything were to happen to de Klerk or Mandela, it could be over in a moment."

Meeting the Conditions

Bush said the South African government had met all the conditions for lifting the sanctions, leaving him no choice but to abide by the 1986 law.

The anti-apartheid law had stated that the sanctions would be lifted once five conditions were met. Those conditions were: The government of South Africa must release from prison all persons, including Mandela, prosecuted for their political beliefs or detained unduly without trial; must repeal the state of emergency in effect and must release all detainees held under such state of emergency; must unban democratic political parties and permit free exercise by South Africans of all races of the right to form political parties, express political opinions, and otherwise participate in the political process; must repeal the Group Areas Act and the Population Registration Act and institute no other measures with the same purpose; and must agree to enter into good-faith negotiations with members of the black majority without precondition.

Critics disputed Bush's determination, with some members questioning whether South Africa had fully met even one of the conditions. For example, they cited reports from international human rights groups that South Africa continued to hold political prisoners, in violation of the law's first, non-negotiable condition.

But administration officials maintained that the only politically motivated prisoners still being held were properly tried for crimes of violence.

Sen. Richard G. Lugar of Indiana, who was a crucial Republican sponsor of the sanctions bill but supported Bush's decision, said the conditions agreed to in 1986 reflected hard-won political compromises. He believed some critics were unfairly seeking to go beyond those original aims.

"But the compromise was the law, the law has been met, and our credibility is at stake," Lugar said.

Critics themselves disagreed on what constituted compliance. For instance, Rep. Ronald V. Dellums, D-Calif., said that the condition requiring that all South Africans be allowed political participation should include granting blacks the right to vote. Wolpe interpreted that condition more narrowly as participation in the constitutional negotiations.

But Wolpe nevertheless called it "pure fantasy" to say the conditions had been met. Critics argued that it was Bush who changed the rules of the game, adopting an excessively narrow definition of the terms to justify ending a policy he had never liked.

Underlying the different opinions on compliance with the five conditions were markedly diverging assessments of how far, and with how much conviction, the white government in Pretoria had moved toward giving non-whites equality.

Black Caucus Reaction

Bush's action met particularly strong opposition from black groups, who had long related South African apartheid to the past enslavement and persistent discrimination faced by blacks in this country.

Several members of the Congressional Black Caucus painted Bush's sanctions decision as part of a broader picture of administration disdain for black concerns. They cited as well the president's threat to again veto civil rights legislation and his nomination of conservative Judge Clarence Thomas to the Supreme Court. *(Thomas confirmation, p. 274)*

"I'm very disappointed in this president's civil rights record," said Conyers. "It's not getting better as time goes on."

Rangel suggested that Bush's critics might need to turn their focus away from Washington, concentrating instead on pressuring corporate America to stay out of South Africa until more progress was made.

Anne Griffin, legislative director for the black foreign policy lobby, TransAfrica, said her group had already begun to concentrate on targeting corporations and building community anti-apartheid movements.

Although groups such as the National Association for the Advancement of Colored People began calling for a new sanctions bill to undo Bush's decision, members were skeptical about re-creating the grass-roots political pressure that spurred Congress to pass the 1986 law.

Recalling there were nationwide demonstrations against apartheid that preceded that action, Dellums said, "You don't see all of that fervor taking place at this point." ■

Fiscal 1991 Intelligence Authorization

The congressional Intelligence committees began 1991 with a significant piece of unfinished business from the year before: On Nov. 30, 1990, in a surprise action, President Bush announced that he was pocket-vetoing the fiscal 1991 intelligence authorization bill.

Almost four years had passed since Oliver L. North enthralled the nation with his testimony about the Iran-contra arms dealings of the Reagan administration. But the veto meant that Congress once again had to grope for legislation to restrict such covert schemes.

In his veto message, Bush complained about the measure's effort to rewrite requirements that the president notify Congress of covert intelligence actions. Bush argued in particular that the measure (S 2834) "purports to regulate diplomacy" by mandating that Congress be notified of requests by U.S. government agencies "to a foreign government or a private citizen to conduct a covert action on behalf of the United States." *(1990 Almanac, p. 791)*

Most of the covert-operations provisions in the vetoed bill had been added by the Senate, where a handful of members worked for years to draft reporting rules to prevent a repeat of the Iran-contra scandal.

Under the re-crafted version of the bill that ultimately was enacted in 1991 (HR 1455 — PL 102-88), the administration for the first time was required by law to report all covert activities to Congress and to authorize the actions in advance with a written presidential "finding."

In the finding, the president had to determine that the covert action was necessary "to support identifiable foreign policy objectives" of the United States. He was not allowed to authorize covert acts that violated the Constitution or any laws.

The measure required the president to notify Congress "in a timely fashion" whenever he failed to provide advance notification of a covert operation. But report language accompanying the measure simply took note of an unresolved dispute between Congress and the president as to whether such notification must be given within a few days.

The bill also authorized appropriations for the Central Intelligence Agency, the National Security Agency and other intelligence-related activities.

The measure was designed to replace a combination of statutes, executive orders and informal understandings that had governed covert actions over the prior decade. However, these had failed to prevent the Reagan administration in the mid-1980s from selling arms to Iran and diverting the proceeds to anti-government rebels in Nicaragua, without informing Congress and in defiance of a congressional ban against contra aid.

BOXSCORE

➡ **Fiscal 1991 Intelligence Authorization (HR 1455 — PL 102-88).** The bill, a revised version of a measure pocket-vetoed in 1991, rewrote requirements that the president notify Congress of covert intelligence actions. Its secret provisions also reportedly authorized about $30 billion in funds for intelligence operations.

Reports — H Rept 102-37; S Rept 102-85; H Rept 102-166.

KEY ACTION

May 1 — The **House** passed HR 1455 by voice vote.

June 28 — The **Senate** passed S 1325 by voice vote.

July 31 — The **House** approved the conference report on HR 1455, 419-4. The same day, the **Senate** cleared the measure by voice vote.

Aug. 14 — President Bush signed HR 1455 — PL 102-88.

HOUSE ACTION

The longstanding dispute between Congress and the White House over reporting covert operations was left unresolved with House passage May 1 of the fiscal 1991 intelligence authorization bill.

The House bill (HR 1455 — H Rept 102-37) sidestepped the issue by dropping the proposed changes in requirements for informing Congress about such secret intelligence activities.

House members said they wanted current law tightened. But they argued that existing law, despite its ambiguities and loopholes, was preferable to settling for new reporting requirements that excluded provisions opposed by Bush.

They were wary that Senate negotiators, in trying to specify what should be reported to Congress and when, could end up weakening requirements by failing to mention certain activities, such as operations conducted by other countries or private individuals.

"The Senate is willing to settle for something that we think is a step back," said Dave McCurdy, D-Okla., who was the newly appointed chairman of the House Intelligence Committee. McCurdy said that the administration had rejected a number of compromise proposals that he had suggested.

Although intelligence programs had been without a specific authorization since the previous Oct. 1, the administration argued that most of the intelligence activities were authorized by the annual defense bill.

The panel's ranking Republican, Bud Shuster, Pa., said there was "a strong feeling that every day that goes by without an intelligence bill really hurts the Intelligence Committee."

Although most provisions were classified, the intelligence bill reportedly authorized $30 billion for the government's intelligence programs. The committee's report said that, with the exception of the oversight language, the bill was virtually identical to the one that Congress cleared late in 1990 but Bush pocket-vetoed.

SENATE ACTION

On June 19, the Senate Intelligence Committee unanimously approved S 1325 (S Rept 102-85), a version of the legislation designed to change the way the executive branch reported to Congress about covert action.

The Senate committee report contained some of the same language that the administration objected to the previous year. But it also included additional phrases clarifying its intent.

The committee's bill required the president to issue a

written "finding" to the Intelligence committees of Congress each time he approved a covert action. The report would usually have to be provided "as soon as possible after approval and prior to the initiation of the covert action."

Under "extraordinary circumstances," the president could wait to notify Congress in a "timely fashion" after the operation began, as long as he explained the delay in writing.

The finding could not authorize any activity that violated the U.S. Constitution nor could it retroactively authorize an ongoing action. The president also would have to find that the covert action was necessary to U.S. national security and was in accordance with identifiable foreign policy objectives.

The administration would have to report to Congress if it "contemplated" any assistance from a third party in covert activity. But, in the case of a foreign government, the administration would not have to reveal the name of the country. The committee report emphasized that the requirement was intended to ensure that agencies inform the president of any such third-party involvement.

These oversight requirements would apply to all government agencies, not only the CIA. That was in response to the Reagan administration's contention that it was not required to tell Congress about the Iran-contra affair because it was managed by the National Security Council.

Committee Chairman David L. Boren, D-Okla., seemed uncertain whether the administration would accept the attempt at compromise.

"We believe we have addressed most of the president's objections," he said. "We are committed to working with the president ... to ensure the legislation will not be vetoed."

Ranking Republican Frank H. Murkowski, R-Alaska, added, "We have devoted many hours to working with the White House on this, and I believe we have reached a reasonable compromise."

Like the House version, the Senate bill reportedly authorized about $30 billion for U.S. intelligence activities for fiscal 1991. On June 28, the Senate quietly approved the bill by voice vote just before members left for an Independence Day recess.

A minor amendment pushed by Sen. Robert C. Smith, R-N.H., clarified that the Intelligence committees had access to intelligence documents on Vietnam prisoners of war and soldiers missing in action.

FINAL ACTION

House and Senate conferees reached agreement on a compromise version of the long-delayed fiscal 1991 intelligence authorization bill on July 24, including the requirements for reporting of covert activities that were the most significant legislative byproduct of the Iran-contra scandal.

With surprisingly little debate, Congress sent the bill to the president on July 31.

The House approved the conference report on the bill (HR 1455 — H Rept 102-166), which also authorized all government intelligence activities for fiscal 1991, by a vote of 419-4. *(Vote 237, p. 58-H)*

About nine hours later, the Senate quickly approved the measure by voice vote, sending it to the White House.

The bill included a few important changes from the measure that Bush had vetoed the year before. As in the bill approved by the Senate, the final version required that the president inform Congress if he anticipated that any third party would participate significantly in a covert action, but it did not require that he identify the participant.

The executive and legislative branches also haggled over setting a time limit for reporting covert actions. Although the bill generally called for notification before a covert action had begun, it maintained an existing provision allowing the president to inform Congress "in a timely fashion" if prior notice was not given.

The administration had opposed report language accompanying the prior year's bill that defined "in a timely fashion" as "within a few days." Bush argued that, while he intended to meet that standard in most instances, the limit was an unconstitutional infringement on his presidential authority.

After eight months of negotiations, Intelligence Committee leaders in effect agreed to disagree with the administration on this point. With what Republican Shuster called "baroque intricacy," the new report stated that conferees still believed that notification should be within a few days, but that they realized the president may assert constitutional authority to withhold notice for a longer period.

Conferees wrote that they "recognize that this is a question that neither they nor the Congress itself can resolve," effectively pushing any potential confrontation into the judicial system.

Ted Weiss, D-N.Y., complained on the House floor that the language provided a loophole that "allows the president still to claim that he can withhold whatever information that he wants."

But Intelligence Committee Chairman McCurdy said that one of the major disputes between the administration and Congress had been over a 1986 Justice Department opinion that the timely notice language gave the president "virtually unfettered discretion to choose the right moment for making the required notification."

McCurdy noted that the conferees specifically rejected that interpretation.

One of the major recommendations of the House and Senate committees that investigated the Iran-contra affair was that the administration be required to report all covert activities to Congress within 48 hours. The Reagan administration waited 10 months to formally notify Congress of covert arms sales to Iran and did so then only after news of the transactions was published in a Beirut magazine.

Rep. Anthony C. Beilenson, D-Calif., who as chairman of the Intelligence Committee in 1990 strongly criticized the Bush veto of the earlier bill, said that he would have preferred tighter restrictions but was not unhappy with the compromise.

"In the final analysis, you have to rely on whether the administration you're dealing with is going to abide by the law, in its letter and spirit," Beilenson said. "The problem with the Reagan administration was that it didn't even comply with all the requirements that were in the law at the time."

The legislation overhauled the intelligence oversight process in a number of ways.

First, it expanded to the entire federal government existing prohibitions against conducting covert actions without both a presidential finding and notification of Congress, which had applied only to the CIA.

Under the bill, the president was generally required to authorize all covert acts in advance with a written finding that the action was needed to achieve a specific foreign policy objective and was important for national security. If immediate action was required, however, the president had up to 48 hours to put his decision into a written finding.

For the most part, the findings were to be given to the two congressional Intelligence committees. In extraordinary cases, however, the president could limit notification to the congressional leadership.

The president also was required to inform Congress of any significant changes in previously approved covert actions.

The bill defined covert action in law for the first time, calling it an action undertaken by the government "to influence political, economic or military conditions abroad, where it is intended that the role of the United States government will not be apparent or acknowledged publicly." Exceptions were provided for what had been generally considered traditional intelligence-gathering, diplomatic, military and law enforcement activities.

The bill specifically prohibited covert actions intended to influence domestic politics, public opinion, policies or the media.

Although most of the other provisions of the bill were classified, it reportedly authorized about $30 billion in fiscal 1991 for the CIA, the National Security Agency, the Defense Intelligence Agency and other intelligence-related activities.

ADMINISTRATION ACTION

On Aug. 14, Bush signed into law the fiscal 1991 intelligence authorization bill (PL 102-88)

In his statement upon signing the measure, however, Bush emphasized that he still opposed efforts to mandate congressional notification of covert activities within a set time. Bush insisted that the Constitution allowed him to wait longer if he thought it necessary to carry out his duties. The president's statement also underscored potential differences over what types of covert military activities were covered by the new reporting law.

Congressional conferees and administration officials worked closely together on conference report language to describe which "traditional" military activities would be exempt from reporting requirements.

But when he signed the measure, Bush caught members by surprise by writing in the accompanying statement: "In determining whether particular military activities constitute covert actions, I shall continue to bear in mind the historic missions of the Armed Forces to protect the United States and its interests, influence foreign capabilities and intentions, and conduct activities preparatory to the execution of operations."

Senate Armed Services Committee Chairman Sam Nunn, D-Ga., objected later that Bush's definition was so broad it "would virtually cover everything the CIA has done that I know anything about in covert activity." Nunn called this a "fundamental difference" from what Congress had intended in the new law.

In September, during the Senate Intelligence Committee's confirmation hearings on Robert M. Gates, Bush's nominee as director of central intelligence, Nunn warned that "we on the Armed Services Committee are going to be watching that very carefully." *(Gates appointment, p. 486)*

Despite Bush's refusal to commit to prompt notification about covert operations without exception, Gates promised that as CIA director he would attempt to notify Congress within 48 hours.

He added: "Should the president decide for some reason involving life and death not to notify the Congress, it is my view that that non-notification should be withheld for no more than a few days at the most. Should it extend beyond that, I would argue or raise it on a daily basis with the president, and if it reached a point where I felt that the non-notification were no longer warranted or that a relationship of trust and confidence between the agency and the Congress was jeopardized, then I would contemplate resignation."

Another lingering area of ambiguity involved a requirement that Congress also be informed of "significant" intelligence activities other than covert operations.

Boren said the committee had made considerable headway in the previous few years working with the administration to clarify just what that meant.

But he said a broader definition would become increasingly important if the CIA devoted less time to covert actions and more to other activities.

"It is in the interest of the committee to expand the universe of what's significant enough for them to tell us about," Boren said. "But how you exactly define that is difficult." ■

Fiscal 1992 Intelligence Authorization

Congress took the first step toward making public the amount of money spent on the nation's intelligence activities in its fiscal 1992 intelligence authorization (HR 2038). That bill included a provision that recommended that President Bush reveal the total spent on intelligence activities — believed by experts to be about $30 billion annually.

The provision originally would have required the president to make the number public. But faced with a veto threat, lawmakers backed down and only "recommended" that he do so.

The measure also halted, at least temporarily, a move by the Central Intelligence Agency to relocate some of its workers to Prince William County in Virginia and to Jefferson County, W.Va. Though the bill authorized the funds to pay for the move, it also imposed strict reporting requirements on the CIA's method of choosing a new site.

The bill established a new program (authorized at $150 million) for U.S. students to learn foreign languages.

A debate over putting new restrictions on covert actions was waged on the fiscal 1991 intelligence authorization bill that was also enacted in 1991 after an initial version was pocket-vetoed at the end of 1990.

HOUSE ACTION

Most of the fiscal 1992 authorization bill for civilian and military intelligence agencies was secret, as was customary. But the public report on the measure (H Rept 102-65), approved 16-0 by the House Intelligence Committee on May 7, urged eliminating duplication and waste among security operations including the CIA, the Defense Intelligence Agency and the National Security Agency.

"We must also grapple with the legacy of the rapid and often uncoordinated expansion of intelligence programs and personnel that occurred in the 1980s," the report said.

Funding levels for intelligence activities were classified and hidden in the Defense Department budget, but they had been estimated at $30 billion annually. The report said its recommendation was "marginally lower than that requested by the president."

The committee had guarded praise for intelligence activities in Operation Desert Shield/Desert Storm, the U.S. troop deployment in the gulf war, but expressed concern about the inability of intelligence officials to predict that Iraq would invade Kuwait. The panel's assessment noted the apparent need for more portable equipment to cope with crises worldwide.

Republicans on the committee filed a minority report that blasted the idea of putting a "top hat" of secure floors on the unfinished U.S. Embassy building in Moscow, which was riddled with espionage devices. Critics wanted the building demolished. *(Moscow Embassy, p. 466)*

BOXSCORE

➡ **Fiscal 1992 Intelligence authorization (HR 2038).** The bill authorized appropriations for fiscal 1992 for intelligence activities of the U.S. government, the Intelligence Community Staff and the Central Intelligence Agency Retirement and Disability System.

Though the amount was officially classified, the bill was estimated to authorize about $30 billion in fiscal 1992 to cover those activities.

Reports: H Rept 102-65, Parts I and II; H Rept 102-327.

KEY ACTION

May 7 — **House** Intelligence Committee approved HR 2038, 16-0.

June 11 — The **House** passed HR 2038 by voice vote.

Oct. 16 — The **Senate** passed HR 2038 after amending the bill to contain the provisions of S 1539.

Nov. 20 — The **House** adopted the conference report by voice vote.

Nov. 20 — The **Senate** cleared the conference report by voice vote.

Dec. 4 — President Bush signed HR 2038 — PL 102-183.

Floor Action

House Republicans, who earlier in the year had complained about a liberal tilt on the Intelligence Committee, succeeded June 11 in winning House approval of a requirement that all committee members and aides sign an oath of secrecy.

The amendment, offered by the committee's ranking Republican, Bud Shuster, Pa., was attached to the fiscal 1992 intelligence authorization bill, which was later approved by voice vote.

Proposals for a secrecy oath first arose in February when some House Republicans complained about the appointment of four liberal Democrats to the panel and implied that they would be prone to leaks. Shuster acknowledged that he had no complaints with the committee's performance.

But Shuster said the oath was needed to encourage intelligence agencies to be more open with the committee and to emphasize members' commitment to protect government secrets.

"This city leaks like a sieve," he said, "and we need to set an example."

Democratic leaders, who tried unsuccessfully to prevent Shuster's amendment from reaching the floor, argued that existing House and committee rules already required secrecy and asserted that most intelligence leaks came from the administration.

Both House and committee rules prohibited members from disclosing any classified information they received while on the panel unless authorized by the committee or the House. Committee aides were required to sign nondisclosure agreements vowing that they would not disclose any secret information unless authorized.

New committee Chairman Dave McCurdy, D-Okla., questioned Shuster's motives and said approval of the oath would set a bad precedent.

"It irritates me because it seems as if people are trying to take partisan advantage . . . by placing people in a position," he said. "If we accept the oath on this, what is next? Polygraphs? And after polygraphs, do we have to do random drug testing of members?"

But Shuster said he did not understand what all the fuss was about: "One would think that we were proposing that members and staff of the Intelligence Committee be strip-searched in the well of the House."

McCurdy successfully raised a point of order against an initial version of Shuster's amendment, arguing that it was not germane to the intelligence bill because it would change House rules.

Shuster then offered a reworded amendment that skirted parliamentary roadblocks by prohibiting intelligence agencies from sharing any classified information with a committee member or aide who had failed to sign a secrecy oath.

After some debate and a commitment from Shuster not to offer similar amendments to other bills, McCurdy agreed to accept the proposal and support it in conference with the Senate.

The bill, which McCurdy said would provide slightly less funding than the administration requested but more than was provided in fiscal 1991, was generally uncontroversial.

In light of a peace agreement earlier that year between rebels and the government of Angola, the measure reportedly cut U.S. aid to the rebels from the $60 million provided in fiscal 1991 to $20 million. The aid was intended solely for non-military uses and, according to one source, could be converted later to overt aid.

By a vote of 169-234, the House rejected an amendment by New York Republican Gerald B. H. Solomon to require the CIA to conduct random drug testing of all its officers and employees.

McCurdy argued that the agency already had extensive procedures for controlling drug use by employees. *(Vote 146, p. 36-H)*

SENATE ACTION

Sen. Howard M. Metzenbaum, D-Ohio, argued that it would be impossible to impose fiscal discipline on the U.S. intelligence community so long as its budget remained secret.

So he proposed that the total budget for intelligence activities be made public. The Senate Intelligence Committee approved Metzenbaum's amendment to the fiscal 1992 intelligence authorization bill that would have required the figure to be declassified beginning in fiscal 1993.

The committee, which met in closed session July 17, also approved the underlying legislation, which authorized funding for intelligence activities in fiscal 1992. That bill, according to Metzenbaum, made a substantial reduction in the Bush administration's budget request for the next fiscal year.

If Metzenbaum's amendment had been enacted, there would not be a need for such vague descriptions of changes in the intelligence budget. The overall figure — the $30 billion a year estimate — would have been publicized, although it would not have included breakdowns for individual agencies.

"The American people are entitled to know what we spend on intelligence," Metzenbaum said. "They deserve to know. This disclosure will in no way harm our national security."

Some former intelligence officials agreed that release of the aggregate total would not compromise security. Adm. Bobby Ray Inman, former deputy director of the CIA, supported disclosure of the overall budget.

But George Carver, a former CIA official, who was with the Center for Strategic and International Studies, called the proposal "an absolutely wretched idea."

Carver said that while release of the budget total would not cause problems initially, other nations could glean important information from the year-to-year changes in the budget. It would also have increased pressure for further disclosures, Carver said. "Pretty soon, the intelligence bill will be like any other bill," he said.

Members of the Senate Intelligence Committee revealed a few of the other provisions contained in the mostly classified authorization measure. The committee's chairman, David L. Boren, D-Okla., along with panel members Sam Nunn, D-Ga., and John W. Warner, R-Va., announced a provision to shift $180 million from more traditional functions in the intelligence budget to create a trust fund aimed at improving the education of American students in international affairs.

In fiscal 1992, $35 million from the trust fund was to be spent for university grants, for graduate fellowships and to enable more U.S. students to matriculate abroad.

According to Boren, the proposal originated from a desire by the committee to improve U.S. intelligence capabilities. "The fact is that America is dangerously ill-prepared to meet the challenges of the post-Cold War era," he said, noting that declining numbers of American college students were learning foreign languages or studying abroad.

Nunn linked the program, called the National Security Education Act, to the U.S.-led war against Iraq. "We had to put 500,000 American men and women in harm's way" because of the failures of the intelligence and diplomatic communities to anticipate and avert the military crisis, he said.

In 1990, there were only 42,000 U.S. college undergraduates studying abroad, while 356,000 international students came to the United States, according to Boren.

In other action, the committee approved a plan by the CIA to relocate nearly two dozen of its offices to new sites in Virginia and West Virginia. The plan, supported by Warner and Robert C. Byrd, D-W.Va., chairman of the Appropriations Committee, had been strongly opposed by Washington, D.C.-area House members, whose districts would lose jobs in the transfer.

Floor Action

With the bitter confirmation battle of Clarence Thomas to the Supreme Court less than 24 hours old, the Senate considered — and quickly rejected — a plan to make three additional top CIA posts subject to congressional approval. *(Thomas confirmation, p. 274)*

Even the sponsor of the proposal, John Glenn, D-Ohio, acknowledged that he had probably picked the "worst time in the history of the nation" to offer his plan.

Glenn's amendment, rejected 38-59, was proposed Oct. 16 during consideration of the fiscal 1992 intelligence authorization bill (HR 2038). The Senate approved the legislation by voice vote and then sent it to a conference committee with the House. *(Vote 225, p. 30-S)*

During Senate floor debate, Glenn argued that the CIA would be more accountable to Congress if its deputy director for intelligence, deputy director for operations and general counsel were confirmed. Under existing law, confirmation was required only for the director, deputy director and inspector general.

Glenn said Senate approval would prevent CIA directors from appointing top assistants "based on political factors or personal and business ties."

He cited CIA Director William J. Casey's appointment in the early 1980s of Max Hugel to head the agency's covert operations. Hugel, a friend of Casey's with no experience in covert operations, was forced to resign after two months on the job because of allegations of business improprieties.

"I believe such an appointment would have never been confirmed by the Senate," Glenn said.

But opponents argued that the confirmation process would make the agency more political as potential candidates tried to curry favor with the White House and Congress.

"Anybody who wants to get ahead in the CIA in the lower echelons is going to know . . . the way to get ahead is make points with the administration, tell them what they want to hear," said John H. Chafee, R-R.I. "That's the danger of this amendment."

He and others noted that one of the most serious allegations lodged against President Bush's successful choice for director of central intelligence, Robert M. Gates, was that he slanted intelligence analyses to bolster the policy goals of the Reagan administration. *(Gates, p. 486)*

Most provisions in the legislation were classified. But the Senate version called for public disclosure for the first time of the overall level of intelligence spending, beginning in fiscal 1993; the House bill did not.

The administration threatened to veto the bill if it included such a provision, arguing that release of the intelligence budget figure could jeopardize national security.

There was little debate about the proposal to release the intelligence budget total, a provision added to the bill in committee by Metzenbaum.

Many members on the panel believed that disclosure of the number would not harm U.S. security and would satisfy the public's right to know how much it was spending on those activities at a time when pressure was great to cut federal spending.

In fact, Gates, during his confirmation hearings before the Intelligence Committee, endorsed the proposal as a way to build public confidence in the intelligence community.

However, the administration and other opponents argued that once the overall budget totals were released, pressure would build for more details. A statement from the White House on Oct. 16 said that annual disclosures "are likely to raise innumerable questions that can only be answered by disclosing classified activities, which, in turn, could ultimately jeopardize U.S. national security."

The White House noted that all members of Congress already had access to the information and that the intelligence budget was reviewed by six congressional committees.

The Senate bill required the annual release of three figures: the amount requested by the president, the amount authorized by Congress and the amount actually spent.

The administration also said it opposed the legislation because of "significant reductions" in the president's intelligence budget request. During Senate floor debate on the defense authorization bill in August, Intelligence Chairman Boren said the panel had cut between $600 million and $700 million in fiscal 1992 intelligence spending. *(Defense authorization p. 393)*

Such cuts "would significantly impact the intelligence community's ability to meet today's intelligence challenges," the White House said.

The legislation also authorized $180 million for a new National Security Education Trust Fund to provide scholarships and grants for foreign language and international studies. Boren said the education assistance would improve the quality of U.S. intelligence gathering.

FINAL ACTION

Completing work on the fiscal 1992 intelligence authorization bill (HR 2038), conferees agreed Nov. 12 to put the brakes on a $1.2 billion plan to move several thousand CIA employees to West Virginia and Prince William County, Va.

Instead, the bill required a public re-evaluation of the proposal, which evolved from secret discussions between CIA officials and Senate leaders, with the considerable influence of Senate Appropriations Committee Chairman Byrd.

House Intelligence Committee members had been especially outraged by the consolidation plan, which the Senate had included in its version of the intelligence bill. In a rare public hearing July 30, House panel members had blasted the CIA for not keeping the committee informed.

Now, said House Intelligence Chairman McCurdy, selection of the new CIA office site "will be an open process."

Conferees decided to approve $10 million for the CIA to purchase property for its relocation effort, but only after the agency had met certain conditions. These included providing a written description of the criteria used in the site selection.

Once these conditions were met, an additional $20 million would be made available, subject to the approval of the House and Senate Intelligence and Armed Services committees.

The relocation plan was intended to consolidate CIA employees scattered throughout the Washington, D.C., area in two new facilities. CIA headquarters in McLean, Va., would not have been affected.

Members representing the Washington suburbs questioned the selection of sites so far from headquarters and said the proposed relocation would have forced affected CIA employees to either move, quit their jobs or resign themselves to lengthy commutes.

Rep. Frank R. Wolf, R, whose Northern Virginia district was home to many of the estimated 3,000 CIA employees slated for the move, was pleased with the conference agreement. He said he thought the new site selection criteria "were very tough" and would force officials to choose a site closer to headquarters.

However, Byrd, who applied his formidable influence to moving federal jobs to his economically hard-pressed state, said in a statement Nov. 13 that he had "no problem" with the conference agreement, and that he was confident the "CIA consolidation proposal will go forward."

Conferees were less successful in opening to public scrutiny the total amount of federal dollars spent each year on intelligence activities, as proposed in the Senate bill.

Faced with a veto threat, conferees agreed to recommend — but not require — that the administration reveal the overall intelligence figure, believed to be about $30 billion a year.

Metzenbaum, sponsor of the provision, said he was confident the administration would decide to make the figure public because newly sworn CIA Director Gates had endorsed the proposal.

Metzenbaum and others had said that the public had a right to know how much it spends on intelligence activities. However, the administration argued that release of the budget total would inevitably force the disclosure of additional details "which, in turn, could ultimately jeopardize U.S. national security."

McCurdy said he and other conferees told Metzenbaum that if the administration did not release the figure, the issue could be addressed in 1992 as part of a congressional effort to reorganize the nation's intelligence network.

Conferees also agreed to authorize $150 million, instead of the $180 million in the Senate version, for a new National Security Education Trust Fund to provide scholarships and grants for foreign language and international studies.

Under the conference agreement, $35 million could be obligated in fiscal 1992 from the trust fund: $15 million in scholarships for undergraduate studies abroad, $10 million for graduate fellowships and $10 million for grants to educational institutions.

To avoid suspicions that recipients might be working undercover on school campuses, the bill prohibited those receiving the funds from conducting U.S. intelligence activities while participating in the program.

"It must be clear to foreign governments and organizations who host U.S. citizens receiving assistance under this program that the individuals concerned are engaged in purely academic pursuits," conferees said in their report.

However, Rep. Don Edwards, D-Calif., said suspicions were likely to persist. He recalled that "great damage was done" to the CIA by its efforts to gain "influence in universities" through covert funding in the 1960s and '70s.

Dropped from the bill was a House provision requiring members of the House Intelligence Committee to take an oath of secrecy. Instead, the committee passed a rule in October requiring the oaths, which were signed by each member.

The conference agreement phased out aid for U.S.-backed rebels in Angola before elections were held there in 1992. The bill provided an estimated $20 million in non-military aid, compared with $60 million in fiscal 1991.

Although the bill made what McCurdy called "significant" cuts in the administration's intelligence request, the exact amount remained secret.

The Senate on Nov. 20 cleared the intelligence measure for the president by voice vote. The House approved the largely classified measure earlier in the day, also by voice vote.

Despite earlier veto threats, President Bush signed the legislation Dec. 4. ■

Gates Confirmed as CIA Director

Robert M. Gates was sworn in as director of central intelligence on Nov. 12, six months after President Bush had nominated his deputy national security adviser to replace retiring Director William H. Webster. Despite weeks of heated testimony that revealed as much about the inner workings of the intelligence community as about the nominee, the Senate confirmed Gates on Nov. 5 with a solid vote of 64-31. *(Vote 243, p. 32-S)*

Supporters said Gates was the best person for the job because of his extensive CIA experience and his close relationship with the president. The director of central intelligence headed the Central Intelligence Agency and oversaw the government's sprawling network of civilian and defense intelligence operations.

But opponents said it was Gates' background that made him exactly the wrong man for the job. While there was no proof of misconduct, they said, there were numerous unanswered questions about his role in the arms-for-hostages dealings of the Reagan administration during the Iran-contra scandal.

At first, it looked like President Bush's choice to head the CIA in 1991 would face much of what he had in 1987, when President Ronald Reagan nominated him for the same job. Doubts about Gates' role in Iran-contra held up Senate action on the nomination at that time, and he eventually withdrew his name.

As events began to unfold in 1991, there was again uncertainty and delay. The Senate Intelligence Committee postponed Gates' nomination hearings, which initially were scheduled to begin in July. Committee Chairman David L. Boren, D-Okla., said there were "facts we'd like to get from other people" because of new revelations in the criminal probe into the Iran-contra scandal by independent counsel Lawrence E. Walsh.

While the hearings, which finally began in September, were held to review Gates' qualifications, they provided new insights into the clandestine world, especially as overseen by CIA Director William J. Casey. Casey died in 1987, leaving many questions about Iran-contra unanswered, including the extent of his, Gates' and others' roles. *(1987 Almanac, p. 61)*

Gates appeared headed for confirmation as director of central intelligence after the initial week of hearings ended Sept. 20, although later revelations put the outcome in doubt, if only briefly.

Perhaps most effective was his opening mea culpa, in which he told the committee that he should have acted more aggressively when, as deputy director of the CIA, he got his first inkling that profits from the sale of arms to Iran were being diverted to fund the Nicaraguan contras.

"Clearly . . . I would do certain things differently," he told the committee.

He also made a vow to quit rather than abuse the trust of the Intelligence panels. "I commit to you," he said, "that should I be confirmed, whatever differences may develop from time to time between the Intelligence committees and the executive branch generally or CIA in particular, I would resign rather than jeopardize that relationship of trust and confidence."

While the hearings initially centered on Gates' role in the Iran-contra scandal, they gradually turned to criticism that he was sometimes an abrasive manager and may have risen too quickly in the ranks of the CIA. Gates became head of the CIA's analysis branch at the age of 38 and deputy director at 42.

Gates also came under fire for some of his analytical work, which had been considered by many to be his strong point.

Although some former CIA colleagues defended Gates, others went public to accuse him of slanting and politicizing the agency's analysis to promote administration policies and his own hard-line views. He was also criticized for his failure to predict the revolutionary changes in the Soviet Union, despite his training as a Soviet specialist. Gates said that his miscalculation of the strength of reform in the Soviet Union had been a "humbling" experience.

Gates survived blows against his past record and managed to sway support in his favor, in part, by promising a more user-friendly CIA if he was confirmed as the nation's director of central intelligence. It was a change that won points on Capitol Hill, where memories of deceit by Casey and other intelligence officials lingered and new concerns had been raised that U.S. intelligence was flabby and ineffective.

Testimony by Gates and other witnesses painted the picture of a generally upright but ambitious career official. There was no concrete evidence that Gates, a 25-year government veteran, acted illegally during or after the Iran-contra affair.

The two members who most actively challenged the nomination — Democrats Bill Bradley of New Jersey and Howard M. Metzenbaum of Ohio — were able to influence only a few committee colleagues.

It was Gates' strengths that were cited by committee members as they voted 11-4 on Oct. 18 to recommend his nomination to the full Senate.

IRAN-CONTRA: RAKING UP THE PAST

Gates' nomination on May 14 was initially greeted with effusive praise by several members of the Senate Intelligence Committee, including Boren, whose trust and friendship Gates had cultivated over several years. But Gates' troubles began when Alan D. Fiers Jr., the former chief of the CIA's Central America Task Force, pleaded guilty in U.S. District Court on July 9 to two misdemeanor counts of unlawfully withholding information from Congress.

Fiers acknowledged that he knew more than he admitted to congressional committees in 1986 about the Iran-contra scandal and that he passed on to his CIA superiors his knowledge about the secret diversion to the contras in Nicaragua of funds from arm sales to Iran.

Although Fiers made no mention of Gates, members of the Senate Intelligence Committee said that Fiers would be asked to testify under oath about any knowledge that Gates — who was the agency's deputy director at the time — might have had of the diversion.

An even more important witness, whose testimony was sought but never secured by the committee, was Clair E. George, the former deputy director for operations at the CIA and Gates' immediate subordinate. According to prosecutors, George had instructed Fiers to lie to Congress when the scandal began to unravel in October 1986.

Gates had contended that he heard no more than

"flimsy speculation" of improper activities before Attorney General Edwin Meese III publicly revealed the Iran-contra affair on Nov. 25, 1986. Yet he found himself in the uncomfortable position of trying to prove a negative — that he knew little or nothing about the scandal — during a period in which testimony had shown that his superiors and subordinates were aware of it.

Going on the offensive to support his nominee, Bush said senators "ought not to panic and run like a covey of quail because somebody has made an allegation against a man whose word I trust, and who, as I understand it, hasn't been fingered by what's coming out."

Gates' Testimony

In his opening two-day appearance before the Senate Intelligence Committee on Sept. 16-17, Gates distanced himself repeatedly from the cloak-and-dagger administrative techniques of former agency boss Casey. *(Text, p. 27-E)*

In response to numerous oral and written questions from committee members, Gates also said he did not recall or had no knowledge of events that could have linked him to Iran-contra.

In areas in which he admitted knowledge but failed to act, Gates told committee members that, in retrospect, he wished he had behaved differently. "I should have asked more questions, and I should have been less satisfied with the answers I received," he said.

Most members appeared more than willing to give the benefit of the doubt to Gates, who had developed a good working relationship with the committee. He was effusively praised for his intelligence and analytical abilities, as well as for his long service with the agency.

His critics felt powerless. "I'm not sure if I stood on my head and sang 'Yankee Doodle Dandy' I could have any influence on the other side of the aisle," Metzenbaum said. Gates said he knew of the arms sales to Iran as early as Dec. 5, 1985, and had some indication that White House aide Oliver L. North was helping to solicit private assistance for the contras. But he said he was unaware of North's direct involvement in aiding the contras and, before Nov. 25, had only "flimsy" evidence that profits from the sale of arms to Iran were going to the rebels.

Gates testified, as he had before, that he received the first word about a possible diversion of funds on Oct. 1, 1986, when he was approached by CIA analyst Charles Allen with suspicions that such transactions might be taking place.

He also testified, as he had previously, that he could not recall a conversation that then-Deputy Director for Intelligence Richard J. Kerr had said he had with Gates in August 1986, in which Kerr passed along similar concerns that Allen had expressed to him. Gates told the committee that he and Kerr had numerous informal discussions every day about dozens of topics.

But Kerr told the committee in a sworn statement, released Sept. 19, and in a personal appearance later, that Gates had responded at the time "that he had heard some reference to this before, rumors."

Gates told the committee that if he had said such a thing, he would have been referring to long-circulating speculation about private and foreign government funding of the contras, not about any diversion involving the Iranian arms sales.

Thomas Polgar, a former CIA official and analyst for the Senate Iran-Contra Committee in 1987, was the first witness to appear in opposition to Gates. He said the nominee's failure to remember the conversation with Kerr should raise questions about his qualifications to be director.

But other witnesses lent credence to Gates' defense that he was largely cut out of the loop on covert operations, an area in which Casey took a special interest. Both of Gates' predecessors as deputy director, John McMahon and retired Adm. Bobby R. Inman, said that it was possible and even probable that Gates did not know of the diversion.

Inman, a strong Gates supporter, said he thought it was "entirely plausible that [Casey] made a conscious decision to keep Bob Gates out of areas" that might be troublesome in order to protect Gates' promising future with the agency.

Fiers testified Sept. 19 on his gradual entanglement in the White House plan to support the contras after Congress had prohibited such aid.

Fiers said it was his impression that Gates understood "the framework" but not the details of White House involvement with funding of the contras.

"He was late to the game," Fiers said, referring to Gates' ascendance to the deputy director's job in April 1986. "I think he got glimpses and snatches and insights into it, enough so that he knew ... there were shoals out there."

Fiers also recounted a meeting in Casey's office on Oct. 9, 1986, at which it was decided that George, not Gates, would testify in Congress the following day about the resupply effort. Fiers admitted that, at George's request, he falsified the testimony to conceal administration involvement.

Two days earlier, Gates had told the panel that he did not recall the meeting, one of many events others recounted but Gates did not remember.

GATES AS MANAGER

As the Senate Intelligence Committee began an unexpected third week of hearings on Oct. 1, the focus shifted to Gates' management style.

As a witness, Gates proved adept at defusing charges that, as deputy director of intelligence, he tampered with agency analysts' work to promote either his own or the administration's position.

Much of the criticism stemmed from testimony from former and current CIA employees in closed session Sept. 25 about accusations that certain analyses produced under Gates' jurisdiction were slanted.

Most disturbing to members were the statements of former Soviet affairs analyst Melvin A. Goodman, who alleged that Gates was instrumental in slanting analyses to exaggerate the Soviet threat and that he unceremoniously squashed dissenting views.

The allegations of bias centered on a number of reports for which Gates was responsible during the mid-1980s. They included a 1985 intelligence estimate on Iran that some said overemphasized Soviet influence and instability in that country and was used as a justification for the administration's sale of arms to Iran. Also discussed was a controversial 1985 report on the possibility of Soviet involvement in the assassination attempt on Pope John Paul II.

The committee, in closed session, also heard testimony about the possibility that Gates was involved in failing to properly inform Congress in the mid-1980s about a CIA initiative to share intelligence information with Iraq in its war against Iran.

Boren said after the session that there was no evidence that the information was illegally withheld from Congress, although he believed that the activity was significant enough that the committee should have been informed.

However, Bradley, one of Gates' most outspoken critics on the committee, said he still thought that a case could be made that some of the action taken was illegal. He said, "It depends on how you interpret" the law at the time governing disclosures to Congress. "I interpret it strictly," he said.

Committee members, including Gates' supporters, considered Goodman's testimony so significant that they decided that it should be presented in open session, along with the views of four other analysts who worked with Gates.

Former Employees Testify

The most emotional and sometimes riveting testimony came from the oldest and the youngest of Gates' former colleagues to appear. Both pleaded with the committee not to approve the nomination.

Harold P. Ford, 70, who joined the CIA in 1950 and worked there on a contract basis at the time of the hearings, said he had initially planned to deliver neutral testimony but changed his mind after hearing the complaints of colleagues he respected, reviewing Gates' record and listening to the nominee's testimony.

"Robert Gates should not be confirmed," said Ford.

Ford added that Gates, a Soviet expert, had been "dead wrong" in not predicting the collapse of the Soviet Union and in his belief of an expanding Soviet role in the Third World.

Jennifer Glaudemans, 32, a former Soviet affairs analyst, told the committee that employees of her office were cowed by their belief that their jobs would be in jeopardy if they did not agree with Gates' view of pervasive Soviet involvement.

"There was and apparently still is an atmosphere of intimidation within the office of Soviet analysis," said Glaudemans, who worked at the agency from 1982 to 1989. "There were times when insufficient evidence was irrelevant as long as a judgment was consistent with what Mr. Gates wanted, as in the case of the Iran estimate."

That estimate — prepared while Gates was the CIA's deputy director for intelligence and chairman of an interagency council responsible for the report — warned that the Soviets would try to increase their influence in Tehran and could begin to sell new arms to that country, despite the judgments of the CIA's Soviet office that such moves were unlikely.

Goodman, Glaudemans' former boss at the CIA who was on the faculty of the National War College when he testified, alleged that Gates' role in drawing up this and other estimates was "to corrupt the process and the ethics of intelligence" as he tried to pander to the strong anti-Soviet views of his boss, Casey.

Goodman charged that this was never more apparent than in the process used in preparing the paper on the papal assassination attempt, which Gates commissioned at Casey's request. Goodman said that contrary evidence was ignored and that Gates rewrote the major findings of the paper to fit his own theory that the Soviets were behind the plot. He said Gates also signed a cover memo that misled policy-makers, including Vice President George Bush, into believing that the study was balanced.

Gates' supporters quickly painted the testimony as the complaints of a few disgruntled employees in a large organization who could not adjust to Gates' tough management style.

"While I know and respect Mel Goodman as a very knowledgeable and experienced Soviet analyst, in all frankness, I do not readily recognize the Bob Gates described in his testimony," testified Graham E. Fuller, the former CIA analyst who had responsibility for the controversial Iran estimate.

Fuller denied that Gates put pressure on him in any way to present a particular point of view in the estimate and said he would have rejected such a suggestion.

Douglas J. MacEachin, who was head of the CIA's Office of Soviet Analysis during that period and became a special assistant to the director for arms control, said that Gates was a hard taskmaster and that there were serious morale problems.

But, MacEachin said, "I found him more ready to ensure treatment of competing hypotheses, honest treatment, than many of the people criticizing him here for imposing his own outlook."

Gates' Rebuttal

Gates gave a 20-point rebuttal in a return appearance before the committee Oct. 3 to many of the charges made against him during the hearings. He said he had watched the proceedings "with some dismay as well as some pain and anger."

He acknowledged that the tone for his tenure as deputy director for intelligence was probably set in 1982, when he first took over and tried to make major changes in the way analysis was produced. At that time, he said, he told employees of the directorate that much of their work was "flabby" and irrelevant to policy-makers.

Gates said that papers he was accused of killing for political reasons were poorly done or did not contribute anything new.

However, Gates did not address Glaudemans' concerns about his 1987 testimony on the Iran estimate, saying he did not recall how the testimony was put together.

He also acknowledged that the cover note on the papal assassination attempt report should have more clearly indicated that it did not "thoroughly examine all the alternatives that were available."

Preparing for the Vote

While the committee's seven Republicans remained firmly behind the nominee and a handful of Democrats were clearly opposed, several committee Democrats said, as public hearings concluded Oct. 4, that they had yet to make up their minds.

Key among these were committee Chairman Boren and Armed Services Chairman Sam Nunn, Ga., whose votes had the potential to determine the fate of the nomination both in committee and on the Senate floor.

However, Boren gave a strong defense Oct. 4 of Gates' track record as an advocate of close relations between the administration and congressional Intelligence committees, which he said should be a key factor in judging the nominee. "No single person in the intelligence community, without exception," has more strongly supported the oversight process, Boren said.

Both sides agreed that the CIA's image had been badly tarnished by the often tumultuous hearings. Their disagreement was over whether Gates was the right man to clean it up.

"What will the people of America think if we confirm for this position a man against whom so many have been willing to come forth?" asked Metzenbaum. "There isn't any question the CIA is under a cloud by reason of these hearings. By confirming Robert Gates, do we remove that cloud or do we only make the cloud a little bit thicker?"

Ernest F. Hollings, D-S.C., who said he entered the hearings inclined to support the nominee but changed his mind after listening to critics' testimony, told Gates that he was "part of the problem put up to solve the problem.... Your experience there is exactly what's disqualified you."

Gates and committee Republicans agreed that the contentious hearings had stripped bare internal tensions in the intelligence agency. But they insisted that he could repair the damage.

"There are a lot of feelings [within the CIA] ... that I could help bring them through what is going to be a difficult period of change," Gates told the committee, "because of my relationship with the Congress, my relationship with the president, that I could give them the kind of leadership and the kind of support that they would need."

Warren B. Rudman, R-N.H., said many of the charges against Gates were "McCarthyism, pure and simple."

At a news conference Oct. 4, President Bush denounced the allegations of slanted analysis as "an outrageous assertion against a very honest man." Dismissing complaints of doctored analysis from within the CIA, Bush, a former director of the agency, said, "Every junior analyst cannot have his or her estimate be the one that comes to the president."

Gates said if he were confirmed he would try to be "more sensitive" to employees and institute procedures to protect against politicization of intelligence reports and to encourage subordinates to bring their complaints to him.

COMMITTEE VOTE

Gates' ability to rebuke the allegations against him and to address the reshaping of the intelligence community for a post-Cold War world were cited by members of the Senate Intelligence Committee as they voted 11-4 on Oct. 18 to recommend his nomination to the full Senate.

Boren said that the new director "will immediately have to plunge into the process of radically changing the intelligence community.... This is no time to bring in a new director from the outside."

But Bradley sharply criticized what he portrayed as Gates' selective candor before the committee: "He is a man who apologizes for undeniable mistakes, recalls possible mistakes only when questioned repeatedly in public, refuses to recall or forgets unproven mistakes."

Officials working on the nomination for the White House speculated that the Senate would not want to engage in another grueling confirmation fight so soon after the divisive debate over Clarence Thomas' appointment to the Supreme Court. *(Thomas confirmation, p. 274)*

Besides strong Republican support, the committee's two most influential Democrats on the subject — Boren and Nunn — voted to report the nomination. However, Nunn acknowledged doubts about the signal the nomination might send to CIA employees concerning "how you get to the top in this town," an apparent reference to allegations that Gates kowtowed to superiors.

In addition to Metzenbaum and Bradley, Democrats Hollings and Dennis DeConcini, Ariz., voted against the nominee. The committee's seven Republicans and Democrats Boren, Nunn, Alan Cranston, Calif.; and John Glenn, Ohio, voted in favor.

SENATE VOTE

As expected, the Senate confirmed Gates on Nov. 5, 64-31. All 42 Republicans voting and 22 Democrats supported Gates. Thirty-one Democrats voted no.

Critics noted prior to the vote that Gates could not recall numerous important meetings others reported having with him to discuss CIA and White House involvement in the Iran-contra affair. Opponents said they found this bothersome for a man considered to be extremely intelligent.

"You cannot make him the smartest and the dumbest all at the same time," said Hollings.

But other lawmakers argued that the president should be given the benefit of the doubt for high-level appointments.

"The question before us is not whether Bob Gates is the best-qualified person in America to hold this job," said Joseph I. Lieberman, D-Conn., but whether, having been nominated, "he is qualified to hold this job. And in my opinion he more than passes that test."

Other supporters, including Democrats Nunn and Patrick J. Leahy of Vermont, said they had reservations but were influenced by Boren's strong support of Gates and by the nominee's pledge to work closely with Congress.

But Leahy, as well as Boren, promised to closely monitor Gates' performance. Leahy said he would push for Gates' removal if evidence emerged that he slanted intelligence, lied to Congress or penalized CIA employees.

Boren noted that Gates had promised to resign from office rather than do anything to jeopardize a relationship of "trust and confidence" he planned to build with Congress. "Having taken the position I have taken on this nomination," Boren said, "I can assure you I would probably be the first person to demand such action if he did not continue to merit the confidence which I and others have expressed in him."

These comments stirred Majority Leader George J. Mitchell, D-Maine, a Gates opponent. "The need for the chairman of the Intelligence Committee to make such a statement is so remarkable and so extraordinary that it speaks for itself," Mitchell said. "It simply should not be necessary for such a commitment to be made."

Mitchell said that if Gates were confirmed "he will owe that confirmation to one person and one person alone, and that is Sen. Boren."

On Nov. 12, Gates was sworn in as director of central intelligence in a ceremony at the CIA. As Gates and Boren had done previously, President Bush used the occasion to talk about the need to develop a new focus for U.S. intelligence operations in the aftermath of the Cold War.

"The intelligence community's new challenge under Bob Gates' leadership is to move beyond the Cold War to the complex problems of the 21st century," Bush said. "We need a strong intelligence community to consolidate and extend freedom's gains against totalitarianism. We need intelligence to verify historic arms reduction accords and we need it to suppress terrorism and drug trafficking. And we must have intelligence to thwart anyone who tries to steal our technology or otherwise refuses to play by fair economic rules. And we must have vigorous intelligence capabilities if we're to stop the proliferation of weapons of mass destruction." ■

No Full-Scale Probe Of 'October Surprise'

For a controversy that was a decade old, the "October surprise" produced a surprising amount of acrimony in Congress during 1991. Both the House and Senate failed to act on resolutions to authorize full-scale investigations into persistent but unproven allegations that Ronald Reagan's presidential campaign had secretly negotiated to delay the release of U.S. hostages held by Iran until after the 1980 election.

A Senate subcommittee persisted in conducting a low-level inquiry into the issue. And the House voted, 217-192, on Feb. 5, 1992, to authorize a 13-member task force to investigate the allegations.

The controversy gained its name from the concern in the Reagan-Bush campaign of 1980 that President Jimmy Carter would pull off an "October surprise," arranging a pre-election release of the U.S. hostages in Iran that would boost his sagging popularity.

The hostage crisis had dragged on since Nov. 4, 1979, when Iranian militants seized U.S. diplomatic personnel and visitors in the U.S. Embassy in Tehran. *(Hostages, 1979 Almanac, p. 97)*

Iran, whose government had been taken over by Islamic fundamentalists, released the hostages on Jan. 20, 1981, when Reagan was taking the oath of office as president. *(Chronology, 1980 Almanac, p. 352)*

The allegations of a secret deal had circulated for years but had been vehemently denied by Reagan and his supporters. The issue was given new life in April 1991 by former Carter administration official Gary Sick.

A former National Security Council staff aide who worked on the hostage crisis, Sick wrote an article in The New York Times outlining a series of possible contacts between Reagan campaign officials and Iranian officials.

Sick, who wrote a book on the subject, acknowledged that he had discovered no "smoking gun" to prove his case.

However, he suggested areas of inquiry that he said could resolve questions about the affair.

Much of the speculation centered on one of the most enigmatic figures of the Reagan years, William J. Casey. The late Casey, a World War II spymaster, served as chairman of Reagan's 1980 campaign and later as his director of central intelligence.

Some news reports placed Casey in Europe at the time the negotiations supposedly took place. Yet some Democrats suspected that Casey — renowned as a covert operator even before he became embroiled in the Iran-contra scandal as Reagan's CIA director — would have eliminated all evidence of any such arrangement.

Seeking Discretion

For many lawmakers, the notion of a discreet congressional investigation into politically explosive allegations would have seemed a contradiction in terms.

But in mid-year, several House Democrats sought a way to quietly pursue the long-simmering questions concerning the Reagan-Bush campaign and Iran.

Rep. Dan Glickman, D-Kan., said there was growing sentiment among House Democrats in favor of a formal investigation, with investigators empowered to subpoena documents and witnesses. But he added that most members of the party wanted an inquiry that would be "far less public" and "far less of a show" than the nationally televised Iran-contra hearings. *(1987 Almanac, p. 61)*

Many Democrats were embarrassed by those hearings, which had the unintended result of transforming Oliver L. North, originally viewed as a culprit in the scandal, into a celebrity victim of congressional interrogators.

Glickman said pursuing the inquiry "has the potential to backfire, but it also has the potential to blow this government wide open."

The proposed probe picked up support in the Senate during the week of June 24, as Al Gore, D-Tenn., introduced a resolution calling for a formal investigation of the allegations.

"Some deals should never be made," Gore said, "whether arms for hostages or hostages for elections."

In a Republican response, House Minority Leader Robert H. Michel of Illinois said June 25 that the evidence revealed to date did not warrant a congressional probe. But if such an inquiry took place, Michel said, he would insist that "the first matter to be investigated" would be separate allegations that President Jimmy Carter's administration tried to arrange an arms-for-hostages deal in October 1980.

On Aug. 5, with more wariness than zeal, congressional Democratic leaders announced that they had decided to investigate the allegations concerning the Reagan-Bush campaign.

Calling the reports "persistent and disturbing," Speaker of the House Thomas S. Foley, D-Wash., and Senate Majority Leader George J. Mitchell, D-Maine, announced parallel probes.

"We have no conclusive evidence of wrongdoing," said a statement by the two leaders, "but the seriousness of the allegations, and the weight of circumstantial information, compel an effort to establish the facts."

Lee H. Hamilton, D-Ind., chairman of the Foreign Affairs Subcommittee on Europe and the Middle East, was named to head a special House task force to investigate the issue. In the Senate, the Foreign Relations Subcommittee on Near Eastern and South Asian Affairs, chaired by Terry Sanford, D-N.C., was asked to conduct the inquiry.

Hamilton — who called himself "a reluctant investigator" — and Sanford vowed to follow the evidence wherever it led. But in announcing the investigations, Mitchell and Foley said that they accepted President Bush's denial of any knowledge of contacts between campaign officials and Iranian representatives.

That assurance clearly did not satisfy most Republicans, who charged that the investigation was politically motivated. Sen. Richard G. Lugar, R-Ind., said in a television interview on Aug. 7 that some Democrats "are extremely frustrated at the success of President Bush, and they really are looking for opportunities, and this is one that came along."

President Bush sounded the Republican skepticism toward the investigation. "I'm sure that Foley and Mitchell do not intend to conduct a political trial of some sort here," he told reporters Aug. 6. "But people are going to be saying, 'What's your evidence. What's the hard evidence here?' "

Committee Action

Although the Democratic leaders in Congress set inquiries into motion, full-scale and fully funded investigations required action by the full Senate and House.

After angry exchanges, the Senate Foreign Relations Committee voted 9-8 on Oct. 29 to approve a resolution (S Res 198) authorizing a probe into the allegations concerning the Reagan-Bush campaign and Iran.

A number of Republicans on the Foreign Relations panel strongly opposed the investigation, saying that there was not enough evidence to warrant spending $596,000, as was to be authorized under the resolution, for an investigation by the committee's Near Eastern and South Asian Affairs Subcommittee.

An angry Lugar said the probe was politically motivated "to embarrass the president. It is a rerun of the campaign of 1980 and [Republicans] will fight this monstrosity."

But panel Democrats said the committee had a responsibility to investigate the charges, which gained new momentum over the summer.

"Elliot Abrams lied to this committee. Alan Fiers lied to this committee. Clair George is indicted for lying to this committee. We have to get to the heart of the matter.... There is a reasonable assumption that something happened," said John Kerry, D-Mass.

Abrams, assistant secretary of State for inter-American affairs from 1985 to 1989, pleaded guilty Oct. 7 to two misdemeanor counts of withholding information from Congress. Fiers, former chief of the CIA's Central American Task Force, pleaded guilty to similar charges July 9; George, former CIA deputy director of operations, was indicted Sept. 6 on 10 counts of lying to Congress.

On Nov. 7, the House Rules Committee endorsed creation of a special Foreign Affairs Committee task force to look into allegations that the Reagan-Bush campaign had been involved in a politically inspired delay in the release of U.S. hostages in Iran.

After an acrimonious hearing and markup, the panel voted, 8-4, along party lines to approve a measure (H Res 258) creating the panel.

The Rules panel rejected a series of Republican attempts to limit the inquiry's duration to six months or broaden it to include allegations that the Carter administration offered to sell arms to Iran in exchange for an early release of the hostages.

Representatives of the General Accounting Office told panel members that the agency could find no evidence to substantiate rumors that then-vice presidential candidate George Bush made a secret trip to Paris in October 1980 to broker a deal with the Iranians. Bush denied any such action.

On Nov. 14, the House Administration Committee voted 14-9 to approve H Res 258.

The committee turned back close to a dozen amendments by Republicans that would have restricted the probe or extended it to Carter's administration.

Floor Debate

On Nov. 22, by a vote of 51-43, the Senate failed to reach the 60 votes needed to cut off debate on the resolution (S Res 198) authorizing a probe into the Reagan-Bush campaign by a Senate Foreign Relations subcommittee. *(Vote 271, p. 35-S)*

Sanford said the Senate "would be derelict" if it spurned requests by some former hostages to look into the allegations. In arguing on behalf of the Senate resolution, Majority Leader Mitchell said, "We know two things: We know that the release of the hostages was delayed until moments after President Reagan took office. And we know that after taking office, President Reagan authorized a secret effort to transfer arms to Iran.

"What we do not know is whether the two events occurred completely independently and totally by coincidence, or whether they were the result of a secret agreement linking them."

But Republicans derided what Frank H. Murkowski, Alaska, called the "granddaddy of all conspiracy theories."

Mitch McConnell, R-Ky., said the Senate resolution would have funded an investigation into "the ravings of channelers, liars, felons and flat-out flakes."

McConnell ridiculed the allegations as a conspiracy theory worthy of a supermarket tabloid headline: "Elvis Is Key Witness in October Surprise Investigation."

In lieu of the well-funded inquiry envisioned under the resolution, Sanford's Senate subcommittee planned to go ahead in 1992 with a less ambitious investigation under its standing authority.

The House adjourned Nov. 27 without considering a resolution (H Res 258) that would have created a task force of members from the Foreign Affairs Committee to look into the allegations.

Robert G. Torricelli, D-N.J., one of the leading advocates of the probe, said that Democratic leaders had previously indicated that the resolution would be the final matter considered before adjournment.

But in the chaotic rush to depart other legislation took precedence, according to several lawmakers. "We ran out of time," Torricelli said.

When the House approved the investigation on Feb. 5, 1992, the 217-192 vote fell mostly along party lines. But 34 Democrats voted against the resolution authorizing the probe, reflecting continuing ambivalence about the wisdom of plunging into the murky allegations. ■

New Committee Created On Vietnam POWs/MIAs

A grainy photo of uncertain origin revived a wrenching, unresolved mystery in 1991. The Senate created a Select Committee on POW/MIA Affairs to investigate the fate of U.S. soldiers, particularly from the Vietnam War, whose fate was never accounted for.

By voice vote, the Senate adopted the resolution creating the panel (S Res 82) on Aug. 2

The committee was instructed to investigate the fate of U.S. prisoners of war (POWs) and those missing in action (MIAs). The chairman of the 12-member panel was Sen. John Kerry, D-Mass., a decorated veteran of the Vietnam War.

The resolution had been approved earlier the same day by the Senate Committee on Rules and Administration. A committee member had predicted that the full Senate would act on the proposal in the fall, but Senate leaders beat that timetable in their apparent eagerness to move on the emotional issue.

The POW/MIA issue brought back painful images of the United States' losing effort to defeat communism in Vietnam, which ended with the humiliating and chaotic evacuation of Saigon in 1975.

Concern about the fate of the long-lost soldiers was revived by the grainy photo, which relatives believed showed several Americans in captivity.

A Defense Department spokesman cautioned on Aug. 6 that such photos had been "phonied up" repeatedly and that the photo in question was being circulated along with several others that were clearly copied from a Soviet publication found in a reading room in Phnom Penh, Cambodia.

At a news conference on Aug. 2, President Bush said the U.S. government should "run down every single lead" concerning the 2,273 Americans classified as POWs and MIAs after the Vietnam War. But he added, "There's no hard evidence of prisoners being alive, and for those who are unscrupulously raising the hopes of families by fraud, that should be really condemned."

Members of Congress prodded the administration to keep up pressure on Vietnam to cooperate in resolving the issue. Robert C. Smith, R-N.H., sponsor of the measure creating the select committee, told the Senate on Aug. 2, "We know where the answers are. They are in Hanoi, they are in Phnom Penh and in Vientiane in Laos. That is where the answers are. We have to go get those answers."

Smith had sought a 12-member panel, evenly divided between Democrats and Republicans. Over Republican protests, Chairman Wendell H. Ford, D-Ky., had amended the bill in committee to give the proposed panel a 6-5 Democratic majority. Facing Republican protests, the Democrats amended the measure on the floor to restore an evenly divided 12-member panel.

Committee Launched

In three days of initial hearings, which ended Nov. 7, the Senate Select Committee on POW/MIA Affairs mostly underscored the limitations of its capabilities.

"There are some who may be looking for this committee to do the impossible — to bring back those who are truly lost or to uncover some hidden file where all the answers to all the unanswered questions are secretly stored," said Kerry.

Kerry said a "more realistic goal" for the panel would be to provide a "full accounting" of the Defense Department's handling of reports that POWs and MIAs were still alive in Southeast Asia a generation after the war.

Families of the missing "want to know whether they can trust what their government tells them," Kerry said.

Defense Secretary Dick Cheney, the leadoff witness on the first day of hearings, was quick to assure the committee that the Pentagon would assist in the investigation. But he strongly refuted charges that his department suppressed information.

Cheney said a full accounting depended on the governments of Southeast Asia.

"Too often our office finds that public pronouncements of increased cooperation by Hanoi do not produce satisfactory arrangements on the ground," he said, referring to a U.S. office set up in Hanoi in July.

Some family members of the missing servicemen agreed.

"The lack of greater results is simply not due to lack of dedication by the United States," said Ann Mills Griffiths, executive director of the National League of Families of American Prisoners and Missing in Southeast Asia. But other family members argued that the Defense Department had moved at a near glacial pace.

Garnett E. Bell, the chief of the Office for POW/MIA Affairs in Hanoi, told the committee that "possibly 10 or less" Americans were left behind in Vietnamese prison camps at the end of the Vietnam conflict, but he said there was no information to suggest any were still alive.

Asked by Kerry if the Defense Department "covered up" knowledge of POWs, Bell said, "I don't think there was a coverup, but the information was not acted on."

Panel member Charles E. Grassley, R-Iowa, said he was convinced the Pentagon had mishandled the MIA files. "There are major discrepancies and follow-up deficiencies in these reports," Grassley said.

The House Foreign Affairs Subcommittee on Asian and Pacific Affairs also held a hearing on the issue Nov. 6, in part to remind the public that its staff had been investigating the POW/MIA issue for 10 years.

Sensitive Relations

During 1991, the POW/MIA issue also arose in Senate debate over proposals to resume diplomatic and economic relations with Vietnam that had been cut off ever since the war years.

On July 29, in passing the State Department authorization bill (HR 1415), the Senate voted to condition better relations on progress in resolving the POW-MIA question. *(State Department, p. 493)*

The Foreign Relations Committee had approved, 12-1, an amendment by Frank H. Murkowski, R-Alaska, calling for the lifting of the longstanding trade embargo against Vietnam and Cambodia. But John McCain, R-Ariz., who as a Navy pilot spent six years in a North Vietnamese prisoner of war camp after his jet was shot down in 1967, succeeded in modifying the measure.

McCain's proposal, which the Senate approved by voice vote, expressed the sense of Congress that the United States should move toward normal relations with its wartime enemies — but only if the "pace and scope" of normalization was linked to Vietnam's cooperation in resolving MIA cases and in settling the war in Cambodia.

McCain did not refer directly to the vigorously disputed reports of live sightings of U.S. servicemen in Vietnam. But he said, "We are first and foremost obligated to the 2,273 Americans who are still classified as missing in action or prisoner of war in Southeast Asia, and their families."

Murkowski argued that more information about POWs and MIAs could be gathered if the United States had normal relations with Vietnam, but he did not challenge the amendment offered by the war hero.

Although Vietnam remained politically rigid, its leaders expressed interest during 1991 in economic change and increased contacts with the West. Change in Southeast Asia also was demonstrated in Cambodia. In Paris on Oct. 23, that country's long-warring forces signed a peace treaty under auspices of the United Nations.

Although enthusiastic about the possibility of peace in Cambodia after a generation of war, some members of Congress expressed misgivings that the U.S.-backed peace plan included the Khmer Rouge, whose brutal forces killed more than 1 million Cambodians in the 1970s. Administration officials argued that the Khmer Rouge were far less dangerous taking part in a transition to democracy than attacking it from outside the process. ■

Nearly $12 Billion Authorized for State

Legislation authorizing almost $12 billion for the State Department and related international agencies for fiscal 1992-93 (HR 1415 — PL 102-138) cleared the House Oct. 8.

But the bill's enduring contribution might have been a provision that was removed from the measure in conference and passed as separate legislation: import sanctions against countries that used chemical or biological weapons and against companies that sold the material and technology needed to build them.

Because of a legislative turf dispute, the sanctions were attached to a trade bill that also adjusted unemployment benefit formulas (HR 1724 — PL 102-182) that the House cleared on Nov. 26.

The State Department measure authorized funding for the department, the U.S. Information Agency and the Board for International Broadcasting. The measure largely reflected the administration's request, although it authorized $630 million, $140 million more than President Bush requested, in refugee assistance. Sponsors said the additional money was needed for unanticipated expenses related to Soviet, Kurdish, Southeast Asian and African refugees.

The bill authorized $130 million in each of the two fiscal years for a new U.S. Embassy in Moscow but left up to the administration the final decision on how this should be done. Options included razing the existing structure, which was riddled with listening devices, and constructing a new one; adding secure floors on top of the existing structure; or building an entirely new embassy next door. *(Moscow embassy, p. 466)*

HOUSE ACTION

After approval by the House Foreign Affairs Committee on April 30, the House passed HR 1415, the State Department authorization bill, by voice vote on May 15.

Most of the debate on the House floor concerned the longstanding dispute over what to do with the Moscow embassy that was laced with eavesdropping devices. Members turned back a determined effort by Olympia J. Snowe, R-Maine, to force the House to vote on her proposal to demolish the partially built, unused embassy chancery.

Instead, they voted, 223-185, to authorize $130 million in fiscal 1992 for some solution to the embassy quandary. But they left it up to the Bush administration to decide whether to tear down the building and start over or adopt the so-called Top Hat approach, which would replace the two top stories of the embassy with four secure floors. *(Vote 90, p. 22-H)*

The House rejected three other amendments to the bill:

- It turned back, 145-265, an effort by Gerald B. H. Solomon, R-N.Y., to subject State Department personnel to random drug tests. *(Vote 93, p. 24-H))*
- It rejected, 189-224, a call by Paul E. Kanjorski, D-Pa., to slash $14 million from the funds for the National Endowment for Democracy (NED). *(Vote 94, p. 24-H)*

The Bush administration requested $30 million for NED in fiscal 1992, and the Foreign Affairs Committee had included that amount in HR 1415. But a General Accounting Office report in March excoriated NED for its accounting practices, and the panel responded by setting aside $5 million of the funding pending serious efforts to revamp its grant-tracking procedures.

- It defeated, 155-248, an attempt by Robert S. Walker, R-Pa., to cut about $500 million from the overall State Department budget for fiscal 1992-93. *(Vote 95, p. 24-H)*

Other provisions of the House-passed bill:

- Authorized $630 million for refugee assistance in fiscal 1992, $140 million more than Bush wanted.
- Expressed the sense of Congress that talks with the Palestine Liberation Organization not be resumed until it recognized Israel's right to exist and amended its charter to reflect this.
- Authorized the U.S. Information Agency for fiscal 1992 only, pending the report of a presidential advisory commission reviewing U.S. government broadcasting activities.
- Created a position of assistant secretary of State for South Asia.
- Rejected an administration request to cancel Radio Free Afghanistan.
- Authorized $2 million in both fiscal 1992 and 1993 to go to the city of Buffalo, N.Y., as partial compensation for the World University Games that were scheduled to take place there in 1993.

SENATE ACTION

As approved by the Senate on July 29, the State Department authorization bill provided for tough sanctions to curb the proliferation of chemical and biological weapons but also included $1 billion in loan guarantees to promote overseas sales by U.S. arms merchants.

Committee Action

On May 14, the Senate Foreign Relations Committee's Subcommittee on Terrorism, Narcotics and International Operations attached to the State Department authorization bill a proposal to curb international arms proliferation.

The proposal was designed to prohibit conventional arms sales to the Middle East until 60 days after the president reported to Congress on the threat to allies in the region, the types of arms needed, and the feasibility of regional security arrangements and an international supplier conference to restrict sales.

It was one of several arms proliferation proposals that were attached to broader legislation or offered as free-standing bills.

On June 12, the Senate Foreign Relations Committee approved the State Department authorization bill, 18-0, after narrowly defeating an attempt to restrict U.S. military aid to El Salvador.

The debate reflected both longstanding divisions over U.S. support for the conservative government in El Salvador and newfound uncertainty about how to encourage peace talks in the war-torn country.

At year's end, on Dec. 31, the government of El Salvador and leaders of leftist guerrilla groups signed a peace agreement at the United Nations. But that outcome had been far from clear when the Senate committee dealt with the issue in midyear.

Christopher J. Dodd, D-Conn., sought to hold back half of the $85 million in aid the administration requested for El Salvador, similar to a limit that was imposed by Congress on fiscal 1991 aid. *(1990 Almanac, p. 779)*

The restrictions were intended to encourage both sides

to end the nation's civil war. It allowed the administration to release the funds if it found that leftist guerrillas were not negotiating in good faith with the government of Alfredo Cristiani.

Dodd said that failing to impose a similar limit on fiscal 1992 aid might disrupt ongoing peace efforts. "What we're trying to do here is maintain the status quo," he said.

But opponents argued that a different message would be sent. They said a move by Congress to restrict aid would be a blow to Cristiani, who was in Washington during the week of June 10 to lobby his cause in meetings with President Bush and congressional leaders.

Richard G. Lugar, R-Ind., said the Salvadoran president had made great strides in organizing his government and controlling the nation's military. "The belief that this money is going to a military run amok is simply untrue," Lugar said.

A tabling motion by Jesse Helms, R-N.C., to kill Dodd's amendment was approved, 10-9.

As approved by the committee, the measure authorized $5.9 billion in fiscal 1992 and $5.3 billion in fiscal 1993 for the State Department, the United States Information Agency and the Board for International Broadcasting. It authorized creating a broadcast network, similar to Radio Free Europe, to promote democracy in China. And it called for $130 million in fiscal 1992 and $85 million in fiscal 1993 to complete the U.S. Embassy in Moscow.

The committee left in the bill the subcommittee proposal for a moratorium on arm sales to the Middle East. But the committee also approved, 11-5, an amendment by Dodd to create a $1 billion loan guarantee program for U.S. companies selling military goods to NATO countries, Japan, Israel, Australia and New Zealand.

A similar proposal by the administration had run into strong opposition, especially in the House. Critics said the guarantees would encourage arms proliferation abroad at a time when the United States was scaling back its defense budget and seeking international arms controls.

"It seems to me there's an inconsistency here," said Sen. Paul S. Sarbanes, D-Md.

But Dodd said the guarantees were needed to help domestic military contractors compete with subsidized foreign firms. John Kerry, D-Mass., argued that continued U.S. involvement in the international arms market would mean "furthering of our clout" when it came to seeking multilateral arms control agreements.

BOXSCORE

➡ **State Department authorization (HR 1415).** The State Department bill authorized almost $12 billion for fiscal 1992-93 for the department and related international agencies.

Reports: H Rept 102-53, S Rept 102-98, H Rept 102-238.

KEY ACTION

May 15 — HR 1415 passed the **House** by voice vote.

July 29 — HR 1415 passed the **Senate**, 86-11.

Oct. 4 — The conference report on HR 1415 was approved in the **Senate** by voice vote after the measure was stripped of import sanctions on countries and companies that contributed to proliferation of chemical and biological weapons.

Oct. 8 — HR 1415 was cleared by the **House** by voice vote.

Oct. 28 — President Bush signed HR 1415 — PL 102-138.

➡ **Chemical weapons sanctions (HR 1724).** Imposed import sanctions on countries and companies that contributed to the proliferation of chemical and biological weapons.

Report: H Rept 102-391.

KEY ACTION

Nov. 26 — The **Senate** approved the conference report on HR 1724, and the **House** cleared it, both by voice vote. The bill, which adjusted unemployment benefit formulas, became the vehicle for the import sanctions.

Dec. 4 — President Bush signed HR 1724 — PL 102-182.

The committee also agreed, 12-1, to an amendment expressing the sense of Congress that the U.S. trade embargo against Vietnam and Cambodia should be lifted. Kerry and Frank H. Murkowski, R-Alaska, said the embargo hurt U.S. firms and had prevented Americans from resolving prisoner-of-war and missing-in-action cases left over from the Vietnam War. "We need access," Murkowski said.

Floor Action

On July 29, the Senate approved, 86-11, the State Department authorization bill (HR 1415). *(Vote 157, p. 21-S)*

The Senate-passed bill demonstrated the difficulties in developing a consistent approach to global weapons proliferation. Although the legislation sought to impose tough sanctions against foreign governments and companies that engaged in the trade of chemical and biological weapons — provisions that were opposed by the Bush administration — it also authorized the $1 billion loan guarantee program to increase overseas sales by U.S. arms manufacturers.

Dodd modified the administration's original proposal with language intended to prevent unstable countries in the Middle East and elsewhere from taking advantage of the program.

Challenging the notion of bolstering the economy by promoting U.S. arms exports, Dale Bumpers, D-Ark., asked on the Senate floor, "We are going to create jobs in the defense industry? And send more and more weapons all over the world? And have those weapons, maybe, ultimately pointed at us? That's what happened . . . in the Persian Gulf War."

Dodd responded that "the hard realities of life" dictated that "there will be defense articles made and produced in Europe and elsewhere around the globe. It is an important industry in this country. And it is our industry that is suffering."

The bill included the committee language calling for a moratorium on U.S. weapons sales to the Middle East unless the administration worked to convene a conference of major arms suppliers to the Middle East. But the State Department made that language moot by meeting with other suppliers in Paris in May.

The Senate took a hard line on the proliferation of chemical and biological weapons, as it approved by voice vote an amendment by Foreign Relations Chairman Claiborne Pell, D-R.I., to impose tough sanctions on companies and countries that facilitated the transfer of such technology.

Under the amendment, the president would be required

to impose sanctions on foreign governments that used chemical or biological weapons. Such countries would face termination of all U.S. assistance and credits, along with restrictions on trade.

Companies that "knowingly and materially contribute" to a foreign government's efforts to "use, develop, produce, stockpile or otherwise acquire" chemical and biological weapons would be barred from trade with the United States.

The chemical weapons provisions had wide support in both chambers. In 1990, the Senate had approved a previous Pell-Helms amendment, 92-0, but Bush pocket-vetoed the legislation revamping export controls in November 1990. *(1990 Almanac, p. 198)*

Although Bush said he shared the objective of halting the spread of such weapons, he maintained that the provisions would "unduly interfere with the president's responsibility for carrying out foreign policy."

But in 1991, the president had won praise from lawmakers for pledging to destroy U.S. chemical stockpiles and declaring that the United States would not retaliate in kind if attacked by chemical weapons. That position encouraged sponsors of the sanctions provision to hope for a compromise with the administration on their measure.

The Senate also touched on the sensitive issue of U.S. servicemen who were declared prisoners of war (POWs) or missing in action (MIA) in the Vietnam War. *(POWs/MIAs, p. 491)*

The Senate approved by voice vote an amendment to Murkowski's provision in the committee bill that called for the lifting of the trade embargoes against Vietnam and Cambodia.

John McCain, R-Ariz., who as a Navy pilot spent six years in a North Vietnamese prisoner-of-war camp after his jet was shot down in 1967, sought the change.

McCain's proposal, which the Senate approved by voice vote, said it was the sense of the Congress that the United States move toward normal relations with its wartime enemies — provided that the "pace and scope" of normalization be linked to Vietnam's cooperation in resolving MIA cases and in settling the war in Cambodia.

The Senate also tackled the knotty question of whether the United States should provide direct assistance to dissident republics in the Soviet Union and Eastern Europe.

An amendment offered by Minority Leader Bob Dole, R-Kan., said it should be U.S. policy, so long as the president deemed it in the national interest, to provide foreign aid directly to democratic governments "that exist within countries which include a communist majority in other republic governments and/or at the federal level."

Dole said his amendment, approved by voice vote, would enable the United States to assist democratic republics in Yugoslavia and the Soviet Union. *(Soviet aid, p. 463)*

The Senate-passed bill also included language:

- Stating that no U.S. officials should negotiate with members of the Palestine Liberation Organization until the PLO recognized Israel's right to exist. A similar provision, which was opposed by the administration, was included in the House version of the foreign aid authorization bill.
- Calling for the appointment of an 11-member commission to study the feasibility of a U.S.-operated radio broadcasting service to the People's Republic of China.
- Calling for the establishment of a special office in the State Department to prosecute "Persian Gulf War criminals," preferably through the United Nations or in concert with gulf war allies.

The provision was opposed by the administration, which said in a statement it would "pose serious legal difficulties and limit the president's diplomatic flexibility."

- Insisting that $5 million of $30 million for the National Endowment for Democracy be withheld until the agency that promoted democracy abroad implemented management changes recommended by the General Accounting Office.

FINAL ACTION

The House approved the conference report on the State Department authorization bill on Oct. 4. The Senate cleared the bill on Oct. 8. But action on the bill was completed only after supporters agreed to strip it of the important provisions imposing trade sanctions on countries and companies deemed to participate in the proliferation of chemical and biological weapons.

The Ways and Means Committee had objected to inclusion of the sanctions on jurisdictional grounds. With the committee's backing, the sanctions were later amended into a bill adjusting unemployment compensation (HR 1724), which cleared the House on Nov. 26.

Conference Committee

On Sept. 26, a House-Senate conference committee on the State Department authorization bill (HR 1415) announced a compromise with the Bush administration on the provisions to punish those who contributed to the spread of chemical and biological weapons.

The conferees had been in conflict with the administration for weeks over the Senate-drafted provision to impose mandatory sanctions on companies and countries that facilitated the development of such weapons.

Ultimately, the conference committee agreed to grant the president authority to waive the sanctions on countries if he determined it to be in the interest of national security.

In return, the president was required to notify the chairmen and ranking Republican members of the Senate Foreign Relations Committee and House Foreign Affairs Committee 15 days before waiving the sanctions. Under such notification procedures, the president customarily refrained from taking actions that were strongly opposed by the committee leaders.

The administration had long resisted congressional attempts to legislate mandatory sanctions as an infringement on the president's authority to make foreign policy. Administration officials had warned that Bush would veto the State Department bill if the provision was not moderated.

Despite agreement with the administration, the conference committee was unable to complete work on the bill because of jurisdictional difficulties raised by leaders of the Ways and Means Committee.

Rep. Sam M. Gibbons, D-Fla., chairman of the Ways and Means Subcommittee on Trade, told the conferees that his panel had not had a chance to consider a key aspect of the sanctions provision. Gibbons asserted that the legislation's proposed ban on U.S. imports from foreign companies and countries selling chemical or biological weapons came under the jurisdiction of Ways and Means.

The conference committee tried to address Gibbons' concerns by introducing a new, stand-alone measure (HR 3409) in the House that incorporated the sanctions and the presidential waiver provisions from the State Department bill.

The House Foreign Affairs Committee quickly moved to approve the sanctions legislation Sept. 26, referring it to Ways and Means.

Rep. William S. Broomfield, Mich., the ranking Republican on Foreign Affairs, said the legislation "does have the strong support of the administration."

The conference committee resolved other differences over the State Department bill. It stripped Dodd's controversial amendment that would have created a $1 billion loan guarantee program to increase overseas sales by U.S. arms manufacturers.

Sarbanes insisted that the United States should not be assisting in the global proliferation of weapons. House members from both parties also opposed the measure.

After considerable debate, the Senate conferees agreed by a one-vote margin to eliminate the provision.

The conference committee also approved a provision, contained in both the House- and Senate-passed bills, to end the last vestiges of an era when foreign visitors were denied entry into the United States on ideological grounds.

The conferees required the State Department to remove anyone who had been excluded from entering the United States on the basis of political beliefs from its list of those who in the past had been barred entry to the country. The report accompanying the Senate bill said there were more than 250,000 names on the department's list of such people.

The conference committee accepted a Senate provision to allow the department up to three years to excise the names from its list, instead of the tougher amendment approved by the House. But Howard L. Berman, D-Calif., author of the House amendment, said approval of the provision represented an important triumph in the area of civil liberties.

The conference committee also:

- Approved a House-passed provision, strongly supported by Berman, to grant the State Department greater flexibility in closing diplomatic posts. Conferees backed the provision over the objection of Pell, a former foreign service officer.
- Approved an amendment, originally offered in the House by Stephen J. Solarz, D-N.Y., to establish a separate State Department bureau for South Asian affairs. At the conference, Solarz asserted that the bureau for Near Eastern and South Asian Affairs was preoccupied with the Middle East and therefore did not have time to properly address issues on the subcontinent.
- Approved an amendment to the Senate legislation, written by Joseph R. Biden Jr., D-Del., to establish a commission to study the feasibility of instituting government-sponsored broadcasting to China.
- Included a provision banning "Israel only" passports, which were offered by the United States to U.S. citizens traveling to that country. Travelers later could use their regular passports, which had no Israeli stamps, to gain entry into Arab nations.

The practice, necessitated by an Arab boycott of Israel, received widespread attention in 1991 when Sen. Frank R. Lautenberg, D-N.J., was denied entry into Saudi Arabia because of an Israeli stamp on his passport. The legislation also called on the administration to negotiate with Arab nations to end the practice.

- Called for the State Department to comply with provisions in its fiscal 1990-91 authorization bill requiring a private study of allegations of sexual harassment within the department.
- Required the State Department to answer questions from members of the Senate Foreign Relations and House Foreign Affairs committees within 21 days of a request.
- Created 15 scholarships each year for residents of Vietnam to study at U.S. colleges and universities.

Floor Action

On Oct. 4, the Senate approved by voice vote the conference report on the State Department authorization bill (HR 1415 — H Rept 102-238).

On Oct. 8, the House cleared the State Department authorization bill (HR 1415) by voice vote.

President Bush signed the State Department authorization bill (PL 102-138) on Oct. 28

The final version of the bill included some new penalties against countries that used weapons of mass destruction and against foreign companies that sold the material and technology needed to build them.

It called for immediate sanctions against any country found by the president to have used, or prepared to use, chemical or biological weapons. These included a cutoff of U.S. aid and the termination of arms sales and assistance. Additional sanctions were required if the country took no action within three months to end its weapons use.

The only sanction that remained in the State Department bill against companies was a cutoff of all U.S. government purchases and contracts, which would affect only some foreign concerns.

But the key provision requiring import sanctions as a penalty still awaited action in separate legislation (HR 3409) that incorporated the entire package of sanctions.

House Ways and Means Committee Chairman Dan Rostenkowski, D-Ill., said he would not mark up the separate sanctions bill without assurances from the Senate that its members would not attach unrelated revenue provisions, such as a controversial proposal for a capital gains tax cut, to the sanctions measure.

Senate leaders were unable to get such a unanimous-consent agreement before members left Oct. 8 for the Columbus Day recess. House and Senate aides said at least one Republican senator had privately objected to the consent agreement.

Import Sanctions

Once Rostenkowski received assurances from the Senate that no tax amendments would be attached, the Ways and Means Committee approved the import sanctions on Nov. 19 and sent them to the House floor, where they were amended on Nov. 20 into a bill adjusting unemployment benefit formulas (HR 1724).

The administration issued a statement on Nov. 20 saying it had "no objection" to the sanctions measure because it allowed the president to waive the penalties.

The bill called for immediate sanctions to be imposed for at least a year on individuals and foreign companies found to be using, or stockpiling chemical and biological weapons or their components.

Those identified would be banned from exporting products from the United States and from selling goods or services to the U.S. government.

Foreign governments found to be stockpiling or using these weapons would be subject to several sanctions immediately, including the termination of foreign aid, arms sales, other high-technology exports and financing supplied by the U.S. government.

If the country continued using or building chemical or biological weapons after 90 days, it would be hit with further sanctions, including a ban on its imports to the United States, a prohibition on U.S bank loans to the country, further restrictions on high-technology exports and downgrading of diplomatic relations.

The Senate passed HR 1724 on Nov. 26 by voice vote, and the House cleared the bill by voice vote later in the day. President Bush signed the measure (PL 102-182) on Dec. 4. ■

CQ

Chapter 10

APPROPRIATIONS

Appropriators Had Easy Task in '91

Budget rules kept lawmakers to a tight script; four supplemental spending bills enacted

Congress had relatively little trouble writing and approving all but one of the 13 regular spending bills needed to keep the federal government in business in fiscal 1992. The job was considered easy because lawmakers were working from a script written in the 1990 White House-congressional budget summit. The budget rules (PL 101-508) set strict caps for defense, domestic and international spending, and they barred Congress from using savings in one category to exceed the limit in another.

Moreover, as long as the appropriators stayed within the caps, they did not have to worry about finding additional ways to cut the deficit. In fact, the caps allowed discretionary spending authority for domestic programs to grow 5.4 percent from the previous year.

The only bill that was not completed before Congress adjourned would have appropriated funds for foreign operations; it was put off until April 1993 to accommodate a request from President Bush that $10 billion in housing loan guarantees for Israel be delayed to allow Middle East peace talks to get under way. In the meantime, a continuing resolution (CR) kept funds flowing for foreign operations through March 31, 1992.

Dividing Up the Money

The process officially began the week of May 13 when the 13 House Appropriations subcommittee chairmen met behind closed doors to divide up the $513.5 billion available for discretionary spending in fiscal 1992. That was about a third of the $1.59 trillion budget. (The remainder went to mandatory spending and interest on the debt, accounts over which the appropriators had no real control.) The full House Appropriations Committee approved the allocations, known as 602bs, by voice vote on May 22.

Senate appropriators approved their subcommittee allocations by voice vote on June 5. The panel did not stray far from the marker laid down in the House; the differences were reconciled by the two committees in July.

The allocations set the stage for detailed work on programs by each of the subcommittees; in some cases, however, the allocations left few choices. The most dramatic example was a decision by House appropriators to cut $1.3 billion for the Subcommittee on VA-HUD and Independent Agencies; the cut forced appropriators to choose either to increase housing and veterans' programs or to substantially fund NASA's space station. In a highly controversial move, the subcommittee voted to cut the space station. The full House reversed that decision, but only by cutting housing money and freezing all other NASA spending at 1991 levels. In the end, Congress approved $2 billion for the space station, but NASA paid a stiff price in funding lost for other programs.

Stopgap Bills

Congress was able to clear three of the 13 bills before leaving for the August recess, but President Bush vetoed the District of Columbia bill over language that would have permitted the District government to pay for abortions with local tax revenues.

By Oct. 1, the start of fiscal 1992, only one more bill had cleared. (A new District of Columbia bill without the abortion provision had also been cleared.) As a result, Congress began the process of passing short-term CRs to keep the remaining federal departments and programs operating until the 10 outstanding bills had been enacted.

The first stopgap bill (H J Res 332 — PL 102-109), good through Oct. 29, sailed through the Senate on Sept. 25 and cleared the House on Sept. 26; both chambers approved it by voice vote. The bill funded agencies at the lowest of three levels: 1991 spending, the amount in the House-passed bill or the amount in the Senate-passed version.

A second CR (H J Res 360 — PL 102-109) kept the government open through Nov. 14, using the same funding formula. The House passed the measure 288-126 on Oct. 24; the Senate approved it by voice vote the same day. The measure made a special exception for the foreign operations bill, extending foreign aid programs at the 1991 level until March 31. *(Vote 340, p. 82-H)*

A third and final 1992 stopgap funding bill (H J Res 374 — PL 102-163) extended spending authority for the Departments of Defense, Education, Labor, and Health and Human Services through Nov. 26, using the same formula as the previous CRs. The House passed the measure by voice vote Nov. 12; the Senate cleared it Nov. 13 on a 91-4 vote. *(Vote 250, p. 33-S)*

Bush signed the last two spending bills — for Defense and Labor-HHS programs — on Nov. 26. He had vetoed an earlier version of the Labor-HHS measure over language that would have stopped the government from enforcing controversial rules barring abortion counseling in federally funded family planning clinics. After the House failed to override the veto, Congress cleared a second version without the contested language.

Supplemental Appropriations

Congress also cleared four supplemental appropriations bills, three of them providing extra spending for fiscal 1991:

- **Desert Shield/Desert Storm.** The first supplemental (HR 1282 — 102-28) provided $42.6 billion for Operation Desert Shield/Desert Storm. *(p. 680)*
- **'Dire emergency.'** A $5.4 billion "dire emergency" supplemental (HR 1281 — PL 102-27) provided emergency money for Israel and Turkey, and paid home-front costs of the Persian Gulf War. *(p. 668)*
- **Iraqi refugees.** Congress also approved a $572 million supplemental (HR 22-51 — PL 102-55), primarily for assistance to refugees in Iraq and elsewhere. *(p. 458)*
- **Natural disasters.** Work on a fourth supplemental spending bill, for domestic disasters (H J Res 157 — PL 102-229) — took so long that what was originally a 1991 measure had to be changed to a fiscal 1992 bill. *(p. 661)* ■

Status of Appropriations

(As of Dec. 6, 1991)

Bill	House	Senate	Final	Story
Agriculture, Rural Development and Related Agencies (HR 2698 — Conference Report H Rept 102-239)	Passed 6/26/91	Passed 7/30/91	Signed 10/28/91 PL 102-142	p. 581
Commerce, Justice, State, Judiciary (HR 2608 — Conference Report H Rept 102-233)	Passed 6/13/91	Passed 7/31/91	Signed 10/28/91 PL 102-140	p. 531
Defense (HR 2521 — Conference Report H Rept 102-328)	Passed 6/7/91	Passed 9/26/91	Signed 11/26/91 PL 102-172	p. 621
District of Columbia (HR 3291 — Conference Report H Rept 102-181)	Passed 9/16/91	Passed 9/16/91	Signed 10/1/91 PL 102-111	p. 616
Energy and Water Development (HR 2427 — Conference Report H Rept 102-177)	Passed 5/29/91	Passed 7/10/91	Signed 8/17/91 PL 102-104	p. 569
Foreign Operations (HR 2621 — H Rept 102-108)	Passed 6/19/91		Funded by Continuing Resolution (H J Res 360) through 3/92	p. 646
Interior and Related Agencies (HR 2686 — Conference Report H Rept 102-256)	Passed 6/25/91	Passed 9/19/91	Signed 11/13/91 PL 102-154	p. 555
Labor, Health and Human Services, Education (HR 3839, formerly HR 2707, — Conference Report H Rept 102-282)	Veto sustained on HR 2707 11/19/91 HR 3839 passed 11/22/91	HR 2707 Passed 9/12/91	Signed 11/26/91 PL 102-170	p. 501
Legislative Branch (HR 2506 — Conference Report H Rept 102-176)	Passed 6/5/91	Passed 7/17/91	Signed 8/14/91 PL 102-90	p. 544
Military Construction (HR 2426 — Conference Report H Rept 102-236)	Passed 5/30/91	Passed 9/16/91	Signed 10/25/91 PL 102-136	p. 640
Transportation and Related Agencies (HR 2942 — Conference Report H Rept 102-243)	Passed 7/24/91	Passed 9/17/91	Signed 10/28/91 PL 102-143	p. 603
Treasury, Postal Service, General Government (HR 2622 — Conference Report H Rept 102-234)	Passed 6/18/91	Passed 7/18/91	Signed 10/28/91 PL 102-141	p. 591
VA, Housing and Urban Development, Independent Agencies (HR 2519 — Conference Report H Rept 102-226)	Passed 6/6/91	Passed 7/18/91	Signed 10/28/91 PL 102-139	p. 516

Abortion Dispute Derails First HHS Bill

It took two tries, but Congress in the closing week of its session finally cleared a fiscal 1992 appropriations bill for the Departments of Labor, Health and Human Services, and Education that was acceptable to President Bush.

The action came Nov. 22, three days after Bush had vetoed the original Labor-HHS funding bill (HR 2707) because it contained a provision to suspend administration regulations that barred abortion counseling in federally funded family planning clinics.

The House on Nov. 19 failed by a dozen votes to override the president's veto, putting an end to the year's fight over the so-called gag rule. *(Abortion issue, p. 339)*

Both chambers then quickly passed a new Labor-HHS spending measure (HR 3839) that was identical to HR 2707 except for the contested language, which was dropped. Bush signed that measure.

Abortion was not the only issue to complicate the Labor-HHS measure. Money problems also plagued efforts to produce the annual spending bill, which funded most of the government's major health, education and social service programs. Because of the spending caps imposed by the 1990 budget agreement between the White House and Congress, appropriators had a particularly difficult time deciding between popular health and education programs. In the end, they reached agreement only by pushing $4.3 billion worth of spending in the bill into fiscal 1993.

The funding device, which opponents labeled a "scam," cut into the margin of support for the bill.

"A combination of budget pressures and anti-choice votes produced the critical mass to keep us under two-thirds," said Les AuCoin, D-Ore., one of the House's abortion rights leaders.

BOXSCORE

➡ **Fiscal 1992 appropriations for the Departments of Labor, Health and Human Services, and Education (HR 3839, formerly HR 2707).** The $205 billion spending bill provided funding for most federal social programs.

Reports: HR 2707: H Rept 102-121; S Rept 102-104; conference report filed in the House, H Rept 102-282.

KEY ACTION

June 26 — HR 2707 passed the **House** by a vote of 353-74.

Sept. 12 — HR 2707 passed the **Senate** by a vote of 78-22.

Oct. 29 — HR 2707 approved by **House-Senate** conference.

Nov. 6 — The **House** approved conference report by a vote of 272-156.

Nov. 7 — The **Senate** cleared conference report by a vote of 73-24.

Nov. 19 — President Bush vetoed HR 2707.

Nov. 22 — **House** passed HR 3839 by a vote of 364-58; **Senate** cleared HR 3839 by voice vote.

Nov. 26 — President Bush signed HR 3839 — PL 102-170.

HOUSE COMMITTEE ACTION

House appropriators on June 20 one-upped Bush's vaunted education initiatives by boosting spending for remedial education and Head Start programs nearly $2 billion beyond his fiscal 1992 budget request. But the additional funds came at the expense of other programs to help low-income people, as members approved cuts in home energy assistance, rural health, substance abuse and mental health counseling and refugee aid.

In the process, the House Appropriations Committee set the stage for a potentially painful floor vote on HR 2707.

Although the $204 billion measure allowed for a $21 billion increase over fiscal 1991 spending, most of that was for entitlement programs such as Medicare and Medicaid, which appropriators did not control. The $59 billion that was subject to their discretion represented only a slight increase over existing spending.

The Appropriations Committee approved the bill by voice vote, essentially ratifying the recommendations of the Labor, HHS-Education Appropriations Subcommittee and its longtime chairman, William H. Natcher, D-Ky. The full committee made only minor changes during a markup that was dominated by a battle over abortion-related policy issues.

Natcher's subcommittee, which drafted the bill in private on June 6, recommended $28.27 billion for the Education Department, $1.7 billion more than Bush requested. About half of that increase went to the department's compensatory education program (Chapter 1) for educationally disadvantaged children, which was slated for $7.08 billion.

The panel also gave a big boost to the popular Head Start program in HHS, which provided health, education and social services to low-income preschool children. The $2.2 billion approved by the committee was $250 million more than the fiscal 1991 appropriation and $150 million more than Bush sought.

To help pay for the increases in education funding, the panel cut funding for programs designed to aid low-income Americans. Among the big losers was the Low Income Home Energy Assistance Program (LIHEAP), which was allocated $1 billion, $415 million less than in fiscal 1991. The committee did include a $600 million "contingency fund" for the program, but the money could be released only if the president declared an energy emergency. Bush sought $75 million less than the committee approved.

Also slated to receive less than in fiscal 1991 were programs to aid refugees, expand rural health programs, and the Alcohol, Drug Abuse, and Mental Health block grant.

The Outlay Crunch

Only in the world of federal budgeting could members complain that a spending bill appropriating $204 billion was not enough — and be taken seriously by their colleagues. But in putting together the second-largest of the 13 regular appropriations bills (defense was the biggest), members faced knotty problems.

The 1990 White House-congressional budget agree-

Labor/HHS/Education

(In thousands of dollars)

	Fiscal 1991 Appropriation	President's Request	House Bill	Senate Bill	Final Bill
Labor Department					
Job-training grants	$ 2,988,382	$ 2,988,382	$ 3,033,382	$ 3,033,382	$ 3,033,382
Job Corps	867,497	887,497	898,497	927,497	919,533
Trade adjustment, allowances	269,500	226,250	226,250	226,250	226,250
Unemployment compensation (trust funds)	*(2,134,441)*	*(2,262,885)*	*(2,262,885)*	*(2,262,885)*	*(2,248,885)*
Employment Standards Administration	1,456,370	1,342,574	1,342,574	1,341,274	1,341,274
Occupational Safety & Health Administration	285,193	302,107	302,107	305,207	304,157
Other	1,674,595	1,589,637	1,632,263	1,651,566	1,651,634
TOTAL, Labor Department	**$ 7,541,537**	**$ 7,336,447**	**$ 7,435,073**	**$ 7,485,176**	**$ 7,476,230**
Health and Human Services					
Public Health					
Family planning	144,311	150,000	—	162,000	150,000
Ryan White AIDS programs	220,553	220,553	246,819	289,165	280,000
Centers for Disease Control	1,311,586	1,396,927	1,390,662	1,540,982	1,504,924
National Institutes of Health	8,276,739	8,774,886	8,824,886	8,978,133	9,010,405
Alcohol/Drug Abuse/Mental Health	2,940,115	3,048,328	2,917,742	3,175,832	3,081,119
Health Care Financing, Social Security					
Medicaid grants to states	54,654,950	63,407,649	63,499,149	63,499,149	63,499,149
Medicare and other Medicaid	35,335,000	39,401,083	39,421,485	39,401,083	39,421,485
Supplemental Security Income	18,003,921	19,166,491	19,166,491	19,169,491	19,169,491
Black lung benefits	832,592	815,336	815,336	815,336	815,336
Public Welfare					
Family-support payments to states (AFDC)	14,295,146	15,862,146	15,862,146	15,901,046	15,901,046
Payments for workfare programs	1,000,000	1,000,000	1,000,000	1,000,000	1,000,000
Low-Income Home Energy Assistance	1,610,235	1,025,000	1,000,000	1,500,000	1,500,000
Community Services Block Grant	427,737	10,832	420,724	453,431	437,418
Child-care grants	744,925	744,925	705,075	838,000	825,000
Social Services Block Grant (Title XX)	2,800,000	2,800,000	2,800,000	2,800,000	2,800,000
Head Start	1,951,800	2,051,800	1,963,800	1,951,800	1,951,800
Programs for the Aging	767,726	766,750	766,750	822,603	804,419
Foster care, adoption	2,611,281	2,614,005	2,614,005	2,614,005	2,614,005
Other	3,752,210	2,400,634	3,718,747	3,891,527	3,846,365
TOTAL, HHS	**$ 151,680,827**	**$ 165,657,345**	**$ 167,121,817**	**$ 168,803,583**	**$ 168,611,962**
Education Department					
Elementary and Secondary Education					
Compensatory education (Chapter 1)	6,075,655	6,224,334	7,075,750	6,436,526	6,707,014
Impact aid	780,720	620,130	764,756	771,708	771,708
State block grants (Chapter 2)	469,408	462,577	474,600	474,600	474,600
Drug-Free Schools	606,349	631,518	607,018	635,603	623,963
Education Excellence (America 2000)	0	690,000	250,000	75,000	100,000
Head Start, other existing programs	—	—	250,000	250,000	325,000
Bilingual, immigrant education	198,014	200,789	249,000	201,814	225,407
Special education	2,616,307	2,729,853	2,822,676	2,860,756	2,854,895
Higher Education					
Pell grants	5,374,282	5,775,121	5,450,000	5,460,000	5,460,000
Guaranteed student loans	34,671	2,866,680	2,866,680	2,860,247	2,860,247
Liquidation and shortfalls	*(5,381,422)*	*(3,105,711)*	*(3,105,711)*	*(3,105,711)*	*(3,105,711)*
Higher education grants	762,638	784,501	821,438	834,557	827,523
Rehabilitation services	1,889,288	2,003,380	1,998,501	2,071,158	2,077,158
Vocational and adult education	1,245,536	1,254,519	1,651,500	1,403,333	1,429,760
Other	2,830,652	2,337,570	2,984,240	3,081,125	3,037,037
TOTAL, Education Department	**$ 22,883,520**	**$ 26,580,972**	**$ 28,266,159**	**$ 27,416,427**	**$ 27,774,312**
Action	191,292	198,552	193,678	201,691	198,592
Corporation for Public Broadcasting	318,636	260,000	253,309	284,000	275,000
Other related agencies	570,022	578,098	583,286	584,392	583,667
GRAND TOTAL	**$ 183,185,834**	**$ 200,611,414**	**$ 203,853,322**	**$ 204,775,269**	**$ 204,919,763**

SOURCE: House Appropriations Committee

ment, which put strict caps on discretionary spending for all domestic programs, put appropriators in a tight spot. Just funding all of the programs in the bill at existing levels would have put the bill $207 million over its allowed ceiling for fiscal 1992 outlays, or the amount to be spent during the fiscal year.

The outlay crunch explained in part the bill's largess for education programs. Because education funding was spent at a slower rate than health and labor programs, the committee could give education programs more new budget authority (the amount that could be obligated during the fiscal year) without breaching the outlay cap.

A second problem involved procedural matters. In the past, Natcher delayed some of the most painful reckoning by deferring funding decisions for programs that Congress had yet to authorize for the coming fiscal year. Instead, he set aside a reserve fund large enough to fund the programs at the previous year's level, but with no increases.

But in 1990, Natcher's counterpart in the Senate, Labor-HHS Subcommittee Chairman Tom Harkin, D-Iowa, said that because the House did not fund the unauthorized programs, it could not ask for funding levels in excess of those provided in the Senate bill. That put Natcher at a disadvantage in House-Senate conference negotiations. So in 1991, Natcher broke with tradition and provided funding in the bill for most of the unauthorized programs.

One notable exception to that practice was the federal family planning program, Title X of the Public Health Service Act. No family planning money was included in the bill because the program was entangled in abortion-related controversy and committee members were sure someone would try to strike its funding on the floor.

Educators Circle the Wagons

Education lobbyists said they understood why non-education groups were unhappy with the bill's dollar distribution. But Edward M. Elmendorf, vice president for government relations of the American Association of State Colleges and Universities, vowed that education groups would "circle the wagons" to fight off attempts by other groups to cut into their increases.

Although the subcommittee's recommendations provided only contingency funding for the president's "America 2000" initiative — unless it was authorized by the end of 1991, the money was to go to existing programs — Education Secretary Lamar Alexander was not complaining. A statement released by his office said: "We're pleased the committee has appropriated funds for America 2000 and look forward to working with the Congress to reform and strengthen American schools."

The only spending fight at the markup came over an amendment offered by Mickey Edwards, R-Okla., who sought to give small businesses a broader exemption from regular safety inspections by the Occupational Safety and Health Administration (OSHA).

The amendment was backed by the National Federation of Independent Business (NFIB), an increasingly active small-business organization, but the committee rejected it on a largely party-line vote of 17-29.

"We're supposed to be subordinate to the American people, not to the NFIB," said David R. Obey, D-Wis.

HOUSE FLOOR ACTION

The House passed HR 2707 on June 26 by a 353-74 vote, without holding a separate vote on whether to overturn the ban on abortion counseling in family planning clinics. *(Vote 200, p. 50-H)*

Abortion rights supporters said the decision by abortion opponents not to try to strike the provision showed that abortion foes feared they lacked enough votes to sustain an anticipated veto.

Supporters of the rules dismissed that assessment, and said that many members who voted for the popular Labor-HHS bill on passage would vote to sustain a veto.

"Vote for the bill, but get ready to support the veto," Vin Weber, R-Minn., an abortion opponent, counseled his colleagues on the floor.

Although they debated several subjects in addition to abortion, members made few changes to the sweeping measure.

Members adopted by voice vote an amendment offered by Timothy J. Penny, D-Minn., to add $12 million to the Head Start program for low-income preschoolers. The funds, supplementing a proposed hike of $250 million already in the bill, were to be offset by an equal reduction in HHS departmental management accounts.

The House rejected, 55-366, an amendment by Robert S. Walker, R-Pa., to reduce each program by 5.9 percent. *(Vote 199, p. 48-H)*

Members complained about the bill's cuts in drug treatment programs and energy assistance to the poor, but an amendment to alter drug funding was ruled out of order, and no substantive changes were made on energy assistance.

Abortion rights backers won two procedural victories during consideration of the Labor-HHS bill.

As predicted, language added to the bill in committee to require that parents be notified before minors could receive abortions was struck for violating the rule forbidding legislating on an appropriations bill.

Patricia Schroeder, D-Colo., also struck from the bill funding for the Adolescent Family Life program, Title XX of the Public Health Service Act. The program, which received $7.8 million in fiscal 1991, provided grants to organizations that sought to discourage teenagers from becoming sexually active.

Unlike the much larger federal family planning program, Title X of the Public Health Service Act, the Adolescent Family Life program forbade abortion counseling and referrals and required parental consent for most services.

Both programs had remained unauthorized since 1985. The House bill included no funding for the main family planning program.

SENATE COMMITTEE ACTION

The Senate Appropriations Committee on July 11 set up a potential showdown with the House over HR 2707.

While the House bill provided large increases for programs in education, mostly at the expense of programs for those with low incomes, the version approved by the Senate committee, 29-0, increased funding to low-income programs by reducing the size of the education increases in the House bill.

Both the House and Senate versions appropriated more for education programs than the $26.6 billion requested by President Bush. But the Senate committee's total of $27.2 billion was nearly $1.1 billion less than the House provided.

Most of the difference was in funding for the Chapter 1 program of compensatory services for educationally disadvantaged students. The committee's proposed funding of

President's Veto Message

Following is the text of President Bush's Nov. 19 veto message on HR 2707, the fiscal 1992 spending bill for the Departments of Labor, Health and Human Services, and Education.

HR 2707 contains a provision that would prohibit implementation of rules related to the Title X family planning program and abortion. I am therefore compelled to disapprove HR 2707. I will sign a bill that does not include language that prohibits implementation of the abortion counseling and referral rule.

I have informed the Congress on numerous occasions that, consistent with the intent of the statute originally establishing Title X, I would veto any legislation that would entangle Title X with abortion. Accordingly, it is my intention to ensure that no federal funds are used to support abortion except in cases where the life of the mother would be endangered if the fetus were carried to term.

Under the regulations upheld by the Supreme Court, pregnant women who seek services from projects funded by Title X are appropriately referred to qualified providers for prenatal care and other social services, including counseling. The administration seeks to ensure the integrity of Title X as a pre-pregnancy family planning program and to ensure that women who are pregnant or have a medical problem are referred to providers who can ensure continuity of care. We do not seek to limit in any way the counseling pregnant women receive when they seek services from those providers.

In a memorandum to Secretary [of Health and Human Services Louis W.] Sullivan on Nov. 5, 1991, I reiterated my commitment to preserving the confidentiality of the doctor-patient relationship and seeing that the operation of the Title X family planning program is compatible with free speech and the highest standards of medical care. My memorandum makes clear that there is no "gag rule" to interfere with the doctor-patient relationship. I have directed that in implementing these regulations, nothing prevent a woman from receiving complete medical information about her condition from a physician. There can be no doubt that my administration is committed to the protection of free speech. The United States Supreme Court specifically found that the regulations in no way violate free speech rights.

HR 2707 contains several provisions that would delay the obligation of over $4.4 billion until the last few weeks of fiscal 1992 and early fiscal 1993. The magnitude of the delays contained in HR 2707 would make it much more difficult to remain within the fiscal 1993 spending limits required by the Budget Enforcement Act. ■

$6.3 billion was $208 million more than the fiscal 1991 appropriation and $60 million more than Bush requested. But it was still $790 million less than the House provided.

The Senate's education total, however, included $325 million for programs that were not strictly educational. That amount, provided under the auspices of Bush's education initiative, America 2000, was to be used in the Senate bill to provide additional funding to three HHS programs: Head Start, Community Health Centers and Comprehensive Child Development Centers. None of the programs were part of the Bush education initiative.

Emphasis on Children

Increased emphasis on programs for children and low-income families was a key goal for Senate appropriators. Labor-HHS Subcommittee Chairman Harkin said at both the subcommittee markup July 11 and the full committee meeting later that day that the aim was "to tip the scales in favor of the next generation of Americans."

To that effect, the bill increased funding over Bush's request and the House bill for a wide variety of programs, including the Maternal and Child Health Block Grant ($686 million, $132 million more than the Bush request and $106 million more than the House); and the Preventive Health Services Block Grant ($150 million, $42.5 million more than the Bush request and $57.3 million more than the House).

The Senate committee bill also funded the controversial federal family planning program, Title X of the Public Health Service Act. The $162 million in the bill was $18 million more than the program received in fiscal 1991 and $12 million more than Bush sought.

The House bill provided no funding for the program, although it, like the Senate committee bill, prohibited the Bush administration from enforcing regulations barring abortion counseling.

The bill appropriated $289 million for programs under the auspices of the 1990 AIDS bill named for Ryan White, the Indiana schoolboy whose battle with the disease drew nationwide attention. The total for the programs, which provided emergency funding to cities hardest hit by the epidemic and for preventive programs, was $69 million more than the amount available in fiscal 1991 (the same as the Bush request) and $42 million more than the House bill. *(1990 Almanac, p. 582)*

Energy Assistance Raised

Although the Senate bill provided more than the House or the Bush request for LIHEAP, backers complained that the total was still not enough.

The committee bill appropriated $1.3 billion for the energy assistance program, up from the House's $1 billion and Bush's request of $925 million.

But not only was the amount down from fiscal 1991's $1.6 billion, $445 million of the Senate total was not to be available until Sept. 30, 1992, the last day of the fiscal year.

That drew cries of outrage from Frost Belt legislators, led by Sen. Warren B. Rudman, R-N.H.

"Some programs are truly safety net programs," said Rudman. "Loss of heating assistance poses life-threatening situations."

But Harkin, while expressing support for the program, said he was limited by the 1990 budget agreement between Congress and the White House. As a result of that agreement, he noted in his opening statement, the $57.8 billion allocation for discretionary programs over which the subcommittee had direct authority was $1 billion less than the amount needed to maintain all programs at fiscal 1991 levels after accounting for inflation, and $87 million less than needed to maintain the programs simply at the fiscal 1991 amounts.

"We're in a straitjacket here," agreed Mark O. Hatfield, Ore., the full committee's ranking Republican, after other members fell into an argument over whether to fund research into AIDS or other diseases. Rather than choosing among basic needs, he said, "we should be arguing heating for the poor vs. chemical weapons."

SENATE FLOOR ACTION

After three days of wide-ranging debate over AIDS, abortion and various domestic spending priorities, the Senate on Sept. 12 overwhelmingly approved HR 2707.

But the 78-22 vote in favor of the measure belied its likely fate. Bush vowed to veto the $204.8 billion bill over several provisions, most notably language that sought to lift the so-called gag rule. Senators also added language permitting federal funding of abortions in certain cases of rape and incest. *(Vote 189, p. 25-S)*

The Senate — like the House before it — declined to take separate votes on the abortion provisions.

The sole abortion-related issue that surfaced during floor debate was the question of whether parents should be notified before a minor could obtain an abortion.

Members overwhelmingly approved a compromise proposal by Nancy Landon Kassebaum, R-Kan., even though it was vehemently opposed by groups on both sides of the abortion question.

Kassebaum's compromise generally required that at least one parent be notified within 48 hours or provide consent before a girl under age 18 could obtain an abortion at any facility that received federal family planning funds.

But Kassebaum's plan allowed exceptions, including cases in which: a physician certified the presence of a health emergency; a judge permitted the girl to obtain the abortion; or a professional counselor with no financial interest in the abortion certified that notification could put the girl at risk of physical abuse or emotional harm.

On another social issue, senators by 99-1 approved an amendment ordering the Labor Department to complete action on standards requiring health workers to observe "universal precautions" to prevent transmitting AIDS, hepatitis B and other blood-borne diseases. *(Vote 184, p. 24-S)*

Funding Debate

For the first time in years, senators seriously debated budget priorities as they tackled the Labor-HHS bill.

Harkin picked a fight with some of the Senate's most influential budget policy-makers with a proposal to shift $3.15 billion to domestic programs from the Pentagon budget.

Harkin's amendment would have channeled the money to 10 domestic programs, including $400 million for the National Cancer Institute, $100 million for immunization programs, $270 million for Pell student aid grants, and $900 million for Head Start, the popular program for low-income preschool children.

Although he was planning the amendment before Congress left for its summer recess in August, Harkin said the sudden crumbling of the Soviet Union and of the communist military threat during the recess further justified defense budget cuts.

His arguments won words of support from fellow Democratic liberals. But the 1990 White House-congressional budget agreement, which prohibited shifting funds from defense to domestic programs, held more sway.

"I have a great deal of sympathy" for the amendment, said Budget Committee Chairman Jim Sasser, D-Tenn. But, he added, "If we can breach the budget-summit agreement for this particular appropriations bill, then clearly we can breach it for a whole host of appropriations bills to follow. [That] is a short-term ticket for fiscal chaos in this body."

The Senate rejected, 28-69, Harkin's effort to waive budget rules. The total fell well short of the 60 votes he needed. *(Vote 182, p. 24-S)*

Appropriations subcommittees were required to keep their bill totals under preordained spending caps, in terms of both budget authority (the amount obligated to programs) and outlays (the amount to be spent in the fiscal year).

Harkin had met his outlay caps and came in well below the authority ceiling. But education groups, angered by what they considered Harkin's underfunding of their programs, enlisted Tim Wirth, D-Colo., to draft a floor amendment to add funds to the subcommittee's leftover budget authority.

Wirth planned a variation on a theme Harkin had been playing since he became chairman of the subcommittee in 1989. Harkin had frequently "borrowed" from the following year's outlay total by adding budget authority to programs but making the money available only at the end of the fiscal year, thus pushing outlays into the following fiscal year.

In 1991 the practice caught up with Harkin, and the fiscal 1992 bill reached its outlay cap with nearly $1 billion in budget authority to spare.

Harkin chafed at the prospect of Wirth's pushing still more outlays into fiscal 1993. Because all of the money in Wirth's original amendment went for education, explained Harkin on Sept. 10, "the problem was that next year, the health community would come out on the short end."

Instead, Harkin drafted his amendment using the defense money to pay for it. But assuming he would not prevail, he also worked out a compromise with Wirth to use up the subcommittee's remaining budget authority. The new version provided an additional $300 million for education programs, $200 million for the low-income energy aid program and $10 million for child immunizations.

After rejecting Harkin's defense transfer plan, the Senate approved his compromise, 79-21. *(Vote 183, p. 24-S)*

Sex Survey

Senators sparred Sept. 12 over whether taxpayers should fund scientific surveys of sexual behavior.

In July, during House consideration of a bill (HR 2507) to reauthorize the National Institutes of Health (NIH), members rejected an amendment to ban a proposed $18 million study of teenagers' sexual habits. Health and Human Services Secretary Louis W. Sullivan had already announced cancellation of the survey. *(NIH reauthorization, p. 346)*

But the Senate went a step further on the Labor-HHS bill, approving an amendment by Jesse Helms, R-N.C., to bar both the teen survey and a planned study of adult sexual behavior.

Instead, the Helms amendment directed that $10 million be taken from the National Institute on Child Health and Human Development (the agency planning the study), to fund the Adolescent Family Life Program, Title XX of the Public Health Service Act.

The House provided no funding for the family life program, which received $7.8 million in fiscal 1991 to provide grants to organizations that sought to discourage teenagers from becoming sexually active. Although the Senate Appropriations Committee provided no funding for it either, an amendment by Slade Gorton, R-Wash., a day earlier had restored the program to the bill, although with no specified amount.

"The results of these surveys can never be trusted because mostly it's a brainwashing job," said Helms, who charged that the studies were part of the "homosexual movement's agenda to legitimize their sexual behavior and thereby gain public acceptance."

On the other hand, he said, the family life program was "the only federally funded sex education program that counsels our children to abstain from sex until they are married."

Continued on p. 513

Labor/HHS/Education Provisions

The second-largest of the 13 regular annual spending bills funded the Departments of Labor, Health and Human Services (HHS), Education and 18 related agencies. Many of the federal government's most popular social programs, such as Head Start for preschoolers and the National Institutes of Health, were included in the bill. (HR 3839 — PL 102-170)

Appropriators had little say over how roughly 70 percent of the bill's $205 billion was spent. That majority was for such mandatory programs as Medicaid, the federal-state health program for the poor, and for unemployment benefits. Other Capitol Hill committees determined eligibility and funding levels for those programs.

For fiscal 1992, appropriators had roughly $59 billion in discretionary funds to parcel out to more than 500 separate programs. The $59 billion was the third-highest allotted in an appropriations bill, trailing the spending bills for defense and for the Departments of Veterans Affairs, Housing and Urban Development, and independent agencies.

As in past years, debate over sensitive social issues largely overshadowed consideration of the bill's funding totals. Fiscal 1992's version of the abortion debate concerned two questions: whether to bar enforcement of an administration ban on abortion counseling in federally funded family planning clinics, and whether to allow federal funding of abortion in certain cases of rape or incest.

Conferees agreed to drop the rape and incest language, as well as a controversial Senate amendment that would have required parents to be notified in certain cases before a minor could obtain an abortion. That left only the identical language approved by both chambers that would block enforcement of the abortion-counseling ban. Upheld by the Supreme Court in May 1991, the regulations were dubbed a "gag rule" by critics who hoped to overturn them by linking the issue to the popular funding bill. But President Bush vetoed the bill, and after the House failed to override, Congress stripped out the "gag rule" language.

On other issues, the Senate overwhelmingly adopted an amendment to require the Labor Department to complete action on standards requiring health workers to take "universal precautions" to prevent the spread of AIDS, hepatitis B and other bloodborne diseases. Senators also voted to block two controversial studies of sexual habits of U.S. citizens. Both amendments were adopted by conferees and included in the final version of the bill.

Also of considerable controversy was more than $3.2 billion appropriated in the bill with the stipulation that funds not be available until Sept. 30, 1992, the last day of the fiscal year. The device effectively pushed most of the actual spending into fiscal 1993; thus, it was not counted against the bill's ceiling for actual budget outlays. Members spread the "delayed obligations" over 50 separate programs.

Members also deferred an additional $1.1 billion by putting off until fiscal 1993 all funding for a program to help states cope with the costs of illegal aliens who were legalized under the 1986 immigration bill.

DEPARTMENT OF LABOR

Training and Employment Services

The Labor Department's Employment and Training Administration oversaw job-training and related skills programs for dislocated and economically disadvantaged workers, primarily through the 1982 Job Training Partnership Act (JTPA), cited during the 1988 presidential campaign by then-Sen. Dan Quayle, R-Ind., as one of his primary legislative achievements.

The program enjoyed bipartisan support, but some lawmakers had complained that it had helped many skilled people who did not need government help to find a job. A reauthorization bill (HR 3033) introduced in 1991 would make program changes aimed at increasing its effectiveness.

The $4.2 billion appropriated in the bill funded a "program year," running from July 1, 1992, through June 30, 1993, rather than the traditional fiscal year that ran from Oct. 1 to Sept. 30.

Also under JTPA was the Job Corps, established during President Lyndon B. Johnson's War on Poverty in the mid-1960s to provide remedial education and job skills to disadvantaged youths. The $920 million in the bill included $73 million to build and expand residential Job Corps centers.

The bill included $395 million for the Community Service Employment for Older Americans program, which provided low-income elderly people about 65,000 jobs in hospitals, libraries and other community facilities.

Jobless Benefits

The bill appropriated $2.2 billion for federal unemployment benefits and the federal government's share of the benefits paid by states. Under existing law, states provided up to 26 weeks of benefits to unemployed workers. Under a separate extended benefits program, if a state's economy was in severe trouble, the state's unemployed workers could qualify for an additional 13 weeks of benefits. Costs of providing that compensation were split 50-50 between the states and the federal government. Most of the funding was an entitlement; that is, any person who met specific requirements could get the benefits.

The bill also provided $1.5 billion for administrative costs of processing unemployment insurance claims.

Employment Standards

The bill appropriated $232 million for the Employment Standards Administration, charged with administering many of the federal government's laws to protect workers. These included the Fair Labor Standards Act, which set the minimum wage and other working conditions, and the Immigration and Nationality Act, which governed the employment of foreign workers.

The agency also enforced non-discrimination laws relating to companies that did business with the federal government and oversaw income maintenance programs for disabled workers not covered by Social Security.

Pension Benefit Guaranty Corporation (PBGC)

Created in 1974, the PBGC was a government-owned corporation chaired by the secretary of Labor. Its mission was to guarantee pension payments for retirees of companies that went out of business or whose plans failed, and it was financed primarily by insurance premiums paid by covered companies. Appropriators determined the amount the corporation could spend on administrative expenses, a figure set at $73 million for fiscal 1992.

Occupational Safety and Health

The bill appropriated $304 million for the Occupational Safety and Health Administration (OSHA), which set and enforced standards to protect workers on the job. It also gathered statistics about on-the-job injuries and illnesses and aided states in administering and enforcing their programs.

Bureau of Labor Statistics

A total of $307 million was provided for the Bureau of Labor Statistics, the federal government agency that collected and analyzed data including unemployment rates and the Consumer Price Index, which measured changes in retail prices.

Mine Safety/Black Lung Benefits

The Labor Department was also responsible for ensuring the safety of workers in the nation's mines. The bill appropriated $185 million for the Mine Safety and Health Administration, which set health and safety standards for, and conducted inspections in, the nation's mines. The department also oversaw the Black Lung Disability Trust Fund, an entitlement program for afflicted coal miners and their families. Financing for the program, estimated to cost $918 million in fiscal 1992, came from an excise tax on coal, payments made by mine operators and contributions from the U.S. Treasury.

DEPARTMENT OF HEALTH AND HUMAN SERVICES

Often referred to as the "people's department," the Department of Health and Human Services (HHS) administered a myriad of programs that touched the lives of virtually every American. Even those who did not contribute a portion of each paycheck for — or collect benefits from — Social Security and Medicare were affected by research funded by the National Institutes of Health or consumed products regulated by the Food and Drug Administration. HHS also administered programs for the poor, including Aid to Families with Dependent Children (the principal federal-state welfare program), Medicaid and Head Start.

With a budget estimated at $525 billion for fiscal 1992, HHS was by far the federal government's largest single agency, accounting for more than a third of the total federal budget. That's even more than the Defense Department's budget of just under $300 billion.

Most of the agency's funding, however, was not included in the department's annual appropriations bill. Funding for the Food and Drug Administration (FDA), for example, was by tradition provided in the Agriculture spending bill. (FDA was part of that department until 1940.) Funding for most of the department's two largest programs — Medicare, the federal health insurance program for 34 million elderly and disabled Americans, and Social Security — did not appear in the spending bill either. More than half the department's budget — an estimated $288 billion in fiscal 1992 — was for Social Security retirement and disability benefits. Another $76 billion was for the hospital portion of Medicare. Both programs had permanent appropriations and were financed directly from the proceeds of the 7.65 percent payroll tax paid by workers and their employers, which were paid into earmarked trust funds.

By contrast, three-quarters of the amount needed to fund Medicare's Part B, which covered physician and other outpatient costs, appeared in the bill. The remaining 25 percent was financed by monthly premiums that beneficiaries paid for the optional program. For fiscal 1992, that was estimated to require $38.7 billion in appropriations.

MANDATORY PROGRAMS

Most of the $168.6 billion in the fiscal 1992 bill for the department was for so-called mandatory programs, over which appropriators had only limited authority.

Under traditional entitlement programs, such as Medicare, the government paid for anyone who qualified, and funds were appropriated according to eligibility and price estimates. Caps for the programs, as well as basic eligibility requirements, were determined by authorizing committees, largely Ways and Means and Energy and Commerce in the House, and Finance in the Senate.

Among the major capped entitlements in the bill were:

- **Social Services Block Grant, Title XX of the Social Security Act** ($2.8 billion cap). States could use their funds, distributed according to population, for services, including child care and aid to the homebound elderly, that were aimed at helping the poor or disabled become self-sufficient.
- **Job Opportunities and Basic Skills (JOBS) Program** ($1 billion cap). The 1988 welfare overhaul (PL 100-485) required states to put into effect JOBS education and training programs in an effort to move adult welfare recipients into full-time jobs.
- **Child care for families** ($300 million cap). This new program, supporting child care for families who needed such care in order to work and were at risk of needing welfare absent available child care, was created in 1990 as part of an omnibus child-care bill folded into the fiscal 1991 budget-reconciliation package (PL 101-508).

The bill included funding for uncapped entitlement programs, which required the government to spend as much as it took to assist all those who qualified. Amounts were determined largely according to estimates. Among the biggest:

- **Medicare Part B.** The bill appropriated $38.7 billion for the optional portion of Medicare, which underwrote part of the costs of physician and outpatient care for 34 million elderly and disabled beneficiaries. Under existing law, the federal government paid 80 percent of Part B costs; beneficiary premiums made up the difference.
- **Medicaid.** The bill provided $59.9 billion for the federal share of Medicaid, the federal-state health program for the poor. Following tradition, that total included funding for the first quarter of fiscal 1993. (This total, as well as the totals for the uncapped entitlements below, also reflected amounts for the first quarter of fiscal 1992 approved in the fiscal 1991 bill). Medicaid would provide benefits for an estimated 29 million people in fiscal 1992. The Medicaid total did not reflect administration-proposed savings of $91.5 million that would come from requiring health facilities to help pay the costs of inspecting them for compliance with Medicaid standards. Such a change would have to be made by the authorizing committees, which had rejected such proposals.
- **Aid to Families with Dependent Children (AFDC).** The bill provided $12.1 billion for the federal share of AFDC, the principal federal-state welfare program. That included funding for the first quarter of fiscal 1993. Another $2.4 billion was included for adjunct programs, among them

child care for families in job-training programs.

• **Supplemental Security Income.** The bill appropriated $17.5 billion for Supplemental Security Income (SSI), the federal welfare program for low-income aged, blind and disabled people. That amount included funding for the first quarter of fiscal 1993.

• **Foster care and adoption assistance.** The bill appropriated $2.6 billion for the foster care and adoption assistance programs, both of which were funded jointly by states and the federal government. The federal government helped states pay foster-care costs of children who would have qualified for welfare if they lived at home. The adoption assistance program supported efforts to find permanent homes for difficult-to-place youngsters.

Although they had little say about overall totals for entitlement programs, appropriators had some authority to allocate some specific sums for set purposes within those programs. Two of the most prominent examples were:

• **Medicare contractors.** The bill allocated $1.5 billion to pay the insurance companies that process claims for Medicare. Another $257 million was set aside in a contingency fund that would become available to meet "unanticipated costs."

• **Social Security administrative costs.** The bill allowed the Social Security Administration to spend up to $4.6 billion to run its programs. The funds, taken from the Social Security trust funds, paid for operation of Social Security old-age and disability programs as well as SSI.

DISCRETIONARY PROGRAMS

Research and Data Programs

By far the largest programs within HHS's discretionary pot paid for research into health and social services.

• **National Institutes of Health (NIH).** The $9 billion appropriated for the 18 research establishments that made up NIH accounted for more than 15 percent of the entire bill's discretionary program total. President Bush asked for $8.77 billion, up from fiscal 1991's $8.3 billion.

NIH had many champions in Congress and long had been a bipartisan favorite of the Labor-HHS Appropriations subcommittees. But along with congressional largess came strings. The House report on the bill devoted 52 of its 214 pages to directives for NIH to follow; the Senate report's NIH section consumed 74 of its 285 pages.

Both chambers emphasized women's and minority health and said NIH was not including enough women and minorities as research subjects and not devoting enough resources to ailments that disproportionately afflicted them.

The Senate report directed that NIH's National Cancer Institute spend at least $40 million on breast, ovarian and uterine cancer, while the House report noted that women's health received the committee's "highest priority" and accounted for more than a third of the increases in the bill. The House also directed the National Institute on Child Health and Human Development to establish a gynecology research program at NIH's campus in Bethesda, Md.

During the conference on the bill, members struggled over how to reconcile the different report language without running afoul of House Chairman William H. Natcher, D-Ky. Natcher had steadfastly refused to earmark funds for specific diseases in the bill. Members ultimately agreed on conference report language noting the increase in the bill for NIH and restating their intention "that funding for direct research on breast, ovarian and prostate cancer receive significant increases as outlined in both" the House and Senate reports. The prostate cancer language was added at the urging of conferee Sen. Ted Stevens, R-Alaska, who had prostate cancer surgery in August 1991.

House and Senate committees also noted NIH steps to address the problem of research institutions, primarily universities, charging the federal government for inappropriate expenses disguised as "indirect costs" of the research. Major universities had been found to use federal funds to purchase art, finance trips and maintain presidents' homes and yachts. But both reports cautioned that further action might be required, and the Senate report directed the department's inspector general to conduct audits "to insure that the reform package proposed by the administration is having the desired effect."

• **Alcohol, Drug Abuse and Mental Health Administration.** ADAMHA was NIH's sister umbrella agency. Unlike NIH, which treated patients only as an adjunct to research, ADAMHA's five components — the National Institute of Mental Health, National Institute on Drug Abuse, National Institute on Alcoholism and Alcohol Abuse, and Offices for Substance Abuse Prevention and Treatment Improvement — did research and funded major mental health and substance abuse treatment and prevention programs.

With a fiscal 1992 appropriation of $3.1 billion, ADAMHA was dwarfed by NIH. Nevertheless, it was the second-largest discretionary health program.

The largest single line item in the ADAMHA budget was the $1.4 billion for the alcohol, drug abuse and mental health block grant, which provided funds to states to help operate prevention, treatment and rehabilitation programs. Funds were allocated according to a formula based on each state's relative wealth, the average age of its residents, how many people lived in urban areas and how much the state received in prior years. Rural legislators had complained that the formula was unfair to their districts.

The bill provided an additional $928 million for mental health, drug abuse and alcohol abuse research programs. In keeping with its emphasis on women's health, the Senate report directed ADAMHA to establish an Office of Women's Health Research and Services, noting that the level of attention paid to women's health issues "does not reflect the fact that the majority of Americans are women." NIH established a similar office in 1990.

Information Gathering

Another key function of the nation's health infrastructure was the gathering, analysis and dissemination of data used to make policy and other decisions.

• **Centers for Disease Control (CDC).** One of the largest of these programs was the $480 million for AIDS-related activities in the Public Health Service's Centers for Disease Control. CDC, whose epidemiologists investigated and responded to outbreaks of contagious diseases nationwide, had become one of the federal government's leaders in combating AIDS. It used its AIDS funds to help track cases of AIDS and HIV, the AIDS virus; to help finance blood testing, counseling and partner notification programs; and to provide information, education and prevention services.

• **Agency for Health Care Policy and Research.** This two-year-old agency was created in the 1989 budget-reconciliation bill (PL 101-239) to study the effectiveness of medical treatments and the organization, financing and delivery of health-care services. It got $102 million in the bill. The agency was also slated to receive an additional $13 million from other Public Health Service agencies as well as $6 million from the Medicare trust fund, bringing its total fiscal 1992 budget to $121 million.

• **National Center for Health Statistics.** The bill appropriated $51 million for the National Center for Health Statistics, which collected, analyzed and disseminated statistics on health, illness and disability, in addition to tracking births, deaths, marriages and divorces. The center was also authorized to receive an additional $29 million from other Public Health Service agency budgets.

Other appropriations for research/data programs included:

• **National Institute on Occupational Safety and Health.** This institute got $107 million to conduct research and set criteria for standards aimed at reducing on-the-job illness and injury.

• **Adoption opportunities program.** $13 million went to this program, which sought to find permanent homes for hard-to-place children and included operation of the National Adoption Clearinghouse, a national adoption information exchange system.

• **National Practitioner Data Bank.** $6 million was appropriated for the data bank, to maintain a nationwide list of physicians and other health-care practitioners who had been found guilty of malpractice, lost their licenses or otherwise been professionally sanctioned.

• **Child welfare research programs.** $7 million was appropriated for studies of child welfare, child care, youth development and family and child development.

Health Delivery Programs

Largely through the department's Health Resources and Services Administration, HHS also operated many programs to provide or help states offer health care.

• **Maternal and Child Health block grant.** This was the second-largest of the block grant programs, after the Alcohol, Drug Abuse and Mental Health services block grant, with a fiscal 1992 appropriation of $650 million. The grant helped state and local health agencies provide a variety of services aimed at reducing infant mortality and improving the health of young children.

• **Community health centers.** The bill appropriated $527 million for a network of more than 500 clinics that provided primary health care to about 5.4 million individuals annually, most of them with low incomes or living in areas with shortages of health professionals.

• **Healthy Start**. The Bush administration's controversial initiative to test comprehensive programs in selected areas with high infant mortality rates received $75 million. Bush requested $139 million. Conferees earmarked $10 million for infant mortality reduction projects at commmunity and migrant health centers, including those not in designated "Healthy Start" communities.

• **Immunizations.** For the CDC's immunization program, the bill appropriated a total of $298 million, the bulk of which provided grants to states to help vaccinate children against preventable diseases, including measles, mumps and polio. The House and Senate reports directed CDC to put more emphasis on vaccinating children under age 2, particularly since they had been the primary victims of sporadic measles outbreaks.

• **AIDS services.** In addition to the funds for AIDS research, the 1990 Ryan White AIDS bill authorized funds for areas hardest hit by the epidemic as well as funds to create networks of comprehensive treatment services for those afflicted with the disease and their families. The bill appropriated $280 million, an increase over the fiscal 1991 total (and fiscal 1992 administration request) of $221 million, but well short of the approximately $880 million authorized in 1990.

• **Family planning.** Appropriators ultimately approved $150 million for the federal family planning program, Title X of the Public Health Service Act — easily the most controversial program in the entire bill. Unauthorized since 1985 due to abortion-related controversies, the program had nevertheless obtained funding each year. The administration requested $150 million for the program but wanted Congress to convert it into a block grant in which funds would only be given to states. In 1991, states could receive funds, but so could individual private, nonprofit agencies, such as affiliates of Planned Parenthood Federation Inc. The biggest controversy surrounding the family planning program in 1991 stemmed from efforts to block administration regulations barring abortion counseling in family planning clinics.

• **National Health Service Corps.** This program, which paid for the education of doctors and other health professionals in exchange for their practicing on Indian reservations or medically underserved rural and inner-city areas, was given $101 million.

• **Sexually transmitted diseases.** CDC's program to prevent sexually transmitted diseases, which made grants to state and local governments as well as private facilities and voluntary health agencies to track, treat and prevent such diseases as syphilis, got $89 million.

• **Breast and cervical cancer.** A program enacted in 1990 to screen women for breast and cervical cancer when they were most treatable got $50 million.

Social Service Delivery Programs

Although its health programs were considerably larger, HHS also oversaw programs that provided social services to specific groups of people. These were separate from HHS programs aimed at those with low incomes, although beneficiaries generally had to meet other specific requirements, such as being disabled or elderly.

• **Administration on Aging.** The largest such programs were those operated by the Administration on Aging under the 1966 Older Americans Act. The bill appropriated $804 million for the programs, which included funds to run senior citizens' centers, to provide hot meals both in seniors' homes and in group settings, to provide legal assistance, and to provide homemaker, home-health and other services needed by frail elderly people to continue living at home.

• **Child-care grants.** The bill appropriated $825 million — the full authorized level — for the child-care grant program Congress approved as part of 1990's budget-reconciliation bill. States could use up to 75 percent of amounts received to pay for child care for families with incomes below 75 percent of the state's median income.

None of the funds, however, were available until Sept. 30, 1992, the last day of the fiscal year.

• **Family crisis.** Another $114 million was appropriated for family crisis programs. These included grants to state and local governments to improve their ability to prevent, detect and treat child abuse and family violence, as well as to address the needs of runaway and homeless youths.

• **Child welfare services.** This $274 million program, Title IV-B of the Social Security Act, gave states funding for services aimed at keeping troubled families together.

• **Developmental disabilities.** This included $90 million for several programs to promote the independence and protect the rights of those with developmental disabilities, including mental retardation and cerebral palsy.

• **Protection and advocacy for the mentally ill.** This was a $20 million program within the National Institute of Mental Health to ensure protection of the rights of mentally ill individuals while they were in institutions and for 90 days after discharge.

Low-Income Programs

Among the largest of HHS's discretionary programs were those aimed at helping the poor become self-sufficient.

• **Head Start.** The largest, best-known and most politically popular of these programs, Head Start provided low-income preschoolers with early education, health, nutrition and social services. The bill appropriated $2.2 billion for the program, enough to enroll an additional 39,000 children over the 596,000 served in fiscal 1991. President Bush requested $2.1 billion. The subject of a bidding war between Congress and the Bush administration, funding for Head Start had nearly doubled over four years, but the program still enrolled fewer than half of all eligible preschoolers.

• **Low Income Home Energy Assistance Program.** LIHEAP, as it was known, was second only to the family planning program in terms of appropriations fights. When the fur stopped flying in 1991, members appropriated $1.5 billion for the program, which helped low-income families pay heating and cooling bills and weatherize their homes. That was a $110 million decrease from fiscal 1991 and well below the program's fiscal 1992 authorization level of $2.23 billion, but more than the $1 billion Bush requested. Still, the total could ultimately be less than it appeared: Conferees used a variety of budget devices to reach their final total. Members actually appropriated only $1.014 billion for the "regular" LIHEAP program for fiscal 1992. Another $405.6 million was appropriated on a delayed basis and would become available on Sept. 30, 1992, the last day of the fiscal year. Members declared an additional $80 million an "emergency," as defined in the 1991 budget bill (PL 101-508). That meant the money did not count toward the subcommittee's budget limits. Finally, members appropriated $300 million that would be available only if the president declared an emergency. Since administration officials had stated in no uncertain terms that such a declaration would not be forthcoming, that final amount was not included in the $1.5 billion total for the program.

LIHEAP was a target for elimination under the Reagan administration and for major cuts under Bush; Frost Belt legislators fought every year to maintain it. But the program had lost two of its most ardent advocates, first with the 1988 defeat of Sen. Lowell P. Weicker Jr., R-Conn., and then the 1991 death of Rep. Silvio O. Conte, R-Mass.

• **Community Services Block Grants.** Another budget-cutting target of the Bush administration kept alive by Congress was this program, which, like Head Start, was one of President Johnson's Great Society social programs. It provided funds to local community action agencies that offered services aimed at helping the poor become self-sufficient. In proposing to end the program, Bush officials said "basic reforms have been institutionalized" and funding increased for other programs with the same goal. The block grant program wound up with an appropriation of $360 million. Bush requested $11 million, enough only to continue the National Youth Sports Program, which provided low-income youth recreation and counseling opportunities through the National Collegiate Athletic Association.

• **Refugee and Entrant Assistance Program.** This provided states with funds to help offset social services and other costs associated with helping settle newcomers during their first months in the United States. The program also funded job-training and English-tutoring programs. It received $411 million.

• **Comprehensive Child Development Centers.** Designed to provide continuous support services for low-income children and their families from birth until they entered school, this program received $24 million, the same as the program received in fiscal 1991 and the amount requested by Bush.

Education and Training Programs

HHS devoted considerable funding and resources to education and training programs for health and social service professionals. It was impossible to come up with a definitive dollar figure, because funding for many was included within larger appropriations for programs that provided services or paid for research as well as training. Other programs, such as the National Health Service Corps, accomplished dual purposes: training of health professionals and services when those professionals paid off their debt by practicing for years in medically underserved areas.

• **Health professions.** The health professions program was the largest of the efforts aimed exclusively at training. The bill appropriated $235 million for two dozen separate programs for education of doctors, dentists and other health professionals. Most programs were aimed at encouraging health professionals to enter primary-care fields such as family medicine and geriatrics, and at increasing the number of minority professionals. Like President Ronald Reagan, Bush proposed eliminating most of the programs, and he sought a total of $84 million.

• **Nurse training.** The bill appropriated another $61 million for nurse training programs, also targeted for elimination in the Bush budget. The programs enabled nursing schools to recruit low-income and minority applicants and offer advanced training in such specialties as anesthesia and obstetrics.

• **Office for Substance Abuse Prevention.** This office in ADAMHA sought to train counselors, health professionals, social workers and others in preventing and treating substance abuse. It got $21 million.

• **Child Development Associate Scholarship Program.** $1.4 million was devoted for funds to help low-income individuals obtain the credential required to teach early-childhood education programs.

• **Mental health training programs.** These got $38 million.

ABORTION

Both the House and Senate bills included language to bar enforcement of controversial Bush administration regulations — upheld by the Supreme Court on May 23 — barring abortion counseling in federally funded family planning clinics. The "funding limitation" language would not overturn the regulations, which dated back to the Reagan administration, because an outright overturn would have been subject to being deleted from the bill on the

House floor for impermissibly legislating on an appropriations bill. But the language was a casualty of Bush's veto.

The Senate added to the bill two other amendments. One would permit federal funding of abortions (principally through Medicaid) in certain cases of rape or incest.

The other abortion-related amendment included in the Senate bill, drafted by Nancy Landon Kassebaum, R-Kan., aimed at requiring parental notification in a minor's decision to obtain an abortion. In an effort to strike a compromise between pro- and anti-notification forces, Kassebaum's language would have required that a parent be told at least 48 hours before the procedure could be performed by any entity receiving federal family planning funds. But it also included exceptions to that rule. For example, states with their own laws on the subject or that had voted not to have a law (as Oregon did in 1990) would be exempt. Parents would also not have to be notified if a physician certified the presence of a health emergency, if the girl obtained the permission of a judge, or if a professional counselor with no financial interest in the abortion certified that notification of a parent would put the girl at risk of physical abuse or emotional harm. The language was opposed by those on both sides of the abortion debate; abortion opponents said it had too many exemptions, while abortion rights groups opposed the entire concept of parental notification. Nevertheless, the Senate approved the language by an overwhelming 92-8. It, too, was ultimately dropped, with Kassebaum saying she would seek to append it instead to a family planning reauthorization bill.

DEPARTMENT OF EDUCATION

The Department of Education was created as a political reward to the nation's teachers for helping elect Jimmy Carter president. It had had a rocky history, however, as Reagan tried to take the department apart during the 1980s. Some education experts said the department had little impact on the quality or content of children's educational experience — particularly since that responsibility rested with state and local governments that spent more than 90 percent of all money going to education. Generally, the department's mission was to focus its elementary and secondary programs on children who were economically disadvantaged and needed remedial help.

Education for the Disadvantaged

Chapter 1, originally Title I of the Elementary and Secondary Education Act of 1965, was given $6.7 billion to provide money to states and local school districts to help educate disadvantaged children. A school might use the money to hire an extra teacher to work with children having trouble reading, writing or learning math. Funds were distributed by formula, based on what a state spent per pupil and on the number of school-age children from low-income families. The Even Start program also received money to teach literacy skills to young children and their parents. Other Chapter 1 funds went to help children of migrant agricultural workers and fishermen.

Impact Aid

This program provided $771.7 million to compensate school districts for the costs of educating children when federal activities had caused increased enrollment or a loss of revenue. For example, a military base in a school district might send hundreds of children to the local schools, but their parents would not pay property taxes that helped run the schools because they lived on the base. Impact aid also helped districts damaged by natural disasters.

School Improvement Programs

The department ran programs to improve the quality of education, particularly in math and science, and to promote drug-free schools. The Chapter 2 state block grants provided direct grants to state education agencies to improve elementary and secondary education in public and private schools. The money could be used to buy books, train teachers and finance programs to help students at risk of failing school. Money also went to the Eisenhower mathematics and science education state grant program, which paid to improve teachers' skills and the quality of instruction. The programs were given $474.6 million.

Educational Excellence (America 2000)

In April, Bush proposed a sweeping education initiative, America 2000. Among his proposals were: voluntary national testing for fourth-, eighth- and 12th-graders; creation of non-traditional schools; allowing parents to choose their children's schools, public or private; and rewarding better teachers with higher pay. Democrats, however, were wary of giving Bush the upper hand in education. And the school choice plan was extremely controversial, with many concerned about sending public dollars to private schools.

By the time appropriators put the finishing touches on the education spending measure, the authorization bill for America 2000 was nowhere near finished.

Congress did appropriate $425 million under an "America 2000" account, but the bulk of those funds were required to be used for other, existing HHS programs: $250 million was earmarked for Head Start; $55 million for Community and Migrant Health Centers; and $20 million for Comprehensive Child Development Centers.

Appropriators did set aside $100 million for America 2000 if it or a comparable authorizing bill was enacted by April 1, 1992. If no such bill was enacted, conferees stipulated that the money be "allocated among existing programs which provide direct assistance to local school districts in reaching the America 2000 education goals," such as Chapter 1, which provided funding by formula and was aimed at disadvantaged children.

Bilingual and Immigrant Education

Federal support for bilingual education, funded at $225 million, came in the form of discretionary grants to local school districts to help them pay for the cost of helping students with limited English.

Special Education

This appropriation of $2.85 billion went to carry out the Individuals with Disabilities Education Act (PL 94-142), which helped states provide all children with disabilities access to a free public education that was appropriate for their needs. The bulk of the money was sent to states in the form of grants, based on the number of disabled children served.

Rehabilitation Services, Disability Research

The Rehabilitation Act of 1973 included a number of programs that helped people with disabilities obtain employment and learn to live independently. Most of the $2.1 billion appropriation went to states as vocational rehabilitation grants. These grants helped pay the cost of job training for people with physical and mental disabilities.

Earmarked in the report was $5.9 million for the Helen Keller National Center for Deaf-Blind Youth and Adults in Sands Point, N.Y. Sen. Tom Harkin, D-Iowa, had a special interest in this field because his brother was deaf. Another $61 million was earmarked for the National Institute on Disability and Rehabilitation Research.

Institutions for People with Disabilities

- **American Printing House for the Blind.** $5.9 million.
- **National Technical Institute for the Deaf.** $39.4 million.
- **Gallaudet University.** $76.5 million.

Vocational and Adult Education

This appropriation went to support the Carl D. Perkins Vocational and Applied Technology Education Act and the Adult Education Act. Most of the funds were spent on basic grants to help states expand and improve vocational education programs.

The newly authorized "tech-prep" program to prepare high school students for postsecondary vocational education received $90 million to provide a link between high schools and postsecondary schools, helping students make a smooth transition between the two.

States also received grants under the Adult Education Act to help educationally disadvantaged adults learn basic skills, such as reading and writing, as well as earning high school equivalency diplomas. And $9.8 million funded literacy training for the homeless. The total appropriation for these programs was $1.4 billion.

Student Financial Assistance

The Higher Education Act of 1965 governed all federal financial aid to college, trade school and graduate students. Congress appropriated $9.7 billion to provide grants, scholarships and loans.

- **Pell grants.** The best-known program was named for Sen. Claiborne Pell, D-R.I. A total of $5.4 billion was being spent on it, with eligible students receiving a maximum of $2,400 annually. Most recipients came from families that earned no more than $30,000 a year. Other programs included Supplemental Educational Opportunity Grants, administered directly by the schools; College Work-Study, funds to schools to pay students for part-time work; Perkins loans, matching funds to schools for long-term, low-interest loans to students; and state student incentive grants, matching grants to states for work-study and grants to needy postsecondary students.
- **Guaranteed student loans.** The federal guaranteed student loan program was designed to give private lenders incentives to provide long-term loans to students. The federal government paid the lenders the interest while a student was in school until the student could take over the payments. There were three types of loan programs. The most popular was the Stafford loan, available to needy students at about 8 percent interest the first four years and 10 percent thereafter. Maximum loan levels were $2,625 for first- and second-year students and $4,000 for other undergraduates. Loan limits for graduate students were $7,500 a year and no more than $54,750 total. Also available were Supplemental Loans for Students (SLS), generally given to graduate and financially independent undergraduate students, and PLUS loans for parents of dependent undergraduates. PLUS and SLS loans were not made based on need, and the federal government did not pay the interest while students were in school. The $2.8 billion funding covered the cost of subsidies on loans made in 1992 and included the amount expected to be spent over the life of the loans.
- **Higher education.** Congress also paid for smaller programs designed to improve historically black colleges and universities as well as other postsecondary schools; to improve minority participation in the sciences; to run a student literacy corps promoting community service; and to foster international education and foreign language studies. These programs received $828 million.
- **Howard University and academic facilities loans.** $8.1 million. Congress traditionally provided money to help run Howard University, a historically black university in Washington, D.C. For fiscal 1992, that appropriation was $212 million. In addition, Congress provided loans to colleges to help build dormitories and academic facilities.
- **Education research, statistics and improvement.** $264 million. This included funding for the Office of Educational Research and Improvement.
- **Libraries.** $148 million, including grants to states to improve and extend library services.
- **Departmental management.** $370 million. Of that amount, $55 million went to the Office for Civil Rights and $26.9 million to the Office of the Inspector General.

RELATED AGENCIES

The bill also made appropriations for 18 related independent agencies. Some, like the Physician Payment Review Commission and National AIDS Commission, were permanent boards that advised Congress and the administration on policy matters. Others, like the National Commission on Children, were created temporarily to produce a single report or study. Still others, like the Federal Mediation and Conciliation Service and Federal Mine Safety and Health Review Commission, performed statutory functions, in these cases arbitrating disputes.

- **Corporation for Public Broadcasting (CPB).** The most prominent of the bill's related agencies, the CPB developed programming and provided funds for the nation's public radio and television stations. Because of planning needs, CPB's funds were provided two years in advance, so the $275 million in the bill was its fiscal 1994 funding. In the fiscal 1991 bill, $319 million was appropriated for the corporation for fiscal 1993, but that total included a one-time payment of $65 million to replace a satellite. Conferees urged the agency to spend the maximum allowable amount to expand public broadcasting to unserved or underserved areas.
- **ACTION.** The bill appropriated $199 million for ACTION, the umbrella agency that oversaw domestic volunteer programs. That included funding for VISTA (Volunteers in Service to America), an anti-poverty program, and the Older American Volunteer Programs, which encouraged activities aimed at both children and the elderly.
- **National Labor Relations Board.** The bill appropriated $162 million for the agency that handled charges of unfair labor practices made by businesses, labor unions and individuals. ■

Continued from p. 505

Helms' opponents both defended the surveys and criticized the family life program.

"I know this is a very nervous-making matter," said Daniel Patrick Moynihan, D-N.Y. Still, he said, the problems of sexually transmitted diseases and the growing number of births to unwed mothers "is something we need to know about."

Meanwhile, Brock Adams, D-Wash., belittled the family life program. "There is no evidence that abstinence-only programs reduce teen pregnancies," he said. "Why waste any more money on programs that don't work?"

Helms prevailed, however, after the Senate rejected, 34-66, a tabling motion to kill his amendment. It was subsequently adopted on a voice vote. *(Vote 188, p. 25-S)*

Other Amendments

The Senate gave voice vote approval to nearly three dozen amendments to the bill. Among them were:

- By Alan Cranston, D-Calif., to earmark $10 million of Health Resources and Services Administration funds to carry out the 1990 Trauma Care System Planning Act (PL 101-590). *(Trauma care, 1990 Almanac, p. 597)*
- By Domenici, to provide an additional $57 million for mental illness research and grants to aid homeless, mentally ill people. The funds were offset in the bill by reductions in the salaries and expense accounts of all three departments.
- By Harry Reid, D-Nev., to add $9.4 million for family violence programs. The funds were offset by reductions in operating expenses for the HHS inspector general.
- By Paul Simon, D-Ill., to add $10 million to the bill for state literacy resource centers. The funds were offset by reductions in the Labor Department's salaries and expense account.
- By Jeff Bingaman, D-N.M., to add $10 million to the bill for a prison literacy program. The funds were offset by reductions in operating expenses for the HHS inspector general.
- By Mark O. Hatfield, R-Ore., to add $6 million in funding for research on a vaccine to prevent AIDS. The funds were offset by reductions to the amounts provided for NIH buildings and facilities.
- By Alfonse M. D'Amato, R-N.Y., to provide an additional $5 million for Centers for Disease Control programs to eradicate tuberculosis. The funds were offset by reductions in program management funds for the Health Care Financing Administration.
- By Hatfield and Harkin, to provide an additional $34 million for research on Alzheimer's disease and services to Alzheimer's patients and their families. The funds were offset by reductions in the NIH director's contingency fund and to amounts provided for NIH buildings and facilities.
- By Ted Stevens, R-Alaska, and Daniel K. Inouye, D-Hawaii, to establish within the National Cancer Institute a Matsunaga-Conte Prostate Cancer Research Center, named for the late Sen. Spark M. Matsunaga, D-Hawaii (House 1963-77; Senate 1977-90), and the late Rep. Silvio O. Conte, R-Mass. (1959-91), who both battled the disease. Stevens underwent prostate cancer surgery during the August recess.
- By Thad Cochran, R-Miss., to exempt certain garments made for display by employees of fabric stores from Labor Department regulations governing workers who sewed garments in their homes.
- By Helms, to bar inmates in state or federal prisons from receiving Pell college aid grants.
- By John Seymour, R-Calif., to earmark $60 million from the Alcohol, Drug Abuse and Mental Health Administration for demonstration projects serving pregnant and post-partum addicts and their infants.

The Senate rejected a Helms amendment that would have barred employers from using hiring quotas. Although it was similar to one defeated during Senate floor consideration of the crime bill (S 1241) in June, this version would have allowed the use of affirmative-action programs intended to entice more women and minorities to apply for jobs. On a 33-67 vote, senators ruled the amendment was not germane to the bill. *(Vote 187, p. 25-S)*

CONFERENCE

After three tense weeks of arguing over scarce dollars, conferees finally reached agreement on HR 2707 on Oct. 29 using an accounting sleight of hand.

A weeklong impasse was broken when House conferees agreed to pare back somewhat their education spending totals, while Senate conferees gave a little on the health programs for which they had been fighting.

But conferees wound up closing most of the gap between totals they had agreed to earlier in the conference by pushing funding into fiscal 1993.

Conferees ultimately included in the bill more than $4 billion worth of "delayed obligations" — appropriating funds that were not to become available until Sept. 30, 1992, the last day of the fiscal year. By pushing most of the spending into fiscal 1993, appropriators inflated program funding totals in the bill without having most of the funds "scored" against their spending limits.

Several conferees complained that such devices would only complicate matters when it came time to produce the fiscal 1993 bill.

Sen. Dale Bumpers, D-Ark., said he used to work with contractors "who used money from the next job to pay for the last job. Most of them ended up in bankruptcy."

And Rep. Neal Smith, D-Iowa, pointed out that if the panel pushed $3.5 billion into fiscal 1993, then got only the projected $2.5 billion increase in its fiscal 1993 allocation, "you won't even have enough money for cost of living increases" for all the other programs.

In the end, though, members quietly agreed to nearly all the delayed funding included in both the House and Senate bills.

"It's an easy way to get money because we won't have to rassle with that gorilla until next year," said Rep. David R. Obey, D-Wis.

Even those who disapproved of the maneuvering on policy grounds, such as House Labor-HHS Chairman Natcher, said the health-vs.-education funding impasse left them little choice.

"It's bad," Natcher agreed, but he noted that Bush in his own fiscal 1992 budget proposed delaying about $580 million in spending. "We're just facing the cold, hard facts," he said of the technique.

Earmarked NIH Funding

By far the most heated debate came over the issue of whether to provide extra funding for two arms of the National Institutes of Health, the National Cancer Institute and National Institute on Aging.

Conferees ultimately agreed to a Senate plan pushed by Ernest F. Hollings, D-S.C., to provide $175 million — out of a total of more than $9 billion — specifically for research on cancer and Alzheimer's disease. The funding, $160 million for cancer and $15 million for Alzheimer's, was not to be available, however, until Sept. 30, 1992, the last day of the fiscal year.

Obey continued to object to the earmarks, not so much because of the forward funding, he said, as because of the precedent of politicians deciding research priorities.

"I'm a passionate supporter of NIH," he said, "but it's dangerous having dollars allocated on the basis of politics." In the 1970s, he pointed out, Congress "poured money into the cancer institute and starved the other institutes to do it."

Obey forced a vote on the issue, which he lost on a 7-1 show of hands. He did not sign the conference agreement.

Members also settled the matter of how to communicate their concern over women's health.

Although both the House and Senate reports specified increased funding for research into breast and ovarian cancer and other diseases afflicting primarily or exclusively women, female legislators wanted the amounts written into the bill. Those efforts were strongly resisted by Natcher, a vehement opponent of earmarking.

Members ultimately accepted compromise language crafted by Sen. Adams and Rep. Steny H. Hoyer, D-Md., stating that conferees "urge, in the strongest way, that the National Cancer Institute make breast, prostate, ovarian and cervical cancer their top priorities," and that funding for related research "receive significant increases as outlined in both the House and Senate reports."

The inclusion of prostate cancer, a male disease, was for Sen. Stevens, who had had prostate cancer surgery in August and complained earlier in the conference that funding for male-specific diseases was also too low.

The female legislators pushing for the extra funding declared victory nevertheless.

"It's peanuts compared to what they spend on other diseases that are epidemic," said Rep. Mary Rose Oakar, D-Ohio. "But it's the first time they've really focused in on these issues."

Abortion Issue Compromise

Conferees quickly resolved the abortion issue, for the short-term, when they agreed to drop from the measure both the parental notification and rape and incest amendments added by the Senate.

Although many opponents of the counseling ban also supported the rape and incest language, they agreed that they had a better chance of blocking the regulations without adding additional complications — and additional reasons for a veto.

"The president, if he's going to veto it, will have to veto it on the basis of the gag rule alone," said Rep. John Porter, R-Ill., author of the language blocking the regulations.

Deferred SLIAG Funding

In addition to approving the delayed obligations that were going to eat into the subcommittee's fiscal 1993 outlay total, members dug the hole deeper still by promising to fund at least part of a $1.12 billion program to help states cope with the public assistance, health and education costs of aliens whose presence was legalized under the 1986 immigration act (PL 99-603). *(1986 Almanac, p. 61)*

In the past three spending bills, members had deferred the final year of funding for the State Legalization Impact Assistance Grants (SLIAG).

Because states were slow in getting their immigration programs up and running, few were affected by the delayed funding, which was pushed ahead to fiscal 1993.

But officials in several states, primarily California, Florida, Texas and New York, began to worry about the ultimate availability of the final year of funds. The Bush administration in its fiscal 1992 budget had proposed rescinding the funding permanently.

At the request of Rep. Edward R. Roybal, D-Calif., members adopted language in effect promising that SLIAG funds would be made available early in fiscal 1993. Roybal's initial language would have required the full amount to be made available, but that was ultimately amended to provide "amounts needed."

Roybal was backed by Sen. Phil Gramm, R-Texas. "States feel — rightly so — a commitment was made that this money be provided," Gramm said. "Come next year, that money needs to be available."

OSHA Exemption

Conferees resolved one lingering policy dispute concerning the Labor Department's Occupational Safety and Health Administration (OSHA).

Under existing law, businesses with fewer than 10 workers were generally exempt from routine OSHA safety inspections if their type of business had a lower-than-average rate of workplace injury. One of the exceptions to that rule was if an accident resulted in the hospitalization of five or more workers.

The Bush administration in its fiscal 1992 budget recommended dropping the inspection exemption. Labor Department officials said the exemption was unnecessary, given the agency's inspection practices.

The House bill kept the exemption but lowered the number of workers who had to be injured before routine inspections could take place to one.

The reason, said Obey, was that if a business had only five workers, "the entire work force would have to be hospitalized before OSHA could come in and inspect."

The Senate bill, with the support of the National Federation of Independent Business, a small-business industry group, kept the number at five.

"There's no data or studies to indicate any changes are needed," said Sen. Thad Cochran, R-Miss., who championed the Senate position.

But Obey insisted that it was "weirdly anomalous" for a Democratic-controlled Congress to appear less concerned about worker protection than the Republican administration.

The matter got even more confusing when Cochran and Rep. Carl D. Pursell, R-Mich., produced a letter from Bush officials disavowing the change.

"I find it quaint that the administration now seems to be abandoning its own budget submission," said Obey.

Members ultimately compromised by lowering the number of workers who would have to be hospitalized before OSHA could make routine inspections from five to two.

FINAL ACTION

Although both chambers the week of Nov. 4 agreed to the conference report on HR 2707, the House did not pass it by enough votes to sustain the expected veto.

The abortion counseling issue and the delayed funding questions dominated debate on the conference report.

"This bill is a fiscal time bomb which will make it all but impossible to meet domestic spending limits in fiscal 1993," said a letter to House Republicans from six Republican members of the House Budget Committee, led by ranking member Bill Gradison of Ohio.

"What we have here is a legislative shell game; now you see it, now you don't, presto, gusto, sleight of hand," said House Minority Leader Robert H. Michel, R-Ill., during floor debate.

Opponents, however, could not keep the delayed spending out of the bill. On three successive votes, members sided with conferees to keep the funds in the bill. *(Votes 381, 382, 383, pp. 92-H, 94-H)*

Still, the funding dispute cost the bill votes on final passage.

Rep. Al McCandless, R-Calif., said in a statement that he supported efforts to block the abortion counseling rules, "but I am not going to be bullied into voting for another budget-buster just because of one paragraph."

Similarly, Rep. Jim Kolbe, R-Ariz., said he would "strongly support" overturning the counseling rules, but nevertheless could not vote for the measure because of "the funding tricks and gimmicks" it contained.

Also voting against the bill were two other Republicans, Alex McMillan, N.C., and Jerry Lewis, Calif., who during committee markups in Appropriations and Energy and Commerce, respectively, voted to block or overturn the counseling rules.

Abortion rights Democrats accused Republicans of using the budget issue as a smoke screen.

"This is giving a lot of people a fig leaf to have it both ways," said Rep. Schroeder.

But Republicans said the budget issue was a real one.

"If the gag rule [reversal] wasn't in it I couldn't vote for this bill," said Porter, a conferee on the bill who spoke out repeatedly against the delayed funding.

At the same time, abortion opponents accused the other side of beefing up its own totals by hiding behind a must-pass spending bill.

"It's a great bill. It's got every popular program under the sun," said Weber, a member of the Labor-HHS Subcommittee who nevertheless sought to persuade colleagues to vote "no" because of the abortion language.

Abortion foes also reminded colleagues that with or without the disputed language, the Labor-HHS bill would become law at some point.

"Do not be misled," said Henry J. Hyde, R-Ill., one of the House's anti-abortion leaders. "All the good things in this bill, and there are good things in this bill, will be retained after the offensive abortion baggage is excised, and the president vetoes it and we sustain his veto."

Veto Sustained

On Nov. 19, Bush finally carried out his veto threat and the House failed to override.

The 276-156 vote put a temporary end to the gag-rule fight that had raged since the Supreme Court upheld the ban on abortion counseling May 23. *(Vote 403, p. 98-H)*

The failure of the override technically killed the bill, putting pressure on members to ensure funding for the popular Labor-HHS programs by rushing through both houses HR 3839, which was identical to HR 2707 but without the contested language. In the statement accompanying the veto, Bush had indicated that he would sign such a bill.

After only perfunctory debate, the House on Nov. 22 approved HR 3839 by a vote of 364-58. Republicans, raising budget-based objections, tried to get the bill sent to committee, but failed on a 148-276 vote. *(Votes 417, 416, pp. 102-H, 100-H)*

The Senate, later the same day, approved the bill by voice vote. ■

Juggling the Demands of Space and Housing

After months of complaining about not having enough money to fund programs for veterans, housing, space and the environment, Congress on Oct. 3 easily cleared an $81 billion spending bill that was laden with special projects for hometown interests.

House and Senate conferees on the fiscal 1992 appropriations measure (HR 2519) had difficulty juggling the competing demands of the space station *Freedom*, housing for the poor and environmental cleanup.

But they did manage to double the amount for pork barrel projects in one housing account to $150 million, as well as order up scores of other projects.

"They went too far," said Jack F. Kemp, secretary of Housing and Urban Development (HUD), who said the 78 projects that conferees earmarked in his department would come at the expense of a new program to help public housing tenants buy their homes. The Senate had previously earmarked 55 projects.

The projects added in conference included six worth a total of $7.45 million to Michigan, home state of Democrat Bob Traxler, who was chairman of the House Appropriations subcommittee responsible for the bill. The money was to go to rehabilitating a historic building in Ypsilanti; water, sewer and roads projects in Boyne City; purchasing communications equipment in Marquette; buying land for a conference center and hotel in Bay City; rehabilitating housing in Benton Harbor; and buying a building for Delta College in Saginaw.

BOXSCORE

➡ **Fiscal 1992 VA-HUD appropriations bill (HR 2519).** The bill provided $81 billion in fiscal 1992 appropriations for the Departments of Veterans Affairs (VA), Housing and Urban Development (HUD) and certain independent agencies, including the National Aeronautics and Space Administration and the Environmental Protection Agency.

Reports: H Rept 102-94; S Rept 102-107; conference report, H Rept 102-226.

KEY ACTION

June 6 — HR 2519 passed the **House** by a vote of 363-39.

July 18 — HR 2519 passed the **Senate** by voice vote.

Oct. 2 — The **House** agreed to conference report by a vote of 390-30; **Senate** agreed to it by voice vote.

Oct. 3 — The **House** cleared bill.

Oct. 28 — President Bush signed HR 2519 — PL 102-139.

The measure also funded the Department of Veterans Affairs (VA) and independent agencies such as the National Aeronautics and Space Administration (NASA) and the Environmental Protection Agency (EPA).

Although HUD Secretary Kemp wanted Bush to veto the measure, the president signed the bill on Oct. 28 because it provided $2.03 billion to the president's highest priority, the space station, an orbiting laboratory that had come under attack for its costs and its flawed design. *(Space station, p. 239)*

The House adopted the conference report Oct. 2 on a 390-30 vote. The Senate gave it voice vote approval the same day, although a disagreement over who should set standards for veterans' medical laboratories delayed final action until Oct. 3. *(Vote 286, p. 70-H)*

HOUSE COMMITTEE ACTION

Given little breathing room for new spending, members of the House Appropriations VA, HUD and Independent Agencies Subcommittee agreed May 15 to kill NASA's beleaguered space station to increase spending for its other domestic accounts.

Meeting privately, the subcommittee informally voted 6-3 against President Bush's $2.03 billion request for the space station in fiscal 1992, according to one member.

"We simply can no longer afford huge new projects with huge price tags while trying to maintain services that the American people expect to be provided," said Traxler.

The space station *Freedom* was one of NASA's highest-profile programs, but its rising cost had undermined support for it.

The agency reduced the project's size and price tag in February 1991 to comply with a request made in 1990 by the Appropriations Committee. But the project was still expected to cost about $40 billion over the next 10 years, according to a report released by the General Accounting Office.

The VA-HUD panel's action came despite a personal lobbying effort by Bush and by Vice President Dan Quayle, who was chairman of the White House National Space Council. Before the subcommittee met, Quayle went to key lawmakers to rally support for the redesigned station.

Bush entered the fray May 14 with a letter to House and Senate Appropriations chairmen asking for special consideration for NASA programs.

But Traxler maintained that the space station was no longer feasible given the limited amount of money for domestic spending allowed by the 1990 White House-congressional budget agreement, as translated by 13 subcommittee chairmen of House Appropriations.

This "college of cardinals," as they were known, met privately May 14 and agreed on spending caps for each of the 10 subcommittees that oversaw domestic spending. Their allocation for the VA-HUD panel was $63.5 billion in new budget authority, $1.2 billion less than Bush requested for the programs.

Subcommittee member Jim Chapman, D-Texas, who sought to continue the space station project, said the committee's action was a sharp blow to space station supporters.

"If we want the space station, we're going to have a battle on our hands," he said.

Besides Chapman, Republicans Bill Lowery of California and Joseph M. McDade of Pennsylvania, whose districts benefited from contracts with NASA, also opposed dropping the space station.

During the markup, subcommittee members were given papers showing two columns — one reading "station in," the other, "station out." Under the column assuming full funding for the space station, almost every other program — space and non-space — was accorded sums far below Bush's budget request.

VA, HUD, Independent Agencies

(In thousands of dollars)

	Fiscal 1991 Appropriation	President's Request	House Bill	Senate Bill	Final Bill
Veterans Affairs					
Compensation and pensions	$ 16,397,135	$ 15,841,620	$ 15,841,620	$ 15,841,620	$15,841,620
Readjustment benefits	752,500	635,400	635,400	635,400	635,400
Loan funds	751,000	624,921	624,921	624,921	624,921
Medical care	12,335,490	13,287,096	13,495,096	13,527,920	13,512,920
Medical research	216,795	216,795	226,795	227,000	227,000
Construction projects	710,640	645,701	711,701	500,551	604,951
Other	1,109,660	1,052,635	1,068,340	1,077,635	1,079,140
Total, VA	**$ 32,273,220**	**$ 32,304,168**	**$ 32,603,873**	**$ 32,435,047**	**$ 32,525,952**
Housing and Urban Development					
HOPE grants	—	865,400	361,000	215,400	136,000
HOME program	—	1,000,000	500,000	2,000,000	1,500,000
Assisted housing	9,525,000	9,065,790	9,985,790	7,917,000	8,070,201
Rescission of deobligations	−535,190	−227,000	−227,000	−227,000	−167,000
Expiring Section 8 subsidies	7,890,800	7,024,589	7,024,589	7,024,589	7,355,128
Low-income housing projects	2,175,000	2,155,844	2,188,844	2,500,000	2,450,000
Federal Housing Administration	317,366	243,911	243,911	243,911	243,911
Limitation on guaranteed loans	*(75,000,000)*	*(62,244,716)*	*(68,651,901)*	*(68,651,901)*	*(68,651,901)*
Drug elimination grants	150,000	165,000	165,000	165,000	165,000
Ginnie Mae (receipts)	—	−273,105	−273,105	−273,105	−273,105
Limitation on guaranteed loans	*(80,000,000)*	*(74,769,293)*	*(74,769,293)*	*(74,769,293)*	*(74,769,293)*
Homeless assistance	339,427	535,733	536,200	449,960	449,960
Community development block grants	3,213,000	2,920,000	3,265,000	3,400,000	3,400,000
Other HUD accounts	541,193	780,899	478,719	490,676	478,701
Total, HUD	**$ 23,616,596**	**$ 24,257,061**	**$ 24,248,948**	**$ 23,906,431**	**$ 23,808,796**
NASA					
Space station	1,894,512	2,028,900	1,900,000	2,028,900	2,030,000
Other research and development	4,129,088	5,169,600	4,123,600	4,520,100	4,383,800
Space flight, control, data communications	6,334,132	5,608,300	5,157,075	4,907,000	5,157,075
Portion applied to debt reduction	−1,209,732	−32,675	−32,675	−32,675	−32,675
Construction of facilities	497,900	480,300	497,900	525,000	525,000
Research and administration	2,222,400	2,466,900	2,222,400	2,356,900	2,256,900
Total, NASA	**$ 13,868,300**	**$ 15,721,325**	**$ 13,868,300**	**$ 14,305,225**	**$ 14,320,100**
Environmental Protection Agency					
Research and development	254,900	313,000	333,875	313,000	323,000
Abatement, control and compliance	1,006,525	1,019,500	1,133,625	1,142,500	1,133,625
Superfund	1,616,228	1,750,000	1,630,000	1,616,228	1,616,228
Construction grants	2,100,000	1,900,000	2,195,000	2,400,000	2,400,000
Salaries, other	1,116,700	1,229,200	1,248,361	1,163,200	1,196,000
Total, EPA	**$ 6,094,353**	**$ 6,211,700**	**$ 6,540,861**	**$ 6,634,928**	**$ 6,668,853**
Independent Agencies					
Emergency Management Agency	562,975	824,334	765,540	773,084	773,084
Disaster relief	(—)	(274,459)	(184,459)	(184,459)	(184,459)
Planning and assistance	(282,624)	(277,827)	(277,827)	(285,827)	(285,827)
Food and shelter program	(134,000)	(100,000)	(134,000)	(134,000)	(134,000)
National Science Foundation	2,316,028	2,722,000	2,720,800	2,645,500	2,577,500
Research, facilities	(1,714,678)	(2,013,500)	(1,980,500)	(1,972,000)	(1,912,000)
Education	(322,350)	(390,000)	(435,000)	(465,000)	(465,000)
Other independent agencies	209,083	189,846	178,379	276,659	266,759
GRAND TOTAL	**$ 78,940,555**	**$ 82,230,434**	**$ 80,926,701**	**$ 80,976,874**	**$ 80,941,044**
FSLIC resolution fund	$ 22,000,000	$ 3,419,000	$ 15,899,000	$ 15,867,000	$ 15,867,000

SOURCE: House Appropriations Committee

By cutting out the $2 billion space station request, the committee recommended $13.7 billion for NASA in fiscal 1992, less than its fiscal 1991 appropriation of $13.8 billion. Bush had requested $15.7 billion for NASA in fiscal 1992. *(1990 Almanac, p. 854)*

Appropriators said they were under great strain to spread their resources to fund a number of domestic initiatives authorized by Congress in 1990, including new housing programs and stepped-up regulatory efforts ordered by the new Clean Air Act. Ongoing programs such as veterans' health care and hospitals also required increased spending, Traxler said.

Kemp's HOPE

HUD Secretary Kemp had threatened to recommend a veto of HR 2519 if his department did not receive the $865 million he sought to start up a housing program called HOPE — Homeownership and Opportunity for People Everywhere — which was to help low-income tenants purchase their homes.

The House subcommittee included no money to sell public housing to tenants, Kemp's favorite component of HOPE, although it did allocate $100 million to help low-income tenants buy their private apartment buildings and $100 million to help low-income people buy single-family homes that had been repossessed by their city, HUD, the Resolution Trust Corporation or the Department of Veterans Affairs.

Kemp maintained that home ownership "empowers" the poor, giving them a stake in their community. But both Traxler and his Senate counterpart, Barbara A. Mikulski, D-Md., questioned the wisdom of selling public housing, as well as whether very poor people could afford to buy their own homes.

Traxler's subcommittee agreed to give some money to the other major housing program created in 1990, advocated primarily by Democrats, called HOME Investment Partnerships.

Bush had requested $1 billion for the block-grant-type program to provide matching funds to state and local governments to expand the supply of affordable housing through construction, rehabilitation and rental vouchers. *(Housing authorization bill, 1990 Almanac, p. 631)*

The subcommittee recommended $500 million for HOME, although the panel's markup papers suggested that it would have gotten that amount even if the space station had been funded.

Meanwhile, the panel agreed to give nearly $1.5 billion more than Bush requested to existing housing programs, such as public and Indian housing, and housing for the elderly and disabled.

In the wake of the new Clean Air Act, the subcommittee gave a boost to regulatory enforcement efforts of the Environmental Protection Agency.

The panel recommended adding $400 million to Bush's $6 billion request for the EPA. That included $121 million earmarked for Clean Air Act compliance, $4 million more than Bush had asked for.

And in the afterglow of the Persian Gulf War, veterans fared far better in the House subcommittee bill than in the administration budget request.

Veterans Affairs was to receive $269 million over Bush's request of $33.2 billion, which included cost of living adjustments and other variables that, according to the Congressional Budget Office, brought the subcommittee recommendation to $32.57 billion.

The full Appropriations Committee approved the panel's work on June 3.

HOUSE ACTION

The House on June 6 reversed the Appropriations Committee's action and voted to continue funding the space station *Freedom,* despite repeated warnings that NASA's flagship project had little merit as a science project. The space station funding was salvaged by freezing every other space program and cutting public housing money for the poor.

The House voted 240-173 on an amendment to restore the $1.9 billion for the station. The final bill passed, 363-39. *(Votes 141, 143, p. 34-H, 36-H)*

The surprise turnaround for the space station came after an all-out lobbying effort by the White House, with phone calls from both Bush and Quayle to key members of Congress. NASA circulated among members a district-by-district breakdown of space station contracts, employment and dollars spent, showing what each would lose if the project were killed.

Members attributed the win to solid bipartisan backing for the multibillion-dollar NASA project and the romantic appeal of manned space exploration. "It clearly caught the imagination of our colleagues," said Lowery, one of the sponsors of the amendment that restored funding for the station.

Some members warned that the House was failing to recognize that the budget would be even tighter in future years. Since 1984 the government had spent $5 billion, although construction had not yet begun. Originally, it was expected to cost about $8 billion and to be finished by 1992. By 1991, cost estimates topped $40 billion, and it was not slated for completion until the end of the century.

In past years, when House members wanted to increase space program spending, they took largely from housing programs for the poor and homeless. But in 1991, space station supporters instead opted to take the majority of the funds from within the space agency and focus the debate on the merits of the space station.

The key amendment to restore space station funding to the spending bill was drafted by the Office of Management and Budget and offered by Chapman and Lowery.

Although there were no NASA facilities or jobs in Lowery's North San Diego district, California aerospace companies had some of the largest contracts to build the station.

Chapman's Texarkana district also received no direct benefits from NASA or the space station. But as a member of the cohesive Texas delegation, Chapman had taken a stand in behalf of his state, which was to receive at least $3.1 billion in contracts for the space station.

Chapman, Lowery and other space station proponents argued that the project was symbolic of America's leadership in space and could lead to groundbreaking discoveries that would inspire students to go into the sciences. They also said that if the United States backed out of the station, it would damage the country's reputation as a partner in international science ventures. Japan, the European Community and Canada had already committed more than $1.5 billion to the station's development. Japan had said that if the United States withdrew from the project, it would be leery of contributing to other U.S. science projects, including the superconducting super collider.

Chapman said medical breakthroughs were on the horizon. "The space station *Freedom* will have a first-class medical laboratory that will allow us to do research in hypertension, diabetes, osteoporosis and research into diseases like cancer and AIDS," he said.

Critics countered that under the current design the scientific capability of the space station could not live up to those promises.

They pointed out that a number of science groups, including the prestigious and nonpartisan National Academy of Sciences, viewed the station's scientific capability as virtually non-existent.

Opponents also complained that NASA's current space station plan was a far cry from its original scope, which envisioned a multitude of purposes for the station: as a space observatory, a life sciences laboratory, a manufacturing facility and a staging area for deep space missions.

Social Programs vs. Science?

When the Appropriations Committee voted to kill the station, it appeared that the House floor debate would pit social programs against science. However, space proponents decided that their best bet for restoring the station would be to avoid that sort of face-off.

In funding the space station, the House cannibalized every other NASA program, including its environmental satellite project, Mission to Planet Earth, and its orbiting observatories.

After the vote, NASA Administrator Richard H. Truly conceded that unless the final fiscal 1992 appropriation for his agency was increased, it would be very difficult to run NASA's other programs.

NASA scientists were more blunt.

"It would be a disaster," said Jeff Dozier, chief scientist for NASA's Earth Observing System program, the centerpiece of Mission to Planet Earth.

The Chapman-Lowery amendment also proposed cutting the funds used to maintain public housing by $250 million, or 10 percent. To sweeten the deal, they proposed adding $33 million to veterans' medical care.

Traxler undercut the sweetener by offering to add the $33 million to veterans himself. The amendment was adopted by voice vote. Chapman then took the $33 million out of his amendment, reducing the public housing cut to $217 million.

Despite the existing surge in sympathy for the homeless, only a few members spoke out vigorously against the reduction in public housing operating subsidies.

Lawrence J. Smith, D-Fla., however, tried to broker a compromise. He offered an amendment to leave housing dollars alone and force NASA to fund the space station entirely from its own budget. It was rejected, 122-296. *(Vote 140, p. 34-H)*

In a second slap at the appropriators, members voted 216-183 to give HUD Secretary Kemp $151 million for his new program to help public housing tenants buy their units. *(Vote 142, p. 34-H)*

Kemp had requested $865 million for his HOPE program. But the Appropriations Committee recommended only $210 million, with no money to sell public housing.

Reps. Jim Kolbe, R-Ariz., and Mike Espy, D-Miss., offered the amendment to take $151 million away from the flexible subsidy housing program, which provided grants and loans to developers to make improvements to their low-income rental housing.

In other action, the House agreed by voice vote to an amendment offered by Science Committee Chairman George E. Brown Jr., D-Calif., to hold contractors liable for the work that they performed for NASA.

SENATE COMMITTEE ACTION

The Senate Appropriations Committee agreed to continue paying for NASA's $40 billion space station *Freedom*, quieting most complaints about the fat target within the strapped spending bill for veterans, housing, the environment and space.

The smooth approval of HR 2519 from both the Appropriations Committee and its subcommittee on VA, HUD and Independent Agencies contrasted starkly with the breast-beating that occurred in the House.

Senate subcommittee members approved the bill by voice vote July 10; the full committee approved the measure, 24-0, a day later.

Appropriations subcommittee Chairman Mikulski said she crafted the bill by taking "small bites" out of numerous programs to pay for the space station. "We were not going to dynamite or pulverize any one program," she said.

Indeed, Mikulski appeared to have found more money for all of the big constituencies:

- For veterans, she increased the medical care appropriation to $13.5 billion, $33 million more than the House and $241 million more than Bush's request.
- For environmentalists, the Environmental Protection Agency was to receive $6.6 billion, almost $100 million more than the House approved and $400 million more than the administration's request.
- For low-income housing advocates, she gave $2 billion to the new HOME Investment Partnerships program. That compared with $500 million recommended by the House and $1 billion recommended by the administration.
- For public housing, the committee gave $2.5 billion to operate the projects. Public housing operating subsidies, which covered the difference between what tenants paid and what it cost to run a project, had been cut in the House to $2.19 billion to help pay for the space station. The Senate bill also provided $3 billion to modernize the public housing projects, compared with $2.5 billion from the House.
- And for HUD Secretary Kemp, Mikulski's committee provided $440 million for his prized HOPE program, including $175 million to help public housing tenants buy their projects. The rest of the money would go to helping low-income families buy single- and multifamily homes. House appropriators had recommended not giving any money to the public housing component of HOPE. But they were rebuffed on the floor when members voted to shift $151 million within HUD to pay for the program.

Despite a few low-key grumbles from Democrats on the subcommittee, the largess to a few key projects seemed to quiet concerns that the space station was gobbling up money needed by social programs. Even NASA boosters said they could live with the amount earmarked for both the space station and the other space science programs. For example, Sen. Jake Garn, R-Utah, the ranking minority member of the VA-HUD Subcommittee, usually complained bitterly that there was not enough money for space programs.

In 1991, however, he had nothing but praise for Mikulski. Garn said: "I think it's a good bill and a dramatic improvement over what the House of Representatives did."

Creative Financing

Besides chipping away at programs here and there, Mikulski used some creative financing to come up with additional money. She said she gathered support for the bill "one senator at a time."

Key to providing more money for new housing programs was a change in the financing rules for an old program, Section 202 housing for the elderly and disabled. In the past, HUD offered loans to groups building housing for the elderly and then provided them with Section 8 rental assistance to pay off those same loans. The 1990 housing act switched it from a loan program to a grant program, eliminating the need to provide rental assistance.

The bill estimated that the change would save at least $1.2 billion.

In addition, Mikulski said she found $565 million in unused money within the housing department. Overall, HUD was to receive $23.9 billion, which was $342.5 million less than the House and $351 million less than the administration's request.

The committee took advantage of an accounting device that would save the government no money but freed up fiscal 1992 cash for others program covered by the bill. In the short term, this accounting change could solve HUD's bookkeeping problems.

The committee's report was extremely critical of HUD's efforts to figure out just how much money it needed for rental assistance contracts, citing a 1990 HUD inspector general report that said in some cases there was an error rate of 95 percent.

Kemp called Mikulski the evening before her subcommittee marked up its bill to say that HUD needed another $1 billion to cover expiring rental subsidy contracts that need to be renewed. Those contracts provided payments to landlords for low-income housing.

An aide to Mikulski said Kemp admitted: "We goofed."

To address the accounting problem, the committee's plan would force HUD to shorten the contracts to three years from five years and harden its estimates of the money needed to provide the housing. Instead of giving Kemp the $1 billion to renew the five-year contracts, the committee instead cut $1.2 billion out of the $2.5 billion account that shored up ongoing rental contracts that had run out of money. The change to a three-year contract allowed the panel to appropriate less money in fiscal 1992.

The change had an added benefit: It freed up the $1.2 billion in budget authority for other programs in fiscal 1992. But the money was likely to come due for the rental contracts three years down the road.

Space Agency Cuts

The $2 billion required in fiscal 1992 to move the space station along did not come without pain. NASA's unmanned space projects suffered numerous cuts and scrapes from Senate appropriators, though they were not as severe as in the House.

The space agency's total budget for fiscal 1992 grew by $437 million over the previous year, bringing the bottom line to $14.3 billion, compared with Bush's request for $15.7 billion.

Mikulski killed the CRAF portion of the CRAF-Cassini project, an unmanned mission to study the composition of a comet, saving $112 million. She joked that the orbiting comet would rotate back some other time and that NASA could then conduct the mission.

She also cut $60 million from the AXAF project, an observatory similar to the Hubble Telescope designed to study the X-ray system. That was expected to cause a one-year delay in the launch date.

The Earth Observing System, one of NASA's premier projects to study the changing climate of the Earth, was to lose $50 million.

Other Agencies Suffer

Other agencies also felt the tug and pull of the fiscal tightening proposed by the Senate committee.

Although the EPA's total budget was to grow, the committee would cut the amount Bush requested for its employees' salaries and expenses by $61 million. EPA officials said that cut could affect the agency's ability to put the Clean Air Act to work. And EPA's "superfund" program to clean up hazardous waste sites was to be frozen at the fiscal 1991 level of $1.6 billion.

Construction of hospitals and nursing homes for veterans received significantly less than the administration or the House recommended. Citing "excessive cost overruns," the committee recommended $309.8 million for veterans construction projects, down from the $522 million House level and the $450 million administration request.

Money for research in the Antarctic, overseen by the National Science Foundation, was slashed, with the committee recommending that the Department of Defense pick up the remainder of the tab. The bill provided $78 million for the research, down from $100 million appropriated in fiscal 1991 and $118 million recommended by both the House and the administration. Logistical support of the project would be cut to $10 million, down from $75 million appropriated in fiscal 1991 and $75 million recommended for fiscal 1992 by the administration and the House.

SENATE ACTION

The space station *Freedom* persevered through another round of name-calling as the Senate voted, 35-64, against killing NASA's top project. Dale Bumpers, D-Ark., led the fight July 17 to cut $1.9 billion of the $2 billion appropriation in HR 2519. *(Vote 132, p. 18-S)*

The Senate gave voice vote approval July 18 to the $80.9 billion bill after two long days of interrupted debate.

Bumpers, driven by the $348 billion budget deficit projected for fiscal 1992, had set out on a crusade to cut down on expensive projects. "It is so huge, so mammoth and so staggering that we don't even talk about it anymore," Bumpers said of the deficit.

The week before, Bumpers tried to cut $509 million intended for the superconducting super collider from the Energy and Water Appropriations measure (HR 2427). That amendment was tabled, 62-37. *(Energy and Water appropriations, p. 569)*

Bumpers complained that the space station had little scientific merit and little cachet with the American people. He proposed cutting $1.9 billion from the project in fiscal 1992 and redistributing $600 million to several NASA programs, the National Science Foundation and veterans' medical care and prosthetic research. The remaining $1.3 billion would have been applied to reducing the deficit.

Bumpers was up against a former astronaut-hero, John Glenn, D-Ohio; a guest-astronaut, Jake Garn, R-Utah; and many other senators with multimillion-dollar NASA contracts and space centers in their states.

Mikulski said that in the past, she had been skeptical about the space station, too. She said she thought it was "a condo in the sky." However, she said the project's design and mission has been streamlined and clarified.

Continued on p. 528

VA, HUD, Independent Agencies Provisions

The appropriations bill for Veterans, Housing and independent agencies was the catchall measure originally intended to cover all non-Cabinet-level agencies. By 1991, however, Veterans Affairs (VA) was not only the third-largest federal agency, it had also achieved Cabinet status. So, too, had the Department of Housing and Urban Development (HUD). And the Environmental Protection Agency (EPA) was on the cusp of becoming a Cabinet department.

Altogether, the $81 billion bill (HR 2519, PL 102-139) funded 25 separate departments, agencies and commissions, from the Interagency Council on the Homeless ($1.1 million) to the VA ($32.5 billion).

Frequently in funding battles, the bill's scientific cast clashed with the social service, humanitarian side. Appropriators had to weigh the needs of the National Aeronautics and Space Administration (NASA) against the needs of the homeless, of low-income families unable to pay their rent, and of veterans seeking quality medical care. In 1991, both the House and Senate spent their time debating the merits of the $40 billion space station Freedom *and whether its existence would drain too much money from the rest of the bill. In the end,* Freedom *won out, and NASA received a $14.3 billion appropriation — 3 percent more than the year before.*

Besides space, housing and veterans, the VA-HUD bill spent close to $16 billion to cover costs previously incurred when the now-defunct Federal Savings and Loan Insurance Corporation (FSLIC) closed 200 failed thrifts in 1988. This amount was not included in the bill's bottom line under an agreement with the administration.

VETERANS AFFAIRS

Elevated to Cabinet-level status in 1989, the VA touched the lives of nearly one-third of the total population of the United States. Its principal mission was to provide U.S. veterans and their families medical care, education loans and grants, discount home mortgages, and pensions and compensation for service-related disabilities. The department was essentially split into two branches — the Veterans Benefits Administration and the Veterans Health Administration. About 53 percent of all veterans spending was mandatory, such as funding for pensions, disability benefits and educational aid. Appropriators controlled the rest.

The Veterans Benefits Administration, funded at $17.1 billion, covered all non-medical benefits to veterans and their families. The administration also paid death compensation for surviving spouses and dependents of service personnel who died while on active duty or from injuries sustained on active duty. Needy veterans who were permanently disabled or older than 65 qualified for pensions, which could go to their families after they died. Other non-medical benefits included: vocational rehabilitation; educational loans and training assistance; home-buying aid; and life insurance programs.

The VA also gave $635.4 million in "readjustment benefits" to finance the education and training of peacetime veterans and for dependents of veterans who died from service-related causes, were missing in action or had a permanent service-related disability. Veterans also could get vocational rehabilitation training and grants to adapt their homes and cars to accommodate their disability.

The Veterans Health Administration, funded at $13.8 billion, maintained a national health-care delivery system for veterans using 172 medical centers, 339 outpatient clinics, 126 nursing homes and 32 soldiers' homes. Appropriators, in report language over the years, had repeatedly criticized the quality of health care provided to veterans.

The Senate report said the committee was "outraged" over problems at the North Chicago Veterans Medical Center, where the poor quality of care led to several deaths. According to the inspector general, problems included misdiagnosis, inappropriate treatment, inappropriate surgical procedures and inadequate supervision of resident doctors. The Senate committee stopped short of mandating changes but said that improving the quality of care at all veterans' hospitals should be the department's top priority.

The Veterans Health Administration was also responsible for medical and prosthetic research and scholarships to study nursing and other health fields in return for a one-year service commitment to the VA.

Among other miscellaneous appropriations for the VA was $796 million to run the agency. This account included operation of the national cemetery system, which provided burial for veterans and their spouses, and maintained their graves in 146 cemeteries across the country. Squirreled away in this departmental administration section of the bill was money to fund large and small construction projects of veterans' hospitals, clinics, nursing homes and parking lots. It was a prime area for earmarks by members of Congress looking out for their districts. For example, the House proposed spending $522 million for major construction projects, the Senate proposed spending $309.9 million, and the conferees agreed on $414 million. That included $16.8 million for an addition to an Ann Arbor, Mich., veterans' clinic — in the home state of VA-HUD Appropriations Subcommittee Chairman Bob Traxler, D.

- **VA drug prices.** The 1990 budget-reconciliation law (PL 101-508) required drug-makers to offer state Medicaid programs for the poor the same discounts they provided to other bulk purchasers. Since that law took effect in January 1991, VA officials said drug companies had eliminated longstanding discounts to the VA to avoid having to sell to Medicaid at such low prices. As a result, the VA projected it would spend an additional $117 million on drugs in fiscal 1991.

The VA-HUD spending bill exempted the VA from the budget law's provision, in the apparent hope that drug-makers would return to the old prices. The exemption would expire on June 30, 1992, or when other legislation was passed to address VA-Medicaid drug pricing.

The bill also directed the secretary of Veterans Affairs "to attempt to negotiate new contracts" to reinstate discount prices in effect before the Medicaid law was enacted.

HOUSING AND URBAN DEVELOPMENT

President John F. Kennedy tried to pull together all the housing-related activities of the federal government into one department but was blocked by the House Rules Committee, whose members did not want to create a new Cabinet department. With the surge of Great Society programs under President Lyndon B. Johnson, Congress approved the creation of HUD in 1965. The department encompassed a wide variety of programs. It was charged with ensuring fair housing opportunities and combating discrimination against home buyers through enforcement of fair housing laws. It provided mortgage credit in order to make more money available to lenders, generally for the benefit of middle-class home buyers. It was responsible for carrying out programs to aid the homeless as well as for providing rental subsidies and other housing assistance for low-income families. For many years it was the principal agent for construction of low-income housing.

With the advent of the Reagan administration, Democrats were unable to get new housing legislation enacted, and they had to fight to protect existing programs from Republican budget-cutters. Debate over housing policy shifted from the Banking committees to the Appropriations committees, where Democrats fought Reagan administration proposals to gut spending for housing programs. In 1990, with President Bush in office and more amenable to housing issues, the time was ripe for the first major housing bill since Community Development Block Grants were created in 1974. Congress examined HUD and sought to shake it up, reorganizing its functions, creating new programs, killing and restructuring old ones and authorizing appropriators to spend far more money on housing. It took Banking Committee members months of work and resulted in little political benefit, according to members who said their constituents did not recognize their housing work. And the final legislation required the marriage of two contradictory proposals: one to expand the supply of affordable housing, the other to sell off the existing stock. While Bush had not slashed housing dollars the way President Ronald Reagan once did, housing groups still complained that he was not willing to spend enough money on the agency. Altogether, Bush recommended spending a total of $24.3 billion for HUD in fiscal 1992, and conferees approved $23.8 billion.

• **New housing programs.** Appropriators had focused on two programs to the exclusion of several other new ideas that were authorized in the National Affordable Housing Act of 1990: Home Ownership and Opportunity for People Everywhere (HOPE) and HOME Investment Partnerships. The HOPE grants, promoted by HUD Secretary Jack F. Kemp, had provoked the most controversy among appropriators. The program had several dimensions, but the best known would give grants to public housing tenants to help them buy the units they lived in. Funds would be distributed through competition among tenant-management groups. Many Democrats had protested that the government should not give away its public housing stock and that very poor public housing tenants were not financially able to become homeowners. Kemp, on the other hand, said that home ownership was the key to stability in blighted urban areas, giving families a stake in their communities. Kemp had hoped to receive $380 million to get HOPE I off the ground. The House recommended $151 million, the Senate recommended $175 million, and the conference provided $161 million.

Other components of the HOPE program included: HOPE II, which would provide grants to help tenants buy private apartment buildings, at $95 million; HOPE III, which would provide grants to help low-income people buy single-family homes, at $95 million; and HOPE for elderly independence, which would offer grants for services to enable elderly people to continue to live on their own, at $10 million.

The HOME Investment Partnerships program was devised in the Senate to provide grants to states and local governments to expand the supply of affordable housing through construction, rehabilitation of existing housing and rental assistance subsidies to low-income families. Primarily the brainchild of Sen. Alan Cranston, D-Calif., it was amended substantially to be acceptable to the administration. The idea behind the program was to leverage private and local funds with federal dollars, leaving the execution to state and local governments. Kemp complained vigorously that the House-Senate conference deleted HOME's matching provision so that state and local governments would not be required to raise any money. To get the program off the ground, Barbara A. Mikulski, D-Md., chairman of the Senate VA-HUD Appropriations Subcommittee, wanted the matching requirement dropped because local governments were struggling with their own financial problems. She promised that the match would be restored in fiscal 1993. The House had recommended $500 million, and the Senate proposed $2 billion for HOME. Conferees approved $1.5 billion.

• **Assisted Housing.** The bulk of housing programs in this category was aimed at directly assisting low-income families without middlemen such as developers. One of the largest was the Section 8 rental assistance program, which provided people with vouchers and certificates to be paid to their landlords. Typically, HUD vouchers were "tenant based," to be used wherever the tenant chose to live. Vouchers were set at a figure designed to reflect a "fair market rent standard" for a community. If a family's rent was higher than the voucher, the family paid the difference. Housing certificates, by contrast, were "project based," available to tenants in certain apartment buildings. Tenants with certificates could not spend more than 30 percent of their monthly income to make up the difference between HUD's contribution and rent.

The conference agreed to add 25,000 additional vouchers and 25,900 additional certificates for new families not already receiving rental subsidies. The total for assisted housing was $8.1 billion.

Besides the new money for "incremental" or additional vouchers and certificates, the bill included $7.36 billion to renew Section 8 contracts that provided subsidies to families who had been receiving vouchers or certificates over the years. Some of those contracts, however, had run out of money, and the bill provided $2.3 billion for Section 8 amendments to fulfill those existing contracts with landlords renting to millions of families. HUD Secretary Kemp angered Appropriations members when he called Mikulski the night before her Senate VA-HUD Appropriations Subcommittee marked up the bill to say that HUD "goofed" and needed an extra $1 billion to renew expiring contracts. The conference responded by providing an extra $330.5 million in fiscal 1992 and $850 million, not to be spent until Oct. 1, 1992.

The Section 202 program provided grants directly to groups to develop housing for the elderly and disabled. This had been a loan program but was changed because the government provided subsidies to pay off the loans, making the program more expensive in the long run.

The bill also provided public housing authorities with operating subsidies to run public housing projects. The operating subsidies were generally the difference between the tenants' rent and what it actually cost to maintain the buildings. Besides operating subsidies, the bill provided $574 million to buy and build new public housing and Indian public housing as well as money to renovate existing public housing. Public and Indian Housing Authorities would receive $2.5 billion to operate existing housing, compared with the $2.1 billion requested by the administration.

Of the total amount provided for assisted housing, the bill designated $50 million to go for a new program under the 1990 housing act to house people with AIDS. Another $50 million would be sent to states and local governments to eliminate lead-based paint in low- and moderate-income rental units.

The bill also set aside $618 million to preserve low-income housing units threatened by the prepayment of subsidized federal mortgages. The 1990 housing bill established new rules for owners who wanted to pay off their mortgages and stop renting to low-income families. The money would be used as incentives for owners to continue renting to low-income families.

Appropriators set aside a record $150 million for "special purpose grants" requested by lawmakers for their districts. That was twice as much as the year before, and Kemp said lawmakers "went too far." These grants, generally considered pork-barrel spending by HUD officials, were earmarked in the final report.

• **Federal Housing Administration (FHA).** The FHA mutual mortgage insurance program had backed loans for more than 15 million homes since Congress first authorized it back in 1934. The program was intended to spur home ownership and stimulate the housing industry by encouraging banks to make loans to people who didn't have the money for a traditional 10 percent to 20 percent down payment. FHA loans required down payments of 3 percent on the first $25,000 and 5 percent on the remainder. Appropriators required the FHA not to make commitments to guarantee loans exceeding $60 billion in fiscal 1992. Administrative costs would come to $189 million and program costs would amount to $54.9 million, for a total of $243.9 million.

• **Anti-drug programs.** The bill provided $165 million for grants to public housing agencies to fight drug-related crime in public housing projects. The money was used for security guards at public housing projects as well as for drug education programs. Of that amount, $10 million would be used for drug-elimination grants for federally assisted, low-income housing.

• **Government National Mortgage Association (Ginnie Mae).** Ginnie Mae was a secondary loan market that guaranteed privately issued securities backed by pools of mortgages. The mortgages involved were backed by the FHA, the VA and the Farmers Home Administration (FmHA). The bill required that new commitments to issue guarantees not exceed $74.7 billion, the amount of risk Congress was willing to accept. The appropriation to carry out the program was $17.8 million.

• **Homeless assistance.** The Stewart B. McKinney Homeless Assistance Act authorized a number of small programs to provide temporary and transitional housing for homeless people. Rep. McKinney, R-Conn., was one of the sponsors of the legislation, and he died before it passed in 1987. The fiscal 1992 funding bill included a total of $450 million for these programs, among them grants to communities to help pay for emergency shelters. Grants could be used to renovate or convert buildings to homeless shelters or to operate emergency shelters and provide social services. Communities had to provide matching funds to participate.

The transitional and supportive housing demonstration program, funded at $150 million, was designed to encourage local groups to develop new approaches to helping homeless people move into temporary housing. Money was targeted particularly to people who were disabled, homeless families and people who had been released from mental institutions. The money went for acquiring and renovating housing for the homeless, in addition to the cost of operating the housing and providing support services for the people living there.

Supplemental Assistance for Facilities to Assist the Homeless, at $11.3 million, was another grant program designed to funnel money to groups providing housing and social services for the homeless.

One of the more popular homeless programs was known as Section 8 single-room occupancy, an effort to provide permanent housing for the homeless.

Many housing advocates believed that the ranks of the homeless increased over the years due to the elimination of "flophouses" or single-room occupancy units in old boardinghouses and hotels as redevelopment projects overtook seedier parts of the inner cities. This $105 million program, for development and renovation of single rooms, was designed to reverse that trend.

Shelter Plus Care was a new program developed in the 1990 housing act to aid homeless people not only with housing but also with social services. The bill used rental assistance and single-room occupancy programs as a way for HUD to enter into contracts with states and local governments. In turn, these governments contracted with nonprofit organizations to provide services such as job training and day care. The bill included $110.5 million.

• **Community Planning and Development.** The Community Development Block Grants program was very popular among lawmakers for sending money back to the states and local governments. The states and communities were given discretion over what to do with the money, but Congress intended for it to be used for economic development, affordable housing and eradicating urban blight.

At least 70 percent of the money was supposed to go to programs benefiting low- and moderate-income people. Critics said that the funds were not carefully distributed and were all too frequently used to build golf courses, swimming pools and other non-essential projects. Republican administrations had frequently requested far less money than Congress ultimately appropriated. The administration recommended $2.9 billion compared with the $3.4 billion provided by the conference.

Miscellaneous

The housing portion of the bill provided $25 million for policy development and research, $438 million for management and administration and $35 million for the office of inspector general. Also included was debt forgiveness from urban renewal projects for a number of communities, including New London, Conn.; Newburyport and Malden, Mass.; Jefferson, Mo.; Calhoun Falls, S.C.; and Soddy Daisy, Tenn.

NASA

Founded in 1958 to do space and aeronautical research for peaceful purposes, the National Aeronautics and Space Administration rose to prominence with the Apollo mission, which landed American astronauts on the moon in 1969. Apollo, begun in 1962 by President Kennedy, marked the beginning of Americans' love affair with space exploration. For nearly a quarter of a century the agency was the golden child of Congress and the country, receiving hefty annual increases in its budget as its spacecraft ranged farther into the solar system, sending back pictures of Mars, Venus and Saturn.

The golden era ended with the 1986 explosion of the space shuttle *Challenger*, which killed seven astronauts and shocked the nation. Since then, NASA had had a succession of mishaps leading to flawed missions, hundreds of millions of dollars in cost overruns and a widespread perception that the agency was adrift.

The agency's flagship project, its $40 billion space station *Freedom*, was slated to be launched at the end of the century. It became the fulcrum of the debate over the fiscal 1992 appropriation for the VA-HUD bill. House appropriators tried to cancel the station to free funds for other NASA projects to grow.

Nearly full funding was restored on the House floor after an all-out lobbying campaign by the White House, NASA and aerospace contractors.

In coming years, however, both the station and other high-dollar NASA projects were likely to come under fire as Congress continued to try to balance the needs of science with those of the VA-HUD bill's other constituencies, veterans, housing for the poor and the environment.

For fiscal 1992, in order to pay for the space station and slow NASA's growth, Congress put the lid on new programs at the agency, refusing to fund most of them, and terminated or cut the administration's budget request for many existing programs. Overall, the agency's budget in fiscal 1992 grew just 3.5 percent to $14.3 billion. By contrast, it grew by nearly 15 percent in 1989 and 12 percent in 1990. About 90 percent of its budget went to pay the contractors who built its spacecraft, launch vehicles, computers, telescopes and other equipment.

NASA had two high-profile areas: space research, which included projects such as the space station *Freedom*, and the shuttle. Within its space research activities NASA had three main missions: conceptualizing space projects, doing the research necessary to design and build them, and getting them to space. In addition, the agency had programs whose goal was to transfer technology learned through the space program to private industry.

The reports of House and Senate VA-HUD subcommittees consisted mainly of lists of individual NASA projects and activities. They told little about the agency's functions. The following description of NASA programs is a synthesis of information from Appropriations committee hearings, the agency's budget documents, House and Senate authorizing committee analyses and the appropriations conference report.

Major Projects

Every major NASA program with the exception of the space shuttle was funded through the $6.41 billion fiscal 1992 appropriation in the research and development account. The major projects were the best known and most expensive of the projects NASA had under way. In several cases, Congress canceled projects altogether or capped the total project costs in an effort to bring the agency's spending under control.

• **Station *Freedom*.** The $40 billion space station was slated to be completed in 2000 and initially would be able to support four astronauts. Its goal was to learn how astronauts withstood long periods in gravity-free environments so that scientists could plan for longer space journeys such as the estimated two years it would take for astronauts to go to Mars.

It would also do research on the effect of low-gravity environments on chemical and other scientific processes. Astronauts would begin assembling the shuttle in space in 1995. Fiscal 1992's appropriation for the project was $2.03 billion, the same amount as the administration requested. The station's fiscal 1993 cost was capped in the bill at $2.25 billion.

• **Mission to Planet Earth.** The series of satellites that would send volumes of environmental information on the oceans, atmosphere and the land to scientists on Earth was known as Mission to Planet Earth. The largest of the satellites, the Earth Observing System, was scheduled for launch in 1997. But over the next five years smaller satellites would feed environmental information to powerful computers that would decipher and catalog it for scientists.

Congress, which had strongly supported the program, ordered NASA in the fiscal 1992 appropriation to cut the $17.5 billion price tag of its biggest satellites by 31 percent. The cut would probably entail abandoning the plan to put in two big platforms carrying eight to 10 scientific instruments. Instead, NASA would send into space a series of satellites, each carrying no more than three or four instruments. The Earth Observing System received $271 million for fiscal 1992, about 80 percent of the funding requested by the administration.

• **'Great Observatories.'** The four space-based "Great Observatories" were powerful scientific instruments that could "see" light in different parts of the light spectrum, including infrared and gamma rays, all of which would give scientists new information about the heavens.

The best known of these, the $1.5 billion Hubble Telescope, was launched in 1990. It was designed to pick up faint light and light from the ultraviolet area of the spectrum. But its mirror was flawed and it could see only half of what it was designed to see. There was no dispute over funding for Hubble.

The Gamma Ray Observatory, launched in April 1991, was able to pick up gamma rays, the highest energy particles in the universe. They usually emanated from the area inside quasars, black holes and supernovas. There had been little controversy over the project's cost — $540 million for construction and $30 million annually for operation.

The Advanced X-Ray Astrophysics Facility (AXAF), scheduled for launch in 1997, was designed to pick up X-rays that would help astronomers study large-scale galactic phenomena such as black holes, the contribution of hot gases to the mass of the universe and clusters of distant galaxies. Its appropriation for fiscal 1992 was $151 million, about 28 percent less than the administration requested; its total cost was expected to be $1.6 billion.

The Space Infrared Telescope Facility, designed to see light at the infrared end of the spectrum, was terminated.

• **CRAF/Cassini.** These were two astronomy programs: One was designed to study a comet and an asteroid; the other project, to fly to Saturn and study one of its moons. The agency was in the midst of revising both projects' flight schedules. As part of their effort to reduce the agency's budget, conferees reduced funding for the two programs to $210.7 million in fiscal 1992, a third less than the Bush administration requested. NASA estimated the total cost of the two projects at $1.6 billion.

• **National Aerospace Plane.** A joint project with the Defense Department, the plane was virtually terminated. The administration proposed spending $72 million to continue research on the aeronautics technology needed to build a plane that could take off from a conventional airport and go straight into low Earth orbit — the same orbit as the shuttle. However, the bill appropriated only $5 million.

Ongoing Research and Development

• **Space science and applications.** Appropriators approved a fiscal 1992 budget of $2.66 billion for NASA's space science and applications division, a 10 percent increase in the program over fiscal 1991. NASA had requested a 20 percent increase. The division's observation systems conducted scientific investigations of the Earth, sun, other planets and the galaxy. Its research also included the development of some space technology.

• **Space transportation.** In fiscal 1992, appropriators approved $597.9 million for development, testing and procurement of hardware to deploy spacecraft into higher orbits than the shuttle. This was nearly $300 million less than the agency requested, and about $5 million less than the fiscal 1991 appropriation. The space shuttle was developed using funds from this account. The highest-profile project in this account, the National Launch System, designed to put heavier spacecraft into orbit, was cut 84 percent from the administration's request of $175 million to $28 million. Appropriators said the agency had not yet made clear the need for a new launch system.

• **Commercial programs.** NASA's commercial programs took off in the early 1980s in the wake of the first flights of the space shuttle. Congress hoped that once space was accessible, private companies would develop space-based industry. However, that proved more difficult than expected. Companies wanted to experiment with manufacturing in space, but the cost of getting there was too high unless the government continued to pay for it. In an effort to get the program off the ground, Congress gave partial funding to 15 "Centers for the Commercial Development of Space." The balance of the funding was provided by private industry and universities. The companies — largely in the aerospace field — designed space experiments with industrial applications at the centers. Two sets of industry experiments were ready to be launched and were waiting for room on the shuttle and on an unmanned rocket.

The division also had six "technology transfer centers," where businesses worked with NASA scientists to learn applications for aerospace technologies.

Over the years, commercial programs also had funded a number of projects requested by individual members of Congress to benefit specific districts. The fiscal 1992 appropriation of $123 million included $9 million for the National Technology Transfer Center at Wheeling (W.Va.) Jesuit College, a project sponsored by Robert C. Byrd, D-W.Va., chairman of the Senate Appropriations Committee.

• **Space research and technology.** Since NASA's beginnings, the Space Research division had been NASA's think tank, charged with dreaming up new projects for the agency. The division's work was largely theoretical and rarely focused on near-term missions.

Over the past two years the division had spearheaded Bush's project to send astronauts back to the moon and to Mars, missions that were a decade or more away. As the budget tightened, members of Congress attempted to cut the division's spending. The fiscal 1992 appropriation of $298 million was about 25 percent less than the administration request; it cut in half Bush's proposal to spend $52 million on moon-Mars research aimed at designing a space mission that would take Americans to Mars.

• **Aeronautical research and technology.** The bread and butter of NASA's work was its research on aeronautics — the science of flight. Nearly half a century before there was a space agency, the National Advisory Committee on Aeronautics coordinated government and industry research in flight dynamics. Its research was folded into NASA when the agency was created. The $574.2 million fiscal 1992 appropriation was just $17 million less than the administration request. The money funded studies in aeronautics technology, safety and materials, and projects that used supercomputers to model air flow and aerodynamics.

Space Flight

The space flight account, which paid for shuttle operations and production, got $5.2 billion, about $400 million less than the administration's request. Although it was a nominal increase over fiscal 1991, the new appropriation represented one of the largest cutbacks from the Bush budget. This account also included the space- and ground-based data and tracking satellites. The satellites transmitted data gathered by spaceships and directed it to computer storage facilities on Earth.

• **Space shuttle.** In fiscal 1992 the shuttle was scheduled for nine trips. However, because the $2.69 billion appropriation was nearly $100 million less than fiscal 1991, NASA said it would be able to afford only eight flights. The space shuttle was the first reusable space vehicle and was designed to carry astronauts, scientific experiments and Defense Department projects. Its annual costs were driven largely by the need for a standing army of 2,500 engineers, aeronautics experts and support staff at Cape Canaveral, Fla., where the shuttle and other spacecraft were launched. NASA's four shuttles — *Columbia*, *Atlantis*, *Discovery* and *Endeavor* — were made by Rockwell International Corp., the agency's largest contractor.

• **Expendable launch vehicles.** The Space Flight Control division also included a $217.4 million appropriation for one-time-only rockets to launch spacecraft carrying scientific projects that did not require special handling by astronauts. The administration sought $341.9 million. These expendable vehicles typically burned up when they re-entered the Earth's atmosphere.

• **Advanced Solid Rocket Motor project.** Aimed at giving the shuttle the ability to carry heavier cargoes into space, this project received $315 million — 30 percent more than the administration requested. The controversial and expensive new launch system was being built by Aerojet-General Corp. and Lockheed Corp. in Yellow Creek, Miss., in the district of House Appropriations Chairman Jamie L. Whitten, D.

Overall, Congress appropriated about $400 million less than NASA requested for this account largely because the Defense Department refused to reimburse the agency for $386 million worth of tracking services.

Construction

The appropriation of $525 million for construction at NASA included modernization, repair and renovation at the agency's eight space flight centers across the country and at other NASA-funded projects. The largest project was construction associated with the production of the

Advanced Solid Rocket Motor test facilities.

Key committee members included about $72.9 million worth of pet projects in this section of the bill. Senate subcommittee Chairman Mikulski earmarked $20 million for the Christopher Columbus Center of Marine Research and Exploration in Baltimore, a new biotechnology lab whose total cost would be about $150 million.

Also, Senate full committee Chairman Byrd got his colleagues to include three projects totaling $29.5 million: $10 million for an independent software validation and verification center at West Virginia University; $6 million to build a teaching facility and $13.5 million to build a technology transfer learning center, both at Wheeling Jesuit College, in addition to the $9 million for programs there. Senate ranking minority member Jake Garn, R-Utah, got $10 million for a space dynamics center at Utah State University.

House subcommittee Chairman Traxler got $3.4 million added to the bill for planning and construction of CIESIN, a consortium in Ann Arbor, Mich., that eventually would employ hundreds of scientists to translate data generated by NASA satellites into a form that could be used by citizens and policy-makers. The bill also earmarked $25 million for the consortium's programs.

The bill included $10 million requested by Sen. Ted Stevens, R-Alaska, to improve the Poker Flats Research Range, a rocket testing facility operated by the University of Alaska at Fairbanks. This was the third year that Stevens had helped the university get money to improve the facility, bringing total funding to $32 million for a project whose costs were estimated at up to $40 million.

Personnel and Administration

This account's $2.24 billion appropriation funded salaries, benefits and travel for NASA employees as well as the overhead for agency facilities. NASA employed a total of 24,800 people at its Washington headquarters and at nine centers scattered across the country.

The appropriation was $210 million less than the administration request, which could have further diminished the agency's already strained ability to store data and maintain buildings and equipment.

ENVIRONMENTAL PROTECTION AGENCY

Created by President Richard M. Nixon in 1970 during the nation's outpouring of concern for the environment, the Environmental Protection Agency (EPA) oversaw regulation of air and water quality, solid and hazardous wastes, pesticides and radioactive materials. Among the agency's most contentious tasks were the supervision of the cleanup of hazardous waste sites under the 1980 "superfund" law, putting into effect new regulations called for under the 1990 revision of the Clean Air Act, guiding the elimination of leaky underground petroleum storage tanks and helping fund the construction of sewage treatment plants nationwide, a costly undertaking that cities increasingly had had to pay for.

The EPA's $6.67 billion total budget far overshadowed those of regulatory agencies such as the Food and Drug Administration's $700 million appropriation and the $300 million for the Occupational Safety and Health Administration. Its importance was underscored by the Senate's Oct. 1 vote to elevate the EPA to Cabinet-level status.

• **Operating programs.** The EPA employed 16,700 people in 10 regional offices and smaller field offices nationwide, for which the Bush administration requested an increase of $115.3 million over fiscal 1991 funding levels, to $1.09 billion. The House approved that amount. But Senate subcommittee Chairman Mikulski complained that staffing levels were too high, noting that the much larger HUD employed 14,000 people. Her panel approved an increase to $1.03 billion. EPA eventually got $1.04 billion, $11 million more than the Senate committee had recommended. Appropriators specifically instructed the EPA's Office of Water to beef up by 10 people its program aimed at preventing generalized runoff from streets and fields (so-called non-point source pollution). And in the wake of publicity over the health hazards associated with lead-based paint, which could lead to brain damage in children, the Senate directed that $1.5 million be funneled into a program to train people to identify these paints in the nation's building stock.

• **Office of the Inspector General.** The EPA's administrative audit and investigative branch received $41.2 million. A big chunk of it — $14.9 million — came from the superfund, the nation's main program for cleaning up hazardous wastes. One of the office's first duties was to monitor the work of private companies and government agencies that had contracted to clean up hazardous wastes. Appropriators criticized the office for not being aggressive enough in ferreting out fraud in the superfund program and demanded increased oversight activities. *(See below)*

• **Research and development.** For all outside research excluding superfund and leaking underground storage tanks, Congress increased the Bush administration budget request by $10 million to $323 million. Beyond the administration's request, appropriators set aside an extra $3.2 million for the Center for Environmental Management and $1.3 million for a demonstration office waste recycling program at Western Michigan University in Kalamazoo. It also continued the global warming research budget at 1991 levels.

• **Anti-pollution programs.** The $1.13 billion abatement, control, compliance and education account was one of the key components of the EPA's anti-pollution programs. The program set standards for air quality, water quality, safe drinking water, hazardous wastes and radiation exposure. It monitored the standards and enforced those regulations. The EPA had requested $285 million in its air program, $264.9 million in its water quality program, $78.5 million in its drinking water program, $203.7 million in its hazardous waste regulation program, $53.2 million in its pesticides program, $21.4 million in its radiation program, $20.6 million in its "multimedia" program (which reviewed federal environmental impact statements), $53.4 million for toxic substances and $38.5 million for management and support.

Congressional appropriators required the administration to spend $37 million for grants to schools for asbestos removal, $7 million for a program to clean up America's lakes and $51.2 million for state grants for controlling polluted runoff coming from generalized sources such as fields and pavement. Congress added $9.5 million for global climate change research but took $17 million out of other accounts.

The bill also steered projects to individual states, such as $2.75 million for three projects in Byrd's home state of West Virginia: a small-community water pollution research center, a demonstration project to design a wastewater treatment technology for small communities and an EPA training center. Mikulski got $1 million for a storm-water control demonstration project on the Patuxent River in Maryland.

• **Buildings and facilities.** For the design, construction and maintenance of EPA-owned facilities, Congress increased the administration's budget request by $26 million. Most of the boost was taken up by $20 million for the site acquisition and design of a Training and Ecology Center in Bay City, Mich., in Traxler's district. The bill prohibited the EPA from spending any money for its proposed Environmental Technology and Engineering Center in Edison, N.J., a provision inserted by Senate VA-HUD Appropriations Committee member Frank R. Lautenberg, D-N.J. The proposed center, which would have researched innovative treatment technologies for hazardous wastes, had drawn local opposition over fears that a community college next door could be exposed to toxic materials. The bill included $6 million for a Christopher Columbus Marine Research and Exploration Center in downtown Baltimore, home of subcommittee Chairman Mikulski. The total appropriations for buildings and facilities was $39.3 million.

• **Superfund.** The 1990 Budget Reconciliation Act extended the superfund through Sept. 30, 1994, and extended the life of the superfund trust fund through 1995. The superfund trust fund was financed by taxes on petroleum, hazardous chemicals, and a broad-based environment tax on corporations as well as appropriations. The fund was established in 1980 to clean up sites where hazardous and toxic materials had been released into the ground or water. The superfund program also was responsible for emergency response to chemical accidents, as well as research into and development of new cleanup techniques. The superfund's priority list included about 1,200 sites; through fiscal 1990, 52 of the sites had been cleaned up. Congress had authorized more than $15.2 billion for the superfund, and as of September 1989, EPA had spent $3.6 billion. Revamped in 1986, the program had been criticized in recent years for spending too much on administration and not enough on cleanups. The appropriators capped administrative expenses at $240 million; that was more than 56 percent higher than 1987 totals. The conferees approved a total of $1.62 billion for fiscal 1992.

• **Leaking Underground Storage Tank Trust Fund.** A growing environmental concern had been the thousands of corroding and leaking underground tanks that were letting gasoline, oil and other toxic liquids seep into the ground. The responsibility for cleanup lay with owners of the tanks. This $75 million program was designed to provide technical support to state and local agencies to help select the best possible cleanup strategy. As in the case of superfund, the bill capped administrative costs, in this case at $6.4 million.

• **Construction grants/state revolving funds.** A key EPA task was to help states and local jurisdictions build plants to treat sewage and other wastewater. Though the EPA once gave municipalities outright grants for these plants, since 1991 most of the construction money had been put into a revolving loan fund, which provided below-market rate loans to states and localities. Appropriators approved an EPA request to give large direct grants to seven cities to pay for new secondary wastewater treatment plants: Boston ($100 million), New York ($70 million), Los Angeles ($55 million), San Diego ($40 million), Seattle ($35 million), Baltimore ($40 million) and Tijuana, Mexico ($49 million). Members were somewhat reluctant to approve money for the Tijuana project, criticizing its rapidly escalating cost. But EPA officials contended the Mexican plant was necessary to keep that city from fouling Southern California waters. Another $46 million was targeted by the House panel to solve another pollution problem: storm-water runoff that could often overwhelm treatment plants. This "wet weather" demonstration project was steered to Wayne County (Detroit), Mich., in the district of Democrat John D. Dingell. The total for this account was $2.4 billion.

• **Administrative provisions.** Reflecting concern with the growth of the EPA's headquarters staff, HR 2519 contained specific language setting personnel levels for the agency in Washington — for example, no more than 51 workers in Administrator William K. Reilly's immediate staff and 45 workers in the office of congressional affairs.

NATIONAL SCIENCE FOUNDATION

With concern mounting nationwide that students were inadequately educated in science, Congress had increased money over the past several years for the National Science Foundation (NSF) to improve math and science teaching for elementary and secondary students. Besides education, NSF's mission was to support basic and applied research through grants and contracts to colleges, universities, nonprofit organizations and other research organizations. The bill provided money to modernize academic research facilities and to upgrade instruments and equipment.

One program within NSF, to study the Antarctic, sparked major disagreement within Congress and the administration. Mikulski cut back the amount of money devoted to Antarctic research and wrote in her report that the Department of Defense should shoulder the bulk of the burden because it benefited from the program, too. That solution, however, violated the budget agreement, which prohibited transfers of money between defense and domestic programs.

NSF spread its money around through competitions for grants, decided by panels of experts.

The appropriations were $1.9 billion for research, $33 million for academic research facilities and instrumentation, $88 million for U.S. Antarctic research activities and logistical support, $465 million for science education and $112.5 million for salaries and expenses.

FEDERAL DEPOSIT INSURANCE

A total of $15.87 billion would go to cover costs previously incurred when the now-defunct Federal Savings and Loan Insurance Corporation (FSLIC) closed 200 failed thrifts in 1988. This amount was not included in the bill's bottom line under an agreement with the administration.

INDEPENDENT AGENCIES

• **American Battle Monuments Commission.** The bill appropriated $18.4 billion for the board responsible for maintaining and building U.S. monuments and memorials commemorating achievements in battle.

• **Commission on National and Community Service.** This board would make grants to states and other groups to create opportunities for students and other young people to perform community service work — $2 million for salaries and expenses of the commission and $73 million for program activities.

• **Consumer Product Safety Commission.** The commission was an independent regulatory agency responsible for protecting the public against unreasonable risks of injury from consumer products and developing uniform safety standards for consumer products — $40.2 million.

• **Court of Veterans Appeals.** The court was established to review decisions of the Board of Veterans Appeals. It had the authority to decide all questions of law and all statutory and regulatory provisions under the Department of Veterans Affairs — $9.1 million.

• **Department of Defense.** This portion of the bill funded the Pentagon's caring for Civil Cemeterial Expenses, Arlington National Cemetery and the Soldier's and Airmen's Home National Cemetery — $12.6 million.

• **Executive Office of the President — Council on Environmental Quality and Office of Environmental Quality.** The council's main responsibility was to advise the president on national and international policies promoting environmental protection — $2.6 million.

• **National Space Council.** The council's job was to advise the president on national space policy, including long-range goals — $1.5 million.

• **Office of Science and Technology**. The office was created to advise the president on science and technology policies — $6 million.

• **The Points of Light Foundation.** The foundation was a governmental nonprofit corporation in the Executive Office of the President. Its job was to promote community service as a way of life for all people — $5 million.

• **Federal Emergency Management Agency (FEMA).** FEMA was responsible for coordinating federal efforts to anticipate and respond to a range of major civil emergencies, such as hurricanes and earthquakes — $773 million for emergency management planning.

• **General Services Administration's Consumer Information Center.** The center was designed to help federal departments and agencies promote and distribute consumer information collected from government programs. The center also distributed catalogs of information to the general public through its distribution center in Pueblo, Colo. — $1.9 million.

• **Department of Health and Human Services Office of Consumer Affairs.** This office was designed to make sure consumers' views were heard throughout federal agencies — $2.1 million.

• **Interagency Council on the Homeless.** This was an independent organization composed of 17 federal agencies to review federal programs to help the homeless. The $1.08 million to be appropriated was delayed by the conference until Sept. 20, 1993.

• **National Commission on Financial Institution Reform, Recovery and Enforcement.** This new commission was created by the 1990 Crime Control Act and was supposed to examine and identify the causes of the savings and loan industry problem — $1 million.

• **National Commission on Native American, Alaska Native and Native Hawaiian Housing.** The 1989 HUD Reform Act created this commission to evaluate the obstacles to affordable housing for American Indians, Alaska Natives and native Hawaiians — $500,000.

• **National Credit Union Administration.** The administration provided funds to help credit unions meet emergency financial needs. Credit unions had to invest in the capital stock of the administration in order to benefit, and those funds were ultimately available to the individual credit unions. The bill limited those loans to $600 million.

• **Neighborhood Reinvestment Corporation.** The corporation assisted local communities in creating partnerships between residents and representatives of the private and public sectors. The partnerships were independent tax-exempt, nonprofit groups promoting affordable housing — $31.9 million.

• **Selective Service System.** The system's mission was to be prepared to supply the armed forces with manpower during a national emergency — $27.48 million. ■

Continued from p. 520

Mikulski, whose state was home to the Goddard Space Flight Center, said she was a convert as well as "a true believer."

And Glenn told of the scientific progress that had been made from space exploration, such as the development of lighter, stronger materials.

"Every single advance we have made has been because someone was curious about the unknown," Glenn said, urging senators to fund the project even though no one knew exactly what would come of it.

Savings and Loan Debacle

A less noticed item in the VA-HUD bill provided $15.867 billion for costs previously incurred when the now-defunct Federal Savings and Loan Insurance Corporation (FSLIC) closed 200 failed thrifts in 1988.

Guaranteeing a return on assets, the FSLIC negotiated nearly 100 deals in which thrifts were handed over to new owners. Those guarantees were paid for with promissory notes coming due in 1991.

In fiscal 1991, the government spent $22 billion to cover those obligations. Under an agreement with the administration, the $15.867 billion was not counted toward the bill's bottom line.

Tim Wirth, D-Colo., said he did not begrudge the appropriation. However, he offered an amendment requiring all regulatory examinations of defunct thrifts to be public information. Wirth also wanted the release of all agreements between the government and successful bidders for those failed thrifts. "When public money is expended, the public ought to know where that money is going."

Bob Kerrey, D-Neb., offered an amendment to Wirth's, which required the release of a Washington law firm's analysis of who tried to buy a majority of thrifts that failed in 1988.

Garn, the ranking minority member of the Banking Committee, strenuously objected to Wirth's proposal.

"The public does have a right to know what happened," Garn said. But he said individual customers' privacy would be violated by disclosing examination reports.

Wirth said he was not interested in consumer car and home loans but in the people who bought the thrifts with generous incentives from the government. The two hit an impasse over the privacy issue, and Garn refused to allow the amendments to come to a roll call vote.

In an agreement worked out by Majority Leader George J. Mitchell, D-Maine, Wirth and Kerrey said they would withdraw their amendments if they failed to get three-fifths of the Senate to vote to invoke cloture and cut off debate.

The cloture vote failed by three votes, 57-40, and Wirth and Kerrey withdrew their amendments. *(Vote 139, p. 19-S)*

Pork Projects

Robert C. Smith, R-N.H., a freshman member of the Senate, complained at length that members of the Appropriations Committee had inserted $72.8 million worth of grants for their states and their friends' states into the bill.

For example, $500,000 was earmarked for the Newark Public Library in New Jersey to develop literacy training and reading rooms at five public housing developments. Frank R. Lautenberg, D-N.J., was a member of the subcommittee.

"How did we determine it would go to Newark?" Smith asked. With no official competition to receive a grant, he said, "the process is terrible, it's unfair, it's unjust."

Smith proposed killing the so-called special purpose grants within the HUD portion of the bill and transferring the $72.8 million to veterans' medical care. But after making his speech and promising to bring the pork subject up at every opportunity, he withdrew his amendment because he said he did not have the votes.

Mikulski noted that her subcommittee tried to choose only projects that would aid low- and moderate-income people and eliminate blight.

CONFERENCE ACTION

House and Senate conferees on the $80.9 billion spending bill for veterans, housing and space programs believed they had found a way to satisfy most of the conflicting demands of those constituencies.

But to do so, appropriators had to use a one-time budgetary windfall to pay for new housing initiatives, cut an array of space programs at NASA to cover the cost of the space station *Freedom*, and trim salaries and expenses for almost every agency, including the EPA.

The result was surprisingly swift agreement Sept. 25 on HR 2519.

"We have tried to balance the compelling needs ... from virtually every agency and interest group from our aging veterans to the pioneers of the new frontiers in space," said Mikulski.

In a Sept. 25 letter to the conference chairmen, HUD Secretary Kemp charged that the House-Senate compromise was a "betrayal of low-income families" and amounted to a return "to the failed scandal-prone housing programs of the past."

Extra Money for Housing

One of the keys to reaching a compromise, conference leaders said, was finding an extra $1.75 billion for housing through a new accounting method. It was a one-time windfall that occurred when the financing rules were changed for a longstanding housing program, known as Section 202, for the elderly and disabled.

In the past, HUD offered loans to those building housing for the elderly and then provided them with rental assistance to pay off the loans. The 1990 housing reauthorization bill switched the housing loan program to a grant program, eliminating the need for long-term rental subsidies.

House Appropriations subcommittee Chairman Traxler acknowledged that the windfall merely put off the day of reckoning for the multifaceted bill. "This is a funding strategy that will not be around next year," he said.

Under the conference agreement, the housing portion of the bill was slated to cost $23.8 billion in fiscal 1992, with almost half — $10.4 billion — of those dollars to be spent on rent subsidies for low-income Americans. It also included money for the more contentious parts of the bill, the new HOME and HOPE housing programs.

The conference allocated $1.5 billion for the HOME program and $361 million for HOPE.

McDade, ranking Republican on the House Appropriations Committee, tried to appease Kemp with an amendment to add $25 million to the section of the HOPE program that was to help public housing tenants buy their units. Conferees agreed to add $10 million but merely shifted it from another section of the HOPE program.

Committee members expressed frustration with Kemp, a former House colleague, saying that he was looking a gift horse in the mouth. "We really are treating the secretary very well," Traxler said.

Mikulski added that the committee had to make up for an unexpected $325 million shortfall in low-income housing subsidies and that Kemp seemed not to appreciate their effort.

Small Boost for NASA

No agency in the bill saw as drastic a change in its fortunes as NASA. The conferees gave the space agency a mere 3 percent overall boost in its funding, bringing its fiscal 1992 budget to $14.3 billion — a sharp contrast to the 10 percent to 14 percent annual increases it had received for the past several years.

The agency's budget was dominated by the space station. The conferees rejected a plea from Bill Green, N.Y., ranking Republican on the House VA-HUD Subcommittee, to split the difference between the House and Senate versions of the space station and put $65 million toward environmental programs.

That produced an ironic moment when Traxler spoke out against Green. Traxler was a strong supporter of NASA's environmental and science programs and had worked with Green to kill the station, which both men believed was a flawed project.

However, once the full House went so strongly on record for the space station, Traxler felt he had to defend that position.

"The irony is that the House bill originally was tilted toward science, but I find myself now defending the space station — contrary to where I was three months ago," he said.

The price the administration had to pay to keep *Freedom* on course included termination of a number of NASA programs and deep cuts in others. Conferees agreed to:

- Terminate the Orbiting Solar Laboratory, the infrared telescope, the new fuel pump for the shuttle and the Flight Telerobotic Servicer.
- Reduce by 80 percent the $175 million request for a new national launch system able to propel spacecraft farther.
- Cut 20 percent from the Earth Observing System, designed to study global climate change.
- Cut 90 percent from the National Aerospace Plane, a project that was saved from termination by an amendment offered by Garn.

The NASA budget was strapped by the Pentagon's refusal to transfer $384 million to the space agency. Conferees had been counting on the money to help offset other NASA cuts.

EPA Salaries Request Cut

The EPA cuts were the most surprising given the political clout of environmental interests. Conferees funded the agency's activities at $6.64 billion, about $423 million more than the president's request.

But they recommended $50 million less than the budget request for the account that paid salaries and expenses — a crucial area for the EPA, which said it had to have a sufficient number of employees to enforce anti-pollution laws.

The reduction was a rebuff to EPA Administrator William K. Reilly, who personally lobbied members of Congress for more generous funding for the salaries account.

The conference total for veterans' programs, which made up the largest portion of the bill, was $32.5 billion. There was little controversy over the funding levels but extensive discussion over a recent directive from VA Secretary Edward J. Derwinski prohibiting the sale of tobacco products at VA hospitals.

The committee agreed to report language directing Derwinski to review the policy.

The conference agreement received only scattered opposition in both chambers, notwithstanding a concession by Traxler that it was "a size 9 shoe with a [size] 12 foot to fit into it."

House Science Committee Chairman Brown said he was "extremely frustrated and unhappy" with the number of pork-barrel projects put in NASA's budget.

"The Appropriations Committee complains about tremendous budgetary pressures but found room for $100 million in special projects," Brown said. "Basically, space science got shortchanged and we actually had to cancel several important new science projects and cut back on others. It's very discouraging."

Traxler, in an interview after the floor debate, said he refrained from pointing out that the bill included three earmarks under the EPA that would benefit Brown's district.

West Virginia Benefits

In the Senate, Mikulski told her colleagues that the subcommittee struggled to meet the needs of each agency. "We had three lists of priorities: what we must do, what we should do and what we would like to do," she said.

The bill sailed through the Senate with virtually no comment.

An aide to Mikulski echoed Traxler's explanation that subcommittees received far more requests for special projects in 1991 than ever before. Traxler attributed the rise to a sour economy. "Most communities do not have the wherewithal to do physical infrastructure projects," he said.

A disproportionate number of the bill's earmarks benefitted West Virginia, home state of Democratic Sen. Robert C. Byrd, chairman of the full Appropriations Committee.

Five West Virginia projects received $4 million from HUD dollars; another $4 million came from the EPA; and $40 million in projects were paid for by the NASA account.

The largest was a $22.5 million earmark for a National Technology Center at Wheeling Jesuit College. The center was to serve as a clearinghouse on federally developed technologies and help transfer them to the private sector. ■

Congress Ducks Call on Moscow Embassy

After yet another fight about what to do with the half-built, bug-riddled U.S. Embassy in Moscow, Congress on Oct. 3 sent the president a $22 billion spending bill (HR 2608) for the Departments of Commerce, Justice and State.

Appropriations Committee conferees had decided on Oct. 2 to resolve the six-year-long question over whether to raze or remodel the embassy by opting to build a new one next door. But angry House members, objecting to the plan's estimated cost of $220 million and saying they were left out of the decision, voted 175-231 the next day to reject the conferees' plan. *(Vote 293, p. 70-H)*

"This is a world-class waste of money," said Olympia J. Snowe, R-Maine, arguing that Washington first should decide what to do with the existing embassy facility.

Instead, the House voted to leave the embassy decision to the State Department, but with the condition that whatever plan was decided upon, the department report back to Congress. Unwilling to tie up the underlying measure, which also funded the federal judiciary, the Senate agreed. Both chambers passed the conference report on HR 2608 by voice votes.

Overall, the measure provided about $2.6 billion more than the fiscal 1991 appropriation, including $9.3 billion for the Department of Justice; $3 billion for Commerce; $3.8 billion for the State Department; and $2.3 billion for the federal judiciary. *(1990 Almanac, p. 881)*

BOXSCORE

➡ **Fiscal 1992 Commerce, Justice, State and federal judiciary appropriations (HR 2608).** The bill provided $22 billion for the programs under the Departments of Commerce, Justice, State, the federal judiciary and related agencies.

Reports: H Rept 102-106; S Rept 102-106; Conference report filed in the House, H Rept 102-233.

KEY ACTION

June 13 — HR 2608 passed the **House** by a vote of 338-80.

July 31 — HR 2608 passed the **Senate** by a vote of 86-13.

Oct. 3 — **House** approved conference report by voice vote; **Senate** approved it also by voice vote.

Oct. 28 — President Bush signed HR 2608 — PL 102-140.

HOUSE COMMITTEE ACTION

When the House Commerce, Justice, State and the Judiciary Appropriations Subcommittee took up the fiscal 1992 spending bill for programs under its jurisdiction, members voted May 30 to pull the plug on TV Marti, a U.S. government-sponsored network that beamed television programs to Cuba.

The roughly $14 million planned for the network — which had started to transmit programs in March 1990 — was stripped from the subcommittee's $21.8 billion spending bill.

Spending limits imposed by the 1990 White House-Capitol Hill budget agreement dominated the panel's work. Chairman Neal Smith, D-Iowa, said the budget squeeze had forced members to hold spending for most programs to a slight increase over fiscal 1991 spending but not enough to cover inflation.

In fiscal 1991, Justice Department funding was $8.5 billion. The State and Commerce departments received $3.3 billion and $2.7 billion, respectively.

For the first time in four years, the panel funded all programs under its jurisdiction. In the past, Smith had refused to fund agencies and programs that were not authorized. He relented, he said, because a conference with the Senate was difficult without a full appropriation and because of a fear that other subcommittees might sop up unappropriated money.

Members included in the bill an administration plan to impose new user fees on radio license holders. The subcommittee projected that $67 million in revenue would be generated from the fees.

The sponsor of the amendment to drop TV Marti funding, Bill Alexander, D-Ark., called the program "a total waste of money." He wanted a subcommittee vote rather than having to offer his amendment on the floor, where support for TV Marti had been overwhelming. Indeed, when he sponsored a floor amendment to the fiscal 1991 bill that would have cut TV Marti to $8 million, it lost by a ratio of nearly 3 to 1. *(1990 Almanac, p. 884)*

During the subcommittee markup, Smith tried to persuade Alexander to wait again for floor action. But Bob Carr, D-Mich., said Alexander did so in 1990 with the understanding that he would get a subcommittee vote in the future. Over Smith's objections, a roll call vote was called, and the amendment was approved 6-5.

But when the full Appropriations Committee met June 11, members restored the funds for TV Marti.

Also during full committee action, Robert L. Livingston, R-La., had pressed amendments to reduce funds for publicly sponsored lawyers who helped death row inmates file petitions in federal courts challenging their cases. The habeas corpus petition process began after an inmate exhausted state appeals of his conviction and sentence.

"The fact is the death penalty is becoming meaningless," Livingston said, complaining about the successive habeas corpus petitions inmates often filed to delay execution. But both of his amendments failed.

HOUSE FLOOR ACTION

The House on June 13 approved nearly $21 billion in spending for the Departments of Commerce, Justice and State and the federal judiciary, after striking funds for the National Endowment for Democracy and easily defeating an amendment that would have made an 8 percent across-the-board cut.

The vote on passage of HR 2608 was 338-80. *(Vote 154, p. 38-H)*

By removing the funds for the National Endowment for Democracy from the bill, on a procedural maneuver, supporters were able to avert a bruising floor debate that could have put members on the line to cut the agency's funding.

The endowment funneled money to foreign political parties, labor unions and other institutions overseas to foster democratic reforms. But since the endowment's in-

Commerce, Justice, State

(In thousands of dollars)

	Fiscal 1991 Appropriation	President's Request	House Bill	Senate Bill	Final Bill
Department of Justice					
Office of Justice programs	$ 686,254	$ 606,479	$ 691,905	$ 696,111	$ 695,611
Legal activities	2,311,934	2,622,110	2,470,061	2,497,100	2,467,156
Organized-crime drug enforcement	328,000	401,974	363,374	380,344	363,374
Federal Bureau of Investigation	1,692,595	2,021,217	1,866,832	1,972,807	1,926,092
Drug Enforcement Administration	694,340	747,957	706,286	740,667	716,653
Immigration and Naturalization Service	897,653	1,008,026	950,041	953,817	941,241
Federal prison system	1,742,208	2,159,649	2,062,610	2,074,946	2,061,231
Other	136,159	177,426	147,673	154,647	152,275
Subtotal	**$ 8,489,143**	**$ 9,744,838**	**$ 9,258,782**	**$ 9,470,439**	**$ 9,323,633**
Related Agencies					
EEOC	201,930	210,271	209,875	210,271	210,271
Federal Communications Commission	116,794	67,929	67,929	126,309	126,309
Federal Trade Commission	56,095	72,296	68,892	70,000	69,200
Securities and Exchange Commission	159,085	225,792	157,485	157,485	157,485
Other	35,969	43,754	37,823	39,179	38,309
Subtotal	**$ 569,873**	**$ 620,042**	**$ 542,004**	**$ 603,244**	**$ 601,574**
The Judiciary					
Supreme Court	22,536	25,093	24,588	25,093	24,588
Courts of Appeals, District Courts and Other Judicial Services	1,927,503	2,407,259	2,287,261	2,199,350	2,218,769
Administrative Office of the U.S. Courts	39,850	51,600	44,681	44,743	44,681
Other	47,492	64,989	54,367	58,675	53,502
Subtotal	**$ 2,037,381**	**$ 2,548,941**	**$ 2,410,897**	**$ 2,327,861**	**$ 2,341,540**
Department of Commerce					
NIST	215,328	248,040	237,655	252,663	246,713
NOAA	1,400,376	1,541,191	1,424,085	1,799,939	1,673,915
Bureau of the Census	382,950	307,495	295,366	272,960	290,290
International Trade Administration	187,120	196,269	194,875	203,814	207,160
Patent and Trademark Office	91,000	94,300	91,887	88,441	88,441
Economic Development Administration	177,018	20,000	28,218	214,147	256,882
Other	228,224	219,989	221,958	250,282	231,355
Subtotal	**$ 2,682,016**	**$ 2,627,284**	**$ 2,494,044**	**$ 3,082,246**	**$ 2,994,756**
Related Agencies					
Maritime Administration	314,000	298,000	295,920	308,961	307,161
Legal Services Corporation	328,186	355,000	0	350,000	350,000
Small Business Administration	469,578	568,687	820,119	811,445	837,325
Other	40,338	26,507	27,867	26,904	27,303
Subtotal	**$ 1,152,102**	**$ 1,248,194**	**$ 1,143,906**	**$ 1,497,310**	**$ 1,521,789**
Department of State					
Administration of Foreign Affairs	2,298,957	2,793,307	2,745,791	2,742,235	2,733,324
International Organizations, Conferences	909,905	1,327,333	981,130	955,113	955,113
Other	61,725	63,473	64,358	66,217	65,711
Subtotal	**$ 3,270,587**	**$ 4,184,113**	**$ 3,791,279**	**$ 3,763,565**	**$ 3,754,148**
Related Agencies					
Arms Control and Disarmament Agency	37,040	47,446	43,527	42,423	44,527
Board for International Broadcasting	205,750	217,960	212,491	212,491	212,491
United States Information Agency	1,010,637	1,059,012	1,033,508	1,080,675	1,087,094
Other	41,749	44,234	44,384	43,234	43,884
Subtotal	**$ 1,295,176**	**$ 1,368,652**	**$ 1,333,910**	**$ 1,378,823**	**$ 1,387,996**
GRAND TOTAL	**$ 19,496,278**	**$ 22,342,064**	**$ 20,974,822**	**$ 22,123,488**	**$ 21,925,436**

SOURCE: House Appropriations Committee

ception under the Reagan administration in 1983, some members had viewed it with suspicion, worried that GOP administrations would use it to support rightist groups. *(1989 Almanac, pp. 528, 569)*

The 1991 fight occurred after Majority Whip William H. Gray III, D-Pa., asserted that the endowment had not distributed $10 million in aid to political groups helping victims of apartheid in South Africa, as Congress had directed in spring 1990. Gray was going to move to cut the endowment's proposed $26 million funding by $10 million. The House's decision to skirt a full debate on the issue meant that the dispute would be played out on a pending State Department authorization bill. *(State Department authorization, p. 493)*

On a number of other potentially controversial issues in the spending bill, members elected to sidestep or postpone debate.

After little discussion, the $335 million in funds for the Legal Services Corporation (LSC) and $246 million for the Economic Development Administration (EDA) were dropped.

The LSC had been the subject of perennial battles over what kinds of cases could be taken by the attorneys it funded. And the Bush administration had been trying to phase out the EDA.

Striking funds for those two programs, on procedural grounds that neither was authorized under separate legislation, spared members from having to thrash out their merits. It was expected that funds for both programs would be restored.

Two special projects remained in the bill, after members defeated, 151-267, a move by Dan Burton, R-Ind., to kill what he called pork barrel spending. *(Vote 153, p. 38-H)*

The bill appropriated $542,000 for a Fish Farming Experimental Laboratory in Stuttgart, Ark., and $394,000 for a semitropical research facility in Key Largo, Fla.

Alexander had sponsored the projects. He was a business partner of the managers of the Key Largo project, but he said he had no financial interest or involvement in the research facility.

The much-debated issue of whether to modify or tear down the bugged U.S. Embassy in Moscow was left in the administration's hands. The bill provided for the embassy the $130 million the administration requested for fiscal 1992. It required the State Department to return to Congress with a plan for the building before any of the funds could be spent.

There was no move during floor debate to challenge the funds for TV Marti, restored in full committee, because the network was popular with many House members, particularly Floridians.

Dick Armey, R-Texas, offered the amendment to strip 8 percent of all of the discretionary funds from the bill. "If we're ever going to get to a balanced budget, we're going to have to accept smaller increases," he told colleagues. But subcommittee Chairman Smith said programs already were pared back to meet the budget resolution. The Armey motion failed 122-295. *(Vote 152, p. 38-H)*

Law and Order

The largest single share of the funds in HR 2608 was for the Justice Department: $9.3 billion. The appropriation was about $490 million short of the administration's request, but the committee report said Justice spending, which would grow by 9.8 percent over fiscal 1991, already was the highest funding priority in the bill.

The top item within the department was money for the opening of five new prisons and several prison expansions. The federal prison system received $2.063 billion under the bill, compared with its fiscal 1991 appropriation of $1.742 billion.

But increases in the FBI and Drug Enforcement Administration (DEA) were modest. FBI spending went up from $1.7 billion to $1.9 billion, gaining only half of the requested Bush administration increase for the bureau. DEA funding increased from $694 million to $706 million.

HR 2608 set aside $3.8 billion for the State Department and $2.5 billion for the Commerce Department, including $1.4 billion for the National Oceanic and Atmospheric Administration.

Judiciary accounts, including money for all federal courts, received $2.4 billion.

The bill included $185 million for federal public defender programs, about $52 million more than amounts enacted in 1991.

Endowment for Democracy

Much of the floor debate focused on the National Endowment for Democracy, even after members struck the agency's funds from the bill on a procedural motion.

Since the mid-1980s, Congress had complained intermittently about the kinds of political projects the endowment undertook and how accountable it was for spending decisions. Although general concerns about the endowment's agenda were raised by members of both parties during floor action, debate mostly centered on the endowment's not carrying out a $10 million aid program for political groups that represented victims of apartheid in South Africa. The money had been approved as part of a 1990 supplemental appropriations bill.

Gray said the money was for vehicles and office supplies so that black South African parties could "sit at the table with the de Klerk government. . . . Now, almost 14 months later, [the funding] has not occurred."

However, although the money was directed to be spent by the endowment, it was appropriated through the State Department and the Agency for International Development. An endowment spokesman said the money had not been turned over.

Gray and Paul E. Kanjorski, D-Pa., who had tried before to cut the endowment's funds, had been ready to move that the quasi-public agency's $26 million proposed appropriation be cut by $10 million. Kanjorski said the agency lacked accountability.

Their motion was set aside after Howard L. Berman, D-Calif., moved to strip the agency funds from the bill because they were not authorized. He said he wanted to avoid a vote to cut the endowment's budget, although he acknowledged that Gray had "a legitimate beef."

SENATE COMMITTEE ACTION

The Senate Appropriations Committee on July 11 approved a $22.1 billion version of HR 2608 that included $130 million to tear down and replace the bug-riddled U.S. Embassy in Moscow.

The action did little, however, to resolve the longstanding dispute over what to do with the partially built embassy.

The Senate committee wanted the building razed. Ernest F. Hollings, D-S.C., chairman of the relevant subcommittee, said, "I don't think we should be asking our own people to work in a building filled with listening devices."

The Senate version of HR 2608 was $1.1 billion more than the House-passed bill. About half of the increase stemmed from the inclusion of funding for three programs dropped during House floor consideration: the Legal Services Corporation ($350 million), Economic Development Administration assistance programs ($227 million) and the National Endowment for Democracy ($30 million).

The committee spent most of its time debating a "Buy American" amendment by Barbara A. Mikulski, D-Md., to require the Department of Defense to buy only U.S.-built ships for the Ready Reserve Force of the Maritime Administration.

Ted Stevens, R-Alaska, said he did not want to preclude the government from purchasing three Danish ships leased to the United States for the Persian Gulf War. Mikulski said she would make an exception for those vessels, and her amendment was adopted by voice vote.

Almost half of the funding in the Senate bill went to the Justice Department — $9.5 billion, or a 12 percent boost over fiscal 1991 funding and about $200 million more than the House voted. About $2.1 billion was for prisons to incarcerate an estimated 9,140 more prisoners during fiscal 1992. The total federal prison population was to be 71,590.

The measure contained no funding for the big anti-crime package the Senate passed July 11. *(Crime bill, p. 262)*

The Department of Commerce received $3.1 billion, including $1.8 billion for the National Oceanic and Atmospheric Administration (NOAA) — almost $400 million more than in fiscal 1991.

Of the total, $344 million was to go to NOAA's environmental satellite, data and information service (up from $274 million) and $100 million was to be used to modernize its aging ship fleet.

State Department budget authority was $3.8 billion under the bill, a $500 million increase. It included $257 million to pay for Radio and TV Marti and Radio Free Europe/Radio Liberty, $11 million more than the House approved.

The federal courts received $2.3 billion, a 14 percent increase, from the fiscal 1991 appropriation of $2 billion.

SENATE FLOOR ACTION

The Senate on July 31 passed HR 2608, which included a hefty 12 percent increase in law enforcement funds, extra money for weather satellites and an order to the State Department to tear down the bugged U.S. Embassy in Moscow.

The fiscal 1992 spending bill was approved, 86-13, after senators rejected two amendments. One would have taken money from a legal aid program and given it to the FBI. Another would have increased the amount of money for border control to keep illegal aliens out of the country. *(Vote 165, p. 22-S)*

As had happened before with the Commerce-Justice-State spending bill, floor debate on July 30-31 became a forum for members' unrelated special interests.

Jesse Helms, R-N.C., successfully amended the bill so that patients who underwent "invasive" medical procedures would be required to undergo AIDS tests except "in emergency situations." It also stipulated that results of the tests be kept confidential and that violators be fined up to $10,000 or imprisoned up to one year.

Helms on July 18 had amended another spending bill to carry prison terms for health-care workers with AIDS who failed to notify their patients. *(Treasury/Postal Service appropriations, p. 591)*

Census Undercount

More directly related to the subject matter of the bill, the Senate adopted, by voice vote, a compromise for addressing an apparent undercount in the 1990 census. *(Census, p. 180)*

Subcommittee Chairman Hollings first proposed adjusting the 1990 census figures by an estimated 5.3 million people through a Census Bureau model. His amendment stated that the adjusted figures could not be used for redistricting, although they would have been used for distribution of federal funds to states based on population figures, causing some states to lose funds and others to gain.

"We shouldn't have to wait another 10 years to get an accurate census," Hollings declared.

Commerce Secretary Robert A. Mosbacher had said that the administration would not adjust the 1990 census to correct its undercount. Bob Kasten, R-Wis., who defended that decision, told Senate colleagues during floor debate that if the Hollings amendment were adopted, President Bush would veto the bill.

The discussion ended when Herb Kohl, D-Wis., said that the matter, affecting $50 billion in funds to states, needed more study and offered a compromise amendment. The Senate adopted the plan, directing the Governmental Affairs Subcommittee on Government Information and Regulation, which Kohl chaired, to study the problem and recommend changes by Feb. 1, 1992.

Bush Request Matched

The $22.1 billion Senate bill increased spending from fiscal 1991 limits by nearly $3 billion and came close in many areas to matching the administration's total $22.3 billion funding request.

For the large departments in the bill, the Senate set aside $9.5 billion for Justice; $3.8 billion for State; $3.1 billion for Commerce; and $2.3 billion for the judiciary.

Hollings said that after law enforcement, the appropriators' chief concern was modernizing NOAA. The agency was to get $1.8 billion, or $400 million more than fiscal 1991, including $410 million for weather satellites. That was $110 million more than the administration's request and $151 million above the House allowance for the satellites.

The bill set aside $130 million for the State Department to tear down and replace the bug-riddled U.S. Embassy in Moscow.

The House had passed its spending bill with the proviso that the administration choose whether the embassy be rebuilt or left as it was and report back to Congress on its decision.

FBI vs. LSC

The Office of Management and Budget had complained about areas in which the Senate bill did not meet the administration's targets, particularly for the FBI.

Bush had requested $2 billion for the FBI. The Senate bill set aside $1.973 billion, compared with the fiscal 1991 appropriation of $1.693 billion. The House gave the FBI $1.867 billion for fiscal 1992.

To accommodate the administration, Phil Gramm, R-

Continued on p. 542

Commerce, Justice, State Provisions

Congress set aside $22 billion for the Departments of Commerce, Justice and State and related agencies for fiscal 1992, about $2.4 billion more than in fiscal 1991. Throughout the past decade the Justice Department and the costs of fighting crime had commanded an increasingly larger share of the bill.

For fiscal 1992, Justice received $9.3 billion. The Commerce Department got $3 billion and the State Department, $3.8 billion. The federal judiciary, also funded in this bill, received $2.3 billion.

Among funding priorities were, again, law enforcement and improvements within the National Oceanic and Atmospheric Administration, particularly the agency's foundering weather satellite program.

JUSTICE DEPARTMENT

The Department of Justice, which was created in 1870 to handle all criminal prosecutions and civil lawsuits in which the United States had an interest, had one of the fastest growing budgets in the government. The department investigated and prosecuted federal violations, carried out immigration law and supervised the federal prison system. The department also interpreted laws under which federal departments acted.

Since President Bush's first year in office, Justice's budget had increased about 75 percent, and it had nearly quadrupled over the past decade. Justice got $9.3 billion for fiscal 1992, compared with $8.5 billion in fiscal 1991. Bush had requested $9.7 billion for 1992.

The increased funding reflected worries over crime and a perennial battle between Democrats and Republicans to claim the mantle of "toughest on crime." Most of the new money was for more investigators, prosecutors and prisons, spread throughout the country at the discretion of the Justice Department, with few exceptions.

Within each division of Justice, most of the money was spent on salaries and related personnel expenses. The number of employees directly funded through the appropriations process had grown at Justice from an estimated 54,600 in 1982 to 83,000 in 1991.

Federal Bureau of Investigation

The FBI, which pursued a broad range of wrongdoing from street-gang crime to international terrorism, received a $1.9 billion appropriation in fiscal 1992, up about 15 percent from fiscal 1991. FBI operations were run out of 56 field headquarters and about 400 local offices throughout the United States and Puerto Rico. The bureau's national priorities were organized crime, drugs, white-collar crime, counterterrorism and foreign counterintelligence. The FBI also coordinated with state and local law enforcement a national crime data bank, fingerprinting system and forensic laboratories, including new standards for DNA research.

Most of the bureau's budget went for salaries and operating expenses (cars, telecommunications, field office equipment) for some 22,000 employees.

Beyond sustaining the FBI's base operations from fiscal 1991, the conference agreement provided $76.7 million for a number of high-priority programs, including:

- **Automated fingerprint identification.** $48 million of the added money went toward developing an automated fingerprint identification system, with another $1.5 million for continuing the relocation and updating of the fingerprinting headquarters at the new FBI building in West Virginia. A 1990 supplemental appropriations bill directed the FBI to move its fingerprinting headquarters to West Virginia.

Officials intended to develop an electronic image system, by which local law enforcement agencies could take an electronic print of a suspect's finger and transmit it to federal headquarters for potential identification. The goal was a two-hour turnaround, compared with the 22 days it took in 1991, with fingerprints sent to the FBI by mail.

The funds went toward designing and developing a system and prototype. Because the money would be pumped into West Virginia, the home state of Senate Appropriations Chairman Robert C. Byrd, some House Republicans tried unsuccessfully during floor consideration of the conference report to strike the $48 million project, arguing that it was a flagrant example of pork-barrel politics. But Kentucky Republican Harold Rogers, who was ranking member on the Appropriations subcommittee that handled Justice projects, said the country "desperately needs" the project.

In addition to the system's relocation and improvement, appropriators provided $12.5 million for more employees to reduce the backlog of fingerprint cards and arrest dispositions sent to the bureau from throughout the country for checks on criminal suspects.

- **Communications.** The bill included $4 million for telephones, computers and other technical support in the FBI field offices.
- **Savings and loan investigations.** $3.5 million was designated for more agents to step up investigations of wrongdoing in savings and loans and the banking industry.

Prisons

The increased effort to put criminals behind bars, combined with Congress' predilection toward mandatory minimum prison sentences, had put tremendous pressure on the federal prison system and the U.S. Marshals Service, which had to find housing for prisoners awaiting trial and sentencing in often overcrowded state and local jails. In the past year, the federal prison population grew by about 10 percent; prisons along the Southwest border and in Florida were among the most crowded, at an estimated 130 percent of capacity. The cost of new buildings was just the first expense, to be followed in future years by the cost of upkeep and care for the additional prisoners. The total federal inmate population for 1992 was projected at 71,590, an increase of 9,140 over fiscal 1991.

The Bureau of Prisons received $2 billion, including $452 million for construction and repair of facilities, up from a total prison budget authority of $1.7 billion in 1991. Most of the bureau's money was spent on salaries and related expenses, of which an estimated $40 million was expected to be spent to support the projected increase in the inmate population. The Justice Department figured that it cost roughly $20,000 per year to confine an inmate.

- **Opening new prisons.** The following prisons were scheduled to open in fiscal 1992: the Seymour Johnson expansion in North Carolina, Guynabo prison in Puerto Rico, Oakdale II in Louisiana, Estill prison in South Carolina and the Florence complex in Colorado. The cost of these prisons was about $100 million and was reflected within the salaries and expenses line of the bureau's budget.

• **Prison expansion.** The bureau sought and received all the money it requested — $452 million — for additions at existing facilities and ongoing construction. Still under construction were a low-security correctional complex in Allenwood, Pa., and medium-security institutions in Minersville, Pa.; Manchester, Ky.; and Cumberland, Md. Appropriators designated within the total construction funds $55 million to begin a new federal prison in Houston and $82 million for a Philadelphia facility. Both were intended to be temporary holding centers for federal prisoners on trial in those urban areas. Modernization and repair of existing prisons was expected to cost $126 million in 1992. The 1992 expansion was intended to yield about 3,600 new prison beds, but it was part of a long-term construction plan for a total of 34,400 new beds over several years.

Immigration and Naturalization (INS)

The INS enforced immigration laws, oversaw the Border Patrol and investigated, apprehended and deported foreigners who were in the United States illegally. In recent years, the INS had added new user fees to offset its appropriations, among them for airport inspections, adjudication of alien status, naturalizations and refugee programs. The total amount expected in fees in fiscal 1992 was $392 million. Still, the agency got its largest appropriation ever — $941 million, compared with fiscal 1991's $898 million — mostly to boost efforts to detect and deport illegal aliens.

The Border Patrol monitored the U.S. perimeter, on foot, on horseback and by car, helicopter and airplane. Close to 90 percent of its work was on the Southwest border. The division was expected to receive $312.5 million for fiscal 1992, including $3 million for new agents.

The Border Patrol's detention and deportation division handled illegal aliens, from the quick-turnaround cases of some 1 million Mexicans who crossed the border each year and were put on a bus home after a few hours of processing, to criminal aliens who had come through court trials and were awaiting arrangements with home countries. The division received $161 million.

Land-border inspections, which took place at designated ports of entry and made up the third-largest INS section, would cost $88 million under the new budget.

The INS said that inspection workloads at ports of entry along southern and northern borders had far outpaced staffing. In 1990, fewer than 1,500 inspectors were responsible for inspecting the more than 400 million persons who entered the country through land crossings. About 800,000 inadmissible aliens were intercepted. The conference agreement provided the full requested increase of $6 million for 135 additional land-border inspectors.

Drug Enforcement Administration (DEA)

The country's "war on drugs" remained a priority for Congress and the Department of Justice. Congress gave the DEA, the lead agency in the federal government's effort to stop illegal drug trafficking, $717 million of the $748 million the Bush administration requested. The fiscal 1991 appropriation was $694 million.

DEA's largest section was the domestic enforcement program, which included the operation of DEA's 19 field divisions and a staff of more than 2,000. Using confidential informants, undercover operations and electronic surveillance, DEA agents identified and penetrated drug trafficking organizations that operated nationally and internationally. The section received $228 million.

• **Special enforcement operations.** Programs aimed at specific problems or organizations, such as the Colombian Medellin cartel, received $74.2 million.

DEA officials told Congress that within the past year, the United States and Colombia competed for the distinction of being the world's No. 2 marijuana producer behind Mexico. Although most of the marijuana consumed in this country came from Mexico, a report showed that 35 percent of the 1989 domestic marijuana consumption was home-grown, compared with 20 percent the previous year. Because of the drug's increasingly higher quality, the DEA said, domestic users were beginning to prefer U.S. marijuana. As a result, appropriators designated $13 million for marijuana plant eradication in the United States.

The foreign cooperative investigations unit got $58 million toward its coordination of the reduction of the importation of illegal drugs. The unit worked out of 70 offices in 48 countries. It maintained a network of informants and developed intelligence intended to lead to cooperative arrests and a diminishing drug supply.

The DEA's efforts to stop the diversion of legally produced chemicals and drugs into illegal trafficking got $40 million; a fund for state and local task forces received $51 million.

Additional anti-drug money was included throughout other Justice divisions for the apprehension and prosecution of individuals involved in secondary drug activities such as money laundering, tax evasion and firearms possession. Justice Department officials estimated that, overall, $4.4 billion had been spent on anti-drug efforts in fiscal 1992.

Office of Justice Programs

A number of separate programs provided resources for state and local police, including those generating research and demonstration programs, building criminal justice statistics and fostering juvenile justice and missing children programs. The total appropriation for these was $696 million. The largest share, $475 million, went to a five-year-old program of anti-drug-abuse grants. The grants were intended for state and local governments to work in partnership with a national drug control approach. Twenty-five percent of the funds were required to be matched by local police agencies.

• **National Crime Information Center.** Appropriators designated $22 million for second-year funding for the modernization of the National Crime Information Center. This was an FBI-managed system that was designed to provide state and local police with instantaneous information on wanted persons, stolen property and criminal history records. The system was the only one by which local police could quickly identify individuals who had committed a crime in one state and subsequently moved to another state.

• **Alternatives to prison.** The conference agreement provided $13 million for grants for correctional options that provided alternatives to traditional modes of incarceration. This new grant program, authorized in the 1990 crime bill, allowed for the development and testing of projects such as house arrest and boot camps.

• **Juvenile justice.** Juvenile justice and delinquency prevention programs got $76 million, with most of it distributed among states based on their population under the age of 18. The money was used to prevent delinquency, and once a youth got into trouble, to provide community-based alternatives to prison.

• **Mariel Cubans.** $5 million was set aside for states' imprisonment of Mariel Cubans convicted of a felony after having been paroled into the United States by the attorney general.

U.S. Attorneys

Spread out through 94 judicial districts, U.S. attorneys were the principal litigators for the federal government. Within each office, attorneys pursued criminal and civil litigation, debt collection, organized-crime eradication and drug enforcement. Their funds had been growing steadily over the previous five years and went up to $721 million for fiscal 1992. The administration had sought more attorneys to handle the increased prosecutions for drug and firearms offenses. All of the money in this section was earmarked for salaries and office expenses.

The Justice Department told appropriators it intended to use the funds to add about 300 positions (roughly half would be attorneys) to bring the department to an estimated 8,500 positions. Most of the new positions would be devoted to criminal litigation.

In their conference report, appropriators urged the attorney general to put more assistant U.S. attorneys into investigating and prosecuting defense procurement fraud, drug abuse, savings and loan fraud and criminal aliens. Conferees also said that telemarketing fraud investigations should get higher priority and ordered the department to report to Appropriations subcommittees by Feb. 1, 1992, on steps toward fighting telemarketing fraud.

• **Legal education.** Congress required that the site of a legal education program to train U.S. attorneys and state and local prosecutors be moved from Washington, D.C., to the campus of the University of South Carolina Law Center, in Columbia.

A Senate committee report acknowledged that relocating the department's legal education program from Washington would be expensive but said, "The committee believes that over the long term the program will benefit from reduced space costs which will allow for larger facilities and reduced per diem costs in South Carolina." This provision was added in the Senate at the urging of the chairman of the Commerce, Justice, State Subcommittee, South Carolina Democrat Ernest F. Hollings, and was estimated to cost an initial $10 million.

Related Agencies

• **Equal Employment Opportunity Commission (EEOC).** The EEOC was created by the 1964 Civil Rights Act to end job discrimination. It enforced the act's prohibition against discrimination on the basis of race, color, religion, sex or national origin by employers of 15 or more workers. The commission most often resolved bias complaints through conciliation or settlement, but in selected cases it went to court to force compliance.

The EEOC's latest mandate came in July 1990 when the Americans with Disabilities Act (PL 101-336) became law. The legislation allowed workers who believed they were victims of discrimination because of physical or mental disabilities to seek redress through the EEOC. The ADA requirements began to take effect on July 26, 1992.

Overall, the EEOC operated 50 enforcement field offices to receive and handle complaints; these accounted for 75 percent of its costs. The EEOC's new budget was $210 million, which was exactly what the administration requested. Most of that increase went toward hiring new workers for the ADA.

• **Securities and Exchange Commission (SEC).** Established by the Securities Exchange Act of 1934, the SEC regulated the sale of securities by requiring traders to disclose financial and other information. It enforced numerous federal laws to prevent fraud and malpractice in the securities markets. Congress provided $158 million for fiscal 1992, compared with $226 million requested by Bush.

The conferees ordered fees for issuers of securities to be raised from one-fiftieth of 1 percent to one-thirty-second of 1 percent of the total dollar amount of the shares registered. Conferees said that the increased fees would generate $68 million for the SEC and when added to the $158 million appropriation would meet the Bush budget goal of $226 million.

• **Federal Communications Commission (FCC).** The FCC oversaw a range of communications technologies and licensed about 3 million firms and individuals in a host of areas. It regulated the rates and terms of service for interstate telephone services; licensed and established rules for television and radio stations; and regulated private radio users, including taxi operators and police departments. Appropriators rejected an administration request to order an increase in fees for FCC licensees and other communications users. The appropriation for the FCC was $126 million, almost twice the $67 million Bush had sought. The administration had recommended the reduced amount, anticipating that the difference would be made up in user-fee collections.

The conference agreement also included language from prior appropriations bills that forbade the FCC from repealing or re-examining policies that gave preference on ownership of broadcasting licenses to minorities and women. The Supreme Court in 1990 ruled that Congress could order preferential treatment of blacks and other minorities to increase their ownership of broadcast licenses. With the court becoming more conservative, there was a chance that such a ruling could be overturned in another case.

• **Federal Trade Commission (FTC).** Charged with promoting competitiveness at home and abroad, the commission monitored trade practices and investigated complaints of monopoly, unfair restraint or deceptive practices. The commission's budget was divided roughly between its mission of maintaining competitiveness (through the regulation of mergers and other potential antitrust activities) and consumer protection. The latter division educated consumers on their rights and businesses on their responsibilities under federal law. Congress appropriated $69.2 million but noted that the anticipated collection of $13.5 million in fees from pre-merger notification filings raised the FTC budget to $82.7 million. Bush had requested $72 million.

THE JUDICIARY

Unlike other budget requests that came to Capitol Hill, the Judiciary request went directly to Congress without first being reviewed by the Office of Management and Budget. The judiciary was in the unique position of constituting the third branch of government but depending on the budgeting process of the other two branches to run its operations. Personnel was the major expense in the federal judiciary, where an estimated 25,000 people worked. The total budget was $2.3 billion for fiscal 1992.

• **Supreme Court.** The highest court in the country, the Supreme Court interpreted the Constitution, federal legislation and treaties. It received $24.6 million, up from $23 million in fiscal 1991. The chief justice had a salary of $160,600; associate justices received $153,600.

• **Courts of Appeals, district courts and other judicial services.** This encompassed all federal trial courts, the 12 circuit courts of appeals and their personnel. Their workload had increased because of rising prosecutions for drug-related crimes and the crackdown on financial fraud. The appropriation was increased to $2.2 billion, including $94.9 million for automation of court files.

Included within the bill were new money for magistrate and bankruptcy judges, $11 million; funds for increased review of savings and loan cases, $4 million; new court clerk personnel, $3.5 million; and probation pretrial personnel, $3.2 million.

• **Court of Appeals for the Federal Circuit.** This court, which reviewed decisions from the Merit Systems Protection Board, Patent and Trademark Office, Court of International Trade and Claims Court, received $10.8 million, up from $9.8 million.

• **U.S. Court of International Trade.** The court, which handled disputes on imports and exports, received $9.4 million.

• **Administrative Office of the U.S. Courts.** This office was the bureaucratic arm of all courts except the Supreme Court. It examined the dockets of the courts, prepared statistical data and reports on the business of the courts. The office, made up of about 800 workers, coordinated support staff, such as clerks and librarians, for the judges and assisted with the automation of judicial records. It found accommodations for the courts and coordinated the building of any new chambers or courthouses. It received $44.7 million.

• **Federal Judicial Center.** The appropriation for this office was $17.8 million. It conducted research on the operations of the federal court system and provided continuing education programs for judges and court personnel.

• **United States Sentencing Commission**. It got $9 million, up from $8.4 million, to develop and monitor guidelines for judges to use in sentencing criminal defendants.

COMMERCE DEPARTMENT

Commerce Department funding had barely held steady during the past decade as the Justice Department had eaten up more and more of the discretionary funds available under this appropriations bill. The Commerce Department, which was established in 1913, was intended to promote economic growth, international trade and technological development. Its contemporary goals included raising the quality of U.S. products and services, directing national export initiatives and making it easier to bring new technologies to market.

The department, made up of a number of multimillion-dollar agencies, received $3 billion for fiscal 1992, compared with $2.7 billion for 1991 and $2.4 billion in fiscal 1981. Bush had requested $2.6 billion. The difference between Bush and Congress rested largely in the administration's proposed gutting of the Economic Development Assistance grants, a perennial idea, and recommended cuts in various environmental, weather and fisheries programs.

National Oceanic and Atmospheric Administration

More than half of the Department of Commerce budget went to NOAA. The total was $1.7 billion for fiscal 1992. This far-ranging agency was responsible for managing current and long-term data on the status of the Earth. Its scientists and researchers followed climate and global changes and managed a worldwide series of experiments and data-gathering programs.

• **Satellite programs.** NOAA observed the environment, using polar orbiting and geostationary satellites (GOES). The former orbited over the poles, producing routine data for weather forecasters. The GOES revolved at a speed synchronized to the Earth's rotation so that they always appeared above the same place on the Earth.

NOAA was in the middle of a $1 billion weather satellite modernization, which had been complicated by the increasing age of existing satellites, for which parts were becoming difficult to obtain. Satellite outages made the prediction of violent weather difficult, and for appropriators, the situation had raised problems about the timing of funding and whether the money was being well spent.

For fiscal 1992 the polar system received $130 million, compared with fiscal 1991's $51 million, because new satellite operations, which were purchased in increments, were going on-line. The GOES observational satellite, which was mostly intended to monitor severe storms, received $118 million. This satellite system had been a problem for appropriators because, they said, a combination of lax government management and poor contractor performance had left the program behind schedule and with cost overruns.

Because the system was foundering, appropriators set aside an additional $110 million in an emergency fund for a "gap filler geostationary satellite," which would monitor severe storms in the interim.

The other satellite funds went to satellite observation services ($48 million) and to LANDSAT operations ($7.6 million). The LANDSAT took pictures of the Earth and tracked vegetation and minerals. Funding for storing all the data collected from satellites was $32.8 million, bringing the total cost of all the satellite systems to $449 million, compared with $275 million in fiscal 1991.

• **National Weather Service.** The weather service maintained stations across the country. Its total appropriation for fiscal 1992 was $445 million (compared with $478 million in fiscal 1991), the bulk of which went to local forecasters and warning systems.

Conferees set aside $132 million for systems acquisitions, the most expensive being equipment for the Next Generation Weather Radar system (NEXRAD). This was intended to replace obsolete weather radars and enhance severe weather and flood warnings. The weather service said nationwide implementation of this advanced doppler radar warning system could increase tornado-warning lead time from the existing average of one to two minutes to 20 to 30 minutes and reduce false warning rates. The NEXRAD project, which in fiscal 1991 got $129 million, received $83.4 million in fiscal 1992.

Conferees also agreed to set aside $9 million for a supercomputer for the National Meteorological Center in Suitland, Md.

• **NOAA fleet.** Creating a new account at the Senate's urging, the bill included $33 million to replace NOAA's aging fleet of ships. Senate appropriators, who had pushed for $100 million, said that without funding, the NOAA fleet would be unseaworthy and mothballed by the year

2000. NOAA vessels conducted operations that supported programs in nautical charting, fisheries research, resource assessment and marine environment. The fleet consisted of 23 vessels, several of which were inactive and many others of which were obsolete and deteriorating. The ships' average age was 28 years. It was expected that the fleet would take up to 10 to 15 years to replace, with appropriations needed every year for the refurbishing.

• **Other NOAA funds.** The National Ocean Service, which managed ocean and coastal resources and was responsible for improving the quality and timeliness of ocean observation data, received $165.5 million ($14 million more than the previous year).

The National Marine Fisheries Service, responsible for making sure fishery stocks continued as a renewable resource and protecting endangered marine species, got $227 million. Oceanic and Atmospheric Research, which conducted research on a range of global change issues at the heart of NOAA's mission, got $213 million.

Census Bureau

The bureau collected and published current and periodic statistics, including economic, social and demographic data on the U.S. population. Its major task was the decennial census. Its budget was $290 million, down from $383 million in fiscal 1991 because most of the work on the 1990 census was completed. Of its appropriation, $125.3 million went to salaries and expenses. Included within that amount was $400,000 earmarked by appropriators for three census reports on cotton, soybeans and sunflower oil seeds.

• **1990 census.** The bill included money for tabulating and distributing information from the 1990 census and other periodic censuses, a total of $165 million. The data provided such information as commuting patterns, income, education and housing patterns. A key issue in dispute was how much money the bureau needed to produce its recently collected data. The Senate had proposed an appropriation of some $20 million less than the House, but after bureau officials complained that certain data would not be processed, all but $10 million of the administration's request was funded. The conference report said the $10 million reduction could be made up with savings and recoveries from prior years.

• **2000 census.** The conference bill included $8.4 million to pay for early planning and testing for the 2000 decennial census. In addition, $1.4 million was set aside for the Department of Commerce to enter into a contract with the National Academy of Sciences to make a comprehensive study of the decennial census. Appropriators had complained that the existing form was too long and complicated, discouraging people from filling it out.

National Institute of Standards and Technology (NIST)

The technology division of the Commerce Department ran the National Institute of Standards and Technology, one of the nation's oldest scientific laboratories, as well as an array of programs aimed at helping industry make use of sophisticated technologies.

The division, whose fiscal 1992 appropriation was $247 million, was gaining a higher profile in Congress, as members became more concerned about the United States losing ground to foreign companies in the world marketplace and especially in fields involving sophisticated technologies. Its mission was expanded in 1988 by the Omnibus Trade and Competitiveness Act (PL 100-418), which specifically charged NIST with assisting industry in the development of cutting-edge technology. In addition to its in-house work, it did research on contract for other government agencies.

NIST research, aimed at helping industry advance in fields such as electronics, chemistry, physics, materials science, optical fibers, supercomputers and microwave communications, was disseminated through the publication of scientific papers and informal programs that brought many scientists from industry to work at NIST labs.

Of NIST's budget, $183 million funded scientific and technical research by its 2,500 staff scientists. In addition, NIST often had as many as 1,000 guest scientists working at its Gaithersburg, Md., and Boulder, Colo., laboratories. More than 200 of those were from industry. The agency also received $100 million in transfers from other agencies for doing research.

• **Advanced Technology Program.** The program provided seed money to companies that wanted to research generic technologies needed to develop commercially viable products. The program was authorized in 1988 to promote the competitiveness of U.S. industry.

The program had proved popular with industry, which had lobbied for it to be funded at its proposed authorization level of $100 million. In the first year the program was funded, there were 249 applications for grants, but the agency had money for just 11. The grants awarded included: research into technology that corrected production flaws caused by the heating and cooling of machine tools, and research into a new form of computer memory storage that had the potential to replace disk drives and magnetic tapes.

Fiscal 1992 was the third year of funding for the program, and it received $47.4 million, a 32 percent increase over fiscal 1991.

• **Manufacturing Technology Centers.** Also known as the "Hollings Centers," for Senate Commerce Committee Chairman Ernest F. Hollings, D-S.C., who encouraged their development, the centers helped small and midsize companies learn to use advanced technologies to become more competitive. The centers, which received $15.1 million in fiscal 1992, were in Columbia, S.C.; Troy, N.Y.; Cleveland; Ann Arbor, Mich.; and Topeka, Kan. The 31 percent increase in funding allowed the establishment of three new centers.

Other Department Agencies

• **Economic Development Administration.** This agency provided public works and technical assistance grants to state and local governments, public institutions, nonprofit organizations and Indian reservations. Its goal was to stimulate growth and create jobs. It received $257 million, up from $177 million in fiscal 1991. The administration had sought to phase out this program.

• **International Trade Administration.** The agency developed trade policy and put in place programs to promote world trade and strengthen U.S. international trade and investments. It received $207 million. Its appropriation included $15.2 million for new research initiatives for the U.S. textile and apparel industries.

• **Patent and Trademark Office.** The office awarded patent protection to qualified inventions and disseminated technological information disclosed in patents. It received $88 million.

• **Other Commerce programs.** Appropriators also provided for the following programs: National Telecommunications and Information Administration, $42.5 million; Economic and Statistical Analysis, $40.4 million; Export Administration, $39.5 million; and Minority Business Development Agency, $40.5 million.

Related Agencies

• **Small Business Administration (SBA).** The SBA provided loans and management advice to small businesses, including programs to help victims of floods and other catastrophes rebuild. It provided financial aid to municipalities for development projects and generated economic and statistical data on small businesses. The SBA received $837 million for fiscal 1992, up from $470 million in fiscal 1991. The increase was due largely to conferees' raising the funds available for business loans to help make sure capital continued to be available to small concerns.

• **Legal Services Corporation.** This was a quasi-governmental corporation that awarded grants to local agencies providing legal services to the poor. It received $350 million.

During his two-term presidency, Ronald Reagan tried to abolish this legal aid program, concerned that the grantee-lawyers were too ideologically liberal.

Although controversy had quieted in the past two years, the Legal Services Corporation had been kept alive only through the appropriations process. The agency had not had a formal authorization for more than 10 years. Its fiscal 1991 appropriation was $328 million.

• **Maritime Administration.** Though this was a division of the Department of Transportation, it was funded in this appropriations bill. It conducted research on shipbuilding and operations, helped secure financing and tax-deferred funds for shipbuilding, and operated the U.S. Merchant Marine Academy in Kings Point, N.Y. It received $307 million.

• **U.S. Trade Representative.** $20.4 million was also provided for the Office of the U.S. Trade Representative.

STATE DEPARTMENT

The bill provided $3.75 billion in fiscal 1992 for the State Department to conduct the foreign affairs of the United States. That figure was $430 million less than the administration's request but $483.6 million more than the fiscal 1991 appropriation.

Most of the funding went toward the nuts and bolts: the salaries of State Department employees and the maintenance and construction of U.S. facilities around the world.

The bill also funded U.S. obligations to the United Nations and other international organizations. U.S. foreign aid was funded through the separate appropriations bill for foreign operations. While that bill was often the subject of intense policy debates, the State Department appropriation was usually handled in a more routine fashion. The one exception in recent years had been the controversy over whether to rebuild or replace the unfinished U.S. Embassy in Moscow.

Salaries and Expenses

More than half of the funding for the State Department's operations, $2 billion, went for salaries and expenses. And more than half of this category, slightly more than $1 billion, was for compensation and benefits for the department's more than 20,000 employees. Among the other expenses included in this category were $219.8 million for rent and $150 million for transportation.

• **Telecommunications.** The House-Senate conference dealt a serious setback to the State Department when it refused to provide any money for a planned $350 million new, state-of-the-art telecommunications network. The network had been intended for internal State Department communications between Washington and U.S. embassies and consulates.

The House, which had been more supportive of the plan than the Senate, included $30 million for the program in the fiscal 1992 bill. The Senate provided no funding for the program.

The conference committee, citing a variety of factors including "national budgetary constraints," provided $15 million, but only for the purpose of enhancing the existing system, and it embargoed that until State set up an office to study options.

• **Congressional Relations.** Both subcommittees had sharply criticized the State Department office with which they had the most frequent contact, the Office of Congressional Relations, but ultimately stopped short of punishing the office.

The department requested $3.7 million for this office in fiscal 1992 as part of its overall budget for salaries and expenses. But the House bill placed a ceiling of $500,000 for expenditures by the office — an effective reduction in its budget of more than 80 percent.

The House report complained that employees from the office were sent to committee meetings but never made substantive contributions. The report said this led the committee to conclude that "they were sent uninvited to such meetings to report upon and ensure that the substantive officials of the department provide only politically correct statements to the committee."

The Senate restored the funding but said the committee's relationship with the office "is serving neither the secretary's nor the committee's interest." The conference committee deleted the House-set ceiling of $500,000 for the office's operations.

U.S. Buildings Abroad

After salaries and expenses, the next single costliest category in the State Department's budget was for the acquisition and maintenance of buildings abroad.

The bill provided $545 million as the first installment on the State Department's ambitious six-year program for rehabilitating dilapidated U.S. facilities around the world and constructing new embassies and chanceries. It was nearly double the $227.7 million appropriated for this program in fiscal 1991.

• **Moscow embassy.** After six years of debate over what to do about the unfinished U.S. Embassy in Moscow, which was riddled with eavesdropping devices, Congress in essence left the matter up to the State Department. The bill provided $100 million for the construction of a new chancery facility, which was expected to eventually cost more than $220 million. But the question was not completely resolved: Congress and the administration still had to resolve the fate of the vacant facility. Construction was halted on that building when the electronic bugs were discovered in 1985.

• **Baltic States.** The conference committee, responding to the sweeping changes in the Soviet Union, agreed to appropriate $30 million for new embassies and facilities in the newly independent Baltic States and other sites in the Soviet Union and Eastern Europe.

• **New facilities.** Among the countries in which the department planned to build new facilities were Colombia, where the Bogota compound "continues to present an unacceptable security situation," according to a State Department document, and Guinea-Bissau, where the embassy building had faulty plumbing.

• **Rehabilitation of facilities.** The department also planned to rehabilitate several U.S. office buildings around the world, including the one in Tel Aviv, Israel, which "fronts the sea and receives intense salt and sea air abuse," according to the department.

Other State Department Programs

• **Protecting foreign missions.** The bill provided $10.5 million for the protection of foreign missions and officials in the United States. The total included $8.3 million to reimburse New York for costs it entailed in providing protection for foreign visitors to the United Nations and other international organizations.

• **Representation allowances.** The bill funded the department's $4.8 million request for what were termed "representation allowances." The funds reimbursed U.S. diplomats for entertainment expenses — including tuxedo rentals and the purchase of wine and flowers — incurred in carrying out their official duties.

International Organizations and Conferences

The bill provided $955.1 million for U.S. payments to international organizations, including $842.4 million in current and past dues and $107.2 million for the U.S. share of maintaining several U.N. peacekeeping forces.

• **United Nations.** The administration asked Congress to fully fund arrearages to the United Nations and other international organizations, most dating back to an era when either the executive branch or Congress would signal its displeasure by withholding annual contributions.

In fiscal 1991, the administration initiated a five-year program for making the back payments. Congress had been supportive of the plan, although lawmakers had balked at the administration's request that the entire appropriation be approved in advance.

More than half of the money appropriated by Congress for current obligations — $533.5 million — went toward the United Nations or its affiliated agencies, such as the World Health Organization. A decade earlier, such an appropriation might have been the subject of bitter partisan and ideological conflict. But the political climate had changed dramatically, with the U.N. Security Council transformed from a forum for superpower competition to an important mediator of international disputes.

Of the $370.9 million in arrearages that the United States owed to international organizations, $322.1 million was owed to the United Nations or affiliated organizations. Approximately one-fourth of the remaining arrearages, $92.7 million, would be paid off in fiscal 1992.

• **Other organizations.** The bill provided $42.3 million for NATO. For the Pan American Health Organization, which coordinated the efforts of nations in the Western Hemisphere to combat disease, the bill provided $42.4 million to meet current obligations and $2.6 million for arrearages.

• **International peacekeeping activities.** The State Department also requested funds for peacekeeping activities carried out by U.N. groups. The bill provided $68.9 million for the U.S. share of funding these operations during fiscal 1992. Additionally, the bill provided $38.4 million for arrearages owed to U.N. agencies for these operations, which included five U.N. peacekeeping groups: The U.N. Disengagement Observer Force on the Golan Heights; the U.N. Interim Force in Lebanon; the U.N. Observer Group in Central America; the U.N. Iran-Iraq Military Observer Group; and the U.N. Angola Verification Mission.

International Commissions and Foundations

The bill provided $40.2 million for the U.S. contribution to other international commissions, including $21.7 million for the International Boundary and Water Commission.

The commission managed water and boundary issues for the U.S.-Mexico border region. In recent years, the commission had been occupied with the increasingly serious environmental problems along the southern border.

The bill provided $25.5 million for a host of miscellaneous international activities, including $16 million for the Asia Foundation, a nonprofit organization that tried to promote democracy in Asia.

RELATED AGENCIES

United States Information Agency (USIA)

Founded in 1953 to tell "America's story to the world," according to a former director, the USIA operated the Voice of America, which broadcast worldwide in 43 languages and provided government-sponsored television programs for a number of countries.

The USIA also managed the government's educational and cultural exchange programs, including the Fulbright Scholarship Program. The National Endowment for Democracy, which attempted to promote democratic values around the world, also fell under the agency's jurisdiction.

With an appropriation of more that $1 billion and nearly 9,000 employees, it was by far the largest independent agency involved in foreign policy. But its mission and perhaps its funding level could be significantly altered as a result of the changes in the world.

The Office of Management and Budget cut the overall USIA request for fiscal 1992 by $159 million. Congress provided $1.09 billion, almost $30 million more than the administration's request, and more than $70 million more than the fiscal 1991 appropriation.

• **Salaries and expenses.** The bulk of USIA's funds — $691.7 million — went to this category.

• **Educational and cultural exchanges**. Few programs were more popular in Congress than USIA's education and cultural exchanges. The conference committee agreed on a figure of $194.2 million, an increase of more than $21 million over the administration's request.

Most of that funding went toward academic exchanges and international visitor programs. The agency indicated that it was shifting funds from programs in Western Europe to expand programs in Eastern Europe, the Soviet Union and Islamic countries.

The bill also included $24.5 million in funding for the East-West Center, a Honolulu, Hawaii-based institution that promoted better relations between the United States and Asia. Sen. Daniel K. Inouye, D-Hawaii, the second-ranking member of the Appropriations Committee, had been a consistent advocate for the center.

• **Broadcasting to Cuba.** The USIA tried to "provide hope to the people of Cuba" through its television and radio broadcasting to the island nation, according to former director Bruce S. Gelb. The controversial Radio Marti and TV Marti programs, first conceived during the Reagan administration, had won strong support from Florida lawmakers. The programs were popular with Cuban-Americans, a large number of whom lived in Florida. But they had been opposed by some in Congress as an unnecessary expenditure. Rep. Bill Alexander, D-Ark., had waged an intense, but unsuccessful, campaign against broadcasting to Cuba for the past few years.

Congress provided $36.9 million for broadcasting to Cuba in fiscal 1992, which included $11 million for Radio Marti and $14.6 million for TV Marti. TV Marti was set back in 1991 when the aerostat balloon that housed the television antenna broke away from its tether. The balloon landed in the Florida Everglades; it would cost nearly $1 million to repair.

- **National Endowment for Democracy.** The endowment was established in 1983 to promote democracy abroad. It had attempted, by funding programs in more than 70 countries, to foster political pluralism and develop political parties and electoral processes.

Endowment programs were ambitious and wide-ranging. During 1990, the endowment contributed to the establishment of a voters' organization in Bangladesh, aid to a group of exiled students from Myanmar, formerly Burma, and training for a human rights monitoring organization in Cambodia.

But the broad agenda and complicated funding arrangement had led to management difficulties. In March 1991, the General Accounting Office compiled a devastating report on the endowment, citing instances of funds "being misused, mismanaged, or not effectively accounted for." Congress provided $27.5 million in fiscal 1992.

Board for International Broadcasting

The failed coup in the Soviet Union was likely to set off a full-fledged debate over the future of the Board for International Broadcasting, which received $212.5 million for fiscal 1992. The board provided funding for Radio Liberty and Radio Free Europe, two institutions that came to symbolize U.S. propaganda efforts during the Cold War. Their mission was to "provide surrogate or proxy domestic broadcasting to the people of the Soviet Union and Eastern Europe," according to the board's presentation to Congress.

Before the coup, there were indications that the administration wanted to substantially reduce the operations of Radio Liberty and Radio Free Europe. The administration requested $218 million for the board in fiscal 1992, which represented a nominal increase over the fiscal 1991 appropriation but a cut in inflation-adjusted dollars.

As a result, the agency eliminated 30 positions in the broadcasting service for three Eastern European countries and shut down the fledgling Radio Free Afghanistan service.

A presidential commission had been studying the future role of government-supported broadcasting abroad, and there were predictions that it would call for a gradual phasing out of Radio Free Europe and Radio Liberty. Board officials had responded by trying to demonstrate that the agency's broadcasts are crucial for the Soviet Union's transition to democracy.

Arms Control and Disarmament Agency (ACDA)

ACDA advised the president and members of the Cabinet on arms control issues. It was assessing the impact of the breakup of the Soviet Union on pending and future agreements to reduce weapons. There was a widespread belief among military analysts prior to the coup in the Soviet Union that the era for major new arms pacts between the United States and the Soviet Union had passed. But the failed coup and Bush's proposals to reduce nuclear arms appeared to have improved prospects for deeper cuts in conventional and nuclear weapons.

The agency's budget was small, as was its staff. The bill provided $44.5 million for ACDA's operations in fiscal 1992, $2.9 million less than requested by the administration. But that represented an increase of nearly 20 percent over the fiscal 1991 appropriation. ACDA had slightly more than 200 employees, although it also used outside consultants. Like the State Department, approximately half of its budget went toward salaries.

International Trade Commission

The International Trade Commission was responsible for conducting investigations and research into trade-related issues. The work of the commission was used by the Office of the U.S. Trade Representative and the Department of Commerce in formulating trade policy. Its investigations focused on alleged unfair trade practices by other countries. Congress provided $42.4 million in fiscal 1992. ■

Continued from p. 534

Texas, proposed transferring $48.4 million from the Legal Services Corporation, which he had in the past accused of funding lawyers who carried out liberal agendas, to the FBI. He said the $48 million would make up the difference with the administration's request. *(1990 Almanac, p. 531)*

The administration had not targeted the LSC, which provided federal funds to state and local legal services for the needy, for cuts. Bush had requested the quasi-independent corporation be given $355,000; the Senate bill gave it $350,000.

Warren B. Rudman, R-N.H., a longtime legal services supporter, argued against the amendment, which Gramm said would provide more money for white-collar investigations.

"The FBI is hardly underfunded," said Rudman, who was the ranking Republican on the Appropriations Subcommittee with jurisdiction over the bill. "We increased FBI funding from last year's level . . . $280 million, or 16.5 percent. I daresay that few other federal agencies will have that kind of an increase."

In contrast, Rudman said, the LSC appropriation would increase in fiscal 1992 by 6.6 percent.

The Senate tabled the Gramm amendment 73-26. *(Vote 163, p. 22-S)*

John Seymour, R-Calif., tried to transfer $40 million within the bill for more money to keep illegal aliens from crossing the Southwestern border of the country. He proposed that all domestic discretionary funds be trimmed slightly to provide funds for additional border patrol agents and vehicles and equipment used for surveillance.

The Border Patrol was slated to get $312 million for fiscal 1992.

Hollings protested the transfer, saying that the Border Patrol's allocation had doubled in the past five years. Rudman acknowledged that illegal immigration to California was a problem but said that other priorities precluded additional money being put to keeping aliens out of the country.

The Seymour amendment was tabled, 56-43. *(Vote 164, p. 22-S)*

In separate action, Edward M. Kennedy, D-Mass., tried to block Helms from his proposal for AIDS tests on patients. "As a matter of sound public health policy, we should be establishing uniform protections for members of the health professions across the United States," said Kennedy, chairman of the Senate Labor and Human Resources Committee. He said Helms' plan would result in a "crazy quilt of different state rules."

Kennedy's effort to table the amendment failed, 44-55. *(Vote 162, p. 22-S)*

Helms also won on an attempt to bar federal prisoners from obtaining Pell grants. "This amendment is not intended to be spiteful," he said. "It is intended to speak for ... all American taxpayers, who wonder why they have to struggle to send their children to school."

Claiborne Pell, D-R.I., for whom the 1972 higher education grants were named, responded, "I believe that the more people who leave jail with some kind of skill or education, the better off we are."

His motion to table Helms' amendment was rejected, 38-60. *(Vote 161, p. 22-S)*

FINAL ACTION

Aside from the fierce debate on Oct. 3 over what to do about the Moscow embassy, and voting to leave that decision to the State Department, House action on the conference report on HR 2608 was devoted to pork barrel projects that Republicans attempted unsuccessfully to strike from the bill — an FBI automated fingerprint-identification laboratory in West Virginia, a new materials-development center in Iowa and grants for small businesses throughout the country.

Embassy Debate

Construction of the Moscow embassy began in 1979, but the discovery of listening devices throughout the building stopped construction in 1985. The embassy had remained in limbo while Congress and the Reagan and Bush administrations debated what to do. *(1990 Almanac, pp. 760, 881)*

Competing proposals had centered on tearing down the embassy and rebuilding it from its foundation or adding new, secure top floors.

In 1990, in the fiscal 1991 appropriation, Congress rebuffed the administration's request for funds for razing and rebuilding the facility and limited the State Department to $3.8 million to begin a design study. Early in 1991, the administration first asked for funds to rebuild.

But House Commerce, Justice, State Appropriations Subcommittee Chairman Smith opposed tearing down the facility as too costly.

To woo Smith, the State Department scaled back its request, supporting the "top hat" approach to add secure floors. The House's bill left the embassy's fate up to the State Department, and ordered it to report to Congress on its decision.

The Senate, however, took a different tack. Its bill directed the department to raze and rebuild the embassy and provided $130 million for that purpose.

Conferees on the measure agreed Oct. 2 on a compromise: $100 million toward a new building.

During House debate the next day, Snowe and others complained that the proposal had been sprung on them and they needed to study it.

"Formal cost estimates or engineering studies have not been conducted as they have in the tear down and rebuild process, for example," said Snowe, who had wanted the building torn down and replaced. Snowe was the ranking Republican on the Foreign Affairs Subcommittee on International Operations.

Defending the deal, Smith said the State Department had estimated that a new, 60,000-square-foot building would cost an eventual $220 million.

Smith added that if the old building were redone there would still be a chance that bugs in the foundation might not be eliminated.

But he did not persuade the majority.

Smith then offered to amend the bill to leave the decision on the embassy to the State Department, with notification to Congress. The amendment was adopted by voice vote.

Pork Barrel Projects

Burton, a frequent opponent of appropriations projects, attacked first a proposed $48 million automated fingerprinting system for the new FBI headquarters in Clarksburg, W.Va. That was in the home state of Senate Appropriations Committee Chairman Robert C. Byrd, whose goal was to bring home at least $1 billion in projects.

Burton accurately predicted that his move to strike the project would be shot down, but he implored the House to send "a signal that we mean business around this place." He added, "We are spending ourselves into disaster."

But his Republican and Democratic colleagues defended the project as important to fighting crime.

Subcommittee Chairman Smith said that the FBI supported the project's location. Smith's motion to accept the Senate amendment for the FBI project was adopted 252-162. *(Vote 290, p. 70-H)*

The House also adopted an amendment for $15.2 million for the Office of Textiles and Apparel and $3 million for a new-materials center in Ames, Iowa, the home district of Smith. The center developed durable metals for construction projects. The vote was 300-111. *(Vote 291, p. 70-H)*

Over arguments from Smith and others that the United States needed to advance in the textile and materials industry, Burton suggested that private corporations or cities and states should foot the bill for such projects.

Burton tried to remove $236 million for the Small Business Administration, which he said contained "truckloads of pork barrel projects" for members' hometowns.

"We believe that every one of these projects has a direct federal purpose," Smith rejoined.

Harold Rogers, Ky., the ranking Republican on the Appropriations subcommittee, added that many of the projects were in economically depressed areas and "will transfer emerging technologies to small businesses, which we all know is the foundation of the American free-enterprise system."

By a 310-106 vote, the House kept the projects in the bill. *(Vote 292, p. 70-H)* ■

Senate Pay Hike Riled Constituents

Lawmakers drew considerable public rebuke when they acted on the fiscal 1992 spending bill (HR 2506) for the legislative branch that gave the Senate a 23 percent pay raise.

The bill equalized House and Senate pay at $125,100, giving senators a $23,200 increase. That was the central feature of a package that was part of the final version of the $2.3 billion spending bill, which the House approved July 31 and the Senate cleared Aug. 2. The fast action made it possible for senators to get their pay increase during the summer recess; the pay provisions took effect as soon as President Bush signed the measure on Aug. 14. *(Senate pay raise, p. 22)*

There was little opposition on the floor. Some in the House groused about the Senate pay raise, and some senators criticized House-crafted rules that eased two-year-old restrictions on acceptance of gifts.

House leaders ushered the bill to the floor in a well-orchestrated move designed to prevent a roll call vote. A few back-bench Republicans tried to force a vote, but the leaders thwarted them by having the chamber — usually almost vacant during debates — packed with 225 loyalists. When Republican freshman Rick Santorum, Pa., requested a recorded vote, only three colleagues supported his request — far less than the required 44.

The new rules allowed senators, representatives and their employees to accept more expensive gifts (worth up to $250) than the previous rules allowed, and an unlimited number of lesser gifts (worth $100 or less). The rules also eliminated almost all of the requirements for publicly disclosing gifts. And the limits on the value of allowable gifts and those that were required to be disclosed was pegged to inflation so that in later years they would increase automatically.

The fiscal 1991 appropriation for the legislative branch totaled $2.2 billion. *(1990 Almanac, p. 894)*

BOXSCORE

➡ **Fiscal 1992 Legislative Branch Appropriations Bill (HR 2506).** The spending bill provided $2.3 billion for the fiscal 1992 operations of the House and Senate and related agencies.

Reports: H Rept 102-82; S Rept 102-81; conference report filed in the House, H Rept 102-176.

KEY ACTION

June 5 — HR 2506 passed the **House** by a vote of 308-110.

July 17 — HR 2506 passed the **Senate** by voice vote.

July 30 — HR 2506 approved by **House-Senate** conference.

July 31 — The **House** approved conference report by voice vote.

Aug. 2 — The **Senate** approved conference report by voice vote.

Aug. 14 — President Bush signed HR 2506 — PL 102-90.

HOUSE COMMITTEE ACTION

The House Appropriations Committee's Legislative Branch Subcommittee approved the House budget for fiscal 1992 on May 22 and included $80 million for mailing costs, indicating that restrictions on House members' use of taxpayer funds for mass mailings appeared to be reducing the cost of the frank.

The figure for the previous four election years ranged between $96 million and $114 million.

Subcommittee members also saw no need to bolster their fiscal 1991 franking appropriation of $59 million, making fiscal 1992 an off-year low and marking the first year in several when there was no embarrassing shortfall of funds.

The subcommittee's spending bill appropriated $1.8 billion for the House's own operations and those of associated agencies. The Senate was expected to add $500 million or more for its activities.

Franking restrictions imposed in 1990 after years of bickering had prompted subcommittee leaders to predict a relatively smooth path for the legislative spending bill in 1991. Chairman Vic Fazio, D-Calif., repeated that prediction at the May 22 markup. *(1990 Almanac, p. 895)*

But as Fazio admitted, he had hoped for the same thing every year, and it had never happened. The bill was routinely attacked by maverick members, usually conservative Republicans trying to highlight what they saw as the self-protectionist ways of House Democrats.

No big issues surfaced at the markup to douse Fazio's wish, though ranking Republican Jerry Lewis of California fired a warning shot.

He complained that some committees were abusing rules allowing them to have General Accounting Office (GAO) investigators detailed to their staff temporarily. Lewis said one House panel — later identified as Energy and Commerce Committee Chairman John D. Dingell's aggressive Investigations Subcommittee — had 21 GAO workers.

Lewis said he would try to work out the matter before the bill came to the floor, where he said some of his colleagues would love for such a "juicy" issue to end up.

Fazio denied that the use of GAO staff was an abuse, and Lewis withheld an amendment on the subject after Fazio said he had the votes to defeat it.

Full Committee

With little debate or controversy, the House Appropriations Committee on May 30 approved HR 2506.

Lewis told the Appropriations Committee that while the bill seemed relatively free of controversy, it could be attacked when it reached the House floor. Republicans usually attacked the bill as too expensive and too protective of incumbent perks.

The bill, approved by voice vote, appropriated $1.8 billion for the House's own operations and several other congressional agencies in fiscal 1992, about $65 million more than in fiscal 1991 and $288 million less than was requested.

The committee approved several minor amendments by voice vote, including one to turn the House's existing child-care center, a private, nonprofit entity, into a government-run center. Lewis hinted that the provision could prompt a floor fight.

Lewis also said that Republicans could offer an amendment on the floor to curb the increasing use by House

Legislative Branch

(In thousands of dollars)

	Fiscal 1991 Appropriation	House Bill	Senate Bill	Final Bill
Senate				
Senators' personal office accounts	$ 171,000	—	$ 185,768	$ 185,768
Payment to widows and heirs	—	—	102	102
Mileage	60	—	60	60
Officers, leadership offices	65,941	—	76,218	76,218
Leadership expense accounts	86	—	86	86
Committees	70,773	—	77,000	77,000
Official mail	30,000	—	32,000	32,000
Other	99,363	—	95,015	95,015
Subtotal, Senate	**$ 437,223**	**—**	**$ 466,249**	**$ 466,249**
House of Representatives				
Members' personal office accounts	273,805	301,100	301,100	301,100
Payment to widows and heirs	125	—	—	—
Mileage	210	210	210	210
Officers, leadership offices (including expense accounts)	49,848	54,659	54,659	54,659
Committees (including computer system)	134,431	141,324	141,324	141,324
Official mail	58,984	80,000	80,000	80,000
Other	130,272	131,918	131,918	131,918
Subtotal, House	**$ 647,675**	**$ 709,211**	**$ 709,211**	**$ 709,211**
Joint Items				
Joint committees	10,147	11,170	11,170	11,170
Office of Attending Physician	1,436	1,509	1,509	1,509
Capitol Police Board	67,619	65,372	66,872	66,122
Capitol Guide Service	1,490	1,603	1,603	1,603
Special Services Office	255	292	292	292
Office of Technology Assessment	19,557	21,025	21,025	21,025
Congressional Budget Office	21,183	22,372	22,789	22,542
Architect of the Capitol	139,806	98,301	140,617	140,013
Congressional Research Service	52,743	55,725	56,000	55,725
Government Printing Office (congressional printing)	79,615	89,941	89,341	89,341
Other	33,240	20	20	20
TOTAL, congressional operations	**$ 1,511,989**	**$ 1,076,541**	**$ 1,586,698**	**$ 1,584,822**
Other Agencies				
Botanic Garden	3,519	2,862	2,862	2,862
Library of Congress	239,924	248,452	244,540	243,224
Copyright Office (net)	(10,258)	(9,844)	(9,844)	(9,844)
Books for the blind and disabled	(48,617)	(41,179)	(41,179)	(41,179)
Architect of the Capitol (library buildings)	15,268	10,187	10,187	10,187
Copyright Royalty Tribunal (net)	127	130	130	130
Government Printing Office (salaries and expenses)	26,500	26,327	26,327	26,327
General Accounting Office	419,130	440,879	434,379	438,679
Other	—	—	200	—
TOTAL, other agencies	**$ 704,468**	**$ 728,837**	**$ 718,625**	**$ 721,409**
GRAND TOTAL	**$ 2,216,457**	**$ 1,805,378**	**$ 2,305,323**	**$ 2,306,231**

NOTES: Numbers based on Appropriations Committee reports; categories have been readjusted to illustrate more precisely how the money is spent, so some figures do not match those in committee charts. Totals may not agree with those in the provisions on pages 113-118 because funds for an activity may be spread among several accounts. The "administration request" category was deleted because the president submits without change requests forwarded from Congress and the agencies. The House bill includes no funding for the Senate because the bill originates in the House and, by tradition, each chamber is solely responsible for its own appropriations.

committees of GAO investigators to supplement their staffs.

HOUSE FLOOR ACTION

As Lewis predicted, House Republicans rebelled against the GAO on June 5, voting overwhelmingly to slash the congressional agency's budget to protest what they alleged was the agency's partisan slant.

Democrats defended the GAO, and their votes defeated the Republicans' proposed cut by a lopsided margin.

The showdown came as the House finished work on HR 2506. The bill was approved 308-110, with most Democrats voting yes and most Republicans voting no. *(Vote 137, p. 34-H)*

As usual, the annual funding bill became a target for conservatives seeking to embarrass the House's majority party. Subcommittee Chairman Fazio characterized the critics' feelings: "They think the only way we can save Congress is to destroy it."

The Democrats rallied to defeat all five Republican-backed amendments, including one offered by a maverick Democrat. All but one would have cut money from the bill. None received more than 200 votes, and each was defeated by a majority of Democrats voting against a majority of Republicans.

Republicans focused most of their fire on the GAO. The agency had long been the subject of bias complaints, but congressional aides could recall no other instance in which it was so openly attacked on the House floor.

The attack came during debate on an amendment by C. Christopher Cox, R-Calif., to cut the agency's budget from $441 million to $333 million.

The Democrats' rebuttal was led by Energy Committee Chairman Dingell, one of the most frequent users of GAO services. "This is a penny-wise, pound-foolish, partisan amendment," Dingell said in an impassioned 10-minute speech. "Billions of dollars have been saved, and audits of things like the safety of the blood supply, audits of things like misbehaviors at colleges and universities and by defense contractors, audits of important questions like rail safety . . . have been carried out by the General Accounting Office."

Cox's amendment was defeated 130-294, with only two Democrats supporting it and 37 Republicans opposing it. *(Vote 136, p. 34-H)*

The Republicans offered only a few specific examples of what they said was GAO bias. GOP Whip Newt Gingrich of Georgia complained that a report issued days earlier endorsed Canada's nationalized health-care system. Minority Leader Robert H. Michel, R-Ill., criticized the GAO's handling of a Democrat-instigated investigation into alleged talks between Ronald Reagan's 1980 presidential campaign and Iranian operatives concerning U.S. hostages.

Lewis, the Legislative Appropriations Subcommittee's ranking Republican, offered another GAO amendment. He wanted to enforce an existing law that limited committees' use of GAO investigators to one year. Scores of GAO workers were detailed to certain committees every year, and some stayed on longer than a year. Among the heaviest users of GAO detailees was Dingell's aggressive Investigations Subcommittee, and much of the Republican ire about alleged GAO abuse clearly was aimed at Dingell.

Lewis withdrew the amendment after the leadership of the House Administration Committee, which was charged with overseeing the use of detailees, promised to look into the matter.

In other action on the bill, the House:

- Rejected, by 150-276, an amendment by Santorum that would have limited the Appropriations Committee's ability to shift excess funds between accounts. Santorum wanted any such excess funds to be used to reduce the deficit. *(Vote 132, p. 32-H)*
- Rejected, by 198-227, an amendment by Timothy J. Penny, D-Minn., to cut the House's mailing budget from $80 million to $59 million, the amount appropriated in fiscal 1991. *(Vote 133, p. 34-H)*
- Rejected, by 171-255, an amendment by Joel Hefley, R-Colo., to cut the bill by 1.4 percent. Hefley said it would have cut $21.4 million in outlays from the bill, reducing its 3.7 percent increase to 2.4 percent. *(Vote 135, p. 34-H)*
- Killed a provision that would have turned the private, nonprofit House child-care center into a government-run operation. The purpose was to offer employees of the center better pay and fringe benefits, said Lewis. Hefley objected to the provision and invoked a rule against including such language in a spending bill to have it removed.

SENATE COMMITTEE ACTION

A week after House Republicans lambasted the GAO for alleged bias, the Senate Appropriations Committee nicked the investigative agency's budget by a few million dollars in what was described as a bipartisan warning shot.

In approving HR 2506 on June 12, committee members also decided to authorize big raises for top Senate employees and ban all aides from accepting honoraria payments. And they approved a 35 percent increase for the office of the president pro tempore, Robert C. Byrd, D-W.Va., who was also chairman of the committee that wrote the bill.

Overall, however, members described the bill as a stingy one. Approved 20-0, it appropriated $2.3 billion. With funds for mandatory accounts, over which appropriators had little control, spending would total about $2.4 billion in fiscal 1992.

"We are short of the money necessary to do what really ought to be done," said Harry Reid, D-Nev., chairman of the Legislative Branch Subcommittee. He said that nearly 80 percent of the requested increases were denied.

The House had approved its version of the bill June 5, after a bruising floor fight by some Republicans who charged that there was bias at the GAO.

Reid, who crafted the spending bill, said the GAO's stance on mining issues rankled him. His bill cut the House-approved GAO budget by $6.5 million — a funding level that would kill a plan to increase GAO staff performance bonuses and require other cuts, the committee said.

Reid later said the cut, which did not prompt debate in the markup, was meant as a warning to the GAO — "a shot across the bow," aides said.

The committee's report on the bill included some of the same complaints that were voiced by House Republicans during the June 5 debate.

Equalizing Staff Salaries

Byrd offered the only substantive amendment to the bill. Approved by voice vote, it banned honoraria for all Senate staff members and allowed raises for top personal and committee aides and the Senate's seven non-member "officers" — the chaplain, the secretary, the sergeant at arms, the legal counsel, the legislative counsel, and the majority and minority secretaries.

Byrd said his amendment was designed to correct an inequity created in 1989 when the Senate opted for a lower pay scale than the House. *(1989 Almanac, p. 51)*

In 1991, most senators were paid $101,900 a year, while most House members received $125,100. Because the maximum salaries of top Senate aides were tied to members' salaries, Senate aides could get no more than about $100,000, said Ted Stevens, R-Alaska, while top House aides could make more than $115,000. Sixty-eight House staff members made more than the Senate cap, he said.

Byrd's amendment allowed senators to raise salaries for top staff to more than $120,000, aides said. Salaries of the Senate's officers (except for the chaplain) would increase from about $100,000 to more than $123,000, a committee aide said.

Byrd noted that his amendment would result in some aides being paid more than their senator-bosses. That could increase pressure for a Senate pay increase.

Byrd said he feared that underpaid Senate staff members would flee to the House. "We're going to see ourselves bled of these staffers," he said. "There is honor in serving the Senate. But honor alone will not carry the mortgage."

Ironically, many in the House complained that they were not allotted enough money to keep their aides from fleeing to the Senate. Partly for that reason, House members in 1991 were allowed a personal office payroll increase of about $40,000 each.

The bill also provided money to expand the staffs of several agencies, including Byrd's president pro tempore office. The bill raised its budget by $108,000, to $419,000, allowing Byrd to add two new aides to his existing staff of seven. By comparison, the majority and minority whips each would get $312,000 under the bill, an $8,000 increase. In 1989, when Byrd became chairman of the Appropriations Committee and president pro tempore, the office's budget was $156,000.

Once largely ceremonial, the office had taken on new responsibilities over the years, the committee said, including "the appointment of legislative boards, commissions and committees, and the administrative oversight of various Senate organizations."

SENATE FLOOR ACTION

When HR 2506 reached the Senate floor it became the vehicle for the pay raise for senators. The Senate passed HR 2506 by voice vote on July 17 in largely the same form as it came out of the Senate Appropriations Committee. Aside from the pay raise issue, the bill was far less contentious than it had been in past years.

"If we lay that to one side, we may very well have set a record for the non-controversial nature of this bill and for the amicability with which it was dealt with here on the floor of the Senate," said Slade Gorton, R-Wash., the ranking minority member of the Legislative Branch Appropriations Subcommittee.

Gorton and subcommittee Chairman Reid agreed to accept all of the nine mostly minor amendments approved by the Senate; none prompted debate or roll call votes. The bill's total of $2.3 billion represented an increase over fiscal 1991 of roughly $90 million, or about 4 percent. Most of the increases went to accounts for the House and Senate.

Reid and Gorton rejected only one amendment. Offered by Pete V. Domenici, R-N.M., it was aimed at double-checking the accuracy and fairness of reports issued by the GAO.

The amendment would have required the GAO to set up a system under which a sampling of GAO reports would have been submitted to outside experts for study. The GAO's head, the comptroller general, would have had to correct any systemic problems identified by the experts.

The amendment was based on a bill (S 1400) sponsored by Domenici and the Republican leadership. Comptroller General Charles A. Bowsher had endorsed the peer-review concept, but there was resistance to the idea in the House.

Reid asked Domenici to withhold the amendment, and it was not offered. Reid and Gorton told Domenici that language in the committee's report and a $6.5 million cut in the GAO's budget should be enough of a message to get the agency to pay attention.

Other amendments included ones by:

- Hank Brown, R-Colo., to cut the account for Senate mail by $2 million, to $32 million. The franking account had often sparked fights, but limits on mass mailings had reduced costs lately. Reid accepted the amendment to avoid another fight over the issue after Brown agreed to reduce the cut from $4 million.
- Gorton, to hike the budgets for the two parties' leadership, policy and conference offices by $730,000.
- Harris Wofford, D-Pa., to cut his own fiscal 1991 mailing account by $150,000, because "I made a promise to the people of my state [that] I would not send out self-promotional mass mailings at public expense."
- John D. Rockefeller IV, D-W.Va., to appropriate $200,000 for the National Commission on Children. The panel, which Rockefeller headed, recently issued its report and sought money to print and distribute it.
- Reid, to turn authority for operating the House's privately run Child Day Care Center over to the House. A similar amendment prompted controversy in the House and was stripped from the bill on the floor. Reid said he inserted the measure into the bill at the request of his House counterparts.
- Reid, to transfer authority over Senate-side Capitol elevator operators and the Senate chamber's public address system from the architect of the Capitol to the sergeant at arms.

FINAL ACTION

House and Senate negotiators completed work on HR 2506 on July 30.

The House approved the conference report the next day by voice vote. The Senate cleared the bill Aug. 2 also by voice vote.

As approved, the bill included a 23 percent pay raise for senators and eased gift rules for all members.

The new rules allowed senators, representatives and their employees to accept from anyone more expensive gifts — worth up to $250 — than existing rules, and an unlimited number of lesser gifts — worth $100 or less.

The new rules prompted officials at Common Cause, the public interest group that successfully lobbied in 1989 for tightened gift rules, to sputter with indignation.

"To start weakening and walking away from ethics reforms 18 months later is an act of bad faith and totally unjustified and just plain wrong," said Fred Wertheimer, president of Common Cause. "There is absolutely no justification for the kind of ripping off that's going on here."

House vs. Senate

An undercurrent of institutional animosity between the chambers was evident as the bill moved toward final pas-

Continued on p. 553

Legislative Branch Provisions

The U.S. government's legislative branch, a 38,000-employee bureaucracy, cost $2.4 billion in fiscal 1992. Though the growth of spending on Congress and its agencies had slowed considerably in recent years, its budget was more than 40 times what it was shortly after World War II.

Almost all the money was contained in the legislative branch's fiscal 1992 spending bill (HR 2506 — PL 102-90). The bill funded the operations of the Senate, the House, a host of congressional support agencies and several other entities that were deemed to be part of the legislative branch. The measure was among the least popular to grace the floors of the House and Senate every year because members must vote to spend money not on the voters back home but on themselves. The embarrassment proved so great from 1978 to 1982, in fact, that Congress declined to enact a separate spending bill for itself, parceling out the money instead among other must-pass measures.

Congress moved to ease the pain somewhat in 1981 by excluding from the bill money for the members' own salaries, approving a permanent appropriation for that purpose starting in fiscal 1983. That action slightly distorted the true cost of legislative branch operations: The fiscal 1992 bill's $2.3 billion total did not include the annual $125,100 salaries and benefits for Congress' 535 members, four delegates and one resident commissioner. Those costs would otherwise add more than $80 million.

Salaries for Congress' other employees ate up more than two-thirds of the money in the bill each year. The rest of the money paid for supplies, building maintenance, rent, computer services and other non-personnel items.

The 1946 measure totaled $54 million, according to "Vital Statistics on Congress," a book compiled by American Enterprise Institute (AEI) researchers. The fiscal 1992 bill was more than five times as large, after adjusting for inflation.

Over the past 15 years, however, legislative branch spending did not keep pace with inflation. The fiscal 1992 bill was 4 percent larger than fiscal 1991's, slightly below the rate of inflation. Vic Fazio, D-Calif., chairman of the House Appropriations subcommittee in charge of the bill, frequently pointed out that since the late 1970s, the executive branch's budget had grown much faster.

But that had not stopped conservatives and mavericks from griping that the bill was bloated, and every year they tried to trim it. Though they had been successful in the past, in 1991 they failed in several attempts on the House floor.

The following is a breakdown of where the money in the fiscal 1992 bill would go and other significant provisions in the bill. The employee counts are estimates based on the AEI's statistics and various government sources.

THE SENATE

Staff and Administrative Expenses

The Senate would spend $466.25 million on itself under the bill. It employed about 7,400 people.

• **Members' offices.** The biggest chunk ($185.8 million) would pay the salaries of up to 4,100 aides on senators' personal staffs — about one-third in senators' home states and the rest in Washington — and expenses to run their Capitol and home-state offices.

Senators were allowed between about $1.3 million and $2.3 million each from this account, depending mainly on the size of their state and its distance from the Capitol.

The bill would allow about half of the senators automatic increases of between $42,000 and $165,000 for hiring staff members.

Senators got the bulk of what they spent operating their offices from this account, but they also got help from other accounts. For example, computers, telephone services and the rent for state offices were paid by the sergeant-at-arms budget, and the architect of the Capitol provided furniture to senators' personal offices.

• **Travel.** Under an 1866 law, Congress every year appropriated a total of $60,000 for 20-cent-per-mile payments to members to compensate each for one round trip home from the Capitol. Payments to senators (and the vice president) ranged from $4 for a Virginian to $2,076 for a Hawaiian.

Senators could also turn to their office accounts, the committee budgets and other pockets of money to pay for trips. There was a separate $125,000 account for foreign travel. Moreover, the Pentagon frequently shuttled members overseas on military planes, but those trips were covered by the defense appropriations bill. An additional permanent appropriation of $440,000 a year — administered by the State Department and established in a 1987 omnibus spending bill — paid for members' trips to international meetings of parliamentary groups. Members also took trips at the expense of corporations, interest groups and foundations.

• **Franking.** Both chambers appropriated money every year to reimburse the Postal Service for official mail costs, most of which paid for members' franked mass mailings. The bill included $32 million for franked Senate mail, which was just slightly below the amount needed to pay for one statewide mailing for each senator and for the mail of committees and Senate officers.

In past years, members' franking rights had been among the most controversial items in the bill. But past reform efforts had limited members' use of the frank and made the cost of each member's mass mailings public, and this had resulted in lower costs for congressional mailings.

• **Committees.** Another big Senate item was the cost of running its committees, which employed 1,400 people. Most of the committees' operations were funded under the bill's "inquiries and investigations" account, which totaled $77 million.

Each Congress, the Senate separately approved budgets for almost all the committees, based on recommendations crafted by the Rules Committee that in turn were based on requests from the committees. The inquiries account each year approved enough money to fund whatever was in the resolution, as well as committee employees' fringe benefits.

LEADERSHIP, ADMINISTRATIVE OFFICES

Other accounts (totaling more than $170 million) covered the salaries, benefits and expenses of another 1,900 Senate employees — those in the leadership offices and the Senate administrative offices.

• **Sergeant-at-Arms.** The biggest of these offices was the Sergeant-at-Arms and Doorkeeper of the Senate, which oversaw the day-to-day operations of most of the Senate's basic support services, sometimes working with the General Services Administration, the executive branch's landlord.

The sergeant-at-arms — in 1991 Martha S. Pope, former chief of staff to Majority Leader George J. Mitchell, D-Maine — maintained the Senate's massive computer system; rented home-state offices for members; oversaw the Senate's phone system; leased cars; printed and mailed news releases and other documents for members; provided members with office equipment; furnished the Capitol's Senate side; and ran the Senate's photographic, audio and video studios.

The office also oversaw Senate pages, doorkeepers, hairstylists, parking lot attendants, tour guides, custodians, cabinetmakers, photographers and video operators, telephone operators, post office workers and folding room workers. A new provision transferred authority over the Senate's elevator operators and public address system from the Architect of the Capitol to the Sergeant-at-Arms. Pope helped oversee the Capitol Police, funded elsewhere in the bill.

The press galleries also fell under the Sergeant-at-Arms' budget, although they were basically autonomous.

In all, the office would employ 913 people in fiscal 1992 at a cost of $32.7 million, not counting benefits. For other expenses, the bill provided $88.8 million, most of which would be spent on computer items. About $10.5 million would be spent on renting office space and mobile offices for members in their home states.

In its report on the bill, the Senate Appropriations Committee criticized the office for the "aimless growth of the computer service in recent years" and pressed Pope to come up with a plan for it in 1992.

• **Secretary of the Senate.** The second-biggest office belonged to Walter J. Stewart, who as secretary of the Senate was the chamber's chief administrative officer. He employed up to 226 employees at a cost of $11.4 million, not counting benefits, and spent almost $2 million more on other expenses.

The office disbursed appropriated funds; kept track of bills; transcribed floor debates for the Congressional Record; maintained public records and documents for inspection and distribution; ran the Senate library, historical office, curator's office and parliamentarian's office; oversaw the office-supply distribution system; provided orientation seminars for members and staff; supplied Senate offices with reference books; and contracted with the District of Columbia for the education of Senate pages.

The secretary's allocation included a new $2 million appropriation to pay for closed-captioning services for the deaf on C-SPAN.

• **Senate lawyers.** The Senate's chief lawyers — the legislative counsel and the legal counsel — would spend $3.9 million and employ nearly 40 people.

• **Chaplain.** The chaplain would get $161,000 for himself and two employees.

• **President Pro Tempore.** Of the leadership offices, perhaps the fastest-growing was that of the president pro tempore — the person who presided over the Senate in the absence of the vice president and was third in line to the presidency, behind the vice president and House Speaker.

The position, which by tradition went to the senior senator of the majority party, in 1991 was held by Robert C. Byrd, D-W.Va., who was also the chairman of the Appropriations Committee. The salary budget for his office in fiscal 1992 would be $419,000 — up from $156,000 when Byrd took both positions in 1989 and enough for about nine employees. The committee's report said the office, once largely ceremonial, had been given many new responsibilities in recent years.

• **Vice President.** Vice President Dan Quayle, who served as president of the Senate, had the biggest single leadership office budget — $1.4 million for a staff of up to 34. The vice president's office got additional money from the spending bill that funded the White House. *(Treasury-Postal Service appropriations, p. 591)*

• **Democratic leadership.** On the surface, Majority Leader Mitchell seemed to have a much smaller budget of just over $1 million.

But the Democratic leadership's power was consolidated. Though Mitchell had shared more of the power than his predecessor (Byrd), he had control over most of the budgets of several other leadership offices — the Democratic Conference, the Democratic Policy Committee and the secretary of the majority's office. These offices' budgets totaled $2.7 million, giving Mitchell almost complete control over $3.7 million and a staff of about 60. Of that, $1.2 million went to the Democratic Policy Committee, whose chair Mitchell shared with Tom Daschle of South Dakota. There were other Democratic leadership offices — the whip (Wendell H. Ford, D-Ky.), with a budget of $312,000, and the secretary of the conference (David Pryor, D-Ark.), with a budget of $175,000.

• **Republican leadership.** Among Republicans, who got the same amount as the Democrats for their party leadership offices, power was much more diffuse. Republican leader Bob Dole of Kansas basically controlled two budgets — the minority leader's ($1 million) and the secretary of the minority's ($530,000). The Republican Conference, headed by Thad Cochran of Mississippi, had a budget of nearly $1 million. The secretary of the conference, Bob Kasten of Wisconsin, got $175,000. The Republican Policy Committee, headed by Don Nickles of Oklahoma, got $1.2 million. And the minority whip, Alan K. Simpson of Wyoming, received $312,000.

• **Consultants.** Various Senate leaders and officers had authority to hire consultants "on a temporary or intermittent basis." Past laws gave such authority to the president pro tempore, the majority and minority leaders and the secretary of the Senate. The fiscal 1992 law added the legislative counsel — the Senate's chief bill drafter — to the list.

The bill allocated $500,000 for this purpose. In effect, the money supplemented the salary budgets of these offices, allowing them to expand their staffs. For example, Republican leader Dole had had a "temporary" consultant on his staff since 1987 — Robert B. Dove, the Senate's parliamentarian in 1981-87.

• **Leadership office expenses.** Some of the leadership office budgets included money for office expenses, while others were limited to money for salaries. But occasionally, according to some members' aides, the lines between different leadership offices (and the leaders' personal offices) blurred, so some expense money allocated to one office might actually be used by another.

A bill provision increased from $75,000 to $275,000 how much the two parties' conference chairmen could shift from their salary account to the office expenses account, which otherwise was limited to $75,000.

Some leaders, including Mitchell, used their leadership

expense allowances (below) for office expenses.

• **Expense allowances.** The leaders from both parties, including the vice president, were allowed some tax-free spending money under laws that did little to define what expenses were allowable. According to aides, the money paid for food at official meetings, office expenses not funded from other accounts and other official expenses. These "expense allowances" totaled $56,000 — $10,000 each to the vice president, president pro tempore and the majority and minority leaders; $5,000 each to the majority and minority whips; and $3,000 each to the chairmen of the majority and minority conference committees.

The majority and minority leaders were also allowed $15,000 each for a vaguely defined "representation allowance" for expenses related to "their appropriate responsibilities" to visiting foreign officials and "intergovernmental organizations." Some Senate officers (the secretary, the sergeant-at-arms and the minority and majority secretaries) got expense allowances, too — $3,000 each. The leaders and officials did not all use their full allowances.

• **Other accounts.** A variety of other items would take up the rest of the Senate's money, including: funds for death benefits for the heirs of deceased employees and members, including Teresa Heinz, widow of Sen. John Heinz, R-Pa., who would get $101,900; $25,000 for receptions for foreign dignitaries; $1.2 million for two Senate observer missions (one for Central America, one for arms control); $250,000 for a fellowship program; $75,000 for the Rules Committee to print calendars; and $336,000 for the Senate's Caucus on International Narcotics Control.

Pay and Income Limits

• **Pay raise.** Although members' salaries were paid for from a separate permanent appropriation, the bill raised senators' pay, bringing the annual salary rate for non-leadership members up to the House level — $125,100, up from $101,900. The raise was effective the day the bill was signed by President Bush, Aug. 14. That meant senators would make about $110,729 for the remainder of 1991.

• **Income limits.** The pay-raise provision also imposed income limits on senators identical to those already in place for House members. It barred senators from supplementing their income by more than 15 percent a year ($18,765) from outside jobs (not counting investment income) or from accepting any speaking or writing fees, known as honoraria.

Though the honoraria ban took effect upon enactment, senators were allowed to keep any such fees already accepted up to the 1991 limit of $23,068. Senators who kept the maximum would earn $133,797, which would be $8,697 more than House members would make.

The bill allowed senators to have up to $2,000 per speech donated to charity, but they could not derive any tax benefits from such transactions.

The provision also barred senators from being paid for: teaching without prior approval from the Ethics Committee; serving on boards of directors; practicing a profession that involved a "fiduciary relationship"; or affiliating with any entity that provided such professional services. Senators also could not let their names be used by such firms.

"Fiduciary" was not defined; the Senate Ethics Committee was charged with interpreting the law. The House Committee on Standards of Official Conduct struggled to define the term for months before issuing a four-page statement in April that said it would consider such matters case by case. In the House, it was generally assumed that virtually any law-firm-related work was barred, an aide said.

• **Staff income.** The provision also meant raises for some top Senate aides and officers because maximum salaries for such employees were pegged just below senators' salaries. It also barred Senate employees from pocketing honoraria. Top aides were also subject to the same outside income and employment restrictions as senators.

• **Fines.** Senators and employees who violated the income and employment limits risked fines of $10,000 or the amount of illegal compensation, whichever was greater, unless they acted in good faith on the advice of the Ethics Committee.

THE HOUSE OF REPRESENTATIVES

The House would spend $709,211,000 on itself under the bill. It employed about 12,500 people.

Staff and Administrative Expenses

• **Members' offices.** Like the Senate, the House spent the biggest chunk of its money on salaries and expenses of its members' offices. The members, delegates and resident commissioner would be allowed $515,760 each for the salaries of up to 22 staff members. That included a $40,760 increase that was approved in the spring by the House Administration Committee, which oversaw such matters. The bill appropriated $218.5 million for this purpose (called "clerk hire"), nearly $48.6 million shy of what would be needed if all members used the maximum; some did not.

In all, that money would pay the salaries of nearly 8,000 employees — about 30 percent of whom were based in district offices.

In addition, members were allowed temporary helpers from the Lyndon Baines Johnson Congressional Intern program, for which $1.1 million was appropriated; about $82.6 million would be spent on members' official expenses. Members would get an average of about $176,000 each; members' allowances ranged between $135,000 and $320,000, depending on their districts' distance from the Capitol and office rental rates in the districts.

More so than in the Senate, House members got most of what they spent running their offices from these two accounts. Some but not many other expenses (such as furniture for their Washington offices, which was provided by the clerk) were funded by other accounts.

• **Travel.** Members got the same 20-cent-per-mile payments as senators for a trip home and back each year. The bill included $210,000 for this purpose. As with senators, members got travel subsidies from a host of other sources, including their office expense account, which also allowed House members to lease cars.

• **Franking.** The bill included $80 million for franked mail. Though an increase over fiscal 1991's $59 million, the fiscal 1992 appropriation was much less than that of past election years, reflecting franking limits enacted for fiscal 1991 to check mass mailings. An attempt on the floor to cut the appropriation back to the fiscal 1991 level failed, apparently because members were satisfied that the reforms were sufficient.

All members received a mail budget big enough to send three items to each home in their district, and how much they spent was disclosed quarterly. Members were allowed to transfer $25,000 a year from other accounts into their mail account.

• **Committees.** Four accounts, totaling $132.7 million,

provided almost all funding for the House's 27 committees, which employed roughly 2,400 people. (Some administrative expenses, such as stenographic services, office supplies and some telephone services, were funded from other accounts.) Budgets ranged from less than $800,000 for most select committees to more than $16 million for the Appropriations Committee, which got almost twice the budget of the next largest, Energy and Commerce.

All but two of the House's standing committees, as well as the Permanent Select Committee on Intelligence, got a base contingent of 30 employees (with up to 10 assigned to the minority in most cases). The Appropriations and Budget committees set their own base staff levels. The biggest of the four accounts paid the salaries of these aides.

The second-biggest account funded the staff and expenses of the other so-called select committees and the expenses and additional staff of the panels funded by the first account — Intelligence and all standing committees except Budget and Appropriations (which got additional money from the two remaining accounts).

Funding from this second account, though part of the spending bill, was approved separately by the House in annual resolutions crafted by the House Administration Committee.

It was the division of money from this account that often drew the ire of House Republicans. Rules for the first account reserved one-third of the staff budget for the minority party, but there was no such protection governing the second account. Funding from it was in effect controlled by the majority party.

In the past, House rules for the second account guaranteed minority committee members either "fair consideration" in staffing splits or at least one-third of the staff money. Currently, minority members were assured only that the ranking minority members of up to six subcommittees would get at least one aide.

House Republicans had pushed in recent years for at least 20 percent of the staff funding in the second account, with an eventual goal of one-third. In 1989, they persuaded the House Administration Committee to endorse that goal.

When the fiscal 1992 committee funding resolution (H Res 92) was approved March 20, the Republicans claimed limited progress: Of the staff the resolution paid for, 19.3 percent was for the GOP, up from less than 18 percent. The balance on particular panels varied widely, Republicans said — Judiciary Republicans got 9 percent of their committee's staff money, while Public Works Republicans got more than 30 percent.

By contrast, Senate rules called for total committee staff to "reflect the relative number of majority and minority members" on each committee.

• **Other accounts.** Various other accounts took up much of the rest of the House's money, including more than $100 million for employee benefits and $25 million for office equipment and supplies, telephone expenses, furniture and other items.

Administrative Offices

There were nine administrative offices in the House. Together, their budgets totaled more than $40 million, and they employed more than 1,200 people.

• **Clerk.** The biggest budget ($20.9 million) was for the clerk, the House's main administrator and the counterpart of the secretary of the Senate, although they did not have identical duties.

The clerk, with more than 570 employees, oversaw the disbursement of most appropriated funds; the distribution of members' office equipment, furniture and supplies; the technical aspects of moving bills through the House; contracting; the House library; the transcribing of committee hearings and floor debates; the recording studio; the telephone system; the House's main institutional lawyers; the House's Fair Employment Practices and Employee Assistance offices; and the public records office, which collected and filed financial disclosure and lobbyist registration documents.

The bill would turn the operation of the House's private child-care center over to the clerk of the House. The bill earmarked $45,000 for the center, but bill drafters warned that it would have to be self-sustaining after fiscal 1992.

• **Doorkeeper.** This office, with nearly 400 workers, would get $10 million.

The doorkeeper's office supervised the doormen who tended the entrances to the House floor and galleries, the pages and the cloakroom workers. It oversaw the document room, which distributed documents to the public, the members' photography and publications distribution service, the hair salon and barbershop. The press galleries fell into the doorkeeper's bailiwick, although, like the Senate's, they were relatively autonomous.

• **Sergeant-at-Arms.** The sergeant-at-arms' budget was $1.3 million. Like his Senate counterpart, he helped oversee the Capitol Police (funded elsewhere) but otherwise had very few of the same duties. His most important other job was to administer the members' payroll and benefits, including insurance and retirement. He also ran the House bank, which provided checking accounts for members only and check-cashing privileges for staff. It would be closed by the end of the 1991 in response to the uproar over members' floating checks.

• **Other offices.** The other offices funded by the bill were the postmaster ($4.4 million); the chaplain ($120,000); the parliamentarian ($946,000); the historian ($361,000); the law revision counsel, which codified enacted laws into the U.S. Code ($1.4 million); and the Legislative Counsel ($4.2 million).

• **House Information Systems.** Unlike the Senate, where the sergeant-at-arms oversaw the computer system, the House's system was run by a standing committee — House Administration, which ran a separate office for that purpose. Called the House Information System, it employed 238 people. Its budget would total $20 million, but only $8.6 million was directly appropriated in the bill; reimbursements from various legislative branch agencies for computer work covered the rest.

Leadership Offices

The five main leadership offices would get about $5.8 million under the bill — $1.5 million for the Speaker (Thomas S. Foley, D-Wash.); $1.1 million for the majority leader (Richard A. Gephardt, D-Mo.); $1.4 million for the minority leader (Robert H. Michel, R-Ill.); $1 million for the majority whip (David E. Bonior, D-Mich.); and $764,000 for the minority whip (Newt Gingrich, R-Ga.). Not counting the Speaker, the budgets for leaders and whips were evenly split between the parties. The money included about 85 employees' salaries.

• **Expense accounts.** Each leader's budget included an automatic annual allowance for official expenses. The Speaker got $25,000; the two leaders $10,000 each; and the whips $5,000 each. The expense money was in addition to their annual salaries, which for the Speaker ($160,600) and two leaders ($138,900) were higher than the other members' 1991 salary of $125,100.

The expense money was paid to each personally in monthly installments, and they did not have to account publicly for how they spent it. However, they had to declare it as income for tax purposes and pay taxes on any amount not used for official expenses.

• **Chief deputy whips.** The whips' budgets also each included money for a chief deputy whip — $308,930 for the Democrats and $93,520 for the Republicans. The Democrats had three chief deputy whips, while the Republicans had two, so presumably the money would be split among them.

• **Other accounts.** These budgets were not all the money and staff at the leaders' disposal. For example, the bill elsewhere included $113,000 for drivers for the leaders.

Moreover, Republican leader Michel had control over six additional employees (for whom $713,000 was appropriated). These employees compensated the minority party for having virtually no control over whom the Democrats picked to be the House's top six administrative employees. Some were given corresponding titles but they were essentially political aides. Minority Doorkeeper William R. Pitts Jr., for instance, was Michel's top floor strategist.

• **Party caucuses.** The two parties each got a pot of money (almost $1.5 million) for their main House organizations. Between the two, they employed 38 employees, and the bill authorized raises for some of them.

Most of the Democrats' money went to the Democratic Steering and Policy Committee (headed by Speaker Foley), the executive arm of the entire Democratic Caucus (headed by Steny H. Hoyer, Md.), which got the rest of the money.

In the bill, the GOP's money was all designated for the Republican Conference (headed by Jerry Lewis, Calif.), but its budget also funded the Republican Policy Committee (headed by Mickey Edwards, Okla.) and the Republican Research Committee (headed by Duncan Hunter, Calif.)

• **Former Speakers.** The House paid for staffs for former Speakers, for which $410,000 was appropriated.

LEGISLATIVE BRANCH AGENCIES

The bill's remainder was divided among agencies and agency divisions that worked only for Congress (such as the joint committees, the Congressional Budget Office and the Library of Congress' Congressional Research Service) and entities with broader purposes (such as the rest of the Library of Congress and the Botanic Garden). Together, their budgets totaled $1.1 billion, and they employed about 19,000 workers. Using the panel's breakdown, direct congressional operations would cost $1.6 billion ($709 million for the House, $466 million for the Senate and $409 million for entities that directly served Congress).

Some of the committee's accounting seemed arbitrary. More than half of the $721 million in the broader-purpose section, for instance, went to the General Accounting Office, which did the great majority of its work directly for Congress. Many entities in the bill had little to do with Congress, including the Copyright Royalty Tribunal and the Library of Congress' Copyright Office.

On the other hand, several agencies that were deemed to be part of the legislative branch were funded in other spending bills, including the U.S. Tax Court and various congressional commissions.

In the descriptions that follow, agencies' total budgets are given regardless of how they were split up in the bill.

• **Joint committees.** The bill funded three committees that had members from both chambers, with a total of 145 employees. The Joint Committee on Taxation, Congress' official estimate-producer for revenue measures, would get $5.8 million. Its request ($6.2 million) was the only one of the three to be cut. The Joint Economic Committee, which studied the nation's economic health on a continuing basis, would get $4 million. The Joint Committee on Printing, which oversaw government printing programs, including the Government Printing Office, would get $1.4 million.

• **Capitol Police.** The budget would be $66 million, almost all of which was for the salaries of about 1,300 employees. The payroll budget was split between the House ($31.7 million) and the Senate ($32.4 million). The police were controlled by the Capitol Police Board, made up of the two sergeants-at-arms and the architect of the Capitol.

• **Capitol Guide Service.** This was the agency that offered tours of the Capitol, helping more than a million visitors a year. Its budget would be $1.6 million, enough to employ about 45 people, including a dozen temporary workers for peak tourist months.

• **Special Services Office.** This office, with a budget of nearly $300,000, helped disabled guests, staffs and visitors.

• **Office of Technology Assessment.** With a budget of $21 million and 143 employees, this was the smallest of Congress' main legislative support agencies (behind the General Accounting Office, the Congressional Budget Office and the Library of Congress' Congressional Research Service). Formed 20 years ago, it studied high-tech issues for Congress.

• **Congressional Budget Office (CBO).** This 226-person agency studied a broad range of budget-related issues for Congress and determined the cost of each bill, providing a counterweight to the White House's Office of Management and Budget. CBO had a budget of $22.5 million.

• **General Accounting Office (GAO).** Aside from the House and the Senate, the GAO had the single largest budget in the bill — about $440 million. The GAO, which investigated and audited government agencies for Congress, had more than 5,000 employees, many of them scattered in offices across the country and overseas.

The GAO was the subject of one of 1991's big controversies on the legislative spending bill. Republicans charged that it was biased against them. Some Western Democratic senators were equally annoyed, and the Senate nicked the GAO's House-approved budget by $6.5 million. Most of that money was restored in conference, and the GAO promised to address the members' concerns. The bill's drafters ordered the agency's head, Comptroller General Charles A. Bowsher, to give monthly reports to Congress' leaders listing all new investigations and audits.

Included in the GAO's budget was $1.8 million to sponsor the triennial Congress of the International Organization of Supreme Audit Institutions in October 1992, a meeting of government auditors from around the world. The meeting of 500 officials from 140 countries would cost the United States more than $4 million over several years.

• **Library of Congress.** The library had a split budget because only the Congressional Research Service (CRS) was considered to directly serve Congress. The library, with about 5,000 employees, would have a $400 million budget, but only about $310 million was included in the legislative branch spending bill — $55.7 million for the CRS, $243.2 million for the rest of the library and $10.2 million, part of the Architect of the Capitol's budget, for maintenance of the library's main buildings in Washington.

The rest of the money would come from fees paid to the library's Copyright Office and for other public services, reimbursements from other government agencies and donations from outside organizations.

The bill included $622,000 to subsidize the sale of card catalogs to public libraries and $41 million to provide special books and audio materials to hundreds of thousands of disabled people.

• **Architect of the Capitol.** The architect maintained the Capitol, its grounds and its power plant and various congressional buildings. The office employed more than 2,000 people and had a budget of $150.2 million, including the $10.2 million for upkeep of the Library of Congress. It also ran the Senate restaurant (but not the House's) and provided custodial services for some parts of the Capitol Hill complex. Another $3 million-plus, funded in the Commerce-State-Justice bill, would be used to maintain the Supreme Court building.

• **Botanic Garden.** The $2.9 million agency, founded in 1820 and run by the Architect of the Capitol, collected and cultivated plants for display and offered tours and horticultural courses. Each member's office could borrow six potted plants; the garden provided flowers and floral centerpieces for official functions. The architect's request for $9 million to begin renovating the garden's dilapidated conservatory near the Capitol was turned down.

• **Copyright Royalty Tribunal.** This obscure agency, which distributed royalties to various copyright holders, had a budget of $865,000, of which $735,000 was offset by fees.

• **Government Printing Office (GPO).** The bill included a total of $115.7 million for the GPO, of which $89.3 million was for congressional printing and binding services. The GPO was actually a much bigger agency than those figures implied. Employing about 5,000 people, it was the federal government's main printer and known as the biggest printing shop in the world — even though more than 75 percent of its work was contracted out to private printers.

The bill also authorized the GPO's revolving fund, which financed its non-congressional printing operations. About $1 billion would flow through the fund in fiscal 1992. Most of that money was from executive branch agencies and was appropriated through other spending bills.

• **Office of the Attending Physician.** Based near the Capitol's Rotunda, Congress' health clinic employed 31 people, including three doctors, 14 nurses and 10 technicians. Its budget came from three accounts and totaled about $2.4 million. It provided health care to the Capitol Hill complex. The bill identified about $1.7 million for the physician's office; more than half reimbursed the Navy for military personnel and equipment.

The rest of the physician's total budget ($700,000 or so) came from the Architect of the Capitol's budget and paid the salaries of the nurses who staffed first aid rooms in various Capitol Hill buildings.

GENERAL PROVISIONS

The bill also included several changes in laws and rules related to Congress. The most significant would:

• Ease rules that limited gifts members and employees of both chambers could accept, as well as gift disclosure laws.

• Allow Senate child-care center employees to get health benefits. ■

Continued from p. 547

sage. Some senators said privately that they suspected the House was trying to embarrass them with the gift rules and punish them by forcing them to outlaw stipends that some senators received for hosting radio shows.

Many House members still were peeved at the many years of bashing they took over the franking issue, which subsided in 1990 when the House accepted Senate demands to limit members' penchant for bombarding constituents with self-promoting, government-paid mass mailings.

Moreover, House members continued to seethe over the Senate's handling of the pay issue in 1989. Senators at the last minute backed away from a two-step, 40 percent salary increase after House members had already approved it for themselves, leaving them to take the heat alone. Some House members also complained because senators did not delay their raise until after the next election, as the House had.

House GOP leader Michel hinted at such ill will in his floor speech on the bill: "We took the honorable course in the last Congress by doing what we did when we did it and how we did it." Democratic Rep. Fazio, a key 1989 pay-raise proponent, agreed.

"I think the House dealt with the pay raise courageously," he said. "We delayed taking the pay until a subsequent election had taken place."

The Senate pay raise gave House members considerable leverage over the particulars of the final bill, and Fazio and his allies got just about everything they wanted.

But the House members allowed their Senate colleagues to walk away with one plum: the $9,000 windfall.

The Senate's pay-raise provision simultaneously barred members from pocketing any more honoraria, the payments for speeches and appearances that the House forswore in 1989 to distance itself from special-interest money.

But the negotiators July 30 decided it would be unfair to require senators to forfeit speaking fees accepted before the bill was signed — letting them keep the full $23,068 allowed by law in 1991.

But the Senate had to pay a price for House approval of its pay raise — a provision barring senators from accepting stipends for hosting radio shows beginning in 1992.

"We want a level playing field," said House subcommittee Chairman Fazio.

Two pairs of senators participated in regular staged radio debates: Alan K. Simpson, R-Wyo., vs. Edward M. Kennedy, D-Mass., which aired five days a week; and Richard G. Lugar, R-Ind., vs. Tom Daschle, D-S.D., which aired 65 times a year, according to an Associated Press story about the practice. All but Kennedy, who declined compensation, were paid about $100 a show, the story said.

The House Committee on Standards of Official Conduct ruled earlier in 1991 that such stipends were prohibited under the House speaking-fee ban. But the Senate Ethics Committee in 1988 had decided that stipends were not honoraria and therefore were not covered by limits on speaking fees.

Simpson, who reported making $37,750 for his 1990 shows, said of the new prohibition, "It doesn't bother me at all."

Dole said he thought Senate rules should allow members to charge interest groups more than $2,000 for a speech, so long as it was donated to charity.

Dole's office said he had given $700,000 in honoraria to charities over the years. In 1990, he reported directing $47,700 to charities, churches and colleges, most in Kansas.

Dole had the support of fellow Republicans Simpson and Ted Stevens of Alaska. "If somebody wants to give $100,000 to the Boy Scouts in my name, what's wrong with that?" Stevens asked House conferees July 30. The House refused to go along.

An earlier effort by Senate Majority Leader George J. Mitchell of Maine to raise the pay for the majority and minority leaders in both chambers and for the Senate president pro tempore was abandoned. All five members made $138,900 after the bill was signed. Mitchell wanted something closer to the House Speaker's $160,600 but reportedly gave up after House leaders refused to agree.

House members also successfully insisted that the Senate bar its members from deriving any tax benefits from honoraria donated to charity. The tax code had blocked such benefits for House members.

No Disclosure

Although the stipend dispute was widely known, the gift-rule change was kept quiet until the last minute. Members of both chambers had complained that the rules for accepting gifts and reporting them on annual financial disclosure forms were confusing, particularly because the rules were different for each chamber.

The rules were toughened in 1989 as part of the same ethics law that boosted House members' pay and banned them from pocketing honoraria. Efforts then to make the rules uniform failed when the Senate refused to go along with a House proposal because senators considered it too strict.

Here is what they did in 1989:

The House barred its members from accepting gifts totaling more than $200 a year from anyone but relatives. That was an increase from $100, but the previous cap only applied to givers with a "direct interest in legislation," a vaguely defined term under House rules. House members also decided to raise the $200 limit automatically every three years to account for inflation.

Senators considered the House threshold too low and set the total for the Senate at $300 annually. But they retained an existing rule barring members from accepting gifts worth more than $100 from anyone with a direct interest in legislation — a term defined more narrowly in Senate rules to generally include only people and organizations with ties to registered lobbyists or political action committees.

Both chambers decided that gifts worth less than $75 did not have to be counted toward those limits, up from $50 in the House and $35 in the Senate.

And both retained governmentwide financial-disclosure requirements with some changes: Members and other officials were required to report who gave them $100 or more in gifts worth more than $75 each. The reporting threshold for travel and entertainment-related gifts was higher: $250.

All that would change under the last-minute deal engineered by Fazio and his Senate counterpart, Reid.

The new rules allowed members to accept up to $250 worth of gifts annually from anyone (up from $200 in the House and up from $100 under the Senate's provision on gifts from people with legislative interests). Members would not have to count gifts worth $100 or less (up from $75).

And all federal officials only had to disclose who gave them more than $250 in gifts (up from $100) worth more than $100 each (up from $75). The separate category for reporting travel and entertainment-related gifts was eliminated.

All of the new thresholds were to be raised automatically every three years to account for inflation in later years.

The disclosure changes meant that members of Congress and their employees had to report gifts they were not allowed to accept or gifts for which they had received waivers.

"If you got a gift that's legal, you don't have to report it," said Fazio.

Reporters regularly perused members' disclosures and publicized gifts, an embarrassing annual event for some members.

Common Cause, the public interest lobby that helped to push through the 1989 gift rules and supported the Senate pay raise because it banned speech fees, disagreed.

"You can accept $100 a day from a person or $100 a week — there's no limit," said Wertheimer, referring to the provision that gifts of $100 or less would not count toward the $250 limit. Wertheimer conceded that such behavior would run afoul of the rules if the member was found to be merely evading the limits. But he asked, "Who's going to enforce it, based on what information, since there's no disclosure?"

Wertheimer accused Congress of breaking the 1989 pay raise-ethics reform deal. "You can't justify this in the name of unifying the rules," he said. "You can't justify this by saying these matters haven't been looked at lately because we just looked at it in 1989. The only way to justify this is to say members are being greedy and grabby."

Common Cause sent telegrams to every member of Congress and stationed lobbyists off the House floor to plead with members to reject the rules. The effort was futile.

The new rules for Congress conflicted with the approach taken by the Office of Government Ethics. Relying on the same 1989 ethics law, the agency July 23 proposed much stricter limits. They sought to prohibit all executive branch employees (except the president and vice president) from accepting anything but the smallest gifts from almost anyone with any interest in the work of the employee's agency. Generally, gifts worth less than $25 would be allowed, but only if one source did not give more than $100 worth a year, with even the smallest gifts counting toward the total.

And even this exemption was limited, the agency said, because "the acceptance of gifts on a recurring or frequent basis, whether from the same or different sources, gives rise to an appearance of use of public office for private gain."

Most GAO Money Restored

The $2.3 billion legislative branch appropriations bill also:

- Increased spending by less than 4 percent over the previous year's $2.2 billion. Most of the increase went to House and Senate operations; the chambers got 10 percent and 7 percent increases, respectively.
- Cut the GAO's House-passed budget by $2.2 million to $438.7 million. Republicans favored the Senate's $6.5 million cut to signal displeasure with the GAO, which had been under fire recently for alleged bias toward Democrats. To address complaints that the agency had not kept Republicans up to date, conferees ordered it to provide leaders of both parties monthly lists of all new investigations. ■

Little New in Hard-Fought Interior Bill

The $12.3 billion conference agreement on the fiscal 1992 appropriations bill (HR 2686) for the Interior Department and related agencies was one of the most contentious in years. But in the end it was generally a lean version of the fiscal 1991 measure, with no major initiatives such as the 1991 bill's offshore oil exploration moratorium.

The fiscal 1991 Interior spending bill had totaled $11.7 billion. *(1990 Almanac, p. 870)*

Senate Appropriations Committee Chairman Robert C. Byrd, D-W.Va., said the fiscal 1992 bill was the most drawn-out he had participated in. The measure was debated for six days on the Senate floor, and the conference met four times over two weeks on more than 1,900 differences between the bills.

The House agreed to the conference report Oct. 24; and the Senate followed suit on Oct. 30 and then finally cleared the bill on Nov. 1.

Despite all the sound and fury, the final bill generally kept the status quo. The National Endowment for the Arts (NEA), often a battlefield over the issue of obscenity in the arts, escaped unscathed. There were no increases in grazing fees on public lands, much to the relief of Western lawmakers. There was no moratorium on mining patent claims, as called for by some members who sought to rewrite the 119-year-old mining law. *(Grazing fees, p. 214; mining patent reform, p. 217)*

There also was no language directing a recovery plan for the threatened northern spotted owl, which resided in the Pacific Northwest's timber-rich old-growth forests. However, Sen. Slade Gorton, D-Wash., won language directing the Fish and Wildlife Service to minimize job losses in considering such a plan. *(Endangered species, p. 209)*

Finally, there was no increase in the administrative costs states had to pay to get their share of royalties from oil and gas wells on public lands — something that would have netted the federal government $68 million but was opposed by Western states. *(Oil and gas royalties, p. 220)*

BOXSCORE

➡ **Fiscal 1992 appropriations for Interior Department and related agencies (HR 2686).** The $12.3 billion measure provided funding for programs under the Interior Department and agencies such as the Smithsonian Institution, National Endowment for the Humanities and National Endowment for the Arts.

Reports: HR 2686: H Rept 102-116; S Rept 102-122; conference report filed in the House, H Rept 102-256.

KEY ACTION

June 25 — HR 2686 passed the **House** by a vote of 345-76.

Sept. 19 — HR 2686 passed the **Senate** by a vote of 93-3.

Oct. 17 — HR 2686 approved by **House-Senate** conference.

Oct. 24 — **House** agreed to conference report by a 310-104 vote.

Oct. 30 — **Senate** agreed to conference report by a 93-4 vote.

Nov. 13 — HR 2686 signed by President Bush — PL 102-154.

HOUSE COMMITTEE ACTION

Western resource users found little to be happy about as the House Appropriations Subcommittee on Interior marked up its $13.2 billion fiscal 1992 spending bill June 6.

Over the objections of Western members, the subcommittee voted to raise grazing fees on public lands by a whopping 33 percent and reduced an already small timber-harvest level in the Northwest.

"This is something that Eastern folks simply don't understand," said Joe Skeen, R-N.M., who tried unsuccessfully to stop the grazing fee increase. He said the move would cost ranchers $10 million annually.

The subcommittee agreed to continue for another year a moratorium on oil drilling off the Pacific and Atlantic coasts and off the Florida Keys.

And the panel approved the first congressional steps to protect the Northwest's threatened salmon, appropriating $1.8 million for habitat improvement on the Columbia River and $7.5 million for management of anadromous fish nationwide.

As the bill was crafted, the Interior Subcommittee began the all-too-familiar struggle with domestic spending caps that were put in place with the 1990 budget agreement.

"It's like trying to put an oak tree back into an acorn," said Sidney R. Yates, D-Ill., the panel's chairman. "It's much more difficult this year because we have no flexibility."

Yates said that pressing needs, such as maintenance of parks and public lands and health care on Indian reservations, remained underfunded in the bill, even though the $13.2 billion total was 4 percent higher than the fiscal 1991 appropriation.

Resource users, however, found no ally in Yates, who wanted to lock in increases in grazing fees for five years and who also moved to lower the federal government's share of costs to administer mining on government lands.

Nonetheless, the Bureau of Land Management at about $909 million, the Parks Service at $1.37 billion and the Bureau of Indian Affairs at $1.57 billion all received slight increases over fiscal 1991 funding.

The Fish and Wildlife Service suffered cuts, receiving $686 million, as did the Bureau of Mines at $176 million and the Forest Service at $2.3 billion.

No program was safe. President Bush's touted tree-planting initiative, for example, was trimmed to $35 million from a requested $90 million.

It was those tight budget realities that prompted Les AuCoin, D-Ore., who feared an acrimonious session, to move to close the markup. The motion was approved, 8-2, with Yates and full committee Chairman Jamie L. Whitten, D-Miss., dissenting.

The Northwest fared relatively well in the deliberations. The panel set a timber sales preparation level of 3 billion board feet of wood in Washington and Oregon, down by about 400 million board feet from fiscal 1991. The average for the previous two years had been about 4 billion board feet.

The panel included language for the committee report directing the Forest Service to follow guidelines limiting below-cost timber sales that were set forth in a recent General Accounting Office report.

Brushing aside a Skeen effort to hold the line on grazing fees, the subcommittee voted 4-3 to raise the fee for ranch-

Interior

(In thousands of dollars)

	Fiscal 1991 Appropriation	President's Request	House Bill	Senate Bill	Final Bill
Interior Department					
Bureau of Land Management					
Management of lands	$ 497,491	$ 525,578	$ 516,865	$ 537,199	$ 532,149
Firefighting	167,880	222,879	122,010	222,879	120,473
Other	244,641	271,130	270,189	260,394	257,826
Subtotal	**$ 910,012**	**$ 1,019,587**	**$ 909,064**	**$ 1,020,472**	**$ 910,448**
Fish and Wildlife Service					
Resource management	473,776	517,137	509,891	526,675	511,905
Construction and anadromous fish	92,625	50,147	71,102	96,750	113,447
Other	127,478	103,023	110,368	120,126	122,827
Subtotal	**$ 693,879**	**$ 670,307**	**$ 691,361**	**$ 743,551**	**$ 748,179**
National Park Service					
Operations	876,699	970,526	969,047	949,976	953,498
Construction	270,446	115,896	237,506	202,097	272,326
Land acquisition, state aid	136,792	117,645	108,365	84,450	105,227
Other	63,968	57,825	62,546	54,395	56,117
Subtotal	**$ 1,347,905**	**$ 1,261,892**	**$ 1,377,464**	**$ 1,290,918**	**$ 1,387,168**
Bureau of Indian Affairs					
Indian programs	1,320,044	750,657	1,283,630	803,489	1,220,503
Construction	167,653	79,879	212,856	103,735	203,565
Education	—	418,616	—	431,541	—
Other	70,844	150,731	106,208	199,516	105,974
Subtotal	**$ 1,558,541**	**$ 1,399,883**	**$ 1,602,694**	**$ 1,538,281**	**$ 1,530,042**
Geological Survey	570,698	563,100	589,499	569,457	582,619
Minerals Management Service	195,995	234,124	208,090	220,614	204,461
Bureau of Mines	181,227	156,123	175,890	172,849	174,464
Office of Surface Mining	309,801	271,993	301,950	299,969	298,984
Territorial affairs	178,997	104,481	157,138	121,611	141,629
Departmental offices	110,543	143,838	129,216	120,581	126,758
TOTAL, Interior Department	**$ 6,057,598**	**$ 5,825,328**	**$ 6,142,366**	**$ 6,098,303**	**$ 6,104,752**
Forest Service (Agriculture Department)					
National forest system	1,298,333	1,377,393	1,280,947	1,379,605	1,342,530
Forest research	167,629	163,230	183,572	176,850	180,509
Firefighting	297,937	302,203	189,803	302,203	187,411
Construction	277,133	286,148	350,420	265,545	271,711
Timber receipts (goes to general Treasury)	(−96,280)	(−94,872)	(−94,872)	(−94,872)	(−94,872)
Other	278,389	354,149	303,774	285,600	277,991
TOTAL, Forest Service	**$ 2,319,421**	**$ 2,483,123**	**$ 2,308,516**	**$ 2,409,803**	**$ 2,260,152**
Energy Department					
Clean coal technology	−565,000	−150,000	—	—	−50,000
Fossil energy research	458,750	227,005	445,989	454,015	444,332
Naval Petroleum Reserve	223,135	222,300	238,200	222,300	232,335
Energy conservation	495,177	325,934	559,661	526,084	536,322
Strategic Petroleum Reserve	200,576	185,858	63,173	63,173	62,377
Other	83,148	99,182	294,822	268,401	104,450
TOTAL, Energy Department	**$ 895,786**	**$ 910,279**	**$ 1,601,845**	**$ 1,533,973**	**$1,329,816**
Other Related Agencies					
Indian Health	1,577,569	1,423,611	1,727,923	1,689,159	1,705,954
Smithsonian Institution	326,117	357,150	342,079	333,124	331,837
National Endowment for the Arts	174,083	174,083	178,200	174,083	175,955
National Endowment for the Humanities	170,005	178,200	178,200	175,000	175,955
Other agencies	226,971	239,381	238,398	231,158	227,846
GRAND TOTAL	**$ 11,747,550**	**$ 11,595,927**	**$ 12,717,527**	**$ 12,644,603**	**$ 12,312,267**

SOURCE: House Appropriations Committee

ers and sheepherders on public lands from $1.97 per animal unit month (AUM) to $2.62. (An AUM was the amount of forage required to feed one cow or five sheep for a month.)

The full House in 1990 adopted an amendment to the fiscal 1991 Interior spending bill that would have increased the grazing fee sharply. But the provision was dropped in conference with the Senate.

There was little controversy over the modestly higher appropriations for the Smithsonian Institution ($342 million), the National Endowment for the Arts and the National Endowment for the Humanities (both at $178.2 million).

The subcommittee also put back into the appropriations bill $150 million for a fifth round of research into clean-burning coal technology that the administration had tried to cut.

Full Committee

The House Appropriations Committee on June 19 approved a $12.9 billion spending bill for the Interior Department and related agencies.

The lack of contention over the spending level for fiscal 1992 was in marked contrast to debate over the fiscal 1991 spending bill, which was defined by furious arguments over spending for the controversial National Endowment for the Arts and a provision seeking to protect the northern spotted owl.

One reason that the committee spent time debating new fees instead of spending levels was that it had very little room in which to maneuver. Two provisions sought to raise more money, however. Most infuriating to Western members was language raising grazing fees for ranchers by 33 percent — to $2.62 a month to graze cattle on public lands.

Skeen had been expected to offer an amendment seeking to strip that provision from the bill. But he chose not to do so when Yates assured him that committee members would not object if Skeen moved to pull the provision from the bill during House floor debate.

Yates said that another fee provision — one to charge mining patent claim holders $100 a year if they wished to keep their claims active — also was expected to face a floor challenge. The goal of the mining fee provision was to ensure that mining claim holders used their claims to tap mineral resources. Program critics said some claim holders were speculators or developers and abused the law to get access to inexpensive land.

Mining claim holders in 1991 had to perform only $100 worth of "work" annually to keep their claims active. Appropriators were critical of the $100 requirement in the committee report and said it "bears no relationship to the serious intent to develop claims."

Provisions to protect the environment from abuse were sprinkled throughout the bill.

For example, with no debate, the committee approved a provision keeping most of the outer continental shelf closed to oil and gas drilling. The moratorium kept funds from being spent for leasing or selling underwater oil fields off the coasts of California, the Florida Panhandle, and in the Gulf of Mexico and the North Atlantic.

"Right now, there's a fence around the whole country," Yates said. "The only coasts where moratoria are not in effect are off the coasts of Alabama, Louisiana, Mississippi and Texas." The moratoriums on drilling were a response to fears that technology was not adequate to protect coastlines and the populations that used them in the event of a massive oil spill.

Despite that concern, the committee voted to chop more than $3 million from an Interior Department program, known as Coastal America, that sought to better coordinate federal efforts to protect coastal environments.

Some committee members said the move was ill-conceived. But appropriators provided money for other new environmental programs, including:

- $348,000 to prepare an environmental impact statement in anticipation of the reintroduction of endangered wolves in Yellowstone National Park — a provision opposed by some ranchers whose livestock roamed nearby.
- $1.75 million to protect the Pacific yew — the bark of which yielded a cancer-suppressing drug. The money, which was to come from the Forest Service budget, was intended to develop a unified federal effort to protect the tree, which previously was considered nothing more than a big weed.
- $35 million for the Fish and Wildlife Service for its endangered species program.

Though there was little debate over the fate of the threatened northern spotted owl, the committee approved several initiatives to regulate the cutting of old-growth forests in the Northwest — home to the nocturnal predator.

The panel recommended that the Northwest timber harvest level be set at 3 billion board feet for 1992, about 400 million board feet less than in 1990.

The panel also banned the export of unprocessed logs harvested from federal lands. In recent years, exports of unprocessed logs had increased. The exports were cited by some as a reason for the decline in the Northwest lumber milling industry.

HOUSE FLOOR ACTION

With Western lawmakers protesting every step of the way, the House on June 25 passed HR 2686, a $12.7 billion fiscal 1992 appropriations bill for the Interior Department and related agencies that would have more than quadrupled grazing fees on public rangelands over four years.

In addition, two attacks on the National Endowment for the Arts failed by large margins.

The most contentious issue in HR 2686, which passed 345-76, was how much to charge Western ranchers to use federal rangelands. *(Vote 196, p. 48-H)*

That was settled when lawmakers adopted, 232-192, an amendment offered by Mike Synar, D-Okla., boosting fees. Members had earlier stripped from the bill language containing a more moderate fee hike after Skeen raised a technical objection. *(Vote 194, p. 48-H)*

Western lawmakers said the existing $1.97 per animal unit month fee was a fair one, even though studies from the General Accounting Office and elsewhere had determined that the average market rate for Western rangeland was $9.22.

Critics of the fee contended that it was an unwarranted subsidy for a select handful of ranchers. They were joined by environmentalists who said the fee encouraged overgrazing and the destruction of the West's fragile environment.

Proponents of an increase in grazing fees — led by Synar, George "Buddy" Darden, D-Ga., and Chester G. Atkins, D-Mass. — focused at first on the economics of what Synar called "one of the gross subsidies throughout this nation's history."

Below-market fees had allowed 2 percent of the nation's herds to chew "their way through $650 million of subsidies over the last five years," Synar said.

The amendment raised fees from $1.97 to $8.70 per AUM by 1995. Synar said the fee increase let the government run the grazing program "like a business."

Western lawmakers vehemently opposed the amendment. Some, such as Skeen, went so far as to say the grazing fees in effect were too high, given the amount of work ranchers had to do to keep up federal rangelands as part of their grazing permit.

But others, such as Pat Williams, D-Mont., acknowledged that the low fees amounted to a subsidy, conceding that they offered a "little bit of help for our cattle people." Williams then argued that the existing system should be retained because it was helping to keep the economy of the West afloat for thousands of small operators and their dependent businesses.

But Atkins attacked the idea of small ranchers depending on grazing fees. "We find that 90 percent of that acreage is controlled by wealthy individuals, by hobby farmers, by corporations, by conglomerates and syndicates," he said.

In the end, when the amendment to increase grazing fees passed, reform proponents lost 19 votes from a similar vote in 1990.

The West, however, fared better under other parts of the bill dealing with public lands. A provision in the bill that would have effectively banned the export of unprocessed logs harvested on federal lands was removed at the urging of Harold L. Volkmer, D-Mo.

No attempts were made on the floor to change a deal worked out in a closed committee session to lower the amount of timber harvested in the old-growth forests of the Northwest to about 3 billion board feet in 1992, a moderate decrease from existing harvest levels.

A provision that would have required mining claim holders to pay a $100 annual holding fee to keep their claims was stripped out of the bill after Nick J. Rahall II, D-W.Va., objected to it.

The existing requirement was that claim holders had to perform only $100 worth of "work" each year on their claims to keep them active. Environmentalists said that claim holders had often scarred their land needlessly to justify the work requirement.

Rahall also objected to a provision that would have raised the state share of mining administration costs by 50 percent.

Slightly less contentious was a last-minute attempt, spearheaded by Philip M. Crane, R-Ill., to kill the $178.2 million appropriation for the NEA. Crane said that the federal government had no business funding the arts and that if it did there would always be the question of government regulation leading to censorship. The amendment failed 66-361. *(Vote 192, p. 48-H)*

Another unsuccessful attack on the NEA, from Cliff Stearns, R-Fla., to strike $7.4 million, or 4.2 percent, of the endowment's $178.2 million appropriation, sent perhaps a stronger message to the endowment. The amendment failed, 196-228, but by a much slimmer margin. *(Vote 193, p. 48-H)*

Though the $12.7 billion spending bill was less than 4 percent higher than the fiscal 1991 appropriation, several members noted that the bill contained an off-budget $213 million in "emergency" firefighting money that in all probability would be used, considering firefighting costs of past years.

Minnesota Democrat Timothy J. Penny said that to label the firefighting appropriation as emergency funding was a "phony and a blatant subversion of the budget agreement."

That was a view shared by the White House, which in a letter to members called the attempt a "gimmick designed to force the president to declare an emergency for clearly anticipated costs."

Penny and Fred Upton, R-Mich., offered an amendment to cut the entire bill by $213 million to put the firefighting money on budget, but it failed, 169-249. *(Vote 195, p. 48-H)*

Overall, because of tight budgetary times, the bill had more losers than winners, said subcommittee Chairman Yates.

He noted that the Bureau of Land Management, the Fish and Wildlife Service, the Bureau of Mines, and the Forest Service all received less money in fiscal 1992 than in fiscal 1991.

SENATE COMMITTEE ACTION

The Senate Appropriations markup July 24 of HR 2686 was not supposed to be controversial: The measure came in at $91 million less than the House version, and it contained no controversial provisions to increase grazing fees, halt mining patents or save the northern spotted owl.

But one provision in the $12.6 billion spending bill so upset Western senators that committee member Pete V. Domenici, R-N.M., darkly warned of a floor fight, and Wyoming Republican Malcolm Wallop sent word that he was considering a filibuster.

The object of the senators' ire was a provision to raise the states' share of the costs of collecting royalties from oil and gas wells on public land — a program administered by the Minerals Management Service (MMS). The change could have cost Domenici's fiscally squeezed state nearly $21 million a year.

Instead of the existing program in which the states paid 25 percent of the program's administration costs, language in the bill increased the percentage to 50 — removing $68.2 million from the royalty fund before it was distributed to the states. Because mineral-rich states such as Wyoming and New Mexico received a higher percentage of the royalties, they would have suffered a disproportionate cut. Domenici said that was unfair because paperwork costs were the same regardless of the value of the fossil fuels extracted.

"This is not a fee, it's a tax," Domenici said.

Domenici told Appropriations Chairman Byrd that Westerners "will not agree to this; we'll have a full-blown argument on the floor over this."

Though no amendments were offered to strip that controversial provision, Don Nickles, R-Okla., the Interior Subcommittee's ranking Republican, said that the proposed collection system might need to be modified.

The Interior appropriations bill was marked up by the subcommittee and approved by the full committee in a six-hour period.

James M. Jeffords, R-Vt., said he was seriously considering sponsoring a grazing fees amendment similar to the one authored by Rep. Ralph Regula, R-Ohio, in the Bureau of Land Management (BLM) reauthorization bill (HR 1096) and passed by the House on July 23. *(BLM reauthorization, p. 216)*

The rest of the bill was relatively free of contention. Chairman Byrd noted that the fiscal squeeze was tighter in the Senate than in the House, despite having the same spending allocation. While the House took $213 million in firefighting expenses and designated them as "emergency"

Continued on p. 565

Interior Provisions

The $12.3 billion spending bill for the Interior Department and related agencies more than any other appropriations measure supported the nation's vast public lands, most of which were in the West.

The bill provided money for the preservation of lands — both for the enjoyment of people and the survival of wildlife. The lands were managed by the Agriculture Department's Forest Service and by the Interior Department's Bureau of Land Management and National Park Service. The bill financed the management of mining and timber cutting on public lands. It provided money for an array of funds that allowed for the purchase of environmentally sensitive land, state recreation grants and the protection of endangered plants and animals. Among them was the Land and Water Conservation Fund, which was established in 1965 and spread $321.4 million among four agencies.

Social and economic development programs for American Indians administered by Interior's Bureau of Indian Affairs got more money than any other Interior agency. Indian health programs were funded in the bill through the Indian Health Service, an arm of the Department of Health and Human Services. Indian education programs were funded through the Education Department. The bill also supported an array of cultural programs at the Smithsonian Institution, the National Gallery of Art and the National Endowments for the Arts and Humanities.

Spending levels included in this summary reflect a 1.26 percent across-the-board cut approved by conferees.

INTERIOR DEPARTMENT

Bureau of Land Management

The Bureau of Land Management was provided $910.4 million to manage 269.5 million acres of federal land, mostly in the West. The lands were used for grazing 4.3 million head of livestock on vast rangeland, logging on 4 million acres of forest and mining of a wide array of minerals and precious metals. Bureau lands also provided more opportunities for recreation in the West than any other agency except the National Forest Service.

• **Land management.** Appropriators provided $532.1 million for the bureau's approximately 10,500 workers to monitor, inventory and keep up the bureau's lands.

• **Wild horses.** Reflecting a controversy that simmered in the mid-1980s over the slaughter of wild horses, the bill had for several years prohibited the bureau from spending money to kill healthy, unadopted wild horses or burros living on its land. The language was pushed by Bill Green, R-N.Y., a member of the House Appropriations Committee, who had long been concerned with animal protection issues. The bureau could still transfer horses, sterilize them or put them up for adoption and was budgeted $14.43 million for wild horse management.

• **Firefighting.** House appropriators set aside $120.5 million to be used for firefighting in 1992. That included non-emergency firefighting, fire prevention and activities such as planned burns, the stockpiling of firefighting equipment and the rehabilitation of scorched land. Appropriators refused to fund $100.9 million in emergency wildfire fighting funds sought by the administration. Instead, House appropriators placed the $100.9 million in a separate "emergency firefighting fund" to be used only if the president declared a budgetary emergency. Conferees agreed that beginning in fiscal 1993, the emergency fund could only be tapped to pay for combating fires if firefighting costs exceeded the 10-year average.

• **Payments to local governments.** To partially offset revenue losses, the bureau provided money known as "payments in lieu of taxes" to local governments that had nontaxpaying federal lands within their boundaries. The funds could be used as local governments saw fit. Appropriators allotted $103.7 million for such payments.

• **Land acquisition.** The bureau was given $25 million to purchase 45 sites across the country, including $700,000 to protect the habitat of the endangered desert tortoise in California. Among other parcels to be purchased were two sites in Washington state: $950,000 for an ecologically sensitive area in Grande Ronde and $2.3 million for the Yakima River Canyon. Norm Dicks, D-Wash., a member of the House Appropriations Interior Subcommittee, called for the purchase of both parcels.

• **Range improvements.** Much of the bureau's land was range that required extensive maintenance. The land had to be be seeded, fenced and weeded. Breeding grounds for fish and wildlife also had to be restored. Appropriators set aside $10.69 million for this effort — funds that came from grazing receipts.

• **Grazing.** The bill contained no increase in the fees ranchers paid the federal government to graze their herds on public lands, despite a strong House vote in June to more than quadruple such fees by 1995. The existing fee was $1.97 an animal unit month (AUM), the amount of forage a cow and a calf typically consumed in that time. The formula used to set fees had not changed since passage of the Public Range Lands Improvement Act in 1978, and fees had actually gone down in recent years. The fee was substantially lower than that charged by private pastures, and the bureau had said grazing fee revenues did not cover program costs. Ranchers contended that grazing fees were fair and reflected costs they incurred maintaining federal land and obeying layers of government regulation. Opponents of low grazing fees said they encouraged overgrazing of fragile arid rangeland and gave Western ranchers an unfair competitive advantage over those who depended upon private rangeland.

House appropriators had proposed increasing the fee to $2.62 an AUM in 1992 — but that was overturned when the whole House approved, 232-192, an amendment by Mike Synar, D-Okla., to raise the fee to $4.35 in fiscal 1992, gradually increasing to $8.70 an AUM by fiscal 1995. But the Senate turned down an amendment by James M. Jeffords, R-Vt., for a more modest boost to $5.13 by fiscal 1996. Conferees chose to stay with the status quo. They directed the Agriculture and the Interior secretaries to issue by April 30, 1992, a revised report on grazing fees. Among issues the report was to examine were alternatives to the existing grazing fee formula and the extent to which Western ranchers depended upon public lands. The last grazing fee report was issued in 1986 and sparked concern about the issue.

• **Oregon and California grant lands.** Some 2.6 million acres in southern Oregon and Northern California were granted to the Oregon and California Railroad Co. in 1866 and reacquired by the federal government in 1916. They provided some of the best timber in the country, and the majority of the 750 million board feet of wood the bureau was targeting for sale in 1991 was found here. But these areas, known as O&C lands, included large swaths of the old-growth forest critical to the survival of the threatened northern spotted owl.

In October, Interior Secretary Manuel Lujan Jr. decided to convene a high-level federal panel, known as the "God Squad," to consider granting an exemption to the Endangered Species Act after weighing a host of economic factors. The committee was called to resolve how much of the forests in this area had to be set aside for the preservation of the owl. Appropriators remained silent about the dispute but did direct in their report that the Forest Service consider the owl in setting timber sale levels. Appropriators gave the bureau an extra $10.1 million to replant forests and cover administrative costs. The total appropriation to tend, build on and buy land for the O&C forests was $89.1 million.

U.S. Fish and Wildlife Service

The Fish and Wildlife Service was allotted $748.2 million to study, conserve, manage and protect sports fisheries and wildlife resources on 91.1 million acres. The land encompassed 482 national wildlife refuges and 28 waterfowl sanctuaries and breeding areas. The service was now emphasizing "biodiversity," the conservation of entire ecosystems, not just individual species. It also was the lead agency in implementing the 1973 Endangered Species Act.

Appropriators allotted $511.9 million for resource management programs. Specific designations included: $500,000 to keep a wetlands advisory office open in Chicago at the request of Rep. Sidney R. Yates, D-Ill., chairman of the Interior Appropriations Subcommittee; $700,000 to keep an urban wetlands project open in the Portland, Ore., district of House Interior Appropriations Subcommittee member Les AuCoin, D, and $1.75 million to continue an ecosystems study project in Washington state that was pushed by Senate appropriator Brock Adams, D-Wash., and supported by House appropriator Dicks.

- **Endangered species.** After appropriators moved to cut the administration's $10.2 million request for listing endangered species, conferees settled on $7.3 million for the program — $3 million higher than fiscal 1991's level. Overall, appropriators penciled in $34.8 million for all endangered species programs. That included a new program that allowed states to apply for grants to operate their own projects to protect endangered species.
- **Gray wolf.** The bill prohibits the Fish and Wildlife Service from spending any money to reintroduce the rare gray wolf into Yellowstone National Park and in central Idaho. In subcommittee, House appropriators had originally directed the service to begin implementing a 1987 plan to reintroduce the wolf into the park. But conferees weakened the language and directed the service to simply keep the plan on the table. The language was inserted at the urging of Rep. Wayne Owens, D-Utah, a longtime proponent of reintroducing the wolf. But House and Senate negotiators directed the service to prepare an environmental impact statement on the topic within 18 months.
- **Endangered trout and salmon.** The Northwest's Snake River steelhead trout and salmon stocks were declining precipitously. Appropriators had made saving them a priority and allotted $10.8 million to build a dozen hatcheries in Idaho and Oregon. The Bonneville Power Administration had agreed to reimburse the government for the hatcheries at the end of fiscal 1992.

Salmon and steelhead trout are born in fresh water but spend adulthood in the ocean.

In order to breed, they make a pilgrimage back to their original spawning ground, something that had been made more difficult by the presence of federal dams backing up the Snake River. Another $52 million was appropriated for hatcheries and fish management nationwide.

- **Construction.** Appropriators added $63.7 million in projects to the $49.7 million in administration projects that they agreed to fund, providing for a $113.4 million appropriation. The districts and states of appropriators were among some of the beneficiaries. Added was an $8.2 million national fishery research center in Seattle at the urging of Dicks of Washington; a $5 million national fish hatchery in Mora, N.M., in the district of Rep. Bill Richardson, D-N.M., who testified for the project; a $12.7 million training facility in Senate Appropriations Committee Chairman Robert C. Byrd's home state of West Virginia; and a $300,000 study of the East Coast's declining striped bass population at the request of Rep. Walter B. Jones, D-N.C., chairman of the Merchant Marine and Fisheries Committee.
- **Natural Resource Damage Assessment and Restoration Fund.** This was a new revolving fund that made money available to federal agencies to assess and map cleanup strategies for environmental disasters such as the 1989 *Exxon Valdez* oil spill. Penalties paid by polluters would be used to replenish the fund. Appropriators specified that the fund be used to pay for a study of the polluted Commencement Bay industrial area in Tacoma, Wash., in the district of House appropriator Dicks. Appropriators provided $4.3 million to start up the fund.
- **Land acquisition.** Appropriators dropped seven administration projects but added 24 of their own by boosting to $98.9 million the administration's request of $62 million for land acquisition. The projects were funded under the Land and Water Conservation Fund, which was established in 1965 to buy land to protect wetlands and fish and wildlife habitats and to provide recreation. Money for the fund came mainly from offshore oil leasing royalties and a motorboat fuel tax. This account garnered a number of member requests, including $2 million to expand the Cypress Creek Wildlife Refuge in Union County, Ill., a project requested by Rep. Glenn Poshard, D-Ill.; $2 million for an environmental training center in Byrd's home state of West Virginia; and $350,000 to buy an easement to protect 50 acres near Walden Pond in the Concord, Mass., district of House Interior Appropriations Subcommittee member Chester G. Atkins, a Democrat.
- **Cooperative Endangered Species Conservation Fund**. The $6.6 million provided for the conservation fund was $900,000 higher than requested by the administration — good news for states eligible to receive money from this fund for the conservation of threatened and endangered species. Appropriators called for most of the extra funding to go to Oregon, Washington and California to help save the northern spotted owl, and to New Mexico, home of the Mexican spotted owl, a threatened cousin.
- **National Wildlife Refuge Fund**. This fund, which came from user fees, went to local governments that had lost revenues because government-owned refuges generated no tax revenues, in the same way the Bureau of Land Management offered payments in lieu of revenues. Appro-

priators allotted $11.8 million. The fees were only expected to raise $5 million. Though this politically popular program had almost doubled since 1988, the service estimated it would only be able to reimburse local governments for 84 percent of their lost tax revenues.

• **Miscellaneous.** The bill allotted $1.2 million for the federal African Elephant Conservation Fund, which was supported by the administration and was a cause of Rep. Anthony C. Beilenson, D-Calif. Appropriators also directed that the Tinicum National Environmental Center in Philadelphia be renamed the John Heinz National Wildlife Refuge in honor of the late Pennsylvania Republican senator, who was killed in a plane crash on April 4.

National Park Service

The National Park Service, founded in 1916, sought to conserve natural conditions, scenery and wildlife in the country's 357 national parks, monuments and reservations, and to make those parks easily accessible to anyone who wished to use them. In 1990, Park Service facilities had a record 258.7 million visitors.

Responding to the deterioration of crowded national parks, appropriators increased the Park Service's maintenance and operation budget by $89 million, to a total of $953.5 million for fiscal 1992. Appropriators took on a continuing dispute over long-term contracts given to park concessionaires. Critics charged that some concessionaires were paying too little for the right to sell goods in national parks and that outdated contracts should be rewritten. Appropriators addressed the issue by directing the Park Service to ensure that new contracts could be ended for good cause and that the Park Service be allowed to keep any improvements, such as stands and buildings, as long as concessionaires were compensated.

• **Urban parks.** Though the administration requested no money for the maintenance of urban parks, lawmakers set aside $4.9 million for the nation's cities, which would match the funds. Recipients included Boston's Revolutionary War-era National Historic Park and San Francisco's Golden Gate National Recreation Area.

• **Manassas Battlefield.** Irked by reports that the Park Service was going out of its way to accommodate the equestrian activities of Vice President Dan Quayle's family and other administration officials at the Civil War battlefield in Manassas, Va., Senate appropriators specifically barred the use of funds to build stables there, and conferees agreed.

• **Land acquisition and roads.** The service operated a network of about 10,000 miles of roads and was expected to receive $95 million in federal highway funds to maintain and operate those roads. Among the larger road construction projects were $11 million for a project in Yellowstone National Park and $6 million to upgrade roads near the monuments in the nation's capital. For buying new land, the Parks Service was allocated $105.2 million, including $6 million requested by Senate appropriator Pete V. Domenici, R-N.M., for the Petroglyphs National Monument project in New Mexico.

• **Construction.** House appropriators set aside a generous $156.4 million over and above the administration's list of construction projects. The administration had requested $115.9 million. Appropriators added $13.7 million for buildings at Crater Lake National Park in Oregon, $4.7 million for building at the Gateway National Recreation Area along the New York-New Jersey border and $3 million for construction of the Lyndon B. Johnson National Historic Park in Texas. The Senate bill set aside $1 million for the renovation of Tad Gormley Stadium in New Orleans in the home state of Senate appropriator J. Bennett Johnston, a Democrat. The $1 million was diverted from several wetlands study funds. Appropriators agreed to provide $272.3 million for construction activities.

• **The Kennedy Center.** The Park Service was responsible for all operations at the John F. Kennedy Center for the Performing Arts in Washington, D.C., that did not deal with the performing arts, such as visitor information and maintenance. Appropriators provided $22.7 million for those activities.

U.S. Geological Survey

The Geological Survey made more maps than any other organization in the United States. It also classified public lands, surveyed groundwater and studied the solar system. The bill altered the agency's name to the United States Geological Survey.

The agency was given an extra $15.9 million to study volcano- and earthquake-prone areas, bringing total funds for such geological studies to $67 million. Lawmakers also added $5.1 million to continue ongoing studies of shoreline areas in Illinois, Massachusetts, Alabama, Mississippi, Louisiana and Texas. Appropriators allotted a total of $582.6 million for the survey for fiscal 1992.

Mineral Management Service

The Mineral Management Service was provided $204.5 million to develop mineral leases, both offshore and on federal and Indian lands, and to collect royalties from them. Appropriators sought to raise to 50 percent the states' share of the cost of collecting these royalties to reap the government an additional $68 million annually. But they were rebuffed on the floor. In the House, Nick J. Rahall II, D-W.Va., objected to the change, saying it amounted to new legislation. In the Senate, Malcolm Wallop, R-Wyo., and other Western lawmakers were able to win approval of an amendment effectively keeping the state share of costs at its existing 25 percent. In conference, negotiators left the fees unchanged. Western states depended on the royalties to fund important programs such as education and were vehemently opposed to any change. Congress did direct the service, in cooperation with the Bureau of Land Management and the Forest Service, to study revising the way in which the royalties were collected and distributed, with an eye to perhaps giving more responsibilities to the states.

• **Offshore oil.** The outer continental shelf begins three miles out from the nation's coastline. In many places, exploration had shown the shelf to have potential for oil and gas production. However, oil spills such as the infamous 1969 blowout of a rig off the California coast near Santa Barbara had led to the banning of offshore leasing and oil exploration — principally through limitations imposed on annual appropriations bills. Appropriators, with the support of the administration, expanded the ban to cover Bristol Bay in Alaska, the eastern Gulf of Mexico off the Florida coast and key areas off the Atlantic and Pacific coasts. Despite the bans, there was still a good deal of exploration and oil extraction in outer continental shelf areas. A total of $102.6 million was appropriated for the program, including administrative costs of leasing the lands and evaluating their resource potential.

Bureau of Mines

Though the administration proposed cutting the bureau's research budget by nearly 25 percent for fiscal 1992, appropriators restored most of the money. Both Yates and Byrd were strong supporters of the nation's coal mining industry and considered mine research an investment in the safety and productivity of the nation's mines. The bureau studied mine safety, disaster prevention and occupational health issues. Appropriators provided the bureau $174.5 million for fiscal 1992.

Surface Mining

The Office of Surface Mining Reclamation and Enforcement issued regulations governing about 3,600 commercial mining operations and oversaw the reclamation of the land once it was mined. Appropriators budgeted $187.8 million for the Abandoned Mine Reclamation Fund, $11.2 million less than fiscal 1991.

The fund was made up of fees levied on coal producers. Appropriators directed that the agency not lay off 23 employees in Wilkes-Barre, Pa., as had been planned. The move came at the request of Yates and fellow Interior Appropriations Subcommittee member John P. Murtha, D-Pa. Lawmakers also criticized agency officials for borrowing money from the states' abandoned mine fund and directed them not to do so in the future. Appropriators set aside $299 million for these activities.

AMERICAN INDIANS

Federal programs for American Indians funded under this bill were administered by Interior's Bureau of Indian Affairs, the Department of Health and Human Services' Indian Health Service and the Education Department.

The Bureau of Indian Affairs was the largest recipient of Interior dollars, providing social service, education and natural resource development to American Indians. The bureau had not been overhauled in recent years despite a November 1989 proposal to drastically reshape it made by the Senate Indian Affairs Special Committee on Investigations, a special investigatory panel set up to probe alleged fraud and abuse in federal Indian programs. Such a change awaited the findings of an intra-agency task force reviewing various reorganization plans, and the bill forbade any reorganization proposal from going forward until that task force reported to Congress, perhaps not until 1993. Yates had long championed the needs of Indians, and his panel was resisting attempts to reorganize the bureau. Appropriators budgeted $1.5 billion for bureau operations.

The Indian Health Service, a division of the U.S. Public Health Service, was committed to providing health and medical services to the 1 million American Indians and native Alaskans. Its fiscal 1992 appropriation of $1.7 billion was slightly larger than the bureau's appropriation.

Appropriators harshly criticized the administration's budget request after citing as "absurd" and "beyond belief" its budget assumptions. Administration officials projected that collections from private health insurers would increase to $129 million in fiscal 1992 from only $3.7 million in fiscal 1990.

- **Indian construction**. Lawmakers provided a $35.9 million boost for bureau construction programs, mainly to build new schools on Indian reservations. Appropriators called for the construction of five new schools — on the Cheyenne River Reservation in South Dakota; in Rock Point, Ariz.; in Philadelphia, Miss.; in Dunseith, N.D.; and in Lawrence, Kan. The administration sought no construction funds for the schools. Appropriators allotted $203.6 million to build roads, fish hatcheries, irrigation systems and buildings on Indian reservations.
- **Navajo-Hopi land dispute.** Since Congress sought to settle a centuries-old land dispute with passage of a 1974 law divvying up disputed land between neighboring Hopi and Navajo tribes in Arizona, the bureau had been attempting to resettle those who ended up on the wrong side of boundary lines. The law guaranteed new housing to resettled Indian families. The Office of Navajo and Hopi Indian Relocation still had to resettle about 900 families into new homes. The bureau also had to provide housing to others who moved before their houses were built. Appropriators provided $25.8 million for the resettlement program.
- **Indian education**. Senate appropriators accepted one of the recommendations of the Senate's special Indian investigatory panel and placed the Bureau of Indian Affairs' education programs in a separate account to increase accountability. House appropriators sought to continue funding the programs through the bureau — a position that eventually prevailed in conference. Indian education programs were budgeted $411.7 million, $132.8 million less than they received in fiscal 1991. Lawmakers also provided $76.5 million for the Education Department's Indian teaching programs.
- **Indian health facilities.** Appropriators provided $274.3 million and dramatically increased funding for the repair, maintenance and building of hospitals to serve Indians in fiscal 1992 through the Indian Health Service. The administration had requested only $12.4 million for such facilities — a drop of $154 million from what appropriators had budgeted in fiscal 1991.

Territories

The Office of Territorial and International Affairs was provided $141.6 million for fiscal 1992 to manage the various Pacific and Caribbean islands administered by or associated with the United States — American Samoa, Guam, Northern Mariana Islands, the uninhabited Palmyra Atoll in the Pacific Ocean and the U.S. Virgin Islands in the Caribbean. It also administered Palau and provided aid to the independent Marshall Islands and Micronesia. Among other projects, appropriators approved an additional $15.5 million to continue to help the Virgin Islands recover from 1989's Hurricane Hugo. Appropriators criticized the government of American Samoa for its deficit. They also set aside $500,000 to control the brown tree snake, a 5- to 10-foot reptile that had decimated Guam's bird population and was feared to be spreading to other islands. Appropriators provided $100,000 to train fruit-sniffing beagles in Hawaii to help detect illegally imported produce.

Department Offices

Appropriators provided $126.8 million for fiscal 1992, an increase of $16.3 million over the fiscal 1991 appropriation for the operation of Interior's offices of the Secretary, Solicitor and Inspector General and for the national Indian Gaming Commission and the Oil Spill Emergency Fund.

RELATED AGENCIES

Forest Service

Appropriators provided the Agriculture Department's Forest Service $2.26 billion for fiscal 1992 to manage 191 million acres of forestland. Its major goal was to conserve forests. Forest Service lands provided about 40 percent of the recreational opportunities available on federal lands. The service also sold its timber resources and allowed private companies to cut down 8.5 billion to 11 billion board feet a year — something that had become increasingly controversial in the old-growth forests of the Pacific Northwest. Its forests and grasslands were used by 11,000 cattle ranching operations and provided about 55 percent of the annual water yields of the Western states.

• **Research.** Lawmakers allotted $180.5 million to study pesticides and ways to protect forests from fire, disease, beetles and other insects. Appropriators added more than 80 small new projects. At the suggestion of Yates, appropriators allotted $1.7 million for research on the Pacific yew, a tree whose bark had been found to be a promising source of the cancer-fighting compound Taxol. Appropriators also directed that money be set aside for programs dealing with biological diversity and low-pesticide pest management and that $7 million be set aside for a program intended to reduce clear-cutting of forests and increase activities to maintain diverse forest plant and animal populations.

• **State and private forests.** Appropriators provided $181.8 million to the Forest Service to help manage, protect from pest infestation and preserve 805 million acres of privately owned forests under cooperative programs with local governments, the forest industry and private landowners.

• **Timber sales.** The Forest Service was allotted $263.7 million to prepare forests for tree cutting and timber sales. Nationally, the Forest Service allowed 10.5 billion board feet of timber to be cut and harvested in 1990. (A board foot is equal to a plank of wood a foot square and an inch thick.) Such sales brought the government a total of $1.05 billion in fiscal 1990, out of which $327 million was paid to states. Appropriators said that the Forest Service, in the wake of allegations that it had engaged in a number of below-cost sales, failed to factor many of its costs when determining what its profits were.

The most controversial timber sales were in the Pacific Northwest, home of the nation's dwindling old-growth forests and the threatened northern spotted owl. It was in this region that appropriators cut $2 million from the administration's request for timber sale preparation, providing $61 million. That spending level would have led to a lower harvest of 2.2 billion to 3 billion board feet, which was about 450 million board feet below the fiscal 1991 harvest target.

Despite litigation initiated by environmental groups seeking to lower timber harvest levels on public lands, the service sought to boost its fiscal 1992 spending to cover timber harvest administration and pipeline costs. Appropriators gave them $124.5 million for sales preparation, $76 million for harvest administration and $20 million to keep a steady flow of timber moving through the system.

Appropriators, however, cut by $4.6 million money for reforestation and timber stand improvement, providing $96.1 million. Lawmakers also directed the Forest Service to give precedence to environmental standards and guidelines when such standards conflicted with timber sales plans. Finally, appropriators directed the Forest Service to strive to reduce by 25 percent by fiscal 1995 the amount of forestland that were clear-cut — a practice that Yates directed the service to halt in Shawnee National Forest in his home state of Illinois.

• **Endangered species.** Appropriators budgeted $29.2 million to protect threatened, endangered and sensitive species. In a move to maintain biological diversity, appropriators emphasized the importance of protecting endangered plants. Appropriators also allotted $200,000 for research on the Rocky Mountain wolf and $27.3 million for maintaining anadromous fish such as the Northwest's threatened Columbia River salmon species.

• **Firefighting.** The bill provided $187.4 million for firefighting. As they did for the Bureau of Land Management's firefighting account, House appropriators allotted an additional $112 million for "emergency" firefighting programs. The money could only be spent if the president declared such an emergency. Under the 1990 congressional-White House budget agreement, such emergency funds did not count against appropriators' spending caps. As in the Bureau of Land Management firefighting request, beginning in fiscal 1993, only firefighting expenses above the 10-year average could be scored as emergency funds.

• **Construction.** The total budget of $271.7 million for construction of roads, trails and facilities represented a decrease of $6 million from the fiscal 1991 appropriation. Funding for timber road construction was closely watched because there could be no timber cutting without roads. More significantly, appropriators cut about $34.7 million from the administration's budget request.

• **Land acquisition.** The land acquisition account was given $88.3 million to provide money for purchasing land in 44 areas, including plots in Idaho's Hells Canyon and in the Shawnee National Forest.

Energy Department

The bill's $1.3 billion for Energy Department programs included those that provided research into clean- and alternative-fuel technologies, energy conservation and the operation of the Strategic Petroleum Reserve. Appropriators such as Yates, while welcoming research into energy conservation, criticized Energy Department efforts to reduce spending for state and local conservation programs and clean-coal technology. They also cited administration resistance to increasing the fuel efficiency of automobiles. Lawmakers expressed dismay that the department was trying to scale back the Naval Petroleum Reserve's profitable oil fields.

• **Clean-coal technology.** Appropriators rejected administration efforts to cut $150 million from this program and kept spending at a previously funded level of $465 million. Under the program, the Energy Department shared the cost of industry demonstration projects of innovative coal-burning technologies. The projects looked for ways to reduce air pollutants from coal-burning power plants, hopeful that it would increase usage of America's most abundant energy resource. Administration officials had argued that they could not spend the $150 million in fiscal 1992 because it was intended for studies that would not get under way until fiscal 1993.

• **Fossil energy.** Lawmakers provided $444.3 million to fund research into fossil fuels, including coal liquefaction, flue-gas cleanup and enhanced oil and gas recovery. Beneficiaries included the Pittsburgh Energy Technology Center, a long-established research center near the district of its champion, House appropriator Murtha; and the University of North Dakota Energy and Environmental Research Center in the home state of Senate Appropriations Committee member Quentin N. Burdick, a Democrat.

• **Alternative fuels.** The major project under this account was the Great Plains Gasification Plant near Beulah, N.D., which was purchased by the Beulah Electric Power Cooperative from the Energy Department in 1988. It was the only synthetic natural gas plant in the country. Burdick successfully got approval of a Senate amendment to allow up to $50 million from the proceeds of the sale to be used to install a costly scrubber to reduce the plant's sulfur dioxide emissions.

• **Naval petroleum and oil-shale reserves.** Appropriators provided $232.3 million for six government-owned oil fields — two in Elk Hills, Calif., one northeast of Casper, Wyo., two in Rifle, Colo., and one in the Utah counties of Carbon and Uintah. The reserves produced 69,000 barrels of oil and liquid products a day and were expected to produce $523 million in revenues in fiscal 1992. The oil reserves had been a bone of contention between the administration and Congress — the administration wanted to sell or lease them, while Congress valued them for their revenue-producing capabilities.

• **Energy conservation.** This program included money to research solar technology, the efficiency of building heating and lighting systems, the production of energy from garbage and the creation of a new generation of batteries. Appropriators fully funded the department's request for $27 million for the U.S. Advanced Battery Consortium — a government-industry effort involving the three largest domestic automakers and other corporations trying to develop a battery capable of efficiently powering an automobile. The bill also allotted $243.4 million for grant programs to state and local governments to support weatherization programs for homes, schools and hospitals.

• **Emergency preparedness.** Appropriators provided $8.2 million for the Energy Department to analyze vulnerability to a sudden disruption in energy supplies and to fashion potential responses.

• **Strategic Petroleum Reserve.** Lawmakers appropriated $62.4 million to operate the Strategic Petroleum Reserve in fiscal 1992. Created in 1975, the reserve was intended to store 750 million barrels of oil in five underground salt domes in Texas and Louisiana and at a ground marine terminal in Louisiana. Appropriators directed that the reserve be filled at a rate of about 57,000 barrels a day in fiscal 1992. The reserve was drawn down during the Persian Gulf War to counter price increases and, according to Energy Secretary James D. Watkins, about 17.3 million barrels were sold to 13 U.S. oil companies, netting the government about $315 million that would be used to replenish the reserve.

Appropriators allotted $274.1 million to buy oil for the reserve. But in a budgetary maneuver, House appropriators directed that only $139 million of that be spent in fiscal 1992. The rest of the money could be spent in future years. Appropriators also prohibited leasing oil from oil companies owned by foreign governments.

CULTURAL PROGRAMS

Smithsonian Institution

Appropriators provided $331.8 million for the Smithsonian to operate 13 museums in Washington and New York. It also ran the National Zoo in Washington; an animal conservation and research center in Front Royal, Va.; an aircraft museum in Suitland, Md.; natural wildlife preserves on the Chesapeake Bay and in Panama; an oceanographic research facility in Fort Pierce, Fla.; and astrophysical observatories in Cambridge, Mass., and Mount Hopkins, Ariz. More than 28 million people visited the museums in fiscal 1990.

Appropriators criticized the Smithsonian for requesting an almost 50 percent increase in its budget. They cited the Smithsonian's inability to fill staff vacancies and meet a backlog of infrastructure requirements. House and Senate negotiators staked out different positions on the construction of a National Air and Space Museum annex. In their conference report, House conferees urged the Smithsonian to competitively bid the project, while Senate negotiators backed museum officials who wanted the annex built at Washington Dulles International Airport.

National Gallery of Art

Created as part of the Smithsonian in 1937 but now operating independently, the two-wing museum grew from the private collection of Andrew W. Mellon, and appropriators provided the museum $52.1 million for fiscal 1992. In 1990, it drew 5.8 million visitors. The museum used its private endowment to make acquisitions.

National Endowment for the Arts

Lawmakers appropriated $176 million for the endowment to support projects and productions in the arts through assistance to groups and individuals. It attracted controversy in recent years and again in 1991 when Sen. Jesse Helms, R-N.C., won an amendment banning the endowment from funding art that depicted "sexual or excretory activities or organs." Despite two non-binding House votes supporting prohibitions against subsidizing "patently offensive" art and performances, conferees dropped the Helms language. In a deal labeled "corn for porn," negotiators agreed to reject stronger anti-obscenity language in federal arts funding in exchange for dropping a proposed boost in grazing fees. The issue was briefly resurrected when the House took up the conference report Oct. 24 but was squelched with a 214-205 vote turning aside an attempt to overturn the deal.

National Endowment for the Humanities

The endowment was given $176 million to advance the humanities by supporting projects in history, literature, foreign languages and other disciplines. 1990's highly acclaimed Public Broadcasting Service series on the Civil War was funded in part by this endowment.

• **Cultural panels.** An educational center and a host of arts and cultural panels were also funded by the bill. Among them were the Woodrow Wilson International Center for Scholars, which was provided $5.74 million to extend educational grants to scholars to pursue research on a variety of subjects in international and cultural fields; the Institute of Museum Services, which was appropriated $26.9 million to support educational programs and the renovation of museums; the Commission of Fine Arts, which was appropriated $722,000 to advise the government on arts and architecture in the nation's capital; a $7 million appropriation to support art programs in the nation's capital; the Advisory Council on Historic Preservation, which got $2.6 million to support preserving historic and cultural resources; and the National Capital Planning Commission, which was given $4.8 million for the planning and renovation of federal facilities. There also were the Franklin Delano Roosevelt Memorial Commission, appropriated $33,000 for planning a $6 million National Park Service memorial to the 32nd president; the Pennsylvania Development Corporation, given $7.9 million to continue upgrading Pennsylvania Avenue between the White House and the Capitol; and the United States Holocaust Memorial Council, appropriated $10.9 million to oversee the construction of a memorial to Holocaust victims. ■

Continued from p. 558

spending, Senate appropriators approved the full administration firefighting request of $524 million.

Because of that, more programs suffered cuts from the House bill, including the National Park Service, the Bureau of Indian Affairs, The Smithsonian Institution, the National Endowment for the Arts and the National Endowment for the Humanities.

The Forest Service, however, was allocated an extra $98 million, including more money for endangered species management. However, the appropriators cut $41 million from the service's road-building budget, a move that delighted environmentalists who said road-building led to log cutting.

The committee report, while not solving the spotted owl crisis, did lower its recommended timber sales level in the Northwest to 3 billion board feet, about 400 million board feet down from fiscal 1991 level, and the same as that recommended by the House.

Though the payment process of the minerals royalty program came under criticism, the committee nonetheless allocated an extra $111 million for the BLM, bringing it up above $1 billion. They did so even though BLM Director Cy Jamison had testified in the past that his bureau was not underfunded.

As approved by the committee, the bill:

- Increased the Bureau of Indian Affairs budget to $1.5 billion, $200 million more than the fiscal 1991 appropriation but $65.8 million less than the House allowance.
- Appropriated $333 million for the Smithsonian Institution, $24 million less than requested by the administration. In a possible foreshadowing of battles to come, the committee sharply criticized the Smithsonian's management priorities, which it said concentrated on grand construction projects while "back at the Mall, there is a steady accretion of unmet needs."
- Provided for continuing payments to Oregon and California land-grant counties affected by decisions related to the northern spotted owl, whose dwindling population had caused a sharp cutback in timber harvests in the Northwest. The provision, in effect, increased the state share of government receipts garnered by timber cutting in the Northwest.
- Attempted to manage problems stemming from the rapid increases in wild horse populations in Nevada and elsewhere. The committee budgeted $15.2 million for their management, including $200,000 for horse-contraception research, and directed that horse adoption programs be streamlined.
- Stripped $1 million from three wetlands studies and used the money to fund renovations at Tad Gormley Stadium in New Orleans, where the Olympic track and field trials were to be held. The amendment was sponsored by J. Bennett Johnston, D-La., whose state was in an uproar over proposed regulations that would further restrict development on wetlands.

SENATE FLOOR ACTION

By combining emotional talk of endangered cowpokes with hard-nosed threats of a filibuster, Westerners were able to hold the line on federal land policies as the Senate passed its $12.7 billion version of HR 2686.

"Wyoming and other Western states felt totally under siege," said Wallop, who led the charge against several attempts to change policies that primarily benefited the West. "All those provisions were like poisonous snakes that kept rising up to bite us in the buns."

During debate on the measure, the Senate considered language and amendments that would have raised public-lands grazing fees, placed a moratorium on mining patent and oil-shale claims, and charged Western states substantially more for oil- and gas-royalty collections. But faced with a united Western front, the Senate approved only the oil-shale provision, and that for just nine months.

The Senate passed the bill 93-3 on Sept. 19 after considering several controversial amendments on the NEA. *(Vote 200, p. 26-S)*

As was true in the House, the most divisive issue was an attempt to increase the federal grazing fee, led in the Senate by Jeffords and Howard M. Metzenbaum, D-Ohio. The existing fee was $1.97 per AUM, which was about 900 pounds. The Jeffords amendment would have raised the fee to $5.13 by 1996. The House-passed bill raised it to $8.70 by 1995.

Jeffords, who was the co-chairman of the Northeast-Midwest Senate Coalition, said he sponsored the amendment to highlight some of the subsidies that went to Western states.

The fee, he said, allowed the 27,000 ranchers with public grazing permits to feed cattle at a far lower cost than ranchers using privately owned land.

Passion Prevails

Western senators fought the increase in grazing fees with a passion that belied its relatively small impact — estimated at $7 million to $8 million in its first year — on the federal budget.

Wallop, a rancher who once grazed his herd on public land, said he found it "difficult to contain my rage" over the Jeffords amendment. He said it was "preposterous for a dairy-state senator to be talking about federal subsidies," asserting that taxpayers foot a far higher bill for dairy subsidies.

Debate on the bill began Sept. 16. Over the next three days, Western senators took the floor one by one to denounce the amendment.

John McCain, R-Ariz., said, "These people are small family farmers, and what the senator is going to do is drive them out of business."

But Metzenbaum said, "The tears are flowing copiously, and all of our handkerchiefs are out for the poor little cattle ranchers." He said that 90 percent of the federal land grazed was leased by 300 wealthy individuals and corporations.

In the end, on Sept. 17 the Senate voted 60-38 to table the amendment in a vote split along ideological and regional lines. *(Vote 195, p. 26-S)*

Jeffords and Metzenbaum said that some increase was likely to come out of the conference committee.

Oil and Gas Royalties

On Sept. 12, the Senate agreed to roll back a proposed increase in the amount that Western states paid to collect royalties from companies extracting oil and gas on federal lands. On Sept. 13, the Senate by 47-46 killed a proposal by Dale Bumpers, D-Ark., to freeze for one year applications for hard-rock mining claims on federal lands. A similar provision passed in the House.

Western senators were pleased with both developments. Wallop had threatened to filibuster over the oil and gas royalty provision and hold up the bill.

"This is a big, big win for Wyoming," Wallop said. "The

mineral royalty program is vital to Wyoming and a handful of other states."

Royalties from oil and gas companies operating on federal lands were shared by the states and the federal government. Western states depended on the money to fund vital state programs such as education.

The oil and gas royalty deal was included in a series of otherwise uncontroversial amendments that were approved by voice vote Sept. 12. Funding for the amendment was to come from the unused allocation that appropriators divvied up for the fiscal 1992 energy and water development appropriation, according to Nickles. *(Energy and water appropriations, p. 569)*

The amendment would leave the royalty collection costs assessed states at the existing level of 25 percent. The defeated provision would have boosted to 50 percent the state's share of collection costs for the royalty program. The House appropriations bill left all collection costs to the federal government.

Appropriations Chairman Byrd, Nickles and Wallop sought to prevent a filibuster and continued negotiations on the deal until the Interior spending bill was brought up on the floor late Sept. 12. In the end, Byrd agreed to roll back the collection costs.

Wallop vowed to seek further changes in the way administrative costs for the royalty program were collected — perhaps allowing states to do collections themselves or changing the way individual state shares were calculated.

Byrd's determination to see the bill move helped derail on Sept. 13 an amendment by John McCain, R-Ariz., to require stricter regulation of water flows from the Glen Canyon Dam on the Colorado River to protect damaged downstream Grand Canyon beaches and marshes. The Senate, however, agreed by voice vote to an amendment offered by Tim Wirth, D-Colo., to place a nine-month moratorium on oil-shale patent applications until mining patent reform legislation could be considered.

CONFERENCE ACTION

A hastily arranged deal that swapped a freeze on federal grazing fees for a truce on arts funding helped wrap up conference consideration of HR 2686 on Oct. 17.

But the compromise on the $12 billion-plus fiscal 1992 bill ignored two House votes in as many days that overwhelmingly supported specific prohibitions against subsidizing "patently offensive" art and performances.

In its consideration of the spending bill, the Senate had adopted an amendment by Jesse Helms, R-N.C., that prevented the $178.2 million arts agency from funding projects that depicted "in a patently offensive way sexual or excretory activities or organs."

House Interior Appropriations Subcommittee Chairman Yates protested during conference that the Senate language was unnecessary. "I regret very much having to face this issue year in and year out," Yates said.

Nickles, while sympathetic, countered that the stricter language was needed to send a message that lawmakers would not tolerate public funding of offensive works.

Yates argued that Helms' language came from an existing law that already prohibited the endowment from funding patently offensive art.

Rep. William E. Dannemeyer, R-Calif., proposed the two non-binding motions, which the House approved, 286-135, on Oct. 16 and 287-133 a day later, saying they were needed to stop the endowment from funding theater groups whose performances depicted homosexual acts. *(Vote 309, p. 74-H; vote 314, p. 76-H)*

In agreeing to the trade-off that was quickly labeled "corn for porn," House and Senate negotiators also rebuffed 68 senators who had voted for the arts funding restrictions sought by Helms during Senate consideration of the Interior spending bill on Sept. 19. Turned aside, too, were 232 lawmakers who had voted to raise grazing fees during House consideration of the spending bill on June 25.

An outraged Dannemeyer called the conference deal "arrogance of the worst order." He staged an unsuccessful effort to recall chief House negotiator Yates and the rest of the House conferees.

But the compromise drew applause from Western ranchers.

At the outset, conferees got under way slowly in their effort to hammer out a final version of the spending bill. The only major issue agreed to during the opening round the week of Oct. 7 was the decision not to change the fees charged states for the collection of oil and gas royalties. Under the agreement, states were to be assessed 25 percent of federal royalty collection costs in fiscal 1992, just as they were in fiscal 1991.

But agreements that would settle disputes over grazing fees, arts funding and a House-approved moratorium on mining patent claims continued to elude negotiators. The logjam did not begin to break until Oct. 16, when Senate conferee Harry Reid, D-Nev., reached an understanding with Sen. Bumpers over the 1872 mining law.

Bumpers, unable to get the Senate to consider revamping the law, won a pledge from Reid that Westerners would allow the issue to be considered by the Energy and Natural Resources Committee. In turn, conferees dropped a House-passed provision calling for a one-year moratorium on mining patent claims.

Republican appropriators also chastised the Smithsonian Institution. Sen. Ted Stevens, R-Alaska, said it had a tendency to hold itself above federal regulations, citing the controversy over its search for a National Air and Space Museum annex.

A request by House appropriator Chester G. Atkins, D-Mass., for an additional $400,000 to maintain the Smithsonian's Amazon Research Project was also jeopardized and left to be resolved. Nickles said the institution had too many other pressing projects.

Conferees also temporarily shelved a Stevens request, made in behalf of the Alaskan Athabaskan Indians, to rename Mount McKinley. The original name had a staunch backer in House appropriator Regula of Ohio, the home state of President William McKinley, the 25th president.

After debating a proposed visitors' center in Iowa's Council Bluffs National Park that was sought by Democratic presidential hopeful Tom Harkin, D-Iowa, negotiators recessed to await the outcome of Dannemeyer's effort. Deluged with similar requests for visitors' centers, appropriators had decided early on to turn them all down, but they ended up making an exception for Harkin.

Chief Senate negotiator Byrd, looking to wrap up the conference, reminded the House conferees that they were not bound by Dannemeyer's effort. But his Republican counterpart, Nickles, pushed hard to retain the Helms language.

When the standoff continued, conferees turned to the issue of grazing and failed to make headway at first. One by one, Western lawmakers expressed opposition to an increase in grazing fees — both a steep increase as proposed by the House spending bill as well as a more modest increase that had been included in a separate bill to reauthorize the BLM.

Finally, Rep. Les AuCoin, D-Ore., who had been siding with the ranchers, broke the impasse Oct. 16. He first offered an unsuccessful proposal that the House drop any increase in grazing fees. AuCoin then suggested a trade-off that called on House negotiators to drop a grazing fee boost in exchange for Senate abandonment of the restrictions on arts funding sought by Helms.

Seizing the compromise as the only viable way to complete action on the bill, House conferees voted, 7-2, for it despite the objections of House appropriator Regula, who branded it an "unholy deal." Senate conferees quickly followed suit.

But a nonplused Regula said, "These things happen in conference. But I'm not sure we've heard the last word on this."

On the final day of negotiation, Sen. Brock Adams, D-Wash., tried to limit forestland set aside to protect the threatened northern spotted owl to a 70-acre area encircling every nest. But in the face of strong opposition from Rep. Gerry E. Studds, D-Mass., and Sen. Patrick J. Leahy, D-Vt., who said the proposal would gut the Endangered Species Act, conferees agreed to a watered-down provision. It urged the government to "minimize employment loss" in any owl-recovery plan.

Negotiators also effectively left in place a ban that blocked the government from leasing oil from foreign producers for the Strategic Petroleum Reserve.

FINAL ACTION

The NEA escaped unscathed, but two projects criticized as pork were axed as the House on Oct. 24 adopted, by a 310-104 vote, the conference report on HR 2686. *(Vote 342, p. 84-H)*

On a 205-214 vote, the House narrowly rejected an effort to strike the so-called corn for porn deal that had been worked out by conferees on Oct. 17, in which a House-approved hike in grazing fees was dropped in exchange for a truce on attempts to rein in the arts agency. *(Vote 341, p. 82-H)*

The vote came after California Republican Bill Lowery, a member of the Interior Appropriations Subcommittee, moved to send the bill back to conference, with House conferees instructed to insist on the amendment, originally offered by Helms, to restrict the NEA from funding materials that depicted "in a patently offensive way, sexual or excretory activities or organs."

Though Lowery acknowledged that the NEA had had a positive effect on the nation's culture, he said he made the move "to send a message." Lowery was supported by Regula, the ranking Republican on the Interior spending subcommittee. Regula said, "The will of the House, the will of the vast majority of the members on my side of the aisle is not reflected with respect to this issue in this conference report."

The House had voted twice on Oct. 17 to include the Helms amendment. Yet the votes were ignored by Interior Subcommittee Chairman Yates and AuCoin, who engineered the corn for porn swap.

On the floor, Yates admitted that he was aware the House had spoken but said, "The House did not instruct me to give up my better judgment. The House did not instruct me to give up my common sense."

As was usual when the embattled arts agency became the subject of congressional debate, tempers flared.

"I am sick and tired of having to write back to postcards asking why I allegedly support pornography," said Rep. Paul B. Henry, R-Mich.

But Rep. Fred Grandy, an Iowa Republican who began his career as an actor, said the Helms amendment was "a hunting license to go after every single sculptor, photographer or painter whose works you find patently offensive."

With restrictions on artistic imagination, he said, "art becomes house painting; it becomes elevator music, it becomes the Congressional Record."

In the end, an unrestricted NEA prevailed.

Some Pork Trimmed

Yates called the spending bill the "most difficult" he had ever worked on, and noted that about 1,900 items had to be resolved in conference, resulting in 226 amendments — including a 1.26 percent across-the-board cut in all but a few programs.

With the cut, the bill totaled $12.3 billion. That included $910.2 million for the Bureau of Land Management; $748.2 million for the Fish and Wildlife Service; $1.39 billion for the National Park Service; $1.53 billion for the Bureau of Indian Affairs; $2.26 billion for the National Forest Service; $331.8 million for the Smithsonian; and $176 million for the NEA.

As Yates and Regula raced through approval of the various amendments to the conference report, they were occasionally tripped up by Rep. Dan Burton, R-Ind., who called the members' attention to various programs he said were unneeded pork-barrel projects.

Burton criticized a $1 million National Park Service grant to renovate Tad Gormley Stadium in New Orleans. He said that the stadium, which was named after a high school football coach, was in a city park, not a national park, and did not deserve the money. The money would be used to get the stadium in shape for the 1994 trials for the 1996 Olympics. Though Burton noted the U.S. Olympic Committee was a private organization, the House voted, 243-164, to retain the project. *(Vote 343, p. 84-H)*

A $4.5 million hardwood manufacturing training center in Mercer County, W.Va., the district of Democrat Nick J. Rahall II, was also attacked. Burton said Senate appropriator Byrd had already sent billions to his state, and enough was enough.

"I don't mind giving a little bit of pork to West Virginia," Burton said, "but not the whole pig."

That apparently struck a chord, and the House voted, 224-178, to cut the project. *(Vote 344, p. 84-H)*

Finally, the House also disapproved a $44.2 million clean-coal technology project near Gillette, Wyo., that had been inserted into the bill by Sen. Alan K. Simpson, R-Wyo. The project had placed 19th out of 33 projects submitted for a $315 million clean-coal program, though first in its particular category of new fuels from highly polluting high-sulfur coal.

The House axed that program on a voice vote. However, the program would have been funded only if unobligated funds had been left over from other clean-coal technology projects.

Senate Approves Deal

The Senate debate on the House-Senate compromise on HR 2686 began when Helms stood on the Senate floor and waved a magazine called Performance Journal, which he said featured a "blown-up" photo of a woman's vagina. The magazine, he said, was partially funded by the NEA.

The debate continued with a ribald account by Byrd of Theodora, a sixth-century version of a performance artist. She would lie naked onstage as geese plucked barley seeds from her "private parts," as Byrd said. Colorado Democrat Wirth then chimed in, warning women and children in the gallery not to look as he unveiled posters of a nude Venus as portrayed by Titian, the 16th-century Venetian master.

But the arguments ended for all practical purposes when the Senate decided the picture it really did not like was one of continued battle with the House over a separate but linchpin issue: whether to sock Western ranchers with higher grazing fees.

Western conservatives, usually Helms' allies, seemed keenly aware of what that vote might portend — a vengeful Rep. Yates. Yates was likely to find a way — using the procedural powers of the House Rules Committee — to reopen the grazing fees issue if the porn for corn deal was broken, Byrd warned.

Yates' revenge was the last thing Western conservatives wanted after winning a bruising fight to keep the fees at their existing low levels. The House had sought a stiff increase in the fees, and there were unsuccessful efforts to raise them on the Senate floor and in conference. But Yates agreed to abandon the proposal when Byrd, who led the Senate conferees, agreed to drop Helms' original Senate amendment on the NEA.

Helms tried to amend the final conference report with identical language, but this time around, a Senate weary of the contentious and long-running bill became the amendment's worst enemy.

In addition to the wavering Westerners, there were liberal Easterners who were incensed at voting on the NEA for the ninth time in two years, despite year-old authorizing legislation that banned it from funding pornographic art.

John H. Chafee, R-R.I., noted that the NEA had taken earlier legislative warnings to heart — and was being sued by artists because of it. "They've got a tough job to do. Let's not make it any tougher," he said.

And after his discussion of the "life of harlotry" of Justinian's wife, Theodora, Byrd observed that restraining the NEA could not be easily legislated. "We try to close one loophole with verbiage, and another opens up," he said. Byrd moved to kill Helms' amendment, and the motion passed, 73-25. *(Vote 241, p. 32-S)*

The Senate acquiesced on several other conference compromises, including cutting $4.5 million for a hardwood manufacturing technology center in Mercer County, W.Va.

But the Senate insisted on a project in Wyoming, pushed by Sens. Simpson and Bob Kasten, R-Wis. Simpson had inserted a directive for the Energy Department to use $44.1 million in unobligated money for a clean-coal project in Wyoming, run by the Wisconsin-based Heartland Development Corp., even though the project had not made the cut in the competitive clean-coal program. Choosing not to second-guess the Energy Department, the House had stripped the language. At Kasten's urging, the Senate on Oct. 31 agreed to give the project $5 million to keep it viable.

But when that proposal went back to the House on Nov. 1, members heeded Rep. Robert S. Walker, R-Pa., who called the deal an unfair "foot in the door." The Senate finally caved later that day, stripping the earmark from the bill. ■

Atom Smasher Funded in Energy Bill

A $21.8 billion fiscal 1992 spending bill for energy and water development was approved by both chambers the week of July 29.

The appropriations bill (HR 2427) provided funding for the nation's nuclear weapons programs, energy research and water projects, as well as for the superconducting super collider, a controversial atom smasher, to be built in Waxahachie, Texas.

The Bush administration had sought more money for the atom smasher and less for water projects it considered wasteful.

House and Senate negotiators agreed to the final version July 30, taking less than two hours to iron out their differences. The House the next day adopted the conference report 393-32. *(Vote 245, p. 60-H)*

The Senate cleared the measure Aug. 2 by voice vote.

In 1991, it took some extra effort to forge the energy spending bill.

When Senate appropriators divided the available money among the 13 spending bills, they allotted almost half a billion dollars more for the energy and water bill than had House leaders. That meant House and Senate conferees could not draft a final version until the two Appropriations committees agreed on how much they could spend.

The compromise allocation, which was slightly different than the actual appropriation, included $11.98 billion for defense-related spending and $9.9 billion for domestic programs.

In 1990, appropriations for energy and water development had totaled $20.2 billion. *(1990 Almanac, p. 861)*

BOXSCORE

➡ **Fiscal 1992 energy and water development appropriations bill (HR 2427).** The bill provided $21.8 billion for energy and water development projects.

Reports: H Rept 102-75; S Rept 102-80; conference report filed in the House, H Rept 102-177.

KEY ACTION

May 29 — HR 2427 passed the **House** by a vote of 392-24.

July 10 — HR 2427 passed the **Senate** by a vote of 96-3.

July 30 — **House-Senate** conference agreed to bill.

July 31 — The **House** agreed to conference report by a vote of 393-32.

Aug. 2 — The **Senate** approved conference report by voice vote.

Aug. 17 — President Bush signed HR 2427 — PL 102-104.

HOUSE COMMITTEE ACTION

Striking a frugal opening note for the fiscal 1992 budget season, House appropriators slashed President Bush's spending request for the giant atom smasher and turned away all requests for new water projects.

Meeting in closed session the morning of May 15, the Appropriations Subcommittee on Energy and Water Development took its traditional position as the first of the 13 subcommittees to draft its spending bill. The panel tentatively approved a $21.5 billion bill, up from the fiscal 1991 total of $20.2 billion and just below the administration's request of $21.6 billion.

Subcommittee Chairman Tom Bevill, D-Ala., described the bill as a stay-even package adjusted for inflation, with "no new anything." An exception was $2 million for a new regional center to research global environmental change at the University of Alabama.

The administration had requested $534 million — more than double the $243 million approved in fiscal 1991 — for the superconducting super collider, expected to cost in excess of $8 billion. *(Super collider, p. 242)*

The subcommittee approved a hefty increase for the project but stopped at $434 million, $100 million shy of the administration's goal.

Jim Chapman, D-Texas, a key panel booster of the atom smasher, raised concerns that the cut would delay construction and drive up costs. Bevill said his panel simply had to pare the money to stay within its spending cap.

In Bevill's subcommittee, roughly half of the spending went for nuclear defense programs. In 1991, members approved $11.8 billion for those programs. That meant the super collider had to compete with water projects and research programs for remaining domestic funds.

In defense spending, the subcommittee included money for the controversial Rocky Flats nuclear weapons plant in Colorado.

But it attached language requiring the Energy Department to first establish the need for that facility to carry out certain plutonium recovery processes before money could be spent on them.

The panel also allocated more money to clean up the Department of Energy's nuclear weapons facilities.

In 1990, Congress appropriated $3.1 billion for environmental cleanup, significantly above the Bush administration request. In 1991, the administration asked for $4.2 billion, and the subcommittee nudged that up to $4.4 billion. That was just a fraction of the total costs, however, which were estimated at $60 billion to $200 billion over the next few decades.

The administration won its full $337 million request for research into fusion energy, a 23 percent increase over fiscal 1991. According to Bevill, the subcommittee also increased Bush's request for solar and renewable energy programs, up to $237 million.

The subcommittee allocated $3.6 billion for ongoing water projects by the Army Corps of Engineers. But it was only the second time in recent years that the subcommittee had not weighted the bill with new water construction projects sought by lawmakers and the administration.

In 1988, the subcommittee also agreed to forgo so-called new starts, but abandoned such frugality the following year. *(1988 Almanac, p. 701)*

Bevill said any temptation to begin a project was cooled by doubts that members could continue funding in the next budget cycle, which was expected to be even tighter.

Full Committee

The House Appropriations Committee on May 22 sent a $21.5 billion spending bill for energy and water development to the House floor but not before reopening the

Energy & Water Development

(In thousands of dollars)

	Fiscal 1991 Appropriation	President's Request	House Bill	Senate Bill	Final Bill
Army Corps of Engineers					
General construction	$ 1,143,086	$ 1,222,357	$ 1,264,991	$ 1,327,441	$ 1,284,142
Operation and maintenance	1,450,669	1,514,935	1,547,855	1,537,265	1,535,229
General investigations	146,435	160,342	200,566	176,211	194,427
Other	562,306	597,550	596,437	596,437	596,437
TOTAL, Corps of Engineers	**$ 3,302,496**	**$ 3,495,184**	**$ 3,609,849**	**$ 3,637,354**	**$ 3,610,235**
Bureau of Reclamation (Interior)					
Construction	667,897	546,279	553,209	564,409	564,209
Operation and maintenance	221,516	258,685	258,685	258,685	258,685
General investigations	13,221	12,614	13,789	13,204	13,554
Other	62,970	65,056	61,535	63,535	63,535
TOTAL, Interior	**$ 965,604**	**$ 882,634**	**$ 887,218**	**$ 899,833**	**$ 899,983**
Energy Department					
Atomic energy defense					
Research, development and testing	1,737,075	1,764,000	1,776,950	1,976,650	1,943,950
Production and surveillance	2,792,354	2,548,500	2,460,478	2,590,478	2,515,478
Materials production	2,341,900	1,876,900	1,876,900	1,891,900	1,876,900
Verification and security	352,408	408,600	403,600	403,600	403,600
Naval reactors	652,000	801,000	801,000	818,000	818,000
Environmental cleanup (defense)	3,044,722	3,705,000	3,748,900	3,640,372	3,680,672
Other	616,555	664,000	700,672	647,000	729,400
Subtotal, atomic energy	**$ 11,537,014**	**$ 11,768,000**	**$ 11,768,500**	**$ 11,968,000**	**$ 11,968,000**
Energy supply R&D					
Solar energy	129,418	142,878	173,503	158,866	175,503
Nuclear energy	304,707	398,658	314,658	346,658	336,658
Environmental cleanup (non-defense)	437,023	523,495	602,495	602,495	602,495
Fusion energy	273,557	337,100	337,100	337,100	337,100
Basic energy sciences	711,760	714,700	714,700	737,700	764,700
Other	523,206	757,972	694,234	751,060	683,447
Subtotal, R&D	**$ 2,527,082**	**$ 2,821,428**	**$ 2,854,053**	**$ 2,940,916**	**$ 2,961,903**
Uranium supply & enrichment	1,340,018	1,547,000	1,337,600	1,367,600	1,313,600
Revenues	−1,450,400	−1,547,000	−1,547,000	−1,547,000	−1,547,000
General science					
Superconducting super collider	242,866	533,700	433,700	508,700	483,700
High-energy physics	588,587	666,449	622,999	637,999	627,999
Nuclear physics	313,329	342,390	342,390	354,390	354,390
Other	33,950	6,400	6,400	6,400	6,400
Subtotal, general science	**$ 1,148,732**	**$ 1,548,939**	**$ 1,405,489**	**$ 1,507,489**	**$ 1,472,489**
Nuclear waste	242,833	305,071	305,071	295,071	275,071
Power Marketing Administration	326,387	387,029	362,029	382,029	362,029
Federal Energy Regulatory Commission	122,750	141,071	141,071	141,071	141,071
Revenues	−122,750	−141,071	−141,071	−141,071	−141,071
Other Energy Department	133,214	173,652	170,555	172,055	161,555
TOTAL, Energy Department	**$ 15,915,262**	**$ 17,004,119**	**$ 16,656,297**	**$ 17,085,660**	**$ 16,967,647**
Independent Agencies					
Appalachian Regional Commission	170,000	100,000	170,000	190,000	190,000
Nuclear Regulatory Commission	465,000	512,500	512,500	512,500	512,500
Revenues	−153,450	−492,538	−492,538	−492,538	−492,538
Tennessee Valley Authority	135,000	91,266	135,000	135,000	135,000
Other agencies	12,798	16,663	16,673	16,673	16,673
GRAND TOTAL	**$ 20,812,710**	**$ 21,609,828**	**$ 21,494,999**	**$ 21,984,482**	**$ 21,839,500**

SOURCE: House Appropriations Committee

debate over how much the government should invest in the super collider.

Bush had requested $534 million for the atom smasher, but Appropriations members accepted the recommendation of the Energy and Water Subcommittee to cut the request by $100 million.

The Energy Department project was expected to cost more than $8 billion to complete, nearly twice as much as advertised when the House voted in June 1989 to break ground at a site 25 miles south of Dallas. Texas pledged to cover $1 billion of the cost, and foreign governments were also expected to kick in, although by 1991 no country had yet proffered a cash contribution. *(1989 Almanac, p. 737)*

Critics complained that the escalating cost of the super collider was crowding out other less expensive, and potentially more fruitful, scientific endeavors. On May 23, Sherwood Boehlert, R-N.Y., a member of the Science Committee, sought permission from the Rules Committee to offer a floor amendment to cap the U.S. investment in the project at $5 billion. He was denied that request because it involved putting legislative language on an appropriations bill.

Meanwhile, at the Appropriations markup, Sidney R. Yates, D-Ill., proposed cutting $43 million more from the super collider appropriation to start upgrading a new particle collider ring at the Fermi National Accelerator Laboratory, located outside Chicago, his hometown.

Subcommittee Chairman Bevill, said funding the new particle injector at Fermi would unravel the subcommittee's pact not to fund any new construction projects. "It would create chaos if we adopted this amendment," he said.

Yates' motion failed 11-32 but not before drawing some sympathy from members who worried about the super collider's rising cost. "This has turned out to be one of the hungriest hogs at the federal trough," said Richard J. Durbin, D-Ill.

HOUSE ACTION

After hours of intense debate over the cost and merits of building the super collider, the House on May 29 decided to go ahead with the Texas project.

Discussion of the super collider dominated floor debate over HR 2427. The energy and water bill, the first of the 13 appropriations bills to come to the floor, passed 392-24. *(Vote 119, p. 30-H)*

A controversial amendment that would have cut the atom smasher's $434 million appropriation failed 165-251. However, its authors considered the outcome a victory because they gained far more support than they had had in the past. *(Vote 117, p. 30-H)*

A similar amendment offered in 1989 garnered just 93 votes. *(1989 Almanac, vote 118, p. 42-H)*

The super collider had come under fire as Energy Department cost estimates had more than doubled from a little more than $4 billion in 1988 to more than $8.2 billion in 1991.

During the House debate, the project was derided by opponents as a "dollar gobbler" and "a Texas Gila monster that would snap up every federal research dollar in sight." As an example, lawmakers pointed to cuts made by the Appropriations Committee for another federal particle collider in Illinois that was included in the administration's budget plan.

But Illinois lawmakers helped to restore $10 million for upgrading that particle collider ring at the Fermi National Accelerator Laboratory.

Appropriations Committee member Yates originally had sought to include the full $43.5 million the administration had recommended for the Fermilab project, taking the money from the super collider appropriation. The Appropriations subcommittee had deleted the money, citing budget constraints.

But after consulting with subcommittee Chairman Bevill and ranking Republican member John T. Myers, Ind., Yates agreed to a compromise: $10 million to do the design work for the planned Fermilab particle injector, without specifying what programs were to be cut to provide the money. By settling for the smaller amount, Yates got Bevill and Myers in his corner and won approval on a voice vote.

The compromise helped lead to the defeat of an amendment offered by Jim Slattery, D-Kan., that would have deleted collider spending and restored the $43.5 million for Fermilab.

Collider supporters argued that the scientific discoveries from the project outweighed its costs and jeopardized more than $748 million already committed.

Proponents also noted that efforts to stop funding for the project would undermine its international profile and make it more difficult for the Energy Department to persuade foreign governments to contribute to the project.

But opponents cited the project's cost. "Congress must insist on knowing the full true cost of this project," said Howard Wolpe, D-Mich., who along with Boehlert led the fight to kill the atom smasher. "Already this project is showing traits similar to those of many white elephants of the past. Costs grow, time frames stretch out. Every estimate that goes awry is replaced by a new and improved version."

Congressional support for the super collider was nearly unanimous in 1987 and 1988 before the Energy Department selected its location in Waxahachie, Texas. But once construction was about to begin, it was increasingly seen as a costly project that largely benefited Texas.

Noting that House floor opponents hailed from many states, Boehlert claimed that its supporters came from "Texas and Texas and Texas and Texas."

But Joe L. Barton, R-Texas, who represented the district in which the collider was located, downplayed the significance of the increased opposition and said opponents would have less ammunition in 1992 when the project was further along.

With the super collider battle behind them, members voted overwhelmingly to pass the overall energy and water spending bill.

Apart from the super collider conflict, there was little floor debate over the spending bill, about half of which went toward nuclear defense production and cleanup activities. Legislators set aside $4.4 billion for cleanup work at federal nuclear facilities, up from $3.5 billion in 1990.

Interior Committee Chairman George Miller, D-Calif., was unhappy with a $20 million payment to New Mexico communities in connection with plans to operate a nuclear waste repository there. *(Nuclear waste, p. 224)*

The Energy Department wanted to operate an underground storage facility for defense-related nuclear waste, known as the Waste Isolation Pilot Plant, WIPP, in New Mexico. The appropriations bill included $20 million in impact aid for the state and affected communities.

Miller said the Interior, Armed Services and Energy and Commerce committees were negotiating with New

Mexico over terms for hosting the waste facility, and it was too soon to know how much the government should pay. But he declined to press the issue during floor debate, instead urging Congress not to go beyond $20 million in the following few years.

Otherwise, the energy and water bill met with the same acceptance that customarily had allowed it to pass quickly on to the Senate.

After the long super collider debate, William E. Dannemeyer, R-Calif., sought to cut about $107 million, or 0.5 percent, from the bill in the interest of deficit reduction. His proposal was rejected 92-320. *(Vote 118, p. 30-H)*

And, in the difficult budget climate, there was no great rush by members to call attention to projects affecting their districts. Vic Fazio, D-Calif., a member of the subcommittee that wrote the bill, remarked on the relative silence, saying, "Most of us . . . do not want to identify how successful we may have been in this legislation."

SENATE COMMITTEE ACTION

Faced with almost half a billion more dollars to spend on energy and water programs than their House counterparts, Senate appropriators boosted spending for two high-profile science projects: nuclear defense laboratories and water construction projects.

The Senate Appropriations Committee on June 12 voted unanimously to approve a $21.98 billion energy and water spending bill, making few changes from the subcommittee bill approved the day before. Roughly half the bill's spending, $11.97 billion, went to nuclear defense programs and cleanup.

In the House, the bill's fiercest battle came over the $434 million appropriation for the superconducting super collider. But Senate appropriators showed no such qualms, approving not only the House spending level but also restoring $75 million of the $100 million that chamber had cut from the administration's request.

J. Bennett Johnston, D-La., who chaired the Senate Appropriations subcommittee with jurisdiction over the bill, said the overall $508.7 million appropriation should allow super collider construction to proceed on schedule.

The Senate committee also added money to upgrade another particle collider at Chicago's Fermi National Accelerator Laboratory, although not the full $43.5 million requested by the president. The House had allotted $10 million to design the project, and Senate appropriators upped that to $25 million.

While the House took the unusually austere step of omitting any new water construction projects, Senate appropriators had $290 million more to spend on non-defense items and found enough money for 14 so-called new starts. Four of the 14 new starts had been recommended by Bush, and most were in states represented by senators on the Appropriations Committee.

The 14 projects were: Homer Spit, Alaska; Bayou La Batre, Ala.; Holbrook, Ariz.; Oceanside, Calif.; Miami Harbor Channels, Fla.; Richard Russell Mitigation, Ga.; Alenaio Streams, Hawaii; West Des Moines-Des Moines, Iowa; Aloha Rigolette, La.; Missouri River, Fort Yates Bridge, North and South Dakota; Rio Grande Floodway, San Acacia to Bosque, N.M.; Atlantic Coast of New York City, Coney Island, N.Y.; Folly Beach, S.C.; and Brazos Island Harbor, Texas.

Senators also increased money for some ongoing construction projects.

Overall, the Senate bill allocated $4.5 billion for the Army Corps of Engineers and Bureau of Reclamation, roughly $40 million more than the House and $159 million above the president's budget. Johnston said the 14 new projects would cost $291 million over a period of several years and did not represent an unreasonable drain on future funds.

In the defense portion of the bill, senators had $200 million to spend above the House bill and allocated most of that to nuclear weapons laboratories in New Mexico and California.

Senate Appropriations members struck controversial language that the House had included in most of its drafts to void a law passed in 1990 requiring chief financial officers to be installed in 23 Cabinet departments and federal agencies and the adoption of a uniform system of financial accountability in the same agencies.

Johnston also inserted language seeking to nullify 1989 federal wetlands rules that had created a furor in many communities. *(Clean water, p. 212)*

He and other critics said they did not disagree with restricting development on wetlands but claimed the 1989 rules so broadened the definition of a wetland as to be unreasonable.

Even with the extra $490 million Senate appropriators had to spend beyond the House bill, there were some hard feelings on the Senate side over what was left out of its bill.

During the full committee markup, Ted Stevens, R-Alaska, warned that buildings in Bethel, Alaska, could be washed out if appropriators did not add $1 million to begin a flood-prevention project there.

Johnston refused to add the money, noting that Alaska had already received one of the 14 precious "new starts." He offered to switch the two, but Stevens protested, saying "to trade them out would be to trade off one emergency for another."

Stevens argued that it was unfair to hold all states to only one new project when Alaska was one-fifth the size of the lower 48 put together. He and Johnston engaged in a lengthy and somewhat heated exchange over the project.

Daniel K. Inouye, D-Hawaii, was the only senator to join the fray, defending the need for the Alaska project and recalling the days of looser budgeting rules by asking, "Is there any way we can get it out of defense?"

Although appropriators used to dip into the defense portion of the energy and water bill to finance civilian projects, the 1990 budget rules had erected a wall between the two pots of money.

Stevens' bid for the project was defeated on a voice vote.

SENATE ACTION

The Senate for the first time July 10 went on record supporting the giant atom smasher, approving $509 million to begin building the Texas project.

The vote came on the Senate version of HR 2427, which was brought to the floor the night of July 9 after senators had deadlocked over provisions of a major crime bill. The next day it became the first of 13 spending bills to pass the Senate, winning approval, 96-3. *(Vote 122, p. 17-S; Crime bill, p. 262)*

It was the first time senators had been forced to stake out a position for or against the $8 billion-plus super collider.

Continued on p. 579

Energy and Water Development Provisions

The key components of the energy and water development spending bill included water projects conducted by the Army Corps of Engineers and the Interior Department's Bureau of Reclamation, and energy research and nuclear weapons programs run by the Energy Department. Operating under new budget rules, appropriators were restricted by fixed spending caps for the two types of programs included in their bill — defense and non-defense — and they could not shift money between the accounts.

The fiscal 1992 bill parceled out a total of $21.8 billion, almost $12 billion of it for nuclear weapons programs. While defense policy debates were generally played out in the defense authorization bills, appropriators held a more central role in shaping national energy and water programs.

ARMY CORPS OF ENGINEERS

The Corps of Engineers' domestically based unit conducted civil works programs to promote commercial navigation and flood control, recreation and natural disaster response. The corps first approved water projects for preliminary study. The studies and subsequent design work showed up as part of the corps' "general investigations" budget. Studies examined the costs, benefits and scope of the project and the ability to secure local funding. Based on the results, projects could later be approved as new construction starts. After the first round of exploratory studies, the cost of subsequent planning and construction work was shared with local groups.

Corps officials were increasingly mindful of the environmental threats posed by ongoing and new water projects. For example, all nine of the new, so-called reconnaissance studies the administration proposed for fiscal 1992 were for environmental restoration work, such as restoring fish and wildlife breeding areas at South Dakota's Big Bend Dam and helping fish spawn in the Susquehanna River in Maryland. Such studies in the past had focused on more traditional lock, dam and waterway construction projects.

The corps was also seeking to shift resources exclusively to projects that were too big for local groups to carry out. As submitted, the president's budget would have phased out the corps' funding category for smaller-scale projects. But many lawmakers protested that small communities were too pinched to pay for such projects alone, and House and Senate appropriators explicitly rejected the administration's attempt to stop the program.

For fiscal 1992, the budget included $3.6 billion for the corps. That amount accounted for one year's worth of work on corps projects, some of which were spread over decades. Because the water projects were public works manna to localities, appropriators typically added their favorites to the administration's initial request.

Construction

The $1.3 billion general construction budget for fiscal 1992 was a case in point. It included funds for 15 new construction projects, only four of which President Bush had requested.

- **Administration requests.** The administration's four requested projects were in Homer Spit, Alaska, costing $3.3 million; Brazos Island Harbor, Texas, $1 million; Bayou La Batre, Ala., $500,000; and Alenaio Stream, Hawaii, $1.9 million.
- **Member requests.** Senate appropriators added money in subcommittee for 10 other projects — eight of them in the states of full committee members: Holbrook, Ariz., $100,000; Miami Harbor Channel, Fla., $400,000; Oceanside Harbor, Calif., $3.1 million; wildlife mitigation at the Richard Russell Dam in Georgia and South Carolina, $10 million; West Des Moines-Des Moines, Iowa, $700,000; Aloha Rigolette, La., $50,000; Rio Grande Floodway, San Acacia to Bosque, N.M., $3 million; Atlantic Coast of New York City, $2 million; Fort Yates Bridge, N.D. and S.D., $2.5 million; Folly Beach, S.C., $600,000. On the Senate floor, Ted Stevens, R-Alaska, also added $5 million for emergency erosion-control work at Bethel, Alaska. House appropriators originally had less money for water projects and included no new construction starts in their version of the bill. In conference they accepted the Senate's 15 new projects.
- **Ongoing projects.** Appropriators shifted even larger amounts of money within some ongoing projects, most notably the Red River Waterway and the Levisa and Tug forks flood-control program in Kentucky and West Virginia. Bush requested $1.2 billion for construction work, virtually all of it for ongoing projects. Appropriators raised that to $1.3 billion. The president also sought $1.5 billion for the operation and maintenance of those projects. Appropriators added about $20 million. The administration for several years had battled with congressional backers of the Red River Waterway, a 25-year-old project to construct a commercial channel from the Mississippi River about 75 miles north of Baton Rouge to Shreveport, La. The initial three locks were virtually complete, but the administration did not want to finish the proposed additional locks. However, congressional appropriators allotted $123.7 million to proceed with the project, up from only $38.3 million included in Bush's fiscal 1992 budget request.

The waterway project affected Arkansas, Louisiana, Oklahoma and Texas, although Louisiana would be the prime beneficiary of the next phase of work. The project lost one of its strongest House advocates with the retirement of Lindy (Mrs. Hale) Boggs, a Louisiana Democrat who sat on the House Appropriations Energy and Water Development panel. However, Rep. Jim Chapman, D-Texas, continued to be a strong advocate for the project on that panel, and Louisiana Sen. J. Bennett Johnston, a Democrat, was chairman of the Senate Energy and Water Appropriations Subcommittee.

Appropriators also split with the administration on a flood-control project for the Upper Cumberland River and two forks of the Big Sandy River — Levisa and Tug forks — in West Virginia, Virginia and Kentucky. House appropriators more than doubled the administration's $13.2 million request to $33.7 million. The Senate then almost doubled the House amount. Conferees settled on $57.8 million.

Of that money, $26 million was earmarked for two elements of the project in West Virginia, home state of Senate Appropriations Chairman Robert C. Byrd, a Democrat. Another $20.5 million was set aside for two Kentucky sections of the project, levee and flood wall construction in Barbourville and river-diversion tunnels in Harlan. The administration had not recommended any new funds for the Harlan and Barbourville work, but House Appropriations member Harold Rogers, R-Ky., appeared before the Energy and Water Subcommittee to argue the merits of the project. Rogers and other Kentucky representatives were accompanied by fellow Kentuckian William H. Natcher, the second-ranking Democrat on the Appropriations Committee, who introduced each to the subcommittee.

• **New Jersey.** Two of the new members of the House Energy and Water Appropriations Subcommittee, Republican Dean A. Gallo and Democrat Bernard J. Dwyer, were from New Jersey, and their influence helped gain money for some home-state projects, particularly the Passaic River flood-control project. The administration requested $5 million for planning work on the project; House appropriators successfully boosted that to $7.2 million.

• **Columbia and Snake rivers dredging.** Lawmakers on the House Appropriations Energy and Water Development Subcommittee expressed concern that planned efforts to protect salmon on the Columbia and Snake rivers could interfere with commercial navigation. They added $8 million, agreed to by Senate appropriators, for one-time dredging on these waterways in Oregon and Washington. The dredging had been a major concern for Northwest lawmakers, including House Speaker Thomas S. Foley of Washington and Oregon's two Appropriations Committee members, Republican Sen. Mark O. Hatfield and Democratic Rep. Les AuCoin.

The bill included numerous other appropriations relating to the fate of salmon in the Columbia and Snake rivers, such as $31.7 million toward building fish ladders at several locks and dams along the rivers.

• **Inland Waterway Trust Fund.** Appropriators cut the $27.6 million the administration had sought for five rehabilitation projects, four of them involving locks and dams along the Mississippi River and the other involving four locks on the Illinois Waterway between Chicago and Grafton, Ill. The administration wanted to pay for half of those projects from the Inland Waterway Trust Fund. The fund came from a fuel tax assessed on navigators who used the inland waterways. But appropriators balked, questioning whether that money could properly be used for rehabilitation work rather than major construction work, as has been typical. Appropriators put the projects on hold while the funding dispute was worked out.

Mississippi River Flood Control

The waterway and flooding problems associated with the lower Mississippi basin were so extensive that the project was in a separate section of the corps' budget. The budget included $353.4 million for this account, about $6.9 million more than Bush requested.

The money would pay for projects such as channel dredging, levee construction and erosion-control projects in appropriators' home states of Arkansas, Illinois, Kentucky, Louisiana, Mississippi, Missouri and Tennessee. Increased spending for the Yazoo Basin in Mississippi, the home state of Democratic House Appropriations Chairman Jamie L. Whitten, accounted for most of the increase. And $400,000 of that boost was earmarked for an ongoing report on the infrastructure and port development needs at Newport, near the Tennessee border in Whitten's district.

Miscellaneous

• **High-speed transit system.** The Corps of Engineers' budget included $8 million toward an interagency project to promote a high-speed transit system consisting of aboveground trains propelled by magnetic currents.

• **Coastal areas.** Lawmakers rebuffed the administration's request for $7 million for the corps' share of an interagency effort to clean up and protect coastal areas. The joint effort would seek strategies to reduce the loss of coastal fish and wildlife habitats and to control pollution. The administration had envisioned a cooperative effort among the Corps of Engineers, the Environmental Protection Agency, the Commerce Department's National Oceanic and Atmospheric Administration, the Interior Department and relevant state and local governments. Lawmakers argued that the corps' budget already included extensive environmental programs.

Regulation

• **Wetlands.** At the instigation of Louisiana's Sen. Johnston, appropriators added language that in effect barred the corps from enforcing its controversial 1989 wetlands rules. Landowners were required to seek a permit to build or alter wetlands. Critics contended that the 1989 rules unfairly expanded the wetlands classification to cover land that was rarely wet or was of little ecological significance.

Under the bill language, the corps could not enforce those rules until it submitted them or a revised version to a public-approval process. The corps could process ongoing permit applications if the landowner opted to continue under the 1989 designation. However, the Bush administration's unveiling of new rules that would ease wetlands restrictions could make the bill language obsolete.

Appropriators refused the corps' request to increase fees for the wetlands permits and related services. They also blocked a proposed fee increase for shoreline management work.

• **Office closures.** Sen. Don Nickles, R-Okla., successfully barred the corps from using any money to proceed with reorganization studies or other work aimed at closing some of its civilian offices. Many lawmakers were skittish about losing corps offices in their districts and said they first wanted to devise a framework for evaluating and approving office closings, perhaps similar to the base-closing commission for military facilities.

BUREAU OF RECLAMATION

Part of the Interior Department, the Bureau of Reclamation was charged with managing water and related land resources in 17 Western states of the continental United States. It was created in 1902 to provide irrigation for the arid West. Since then, its mission had expanded greatly. Projects included irrigation, water supply, hydroelectric power generation, flood control, and recreation and wildlife habitat protection. For fiscal 1992, the budget included $13.6 million for investigations, $338.4 million for construction work.

Plentiful and inexpensive bureau water had become a way of life in the West. But the program had come increasingly under attack from environmentalists and urban-minded politicians in Congress. The first priority of reformers was blocking large farms from getting around acreage limitations that restricted eligibility for subsidized water. And reformers had shown they were ready to hold up authorization for new bureau projects until the dispute was settled.

• **Construction.** The bureau's general construction budget for fiscal 1992 was $338.4 million. Almost $39 million of that was for California's Central Valley Project, a massive water project begun in 1936 that generated hydropower and supplied water to farms and municipalities.

Another large appropriation within the bureau's construction budget was for the controversial Garrison Diversion Unit in North Dakota, a massive irrigation and water supply project first authorized in 1965 and since under fire as unaffordable and environmentally unsound. Having failed in previous attempts to abandon the Garrison project, the administration requested $25 million toward completing a more limited plan in fiscal 1992. But Senate appropriators, including Quentin N. Burdick, D-N.D., added another $10 million for the project. Conferees settled on an extra $8 million, for a total of $33 million, in the final bill.

• **Colorado River storage.** The bureau also ran several large projects in the Colorado River Basin, which were funded from separate accounts. One such project was the Colorado River Storage Project, which sought to secure dependable water supplies for the Upper Colorado Basin. Appropriators provided $123.4 million for the project, up from the $115.4 million requested by the administration for fiscal 1992.

• **Central Utah Project.** Authorizing legislation for a part of the Colorado storage account — the Central Utah Project — died in the 101st Congress. But appropriators insisted that the Central Utah Project advance. They approved $66.1 million for it for fiscal 1992, $8 million more than Bush requested. Propelling the project was the growing water demand of sprawling Salt Lake City. Senate appropriators, including Jake Garn, R-Utah, prevailed in directing most of that increase toward building an aqueduct instead of toward fish and wildlife facilities, as the House had outlined. Appropriators also specified that ongoing local payments for the project could be credited toward cost-sharing mandates once the program was authorized.

• **Central Arizona Project.** Appropriators allocated $132.7 million for the Central Arizona Project, which included a hydropower generating facility and a massive aqueduct and pumping system that would deliver water to farms, municipalities and Indian reservations in central and southern Arizona. When completed, it would carry Colorado River water as far as Tucson and was meant to ease pressure on the state's groundwater supplies.

• **Bureau of Indian Affairs dam repairs.** The administration's request for $12 million for safety repairs on dams managed by the Bureau of Indian Affairs was turned down. Appropriators did provide money for dam repairs but left the account where it had been — in the spending bill for the Interior Department.

It was the second time the administration had sought to shift the repair program to the Bureau of Reclamation. Congress had turned down the request for fiscal 1991, citing objections from tribes that feared it would undermine the Bureau of Indian Affairs and possibly endanger existing contracts for the program.

ENERGY DEPARTMENT

The department's responsibilities included regulating domestic energy industries, managing nuclear waste, and researching and developing energy technologies and nuclear weaponry. The energy and water spending bill included just under $17 billion for the department, the bulk of the agency's budget. The department's fossil fuel programs were funded in a separate bill, with appropriations for the Interior Department.

Research and Development

The bill provided just under $3 billion for an array of Energy Department programs to promote energy sources, such as solar and nuclear power, and related research and environmental cleanup work at the department's non-military facilities.

Appropriators typically included money for specific universities, including construction projects related to energy research. In final negotiations for fiscal 1992, House and Senate conferees directed that almost $85 million of research and development money go to 10 university construction projects — most of them located in appropriators' states.

That list included $10 million for a micromanufacturing institute at Louisiana Tech University; $10 million for an ambulatory research and education building at the Oregon Health Sciences University; $10 million to build a cancer research center at the Indiana University School of Medicine at Indianapolis; $10 million for a high-tech education center at Bridgewater State College in Massachusetts; $10 million for a molecular electronics center at the University of Missouri-St. Louis; $10 million to build a research institute at the Loma Linda University Medical Center in California; $10 million to expand a science research building at the University of Alabama; $6 million to complete a center for cardiovascular disease, molecular biology and neurobiology at the Biomedical Research Institute of Louisiana State University in Shreveport; $4.8 million for a cancer center at the Medical University of South Carolina; and $4 million for the technology complex at Pittsburg State University in Kansas.

• **Solar and renewables.** The program promoted the development of various forms of solar energy, as well as photovoltaics, wind, ocean energy and biofuels. It accounted for about half a billion dollars in 1981, but under the Reagan and early Bush administrations dwindled to less than $100 million. The oil jitters created by the Persian Gulf War focused greater attention on this program to develop alternative energy sources. Bush requested $143 million for fiscal 1992. The account grew as it went through the appropriations process, ending at $175.5 million for fiscal 1992.

Geothermal and hydropower programs were considerably smaller and did not grow as much. Appropriation: $27 million for geothermal technology development and $1 million for hydropower development.

• **Environment, safety and health.** The bill provided $159.7 million in fiscal 1992 for this Energy Department office that was responsible for ensuring that all department programs conform with environmental laws and safeguard workers and the public health against safety hazards. The office conducted assessments, known as the Tiger Team program, of how well Energy Department operating facilities complied with relevant environmental and safety laws.

• **Electric energy systems and storage.** The bill provided $38 million for researching the health effects of electricity transmission, as well as developing improved transmission, distribution and storage systems.

• **Nuclear.** Provided in the bill was $337 million to promote civilian nuclear power plants and space and defense nuclear power systems and to find ways to manage civilian nuclear waste.

The program included $62.5 million to develop improved technology for light-water reactors and another $60 million to promote other advanced reactor technologies, including a high-temperature gas reactor and liquid-metal reactor.

General Electric and Asea Brown Boveri's Combustion Engineering subsidiary, both based in Connecticut, and the Pittsburgh-based Westinghouse Corp. were the major contractors for the advanced light-water reactor program. All three were also involved with elements of the advanced reactor program, as were Bechtel National of San Francisco, General Atomics of San Diego and several other contractors.

Defense- and space-related spending included $40 million for space reactor power systems and $51 million to provide radioisotope thermoelectric generators for the government's space agency and defense programs. Much of the money for the radioisotope program went for plutonium processing at the department's Savannah River complex in South Carolina.

There was also $5 million for a new Space Exploration Initiative, a cooperative program with the National Aeronautics and Space Administration to develop and test a power system to support human exploration of the moon and Mars. House appropriators originally left this project out of the bill, citing budget constraints and concern that the Energy Department did not have a clearly defined role in the space-related projects. Senate appropriators had advocated $10 million, saying the Energy Department should be involved in the project.

• **Fusion**. The program, designed to promote magnetic fusion energy, had a goal of running a demonstration plant by 2025 or sooner. Advocates hoped fusion energy could provide safer and cheaper nuclear power without the hazardous waste created by nuclear fission. The total budget for the fusion program was $337.1 million for fiscal 1992, a $64 million increase over fiscal 1991, as requested by the administration. The Princeton Plasma Physics Laboratory in New Jersey was a leading contractor for the fusion program.

The fusion budget included U.S. participation in an international effort to develop fusion energy in concert with Japan, the European Community and the Soviet Union.

• **Biological and environmental research.** The bill provided $353 million for a program to study the health and environmental impact of energy use and to employ the Energy Department's scientific and technological resources to help solve medical and biological problems.

It included a project to study global warming, funded at $74.5 million for fiscal 1992. Of that, $11 million was for the National Institute for Global Environmental Change, with $2 million earmarked for a new Southeastern Regional Center at the University of Alabama, the alma mater of House Appropriations Energy and Water Development Subcommittee Chairman Tom Bevill, D-Ala.

Another large item was the human genome project to study the genetic coding that guided human development and functioning. The project was being pursued jointly by the Energy Department and the National Institutes of Health, although the institutes' budget for the project had been almost twice that of the Energy Department's. The bill provided almost $57 million for Energy's share of the project in fiscal 1992, $11 million more than in fiscal 1991. Energy's genome research took place at three of its national laboratories: the Lawrence Livermore and Lawrence Berkeley laboratories in California and the Los Alamos laboratory in New Mexico.

This section of the bill also included money for various nuclear medicine programs, which explored the use of nuclear-related technologies to diagnose and treat diseases such as cancer.

• **Supporting research and analysis**. The bill provided $867 million for Energy Department support for basic research in the physical, biological and engineering sciences that could help supply energy. It supported the government's national energy laboratories and some private universities that served a variety of programs.

The Energy Department was part of an interagency effort to develop high-performance computing, or supercomputers. Appropriators allotted $93 million for programs related to the effort and urged that the department be given a clearer and preferably larger role in the joint effort.

The budget also included $90 million toward building the so-called 6-7 GeV Synchrotron Radiation sources at the Argonne National Laboratory in Argonne, Ill. The new synchrotron would provide brilliant X-ray beams that could penetrate matter to determine its structure — information of use to many scientific and technological fields.

• **Non-defense cleanup**. This account allotted $602.5 million for an array of environmental cleanup programs related to the Energy Department's non-military programs.

One major section of the account was a program to clean up 24 former uranium ore processing sites and adjacent properties, most in the West. Appropriators gave the program $139.9 million for fiscal 1992, and the House Energy Appropriations Subcommittee called for more work on several affected sites in Colorado.

Another $104 million was allotted for a West Valley, N.Y., nuclear waste storage project. The West Valley demonstration project would process high-level nuclear waste, some of it in liquid form, into a solid that was easier to store.

The account also included $79 million to continue to operate the Fast Flux Test Reactor at Hanford in Washington state for another year. The administration had sought to shut down the Fast Flux reactor, but Washington lawmakers and other supporters of the facility were pushing to develop it into a joint venture, with the private sector helping to underwrite costs in exchange for industrial and medical isotopes and irradiation services.

Uranium Supply and Enrichment

This program supplied enriched uranium for use in civilian nuclear power plants, domestic and foreign, and for other governmental needs, including defense.

The administration and some members wanted to privatize the project, and the administration's total budget request of roughly $1.6 billion included extra money to begin that process. But House and Senate appropriators said the Energy Department could not begin to privatize the enrichment process without enabling legislation. They cut the program appropriation accordingly, to $1.3 billion.

The program also included research into uranium atomic vapor laser isotope separation, or AVLIS, a new and potentially preferable technique for enriching uranium. The administration had sought $214 million for fiscal 1992 for the AVLIS research, but appropriators agreed to provide only $164 million.

Program costs were recouped through the sale of the enriched uranium.

General Science and Research

• **High-energy physics.** The bill provided $628 million for research in particle physics, particularly by studying particle collisions produced by colliders or accelerators. Included was $15 million toward construction of a new collider ring at the Fermi National Laboratory.

• **Nuclear physics.** Appropriators allocated $354 million to investigate the structure and interactions of atomic particles and the possible applications to astrophysics. This account included money to continue building the Relativistic Heavy Ion Collider at Brookhaven, N.Y., and the Continuous Electron Beam Accelerator Facility at Newport News, Va.

• **Superconducting super collider.** The administration had sought $534 million for fiscal 1992 for a giant atom-smasher being built in Waxahachie, Texas, for an eventual cost of more than $8 billion. Scientists were hopeful the collider would unlock valuable secrets about the building blocks of matter, but critics had derided the project as a white elephant. Appropriators cut fiscal 1992 funding to $484 million after attempts in both chambers to cut all funding for the 54-mile tunnel.

Miscellaneous

• **Nuclear waste.** The bill provided $275 million to proceed with various projects to handle nuclear waste from civilian power plants.

The largest expenses were studies of Yucca Mountain in Nevada as a possible site for a high-level civilian nuclear waste dump. The budget included $12.5 million for Nevada's universities and its state and local governments to monitor the work, which had been highly controversial in Nevada.

The disposal fund also covered smaller programs to design and site a temporary waste dump, known as monitored retrievable storage, as well as waste transportation systems.

• **Isotope fund.** The Energy Department supplied radioactive and stable isotope products and services to a range of customers in the United States and abroad. The isotopes could be used in fields such as medical research, manufacturing, agriculture and defense activities. The program operated under a revolving fund, which was granted an initial $16.2 million appropriation in fiscal 1990 and now operated on revenues. For fiscal 1992, the program received $8.5 million in borrowing authority to finance three new medical and industrial product initiatives, to be repaid through sales.

• **Departmental administration.** The bill included a net appropriation of $122 million, after revenues were deducted, to pay for department salaries and other administrative expenses, as well as cooperation in international energy activities such as nuclear non-proliferation programs.

About one-third of the $12 billion atomic defense program was for cleaning up nuclear weapons facilities, such as the Savannah River facility in South Carolina.

• **Inspector general.** Appropriators allocated $31 million for the department's oversight office, which conducted audits and investigations to correct fraud, waste or mismanagement.

• **Power marketing administrations.** The bill provided funding for four regional power authorities that developed and marketed power from federal hydroelectric facilities. They were the Alaska Power Administration, $3.2 million; Southeastern Power Administration, $23.7 million; Southwestern Power Administration, $28.5 million; and the Western Area Power Administration, $306.5 million.

It also authorized the Northwest's Bonneville Power Authority, which was self-supporting, to spend its revenues.

The administration had sought to decrease federal subsidies for power authority customers, but lawmakers had repeatedly resisted such a move and for fiscal 1992 explicitly blocked the administration from conducting any studies aimed at raising the electric rates. According to the appropriators' report, such rate changes could damage the affected economies too severely and possibly jeopardize federal revenues by driving energy-intensive industries from the regions.

• **Federal Energy Regulatory Commission.** Appropriators set aside $141 million to run the Federal Energy Regulatory Commission, which oversaw regulations affecting oil and natural gas, hydroelectric power and electric utilities. Budgeted expenses were entirely offset by projected revenues from license fees and other charges.

• **Geothermal resources development fund.** This was a federal loan guarantee fund to help encourage the commercial production of geothermal energy by guaranteeing lenders against losses on loans to qualified geothermal projects. The Energy Department in 1982 announced it would begin closing out the program. Administrators said they had processed all pending applications, and no new money was budgeted for the program.

Independent Agencies

• **Appalachian Regional Commission.** The bill allotted $190 million for infrastructure and other development work in 13 states of the Appalachian region. Of that money, about $23 million was earmarked for road construction in Alabama, $16 million for work in Mississippi and $58 million for roads in West Virginia.

The Reagan administration repeatedly tried to zero out this program, founded in 1965, but Bevill and other strong congressional supporters kept it alive through the 1980s. For fiscal 1992, appropriators almost doubled the administration's request of $100 million.

• **Tennessee Valley Authority.** The authority oversaw an array of public lands and facilities connected with the vast public utility project. Its operations paid for themselves, but the federal agency spent money on environmental management, rural development and the National Fertilizer and Environmental Research Center. Appropriators gave the authority $135 million for fiscal 1992, almost $44 million more than the administration requested. They emphasized that the authority should promote broader economic development in the area.

• **Nuclear Regulatory Commission.** The commission was charged with overseeing the nuclear power industry, particularly by reviewing nuclear power plant license applications and promoting plant safety. Appropriators allocated $512.5 million for commission expenses, most of which would be offset by projected revenues from fees. Lawmakers approved a net appropriation of just under $20 million.

• **River commissions.** The bill also budgeted money for several regional river basin commissions that the federal government helped to support: Delaware River Basin Commission, $775,000; Potomac River Basin, $510,000; Susquehanna River Basin Commission, $594,000.

• **Defense Nuclear Facilities Safety Board.** The

board oversaw the standards governing most nuclear defense facilities and was charged with investigating any health or safety issues at the facilities. It was created in late 1988 as an independent agency that could make recommendations to the Energy secretary, but was not under his direction. The board's fiscal 1992 allocation was $11.5 million.

• **Nuclear Waste Technical Review Board**. The 11-member board was created by the 1987 amendments to the Nuclear Waste Policy Act to oversee the technical and scientific soundness of the Energy Department's civilian nuclear waste program. For instance, the board monitors the department's politically controversial work to site a permanent waste dump at Nevada's Yucca Mountain. The board received the full $3.3 million it sought in its first budget request to pay for a full-time staff of 22 people and other expenses.

NUCLEAR DEFENSE PROGRAMS

The Energy Department helped build the nation's nuclear arsenal at more than a dozen complexes across the country. Since the late 1980s, the program had been beset by safety, environmental and management problems. The department's tritium production reactors at Savannah River had been shut since 1988, and the Rocky Flats plant, which produced the plutonium triggers for hydrogen bombs, had been closed since early 1990.

Secretary James D. Watkins took over the department in 1989 pledging a "new culture" that would emphasize safety and environmental concerns, reflect the changing defense needs of the post-Cold War era and restore the program's credibility. The department's recommendations for reconfiguring the weapons complex, submitted to Congress in February 1991, envisioned a smaller nuclear stockpile and fewer and more efficient weapons complexes. Under the reconfiguration plan, more of the program's non-nuclear work would be transferred to the private sector.

The president's 1992 budget, generally adopted by Congress, reflected some of those new priorities. There was more money for environmental cleanup and arms control verification. Within research and production accounts, there was a greater emphasis on safety and waste reduction.

Critics believed the atomic defense program was still badly managed and skewed toward production. But some of the most controversial projects could be up for review in the wake of Bush's plans — announced in late September — for a new round of nuclear arms cuts.

Research, development and testing activities took place at four installations: the Lawrence Livermore National Laboratory in California, the Los Alamos National Laboratory in New Mexico, the Sandia national laboratories in New Mexico and California, and the Nevada test site.

The Mound plant in Ohio, the Kansas City plant and the Pinellas plant in Florida all manufactured non-nuclear components for nuclear weaponry.

Nuclear materials production and manufacturing, as well as some non-nuclear work, took place at the Hanford plant in Washington, the Oak Ridge plant in Tennessee, the Savannah River site in South Carolina, the Pantex plant in Texas, the Rocky Flats plant in Colorado and the Idaho National Engineering Laboratory.

Appropriators provided $12 billion for the Energy Department's nuclear defense program.

Research, Development and Testing

Nuclear weapons research and development encompassed designing new weaponry, as well as increasing the safety of nuclear weapons and inventing new design concepts such as reusing explosive warhead triggers. Planners wanted to make the weapons manufacturing more compact and efficient, and generate less waste.

• **Nuclear fusion.** One of the largest projects within the research program was one of the Energy Department's efforts on nuclear fusion, known as inertial confinement fusion. The project was an effort to create a controlled thermonuclear explosion through fusion to study the process and consider its potential for weaponry and as an energy source. The bill contained $195 million for the fusion project, about $12 million more than the administration had requested. House appropriators earmarked about $20 million of that to upgrade the OMEGA laser at the University of Rochester, more than twice the amount the administration had sought for the laser upgrade.

• **Plutonium processing.** The bill allocated $15 million to continue work at the Lawrence Livermore National Laboratory toward developing an advanced chemical processing technology that could enable the department to process plutonium with less waste. Senate appropriators inserted the $15 million, arguing that the laboratory has assembled an accomplished scientific team on plutonium processing whose expertise would be lost if allowed to disband.

• **Testing.** The account included just under $500 million for testing, somewhat more than requested by the administration but about $20 million less than recommended by Senate authorizers to accommodate the new emphasis on safety and innovative designs.

Underground nuclear tests were conducted at a nuclear test site in southern Nevada. The testing account also paid for health and environmental monitoring on the Marshall Islands, in connection with past U.S. atmospheric tests there.

• **Production and surveillance.** This account funded many of the nuclear weapons production facilities, including the troubled Rocky Flats complex in Colorado. The $2.5 billion account included programs to address health and environmental concerns at the bomb factories. The administration had requested $88 million to develop a short-range attack missile, called the SRAMT, and a nuclear depth-strike bomb. But those projects had been sidelined. Conferees deleted $33 million for the two weapons and specified that the rest of the money be shifted to cover the cost of retiring weapons and other ongoing expenses.

• **Materials production.** The bill provided nuclear materials for weaponry as well as for government and civilian research, commercial and medical applications. The materials production operations had been concentrated primarily at the Savannah River site, the Hanford complex and the Idaho National Engineering Laboratory.

This account was decreasing due to a shrinking nuclear arsenal, and, as some facilities were shut down, their expenses were transferred to a cleanup program. The program was allotted $1.9 billion in the budget, compared with $2.3 billion in fiscal 1991. However, House appropriators had complained that operating expenses were not dropping in proportion to the smaller overall mission and budget of these facilities.

• **Verification and security.** The bill included $403.6 million for arms control verification programs and measures to safeguard the nuclear defense program, about $50 million more than in fiscal 1991. Most of that increase was allocated for arms control verification to carry out the Threshold Test Ban Treaty and Peaceful Nuclear Explosions Treaty and the technology development for treaty verification.

• **New production reactors.** The bill allotted $515.5 million for the new production reactor program, designed to ensure a supply of tritium gas for nuclear warheads. No new tritium had been produced since the 1988 shutdown of the production reactors at Savannah River. The new reactor, once built, would provide a reliable new source of tritium.

The Energy Department had originally proposed building a heavy water reactor at the Savannah River complex in South Carolina and a high-temperature gas reactor at the Idaho National Engineering Laboratory. The department proposing building only one reactor and was expected to choose both the site and the technology in late 1991 or early 1992.

The design choice would no longer predetermine where the reactor would be built, and both the Idaho and South Carolina delegations were expected to lobby fiercely for their respective sites.

As a contingency, the Energy Department was also exploring producing tritium in a partially completed light water reactor at the Hanford nuclear weapons complex in Washington state. The appropriations bill set aside $15.5 million for that light water reactor project. Senate authorizers were concerned that the reactor program was falling behind schedule and had recommended $552 million for fiscal 1992 to keep it on track.

• **Naval reactors.** The program conducted the research, development and oversight of nuclear propulsion plants and reactor cores for the nation's nuclear fleet, predominantly submarines but also large surface ships. One major project was to build an advanced reactor to power the politically troubled *Seawolf*-class attack submarine, being built by Electric Boat Co. in Connecticut. The program also included uranium enrichment to manufacture the fuel needed for the cores in naval ships powered by nuclear reactors.

Program costs had been increasing due to environmental and safety concerns at the test reactor at the Idaho National Engineering Laboratory. In keeping with the recommendations of the defense authorization bill, appropriators allotted $818 million for this program, $17 million more than the administration had requested.

• **Cleanup.** Almost one-third of the atomic defense program for fiscal 1992 was for cleaning up the nuclear weapons facilities and developing waste management technologies. The account was the fastest growing item in the program budget, jumping to $3.7 billion in fiscal 1992 from $3 billion in fiscal 1991. However, Senate appropriators cut back the even higher amounts recommended by the administration and House appropriators.

Although the total cleanup was ultimately expected to require many billions of dollars, some Senate appropriators argued that cleanup officials needed more time to decide how best to spend so much money.

Environmental restoration work was under way at virtually all of the Energy Department complexes involved with nuclear defense, with particularly extensive work to be done at Hanford, Rocky Flats, Oak Ridge, Savannah River and the Idaho National Engineering Laboratory. The department stopped production work at the Feed Materials Production Center in Fernald, Ohio, in late 1989, and that facility was slated for extensive cleanup operations.

The bill earmarked $79.2 million of the cleanup money for the Hanford waste vitrification plant, to process nuclear waste into a less hazardous solid. The Energy Department had initially sought only $37 million for the project but subsequently agreed to spend the extra $42.2 million as part of an agreement with Washington state and the Environmental Protection Agency on cleanup at the Hanford plant.

Another $17.1 million was set to build a new environmental and molecular sciences lab at Hanford that would research molecular processes in the environment that might have a bearing on cleanup work.

The defense cleanup account included $142 million for work at the Waste Isolation Pilot Plant , which was being built near Carlsbad, N.M., to store waste from nuclear bomb facilities. Conferees also targeted $20 million for state and local aid in connection with the waste plant.

The administration had been seeking congressional approval to begin trial storage, but as of early October took steps to proceed on its own authority. Under the appropriations bill, the $20 million in impact aid would become available once that testing had begun.

• **Training and technology transfer.** The bill provided just under $50 million to train workers for the nuclear defense program and to promote the commercialization of program technologies. The Energy Department's nuclear defense research program included another $50 million for promoting commercial applications. ■

Continued from p. 572

When the bill came to the floor, Dale Bumpers, D-Ark., proposed eliminating funding for it.

Bumpers belittled the necessity of the super collider, which scientists believed would help them discover the building blocks of matter, and said it was unlikely that the project would provide commercial spinoffs. He argued that the tight economic times overshadowed any scientific merit.

But subcommittee Chairman Johnston and both Texas senators sprang to the project's defense.

They argued that the United States could ill-afford to turn its back on the scientific and technical promise of the project. Phil Gramm, R-Texas, cast it as a choice between investing in future technological competitiveness or spending programs with more immediate political popularity.

Bumpers was the only senator to speak in favor of his amendment and acknowledged that he lacked the votes for passage. The Senate eventually voted 62-37 to reject the proposal, but Bumpers did win some prominent votes, including Majority Leader George J. Mitchell, D-Maine, and Assistant Minority Leader Alan K. Simpson, R-Wyo. *(Vote 121, p. 17-S)*

The Senate more narrowly rejected an amendment to shift $118 million from nuclear weapons research and production to cleaning up the sites where those weapons were made.

The change would have more than restored the $108 million Senate appropriators had cut from the House cleanup budget of $3.7 billion, while leaving the weapons research and production budget above the House level.

Amendment supporters argued that the Cold War was over and that the government should shift its resources out of nuclear weapons building and into repairing the environmental damage caused by those programs. John Glenn, D-Ohio, an amendment sponsor, said the ongoing cleanup program would be hampered without extra money.

But Johnston said the cleanup account had grown so

rapidly that the Energy Department probably would not be able to spend it all properly. "You do not spread dollar bills out on the ground, and they do not automatically absorb nuclear waste."

Johnston said additional money for weapons production and research was needed to make the weapons program safer, rather than to build new bombs.

Glenn's amendment was tabled (killed), 54-43. *(Vote 119, p. 16-S)*

Senators also agreed to ease the 1989 federal wetlands rules that some senators believed defined wetlands too broadly and placed unfair restrictions on landowners.

The Senate, on a voice vote, approved an amendment that would require the Army Corps of Engineers to return to a weaker definition of a wetland. The provision allowed some landowners to alter their property without first seeking a permit but specifically sought not to stall any ongoing projects. The action came after Johnston revised an earlier amendment, approved by the Appropriations Committee, that would have barred any enforcement of the rules and could have hampered pending projects.

The Senate bill also included 14 so-called new starts. It also dramatically boosted spending on some existing projects, including the Red River Waterway in Louisiana and the Levisa and Tug Forks projects in Kentucky and West Virginia.

On the floor, senators added another water-construction project: $5 million for urgent erosion-control work in Bethel, Alaska, where according to Alaska's Stevens a river threatened to wash away vital buildings.

Senators added a number of smaller earmarks, including $850,000 for the Wyoming River Valley levees in Pennsylvania and $500,000 to study a wastewater delivery system in Cranston, R.I.

Other amendments approved by voice vote included:

- By Wyche Fowler Jr., D-Ga., and James M. Jeffords, R-Vt., to restore $14.7 million cut from the House budget to promote the commercial use of renewable energy, including solar energy, photovoltaics, biofuels and wind energy. The money was to come from the Energy Department's general research and development account.
- By Don Nickles, R-Okla., to block the Army Corps of Engineers from increasing certain fees on lakefront property.
- By Tim Wirth, D-Colo., to add $500,000 to a program to help civilian nuclear reactors switch to fuel that could not be used for atomic weaponry.

CONFERENCE ACTION

House and Senate negotiators agreed to the final $21.8 billion version of the energy and water spending bill July 30. The House adopted the conference report the next day.

During the July 31 House debate, Dan Burton, R-Ind., forced a separate vote Aug. 1, complaining that House negotiators had agreed to some non-essential projects inserted by the Senate. He unsuccessfully sought to delete two of 14 new water construction projects tacked on in the Senate and retained by conferees.

House appropriators originally had refrained from approving any of the coveted new starts. But House subcommittee Chairman Bevill said House conferees did not mind including the 14 projects after they were given more money to spend during conference.

On the floor, members rejected Burton's challenge and voted, 338-80, to accept the disputed provision containing the two new water projects. That cleared the way for the bill to go to the Senate. *(Vote 249, p. 60-H)*

The compromise allocation, which was slightly different from the actual appropriation, included $11.98 billion for defense-related spending and $9.9 billion for domestic programs. That included all of the Senate's additional defense money, $200 million, and half of the extra domestic funds, $145 million of the original $290 million.

Within the defense account, conferees shifted $40 million more toward cleaning up the nation's nuclear weapons facilities, for a total of $3.68 billion. That figure was still somewhat below the House-approved amount and the administration's request.

That account included about $80 million for a nuclear waste vitrification project at the Hanford nuclear facility in Washington state, roughly twice the administration's original request. Vitrification was a process of treating radioactive materials and allowing them to harden into a solid.

On the domestic side of the ledger, negotiators cut a little deeper into the superconducting super collider. Conferees settled on $484 million for the project, a compromise between the House and Senate amounts that was $50 million less than Bush had sought.

That amount was still roughly twice the super collider's appropriation for fiscal 1991.

Members also cut to $275 million the Energy Department's budget to pursue building a nuclear waste dump at Yucca Mountain, Nev. The Senate had cut $10 million from the administration request, and conferees took another $20 million. *(Yucca Mountain dump site, p. 226)*

The Senate also yielded to some House preferences; for instance, agreeing to restore money cut from a flood control project along New Jersey's Passaic River. Two of the 11 House conferees, Democrat Bernard J. Dwyer and Republican Dean A. Gallo, were from New Jersey.

Conferees agreed to retain a measure inserted by Senate subcommittee Chairman Johnston aimed at blocking implementation of 1989 federal wetlands rules that many members believed were too stringent. The bill banned the Army Corps of Engineers from enforcing the rules in most cases, unless it first submitted them or new regulations to a public review process. ■

Record Amounts To Aid Women, Children

The Senate on Oct. 16 cleared for the president's signature a $52.5 billion fiscal 1992 appropriations bill (HR 2698) for the Agriculture Department and related agencies.

Senators voted 88-10 to adopt a conference report on the bill, which included record appropriations for nutrition programs for needy women and children and new funding for environmental programs authorized by the 1990 farm bill. *(Vote 223, p. 29-S)*

The House had agreed to the conference report on Oct. 8 by voice vote.

Food stamps, school lunches and the Women, Infants and Children (WIC) feeding program accounted for $32 billion of the bill's spending, 62 percent of the total.

The bill earmarked $7.25 billion on farm subsidies and price supports through the Commodity Credit Corporation (CCC).

It included no restrictions on crop insurance or spending for the Export Enhancement Program, an incentive program for selling farm commodities overseas.

Farm-state lawmakers had hoped the spending bill would provide money for a Rural Development Administration within the Agriculture Department, as was authorized in the 1990 farm bill.

Jamie L. Whitten, D-Miss., chairman of the House Appropriations Committee and its Agriculture Subcommittee, had attempted to block the Agriculture Department from spending any money on the new agency. He later dropped the funding ban, but the bill still provided no money for it.

Environmentalists had hoped for more money for new environmental programs included in the 1990 farm bill but were satisfied that most received at least enough money to get started.

BOXSCORE

➡ **Fiscal 1992 appropriations for the Agriculture Department and related agencies (HR 2698).** The $52.5 billion measure provided funding for the Agriculture Department, the Food and Drug Administration, and food for international programs.

Reports: HR 2698: H Rept 102-119; S Rept 102-116; conference report filed in the House, H Rept 102-239.

KEY ACTION

June 26 — HR 2698 passed the **House** by a vote of 368-48.

July 30 — HR 2698 passed the **Senate** by a vote of 92-7.

Oct. 3 — HR 2698 approved by **House-Senate** conference.

Oct. 8 — The **House** agreed to conference report by a voice vote.

Oct. 16 — The **Senate** agreed to conference report by a 88-10 vote.

Oct. 28 — President Bush signed HR 2698 — PL 102-142.

HOUSE COMMITTEE ACTION

The House Appropriations Committee on June 20 approved a $52.6 billion fiscal 1992 spending bill for the Department of Agriculture that undercut much of the Bush administration's effort to get the government out of the business of extending direct loans to farmers.

HR 2698 was $1.5 billion less than the department's fiscal 1991 spending bill, but the reduction did not represent real savings. It was the result of bookkeeping changes required by the 1991 Credit Reform Act, which called for a new accounting of loans to reveal their actual annual costs. *(1990 Almanac, p. 867)*

The committee appropriated $31.5 billion for domestic food programs — the largest portion of the bill. That was $2.4 billion more than the fiscal 1991 spending level and about $954 million less than requested by President Bush. However, the panel provided $26 million more than Bush requested for the WIC feeding program.

Committee Chairman Whitten boasted that despite the fiscal 1992 budget constraints, he had managed to satisfy many lawmakers' requests for special projects. The spending bill traditionally was flush with money earmarked for lawmakers' special farming projects throughout the country.

For example, $1 million in the fiscal 1992 bill was for improvement of sugar cane research facilities in Hawaii, $175,000 was for swine research at the University of Minnesota and $70,000 was for an Ohio State University research project on why white mold attacked soybeans.

"We've tried to deal fairly with all the members and their problems," Whitten said. "And, when I say members, I mean sections of the United States."

The most sweeping changes came in spending for the Farmers Home Administration, which administered rural housing loan programs and farm operating loans, farmland loans and loans for rural water and sewer systems.

The administration had proposed requiring the federal government to guarantee most of the loans, rather than directly lending to borrowers. The Agriculture Department also set up a Rural Development Administration to administer a number of the rural loan programs.

But the committee reversed the administration's move to put the bulk of the Farmers Home Administration loan money into loan guarantees and refused to fund the new agency.

The committee gave the administration leeway to guarantee a large number of private bank loans but also restored funding for the program that made loans directly from the Treasury.

In a move that Agriculture Department officials said would diminish interest in the loan program, appropriators refused to fund a loan subsidy program that allowed the government to pay a portion of the interest rates on private loans to make them less expensive and more attractive to borrowers.

The panel action returned the Farmers Home Administration's loan program to what it had been since its inception in the 1930s, when it was set up as a lender of last resort for farmers.

The committee also refused to fund two environmental initiatives included in the 1990 farm reauthorization bill (PL 101-624). They were the Wetlands Reserve Program, designed to restore and protect 1 million acres of wetlands between 1991 and 1995, and the Organic Standards Board, which was created in 1990 to oversee the farming and

Agriculture & Rural Development

(In thousands of dollars)

	Fiscal 1991 Appropriation	President's Request	House Bill	Senate Bill	Final Bill
Agriculture Programs					
Agricultural Research Service	$ 665,101	$ 709,227	$ 710,397	$ 693,461	$ 711,443
Cooperative State Research	451,356	409,151	479,415	480,557	505,981
Extension Service	398,478	410,817	417,057	412,129	419,325
Animal and plant inspection	415,516	433,700	448,299	436,887	452,335
Food safety and inspection	448,882	473,512	473,512	473,512	473,512
Crop Insurance	677,365	631,652	544,370	583,370	583,370
Commodity Credit Corporation (CCC)	5,001,400	9,000,000	8,450,000	8,450,000	7,250,000
Other	507,885	530,451	1,217,666	473,084	1,224,545
Subtotal	**$ 8,565,983**	**$ 12,598,510**	**$ 12,740,716**	**$12,003,000**	**$11,620,511**
Conservation Programs					
Soil Conservation Service	771,257	808,740	849,950	848,698	849,978
Conservation Reserve Program	1,314,926	1,642,760	1,642,760	1,611,277	1,611,277
Other conservation	241,521	346,101	254,347	331,044	293,204
Subtotal	**$ 2,327,704**	**$ 2,797,601**	**$ 2,747,057**	**$ 2,791,019**	**$ 2,754,459**
Rural Development Programs					
Farmers Home Administration					
Rural Housing Fund					
New budget authority	2,975,286	1,121,484	1,382,182	1,298,746	1,333,836
(Loan authorization)	*(1,978,581)*	*(1,905,350)*	*(2,512,581)*	*(2,088,581)*	*(2,476,630)*
Agricultural Credit					
New budget authority	6,018,106	487,039	642,865	555,768	557,626
(Loan authorization)	*(4,868,100)*	*(3,488,000)*	*(4,918,100)*	*(3,395,740)*	*(4,200,240)*
Rural Development					
New budget authority	1,666,160	130,663	173,991	146,205	161,185
(Loan authorization)	*(760,000)*	*(615,700)*	*(860,000)*	*(760,000)*	*(860,000)*
Other Farmers Home	1,138,127	499,675	494,976	499,539	501,411
Rural Electrification Administration					
New budget authority	334,632	171,303	293,949	214,882	220,974
(Loan authorization)	*(1,794,375)*	*(1,426,700)*	*(2,522,075)*	*(2,288,075)*	*(2,775,604)*
Other rural development	530	14,443	552	572	572
Subtotal	**$ 12,132,841**	**$ 2,424,607**	**$ 2,988,535**	**$ 2,715,692**	**$ 2,775,604**
Domestic Food Programs					
Food stamp program	20,550,901	23,162,975	22,162,975	23,662,975	23,362,975
Child nutrition programs	5,577,199	6,064,803	6,067,386	6,068,743	6,068,315
Transfer from customs receipts	(4,696,501)	(4,675,092)	(4,675,092)	(4,675,092)	(4,675,092)
Women, Infants and Children (WIC)	2,350,000	2,573,400	2,600,000	2,573,400	2,600,000
Other food programs	638,520	647,483	663,146	649,235	658,313
Subtotal	**$ 29,116,620**	**$ 32,448,661**	**$ 31,493,507**	**$ 32,954,353**	**$ 32,689,603**
International Programs					
PL 480 (Food for Peace)	1,010,853	1,301,921	1,400,585	1,486,000	1,486,000
(Program level)	(1,576,000)	(1,400,000)	(1,521,759)	(1,607,500)	(1,607,485)
CCC export loan subsidy	—	155,524	155,524	155,524	155,524
(loan authorization)	*(5,500,000)*	*(5,700,000)*	*(5,700,000)*	*(5,700,000)*	*(5,700,000)*
Other	113,489	119,515	122,297	116,338	121,090
Subtotal	**$ 1,124,342**	**$ 1,576,960**	**$ 1,678,406**	**$ 1,757,862**	**$ 1,762,614**
Related Agencies					
Food and Drug Administration	690,481	572,716	761,924	738,696	759,924
Other	133,960	160,891	159,906	159,203	159,906
TOTALS					
New budget authority	**$ 54,089,588**	**$ 52,579,946**	**$ 52,570,051**	**$ 53,120,030**	**$ 52,522,621**
Direct and insured loan level	*5,129,536*	*2,729,050*	*5,200,826*	*5,011,326*	*5,189,625*
Guaranteed loan level	*4,390,620*	*3,038,800*	*4,385,620*	*3,236,126*	*3,750,916*

SOURCE: House Appropriations Committee

marketing of organic foods. *(1990 Almanac, p. 323)*

Bush had requested $124.4 million for the wetlands program but did not request funding for the organic board.

The federal Crop Insurance Program, which Whitten had tried to eliminate in past years, remained intact. The committee agreed to fund it at the level requested by the administration — $322.9 million.

The committee approved $8.45 billion to cover losses in farm-subsidy programs funded through the CCC. That was $550 million less than the administration estimated was to be needed in fiscal 1992.

In the past, when the CCC came up short of funds, lawmakers had been required to provide supplemental appropriations to keep farm programs from shutting down. In an unusual move, Whitten inserted $720 million in direct appropriations for salaries and expenses that were normally paid out of CCC accounts.

HOUSE FLOOR ACTION

The House on June 27 passed with relatively little controversy a $52.6 billion version of HR 2698.

The measure, which passed 368-48, included $31.5 billion for the food stamp and WIC programs and $12.7 billion for farm price supports. *(Vote 201, p. 50-H)*

After the vote, the White House's Office of Management and Budget (OMB) issued a sharply worded statement that stopped short of a veto threat.

OMB strongly objected to provisions for the Rural Electrification Administration and the Farmers Home Administration, both of which undercut administration efforts to reduce the number of direct loans to farmers and rural borrowers.

During House debate, the only serious controversy came over a one-line provision prohibiting the Agriculture secretary from spending any money on the Rural Development Administration, created by the 1990 farm bill.

The move drew particularly heavy fire from Agriculture Committee members, who had created the agency in the 1990 farm bill, as they sought to maintain control over farm policy.

E. "Kika" de la Garza, D-Texas, chairman of the Agriculture Committee, offered a successful amendment that allowed spending for the agency. Although the bill still provided no money for it, the amendment allowed any excess funds to be spent on the program.

Debate also was sparked by another program designed to improve water quality that the Agriculture Committee had placed in the farm bill but that the Appropriations Committee had not funded. An amendment offered by Jim Jontz, D-Ind., a member of the House Agriculture Committee, reinstated $3.5 million for the program — a fraction of the $124 million requested by the administration.

SENATE COMMITTEE ACTION

The Senate Appropriations Committee on July 23 approved HR 2698, a $53.12 billion version of the agriculture spending bill that boosted spending for environmental programs and undercut the Bush administration's effort to reduce direct lending to farmers.

The Senate had $434 million less than the House to spend on discretionary programs funded by the bill. However, Whitten and Senate Appropriations Committee Chairman Robert C. Byrd, D-W.Va., resolved much of that difference on July 25 by agreeing to increase the Senate's spending outlay limit for agriculture by $350 million.

The Senate rejected, as did the House, the administration's request to fund the $167 million administrative budget of the Food and Drug Administration through user fees. Both bills held the money in reserve and made it available only if the president requested it and agreed that some of it could be considered emergency spending.

The Senate version of the measure was $970 million less than the department's fiscal 1991 spending bill, but the reduction was primarily the result of bookkeeping changes required by the 1991 Credit Reform Act.

The largest portion of the Senate bill appropriated nearly $33 billion for domestic food programs, about $4 billion more than the fiscal 1991 appropriation and $1.46 billion more than the House approved.

More than $3 billion of the increase was in the $23.7 billion request for the food stamp program, considered mandatory spending outside of appropriators' discretion. Demand was rising because there were an increasing number of qualified people applying for the benefits.

Despite the tight constraint on spending, there was room for numerous special projects in lawmakers' districts.

The bill included $300,000 under rural health care for a feasibility study for a pediatric clinic in Pittsburgh requested by Appropriations Committee member Arlen Specter, R-Pa.

It also included $400,000 to expand aquaculture research at Louisiana State University to include redfish and alligators and $200,000 for research at Texas A&I University in Kingsville into the cultivation of mesquite and prickly pear trees, whose wood was used for smoking meats and fish.

Thad Cochran of Mississippi, ranking Republican on the Agriculture Appropriations Subcommittee, said that requests from senators exceeded the amount of money available to the Appropriations Committee in 1991. "We have had many requests for funding of research programs, and there simply has not been enough money to go around," he said.

The biggest difference between the Senate and House versions of the bill was in spending for high-profile environmental and conservation programs authorized by the 1990 farm bill, which was vaunted as a "green" farm bill.

The Senate bill appropriated $91 million for the Wetlands Reserve Program to preserve 1 million acres of wetlands as habitat for animals and migratory birds; the House did not fund the program. The Senate also approved the Organic Standards Board.

Both chambers refused to fund a new Rural Development Administration, also created by the 1990 farm bill, although a deal worked out in the House allowed the Agriculture Department to fund the agency through other means.

The Senate, like the House, opposed the Bush administration's funding proposals for loans to farmers and for the Farmers Home Administration. The Bush administration proposed allowing the federal government to guarantee loans to farmers rather than directly lending to them. But the Senate largely opposed that move and restored much of the direct lending program.

The Senate approved the same amount — $322 million — for the crop insurance program as did the House.

The program was a favorite of Senate Agriculture Appropriations Subcommittee Chairman Quentin N. Burdick, D-N.D. In the past Burdick had repeatedly saved the program

Continued on p. 590

Agriculture and Rural Development Provisions

The appropriations bill for agriculture, rural development and related agencies covered a vast array of programs that directly or indirectly affected the price, quality and safety of American food and the quality of life in rural communities.

More than half of the funds in the bill were devoted to helping provide food for needy people, largely through the $23.4 billion food stamp program, which was run by the Agriculture Department. Farm-oriented groups were more interested in the bill's spending for commodity price supports, farm lending and other farmer-support services.

Other agencies funded by the bill included the Food and Drug Administration, which was part of the Department of Health and Human Services.

The bill includeed discretionary appropriations and entitlement programs, in which spending levels were determined by eligibility criteria already set by law. Entitlements accounted for about 60 percent of the bill's $52.5 billion price tag; they included food stamps and the crop-subsidy payments made to farmers through the Agriculture Department's Commodity Credit Corporation.

AGRICULTURE PROGRAMS

Commodity Credit Corporation (CCC)

Created in 1933 as part of Franklin D. Roosevelt's New Deal, the CCC was the centerpiece of the government's price-support program for agriculture. It essentially functioned as the Agriculture Department's bank. It was the financial entity that paid farm subsidies and disposed of surplus commodities acquired under the programs. It also paid subsidies to exporters through the Export Enhancement Program — one of the programs the department used to challenge foreign competitors in overseas markets.

During the course of the fiscal year, the CCC paid out loans and subsidies and took in payments as previous years' loans were repaid; Congress then made up the difference. The CCC had authority to borrow up to $30 billion to cover its expenses, with the shortfall reimbursed by Congress. For fiscal 1992, Congress appropriated $7.2 billion to reimburse the CCC for its losses.

If the Agriculture Department's estimate of the CCC's annual need turns out to be too low (the result of unexpected bad weather, the consequent crop losses and then price decreases), the CCC can exhaust all of its borrowing authority; in that case Congress must come back with a supplemental appropriation in the middle of the fiscal year to cover the shortfall. If the CCC runs out of money and borrowing authority with no new appropriation, the Agriculture Department must stop payment on all price-support checks to farmers. (This scenario was a recurring problem at the height of the farm crisis in the mid-1980s, but in the past four years, the CCC had not even come close to hitting its borrowing limit.)

The Reagan and Bush administrations had sought repeatedly to make the CCC reimbursement a "permanent" appropriation by taking the discretionary funding decision away from Congress and allowing the department to spend money as needed to carry out farm law. But House Appropriations Chairman Jamie L. Whitten, D-Miss., had always wanted to keep a firm hand on the CCC's purse strings and had opposed such a move. In the past, Whitten used the need for a CCC supplemental as leverage to advance a supplemental spending bill that was padded with pet projects of individual members.

Conservation Reserve Program

The Conservation Reserve Program was the most ambitious, and thus most expensive, of the conservation programs run by the government. Under the program, the government paid farmers to take erodible land out of production for 10 years and plant it with cover crops that discouraged erosion. By 1991 nearly 36 million acres had gone under contract since the program was created by Congress in 1985.

For fiscal 1992, Congress appropriated $1.6 billion for the program, enough to pay for 357,000 existing contracts and the 17,000 new contracts the department expected to write.

Crop Insurance

Crop insurance costs were established through an eligibility formula and thus did not fall within the discretion of appropriators. The bill provided $260.5 million for this program in fiscal 1992.

The Federal Crop Insurance Corporation was created in 1938 after the catastrophic dust bowl years to help farmers cope financially with the destruction of their crops by natural disasters. It paid farmers 30 percent of the cost of buying insurance to protect them from losses. The insurance was provided by private firms and underwritten by the corporation. Losses were apportioned between private insurers and the federal government.

For much of the 1980s the crop insurance program operated in the red, spending $1.45 for every $1 that it earned in premiums. It had drawn criticism from the Reagan and Bush administrations as well as from House Chairman Whitten, who would have liked the government to run it rather than private insurance companies. In contrast, Sen. Quentin N. Burdick, D-N.D., chairman of the Senate Appropriations Subcommittee on Agriculture, was a staunch defender of the crop insurance program. In his home state, 82 percent of the eligible acres were enrolled in the program. In Mississippi, Whitten's home state, only 27 percent of eligible acres were enrolled.

This regional split in participation was reflected nationwide. Midwest and Great Plains farmers purchased crop insurance in far greater numbers than did Southern or New England farmers. One explanation: Farms in the Plains states were limited to fewer crops and so were more vulnerable to natural disasters. Southern farmers often planted more than one crop a year on their acreage, giving them more opportunity to make up losses on one bad crop.

Overall, only 40 percent of the acres eligible for insurance were in the program, mainly because the program's coverage overlapped with other federal disaster-aid programs that farmers received at little or no cost.

Other Agriculture Programs

• **Soil Conservation Service.** This was the grandfather of the New Deal agriculture programs. It was created in 1935, the height of the Depression, and marked the first time that a farmer's eligibility for federal financial support was linked to his use of farm practices that conserved soil and water.

Congress appropriated $850 million for the program in fiscal 1992. The money was funneled through the Soil Conservation Service's 3,000 county field offices, where government experts helped land users design and apply conservation techniques — dams, windbreaks, terraces, irrigation systems and ponds — that improved water quality, preserved wetlands and topsoil and reduced flooding.

• **Agricultural Stabilization and Conservation Service (ASCS).** The ASCS administered the farm subsidy and price support programs of the Agriculture Department and the CCC. In addition, the agency administered two of the department's principal conservation programs: the Conservation Reserve Program and the Agriculture Conservation Program. The latter had a variety of cost-sharing arrangements for farmers to help them buy technology to conserve and improve water quality and prevent erosion.

The ASCS had offices in almost every county in the country and employed 130,000 people. The $720.5 million appropriation for fiscal 1992 covered administration and salary expenses of the agency over and above the contract expenditures of the CCC and the Conservation Reserve Program. Thus in fiscal 1992, the agency would administer a total of $9.8 billion.

• **Agricultural Research Service.** The Agricultural Research Service was responsible for conducting basic, applied and developmental research on soil and water conservation, plant and animal productivity and genetics, and human nutrition.

Most of the agency's $709 million budget for operations and construction would go to federal agricultural research laboratories, as well as to private and state universities conducting the research. The Appropriations committees' practice of specifying which university or universities should receive research grants was known as earmarking. It was the most common form of pork-barrel spending in the agriculture bill, although only a small portion ($29 million) of the agency's budget was so designated. The agency parceled out the rest of the money based on existing research priorities and on competitive grants.

Earmarked projects in the fiscal 1992 bill included: a $900,000 grant requested by Rep. Bob Traxler, D-Mich., for global climate change research at the Consortium for the International Earth Science Information Network in Ann Arbor, Mich.; a $300,000 research grant requested by Sen. Robert C. Byrd, D-W.Va., for a lab in Beckley, W.Va., to develop methods to use byproducts from coal-powered electric plants as a substitute for lime fertilizer; a $250,000 grant requested by Sen. Mark O. Hatfield, R-Ore., to expand research in grape and berry production and post-harvest technology at a lab in Corvallis, Ore.; a grant for $1.1 million, requested by Sen. Thad Cochran, R-Miss., to complete planning, design and continue construction of the National Center for Warm Water Aquaculture in Stoneville, Miss., at Mississippi State University.

• **Food Safety and Inspection Service.** Congress appropriated $473.5 million in fiscal 1992 for the agency, which inspected meat and poultry slaughter and processing facilities to make sure that when the meat came to market, it was sanitary. Most of the agency's money was spent on salaries for the nearly 7,200 inspectors at the 6,171 slaughter and processing plants nationwide. Slaughter facilities also had a department veterinarian on staff and the agency paid for laboratory tests to detect disease. When meat in the grocery store was stamped "USDA inspected," it referred to the meat plant inspection. However, high-speed slaughter technology had reduced the scrutiny given to each animal carcass. It was now routine in poultry plants for 40 to 60 carcasses a minute to move down the line, making it difficult, some critics said, for inspectors to do much more than eyeball each bird.

• **Animal and Plant Health Inspection Service.** A total of $430.9 million in fiscal 1992 would go to monitor animal health and conduct programs to control and eradicate pests, such as fire ants, and citrus canker and foot-and-mouth disease. The agency also regulated animal care at research facilities and inspected cargoes coming into the United States to prevent the introduction of exotic diseases.

This was another program in which members earmarked several million dollars in projects for local constituencies. Among them was a $400,000 grant for the state of Hawaii to purchase and install new electronic baggage handling equipment at its airports. The money, requested by Sen. Daniel K. Inouye, D-Hawaii, had been sought (and obtained) for the past three years by his Senate counterpart, Daniel K. Akaka, D-Hawaii, then a member of the House Agriculture Appropriations Subcommittee, who was trying to ensure that the airports had the most sophisticated electronic equipment possible to detect agricultural pests on fruit or vegetables.

However, a number of international airports, including Kennedy Airport in New York, used an alternative and lower-technology method to detect agricultural pests: teams of beagles, trained to sniff out fruits, vegetables and meats. The dogs walked along the lines of passengers waiting to go through customs and when the dogs smelled a fruit, vegetable or meat product, they sat quietly with their paw on the piece of luggage.

A $100,000 grant for North Dakota was secured by Senate Chairman Burdick to create a blackbird habitat to divert the birds from the state's sunflower crop, which they had ravaged in recent years.

• **Cooperative State Research Service.** The U.S. government would spend $430.7 million in fiscal 1992 to coordinate research projects that were funded jointly by the Agriculture Department, the states' land grant schools and private-sector agribusiness.

Of the projects funded by the agency, Congress earmarked about $74 million (17 percent) for specific projects in lawmakers' districts. Among those in the bill were a grant of $100,000 for Texas A & I University in the district of Rep. Solomon P. Ortiz, D-Texas, to research the commercial utilization of mesquite and prickly pear wood; a $45,000 grant for Oregon State University to do mink research, requested by Rep. Bob Smith, R-Ore.; and a $390,000 grant for Louisiana State University, requested by Sen. J. Bennett Johnston, D-La., to research the raising of redfish and alligators as food.

• **Extension Service.** $419.3 million would go to this program, the best known of the outreach programs operated by the Agriculture Department. The nearly 15,000 county extension agents in 3,150 counties across the country taught rural residents everything from how to apply pesticides to how to start a home sewing business. The service also had staff members overseas, including a team of people working in Poland to help its new government set up an extension service modeled on the U.S. system.

For decades, the Extension Service was the only contact farmers in rural areas had with the outside world. It provided information on the latest planting methods, on preserving fresh foods and on home economics. The service continued to pay a portion of the cost of running 4-H clubs for rural youth.

• **National Agricultural Statistics Service.** The Agriculture Department agency would spend $82.6 million in fiscal 1992 gathering statistics on production, supply, price and other aspects of the agricultural economy. The statistics, which were released in weekly and monthly reports by the agency and were gathered by employees throughout the country, were treated as gospel by futures market analysts who used the information to forecast crop yields and market prices. They were also used by farmers, Congress and the Agriculture Department to estimate the size of U.S. crop subsidies.

• **Economic Research Service.** This was the Agriculture Department's own think tank, and its 434 economists and academic experts analyzed economic and other social science information on agricultural prices, world markets, crop production, the rural economy and related issues. The information was disseminated to the general public through technical papers, professional journals, general-reader magazines and direct computer access. The 1992 appropriation was $58.7 million. Another $2.4 million went to the World Agricultural Outlook board, which provided estimates of foreign crop conditions, particularly those of the Soviet Union and China, which were major markets for U.S crops. The agency's information came from an array of sources, including the CIA, and was considered a cornerstone of the country's economic intelligence as well as a critical factor in establishing the price of U.S. commodities.

• **Agricultural Marketing Service.** The $56.6 million appropriation for this agency helped promote the sale of U.S. commodities through an array of programs. One of its largest activities involved the distribution of nearly $400 million of food annually for the federally run school lunch program. It also collected information on the supply, inventories and prices of agricultural commodities for the commodity trade.

The service also ran the controversial program that set the standards for the quality of fresh produce sold in the nation's food stores. Environmental groups charged that the standards encouraged farmers to use pesticides and other agricultural chemicals to make sure their products' appearance made the grade. Department officials disputed such charges and had decided against carrying out a study mandated by the 1990 farm bill to determine whether its standards discouraged farmers from reducing their pesticide applications.

• **National Agricultural Library.** As old as the Agriculture Department, which was established in 1862, the National Agricultural Library was one of three national libraries funded by Congress. (The others were the Library of Congress and the National Library of Medicine.) Its headquarters in Beltsville, Md., north of Washington, held 2.1 million volumes primarily covering current topics but also including historical information, as well as 27,000 journals in more than 50 languages. Topics covered included everything from botany and forestry to human nutrition and rural life. The library cooperated extensively with the agricultural data base run by the United Nations, in addition to working with universities nationwide. Its fiscal 1992 appropriation was $17.7 million.

RURAL DEVELOPMENT PROGRAMS

Two Agriculture Department agencies, the Farmers Home Administration (FmHA) and Rural Electrification Administration (REA), administered the bulk of the money that the government spent in rural America. Both agencies were rooted in the Great Depression, when farmers, especially in the rural South, could not get credit from overextended private banks.

The FmHA's mission was to extend loans to farmers to buy farms and finance their operations. It had become known as the "lender of last resort" for farmers who could not get credit from commercial banks or the quasi-governmental Farm Credit System.

The REA's mission was to finance electric and telephone service to rural communities where private companies were reluctant to do business.

During the farm crisis of the early 1980s, the FmHA lost billions when thousands of farmers defaulted on their loans. The Reagan administration, to try to bring the agency's costs under control, wanted Congress to stop making direct loans to farmers and instead to guarantee loans made by private lenders. The Reagan policies (supported to a great extent by Bush officials) would have halted most lending to new farmers and to those on shaky financial ground, concentrating instead on FmHA's older and more stable customers. Although Congress in the 1985 farm bill and again in the 1990 budget agreement approved a gradual shift in loan policy from direct to guaranteed loans, the Appropriations committees had been reluctant to pursue that course as aggressively as the administration wanted.

Congress and the Bush administration were continuing to battle over whether to convert from direct loans to guaranteed loans. In fiscal 1992, the Appropriations committees flouted the Bush request, which would have drastically reduced the total amount of FmHA and REA loans from $9.4 billion in fiscal 1991 to $5.7 billion, with a majority ($3 billion) switched to guaranteed loans. Instead, Congress approved $5.2 billion in direct loans and $4.3 billion in guaranteed loans.

Farmers Home Administration

The FmHA operated four "revolving loan" accounts for farm lending. The Appropriations committees set limits on the amount of loans that could be issued from each account. In the past, the appropriation for each account reflected the difference between the amount of loans issued each year and the amount that was repaid from previous years, with Congress making up the losses incurred from subsidizing interest rates or when borrowers failed to repay loans. Critics of these and other credit programs throughout the federal government charged that this procedure never gave an accurate picture of the actual government subsidy in the loan programs, since Congress could (and often did) appropriate less than was actually needed during the fiscal year, forcing the FmHA to use its borrowing authority to cover the remaining losses.

The 1991 Credit Reform Act (PL 101-508) established new accounting practices for revolving loan accounts such as the FmHA. The fiscal 1992 agriculture spending bill continued to establish loan ceilings for each revolving account, but the actual appropriation now reflected Congress' estimate of the current and future losses, called the loan subsidy. The effect was to reduce the annual appropriations for loan programsin fiscal 1992, but as losses mounted there was supposed to be a more accurate reflection of the government's year-to-year liability.

• **Agricultural Credit Insurance Fund.** This was the most controversial of the FmHA funds because it was left holding the bag during the 1980s when farmers defaulted on billions of dollars in loans. The FmHA was criticized for lending to borrowers who, even under the best of circumstances, would not have had the money to repay the loans. Its biggest programs helped farmers finance the purchase of farmland as well as their farm operations. The fund was also used for disaster loans. Congress in fiscal 1992 authorized direct and guaranteed loans of up to $4.2 billion, which required an appropriation of $323.7 million to cover the estimated loan subsidies. The total appropriation, including salaries and other expenses, was $557.6 million.

• **Rural Development Insurance Fund.** This fund provided loans to rural communities to improve water and sewer systems and build community facilities such as firehouses, clinics and centers that provided social and cultural services. The fund included $100 million for economic development projects. The bill authorized up to $860 million in loans, requiring an appropriation of $108.9 million to cover the loan subsidy. The total appropriation for this account was $161.2 million.

• **Rural Housing Insurance Fund.** This program provided loans to rural residents for home building, rural rental housing and low-income home repair. Loan programs were limited to communities of fewer than 20,000 population. The bill authorized up to $2.5 billion in loans, with an appropriation of $586.8 million for the loan subsidies. The total appropriation was $1.33 billion.

• **Miscellaneous grant programs.** The bill appropriates $445.5 million for a grab bag of FmHA grant programs, including ones for home repair for the elderly poor, community fire protection facilities and home rehabilitation for low-income families. A $20.8 million rural development grant program spread its dollars to economic development projects in rural areas across the country, including member requests for nearly a dozen specific projects. Sen. Bob Dole, R-Kan., requested $400,000 for his hometown of Russell to build, with the help of a local grain elevator and a farmers' cooperative, a plant that extracted gluten from wheat. Sen. Patrick J. Leahy, D-Vt., requested $400,000 for Vermont state colleges to build community centers and link them, using telecommunications.

Rural Electrification Administration

The REA was created by an executive order of President Franklin D. Roosevelt in 1935 to bring electricity to rural America. Subsequently it also subsidized telephone service for rural communities. Although most communities in the United States now had electricity and telephone service, the REA continued to provide loans to companies that maintained and replaced aging power lines and upgraded telephone technology. It also provided low-interest loans to companies to do rural economic development and job creation programs.

In recent years, the REA had come under fire from the Reagan and Bush administrations as well as the General Accounting Office, Congress' chief auditor. They had charged that many of the loan programs were poorly managed, resulting in defaults on loan payments that had the potential to cost the government millions of dollars. The REA also had been criticized for making subsidized loans to companies that were already highly profitable — such as telecommunications giant GTE Corp.. Congressional defenders of the REA said the agency was still needed to help remote rural areas maintain their telephone and electric service because private companies would refuse to serve them without the government assistance. Like the FmHA, the REA operated three revolving loan accounts whose accounting had also changed under the Credit Reform Act.

• **Rural Electrification and Telephone Loans.** As with the FmHA, loan assistance by the REA was either done with loan guarantees or subsidized direct loans, which offered reduced interest rates to borrowers. The administration would have liked Congress to increase the proportion of loan guarantees in relation to direct loans, but of the $2.29 billion in loans authorized in fiscal 1992, virtually all were in direct loans. The $201 million appropriation for this account included $171.8 million for the estimated loan subsidies.

• **Rural Telephone Bank.** This program, created in 1971, had somewhat different criteria from the REA telephone loan program. It was designed as an incentive for companies that were too well financed to qualify for the very low interest loans offered through the REA's Electrification and Telephone Revolving Loan Fund. The loans offered through the Rural Telephone Bank offered less of a subsidy and had been used by such telecommunications giants as GTE.

The bill authorized up to $210.5 million in loans in this account, but not less than $177 million, appropriating $3.6 million to cover the loan subsidies. The total appropriation was $12.2 million.

• **Rural Economic Development.** This program allowed some of the unused money in the REA loan account to be used by REA borrowers for rural economic development programs and job creation projects. The bill authorized up to $8.4 million in loans, with an appropriation of $2.55 million for the loan subsidies. The total appropriation was $2.79 million.

FOOD AND NUTRITION PROGRAMS

These Agriculture Department programs accounted for $32.7 billion, or 62 percent, of the bill's cost. The biggest item, at $23.1 billion, went to pay for the food stamp program, which serveed more poor people than any other government benefit except Medicaid. In 1990, 20 million people received food stamps, and that number was expected to rise to 22.3 million in 1991.

Food stamps and the school lunch program were created as pilot programs in part to dispose of surplus food. Recognizing the potential for political benefits, President Lyndon B. Johnson took what had been a modest demonstration program under President John F. Kennedy and turned it into a pillar of his Great Society. The nutrition programs turned out to be a boon for farm-state legislators, who needed to protect controversial farm programs from an increasingly urban Congress. A new constituency base — the urban poor — joined the traditional farm coalition when farm and nutrition programs were married in the same bill.

The continued expansion of nutrition programs was why farm bills regularly passed the urbanized House by wide margins. Although the 1990 budget-summit agreement placed the food stamp and school lunch programs under the "mandatory" spending category (any citizen who met the eligibility criteria could get them, so Congress had little discretion over annual funding levels), House Chairman Whitten maintained that appropriators still had the final say, and he routinely tried to exert some degree of control over spending levels. His main complaint about the programs was that the administration had for several years understated their cost by several billion dollars.

Food Stamps

The bill provided $23.4 billion for fiscal 1992, which

was the Agriculture Department's estimate of the demand for food stamps under the Bush administration's existing economic scenario. If the economy worsened, driving more people out of work and raising the need for food stamps, the department would have to seek a supplemental appropriation from Congress to meet the increased demand.

Whitten argued that the administration request would not be enough even if the economy did not fluctuate. The conference approved $1.5 billion less than the administration request for fiscal 1992, but made that much available subject to a special request by the administration justifying its need.

- **Puerto Rico.** Since 1981, Puerto Rico had received a special block grant rather than food stamps. The bill provided $1 billion for this purpose in fiscal 1992. The commonwealth distributed the money directly to eligible individuals: About 45 percent of the island's population received the cash benefits, according to the Agriculture Department. The program's guidelines were looser than those for mainland states, leaving to the discretion of recipients what the money was used for.

The only special condition imposed by Congress was that the department spend $10.8 million from this account on cattle tick eradication on the island, to be carried out by the department's Animal and Plant Health Inspection Service.

Child Nutrition Programs

Congress appropriated $6.1 billion for supplemental feeding programs such as school lunches and breakfasts, summer food service and food programs for homeless children and the elderly poor. Schools that served subsidized breakfasts and lunches to poor children were reimbursed through their local school districts. States administered the other child nutrition programs and were reimbursed by the federal government. In fiscal 1991, 25 million children were served by the school lunch program, and 4 million were served by the school breakfast program.

Women, Infants and Children (WIC)

Congress had much more direct control over the funding of this supplemental feeding program, and historically it had been a bone of contention between urban and rural lawmakers. For urban members it was often the only discretionary item in the agriculture bill that sent money to their districts. But for rural lawmakers, the more money that went to WIC, the less there was for the traditional pork-barrel projects that helped farm communities and rural areas.

The states administered this program, but they were fully reimbursed by the federal government. Women with children under age 5 became eligible for WIC vouchers only after a health-care professional certified that the children had nutritional deficiencies and a state WIC caseworker certified that they were financially needy. The vouchers were exchanged at grocery stores for eggs, milk and other dairy products, infant formula and cereal.

The appropriation for WIC was $2.6 billion, up from $2.35 billion in fiscal 1991. Fiscal 1991's funding level was enough to serve about 4.7 million individuals, but according to the Congressional Budget Office, that was just 54 percent of those who were eligible for WIC benefits.

WIC got special attention in fiscal 1992 — and more support on Capitol Hill — after the chief executive officers of five large corporations testified before the House Budget Committee that full funding was crucial to the health of young Americans and the future of the U.S. economy.

Other Food and Nutrition Programs

- **Commodity Supplemental Food Program.** The $90 million appropriated for this program provided food to a targeted poor population similar to that of the WIC program, but also was available to the elderly and to women with children up to age 6. Instead of the vouchers used in the WIC program, the Agriculture Department contracted, through state human services agencies, with nonprofit church and other social service groups to distribute food packages containing approved groceries such as iron-fortified infant formula, rice, cereal, canned juice, evaporated milk or nonfat dry milk, canned vegetables or fruits, peanut butter and dry beans.
- **Temporary Emergency Food Assistance Program.** The bill provided $45 million for the TEFAP program, which distributed food commodities and cash subsidies free of charge to soup kitchens, hunger centers, food banks and similar nonprofit food-distribution centers whose goal was to relieve situations of emergency and distress.
- **Human Nutrition Service.** As the lead government agency providing dietary guidance to the general public, this Agriculture Department division tracked Americans' food consumption patterns and the nutrient content of the nation's food supply. The department's role was expanded in 1991 when Congress passed a nutrition monitoring bill (PL 101-445) to develop a 10-year plan to determine what kinds of food Americans ate and their nutritional value. The fiscal 1992 appropriation was $10.8 million.

FOREIGN ASSISTANCE

Commodity Distributions

- **Food for Peace (PL 480).** The Food For Peace program, which was known almost worldwide by its public law number from the 83rd Congress, was the nation's main way of distributing surplus crops to less developed or famine-stricken regions of the world. Created in 1954 and overhauled most recently by the 1990 farm bill, its goal was twofold: to provide humanitarian hunger relief and to develop new markets for U.S. commodities in the Third World. The program was administered jointly by the Agriculture Department and the State Department's Agency for International Development. The food was provided to the countries through low interest, long-term loans and outright grants.

The total appropriation, including the grant program, shipping costs and salaries and expenses, was $1.5 billion. The "program level" that the government would regulate was capped at $1.6 billion.

- **Credit Guarantee Program.** The government's largest means for stimulating overseas commodity sales was its program to guarantee loans made to approved foreign buyers. The guarantees were provided to foreign governments that were short on cash or were otherwise perceived as credit risks by private lenders. The U.S. guarantee made it easier for the countries to obtain a loan.

The 1990 farm bill required that the Agriculture Department provide loan guarantees of not less than $5 billion a year. The bill authorized short-term, intermediate-term and emergency loans of up to $5.7 billion in fiscal 1992.

The appropriation was governed by the 1990 Credit

Reform Act, which required Congress to estimate the current and future losses of loans. The bill provided $155.5 million for loan subsidies as part of a total appropriation of $158.8 million.

• **Export Enhancement Program.** The government's main program to stimulate overseas sales of U.S. commodities, the Export Enhancement Program reimbursed exporters who sold U.S. commodities — grains, oils and dairy products — into selected foreign markets at below the world market price. The Agriculture Department covered exporters' losses by giving them certificates that could be traded for government-owned surplus commodities that were worth the amount of the discount. The exporters could then sell those commodities to make up for their losses. The goal of the program was to gain market share in overseas markets by undercutting the prices foreign countries, particularly the European Community, charged for their agricultural products.

No appropriation was required for the program since the Office of Management and Budget said it had no net cost to the Treasury. However, in fiscal 1992 the department expected to spend $1.2 billion on the surplus commodities it would give to exporters in the program.

Foreign Agricultural Service

Operating much like a mini-State Department, the service administered $8.5 billion worth of programs, most of which were paid for through the Commodity Credit Corporation. The Appropriations committees had little control over spending for them; however, they did control the salaries and expenses of the service. In fiscal 1992, Congress appropriated $110 million for the agency's administration. The FAS also administered PL 480.

• **Personnel.** Foreign Agricultural Service officers — 120 Americans and 150 foreign nationals — worked until 1954 as agricultural attachés reporting to the State Department. They now reported to the Agriculture Department in the 73 countries where they were posted, as well as an additional 35 countries, and their reports were sometimes used by government intelligence agencies.

• **Market promotion.** Whitten had been a critic of the agency's Marketing Promotion Program, which spent about $200 million annually to promote sales of U.S. products overseas. Among the generic products the agency promoted were Kentucky bourbon at a cost of $3 million a year; mink at a cost of $2.3 million a year and Wisconsin ginseng root at a cost of $158,000 a year.

The agency promoted brand-name products in overseas markets through television and print advertising. It spent over $9 million 1991 to promote Sunkist oranges, which was the lion's share of the $10.1 million promotion budget for brand-name citrus products; and it spent $5.1 million to promote Gallo wine, which represented about half the budget for brand-name wine promotions.

For fiscal 1992, the House report instructed the agency to use $500,000 for Ameri Flora '92, an international horticulture exposition that would be held in Columbus, Ohio, and had been sanctioned by the U.S. Christopher Columbus Quincentenary Jubilee Commission and the International Association of Horticulture Producers.

The Senate report instructed the department to allocate up to $500,000 to allow the Georgia Department of Agriculture to establish, in cooperation with peanut grower groups and processors, a peanut marketing program in Eastern Europe. The Senate report also instructed the department to pay special attention to pecans and peanuts when it allocated the money spent through its Market Promotion Program.

• **Export promotion.** Whitten also had criticized the export promotion program, which spent nearly $900 million annually to promote the sale of agricultural commodities overseas. Most of the money went in the form of commodity certificates to the nation's three largest grain merchants (which were also some of the largest corporations in the United States): Cargill Inc., Continental Grain Co. and Louis Dreyfus Corp.

Many members of Congress had criticized the agency's administration of U.S. agricultural loans to Iraq. For years, they said, agency officials allowed Iraq to buy commodities through the loan program without raising questions about Iraq's stability or its record of human rights abuses. When Iraq invaded Kuwait in August 1991, it defaulted on loan payments for $2 billion worth of U.S. commodities.

RELATED AGENCIES

Food and Drug Administration (FDA)

The FDA's responsibility was consumer protection. It set standards for food content, tests drugs and medical technology before they were marketed and conducted safety studies on an array of products. The agency also ensured that the nation's blood supply was clean and safe and that products were clearly and accurately labeled.

The Bush administration i9n fiscal 1991 sought to pay for some of the agency's expenses through user fees, a move that brought swift retaliation from the Senate. Under the conference agreement, the FDA got $759.9 million, nearly its full request. But conferees slapped the administration's wrist for requesting user fees, adding language to require the FDA to make a special request later in the year for $188 million of its appropriation.

Commodity Futures Trading Commission (CFTC)

The CFTC regulated the commodity futures markets, including the Chicago and Kansas City boards of trade. Its employees conducted market surveillance analysis and research, enforcement, audits and registrations of futures firms. The agency's $47.3 million appropriation covered the salaries of employees and commissioners, but the majority of its operational costs were covered by fees paid by commodity trading firms.

Farm Credit Administration

The Farm Credit Administration was an independent federal agency that regulated the Farm Credit System, a federally chartered network of agricultural lending institutions. Those institutions included land banks, production credit associations and banks for cooperatives. The regulatory agency's $40.2 million operating budget was paid for by fees on the banks, although Congress set an overall limit on the agency's expenses.

• **Farm Credit System bailout.** The bill also included $112.6 million as part of the 1987 federal bailout of the Farm Credit System. The Treasury currently covered the interest payments on $1.2 billion in debt that the system sold to finance the bailout. The new appropriation brought taxpayer contributions to $259 million.

In addition, the system had to borrow $388 million to liquidate the long-term credit bank in Jackson, Miss., but no congressional appropriations for that debt were anticipated. ■

Continued from p. 583
from the scythe of the House, which usually opposed it.

SENATE FLOOR ACTION

The Senate on July 30 passed HR 2698, a $53.1 billion fiscal 1992 agriculture spending bill that was changed from the committee bill to incorporate modified administration goals.

The administration had hoped appropriators would take the 1990 farm bill as a guide in setting spending priorities, especially in the areas of farm credit and the environment. The Senate voted 92-7 in favor of an appropriations bill that, unlike the House's, allowed a slight reduction in direct loans to farmers and funded several new environmental programs. *(Vote 160, p. 21-S)*

The Senate bill was $549.9 million higher than the House version because of a higher estimate of the cost of entitlement programs such as food stamps. The largest portion of the Senate bill, $37.9 billion, went for such programs, most slated to be spent on food stamps.

The Senate Appropriations Committee bill had nearly $434 million less in discretionary spending than the House version. Much of the difference was resolved two days later when the chairmen of the House and Senate Appropriations panels, Whitten and Byrd, worked out a deal that resulted in a $350 million increase in the Senate's spending pot.

Increase for FDA

An amendment offered by Orrin G. Hatch, R-Utah, and approved on a voice vote appropriated an additional $168 million for the Food and Drug Administration, bringing the total request that could be spent in fiscal 1992 to $705 million. The administration had requested $734 million, but $197.5 million of that was to be paid by unpopular user fees. The Senate Appropriations Committee had retaliated by making $168 million of its $705 million request conditional on an emergency request. The Hatch amendment freed money from those restraints.

The Senate also gave voice vote approval to an amendment offered by Burdick to move $100 million in direct government loans to guarantees of private loans in one of the Farmers Home Administration accounts. The measure brought the Senate bill closer to the administration's request, but it still fell far short of the administration's goal of cutting by half the direct loans to farmers. The administration had proposed that $410 million be appropriated in fiscal 1992 for direct loans, in contrast to the $900 million appropriated in fiscal 1991. The Senate bill appropriated $740 million.

Two other amendments altered provisions for environmental programs authorized by the 1990 farm bill.

An amendment to the Wetlands Reserve Program offered by Agriculture Committee Chairman Patrick J. Leahy, D-Vt., which passed 76-22, bolstered the program by requiring that leases on wetlands extend for at least 30-year periods. This administration-backed program was designed to take wetlands out of production so that their natural vegetation could return. *(Vote 159, p. 21-S)*

The committee version permitted 15-year leases, which environmentalists argued was too short a period for a wetland to be restored. The House did not provide any funding for the wetlands program.

An amendment by Tom Harkin, D-Iowa, increased the appropriation for the Water Quality Incentive Program from $3.5 million to $10 million. The House version spent $3.5 million on the program.

CONFERENCE

House and Senate conferees on HR 2698 spent most of the their time Oct. 3 bickering over local matters, such as whether to move money from mechanical tomato harvesting research at Pennsylvania State University to the school's dairy management program. That was because the big differences between the House and Senate versions of the spending measure — how much to spend on farm loans, wetlands protection and the Food and Drug Administration (FDA) — had already been ironed out in private negotiations.

Members subsequently approved a conference report in short order, never mentioning the $200 million difference between House and Senate recommendations for agricultural loans, or a $100 million difference in funding for the FDA, or a $91 million difference in funding for the Wetlands Reserve program.

As it turned out, Whitten and Burdick were able to resolve the big money differences with the unlikely help of the White House budget office.

The House had started out with a higher allocation for agriculture than the Senate. But it turned out that the Senate had figured less for expected farm loan losses because it had used the estimates of the Office of Management and Budget (OMB). The House bill had used higher loan-loss estimates by the Congressional Budget Office (CBO). *(New budget rules, p. 73)*

Taking OMB's numbers essentially allowed the House and Senate to work from the same balance sheet. The House could then increase spending for some programs it had cut, and the Senate could take full advantage of an increase in its allocation.

Under the conference agreement, the FDA received $725 million, nearly its full request. The Senate had approved $705 million but ordered the agency not to spend $51 million until the end of the fiscal year. It also made another $45 million contingent on an emergency request from the administration.

Conferees slapped the administration's wrist for requesting that a part of the agency's funding be paid with user fees. Appropriators strongly opposed user fees, and to underscore that point, conferees approved language to require the FDA to make a special request for $188 million of its appropriation.

Environmental Programs Gain

Several environmental programs also got a boost. Conferees agreed to provide $46 million for a new Wetlands Reserve Program, which paid farmers to take wetlands out of production for 30 years or more. That was only half the amount that the Senate wanted; the House had provided no funds. The final bill limited the program to 50,000 acres in five state pilot projects.

Conferees also compromised on two other programs with strong support from environmental groups. They split the difference between House and Senate bills and approved $6.7 million for a water quality improvement program. The House also dropped its previous refusal to provide $120,000 for the National Organic Standards Board.

Despite the constraints imposed by the fiscal 1992 budget, conferees found room to increase Cooperative State Research Grants — projects of special interest to individual members — to nearly $74 million, about $10 million more than had been allotted in either bill. ■

Postal Subsidies Posed Difficult Issue

After House and Senate conferees discarded controversial campaign finance language, the Senate on Oct. 3 easily cleared for the president by voice vote a $19.9 billion fiscal 1992 spending bill (HR 2622) for the Treasury Department, U.S. Postal Service and other government operations.

The House had adopted the conference report, also by voice vote, earlier in the day.

The bill had faced major Republican opposition in the House and Senate over an amendment added to it during a conference between appropriators Sept. 27.

The amendment was designed to ensure that Democratic presidential candidates could collect more federal dollars for their primary campaigns than allowed under new Treasury Department regulations. It was offered by Senate Treasury, Postal Service and General Government Appropriations Subcommittee Chairman Dennis DeConcini, D-Ariz., on behalf of Majority Leader George J. Mitchell, D-Maine.

Treasury regulations approved in 1991 set aside money in the taxpayer-supported checkoff fund for the major-party conventions and general election candidates. The rules were to ensure that these two areas received full funding before any money was made available to candidates in the primaries.

BOXSCORE

➡ **Fiscal 1992 appropriations for Treasury Department, U.S. Postal Service and general government (HR 2622).** The $19.9 billion bill provided funding for agencies under the Treasury Department, including the Internal Revenue Service, General Services Administration and U.S. Customs Service. It also funded the U.S. Postal Service and the executive branch.

Reports: H Rept 102-109; S Rept 102-95; Conference report filed in the House, H Rept 102-234.

KEY ACTION

June 18 — HR 2622 passed the **House** by a vote of 349-48.

July 18 — HR 2622 passed the **Senate** by a vote of 91-8.

Sept. 27 — HR 2622 approved by **House-Senate** conference.

Oct. 3 — The **House** approved conference report by voice vote; **Senate** cleared it by voice vote.

Oct. 28 — President Bush signed HR 2622 — PL 102-141.

The larger field of Democratic candidates was to be most affected by the rules. Democrats said that the laws favored President Bush, a strong incumbent who lacked significant competition.

Republicans accused Democrats of trying to change the rules after electioneering had begun and threatened floor battles.

In an informal conference Oct. 2, conferees decided to strike the amendment to avoid a lengthy floor fight with Republicans the following day.

Another issue that dogged conferees almost up until the bill reached the House floor was how to weigh protection from the AIDS virus with basic constitutional rights.

On July 18, Sen. Jesse Helms, R-N.C., had successfully offered an amendment calling for prison terms for health-care workers with AIDS who failed to notify their patients before performing "invasive" procedures such as surgery or dentistry.

Also passed was a leadership-preferred amendment by Minority Leader Bob Dole, R-Kan.; Mitchell; Edward M. Kennedy, D-Mass.; and Orrin G. Hatch, R-Utah. It required states to adopt within a year guidelines on AIDS and health-care workers issued July 15 by the federal Centers for Disease Control (CDC).

The Helms amendment was removed by conferees Sept. 27. House appropriators, including Edward R. Roybal, D-Calif., chairman of the House Treasury, Postal Service and General Government Subcommittee, wanted the leadership amendment taken out as well, but DeConcini warned that since the Helms amendment passed by a strong majority in the Senate, the issue should be addressed.

After lengthy negotiations, Roybal and DeConcini agreed to include the leadership language. Not all appropriators were satisfied with the decision. Rep. David E. Skaggs, D-Colo., said both amendments should have been left out.

"We were forced by Senate negotiators to accept alternative language," he said. "I can't associate myself with that provision."

Skaggs said the amendment violated jurisdictional rules because the bill provided no funding for needed AIDS research or health care.

Roybal said the most difficult issue for appropriators to resolve was how much to provide for the U.S. Postal Service to pay for mail subsidies to nonprofit groups and associations.

The final bill included $470 million for the subsidies. The Senate had asked for $383 million; the House, $649.3 million.

A House aide said that the higher subsidies pushed the final bill's cost above a previous calculation of $19.7 billion.

The Bush administration had requested $182.8 million in an attempt to force Congress to pass reform legislation to eliminate the profit-oriented uses of the subsidies.

The measure called for an increase of 2.2 cents in the reduced postage for larger, magazine-size pieces of mail. Members predicted that many of the nonprofit groups who used the reduced postage would downsize their larger magazines to save money.

Besides resolving the few controversial issues that temporarily stalled the bill, appropriators on the House and Senate Treasury-Postal subcommittees had trouble finding the dollars to fund all of the programs under the bill.

Members had to divide up the money with a budget allocation of $1 billion less than the fiscal 1991 level.

As cleared, HR 2622:

- Provided $9.6 billion for the Treasury Department, including appropriations for the two big revenue-producing agencies under the bill — the Internal Revenue Service (IRS) and the U.S. Customs Service.

The IRS received $6.7 billion, up from $6.1 billion in fiscal 1991, and Customs received $1.5 billion, compared with $1.3 billion in fiscal 1991. The president had requested $6.7 billion for the IRS and $1.4 billion for Customs.

- Funded the Executive Office of the President and the offices that supported the presidency. Appropriators provided $298.3 million for the office, which included $200,000

Treasury, Postal Service

(In thousands of dollars)

	Fiscal 1991 Appropriation	President's Request	House Bill	Senate Bill	Final Bill
Treasury Department					
U.S. Customs Service					
Salaries and expenses	$ 1,137,786	$ 1,261,814	$ 1,226,514	$ 1,270,005	$ 1,266,305
Operations, air interdiction	110,347	121,432	109,432	176,932	175,932
Air facilities construction	—	—	—	26,600	12,100
Other	17,007	17,981	17,981	17,981	17,981
Subtotal, Customs	**$ 1,265,140**	**$ 1,401,227**	**$ 1,353,927**	**$ 1,491,518**	**$ 1,472,318**
Internal Revenue Service					
Administration and management	142,279	144,503	144,503	141,653	141,372
Processing tax returns, assistance	1,521,595	1,661,298	1,661,298	1,661,298	1,657,944
Tax law enforcement	3,501,119	3,632,384	3,606,124	3,582,485	3,579,879
Information systems	942,932	1,294,713	1,294,713	1,294,713	1,294,713
Subtotal, IRS	**$ 6,107,925**	**$ 6,732,898**	**$ 6,706,638**	**$ 6,680,149**	**$ 6,673,908**
Bureau of Alcohol, Tobacco and Firearms	303,882	316,796	316,796	341,040	336,040
U.S. Secret Service	411,606	475,423	475,423	475,423	475,423
Bureau of the Public Debt	175,139	192,270	192,270	185,659	189,000
Financial Management Service	218,742	233,895	189,195	228,968	231,500
Other	244,903	247,005	239,469	257,305	244,857
TOTAL, Treasury Department	**$ 8,727,337**	**$ 9,599,514**	**$ 9,473,718**	**$ 9,660,062**	**$ 9,623,046**
Postal Service					
Postal subsidies	472,592	182,778	649,301	383,000	470,000
Non-funded liabilities	38,142	40,575	40,575	40,575	40,575
TOTAL, Postal Service	**$ 510,734**	**$ 223,353**	**$ 689,876**	**$ 423,575**	**$ 510,575**
Executive Office of the President					
President's compensation	250	250	250	250	250
Administration and residence	69,291	70,689	69,189	70,689	70,689
Vice president's residence	626	324	324	324	324
Council of Economic Advisers	3,064	3,345	3,345	3,345	3,345
National Security Council	5,893	6,145	6,145	6,145	6,145
Office of Management and Budget	48,343	53,434	50,470	53,434	51,934
Office of National Drug Control Policy	145,000	146,222	146,122	180,019	157,622
Other activities	7,709	7,994	7,994	7,994	7,994
TOTAL, Executive Office	**$ 280,176**	**$ 288,403**	**$ 283,839**	**$ 322,200**	**$298,303**
Independent Agencies					
General Services Administration					
Operations and supplies	183,365	192,390	199,390	191,400	196,124
Building construction, repairs	1,645,733	232,823	117,218	301,000	271,000
Limitation on use of revenues	*(5,339,948)*	*(4,246,951)*	*(4,131,346)*	*(4,027,836)*	*(4,152,613)*
Subtotal, GSA	**$ 1,829,098**	**$ 425,213**	**$ 316,608**	**$ 492,400**	**$ 467,124**
Office of Personnel Management					
Annuitants, health benefits	3,509,563	2,503,535	2,503,535	2,503,535	2,503,535
Annuitants, life insurance	8,700	14,249	14,249	14,249	14,249
Civil Service retirement and disability	5,687,105	6,078,686	6,078,686	6,078,686	6,078,686
Salaries and expenses	119,068	122,011	3,118	120,611	120,611
Subtotal, OPM	**$ 9,324,436**	**$ 8,718,481**	**$ 8,599,588**	**$ 8,717,081**	**$ 8,717,081**
Federal Election Commission	17,150	18,808	18,808	18,808	18,808
National Archives	138,219	152,143	152,143	154,143	152,143
U.S. Tax Court	31,598	33,050	33,050	32,050	32,050
Other agencies	56,229	63,072	63,072	63,225	63,225
TOTAL, Independent agencies	**$ 11,396,730**	**$ 9,410,767**	**$ 9,183,269**	**$ 9,477,707**	**$9,450,431**
GRAND TOTAL	**$ 20,914,977**	**$ 19,522,037**	**$ 19,630,702**	**$ 19,883,544**	**$ 19,882,355**

SOURCE: House Appropriations Committee

for the president's salary and $50,000 for official expenses, the same amount as in fiscal 1991. The Office of Management and Budget received $51.9 million, an increase of $3.6 million over fiscal 1991. *(1990 Almanac, p. 886)*

HOUSE COMMITTEE ACTION

The House Appropriations subcommittee that provided funding for the Treasury Department and other government operations resorted to extreme measures in 1991 to come within its $19.7 billion limit: Members declined to approve any new pork barrel projects.

"I've never seen it this tight," said Steny H. Hoyer, D-Md., after a closed-door markup by the Treasury, Postal Service and General Government Subcommittee on May 29.

Members gave voice vote approval to HR 2622 that funded agencies such as the IRS, the General Services Administration (GSA) and the White House.

Hoyer said subcommittee Chairman Roybal made the decision not to accept any members' requests to fund pet construction projects by GSA because the subcommittee was having trouble meeting basic budget requests from the agencies.

In all, according to a subcommittee aide, from $160 million to $180 million in requests was denied.

Hoyer, for his part, had wanted to include a grant to continue development of the Christopher Columbus Center on Marine Research and Exploration in Baltimore, which received $5 million in 1990.

Even Roybal had to forgo a request to fund construction of a building to be named for former Rep. Augustus F. Hawkins, D-Calif. (1963-91), at Charles R. Drew University of Medicine and Science in Los Angeles.

"The chairman's view was that if we can't fund a significant number except by pirating money from other projects, then we shouldn't fund any," Hoyer said.

"The rest of the committee felt that the chairman's idea made sense."

The Treasury Subcommittee was working against tight spending constraints imposed by the full Appropriations Committee, which ordered it to make cuts of $1.2 billion from the fiscal 1991 appropriation of $20.9 billion.

Most of those cuts had to be made in the subcommittee's discretionary budget: Bush had requested $10.81 billion in discretionary spending for the bill, which was nearly $1 billion below the fiscal 1991 level. The full committee cut that to $10.75 billion.

Besides cutting GSA construction, members also resorted to some budgetary sleight-of-hand to make ends meet. While giving Bush nearly all of the $600 million increase he requested for the IRS, the panel also sought to keep the agency from spending much of the money.

According to subcommittee staff, the panel approved $6.7 billion in new budget authority for the IRS — only $26 million less than requested — but also ordered the agency to cut $417 million in fiscal 1992 outlays, which represented the actual spending from existing and previous appropriations.

An aide said the agency was expected to make the cut by holding off for one year on plans to modernize its computer systems.

Few agencies escaped the knife. The White House Office of National Drug Control Policy, for instance, had included in its $69.2 million budget request an additional $200,000 to pay for private drivers for agency officials, who took cabs or drove themselves to official meetings. Although many other agency officials had such drivers, the drug office request for drivers was denied.

Full Committee

The U.S. Customs Service received a boost, but salary and expenses at some government agencies, including the Office of Management and Budget, faced cuts under the $19.7 billion version of HR 2622 approved by the House Appropriations Committee on June 12.

Customs, the only area to get an increase from the committee, gained nearly $89 million over its fiscal 1991 appropriation of $1.3 billion. Because of budget constraints, the fiscal 1992 spending total was $1.2 billion less than the fiscal 1991 appropriation of $20.9 billion.

Ronald D. Coleman, D-Texas, offered an amendment, adopted by voice vote, to provide $6 million more than the $1.2 billion in salaries and expenses for customs approved May 29 by the Treasury-Postal Service Appropriations Subcommittee.

Coleman said he was concerned that Customs, which handled border traffic in his Texas district, had been "grossly underfunded" in the subcommittee bill. He said the money could be used to hire 100 additional Customs employees.

"I think the gentleman makes a very convincing argument," said Roybal. "We do need 100 more agents, providing they don't all go to Texas."

Under the Coleman amendment, the Office of Administration was cut from $24.5 million to $23 million. OMB spending increases were cut from $52.4 million to $50.4 million. Cuts were made in repair and improvement costs for the main Treasury building and other related areas, from $68.9 million to $67.5 million.

In addition, the amendment cut increases in expenses for the International Affairs division of the Treasury Department. The account, which included travel expenses and computer modernization costs, was cut from $33.9 million to $32.8 million.

The bill included a rider to prohibit the use of any money to fund agency chief financial officers. Appropriations Committee Jamie L. Whitten, D-Miss., was concerned that the Chief Financial Officers Act of 1990 (PL 101-576) would aid the administration in the ongoing struggle between Congress and the president for control of the agencies. *(CFO act, 1990 Almanac, p. 416)*

HOUSE FLOOR ACTION

House members, led by Democrats, seized an opportunity to win points with middle-class and lower-income constituents June 18 when they voted to give the IRS more money to audit high-income taxpayers.

The action was part of the action on HR 2622, which provided $19.7 billion for the Treasury Department and other government operations. The House passed the bill 349-48. *(Vote 164, p. 40-H)*

At the same time, members incurred the wrath of James A. Traficant Jr., D-Ohio, when they voted against including language he designed to protect taxpayers from IRS harassment. This set in motion a marathon procedural assault by Traficant. For several hours, he held up passage by repeatedly raising points of order under House rules throughout the 86-page bill. He said sections of the bill overstepped the boundaries for appropriators and should have been left to the authorizing committees.

When the House finally completed consideration of the largely non-controversial measure after 10 hours, Traficant had succeeded in striking a substantial portion of the bill's language, including sections to prohibit the president from using funds appropriated for official expenses for other purposes. Also stricken were committee directions on dozens of items, including funding for the Resolution Trust Corporation and White House repairs.

Subcommittee Chairman Roybal offered amendments to replace the actual appropriation while leaving out the legislative language. But for the most part, he was forced to concede to Traficant's points of order. An aide to the chairman said Roybal hoped that the Senate would replace the language Traficant had struck.

In another struggle, House Appropriations Committee Chairman Whitten lost a fight over 1990 legislation that required the appointment of a chief financial officer in 23 government departments and agencies.

Whitten opposed the plan and had instructed Appropriations subcommittee chairmen to block the appointments. But John Conyers Jr., D-Mich., successfully offered an amendment, approved 341-52, to allow funds for the officers, thereby blocking Whitten's efforts to strike the funds. *(Vote 163, p. 40-H)*

Traficant's Mission

For two Congresses, Traficant, who had been the focus of an IRS audit, had tried to push through legislation to protect taxpayers from IRS harassment. Traficant said he was a victim of IRS harassment in 1987 when a federal tax court held him liable for back taxes, interest and civil penalties after ruling that he had accepted $108,000 in bribes from organized crime figures while serving as sheriff of Mahoning County, Ohio.

Traficant was successful in 1990 in getting an amendment passed to fund a program to teach IRS employees to be more polite to taxpayers. The Treasury Appropriations Subcommittee accepted language that would have required the IRS to establish a program to ensure that taxpayers "are not abused, intimidated, or scared to death."

The Ways and Means Committee did not challenge the measure, and the amendment passed with some members strongly supporting Traficant. However, under objections from the IRS, the provision was removed in conference with the Senate. The IRS said it already had such a program in place.

In 1991, Traficant's amendment directed the IRS to submit a report to Congress on its program, complete with an analysis of its effectiveness.

Traficant said on the House floor that he had an agreement with Roybal to include the language in the bill over the objections of influential staff members.

The fight began when the House passed, 252-163, the rule that allowed consideration of the auditing amendment, sponsored by Majority Leader Richard A. Gephardt, Mo., and fellow Democrats David R. Obey of Wisconsin and Byron L. Dorgan of North Dakota. *(Vote 158, p. 38-H)*

The Gephardt amendment, subsequently passed 411-1, directed the IRS to transfer the difference between the fiscal 1992 appropriation and the fiscal 1991 funding for its information reporting program — about $13 million — for use in auditing the tax returns of high-income taxpayers. *(Vote 159, p. 40-H)*

Gephardt said the language was sparked by a General Accounting Office report that found that the IRS had a policy of primarily focusing on audits of middle-income people.

Republicans, including Robert S. Walker of Pennsylvania, chief deputy minority whip, objected to the language but ended up voting for it. Republicans argued, however, that the Traficant amendment on taxpayer protection should be added to balance the Gephardt amendment.

Both Traficant and Roybal had requested the necessary waiver from the Rules Committee to allow them to add language that technically violated a House rule against putting authorizing language in an appropriations bill. However, a last-minute letter from Dan Rostenkowski, D-Ill., chairman of the tax-writing Ways and Means Committee, influenced the Rules Committee not to grant the waiver for the Traficant provision.

Rostenkowski said Ways and Means was "the appropriate forum for considering issues related to IRS treatment of taxpayers." He said, however, that he had addressed Traficant's concerns by agreeing to hold a hearing on taxpayer rights and inviting Traficant to testify.

Because Rostenkowski did not block the Gephardt amendment, Traficant was not appeased.

"It was a blatant use of power" by Democratic leaders, Traficant said. "Meanwhile they overlooked someone who has about had it.

SENATE COMMITTEE ACTION

Mail subsidies for the U.S. Postal Service were targeted for cuts as the Senate Appropriations Committee on June 26 approved a $19.6 billion version of HR 2622.

Citing budget restrictions, a Senate Appropriations subcommittee agreed June 25 to cut funding for the mail subsidy to $383 million, $266 million less than the House version.

The Bush administration had proposed $183 million for postal subsidies in fiscal 1992. But that was to be contingent upon Congress tightening up rules that set who was eligible for the special mail rates. And that was not expected to happen quickly.

The Senate bill, approved 26-0, budgeted $48.7 million less than the House bill passed June 18.

As expected, the Senate committee put back into its bill pages' worth of language that Traficant had removed during House floor consideration of the bill.

The Senate also added $186 million more to the Treasury Department than the House bill, bringing the total for the department to $9.7 billion.

Although the Internal Revenue Service received $6.7 billion, $26.5 million less than in the House bill, other agencies under the Treasury Department benefited, including the U.S. Customs Service, which received $1.5 billion, an increase of $137.6 million over the House version. The Bureau of Alcohol, Tobacco and Firearms was given $341 million, $24 million more than in the House bill.

The Executive Office of the President received $322 million under the Senate bill, $38 million more than the House bill. Within the Executive Office, the Office of Management and Budget gained $3 million. In addition, the Office of National Drug Control Policy received $180 million, gaining $34 million under the Senate version.

But cuts to the Postal Service were already causing tremors among nonprofit groups that received special mail rates. The Postal Service funded most of its own activities but received an annual federal payment to compensate for the amount lost each year because nonprofit and other groups received free or lower rates for mail.

In fiscal 1991, almost $473 million was provided for this subsidy — $90 million more than was requested by the Senate.

Continued on p. 600

Treasury, Postal Service Provisions

Nothing is as certain as debt and taxes, and HR 2622 covered both. It officially authorized the payment of $304 billion as interest on the national debt, and it funded the activities of the Internal Revenue Service (IRS), which was expected to bring in $1.09 trillion in fiscal 1992.

However, tight limits set by the 1990 budget summit agreement kept appropriators from much expansion in activities, including drug-enforcement efforts. Members and staff of the Treasury-Postal subcommittees called this the tightest year in memory.

The largest amount — $6.7 billion — went to the IRS, the agency that generated more revenues for the U.S. Treasury than any other agency under the bill. More than half of the IRS budget, $3.6 billion, was used for tax law enforcement, including tax fraud and financial investigation, examination, appeals and tax litigation.

While funds for the Treasury Department and its agencies, including the IRS, constituted about half of the bill's funding — $9.6 billion — the Postal Service accounted for a small portion, since it went private in 1971.

This bill also funded the presidency and its many offices at a level of $298.3 million.

Almost as large as the IRS budget was the money paid for federal employee benefits. The bill provided $6 billion for government workers' retirement and disability funding and $2.5 billion for health benefits.

It takes money to make money, and in addition to funds for the IRS, HR 2622 included money for the U.S. Customs Service, another revenue-builder.

The Customs Service, funded in fiscal 1992 at $1.5 billion, generated funds through collections of taxes and duties. It was expected to take in $19 billion in fiscal 1991.

Lawmakers generally looked toward the major construction account of the General Services Administration Administration (GSA) for possible projects to locate back home. For fiscal 1992, House subcommittee Chairman Edward R. Roybal, D-Calif., denied requests from members for funding grants for projects for their districts. Previously, members had pushed through grants for city projects, colleges and charitable organizations.

In fiscal 1992, member requests were limited to construction of federal buildings. Appropriators provided $548.5 million for construction and acquisition of federal buildings for the agencies and the federal courts.

They also included $1.6 billion for rental of space for the agencies and $144.6 million for design and construction services for new buildings. New budget authority for GSA was slated to reach $271 million in fiscal 1992. That figure included a list of projects, mostly federal court buildings, requested by members.

Restricted spending forced appropriators to cut 5 percent from travel expenses for all agencies under the bill. Hard hit by this was the U.S. Secret Service, which was required to step up travel activities during the 1992 presidential campaign, and agencies such as the Customs Service that were involved in illegal drug interdiction.

TREASURY DEPARTMENT

The Treasury Department was responsible for the financial workings of the nation and had under its umbrella a number of agencies set up to regulate the country's economic affairs. The principal agencies were the Internal Revenue Service; U.S. Customs Service; Bureau of Alcohol, Tobacco and Firearms; and the U.S. Secret Service.

Appropriators provided about $9.6 billion for the department, the amount the president requested. Almost all of the money went to the programs; the Treasury Department headquarters had only 1,105 employees, at a cost of about $101.6 million for departmental expenses including salaries and benefits.

The bill also provided some payments under permanent authority that did not require consideration by Congress in the normal appropriations process. The largest item was the Treasury Department's payment of interest on the public debt, which was expected to reach $304 billion in fiscal 1992.

Bureau of Alcohol, Tobacco and Firearms

The bureau had broad responsibility for reducing the criminal use of firearms (including trafficking in illegal firearms and explosives) and combating arson-for-profit schemes. The agency also combatted illegal trade practices in the alcoholic beverage industry as well as the manufacture and sale of untaxed alcoholic beverages. It assured collection of taxes on alcohol and tobacco and tried to prevent organized crime from entering the alcohol and tobacco industries.

Lawmakers provided $336 million for the agency. About $19 million would fund enforcement of federal alcohol laws, $1 million of which could be used for attorneys' fees. The funding paid for salaries for 4,109 full-time employees.

- **Armed Career Criminal Apprehension Program.** The program was created by the 1984 Armed Career Criminal Act and later expanded by the sweeping Anti-Drug Abuse Act of 1986. It was designed to facilitate the capture, prosecution and conviction of repeat offenders, especially those involved with drugs. Program-sponsored task forces in 16 cities helped capture suspects and confiscated thousands of illegal weapons and paraphernalia. Appropriators provided funding in fiscal 1992 for task forces in four additional cities: Atlanta; Charleston, S.C.; Milwaukee; and Portland, Ore. The budget provided for $100 million and 1,127 employees.
- **Project Outreach.** The BATF budget also provided $800,000 for two full-time employees and operational expenses for Project Outreach, a "pilot gang prevention task force" in Phoenix, to educate young people about the dangers of gangs and gang membership. One half of the money was to be used to compensate state and local officials for their participation.

U.S. Customs Service

Mandated by Congress to enforce U.S. border laws governing international traffic and trade and to collect tariffs and duties, the Customs Service was divided into seven regions with 42 districts and was responsible for more than 300 ports of entry into the United States.

Customs agents' duties included protecting Americans and the environment against hazardous products. In addition, the service was directed to safeguard U.S. industries and workers from unfair competition from foreign manufacturers.

Funds were used for investigation and interdiction of all contraband, including illegal drugs, arms and toxic products. It was the lead agency for drug interdiction in territorial waters, with an authorized fleet of 200 vessels. It also had major forces directed at combating drug smuggling in the air and on land.

The service received a total of $1.5 billion, including salaries and expenses, construction and drug interdiction costs. The president had requested $1.4 billion. The agency was expected to bring in $19 billion in fiscal 1991 from its collections of tariffs and duties.

Funding in fiscal 1992 would pay for salaries of 17,411 employees, including more than 5,000 for drug enforcement. Also provided in the budget were: $438 million for inspection and control; $437 million for enforcement activities; $395 million for tax and trade programs; $175.9 million for the air interdiction program; $12.1 million for construction of air facilities; $2.9 million to provide customs services at small airports.

- **Drug enforcement/interdiction.** Fighting illegal drugs was a major focus for some appropriators, especially for Senate subcommittee Chairman Dennis DeConcini, D-Ariz., and ranking Republican Pete V. Domenici of New Mexico. Both represented Southwestern states bordering Mexico and were concerned about the flow of illegal drugs across the border. Appropriators included a total of $1 billion for drug interdiction efforts.

Of that amount, $158 million would be spent for anti-drug enforcement activities under customs; $259 million for anti-drug inspection and control; $418 million for salaries and expenses for drug enforcement activities; $177 million for maintenance and operating expenses for air and water interdiction programs. The funding would pay for operations and maintenance of aircraft, boats, radar, equipment and facilities. It also included funds for equipment purchasing and training. An additional $10 million was added for support helicopters to help with investigations and other enforcement activities. For construction and improvements for air interdiction facilities, lawmakers provided $12.1 million and $3.5 million for renovation and expansion of a center to train dogs for sniffing out drugs.

- **Southwest border.** Appropriators designated the Southwest border of the United States as a "high-intensity drug trafficking area," one of a number of areas in the country that had been ravaged by the drug trade. Other areas were New York, Houston, Miami and Los Angeles. Consequently, $3.5 million was provided for an extra 30 full-time employees for the air interdiction program for the border.

Internal Revenue Service

Because of its potential to make money for the federal Treasury through tax collection, the IRS usually made a good case with appropriators for funding increases. For fiscal 1992, however, lawmakers said they were forced to make some cuts because of budget constraints. The $6.7 billion provided for the agency was $58.9 million below the president's request.

- **Administration and management.** Appropriators provided $141.4 million to administer and manage the operations of the agency. In addition to covering routine salaries and expenses, the money was designated for policy development covering internal audits and security investigations "critical to protecting the public confidence in the integrity of the Internal Revenue Service."

- **Tax returns.** For processing tax returns, providing assistance to taxpayers and issuing refunds and notices, lawmakers included $1.7 billion. Of that figure, $3 million was designated for tax counseling for the elderly.
- **Tax law enforcement.** Appropriators included $3.6 billion for tax law enforcement, including tax fraud and financial investigations, examination, appeals and tax litigation. In addition, the enforcement division provided technical assistance and training to foreign governments and gave taxpayer service and compliance support to Puerto Rico, the Virgin Islands and a number of other Pacific islands. The money was earmarked for monitoring employee pensions and determining eligibility of organizations seeking tax-exempt status.
- **Tax Fraud and Financial Investigations Division.** For investigation of money laundering, especially high-level schemes, tax fraud and drug-related crimes, the bill included $298 million. Of that figure, $6 million was slated to be used for operations and salaries for 60 full-time employees for the program operating within the Office of National Drug Control Policy's special forfeiture fund.
- **Computer systems.** The bill included $1.3 billion for information systems, including tax systems modernization, implementation of a redesigned system and replacement of equipment at the agency's two corporate sites at Martinsburg, W.Va., and Detroit.

U.S. Secret Service

The Secret Service protected the president, vice president and their immediate families, visiting heads of state and their families, former presidents and their spouses as well as widows of presidents until they remarried. In addition, the Secret Service was responsible for investigating and apprehending those engaged in counterfeiting or forging U.S. and foreign securities, credit card fraud, computer fraud, food stamp fraud and fraudulent use of government identification. Its uniformed division protected the White House and grounds and other buildings where White House offices were located.

For salaries and expenses, the bill provided $475.4 million, the same figure the president requested, an increase of more than $60 million over fiscal 1991. The funds would allow the service to continue employing 4,531 full-time staffers.

Additional funds would pay for security for candidates running for president in 1991-92. At the time, Secret Service officials were uncertain about how much money or manpower the agency would need to protect them, since the field of contenders was continuing to grow.

- **Security posts.** Appropriators provided $2.5 million for renovation of a Secret Service command post at the U.S. Naval Observatory in the District of Columbia, where the vice president's residence was located. A Secret Service official said the command post building was termite-infested and needed extensive repair. Another $1.6 million would pay for renovations of the service's New York field office.

Other Divisions

- **International Affairs.** This division provided staff analysis for the Treasury secretary and other senior officials responsible for determining and implementing economic and financial policies overseas. The staff handled issues including relations with the oil-producing countries of the Middle East, international monetary affairs and economic analysis, international trade and investment policy.

Appropriators agreed to provide $33.3 million for the division, including about $2.5 million for computer modernization, $2 million for official travel expenses and $73,000 for official receptions. The funding also paid for car rental and insurance policies on properties owned or leased for official business by the United States overseas.

• **Office of Foreign Assets Control.** This office administered economic sanctions against foreign countries in the interest of national security. Its staff implemented trade and economic sanctions against Iran, Nicaragua and South Africa and administered frozen assets and embargoes against Iraq, Cuba, North Korea, Vietnam, Cambodia, Libya and Panama.

Appropriators provided $2.5 million for office operations and salaries for its 40 full-time employees, including at least five criminal investigators.

• **Office of the Inspector General.** Considered the congressional watchdog for the department, this office received $24.8 million for salaries and expenses for 326 full-time staffers, 27 more than last year at an additional cost of $3.5 million. The money also paid for expanded investigation and oversight activities and restored fiscal 1991 funding cuts to pay for mandatory spending. Up to $2 million of the total was earmarked for official travel expenses and as much as $100,000 for "unforeseen emergencies of a confidential nature." Unforeseen emergencies included cash for drug and other sting operations.

• **Financial Crimes Enforcement Network (FinCEN).** The network was established in fiscal 1991 as a component of the administration's national drug control strategy to fight money laundering. It was a multi-agency network that helped coordinate investigations of federal, state, local and foreign law enforcement and regulatory agencies. Lawmakers provided $18 million for FinCEN operations, including salaries for 151 employees, an increase of three full-time staffers. Funding included $945,000 for computer systems. The office received $16.5 million in fiscal 1991.

• **Federal Law Enforcement Training Center.** The center provided facilities, equipment and support services for basic training of federal law enforcement personnel at three sites. State and local governments could use the facilities if space was available.

Appropriators provided $39.6 million for the center's operations. An additional $8.3 million would pay for construction (permanent driving and firearms ranges, etc.), improvements and other related costs for center facilities in Glynco, Ga.; Marana, Ariz.; and Artesia, N.M. The funding would also be used to buy up to 52 vehicles.

• **Financial Management Service.** The service managed and monitored the movement of all federal dollars and monitored overall financial operations of the federal government with financial and accounting services. Its customers were Congress, the agencies, financial institutions and the public. The service managed about $2 trillion a year in payments and collections.

Appropriators provided $231.5 million for salaries and expenses for the service, compared with $218.7 million in fiscal 1991. Funding paid for 2,216 full-time employees, the same number as fiscal 1991. The cuts deferred a number of service initiatives, including credit reform and guaranteed loan management.

• **U.S. Mint.** The Washington, D.C.-based Mint made coins, protected the federal government's supply of metals and received gold and silver bullion. The funding appropriated in the fiscal 1992 budget permitted production of 15 billion coins. Members provided $52.5 million to pay for salaries of 879 full-time staffers and expenses for the Mint, an increase of $1 million, the same as the House version and the president's request.

• **Bureau of the Public Debt.** The bureau administered laws on public debt financing. Its major focus was the issuing, servicing and retiring of public debt securities.

Appropriators provided $189 million, $3.3 million less than the president's request. The money would pay for operating costs of the bureau (including salaries for 1,970 full-time positions) and the U.S. Savings Bonds Division. The division promoted the sale and retention of U.S. Savings Bonds to reduce government borrowing on private markets. Funding was also to be used to reimburse the Federal Reserve Banks for providing services as fiscal agents for the federal government and to pay the U.S. Postal Service for delivering securities.

In 1991, the bureau, which already had located some of its operations in an office in Parkersburg, W.Va., decided to move all Washington, D.C.-based activities to West Virginia, home of Senate Appropriations Committee Chairman Robert C. Byrd, a Democrat. By 1995, the bureau planned to have relocated 700 of its 824 Washington employees to West Virginia.

For years, members had railed about the steady stream of federal agencies and jobs moving each year to West Virginia. With this sizable move of the bureau, appropriators led by Steny H. Hoyer, D-Md., and including the House subcommittee's ranking Republican , Frank R. Wolf of Virginia, fought back with a provision designed to protect employees, many of whom were Washington-area constituents of Wolf or Hoyer. The provision ensured that any employee who did not want to move would be given another metro-area job within the Treasury Department.

U.S. POSTAL SERVICE

The quasi-private postal agency had funded its own operations since 1971, when legislation was enacted that converted the 141-year-old Post Office Department into the U.S. Postal Service. The only postal funding Congress now provided was an annual payment to subsidize free or discounted delivery to qualified organizations such as nonprofit groups. Attempts by the Senate to trim those postal rate subsidies in fiscal 1992 drew immediate fire from organizations that depended on reduced-rate mailings.

Appropriators included $470 million in mail subsidies. The House version would have funded the Postal Service's request for $649.3 million. Bush had proposed $182.8 million, a large drop from the fiscal 1991 level of $472.6 million, hoping to force Congress to move on reform legislation to eliminate the profit-oriented uses of the subsidies.

Although major reforms were under way, appropriators did call for an increase of 2.2 cents in the reduced postage for larger magazine-sized pieces of mail, which cost more to process.

Attempting to protect rural and other small post offices from the ax of budget cuts, appropriators included language specifying that none of the funding provided by the bill would be used to "consolidate or close" the small post offices in fiscal 1992.

EXECUTIVE OFFICE OF THE PRESIDENT

For accounts listed under the Executive Office of the President, appropriators included $298.3 million.

• **President's salary and compensation.** The president received a yearly salary of $200,000 and $50,000 for official expenses. Any unused expense funds reverted to the Treasury.

Appropriators also provided $2.1 million to pay for pensions, office staff and travel for former Presidents Richard M. Nixon, Gerald R. Ford, Jimmy Carter and Ronald Reagan, and for a pension and postal franking privileges for former first lady Lady Bird Johnson. The figure was up from $2 million in fiscal 1991.

• **Office of Administration.** Appropriators included $24.5 million to provide common services (such as personnel management, recruitment, training, payroll, printing and graphics) to all White House agencies. The money also funded operations for the Automated Systems Division, which would gain 12 additional full-time employees and paid for a new computer system, accounting system, and the development of a child-care facility. Another $34.9 million was included for 401 full-time positions for administrative and support services for the president.

• **White House residence.** Appropriators provided $8.4 million for care, maintenance and repair, heating, lighting and other requirements for the White House. That amount was requested by the president. The funding paid the salaries of 97 people who maintained the 132-room residence and grounds.

The maintenance staff included domestic workers such as cooks and housekeepers; skilled people, including plumbers, carpenters and painters; as well as a specialized staff of 15 made up of five curators, five florists and five calligraphers.

• **Vice president's residence.** For the operation of the vice president's home — including heating, lighting and refurnishing — the bill included $324,000. Starting in fiscal 1992, the costs of renovating the residence would be paid by the Department of the Navy.

• **Council of Economic Advisers.** Appropriators provided $3.3 million for salaries and expenses for the council and its 41 full-time employees. The council was a group of economists who provided economic advice to the president, including administration economic assumptions to guide budget decisions.

• **Office of Policy Development.** The budget provided $3.7 million for this office, which advised the president on long-range economic and domestic policy. It also funded the salaries of 51 employees for fiscal 1992.

• **National Critical Materials Council.** The council was established by legislation in 1984 to help coordinate federal policy, programs and research on critical materials such as manganese, cobalt and platinum. These materials needed for industrial manufacturing processes in the United States had to be imported from other countries, such as South Africa, which had a large share of the world's manganese. There was some criticism that the council had repeatedly ignored its directives from Congress. Even so, appropriators provided $235,000 for operations and salaries for the council, the amount the president requested. The fiscal 1991 appropriation was $400,000.

• **National Security Council (NSC).** The NSC advised the president on domestic, foreign and military policies dealing with national security. It also coordinated defense and intelligence activities of the Departments of State and Defense.

Appropriators provided $6.1 million, the amount requested by the president. The funding would pay for operations and salaries for 60 staff members.

• **Office of Management and Budget (OMB).** OMB helped the president prepare and implement the federal budget. For years, the office had been at the center of a fight between Congress and the executive branch over control of the agencies and departments. It had often been criticized by members who said the agency tried to circumvent the will of Congress by doctoring testimony of witnesses before congressional committees and interfering in regulatory matters that should be left to the agencies. House and Senate bills included specific language forbidding OMB to interfere in a number of areas. For example, bill language prohibited the office from using appropriated funds to change the testimony of witnesses or review agricultural marketing orders of the Department of Agriculture. The bill language also forbade the office to use its funds to alter publication of statistical data on alcohol abuse and other public health and industrial safety issues relating to the alcohol and tobacco industries. Congress had often criticized OMB for changing testimony of agency officials to match the policy goals of the administration.

Appropriators included $51.9 million for staff and operating expenses. The House version of the bill would have granted $50.5 million; the Senate, $53.4 million, the amount requested by the president. The fiscal 1991 appropriation was $48.3 million.

• **Office of National Drug Control Policy.** Public fear of the spread of illegal drugs and violence in American communities and schools spawned the wave of legislative action that created the Drug Control Policy Office in 1988. Its responsibilities included developing an annual national drug-control strategy and coordinating all federal anti-drug programs and policies. The 1988 law was amended in 1990 to add a Counter-Drug Technology Assessment Center within the office, to serve as the center of anti-drug enforcement research and development for the federal government.

In 1991, former Florida Gov. Bob Martinez, a Republican, was confirmed as director of the agency, replacing the controversial William J. Bennett. Martinez, who some Democrats had predicted would be a caretaker in the office, asked for about $30 million less than fiscal 1991's appropriation of $99 million. Appropriators provided $105.1 million, with the extra funding going to the IRS for tax law enforcement as well as to the Alcohol, Drug Abuse and Mental Health Administration for drug treatment programs.

The office was closely watched by DeConcini and Domenici, both from Southwestern border states. (DeConcini, known for a long career of anti-drug work, declined Bush's offer to be the first director of the office in 1989.) House Chairman Roybal represented a Los Angeles district that had been plagued by the drug trade and drug-related gang violence. Los Angeles was also designated under the bill as one of five "high intensity drug trafficking areas."

Included was a Senate plan to provide $50 million for the areas most afflicted by drug trafficking — New York, Miami, Houston, Los Angeles and the Southwest border. Members stipulated that $35 million be used to assist state and local drug enforcement agencies — $15 million for the Southwest border and $20 million for the four other areas marked as having a concentrated drug trade.

Appropriators included $52.5 million from the special forfeiture fund for anti-drug efforts. The committees directed how the funds should be spent, including:

• $6 million to be transferred to the IRS for tax law enforcement.

• $19 million to be transferred to the Alcohol, Drug Abuse and Mental Health Administration's substance abuse prevention division for programs including the establishment of up to 10 demonstration projects to help women substance abusers.

• $20 million for the Counter-Drug Technology Assessment Center.

• $5 million for the U.S. Secret Service for a West African task force drug initiative.

• **Contingency funds for the president.** In 1940, Congress began appropriating additional funding for the president for unplanned expenses that were not otherwise part of the budget. Originally called the "emergency fund for the president," the name was changed to "unanticipated needs" in 1975. The director of the Office of Management and Budget was responsible for assuring that the money was only spent for proper expenses. Appropriators included $1 million for fiscal 1992.

INDEPENDENT AGENCIES

• **Administrative Conference of the United States.** The conference was responsible for improving administrative procedures for all government agencies, the president and Congress. It conducted studies, issued recommendations and encouraged their implementation through congressional, agency or judicial action. Appropriators provided $2.2 million to improve administrative procedures and for salaries for 24 full-time staff.

• **Advisory Commission on Intergovernmental Relations.** The commission was an independent bipartisan body whose mission was to identify and analyze the causes of intergovernmental conflicts between federal, state and local governments and suggest ways to improve the system.

It consisted of representatives of the executive, legislative and administrative branches of federal, state and local governments as well as the general public. Appropriators included $1.3 million.

• **Committee for Purchase From the Blind and Other Severely Handicapped.** The committee was established in 1971 to increase the employment opportunities for the blind and others with severe physical or mental disabilities. The federal government purchased at fair market rates many of the products made and services offered by the blind and severely handicapped.

The committee published a procurement list of services available and supervised the selection of new goods and services and helped set pricing guidelines. Appropriators provided $1.4 million for committee operations and salaries for 18 employees.

• **Federal Election Commission.** The commission was responsible for enforcement of the Federal Election Campaign Act, including advancing public disclosure of campaign financing, as well as informing the press and the public about the law and about campaign financing.

The commission also enforced compliance with the act through investigations, audits and litigation if necessary. Appropriators included $18.8 million for its operations and a staff of 266.

OTHER AGENCIES

General Services Administration (GSA)

Appropriators included $1.6 billion for rental of space for various agencies and $112.3 million for design and construction services for new buildings.

Appropriators also gave $548.5 million for construction and acquisition of federal buildings. The House proposed $371.4 million in funding, the Senate $385.1 million, and the administration had requested $477 million.

Members had traditionally used the GSA account to bring home projects for their individual districts or states. In 1991, for the first time in recent memory, House subcommittee Chairman Roybal announced that because of the low allocation of funds from the full House Appropriations Committee, all requests from members for grants would be denied — more than $170 million worth. However, some members still managed to push through federal building projects for their areas.

National Archives, Records Administration

Appropriators included $152.1 million, the amount requested by the president, for operations and management of the federal government's records and archives, grants for historical publications, operating expenses for presidential libraries and reviews necessary to declassify classified material.

Office of Government Ethics

The office, which became an independent agency of the executive branch in 1989, was established to help prevent conflicts of interest in the executive branch and to promote public confidence in federal officials.

The office develops rules and regulations on such issues as post-government employment restrictions, conflicts of interests and financial disclosure requirements.

The office also determined whether violations had occurred and recommended remedies. Members approved the administration's request of $6.3 million.

Office of Personnel Management

Like personnel offices at corporations, the OPM handled matters relating to the recruitment and retention of government employees.

The office also developed job qualifications for all government personnel as well as standards and policies for pay and leave. Appropriators included $116.6 million for salaries and operations of the office, up from $114.5 million; and a total of $8.7 billion for the office, down from $9.3 billion in fiscal 1991.

• **Office of Inspector General.** The office was responsible for preventing and investigating waste, fraud and abuse at OPM. Appropriators provided $4 million for salaries for 118 staff members and operations of the office. The fiscal 1991 appropriation was $4.6 million.

• **Health benefits for employees and retirees.** Appropriators provided $2.5 billion for the government's share of payments for health benefits for federal employees and retirees, administered through two trust funds. The funds paid insurance carriers for health benefits protection, salaries and expenses for the account and contributions to private health insurance plans under the Retired Employees Health Benefits Program.

• **Life insurance for employees and retirees.** The federal government was required to contribute one-third of the cost of the premium for basic coverage for federal employees' group life insurance. Appropriators included $14.2 million, as the president requested.

• **Civil Service Retirement and Disability Fund.** The fund was created in 1920 to administer the financing and payment of annuities to retired federal workers and their survivors. The fund would serve about 2.9 million former employees and 1.7 million survivors in fiscal 1992, providing benefits of more than $34 billion. Appropriators provided $6 billion for the fund.

The fund itself worked much like Social Security. Federal employees contributed 8.5 percent of their salaries to the fund, and the federal government matched that figure. Congress had to appropriate additional funding each year, the unfunded liability, to make up for pay raises, new benefits and increases in current benefits.

• **Merit Systems Protection Board.** The board was an independent agency responsible for safeguarding the federal civil service against political partisanship and other unfair practices. The board, a quasi-judicial agency, also protected employees from management abuse and required federal agencies to hire and promote based on merit. It received $23.4 million.

• **Office of Special Counsel.** This office of the Merit Systems Protection Board was established to investigate and prosecute government personnel involved in activities prohibited by law, including illegal personnel practices and political participation. The office also gave federal employees a protected confidential means of disclosing information about wrongdoing within the agencies. Members included $7.8 million for operations for the office, including salaries for 101 staff members.

• **Federal Labor Relations Authority.** The authority was created to resolve disputes between employees and management within the federal agencies. A division of the office, the Federal Service Impasses Panel, helped federal agencies and federal employee unions settle impasses arising in labor negotiations. Appropriators provided $20.8 million.

• **Pay issues.** Fiscal 1991's Treasury-Postal spending bill included sweeping salary provisions that provided for increased pay to federal employees. The increases were an attempt to bring federal pay more in line with the private sector in order to retain and attract the most qualified individuals.

In addition to the general increase, the fiscal 1991 bill also authorized geographic pay increases to federal workers in the New York, San Francisco and Los Angeles metropolitan areas. House and Senate appropriators remained concerned about disparities in pay in other costly metropolitan areas, including Washington, D.C., and Baltimore. In committee reports, they directed OPM to submit a report to the president no later than December 1991 on the pay gaps in other cities. Appropriators instructed that after the review was completed, OPM should recommend to the president whether additional geographic adjustments should be provided in fiscal 1992.

Miscellaneous

• **U.S. Tax Court.** The court, an independent, judicial body of the legislative branch, decided cases involving federal estate, income and gift tax problems and excise taxes involving public charities, qualified pension plans and private foundations. The court was made up of a chief judge and 18 judges. Members included $32 million for the court, $1 million less than the president requested.

General Provisions

In the general provisions, listed on the final pages of the bill, members gave specific directions to the agencies on issues of their choosing, mandating that they act or refrain from action on certain matters.

The provisions generally constituted legislating on an appropriations bill, which was against the rules of the House and Senate. However, unless a point of order was raised — which was rarely done — the provisions bacame law. In 1991, for the first time, a member of the House, James A. Traficant Jr., D-Ohio, raised dozens of points of order on the bill and the provisions were removed on the House floor. The bill was left in tatters and the Senate restored the language.

One such provision involved the hiring of Chinese nationals. Under existing law, the federal government could not employ non-citizens of the United States.

However, a number of exceptions had been put into law, including citizens or refugees from Cuba, Poland, Laos and the Baltic countries. The amendment pushed through by Sen. Hank Brown, R-Colo., added to the list "nationals of the People's Republic of China."

Brown became interested in the issue when he hired a Chinese intern, a former leader of the Chinese student democracy movement, but could not pay the person wages, because natives of China were not included in the exemptions. Brown pushed through the language in order to pay the intern and assist others seeking federal employment. ■

Continued from p. 594

Subcommittee Chairman DeConcini said that the cuts were deep but unavoidable. "We were unable to fund any of the programs at levels we'd like."

Overall, the panel had $1.2 billion less to work with than in fiscal 1991, requiring members to look for places to cut. The mail subsidy had traditionally been the first place tapped. During the Reagan administration, attempts were made almost every year to reduce mail subsidies.

In 1990, language included in the bill terminated mail subsidies for groups advertising travel, insurance or certain credit card sales. DeConcini said the move saved $30 million.

Although the 1991 cut sent nonprofit groups scurrying to lobby members, the Appropriations panel was nearly united against an increase. Only one member, Nebraska Democrat Bob Kerrey, voted against the measure at the subcommittee level, citing the cut in subsidized mail.

Other members seemed resigned to the cut. "The consensus was, the money's not there," a staff member said.

Language in the report accompanying the Senate bill did not allow the Postal Service to cut free mailing for the blind or overseas voting. In addition, six-day delivery of bulk mail and delivery of mail to rural areas could not be scaled back because of the cuts.

Some nonprofit organizations banded together to form the Alliance of Non-Profit Mailers, which was made up of about 120 groups.

Dan Doherty, a spokesman for the group, said that many of the alliance's members reported that they would be forced to cut back mailing or lay off workers if postal rates went up as a result of a subsidy cut.

SENATE FLOOR ACTION

When the full Senate took up HR 2622 on July 18, members voted to amend the bill to include language calling for prison terms for health-care workers with AIDS who failed to notify their patients. The amendment was offered by Helms.

By 81-18, the Senate voted to include the amendment

before passing the $19.6 billion spending bill, 91-8. *(Votes 136, 138, pp. 18-S, 19-S)*

The Helms amendment took much of the attention away from the provisions of the appropriations bill by focusing on the emotional issue of people who contracted AIDS from health-care professionals.

Under the amendment, medical workers who performed "invasive" medical procedures such as surgery or dentistry and who also knew that they had the AIDS virus but did not tell their patients could be sentenced to 10 years in prison and a minimum $10,000 fine.

Helms said he was prompted to act after hearing the stories of five Florida residents who acquired the disease from their dentist, particularly that of 23-year-old Kimberly Bergalis, who had gone public with her story in national magazines.

Edward M. Kennedy, D-Mass., argued that the amendment would "do more harm than good" by discouraging health-care workers from being tested for AIDS for fear of losing their jobs.

The Senate also adopted, 99-0, a leadership-preferred amendment by Minority Leader Dole, Majority Leader Mitchell, Kennedy and Hatch. It required states to adopt within a year guidelines on AIDS and health-care workers issued July 15 by the federal Centers for Disease Control (CDC). *(Vote 137, p. 19-S)*

Unlike Helms' amendment, which defined invasive procedures as "invasive physical contact" between the patient and the health-care worker, the federal guidelines suggested that workers with AIDS or the HIV virus refrain from performing "exposure-prone" procedures. Such procedures included those during which the worker could be cut or injured, exposing the patient to infected blood.

The CDC guidelines also emphasized the use by all health-care workers of "universal precautions," which included thorough sterilization of equipment, careful handling and disposal of needles and other sharp objects and the wearing of gloves when appropriate.

Helms insisted that the two amendments did not conflict. "They complement each other. One addresses the criminality. The other addresses what states must do in order to receive federal funds."

Helms also offered an amendment that mandated prison terms for selling child pornography. It was adopted, 99-0. *(Vote 135, p. 18-S)*

The Easy Ones

Other provisions in the bill sailed through the Senate, even though Treasury Appropriations Subcommittee Chairman DeConcini and ranking Republican Pete V. Domenici of New Mexico said they were plagued during the appropriations process by tougher-than-usual budget constraints.

The bill provided $322 million for the Executive Office of the President, while the House version provided $284 million.

The Office of National Drug Control Policy received $180 million, about $54 million more than in the House bill.

The measure also included $563 million in mail subsidies for the U.S. Postal Service — good news for thousands of nonprofit groups, associations and libraries who depended heavily on the funding, which the Senate Appropriations Committee had previously trimmed.

The Senate settled the issue by approving, 98-0, an amendment to add $180 million to the committee request in postal subsidies depended upon by nonprofit groups, associations and libraries. *(Vote 124, p. 17-S)*

The Bush administration had proposed $183 million for postal rate subsidies in fiscal 1992 contingent upon Congress tightening rules that determined who was eligible for special mail rates. Democrats said the Bush administration had promised to submit legislation on mail subsidies but had not done so, forcing Congress to act.

The Senate adopted a compromise amendment offered by DeConcini and Domenici that would charge nonprofit groups more to mail magazine-size material. The groups were to be charged existing rates for smaller pieces of mail.

DeConcini said the move would add $180 million to the $383 million already provided in the bill for mail subsidies. Mail for the blind and for overseas voting remained free under the bill. Rural newspapers were also protected from increases.

DeConcini said the amendment attempted to balance the concerns of appropriators about keeping the cost of the bill down, while protecting organizations that could be hurt by an increase in mailing expenses.

The bill also included $9.7 billion for the Treasury Department, $186 million more than the House version. However, one of its agencies, the IRS, received $6.7 billion, $26.5 million less than the House bill. Members' attempts to add money to the agency's budget were unsuccessful.

Herb Kohl, D-Wis., offered an amendment to move $30 million from the budget for the U.S. Customs Service's air drug interdiction program to fund IRS efforts to go after high-income and corporate tax cheaters. Members agreed to kill the amendment on a tabling motion by a vote of 78-16. *(Vote 126, p. 17-S)*

Those voting against the motion to table included John Glenn, D-Ohio, chairman of the Governmental Affairs Committee, and Al Gore, D-Tenn.

Freshman member Robert C. Smith, R-N.H., also suffered a resounding defeat at Mitchell's hands on a controversial interstate issue.

Smith offered an amendment to stop the federal government from withholding Maine state income taxes from the pay of New Hampshire residents who worked at the Portsmouth Naval Shipyard, a federal facility.

Smith said the federal government withheld Maine state income taxes from the federal paychecks of more than 4,000 New Hampshire workers at the shipyard. However, he said, the shipyard was between the border of New Hampshire and Maine, and the boundaries were disputed.

While he was not attempting to repeal the tax, Smith said he wanted the government to stop the tax until the matter was resolved.

Mitchell fiercely defended his state and the government's practice, arguing that the shipyard was in Maine. No boundary dispute existed, he said, because it was settled by a 1975 Supreme Court ruling.

The Senate voted 72-22 to table the amendment, with Republican William S. Cohen of Maine voting with Mitchell. *(Vote 127, p. 17-S)*

There's the Pork

Despite the difficulty in bringing home the big-dollar building projects, some members managed to include in the Senate bill funding for federal buildings for their states. The bill included millions of dollars in funding for federal building projects requested by members.

Barbara A. Mikulski, D-Md., a member of the Appropriations Committee, had lobbied hard for funding for a $200 million Food and Drug Administration building in her state, according to a spokesman.

Democratic Appropriations Committee Chairman Robert C. Byrd of West Virginia requested a $25 million federal building and courthouse in Beckley, W.Va.

The bill also included a $10 million federal courthouse for Wichita, Kan., asked for by Dole.

The Senate took out a number of projects favored by House members and included in the House version of the bill, including a $1.9 million federal building and courthouse in Monterey, Calif., requested by House Budget Committee Chairman Leon E. Panetta, D-Calif.

However, a $30 million building and courthouse requested by House Majority Leader Gephardt survived.

CONFERENCE

House and Senate conferees completed action late Sept. 27 on a $19.7 billion version of HR 2622.

Conferees approved $470 million for postal subsidies. The Bush administration had requested $182.8 million, although the Postal Service said it needed $649.3 million to recover the costs of lower mail rates for those groups.

Nonprofit groups won a small victory when conferees agreed not to substantially reduce mail subsidies for the Postal Service. The groups had lobbied hard against cuts proposed by the Bush administration and those included in the Senate version of the bill.

In fiscal 1991, the Postal Service received $472.6 million in subsidies. It would have received $649.3 million under the House version of the bill passed June 18.

While the Senate did not cut the rates as low as the president requested, the Senate version included $383 million in subsidies. DeConcini said the Postal Service would also save $186 million because of bill language directing it to charge more for certain larger pieces of mail.

But House subcommittee Chairman Roybal said many senators who voted for the lower Senate number had since said they supported a higher appropriation.

"Members of the Senate believed they were voting for a higher figure," he said, because they thought $180 million described by DeConcini on the Senate floor was being added to the $383 million.

Conferees disagreed in principle over whether the federal government should subsidize the mailings. But most agreed that authorizing committees needed to pass reform legislation to deal with the problem.

Domenici said taxpayers should not help pay for mailings for such enterprises as the publications of Harvard University or the Heritage Foundation, a conservative Washington-based think tank.

"It's absurd that we are subsidizing these kinds of mail to the tune of $600 million a year," he said.

Roybal said he was concerned about the effects that cuts could have on hospitals and charities that depended on the assistance for their mailings.

Delaying Outlays

Conferees also debated the merits of the practice of providing new budget authority to agencies but not allowing them to spend it until the end of the fiscal year, thus pushing the actual outlays into the next fiscal year. The result was to give the subcommittee more room to fund programs that had higher outlay levels.

The practice of limiting appropriations to the end of the fiscal year was becoming more frequent as appropriators scrambled to meet more immediate spending demands.

For hours, conferees haggled over where to find the money to fund the postal subsidies at a level of $470 million.

Both sides suggested configurations that would have provided relatively small amounts of funding to the IRS and the Customs Service, without allowing them to use it until the end of fiscal 1992.

Domenici, who was the ranking Republican on the Senate Budget Committee, was the most passionate dissenter on the issue.

"You lose me on any bill that has this kind of gimmick in it," he said. "It's as close as you can get to cheating under the act."

In addition, he said, pushing outlays into fiscal 1993 would not get appropriators off the hook for long. "We're going to face this problem next year," he said.

DeConcini said he understood Domenici's concern, but "I don't have quite the same strong feeling that Pete does on this."

Conferees finally agreed to settle the matter with some small cuts and delays in some funding.

The largest amount of funding to be delayed involved $80 million for an IRS computer systems modernization program. Bill Smith, an aide to Roybal, said the IRS preferred that the money be appropriated that way because it did not know exactly when it would be spent but it needed the appropriation in order to write contracts for the work.

Constitutional concerns led to the scrapping of one $5 million project that the Senate had favored. The project was dropped after the House attacked it.

The Bureau of Alcohol, Tobacco and Firearms had proposed to establish a Gang Analysis Information Center to track information on youth gangs. The center was to share the information with state and local authorities.

The project, passed in the Senate, was opposed by Government Operations Committee Chairman Conyers and Don Edwards, D-Calif., chairman of the Judiciary Subcommittee on Civil and Constitutional Rights, on the grounds that the rights of some young people could be ignored if they were improperly identified by police as gang members.

Conyers and Edwards wanted the term "gang" defined before the money was appropriated.

Under the plan contained in the Senate bill, the term gang would have been defined by Justice Department officials and others during establishment of the program.

Roybal fought hard against the project, arguing that some youths in his Los Angeles district were being falsely identified as gang members. DeConcini suggested that appropriators provide the money without allowing it to be spent, but Roybal would not agree.

Agency representatives who had been lobbying members for months were not pleased with the outcome of the conference, but most were thankful that cuts were not deeper.

None expected much, given the frequent forecasts from the subcommittee chairmen earlier in the year.

DeConcini began the conference by outlining the difficulties both sides had in trying to fund agency requests.

In addition, conferees had to decide whether to include the controversial amendment by Sen. Helms, calling for prison terms for health-care workers with AIDS who failed to notify their patients.

According to a House aide, appropriators finally agreed to take out the Helms amendment late on the second day of the conference. ■

Boosts for Highway and Transit Programs

Despite general belt-tightening, 1991 was a banner year for transportation. Spending on federal highways, aviation programs, mass transit and the Coast Guard received a boost in the $14.3 billion fiscal 1992 transportation appropriations bill (HR 2942) cleared by the Senate on Oct. 16.

The rosy outcome was in large part due to a fortuitous coincidence: a multiyear authorization for federal highway and transit programs also moved through Congress. *(Transportation reauthorization, p. 137)*

Major changes in federal transportation policy were promised in 1991 as lawmakers on the committees with jurisdiction over public works hashed out a $151 billion measure. That bill (HR 2950 — PL 102-240) was signed by the president Dec. 18.

Under the spending bill, motorists in New Jersey, New York, Michigan and Florida were to benefit the most from $139.8 million approved for high-technology highway projects intended to ease traffic congestion and cut safety problems. These states were also represented by key members of the Appropriations committees.

Pilot projects for so-called intelligent vehicle-highway systems (IVHS) were already under way in California, Florida and Illinois. Those projects were being financed by the automobile industry, telecommunications firms and state governments after winning initial federal funding in past years.

Among other devices, the new technology employed satellites, video cameras and sensors buried under highways to monitor traffic tie-ups. The information was to be at drivers' fingertips, relayed by dashboard video screens. A system in place in Orlando, Fla., also offered weary drivers hotel and restaurant advice.

Congress began funding high-tech highways in earnest when it provided $2.3 million in fiscal 1990. A year later that amount climbed to $20 million. The $139.8 million for smart highway and vehicle technology in the fiscal 1992 transportation bill contained $119.8 million for 20 projects in the states of senators or representatives with seats on the Transportation Appropriations subcommittees. The other $20 million went toward basic research.

The House had approved the conference report on Oct. 9, 374-49, after controversy involving $588 million for 127 new and ongoing highway "demonstration" projects requested by House and Senate lawmakers. The Senate cleared it, 95-3. *(House vote 299, p. 72-H; Senate vote 224, p. 29-S)*

During House consideration of the conference report, Republicans Dan Burton of Indiana, Robert S. Walker of Pennsylvania and Harris W. Fawell of Illinois argued that most of the bill's demonstration projects were wasteful, were not authorized by the appropriate committees and bypassed state planning priorities.

BOXSCORE

➡ **Fiscal 1992 appropriations for the Department of Transportation and related agencies (HR 2942).** The $14.3 billion spending bill provided funding for highway and mass transit programs.

Reports: HR 2942: H Rept 102-156; S Rept 102-148; conference report filed in the House, H Rept 102-243.

KEY ACTION

July 24 — HR 2942 passed the **House** by a 379-47 vote.

Sept. 17 — HR 2942 passed the **Senate** by a vote of 95-3.

Oct. 7 — HR 2942 approved by **House-Senate** conference.

Oct. 9 — **House** approved conference report by a 374-49 vote.

Oct. 16 — **Senate** cleared conference report by a 95-3 vote.

Oct. 28 — HR 2942 signed by President Bush — PL 102-143.

The Republicans implored the House to reject a conference amendment providing $249.1 million for 89 of the projects. But the House refused, voting 330-96 for the projects. *(Vote 300, p. 72-H)*

The fiscal 1991 spending bill had provided $12.9 billion for transportation programs. *(1990 Almanac, p. 876)*

HOUSE COMMITTEE ACTION

Mass transit received its biggest boost in nearly a decade under a $14.2 billion version of HR 2942 approved July 10 by the House Transportation Appropriations Subcommittee.

Approved by voice vote, the measure provided $3.85 billion for transit programs, compared with $3.26 billion in fiscal 1991.

Transit programs last received an increase of that magnitude in fiscal 1983, but it was followed by seven years of spending cuts under the Reagan administration.

The appropriations bill raised the limit on spending from the Highway Trust Fund to $16.2 billion, up from the fiscal 1991 level of $14.6 billion. That level was higher than the $15.8 billion proposed by the Bush administration.

The Federal Aviation Administration (FAA) received a slight increase to $4.3 billion, up from $4 billion appropriated in 1991. The panel proposed cutting the Federal Railroad Administration's budget to $793.5 million from $893.8 million in fiscal 1991. Amtrak subsidies jumped to $649 million from $625 million in fiscal 1991.

The bill included at least 32 new highway demonstration projects costing more than $80 million. Among the more costly projects was $9.3 million for rebuilding the 77th Street bridge in Minneapolis.

Several states and cities received new mass transit projects under the bill. Among them was New Jersey, which was to get $65 million for a new rail corridor connecting downtown Newark with its international airport. San Francisco received $60 million to extend its BART transit system, and Boston received $25 million for a new transit project.

Efforts by Houston city leaders to build a $1.2 billion, 24-mile monorail system were dealt a severe blow when Tom DeLay, R-Texas, opposed the project because of projected low ridership levels and high costs.

DeLay won a commitment that the fiscal 1991 appropriation of $146 million remained available to Houston. To mollify local critics, DeLay also persuaded Transportation Subcommittee Chairman William Lehman, D-Fla., to agree to an additional $10 million for Houston's bus system.

Full Committee

The House Appropriations Committee on July 18 approved HR 2942 by voice vote. The bill provided $92.9 million for 33 new highway demonstration projects and

Transportation

(In thousands of dollars)

	Fiscal 1991 Appropriation	President's Request	House Bill	Senate Bill	Final Bill
Transportation Department					
Office of the Secretary	$ 172,271	$ 159,504	$ 183,080	$ 184,470	$ 183,306
Rural airline subsidies	26,600	*(38,600)* [1]	*(38,600)* [1]	*(38,600)* [1]	*(38,600)* [1]
Coast Guard					
Operating expenses	2,039,839	2,539,600	2,483,800	2,222,000	2,230,272
Acquisition, construction	406,331	422,978	365,031	407,470	390,000
Retired pay	451,800	487,700	487,700	487,700	487,700
Other	159,553	176,400	172,300	100,800	211,750
Subtotal, Coast Guard	**$ 3,057,523**	**$ 3,626,678**	**$ 3,508,831**	**$ 3,217,970**	**$ 3,319,722**
Federal Aviation Administration					
Operations	4,037,000	4,457,000	4,342,000	4,382,058	4,360,000
Facilities and equipment	2,095,407	2,700,000	2,469,500	2,557,807	2,394,000
Research, engineering, development	205,000	210,000	218,000	225,120	218,135
Other	−200,000	150	150	150	150
Subtotal, FAA	**$ 6,137,407**	**$ 7,367,150**	**$ 7,029,650**	**$ 7,165,135**	**$ 6,972,285**
Airport Trust Fund ceiling	*(1,800,000)*	*(1,900,000)*	*(1,900,000)*	*(1,900,000)*	*(1,900,000)*
Federal Highway Administration					
Ongoing demonstration projects	332,487	—	211,390	191,535	363,881
New demonstration projects	119,658	—	88,290	196,000	225,193
Other	64,900	56,317	66,687	53,000	64,605
Subtotal, FHwA	**$ 517,045**	**$ 56,317**	**$ 366,367**	**$ 440,535**	**$ 653,679**
Highway Trust Fund ceiling	*(14,571,500)*	*(15,817,000)*	*(16,270,000)*	*(17,173,960)*	*(16,875,000)*
National Highway Traffic Safety Administration	118,713	127,207	118,352	121,986	122,700
Highway Trust Fund ceiling	*(134,635)*	*(165,000)*	*(135,000)*	*(160,000)*	*(138,000)*
Federal Railroad Administration					
Amtrak	625,080	480,000	648,900	656,000	651,000
Northeast Corridor improvement	179,000	—	36,000	260,000	205,000
Other	89,730	85,540	108,626	80,409	105,079
Subtotal, railroads	**$ 893,810**	**$ 565,540**	**$ 793,526**	**$ 996,409**	**$ 961,079**
Urban Mass Transportation Administration					
Formula grants	1,605,000	2,599,908	1,600,000	1,190,000	1,520,000
Discretionary grants	—	—	—	775,000	—
Interstate transfer grants	160,000	160,000	160,000	—	160,000
Washington Metro	64,100	80,000	124,000	124,000	124,000
Other	40,583	139,591	63,000	—	63,000
Subtotal, UMTA	**$ 1,869,683**	**$ 2,979,499**	**$ 1,947,000**	**$ 2,089,000**	**$ 1,867,000**
Highway Trust Fund ceiling	*(1,400,000)*	*(350,000)*	*(1,900,000)*	*(1,605,500)*	*(1,900,000)*
Other Transportation Department	69,000	87,333	82,659	81,935	81,574
TOTAL, Transportation Department	**$ 12,862,052**	**$ 14,969,228**	**$ 14,029,465**	**$14,297,440**	**$14,161,345**
Related Agencies					
Architectural and Transportation Barriers Compliance Board	2,700	2,980	2,900	2,980	2,940
National Transportation Safety Board	31,470	34,176	34,176	35,676	35,676
Interstate Commerce Commission	43,777	41,373	40,923	41,373	40,923
Panama Canal Commission *(limitation on expenses)*	*(519,000)*	*(461,318)*	*(519,000)*	*(500,000)*	*(509,500)*
St. Lawrence Seaway Toll Rebate	10,500	10,703	10,250	10,250	10,250
Washington Metro (interest payments)	51,663	51,663	51,663	51,663	51,663
GRAND TOTALS					
New budget authority	**$ 13,002,162**	**$ 15,110,123**	**$ 14,169,377**	**$ 14,439,382**	**$ 14,301,797**
Trust fund limitations	*($ 17,906,610)*	*($ 18,271,075)*	*($ 20,244,075)*	*($ 20,908,535)*	*($ 20,852,075)*

[1] *Payments to rural air carriers beginning in fiscal 1992 would be paid from the Airport and Airway Trust Fund.*

SOURCE: House Appropriations Committee

$216.5 million for 33 ongoing projects. The federal government would fund 80 percent of the new projects.

"There's something in here for darn near everyone," said Lawrence Coughlin, R-Pa., ranking member of the Transportation Subcommittee. The so-called demonstration projects accounted for 2 percent of the bill's funding.

The bill also included "an unusually high number of requests for new starts" for mass transit projects, said Lehman. It provided $560 million for transit systems in 26 cities, compared with $440 million appropriated in fiscal 1991 and $300 million in the president's fiscal 1992 budget request.

Virtually all transportation programs received funding increases in the bill. Mass transit was increased to $3.8 billion, a 16.5 percent boost over fiscal 1991. The FAA budget for facilities and equipment was boosted to $2.5 million, or 18 percent.

Spending from the highway and aviation trust funds was accelerated under the bill. The Highway Trust Fund limit on spending was increased to $16.3 billion from $14.6 billion in fiscal 1991. Spending from the Airport and Airways Trust Fund was increased to $1.9 billion from $1.8 billion in fiscal 1991.

Nineteen airports received $84 million in grants to replace air-traffic control terminal facilities.

The National Highway Traffic Safety Administration received a modest increase to $253.3 million, $38.9 million less than the level proposed by President Bush.

There was little debate over the bill. In one exchange, Charles Wilson, D-Texas, got an assurance from Lehman that the committee would look favorably on future mass transit needs for Houston in the wake of DeLay's decision not to seek funding for a proposed Houston monorail system.

HOUSE FLOOR ACTION

The House on July 24 passed a $14.2 billion version of HR 2942 after voting to keep 63 demonstration projects as well as recommended funding increases for the offices of Transportation Secretary Samuel K. Skinner.

The bill, which passed on a 379-47 vote, provided $1.17 billion more than was appropriated in fiscal 1991, but was nearly $1 billion less than was requested by Bush because of different ways of accounting for mass transit funds. *(Vote 224, p. 54-H)*

The bill provided $3.85 billion for mass transit programs, compared with $3.27 billion in fiscal 1991. It also raised spending from the Highway Trust Fund to $16.3 billion from $14.6 billion in fiscal 1991.

Debate over so-called demonstration projects dominated floor action.

Lawmakers increasingly used such earmarks to steer federal dollars toward specific local road projects, bypassing the traditional formula funding process. The bill contained $309 million in 66 new and ongoing demonstration projects.

Illinois Republican Fawell led an assault against 63 projects funded in the bill at $243.3 million. Those projects did not receive the authorizing scrutiny of the Public Works Committee, which was working on its own, $6.8 billion list of demonstration projects.

"We're wasting a hell of a lot of money," agreed Burton. "A lot of these demonstration projects here are pork."

Bob Carr, D-Mich., a member of the Transportation Appropriations Subcommittee, came to the defense of the earmarks. "The people who die on our highways, the people who sit in congestion on our highways ... should resent your calling them pigs and hogs," Carr said. "They're not hogs, they're not pigs and they do not regard this as pork."

The Fawell amendment was defeated on a 61-365 vote. *(Vote 221, p. 54-H)*

Popularity Vote

Another amendment, by Timothy J. Penny, D-Minn., and Byron L. Dorgan, D-N.D., became a referendum on Skinner's popularity.

As approved in committee, the bill boosted funding for Skinner's office by 18 percent to $1.4 million; for the deputy secretary by 33 percent to $550,000; and for the assistant secretary for budget, by 15 percent to $2.7 million.

Penny and Dorgan sought to cut those increases to 9 percent.

Skinner, one of the best-liked Cabinet members among lawmakers, had received unfavorable press attention for using a military jet for a golf trip. A licensed pilot, Skinner also came under criticism when it was reported that he received flight instruction from FAA officials at a reported cost to taxpayers of $40,000.

"This amendment to me seems to be aimed directly at him," said William O. Lipinski, D-Ill., from Skinner's hometown of Chicago.

Lehman said the amendment "would do serious harm to the good relations we have enjoyed between Congress and Secretary Skinner."

The House rejected the amendment, 84-339. *(Vote 220, p. 54-H)*

SENATE COMMITTEE ACTION

Senate appropriators treated their colleagues to 63 special road projects — including $165 million for one West Virginia highway — and gave big boosts to highway and mass transit programs in a $14.4 billion version of HR 2942 approved by the Appropriations Committee on Sept. 12.

The bill was approved by voice vote just hours after action by the Transportation Subcommittee.

West Virginia fared the best in the scramble for special road projects. Appropriations Chairman Robert C. Byrd, D-W.Va., earmarked $165 million for an Appalachian highway called Corridor G that traversed the western part of the rural state.

Appropriators set aside $168 million for 40 "highway construction demonstration projects" for other senators — just slightly more than Byrd received for his single project. Corridor G was listed in a separate category with four other demonstration projects for other states that would total $31 million.

Byrd's project more than doubled the amount that West Virginia received in annual highway formula funds. He steered home $137 million for four special road projects in fiscal 1991.

The state also received $5.5 million to study four future projects, including $600,000 for roads leading to the new FBI fingerprinting complex that Byrd won for the state in 1990.

The bill provided $23.5 million to study a total of 18 new projects, including the four in West Virginia.

Transportation Appropriations Subcommittee Chairman Frank R. Lautenberg, D-N.J., said he received 578 requests for special highway, transit, aviation and other transportation projects from 85 senators. "Obviously, we

Continued on p. 613

Transportation Provisions

The appropriations bill for the Department of Transportation and related agencies provided annual funding to operate, build and improve the nation's highways, airports and mass transit systems. It also provided procurement and operating funds for the Coast Guard and the Federal Aviation Administration, subsidized the Amtrak passenger rail corporation and paid for safety programs aimed at all transportation modes.

In addition to the $14.3 billion in new budget authority for fiscal 1992, Congress approved up to $20.8 billion worth of pledges to pay for future projects out of a variety of user-funded trust funds.

The measure would raise the limit on spending from the Highway Trust Fund, which got its money from gasoline taxes, for highway construction and safety programs by 15.9 percent, from $14.6 billion in fiscal 1991 to $16.8 billion.

On top of that, the bill included $589 million for 127 highway "demonstration projects." These were new and ongoing road projects — in some respects a classic form of pork-barreling — that typically circumvented state planning priorities, but that members had argued were needed to address traffic and safety concerns back home. In addition, Congress in fiscal 1992 will spend $139.8 million for "intelligent" highways and vehicles research along selected highways.

In fiscal 1992 Congress will spend $4.4 billion — an 8.9 percent increase — to operate the Federal Aviation Administration. The figure included funding for 450 new traffic controllers, 136 new safety inspectors and 178 new aviation security positions. The bill provided $2.4 billion to upgrade air-traffic control centers, airport towers and flight service facilities.

Mass transit operating assistance would be the same as fiscal 1991 — $802 million — and $565 million would be spent on new rail transit systems in 23 cities. Another $550 million went toward modernizing and expanding existing transit systems and $117 million toward improving mass transit in rural areas.

The Coast Guard received $3.3 billion, up $262 million from fiscal 1991. And the Federal Railroad Administration got $961 million, up from $894 million in fiscal 1991 — with new emphasis placed on upgrading the Northeast rail corridor, a project aimed at speeding travel times among cities on the upper East Coast.

Congress also made a number of policy changes. Transportation workers in safety-sensitive positions would have to submit to random drug and alcohol tests. Aging aircraft would have stepped-up inspection regimes. And radar detectors were banned for all interstate commercial truck and bus drivers.

ROADS

Federal Highway Administration

The FHwA worked with states to administer the federal-aid highway construction program, which included 274,000 bridges, the 44,328-mile Interstate system and 804,428 miles of roads classified as primary, secondary and urban systems. It regulated and enforced federal safety requirements for commercial trucks engaged in interstate or international commerce. The agency also governed the safety of moving dangerous cargoes and hazardous materials over the nation's highways.

Most federal aid to state highway programs came from the Highway Trust Fund, which was fed by a 14.1-cents-per-gallon tax on motor fuels. Many local road demonstration projects were funded from general revenues.

Federal funds for highway construction and safety grants were promised to states through contract authority, which allowed states to enter into contracts for road and bridge work and obtain reimbursement out of the Highway Trust Fund.

Because of budget constraints, the executive branch since 1966 — and Congress since 1976 — had put limits on the amount of new contract authority that could be obligated from the trust fund. This trust fund "ceiling" did not limit the amount of cash available for reimbursement to states, but it limited the amount made available to states for new obligations during any one fiscal year for future road work. In fiscal 1992, Congress put a $16.8 billion cap on contract authority obligations for road construction, with a total program level of $17.5 billion. The total program level for fiscal 1991 was $15 billion, with contract authority capped at $14.6 billion. The money was divided among the states through various highway programs, each using different formulas that included factors such as population, the number of miles of highway in a state and postal route mileage.

Not included in that amount were operating expenses paid out of the general Treasury that included funds for FHwA salaries, expenses and research and development programs. Congress agreed to spend $419 million on this area for fiscal 1992, $139.8 million of which was earmarked for research and projects that demonstrated the latest technology for intelligent vehicles and highways.

Congress appropriated the following amounts for other spending categories from the trust fund: grants to 70 university transportation centers, $5 million; highway-related safety grants, $20 million in contract authority; railroad-highway crossings demonstration projects, $12 million, of which $8 million would come from the trust fund; federal truck safety program, $47.6 million; grants to states for truck safety programs, $65 million. Another $42.5 million would be spent from the trust fund in the form of cash advances to states for acquiring rights of way for highway construction, so that property values would not increase while the state waited for construction to begin. States would reimburse the funds once construction got under way.

A final bookkeeping note: The $17.5 billion highway appropriation represented decisions on highway priorities. The FHwA would cut checks for another $15.4 billion pledged in previous years — a process known as "liquidation of contract authority" — for federal-aid highways, as well as $20 million for highway-related safety grants and $65 million for truck safety grants.

• **Demonstration projects.** No aspect of transportation spending was more controversial than the demonstration projects that lawmakers funded to build roads and bridges back home. The fiscal 1992 transportation appropriations bill provided $589 million for 127 special projects — less than the fiscal 1991 record of $751.4 million, but consistent with the explosion in such projects that began a little more than a decade before.

Demonstration projects were controversial for several reasons. Most had not been authorized by House and Senate Public Works committees. In addition, state transportation officials often disliked these projects because they bypassed the traditional highway funding method of lump-sum grants, which let states decide how to spend the money. Critics said the projects rarely "demonstrate" novel road-building techniques and force states to put up matching funds to pay for work not considered by state officials to be of priority. Members of Congress defended the spending, saying they often know local road needs better than state transportation officials.

Not surprisingly, the bulk of the projects funded tended to be those favored by the most powerful lawmakers. The five states that received the most earmarked funds were represented by chairmen, ranking members or key members on the Appropriations panels and transportation subcommittees: West Virginia ($162.7 million), Michigan ($46 million), Pennsylvania ($36.3 million), New Jersey ($35.7 million) and New York ($33.9 million).

Consistent with past practice, conferees agreed to accept all of the projects approved in the House and Senate bills, but they cut funding across-the-board by 10 percent for most ongoing projects and by 20 percent for most new projects.

By far the most expensive project was a West Virginia highway improvement project won by Appropriations Chairman Robert C. Byrd, D-W.Va. Known as Corridor G, it was first funded in fiscal 1990 and for fiscal 1992 would receive $148.5 million. A list of the 74 new projects totaling $207 million appears on page 129.

- **Intelligent vehicles.** Congress agreed to spend $139.8 million on intelligent vehicle-highway systems (IVHS) research, to find new ways to reduce traffic congestion, improve safety and aid motorists through electronic communication. The amount was $90 million more than the administration requested. Examples of these technologies included electronic toll-charging devices, message signs along highways and automobile navigation devices that could "read" road and traffic conditions and suggest alternate routes.

Of the total, $20 million would go toward research and $119.8 million toward specific applications. Of the latter amount, $109 million was earmarked for highways in the states of key appropriators. House appropriators steered $42.5 million toward highways in 11 cities in Michigan, Illinois, Florida, Minnesota, Texas, Pennsylvania and California. Senators added $44 million for high-technology corridors in New Jersey, $20 million for the Southern State Parkway in New York and $2.5 million for Maryland roads.

- **Other highway research.** Congress agreed to spend $28.5 million for other highway research, development and technology. Senate appropriators directed that up to $2 million of those funds go to a research project on why truck drivers lost alertness at the wheel, including $500,000 to evaluate the adequacy of public and private places for truckers to stop and rest. Of the research funds, $1 million was earmarked for the Constructed Facilities Center at West Virginia University. The remainder of funds would be allocated by the highway administration.

- **Radar detectors.** The House agreed to accept a provision in the Senate bill that banned radar detectors in commercial interstate trucking operations, and required the Transportation secretary to issue, by Jan. 15, 1992, a notice of proposed rulemaking on a ban.

- **Emergency relief.** Congress also agreed to advance to the state of Washington as much emergency relief funding as necessary to repair the I-90 bridge between Seattle and Bellevue, which was damaged during a severe storm. Should courts eventually find the damage was caused by human error, the funds would have to be repaid.

National Highway Traffic Safety Administration

Established in 1970, the NHTSA had as a main goal to reduce deaths, injuries and economic losses from traffic accidents on the nation's highways. The agency also worked to improve automotive fuel economy and aid consumers who bought automobiles.

Appropriators agreed to spend $260.7 million for NHTSA programs, which included $122.7 million for operations and research (with $44.1 million from the Highway Trust Fund), and obligation limits set at $130 million for highway traffic safety grants and $20 million for alcohol safety incentive grants. The total was up from the fiscal 1991 level of $253.3 million.

- **Operations and research.** The request by President Bush of $127.2 million for this category was reduced to $122.7 million, largely by holding travel costs to fiscal 1991 levels. The House report added to the agency's funding $3 million for more aggressive biomechanical research that would lead to better automobile side-impact protection and $2 million for the continued development of a trauma research center at Jackson Memorial Hospital in Miami, Fla., in the district of Republican Rep. Ileana Ros-Lehtinen.

- **Highway traffic safety grants.** Appropriators spent $130 million, $26 million less than the administration request, on state and community highway safety grants, school bus driver training grants and alcohol safety-incentive grants. Congress did not fund a proposed safety bonus grant program, as the Bush administration requested, because the program was not authorized. Included was $20 million for state grants to encourage safety belt and motorcycle helmet use.

RAILROADS

Federal Railroad Administration

The FRA, established as a separate agency in 1967, was responsible for carrying out safety programs for the freight and passenger railroad industries, and to rehabilitate and improve passenger railroads through financial aid programs and grants to the National Railroad Passenger Corporation (Amtrak). Appropriators agreed to spend $961 million for FRA activities, more than half of which would go to Amtrak. Amtrak got a funding increase, but it came with a scolding from appropriators about the quality of service.

FRA funding also included local rail-freight assistance, railroad safety and research programs. The total appropriation for FRA was $395.5 million more than the president's request and $67.3 million more than was spent in fiscal 1991.

The railroad industry, partly deregulated in 1980, was highly dependent on coal, heavy industry and agriculture for much of its traffic base. Appropriators did not share entirely the administration's optimistic assessment of the industry's health, and had continued to provide grants to local rail lines.

• **Amtrak**. Congress gave $506 million for Amtrak operating and capital expenses, up from $475 million in fiscal 1991 and from an administration request of $330 million. Included in that amount was a $331 million operating grant to offset losses expected by the public-private train system in fiscal 1992.

Amtrak hoped to recover more than 80 percent of its operating costs during 1991 and had a goal of becoming self-sufficient by the end of the decade.

Appropriators included $5 million for Amtrak officials to use to take a more aggressive marketing stand. The House report said Amtrak "did not take sufficient advantage of the recent slowdown in air travel to attract new ridership."

The lawmakers also expressed concern about a 40 percent increase in complaints about Amtrak service over the past year. "Amtrak is not likely to improve revenues significantly if it continues to disenchant its customers at an increasing rate," the House report said.

Congress provided $175 million for capital expenses, 33 percent above the fiscal 1991 level. Most new spending would be for new locomotives and passenger cars.

Rep. William H. Gray III, D-Pa., who was chairman of the Appropriations subcommittee when he resigned in September, won $7 million in demonstration funds to convert track bed and other railroad assets to Amtrak's use at the 30th Street station area in Philadelphia.

Also included was $500,000 for a feasibility study of high-speed rail service between Chicago and St. Louis.

• **Local rail service assistance.** This program, established for the Northeast in 1973 and expanded to all states in 1976, provided financial support to states to allow continuation of rail-freight service on abandoned lines. Congress provided $11.5 million, up by $1.5 million from the fiscal 1991 level. The Bush administration requested no funding, arguing that regional railroads now were a growth industry and no longer needed federal help.

• **Railroad safety.** Congress provided $37.7 million to encourage safe operation of passenger and freight trains, a 9 percent increase over fiscal 1991 but $3.3 million less than recommended by Bush. The funding paid for federal enforcement, track inspection and safety education programs.

Congress did not provide $1 million in FRA-requested funds to carry out railroad provisions of the 1990 Sanitary Food Transportation Act (PL 101-500) that ensured that food was not transported in vehicles that had previously carried garbage or hazardous materials. Appropriators said testimony showed that the problem was not widespread and that the Transportation Department had little experience in food safety regulation.

• **Research and development.** Congress provided $22.3 million for research activities geared toward reducing railroad accidents.

• **Magnetic levitation and high-speed rail.** Magnetically levitated trains, which would operate on an electromagnetic field, and steel-on-steel high-speed rail systems were competing to become the dominant new trend in mass transit. Senate appropriators attempted to provide $30 million in funding for a National Magnetic Levitation Design Program, but they dropped their bid during the House-Senate conference because the program had yet to be authorized by the Senate highway authorization bill (S 1204).

Conferees agreed to $12 million for magnetic levitation and high-speed rail research, of which $800,000 was for national laboratories managed by the Department of Energy to study the technology. Also included in the total was $500,000 each for magnetic levitation state planning grants for five corridors: Baltimore-Washington (Maryland Department of Transportation), New York City-Albany-Boston (New York DOT), Milwaukee-Chicago (Wisconsin DOT), the Pittsburgh metropolitan area and Las Vegas. State or local governments, or other non-federal concerns, would have to provide dollar-for-dollar matching money.

• **Northeast Corridor Improvement Program.** The administration sought no funds for a multi-year program to improve track and facilities in the Northeast Corridor, but Congress provided $205 million, up from $179 million in fiscal 1991. Of that amount, $150 million would be used to continue electrifying the rail line between New Haven, Conn., and Boston, which would reduce travel time between New York City and Boston from three hours, 55 minutes to three hours.

MASS TRANSIT

Urban Mass Transportation Administration

UMTA provided federal financial aid for planning, developing and improving mass-transportation systems in urban and rural areas.

Few transit systems could survive without government assistance, but even though transit ridership reached a record level of about 9 billion passengers in 1991, federal funding for mass transit had declined by about 50 percent over the past decade. Another $6 billion to $11 billion would be needed over the next five years to address a backlog of projects placed on hold because of funding shortages, according to the American Public Transit Association.

Congress and the administration clashed in 1991 over the role the federal government should play to keep transit systems operating.

The administration proposed only a negligible funding increase for mass transit and pushed to eliminate operating assistance to transit systems in urban areas, in line with positions held since the beginning of the Reagan administration. Instead, appropriators gave mass transit its biggest boost since 1983 — up 13 percent over fiscal 1991 levels. The increase came in the form of grants to specific mass transit systems.

Total funding for mass transit was $3.8 billion; the Bush administration had requested $3.3 billion. Fiscal 1991's total spending was $3.3 billion.

Funds to local mass transit authorities were available in two forms. Formula grants helped with routine capital and operating expenses and programs for the elderly and handicapped. Discretionary grants were project-specific funds for bus facilities, rail modernization, new rail systems and research at university transportation centers.

About 30 percent of UMTA funds came from the mass transit account of the Highway Trust Fund, which received 1.5 cents of the 14.1-cents-per-gallon gasoline tax. The remainder came from general revenues. To lessen the burden on the general Treasury, the Bush administration proposed funding the entire UMTA budget through the trust fund, except for $80 million for the Washington, D.C., Metro. Appropriators rejected that idea, choosing to retain the existing mix of trust fund spending.

• **Formula grants**. Congress provided $1.5 billion for capital and operating assistance in urban and rural areas, which was $85 million less than fiscal 1991 levels.

Grants could be used to buy and repair buses, modernize bus stations and garages, improve rail service equipment and maintain or expand service for the elderly and handicapped. Congress applied $802 million of the formula grant program toward operating assistance, the same as the fiscal 1991 level. The administration had proposed $298 million. The money was divided among the nation's mass transit systems based on formulas that used factors such as population, population density, how many route miles were in a transit system and how much revenue was earned from each vehicle.

• **Discretionary grants.** Congress designated $1.9 billion for discretionary grants, with the entire amount coming from the trust fund. Grants went toward building new "fixed guideway" (rail) systems, major bus fleet expansions and rail modernization for existing systems.

For new rail systems and extensions, Congress provided $565 million for preliminary engineering, right of way acquisition, project oversight and construction, apportioned among 23 urban areas: Los Angeles, $135 million; Atlanta, $20 million; St. Louis, $35 million; San Francisco, $55 million; Honolulu, $40 million; Houston, $30 million; Dallas, $40 million; Baltimore, $5 million; Jacksonville, Fla., $10 million; Cleveland, $1 million; New Jersey urban core, $70 million; Chicago, $21 million; Miami, $11 million; Salt Lake City, $5 million; San Diego, $1 million; Pittsburgh, $15 million; Portland, Ore., $26 million; New York, $11 million; Boston, $21 million; Kansas City, Mo., $1 million; Philadelphia, $1 million; Seattle-Tacoma, $10 million; Orlando, Fla., $1 million.

Rail modernization grants totaled $550 million, and funding went primarily to nine areas: New York, northern New Jersey, southern Connecticut, Chicago, Philadelphia, Pittsburgh, Boston, Cleveland and San Francisco.

Bus facilities received $230 million, including special earmarks from the House for systems in East Texas ($10 million), Raleigh, N.C. ($311,000), Baltimore ($13 million), Spokane, Wash. ($4.2 million) and Buffalo, N.Y. ($5 million). Those cities could use the funds to buy or improve buses and to build or upgrade bus facilities.

Senate earmarks for bus facilities included funds for the following transit authorities: New Jersey Transit fleet expansion ($21 million); Maryland Mass Transit Authority fleet expansion ($13 million); Hamilton, N.J., "intermodal" facility ($3 million); Atlantic City, N.J., bus facility ($3 million); Tucson, Ariz., ($3 million) for up to five alternative fuel vehicles, plus $4 million for the Tucson dial-a-ride program; and Eugene, Ore., ($3.5 million) for a bus transfer station.

• **Administrative expenses.** The General Accounting Office and the Office of the Inspector General had been critical of UMTA's oversight of about $32 billion in active grants. The Inspector General questioned about $340 million in grants over the past four years, including cases in which local transit authorities double-billed the administration or failed to reimburse the agency when costs were less than expected. The $37 million Congress provided for administrative expenses included funds for 31 new full-time positions for oversight of the national grant program.

• **Planning and technical studies.** Congress spent $45 million for planning and technical studies, with six transit systems earmarked for planning funds: Sacramento, Calif. ($2.5 million); Lackawanna and Monroe counties, Pa. ($200,000); North Carolina ($750,000); Charlotte, N.C. ($500,000); Jefferson County, Mo. ($80,000); and Buffalo, N.Y. (as necessary).

• **Washington, D.C., Metro.** The bill included $124 million for expansion of the Washington, D.C., Metrorail system, nearly double the $64.1 million amount appropriated in fiscal 1991 and $44 million more than the administration requested.

MARITIME

Coast Guard

The Coast Guard, established in 1915, enforced federal laws on the high seas and waterways within U.S. jurisdiction. Agency missions also included drug interdiction, search and rescue, vessel and shore facility inspections, boating safety, protecting the marine environment and maintaining a state of readiness to function as a specialized service of the Navy during wartime.

In fiscal 1992, Congress provided $3.3 billion in new budget authority. Of the total, $2.3 billion was for operating expenses, including the operation and maintenance of vessels, aircraft and shore units and drug interdiction, and $390 million would be spent to acquire new vessels, aircraft and other items.

The Coast Guard performed support missions for the Operation Desert Shield buildup and Desert Storm hostilities overseas and at home, including port security and anti-terrorism activities, assisting the Navy with Coast Guard active-duty law enforcement ship-boarding teams, and logistics and medevac flights in the United States.

• **Operating expenses.** Congress provided $2.3 billion for the operation and maintenance of vessels, aircraft and shore units along the coasts and inland waterways within the United States and in selected areas overseas.

Of the total, $31.9 million would come from the oil spill liability trust fund, which was fed by a 5-cents-a-barrel oil tax, to assist in preventing and cleaning up oil spills.

For fiscal 1992, drug interdiction activities received $603.4 million, an increase of $821,000 over fiscal 1991. But that compared with a fiscal 1990 amount of $665 million. Drug interdiction had been increasingly a Coast Guard responsibility, accounting for about one-fourth of the agency's operating expenses. With increased involvement of the Defense Department in that area, appropriators and Coast Guard officials said they were attempting to "restore balance" by putting more emphasis on traditional missions and less on drug interdiction.

Also as part of this effort, appropriators prevented Coast Guard funds from being spent to operate land- and sea-based stationary balloons or drug interdiction aircraft.

The operating expense account category would pay the salaries for 38,262 military positions and 5,206 civilian positions — an increase of 515 military personnel and 386 civilians over fiscal 1991.

• **Acquisition, construction and improvements.** Congress would spend $390 million (down from $406.3 million in fiscal 1991) to pay for new vessels, aircraft, shore units and aids to navigation in fiscal 1992. The Coast Guard operated about 250 vessels, ranging from tugboats to polar ice-breakers, and more than 210 helicopters and fixed-wing aircraft. The Coast Guard also operated more than 600 stations, support and supply centers, communications facilities and other shore units. Navigational aids included roughly 48,000 buoys, lighthouses and radio navigation stations.

Included in the total amount were $26.4 million to buy

equipment needed to clean up future oil spills, $60.4 million to acquire new aircraft and increase aviation capability, and $144.2 million to acquire, repair and improve Coast Guard ships. The agency also would buy about $48.8 million worth of new equipment such as computer networking devices and communications equipment.

Improvements at Coast Guard stations and other navigation facilities would be made at a cost of $102.7 million.

The Coast Guard also could spend $34 million, an $8.4 million decrease from the administration request, on administrative personnel. Appropriators rejected a Coast Guard request for 90 new staff positions, with 71 of them military positions. Rather, the appropriation allowed only 35 new staff positions. The House report cited a Coast Guard study that found the ship acquisition process "already bloated with too many personnel, and that those personnel do not share a common vision of program objectives."

- **Environmental compliance and restoration**. The bill provided $21.5 million, $3.6 million less than the administration request, to bring Coast Guard facilities in line with federal, state and local environmental regulations.
- **Alteration of bridges**. The bill designated $11.1 million to alter or remove bridges that obstructed commercial ship travel. The bridges were in Pascagoula, Miss.; Burlington, Iowa; and Brunswick, Ga.
- **Retired pay**. The bill spent $487.7 million, including payments under the Retired Serviceman's Family Protection and Survivor Benefits Plans and payments for medical care of retired personnel and their dependents under the Dependents Medical Care Act.
- **Reserve training**. The bill provided $25 million for the Coast Guard Reserve. Members were available for active duty in time of war or national emergency. The funds included maintenance and operation of facilities, supplies, equipment and services.
- **Research, development, evaluation**. Appropriators spent $29.2 million for applied scientific research, development, testing and evaluation; maintenance, rehabilitation, lease and operation of facilities and equipment. Examples included $75,000 for a search-and-rescue hovercraft near Anchorage, Alaska, won by Sen. Ted Stevens, R-Alaska, and $300,000 for a grant to the New Jersey Marine Sciences Consortium to develop educational materials on fishing boat safety, won by Sen. Frank R. Lautenberg, D-N.J.
- **Boat safety**. The Aquatic Resources Trust Fund could spend $35 million, the same amount as was spent in fiscal 1991 and the same as the administration's request, for grants to states for boat-safety education programs.

AIR

Federal Aviation Administration

The FAA, established in 1958, was responsible for the safety and development of civil aviation and the evolution of a national system of airports. Total funding for FAA activities came to $8.9 billion, an increase of 10.5 percent over fiscal 1991 levels, but a $395 million cut from the administration request.

The FAA got its money from the general Treasury and the Airport and Airway Trust Fund, which was fed mostly by a 10 percent tax on airline tickets. Airport development and planning grants were made from the trust fund, with money available for grants capped at $1.9 billion, up from $1.8 billion in fiscal 1991. Direct appropriations totaled $7 billion and paid for operations, facilities and equipment, research and an aircraft purchase loan guarantee program.

In addition to the $1.9 billion in airport grants, another $2.4 billion from the Airport and Airway Trust Fund would be spent to modernize and improve air-traffic control and airway facilities.

- **Airport grants.** The money for airport development and planning grants was issued in the form of contract authority, which amounted to a promise to airports that federal funds would be available to reimburse them for construction or improvement projects. Congress had pledged up to $1.9 billion for such grants in fiscal 1992. It also provided $1.52 billion in "contract authority liquidation" — money pledged to airports in past years for construction payments that were coming due.

House and Senate appropriators recommended in the report a list of 84 airports that should get priority consideration for grant applications. The list did not include funding levels for individual airports.

- **Operations**. Nearly half of the FAA's spending — $4.4 billion — would go to operate and maintain the nation's air-traffic control and navigation systems, including research and development and maintenance of aircraft. Operations money included:
- **Air-traffic control.** Congress appropriated $2 billion to operate the nation's air-traffic control system, $133 million more than in fiscal 1991. The increase paid for 17,945 air-traffic controllers, 450 more than in fiscal 1991. The increase was requested by the administration before Mideast hostilities reduced air travel. Still, FAA Administrator James B. Busey said in hearings after the war that he wanted to continue building the work force to meet future needs.

Perhaps more important than the number of controllers was the experience level: Busey said a growing number of highly experienced controllers had led to decreased flight delays and a declining operation error rate for every year since 1984. The agency had been recovering from a nationwide air-traffic controller strike in 1981, when more than 11,000 striking controllers were fired.

Of the total amount, $1.5 billion went toward air-traffic control centers and towers, including staffing more than 22,000 positions, and $250 million went toward the operation of flight service stations.

Congress added $1.6 million above the administration request to install new control towers in Kenosha, Wis.; Athens, Ga.; Norman, Okla.; Jackson, Tenn.; and Gary, Ind.

- **Telecommunications upgrade.** The bill aimed to speed up the FAA's effort to develop a new telephone backup system in the wake of a Sept. 18 New York City phone-switching failure that froze airport operations. The House bill, drafted before the outage, had denied the FAA's $18.4 million request to develop a better telecommunications system, citing the General Services Administration's (GSA) withdrawal of permission for the FAA to seek bids for an upgraded system. Funds were included after the GSA on Sept. 26 allowed the contract bidding, at the urging of Alfonse M. D'Amato, N.Y., ranking Republican on the Senate Transportation Appropriations Subcommittee.

Congress also boosted FAA funding for leased telecommunications services by $60 million to $348.2 million, including the costs to upgrade the FAA phone system.

- **Aviation safety inspections.** The FAA would add 57

general aviation and 43 air carrier inspector positions, raising the total number of inspector positions to 3,158. This was an increase of 96 percent since fiscal 1985. The FAA said the quality of inspections was improving, partly attributed to the hiring of inspectors who once worked for airlines that had since gone bankrupt.

Aviation security. About $65.7 million would be spent on security personnel, including 178 new positions.

Flight service stations. Congress agreed to language, at the urging of Sen. Barbara A. Mikulski, D-Md., banning the consolidation of most flight service stations for a period of nine months following submission to Congress of a new consolidation plan. Such stations monitored local weather and gave flight information to nearby pilots.

The language allowed Mikulski to save a flight service station in Salisbury, Md., and 111 others from closure. The FAA wanted pilots to use newer, state-of-the-art control centers. Mikulski argued that the Salisbury station was critical to the Chesapeake Bay area, where weather fronts could change in minutes between the bay and the Atlantic Ocean.

- **Facilities and equipment.** Congress provided $2.4 billion to buy new equipment and build and modernize facilities. The amount fell $300 million short of what the FAA requested to carry out its comprehensive "national airspace system" — a master plan to modernize and coordinate all airport activities. Spending included:

Air-traffic control. The amount included $889.6 million for upgrading equipment at air-traffic control centers across the country, $664.1 million for equipment for airport traffic control towers, $52.7 million for flight service stations and $57.4 million for aircraft and related equipment.

The FAA would spend $21 million to pay its share of the Next Generation Weather Radar (NEXRAD) program, which came under fire during the appropriations process because of trouble with the contractor, Unisys. The FAA shared 20 percent of the costs for the project, along with the Departments of Defense and Commerce.

The control tower at the Roswell, N.M., airport would get a new radar system ($11 million); the Eastern West Virginia Airport in Martinsburg would get an upgraded approach radar system ($14 million).

Airway sciences program. Congress provided $20 million, $3 million above the requested amount, for the airway sciences curriculum program to train the next generation of airways operators, managers and technicians. Funds were earmarked for Dowling College of New York ($3 million), Middle Tennessee State University ($250,000), North Dakota State University ($989,000), the University of North Dakota ($2 million), Northeast Louisiana University ($4 million) for a new airway science center, and Southern University in Shreveport, La. ($3 million). The Senate report also asked that priority consideration be given to expanding airway science facilities at Daniel Webster College in Nashua, N.J. ($3 million).

The FAA would spend $26 million to procure 16 new flight inspection aircraft, of which 11 would replace aging aircraft and five would be added to meet expanded needs. The existing fleet of 36 aircraft was used to certify navigation equipment, check out new flight procedures and analyze radio signals.

- **Research, engineering and development.** Congress spent $218.1 million for research on air-traffic control, advanced computers, navigation, aviation weather, medicine, safety and the environment.

- **Aircraft purchase loan guarantee program.** The bill provided $1.2 million, plus accrued interest of $150,000, to repay the Treasury for loans made to pay the banks of five airlines that were in some form of bankruptcy: Big Sky, Dorado Wings, Midway, Mid Pacific and Pocono airlines. These airlines defaulted on federally guaranteed loans, sticking the federal government for the bill.

The Transportation secretary would be allowed to borrow up to $9.97 million from the Treasury to pay airlines' defaulted loans, the same as the fiscal 1991 level.

- **Aging aircraft safety.** As part of the 1992 appropriation, Congress ordered the FAA administrator to issue a rule within 180 days of enactment to ensure the continuing airworthiness of aging aircraft. At a minimum, the rule would require the administrator to determine that aircraft used by air carriers were in safe condition and were properly maintained. The inspections would be carried out as part of each heavy maintenance check of aircraft in service for 15 years or more.

The administrator also was required to encourage foreign governments and relevant international organizations to develop standards and requirements to inspect the airworthiness of aging aircraft.

DEPARTMENT ADMINISTRATION

Office of the Secretary

Appropriations for the Office of the Secretary included budgets for Transportation Secretary Samuel K. Skinner, five assistant Department of Transportation (DOT) secretaries, the Office of General Counsel and other administrative offices. For fiscal 1992 Congress provided $64 million for these administrators to run the DOT, an 8.8 percent increase over fiscal 1991.

- **Secretary's office.** Skinner got $1.4 million to run his office, the level requested by the administration. The secretary's travel budget was increased to $160,000. Though only $54,000 was appropriated in fiscal 1990, Skinner and his staff spent $133,000 on foreign and domestic travel after transferring the extra funds from other accounts. Skinner spokesman Bob Marx said the travel increase reflected the secretary's "outreach style" as opposed to predecessor Jim Burnley. Burnley's actual travel expenses in fiscal 1989 were $57,000.
- **Planning, research and development.** The secretary's office could spend $3.1 million for activities that included the collection of national transportation statistics. Continued emphasis would be made on research on sleep and fatigue while operating planes, trains, trucks and other forms of transportation.
- **Commercial space transportation.** Congress appropriated $4.3 million for operations and research, 20 percent more than in fiscal 1991. Still, the House Transportation Appropriations Subcommittee expressed concern that the Office of Commercial Space Transportation inflated the numbers of projected commercial launches to justify its office staffing. In 1990, the office estimated 40 launches would take place in fiscal 1991, but only about 13 would have taken place — four of them as Defense Department experiments.
- **Essential Air Service program.** The bill spent $38.6 million from the Airport and Airway Trust Fund to pay air carriers to serve unprofitable rural locations that needed air transportation. Congress limited the funds only to communities that already were receiving the service.

One exception was won by Transportation Appropriations panelist Martin Olav Sabo, D-Minn., to allow an airport in Fergus Falls, Minn., to join the Essential Air Service program.

Research, Special Programs Administration

This agency was set up in 1977 as a research and technical development arm of the department for all modes of transportation but with emphasis on pipeline safety and transportation of hazardous cargo.

Congress provided $34 million for the agency, $7.1 million more than in fiscal 1991 and $3.8 million less than the administration request.

The Senate report came down hard on the agency for reprogramming funds away from the Office of Hazardous Materials Transportation to management and administrative offices.

Hazardous-materials program funds were shifted to administrative uses, the report said, which led to a "degradation of critical regulatory functions." The funds were used to finance, among other items, "a consulting contract to provide the administrator and deputy administrator with professional coaching on the proper dress, demeanor, speech and gestures for radio and TV interviews."

Funds were also found to replace furniture within the Office of the Administrator and conduct staff retreats in Annapolis, Md., and other locations in which lodging and food costs for numerous staff members were covered by the agency.

As a result, Senate report language adopted by conferees restructured the agency's funding to keep better track of spending. Included in the funding level was $12 million for hazardous materials safety and $13.47 million for pipeline safety.

Inspector General

The inspector general's office was set up in 1978 to provide independent oversight for detecting and preventing waste, fraud and abuse. The bill appropriated $37 million, $1.6 million less than the administration request. It supported an 8 percent staffing increase over fiscal 1991.

RELATED TRANSPORTATION AGENCIES

Architectural and Transportation Barriers Compliance Board

The board ensured compliance with standards prescribed by the 1968 Architectural Barriers Act (PL 90-480), which mandated that public conveyances be readily accessible to handicapped people.

The bill provided $2.9 million for the agency. The amount was a $240,000 increase over fiscal 1991, allowing for more staffing to carry out 1990's Americans with Disabilities Act (PL 101-336).

National Transportation Safety Board

The NTSB, set up in 1974, was responsible for improving transportation safety by investigating accidents, conducting studies and recommending ways to prevent accidents. It also evaluated the transportation safety programs of other agencies and reviewed appeals of actions filed against certificates or licenses issued by the department.

In fiscal 1991, the board estimated that it would have completed six major aviation accident reports and 2,440 minor aviation field reports. The board also reported on highway, rail and water accidents. For fiscal 1992 Congress provided $34.7 million for the board, the amount requested by the administration and $3.2 million more than in fiscal 1991. Sixteen new full-time positions were funded over fiscal 1991 levels.

Interstate Commerce Commission

The ICC was an independent agency that regulated the nation's commercial railroads, trucking companies, bus lines, water carriers, one coal slurry pipeline, freight forwarders and transportation brokers. Its goal was to ensure that the public had an adequate, efficient transportation system for moving goods.

The bill provided $40.9 million in fiscal 1992 for the agency. That figure was $2.8 million less than in fiscal 1991.

Omnibus Transportation Employee Testing

Congress required that within a year of the bill's enactment the Transportation Department and the Federal Aviation Administration require drug and alcohol testing for aviation, rail, trucking, bus and mass transit employees performing safety-sensitive jobs. Such jobs would be defined in upcoming regulations, but presumably would include operating, inspecting or maintaining trains, planes and trucks, and conducting security checks at airports.

The tests would be required at any of four different points: before hiring; if there was reasonable cause to suspect drug or alcohol usage; at a random time; and after involvement in an accident.

The Transportation secretary or FAA administrator would have to fire or suspend any employees who tested positive in violation of law or federal regulations regarding alcohol or drug use.

Any person who was determined to have violated federal laws or regulations by using alcohol or drugs would be banned from working at his job unless he completed a rehabilitation program.

Congress specified that the drug and alcohol testing procedures should promote individual privacy in the collection of specimen samples and should follow Department of Health and Human Services guidelines regarding standards for laboratory testing, including the best available technology and strict procedures governing the chain of custody of samples.

The Bush administration since 1990 had required random tests for drugs — but not for alcohol — for aviation, trucking and rail employees in safety-sensitive positions.

But the U.S. Court of Appeals for the District of Columbia Circuit ruled in January 1990 that the Urban Mass Transporation Administration lacked the regulatory authority to force its drug-testing rules on mass transit systems. ■

Continued from p. 605
were not able to provide for every request," he said.

The committee bill spent $524 million for new rail systems in 22 cities. The projects closely tracked recommendations in the House bill, but the Senate bill provided less funding for such projects in 13 cities.

At the urging of Lloyd Bentsen, D-Texas, the Senate panel opted to spend $30 million to begin construction on a controversial Houston monorail system. The House had decided not to fund the project.

The bill raised the ceiling on spending from the Highway Trust Fund to $17.2 billion, from $14.6 billion in fiscal 1991. The House bill had raised the cap to $16.3 billion.

Mass transit operating assistance, at $802 million, also was to be continued, despite Bush administration calls to eliminate the aid.

Sponsors also added a provision that required random drug and alcohol testing of mass transit, aviation, bus and rail workers. *(Drug testing for transportation workers, p. 151)*

SENATE FLOOR ACTION

Senators usually accepted early on that Byrd, as Appropriations Committee chairman, would bring home the bacon. But every now and then there was a freshman who challenged political reality. That was the case Sept. 17 when first-year Sen. Robert C. Smith, R-N.H., decided to take on Byrd and other key appropriators who had steered some $387 million in special road projects homeward — including a hefty $182 million for West Virginia.

Smith offered an amendment to the $14.4 billion version of HR 2942 that sought to more equitably distribute the road money nationwide. The amendment failed, 84-14, and the Senate later passed the appropriations bill, 95-3. *(Votes 193, 194, p. 26-S)*

"Stand up and say the process is wrong," Smith implored his colleagues. He railed that West Virginia received nearly half of the special road funds, including $165 million for a single highway corridor and $12.9 million for roads to a new FBI fingerprinting complex that Byrd secured for his home state.

Twenty-three states, including New Hampshire, California and Texas, received no special road projects under the bill. Smith's amendment would have given all but 11 states a boost in highway dollars. West Virginia's amount would have been slashed to $4.8 million.

Nonetheless, most senators opted against giving their states more money and cast their votes for the status quo.

Smith conceded that his amendment did not make him "popular." But he gambled more than just good will by challenging those who held the purse strings.

Alfonse M. D'Amato, R-N.Y., ranking member of the Transportation Appropriations Subcommittee, in a not-so-veiled warning, reminded Smith that Daniel Webster College in Nashua, N.H., was seeking $3.9 million to expand its aviation sciences facilities.

The only members of the Appropriations panel to vote with Smith were longtime government-spending critic Phil Gramm, R-Texas, and Arlen Specter, R-Pa., who had an ongoing feud with Transportation Appropriations Subcommittee Chairman Lautenberg over not being consulted on recent Pennsylvania transit projects.

The only Democrat to side with Smith was Joseph R. Biden Jr. of Delaware. Delaware would have received $2 million in extra road funds. A Biden spokesman said the senator had no comment on the vote.

Under the bill as passed by the Senate, spending from the Highway Trust Fund for construction programs, limited in fiscal 1991 to $14.5 billion, was increased to $17.2 billion. The bill was amended by voice vote to decrease the cap by $5.8 million to bring it in line with revised spending limits issued by the Senate Budget Committee the week of Sept. 9.

The Senate also went on record against any increase in gasoline taxes by passing a non-binding resolution, sponsored by Daniel R. Coats, R-Ind., as an amendment to the appropriations bill.

The resolution, which was passed by voice vote, came one day before House leaders abandoned their proposal to raise the tax by a nickel. House tax and transportation committees sought to work out an alternative that would raise more revenues for that chamber's then-paralyzed bill to reauthorize federal highway and mass transit programs (HR 2950).

"The issue of the gasoline tax should be moot now," conceded Daniel Patrick Moynihan, D-N.Y., author of the Senate-passed reauthorization bill, which contained no gas-tax increase (S 1204).

In other action on the bill, Minority Leader Bob Dole, R-Kan., withdrew an amendment that would have repealed a 1979 law limiting use of Dallas' Love Field airport only to those who traveled from Texas and adjoining states. The intention of the law was to encourage national traffic to use the Dallas-Fort Worth International Airport.

Dole, who complained that the law was no longer needed and inconvenienced Kansas air passengers, said he would offer the amendment on a fiscal 1991 supplemental appropriations bill unless he could reach a compromise with Texas senators who opposed his measure.

Other differences between the House and Senate bills included:

- A House cap of $16.2 billion on highway programs, lower than the $17.1 billion proposed in the Senate bill.
- A $260 million Senate appropriation for the Amtrak Northeast Corridor, $193.8 million of which was to be used to continue electrifying the rail line between New Haven, Conn., and Boston. Travel time from New York City to Boston would be shortened from four hours and 40 minutes to less than three hours.

The House bill provided only $36 million for routine capital expenses. House appropriators provided no funding for the New Haven-Boston rail upgrade. "Before a decision is made on further financing for this project, the committee needs to understand the total costs estimated," said the House report.

- A $30 million Senate appropriation for a National Magnetic Levitation Design Program, which was authorized in that chamber's version of the highway reauthorization bill.

The program was to weigh competing bids to design and develop a prototype magnetic levitation train system.

The House report said steel-on-steel, high-speed rail systems, as opposed to magnetic levitation, remained the committee's preferred new technology and that "it would appear that the prospects for implementation of advanced technology 'maglev' systems in the United States are very dim."

The House bill provided $3 million for maglev safety research and $1 million for high-speed rail research.

- Differences over several Coast Guard and FAA special projects, which came on top of each chamber's list of special highway and transit projects. The Senate, for example, wanted $4.4 million to build an indoor swimming pool in Kodiak, Alaska, for Coast Guard personnel.
- A $15 million House appropriation for an additional Jayhawk helicopter for the Coast Guard, as well as $20

million to replace the Coast Guard's primary long-range command and control aircraft, the 20-year-old VC-11A. Senate appropriators objected to the items.

- A $29.3 million Senate appropriation for Coast Guard public family housing funds, including $15 million for a housing project in Puerto Rico that included a day-care facility, an outdoor swimming pool and a recreation center. The House rejected funding for the center.
- A House attempt to cut a 5 percent pay increase, over a two-year period, for 29,000 FAA employees, including air-traffic controllers. The House report branded the raises a reward for those air-traffic controllers who did not strike. Senate appropriators directed that the funds be restored, saying no hearings were held on the issue.

CONFERENCE

Truckers, mass transit workers and airline employees faced more stringent drug-testing and safety rules under an Oct. 2 conference agreement on HR 2942, a $14.3 billion fiscal 1992 transportation appropriations bill.

House appropriators, led by Lehman, dropped their past opposition and accepted a Senate provision mandating random drug and alcohol testing of transportation workers in safety-sensitive jobs. They also adopted Senate language to ban interstate truckers and bus drivers from using radar detectors.

Senate appropriators, led by Lautenberg, in turn agreed to a House provision to bolster inspections of aging aircraft.

HR 2942 raised the ceiling on spending from the Highway Trust Fund to $16.8 billion in fiscal 1992, up from $14.6 billion in fiscal 1991. Trust fund spending was not part of the $13.8 billion in new budget authority that was provided by the bill.

Atop money for highway formula grants, appropriators included roughly $600 million — mostly from general revenues — for 127 new and ongoing demonstration projects for specific lawmakers' districts and states.

As in the past, conferees accepted each others' lists of road construction projects and reduced overall funding. The 1991 cut was 20 percent for new construction projects and 10 percent for ongoing ones.

The bill also gave $3.76 billion to mass transit programs, including $565 million to build new rail transit systems in 23 specified cities. Such mass transit programs received $3.26 billion in fiscal 1991.

The biggest fight was over whether to give Houston $30 million to build a monorail system. House appropriator DeLay opposed Texas senators and fought to reject the funds.

Ultimately, a compromise was worked out under which Houston received the money but could not spend it until the city reached an agreement on a rail system.

Appropriators also discovered another way to send road funds home, providing $139.8 million for a new "intelligent vehicle-highway systems" research program. The program sought high-technology solutions to the nation's traffic problems, including computerized highway traffic monitoring and in-car navigation systems.

Federal funding for the research program began at $2.3 million in fiscal 1990 and grew to $20 million in fiscal 1991. HR 2942's $139.8 million program included $119.8 million steered toward specific highways, universities and regions in the districts and states of appropriators, including New Jersey, Maryland and New York.

An administration statement complained about the special projects and said the selection of recipients for research funds should be left to the Transportation Department.

Without the usual fight from key drug-testing opponents such as Energy and Commerce Chairman John D. Dingell, D-Mich., the House passed a non-binding motion Sept. 24 to instruct conferees to accept mass transit drug-testing language sponsored by Sen. D'Amato. The motion carried by an overwhelming 413-5. *(Vote 273, p. 66-H)*

Conferees, who in 1990 rejected similar D'Amato language, went a step further in 1991. They adopted a broader bill by Sen. Ernest F. Hollings, D-S.C., that mandated random drug and alcohol tests on all transportation workers in safety-sensitive positions.

House negotiators also agreed to a Senate provision that required the Transportation secretary to issue rules by Jan. 15 prohibiting the use of radar detectors in all interstate commercial trucks and buses. In 1990, Senate conferees bowed to objections by the House and dropped a similar provision from the final bill.

And Senate appropriators agreed to a House proposal calling for stepped-up inspections of aging aircraft. The House had twice passed legislation calling for such inspections — in 1990 and again in April — but had failed to see action in the Senate. *(Aging aircraft inspection, p. 153)*

The measure directed the FAA to require special safety inspections of planes 15 years old or older that were down for heavy maintenance checks.

Democratic Sen. Jim Sasser won report language directing the FAA to consider factors that could lead to less burdensome inspection requirements for cargo air carriers. Federal Express Corp. was headquartered in Memphis in Sasser's home state.

Magnetic Levitation Funds Cut

Appropriators went into the conference with few other major differences between the two bills.

The Senate failed in its bid to spend $30 million on a pilot program for a magnetic levitation train able to travel at high speeds by floating on an electromagnetic field.

House appropriators prevailed, saying in their report that prospects for carrying out such a pilot program were "very dim." House lawmakers sided with the Federal Railroad Administration in favoring steel-on-steel, high-speed rail over magnetic levitation.

Conferees agreed to spend $205 million, close to Senate-recommended funding levels, for a Northeast Corridor rail-improvement program.

The program included funding to electrify the line from New Haven, Conn., to Boston — a measure that proponents said would decrease to three hours the travel time from New York to Boston. The House bill had originally recommended no funding for the electrification project.

Other issues settled in conference included:

- Sen. Bob Kasten, R-Wis., won an amendment exempting states from having to take down 65 mph speed limit signs until a new highway authorization bill was enacted.

Federal authority for the 65 mph limit on non-Interstate, four-lane roads expired Sept. 30 with the rest of the federal highway program.

- Rep. Carr won report language directing the National Highway Traffic Safety Administration to study the usefulness of crash-test data and explore ways to standardize the types of crash dummies in tests. Carr argued that older-model crash dummies could skew results and make cars appear less safe.
- Rep. Martin Olav Sabo, D-Minn., won an exception for

a home-state airport that had been prevented from joining a program that gave subsidies to air carriers servicing low-traffic rural airports. The bill banned the program from being expanded to new airports, but Sabo won language exempting the Fergus Falls, Minn., airport.

- Rep. Richard J. Durbin, D-Ill., failed to persuade conferees to reinstate dropped language to provide more take-off and landing slots for carriers serving rural communities from Chicago O'Hare Airport.

FINAL ACTION

When the House approved the conference agreement on Oct. 9, members rejected moves to cut the $588 million targeted for special highway projects.

Republicans Burton, Walker and Fawell argued that the bulk of the 127 projects were wasteful, were not authorized by the appropriate committees and bypassed state planning priorities. But the House rejected their attempt to cut both the funds for and the number of the projects.

Burton, Walker and Fawell then focused on Byrd, who had secured $162.7 million in road projects for West Virginia, including $148.5 million for Corridor G in the southwestern part of the state.

Burton first appealed to lawmakers to reject $18.4 million in feasibility studies inserted in the bill by the Senate, but the effort failed by voice vote. Of that amount, $15.1 million was earmarked for West Virginia and New Jersey, home states of Byrd and Senate Transportation Appropriations Subcommittee Chairman Lautenberg.

Burton then launched an unsuccessful effort to delete funding for Corridor G, which ran through Appalachia. The House accepted the road project on a vote of 238-186, assembling a much narrower margin than it had on the previous vote to cut both chambers' special projects. *(Vote 301, p. 72-H)*

"If that ain't pork, what is?" Burton asked. "He [Byrd] doesn't want to bring home the bacon; he wants to bring home the whole pig."

In their floor attacks of Byrd, Burton and Walker were frequently reminded by the presiding officer that making personal references to senators violated House rules.

During the debate, Lehman urged lawmakers to support Byrd's projects or risk killing the measure.

"It takes votes in both chambers to pass an appropriations bill," Lehman said. "We have to deal with the Senate in good faith."

High-Technology Highways

Along with the demonstration projects that brought funds to appropriators' home states, the spending bill also included a number of high-technology research projects that funneled additional money home. Of the total fiscal 1992 funding for the research program, more than half went to New Jersey and New York — homes to the chairman and ranking member, respectively, of the Senate Transportation Appropriations Subcommittee.

Some of the projects receiving funding were already well-established, such as a system in Chicago that received $7.5 million under the bill and cost $40 million over five years. Under the project, Motorola Inc. and other technology companies were to equip as many as 5,000 vehicles with in-car navigation systems that used satellites to help divert drivers from bottlenecks.

But many other projects were new, and their locations were picked by appropriators who circumvented competitive bidding procedures to select home-state recipients. The FAA, which had a research office, typically decided the location of such projects based on bids from states. For example:

- New Jersey, home of Senate Transportation Appropriations Chairman Lautenberg, received $44 million to make his state's highways and toll roads smart.

Of that, $25 million was to be spent equipping the state's toll roads with electronic sensing devices. Automobiles would speed by toll booths, and sensors would automatically charge the toll to the drivers' credit cards.

The remainder of funds were to be spent on advanced traffic monitoring equipment for roads across the state.

- New York, home of ranking Republican D'Amato, received $20 million to install automated traffic management devices on the Southern State Parkway.
- Michigan, home of House Transportation Appropriations member Carr, received $11.5 million for three pilot projects in Detroit and outlying Oakland County.
- In Minnesota, an ongoing project called Guidestar was given $10 million. It was won by House Transportation Appropriations Democrat Sabo.
- Miami received $5 million for a new traffic surveillance system called FLAMINGO. Miami was the home of House Transportation Appropriations Chairman Lehman.
- Maryland Democratic appropriator Barbara A. Mikulski brought home $2.5 million for highways and major arteries in her state.
- Houston, home of House Transportation Appropriations Republican DeLay, and Philadelphia, home of former Democratic panelist William H. Gray III, received $2 million each for projects that were not yet planned in 1991.

Urban areas such as Charlotte, N.C., Dallas and San Antonio, which were projected to have more-serious congestion problems by 2005 than most of the highways targeted by appropriators, received no specific funding.

Earmarking Attacked

The Bush administration opposed all special highway projects, but its statement on the appropriations bill singled out the high-tech highway projects for criticism. The Transportation Department "should be given the discretion to fund appropriate research and development of IVHS without special-interest earmarking," said the administration.

Lester P. Lamm, president of the Highway Users Federation and a member of IVHS America, an industry-university-government consortium, called it "presumptuous" for lawmakers to claim to know the best places to test the technology.

"It bothers the entire leadership of IVHS America. It's very difficult to predict right now what technology is going to come off the shelf in the next three to four years, let alone to predict what highway corridor is the best place for testing," he said.

Defending the earmarking process, New Jersey Department of Transportation Commissioner Thomas M. Downs said the industry should be thankful that it had an ally such as Lautenberg in Congress.

"He's pushing resources at the industry as fast as it can take it. I don't think there has been much of a recognition of his interest in IVHS from the industry," he said.

Another criticism leveled by those in the industry was that state highway officials would not use the federal money for groundbreaking technology, but steer it toward more conventional road projects such as electronic traffic signs and computerized traffic signals. ■

D.C. Bill Passed After Abortion Veto

Congress — with remarkable ease — approved a record $630.5 million federal payment in the fiscal 1992 appropriations bill for the District of Columbia, despite a presidential veto and a battle between the two chambers over a pet project.

The city's relationship with Congress improved notably in 1991 under the new administration of Mayor Sharon Pratt Kelly (inaugurated as Sharon Pratt Dixon, on Dec. 7 she married Washington businessman James R. Kelly III and changed her name). Her style was considered a vast improvement over former Mayor Marion S. Barry Jr., who began serving a six-month jail term on Oct. 26 on one misdemeanor count of cocaine possession. *(Congress and the District of Columbia, p. 190)*

Two versions of the spending bill went to President Bush in 1991. He vetoed the first one (HR 2699) over language that would have allowed the city to use locally raised revenue to fund abortions for poor women.

Congress removed the abortion language from the second bill (HR 3291), and the president signed it. Lacking the votes for an override, congressional leaders agreed to drop the offending abortion language without a fight in order to pass the measure before the Oct. 1 start of the District's fiscal year.

In 1989, abortion rights activists put up a bitter fight to retain the liberalized abortion language, prompting two presidential vetoes and delaying enactment of the bill until Nov. 20. *(1989 Almanac, p. 757)*

In 1991, House District of Columbia Appropriations Subcommittee Chairman Julian C. Dixon, D-Calif., agreed to strip the abortion language without a new series of markups or floor fights. While Dixon refused to wage another prolonged fight, he remained critical of Bush's position.

"The president is saying that the city of Washington cannot do what other jurisdictions are permitted to do as it relates to abortions," he said during the brief debate on the new bill.

The second bill, even devoid of abortion language, snagged on a pet issue — funding for George Washington University, the alma mater of Hawaii Democrat Daniel K. Inouye. The senator did not recede from his amendment until Sept. 26, when it finally cleared Congress.

As signed into law, HR 3291 provided the much-touted $630.5 million payment to the District government. The federal payment to the District government was to compensate the city for lost taxes and other costs of hosting the federal government. The measure totaled $4.6 billion because it also allowed the city to raise $3.9 billion in local revenue.

BOXSCORE

➡ **Fiscal 1992 appropriations for the District of Columbia. (HR 3291, HR 2699)** The $4.6 billion spending bill provided a $630.5 million federal payment to the District and allowed the city to raise $3.9 billion in local revenue. HR 2699 was vetoed by President Bush over abortion-related language.

Reports: HR 2699: H Rept 102-120; S Rept 102-105; conference report filed in the House, H Rept 102-181.

KEY ACTION

June 26 — HR 2699 passed the **House** by a vote of 300-123.

July 18 — HR 2699 passed the **Senate** by voice vote.

July 31 — HR 2699 approved by **House-Senate** conference.

Aug. 1 — **House** approved conference report by a 239-180 vote.

Aug 2 — **Senate** cleared conference report by voice vote.

Aug. 17 — President Bush vetoed HR 2699.

Sept. 16 — HR 3291 passed the **House** by voice vote; HR 3291 passed the **Senate** by voice vote.

Oct. 1 — HR 3291 signed by Bush — PL 102-111.

In fiscal 1991, the city received a $430.5 million federal payment as part of an overall $4.4 billion spending bill. An additional $100 million was added in the supplemental appropriations bill (HR 1281 — PL 102-27) cleared by the Senate on March 22. *(1990 Almanac, p. 891; 1991 supplemental spending bill, p. 668)*

HOUSE COMMITTEE ACTION

The House District of Columbia Appropriations Subcommittee voted June 13 to increase the federal payment to the capital city for the first time in five years. By voice vote, the subcommittee approved $695.8 million in federal funds for fiscal 1992, including a $630.5 million federal payment for the city government.

The main subject of controversy during consideration of the District of Columbia bill was not how much money to allocate for the city but whether any of it could be spent to pay for abortions.

Subcommittee Chairman Dixon won unanimous approval for adoption of the strictest language on banning the use of federal funds for abortion, while leaving the bill silent on the use of the District's locally raised revenue. Since 1989, the House had approved in the District's appropriations bill the use of federal funds for abortion in cases of rape, incest or when the woman's life was in danger. But Bush had vetoed all bills that permitted abortion funding except to save the woman's life.

For the first time, Dixon took Bush's position on federal spending but challenged him on the issue of home rule by not blocking the use of local funds for abortion. Dixon said that he would challenge Bush once on this issue but would not subject the bill to a lengthy delay over abortion language.

Full Committee

The House Appropriations Committee on June 20 approved, by voice vote, $699.8 million in federal funds for the District of Columbia for fiscal 1992 without any debate or amendments.

"May we always have such uneventful 30-second appropriations markups," said Del. Eleanor Holmes Norton, D-D.C., who was not a member of the committee but who followed the funding bill closely.

While subcommittee Chairman Dixon expected a floor fight over the bill's abortion language, he did not expect it to short-circuit additional funding for the District.

As approved by the committee, HR 2699 included the $630.5 million federal payment. The appropriations bill

Continued on p. 618

District of Columbia

(In thousands of dollars)

	Fiscal 1991 Appropriation	President's Request	House Bill	Senate Bill	Final Bill
Appropriations to D.C.					
Federal payment	$430,500	$ 484,000	$ 630,500	$ 630,500	$ 630,500
Contributions to retirement fund	52,070	52,070	52,070	52,070	52,070
Other	67,130	0	13,227	13,754	13,280
Subtotal	**$549,700**	**$ 536,070**	**$ 695,797**	**$ 696,324**	**$ 695,850**
Other Appropriations					
D.C. Institute for Mental Health		0	1,000	426	1,000
Children's National Medical Center		0	3,000	3,000	3,000
GWU Medical Center	0	0	0	250	0
Total, New Budget Authority	**$549,700**	**$ 536,070**	**$ 699,797**	**$ 700,000**	**$ 699,850**
District-raised funds	$3,862,574	$ 3,879,867	$ 3,894,194	$ 3,894,021	$ 3,895,772
Total D.C. budget	**$4,412,274**	**$ 4,415,937**	**$ 4,593,991**	**$ 4,594,021**	**$ 4,595,622**

SOURCE: House Appropriations Committee

District of Columbia Provisions

The District of Columbia appropriations bill (HR 3291 — PL 102-111) was a relic of the days when Congress directly ran the city where the nation's lawmakers gathered. Home rule came in 1973, but the District faced unusual expenses by continuing to host the federal government and by needing to provide the services of both a city and a state. The bulk of the $630.5 million in fiscal 1992 federal funds for the District was given without strings attached, but some money was earmarked for specific departments for designated purposes.

The process of providing federal funds for the capital city followed a pattern similar to the one for federal agencies. The mayor prepared a budget and submitted it to the Office of Management and Budget (OMB), which submitted it to Congress along with the rest of the president's request for government spending. At the time the president's request went to Congress, the District's proposed budget also went to the City Council.

The budget agency usually submitted the request as prepared by the mayor. Since 1988, however, OMB had added language to the D.C. budget request requiring that no locally raised funds be used to pay for abortion except to save the woman's life. (1988 Almanac, p. 713)

FEDERAL PAYMENT

Appropriators provided a federal payment of $630.5 million to the District of Columbia for fiscal 1992, up from $430.5 million in fiscal 1991. The funds were given to the city government to compensate for costs associated with hosting the federal government, mainly as payment in lieu of taxes for the use of District land.

The 1973 Home Rule Bill fixed the federal payment at a minimum of $425 million for 1985 and beyond. But as a percentage of the city's budget, the federal payment had varied widely.

In 1990, the federal payment made up 13.9 percent of the city's total budget. The $630.5 million for fiscal 1992 equaled 19.1 percent of the city's budget, a record.

The 1991 law authorizing that it be set at 24 percent of local tax revenue would take effect in fiscal 1993.

The increase for fiscal 1992 was important because of the city's financial woes: It had an estimated deficit of $332 million in fiscal 1991. In August, Congress cleared a separate bill (HR 2969 — PL 102-106) allowing the District to sell 12-year bonds to refinance its deficit. It also allowed the mayor to cut the budgets of 17 independent city agencies and lay off more than 2,000 city employees over 18 months.

On Oct. 1, the mayor began the process of cutting the work force.

The federal payment went into the general fund of the District government, to be used in the same way as any other revenue that was controlled by the mayor and the City Council.

In addition to the federal payment, the appropriations measure also provideed funds for the following specific programs:

Retirement Funds

For the federal contribution to the city's police officers', firefighters', teachers' and judges' retirement funds, appropriators provided $52.1 million. The federal government agreed in 1979 to provide $52 million annually for 25 years to cover unfunded pension liability from the days before home rule, when these employees worked for the federal government.

Metropolitan Police Department

The measure provided $75,000 to the city's police department, of which $25,000 was earmarked for an accreditation study and $50,000 was for programs boosting community policing programs. The two-year accrediting routine included a self-examination by the police department to see if it met certain nationwide criteria for large-city police operations. An accrediting team then would visit the department to evaluate it.

The total city budget for the police department was $253.5 million.

Board of Education

The measure appropriated $3.2 million to the Board of Education, of which $2.1 million was to be used to renovate public school athletic and recreational grounds and facilities under a priority list set by the Board of Education. The total education budget was $519.3 million.

The remaining funds were to be spent as follows:

- $330,000 for the Options Program, an intensive drop-out-prevention program for youths 12 to 15 years of age who were at least two years behind their appropriate grade level.
- $250,000 for the Parents as Teachers Program, which encouraged parental involvement as an important part of a child's education.
- $500,000 for maintenance, improvements and repairs to public school facilities under the Direct Activity Purchase System (DAPS). The bill also provided that the $500,000 included for DAPS was to be returned to the U.S. Treasury on Oct. 1, 1992, if the amount spent by the city out of its own funds under DAPS for maintenance, improvements and repairs to public school facilities in fiscal 1992 was less than the amount spent by the District out of its own funds for such purposes in fiscal 1991.
- Although the measure provided $3.2 million for the Board of Education for fiscal 1992, $1.5 million was not allowed to be spent until fiscal 1993.

D.C. General Hospital

The measure provided $9.5 million for D.C. General Hospital, of which $8.5 million was not to be spent until fiscal 1993.

The funds were to be used to upgrade existing facilities at the public hospital.

The conferees also required hospital officials to direct some of the funds to high-priority areas such as physical examinations and immunizations for 10,000 preschool and school-age children and the establishment of outpatient HIV service for infants and children.

Department of Human Services

Appropriators provided $500,000 to the city's Department of Human Services for the breast and cervical cancer screening program for women in the District who had no insurance and did not qualify for Medicare. The funds would allow the District to continue to contract for a second year with the D.C. Cancer Consortium, which provided the breast and cervical cancer screening.

D.C. Institute for Mental Health

The measure provided $1 million in federal funds to the D.C. Institute for Mental Health (St. Elizabeths Hospital) to provide mental health care to low-income, underinsured and indigent children, adults and families in the District. In October 1987, St. Elizabeths was transferred from federal to local control. At the time of the transfer, the U.S. government pledged to provide some funding for the institution through fiscal 1991. It received $10 million in fiscal 1991. Appropriators decided to continue the subsidy in fiscal 1992 at a reduced level.

Children's National Medical Center

Appropriators provided $3 million in federal funds to the Children's National Medical Center for a cost-shared National Child Protection, Trauma and Research Center.

D.C. Funds - Division of Expenses

Appropriators also approved allowing the city to raise $3.9 billion of its own funds through taxes and the city lottery. The measure also directed the D.C. government on how to spend some of these locally raised funds, although, in most cases, the allocation of the funds had already been approved by the mayor and the City Council.

For example, the measure directed the D.C. government to use $100,000 of the general fund to reimburse Fairfax County and Prince William County, Va., for expenses incurred by the counties in relation to the city's Lorton prison complex. The measure also required the District government to maintain a free, 24-hour telephone information service so that residents of the area surrounding the Lorton prison complex could obtain information on all disturbances at the prison, including escapes, fires, riots and similar incidents. It also allocated $41.1 million to be used to help eliminate the general fund deficit of $332 million. ■

Continued from p. 616

also approved $3.9 billion to come from the District of Columbia's own locally raised revenue.

The bill was identical to the measure approved June 13 by the Appropriations subcommittee, which had restored to the initial request of $695.8 million: $1 million for the District of Columbia Institute for Mental Health and $3 million for the Children's National Medical Center.

The measure banned the use of federal funds for abortions except to save the woman's life but placed no restrictions on the use of the District's locally raised revenue.

Norton said the fiscal 1992 spending bill was consistent with Bush's support for giving state and local jurisdictions more responsibility in deciding how funds should be spent.

"The president has jurisdiction over federal dollars," Norton said. "We haven't asked to use federal dollars, we have only asked to use our money for abortion."

HOUSE FLOOR ACTION

The House on June 26 passed, 300-123, a record $699.8 million fiscal 1992 spending bill for the District of Columbia, providing the city with much-sought-after additional funds but also setting up a confrontation with Bush over controversial abortion language. *(Vote 198, p. 48-H)*

As passed, HR 2699 banned the use of federal funds for abortions except to save a woman's life but challenged Bush's position on abortion funding by placing no restrictions on the use of the District's locally raised revenue.

Rather than fighting the language, House abortion opponents said they would rely on Bush to make good on his threat to veto any bill that loosened existing abortion funding restrictions.

Fights over abortion language in the District's appropriations measure had become routine as Congress also wrangled over how much to allocate to the city.

HR 2699 included the $630.5 million federal payment to the District government and an additional $69.3 million for District services, including $52.1 million for civil servant retirement funds and $12 million for the D.C. General Hospital.

The measure also approved the spending of $3.9 billion in locally raised revenues.

Before passing the measure, the House approved an amendment by James A. Traficant Jr., D-Ohio, mandating that all D.C. government purchases be in accordance with the 1933 Buy American Act, which stipulated that U.S. government agencies should favor domestic purchases.

The House rejected two amendments offered by Dana Rohrabacher, R-Calif., who said Congress needed to act to reduce the federal deficit. The first, rejected 153-270, would have reduced the federal payment to the District to $611 million. *(Vote 197, p. 48-H)*

A second amendment, to cut $13.2 million in federal funds to the District, including $12 million for the D.C. General Hospital, was rejected by voice vote.

SENATE COMMITTEE ACTION

The Senate Appropriations Committee approved HR 2699, by a 24-0 vote and without amendments, on July 11. As approved by the committee, the bill provided the District of Columbia and local facilities with a record $700 million in federal funds.

The Senate District of Columbia Appropriations Subcommittee had approved the bill by voice vote on July 10.

Like the House measure, the Senate bill barred the use of federal funds for abortions but allowed the city to use locally raised revenue for the procedure.

While abortion opponents decried the language, they made no effort to strip it from the bill. They said they would leave it to Bush to veto any legislation that loosened existing abortion funding restrictions.

"I don't know if we'd have the votes to override a veto," said Brock Adams, D-Wash., chairman of the Appropriations subcommittee.

The Senate measure also included a $630.5 million federal payment to the city government.

"This is not a bailout of the local government; this is not a gift," said Adams. "What it is is recognition that fully two-thirds of the local economy is beyond taxation."

Slade Gorton, R-Wash., blasted the $100 million increase in the federal payment over fiscal 1991. "If there's another item that's received such a large increase over last year, I don't know of it." Even so, Gorton voted for the measure in subcommittee.

The Senate version differed slightly from the House-passed measure. Adams' panel included $799,000 for a fire station near the Capitol that the city had recommended closing. It also gave approval to District plans to sell $332 million in municipal bonds.

Inouye's Request for GWU

In addition, the Senate bill provided $250,000 for the renovation of George Washington University Hospital. The line item was included at the request of Inouye, who was the No. 2 Democrat on the Appropriations panel.

Inouye had recently resigned from the George Washington University Board of Trustees.

The Senate panel scrapped two amendments approved during House floor debate. One amendment would have mandated that District government purchases favor products made in the United States. The second would have barred the use of local or federal funds to renovate the Eastern Market shopping area in the city. District officials

Text of Veto of D.C. Bill

Following is the text of President Bush's Aug. 17 veto message of HR 2699, the fiscal 1992 appropriations bill for the District of Columbia, which he objected to because of abortion language.

I am withholding my approval of HR 2699, a bill providing appropriations for fiscal year 1992 for the District of Columbia.

While I do not object to the underlying legislation and the funding the bill would provide, language concerning the use of funds provided by the bill for abortion is unacceptable. I have stated my intention to veto any bill that does not contain language that prohibits the use of all congressionally appropriated funds to pay for abortions other than those in which the life of the mother would be endangered if the fetus were carried to term. The limitation I propose is identical to the one included in the District of Columbia Appropriations Act of FY 1989, FY 1990 and FY 1991.

HR 2699 would place such a limitation on the use of federal funds to pay for abortion, but would permit congressionally appropriated local funds to be used for abortions on demand with no restriction whatsoever. As a matter of law, the use of local funds in the District of Columbia must be approved by the Congress and the president through enactment of an appropriation act. Under these circumstances, the failure of HR 2699 to prohibit the use of all funds appropriated by the bill to pay for abortion, except in the limited circumstances mentioned above, is unacceptable.

From the outset of my administration, I have repeatedly stated my deep personal concern about the tragedy in America of abortion on demand. As a nation, we must protect the unborn. HR 2699 does not provide such protection. I am, therefore, withholding my approval of HR 2699.

The adjournment of the Congress has prevented my return of HR 2699 within the meaning of Article I, Section 7, Clause 2 of the Constitution. Accordingly, my withholding of approval from the bill precludes its becoming law. (The *Pocket Veto Case*, 279 U.S. 655, 1929) Because of the questions raised in options issued by the U.S. Court of Appeals for the District of Columbia Circuit, I am sending HR 2699 with my objections to the clerk of the House of Representatives.

GEORGE BUSH

The White House
Aug. 17, 1991

had complained the amendment amounted to undue congressional meddling in District affairs.

SENATE FLOOR ACTION

Without a word of dissent and with nothing but praise for Mayor Dixon, the Senate on July 18 gave voice-vote approval to HR 2699.

The measure included the much-sought $630.5 million federal payment to the city to compensate for costs associated with hosting the federal government, a $100 million increase over what the city received in fiscal 1991.

Calling it a home-rule issue, both the House and Senate versions of the bill banned the use of federal funds for abortions but reversed existing law and allowed the city to use locally raised revenue for the procedure.

Little mention had been made of the abortion language in either chamber during committee or floor debate, with both sides of the abortion issue holding their fire in anticipation of a probable veto.

CONFERENCE ACTION

The conference report on HR 2699 was approved, 239-180, by the House on Aug. 1, and the Senate cleared it by voice vote a day later. *(Vote 251, p. 62-H)*

The House and Senate conference on the $700 million bill had approved its report July 31.

White House opposition to the fiscal 1992 spending bill for the District was clear-cut because conferees had agreed to let language remain that barred the use of federal funds for abortions in the District but allowed the city to use locally raised revenue for the procedure.

Although conferees agreed on the most substantial parts of the bill, two provisions provoked amiable debate.

The Senate bill provided $250,000 in fiscal 1992 to George Washington University Hospital for renovations and made a commitment to provide $50 million to the hospital over four years. Inouye, who had included the language, was not a conferee. House conferees did not want the provision, and the Senate finally caved on the request when it went back to the floor for a vote.

The Senate conferees also fought for $799,000 for a fire station near the Capitol that the city had recommended closing. Conferees agreed to keep the station open but did not commit any funds to it.

FINAL ACTION

As expected, Bush vetoed HR 2699 on Aug. 17. In his veto message, he said, "While I do not object to the underlying legislation and the funding the bill would provide, language concerning the use of funds provided by the bill for abortion is unacceptable." *(Veto message, p. 619)*

After the president's veto, the House passed a new District spending bill (HR 3291) by voice vote Sept. 16. But the measure hit a snag in the Senate that afternoon, when Inouye tacked on his amendment to provide $50 million over four years for the George Washington University Hospital.

To drive home the depth of House opposition to the amendment, Dixon called for a recorded vote on his motion to disagree with the Senate amendment. Dixon's motion passed 405-0 on Sept. 17. *(Vote 268, p. 64-H)*

The Senate finally cleared the second version of the D.C. spending bill, HR 3291, Sept. 26. The $4.6 billion bill, which provided a $630.5 million record payment to the District government, was stalled because of Senate amendments that would have provided $50 million over four years for renovations at the George Washington University Medical Center.

The Senate finally receded from the amendments and cleared the bill by voice vote. The amendments had been added by Inouye because he wanted to give the medical center $250,000 in fiscal 1992 to begin the renovations. He proposed taking the $250,000 from federal funds provided for the District of Columbia General Hospital.

The House, however, had objected to giving such funds to a private hospital at a time when the District government faced pressing financial needs. ■

SDI, Stealth Bomber Cut Back

The Senate on Nov. 23 sent to President Bush the $270 billion fiscal 1992 defense appropriations bill, approving the conference report on the measure by a vote of 66-29. As usual, the measure (HR 2521) funded without significant change the bulk of Bush's Pentagon budget request. Also typically, its most significant departures from Bush's defense program echoed changes already incorporated in the companion defense authorization bill, cleared for the president Nov. 22. *(Vote 272, p. 35-S; Defense authorization, p. 393)*

BOXSCORE

➡ **Fiscal 1992 appropriations for the Defense Department (HR 2521).** The $270 billion spending bill provided funds for the Pentagon.

Reports: HR 2521: H Rept 102-95; S Rept 102-154; conference report filed in the House, H Rept 102-328.

KEY ACTION

June 7 — HR 2521 passed the **House** by a vote of 273-105.

Sept. 26 — HR 2521 passed the **Senate** by voice vote.

Nov. 15 — HR 2521 approved by **House-Senate** conference.

Nov. 20 — **House** approved conference report by voice vote.

Nov. 23 — **Senate** cleared conference report by a vote of 66-29.

Nov. 26 — HR 2521 signed by President Bush — PL 102-172.

Despite that kinship, the extraordinarily strong opposition to the appropriations conference report was spearheaded by some of the leading architects of the authorization bill: Armed Services Committee Chairman Sam Nunn, D-Ga., and 13 other members of the 20-member committee.

Nunn protested that the appropriations bill circumvented the role of the House and Senate authorizing committees by providing a total of nearly $5 billion more than was authorized for about 170 projects, even though the authorization process generally was understood to set caps on spending.

"If the Appropriations Committee can come in under the authorized level," Nunn said, "and they can also exceed the authorized level, then clearly there is no point in having an authorization."

Defense Appropriations Subcommittee Chairman Daniel K. Inouye, D-Hawaii, and Ted Stevens of Alaska, the panel's ranking Republican, countered that the unauthorized increases, accounting for a small fraction of the bill, were the inevitable result of having to hammer out a compromise.

"In trying to work out an agreement with House members ... we had to make significant concessions on small items," Stevens said. "They are very small items." The House had approved the conference report by voice vote on Nov. 20.

Nunn and his allies also objected that the appropriations bill earmarked $95 million in Pentagon research funds for 16 colleges and universities, explicitly waiving laws that required that such funds be awarded only on a competitive basis. Earmarks had been a bone of contention for years, with Nunn and others objecting that they circumvented the process of "peer review," by which committees of noted researchers allocated funds among competing schools.

But critics dismissed that process as the product of an "old boys' network" of established scholars who channeled research funds to each other's schools, freezing out "have-not" institutions.

Major Weapons

Combined with funds appropriated separately for military construction and for defense-related nuclear programs conducted by the Energy Department, the defense spending bill brought the total defense budget for fiscal 1992 to $290.5 billion, slightly less than Bush requested. The fiscal 1991 defense spending measure provided $269 billion for the Pentagon and a total defense budget of $288.3 billion. *(1990 Almanac, p. 812)*

Like the defense authorization bill (HR 2100), the appropriations measure trimmed Bush's request for major strategic weapons, providing:

- $1.8 billion to keep alive the production line for the B-2 stealth bomber but requiring subsequent congressional approval for work on planes in addition to the 15 previously authorized.
- $4.15 billion, instead of the $5.15 billion requested, to develop anti-missile defenses under the Strategic Defense Initiative (SDI).

Many of the appropriations bill's significant add-ons to Bush's request mirrored those previously authorized, including:

- $315 million to modernize the Army's fleet of M-1 tanks.
- $625 million to continue development of the V-22 Osprey, a hybrid airplane/helicopter designed as a troop-carrier for the Marine Corps.

Of the $5 billion in unauthorized funding for procurement and research programs, more than 40 percent was concentrated in a handful of major projects, including fast cargo ships ($600 million), F-15 fighters ($335 million) and air-cushion landing barges ($238 million).

About half of the 170 programs increased were boosted by $10 million or less.

'Floors' and Ceilings

In a previous round of their chronic turf fight, leaders of the Senate Armed Services and Appropriations committees signed a formal agreement delineating their respective roles.

Among other provisions, it stipulated that Armed Services would not write into its bill "floors," minimum funding levels that had to be appropriated. But it also provided that Appropriations would not appropriate more than the ceiling that was authorized, unless the added funds were made subject to subsequent authorization.

As Inouye and his allies pointed out, however, the agreement did not bind members of the House. It also was unclear whether it applied only to funding levels for large budget accounts or for the specific projects within each account.

However, even considering only the totals for each account, Nunn said, the appropriations bill exceeded authorized limits by more than $3.3 billion.

HOUSE FLOOR ACTION

On two prominent defense issues — the B-2 and SDI — the $270.6 billion defense appropriations bill passed by the House on June 7 mirrored the companion authorization bill

Defense

(In thousands of dollars)

	Fiscal 1991 Appropriation	President's Request	House Bill	Senate Bill	Final Bill
Personnel					
Army	$ 23,927,226	$ 24,226,100	$ 24,526,100	$ 24,136,000	$ 24,176,100
Navy	19,111,067	19,597,700	19,577,700	19,603,025	19,602,967
Marines	5,911,602	6,066,800	6,086,800	6,055,360	6,065,560
Air Force	19,786,172	18,905,500	18,905,500	18,838,800	18,868,300
National Guard and reserves	9,509,400	9,220,800	9,657,000	9,532,800	9,553,400
Subtotal	**$ 78,245,467**	**$ 78,016,900**	**$ 78,753,100**	**$ 78,165,985**	**$ 78,266,327**
Operations and maintenance					
Army	21,571,694	21,886,800	18,362,945	20,913,805	17,722,903
Navy	23,308,647	23,934,200	21,394,932	23,012,390	21,079,548
Marines	1,892,200	1,894,600	2,082,500	2,109,665	1,892,110
Air Force	20,092,735	20,342,900	17,660,213	19,242,014	17,180,259
Defense agencies	8,498,957	8,794,800	18,599,037	8,635,768	16,408,161
National Guard and reserves	7,285,400	7,273,100	7,439,500	7,363,600	7,361,200
Environmental restoration	1,062,527	1,252,900	2,152,900	1,183,900	1,183,900
Other	25,400	23,500	28,500	1,026,500	530,500
Subtotal	**$ 83,737,560**	**$ 85,402,800**	**$ 87,720,527**	**$ 83,487,642**	**$ 83,358,581**
Procurement					
Army	9,307,231	7,956,200	8,311,489	7,991,971	8,243,237
Navy	29,423,587	27,512,100	29,580,700	25,669,694	27,096,991
Marines	719,141	1,039,400	1,043,218	1,100,570	1,079,951
Air Force	22,858,343	24,773,400	20,689,486	23,541,363	23,715,904
National Guard and reserves	2,463,700	—	1,292,500	667,300	1,877,800
Defense agencies	2,354,646	2,089,600	2,708,446	2,087,400	2,250,826
Defense Production Act	50,000	—	25,000	—	—
Sealift and prepositioning	—	—	995,000	2,000,000	—
Subtotal	**$ 67,176,648**	**$ 63,370,700**	**$ 64,645,839**	**$ 63,058,298**	**$ 64,264,709**
Research, development and testing					
Army	5,607,379	6,307,300	6,241,621	6,280,361	6,562,672
Navy	9,037,684	7,342,633	7,464,910	7,666,142	8,557,635
Air Force	11,961,310	15,032,600	14,263,941	14,123,675	14,077,834
Other	9,368,419	10,539,000	9,214,641	9,623,506	10,203,782
Subtotal	**$ 35,974,792**	**$ 39,221,533**	**$ 37,185,113**	**$ 37,693,684**	**$ 39,401,923**
Intelligence programs					
CIA retirement and disability	164,600	164,100	164,100	164,100	164,100
Intelligence community staff	28,900	30,719	30,719	28,819	28,819
Subtotal	**$ 193,500**	**$ 194,819**	**$ 194,819**	**$ 192,919**	**$ 192,919**
Other programs					
Revolving and management funds	1,984,200	3,400,200	2,444,100	3,400,200	3,424,200
Chemical agents destruction	292,700	474,800	451,800	474,800	374,398
Drug interdiction	1,084,100	1,158,600	1,155,994	1,117,075	1,188,600
Inspector general	99,500	116,200	121,900	116,200	116,200
Rescissions, reductions, miscellaneous adjustments	**−400,391**	**−420,230**	**−2,107,400**	**−2,550,944**	**−676,617**
Operations Desert Shield/Desert Storm	**$ 15,000,000**	—	—	—	—
GRAND TOTAL	**$ 283,388,076**	**$ 270,936,322**	**$ 270,565,792**	**$ 270,257,747**	**$ 269,911,240**

SOURCE: House and Senate Appropriations committees

passed two weeks earlier. The House Appropriations Committee had reported out HR 2521 on June 4.

Despite threats of a veto, the bill appropriated none of the $3.2 billion Bush had requested to continue production of the B-2 stealth bomber, and it slashed $1.6 billion from Bush's funding request for the anti-missile Strategic Defense Initiative.

Both bills approved $1.56 billion to continue B-2 development, $2.66 billion for SDI and an additional $787 million for a separate program to develop defenses against short-range (or "tactical") missiles.

But the appropriations measure also challenged the administration's defense program on two other key fronts:

- It froze the size of the National Guard and reserve components, rejecting out of hand Bush's proposal to slice their number by nearly 108,000 in fiscal 1992. That personnel action plus the addition of unbudgeted equipment for Guard and reserve units added nearly $2 billion to the budget request.
- And the bill also provided almost $4 billion, not requested in the budget, for ships and aircraft intended to speed the deployment of U.S.-based forces to distant trouble spots.

The House-passed version of the defense authorization bill allowed about one-third of Defense Secretary Dick Cheney's proposed cut in Guard and reserve personnel. But House Defense Appropriations Subcommittee Chairman John P. Murtha, D-Pa., took a hard line against any cutback in 1991 in the politically well-connected reserve components.

For one thing, Murtha insisted that the Pentagon should first draw up a detailed plan of what active-duty and reserve units it wanted to retain at the end of the long-term budget cutback that was in progress.

The House passed the defense bill 273-105 after deleting on procedural grounds a provision that would have allowed women in the service or military dependents stationed abroad to undergo abortions at U.S. military hospitals overseas at their own expense. *(Vote 145, p. 36-H)*

The House had approved the same provision as an amendment to the defense authorization bill May 22.

The House rejected, 155-229, an amendment by Barney Frank, D-Mass., that would have deleted $260 million earmarked to complete development of a rail-mobile version of the MX intercontinental ballistic missile. *(Vote 144, p. 36-H)*

It adopted by voice vote two amendments by James A. Traficant Jr., D-Ohio, which:

- Barred Pentagon purchases from any country that the secretary of Defense found to be in violation of a reciprocal trade agreement with the United States.
- Limited to $1 billion the amount the Defense Department could spend on consultants, a reduction of about $150 million, according to Traficant.

In addition to cutting Bush's requests for the B-2 and SDI, the bill cut the Navy's budget request by $851 million, approving four of a requested five destroyers.

And it trimmed more than $1 billion from various accounts that were perennial targets for congressional budgeteers. For instance, a $195 million cut was intended to reduce employee travel, a $315 million reduction was intended to pare the size of headquarters, and the payroll for foreigners employed at overseas bases was cut by $202 million.

On the other side of the ledger, the actions related to reserve forces and transportation equipment accounted for the preponderance of unbudgeted congressional initiatives funded by the bill.

But it also included nearly $1.3 billion for three weapons programs the administration wanted to cancel: the Army's M-1 tank, the Navy's F-14 fighter jet and the Osprey — a hybrid airplane/helicopter wanted by the Marine Corps as a troop transport.

Following are key provisions of HR 2521 as passed by the House:

Guard and Reserves

The Appropriations Committee buttressed its case against deep cuts in Guard and reserve manpower by citing in its report praise for their contribution to the Persian Gulf victory by Bush and Gen. Colin L. Powell Jr., chairman of the Joint Chiefs of Staff.

"Many believe using the reserve components early in the conflict was one of the main ingredients for the overwhelming support the war in the Persian Gulf received," the panel said.

Most observers agreed that reserve units assigned to critical supply jobs and air combat missions performed up to snuff in the gulf war. What the skeptics questioned, for the most part, was the policy of assigning reserve units to front-line, ground-combat missions with only a few weeks of post-mobilization refresher training.

Three Army divisions were deployed to the gulf without National Guard brigades that supposedly were attached to them. The three Guard units, meanwhile, were sent to prolonged training programs during which the commander and some other officers in a Georgia brigade were replaced.

Guard and reserve advocates complained that the three brigades were sandbagged by active-duty officers intent on discrediting reserve units. But Powell and Cheney insisted that the travails of the three Guard brigades reflected the impossibility of part-time infantrymen keeping pace with full-timers in the physically wearing ground-combat role.

The bill included $645 million to add 1,065 members to the Guard and reserves rather than cutting membership by 107,526, as Cheney proposed.

The bill also included a provision barring the Pentagon from disbanding any Guard or reserve unit. The Appropriations Committee said it intended to freeze the existing organizational structure until the Pentagon spelled out in detail which active duty and reserve units were to be disbanded as part of the long-term cutback.

Eventually, reserve manpower was to be cut and some reserve units disbanded, the panel conceded. But it served notice that any such cutbacks would have to pass muster politically "to insure that one area of the country is not taking an inordinate amount of the cutbacks."

The Pentagon's budget request earmarked equipment for Guard and reserve units worth $1.45 billion. But the Appropriations Committee complained that no major weapons were included in that tally. So it added to the bill $1.29 billion worth of Guard and reserve equipment, including $374 million for 14 C-130 transport planes and $205 million for improvements in Guard and reserve fighter planes.

Other Personnel

The bill added $300 million to the Army's budget request for military personnel. With that increase, the committee said, the Army could forgo plans to give some personnel involuntary discharges.

The panel also warned the services to be more frugal in

assigning some of their expensively trained specialists, complaining that the Air Force had 1,000 pilots in jobs that did not involve flying.

The bill included a provision that ruled out the assignment of military physicians to command medical facilities unless they were trained administrators.

Several other provisions also dealt with medical care issues, including:

- A ban on personnel cuts at any medical facility.
- An additional $44 million above the amount requested to continue medical care at Letterman Army Hospital in San Francisco, located on a base that was scheduled to be closed.
- An additional $10 million above the amount requested to expand a bonus program aimed at recruiting nurses with training in key specialties, such as anesthesiology.

The bill included a provision that would phase out by 1997 the Pentagon's medical school in Bethesda, Md. House Appropriations had tried unsuccessfully to close the school in 1990, complaining that its costs per student were four and a half times as high as private medical schools.

The Bethesda school was established in the early 1970s under the sponsorship of Rep. F. Edward Hebert, D-La. (1941-77), who was then chairman of the House Armed Services Committee. In its report on the fiscal 1992 bill, House Appropriations members told the Pentagon to name its several medical school scholarship programs after Hebert.

Transport

The $1.3 billion for new cargo ships that House Appropriations added to the bill nearly doubled the amount that was already awaiting a Pentagon decision on how to expand the sealift fleet: $1.28 billion appropriated for that purpose in fiscal 1991 had not yet been spent.

The bill left it to the Pentagon to decide how much of those funds should be spent on high-speed ships based in the United States and how much on ships that would be stocked with tanks and other combat gear and "pre-positioned" around the world near potential trouble spots.

But in its report, the Appropriations Committee demanded that the Pentagon make the decision quickly and start buying ships, telling the department that it anticipated a detailed spending plan within a month.

The bill also included $995 million not requested by the Pentagon, which was earmarked to replace some of the older equipment stocked in the 13 pre-positioning ships that had been deployed since the mid-1980s. For example, the Appropriations panel said, the 1970s-vintage M-60 tanks that were landed in Saudi Arabia from those ships during the gulf crisis could not shoot as far as the Soviet-built T-72 tanks driven by some Iraqi units.

One rough spot in the mobilization for war with Iraq was the so-called Ready Reserve Fleet of mothballed freighters, many of which took longer to put in service than was planned. To pay for more frequent training exercises to reveal shortcomings in those ships, the bill added $30 million to the budget request.

In the transportation category, the remainder of the bill's major additions to the budget request were to beef up the amphibious landing fleet, which was designed to let Marine Corps units fight their way ashore in the face of hostile fire. The corps had many friends on Capitol Hill, none more staunch than Murtha, who had commanded a Marine unit in combat in Vietnam.

These additions to the budget request included:

- $972 million for a ship the size of a World War II aircraft carrier, designated an LHD, which could carry nearly 2,000 Marines and 20 to 30 helicopters to haul them ashore. The bill also included the $245 million requested for a smaller amphibious ship, designated an LSD.
- $541 million for 24 big hovercraft, designed to haul tanks ashore at 50 mph. Added to the dozen such craft requested in the budget, this brought the total appropriation for these so-called LCACs to $807 million for 36 vessels.
- $625 million to begin building Osprey troop carriers. Since 1989, Cheney had tried on grounds of budgetary limits to kill this aircraft, built to take off like a helicopter and fly like a conventional airplane. The bill added to this amount $365 million previously appropriated for the Osprey program, which Cheney had declined to spend.
- $455 million for 20 CH-53 troop-carrying helicopters, in addition to the $137 million requested for 12 of these big aircraft. Saying this would fill the Marine Corps' needs, the committee dropped from the bill $54 million requested for components that were to be used to build CH-53Es in future years.

Of these four add-ons, only the one for the Osprey was included in the House-passed authorization bill.

The appropriations bill also included with minor changes the amounts requested for several kinds of cargo aircraft, including $1.98 billion for six C-17, long-range, wide-body planes, $245 million for eight shorter-range C-130 Hercules transports and $334 million for 60 Blackhawk helicopters, used by the Army to haul infantry squads.

Ground Combat

Like the companion authorization bill, HR 2521 rejected the Pentagon's plan to suspend tank production, pending development of a new tank designated "block III," which the Army hoped to put into production late in the 1990s.

The appropriations bill added to the budget request $90 million to buy 60 additional copies of the so-called M-1A2 tank, and it added $266 million to set up a production line that could convert existing M-1s to the new model.

The bill also included only $323 million of the $401 million requested for a project intended to develop the block III tank and several other types of new armored vehicles. Echoing the stance taken by other congressional committees that were dealing with the defense budget, House Appropriations was skeptical of the Army's plan to equip the new block III tank with a gun firing a shell 140mm in diameter, rather than the 120mm gun equipping late-model M-1s.

In its report, the committee warned that tanks that needed such unwieldy ammunition would complicate the Army's supply system. And it touted new weapons technologies that could give the new tank as much punch as the cannon but in a smaller package. To accelerate work on one of those new approaches — a high-powered gun fired by electric current — the committee included in the bill $22 million more than the $92 million requested by the Pentagon.

The bill also denied the $43 million requested by the Army to choose off the shelf a lightly armored vehicle with a 105mm cannon. If it really needed such a weapon, the Appropriations Committee said, the Army should buy a version of the LAV armored car used by the Marine Corps.

The bill also included $58 million not requested to buy 16,000 MLRS artillery rockets. The Pentagon had planned

Continued on p. 631

Defense Provisions

The $270 billion Defense appropriations bill included 95 percent of the total amount provided for defense-related activities in fiscal 1992. An additional $8.56 billion was provided by the companion Military Construction bill to build military facilities and to build and maintain military family housing units. Most of the rest of the defense budget was made up of the $11.97 billion included in the Energy and Water Development appropriations bill for Energy Department programs to develop and manufacture nuclear weapons and nuclear power plants for warships.

More than 60 percent of the funds provided by the Defense bill went to cover recurring costs of day-to-day Defense Department operations, including the military payroll, operations and maintenance. Less than 40 percent was for capital investment in the form of procurement of weapons and major equipment (24 percent) and research and development (15 percent).

Although the bill appropriated slightly more than $271 billion for defense programs in fiscal 1992, budget experts scored it as costing only $269.9 billion in new budget authority. The balance of $1.1 billion was covered by funds from previous Defense appropriations which this bill rescinded (canceled).

MILITARY PERSONNEL

In all, 40 percent of the $290 billion defense budget was for compensation of military personnel and civilian Pentagon employees. That included a 4.2 percent annual pay raise recommended by President Bush.

The Pentagon employed more than 900,000 civilians, and most of their $35 billion in pay and benefits was scattered throughout the defense bill, with a small portion covered by the companion military construction bill. All compensation for uniformed personnel was included in the defense bill's $78 billion military personnel title, including nearly $3 billion for the travel expenses of personnel transferred between posts.

• **Active-duty personnel.** For 1.89 million active-duty service members, it included nearly $66 billion: $45 billion in pay, more than $6 billion in fringe benefits and nearly $15 billion in payments to the military retirement system.

• **Reserves, National Guard.** The 1.14 million members of reserve and National Guard units were paid at the same rates as their active-duty counterparts but only when they were on duty, which was typically for one weekend training session each month and for a two-week session once a year. For Guard and reserve compensation (and for student stipends for the Reserve Officers Training Corps), the title included $9.4 billion for pay, benefits and retirement contributions. Reflecting Congress' resistance to the Bush administration's plan to sharply cut back Guard and reserve forces, this was $333 million more than the budget requested.

• **Officers.** Nearly 29 percent of the amount for active-duty compensation was earmarked for the more than 283,000 officers who made up nearly 15 percent of the force. An additional $118.3 million was for the nearly 13,000 cadets and midshipmen who were training at West Point, Annapolis and the Air Force Academy to become officers. The remaining $46.6 billion was for the 1.63 million enlisted personnel.

The ratio of officers to enlisted members varied among the services. For instance, the Marine Corps' complement of more than 19,500 officers made up only 10 percent of that service, reflecting its limited dependence on high-tech weaponry and the fact that it was part of the Navy, which provided Marines with non-combat support in such officer-rich fields as medical care. At the other end of the technology spectrum, the more than 95,000 officers in the Air Force made up 19 percent of that service.

Pay and Benefits

Sorting out what the military personnel appropriation paid for was complicated by the lack of a simple answer to the question, "What does a colonel get paid?" The military compensation system was built around a backbone of "basic pay," which was pegged to rank and seniority. But that accounted for less than two-thirds of a service member's take-home pay because take-home pay also included an array of other allowances and bonus payments.

• **Basic pay.** In the fiscal 1992 bill, a total of $35.1 billion was for active-duty basic pay. To illustrate how that sum was parceled out:

—Each of the 35 four-star generals and admirals at the apex of the largest organization in the industrialized democracies would receive slightly more than $100,000 in basic pay, with a bonus of about $11,000 for the six who sat on the Joint Chiefs of Staff.

—The 13,379 colonels and Navy captains standing on the top rung of the services' middle management, who typically had 22 to 30 years of experience and might command a billion-dollar warship or a combat brigade, would receive roughly $61,000.

—The 102,033 captains and Navy lieutenants, typically with six to eight years of service, would collect about $34,000.

—At the top of the enlisted ranks stood 14,536 sergeant majors and master chief petty officers with more than 20 years of experience, whose average basic pay would be nearly $34,000.

—The most numerous ranks were the 418,384 corporals and third-class petty officers who typically had served three years or more and whose average basic pay would be more than $13,000.

• **Housing allowances.** Traditionally, the government also had provided housing for military personnel as well as meals for all enlisted members and, under some circumstances, for officers. In lieu of those in-kind contributions, service members who obtained housing privately were paid allowances that varied with their rank and whether they were living with dependents.

The bill included $4.7 billion to pay active-duty members their "basic allowance for quarters." For example, a colonel with dependents would receive nearly $9,100; a Navy lieutenant without dependents, about $5,400; a corporal with dependents nearly $4,100.

An additional $1.2 billion in the bill was for an extra allowance paid to personnel who were stationed in areas with particularly high local housing costs. Nearly half of these payments were to Navy personnel, who were concentrated in major seaports, which typically were high-cost areas.

• **Subsistence allowance.** To pay allowances for meals (referred to as "subsistence," in Pentagon argot), the bill provided $2.9 billion. Most of that sum was for enlisted members who did not live on bases and were authorized to dine at their own expense rather than eating in mess halls or aboard Navy ships. Their annual allowance was slightly more than $2,300, or $6.34 per day.

• **Bonuses.** $3.2 billion was provided for an array of additional payments intended to attract and retain active-duty personnel in job specialties that were particularly hazardous or were highly paid in civilian life.

That total included $508 million for aircraft crew members. The payments varied with seniority, but for officers with between six and 18 years of experience, flight pay could amount to $7,800 annually. Moreover, experienced pilots who contracted to remain in the service for a certain number of years could receive an additional payment of more than $10,000 annually.

Another large chunk of special pay went to physicians, nurses, dentists and other medical professionals, for whom the bill contained $486 million. A physician could qualify to receive concurrently several different medical bonuses, one of which paid up to $29,000 annually. A nurse could receive an additional $6,000 per year.

Also included in the bill was $292 million for crew members of Navy ships and an additional $108 million for submarine crews. A Navy captain commanding a nuclear sub would receive sea pay amounting to nearly $3,500 and an additional $7,140 for serving in a submarine. The top-ranking petty officers in his crew would receive more than $4,800 for sea pay and nearly $4,300 for sub duty.

A total of $56 million was included for enlistment bonuses, and $472 million for re-enlistment bonuses for hard-to-fill job specialties. The maximum enlistment bonus was $12,000 for a four-year enlistment, not more than $7,000 of which could be paid in an initial lump sum. In general, the maximum bonus for re-enlisting was $20,000, although up to 10 percent of recipients could receive up to $45,000.

OPERATIONS AND MAINTENANCE

The largest of the major slices in the defense funding pie was the $83.4 billion appropriation for operations and maintenance, referred to as O&M. Other than the military payroll, this title of the bill covered most of the day-to-day costs of military operations, including most of the $35 billion civilian payroll.

It involved the gamut of Pentagon activities — from operation of the B-1 bomber fleet ($271 million) to the Naval Observatory in Washington, D.C. ($11 million).

The net reduction of $2 billion, which the Appropriations committees made in budget requests for O&M, included some additions and subtractions that the services had to allocate among specific parts of their operating budgets. But those changes likely did not change the basic proportions of the O&M budget as it was submitted to Congress in February 1991. By the Pentagon's accounting, more than three-quarters of its $85.4 billion O&M budget request was tied to seven major categories:

—Strategic forces. 5 percent of the O&M request. These were spearheaded by more than 200 long-range bombers and the midair refueling tankers that supported them, 920 intercontinental ballistic missiles (ICBMs) and 29 missile-launching submarines.

—Conventional forces. 28 percent. These "general purpose forces," as the Pentagon called them, included 14 active-duty divisions in the Army and three in the Marine Corps, 424 naval vessels (among which were 13 aircraft carriers, 135 surface warships and 88 attack submarines), and nearly 2,600 fighter jets in 153 squadrons.

—Airlift, sealift. 3 percent. This funded nearly 350 long-range transport planes, more than 400 medium-range Hercules transports and 72 tanker and cargo ships.

—Communications, intelligence. 11 percent.

—Maintenance, supply. 17 percent. This included overhauls, spare parts depots and other major maintenance and supply activity.

—Training. 3 percent.

—Medical. 9 percent. This included medical programs serving an eligible population of 8.5 million people, including active-duty personnel, military retirees and their dependents and survivors.

Operating Tempo

For more than a decade, congressional critics of high-tech weapons procurement had touted O&M funding as a higher priority, on grounds that it contributed directly to the "combat readiness" of U.S. forces.

In fact, the operations and maintenance appropriation paid for a wide range of activities engaged in by a bureaucracy of nearly 3 million uniformed and civilian members. The portion that related most closely to combat readiness of units in the field was the funding of operating tempo.

"Op tempo" was the Pentagon's term for the pace at which combat units practiced their craft, using fuel and other consumables in the process. It was measured crudely by how much vehicles were driven, ships were steamed and planes and helicopters flown:

• **Army, Marines.** The defense bill included nearly $5 billion for operations of active-duty Army combat units and nearly $300 million for the Marines. For the year, that permitted each battalion to log, on average, 800 miles in its M-1 tanks, 742 miles in its Bradley armored troop carriers and more than 4,100 miles in its jeeplike HMMWV trucks.

Army Reserve and National Guard units were to operate at one-quarter to one-third of the active-duty tempo.

• **Navy.** To operate 417 ships manned by active-duty crews, the Navy received $4.9 billion. Steaming time traditionally was measured in terms of the average number of days per quarter of the year that a ship spent underway. The bill complied with the budget request by allowing ships assigned to the 6th Fleet in the Mediterranean and the 7th Fleet in the Far East to operate an average of 50.5 days per quarter while ships assigned to the U.S.-based fleets would steam an average of 29 days per quarter.

For the 40 frigates, minesweepers and amphibious landing ships crewed largely by reservists, the bill included $72 million for an average of 18 steaming days per quarter.

• **Flight operations.** A total of nearly $7 billion was provided for more than 6 million hours of flight operations by active-duty units. That permitted crews for the nearly 4,600 Army aircraft, most of which were helicopters, to fly an average of 14.5 hours per month. In the Air Force, bomber crews would fly an average of 17.8 hours monthly, fighter crews 19.3 hours and cargo crews 27.7 hours. Navy and Marine fighter crews would average more than 24 hours per month. The Navy said its higher standard reflected the difficulty its pilots faced in landing on aircraft carriers.

Reserve and National Guard flight crews were to fly at about half the tempo of their active-duty counterparts.

Base Operating Support

The bill made no major changes in the $11.2 billion budget request for operating 295 active-duty bases and 19 reserve bases in the United States and 185 bases overseas.

However, it boosted to $4.5 billion the funding that was dedicated to facilities maintenance. Of that amount, $56.4 million was budgeted to maintain buildings of historic interest on Army and Air Force bases.

The nearly 155,000 military personnel assigned to keep the bases humming were paid out of the military personnel account. But the base operations fund in the O&M title paid the 142,500 civilians who held similar jobs.

• **Historic ships.** The Navy's real property maintenance appropriation includeed $4 million for "Old Ironsides," the sail frigate *Constitution*, which played a stellar role in the War of 1812 and was a historic relic floating in Boston Harbor. An additional $345,000 was earmarked for maintenance of the *Nautilus*, the first nuclear-powered submarine, which was maintained as a historic ship in Groton, Conn.

Supply and Maintenance

Within the O&M appropriation, the bill earmarked a minimum of $7.3 billion for major equipment overhauls performed at central depots rather than at the installations where the equipment usually was based. The depot maintenance allowances were:

—$978 million for the Army
—$99 million for the Marine Corps
—$1.68 billion for the Air Force
—$4.54 billion for the Navy, which included more than $500 million budgeted for retiring 76 ships, including 34 frigates commissioned around 1970 and 11 nuclear-powered submarines.

Revolving Fund

The Defense Business Operations Fund was covered by a separate title of the bill but inextricably connected to O&M funding. This was a revolving fund that bought fuel and other supplies on the commercial market and operated Defense Department maintenance depots. The fund was reimbursed by operating units that "bought" goods and services from it.

The centralized fund was created in fiscal 1992 by consolidating several funds of more limited scope. To cover overhead costs of the operation, the bill appropriated $3.4 billion.

• **Commissaries.** The fund included $980 million to subsidize the worldwide network of 422 commissaries, which sold groceries and certain personal-care items to active-duty and retired personnel at prices as much as 20 percent lower than those at commercial stores. The stores projected sales totaling $6.5 billion in fiscal 1992.

Recruiting and Training

The bill provided $555 million for recruiting costs, including advertising. The active-duty forces planned to take in nearly 216,000 fresh recruits during fiscal 1992 and to sign up an additional 2,500 people with prior military experience.

The bill made no direct change in the $2.9 billion requested for training and eduction, which included:

—$39 million for basic training of enlisted recruits.
—$629 million to train enlisted personnel in job specialties.
—$321 million to train officer cadets and midshipmen.
—$247 million for mid-career training programs for officers.
—$837 million for flight training.

Medical Program

The 2 million active-duty personnel were entitled to unlimited care in the 163 hospitals and 586 clinics run by the military services.

The 2.6 million military dependents, 1.7 million military retirees and their 2.3 million dependents and survivors could receive treatment in military facilities if space and time permitted. Otherwise, their treatment in private facilities was covered by the Civilian Health and Medical Program of the Uniformed Services (commonly known as CHAMPUS), which was the Pentagon's medical and hospitalization insurance program for dependents and retirees.

Beneficiaries paid no premium for CHAMPUS coverage but had to pay deductibles in each fiscal year.

Of the $8.1 billion included in the bill for medical programs, $4.5 billion was for the services' in-house medical activities. The hospitals projected an average daily admission rate during the year of nearly 2,300 patients and an average daily inpatient load of more than 11,500 patients. The system anticipated more than 49 million outpatient visits and more than 45 million dental procedures.

The $3.6 billion CHAMPUS appropriation would cover 326,000 admissions to civilian hospitals and more than 12 million outpatient treatments.

Morale and Welfare

The bill made no direct change in the budget request for $954 million to subsidize recreational and welfare programs, some of which were paid for in part by user fees. The two largest funding categories were:

• **Day-care and child-development centers.** $160 million.

• **Gymnasiums.** $137 million.

In a separate account, the bill provided $1.2 billion for the network of elementary and secondary schools available at no charge to dependents of military personnel stationed abroad or in isolated areas.

Other Programs

The Operations and Maintenance title also provided for:

• **Environmental cleanup.** Funds to clean up operating and abandoned military installations, $1.18 billion.

• **Drug interdiction**. Operations by military units, $779 million.

• **Defense Contract Audit Agency**. $330 million.

• **Office of the department's Inspector General**. $116 million.

PROCUREMENT

The bill's $64 billion procurement appropriation covered the purchase of durable goods ranging from Navy destroyers ($4.2 billion for four ships of the *Arleigh Burke* class) to forklifts ($24 million).

Slightly less than half of that total was to be used for major weapons — planes, missiles, ships, ammunition and other big-ticket items. The remainder was earmarked for spare parts, so-called support equipment (such as the forklifts) and modification of existing weapons. Modifications likely would account for a larger share of the procurement budget in the next decade, as tight budgets drove the services to upgrade existing equipment rather than buy new types.

In principle, Congress appropriated the complete cost of an item in the first year, even though the funds would be doled out to contractors over the several years that were required to build a jet plane or a warship. The chief exception to this "full-funding" principle was that, a year or more in advance of funding certain ships and planes, Congress appropriated funds to buy so-called long lead-time items. These were components such as engines or electronic gear that had to be in hand early in the process of construction.

Aircraft

Of the $19 billion appropriated for aircraft procurement, about two-thirds was earmarked to buy planes and helicopters, with the rest going for spare parts, modifications and support equipment.

• **B-2s.** The largest amount for a single program was the $2.8 billion to continue production of the controversial B-2 stealth bomber. Of that amount, $1.8 billion was earmarked to keep the production line warm by buying components and spare parts. The remaining $1 billion could be used to buy a 16th plane of this type, but only if Congress first passed a bill approving that expenditure.

• **Tactical fighters.** $3.8 billion was provided to buy fighter jets: $1.78 billion for 39 Navy F/A-18s (plus $150 million for long-lead funding); $1.1 billion for 48 Air Force F-16s (plus $78 million for long-lead); $505 million to close out production of the larger Air Force F-15, with six more planes plus support equipment; $173 million to shut down production of the Navy's F-14 and $40 million to rebuild two of the Marine Corps' Harrier vertical-takeoff jets.

• **Cargo planes.** For two types of cargo planes, the bill provided $2.9 billion: $1.5 billion for four C-17 wide-body jets of intercontinental range and $1.2 billion for 42 of various models of the C-130 Hercules medium-range turboprop, most of them earmarked for Guard and reserve units.

• **Helicopters.** Nearly $2 billion was provided for helicopters, almost two-thirds of it for troop and cargo carriers including:

—$424 million for 47 Blackhawks used by the Army to carry 11-man infantry squads, plus long lead-time items.

—$24 million for six Blackhawks for the Navy and Air Force, equipped to rescue downed pilots.

—$340 million for 16 of the much larger CH-53Es for the Marine Corps, designed to carry 55 Marines or a 14-ton armored car.

The rest of the helicopter funds were for armed craft, with most of the money — $494 million — earmarked for two dozen Navy Seahawks (plus long-lead). This was a ship-based version of the Blackhawk, equipped to launch torpedoes at submarines. In addition, $129 million was earmarked for a dozen Cobra helicopters, which carried anti-tank missiles, for the Marines. And $138 million was to pay for overhead costs and training equipment as production of 807 Apache tank-hunting helicopters wound down.

• **Electronic warfare planes.** These aircraft, intended either to detect enemy targets or to shield U.S. forces from enemy detection, consumed more than $900 million of the appropriation, including:

—$540 million for six Navy Hawkeyes (plus long-lead), smaller counterparts of the AWACS radar plane, built to operate off carriers.

—$190 million for six Army Guardrail aircraft. These were small, twin-engine executive planes packed with electronic eavesdropping gear to pin down enemy radios and radars.

—$115 million to upgrade existing EA-6B carrier-based radar-jammers.

—$125 million to gear up for production of JSTARS radar planes, converted jetliners rigged with powerful radars to detect tank columns and other ground targets more than 200 miles away.

• **Modifications.** The $4.5 billion appropriated for aircraft modifications would touch on practically every type of aircraft in the Pentagon's fleet. But nearly half of the funds went to seven major programs.

Three of the seven programs were for relatively routine upgrades in F-15 fighters ($297 million), F-16 fighters ($254 million) and B-1 bombers ($97 million).

The bill also provided:

—$587 million to put more powerful engines on 1960s-vintage midair refueling tankers slated to remain in service for another 30 years.

—$257 million for the final increment of a multi-year program to beef up the Army's 472 Chinook helicopters, used to haul cannons, ammunition and other heavy cargo around the battlefield.

—$312 million to equip Chinook and Blackhawk helicopters with radar and night-vision gear so they could carry special operations units low over enemy territory at night.

—$272 million to equip "scout" helicopters with air-to-air and anti-tank missiles.

Missiles, Satellites and Torpedoes

The $10.5 billion appropriation for procurement of missiles and certain categories of weapons included $5.1 billion for combat missiles and $985 million for space satellites and satellite launch rockets. It also included $2.3 billion for secret projects — the largest pot of money for classified programs in the procurement budget.

The missile appropriations also included: $233 million for spare parts, $538 million to modify missiles already in the inventory, and $549 million for related items such as aerial target drones ($202 million).

• **Strategic weapons.** Nearly $2 billion of the missile total was for long-range nuclear-armed (or "strategic") weapons, with nearly 60 percent of those funds ($1.2 billion) earmarked for 28 Trident II submarine-launched missiles (plus long lead-time components). The other large appropriation in this category was $502 million for 120 2,000-mile-range stealth cruise missiles to be carried by bombers (plus long lead-time items).

• **Tomahawk missiles.** The bill allocated to the Navy $411 million for 176 more of the Tomahawk cruise missiles, which had been deployed in the past decade to greatly extend the reach of most U.S. warships. When equipped with a 1,000-pound conventional warhead, as were the nearly 300 Tomahawks launched against Iraq, this extremely accurate weapon had a range of more than 300 miles.

• **Artillery rockets.** More than $500 million was provided for Army artillery rockets: $171 million for 300 ATACMS missiles (plus long lead-time) with a range of more than 60 miles, and $353 million for 20-mile-range MLRS rockets — which were fired in salvos of up to a dozen — and their launchers. Both weapons blanketed their targets with hundreds of fist-sized "bomblets" designed to kill troops and damage any vehicles that were not heavily armored.

• **Short-range missiles.** More than $300 million was provided for short-range missiles designed to punch through tank armor. This included $20 million for 119 four-mile range Hellfires, carried by helicopters; and $231 million for 12,400 TOWs, launched from several types of vehicles or from a simple tripod.

• **Anti-aircraft weapons.** The bill included more than $700 million for anti-aircraft weapons, nearly half of it ($332 million) to buy 330 Standard missiles, used by the Navy. An additional $185 million was for 149 turrets carrying clusters of 3-mile-range Stinger missiles (plus long lead-time), to be mounted in the back of pickup trucks. Also included was $25 million for Patriot anti-aircraft missiles modified to counter short-range (or "tactical") ballistic missiles, such as the Iraqi Scuds that Patriots took on during the Persian Gulf War. An additional $78 million was to prepare the Patriot production line for further production of anti-missile versions.

• **Air-to-ground missiles.** For such missiles (other than the anti-tank Hellfire), the bill provided more than $600 million. More than half ($324 million) was earmarked for more than 1,200 HARM missiles, designed to home in on anti-aircraft missile radars.

Also included was: $70 million for 120 TV-guided AGM-130s, with a 1-ton warhead and a range of more than 25 miles, designed to be carried by fighter planes; $35 million for 32 copies of the Israeli-designed "Have Nap" missile, a larger TV-guided weapon with a 1-ton warhead and a 50-mile range, intended to be carried by B-52 bombers; and $168 million for 150 additional SLAMs — a TV-guided version of the Navy's Harpoon missile, with a 570-pound warhead and a 60-mile range.

• **AMRAAM missiles.** The bill included $740 million for nearly 900 AMRAAM radar-guided air-to-air missiles, with a range of more than 30 miles; they were carried by all types of Air Force, Navy and Marine Corps fighters.

• **Space satellites.** The $985 million provided for space satellites and related equipment included $296 million for Titan IV launch rockets and $222 million for smaller Atlas-Centaur launchers.

• **Others.** The spending for missiles, satellites and torpedoes included:
—$283 million for Navy communications satellites.
—$56 million for general-use communications satellites.
—$189 million for navigation satellites.
—$108 million for weather detection satellites.

The bill included $689 million for homing torpedoes and related equipment: $295 million for the 108 copies of the 20-mile-range Mark 48 (plus long lead-time), a 3,000-pound weapon carried only by submarines; and $262 million for 246 of the 800-pound Mark 50s, carried by aircraft. To catch the high-speed Soviet submarines commissioned since the mid-1970s, both weapons were designed to travel more than 60 mph.

Ships

The bill provided $8.3 billion for Navy vessels, plus $464 million to cover inflation-driven increases in the cost of ships funded in earlier budgets and $389 million to put the finishing touches on ships nearing delivery (for instance, stocking them with spare parts and supplies).

• **Warships.** Six front-line warships were funded:

For the third in the class of *Seawolf* nuclear-powered submarines, designed to quietly hunt other subs, the bill included $1.5 billion, with an additional $376 million earmarked for long lead-time components to be used in subs to be funded in future budgets.

For five *Arleigh Burke*-class destroyers, the bill included $4.1 billion, plus $16 million for long lead-time items. More than half the cost of each ship was for its Aegis anti-aircraft system, an anti-aircraft missile battery controlled by a network of powerful radars and computers.

• **Other vessels.** The bill provided:
—$600 million to buy existing cargo ships or build new ones to enlarge the "sealift" fleet intended to haul U.S.-based combat forces to distant trouble spots.
—$504 million for 24 air-cushion landing barges, able to carry a 60-ton tank at nearly 50 mph.
—$341 million for three minesweepers, each equipped with a 1-ton robot submarine to blow up mines.
—$500 million for a giant supply ship, designed to replenish a carrier and its escorts in mid-ocean with fuel, supplies and ammunition.
—$100 million for two oceanographic research ships, to be used for charting the sea bottom.

• **Modernization.** In addition to the funds for ship construction, the bill provided more than $3 billion for equipment for new vessels and to modernize ships already in service. This included $106 million for radars and more than $1 billion for sonars and other electronic devices used by submarines and anti-sub vessels. An additional $70 million was provided for sonobouys, which were disposable sonars dropped from sub-hunting aircraft.

Tanks, Guns and Ammunition

The bill included $2.7 billion for ammunition, aerial bombs and munitions production plants and an additional $1.3 billion for tanks, combat vehicles, cannon and personal firearms.

• **M-1 tanks.** This included $90 million to buy 60 M-1A2 tanks for the Army and $225 million to upgrade older M-1s to M-1A1s, with a larger cannon and sophisticated electronic gear so they could be operated in the dark. Civilian Pentagon leaders had balked at the cost, but Army brass and the congressional defense committees hoped eventually to upgrade all of the more than 3,200 older M-1s.

• **Others.** The bill also included:
—$127 million to modernize self-propelled 155mm howitzers so that they could shoot farther, more quickly and more accurately, and could be driven at night.
—$36 million for 86 British-designed 105mm lightweight guns.
—$31 million for nearly 68,000 M-16 rifles.

National Guard and Reserve Equipment

In the past decade, it had become routine for Congress to add to the annual defense bills hundreds of millions of dollars for equipment earmarked for National Guard and reserve units. Though the Guard and reserves had been assigned many high-priority missions, congressional backers insisted that the services routinely shortchanged them at budget time.

The Bush administration's fiscal 1992 request included $1.4 billion for equipment to be issued to the Guard and reserves, but none of it for major items. The Appropriations bill added to that amount $1.9 billion. Nearly two-thirds of the congressional increase was earmarked to provide the Guard and reserves with major weapons: 31 Hercules transports and cargo planes ($866 million),

MLRS rockets and launchers ($158 million), six Cobra anti-tank helicopters ($71 million), four Blackhawk search and rescue helicopters ($35 million) and four minesweeping helicopters for the Naval Reserve ($129 million).

Other Procurement

• **Communications.** To buy myriad types of communications and electronic equipment, the bill provided nearly $5 billion. One of the largest slices of this pie was the $286 million appropriated for SINCGARS, the Army's network of battlefield radios designed to foil enemy jamming efforts by rapid changes of frequency. Another large appropriation was for components of Milstar ($264 million), a satellite-based global communications system scheduled to enter service in the mid-1990s.

• **Vehicles.** More than $800 million was provided for non-armored vehicles for use on the battlefield, including:
—$322 million for nearly 8,600 High-Mobility Multipurpose Wheeled Vehicles (HMMWVs) — nicknamed "humvees" or "hummers" — boxy, four-wheel drive vehicles that are the more muscular successors to the venerable jeep. They are used by the Army, Marine Corps and Air Force as everything from ambulances to missile-armed tank-hunters.
—$160 million for huge "low-boy" tractor-trailers, designed to save wear and tear on 70-ton M-1 tanks by hauling them to the battlefield.
—$100 million for 281 heavy-duty ammunition trucks, able to carry more than 30 tons of munitions and equipped with rapid unloading equipment.
—$130 million for 5-ton and 10-ton cargo trucks.

• **Miscellaneous.** The bill also provided:
—$151 million for equipment to dismantle and neutralize obsolete chemical weapons.
—$219 million for medical equipment.
—$154 million for a data processing network to streamline management and mobilization planning for reserve and National Guard units.
—$179 million for night-vision equipment.
—$17 million for 42 water-distillation units designed to purify 3,000 gallons per hour.
—$9 million for 85 mobile laundry trailers to accompany Army field units.

RESEARCH AND DEVELOPMENT

The $39.4 billion appropriation for Pentagon research and development accounted for slightly more than half of all R&D funding in the federal government's fiscal 1992 budget.

By the Defense Department's accounting, $4.3 billion of the total was for basic research and $6.5 billion for development of technologies not yet linked to a particular weapons development program.

Development programs related to strategic arms consumed $4.7 billion, conventional weapons programs $14.8 billion and communications and intelligence programs $5.2 billion.

An additional $3.9 billion was for overhead and support costs that underwrote the overall defense R&D effort.

Aside from the cost of operating the military's test ranges, some of the largest single support programs funded by the bill were to develop satellite launch rockets: $145 million to continue refining the Titan IV, designed to orbit 20-ton payloads; and $55 million to develop a new "advanced launch system" with four times the Titan's lifting power.

Taken together, basic research and technology development — which the Pentagon regarded as an investment in its technology base — accounted for more than 25 percent of the R&D total, while strategic arms programs accounted for less than 12 percent.

But those figures were disputed by critics who complained that the Bush administration invested too heavily in strategic programs that had been overtaken by the collapse of communist power.

At issue was the status of the largest single program in the Pentagon research budget: the $4.15 billion anti-missile defense program known as the Strategic Defense Initiative (SDI).

Pentagon officials argued that many of the dozens of projects under the SDI umbrella were so futuristic that, by the usual standards, they qualified as "technology development" rather than being tied to a particular weapons program. Moreover, many of these projects would prove applicable to conventional weaponry and civilian technology.

The critics' argument was that Presidents Ronald Reagan and Bush had given SDI a particularly tight focus, driving it strongly toward deployment of anti-missile weapons in the relatively near future. Following that logic — counting SDI funding as a "strategic" program rather than "technology development" — the bill earmarked about 17 percent of the R&D appropriation for basic research and technology development. And the strategic programs' share of the pie nearly doubled to more than 22 percent.

Strategic Programs

Aside from the $4.15 billion for SDI, the lion's share of the strategic weapons R&D was for the Air Force ($3.9 billion). In turn, most of that money was to continue develement of a handful of major programs: the B-2 bomber ($1.6 billion), the Milstar communications satellite ($1.1 billion) and the stealth cruise missile ($29 million). Most of the remainder ($434 million) was to develop a small single-warhead intercontinental ballistic missile (ICBM).

Nicknamed Midgetman, this weapon originally was planned to go in a launcher carried by a huge off-road vehicle. But Bush scrapped all mobile ICBM programs in his nuclear arms reduction initiative unveiled Sept. 27.

After that, Midgetman survived as a potential replacement for the aging Minuteman missiles based in armored underground silos.

Other weapons that were in the president's R&D budget request but were dropped after his arms proposal were a rail-mobile launcher for the much larger MX missile ($260 million) and the SRAM II supersonic bomber-launched missile ($166 million).

Only $328 million of the Army and Navy appropriations were for strategic R&D, including:
—$51 million for the Army's ground-launched anti-satellite missile.
—$54 million to continue development of the Trident II sub-launched missile.
—$30 million for work on lasers and other techniques for communicating with submerged missile-launching submarines.

An additional $464 million was for strategic arms research by other Pentagon agencies.

Conventional Weapons

The $15 billion appropriated by the bill to develop conventional arms was parceled out among hundreds of programs. But 18 major projects — five in the Army, six in the Air Force and seven in the Navy — absorbed more than 40 percent of the total.

• **Army.** The Army's largest program ($500 million) was to develop the Comanche (formerly designated LH), a missile-armed scout helicopter intended to be smaller, faster and harder to detect than Apaches or the scout helicopters in existing use.

Another of the Army's five projects was the Longbow system, a target-finding radar coupled with a radar-guided version of the Hellfire anti-tank missile ($254 million).

The Hellfire was designed to home in on the reflection off its target of a laser beam aimed by the launching Apache or by a scout helicopter. If it worked out, the Longbow would be able to find targets in smoke and haze that would blind a laser.

Moreover, because the modified Hellfires would be guided to the target by their own tiny radars, the launching helicopter could dodge away from hostile fire as soon as it launched the missiles.

Other major Army programs included:

—$301 million for the $60 billion "armored systems modernization" program, intended to develop and field a "family" of 6,000 armored combat vehicles, including a new tank and five other types using common automotive parts.

However, citing the success of the M-1 tank in the gulf war, Congress ordered the Army to slow its work on the proposed new tank, emphasizing instead development of a new mobile cannon.

—$151 million for the SADARM anti-tank warhead to be dispensed by artillery shells or rockets. It was intended to blast through the roof of a tank, where the armor was relatively thin.

—$131 million for "joint tactical fusion," an information network designed to help a commander integrate information from different intelligence sources.

• **Navy.** The Navy's seven largest conventional arms development programs accounted for more than a third of its $5.6 billion conventional R&D total.

The largest, by a good margin, was one Congress had kept alive for two years over the objections of Defense Secretary Dick Cheney: $625 million to continue development of the V-22 Osprey — a hybrid airplane/helicopter designed as a troop carrier for the Marine Corps.

The bill's next largest Navy program earmarked $420 million to develop an enlarged version of the F/A-18 fighter. This "stretched" version — to be designated the "E" and "F" models — was intended to replace the larger F-14 as it began to wear out late in the 1990s.

Two of the largest Navy programs related to the *Seawolf*-class subs under construction: The bill included $157 million to continue development of the design and $267 million for the "submarine combat system," an electronic nervous system to link the new subs' weapons launchers with target detection gear.

The bill also provided $238 million for the "fixed distributed system," a network of submarine detectors anchored to the sea bottom. This was intended to replace the SOSUS listening systems deployed around the Northern Hemisphere, which reportedly could detect subs hundreds of miles away.

The conferees consolidated into one project several programs listed separately in the budget request — some of them secret — that were aimed at improving the self-defense capability of ships. It earmarked $221 million for the combined project.

The bill also provided $177 million, as requested, for the ambiguously labeled "joint advanced systems." Circumstantial evidence suggested that this project was the development of an air-launched cruise missile with a conventional warhead.

• **Air Force.** The $1.6 billion appropriated for the fiscal 1992 installment toward development of the F-22 fighter plane accounted for nearly one-third of the Air Force's conventional weapons development budget. Designed to combine agility and stealthiness, the plane was intended to supplant the F-15 as the service's premier air-to-air fighter.

Two other large appropriations were to continue development of planes slated to enter service in the next few years:

—$376 million for the C-17 wide-body cargo plane, the prototype of which first flew Sept. 15.

—$312 million for the JSTARS radar plane, designed to detect tank columns and other ground targets at a range of hundreds of miles.

The remaining three of the largest Air Force projects were to improve planes that had been in service for a decade or more:

—$202 million for AWACS radar planes.

—$160 million for F-16 fighters.

—$113 million for the ground-attack "E" model of the F-15. ■

Continued from p. 624

to suspend MLRS production while it developed a new anti-tank warhead for these 20-mile-range missiles. But the Appropriations panel contended that it would be cheaper to keep the production line running. Underscoring that point, the bill included only $154 million of the $178 million requested to buy 43 launchers for these rockets. According to the committee, most of the reduction reflected efficiencies that would result from keeping the rockets in production.

The bill included the $47 million requested to develop the new tank-busting warhead intended for MLRS.

The bill also included:

• $147 million for 300 longer-range ATACMS artillery rockets, a $4 million reduction from the request.

• $127 million of the $162 million requested to modernize existing mobile artillery pieces, a reduction mandated by the authorization bill.

The bill also included $60 million for 80 armored ammunition carriers, designed to replenish artillery batteries under fire. The vehicles, designated FAASVs, were built in York, Pa., by Harsco Corp.

Like House Armed Services, the Appropriations Committee told the Army to streamline its plans for upgrading the fleet of Apache missile-armed anti-tank helicopters. The appropriations bill included the $244 million requested to develop a new target-finding radar, called Longbow, which was to be the keystone of the upgraded helicopter. But it denied $83 million requested to perform a limited upgrade on some Apaches that later would be given the Longbow. The committee told the Army to modernize the fleet in one step.

The bill included $200 million to equip 36 of the Army's small "scout" helicopters with new target-finding equipment, a program the Pentagon wanted to terminate because of budgetary limits. But the committee dropped from the bill $19 million requested to develop a modification package to arm with missiles the 243 scout helicopters that already had been given the new electronics. The committee acknowledged that the small force of armed scouts had been highly effective in the gulf war but asked the Army to review the necessity of arming the entire fleet.

The bill included the $508 million requested to continue development of the new Comanche helicopter (formerly designated LH), which the Army selected in April as its next armed chopper. But the committee ordered the Army to use at least $5 million of that amount to review the losing design in the LH competition for technologies that could be incorporated in the Comanche.

The bill included $75 million not in the budget request to buy 1,800 Stinger shoulder-launched anti-aircraft missiles. It also included the $132 million requested to equip 149 pickup trucks with clusters of Stinger launchers.

Aerial Combat

Lamenting what it called the "collapse" of the Navy's plans to modernize its air squadrons, the Appropriations Committee added funds to the budget request for several naval air projects.

Following the authorization bill, the appropriations measure included $504 million to begin rebuilding F-14 fighters with new engines and radars. The administration had requested only $173 million for lesser modifications.

The Appropriations panel said it had "mixed feelings" about the Navy's plan to begin developing a new carrier-based bomber, designated A-X, by using $138 million that was appropriated in prior budgets to begin building the A-12. The A-12 was a carrier-based bomber that Cheney canceled in January 1991 because of delays and cost increases.

Like the A-12, the A-X was intended to replace the A-6Es that were the Navy's heaviest carrier-based bombers.

Many problems with the A-12 program had their roots in the department's use of a design and exotic materials intended to make the plane extremely "stealthy" — able to evade enemy detection until the last possible moment.

The committee acquiesced in the transfer of the leftover A-12 funds. But it demanded that the Navy consider possible trade-offs between making the new bomber stealthy and equipping a less stealthy plane with accurate "stand-off" missiles that could be fired at targets from beyond the reach of anti-aircraft defenses.

The committee also insisted that the A-X design be adaptable to the Air Force's need for a plane to replace its aging F-111 ground-attack planes.

The bill also added to the budget request:

- $50 million to develop a version of the Air Force's new F-22 fighter plane that could operate from aircraft carriers.
- $30 million to upgrade A-6Es that would have to stay in service longer than had been planned because of the delay in fielding a replacement.
- $50 million to develop a version of the F-14 that could fill the A-X role.
- $40 million to rebuild two AV-8B Harriers, vertical-takeoff jets used by the Marines as bombers. Cheney had planned to buy no new Harriers after fiscal 1991; the Appropriations panel described its Harrier add-on as a test of whether existing planes could be significantly upgraded.

The bill funded most major Air Force programs for tactical aircraft essentially as requested, including $1.64 billion to continue developing the F-22 and $1.1 billion for 48 additional F-16 fighters.

As authorized, the bill added to the budget request $83 million to upgrade F-117 stealth fighters. Like House Armed Services, the Appropriations panel also ordered the Air Force to continue buying F-16s at the rate of 48 annually, rather than phasing out production in 1993 as planned.

Not included in the bill was $106 million requested to develop an upgraded version of the F-16. Before approving this project, the committee said, it wanted a detailed explanation of how it fit in with long-term Air Force plans for a "low-end" fighter to be built in the next decade to complement the "high-end" F-22.

The bill included $974 million for nearly 1,200 AMRAAM air-to-air missiles, an increase of $115 million (and 300 missiles) over the budget request. Citing recent successful tests, the committee said that the long-gestating project was ready to go into full-scale production. The committee added to the bill a provision that waived an existing law that had delayed full-scale production.

But the bill denied $89 million requested to develop a long-range air-to-air missile (designated AAAM). It was intended as a lighter-weight replacement for the half-ton, 100-mile-range Phoenix missile, which was carried only by F-14s. The committee ordered the Navy to use instead the Air Force-developed AMRAAM, which had a range of about 40 miles.

Naval Forces

The bill's largest single change in the Navy's budget was its approval of $3.31 billion for four destroyers equipped with the Aegis anti-aircraft system — a reduction of one ship (at $851 million) from the request.

Many of the other major naval programs adjusted by the bill dealt with anti-submarine warfare. The bill included the $1.53 billion requested for the third *Seawolf*-class sub-hunting submarine and $482 million, as requested, to buy two types of anti-sub torpedoes. But it also added to the budget request:

- $42 million to study an improved version of the P-3C land-based anti-sub patrol plane.
- $20 million to continue developing the Sea Lance missile, designed to be fired from surface ships or submarines at subs more than 60 miles away.

In hope of fielding an interim anti-sub weapon while Sea Lance was being developed, the committee also ordered the Pentagon to continue testing a modified version of the short-range ASROC missile, using funds appropriated for that purpose in fiscal 1989 but not yet spent.

- $100 million for research on methods for detecting submarines through means other than sound.
- $149 million for a surveillance ship, built to tow a mile-long row of underwater microphones designed to detect submarines at a great distance. The Navy planned to include such a ship in the fiscal 1993 budget request, but the Appropriations panel said it should be funded in fiscal 1992 to take advantage of a limited-time option in the contract for surveillance ships already under construction.

The bill included $500 million of the $540 million requested for a high-speed supply ship, intended to carry fuel, food and ammunition for a carrier and its escorts. And it included $41 million for one oceanographic research ship. The budget requested $130 million for two research ships, one of which was to be built to operate in ice-choked waters. According to the committee, the ice-hardened ship was rendered superfluous by a recent administration decision to buy for the Coast Guard a new icebreaker equipped for oceanographic work.

Space Launchers

The bill denied more than half a billion dollars requested for space launchers designed to boost very heavy payloads into orbit.

It included only $800 million of the $1.2 billion requested to continue developing and building Titan IV launchers and the associated Centaur upper stages. For one thing, the Appropriations Committee complained that the Pentagon had been stocking up on Titan IV boosters faster than it was scheduling launches.

More fundamentally, however, the committee was unhappy over test failures that had dogged both the Centaur program and the effort to develop powerful booster rockets that could be strapped in pairs to the side of a Titan IV to launch very heavy payloads, such as secret reconnaissance satellites.

The bill also slashed the funding requested to develop a new space launcher that could carry even heavier loads into orbit. In addition to $172 million requested in the Pentagon budget, the administration asked for $175 million in the NASA budget for the so-called National Launch System.

The Appropriations Committee said there was no defense payload in prospect large enough to require the proposed new system.

Of the $172 million in the Pentagon request, the defense bill included only $25 million. Moreover, the committee said that money should be used only to improve the Titan IV's performance.

SENATE COMMITTEE ACTION

Pentagon funding for the B-2 stealth bomber received conditional approval from the Senate Defense Appropriations Subcommittee on Sept. 19 and from the full committee the following day as part of the $270.4 billion Senate version of HR 2521. But critics of the B-2, led by Jim Sasser, D-Tenn., and Patrick J. Leahy, D-Vt., said they would mount their attack on the bomber's funding when the measure reached the Senate floor.

On Aug. 1, the Senate rejected 42-57 an amendment by Leahy that would have cut off B-2 production at the 15 planes previously funded, dropping from the companion defense authorization bill (S 1507) the $3.2 billion earmarked for additional B-2 production.

But three weeks after that vote, the hard-line Communist coup in Moscow had collapsed, the Soviet state was in the throes of rapid decentralization and the decline of Soviet military power seemed to have dramatically accelerated.

B-2 supporters had touted the plane's potential for pinpoint attacks at distant, non-Soviet targets with "smart," non-nuclear weapons, such as those dropped on Baghdad by the smaller F-117 stealth fighter. But Leahy and other B-2 critics insisted that the plane, with its expensive radar-spoofing design and materials, was much harder to justify as the prospect of war with the Soviet Union was becoming much less plausible.

B-2 supporters got a second jolt the week of Sept. 16, when the Pentagon informed Congress that a radar had detected a B-2 more easily than expected during a July 26 test flight. While details were secret, Air Force officials maintained that the problem could be fixed.

"The once highly visible Soviet Union has disappeared, and the once invisible B-2 has appeared," Leahy said at the subcommittee markup Sept. 19.

As reported to the floor, the bill included $3.2 billion for B-2 production. But to ease senators' concerns about the B-2's technical problems, subcommittee Chairman Inouye and ranking Republican Stevens, both staunch B-2 supporters, erected what Inouye called "a large and tall fence" around the production funds. Though officially appropriated for B-2 procurement and thus protected from diversion to other projects, the bill stipulated that the new money could not be spent until Congress gave its approval in a supplemental appropriations bill in 1992.

Shipbuilding Issues

Under concerted pressure from New England senators and the Navy, Inouye backed off from an effort to suspend funding for the Navy's costly new *Seawolf*-class attack submarine, designed to leapfrog anticipated improvements in Soviet subs. So as reported, the committee bill included the $1.53 billion requested for the third of the ships.

The Defense Subcommittee had recommended building two more *Los Angeles*-class nuclear submarines ($2.63 billion) instead of the requested *Seawolf*, which was the third of its type.

When the subcommittee marked up the bill Sept. 19, Inouye pointed out that both of the *Seawolf*-class ships funded in earlier years were in trouble: Because of defective welds, the partly constructed first vessel was being rebuilt, and court battles had delayed award of a contract for the second. But Inouye also suggested that the *Seawolf* design — intended to surmount anticipated improvements in Soviet subs — was too expensive. The Navy was designing a less expensive sub, the *Centurion*, to replace some planned *Seawolf*-class ships.

Since 1972, *Los Angeles*-class subs had been built by two contractors: a General Dynamics shipyard in Groton, Conn., and a Tenneco Corp. yard in Newport News, Va.

But because of the *Seawolf's* cost, the Navy planned to build only one ship annually, and for efficiency, the Pentagon hoped to have all of them built in Connecticut, driving the Virginia yard out of the nuclear sub market.

Inouye and Stevens contended that buying two of the less expensive *Los Angeles* subs would keep both yards in the submarine business — and thus able to bid competitively on the *Centurion* — while the Navy sorted out its long-term sub-building plans.

By the time the full Appropriations Committee took up the defense bill Sept. 20, however, Inouye and Stevens ran up the white flag under pressure from *Seawolf* proponents:

"In the past 48 hours, I must have spent 20 hours on *Seawolf*," Inouye lamented. This included sessions with New Hampshire Republican Warren B. Rudman "pounding on my back" and with Connecticut Democrats Christopher J. Dodd and Joseph I. Lieberman.

SENATE FLOOR ACTION

Political support for costly strategic arms programs showed heavy erosion during Senate debate on HR 2521 on Sept. 25-26.

The B-2 bomber and Strategic Defense Initiative narrowly survived attacks, and the Senate voted to kill the plan to mount MX missiles on rail cars. The debate reflected Congress' increasing doubts about big defense budgets as Democrats sought to protect domestic spending and members of both parties responded to the anti-communist upheaval in the Soviet Union.

The sea change in attitudes toward defense was ratified

Sept. 27, a day after the Senate passed the defense spending bill by voice vote, when Bush made his boldest proposals to dismantle the nuclear arsenals of the Cold War.

In the Senate, continued production of the B-2 stealth bomber was approved 51-48, but opponents rounded up six more votes to kill the program than they had mustered only seven weeks earlier in action on the companion defense authorization bill.

Similarly, a proposal to provide SDI with $3.5 billion, rather than the $4.6 billion in the bill, was rejected 50-49. However, the amendment was supported by three senators who had opposed a similar cut in the authorization bill. In each case, all of the senators who switched positions were Democrats. *(Votes 206, 207, p. 27-S)*

The Senate killed one relatively minor program by a lopsided margin, voting 67-33 to end development of a rail-based launcher for the MX intercontinental ballistic missile (ICBM). The Pentagon planned to test the system and then mothball it. It had survived a challenge in August by one vote. *(Vote 208, p. 27-S)*

The defense spending bill provided $2.7 billion less than the House approved and $1.6 billion less than the Bush administration requested.

After the Coup . . .

With the collapse of the hard-line Soviet coup in mid-August and the subsequent eclipse of communist power in that country, critics insisted on a more radical change in the U.S. defense posture than the 25 percent reduction through fiscal 1995 that was already in progress.

For J. Bennett Johnston, La. — a conservative Democrat who was among those who switched positions on the B-2 bomber — the transformed international situation was symbolized by the removal from a Moscow square of a huge statue of Feliks Dzerzhinsky, founder of the Soviet secret police.

"With the toppling of that statue . . . goes, in effect, the danger of the Soviet Union," Johnston told the Senate.

Defense Appropriations Subcommittee Chairman Inouye warned repeatedly during the debate against too rapid a cutback. The Soviet nuclear arsenal required continued U.S. vigilance, and the turmoil from the Soviet collapse would bring new dangers to the fore, he said.

But Inouye acknowledged that senators' changed votes reflected a different perspective. "It's part of the national euphoria that the Cold War is over," he said, adding, "At least, they think so."

In a televised speech Sept. 27, Bush called for reductions in the U.S. and Soviet nuclear arsenals that went far beyond the cuts of roughly 30 percent required by the Strategic Arms Reduction Treaty (START), signed in July and expected to be considered by the Senate in 1992.

Echoing the Senate action, Bush shelved the effort to develop a rail-mobile version of the MX. He also proposed elimination of all long-range, land-based missiles armed with multiple warheads, long regarded by U.S. officials as the most dangerous element of the U.S.-Soviet nuclear balance.

Bush said he would remove all tactical nuclear weapons from warships and submarines. He would also scrap all short-range nuclear missiles and artillery shells and dismantle their warheads. *(Bush's arms reduction plan, p. 421)*

. . . After the Budget Deal

The senators' sense that the Soviet threat had faded was complemented by their desire to cut major weapons programs as a down payment on larger defense cuts to relieve long-term budget restraints on domestic programs.

That was the explicit goal of Budget Committee Chairman Sasser, who led the attack on the B-2, SDI and rail-mobile MX. He was powerfully seconded by Appropriations Committee Chairman Robert C. Byrd, D-W.Va.

Sasser usually had supported defense cuts, while Byrd usually had been in the opposite corner. But this time, they worked side by side.

Faced with pressing domestic needs, Byrd said, "I can no longer support these big-ticket items, which seem to have a life of their own."

In fact, the B-2 and SDI debates were early skirmishes in a battle over budget shares for defense and domestic programs in fiscal 1994-95. It was a battle that was practically guaranteed by the 1990 budget act.

The 1990 deficit-reduction act set ceilings on the amounts that could be appropriated in fiscal 1991-93 for defense, foreign aid and domestic programs. It also limited total fiscal 1994 and 1995 appropriations for those programs but without dividing the total.

Under Bush's plan, the defense budget was to decline in inflation-adjusted terms by the amounts required by the defense spending caps for fiscal 1991-93. It was to continue to decline in real terms through fiscal 1995.

But Sasser and Byrd argued that the budget act contained no restriction on cutting the defense budget even more deeply than it anticipated. "It was well-known to the negotiators [of the 1990 budget deal] that when we got to the outyears . . . there was very likely to be some competition between defense, domestic discretionary and international spending," Sasser said.

To set the stage for more defense cuts later, he argued, it was necessary then to kill expensive, long-term programs such as the B-2.

On Sept. 26, Bill Bradley, D-N.J., offered an amendment that would have required the Pentagon to submit with its fiscal 1993 budget and long-term spending plan an alternative budget proposal showing how it would accommodate an additional reduction of $80 billion.

"It's inevitable that we're going to cut the defense budget," Bradley said. "Why do it blind?"

Inouye branded the proposal a request for the Pentagon to draw up a "hit list" for its foes. The amendment was rejected 58-41. *(Vote 210, p. 28-S)*

Stealth Bomber

The controversial B-2 came before the Senate on Sept. 25 with the additional handicap of having failed one test of its ability to evade radar detection — the very rationale for its exotic and costly design and construction.

In hope of assuaging uncertainty about the test problem, the Appropriations Committee had included in the bill the $3.2 billion that Bush requested for four additional B-2s, but with the proviso that the money could not be spent until Congress approved its release in a 1992 supplemental appropriations bill.

The House versions of the defense authorization and appropriations bills included no B-2 production funds and therefore would end B-2 production with the 15 planes already funded.

After the war with Iraq, however, the plane gained some House supporters as the Air Force touted the B-2's value for precision attacks against such non-Soviet adversaries with non-nuclear weapons.

Echoing that theme on the Senate floor, Christopher S.

Bond, R-Mo., said, "It is more, not less, likely that we will be faced with conflicts around the globe. The United States . . . will need to be prepared to deal with these conflicts when they arise, and the B-2 bomber is one weapon that is well-suited."

But others cited the collapse of the historic Soviet adversary in arguing to kill the program: "The superpower that the B-2 was slated to engage is now no more," insisted Sasser.

Besides Johnston and Byrd, the senators who voted for the B-2 in August but against it Sept. 25 were Democrats Wendell H. Ford, Ky.; Terry Sanford, N.C.; John B. Breaux, La.; and Richard H. Bryan, Nev.

The senators who had opposed an effort to cut SDI funds in the authorization bill but supported the $1.1 billion cut proposed Sept. 25 were Democrats Byrd, Breaux and Kent Conrad of North Dakota.

By voice vote, the Senate adopted an amendment by Democrat Dale Bumpers of Arkansas that trimmed from $625 million to $425 million the portion of the $4.6 billion SDI appropriation that could be spent to develop the space-based interceptor missiles known as Brilliant Pebbles.

Submarine Budgets

But the Senate swamped, 10-90, a budget-driven attack on another costly weapon: an amendment by John McCain, R-Ariz., that would have killed the *Seawolf*-class nuclear submarine. *(Vote 209, p. 28-S)*

The president's budget included $1.53 billion for the third ship of that class, which was designed with the speed and firepower to leapfrog anticipated improvements in Soviet sub design. The Defense Appropriations Subcommittee objected that the *Seawolf* design was too expensive and recommended instead constructing two more of the older *Los Angeles*-class ships.

But the initiative to stop the *Seawolf* was overturned by the full Appropriations panel under strong pressure from the Navy, senators from New England and officials of General Dynamics' Electric Boat Division in Groton, Conn., which probably would build all the *Seawolf*-class ships.

So the bill reported to the Senate included the requested $1.53 billion for a *Seawolf.* It also included $375 million for components to be used in future submarines of any type.

The bill also included $50 million to develop the less expensive *Centurion*, which the Navy hoped to build by the end of the decade.

McCain's amendment would have barred constructing an additional *Seawolf*, freeing $1.8 billion in the bill to pay the costs of killing that contract, building one *Los Angeles* and developing a new sub design.

McCain ally Trent Lott, R-Miss., who said he was speaking against a weapons system for the first time in his 19 years in Congress, called the *Seawolf* "a Cold War weapon . . . overdeveloped for a post-Cold War [defense] posture."

But the four senators from Connecticut and Rhode Island touted the newer design for the new international situation.

With a higher speed, larger weapons load and quieter power plant than the *Los Angeles* type, argued Joseph I. Lieberman, D-Conn., a *Seawolf* could covertly gather intelligence, land special operations forces, lay mines or launch long-range cruise missiles in "regional" conflicts.

Middle East Politics

A Byrd amendment authorizing the Pentagon to store fuel in Israel for use by U.S. forces was adopted by voice vote. The amendment permitted Israel to draw on the supply in case of an emergency, provided the U.S. government concurred and was reimbursed by Israel.

By a vote of 99-0, an amendment by Tim Wirth, D-Colo., was adopted that required Pentagon contractors to certify that they did not participate in the Arab boycott of Israel. The skids were greased for approval of the measure when Wirth agreed to exempt contracts for the purchase of food, fuel and services. *(Vote 211, p. 28-S)*

By voice vote, a Bumpers amendment was accepted that barred imports from companies that the president certified had knowingly contributed to Iraq's development of nuclear, chemical or biological weapons.

Other Amendments

Among the other provisions added to the bill by voice vote were amendments:

- By Majority Leader George J. Mitchell, D-Maine, to earmark $5 million to operate an office of POW/MIA affairs in Hanoi, Vietnam.
- By David L. Boren, D-Okla., to establish scholarships and fellowships in foreign languages, area studies and other academic specialties relevant to national security.

The major provisions of HR 2521, as approved by the Senate follow:

Military Personnel

The bill adopted the administration's proposal to reduce the number of active-duty military personnel by more than 106,000, to 1.89 million men and women. It also included the requested 4.2 percent military pay hike.

In its report on the bill, the Appropriations Committee reluctantly agreed with the Pentagon's contention that the large personnel cuts in prospect would require the dismissal of some career service personnel before they completed the 20 years of active duty that qualified them for a pension.

To forestall such dismissals, the House included in its version of the bill $300 million more for military personnel costs than the budget requested.

Because the dollar's value had risen against many foreign currencies, the bill reduced by $197 million the amount earmarked for special allowances paid to some personnel stationed overseas.

On the other hand, HR 2521 included $69 million more than was requested because the war with Iraq had delayed the planned decommissioning of two battleships and an aircraft carrier.

More than $8 billion was appropriated for the Pentagon's medical-care programs. The Senate bill rejected House provisions to:

- Consolidate medical operations of the separate services;
- Close the military medical school;
- Earmark $2.5 million to operate a federal nursing school in collaboration with a small college in the district of House Defense Appropriations Subcommittee Chairman Murtha; and
- Reverse a planned phase-down of Letterman Army Hospital at the Presidio of San Francisco, a base that was slated to be closed. The House added to the bill $44 million to keep operating Letterman as a 185-bed hospital, instead of the 100-bed facility planned.

The bill reduced the National Guard and reserve forces

by 35,166 to a new total of 1,140,760. That was only about one-third the cutback of 107,526 sought in the president's budget. To pay the additional personnel, the Senate bill included $306 million more than the budget requested for Guard and reserve payrolls.

For arms and equipment earmarked for Guard and reserve units, the bill included $936 million that was not requested. The largest share of that was $546 million for 20 C-130 transport and tanker planes.

Operations and Maintenance

The bill provided $83.5 billion for day-to-day operations, training and maintenance, a reduction of $1.9 billion from the amount requested.

According to the Appropriations panel, more than $1.6 billion sliced from the budget request merely reflected changed economic conditions and thus had no impact on Pentagon operations. This included reductions of:

- $797 million to take account of the purchasing power of the dollar overseas;
- $400 million to draw down surplus cash that had accumulated in revolving funds that the services used to purchase supplies and industrial services;
- $238 million budgeted for civilian Pentagon jobs that were vacant because of a hiring freeze; and
- $188 million because inflation was lower than had been assumed when the budget was drawn up.

Other cuts in the Pentagon funding request were aimed at traditional targets of congressional budgeters. For example, the bill cut $78 million by trimming headquarters staffs. And it cut an additional $184 million by requiring Pentagon personnel and weapons contractors traveling on government business to take advantage of discount air fares.

The bill also denied $345 million for expenses that the Appropriations Committee said should be paid for with allied contributions to cover the cost of the Persian Gulf War.

Strategic Forces

In addition to its action on the B-2, the bill trimmed the funding requests to modify two other types of bombers already in service. For B-1s, which were built in the mid-1980s, it approved $116 million for safety-related improvements but denied $143 million requested for other modifications.

For the 1960s-vintage B-52s, it approved $31 million of the $57 million requested for modifications.

The bill included $434 million for 120 stealth cruise missiles intended to be carried by B-1Bs and $177 million to gear up for production of the shorter-range SRAM II bomber-carried missile.

No funds were provided to develop a tactical version of the nuclear-tipped SRAM II — designated SRAM-T — that was intended to be carried by fighter planes. The Pentagon had requested $34 million.

Like the Senate version of the companion defense authorization bill, the appropriations measure included $1.2 billion for 49 Trident II submarine-launched missiles — $222 million and 21 missiles more than the budget requested.

The two Senate bills also were in agreement in funding production of 12 additional MX missiles, for which the appropriations bill earmarked $371 million in new funds and $236 million in unspent money from earlier budgets.

The $4.6 billion included in the bill for anti-missile defenses was the same amount the Senate had authorized for SDI and $600 million less than the administration requested.

However, the appropriations bill deferred spending for an interceptor missile designated THAAD and a ground-based radar, both of which were intended to deal with so-called tactical (or short-range) missiles.

The appropriations bill also reduced the amount earmarked for developing anti-bomber defenses by $109 million, approving $164 million.

As requested, the bill provided $296 million to buy Titan IV satellite launchers and $222 million to buy smaller Atlas-Centaur launchers. But it sliced $98 million from the request to develop a launch rocket for extra-heavy satellites, approving $50 million. And the bill contained none of the $232 million requested to develop a space plane, designed to take off like a jetliner and fly into Earth orbit.

Ground Combat

Claiming the program was too expensive, senior Pentagon officials had resisted congressional pressure to begin converting the oldest M-1 tanks to M-1A1 models carrying a larger cannon. But the Senate appropriations bill included $225 million for such conversions.

However, the Appropriations Committee said it was skeptical of the Armed Services Committee's proposal for a more expensive program, which would further upgrade the tanks to M-1A2s carrying more sophisticated electronic gear so that they could operate at night. Because the Persian Gulf War had shown the superiority of the M-1A1 over any existing tank, the Appropriations panel contended, the purpose of the upgrade program was not so much to improve the combat power of the tanks as it was to keep the tank plants in business pending development of a future tank.

But that new tank — the block III — was a less pressing military necessity than a new mobile cannon, the committee insisted. So it trimmed $125 million from the funding requested to develop the block III and boosted by $63 million (to $111 million) funding to develop a new cannon.

So the Army could field some lightweight mobile cannons pending development of the new gun, the bill included the $43 million requested to select such a weapon "off the shelf" to replace the obsolescent Sheridan light tanks used by the 82nd Airborne Division.

To develop the Comanche combat helicopter armed with anti-tank missiles (formerly designated LHX), the bill provided $500 million, trimming from the request $8 million earmarked for adding to its design a new target-finding radar dubbed Longbow.

But the bill also included the $233 million requested to develop Longbow, which was to be added to existing Apache attack helicopters.

To arm existing scout helicopters, the bill included $139 million, a reduction of $45 million from the budget request.

For the two most powerful anti-tank missiles in service, the bill approved the amounts requested: $201 million for 10,000 TOWs, launched from helicopters, various ground vehicles and simple tripod launchers; and $20 million for 112 larger Hellfires, carried by Apache helicopters.

The bill also fully funded development of two new tank-killers: It approved the $152 million requested for the LOSAT, carrying ultra-high-speed rockets designed to punch through a tank's armor. And it also approved the use of $25 million left over from earlier budgets to restart work on the FOG-M missile, which had been suspended. A TV camera in the nose of the FOG-M was linked by a hair-thin fiber-optic cable to a ground operator, who could direct the missile onto a tank miles away.

The administration's budget sought to end production of the 20-mile-range MLRS artillery rocket. But the Senate bill included $134 million to continue production of the rockets, averting the need to negotiate a multi-year production contract.

Because the existing contract was preserved, $160 million could purchase 52 launchers for MLRS rockets, compared with $178 million to buy 43 launchers in the president's budget request.

For 300 longer-range ATACMS bombardment rockets, the bill included $147 million, a $4 million reduction from the request.

To speed up development of an anti-aircraft version of the large armored cars used by the Marine Corps, the bill increased funds for the program by $7 million, to $28 million.

As requested, the bill included $133 million to buy 149 anti-aircraft systems consisting of clusters of Stinger missiles mounted on the backs of pickup trucks.

Air Combat

The bill slowed the Navy's project to refurbish its carrier air squadrons. The plans were drawn up after Defense Secretary Cheney canceled in January 1991 the planned A-12 bomber, which had been intended to replace the 1970s-vintage A-6Es that were currently deployed on carriers.

For the near term, the Navy's plan was to buy additional F/A-18s, designed to hit both air and ground targets. By the late 1990s, the Navy hoped to develop and begin building enlarged F/A-18s — the E and F models — which would replace the aging F-14s that were deployed as long-range interceptors. A new carrier-based bomber to replace the A-6, designated A-X, was to enter service early in the next decade. *(A-12 bomber, p. 431)*

But the Appropriations Committee questioned the need to expand the F/A-18 fleet, considering that the Navy was retiring at least two carriers. Instead of the 48 F/A-18s requested in the budget (costing $1.98 billion), the appropriations bill funded only 39 of the planes ($1.78 billion).

Moreover, the panel warned that future Navy budgets likely could not afford to develop both the F/A-18 E/F models and the A-X. The panel strongly suggested that it wanted the Navy to pick an A-X design that could handle both ground and air targets, thus eliminating the need to develop the F/A-18 E/F for the air-combat role.

The bill reduced the F/A-18 E/F development program by $133 million, providing $250 million.

Like the budget request, the Senate bill included no funds to modernize F-14s into F-14Ds with more powerful engines and radars. The House appropriations bill included $331 million for that project.

Consistent with the Senate authorization bill, the Senate appropriations measure provided none of the 48 F-16 Air Force fighters requested in the budget ($1.07 billion), thus terminating that program. Instead, the bill added to the budget $1.03 billion for 24 additional F-117 stealth fighters.

The bill also provided $100 million to develop and install on F-117s reconnaissance equipment that could instantaneously transmit back to headquarters detailed pictures of ground targets. During the gulf war, U.S. commanders complained that it took too long to develop the pictures taken by Vietnam War-era reconnaissance jets.

Though the administration planned no further production of F-15E fighters in 1992 or beyond, the bill included a provision ordering the Pentagon to buy an additional 12 planes with the proceeds of a sale to Saudi Arabia of 24 older-model F-15s.

The bill also included $772 million, not requested, to buy spare parts and support equipment for the additional planes.

It also added to the bill $5.5 million to equip U.S. fighters with advanced video recorders so that the results of their bomb attacks could be assessed more accurately.

The bill included $703 million for 891 AMRAAM air-to-air missiles, used by Navy and Air Force fighters, a reduction of $271 million (300 missiles) from the budget request.

It also included the $89 million requested to develop a longer-range air-to-air missile, designated AAAM.

On the other hand, it included only $14 million of the $26 million requested to develop new versions of the short-range Sidewinder air-to-air missile, urging the Air Force to concentrate on modest improvements while deferring a more radical redesign.

The budget requested $324 million for more than 1,200 HARM anti-radar missiles, but the bill provided no funds. The committee recommended that additional purchases be deferred because a less expensive version of the missile was nearing production.

Naval Forces

The bill's $7.72 billion appropriation for shipbuilding was $768 million less than the budget request. The largest single reduction was the omission of the $540 million requested for a large fuel and ammunition ship designed to resupply in mid-ocean an aircraft carrier and its escorts. Noting that the Navy had diverted to other purposes the funds appropriated for this ship in the fiscal 1991 budget, the committee reasoned that the service placed a low priority on the supply vessel.

One potentially controversial provision involved funds appropriated in fiscal 1991: Congress had earmarked money to put the aircraft carrier *John F. Kennedy* through the Philadelphia Naval Shipyard's service life extension program (SLEP), a thorough reconstruction intended to render the ship fit for 15 more years of service.

But Navy officials insisted that a less expensive overhaul, good for an additional five years of service — and providing fewer jobs at the Philadelphia facility — would suffice because the Navy planned to reduce the number of carriers in service.

The Senate bill included a provision approving use of the SLEP funds for an overhaul at Philadelphia. But the provision, crafted by Arlen Specter, R-Pa., also stipulated that the overhaul render the carrier fit for service through the year 2010.

For five destroyers equipped with the Aegis anti-aircraft system, the bill included $4.09 billion, a reduction of only $74 million from the request.

The bill included $415 million for 525 Standard anti-aircraft missiles and $454 million for 236 Tomahawk long-range cruise missiles, designed to attack ships and land targets. Both amounts met the budget request.

As requested, the bill included nearly half a billion dollars to buy anti-sub torpedoes: $221 million for the one-ton Mark 48s, carried only by submarines, and $262 million for 246 of the smaller Mark 50s, which were carried by helicopters and planes.

It also included $20 million to develop a guided missile that could be fired from warships or submarines at distant, submerged subs.

For 18 Seahawk sub-hunting helicopters, carried by many types of warships, the bill included $408 million, as requested.

To develop improvements for the fleet of P-3C land-based patrol planes, the bill included $51 million, a $10 million increase over the budget request. The Appropriations panel ruled out as too expensive a planned upgrade of the planes' electronics, but added funds to develop new engines.

Noting problems that the Navy and Marine Corps had clearing Iraqi mines in the Persian Gulf, the Appropriations Committee made minesweeping a priority in the bill. The measure included funds for three minesweepers ($361 million) rather than the two requested ($261 million). Moreover, it increased by $34 million the amount earmarked for developing anti-mine countermeasures, including Magic Lantern, a helicopter-borne laser to hunt underwater mines.

Air and Sea Transport

Four additional C-17 long-range cargo planes were funded by the bill ($1.42 billion) rather than the six planes requested, a reduction of $551 million. But the measure included the $377 million requested to continue development of the wide-body jet, the prototype of which made its first flight in September 1991.

It included the $257 million requested to upgrade the Army's Chinook cargo helicopters. But it provided funds for only 47 new Blackhawk troop-carrying helicopters ($251 million), a reduction of 13 aircraft and $83 million from the request.

The bill added to the budget $2 billion to be spent on cargo ships intended to support the rapid deployment of ground-combat units to distant trouble spots.

With only minor reductions, the measure funded administration requests for amphibious vessels designed to land Marine Corps combat units on enemy-held beaches. It provided $241 million for a so-called LSD built to carry tanks and other heavy combat gear as well as the barges to haul them ashore. And it included $254 million for a dozen air-cushion landing barges, built to carry a tank at up to 50 mph.

Pursuant to the budget request, the bill transferred $165 million appropriated in prior budgets for the V-22 Osprey to fund continued development of that aircraft in fiscal 1992. The Osprey was a hybrid airplane/helicopter designed to haul Marine troops ashore. Since 1989, Cheney had tried to kill the program on budgetary grounds, although it had vigorous congressional support.

The bill also included $575 million to resume production of the CH-46E, which the Osprey was intended to replace. This allowed the Marines to replace some of their aging CH-46Es while Congress and the Pentagon continued to wrestle over the Osprey.

Cheney proposed the larger CH-53E helicopter to replace the V-22, but the bill included none of the $455 million requested for 32 of those craft. The measure did, however, add to the budget $129 million for four CH-53Es modified to serve as minesweepers.

Other Provisions

The bill included the $1.25 billion requested for the Defense Environmental Restoration Account (DERA), which funded the Pentagon's long-term plan to clean up toxic waste on military bases. But the bill earmarked $69 million to be used solely to clean up bases that were being closed.

In addition to the DERA funds, the bill included $885 million for environmental restoration, which the Appropriations Committee said should be used for actual cleanup operations rather than for studies and analysis.

For military drug interdiction operations, the bill included $1.12 billion of the $1.16 billion requested. However, the Senate allowance included $58 million for the Defense Department to take over certain airborne anti-smuggling radars run by the Coast Guard.

The bill also included funds for other operations which, the administration insisted, were not properly covered by the defense budget, including $318 million for other Coast Guard operations and $75 million for support of National Science Foundation research in Antarctica.

The bill also included:

- $289 million, not requested, to pay damage claims by U.S. personnel evacuated from the Philippines when Mount Pinatubo erupted.
- $28 million for AIDS research by the military, a $25 million increase over the budget request.
- A provision requiring that closed military bases be given free to state or local governments. Through fiscal 1995, according to the Bush administration, this could cost the Pentagon $1.9 billion in anticipated revenues that had been earmarked to fund future base closures.

CONFERENCE ACTION

The $271 billion version of HR 2521 that was wrapped up Nov. 15 by Senate-House conferees funded most major weapons as requested in Bush's budget, with the few major exceptions that had been hammered out in the companion defense authorization bill.

HR 2521 echoed the authorization measure by including $1.8 billion to keep alive the production line for the controversial B-2 stealth bomber but approving no funds to begin work on additional planes beyond the 15 previously authorized. Similarly, the bill appropriated $4.15 billion of the $5.2 billion requested to develop anti-missile defenses under SDI.

However, the appropriations conferees rejected a Senate-backed initiative in the authorization bill that would have resumed production of the F-117, a small stealth bomber used successfully in the Persian Gulf War.

Combined with amounts provided in other appropriations bills covering military construction projects and defense nuclear programs conducted by the Energy Department, HR 2521 brought the total defense budget for fiscal 1992 to $291 billion, essentially the amount requested.

Guard and Reserve Cuts

On one of the most highly charged issues facing the conferees, they approved a reduction of only 37,000 members in the politically influential National Guard and reserves. This was about one-third as deep a cut as the administration sought.

However, the conference report also gave the Pentagon leeway to cut Guard and reserve manpower by an additional 2 percent, permitting a total cutback in fiscal 1992 of roughly 60,000.

The House and Senate each had approved the budget

proposal to cut by 106,000 the armed services' active-duty payroll of 1.9 million members. But House Defense Appropriations Subcommittee Chairman Murtha and others balked at the recommended cut of nearly 108,000, or about 10 percent, in Guard and reserve manpower.

Far from approving the requested reduction, the House version of the appropriations bill would have mandated a slight increase in the Guard and reserves.

Murtha said Nov. 15 that the provision approved by the conferees protected the Guard and reserves from draconian cuts for a year.

"You can't cut all regulars and not cut reserves, particularly the [Guard and reserve] units that are related to regular units," he acknowledged. But before Congress approved any far-reaching cutback in Guard and reserve forces, he added, "we want to see a plan first."

House Defense Subcommittee member Norm Dicks, D-Wash., who backed the administration on the Guard and reserve issue, applauded the conference deal as "a significant step in the right direction." However, he predicted that Congress would approve deeper Guard and reserve reductions in future years only if it could insulate the process from constituent pressures to save local jobs.

"We're going to have to have another commission," Dicks said, referring to the commission established in 1990 that had greased the skids to close domestic military bases.

Abortions Overseas

In the face of a veto threat by Bush, the conferees dropped a Senate provision that would have permitted military personnel and dependents stationed overseas to obtain abortions in military hospitals, if they paid for the procedure.

Such abortions had been allowed until 1988, when the Reagan administration banned them by administrative order. *(Abortion issue, p. 339)*

In May 1991, the House voted 220-208 to add to the defense authorization bill an amendment by Les AuCoin, D-Ore., allowing such privately funded abortions overseas. The Senate approved the same provision with 58 votes in support, but the amendment was withdrawn on Aug. 2 under threat of a filibuster.

Abortion rights advocates had agreed to drop the provision from the defense authorization conference report but pinned their hopes on securing its inclusion in the defense appropriations measure.

"We know the president doesn't want to veto the defense [appropriations] bill," said Linda Heller Kamm of the Women's Legal Defense Fund.

Sen. Frank R. Lautenberg, D-N.J., added the overseas abortion provision to the Senate version of the appropriations bill. In the House, it faced strong opposition from Murtha and was dropped on procedural grounds.

AuCoin and Lautenberg protested Nov. 15 that their opponents had killed the provision in conference by lining up the votes of senior members of the Senate and House Appropriations committees. The chairmen and ranking members sat on all subcommittees ex officio but rarely played an active role in conferences on the annual defense bill.

"What was said to servicewomen," Lautenberg said, "is that your rights are different from other Americans'." ■

Domestic Military Projects Win Out

The Senate on Oct. 16 cleared an $8.56 billion measure to fund construction projects and family housing at U.S. military facilities.

The military construction appropriations bill for fiscal 1992 (HR 2426) was sent to the president on a 99-0 vote. The House on Oct. 8 had approved the conference report on the bill by voice vote.

The measure was $55.7 million less than President Bush had requested and about $200 million more than Congress appropriated in fiscal 1991. It included funds to close domestic military bases that had been deemed surplus and to clean up environmental problems at the facilities. *(Fiscal 1991 appropriations, 1990 Almanac, p. 826)*

Congress reduced the funding the administration had sought for overseas bases, shifting more funds to domestic projects and in particular to facilities for the National Guard and reserves.

Like the fiscal 1991 military construction bill, the measure opposed U.S. contributions toward a NATO air base being built at Crotone, Italy. "We simply do not need to build a new full-service air base in southern Italy when we will be closing bases all over Europe and inside the United States," Jim Sasser, D-Tenn., chairman of the Appropriations Subcommittee on Military Construction, told the Senate.

BOXSCORE

➡ **Fiscal 1992 military construction appropriations (HR 2426).** The bill provided $8.56 billion in funds for construction projects and housing at U.S. military facilities.

Reports: H Rept 102-74; S Rept 102-147; conference report filed in the House, H Rept 102-236.

KEY ACTION

May 30 — HR 2426 passed the **House** by a vote of 392-18.

Sept. 16 — HR 2426 passed the **Senate** by voice vote.

Oct. 3 — HR 2426 approved by **House-Senate** conference.

Oct. 8 — **House** approved conference report by voice vote.

Oct. 16 — **Senate** approved conference report by a vote of 99-0.

Oct. 25 — President Bush signed HR 2426 — PL 102-136.

HOUSE COMMITTEE ACTION

Keeping Pentagon dollars at home was a prominent theme in the debate on the military construction spending bill reported May 22 by the House Appropriations Committee.

As approved by the committee, HR 2426 cut more than $240 million from the administration's budget request for overseas construction. But those cuts were more than offset by funds added to the bill for domestic facilities, including $189 million for the politically well-connected National Guard and reserves.

President Bush requested a military construction appropriation of $8.14 billion. But in his request for the companion appropriations bill covering the bulk of the Pentagon budget, he sought an additional $420 million for construction and repair of facilities. *(Defense appropriations, p. 621)*

The House Appropriations and Armed Services panels both treated the additional sum as part of a military construction request totaling $8.56 billion.

The bill approved by the Appropriations panel May 22 funded $8.67 billion worth of projects.

But of that total, $190 million would come from rescinding appropriations made in earlier budgets, mostly from strategic weapons projects that the Bush administration had canceled.

Taking account of the funds made available by the rescissions and other minor bookkeeping adjustments, the bill drafted by the Military Construction Appropriations Subcommittee provided $8.48 billion in new budget authority — $121 million more than was appropriated in fiscal 1991 but $85 million less than Bush requested.

The Appropriations Committee approved the subcommittee's bill with only minor amendments by voice vote.

Burden-Sharing

In its most sweeping action to cut U.S. construction spending overseas, the committee, following the lead of House Armed Services, approved only $159 million of the $359 million requested for the annual U.S. contribution to NATO's so-called infrastructure fund.

U.S. contributions were supposed to account for 28 percent of the fund, which was used to build facilities of benefit to the alliance. Previously, infrastructure funds were earmarked almost exclusively for projects in Europe. But for fiscal 1991, according to the Appropriations panel, $100 million was programmed for projects in the United States.

Among programs for which the committee denied Bush's appropriations request was one that the panel said would be paid for by the NATO funds: a $36.5 million project to replace some trestles at a Navy ammunition loading port at Earle, N.J.

The committee approved $171 million of the $214 million requested for specific projects in foreign countries. The bill included only $2.5 million of the $21.8 million requested for projects in South Korea. The South Korean government had offered to subsidize construction of U.S. military facilities on its territory, and the House panel urged the Pentagon to propose legislation that would clear the way for such an arrangement.

The bill contained no provisions related to a NATO-funded air base at Crotone, Italy. It was intended to house a wing of U.S. fighter planes being evicted by the Spanish government from a base near Madrid. The House-passed version of the defense authorization bill included a provision to bar using any funds to transfer the U.S. unit.

The committee approved $759 million to pay for shutting down superfluous military bases and transferring units to other installations, a $25 million increase over Bush's request.

Within that total, the panel earmarked $201 million, $25 million more than requested, to clean up toxic and hazardous wastes on abandoned sites.

HOUSE FLOOR ACTION

The House approved HR 2426 May 30, providing $8.5 billion in fiscal 1992 for construction of military facilities and family housing.

Continued on p. 644

Military Construction

(In thousands of dollars)

	Fiscal 1991 Appropriation	President's Request [1]	House Bill	Senate Bill	Final Bill
Military Construction					
Army	$ 746,137	$ 870,170	$ 877,585	$ 798,770	$ 880,820
Navy	1,132,608	879,420	848,429	878,211	883,859
Air Force	949,094	1,151,020	1,129,420	967,570	1,005,954
Defense agencies	601,288	725,700	745,990	654,330	724,740
NATO infrastructure	192,700	358,800	158,800	254,400	225,000
National Guard and reserves	690,117	281,400	470,531	662,703	628,672
Subtotal	**$ 4,069,488**	**$ 4,266,510**	**$ 4,230,755**	**$ 4,215,984**	**$ 4,349,045**
Family housing					
Army	1,538,267	1,534,425	1,579,245	1,508,975	1,557,245
Navy	866,018	879,900	908,140	860,900	902,140
Air Force	934,399	1,093,800	1,085,983	991,283	1,075,283
Defense agencies	21,014	26,200	26,200	26,200	26,200
Homeowners Assistance Fund	5,100	84,000	84,000	84,000	84,000
Subtotal	**$ 3,364,798**	**$ 3,618,325**	**$ 3,683,568**	**$ 3,471,358**	**$ 3,644,868**
Base realignment and closure	**$ 998,100**	**$ 733,600**	**$ 758,600**	**$ 971,600**	**$ 758,600**
TOTALS					
Appropriation	8,674,840	8,618,435	8,672,923	8,658,942	8,752,513
Rescissions [2]	−312,419	—	−189,792	−189,792	−189,792
Debt reduction	−250	−125	−125	−125	−125
Net New Budget Authority	**$8,362,171**	**$ 8,563,030**	**$ 8,483,006**	**$ 8,469,025**	**$8,562,596**

[1] *Includes $420,230,000 that the president requested for the companion defense appropriations bill but was transferred by the House Appropriations Committee.*
[2] *Rescissions of prior-year appropriations are subtracted from individual accounts.*

SOURCE: House Appropriations Committee

Military Construction Provisions

The bill, HR 2426, paid for the cost of building military bases in the United States and around the world, for housing military personnel and their families and — in an activity that began in 1989 and was certain to become more common in the future — for the cost of closing unneeded military bases. So even as the size of the military had started to decrease, the bill's $8.75 billion was close to fiscal 1991's $8.67 billion.

CONSTRUCTION PROJECTS

Loaded into this category — which received $4.16 billion in fiscal 1992 — were many popular construction projects that a member of Congress could bring home to his or her district. Most of the funds would end up being contracted out to local companies to build the various structures on the military bases.

Hospitals

The bill appropriated $223.8 million for hospital construction projects in fiscal 1992. (This did not include funds provided to improve or replace hospitals that were affected by base closings, which were in a separate base closings account.)

The Pentagon maintained 125 hospitals across the country that provided free medical care to members of the military and their dependents and to retired military personnel. Construction of hospitals was one of the big-ticket items in the annual military construction bill. Many of the hospitals were multimillion-dollar projects whose funding was spread over several years.

For example, a replacement for Portsmouth Naval Hospital in Virginia received $40 million in fiscal 1992. But that covered only Phase III of the operation. In fiscal 1990 and 1991, Congress appropriated $48.5 million for the first two phases of the hospital replacement. When it is finished, the hospital will have cost $301.5 million over the seven years of construction.

- **Other projects.** Major hospital projects and their fiscal 1992 funding included $34 million for a new hospital for the Marines at Cherry Point, N.C., and $37 million for a new hospital complex for the Army's Fort Sam Houston, Texas.

Barracks

Despite a planned 25 percent reduction in troop levels over the next five years, Congress and the Pentagon wanted to spend hundreds of millions of dollars to repair troop housing and to build new barracks.

Barracks is housing for "unaccompanied" or single members of the military. Congress appropriated $287.5 million for barracks construction. That covered 42 projects in 18 states.

House and Senate reports emphasized their opinion that the quality of life for members of the military constantly needed improvement, even in an era of shrinking forces.

• **Major projects.** The costs for barracks projects in fiscal 1992 ranged from $30.2 million to modernize the quarters at Fort Hood in Texas to $997,000 for a training site and officer and enlisted quarters at Camp Rilea Army National Guard in Oregon.

Reserve and National Guard

Virtually every year, the president's military construction request undergoes major surgery by the House and Senate. One of the major operations transfers money from overseas construction projects to build structures for the popular reserve and National Guard troops back home. Fiscal 1992 was no different.

Congress appropriated $629 million for non-active duty forces, more than twice the amount requested by President Bush. The funds went for construction of training facilities, maintenance shops for on-site weapons and storage buildings.

Of the $629 million for the National Guard and reserves, $71.85 million went for new armories at 30 sites across the country. For Guard and reserve troops, an armory functions as a drill hall and also contains offices.

Special Weapons Construction

To accommodate new military planes, weapons and other hardware, specialized structures frequently are needed. Each new plane calls for different types of runways and hangars, for example. To keep up with technology, the military construction bill funded projects to house the new weapons that were purchased through the defense appropriations bill.

• **C-17 facilities.** The fiscal 1992 bill included $55.1 million for specialized construction for the new C-17 airplane at Altus Air Force Base in Oklahoma. That money would build a 9,000-foot runway for the cargo plane ($30 million), a corrosion control and maintenance shop especially for the C-17 ($13.8 million), more airplane parking spots with access to fueling hydrants ($6.7 million), and parachute packing and maintenance space ($3.8 million).

Charleston Air Force Base in South Carolina also got funds for construction to support the C-17: $21.9 million to support a fire and crash rescue station for the cargo plane and to add more parking spaces for the plane next to fueling hydrants.

• **B-2 facilities.** Particular appropriations can get bogged down because of fights over the weapons systems that they are designed to accommodate. In fiscal 1992, the Bush administration requested $49.5 million for special construction at Whiteman Air Force Base in Missouri to help house the new, controversial B-2 stealth bomber. Neither the House nor the Senate approved full funding of this request because of questions about the future of the bomber. Conferees agreed to give the president $29.5 million for the Missouri project.

• **Other projects.** Major special weapons construction funds included: $80 million for construction of a testing site for solid-propellant (J-6) rocket motors at Arnold Engineering Development Center, Tenn., and $39 million for new hangars for the F-117A fighter plane at Holloman Air Force Base in New Mexico.

Child-Care Centers

These centers are a new feature on many military bases. The Pentagon justified the centers in its budget documents as "a necessary element in today's volunteer force, as their availability alleviates many problems incurred by military parents who are single, who both work or who have other special needs."

Each center was relatively inexpensive in comparison with other military facilities in the bill. Congress appropriated $42.8 million for construction of 18 child-care centers in fiscal 1992. They ranged from a $4 million project at the Orlando Naval Training Center in Florida to build two centers to $900,000 for one center at Fort Story in Virginia that would accommodate about 60 children.

Physical Fitness Centers

Not surprisingly, the military is concerned with the shape its soldiers are in, and most U.S. domestic bases have physical training centers.

These gyms have the typical equipment — stationary bicycles, treadmills and weight-training apparatus. The bill for fiscal 1992 gave $33.9 million to the military for construction and improvements on these centers.

Overseas Construction

For construction projects overseas, the bill provided $811.3 million. Of that, $368 million went for projects that were too small to be listed separately but together with other overseas construction projects made up close to 10 percent of the bill's costs. The measure also included nearly $21 million for classified overseas construction.

The bill provided $198 million for specific construction projects abroad.

• **Kwajalein Atoll.** The biggest project — $47.4 million for Kwajalein Atoll in the Pacific — would provide housing for 100 personnel ($9.6 million), add an electric power generator ($33 million), build a cold storage warehouse for frozen and chilled food products ($10.2 million) and build a controlled-humidity warehouse for food, supplies and equipment that were temperature- or humidity-sensitive ($9.9 million) and several other items. President Bush had originally asked for $77.4 million for this project. While members gave him only $47.4 million of that, they did not specify how the reduction should be apportioned among the various improvements.

Kwajalein was an Army base that primarily conducted intelligence operations. Existing housing at the base was old, cramped and uncomfortable. That, plus the isolation of the base (located about 2,000 miles southwest of Hawaii), had led to high turnover in staff.

• **NATO fund.** The bill would also provide $225 million for NATO's infrastructure fund, the pooled contributions that paid for construction of bases used by the North Atlantic Treaty Alliance.

Miscellaneous

The measure included $85.5 million for construction of water-pollution controls and another $30 million to make operations at bases more energy-efficient. The rest of the construction funds not otherwise accounted for paid for projects such as new roads, upkeep on firing ranges and fire stations.

• **By service.** The Army received $881 million for military construction in fiscal 1992, the Navy got $884 million, and the Air Force received $1 billion.

FAMILY HOUSING

Because of the low pay for members of the military, Congress and the executive branch consistently supplemented military paychecks with benefits such as imminent danger pay to make serving in the armed forces more attractive. One such perquisite was government aid in finding and paying for housing.

Depending on the location, the military would either provide housing on-base for a soldier and his or her family or give an allowance to help pay for housing in the surrounding civilian community.

Once on-base housing was full, the services looked first to communities that surrounded the base. But in some cases, renting or buying existing houses was very expensive, and construction of more government-owned buildings was considered a better value.

The Pentagon asked for $3.62 billion for construction of family housing, operations and maintenance costs and rental expenses for fiscal 1992, $324 million more than appropriated in fiscal 1991.

That amount would fund construction of 1,503 new units of housing. The military owned a total of 377,249 units of housing in fiscal 1990.

Congress approved $3.64 billion, buying 2,113 new housing units.

Construction

Of the funds for housing, $537.9 million would go to pay for construction of new family housing projects, improvements to existing housing and planning and design costs.

• **Oahu housing.** Reports accompanying the bill highlighted in particular the situation in Oahu, Hawaii. The cost of living, and especially the high cost of housing on the island, had seriously affected the lives of members of the military stationed there.

According to the Senate report, "To rent quarters [in] the local economy, families must expend 40 to 55 percent of their total monthly household income. . . . Today, the families of junior enlisted personnel of all military services comprise the most numerous user group of food stamps on Oahu."

Both the House and Senate provided money to build more military homes on Oahu — $41.5 million and $16.5 million, respectively. The final bill gave the Pentagon $41.5 million for 360 units of family housing for the Army on the island.

• **Other projects.** Examples of family housing expenditures in fiscal 1992 included: $11.6 million for an additional 130 units of housing at Hill Air Force Base in Utah and $29.8 million to build 260 units of housing for naval personnel in San Diego. The base had 6,289 units, which met only 15 percent of the demand for family housing.

Operation Costs

The government picked up the tab for running the housing. Military personnel living in on-base housing paid neither rent nor utilities. The cost for utilities in fiscal 1992 was $768 million.

For other maintenance costs, which made up the bulk of family housing expenditures, Congress appropriated $2.25 billion.

The money went for items such as furniture ($155 million) and management costs ($199 million) associated with the base housing. That account also paid for off-base family housing units that the Pentagon leased for members of the military ($593 million).

• **Homeowners' assistance.** The bill included $84 million for the Homeowners Assistance Fund. That account helped members of the military who, because of base closings or related activities, had to sell their houses at a loss. Owners were able to recapture up to 95 percent of the value of their houses through this assistance.

• **By service:** The bill appropriated $1.6 billion for Army family housing, $902 million for the Navy and $1.1 billion for the Air Force.

Base Closings

In order to save money, you have to spend money — at least, that was the prevailing wisdom when it came to closing U.S. military bases.

• **1989 closing list.** Congress in 1989 approved a list of 86 military bases for closure or realignment; that process would cost $658.6 million in fiscal 1992.

Although neither the Senate nor the House report detailed how this money was to be spent, the following breakdown was in the Pentagon budget justification submitted in February:

Of the $658.6 million, $341.7 million was slated to go to the Army for eight consolidation moves resulting from the base closures.

The Air Force got $265.9 million for closures at five bases. And the Navy portion of the total was $19.8 million for two projects.

When a base was closed, whatever medical facilities were on the base generally were closed. That frequently meant that other military medical facilities surrounding the base got a bigger workload and thus needed more space. In fiscal 1992, $33.4 million was given to the Pentagon from the base closings account to pay for upgrades and new construction at military hospitals.

More than a quarter of the base closing costs came from the need to clean up environmental problems on the installations before they could be used for anything else. Many of the bases had enormous environmental problems, requiring intensive cleanup efforts. The bill required the Pentagon to spend at least $220 million of the $658.6 million on environmental restoration, more than twice what was spent in fiscal 1991.

• **1991 closing list.** Congress set up a second base closing account in 1990 as part of the fiscal 1991 defense authorization (PL 101-510). This account would be used for the closing of 34 bases that were thus approved earlier in 1991. Because the Bush administration did not know when it prepared its budget which bases would be approved for closure, the Pentagon asked for $100 million for this account for planning and design costs, surveys and community planning.

Congress appropriated $100 million for this account, but it warned the Defense Department that more funds would be needed in future fiscal years to speed up the environmental cleanup at the bases that were being closed. ■

Continued from p. 640

The popular measure, which was the second of the 13 annual appropriations bills to be considered by the House in 1991, was approved, 392-18, after a brief debate. *(Vote 121, p. 30-H)*

The bill reduced by $200 million the $359 million requested for the annual U.S. contribution to NATO's infrastructure fund.

It appropriated $759 million for costs associated with shutting down U.S. military bases, $25 million more than requested. Of this amount, at least $201 million was set aside for toxic and hazardous waste cleanup at abandoned sites.

The bill also provided $78 million more than requested for family housing projects and $189 million more for National Guard and reserve construction. The latter amount was $220 million less than appropriated in fiscal 1991.

"We can and have cut military construction, but it cannot be axed," said Bill Lowery of California, ranking Republican on the Military Construction Appropriations Subcommittee.

The bill provided $40 million, $10 million less than requested, for construction of a facility to house the B-2 bomber at Whiteman Air Force Base in Missouri.

SENATE COMMITTEE ACTION

The fiscal 1992 military construction spending bill that the Senate Appropriations Committee approved Sept. 12 substantially "altered priorities" in the president's budget request, said subcommittee Chairman Sasser.

The committee unanimously approved the $8.4 billion measure with little debate and no amendments.

The Senate bill provided $8.673 billion in new budget authority, with almost $190 million coming from rescissions of prior-year appropriations. That was $149 million less than the president's request and $69 million less than the House-passed version of HR 2426. The fiscal 1992 figure compared with a fiscal 1991 total of $8.36 billion.

The panel slashed more than $250 million from the president's overseas construction requests.

Military Construction Subcommittee Chairman Sasser categorized much of the Bush administration's foreign construction plans as "extravagant" in light of the end of the Cold War and the disintegration of the Soviet Union.

The bill was not formally considered by the subcommittee. Panel members could not find a time to meet before the markup, Sasser said.

Instead, the subcommittee voted in writing, 6-0, to report the bill to the full committee.

Of the $8.4 billion in the bill, $3.5 billion was for family housing construction for the military.

The Senate committee's single deepest cut was from funding for the NATO infrastructure account. The Senate panel pared that to $254 million, a middle ground between the $358.8 million requested by Bush and the House-passed figure of $158.8 million.

The savings were redirected to facilities for the popular National Guard and reserve forces, with an instruction to Defense Secretary Dick Cheney by committee members to send them a detailed overseas base plan.

As in past years, the committee opposed the use of U.S. funds for the NATO air base under construction in Crotone, Italy. "The bottom line is we're closing bases all over the United States" said Texas Republican Phil Gramm, ranking member of the Military Construction panel, in explaining why he opposed the Crotone project.

One of the biggest increases the panel made to the Bush budget and the House bill was for the closure of domestic military bases. The panel approved $970 million to close bases in fiscal 1992, $238 million more than Bush wanted and $213 million more than the House version.

In the report accompanying the bill, members noted that the Defense Base Closure and Realignment Commission estimated that it would take $4.1 billion to close bases on the list it approved in 1991. Members provided the additional money to speed up the closing process and allow affected communities to reuse the property as soon as possible.

SENATE FLOOR ACTION

Showing why the annual spending bill for military construction rarely encountered resistance on Capitol Hill, the Senate on Sept. 16 passed an $8.47 billion version of HR 2426.

The measure, approved by voice vote after less than an hour of debate, provided funds for building hospitals, schools and child-care centers across the nation. One amendment, offered by Minority Leader Bob Dole, R-Kan., funded such projects at McConnell Air Force Base in Wichita, Kan.

Although it added $55 million to the bill's total, the Senate approved Dole's amendment by voice vote. The base suffered severe tornado damage in April. The storms rendered a school and a hospital useless and left many members of the military without houses, Dole said.

Though funds for the air base were also contained in a supplemental spending bill for fiscal 1991, President Bush had threatened to veto that measure. Dole sought to ensure that the base would get the money by adding it to the military construction bill. *(1991 supplemental, p. 668)*

The bill was otherwise virtually unchanged from the recommendations of the Senate Appropriations Committee.

The Senate bill contained $44.85 million for construction projects in West Virginia. The Bush request and the House-passed version of the bill contained only $550,000 for the home state of Robert C. Byrd, Democratic chairman of the Senate Appropriations Committee.

The Pentagon had said it would seek $4.2 million for West Virginia in the future but had no plans for the remainder of Byrd's wish list.

The Senate bill provided $25.1 million to the military base in Martinsburg, W.Va., for construction of support facilities for C-130 cargo aircraft.

But another plane, the controversial B-2 stealth bomber, was not so well provided for. The Senate bill appropriated none of the $49.5 million that the Pentagon wanted to house the B-2 at Whiteman Air Force Base in Missouri.

The House included $39.5 million for the B-2 facility.

In their report, members of the Senate Military Construction Appropriations Subcommittee said they would review the B-2 request again once the conferees on the fiscal 1992 defense authorization bill (HR 2100) had reached a decision on procurement of the bomber. *(Defense authorization, p. 393)*

Another item to be dealt with by the House-Senate conference was how much to appropriate to clean up military bases slated to close over the following five years. The Senate bill contained $971.6 million for this, $213 million more than the House measure.

"If anyone ever thought closing bases would be cheap, I think they now realize they are living in a dream world," said Sasser.

The additional funds were for the "acceleration of environmental cleanup activities," he said. And he urged the Pentagon to include more funds in its base-closing accounts for fiscal 1993.

Another issue that was to be decided in conference was whether to provide funds for construction of a trestle at Earle Naval Weapons Station in New Jersey. While the House denied funds for the project, the Senate provided the full $36.5 million request. The base was used by NATO forces, and the alliance was to pay 50 percent of the construction costs for the Navy ammunition loading port.

CONFERENCE

House and Senate conferees took only seven minutes Oct. 3 to adopt a compromise version of HR 2426. The committee staff had crafted compromises on more than 300 items that were in disagreement on the $8.5 billion bill.

The conference went by so quickly that Lowery, ranking member on the House Appropriations subcommittee, nearly missed it by arriving a few minutes late.

One of the few topics of discussion at the conference was technical language concerning a new road into Andrews Air Force Base in Maryland. At issue was a waiver that was left out of the draft version but that House subcommittee Chairman W. G. "Bill" Hefner, D-N.C., wanted included.

The provision was to waive a requirement that the secretary of Defense certify the need for the road project at Andrews. The $6 million for the project was already included in the bill, but the waiver provision that conferees adopted was necessary to proceed with the construction.

Overseas Cuts

The bill provided only a portion of the amount Bush wanted for overseas construction projects and for the annual U.S. contribution to NATO's infrastructure account. Savings from these cuts were to go to domestic programs — largely for National Guard and reserve units.

While Bush wanted $358.8 million for the NATO account, the conference agreed to give him only $225 million. That amount was $66 million more than the House originally proposed and $29 million less than the Senate bill provided.

As in previous years, the conference report contained language to prevent any unobligated funds in the NATO account from being spent on an air base in Crotone, Italy. Congress was opposed to the project because of its high cost — especially when domestic bases across the country were being closed to save money.

As for other overseas projects, the conference cut more than a third from the $289 million Bush had requested. The biggest, to build better family housing at Kwajalein Atoll in the Pacific, received $47.4 million of the $77.4 million the Pentagon wanted.

Because of the closure of some overseas bases, the conferees also made across-the-board reductions in worldwide construction projects for the services. Of the $478.9 million Bush wanted for small, unspecified jobs, the conferees approved $362.98 million.

The Defense Department also received less than it wanted to house the B-2 stealth bomber. Bush asked for $49.5 million for weapons storage areas, a survival equipment facility and other support structures for the controversial plane.

The House approved each of the 14 construction projects for the B-2 but made a $10 million across-the-board reduction. The Senate included no money in its bill for the project. The conferees provided $29.5 million.

The conference deleted funds that the administration had requested in February 1991 for bases that the Defense Base Closure and Realignment Commission had voted to close, and the conferees shifted those funds to the bases the commission spared.

The Orlando, Fla., Naval Training Center, which had been slated for closure by the Pentagon but was spared by the commission, received $21.4 million for two child-care centers, new barracks, a warehouse and a mess hall.

But $5 million that had been requested for the Air National Guard units at Rickenbacker Air Force Base in Ohio was deleted from the bill. Rickenbacker was scheduled to close within five years.

Most of the projects that were included in one chamber's version of the bill but not in the other's managed to survive the conference. For example, the $44.3 million in the Senate bill for projects in West Virginia, home state of Appropriations Committee Chairman Byrd, made the cut. So did a $22.2 million, House-passed project for barracks at Fort Bliss, Texas. Members paid for these programs with cuts in the overseas construction accounts.

In addition to resolving the items in disagreement, the conference included more than $16 million in additional projects in the final report that were not in either the House or Senate measures.

Of that, $9.6 million went to build an aerial cable range, strung between mountains, for target practice at White Sands Missile Range in New Mexico. The rest went for firing-range improvements at Army National Guard locations in California and Mississippi.

While Hefner acknowledged the need to move forward on the environmental cleanup of domestic bases that were closing, the House did not agree to the Senate funding level.

Sasser wanted to provide $971.6 million for base-closing procedures, but the House had approved $758.6 million. The conference took the House-passed figure, which was $25 million more than Bush requested. ■

Foreign Aid Funded by Short-Term Bill

Congress in 1991 provided for six months of funding for foreign aid through a continuing resolution (H Con Res 360) that expired at the end of March 1992.

The measure provided only $14.3 billion in budget authority — compared with $15.4 billion requested by the administration for fiscal 1992 and $15.2 billion included in a full-year appropriations bill (HR 2621) that was approved by the House in June.

Action on HR 2621 was deferred by the Senate under an agreement with the administration to delay consideration of Israel's request for $10 billion in loan guarantees. *(Mideast peace talks, p. 460)*

Because Congress did not act on a full appropriations bill during 1991, State Department officials had to improvise in allocating military and economic aid for individual countries. Some decisions were easy: Aid levels for the two biggest recipients had been at the same level for several years — $3 billion in military and economic assistance for Israel and $2.15 billion for Egypt on an annual basis — and were not changed.

But the situation was murkier for other countries and programs. Several administration officials said funds would be spent slowly while the continuing resolution was in effect — in case congressional priorities changed.

Under the formula for the short-term measure, funding was either at the level in the House-passed measure or the fiscal 1991 foreign operations bill, whichever was lower. Foreign operations received $15.4 billion in fiscal 1991. *(1990 Almanac, p. 830)*

BOXSCORE

➡ **Fiscal 1992 Foreign Operations appropriations. (HR 2621 and H J Res 360).** The $14.3 billion in budget authority for foreign operations was provided for in a continuing resolution (H J Res 360). The House had also approved a free-standing spending bill (HR 2621) for foreign operations.
Report: HR 2621: H Rept 102-108.

KEY ACTION

June 19 — HR 2621 passed the **House** by a vote of 301-102.

Oct. 24 — H J Res 360 passed the **House** by a vote of 288-126; passed the **Senate** by voice vote.

Oct. 28 — H J Res 360 signed by President Bush — PL 102-145.

HOUSE COMMITTEE ACTION

As everyone from visiting Soviet officials to teams of U.S. economists debated how much Western economic aid the Soviet Union needed to salvage its crumbling economy, a key House panel also left its imprint on the debate. *(Soviet aid, p. 463)*

The House Appropriations Foreign Operations Subcommittee made no effort to put a price tag on Soviet aid. But the appropriators offered policy guidelines for providing assistance to Moscow as they approved by voice vote May 29 a $15.3 billion foreign aid spending plan for fiscal 1992.

Although only a recommendation (the guidelines were included in the report accompanying the legislation) the subcommittee's proposal took on political heft because it was strongly supported by Majority Leader Richard A. Gephardt, D-Mo.

Briefing reporters the next day, Gephardt and subcommittee Chairman David R. Obey, D-Wis., asserted that Western nations had not yet developed a coordinated response to the Soviet economic crisis.

Secretary of State James A. Baker III reportedly told Soviet officials that they had to undertake economic and political reforms before the United States would consider providing direct economic aid.

The proposal approved by the subcommittee, by contrast, gave equal weight to the carrot and the stick.

The plan, which was supported by Mickey Edwards, Okla., the subcommittee's ranking Republican, called for "specifically spelling out what kind of Western economic assistance" would be provided by the United States and its allies in return for "meaningful concrete Soviet actions."

Gephardt charged that the Bush administration, concerned about possible political ramifications, had displayed "an abundance of caution." Although the administration appeared to be edging toward agreeing to a request from Moscow for $1.5 billion in agricultural credits, such piecemeal assistance would only "paper over the problem for three or four months," Gephardt said.

Under the subcommittee's proposal, the Soviet Union was required to hold free elections and grant the dissident Baltic States "a legitimate opportunity to determine" their future relationship with the central government.

Aid was also tied to completion of arms control pacts and "a changed pattern" of Soviet conduct in the Western Hemisphere.

While the proposal was silent on the amount of aid needed, Gephardt speculated that the U.S. share could reach $2 billion to $3 billion a year.

For Obey, the proposal was part of his own emerging version of what President Bush called the new world order, at least as far as foreign aid was concerned. For the second consecutive year, Obey guided his panel in reducing the administration's military aid request, shifting much of the money to economic aid programs.

The panel approved $4.1 billion in foreign military grant aid, a $500 million reduction from the administration's request and $159.9 million below fiscal 1991.

Overall, the panel's budget was more than $100 million under the administration's request and more than $600 million below the assistance provided during fiscal 1991. Foreign aid had soared in 1991, as Congress approved $850 million in supplemental war-related aid for Israel and Turkey.

The subcommittee accepted Obey's recommendations for increasing population aid from its existing level of $250 million to $300 million. Funding for refugee and disaster aid increased by nearly $200 million to $750 million.

U.N. Population Fund

But the panel's efforts could have been jeopardized by an issue that had sidetracked previous foreign aid measures: abortion. *(Abortion issue, p. 339)*

To Obey's chagrin, the panel approved an amendment by Republicans Bill Green, N.Y., and John Porter, Ill., that

Foreign Operations

(In thousands of dollars)

	Fiscal 1991 Appropriation	President's Request	House Bill	Continuing Resolution
Multilateral Aid				
World Bank				
Paid-in capital	$ 110,592	$ 70,126	$ 70,126	$ 70,126
Limitation on callable capital	*(2,899,610)*	*(2,267,418)*	*(2,267,418)*	*(2,267,418)*
Global Environmental Facility	—	—	50,000	—
International Development Association	1,064,150	1,060,000	1,060,000	1,060,000
International Finance Corporation	40,331	—	40,331	40,331
Inter-American Development Bank	91,299	90,389	90,389	90,389
Limitation on callable capital	*(2,235,077)*	*(2,235,077)*	*(2,235,077)*	*(2,235,077)*
Enterprise for the Americas investment fund	—	100,000	100,000	—
Asian Development Bank	—	25,526	25,526	—
Asian Development Fund	126,854	174,955	158,793	126,854
African Development Bank	10,136	8,987	8,987	8,987
African Development Fund	105,452	—	135,000	105,452
European Development Bank	70,021	70,021	70,021	70,021
International Monetary Fund (U.S. quota increase)	—	12,158,000	—	—
State Department international programs	284,730	250,212	300,612	284,730
Other	10,601	185,001	3,001	10,602
TOTAL, Multilateral Aid	**$ 1,914,166**	**$ 14,193,217**	**$ 2,112,786**	**$ 1,867,492**
Bilateral Aid				
Agency for International Development (AID)				
Development assistance	1,313,683	1,277,000	1,376,635	1,313,683
Sub-Saharan Africa, development aid	800,000	800,000	1,000,000	800,000
Operating expenses	474,884	521,039	519,039	474,884
Enterprise for the Americas: debt reduction	—	304,340	65,000	—
Economic Support Fund	3,991,000	3,228,000	3,216,624	3,216,624
Assistance for Philippines	100,000	160,000	260,000	100,000
Assistance for Eastern Europe	369,675	400,000	400,000	369,675
Other	281,341	170,218	237,218	233,385
Subtotal, AID	**$ 7,330,583**	**$ 6,860,597**	**$ 7,074,516**	**$ 6,508,251**
State Department				
International narcotics control	150,000	171,500	150,000	150,000
Migration and refugee aid	663,648	510,557	680,000	610,648
Anti-terrorism assistance	12,026	15,000	15,000	12,026
Subtotal, State Department	**$ 825,674**	**$ 697,057**	**$ 845,000**	**$ 772,674**
Peace Corps	186,000	200,000	200,000	186,000
Overseas Private Investment Corp. *(loan levels)*	*(290,000)*	*(400,000)*	*(400,000)*	*(275,000)*
Other	38,000	74,393	53,143	47,399
TOTAL, bilateral aid	**$ 8,380,257**	**$ 7,832,047**	**$ 8,172,659**	**$ 7,514,324**
Bilateral Military Aid (appropriated to the president)				
Foreign military financing	4,663,420	4,640,000	4,150,900	4,150,900
Estimated loan program	—	*(313,961)*	*(404,000)*	*(404,000)*
International military education and training	47,196	52,500	47,196	47,196
Special defense acquisition *(limitation on obligations)*	*(350,000)*	*(275,000)*	*(275,000)*	*(275,000)*
Other	664,862	48,000	38,000	38,000
TOTAL, military aid	**$ 5,375,478**	**$4,740,500**	**$ 4,236,096**	**$4,236,096**
Export Assistance				
Export-Import Bank	750,000	555,778	650,613	650,613
Export assistance *(loan levels)*	—	*(9,525,000)*	*(11,000,000)*	*(11,000,000)*
Trade and development	35,000	35,000	40,000	35,000
Deficit reduction	—	—	135,000	—
GRAND TOTAL	**$ 16,455,401** [1]	**$ 27,626,542** [2]	**$ 15,196,532**[3]	**$14,303,525**

[1] *Fiscal 1991 total included $500,000 in other assistance for Eastern Europe.*
[2] *Administration request included $270 million to refinance already concluded foreign military sales.*
[3] *House total included a 1 percent across-the-board cut, excepting narcotics control, earmarked aid and deficit reduction.*

SOURCE: House Appropriations Committee

provided $20 million to the United Nations Population Fund. Bush had pledged to veto any bill that included funding for the agency because it operated in China, which had been condemned for its policy of forced abortions.

Green tried to address the administration's objections by directing that the $20 million could be used only for "the procurement of contraceptive commodities." The White House offered no specific comment on the amendment, but similar measures in the past had triggered vetoes.

Disregarding Obey's plea not to be "devoured by the abortion issue," the panel approved Green's amendment, 8-3. Obey chided the White House for opposing funds for the U.N. agency because of its involvement with China, while at the same time backing most-favored-nation (MFN) trading status for China.

Trade status was "the issue we ought to fight on China this year," he said, "not this one [on family planning]."

Tracking Foreign Affairs

On the U.N. family planning funds and other issues, the subcommittee backed proposals of the House Foreign Affairs Committee, which had nearly finished work on legislation authorizing foreign aid for fiscal 1992-93. *(Foreign aid authorization, p. 470)*

Following the lead of the Foreign Affairs Committee, the Appropriations panel reduced the administration's request for foreign military grant aid for Turkey by $125 million. In maintaining the program at its fiscal 1991 level of $500 million, the subcommittee preserved Congress' customary formula of $7 in military aid for Greece for every $10 that went to Turkey.

Edwards offered an amendment that would have removed ceilings on military aid for Greece, Turkey and Portugal — effectively enabling the administration to scrap the 7-10 ratio — but the panel rejected it, 4-6.

After some debate, the subcommittee also endorsed the Middle East arms control regime developed by members of Foreign Affairs. The lawmakers' efforts were overshadowed by Bush, who offered his own regional non-proliferation initiative the same day. *(Arms control, p. 415)*

In an example of partisan wrangling over arms control, Edwards said he might oppose the provision, which provided for an indefinite moratorium on arms sales to the region, when the legislation was considered by the full Appropriations Committee.

While approving the regional arms control plan, the panel retained existing levels of military and economic aid for Israel and Egypt, which together received about one-third of all U.S. foreign aid.

The subcommittee approved $1.8 billion in military assistance grants and $1.2 billion in economic support fund (ESF) aid for Israel. Egypt received $1.3 billion in military grants and $815 million in ESF aid. But the legislation required the Egyptian government to undertake more stringent economic reforms than in past years.

Like the Foreign Affairs panel, the subcommittee essentially deferred the nettlesome issue of military aid to El Salvador. Obey said he agreed to a request from a U.N. official, who was attempting to mediate a cease-fire in the country's long-running civil war, not to "rock the boat" with a contentious debate over military aid. But the chairman indicated that if peace talks failed, he might offer an amendment that would effectively cut by half the administration's $85 million aid request.

The panel also approved a proposal initiated by members of the Congressional Black Caucus to increase the administration's request for the Development Fund for Africa by $200 million — $400 million over the funding enacted just two years previously — to $1 billion.

Enterprise for the Americas

The subcommittee sharply diverged from the authorizing panel, however, in funding the Enterprise for the Americas Initiative, the administration's program for stimulating private investment and economic reform in the Western Hemisphere.

The appropriations panel cut from $304.3 million to $65 million the administration's program to reduce the official debt owed by countries in the region. The Foreign Affairs Committee had approved $243 million to fund that aspect of the initiative.

Edwards and other subcommittee members were still bitter over the administration's grant of debt forgiveness for Egypt, enacted in 1990 over the opposition of many House lawmakers. Obey asserted that there was "minimum high regard" for debt relief in the House.

The chairman reiterated his contention that even if Enterprise for the Americas were fully funded, it would have a negligible impact on the region's $430 billion foreign debt. "It's a marginal write-down," he said.

If the administration heeded the suggestion of Charles Wilson, D-Texas, most of the $65 million in debt-reduction funding was to be directed toward one nation, Jamaica. Wilson and William H. Gray III, D-Pa., included report language singling out the island for special consideration.

Edwards and Obey combined to provide the bill with a unique feature: The two men agreed to set aside $135 million for a contribution to the federal deficit. Obey said the measure was designed to "bring the [budget] summit back to reality." While there were no objections to the plan, several members of the subcommittee said they believed that Senate appropriators would merely use the unspent funds for their own purposes.

The legislation approved by the subcommittee also included the following provisions:

- The lawmakers retained restrictions on aid to Pakistan. Aid was suspended in October 1990, when Bush failed to certify that the Pakistani government did not possess a nuclear weapon. The administration had lobbied to lift the certification requirement while vowing to continue to live by the spirit of the provision.
- With no debate, the subcommittee followed Obey's recommendation and rejected the administration's request for a $12.1 billion increase in the U.S. share of the lending authority of the International Monetary Fund (IMF). While the increase required no budgetary outlays, Obey had opposed IMF lending policies. The report accompanying the bill also noted that Bush had not provided a letter outlining reasons why the increase was needed.

Full Committee

The $15.3 billion spending measure was approved by the House Appropriations Committee by voice vote on June 12. Anti-abortion House Republicans faced a unique dilemma as Obey found a way to link the seemingly disparate issues of trade with China and funding for an international family planning agency.

If they backed the president's request to grant preferential trade status to China, they also ran the risk of aiding the U.N. Population Fund. For years, most Republicans had

Continued on p. 657

Foreign Operations Provisions

Congress did not enact a full-year foreign operations appropriations measure on a normal schedule. Instead, it funded foreign operations through a continuing resolution. That measure (H J Res 360), which was approved by both chambers on Oct. 24, provided funding through March 31, 1992, because a fiscal 1992 bill was not enacted before then.

Like the full-year bill, the continuing resolution paid for foreign aid and U.S. participation in a variety of international military and economic efforts.

More than three-quarters of the money in the bill went toward bilateral military and economic assistance programs. The legislation also funded U.S. quotas in multilateral banks and development institutions as well as export assistance programs.

Most activities of the Agency for International Development, the primary provider of U.S. foreign aid, were funded in the bill. Most of the State Department's budget and dues for international organizations such as the United Nations were in the Commerce, Justice, State and the judiciary appropriations measure, but some of the department's foreign policy operations were funded in the foreign operations bill.

For fiscal 1992, the House approved a $15.2 billion foreign operations bill on June 19 (HR 2621). But the Senate, as part of an agreement with the administration to defer consideration of Israel's request for $10 billion in loan guarantees, delayed action on its bill.

Under the continuing resolution (CR), funding was either at the level enacted for foreign operations in fiscal 1991 (PL 101-513) or the House-passed level, whichever was lower. The funding was provided under the authority and conditions contained in the fiscal 1991 bill.

Administration officials had said that they would fund programs conservatively under the CR because of uncertainty over spending demands that might be made by the full-year bill that had yet to be crafted.

The CR included funding but no legislative language. It lacked the usual congressional earmarks — requirements that the administration provide a minimum level of funding for a certain program or country.

But rather than defy congressional preferences, the administration probably operated as if most longstanding earmarks — such as those setting aid levels for Egypt and Israel — were in place. Several officials said they expected such earmarks to be included in a fiscal 1992 bill, assuming one was enacted, or for the fiscal 1991 earmarks to be binding if a full-year CR was enacted.

Total funding in the CR was $14.3 billion, compared with a funding level of $15.2 billion in the House-passed version of the full-year bill. The administration had requested $27.6 billion, including $12.2 billion for an increased U.S. contribution to the International Monetary Fund.

AGENCY FOR INTERNATIONAL DEVELOPMENT

The Agency for International Development (AID) had the politically unappealing responsibility of taking the lead in providing economic assistance to other countries.

The continuing resolution provided $6.5 billion for AID's operations. AID's total funding was cut substantially because the continuing resolution took the lesser amounts from individual accounts in the fiscal 1991 bill or the House-passed measure for fiscal 1992. The $6.5 billion was nearly $600 million lower than the House-passed bill, and more than $800 million lower than the fiscal 1991 level.

Established in 1961, AID's mission had undergone major changes. During the war in Vietnam, the agency supported extensive operations in Southeast Asia. In recent years, AID had significantly increased its aid programs in Eastern Europe, and it was expected that it could soon be asked to begin carrying out similar programs in the Soviet Union.

Congressional support for AID usually had been unenthusiastic. Not much had changed since 1969, when three Republican House members urged their colleagues to cut funding for "the hydra-headed monster called foreign assistance."

AID's unpopularity had been due in part to periodic revelations of waste or corruption. Like the Pentagon's overpriced toilet seats, foreign aid programs were often cited by lawmakers as examples of government squandering.

AID and its administrator, Ronald W. Roskens, had come under new criticism. AID Inspector General Herbert L. Beckington alleged that Roskens violated ethics laws when he accepted compensation from companies with an interest in AID contracts. The White House cleared Roskens of any serious wrongdoing, but the General Accounting Office was investigating the matter.

AID officials had conceded that management controls could be tightened. But they blamed some of the problems on budget constraints, which had forced the agency to rely increasingly on outside contractors.

Providing foreign assistance had become a thriving business for some U.S. companies, universities and private volunteer organizations. AID officials estimated that 65 percent of the funding for development assistance and the separate Development Fund for Africa was for programs managed by U.S.-based institutions.

There was little available information on the total number of outside contractors retained by the agency. Beckington said in May 1991 that "neither the administrator nor I as the inspector general can ask for and receive an accurate, complete and up-to-date list of the agency's outstanding and active grants." In October, Beckington's office confirmed that that was still the case.

The continuing resolution provided $441 million for AID's operating expenses, most of which would fund salaries for the agency's directly hired employees. The agency had 4,308 such employees during fiscal 1990, the most recent year for which statistics were available. Nearly half, 2,053, were based in Washington, while the rest worked in AID missions around the world.

Development Assistance

Development assistance was what most Americans thought of as foreign aid: projects throughout the world to reduce infant mortality and increase crop yields, to build roads and bridges, and to improve the education of children in developing countries.

The continuing resolution provided $1.31 billion in development assistance, an amount derived from the fiscal

1991 spending level because it was lower than that in the fiscal 1992 House-passed bill. The administration had requested $1.28 billion in development assistance for fiscal 1992, while the full-year House bill would provide $1.38 billion.

The administration had sought increased flexibility in expending development aid and asked that the assistance be provided through one general account. Instead, the CR retained fiscal 1991 spending levels, under which funding was specifically set for a range of development aid programs:

- **Health/Child Survival.** The continuing resolution provided funding at an annual rate of $287 million for international health and child survival activities. The House bill earmarked $345 million for these programs during fiscal 1992, a $53 million increase over the administration request.

The report accompanying the House bill took the administration to task for its efforts in these areas. "The Congress is taking the lead in children's programs," the report said, "and the administration is ignoring the priorities that have been set."

AID had cited several initiatives taken on behalf of children's health during the past few years. The agency said it would spend over $50 million over the next five years to reduce deaths from measles and would work with private volunteer organizations to improve infant nutrition.

- **AIDS.** Within the funding for health programs, the CR included $52 million for international AIDS prevention and control. The House bill earmarked $65 million, while the administration requested $55 million.

According to AID officials, up to half of all adult inpatients at many African hospitals were afflicted with the HIV virus, which caused AIDS.

One aim of the AIDS programs was to increase awareness of the disease. An agency budget justification document maintained that the president of Uganda "changed his position to support condom promotion" after viewing an AID presentation.

- **Agriculture.** The CR provided $481.6 million for agricultural development assistance. Much of this funding was typically provided to U.S. agribusinesses and universities that carried out programs on behalf of the agency.

AID actively promoted such programs as benefiting Americans. U.S. land-grant colleges and universities performed much of the agricultural research. "American farmers and consumers were among the big winners" from such research, an AID budget document said.

- **Family planning.** The CR provided $250 million for family planning assistance. That was $22 million above the level sought by the administration but $50 million less than the House-passed level.

AID population programs were aimed at ensuring the availability of family planning services while adhering to the "Mexico City" policy, which barred aid for any organization that "performs or actively promotes" abortion as a means of family planning.

The policy was named after the city where the policy was announced by the Reagan administration during an international conference in 1984.

Sub-Saharan Africa

The Development Fund for Africa was created in 1987 to provide more stability in development assistance for Africa south of the Sahara Desert.

For many administration officials and members of Congress, the fund was a model for how assistance programs should be managed. AID officials asserted that because the fund was virtually exempt from earmarks, they had greater flexibility to meet the needs of the more than 40 countries that received aid.

The continuing resolution funded the program at the fiscal 1991 level of $800 million, the administration request for fiscal 1992. The House bill would provide $1 billion for the Development Fund, a level that was strongly backed by members of the Congressional Black Caucus.

While its funding level had nearly doubled since its inception, the program had not been enough to stem the overall decline in aid for Africa since the early 1980s.

Schools and Hospitals Abroad

The American Schools and Hospitals Abroad (ASHA) program provided assistance to American-based overseas institutions. The continuing resolution provided $29 million, the fiscal 1991 level, for the program.

This program had frequently been the subject of intense lobbying by lawmakers eager to help U.S.-based overseas institutions. In recent years the practice of earmarking particular projects within this account had ceased, but reports accompanying bills often singled out certain institutions as worthy candidates.

- **Favorite recipients.** From fiscal 1986 through fiscal 1990, the American University in Beirut was awarded $25 million in grants, the most funding to any single institution.

In recent years, Chinese institutions had been awarded increasing amounts of ASHA funding. But in fiscal 1991 Sen. Jesse Helms, R-N.C., blocked AID funding for two Chinese institutions whose programs he opposed.

International Disaster Assistance

The virtually impossible task of planning for disasters was the mission of AID's Office of U.S. Foreign Disaster Assistance, in essence the international counterpart to the Federal Emergency Management Agency.

Earlier in 1991, the office was simultaneously trying to provide assistance to Kurdish refugees fleeing the postwar turmoil in Iraq, forestall a massive famine in the Horn of Africa, help hundreds of thousands of cyclone victims in Bangladesh and deal with an outbreak of cholera in Latin America — all on a regular appropriation for fiscal 1991 of $40 million.

An emergency supplemental appropriation (PL 102-55) was enacted in June to provide an additional $67 million for disaster relief activities in the Middle East and elsewhere during fiscal 1991.

In its report accompanying the House-passed foreign aid bill, the House Foreign Operations Subcommittee accused the administration of deliberately underfunding disaster relief assistance. The continuing resolution provided funding at an annual rate of $70 million — the House-passed figure — which was a $30 million increase over the administration request.

Credit Guarantee Programs

The U.S. government guaranteed the entire amount of loans under two credit guarantee programs, the Housing Guaranty Program and the Private Sector Investment Program.

With those guarantees in hand, recipient governments could borrow funds from commercial lenders at lower interest rates than they could otherwise obtain because the U.S.

government assumed the risk.

• **Housing Guaranty Program.** The housing program originally was devoted to private-sector financing for low-income housing in developing countries. But it was significantly broadened during fiscal 1991, when AID authorized $400 million in guarantees for Israel, boosting the size of the program to $550 million.

Israel requested $10 billion in new guarantees over the next five years in September, but President Bush sought and received assurances from congressional leaders to delay consideration of the request until early 1992.

The continuing resolution included the House-passed loan level of $150 million, $50 million more than the administration's request. The CR provided an appropriation of $17.9 million to cover the estimated subsidy behind the loans.

The subsidy appropriation was required under the 1990 Credit Reform Act (PL 101-508), which established new accounting practices for such revolving loan accounts. The actual appropriation therefore reflected Congress' estimate of the program's current and future losses.

In the past, the appropriations were based on the difference between the amount of loans issued each year and the amount repaid from previous years, with Congress making up the losses incurred from subsidizing interest rates or when borrowers failed to repay loans. Critics charged that such procedures never gave an accurate picture of the actual government subsidies in the loan programs.

• **Private Sector Investment Program.** The fund promoted a free-market approach to economic development by providing guarantees for loans to small businesses.

The program targeted businesses in developing countries that had difficulty getting credit. The continuing resolution set a limit of $67 million on guaranteed and direct loans provided under the program. The House had recommended a level of $114 million for guaranteed loans in fiscal 1992.

Enterprise for Americas

The enterprise was a multifaceted U.S. government program of investment and debt reduction in support of market-oriented economic reforms in Latin America. The continuing resolution provided no funding for this program because it was not funded in the fiscal 1991 bill.

The administration had requested $304.3 million to reduce official debt owed by Latin American countries to the United States. The House bill would provide only $65 million for debt reduction.

Foreign Operations Appropriations Subcommittee Chairman David R. Obey, D-Wis., and other House members who objected in 1990 to the administration's grant of debt relief for Egypt also opposed large-scale forgiveness of the debt of Latin American nations.

Economic Support Fund

The Economic Support Fund (ESF) had been called one of the most important foreign policy tools available to the president. But critics described ESF as little more than international "walking around money" — payoffs to ensure that nations remained loyal.

Unlike other economic aid programs, in which goods or services were provided, ESF was usually given directly in cash or by financing a country's imports of U.S. commodities.

The continuing resolution provided the House-passed level of $3.216 billion in ESF assistance. That figure was less than $12 million below the administration request for fiscal 1992.

But administration officials had said they would be unable to set allocations of ESF aid for individual countries until a fiscal 1992 bill was enacted. Typically, two-thirds of ESF aid had gone to Israel and Egypt.

A group of powerful senators, which included Appropriations Chairman Robert C. Byrd, D-W.Va., favored limiting the amount of cash aid in the ESF program, instead increasing "tied aid," the amount tied to specific projects. U.S. firms would then be eligible to win contracts generated by the projects.

The issue was expected to arise again when the Senate took up the fiscal 1992 foreign operations bill in January 1992.

• **Israel.** As in past years, the House bill earmarked $1.2 billion for Israel. The administration was not bound by the earmark for the duration of the CR but was likely to provide that level of ESF assistance for Israel.

The House-passed legislation, like previous foreign operations bills, would require that Israel's total ESF aid be made available on a grant basis in cash within 30 days after the enactment of the bill.

Administration officials had estimated that the expedited disbursement of aid enabled the Israeli government to earn as much as $70 million in annual interest on its ESF assistance, depending on prevailing interest rates.

But the administration, citing the uncertainties of funding programs after the expiration of the continuing resolution, broke with that policy. It provided only half of the $1.2 billion to Israel in expedited payments.

Israel used much of its ESF aid to repay outstanding loans to the United States. Since fiscal 1985, Congress had required that ESF aid be at least equal to Israel's principal and interest payments to the United States.

• **Egypt.** The continuing resolution also enabled the administration to provide $815 million in ESF aid to Egypt, the level earmarked by the House. Of that aid, $200 million was to go to finance commodity imports. The House bill tied the aid to continued economic reforms by the Egyptian government.

• **Other earmarks.** The House bill would require that the administration provide at least $15 million for Cyprus and $16 million for programs run by private volunteer organizations for Palestinians in Israeli-occupied West Bank and Gaza Strip.

The bill, drafted before the dramatic changes that had reshaped the Soviet Union, also would provide aid to what were Soviet republics. The bill included $15 million, to be divided between the Baltic States and other republics whose governments were freely chosen.

But the continuing resolution did not specifically earmark funding for either program.

• **Prohibitions.** The continuing resolution provided assistance under conditions contained in the fiscal 1991 bill. That bill, like the House-passed legislation, barred any ESF aid for Zaire because of that country's record of human rights abuses.

Both the fiscal 1991 bill and House-passed measure also included a standard provision barring any assistance or guaranteed loans for the governments of Angola, Cambodia, Cuba, Iran, Iraq, Libya, Syria or Vietnam.

• **Andean Initiative.** It was not clear what impact the continuing resolution would have on the State Department's plans to provide ESF assistance to other key allies.

According to its fiscal 1992 budget, the administration

intended to provide $275 million to support anti-narcotics activities in the Andean countries of South America. In addition, the administration indicated that it would provide $150 million in ESF aid to Nicaragua and $120 million to El Salvador.

Multilateral Initiatives

• **Eastern Europe.** The continuing resolution included $369.7 million, the fiscal 1991 funding level, in assistance for the emerging democracies of Eastern Europe.

Under the program, aid was directed toward functional programs for the region rather than for individual countries. The fiscal 1991 bill had required that $113.7 million be spent on technical aid and training; $75 million for environment and energy activities; and $90 million for the Polish-American and Hungarian-American Enterprise Funds.

The funding was $30.3 million less than was requested by the administration for fiscal 1992 and would be provided in the House-passed bill. State Department officials had said they would be forced to operate at a lower funding level at a time when more countries had become eligible for aid under the Eastern European program. Romania, Bulgaria, Albania and the former Soviet republics of Latvia, Lithuania and Estonia had all recently become eligible for such assistance.

• **Philippines.** The United States also provided aid for the Philippines in coordination with other nations as part of the Multilateral Assistance Initiative.

The continuing resolution provided $100 million for the Multilateral Initiative, the fiscal 1991 level. The House had agreed to provide the full administration request of $160 million for the initiative in fiscal 1992.

The House bill was approved before the rejection by the Philippine Senate of a treaty that would have allowed the United States to maintain bases in the country for the next decade. In the wake of that rebuff, there was substantial sentiment in Congress to sharply reduce aid for the Philippines.

• **Fund for Ireland.** The continuing resolution also provided $20 million for the International Fund for Ireland. The fund was established in 1986 to support the Anglo-Irish Accord on Northern Ireland.

The fund, which was strongly backed by Irish-American members of Congress, promoted economic development in Northern Ireland and the portion of the Republic of Ireland that bordered Northern Ireland.

STATE DEPARTMENT, RELATED AGENCIES

Most State Department operations were funded under the separate appropriation for the Departments of Commerce, Justice and State, the judiciary and related agencies. But the foreign operations appropriations bill funded those activities deemed to have a particular foreign policy component, and those programs were included under the "Economic Assistance" section of the bill.

Refugee Assistance

Most U.S. aid for displaced persons around the world was provided under the State Department's migration and refugee assistance account. The House recommended $630 million for these activities in fiscal 1992, a 28 percent increase over the administration's request of $490.6 million. But the continuing resolution put funding at the fiscal 1991 level of $560.6 million.

In response to the turmoil in the Middle East and elsewhere, funding for the migration and refugee account was increased about 31 percent in fiscal 1991 over the fiscal 1990 level. Obey's panel alleged that the administration had provided insufficient aid for refugees just as it had underfunded AID's Office of Disaster Assistance.

• **Israel's immigrants.** The House earmarked $80 million of the refugee assistance — twice the administration's request — to help Israel resettle an estimated 1 million immigrants from Eastern Europe and the Soviet Union who were expected to arrive in the country by 1995. The continuing resolution did not set a specific spending level for these activities.

• **Overseas programs.** Although the continuing resolution was silent, the House bill also earmarked $315 million for the department's overseas programs, an increase of $81.6 million over the administration request. Much of that aid would be provided through international agencies, such as the Office of the United Nations High Commissioner for Refugees.

• **Emergency fund.** The continuing resolution provided a separate appropriation of $50 million, the House-passed level, for the U.S. Emergency Migration and Refugee Fund. That was more than twice the administration request of $20 million but well below the fiscal 1991 level of $103 million.

The president could draw down the account to meet "unexpected urgent refugee and migration needs."

International Narcotics Control

The State Department's Bureau for International Narcotics Matters (INM) was the lead agency in the government's efforts outside U.S. borders to stem the international trade in illegal narcotics.

But in recent years, more attention and resources had been devoted to the president's Andean Initiative, aimed specifically at the world's largest producers of cocaine: Colombia, Bolivia and Peru. A key aspect of the initiative — providing military and Economic Support Fund assistance to the three countries — had been implemented by other State Department bureaus and the Defense Department.

The CR provided $150 million for INM activities, the same level that was funded in the House bill and during fiscal 1991.

• **Enforcement.** Most of INM's funding in fiscal 1991 — $95.4 million — was devoted to bolstering the enforcement capabilities of the governments of the nations where drugs were produced. In Colombia, INM provided $12 million for aircraft support. The bureau had also provided the government of Mexico with UH-1H helicopters for drug interdiction.

• **Airwing.** The department managed its own fleet of 51 helicopters and fixed-wing aircraft for operations in drug-producing countries. In fiscal 1991, the agency's interregional aviation budget was $33.5 million.

The Airwing, as it was called, was based at Patrick Air Force Base in Florida. According to the bureau's budget request, the Airwing flew more than 16,000 hours in fiscal 1990, the most recent year for which data was available.

• **Crop control.** In fiscal 1991, the bureau spent $22.3 million on drug crop eradication programs. The INM said it would upgrade its campaign in Mexico.

Anti-Terrorism

The top priority of the State Department's anti-terrorism program was to aid countries that were said to be confronting significant terrorism activity. The continuing resolution provided $12 million for anti-terrorist activities.

Most of that funding ($3.6 million) would go toward airport security, followed by other anti-terrorism support ($3.5 million) and dogs trained to detect explosives ($3.3 million).

Peace Corps

The Peace Corps was an independent agency that trained American volunteers and placed them at work in development and education projects around the world. No other agency embodied President John F. Kennedy's New Frontier more than the Peace Corps, 30 years old in 1991.

The continuing resolution provided $186 million, the fiscal 1991 level for the Peace Corps. The House bill included $200 million.

Most of the Peace Corps' budget — $116.7 million in fiscal 1992, according to the agency's budget — went to train and support its volunteers.

During fiscal 1990, 3,058 trainees were placed in programs serving 75 countries around the world. A typical program was the Peace Corps operation in Senegal, where 62 trainees were expected to work in fiscal 1992: 14 in agriculture, 24 on environmental programs, 11 on health projects and 13 on small-business development.

Independent Agencies

Most of the independent agencies involved in foreign policy were funded under the Commerce, Justice, State and judiciary appropriation. The foreign operations bill provided funding for three agencies:

- **African Development Foundation.** The foundation was established by Congress to support grass-roots development on the continent. The foundation anticipated that it would fund 100 new projects in 29 African countries in fiscal 1992. The continuing resolution provided $13 million.
- **Inter-American Foundation.** The foundation, established in 1969, fulfilled a similar mission in Latin America. The continuing resolution included $25 million.
- **Overseas Private Investment Corporation (OPIC).** OPIC provided insurance for U.S. investors abroad against losses resulting from political upheaval in foreign countries. The corporation also provided financing for investment projects overseas through loan guarantees or direct loans.

The continuing resolution provided $9.4 million — the House-passed level — for OPIC. The continuing resolution set a limit on guaranteed loans of $250 million and a limit on direct loans of $25 million.

BILATERAL MILITARY ASSISTANCE

The continuing resolution provided $4.24 billion in military assistance, the level in the the House-passed measure.

As recently as fiscal 1987, military aid accounted for 37 percent of the foreign operations appropriations bill. In the House-passed bill, by contrast, military assistance only made up 28 percent of the spending in the bill.

The reduction represented a significant shift away from the Reagan-era policy of arming key allies as bulwarks against Soviet influence. But many lawmakers had begun to press for even deeper cuts in spending on military assistance.

Still, such assistance had a constituency in Congress because it brought undeniable benefits to some U.S. arms manufacturers. With military spending for U.S. strategic needs in decline, those manufacturers had begun increasingly to look abroad for markets.

Foreign Military Financing

This was by far the most important and costliest U.S. military assistance program. Primarily managed by the Pentagon's Defense Security Assistance Agency, Foreign Military Financing (FMF) enabled key allies to purchase U.S. military equipment, training and services.

The continuing resolution provided $4.15 billion for Foreign Military Financing.

Arguing for the domestic advantages of the FMF program, the administration's budget request said, "That part of the production of U.S. defense industry which is composed of arms sales provides jobs for American workers and increases exports to help the U.S. balance of trade."

With a few exceptions, FMF aid had to be spent on U.S. goods and services.

- **Grants.** Until the mid-1980s, FMF was provided almost entirely in the form of government guarantees for commercial loans. But because of high interest rates in the early part of the decade, countries had difficulty making repayments, in some cases requiring the Treasury to repay the private lenders.

In fiscal 1985, the United States forgave FMF debts of many allies, including Egypt and Israel. It also acted to avoid possible repayment problems by gradually transforming FMF into a mostly grant program. During fiscal 1991, 91 percent of the $4.7 billion FMF program was in the form of grants.

The continuing resolution included the House-passed level of $4.1 billion for the grant assistance. The administration had requested $4.6 billion for fiscal 1992.

- **Loans.** To partly compensate for the sharp reduction in grant aid funding, the continuing resolution — like the House-passed bill — provided for $404 million in low-interest "concessional" loans, $90 million more than the administration request. These loans had an interest rate of about 5 percent.

Under 1990's Credit Reform Act, requiring an estimate of the costs of current and future losses, the continuing resolution included $50.9 million to cover loan subsidies.

- **Israel/Egypt.** For years, Congress had earmarked most of the funding in the FMF program for Israel and Egypt. The continuing resolution would enable the administration to provide the customary levels of $1.8 billion in grants for Israel and $1.3 billion for Egypt. For several years, foreign operations bills had stipulated that, as in the case of ESF aid for Israel, grant military aid for the country had to be provided within 30 days of the enactment of the legislation.

As with ESF aid, the administration chose to deliver only half of $1.8 billion in military aid to Israel under the continuing resolution.

- **Non-U.S. purchases.** The House bill specifically would allow Israel to use $475 million of its FMF assistance on procurement in Israel of defense articles and services. In addition, a small group of countries other than Israel and Egypt was able to spend a total of $300 million of their FMF aid on research and development on non-U.S. defense items.

Although the fiscal 1991 bill also included those provisions, the continuing resolution did not address those issues.

- **Greece/Turkey.** The House bill would give up to

$350 million for Greece and $500 million for Turkey. In setting a ceiling for FMF assistance for Greece and Turkey, the House continued the congressional custom of providing military aid for the two governments in a rough 7-to-10 ratio. In order to maintain the ratio, the bill would cut the administration's request for Turkey from $625 million to $500 million.

The administration had long opposed the ratio. The issue was not addressed in the continuing resolution, but the administration was expected to abide by the ratio to avoid a confrontation with Congress over the issue.

While all of Turkey's FMF assistance during fiscal 1991 was provided in grant form, Greece received only $30 million in grants and the rest in loans.

Supporters of Greece, led by Sen. Paul S. Sarbanes, D-Md., favor phasing out the loan program entirely. That could force the administration to increase grant assistance to Greece.

But the administration and some House members were opposed to turning FMF into an all-grant program. Administration officials said that loans required far less appropriated funding than grants, enabling the United States to assist more countries.

Special Defense Acquisition Fund

The Special Defense Acquisition Fund enabled the Defense Department to purchase certain high-demand military items in anticipation of their eventual sale to key U.S. allies. In essence, the Pentagon warehoused these items until they were sold.

Administration officials said the program proved particularly useful during the Persian Gulf War, when the United States was able to sell needed equipment at short notice to its allies against Iraq.

The continuing resolution set a ceiling of $275 million, the level in the House bill, for obligations in this program during fiscal 1992. While funding was provided each fiscal year, the fund sustained itself with sales of equipment.

Thus, no new budget authority or new outlays were provided in the bill.

Military Education and Training

Since 1950, more than a half-million foreign military officers had studied in the United States under the International Military Education and Training (IMET) program and its predecessor.

While the students came for military training, the Pentagon stressed the exposure that the officers received to democratic institutions in the United States.

- **Funding.** The continuing resolution provided the House-passed level of $47.2 million for the IMET program in fiscal 1992. Like the fiscal 1991 bill, the legislation stipulated that medium- and high-income countries (those with per capita GNPs of over $2,349 a year) receive no assistance. Those nations would have to spend their own money to send officers.
- **Countries.** The Pentagon expected to train more than 6,400 foreign officers under the IMET program during fiscal 1992. More than half (3,164) would come from Latin America and the Caribbean. Colombia would send the largest contingent, 1,375 officers.

Other Military Assistance

- **Drawdown.** The House bill would retain a provision enabling the administration to provide Israel with up to $700 million worth of equipment from Defense Department stocks. The amendment, originally attached to the fiscal 1991 bill, was intended to bolster Israel's security during the Persian Gulf crisis.

The Pentagon had promised to continue the program until the $700 million ceiling was reached.

- **Stockpiles.** Another provision of the fiscal 1991 bill authorized the Defense Department to stockpile as much as $300 million worth of defense equipment in Israel. The continuing resolution did not address the matter, but the administration previously had pledged to meet the target.

Peacekeeping Operations

The continuing resolution also included $28 million to support international peacekeeping operations.

- **Multinational forces.** The continuing resolution would enable the administration to provide $19.5 million for the Multinational Force and Observers in the Sinai, the independent organization set up to monitor the 1979 Israel-Egypt Peace Treaty.

The administration also intended to provide $8.5 million for the U.N. force in Cyprus, which monitored the truce between Turkey and Greece on the island nation.

MULTILATERAL ORGANIZATIONS

Multilateral lending institutions

A large share of the foreign aid appropriation would go with virtually no strings attached to six large international lending institutions. They sought to promote economic development abroad through a variety of lending programs aimed at the needs of poor and middle-income Third World countries.

The amounts going to the multinational lenders in the continuing resolution were derived from the fiscal 1991 foreign operations bill. The House-passed bill for fiscal 1992 would appropriate slightly larger sums, chiefly because three programs that would be aided by that measure received no money in fiscal 1991.

The new budget authority for the multilateral banks in the continuing resolution totaled $6.4 billion. But only $1.6 billion of that was paid directly to the banks — and only that amount typically was included in calculations of foreign aid appropriations.

Almost three-fourths of the total — $4.8 billion — was pledged as "callable capital." Although the banks could use this as collateral for borrowing on world markets, the United States would only pay the money if a development bank faced default, an extremely unlikely event. As a result, the $4.8 billion did not translate into any outlays.

Most loans went to government borrowers for specific projects, from roads and dams to irrigation systems and housing. Loans to better-off countries typically were made at or near market terms; poorer countries generally got "concessional loans" at zero interest with long payback periods — often 30 or 40 years.

Increasingly, the banks were making loans that were not tied to specific projects, and some countries had used the money to repay commercial banks, a practice that had raised the ire of Congress. Several of the banks had special lending arms that financed private-sector development.

The United States was also a major participant in the International Monetary Fund (IMF), a sister institution of the World Bank that promoted international currency stability as well as sustained growth in the developing world. IMF loans were usually tied to specific economic changes in the borrowing country.

U.S. payments to these institutions corresponded generally to the relative role the United States played in running them. Typically, the United States had a 10 percent to 20 percent stake and a similar share of the vote. In some cases, the United States had enough votes — especially when it teamed with other countries — to block or place conditions on a loan application. But it could not always do so.

Congress sometimes tried to influence lending by the multilateral banks, but its reach was limited. Since the 1989 Tiananmen Square massacre, for example, Congress had tried to discourage certain World Bank loans to China by requiring the United States to withhold an amount equivalent to its share (about 22 percent) of any such loan that was not for "basic human needs."

Authorizations for increased U.S. contributions to several of these multilateral institutions were pending in a broad multilateral lending authorization bill (HR 3428) that could be mired permanently in the House Banking Committee. They were also included in the conference agreement of a comprehensive foreign aid authorization bill (HR 2508) that the House killed Oct. 30. Thus, the CR was enacted with funds for the multilateral lending institutions but with no authorizing language in effect.

In those years when no authorization bill was enacted — a not-uncommon fate for multilateral authorizations — the foreign aid appropriations bill was sometimes amended in conference to include authorizing language.

• **International Monetary Fund.** The United States had agreed to participate in a 50 percent increase in financial backing for the IMF, but neither the continuing resolution nor the House-passed foreign aid bill included the $12.2 billion needed to cover the U.S. share. Such an appropriation would not result in any budget outlays because once the money was paid to the IMF, the United States would receive an equivalent increase in its interest-bearing reserves held by the fund.

Because the continuing resolution carried forward fiscal 1991 foreign aid appropriations, it gave $10.6 million to a special interest-rate subsidy program of the IMF, the so-called Enhanced Structural Adjustment Facility. This program was not supposed to receive any money after fiscal 1991, and it was expected that the Treasury Department would simply not forward the money to the IMF.

• **World Bank.** The continuing resolution included four specific appropriations for the World Bank. The World Bank was the largest and oldest of the multilateral lenders, founded in 1945 following the Bretton Woods conference that also created the IMF.

The International Bank for Reconstruction and Development (as the World Bank was officially known) got $70.1 million in paid-in capital and $2.3 billion in callable capital. That was the third installment of a five-year pledged capital increase for the bank, which made market-rate loans, mostly to middle-income countries.

The continuing resolution did not provide funds for a new Global Environmental Fund, which would receive $50 million in the House-passed bill. The fund was intended to reduce global warming, promote biological diversity and prevent ozone depletion. The administration had planned to finance three $50 million contributions to the fund through in-kind efforts by the Agency for International Development (AID). The House Foreign Operations Appropriations Subcommittee put separate funding in the House measure for fiscal 1992 to ensure that the administration would commit new money to the effort rather than claim credit for previously scheduled AID environmental projects.

The International Development Association (IDA), the World Bank's concessional lending arm for the poorest countries, would receive just under $1.1 billion, the second of three annual installments promised to that lending agency.

Because the agency made long-term, no-interest loans, it was not practical for it to borrow the money. Instead, it relied on donor countries for its capital.

The continuing resolution did not include a provision from the House-passed bill on loans to China. The provision would reduce the U.S. contribution if the IDA made loans to China other than for basic human needs, but only if the United States denied most-favored-nation status to China.

The continuing resolution included $40.3 million for the International Finance Corporation, the private-sector promotional arm of the World Bank. This money was supposed to be an installment toward a $1 billion capital increase for the agency — of which the U.S. share was 25 percent. As a technical matter, the appropriation could not be earmarked for that purpose until a permanent appropriations bill was enacted, but the United States could advance the money anyway. The House-passed bill would have imposed a $6.1 million spending cap in fiscal 1992 (although the balance would be available in future years).

• **Inter-American Development Bank.** The IADB — established in 1959 to promote Latin American development — got $57.3 million in paid-in capital and $2.2 billion in callable capital in the continuing resolution as the second installment of a five-year capital increase for the bank. In addition, the IADB's Fund for Special Operations — its concessional lending arm — got $20.6 million. The continuing resolution did not include a provision from the House-passed bill that would have required that the United States oppose loans from the fund to countries that discriminated on the basis of nationality in their purchases of goods and services.

The Inter-American Investment Corporation, which loaned to small and midsize companies in the region, got $12.5 million, the final part of a U.S. commitment of $51 million.

The continuing resolution did not include money for the newly created Enterprise for the Americas Multilateral Investment Fund. In the House-passed bill, it would have received $100 million, the first of five equal installments. The fund would promote broad-scale private-sector development in the region. A third of its money was to come from the United States, a third from Japan and the balance from other countries.

• **Asian Development Bank.** The continuing resolution made one appropriation to the bank, which was founded in 1966 to lend throughout Asia. The House-passed bill, however, contained three appropriations for the bank.

The Asian Development Fund, the bank's concessional lending arm, would receive $126.9 million toward the U.S. share of a replenishment of the fund. The House-passed bill would provide $158.8 million, which would nearly complete the replenishment, leaving about $16.2 million in arrears. The House-passed bill would make the appropriation subject to a certification to the House and Senate Appropriations committees that none of the money would go to China.

The House-passed bill, but not the continuing resolution, would provide $25.5 million in paid-in capital and $187 million in callable capital for the Asian Bank's market-rate lending operation, which constituted the first half of the U.S. share of a special capital increase for the bank.

The bill made the money available subject to restrictions on loans to China identical to those that it would impose on the World Bank's IDA appropriation.

• **African Development Bank and African Development Fund.** The continuing resolution made two appropriations to the African Bank, which was founded in 1964 to make market-rate loans to countries on that continent. The United States joined the bank in 1983. The bank got $9 million in paid-in capital and $134.8 million in callable capital, the last of five payments on a capital increase.

The continuing resolution also included $105.5 million for the African Development Fund, a separate, concessional lending operation founded in 1973 that aided the poorest countries in Africa. Under the House-passed bill this appropriation would total $135 million, as the first of three scheduled installments of a new replenishment for the fund. The smaller amount in the continuing resolution was derived from the fiscal 1991 U.S. payment on the previous replenishment of the fund. The new replenishment was subject to a separate authorization. As a technical matter, the appropriation could not be earmarked for the new replenishment until a permanent appropriations bill was enacted, but the United States could advance the money anyway.

• **European Bank for Reconstruction and Development.** The European Bank was created in 1990 to aid the emerging democracies of Eastern and Central Europe. A paid-in capital contribution of $70 million and a callable capital contribution of $163.4 million would constitute the second of five installments of the bank's initial capitalization.

• **Environmental controls.** The continuing resolution did not include language from the House-passed bill that would direct the U.S. executive directors of multilateral institutions — especially of the Asian Development Bank — to promote energy conservation, energy efficiency and renewable energy programs and to seek to require environmental impact statements early in the planning for energy projects. The House bill also would require the Treasury secretary to promote environmental reforms at the IMF before committing additional money to that institution and to insist that a portion of loans made by the European Bank for Reconstruction and Development go for environmental protection and restoration. The Treasury secretary would have to report to Congress by March 1992 on progress the United States had made in getting multilateral institutions to increase their environmental efforts.

• **Anti-terrorist loans.** The House-passed bill, but not the continuing resolution, would require the United States to vote against any loan that would go to or benefit a country identified as "terrorist" by the secretary of State.

INTERNATIONAL ORGANIZATIONS

The continuing resolution provided $284.7 million for voluntary contributions to a number of international organizations, $34.5 million over the administration's request. The House bill would provide $300.6 million for international organizations. The separate Commerce, Justice, State appropriation funds assessed contributions — in effect, dues — for organizations such as the United Nations.

The continuing resolution set no funding level for specific organizations.

• **UNICEF.** The House bill would increase funding over levels sought by the administration for most programs targeted at improving the lot of the world's children.

The House subcommittee chastised the administration for failing to provide more funding for the United Nations Children's Fund (UNICEF), which it described in its report as "the universally acclaimed agency that saves children's lives."

After enactment of the continuing resolution, the administration reportedly agreed to provide $75 million for UNICEF, $10 million below the House-passed level.

• **UNDP, UNEP.** The House bill would provide funding for the United Nations Development Program (UNDP) and the United Nations Environment Program (UNEP). The House bill included $120.7 million for the UNDP, which provided technical development assistance to the world's poorest countries.

That bill included $20 million for the UNEP, which coordinated international agreements and conventions on the environment.

EXPORT ASSISTANCE

Export-Import Bank

The Export-Import Bank was a federal agency that financed overseas purchases of U.S. goods through low-interest direct loans, loan guarantees and export credit insurance. Financing was arranged with foreign governments, private companies and U.S. exporters for a wide range of products that in the past had included power plants, locomotives, aircraft, mining equipment and sugar refineries.

As an example of the bank's lending activities, in fiscal 1990, its direct loans totaled $612.4 million; the bank made $3.3 billion in loan guarantees; and it provided $4.8 billion in export credit insurance.

The credit insurance program was intended for exporters who provided their own favorable, short-term credit to foreign buyers. Guarantees assured repayment of loans made through commercial lenders.

Congress and the Bush administration agreed that the bank, which had suffered annual losses throughout the past decade, was in bad financial shape. Current estimates suggested that $5.3 billion in outstanding loans — 44 percent of the bank's portfolio — would never be paid back.

• **Program funding.** The continuing resolution provided $650.6 million for the Ex-Im Bank, the same level as in the House bill. Of that, $612 million would be used to underwrite the bank's lending programs in fiscal 1992. That represented Congress' estimate of what it would cost the bank to offer up to $11 billion in assistance during the year ahead, a calculation required by the 1991 Credit Reform Act.

Specifically, it covered the expected cost to the bank of offering below-market interest rates and an amount set aside to cover future defaults.

The Bush administration requested $517.2 million, which would have enabled the bank to provide $9.5 billion in financing. In recent years, Congress had regularly appropriated more for the Ex-Im Bank than requested by the White House. The increase reflected the efforts of House subcommittee Chairman Obey to give the agency a modest increase, partly to finance the rebuilding of Kuwait and an expected increase in loan activity for the Soviet Union and Eastern Europe.

• **Overhead.** The continuing resolution appropriated $25.1 million for administrative expenses, including salaries for the bank's 360 employees, travel and other costs of running the bank.

• **Credit insurance.** An additional $13.5 million was included for the bank's export credit insurance program. It was administered by the Foreign Credit Insurance Association, which was made up of several insurance companies, but the Ex-Im Bank assumed all the risk.

• **Accounting changes.** A new formula was being used to determine the level of appropriations necessary to cover Ex-Im Bank operations. Changes enacted as part of the 1990 Credit Reform Act (PL 101-508) required appropriators to provide funding to cover the estimated future cost, including losses, of loans made or guaranteed during fiscal 1992.

In the past, Congress provided a lump sum to cover the difference between the amount of new loans to be issued during the year and the repayments the bank was expected to receive for past loans.

Appropriators had made one other change in the bank's operation. In the past, the committee set caps on the various forms of financing the bank could offer each year.

But the caps constrained the Ex-Im Bank's ability to provide financing once it hit a particular cap.

Under the continuing resolution, the caps were lifted. The bank was free to allocate the $11 billion as it wanted among loans, guarantees and other financing. The idea was to allow the bank to offer whatever financing the export market demanded.

• **Military sales.** The Bush administration earlier in 1991 had asked Congress to authorize the Ex-Im Bank to use up to $1 billion in fiscal 1992 to finance overseas sales of U.S. military hardware.

It said the loans were needed to help military contractors boost their foreign sales at a time when the U.S. defense budget was decreasing. The bank had been barred since 1968 from underwriting arms sales to developing countries and had a longstanding policy against such loans to developed nations.

But Congress opened the door in 1990 by authorizing a $1.2 billion guarantee for the sale of military helicopters to Turkey.

Rebuffing the administration's request, the House bill would explicitly prohibit the Ex-Im Bank from financing military items included on the United States Munitions List, the government's list of military hardware and other products that required licenses for export.

The continuing resolution was silent on the subject, and the matter was likely to arise again when the Senate marked up its bill.

• **Tied aid.** The House bill would encourage the bank to use the full $200 million in loan funds authorized for the Ex-Im Bank's so-called tied-aid war chest.

Countries that received tied-aid credits or grants were required to use the funds to contract with U.S. firms for construction projects or to buy U.S. goods. The official purpose of the war chest, authorized in 1989, was to combat the use of tied aid by U.S. competitors.

Of $9.3 billion in export assistance that the bank provided in fiscal 1991, $3.6 billion went to Latin America, $3 billion to Europe and Canada, $1.2 billion to Asia and the rest to Africa, the Middle East and other locations.

Trade and Development Program

This program, run by the International Development Cooperation Agency, a U.S. government program, helped plan development projects in the Third World, employing staff experts as well as private consultants. The continuing resolution provided $40 million in fiscal 1992, an increase of $5 million over fiscal 1991. ■

Continued from p. 648

strongly opposed any U.S. funding for the U.N. agency, on the grounds that it supported China's policy of forced abortions.

Obey joined the subjects in an amendment to HR 2621.

Obey sardonically called his amendment the "Hypocrisy Reduction Act of 1991." It made this connection: $20 million would be provided for the U.N. family planning fund but only if Congress extended most-favored-nation (MFN) trade status to China. If MFN was denied, then no assistance was to be provided for the fund.

The administration had been conducting an intensive lobbying campaign seeking congressional approval of MFN for China. At the same time, Bush had reiterated the Reagan administration policy of pledging to veto any bill that included aid for the U.N. agency — because it operated in China. *(China trade status, p. 121)*

Obey's subcommittee had approved $20 million for the U.N. agency on May 29. At the full Appropriations Committee markup, Vin Weber, R-Minn., offered an amendment to strike the funding.

Instead, the committee supported Obey's substitute amendment, 30-19. He threatened to offer a similar amendment to the MFN legislation, conditioning preferred trade status on a certification by Bush that China did not have a policy of forced abortion. "If we're going to isolate China," Obey said, "we ought to isolate them across the board."

Weber conceded that linking the two issues could create problems for the administration as it tried to drum up Republican support for MFN status. "It cross-pressures a lot of Republicans," said Weber. "It would be hard for me not to support [Obey's amendment] on the floor."

Christopher H. Smith, R-N.J., perhaps the leading anti-abortion member of the House, agreed. Smith said that while he hesitated to bring the family planning dispute into the trade debate, Obey's amendment "will shed further light on the outrages of the Chinese [abortion] program."

Obey said he devised his strategy because the administration was inconsistent on China and reluctant to work toward passage of a foreign aid bill.

Describing the president as "at war with himself on this issue," Obey said, "The right-to-lifers are not being inconsistent; George Bush is."

Less Controversial Issues

Aside from disputes over family planning, which also bogged down the foreign aid authorization measures moving through both chambers, the appropriations process had been largely free of controversy.

Edwards, the ranking minority member on Obey's subcommittee, called the House Appropriations measure "a good bill for where we are in the process."

The full committee endorsed, without debate, the bulk of the subcommittee's recommendations, including a $504 million reduction in the administration's military assistance request for fiscal 1992. The subcommittee used that money to increase development and population aid and to provide $1 billion for the Development Fund for Africa, $200 million more than the administration's request.

Deputy Secretary of State Lawrence S. Eagleburger sent a letter to committee members warning that "we particularly oppose" the reduction in the administration's request for $625 million in military aid for Turkey. But the full committee followed the lead of the subcommittee, maintaining military aid for Turkey at its fiscal 1991 level of $500 million.

Some members expressed concern over report language, approved by the panel, urging the president to detail the aid the West would provide in return for "meaningful concrete actions" by the Soviet Union in implementing political and economic reforms.

Steny H. Hoyer, D-Md., said he worried about the impact the proposal would have on the democracy-minded Baltic States. But Edwards insisted that the subcommittee did little more than recommend that the president consider providing aid "when the Soviet Union becomes one of us" — a Western-style democracy.

HOUSE FLOOR ACTION

With a strong vote of approval that belied serious divisions, the House on June 19 approved HR 2621.

The $15.2 billion legislation, approved 301-102, reduced by $500 million the administration's request for a key category of military assistance. It increased funds for development and population aid, along with a range of programs aimed at helping children. *(Vote 181, p. 44-H)*

Obey called the bill the second installment "in a five-year plan to adjust foreign aid spending to the end of the Cold War."

The bill included an ambitious plan to stem the flow of arms to the Middle East, which could require the administration to temporarily halt weapons sales to the region. While providing $15 million in aid for the Soviet Union's Baltic republics, the legislation also provided guidelines for changes by the Soviet central government that would merit aid from the West.

Obey and Edwards were perhaps most proud that the legislation set aside $135 million to reduce the federal deficit. Edwards called the provision "one of the most important of the entire bill."

The administration all but ignored Obey's unique proposal providing $20 million to the U.N. Population Fund only if Congress backed the administration's request to grant MFN status to China and reiterated the threat of a veto if the bill remained in its existing form. But the administration and its congressional supporters refrained from a full-scale battle in the House over the issue, hoping that the provision would be stripped from the bill in a House-Senate conference on the legislation.

"This is not the final step for this bill," Edwards said. Obey insisted that a veto threat would not have been necessary if White House Chief of Staff John H. Sununu had heeded his plea to reach a compromise with backers of aid to the U.N. agency. He said he would have supported any such compromise "sight unseen."

But Obey said the administration did not try to negotiate a compromise until one hour after his subcommittee began marking up the bill, "obviously too late to have an effect on anybody or anything."

Limiting Amendments

For many Republicans, the continuing dispute over population fund aid was secondary to the frustrations they encountered in attempting to amend the bill once it was on the floor. Many chafed under what they viewed as an overly restrictive rule that barred floor amendments that had not been submitted in advance.

The night before the House took up HR 2621, Minority Whip Newt Gingrich, R-Ga., interrupted debate on another bill to lambaste the rule, calling it "an absolute assault on the middle class" because it prevented lawmakers from cutting spending from the appropriations measure.

But Obey defended the restrictions, noting that in recent years the House had generally limited debate on foreign aid spending bills. In addition, he said that the administration had sought most of the items in the bill and benefited from a more restricted debate.

Minority Leader Robert H. Michel, R-Ill., complained that the rule violated a "time-honored tradition" by failing to allow members to strike provisions from the bill. But he said he settled for Democratic assurances that such restrictions were to be used more sparingly in the future. The House voted, 264-145, to accept the restrictive rule. *(Vote 180, p. 44-H)*

Coincidentally, the House also resumed consideration of the foreign aid authorization bill (HR 2508) — with virtually no restrictions on debate — during the week of June 17.

The contrast in the way in which the House dealt with the two bills could not have been more striking: While lawmakers spent five days on the authorization bill, conducting scores of recorded votes, the appropriations measure breezed through with minimal debate in less than three hours.

Even potentially contentious issues, such as assistance to Jordan, were resolved with little fuss. The House approved an amendment by Harold L. Volkmer, D-Mo., to cut off all military aid to Jordan for fiscal 1992. The administration had requested $27 million in military assistance for the kingdom.

But Obey modified the amendment significantly, allowing the president to provide the assistance if he determined that it was "in the U.S. national interest" and certified that Jordan had terminated aid for Iraq and was backing the Middle East peace process. The authorization bill included much tougher conditions on assistance to Jordan.

The other amendments added during House debate were uncontroversial. An expected battle over military assistance for Turkey never took place. The bill reduced the administration's aid request for Ankara from $625 million to $500 million.

Edwards had considered an amendment that would have permitted the administration to lift the ceiling on military aid for Turkey. But he avoided forcing a divisive debate on the issue, hoping that the Senate would restore the administration's full request. The chairman of the Senate Appropriations Committee, Robert C. Byrd, D-W.Va., was Turkey's strongest congressional backer.

In what had become something of a tradition, the House approved by voice vote an amendment offered by James A. Traficant Jr., D-Ohio, that required an across-the-board cut of 1 percent in foreign aid funding. Obey modified that amendment as well, exempting countries whose aid levels were set by Congress — nations that received earmarked assistance — from the 1 percent cut.

Without that change, Israel, Egypt and Turkey would have been subject to the aid reduction. Traficant had already exempted anti-narcotics funding and the deficit-reduction provision from the cut.

The House approved Edwards' proposal to increase the amount provided to the Democracy Contingency Fund, an account the president could tap to aid emerging democracies, from $25 million to $50 million. The administration had requested $100 million for the fund.

Like all of the amendments considered, it was approved by voice vote.

Changing Priorities

The basic thrust of the foreign aid spending plan approved by the Foreign Operations Subcommittee was unchanged by the full House. It set significantly different priorities than the administration's foreign aid request.

"The committee believes that the priorities in the administration's budget do not address the real challenges and opportunities" the United States is confronting in a world that is "undergoing rapid changes," said the report accompanying the bill. The panel urged the administration to "present a more realistic budget for next year."

The bill reduced the administration's request for foreign military financing grants by $500 million, from $4.6 billion to $4.1 billion. While the legislation enabled the administration to provide $404 million in low-interest loans, almost $100 million more than the administration's request, the total for military grants and loans was nearly $410 million below the request.

In its statement on the bill, the Office of Management and Budget said the reduction would "hinder the president in fulfilling U.S. commitments to our key friends and allies."

Aside from Turkey, military aid for two other European nations where the United States had military bases — Portugal and Greece — was to be fixed at fiscal 1991 levels. Portugal received $100 million, $25 million under the request. Greece received $350 million, the amount sought by the administration.

The bill also transferred half of the military aid requested for the Philippines, another country where the United States had base rights, to development assistance. The legislation fully funded the administration's $160 million request for a multilateral assistance initiative for the Philippines, but it shifted $100 million of the $200 million military aid request to development assistance. *(Philippine base closings, p. 433)*

That pattern extended throughout the legislation. In reducing overall spending on military assistance, the bill increased funds for most development aid, as well as health and child survival programs.

The primary program supporting Africa's development needs, the Development Fund for Africa, was funded at $1 billion, $200 million more than the administration's request. And the bill provided $400 million in aid to Eastern Europe, a slight increase over the administration's $369.7 million request.

The legislation provided a $104 million increase over the administration's $479 million request for children's health and welfare programs, including the United Nation's Children's Fund, programs to combat AIDS and specific programs in Cambodia, Romania and Laos.

The bill also provided $680 million, nearly $170 million more than the administration had sought, to aid refugees around the world. The report accompanying the bill noted that the administration made its estimate of refugee needs in late 1990, well before the massive outpouring of refugees from Iraq in the immediate aftermath of the Persian Gulf War.

In addition to slashing requests for increased military aid, the House also rejected the administration's request for a $12.2 billion contribution to the International Monetary Fund.

In a reflection of continuing congressional hostility to any form of debt forgiveness, the legislation provided only $65 million of the $304 million sought by the administration for the debt-reduction portion of the Enterprise for the Americas Initiative.

And the House retained existing prohibitions barring the Export-Import Bank from financing arms sales overseas.

The Middle East

As had been the case for several years, approximately one-third of the funding in the foreign aid bill was directed toward Israel and Egypt. Israel received $3 billion, all of it in security-related aid — the same amount that was provided in fiscal 1991.

In addition, the bill retained a provision, first included in the 1990 appropriations bill (PL 101-513) under which Israel was eligible to receive up to $700 million in military equipment drawn down from U.S. stocks. Any materiel provided during the current fiscal year would be deducted from that total.

The bill also extended a provision granting the president the authority to locate up to $300 million in military stockpiles in Israel during fiscal 1992. The legislation earmarked $80 million in refugee aid for the resettlement of Jews from the Soviet Union and Eastern Europe who had emigrated to Israel.

Egypt received $2.15 billion in security-related aid, $1.3 billion in foreign military financing grants and $815 million in economic support assistance — the same amount provided during fiscal 1991.

Other Issues

The House bill also:

- Deferred the divisive issue of military aid to El Salvador until September at the administration's request. During floor debate, Matthew F. McHugh, D-N.Y., said the action was delayed to allow both sides to negotiate a truce in the country's long-running civil war.

"If either side fails to negotiate in good faith or acts to scuttle the talks, it should have a profound effect on our decision in the fall," McHugh said.

- Approved $20 million in development and humanitarian aid for Cambodians, in addition to the $5 million in assistance for Cambodian children.

But the report accompanying the bill expressed frustration that the administration had thus far provided aid only to the non-communist resistance in Cambodia, which had cooperated militarily with the Khmer Rouge rebels. The Khmer Rouge had killed more than a million Cambodians during its rule of the country from 1975 to 1979.

The report said the committee "would expect" the president to certify that no cooperation was occurring between the Khmer Rouge and the resistance before more aid could go to the resistance. In addition, the report strongly urged the administration to make "a genuine effort" to support civilians other than those involved with the resistance.

- Retained the existing restriction on aid to Pakistan, which the administration had sought to have lifted. The president was required to certify that Pakistan did not possess a nuclear device before Islamabad was eligible to receive U.S. aid.

CONTINUING RESOLUTION

Both chambers approved an omnibus continuing resolution Oct. 24 (H J Res 360) that included funds for foreign aid through the end of March 1992. Under the resolution, funding was to be provided at the level approved by the House in June or the fiscal 1991 level, whichever was lower. The House passed the legislation by a vote of 288-126; and the Senate cleared it by voice vote. *(Vote 340, p. 82-H)*

Although the House passed HR 2621 on June 19, Senate leaders deferred action on the fiscal 1992 foreign aid bill as part of an agreement with the administration to delay for four months consideration of Israel's request for $10 billion in loan guarantees.

In pressing for the delay, however, Bush earned the enmity of pro-Israel lawmakers and powerful U.S. organizations that lobbied for the Jewish state, perhaps setting the stage for a bitter confrontation over fiscal 1992 foreign aid spending.

Bush put his prestige on the line, saying Sept. 6 that he would "ask every single member of Congress to defer for just 120 days consideration" of the aid package.

Highlighting the importance of the issue for his administration, Bush said during a White House photo opportunity, "I know it is in the best interest of world peace to have this deferred."

Secretary of State Baker had asked Israeli Prime Minister Yitzhak Shamir to hold off on requesting the guarantees until after a Middle East peace conference held in the fall.

But Shamir rejected Baker's plea, and on Sept. 6 Israel formally requested the guarantees, which were to be used to back loans to help the Israeli government absorb an estimated 1 million immigrants from the Soviet Union and Eastern Europe over five years.

The day before, Bush had sought and received the assurance of Patrick J. Leahy, D-Vt., chairman of the Senate Appropriations Subcommittee on Foreign Operations, that he would postpone a confrontation on the issue by delaying consideration of the entire foreign aid appropriations bill.

Leahy said in a statement that he "strongly supported" providing the loan guarantees. "At the same time," he said, "if the president of the United States asks for a delay in the guarantees to help the chances for peace in the Middle East, I believe I should support him."

But congressional Democrats made significant concessions in accepting the delay on the spending bill and agreeing to continue funding in the continuing resolution. Liberals were reportedly disappointed that they lost the opportunity, for perhaps as long as six months, to place new restrictions on military aid to El Salvador.

Deputy Secretary of State Eagleburger wrote members of the Appropriations committees assuring them that the administration would abide by existing restrictions on El Salvador, imposed in the 1990 spending bill. Until a 1992 bill was passed, he said, the administration intended to provide no more than $3.5 million a month in military aid to the Salvadoran government.

Eagleburger said aid could be increased only if there was a "radical change in the military situation in El Salvador." During fiscal 1991 the administration waived conditions on aid, over the objections of some Senate Democrats.

Sen. Patrick J. Leahy, D-Vt., cosponsor of the 1990 restrictions, put the best face on the arrangement, saying the Senate still had the right to "seek new conditions on military aid if that is the will of this body."

Some lawmakers were also concerned that adoption of the continuing resolution meant that Congress would not have a foreign aid spending bill to use as a vehicle for aid to the Soviet Union. The House bill, approved before the dramatic changes in the Soviet Union, had included $15 million for the Baltic States and democratically elected republics.

Administration Split

There was also a split in the administration over what strategy to pursue on foreign aid. Treasury Secretary Nicholas F. Brady, upset that the continuing resolution did not provide for a $12.2 billion increase in the U.S. quota in the International Monetary Fund, had asked lawmakers to include that provision in the stopgap bill.

Treasury also had hoped that some funding would be provided for the debt-reduction portion of the Enterprise for the Americas Initiative.

But the State Department, afraid that any amendments to the continuing resolution could have opened the way for unwanted provisions on Israel and El Salvador, reportedly was successful in overruling Treasury.

State Department officials said that foreign aid might have to be increased substantially in 1992. In addition to possible Soviet aid and the Israeli guarantees — which probably would have to be backed with appropriated funds — the United States was likely to bear some costs of a U.N. peacekeeping force in Cambodia. A peace treaty was signed in Paris on Oct. 23 by Cambodia's warring factions.

Leahy, chairman of the Senate Appropriations Subcommittee on Foreign Operations, vowed to act on a 1992 spending bill "well before" the continuing resolution expired.

But the decision to defer action set up the fact that lawmakers would be confronted with two foreign aid bills — for fiscal 1992 and 1993 — within a six-month period during an election year. ■

Fiscal 1992 Natural Disasters Bill Signed

Congress cleared yet another "dire emergency" supplemental spending bill (H J Res 157 — PL 102-229), but action on the measure took so long that what had begun as a fiscal 1991 measure had to be turned into the first supplemental appropriations for fiscal 1992.

Technically, the bill appropriated $6.9 billion for farmers and communities that had been hit by natural disasters, and for the mop-up costs of Persian Gulf activities during Operation Desert Shield/Desert Storm. But in a compromise that helped guarantee that President Bush would sign the bill, appropriators agreed to make only $6 billion available unconditionally. The remaining $898 million could be spent — for disaster aid to communities and crop-loss money for farmers — only if the White House requested it and designated it as emergency funds.

The bargain gave both sides a political advantage: Appropriators could say they tried to make the full amount available but were blocked by the White House; the Bush administration could insist that it put a lid on runaway congressional spending.

Once Congress and the Bush administration had negotiated the truce, the House voted 303-114 to pass the measure Nov. 27; the Senate cleared it later that day by voice vote. Bush signed it (PL 102-229) on Dec. 12. The bill's progress had been blocked for months by a dispute between Congress and the White House over the price tag, and more important, how much of the bill should be classified as emergency spending. Under budget rules adopted in 1990, spending that both Congress and the White House designated as an emergency was not counted under the strict caps that limited discretionary appropriations.

BOXSCORE

➡ **Fiscal 1992 Supplemental (H J Res 157)** The bill appropriated $6.9 billion for farmers and communities that had been hit by natural disasters, and for the mop-up costs of Operation Desert Shield/Desert Storm.

Reports: H Rept 102-394; H Rept 102-255; S Rept 102-216.

KEY ACTION

Oct. 17 — The **House** Appropriations Committee approved HR 3543 by voice vote.

Oct. 29 — The **House** approved HR 3543, 252-162.

Nov. 15 — The **Senate** Appropriations Committee approved H J Res 157, 26-3.

Nov. 22 — The **Senate** approved H J Res 157, 75-17.

Nov. 27 — The **House-Senate** conference report on H J Res 157 was filed; The **House** approved it by a vote of 303-114; the **Senate** cleared it later that day by voice vote.

Dec. 12 — President Bush signed H J Res 157 — PL 102-229.

President's Request

Bush asked June 28 for $3.6 billion in supplemental appropriations, the largest chunk of which was $2.9 billion in 1991-92 funding for incremental costs of Operation Desert Shield/Desert Storm, primarily to replace or repair materiel lost, consumed or damaged in combat. The White House also requested $839.5 million in 1991-92 disaster assistance funds to help the Federal Emergency Management Agency (FEMA) meet unpaid bills for numerous domestic natural disasters and to allow the Defense Department to restore facilities destroyed or damaged by a tornado at an Air Force base in Kansas.

FEMA had already provided some assistance to families and individuals; this money was to help state and local governments repair or replace public facilities, such as roads and bridges, or to clean up debris.

The administration agreed to designate the military funding and $151 million of the FEMA money as emergency funds. It proposed that the rest be offset by spending cuts, including $542 million worth of cuts in funding for the Economic Development Administration and the Department of Housing and Urban Development.

HOUSE COMMITTEE ACTION

The House Appropriations Committee put the year's fourth supplemental on a fast track in early July, aiming to complete House action by the end of the month. But the appropriators quickly backed off, frustrated by White House veto threats over the emergency spending issue.

Appropriations Subcommittees

The subcommittee chairmen, known as the College of Cardinals, put themselves on a collision course with the White House, deciding on July 10 that they wanted all the non-defense money in the bill counted as emergency spending. They quickly set about creating a measure that would do just that, adding emergency items of their own and rejecting administration requests for offsetting spending cuts.

The Commerce, Justice, State Subcommittee met the same day and refused to approve a White House request to rescind $115 million in previously approved 1991 spending for the Economic Development Administration.

The subcommittee also added another $3.3 million in emergency spending for the National Oceanic and Atmospheric Administration to replace a destroyed computer system and reimburse the agency for work done in assessing the *Exxon Valdez* oil spill.

The next day, the Agriculture Subcommittee added $1.75 billion in emergency funding for crop-loss payments to farmers hit by freezes, floods and other agricultural disasters. The Interior Subcommittee added $10.3 million in emergency funding for abandoned mine reclamation, and the Energy and Water Subcommittee added $15 million for emergency repairs to four flood-weakened dams in Mississippi. None of the subcommittees proposed offsets for any of the additional funds.

Full Appropriations Committee

The full House Appropriations Committee was set to mark up the bill July 18 and send it to the House floor a week later, hoping to leave time for Senate action and a House-Senate conference before the August recess. The panel planned to include language designating all of the

Disasters/Gulf War Supplemental

On Nov. 27, Congress cleared a "dire emergency" fiscal 1992 supplemental spending bill (H J Res 157) that included help for farmers and communities hit by natural disasters and money for mop-up costs of Operation Desert Shield/Desert Storm. Non-emergency FEMA and CCC money in the final bill could only be spent if the White House requested it and designated it as emergency funds.

Amounts in parentheses were transferred from other accounts and did not require new budget authority. Amounts are in millions of dollars; totals may not add due to rounding.

	President's Request	House Passed	Senate Passed	Final Bill
Operation Desert Shield/Desert Storm				
Defense				
Procurement	—	—	$10.1	$113.1
National Guard personnel *	—	40.2	—	—
Operations and maintenance *	$227.3	$425.7	572.3	665.7
Procurement *	1,472.9	1,536.7	1,852.6	2,028.6
Research, development, test and evaluation *	108.5	108.5	106.3	106.3
Supply operations *	1,140.0	1,140.0	1,140.0	1,140.0
Transportation				
Coast Guard *	—	10.5	17.9	17.9
Veterans				
Medical care *	—	—	10.0	10.0
Defense (from previously appropriated funds)				
Military personnel	(951.0)	(951.0)	(951.0)	(951.0)
Operations and maintenance	(5,622.4)	(5,331.4)	(5,331.4)	(5,331.4)
General provision				
Protection, relief for Kurds *	—	—	115.0	115.0
Natural Disasters				
Independent Agencies				
Federal Emergency Management Agency (FEMA)				
(Emergency)	151.0	943.0	943.0	800.0
(Non-emergency or by special request)	542.0			143.0
Agriculture				
Commodity Credit Corporation (CCC)				
(Emergency)	—	1,750.0	1,750.0	995.0
(Non-emergency or by special request)	—	—	—	755.0
Soil Conservation Service	—	50.0	28.0	28.0
Emergency conservation program	—	5.0	—	—
Defense — Civil				
Corps of Engineers flood control	—	30.0	40.0	—
Interior				
Abandoned mine reclamation fund	—	10.3	—	—
Bureau of Reclamation	—	15.0	—	—
Geological Survey	—	5.0	—	—
Forest Service	—	25.0	—	—
Justice (by transfer)				
Community Relations Service	(7.7)	—	—	—
Commerce				
National Oceanic and Atmospheric Administration	—	1.3	0.3	—
Children				
Agriculture				
Women, Infants and Children	—	100.0	100.0	—
Health and Human Services				
Head Start	—	1,200.0	1,200.0	—
Childhood Immunization Program	—	90.0	90.0	—
Miscellaneous				
State Department emergencies	—	—	5.0	—
U.S. Information Agency	—	—	(5.6)	
Fish and Wildlife Service	—	—	(1.0)	(1.0)
Rescissions				
Economic Development Administration	115.0	—	—	—
Housing assistance	427.0	—	—	—
TOTAL				
New budget authority	$3,641.7	$7,486.3	$7,980.5	$6,889.6
(By transfer)	(6,581.1)	(6,282.4)	(6,289.0)	(6,283.4)

* *From the Defense Cooperation Account or the Persian Gulf Regional Defense Fund*

SOURCE: House Appropriations Committee

funding as emergency spending.

But that plan came unglued when Chairman Jamie L. Whitten, D-Miss., received a veto threat from Office of Management and Budget (OMB) Director Richard G. Darman. Whitten called off the markup and sought a meeting with Bush on the measure.

Much of Darman's veto warning concerned the $1.75 billion that Whitten's Agriculture Appropriations Subcommittee had added for disaster payments to farmers and ranchers. Whitten believed the money was fully justified as emergency spending; Darman called it "unwarranted" and said it would not qualify for emergency designation.

With appropriators divided over whether to force a test of wills with Bush, House leaders opted to try negotiating with the White House. Whitten talked with Bush and met with top administration officials, but the White House did not indicate any willingness to budge. With no compromise in sight, Whitten announced in late July that action would be postponed until after the August recess.

Markup sessions were scheduled in September, only to be canceled and rescheduled. In an attempt to jump-start the bill, Senate Appropriations Chairman Robert C. Byrd, D-W.Va., wrote to Whitten in late September suggesting that the House adopt a series of spending offsets due to expire at the end of fiscal 1991. But Whitten responded that he still intended to move a straight emergency bill.

On Oct. 17, the House Appropriations Committee finally approved a $5.8 billion bill (HR 3543) by voice vote. Defying veto threats, the panel sent the measure to the full House with no spending offsets. But members acknowledged that it almost certainly would not get far enough in that form to face a veto. Instead, it was assumed that once the bill got to conference, appropriators would bargain with OMB to fashion a bill acceptable to both sides.

In the meantime, House appropriators tried to embarrass the White House into declaring more of the funding as emergency money. Committee Chairman Whitten noted that Bush had approved more than $1 billion in emergency appropriations for other nations in 1991 but only about $39 million for domestic needs. "We have to take care of our own country," Whitten said. "The chips are down."

Before the bill came to the full committee, it had been revised, largely by dropping a few small spending items and adding an official finding of emergency conditions to justify the committee's insistence that the bill be designated as emergency spending.

Two significant amendments were approved by the full committee:

- A rider by John P. Murtha, D-Pa., chairman of the Defense Appropriations Subcommittee, added $447.8 million to allow the Air Force to replace F-15 fighter jets and laser-guided bomb kits lost or expended during Operation Desert Storm. The amendment was approved by voice vote.
- Vic Fazio, D-Calif., offered an amendment to change the way presidential candidates got money from the fund fueled by the $1 checkoff on income tax returns.

Under existing rules, money in the fund was set aside first for the general elections and the party conventions, leaving comparatively little in January through March for primary elections. Democrats worried that, given his much greater fundraising capacity, Bush would soak up most of the matching funds in January, long before his Democratic rivals had raised comparable amounts of money.

Fazio's provision required that funds be made available on the basis of tax returns anticipated in March, April and May, making more money available to Democratic challengers during the intensive January-to-March primary season. Fazio said the change would "level the playing field." Republicans denounced it as partisan politics and warned that it would draw a sure White House veto. The amendment was adopted on a 19-15 show of hands.

Authorization for Disaster Relief

The House on July 25 overwhelmingly passed a bill (HR 2893), 328-67, to authorize $1.75 billion in disaster spending for farmers that was part of the supplemental spending request. HR 2893 sought to extend the disaster provisions included in the 1990 Farm Bill (PL 101-624) to the 1991 disasters that hit farmers from Kansas to California. Relief payments were to be limited to $100,000 per person. The bill also prohibited assistance to farmers with gross revenues of more than $2 million a year.*(Vote 225, p. 54-H)*

The bill was referred to the Senate Agriculture Committee, which reported it with amendments on Oct. 25.

HOUSE FLOOR ACTION

The House approved HR 3543 on Oct. 29 — but not before loading it with add-ons that the administration warned would guarantee a veto. The measure passed by a vote of 252-162. *(Vote 352, p. 86-H)*

Beginning with the $5.8 billion measure reported by the Appropriations Committee, members added another $1.7 billion — chiefly aid for low-income children. The result was a $7.5 billion measure, nearly $4 billion more than what the administration had originally sought.

The bill "doesn't have a chance of seeing the light of day," warned Appropriations Committee ranking Republican Joseph M. McDade of Pennsylvania, who charged that Democrats had fattened it with spending that had nothing to do with emergency needs. McDade noted that OMB had issued not just one but two veto threats, one over the extra money and another over the campaign finance provision.

Whitten conceded that some of the spending added by the House would cause trouble with the White House, but he asked his colleagues to pass the measure anyway. "This is not the last chance to correct things in this bill, because now it goes to the Senate," Whitten said.

"There'll be a compromise," predicted Vin Weber, R-Minn., secretary of the House Republican Conference, who said that sustaining a veto in the House — presuming the campaign finance language had been eliminated — could be a "very dicey situation."

While there was widespread belief that the final bill would be a compromise, it was unclear how such a deal could evolve. Under the 1990 budget rules, appropriators had a fixed amount of money to spend in fiscal 1992, and the regular appropriations bills had used all but a very small portion of that. If the White House insisted on offsets, lawmakers had virtually nowhere to go but to the regular 1992 spending bills, which appropriators insisted were too tight already.

In a motion to send the bill back to committee, McDade proposed that offsets be included, but he was turned down, 180-232. He warned that unless the supplemental was modified, the administration could implement such a cut in the form of a disciplinary sequester under the budget rules. *(Vote 351, p. 86-H)*

During the course of the debate on Oct. 29, the House considered several topics unrelated to emergency spending. Included were:

- Three amendments by Joe L. Barton, R-Texas, that

sought to provide $50,000 to establish a mandatory drug-testing program for members of Congress. Opponents successfully challenged Barton's first two amendments on points of order that held that they constituted legislation on an appropriations bill. Barton's third amendment passed, 226-190, but it simply provided an additional $50,000 in internal spending for the House, with no direction as to how it should be spent. *(Vote 349, p. 84-H)*

- An amendment by John A. Boehner, R-Ohio, to cancel a $250,000 loan to Aristotle Industries to develop lists of registered voters to help House members more carefully target their government-paid mailings to constituents. The amendment failed, 182-231. *(Vote 350, p. 86-H)*

House Bill Highlights

As passed by the House, HR 3543 included:

- $3.3 billion for Operation Desert Shield/Desert Storm, primarily to replace or repair materiel lost, consumed or damaged during the war with Iraq.
- $1.75 billion for emergency payments to farmers and ranchers hard-hit by drought, floods and other natural disasters.
- $1.39 billion for three programs aimed primarily at low-income children: the Head Start preschool education program, the Women, Infants and Children nutrition program, and the Childhood Immunization program. The bulk of the money, $1.2 billion, was for Head Start. All of the money was added on the floor by Patricia Schroeder, D-Colo., on an amendment that passed 243-180. *(Vote 347, p. 84-H)*
- $943 million to enable FEMA to help communities cope with the costs of fires, floods, ice storms and other recent disasters.

When the bill left the Appropriations Committee, it included $693 million for FEMA. Whitten added another $250 million on the floor, primarily to cope with the costs of fires in Oakland, Calif., and in the states of Washington and Virginia. Whitten's amendment, which included another $85 million in emergency funds for five other agencies, was approved on a voice vote.

- The language changing the way presidential candidates received matching money from the taxpayer checkoff fund.

SENATE COMMITTEE ACTION

The Senate Appropriations Committee approved a nearly identical bill by a vote of 26-3 on Nov. 15, setting up a showdown with the White House. The price tag on the bill was slightly higher — $7.6 billion compared with $7.5 billion for the House bill.

Senate appropriators had been widely expected to pare the bill to meet administration objections, but they threw their House colleagues a legislative curveball. Ignoring the House-passed bill, they picked up a dormant measure sent to the Senate earlier in the year (H J Res 157), stripped it and built their own version of the emergency spending bill in the shell.

That allowed the Senate committee to drop the controversial House-passed checkoff fund language. "I didn't want it on our bill," said Chairman Byrd, who added that the provision would have opened the way for tax amendments and would have provoked "a sure filibuster" on the Senate floor.

Instead of scaling back the bill, the panel accepted virtually everything the House had passed and added a little military spending of its own. Thad Cochran, R-Miss., a committee member and a chief supporter of the farm aid provision, said the House had "sort of set the Senate up to be the heavy" by raising expectations that senators would cut the bill down to size.

As approved by the Senate Appropriations Committee, the bill included about $3.5 billion in mop-up costs for Operation Desert Shield/Desert Storm, $1.75 billion for crop-loss assistance to farmers and ranchers, $943 million for FEMA, $1.4 billion for three children's-assistance programs and smaller sums for other priorities.

The Senate panel also included a provision to bar military sales to Saudi Arabia and Kuwait until those countries paid an estimated $3.29 billion still owed the United States for expenses connected with the gulf war.

Like the House, the Senate provided no spending offsets. But Byrd added a twist of his own, including language that would have blocked spending any of the money unless the president declared it an emergency at the time he signed the bill. That would have prevented Bush from signing the measure, spending the money and then ordering an across-the-board spending cut in other domestic programs to pay for it — something he could have done with the House bill.

But the language would have opened the way for Bush to selectively designate emergency items in the bill, letting the others expire for lack of funds.

SENATE FLOOR ACTION

The Senate approved an $8 billion version of the dire emergency supplemental (H J Res 157) on Nov. 22, leaving little time before the end of the session for a critical House-Senate conference. The vote was 75-17. *(Vote 270, p. 35-S)*

Through much of the day, final passage seemed very much in doubt. With adjournment looming and senators increasingly desperate for a vehicle to carry their unfinished legislative business, the bill was the target for dozens of largely unrelated amendments.

By evening, Byrd began warning colleagues that the House would not accept any amendments that constituted legislation on an appropriations bill.

Byrd urged senators to offer their amendments, but when he found himself all but alone on the floor, he gave his colleagues 10 minutes to come forward or lose their chance. When the time expired, virtually all amendments had melted away, and Byrd moved the bill to final passage hours earlier than most participants had been predicting. As approved by the Senate, the supplemental increased mop-up funding for Operation Desert Shield/Desert Storm to $3.8 billion and included $1.75 billion in crop-loss payments for farmers and ranchers, $943 million for FEMA, $1.39 billion in additional funding for various children's programs, and smaller amounts for other priorities.

During floor action, the Senate also:

- By voice vote added controversial language to allow military servicewomen and dependents to obtain abortions in overseas military health facilities if they paid for the procedure. Approval of the language, offered by Frank R. Lautenberg, D-N.J., and amended by Tim Wirth, D-Colo., came after the Senate rejected, 40-57, a ruling by the chair that the amendment was out of order as legislation on an appropriations bill. *(Vote 268, p. 35-S)*
- Voted 47-51 to reject a dairy amendment offered by Agriculture Committee Chairman Patrick J. Leahy, D-Vt., that would have increased milk price supports by $1 per 100 pounds of milk and created a program to raise milk prices by cutting production. *(Vote 266, p. 35-S)*
- Voted 66-31 to table an amendment by Arlen Specter, R-Pa., and Pete V. Domenici, R-N.M., that would have permitted penalty-free withdrawals of up to $10,000 from

Continued on p. 667

Fiscal 1992 Natural Disaster Bill Provisions

Before adjourning Nov. 27, Congress cleared a fiscal 1992 "dire emergency" supplemental spending bill (H J Res 157) providing aid for communities hit by disasters, crop-loss money for farmers and mop-up funds for Operation Desert Shield/Desert Storm. Of the $6.9 billion appropriated in the bill, $6 billion was available unconditionally. The remaining $898 million could be spent only if the White House requested it and designated it as emergency spending.

The law (PL 102-229), signed on Dec. 12:

SUPPLEMENTAL APPROPRIATIONS

Appropriated, from funds still available under the fiscal 1992 defense spending cap, $180.1 million, to be divided as follows:

- **Patriot missiles.** $145 million to acquire additional Patriot missiles. The amount included $67 million from contract savings on the Maverick missile.
- **Navy shipbuilding and conversion.** $25 million for advance procurement of engines and generators for the cargo variant of the LSD-41 dock landing ship.
- **Air National Guard helicopter.** $10.1 million for one MH-60G helicopter.

DESERT SHIELD/DESERT STORM EMERGENCY

Appropriated $4 billion from the Defense Cooperation Account (made up of contributions from U.S. allies toward the cost of Operation Desert Shield/Desert Storm) or the Persian Gulf Regional Defense Fund (an account designed for temporary use when the Defense Cooperation Account was depleted due to slow payments by allies or other problems) for the following items:

Defense

- **Operations and maintenance.** A total of $665.7 million, to be divided as follows:

Army	$227.3 million
Navy	$270.0 million
Marine Corps	$75.0 million
Army Reserve	$23.2 million
Naval Reserve	$28.3 million
Army National Guard	$41.9 million

- **Procurement.** A total of $2 billion, to be divided as follows:

Army aircraft. $270.8 million to purchase 19 helicopters and modifications for 14 helicopters.

Army missiles. $21.8 million for restocking TOW and Stinger missiles.

Army tanks. $63 million to purchase 18 M-1A1 tanks.

Army vehicles. $80.5 million for 794 trucks and other vehicles.

Navy aircraft. $521 million to purchase 18 helicopters and attack and fighter jets, plus various aircraft modifications.

Navy weapons. $8.1 million for one 5-inch gun mount.

Navy equipment. $112.7 million for civil engineering equipment, mine-clearing sleds, trucks and medical support equipment.

Marine Corps vehicles. $4.3 million for four light armored vehicles.

Air Force aircraft. $268.8 million for three F-15E jet aircraft and $40.7 million for F-117A stealth aircraft.

Air Force munitions. $460.0 million for laser-guided bomb kits and $100 million for combined effects munitions.

Special Operations Command aircraft. $76.9 million for one AC-130 "U" model aircraft and one UH-60L helicopter.

- **Research, development, test and evaluation.** A total of $106.3 million, to be divided as follows:

Army: $7.5 million for development of chemical-biological defense equipment.

$8 million for development of a night vision system.

$1.3 million for technologies for defeating chemical/smoke equipment.

$1.6 million for a classified Army program.

$1.1 million for combat vehicle and automotive technology.

$1.1 million for military engineering technology.

$2.1 million for "TRACTOR HOLE," a classified program.

$2.1 million for development of logistics and engineer equipment.

$1.4 million for Army test ranges.

$6.2 million for exploitation of foreign intelligence items.

$1.7 million for land-mine war/barrier technology.

$13.7 million for various programs under $1 million each.

Navy: $1.3 million for a tactical command system.

$2.2 million for mine countermeasures.

$2.6 million for various programs under $1 million each.

Air Force: $7.3 million for the Airborne Warning and Control System (AWACS).

$1.8 million for electronic warfare development.

$3.3 million for a joint surveillance system.

$3.8 million for an intelligence program called Constant Source.

$0.7 million for armament ordnance development.

$3.4 million for surface defense suppression.

$4.0 million for various programs under $1 million each.

Defense agencies: $10.3 million for Flying Carpet, a classified program.

$5.6 million for DART, also classified.

$6.3 million for the Defense Advanced Research Project Agency.

$2.8 million for the Office of the Secretary of Defense.

$0.3 million for the Defense Communications Agency.

$2.7 million for the Special Operations Command.

$0.1 million for the Defense Support Project Office.

- **Defense Business Operations Fund.** A total of $1.1 billion, to be divided as follows:

Army supply operations	$410 million
Navy supply operations	$450 million
Air Force supply operations	$280 million

Transportation Department

- **Coast Guard.** $17.9 million for Coast Guard operating expenses.

Veterans Affairs

- **Veterans Health Administration.** $10 million for medical care.

Defense Department

In addition, $6.3 billion would be reallocated from money previously appropriated for Operation Desert Shield/Desert Storm for fiscal 1991 expenses, to allow the money to be used in fiscal 1992, as follows:

- **Military personnel.** $951 million for military personnel, to be divided as follows:

Army	$685 million
Navy	$70 million
Marine Corps	$18 million
Air Force	$81 million
Army Reserve	$80 million
Air Force Reserve	$4 million
Army National Guard	$10 million
Air Force National Guard	$3 million

- **Operation and maintenance.** $5.3 billion for operation and maintenance, to be divided as follows:

Army	$2.7 billion
Navy	$1.1 billion
Marine Corps	$165.0 million
Air Force	$1.2 billion
Army Reserve	$6.0 million
Air Force Reserve	$59.2 million
Army National Guard	$3.6 million
Air National Guard	$58.7 million

NATURAL DISASTERS EMERGENCY

Agriculture Department

- **Disaster relief.** Appropriated $1.8 billion for disaster payments to farmers and ranchers to compensate them for losses due to natural disasters during crop years 1990-92.

Of that amount, $995 million was available immediately, for losses in either 1990 or 1991. The other $755 million was available for losses in crop years 1990-92, but only if the president specifically requested it and designated the money as emergency spending under the budget rules. The $755 million included $100 million for program crops planted in 1991 for harvest in 1992; this provision was reportedly inserted at the request of Senate Minority Leader Bob Dole, R-Kan., to cover winter wheat.

• **Animal and Plant Health Inspection Service (APHIS).** Earmarked $530,000 in previously appropriated funds for a grant to the Maine Department of Agriculture, Food and Rural Resources for potato disease detection, control, prevention, eradication and related efforts, including compensation to persons for economic losses associated with such efforts.

Federal Emergency Management Agency (FEMA)

• **Disaster relief.** Provided $943 million, of which $800 million was available as emergency funding outside the budget caps. The other $143 million would be available only upon further presidential request. The money allowed FEMA to assist state and local governments throughout the United States and its territories in coping with the costs of natural disasters.

Future requests for emergency funding for disaster relief were tobe designated "emergency" funds outside the budget caps only to the extent that they exceeded either $320 million a year or the amount requested in the president's budget that year for disaster relief. The Bush administration had charged that congressional appropriators consistently and deliberately underfunded disaster relief accounts and relied on emergency requests to bail them out. This provision put substantial pressure on the appropriators to annually appropriate what the Bush administration said was the historical average amount needed for disaster relief.

GENERAL PROVISIONS

• **Congressional finding of emergency.** Found that the president had asked for more than $1.1 billion in emergency funds for foreign nations, but that meanwhile, floods, droughts, tornadoes, hurricanes, earthquakes, freezes and typhoons had created catastrophic situations in the United States. The bill found further that since October 1990, there had been 44 domestic disasters declared by the president and 89 by the secretary of Agriculture for which federal funds were not available to meet emergency needs. The combined effects of these disasters and the ongoing recession constituted a "dire emergency situation."

• **Congressional designation of emergency.** Provided a congressional designation of all the funds in Titles I and II as "emergency requirements." If the president also made such a finding in signing the bill, the money would not be counted under discretionary spending caps in the budget rules, which meant it would not trigger an across-the-board spending cut.

• **Soviet nuclear weapons dismantling.** Permitted the transfer of $400 million from fiscal 1992 defense spending to assist in the dismantling of Soviet nuclear weapons, provided that the readiness of U.S. military forces was not thereby diminished.

• **Soviet humanitarian assistance.** Permitted the transfer of $100 million from fiscal 1992 defense spending to transport food, medical supplies and other humanitarian assistance to the Soviet Union, its republics, or any localities, provided that the readiness of U.S. military forces was not thereby diminished.

• **Kurdish Protection Force.** Appropriated from funds available for Operation Desert Shield/Desert Storm, $100 million for the 1991 and 1992 costs of the U.S. military forces in Iraq and Turkey to protect Iraqi Kurds.

• **Middle East humanitarian relief.** Made available up to $15 million of the $100 million appropriated for the Kurdish Protection Force to pre-position relief supplies to meet Kurdish and other Iraqi-related emergency humanitarian needs. The Defense secretary could also transfer another $15 million for this purpose from funds available for the costs of Operation Desert Shield/Desert Storm.

• **Arms sales to Saudi Arabia and Kuwait.** Banned, beginning 120 days after enactment, arms sales to Saudi Arabia and Kuwait until those countries had finished paying the money they pledged as contributions toward the cost of Operation Desert Shield/Desert Storm.

• **Saudi and Kuwaiti parking tickets.** Warned the governments of Saudi Arabia and Kuwait that Congress was aware that Saudi diplomats owed thousands of dollars in parking fines in New York City and Washington, D.C., and that Kuwaiti diplomats still had outstanding fines in Washington, D.C., and that "continued failure to pay parking fines by foreign diplomats would result in legislative consideration of measures both to restrict benefits granted to such countries and to restrict diplomatic privileges enjoyed by such countries."

• **Repeal CRAF/Cassini cap.** Repealed the development cost cap on the Comet Rendezvous Asteroid Flyby/Cassini contained in the 1990 VA-HUD appropriations bill. A new development cost cap would be transmitted to Congress with the 1992 NASA operating plan.

• **National Commission on Severely Distressed Housing.** Transferred to the National Commission on Severely Distressed Housing $250,000 from the salaries and expenses account of the Department of Housing and Urban Development, to allow the commission to complete its work.

• **TWA pension fund.** Amended the Employment Retirement Income Security Act of 1974 in such a way as to prevent Carl C. Icahn, owner of Trans World Airlines, from being relieved of accountability for TWA's unfunded pension liabilities as long as Icahn had assets available and either owned TWA or controlled its board and management.

According to one of its sponsors, Sen. John C. Danforth, R-Mo., this provision was designed to block a proposal by Icahn to TWA's creditors that would involve reducing his ownership in TWA below 80 percent, the legal threshold for being "in control" of the airline, while still retaining his control of the TWA board and management.

• **Aid to Kenya.** Prohibited the use of any money appropriated by this bill or any money made available by the Economic Support Fund or the Foreign Military Financing Program to go to Kenya unless the president certified to Congress that the government of Kenya had improved its human rights behavior, including taking significant steps toward allowing the freedom to advocate the establishment of political parties and organizations.

During fiscal 1992, foreign assistance to Kenya could be made available only for new projects that met certain tests, such as promoting basic human needs or improving the performance of democratic institutions.

• **Ukrainian independence.** Expressed the sense of the Senate that the president should recognize Ukraine's independence and take steps toward establishing full diplomatic relations with Ukraine should the Dec. 1, 1991, referendum confirm the Ukrainian Parliament's independence declaration [which it did]. The bill also said that the president should use U.S. assistance, trade and other programs to support the government of Ukraine and encourage the further development of democracy and a free market in that country.

• **Botanic Garden renovation.** Provided that not more than $2 million in donated funds could be accepted or obligated to prepare working drawings, specifications and cost estimates for renovation of the Botanic Garden conservatory.

• **National Garden.** Authorized the Architect of the Capitol to construct a National Garden, which would demonstrate the diversity of U.S. plants, including the national flower, the rose. The garden would be constructed at the foot of Capitol Hill, between Maryland and Independence avenues S.W., extending from the Botanic Garden Conservatory to Third St. S.W. The Architect of the Capitol was authorized to accept gifts of money or non-compensated personal services for this project.

• **Senate ethics requirement.** Delayed until May 1, 1992, implementation of a new rule prohibiting senators from using campaign funds to pay for official expenses, such as furnishing and operating Senate offices or generating constituent newsletters. The fiscal 1991 legislative branch appropriations bill originally set a Jan. 3, 1992, deadline, but senators complained that they needed more time to understand how the new rule would affect them.

• **Exxon Valdez settlement.** Provided that funds received by the U.S. government from the settlement with Exxon over the *Exxon Valdez* oil spill be deposited in the Interior Department's Natural Resource Damage Assessment and Restoration Fund instead of into the Oil Spill Liability Trust Fund. The bill also provided for use of the funds to carry out the terms of the settlement.

- **Use of U.S. Senate seal.** Established protection and criminal penalties of a $250 fine and six months in prison for unauthorized use of any likeness of the seal of the U.S. Senate.
- **Four-ton dolly jacks — Buy American.** Prohibited buying four-ton dolly jacks outside the United States unless the Defense secretary waived the provision in the interest of national security.
- **Court of Veterans Appeals.** Provided that up to $950,000 of fiscal 1992 funding for the Court of Veterans Appeals be available for a demonstration program that would permit the Legal Services Corporation to make grants to organizations that assisted veterans in representing themselves before the court.
- **EPA wastewater treatment funds.** Provided that up to 1.5 percent of the funds appropriated for wastewater treatment facilities be made available by the Environmental Protection Agency for direct grants to Indian tribes.
- **Fishing vessel obligation guarantees.** Changed, from $10 million to $24 million, the limitation for the loan guarantee program level under "Fishing Vessel Obligation Guarantees" in the fiscal 1992 Commerce, Justice, State appropriations bill (PL 102-140).
- **U.S. Fish and Wildlife Service.** Transferred $965,000 from the $3.8 million in the U.S. Fish and Wildlife Service land acquisition account for acquisition of water rights in the Stillwater National Wildlife Refuge in Nevada. The money would instead go to Fish and Wildlife's resource management account to be used for various activities under the Truckee-Carson-Pyramid Lake Settlement Act.
- **Composite medical replacement facility.** Directed the secretary of Defense to continue construction of a composite medical replacement facility at Nellis Ar Force Basein Nevada.
- **Bridges in Vermont.** Earmarked funds, previously appropriated, for repair of the following bridges in Vermont: $350,000 to the city of Barre for the Granite Street Bridge; $350,000 to the city of Montpelier for the Bailey Avenue Bridge; $90,000 to the town of Brandon for the replacement of the Dean Bridge; and $90,000 to the town of Williston and $110,000 to the town of Essex for the North Williston Road Bridge. ■

Continued from p. 664

individual retirement accounts as long as the money was used to buy a home, an auto, home improvements or major appliances. *(Vote 269, p. 35-S)*

- By voice vote to approve an amendment by Edward M. Kennedy, D-Mass., to give Saudi Arabia and Kuwait a 120-day grace period before implementing the provision banning arms sales to those nations until they finished paying the $3.3 billion they owed in unpaid pledges for the cost of Operation Desert Shield/Desert Storm. Kennedy's intention was to avoid harm to U.S. arms manufacturers with pending sales to those countries.

CONFERENCE, FINAL ACTION

Nearly five months after it had begun work, Congress cleared a $6.9 billion version of the supplemental spending bill. The cost had been pared by House and Senate conferees in last-minute bargaining with the White House that budged both from positions that had changed little since Bush first asked for the funds.

In a key compromise, appropriators agreed to make only $6 billion in the bill available without conditions. The remaining $898 million could be spent — for disaster aid to communities and crop-loss money for farmers — only if the White House requested it and designated the money as emergency funds. A White House official said that was unlikely.

The House then quickly voted 303-114 to pass the conference report Nov. 27, and the Senate cleared it later that day by voice vote. *(Vote 438, p. 106-H)*

During the House-Senate conference that began on Nov. 25, White House pressure forced conferees to drop two controversial amendments, one on overseas abortions for U.S. military personnel and their dependents and another that would have changed the way presidential candidates could get financing from the taxpayer checkoff fund. Both had drawn veto warnings.

Administration pressure also forced conferees to sharply scale back the bill's size. They dropped the entire $1.39 billion in funding for children's programs added by the House and slashed the unconditionally available emergency funding for farmers and disaster-struck communities.

Overall, conferees cut more than $2 billion from the $8 billion measure passed by the Senate, but add-backs for Operation Desert Shield/Desert Storm and other Pentagon spending yielded a total of $6 billion to be available without a special presidential request. As part of the compromise, all the money immediately available under the measure was to be designated emergency spending, exempting it from the discretionary spending caps.

Conference Decisions

Key provisions in the final bill included:

- Of the $1.75 billion the House and Senate originally approved for crop-loss payments to farmers, $995 million was made available without additional White House action. The remaining $755 million included $100 million for certain crops planted in 1991 for harvest in 1992 — a provision reportedly added at the behest of Senate Minority Leader Bob Dole, R-Kan., for winter wheat.
- Of the $943 million originally approved to enable FEMA to help communities recover from natural disasters, $800 million was made available unconditionally. The other $143 million required a presidential request.

In exchange for the $800 million, OMB extracted a concession forcing the House and Senate VA-HUD Appropriations subcommittees (which handled FEMA money) to henceforth appropriate $320 million a year for domestic disasters. OMB had complained that the subcommittees consistently underfunded the FEMA account and relied on subsequent emergency supplementals to bail them out.

- The least contentious major provision provided $4.1 billion in mop-up costs for Operation Desert Shield/Desert Storm, primarily to replace or repair munitions or equipment expended, destroyed or damaged during the war with Iraq.
- The bill authorized the transfer of $400 million in previously appropriated Defense Department funds to help the Soviet Union dismantle its nuclear weapons. Another $100 million could be transferred to defray the cost of using U.S. military equipment and personnel to transport humanitarian aid to the Soviets. *(Soviet aid, p. 463)*

The bill also included provisions that:

- Banned arms sales to Saudi Arabia and Kuwait beginning 120 days after enactment unless those countries finished paying the $3.3 billion in outstanding pledges to underwrite Operation Desert Shield/Desert Storm.
- Banned security assistance to Kenya pending improvements in that government's human rights performance. ■

Fiscal 1991 'Dire Emergency' Bill Passed

In March, Congress passed a "dire emergency" supplemental spending bill for fiscal 1991 to pay for extra civilian costs that grew out of the Persian Gulf War.

The dire emergency bill moved through Congress in tandem with a separate and much larger Desert Storm supplemental measure (HR 1282 — PL 102-28) that covered the military costs of the war.

The bill, which began with administration requests totaling $3.7 billion, grew to $5.4 billion by the time it cleared.

About $1.6 billion of that was classified as emergency expenditures exempt from spending ceilings that had been agreed to as part of the 1990 budget deal.

The White House asked, and the congressional leadership agreed, that the Desert Storm measure be kept free of any add-ons, leaving the dire emergency bill as the vehicle for additional home-front war costs and other matters that Congress felt could not wait for the next round of regular appropriations bills. *(Desert Storm supplemental, p. 680)*

In the final analysis, the restraining hand of the White House appeared throughout the scores of provisions in HR 1281, scaling back many of lawmakers' more ambitious attempts at spending money.

Key items in the final bill included $650 million in emergency foreign aid for Israel and $200 million for Turkey, both of which stood by the United States during the war.

BOXSCORE

➡ **Fiscal 1991 Supplemental (HR 1281).** The bill provided $5.4 billion in new budget authority in fiscal 1991 for dozens of spending programs, some related to the war. The items included $1.5 billion for food stamps, $650 million for Israel, $200 million for Turkey and a $100 million payment for the District of Columbia.

Report: H Rept 102-29.

KEY ACTION

March 5 — The **House** Appropriations committee approved the supplemental by voice vote.

March 7 — The **House** approved a $4.1 billion version of the supplemental by a vote of 365-43.

March 14 — The **Senate** Appropriations Committee voted 24-0 to approve a $5.2 billion version of the bill.

March 20 — The **Senate** approved the dire emergency supplemental 92-8.

March 22 — The **House** approved the conference report on the $5.4 billion dire supplemental 340-48; the **Senate** cleared the bill by voice vote.

April 10 — President Bush signed HR 1281 — PL 102-27.

Veterans Assistance

The measure contained more than $1.3 billion worth of salary increases and education, health and other benefits for veterans. This included a $655 million package specifically for gulf war veterans, which was to be paid for out of contributions by U.S. allies in the war. It also included $659.5 million to provide for a cost of living pay increase and for other needs for all veterans. *(Gulf veterans benefits, p. 320)*

The final bill eliminated nearly $600 million in defense funding that had been approved in the House version.

Much of the money would have gone to buy Patriot missiles and other weapons in quantities greater than the Defense Department said were needed to replace items used during the war.

Congress also rejected a proposal urged by Department of Housing and Urban Development (HUD) Secretary Jack F. Kemp to jump-start a trio of new housing programs. Similar proposals had failed on the House floor and in the House and Senate Appropriations committees, beaten back by Democrats who insisted that Kemp wait for the fiscal 1992 funding cycle to begin the programs.

HOUSE SUBCOMMITTEE ACTION

The dire emergency supplemental was pieced together largely from White House requests. President Bush asked for more than $2 billion in net, non-emergency supplemental spending when he submitted his fiscal 1992 budget on Feb. 4.

The White House asked for an additional $89.8 million in 1991 emergency spending in a request Feb. 22. The money was to offset the costs of increased security and other activities related to the gulf war.

House Appropriations subcommittees launched a blitzkrieg round of markups Feb. 27.

White House Scenario

Members worked almost exclusively from the script provided by the White House, shaving or slashing administration requests here and there but adding little new spending. The following are highlights of subcommittee action:

- **VA/HUD.** The Subcommittee on Veterans Affairs and Housing and Urban Development handed Kemp a disappointing setback, rejecting his plan to shift nearly $800 million in previously approved 1991 funding away from various housing programs — primarily public housing construction — to provide money for HOPE (Home Ownership and Opportunity for People Everywhere), an administration initiative to allow public housing tenants to buy their units; HOME Investment Partnerships, a block-grant-like Democratic plan to provide housing funds to states and cities; and Shelter Plus Care, a program to provide shelter and social services to the homeless.

However, the panel did cut $275.8 million from Section 8 rental subsidies that were slated to be used for housing for the elderly and disabled. Of that amount, $155.8 million was transferred into Section 8 rental subsidy contract renewals and $75 million for public housing operating subsidies.

The subcommittee also added $58 million for the Department of Veterans Affairs (VA) — $46 million for medical care and $12 million for operating expenses. According to a subcommittee aide, the VA had asked for money for medical care but was turned down by the Office of Management and Budget (OMB), which declined to include the funding in the supplemental request.

The subcommittee added it anyway and indicated that

it wanted the $58 million counted as emergency Operation Desert Storm money not subject to spending caps. The subcommittee also approved a much larger amount of veterans money — $303.1 million — but did this merely to fulfill a pre-agreed upon plan to give disabled veterans a cost of living adjustment called for in the president's budget and approved by Congress (HR 3) in January.

• **Labor/HHS.** The Subcommittee on Labor and Health and Human Services doubled an administration request for $100 million to help states handle the administrative costs of running unemployment insurance programs.

The subcommittee approved an administration request for $232 million for reviews of cases in which disabled children were denied Supplemental Security Income (SSI) payments. The reviews were ordered by the Supreme Court in 1990.

In action the administration did not request, the panel also voted to release $100 million from the regular Social Security contingency fund for processing and review of disability claims.

The subcommittee also provided $25 million in 1991 funds to start up an infant mortality initiative included in Bush's 1992 budget.

However, subcommittee members specifically rejected an administration request to divert $33.7 million from other maternal and child health programs to start the new program.

• **Commerce/Justice/State.** The subcommittee approved $61.1 million in war-related emergency funding for the Departments of Justice and State and for the U.S. Information Agency, tracking the administration's request. The administration had asked for funding to handle, among other things, the evacuation of employees and increased security costs.

The subcommittee also approved $186.8 million in supplemental appropriations unrelated to Desert Storm, including funds for judges' salaries and witness fees, again tracking requests by the administration.

The only money the subcommittee added was $2 million for the Federal Trade Commission.

• **Energy/Water.** The Subcommittee on Energy and Water Development approved $482.5 million of the $623 million in the administration's supplemental requests.

The panel approved the full administration request for $340 million to clean up nuclear wastes at various defense facilities. But it cut from $283 million to $142.5 million a request for money to resume plutonium operations at the Rocky Flats Plant in Colorado. The subcommittee added $30 million the administration had not requested for emergency drought relief. Vic Fazio, D-Calif., said the money was needed because parts of the West were entering their seventh year of drought.

Of the money, $10 million was for drilling wells and buying water for wildlife refuges and $10 million was for alternative water sources for communities as well as streams and wildlife refuges.

The remaining $10 million was to be used for new equipment for Bureau of Reclamation project facilities to assure water deliveries when reservoirs were low and to construct saltwalter intrusion barriers in the Sacramento-San Joaquin Delta. An aide said the money would come from unused fiscal 1991 funds.

• **Defense.** The subcommittee added $333.6 million in emergency funding — $224 million to build 342 Patriot missiles, $45.3 million to buy 2,500 TOW anti-tank missiles, $29.6 million to pay for 120mm mortar ammunition for the Army and $34.7 million for modifications to Marine Corps Hawk missiles. It assumed that the money for these expenditures would come from the Defense Cooperation Account, set up to receive contributions from U.S. allies in the gulf war.

The subcommittee also added $407.5 million in non-emergency money for operations and maintenance and research and development, including $58 million for Patriot missile upgrades, $79.5 million for depot maintenance and $270 million for CHAMPUS (the Civilian Health and Medical Program of the Uniformed Services, the military's health-care system for active-duty personnel and their dependents).

The committee agreed to require the Defense Department to spend previously appropriated funds for building the V-22 Osprey tilt-rotor troop transport aircraft in Texas; and paying for the Service Life Extension Program for the aircraft carrier USS *Kennedy* at the Philadelphia Naval Shipyard.

• **Agriculture.** The subcommittee had little choice but to approve an administration request for $200 million in increased spending for the mandatory food stamp program. The panel rejected an administration request to rescind $10 million in 1991 spending authority for the Soil Conservation Service, and it added $46.9 million for the Agricultural Stabilization and Conservation Service, money the administration would have transferred from another account.

• **Military Construction.** The subcommittee approved language lifting a moratorium on construction projects imposed in 1990 by Defense Secretary Dick Cheney. Work could begin on bases not included in an April 15, 1991, list of bases to be closed or realigned.

• **District of Columbia.** The subcommittee approved $3.6 million in extra 1991 funding to help the District government cope with the possible threats of terrorism related to the gulf war.

• **Transportation.** The subcommittee approved $18.9 million for Operation Desert Storm funding for the Coast Guard and $14.5 million for the Coast Guard retired pay account.

FULL COMMITTEE

The full committee approved the supplemental by voice vote March 5, after agreeing to add $650 million in emergency assistance requested by the administration for Israel and making several other smaller changes. The committee also accepted an amendment by John P. Murtha, D-Pa., to prevent the Labor Department from using funds to implement or administer regulations creating a new category of low-wage "helpers" in the construction industry; the regulations modified the Davis-Bacon Act, which required federal contractors to pay prevailing wage rates, typically the union scale.

And it agreed to require the Navy to pay Grumman Industries, within 30 days of enactment, $987 million in previously appropriated money to upgrade F-14 aircraft.

Also added was a $100 million federal payment to the District of Columbia to help meet the costs of hosting the federal government. *(D.C. appropriations, p. 616)*

FLOOR ACTION

The House approved a $4.1 billion version of the supplemental March 7 by a vote of 365-43. *(Vote 35, p. 10-H)*

1991 'Dire Emergency' Supplemental . . .

(Budget authority of HR 1281 in millions of dollars)

	President's request	House	Senate	Final
EMERGENCY				
Commerce				
International Trade Administration	—	$ 3.0	$ 0.3	—
National Oceanic and Atmospheric Administration	—	2.8	0.6	—
National Institute of Standards and Technology	—	1.6	—	—
Justice				
FBI, INS terrorism-related costs	7.7	7.7	7.7	7.7
State				
Salaries, emergency costs	49.0	49.0	49.0	49.0
U.S. Information Agency	4.4	5.4	4.4	4.4
By transfer	—	(1.4) [1]	(1.4) [1]	(1.4) [1]
Defense Department				
TOW, Patriot missiles	—	(269.3) [2]	—	—
Army ammunition	—	(29.6) [2]	—	—
Hawk missile modification	—	(34.7) [2]	—	—
District of Columbia				
Costs tied to protests, security	3.6	3.6	3.6	3.6
Funds appropriated to the president				
AID employee evacuations	6.0	6.0	6.0	6.0
Aid to Israel	650.0	650.0	650.0	650.0
Aid to Turkey	200.0	—	200.0	200.0
Legislative Branch				
Capitol police security	11.5	7.1	7.5	7.3
Library of Congress security	0.6	—	0.4	0.1
Panama Canal Revolving Fund				
(limit on expenses)	—	(60.0)	(60.0)	(60.0)
Treasury				
BATF explosives training, bomb-threat management	$ 2.0	$ 2.0	$ 2.0	$ 2.0
Customs Service	—	—	$ 1.8	$ 1.8
Secret Service	4.9	4.9	4.9	4.9
Veterans				
VA medical care	—	46.0	25.0	25.0
VA operating expenses	—	12.0	12.0	12.0
Military Benefits	—	—	(500.0) [2]	(655.0) [2]
	—	—	50.0	50.0
NON-EMERGENCY				
Justice				
Legal activities	9.2	9.2	13.2	11.2
By transfer	(6.1) [1]	(6.1) [1]	(6.1) [1]	(6.1) [1]
Equal Employment Opportunity Commission	—	1.0	2.0	3.6
Legal Services Corporation	—	1.0	1.0	1.0
Judiciary				
Salaries, fees, expenses	79.9	79.9	78.3	79.1
Commerce				
Census Bureau	—	(1.0) [1]	(1.0) [1]	(1.0) [1]
Economic and Statistical Analysis	—	1.0	—	1.0
Economic Development Administration rescission	—	−9.6	−20.0	−24.0
National Oceanic and Atmospheric Administration	—	—	3.0	3.0
Federal Communications Commission	—	1.0	1.0	1.0
Federal Trade Commission	—	2.0	1.0	2.0
International Trade Administration	—	1.5	1.5	1.5
Export Administration	—	—	—	1.4
U.S. Travel and Tourism Administration	—	—	—	1.1
Securities and Exchange Commission	—	$ 2.0	$ 1.0	$ 1.6
Small Business Administration	—	(1.5) [1]	(1.5) [1]	(1.5) [1]

[1] *By transfer from other accounts; does not add to total*
[2] *By transfer from the Defense Cooperation Account, which contains allied war contributions*

The Bush administration challenged several of the spending proposals designated by the House as war-related emergencies. Budget rules enacted in the fiscal 1991 reconciliation bill (HR 5835 — PL 101-508) exempted appropriations for the military buildup and war in the gulf or for other presidentially defined emergencies from strict spending caps.

But the White House warned that it would take a hard line on which costs qualified for exemptions. The distinction had important implications: Non-emergency discretionary spending had to stay within the fiscal 1991 budget caps; if it did not, it would trigger an across-the-board cut, or sequester.

OMB objected to a House decision to provide $8.3 million more than the White House requested for the U.S. Information Agency and for a variety of Commerce Department agencies, some of it to pay for evacuating agency personnel because of the war. OMB also argued that most of the extra money for VA medical care could not be justified as emergency spending because the war did not create "an unmanageable burden" of casualties.

OMB said preliminary estimates showed that the House bill would trigger an automatic $53 million sequester in domestic discretionary spending.

Highlights of floor action follow:

- **Aid to Israel.** Some of the sharpest exchanges occurred over the proposed $650 million for Israel. The funding underwent a rhetorical shelling but easily survived four attempts to cut it back or kill it.

Tim Valentine, D-N.C., proposed deleting the entire

. . . Funds Emergency, Other Programs

(Budget authority of HR 1281 in millions of dollars)

	President's request	House	Senate	Final
State				
Board for International Broadcasting	$ 8.0	$ 8.0	$ 8.0	$ 8.0
International fisheries commissions	—	0.1	0.1	0.1
Defense				
Operations and maintenance, R&D	—	407.5	—	150.0
District of Columbia				
Essential municipal services	—	100.0	100.0	100.0
Interior				
Bureau of Reclamation	—	30.0	20.0	25.0
Energy				
Atomic Energy defense activities	623.0	603.0	623.0	623.0
Delaware/Susquehanna River Basin Commissions	—	0.1	0.1	0.1
Labor				
State unemployment insurance programs (limit on transfers)	(100.0)	(200.0)	(150.0)	(150.0)
Health, Human Services				
Infant mortality initiative	—	25.0	25.0	25.0
Social Security	232.0	232.0	232.0	232.0
(Limit on administrative expenses)	(232.0)	(232.0)	(232.0)	(232.0)
Vaccine injury compensation	—	—	17.0	17.0
Legislative branch				
Gratuities, deceased members	—	0.1	0.1	0.1
Agriculture				
Cooperative State Research Service	—	—	(0.1) [1]	(0.1) [1]
Animal, plant inspection	13.0	13.0	13.0	13.0
Food Safety and Inspection Service	8.0	8.0	8.0	8.0

	President's request	House	Senate	Final
Agricultural Stabilization and Conservation Service	$ (86.9) [1]	$ 46.9	$ 46.9	$ 46.9
Commodity Credit Corporation	—	—	1.4	1.4
Soil Conservation Service rescission	−10.0	—	—	—
Food Stamps	1,500.0	1,500.0	1,500.0	1,500
Transportation				
Coast Guard, retired pay	14.5	14.5	14.5	14.5
Maritime Administration	—	—	20.0	20.0
Highway Traffic Safety Administration	—	—	(10.0)	(10.0)
Veterans				
Compensation and pensions	303.1	303.1	712.6	712.6
Readjustment benefits	—	—	250.0	250.0
Housing and Urban Development				
Renewal of Section 8 contracts	(155.8) [1]	155.8	155.8	155.8
HOPE grants	165.0	—	—	—
HOME Investment Partnerships	500.0	—	—	—
Section 8 moderate rehabilitation	(24.0) [1]	—	—	—
Section 202 rental assistance	18.0	—	—	—
Homeless rental housing assistance	80.0	—	—	—
Public housing	−539.1	−275.8	−275.8	−298.8
Public housing operating subsidies	—	75.0	75.0	75.0
Rental rehabilitation grants	−70.0	—	—	—
Congregate services program	−9.5	—	—	—
Urban development action grants	−13.5	—	—	—
Urban homesteading	−13.4	—	—	—
Rehabilitation loan fund	−135.0	—	—	—
TOTAL	3,702.9	4,136.4	4,654.0	4,786.1
By transfer	(272.8)	(10.0)	(11.1)	(11.1)
By transfer, Defense Cooperation Account	—	(333.6)	(500.0)	(655.00)

[1] *By transfer from other accounts; does not add to total*
[2] *By transfer from the Defense Cooperation account, which contains allied war contributions; does not add to total*

amount. He insisted he was a strong Israel supporter, but he argued that "foreign aid is out of control."

David R. Obey, D-Wis., chairman of the Foreign Operations Appropriations Subcommittee, defended the aid as "part of the price we're going to have to pay" in the aftermath of the war. Obey said the aid was conditioned on a pledge by Israel not to request any more funds until after Labor Day, Sept. 2, less than a month before the start of fiscal 1992. Other members argued that the aid was more than justified by Israel's years of staunch support for the United States and the punishment it suffered from Iraqi Scud missiles during the gulf war. The House rejected Valentine's aid cut 24-397. *(Vote 30, p. 8-H)*

James A. Traficant Jr., D-Ohio, offered three more amendments to cut the Israel aid — by $250 million, $50 million and $13 million. The House rejected all three on voice votes.

- **Philadelphia Shipyard.** Members rejected, 105-315, an amendment by Dan Burton, R-Ind., that would have eliminated the provision directing the Navy to begin spending 1991 funds to overhaul the USS *Kennedy* at the Philadelphia Naval Shipyard. *(Vote 32, p. 8-H)*
- **HUD programs.** The House voted 177-240 to reject an amendment by Jim Kolbe, R-Ariz., that would have allowed Kemp to reshuffle 1991 funding to start housing programs authorized by Congress the previous year. Kemp, a former GOP House member from Buffalo, N.Y., came to the floor to lobby in person for the amendment, but to no avail. *(Vote 33, p. 8-H)*

Kolbe and others argued that Kemp should be allowed

to get HOPE and HOME up and running, instead of waiting until fiscal 1992. But Bob Traxler, D-Mich., chairman of the VA/HUD Appropriations Subcommittee, said it was premature to fund the programs before determining whether there would be enough money to keep them going in 1992.

• **Helpers.** The House rejected, 173-244, an amendment by Charles W. Stenholm, D-Texas, to eliminate the provision barring the use of money to implement regulations that would permit the use of helpers on federally funded construction projects. Arguing against the Stenholm amendment, Education and Labor Committee Chairman William D. Ford, D-Mich., said the the regulations would create a new classification of workers not protected by the Davis-Bacon Act and that the appropriate vehicle for such a fundamental change was authorizing legislation, not executive regulations. *(Vote 34, p. 8-H)*

• **Rocky Flats Plant.** John T. Myers, R-Ind., won voice-vote approval of an amendment to restore $120.5 million of the $140.5 million cut from the administration request for money to resume plutonium operations at the Rocky Flats Plant. Myers argued that the money was critical to allow the plant to resume production of triggers for nuclear weapons.

• **Highway Trust Fund.** Public Works Committee Chairman Robert A. Roe, D-N.J., succeeded in enforcing a point of order to remove language from the supplemental that he argued would have changed the way the Department of Transportation (DOT) handled certain unspent money from the Highway Trust Fund. Instead of mandating that the money be reallocated to the states every year, the language would have permitted DOT to keep the money in the trust fund.

SENATE COMMITTEE ACTION

The Senate Appropriations Committee performed major surgery on the House-passed bill March 14, slicing out more than $700 million in what it said was unjustified defense spending and adding $1.2 billion in benefits for veterans and active-duty troops.

The Senate panel also added $200 million in aid to Turkey as a reward for that nation's role as a key U.S. ally during the gulf war and the prewar confrontation with Iraq, in addition to approving the House-passed grant of $650 million to Israel. The Senate also left intact the $100 million House increase for the District of Columbia.

In further agreement with the House, the committee rejected Kemp's proposal to shuffle nearly $800 million in housing funding to provide start-up money for new housing programs. Supporters vowed to seek an amendment on the Senate floor to provide the HUD money.

The action came as the committee voted 24-0 to approve a $5.2 billion version of the bill.

Defense/Veterans

The committee jettisoned hundreds of millions of dollars in spending proposals and substituted many of its own ideas.

In a significant departure from the House-passed bill, the Senate committee disallowed $741.1 million in spending the House had approved for military hardware, including the Patriot and TOW missiles, and other Defense Department expenses.

The Senate committee noted that it had already provided money in the Desert Storm supplemental to buy enough of both missiles to replace those shot off during the war with Iraq, and it refused to go along with the House in buying more. The panel likewise refused to include spending authority for mortar ammunition and HAWK missile modifications, on the grounds that neither item was requested by the Defense Department.

The Senate appropriators also zeroed out $407.5 million provided by the House to the Defense Department accounts for operation and maintenance and for research, development, testing and evaluation, also on the grounds that the Defense Department had requested none of the money.

While they slashed House-passed defense spending, the Senate appropriators approved three amendments that tracked House provisions to make sure the Pentagon spent money for defense projects that the military thought it could live without — but that had tenacious congressional backing because they provided jobs in four states.

The committee agreed to require the Defense Department to spend previously appropriated funds to upgrade F-14 fighter jets, a move designed to keep Grumman Corp. plants on Long Island and Maryland's Eastern Shore in business; to build the V-22 Osprey, which provided business for the Boeing Co. and Textron Inc. in Pennsylvania and Texas; and to pay for the Service Life Extension Program for the aircraft carrier USS *Kennedy* at the Philadelphia Naval Shipyard.

After taking military money out of the supplemental, the Senate panel added back $1.2 billion in benefits for veterans and for active-duty military personnel and their dependents.

In response to a VA request that came a day before the markup, the panel added $409.5 million to House-approved funds to account for revised caseload and cost estimates for veterans compensation payments. The committee also provided $250 million above the House amount for readjustment benefits to handle higher-than-expected payments to regular military personnel who left the service in 1991.

The committee also provided $550 million for benefits authorized the same day by the full Senate in a bill (S 578) aimed at increasing pay and other benefits for military personnel who served in the Persian Gulf. The bulk of the money, $500 million, was to be paid for out of the Defense Cooperation Account by funds provided by U.S. allies in the war against Iraq. But $50 million for family education and support and for child-care assistance was to come from U.S. funds.

Other Action

Other highlights of the Senate committee's action on the dire emergency supplemental included:

• **Aid to Turkey.** When it saw the House approve $650 million in aid to Israel, Turkey asked the Bush administration for at least the same amount, according to Richard G. Darman, director of OMB. Darman and Byrd, a longtime Turkey supporter, dickered over the figure, ultimately arriving at $200 million. Like the aid to Israel, the money for Turkey was designated as emergency spending not subject to caps on foreign aid.

• **State unemployment insurance administration.** The Senate worked out a compromise with the administration to provide $150 million in extra money to the states to help administer unemployment insurance programs, which had come under heavy pressure during the recession. The

Continued on p. 678

'Dire Emergency' Supplemental Provisions

Following are provisions of the 'Dire Emergency' Supplemental spending bill (HR 1281) as signed by President Bush on April 10:

EMERGENCY SUPPLEMENTAL APPROPRIATIONS

Justice

• **FBI.** Appropriated $4.633 million for salaries and expenses for the FBI to supplement counterterrorism programs.

• **INS.** Appropriated $3.103 million for the Immigration and Naturalization Service (INS) for salaries and expenses to cover the cost of overtime and security upgrades resulting from enhanced INS inspections at ports of entry and from heightened investigations of Iraqi non-immigrants.

State

• Appropriated $39.7 million to reimburse the State Department for additional security, communications, evacuation claims, emergency travel support and crisis requirements.

• Appropriated $9.3 million for emergencies in the diplomatic and consular service. The money was to cover evacuations of U.S. citizens from the Middle East and Africa.

U.S. Information Agency

• Appropriated $5.8 million for the U.S. Information Agency (USIA), of which $1.4 million would be transferred from USIA's radio construction account, subject to the Defense Department waiving reimbursement for the costs of setting up a temporary broadcast facility for the Voice of America (VOA) in Bahrain. The money would reimburse USIA for emergency evacuation costs and allow expanded VOA broadcasting in the Persian Gulf.

District of Columbia

• Appropriated $3.565 million for the District of Columbia to reimburse the D.C. government for expenses related to demonstrations and increased security for diplomats and for federal facilities and officials.

Agency for International Development

• Appropriated $6 million for the Agency for International Development, to be available only for the costs of evacuating U.S. government employees and personal services contractors and their dependents, and for subsistence payments.

Aid to Israel and Turkey

• Appropriated $850 million for the Economic Support Fund, of which $650 million would be made available for Israel and $200 million for Turkey. The money, in cash grants, would remain available until Sept. 30, 1991. The money could be used by Israel and Turkey to meet the incremental costs of the conflict in the Persian Gulf.

Legislative Branch

• Appropriated $6.239 million for salaries for the Capitol Police, of which $3.143 million would be for the Sergeant-at-Arms of the House, and $3.096 million for the Sergeant-at-Arms and Doorkeeper offices of the Senate. The money provided funds for six police K-9 positions, to be filled by vacancies or by upgrading current patrols. There were also funds to add 10 freight-handler positions for the off-site delivery center, which screened deliveries to the Capitol.

• Appropriated $1.081 million for general expenses for the Capitol Police. Included in that sum was $103,000 to equip six additional K-9 teams, including $15,000 to buy dogs.

Library of Congress

• Appropriated $74,000 for salaries and expenses for the Library of Congress to allow the library to fill nine authorized but previously unfunded police positions.

Panama Canal Commission

• Increased by $60 million the fiscal 1991 obligation on non-administrative and capital programs to meet the unexpectedly high traffic from disruptions in world markets caused by the Middle East crisis.

Treasury

• **BATF.** Appropriated $2.028 million for salaries and expenses for the Bureau of Alcohol, Tobacco and Firearms (BATF). The money was to help BATF enhance its bomb and explosives investigative capabilities to counter increased terrorist threats in the United States as a result of the war with Iraq. The funds were to pay for command center trucks, bomb disposal trucks, all-terrain vehicles, X-ray equipment, overtime and travel, cellular telephones and bomb-disposal suits.

• **Customs.** Appropriated $1.825 million for the U.S. Customs Service for salaries and expenses. The money included amounts to increase security at small ports of entry, protect customs personnel and facilities, increase enforcement of illegal export of munitions, operate crisis watch centers and provide overtime for air staffing.

• **Secret Service.** Appropriated $4.906 million for salaries and expenses for the U.S. Secret Service to pay for increased overtime, expanded protective details and other security activities.

Veterans Affairs

• Appropriated $25 million to provide for unbudgeted medical expenses for the Veterans Health Service and Research Administration resulting from Operation Desert Shield/Desert Storm.

• Appropriated $12 million for the Veterans Benefits Administration for general operating expenses generated by unbudgeted costs from Operation Desert Shield/Desert Storm.

Agriculture

• Repealed the cap of $425 million on the Export Enhancement Program (EEP), which was used primarily to subsidize and promote the sale of U.S. wheat in foreign markets. The Agriculture Department estimated that with no cap on EEP, it would spend about $900 million in fiscal 1991 to subsidize exports of wheat and other commodities.

House and Senate conferees said in the conference report that they expected the Agriculture Department to use the Commodity Credit Corporation and other authority to remove surplus milk products from the domestic market and donate them as a bonus (in addition to regular purchases) to various domestic feeding programs, such as the Women, Infants and Children nutrition program.

The conferees also strongly urged the Agriculture Department to use the Export Enhancement Program to export 100 million pounds of nonfat dry milk and 100 million pounds of butter during the remainder of 1991. The conferees asked that added emphasis be given to the export of oils, poultry and rice under the export program.

SUPPLEMENTAL APPROPRIATIONS

Commerce

• **Census Bureau.** Transferred $1 million from the periodic censuses and programs appropriations to provide salaries and expenses for the Census Bureau.

• **Economic analysis.** Appropriated $1 million for salaries and expenses for the Bureau of Economic Analysis to improve international economic statistics.

• **Economic Development Administration.** Rescinded $24 million from unobligated balances in the Economic Development Administration's revolving loan fund, money that exceeded the levels needed to handle liabilities on outstanding loan guarantees.

• **International Trade Administration.** Appropriated $1.5 million for operations and administration for the International Trade Administration to allow the processing of an increased number of anti-dumping/countervailing duty cases.

• **Export Administration.** Appropriated $1.4 million for operations and administration for the Export Administration for certain ongoing costs arising from the Persian Gulf conflict, including additional review of license applications to Third World countries and the Middle East, support for the Gulf Reconstruction Center, and additional training and workload requirements for special agents in export enforcement activities.

• **Travel and tourism.** Appropriated $1.1 million for the U.S. Travel and Tourism Administration, to reimburse the Treasury Department for a judgment against the United States for certain construction costs of the U.S. pavilion at the Louisiana World's Fair in 1984.

• **NOAA.** Appropriated $3 million for operations, research and facilities for the National Oceanic and Atmospheric Administration (NOAA). The money included funding for increased fuel costs for P-3 hurricane hunter aircraft and steaming hours for NOAA ocean and fisheries research vessels. Also included was money to replace furniture and computers damaged in a recent fire at a NOAA facility in Germantown, Md., and to rent temporary space for employees displaced by the fire.

• **Micronesia.** Required that $750,000 in funding for the Census Bureau be available to provide the Federated States of Micronesia technical assistance and training for census-taking and other data collection efforts.

Justice

• **General legal activities.** Appropriated $5.18 million, including a transfer of $3.18 million from an existing appropriation for federal prisons. Most of the money was to be used to comply with the Americans with Disabilities Act (PL 101-336) or to provide technical assistance for implementation of the act. Money was also provided for protection of witnesses and for a Geographical Information System.

• **U.S. attorneys.** Transferred $1.903 million from an existing appropriation for general legal activities to pay for salaries and expenses for U.S. attorneys.

• **U.S. Marshals Service.** Transferred $1.025 million from an existing appropriation for federal prisons to pay for salaries and expenses for the U.S. Marshals Service.

• **Witness protection.** Appropriated $9.203 million to implement several new security initiatives in the witness protection program, provide short-term witness security services in the District of Columbia, and increase fees paid to fact witnesses, as mandated by the Judicial Improvements Act of 1990 (PL 101-650).

• **Assets Forfeiture Fund.** Amended the law relating to the Assets Forfeiture Fund by stating that, subject to certain conditions, any unobligated balances in the fund on Sept. 30, 1991, and Sept. 30, 1992, be available to the attorney general to buy vehicles, equipment and other non-construction capital investment items for Justice Department activities in the war on drugs and violent crime.

• **Witness fees for prisoners.** Prohibited the use of any funds appropriated to the Justice Department in fiscal 1991 or any prior year to pay a fact witness fee to a prisoner testifying in a federal court. The prohibition responded to a Jan. 8, 1991, Supreme Court holding that imprisoned fact witnesses are entitled to reimbursement for their testimony in federal cases, and the provision specifically exempted the witness fee paid in that case.

State

• **Motor vehicles.** Permitted the State Department to use fiscal 1991 funds to buy special purpose motor vehicles for overseas posts without regard to price limits established by law. The vehicles were needed to maintain diplomatic security for U.S. personnel.

• **Fisheries commissions.** Appropriated $100,000 for international fisheries commissions to allow the United States to make its full contribution to the United States-Canada Pacific Salmon Commission.

The Judiciary

• **Supreme Court.** Appropriated $54,000 for salaries and expenses for the Supreme Court to cover a January 1991 pay increase for the justices and increased Medicare contributions.

• **Court of Appeals.** Appropriated $51,000 for salaries and expense for the U.S. Court of Appeals for the Federal Circuit to cover the January 1991 pay increase for the judges and increased Medicare contributions.

• **Court of International Trade.** Appropriated $36,000 for salaries and expenses for the U.S. Court of International Trade to cover the January 1991 pay increase for the judges and increased Medicare contributions.

• **Other courts.** Appropriated $68.73 million for courts of appeals, district courts and other judicial services to pay for the fiscal 1991 judges' pay raise, the cost of 20 judges to be appointed in fiscal 1991, geographical pay increases and implementation of the Judicial Improvements Act of 1990. The provision also transferred $750,000 to the National Commission on Judicial Discipline and Removal.

• **Juror fees.** Appropriated $5.6 million to provide for a mandated increase in the daily fee for jurors.

• **Court security.** Appropriated $530,000 to cover the additional court security costs mandated by the Federal Judgeship Act of 1990.

• **Administrative Office.** Appropriated $2.45 million for the Administrative Office of the U.S. Courts to support development and implementation of the civil justice expense and delay reduction plan mandated by the Civil Justice Reform Act of 1990 and for staffing to handle the additional work associated with new judgeships authorized in the Federal Judgeship Act of 1990.

• **Federal Judicial Center.** Appropriated $1.633 million for the Federal Judicial Center to cover costs associated with the development and implementation of civil justice expense and delay reduction plans mandated by the Civil Justice Reform Act of 1990.

Related Agencies

• **Board for International Broadcasting.** Appropriated $8 million for the Board for International Broadcasting for grants to Radio Free Europe to partly offset the depreciation of the U.S. dollar overseas.

• **EEOC.** Appropriated $3.63 million for the Equal Opportunity Employment Commission (EEOC) to provide technical assistance for implementation of the Americans with Disabilities Act.

• **FCC.** Appropriated $1 million for the Federal Communications Commission (FCC) to acquire computers and related equipment to improve staff productivity and handle an increased workload.

• **Federal Trade Commission.** Appropriated $2 million for the Federal Trade Commission to achieve a base staffing level of 950 full-time-equivalent positions.

• **Legal Services.** Appropriated $1 million to supplement previous appropriations for the Legal Services Corporation's basic field programs. The money was to be used to increase by an equal percentage the amount by which each grantee's 1991 funding fell below $17.68 per poor person within its geographical area under the 1980 census.

• **SEC.** Appropriated $1.6 million to help the Securities and Exchange Commission (SEC) deal with additional requirements imposed by the Market Reform Act of 1990 (PL 101-432) and the Securities Enforcement Remedies and Penny Stock Reform Act of 1990 (PL 101-429). The bill also made available to the SEC the full $30 million in offsetting collections from increased fees, restoring to the SEC fees collected between Oct. 1 and Nov. 4, 1990.

• **SBA.** Transferred $1.5 million from the disaster loan fund to the Small Business Administration (SBA) to help the SBA respond more effectively to higher than anticipated activity in agency loan programs. The bill also forbade the SBA administrator to withhold disaster assistance under Section 7 of the Small Business Act to nurseries and greenhouses that suffered damage from disasters that occurred between Oct. 1, 1990, and March 1, 1991. The provision was aimed at greenhouses and nurseries damaged by floods in the state of Washington in November 1990.

Defense — Military

• **CHAMPUS.** Appropriated the following amounts for operation and maintenance: $56 million for the Army, $62 million for the Navy and $32 million for the Air Force. The money was to be used for increased CHAMPUS (Civilian Health and Medical Program for the Uniformed Services) costs associated with Operation Desert Shield/Desert Storm. Of the money provided to the Army, $5 million could only be used to pay the increased costs of the Fort Bragg (N.C.) Mental Health Demonstration Project.

• **Special Olympics.** Directed the Department of Defense to make $500,000 available for logistical support and personnel services for the Special Olympics Games in Minnesota in July 1991 from funds previously appropriated for the 1990 Goodwill Games.

• **Air battle captain.** The conferees agreed that the Army should continue for the remainder of fiscal 1991 its demonstration program to place helicopter pilots graduated from the University of North Dakota in advanced helicopter pilot training.

• **Ready Reserve Force vessels.** The conferees directed that at least half of 71 Ready Reserve Force vessels slated for deactivation after being used by the Navy for Operation Desert Shield be allocated to Navy shipyards to perform the required repair and refurbishment.

• **Civil Air Patrol.** The conferees strongly supported House report language insisting that the Air Force not realign $3.294 million earmarked for operations of the Civil Air Patrol. The conferees further directed the Air Force to provide the Civil Air Patrol with its 1991 funds in a timely manner and to work with the Civil Air Patrol on its funding requirement for fiscal 1992.

• **Gulf environmental damage.** Conferees strongly urged the director of the Central Intelligence Agency to assemble a task force to identify intelligence assets capable of assessing the environmental damage caused by Iraqi sabotage of Kuwaiti oil wells and to conduct that assessment. The CIA director was asked to make a preliminary report on the findings within 60 days of enactment.

• **Off-island leave program.** Required that, of the money available for chemical agents and munitions destruction, $2 million must be available only for an off-island leave program.

• **USS *Kennedy*.** Required that funds available to the Defense Department for advance procurement of materials and other efforts associated with the aircraft carrier USS *Kennedy* be used for no purpose other than a service life extension program for the carrier at the Philadelphia Naval Shipyard.

• **F-14 remanufacturing.** Required that $987.936 million of the money previously appropriated for fiscal 1991 Navy aircraft procurement be obligated for the remanufacture of 12 F-14 aircraft within 30 days of enactment. The provision was designed to help protect more than 4,000 jobs at Grumman Corp., Long Island's largest employer, according to Sen. Alfonse M. D'Amato, R-N.Y.

• **V-22 Osprey.** Required that $200 million in previously appropriated fiscal 1989 funds be obligated within 60 days of enactment for the V-22 Osprey tilt-rotor program.

• **AOE combat support ships.** Transferred $237 million from Fast Combat Support Ship (AOE) program funded in 1991 to other AOE ships funded in prior years to provide for potential cost overruns. The ships accompanied and provided fuel and supplies to aircraft carriers and their escorts. The conferees directed the General Accounting Office (GAO) to monitor the resolution of cost overrun claims. The Navy was forbidden to obligate any funds for payment of claims until the GAO determined that each specific obligation was an appropriate government cost.

• **Loyola University.** Transferred $8 million to the Education Department from a Defense Department appropriation for research, development, testing and evaluation. The money was to be given as a grant for the Center for Commerce and Industrial Expansion at Loyola University of Chicago. A House aide said the money was transferred from the Defense Department to the Education Department at the request of Rep. Dan Rostenkowski, D-Ill., who was in turn doing a favor for Loyola officials, who worried that accepting money from the Defense Department eventually could require the center to conduct defense-related research. On April 25, the Office of Management and Budget found that the transfer of the money from defense to domestic spending had breached the 1991 domestic discretionary spending cap by $7.3 million, triggering an across-the-board spending cut ("sequester") of that amount from 1991 domestic spending programs.

Defense — Civil

• **Los Angeles-Long Beach Harbor.** Provided that 1991 funds appropriated for general investigations for the initiation of preconstruction engineering and design for the Los Angeles-Long Beach Harbor, Calif., project could be used for completion of the feasibility study for that project.

• **Passaic River Main Stem.** Provided that, of 1991 funds for general investigations, at least $5.8 million had to be available only for the Passaic River Main Stem project in New Jersey.

• **Louisiana wetlands.** Required the secretary of Defense to make available $300,000 to implement the provisions of the Coastal Wetlands Planning, Protection and Restoration Act (PL 101-646). The provision, sponsored by Sen. J. Bennett Johnston, D-La., spared Louisiana from having to pay half the costs borne by the U.S. Army Corps of Engineers in identifying priority wetlands for federally funded restoration. The measure funded operations of the Louisiana Coastal Wetlands Conservation and Restoration Task Force through Oct. 31, until money was scheduled to become available from a new federal wetlands trust fund, funded by the federal gasoline tax on off-road vehicles and equipment. The trust fund was expected to receive at least $50 million a year, 70 percent of which is to go to Louisiana.

District of Columbia

• Appropriated $100 million as an addition to the fiscal 1991 federal payment to the District of Columbia. The money had to be transferred to the District government by May 1, 1991, but it could not be turned over until the mayor had certified that the city had begun to implement $216 million in spending cuts and revenue increases and had received all the necessary approvals for those cuts and increases from the D.C. City Council.

Interior

• **Bureau of Reclamation construction program.** Appropriated $25 million to meet emergency needs of areas affected by the continuing drought in the West.

• **Buffalo Bill Dam.** Provided that up to $11.93 million in 1991 funds be available for the Buffalo Bill Dam modification project in Wyoming.

Energy

• **Hawaiian geothermal energy.** Required the secretary of Energy to use such sums as necessary to conduct an environmental assessment and/or an environmental impact statement on ongoing activity to verify and characterize the nature of geothermal energy potential in Hawaii. Although the ongoing work did not constitute a "major federal action" and did not require an environmental impact statement, the conferees felt that the sensitivity of the activity was so acute that an impact statement process was necessary anyway.

• **Atomic energy defense activities.** Appropriated $623 million for atomic energy defense activities, including $283 million for activities at the Rocky Flats Plant and $340 million for environmental restoration and waste management activities at Energy Department nuclear facilities. The Rocky Flats Plant in Colorado, a critical part of the nation's nuclear weapons complex, provided key components for nuclear bombs.

• **Colorado communities affected by the Rocky Flats Plant.** Provided up to $10 million in community impact assistance from existing Department of Energy (DOE) waste management funds to assist the Colorado communities of Broomfield, Westminster, Thornton and Northglenn in the construction of a water diversion project to protect the communities' drinking water supply. The project was intended to protect the drinking water from contamination from runoff from the plutonium operations at the Rocky Flats Plant.

DOE felt that it did not have sufficient authorization to make initial payments to the communities to defray their expenses in connection with the water diversion project; the amendment, which was sponsored by Colorado Sens. Tim Wirth, D, and Hank Brown, R, provided such authorization.

Independent Agencies

• **Delaware River Basin Commission.** Appropriated $39,000 to cover increased salaries and benefit costs resulting from January 1991 executive pay increases.

• **Susquehanna River Basin Commission.** Appropriated

$39,000 to cover increased salaries and benefit costs resulting from January 1991 executive pay increases.

Labor

• **State unemployment insurance.** Appropriated $150 million from the Unemployment Trust Fund for state unemployment insurance administration. The money was to provide extra funding to states for operating unemployment programs with sufficient staff to avoid lengthy delays in the processing of claims. The recession and the resulting increase in unemployment had strained many state unemployment programs, leading to lengthy delays in getting benefits to those qualified to receive them. The Bush administration agreed to score this money as emergency funding.

• **Transition Assistance Program.** Appropriated $4 million from the Unemployment Trust Fund for a Transition Assistance Program for returning veterans.

• **PBGC.** Approved language that would enable the Pension Benefit Guaranty Corporation (PBGC) to spend outside its administrative expense limit for any purpose related to the termination of pension plans. The language permitted the PBGC to limit losses by immediately taking over a pension plan without undergoing the usual time delay for the appropriations process.

Health and Human Services

• **Infant mortality initiative.** Appropriated $25 million for a targeted infant mortality initiative. No funds appropriated for rural health outreach grants could be used to provide forward or multi-year funding, and no funds appropriated for ongoing activities within community health centers or maternal- and child-health block grant programs could be reprogrammed, redirected or reallocated for any other purposes.

• **Vaccine injury compensation.** Appropriated $17 million for the vaccine compensation program, which paid families for injuries or deaths resulting from immunizations. A Senate aide said Congress already had appropriated $63 million for the program; the Senate Appropriations Committee wanted to increase that to a total of $163 million. But White House budget officials balked, saying they would score anything over the authorized level of $80 million against spending caps — a move that could have triggered automatic domestic program cuts. The extra $17 million brought the program up to its authorized level. The bill also appropriated $1 million from the Vaccine Compensation Trust Fund for administrative costs of the program.

• **Supplemental Security Income program.** Appropriated $232 million for payment to the Social Security trust funds to cover administrative costs necessary to implement the *Sullivan v. Zebley* Supreme Court decision. The decision called for the Social Security Administration to re-evaluate childhood disability claims for Supplemental Security Income benefits that were denied because the child's functional limitations were not considered in evaluating the severity of the impairment. An estimated 200,000 to 300,000 new disability determinations were expected to result. Funds would remain avail

the regular appropriation for Supplemental Security Income. Retroactive benefits could total $1.4 billion, and ongoing monthly payments were estimated at several hundred million dollars a year.

• **Family Support Administration.** Permitted amounts provided under refugee and entrant assistance for cash and medical assistance to be used for grants to private nonprofit agencies for private-sector resettlement activities.

Education

• **Tribal vocational schools.** Provided that previously appropriated funds for tribally controlled vocational schools be awarded no later than June 1, 1991. Certain administrative requirements were to be waived to permit an accelerated review process.

• **National Board for Professional Teaching Standards.** Waived the requirement that there be an authorization to allow the expenditure of $5 million previously appropriated for the National Board for Professional Teaching Standards but required that the funds be spent as they would have been if the House-passed authorization bill had become law.

Legislative Branch

• **Corinne L. Conte.** Appropriated $125,100 for payment to Corinne L. Conte, widow of Rep. Silvio O. Conte, R-Mass.

• **Mobile office identification.** Eliminated, for security purposes, the requirement that a senator's mobile office have an inscription identifying it as the office of a senator.

• **Spending by Senate leaders.** Provided that, upon written request from the majority or minority leader of the Senate, the secretary of the Senate transfer funds from the appropriations accounts for officers' and employees' salaries or for offices of the majority and minority leaders. The money was to go to the miscellaneous items appropriations account. The majority and minority leaders were each authorized to spend "as may be necessary or appropriate" from that account.

• **Library of Congress.** Permitted the Architect of the Capitol to lease temporary storage space to accommodate overflow from the Library of Congress, subject to enactment of authorizing legislation.

• **Library of Congress.** Exempted previously obligated funds for Library of Congress' books for the blind and physically handicapped account from certain limitations. The effect was to extend the availability of certain unused funds for research and development of talking book machines.

Defense — Military Construction

• **Disapproval of deferrals.** Disapproved, effective April 16, 1991, the Defense Department's deferrals of contracts for military construction and family housing. The General Accounting Office found that the department's moratorium/prohibition on construction was an illegal and unreported impoundment of funds. The requirement that deferred funds be made available did not apply to projects at bases recommended for closure by the secretary of Defense in his April 15, 1991, report to Congress. The conferees objected to the Defense Department's continued disregard for the impoundment control process, which required that deferral of budget authority be reported to Congress.

• **Missouri Housing Development Commission.** Provided for the conveyance of surplus land and facilities known as the U.S. Army Charles Melvin Price Support Center Wherry Housing Annex. Within 90 days of enactment, the land was to be conveyed to the Missouri Housing Development Commission on the condition that it be used for low-income and transitional housing for the homeless.

Agriculture

• **University of Maine.** Transferred $93,000 from a Cooperative State Research Service (CSRS) account to a special CSRS research grants program to allow the University of Maine to buy scientific instruments to help carry out agricultural research.

• **Maine potato virus.** Earmarked up to $1 million from previously appropriated funds for the Animal and Plant Health Inspection Service to carry out, in the state of Maine, an inspection, quarantine, eradication and control program aimed at a particular strain of potato virus that causes little or no damage to potatoes, but which could be devastating to other crops, particularly tomatoes and tobacco.

• **APHIS.** Permitted the Animal and Plant Health Inspection Service (APHIS) to use up to $13 million from the agricultural quarantine inspection user fee account in order to continue inspection activities at ports and airports outside usual duty hours.

• **Food Safety and Inspection Service.** Appropriated $8 million to carry on inspection services authorized by the Federal Meat Inspection Act and the Poultry Products Inspection Act.

• **Agricultural Stabilization and Conservation Service.** Appropriated $46.9 million, in part to implement 1990 farm bill provisions for mandatory commodity and conservation program activities.

• **Commodity Credit Corporation.** Provided $1.4 million for disaster payments for producers who suffered crop losses resulting from Hurricane Hugo, which struck the Carolinas, Puerto Rico and the Virgin Islands in 1989.

• **Farmers Home Administration.** Made available, from loan funds previously made available under Title V of the Housing Act of 1949, up to $35 million for a rural housing deferred mortgage demonstration program.

• **Food stamp program.** Provided an additional $200 million for benefits to individuals under the Food Stamp Act. An additional $1.3 billion was available but only if a budget request for a specific dollar amount were sent to Congress by the White House.

• **PL 480.** Allowed the president to renegotiate payment on debt incurred under the PL 480 Food for Peace program by eligible countries in Latin America, the Caribbean and sub-Saharan Africa.

Transportation

• **Coast Guard retired pay.** Appropriated $14.5 million to pay full retirement benefits for all eligible Coast Guard retirees.

• **Federal Highway Administration.** Extended the availability of funds for a trade enhancement demonstration in Arizona.

• **National Highway Traffic Safety Administration.** Appropriated $4.98 million for highway traffic safety grants and increased the limitation on obligations for alcohol safety incentive grants by $4.98 million.

• **Federal Railroad Administration.** Extended the availability of funds for mandatory passenger rail service payments.

• **Maritime Administration — Ready Reserve Force.** Appropriated $20 million to upgrade two or three National Defense Reserve Fleet ships to operational status and to add these to the inventory of the Ready Reserve Force. The work was to be carried out at U.S. Navy shipyards.

General Services Administration (GSA)

Required the GSA to have advance approval in writing from the House Committee on Public Works and Transportation, the Senate Committee on Environment and Public Works and the House and Senate Appropriations committees before awarding a final contract for site acquisition or construction of the Naval Systems Command Headquarters project. The provision also required the GSA, in consultation with the General Accounting Office, to report to Congress within 30 days to indicate whether modifying or canceling the existing solicitation for offers for the headquarters in Northern Virginia was in the best interests of the United States.

Executive Office of the President

• **Vice president's residence.** Made $330,000 in previously appropriated funds for refurbishing the vice president's official residence available until spent. The House had sought to limit the availability of the money.

Veterans Affairs

• **Compensation and pensions.** Appropriated $712.584 million for veterans compensation, benefits and burial benefits. Of the total, $303.084 million was to pay for the recently enacted 5.4 percent cost of living increase for compensation payments to veterans and survivors. Another $317.5 million reflected revised caseload and cost estimates for compensation payments. Another $87 million was to pay for an increased average cost per beneficiary. And the remaining $5 million was for burial benefits.

• **Readjustment benefits.** Appropriated $250 million for readjustment benefits to fully fund higher-than-expected benefit payments to a greater number of trainees, primarily because of an increase in participation from regular military personnel who were to leave the service in 1991.

Housing and Urban Development (HUD)

• **Assisted housing.** Rescinded $298.815 million in the annual contribution to assisted housing, which provided subsidies to low-income renters.

• **Expiring Section 8 subsidy contracts.** Added $155.815 million to the $7.7 billion provided in the fiscal 1991 spending bill to renew expiring rent subsidy contracts. That included money for families receiving rental certificates and vouchers, as well as loan-management funds to run project-based Section 8 contracts.

• **Congregate services.** Required any unobligated funds for congregate services to be used to continue existing programs, as well as to start new ones. Congregate services included a number of social services to low-income housing residents.

• **Low-income housing projects.** Provided $75 million to operate low-income housing projects. The funds were to remain available until Sept. 30, 1992.

• **Research and technology.** Required that $500,000 of the 1991 research and technology appropriation be used for the National Commission on Manufactured Housing. The commission was created as a compromise when Congress refused to change the law governing manufactured housing when writing the 1990 National Affordable Housing Act (PL 101-625).

• **Administrative provisions.** Increased the number of disabled people allowed to live in a supportive housing facility from 20 to 24.

• Exempted the city of West Hollywood, Calif., from rent control restrictions when using rental renovation funds.

• Required that any money not spent by March 20, 1991, under the Supplemental Assistance for Facilities to Assist the Homeless program would remain available for that program. The program provided money to local communities for innovative homeless projects.

• Required that money previously appropriated to HUD for Community Development grants and Urban Development Action Grants remain available until spent.

• Rescinded $23 million set aside for the Section 202 elderly and disabled construction program and applied it to Community Development Block Grants and Urban Development Action Grants. The elderly and disabled construction program was changed from a loan guarantee program to a direct grant program, requiring the shifting of funds.

General Provisions

• **Medium Range Recovery Helicopter.** Provided that funds appropriated for the Transportation Department for fiscal 1991 may be used to initiate a multi-year contract for the Medium Range Recovery Helicopter (HH-60J) program.

• **Davis-Bacon regulations.** Prohibited the Labor Department from implementing or administering regulations under the Davis-Bacon Act pertaining to the helper category of workers, as well as certain new regulations affecting apprenticeship programs in the construction industry. The Davis-Bacon law required that workers be paid the prevailing local wage rate on federal contracts.

• **Payment of allied war pledges.** Expressed the sense of Congress that pledges from U.S. allies to help pay for the war against Iraq were appreciated but that the six nations that had pledged money should either pay or agree on a payment schedule by April 15, 1991. If nations did not meet their commitments, Congress may consider appropriate action.

• **Lawrence Welk birthplace.** Prohibited the use of any appropriated funds to restore the birthplace of Lawrence Welk. This provision was added by the House to strip an amendment to the fiscal 1991 Agriculture appropriations bill that earmarked $500,000 for restoration of the Welk birthplace near Strasburg, N.D. House critics called the earmark an abuse of the process, arguing that it was inserted by the Senate with no House consideration. Quentin N. Burdick, D-N.D., who oversaw addition of the Welk amendment in 1990, declined to remove this provision when the supplemental came to the Senate in March 1991. A Burdick aide said that because the Welk birthplace already had been restored with private funds, the new provision had no practical effect. North Dakota officials were seeking Farmers Home Administration approval of the grant for $500,000 to promote rural economic development around the Welk home. Officials argued that the area was economically depressed after years of drought and qualified for the grant.

• **White House conference on Indian education.** Extended the deadline for the president to call and conduct a conference on Indian education, from Sept. 30, 1991, to no later than 12 months after an advisory committee met to help plan the conference.

• **Stormwater discharge regulations.** Prohibited the Environmental Protection Agency from enforcing the March 18, 1991, deadline for group applications for stormwater discharges until that deadline was extended to Sept. 30, 1991.

The provision provided a temporary extension for submission of group applications for stormwater discharge permits by municipalities. It also allowed other local units of government and operators of industrial sites extra time to use this streamlined regulatory procedure.

• **Tropical forests.** Prohibited use of funds of the Agency for International Development for projects involving commercial timber extraction in primary tropical forest areas unless certain conditions were met.

• **Environmental monitoring in the Persian Gulf.** Encouraged the president to seek an international agreement to provide for environmental monitoring, assessment, remediation and restoration in the Persian Gulf region. Costs were to be paid by the host country, and the administration was required to submit a report to Congress within 60 days of enactment to identify actions taken to implement this amendment. By March 1, 1992, the Environmental Protection Agency was required to report to Congress on the environmental effects of the Persian Gulf War.

• **Child Care and Development Block Grant Act of 1990.** Made a technical change to the act to require that funds be obligated but not necessarily spent by states by the end of the year following the appropriation.

• **Syria.** Expressed the sense of Congress that Syria undermined peace and good will in the Middle East by depriving the 4,000 Jews living in Syria of the right to emigrate. Congress condemned the government of Syria for continuing to deny the basic human right of free emigration and called upon the government to allow Jews to emigrate freely and to release Jews from prison who were suspected of having traveled illegally or having planned to do so. Congress called on the Bush administration to press human rights issues with the Syrian government.

• **Real estate settlement procedures.** Amended the Real Estate Settlement Procedures Act of 1974, changing some of the terms of liability for the originator or servicer of a federally related mortgage loan, effective April 20, 1991.

• **Defense Cooperation Account.** Required the secretary of Defense to notify the Armed Services and Appropriations committees of the House and the Senate before transferring any funds from the Defense Cooperation Account. No transfer could be made until the seventh day after the committees received such notification.

• **Jordan.** Prohibited foreign assistance to Jordan from the fiscal 1991 Foreign Operations Appropriations Act, except under conditions spelled out in this provision. Exceptions were provided for aid to refugees and assistance to finance the ongoing training or studies of students outside Jordan. The president could waive the prohibition if he determined and certified that Jordan had taken steps to advance the peace process in the Middle East or that providing such assistance to Jordan would be beneficial to the peace process.

Military Personnel, Veterans' Benefits

• **General authority.** Appropriated $655 million from the Defense Cooperation Account (which contained contributions from U.S. allies to defray costs of the Persian Gulf War) to pay for benefits for military personnel and veterans. The money was scored as emergency spending not subject to spending caps. Individual appropriations were as follows, combined for all services, with all numbers for fiscal 1991:

• $25 million for special death gratuities for service members participating in the Servicemen's Group Life Insurance Program.

• $5 million for an additional amount for the payment of death gratuities.

• $173 million for a temporary increase in the rate of special pay for duty subject to hostile fire or imminent danger.

• $10 million for special pay for health professionals recalled to active duty or involuntarily retained on active duty.

• $980,000 for increased amounts attributable to removal of the 60-day limitation on the amount of leave that could be paid to survivors of military members who die on active duty.

• $91,000 to pay retired members of the armed forces recalled to active duty during a war or national emergency at the highest grade previously held and to allow these members to retire in the highest grade held.

• $36 million for the basic allowance for quarters for military reservists without dependents.

• $51 million for family separation allowances.

• $48 million for increased costs for the Civilian Health and Medical Program of the Uniformed Services (CHAMPUS).

• $25 million to provide transitional health-care coverage upon deactivation for reservists on active duty during the Persian Gulf conflict.

• **Guaranteed student loans.** Transferred about $12.3 million from the Defense Cooperation Account for the additional fiscal 1991-95 costs of guaranteed student loans.

• **Student financial assistance.** Transferred $13.95 million from the Defense Cooperation Account for the additional fiscal 1991-95 costs of student financial assistance.

• **Veterans benefits administration.** Transferred $2.9 million from the Defense Cooperation Account for the additional fiscal 1991-95 costs of compensation and pensions.

• **Veterans' education benefits.** Transferred $655 million — minus all additional fiscal 1991-95 costs under this section of the bill — for the additional fiscal 1991-95 costs of veterans' education benefits.

• **Family assistance.** Appropriated $50 million, of which $30 million could be made available for Family Education and Support Services, as authorized by the Persian Gulf Conflict Supplemental Authorization and Personnel Benefits Act of 1991. The remaining $20 million could be made available for child-care assistance, as authorized in the same act.

Technical Corrections

• **1991 Foreign Operations Appropriations Act.** Corrected an error in the 1991 Foreign Operations Appropriations Act (PL 101-513) that resulted in a sequester of roughly $400 million. Upon correcting the error, the sequester order issued by the president was to be rescinded and any action to implement that sequester reversed.

• **Other corrections.** Made technical corrections to fiscal 1991 appropriations bills for military construction (PL 101-519), Treasury, Postal Service (101-509) and Transportation (101-516). ■

Continued from p. 672

House had doubled the administration request, providing $200 million. In exchange for the lower figure, the administration agreed to treat the money as emergency spending not subject to spending caps.

• **Export Enhancement Program (EEP).** The committee included in its version of the bill a proposal to help wheat farmers by repealing the cap on the Export Enhancement Program (EEP), an export subsidy program that went primarily to promote wheat sales abroad.

Patrick J. Leahy, D-Vt., complained that cost estimates from the Congressional Budget Office indicated that the repeal could cost $380 million. The administration stuck by OMB estimates that showed no extra cost. Leahy said he would not challenge the EEP expansion but warned that he would bring to the floor an amendment to provide similar help for dairy farmers, who he argued had been harmed even more by falling prices for their commodity. *(Export enhancement, p. 172)*

FLOOR ACTION

The Senate approved the dire emergency supplemental 92-8 on March 20 after two days of floor action, much of it dissipated in quorum calls. *(Vote 40, p. 6-H)*

In the end, the Senate approved several changes and additions to the House-passed supplemental.

The following are highlights of the Senate action:

• Leahy won a 60-40 vote in favor of his dairy farmer bailout plan March 19, after convincing his colleagues that beleaguered dairy farmers needed relief from deteriorating milk prices. *(Vote 32, p. 5-H)*

• Don Nickles, R-Okla., won support for an amendment to cut $57.2 million in previously approved fiscal 1991 economic and military aid to Jordan. The amendment permitted continued refugee assistance to Jordan, along with more than $200 million in aid already in the pipeline. The administration strongly objected to the measure, insisting that congressional micromanagement of foreign policy would complicate Bush's efforts to forge a postwar Mideast peace. But the Senate failed to table (kill) the Nickles amendment, 43-57, and then approved it on a voice vote. *(Vote 36, p. 6-S)*

• Alfonse M. D'Amato, R-N.Y., failed in two attempts to provide funds for Kemp's housing programs. *(Votes 33, 34, p. 6-S)*

• Daniel R. Coats, R-Ind., succeeded in stripping the House language requiring the Pentagon to overhaul the aircraft carrier USS *Kennedy* at the Philadelphia Naval Shipyard. Coats argued that the expensive overhaul was a money-waster the Navy would be better off without. Arlen Specter, R-Pa., countered that canceling the overhaul could lead to closure of the Philadelphia yard, whose continued existence he said was vital to national security. Democrat Frank R. Lautenberg, from neighboring New Jersey, said cancellation would save money in the short run but ultimately would be far more costly because a less expensive overhaul would extend the carrier's life only five years, as opposed to 15 years. The Senate failed to table (kill) Coats' amendment 44-56 and then approved it by voice vote. *(Vote 39, p. 6-S)*

• Nickles failed in an effort to strike the language barring money to expand the use of helpers on federally funded construction projects. *(Vote 35, p. 6-S)*

FINAL ACTION

Congress cleared the dire emergency supplemental, along with the Desert Storm bill, March 22, but not before knuckling under to administration demands to throw out or modify provisions the White House found unacceptable.

Working under the cloud of a strong veto warning from OMB Director Darman and badgered by colleagues champing at the bit to go home for the two-week Easter recess, House and Senate negotiators meeting March 21 junked Leahy's dairy program and softened the provision cutting military and economic aid to Jordan.

After being warned that the spending exceeded budget ceilings and would eventually trigger automatic cuts, conferees agreed to trim their spending plans to meet administration guidelines.

When the conferees had finished, the White House dropped its veto threat. That opened the way for floor passage of both the Operation Desert Storm supplemental and the $5.4 billion dire emergency supplemental.

The House approved the conference report on the dire supplemental 340-48; the Senate cleared the bill by voice vote. *(House vote 61, p. 16-H)*

KEY CONFERENCE ACTION

When it came to confrontations over extra spending, the administration appeared to win more often than it lost.

For instance, just two days after winning a Senate floor vote in favor of his dairy farmer bailout plan, Leahy was forced to abandon the program. Darman sent negotiators a letter warning that the dairy provision could help trigger a veto recommendation from Bush's top staff. He contended the provision would increase milk prices 32 cents a gallon, costing consumers $1.36 billion and raising costs of the Women, Infants and Children nutrition program enough to force 135,000 participants off the rolls. Ripple effects from the milk price increase would also raise food stamp program costs and Commodity Credit Corporation dairy program outlays and that could trigger automatic spending cuts, Darman said.

The death blow for the Leahy proposal appeared to come when Senate Appropriations Chairman Robert C. Byrd, D-W.Va., who had earlier supported Leahy on the floor, cited Darman's spending-cut threat as sufficient reason to abandon Leahy's proposal in conference.

That prompted strenuous complaints from Leahy and dairy ally Obey, that mere threats to unleash automatic spending cuts gave OMB, in effect, a line-item veto over congressional spending proposals.

Other conference highlights:

• **Jordan.** Nickles' amendment on the Senate floor to cut previously approved fiscal 1991 aid to Jordan became a key element in the administration's veto threat. Conferees ultimately agreed to soften the restrictions, giving Bush substantial flexibility to restart the aid, which he had suspended, if he believed that it would assist the peace process.cw0

• **Defense.** Conferees agreed to strip out nearly $600 million in House-approved defense funding for Patriot missiles and other weapons in quantities greater than the Defense Department said were needed to replace items used during the war.

• **USS *Kennedy*.** The conferees restored the House provision calling for a Service Life Extension Program for the USS *Kennedy*.

• **Export Enhancement Program.** Leahy had attached his doomed dairy price increase plan to a provision added by the Senate appropriators repealing the cap on the Export Enhancement Program, which primarily aided wheat farmers. For a while, it seemed that the efforts to kill the milk price increase would also doom the EEP expansion.

But the administration wanted the EEP subsidy as a bargaining tool to counter foreign agricultural subsidies in the international negotiations over the General Agreement on Tariffs and Trade, and Senate Republicans — particularly Minority Leader Bob Dole of Kansas — were vitally interested in boosting the fortunes of wheat farmers.

After nearly canceling the EEP provision, the conference took a break to regroup and came back to approve the plan. In a last-ditch attempt to win something for dairy farmers, Leahy managed to attach report language urging the secretary of Agriculture to use EEP to sell 100 million pounds of nonfat dry milk and 100 million pounds of butter. It was not what he wanted, Leahy said, but it was better than nothing.

• **State unemployment insurance programs.** Conferees adopted the Senate plan to give states an extra $150 million to help administer the unemployment benefits program. Bush had requsted $100 million; the House had doubled that to $200 million.

• **NOAA.** Conferees agreed to a Senate item providing $3 million in non-emergency spending authority for the National Oceanic and Atmospheric Administration (NOAA) but deleted $2.8 million in emergency funds that had been approved by the House.

• **Veterans.** Conferees accepted a Senate provisions of $25 million for VA medical care, rather than the $46 million approved by the House. They increased the military benefits package from $500 million to $655 million. ■

War Expense Bill Passes With Ease

Prodded to quick action by the fiscal necessities of the Persian Gulf War and the political popularity of victory, Congress swiftly and enthusiastically enacted HR 1282, a supplemental appropriations measure providing $42.6 billion to cover the costs of waging the Persian Gulf War.

The funds were to be drawn from an account composed of money pledged by foreign governments for the war effort, plus an additional $15 billion in U.S. funds. The bill required that U.S. costs be covered by the foreign contributions to the extent they materialized. The $15 billion in U.S. funds was to be used to cover immediate costs pending receipt of foreign contributions, with any portion left over to be returned to the U.S. Treasury.

Spending restrictions set by the Budget Enforcement Act of 1990 (PL 101-508) exempted from budget caps the direct costs of the war.

The Bush administration requested on Feb. 22 a supplemental appropriations bill that would have provided $15 billion in U.S. funds and authority to spend an additional $52.5 billion provided by allies. The funds were to cover the war effort, Operation Desert Storm, and the prewar deployment known as Operation Desert Shield.

Congress ultimately reduced the total and placed more restrictions than the administration had proposed on how the money would be apportioned to pay for operating expenses of the war and replenishment of weapons. But members, their customary spending instincts held in check by the high popularity of the war effort, resisted the temptation to slow the bill or burden it with unrelated provisions. Instead, they loaded some of those provisions onto a separate "dire emergency" spending bill (HR 1281 — PL 102-27). *(1991 supplemental, p. 668)*

BOXSCORE

➡ **Desert Storm Supplemental Appropriations (HR 1282).** The bill provided $42.6 billion to cover the costs of the war and required that those costs be paid from $53.5 billion pledged by foreign governments, to the extent such funds materialized.

Report: Conference Report H Rept 102-30.

KEY ACTION

March 5 - The **House** Appropriations Committee approved the $42.6 billion measure.

March 7 - The **House** passed a $43 billion bill, 380-19.

March 14 - The **Senate** Appropriations Committee approved it with only minor changes.

March 19 - The **Senate** passed its version, 98-1.

March 21 - **Senate-House** conferees reached agreement.

March 22 - The **House** adopted the conference report, 379-11; the **Senate** followed, clearing the $42.6 billion measure for the president by voice vote.

April 10 - President Bush signed HR 1282 — PL 102-28.

Administration Request

The administration's plan for funding the war effort would provide $71 billion, with $54 billion — more than three-fourths of the total — coming from allied governments.

In the fall of 1990 Congress approved the $2 billion in budget authority that the administration had requested for the initial stages of the U.S. deployment that followed Iraq's invasion of Kuwait on Aug. 2. Congress also approved during 1990 the expenditure of $1 billion contributed by foreign governments to the gulf effort.

On Feb. 22, the Bush administration asked Congress to appropriate an additional $15 billion to cover the costs of the Persian Gulf War and for authority to spend an additional $53 billion contributed by allied countries to offset U.S. costs.

By late February, the total contributed by foreign governments had grown to $12.2 billion in cash as well as in-kind contributions — supplies, equipment and services — valued at $2.7 billion, budget director Richard G. Darman told reporters.

But Darman did not purport to offer the $71 billion as a firm estimate of the U.S. cost of conducting a war that was then under way and whose length and nature was not yet clear. He said the daily cost of combat could range from $150 million to $1.65 billion, depending on the tempo of operations.

Darman rejected complaints from Congress that the allies were dragging their feet on delivering their promised contributions. "We've had very good results to date," he said. "We expect the commitments to be honored."

HOUSE COMMITTEE ACTION

The supplemental funding bill provided an opportunity for Congress to reclaim a modest role after weeks on the sidelines of the war. Even as the U.S.-led juggernaut smashed the Iraqi army occupying Kuwait, Congress began to face the thankless but indispensable task of paying the costs of the operation.

The war's extraordinarily quick and successful end meant that the conflict cost less than initially anticipated — and the U.S. military's success swept up lawmakers in a burst of enthusiasm for the Pentagon and its programs.

Members backed away from initial plans to tack on to the virtually veto-proof bill additional funding for Israel and a bevy of domestic programs. By March 1, Democratic congressional leaders decided not to risk charges that they had larded up the Pentagon request.

Instead, other supplemental funding was packaged in a grab bag measure (PL 102-27) of emergency and nonemergency spending for everything from beefed-up wartime security in the halls of Congress to drought relief in California.

In requesting the Desert Storm supplemental, the Pentagon insisted that it could not provide a detailed "line-item" request because many costs of the ongoing operation could not yet be calculated. Instead, it provided what the Defense Department called "illustrative," examples of the costs that were anticipated. Still, some of these estimates were fairly firm:

- $21.4 billion for the costs incurred in the six months beginning the previous Oct. 1 in deploying 539,000 U.S. personnel and their equipment in the gulf region and operating there (but not including combat operations).

- $7 billion for personnel and operating costs while winding down the deployment after the war.
- $5.2 billion to return the forces to their home bases.

But two other parts of the cost estimate were more speculative or what the Pentagon referred to as "notional":

- The cost of combat operations was dependent on the duration of the war and its intensity, with daily expenses running from $150 million to 11 times that amount, depending on the number of tanks, planes and ships destroyed.
- $6.4 billion was penciled in to replace missiles and ammunition used in combat.

Foreign Pledges

Some members of Congress expressed concern that U.S. allies were too slow to deliver on their pledges of assistance in paying the costs of war, and some demanded that they pay the full tab. "The United States ought to have the entire cost of this war borne by others," Senate Appropriations member Arlen Specter, R-Pa., said Feb. 26.

But when the House Defense Appropriations Subcommittee marked up its version of the supplemental bill Feb. 28, it took a different approach. "We don't want the foreign countries to think we're not coming up with the money," said Chairman John P. Murtha, D-Pa.

Meeting behind closed doors, Murtha's panel approved the requested $15 billion in U.S. funds plus authority to spend foreign contributions up to $43 billion.

President Bush had asked Congress to provide the additional funding in a lump sum, although administration witnesses promised to keep congressional committees apprised of how it was spent.

Instead, Murtha's subcommittee divvied up the $43 billion among specific expenses listed in the Pentagon's illustrative cost estimate. For several items it deemed fully justified, the panel approved the full amount requested.

But the panel arbitrarily reduced the amount approved for parts of the Pentagon request when the ultimate cost was uncertain. "What they called notional costs we funded with notional money," quipped Murtha.

The subcommittee bill called for:

- $21.4 billion for six months of deployment costs, excluding the cost of combat, as requested.
- $12 billion for winding down the operation and sending the forces back to their bases, as requested.
- $3.2 billion — half the Pentagon's request — to restock missiles and ammunition.
- $6.3 billion for the cost of combat operations, calculated at a daily rate of $150 million for 42 days.

Missile Purchases

A particularly controversial item in the Pentagon cost estimate was that nearly $3 billion would be spent to buy eight types of missiles.

All eight types were used during the war. In some cases, however, fewer were actually used than the Pentagon said it might purchase with supplemental funds.

Several members of Congress complained that the missile shopping list exceeded what would be needed to restock Pentagon arsenals to the level necessary for the smaller force in prospect by the mid-1990s.

But Pentagon officials denied any intention of using the war's popularity to stock up on weaponry. Some of the illustrative procurement requests were based on the assumption of a longer war than occurred, they said. In other cases, large production runs were suggested because contractors had sped up their normal production run for fiscal 1991 and would face an expensive gap in production if they had to wait for fiscal 1992 funds to become available.

In light of the unanticipated brevity of the ground war, the Pentagon promised to send Congress a scaled-down list of missiles and ammunition to replenish U.S. stockpiles.

The Pentagon's original request made allowance for: $324 million for 500 anti-missile versions of the Patriot; $50 million for 87 ATACMS long-range bombardment missiles; $425 million for 60,000 MLRS artillery rockets; $110 million for 2,760 Hellfire anti-tank missiles; $244 million for 9,600 TOW anti-tank missiles; $454 million for more than 2,000 HARM air-launched anti-radar missiles; $545 million for 400 Tomahawk Navy cruise missiles; and $540 million for 9,000 Maverick air-to-ground missiles.

Appropriators Set Limits

The full House Appropriations Committee, acting March 5, essentially approved its subcommittee's action.

The Appropriations Committee rejected Bush's request for the $15 billion in U.S. funds to be appropriated in a lump sum and for the Pentagon to be given unlimited authority to spend foreign contributions, whatever they might total. Instead, the committee limited expenditures from both sources to $42.6 billion, apportioning that among Pentagon accounts as with any other defense funding bill.

The committee's allocations were based on the cost breakdown that the Pentagon had insisted was merely "illustrative" pending a full accounting of the war's costs.

In one crucial category, the Appropriations panel sliced the Pentagon estimate by almost half: It approved only $2.9 billion of the $6.4 billion requested to pay for some weapons modifications and to replenish stocks of missiles, ammunition and bombs used during the campaign.

The reduction, negotiated with the Pentagon, was aimed at ensuring that the supplemental spending bill bought only enough weapons to restock U.S. arsenals to the level that would be needed for the smaller U.S. force in prospect by the mid-1990s.

Furthermore, the committee rejected the administration's claim that the Desert Storm exemption from the budget cap should extend to funds offsetting the increased fuel costs of U.S. forces not directly involved in the Persian Gulf campaign.

The increased costs were a result of the worldwide increase in oil prices after Iraq seized Kuwait.

On the other hand, the panel added nearly $11 million to the bill: $350,000 toward the cost of a Memorial Day parade to welcome home the victorious troops and $10.5 million to beef up services to military dependents in coastal Virginia, home to a large number of personnel deployed to the gulf on short notice.

HOUSE FLOOR ACTION

Silence sometimes speaks volumes, as the House demonstrated March 7 in its quick and perfunctory debate before approving the $43 billion supplemental appropriations bill to pay for the gulf war.

The measure passed by a vote of 380-19. *(Vote 36, p. 10-H)*

The virtually undisputed passage of the measure was another striking affirmation of the popularity of the war and of the commander in chief. The action came the day after Bush received a clamorous reception for his postwar address to a joint session of Congress. *(Text, p. 9-E)*

As a rule, such supplemental appropriations bills loom

like giant sequoias in a forest of legislative Christmas trees that droop with ornaments to meet particular constituents' needs. And members had especially powerful incentives to pile extra projects onto the bill funding Operations Desert Shield and Desert Storm.

The measure offered one of the few routes by which members could slide additional funding past extraordinarily stringent budget limits.

A budget summit agreement between the administration and congressional leaders set strict caps for fiscal 1991 and future years on the totals that could be spent for domestic programs, defense and foreign aid. But it also exempted from the defense cap the direct costs of the Persian Gulf campaign.

Moreover, the bill was practically veto-proof: With fiscal 1991 less than half over, the Marine Corps and the Army had covered most of their wartime costs by stretching nearly to the limit budgets that were drawn up for peacetime operations.

Nevertheless, Bush's supplemental funding request for Desert Storm went through the House almost as fast as Desert Storm commander Gen. H. Norman Schwarzkopf's tanks went through Iraq's Republican Guards — and absorbed almost as little damage in the process.

"I think there is a core of war-related issues that would be very dangerous to oppose the president on," said centrist Democrat Jim Cooper of Tennessee.

By contrast, members had no hesitation in loading favorite programs onto the separate supplemental appropriations measure to cover non-defense war costs. And they also fashioned generous packages of benefits for Desert Storm troops and for veterans. *(Gulf veterans benefits, p. 320)*

As it passed the House, the Desert Storm supplemental appropriations bill was written to:

- Appropriate $42.6 billion for the "incremental" costs of the Persian Gulf deployment — that is, costs in excess of those the Pentagon would have incurred had Bush not dispatched U.S. forces to drive Iraq out of Kuwait.
- Require that those appropriations be funded from amounts pledged by foreign governments to offset U.S. war costs to the extent such funds are available.
- Appropriate $15 billion in U.S. funds to cover expenses within the appropriated totals, if necessary, pending collection of the balances pledged by other governments. Should these funds be used, the bill required that they be replenished as the foreign contributions were paid. Any U.S. funds remaining after all covered expenses were met were to revert to the Treasury.

Desert Storm Appropriation

Here are major categories of HR 1282, as cleared for the president on March 22. The House had approved its version on March 7 and the Senate on March 19 *(in millions of dollars)*:

	House Bill	Senate Bill	Final Bill
Personnel	$ 7,923	$ 7,890	$ 7,923
Operations and maintenance	25,120	21,768	23,021
Procurement	2,919	2,893	3,415
Research and development	1	0	69
Revolving funds	271	271	271
Combat operations	6,300	9,750	7,873
Military construction	35	35	35
Coast Guard operations	19	19	19
TOTAL	**$ 42,588**	**$ 42,626**	**$ 42,627**

SENATE COMMITTEE ACTION

The Senate Appropriations Committee made only minor changes in approving the supplemental spending bill on March 14, adding $37 million to the amount approved by the House.

The panel criticized the United Arab Emirates for contributing too little in light of its closeness to Iraq and its ability to pay, echoing a theme sounded earlier by committee Chairman Robert C. Byrd, D-W.Va.

The Bush administration had tried to secure $7 billion from the country, the committee said.

The panel urged the administration not to seek congressional approval of any arms sales to the United Arab Emirates until it agreed to pay a larger share of U.S. war expenses.

Also included in the bill was a more general provision to bar U.S. arms sales to any country that had not paid its full promised amount.

"If the promisor nation has the money to buy arms from us," the committee said in its report, "it can first use that money to fulfill its pledge to defray some of our costs."

In the first concrete effort to implement congressional demands to limit arms sales in the Middle East, the committee also added to the bill provisions that would require congressional approval of any transfer of U.S.-controlled weapons to other countries.

It specifically mentioned within that provision Iraqi equipment, which included types used by many other Arab states, captured during the war.

To facilitate the deployment of U.S. forces to Saudi Arabia in any future military crisis, Defense Secretary Dick Cheney and other officials had suggested that U.S. forces might leave behind enough tanks and other heavy gear to equip one or two divisions. The committee said it would not object to such "prepositioning," provided the equipment remained U.S. property and was reserved for use by U.S. forces.

The panel also asked the Pentagon for a report on its plans to preposition equipment in the gulf region.

Combat Costs Allocated

One significant change made by the Senate committee was in the allocation of funds for combat operations.

The Pentagon estimated before ground combat began that daily costs could range widely from $150 million to $1.65 billion.

The House bill appropriated $6.3 billion for combat operations: the lowest daily rate ($150 million) multiplied by 42 days of battle. But the Senate panel boosted the combat funding to $9.75 billion, partly to cover the cost of aircraft lost during the war.

Senate Appropriations also deleted from the House bill:

- $1.28 billion for higher fuel prices resulting from the gulf crisis that were incurred by U.S. forces not participating in the gulf deployment.
- $2.09 billion for food, housing, construction equipment

and other items given by allies as in-kind contributions.

- $350,000 for a Memorial Day celebration.
- $11 million to improve services to military dependents in coastal Virginia.

SENATE FLOOR ACTION

On March 19, the Senate approved its version of the bill, 98-1. *(Vote 31, p. 5-S)*

In the brief debate preceding Senate passage, Byrd renewed his earlier criticism of allied governments that were slow to pay their pledged contributions to U.S. costs.

He singled out Germany for particularly scathing comment. An opposition parliamentarian in Germany had urged his government to withhold some of its promised funds on the grounds that the United States might collect more from its allies than it had spent on the war.

The critic's analysis was based on simple arithmetic: Allies had pledged $54 billion, but Congress was appropriating less than $43 billion to pay for the conflict, implying a surplus of $11 billion if all allied funds were paid.

A German government spokesman announced that Bonn would ask the Bush administration to spell out its estimates of U.S. war costs.

But he also pointed out that the amount appropriated by HR 1282 would not cover the continuing cost of withdrawing U.S. forces from the Persian Gulf in an orderly fashion.

White House spokesman Marlin Fitzwater assured reporters that the United States would not make a profit on the war.

Reflecting Byrd's insistence that foreign governments pay up, the Senate-passed version of the Desert Storm bill included a provision barring any arms sales to countries that had not made their promised contributions.

FINAL ACTION

Senate-House conferees on HR 1282 hammered out the final version of the bill March 21.

The administration's request for the supplemental spending bill, submitted just before the U.S.-led coalition launched its ground assault against Iraqi forces, included an "illustrative" list of expected costs.

According to the conference report on HR 1282, the final bill reflected more detailed Pentagon estimates of some costs, such as the number of missiles and other weapons that were needed to replenish stockpiles depleted by combat.

The administration objected that Byrd's provision banning arms sales to countries that had not made promised contributions was too rigid.

In some cases, administration officials argued, foreign payments were awaiting the Pentagon's calculations of specific U.S. costs.

"There can thus be 'delays' caused by U.S. action or inaction," Office of Management and Budget officials told the conferees on the bill.

The conferees responded by making an apparently minor change in the provision, providing in the final bill that arms sales were banned to any country "that has not fulfilled its commitment" to contribute to U.S. costs.

"It means the same thing," Byrd told the Senate on March 22.

That day, the conference report on the war funding measure was adopted by the House on a vote of 379-11. Soon after, the Senate approved the report by voice vote, clearing the measure for the president. *(Vote 62, p. 16-H)*

Bush signed the measure, PL 102-28, on April 10.

FINAL PROVISIONS

The Desert Storm supplemental spending bill, HR 1282 (PL 102-28) appropriated $42.6 billion to cover the "incremental" costs of the Persian Gulf deployment — that is, costs in excess of those the Pentagon would have incurred if Bush had not dispatched U.S. forces to drive Iraqi forces from Kuwait.

The account was to be funded by money pledged by foreign governments for that purpose, plus an additional $15 billion in U.S. funds.

The bill also required that the U.S. costs be covered by foreign contributions, insofar as they were available. The $15 billion in U.S. funds was to be used only as a "bridge loan," to cover immediate costs pending collection of the foreign pledges.

Any of the $15 billion that was left unspent after all Persian Gulf costs had been paid would revert to the U.S. Treasury.

To replenish weapons used in the war, the bill provided:

- $378 million for 291 Tomahawk ship-launched cruise missiles.
- $166 million for 283 Patriot anti-missile missiles. The bill also included an additional $146 million for various projects related to production and improvement of Patriots.
- $420 million for 2,041 HARM air-launched missiles, designed to home in on anti-aircraft radars.
- $392 million for 5,291 Maverick air-to-ground missiles.
- $152 million for 20,286 MLRS artillery rockets.
- $202 million for "smart" bombs, precision-guided to their targets by lasers and television cameras.

The bill also paid for modifications made in anticipation of the war to adapt existing weapons to combat in the desert and at night, including $15 million to equip Marine Corps helicopters with night-vision equipment.

And it included funds for the cost of using in combat some high-tech prototypes that were still undergoing preproduction tests: $47 million for the JSTARS radar surveillance plane, able to locate ground targets far behind enemy lines; and $9 million for a helicopter-borne laser called "Magic Lantern," designed to locate underwater mines.

The final version of the bill permitted the Pentagon to use foreign contributions — but not the $15 billion in U.S. funds — to cover the increased fuel costs resulting from the gulf crisis.

In other provisions, the bill:

- Earmarked $25 million for emergency loans to small businesses in communities that were hard hit by the deployment of troops to the Persian Gulf. The loans were to come from a $200 million economic adjustment fund created in 1990 to cushion the economic impact of the downturn in defense spending.
- Required notice to Congress before any transfer or sale to other countries of U.S. equipment deployed to the region or Iraqi equipment captured by U.S. forces. The procedure, allowing Congress to block any transfer by enacting a joint resolution, followed existing law on arms sales.

The administration had objected to a Senate-passed provision that would have barred any transfers to other countries of deployed or captured weapons unless approved by legislation. ■

CQ

Appendix A

POLITICAL REPORT

Voters Expressed Dissatisfaction

Lagging economy, concern over nation's health-care needs made for anti-incumbent sentiment

Concern about the economy and health care, as well as growing anti-incumbent sentiment, produced a pair of major election upsets in 1991 and had a significant impact on the campaign agenda for 1992. It also helped fuel a nationwide movement toward term limits for state officials and members of Congress.

The upsets came in Mississippi, where voters lashed out at Democratic Gov. Ray Mabus and easily elected conservative Republican Kirk Fordice, and in Pennsylvania, where voters picked appointed Sen. Harris Wofford, a liberal Democrat, over former Attorney General and Gov. Dick Thornburgh. Economic issues were a major concern in both states.

Thornburgh started out as the heavy favorite. He had been urged by President Bush to run for the seat vacated when Republican John Heinz was killed in a plane crash.

Bush and other administration officials, campaigning for Thornburgh, initially understimated the low-key and little-known Wofford, who managed to turn the election into a referendum on Bush's economic record. Wofford also scored major gains by tapping into widespread public concerns over the cost and availability of health care.

In Mississippi, Mabus' ouster capped a broader incumbent purge that had begun in the Sept. 17 primary. In all, 29 state legislators failed to win either renomination or re-election.

Anti-incumbent fervor of a different kind was obvious in Kentucky when Democratic Lt. Gov. Brereton Jones scored a crushing victory over GOP Rep. Larry J. Hopkins. Hopkins was hurt badly by revelations that he was one of many House members who had floated checks at the House bank. *(Ethics scandals, p. 39)*

The five special elections for House seats in 1991 produced one turnover: Democrat John Olver picked up the Massachusetts seat of Republican Silvio O. Conte, who died Feb. 8.

Texas state Rep. Sam Johnson, a Republican, beat Tom Pauken to take the 3rd District seat of Republican Steve Bartlett, who resigned to run for mayor of Dallas.

In Illinois' safely Republican 15th District, GOP state Rep. Thomas W. Ewing breezed to victory over Democratic former state Rep. Gerald Bradley to succeed Republican Edward Madigan, who resigned in March to become President Bush's new secretary of Agriculture.

Democrat Ed Pastor became Arizona's first Hispanic member of Congress with a comfortable victory over his Republican opponent in the special election in the state's 2nd District. Pastor succeeded Democratic Rep. Morris K. Udall, who represented the 2nd for 30 years before resigning May 4 due to failing health.

In Pennsylvania's 2nd District, Democrat Lucien Blackwell, a former city councilman, beat out a crowd of Democratic challengers to take the seat previously held by William H. Gray III, who stepped down to become president of the United Negro College Fund.

And in Virginia, state Delegate George F. Allen kept the 7th District in the Republican column, defeating Democrat Kay Slaughter by a nearly 2-to-1 margin in the Nov. 5 special election to replace Republican Rep. D. French Slaughter Jr.

Throughout 1991, an anti-incumbent sentiment — perceived and real — helped spark a movement to impose term limits on state officials and members of Congress. But in a key test of the issue, voters in Washington state confounded expectations and rejected a stringent term-limit ballot initiative. *(Term limits, p. 12-A)*

Gubernatorial Races

KENTUCKY

After a long boisterous battle for the governorship in Kentucky, Democratic Lt. Gov. Brereton Jones scored a crushing victory over GOP Rep. Larry J. Hopkins in the Nov. 5 gubernatorial contest.

Official returns:

Jones (D)	540,468	64.7%
Hopkins (R)	294,452	35.3%

Jones' 64.7 percent tally against Hopkins was an ironic ending to a race that initially appeared to be a good chance for Republicans to reclaim the office. Though the Democratic Party had a voter registration advantage of more than 2 to 1 in Kentucky, many of those Democrats frequently voted Republican: Ronald Reagan in 1984 and George Bush in 1988 easily carried Kentucky.

Throughout the gubernatorial race, Jones' personal finances were the major focus; He refused to release his tax returns, and would not disclose whether he had paid income taxes every year.

In the end, however, revelations about Hopkins' check-bouncing at the House bank gave Jones the victory. Jones won 107 of 120 counties, including every county in Hopkins' 6th District.

Jones, 52, first held public office in West Virginia as a Republican state representative. He moved to Kentucky in the early 1970s, switched parties, and in 1987 was elected lieutenant governor.

Jones won that race by a comfortable margin and he seemed a natural successor to Democratic Gov. Wallace G. Wilkinson, who was barred by law from seeking a second consecutive term, but the road to victory was bumpy from the start for Jones. He had a difficult primary and spent much time batting away queries about his personal financial affairs.

Hopkins served in the state House and Senate before taking the north-central 6th Congressional District from Democratic hands in 1978. He won that race with 51 percent of the vote, but had since been re-elected with ease; he was unopposed in 1990. He was a member of both the Agriculture and Armed Services committees.

But Hopkins, like Jones, endured a bruising primary for the GOP gubernatorial nomination and had trouble getting Republicans united behind him. Nevertheless, polls showed him within striking distance of Jones by the end of September.

Hopkins whittled away at Jones' advantage as a Democrat in Kentucky by running a television advertisement ridiculing Jones' refusal to release his tax returns. Jones, a wealthy horse breeder from Woodford County (just west of Lexington), contended that if he released his tax information, his opponents would distort it; and he cited tax summaries that he filed since 1987 with the state Financial Disclosure Review Commission.

Hopkins also raised questions about a 1985 barn fire that killed 15 horses at Jones' farm; the fire occurred after an outbreak of an equine disease strained the finances of Jones' horse-breeding operation. Fire investigators looked into the incident, but no charges were brought.

Jones, who criticized the influence of special-interest money in state politics, had tried to make campaign finance reform a centerpiece of his pitch. But an array of contributors — including mining and tobacco company executives and construction contractors — fattened his campaign treasury; Going into October, Jones had $1.8 million cash on hand — roughly twice as much as Hopkins.

Hopkins accused Democrats of being beholden to special-interest contributors. He decried what he referred to as the "For Sale" sign on the state Capitol. But Hopkins had his own set of finance questions to contend with; he was dogged by what the local media referred to as the "$660,000 question" — namely, if he lost the gubernatorial race and then did not seek re-election to Congress in 1992, would he pocket more than $660,000 in cash that was in his campaign fund? House rules allowed Hopkins to convert the political money to personal use.

Kentucky voters had long been familiar with furor and fussing over money and politics. In 1888, state Treasurer James William "Honest Dick" Tate vanished with $250,000 from the state till, an act that prompted adoption of an amendment to the Kentucky Constitution barring state officials from serving successive terms.

Hopkins' campaign, however, did not go into free fall until he admitted bouncing 32 checks at the House bank.

Primary Battles

Both Jones and Hopkins faced difficult primaries before going head-to-head with each other.

A number of people — including Wilkinson's wife, Martha — lined up to challenge Jones in the May gubernatorial primary. She pulled out of the race shortly before the primary amid controversy over connections between her campaign financing and her husband. Her campaign had raised several million dollars, much of it from contractors doing business with the state under no-bid contracts.

Although Democrats had controlled Kentucky's governorship without interruption since 1971, Jones kept himself apart from that record of incumbency with the fallout over Wilkinson. One of his TV ads showed him telling a group, "I just don't think Frankfort ought to be run by wealthy special interests," and he supported sharply lower limits on campaign contributions — even as he was raising a state-record campaign treasury of $7.7 million.

In the primary, Jones was able to stave off a late surge by Lexington Mayor Scotty Baesler; he won the nomination with 38 percent of the vote to Baesler's 30 percent.

Hopkins, 58, had an equally difficult primary for the Republican nomination. Hopkins rejected party overtures to run for governor in 1983 and 1987 before embarking on his 1991 bid. He began the primary season as the clear GOP favorite, but the unexpected candidacy of Lexington lawyer Larry L. Forgy scrambled the picture. Forgy was state chairman for President Ronald Reagan's 1980 and 1984 campaigns, and he dropped out of the 1987 gubernatorial campaign. The primary promised to be the stiffest GOP contest since 1967, the last time a Republican won the governor's office.

One month before Kentucky's GOP May 28 gubernatorial primary, Hopkins came under fire for résumé inaccuracies regarding his military service and education.

Credited in the past as a Korean War veteran, Hopkins touted his veteran status during the fractious campaign, contrasting it with Forgy's student and family deferments.

But Forgy battled back, noting that Hopkins did not join the Marines until a year after the fighting in Korea was over. When asked during an April 19 news conference to clarify the matter, Hopkins said he served "in the latter part of the Korean War conflict" — although not as a combat soldier.

Marine Corps records indicated that Hopkins enlisted in June 1954, about 11 months after the fighting ended. He served two years in the United States and was honorably discharged in June 1956. An aide to Hopkins said that the federal law governing veterans' benefits defined the Korean conflict as lasting through January 1955. Hopkins later acknowledged that he did not visit Korea until he traveled there as a House member in 1981.

Hopkins' biography had also previously listed him as a member of the Veterans of Foreign Wars, which required overseas service. Hopkins was actually a member of the American Legion, which did not have the same requirement. Hopkins' office attributed this switch to staff error.

Hopkins' résumé had in the past cited attendance at Murray State University, Purdue University and Southern Methodist University. But in 1985, "Politics in America" deleted Purdue and SMU, on information from Hopkins' office; two years later, "The Almanac of American Politics" also did so. The Louisville Courier-Journal reported that Purdue and SMU had no record of Hopkins' attendance, though Hopkins, a stockbroker by profession, said he took securities courses at both.

In the end, Hopkins eked out a narrow victory, running more poorly than expected outside his base in the 6th and neighboring 4th districts.

MISSISSIPPI

Troubled by a stagnant economy and a high unemployment rate, Mississippi voters lashed out Nov. 5, giving conservative Republican Kirk Fordice an upset victory over Democratic Gov. Ray Mabus.

Mabus' ouster capped a broader incumbent purge that began in Mississippi's Sept. 17 primary. Three-term Democratic Lt. Gov. Brad Dye also lost Nov. 5; all told, 29 state legislators failed to win either renomination or re-election.

Fordice's victory made him the first Republican elected governor in Mississippi since Reconstruction. Georgia stood out as the only Southern state not to elect a GOP governor since then.

Official returns:

Fordice (R)	361,500	50.8%
Mabus (D)	338,435	47.6
Shawn O'Hara (I)	11,253	1.6

Fordice, a Vicksburg construction executive, carried 49

of the state's 82 counties; he won by more than 2 to 1 in populous Rankin County, which included suburbs of Jackson, and stayed close to Mabus in Hinds County (Jackson). He also ran up big margins in the more conservative and Republican southern part of the state, between Jackson and the Gulf Coast.

Fordice, who never held public office and touted himself as an outsider, was aided by an anti-incumbent feeling among the state's voters. By positioning himself as an "anti-politician," Fordice overcame a huge deficit in early polls to defeat state Auditor Pete Johnson in the Oct. 8 GOP runoff. And it continued to work against Mabus, who spent five times as much as Fordice on the campaign.

Mabus spent heavily from his campaign treasury in the Democratic primary, but he still had the resources for a showdown with Fordice. He ran ads portraying Fordice as a tool of business interests. Referring to Fordice's tenure as president of the Associated General Contractors, a large trade association that represented the heavy construction industry, the Mabus campaign ads claimed that Fordice peddled his influence "to help himself and his rich friends in industry."

But Mabus, who was the first governor to attempt to take advantage of a 1987 change in state law that permitted the chief executive to serve two consecutive terms, had his own problems to contend with: he showed signs of vulnerability in the primary. Facing a challenge for the Democratic nomination from former U.S. Rep. Wayne Dowdy (1981-89), the governor barely managed to avoid a runoff.

Industrial plant closings and Mississippi's 8 percent unemployment rate already left the electorate uneasy and receptive to Fordice's overtures. Promising economic development and fiscal responsibility, Fordice called for welfare reform and suggested consolidation of some state colleges.

Some Democrats charged that Fordice — who opposed affirmative action and racial quotas in hiring — resorted to subtle racial appeals; Fordice's critics cited one of his TV ads on welfare reform that portrayed a black woman holding her child.

Observers had said the heavy black support that pushed Mabus over the top in the 1987 gubernatorial race would be key to the race, particularly since Fordice was not expected to get the minority vote. In 1987, Mabus won with 53 percent of the vote with his promise that "Mississippi would never be last again." He had vowed to end the state's national notoriety for its low levels of achievement in education and social programs.

Though Mabus won national notice for his child-care and education reform efforts, the recognition had not translated into votes or political clout. He alienated himself from many Democratic legislators — who had been accusing him of governing in an imperious style and of being aloof — by refusing to raise taxes for new programs after the legislators balked at his lottery proposal.

But it was tepid voter turnout in the heavily black Delta counties that proved Mabus' undoing. Blacks make up 36 percent of the state population and Mabus carried every county along the Mississippi River except Warren (Fordice's home), but his total vote could not compensate for the losses he suffered among rural white voters — particularly in the traditional Democratic strongholds of northeast Mississippi's hill country.

Primary Battle

In the Democratic primary Sept. 17, Mabus had beaten Dowdy to win. But, Mabus took just 51 percent of the vote, barely enough to avoid a runoff with Dowdy, who ran about 9 percentage points back. George "Wagon Wheel" Blair, a retired National Guardsman, drew the rest of the Democratic vote.

Mabus began the campaign in a precarious position — alienated from state legislators and facing an aggressive intraparty challenge from Dowdy, a four-term congressman from southwest Mississippi's 4th District who stepped down in 1988 to run for the Senate.

Dowdy aimed to capitalize on anti-Mabus sentiment, presenting himself as a folksy populist. Early polls indicated a dogfight, with Dowdy close on Mabus' heels.

But the contest failed to generate much excitement in the state, and Dowdy's cash-strapped campaign was not able to match Mabus' hard-hitting negative ads in the final weeks.

Midsummer financial reports indicated that Mabus had raised 10 times as much as Dowdy; Dowdy ended up being outspent 5 to 1.

While Dowdy's bid was fading in the final weeks of the primary, the Republican race was heating up. With two GOP senators securely ensconced and a strong showing in the 1987 gubernatorial race, Republicans were heartened about party prospects for 1991.

Three candidates stepped forward to vie in the Sept. 17 Republican primary: Fordice, Johnson, who was elected in 1987 as a Democrat, but switched parties in 1989, and Bobby Clanton, a tough-talking Jackson businessman who proposed the death penalty for convicted second-time drug dealers.

Johnson, considered the GOP front-runner going into the primary, had the name recognition: His uncle and grandfather both served as governor and Johnson himself had an unsuccessful bid for the Democratic nomination for the 2nd District in 1982.

Fordice and Clanton — both of whom had never held public office — chipped away at Johnson's lead by deriding him as a professional politician.

As the race tightened, Johnson went on the offensive, running negative television ads. But he could not halt Fordice's advance with his "outsider" campaign.

The GOP primary was tight, with Fordice running ahead of Johnson by less than 2 percentage points. Clanton was a distant third. Since neither Fordice nor Johnson won more than 50 percent in the GOP primary, but were the top two finishers, they competed in an Oct. 8 runoff.

Fordice pummeled Johnson in the Republican gubernatorial runoff. He outpaced Johnson with more than 60 percent of the vote.

Senate Races

PENNSYLVANIA

If there was ever a Senate race that appeared to be a sure bet for a Republican candidate to win, it would have been the Pennsylvania 1991 special election.

A Democrat had not won a Senate race in Pennyslvania since Joseph S. Clark in 1962, and a Republican seemed the likely choice to fill the vacancy created by the death of popular Republican John Heinz.

Heinz, a fierce defender of Pennsylvania's economic interests and an outspoken advocate of the elderly, died April 4 when his charter plane collided with a helicopter and crashed in a suburban Philadelphia schoolyard. Republican Dick Thornburgh, President Bush's attorney general who served two terms as Pennsylvania's governor, was clearly the favored candidate to fill the three years remaining in Heinz's term.

But Pennsylvania's two-party heritage and the backdrop of economic recession lent an element of unpredictability to the outcome. On Election Day, appointed Democratic Sen. Harris Wofford — who successfully tapped public anxieties about the health-care squeeze — won the election by a margin of nearly 340,000 votes. It was his first run for an elective office.

Official returns:

Harris Wofford (D)	1,860,760	55.0%
Dick Thornburgh (R)	1,521,986	45.0%

Wofford was known to insiders as a civil rights adviser to President John F. Kennedy, a founder of the Peace Corps, the president of Bryn Mawr College in suburban Philadelphia and the secretary of Labor and Industry in the Cabinet of Democratic Gov. Robert P. Casey.

But the 65-year-old Wofford was not widely known by Pennsylvania voters when he was appointed in May by Casey to fill the vacancy created by the death of Heinz. He was not even Casey's first choice. Chrysler Corp. Chairman Lee A. Iacocca, an Allentown native who had lived nearly all of his adult life in Michigan, was first offered the appointment but turned it down, noting that he "was not prepared to make the commitment necessary to fill the heavy responsibilities of a United States senator."

Yet Wofford proved to be an effective vehicle of protest for voters in economically sluggish Pennsylvania, using a call for national health care as the centerpiece of a campaign pitched to middle-class voters. His tag line: "It's time to take care of our own." Wofford's pitch for national health insurance also resonated powerfully because he managed to use it as a metaphor for his patriotism and values and even his views on the status quo and on crime. One of the most talked-about of his television ads hit all of these buttons: Wofford looked into the camera to say: "If criminals have the right to a lawyer, I think working Americans should have the right to a doctor."

His success in a state with an unemployment rate of 6.5 percent, almost identical to the national average at the time, gave Democratic strategists some tangible evidence that the "middle class squeeze" issue might provide the party with a workable thematic blueprint for the 1992 presidential campaign.

The race was seen in some quarters as a referendum on Bush and his domestic policies. Thornburgh, who had served as attorney general for three years before resigning in August to run for the Senate, had headed Bush's Domestic Policy Council and had been the beneficiary of several presidential campaign visits to Pennsylvania in his behalf before the special election.

Wofford was able to chop into Thornburgh's huge early lead with an aggressive "anti-Washington" message that the better-known Republican actually encouraged by portraying himself at the start as a well-connected Washington insider. By the final days of the campaign, polls showed that Wofford had pulled even. Wofford built a constituency that featured, but was not limited to, the old New Deal coalition of ethnics, minorities and liberals. He easily carried Pennsylvania's Democratic keystones — liberal Philadelphia and the most socially conservative blue-collar coal and steel country of western Pennsyvania.

There was little passion in the Thornburgh campaign. While Wofford seized on the pocketbook concerns of middle-class voters, Thornburgh emphasized the need for fiscal responsibility. He tried to link Wofford with Casey and the massive package of tax increases that the governor had gotten enacted earlier in the year.

Early on, Republicans began to refer to Wofford as a liberal. But Wofford sought to put the best twist on the term, emphasizing his support for New Deal-style job-creating programs.

Wofford was careful in his statements on social issues. He said that he backed Casey's decision in 1990 to sign one of the nation's strictest abortion-control laws, but declined to discuss his views on abortion "outside of a thoughtful context."

How the Race Developed

Shortly after Heinz's death, Pennsylvania Republican leaders agreed the party nomination was for Heinz's widow, Teresa. But, after discussing the matter with her three sons, she announced April 23 that she would not run because she had "too much healing to do, too many family responsibilities." Her announcement opened up the possibilities for a competitive race, but one that would have to undergo more hurdles — in the form of court rulings — before the Nov. 5 special election.

Following a challenge to the state's special election statute, a federal appeals court ruled Aug. 6 that the selection of nominees for special elections was left to the discretion of the states, overturning a lower court ruling that the state's special election statute was unconstitutional.

The ruling all but guaranteed a Nov. 5 showdown between Thornburgh and Wofford.

For Wofford, who had never run for public office but had headed the Democratic state committee, it meant a daunting task of trying to win a race in a state in which Democrats had lost nine straight Senate elections.

But Thornburgh would not have a cakewalk against the lesser-known Wofford. Both parties appeared united; both candidates had plenty of money.

Thornburgh enjoyed a generally favorable reputation among Pennsylvania voters. He left the governorship in 1987 on a high note, with a state budget surplus, a "Mr. Clean" image and a reputation as a cool, efficient manager that was forged early in his administration with his calm response to the crisis at the crippled Three Mile Island nuclear plant near Harrisburg in 1979.

But Thornburgh's reviews as attorney general were mixed. Appointed by President Ronald Reagan in 1988 to replace the embattled Edwin Meese III, Thornburgh drew praise for increasing the professionalism of the office.

But he drew criticism for a style that had been variously described as imperious, cipherlike and secretive. And some of his personnel decisions backfired; before the election, a former top aide was convicted of cocaine use.

A key question in the race was whether Thornburgh's vote-getting appeal was overrated. After initially winning the governorship in 1978 with 52.5 percent of the vote, Thornburgh won re-election in 1982 with a mere 50.8 percent against little-known Democratic Rep. Allen E. Ertel. When Thornburgh was on the ballot in 1982, it was his strong showing in western Pennsylvania that bailed him out. Wofford had no ties to western Pennsylvania. He was born in New York City and called the Philadelphia suburbs home.

Republicans blamed the recession for Thornburgh's mediocre showing and contended that it was a considerable feat for him to win at all that year when Republicans were losing a number of governorships across the industrial Frost Belt.

But Wofford was backstopped by an experienced campaign team that featured James Carville, a political consultant with a reputation for hardball politics; he managed Casey's winning gubernatorial campaigns in 1986 and 1990 and New Jersey's Democratic Sen. Frank R. Lautenberg's re-election victory in 1988.

As the election neared, the race turned to pocketbook issues; concerns about job maintenance and job creation were nearly always on the political front burner in Pennsylvania.

The state had been in the process of making the slow, and often painful, transition from an economy based on heavy industry to one more rooted in service and high-technology jobs.

Wofford blamed the policies of the Reagan and Bush administrations over the previous decade for putting Pennsylvania behind the economic eight ball.

He characterized Thornburgh as "a do-nothing Washington insider" who boasted of his leadership experience but failed to develop programs that would aid Pennsylvania when he headed the president's Domestic Policy Council.

The issue on which Wofford and Thornburgh seemed to joust most vigorously was the proposed free-trade agreement with Mexico. Wofford was an unabashed protectionist. Thornburgh argued the other side, backing the free-trade agreement and debunking Wofford for applying 1960s thinking to the '90s.

"I'm not afraid of trading with the rest of the world," Thornburgh said.

But Wofford, armed with the support of organized labor, the power of the trade issue, and the backdrop of recession, sailed on to victory.

House Special Elections

TEXAS — 3RD

When Republican Steve Bartlett announced he was giving up his safe House seat to run for mayor of Dallas, the only real question was which Republican would succeed him. The 3rd District, dominated by affluent neighborhoods in Dallas and fast-growing suburbs to the north, was overwhelmingly Republican and likely to stay that way.

The answer turned out to be state Rep. Sam Johnson, who won the first special election of the 102nd Congress by narrowly defeating Dallas businessman Tom Pauken in a May 18 runoff. On May 22, Johnson was sworn in.

Official returns:

Johnson	24,004	52.6%
Pauken	21,647	47.4

Johnson's victory reversed the result of the May 4 primary, in which Pauken had come out on top of a 12-person field, leading Johnson, 27 percent to 20 percent. Eleven of the 12 primary candidates were Republicans.

The lone Democrat, Wayne E. Putnam, ran a distant seventh.

Though Pauken won the first round, Johnson, a highly decorated former Vietnam prisoner of war, roared past him in the runoff, buoyed by endorsements from a trio of losing candidates in the primary and strong support from his home base, fast-growing Collin County.

Although the Collin County portion cast just one-fifth of the runoff ballots, Johnson represented much of the county in the Texas House and swept it with 75 percent of the vote. In the populous Dallas County portion where the rest of the ballots were cast, Johnson drew a respectable 47 percent. That marked a considerable improvement from May 4, when he finished fourth in Dallas County with barely 10 percent.

Pauken's failure to carry Dallas County more decisively in the runoff was a major disappointment to his campaign. He had fashioned his political career in the county, narrowly losing previous bids for Congress in 1978 and 1980 in a district that covered the eastern portion of Dallas County, and in 1990 had led the successful campaign to "Just Say No! to 14-1," a minority-preferred council redistricting plan in the city of Dallas.

But that redistricting campaign demonstrated the outspoken Pauken's bent for controversy. Consequently, in the wake of the May 4 vote, the third-, fourth- and sixth-place finishers — former state Rep. Bill Hammond, Paul Zane Pilzer and Pete Sessions, respectively — all endorsed Johnson rather than Pauken.

Johnson featured the endorsements in radio advertising and direct mail, and on the day of the runoff election, both Pilzer and Sessions (the son of FBI Director William S. Sessions) greeted voters on Johnson's behalf at their polling places.

The Pauken camp discounted the value of the endorsements, pointing to grass-roots workers whom their candidate had lured from the other campaigns.

Pauken went on the offensive in the runoff, accusing Johnson of backing a controversial school financing plan that would redistribute funds from more affluent school districts in Texas to poorer ones. Critics of the plan abounded in the 3rd District, and it was widely known as the "Robin Hood" plan.

Johnson argued that he had favored a procedural move to send the measure to committee for revisions but had opposed it once it came back to the floor of the Texas House.

Meanwhile, Johnson spotlighted his military record. He ran a television spot that featured footage of President Bush lauding Johnson at a ceremony at a Vietnam veterans memorial in the Dallas area.

And on the day before the runoff, a fellow Vietnam War pilot, freshman GOP Rep. Randy "Duke" Cunningham of California, came to the Texas 3rd to campaign in Johnson's behalf.

Turnout on May 18 was low across the district. Although the Texas 3rd was one of the faster-growing districts in the country — with a 35 percent population growth in the 1980s — barely 45,000 votes were cast in the runoff.

That was a lower total than for all but two of the special House elections held thus far during the Bush presidency. The two lower turnouts came in urban, minority-dominated districts — the Houston-based Texas 18th and the New York 18th in the South Bronx — where population growth in the 1980s was slow at best.

MASSACHUSETTS — 1ST

Democrats claimed a seat they had not held since 1892 when state Sen. John Olver, a liberal, held off conservative Republican Steven D. Pierce in the June 4 special election in the 1st District of western Massachusetts.

Olver, a former professor of chemistry at the University of Massachusetts at Amherst and a state legislator since 1969, claimed the seat vacated by the Feb. 8 death of Republican Rep. Silvio O. Conte, who was in his 17th term. Olver's election made for an all-Democratic Massachusetts delegation in Congress: 11 Democrats in the House and two in the Senate.

Official returns:

John Olver (D)	70,022	49.6%
Steven D. Pierce (R)	68,052	48.2
Patrick Joseph Armstrong (I)	1,859	1.3
Dennis Kelly (I)	880	0.6
Thomas Boynton (I)	250	0.2

Olver, 54, was the presumed favorite after winning the nomination in the April 30 primary. Although the largely rural district had historically belonged to the GOP and Conte had won in past elections with staggering margins, the district's registration was nearly one-half independent, and Democrats outnumbered Republicans among those picking a party.

The critical vote in the election came as expected from the state's westernmost county of Berkshire — the portion of the district neither Olver nor Pierce had represented. Olver's advantage in the blue-collar precincts of Pittsfield was nearly equal to his margin of victory.

Olver started from a strong base. His Senate district comprised about 150,000 residents in Franklin and Hampshire counties, at the geographic center of the 1st District. Pierce benefited from unusually heavy voting in his hometown of Westfield, in Hampden County west of Springfield.

Both candidates agreed that the No. 1 issue in the special election was western Massachusetts' slumping economy. In recent years, the loss of jobs in manufacturing and at the myriad educational institutions that dotted the 1st District — which extended from the populous Connecticut River Valley across the Berkshire Hills to the New York border — had sent the unemployment rate in many western Massachusetts communities soaring into double digits.

Pierce tried to link the loss of jobs to high tax levels and sought to tie both to Olver, who as Senate chairman of the legislature's Taxation Committee could scarcely disassociate himself from the reign of former Gov. Michael S. Dukakis. Pierce called Olver "Dr. Taxes." Said Pierce: "My opponent was one of the boys who stood by silent when the state went down the drain fiscally."

Olver responded that the money his committee raised went to support social programs for education and the environment that district residents supported — and that Pierce had opposed. He also made sure voters did not forget the "right-wing ideologue" label attached to Pierce in 1990 by a GOP rival, William F. Weld, who went on to be elected governor.

Weld later named Pierce to his Cabinet and endorsed his bid for Congress. Nonetheless, Olver recycled several of Weld's 1990 criticisms of Pierce on child care and a variety of other issues.

The one non-economic issue stressed by both candidates was abortion. Polls showed the district to be strongly pro-abortion rights. The National Abortion Rights Action League (NARAL) mounted an independent campaign in Olver's behalf in the primary (when Olver's principal rival was a female legislator who opposed abortion) and did so again for the June vote.

Pierce, who favored allowing abortion in cases of rape, incest or a threat to the mother's life, said Olver and NARAL were distorting his position to make it appear extreme. Pierce also attacked a Supreme Court decision denying federal funds to family planning counseling programs that included abortion information.

In the closing days of the campaign, Pierce heavily publicized his criticism of that court ruling.

Primaries

Pierce, popular with party activists, won the three-way Republican primary with 56 percent. Conte had been among the House's most liberal Republicans and regularly voted with the Democrats.

Pierce, 41, a former minority leader in the state House and an unsuccessful gubernatorial candidate in 1990, was hardly cut from Conte's old-fashioned cloth, hailing instead from the state party's New Right wing. Critics said Pierce was too conservative for a district that voted for the Democratic presidential candidate in three of the past four elections.

Nevertheless, in the weeks after he had dismissed two rivals in the GOP primary, Pierce softened his ideological edge, sharpened his rhetoric and on Election Day came within fewer than 2,000 votes of an upset. He was aided by a strong show of support from national GOP figures; Barbara Bush, Conte's widow, Corinne (who endorsed him after favoring another candidate in the primary) and Senate GOP leader Bob Dole of Kansas all campaigned for him.

Olver was a comfortable winner in the crowded Democratic primary, with just under one-third of the vote. After besting a big field in the primary, he collected endorsements from his rivals to go with those of labor unions, teachers, environmentalists, women's groups and supporters of abortion rights.

The Democratic vote was sharply divided in the primary, but Olver benefited from the fact that in the course of his long legislative career, he had represented almost half the towns in the district. Olver carried about 55 communities in the Democratic primary, including virtually all of those in Hampshire County, rural Franklin County and the portion of Worcester County in the 1st.

Other Democratic candidates had trouble breaking out of their more limited bases. Linda J. Melconian ran well in the Springfield area, home of her state Senate district. But her efforts to sell herself across the district as an experienced political insider, with nearly a decade on the staff of former House Speaker Thomas P. O'Neill Jr., were blunted.

Her anti-abortion rights stance drew an independently financed media campaign against her by the National Abortion Rights Action League, and she was unable to shake charges of carpetbagging. Melconian moved from Springfield in the 2nd District to West Springfield in the 1st to make the race.

Over the hills in Berkshire County, two Democratic, local candidates split the vote — state Rep. Christopher J. Hodgkins and former state Rep. Sherwood Guernsey.

ILLINOIS — 15TH

Running in Illinois' dependably Republican 15th District, GOP state Rep. Thomas W. Ewing breezed to victory in a July 2 special election. Ewing defeated Democratic former state Rep. Gerald Bradley to succeed Republican Edward Madigan, who resigned in March to become Presi-

dent Bush's new secretary of Agriculture.
Official returns:

Ewing	25,675	66.4%
Bradley	13,011	33.6

The heavily rural east-central Illinois district's GOP tendencies had made Ewing, 55, a solid favorite. Ewing, who stepped down as deputy Republican leader in the state House to run for Congress, appeared to be a prime example of a Midwestern "Main Street Republican." A lawyer, he was a member of the Elks, Masonic and Moose lodges in Pontiac and had served as treasurer of the state Republican Party.

First elected to the state House in 1974, Ewing — a former executive director of the Pontiac Chamber of Commerce — hewed to a pro-business line. As co-chairman of the legislature's Economic and Fiscal Committee, Ewing had taken a conservative stance on budget issues.

Ewing pledged to rural voters that he would seek a seat on the Agriculture Committee. Madigan was ranking Republican on that panel before his Cabinet appointment.

Although Bradley, 63, a Bloomington businessman, also had a long state House tenure (1969-83), Ewing's strong advantages in name recognition and fundraising cinched his victory. Bradley predicated his campaign on the likelihood of a low turnout — the election fell during growing season and on the eve of the Fourth of July weekend — and focused his campaign on the district's few Democratic pockets.

The 15th was typical of a number of districts in the Midwestern Corn Belt, filled with small towns; flat, productive farmland, and plenty of Republicans. In every election since he had won the seat in 1972, Madigan had been re-elected with more than 65 percent of the vote. Republican presidential candidates routinely swept the district with a percentage nearly that large.

The district included all or part of 13 counties from the center of Illinois east to the Indiana line.

A member of local Young Republican organizations, Ewing entered the public arena in 1968 as an assistant state's attorney for Livingston County. As he rose through the leadership ranks — to assistant House minority leader and then to the deputy's position — Ewing remained a partisan activist. He was a delegate to the 1980, 1984 and 1988 Republican national conventions, and was elected treasurer of the state GOP in 1990.

Primaries

Ewing started in a much stronger position than Bradley. As a GOP insider in Springfield, Ewing quickly emerged as the GOP's consensus choice. That freed the party to become actively involved in Ewing's campaign, and when Vice President Dan Quayle went to Chicago in mid-April to help open the White Sox's new Comiskey Park, he also held a fundraiser for Ewing that raised roughly $30,000.

Still, some Democrats believed that Ewing could be beaten. They pointed to the unpredictability of low-turnout special elections, his low name familiarity in parts of the district, and a series of recent successes Democrats had in picking off traditionally Republican seats in downstate Illinois. But neither Bradley nor his opponent in the May 21 primary, former Rep. Tim Lee Hall (1975-77), seemed capable of overcoming GOP orientation in the district.

In previous congressional bids, each showed limited vote-getting appeal.

Bradley challenged House Minority Leader Robert H. Michel in 1984 in the neighboring 18th District and was beaten by a ratio of better than 3 to 2.

Hall was elected once to Congress in a district that overlapped the central part of the current 15th. But his win was largely regarded as a fluke. He captured the seat of retiring GOP Rep. Leslie C. Arends in 1974, the election held in the wake of the Watergate scandal, when a number of traditionally Republican seats across the country toppled into Democratic hands.

Once in Congress, Hall did not try to mute his liberal, pro-labor instincts and two years after his unexpected victory, he was voted out of office.

Bradley, who emphasized the need for fiscal responsibility, enjoyed wider support from party leaders and was considered the front-runner in the Democratic primary. So it was no surprise that he won the low-key, low-cost and low-turnout primary. Bradley enjoyed nearly a 3-to-2 advantage in the primary over Hall.

ARIZONA — 2ND

Democrat Ed Pastor became Arizona's first Hispanic member of Congress with a comfortable victory over his Republican opponent in the Sept. 24 special election in the state's 2nd District.

A Maricopa County (Phoenix) supervisor, Pastor, 48, who resigned to run for the House defeated former Yuma County Supervisor Pat Conner. He succeeded Democratic Rep. Morris K. Udall, who represented the 2nd for 30 years before resigning May 4 due to failing health.

Official returns:

Ed Pastor (D)	32,289	55.5%
Pat Conner (R)	25,814	44.4

With the special election the only contest on the ballot, turnout was extremely light: About 23 percent of the registered voters in the 2nd cast ballots — about 11,600 more votes than were cast in the Aug. 13 Democratic and GOP primaries.

While Pastor's winning tally did not approach that typically posted by the warmly regarded Udall (who topped 65 percent in his last five elections), Pastor matched the 1988 showing in the 2nd District of Democratic presidential nominee Michael S. Dukakis. The 2nd was Arizona's only district represented by a Democrat, and it was the state's most Hispanic district, with more than 45 percent of its residents of Hispanic origin.

Running in a district where Democrats outnumbered Republicans by 2 to 1, Pastor, was heavily favored over Conner. By carrying Maricopa and Pima each by more than 4,800 votes, Pastor more than offset Conner's 2-to-1 showing in his home county of Yuma.

Pastor's election also marked the end of Tucson's monopoly on the 2nd District seat. Maricopa County (Phoenix) and Pima County (Tucson) had nearly equal shares of voters in the district, but both Udall and his predecessors in the 2nd, brother Stewart L. Udall (1955-61) and Harold A. Patten (1949-55), called Tucson home. Pastor's four primary challengers — including the mayor of Tucson — also listed Tucson as their hometown.

Neither Pastor nor Conner began the campaign well-known beyond his own county; each won his party's primary with less than 40 percent of the vote. Pastor's profile in populous Maricopa, coupled with Democratic dominance in Pima, more than made up for Conner's strong performance in Yuma. Three out of four votes cast in the special election came from Maricopa or Pima; Yuma accounted for a fifth of the vote.

Pastor campaigned for improved health care and health insurance. He supported giving women the option to choose an abortion. In February 1990, he testified before the Senate Finance Committee in favor of the proposed U.S.-Mexico free-trade agreement.

Pastor, who served a Maricopa County supervisory district that extended from Tempe to Gila Bend, emphasized his 15 years of public service during his House campaign. A former chemistry teacher, Pastor had been an aide to Democratic Gov. Raul Castro (1975-77) before serving four terms on the the Maricopa County Board of Supervisors.

Pastor got endorsements from leading officeholders — Hispanic and Anglo — during the primary, emerging as the candidate of the political establishment. (His two major primary opponents ran anti-establishment campaigns.) He won the Aug. 13 Democratic primary with 37 percent of the vote; his nearest foe had 32 percent.

Conner, 48, a real estate broker and owner of two car washes in Yuma, served six and a half years on the county board. Running on an anti-government, anti-regulatory platform, he contended that government bureaucracy had hamstrung small business.

Conner enlisted the aid of the National Republican Congressional Committee to counter Pastor's dominant campaign treasury. His TV and radio ads attacked Pastor for accepting campaign donations during his successful 1988 race for county supervisor from savings and loan executive Charles H. Keating Jr. and for receiving a $1,000 set of golf clubs from a lobbyist later indicted in a political corruption probe. Pastor sent the Keating contribution to the U.S. Treasury and returned the golf clubs.

Primaries

Five Democrats and five Republicans met the June 14 filing deadline to fill Udall's seat. But in a district where Democrats outnumbered Republicans in registration by about 2 to 1, most of the attention was on the Aug. 13 Democratic primary.

The five-way race came down to a turf battle between Pastor and Tom Volgy, the mayor of Tucson (Pima County), whose residents had long considered the seat theirs.

Although Volgy ran well in his home county, he could not dent Pastor's base in Maricopa County, where he ran a distant third, behind Virginia Yrun, on leave as executive director of Planned Parenthood of Southern Arizona.

In contrast, Pastor — who enjoyed a fundraising edge that permitted him to run TV and radio ads — picked up half as many votes in Pima County as he garnered in his own county.

Rounding out the Democratic field were Joseph Sweeney, administrator of an unaccredited Tucson law school and Craig Runyon, a real estate broker.

First elected to his county post in 1975, Pastor resigned to run for the House. Competing in a strongly Hispanic district, Pastor had an automatic entree to a crucial Democratic voting bloc. His district as supervisor covered much of the 2nd's portion of Maricopa County, stretching from southern Phoenix to outlying rural areas.

Volgy may not have had the ethnic bond Pastor could boast — he was born in Budapest, Hungary — but he hailed from Pima County (Tucson), home to the University of Arizona, where he taught political science. First elected mayor in 1987 after 10 years on the City Council, Volgy had already decided not to seek re-election in 1991. In 1976, with Udall running for president, Volgy briefly ran for the Democratic House nomination; he withdrew once Udall returned to run for his seat.

Both Volgy and Pastor had touted similar causes, voicing support for economic development in Arizona, national health care, protection of the environment and reform of the nation's educational system. Volgy had also pushed campaign finance reform: When he launched his campaign, he called on his primary challengers to adhere to a spending cap of $175,000.

Pastor's campaign was the most flush in the Democratic field, having raised nearly $200,000. He ran some TV ads early in the campaign and radio, cable and network TV ads in the remaining weeks. He also accrued support from some leading district politicians.

On the Republican side, there were also five candidates. Conner took 4,253 votes (32.6 percent) to edge John Kaites' 3,822 votes (29.3 percent); Kaites was a Phoenix lawyer who had also been a substitute TV weatherman.

First-time candidate Don Shooter, a Yuma asparagus and date farmer, gained a surprising tally of 2,727 votes (20.9 percent), outdistancing former Douglas Mayor Albert Rodriguez's 1,497 votes (11.5 percent) and Paradise Valley businessman Elliott Glasser's 713 votes (5.4 percent).

PENNSYLVANIA — 2ND

When Majority Whip William H. Gray III announced June 20 that he was stepping down as the No. 3 Democrat in the House to be president of the United Negro College Fund, the news rekindled a bitter feud that had split black Democrats in the Philadelphia mayoral primary just a month earlier.

On the ballot for the Nov. 5 special House election were: Democrat Lucien Blackwell, a former city councilman; Consumer Party candidate Chaka Fattah, 34, a freshman state senator; independent John F. White Jr., 42, the former state welfare department head; and Republican Nadine G. Smith-Bulford, 37, a minister.

In the end, Blackwell won the race and the remaining year of Gray's term.

Official returns:

Blackwell (D)	51,820	39.2%
Fattah (D)	37,068	28.0
White (D)	36,469	27.6
Smith-Bulford (R)	6,928	5.2

Anchored in North and West Philadelphia, the 2nd was one of the most Democratic districts in the country. Eighty percent black, it gave Democratic presidential nominee Michael S. Dukakis 91 percent of the vote in 1988.

More than one-third of the district's residents were poor, and they were concentrated in North Philadelphia. Voters there comprised Blackwell's core support in his successful bids for the City Council.

But, the race among the Democrats was competitive. Fattah, considered to be a rising star in Philadelphia politics, represented about 250,000 constituents in a Senate district that included parts of North and West Philadelphia, in addition to Manayunk, East Falls and Germantown. Fattah also had a stronger grass-roots organization in that area, built for his three successful state House campaigns and the 1988 state Senate race.

Fattah and White counted heavily on backing from the district's younger, more affluent blacks and from whites, who made up about one-fifth of the electorate. But, Fattah and White ran almost equally well among their targeted voters; as a result, neither was able to get within striking distance of Blackwell.

Blackwell Not Gray's Choice

Blackwell's victory in the Nov. 5 election to succeed Gray gave an ironic twist in the chilly relationship between him and Gray. Gray had repeatedly used his influence to block Blackwell's political career.

Earlier in 1991, when Blackwell announced his mayoral bid; Gray backed another black candidate. In the state's May Democratic mayoral primary, the black vote split so much that Ed Rendell, a prominent white Democrat, won the party nomination to succeed W. Wilson Goode, the city's first black mayor.

When Gray announced his resignation, Blackwell immediately launched his candidacy and because he had already built a citywide organization, was immediately favored to win.

But then intense political and legal maneuvering began, with Gray taking an active role.

Gray delayed setting a date for his resignation, which prevented the scheduling of a special election. Under Pennsylvania law, it appeared necessary for 60 days to elapse between the occurrence of the vacancy and the holding of a special election.

Gray had to resign by Sept. 5 to satisfy the 60-day rule and allow for a Nov. 5 election. Instead, Gray stepped down Sept. 11 — a move many suggested was designed to disadvantage Blackwell, a longtime Gray rival, from capitalizing on his strength with ward leaders to secure quick nomination.

State Democrats and many party loyalists in Philadelphia hoped for a Nov. 5 election to coincide with the special Senate election and with voting for local offices. These Democrats felt that a special House election Nov. 5 would increase black voter turnout in the 2nd, boosting other Democratic candidates on the ballot that day.

It took a convoluted series of court cases to get around the 60-day rule, but on Oct. 1, the courts agreed to permit the election in November. Democratic ward leaders acted immediately on the ruling, giving Blackwell the Democratic nomination. Lingering bitterness over Gray's attempt to block Blackwell helped fuel Blackwell's support.

The news from Democratic Party leaders sent several candidates scrambling. Some got out of the race, while others decided to take different routes.

White and Fattah filed to run as independents, but Fattah moved to the Consumer Party line.

VIRGINIA — 7TH

State Delegate George F. Allen kept Virginia's 7th District in the Republican column, defeating Democrat Kay Slaughter by a nearly 2-to-1 margin in the Nov. 5 special election to replace Republican Rep. D. French Slaughter Jr.

Slaughter had announced his resignation in July, effective Nov. 5, because of health problems. He suffered a series of mild strokes in the weeks prior to his announcement. Slaughter said his resignation was timed so a special election could be held when Virginia voters went to the polls for state legislative elections.

Official returns:

George F. Allen (R)	106,745	62.0%
Kay Slaughter (D)	59,655	34.7
John Torrice (I)	5,566	3.3

Since 1982, Allen, 40, had represented a state House district containing most of Albemarle County, in the southwestern corner of the 7th. He was the son and namesake of the late coach of professional football's Washington Redskins, a team with a sizable following in Virginia.

With 16 entire counties, parts of two others and five independent cities, the 7th was larger in area than three states: Rhode Island, Delaware and Connecticut. The district ran from Richmond's northern suburbs across the Blue Ridge Mountains and up the Shenandoah Valley to Winchester. To the east, it took in Fredericksburg and the northwestern portion of Prince William County, in the suburban orbit of Washington.

Early on, Allen was regarded as a heavy favorite to win, but then Democrats nominated a candidate with high name recognition: Slaughter, the incumbent's first cousin. Because of her familiar surname (French Slaughter's political career spanned more than 30 years) and most voters' unfamiliarity with the two contestants, Slaughter led in early polls.

Allen attacked Slaughter as an out-of-the-mainstream liberal. Slaughter, in her first term on the Charlottesville City Council, ran as a political outsider, saying Allen was a career politician. Allen devoted himself to dispelling the notion that his opponent shared Rep. Slaughter's conservative Republican pedigree. But it took some time for that message to penetrate.

Rep. Slaughter lent his name to the effort, endorsing Allen in a statement released by the National Republican Congressional Committee and calling his cousin "an extremely liberal Democrat."

But the biggest asset for Allen's House campaign was the recent voting history of the 7th.

For generations, the district spawned and supported conservative Democrats — one of its cities, Winchester, was the home of Virginia's political dynasty, the Byrd family — but in recent years it had emerged as the state's foremost Republican stronghold. George Bush got 66 percent of its vote in the 1988 presidential election.

Allen drew some media criticism during the campaign for seemingly fuzzing his views on several issues. Allen had said that laws on abortion should be determined on the state level, not the federal level, a position that brought accusations that he was trying to avoid taking a stand. Allen initially opposed term limits for members of Congress, but later said he would support a law allowing states to limit members' terms.

The closing weeks of the campaign saw Allen pull ahead, helped by an almost 2-to-1 fundraising advantage that enabled him to run a flurry of TV ads, including one that Slaughter contended questioned her patriotism. The ad superimposed a photo of Slaughter over footage from an anti-gulf war rally where a banner reading "Victory to Iraq" was clearly visible. Slaughter had advocated economic sanctions against Iraq and attended a rally protesting the war, but not the one pictured in the ad.

Getting the Nod

To secure the GOP nomination, Allen had to get past the incumbent's son, D. French Slaughter III. The younger

Slaughter, a Charlottesville lawyer, had been active in local politics and was a member of the Republican state central committee.

But the Allen campaign outmuscled Slaughter's forces in local "mass meetings" — the equivalent of party caucuses. Slaughter withdrew Aug. 9, giving his endorsement to Allen.

On the Democratic side, Kay Slaughter, 51, easily dispatched two rivals at the party convention in Culpeper on Sept. 7.

Her opponents — Wilke Green, a Winchester lawyer and Senate staff member, and T. Dean Reed, a public relations executive — both withdrew after it became apparent that Slaughter had enough delegates' support to ensure her nomination. Having started late in the election cycle, the two were unable to effectively challenge her.

Slaughter promoted herself as a pro-abortion rights environmentalist, but she also noted her support for a balanced-budget constitutional amendment and a line-item presidential veto, two fiscal tools long promoted by Presidents Reagan and Bush. ■

Drive To Limit Terms Loses Key Test

Washington state voters confounded expectations on Nov. 5 when they rejected a stringent term-limit ballot initiative that could have terminated the career of House Speaker Thomas S. Foley.

The measure, Initiative 553, had ridden high in opinion polls, and local observers had considered it certain to win approval. Even the opposition organization's polling had showed 72 percent of the state in favor of term limits earlier in the fall.

But in heavy turnout — about 60 percent of the state's 2.2 million registered voters — Initiative 553 was rejected by 54 percent to 46 percent. Opposition to the measure was led in the closing days of the campaign by Foley and other members of the state's congressional delegation.

The initiative would have held members of Congress to three consecutive terms and senators to two consecutive terms — imposing the limits retroactively. That would have meant that all eight members of Washington's House delegation would have had to retire by the end of 1994.

The Washington measure was the most far-reaching of a spate of similar proposals across the country that underscored the extent to which the public had grown to mistrust Congress. Colorado imposed limits on its congressional delegation in 1990, but they were not set to apply until 2002. California and Oklahoma had adopted limits on state officials in 1990 and faced proposals to vote on congressional limits in 1992.

In 1991, term limits in various forms were introduced as bills in 45 states, according to the National Council of State Legislatures. In many states, supporters were pushing congressional term-limit initiatives onto 1992 ballots.

The California Supreme Court on Oct. 10 upheld that state's 1990 election law tightly limiting the length of state legislators' careers. While the law did not apply to federal officeholders, the 6-1 ruling in its favor was sweeping enough to raise the blood pressure of incumbents everywhere.

The California ruling held that there was no constitutional right, federal or state, to run for a given office or to vote for a given person. The court said term limits were valid protection "against an entrenched, dynastic legislative bureaucracy."

Washington Protects Seniority

An Associated Press poll taken the week before the election found that about two-thirds of those surveyed nationwide favored the concept of a 12-year limit for members of Congress. The poll surveyed 1,006 adults and had a margin of sampling error of plus or minus 3 percent. In Washington, polls had shown as much as 73 percent support for Initiative 553 before the opposition geared up in the closing weeks.

The opposition drive, capped by a three-day broadcast blitz by Foley in the closing days of the campaign, accepted the voters' apparent animus against the federal government and posed new questions:

What would the federal bureaucracy do with Washington's water, cheap electric power and protected environment if the state had no senior, powerful representatives of its own in Congress? Who would hold the thirsty, expanding colossus of California at bay?

The No on 553 Committee raised about $300,000 — mostly from unions, civic organizations such as the League of Women Voters and Washington Grange, various Democratic campaign funds and such interest groups as alcohol and tobacco companies and the National Rifle Association.

Foley appeared on every network-affiliate TV and radio station in Spokane and Seattle, as well as many others, denouncing 553 as "an arrogant insult to the electorate." He warned that it would leave the state defenseless against other delegations, which could use their size and seniority in Congress to shove onerous legislation down the throat of a neophyte Washington contingent.

Despite support for term limits from President Bush and Vice President Dan Quayle, the state GOP did not endorse the measure, and Republican Rep. Sid Morrison campaigned vigorously against it from the beginning.

Most of the action was on the Democratic side of the delegation, however. Democrat Norm Dicks, whose district lay athwart Puget Sound, warned that the federal government might lift its ban on heavy tankers in the sound unless senior, powerful members were on hand to preserve it. Dicks also warned that offshore oil drilling proposed by the Department of Energy could occur if Pacific Northwest legislators suddenly lacked the clout to stop it.

Also pivotal in the late campaign were the speeches of Rep. Al Swift, D-Wash., who shed the appearance of self-interest by announcing Oct. 25 that he would not run after 1992, partly in order to campaign against the limits, and a House floor speech given Oct. 28 by Rep. Jim McDermott, D-Wash., focusing on Citizens for Congressional Reform (CCR), a national organization based in Washington, D.C., that provided most of the funding for the Washington campaign. McDermott said that at that time CCR had contributed more than $600,000 of the $760,000 spent to promote 553 (according to the state's Public Disclosure Commission). More recent commission figures showed CCR providing 71.5 percent of a total of $850,000 spent.

Reaction From Proponents

Limit proponents, both local and national, were stung

by the defeat of the measure. They accused Foley of panicking voters with exaggerated tales of calamity.

"Scare tactics and lies," said Sherry Bockwinkel, cofounder of Legislative Initiative Mandating Incumbent Terms (LIMIT), which drafted 553 early in 1991. She began the drive after a candidate she had worked for, Mike Collier, was easily dispatched by veteran Rep. Dicks in the 1990 Democratic primary.

"The people of Washington state just really got scared, and I understand that," said Mary Ann Best, executive director of CCR.

"Obviously, Speaker Foley pulled out all the stops to derail the initiative," said Clayton Yeutter, chairman of the Republican National Committee and a term-limit backer. "And clearly that initiative could have been improved by better draftsmanship" — a reference to the retroactivity of 553.

Yeutter and other term-limit advocates predicted that the Washington vote would not slow the movement nationally.

On the Floor

A day after the Washington vote, the issue spilled onto the floor of the U.S. House. On Nov. 6, Republicans protested a House counsel's brief that argued that congressional term limits were unconstitutional. The brief was filed with the Florida Supreme Court, which was reviewing the constitutionality of a term-limit measure slated for that state's ballot in 1992.

The resolution (H Res 268) would have declared that Congress had no official opinion on term limits. With Democratic leaders leading the charge, it was tabled on a near-perfect party-line vote of 265-160. *(Vote 377, p. 92-H)*

The debate began with a resolution offered by C. Christopher Cox, R-Calif., "regretting" a legal brief against term limits written by the House counsel in the Florida case and trying to neutralize it. Cox would not be placated with the suggestion that the counsel might also file a brief defending the limits in behalf of members so inclined. Cox called that "a silly gesture."

The debate centered on whether the House counsel had erred by writing the brief for Lawrence J. Smith, D-Fla., which Smith then submitted to the Florida Supreme Court.

Democrats — and a few Republicans — said it was the counsel's job to provide members with legal advice on questions of law that touched on the House as an institution. ■

Term Limits Debated On Constitutionality

Did states have the power to limit terms of service in Congress? Many legal scholars said no. But others thought the Supreme Court might not automatically rule them invalid.

Argument centered on the first Article of the Constitution, which declared: "Each house shall be the judge of the election, returns and qualifications of its own members."

That meant, according to experts skeptical of term limits, that the states and Congress could not set qualifications beyond those explicit in the Constitution: age, citizenship, residency. In addition, many experts said, by restricting voters' choice, term limits violated the Constitution's democratic principles.

"It would take a constitutional amendment to do it — I think that's abundantly clear," said Walter Berns, a Georgetown Law Center professor and adjunct scholar at the American Enterprise Institute.

The issue was considered explicitly when the Constitution was written.

"Given that we have evidence that the framers did consider and did in fact reject term limits, it is much harder to make the case that term limits would be constitutional without an amendment," said Robert A. Katzmann, a visiting fellow in governmental studies at the Brookings Institution.

But some experts thought there was room for debate. Wallace M. Rudolph, a constitutional law professor at the University of Puget Sound Law School in Tacoma, Wash., said that although most of the focus was put on the three explicit qualifications for office, the Constitution also recognized a prohibition against holding other federal offices while serving in Congress. Many states also had barred felons from running for office or even voting.

"We see the constitutional qualifications as a minimum — not a maximum — number for federal representatives," said Rudolph. "I think we can show historically there have been all kinds of ballot qualifications imposed and enforced and upheld."

1969: *Powell v. McCormack* Ruling

The major modern test of the constitutionality of limits on members' qualifications came in 1969, when the U.S. Supreme Court ruled in *Powell v. McCormack* that the Congress had unlawfully refused to seat a member who met the simple qualifications for office set forth in Article I. By doing so, the court found, Congress added to the constitutional qualifications for office.

The case arose after the House voted in 1967 to exclude Adam Clayton Powell Jr., D-N.Y., who had represented Harlem for 22 years, beginning in World War II. Powell was a controversial figure, repeatedly prosecuted for tax evasion and other alleged offenses and held in contempt of court. He was also criticized for lavish travel at government expense and for various abuses of his office accounts.

After an investigation found Powell misusing Education and Labor Committee funds, the House Democratic Caucus voted in January 1967 to remove him from the committee chairmanship. Powell called the action "a lynching, Northern style."

But his problems were far from over. The next day, Jan. 10, the House adopted a resolution (offered by Republican leader Gerald R. Ford of Michigan) denying Powell his seat, pending an investigation of his conduct by a select committee. The vote was 363-65, with a majority of both parties in support.

A select committee held hearings in February and submitted a report recommending that Powell be stripped of his seniority, censured for "gross misconduct" and fined $40,000 (a punishment without precedent in congressional history). The House rejected those recommendations and instead voted 307-116 (with Southern Democrats joining Republicans) to deny Powell his seat for the duration of that Congress (1967-68).

At the hearings, Powell would answer only questions regarding his age, citizenship and residency. He and his lawyers contended that those were the only questions relevant to his being seated as a duly elected member.

After his exclusion, Powell sued (naming Speaker John W. McCormack, D-Mass., among other defendants). His suit eventually was heard by the Supreme Court, which ruled 7-1 on June 16, 1969, that Powell had been improperly excluded because Congress could not add to the basic three qualifications set forth by the Constitution (25 years of age, seven years of citizenship and residency in the state to be represented).

The court's opinion was written by Chief Justice Earl Warren. It held that Powell was elected by the voters and "was not ineligible to serve under any provision of the Constitution," referring specifically to the basic three qualifications. So, the court ruled, "the House was without power to exclude him from its membership."

The only dissent came from Justice Potter Stewart, who said the case was moot because the 90th Congress had ended and the court should let such sensitive matters alone.

After the decision, Powell was sworn in and seated (having been re-elected in the interim). But he rarely attended, preferring to stay at his retreat in Bimini. In 1970, Charles B. Rangel defeated Powell in the Democratic primary to claim the seat. Powell died in Miami in 1972.

Powell stops "one step short" of disposing of term limits, according to A. E. Dick Howard, a constitutional law professor at the University of Virginia.

"*Powell* clearly limits what the House might do, but it does not necessarily answer the question of what a state might do," says Howard.

Amending the Constitution

It was thought that strong public support for term limits could create a climate in which Congress and the legislatures would move to amend the Constitution.

Much the same progression of efforts led to the 17th Amendment, which provided for the direct election of U.S. senators by the voters rather than by the state legislatures.

Agitation for direct election of senators commenced at the beginning of the Republic. But it picked up in the Civil War era and gained steam with each decade, becoming part of the Democratic Party platform in 1900.

Some state legislatures regularly called for a constitutional convention on the issue. The House began to pass measures calling for a constitutional amendment.

Finally, in 1912, the necessary two-thirds vote of the Senate was obtained. Within a year, the necessary three-fourths of the state legislatures had ratified the amendment.

Eleven bills to limit terms were introduced in the House in 1991; each proposed a constitutional amendment.

The only term-limit votes taken in Congress were in the Senate. One came in 1947, when Sen. W. Lee "Pappy" O'Daniel, a Texas Democrat, proposed amending the two-term limit on presidents (then being debated) to apply a single six-year term to all federal elected officials. His proposal failed on a vote of 1-82. In 1991, freshman Republican Sen. Hank Brown of Colorado tried to amend the campaign finance bill (S 3) to impose a two-term limit on senators who used public campaign funding. It was tabled (killed) on a 68-30 vote. *(Campaign financing, p. 13)* ■

Vote Studies

Bush's Popularity Didn't Hold on Hill

Despite boost from gulf war, president's success rate in Congress was a modest 54 percent for 1991

It sounded so easy in the warm afterglow of the Persian Gulf victory. Send me the crime and transportation bills in 100 days, President Bush told a joint session of Congress on March 6. "And then let's build on our success with those and enact the rest of our agenda."

Members cheered wildly and waved flags as the president declared the war won. They rushed to his side when he finished speaking.

But a day later the president with the highest approval rating ever measured by a Gallup Poll, 89 percent in early March, learned how little his newly minted currency would buy in Congress. The House overwhelmingly approved $42.6 billion in new spending to pay for the popular war — but not before rejecting 177-240 the administration's request to shift money to favored housing programs.

The 24 hours set the tone for Bush's year on Capitol Hill. According to Congressional Quarterly's annual study of voting in Congress, Bush prevailed on 54 percent of the 192 roll call votes in the House and Senate on which he took a stand in 1991, only a modest improvement over his dismal 47 percent success rate in 1990.

To be sure, Bush often won when it counted. For instance, he carried 15 of the 23 "key votes," as selected by CQ editors, on which he took a stand. *(Key votes, p. 34-B)*

But by the broader measure of all roll calls, 1991 was the third straight year in which Bush scored below his predecessors at similar points in a first term. CQ began the annual study in 1953. *(Graph, p. 8-B)*

Bush's year offered striking evidence that the president's popularity did not determine his success with Congress. Victory in the Persian Gulf propelled his public stock to new heights in the winter of 1990; a stagnant economy began bringing it back to earth as the following summer turned to fall.

But when Bush was up, it did not bolster his hand: He got his way roughly half the time on the 129 roll call votes cast before Sept. 1, slightly below his average for the year. And when he began falling, he actually did a little better: He won on nearly three-fifths of the 63 roll call votes cast after Sept. 1.

While this seemed counterintuitive, it was to be expected. "We've analyzed popularity and success every way you can think of, and, basically, popular presidents don't win that much more than unpopular presidents," said Jon R. Bond, a Texas A&M University political scientist and co-author with Richard Fleisher of the 1990 book, "The President in the Legislative Arena."

"The proposition that a president's popularity systematically alters congressional support is based on a rather naive theory of democracy and representation that assumes citizen knowledge and interest that rarely exist," Bond and Fleisher wrote. Voters do not track each roll call vote or the president's position. Rather, they form impressions about a member's voting record from his ideology and party. "Incumbents seldom lose because they support a popular president too little or support an unpopular president too much; they are more likely to lose because they are too liberal or conservative for their constituencies."

Consider two Democrats, Sen. Richard C. Shelby of Alabama and Rep. Lane Evans of Illinois. The two were at

Guide to Vote Studies

Since 1945, Congressional Quarterly has analyzed the voting behavior of members of Congress. The present studies have become references for academics, journalists, politicians and students of how Congress behaves as an institution and how individual members vote.

Leading Scorers: Presidential Support

Highest Scorers — Support

Those who in 1991 voted most often (based on actual votes cast) for President Bush's position:

Senate

Heflin

Dole

Democrats		Republicans	
Heflin, Ala.	74%	Dole, Kan.	96%
Shelby, Ala.	69	Gramm, Texas	96
Breaux, La.	66	Domenici, N.M.	94
Boren, Okla.	60	Lugar, Ind.	93
Nunn, Ga.	60	McConnell, Ky.	93
Robb, Va.	59	Garn, Utah	92
Dixon, Ill.	58	Hatch, Utah	92
Bentsen, Texas	57	Cochran, Miss.	91
Ford, Ky.	57	Craig, Idaho	91
		Nickles, Okla.	91
		Symms, Idaho	91

House

Hall

Michel

Democrats		Republicans	
Hall, Texas	67%	Michel, Ill.	90%
Montgomery, Miss.	66	McCrery, La.	88
Stenholm, Texas	66	Armey, Texas	86
Barnard, Ga.	63	Broomfield, Mich.	86
Ray, Ga.	62	Ewing, Ill.	86
Huckaby, La.	61	Goss, Fla.	86
Hutto, Fla.	60	Hyde, Ill.	86
Orton, Utah	60	Livingston, La.	86

Highest Scorers — Opposition

Those who in 1991 voted most often (based on actual votes cast) against President Bush's position:

Senate

Harkin

Jeffords

Democrats		Republicans	
Harkin, Iowa	77%	Jeffords, Vt.	44%
Wellstone, Minn.	77	Hatfield, Ore.	40
Adams, Wash.	74	Chafee, R.I.	36
Daschle, S.D.	73	Cohen, Maine	33
Kerry, Mass.	72	Specter, Pa.	32
Leahy, Vt.	72	Packwood, Ore.	31
Metzenbaum, Ohio	72		
Wofford, Pa.	71		

House

Evans

Green

Democrats		Republicans	
Evans, Ill.	85%	Green, N.Y.	59%
Schroeder, Colo.	82	Morella, Md.	56
Mrazek, N.Y.	81	Gilman, N.Y.	50
Mink, Hawaii	80	Snowe, Maine	50
Moody, Wis.	80	Machtley, R.I.	47
Olver, Mass.	80	Horton, N.Y.	46
Scheuer, N.Y.	80	Fish, N.Y.	45

opposite extremes in their support for the president: Shelby often sided with Bush, Evans almost never did. Still, they reached their destinations by traveling similar roads. Each said he voted his ideology and constituency and did not calculate what would be gained or lost by supporting or opposing the president. *(Leading scorers, p. 4-B)*

Shelby sided with Bush on 69 percent of roll call votes in 1991, second only among Democrats to his Alabama colleague Howell Heflin.

"I could care less whether it is an administration issue," Shelby said of roll call votes. "What counts is, if it's a substantive issue, how does it play? What are the merits? How do I feel? How do my people feel about it?"

Evans was a liberal who through five terms had been a consistent leading opponent of Republican Presidents Ronald Reagan and Bush.

"I have fought for and defended my positions," Evans said. "Republican opponents have tried to raise [my voting scores] as issues, and it is covered fairly substantially in the media." But voters "understand that I don't get up every day and say, 'This is another day to take on the president.' "

R. MICHAEL JENKINS

President Bush's popularity soared after the Persian Gulf War, then dove when the economy didn't improve. Neither had much effect on his success rate in Congress.

What Really Matters

If popularity did not regulate a president's success, what did?

As Evans' and Shelby's comments indicated, Congress' ideological makeup was a critical factor. Hence, presidential success was determined mostly by the last election, by "how many Democrats and Republicans there are in Congress," Bond said.

So while George Bush was the architect of New World Order abroad, he was captive to the Old World Order in Washington. He took office with fewer Republicans in Congress than any other newly elected GOP president in the century. Republicans then lost seats in 1990 midterm elections, leaving Bush to face even stronger Democratic majorities in the House and Senate in 1991.

Moreover, Bush hurt himself by failing to define the domestic legislative agenda. Instead of playing offense, he played defense, and relied heavily on the veto or the threat of a veto to shape legislation.

That was the worst possible posture for building a winning record, according to Cary R. Covington, an Iowa University political scientist who studied congressional-presidential relations. Presidents fared best when they set the agenda, even if the opposition party controlled Congress. Conversely, they fared worst when they were reacting to the opposition's agenda. "The more agenda space he absorbs, the less there is for somebody else to take," Covington said.

Bush's veto strategy was redefining what constituted success. In all, he had vetoed 24 bills since taking office and defeated all 16 attempts to override him. In 1991, he vetoed three measures and defeated the two override attempts. The vetoes made scorekeeping quirky.

For example, the House in August 1991 passed a District of Columbia spending bill with abortion language opposed by the White House. Bush vetoed the bill, and there was no attempt to override. The offending language was removed, and the new measure passed by voice votes in the House and Senate. CQ gave the president a defeat for the initial loss but assigned no credit for the eventual victories because there were no subsequent roll call votes.

It was one reason why Frederick D. McClure, the chief White House lobbyist, said Bush's record was not fully reflected by the success tally.

Of the veto strategy, he said, "We play that game quite frequently. It's one of the things you have to do when you don't control either House."

Even so, House Speaker Thomas S. Foley of Washington was irked by the notion that sustaining a veto was equated with winning. The president had only to muster one-third plus one of the votes in either chamber to sustain his position.

"My perspective is that the president should get no particular credit for sustaining a veto and a lot of blame if he gets overriden, because it's not a level playing field to begin with," Foley said. "It's routine that the president should be able to sustain the veto. It's extraordinary that he should lose one."

The CQ Method

CQ's study examined roll call votes on which the president took a clear position. This offered a limited, statistical look at the relationship between the president and Congress by addressing two factors:

- **Presidential success.** How often did the president get his way on roll call votes in the House and Senate?
- **Members' support.** How often did individual members side with the president, regardless of whether his position prevailed?

These numbers pointed to the Senate and national security issues as Bush's sources of strength. His 69 percent overall success rate in the Senate (56 of 81 votes) pulled up

1991 Senate Presidential Position Votes . . .

The following is a list of Senate and House votes in 1991 on which there was a clear presidential position, listed by roll call number with a brief description and categorized by topic. *(Definition, p. 9-B)*

Domestic Policy

Vote #	Description
16 Victories	
5	Veterans' benefits
9	Agent Orange benefits
45	CFTC reauthorization
102	Crime bill/death penalty
106	Crime bill/death penalty
107	Crime bill/death penalty
108	Crime bill/death penalty
121	Superconducting super collider
132	Space station funding
177	Overseas military abortions
191	Mining patents
221	Unemployment benefits
238	Civil Rights Act
248	Older Americans Act/pensions
254	Unemployment benefits
278	Crime bill
19 Defeats	
32	Dairy price supports
33	Housing programs funding
34	Housing programs funding
35	Labor regulations
85	Campaign finance
88	Telecommunications equipment/domestic content
89	Telecommunications equipment
96	Federal highway funding
103	Crime bill
104	Crime bill/search and seizure
128	Family planning
201	Unemployment benefits
205	Unemployment benefits
213	Unemployment benefits
215	Family and Medical Leave Act
237	Civil Rights Act/Senate employees
246	Labor-HHS appropriations/abortion

Defense and Foreign Policy

Vote #	Description
24 Victories	
1	Sanctions against Iraq
2	Force against Iraq
15	Parents in combat
30	Desert Storm spending
56	Seafarers Standards Treaty
57	Ship Pollution Treaty
58	Safety and Load Line Treaty
59	Forced Labor Treaty
149	Foreign aid/IMF
154	State Department funding/Worldnet
168	SDI deployment
169	ABM deployment
171	SDI funding
172	ABM deployment
173	SDI funding
174	B-2 bomber
176	SRAM-T missile
182	Defense to domestic spending transfer
206	B-2 bomber
207	SDI funding
209	Seawolf-class submarine
210	Defense spending
225	CIA appointments
273	Conventional Forces in Europe Treaty
7 Defeats	
36	Foreign aid/Jordan
146	Foreign aid/cargo preference
147	Foreign aid/"tied aid"
148	Foreign aid/El Salvador
152	Foreign aid/Middle East arms sales
153	Foreign aid
219	Foreign aid

Nominations

Vote #	Description
6 Victories	
11	Lynn Martin confirmation
24	Edward Madigan confirmation
41	Bob Martinez confirmation
220	Clarence Thomas confirmation
243	Robert M. Gates confirmation
260	Carol T. Crawford confirmation

Economic Affairs and Trade

Vote #	Description
10 Victories	
10	Gramm-Rudman suspension
21	RTC financing
22	RTC restructuring
23	RTC financing
25	RTC financing
46	Social Security tax cuts
55	Gramm-Rudman suspension
86	Fast-track procedures
198	Gramm-Rudman suspension
252	Banking reform
1 Defeat	
142	China MFN status

. . . And House Position Votes, by Category

Vote #	Description
	Domestic Policy
17 Victories	
14	Veterans' benefits
16	Agent Orange benefits
72	Railroad labor dispute
117	Superconducting super collider
127	Civil Rights Act/damages
140	Space station funding
141	Space station funding
264	Unemployment benefits
312	Crime bill/death penalty
313	Crime bill/death penalty
320	Crime bill/search and seizure
322	Crime bill/death penalty
324	Crime bill/death penalty
386	Civil Rights Act
396	Unemployment benefits
403	Labor-HHS appropriations/veto override
417	Labor-HHS appropriations
30 Defeats	
18	VA physicians' salaries
33	Housing programs funding
34	Labor regulations
89	Niobrara River designation
109	Overseas military abortions
128	Civil Rights Act
131	Civil Rights Act
187	Water projects
194	Grazing fee increase
198	D.C. appropriations/abortion
213	Striker replacement
229	NIH reauthorization
250	Flight attendant duty time
251	D.C. appropriations/abortion
253	Unemployment benefits
267	Unemployment benefits
280	Unemployment benefits
282	Lumbee Tribe recognition
285	Unemployment benefits
306	Flint Hills Prairie Monument
316	Crime bill/habeas corpus
326	Crime bill/habeas corpus
338	Surface transportation reauthorization
380	Labor-HHS appropriations/abortion
393	Family and medical leave
407	Medicaid rules moratorium
420	California desert protection
427	Campaign finance
435	California desert protection
443	Crime bill
	Defense and Foreign Policy
17 Victories	
8	Sanctions against Iraq
9	Force against Iraq
17	Military benefits
29	Defense Production Act
30	Foreign aid/Israel
36	Desert Storm funding
58	Desert Storm funding
90	Moscow Embassy
97	SDI funding
101	Troops overseas
103	Troops in South Korea
106	ICBM funding
144	MX missile rail garrison
168	Foreign aid/Jordan
169	Foreign aid/Jordan
232	Military base closings
354	Foreign aid/abortion
16 Defeats	
7	War powers
48	Desert Storm spending
99	Defense spending
110	Defense spending
145	Defense appropriations
148	Foreign aid/U.N. Population Fund
149	Foreign aid/abortion
150	Foreign aid/agricultural products
151	Foreign aid/Pakistan
155	Foreign aid/India
167	Foreign aid/unused funds
170	Foreign aid/Jordan
171	Foreign aid/Jordan
176	Foreign aid/Soviet Union
185	Foreign aid
231	Overseas base closings
	Economic Affairs and Trade
14 Victories	
27	CFTC reauthorization
39	RTC financing
41	RTC financing
50	RTC financing
51	RTC financing
56	RTC financing
115	Fast-track procedures
368	Banking reform
369	Banking reform
375	Banking reform
398	Banking reform
410	Soviet Union MFN status
411	Hungary MFN status/unemployment benefits
415	Banking reform
17 Defeats	
3	CBO scorekeeping
4	CBO scorekeeping
5	CBO scorekeeping
40	RTC financing
42	RTC financing
45	Deficit scorekeeping
70	President's budget
74	CBO scorekeeping
203	China MFN status
205	China MFN status
206	Technology loan fund
207	Technology loan fund
364	Banking reform
374	Banking reform
399	Banking reform
405	CBO scorekeeping
436	China MFN status

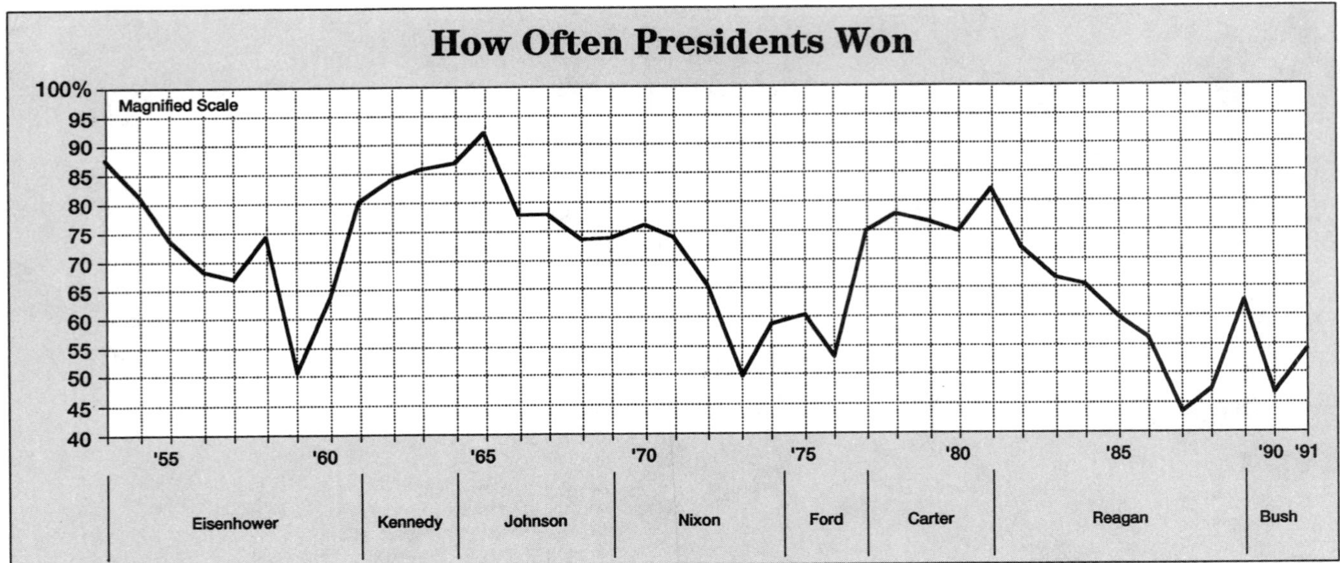

the 43 percent success rate in the House (48 of 111 votes).

Bush did worst on domestic issues. He won 49 percent overall: 64 percent in the Senate, 40 percent in the House.

He made up lost ground on national security issues. He won 63 percent overall, bolstered by a 76 percent success rate in the Senate. Action on treaties and war-related measures boosted his score. His Achilles' heel was foreign aid: Of his 23 defense and foreign policy defeats in the House and Senate, 17 concerned foreign aid.

As usual, the president's most ardent supporters were Senate Republicans, who backed him 83 percent of the time. House Republicans voted with him 72 percent of the time. Bush only rarely failed to carry his own party, a critical factor in presidential defeats. He carried a majority of Republicans on all but 16 of his 63 defeats in the House and four of 25 defeats in the Senate.

The veto strategy increased the impetus for Republican unity. The White House often won votes from wavering Republicans by persuading them that solidarity was essential to make veto threats stick.

True to their role as the "president's men" on Capitol Hill, the House and Senate minority leaders, Sen. Bob Dole of Kansas (96 percent) and Rep. Robert H. Michel of Illinois (90 percent) were the president's leading supporters in their respective chambers. But the House GOP whip, Newt Gingrich, was far less supportive (81 percent). That was indicative of the broader troubles Bush had with House conservatives.

Support for the president was not always a good gauge of a member's party. Fifty-four Democrats had higher support scores than Republican Bill Green, N.Y., with 41 percent. Small wonder. Fewer than one in five of Green's Manhattan constituents were Republicans.

Some of Bush's strongest Democratic supporters in the Senate, moreover, were members of the Democratic leadership.

Charles S. Robb of Virginia, the chairman of the Democratic Senatorial Campaign Committee (59 percent); Alan J. Dixon of Illinois, the chief deputy majority whip (58 percent); and Wendell H. Ford of Kentucky, the majority whip (57 percent); all supported the president more frequently than Republican James M. Jeffords of Vermont (56 percent). Contrast this with Senate Majority Leader George J. Mitchell of Maine's score (35 percent).

Unlike his predecessors, Bush could not depend on a conservative coalition of Republicans and Southern Democrats to sustain him. The conservative coalition was defined by CQ as a bloc consisting of a majority of Republicans and a majority of Southern Democrats voting against a majority of Northern Democrats. As late as 1981, it gave Reagan a working majority in the House on key budget votes. But a decade later, it appeared on only 17 percent of the votes where Bush took a stand. He won all but two of them. "In the early 1980s, it was a very different kind of context," said Rep. Robert S. Walker, R-Pa., the chief deputy minority whip. "There was a conservative coaliton that was real and thought of itself as a governing coalition in the House and capable of passing legislation. Now it wasn't always the happiest of arrangements and alliances, but we had the strength to govern when we chose to do so. [Lacking that] the president has had to resort to a veto strategy."

Some Caveats

In general, analysts who use the CQ study should do so cautiously, taking into account its strengths and weaknesses. It is a useful gauge of long-term trends in presidential-congressional relations, and it serves as a yardstick for political scientists.

The study's usefulness diminishes, however, as the need for detail rises. It masks controversies that never reached a roll call vote on the floor. In the Senate, particularly, legislation of considerable substance often passed by voice vote. When a committee killed a bill the president supported, this went unrecorded in the vote study.

It is also important to consider the matters that did make it to the floor. For example, 10 votes on treaties and nominations in the Senate tended to push Bush's score higher in that chamber. Meanwhile, the 1990 budget summit prevented much of the usual controversy over the budget.

The study also gave equal weight to every vote, no matter its actual importance. So the Senate's adoption of a routine treaty on shipping matters May 14 by a 97-0 votes was given equal weight to the Senate's Jan. 12 vote authorizing the war with Iraq. ■

Presidential Support Definitions

Congressional Quarterly determined presidential positions on congressional votes by examining the statements made by President Bush or his authorized spokesmen. *Support* measures the percentage of the time members voted in accord with the position of the president. *Opposition* measures the percentage of the time members voted against the president's position. *Success* measures the percentage of the contested votes on which the president prevailed. Absences lowered parties' scores.

National Security vs. Domestic Issues

1991 presidential success scores broken down into domestic and national security issues, with national security including foreign policy and defense. Scores for 1990 are in parentheses:

	National Security		Domestic		Average	
Senate	76%	(78)	64%	(56)	69%	(63)
House	50	(39)	40	(31)	43	(32)
Average	63	(60)	49	(41)	54	(47)

Average Scores

Scores for 1990 are in parentheses:

Support

	Democrats		Republicans	
Senate	41%	(38)	83%	(70)
House	34	(25)	72	(63)

Opposition

	Democrats		Republicans	
Senate	56%	(60)	16%	(27)
House	62	(70)	25	(34)

Regional Averages

Scores for 1990 are in parentheses:

Support

	East		West		South		Midwest	
Democrats								
Senate	35%	(31)	40%	(38)	51%	(49)	35%	(33)
House	29	(21)	31	(21)	41	(34)	31	(22)
Republicans								
Senate	73%	(61)	84%	(69)	89%	(79)	84%	(73)
House	64	(52)	76	(67)	74	(68)	74	(65)

Opposition

	East		West		South		Midwest	
Democrats								
Senate	64%	(68)	56%	(58)	45%	(50)	61%	(65)
House	67	(73)	63	(76)	55	(62)	67	(75)
Republicans								
Senate	26%	(37)	14%	(26)	9%	(20)	14%	(25)
House	34	(45)	22	(29)	21	(29)	23	(31)

(CQ defines regions of the United States as follows: ***East:*** *Conn., Del., Maine, Md., Mass., N.H., N.J., N.Y., Pa., R.I., Vt., W.Va.* ***West:*** *Alaska, Ariz., Calif., Colo., Hawaii, Idaho, Mont., Nev., N.M., Ore., Utah, Wash., Wyo.* ***South:*** *Ala., Ark., Fla., Ga., Ky., La., Miss., N.C., Okla., S.C., Tenn., Texas, Va.* ***Midwest:*** *Ill., Ind., Iowa, Kan., Mich., Minn., Mo., Neb., N.D., Ohio, S.D., Wis.)*

Success Rate History

Eisenhower	
1953	89.0%
1954	82.8
1955	75.0
1956	70.0
1957	68.0
1958	76.0
1959	52.0
1960	65.0

Kennedy	
1961	81.0%
1962	85.4
1963	87.1

Johnson	
1964	88.0%
1965	93.0
1966	79.0
1967	79.0
1968	75.0

Nixon	
1969	74.0%
1970	77.0
1971	75.0
1972	66.0
1973	50.6
1974	59.6

Ford	
1974	58.2%
1975	61.0
1976	53.8

Carter	
1977	75.4%
1978	78.3
1979	76.8
1980	75.1

Reagan	
1981	82.4%
1982	72.4
1983	67.1
1984	65.8
1985	59.9
1986	56.1
1987	43.5
1988	47.4

Bush	
1989	62.6%
1990	46.8
1991	54.2

Presidential Support, Presidential Opposition: House

1. Bush Support Score, 1991. Percentage of 111 recorded votes in 1991 on which President Bush took a position and on which a representative voted "yea" or "nay" *in agreement* with the president's position. Failures to vote lowered both support and opposition scores.

2. Bush Opposition Score, 1991. Percentage of 111 recorded votes in 1991 on which President Bush took a position and on which a representative voted "yea" or "nay" *in disagreement* with the president's position. Failures to vote lowered both support and opposition scores.

3. Bush Support Score, 1991. Percentage of 111 recorded votes in 1991 on which President Bush took a position and on which a representative was present and voted "yea" or "nay" *in agreement* with the president's position. In this version of the study, absences were not counted; therefore, failures to vote did not lower support or opposition scores. Opposition scores, not listed here, are the inverse of the support score; i.e., the opposition score is equal to 100 percent minus the individual's support score.

[1] *Ed Pastor, D-Ariz., was sworn in Oct. 3, 1991, to succeed Morris K. Udall, D, who resigned May 4, 1991. Udall was eligible for 29 presidential support votes in 1991. His presidential support score in 1991 was 0 percent; his opposition score was 100 percent; and his support score, adjusted for absences, was 0 percent in 1991. Pastor was eligible for 33 of the 111 presidential support votes in 1991.*

[2] *Thomas W. Ewing, R-Ill., was sworn in July 10, 1991, to succeed Edward Madigan, R, who resigned March 8, 1991, after being appointed secretary of Agriculture. Madigan was eligible for 16 presidential support votes in 1991. His presidential support score was 75 percent; his opposition score was 6 percent; and his support score, adjusted for absences, was 92 percent in 1991. Ewing was eligible for 49 presidential support votes in 1991.*

[3] *John Olver, D-Mass., was sworn in June 18, 1991, to succeed Silvio O. Conte, R, who died Feb. 8, 1991. Conte was eligible for 10 presidential votes in 1991. His presidential support score was 60 percent; his opposition score was 40 percent; and his support score, adjusted for absences, was 60 percent in 1991. Olver was eligible for 59 presidential votes in 1991.*

[4] *Lucien E. Blackwell, D-Pa., was sworn in Nov. 13, 1991, to succeed William H. Gray III, D, who resigned Sept. 11, 1991. Gray was eligible for 73 presidential support votes in 1991. His presidential support score was 23 percent; his opposition score was 56 percent; and his support score, adjusted for absences, was 29 percent in 1991. Blackwell was eligible for 16 presidential support votes in 1991.*

[5] *Sam Johnson, R-Texas, was sworn in May 22, 1991, to succeed Steve Bartlett, R, who resigned March 11, 1991. Bartlett was eligible for 16 presidential support votes in 1991. His presidential support score was 94 percent; his opposition score was 6 percent; and his support score, adjusted for absences, was 94 percent in 1991. Johnson was eligible for 76 presidential support votes in 1991.*

[6] *George F. Allen, R-Va., was sworn in Nov. 12, 1991, to succeed D. French Slaughter Jr., R, who resigned Nov. 5, 1991. Slaughter was eligible for 94 presidential support votes in 1991. His presidential support score was 68 percent; his opposition score was 12 percent; and his support score adjusted for absences was 85 percent in 1991. Allen was eligible for 16 presidential support votes in 1991.*

[7] *Thomas S. Foley, D-Wash., as Speaker of the House, voted at his discretion. Foley was eligible for eight presidential support votes in 1991.*

KEY

† Not eligible for all votes or voted "present" to avoid conflict of interest on one or more votes in 1991. Ineligible votes are excluded from calculation of scores.

Democrats ***Republicans***
Independent

	1	2	3
Alabama			
1 ***Callahan***	65	25	72
2 ***Dickinson***	72	23	75
3 Browder	41	58	41
4 Bevill	42	55	44
5 Cramer	38	61	38
6 Erdreich	40	60	40
7 Harris	41	59	41
Alaska			
AL ***Young***	66	26	72
Arizona			
1 ***Rhodes***	82	15	84
2 Pastor [1]	33	67	33
3 ***Stump***	78	22	78
4 ***Kyl***	81	19	81
5 ***Kolbe***	76	21	79
Arkansas			
1 Alexander	37	54	41
2 Thornton	35	61	36
3 ***Hammerschmidt***	71	19	79
4 Anthony	44	50	47
California			
1 ***Riggs***	72	28	72
2 ***Herger***	68	30	70
3 Matsui	28	60	32
4 Fazio	34	61	36
5 Pelosi	24	69	26
6 Boxer	21	66	24
7 Miller	23	73	24
8 Dellums	25	69	27
9 Stark	24	71	25
10 Edwards	26	71	27
11 Lantos	30	65	31
12 ***Campbell***	61	28	69
13 Mineta	30	68	31
14 ***Doolittle***	73	22	77
15 Condit	36	61	37
16 Panetta	35	64	35
17 Dooley	38	62	38
18 Lehman	38	59	39
19 ***Lagomarsino***	85	14	85
20 ***Thomas***	72	22	77
21 ***Gallegly***	81	18	82
22 ***Moorhead***	82	15	84
23 Beilenson	32	66	33
24 Waxman	27	63	30
25 Roybal	29	65	31
26 Berman	32	63	33
27 Levine	18	44	29
28 Dixon	26	66	28
29 Waters	23	70	25
30 Martinez	31	52	37
31 Dymally	21	54	28
32 Anderson	41	59	41
33 ***Dreier***	84	15	85
34 Torres	25	70	26
35 ***Lewis***	81	16	83
36 Brown	38	59	39
37 ***McCandless***	85	14	85
38 ***Dornan***	76	17	82
39 ***Dannemeyer***	71	21	77
40 ***Cox***	77	23	77
41 ***Lowery***	83	17	83
42 ***Rohrabacher***	70	30	70
43 ***Packard***	83	17	83
44 ***Cunningham***	78	22	78
45 ***Hunter***	80	16	83
Colorado			
1 Schroeder	18	81	18
2 Skaggs	36	63	36
3 Campbell	34	56	38
4 ***Allard***	80	20	80
5 ***Hefley***	71	29	71
6 ***Schaefer***	71	27	72
Connecticut			
1 Kennelly	30	70	30
2 Gejdenson	23	77	23
3 DeLauro	26	72	27
4 ***Shays***	58	42	58
5 ***Franks***	74	24	75
6 ***Johnson***	63	35	64
Delaware			
AL Carper	37	63	37
Florida			
1 Hutto	59	40	60
2 Peterson	37	63	37
3 Bennett	33	67	33
4 ***James***	66	34	66
5 ***McCollum***	76	21	79
6 ***Stearns***	71	29	71
7 Gibbons	41	59	41
8 ***Young***	73	23	76
9 ***Bilirakis***	78	19	81
10 ***Ireland***	81	14	85
11 Bacchus	35	64	35
12 ***Lewis***	73	25	74
13 ***Goss***	86	14	86
14 Johnston	32	64	33
15 ***Shaw***	80	17	82
16 Smith	29	67	30
17 Lehman	26	52	33
18 ***Ros-Lehtinen***	67	32	67
19 Fascell	37	63	37
Georgia			
1 Thomas	51	49	51
2 Hatcher	43	41	51
3 Ray	60	37	62
4 Jones	27	73	27
5 Lewis	22	71	23
6 ***Gingrich***	78	19	81
7 Darden	49	50	49
8 Rowland	50	47	51
9 Jenkins	45	50	47
10 Barnard	60	36	63
Hawaii			
1 Abercrombie	21	78	21
2 Mink	19	77	20
Idaho			
1 LaRocco	41	55	42
2 Stallings	50	47	52
Illinois			
1 Hayes	23	77	23
2 Savage	25	68	27
3 Russo	31	68	31
4 Sangmeister	24	64	28
5 Lipinski	38	59	39
6 ***Hyde***	85	14	86
7 Collins	23	73	24
8 Rostenkowski	36	52	41
9 Yates	23	68	26
10 ***Porter***	67	30	69
11 Annunzio	39	61	39
12 ***Crane***	71	20	78
13 ***Fawell***	75	22	78
14 ***Hastert***	84	14	85
15 ***Ewing*** [2]	86	14	86
16 Cox	28	72	28
17 Evans	15	85	15
18 ***Michel***	81	9	90
19 Bruce	30	70	30
20 Durbin	25	73	26
21 Costello	34	65	35
22 Poshard	30	70	30
Indiana			
1 Visclosky	29	71	29
2 Sharp	28	67	30
3 Roemer	43	56	44

	1	2	3
4 Long	32	68	32
5 Jontz	23	76	24
6 ***Burton***	75	23	76
7 ***Myers***	75	22	78
8 McCloskey	29	70	29
9 Hamilton	43	57	43
10 Jacobs	27	68	28
Iowa			
1 ***Leach***	59	41	59
2 ***Nussle***	80	20	80
3 Nagle	29	69	29
4 Smith	37	54	41
5 ***Lightfoot***	81	19	81
6 ***Grandy***	83	17	83
Kansas			
1 ***Roberts***	82	17	83
2 Slattery	38	62	38
3 ***Meyers***	68	32	68
4 Glickman	35	61	36
5 ***Nichols***	77	23	77
Kentucky			
1 Hubbard	37	61	38
2 Natcher	35	65	35
3 Mazzoli	38	62	38
4 ***Bunning***	76	23	77
5 ***Rogers***	70	25	74
6 ***Hopkins***	35	12	75
7 Perkins	28	72	28
Louisiana			
1 ***Livingston***	86	14	86
2 Jefferson	26	63	29
3 Tauzin	53	44	55
4 ***McCrery***	84	12	88
5 Huckaby	57	36	61
6 ***Baker***	79	14	85
7 Hayes	54	40	58
8 ***Holloway***	60	22	74
Maine			
1 Andrews	23	76	23
2 ***Snowe***	47	47	50
Maryland			
1 ***Gilchrest***	70	30	70
2 ***Bentley***	60	36	63
3 Cardin	32	67	33
4 McMillen	40	60	40
5 Hoyer	33	67	33
6 Byron	51	49	51
7 Mfume	23	76	24
8 ***Morella***	43	54	44
Massachusetts			
1 Olver [3]	20	80	20
2 Neal	26	71	27
3 Early	27	68	29
4 Frank	29	68	30
5 Atkins	25	75	25
6 Mavroules	34	63	35
7 Markey	23	76	23
8 Kennedy	24	74	25
9 Moakley	32	66	32
10 Studds	20	76	21
11 Donnelly	25	67	27
Michigan			
1 Conyers	23	75	24
2 ***Pursell***	65	27	71
3 Wolpe	23	74	24
4 ***Upton***	60	40	60
5 ***Henry***	64	35	65
6 Carr †	34	61	36
7 Kildee	29	71	29
8 Traxler	28	65	30
9 ***Vander Jagt***	78	19	81
10 ***Camp***	71	29	71
11 ***Davis***	62	28	69
12 Bonior	30	68	30
13 Collins	23	77	23
14 Hertel	24	76	24
15 Ford	22	73	23
16 Dingell	28	67	30
17 Levin	28	72	28
18 ***Broomfield***	83	14	86
Minnesota			
1 Penny	50	50	50
2 ***Weber***	73	25	74
3 ***Ramstad***	65	34	65
4 Vento	26	70	27

	1	2	3
5 Sabo	30	68	30
6 Sikorski	22	76	22
7 Peterson	39	60	39
8 Oberstar	30	59	33
Mississippi			
1 Whitten	39	55	41
2 Espy	32	67	32
3 Montgomery	66	33	66
4 Parker	58	41	59
5 Taylor	55	42	56
Missouri			
1 Clay	24	69	26
2 Horn	30	70	30
3 Gephardt	30	68	31
4 Skelton	52	47	53
5 Wheat	23	77	23
6 ***Coleman***	77	21	79
7 ***Hancock***	79	19	81
8 ***Emerson***	71	29	71
9 Volkmer	49	50	49
Montana			
1 Williams	31	61	33
2 ***Marlenee***	65	26	71
Nebraska			
1 ***Bereuter***	79	21	79
2 Hoagland	42	58	42
3 ***Barrett***	84	14	85
Nevada			
1 Bilbray	41	57	42
2 ***Vucanovich***	84	14	85
New Hampshire			
1 ***Zeliff***	80	20	80
2 Swett	46	53	46
New Jersey			
1 Andrews	35	64	35
2 Hughes	29	68	30
3 Pallone	33	66	34
4 ***Smith***	62	37	63
5 ***Roukema***	54	41	57
6 Dwyer	30	64	32
7 ***Rinaldo***	62	38	62
8 Roe	37	59	39
9 Torricelli	33	60	36
10 Payne	24	72	25
11 ***Gallo***	67	31	69
12 ***Zimmer***	60	39	61
13 ***Saxton***	69	29	71
14 Guarini †	33	64	34
New Mexico			
1 ***Schiff***	67	33	67
2 ***Skeen***	75	25	75
3 Richardson	33	67	33
New York			
1 Hochbrueckner	29	68	30
2 Downey	25	75	25
3 Mrazek	13	55	19
4 ***Lent***	77	20	79
5 ***McGrath***	57	41	58
6 Flake	23	65	27
7 Ackerman	25	64	28
8 Scheuer	19	77	20
9 Manton	35	58	38
10 Schumer	28	70	28
11 Towns	21	69	23
12 Owens	21	77	21
13 Solarz	31	68	31
14 ***Molinari***	62	33	65
15 ***Green***	39	57	41
16 Rangel	25	71	26
17 Weiss	20	70	22
18 Serrano	19	71	21
19 Engel	27	71	28
20 Lowey	24	74	25
21 ***Fish***	52	43	55
22 ***Gilman***	50	50	50
23 McNulty	31	68	31
24 ***Solomon***	71	25	74
25 ***Boehlert***	58	41	58
26 ***Martin***	70	22	76
27 ***Walsh***	70	28	72
28 McHugh	32	67	32
29 ***Horton***	52	45	54
30 Slaughter	25	73	26
31 ***Paxon***	75	23	77

	1	2	3
32 LaFalce	32	67	33
33 Nowak	32	67	32
34 ***Houghton***	71	27	72
North Carolina			
1 Jones	40	55	42
2 Valentine	45	51	47
3 Lancaster	40	60	40
4 Price	40	60	40
5 Neal	38	58	40
6 ***Coble***	70	30	70
7 Rose	29	63	31
8 Hefner	34	59	37
9 ***McMillan***	78	22	78
10 ***Ballenger***	79	17	82
11 ***Taylor***	84	16	84
North Dakota			
AL Dorgan	30	69	30
Ohio			
1 Luken	50	50	50
2 ***Gradison***	77	17	82
3 Hall	35	61	36
4 ***Oxley***	79	20	80
5 ***Gillmor*** †	73	26	74
6 ***McEwen***	78	18	81
7 ***Hobson***	77	23	77
8 ***Boehner***	84	14	85
9 Kaptur	29	67	30
10 ***Miller***	66	19	78
11 Eckart	22	77	22
12 ***Kasich***	77	23	77
13 Pease	39	61	39
14 Sawyer	31	69	31
15 ***Wylie***	83	16	84
16 ***Regula***	69	30	70
17 Traficant	26	74	26
18 Applegate	41	59	41
19 Feighan	28	70	28
20 Oakar	30	68	31
21 Stokes	24	74	25
Oklahoma			
1 ***Inhofe***	68	27	72
2 Synar	28	70	28
3 Brewster	45	54	45
4 McCurdy	41	55	42
5 ***Edwards***	74	22	77
6 English	43	56	44
Oregon			
1 AuCoin	26	69	27
2 ***Smith***	78	19	81
3 Wyden	31	68	31
4 DeFazio	26	70	27
5 Kopetski	37	63	37
Pennsylvania			
1 Foglietta	23	72	25
2 Blackwell [4]	31	69	31
3 Borski	36	59	38
4 Kolter	36	58	38
5 ***Schulze***	73	22	77
6 Yatron	36	52	41
7 ***Weldon***	54	41	57
8 Kostmayer	26	72	27
9 ***Shuster***	68	28	71
10 ***McDade***	68	25	73
11 Kanjorski	37	63	37
12 Murtha	44	52	46
13 ***Coughlin***	66	33	66
14 Coyne	28	70	28
15 ***Ritter***	70	30	70
16 ***Walker***	81	19	81
17 ***Gekas***	74	25	75
18 ***Santorum***	72	28	72
19 ***Goodling***	68	23	74
20 Gaydos	36	57	39
21 ***Ridge***	58	41	59
22 Murphy	34	53	39
23 ***Clinger***	76	23	76
Rhode Island			
1 ***Machtley***	52	47	53
2 Reed	29	71	29
South Carolina			
1 ***Ravenel***	57	43	57
2 ***Spence***	74	19	80
3 Derrick	41	58	41
4 Patterson	39	61	39
5 Spratt	40	59	40
6 Tallon	47	53	47

	1	2	3
South Dakota			
AL Johnson	34	66	34
Tennessee			
1 ***Quillen***	68	25	73
2 ***Duncan***	65	34	65
3 Lloyd	37	44	46
4 Cooper †	49	51	49
5 Clement	43	56	44
6 Gordon	37	62	37
7 ***Sundquist***	74	19	80
8 Tanner	41	53	44
9 Ford	20	62	24
Texas			
1 Chapman †	40	49	45
2 Wilson	32	52	38
3 ***Johnson*** [5]	84	16	84
4 Hall	66	32	67
5 Bryant	21	73	22
6 ***Barton***	70	23	76
7 ***Archer***	84	14	85
8 ***Fields***	79	18	81
9 Brooks †	31	61	33
10 Pickle	41	56	42
11 Edwards	41	56	43
12 Geren	49	48	50
13 Sarpalius	58	41	59
14 Laughlin	49	50	50
15 de la Garza	38	54	41
16 Coleman	34	65	35
17 Stenholm	66	33	66
18 Washington	23	70	24
19 ***Combest***	77	23	77
20 Gonzalez	32	67	32
21 ***Smith***	75	23	77
22 ***DeLay***	75	20	79
23 Bustamante	32	57	36
24 Frost	35	61	36
25 Andrews	47	50	48
26 ***Armey***	86	14	86
27 Ortiz	41	53	44
Utah			
1 ***Hansen***	82	15	84
2 Owens	38	59	39
3 Orton	58	39	60
Vermont			
AL *Sanders*	22	77	22
Virginia			
1 ***Bateman***	82	17	83
2 Pickett	52	46	53
3 ***Bliley***	81	19	81
4 Sisisky	45	49	48
5 Payne	47	50	48
6 Olin	45	51	47
7 ***Allen*** [6]	69	31	69
8 Moran	40	58	41
9 Boucher	34	62	36
10 ***Wolf***	81	18	82
Washington			
1 ***Miller***	63	33	65
2 Swift	31	68	31
3 Unsoeld	25	72	26
4 ***Morrison***	68	29	70
5 Foley [7]			
6 Dicks	36	59	38
7 McDermott	27	70	28
8 ***Chandler***	73	23	76
West Virginia			
1 Mollohan	41	59	41
2 Staggers	32	65	33
3 Wise	26	70	27
4 Rahall	36	59	38
Wisconsin			
1 Aspin	38	54	41
2 ***Klug***	68	32	68
3 ***Gunderson***	68	31	69
4 Kleczka	23	75	24
5 Moody	19	74	20
6 ***Petri***	68	32	68
7 Obey	29	71	29
8 ***Roth***	69	29	71
9 ***Sensenbrenner***	66	33	66
Wyoming			
AL ***Thomas***	77	16	83

	1	2	3
Alabama			
Heflin	73	26	74
Shelby	69	31	69
Alaska			
Murkowski	89	11	89
Stevens	83	14	86
Arizona			
DeConcini	41	54	43
McCain	86	14	86
Arkansas			
Bumpers	40	59	40
Pryor	19	31	38
California			
Cranston	23	53	31
Seymour	84	14	86
Colorado			
Wirth	36	58	38
Brown	75	23	76
Connecticut			
Dodd	49	49	50
Lieberman	49	46	52
Delaware			
Biden	33	65	34
Roth	83	16	84
Florida			
Graham	47	51	48
Mack	86	14	86
Georgia			
Fowler	44	54	45
Nunn	57	38	60
Hawaii			
Akaka	35	64	35
Inouye	51	47	52
Idaho			
Craig	91	9	91
Symms	91	9	91
Illinois			
Dixon	57	42	58
Simon	32	67	33
Indiana			
Coats	85	15	85
Lugar	93	7	93
Iowa			
Harkin	19	62	23
Grassley	75	25	75
Kansas			
Dole	96	4	96
Kassebaum	79	20	80
Kentucky			
Ford	57	43	57
McConnell	93	7	93
Louisiana			
Breaux	65	33	66
Johnston	56	43	56
Maine			
Mitchell	35	65	35
Cohen	67	33	67
Maryland			
Mikulski	33	67	33
Sarbanes	30	70	30
Massachusetts			
Kennedy	31	67	32
Kerry	28	72	28
Michigan			
Levin	37	63	37
Riegle	33	67	33
Minnesota			
Wellstone	22	75	23
Durenberger	83	17	83
Mississippi			
Cochran	90	9	91
Lott	88	10	90
Missouri			
Bond	85	11	88
Danforth	77	16	83
Montana			
Baucus	40	58	41
Burns	89	11	89
Nebraska			
Exon	52	48	52
Kerrey	32	52	38
Nevada			
Bryan	47	53	47
Reid	51	49	51
New Hampshire			
Rudman	85	15	85
Smith	85	14	86
New Jersey			
Bradley	32	64	33
Lautenberg	31	69	31
New Mexico			
Bingaman	51	48	51
Domenici	93	6	94
New York			
Moynihan	35	65	35
D'Amato	79	21	79
North Carolina			
Sanford	33	65	34
Helms	84	11	88
North Dakota			
Burdick	37	62	38
Conrad	36	63	36
Ohio			
Glenn	41	56	42
Metzenbaum	27	69	28
Oklahoma			
Boren	60	40	60
Nickles	89	9	91
Oregon			
Hatfield	59	40	60
Packwood	68	31	69
Pennsylvania			
Wofford [1]	27	67	29
Specter	68	32	68
Rhode Island			
Pell	32	68	32
Chafee	62	35	64
South Carolina			
Hollings	56	44	56
Thurmond	88	10	90
South Dakota			
Daschle	27	73	27
Pressler	88	12	88
Tennessee			
Gore	46	54	46
Sasser	36	64	36
Texas			
Bentsen	56	42	57
Gramm	93	4	96
Utah			
Garn	85	7	92
Hatch	86	7	92
Vermont			
Leahy	28	72	28
Jeffords	54	43	56
Virginia			
Robb	59	41	59
Warner	89	11	89
Washington			
Adams	26	74	26
Gorton	86	14	86
West Virginia			
Byrd	49	51	49
Rockefeller	36	64	36
Wisconsin			
Kohl	41	59	41
Kasten	84	16	84
Wyoming			
Simpson	86	11	89
Wallop	86	10	90

KEY

Democrats ***Republicans***

Presidential Support and Opposition: Senate

1. Bush Support Score, 1991. Percentage of 81 recorded votes in 1991 on which President Bush took a position and on which a senator voted "yea" or "nay" *in agreement* with the president's position. Failures to vote lowered both support and opposition scores.

2. Bush Opposition Score, 1991. Percentage of 81 recorded votes in 1991 on which President Bush took a position and on which a senator voted "yea" or "nay" *in disagreement* with the president's position. Failures to vote lowered both support and opposition scores.

3. Bush Support Score, 1991. Percentage of 81 recorded votes in 1991 on which President Bush took a position and on which a senator was present and voted "yea" or "nay" *in agreement* with the president's position. In this version of the study, absences are not counted; therefore, failures to vote did not lower support or opposition scores. Opposition scores, not listed here, are the inverse of the support score; i.e., the opposition score is equal to 100 percent minus the individual's support score.

[1] Sen. Harris Wofford, D-Pa., was sworn in May 9, 1991, to succeed John Heinz, R, who died in a plane crash April 4, 1991. Heinz was eligible for 19 presidential support votes in 1991. His presidential support score was 79 percent; his opposition score was 21 percent; and his support score, adjusted for absences, was 79 percent in 1991. Wofford was eligible for 60 of the 81 presidential support votes in 1991.

Individualists Found the Going Rough

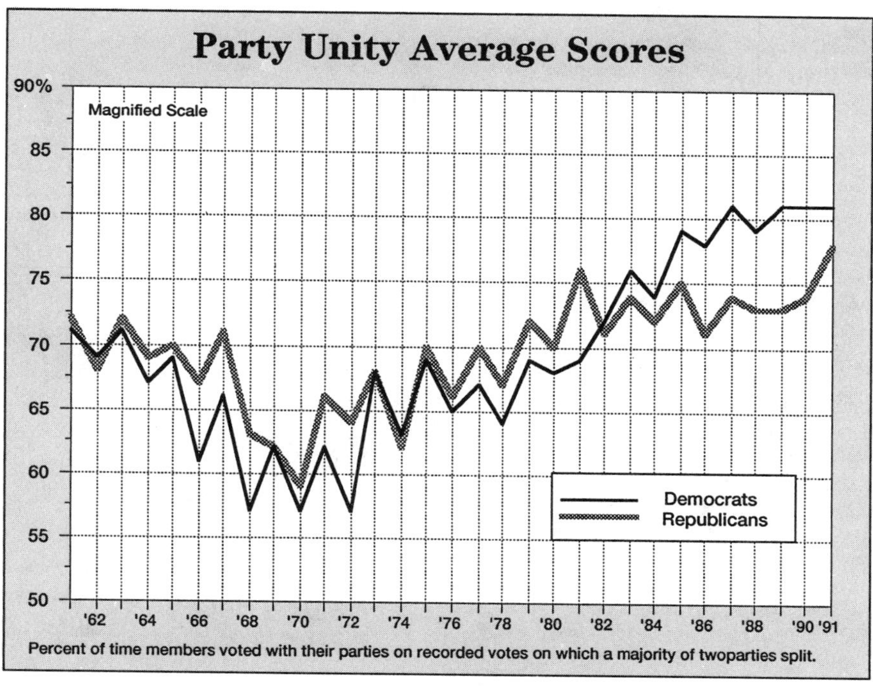

Percent of time members voted with their parties on recorded votes on which a majority of twoparties split.

Pity the congressional maverick, a dwindling yet hardy breed.

New York Rep. Bill Green voted with the Democrats so often he was practically a Republican in name only. Once, he recalled, former White House chief of staff John H. Sununu "threatened to bury me in the Giants' end zone."

From the other side of the aisle came this lament from Mississippi Democratic Rep. Mike Parker, whose vote Republicans counted in their tally half the time: "Maybe that's why I'm not on the leadership track."

Parker and Green operated on their parties' increasingly lonely outer edges. While large factions in Congress once voted against the party line with regularity and impunity, more and more members were moving closer to the middle of their party's congressional makeup.

The result was more party loyalty than Congress had seen in several decades. "The parties have become more internally similar and more different from one another; the reason for it is the mavericks," said David Rohde, a Michigan State University political scientist who had studied the phenomenon.

Twenty years ago, Democrats and Republicans voted with the majority of their party less than 70 percent of the time, according to Congressional Quarterly's voting studies. Hordes of independent-minded members rejected party positions on such touchstone issues as civil rights and urban ills.

A decade later, Ronald Reagan's ascendance to the presidency helped reduce the number of Republican defections. Democrats' loyalty also improved, but the conservative revolution persuaded some of them to abandon the majority of their party colleagues an average of 30 percent of the time.

In 1991, the trend to greater party unity continued: On votes where a majority of Republicans opposed a majority of Democrats, members in both chambers voted with their party about 80 percent of the time — a historically high figure that translated to many victories for Democrats, who had the majority in both chambers.

Meanwhile, over the same two decades the parties also tended to vote against each other more frequently.

In 1971, majorities of the two parties opposed each other 40 percent of the time; in 1981, the score edged up to 43 percent. But by 1991, Democrats and Republicans lined up against each other 53 percent of the time.

Rohde said simple political math was behind the increase of party loyalty in Congress: Conservative Southern Democrats had been replaced, either by more moderate Democrats or by Republicans. Mississippi traded Democratic Sen. John Stennis for Republican Trent Lott, for example.

Meanwhile, liberal Northern Republicans had been replaced by Democrats: Witness Massachusetts, which had five Republicans in Congress 20 years ago and in 1991 lost its last when Rep. Silvio O. Conte died and was succeeded by Democrat John Olver.

"If you remove mavericks from the party," Rohde said, "party loyalty goes up."

Two and Only Two Parties

Still, the voting behavior of the remaining mavericks and the handful of new ones provided a snapshot of how the party system operated in Congress.

In the past, there was something akin to four parties — the two main parties, plus the Boll Weevil Democrats and the "Rockefeller Republicans" — generally Northeastern liberals in the vein of the late New York Gov. Nelson Rockefeller.

But in 1991, a more concrete two-party divide had re-emerged. All that remained of the alternative factions were small clusters of mavericks who often wandered from the fold but were more easily called back on key party votes.

In nearly a score of interviews, this portrait of the nonconformists developed:

They saw themselves as independents, but only a couple had ever seriously considered abandoning their party. And most were more willing to support their leaders on key votes, especially on procedural matters, for they acknowledged that the party was still their main source of power and influence within the institution.

But when they strayed, it was to make a point: Most wanted their parties to move toward what they considered the political center on major issues.

Many GOP mavericks feared their party was on the wrong side of the abortion question and other social issues.

"We don't have majority status [because] the majority of the minority is too far right," said Rep. Sherwood Boehlert, R-N.Y.

The Democratic mavericks, meanwhile, thought their

party was too soft on crime and national security issues. "The party needs people like me to help balance out the opposite liberal extreme," said Rep. W. J. "Billy" Tauzin, D-La.

Most saw measures of success in shifting their parties and reported a level of tolerance among leaders.

"They know I have a district that is only 18 percent Republican," said Rep. Green.

But others were quite pessimistic and complained that they were ignored or punished. Rep. Jimmy Hayes, D-La., who supported the Democrats only 60 percent of the time and felt he was not well suited politically for either party, said the Democratic leadership used to "pretend I didn't exist" only some of the time. In 1991, he said, "I'm not included at all."

All the rebels defended their votes in similar terms, some more defiantly than others. Democrat Parker explained his low party-support score — and high presidential-support score — this way: "That's because they're correct 51 percent of the time. [Bush] is correct 59 percent of the time. I happen to be correct 100 percent of the time."

"I think my voting record represents a majority of the Democrats in the United States," Parker added. "And I know it represents a majority of Democrats in the 4th District."

Two House Mavericks

Stenholm, D-Texas

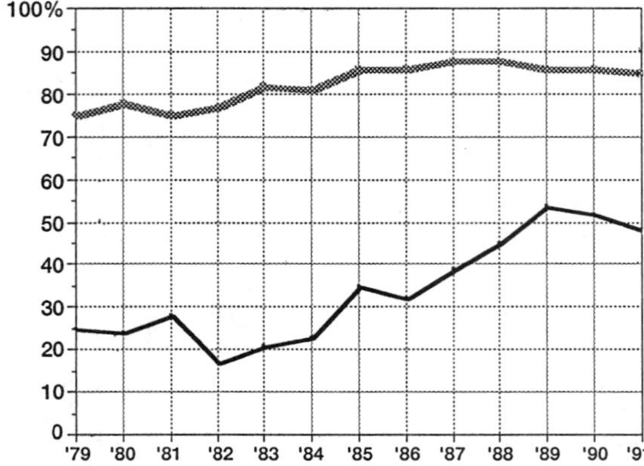

Green, R-N.Y.

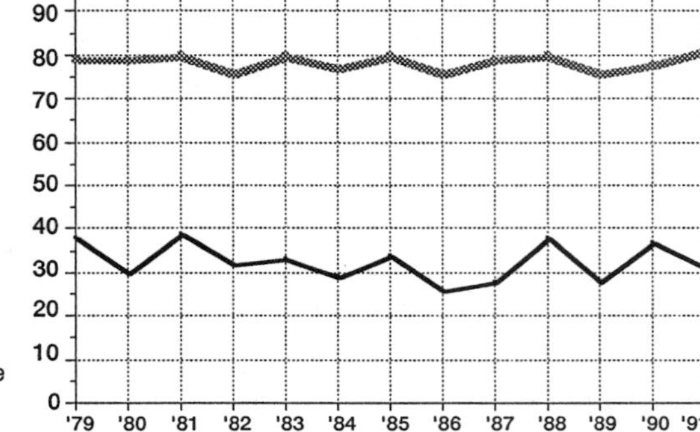

Party's Average Support Score
Individual Support Score

Graphs show that Charles W. Stenholm of Texas and Bill Green of New York have often strayed from positions taken by a majority of their party colleagues.

Fear of Consequences

The attrition of schismatic members had had residual effects that further strengthened party unity: The remaining mavericks in the Democratic Party had seen their ability to form winning coalitions with Republicans diminish along with Congress' GOP membership.

So Democratic mavericks had moderated their ways rather than opposing the party and suffering the consequences — losing some of the perks that came with loyalty, such as leadership appointments and plum committee assignments. Conservatives pointed to the appointment of Rep. Butler Derrick, D-S.C., as a chief deputy whip as evidence that it paid to toe the party line.

Derrick voted with the party 85 percent of the time. Like many others in the House, his score had increased in the previous years, but his loyalty had always been above average for Southern members — which conservative Democrats said explained why the leadership chose him when looking South to round out its team.

The leaders kept close tabs on who voted how and at times came down hard on those perceived to have strayed too often. Former Rep. Tony Coelho, D-Calif., majority whip from 1986 until 1989, developed a list of disloyal members. "In effect, you don't count them, and you don't count on them," he said in an interview.

Coelho said it was Louisiana's Buddy Roemer — once a Democratic House member, in 1991 a defeated Republican governor — who helped frame his approach to maverick Democrats. The last time he asked Roemer for his vote, Coelho said, Roemer responded, "OK, I'm with you."

Coelho: "Can I count on you?"

Roemer: "No. I'm with you right now, but I'll be having lots of other discussions, and it might mean that I'll change my vote at some other point."

Coelho: "I'll never talk to you again about another vote."

Increased Cohesion

Coelho's strategy changed only on procedural votes — the roll calls that allowed the Democrats to run the House as they wished. "That's when you really get aggressive," he said.

New Hampshire Rep. Dick Swett, a rare conservative Northeastern Democrat who recalled crossing the leadership on one such vote, said, "I have been cornered and, I wouldn't say scolded, but dealt with forcefully and my motives have been questioned."

The increased cohesion among the Democrats forced the Republicans to act more and more like a classic minority party — voting as a bloc, either to protest or obstruct.

Pressure came from the top. Two years earlier, South Carolina Rep. Arthur Ravenel Jr., a Republican moderate, said party leaders tried to punish him for his voting record (especially on environmental issues) by denying him a seat on the little-noticed Merchant Marines and Fisheries Committee — a slot no other Republican even wanted. He said

Leading Scorers: Party Unity

Support indicates those who in 1991 most consistently voted with their party's majority against the majority of the other party; opposition shows how often members voted against their party's majority. Scores are based on actual votes cast; absences were not counted. Members not eligible for half the votes are not listed.

Highest Scorers — Support

Senate

Adams

Craig

Democrats		Republicans	
Adams, Wash.	96%	Craig, Idaho	97%
Harkin, Iowa	96	Symms, Idaho	97
Sarbanes, Md.	96	Wallop, Wyo.	96
Simon, Ill.	95	Garn, Utah	95
Wellstone, Minn.	95	Gramm, Texas	95
Metzenbaum, Ohio.	94	McConnell, Ky.	95
Kennedy, Mass.	93	Helms, N.C.	94
Moynihan, N.Y.	93	Smith, N.H.	94
Riegle, Mich.	93	Burns, Mont.	93
Sanford, N.C.	93	Dole, Kan.	93
		Hatch, Utah	93
		Lott, Miss.	93
		Thurmond, S.C.	93

House

Olver

Armey

Democrats		Republicans	
Olver, Mass.	99	Armey, Texas	99%
Abercrombie, Hawaii	98	Gallegly, Calif.	97
Boxer, Calif.	98	Hancock, Mo.	97
Collins, Ill.	98	Moorhead, Calif.	97
Conyers, Mich.	98	Rhodes, Ariz.	97
Lewis, Ga.	98	Stump, Ariz.	97
Mrazek, N.Y.	98	Walker, Pa.	97
Payne, N.J.	98		
Rangel, N.Y.	98		
Scheuer, N.Y.	98		
Studds, Mass.	98		

Highest Scorers — Opposition

Heflin

Jeffords

Democrats		Republicans	
Heflin, Ala.	50%	Jeffords, Vt.	62%
Shelby, Ala.	46	Hatfield, Ore.	49
Breaux, La.	39	Chafee, R.I.	46
Hollings, S.C.	37	Cohen, Maine	41
Boren, Okla.	34	Packwood, Ore.	40
Johnston, La.	34	Specter, Pa.	33
Ford, Ky.	33	Durenberger, Minn.	30
Exon, Neb.	32	Kassebaum, Kan.	30
Dixon, Ill.	30		
Nunn, Ga.	30		

Hall

Green

Democrats		Republicans	
Hall, Texas	53%	Green, N.Y.	69%
Stenholm, Texas	50	Horton, N.Y.	65
Taylor, Miss.	50	Gilman, N.Y.	61
Parker, Miss.	49	Morella, Md.	60
Hutto, Fla.	48	Fish, N.Y.	57
Tauzin, La.	48	Boehlert, N.Y.	54
		McGrath, N.Y.	52

he had to threaten to switch parties to get his way.

Senate Republicans also saw party unity as their best alternative. "If we're going to be a force here, we have to be together — you hear that more and more," said the man who usually delivered that message, Republican Senate Whip Alan K. Simpson of Wyoming.

That message, in turn, further hardened Democratic resolve, especially when it came to votes to fend off threatened Republican filibusters on the Senate floor. It took 60 votes to invoke cloture, which meant that a minority of 41 members could stall any bill. There were 43 Republicans in the Senate.

Sen. Jim Exon, a somewhat conservative Nebraska Democrat, said he sometimes voted for cloture even when he was against the bill just to keep the Republicans in check.

"If you don't take that attitude," he says, "you will always need 60 votes to prevail."

Louisiana's John B. Breaux, one of the Senate's most conservative Democrats, said that during the 1970s, there was less emphasis on loyalty. "Now I think you see party leaders much more involved in reminding members that they are part of a party."

When Partisanship Flares

In the House, Democratic conservatives also had been known to put aside their ideological leanings in rebellion against Republican intransigence.

The 1991 crime bill passed the House by 205-203 on Nov. 27 because Southern Democrats supported it by a 63-16 margin — even though Republicans called it a "criminal rights" bill. The conservative Democrats resented what they saw as a partisan attempt by the GOP to blame their party for failing to pass a crime bill.

The measure died later that day at the hands of a near-solid Republican bloc in the Senate — including many moderates who likely would have much preferred it over the harsher GOP alternative. A cloture motion failed 49-38, far short of the required 60 votes.

There were other, unrelated explanations for the trend of increased party unity. For example, the continuing deficit crisis had stifled spending opportunities, giving liberal Republicans fewer initiatives to vote for and conservative Democrats fewer to vote against.

And there was evidence that the parties were trying harder to accommodate minority views within their ranks.

When the Democratic conservatives threatened to pitch a fit on 1991's campaign finance bill because they opposed public financing, Democratic leaders stripped the bill of the tax revenues needed to pay for it. The bill passed Nov. 25 by 273-156, and only a dozen Democrats jumped ship.

Said Rep. Charles W. Stenholm, D-Texas, who was among those objecting to the original bill: "We try to pull them to the center, and if they come far enough, we try to work with them; I think we're accomplishing our goal, no question about it."

Then and Now

Stenholm exemplified the trend among those long-term mavericks who had become more loyal to their party. He only voted with his party 28 percent of the time in 1981, when scores of Boll Weevils bolted the party to support Reagan's conservative agenda.

In 1991, Stenholm was part of the Democrats' whip organization and agreed with his party almost twice as often as he used to — 48 percent of the time.

Two pairs of his votes were illustrative: He opposed his party when President Bush wanted to go to war against Iraq but rejected the president's defense budget. He voted with Republicans on just about every vote on the crime bill but then abandoned them to give Democrats the narrow victory on approving the final version.

"Some of my people at home think I've gone too far to the left, but I think our party has moved more to the center," Stenholm said.

That was the explanation many conservative Democrats gave for their increased loyalty — that is, their party had shifted, not them. "The Democratic Party's position is moderating significantly," said Sen. Harry Reid, D-Nev., who abandoned his party's position 25 percent of the time.

> **"If we're going to be a force here, we have to be together — you hear that more and more."**
>
> **—Alan K. Simpson**

As evidence of a shift, some pointed to the House's newer conservative-minded Democrats. Two came from the Northeast, Swett of New Hampshire and Frank Pallone Jr. of New Jersey. Another pair, Pete Geren and Gary Condit, represented the districts of two retired liberal House leaders — Speaker Jim Wright of Texas and whip Coelho, respectively.

Political scientists, however, downplayed the notion that there had been significant shifts in either party.

The new mavericks were best explained by this well-established thesis: "The people who are most likely to be mavericks are those who have constituencies that are atypical of their party constituencies," said University of California Professor Gary W. Cox. In other words, conservative Democrats came from Republican-leaning districts, and liberal Republicans came from Democratic-leaning districts.

Both parties made much of the notion that they were "big tents" with room enough for a range of views.

Democrats started using that philosophy long ago, but only to explain the Boll Weevils' flight to Reagan's side, not to accommodate them. Republicans adopted the big-tent rhetoric in later years to stop abortion rights advocates from abandoning the party.

The Republicans also were being more accommodating to their mavericks, especially in the face of threats to Bush's perfect record of successful vetoes. The party was being pushed slightly to the left as a result.

So many Republicans bolted on a series of jobless-benefits votes — up to 13 in the Senate and up to 55 in the House — that the administration was forced to compromise amid fears that its veto strategy would not hold indefinitely. Likewise, though the House's 273-158 vote on 1991's civil rights bill was a dozen-plus short of a veto-override margin, enough Republican moderates in the Senate were upset with the administration's stance that Bush agreed to compromise. ■

Party-Unity Definitions

Party-unity votes. Recorded votes in the Senate or the House that split the parties, with a majority of voting Democrats opposing a majority of voting Republicans.

Party-unity scores. Percentage of party-unity votes on which a member voted "yea" or "nay" *in agreement* with a majority of his party. Failures to vote lowered scores for chambers and parties.

Opposition-to-party scores. Percentage of party-unity votes on which a member voted "yea" or "nay" *in disagreement* with a majority of his party. Failures to vote lowered scores for chambers and parties.

Average Scores by Party

	1991		1990	
	Dem.	**Rep.**	**Dem.**	**Rep.**
Party Unity	81%	78%	81%	74%
Senate	80	81	80	75
House	81	77	81	74

	1991		1990	
	Dem.	**Rep.**	**Dem.**	**Rep.**
Opposition	14%	18%	13%	21%
Senate	17	17	18	22
House	14	18	13	21

Sectional Support, Opposition

SENATE	**Support**	**Opposition**
Northern Democrats	85%	13%
Southern Democrats	70	26
Northern Republicans	79	19
Southern Republicans	88	9

HOUSE	**Support**	**Opposition**
Northern Democrats	85%	10%
Southern Democrats	74	21
Northern Republicans	76	20
Southern Republicans	80	13

1991 Victories, Defeats

	Senate	**House**	**Total**
Democrats won, Republicans lost	81	197	278
Republicans won, Democrats lost	57	39	96

Unanimous Voting by Parties

The number of times each party voted unanimously on 1991 party-unity votes. Scores for 1991 are in parentheses:

	Senate	**House**	**Total**
Democrats voted unanimously	19 (28)	11 (13)	30 (41)
Republicans voted unanimously	15 (5)	18 (17)	33 (22)

Party-Unity Average Scores

Year	**Democrats**	**Republicans**	**Year**	**Democrats**	**Republicans**
1991	81%	78%	1975	69%	70%
1990	81	74	1974	63	62
1989	81	73	1973	68	68
1988	79	73	1972	57	64
1987	81	74	1971	62	66
1986	78	71	1970	57	59
1985	79	75	1969	62	62
1984	74	72	1968	57	63
1983	76	74	1967	66	71
1982	72	71	1966	61	67
1981	69	76	1965	69	70
1980	68	70	1964	67	69
1979	69	72	1963	71	72
1978	64	67	1962	69	68
1977	67	70	1961	71	72
1976	65	66			

Breakdown of Party-Unity Votes

Following are the votes, listed by roll call number, on which a majority of Democrats voted against a majority of Republicans.

House

(236 of 428 votes)

2	51	94	129	158	203	235	289	319	352	387	424
3	54	95	130	165	204	250	290	320	353	388	425
4	56	99	131	166	206	251	291	321	354	389	426
5	60	100	132	167	207	254	292	322	355	390	427
6	67	101	133	169	208	258	293	324	356	391	428
7	69	103	135	174	209	259	295	326	357	392	429
8	70	104	136	178	210	260	296	331	358	393	430
9	71	105	137	179	212	261	297	332	362	398	431
32	73	107	141	180	213	266	301	333	363	399	432
33	74	108	142	183	215	267	303	340	364	401	433
34	77	109	144	185	216	269	304	341	366	403	435
39	81	110	146	188	217	270	305	343	371	405	437
40	82	111	148	190	218	272	306	344	374	406	441
42	83	112	149	191	226	279	308	345	376	413	442
43	85	114	150	193	227	280	310	346	377	416	443
44	87	115	151	194	228	281	313	347	379	418	444
45	88	125	152	195	229	282	315	348	380	419	
46	90	126	153	197	230	283	316	349	381	420	
47	91	127	156	198	233	284	317	350	382	421	
50	93	128	157	202	234	285	318	351	383	422	

Senate

(138 of 280 votes)

1	34	63	74	86	113	131	154	177	201	215	248
2	35	64	75	88	114	132	156	179	202	216	252
15	36	65	76	91	115	134	162	180	203	219	256
16	37	66	78	97	116	139	163	181	204	220	257
17	38	67	79	102	117	140	164	185	205	221	259
18	46	68	80	103	118	141	168	187	206	225	260
19	47	69	81	104	119	142	169	188	207	229	262
22	52	70	82	105	120	146	171	190	208	233	266
26	53	71	83	108	127	148	172	191	210	234	268
32	54	72	84	110	128	150	173	195	212	237	269
33	60	73	85	111	130	151	174	196	213	242	271
						152	176	199	214	243	278

Proportion of Partisan Roll Calls

How often a majority of Democrats voted against a majority of Republicans:

Year	House	Senate	Year	House	Senate
1954	38%	47%	1973	42%	40%
1955	41	30	1974	29	44
1956	44	53	1975	48	48
1957	59	36	1976	36	37
1958	40	44	1977	42	42
1959	55	48	1978	33	45
1960	53	37	1979	47	47
1961	50	62	1980	38	46
1962	46	41	1981	37	48
1963	49	47	1982	36	43
1964	55	36	1983	56	44
1965	52	42	1984	47	40
1966	41	50	1985	61	50
1967	36	35	1986	57	52
1968	35	32	1987	64	41
1969	31	36	1988	47	42
1970	27	35	1989	55	35
1971	38	42	1990	49	54
1972	27	36	1991	55	49

Democrats *Republicans*

	1	2	3
Alabama			
Heflin	49	50	50
Shelby	54	46	54
Alaska			
Murkowski	88	10	90
Stevens	78	20	80
Arizona			
DeConcini	75	23	76
McCain	87	11	89
Arkansas			
Bumpers	82	16	84
Pryor	33	7	84
California			
Cranston	78	7	92
Seymour	81	14	85
Colorado			
Wirth	81	15	84
Brown	85	14	86
Connecticut			
Dodd	83	16	84
Lieberman	80	19	81
Delaware			
Biden	88	8	92
Roth	78	20	79
Florida			
Graham	80	18	82
Mack	88	11	89
Georgia			
Fowler	79	20	80
Nunn	69	29	70
Hawaii			
Akaka	91	9	91
Inouye	77	19	80
Idaho			
Craig	97	3	97
Symms	93	3	97
Illinois			
Dixon	69	30	70
Simon	94	5	95
Indiana			
Coats	91	9	91
Lugar	88	11	89
Iowa			
Harkin	75	3	96
Grassley	83	17	83
Kansas			
Dole	93	7	93
Kassebaum	69	30	70
Kentucky			
Ford	67	33	67
McConnell	95	5	95
Louisiana			
Breaux	59	37	61
Johnston	65	34	66
Maine			
Mitchell	92	8	92
Cohen	59	41	59
Maryland			
Mikulski	91	8	92
Sarbanes	96	4	96
Massachusetts			
Kennedy	92	7	93
Kerry	92	8	92
Michigan			
Levin	90	10	90
Riegle	93	7	93
Minnesota			
Wellstone	91	5	95
Durenberger	68	30	70
Mississippi			
Cochran	89	9	90
Lott	91	7	93
Missouri			
Bond	86	12	88
Danforth	72	24	75
Montana			
Baucus	83	17	83
Burns	93	7	93
Nebraska			
Exon	68	32	68
Kerrey	70	13	84
Nevada			
Bryan	78	22	78
Reid	75	25	75
New Hampshire			
Rudman	75	25	75
Smith	93	6	94
New Jersey			
Bradley	84	11	89
Lautenberg	89	11	89
New Mexico			
Bingaman	78	20	79
Domenici	88	11	89
New York			
Moynihan	92	7	93
D'Amato	75	25	75
North Carolina			
Sanford	91	7	93
Helms	78	5	94
North Dakota			
Burdick	88	9	90
Conrad	72	26	74
Ohio			
Glenn	83	14	85
Metzenbaum	93	6	94
Oklahoma			
Boren	65	33	66
Nickles	88	9	90
Oregon			
Hatfield	51	49	51
Packwood	59	40	60
Pennsylvania			
Wofford [1]	87	9	91
Specter	67	33	67
Rhode Island			
Pell	89	10	90
Chafee	52	45	54
South Carolina			
Hollings	63	37	63
Thurmond	92	7	93
South Dakota			
Daschle	90	9	91
Pressler	89	10	90
Tennessee			
Gore	86	14	86
Sasser	91	9	91
Texas			
Bentsen	74	24	76
Gramm	92	5	95
Utah			
Garn	88	5	95
Hatch	90	7	93
Vermont			
Leahy	90	10	90
Jeffords	36	58	38
Virginia			
Robb	74	26	74
Warner	82	18	82
Washington			
Adams	96	4	96
Gorton	82	18	82
West Virginia			
Byrd	76	24	76
Rockefeller	91	8	92
Wisconsin			
Kohl	83	17	83
Kasten	82	18	82
Wyoming			
Simpson	88	11	89
Wallop	94	4	96

Party Unity and Party Opposition: Senate

1. Party Unity, 1991. Percentage of 138 party-unity recorded votes in 1991 on which a senator voted "yea" or "nay" *in agreement* with a majority of his or her party. (Party-unity roll calls are those on which a majority of voting Democrats opposed a majority of voting Republicans.) Failures to vote lowered both party-unity and party-opposition scores.

2. Party Opposition, 1991. Percentage of 138 party-unity recorded votes in 1991 on which a senator voted "yea" or "nay" *in disagreement* with a majority of his or her party. Failures to vote lowered both party-unity and party-opposition scores.

3. Party Unity, 1991. Percentage of 138 party-unity recorded votes in 1991 on which a senator was present and voted "yea" or "nay" *in agreement* with a majority of his or her party. In this version of the study, absences were not counted; therefore, failures to vote did not lower unity or opposition scores. Opposition scores, not listed here, are the inverse of the unity score; i.e., the opposition score is equal to 100 percent minus the individual's unity score.

[1] *Sen. Harris Wofford, D-Pa., was sworn in May 9, 1991, to succeed John Heinz, R, who died in a plane crash April 4, 1991. Heinz was eligible for 16 of the 138 party-unity votes in 1991. His party-unity score was 63 percent; opposition score was 38 percent; unity score, adjusted for absences, was 63 percent in 1991. Wofford was eligible for 117 of the party-unity votes in 1991.*

Party Unity and Party Opposition: House

1. Party Unity, 1991. Percentage of 236 party-unity recorded votes in 1991 on which a representative voted "yea" or "nay" *in agreement* with a majority of his or her party. (Party-unity roll calls are those on which a majority of voting Democrats opposed a majority of voting Republicans.) Failures to vote lowered both party-unity and party-opposition scores.

2. Party Opposition, 1991. Percentage of 236 party-unity recorded votes in 1991 on which a representative voted "yea" or "nay" *in disagreement* with a majority of his or her party. Failures to vote lowered both party-unity and party-opposition scores.

3. Party Unity, 1991. Percentage of 236 party-unity recorded votes in 1991 on which a representative was present and voted "yea" or "nay" *in agreement* with a majority of his or her party. In this version of the study, absences were not counted; therefore, failures to vote did not lower unity or opposition scores. Opposition scores, not listed here, are the inverse of the unity score; i.e., the opposition score is equal to 100 percent minus the individual's unity score.

[1] *Ed Pastor, D-Ariz., was sworn in Oct. 3, 1991, to succeed Morris K. Udall, D, who resigned May 4, 1991. Udall was eligible for 30 of the 236 party-unity votes in 1991. His party-unity score was 13 percent; his opposition score was 0 percent; and his unity score, adjusted for absences, was 100 percent in 1991. Pastor was eligible for 95 party-unity votes in 1991.*

[2] *Thomas W. Ewing, R-Ill., was sworn in July 10, 1991, to succeed Edward Madigan, R, who resigned March 8, 1991, after being appointed secretary of Agriculture. Madigan was eligible for 11 of the 236 party-unity votes in 1991. His party-unity score was 73 percent; his opposition score was 9 percent; and his unity score, adjusted for absences, was 89 percent in 1991. Ewing was eligible for 136 party-unity votes in 1991.*

[3] *John Olver, D-Mass., was sworn in June 18, 1991, to succeed Silvio O. Conte, R, who died Feb. 8, 1991. Conte was eligible for eight of the 236 party-unity votes in 1991. His party-unity score was 50 percent; his opposition score was 50 percent; and his unity score, adjusted for absences, was 50 percent in 1991. Olver was eligible for 157 party-unity votes in 1991.*

[4] *Lucien E. Blackwell, D-Pa., was sworn in Nov. 13, 1991, to succeed William H. Gray III, D, who resigned Sept. 11, 1991. Gray was eligible for 123 of the 236 party-unity votes in 1991. His party-unity score was 75 percent; his opposition score was 2 percent; and his unity score, adjusted for absences, was 98 percent in 1991. Blackwell was eligible for 34 party-unity votes in 1991.*

[5] *Sam Johnson, R-Texas, was sworn in May 22, 1991, to succeed Steve Bartlett, R, who resigned March 11, 1991. Bartlett was eligible for 11 of the 236 party-unity votes in 1991. His party-unity score was 82 percent; his opposition score was 9 percent; and his unity score, adjusted for absences, was 90 percent in 1991. Johnson was eligible for 189 party-unity votes in 1991.*

[6] *Bernard Sanders, I-Vt., voted as an independent. Had he voted as a Democrat, his party-unity score would have been 84 percent; his opposition score would have been 8 percent; and his unity score, adjusted for absences, would have been 92 percent.*

[7] *George F. Allen, R-Va., was sworn in Nov. 12, 1991, to succeed D. French Slaughter Jr., R, who resigned Nov. 5, 1991. Slaughter was eligible for 200 of the 236 party-unity votes in 1991. His party-unity score was 57 percent; his opposition score was 9 percent; and his unity score, adjusted for absences, was 86 percent in 1991. Allen was eligible for 35 party-unity votes in 1991.*

[8] *Thomas S. Foley, D-Wash., as Speaker of the House, voted at his discretion. He voted on eight of the 236 party-unity votes.*

KEY

† Not eligible for all votes or voted "present" to avoid conflict of interest on one or more votes in 1991. Ineligible votes are excluded from calculation of scores.

Democrats ***Republicans***
Independent

	1	2	3
Alabama			
1 ***Callahan***	72	15	83
2 ***Dickinson***	79	12	87
3 Browder	74	23	76
4 Bevill	73	23	76
5 Cramer	77	22	77
6 Erdreich	72	26	74
7 Harris	73	25	75
Alaska			
AL ***Young***	66	24	73
Arizona			
1 ***Rhodes***	93	3	97
2 Pastor [1]	92	7	93
3 ***Stump***	97	3	97
4 ***Kyl***	95	5	95
5 ***Kolbe***	83	15	85
Arkansas			
1 Alexander	79	13	86
2 Thornton	84	12	88
3 ***Hammerschmidt***	70	22	76
4 Anthony	77	17	82
California			
1 ***Riggs***	81	14	85
2 ***Herger***	86	8	91
3 Matsui	78	5	94
4 Fazio	87	9	91
5 Pelosi	89	4	95
6 Boxer	76	1	98
7 Miller	92	3	97
8 Dellums	90	3	96
9 Stark	87	3	96
10 Edwards	92	6	94
11 Lantos	89	6	94
12 ***Campbell***	69	19	78
13 Mineta	92	4	96
14 ***Doolittle***	89	5	95
15 Condit	62	33	65
16 Panetta	87	12	88
17 Dooley	84	16	84
18 Lehman	84	11	88
19 ***Lagomarsino***	92	8	92
20 ***Thomas***	80	12	87
21 ***Gallegly***	94	3	97
22 ***Moorhead***	95	3	97
23 Beilenson	84	12	87
24 Waxman	84	6	93
25 Roybal	88	4	95
26 Berman	83	7	92
27 Levine	59	5	93
28 Dixon	88	4	95
29 Waters	85	3	96
30 Martinez	71	10	88
31 Dymally	74	3	97
32 Anderson	86	13	87
33 ***Dreier***	89	10	90
34 Torres	94	3	97
35 ***Lewis***	78	16	83
36 Brown	83	7	92
37 ***McCandless***	94	6	94
38 ***Dornan***	87	5	94
39 ***Dannemeyer***	87	4	95
40 ***Cox***	85	10	89
41 ***Lowery***	79	12	87
42 ***Rohrabacher***	91	8	92
43 ***Packard***	84	12	87
44 ***Cunningham***	89	9	91
45 ***Hunter***	84	6	93
Colorado			
1 Schroeder	80	18	81
2 Skaggs	91	8	91
3 Campbell	75	21	78
4 ***Allard***	94	6	94
5 ***Hefley***	88	9	90
6 ***Schaefer***	90	9	91
Connecticut			
1 Kennelly	94	6	94
2 Gejdenson	96	3	97
3 DeLauro	95	5	95
4 ***Shays***	65	35	65
5 ***Franks***	87	12	88
6 ***Johnson***	53	46	53
Delaware			
AL Carper	75	23	76
Florida			
1 Hutto	50	46	52
2 Peterson	84	15	85
3 Bennett	78	22	78
4 ***James***	81	18	82
5 ***McCollum***	81	13	86
6 ***Stearns***	88	10	90
7 Gibbons	82	15	85
8 ***Young***	72	22	76
9 ***Bilirakis***	81	14	86
10 ***Ireland***	86	8	92
11 Bacchus	86	12	88
12 ***Lewis***	88	10	90
13 ***Goss***	90	10	90
14 Johnston	83	11	88
15 ***Shaw***	78	16	83
16 Smith	87	4	95
17 Lehman	64	4	94
18 ***Ros-Lehtinen***	75	22	78
19 Fascell	92	8	92
Georgia			
1 Thomas	74	22	77
2 Hatcher	70	14	83
3 Ray	59	36	62
4 Jones	88	10	90
5 Lewis	96	2	98
6 ***Gingrich***	88	7	92
7 Darden	81	18	82
8 Rowland	70	21	77
9 Jenkins	72	19	79
10 Barnard	62	32	66
Hawaii			
1 Abercrombie	95	2	98
2 Mink	96	3	97
Idaho			
1 LaRocco	81	18	82
2 Stallings	68	27	72
Illinois			
1 Hayes	96	3	97
2 Savage	76	7	92
3 Russo	86	11	89
4 Sangmeister	80	13	86
5 Lipinski	72	22	77
6 ***Hyde***	83	13	87
7 Collins	88	2	98
8 Rostenkowski	80	10	89
9 Yates	90	3	97
10 ***Porter***	69	27	72
11 Annunzio	89	10	90
12 ***Crane***	87	5	95
13 ***Fawell***	80	16	84
14 ***Hastert***	90	6	94
15 ***Ewing*** [2]	81	15	84
16 Cox	90	8	91
17 Evans	95	4	96
18 ***Michel***	78	10	88
19 Bruce	88	11	89
20 Durbin	92	6	94
21 Costello	77	22	78
22 Poshard	79	19	80
Indiana			
1 Visclosky	92	8	92
2 Sharp	81	12	87
3 Roemer	75	25	75

	1	2	3
4 Long	85	15	85
5 Jontz	94	6	94
6 ***Burton***	92	6	94
7 ***Myers***	66	29	69
8 McCloskey	91	4	96
9 Hamilton	80	20	80
10 Jacobs	61	34	64
Iowa			
1 ***Leach***	61	35	63
2 ***Nussle***	85	14	85
3 Nagle	89	7	93
4 Smith	81	12	87
5 ***Lightfoot***	86	12	88
6 ***Grandy***	81	19	81
Kansas			
1 ***Roberts***	90	6	93
2 Slattery	71	26	73
3 ***Meyers***	73	27	73
4 Glickman	70	22	76
5 ***Nichols***	82	17	83
Kentucky			
1 Hubbard	67	31	68
2 Natcher	88	12	88
3 Mazzoli	88	11	89
4 ***Bunning***	94	4	96
5 ***Rogers***	76	21	79
6 ***Hopkins***	33	4	90
7 Perkins	89	10	90
Louisiana			
1 ***Livingston***	77	20	79
2 Jefferson	82	5	95
3 Tauzin	50	45	52
4 ***McCrery***	78	15	84
5 Huckaby	55	36	61
6 ***Baker***	88	6	94
7 Hayes	55	37	60
8 ***Holloway***	69	7	91
Maine			
1 Andrews	93	6	94
2 ***Snowe***	52	47	53
Maryland			
1 ***Gilchrest***	78	21	79
2 ***Bentley***	72	25	75
3 Cardin	91	8	92
4 McMillen	84	14	85
5 Hoyer	90	7	93
6 Byron	63	33	65
7 Mfume	89	6	93
8 ***Morella***	39	58	40
Massachusetts			
1 Olver [3]	96	1	99
2 Neal	89	6	94
3 Early	81	15	84
4 Frank	90	7	93
5 Atkins	93	5	95
6 Mavroules	85	9	91
7 Markey	94	3	97
8 Kennedy	94	3	97
9 Moakley	90	7	93
10 Studds	96	2	98
11 Donnelly	84	12	87
Michigan			
1 Conyers	91	2	98
2 ***Pursell***	64	27	70
3 Wolpe	96	3	97
4 ***Upton***	78	21	79
5 ***Henry***	74	24	75
6 Carr †	79	14	85
7 Kildee	95	5	95
8 Traxler	83	9	90
9 ***Vander Jagt***	79	15	84
10 ***Camp***	88	12	88
11 ***Davis***	53	38	59
12 Bonior	94	5	95
13 Collins	93	3	97
14 Hertel	94	3	97
15 Ford	84	3	97
16 Dingell	81	11	88
17 Levin	95	5	95
18 ***Broomfield***	75	19	80
Minnesota			
1 Penny	66	32	67
2 ***Weber***	84	11	88
3 ***Ramstad***	81	18	82
4 Vento	94	4	96
5 Sabo	91	5	95
6 Sikorski	87	11	88
7 Peterson	76	20	79
8 Oberstar	83	8	91
Mississippi			
1 Whitten	78	15	84
2 Espy	83	11	88
3 Montgomery	53	44	54
4 Parker	50	47	51
5 Taylor	50	49	50
Missouri			
1 Clay	80	10	89
2 Horn	92	8	92
3 Gephardt	90	5	95
4 Skelton	65	32	67
5 Wheat	97	3	97
6 ***Coleman***	79	19	81
7 ***Hancock***	95	3	97
8 ***Emerson***	71	28	72
9 Volkmer	71	28	71
Montana			
1 Williams	75	14	85
2 ***Marlenee***	74	13	85
Nebraska			
1 ***Bereuter***	77	22	77
2 Hoagland	83	17	83
3 ***Barrett***	92	6	94
Nevada			
1 Bilbray	81	16	84
2 ***Vucanovich***	87	9	90
New Hampshire			
1 ***Zeliff***	86	11	89
2 Swett	72	25	74
New Jersey			
1 Andrews	78	18	81
2 Hughes	79	18	81
3 Pallone	75	24	76
4 ***Smith***	58	40	59
5 ***Roukema***	56	37	60
6 Dwyer	87	6	93
7 ***Rinaldo***	53	46	53
8 Roe	83	9	90
9 Torricelli	81	10	89
10 Payne	95	2	98
11 ***Gallo***	67	30	69
12 ***Zimmer***	79	19	80
13 ***Saxton***	76	19	80
14 Guarini †	82	14	86
New Mexico			
1 ***Schiff***	64	33	66
2 ***Skeen***	69	30	70
3 Richardson	91	8	91
New York			
1 Hochbrueckner	91	6	93
2 Downey	96	3	97
3 Mrazek	63	1	98
4 ***Lent***	66	26	72
5 ***McGrath*** †	46	50	48
6 Flake	87	4	96
7 Ackerman	86	3	96
8 Scheuer	92	2	98
9 Manton	86	6	93
10 Schumer	89	6	93
11 Towns	83	3	96
12 Owens	87	3	97
13 Solarz	91	8	92
14 ***Molinari***	72	26	73
15 ***Green***	31	68	31
16 Rangel	92	2	98
17 Weiss	85	3	97
18 Serrano	86	3	97
19 Engel	93	4	96
20 Lowey	95	3	97
21 ***Fish***	40	53	43
22 ***Gilman***	39	61	39
23 McNulty	93	6	94
24 ***Solomon***	89	8	92
25 ***Boehlert***	46	54	46
26 ***Martin***	72	16	82
27 ***Walsh***	67	32	68
28 McHugh	89	8	92
29 ***Horton***	34	63	35
30 Slaughter	93	3	97
31 ***Paxon***	90	7	93
32 LaFalce	89	8	91
33 Nowak	89	8	92
34 ***Houghton***	58	37	61
North Carolina			
1 Jones	80	14	85
2 Valentine	59	35	63
3 Lancaster	74	23	76
4 Price	86	12	88
5 Neal	68	23	75
6 ***Coble***	89	8	92
7 Rose	84	8	91
8 Hefner	79	16	83
9 ***McMillan***	85	14	85
10 ***Ballenger***	93	3	96
11 ***Taylor***	91	7	93
North Dakota			
AL Dorgan	75	23	76
Ohio			
1 Luken	67	31	68
2 ***Gradison***	76	19	80
3 Hall	86	11	89
4 ***Oxley***	83	16	84
5 ***Gillmor*** †	67	30	69
6 ***McEwen***	86	11	89
7 ***Hobson***	85	15	85
8 ***Boehner***	96	4	96
9 Kaptur	85	8	92
10 ***Miller***	84	8	91
11 Eckart	92	6	94
12 ***Kasich***	81	17	83
13 Pease	82	14	85
14 Sawyer	91	6	94
15 ***Wylie***	81	16	84
16 ***Regula***	70	29	71
17 Traficant	82	17	82
18 Applegate	66	31	68
19 Feighan	91	4	96
20 Oakar	90	6	94
21 Stokes	90	4	96
Oklahoma			
1 ***Inhofe***	90	6	93
2 Synar	93	5	95
3 Brewster	71	26	73
4 McCurdy	75	20	79
5 ***Edwards***	82	11	88
6 English	62	36	63
Oregon			
1 AuCoin	86	6	94
2 ***Smith***	88	10	90
3 Wyden	94	5	95
4 DeFazio	88	8	91
5 Kopetski	86	11	88
Pennsylvania			
1 Foglietta	92	3	97
2 Blackwell [4]	94	6	94
3 Borski	89	9	91
4 Kolter	76	19	80
5 ***Schulze***	70	19	79
6 Yatron	69	16	81
7 ***Weldon***	71	24	75
8 Kostmayer	89	8	92
9 ***Shuster***	75	20	79
10 ***McDade***	56	36	61
11 Kanjorski	85	14	86
12 Murtha	82	15	85
13 ***Coughlin***	65	31	68
14 Coyne	93	4	96
15 ***Ritter***	72	24	75
16 ***Walker***	96	3	97
17 ***Gekas***	84	14	86
18 ***Santorum***	88	12	88
19 ***Goodling***	70	20	77
20 Gaydos	70	17	81
21 ***Ridge***	66	27	71
22 Murphy	63	28	69
23 ***Clinger***	66	32	68
Rhode Island			
1 ***Machtley***	58	39	60
2 Reed	92	7	93
South Carolina			
1 ***Ravenel***	55	43	56
2 ***Spence***	75	18	81
3 Derrick	82	14	85
4 Patterson	66	33	67
5 Spratt	82	15	84
6 Tallon	68	30	69
South Dakota			
AL Johnson	80	19	80
Tennessee			
1 ***Quillen***	64	27	71
2 ***Duncan***	84	14	85
3 Lloyd	52	28	65
4 Cooper †	72	26	74
5 Clement	80	19	81
6 Gordon	89	11	89
7 ***Sundquist***	84	9	90
8 Tanner	64	26	71
9 Ford	74	5	94
Texas			
1 Chapman †	68	21	76
2 Wilson	61	23	72
3 ***Johnson*** [5]	86	10	90
4 Hall	46	51	47
5 Bryant	88	6	94
6 ***Barton***	81	13	86
7 ***Archer***	85	11	88
8 ***Fields***	92	5	95
9 Brooks †	82	10	89
10 Pickle	78	17	83
11 Edwards	78	20	79
12 Geren	58	38	60
13 Sarpalius	60	38	61
14 Laughlin	61	34	64
15 de la Garza	78	14	85
16 Coleman	88	11	89
17 Stenholm	48	49	50
18 Washington	80	4	95
19 ***Combest***	82	17	83
20 Gonzalez	93	7	93
21 ***Smith***	84	11	88
22 ***DeLay***	89	5	95
23 Bustamante	83	6	93
24 Frost	80	10	89
25 Andrews	75	24	76
26 ***Armey***	97	1	99
27 Ortiz	76	19	80
Utah			
1 ***Hansen***	89	7	93
2 Owens	83	11	88
3 Orton	57	37	60
Vermont			
AL *Sanders* [6]	—	—	—
Virginia			
1 ***Bateman***	69	26	72
2 Pickett	70	26	73
3 ***Bliley***	88	9	90
4 Sisisky	68	25	73
5 Payne	66	30	69
6 Olin	74	22	77
7 ***Allen*** [7]	86	14	86
8 Moran	79	16	83
9 Boucher	84	10	90
10 ***Wolf***	81	17	82
Washington			
1 ***Miller***	69	26	73
2 Swift	89	8	92
3 Unsoeld	93	5	95
4 ***Morrison***	53	44	55
5 Foley [8]			
6 Dicks	85	9	90
7 McDermott	95	5	95
8 ***Chandler***	79	17	83
West Virginia			
1 Mollohan	79	17	82
2 Staggers	83	11	88
3 Wise	90	6	93
4 Rahall	85	11	88
Wisconsin			
1 Aspin	79	14	85
2 ***Klug***	67	31	68
3 ***Gunderson***	68	31	68
4 Kleczka	89	4	96
5 Moody	78	8	91
6 ***Petri***	69	30	70
7 Obey	92	6	94
8 ***Roth***	81	17	83
9 ***Sensenbrenner***	87	11	88
Wyoming			
AL ***Thomas***	93	6	94

Conservative Coalition Clearly On the Wane

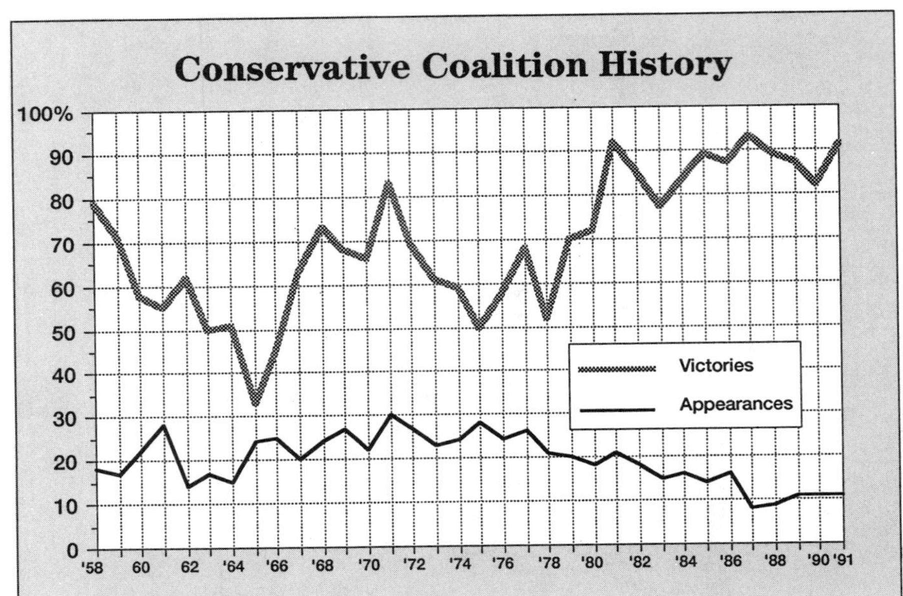

The conservative coalition, the confluence of Republicans and Southern Democrats who made up an immutable force in American politics for half a century, was in 1991 little more than an academic phenomenon in Congress. It still appeared on a few votes, but it had little political impact on most legislation.

"The conservative coalition as a working political force is really a statistical artifact," said Burdett Loomis, professor of political science at the University of Kansas.

"At one time, in the '30s, '40s, '50s, there was a real conservative coalition that had an ideology and talked to each other. Now, you may have some conservative Democrats talking to some conservative Republicans, but it's not a formalized thing."

Nonetheless, the continuing appearance of the coalition — primarily on crime and defense votes in 1991 — suggested that at least on certain issues, the conservative heritage of the South continued to be reflected in the day's politics despite increased participation by blacks and other minorities.

"There is still a clear tendency of a majority of Southerners to tend to go along with Republicans," said Rep. John Bryant, D-Texas.

The conservative coalition, as defined and measured by Congressional Quarterly since the Eisenhower administration, was a voting bloc in the House and Senate consisting of a majority of Republicans and a majority of Southern Democrats, when combined against a majority of Northern Democrats. In 1991, it appeared on 37 of 428 House votes, or 9 percent of the time, and on 40 of 280 Senate votes, or 14 percent of the time, for a combined rate of 11 percent.

That was the same rate as in 1989 and 1990, when the conservative coalition appeared on 11 percent of all votes. In 1988, the appearance rate was 9 percent.

When the conservative coalition did occur, it generally won because the total of Republicans and Southern Democrats constituted a majority of the lawmakers in both chambers. In 1991 it lost on only a handful of votes in each chamber.

The conservative coalition was an obstacle to passage of civil rights laws in the 1960s. Throughout the 1970s, it appeared on one in every five votes in Congress, peaking at 30 percent in 1971. It was credited with helping President Ronald Reagan cut federal taxes in 1981.

During the first four years after Reagan, however, issues on which it appeared were increasingly difficult to identify with an ideological bent. And, increasingly, it was political forces such as loyalty to committee chairmen or to the state delegation that influenced lawmakers' allegiances, said members and academics.

Republicans said they no longer counted on Southern Democrats as a supportive voting bloc. Instead, they tried to build coalitions with any combination of Democrats who would back the president's position.

"It is very much an issue-oriented thing," said Pennsylvania's Robert S. Walker, a member of the House Republican leadership. "A lot of the people voting with us on crime were hard-core ethnic Northern Democrats. Then there are some people who voted with us on social issues but not on labor issues, and some people who backed us on business- and labor-related issues."

United by Crime, Defense

The two areas in which the conservative coalition emerged most frequently were votes related to defense spending and anti-crime initiatives, which together accounted for 16 of its 40 appearances in the Senate and 16 of its 37 appearances in the House.

In the Senate, there were 10 defense votes on which the coalition appeared, and in the House there were seven.

The defense votes, in particular, seemed to reflect Southern Democrats' continuing allegiance to the commander in chief in the White House, whether he was a Republican or Democrat. "If I'm sort of undecided, I'll vote with the Democrats," said Sen. Howell Heflin, D-Ala., who voted 90 percent of the time with the conservative coalition. But on defense, he said, "I went with every Republican position."

Five other defense votes in the Senate involved cuts in funding for deployment of advanced ballistic missiles, the B-2 bomber and development of the Strategic Defense Initiative. Once again, the conservative coalition provided the majority to block the cuts.

The coalition also enabled J. Bennett Johnston, D-La., to quash an effort by John Glenn, D-Ohio, to move money out of the Energy Department's nuclear weapons building budget and into environmental cleanup.

Yet, while Southerners' continued support for the president's defense spending requests demonstrated a conservative philosophy, the votes had economic and regional undertones as well.

According to Michigan State University's David Rohde,

Leading Scorers: Conservative Coalition

High scorers in support are those who in 1991 voted most often with the conservative coalition. Opposition figures are for those who voted most often against the conservative coalition. Scores are based on actual votes cast; absences were not counted. Members who were not eligible for half the votes are not listed.

Highest Scorers — Support

Senate

Ford

Dole

Dixon

Southern Democrats

Ford, Ky.	95%	Johnston, La.	82%
Heflin, Ala.	90	Boren, Okla.	79
Breaux, La.	87	Pryor, Ark.	79
Nunn, Ga.	85	Bentsen, Texas	78
Shelby, Ala.	83		

Republicans

Dole, Kan.	98	Cochran, Miss.	95
McConnell, Ky.	98	Helms, N.C.	95
Thurmond, S.C.	98	Lott, Miss.	95
Gramm, Texas	97	Symms, Idaho	95
Burns, Mont.	95	Warner, Va.	95

Northern Democrats

Dixon, Ill.	77	Byrd, W.Va.	68
Exon, Neb.	77	Bingaman, N.M.	65
Bryan, Nev.	73	Reid, Nev.	62

House

Geren

Archer

Skelton

Southern Democrats

Geren, Texas	100%	Thomas, Ga.	97%
Huckaby, La.	100	Edwards, Texas	95
Hall, Texas	97	Laughlin, Texas	95
Montgomery, Miss.	97	Stenholm, Texas	95
Parker, Miss.	97	Tauzin, La.	95
Sarpalius, Texas	97		

Republicans

Archer, Texas	100	DeLay, Texas	100	McCandless, Calif.	100
Armey, Texas	100	Dickinson, Ala.	100	Michel, Ill.	100
Baker, La.	100	Doolittle, Calif.	100	Moorhead, Calif.	100
Ballenger, N.C.	100	Dreier, Calif.	100	Myers, Ind.	100
Barrett, Neb.	100	Ewing, Ill.	100	Nichols, Kan.	100
Bliley, Va.	100	Fields, Texas	100	Shaw, Fla.	100
Boehner, Ohio	100	Hancock, Mo.	100	Sundquist, Tenn.	100
Combest, Texas	100	Livingston, La.	100	Vander Jagt, Mich.	100
Dannemeyer, Calif.	100	Martin, N.Y.	100		

Northern Democrats

Skelton, Mo.	94	Volkmer, Mo.	89
Byron, Md.	92	Bilbray, Nev.	81

Highest Scorers — Opposition

Senate

Gore

Jeffords

Harkin

Southern Democrats

Gore, Tenn.	65%	Graham, Fla.	40%
Sasser, Tenn.	60	Fowler, Ga.	38
Sanford, N.C.	56		

Republicans

Jeffords, Vt.	61	Hatfield, Ore.	52
Chafee, R.I.	54	Cohen, Maine	43

Northern Democrats

Harkin, Iowa	94	Kerry, Mass.	90
Wellstone, Minn.	92	Lautenberg, N.J.	90
Adams, Wash.	90	Metzenbaum, Ohio	90

House

Lewis

Green

Dymally

Southern Democrats

Lewis, Ga.	97%	Lehman, Fla.	92%
Washington, Texas	97	Smith, Fla.	89
Ford, Tenn.	94		

Republicans

Green, N.Y.	72	Gilman, N.Y.	43
Morella, Md.	58	Shays, Conn.	43
Fish, N.Y	43		

Northern Democrats

Dymally, Calif.	100	Rangel, N.Y.	100
Flake, N.Y.	100	Scheuer, N.Y.	100
Owens, N.Y.	100	Stokes, Ohio	100
Payne, N.J.	100	Weiss, N.Y.	100

a political scientist who had studied the conservative coalition, a vote for defense spending was also a jobs vote. "Defense bases and industry are disproportionately Southern," said Rohde.

The result was that in depressed Southern states such as Louisiana, Mississippi and Arkansas, Southern politicians voted to maintain or increase military spending because it was linked to the economic health of the region.

In the House, Southerners were similarly enthusiastic defenders of defense spending. Two of the defense votes involved the Iraq war; the other four, defense spending.

Rep. Butler Derrick of South Carolina, who was appointed Democratic deputy whip in 1991, said that along with having a lot of military bases, Southerners had a 200-year history of supporting defense. And, distant as it sounded, the experience of the Civil War remained a potent symbol in the South of the need for a strong defense.

"Southerners tend to be more defense-oriented. It's inbred in the Southern mind," Derrick said. "After all, we're the only part of the country that's ever been invaded."

Academics and members of Congress believed the conservative coalition was likely to remain in eclipse, particularly if the economy remained shaky.

Crime's Influence

On crime issues, the conservative coalition appeared on six votes in the Senate and nine in the House.

The House crime votes largely involved the death penalty and gun control. Opinion was deeply divided among members, however, about the significance of those votes.

"If there is any issue that brings the Democratic moderate into a more conservative position, it is crime and the threat of crime," said Rep. William Lehman, D-Fla. "The more crime in the streets, the more conservative Democrats become."

Members and academics agreed that taking a tough stand on crime — once viewed as a vote representative of conservative whites — now also drew support from urban and rural blacks who feared crime in their neighborhoods.

"People, both white and black and yellow and red and of every economic background, are concerned about crime," said Michigan State's Rohde.

"They want government to do something to protect them against crime, and civil liberties are not a big concern in that equation."

When the vote came on the death penalty, black constituents were willing to back politicians who supported it even though proportionally many more blacks than whites were on death row.

"One of the peculiarities of civil liberties is that they don't have popular support. They are an issue primarily for elites," Rohde said.

Moreover, the death penalty was getting increasing support nationwide, said House leadership staff members. One vote in 1991 was on whether to drop the death penalty for drug kingpins. Southern conservatives overwhelmingly voted to retain it, but so did nearly half of the 177 Northern Democrats who cast a vote on that issue.

"What we can't figure out is why anybody votes against the death penalty," said a Democratic House leadership staff member. "Everybody is on that bandwagon. We don't view death penalty support as a particularly Southern conservative position."

On gun control, although the conservative coalition stood squarely against federal intervention, House politics on the issue was perceived as breaking more along urban-rural lines, said staff and academics.

Indeed, one of the most conservative of the anti-gun control initiatives offered in 1991 came from a rural Northern Democrat, Rep. Harold L. Volkmer, Mo. Volkmer was successful in getting the House to drop a prohibition on the sale of 13 types of semiautomatic assault weapons and provisions that would have made it illegal to own or sell ammunition clips of more than seven rounds.

In the Senate, conservative Southern Democrats played perhaps their most crucial role on a vote where the conservative coalition did not actually emerge. That was the confirmation of Bush's nominee to the Supreme Court, Clarence Thomas.

Southern Democrats split on that highly charged, 52-48 vote — eight voted for Thomas' confirmation, and nine voted against him. So even though a majority of Southern Democrats voted with a majority of Northern Democrats, it was the Southern conservatives who provided the margin of victory for the president.

In the absence of those votes, Thomas would not have been confirmed.

By casting a vote for Thomas, conservative Southern Democrats had a rare chance to support both the White House position and the preference of their black constituents.

Polls on support for Thomas among blacks showed that despite Professor Anita F. Hill's charges of sexual harassment, the majority of blacks believed Thomas should be confirmed.

Sometimes the influence of Southern Democrats was most significant when the conservative coalition was invisible. For example, the House Democratic leadership's bill to overhaul campaign finance laws was delayed for months until the leadership framed it in such a way that it would draw Southern Democrats' support.

Those flashes of influence, however, were just flashes. And academics and members of Congress believed the conservative coalition was likely to remain in eclipse, particularly if the economy remained shaky.

"Historically, economic issues are some of the few areas on which Northern and Southern Dems do agree," said Rohde, who predicted that the economy would help unify the parties and militate against any revival of the conservative coalition.

Rep. Rick Boucher, D-Va., who represented a rural district, said even his most conservative, white constituents cared most about seeing more federal money spent at home.

"The phenomenon at play in my area is that, as the recession worsens, people have seen the need for federal assistance more clearly," Boucher said. "Even people who in better times might have had a more conservative view are putting that aside in favor of a more practical approach." ■

Conservative Coalition Definitions

Conservative coalition. As used in this study, "conservative coalition" means a voting alliance of Republicans and Southern Democrats against the Northern Democrats in Congress. This meaning, rather than any philosophic definition of the conservative position, provides the basis for CQ's selection of coalition votes.

Conservative coalition support score. Percentage of conservative coalition votes on which a member voted "yea" or "nay" *in agreement* with the position of the conservative coalition. Failures to vote, even if a member announced a stand, lowered the score. (Scores for individual members were also computed that exclude absences.)

Conservative coalition vote. Any vote in the Senate or the House on which a majority of voting Southern Democrats and a majority of voting Republicans opposed the stand taken by a majority of voting Northern Democrats. Votes on which there was an even division within the ranks of voting Northern Democrats, Southern Democrats or Republicans were not included.

Conservative coalition opposition score. Percentage of conservative coalition votes on which a member voted "yea" or "nay" *in disagreement* with the position of the conservative coalition. Failures to vote, even if a member announced a stand, lowered the score. (Scores for individual members were also computed that exclude absences.)

Average Scores

Scores for 1990 are in parentheses:

Coalition Support	Southern Democrats		Republicans		Northern Democrats	
Senate	67%	(69)	81%	(80)	32%	(28)
House	66	(66)	86	(82)	29	(26)

Coalition Opposition	Southern Democrats		Republicans		Northern Democrats	
Senate	28%	(29)	16%	(16)	65%	(70)
House	30	(30)	10	(14)	67	(70)

Regional Scores

Scores for 1990 are in parentheses:

Regional Support

	East		West		South		Midwest	
Democrats								
Senate	24%	(20)	41%	(32)	67%	(69)	35%	(34)
House	27	(25)	26	(23)	66	(66)	34	(29)
Republicans								
Senate	65%	(63)	83%	(80)	93%	(95)	80%	(81)
House	78	(68)	90	(87)	88	(91)	89	(83)

Regional Opposition

	East		West		South		Midwest	
Democrats								
Senate	75%	(78)	55%	(64)	28%	(29)	61%	(65)
House	70	(69)	67	(74)	30	(30)	63	(67)
Republicans								
Senate	33%	(35)	13%	(13)	5%	(4)	18%	(16)
House	20	(28)	7	(10)	5	(6)	10	(13)

(CQ defines regions of the United States as follows: ***East:*** *Conn., Del., Maine, Md., Mass., N.H., N.J., N.Y., Pa., R.I., Vt., W.Va.* ***West:*** *Alaska, Ariz., Calif., Colo., Hawaii, Idaho, Mont., Nev., N.M., Ore., Utah, Wash., Wyo.* ***South:*** *Ala., Ark., Fla., Ga., Ky., La., Miss., N.C., Okla., S.C., Tenn., Texas, Va.* ***Midwest:*** *Ill., Ind., Iowa, Kan., Mich., Minn., Mo., Neb., N.D., Ohio, S.D., Wis.)*

Conservative Coalition History

Following is the percentage of the recorded votes for both chambers of Congress on which the coalition appeared and its percentage of victories:

Year	Appearances	Victories	Year	Appearances	Victories
1991	11%	91%	1980	18%	72%
1990	11	82	1979	20	70
1989	11	87	1978	21	52
1988	9	89	1977	26	68
1987	8	93	1976	24	58
1986	16	87	1975	28	50
1985	14	89	1974	24	59
1984	16	83	1973	23	61
1983	15	77	1972	27	69
1982	18	85	1971	30	83
1981	21	92	1970	22	66

Conservative Coalition Vote Breakdown

Following is a list of votes, by roll call number, cast in 1991 on which a majority of Southern Democrats and a majority of Republicans voted against a majority of all other Democrats.

House

32 Victories

Vote #	Vote Captions
8	Sanctions against Iraq
9	Force against Iraq
41	RTC financing
56	RTC financing
97	SDI funding
101	Troops overseas
103	Troops in South Korea
114	Fast-track procedures
127	Civil Rights Act
140	Space station funding
141	Space station funding
144	MX missile rail garrison
155	Foreign aid/India
175	Foreign aid/Soviet Union
183	Foreign aid/South Africa
261	Defense authorization
308	Arts funding restrictions
309	Arts funding restrictions
311	Crime bill/death penalty
312	Crime bill/death penalty
314	Arts funding restrictions
318	Crime bill/assault weapons
319	Crime bill/death penalty
320	Crime Bill/search and seizure
322	Crime bill/death penalty
324	Crime bill/death penalty
335	Minority preferences
348	Wetlands
354	Foreign aid/abortion
356	Export controls
366	Banking reform
429	California desert protection/hunting

5 Defeats

Vote #	Vote Captions
81	Handgun waiting period
83	Handgun waiting period
193	Arts funding restrictions
250	Flight attendant duty time
341	Arts funding restrictions

Senate

38 Victories

Vote #	Vote Captions
15	Parents in combat
21	RTC financing
39	Navy funding USS *Kennedy*
44	CFTC reauthorization
46	Social Security tax cuts
49	Defense spending
50	Defense spending
51	Defense spending
74	Campaign finance
90	Federal highway funding
91	Federal highway funding
102	Crime bill/death penalty
106	Crime bill/death penalty
108	Crime bill/death penalty
109	Crime bill/death penalty
111	Crime bill/death penalty
117	Crime bill/prisoner literacy
119	Defense nuclear waste
121	Superconducting super collider
161	Prisoners' Pell grants
162	HIV testing
168	SDI deployment
171	SDI funding
172	ABM deployment
174	B-2 bomber
176	SRAM-T missile
179	Tobacco products
182	Defense to domestic spending transfer
188	Sex survey funding
195	Grazing fees
197	Arts funding restrictions
243	Robert M. Gates confirmation
248	Older Americans Act/pensions
257	Banking reform
262	Banking reform
266	Dairy price supports
267	Light trucks tariffs
280	RTC funding

2 Defeats

Vote #	Vote Captions
97	Federal highway funding
242	National energy policy

	1	2	3
Alabama			
Heflin	88	10	90
Shelby	83	18	83
Alaska			
Murkowski	90	10	90
Stevens	85	10	89
Arizona			
DeConcini	48	45	51
McCain	90	8	92
Arkansas			
Bumpers	70	30	70
Pryor	28	8	79
California			
Cranston	15	65	19
Seymour	90	8	92
Colorado			
Wirth	20	75	21
Brown	85	13	87
Connecticut			
Dodd	43	58	43
Lieberman	38	63	38
Delaware			
Biden	10	85	11
Roth	68	28	71
Florida			
Graham	60	40	60
Mack	90	8	92
Georgia			
Fowler	63	38	63
Nunn	83	15	85
Hawaii			
Akaka	25	75	25
Inouye	50	43	54
Idaho			
Craig	90	8	92
Symms	93	5	95
Illinois			
Dixon	75	23	77
Simon	18	80	18
Indiana			
Coats	85	15	85
Lugar	83	10	89
Iowa			
Harkin	5	75	6
Grassley	83	18	83
Kansas			
Dole	98	3	98
Kassebaum	75	23	77
Kentucky			
Ford	95	5	95
McConnell	98	3	98
Louisiana			
Breaux	83	13	87
Johnston	80	18	82
Maine			
Mitchell	20	80	20
Cohen	58	43	58
Maryland			
Mikulski	33	65	33
Sarbanes	13	88	13
Massachusetts			
Kennedy	13	88	13
Kerry	10	90	10
Michigan			
Levin	30	70	30
Riegle	28	73	28
Minnesota			
Wellstone	8	88	8
Durenberger	65	35	65
Mississippi			
Cochran	95	5	95
Lott	93	5	95
Missouri			
Bond	85	15	85
Danforth	68	28	71
Montana			
Baucus	45	55	45
Burns	95	5	95
Nebraska			
Exon	75	23	77
Kerrey	45	35	56
Nevada			
Bryan	73	28	73
Reid	60	38	62
New Hampshire			
Rudman	80	20	80
Smith	85	15	85
New Jersey			
Bradley	15	83	15
Lautenberg	10	90	10
New Mexico			
Bingaman	65	35	65
Domenici	88	10	90
New York			
Moynihan	25	75	25
D'Amato	80	20	80
North Carolina			
Sanford	43	55	44
Helms	90	5	95
North Dakota			
Burdick	38	58	39
Conrad	43	58	43
Ohio			
Glenn	38	63	38
Metzenbaum	10	90	10
Oklahoma			
Boren	75	20	79
Nickles	93	8	93
Oregon			
Hatfield	48	52	48
Packwood	75	23	77
Pennsylvania			
Wofford [1]	22	72	23
Specter	75	25	75
Rhode Island			
Pell	20	78	21
Chafee	45	52	46
South Carolina			
Hollings	65	35	65
Thurmond	98	3	98
South Dakota			
Daschle	38	63	38
Pressler	85	15	85
Tennessee			
Gore	35	65	35
Sasser	40	60	40
Texas			
Bentsen	78	23	78
Gramm	90	3	97
Utah			
Garn	70	10	88
Hatch	88	10	90
Vermont			
Leahy	18	80	18
Jeffords	35	55	39
Virginia			
Robb	70	30	70
Warner	95	5	95
Washington			
Adams	10	90	10
Gorton	80	20	80
West Virginia			
Byrd	68	33	68
Rockefeller	28	73	28
Wisconsin			
Kohl	40	58	41
Kasten	78	23	78
Wyoming			
Simpson	88	10	90
Wallop	83	10	89

Democrats ***Republicans***

Conservative Coalition Support and Opposition: Senate

1. Conservative Coalition Support, 1991. Percentage of 40 recorded votes in 1991 on which the conservative coalition appeared and on which a senator voted "yea" or "nay" *in agreement* with the position of the conservative coalition. Failures to vote lowered both support and opposition scores.

2. Conservative Coalition Opposition, 1991. Percentage of 40 recorded votes in 1991 on which the conservative coalition appeared and on which a senator voted "yea" or "nay" *in disagreement* with the position of the conservative coalition. Failures to vote lowered both support and opposition scores.

3. Conservative Coalition Support, 1991. Percentage of 40 recorded votes in 1991 on which the conservative coalition appeared and on which a senator was present and voted "yea" or "nay" *in agreement* with the position of the conservative coalition. In this version of the study, absences were not counted; therefore, failures to vote did not lower support or opposition scores. Opposition scores, not listed here, are the inverse of the support score; i.e., the opposition score is equal to 100 percent minus the individual's support score.

[1] *Harris Wofford, D-Pa., was sworn in May 9, 1991, to succeed John Heinz, R, who died in a plane crash April 4, 1991. Heinz was eligible for three of the 40 conservative coalition votes in 1991. His conservative coalition support score was 33 percent; his opposition score was 67 percent; and his support score, adjusted for absences, was 33 percent in 1991. Wofford was eligible for 32 of the 40 conservative coalition votes in 1991.*

Conservative Coalition Support and Opposition: House

1. Conservative Coalition Support, 1991. Percentage of 37 recorded votes in 1991 on which the conservative coalition appeared and on which a representative voted "yea" or "nay" *in agreement* with the position of the conservative coalition. Failures to vote lowered both support and opposition scores.

2. Conservative Coalition Opposition, 1991. Percentage of 37 recorded votes in 1991 on which the conservative coalition appeared and on which a representative voted "yea" or "nay" *in disagreement* with the position of the conservative coalition. Failures to vote lowered both support and opposition scores.

3. Conservative Coalition Support, 1991. Percentage of 37 recorded votes in 1991 on which the conservative coalition appeared and on which a representative was present and voted "yea" or "nay" *in agreement* with the position of the conservative coalition. In this version of the study, absences were not counted; therefore, failures to vote did not lower support or opposition scores. Opposition scores, not listed here, are the inverse of the support score; i.e., the opposition score is equal to 100 percent minus the individual's support score.

[1] *Ed Pastor, D-Ariz., was sworn in Oct. 3, 1991, to succeed Morris K. Udall, D, who resigned May 4, 1991. Udall was eligible for four of the 37 conservative coalition votes in 1991. He voted on none of them. Pastor was eligible for 17 conservative coalition votes in 1991.*

[2] *Thomas W. Ewing, R-Ill., was sworn in July 10, 1991, to succeed Edward Madigan, R, who resigned March 8, 1991, after being appointed secretary of Agriculture. Madigan was eligible for two of the conservative coalition votes in 1991. His conservative coalition support score was 100 percent; his opposition score was 0 percent; and his support score, adjusted for absences, was 100 percent in 1991. Ewing was eligible for 19 conservative coalition votes in 1991.*

[3] *John Olver, D-Mass., was sworn in June 18, 1991, to succeed Silvio O. Conte, R, who died Feb. 8, 1991. Conte was eligible for two of the 37 conservative coalition votes in 1991. His conservative coalition support score was 0 percent; his opposition score was 100 percent; and his support score, adjusted for absences, was 0 percent in 1991. Olver was eligible for 22 conservative coalition votes in 1991.*

[4] *Lucien E. Blackwell, D-Pa., was sworn in Nov. 13, 1991, to succeed William H. Gray III, D, who resigned Sept. 11, 1991. Gray was eligible for 19 of the 37 conservative coalition votes in 1991. His conservative coalition support score was 11 percent; his opposition score was 53 percent; and his support score, adjusted for absences, was 17 percent in 1991. Blackwell was eligible for one conservative coalition vote in 1991.*

[5] *Sam Johnson, R-Texas, was sworn in May 22, 1991, to succeed Steve Bartlett, R, who resigned March 11, 1991. Bartlett was eligible for two of the 37 conservative coalition votes in 1991. His conservative coalition support score was 100 percent; his opposition score was 0 percent; and his support score, adjusted for absences, was 100 percent in 1991. Johnson was eligible for 28 conservative coalition votes in 1991.*

[6] *George F. Allen, R-Va., was sworn in Nov. 12, 1991, to succeed D. French Slaughter Jr., R, who resigned Nov. 5, 1991. Slaughter was eligible for 36 of the 37 conservative coalition votes in 1991. His conservative coalition support score was 56 percent; his opposition score was 3 percent; and his support score, adjusted for absences, was 95 percent in 1991. Allen was eligible for one conservative coalition vote in 1991.*

[7] *Thomas S. Foley, D-Wash., as Speaker of the House, voted at his discretion on two of the 37 conservative coalition votes in 1991, for a support score of 0 percent.*

KEY

† Not eligible for all votes or voted "present" to avoid conflict of interest on one or more votes in 1991. Ineligible votes are excluded from calculation of scores.

Democrats ***Republicans***
Independent

	1	2	3
Alabama			
1 ***Callahan***	70	3	96
2 ***Dickinson***	95	0	100
3 Browder	92	5	94
4 Bevill	92	8	92
5 Cramer	89	11	89
6 Erdreich	86	14	86
7 Harris	89	11	89
Alaska			
AL ***Young***	86	11	89
Arizona			
1 ***Rhodes***	92	3	97
2 Pastor [1]	24	76	24
3 ***Stump***	97	3	97
4 ***Kyl***	97	3	97
5 ***Kolbe***	89	11	89
Arkansas			
1 Alexander	54	43	56
2 Thornton	65	30	69
3 ***Hammerschmidt***	89	3	97
4 Anthony	59	38	61
California			
1 ***Riggs***	78	19	81
2 ***Herger***	95	3	97
3 Matsui	16	62	21
4 Fazio	24	68	26
5 Pelosi	3	86	3
6 Boxer	8	73	10
7 Miller	3	89	3
8 Dellums	3	92	3
9 Stark	8	86	9
10 Edwards	8	89	8
11 Lantos	35	62	36
12 ***Campbell***	62	30	68
13 Mineta	5	92	6
14 ***Doolittle***	95	0	100
15 Condit	73	27	73
16 Panetta	24	73	25
17 Dooley	62	38	62
18 Lehman	46	51	47
19 ***Lagomarsino***	95	5	95
20 ***Thomas***	95	3	97
21 ***Gallegly***	95	3	97
22 ***Moorhead***	95	0	100
23 Beilenson	16	84	16
24 Waxman	14	70	16
25 Roybal	11	76	13
26 Berman	14	81	14
27 Levine	22	51	30
28 Dixon	14	84	14
29 Waters	5	84	6
30 Martinez	30	43	41
31 Dymally	0	76	0
32 Anderson	38	59	39
33 ***Dreier***	100	0	100
34 Torres	14	84	14
35 ***Lewis***	84	5	94
36 Brown	30	65	31
37 ***McCandless***	97	0	100
38 ***Dornan***	95	5	95
39 ***Dannemeyer***	86	0	100
40 ***Cox***	89	8	92
41 ***Lowery***	89	5	94
42 ***Rohrabacher***	89	11	89
43 ***Packard***	92	5	94
44 ***Cunningham***	97	3	97
45 ***Hunter***	92	5	94
Colorado			
1 Schroeder	11	89	11
2 Skaggs	24	76	24
3 Campbell	62	24	72
4 ***Allard***	95	5	95
5 ***Hefley***	95	5	95
6 ***Schaefer***	92	5	94
Connecticut			
1 Kennelly	24	76	24
2 Gejdenson	11	89	11
3 DeLauro	19	78	19
4 ***Shays***	57	43	57
5 ***Franks***	97	3	97
6 ***Johnson***	68	32	68
Delaware			
AL Carper	59	38	61
Florida			
1 Hutto	92	5	94
2 Peterson	73	27	73
3 Bennett	59	41	59
4 ***James***	86	14	86
5 ***McCollum***	86	3	97
6 ***Stearns***	95	5	95
7 Gibbons	49	51	49
8 ***Young***	78	16	83
9 ***Bilirakis***	78	14	85
10 ***Ireland***	92	3	97
11 Bacchus	51	49	51
12 ***Lewis***	95	3	97
13 ***Goss***	86	14	86
14 Johnston	24	70	26
15 ***Shaw***	97	0	100
16 Smith	11	86	11
17 Lehman	5	62	8
18 ***Ros-Lehtinen***	73	24	75
19 Fascell	32	68	32
Georgia			
1 Thomas	97	3	97
2 Hatcher	68	22	76
3 Ray	89	11	89
4 Jones	32	65	33
5 Lewis	3	89	3
6 ***Gingrich***	95	5	95
7 Darden	89	11	89
8 Rowland	84	5	94
9 Jenkins	84	5	94
10 Barnard	89	5	94
Hawaii			
1 Abercrombie	8	92	8
2 Mink	3	97	3
Idaho			
1 LaRocco	59	35	63
2 Stallings	76	19	80
Illinois			
1 Hayes	5	95	5
2 Savage	5	73	7
3 Russo	43	57	43
4 Sangmeister	43	51	46
5 Lipinski	68	30	69
6 ***Hyde***	92	8	92
7 Collins	5	89	6
8 Rostenkowski	51	43	54
9 Yates	5	92	6
10 ***Porter***	78	22	78
11 Annunzio	51	49	51
12 ***Crane***	89	5	94
13 ***Fawell***	84	11	89
14 ***Hastert***	95	3	97
15 ***Ewing*** [2]	100	0	100
16 Cox	16	84	16
17 Evans	11	89	11
18 ***Michel***	95	0	100
19 Bruce	54	46	54
20 Durbin	30	70	30
21 Costello	68	32	68
22 Poshard	57	43	57
Indiana			
1 Visclosky	32	68	32
2 Sharp	38	57	40
3 Roemer	76	24	76

	1	2	3
4 Long	59	41	59
5 Jontz	22	78	22
6 ***Burton***	97	3	97
7 ***Myers***	100	0	100
8 McCloskey	30	70	30
9 Hamilton	57	43	57
10 Jacobs	32	65	33
Iowa			
1 ***Leach***	59	41	59
2 ***Nussle***	81	19	81
3 Nagle	24	73	25
4 Smith	41	54	43
5 ***Lightfoot***	95	5	95
6 ***Grandy***	76	24	76
Kansas			
1 ***Roberts***	97	3	97
2 Slattery	76	24	76
3 ***Meyers***	76	22	78
4 Glickman	62	30	68
5 ***Nichols***	100	0	100
Kentucky			
1 Hubbard	78	19	81
2 Natcher	57	43	57
3 Mazzoli	35	65	35
4 ***Bunning***	97	3	97
5 ***Rogers***	86	5	94
6 ***Hopkins***	30	3	92
7 Perkins	43	57	43
Louisiana			
1 ***Livingston***	100	0	100
2 Jefferson	19	68	22
3 Tauzin	95	5	95
4 ***McCrery***	95	3	97
5 Huckaby	86	0	100
6 ***Baker***	92	0	100
7 Hayes	86	11	89
8 ***Holloway***	68	3	96
Maine			
1 Andrews	8	92	8
2 ***Snowe***	89	11	89
Maryland			
1 ***Gilchrest***	86	14	86
2 ***Bentley***	84	14	86
3 Cardin	22	78	22
4 McMillen	62	38	62
5 Hoyer	19	81	19
6 Byron	89	8	92
7 Mfume	5	95	5
8 ***Morella***	41	57	42
Massachusetts			
1 Olver[3]	5	95	5
2 Neal	19	81	19
3 Early	32	65	33
4 Frank	16	84	16
5 Atkins	16	84	16
6 Mavroules	32	59	35
7 Markey	11	89	11
8 Kennedy	14	86	14
9 Moakley	22	73	23
10 Studds	5	92	6
11 Donnelly	30	65	31
Michigan			
1 Conyers	3	89	3
2 ***Pursell***	78	14	85
3 Wolpe	3	97	3
4 ***Upton***	86	14	86
5 ***Henry***	78	22	78
6 Carr	43	41	52
7 Kildee	14	86	14
8 Traxler	41	49	45
9 ***Vander Jagt***	92	0	100
10 ***Camp***	95	5	95
11 ***Davis***	92	5	94
12 Bonior	8	89	8
13 Collins	5	95	5
14 Hertel	14	86	14
15 Ford	16	73	18
16 Dingell	51	49	51
17 Levin	8	92	8
18 ***Broomfield***	86	14	86
Minnesota			
1 Penny	57	41	58
2 ***Weber***	92	8	92
3 ***Ramstad***	86	14	86
4 Vento	5	86	6

	1	2	3
5 Sabo	8	89	8
6 Sikorski	11	89	11
7 Peterson	57	43	57
8 Oberstar	16	76	18
Mississippi			
1 Whitten	57	27	68
2 Espy	41	57	42
3 Montgomery	97	3	97
4 Parker	95	3	97
5 Taylor	86	14	86
Missouri			
1 Clay	3	86	3
2 Horn	43	57	43
3 Gephardt	22	70	24
4 Skelton	92	5	94
5 Wheat	5	95	5
6 ***Coleman***	78	16	83
7 ***Hancock***	100	0	100
8 ***Emerson***	97	3	97
9 Volkmer	89	11	89
Montana			
1 Williams	32	51	39
2 ***Marlenee***	89	3	97
Nebraska			
1 ***Bereuter***	78	22	78
2 Hoagland	54	46	54
3 ***Barrett***	97	0	100
Nevada			
1 Bilbray	78	19	81
2 ***Vucanovich***	95	5	95
New Hampshire			
1 ***Zeliff***	97	3	97
2 Swett	78	22	78
New Jersey			
1 Andrews	41	59	41
2 Hughes	41	59	41
3 Pallone	54	46	54
4 ***Smith***	73	24	75
5 ***Roukema***	62	35	64
6 Dwyer	27	68	29
7 ***Rinaldo***	81	19	81
8 Roe	30	65	31
9 Torricelli	38	54	41
10 Payne	0	97	0
11 ***Gallo***	84	14	86
12 ***Zimmer***	89	11	89
13 ***Saxton***	86	11	89
14 Guarini	54	43	56
New Mexico			
1 ***Schiff***	86	14	86
2 ***Skeen***	89	11	89
3 Richardson	54	46	54
New York			
1 Hochbrueckner	32	68	32
2 Downey	8	92	8
3 Mrazek	3	70	4
4 ***Lent***	81	11	88
5 ***McGrath***	68	24	74
6 Flake	0	95	0
7 Ackerman	8	78	9
8 Scheuer	0	97	0
9 Manton	22	76	22
10 Schumer	19	78	19
11 Towns	3	86	3
12 Owens	0	97	0
13 Solarz	24	76	24
14 ***Molinari***	76	24	76
15 ***Green***	27	70	28
16 Rangel	0	97	0
17 Weiss	0	97	0
18 Serrano	5	89	6
19 Engel	14	86	14
20 Lowey	8	92	8
21 ***Fish***	57	43	57
22 ***Gilman***	57	43	57
23 McNulty	35	65	35
24 ***Solomon***	95	3	97
25 ***Boehlert***	62	38	62
26 ***Martin***	84	0	100
27 ***Walsh***	76	22	78
28 McHugh	24	76	24
29 ***Horton***	68	32	68
30 Slaughter	24	73	25
31 ***Paxon***	97	3	97

	1	2	3
32 LaFalce	22	78	22
33 Nowak	22	78	22
34 ***Houghton***	65	30	69
North Carolina			
1 Jones	78	19	81
2 Valentine	89	8	92
3 Lancaster	78	22	78
4 Price	59	41	59
5 Neal	62	24	72
6 ***Coble***	86	11	89
7 Rose	38	57	40
8 Hefner	78	19	81
9 ***McMillan***	92	8	92
10 ***Ballenger***	100	0	100
11 ***Taylor***	95	5	95
North Dakota			
AL Dorgan	51	49	51
Ohio			
1 Luken	76	24	76
2 ***Gradison***	84	8	91
3 Hall	38	62	38
4 ***Oxley***	95	5	95
5 ***Gillmor***	95	5	95
6 ***McEwen***	95	3	97
7 ***Hobson***	95	5	95
8 ***Boehner***	97	0	100
9 Kaptur	41	54	43
10 ***Miller***	86	8	91
11 Eckart	19	81	19
12 ***Kasich***	97	3	97
13 Pease	30	70	30
14 Sawyer	14	86	14
15 ***Wylie***	89	11	89
16 ***Regula***	86	14	86
17 Traficant	46	54	46
18 Applegate	65	30	69
19 Feighan	8	92	8
20 Oakar	22	78	22
21 Stokes	0	100	0
Oklahoma			
1 ***Inhofe***	97	3	97
2 Synar	19	78	19
3 Brewster	84	14	86
4 McCurdy	84	14	86
5 ***Edwards***	84	3	97
6 English	86	14	86
Oregon			
1 AuCoin	8	89	8
2 ***Smith***	95	5	95
3 Wyden	24	73	25
4 DeFazio	27	68	29
5 Kopetski	27	70	28
Pennsylvania			
1 Foglietta	5	89	6
2 Blackwell[4]	0	100	0
3 Borski	38	54	41
4 Kolter	62	35	64
5 ***Schulze***	92	3	97
6 Yatron	54	38	59
7 ***Weldon***	76	22	78
8 Kostmayer	16	81	17
9 ***Shuster***	92	3	97
10 ***McDade***	70	19	79
11 Kanjorski	59	41	59
12 Murtha	62	35	64
13 ***Coughlin***	84	16	84
14 Coyne	16	81	17
15 ***Ritter***	97	3	97
16 ***Walker***	97	3	97
17 ***Gekas***	97	3	97
18 ***Santorum***	97	3	97
19 ***Goodling***	78	8	91
20 Gaydos	51	35	59
21 ***Ridge***	89	8	92
22 Murphy	51	38	58
23 ***Clinger***	81	16	83
Rhode Island			
1 ***Machtley***	59	38	61
2 Reed	27	70	28
South Carolina			
1 ***Ravenel***	84	16	84
2 ***Spence***	86	8	91
3 Derrick	46	51	47
4 Patterson	86	14	86
5 Spratt	73	27	73
6 Tallon	81	19	81

	1	2	3
South Dakota			
AL Johnson	54	46	54
Tennessee			
1 ***Quillen***	92	3	97
2 ***Duncan***	86	11	89
3 Lloyd	78	8	91
4 Cooper †	78	22	78
5 Clement	78	22	78
6 Gordon	68	32	68
7 ***Sundquist***	95	0	100
8 Tanner	81	5	94
9 Ford	5	84	6
Texas			
1 Chapman	84	8	91
2 Wilson	86	5	94
3 ***Johnson***[5]	93	4	96
4 Hall	95	3	97
5 Bryant	38	57	40
6 ***Barton***	89	5	94
7 ***Archer***	100	0	100
8 ***Fields***	97	0	100
9 Brooks	62	30	68
10 Pickle	54	43	56
11 Edwards	95	5	95
12 Geren	100	0	100
13 Sarpalius	97	3	97
14 Laughlin	95	5	95
15 de la Garza	51	38	58
16 Coleman	54	43	56
17 Stenholm	95	5	95
18 Washington	3	92	3
19 ***Combest***	100	0	100
20 Gonzalez	16	84	16
21 ***Smith***	95	5	95
22 ***DeLay***	92	0	100
23 Bustamante	41	43	48
24 Frost	54	43	56
25 Andrews	81	16	83
26 ***Armey***	100	0	100
27 Ortiz	73	24	75
Utah			
1 ***Hansen***	95	3	97
2 Owens	27	68	29
3 Orton	68	27	71
Vermont			
AL *Sanders*	14	86	14
Virginia			
1 ***Bateman***	86	11	89
2 Pickett	89	8	92
3 ***Bliley***	97	0	100
4 Sisisky	76	14	85
5 Payne	84	14	86
6 Olin	65	35	65
7 ***Allen***[6]	100	0	100
8 Moran	30	68	31
9 Boucher	43	49	47
10 ***Wolf***	92	8	92
Washington			
1 ***Miller***	65	27	71
2 Swift	16	81	17
3 Unsoeld	19	78	19
4 ***Morrison***	86	14	86
5 Foley[7]			
6 Dicks	43	54	44
7 McDermott	8	92	8
8 ***Chandler***	84	11	89
West Virginia			
1 Mollohan	62	38	62
2 Staggers	38	62	38
3 Wise	41	54	43
4 Rahall	49	46	51
Wisconsin			
1 Aspin	51	49	51
2 ***Klug***	76	22	78
3 ***Gunderson***	92	8	92
4 Kleczka	22	73	23
5 Moody	16	81	17
6 ***Petri***	89	11	89
7 Obey	24	73	25
8 ***Roth***	84	16	84
9 ***Sensenbrenner***	86	14	86
Wyoming			
AL ***Thomas***	92	3	97

Voting Participation At Record High

Congress may not have received good grades from the public for its performance in 1991, but members could at least say they rarely missed a class. Congressional voting participation continued at a record high in 1991.

For the third straight year, members of both chambers on average voted on 95 percent of all roll call votes. This remained the highest level of voting participation for Congress since Congressional Quarterly began tracking recorded votes in 1953.

Senators on average voted 97 percent of the time, the same rate as in 1990.

House members averaged 95 percent, a 1 percentage-point increase over 1990.

Since voting participation hit a low of 79 percent in 1970, scores had made a dramatic comeback, peaking in the past three years. The indicator struck home with voters, and it could cost dearly at the polls if a member missed many votes, according to members and congressional observers. It was also a factor over which members had control.

"Voters view [voting participation] as a significant statement about a member's performance," said Rep. Timothy J. Penny, D-Minn., who had consistently scored perfect or near perfect participation since taking office in 1983.

"If the anti-incumbent mood persists, it's an issue that members would just as soon not have raised."

Voting participation scores were often used to gauge a member's dedication to his or her job. But they were meant only to give a rough approximation of members' attendance during a given year.

Committee hearings, bill drafting sessions, bill conferences and meetings with constituents all competed for members' time, and members had to decide which activities were most important to constituents.

In recent years, congressional challengers had effectively used low scores in their campaigns against incumbents.

While running for governor in 1991, Rep. Larry J. Hopkins, R-Ky., chalked up a House-low 38 percent attendance for roll call votes. Hopkins' opponent accused him of abandoning his job in Washington, and the issue became a factor in the race that Hopkins eventually lost by almost 30 percentage points.

Congressional leaders had boosted participation scores by scheduling almost 90 percent of the votes in 1991 between Tuesday and Thursday. This allowed members to spend long weekends visiting their constituents.

"Since [House Speaker Thomas S.] Foley took over, the schedule has become more predictable," Penny said. "It has helped members to plan their lives better, knowing what day of the week to be in town."

Members were also called to the floor less often in 1991. Congress recorded one of the lowest number of roll call votes in 20 years. The Senate took 280 recorded votes, 46 fewer than in 1990 and the lowest number since 1969. The House took 428 votes, a drop-off of 83 votes from 1990 and also one of the lowest in 20 years.

Perfect Scores

Twenty-nine members of Congress participated in every recorded vote in 1991. Eight House members scored 100 percent. The 37-year record of William H. Natcher, D-Ky., remained unblemished. He had not missed a vote in his career, voting 13,055 times since 1954.

Twenty-one senators voted on every roll call in 1991. Robert C. Byrd, D-W.Va., had not missed a recorded vote since the Democrats regained control of the Senate in 1987.

In non-election years, members tended to vote more often because they did not need to return home to campaign.

But in 1991, campaigning took its toll on the voting participation of 16 members who either ran for higher office or were expected to do so in 1992. The 16 members on average took part in 82 percent of the votes, 13 points below the congressional average.

Two presidential hopefuls in the Senate, Tom Harkin, D-Iowa, and Bob Kerrey, D-Neb., scored 75 percent and 77 percent, respectively.

Only three other senators scored below 90 percent. Two were absent for health concerns: David Pryor, D-Ark., had a heart attack on April 16, and Alan Cranston, D-Calif., was recovering from prostate cancer. They scored 44 percent and 83 percent, respectively. Jesse Helms, R-N.C., scored 87 percent. His score suffered significantly when he returned to North Carolina briefly following a death in his family.

Five of the eight lowest scorers in the House were candidates in 1991 for other offices or were likely to be candidates for higher office in 1992.

Another low scorer, Democrat Harold E. Ford of Tennessee, had been indicted for bank, mail and tax fraud and was awaiting a new trial in his home state.

William Lehman, D-Fla., and Mervyn M. Dymally, D-Calif., both missed a significant number of votes due to illness. ■

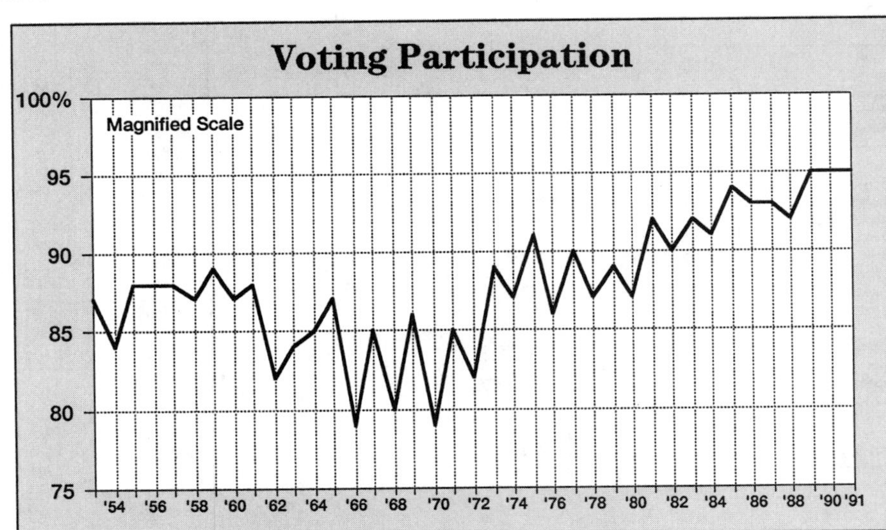

	1
Alabama	
Heflin	99
Shelby	100
Alaska	
Murkowski	99
Stevens	97
Arizona	
DeConcini	96
McCain	98
Arkansas	
Bumpers	99
Pryor #	44
California	
Cranston #	83
Seymour	96
Colorado	
Wirth	95
Brown	98
Connecticut	
Dodd	99
Lieberman	98
Delaware	
Biden	96
Roth	98
Florida	
Graham	98
Mack	99
Georgia	
Fowler	99
Nunn	98
Hawaii	
Akaka	99
Inouye	96
Idaho	
Craig	99
Symms	97
Illinois	
Dixon	97
Simon	99
Indiana	
Coats	99
Lugar	98

	1
Iowa	
Harkin	75
Grassley	100
Kansas	
Dole	100
Kassebaum	98
Kentucky	
Ford	99
McConnell	100
Louisiana	
Breaux	95
Johnston	99
Maine	
Mitchell	100
Cohen	100
Maryland	
Mikulski	99
Sarbanes	100
Massachusetts	
Kennedy	99
Kerry	100
Michigan	
Levin	100
Riegle	99
Minnesota	
Wellstone	98
Durenberger	98
Mississippi	
Cochran	99
Lott	98
Missouri	
Bond	98
Danforth #	94
Montana	
Baucus	99
Burns	99
Nebraska	
Exon	99
Kerrey	77
Nevada	
Bryan	100
Reid	99

	1
New Hampshire	
Rudman	100
Smith	99
New Jersey	
Bradley #	95
Lautenberg	100
New Mexico	
Bingaman	98
Domenici	98
New York	
Moynihan	99
D'Amato	99
North Carolina	
Sanford	99
Helms #	87
North Dakota	
Burdick	98
Conrad	99
Ohio	
Glenn	97
Metzenbaum	99
Oklahoma	
Boren	99
Nickles	97
Oregon	
Hatfield	99
Packwood	97
Pennsylvania	
Wofford [1]	92
Specter #	99
Rhode Island	
Pell	99
Chafee	98
South Carolina	
Hollings	100
Thurmond	99
South Dakota	
Daschle	99
Pressler	99
Tennessee	
Gore	100
Sasser	100

KEY

\# Member absent a day or more in 1991 due to illness, or illness or death in family.

Democrats ***Republicans***

	1
Texas	
Bentsen	97
Gramm	97
Utah	
Garn	92
Hatch #	95
Vermont	
Leahy	99
Jeffords	94
Virginia	
Robb	100
Warner	100
Washington	
Adams	100
Gorton	100
West Virginia	
Byrd	100
Rockefeller	99
Wisconsin	
Kohl	99
Kasten	100
Wyoming	
Simpson	99
Wallop	96

Voting Participation: Senate

1. Voting Participation, 1991. Percentage of 280 recorded votes in 1991 on which a senator voted "yea" or "nay."

[1] Harris Wofford, D-Pa., was sworn in May 9, 1991, to succeed John Heinz, R, who died in a plane accident April 4, 1991. Heinz was eligible for 41 votes in 1991. Wofford was eligible for 226 of the 280 votes in 1991.

NOTE: In the past CQ has reported voting participation scores excluding sergeant-at-arms votes in the Senate. In 1991, the Senate took only one sergeant-at-arms vote.

Scores are rounded to nearest percentage, except that no scores are rounded up to 100 percent.

Voting Participation: House

1. Voting Participation, 1991. Percentage of 428 recorded votes in 1991 on which a representative voted "yea" or "nay."

2. Voting Participation, 1991. Percentage of 407 recorded votes in 1991 on which a representative voted "yea" or "nay." In this version of the study, votes of approval of the House Journal were not included.

[1] *Ed Pastor, D-Ariz., was sworn in Oct. 3, 1991, to succeed Morris K. Udall, D, who resigned May 4, 1991. Udall was eligible for 74 votes in 1991 — 70 not including votes to approve the Journal. Pastor was eligible for 152 votes in 1991, 148 not including votes to approve the Journal.*

[2] *Thomas W. Ewing, R-Ill., was sworn in July 10, 1991, to succeed Edward Madigan, R, who resigned March 8, 1991, after being appointed secretary of Agriculture. Madigan was eligible for 34 votes in 1991, 33 not including votes to approve the Journal. Ewing was eligible for 233 votes in 1991, 222 not including votes to approve the Journal.*

[3] *John Olver, D-Mass., was sworn in June 18, 1991, to succeed Silvio O. Conte, R, who died Feb. 8, 1991. Conte was eligible for 20 votes in 1991, 19 not including votes to approve the Journal. Olver was eligible for 278 votes in 1991, 265 not including votes to approve the Journal.*

[4] *Lucien E. Blackwell, D-Pa., was sworn in Nov. 13, 1991, to succeed William H. Gray III, D, who resigned Sept. 11, 1991. Gray was eligible for 243 votes in 1991, 231 not including votes to approve the Journal. Blackwell was eligible for 54 votes in 1991, 53 not including votes to approve the Journal.*

[5] *Sam Johnson, R-Texas, was sworn in May 22, 1991, to succeed Steve Bartlett, R, who resigned March 11, 1991. Bartlett was eligible for 34 votes in 1991, 33 not including votes to approve the Journal. Johnson was eligible for 328 votes in 1991, 313 not including votes to approve the Journal.*

[6] *George F. Allen, R-Va., was sworn in Nov. 12, 1991, to succeed D. French Slaughter Jr., R, who resigned Nov. 5, 1991. Allen was eligible for 55 votes in 1991, 53 not including votes to approve the Journal. Slaughter was eligible for 370 votes in 1991, 352 not including votes to approve the Journal.*

[7] *Thomas S. Foley, D-Wash., as Speaker of the House, voted at his discretion.*

NOTE: Scores are rounded to the nearest percentage, except that no scores are rounded up to 100 percent.

KEY

† Not eligible for all votes or voted "present" to avoid conflict of interest on one or more votes in 1991. Ineligible votes are excluded from calculation of scores.

\# Member absent a day or more due to illness, or illness or death in family.

Democrats ***Republicans***
Independent

	1	2
Alabama		
1 ***Callahan***	88	88
2 ***Dickinson***	91	91
3 Browder	98	98
4 Bevill	96	96
5 Cramer	99	99
6 Erdreich	99	99
7 Harris	99	99
Alaska		
AL ***Young***	92	93
Arizona		
1 ***Rhodes*** #	96	96
2 Pastor [1]	98	99
3 ***Stump***	100	100
4 ***Kyl***	100	100
5 ***Kolbe***	98	98
Arkansas		
1 Alexander	91	92
2 Thornton	96	97
3 ***Hammerschmidt***	93	93
4 Anthony	93	94
California		
1 ***Riggs***	96	97
2 ***Herger***	95	95
3 Matsui #	85	85
4 Fazio	96	97
5 Pelosi	93	94
6 Boxer	80	80
7 Miller	96	96
8 Dellums	93	94
9 Stark	93	94
10 Edwards	98	98
11 Lantos	94	94
12 ***Campbell***	88	88
13 Mineta	98	98
14 ***Doolittle***	94	94
15 Condit	96	97
16 Panetta	99	99
17 Dooley	99	99
18 Lehman	94	94
19 ***Lagomarsino*** #	99	99
20 ***Thomas***	91	92
21 ***Gallegly***	96	97
22 ***Moorhead***	98	98
23 Beilenson	97	98
24 Waxman	89	90
25 Roybal	92	92
26 Berman	90	91
27 Levine	60	59
28 Dixon	91	92
29 Waters	88	90
30 Martinez	82	84
31 Dymally #	74	74
32 Anderson	99	99
33 ***Dreier***	97	98
34 Torres	94	94
35 ***Lewis***	93	94
36 Brown	92	93
37 ***McCandless***	98	98
38 ***Dornan*** #	92	93
39 ***Dannemeyer***	92	92
40 ***Cox***	96	97
41 ***Lowery***	93	95
42 ***Rohrabacher***	99	99
43 ***Packard***	98	98
44 ***Cunningham***	99	99
45 ***Hunter***	90	92
Colorado		
1 Schroeder	99	99
2 Skaggs	99	99
3 Campbell #	92	92
4 ***Allard***	99	99
5 ***Hefley***	98	98
6 ***Schaefer***	99	99
Connecticut		
1 Kennelly	99	99
2 Gejdenson	99	99
3 DeLauro	99	99
4 ***Shays***	100	100
5 ***Franks***	98	99
6 ***Johnson***	98	98
Delaware		
AL Carper	98	98
Florida		
1 Hutto	96	97
2 Peterson	99	99
3 Bennett	100	100
4 ***James***	98	98
5 ***McCollum***	94	95
6 ***Stearns***	99	99
7 Gibbons	97	97
8 ***Young*** #	96	97
9 ***Bilirakis***	95	95
10 ***Ireland***	92	93
11 Bacchus	97	97
12 ***Lewis*** #	96	96
13 ***Goss***	100	100
14 Johnston	94	94
15 ***Shaw***	95	96
16 Smith #	91	92
17 Lehman #	71	72
18 ***Ros-Lehtinen***	97	98
19 Fascell	99	99
Georgia		
1 Thomas	97	98
2 Hatcher	82	83
3 Ray #	94	95
4 Jones	97	98
5 Lewis	96	96
6 ***Gingrich***	93	93
7 Darden	98	98
8 Rowland #	93	93
9 Jenkins	93	93
10 Barnard	93	93
Hawaii		
1 Abercrombie	98	98
2 Mink	98	98
Idaho		
1 LaRocco	98	98
2 Stallings	95	95
Illinois		
1 Hayes	99	99
2 Savage #	84	85
3 Russo	98	98
4 Sangmeister #	92	92
5 Lipinski	95	96
6 ***Hyde***	96	97
7 Collins	90	90
8 Rostenkowski	89	89
9 Yates #	92	92
10 ***Porter***	96	97
11 Annunzio	99	99
12 ***Crane***	92	93
13 ***Fawell*** #	95	95
14 ***Hastert***	96	96
15 ***Ewing*** [2]	98	98
16 Cox	99	99
17 Evans	99	99
18 ***Michel*** #	90	90
19 Bruce	99	99
20 Durbin	98	98
21 Costello	99	99
22 Poshard	98	98
Indiana		
1 Visclosky	99	99
2 Sharp	94	94
3 Roemer	99	99

	1	2
4 Long	99	99
5 Jontz	99	99
6 ***Burton***	98	98
7 ***Myers*** #	95	95
8 McCloskey	96	97
9 Hamilton	99	99
10 Jacobs	93	94
Iowa		
1 ***Leach***	97	97
2 ***Nussle***	99	99
3 Nagle #	96	96
4 Smith	94	94
5 ***Lightfoot***	99	99
6 ***Grandy***	99	99
Kansas		
1 ***Roberts***	97	98
2 Slattery	98	99
3 ***Meyers***	99	99
4 Glickman #	96	96
5 ***Nichols***	99	99
Kentucky		
1 Hubbard	96	96
2 Natcher	100	100
3 Mazzoli	99	99
4 ***Bunning***	97	97
5 ***Rogers***	96	97
6 ***Hopkins***	38	38
7 Perkins	99	99
Louisiana		
1 ***Livingston***	96	97
2 Jefferson #	89	90
3 Tauzin	95	95
4 ***McCrery***	94	94
5 Huckaby	93	93
6 ***Baker***	94	94
7 Hayes	91	91
8 ***Holloway***	79	79
Maine		
1 Andrews	98	98
2 ***Snowe*** #	96	96
Maryland		
1 ***Gilchrest***	99	99
2 ***Bentley***	97	97
3 Cardin	99	99
4 McMillen	99	99
5 Hoyer	98	99
6 Byron	97	98
7 Mfume	95	96
8 ***Morella***	97	98
Massachusetts		
1 Olver [3]	98	98
2 Neal	95	95
3 Early	96	96
4 Frank	96	96
5 Atkins	98	99
6 Mavroules	94	95
7 Markey	97	97
8 Kennedy	96	97
9 Moakley	97	98
10 Studds	97	97
11 Donnelly	95	95
Michigan		
1 Conyers	93	94
2 ***Pursell***	92	93
3 Wolpe	98	98
4 ***Upton***	99	99
5 ***Henry***	98	98
6 Carr †	93	93
7 Kildee	100	100
8 Traxler	92	91
9 ***Vander Jagt***	95	97
10 ***Camp***	99	99
11 ***Davis*** #	92	93
12 Bonior	98	99
13 Collins	97	99
14 Hertel	97	98
15 Ford #	90	92
16 Dingell	93	94
17 Levin	99	99
18 ***Broomfield***	96	96
Minnesota		
1 Penny	99	99
2 ***Weber***	96	97
3 ***Ramstad***	99	99
4 Vento #	98	98
5 Sabo	97	97
6 Sikorski	98	98
7 Peterson	97	98
8 Oberstar	88	88
Mississippi		
1 Whitten	94	94
2 Espy	96	96
3 Montgomery	98	98
4 Parker	97	98
5 Taylor	99	99
Missouri		
1 Clay	90	90
2 Horn	99	99
3 Gephardt	94	95
4 Skelton #	97	97
5 Wheat	99	99
6 ***Coleman***	98	98
7 ***Hancock***	98	99
8 ***Emerson***	99	99
9 Volkmer	97	97
Montana		
1 Williams	90	90
2 ***Marlenee***	84	85
Nebraska		
1 ***Bereuter***	99	99
2 Hoagland	99	99
3 ***Barrett***	99	99
Nevada		
1 Bilbray #	96	97
2 ***Vucanovich***	97	98
New Hampshire		
1 ***Zeliff***	98	99
2 Swett	98	98
New Jersey		
1 Andrews	98	98
2 Hughes	97	97
3 Pallone	99	99
4 ***Smith***	98	98
5 ***Roukema***	94	94
6 Dwyer	90	89
7 ***Rinaldo***	99	99
8 Roe	95	95
9 Torricelli	91	92
10 Payne	95	96
11 ***Gallo*** #	97	98
12 ***Zimmer***	99	99
13 ***Saxton*** #	96	97
14 Guarini †	95	95
New Mexico		
1 ***Schiff***	98	99
2 ***Skeen***	99	99
3 Richardson	99	99
New York		
1 Hochbrueckner	97	98
2 Downey	98	98
3 Mrazek	63	64
4 ***Lent***	93	93
5 ***McGrath*** †	96	96
6 Flake	90	91
7 Ackerman	88	87
8 Scheuer	95	95
9 Manton #	94	94
10 Schumer	96	97
11 Towns	86	87
12 Owens	91	93
13 Solarz	97	97
14 ***Molinari***	97	97
15 ***Green***	96	96
16 Rangel	94	96
17 Weiss #	87	88
18 Serrano	87	88
19 Engel	96	97
20 Lowey	97	98
21 ***Fish***	94	94
22 ***Gilman*** #	99	99
23 McNulty	99	99
24 ***Solomon***	97	98
25 ***Boehlert***	99	99
26 ***Martin*** #	89	89
27 ***Walsh***	98	98
28 McHugh	96	98
29 ***Horton***	95	95
30 Slaughter	96	97
31 ***Paxon***	98	98
32 LaFalce	96	97
33 Nowak	98	98
34 ***Houghton***	94	95
North Carolina		
1 Jones	94	95
2 Valentine	96	96
3 Lancaster	97	97
4 Price	98	98
5 Neal	89	89
6 ***Coble***	98	98
7 Rose	92	92
8 Hefner #	92	92
9 ***McMillan***	99	99
10 ***Ballenger***	96	96
11 ***Taylor***	99	99
North Dakota		
AL Dorgan	97	97
Ohio		
1 Luken	98	98
2 ***Gradison***	95	95
3 Hall	97	98
4 ***Oxley***	97	97
5 ***Gillmor*** †	97	98
6 ***McEwen***	96	96
7 ***Hobson***	100	100
8 ***Boehner***	99	99
9 Kaptur	93	94
10 ***Miller*** #	89	89
11 Eckart	98	98
12 ***Kasich***	98	99
13 Pease	97	97
14 Sawyer	98	99
15 ***Wylie***	98	98
16 ***Regula***	99	99
17 Traficant	99	99
18 Applegate	97	98
19 Feighan	93	94
20 Oakar	97	98
21 Stokes #	93	94
Oklahoma		
1 ***Inhofe***	97	97
2 Synar	98	98
3 Brewster	97	98
4 McCurdy	95	95
5 ***Edwards***	92	93
6 English	99	99
Oregon		
1 AuCoin	90	91
2 ***Smith***	99	99
3 Wyden	99	99
4 DeFazio	97	97
5 Kopetski	98	98
Pennsylvania		
1 Foglietta	95	96
2 Blackwell [4]	100	100
3 Borski	97	98
4 Kolter	94	95
5 ***Schulze***	91	92
6 Yatron #	84	84
7 ***Weldon*** #	94	95
8 Kostmayer	97	98
9 ***Shuster***	96	96
10 ***McDade*** #	93	93
11 Kanjorski	99	99
12 Murtha	97	97
13 ***Coughlin***	97	97
14 Coyne	98	99
15 ***Ritter***	97	98
16 ***Walker***	99	99
17 ***Gekas***	98	98
18 ***Santorum***	98	98
19 ***Goodling***	92	92
20 Gaydos	90	91
21 ***Ridge*** #	93	94
22 Murphy	90	91
23 ***Clinger***	98	98
Rhode Island		
1 ***Machtley***	98	99
2 Reed	99	99
South Carolina		
1 ***Ravenel***	98	99
2 ***Spence***	91	92
3 Derrick	97	97
4 Patterson	99	99
5 Spratt	97	98
6 Tallon	98	98
South Dakota		
AL Johnson	99	99
Tennessee		
1 ***Quillen***	91	91
2 ***Duncan*** #	98	98
3 Lloyd #	81	82
4 Cooper †	99	99
5 Clement	98	98
6 Gordon	98	98
7 ***Sundquist***	92	92
8 Tanner	92	92
9 Ford	76	77
Texas		
1 Chapman †	90	91
2 Wilson	84	86
3 ***Johnson*** [5]	97	98
4 Hall	98	98
5 Bryant	93	94
6 ***Barton***	94	95
7 ***Archer***	97	98
8 ***Fields***	96	96
9 Brooks †	92	93
10 Pickle	94	95
11 Edwards	98	98
12 Geren	96	97
13 Sarpalius	96	97
14 Laughlin	96	96
15 de la Garza	89	90
16 Coleman	98	99
17 Stenholm	97	97
18 Washington	83	85
19 ***Combest***	99	99
20 Gonzalez	99	99
21 ***Smith***	95	95
22 ***DeLay***	93	93
23 Bustamante	86	86
24 Frost #	92	93
25 Andrews	98	98
26 ***Armey***	98	98
27 Ortiz #	94	94
Utah		
1 ***Hansen***	97	97
2 Owens	95	95
3 Orton	95	95
Vermont		
AL Sanders	92	95
Virginia		
1 ***Bateman***	96	97
2 Pickett	96	96
3 ***Bliley***	98	98
4 Sisisky	95	95
5 Payne	97	98
6 Olin	96	97
7 ***Allen*** [6]	100	100
8 Moran	96	96
9 Boucher	94	95
10 ***Wolf***	99	99
Washington		
1 ***Miller***	96	97
2 Swift	98	99
3 Unsoeld	98	98
4 ***Morrison***	98	98
5 Foley [7]		
6 Dicks	94	95
7 McDermott	98	98
8 ***Chandler***	95	96
West Virginia		
1 Mollohan	97	99
2 Staggers	95	96
3 Wise	95	96
4 Rahall #	96	96
Wisconsin		
1 Aspin	92	93
2 ***Klug***	97	98
3 ***Gunderson*** #	98	98
4 Kleczka	94	94
5 Moody	90	90
6 ***Petri***	99	99
7 Obey	99	99
8 ***Roth***	98	98
9 ***Sensenbrenner*** #	99	99
Wyoming		
AL ***Thomas***	97	98

Key Votes: Economy, Events Overseas Drive '91 Confrontations

Congress found itself reacting to outside forces, with few opportunities to shape new policies or priorities

Some of the major confrontations that come to a head in votes on the House and Senate floors are forged by members trying to change policy; others are forced on members by events outside their control. In 1991, there were far more of the latter than the former.

The year of key votes began on a somber note, as Congress voted to authorize the use of force in the Persian Gulf; four days later, U.S. planes were bombing Iraq. The last key vote was also on foreign policy, as the Senate agreed to give more aid to citizens of the crumbling Soviet empire.

In between were dozens of domestic votes, many driven by concern over the economy.

CQ's 1991 compilation of key votes found Congress responding to the recession by extending unemployment benefits and by pumping money into a highway bill.

There were frequent battles over funding — for defense, for the space station, for the superconducting super collider; most were a result of the 1990 budget deal, which left Congress with a set number of dollars to spread around.

Attempts to change longstanding policy on grazing fees, gun control, energy policy and family leave prompted some heated battles, but all fell short of enactment, though Congress did overwhelmingly approve a major civil rights bill once a compromise had been negotiated with the White House.

There were heated battles with President Bush over nominees Clarence Thomas and Robert M. Gates, most-favored-nation status for China and the abortion "gag rule." Bush won on those issues but lost many of the funding battles.

Congress was also forced to look inward, tackling key votes on campaign finance and the question of honoraria.

Following is a rundown of the key votes of 1991.

How CQ Picked Votes

Starting in 1945, Congressional Quarterly each year selected a series of key votes on major issues of the year.

An issue was judged by the extent that it represented:

- A matter of major controversy.
- A matter of presidential or political power.
- A matter of potentially great impact on the nation and lives of Americans.

For each group of related votes on an issue, one key vote usually was chosen — one that, in the opinion of CQ editors, was most important in determining the outcome.

Charts showing how each member of Congress voted on these issues in 1991 can be found as follows:

House key votes 1-8 .... 50-B
House key votes 9-16 .... 52-B
Senate key votes 1-8.................... 54-B
Senate key votes 9-16.................... 55-B

KEY HOUSE VOTES

1. Persian Gulf War

After one of its longest and most moving debates in recent memory, Congress on Jan. 12 approved a resolution (H J Res 77) authorizing President Bush to use military force to reverse Iraq's occupation of Kuwait. Four days later, Bush did just that, ordering the aerial bombardment of Iraq.

On Feb. 27, following six weeks of devastating air strikes and a brief but bloody ground campaign, Bush announced: "Our military objectives are met." Kuwait was liberated and Iraq had been defeated, Bush said.

In the House, opponents of the war resolution, led by Speaker Thomas S. Foley, D-Wash., knew going into the debate that they were facing an uphill struggle.

For several months, Foley and other Democratic leaders had urged the president to stay the course with economic sanctions that had been imposed on Iraq after it invaded Kuwait on Aug. 2, 1990. But in the weeks leading up to the climactic vote, some key members of the party expressed skepticism that sanctions alone would ever force Iraqi leader Saddam Hussein to withdraw his forces from the tiny, oil-rich emirate.

Armed Services Committee Chairman Les Aspin, D-Wis., had predicted that the United States and it allies could achieve victory over Iraq without sustaining heavy casualties. Stephen J. Solarz, D-N.Y., typified a small group of Northern liberals — most of whom were strong supporters of Israel — who also supported an early resort to force against Saddam.

But the likelihood that the resolution would be approved did little to diminish the tension and emotion that permeated the three-day debate on the issue.

In a rare speech from the well, Foley told his colleagues, "In 26 years in the House of Representatives, I have never seen this House more serious nor determined to speak its heart and mind on a question than they are at this time on this day."

The Senate voted first to approve its war resolution. Minutes later, the House voted 250-183 for H J Res 77, an identical resolution that authorized the president to use military force pursuant to U.N. Security Council Resolution 678. The U.N. resolution, approved in November 1990, had authorized member states "to use all necessary means" to force Iraq out of Kuwait by Jan. 15.

While congressional leaders had urged members to vote their consciences, the vote was split largely along partisan lines: R 164-3; D 86-179 (ND 33-147; SD 53-32); I 0-1.

Pro-defense Democrats from the South joined with Republicans and a handful of liberals to provide the margin of victory. Key committee chairmen — such as Aspin, John D. Dingell, D-Mich., of Energy and Commerce, and Dan Rostenkowski, D-Ill., of Ways and Means — supported H J Res 77.

After the vote, most House members put aside partisan differences and closed ranks in support of the president and hundreds of thousands of U.S. servicemen who were poised for battle in the Persian Gulf.

During the dramatic debate on the measure, Majority Leader Richard A. Gephardt, D-Mo., had said, "Whatever our decision, we will leave this room one again and whole again."

2. Thrift Bailout

Paying for past mistakes is never fun, and the savings and loan debacle was about the biggest mess in Congress' back yard. So it was not surprising that when it came time to ante up the taxpayers' money to cover insured deposits in failed thrifts, members did so reluctantly.

That was never demonstrated more aptly than in March, when the House defeated a succession of plans to give money to the Resolution Trust Corporation (RTC), the thrift bailout agency created in August 1989.

The March votes were required because a bill to give the RTC additional money had failed in the final hours of the 101st Congress. The agency had gotten $50 billion when it was created, a sum that the Bush administration persisted in claiming would be enough. By the summer of 1990, however, administration officials said the cost would range from $89 billion to $132 billion.

So, at the beginning of the 102nd Congress, the House and Senate Banking committees began work on bills to give the RTC another $30 billion — enough, it was plain by then, to last only through 1991, not to finish the job.

In February, the House Banking Committee marked up a bill and then could not summon up the votes to send the measure to the floor. On March 7, it voted to send not one but two bills to the floor.

Eventually, the House voted four times on the two committee options — and variations on their themes — rejecting all four. The final vote, on March 12, was on a "clean" bill (HR 1315) sponsored by ranking committee Republican Chalmers P. Wylie of Ohio, which did little more than provide the needed $30 billion. But even that measure failed on a vote of 201-220: R 120-42; D 81-177 (ND 44-132, SD 37-45); I 0-1.

The clean bill did get more votes than any of the three alternatives, which contained a variety of low-income housing, management reform and so-called pay-as-you-go provisions. These bells and whistles were intended to pick up the votes of disaffected members, but they also generated opposition.

The day after Wylie's bill was rejected, House Democratic and Republican leaders cut a deal with Treasury Secretary Nicholas F. Brady to call up a Senate-passed bill (S 419) that was similarly devoid of controversial amendments and add a few low-income housing provisions to it. The compromise managed to hold the line on Republican support and picked up enough Democratic votes to pass. A conference committee reconciled the two similarly stripped-down versions in about 15 minutes, and both chambers adopted the conference agreement without difficulty.

That did not mean the story was over, however. By the summer of 1991, the administration was asking for $80 billion more. And in the final hours of the 1991 session, almost as its last act, Congress cleared a bill (HR 3435) providing another $25 billion for the RTC and restructuring the agency. It was not at all certain until the end that the second thrift bailout bill of the year would pass either chamber. And with the limited amount of money it contained, Congress set itself up for yet another showdown on the issue in 1992.

3. Gun Control

A May vote on the Brady bill revealed a significant shift in attitudes on gun control in the House and handed the National Rifle Association a rare defeat. Legislation for a waiting period on handgun purchases (HR 7) passed the House on May 8 by a surprising 53-vote margin, 239-186: R 60-102; D 179-83 (ND 138-41, SD 41-42); I 0-1.

Brady

Although Democrats were more inclined to back the legislation, the vote was bipartisan. Three years earlier, the powerful gun lobby had blocked a similar measure by 46 votes.

The handgun proposal, which also passed the Senate in 1991, was on hold at the end of the session after having been modified and rolled into an omnibus crime bill (HR 3371), which was held up over partisan differences. Nonetheless, because of the strong votes for the Brady bill in both chambers, many members expected the provision to become law in 1992.

HR 7 would have required a seven-day waiting period on the purchase of handguns for a background check. The compromise version that became part of the crime bill was for a five-business-day wait.

Its supporters chalked up the win in the House to constituent pressure on members in the face of increasing violent crime. Polls had been showing resounding support for firearms restrictions, and swing voters said they were persuaded to back down on their no-gun-control positions by local police and worried constituents.

The waiting-period language was named for former presidential press secretary James S. Brady, who was wounded in a 1981 assassination attempt on Ronald Reagan.

Brady made several appearances on Capitol Hill in his wheelchair, with his determined wife, Sarah. They were ubiquitous at the Capitol in the days leading up to the vote and had a strong influence on the legislation.

The Bradys became a poignant contrast to the powerful NRA, which boasted among its members several House leaders, including Speaker Thomas S. Foley, D-Wash.

Under then-current law, a gun buyer had to sign a statement that he was not a felon, fugitive, drug addict or mentally ill. But because the form never left the dealer's shop, buyers acted on their honor. Under the Brady bill, gun dealers would have to send that form to the police, who would check the buyer's background to make sure the purchase was legal. HR 7 did not require the police to make the background check, but the new version in the crime bill did.

Before the House passed the Brady bill, it rejected an alternative offered by Harley O. Staggers Jr., D-W.Va. That would have ordered states to set up an instant check system within six months, under which a gun dealer could find out by telephone whether a would-be buyer had a criminal record. The amendment was devised largely to block the Brady bill. Opponents of the Staggers plan pointed to studies showing that because state criminal justice records are not fully computerized, it would take years to put the telephone-check system in place. The House defeated the Staggers substitute, also on May 8, by a strong 193-234.

Overwhelming passage of HR 7, which was offered by Edward F. Feighan, D-Ohio, put pressure on the Senate to develop a similar measure.

The bipartisan compromise was endorsed by the Bradys and adopted in that chamber June 28 by a secure, 67-32 vote as part of a Senate crime bill (S 1241). *(Related Senate key vote 3, p. 43-B)*

4. Strategic Defense Initiative

Since 1985, Congress had routinely slashed the annual funding request for the anti-missile research program called the Strategic Defense Initiative (SDI). And since 1987, it had consistently opposed deployment of space-based anti-missile weapons that would violate the 1972 U.S.-Soviet treaty limiting anti-ballistic missile (ABM) systems.

Despite those hotly contested annual fights over funding and treaty compliance, however, Congress had approved spending at least a few billion dollars annually on a program of anti-missile defense research that was strongly oriented toward eventual deployment of ABM weapons.

President Ronald Reagan launched SDI in 1983, arguing that an array of anti-missile devices could render nuclear weapons obsolete and end the superpower arms race. But many leading arms control advocates had opposed the program on the grounds that missile defenses could stimulate escalating deployments of offensive weapons intended to nullify such defenses.

In past years, some liberals, led by Ronald V. Dellums, D-Calif., had proposed deep reductions in SDI funds that essentially would have limited the program to laboratory research. But most arms control activists had thrown more of their energy into a pragmatic effort to win more modest cuts in SDI. On the other side, conservatives had pushed for rapid deployment of a nationwide anti-missile defense regardless of the 1972 ABM Treaty.

In 1991, the House Armed Services Committee sliced Bush's $5.2 billion request for anti-missile work to $3.5 billion in its version of the fiscal 1992 defense authorization bill. When the House took up the measure in May, no middle-ground amendment was offered to make a relatively moderate additional SDI reduction. However, Dellums offered an amendment that would have sliced the total to $1.1 billion while disbanding the SDI program office and limiting the project to laboratory work.

Dellums' amendment was an effort to draw the line against the kind of ground-based defense against limited missile attacks that had been endorsed by prominent Democratic centrists, including House Armed Services Committee Chairman Les Aspin, Wis. Demonstrating the weakness of the outright opponents of SDI, the amendment was rejected 118-266: R 2-149; D 115-117 (ND 104-55; SD 11-62); I 1-0.

By final passage of the defense authorization bill (HR 2100 — PL 102-190) in November, the House acquiesced in a Senate-forged deal that gave a congressional endorsement to a limited SDI deployment. It provided for rapid deployment of a ground-based anti-missile defense at one site and for negotiations with leaders of the former Soviet Union to revise the ABM Treaty in order to permit a more extensive SDI system.

5. Fast-Track Trade Procedures

Democrats in Congress complained regularly that President Bush's trade policy was ineffective and unsound, but they passed up a rare chance to do more of the job themselves. Influential Democrats decided it was wiser to remain in the back seat shouting directions than to take the wheel.

In what had become a referendum on Bush's controversial decision to begin negotiations with Mexico to create a North American free-trade zone, the House agreed May 23 to continue so-called fast-track procedures that bar lawmakers from amending trade pacts submitted for congressional approval. The Senate followed suit a day later.

During weeks of intensive lobbying, the Bush administration had argued that the two-year extension was imperative not only to begin the U.S.-Mexico talks but also to revive negotiations on strengthening the General Agreement on Tariffs and Trade (GATT), the multilateral accord governing most world trade. No country would negotiate with the United States, officials said, if Congress reserved the right to alter the resulting accord.

The vote was a bitter disappointment to organized labor. The AFL-CIO had campaigned hard to convince members that removing trade and investment barriers with Mexico would cause U.S. workers to lose their jobs as companies headed south to take advantage of cheaper labor and lax environmental laws. Defeat of the extension was the organization's top legislative priority, and it was counting on its close ties with Democrats to produce the votes.

In the end, a majority of House Democrats voted against the extension. Midwestern lawmakers were strongly opposed, arguing that a U.S.-Mexico pact would hurt industries such as automobiles, electronics and glassware. Also voting against the extension were members from states with industries such as agriculture and textiles, which feared that a GATT accord would eliminate U.S. laws that had long shielded them from foreign competition.

But key party members — including Majority Leader Richard A. Gephardt, D-Mo., to whom opponents had looked for leadership, and Ways and Means Committee Chairman Dan Rostenkowski, D-Ill. — voted with the president. They did so after the White House issued an "action plan" promising to uphold U.S. environmental laws, phase in changes affecting farmers and industries worried about being swamped by Mexican imports, and assist workers who lost their jobs as a result of the pact.

Gephardt, the Democrats' leading trade warrior, defended his vote, saying he reserved the right to oppose the final agreement with Mexico if it was not protective enough of U.S. workers and industries. Even with the fast track, Gephardt insisted, lawmakers could amend the terms of any trade deal Bush sent them if they wanted.

The defeat of a resolution that would have terminated the fast track was a victory for Bush, who won endorsement from the Democratic controlled Congress for his free-trade agenda in the middle of a recession.

Equally important, Bush persuaded Congress to leave the negotiating to him, knowing that, if he succeeded, he also would get the credit.

The House defeated the resolution by a vote of 192-231: R 21-140; D 170-91 (ND 128-50, SD 42-41); I 1-0.

6. Superconducting Super Collider

Despite increased opposition and resistance from respected members of the Science and Budget committees, the $8 billion atom smasher being built in Waxahachie, Texas, continued to attract substantial House support.

Enthusiasm for the project was evident May 29 when supporters soundly defeated an attempt to drop federal funding for the project. The vote came during debate on the fiscal 1992 energy and water appropriations bill when the House rejected, 165-251, an amendment by Jim Slattery, D-Kan., that would have eliminated funding for the project: R 58-101; D 106-150 (ND 86-87; SD 20-63); I 1-0.

Boehlert

Still, the vote revealed that the project's popularity had eroded considerably since 1989 — when there were 93 votes to cut funding for the collider — and it suggested that in future years opponents might be able to muster the votes necessary to kill it.

The House version called for allotting $434 million for the atom smasher in fiscal 1992, about $100 million less than the Bush administration's budget request. The super collider was designed to hurl subatomic particles through a 54-mile underground tunnel; scientists hoped that studying particle collisions would help them trace the origins of matter and yield scientific discoveries.

Opposition to the collider was growing in the House among science supporters who feared that its high price tag could cannibalize other science projects and among Budget Committee members who considered it too costly. Joining Slattery's attack were Howard Wolpe, D-Mich., who headed the Science Investigation and Oversight Subcommittee, and Sherwood Boehlert, R-N.Y., ranking member on the subcommittee. Boehlert called the collider a "Texas gila monster" and said support for it came from "Texas and Texas and Texas and Texas."

Boehlert might have added to his short list another 42 states and 1600 Pennsylvania Ave. President Bush had long been an advocate for the project and met personally last year with Tom Bevill, D-Ala., who headed the Appropriations panel with jurisdiction over the project. Bevill, originally a skeptic, had become a strong supporter. Since that meeting with Bush, the White House had been less inclined to oppose additional water projects in the appropriations bill Bevill shepherded through the House. Additional political ballast for the project came from about 8,500 contracts worth hundreds of millions of dollars that had been doled out to 43 states. The contracts had sparked support for the atom smasher from members who otherwise would have had little interest in the project.

In the 1991 debate, supporters of the project were led by the good-natured Joe L. Barton, R-Texas, whose home is just a couple of miles from the collider site. They argued that the atom smasher was likely to produce many lucrative spinoffs and that it was already too far along to stop. The latter was an argument often used by supporters of big, multi-year weapons or science projects.

The 1991 vote was significant because it marked the resurrection of opposition to the project, which had dissipated in 1990. In the tight budget climate that was likely to dominate the decade, high-cost projects had become the target of budget cutters. Supporters also said the vote was key because it provided funds meant to begin construction of the project's tunnel.

7. Civil Rights

An initial blow to civil rights legislation came in late spring when the House failed to gather a two-thirds majority for a bill President Bush was threatening to veto. Bush, who asserted that HR 1 would lead to quota hiring of minorities and women, had vetoed a similar bill in 1990.

The June 5 House vote was the first test of a reconstituted anti-discrimination bill. The vote was largely partisan: 273-158: R 22-143; D 250-15 (ND 177-4, SD 73-11); I 1-0. The 273 votes were 15 short of the two-thirds needed to override a veto; the 1990 House tally on the job-rights conference report was 12 short.

The failure to reach two-thirds effectively stalled HR 1 but paved the way for more intense negotiations among Senate moderates on a separate bill. In the end, a compromise was brokered in the wake of the Senate's Supreme Court nomination hearings involving Clarence Thomas and Anita F. Hill. Workplace protections, similar to those proposed in HR 1, had since become law.

The bill was intended to offer workers more protection against bias, largely by reversing a series of Supreme Court decisions that narrowed the reach of anti-bias laws. It would have for the first time allowed limited money damages for victims of harassment and other intentional discrimination based on sex, religion or disability. Minorities already could win unlimited money damages for racial discrimination under a separate post-Civil War law. HR 1 would have reversed more court cases and been more generous to workers than the legislation eventually enacted.

The House vote came at a time when the political and substantive problems with the job-rights bill were near their height. Republicans had been pounding away on the message that the measure would force employers to use quotas to avoid costly lawsuits. They struck a nerve with white constituents worried about holding onto their jobs in a frail economy.

Democrats, meanwhile, struggled with how to convey the importance of workplace protections. They had tried to appeal to women by adding a study of pay equity and other items designed to appeal to working women. They also tried to defuse the quota issue by inserting language for an outright ban on quotas. Because the Supreme Court had ruled that hiring by the numbers is illegal, the move appeared to be motivated by attempts to give political cover to members who wanted to vote for the bill but faced constituent complaints about "reverse discrimination."

Before the vote on HR 1, the House rejected two other civil rights proposals — a White House plan and a hard-line effort from liberal Democrats that included unlimited money damages in intentional-bias suits.

Only one House member who voted against the 1990 bill switched to support the 1991 version. He was Democrat Bill Sarpalius of Texas.

Sarpalius' switch was more than offset by the one Democrat (Jimmy Hayes of Louisiana) and nine Republicans who voted for the 1990 rights bill but opposed HR 1. *(Related Senate key vote 13, p. 48-B)*

8. Space Station

Bob Traxler, D-Mich., knew he was going out on a limb when he persuaded the House Appropriations Committee to eliminate fiscal 1992 funding for NASA's premier space enterprise, the orbiting space station *Freedom.* He was afraid the massive construction project would take too big a bite out of the $64 billion in discretionary spending allocated to the Subcommittee on Veterans Affairs (VA), Housing and Urban Development (HUD) and Independent Agencies, which oversaw the space agency's funding. At risk were other, smaller space and science projects as well as the many low-income housing, veterans' medical care and environmental programs under the panel's jurisdiction.

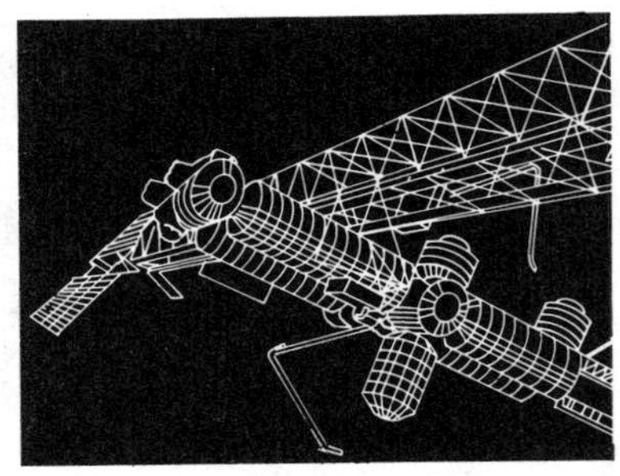

Meeting privately, the subcommittee on May 15 informally voted 6-3 against President Bush's $2.03 billion request for the space station in the fiscal 1992 spending bill (HR 2519). The full committee, at Traxler's request, deferred debate until the House floor, where Traxler believed all members should be put to the test. "We simply can no longer afford huge new projects with huge price tags while trying to maintain services that the American people expect to be provided," he said.

The subcommittee action touched off a lobbying firestorm. Low-income housing groups and environmentalists, in particular, began urging representatives to ratify the subcommittee's bill. They feared that if money was put back in, it would come out of their appropriations.

Also lobbying members were NASA officials, aerospace contractors and members of the House Science Committee. The agency passed out maps showing each House member how many jobs and how many dollars flowed into the districts from space station contracts and subcontracts. *Freedom's* proponents, including Bush, also painted the project as having the potential for scientific breakthroughs with research in space. "It clearly caught the imagination of our colleagues," said Bill Lowery, R-Calif.

But others viewed the space station, estimated to cost a total of $40 billion, as a boondoggle. "If we fund this, it's clearly not for scientific reasons, it's for the contractors who work on the project," said Richard J. Durbin, D-Ill.

The key vote came June 6 on an amendment to restore nearly $2 billion in space station funding. The amendment was drafted by the White House Office of Management and Budget and offered by Jim Chapman, D-Texas, and Lowery, two VA-HUD subcommittee members.

In order to avoid the appearance that the space station would be taking money away from the poor, the amendment primarily cannibalized every other NASA program, including the environmental satellite project, Mission to Planet Earth. But it also proposed cutting $217 million, or nearly 10 percent, of the funds used to maintain public housing.

The House agreed to restore the space station's funding nearly to the level Bush requested by a vote of 240-173: R 133-27; D 107-145 (ND 55-114, SD 52-31); I 0-1.

Sending the bill on to the Senate, *Freedom* proponents knew their project would be protected by Barbara A. Mikulski, D-Md., chairman of the Senate VA-HUD Subcommittee.

Yet in a roundabout way the vote was a victory for Traxler, who may have succeeded in isolating NASA's budget from non-space programs. Space station proponents were so frightened of being cast as foes of the poor that they primarily took from other NASA programs to pay for *Freedom's* appropriation.

9. Grazing Fees

If any issue encapsulated the growing conflict among users of the country's vast public lands, it was grazing fees, a subject that produced much heated debate on public lands policy in 1991.

By almost any measure, the fees ranchers paid to graze their cattle on public land were lower than those paid by ranchers who grazed their cattle on private pastures. The inevitable result, argued some lawmakers and environmentalists, was overgrazing of arid Western rangeland and millions of dollars in lost revenue yearly.

Synar

But Western lawmakers had turned the issue into a symbolic lightning rod, imbuing it with images of another kind of endangered species: struggling ranchers, said to be the backbone of the old West. And they noted that the Bureau of Land Management in its 1990 "State of the Public Rangelands" report said the nation's rangelands were in better shape than at any time in this century.

The rhetoric and lobbying by environmentalists reached a new emotional pitch on June 25 when Mike Synar, D-Okla., proposed an amendment to raise grazing fees from $1.97 to $8.70 per animal unit month by 1995. (Studies from the General Accounting Office had determined that the average private market rate for Western rangeland is $9.22.) The House voted 232-192 to add the amendment to the fiscal 1992 Interior appropriations bill: R 47-114; D 184-78 (ND 140-38, SD 44-40); I 1-0.

Synar's amendment actually passed by a smaller margin than had a similar Synar amendment a year before. On Oct. 15, 1990, the House voted 251-155 to increase grazing fees.

What made the 1991 vote key was that it emboldened Senate supporters of a fee hike, who for the first time since 1978 pushed for a vote in their chamber. The Senate effort, led by James M. Jeffords, R-Vt., ultimately failed, showing that there is a solid phalanx of Western conservatives determined to block a hike in grazing fees. And when the matter reached conference, it became clear that even the House was not willing to place a high enough priority on higher fees to make them stick.

The Senate voted on Sept. 17, 60-38, to table (kill) the Jeffords amendment, which would have raised grazing fees to $5.13 by 1996.

And in conference the House amendment capsized under a deal that became known as "corn for porn." It preserved low grazing fees in exchange for no new restrictions on federal arts funding.

10. Defense Budget Cuts

The 1990 deficit-reduction act proved a formidable obstacle to those members — mostly liberal Democrats — who wanted to cut President Bush's $291 billion defense budget request. The law limited the allowable deficit each year through fiscal 1995. And it limited through fiscal 1993 annual discretionary spending for defense, international affairs and domestic programs. Funds cut from defense could not be transferred to popular domestic programs without violating the cap on domestic spending.

When the House returned from its August recess, some Pentagon critics, led by Barney Frank, D-Mass., calculated that events might have shifted the political equation in their favor. The unsuccessful mid-August coup attempt in Moscow by hard-line communists had been followed by a total collapse of communist power in the Soviet Union and a powerful surge of separatist sentiment in most of the republics that made up the U.S.S.R. The communist superpower's military might had been the motivating threat behind U.S. defense plans for more than 40 years. Therefore, Frank and his allies contended, the passing of that threat called for a fundamental revision of the budget deal.

But Defense Secretary Dick Cheney warned that the defense establishment would suffer far-reaching damage if Congress forced a more rapid cutback than his program to reduce the force by roughly 25 percent by fiscal 1995.

And many House Democratic leaders were aligned with Cheney in opposing any effort to depart significantly from the existing budget deal, although some were willing to renegotiate the budget deal in 1992. House Budget Committee Chairman Leon E. Panetta, D-Calif., and others expressed fear that the political pressures for an array of domestic programs were so powerful that any effort to tamper with the existing arrangement would risk a bidding war that would torpedo the budget deal, endanger the economy and subject the Democrats to taunts that they were addicted to big spending.

When the House appointed conferees on the defense authorization bill (HR 2100 — PL 102-190) Sept. 16, Frank intended to propose a motion instructing them to back the lower of the amounts authorized by the two chambers for any conventional weapons program, "consistent with emerging national security needs." But he was blocked from offering that defense-cutting motion by a procedural vote, which he lost 220-145: R 136-4; D 84-140 (ND 30-124; SD 54-16); I 0-1.

11. Unemployment Benefits

For the first part of the year, congressional Democrats and President Bush sparred over whether the country needed a bill to provide extended unemployment benefits for the long-term jobless. But as the economy worsened and unemployment hovered near 6.8 percent during the summer and fall, Bush stopped talking about whether a bill would be prudent. Instead, he criticized Congress for trying to pay for a multibillion-dollar bill through deficit spending. Congress, Bush maintained, wanted to "bust the budget agreement."

Bush had already blocked one bill in August that would have declared unemployment an emergency and therefore not subject to the budget agreement's pay-as-you-go rules. Bush signed that legislation but not an accompanying emergency designation that would have released the funds.

Democrats vowed to try again. They pointed to the $8 billion surplus in revenues from unemployment taxes paid by employers, which they maintained was being used to help mask the overall federal deficit.

They insisted that the budget agreement allowed Congress to spend money without offsetting tax increases or spending cuts if both Congress and the president declared an emergency. So Democrats pushed through a second bill (HR 3040), which would have automatically triggered spending of $6.3 billion in extended benefits if Bush had signed it into law.

The second time, on Sept. 17, the House voted 283-125: R 48-107; D 234-18 (ND 172-2, SD 62-16); I 1-0. The vote gave Democrats 11 more ayes than necessary to exceed the two-thirds margin needed to override Bush. Despite Bush's opposition, 48 Republicans supported the bill, eight more than Democrats had predicted.

The vote was a key one because it signaled to the administration that Democrats had momentum on their side. More and more members were complaining about the economy — Republicans as well as Democrats. With the override strength apparent, the administration began to accept that negotiations would be necessary in order to reach a compromise and get the unemployment issue off the domestic agenda.

Ultimately, after a four-month political standoff, Congress sent Bush a $5.3 billion bill to extend unemployment benefits for nearly 3 million people. Bush signed the measure the same day he received it, Nov. 15. The bill was paid for by tightening a loophole on those paying quarterly taxes; extending a law allowing Internal Revenue Service collection of debts owed the federal government; extending the federal unemployment tax at 0.08 percent; and garnisheeing the wages of those who defaulted on student loans.

12. Surface Transportation

Congress' biggest legislative achievement of the session, a six-year, $151 billion highway and mass transit bill, began the year mired in controversy. But when the final bill came to the House floor on Oct. 23, it passed swiftly after only a single day of debate.

The smooth sailing was aided by the tight rein the Democrat-dominated Rules Committee kept on items open to floor consideration. Despite Republican protests, the committee limited debate to only a dozen amendments and squelched 41 others. On the floor, Republicans forced three procedural roll call votes in protest. In the end, the House adopted the rule, 323-102, with significant help from Republicans: R 66-97; D 257-4 (ND 174-4, SD 83-0); I 0-1.

Votes on rules typically are procedural matters. But this vote was significant because Democrats succeeded in crafting a "stealth" bill that evaded all controversial issues. Despite the small group of dissenting Republicans, most lawmakers went along because the bill included authority for hundreds of local projects.

The roads and transit measure first faced trouble when House sponsors proposed hiking gasoline taxes by a nickel. The plan met with staunch opposition from both parties, and an early version of the bill was pulled from the floor calendar in August. Leaders of the Public Works and Transportation Committee dropped the nickel increase, opting instead to extend 2.5 cents of a 1990 nickel increase that was set to expire after fiscal 1995.

With that issue out of the way, other potential floor fights loomed: Some lawmakers, particularly from states that paid more in gas taxes than they received in highway funds, were upset that much of the $5.4 billion for 489 special road projects ended up in the states and districts of bill sponsors. Others objected to the new gas-tax plan.

But the Public Works panel, with help from the Rules Committee, managed to keep every controversial issue from coming to a floor vote. Almost every amendment blocked by the Rules panel dealt with potentially explosive issues that had tied up highway bills in the past, including a limit on billboard construction, a repeal of the national speed limit, a weakening of motorcycle helmet laws and a strengthening of drunken driving laws.

"This rule is truly unprecedented, unjustified and unfair," said Gerald B. H. Solomon, R-N.Y., ranking member of the Rules panel.

Republicans, including Rules Committee member Bob McEwen of Ohio, Robert S. Walker of Pennsylvania and Dan Burton of Indiana, opened their assault on the bill by attacking the rule. The Rules Committee had denied Burton's attempts to cut seven special road projects expected to cost $67.1 million.

But the Republican effort to overturn the rule failed in large part because lawmakers feared retaliation from bill sponsors, and they were not eager to lose funding for their hometown road projects.

The Public Works and Transportation Committee's hold over the bill's amendments continued as the bill went to conference with the Senate. The only amendment to pass was one by Anthony C. Beilenson, D-Calif., that would have allowed states to include a warranty clause in highway contracts. Despite the overwhelming approval of the amendment, 400-26, Public Works leaders opposed it, and it was dropped in conference.

13. Foreign Aid

When House members rejected the foreign aid bill on Oct. 30, they were signaling their clear displeasure with helping other nations during a period of economic crisis in this country.

The key vote came when the House defeated the conference report on the bill (HR 2508, H Rept 102-225), 159-262: R 28-134; D 131-127 (ND 105-73, SD 26-54); I 0-1.

It was a dramatic mood change from June, when the House had approved the original foreign aid authorization bill by 136 votes (274-138).

President Bush had vowed to veto the bill on several grounds. In particular he objected that the measure would have repealed abortion-related restrictions on aid to international family planning organizations and would have included a "cargo preference" provision requiring that a certain percentage of exports be transported on U.S.-flagged vessels.

But those red flag provisions had also been part of the original bill that won House approval.

House Foreign Affairs Committee Chairman Dante B. Fascell, D-Fla., the manager of the bill, described what had changed since the June vote: "The big difference is the change in attitude toward domestic issues."

Moreover, there was virtually no downside for members who wanted to cast an anti-foreign aid vote. Foreign aid funding for the first six months had been ensured with the passage of a continuing resolution Oct. 24. "It was almost a free vote," Fascell said.

Democrats had political incentives to oppose the bill. Party leaders had been hammering away at Bush as being more concerned with foreign policy than the domestic economy.

With an eye on the 1992 campaign, Democrats did not want to muddle that message with strong backing for a foreign aid bill.

In an unlikely combination, socialist Bernard Sanders, I-Vt., and bedrock conservative Gerald B. H. Solomon, R-N.Y., attacked a provision — supported by the administration — that would have increased the U.S. contribution in the International Monetary Fund by $12.2 billion.

The failure to enact an authorization bill was hardly unprecedented; no such measure had become law since 1985. But several lawmakers said the vote could be a harbinger of congressional opposition to more significant legislation.

One of the first items on the agenda in the new year was to be the fiscal 1992 foreign aid appropriations bill, which was delayed over the controversy surrounding Israel's request for $10 billion in loan guarantees.

14. Banking Overhaul

On Nov. 4, the House overwhelmingly rejected a comprehensive banking bill that had been debated, amended, negotiated and prayed over for nine months. The vote marked the beginning of the end for the Bush administration's hopes to overhaul the banking industry in 1991.

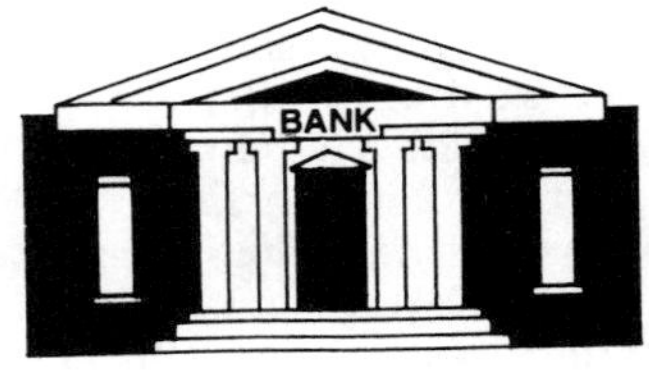

The bill (HR 6) had survived hundreds of amendments and two extensive markup sessions in the House Banking Committee, yet emerged much as the administration had wanted. It had been attacked in the Energy and Commerce Committee because of provisions involving the ownership of banks and bank affiliations with securities firms. So those major controversial elements were dropped or revised in post-markup negotiations between Banking Chairman Henry B. Gonzalez, D-Texas, and Energy and Commerce Chairman John D. Dingell, D-Mich.

On the floor a third controversial element — allowing banks to move freely across state lines — was curtailed by giving states power to limit interstate branching.

Yet, in the end, after all the changes and negotiations, members were still far from satisfied. Some regarded the measure as too restrictive; others thought it still too expansive. The bill was rejected by a vote of 89-324: R 6-153; D 83-170 (ND 69-105, SD 14-65); I 0-1.

Before the bill even got to final passage, it was nearly sidetracked when the rule permitting floor debate was adopted on a 210-208 vote. The rule came close to defeat, but the vote was turned around by the personal lobbying of Speaker Thomas S. Foley, D-Wash., who had promised Treasury Secretary Nicholas F. Brady that he would keep the bill on track. However, after it became clear that the bill would not be changed on the floor to its liking, the administration joined big banks in working to kill the measure outright.

It took two more tries on the floor before the House finally approved a banking bill.

The second failed attempt was on a bill (HR 2094) that began as a stripped-down measure to replenish the Federal Deposit Insurance Corporation's Bank Insurance Fund and overhaul the deposit insurance system. But at the administration's insistence, provisions allowing interstate branching were added back on the floor. Beyond providing the nearly insolvent insurance fund with a line of credit at the Treasury so it could stay in business closing failed banks, the administration's top priority was to improve bank profitability. Allowing nationwide interstate branching was seen as the best way to improve bank efficiency, spead risk and increase profits.

The third bill (HR 3768), which finally passed the House, was limited to refinancing and overhauling the deposit insurance system.

The Senate went through much the same torment, though mostly in behind-the-scenes negotiations. As the progression of House bills got narrower, so did a parallel Senate measure (S 543), which in a series of floor amendments was pared of its language permitting bank affiliations with securities firms and other contentious provisions. The Senate did manage to pass a bill that would have permitted interstate branching. But in conference, the House's overwhelming rejection of anything but the narrowest bill that focused on the deposit insurance system remained the controlling factor.

House and Senate conferees produced a compromise version of S 543 on the final day of the session, Nov. 27, that was essentially the same as HR 3768.

The conference agreement was adopted easily and sent to the president.

15. Abortion 'Gag Rule'

Abortion rights advocates thought the Supreme Court's May 23 ruling in *Rust v. Sullivan* could be a blessing in disguise. Although they strenuously disagreed with the court's ruling — that controversial regulations issued in 1988 banning abortion counseling in federally funded family planning clinics did not violate the Constitution — they thought they finally had an issue that could transcend the traditional pro-choice and anti-abortion debates. Indeed, shortly after the court ruling, many abortion opponents in Congress declared that what opponents dubbed the "gag rule" in their view violated free speech rights by limiting discussion between patients and doctors and other health-care providers.

Opponents of the rules adopted a two-track strategy. One track consisted of legislation that would permanently overturn the rules and write into law the counseling and referral guidelines in effect between 1981 and 1988. The Senate in July passed a free-standing bill (S 323) to do just that, while the House Energy and Commerce Committee in August approved legislation to reauthorize the family planning program (HR 3090) that included provisions to overturn the rules.

But all along, proponents knew their best chance of success lay in the other half of the strategy: inserting language to block enforcement of the rules for one year into the popular spending bill (HR 2707) for the Departments of Labor, Health and Human Services, and Education. Procedural rules governing appropriations measures prevented inclusion of language to overturn the regulations outright.

But while abortion rights advocates were telling colleagues that the issue was not abortion but free speech, abortion opponents were stressing exactly the opposite. Together many of the groups formed the "Abortion is Not Family Planning Coalition," which bought newspaper ads to, in their words, clear up misconceptions about the rules and the effect they would have on federally funded family planning clinics.

The preliminary test on the issue came when the House Nov. 9 approved the conference report on the bill by a vote of 272-156, well short of the two-thirds needed to override Bush's promised veto. But the matter was complicated by a budget issue. Several Republicans who had already come out against the counseling ban said they could not vote for the bill because it pushed more than $4 billion worth of spending into fiscal 1993, thus threatening the viability of the 1990 budget agreement between the White House and Congress.

In his Nov. 19 veto message, Bush eliminated the budget issue. Although he mentioned the matter, he made it clear that the veto was primarily if not exclusively because of the abortion language.

The House Democratic leadership, including anti-abortion Majority Whip David E. Bonior, Mich., worked the issue hard, and a day before the vote Speaker Thomas S. Foley, Wash., predicted that the veto would be overridden.

But the votes that were picked up with the elimination of the budget issue were not enough to offset votes lost by abortion opponents, particularly 43 anti-abortion Democrats.

Members ultimately fell 12 votes short of the 288 they would have needed to override in the 276-156 tally: R 53-113; D 222-43 (ND 155-26, SD 67-17); I 1-0.

16. Campaign Finance

What isn't in a bill is often as important to its fate as what is. So it was in 1991 with campaign finance legislation in the House.

For the second straight year, House Democratic leaders pushed for legislation to limit campaign spending. But the 1991 version (HR 3750 — H Rept 102-340) contained something the 1990 bill avoided: direct public subsidies of campaigns.

The bill would set a $600,000 optional spending limit for House races in primary and general elections. Candidates who agreed to obey the limit would get benefits, including cut-rate postage and up to $200,000 in public financing doled out to match the first $200 of each individual contribution. The measure would also place a $200,000 aggregate cap on how much a candidate could accept from political action committees and a $200,000 aggregate cap on individual contributions of more than $200.

Given the partisan nature of the issue, the Democratic leadership did not want to risk bringing the measure to the floor without enough Democratic votes to assure its passage. So when conservative Democrats began raising objections to the public financing provisions, Sam Gejdenson, D-Conn., the chairman of a special task force on campaign finance, began giving ground.

Public financing had become the touchstone of opposition to the Senate bill earlier in the year when Republicans ridiculed a Democratic measure (S 3) as "food stamps for politicians." Democrats in both chambers countered that public financing was a small price to pay to control campaign costs and diminish the clout of special interests. But Southern Democrats in the House feared that they could not justify launching a new spending program for campaigns at an estimated cost of $75 million every two years when other needs were going unmet and the deficit was soaring.

Gejdenson sought to meet the objections even before introducing the measure Nov. 12. He rewrote draft language to keep the mechanism for raising the revenue vague, leaving that detail to a future tax bill. Instead, the bill as introduced said the money should be raised by limiting the tax deductions that organizations take for lobbying, an effort to make special interests bear the costs.

That still went too far for some, as it designated tax revenues for campaigns. So Gejdenson bent again. Before floor consideration, the bill was stripped of any meaningful way to pay for public financing of campaigns. In effect, the fight over how to pay for public financing was left for another day.

The change ensured widespread Democratic backing for the bill, and on Nov. 26 it easily passed, 273-156: R 21-144; D 251-12; (ND 176-4; SD 75-8); I 1-0.

KEY SENATE VOTES

1. Persian Gulf War

It was one of the rare instances when the mood of the Senate was as grave as the momentous matter being considered.

One by one, senators rose from their chairs to vote on H J Res 77, authorizing the president to use "all necessary means" to reverse Iraq's occupation of Kuwait. When the "yeas" and "nays" were called on Saturday afternoon Jan. 12, the resolution was approved 52-47: R 42-2; D 10-45 (ND 3-35, SD 7-10).

President Bush, after refusing for months to acknowledge that Congress had a formal role in the ultimate decision of whether to go to war, on Jan. 8 finally requested a congressional resolution authorizing force.

It marked the first such request by a president since the 1964 Gulf of Tonkin resolution, which had authorized U.S. military action during the Vietnam War.

But the administration was forced to scramble for votes even after the president made his request. An early projection by Minority Leader Bob Dole, R-Kan., that the resolution would receive 60 votes proved optimistic. By Jan. 10, Sen. Charles S. Robb, Va., a Democratic supporter of the measure, said the resolution stood only a "50-50 chance" of passing the Senate.

The issue was so much in doubt that the administration's allies delayed the introduction of the war resolution until Jan. 11 — the second day of the Senate debate on the issue.

The opposition was led by Senate Majority Leader George J. Mitchell, D-Maine. In opening the debate on the measure, Mitchell had pleaded with his colleagues to allow economic sanctions — imposed on Iraq after its invasion of Kuwait — more time to work.

Mitchell noted that hundreds of thousands of Americans were then preparing for battle in the gulf. "And the truly haunting question," he said, "which no one will ever be able to answer, will be: Did they die unnecessarily? For if we go to war now, no one will ever know if sanctions would have worked if given a full and fair chance."

Proponents of continued reliance on sanctions received important backing from Sam Nunn, D-Ga., the conservative chairman of the Armed Services Committee. Nunn's panel had held a series of hearings on the gulf that had featured the testimony of former generals and admirals, most of whom cautioned against a precipitous rush to war.

But in the end, a slim majority of senators agreed that the authorization of war represented, in the words of the president, "the last best chance for peace." Joseph I. Lieberman of Connecticut, who emerged as the leading Senate Democrat in support of the president's position, quoted the Greek historian Herodotus: "To have peace, you must prepare for war."

After the vote and the war's successful conclusion, Mitchell and other Democratic opponents of the resolution tried to minimize their differences with the administration. They emphasized that they would have been willing to ultimately support the use of force, provided that economic sanctions had been given more of a chance first.

But Sen. Phil Gramm, Texas, the combative chairman of the National Republican Senatorial Committee, predicted that voters would recall Democratic opposition to the war in 1992. "They are going to pay for that vote," Gramm said.

2. Highway Funding

To Trent Lott, R-Miss., the amendment was simple: Keep the federal government's share for Interstate maintenance and bridge projects at 90 percent and 80 percent, respectively. That way, states would continue to have funds and incentives to repair those roads.

Moynihan

But to New York Democrat Daniel Patrick Moynihan, principal author of the then-$124 billion surface transportation authorization (S 1204), the Lott amendment meant a relapse of a "public sector disease" — an ailment that caused public funds to be wasted when awarded with too few strings attached.

Despite intense lobbying pressure from state highway officials, the Senate on June 19 narrowly agreed, 53-44, to a Moynihan motion to table the Lott amendment: R 20-23, D 33-21 (ND 30-9, SD 3-12).

The vote on the amendment marked the end of the Interstate highway era, which was launched in 1956 based on a federal promise to pay 90 percent of all road-building costs. By rejecting it, senators showed they were prepared to abandon a 35-year-old policy of channeling highway funds to states at little or no cost. It also set the stage for Congress to clear for the president the sweeping final highway and transit bill on Nov. 26.

Along with lower federal shares, the legislation would force states and urban areas to compete for funds by tying the money to metropolitan planning requirements, giving urban areas more power and giving states flexibility to spend money on roads or transit.

Competition and productivity were central tenets of Moynihan's bill. He viewed his measure as his only chance to make good on a 31-year mission to stop states from blindly pouring concrete and ruining urban neighborhoods.

"The demand for 90-10 highway funds is so great that there is almost nothing, however sensible, that local governments would not do to get their share," Moynihan wrote in a 1960 essay.

Under the new bill, the federal government was to pay 80 percent for most road and mass transit projects. The government would shoulder 75 percent of the cost of building roads and bridges that added lanes for single-occupancy vehicles. The Bush administration wanted a 60-percent federal share for most road programs, but Moynihan refused to go that far because of the fiscal constraints facing states.

Lott had argued that current federal shares should be continued because states could not afford to pay more for road and bridge projects. "It is very important that we not shift more of the burden for these Interstate highways back to the states," Lott said.

After the vote, Moynihan said at least 15 senators told him that state transportation officials had urged them to vote for the crippling amendment. "Of course they did.... How can you say no to free money?" Moynihan asked. "Has no one heard anything we've said?"

3. Gun Control

After weeks of negotiations among Senate leaders, a compromise on the Brady bill was offered late June 28 and won a decisive 67-32 vote. It was the first time the Senate had approved a provision for a waiting period for handgun purchases, and adoption of it into an omnibus crime bill (S 1241) came amid constituent fears of escalating street violence.

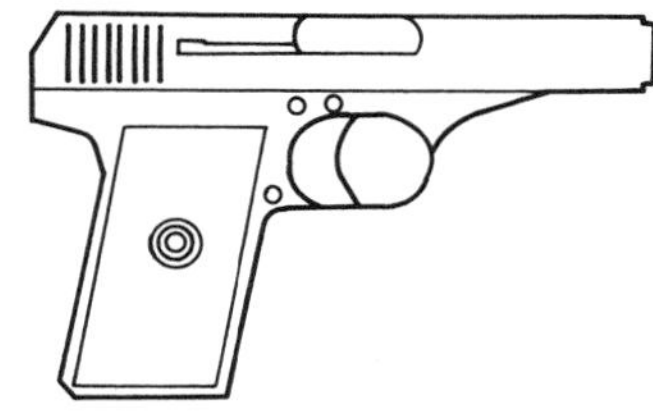

Phil Gramm, R-Texas, one of the strongest opponents of the provision, said at the time, "Our bleeding nation cries out for us to do something about crime." The provision required a five-business-day waiting period for handgun purchases and a plan for an immediate national background check of buyers that would take effect in two-and-a-half years. It superseded a House-passed measure (HR 7) for a seven-day wait with no timetable for an instantaneous check.

The proposal was named for former presidential press secretary James S. Brady, who was wounded in a 1981 assassination attempt on Ronald Reagan. Like many other elements of the Senate crime bill, it was folded into a conference committee crime bill (HR 3371) in November. That legislation stalled at the end of the first session of the 102nd Congress because of partisan differences largely unrelated to gun control.

Senate adoption of the gun-control measure came after opponents of the waiting period backed away from filibuster threats. Recognition that they could not gather the votes to defeat the bill came early June 28, when senators defeated, 44-54, an attempt to strip the Brady provision from the crime bill.

In addition to local crime concerns, the insertion of a timetable for an instantaneous check appeared to be a key factor in winning strong support for the compromise measure. Although the 67-32 vote was bipartisan, it was mostly Republicans who were fighting the Brady bill: R 19-24; D 48-8 (ND 37-3; SD 11-5).

Current law made it illegal for felons and people who have been adjudged mentally ill to buy guns. But there was no nationwide system in place to ensure that people who completed firearm purchase forms are not lying. For four years, a handful of lawmakers had been pushing for a waiting period.

They gained momentum in May when the House approved a related bill (HR 7) by a resounding 53 votes. *(House key vote 3, p. 35-B)*

That put the spotlight on the Senate, and Majority Leader George J. Mitchell, D-Maine, played a major role in the drive for a Senate version that shortened the waiting period from seven days to five business days and required a police background check.

Having the credibility that comes from representing a big sporting state, Mitchell worked on fellow Democrats to support the Brady bill. At the same time, Brady and his wife, Sarah, kept up their emotional pressure on wavering members.

Senate Minority Leader Bob Dole, R-Kan., helped craft the final compromise to help speed action on the crime bill, as did Howard M. Metzenbaum, D-Ohio, who had proposed the original seven-day waiting period in the Senate.

4. Superconducting Super Collider

For the first time, the Senate went on record in support of the superconducting super collider — the giant atom smasher under construction in Waxahachie, Texas, and a symbol of government investment in "big science" projects.

Senate supporters July 10 handily rallied to back the project, which could take until the end of the century and cost at least $8 billion to complete. But it was clear that the 1991 battle, sparked by an effort to kill the smasher, would be the first of many such attempts to derail it.

The Senate vote came during debate on the fiscal 1992 energy and water development appropriations bill (PL 102-104). J. Bennett Johnston, D-La., a strong collider supporter, moved to kill on a tabling motion an amendment offered by Dale Bumpers, D-Ark., that would have eliminated $509 million in funding for the atom smasher. Bumpers' attempt failed when the motion carried, 62-37: R 33-10; D 29-27 (ND 19-21, SD 10-6).

The vote was critical not only because it put the Senate on record for the first time in support of the project but also because it set the stage for what is likely to become an annual debate about the project's cost and scope. The vote also cleared the way to begin construction on the project.

The super collider was to use powerful magnets to hurl protons — particles of matter smaller than atoms — through a 54-mile underground tunnel. Scientists planned to use powerful computers to analyze the debris in an effort to unlock the secrets of the building blocks of matter.

Bumpers argued that the scientific knowledge likely to be yielded by the project was too uncertain given the nation's tight economic times. In addition, he said, supporters had overstated the potential commercial spinoffs to flow from research on the atom smasher. "It would be nice to know the origin of matter," said Bumpers. "It would also be nice to have a balanced budget."

Johnston, who wielded considerable political clout because of his chairmanship of the Energy and Water Development Appropriations Subcommittee, jumped to the project's defense along with both Texas senators. They argued that the project would provide a crucial step in our nation's search for knowledge and would augment U.S. competitiveness.

Perhaps as important to the success of those who quashed the Bumpers amendment was the promise of lucrative research projects linked to the atom smasher and expected to be spread over 43 states. Supporters asserted that a total of 60,000 jobs nationwide were on the line. The White House also lobbied hard for the project.

Though unsuccessful, the attack on the project's funding signaled an end to an era of uncritical support for big-science projects. Opponents several weeks later launched a similar attack on funding for the space station *Freedom*. In the end, the Senate backed the space station by a two-thirds margin, but the vote was the first time the Senate had questioned space station funding.

Although just 37 senators voted against Johnston's motion regarding the super collider, the group included some prominent Republicans, suggesting that the pro-collider lobbying effort launched by the White House lacked full Republican support. Among Republicans voting against Johnston's motion were Republican Whip Alan K. Simpson of Wyoming and Richard G. Lugar of Indiana. Among Democrats, support for Bumpers' effort to eliminate funding came largely from states in the northern Midwest, Great Plains and East, where the project was not expected to generate contract dollars.

5. Honoraria Ban

Historians will mark July 17, 1991, as the day the Senate finally outlawed what critics called a legally sanctioned form of bribery: the acceptance by lawmakers of whopping fees for throw-away speeches from favor-seeking interest groups. "There is nothing honorable about honoraria," said Robert C. Byrd, D-W.Va., the Senate patriarch and a converted one-time defender of the system.

Robert C. Byrd

Senators had twice previously approved the outright ban on all honoraria, but only on purely symbolic votes void of effect. To make it stick required an incentive, a quid pro quo, in fact — a $23,200 pay raise to compensate members for the forgone honoraria income.

The Senate was the last institution in the federal government that continued to allow officials to accept the speaking fees. For years, ethics purists had been complaining about the practice, which defenders argued had ancient traditions. The critics made some headway in the 1970s, persuading Congress to limit the size of the fees and the total amount that could be pocketed each year. But tales of $2,000 breakfast appearances kept the issue alive for years.

After vacillating on the matter for more than a decade, Congress in 1989 barred every employee but those in the Senate from accepting the fees as of Jan. 1, 1991. The Senate balked because leaders could not persuade a majority to accept a House-passed, 40 percent pay raise. Instead, senators took a much smaller pay raise and voted to phase out honoraria slowly as their government salaries grew with future automatic annual increases.

That decision created the pressure that eventually killed the practice. Senators resented being paid less than House members; as of Jan. 1, their annual salary was $101,900, compared with $125,100 for House members. The vagaries of the rules under which congressional aides were paid provided an additional slap: Some top House staffers were being paid more than senators.

As the annual legislative branch spending bill (HR 2506) began making its way toward the floor, Sen. Christopher J. Dodd, D-Conn., and Patrick J. Leahy, D-Vt., publicly mulled offering the honoraria-ban amendment to that must-pass measure. That prompted Byrd to act.

Byrd had laid the groundwork earlier — though he denied a connection — by inserting a provision in the bill to bar Senate staff from accepting honoraria and to allow top aides to earn more than their bosses. The effect was more than symbolic: Senators would be almost totally isolated as virtually the only 100 employees among millions in the federal government still allowed to accept speaking fees.

The former majority leader methodically gathered votes in favor of an honoraria-ban/pay-raise amendment. He gave members up for re-election in 1992 a pass, and in the end, only seven of those 33 voted for the amendment. To compensate, Byrd pressed the chamber's richest members the hardest, persuading a few to reverse their longstanding opposition to pay raises.

Floor consideration of the spending bill was delayed until Byrd had a majority of both parties ready to vote yea. As dusk approached July 17, he confirmed he had the votes by double-checking each at an invitation-only kaffeeklatsch in his office.

A pending bill was abruptly pulled from the floor at 7 p.m., and the legislative-branch spending bill was brought up without notice to the press or the public. Debate was perfunctory on Byrd's amendment.

The amendment passed, 53-45: R 25-18; D 28-27 (ND 22-18, SD 6-9). The House later accepted the provision but not before insisting that the Senate tighten its definition on what constituted honoraria and agree to loosen congressional gift-acceptance rules.

6. China MFN

Majority Leader George J. Mitchell, D-Maine, won Senate approval for a bill requiring China's communist regime to make deep reforms in order to qualify for a renewal of its low-tariff, most-favored-nation (MFN) trade status in 1992.

But while a majority of senators favored the bill, the July 23 vote fell short of the two-thirds necessary to overcome a promised veto, signaling the failure of Mitchell's effort to retaliate for the Chinese government's brutal attack on pro-democracy protesters in Tiananmen Square two years before.

President Bush had made it clear that he would reject any interference from Congress in his handling of Beijing and its octogenarian communist leaders.

Two weeks earlier, the House had voted by a wide margin to set stiff conditions on an MFN renewal. But there was never any question about the bill's fate in the House, which had shown strong support for conditions in 1990. As a result, the White House largely ignored the House and concentrated its efforts on the Senate. Since there was no chance of the bill being defeated in that chamber, the administration opted from the beginning for a veto strategy — getting enough votes to prevent the president from being overridden and holding on to them at all costs.

Mitchell's bill would have required China to account for and release demonstrators arrested during the Tiananmen Square protests as well as to make progress toward lowering its trade deficit with the United States, improving the treatment of dissidents and religious groups and ending exports of missiles and other weapons. The bill contained a variety of other conditions as well.

Before and during floor consideration, Mitchell accepted numerous modifications in an effort to get enough votes to override a veto. By the end, the bill had become a lengthy laundry list, tying MFN renewal to, among other things, China ending assistance for the Khmer Rouge in Cambodia, providing better protection for U.S. patents, reducing assistance to Cuba and ending forced abortions.

Despite the amendment fest, Mitchell could not overcome two factors: First, Bush, a former U.S. envoy to Beijing, enjoyed a deep well of loyalty among Republicans, who were inclined to give his China policy the benefit of the doubt. Second, farm-state Democrats feared that withdrawing China's MFN status would mean the loss of the lucrative Chinese market, which accounted for more than $500 million in U.S. wheat sales last year.

Imitating a strategy that had been successful during the fight over U.S.-Mexico free trade negotiations, the White House pledged to take a series of steps to bring pressure on China — and thus lessen the pressure on Congress to act.

It worked better than the White House might have expected.

After the Senate acted in July, the bill languished until November, when a House-Senate conference was convened to negotiate a final version of the bill.

Only the House voted on the conference report. With no hope of overriding a veto, the Senate did not act on the bill.

In the July vote, a bloc of six conservative Republicans joined 49 Democrats in voting for Mitchell's bill. The vote was 55-44: R 6-37; D 49-7 (ND 36-4; SD 13-3).

7. Women in Combat

Inspired by the prominent role women played in the armed services during the Persian Gulf War, critics of the law that barred assignment of women to certain combat roles began to chip away at that barrier. The law prohibited the assignment of women to Navy warships or to combat aircraft in the Navy, Marine Corps or Air Force. No law prohibited the assignment of Army women to combat jobs, but such assignments were ruled out as a matter of policy.

Female officers long had argued that their career prospects were limited by their inability to serve in combat units that were at the core of their services' missions. Their cause gained clout from the generally glowing reviews of the job performance of women deployed to the gulf region — including women who flew airplanes and helicopters behind enemy lines on ostensibly non-combat missions.

By highlighting the threat posed by ballistic missiles and chemical weapons to warriors far behind the traditional "front lines," the gulf war also called into question the assumption that women assigned to traditionally non-combatant military jobs would be safe.

When the House Armed Services Committee marked up the fiscal 1992 defense authorization bill in May, critics of the combat exclusion law proposed a repeal of the ban on assigning women to combat aircraft. Since all military aviators were volunteers, proposing the change for that group finessed the argument that dropping the law might have forced women into combat against their will.

The committee accepted the provision, and no effort was made on the House floor to delete it before the authorization bill was passed.

But a majority of the Senate Armed Services Committee, led by John Glenn, D-Ohio, and John McCain, R-Ariz., opposed immediate repeal of the combat exclusion law for pilots. As an alternative, the panel included in its version of the authorization bill a provision establishing a blue-ribbon presidential commission to study issues that would be raised by assigning women to combat roles.

When the Senate took up the bill, Glenn and McCain sweetened their alternative by offering an amendment allowing the Pentagon to waive the combat exclusion laws on a trial basis so women would be assigned to any kind of combat unit to provide data for the commission's study. But after accepting that amendment 96-3, the Senate on July 31 also adopted an amendment by Edward M. Kennedy, D-Mass., and William V. Roth Jr., R-Del., waiving the combat exclusion law for women on aircrews in the Navy, Marine Corps and Air Force. A motion to table (kill) the Kennedy-Roth amendment was rejected 30-69: R 14-29; D 16-40 (ND 6-34; SD 10-6).

Although President Bush signed into law the defense authorization measure (HR 2100 — PL 102-190), a Pentagon spokesman said the Defense Department was not likely to make any move to revise its policies banning women from combat until the commission created by the bill completed its work late in 1992.

8. Strategic Defense Initiative

Even before President Reagan launched the Strategic Defense Initiative (SDI) in 1983, Sen. Malcolm Wallop, R-Wyo., and other proponents contended that missile defense would be a winning political issue if it ever got onto the national agenda.

Wallop

The congressional debate on SDI did not get under way in earnest until 1986. Despite critics who ridiculed the idea as a costly and dangerous "Star Wars" fantasy, Wallop's judgment appeared vindicated by Congress' repeated votes to fund the program. Although Congress annually sliced by one-third or more the amounts requested by Reagan and Bush for anti-missile research, lawmakers repeatedly rejected proposals to make more far-reaching cuts that would have restricted SDI to laboratory-based research.

Reagan presented SDI as a revolutionary improvement in national security that would supplant the balance of nuclear terror as the central influence in the U.S.-Soviet military rivalry. SDI officials and conservative missile defense advocates such as Wallop envisioned a network of space-based weapons intended to intercept Soviet missiles in the first few minutes of flight, before they dispensed multiple warheads and swarms of decoys.

But that approach alienated a cadre of key Democrats, including Senate Armed Services Committee Chairman Sam Nunn, Ga., and his House counterpart, Les Aspin, Wis. These centrist critics deemed Reagan's vision of SDI technically infeasible. Moreover, they warned that a U.S. effort to defend against all-out Soviet attack would foster a more vigorous Soviet effort to develop new strategic weapons intended to circumvent SDI.

As an alternative, Nunn and Aspin promoted a more modest anti-missile program: Designed to avoid the appearance of threatening Moscow's retaliatory capacity, this defense would be intended to protect U.S. territory, overseas forces and allies against "limited" attacks, which might be launched by a Third World country or by a renegade military unit. In 1991, the war with Iraq underscored the potential threat of radical Third World regimes armed with ballistic missiles and nuclear or chemical warheads. And the political disintegration of the Soviet Union highlighted the possibility that Moscow's tight rein on its nuclear weapons might slacken.

President Bush's fiscal 1992 budget request recast SDI toward that kind of mission. But he retained the controversial space-based weapons as a key part of the program.

In shaping the annual defense authorization bill (HR 2100 — PL 102-190), Senate Armed Services Republicans led by John W. Warner, Va., hammered out a compromise SDI package with conservative and centrist Democrats: The new approach put aside plans to deploy space-based weapons while providing funds to continue research on them. It directed the president to deploy by 1996 a ground-based anti-missile system at a single site that would comply with the 1972 treaty limiting anti-ballistic missiles (ABMs). And it called on the president to negotiate with the Soviet Union changes in the ABM Treaty that would allow more extensive ABM testing and deployment.

The compromise provision contained a strong implication that the United States should abrogate the ABM Treaty if the Soviet Union did not agree to amend the pact. On the Senate floor, Jeff Bingaman, D-N.M., offered an amendment intended to dilute that threat by declaring that the maintenance of strategic stability between the U.S. and Soviet arsenals was the overriding goal and by deleting references to the deployment of ground-based weapons at a single site as an "initial" deployment. But Bingaman's amendment was rejected July 31 by a vote of 43-56: R 2-41; D 41-15 (ND 33-7; SD 8-8).

9. Domestic Spending

When Congress returned from its August recess, the world had been transformed. Plotters in the Soviet Union had tried to mount a coup and failed; the collapse of the Soviet empire appeared assured. The Soviet military threat that the United States had been girding to fight for 50 years had evaporated, and if ever there were a time to cut back on defense spending, this seemed to be it.

Harkin

It certainly looked that way to Sen. Tom Harkin, D-Iowa, who had started before the recess to push an amendment to the fiscal 1992 Labor-HHS appropriations bill taking $3.15 billion out of defense to beef up spending for 10 domestic programs that he insisted had been underfunded.

As chairman of the Senate Labor-HHS Appropriations Subcommittee, Harkin said an inadequate allocation at the beginning of the year had forced him to give short shrift to such line items as the National Cancer Institute, child immunization programs, Pell student aid grants and Head Start, the widely acclaimed program for low-income preschool children.

Now was the time to right that wrong, Harkin argued. He proposed to rescind sufficient 1992 defense outlays and prior-year unobligated defense balances to pay for the domestic spending increases. "Do we start investing in solutions to our nation's critical problems?" Harkin asked. "Or, in the aftermath of the events of the past month, do we continue to pour billions of dollars into the subsidy of Europe's defense against a now-nonexistent Soviet Union?"

Harkin had a problem, however. Under the terms of the 1990 budget summit agreement, any reduction in defense spending could be used only for deficit reduction — it could not be used to increase spending for domestic programs, as he was proposing. So, before he could get a straight, up-or-down vote on his amendment, he first had to convince three-fifths of the Senate — 60 senators — to agree to waive the Budget Act.

That brought defenders of the budget agreement to the floor, warning that while they might agree with Harkin's desire to increase spending for important programs, it would be far too dangerous to break the budget deal.

"I have a great deal of sympathy" for the amendment, said Budget Committee Chairman Jim Sasser, D-Tenn. But "if we can breach the budget summit agreement for this particular appropriations bill, then clearly we can breach it for a whole host of appropriations bills to follow. [That] is a short-term ticket for fiscal chaos in this body."

Harkin received an even more direct rebuke from Appropriations Committee Chairman Robert C. Byrd, D-W.Va., who spent the better part of an hour warning that the amendment could put all domestic appropriations spending at risk of an across-the-board spending cut. "The amendment would destroy the budget agreement," Byrd said. "I ask all senators not to go down this road of chaos."

In the end, the politically attractive trade-off in Harkin's package could not overcome the Senate's reluctance to break the budget deal they had agreed to less than two years before. The motion was rejected, 28-69: (R 3-39; D 25-30 (ND 24-14, SD 1-16), Sept. 10, 1991.

The budget agreement's defenders had mounted a major effort to convincingly defeat Harkin so that others with similar ideas would think twice. This turned out to be the clearest test of the strength of the budget deal, which remained intact through the end of the year.

10. Unemployment Benefits

Throughout the long debate over providing extra weeks of unemployment benefits to the long-term jobless, the Senate took a more conservative approach than the House. Congress first passed an unemployment bill in August but was blocked by President Bush. During Congress' second attempt to enact a bill, the House wanted to require Bush to pay for the measure through deficit spending. Simply signing the bill would have been the equivalent of declaring a budget emergency, and the money would have flowed to the long-term unemployed.

The Senate, on the other hand, said Bush should decide whether there was an emergency and whether the money should be spent. Senators voted 69-30 on Sept. 24 in favor of that approach.

But Congress had already tried that in August. Bush had refused to declare an emergency, and most unemployed workers were receiving no more than 26 weeks of state benefits. Few federal benefits were finding their way into the hands of the unemployed through the standard extended benefits program.

In a House-Senate conference, House Democrats insisted on forcing Bush to sign or veto the measure without any wiggle room. That way, at least, Congress would have a chance to override a veto. The conference report was sent back to the Senate, where many Republicans were angry with the change from the bill they had just passed. Congress' ability to override an expected veto rested with 13 Republican senators who had initially supported the measure. If just four Republicans changed their votes, the Senate would not have the 67 votes needed to override, and Bush's veto would prevail.

The $6.4 billion bill that came back from conference would have given an additional seven weeks of unemployment benefits to workers in 30 states and the District of Columbia, an additional 13 weeks to workers in 14 states and an additional 20 weeks to workers in six states where unemployment exceeded 8 percent.

The vote was a test of loyalty to the president, but the White House was confident of GOP senators' support and barely lifted a finger to lobby them. Rather, the Senate minority leader, Bob Dole of Kansas, worked the issue extensively. Ultimately, the House language on emergency spending was the reason that five Republicans who had voted for the earlier Democratic bill changed their votes on the conference report. They were: John C. Danforth and Christopher S. Bond of Missouri; John Seymour of California; Conrad Burns of Montana; and David Durenberger of Minnesota. The conference report passed by 65-35 on Oct. 1, two votes short of the number needed to override a veto: R 8-35; D 57-0 (ND 40-0, SD 17-0).

It was a key vote because it finally convinced Senate Democrats that it was time to negotiate with the administration — particularly over finding a way to pay for the measure.

By Nov. 15, Congress sent Bush a $5.4 billion bill to extend unemployment benefits for nearly 3 million people. Bush signed the bill the same day he received it.

11. Family and Medical Leave

It was the second go-round for legislation to require businesses to allow their workers to take unpaid leave for the birth or adoption of a child or for their own serious illness or that of an immediate family member. Democrats had promoted the issue as their own kinder, gentler vision for the country's middle class. But businesses had responded with stiff opposition to being told what to do.

The legislation had already failed to be enacted in 1990; senators had never gone on record voting for or against the measure; and House and Senate leaders knew they did not have the votes in 1991 to override a promised veto. Enter Christopher S. Bond, R-Mo., and bill sponsor Christopher J. Dodd, D-Conn. The pair forged a slightly modified compromise to attract the votes needed for a two-thirds majority — 67 votes.

The Bond-Dodd compromise raised the number of hours an employee had to work from 1,000 hours to 1,250 hours per year in order to qualify for the unpaid leave. It also allowed employers to deny leave to "key employees," defined as those who were the highest paid 10 percent of the company's work force. That provision was included in the House bill (HR 2) but not in the Senate version.

The bill itself would mandate that businesses with more than 50 workers give workers up to 12 weeks of unpaid leave for the birth or adoption of a child or for the serious illness of the worker or an immediate family member.

The compromise came before the Senate Oct. 2 amid intensive lobbying — by women's groups and unions for the measure and by business organizations against it. In 1990, the Senate approved a Family and Medical Leave bill by voice vote. When Bush vetoed the bill, the House sustained him, and senators were never subject to a recorded vote. In 1991, members voted 65-32 for the compromise language: R 15-28; D 50-4 (ND 38-0, SD 12-4). It was two short of the 67 needed for the two-thirds majority that could override a veto. But both supporters and opponents assumed that all three absent Democrats — David Pryor, Ark., and presidential candidates Tom Harkin, Iowa, and Bob Kerrey, Neb. — would have voted for the substitute.

Despite the big vote, senators were not sanguine that they could force the bill into law over Bush's objections. The House had not been able to attract as much support for the compromise language, and many Republicans who had voted for the measure might have buckled on an override vote. "People understand the loyalty factor" and don't punish those who switch votes to support their party's president, said Orrin G. Hatch, R-Utah. In 1992, the House and Senate were to reconcile their two bills and send them back to their chambers for approval before shipping the final version to the president.

12. Thomas Confirmation

Politics and increasing conflicts between the court and Congress converged to give Clarence Thomas, President Bush's second high court nominee, the closest Supreme Court confirmation vote in more than a century.

After two sets of divisive hearings before the Senate Judiciary Committee, the full Senate voted on Oct. 15 to approve Thomas, 52-48: R 41-2; D 11-46 (ND 3-37, SD 8-9).

While Thomas, 43, became only the second black justice on the court, his confirmation was likely to be remembered more for the upheaval over sexual harassment allegations. Senators were to vote on Thomas' nomination Oct. 8. But two days before that scheduled vote, University of Oklahoma law professor Anita F. Hill went public with allegations that Thomas had sexually harassed her when she worked for him at the Department of Education and Equal Employment Opportunity Commission (EEOC).

The Senate Judiciary Committee reconvened to produce three days of nationally televised hearings that, because of their explicit subject matter and window into Senate discord, became the talk of the country.

Both sides estimated that Thomas lost about 10 votes that he might have had before the Hill allegations emerged — narrowing an outcome that still would have been one of the closest in history. But only three senators publicly shifted positions. Democrats Richard H. Bryan, Nev., Joseph I. Lieberman, Conn., and Harry Reid, Nev., withdrew their support. They said they were influenced by Hill's testimony.

The vote ended up being largely partisan, although 11 Democrats, mostly Southerners, made up the margin of difference needed to seat Thomas, a federal appeals court judge who had worked in the Bush and Ronald Reagan administrations for eight years.

Most opponents said Thomas was too conservative and lacked the qualifications for the high court. They also accused Bush of nominating Thomas more for his color than for his credentials. As a black conservative, Thomas' nomination effectively split the minority community and made it difficult for the liberal groups that traditionally opposed conservative nominees to drum up support.

Sen. John C. Danforth, R-Mo., for whom Thomas had twice worked, was credited with keeping the nomination on track.

In many ways, the court's conservative tilt raised the stakes on the nomination and led to the storm over Thomas. Before Thomas was nominated to fill the seat of retiring Justice Thurgood Marshall, Bush and Reagan had named a total of six conservative jurists, including the 1986 elevation of William H. Rehnquist to chief justice. A majority on the high court was lining up with the administration in favor of law enforcement over defendants' rights and on many questions involving whether state authority should supersede individual protections, such as on free speech and abortion.

The Democratic majority in Congress was increasingly finding itself on the other side of battles against the administration and the Court, and Senate Democrats said they were not inclined to give another conservative nominee the benefit of the doubt.

13. Civil Rights

The Senate's overwhelming vote on a compromise job-rights bill was not as dramatic as what had come before: a week of sudden and intense negotiations between the White House and senators to produce a compromise on the hard-fought legislation. The bill was approved by the Senate Oct. 30 by a vote of 93-5: R 38-5; D 55-0 (ND 38-0, SD 17-0).

The deal ended a two-year struggle to reinstate protections for victims of job bias that had been narrowed by the Supreme Court. It also closed a chapter of racial politicking in Congress and the White House that earlier in the year had seemed so divisive as to preclude agreement on a bill. President Bush had vetoed a related bill in 1990.

What changed was the political dynamic. The issue of sexual harassment had been elevated on the national agenda by the Clarence Thomas-Anita F. Hill hearings. The Republican White House also was concerned about fallout from the primary success of Louisiana gubernatorial candidate David Duke, a Republican and former Ku Klux Klansman. (Duke eventually lost but declared his candidacy for president.)

The confluence of those October events intensified gender and racial politics and shifted the atmosphere. Sensing that Bush could no longer count enough GOP senators to sustain another veto, the White House cut a deal with Senate proponents the week of Oct. 21.

The final pact involved the liberal Democrats who began the push for the legislation in 1989 (led by Edward M. Kennedy, D-Mass.) and key moderate Republicans who kept negotiations going with the White House while warnings of quota hiring swirled (led by John C. Danforth, R-Mo.). Bush had charged that earlier versions of the bill would have forced businesses to hire set numbers of minorities and women to avoid lawsuits.

Both Democrats and Republicans tried to claim that they had won the better deal. Indeed, each side made concessions. But the bottom line was that overall, most of the original plan to reverse the court and to give victims of harassment and other intentional discrimination money damages prevailed.

Although workers were likely to be better off under the bill, to what degree was still uncertain because the final agreement left some of the toughest issues to be resolved in the federal courts. The new law, signed by Bush on Nov. 21, countered the effects of nine Supreme Court decisions and made it easier for victims of bias to bring lawsuits to enforce protections already on the books. A key to the compromise was an open-ended provision on how businesses might justify the discriminatory effects of seemingly fair hiring practices, such as tests and academic requirements. Those practices would have to be job-related and necessary to a business' operation. It would be up to the courts to interpret the new standard.

The law also allowed, for the first time, limited money damages for victims of harassment and other intentional discrimination based on sex, religion or disability. Racial minorities already could win money damages under a Reconstruction-era law.

The compromise set caps on damages for intentional bias, ranging from $50,000 for companies with 100 or fewer workers to $300,000 for employers with more than 500 workers.

Democrats in both chambers said that in 1992 they would push legislation to lift such limits.

14. Energy Policy

The oil concerns of the Persian Gulf War created a legislative push for new energy policy early in 1991. But a massive Senate energy bill was eventually slowed by controversy and, when it finally went to the floor late in the year, lawmakers voted to kill the measure — at least temporarily.

The energy bill (S 1220) was crafted by Louisiana Democrat J. Bennett Johnston, and it sped through the Energy and Natural Resources Committee he chaired. The bill would have touched almost every sector of energy policy. But it became best known for proposing to open Alaska's Arctic National Wildlife Refuge to drilling and for failing to mandate specific increases in federal gas mileage standards. Other provisions would have streamlined the licensing of nuclear power plants, eased federal regulation of the electric industry and mandated certain conservation measures and the use of non-gasoline transportation fuels.

Johnston and other advocates said the bill was politically balanced and would have made a critical move toward reducing U.S. dependence on oil imports. But environmental groups and their congressional allies put the bill at the top of their hit list, saying it would have encouraged environmentally damaging production measures and done little to promote energy efficiency and conservation. Many Democrats in particular were cool to the bill, which they saw as kin to a controversial Bush administration policy unveiled early in 1991.

Johnston fought hard to get the bill to the floor, despite a filibuster led by a group of junior Democrats opposed to the Alaska drilling provision. On Nov. 1, the Senate voted 50-44 to shut off debate, 10 votes short of the 60 needed to invoke cloture: R 32-9; D 18-35 (ND 9-28, SD 9-7).

The vote was a powerful setback in the push to enact new energy legislation. It also represented a stunning defeat for

Johnston and the administration, which had endorsed the measure. While acknowledging that the bill included many controversial provisions, Johnston had repeatedly insisted he had enough votes to bring it up for debate. Even opponents had not expected to win by such a large margin.

Environmental groups seized upon the outcome as a mandate for a new approach to energy legislation that would stress efficiency, conservation and environmental protection. Opposition to Alaska drilling did provide the fervor behind the filibuster effort and many of the votes against cloture. Opponents promised to return with a new, more progressive energy bill.

However, the message behind the final tally was considerably more muddled. The filibuster also won support from utilities opposed to the bill's electric industry restructuring and from some auto interests who feared it would become a vehicle for boosting federal fuel-efficiency mandates. Johnston had ignited some turf battles by refusing to refer the bill to several committees that shared jurisdiction on certain energy issues, and nine committee chairmen were among those voting against cloture.

Some of the bill's proponents criticized the vote as proof that Congress, absent an imminent oil crisis, did not have the courage to enact energy policy. However, both Johnston and some of his critics said they would try to move some energy bill early in 1992.

15. Gates Confirmation

When Robert M. Gates was nominated in May to be director of central intelligence, administration officials bargained that lawmakers would be so weary of investigating the involvement of Gates and others in the Iran-contra affair that he would quickly be confirmed.

Gates

They might have been right, had a former CIA official not pleaded guilty on July 9 to unlawfully withholding from Congress information about the agency's role in the 1986 scandal. That plea rekindled a question that had forced Gates to withdraw his name from consideration for the No. 1 job in 1987: As the No. 2 man at the CIA, just how much *had* he known about the illegal diversion of funds from Iranian arms sales to help the contra rebels in Nicaragua?

The Senate Intelligence Committee delayed Gates' confirmation hearings, initially set to begin July 15, for two months to try to determine what role the CIA had played in the diversion. When the hearings opened, the panel had compiled an exhaustive record revealing numerous inconsistencies between Gates' account of events and the accounts of others.

But it quickly became clear from Gates' testimony and that of other witnesses that it would come down to a question of his word against theirs. The same was true of allegations from former and current subordinates of Gates at the CIA that he had forced agency analysts to slant their reports to bolster administration policy objectives.

In the end, the nominee had a lot going for him. He had solid support from Republicans who vowed to stick with the president's nominee unless convinced otherwise. He also had the strong backing of Chairman David L. Boren, D-Okla., who had worked closely with Gates and had found him extremely candid with Congress.

Gates promised that as the nation's chief intelligence official he would work closely with Congress in its oversight role as he put in place massive changes in the way the intelligence community conducted business in the post-Cold War era. Gates' supporters argued that while he may have made some past errors in judgment, he was the best man for the job because of his intellect, lengthy government service and close ties with President Bush.

Some Democrats, led by New Jersey's Bill Bradley, tried to attack Gates' credibility and questioned how the agency could attain an image of openness and honesty with a leader whose record was tainted. But the arguments fell on deaf ears.

A crucial factor was the timing of the Gates vote, just three weeks after the tumultuous debate over Bush's nomination of Clarence Thomas to the Supreme Court. Few members had any desire to take on another key nomination so soon, especially when there was no clear-cut proof that Gates had behaved illegally or unethically. Gates was confirmed on Nov. 5 by a vote of 64-31: R 42-0; D 22-31 (ND 11-25, SD 11-6).

16. Soviet Aid

In a remarkable reversal, Congress agreed in the last hours of its session to give the president the authority to spend up to $500 million in defense funds to help the transformation of the former Soviet Union.

The action was remarkable because just two weeks earlier the chairmen of the Armed Services committees — Rep. Les Aspin, D-Wis., and Sen. Sam Nunn, D-Ga. — had to withdraw a $1 billion aid proposal because of lawmakers' reluctance to spend money on a former enemy when so many domestic needs were not being met. And President Bush, under attack from Democrats for devoting too much attention to foreign policy, refused to endorse the proposal.

But only days before adjournment, a bipartisan group of senior senators decided to give it one last try. These senators — led by Nunn and Richard G. Lugar, R-Ind. — crafted a scaled-back proposal that targeted the funds toward helping the Soviets and the republics dismantle some of the 27,000 nuclear weapons inside their territories. The group argued that the assistance was not "foreign aid" but a defensive move to reduce the nuclear threat against the United States. The senators cited a Harvard study that detailed the potential disaster that could result if the weapons fell into the wrong hands.

Repeated attempts by the senators to elicit White House support for the plan failed, although sponsors said they had been encouraged privately by administration officials. On the Senate floor, however, the proposal received an unusually warm welcome, a tribute to the high regard in which Nunn, Lugar and other sponsors were held by their colleagues, not to mention to their success in repackaging what had been an unpopular proposal. The proposal was adopted on Nov. 25 by a vote of 86-8: R 34-8; D 52-0 (ND 36-0, SD 16-0).

A subsequent amendment to allow another $200 million in aid to help the Soviets transport food and medical supplies to survive the winter was also approved, 87-7.

With the overwhelming backing of the Senate, the proposal had little trouble in the House. The proposal, modified to provide a total of $500 million for both the demilitarization and humanitarian aid, was approved by voice vote in the early morning hours of Nov. 27.

The Senate cleared the legislation later that day by voice vote.

Eleven days later the administration endorsed it.

HOUSE KEY VOTES 1, 2, 3, 4, 5, 6, 7, 8

Following are 1991 votes selected by Congressional Quarterly as key votes (explanation of key votes on page 34-B). Original vote number is provided in parentheses.

1. H J Res 77. Use of Force against Iraq/Passage. Passage of the joint resolution to authorize the use of military force if Iraq has not withdrawn from Kuwait and complied with U.N. Security Council resolutions by Jan. 15. The resolution authorizes the use of force and the expenditure of funds under the War Powers Act. Passed 250-183: R 164-3; D 86-179 (ND 33-147, SD 53-32); I 0-1, Jan. 12, 1991 (House vote 9). A "yea" was a vote supporting the president's position. *(Story, p. 34-B)*

2. HR 1315. RTC Financing/Passage. Passage of the bill to provide $30 billion to the Resolution Trust Corporation to cover fiscal 1991 losses of failed thrifts; also requires that requests for more money for the RTC be accompanied by a spending plan. Rejected 201-220: R 120-42; D 81-177 (ND 44-132, SD 37-45); I 0-1, March 12, 1991 (House vote 42). A "yea" was a vote supporting the president's position. *(Story, p. 35-B)*

3. HR 7. Handgun Waiting Period/Passage. Passage of the bill to require a seven-day waiting period for handgun purchases, allowing local law enforcement authorities to check the background of prospective buyers to determine whether they have a criminal record. The waiting period requirement would end when a national computer system for instant checks became operational. Passed 239-186: R 60-102; D 179-83 (ND 138-41, SD 41-42); I 0-1, May 8, 1991 (House vote 83). *(Story, p. 35-B)*

4. HR 2100. Fiscal 1992 Defense Authorization/SDI. Dellums, D-Calif., amendment to terminate the Strategic Defense Initiative program and permit only a basic SDI research program funded at $1.1 billion. Rejected 118-266: R 2-149; D 115-117 (ND 104-55, SD 11-62); I 1-0, May 20, 1991 (House vote 97). A "nay" was a vote supporting the president's position. *(Story, p. 36-B)*

5. H Res 101. Disapproval of Fast-Track Procedures/Adoption. Adoption of the resolution to disapprove the president's request to extend for two more years fast-track procedures that would require legislation implementing trade agreements to be considered within 60 days of introduction under limited debate and with no amendments permitted. Rejected 192-231: R 21-140; D 170-91 (ND 128-50, SD 42-41); I 1-0, May 23, 1991 (House vote 115). A "nay" was a vote supporting the president's position. *(Story, p. 36-B)*

6. HR 2427. Fiscal 1992 Energy and Water Appropriations/Superconducting Super Collider. Slattery, D-Kan., amendment to eliminate all funding for the superconducting super collider, $434 million, primarily by reducing the bill's funding level for general science and research activities. Rejected 165-251: R 58-101; D 106-150 (ND 86-87, SD 20-63); I 1-0, May 29, 1991 (House vote 117). A "nay" was a vote supporting the president's position. *(Story, p. 37-B)*

7. HR 1. Civil Rights Act of 1991/Passage. Passage of the bill to reverse or modify a series of Supreme Court rulings that narrowed the reach and remedies of job discrimination laws and to authorize compensatory and punitive damages for victims of discrimination based on sex, religion or disability. Passed 273-158: R 22-143; D 250-15 (ND 177-4, SD 73-11); I 1-0, June 5, 1991 (House vote 131). A "nay" was a vote supporting the president's position. *(Story, p. 37-B)*

8. HR 2519. Fiscal 1992 VA and HUD Appropriations/Restore Space Station Funding. Chapman, D-Texas, en bloc amendments to provide $1.9 billion for the space station *Freedom*, restoring its funding to the fiscal 1991 level, and to offset the increase by holding all NASA programs to fiscal 1991 levels — a decrease of $1.7 billion — and by cutting $217 million from public housing operating subsidies. Adopted 240-173: R 133-27; D 107-145 (ND 55-114, SD 52-31); I 0-1, June 6, 1991 (House vote 141). A "yea" was a vote supporting the president's position. *(Story, p. 38-B)*

KEY

Y Voted for (yea).
\# Paired for.
\+ Announced for.
N Voted against (nay).
X Paired against.
\- Announced against.
P Voted "present."
M Not yet a member of Congress when vote was taken.
? Did not vote or otherwise make a position known.

Democrats ***Republicans***
Independent

	1	2	3	4	5	6	7	8
ALABAMA								
1 ***Callahan***	Y	Y	N	N	N	N	N	Y
2 ***Dickinson***	Y	Y	N	N	N	Y	N	Y
3 Browder	Y	N	N	N	#	N	Y	Y
4 Bevill	Y	N	N	N	Y	N	Y	Y
5 Cramer	Y	N	N	N	Y	N	Y	Y
6 Erdreich	Y	Y	N	N	Y	N	Y	Y
7 Harris	Y	N	N	N	Y	N	Y	Y
ALASKA								
AL ***Young***	Y	Y	N	N	N	N	N	Y
ARIZONA								
1 ***Rhodes***	Y	Y	N	N	N	N	N	Y
2 Pastor	M	M	M	M	M	M	M	M
3 ***Stump***	Y	Y	N	N	N	N	N	Y
4 ***Kyl***	Y	Y	N	N	N	N	N	Y
5 ***Kolbe***	Y	Y	N	N	N	Y	N	N
ARKANSAS								
1 Alexander	N	Y	N	?	Y	N	Y	N
2 Thornton	Y	N	N	N	N	N	Y	Y
3 ***Hammerschmidt***	Y	?	N	N	N	N	N	Y
4 Anthony	N	Y	Y	?	N	N	Y	N
CALIFORNIA								
1 ***Riggs***	N	Y	Y	N	N	N	N	Y
2 ***Herger***	Y	N	N	N	N	Y	N	Y
3 Matsui	N	?	Y	Y	N	N	Y	Y
4 Fazio	N	Y	Y	N	N	N	Y	Y
5 Pelosi	N	N	Y	Y	N	N	Y	N
6 Boxer	N	N	Y	Y	Y	Y	Y	N
7 Miller	N	N	Y	Y	Y	Y	Y	N
8 Dellums	N	N	Y	Y	Y	N	Y	N
9 Stark	N	N	Y	Y	Y	Y	Y	N
10 Edwards	N	Y	Y	Y	Y	N	Y	Y
11 Lantos	Y	N	Y	N	Y	Y	Y	Y
12 ***Campbell***	Y	Y	Y	+	N	Y	Y	Y
13 Mineta	N	Y	Y	Y	Y	N	Y	Y
14 ***Doolittle***	Y	Y	N	X	N	N	N	Y
15 Condit	Y	N	N	Y	Y	N	Y	N
16 Panetta	N	Y	Y	Y	N	N	Y	N
17 Dooley	N	N	Y	N	N	Y	Y	Y
18 Lehman	Y	Y	Y	?	Y	N	Y	Y
19 ***Lagomarsino***	Y	Y	Y	N	N	N	N	Y
20 ***Thomas***	Y	Y	Y	N	N	N	N	Y
21 ***Gallegly***	Y	Y	Y	N	N	N	N	Y
22 ***Moorhead***	Y	Y	N	N	N	Y	N	Y
23 Beilenson	N	Y	Y	Y	N	Y	Y	N
24 Waxman	N	Y	Y	Y	Y	N	Y	N
25 Roybal	N	N	?	?	N	N	Y	N
26 Berman	Y	Y	Y	Y	N	N	Y	N
27 Levine	Y	Y	Y	Y	?	N	Y	Y
28 Dixon	N	N	Y	?	Y	N	Y	Y
29 Waters	N	N	Y	Y	Y	Y	Y	N
30 Martinez	N	N	Y	?	Y	N	Y	?
31 Dymally	-	N	Y	Y	Y	N	Y	#
32 Anderson	Y	Y	Y	?	N	N	Y	Y
33 ***Dreier***	Y	Y	N	N	N	N	N	Y
34 Torres	N	N	Y	+	Y	N	Y	Y
35 ***Lewis***	Y	Y	N	N	N	N	N	Y
36 Brown	N	N	Y	N	Y	N	Y	Y
37 ***McCandless***	Y	Y	N	N	N	N	N	Y
38 ***Dornan***	Y	Y	Y	N	X	N	N	Y
39 ***Dannemeyer***	Y	Y	N	N	N	N	N	Y
40 ***Cox***	Y	N	N	N	N	N	N	Y
41 ***Lowery***	Y	Y	Y	N	N	N	N	Y
42 ***Rohrabacher***	Y	N	N	N	N	Y	N	Y
43 ***Packard***	Y	N	Y	N	N	N	N	Y
44 ***Cunningham***	Y	N	N	N	N	N	N	Y
45 ***Hunter***	Y	Y	N	N	Y	N	N	Y
COLORADO								
1 Schroeder	N	N	Y	Y	N	Y	Y	N
2 Skaggs	N	Y	Y	Y	N	N	Y	N
3 Campbell	Y	N	N	?	Y	Y	Y	?
4 ***Allard***	Y	N	N	N	N	N	N	Y
5 ***Hefley***	Y	N	N	N	N	Y	N	Y
6 ***Schaefer***	Y	N	N	N	N	Y	N	Y
CONNECTICUT								
1 Kennelly	N	N	Y	N	N	N	Y	Y
2 Gejdenson	N	N	Y	Y	Y	Y	Y	Y
3 DeLauro	N	N	Y	Y	Y	N	Y	N
4 ***Shays***	Y	Y	Y	Y	N	Y	Y	N
5 ***Franks***	Y	Y	N	N	N	N	N	Y
6 ***Johnson***	Y	Y	Y	N	N	Y	N	Y
DELAWARE								
AL Carper	Y	Y	Y	Y	N	N	Y	N
FLORIDA								
1 Hutto	Y	N	Y	N	N	N	N	Y
2 Peterson	N	N	N	N	Y	Y	Y	Y
3 Bennett	N	N	Y	N	N	Y	Y	Y
4 ***James***	Y	N	Y	N	N	Y	N	Y
5 ***McCollum***	Y	Y	N	N	X	N	N	Y
6 ***Stearns***	Y	N	Y	N	Y	N	N	Y
7 Gibbons	N	N	Y	N	N	N	Y	Y
8 ***Young***	Y	N	Y	N	N	N	N	Y
9 ***Bilirakis***	Y	Y	Y	N	N	Y	N	Y
10 ***Ireland***	Y	Y	N	N	N	N	N	Y
11 Bacchus	Y	N	Y	N	N	?	Y	Y
12 ***Lewis***	Y	N	N	N	N	N	N	Y
13 ***Goss***	Y	Y	Y	N	N	N	N	Y
14 Johnston	N	Y	Y	Y	Y	Y	Y	N
15 ***Shaw***	Y	Y	N	N	N	N	N	Y
16 Smith	N	Y	Y	Y	Y	N	Y	N
17 Lehman	N	Y	?	#	?	N	Y	N
18 ***Ros-Lehtinen***	Y	Y	Y	N	N	Y	Y	N
19 Fascell	Y	Y	Y	N	N	N	Y	Y
GEORGIA								
1 Thomas	Y	Y	N	N	Y	N	Y	Y
2 Hatcher	Y	Y	Y	N	Y	N	Y	N
3 Ray	Y	Y	N	N	Y	N	Y	N
4 Jones	Y	N	Y	N	Y	Y	Y	N
5 Lewis	N	N	Y	?	Y	Y	Y	N
6 ***Gingrich***	Y	Y	N	N	N	N	N	Y
7 Darden	Y	Y	Y	N	Y	N	N	Y
8 Rowland	Y	Y	Y	N	Y	N	Y	N
9 Jenkins	N	Y	N	N	Y	N	N	Y
10 Barnard	Y	Y	N	N	Y	N	N	Y
HAWAII								
1 Abercrombie	N	N	Y	Y	Y	N	Y	N
2 Mink	N	N	Y	Y	Y	N	Y	N
IDAHO								
1 LaRocco	N	N	N	?	N	N	Y	Y
2 Stallings	N	N	N	N	Y	N	Y	Y
ILLINOIS								
1 Hayes	N	N	Y	Y	Y	Y	Y	N
2 Savage	N	N	Y	Y	Y	N	Y	N
3 Russo	N	N	Y	Y	Y	Y	N	N
4 Sangmeister	N	N	Y	Y	Y	Y	Y	N
5 Lipinski	N	N	Y	N	Y	Y	N	Y
6 ***Hyde***	Y	Y	Y	N	N	N	N	Y
7 Collins	N	N	Y	Y	Y	Y	Y	N
8 Rostenkowski	Y	Y	Y	N	N	Y	Y	N
9 Yates	N	N	Y	Y	Y	N	Y	N
10 ***Porter***	Y	Y	Y	N	N	Y	N	Y
11 Annunzio	N	N	Y	N	Y	N	N	Y
12 ***Crane***	Y	N	N	?	N	?	N	Y
13 ***Fawell***	Y	Y	Y	N	N	N	N	Y
14 ***Hastert***	Y	Y	N	N	N	N	N	Y
15 ***Ewing***	M	M	M	M	M	M	M	M
16 Cox	N	Y	Y	Y	N	Y	Y	N
17 Evans	N	N	Y	Y	Y	Y	Y	N
18 ***Michel***	Y	Y	?	N	N	N	N	Y
19 Bruce	N	N	N	Y	Y	N	Y	N
20 Durbin	N	Y	Y	Y	Y	Y	Y	N
21 Costello	N	N	N	N	Y	N	Y	N
22 Poshard	N	N	N	Y	Y	Y	Y	N
INDIANA								
1 Visclosky	N	N	Y	N	Y	Y	Y	N
2 Sharp	N	N	Y	-	N	Y	Y	N
3 Roemer	N	N	Y	N	Y	N	Y	N

ND Northern Democrats SD Southern Democrats

	1	2	3	4	5	6	7	8
4 Long	N	N	N	Y	Y	Y	Y	Y
5 Jontz	N	N	N	Y	Y	Y	Y	N
6 ***Burton***	Y	Y	N	N	N	Y	N	Y
7 ***Myers***	Y	Y	N	N	N	N	N	Y
8 McCloskey	N	N	Y	N	Y	N	Y	N
9 Hamilton	N	Y	Y	N	N	Y	Y	N
10 Jacobs	N	N	Y	Y	Y	Y	Y	N
IOWA								
1 ***Leach***	Y	Y	Y	Y	N	Y	Y	N
2 ***Nussle***	Y	N	N	N	N	N	N	N
3 Nagle	N	N	N	?	Y	N	Y	N
4 Smith	N	Y	N	N	N	N	Y	N
5 ***Lightfoot***	Y	Y	N	N	N	N	N	Y
6 ***Grandy***	Y	Y	N	N	N	Y	N	N
KANSAS								
1 ***Roberts***	Y	Y	N	N	N	N	N	Y
2 Slattery	Y	N	N	N	N	Y	Y	Y
3 ***Meyers***	Y	Y	Y	N	Y	Y	N	Y
4 Glickman	Y	N	Y	N	Y	Y	Y	Y
5 ***Nichols***	Y	Y	N	N	N	N	N	Y
KENTUCKY								
1 Hubbard	Y	Y	Y	?	N	N	Y	Y
2 Natcher	N	N	N	N	Y	N	Y	N
3 Mazzoli	N	N	Y	N	N	N	Y	N
4 ***Bunning***	Y	Y	N	N	N	Y	N	N
5 ***Rogers***	Y	N	N	-	N	N	N	Y
6 ***Hopkins***	Y	N	N	?	?	?	N	Y
7 Perkins	N	N	N	Y	Y	N	Y	Y
LOUISIANA								
1 ***Livingston***	Y	Y	N	N	N	N	N	Y
2 Jefferson	N	N	Y	Y	N	N	Y	Y
3 Tauzin	Y	N	N	N	N	N	Y	Y
4 ***McCrery***	Y	Y	N	N	N	N	N	Y
5 Huckaby	Y	Y	N	N	N	N	N	?
6 ***Baker***	Y	Y	N	N	N	N	N	Y
7 Hayes	Y	P	N	N	Y	N	N	Y
8 ***Holloway***	Y	Y	N	N	Y	N	N	Y
MAINE								
1 Andrews	N	N	Y	Y	Y	Y	Y	N
2 ***Snowe***	Y	Y	N	N	Y	Y	Y	Y
MARYLAND								
1 ***Gilchrest***	Y	Y	Y	N	N	N	N	Y
2 ***Bentley***	Y	N	Y	N	Y	N	N	Y
3 Cardin	N	Y	Y	N	N	N	Y	Y
4 McMillen	Y	N	Y	N	N	N	Y	Y
5 Hoyer	N	Y	Y	N	N	N	Y	N
6 Byron	Y	Y	N	N	N	N	Y	Y
7 Mfume	N	N	Y	Y	Y	Y	Y	Y
8 ***Morella***	N	Y	Y	N	N	Y	Y	Y
MASSACHUSETTS								
1 Olver	M	M	M	M	M	M	M	M
2 Neal	N	N	Y	Y	Y	Y	Y	Y
3 Early	N	N	Y	Y	Y	Y	Y	N
4 Frank	N	N	Y	Y	Y	Y	Y	N
5 Atkins	N	N	Y	Y	N	Y	Y	N
6 Mavroules	N	N	Y	Y	Y	N	Y	N
7 Markey	N	N	Y	Y	Y	Y	Y	N
8 Kennedy	N	N	Y	Y	Y	N	Y	N
9 Moakley	N	N	Y	Y	Y	N	Y	N
10 Studds	N	N	Y	?	Y	Y	Y	N
11 Donnelly	N	N	Y	Y	N	Y	Y	N
MICHIGAN								
1 Conyers	N	N	Y	?	Y	Y	Y	N
2 ***Pursell***	Y	N	Y	N	N	N	N	N
3 Wolpe	N	N	Y	Y	Y	Y	Y	N
4 ***Upton***	Y	N	Y	N	N	Y	N	N
5 ***Henry***	Y	N	Y	N	N	Y	Y	N
6 Carr	N	N	N	N	N	Y	Y	N
7 Kildee	N	N	Y	Y	Y	N	Y	N
8 Traxler	N	Y	N	Y	Y	Y	Y	N
9 ***Vander Jagt***	Y	Y	N	N	N	Y	N	Y
10 ***Camp***	Y	N	N	N	N	Y	N	N
11 ***Davis***	Y	Y	N	N	N	Y	Y	Y
12 Bonior	N	Y	Y	Y	Y	?	Y	N
13 Collins	N	N	Y	Y	Y	Y	Y	N
14 Hertel	N	N	Y	Y	Y	Y	Y	N
15 Ford	N	N	Y	Y	Y	Y	Y	N
16 Dingell	Y	Y	N	N	Y	Y	Y	N
17 Levin	N	Y	Y	Y	Y	Y	Y	N
18 ***Broomfield***	Y	Y	Y	N	N	Y	N	Y
MINNESOTA								
1 Penny	N	N	N	N	N	Y	Y	N
2 ***Weber***	Y	Y	N	N	N	N	N	Y
3 ***Ramstad***	Y	N	N	N	N	#	N	N
4 Vento	N	Y	Y	Y	Y	Y	Y	X
5 Sabo	N	Y	Y	Y	Y	Y	Y	N
6 Sikorski	N	N	Y	Y	Y	Y	Y	N
7 Peterson	N	N	N	Y	Y	Y	Y	N
8 Oberstar	N	N	N	Y	Y	Y	Y	N
MISSISSIPPI								
1 Whitten	Y	N	?	?	Y	N	Y	N
2 Espy	N	N	N	Y	N	Y	Y	N
3 Montgomery	Y	Y	N	N	N	N	N	N
4 Parker	Y	Y	N	?	N	Y	N	N
5 Taylor	N	N	N	N	Y	N	N	Y
MISSOURI								
1 Clay	N	N	Y	Y	Y	N	Y	N
2 Horn	N	N	Y	N	Y	Y	Y	Y
3 Gephardt	N	Y	Y	Y	N	N	Y	Y
4 Skelton	Y	N	N	N	N	N	Y	N
5 Wheat	N	N	Y	Y	Y	N	Y	N
6 ***Coleman***	Y	Y	Y	?	N	N	N	Y
7 ***Hancock***	Y	Y	N	N	N	Y	N	Y
8 ***Emerson***	Y	Y	N	N	N	N	N	Y
9 Volkmer	Y	N	N	N	Y	N	Y	Y
MONTANA								
1 Williams	N	N	N	Y	#	Y	Y	?
2 ***Marlenee***	Y	N	N	N	Y	?	N	Y
NEBRASKA								
1 ***Bereuter***	Y	Y	N	N	N	Y	N	N
2 Hoagland	Y	Y	Y	N	Y	Y	Y	N
3 ***Barrett***	Y	Y	N	N	N	N	N	Y
NEVADA								
1 Bilbray	Y	N	N	N	Y	Y	Y	?
2 ***Vucanovich***	Y	Y	N	N	-	N	N	Y
NEW HAMPSHIRE								
1 ***Zeliff***	Y	Y	N	N	N	Y	N	Y
2 Swett	Y	Y	Y	N	Y	Y	Y	Y
NEW JERSEY								
1 Andrews	N	N	Y	N	Y	N	Y	Y
2 Hughes	Y	Y	Y	N	N	N	Y	N
3 Pallone	Y	N	Y	N	Y	Y	Y	Y
4 ***Smith***	Y	Y	Y	Y	N	N	N	Y
5 ***Roukema***	Y	Y	Y	N	N	Y	N	N
6 Dwyer	N	Y	Y	N	Y	N	Y	N
7 ***Rinaldo***	Y	N	Y	N	N	N	Y	Y
8 Roe	N	N	Y	N	Y	N	Y	Y
9 Torricelli	Y	N	Y	N	N	N	Y	Y
10 Payne	N	N	Y	?	Y	Y	Y	N
11 ***Gallo***	Y	Y	Y	N	N	N	N	?
12 ***Zimmer***	Y	Y	N	N	N	Y	Y	N
13 ***Saxton***	Y	Y	Y	N	N	N	N	Y
14 Guarini	N	N	Y	N	N	N	Y	N
NEW MEXICO								
1 ***Schiff***	Y	Y	N	N	N	N	Y	Y
2 ***Skeen***	Y	Y	N	N	N	N	N	Y
3 Richardson	N	N	N	N	N	N	Y	Y
NEW YORK								
1 Hochbrueckner	N	N	Y	N	Y	N	Y	Y
2 Downey	N	N	Y	Y	N	N	Y	Y
3 Mrazek	N	?	Y	Y	N	?	Y	?
4 ***Lent***	Y	Y	Y	?	N	N	N	Y
5 ***McGrath***	Y	N	Y	N	N	N	N	Y
6 Flake	N	?	Y	Y	Y	Y	Y	N
7 Ackerman	Y	N	Y	Y	Y	?	Y	X
8 Scheuer	N	N	Y	Y	Y	Y	Y	N
9 Manton	N	N	Y	N	Y	N	Y	N
10 Schumer	N	Y	Y	Y	N	N	Y	N
11 Towns	N	N	Y	Y	Y	N	Y	N
12 Owens	N	N	Y	Y	Y	Y	Y	N
13 Solarz	Y	N	Y	Y	N	Y	Y	N
14 ***Molinari***	Y	Y	Y	N	N	N	N	N
15 ***Green***	Y	Y	Y	N	N	N	Y	N
16 Rangel	N	N	Y	#	Y	N	Y	N
17 Weiss	N	N	Y	Y	Y	Y	Y	N
18 Serrano	N	N	Y	Y	Y	N	Y	N
19 Engel	Y	N	Y	Y	Y	?	Y	N
20 Lowey	N	N	Y	Y	Y	Y	Y	N
21 ***Fish***	Y	Y	Y	N	N	Y	Y	N
22 ***Gilman***	Y	Y	Y	N	Y	Y	Y	N
23 McNulty	Y	N	Y	N	Y	N	Y	N
24 ***Solomon***	Y	Y	N	N	Y	Y	N	#
25 ***Boehlert***	Y	Y	Y	N	N	Y	Y	Y
26 ***Martin***	Y	Y	?	N	N	Y	N	?
27 ***Walsh***	Y	Y	Y	N	N	N	Y	Y
28 McHugh	N	Y	Y	Y	N	N	Y	N
29 ***Horton***	Y	Y	N	N	N	?	Y	Y
30 Slaughter	N	N	Y	N	Y	Y	Y	-
31 ***Paxon***	Y	Y	N	N	N	Y	N	N
32 LaFalce	N	N	Y	Y	Y	Y	Y	N
33 Nowak	N	N	Y	N	Y	Y	Y	N
34 ***Houghton***	Y	Y	N	N	N	N	Y	Y
NORTH CAROLINA								
1 Jones	Y	N	Y	N	Y	N	Y	Y
2 Valentine	Y	N	Y	N	Y	Y	Y	Y
3 Lancaster	Y	N	Y	N	Y	Y	Y	N
4 Price	N	Y	Y	N	N	N	Y	N
5 Neal	N	N	Y	?	Y	Y	Y	N
6 ***Coble***	Y	N	N	N	Y	Y	N	N
7 Rose	N	Y	Y	Y	Y	N	Y	N
8 Hefner	N	N	Y	N	Y	N	Y	N
9 ***McMillan***	Y	Y	Y	N	N	N	N	N
10 ***Ballenger***	Y	Y	N	N	Y	N	N	Y
11 ***Taylor***	Y	Y	N	N	Y	N	N	Y
NORTH DAKOTA								
AL Dorgan	N	N	N	Y	Y	Y	Y	N
OHIO								
1 Luken	Y	N	Y	N	N	N	Y	N
2 ***Gradison***	Y	Y	Y	N	N	Y	N	Y
3 Hall	N	?	Y	Y	N	Y	Y	Y
4 ***Oxley***	Y	Y	Y	N	N	N	N	Y
5 ***Gillmor***	Y	Y	N	N	N	Y	N	Y
6 ***McEwen***	Y	Y	N	N	N	N	N	Y
7 ***Hobson***	Y	Y	N	N	N	N	Y	Y
8 ***Boehner***	Y	Y	N	N	N	N	N	Y
9 Kaptur	N	N	Y	N	Y	N	Y	N
10 ***Miller***	Y	?	N	N	Y	N	N	Y
11 Eckart	N	N	Y	Y	Y	Y	Y	Y
12 ***Kasich***	Y	N	N	N	N	N	N	Y
13 Pease	N	Y	Y	Y	Y	N	Y	Y
14 Sawyer	N	N	Y	Y	N	Y	Y	Y
15 ***Wylie***	Y	Y	Y	N	N	N	N	Y
16 ***Regula***	Y	Y	Y	N	N	Y	N	Y
17 Traficant	N	N	Y	Y	Y	N	Y	Y
18 Applegate	N	N	N	?	Y	N	Y	Y
19 Feighan	N	N	Y	Y	Y	Y	Y	Y
20 Oakar	N	N	Y	Y	Y	N	Y	Y
21 Stokes	N	N	Y	Y	Y	N	Y	N
OKLAHOMA								
1 ***Inhofe***	Y	N	N	N	N	N	N	Y
2 Synar	N	N	Y	Y	N	Y	Y	N
3 Brewster	Y	N	N	?	Y	N	Y	Y
4 McCurdy	Y	N	Y	N	N	Y	Y	Y
5 ***Edwards***	Y	Y	N	N	N	N	N	Y
6 English	N	N	N	N	Y	N	Y	Y
OREGON								
1 AuCoin	N	Y	Y	Y	Y	?	Y	N
2 ***Smith***	Y	N	N	N	N	N	N	Y
3 Wyden	N	N	Y	Y	N	Y	Y	N
4 DeFazio	N	N	N	Y	Y	Y	Y	Y
5 Kopetski	N	Y	N	Y	N	N	Y	Y
PENNSYLVANIA								
1 Foglietta	N	N	Y	Y	Y	N	Y	N
2 Blackwell	M	M	M	M	M	M	M	M
3 Borski	Y	N	Y	N	Y	N	Y	?
4 Kolter	N	N	N	?	Y	N	Y	Y
5 ***Schulze***	Y	N	N	N	N	Y	Y	Y
6 Yatron	N	N	N	?	Y	N	Y	Y
7 ***Weldon***	Y	N	Y	N	N	Y	N	N
8 Kostmayer	N	Y	Y	Y	N	Y	Y	?
9 ***Shuster***	Y	N	N	N	Y	Y	N	?
10 ***McDade***	Y	Y	Y	N	Y	N	N	Y
11 Kanjorski	N	N	N	N	Y	Y	Y	N
12 Murtha	Y	Y	N	N	Y	N	Y	N
13 ***Coughlin***	Y	Y	Y	N	N	Y	N	N
14 Coyne	N	N	Y	?	N	N	Y	N
15 ***Ritter***	Y	Y	N	N	N	N	Y	N
16 ***Walker***	Y	Y	N	N	N	N	N	Y
17 ***Gekas***	Y	Y	N	N	N	N	N	Y
18 ***Santorum***	Y	N	N	N	N	Y	N	Y
19 ***Goodling***	Y	Y	Y	N	Y	Y	N	Y
20 Gaydos	N	N	Y	N	Y	N	Y	Y
21 ***Ridge***	Y	N	N	?	N	Y	N	Y
22 Murphy	N	N	N	?	Y	Y	Y	N
23 ***Clinger***	Y	Y	N	N	N	N	N	Y
RHODE ISLAND								
1 ***Machtley***	Y	N	Y	N	N	Y	Y	Y
2 Reed	N	N	Y	Y	Y	Y	Y	N
SOUTH CAROLINA								
1 ***Ravenel***	Y	N	N	N	Y	Y	N	N
2 ***Spence***	Y	N	N	N	Y	N	N	Y
3 Derrick	Y	Y	Y	N	Y	Y	Y	N
4 Patterson	Y	N	N	N	Y	Y	Y	N
5 Spratt	Y	Y	Y	N	Y	Y	Y	N
6 Tallon	Y	N	N	N	Y	Y	Y	Y
SOUTH DAKOTA								
AL Johnson	N	N	N	N	Y	Y	Y	N
TENNESSEE								
1 ***Quillen***	Y	N	N	N	Y	N	N	Y
2 ***Duncan***	Y	N	N	?	Y	Y	N	N
3 Lloyd	Y	N	Y	N	Y	N	Y	Y
4 Cooper	Y	Y	Y	N	N	N	Y	Y
5 Clement	Y	N	Y	N	N	Y	Y	N
6 Gordon	Y	N	Y	N	N	Y	Y	Y
7 ***Sundquist***	Y	Y	N	?	N	Y	N	Y
8 Tanner	Y	N	N	N	N	N	Y	Y
9 Ford	N	N	Y	Y	Y	N	Y	N
TEXAS								
1 Chapman	Y	Y	Y	?	N	N	Y	Y
2 Wilson	Y	?	N	?	N	N	Y	Y
3 ***Johnson***	M	M	M	M	N	N	N	N
4 Hall	Y	?	N	N	N	N	N	Y
5 Bryant	N	N	Y	Y	N	N	Y	Y
6 ***Barton***	Y	Y	N	X	N	N	N	Y
7 ***Archer***	Y	Y	N	N	N	N	N	Y
8 ***Fields***	Y	Y	N	N	N	N	N	Y
9 Brooks	Y	Y	N	N	Y	N	Y	Y
10 Pickle	N	Y	Y	N	N	N	Y	Y
11 Edwards	Y	Y	N	N	N	N	Y	Y
12 Geren	Y	Y	N	N	N	N	Y	Y
13 Sarpalius	Y	Y	N	N	N	N	Y	Y
14 Laughlin	Y	N	N	N	N	N	Y	Y
15 de la Garza	Y	N	N	N	N	?	Y	Y
16 Coleman	N	N	N	N	N	N	Y	Y
17 Stenholm	Y	Y	Y	N	N	N	N	Y
18 Washington	N	N	Y	?	Y	N	Y	N
19 ***Combest***	Y	Y	N	N	N	N	N	Y
20 Gonzalez	N	N	Y	Y	Y	N	Y	N
21 ***Smith***	Y	Y	N	N	N	N	N	Y
22 ***DeLay***	Y	Y	N	N	N	N	N	Y
23 Bustamante	N	N	N	N	N	N	Y	Y
24 Frost	Y	Y	Y	N	Y	N	Y	Y
25 Andrews	Y	N	Y	N	N	N	Y	Y
26 ***Armey***	Y	Y	N	N	N	N	N	Y
27 Ortiz	Y	N	N	N	N	N	Y	Y
UTAH								
1 ***Hansen***	Y	Y	N	N	N	N	N	Y
2 Owens	N	Y	Y	?	N	N	Y	N
3 Orton	Y	Y	N	N	N	N	N	N
VERMONT								
AL *Sanders*	N	N	N	Y	Y	Y	Y	N
VIRGINIA								
1 ***Bateman***	Y	Y	Y	N	N	N	N	Y
2 Pickett	Y	Y	N	N	N	N	Y	Y
3 ***Bliley***	Y	Y	N	N	N	N	N	Y
4 Sisisky	Y	Y	N	N	Y	Y	?	?
5 Payne	Y	Y	N	N	Y	N	Y	N
6 Olin	N	Y	N	N	N	N	Y	N
7 ***Allen***	M	M	M	M	M	M	M	M
8 Moran	N	Y	Y	N	N	Y	Y	Y
9 Boucher	N	Y	N	Y	N	N	Y	Y
10 ***Wolf***	Y	Y	Y	N	N	N	N	Y
WASHINGTON								
1 ***Miller***	Y	Y	Y	N	N	N	N	+
2 Swift	N	Y	Y	Y	N	Y	Y	Y
3 Unsoeld	N	Y	N	Y	Y	Y	Y	N
4 ***Morrison***	Y	Y	Y	N	N	N	N	Y
5 Foley	N						Y	
6 Dicks	N	Y	Y	N	N	N	Y	Y
7 McDermott	N	Y	Y	Y	N	Y	Y	N
8 ***Chandler***	Y	Y	Y	N	N	X	N	Y
WEST VIRGINIA								
1 Mollohan	Y	N	N	N	Y	N	Y	Y
2 Staggers	N	N	N	N	Y	?	Y	N
3 Wise	N	N	N	N	Y	Y	Y	Y
4 Rahall	Y	N	N	Y	Y	N	Y	Y
WISCONSIN								
1 Aspin	Y	N	Y	N	Y	?	Y	Y
2 ***Klug***	Y	Y	Y	?	N	N	Y	Y
3 ***Gunderson***	Y	Y	N	N	N	N	N	Y
4 Kleczka	N	N	Y	Y	Y	Y	Y	N
5 Moody	N	N	Y	Y	Y	Y	Y	N
6 ***Petri***	Y	N	N	N	N	Y	N	Y
7 Obey	N	N	N	Y	Y	Y	Y	N
8 ***Roth***	Y	N	N	N	N	Y	N	N
9 ***Sensenbrenner***	Y	N	Y	N	N	Y	N	Y
WYOMING								
AL ***Thomas***	Y	Y	N	?	N	Y	N	Y

Southern states - Ala., Ark., Fla., Ga., Ky., La., Miss., N.C., Okla., S.C., Tenn., Texas, Va.

HOUSE KEY VOTES 9, 10, 11, 12, 13, 14, 15, 16

9. HR 2686. Fiscal 1992 Interior Appropriations/Grazing Fees. Synar, D-Okla., amendment to increase over four years the domestic livestock grazing fee on public lands administered by the Bureau of Land Management from $1.97 to $8.70 per animal unit month or to fair market value, whichever is higher, by fiscal 1995. Adopted 232-192: R 47-114; D 184-78 (ND 140-38, SD 44-40); I 1-0, June 25, 1991 (House vote 194). A "nay" was a vote supporting the president's position. *(Story, p. 38-B)*

10. HR 2100. Fiscal 1992 Defense Authorization. Dickinson, R-Ala., motion to order the previous question (thus ending debate and the possibility of amendment) on the Dickinson motion to instruct the House conferees on the fiscal 1992 defense authorization bill to insist on the House position to make permanent certain changes in benefits for military personnel who served in Operation Desert Shield/Storm. Motion agreed to 220-145: R 136-4; D 84-140 (ND 30-124, SD 54-16); I 0-1, Sept. 16, 1991 (House vote 261). *(Story, p. 39-B)*

11. HR 3040. Unemployment Benefits Extension/Passage. Passage of the bill to permanently extend unemployment benefits to long-term unemployed workers for up to 20 additional weeks at an estimated cost of $6.3 billion through fiscal 1996. The bill automatically declares the benefits to be emergency spending and would not require a presidential declaration to be exempt from the spending requirements of last year's budget agreement. Passed 283-125: R 48-107; D 234-18 (ND 172-2, SD 62-16); I 1-0, Sept. 17, 1991 (House vote 267). A "nay" was a vote supporting the president's position. *(Story, p. 39-B)*

12. HR 3566. Surface Transportation Reauthorization/Rule. Adoption of the rule (H Res 252) to provide for House floor consideration of the bill to authorize $151 billion for highway and mass transit programs in fiscal 1992-97 and extend through fiscal 1999 half of the nickel added to the federal gasoline tax in 1990. Adopted 323-102: R 66-97; D 257-4 (ND 174-4, SD 83-0); I 0-1, Oct. 23, 1991 (House vote 332). *(Story, p. 39-B)*

13. HR 2508. Fiscal 1992-93 Foreign Aid Authorization/Conference Report. Adoption of the conference report to authorize $25 billion in fiscal 1992-93 for foreign economic and military assistance. Rejected 159-262: R 28-134; D 131-127 (ND 105-73, SD 26-54); I 0-1, Oct. 30, 1991 (House vote 354). A "nay" was a vote supporting the president's position. *(Story, p. 40-B)*

14. HR 6. Bank Reform/Passage. Passage of the bill to restructure the banking industry, overhaul the federal bank deposit insurance system and allow the Federal Deposit Insurance Corporation to borrow $30 billion to cover losses in failed banks. Rejected 89-324: R 6-153; D 83-170 (ND 69-105, SD 14-65); I 0-1, Nov. 4, 1991 (House vote 375). A "nay" was a vote supporting the president's position. *(Story, p. 40-B)*

15. HR 2707. Fiscal 1992 Labor, HHS, and Education Appropriations/Passage. Passage, over President Bush's Nov. 19 veto, of the appropriations bill for the Departments of Labor, Health and Human Services, and Education. The measure would block enforcement of the administration rule, known as the "gag rule," barring abortion counseling in federally funded family planning clinics. Rejected 276-156: R 53-113; D 222-43 (ND 155-26, SD 67-17); I 1-0, Nov. 19, 1991 (House vote 403). A two-thirds majority of those present and voting (288 in this case) of both chambers is required to override a veto. A "nay" was a vote supporting the president's position. *(Story, p. 41-B)*

16. HR 3750. Campaign Finance/Passage. Passage of the bill to provide lower mail costs and up to $200,000 in public matching funds for the first $200 of individual contributions for House candidates who have raised more than $60,000 in individual contributions of less than $200 and agreed to a voluntary spending limit of $600,000. All House candidates would be limited to $200,000 in contributions from political action committees. Passed 273-156: R 21-144; D 251-12 (ND 176-4, SD 75-8); I 1-0, Nov. 25, 1991 (House vote 427). A "nay" was a vote supporting the president's position. *(Story, p. 41-B)*

KEY

- Y Voted for (yea).
- # Paired for.
- + Announced for.
- N Voted against (nay).
- X Paired against.
- \- Announced against.
- P Voted "present."
- C Voted "present" to avoid possible conflict of interest.
- ? Did not vote or otherwise make a position known.

Democrats ***Republicans***
Independent

	9	10	11	12	13	14	15	16
ALABAMA								
1 ***Callahan***	N	Y	N	Y	N	N	N	N
2 ***Dickinson***	N	Y	N	Y	N	N	N	N
3 Browder	N	Y	Y	Y	N	N	Y	Y
4 Bevill	N	Y	Y	Y	N	N	Y	Y
5 Cramer	N	Y	Y	Y	N	N	Y	Y
6 Erdreich	Y	Y	Y	Y	N	N	Y	Y
7 Harris	N	Y	Y	Y	N	N	Y	Y
ALASKA								
AL ***Young***	N	Y	Y	Y	Y	N	N	N
ARIZONA								
1 ***Rhodes***	-	?	N	N	N	N	N	N
2 Pastor				Y	Y	N	Y	Y
3 ***Stump***	N	Y	N	N	N	N	N	N
4 ***Kyl***	N	Y	N	N	N	N	N	N
5 ***Kolbe***	N	Y	N	N	Y	N	Y	N
ARKANSAS								
1 Alexander	N	N	?	Y	N	N	Y	N
2 Thornton	?	N	Y	Y	N	N	Y	Y
3 ***Hammerschmidt***	N	Y	N	Y	N	N	N	N
4 Anthony	N	N	Y	Y	N	N	Y	N
CALIFORNIA								
1 ***Riggs***	N	?	N	Y	Y	N	Y	N
2 ***Herger***	N	?	?	N	N	N	N	N
3 Matsui	Y	N	Y	Y	?	Y	Y	Y
4 Fazio	Y	?	Y	Y	Y	Y	Y	Y
5 Pelosi	Y	N	Y	Y	Y	Y	Y	Y
6 Boxer	Y	N	Y	Y	?	N	Y	Y
7 Miller	Y	?	Y	Y	N	N	Y	Y
8 Dellums	Y	N	Y	Y	Y	N	Y	Y
9 Stark	Y	N	Y	Y	N	N	Y	Y
10 Edwards	Y	N	Y	Y	Y	Y	Y	Y
11 Lantos	Y	?	#	Y	Y	N	Y	Y
12 ***Campbell***	Y	?	N	N	Y	N	Y	N
13 Mineta	Y	N	Y	Y	Y	N	Y	Y
14 ***Doolittle***	N	?	X	N	N	N	N	N
15 Condit	N	N	Y	Y	N	N	Y	Y
16 Panetta	N	N	Y	Y	Y	Y	Y	Y
17 Dooley	N	Y	Y	Y	N	N	Y	Y
18 Lehman	N	N	Y	Y	N	Y	Y	Y
19 ***Lagomarsino***	N	Y	N	N	N	N	N	N
20 ***Thomas***	N	?	X	Y	N	?	Y	N
21 ***Gallegly***	N	Y	N	N	N	N	N	N
22 ***Moorhead***	N	Y	N	N	N	N	N	N
23 Beilenson	Y	N	Y	Y	Y	Y	Y	Y
24 Waxman	Y	N	Y	Y	Y	Y	Y	Y
25 Roybal	Y	?	Y	Y	Y	Y	Y	Y
26 Berman	Y	?	?	Y	Y	Y	Y	Y
27 Levine	?	?	?	Y	Y	N	?	Y
28 Dixon	Y	N	Y	Y	Y	?	Y	Y
29 Waters	Y	N	Y	?	N	N	Y	Y
30 Martinez	N	?	Y	N	Y	N	Y	Y
31 Dymally	N	?	?	Y	Y	Y	Y	Y
32 Anderson	Y	Y	Y	Y	N	N	Y	Y
33 ***Dreier***	Y	Y	N	N	N	N	N	N
34 Torres	Y	N	Y	?	Y	Y	Y	Y
35 ***Lewis***	N	?	X	Y	N	N	N	N
36 Brown	Y	N	Y	Y	Y	N	Y	Y
37 ***McCandless***	N	Y	N	Y	N	N	N	N
38 ***Dornan***	N	Y	N	N	N	N	N	N
39 ***Dannemeyer***	N	Y	N	N	N	-	N	N
40 ***Cox***	Y	Y	N	N	N	N	N	N
41 ***Lowery***	N	?	N	Y	N	N	N	N
42 ***Rohrabacher***	Y	Y	N	N	N	N	N	N
43 ***Packard***	N	?	N	Y	N	N	N	N
44 ***Cunningham***	N	Y	N	N	N	N	N	N
45 ***Hunter***	N	?	?	N	N	N	N	N
COLORADO								
1 Schroeder	Y	N	Y	N	Y	Y	Y	Y
2 Skaggs	Y	N	Y	Y	Y	N	Y	Y
3 Campbell	N	Y	Y	Y	N	?	Y	N
4 ***Allard***	N	Y	N	N	N	N	N	N
5 ***Hefley***	N	Y	N	N	N	N	N	N
6 ***Schaefer***	N	Y	N	N	N	N	N	N
CONNECTICUT								
1 Kennelly	Y	Y	Y	Y	Y	Y	Y	Y
2 Gejdenson	Y	N	Y	Y	Y	N	Y	Y
3 DeLauro	Y	Y	Y	Y	Y	Y	Y	Y
4 ***Shays***	Y	N	N	N	Y	N	Y	Y
5 ***Franks***	N	Y	Y	N	N	N	Y	N
6 ***Johnson***	Y	Y	Y	Y	Y	N	Y	N
DELAWARE								
AL Carper	Y	Y	Y	Y	Y	N	Y	Y
FLORIDA								
1 Hutto	N	?	N	Y	N	N	N	Y
2 Peterson	N	Y	Y	Y	Y	N	Y	Y
3 Bennett	Y	Y	Y	Y	N	N	N	N
4 ***James***	Y	Y	N	N	N	N	N	Y
5 ***McCollum***	N	?	N	N	N	N	N	N
6 ***Stearns***	N	Y	Y	N	N	N	N	N
7 Gibbons	Y	N	Y	Y	Y	Y	Y	Y
8 ***Young***	?	Y	Y	N	N	N	N	Y
9 ***Bilirakis***	N	Y	N	N	N	N	N	Y
10 ***Ireland***	Y	Y	N	N	N	N	N	N
11 Bacchus	Y	Y	Y	Y	Y	N	Y	Y
12 ***Lewis***	N	Y	Y	Y	N	N	N	N
13 ***Goss***	Y	Y	N	N	N	N	N	N
14 Johnston	Y	N	?	Y	Y	Y	Y	Y
15 ***Shaw***	N	Y	N	Y	N	N	N	N
16 Smith	Y	N	Y	Y	Y	#	Y	Y
17 Lehman	Y	?	?	Y	Y	Y	Y	Y
18 ***Ros-Lehtinen***	Y	Y	Y	N	N	N	N	N
19 Fascell	Y	Y	Y	Y	Y	Y	Y	Y
GEORGIA								
1 Thomas	N	Y	Y	Y	N	N	Y	Y
2 Hatcher	N	?	Y	Y	N	N	?	Y
3 Ray	N	Y	N	Y	N	N	N	?
4 Jones	Y	N	Y	Y	Y	Y	Y	Y
5 Lewis	Y	N	Y	Y	Y	Y	Y	Y
6 ***Gingrich***	N	Y	N	N	N	N	N	N
7 Darden	Y	Y	Y	Y	N	N	Y	Y
8 Rowland	Y	?	#	Y	?	N	Y	Y
9 Jenkins	Y	?	Y	Y	N	N	Y	Y
10 Barnard	Y	Y	N	Y	N	N	N	Y
HAWAII								
1 Abercrombie	Y	N	Y	Y	Y	Y	Y	Y
2 Mink	Y	N	Y	Y	Y	Y	Y	Y
IDAHO								
1 LaRocco	N	N	Y	Y	N	N	+	Y
2 Stallings	N	?	Y	Y	N	N	N	Y
ILLINOIS								
1 Hayes	Y	N	Y	Y	N	Y	Y	Y
2 Savage	Y	N	Y	Y	N	N	Y	Y
3 Russo	Y	N	Y	Y	N	N	Y	Y
4 Sangmeister	Y	N	Y	Y	N	?	Y	Y
5 Lipinski	Y	Y	Y	Y	N	N	N	Y
6 ***Hyde***	N	Y	N	Y	N	N	N	N
7 Collins	Y	N	Y	Y	N	Y	Y	Y
8 Rostenkowski	Y	N	Y	Y	Y	N	Y	Y
9 Yates	Y	N	Y	Y	Y	Y	Y	Y
10 ***Porter***	?	Y	N	N	Y	N	Y	N
11 Annunzio	Y	N	Y	Y	N	Y	N	Y
12 ***Crane***	Y	Y	N	N	N	N	N	N
13 ***Fawell***	Y	Y	N	N	N	N	Y	N
14 ***Hastert***	N	Y	N	Y	N	N	N	N
15 ***Ewing***		Y	N	Y	N	N	N	N
16 Cox	Y	N	Y	Y	Y	N	Y	Y
17 Evans	Y	N	Y	N	Y	N	Y	Y
18 ***Michel***	N	Y	N	?	N	?	N	N
19 Bruce	Y	N	Y	Y	N	Y	Y	Y
20 Durbin	Y	N	Y	Y	N	N	Y	Y
21 Costello	Y	Y	Y	Y	N	N	N	Y
22 Poshard	Y	N	Y	Y	N	N	N	Y
INDIANA								
1 Visclosky	Y	N	Y	Y	Y	N	Y	Y
2 Sharp	Y	?	Y	Y	N	N	Y	Y
3 Roemer	Y	Y	Y	Y	N	N	Y	Y

ND Northern Democrats SD Southern Democrats

	9	10	11	12	13	14	15	16
4 Long	N	N	Y	Y	N	N	Y	Y
5 Jontz	Y	N	Y	Y	N	N	Y	Y
6 ***Burton***	N	Y	N	N	N	N	N	N
7 ***Myers***	N	Y	N	Y	N	N	Y	N
8 McCloskey	Y	N	Y	Y	N	N	Y	Y
9 Hamilton	Y	N	Y	Y	Y	N	Y	Y
10 Jacobs	Y	N	Y	N	N	Y	Y	Y
IOWA								
1 ***Leach***	N	Y	Y	Y	N	Y	Y	Y
2 ***Nussle***	N	Y	N	Y	N	N	N	N
3 Nagle	N	N	Y	Y	Y	N	Y	N
4 Smith	N	N	Y	Y	Y	N	Y	Y
5 ***Lightfoot***	N	Y	N	N	N	N	N	N
6 ***Grandy***	N	Y	N	Y	N	N	Y	N
KANSAS								
1 ***Roberts***	N	Y	N	N	N	N	N	N
2 Slattery	Y	N	Y	Y	N	Y	Y	Y
3 ***Meyers***	Y	Y	N	N	Y	Y	Y	N
4 Glickman	Y	N	Y	Y	#	Y	Y	Y
5 ***Nichols***	N	Y	N	Y	N	N	N	N
KENTUCKY								
1 Hubbard	N	Y	Y	Y	N	N	Y	Y
2 Natcher	N	Y	Y	Y	N	N	Y	Y
3 Mazzoli	Y	Y	Y	Y	N	N	N	Y
4 ***Bunning***	N	Y	N	N	N	N	N	N
5 ***Rogers***	N	Y	Y	Y	N	N	N	N
6 ***Hopkins***	N	?	?	?	?	?	N	N
7 Perkins	N	N	Y	Y	N	N	Y	N
LOUISIANA								
1 ***Livingston***	N	Y	N	N	N	N	N	N
2 Jefferson	Y	Y	Y	Y	#	N	Y	Y
3 Tauzin	Y	Y	Y	Y	N	N	N	Y
4 ***McCrery***	Y	?	N	Y	N	N	N	N
5 Huckaby	Y	Y	Y	Y	N	N	N	Y
6 ***Baker***	N	Y	N	N	N	N	N	N
7 Hayes	Y	Y	N	Y	N	N	N	Y
8 ***Holloway***	N	?	?	N	N	N	N	N
MAINE								
1 Andrews	Y	N	Y	Y	Y	N	Y	Y
2 ***Snowe***	Y	Y	Y	N	Y	N	Y	Y
MARYLAND								
1 ***Gilchrest***	N	Y	Y	N	Y	N	Y	N
2 ***Bentley***	N	Y	Y	Y	N	N	Y	N
3 Cardin	Y	N	Y	Y	Y	N	Y	Y
4 McMillen	Y	Y	Y	Y	Y	N	Y	Y
5 Hoyer	Y	N	Y	Y	Y	Y	Y	Y
6 Byron	Y	Y	Y	Y	N	N	Y	Y
7 Mfume	Y	N	Y	Y	N	N	Y	Y
8 ***Morella***	Y	N	Y	Y	Y	N	Y	Y
MASSACHUSETTS								
1 Olver	Y	N	Y	Y	Y	Y	Y	Y
2 Neal	Y	N	Y	Y	N	Y	Y	Y
3 Early	Y	N	Y	Y	N	Y	Y	Y
4 Frank	Y	N	Y	Y	Y	N	Y	Y
5 Atkins	Y	N	Y	Y	Y	Y	Y	Y
6 Mavroules	Y	?	Y	Y	N	Y	N	Y
7 Markey	Y	N	Y	Y	Y	Y	Y	Y
8 Kennedy	Y	N	Y	Y	Y	N	Y	Y
9 Moakley	Y	N	Y	Y	N	Y	Y	Y
10 Studds	Y	N	Y	Y	Y	Y	Y	Y
11 Donnelly	Y	N	Y	Y	N	Y	N	Y
MICHIGAN								
1 Conyers	Y	?	Y	Y	N	N	Y	Y
2 ***Pursell***	?	?	Y	Y	N	N	Y	N
3 Wolpe	Y	N	Y	Y	Y	Y	Y	Y
4 ***Upton***	Y	Y	Y	Y	N	N	Y	N
5 ***Henry***	Y	Y	Y	Y	N	N	N	N
6 Carr	N	?	Y	Y	Y	N	Y	N
7 Kildee	Y	N	Y	Y	N	Y	N	Y
8 Traxler	Y	N	Y	Y	N	Y	Y	Y
9 ***Vander Jagt***	N	Y	N	Y	N	N	N	N
10 ***Camp***	N	Y	Y	N	N	N	N	N
11 ***Davis***	N	Y	Y	Y	N	N	N	N
12 Bonior	Y	N	Y	Y	Y	Y	Y	Y
13 Collins	N	N	Y	Y	N	Y	Y	Y
14 Hertel	Y	Y	Y	Y	Y	Y	Y	Y
15 Ford	Y	?	Y	Y	N	N	Y	Y
16 Dingell	Y	N	Y	Y	Y	Y	Y	Y
17 Levin	Y	N	Y	Y	Y	Y	Y	Y
18 ***Broomfield***	N	Y	N	N	N	N	N	N
MINNESOTA								
1 Penny	N	?	N	Y	Y	Y	Y	Y
2 ***Weber***	N	Y	N	N	N	N	N	N
3 ***Ramstad***	Y	Y	N	N	N	N	Y	N
4 Vento	Y	N	Y	Y	Y	Y	Y	Y

	9	10	11	12	13	14	15	16
5 Sabo	Y	?	Y	Y	Y	Y	Y	Y
6 Sikorski	Y	N	Y	Y	Y	Y	Y	Y
7 Peterson	N	N	Y	Y	N	N	N	Y
8 Oberstar	N	N	Y	Y	N	N	N	Y
MISSISSIPPI								
1 Whitten	N	?	Y	Y	N	N	Y	Y
2 Espy	N	N	Y	Y	N	N	Y	Y
3 Montgomery	N	Y	N	Y	N	N	N	Y
4 Parker	N	Y	N	Y	N	N	N	Y
5 Taylor	N	Y	N	Y	N	N	N	Y
MISSOURI								
1 Clay	Y	?	Y	Y	N	N	Y	Y
2 Horn	Y	N	Y	Y	N	N	Y	Y
3 Gephardt	Y	N	Y	Y	Y	Y	Y	Y
4 Skelton	N	Y	Y	Y	N	N	Y	Y
5 Wheat	Y	N	Y	Y	Y	N	Y	Y
6 ***Coleman***	N	Y	N	N	N	N	Y	N
7 ***Hancock***	N	Y	N	N	N	N	N	N
8 ***Emerson***	N	Y	Y	Y	N	N	N	N
9 Volkmer	N	Y	Y	Y	N	N	N	Y
MONTANA								
1 Williams	N	?	Y	Y	N	N	Y	Y
2 ***Marlenee***	N	?	?	N	N	N	N	Y
NEBRASKA								
1 ***Bereuter***	N	Y	N	Y	N	N	Y	N
2 Hoagland	Y	N	Y	Y	Y	N	Y	Y
3 ***Barrett***	N	Y	N	N	N	N	N	N
NEVADA								
1 Bilbray	N	Y	Y	Y	N	N	Y	Y
2 ***Vucanovich***	N	Y	N	N	N	N	N	N
NEW HAMPSHIRE								
1 ***Zeliff***	Y	Y	N	N	N	N	Y	N
2 Swett	Y	Y	Y	Y	Y	N	Y	Y
NEW JERSEY								
1 Andrews	N	Y	Y	Y	Y	N	Y	Y
2 Hughes	Y	N	Y	Y	N	N	Y	Y
3 Pallone	Y	Y	Y	Y	Y	N	Y	Y
4 ***Smith***	Y	?	Y	Y	N	N	N	Y
5 ***Roukema***	Y	N	Y	Y	Y	Y	Y	N
6 Dwyer	Y	N	Y	Y	Y	?	Y	Y
7 ***Rinaldo***	Y	Y	Y	Y	N	N	N	Y
8 Roe	N	N	Y	Y	N	N	N	Y
9 Torricelli	Y	N	Y	Y	Y	N	Y	Y
10 Payne	Y	N	Y	Y	Y	N	Y	Y
11 ***Gallo***	Y	Y	Y	Y	Y	N	Y	N
12 ***Zimmer***	Y	Y	Y	N	Y	N	Y	N
13 ***Saxton***	Y	?	?	N	Y	N	N	N
14 Guarini	Y	N	Y	Y	N	N	Y	Y
NEW MEXICO								
1 ***Schiff***	N	Y	N	N	Y	N	Y	N
2 ***Skeen***	N	Y	N	N	Y	N	Y	N
3 Richardson	N	Y	Y	Y	Y	N	Y	Y
NEW YORK								
1 Hochbrueckner	Y	Y	Y	Y	Y	Y	Y	Y
2 Downey	Y	N	Y	?	Y	Y	Y	Y
3 Mrazek	Y	?	Y	Y	Y	?	Y	?
4 ***Lent***	N	Y	N	Y	N	N	N	N
5 ***McGrath***	Y	?	Y	Y	?	N	N	N
6 Flake	Y	N	Y	Y	Y	N	Y	Y
7 Ackerman	Y	?	Y	Y	Y	N	Y	Y
8 Scheuer	Y	N	Y	Y	Y	Y	Y	Y
9 Manton	Y	N	Y	Y	N	Y	N	Y
10 Schumer	Y	N	Y	Y	Y	Y	Y	Y
11 Towns	Y	N	Y	Y	Y	Y	Y	Y
12 Owens	Y	N	Y	Y	Y	N	Y	Y
13 Solarz	Y	Y	Y	Y	Y	Y	Y	Y
14 ***Molinari***	N	Y	Y	Y	Y	N	Y	N
15 ***Green***	Y	N	N	Y	Y	?	Y	Y
16 Rangel	Y	N	Y	Y	Y	N	Y	Y
17 Weiss	Y	N	Y	Y	Y	Y	Y	Y
18 Serrano	Y	N	Y	Y	Y	N	Y	Y
19 Engel	Y	N	Y	Y	Y	Y	Y	Y
20 Lowey	Y	N	Y	Y	Y	Y	Y	Y
21 ***Fish***	Y	Y	Y	Y	Y	N	Y	Y
22 ***Gilman***	Y	Y	Y	Y	Y	N	Y	Y
23 McNulty	Y	Y	Y	Y	Y	N	Y	Y
24 ***Solomon***	Y	Y	N	N	N	N	N	N
25 ***Boehlert***	Y	Y	Y	Y	Y	N	Y	Y
26 ***Martin***	N	?	Y	N	N	N	Y	N
27 ***Walsh***	N	Y	Y	N	N	Y	N	N
28 McHugh	Y	N	Y	Y	Y	N	Y	Y
29 ***Horton***	N	Y	Y	Y	N	N	Y	N
30 Slaughter	Y	N	Y	Y	N	N	Y	Y
31 ***Paxon***	N	Y	Y	N	N	N	N	N

	9	10	11	12	13	14	15	16
32 LaFalce	Y	N	Y	Y	N	N	N	Y
33 Nowak	Y	N	Y	Y	N	N	N	Y
34 ***Houghton***	N	?	Y	Y	Y	N	Y	N
NORTH CAROLINA								
1 Jones	N	?	?	Y	N	N	Y	Y
2 Valentine	Y	Y	N	Y	N	N	Y	Y
3 Lancaster	Y	Y	Y	Y	Y	Y	Y	Y
4 Price	Y	N	Y	Y	Y	N	Y	Y
5 Neal	Y	Y	Y	?	N	N	Y	Y
6 ***Coble***	N	Y	N	N	N	N	N	N
7 Rose	N	N	Y	Y	Y	N	Y	Y
8 Hefner	Y	Y	Y	Y	N	N	Y	Y
9 ***McMillan***	N	Y	N	N	N	N	N	N
10 ***Ballenger***	N	Y	N	N	N	N	N	N
11 ***Taylor***	N	Y	N	N	N	N	N	N
NORTH DAKOTA								
AL Dorgan	N	N	Y	Y	N	N	Y	Y
OHIO								
1 Luken	Y	Y	Y	Y	N	Y	N	Y
2 ***Gradison***	Y	?	N	N	N	N	Y	N
3 Hall	Y	Y	Y	Y	Y	N	N	Y
4 ***Oxley***	N	Y	N	Y	N	N	N	N
5 ***Gillmor***	N	Y	Y	Y	N	N	N	N
6 ***McEwen***	N	?	N	N	N	?	N	N
7 ***Hobson***	N	Y	N	Y	N	N	Y	N
8 ***Boehner***	N	Y	N	N	N	N	N	N
9 Kaptur	Y	N	Y	Y	N	N	Y	Y
10 ***Miller***	Y	Y	N	N	N	N	N	N
11 Eckart	Y	N	Y	Y	Y	Y	Y	Y
12 ***Kasich***	Y	Y	N	Y	N	N	N	N
13 Pease	Y	N	Y	Y	N	Y	Y	Y
14 Sawyer	Y	N	Y	Y	Y	Y	Y	Y
15 ***Wylie***	N	Y	N	Y	N	N	N	N
16 ***Regula***	N	Y	Y	Y	N	N	Y	N
17 Traficant	N	N	Y	Y	N	N	Y	Y
18 Applegate	Y	N	Y	Y	N	N	N	Y
19 Feighan	Y	N	Y	Y	Y	N	Y	Y
20 Oakar	Y	N	Y	Y	Y	Y	Y	Y
21 Stokes	Y	N	Y	Y	Y	N	Y	Y
OKLAHOMA								
1 ***Inhofe***	N	Y	N	Y	N	N	N	N
2 Synar	Y	N	Y	Y	Y	Y	Y	Y
3 Brewster	N	Y	N	Y	Y	N	Y	Y
4 McCurdy	Y	Y	Y	Y	Y	N	Y	Y
5 ***Edwards***	N	Y	?	N	?	N	N	N
6 English	N	Y	Y	Y	N	N	Y	Y
OREGON								
1 AuCoin	N	N	Y	Y	Y	N	Y	Y
2 ***Smith***	N	Y	Y	N	N	N	N	N
3 Wyden	Y	N	Y	Y	Y	Y	Y	Y
4 DeFazio	N	N	Y	Y	N	N	Y	Y
5 Kopetski	N	+	Y	Y	Y	N	Y	Y
PENNSYLVANIA								
1 Foglietta	Y	Y	Y	Y	Y	?	Y	Y
2 Blackwell	M	M	M	M	M	M	Y	Y
3 Borski	Y	N	Y	Y	Y	Y	N	Y
4 Kolter	?	N	Y	Y	N	N	N	Y
5 ***Schulze***	N	?	N	Y	N	N	N	N
6 Yatron	Y	?	?	Y	Y	N	N	Y
7 ***Weldon***	Y	Y	Y	N	N	N	N	Y
8 Kostmayer	Y	N	Y	Y	Y	Y	Y	Y
9 ***Shuster***	N	Y	Y	Y	N	N	N	?
10 ***McDade***	N	?	Y	Y	N	N	N	N
11 Kanjorski	Y	N	Y	Y	N	N	N	Y
12 Murtha	Y	Y	Y	Y	N	N	Y	Y
13 ***Coughlin***	N	Y	Y	Y	N	N	Y	N
14 Coyne	Y	N	Y	Y	Y	Y	Y	Y
15 ***Ritter***	Y	Y	Y	Y	N	N	N	N
16 ***Walker***	Y	Y	N	N	N	N	N	N
17 ***Gekas***	N	Y	Y	Y	N	Y	Y	N
18 ***Santorum***	N	Y	N	Y	N	N	N	N
19 ***Goodling***	N	Y	N	Y	N	N	Y	N
20 Gaydos	N	?	Y	Y	N	N	Y	N
21 ***Ridge***	N	Y	Y	Y	N	N	Y	N
22 Murphy	N	Y	Y	Y	N	X	N	Y
23 ***Clinger***	Y	Y	Y	Y	N	N	Y	N
RHODE ISLAND								
1 ***Machtley***	Y	Y	Y	Y	Y	Y	Y	N
2 Reed	N	N	Y	Y	Y	Y	Y	Y
SOUTH CAROLINA								
1 ***Ravenel***	Y	Y	Y	N	Y	N	Y	Y
2 ***Spence***	N	Y	N	N	N	N	N	N
3 Derrick	Y	?	Y	Y	N	N	Y	Y
4 Patterson	Y	Y	Y	Y	N	N	Y	Y
5 Spratt	Y	Y	Y	Y	N	N	Y	Y
6 Tallon	N	Y	Y	Y	N	N	N	Y

	9	10	11	12	13	14	15	16
SOUTH DAKOTA								
AL Johnson	N	N	Y	Y	Y	N	Y	Y
TENNESSEE								
1 ***Quillen***	N	Y	N	Y	N	N	N	N
2 ***Duncan***	N	Y	N	N	N	N	N	Y
3 Lloyd	Y	Y	?	Y	X	N	Y	Y
4 Cooper	Y	Y	N	Y	N	C	Y	Y
5 Clement	Y	Y	Y	Y	N	N	Y	Y
6 Gordon	Y	Y	Y	Y	Y	N	Y	Y
7 ***Sundquist***	N	Y	N	N	N	N	N	N
8 Tanner	Y	Y	N	Y	X	N	Y	Y
9 Ford	Y	N	Y	Y	N	?	Y	?
TEXAS								
1 Chapman	N	Y	Y	Y	N	?	Y	Y
2 Wilson	Y	?	Y	Y	N	N	Y	Y
3 ***Johnson***	N	Y	N	N	N	N	N	N
4 Hall	N	Y	N	Y	?	N	N	N
5 Bryant	Y	?	Y	Y	N	?	Y	Y
6 ***Barton***	N	Y	N	N	N	N	N	N
7 ***Archer***	Y	Y	N	N	N	N	N	N
8 ***Fields***	N	Y	N	N	N	N	N	N
9 Brooks	Y	N	Y	Y	N	P	Y	Y
10 Pickle	N	?	?	Y	Y	Y	Y	Y
11 Edwards	N	Y	Y	Y	N	N	Y	Y
12 Geren	N	Y	Y	Y	N	N	Y	Y
13 Sarpalius	N	Y	N	Y	N	N	N	N
14 Laughlin	N	Y	N	Y	N	N	Y	Y
15 de la Garza	N	?	Y	Y	Y	N	N	Y
16 Coleman	N	Y	Y	Y	N	N	Y	Y
17 Stenholm	N	Y	N	Y	N	N	N	Y
18 Washington	Y	?	Y	?	N	N	Y	Y
19 ***Combest***	N	Y	N	N	N	N	N	N
20 Gonzalez	N	Y	Y	Y	Y	Y	Y	Y
21 ***Smith***	Y	Y	N	N	Y	N	Y	N
22 ***DeLay***	Y	?	N	N	N	N	N	N
23 Bustamante	N	?	Y	Y	Y	N	Y	Y
24 Frost	N	Y	Y	Y	Y	Y	Y	Y
25 Andrews	Y	Y	Y	Y	Y	N	Y	Y
26 ***Armey***	N	Y	N	N	N	N	N	N
27 Ortiz	N	Y	Y	Y	N	Y	N	Y
UTAH								
1 ***Hansen***	N	Y	N	N	N	N	N	N
2 Owens	N	N	Y	Y	Y	N	Y	Y
3 Orton	N	Y	N	Y	N	N	N	Y
VERMONT								
AL *Sanders*	Y	N	Y	N	N	N	Y	Y
VIRGINIA								
1 ***Bateman***	N	Y	N	Y	N	N	N	N
2 Pickett	Y	Y	Y	Y	N	N	Y	N
3 ***Bliley***	N	Y	N	N	N	N	N	N
4 Sisisky	Y	Y	Y	Y	Y	N	Y	N
5 Payne	Y	Y	Y	Y	Y	N	Y	Y
6 Olin	N	Y	N	Y	Y	N	Y	Y
7 ***Allen***	M	M	M	M	M	M	Y	N
8 Moran	N	N	Y	Y	Y	Y	Y	Y
9 Boucher	Y	?	Y	Y	N	Y	Y	Y
10 ***Wolf***	N	Y	N	N	N	N	N	N
WASHINGTON								
1 ***Miller***	Y	Y	N	N	Y	N	Y	Y
2 Swift	N	N	Y	Y	Y	N	Y	Y
3 Unsoeld	Y	N	Y	Y	Y	N	Y	Y
4 ***Morrison***	N	Y	N	N	N	N	Y	Y
5 Foley							Y	
6 Dicks	Y	Y	Y	Y	Y	N	Y	Y
7 McDermott	Y	N	Y	Y	Y	N	Y	Y
8 ***Chandler***	N	Y	N	N	Y	N	Y	N
WEST VIRGINIA								
1 Mollohan	N	Y	Y	Y	N	N	N	Y
2 Staggers	N	N	Y	Y	N	N	N	Y
3 Wise	Y	N	Y	Y	Y	N	Y	Y
4 Rahall	Y	?	#	Y	N	N	Y	Y
WISCONSIN								
1 Aspin	Y	N	Y	Y	Y	N	Y	Y
2 ***Klug***	N	Y	N	N	N	N	Y	Y
3 ***Gunderson***	N	Y	Y	N	N	N	Y	N
4 Kleczka	Y	?	Y	Y	N	Y	Y	Y
5 Moody	Y	?	Y	Y	Y	Y	Y	-
6 ***Petri***	Y	Y	N	Y	N	N	N	Y
7 Obey	Y	N	Y	Y	N	N	Y	Y
8 ***Roth***	N	Y	N	N	N	N	N	N
9 ***Sensenbrenner***	Y	Y	N	N	N	N	N	N
WYOMING								
AL ***Thomas***	N	Y	N	N	N	N	N	N

Southern states - Ala., Ark., Fla., Ga., Ky., La., Miss., N.C., Okla., S.C., Tenn., Texas, Va.

KEY

- Y Voted for (yea).
- # Paired for.
- + Announced for.
- N Voted against (nay).
- X Paired against.
- \- Announced against.
- P Voted "present."
- M Not yet a member of Congress when vote was taken.
- ? Did not vote or otherwise make a position known.

Democrats *Republicans*

	1	2	3	4	5	6	7	8
ALABAMA								
Heflin	Y	N	N	Y	N	Y	Y	N
Shelby	Y	N	N	Y	N	N	Y	N
ALASKA								
Murkowski	Y	Y	N	Y	Y	N	N	N
Stevens	Y	Y	N	Y	Y	N	N	N
ARIZONA								
DeConcini	N	?	N	N	N	Y	N	Y
McCain	Y	N	N	Y	N	N	Y	N
ARKANSAS								
Bumpers	N	N	Y	N	N	Y	Y	Y
Pryor	N	?	?	?	#	?	?	?
CALIFORNIA								
Cranston	-	Y	Y	N	Y	Y	N	Y
Seymour	Y	N	Y	Y	N	N	N	N
COLORADO								
Wirth	N	Y	Y	N	Y	Y	N	Y
Brown	Y	Y	N	Y	N	N	N	N
CONNECTICUT								
Dodd	N	Y	Y	Y	N	Y	N	Y
Lieberman	Y	Y	Y	Y	Y	Y	N	Y
DELAWARE								
Biden	N	Y	Y	N	Y	Y	N	Y
Roth	Y	Y	Y	Y	Y	N	N	N
FLORIDA								
Graham	Y	N	Y	Y	N	Y	N	Y
Mack	Y	N	N	Y	N	Y	N	N
GEORGIA								
Fowler	N	Y	Y	N	N	Y	Y	Y
Nunn	N	?	Y	Y	Y	Y	Y	N
HAWAII								
Akaka	N	Y	Y	Y	Y	Y	N	N
Inouye	N	Y	Y	Y	Y	Y	Y	N
IDAHO								
Craig	Y	Y	N	Y	Y	N	Y	N
Symms	Y	Y	N	Y	Y	N	Y	N
ILLINOIS								
Dixon	N	Y	Y	Y	N	Y	N	N
Simon	N	Y	Y	Y	Y	Y	N	Y
INDIANA								
Coats	Y	N	Y	N	N	N	N	N
Lugar	Y	N	Y	N	Y	N	N	N
IOWA								
Harkin	N	Y	Y	N	Y	Y	N	Y
Grassley	N	N	N	Y	N	N	N	N
KANSAS								
Dole	Y	N	Y	Y	Y	N	N	N
Kassebaum	Y	N	Y	N	Y	N	N	N
KENTUCKY								
Ford	N	N	Y	Y	X	Y	N	N
McConnell	Y	N	N	Y	N	N	N	N
LOUISIANA								
Breaux	Y	N	N	Y	Y	N	Y	Y
Johnston	Y	N	N	Y	Y	N	Y	Y
MAINE								
Mitchell	N	Y	Y	N	Y	Y	N	Y
Cohen	Y	N	Y	N	N	N	N	N
MARYLAND								
Mikulski	N	Y	Y	Y	N	Y	N	Y
Sarbanes	N	Y	Y	Y	Y	Y	N	Y
MASSACHUSETTS								
Kennedy	N	Y	Y	N	Y	Y	N	Y
Kerry	N	Y	Y	N	N	Y	N	Y
MICHIGAN								
Levin	N	N	Y	N	N	Y	N	Y
Riegle	N	N	Y	N	N	Y	N	Y
MINNESOTA								
Wellstone	N	Y	Y	N	N	Y	N	Y
Durenberger	Y	Y	Y	Y	Y	N	N	N
MISSISSIPPI								
Cochran	Y	N	N	Y	Y	N	N	N
Lott	Y	N	N	Y	Y	N	Y	N
MISSOURI								
Bond	Y	N	N	N	N	N	Y	N
Danforth	Y	N	N	Y	Y	N	N	N
MONTANA								
Baucus	N	Y	N	Y	Y	N	N	Y
Burns	Y	N	N	N	Y	N	Y	N
NEBRASKA								
Exon	N	Y	Y	N	Y	N	N	N
Kerrey	N	Y	Y	N	Y	Y	N	Y
NEVADA								
Bryan	Y	N	Y	N	N	Y	Y	Y
Reid	Y	Y	Y	Y	N	Y	N	Y
NEW HAMPSHIRE								
Rudman	Y	Y	Y	Y	Y	N	Y	N
Smith	Y	Y	N	N	Y	Y	Y	N
NEW JERSEY								
Bradley	N	Y	Y	N	N	Y	N	Y
Lautenberg	N	Y	Y	N	N	Y	N	Y
NEW MEXICO								
Bingaman	N	N	Y	Y	Y	Y	N	Y
Domenici	Y	Y	Y	Y	Y	N	N	N
NEW YORK								
Moynihan	N	Y	Y	Y	Y	Y	Y	Y
D'Amato	Y	Y	Y	Y	N	Y	N	N
NORTH CAROLINA								
Sanford	N	Y	Y	N	N	Y	Y	Y
Helms	Y	N	N	Y	N	Y	Y	N
NORTH DAKOTA								
Burdick	N	Y	Y	Y	Y	N	N	Y
Conrad	N	N	Y	N	N	N	Y	Y
OHIO								
Glenn	N	N	Y	Y	N	Y	Y	N
Metzenbaum	N	N	Y	N	Y	Y	N	Y
OKLAHOMA								
Boren	N	N	Y	Y	Y	Y	Y	N
Nickles	Y	Y	N	Y	N	N	N	N
OREGON								
Hatfield	N	N	Y	Y	Y	N	N	N
Packwood	Y	N	Y	Y	N	N	N	N
PENNSYLVANIA								
Wofford	M	N	Y	Y	N	Y	N	Y
Specter	Y	N	N	Y	N	N	N	N
RHODE ISLAND								
Pell	N	Y	Y	Y	Y	Y	N	Y
Chafee	Y	Y	Y	N	Y	N	N	Y
SOUTH CAROLINA								
Hollings	N	N	N	N	N	Y	Y	N
Thurmond	Y	N	Y	Y	Y	N	Y	N
SOUTH DAKOTA								
Daschle	N	N	Y	Y	N	Y	N	Y
Pressler	Y	Y	N	Y	N	N	N	N
TENNESSEE								
Gore	Y	N	Y	N	N	Y	N	Y
Sasser	N	N	Y	N	N	Y	N	Y
TEXAS								
Bentsen	N	Y	Y	Y	Y	Y	N	N
Gramm	Y	Y	N	Y	N	N	Y	N
UTAH								
Garn	Y	Y	N	Y	Y	Y	Y	N
Hatch	Y	N	N	Y	N	N	N	N
VERMONT								
Leahy	N	Y	N	N	Y	Y	N	N
Jeffords	Y	Y	Y	N	Y	N	N	Y
VIRGINIA								
Robb	Y	N	Y	Y	Y	Y	N	N
Warner	Y	N	Y	Y	Y	N	Y	N
WASHINGTON								
Adams	N	Y	Y	N	N	Y	N	Y
Gorton	Y	Y	Y	Y	Y	N	N	N
WEST VIRGINIA								
Byrd	N	Y	Y	Y	Y	Y	Y	N
Rockefeller	N	Y	Y	Y	Y	Y	N	Y
WISCONSIN								
Kohl	N	Y	Y	N	N	Y	N	Y
Kasten	Y	N	Y	Y	N	N	N	N
WYOMING								
Simpson	Y	Y	N	N	Y	N	N	N
Wallop	Y	Y	N	Y	Y	Y	Y	N

ND Northern Democrats SD Southern Democrats

Southern states - Ala., Ark., Fla., Ga., Ky., La., Miss., N.C., Okla., S.C., Tenn., Texas, Va.

1. S J Res 2. Use of Force Against Iraq/Passage. Passage of the joint resolution to authorize military force if Iraq has not withdrawn from Kuwait and complied with U.N. Security Council resolutions by Jan. 15. The resolution authorizes using force and expending funds under the War Powers Act. Passed 52-47: R 42-2; D 10-45 (ND 3-35, SD 7-10), Jan. 12, 1991 (Senate vote 2). A "yea" was a vote supporting the president's position. *(Story, p. 42-B)*

2. S 1204. Surface Transportation Reauthorization/Interstate Maintenance. Moynihan, D-N.Y., motion to table (kill) the Lott, R-Miss., amendment to retain the current 90 percent federal share for Interstate maintenance and 80 percent for bridge projects. Motion agreed to 53-44: R 20-23; D 33-21 (ND 30-9, SD 3-12), June 19, 1991 (Senate vote 97). *(Story, p. 42-B)*

3. S 1241. Crime Bill/Handgun Waiting Period. Dole, R-Kan., amendment to require a waiting period of five business days before handgun purchases, during which time a mandatory background check of the prospective handgun buyers would be conducted, and to require the attorney general within six months of enactment to select a system and computer software for a National Instant Check system that within five years would be able to provide a record of criminal activity. Adopted 67-32: R 19-24; D 48-8 (ND 37-3, SD 11-5), June 28, 1991 (Senate vote 115). *(Story, p. 43-B)*

4. HR 2427. Fiscal 1992 Energy and Water Appropriations/Superconducting Super Collider. Johnston, D-La., motion to table (kill) the Bumpers, D-Ark., amendment to eliminate all funding for the superconducting super collider by reducing the bill's funding level for the General Science and Research Activities account by $508,700,000. Motion agreed to 62-37: R 33-10; D 29-27 (ND 19-21, SD 10-6), July 10, 1991 (Senate vote 121). A "yea" was a vote supporting the president's position. *(Story, p. 43-B)*

5. HR 2506. Fiscal 1992 Legislative Branch Appropriations/Pay Raise. Byrd, D-W.Va., amendment to raise senators' pay from $101,900 to $125,100, ban senators' honoraria and limit outside earned income to 15 percent of a senator's base pay. Adopted 53-45: R 25-18; D 28-27 (ND 22-18, SD 6-9), July 17, 1991 (Senate vote 133). *(Story, p. 44-B)*

6. HR 2212. Conditional MFN for China in 1992/Passage. Passage of the bill to prohibit the president from granting China most-favored-nation status for the 12-month period beginning July 3, 1992, unless he reports that China has accounted for and released all political prisoners and made progress in human rights, among other conditions. Passed 55-44: R 6-37; D 49-7 (ND 36-4, SD 13-3), July 23, 1991 (Senate vote 142). A "nay" was a vote supporting the president's position. *(Story, p. 44-B)*

7. S 1507. Fiscal 1992-93 Defense Authorization/Women in Combat Pilot Positions. Glenn, D-Ohio, motion to table (kill) the Roth, R-Del., amendment to repeal the 1948 law that prohibits women from flying in combat pilot positions. Motion rejected 30-69: R 14-29; D 16-40 (ND 6-34, SD 10-6), July 31, 1991 (Senate vote 167). (The Roth amendment was subsequently adopted by voice vote.) *(Story, p. 45-B)*

8. S 1507. Fiscal 1992-93 Defense Authorization/Strategic Stability. Bingaman, D-N.M., amendment to state that it is the United States' goal to maintain strategic stability with the Soviet Union while deploying an anti-ballistic missile system with one or more ground-based sites and space-based sensors. The amendment would clarify that current actions by the United States are treaty compliant. Rejected 43-56: R 2-41; D 41-15 (ND 33-7, SD 8-8), July 31, 1991 (Senate vote 169). A "nay" was a vote supporting the president's position. *(Story, p. 45-B)*

	9	10	11	12	13	14	15	16
ALABAMA								
Heflin	N	Y	N	N	Y	Y	Y	Y
Shelby	N	Y	N	Y	Y	Y	Y	Y
ALASKA								
Murkowski	N	N	Y	Y	Y	Y	Y	Y
Stevens	N	N	Y	Y	Y	Y	Y	Y
ARIZONA								
DeConcini	?	Y	Y	Y	Y	Y	N	Y
McCain	N	N	Y	Y	Y	Y	Y	Y
ARKANSAS								
Bumpers	N	Y	Y	N	Y	Y	N	Y
Pryor	N	Y	?	N	Y	Y	N	?
CALIFORNIA								
Cranston	?	Y	Y	N	Y	N	?	Y
Seymour	N	N	N	Y	Y	Y	Y	N
COLORADO								
Wirth	Y	Y	Y	N	Y	N	+	Y
Brown	N	N	N	Y	Y	Y	Y	N
CONNECTICUT								
Dodd	N	Y	Y	N	Y	Y	N	Y
Lieberman	N	Y	Y	N	Y	N	Y	Y
DELAWARE								
Biden	Y	Y	Y	N	Y	N	N	Y
Roth	?	N	Y	Y	Y	N	Y	Y
FLORIDA								
Graham	N	Y	Y	N	Y	N	Y	Y
Mack	N	N	N	Y	Y	N	Y	Y
GEORGIA								
Fowler	N	Y	Y	Y	Y	N	N	Y
Nunn	N	Y	Y	Y	Y	Y	Y	Y
HAWAII								
Akaka	Y	Y	Y	N	Y	Y	Y	+
Inouye	N	Y	Y	N	Y	Y	Y	Y
IDAHO								
Craig	N	N	N	Y	Y	Y	Y	N
Symms	N	N	N	Y	N	Y	Y	N
ILLINOIS								
Dixon	N	Y	Y	Y	Y	N	N	?
Simon	Y	Y	Y	N	Y	N	N	Y
INDIANA								
Coats	N	N	Y	Y	N	Y	Y	Y
Lugar	N	N	N	Y	Y	Y	Y	Y
IOWA								
Harkin	Y	Y	?	N	Y	N	N	?
Grassley	N	N	N	Y	Y	N	Y	Y
KANSAS								
Dole	N	N	N	Y	Y	Y	Y	Y
Kassebaum	N	N	N	Y	Y	Y	Y	Y
KENTUCKY								
Ford	N	Y	Y	N	Y	Y	Y	Y
McConnell	N	N	N	Y	Y	Y	Y	Y
LOUISIANA								
Breaux	N	Y	Y	Y	Y	Y	Y	Y
Johnston	N	Y	Y	Y	Y	Y	Y	Y
MAINE								
Mitchell	Y	Y	Y	N	Y	Y	N	Y
Cohen	N	Y	Y	Y	Y	N	Y	Y
MARYLAND								
Mikulski	N	Y	Y	N	Y	N	Y	Y
Sarbanes	Y	Y	Y	N	Y	N	N	Y
MASSACHUSETTS								
Kennedy	Y	Y	Y	N	Y	N	N	Y
Kerry	Y	Y	Y	N	Y	N	N	Y
MICHIGAN								
Levin	N	Y	Y	N	Y	N	N	Y
Riegle	Y	Y	Y	N	Y	N	N	Y
MINNESOTA								
Wellstone	Y	Y	Y	N	Y	N	N	Y
Durenberger	N	N	Y	Y	Y	N	Y	Y
MISSISSIPPI								
Cochran	N	N	N	Y	Y	Y	Y	Y
Lott	N	N	N	Y	Y	N	Y	Y
MISSOURI								
Bond	N	N	Y	Y	Y	N	Y	Y
Danforth	N	N	Y	Y	Y	Y	Y	Y
MONTANA								
Baucus	Y	Y	Y	N	Y	N	N	Y
Burns	N	N	N	Y	Y	Y	Y	Y
NEBRASKA								
Exon	N	Y	Y	Y	Y	N	N	Y
Kerrey	N	Y	?	N	?	X	?	?
NEVADA								
Bryan	N	Y	Y	N	Y	N	Y	Y
Reid	N	Y	Y	N	Y	N	Y	Y
NEW HAMPSHIRE								
Rudman	N	N	N	Y	Y	Y	Y	Y
Smith	N	N	N	Y	N	N	Y	N
NEW JERSEY								
Bradley	Y	Y	Y	N	Y	N	N	Y
Lautenberg	Y	Y	Y	N	Y	N	N	Y
NEW MEXICO								
Bingaman	N	Y	Y	N	Y	Y	N	Y
Domenici	N	N	N	Y	Y	Y	Y	Y
NEW YORK								
Moynihan	N	Y	Y	N	Y	N	N	Y
D'Amato	N	Y	Y	Y	Y	Y	Y	Y
NORTH CAROLINA								
Sanford	N	Y	Y	N	Y	N	Y	Y
Helms	N	N	N	Y	N	Y	Y	?
NORTH DAKOTA								
Burdick	Y	Y	Y	N	Y	N	N	Y
Conrad	Y	Y	Y	N	Y	Y	N	Y
OHIO								
Glenn	N	Y	Y	N	Y	N	Y	Y
Metzenbaum	Y	Y	Y	N	Y	N	N	Y
OKLAHOMA								
Boren	N	Y	N	Y	Y	?	Y	Y
Nickles	N	N	N	Y	Y	Y	Y	N
OREGON								
Hatfield	Y	Y	Y	Y	Y	Y	Y	Y
Packwood	Y	Y	Y	N	Y	Y	Y	Y
PENNSYLVANIA								
Wofford	Y	Y	Y	N	?	?	?	Y
Specter	Y	Y	Y	Y	Y	Y	Y	Y
RHODE ISLAND								
Pell	Y	Y	Y	N	Y	#	Y	Y
Chafee	N	Y	Y	Y	Y	N	Y	Y
SOUTH CAROLINA								
Hollings	Y	Y	N	Y	Y	N	N	Y
Thurmond	N	N	N	Y	Y	Y	Y	Y
SOUTH DAKOTA								
Daschle	Y	Y	Y	N	Y	Y	N	Y
Pressler	N	N	N	Y	Y	Y	Y	N
TENNESSEE								
Gore	N	Y	Y	N	Y	N	N	Y
Sasser	N	Y	Y	N	Y	N	N	Y
TEXAS								
Bentsen	N	Y	Y	N	Y	Y	Y	Y
Gramm	N	N	N	Y	Y	?	Y	Y
UTAH								
Garn	N	N	N	Y	Y	Y	Y	Y
Hatch	N	N	N	Y	Y	Y	+	Y
VERMONT								
Leahy	Y	Y	Y	N	Y	N	Y	Y
Jeffords	N	Y	Y	N	Y	?	Y	Y
VIRGINIA								
Robb	N	Y	Y	Y	Y	N	Y	Y
Warner	N	N	N	Y	Y	Y	Y	Y
WASHINGTON								
Adams	Y	Y	Y	N	Y	N	N	Y
Gorton	N	N	N	Y	Y	Y	Y	Y
WEST VIRGINIA								
Byrd	N	Y	Y	N	Y	Y	Y	Y
Rockefeller	Y	Y	Y	N	Y	N	N	Y
WISCONSIN								
Kohl	Y	Y	Y	N	Y	N	Y	Y
Kasten	N	Y	N	Y	Y	Y	Y	Y
WYOMING								
Simpson	N	N	N	Y	Y	Y	Y	Y
Wallop	N	N	N	Y	N	Y	Y	N

KEY

- Y Voted for (yea).
- # Paired for.
- + Announced for.
- N Voted against (nay).
- X Paired against.
- \- Announced against.
- P Voted "present."
- M Not yet a member of Congress when vote was taken.
- ? Did not vote or otherwise make a position known.

Democrats *Republicans*

ND Northern Democrats SD Southern Democrats

Southern states - Ala., Ark., Fla., Ga., Ky., La., Miss., N.C., Okla., S.C., Tenn., Texas, Va.

9. HR 2707. Fiscal 1992 Labor, HHS, and Education Appropriations/Budget Waiver. Harkin, D-Iowa, motion to waive the Budget Act with respect to the Harkin amendment to the committee amendment, to rescind $3.148 billion in budget authority from unobligated balances in Defense Department accounts from fiscal 1988-91, and transfer the $3.148 billion in budget authority to domestic programs. Motion rejected 28-69: R 3-39; D 25-30 (ND 24-14, SD 1-16), Sept. 10, 1991 (Senate vote 182). A "nay" was a vote supporting the president's position. *(Story, p. 46-B)*

10. S 1722. Unemployment Benefits Extension/Conference Report. Adoption of the conference report to provide an estimated $6.4 billion for up to 20 additional weeks of unemployment benefits based on a state's unemployment rate. The conference report designates the spending as an emergency and would not require a presidential declaration to be exempt from budget agreement limits. Adopted 65-35: R 8-35; 57-0 (ND 40-0, SD 17-0), Oct. 1, 1991 (Senate vote 213). A "nay" was a vote supporting the president's position. *(Story, p. 46-B)*

11. S 5. Family and Medical Leave Act/Substitute. Bond, R-Mo., substitute amendment to raise the number of hours an employee must work in order to be eligible for up to 12 weeks of unpaid leave for the birth or adoption of a child or for the serious illness of the worker or an immediate family member. Adopted 65-32: R 15-28; D 50-4 (ND 38-0, SD 12-4), Oct. 2, 1991 (Senate vote 215). A "nay" was a vote supporting the president's position. *(Story, p. 47-B)*

12. Thomas Nomination/Confirmation. Confirmation of President Bush's nomination of Clarence Thomas of Georgia to be an associate justice of the U.S. Supreme Court. Confirmed 52-48: R 41-2; D 11-46 (ND 3-37, SD 8-9), Oct. 15, 1991 (Senate vote 220). A "yea" was a vote supporting the president's position. *(Story, p. 47-B)*

13. S 1745. Civil Rights Act of 1991/Passage. Passage of the bill to make it easier to sue for employment discrimination and permit women, religious minorities and the disabled to win compensatory and punitive damages for intentional discrimination, mainly by reversing several recent Supreme Court decisions and by expanding Title VII of the 1964 Civil Rights Act. Passed 93-5: R 38-5; D 55-0 (ND 38-0, SD 17-0), Oct. 30, 1991 (Senate vote 238). A "yea" was a vote supporting the president's position. *(Story, p. 48-B)*

14. S 1220. National Energy Policy/Cloture. Mitchell, D-Maine, motion to invoke cloture (thus limiting debate) on the motion to proceed to the bill to allow drilling in the Arctic National Wildlife Refuge, mandate that federal and private vehicle fleets use alternative fuels and direct the secretary of Transportation to adopt new corporate average fuel economy (CAFE) standards, and enact other programs related to energy production and consumption. Motion rejected 50-44: R 32-9; D 18-35 (ND 9-28, SD 9-7), Nov. 1, 1991 (Senate vote 242). A three-fifths majority (60) of the total Senate is required to invoke cloture. *(Story, p. 48-B)*

15. Gates Nomination/Confirmation. Confirmation of President Bush's nomination of Robert M. Gates of Virginia to be director of central intelligence. Confirmed 64-31: R 42-0; D 22-31 (ND 11-25, SD 11-6), Nov. 5, 1991 (Senate vote 243). A "yea" was a vote supporting the president's position. *(Story, p. 49-B)*

16. HR 3807. CFE Treaty Implementation/Dismantlement of Soviet Weapons. Nunn, D-Ga., amendment to authorize $500 million in defense funds to assist the Soviet Union and its republics with the dismantlement of Soviet nuclear, chemical and other weapons. Adopted 86-8: R 34-8; D-52-0 (ND 36-0, SD 16-0), Nov. 25, 1991 (Senate vote 274). *(Story, p. 49-B)*

CQ

PUBLIC LAWS

Public Laws, 102nd Congress, 1st Session

PL 102-1 (H J Res 77) Authorize the use of U.S. armed forces pursuant to United Nations Security Council Resolution 678. Introduced by MICHEL, R-Ill., Jan. 12, 1991. House passed Jan. 12. Senate passed Jan. 12. President signed Jan. 14, 1991.

PL 102-2 (HR 4) Extend the time for performing certain acts under the internal revenue laws for individuals performing services as part of Operation Desert Shield. Introduced by ROSTENKOWSKI, D-Ill., Jan. 3, 1991. Ways and Means reported, amended, Jan. 23 (H Rept 102-2). House passed, amended, under suspension of the rules Jan. 23. Senate passed Jan. 24. President signed Jan. 30, 1991.

PL 102-3 (HR 3) Amend Title 38, United States Code, to revise, effective Jan. 1, 1991, the rates of disability compensation for veterans with service-connected disabilities and the rates of dependency and indemnity compensation for survivors of such veterans. Introduced by MONTGOMERY, D-Miss, Jan. 3, 1991. House passed, under suspension of the rules, Jan. 23. Senate passed Jan. 24. President signed Feb. 6, 1991.

PL 102-4 (HR 556) Provide for the Secretary of Veterans Affairs to obtain independent scientific review of the available scientific evidence regarding associations between diseases and exposure to dioxin and other chemical compounds in herbicides. Introduced by MONTGOMERY, D-Miss., Jan. 17, 1991. House passed, amended, under suspension of the rules, Jan. 29. Senate passed Jan. 30. President signed Feb. 6, 1991.

PL 102-5 (H J Res 30) Designate Feb. 7, 1991, as National Girls and Women in Sports Day. Introduced by SNOWE, R-Maine, Jan. 3, 1991. House Post Office and Civil Service discharged. House passed Feb. 6. Senate passed Feb. 6. President signed Feb. 15, 1991.

PL 102-6 (S J Res 76) Commend the Peace Corps and the current and former Peace Corps volunteers on the 30th anniversary of the establishment of the Peace Corps. Introduced by DODD, D-Conn., Feb. 21, 1991. Senate passed Feb. 21. House passed Feb. 26. President signed March 1, 1991.

PL 102-7 (S J Res 51) Designate the week beginning March 4, 1991, as Federal Employees Recognition Week. Introduced by SARBANES, D-Md., Jan. 29, 1991. Senate Judiciary discharged. Senate passed Feb. 21. House Post Office and civil Service discharged. House passed Feb. 27. President signed March 5, 1991.

PL 102-8 (S J Res 55) Commemorate the 200th anniversary of United States-Portuguese diplomatic relations. Introduced by PELL, D-R.I., Jan. 30, 1991. Senate Judiciary discharged. Senate passed Feb. 20. House Foreign Affairs discharged. House Post Office and Civil Service discharged. House passed, under suspension of the rules, Feb. 27. President signed March 8, 1991.

PL 102-9 (S J Res 58) Designate March 4, 1991, as Vermont Bicentennial Day. Introduced by LEAHY, D-Vt., Jan. 31, 1991. Senate Judiciary discharged. Senate passed Feb. 6. House Post Office and Civil Service discharged. House passed Feb. 27. President signed March 11, 1991.

PL 102-10 (S 379) Make certain technical amendments to the National and Community Service Act. Introduced by KENNEDY, D-Mass., Feb. 6, 1991. Senate passed Feb. 6. House Education and Labor discharged. House passed Feb. 26. President signed March 12, 1991.

PL 102-11 (S J Res 84) Disapprove the action of the District of Columbia Council in approving the Schedule of Heights Amendment Act of 1990. Introduced by LEVIN, D-Mich., Feb. 28, 1991. Senate Governmental Affairs discharged. Senate passed March 5. House passed March 6. President signed March 12, 1991.

PL 102-12 (HR 555) Amend the Soldiers' and Sailors' Civil Relief Act or 1940 to improve and clarify the protections provided by that act, and to amend Title 38, U.S. Code, to clarify veterans' re-employment rights and to improve veterans' rights to reinstatement of health insurance. Introduced by MONTGOMERY, D-Miss., Jan. 17, 1991. House passed, amended, under suspension of the rules, Jan. 29. Senate Veterans' Affairs discharged. Senate passed, amended, Feb. 21. House agreed to Senate amendment Feb. 27. President signed March 18, 1991.

PL 102-13 (H J Res 98) Designate March 4-10, 1991, as National School Breakfast Week. Introduced by BOEHLERT, R-N.Y., Jan. 30, 1991. House Post Office and Civil Service discharged. House passed Feb. 27. Senate passed March 7. President signed March 18, 1991.

PL 102-14 (H J Res 104) Designate March 26, 1991, as Education Day, U.S.A. Introduced by MICHEL, R-Ill., Jan. 31, 1991. House Post Office and Civil Service discharged. House passed March 5. Senate passed March 7. President signed March 20, 1991.

PL 102-15 (H J Res 133) Authorize and request the president to designate the second full week in March 1991 as National Employ the Older Worker Week. Introduced by SOLOMON, R-N.Y., Feb. 19, 1991. House Post Office and Civil Service discharged. House passed March 5. Senate Judiciary discharged. Senate passed March 14. President signed March 21, 1991.

PL 102-16 (HR 180) Amend Title 38, U.S. Code, with respect to veterans' education and employment programs. Introduced by PENNY, D-Minn., Jan. 3, 1991. House passed, under suspension of the rules, Feb. 5. Senate Veterans' Affairs discharged. Senate passed March 7. President signed March 22, 1991.

PL 102-17 (H J Res 167) Designate June 14, 1991, as Baltic Freedom Day. Introduced by HERTEL, D-Mich., March 4, 1991. House Post Office and Civil Service discharged. House passed, amended, March 5. Senate passed March 7. President signed March 22, 1991.

PL 102-18 (S 419) Amend the Federal Home Loan Bank Board Act to enable the Resolution Trust Corporation to meet its obligations to depositors and others by the least expensive means. Introduced by RIEGLE, D-Mich., Feb. 19, 1991. Senate Banking, Housing, and Urban Affairs reported Feb. 14 (S Rept 102-13). Considered Feb. 26, 27, March 5 and 6. Senate passed, amended, March 7. House passed, amended, March 13. Senate agreed to conference report March 19 (H Rept 102-27). House agreed to conference report March 21. President signed March 23, 1991.

PL 102-19 (S J Res 59) Designate March 25, 1991, as Greek Independence Day: A National Day of Celebration of Greek and American Democracy. Introduced by SPECTER, R-Pa., Jan. 31, 1991. Senate Judiciary discharged. Senate passed Feb. 21. House Post Office and Civil Service discharged. House passed, amended, March 20. Senate agreed to House amendment March 21. President signed March 25, 1991.

PL 102-20 (HR 1176) Provide supplemental authorization of appropriations for fiscal year 1991 for the Department of State for certain emergency costs associated with the Persian Gulf conflict. Introduced by BERMAN, D-Calif., Feb. 28, 1991. House passed, amended, under suspension of the rules, March 5. Senate passed March 13. President signed March 27, 1991.

PL 102-21 (HR 1284) Authorize emergency supplemental assistance for Israel for additional costs incurred as a result of the Persian Gulf conflict. Introduced by FASCELL, D-Fla., March 6, 1991. House Foreign Affairs discharged. House passed March 6. Senate passed March 13. President signed March 28, 1991.

PL 102-22 (HR 1316) Amend Chapter 54 of Title 5, U. S. Code, to extend and improve the performance management and recognition system. Introduced by ACKERMAN, D-N.Y., March 7, 1991. House Post Office and Civil Service reported March 14 (H Rept 102-20). House passed, under suspension of the rules, March 19. Senate passed March 19. President signed March 28, 1991.

PL 102-23 (S J Res 53) Designate April 9, 1991, and April 9, 1992, as National Former Prisoner of War Recognition Day. Introduced by GRAHAM, D-Fla., Jan. 30, 1991. Senate Judiciary discharged. Senate passed Feb. 21. House Post Office and Civil Service discharged. House passed March 20. President signed March 28, 1991.

PL 102-24 (S J Res 83) Enact a National Day of Prayer and Thanksgiving. Introduced by DOLE, R-Kan. (on behalf of Coats, R-Ind.), Feb. 28, 1991. Senate passed Feb. 28. House passed March 20. President signed March 28, 1991.

PL 102-25 (S 725) Enact the Persian Gulf Conflict Supplemental Authorization and Personnel Benefits Act of 1991. Introduced by MITCHELL, D-Maine, March 21, 1991. Senate passed March 21. House passed March 21. President signed April 6, 1991.

PL 102-26 (HR 1285) Resolve legal and technical issues relating to federal post-secondary student assistance programs and prevent undue burdens on participants in Operation Desert Storm.

Introduced by FORD, D-Mich., March 6, 1991. House passed, amended, under suspension of the rules, March 19. Senate passed March 21. President signed April 9, 1991.

PL 102-27 (HR 1281) Make dire emergency supplemental appropriations for the consequences of Operation Desert Shield/Desert Storm, food stamps, unemployment compensation administration, veterans' compensation and pensions, and other urgent needs for the fiscal year ending September 30, 1991. Introduced by WHITTEN, D-Miss., March 5, 1991. House Appropriations reported March 5 (H Rept 102-9). House passed, amended, March 7. Senate Appropriations reported, amended, March 14 (S Rept 102-24). Senate considered March 19. Senate passed, amended, March 20. House agreed to conference report March 22 (H Rept 102-29). Senate agreed to conference report March 22. President signed April 10, 1991.

PL 102-28 (HR 1282) Make supplemental appropriations and transfers for Operation Desert Shield/Storm for fiscal year ending September 30, 1991. Introduced by WHITTEN, D-Miss., March 5, 1991. House Appropriations reported March 5 (H Rept 102-10). House passed March 7. Senate Appropriations reported, amended, March 14 (S Rept 102-23). Senate passed, amended, March 19. House agreed to conference report March 22 (H Rept 102-30). Senate agreed to conference report March 22. President signed April 10, 1991.

PL 102-29 (H J Res 222) Provide for a settlement of the railroad labor-management disputes between certain railroads represented by the National Carriers' Conference Committee of the National Railway Labor Conference and certain of their employees. Introduced by DINGELL, D-Mich., April 17, 1991. House Energy and Commerce discharged. House passed, amended, April 17. Senate passed April 17. President signed April 18, 1991.

PL 102-30 (H J Res 134) Designate the weeks of April 14, 1991, and May 3, 1992, as Jewish Heritage Week. Introduced by GILMAN, R-N.Y., Feb. 20, 1991. House Post Office and Civil Service discharged. House passed April 11. Senate passed April 11. President signed April 18, 1991.

PL 102-31 (H J Res 197) Designate the week of April 15, 1991, as National Education First Week. Introduced by LEVINE, D-Calif., March 20, 1991. House Post Office and Civil Service discharged. House passed April 11. Senate passed April 11. President signed April 18, 1991.

PL 102-32 (S 534) Authorize the president to award a gold medal on behalf of Congress to Gen. H. Norman Schwarzkopf and provide for the production of bronze duplicates of such medal for sale to the public. Introduced by LOTT, R-Miss., Feb. 28, 1991. Senate Banking, Housing, and Urban Affairs reported March 14. Senate passed March 21. House passed, under suspension of the rules, April 11. President signed April 23, 1991.

PL 102-33 (S 565) Authorize the president to award a gold medal on behalf of the Congress to Gen. Colin L. Powell and provide for the production of bronze duplicates of such medal for sale to the public. Introduced by WARNER, R-Va., March 5, 1991. Senate Banking, Housing, and Urban Affairs reported March 14. Senate passed March 21. House passed, under suspension of the rules, April 11. President signed April 23, 1991.

PL 102-34 (S J Res 119) Designate April 22, 1991, as Earth Day to promote the preservation of the global environment. Introduced by ROTH, R-Del., April 11, 1991. Senate passed April 11. House Post Office and Civil Service discharged. House passed April 17. President signed April 23, 1991.

PL 102-35 (S J Res 16) Designate the week of April 21, 1991, as National Crime Victims' Rights Week. Introduced by THURMOND, R-S.C., Jan. 14, 1991. Senate Judiciary discharged. Senate passed April 9. House Post Office and Civil Service discharged. House passed April 17. President signed April 24, 1991.

PL 102-36 (H J Res 218) Designate the week beginning April 21, 1991, and the week beginning April 19, 1992, each as National Organ and Tissue Donor Awareness Week. Introduced by MORRISON, R-Wash., April 11, 1991. House Post Office and Civil Service discharged. House passed April 17. Senate passed April 18. President signed April 26, 1991.

PL 102-37 (S J Res 64) Authorize the president to proclaim the last Friday of April as National Arbor Day. Introduced by BRADLEY, D-N.J., Feb. 5, 1991. Senate Judiciary discharged. Senate passed, amended, Feb. 26. House Post Office and Civil Service discharged. House passed April 17. President signed April 26, 1991.

PL 102-38 (S J Res 98) Express appreciation for the benefit brought to the nation by Amtrak during its 20 years of existence. Introduced by EXON, D-Neb., March 20, 1991. Senate Commerce, Science and Transportation discharged. Senate passed April 23. House passed April 24. President signed May 3, 1991.

PL 102-39 (S J Res 102) Designate the second week in May 1991 as National Tourism Week. Introduced by ROCKEFELLER, D-W.Va., March 21, 1991. Senate Judiciary discharged. Senate passed April 17. House Post Office and Civil Service discharged. House passed April 24. President signed May 3, 1991.

PL 102-40 (HR 598) Amend Title 38, U.S. Code, to improve the capability of the Department of Veterans Affairs to recruit and retain physicians and dentists through increases in special pay authorities and to authorize collective bargaining over conditions of employment for health-care employees of the Department of Veterans Affairs. Introduced by MONTGOMERY, D-Miss., Jan. 23, 1991. House passed, amended, under suspension of the rules, Jan. 30. Senate passed, amended, April 17. House agreed to Senate amendment, under suspension of the rules, April 23. President signed May 7, 1991.

PL 102-41 (H J Res 214) Recognize the Astronauts Memorial at the John F. Kennedy Space Center as the national memorial to astronauts who die in the line of duty. Introduced by BACCHUS, D-Fla., April 11, 1991. House Administration discharged. House passed, amended, April 30. Senate passed May 6. President signed May 8, 1991.

PL 102-42 (H J Res 173) Designate May 1991 and May 1992 as Asian/Pacific American Heritage Month. Introduced by HORTON, R-N.Y., March 5, 1991. House Post Office and Civil Service discharged. House passed April 24. Senate passed April 25. President signed May 14, 1991.

PL 102-43 (H J Res 194) Designate May 12, 1991, as Infant Mortality Awareness Day. Introduced by HARRIS, D-Ala., March 19, 1991. House Post Office and Civil Service discharged. House passed May 2, 1991. Senate passed May 7. President signed May 14, 1991.

PL 102-44 (H J Res 109) Designate the week beginning May 12, 1991, as Emergency Medical Services Week. Introduced by MANTON, D-N.Y., Feb. 5, 1991. House Post Office and Civil Service discharged. House passed, amended, May 2. Senate Judiciary discharged. Senate passed May 9. President signed May 15, 1991.

PL 102-45 (HR 2122) Authorize emergency humanitarian assistance for fiscal year 1991 for Iraqi refugees and other persons in and around Iraq who are displaced as a result of the Persian Gulf conflict. Introduced by BERMAN, D-Calif., April 29, 1991. House passed, under suspension of the rules, April 30. Senate passed May 9. President signed May 17, 1991.

PL 102-46 (S 258) Correct an error in the Solar, Wind, Waste, and Geothermal Power Production Incentives Act of 1990. Introduced by JOHNSTON, D-La., Jan. 23, 1991. Senate Energy and Natural Resources reported Feb. 7 (S Rept 102-11). Senate passed April 11. House passed, under suspension of the rules, April 30. President signed May 17, 1991.

PL 102-47 (H J Res 154) Designate the month of May 1991 as National Foster Care Month. Introduced by MATSUI, D-Calif., Feb. 27, 1991. House Post Office and Civil Service discharged. House passed April 24. Senate Judiciary discharged. Senate passed May 8. President signed May 20, 1991.

PL 102-48 (S J Res 134) Designate May 22, 1991, as National Desert Storm Reservists Day. Introduced by BENTSEN, D-Texas, April 25, 1991. Senate Judiciary discharged. Senate passed May 14. House Post Office and Civil Service discharged. House passed May 15. President signed May 21, 1991.

PL 102-49 (S J Res 127) Designate the month of May 1991 as National Huntington's Disease Awareness Month. Introduced by KASSEBAUM, R-Kan., April 23, 1991. Senate Judiciary discharged. Senate passed May 8. House Post Office and Civil Service discharged. House passed May 15. President signed May 22, 1991.

PL 102-50 (S 248) Amend the Wild and Scenic Rivers Act to designate certain segments of the Niobrara River in Nebraska and a segment of the Missouri River in Nebraska and South Dakota as components of the Wild and Scenic Rivers System. Introduced by EXON, D-Neb., Jan. 23, 1991. Senate Energy and Natural Resources reported, amended, March 7 (S Rept 102-19). Senate passed, amended, April 17. House Interior and Insular Affairs reported May 7 (H Rept 102-51, Part I). House Merchant Marine and Fisheries discharged. House passed May 14. President signed May 24, 1991.

PL 102-51 (H J Res 141) Designate the week beginning May 13, 1991, as National Senior Nutrition Week. Introduced by DOWNEY, D-N.Y., Feb. 21, 1991. House Post Office and Civil Service discharged. House passed May 2. Senate Judiciary discharged. Senate passed May 17. President signed May 29, 1991.

PL 102-52 (HR 2127) Amend the Rehabilitation Act of 1973 to extend the programs of such act. Introduced by OWENS, D-N.Y., April 29, 1991. House passed, amended, under suspension of the rules, May 20. Senate passed May 21. President signed June 6, 1991.

PL 102-53 (HR 831) Designate the Owens Finance Station of the U.S. Postal Service in Cleveland, Ohio, as the Jesse Owens Building of the U.S. Postal Service. Introduced by STOKES, D-Ohio, Feb. 5, 1991. House passed, under suspension of the rules, March 19. Senate Governmental Affairs discharged. Senate passed May 24. President signed June 10, 1991.

PL 102-54 (HR 232) Amend Title 38, U.S. Code, with respect to veterans' programs for housing and memorial affairs. Introduced by STAGGERS, D-W.Va., Jan. 3, 1991. House passed, amended, under suspension of the rules, Feb. 6. Senate Veterans' Affairs discharged. Senate passed, amended, May 16. House agreed to Senate amendments May 22. President signed June 13, 1991.

PL 102-55 (HR 2251) Make dire emergency supplemental appropriations from contributions of foreign governments and/or interest for humanitarian assistance to refugees and displaced people in and around Iraq as a result of the recent invasion of Kuwait and for peacekeeping activities, and for other urgent needs for the fiscal year ending Sept. 30, 1991. Introduced by WHITTEN, D-Miss., May 8, 1991. House passed, amended, May 9. Senate passed, amended, May 9. House adopted conference report May 22 (H Rept 102-71). Senate adopted conference report May 22. President signed June 13, 1991.

PL 102-56 (H J Res 219) Designate the second week in June as National Scleroderma Awareness Week. Introduced by DWYER, D-N.J., April 16, 1991. House Post Office and Civil Service discharged. House passed, amended, June 5. Senate passed June 6. President signed June 13, 1991.

PL 102-57 (H J Res 91) Designate June 10 through 16, 1991 as Pediatric AIDS Awareness Week. Introduced by SERRANO, D-N.Y., Jan. 24, 1991. House Post Office and Civil Service discharged. House passed June 5. Senate Judiciary discharged. Senate passed June 11. President signed June 18, 1991.

PL 102-58 (HR 971) Designate the facility of the U.S. Postal Service at 630 East 105th St., Cleveland, Ohio, as the Luke Easter Post Office. Introduced by HORTON, R-N.Y., Feb. 19, 1991. House passed, under suspension of the rules, March 19. Senate Governmental Affairs discharged. Senate passed, amended, May 24. House agreed to Senate amendments June 3. President signed June 18, 1991.

PL 102-59 (S 483) Enact the Taconic Mountains Protection Act of 1991. Introduced by LEAHY, D-Vt., Feb. 26, 1991. Senate Agriculture, Nutrition, and Forestry reported March 12 (S Rept 102-21). Senate passed, amended, March 14. House Agriculture reported June 3 (H Rept 102-90). House passed, under suspension of the rules, June 3. President signed June 18, 1991.

PL 102-60 (S J Res 111) Marking the 75th anniversary of chartering, by act of Congress, of the Boy Scouts of America. Introduced by BRADLEY, D-N.J., March 22, 1991. Senate Judiciary discharged. Senate passed May 22. House Judiciary discharged. House passed June 12. President signed June 18, 1991.

PL 102-61 (S 292) Expand the boundaries of the Sanguaro National Monument. Introduced by McCAIN, R-Ariz., Jan. 30, 1991. Senate Energy and Natural Resources reported, amended, April 23 (S Rept 102-44). Senate passed, amended, April 25. House Interior and Insular Affairs reported June 3 (H Rept 102-88). House passed, under suspension of the rules, June 3. President signed June 19, 1991.

PL 102-62 (S 64) Provide for the establishment of a National Commission on a Longer School Year. Introduced by KENNEDY, D-Mass., Jan. 14, 1991. Senate Labor and Human Resources reported, amended, March 19 (S Rept 102-26). Senate passed, amended, April 17. House passed, amended, June 10. House adopted conference report June 13 (H Rept 102-110). Senate adopted conference report June 14. President signed June 27, 1991.

PL 102-63 (S J Res 159) Designate the month of June 1991 as National Forest System Month. Introduced by SIMPSON, R-Wyo., June 11, 1991. Senate Judiciary discharged. Senate passed June 13. House Post Office and Civil Service discharged. House passed June 26. President signed June 28, 1991.

PL 102-64 (S 909) Amend Chapter 9 of Title 17, U.S. Code, regarding protection extended to semiconductor chip products of foreign entities. Introduced by LEAHY, D-Vt., April 23, 1991. Senate Judiciary reported June 11 (S Rept 102-78). Senate passed June 12. House Judiciary discharged. House passed June 25. President signed June 28, 1991.

PL 102-65 (HR 2332) Amend the Immigration Act of 1990 to extend for four months the applications deadline for special temporary protected status for Salvadorans. Introduced by MOAKLEY, D-Mass., May 14, 1991. House Judiciary reported, amended, June 21 (H Rept 102-123). House passed, amended, under suspension of the rules, June 25. Senate passed June 28. President signed July 2, 1991.

PL 102-66 (H J Res 259) Designate July 2, 1991, as National Literacy Day. Introduced by PAYNE, D-N.J., May 22, 1991. House Post Office and Civil Service discharged. House passed June 26. Senate passed June 27. President signed July 2, 1991.

PL 102-67 (HR 749) Authorize the secretary of the Interior to accept a donation of land for addition to the Ocmulgee National Monument in Georgia. Introduced by ROWLAND, D-Ga., Jan. 30, 1991. House Interior and Insular Affairs reported April 22 (H Rept 102-35). House passed, under suspension of the rules, April 24. Senate Energy and Natural Resources reported June 21 (S Rept 102-89). Senate passed June 25. President signed July 9, 1991.

PL 102-68 (H J Res 72) Designate Dec. 7, 1991, as National Pearl Harbor Remembrance Day. Introduced by HASTERT, R-Ill., Jan. 11, 1991. House Post Office and Civil Service discharged. House passed May 29. Senate Judiciary discharged. Senate passed June 26. President signed July 9, 1991.

PL 102-69 (H J Res 138) Designate the week beginning July 21, 1991, as Lyme Disease Awareness Week. Introduced by HOCHBRUECKNER, D-N.Y., Feb. 20, 1991. House Post Office and Civil Service discharged. House passed May 29. Senate Judiciary discharged. Senate passed June 26. President signed July 10, 1991.

PL 102-70 (H J Res 149) Designate March 1991 and March 1992 both as Women's History Month. Introduced by SCHROEDER, D-Colo., Feb. 27, 1991. House Post Office and Civil Service discharged. House passed March 20. Senate Judiciary discharged. Senate passed June 26. President signed July 10, 1991.

PL 102-71 (S 674) Designate the U.S. Post Office at 304 W. Commercial Ave. in Monterey, Tenn., as the J. E. "Eddie" Russell Post Office. Introduced by GORE, D-Tenn., March 14, 1991. Senate passed March 14. House passed, amended, under suspension of the rules, June 24. Senate agreed to House amendments June 26. President signed July 10, 1991.

PL 102-72 (H J Res 255) Designate the week beginning July 21, 1991, as the Korean War Veterans Remembrance Week. Introduced by SANGMEISTER, D-Ill., May, 15, 1991. House Post Office and Civil Service discharged. House passed July 16. Senate passed July 17. President signed July 23, 1991.

PL 102-73 (HR 751) Enhance the literacy and basic skills of adults to ensure that all adults in the United States acquire the basic skills necessary to function effectively and achieve the greatest possible opportunity in their work and in their lives, and to strengthen and coordinate adult literacy programs. Introduced by SAWYER, D-Ohio, Jan. 30, 1991. House Education and Labor reported, amended, March 18 (H Rept 102-23). House passed, amended, under suspension of the rules, March 19. Senate passed, amended, June 26. House agreed to Senate amendments 1 and 2 with amendments and agreed to Senate amendment 3 on July 11. Senate agreed to House amendments to Senate amendments 1 and 2 on July 15. President signed July 25, 1991.

PL 102-74 (H J Res 279) Declare it to be the policy of the United States that there should be a renewed and sustained commitment by the federal government and the American people to the importance of adult education. Introduced by COLEMAN, R-Mo., June 20, 1991. House passed, under suspension of the rules, July 9. Senate passed July 11. President signed July 26, 1991.

PL 102-75 (HR 427) Disclaim any interests of the United States in certain lands on San Juan Island, Wash. Introduced by

SWIFT, D-Wash., Jan. 3, 1991. House Interior and Insular Affairs reported, amended, April 22 (H Rept 102-34). House passed, amended, under suspension of the rules, April 24. Senate Energy and Natural Resources reported July 2 (S Rept 102-94). Senate passed July 17. President signed July 26, 1991.

PL 102-76 (HR 998) Redesignate the Vacherie Post Office at 2747 Highway 20 in Vacherie, La., as the John Richard Haydel Post Office. Introduced by HOLLOWAY, R-La., Feb. 20, 1991. House passed, amended, under suspension of the rules, July 15. Senate passed July 17. President signed July 26, 1991.

PL 102-77 (HR 2347) Redesignate the Midland General Mail Facility in Midland, Texas, as the Carl O. Hyde General Mail Facility. Introduced by SMITH, R-Texas, May 15, 1991. House passed, amended, under suspension of the rules, July 15. Senate passed July 17. President signed July 26, 1991.

PL 102-78 (S J Res 121) Designate Sept. 12, 1991, as National DARE Day. Introduced by DeCONCINI, D-Ariz., April 16, 1991. Senate Judiciary discharged. Senate passed June 26. House Post Office and Civil Service discharged. House passed July 24. President signed Aug. 2, 1991.

PL 102-79 (H J Res 181) Designate the third Sunday of August 1991, as National Senior Citizens Day. Introduced by SMITH, D-Fla., March 6, 1991. House Post Office and Civil Service discharged. House passed July 16. Senate Judiciary discharged. Senate passed July 23. President signed Aug. 6, 1991.

PL 102-80 (S J Res 40) Designate the period commencing Sept. 8, 1991, and ending on Sept. 14, 1991, as National Historically Black Colleges Week. Introduced by THURMOND, R-S.C., Jan. 15, 1991. Senate Judiciary discharged. Senate passed June 26. House Post Office and Civil Service discharged. House passed, amended, July 24. Senate agreed to House amendments July 25. President signed Aug. 6, 1991.

PL 102-81 (S J Res 142) Designate the week beginning July 28, 1991, as National Juvenile Arthritis Awareness Week. Introduced by SHELBY, D-Ala., May 9, 1991. Senate Judiciary discharged. Senate passed June 26. House Post Office and Civil Service discharged. House passed July 24. President signed Aug. 6, 1991.

PL 102-82 (HR 153) Make technical amendments to the Veterans' Judicial Review Act. Introduced by MONTGOMERY, D-Miss., Jan. 3, 1991. House passed, amended, under suspension of the rules, Feb. 20. Senate Veterans' Affairs reported, amended, July 15. Senate passed, amended, July 16. House agreed to Senate amendments July 24. President signed Aug. 6, 1991.

PL 102-83 (HR 2525) Amend Title 38, U.S. Code, to codify the provisions of law relating to the establishment of the Department of Veterans Affairs and to restate and reorganize certain provisions of that title. Introduced by MONTGOMERY, D-Miss., June 4, 1991. House passed, amended, under suspension of the rules, June 25. Senate passed July 22. President signed Aug. 6, 1991.

PL 102-84 (HR 1779) Designate the federal building being built at 77 West Jackson Blvd. in Chicago as the Ralph H. Metcalfe Federal Building. Introduced by SAVAGE, D-Ill., April 16, 1991. House Public Works and Transportation reported July 26 (H Rept 102-168). House passed, under suspension of the rules, July 29. Senate Environment and Public Works reported July 31. Senate passed July 31. President signed Aug. 10, 1991.

PL 102-85 (S J Res 179) Designate the week beginning Aug. 25, 1991, as National Parks Week. Introduced by WALLOP, R-Wyo., July 16, 1991. Senate Judiciary discharged. Senate passed July 31. House Post Office and Civil Service discharged. House passed Aug. 1. President signed Aug. 10, 1991.

PL 102-86 (HR 1047) Amend Title 38, U.S. Code, to make miscellaneous improvements in veterans compensation and pension programs. Introduced by APPLEGATE, D-Ohio, Feb. 21, 1991. House passed, amended, under suspension of the rules, April 11. Senate Veterans' Affairs discharged. Senate passed, amended, July 25. House agreed to Senate amendments July 29. President signed August 14, 1991.

PL 102-87 (HR 1448) Amend the Act of May 12, 1920 (41 Stat. 596), to allow the city of Pocatello, Idaho, to use certain lands for a correctional facility for women. Introduced by STALLINGS, D-Idaho, March 14, 1991. House Interior and Insular Affairs reported, amended, June 24 (H Rept 102-127). House passed, amended, under suspension of the rules, June 24. Senate Energy and Natural Resources reported, July 25 (S Rept 102-121). Senate passed July 31. President signed Aug. 14, 1991.

PL 102-88 (HR 1455) Authorize appropriations for fiscal year 1991 for the intelligence activities of the U.S. government, the Intelligence Community Staff, and the Central Intelligence Agency Retirement and Disability System. Introduced by McCURDY, D-Okla., March 18, 1991. House Intelligence reported, amended, April 22 (H Rept 102-37). House passed, amended, May 1. Senate passed, amended, June 28. House agreed to conference report July 31 (H Rept 102-166). Senate agreed to conference report July 31. President signed Aug. 14, 1991.

PL 102-89 (HR 2031) Amend Title I of the Employee Retirement Income Security Act of 1974 to provide for equal treatment of telephone and electric cooperative welfare plans for the purposes of pre-emption. Introduced by WILLIAMS, D-Mont., April 23, 1991. House Education and Labor reported, amended, July 15 (H Rept 102-150). House passed, amended, under suspension of the rules, July 16. Senate passed July 24. President signed Aug. 14, 1991.

PL 102-90 (HR 2506) Make appropriations for the legislative branch for the fiscal year ending Sept. 30, 1992. Introduced by FAZIO, D-Calif., May 30, 1991. House Appropriations reported May 30 (H Rept 102-82). House passed June 5. Senate Appropriations reported, amended, June 12 (S Rept 102-81). Senate passed, amended, July 17. House agreed to conference report July 31 (H Rept 102-176). Senate agreed to conference report Aug. 2. President signed Aug. 14, 1991.

PL 102-91 (HR 2901) Authorize the transfer by lease of four vessels to the government of Greece. Introduced by FASCELL, D-Fla., July 16, 1991. House passed, under suspension of the rules, July 29. Senate passed July 31. President signed Aug. 14, 1991.

PL 102-92 (H J Res 166) Designate September 13, 1991, as Commodore John Barry Day. Introduced by GILMAN, R-N.Y., March 4, 1991. House Post Office and Civil Service discharged. House passed Aug. 1. Senate passed Aug. 2. President signed Aug. 14, 1991.

PL 102-93 (H J Res 264) Designate Aug. 1, 1991, as Helsinki Human Rights Day. Introduced by HOYER, D-Md., June 4, 1991. House passed, amended, under suspension of the rules, July 29. Senate passed July 31. President signed Aug. 14, 1991.

PL 102-94 (H J Res 309) Designate Aug. 29, 1991, as National Sarcoidosis Awareness Day. Introduced by SLATTERY, D-Kan., July 18, 1991. House Post Office and Civil Service discharged. House passed Aug. 1. Senate passed Aug. 2. President signed Aug. 14, 1991.

PL 102-95 (S 1593) Improve the operation and effectiveness of the National Commission on Libraries and Information Science. Introduced by PELL, D-R.I., July 30, 1991. Senate passed July 30. House Education and Labor discharged. House passed Aug. 1. President signed Aug. 14, 1991.

PL 102-96 (S 1594) Honor and commend the efforts of Terry Beirn to amend the Public Health Service Act to resume and make technical amendments to the community-based AIDS research initiative. Introduced by KENNEDY, D-Mass., July 30, 1991. Senate Labor and Human Resources discharged. Senate passed July 31. House passed Aug. 2. President signed Aug. 14, 1991.

PL 102-97 (S J Res 72) Designate the week of Sept. 15, 1991, through Sept. 21, 1991, as National Rehabilitation Week. Introduced by SPECTER, R-Pa., Feb. 19, 1991. Senate Judiciary discharged. Senate passed June 26. House Post Office and Civil Service discharged. House passed Aug. 1. President signed Aug. 14, 1991.

PL 102-98 (HR 904) Direct the Interior secretary to prepare a national historic landmark theme study on African-American History. Introduced by LEWIS, D-Ga., Feb. 6, 1991. House Interior and Insular Affairs reported May 6 (H Rept 102-49). House passed, under suspension of the rules, May 7. Senate Energy and Natural Resources reported, amended, June 21 (S Rept 102-90). Senate passed, amended, June 25. House agreed to Senate amendments Aug. 1. President signed Aug. 17, 1991.

PL 102-99 (HR 991) Extend the expiration date of the Defense Production Act of 1950. Introduced by CARPER, D-Del., Feb. 20, 1991. House Banking, Finance and Urban Affairs reported, amended, March 4 (H Rept 102-7). House passed, amended, March 6. Senate passed, amended, March 7. House agreed to conference report Aug. 2 (H Rept 102-186). Senate agreed to conference report Aug. 2. President signed Aug. 17, 1991.

PL 102-100 (HR 1006) Authorize appropriations for fiscal year 1992 for the Federal Maritime Commission. Introduced by JONES, D-N.C., Feb. 20, 1991. House Merchant Marine and Fisheries reported May 23 (H Rept 102-80). House passed, amended, under suspension of the rules, June 24. Senate Commerce, Science and Transportation reported, amended, Aug. 1 (S Rept 102-134). Senate passed, amended, Aug. 1. House agreed to Senate amendment Aug. 2. President signed Aug. 17, 1991.

PL 102-101 (HR 1143) Authorize a study of nationally significant places in American labor history. Introduced by McNULTY, D-N.Y., Feb. 27, 1991. House Interior and Insular Affairs reported May 6, 1991 (H Rept 102-50). House passed, under suspension of the rules, May 7. Senate Energy and Natural Resources reported, amended, June 21 (S Rept 102-91). Senate passed, amended, June 25. House agreed to Senate amendments Aug. 1. President signed Aug. 17, 1991.

PL 102-102 (HR 2123) Amend the District of Columbia Self-Government and Governmental Reorganization Act to establish a predictable and equitable method for determining the amount of the annual federal payment to the District of Columbia. Introduced by DELLUMS, D-Calif., April 29, 1991. House District of Columbia reported June 3 (H Rept 102-92). House passed June 11. Senate Governmental Affairs discharged. Senate passed Aug. 2. President signed Aug. 17, 1991.

PL 102-103 (HR 2313) Amend the School Dropout and Demonstration Assistance Act of 1988 to extend authorization of appropriations through fiscal year 1993. Introduced by KILDEE, D-Mich., May 14, 1991. House Education and Labor reported May 23 (H Rept 102-77). House passed, amended, under suspension of the rules, June 3. Senate passed, amended, July 30. House agreed to Senate amendment Aug. 1. President signed Aug. 17, 1991.

PL 102-104 (HR 2427) Make appropriations for energy and water development for the fiscal year ending Sept. 30, 1992. Introduced by BEVILL, D-Ala., May 22, 1991. House Appropriations reported May 22 (H Rept 102-75). House passed, amended, May 29. Senate Appropriations reported, amended, June 12 (S Rept 102-80). Senate considered July 9. Senate passed, amended, July 10. House agreed to conference report July 31 (H Rept 102-177). House receded and concurred in Senate amendments Aug. 1. House receded and concurred with amendments in Senate amendments Aug. 1. Senate agreed to conference report Aug. 2. Senate agreed to House amendments to Senate amendments Aug. 2. President signed Aug. 17, 1991.

PL 102-105 (HR 2968) Waive the period of congressional review of certain District of Columbia acts. Introduced by DELLUMS, D-Calif., July 23, 1991. House District of Columbia reported, amended, July 26 (H Rept 102-169). House passed, amended, July 29. Senate Governmental Affairs discharged. Senate passed Aug. 2. President signed Aug. 17, 1991.

PL 102-106 (HR 2969) Permit the mayor of the District of Columbia to reduce the budgets of the Board of Education and other independent agencies of the District, and to permit the District of Columbia to carry out a program to reduce the number of employees of the District government. Introduced by BLILEY, R-Va., July 23, 1991. House District of Columbia reported July 26 (H Rept 102-170). House passed July 29. Senate Governmental Affairs discharged. Senate passed Aug. 2. President signed Aug. 17, 1991.

PL 102-107 (HR 3201) Provide emergency unemployment compensation. Introduced by ROSTENKOWSKI, D-Ill., Aug. 2, 1991. House Ways and Means reported Aug. 2 (H Rept 102-184). House passed Aug. 2. Senate passed Aug. 2. President signed Aug. 17, 1991.

PL 102-108 (S 1608) Make technical amendments to the Nutrition Information and Labeling Act. Introduced by METZENBAUM, D-Ohio, July 31, 1991. Senate passed July 31. House passed Aug. 2. President signed Aug. 17, 1991.

PL 102-109 (H J Res 332) Make continuing appropriations for the fiscal year 1992. Introduced by WHITTEN, D-Miss., Sept. 24, 1991. House Appropriations reported Sept. 24 (H Rept 102-216). House passed Sept. 25. Senate passed, amended, Sept. 25. House agreed to Senate amendment Sept. 26. President signed Sept. 30, 1991.

PL 102-110 (S 296) Amend the Immigration and Nationality Act to provide for special immigrant status for certain aliens who have served honorably (or are enlisted to serve) in the Armed Forces of the United States for at least 12 years. Introduced by KENNEDY, D-Mass., Jan. 30, 1991. Senate passed Jan. 30. House Judiciary reported, amended, Aug. 2 (H Rept 102-195). House passed, amended, under suspension of the rules, Sept. 16. Senate agreed to House amendment with amendment Sept. 24. House agreed to Senate amendment to the House amendment Sept. 26. President signed Oct. 1, 1991.

PL 102-111 (HR 3291) Make appropriations for the government of the District of Columbia and other activities chargeable in whole or in part against the revenues of said District for the fiscal year ending Sept. 30, 1992. Introduced by DIXON, D-Calif., Sept. 11, 1991. House passed Sept 16. Senate passed, amended, Sept. 16. House disagreed to Senate amendments Sept. 17. Senate receded from its amendments Sept. 26. President signed Oct. 1, 1991.

PL 102-112 (H J Res 23) Authorize the president to issue a proclamation designating the weeks beginning on Nov. 24, 1991, and Nov. 22, 1992, as National Family Week. Introduced by MYERS, R-Ind., Jan. 3, 1991. House Post Office and Civil Service discharged. House passed July 10. Senate Judiciary discharged. Senate passed Sept. 24. President signed Oct. 3, 1991.

PL 102-113 (H J Res 233) Designate Sept. 20, 1991, as National POW/MIA Recognition Day, and authorize display of the National League of Families POW/MIA flag. Introduced by LAGOMARSINO, R-Calif., April 24, 1991. House Post Office and Civil Service and Veterans' Affairs discharged. House passed Sept. 16. Senate passed Sept. 18. President signed Oct. 3, 1991.

PL 102-114 (S J Res 73) Designate October 1991 as National Domestic Violence Awareness Month. Introduced by SPECTER, R-Pa., Feb. 19, 1991. Senate Judiciary discharged. Senate passed June 26. House Post Office and Civil Service discharged. House passed Sept. 24. President signed Oct. 3, 1991.

PL 102-115 (S J Res 125) Designate October 1991 as Polish-American Heritage Month. Introduced by SIMON, D-Ill., April 17, 1991. Senate Judiciary discharged. Senate passed June 26. House Post Office and Civil Service discharged. House passed Sept. 24. President signed Oct. 3, 1991.

PL 102-116 (S J Res 126) Designate the second Sunday in October of 1991 as National Children's Day. Introduced by HATFIELD, R-Ore., April 18, 1991. Senate Judiciary discharged. Senate passed June 26. House Post Office and Civil Service discharged. House passed Sept. 16. President signed Oct. 3, 1991.

PL 102-117 (S J Res 151) Designate Oct. 6, 1991, and Oct. 6, 1992, as German-American Day. Introduced by RIEGLE, D-Mich., May 23, 1991. Senate Judiciary discharged. Senate passed June 26. House Post Office and Civil Service discharged. House passed Sept. 16. President signed Oct. 3, 1991.

PL 102-118 (S 363) Authorize the addition of 15 acres to Morristown National Historical Park. Introduced by BRADLEY, D-N.J., Feb. 6, 1991. Senate Energy and Natural Resources reported April 23 (S Rept 102-45). Senate passed April 25. House Interior and Insular Affairs reported Sept. 23 (H Rept 102-212). House passed, under suspension of the rules, Sept. 24. President signed Oct. 4, 1991.

PL 102-119 (S 1106) Amend the Individuals with Disabilities Education Act to strengthen such act. Introduced by HARKIN, D-Iowa, May 21, 1991. Senate Labor and Human Resources reported June 18 (S Rept 102-84). Senate passed, amended, June 24. House Education and Labor discharged. House passed, amended, Sept. 11. Senate agreed to House amendment Sept. 16. President signed Oct. 7, 1991.

PL 102-120 (S J Res 95) Designate October 1991 as National Breast Cancer Awareness Month. Introduced by PELL, D-R.I., March 14, 1991. Senate Judiciary discharged. Senate passed June 26. House Post Office and Civil Service discharged. House passed Sept. 24. President signed Oct. 7, 1991.

PL 102-121 (S J Res 78) Designate the months of November 1991 and 1992 as National Hospice Month. Introduced by BENTSEN, D-Texas, Feb. 27, 1991. Senate Judiciary discharged. Senate passed June 26. House Post Office and Civil Service discharged. House passed Sept. 30. President signed Oct. 8, 1991.

PL 102-122 (S J Res 156) Designate the week of Oct. 6, 1991, through Oct. 12, 1991, as Mental Illness Awareness Week. Introduced by SIMON, D-Ill., June 6, 1991. Senate Judiciary discharged. Senate passed June 26. House Post Office and Civil Service discharged. House passed Sept. 30. President signed Oct. 8, 1991.

PL 102-123 (S J Res 172) Authorize and request the president to proclaim the month of November 1991, and the month of each November thereafter, as National American Indian Heritage Month. Introduced by INOUYE, D-Hawaii, June 27, 1991. Senate Judiciary discharged. Senate passed, amended, Sept. 26. House passed Sept. 30. President signed Oct. 9, 1991.

PL 102-124 (S 1773) Extend for a period of 31 days the legislative reinstatement of the power of Indian tribes to exercise criminal jurisdiction over Indians. Introduced by INOUYE, D-Hawaii, Sept. 30, 1991. Senate passed Sept. 30. House passed, amended, Oct. 3. Senate agreed to House amendments Oct. 3. President signed Oct. 9, 1991.

PL 102-125 (H J Res 189) Designate Oct. 8, 1991, as National Firefighters Day. Introduced by WELDON, R-Pa., March 13, 1991. House Post Office and Civil Service discharged. House passed Oct. 2. Senate passed Oct. 3. President signed Oct. 10, 1991.

PL 102-126 (H J Res 305) Designate the month of October 1991 as Country Music Month. Introduced by CLEMENT, D-Tenn., July 17, 1991. House Post Office and Civil Service discharged. House passed Sept. 16. Senate Judiciary discharged. Senate passed Oct. 1. President signed Oct. 10, 1991.

PL 102-127 (S 868) Amend Title 10, U.S. Code, and Title 38, U.S. Code, to improve educational assistance benefits for members of the Selected Reserve of the Armed Forces who served on active duty during the Persian Gulf War. Introduced by CRANSTON, D-Calif., April 18, 1991. Senate Veterans' Affairs reported, amended, July 26 (S Rept 102-124). Senate passed, amended, Aug. 2. House passed Sept. 16. President signed Oct. 10, 1991.

PL 102-128 (S J Res 132) Designate the week of Oct. 13, 1991, through Oct. 19, 1991, as National Radon Action Week. Introduced by LAUTENBERG, D-N.J., April 25, 1991. Senate Judiciary discharged. Senate passed June 26. House Post Office and Civil Service discharged. House passed Oct. 2. President signed Oct. 10, 1991.

PL 102-129 (HR 2935) Designate the building at 6600 Lorain Ave. in Cleveland as the Patrick J. Patton U.S. Post Office Building. Introduced by OAKAR, D-Ohio, July 17, 1991. House passed, under suspension of the rules, Sept. 30. Senate passed Sept. 30. President signed Oct. 15, 1991.

PL 102-130 (HR 2387) Authorize appropriations for certain programs for the conservation of striped bass. Introduced by STUDDS, D-Mass., May 17, 1991. House Merchant Marine and Fisheries reported, amended, July 9 (H Rept 102-144). House passed, amended, under suspension of the rules, July 9. Senate Commerce, Science and Transportation reported Sept. 11 (S Rept 102-145). Senate Environment and Public Works discharged. Senate passed Oct. 2. President signed Oct. 17, 1991.

PL 102-131 (H J Res 303) Designate October 1991 as Crime Prevention Month. Introduced by PRICE, D-N.C., July 16, 1991. House Post Office and Civil Service discharged. House passed Sept. 24. Senate Judiciary discharged. Senate passed Oct. 4. President signed Oct. 17, 1991.

PL 102-132 (HR 3259) Authorize appropriations for drug abuse education and prevention programs relating to youth gangs and to runaway and homeless youths. Introduced by MARTINEZ, D-Calif., Aug. 2, 1991. House Education and Labor reported, amended, Sept. 26 (H Rept 102-222). House passed, amended, under suspension of the rules, Sept. 30. Senate passed Oct. 2. President signed Oct. 18, 1991.

PL 102-133 (S J Res 107) Designate Oct. 15, 1991, as National Law Enforcement Memorial Dedication Day. Introduced by MOYNIHAN, D-N.Y., March 21, 1991. Senate Judiciary discharged. Senate passed Oct. 8. House Post Office and Civil Service discharged. House passed Oct. 9. President signed Oct. 18, 1991.

PL 102-134 (H J Res 230) Designate Oct. 16, 1991, and Oct. 16, 1992, each as World Food Day. Introduced by GILMAN, R-N.Y., April 23, 1991. House Post Office and Civil Service discharged. House passed Oct. 2. Senate passed Oct. 8. President signed Oct. 21, 1991.

PL 102-135 (HR 3280) Provide for a study, to be conducted by the National Academy of Sciences, on how the government can improve the decennial census of population. Introduced by SAWYER, D-Ohio, Aug. 2, 1991. House Post Office and Civil Service reported, amended, Sept. 30 (H Rept 102-227). House passed, amended, under suspension of the rules, Sept. 30. Senate passed, amended, Oct. 3. House agreed to Senate amendments Oct. 9. President signed Oct. 24, 1991.

PL 102-136 (HR 2426) Make appropriations for military construction for the Department of Defense for the fiscal year ending Sept. 30, 1992. Introduced by HEFNER, D-N.C., May 22, 1991. House Appropriations reported May 22 (H Rept 102-74). House passed May 30. Senate Appropriations reported, amended, Sept. 12 (S Rept 102-147). Senate passed, amended, Sept. 16. House agreed to conference report Oct. 8 (H Rept 102-236). House receded and concurred in Senate amendments Oct. 8. House receded and concurred with amendments in Senate amendments Oct. 8. Senate agreed to conference report Oct. 16. Senate agreed to House amendments to Senate amendments Oct. 16. President signed Oct. 25, 1991.

PL 102-137 (HR 972) Make permanent the legislative reinstatement, following the decision of *Duro v. Reina* (58 U.S.L.W. 4643, May 29, 1990), of the power of Indian tribes to exercise criminal jurisdiction over Indians. Introduced by RICHARDSON, D-N.M., Feb. 19, 1991. House Interior and Insular Affairs reported, May 14 (H Rept 102-61). House passed, under suspension of the rules, May 14. Senate Indian Affairs reported, amended, Sept. 19 (S Rept 102-153). Senate passed, amended, Sept. 23. Senate agreed to conference report Oct. 17 (H Rept 102-261). House agreed to conference report Oct. 22. President signed Oct. 28, 1991.

PL 102-138 (HR 1415) Authorize appropriations for fiscal years 1992 and 1993 for the Department of State. Introduced by BERMAN, D-Calif., March 13, 1991. House Foreign Affairs reported, amended, May 8 (H Rept 102-53). House considered May 14. House passed, amended, May 15. Senate Foreign Relations discharged. Senate passed, amended, July 29. Senate agreed to conference report Oct. 4 (H Rept 102-238). House agreed to conference report Oct. 8. President signed Oct. 28, 1991.

PL 102-139 (HR 2519) Make appropriations for the Departments of Veterans Affairs and Housing and Urban Development, and for sundry independent agencies, commissions, corporations, and offices for the fiscal year ending Sept. 30, 1992. Introduced by TRAXLER, D-Mich., June 3, 1991. House Appropriations reported June 3 (H Rept 102-94). House passed, amended, June 6. Senate Appropriations reported, amended, July 11 (S Rept 102-107). Senate considered July 17. Senate passed, amended, July 18. House agreed to conference report Oct. 2 (H Rept 102-226). House receded and concurred in Senate amendments Oct. 2. House receded and concurred with amendments in Senate amendments Oct. 2. Senate agreed to conference report Oct. 2. Senate agreed to House amendments to Senate amendments Oct. 2. Senate agreed to House amendment to Senate amendment with amendment Oct. 2. House agreed to Senate amendment to House amendment to Senate amendment Oct. 3. President signed Oct. 28, 1991.

PL 102-140 (HR 2608) Make appropriations for the Departments of Commerce, Justice and State, the judiciary and related agencies for the fiscal year ending Sept. 30, 1992. Introduced by SMITH, D-Iowa, June 11, 1991. House Appropriations reported June 11 (H Rept 102-106). House passed, amended, June 13. Senate Appropriations reported, amended, July 11 (S Rept 102-106). Senate considered July 30. Senate passed, amended, July 31. House agreed to conference report Oct. 3 (H Rept 102-233). House receded and concurred in Senate amendments Oct. 3. House receded and concurred with amendments in Senate amendments Oct. 3. House insisted on its disagreement to a Senate amendment Oct. 3. Senate agreed to conference report Oct. 3. Senate agreed to House amendments to Senate amendments Oct. 3. Senate receded from its amendment Oct. 3. President signed Oct. 28, 1991.

PL 102-141 (HR 2622) Make appropriations for the Treasury Department, the U.S. Postal Service, the Executive Office of the President and certain independent agencies, for the fiscal year ending Sept. 30, 1992. Introduced by ROYBAL, D-Calif., June 12, 1991. House Appropriations reported June 12 (H Rept 102-109). House passed, amended, June 18. Senate Appropriations reported, amended, July 2 (S Rept 102-95). Senate considered July 11 and 15. Senate passed, amended, July 18. House agreed to conference report Oct. 3 (H Rept 102-234). House receded and concurred in Senate amendments Oct. 3. House receded and concurred with amendments in Senate amendments Oct. 3. Senate agreed to conference report Oct. 3. Senate agreed to House amendments to Senate amendments Oct. 3. President signed Oct. 28, 1991.

PL 102-142 (HR 2698) Make appropriations for Agriculture, Rural Development, Food and Drug Administration and related agencies programs for the fiscal year ending Sept. 30, 1992. Introduced by WHITTEN, D-Miss., June 20, 1991. House Appropriations reported June 20 (H Rept 102-119). House passed, amended,

June 26. Senate Appropriations reported, amended, July 23 (S Rept 102-116). Senate considered July 29. Senate passed, amended, July 30. House agreed to conference report Oct. 8 (H Rept 102-239). House receded and concurred in Senate amendments Oct. 8. House receded and concurred with amendments in Senate amendments Oct. 8. Senate agreed to conference report Oct. 16. Senate agreed to House amendments to Senate amendments Oct. 16. President signed Oct. 28, 1991.

PL 102-143 (HR 2942) Make appropriations for the Department of Transportation and related agencies for the fiscal year ending Sept. 30, 1992. Introduced by LEHMAN, D-Fla., July 18, 1991. House Appropriations reported July 18 (H Rept 102-156). House passed, amended, July 24. Senate Appropriations reported, amended, Sept. 12 (S Rept 102-148). Senate passed, amended, Sept. 17. House agreed to conference report Oct. 9 (H Rept 102-243). House receded and concurred in Senate amendments Oct. 9. House receded and concurred with amendments in Senate amendments Oct. 9. Senate agreed to conference report Oct. 16. Senate agreed to House amendments to Senate amendments Oct. 16. President signed Oct. 28, 1991.

PL 102-144 (H J Res 340) Designate Oct. 19-27, 1991, as National Red Ribbon Week for a Drug-Free America. Introduced by HORN, D-Mo., Oct. 2, 1991. House Post Office and Civil Service discharged. House passed Oct. 17. Senate passed Oct. 22. President signed Oct. 28, 1991.

PL 102-145 (H J Res 360) Make further continuing appropriations for the fiscal year 1992. Introduced by WHITTEN, D-Miss., Oct. 23. House Appropriations reported Oct. 23 (102-266). House passed Oct. 24. Senate passed Oct. 24. President signed Oct. 28, 1991.

PL 102-146 (S J Res 131) Designate October 1991 as National Down's Syndrome Awareness Month. Introduced by LUGAR, R-Ind., April 25, 1991. Senate Judiciary discharged. Senate passed Oct. 1. House Post Office and Civil Service discharged. House passed Oct. 17. President signed Oct. 28, 1991.

PL 102-147 (S J Res 192) Designate Oct. 30, 1991, as Refugee Day. Introduced by SMITH, R-N.H. (on behalf of Kassebaum, R-Kan.), Aug. 2, 1991. Senate passed Aug. 2. House Post Office and Civil Service discharged. House passed Oct. 24. President signed Oct. 28, 1991.

PL 102-148 (HR 470) Authorize the secretary of Transportation to release the restrictions, requirements and conditions imposed in connection with the conveyance of certain lands to the city of Gary, Ind. Introduced by VISCLOSKY, D-Ind., Jan. 9, 1991. House Public Works and Transportation reported, amended, June 7 (H Rept 102-102). House passed, amended, under suspension of the rules, June 24. Senate Commerce, Science and Transportation reported Oct. 17 (S Rept 102-193). Senate passed Oct. 23. President signed Oct. 30, 1991.

PL 102-149 (S J Res 160) Designate the week beginning Oct. 20, 1991, as World Population Awareness Week. Introduced by KERRY, D-Mass., June 13, 1991. Senate Judiciary discharged. Senate passed Oct. 8. House Post Office and Civil Service discharged. House passed Oct. 22. President signed Oct. 30, 1991.

PL 102-150 (HR 1720) Amend the St. Elizabeths Hospital and District of Columbia Mental Health Services Act to permit the secretary of Health and Human Services to enter into an agreement with the mayor of the District of Columbia with respect to capital improvements necessary for the delivery of mental health services in the District. Introduced by DELLUMS, D-Calif., April 11, 1991. House District of Columbia reported June 3 (H Rept 102-91). House passed, amended, June 11. Senate Governmental Affairs discharged. Senate passed Oct. 16. President signed Oct. 31, 1991.

PL 102-151 (S 1823) Amend the Veterans' Benefit and Services Act of 1988 to authorize the Department of Veterans Affairs to use for the operation and maintenance of the National Memorial Cemetery of Arizona funds appropriated during fiscal 1992 for the National Cemetery System. Introduced by DeCONCINI, D-Ariz., Oct. 8, 1991. Senate passed Oct. 8. House passed, amended, Oct. 22. Senate agreed to House amendment Oct. 28. President signed Nov. 5, 1991.

PL 102-152 (HR 1046) Amend Title 38, U.S. Code, to increase, effective Dec. 1, 1991, the rates of disability compensation for veterans with service-connected disabilities and the rates of dependency and indemnity compensation for survivors of such veterans. Introduced by APPLEGATE, D-Ohio, Feb. 21, 1991. House Veterans' Affairs reported, amended, July 25 (H Rept 102-164). House passed, amended, under suspension of the rules, July 29. Senate Veterans' Affairs discharged. Senate passed, amended, Oct. 28. House agreed to Senate amendment Oct. 30. President signed Nov. 12, 1991.

PL 102-153 (H J Res 280) Designate the week beginning Nov. 10, 1991, as Hire a Veteran Week. Introduced by BROWN, D-Calif., June 25, 1991. House Post Office and Civil Service discharged. House passed Oct. 31. Senate passed Nov. 1. President signed Nov. 12, 1991.

PL 102-154 (HR 2686) Make appropriations for the Department of the Interior and related agencies for the fiscal year ending Sept. 30, 1992. Introduced by YATES, D-Ill., June 19, 1991. House Appropriations reported June 19 (H Rept 102-116). House considered June 24. House passed, amended, June 25. Senate Appropriations reported, amended, July 25 (S Rept 102-122). Senate considered Sept. 12, 13, 16, 17 and 18. Senate passed, amended, Sept. 19. House agreed to conference report Oct. 24 (H Rept 102-256). House receded and concurred in Senate amendments Oct. 24. House receded and concurred with amendments in Senate amendments Oct. 24. House insisted on its disagreement to Senate amendments Oct. 24. Senate agreed to conference report Oct. 30. Senate agreed to House amendments to Senate amendments Oct. 30. Senate agreed to House amendments to Senate amendments Oct. 31. Senate receded from its amendments Oct. 31. Senate agreed with amendment to House amendment to Senate amendment Oct. 31. House disagreed to Senate amendment to House amendment to Senate amendment Nov. 1. Senate receded from its amendment to House amendment to Senate amendment Nov. 1. Senate agreed to House amendment to Senate amendment Nov. 1. President signed Nov. 13, 1991.

PL 102-155 (H J Res 175) Designate the weeks beginning Dec. 1, 1991, and Nov. 29, 1992, as National Home Care Week. Introduced by PANETTA, D-Calif., March 5, 1991. House Post Office and Civil Service discharged. House passed Oct. 31. Senate passed Nov. 1. President signed Nov. 13, 1991.

PL 102-156 (H J Res 177) Designate Nov. 16, 1991, as Dutch-American Heritage Day. Introduced by VANDER JAGT, R-Mich., March 5, 1991. House Post Office and Civil Service discharged. House passed Oct. 31. Senate passed Nov. 1. President signed Nov. 13, 1991.

PL 102-157 (H J Res 281) Approve the extension of nondiscriminatory treatment with respect to the products of the Mongolian People's Republic. Introduced by GEPHARDT, D-Mo., June 25, 1991. House Ways and Means reported Oct. 22 (H Rept 102-263). House passed, under suspension of the rules, Oct. 29. Senate passed Oct. 31. President signed Nov. 13, 1991.

PL 102-158 (H J Res 282) Approve the extension of nondiscriminatory treatment with respect to the products of the People's Republic of Bulgaria. Introduced by GEPHARDT, D-Mo., June 25, 1991. House Ways and Means reported Oct. 22 (H Rept 102-264). House passed, under suspension of the rules, Oct. 29. Senate passed Oct. 31. President signed Nov. 13, 1991.

PL 102-159 (S 1848) Restore the authority of the secretary of Education to make certain preliminary payments to local educational agencies. Introduced by KENNEDY, D-Mass., Oct. 22, 1991. Senate Labor and Human Resources discharged. Senate passed Oct. 25. House passed Nov. 1. President signed Nov. 13, 1991.

PL 102-160 (S J Res 36) Designate the months of November 1991 and November 1992 as National Alzheimer's Disease Month. Introduced by PRESSLER, R-S.D., Jan. 14, 1991. Senate Judiciary discharged. Senate passed June 26. House Post Office and Civil Service discharged. House passed Nov. 6. President signed Nov. 13, 1991.

PL 102-161 (S J Res 145) Designate the week beginning Nov. 10, 1991, as National Women Veterans Recognition Week. Introduced by CRANSTON, D-Calif., May 14, 1991. Senate Judiciary reported Oct. 31. Senate passed Nov. 1. House Post Office and Civil Service discharged. House passed Nov. 6. President signed Nov. 13, 1991.

PL 102-162 (S J Res 188) Designate November 1991 as National Red Ribbon Month. Introduced by LAUTENBERG, D-N.J., Aug. 2, 1991. Senate Judiciary reported Oct. 31. Senate passed Nov. 1. House Post Office and Civil Service discharged. House passed Nov. 6. President signed Nov. 13, 1991.

PL 102-163 (H J Res 374) Make further continuing appropriations for fiscal 1992. Introduced by WHITTEN, D-Miss., Nov. 12, 1991. House passed Nov. 12. Senate passed Nov. 13. President signed Nov. 15, 1991.

PL 102-164 (HR 3575) Provide a program of federal supplemental compensation. Introduced by ROSTENKOWSKI, D-Ill., Oct. 17, 1991. House Ways and Means reported, amended, Oct. 24 (H Rept 102-273). House passed, amended, Nov. 14. Senate passed Nov. 15. President signed Nov. 15, 1991.

PL 102-165 (H J Res 140) Designating Nov. 19, 1991, as National Philanthropy Day. Introduced by BURTON, R-Ind., Feb. 21, 1991. House Post Office and Civil Service discharged. House passed Oct. 31. Senate passed Nov. 1. President signed Nov. 18, 1991.

PL 102-166 (S 1745) Amend the Civil Rights Act of 1964 to strengthen and improve federal civil rights laws, to provide for damages in cases of intentional employment discrimination, and to clarify provisions regarding disparate impact actions. Introduced by DANFORTH, R-Mo., Sept. 24, 1991. Senate considered Oct. 25. Senate passed, amended, Oct. 30. House passed Nov. 7. President signed Nov. 21, 1991.

PL 102-167 (HR 3350) Extend the U.S. Commission on Civil Rights. Introduced by EDWARDS, D-Calif., Sept. 17, 1991. House passed, under suspension of the rules, Sept. 30. Senate passed, amended, Oct. 28. House considered Senate amendment, under suspension of the rules, Nov. 5. House agreed to Senate amendment, under suspension of the rules, Nov. 6. President signed Nov. 26, 1991.

PL 102-168 (HR 3402) Amend the Public Health Service Act to revise and extend certain programs regarding health information and health promotion. Introduced by WAXMAN, D-Calif., Sept. 24, 1991. House Energy and Commerce reported Oct. 24 (H Rept 102-270). House passed, amended, under suspension of the rules, Nov. 5. Senate passed Nov. 12. President signed Nov. 26, 1991.

PL 102-169 (H J Res 215) Acknowledge the sacrifices that military families have made on behalf of the nation and designate Nov. 25, 1991, as National Military Families Recognition Day. Introduced by ESPY, D-Miss., April 11, 1991. House Post Office and Civil Service discharged. House passed Aug. 1. Senate Judiciary discharged. Senate passed Nov. 12. President signed Nov. 26, 1991.

PL 102-170 (HR 3839) Make appropriations for the Departments of Labor, Health and Human Services, and Education, and related agencies, for the fiscal year ending Sept. 30, 1992. Introduced by NATCHER, D-Ky., Nov. 21, 1991. House passed Nov. 22. Senate passed Nov. 22. President signed Nov. 26, 1991.

PL 102-171 (S 374) Settle all claims of the Aroostook Band of Micmacs resulting from the band's omission from the Maine Indian Claims Settlement Act of 1980. Introduced by COHEN, R-Maine, Feb. 6, 1991. Senate Indian Affairs reported Aug. 2 (S Rept 102-136). Senate passed Sept. 19. House passed Nov. 12. President signed Nov. 26, 1991.

PL 102-172 (HR 2521) Make appropriations for the Department of Defense for the fiscal year ending Sept. 30, 1992. Introduced by MURTHA, D-Pa., June 4, 1991. House Appropriations reported June 4 (H Rept 102-95). House passed, amended, June 7. Senate Appropriations reported, amended, Sept. 20 (S Rept 102-154). Senate considered Sept. 23, 25. Senate passed, amended, Sept. 26. House agreed to conference report Nov. 20 (H Rept 102-328). Senate agreed to conference report Nov. 23. President signed Nov. 26, 1991.

PL 102-173 (S 1475) Amend the Protection and Advocacy for Mentally Ill Individuals Act of 1986 to reauthorize programs under such act. Introduced by HARKIN, D-Iowa, July 15, 1991. Senate Labor and Human Resources reported July 22 (S Rept 102-114). Senate passed July 31. Energy and Commerce reported Nov. 15 (H Rept 102-319). House passed, under suspension of the rules, Nov. 19. President signed Nov. 27, 1991.

PL 102-174 (S J Res 207) Designate the period commencing on Dec. 1, 1991, and ending on Dec. 7, 1991, and the period commencing on Nov. 29, 1992, and ending on Dec. 5, 1992, each as National Adoption Week. Introduced by HATCH, R-Utah, Oct. 1, 1991. Senate Judiciary discharged. Senate passed Nov. 4. House Post Office and Civil Service discharged. House passed Nov. 22. President signed Nov. 27, 1991.

PL 102-175 (HR 2270) Amend certain provisions of Title 5, U.S. Code, relating to the Senior Executive Service. Introduced by SIKORSKI, D-Minn., May 8, 1991. House passed, amended, under suspension of the rules, Nov. 12. Senate passed Nov. 20. President signed Dec. 2, 1991.

PL 102-176 (H J Res 125) Designate the week of Nov. 24, 1991, and the week of Nov. 22, 1992, each as National Family Caregivers Week. Introduced by SNOWE, R-Maine, Feb. 6, 1991. House Post Office and Civil Service discharged. House passed Nov. 6. Senate Judiciary discharged. Senate passed Nov. 23. President signed Dec. 2, 1991.

PL 102-177 (H J Res 130) Designate Jan. 1 as National Ellis Island Day. Introduced by GUARINI, D-N.J., Feb. 19, 1991. House Post Office and Civil Service discharged. House passed, amended, July 10. Senate Judiciary discharged. Senate passed Nov. 18. President signed Dec. 2, 1991.

PL 102-178 (H J Res 327) Designate 1992 as the Year of the Gulf of Mexico. Introduced by LAUGHLIN, D-Texas, Sept. 17, 1991. House Post Office and Civil Service discharged. House passed Oct. 22. Senate Judiciary discharged. Senate passed Nov. 18. President signed Dec. 2, 1991.

PL 102-179 (S 1568) Amend the act incorporating the American Legion so as to redefine eligibility for membership therein. Introduced by BIDEN, D-Del., July 26, 1991. Senate Judiciary discharged. Senate passed July 29. House passed, amended, under suspension of the rules, Nov. 18. President signed Dec. 2, 1991.

PL 102-180 (S 1720) Amend PL 93-531 (25 U.S. Code 640d, et seq.) to reauthorize appropriations for the Navajo-Hopi relocation housing program for fiscal 1992-95. Introduced by INOUYE, D-Hawaii, Sept. 17, 1991. Senate Indian Affairs reported, amended, Oct. 7 (S Rept 102-176). Senate passed, amended, Oct. 25. House Interior and Insular Affairs reported Nov. 18 (H Rept 102-321). House passed, under suspension of the rules, Nov. 18. President signed Dec. 2, 1991.

PL 102-181 (HR 3728) Provide for a six-month extension of the Commission on the Bicentennial of the Constitution. Introduced by CRANE, R-Ill., Nov. 7, 1991. House passed, under suspension of the rules, Nov. 18. Senate Judiciary discharged. Senate passed Nov. 21. President signed Dec. 3, 1991.

PL 102-182 (HR 1724) Provide for the termination of the application of Title IV of the Trade Act of 1974 to Czechoslovakia and Hungary. Introduced by GIBBONS, D-Fla., April 11, 1991. House Ways and Means reported Sept. 26 (H Rept 102-223). House passed, under suspension of the rules, Oct. 8. Senate Finance discharged. Senate passed, amended, Nov. 15. House agreed to Senate amendment with amendment Nov. 20. House agreed to conference report Nov. 26 (H Rept 102-391). Senate agreed to conference report Nov. 26. President signed Dec. 4, 1991.

PL 102-183 (HR 2038) Authorize appropriations for fiscal 1992 for intelligence activities of the U.S. government, the intelligence community staff, and the Central Intelligence Agency retirement and disability system. Introduced by McCURDY, D-Okla., April 24, 1991. House Intelligence reported, amended, May 15 (H Rept 102-65, Part I). House Armed Services reported June 4 (H Rept 102-65, Part II). House passed, amended, June 11. Senate Intelligence discharged. Senate passed, amended, Oct. 16. House agreed to conference report Nov. 20 (H Rept 102-327). Senate agreed to conference report Nov. 20. President signed Dec. 4, 1991.

PL 102-184 (HR 3394) Amend the Indian Self-Determination and Education Assistance Act. Introduced by MILLER, D-Calif., Sept. 24, 1991. House Interior and Insular Affairs reported, amended, Nov. 18 (H Rept 102-320). House passed, amended, under suspension of the rules, Nov. 18. Senate passed Nov. 19. President signed Dec. 4, 1991.

PL 102-185 (HR 3624) Amend the Tariff Act of 1930 to provide appropriate procedures for the appointment of the chairman of the U.S. International Trade Commission. Introduced by ROSTENKOWSKI, D-Ill., Oct. 24, 1991. House Ways and Means reported Oct. 30 (H Rept 102-279). House passed, under suspension of the rules, Nov. 5. Senate Finance discharged. Senate passed Nov. 20. President signed Dec. 4, 1991.

PL 102-186 (S 1563) Authorize appropriations to carry out the National Sea Grant College Program Act. Introduced by KERRY, D-Mass., July 25, 1991. Senate Commerce, Science and Transportation and Senate Labor and Human Resources jointly reported Sept. 23 (S Rept 102-155). Senate passed Oct. 3. House passed, amended, under suspension of the rules, Nov. 5. Senate agreed to House amendment Nov. 19. President signed Dec. 4, 1991.

PL 102-187 (S J Res 187) Make a technical correction in PL 101-549. Introduced by BREAUX, D-La., Aug. 1, 1991. Senate passed Aug. 1. House passed, under suspension of the rules, Nov. 25. President signed Dec. 4, 1991.

PL 102-188 (S J Res 217) Authorize and request the president to proclaim 1992 as the Year of the American Indian. Introduced by HATFIELD, R-Ore., Oct. 22, 1991. Senate Judiciary reported Oct. 31. Senate passed Nov. 1. House Post Office and Civil Service discharged. House passed Nov. 22. President signed Dec. 4, 1991.

PL 102-189 (H J Res 201) Designate the week beginning Dec. 1, 1991, and the week beginning Nov. 15, 1992, each as Geography Awareness Week. Introduced by PANETTA, D-Calif., March 20, 1991. House Post Office and Civil Service discharged. House passed Nov. 22. Senate passed Nov. 26. President signed Dec. 4, 1991.

PL 102-190 (HR 2100) Authorize appropriations for fiscal 1992-93 for military functions of the Department of Defense and prescribe military personnel levels for fiscal 1992-93. Introduced by ASPIN, D-Wis., April 25, 1991. House Armed Services reported, amended, May 13 (H Rept 102-60). House considered May 20, 21. House passed, amended, May 22. Senate Armed Services discharged. Senate passed, amended, Aug. 2. House agreed to conference report Nov. 18 (H Rept 102-311). Senate considered conference report Nov 20, 21. Senate agreed to conference report Nov. 22. President signed Dec. 5, 1991.

PL 102-191 (HR 2629) Amend the Small Business Act to assist the development of small business concerns owned and controlled by women. Introduced by LaFALCE, D-N.Y., June 12, 1991. House Small Business reported, amended, July 31 (H Rept 102-178). House passed, amended, under suspension of the rules, Oct. 8. Senate Small Business discharged. Senate passed, amended, Nov. 20. House agreed to Senate amendment Nov. 21. President signed Dec. 5, 1991.

PL 102-192 (S J Res 184) Designate the month of November 1991 as National Accessible Housing Month. Introduced by DOLE, R-Kan., July 26, 1991. Senate Judiciary discharged. Senate passed Oct. 4. House Post Office and Civil Service discharged. House passed Nov. 22. President signed Dec. 5, 1991.

PL 102-193 (HR 3919) Temporarily extend the Defense Production Act of 1950. Introduced by CARPER, D-Del., Nov. 25, 1991. House Banking, Finance and Urban Affairs discharged. House passed, amended, Nov. 27. Senate passed Nov. 27. President signed Dec. 6, 1991.

PL 102-194 (S 272) Provide for a coordinated federal research program to ensure continued U.S. leadership in high-performance computing. Introduced by GORE, D-Tenn., Jan. 24, 1991. Senate Commerce, Science and Transportation reported, amended, May 16 (S Rept 102-57). Senate passed, amended, Sept. 11. House passed, amended, Nov. 20. Senate agreed to House amendments Nov. 22. President signed Dec. 9, 1991.

PL 102-195 (HR 1988) Authorize appropriations to the National Aeronautics and Space Administration for research and development, space flight, control and data communications, construction of facilities, research and program management, and inspector general. Introduced by BROWN, D-Calif., April 23, 1991. House Science, Space and Technology reported, amended, April 25 (H Rept 102-41). House passed, amended, May 2. Senate Commerce, Science and Transportation reported, amended, July 2 (S Rept 102-97). Senate passed, amended, Sept. 27. House agreed to Senate amendment with amendment Nov. 7. Senate agreed to House amendment to Senate amendment Nov. 22. President signed Dec. 9, 1991.

PL 102-196 (HR 3370) Direct the secretary of the Interior to carry out a study and make recommendations to Congress regarding the feasibility of establishing a Native American cultural center in Oklahoma City. Introduced by ENGLISH, D-Okla., Sept. 23, 1991. House Interior and Insular Affairs reported, amended, Nov. 22 (H Rept 102-353). House passed, amended, under suspension of the rules, Nov. 23. Senate passed Nov. 25. President signed Dec. 9, 1991.

PL 102-197 (H J Res 346) Approve the extension of nondiscriminatory treatment with respect to the products of the Soviet Union. Introduced by GEPHARDT, D-Mo., Oct. 9, 1991. House Ways and Means reported Nov. 19 (H Rept 102-338). House passed, under suspension of the rules, Nov. 20. Senate passed Nov. 25. President signed Dec. 9, 1991.

PL 102-198 (S 1284) Make certain technical corrections in the Judicial Improvements Act of 1990. Introduced by SYMMS, R-Idaho, June 12, 1991. Senate passed June 12. House Judiciary reported, amended, Nov. 18 (H Rept 102-322). House passed, amended, under suspension of the rules, Nov. 19. Senate agreed to House amendments Nov. 22. President signed Dec. 9, 1991.

PL 102-199 (HR 525) Amend the federal charter for the Boys' Clubs of America to reflect the change of the name of the organization to the Boys and Girls Clubs of America. Introduced by MOLINARI, R-N.Y., Jan. 14, 1991. House Judiciary reported, amended, Aug. 2 (H Rept 102-197). House passed, amended, under suspension of the rules, Nov. 18. Senate Judiciary discharged. Senate passed Nov. 26. President signed Dec. 10, 1991.

PL 102-200 (HR 829) Amend Title 28, U.S. Code, to make changes in the composition of the eastern and western districts of Virginia. Introduced by SLAUGHTER, R-Va., Feb. 5, 1991. House Judiciary reported Nov. 25 (H Rept 102-370). House passed, under suspension of the rules, Nov. 25. Senate passed Nov. 26. President signed Dec. 10, 1991.

PL 102-201 (HR 848) Authorize the establishment of a memorial at Custer Battlefield National Monument to honor the Indians who fought in the Battle of the Little Bighorn. Introduced by CAMPBELL, D-Colo., Feb. 6, 1991. House Interior and Insular Affairs reported, amended, June 24 (H Rept 102-126). House passed, amended, under suspension of the rules, June 24. Senate Energy and Natural Resources reported Oct. 3 (S Rept 102-173). Senate passed, amended, Nov. 22. House agreed to Senate amendment, under suspension of the rules, Nov. 25. President signed Dec. 10, 1991.

PL 102-202 (HR 990) Authorize additional appropriations for the land acquisition at Monocacy National Battlefield, Md. Introduced by BYRON, D-Md., Feb. 20, 1991. House Interior and Insular Affairs reported, amended, June 3 (H Rept 102-85). House passed, amended, under suspension of the rules, June 3. Senate Energy and Natural Resources reported Nov. 23 (S Rept 102-237). Senate passed Nov. 26. President signed Dec. 10, 1991.

PL 102-203 (HR 3322) Designate the Wellston Station facility of the U.S. Postal Service in St. Louis as the Gwen B. Giles Post Office Building. Introduced by CLAY, D-Mo., Sept. 12, 1991. House passed, amended, under suspension of the rules, Sept. 30. Senate Governmental Affairs reported Nov. 25. Senate passed Nov. 26. President signed Dec. 10, 1991.

PL 102-204 (HR 3531) Authorize appropriations for the Patent and Trademark Office in the Department of Commerce for fiscal 1992. Introduced by HUGHES, D-N.J., Oct. 9, 1991. House Judiciary reported, amended, Nov. 25 (H Rept 102-382). House passed, amended, under suspension of the rules, Nov. 25. Senate passed Nov. 27. President signed Dec. 10, 1991.

PL 102-205 (HR 3709) Waive the period of congressional review for certain District of Columbia acts and to permit the City Council of the District of Columbia to enact laws relating to attorneys and the representation of indigents in criminal cases. Introduced by DELLUMS, D-Calif., Nov. 5, 1991. House District of Columbia reported, amended, Nov. 8 (H Rept 102-298). House passed, amended, under suspension of the rules, Nov. 12. Senate Governmental Affairs discharged. Senate passed Nov. 26. President signed Dec. 10, 1991.

PL 102-206 (H J Res 191) Designate the week of Jan. 5, 1992, as National Law Enforcement Training Week. Introduced by ASPIN, D-Wis., March 19, 1991. House Post Office and Civil Service discharged. House passed Sept. 30. Senate Judiciary discharged. Senate passed Nov. 26. President signed Dec. 10, 1991.

PL 102-207 (H J Res 212) Designate the week beginning Feb. 16, 1992, as National Visiting Nurse Associations Week. Introduced by OAKAR, D-Ohio, April 10, 1991. House Post Office and Civil Service discharged. House passed Nov. 22. Senate passed Nov. 26. President signed Dec. 10, 1991.

PL 102-208 (H J Res 300) Designate the month of May 1992 as National Trauma Awareness Month. Introduced by LEHMAN, D-Fla., July 16, 1991. House Post Office and Civil Service discharged. House passed Nov. 22. Senate passed Nov. 26. President signed Dec. 10, 1991.

PL 102-209 (H J Res 356) Designate December 1991 as Bicentennial of the District of Columbia Month. Introduced by BLILEY, R-Va., Oct. 22, 1991. House Post Office and Civil Service discharged. House passed Nov. 26. Senate passed Nov. 27. President signed Dec. 10, 1991.

PL 102-210 (H J Res 372) Designate Dec. 21, 1991, as

Basketball Centennial Day. Introduced by NEAL, D-Mass., Nov. 7, 1991. House Post Office and Civil Service discharged. House passed Nov. 26. Senate passed Nov. 27. President signed Dec. 10, 1991.

PL 102-211 (HR 690) Authorize the National Park Service to acquire and manage the Mary McLeod Bethune Council House National Historic Site. Introduced by LEWIS, D-Ga., Jan. 29, 1991. House Interior and Insular Affairs reported, amended, April 22 (H Rept 102-36). House passed, amended, under suspension of the rules, April 24. Senate Energy and Natural Resources reported June 21 (S Rept 102-88). Senate passed, amended, Oct. 24. House disagreed to Senate amendment, under suspension of the rules, Nov. 25. Senate receded from its amendment Nov. 26. President signed Dec. 11, 1991.

PL 102-212 (HR 794) Establish the Connecticut River National Fish and Wildlife Refuge. Introduced by CONTE, R-Mass., Feb. 5, 1991. House Merchant Marine and Fisheries reported, amended, May 13 (H Rept 102-58). House passed, amended, under suspension of the rules, May 14. Senate Environment and Public Works reported, amended, Sept. 30 (S Rept 102-165). Senate passed, amended, Nov. 23. House agreed to Senate amendments Nov. 25. President signed Dec. 11, 1991.

PL 102-213 (HR 948) Designate the U.S. courthouse at 120 N. Henry St. in Madison, Wis., as the Robert W. Kastenmeier U.S. Courthouse. Introduced by OBEY, D-Wis., Feb. 6, 1991. House Public Works and Transportation reported July 26 (H Rept 102-167). House passed, under suspension of the rules, July 29. Senate Environment and Public Works discharged. Senate passed Nov. 27. President signed Dec. 11, 1991.

PL 102-214 (HR 1099) Amend the Wild and Scenic Rivers Act by designating segments of the Lamprey River in the state of New Hampshire for study for potential addition to the National Wild and Scenic Rivers System. Introduced by ZELIFF, R-N.H., Feb. 21, 1991. House Interior and Insular Affairs reported Nov. 22 (H Rept 102-348). House passed, amended, under suspension of the rules, Nov. 23. Senate passed Nov. 26. President signed Dec. 11, 1991.

PL 102-215 (HR 3012) Amend the Wild and Scenic Rivers Act by designating the White Clay Creek in Delaware and Pennsylvania for study for potential addition to the National Wild and Scenic Rivers System. Introduced by CARPER, D-Del., July 24, 1991. House Interior and Insular Affairs reported Nov. 21 (H Rept 102-344). House passed, under suspension of the rules, Nov. 23. Senate passed Nov. 26. President signed Dec. 11, 1991.

PL 102-216 (HR 3169) Lengthen from five to seven years the expiration period applicable to legislative authority relating to construction of commemorative works on federal lands in the District of Columbia and its environs. Introduced by CLAY, D-Mo., Aug. 1, 1991. House Interior and Insular Affairs reported, amended, Oct. 21 (H Rept 102-257). House passed, amended, under suspension of the rules, Oct. 21. Senate Energy and Natural Resources reported Nov. 12 (S Rept 102-211). Senate passed Nov. 27. President signed Dec. 11, 1991.

PL 102-217 (HR 3245) Designate certain National Forest System lands in the state of Georgia as wilderness. Introduced by JENKINS, D-Ga., Aug. 2, 1991. House Interior and Insular Affairs reported, amended, Nov. 21 (H Rept 102-345, Part I). House Agriculture reported, amended, Nov. 23 (H Rept 102-345, Part II). House passed, amended, under suspension of the rules, Nov. 23. Senate passed Nov. 27. President signed Dec. 11, 1991.

PL 102-218 (HR 3327) Amend Title 39, U.S. Code, to provide for the designation of an assistant secretary of the Department of Veterans Affairs as the chief minority affairs officer of the department. Introduced by MONTGOMERY, D-Miss., Sept. 12, 1991. House Veterans' Affairs reported Nov. 22 (H Rept 102-347). House passed, amended, under suspension of the rules, Nov. 25. Senate passed Nov. 27. President signed Dec. 11, 1991.

PL 102-219 (HR 3387) Amend the Pennsylvania Avenue Development Corporation Act of 1972 to authorize appropriations for implementation of the development plan for Pennsylvania Avenue between the Capitol and the White House. Introduced by KOSTMAYER, D-Pa., Sept. 24, 1991. House Interior and Insular Affairs reported, amended, Nov. 5 (H Rept 102-286). House passed, amended, under suspension of the rules, Nov. 5. Senate Energy and Natural Resources reported Nov. 23 (S Rept 102-239). Senate passed Nov. 26. President signed Dec. 11, 1991.

PL 102-220 (HR 3604) Direct acquisitions within the Eleven Point Wild and Scenic River and establish the Greer Spring Special Management Area in Missouri. Introduced by EMERSON, R-Mo., Oct. 22, 1991. House Agriculture reported, amended, Nov. 21 (H Rept 102-346, Part I). House Interior and Insular Affairs reported, amended, Nov. 22 (H Rept 102-346, Part II). House passed, amended, Nov. 22. Senate passed Nov. 26. President signed Dec. 11, 1991.

PL 102-221 (HR 3932) Improve the operational efficiency of the James Madison Memorial Fellowship Foundation. Introduced by SISISKY, D-Va., Nov. 26, 1991. House passed, under suspension of the rules, Nov. 26. Senate passed Nov. 26. President signed Dec. 11, 1991.

PL 102-222 (S 2050) Ensure that the ceiling established with respect to health education assistance loans does not prohibit the provision of federal loan insurance to new and previous borrowers under such loan program. Introduced by KENNEDY, D-Mass., Nov. 25, 1991. Senate passed Nov. 25. House passed, amended, Nov. 26. Senate agreed to House amendment Nov. 26. President signed Dec. 11, 1991.

PL 102-223 (S 2098) Authorize the president to appoint Maj. Gen. Jerry Ralph Curry to the Office of Administrator of the Federal Aviation Administration. Introduced by FORD, D-Ky., Nov. 26, 1991. Senate passed Nov. 26. House passed Nov. 27. President signed Dec. 11, 1991.

PL 102-224 (S J Res 198) Recognize contributions federal civilian employees provided during the attack on Pearl Harbor and during World War II. Introduced by AKAKA, D-Hawaii, Sept. 18, 1991. Senate Judiciary discharged. Senate passed, amended, Nov. 22. House Post Office and Civil Service discharged. House passed Nov. 26. President signed Dec. 11, 1991.

PL 102-225 (HR 3881) Expand the boundaries of Stones River National Battlefield, Tenn. Introduced by GORDON, D-Tenn., Nov. 22, 1991. House passed, under suspension of the rules, Nov. 23. Senate passed Nov. 26. President signed Dec. 11, 1991.

PL 102-226 (HR 2105) Designate the area in Calhoun County, Texas, known as Rancho La Bahia, as the Myrtle Foester Whitmire National Wildlife Refuge. Introduced by LAUGHLIN, D-Texas, April 25, 1991. House Merchant Marine and Fisheries reported, amended, Oct. 10 (H Rept 102-249). House passed, amended, under suspension of the rules, Oct. 15. Senate Environment and Public Works discharged. Senate passed Nov. 26. President signed Dec. 11, 1991.

PL 102-227 (HR 3909) Amend the Internal Revenue Code of 1986 to extend certain expiring provisions. Introduced by ROSTENKOWSKI, D-Ill., Nov. 25, 1991. House Ways and Means reported Nov. 25 (H Rept 102-377). House considered, under suspension of the rules, Nov. 26. House passed Nov. 27. Senate passed Nov. 27. President signed Dec. 11, 1991.

PL 102-228 (HR 3807) Amend the Arms Export Control Act to authorize the president to transfer battle tanks, artillery pieces and armored combat vehicles to member countries of NATO in conjunction with implementations of the Treaty on Conventional Armed Forces in Europe. Introduced by FASCELL, D-Fla., Nov. 19, 1991. House passed, under suspension of the rules, Nov. 19. Senate passed, amended, Nov. 25. House agreed to Senate amendments with amendments Nov. 27. Senate agreed to House amendments to Senate amendments Nov. 27. President signed Dec. 12, 1991.

PL 102-229 (H J Res 157) Make technical corrections and correct enrollment errors in certain acts making appropriations for the fiscal year ending Sept. 30, 1991. Introduced by WHITTEN, D-Miss., Feb. 28, 1991. House passed Feb. 28. Senate Appropriations reported, amended, Nov. 15 (S Rept 102-216). Senate passed, amended, Nov. 22. House agreed to conference report Nov. 27 (H Rept 102-394). Senate agreed to conference report Nov. 27. President signed Dec. 12, 1991.

PL 102-230 (HR 3576) Amend the Cranston-Gonzalez National Affordable Housing Act to reserve assistance under the HOME Investment Partnerships Act for certain insular areas. Introduced by GONZALEZ, D-Texas, Oct. 17, 1991. House passed, under suspension of the rules, Oct. 21. Senate Banking, Housing, and Urban Affairs discharged. Senate passed, amended, Nov. 23. House agreed to Senate amendment Nov. 26. President signed Dec. 12, 1991.

PL 102-231 (HR 1476) Provide for the divestiture of certain properties of the San Carlos Indian Irrigation Project in the state of Arizona. Introduced by KOLBE, R-Ariz., March 19, 1991.

House Interior and Insular Affairs reported, amended, Nov. 23 (H Rept 102-360). House passed, amended, under suspension of the rules, Nov. 23. Senate passed Nov. 25. President signed Dec. 12, 1991.

PL 102-232 (HR 3049) Amend the Immigration and Nationality Act to restore authority in courts to naturalize persons as citizens. Introduced by MAZZOLI, D-Ky., July 25, 1991. House Judiciary reported, amended, Nov. 5 (H Rept 102-287). House passed, amended, under suspension of the rules, Nov. 12. Senate Judiciary discharged. Senate passed, amended, Nov. 26. House agreed to Senate amendments Nov. 27. President signed Dec. 12, 1991.

PL 102-233 (HR 3435) Provide funding for the resolution of failed savings associations and working capital for the Resolution Trust Corporation and for restructuring the Oversight Board and the Resolution Trust Corporation. Introduced by GONZALEZ, D-Texas, Sept. 30, 1991. House Banking, Finance, and Urban Affairs reported, amended, Nov. 22 (H Rept 102-358). Supplemental report filed Nov. 25 (H Rept 102-358, Part II). House passed, amended, Nov. 27. Senate passed Nov. 27. President signed Dec. 12, 1991.

PL 102-234 (HR 3595) Delay until Sept. 30, 1992, the issuance of any regulations by the secretary of Health and Human Services changing the treatment of voluntary contributions and provider-specific taxes by states as a source of a state's expenditures for which federal financial participation is available under the Medicaid program, and maintain the treatment of intergovernmental transfers as such a source. Introduced by WAXMAN, D-Calif., Oct. 21, 1991. House Energy and Commerce reported, amended, Nov. 12 (H Rept 102-310). House passed, amended, Nov. 19. Senate Finance reported, amended, Nov. 23. Senate passed, amended, Nov. 26. House agreed to conference report Nov. 27 (H Rept 102-409). Senate agreed to conference report Nov. 27. President signed Dec. 12, 1991.

PL 102-235 (S 367) Amend the Job Training Partnership Act to encourage a broader range of training and job placement for women. Introduced by METZENBAUM, D-Ohio, Feb. 6, 1991. Senate Labor and Human Resources reported May 24 (S Rept 102-65). Senate passed Nov. 26. House passed Nov. 27. President signed Dec. 12, 1991.

PL 102-236 (S 1532) Revise and extend the programs under the Abandoned Infants Assistance Act of 1988. Introduced by METZENBAUM, D-Ohio, July 23, 1991. Senate Labor and Human Resources reported, amended, Sept. 25 (S Rept 102-161). Senate passed, amended, Oct. 29. House passed, amended, Nov. 19. Senate agreed to House amendments with amendment Nov. 26. House agreed to Senate amendment to House amendment Nov. 27. President signed Dec. 12, 1991.

PL 102-237 (HR 3029) Entitled, Food, Agriculture, Conservation and Trade Act Amendments of 1991. Introduced by de la GARZA, D-Texas, July 25, 1991. House Agriculture reported, amended, July 30 (H Rept 102-175). House considered, under suspension of the rules, July 30. House passed, amended, under suspension of the rules, July 31. Senate Agriculture, Nutrition and Forestry reported, amended, Nov. 21. Senate, passed, amended, Nov. 22. House agreed to Senate amendment with amendment Nov. 26. Senate agreed to House amendment to Senate amendment Nov. 26. President signed Dec. 13, 1991.

PL 102-238 (S 1193) Make technical amendments to various Indian laws. Introduced by INOUYE, D-Hawaii, May 24, 1991. Senate Indian Affairs reported May 24 (S Rept 102-66). Senate passed, amended, June 4. House passed, amended, under suspension of the rules, July 29. Senate agreed to House amendment with amendments Sept. 24. Senate agreed to House amendment with amendment Oct. 8. House agreed to Senate amendment to House amendment with amendment, under suspension of the rules, Nov. 23. Senate agreed to House amendment to Senate amendment to House amendment Nov. 25. President signed Dec. 17, 1991.

PL 102-239 (S 1891) Permit the secretary of Health and Human Services to waive certain recovery requirements with respect to the construction or remodeling of facilities. Introduced by THURMOND, R-S.C., Oct. 29, 1991. Senate passed Oct. 30. House Energy and Commerce reported, amended, Nov. 23 (H Rept 102-359). House passed, amended, under suspension of the rules, Nov. 23. Senate agreed to House amendment Nov. 25. President signed Dec. 17, 1991.

PL 102-240 (HR 2950) Develop a national intermodal surface transportation system to authorize funds for construction of highways, highway safety programs and mass transit programs. Introduced by MINETA, D-Calif., July 18, 1991. House Public Works and Transportation reported, amended, July 26 (H Rept 102-171, Part I). House Ways and Means reported, amended, Aug. 2 (H Rept 102-171, Part II). House passed, amended, Oct. 23. Senate passed, amended, Oct. 31. House agreed to conference report Nov. 27 (H Rept 102-404). Senate agreed to conference report Nov. 27. President signed Dec. 18, 1991.

PL 102-241 (HR 1776) Authorize for fiscal 1992 the U.S. Coast Guard budget. Introduced by TAUZIN, D-La., April 16, 1991. House Merchant Marine and Fisheries reported, amended, June 26 (H Rept 102-132). House passed, amended, July 18. Senate Commerce, Science and Transportation discharged. Senate passed, amended, Nov. 21. House agreed to Senate amendment with amendment Nov. 25. Senate agreed to House amendment to Senate amendment Nov. 27. President signed Dec. 19, 1991.

PL 102-242 (S 543) Reform the federal deposit insurance system, protect the deposit insurance funds and improve supervision and regulation of the disclosure relating to federally insured depository institutions. Introduced by RIEGLE, D-Mich., March 5, 1991. Senate Banking, Housing, and Urban Affairs reported, amended, Oct. 1 (S Rept 102-167). Senate considered Nov. 13, 14, 18, 19. Senate passed, amended, Nov. 21. House passed, amended, Nov. 23. House agreed to conference report Nov. 27 (H Rept 102-407). Senate agreed to conference report Nov. 27. President signed Dec. 19, 1991.

PL 102-243 (S 1462) Amend the Communications Act of 1934 to prohibit certain practices involving the use of telephone equipment for advertising and solicitation purposes. Introduced by HOLLINGS, D-S.C., July 11, 1991. Senate Commerce, Science and Transportation reported, amended, Oct. 8 (S Rept 102-178). Senate passed, amended, Nov. 7. House passed, under suspension of the rules, amended, Nov. 26. Senate agreed to House amendment Nov. 27. President signed Dec. 20, 1991. ■

Appendix D

CONGRESS AND ITS MEMBERS

Characteristics of Congress

Following is a compilation of information about individual members of the 102nd Congress — their birth dates, occupations, religion and seniority.

The average age of members of the new Congress is 55, slightly higher than in the two previous Congresses.

As in other years, the biggest single occupational group in Congress is lawyers. Nearly half the members — 245 — listed law as their profession. Businessmen and bankers make up the next-largest category, with 194 members falling into those groups.

Roman Catholic members make up the largest religious group, followed by members of the Methodist, Episcopal and Baptist faiths.

The data below, and the composition of Senate and House committees, reflect information received as of Nov. 27, 1991.

Senate — Birth Dates, Occupations, Religions, Seniority

(Seniority rank is within the member's party.)

ALABAMA

Heflin (D)—June 19, 1921. Occupation: lawyer, judge, government and political science lecturer. Religion: Methodist. Seniority: 26.

Shelby (D)—May 6, 1934. Occupation: lawyer. Religion: Presbyterian. Seniority: 45.

ALASKA

Stevens (R)—Nov. 18, 1923. Occupation: lawyer. Religion: Episcopalian. Seniority 3.

Murkowski (R)—March 28, 1933. Occupation: banker. Religion: Roman Catholic. Seniority: 26.

ARIZONA

DeConcini (D)—May 8, 1937. Occupation: lawyer. Religion: Roman Catholic. Seniority: 19.

McCain (R)—Aug. 29, 1936. Occupation: Naval officer, beer distributor. Religion: Episcopalian. Seniority: 32.

ARKANSAS

Bumpers (D)—Aug. 12, 1925. Occupation: farmer, hardware company executive, lawyer. Religion: Methodist. Seniority: 14.

Pryor (D)—Aug. 29, 1934. Occupation: newspaper publisher, lawyer. Religion: Presbyterian. Seniority: 23.

CALIFORNIA

Cranston (D)—June 19, 1914. Occupation: author, journalist, real estate executive. Religion: Protestant. Seniority: 7.

Seymour (R)—Dec. 3, 1937. Occupation: real estate broker. Religion: Episcopalian. Seniority: 43.

COLORADO

Wirth (D)—Sept. 22, 1939. Occupation: education official. Religion: Episcopalian. Seniority: 41.

Brown (R)—Feb. 12, 1940. Occupation: tax accountant, meatpacking company executive, lawyer. Religion: United Church of Christ. Seniority: 41.

CONNECTICUT

Dodd (D)—May 27, 1944. Occupation: lawyer. Religion: Roman Catholic. Seniority: 30.

Lieberman (D)—Feb. 24, 1942. Occupation: lawyer. Religion: Jewish. Seniority: 53.

DELAWARE

Roth (R)—July 22, 1921. Occupation: lawyer. Religion: Episcopalian. Seniority: 6.

Biden (D)—Nov. 20, 1942. Occupation: lawyer. Religion: Roman Catholic. Seniority: 11.

FLORIDA

Graham (D)—Nov. 9, 1936. Occupation: developer, cattleman. Religion: United Church of Christ. Seniority: 48.

Mack (R)—Oct. 29, 1940. Occupation: banker. Religion: Roman Catholic. Seniority: 38.

GEORGIA

Nunn (D)—Sept. 8, 1938. Occupation: farmer, lawyer. Religion: Methodist. Seniority: 9.

Fowler (D)—Oct. 6, 1940. Occupation: lawyer. Religion: Presbyterian. Seniority: 43.

HAWAII

Inouye (D)—Sept. 7, 1924. Occupation: lawyer. Religion: Methodist. Seniority: 5.

Akaka (D)—Sept. 11, 1924. Occupation: elementary school teacher, principal, state program administrator. Religion: Congregationalist. Seniority: 55.

IDAHO

Symms (R)—April 23, 1938. Occupation: fruit grower, fitness club owner. Religion: Methodist. Seniority: 23.

Craig (R)—July 20, 1945. Occupation: farmer, real estate salesman. Religion: Methodist. Seniority: 41.

ILLINOIS

Dixon (D)—July 7, 1927. Occupation: lawyer. Religion: Presbyterian. Seniority: 31.

Simon (D)—Nov. 29, 1928. Occupation: author, newspaper publisher. Religion: Lutheran. Seniority: 35.

INDIANA

Lugar (R)—April 4, 1932. Occupation: agricultural industries executive. Religion: Methodist. Seniority: 12.

Coats (R)—May 16, 1943. Occupation: lawyer. Religion: Presbyterian. Seniority: 37.

IOWA

Grassley (R)—Sept. 17, 1933. Occupation: farmer. Religion: Baptist. Seniority: 24.

Harkin (D)—Nov. 19, 1939. Occupation: lawyer. Religion: Roman Catholic. Seniority: 35.

KANSAS

Dole (R)—July 22, 1923. Occupation: lawyer. Religion: Methodist. Seniority: 4.

Kassebaum (R)—July 29, 1932. Occupation: broadcasting executive. Religion: Episcopalian. Seniority: 16.

KENTUCKY

Ford (D)—Sept. 8, 1924. Occupation: insurance executive. Religion: Baptist. Seniority: 13.

McConnell (R)—Feb. 20, 1942. Occupation: lawyer. Religion: Baptist. Seniority: 31.

LOUISIANA

Johnston (D)—June 10, 1932. Occupation: lawyer. Religion: Baptist. Seniority: 10.

Breaux (D)—March 1, 1944. Occupation: lawyer. Religion: Roman Catholic. Seniority: 40.

MAINE

Cohen (R)—Aug. 28, 1940. Occupation: lawyer. Religion: Unitarian. Seniority: 20.

Mitchell (D)—Aug. 20, 1933. Occupation: lawyer, judge. Religion: Roman Catholic. Seniority: 29.

MARYLAND

Sarbanes (D)—Feb. 3, 1933. Occupation: lawyer. Religion: Greek Orthodox. Seniority: 18.

Mikulski (D)—July 20, 1936. Occupation: social worker. Religion: Roman Catholic. Seniority: 43.

MASSACHUSETTS

Kennedy (D)—Feb. 22, 1932. Occupation: lawyer. Religion: Roman Catholic. Seniority: 4.

Kerry (D)—Dec. 22, 1943. Occupation: lawyer. Religion: Roman Catholic. Seniority: 34.

MICHIGAN

Riegle (D)—Feb. 4, 1938. Occupation: business executive, professor. Religion: Methodist. Seniority: 17.

Levin (D)—June 28, 1934. Occupation: lawyer. Religion: Jewish. Seniority: 26.

MINNESOTA

Durenberger (R)—Aug. 19, 1934. Occupation: adhesives manufacturing executive, lawyer. Religion: Roman Catholic. Seniority: 15.

Wellstone (D)—July 21, 1944. Occupation: college professor. Religion: Jewish. Seniority: 56.

MISSISSIPPI

Cochran (R)—Dec. 7, 1937. Occupation: lawyer. Religion: Baptist. Seniority: 17.

Lott (R)—Oct. 9, 1941. Occupation: lawyer. Religion: Baptist. Seniority: 35.

MISSOURI

Danforth (R)—Sept. 5, 1936. Occupation: lawyer, clergyman. Religion: Episcopalian. Seniority: 10.

Bond (R)—March 6, 1939. Occupation: lawyer. Religion: Presbyterian. Seniority: 33.

MONTANA

Baucus (D)—Dec. 11, 1941. Occupation: lawyer. Religion: United Church of Christ. Seniority: 22.

Burns (R)—Jan. 25, 1935. Occupation: radio and television broadcaster. Religion: Lutheran. Seniority: 39.

NEBRASKA

Exon (D)—Aug. 9, 1921. Occupation: office equipment dealer. Religion: Episcopalian. Seniority: 24.

Kerrey (D)—Aug 27, 1943. Occupation: restaurateur. Religion: Congregationalist. Seniority: 50.

NEVADA

Reid (D)—Dec. 2, 1939. Occupation: lawyer. Religion: Mormon. Seniority: 47.

Bryan (D)—July 16, 1937. Occupation: lawyer. Religion: Episcopalian. Seniority: 50.

NEW HAMPSHIRE

Rudman (R)—May 18, 1930. Occupation: lawyer. Religion: Jewish. Seniority: 22.

Smith (R)—March 30, 1941. Occupation: real estate broker, teacher. Religion: Roman Catholic. Seniority: 40.

NEW JERSEY

Bradley (D)—July 28, 1943. Occupation: professional basketball player, author. Religion: Protestant. Seniority: 26.

Lautenberg (D)—Jan. 23, 1924. Occupation: computer firm executive. Religion: Jewish. Seniority: 32.

NEW MEXICO

Domenici (R)—May 7, 1932. Occupation: lawyer. Religion: Roman Catholic. Seniority: 7.

Bingaman (D)—Oct. 3, 1943. Occupation: lawyer. Religion: Methodist. Seniority: 33.

NEW YORK

Moynihan (D)—March 16, 1927. Occupation: author, government professor. Religion: Roman Catholic. Seniority: 19.

D'Amato (R)—Aug. 1, 1937. Occupation: lawyer. Religion: Roman Catholic. Seniority: 26.

NORTH CAROLINA

Helms (R)—Oct. 18, 1921. Occupation: journalist, broadcasting executive, bank executive, congressional aide. Religion: Baptist. Seniority: 7.

Sanford (D)—Aug. 20, 1917. Occupation: FBI agent, lawyer, university president. Religion: Methodist. Seniority: 39.

NORTH DAKOTA

Burdick (D)—June 19, 1908. Occupation: lawyer. Religion: United Church of Christ. Seniority: 2.

Conrad (D)—March 12, 1948. Occupation: management and personnel director. Religion: Unitarian. Seniority: 49.

OHIO

Glenn (D)—July 18, 1921. Occupation: astronaut, soft drink company executive. Religion: Presbyterian. Seniority: 12.

Metzenbaum (D)—June 4, 1917. Occupation: newspaper publisher, parking lot executive, lawyer. Religion: Jewish. Seniority: 16.

OKLAHOMA

Boren (D)—April 21, 1941. Occupation: lawyer. Religion: Methodist. Seniority: 24.

Nickles (R)—Dec. 6, 1948. Occupation: machine company executive. Religion: Roman Catholic. Seniority: 26.

OREGON

Hatfield (R)—July 12, 1922. Occupation: political science professor. Religion: Baptist. Seniority: 2.

Packwood (R)—Sept. 11, 1932. Occupation: lawyer. Religion: Unitarian. Seniority: 5.

PENNSYLVANIA

Specter (R)—Feb. 12, 1930. Occupation: lawyer, law professor. Religion: Jewish. Seniority: 27.

Wofford (D)—April 9, 1926. Occupation: lawyer, educator. Religion: Roman Catholic. Seniority: 57.

RHODE ISLAND

Pell (D)—Nov. 22, 1918. Occupation: investment executive. Religion: Episcopalian. Seniority: 3.

Chafee (R)—Oct. 22, 1922. Occupation: lawyer. Religion: Episcopalian. Seniority: 11.

SOUTH CAROLINA

Thurmond (R)—Dec. 5, 1902. Occupation: lawyer, teacher, coach, education administration. Religion: Baptist. Seniority: 1.

Hollings (D)—Jan. 1, 1922. Occupation: lawyer. Religion: Lutheran. Seniority: 6.

SOUTH DAKOTA

Pressler (R)—March 29, 1942. Occupation: lawyer. Religion: Roman Catholic. Seniority: 21.

Daschle (D)—Dec. 9, 1947. Occupation: congressional aide. Religion: Roman Catholic. Seniority: 45.

TENNESSEE

Sasser (D)—Sept. 30, 1936. Occupation: lawyer. Religion: Protestant. Seniority: 19.

Gore (D)—March 31, 1948. Occupation: journalist, home builder. Religion: Baptist. Seniority: 37.

TEXAS

Bentsen (D)—Feb. 11, 1921. Occupation: financial executive, lawyer. Religion: Presbyterian. Seniority: 8.

Gramm (R)—July 8, 1942. Occupation: economics professor. Religion: Episcopalian. Seniority: 30.

UTAH

Garn (R)—Oct. 12, 1932. Occupation: insurance executive. Religion: Mormon. Seniority: 9.

Hatch (R)—March 22, 1934. Occupation: lawyer. Religion: Mormon. Seniority: 12.

VERMONT

Leahy (D)—March 31, 1940. Occupation: lawyer. Religion: Roman Catholic. Seniority: 15.

Jeffords (R)—May 11, 1934. Occupation: lawyer. Religion: Congregationalist. Seniority: 36.

VIRGINIA

Warner (R)—Feb. 18, 1927. Occupation: farmer, lawyer. Religion: Episcopalian. Seniority: 19.

Robb (D)—June 26, 1939. Occupation: lawyer. Religion: Episcopalian. Seniority: 50.

WASHINGTON

Adams (D)—Jan. 13, 1927. Occupation: lawyer. Religion: Episcopalian. Seniority: 41.

Gorton (R) Jan. 8, 1928. Occupation: lawyer. Religion: Episcopalian. Seniority: 34.

WEST VIRGINIA

Byrd (D)—Nov. 20, 1917. Occupation: lawyer. Religion: Baptist. Seniority: 1.

Rockefeller (D)—June 18, 1937. Occupation: public official. Religion: Presbyterian. Seniority: 38.

WISCONSIN

Kasten (R)—June 19, 1942. Occupation: shoe company executive. Religion: Presbyterian. Seniority: 25.

Kohl (D) Feb. 7, 1935. Occupation: businessman; professional basketball team owner. Religion: Jewish. Seniority: 53.

WYOMING

Wallop (R)—Feb. 27, 1933. Occupation: rancher, meatpacking executive. Religion: Episcopalian. Seniority: 12.

Simpson (R)—Sept. 2, 1931. Occupation: lawyer. Religion: Episcopalian. Seniority: 18.

House — Birth Dates, Occupations, Religions, Seniority

(Seniority rank is within the member's party.)

ALABAMA

1 **Callahan (R)**—Sept. 11, 1932. Occupation: moving and storage company executive. Religion: Roman Catholic. Seniority: 95.

2 **Dickinson (R)**—June 5, 1925. Occupation: railroad executive, lawyer, judge. Religion: Methodist. Seniority: 6.

3 **Browder (D)**—Jan. 15, 1943. Occupation: professor. Religion: Methodist. Seniority: 234.

4 **Bevill (D)**—March 27, 1921. Occupation: lawyer. Religion: Baptist. Seniority: 22.

5 **Cramer (D)**—Aug. 22, 1947. Occupation: lawyer. Religion: Methodist. Seniority: 244.

6 **Erdreich (D)**—Dec. 9, 1938. Occupation: lawyer. Religion: Jewish. Seniority: 129.

7 **Harris (D)**—June 29, 1940. Occupation: lawyer, judge. Religion: Baptist. Seniority: 189.

ALASKA

AL **Young (R)**—June 9, 1933. Occupation: elementary school teacher, riverboat captain. Religion: Episcopalian. Seniority: 24.

ARIZONA

1 **Rhodes (R)**—Sept. 8, 1943. Occupation: lawyer. Religion: Protestant. Seniority: 111.

2 **Pastor (D)**—June 28, 1943. Occupation: teacher; public official. Religion: Roman Catholic. Seniority: 267.

3 **Stump (R)**—April 4, 1927. Occupation: cotton farmer. Religion: Seventh-day Adventist. Seniority: 31.

4 **Kyl (R)**—April 25, 1942. Occupation: lawyer. Religion: Presbyterian. Seniority: 111.

5 **Kolbe (R)**—June 28, 1942. Occupation: real estate consultant. Religion: Methodist. Seniority: 95.

ARKANSAS

1 **Alexander (D)**—Jan. 16, 1934. Occupation: lawyer. Religion: Episcopalian. Seniority: 25.

2 **Thornton (D)**—July 16, 1928. Occupation: lawyer. Religion: Church of Christ. Seniority: 242.

3 **Hammerschmidt (R)**—May 4, 1922. Occupation: lumber company executive. Religion: Presbyterian. Seniority: 8.

4 **Anthony (D)**—Feb. 21, 1938. Occupation: lawyer. Religion: Episcopalian. Seniority: 90.

CALIFORNIA

1 **Riggs (R)**—Sept. 5, 1950. Occupation: real estate developer. Religion: Episcopalian. Seniority: 146.

2 **Herger (R)**—May 20, 1945. Occupation: rancher, gas company president. Religion: Mormon. Seniority: 111.

3 **Matsui (D)**—Sept. 17, 1941. Occupation: lawyer. Religion: Methodist. Seniority: 90.

4 **Fazio (D)**—Oct. 11, 1942. Occupation: journalist. Religion: Episcopalian. Seniority: 90.

5 **Pelosi (D)**—March 26, 1940. Occupation: public relations consultant. Religion: Roman Catholic. Seniority: 212.

6 **Boxer (D)**—Nov. 11, 1940. Occupation: stockbroker, journalist. Religion: Jewish. Seniority: 129.

7 **Miller (D)**—May 17, 1945. Occupation: lawyer, legislative aide. Religion: Roman Catholic. Seniority: 49.

8 **Dellums (D)**—Nov. 24, 1935. Occupation: psychiatric social worker. Religion: Protestant. Seniority: 32.

9 **Stark (D)**—Nov. 11, 1931. Occupation: banker. Religion: Unitarian. Seniority: 37.

10 **Edwards (D)**—Jan. 6, 1915. Occupation: title company executive, lawyer, FBI agent. Religion: Unitarian. Seniority: 10.

11 **Lantos (D)**—Feb. 1, 1928. Occupation: economics professor. Religion: Jewish. Seniority: 108.

12 **Campbell (R)**—Aug. 14, 1952. Occupation: professor, economist. Religion: Roman Catholic. Seniority: 131.

13 **Mineta (D)**—Nov. 12, 1931. Occupation: insurance executive. Religion: Methodist. Seniority: 49.

14 **Doolittle (R)**—Oct. 30, 1950. Occupation: lawyer. Religion: Mormon. Seniority: 146.

15 **Condit (D)**—April 21, 1948. Occupation: public official. Religion: Baptist. Seniority: 235.

16 **Panetta (D)**—June 28, 1938. Occupation: lawyer. Religion: Roman Catholic. Seniority: 71.

17 **Dooley (D)**—Jan. 11, 1954. Occupation: farmer. Religion: Protestant. Seniority: 244.

18 **Lehman (D)**—July 20, 1948. Occupation: legislative aide. Religion: Lutheran. Seniority: 129.

19 **Lagomarsino (R)**—Sept. 4, 1926. Occupation: lawyer. Religion: Roman Catholic. Seniority: 25.

20 **Thomas (R)**—Dec. 6, 1941. Occupation: political science professor. Religion: Baptist. Seniority: 40.

21 **Gallegly (R)**—March 7, 1944. Occupation: real estate broker. Religion: Protestant. Seniority: 111.

22 **Moorhead (R)**—May 6, 1922. Occupation: lawyer. Religion: Presbyterian. Seniority: 19.

23 **Beilenson (D)**—Oct. 26, 1932. Occupation: lawyer. Religion: Jewish. Seniority: 71.

24 **Waxman (D)**—Sept. 12, 1939. Occupation: lawyer. Religion: Jewish. Seniority: 49.

25 **Roybal (D)**—Feb. 10, 1916. Occupation: social worker, public health educator. Religion: Roman Catholic. Seniority: 10.

26 **Berman (D)**—April 15, 1941. Occupation: lawyer. Religion: Jewish. Seniority: 129.

27 **Levine (D)**—June 7, 1943. Occupation: lawyer. Religion: Jewish. Seniority: 129.

28 **Dixon (D)**—Aug. 8, 1934. Occupation: legislative aide, lawyer. Religion: Episcpalian. Seniority: 90.

29 **Waters (D)**—Aug. 31, 1938. Occupation: Head Start official. Religion: Christian. Seniority: 244.

30 **Martinez (D)**—Feb. 14, 1929. Occupation: upholstery company owner. Religion: Roman Catholic. Seniority: 126.

31 **Dymally (D)**—May 12, 1926. Occupation: special education teacher. Religion: Episcopalian. Seniority: 108.

32 **Anderson (D)**—Feb. 21, 1913. Occupation: banker, home builder. Religion: Episcopalian. Seniority: 25.

33 **Dreier (R)**—July 5, 1952. Occupation: real-estate developer. Religion: Christian Scientist. Seniority: 55.

34 **Torres (D)**—Jan. 27, 1930. Occupation: auto worker, labor official, international trade executive. Religion: Roman Catholic. Seniority: 129.

35 **Lewis (R)**—Oct. 21, 1934. Occupation: insurance executive. Religion: Presbyterian. Seniority: 40.

36 **Brown (D)**—March 6, 1920. Occupation: physicist, management consultant. Religion: Methodist. Seniority: 36.

37 **McCandless (R)**—July 23, 1927. Occupation: automobile dealer. Religion: Protestant. Seniority: 77.

38 **Dornan (R)**—April 3, 1933. Occupation: broadcast journalist and producer. Religion: Roman Catholic. Seniority: 94.

39 **Dannemeyer (R)**—Sept. 22, 1929. Occupation: lawyer. Religion: Lutheran. Seniority: 40.

40 **Cox (R)**—Oct. 16, 1952. Occupation: White House counsel. Religion: Roman Catholic. Seniority: 131.

41 **Lowery (R)**—May 2, 1947. Occupation: public relations executive. Religion: Roman Catholic. Seniority: 55.

42 **Rohrabacher (R)**—June 21, 1947. Occupation: White House speechwriter, journalist. Religion: Baptist. Seniority: 131.

43 Packard (R)—Jan. 19, 1931. Occupation: dentist. Religion: Mormon. Seniority: 77.

44 Cunningham (R)—Dec. 1941. Occupation: businessman. Religion: Baptist. Seniority: 146.

45 Hunter (R)—May 31, 1948. Occupation: lawyer. Religion: Baptist. Seniority: 55.

COLORADO

1 Schroeder (D)—July 30, 1940. Occupation: lawyer, law instructor. Religion: United Church of Christ. Seniority: 37.

2 Skaggs (D)—Feb. 22, 1943. Occupation: lawyer, congressional aide. Religion: Congregationalist. Seniority: 189.

3 Campbell (D)—April 13, 1933. Occupation: rancher, jewelry designer, horse trainer, teacher. Religion: Unspecified. Seniority: 189.

4 Allard (R)—Dec. 2, 1943. Occupation: veterinarian. Religion: Protestant. Seniority: 146.

5 Hefley (R)—April 18, 1935. Occupation: community planner. Religion: Presbyterian. Seniority: 111.

6 Schaefer (R)—Jan. 25, 1936. Occupation: public relations consultant. Religion: Roman Catholic. Seniority: 92.

CONNECTICUT

1 Kennelly (D)—July 10, 1936. Occupation: public official. Religion: Roman Catholic. Seniority: 129.

2 Gejdenson (D)—May 20, 1948. Occupation: dairy farmer. Religion: Jewish. Seniority: 108.

3 DeLauro (D)—March 2, 1943. Occupation: political activist. Religion: Roman Catholic. Seniority: 244.

4 Shays (R)—Oct. 18, 1945. Occupation: real estate broker. Religion: Christian Scientist. Seniority: 128.

5 Franks (R)—Feb. 9, 1953. Occupation: real estate investor. Religion: Baptist. Seniority: 146.

6 Johnson (R)—Jan. 5, 1935. Occupation: civic leader. Religion: Unitarian. Seniority: 77.

DELAWARE

AL Carper (D)—Jan. 23, 1947. Occupation: public official. Religion: Presbyterian. Seniority: 129.

FLORIDA

1 Hutto (D)—May 12, 1926. Occupation: high school English teacher, advertising and broadcast executive, sportscaster. Religion: Baptist. Seniority: 90.

2 Peterson (D)—June 26, 1935. Occupation: educational administrator. Religion: Roman Catholic. Seniority: 244.

3 Bennett (D)—Dec. 2, 1910. Occupation: lawyer. Religion: Disciples of Christ. Seniority: 2.

4 James (R)—May 5, 1941. Occupation: lawyer. Religion: Baptist. Seniority: 131.

5 McCollum (R)—July 12, 1944. Occupation: lawyer. Religion: Episcopalian. Seniority: 55.

6 Stearns (R)—April 16, 1941. Occupation: motel company executive. Religion: Presbyterian. Seniority: 131.

7 Gibbons (D)—Jan. 20, 1920. Occupation: lawyer. Religion: Presbyterian. Seniority: 10.

8 Young (R)—Dec. 16, 1930. Occupation: insurance executive. Religion: Methodist. Seniority: 15.

9 Bilirakis (R)—July 16, 1930. Occupation: lawyer, restaurant owner. Religion: Greek Orthodox. Seniority: 77.

10 Ireland (R)—Aug. 23, 1930. Occupation: banker. Religion: Episcopalian. Seniority: 31.

11 Bacchus (D)—June 21, 1949. Occupation: lawyer, journalist. Religion: Presbyterian. Seniority: 244.

12 Lewis (R)—Oct. 26, 1924. Occupation: real estate broker, aircraft testing specialist. Religion: Methodist. Seniority: 77.

13 Goss (R)—Nov. 26, 1938. Occupation: small-business man, newspaper founder, CIA agent. Religion: Presbyterian. Seniority: 131.

14 Johnston (D)—Dec. 2, 1931. Occupation: lawyer. Religion: Presbyterian. Seniority: 217.

15 Shaw (R)—April 19, 1939. Occupation: nurseryman, lawyer. Religion: Roman Catholic. Seniority: 55.

16 Smith (D)—April 25, 1941. Occupation: lawyer. Religion: Jewish. Seniority: 129.

17 Lehman (D)—Oct. 5, 1913. Occupation: high school English teacher, automobile dealer. Religion: Jewish. Seniority: 37.

18 Ros-Lehtinen (R)—July 15, 1952. Occupation: teacher, private school administrator. Religion: Roman Catholic. Seniority: 144.

19 Fascell (D)—March 9, 1917. Occupation: lawyer. Religion: Protestant. Seniority: 5.

GEORGIA

1 Thomas (D)—Nov. 20, 1943. Occupation: farmer, investment banker. Religion: Methodist. Seniority: 129.

2 Hatcher (D)—July 1, 1939. Occupation: lawyer, teacher. Religion: Episcopalian. Seniority: 108.

3 Ray (D)—Feb. 2, 1927. Occupation: exterminator, Senate aide. Religion: Methodist. Seniority: 129.

4 Jones (D)—Aug. 30, 1941. Occupation: actor. Religion: Baptist. Seniority: 217.

5 Lewis (D)—Feb. 21, 1940. Occupation: civil rights activist. Religion: Baptist. Seniority: 189.

6 Gingrich (R)—June 17, 1943. Occupation: history professor. Religion: Baptist. Seniority: 40.

7 Darden (D)—Nov. 22, 1943. Occupation: lawyer. Religion: Methodist. Seniority: 175.

8 Rowland (D)—Feb. 3, 1926. Occupation: physician. Religion: Methodist. Seniority: 129.

9 Jenkins (D)—Jan. 4, 1933. Occupation: lawyer. Religion: Baptist. Seniority: 71.

10 Barnard (D)—March 20, 1922. Occupation: banker. Religion: Baptist. Seniority: 71.

HAWAII

1 Abercrombie (D)—June 26, 1938. Occupation: community activist. Religion: Unspecified. Seniority: 243.

2 Mink (D)—Dec. 6, 1927. Occupation: lawyer. Religion: Protestant. Seniority: 240.

IDAHO

1 LaRocco (D)—Aug. 25, 1946. Occupation: stockbroker. Religion: Roman Catholic. Seniority: 244.

2 Stallings (D)—Oct. 7, 1940. Occupation: history professor. Religion: Mormon. Seniority: 178.

ILLINOIS

1 Hayes (D)—Feb. 17, 1918. Occupation: labor official, packinghouse worker. Religion: Baptist. Seniority: 189.

2 Savage (D)—Oct. 30, 1925. Occupation: newspaper publisher. Religion: Baptist. Seniority: 108.

3 Russo (D)—Jan. 23, 1944. Occupation: lawyer. Religion: Roman Catholic. Seniority: 49.

4 Sangmeister (D) Feb. 16, 1931. Occupation: lawyer. Religion: United Church of Christ. Seniority: 217.

5 Lipinski (D)—Dec. 22, 1937. Occupation: parks supervisor. Religion: Roman Catholic. Seniority: 129.

6 Hyde (R)—April 18, 1924. Occupation: lawyer. Religion: Roman Catholic. Seniority: 26.

7 Collins (D)—Sept. 24, 1931. Occupation: auditor. Religion: National Baptist. Seniority: 44.

8 Rostenkowski (D)—Jan. 2, 1928. Occupation: insurance executive. Religion: Roman Catholic. Seniority: 7.

9 Yates (D)—Aug. 27, 1909. Occupation: lawyer. Religion: Jewish. Seniority: 14.

10 Porter (R)—June 1, 1935. Occupation: lawyer. Religion: Presbyterian. Seniority: 54.

11 Annunzio (D)—Jan. 12, 1915. Occupation: high school teacher, labor official. Religion: Roman Catholic. Seniority: 15.

12 Crane (R)—Nov. 3, 1930. Occupation: history professor, author. Religion:

Protestant. Seniority: 14.
13 **Fawell (R)**—March 25, 1929. Occupation: lawyer. Religion: Methodist. Seniority: 95.
14 **Hastert (R)**—Jan. 2, 1942. Occupation: teacher, restaurateur. Religion: Protestant. Seniority: 111.
15 **Ewing (R)**—Sept. 19, 1935. Occupation: Lawyer. Religion: Methodist. Seniority: 165.
16 **Cox (D)**—July 10, 1947. Occupation: lawyer. Religion: Roman Catholic. Seniority: 244.
17 **Evans (D)**—Aug. 4, 1951. Occupation: lawyer. Religion: Roman Catholic. Seniority: 129.
18 **Michel (R)**—March 2, 1923. Occupation: congressional aide. Religion: Apostolic Christian. Seniority: 1.
19 **Bruce (D)**—March 25, 1944. Occupation: farmer, lawyer. Religion: Methodist. Seniority: 178.
20 **Durbin (D)**—Nov. 21, 1944. Occupation: lawyer. Religion: Roman Catholic. Seniority: 129.
21 **Costello (D)**—Sept. 25, 1949. Occupation: law enforcement administrator. Religion: Roman Catholic. Seniority: 215.
22 **Poshard (D)**—Oct. 30, 1945. Occupation: educator. Religion: Baptist. Seniority: 217.

INDIANA

1 **Visclosky (D)**—Aug. 13, 1949. Occupation: lawyer. Religion: Roman Catholic. Seniority: 178.
2 **Sharp (D)**—July 15, 1942. Occupation: political science professor. Religion: Methodist. Seniority: 49.
3 **Roemer (D)**—Oct. 30, 1956. Occupation: congressional aide, former college instructor. Religion: Roman Catholic. Seniority: 244.
4 **Long (D)**—July 15, 1952. Occupation: professor. Religion: Methodist. Seniority: 233.
5 **Jontz (D)**—Dec. 18, 1951. Occupation: public official. Religion: Methodist. Seniority: 189.
6 **Burton (R)**—June 21, 1938. Occupation: insurance and real estate agent. Religion: Protestant. Seniority: 77.
7 **Myers (R)**—Feb. 8, 1927. Occupation: banker, farmer. Religion: Episcopalian. Seniority: 8.
8 **McCloskey (D)**—June 12, 1939. Occupation: lawyer, journalist. Religion: Roman Catholic. Seniority: 129.
9 **Hamilton (D)**—April 20, 1931. Occupation: lawyer. Religion: Methodist. Seniority: 15.
10 **Jacobs (D)**—Feb. 24, 1932. Occupation: lawyer, police officer. Religion: Roman Catholic. Seniority: 47.

IOWA

1 **Leach (R)**—Oct. 15, 1942. Occupation: foreign service officer, congressional aide, propane gas company executive. Religion: Episcopalian. Seniority: 31.
2 **Nussle (R)**—June 27, 1960. Occupation: lawyer. Religion: Lutheran. Seniority: 146.
3 **Nagle (D)**—April 15, 1943. Occupation: lawyer. Religion: Roman Catholic. Seniority: 189.
4 **Smith (D)**—March 23, 1920. Occupation: farmer, lawyer. Religion: Methodist. Seniority: 7.
5 **Lightfoot (R)**—Sept. 27, 1938. Occupation: radio broadcaster, store owner, police officer. Religion: Roman Catholic. Seniority: 95.
6 **Grandy (R)**—June 29, 1948. Occupation: actor, congressional aide. Religion: Episcopalian. Seniority: 111.

KANSAS

1 **Roberts (R)**—April 20, 1936. Occupation: journalist, congressional aide. Religion: Methodist. Seniority: 55.
2 **Slattery (D)**—Aug. 4, 1948. Occupation: realtor. Religion: Roman Catholic. Seniority: 129.
3 **Meyers (R)**—July 20, 1928. Occupation: homemaker, community volunteer. Religion: Methodist. Seniority: 95.
4 **Glickman (D)**—Nov. 24, 1944. Occupation: lawyer. Religion: Jewish. Seniority: 71.
5 **Nichols (R)**—April 29, 1926. Occupation: banker. Religion: Methodist. Seniority: 150.

KENTUCKY

1 **Hubbard (D)**—July 7, 1937. Occupation: lawyer. Religion: Baptist. Seniority: 49.
2 **Natcher (D)**—Sept. 11, 1909. Occupation: lawyer. Religion: Baptist. Seniority: 4.
3 **Mazzoli (D)**—Nov. 2, 1932. Occupation: lawyer, law professor. Religion: Roman Catholic. Seniority: 32.
4 **Bunning (R)**—Oct. 23, 1931. Occupation: investment broker, professional baseball player. Religion: Roman Catholic. Seniority: 111.
5 **Rogers (R)**—Dec. 31, 1937. Occupation: lawyer. Religion: Baptist. Seniority: 55.
6 **Hopkins (R)**—Oct. 25, 1933. Occupation: stockbroker. Religion: Methodist. Seniority: 40.
7 **Perkins (D)**—Aug. 6, 1954. Occupation: lawyer. Religion: Baptist. Seniority: 177.

LOUISIANA

1 **Livingston (R)**—April 30, 1943. Occupation: lawyer. Religion: Episcopalian. Seniority: 38.
2 **Jefferson (D)**—March 14, 1947. Occupation: lawyer. Religion: Baptist. Seniority: 244.
3 **Tauzin (D)**—June 14, 1943. Occupation: lawyer. Religion: Roman Catholic. Seniority: 107.
4 **McCrery (R)**—Sept. 18, 1949. Occupation: lawyer, corporate government affairs executive. Religion: Methodist. Seniority: 129.
5 **Huckaby (D)**—July 19, 1941. Occupation: farmer, engineer. Religion: Methodist. Seniority: 71.
6 **Baker (R)**—May 22, 1948. Occupation: real estate broker. Religion: Methodist. Seniority: 111.
7 **Hayes (D)**—Dec. 21, 1946. Occupation: lawyer, real estate developer. Religion: Methodist. Seniority: 174.
8 **Holloway (R)**—Nov. 28, 1943. Occupation: nursery owner. Religion: Baptist. Seniority: 111.

MAINE

1 **Andrews (D)**—March 27, 1953. Occupation: association director, political activist. Religion: Unitarian. Seniority: 244.
2 **Snowe (R)**—Feb. 21, 1947. Occupation: concrete company executive, public official. Religion: Greek Orthodox. Seniority: 40.

MARYLAND

1 **Gilchrest (R)**—April 15, 1946. Occupation: high school history and government teacher. Religion: Methodist. Seniority: 146.
2 **Bentley (R)**—Nov. 28, 1923. Occupation: journalist, international trade consultant. Religion: Greek Orthodox. Seniority: 95.
3 **Cardin (D)**—Oct. 5, 1943. Occupation: lawyer. Religion: Jewish. Seniority: 189.
4 **McMillen (D)**—May 26, 1952. Occupation: communications equipment distributor, professional basketball player. Religion: Roman Catholic. Seniority: 189.
5 **Hoyer (D)**—June 14, 1939. Occupation: lawyer. Religion: Baptist. Seniority: 124.
6 **Byron (D)**—July 27, 1932. Occupation: civic leader. Religion: Episcopalian. Seniority: 90.
7 **Mfume (D)**—Oct. 24, 1948. Occupation: radio station program director, talk show host, assistant professor of political science and communications. Religion: Baptist. Seniority: 189.
8 **Morella (R)**—Feb. 12, 1931. Occupation: English literature professor. Religion: Roman Catholic. Seniority: 111.

MASSACHUSETTS

1 **Olver (D)**—Sept. 3, 1936. Occupation: educator, legislator. Religion: Unspecified. Seniority: 266.
2 **Neal (D)**—Feb. 14, 1949. Occupation: public official. Religion: Roman Catholic. Seniority: 217.
3 **Early (D)**—Jan. 31, 1933. Occupation:

teacher, basketball coach. Religion: Roman Catholic. Seniority: 49.

4 Frank (D)—March 31, 1940. Occupation: lawyer. Religion: Jewish. Seniority: 108.

5 Atkins (D)—April 14, 1948. Occupation: public official. Religion: Unitarian. Seniority: 178.

6 Mavroules (D)—Nov. 1, 1929. Occupation: personnel supervisor. Religion: Greek Orthodox. Seniority: 90.

7 Markey (D)—July 11, 1946. Occupation: lawyer. Religion: Roman Catholic. Seniority: 70.

8 Kennedy (D)—Sept. 24, 1952. Occupation: energy company executive. Religion: Roman Catholic. Seniority: 189.

9 Moakley (D)—April 27, 1927. Occupation: lawyer. Religion: Roman Catholic. Seniority: 37.

10 Studds (D)—May 12, 1937. Occupation: high school teacher. Religion: Episcopalian. Seniority: 37.

11 Donnelly (D)—March 2, 1946. Occupation: high school teacher. Religion: Roman Catholic. Seniority: 90.

MICHIGAN

1 Conyers (D)—May 16, 1929. Occupation: lawyer. Religion: Baptist. Seniority: 15.

2 Pursell (R)—Dec. 19, 1932. Occupation: high school teacher, real estate salesman, office supply business owner. Religion: Protestant. Seniority: 31.

3 Wolpe (D)—Nov. 2, 1939. Occupation: political science professor. Religion: Jewish. Seniority: 90.

4 Upton (R)—April 23, 1953. Occupation: congressional aide; budget analyst. Religion: Protestant. Seniority: 111.

5 Henry (R)—July 9, 1942. Occupation: political science professor. Religion: Christian Reformed. Seniority: 95.

6 Carr (D)—March 27, 1943. Occupation: lawyer. Religion: Baptist. Seniority: 127.

7 Kildee (D)—Sept. 16, 1929. Occupation: teacher. Religion: Roman Catholic. Seniority: 71.

8 Traxler (D)—July 21, 1931. Occupation: lawyer. Religion: Episcopalian. Seniority: 46.

9 Vander Jagt (R)—Aug. 26, 1931. Occupation: lawyer. Religion: Presbyterian. Seniority: 7.

10 Camp (R)—July 9, 1953. Occupation: lawyer, congressional aide. Religion: Roman Catholic. Seniority: 146.

11 Davis (R)—July 31, 1932. Occupation: funeral director. Religion: Episcopalian. Seniority: 40.

12 Bonior (D)—June 6, 1945. Occupation: probation officer. Religion: Roman Catholic. Seniority: 71.

13 Collins (D)—April 13, 1939. Occupation: public official. Religion: Shrine of the Black Madonna (Pan-African Orthodox Christian). Seniority: 244.

14 Hertel (D)—Dec. 7, 1948. Occupation: lawyer. Religion: Roman Catholic. Seniority: 108.

15 Ford (D)—Aug. 6, 1927. Occupation: lawyer. Religion: United Church of Christ. Seniority: 15.

16 Dingell (D)—July 8, 1926. Occupation: lawyer. Religion: Roman Catholic. Seniority: 6.

17 Levin (D)—Sept. 6, 1931. Occupation: lawyer. Religion: Jewish. Seniority: 129.

18 Broomfield (R)—April 28, 1922. Occupation: insurance executive. Religion: Presbyterian. Seniority: 1.

MINNESOTA

1 Penny (D)—Nov. 19, 1951. Occupation: sales representative. Religion: Lutheran. Seniority: 129.

2 Weber (R)—July 24, 1952. Occupation: congressional aide, publisher. Religion: Roman Catholic. Seniority: 55.

3 Ramstad (R)—May 6, 1946. Occupation: legislative aide, lawyer. Religion: Protestant. Seniority: 146.

4 Vento (D)—Oct. 7, 1940. Occupation: science teacher. Religion: Roman Catholic. Seniority: 71.

5 Sabo (D)—Feb. 28, 1938. Occupation: public official. Religion: Lutheran. Seniority: 90.

6 Sikorski (D)—April 26, 1948. Occupation: lawyer. Religion: Roman Catholic. Seniority: 129.

7 Peterson (D)—June 29, 1944. Occupation: accountant. Religion: Lutheran. Seniority: 244.

8 Oberstar (D)—Sept. 10, 1934. Occupation: language teacher, congressional aide. Religion: Roman Catholic. Seniority: 49.

MISSISSIPPI

1 Whitten (D)—April 18, 1910. Occupation: author, lawyer, grammar school teacher and principal. Religion: Presbyterian. Seniority: 1.

2 Espy (D)—Nov. 30, 1953. Occupation: lawyer, businessman. Religion: Baptist. Seniority: 189.

3 Montgomery (D)—Aug. 5, 1920. Occupation: insurance executive. Religion: Episcopalian. Seniority: 22.

4 Parker (D)—Oct. 31, 1949. Occupation: funeral director. Religion: Presbyterian. Seniority: 217.

5 Taylor (D)—Sept. 17, 1953. Occupation: sales representative. Religion: Roman Catholic. Seniority: 237.

MISSOURI

1 Clay (D)—April 30, 1931. Occupation: real estate salesman, insurance executive. Religion: Roman Catholic. Seniority: 25.

2 Horn (D)—Oct. 18, 1936. Occupation: political research and consulting firm president. Religion: Roman Catholic. Seniority: 244.

3 Gephardt (D)—Jan. 31, 1941. Occupation: lawyer. Religion: Baptist. Seniority: 71.

4 Skelton (D)—Dec. 20, 1931. Occupation: lawyer. Religion: Christian Church. Seniority: 71.

5 Wheat (D)—Oct. 16, 1951. Occupation: legislative aide, federal economist. Religion: Church of Christ. Seniority: 129.

6 Coleman (R)—May 29, 1943. Occupation: lawyer. Religion: Protestant. Seniority: 30.

7 Hancock (R)—Sept. 14, 1929. Occupation: businessman. Religion: Church of Christ. Seniority: 131.

8 Emerson (R)—Jan. 1, 1938. Occupation: government relations executive. Religion: Presbyterian. Seniority: 55.

9 Volkmer (D)—April 4, 1931. Occupation: lawyer. Religion: Roman Catholic. Seniority: 71.

MONTANA

1 Williams (D)—Oct. 30, 1937. Occupation: elementary and secondary school teacher. Religion: Roman Catholic. Seniority: 90.

2 Marlenee (R)—Aug. 8, 1935. Occupation: rancher. Religion: Lutheran. Seniority: 31.

NEBRASKA

1 Bereuter (R)—Oct. 6, 1939. Occupation: city planner. Religion: Lutheran. Seniority: 40.

2 Hoagland (D)—Nov. 17, 1941. Occupation: lawyer. Religion: Episcopalian. Seniority: 217.

3 Barrett (R)—Feb. 9, 1929. Occupation: insurance and real estate company owner. Religion: Presbyterian. Seniority: 146.

NEVADA

1 Bilbray (D)—May 19, 1938. Occupation: lawyer. Religion: Roman Catholic. Seniority: 189.

2 Vucanovich (R)—June 22, 1921. Occupation: travel agent, franchise owner, congressional aide. Religion: Roman Catholic. Seniority: 77.

NEW HAMPSHIRE

1 Zeliff (R)—June 12, 1936. Occupation: hotel owner. Religion: Protestant. Seniority: 146.

2 Swett (D)—May 1, 1957. Occupation: architect. Religion: Mormon. Seniority: 244.

NEW JERSEY

1 Andrews (D)—Aug. 4, 1957. Occupation: law professor. Religion: Episcopalian. Seniority: 241.

2 Hughes (D)—Oct. 17, 1932. Occupation: lawyer. Religion: Episcopalian. Seniority: 49.

3 **Pallone (D)**—Oct. 30, 1951. Occupation: lawyer. Religion: Roman Catholic. Seniority: 216.
4 **Smith (R)**—March 4, 1953. Occupation: sporting goods wholesaler. Religion: Roman Catholic. Seniority: 55.
5 **Roukema (R)**—Sept. 19, 1929. Occupation: high school history and government teacher. Religion: Protestant. Seniority: 55.
6 **Dwyer (D)**—Jan. 24, 1921. Occupation: insurance salesman and executive. Religion: Roman Catholic. Seniority: 108.
7 **Rinaldo (R)**—Sept. 1, 1931. Occupation: management consultant, lecturer. Religion: Roman Catholic. Seniority: 19.
8 **Roe (D)**—Feb. 28, 1924. Occupation: construction company owner, engineer. Religion: Roman Catholic. Seniority: 31.
9 **Torricelli (D)**—Aug. 26, 1951. Occupation: lawyer. Religion: Methodist. Seniority: 129.
10 **Payne (D)**—July 16, 1934. Occupation: community development executive. Religion: Baptist. Seniority: 217.
11 **Gallo (R)**—Nov. 23, 1935. Occupation: real estate broker. Religion: Methodist. Seniority: 95.
12 **Zimmer (R)**—Aug. 16, 1944. Occupation: lawyer. Religion: Jewish. Seniority: 146.
13 **Saxton (R)**—Jan. 22, 1943. Occupation: real estate broker, elementary school teacher. Religion: Methodist. Seniority: 93.
14 **Guarini (D)**—Aug. 20, 1924. Occupation: lawyer. Religion: Roman Catholic. Seniority: 90.

NEW MEXICO

1 **Schiff (R)**—March 18, 1947. Occupation: lawyer. Religion: Jewish. Seniority: 131.
2 **Skeen (R)**—June 30, 1927. Occupation: rancher. Religion: Roman Catholic. Seniority: 55.
3 **Richardson (D)**—Nov. 15, 1947. Occupation: business consultant. Religion: Roman Catholic. Seniority: 129.

NEW YORK

1 **Hochbrueckner (D)**—Sept. 20, 1938. Occupation: aerospace engineer. Religion: Roman Catholic. Seniority: 189.
2 **Downey (D)**—Jan. 28, 1949. Occupation: personnel manager. Religion: Methodist. Seniority: 49.
3 **Mrazek (D)**—Nov. 6, 1945. Occupation: congressional aide. Religion: Methodist. Seniority: 129.
4 **Lent (R)**—March 23, 1931. Occupation: lawyer. Religion: Methodist. Seniority: 15.
5 **McGrath (R)**—March 27, 1942. Occupation: physical education teacher. Religion: Roman Catholic. Seniority: 55.
6 **Flake (D)**—Jan. 30, 1945. Occupation: minister. Religion: African Methodist Episcopal. Seniority: 189.
7 **Ackerman (D)**—Nov. 19, 1942. Occupation: advertising executive; publisher and editor; social studies teacher. Religion: Jewish. Seniority: 173.
8 **Scheuer (D)**—Feb. 6, 1920. Occupation: lawyer. Religion: Jewish. Seniority: 47.
9 **Manton (D)**—Nov. 3, 1932. Occupation: lawyer. Religion: Roman Catholic. Seniority: 178.
10 **Schumer (D)**—Nov. 23, 1950. Occupation: lawyer. Religion: Jewish. Seniority: 108.
11 **Towns (D)**—July 21, 1934. Occupation: hospital administrator. Religion: Independent Baptist. Seniority: 129.
12 **Owens (D)**—June 28, 1936. Occupation: librarian. Religion: Baptist. Seniority: 129.
13 **Solarz (D)**—Sept. 12, 1940. Occupation: public official. Religion: Jewish. Seniority: 49.
14 **Molinari (R)**—March 27, 1958. Occupation: public official. Religion: Roman Catholic. Seniority: 145.
15 **Green (R)**—Oct. 16, 1929. Occupation: state government lawyer, federal housing official. Religion: Jewish. Seniority: 39.
16 **Rangel (D)**—June 11, 1930. Occupation: lawyer. Religion: Roman Catholic. Seniority: 32.
17 **Weiss (D)**—Sept. 17, 1927. Occupation: lawyer. Religion: Jewish. Seniority: 71.
18 **Serrano (D)**—Oct. 24, 1943. Occupation: public official. Religion: Roman Catholic. Seniority: 239.
19 **Engel (D)**—Feb 18, 1947. Occupation: public official, teacher. Religion: Jewish. Seniority: 217.
20 **Lowey (D)**—July 5, 1937. Occupation: public official. Religion: Jewish. Seniority: 217.
21 **Fish (R)**—June 3, 1926. Occupation: lawyer. Religion: Episcopalian. Seniority: 12.
22 **Gilman (R)**—Dec. 6, 1922. Occupation: lawyer. Religion: Jewish. Seniority: 19.
23 **McNulty (D)**—Sept. 16, 1947. Occupation: public official. Religion: Roman Catholic. Seniority: 217.
24 **Solomon (R)**—Aug. 14, 1930. Occupation: insurance executive. Religion: Presbyterian. Seniority: 40.
25 **Boehlert (R)**—Sept. 28, 1936. Occupation: congressional aide, public relations manager. Religion: Roman Catholic. Seniority: 77.
26 **Martin (R)**—April 26, 1944. Occupation: lawyer. Religion: Roman Catholic. Seniority: 55.
27 **Walsh (R)**—June 19, 1947. Occupation: businessman. Religion: Roman Catholic. Seniority: 131.
28 **McHugh (D)**—Dec. 6, 1938. Occupation: lawyer. Religion: Roman Catholic. Seniority: 49.
29 **Horton (R)**—Dec. 12, 1919. Occupation: lawyer. Religion: Presbyterian. Seniority: 3.
30 **Slaughter (D)**—Aug. 14, 1929. Occupation: market researcher. Religion: Episcopalian. Seniority: 189.
31 **Paxon (R)**—April 29, 1954. Occupation: public official. Religion: Roman Catholic. Seniority: 131.
32 **LaFalce (D)**—Oct. 6, 1939. Occupation: lawyer. Religion: Roman Catholic. Seniority: 49.
33 **Nowak (D)**—Feb. 21, 1935. Occupation: lawyer. Religion: Roman Catholic. Seniority: 49.
34 **Houghton (R)**—Aug. 7, 1926. Occupation: glassworks company executive. Religion: Episcopalian. Seniority: 111.

NORTH CAROLINA

1 **Jones (D)**—Aug. 19, 1913. Occupation: office supply company owner. Religion: Baptist. Seniority: 21.
2 **Valentine (D)**—March 15, 1926. Occupation: lawyer. Religion: Baptist. Seniority: 129.
3 **Lancaster (D)**—March 24, 1943. Occupation: lawyer. Religion: Presbyterian. Seniority: 189.
4 **Price (D)**—Aug. 17, 1940. Occupation: political science and public policy professor. Religion: American Baptist. Seniority: 189.
5 **Neal (D)**—Nov. 7, 1934. Occupation: newspaper publisher, mortgage banker. Religion: Presbyterian. Seniority: 49.
6 **Coble (R)**—March 18, 1931. Occupation: lawyer, insurance agent. Religion: Presbyterian. Seniority: 95.
7 **Rose (D)**—Aug. 10, 1939. Occupation: lawyer. Religion: Presbyterian. Seniority: 37.
8 **Hefner (D)**—April 11, 1930. Occupation: broadcasting executive. Religion: Baptist. Seniority: 49.
9 **McMillan (R)**—May 9, 1932. Occupation: food store executive. Religion: Presbyterian. Seniority: 95.
10 **Ballenger (R)**—Dec. 6, 1926. Occupation: president of plastics packaging company. Religion: Episcopalian. Seniority: 110.
11 **Taylor (R)**—Jan. 23, 1941. Occupation: tree farmer, banker. Religion: Baptist. Seniority: 146.

NORTH DAKOTA

AL **Dorgan (D)**—May 14, 1942. Occupation: public official. Religion: Lutheran. Seniority: 108.

OHIO

1 **Luken (D)**—July 17, 1951. Occupation: lawyer. Religion: Roman Catholic. Seniority: 244.
2 **Gradison (R)**—Dec. 28, 1928. Occupation: investment broker, federal official. Religion: Jewish. Seniority: 26.
3 **Hall (D)**—Jan. 16, 1942. Occupation: real estate salesman. Religion: Christian. Seniority: 90.

4 **Oxley (R)**—Feb. 11, 1944. Occupation: FBI agent, lawyer. Religion: Lutheran. Seniority: 76.
5 **Gillmor (R)**—Feb. 1, 1939. Occupation: lawyer. Religion: Protestant. Seniority: 131.
6 **McEwen (R)**—Jan. 12, 1950. Occupation: real estate developer. Religion: Protestant. Seniority: 55.
7 **Hobson (R)**—Oct. 17, 1936. Occupation: real estate and mortgage executive. Religion: Methodist. Seniority: 146.
8 **Boehner (R)**—Nov. 17, 1949. Occupation: plastics and packaging sales company president. Religion: Roman Catholic. Seniority: 146.
9 **Kaptur (D)**—June 17, 1946. Occupation: urban planner, White House staff member. Religion: Roman Catholic. Seniority: 129.
10 **Miller (R)**—Nov. 1, 1917. Occupation: electrical engineer. Religion: Methodist. Seniority: 8.
11 **Eckart (D)**—April 6, 1950. Occupation: lawyer. Religion: Roman Catholic. Seniority: 108.
12 **Kasich (R)**—May 13, 1952. Occupation: legislative aide. Religion: Roman Catholic. Seniority: 77.
13 **Pease (D)**—Sept. 26, 1931. Occupation: newspaper editor. Religion: Methodist. Seniority: 71.
14 **Sawyer (D)**—Aug. 15, 1945. Occupation: teacher. Religion: Presbyterian. Seniority: 189.
15 **Wylie (R)**—Nov. 23, 1920. Occupation: lawyer. Religion: Methodist. Seniority: 8.
16 **Regula (R)**—Dec. 3, 1924. Occupation: lawyer. Religion: Episcopalian. Seniority: 19.
17 **Traficant (D)**—May 8, 1941. Occupation: county drug program director, sheriff. Religion: Roman Catholic. Seniority: 178.
18 **Applegate (D)**—March 27, 1928. Occupation: real estate broker. Religion: Presbyterian. Seniority: 71.
19 **Feighan (D)**—Oct. 22, 1947. Occupation: lawyer. Religion: Roman Catholic. Seniority: 129.
20 **Oakar (D)**—March 5, 1940. Occupation: high school English and speech teacher. Religion: Roman Catholic. Seniority: 71.
21 **Stokes (D)**—Feb. 23, 1925. Occupation: lawyer. Religion: African Methodist Episcopal. Seniority: 25.

OKLAHOMA

1 **Inhofe (R)**—Nov. 17, 1934. Occupation: real estate developer, insurance company executive. Religion: Presbyterian. Seniority: 111.
2 **Synar (D)**—Oct. 17, 1950. Occupation: lawyer, rancher, real estate broker. Religion: Episcopalian. Seniority: 90.
3 **Brewster (D)**—Nov. 8. 1941. Occupation: pharmacist, rancher, real estate company owner. Religion: Baptist. Seniority: 244.
4 **McCurdy (D)**—March 30, 1950. Occupation: lawyer. Religion: Lutheran. Seniority: 108.
5 **Edwards (R)**—July 12, 1937. Occupation: journalist, lawyer. Religion: Episcopalian. Seniority: 31.
6 **English (D)**—Nov. 30, 1940. Occupation: petroleum landman. Religion: Methodist. Seniority: 49.

OREGON

1 **AuCoin (D)**—Oct. 21, 1942. Occupation: journalist, public relations executive. Religion: Protestant. Seniority: 49.
2 **Smith (R)**—June 16, 1931. Occupation: cattle rancher. Religion: Presbyterian. Seniority: 77.
3 **Wyden (D)**—May 3, 1949. Occupation: public interest lawyer, professor of gerontology, public interest group executive, campaign aide. Religion: Jewish. Seniority: 108.
4 **DeFazio (D)**—May 27, 1947. Occupation: congressional aide. Religion: Roman Catholic. Seniority: 189.
5 **Kopetski (D)**—Oct. 27. 1949. Occupation: advertising executive. Religion: Unspecified. Seniority: 244.

PENNSYLVANIA

1 **Foglietta (D)**—Dec. 3, 1928. Occupation: lawyer. Religion: Roman Catholic. Seniority: 108.
2 **Blackwell (D)**—Aug. 1, 1931. Occupation: labor official. Religion: Baptist. Seniority: 268.
3 **Borski (D)**—Oct. 20, 1948. Occupation: stockbroker. Religion: Roman Catholic. Seniority: 129.
4 **Kolter (D)**—Sept. 3, 1926. Occupation: accountant. Religion: Roman Catholic. Seniority: 129.
5 **Schulze (R)**—Aug. 7, 1929. Occupation: household appliance dealer. Religion: Presbyterian. Seniority: 26.
6 **Yatron (D)**—Oct. 16, 1927. Occupation: professional boxer, ice cream manufacturer. Religion: Greek Orthodox. Seniority: 25.
7 **Weldon (R)**—July 22, 1947. Occupation: teacher. Religion: Protestant. Seniority: 111.
8 **Kostmayer (D)**—Sept. 27, 1946. Occupation: public relations consultant. Religion: Episcopalian. Seniority: 128.
9 **Shuster (R)**—Jan. 23, 1932. Occupation: computer industry executive. Religion: United Church of Christ. Seniority: 19.
10 **McDade (R)**—Sept. 29, 1931. Occupation: lawyer. Religion: Roman Catholic. Seniority: 3.
11 **Kanjorski (D)**—April 2, 1937. Occupation: lawyer. Religion: Roman Catholic. Seniority: 178.
12 **Murtha (D)**—June 17, 1932. Occupation: car wash operator. Religion: Roman Catholic. Seniority: 45.
13 **Coughlin (R)**—April 11, 1929. Occupation: lawyer. Religion: Episcopalian. Seniority: 12.
14 **Coyne (D)**—Aug. 24, 1936. Occupation: accountant. Religion: Roman Catholic. Seniority: 108.
15 **Ritter (R)**—Oct. 21, 1940. Occupation: engineering consultant, professor. Religion: Unitarian. Seniority: 40.
16 **Walker (R)**—Dec. 23, 1942. Occupation: high school teacher, congressional aide. Religion: Presbyterian. Seniority: 31.
17 **Gekas (R)**—April 14, 1930. Occupation: lawyer. Religion: Greek Orthodox. Seniority: 77.
18 **Santorum (R)**—May 10, 1958. Occupation: lawyer, legislative aide. Religion: Roman Catholic. Seniority: 146.
19 **Goodling (R)**—Dec. 5, 1927. Occupation: public school superintendent. Religion: Methodist. Seniority: 26.
20 **Gaydos (D)**—July 3, 1926. Occupation: lawyer. Religion: Roman Catholic. Seniority: 24.
21 **Ridge (R)**—Aug. 26, 1945. Occupation: lawyer. Religion: Roman Catholic. Seniority: 77.
22 **Murphy (D)**—June 17, 1927. Occupation: lawyer. Religion: Roman Catholic. Seniority: 71.
23 **Clinger (R)**—April 4, 1929. Occupation: lawyer. Religion: Presbyterian. Seniority: 40.

RHODE ISLAND

1 **Machtley (R)**—July 13, 1948. Occupation: lawyer. Religion: Presbyterian. Seniority: 131.
2 **Reed (D)**—Nov. 12. 1949. Occupation: lawyer. Religion: Roman Catholic. Seniority: 244.

SOUTH CAROLINA

1 **Ravenel (R)**—March 29, 1927. Occupation: businessman. Religion: French Huguenot. Seniority: 111.
2 **Spence (R)**—April 9, 1928. Occupation: lawyer. Religion: Lutheran. Seniority: 15.
3 **Derrick (D)**—Sept. 30, 1936. Occupation: lawyer. Religion: Episcopalian. Seniority: 49.
4 **Patterson (D)**—Nov. 18, 1939. Occupation: legislative aide, Peace Corps recruiting officer, Head Start official. Religion: Methodist. Seniority: 189.
5 **Spratt (D)**—Nov. 1, 1942. Occupation: lawyer, insurance agency owner. Religion: Presbyterian. Seniority: 129.
6 **Tallon (D)**—Aug. 8, 1946. Occupation: clothing store owner. Religion: Methodist. Seniority: 129.

SOUTH DAKOTA

AL **Johnson (D)**—Dec. 28, 1946. Occupation: lawyer. Religion: Lutheran. Seniority: 189.

TENNESSEE

1 **Quillen (R)**—Jan. 11, 1916. Occupation:

newspaper publisher, real estate and insurance salesman, banker. Religion: Methodist. Seniority: 3.

2 **Duncan (R)**—July 21, 1947. Occupation: lawyer, judge. Religion: Presbyterian. Seniority: 130.

3 **Lloyd (D)**—Jan. 3, 1929. Occupation: radio station owner and manager. Religion: Church of Christ. Seniority: 49.

4 **Cooper (D)**—June 19, 1954. Occupation: lawyer. Religion: Episcopalian. Seniority: 129.

5 **Clement (D)**—Sept. 23, 1943. Occupation: college president. Religion: Methodist. Seniority: 213.

6 **Gordon (D)**—Jan. 24, 1949. Occupation: lawyer. Religion: Methodist. Seniority: 178.

7 **Sundquist (R)**—March 15, 1936. Occupation: printing, advertising and marketing firm owner. Religion: Lutheran. Seniority: 77.

8 **Tanner (D)**—Sept. 22, 1944. Occupation: lawyer, banker. Religion: Disciples of Christ. Seniority: 217.

9 **Ford (D)**—May 20, 1945. Occupation: mortician. Religion: Baptist. Seniority: 49.

TEXAS

1 **Chapman (D)**—March 8, 1945. Occupation: lawyer. Religion: Methodist. Seniority: 187.

2 **Wilson (D)**—June 1, 1933. Occupation: lumberyard manager. Religion: Methodist. Seniority: 37.

3 **Johnson (R)**—Oct. 11, 1930. Occupation: home builder. Religion: Methodist. Seniority: 164.

4 **Hall (D)**—May 3, 1923. Occupation: businessman, lawyer. Religion: Methodist. Seniority: 108.

5 **Bryant (D)**—Feb. 22, 1947. Occupation: lawyer. Religion: Methodist. Seniority: 129.

6 **Barton (R)**—Sept. 15, 1949. Occupation: engineering consultant. Religion: Methodist. Seniority: 95.

7 **Archer (R)**—March 22, 1928. Occupation: lawyer, feed company executive. Religion: Roman Catholic. Seniority: 15.

8 **Fields (R)**—Feb. 3, 1952. Occupation: lawyer, cemetery executive. Religion: Baptist. Seniority: 55.

9 **Brooks (D)**—Dec. 18, 1922. Occupation: lawyer. Religion: Methodist. Seniority: 3.

10 **Pickle (D)**—Oct. 11, 1913. Occupation: public relations and advertising executive. Religion: Methodist. Seniority: 13.

11 **Edwards (D)**—Nov. 24, 1951. Occupation: radio station owner. Religion: Methodist. Seniority: 244.

12 **Geren (D)**—Jan. 29, 1952. Occupation: lawyer. Religion: Baptist. Seniority: 235.

13 **Sarpalius (D)**—Jan. 10, 1948. Occupation: agricultural consultant. Religion: Methodist. Seniority: 217.

14 **Laughlin (D)**—Jan. 21, 1942. Occupation: lawyer. Religion: Methodist. Seniority: 217.

15 **de la Garza (D)**—Sept. 22, 1927. Occupation: lawyer. Religion: Roman Catholic. Seniority: 15.

16 **Coleman (D)**—Nov. 29, 1941. Occupation: lawyer. Religion: Presbyterian. Seniority: 129.

17 **Stenholm (D)**—Oct. 26, 1938. Occupation: cotton grower. Religion: Lutheran. Seniority: 90.

18 **Washington (D)**—Oct. 12, 1941. Occupation: lawyer. Religion: Baptist. Seniority: 238.

19 **Combest (R)**—March 20, 1945. Occupation: congressional aide, electronics wholesaler, farmer, stockman, agricultural specialist. Religion: Methodist. Seniority: 95.

20 **Gonzalez (D)**—May 3, 1916. Occupation: business consultant, translator. Religion: Roman Catholic. Seniority: 9.

21 **Smith (R)**—Nov. 19, 1947. Occupation: rancher, lawyer. Religion: Christian Scientist. Seniority: 111.

22 **DeLay (R)**—April 8, 1947. Occupation: pest control company owner. Religion: Baptist. Seniority: 95.

23 **Bustamante (D)**—April 8, 1935. Occupation: teacher. Religion: Roman Catholic. Seniority: 178.

24 **Frost (D)**—Jan. 1, 1942. Occupation: lawyer. Religion: Jewish. Seniority: 90.

25 **Andrews (D)**—Feb. 7, 1944. Occupation: lawyer. Religion: Episcopalian. Seniority: 129.

26 **Armey (R)**—July 7, 1940. Occupation: economist. Religion: Presbyterian. Seniority: 95.

27 **Ortiz (D)**—June 3, 1937. Occupation: law enforcement official. Religion: Methodist. Seniority: 129.

UTAH

1 **Hansen (R)**—Aug. 14, 1932. Occupation: insurance executive, land developer. Religion: Mormon. Seniority: 55.

2 **Owens (D)**—May 2, 1937. Occupation: lawyer. Religion: Mormon. Seniority: 188.

3 **Orton (D)**—Sept. 22, 1949. Occupation: lawyer. Religion: Mormon. Seniority: 244.

VERMONT

AL **Sanders (I)**—Sept. 8, 1941. Occupation: free-lance writer, college professor. Religion: Jewish. Seniority: none.

VIRGINIA

1 **Bateman (R)**—Aug. 7, 1928. Occupation: lawyer. Religion: Protestant. Seniority: 77.

2 **Pickett (D)**—Aug. 31, 1930. Occupation: lawyer, accountant. Religion: Baptist. Seniority: 189.

3 **Bliley (R)**—Jan. 28, 1932. Occupation: funeral director. Religion: Roman Catholic. Seniority: 55.

4 **Sisisky (D)**—June 9, 1927. Occupation: beer and soft drink distributor. Religion: Jewish. Seniority: 129.

5 **Payne (D)**—July 9, 1945. Occupation: developer, businessman. Religion: Presbyterian. Seniority: 214.

6 **Olin (D)**—Feb. 28, 1920. Occupation: electronics company executive. Religion: Unitarian. Seniority: 129.

7 **Allen (R)**—March 8, 1952. Occupation: lawyer. Religion: Presbyterian. Seniority: 166.

8 **Moran (D)**—May 16, 1945. Occupation: investment banker. Religion: Roman Catholic. Seniority: 244.

9 **Boucher (D)**—Aug. 1, 1946. Occupation: lawyer. Religion: Methodist. Seniority: 129.

10 **Wolf (R)**—Jan. 30, 1939. Occupation: lawyer. Religion: Presbyterian. Seniority: 55.

WASHINGTON

1 **Miller (R)**—May 23, 1938. Occupation: lawyer. Religion: Jewish. Seniority: 95.

2 **Swift (D)**—Sept. 12, 1935. Occupation: broadcaster, congressional aide. Religion: Unitarian. Seniority: 90.

3 **Unsoeld (D)**—Dec. 3, 1931. Occupation: public official. Religion: Theist. Seniority: 217.

4 **Morrison (R)**—May 13, 1933. Occupation: fruit grower, nurseryman. Religion: Methodist. Seniority: 55.

5 **Foley (D)**—March 6, 1929. Occupation: lawyer. Religion: Roman Catholic. Seniority: 15.

6 **Dicks (D)**—Dec. 16, 1940. Occupation: lawyer, congressional aide. Religion: Lutheran. Seniority: 71.

7 **McDermott (D)**—Dec. 28, 1936. Occupation: psychiatrist. Religion: Episcopalian. Seniority: 217.

8 **Chandler (R)**—July 13, 1942. Occupation: public relations consultant, newscaster, banker. Religion: Protestant. Seniority: 77.

WEST VIRGINIA

1 **Mollohan (D)**—May 14, 1943. Occupation: lawyer. Religion: Baptist. Seniority: 129.

2 **Staggers (D)**—Feb. 22, 1951. Occupation: lawyer. Religion: Roman Catholic. Seniority: 129.

3 **Wise (D)**—Jan. 6, 1948. Occupation: lawyer. Religion: Episcopalian. Seniority: 129.

4 **Rahall (D)**—May 20, 1949. Occupation: broadcasting executive, travel agent. Religion: Presbyterian. Seniority: 71.

WISCONSIN

1 **Aspin (D)**—July 21, 1938. Occupation: economics professor. Religion: Episcopalian. Seniority: 32

2 Klug (R)—Jan. 16, 1953. Occupation: business development firm vice president. Religion: Roman Catholic. Seniority: 146.

3 Gunderson (R)—May 10, 1951. Occupation: public official. Religion: Lutheran. Seniority: 55.

4 Kleczka (D)—Nov. 26, 1943. Occupation: accountant. Religion: Roman Catholic. Seniority: 176.

5 Moody (D)—Sept. 2, 1935. Occupation: economist. Religion: Protestant. Seniority: 129.

6 Petri (R)—May 28, 1940. Occupation: lawyer. Religion: Lutheran. Seniority: 53.

7 Obey (D)—Oct. 3, 1938. Occupation: real estate broker. Religion: Roman Catholic. Seniority: 30.

8 Roth (R)—Oct. 10, 1938. Occupation: real estate broker. Religion: Roman Catholic. Seniority: 40.

9 Sensenbrenner (R)—June 14, 1943. Occupation: lawyer. Religion: Episcopalian. Seniority: 40.

WYOMING

AL Thomas (R)—Feb. 17, 1933. Occupation: businessman. Religion: Methodist. Seniority: 143. ∎

Seniority in the Senate

Senate rank generally is determined according to the official date of the beginning of a member's service, except in the case of new members sworn in at times other than the beginning of a Congress. For those appointed or elected to fill unexpired terms, the date of the appointment, certification or swearing-in determines the senator's rank.

When members are sworn in on the same day, custom decrees that those with prior political experience take precedence. Counted as political experience, in order of importance, is senatorial, House and gubernatorial service. Information on prior experience is given where applicable to seniority ranking. The dates following senators' names refer to the beginning of their present service. Senators elected Nov. 6 were sworn in Jan. 3.

DEMOCRATS

1. Byrd (W.Va.)—Jan. 3, 1959
2. Burdick (N.D.)—Aug. 8, 1960
3. Pell (R.I.)—Jan. 3, 1961
4. Kennedy (Mass.)—Nov. 7, 1962
5. Inouye (Hawaii)—Jan. 3, 1963
6. Hollings (S.C.)—Nov. 9, 1966
7. Cranston (Calif.)—Jan. 3, 1969
8. Bentsen (Texas)—Jan. 3, 1971
9. Nunn (Ga.)—Nov. 8, 1972
10. Johnston (La.)—Nov. 14, 1972
11. Biden (Del.)—Jan. 3, 1973
12. Glenn (Ohio)—Dec. 24, 1974
13. Ford (Ky.)—Dec. 28, 1974
14. Bumpers (Ark.) (ex-governor)—Jan. 3, 1975
15. Leahy (Vt.)—Jan. 3, 1975
16. Metzenbaum (Ohio)—Dec. 29, 1976
17. Riegle (Mich.)—Dec. 30, 1976
18. Sarbanes (Md.) (ex-rep.)—Jan. 4, 1977
19. DeConcini (Ariz.)—Jan. 4, 1977
    Moynihan (N.Y.)—Jan. 4, 1977
    Sasser (Tenn.)—Jan. 4, 1977
22. Baucus (Mont.)—Dec. 15, 1978
23. Pryor (Ark.) (ex-rep.)—Jan. 15, 1979
24. Boren (Okla.) (ex-governor)—Jan. 15, 1979
    Exon (Neb.) (ex-governor)—Jan. 15, 1979
26. Bradley (N.J.)—Jan. 15, 1979
    Heflin (Ala.)—Jan. 15, 1979
    Levin (Mich.)—Jan. 15, 1979
29. Mitchell (Maine)—May 19, 1980
30. Dodd (Conn.) (ex-rep.)—Jan. 5, 1981
31. Dixon (Ill.)—Jan. 5, 1981
32. Lautenberg (N.J.)—Dec. 27, 1982
33. Bingaman (N.M.)—Jan. 3, 1983
34. Kerry (Mass.)—Jan. 2, 1985
35. Harkin (Iowa) (ex-rep., five House terms)—Jan. 3, 1985
    Simon (Ill.) (ex-rep., five House terms)—Jan. 3, 1985
37. Gore (Tenn.) (ex-rep., four House terms)—Jan. 3, 1985
38. Rockefeller (W.Va.)—Jan. 15, 1985
39. Sanford (N.C.)—Nov. 5, 1986
40. Breaux (La.) (ex-rep., eight House terms)—Jan. 6, 1987
41. Adams (Wash.) (ex-rep., six House terms)—Jan. 6, 1987
    Wirth (Colo.) (ex-rep., six House terms)—Jan. 6, 1987
43. Fowler (Ga.) (ex-rep., five House terms)—Jan. 6, 1987
    Mikulski (Md.) (ex-rep., five House terms)—Jan. 6, 1987
45. Daschle (S.D.) (ex-rep., four House terms)—Jan. 6, 1987
    Shelby (Ala.) (ex-rep., four House terms)—Jan. 6, 1987
47. Reid (Nev.) (ex-rep., two House terms)—Jan. 6, 1987
48. Graham (Fla.) (ex-governor)—Jan. 6, 1987
49. Conrad (N.D.)—Jan. 6, 1987
50. Bryan (Nev.) (ex-governor)—Jan. 3, 1989
    Kerrey (Neb.) (ex-governor)—Jan. 3, 1989
    Robb (Va.) (ex-governor)—Jan. 3, 1989
53. Kohl (Wis.)—Jan. 3, 1989
    Lieberman (Conn.)—Jan. 3, 1989
55. Akaka (Hawaii) (ex-rep.)—April 28, 1990
56. Wellstone (Minn.)—Jan. 3, 1991
57. Wofford (Pa.)—May 8, 1991

REPUBLICANS

1. Thurmond (S.C.)—Nov. 7, 1956*
2. Hatfield (Ore.)—Jan. 10, 1967
3. Stevens (Alaska)—Dec. 24, 1968
4. Dole (Kan.) (ex-rep.)—Jan. 3, 1969
5. Packwood (Ore.)—Jan. 3, 1969
6. Roth (Del.)—Jan. 1, 1971
7. Helms (N.C.)—Jan. 3, 1973
   Domenici (N.M.)—Jan. 3, 1973
9. Garn (Utah)—Dec. 21, 1974
10. Danforth (Mo.)—Dec. 27, 1976
11. Chafee (R.I.)—Dec. 29, 1976
12. Hatch (Utah)—Jan. 3, 1977
    Lugar (Ind.)—Jan. 3, 1977
    Wallop (Wyo.)—Jan. 3, 1977
15. Durenberger (Minn.)—Nov. 8, 1978
16. Kassebaum (Kan.)—Dec. 23, 1978
17. Cochran (Miss.)—Dec. 27, 1978
18. Simpson (Wyo.)—Jan. 1, 1979
19. Warner (Va.)—Jan. 2, 1979
20. Cohen (Maine) (ex-rep., three House terms)—Jan. 15, 1979
21. Pressler (S.D.) (ex-rep., two House terms)—Jan. 15, 1979
22. Rudman (N.H.)—Dec. 29, 1980
23. Symms (Idaho) (ex-rep., four House terms)—Jan. 5, 1981
24. Grassley (Iowa) (ex-rep., three House terms)—Jan. 5, 1981
25. Kasten (Wis.) (ex-rep., two House terms)—Jan. 5, 1981
26. D'Amato (N.Y.)—Jan. 5, 1981
    Murkowski (Alaska)—Jan. 5, 1981
    Nickles (Okla.)—Jan. 5, 1981
    Specter (Pa.)—Jan. 5, 1981
30. Gramm (Texas) (ex-rep.)—Jan. 3, 1985
31. McConnell (Ky.)—Jan. 3, 1985
32. McCain (Ariz.) (ex-rep.)—Jan. 6, 1987
33. Bond (Mo.) (ex-governor)—Jan. 6, 1987
34. Gorton (Wash.) (ex-senator)—Jan. 3, 1989
35. Lott (Miss.) (ex-rep., eight House terms)—Jan. 3, 1989
36. Jeffords (Vt.) (ex-rep., seven House terms)—Jan. 3, 1989
37. Coats (Ind.) (ex-rep., four House terms)—Jan. 3, 1989
38. Mack (Fla.) (ex-rep., three House terms)—Jan. 3, 1989
39. Burns (Mont.)—Jan. 3, 1989
40. Smith (N.H.)—Dec. 7, 1990
41. Brown (Colo.) (ex-rep., five House terms)—Jan. 3, 1991
    Craig (Idaho) (ex-rep., five House terms)—Jan. 3, 1991
43. Seymour (Calif.)—Jan. 7, 1991

* *Thurmond began his Senate service Nov. 7, 1956, as a Democrat. He became a Republican Sept. 16, 1964. The Republican Conference allowed his seniority to count from his 1956 election to the Senate.*

Seniority in the House

House rank generally is determined according to the official date of the beginning of a member's service, except in the case of members elected to fill vacancies, in which instance the date of election determines rank.

When members enter the House on the same day, those with prior House experience take precedence, starting with those with the longest consecutive service. Experience as a senator or governor is disregarded. Prior experience is given where applicable to seniority ranking. The dates following members' names refer to the beginning of their present service.

Bernard Sanders of Vermont was the lone independent in the House during the first session of the 102nd Congress.

DEMOCRATS

1. Whitten (Miss.)—Nov. 4, 1941
2. Bennett (Fla.)—Jan. 3, 1949
3. Brooks (Texas)—Jan. 3, 1953
4. Natcher (Ky.)—Aug. 1, 1953
5. Fascell (Fla.)—Jan. 3, 1955
6. Dingell (Mich.)—Dec. 13, 1955
7. Rostenkowski (Ill.)—Jan. 7, 1959
Smith (Iowa)—Jan. 7, 1959
9. Gonzalez (Texas)—Nov. 4, 1961
10. Edwards (Calif.)—Jan. 9, 1963
Gibbons (Fla.)—Jan. 9, 1963
Roybal (Calif.)—Jan. 9, 1963
13. Pickle (Texas)—Dec. 21, 1963
14. Yates (Ill.) (seven terms previously) —Jan. 4, 1965
15. Annunzio (Ill.)—Jan. 4, 1965
Conyers (Mich.)—Jan. 4, 1965
de la Garza (Texas)—Jan. 4, 1965
Foley (Wash.)—Jan. 4, 1965
Ford (Mich.)—Jan. 4, 1965
Hamilton (Ind.)—Jan. 4, 1965
21. Jones (N.C.)—Feb. 5, 1966
22. Bevill (Ala.)—Jan. 10, 1967
Montgomery (Miss.)—Jan. 10, 1967
24. Gaydos (Pa.)—Nov. 5, 1968
25. Alexander (Ark.)—Jan. 3, 1969
Anderson (Calif.)—Jan. 3, 1969
Clay (Mo.)—Jan. 3, 1969
Stokes (Ohio)—Jan. 3, 1969
Yatron (Pa.)—Jan. 3, 1969
30. Obey (Wis.)—April 1, 1969
31. Roe (N.J.)—Nov. 4, 1969
32. Aspin (Wis.)—Jan. 21, 1971
Dellums (Calif.)—Jan. 21, 1971
Mazzoli (Ky.)—Jan. 21, 1971
Rangel (N.Y.)—Jan. 21, 1971
36. Brown (Calif.) (four terms previously)—Jan. 3, 1973
37. Lehman (Fla.)—Jan. 3, 1973
Moakley (Mass.)—Jan. 3, 1973
Rose (N.C.)—Jan. 3, 1973
Schroeder (Colo.)—Jan. 3, 1973
Stark (Calif.)—Jan. 3, 1973
Studds (Mass.)—Jan. 3, 1973
Wilson (Texas)—Jan. 3, 1973
44. Collins (Ill.)—June 5, 1973
45. Murtha (Pa.)—Feb. 5, 1974
46. Traxler (Mich.)—April 16, 1974
47. Jacobs (Ind.) (four terms previously)—Jan. 14, 1975
Scheuer (N.Y.) (four terms previously)—Jan. 14, 1975
49. AuCoin (Ore.)—Jan. 14, 1975
Derrick (S.C.)—Jan. 14, 1975
Downey (N.Y.)—Jan. 14, 1975
Early (Mass.)—Jan. 14, 1975
English (Okla.)—Jan. 14, 1975
Ford (Tenn.)—Jan. 14, 1975
Hefner (N.C.)—Jan. 14, 1975
Hubbard (Ky.)—Jan. 14, 1975
Hughes (N.J.)—Jan. 14, 1975
LaFalce (N.Y.)—Jan. 14, 1975
Lloyd (Tenn.)—Jan. 14, 1975
McHugh (N.Y.)—Jan. 14, 1975
Miller (Calif.)—Jan. 14, 1975
Mineta (Calif.)—Jan. 14, 1975
Neal (N.C.)—Jan. 14, 1975
Nowak (N.Y.)—Jan. 14, 1975
Oberstar (Minn.)—Jan. 14, 1975
Russo (Ill.)—Jan. 14, 1975
Sharp (Ind.)—Jan. 14, 1975
Solarz (N.Y.)—Jan. 14, 1975
Waxman (Calif.)—Jan. 14, 1975
70. Markey (Mass.)—Nov. 2, 1976
71. Applegate (Ohio)—Jan. 4, 1977
Barnard (Ga.)—Jan. 4, 1977
Beilenson (Calif.)—Jan. 4, 1977
Bonior (Mich.)—Jan. 4, 1977
Dicks (Wash.)—Jan. 4, 1977
Gephardt (Mo.)—Jan. 4, 1977
Glickman (Kan.)—Jan. 4, 1977
Huckaby (La.)—Jan. 4, 1977
Jenkins (Ga.)—Jan. 4, 1977
Kildee (Mich.)—Jan. 4, 1977
Murphy (Pa.)—Jan. 4, 1977
Oakar (Ohio)—Jan. 4, 1977
Panetta (Calif.)—Jan. 4, 1977
Pease (Ohio)—Jan. 4, 1977
Rahall (W.Va.)—Jan. 4, 1977
Skelton (Mo.)—Jan. 4, 1977
Vento (Minn.)—Jan. 4, 1977
Volkmer (Mo.)—Jan. 4, 1977
Weiss (N.Y.)—Jan. 4, 1977
90. Anthony (Ark.)—Jan. 15, 1979
Byron (Md.)—Jan. 15, 1979
Dixon (Calif.)—Jan. 15, 1979
Donnelly (Mass.)—Jan. 15, 1979
Fazio (Calif.)—Jan. 15, 1979
Frost (Texas)—Jan. 15, 1979
Guarini (N.J.)—Jan. 15, 1979
Hall (Ohio)—Jan. 15, 1979
Hutto (Fla.)—Jan. 15, 1979
Matsui (Calif.)—Jan. 15, 1979
Mavroules (Mass.)—Jan. 15, 1979
Sabo (Minn.)—Jan. 15, 1979
Stenholm (Texas)—Jan. 15, 1979
Swift (Wash.)—Jan. 15, 1979
Synar (Okla.)—Jan. 15, 1979
Williams (Mont.)—Jan. 15, 1979
Wolpe (Mich.)—Jan. 15, 1979
107. Tauzin (La.)—May 17, 1980
108. Coyne (Pa.)—Jan. 5, 1981
Dorgan (N.D.)—Jan. 5, 1981
Dwyer (N.J.)—Jan. 5, 1981
Dymally (Calif.)—Jan. 5, 1981
Eckart (Ohio)—Jan. 5, 1981
Foglietta (Pa.)—Jan. 5, 1981
Frank (Mass.)—Jan. 5, 1981
Gejdenson (Conn.)—Jan. 5, 1981
Hall (Texas)—Jan. 5, 1981
Hatcher (Ga.)—Jan. 5, 1981
Hertel (Mich.)—Jan. 5, 1981
Lantos (Calif.)—Jan. 5, 1981
McCurdy (Okla.)—Jan. 5, 1981
Savage (Ill.)—Jan. 5, 1981
Schumer (N.Y.)—Jan. 5, 1981
Wyden (Ore.)—Jan. 5, 1981
124. Hoyer (Md.)—May 19, 1981
125. Kennelly (Conn.)—Jan. 12, 1982
126. Martinez (Calif.)—July 13, 1982
127. Carr (Mich.) (three terms previously)—Jan. 3, 1983
128. Kostmayer (Pa.) (two terms previously)—Jan. 3, 1983
129. Andrews (Texas)—Jan. 3, 1983
Berman (Calif.)—Jan. 3, 1983
Borski (Pa.)—Jan. 3, 1983
Boucher (Va.)—Jan. 3, 1983
Boxer (Calif.)—Jan. 3, 1983
Bryant (Texas)—Jan. 3, 1983
Carper (Del.)—Jan. 3, 1983
Coleman (Texas)—Jan. 3, 1983
Cooper (Tenn.)—Jan. 3, 1983
Durbin (Ill.)—Jan. 3, 1983
Erdreich (Ala.)—Jan. 3, 1983
Evans (Ill.)—Jan. 3, 1983
Feighan (Ohio)—Jan. 3, 1983
Kaptur (Ohio)—Jan. 3, 1983
Kolter (Pa.)—Jan. 3, 1983
Lehman (Calif.)—Jan. 3, 1983
Levin (Mich.)—Jan. 3, 1983
Levine (Calif.)—Jan. 3, 1983
Lipinski (Ill.)—Jan. 3, 1983
McCloskey (Ind.)—Jan. 3, 1983
Mollohan (W.Va.)—Jan. 3, 1983
Moody (Wis.)—Jan. 3, 1983
Mrazek (N.Y.)—Jan. 3, 1983
Olin (Va.)—Jan. 3, 1983
Ortiz (Texas)—Jan. 3, 1983
Owens (N.Y.)—Jan. 3, 1983
Penny (Minn.)—Jan. 3, 1983
Ray (Ga.)—Jan. 3, 1983
Richardson (N.M.)—Jan. 3, 1983
Rowland (Ga.)—Jan. 3, 1983
Sikorski (Minn.)—Jan. 3, 1983
Sisisky (Va.)—Jan. 3, 1983
Slattery (Kan.)—Jan. 3, 1983
Smith (Fla.)—Jan. 3, 1983
Spratt (S.C.)—Jan. 3, 1983
Staggers (W.Va.)—Jan. 3, 1983
Tallon (S.C.)—Jan. 3, 1983
Thomas (Ga.)—Jan. 3, 1983
Torres (Calif.)—Jan. 3, 1983
Torricelli (N.J.)—Jan. 3, 1983
Towns (N.Y.)—Jan. 3, 1983
Valentine (N.C.)—Jan. 3, 1983
Wheat (Mo.)—Jan. 3, 1983
Wise (W.Va.)—Jan. 3, 1983
173. Ackerman (N.Y.)—March 1, 1983
174. Hayes (Ill.)—Aug. 23, 1983
175. Darden (Ga.)—Nov. 8, 1983
176. Kleczka (Wis.)—April 3, 1984
177. Perkins (Ky.)—Nov. 6, 1984

178. Atkins (Mass.)—Jan. 3, 1985
Bruce (Ill.)—Jan. 3, 1985
Bustamante (Texas)—Jan. 3, 1985
Gordon (Tenn.)—Jan. 3, 1985
Kanjorski (Pa.)—Jan. 3, 1985
Manton (N.Y.)—Jan. 3, 1985
Stallings (Idaho)—Jan. 3, 1985
Traficant (Ohio)—Jan. 3, 1985
Visclosky (Ind.)—Jan. 3, 1985
187. Chapman (Texas)—Aug. 3, 1985
188. Owens (Utah) (one term previously)—Jan. 6, 1987
189. Bilbray (Nev.)—Jan. 6, 1987
Campbell (Colo.)—Jan. 6, 1987
Cardin (Md.)—Jan. 6, 1987
DeFazio (Ore.)—Jan. 6, 1987
Espy (Miss.)—Jan. 6, 1987
Flake (N.Y.)—Jan. 6, 1987
Harris (Ala.)—Jan. 6, 1987
Hayes (La.)—Jan. 6, 1987
Hochbrueckner (N.Y.)—Jan. 6, 1987
Johnson (S.D.)—Jan. 6, 1987
Jontz (Ind.)—Jan. 6, 1987
Kennedy (Mass.)—Jan. 6, 1987
Lancaster (N.C.)—Jan. 6, 1987
Lewis (Ga.)—Jan. 6, 1987
McMillen (Md.)—Jan. 6, 1987
Mfume (Md.)—Jan. 6, 1987
Nagle (Iowa)—Jan. 6, 1987
Patterson (S.C.)—Jan. 6, 1987
Pickett (Va.)—Jan. 6, 1987
Price (N.C.)—Jan. 6, 1987
Sawyer (Ohio)—Jan. 6, 1987
Skaggs (Colo.)—Jan. 6, 1987
Slaughter (N.Y.)—Jan. 6, 1987
212. Pelosi (Calif.)—June 2, 1987
213. Clement (Tenn.)—Jan. 19, 1988
214. Payne (Va.)—June 14, 1988
215. Costello (Ill.)—Aug. 9, 1988
216. Pallone (N.J.)—Nov. 8, 1988
217. Engel (N.Y.)—Jan. 3, 1989
Hoagland (Neb.)—Jan. 3, 1989
Johnston (Fla.)—Jan. 3, 1989
Jones (Ga.)—Jan. 3, 1989
Laughlin (Texas)—Jan. 3, 1989
Lowey (N.Y.)—Jan. 3, 1989
McDermott (Wash.)—Jan. 3, 1989
McNulty (N.Y.)—Jan. 3, 1989
Neal (Mass.)—Jan. 3, 1989
Parker (Miss.)—Jan. 3, 1989
Payne (N.J.)—Jan. 3, 1989
Poshard (Ill.)—Jan. 3, 1989
Sangmeister (Ill.)—Jan. 3, 1989
Sarpalius (Texas)—Jan. 3, 1989
Tanner (Tenn.)—Jan. 3, 1989
Unsoeld (Wash.)—Jan. 3, 1989
233. Long (Ind.)—March 28, 1989
234. Browder (Ala.)—April 4, 1989
235. Condit (Calif.)—Sept. 12, 1989
Geren (Texas)—Sept. 12, 1989
237. Taylor (Miss.)—Oct. 17, 1989
238. Washington (Texas)—Dec. 9, 1989
239. Serrano (N.Y.)—March 20, 1990
240. Mink (Hawaii)—Sept. 22, 1990
241. Andrews (N.J.)—Nov. 6, 1990
242. Thornton (Ark.) (three terms previously)—Jan. 3, 1991
243. Abercrombie (Hawaii) (one term previously)—Jan. 3, 1991
244. Andrews (Maine)—Jan. 3, 1991
Bacchus (Fla.)—Jan. 3, 1991
Brewster (Okla.)—Jan. 3, 1991
Collins (Mich.)—Jan. 3, 1991
Cox (Ill.)—Jan. 3, 1991
Cramer (Ala.)—Jan. 3, 1991
DeLauro (Conn.)—Jan. 3, 1991
Dooley (Calif.)—Jan. 3, 1991
Edwards (Texas)—Jan. 3, 1991
Horn (Mo.)—Jan. 3, 1991
Jefferson (La.)—Jan. 3, 1991
Kopetski (Ore.)—Jan. 3, 1991
LaRocco (Idaho)—Jan. 3, 1991
Luken (Ohio)—Jan. 3, 1991
Moran (Va.)—Jan. 3, 1991
Orton (Utah)—Jan. 3, 1991
Peterson (Fla.)—Jan. 3, 1991
Peterson (Minn.)—Jan. 3, 1991
Reed (R.I.)—Jan. 3, 1991
Roemer (Ind.)—Jan. 3, 1991
Swett (N.H.)—Jan. 3, 1991
Waters (Calif.)—Jan. 3, 1991
266. Olver (Mass.)—June 4, 1991
267. Pastor (Ariz.)—Sept. 24, 1991
268. Blackwell (Pa.)—Nov. 5, 1991

REPUBLICANS

1. Broomfield (Mich.)—Jan. 3, 1957
Michel (Ill.)—Jan. 3, 1957
3. Horton (N.Y.)—Jan. 9, 1963
McDade (Pa.)—Jan. 9, 1963
Quillen (Tenn.)—Jan. 9, 1963
6. Dickinson (Ala.)—Jan. 4, 1965
7. Vander Jagt (Mich.)—Nov. 8, 1966
8. Hammerschmidt (Ark.)—Jan. 10, 1967
Miller (Ohio)—Jan. 10, 1967
Myers (Ind.)—Jan. 10, 1967
Wylie (Ohio)—Jan. 10, 1967
12. Coughlin (Pa.)—Jan. 3, 1969
Fish (N.Y.)—Jan. 3, 1969
14. Crane (Ill.)—Nov. 25, 1969
15. Archer (Texas)—Jan. 21, 1971
Lent (N.Y.)—Jan. 21, 1971
Spence (S.C.)—Jan. 21, 1971
Young (Fla.)—Jan. 21, 1971
19. Gilman (N.Y.)—Jan. 3, 1973
Moorhead (Calif.)—Jan. 3, 1973
Regula (Ohio)—Jan. 3, 1973
Rinaldo (N.J.)—Jan. 3, 1973
Shuster (Pa.)—Jan. 3, 1973
24. Young (Alaska)—March 6, 1973
25. Lagomarsino (Calif.)—March 5, 1974
26. Goodling (Pa.)—Jan. 14, 1975
Gradison (Ohio)—Jan. 14, 1975
Hyde (Ill.)—Jan. 14, 1975
Schulze (Pa.)—Jan. 14, 1975
30. Coleman (Mo.)—Nov. 2, 1976
31. Edwards (Okla.)—Jan. 4, 1977
Ireland (Fla.)—Jan. 4, 1977*
Leach (Iowa)—Jan. 4, 1977
Marlenee (Mont.)—Jan. 4, 1977
Pursell (Mich.)—Jan. 4, 1977
Stump (Ariz.)—Jan. 4, 1977*
Walker (Pa.)—Jan. 4, 1977
38. Livingston (La.)—Aug. 27, 1977
39. Green (N.Y.)—Feb. 14, 1978
40. Bereuter (Neb.)—Jan. 15, 1979
Clinger (Pa.)—Jan. 15, 1979
Dannemeyer (Calif.)—Jan. 15, 1979
Davis (Mich.)—Jan. 15, 1979
Gingrich (Ga.)—Jan. 15, 1979
Hopkins (Ky.)—Jan. 15, 1979
Lewis (Calif.)—Jan. 15, 1979
Ritter (Pa.)—Jan. 15, 1979
Roth (Wis.)—Jan. 15, 1979
Sensenbrenner (Wis.)—Jan. 15, 1979
Snowe (Maine)—Jan. 15, 1979
Solomon (N.Y.)—Jan. 15, 1979
Thomas (Calif.)—Jan. 15, 1979
53. Petri (Wis.)—April 3, 1979
54. Porter (Ill.)—Jan. 22, 1980
55. Bliley (Va.)—Jan. 5, 1981
Dreier (Calif.)—Jan. 5, 1981
Emerson (Mo.)—Jan. 5, 1981
Fields (Texas)—Jan. 5, 1981
Gunderson (Wis.)—Jan. 5, 1981
Hansen (Utah)—Jan. 5, 1981
Hunter (Calif.)—Jan. 5, 1981
Lowery (Calif.)—Jan. 5, 1981
Martin (N.Y.)—Jan. 5, 1981
McCollum (Fla.)—Jan. 5, 1981
McEwen (Ohio)—Jan. 5, 1981
McGrath (N.Y.)—Jan. 5, 1981
Morrison (Wash.)—Jan. 5, 1981
Roberts (Kan.)—Jan. 5, 1981
Rogers (Ky.)—Jan. 5, 1981
Roukema (N.J.)—Jan. 5 1981
Shaw (Fla.)—Jan. 5, 1981
Skeen (N.M.)—Jan. 5, 1981
Smith (N.J.) Jan. 5, 1981
Weber (Minn.)—Jan. 5, 1981
Wolf (Va.)—Jan. 5, 1981
76. Oxley (Ohio)—June 25, 1981
77. Bateman (Va.)—Jan. 3, 1983
Bilirakis (Fla.)—Jan. 3, 1983
Boehlert (N.Y.)—Jan. 3, 1983
Burton (Ind.)—Jan. 3, 1983
Chandler (Wash.)—Jan. 3, 1983
Gekas (Pa.)—Jan. 3, 1983
Johnson (Conn.)—Jan. 3, 1983
Kasich (Ohio)—Jan. 3, 1983
Lewis (Fla.)—Jan. 3, 1983
McCandless (Calif.)—Jan. 3, 1983
Packard (Calif.)—Jan. 3, 1983
Ridge (Pa.)—Jan. 3, 1983
Smith, Robert F. (Ore.)—Jan. 3, 1983
Sundquist (Tenn.)—Jan. 3, 1983
Vucanovich (Nev.)—Jan. 3, 1983
92. Schaefer (Colo.)—March 29, 1983
93. Saxton (N.J.)—Nov. 6, 1984
94. Dornan (Calif.) (three terms previously)—Jan. 3, 1985
95. Armey (Texas)—Jan. 3, 1985
Barton (Texas)—Jan. 3, 1985
Bentley (Md.)—Jan. 3, 1985
Callahan (Ala.)—Jan. 3, 1985
Coble (N.C.)—Jan. 3, 1985
Combest (Texas)—Jan. 3, 1985
DeLay (Texas)—Jan. 3, 1985
Fawell (Ill.)—Jan. 3, 1985
Gallo (N.J.)—Jan. 3, 1985
Henry (Mich.)—Jan. 3, 1985
Kolbe (Ariz.)—Jan. 3, 1985
Lightfoot (Iowa)—Jan. 3, 1985
McMillan (N.C.)—Jan. 3, 1985
Meyers (Kan.)—Jan. 3, 1985
Miller (Wash.)—Jan. 3, 1985
110. Ballenger (N.C.)—Nov. 4, 1986
111. Baker (La.)—Jan. 6, 1987
Bunning (Ky.)—Jan. 6, 1987
Gallegly (Calif.)—Jan. 6, 1987

Grandy (Iowa)—Jan. 6, 1987
Hastert (Ill.)—Jan. 6, 1987
Hefley (Colo.)—Jan. 6, 1987
Herger (Calif.)—Jan. 6, 1987
Holloway (La.)—Jan. 6, 1987
Houghton (N.Y.)—Jan. 6, 1987
Inhofe (Okla.)—Jan. 6, 1987
Kyl (Ariz.)—Jan. 6, 1987
Morella (Md.)—Jan. 6, 1987
Ravenel (S.C.)—Jan. 6, 1987
Rhodes (Ariz.)—Jan. 6, 1987
Smith (Texas)—Jan. 6, 1987
Upton (Mich.)—Jan. 6, 1987
Weldon (Pa.)—Jan. 6, 1987
128. Shays (Conn.)—Aug. 18, 1987
129. McCrery (La.)—April 16, 1988
130. Duncan (Tenn.)—Nov. 8, 1988
131. Campbell (Calif.)—Jan. 3, 1989
Cox (Calif.)—Jan. 3, 1989
Gillmor (Ohio)—Jan. 3, 1989
Goss (Fla.)—Jan. 3, 1989
Hancock (Mo.)—Jan. 3, 1989
James (Fla.)—Jan. 3, 1989
Machtley (R.I.)—Jan. 3, 1989
Paxon (N.Y.)—Jan. 3, 1989
Rohrabacher (Calif.)—Jan. 3, 1989
Schiff (N.M.)—Jan. 3, 1989
Stearns (Fla.)—Jan. 3, 1989
Walsh (N.Y.)—Jan. 3, 1989
143. Thomas (Wyo.)—April 26, 1989
144. Ros-Lehtinen (Fla.)—Aug. 29, 1989
145. Molinari (N.Y.)—March 20, 1990
146. Allard (Colo.)—Jan. 3, 1991
Barrett (Neb.)—Jan. 3, 1991
Boehner (Ohio)—Jan. 3, 1991
Camp (Mich.)—Jan. 3, 1991
Cunningham (Calif.)—Jan. 3, 1991
Doolittle (Calif.)—Jan. 3, 1991
Franks (Conn.)—Jan. 3, 1991
Gilchrest (Md.)—Jan. 3, 1991
Hobson (Ohio)—Jan. 3, 1991
Klug (Wis.)—Jan. 3, 1991
Nichols (Kan.)—Jan. 3, 1991
Nussle (Iowa)—Jan. 3, 1991
Ramstad (Minn.)—Jan. 3, 1991
Riggs (Calif.)—Jan. 3, 1991
Santorum (Pa.)—Jan. 3, 1991
Taylor (N.C.)—Jan. 3, 1991
Zeliff (N.H.)—Jan. 3, 1991
Zimmer (N.J.)—Jan. 3, 1991
164. Johnson (Texas)—May 18, 1991
165. Ewing (Ill.)—July 2, 1991
166. Allen (Va.)—Nov.5, 1991

** Ireland and Stump began House service Jan. 4, 1977, as Democrats, but later switched parties. The Republican Conference let their seniority count from 1977.*

The Committees: Influence and Power

The bulk of congressional work is done in committees, not on the floor of the House or Senate. Legislation is written by committees; hearings are held by committees; oversight investigations are conducted by committees.

Especially in the House, influence often is closely related to the committee or committees on which a member serves. Assignment to a powerful committee virtually guarantees large campaign contributions.

While many members seek a particular committee because they have an interest in issues within that panel's jurisdiction, others' preferences are based on political need. Members from large agricultural districts gravitate toward the Agriculture committees. Those from districts with major military installations often seek out the Armed Services panels.

Traditionally, the premier committees sought by representatives to the House have been Appropriations, Ways and Means, and Rules, although Rules had lost some of its attraction in recent years. In the last several years, members have also sought seats on Budget and on Energy and Commerce.

In the Senate, where the members serve on more panels, the most popular committees have traditionally been Appropriations and Finance. Both the Budget and Armed Services committees have also been in demand.

Some panels wax and wane, but Finance, Appropriations, and Ways and Means are never eclipsed because they control the flow of money into and out of federal coffers. These committees have been thrust to the center of action by Congress' recent tendency to pile much of its legislative work onto a handful of fiscal measures.

Those members on panels that draft omnibus bills — such as continuing appropriations resolutions and debt-limit legislation — enjoy privileged access to the bulk of Congress' work.

Major vs. Minor

In both chambers, committees are ranked as major and minor. In the House, Energy and Commerce is a major committee, while Post Office and Civil Service is a minor committee. Agriculture, Nutrition and Forestry is a major Senate committee, while Small Business is minor.

In most cases the distinction is based on the traditional importance of the panel. But both the House and Senate Budget committees are classified as minor, even though they often have been in the limelight in recent years.

The House also has three "exclusive" committees — Appropriations, Rules, and Ways and Means — whose members generally cannot serve on other committees. In addition to these three, the House has eight major and 10 minor committees.

In the Senate, there are 12 major and 10 minor committees. While representatives generally serve on only two panels — and sometimes just one — senators often serve on four. The feeling that senators were stretched too thin by serving on too many panels led Senate leaders to seek stricter enforcement in 1985 of the Senate rule that limited senators to two major committees and one minor panel. Usually, the chairman of a committee is the member of the majority party with the most committee seniority.

Senate

Senate Democrats were able to make the all-important majority assignments for the 102nd Congress and the two previous ones, having won back majority status in the 1986 elections.

The number of senators on each committee, as well as the ratio of Republicans to Democrats, is generally determined through negotiations between leaders of the parties. The majority party, however, clearly holds the upper hand.

Democratic senators are assigned to committee openings by the Democratic Steering Committee, which bases its assignments on members' desires and seniority.

A question of seniority arose in 1987 in the Republican ranks when Senate Republicans named Jesse Helms of North Carolina ranking minority member of the Foreign Relations committee, defeating Richard G. Lugar of Indiana, who had served as the panel's chairman since 1985. Both men joined the committee on the same day in 1979, but Helms claimed seniority by virtue of his longer service in the Senate.

Lugar had argued that a reform voted for by Senate Republicans in 1973 had eliminated the traditional requirements that seniority be the sole criterion by which committee chairmen and ranking members were chosen.

Helms, however, said seniority was the issue and other Republicans obviously agreed. Lugar immediately took the position of ranking Republican on the Agriculture Committee, which Helms had chaired when the Republicans controlled the Senate.

House

Democrats are assigned to House committees by the 33-member Democratic Steering and Policy Committee, chaired by Speaker of the House Thomas S. Foley, Wash. The committee consists of 12 members elected by region, nine appointed by Foley and 12 who hold party leadership jobs.

A member seeking a particular committee must be nominated by a member of Steering and Policy, so it helps to have a patron on the inside.

House Republicans get their assignments from the Republican Committee on Committees, chaired by Minority Leader Robert H. Michel, R-Ill. It has 21 members: Michel and the whip, representatives elected from the freshman and sophomore classes, and members elected according to the voting strength of their states. ■

Key to Listings, Abbreviations

Order of Lists

In the committee sections, Democrats are listed on the left in roman type. Republicans are on the right *in italics.*

Members of legislative committees and subcommittees are listed in order of their seniority on those panels.

Members of party committees are listed alphabetically.

Room and Telephone Numbers

Phone and room numbers are listed for each committee and subcommittee, and for the key staffers of committees. All mail should be addressed to the main committee rooms. Phone and room numbers for all members on Congress may be found on pages 68-D and 69-D.

To reach the U.S. Capitol switchboard, call (202) 224-3121.

Buildings, Addresses, ZIP codes

The following abbreviations are used for congresssional office buildings:

- SD — Dirksen Senate Office Building
- SH — Hart Senate Office Building
- SR — Russell Senate Office Building
- CHOB — Cannon House Office Building
- LHOB — Longworth House Office Building
- RHOB — Rayburn House Office Building
- OHOB — O'Neill House Office Building
- FHOB — Ford House Office Building

A map of Capitol Hill showing the location of each building appears on page 73-D.

The ZIP code for all mail addressed to offices of the Senate is 20510; for the House, 20515.

Joint Committees, 102nd Congress

(As of Nov. 27, 1991)

JOINT ECONOMIC

Phone: 224-5171 Room: SD-G01

Executive Director: Steve Quick 224-5171 SD-G01
Minority Staff Director: Edward Gillespie 224-0374 SH-805

Studies and investigates all recommendations in the president's annual Economic Report to Congress. Reports findings and recommendations to the House and Senate.

Senate Members

Paul S. Sarbanes, Md., chairman	*William V. Roth Jr., Del.*
Lloyd Bentsen, Texas	*Steve Symms, Idaho*
Edward M. Kennedy, Mass.	*Connie Mack, Fla.*
Jeff Bingaman, N.M.	*Robert C. Smith, N.H.*
Al Gore, Tenn.	
Richard H. Bryan, Nev.	

House Members

Lee H. Hamilton, Ind., vice chairman	*Dick Armey, Texas*
David R. Obey, Wis.	*Chalmers P. Wylie, Ohio*
James H. Scheuer, N.Y.	*Olympia J. Snowe, Maine*
Pete Stark, Calif.	*Hamilton Fish Jr., N.Y.*
Stephen J. Solarz, N.Y.	
Kweisi Mfume, Md.	

SUBCOMMITTEES

Economic Goals and Intergovernmental Policy

Phone: 224-5171 **Room: SD-G01**

Hamilton, chairman	*Roth*
Bentsen	*Wylie*
Mfume	*Snowe*
Kennedy	

Economic Growth, Trade and Taxes

Phone: 224-5171 **Room: SD-G01**

Bentsen, chairman	*Roth*
Hamilton	*Wylie*
Stark	*Mack*
Solarz	*Fish*

Economic Resources and Competitiveness

Phone: 224-5171 **Room: SD-G01**

Obey, chairman	*Armey*
Sarbanes	*Symms*
Solarz	
Bingaman	
Gore	
Bryan	

Education and Health

Phone: 224-5171 **Room: SD-G01**

Scheuer, chairman
Bentsen
Bingaman
Gore

Snowe
Smith
Fish

Fiscal and Monetary Policy

Phone: 224-5171 **Room: SD-G01**

Kennedy, chairman
Obey
Stark

Fish
Symms
Smith

International Economic Policy

Phone: 224-5171 **Room: SD-G01**

Sarbanes, chairman
Hamilton
Kennedy
Solarz

Roth
Mack
Wylie
Snowe

Investment, Jobs and Prices

Phone: 224-5171 **Room: SD-G01**

Stark, chairman
Gore
Scheuer
Bryan

Armey
Symms

Technology and National Security

Phone: 224-5171 **Room: SD-G01**

Bingaman, chairman
Obey
Sarbanes
Scheuer
Bryan
Mfume

Mack
Armey
Smith

JOINT LIBRARY

Phone: 226-7633 **Room: SR-305**

Staff Director: William Cochrane 224-6352 SR-305
Vice Staff Director: Hilary Lieber 226-7633 103 HOB1

Management and expansion of the Library of Congress; receipt of gifts for the benefit of the library; development and maintenance of the Botanic Garden; placement of statues and other works of art in the Capitol.

Senate Members

Claiborne Pell, R.I., chairman
Dennis DeConcini, Ariz.
Daniel Patrick Moynihan, N.Y.

Mark O. Hatfield, Ore.
Ted Stevens, Alaska

House Members

Charlie Rose, N.C, vice chairman
Joe Kolter, Pa.
Thomas J. Manton, N.Y.

Bill Barrett, Neb.
Pat Roberts, Kan.

JOINT PRINTING

Phone: 224-5241 **Room: SH-818**

Staff Director: John Merritt 224-5241 SH-818

Probes inefficiency and waste in the printing, binding and distribution of federal government publications. Oversees arrangement and style of the Congressional Record.

Senate Members

Wendell H. Ford, Ky., vice chairman
Dennis DeConcini, Ariz.
Al Gore, Tenn.

Ted Stevens, Alaska
Mark O. Hatfield, Ore.

House Members

Charlie Rose, N.C., chairman
Sam Gejdenson, Conn.
Gerald D. Kleczka, Wis.

Pat Roberts, Kan.
Newt Gingrich, Ga.

JOINT TAXATION

Phone: 225-3621 **Room: 1015 LHOB**

Chief of Staff: Harry L. Gutman 225-3621 1015 LHOB

Operation, effects and administration of the federal system of internal revenue taxes; measures and methods for simplification taxes.

Senate Members

Lloyd Bentsen, Texas, vice chairman
Daniel Patrick Moynihan, N.Y.
Max Baucus, Mont.

Bob Packwood, Ore.
Bob Dole, Kan.

House Members

Dan Rostenkowski, Ill., chairman
Sam M. Gibbons, Fla.
J.J. Pickle, Texas

Bill Archer, Texas
Guy Vander Jagt, Mich.

Party Committees

SENATE DEMOCRATS

President Pro Tempore .... Robert C. Byrd, W.Va.
Majority Leader .... George J. Mitchell, Maine
Majority Whip.......................... Wendell H. Ford, Ky.
Conference Chairman............. George J. Mitchell, Maine
Conference Secretary...................... David Pryor, Ark.
Assistant Floor Leader................ Wyche Fowler Jr., Ga.
Chief Deputy Whip .... Alan J. Dixon, Ill.

Deputy Whips (by region, each with an assistant deputy whip):

East.................................. Patrick J. Leahy, Vt.
Barbara A. Mikulski, Md.

South .... Bob Graham, Fla.
Charles S. Robb, Va.

Midwest .... Tom Harkin, Iowa
Tom Daschle, S.D.

West .... Tim Wirth, Colo.
Brock Adams, Wash.

Policy Committee

Phone: 224-5551 **Room: S-118**

Schedules legislation, reviews legislative proposals and provides recommendations.

George J. Mitchell, Maine, chairman
Tom Daschle, S.D., co-chairman
Jeff Bingaman, N.M., vice chairman
John Glenn, Ohio, vice chairman
Terry Sanford, N.C., vice chairman
Paul S. Sarbanes, Md., vice chairman

Richard H. Bryan, Nev.
Dale Bumpers, Ark.
Quentin N. Burdick, N.D.
Wendell H. Ford, Ky.
Howell Heflin, Ala.
Ernest F. Hollings, S.C.
Herb Kohl, Wis.
Frank R. Lautenberg, N.J.
Daniel Patrick Moynihan, N.Y.
Claiborne Pell, R.I.
David Pryor, Ark.
Donald W. Riegle Jr., Mich.
Charles S. Robb, Va.
John D. Rockefeller IV, W.Va.
Tim Wirth, Colo.

Steering Committee

Phone: 224-3735 **Room: S-309**

Makes Democratic committee assignments.

Daniel K. Inouye, Hawaii, chairman

Brock Adams, Wash.
Max Baucus, Mont.
Lloyd Bentsen, Texas
Joseph R. Biden Jr., Del.
David L. Boren, Okla.
Robert C. Byrd, W.Va.
Bob Graham, Fla.
Tom Harkin, Iowa
Edward M. Kennedy, Mass.
John Kerry, Mass.
Patrick J. Leahy, Vt.
Carl Levin, Mich.
Kent Conrad, N.D.
Alan Cranston, Calif.
Dennis DeConcini, Ariz.
Christopher J. Dodd, Conn.
Jim Exon, Neb.
Wendell H. Ford, Ky.
Wyche Fowler Jr., Ga.
Howard M. Metzenbaum, Ohio
George J. Mitchell, Maine
Sam Nunn, Ga.
David Pryor, Ark.
Jim Sasser, Tenn.

Democratic Senatorial Campaign Committee

Phone: 224-2447 **430 S. Capitol St., S.E. 20003**

Campaign support committee for senatorial candidates.

Charles S. Robb, Va., chairman

George J. Mitchell, Maine
John D. Rockefeller IV, W.Va.
Richard H. Bryan, Nev.
Bob Graham, Fla.
David Pryor, Ark.
Paul Simon, Ill.
Lloyd Bentsen, Texas
Joseph R. Biden Jr., Del.
Bill Bradley, N.J.
John B. Breaux, La.
Alan Cranston, Calif.
Tom Daschle, S.D.
Christopher J. Dodd, Conn.
Wyche Fowler Jr., Ga.
Al Gore, Tenn.
Daniel K. Inouye, Hawaii
J. Bennett Johnston, La.
Edward M. Kennedy, Mass.
Bob Kerrey, Neb.
John Kerry, Mass.
Herb Kohl, Wis.
Frank R. Lautenberg, N.J.
Joseph I. Lieberman, Conn.
Howard M. Metzenbaum, Ohio
Barbara A. Mikulski, Md.
Sam Nunn, Ga.
Donald W. Riegle Jr., Mich.
Jim Sasser, Tenn.
Paul Wellstone, Minn.

SENATE REPUBLICANS

Minority Leader .... Bob Dole, Kan.
Assistant Minority Leader .... Alan K. Simpson, Wyo.
Conference Chairman................... Thad Cochran, Miss.
Conference Secretary...................... Bob Kasten, Wis.

Deputy Whips:

Christopher S. Bond, Mo.
Dave Durenberger, Minn.
Nancy Landon Kassebaum, Kan.
John McCain, Ariz.
Frank H. Murkowski, Alaska
Larry Pressler, S.D.
Arlen Specter, Pa.

Policy Committee

Phone: 224-2946 **Room: SR-347**

Advises on party action and policy.

Don Nickles, Okla., chairman

John H. Chafee, R.I.
Thad Cochran, Miss.
John C. Danforth, Mo.
Bob Dole, Kan.
Trent Lott, Miss.
Richard G. Lugar, Ind.
Frank H. Murkowski, Alaska
Bob Packwood, Ore.

Pete V. Domenici, N.M.
Jake Garn, Utah
Phil Gramm, Texas
Orrin G. Hatch, Utah
Mark O. Hatfield, Ore.
Jesse Helms, N.C.
Bob Kasten, Wis.
William V. Roth Jr., Del.
Alan K. Simpson, Wyo.
Ted Stevens, Alaska
Strom Thurmond, S.C.
Malcolm Wallop, Wyo.
John W. Warner, Va.

Committee on Committees

Phone: 224-6253 **SR-487**

Makes Republican committee assignments.

Trent Lott, Miss., chairman

Connie Mack, Fla.
Frank H. Murkowski, Alaska
Robert C. Smith, N.H.

National Republican Senatorial Committee

Phone: 675-6000 **425 Second St., N.E. 20002**

Campaign support committee for Republican senatorial candidates.

Phil Gramm, Texas, chairman

Christopher S. Bond, Mo.
Hank Brown, Colo.
Conrad Burns, Mont.
Larry E. Craig, Idaho
Charles E. Grassley, Iowa
Trent Lott, Miss.
Connie Mack, Fla.
Don Nickles, Okla.
Robert C. Smith, N.H.
Steve Symms, Idaho

HOUSE DEMOCRATS

Speaker of the House .... Thomas S. Foley, Wash.
Majority Leader .... Richard A. Gephardt, Mo.
Majority Whip .... David E. Bonior, Mich.
Caucus Chairman .... Steny H. Hoyer, Md.
Caucus Vice Chairman .... Vic Fazio, Calif.
Chief Deputy Whips .... Butler Derrick, S.C.
Barbara B. Kennelly, Conn.
John Lewis, Ga.

Deputy Whips:

Tom Bevill, Ala.
Dennis E. Eckart, Ohio
Martin Frost, Texas
W. G. "Bill" Hefner, N.C.
Peter H. Kostmayer, Pa.
Norman Y. Mineta, Calif.
Charles B. Rangel, N.Y.
Marty Russo, Ill. (Floor Whip)
Martin Olav Sabo, Minn.
Patricia Schroeder, Colo.
Lawrence J. Smith, Fla.
Charles W. Stenholm, Texas
Esteban E. Torres, Calif.
Pat Williams, Mont.

Whip Task Force Chairmen:

Bart Gordon, Tenn.
David R. Obey, Wis.
Leon E. Panetta, Calif.

At-Large Whips:

Les Aspin, Wis.
Chester G. Atkins, Mass.
Les AuCoin, Ore.
Howard L. Berman, Calif.
Barbara Boxer, Calif.
Rick Boucher, Va.
Terry L. Bruce, Ill.
Benjamin L. Cardin, Md.
Bob Carr, Mich.
George "Buddy" Darden, Ga.
Rosa DeLauro, Conn.
Norm Dicks, Wash.
Brian Donnelly, Mass.
Byron L. Dorgan, N.D.
Richard J. Durbin, Ill.
Don Edwards, Calif.
Mike Espy, Miss.
Lane Evans, Ill.
William D. Ford, Mich.
Barney Frank, Mass.
Sam Gejdenson, Conn.
Dan Glickman, Kan.
Frank J. Guarini, N.J.
Ed Jenkins, Ga.
Ben Jones, Ga.
Dale E. Kildee, Mich.
H. Martin Lancaster, N.C.
Richard H. Lehman, Calif.
Mel Levine, Calif.
Nita M. Lowey, N.Y.
Robert T. Matsui, Calif.
Frank McCloskey, Ind.
Dave McCurdy, Okla.
Michael R. McNulty, N.Y.
George Miller, Calif.
James P. Moran Jr., Va.
Robert J. Mrazek, N.Y.
John P. Murtha, Pa.
Richard E. Neal, Mass.
Mary Rose Oakar, Ohio
James L. Oberstar, Minn.
Timothy J. Penny, Minn.
David Price, N.C.
Bill Richardson, N.M.
Charlie Rose, N.C.
Dan Rostenkowski, Ill.
Charles E. Schumer, N.Y.
Jose E. Serrano, N.Y.
Philip R. Sharp, Ind.
Gerry Sikorski, Minn.
Norman Sisisky, Va.
David E. Skaggs, Colo.
Louise M. Slaughter, N.Y.
John M. Spratt Jr., S.C.
Harley O. Staggers Jr., W.Va.
Al Swift, Wash.
Mike Synar, Okla.
W. J. "Billy" Tauzin, La.
Robert G. Torricelli, N.J.
Peter J. Visclosky, Ind.
Bruce F. Vento, Minn.
Harold L. Volkmer, Mo.
Craig Washington, Texas
Bob Wise, W.Va.
Howard Wolpe, Mich.
Ron Wyden, Ore.

Assistant Whips (by zone number):

1. Nancy Pelosi, Calif.; Matthew G. Martinez, Calif.
2. Jim McDermott, Wash.
3. Tim Johnson, S.D.
4. Sidney R. Yates, Ill.
5. Jim Slattery, Kan.
6. Ronald D. Coleman, Texas; John Bryant, Texas
7. Gerry E. Studds, Mass.
8. Gary L. Ackerman, N.Y.; Thomas J. Downey, N.Y.
9. Paul E. Kanjorski, Pa.
10. Sander M. Levin, Mich.; Tom Sawyer, Ohio
11. Carroll Hubbard Jr., Ky.
12. Liz J. Patterson, S.C.
13. Bud Cramer, Ala.
14. Harry A. Johnston, Fla.

Steering and Policy Committee

Phone: 225-8550 **Room: H-324**

Scheduling of legislation and Democratic committee assignments.

Thomas S. Foley, Wash., chairman
Richard A. Gephardt, Mo., vice chairman
Steny H. Hoyer, Md., second vice chairman

David E. Bonior, Mich.
Albert G. Bustamante, Texas
Butler Derrick, S.C.
Dennis E. Eckart, Ohio
Vic Fazio, Calif.
Martin Frost, Texas
Sam Gejdenson, Conn.
Dan Glickman, Kan.
Barbara B. Kennelly, Conn.
Gerald D. Kleczka, Wis.
John Lewis, Ga.
Thomas J. Manton, N.Y.
Robert T. Matsui, Calif.
Romano L. Mazzoli, Ky.
Matthew F. McHugh, N.Y.
Joe Moakley, Mass.
John P. Murtha, Pa.
Leon E. Panetta, Calif.
Dan Rostenkowski, Ill.
J. Roy Rowland, Ga.
Marty Russo, Ill.
Norman Sisisky, Va.
Lawrence J. Smith, D-Fla.
Al Swift, Wash.
Mike Synar, Okla.
W. J. "Billy" Tauzin, La.
Ray Thornton, Ark.
Alan Wheat, Mo.
Jamie L. Whitten, Miss.
Pat Williams, Mont.

Personnel Committee

Phone: 225-4068 **Room: B343**

Selects, appoints and supervises Democratic patronage positions.

Jack Brooks, Texas, chairman

Democratic Congressional Campaign Committee

Phone: 863-1500 **430 S. Capitol St. S.E. 20003**

Campaign support committee for Democratic House candidates.

Vic Fazio, Calif., chairman
Dan Rostenkowski, Ill., vice chairman
Michael A. Andrews, Texas, co-chairman
Richard J. Durbin, Ill., co-chairman
Dennis E. Eckart, Ohio, co-chairman
Thomas J. Manton, N.Y., co-chairman
Nancy Pelosi, Calif., co-chairman
Lawrence J. Smith, Fla., co-chairman
Jack Brooks, Texas, co-chairman, Chairman's Council
John D. Dingell, Mich., co-chairman, Chairman's Council
Robert G. Torricelli, N.J., co-chairman, House and Senate Council
Barbara B. Kennelly, Conn., co-chairman, Professional Business Forum

Neil Abercrombie, Hawaii
Gary L. Ackerman, N.Y.
Bill Alexander, Ark.
Thomas H. Andrews, Maine
Les Aspin, Wis.
Les AuCoin, Ore.
Howard L. Berman, Calif.
Tom Bevill, Ala.
Larry LaRocco, Idaho
Nita M. Lowey, N.Y.
Frank McCloskey, Ind.
Alan B. Mollohan, W.Va.
John P. Murtha, Pa.
Dave Nagle, Iowa
Richard E. Neal, Mass.
Eleanor Holmes Norton, D.C.
James Bilbray, Nev.
Rick Boucher, Va.
Bill Brewster, Okla.
Terry L. Bruce, Ill.
Beverly B. Byron, Md.
Thomas R. Carper, Del.
Ron de Lugo, Virgin Islands
Norm Dicks, Wash.
John D. Dingell, Mich.
Byron L. Dorgan, N.D.
Mike Espy, Miss.
Eni F. H. Faleomavaega, American Samoa
Edward F. Feighan, Ohio
Jaime B. Fuster, Puerto Rico
Bart Gordon, Tenn.
Frank J. Guarini, N.J.
Lee H. Hamilton, Ind.
Jimmy Hayes, La.
W. G. "Bill" Hefner, N.C.
Peter Hoagland, Neb.
Ed Jenkins, Ga.
Tim Johnson, S.D.
Barbara B. Kennelly, Conn.
H. Martin Lancaster, N.C.
Mary Rose Oakar, Ohio
James L. Oberstar, Minn.
David R. Obey, Wis.
Wayne Owens, Utah
Ed Pastor, Ariz.
Carl C. Perkins, Ky.
Pete Peterson, Fla.
John F. Reed, R.I.
Bill Richardson, N.M.
Martin Olav Sabo, Minn.
Patricia Schroeder, Colo.
Jim Slattery, Kan.
Neal Smith, Iowa
John M. Spratt Jr., S.C.
Charles W. Stenholm, Texas
Dick Swett, N.H.
Mike Synar, Okla.
W. J. "Billy" Tauzin, La.
Esteban E. Torres, Calif.
Harold L. Volkmer, Mo.
Craig Washington, Texas
Maxine Waters, Calif.
Pat Williams, Mont.
Ron Wyden, Ore.

HOUSE REPUBLICANS

Minority Leader .... Robert H. Michel, Ill.
Minority Whip .... Newt Gingrich, Ga.
Conference Chairman .... Jerry Lewis, Calif.
Conference Vice Chairman .... Bill McCollum, Fla.
Conference Secretary .... Vin Weber, Minn.
Chief Deputy Whips .... Steve Gunderson, Wis.
Robert S. Walker, Pa.

Deputy Whips:

Joe L. Barton, Texas
Andy Ireland, Fla.
Gerald B. H. Solomon, N.Y.
Fred Upton, Mich.

Assistant Deputy Whips:

Thomas J. Bliley Jr., Va.
Olympia J. Snowe, Maine
Bill Paxon, N.Y.

Regional Whips:

Dean A. Gallo, N.J.
Dennis Hastert, Ill.
Robert L. Livingston, La.
John Miller, Wash.

Committee on Committees

Phone: 225-0600 **Room: H-230**

Makes Republican committee assignments.

Robert H. Michel, Ill., chairman

Wayne Allard, Colo.
Bill Archer, Texas
Rod Chandler, Wash.
Bill Dickinson, Ala.
Mickey Edwards, Okla.
Newt Gingrich, Ga.
Dennis Hastert, Ill.
Frank Horton, N.Y.
Jim McCrery, La.
Joseph M. McDade, Pa.
Ron Packard, Calif.
Tom Petri, Wis.
Carl D. Pursell, Mich.
Ralph Regula, Ohio
Matthew J. Rinaldo, N.J.
Harold Rogers, Ky.
Cliff Stearns, Fla.
Bob Stump, Ariz.
Don Young, Alaska
C.W. Bill Young, Fla.

Policy Committee

Phone: 225-6168 **Room: 1616**

Advises on party action and policy.

Mickey Edwards, Okla., Chairman

Bill Archer, Texas
Doug Bereuter, Neb.
John A. Boehner, Ohio
Jim Bunning, Ky.
Tom Campbell, Calif.
William E. Dannemeyer, Calif.
Gary Franks, Conn.
Dean A. Gallo, N.J.
Paul E. Gillmor, Ohio
Newt Gingrich, Ga.
Bill Goodling, Pa.
Bill Gradison, Ohio
Fred Grandy, Iowa
Bill Green, N.Y.
Steve Gunderson, Wis.
Dennis Hastert, Ill.
Paul B. Henry, Mich.
Duncan Hunter, Calif.
Jerry Lewis, Calif.
Bill McCollum, Fla.
Jim McCrery, La.
Joseph M. McDade, Pa.
Jan Meyers, Kan.
Robert H. Michel, Ill.
John J. Rhodes III, Ariz.
Ileana Ros-Lehtinen, Fla.
Lamar Smith, Texas
Gerald B. H. Solomon, N.Y.
Floyd D. Spence, S.C.
Craig Thomas, Wyo.
Guy Vander Jagt, Mich.
James T. Walsh, N.Y.
Vin Weber, Minn.

Research Committee

Phone: (202) 225-0871 **Room: LHOB 1622**

At leadership's request, provides information and recommendations on specific policy issues likely to come before Congress. All Republican representatives are members of the committee. The Executive Committee is as follows:

Duncan Hunter, Calif., chairman

Wayne Allard, Colo.
Helen Delich Bentley, Md.
Michael Bilirakis, Fla.
Sherwood Boehlert, N.Y.
Ben Blaz, Guam
Dave Camp, Mich.
Tom Campbell, Calif.
Rod Chandler, Wash.
William F. Clinger, Pa.
Robert J. Lagomarsino, Calif.
Ronald K. Machtley, R.I.
Bill McCollum, Fla.
Jim McCrery, La.
Bob McEwen, Ohio
Alex McMillan, N.C.
Susan Molinari, N.Y.
Michael G. Oxley, Ohio
Ron Packard, Calif.
Randy "Duke" Cunningham, Calif.
Christopher C. Cox, Calif.
William E. Dannemeyer, Calif.
Tom DeLay, Texas
Robert K. Dornan, Calif.
David Dreier, Calif.
Bill Emerson, Mo.
Bill Goodling, Pa.
Porter J. Goss, Fla.
Steve Gunderson, Wis.
Mel Hancock, Mo.
Dennis Hastert, Ill.
Frank Horton, N.Y.
Andy Ireland, Fla.
Nancy L. Johnson, Conn.
Jon Kyl, Ariz.
John J. Rhodes III, Ariz.
Frank Riggs, Calif.
Don Ritter, Pa.
Dana Rohrabacher, Calif.
H. James Saxton, N.J.
Steven H. Schiff, N.M.
F. James Sensenbrenner Jr., Wis.
Charles H. Taylor, N.C.
Clay E. Shaw Jr., Fla.
Bud Shuster, Pa.
D. French Slaughter Jr., Va.
Christopher H. Smith, N.J.
Craig Thomas, Wyo.
Bill Zeliff, N.H.

National Republican Congressional Committee

Phone: (202) 479-7000 **Room: 320 First St., S.E. 20003**

Campaign support committee for Republican House candidates.

Guy Vander Jagt, Mich., chairman

Bill Barrett, Neb.
Michael Bilirakis, Fla.
Ben Blaz, Guam
Dan Burton, Ind.
Sonny Callahan, Ala.
Dave Camp, Mich.
Lawrence Coughlin, Pa.
David Dreier, Calif.
Mickey Edwards, Okla.
Bill Emerson, Mo.
Harris W. Fawell, Ill.
Jack Fields, Texas
Gary Franks, Conn.
Paul E. Gillmor, Ohio
Newt Gingrich, Ga.
John Paul Hammerschmidt, Ark.
James V. Hansen, Utah
Larry J. Hopkins, Ky.
Amo Houghton, N.Y.
Duncan Hunter, Calif.
James M. Inhofe, Okla.
Scott L. Klug, Wis.
Jim Kolbe, Ariz.
Jerry Lewis, Calif.
Robert L. Livingston, La.
Ronald K. Machtley, R.I.
Ron Marlenee, Mont.
Robert H. Michel, Ill.
Bill McCollum, Fla.
Constance A. Morella, Md.
Sid Morrison, Wash.
Jim Nussle, Iowa
Michael G. Oxley, Ohio
Arthur Ravenel Jr., S.C.
Frank Riggs, Calif.
Pat Roberts, Kan.
Marge Roukema, N.J.
Rick Santorum, Pa.
Dan Schaefer, Colo.
Joe Skeen, N.M.
Bob Smith, Ore.
Olympia J. Snowe, Maine
Don Sundquist, Tenn.
Charles H. Taylor, N.C.
Craig Thomas, Wyo.
Barbara F. Vucanovich, Nev.
Vin Weber, Minn.
Frank R. Wolf, Va.
Don Young, Alaska
Bill Zeliff, N.H.

Senate Committees, 102nd Congress

(As of Nov. 27, 1991)

AGRICULTURE, NUTRITION AND FORESTRY

Phone: 224-2035 **Room: SR-328A**

Majority Chief of Staff: Charles Riemenschneider 224-2035 SR-328A
Minority Staff Director: Chuck Conner 224-0019 SR-328

Agriculture in general; animal industry and diseases; crop insurance and soil conservation; farm credit and farm security; food from fresh waters; food stamp programs; forestry in general; home economics; human nutrition; inspection of livestock, meat and agricultural products; pests and pesticides; plant industry, soils and agricultural engineering; rural development, rural electrification and watersheds; school nutrition programs; matters relating to food, nutrition, hunger and rural affairs. Chairman and ranking minority member are members ex officio of all subcommittees of which they are not regular members.

Party Ratio: D 10 — R 8

Patrick J. Leahy, Vt., chairman	*Richard G. Lugar, Ind., ranking member*
David Pryor, Ark.	*Bob Dole, Kan.*
David L. Boren, Okla.	*Jesse Helms, N.C.*
Howell Heflin, Ala.	*Thad Cochran, Miss.*
Tom Harkin, Iowa	*Mitch McConnell, Ky.*
Kent Conrad, N.D.	*Larry E. Craig, Idaho*
Wyche Fowler Jr., Ga.	*John Seymour, Calif.*
Tom Daschle, S.D.	*Charles E. Grassley, Iowa*
Max Baucus, Mont.	
Bob Kerrey, Neb.	

SUBCOMMITTEES

Agricultural Credit

Phone: 224-2035 **Room: SR-328A**

Conrad, chairman	*Grassley*
Boren	*Craig*
Daschle	

Agricultural Production and Stabilization of Prices

Phone: 224-2035 **Room: SR-328A**

Pryor, chairman	*Helms*
Baucus	*Dole*
Kerrey	*Seymour*
Boren	*Grassley*
Heflin	*Cochran*
Harkin	*McConnell*
Conrad	

Agricultural Research and General Legislation

Phone: 224-2035 **Room: SR-328A**

Daschle, chairman	*Seymour*
Kerrey	*Dole*

Conservation and Forestry

Phone: 224-2035 **Room: SR-328A**

Fowler, chairman	*Craig*
Heflin	*Helms*
Baucus	

Domestic and Foreign Marketing and Product Promotion

Phone: 224-2035 **Room: SR-328A**

Boren, chairman	*Cochran*
Pryor	*Helms*
Fowler	*Seymour*
Baucus	*Grassley*
Harkin	*McConnell*
Conrad	

Nutrition and Investigations

Phone: 224-2035 **Room: SR-328A**

Harkin, chairman	*McConnell*
Fowler	*Dole*
Kerrey	*Helms*
Pryor	

Rural Development and Rural Electrification

Phone: 224-2035 **Room: SR-328A**

Heflin, chairman	*Cochran*
Daschle	*Craig*
Pryor	

APPROPRIATIONS

Phone: 224-3471 **Room: S-128 Capitol**

Majority Staff Director: Jim English 224-7200 S-128 Capitol
Minority Staff Director: J. Keith Kennedy 224-7335 SD-135

Appropriation of revenue; rescission of appropriations; new spending authority under the Budget Act. Chairman and ranking minority member are members ex officio of all subcommittees.

Party Ratio: D 16 — R 13

Robert C. Byrd, W.Va., chairman	*Mark O. Hatfield, Ore., ranking member*
Daniel K. Inouye, Hawaii	*Ted Stevens, Alaska*
Ernest F. Hollings, S.C.	*Jake Garn, Utah*
J. Bennett Johnston, La.	*Thad Cochran, Miss.*
Quentin N. Burdick, N.D.	*Bob Kasten, Wis.*
Patrick J. Leahy, Vt.	*Alfonse M. D'Amato, N.Y.*
Jim Sasser, Tenn.	*Warren B. Rudman, N.H.*
Dennis DeConcini, Ariz.	*Arlen Specter, Pa.*
Dale Bumpers, Ark.	*Pete V. Domenici, N.M.*
Frank R. Lautenberg, N.J.	*Don Nickles, Okla.*
Tom Harkin, Iowa	*Phil Gramm, Texas*

Barbara A. Mikulski, Md.	*Christopher S. Bond, Mo.*
Harry Reid, Nev.	*Slade Gorton, Wash.*
Brock Adams, Wash.	
Wyche Fowler Jr., Ga.	
Bob Kerrey, Neb.	

SUBCOMMITTEES

Agriculture, Rural Development and Related Agencies

Phone: 224-7240 **Room: SD-140**

Burdick, chairman	*Cochran*
Bumpers	*Kasten*
Harkin	*Specter*
Adams	*Nickles*
Fowler	*Bond*
Kerrey	

Commerce, Justice, State and Judiciary

Phone: 224-7277 **Room: S-146A Capitol**

Hollings, chairman	*Rudman*
Inouye	*Stevens*
Bumpers	*Hatfield*
Lautenberg	*Kasten*
Sasser	*Gramm*
Adams	

Defense

Phone: 224-7236 **Room: SD-119**

Inouye, chairman	*Stevens*
Hollings	*Garn*
Johnston	*Kasten*
Byrd	*D'Amato*
Leahy	*Rudman*
Sasser	*Cochran*
DeConcini	*Specter*
Bumpers	*Domenici*
Lautenberg	
Harkin	

District of Columbia

Phone: 224-7260 **Room: S-205 Capitol**

Adams, chairman	*Bond*
Fowler	*Gorton*
Kerrey	

Energy and Water Development

Phone: 224-0335 **Room: SD-132**

Johnston, chairman	*Hatfield*
Byrd	*Garn*
Hollings	*Cochran*
Burdick	*Domenici*
Sasser	*Specter*
DeConcini	*Nickles*
Reid	

Foreign Operations

Phone: 224-7209 **Room: SD-136**

Leahy, chairman	*Kasten*
Inouye	*Hatfield*
Johnston	*D'Amato*
DeConcini	*Rudman*
Lautenberg	*Specter*
Harkin	*Nickles*
Mikulski	

Interior

Phone: 224-7233 **Room: SD-127**

Byrd, chairman	*Nickles*
Johnston	*Stevens*
Leahy	*Garn*
DeConcini	*Cochran*
Burdick	*Rudman*
Bumpers	*Domenici*
Hollings	*Gorton*
Reid	

Labor, Health and Human Services, Education

Phone: 224-7283 **Room: SD-186**

Harkin, chairman	*Specter*
Byrd	*Hatfield*
Hollings	*Stevens*
Burdick	*Rudman*
Inouye	*Cochran*
Bumpers	*Gramm*
Reid	*Gorton*
Adams	

Legislative Branch

Phone: 224-7338 **Room: SD-132**

Reid, chairman	*Gorton*
Mikulski	*Bond*
Adams	

Military Construction

Phone: 224-7276 **Room: SD-131**

Sasser, chairman	*Gramm*
Inouye	*Garn*
Reid	*Stevens*
Fowler	

Transportation

Phone: 224-7281 **Room: SD-156**

Lautenberg, chairman	*D'Amato*
Byrd	*Kasten*
Harkin	*Domenici*
Sasser	*Hatfield*
Mikulski	

Treasury, Postal Service and General Government

Phone: 224-6280 **Room: SD-190**

DeConcini, chairman — *Domenici*
Mikulski — *D'Amato*
Kerrey

VA, HUD and Independent Agencies

Phone: 224-7211 **Room: SD-142**

Mikulski, chairman — *Garn*
Leahy — *D'Amato*
Johnston — *Nickles*
Lautenberg — *Gramm*
Fowler — *Bond*
Kerrey

ARMED SERVICES

Phone: 224-3871 **Room: SR-228**

Majority Staff Director: Arnold Punaro 224-3871 SR-228
Minority Staff Director: Patrick Tucker 224-9348 SR-228

Defense and defense policy generally; aeronautical and space activities peculiar to or primarily associated with the development of weapons systems or military operations; maintenance and operation of the Panama Canal, including the Canal Zone; military research and development; national security aspects of nuclear energy; naval petroleum reserves (except Alaska); armed forces generally; Selective Service System; strategic and critical materials. Chairman and ranking minority member are non-voting members ex officio of all subcommittees of which they are not regular members.

Party Ratio: D 11 — R 9

Sam Nunn, Ga., chairman	*John W. Warner, Va., ranking member*
Jim Exon, Neb.	*Strom Thurmond, S.C.*
Carl Levin, Mich.	*William S. Cohen, Maine*
Edward M. Kennedy, Mass.	*John McCain, Ariz.*
Jeff Bingaman, N.M.	*Malcolm Wallop, Wyo.*
Alan J. Dixon, Ill.	*Trent Lott, Miss.*
John Glenn, Ohio	*Daniel R. Coats, Ind.*
Al Gore, Tenn.	*Connie Mack, Fla.*
Tim Wirth, Colo.	*Robert C. Smith, N.H.*
Richard C. Shelby, Ala.	
Robert C. Byrd, W.Va.	

SUBCOMMITTEES

Conventional Forces and Alliance Defense

Phone: 224-3871 **Room: SR-228**

Levin, chairman — *Wallop*
Dixon — *Thurmond*
Glenn — *Cohen*
Wirth — *McCain*
Shelby — *Coats*
Byrd

Defense Industry and Technology

Phone: 224-3871 **Room: SR-228**

Bingaman, chairman — *Coats*
Gore — *Mack*
Wirth — *Smith*
Byrd

Manpower and Personnel

Phone: 224-3871 **Room: SR-228**

Glenn, chairman — *McCain*
Exon — *Wallop*
Kennedy — *Smith*
Byrd

Projection Forces and Regional Defense

Phone: 224-3871 **Room: SR-228**

Kennedy, chairman — *Cohen*
Exon — *McCain*
Dixon — *Lott*
Gore — *Mack*
Shelby

Readiness, Sustainability and Support

Phone: 224-3871 **Room: SR-228**

Dixon, chairman — *Lott*
Levin — *Thurmond*
Bingaman — *Coats*
Wirth — *Mack*
Shelby

Strategic Forces and Nuclear Deterrence

Phone: 224-3871 **Room: SR-228**

Exon, chairman — *Thurmond*
Levin — *Cohen*
Kennedy — *Wallop*
Bingaman — *Lott*
Glenn — *Smith*
Gore

BANKING, HOUSING AND URBAN AFFAIRS

Phone: 224-7391 **Room: SD-534**

Majority Staff Director: Steven Harris 224-7391 SD-534
Minority Staff Director: Lamar Smith 224-7391 SD-534

Banks, banking and financial institutions; price controls; deposit insurance; economic stabilization and growth; defense production; export and foreign trade promotion; export controls; federal monetary policy, including Federal Reserve System; financial aid to commerce and industry; issuance and redemption of notes; money and credit, including currency and coinage; nursing home construction; public and private housing, including veterans' housing; renegotiation of government contracts; urban development and mass transit; international economic policy. Chairman and ranking minority member are members ex officio of all subcommittees of which they are not regular members.

Party Ratio: D 12 — R 9

Donald W. Riegle Jr., Mich., chairman	*Jake Garn, Utah, ranking member*
Alan Cranston, Calif.	*Alfonse M. D'Amato, N.Y.*
Paul S. Sarbanes, Md.	*Phil Gramm, Texas*
Christopher J. Dodd, Conn.	*Christopher S. Bond, Mo.*
Alan J. Dixon, Ill.	*Connie Mack, Fla.*
Jim Sasser, Tenn.	*William V. Roth Jr., Del.*
Terry Sanford, N.C.	*Pete V. Domenici, N.M.*
Richard C. Shelby, Ala.	*Nancy Landon Kassebaum, Kan.*
Bob Graham, Fla.	*John H. Chafee, R.I.*
Tim Wirth, Colo.	
John Kerry, Mass.	
Richard H. Bryan, Nev.	

SUBCOMMITTEES

Consumer and Regulatory Affairs

Phone: 224-1563 **Room: SD-537**

Dixon, chairman	*Bond*
Kerry	
Bryan	

Housing and Urban Affairs

Phone: 224-6348 **Room: SD-535**

Cranston, chairman	*D'Amato*
Sasser	*Gramm*
Sanford	*Bond*
Graham	*Mack*
Kerry	*Roth*
Bryan	*Domenici*
Sarbanes	*Kassebaum*
Dodd	
Shelby	

International Finance and Monetary Policy

Phone: 224-1564 **Room: SD-537**

Sarbanes, chairman	*Mack*
Dixon	*Domenici*
Graham	*Kassebaum*
Wirth	

Securities

Phone: 224-9213 **Room: SD-541**

Dodd, chairman	*Gramm*
Shelby	*Roth*
Wirth	*D'Amato*
Cranston	*Bond*
Sasser	*Mack*
Sanford	

BUDGET

Phone: 224-0642 **Room: SD-621**

Majority Staff Director: Larry Stein 224-0553 SD-621
Minority Staff Director: Bill Hoagland 224-0769 SD-634A

Federal budget generally; concurrent budget resolutions; Congressional Budget Office.

Party Ratio: D 12 — R 9

Jim Sasser, Tenn., chairman	*Pete V. Domenici, N.M., ranking member*
Ernest F. Hollings, S.C.	*Steve Symms, Idaho*
J. Bennett Johnston, La.	*Charles E. Grassley, Iowa*
Donald W. Riegle Jr., Mich.	*Bob Kasten, Wis.*
Jim Exon, Neb.	*Don Nickles, Okla.*
Frank R. Lautenberg, N.J.	*Phil Gramm, Texas*
Paul Simon, Ill.	*Christopher S. Bond, Mo.*
Terry Sanford, N.C.	*Trent Lott, Miss.*
Tim Wirth, Colo.	*Hank Brown, Colo.*
Wyche Fowler Jr., Ga.	
Kent Conrad, N.D.	
Christopher J. Dodd, Conn.	

COMMERCE, SCIENCE AND TRANSPORTATION

Phone: 224-5115 **Room: SD-508**

Majority Chief Counsel & Staff Director: Kevin Curtin 224-0427 SR-254
Minority Chief Counsel & Staff Director: William B. McCormick Jr. 224-5183 SD-554

Interstate commerce and transportation generally; Coast Guard; coastal zone management; communications; highway safety; inland waterways, except construction; marine fisheries; Merchant Marine and navigation; non-military aeronautical and space sciences; oceans, weather and atmospheric activities; interoceanic canals generally; regulation of consumer products and services; science, engineering and technology research, development and policy; sports; standards and measurement; transportation and commerce aspects of Outer Continental Shelf lands. Chairman and ranking minority member are non-voting members ex officio of all subcommittees of which they are not regular members.

Party Ratio: D 11 — R 9

Ernest F. Hollings, S.C., chairman	*John C. Danforth, Mo., ranking member*
Daniel K. Inouye, Hawaii	*Bob Packwood, Ore.*
Wendell H. Ford, Ky.	*Larry Pressler, S.D.*
Jim Exon, Neb.	*Ted Stevens, Alaska*
Al Gore, Tenn.	*Bob Kasten, Wis.*
John D. Rockefeller IV, W.Va.	*John McCain, Ariz.*
Lloyd Bentsen, Texas	*Conrad Burns, Mont.*
John Kerry, Mass.	*Slade Gorton, Wash.*
John B. Breaux, La.	*Trent Lott, Miss.*

Richard H. Bryan, Nev.
Charles S. Robb, Va.

SUBCOMMITTEES

Aviation

Phone: 224-9350 **Room: SH-428**

Ford, chairman	*McCain*
Exon	*Stevens*
Inouye	*Kasten*
Kerry	*Gorton*
Bentsen	

Communications

Phone: 224-9340 **Room: SH-227**

Inouye, chairman	*Packwood*
Hollings	*Pressler*
Ford	*Stevens*
Gore	*McCain*
Exon	*Burns*
Kerry	*Gorton*
Bentsen	
Breaux	

Consumer

Phone: 224-0415 **Room: SH-227**

Bryan, chairman	*Gorton*
Gore	*McCain*
Ford	*Kasten*
Robb	

Foreign Commerce and Tourism

Phone: 224-9325 **Room: SH-428**

Rockefeller, chairman	*Burns*
Hollings	*Packwood*
Bryan	

Merchant Marine

Phone: 224-4914 **Room: SH-425**

Breaux, chairman	*Lott*
Inouye	*Stevens*
Bentsen	

National Ocean Policy Study

Phone: 224-4912 **Room: SH-425**

Hollings, chairman	*Stevens*
Kerry	*Danforth*
Inouye	*Packwood*
Ford	*Kasten*
Gore	*Pressler*
Bentsen	*Gorton*
Breaux	*Lott*
Robb	

Science, Technology and Space

Phone: 224-9360 **Room: SH-427**

Gore, chairman	*Pressler*
Rockefeller	*Stevens*
Bentsen	*Kasten*
Kerry	*Lott*
Bryan	
Robb	

Surface Transportation

Phone: 224-9350 **Room: SH-428**

Exon, chairman	*Kasten*
Rockefeller	*Packwood*
Hollings	*Pressler*
Inouye	*Burns*
Gore	*Lott*
Breaux	
Robb	

ENERGY AND NATURAL RESOURCES

Phone: 224-4971 **Room: SD-364**

Majority Staff Director: Benjamin Cooper 224-4971 SD-360
Minority Staff Director: G. Robert Wallace 224-1017 SD-312

Energy policy, regulation, conservation, research and development; coal; energy-related aspects of deep-water ports; hydroelectric power, irrigation and reclamation; mines, mining and minerals generally; national parks, recreation areas, wilderness areas, wild and scenic rivers, historic sites, military parks and battlefields; naval petroleum reserves in Alaska; non-military development of nuclear energy; oil and gas production and distribution; public lands and forests; solar energy systems; territorial possessions of the United States. Chairman and ranking minority member are members ex officio of all subcommittees of which they are not regular members.

Party Ratio: D 11 — R 9

J. Bennett Johnston, La., chairman	*Malcolm Wallop, Wyo., ranking member*
Dale Bumpers, Ark.	*Mark O. Hatfield, Ore.*
Wendell H. Ford, Ky.	*Pete V. Domenici, N.M.*
Bill Bradley, N.J.	*Frank H. Murkowski, Alaska*
Jeff Bingaman, N.M.	*Don Nickles, Okla.*
Tim Wirth, Colo.	*Conrad Burns, Mont.*
Kent Conrad, N.D.	*Larry E. Craig, Idaho*
Daniel K. Akaka, Hawaii	*John Seymour, Calif.*
Wyche Fowler Jr., Ga.	*Jake Garn, Utah*
Richard C. Shelby, Ala.	
Paul Wellstone, Minn.	

SUBCOMMITTEES

Energy Regulation and Conservation

Phone: 224-4756 **Room: SH-212**

Wirth, chairman	*Nickles*
Akaka	*Domenici*

Bradley	*Murkowski*
Fowler	*Seymour*
Shelby	*Hatfield*
Wellstone	

Energy Research and Development

Phone: 224-7569 **Room: SH-312**

Ford, chairman	*Domenici*
Shelby	*Garn*
Bumpers	*Nickles*
Bingaman	*Burns*
Akaka	*Craig*
Fowler	
Wellstone	

Mineral Resources Development and Production

Phone: 224-7568 **Room: SD-364**

Bingaman, chairman	*Craig*
Bumpers	*Murkowski*
Ford	*Nickles*
Conrad	*Garn*
Shelby	

Public Lands, National Parks and Forests

Phone: 224-7934 **Room: SD-308**

Bumpers, chairman	*Murkowski*
Fowler	*Garn*
Bradley	*Hatfield*
Bingaman	*Domenici*
Wirth	*Burns*
Conrad	*Craig*
Akaka	*Seymour*
Wellstone	

Water and Power

Phone: 224-6836 **Room: SD-306**

Bradley, chairman	*Burns*
Conrad	*Hatfield*
Ford	*Seymour*
Wirth	

ENVIRONMENT AND PUBLIC WORKS

Phone: 224-6176 **Room: SD-458**

Majority Staff Director: David M. Strauss 224-7845 SD-458
Minority Staff Director: Steve Shimberg 224-7854 SD-410

Environmental policy, research and development; air, water and noise pollution; construction and maintenance of highways; environmental aspects of Outer Continental Shelf lands; environmental effects of toxic substances, other than pesticides; fisheries and wildlife; flood control and improvements of rivers and harbors; non-military environmental regulation and control of nuclear energy; ocean dumping; public buildings and grounds; public works, bridges and dams; regional economic development; solid waste disposal and recycling; water resources.

Party Ratio: D 10 — R 7

Quentin N. Burdick, N.D., chairman	*John H. Chafee, R.I., ranking member*
Daniel Patrick Moynihan, N.Y.	*Alan K. Simpson, Wyo.*
George J. Mitchell, Maine	*Steve Symms, Idaho*
Max Baucus, Mont.	*Dave Durenberger, Minn.*
Frank R. Lautenberg, N.J.	*John W. Warner, Va.*
Harry Reid, Nev.	*James M. Jeffords, Vt.*
Bob Graham, Fla.	*Robert C. Smith, N.H.*
Joseph I. Lieberman, Conn.	
Howard M. Metzenbaum, Ohio	
Harris L. Wofford Jr., Pa.	

SUBCOMMITTEES

Environmental Protection

Phone: 224-6691 **Room: SH-408**

Baucus, chairman	*Chafee*
Moynihan	*Simpson*
Mitchell	*Durenberger*
Lautenberg	*Warner*
Graham	*Jeffords*
Lieberman	*Symms*
Metzenbaum	

Gulf Pollution

Phone: 224-6176 **Room: SD-458**

Lieberman, chairman	*Chafee*
Burdick	

Nuclear Regulation

Phone: 224-5031 **Room: SH-415**

Graham, chairman	*Simpson*
Moynihan	*Symms*
Reid	

Superfund, Ocean and Water Protection

Phone: 224-5031 **Room: SH-415**

Lautenberg, chairman	*Durenberger*
Mitchell	*Simpson*
Baucus	*Smith*
Metzenbaum	
Wofford	

Toxic Substances, Environmental Oversight, Research and Development

Phone: 224-3597 **Room: SH-508**

Reid, chairman	*Warner*
Baucus	*Jeffords*
Lieberman	
Wofford	

Water Resources, Transportation and Infrastructure

Phone: 224-3597 **Room: SH-508**

Moynihan, chairman
Mitchell
Lautenberg
Reid
Graham
Lieberman
Metzenbaum

Symms
Warner
Jeffords
Durenberger
Smith
Chafee

FINANCE

Phone: 224-4515 **Room: SD-205**

Majority Staff Director & Chief Counsel: Vanda B. McMurty 224-4515 SD-205
Minority Chief of Staff: Edward J. Mihalski 224-5315 SH-203

Revenue measures generally; taxes; tariffs and import quotas; foreign trade agreements; customs; revenue sharing; federal debt limit; Social Security; health programs financed by taxes or trust funds. Chairman and ranking minority member are members ex officio of all subcommittees of which they are not regular members.

Party Ratio: D 11 — R 9

Lloyd Bentsen, Texas, chairman
Daniel Patrick Moynihan, N.Y.
Max Baucus, Mont.
David L. Boren, Okla.
Bill Bradley, N.J.
George J. Mitchell, Maine
David Pryor, Ark.
Donald W. Riegle Jr., Mich.
John D. Rockefeller IV, W.Va.
Tom Daschle, S.D.
John B. Breaux, La.

Bob Packwood, Ore., ranking member
Bob Dole, Kan.
William V. Roth Jr., Del.
John C. Danforth, Mo.
John H. Chafee, R.I.
Dave Durenberger, Minn.
Steve Symms, Idaho
Charles E. Grassley, Iowa
Orrin G. Hatch, Utah

SUBCOMMITTEES

Deficits, Debt Management and International Debt

Phone: 224-4515 **Room: SD-205**

Bradley, chairman
Riegle

Hatch

Energy and Agricultural Taxation

Phone: 224-4515 **Room: SD-205**

Daschle, chairman
Boren
Breaux

Symms
Dole

Health for Families and the Uninsured

Phone: 224-4515 **Room: SD-205**

Riegle, chairman
Bradley
Mitchell
Rockefeller

Chafee
Roth
Durenberger
Hatch

International Trade

Phone: 224-4515 **Room: SD-205**

Baucus, chairman
Bentsen
Moynihan
Boren
Bradley
Mitchell
Riegle
Rockefeller
Daschle
Breaux

Danforth
Packwood
Roth
Chafee
Symms
Grassley
Hatch

Medicare and Long Term Care

Phone: 224-4515 **Room: SD-205**

Rockefeller, chairman
Bentsen
Baucus
Mitchell
Pryor
Daschle

Durenberger
Packwood
Dole
Chafee
Danforth
Grassley

Private Retirement Plans and Oversight of the Internal Revenue Service

Phone: 224-4515 **Room: SD-205**

Pryor, chairman
Moynihan

Grassley

Social Security and Family Policy

Phone: 224-4515 **Room: SD-205**

Moynihan, chairman
Breaux

Dole
Durenberger

Taxation

Phone: 224-4515 **Room: SD-205**

Boren, chairman
Bentsen
Baucus
Pryor

Roth
Packwood
Danforth
Symms

FOREIGN RELATIONS

Phone: 224-4651 Room: SD-446

Majority Staff Director: Geryld B. Christianson 224-3953 SD-446
Minority Staff Director: James Lucier 224-3941 SD-452

Relations of the United States with foreign nations generally; treaties; foreign economic, military, technical and humanitarian as-

sistance; foreign loans; diplomatic service; International Red Cross; international aspects of nuclear energy; International Monetary Fund; intervention abroad and declarations of war; foreign trade; national security; oceans and international environmental and scientific affairs; protection of U.S. citizens abroad; United Nations; World Bank and other development assistance organizations. Chairman and ranking minority member are members ex officio of all subcommittees of which they are not regular members.

Party Ratio: D 8 — R 6

Claiborne Pell, R.I., chairman
Joseph R. Biden Jr., Del.
Paul S. Sarbanes, Md.
Alan Cranston, Calif.
Christopher J. Dodd, Conn.
John Kerry, Mass.
Paul Simon, Ill.
Terry Sanford, N.C.
Daniel Patrick Moynihan, N.Y.
Charles S. Robb, Va.
Harris L. Wofford Jr., Pa.

Jesse Helms, N.C., ranking member
Richard G. Lugar, Ind.
Nancy Landon Kassebaum, Kan.
Larry Pressler, S.D.
Frank H. Murkowski, Alaska
Mitch McConnell, Ky.
Hank Brown, Colo.
James M. Jeffords, Vt.

SUBCOMMITTEES

African Affairs

Phone: 224-4651 **Room: SD-446**

Simon, chairman
Sanford
Moynihan

Kassebaum
Helms

East Asian and Pacific Affairs

Phone: 224-4651 **Room: SD-446**

Cranston, chairman
Biden
Dodd
Kerry
Robb

Murkowski
Lugar
McConnell
Brown

European Affairs

Phone: 224-4651 **Room: SD-446**

Biden, chairman
Sarbanes
Simon

Pressler
Brown

International Economic Policy, Trade, Oceans and Environment

Phone: 224-4651 **Room: SD-446**

Sarbanes, chairman
Biden
Cranston
Dodd
Pell
Wofford

McConnell
Lugar
Murkowski
Kassebaum

Near Eastern and South Asian Affairs

Phone: 224-4651 **Room: SD-446**

Sanford, chairman
Sarbanes
Moynihan
Robb
Wofford

Jeffords
Pressler
Murkowski

Terrorism, Narcotics and International Operations

Phone: 224-4651 **Room: SD-446**

Kerry, chairman
Simon
Moynihan
Pell

Brown
McConnell
Jeffords

Western Hemisphere and Peace Corps Affairs

Phone: 224-4651 **Room: SD-446**

Dodd, chairman
Cranston
Kerry
Sanford
Robb
Wofford

Lugar
Kassebaum
Helms
Jeffords

GOVERNMENTAL AFFAIRS

Phone: 224-4751 **Room: SD-340**

Majority Staff Director: Leonard Weiss 224-4751 SD-340
Minority Staff Director: Franklin G. Polk 224-2627 SD-350

Budget and accounting measures; census and statistics; federal civil service; congressional organization; intergovernmental relations; government information; District of Columbia; organization and management of nuclear export policy; executive branch reorganization; Postal Service; efficiency, economy and effectiveness of government. Chairman and ranking minority member are non-voting members ex officio of all subcommittees of which they are not regular members.

Party Ratio: D 8 — R 6

John Glenn, Ohio, chairman
Sam Nunn, Ga.
Carl Levin, Mich.
Jim Sasser, Tenn.
David Pryor, Ark.
Herb Kohl, Wis.
Joseph I. Lieberman, Conn.
Daniel K. Akaka, Hawaii

William V. Roth Jr., Del., ranking member
Ted Stevens, Alaska
William S. Cohen, Maine
Warren B. Rudman, N.H.
John Seymour, Calif.
<Vacancy>

SUBCOMMITTEES

Federal Services, Post Office and Civil Service

Phone: 224-2254 **Room: SH-601**

Pryor, chairman

Stevens

Sasser — *Seymour*
Akaka

General Services, Federalism and The District of Columbia

Phone: 224-4718 — **Room: SH-432**

Sasser, chairman — *Seymour*
Lieberman — *Stevens*
Akaka

Government Information and Regulation

Phone: 224-9000 — **Room: SH-605**

Kohl, chairman — *Rudman*
Nunn — *Cohen*
Levin — *Seymour*
Lieberman

Oversight of Government Management

Phone: 224-3682 — **Room: SH-442**

Levin, chairman — *Cohen*
Pryor — *Rudman*
Kohl — *Seymour*
Lieberman — *Stevens*
Akaka
Nunn

Permanent Investigations

Phone: 224-3721 — **Room: SR-100**

Nunn, chairman — *Roth*
Glenn, vice chairman — *Stevens*
Levin — *Cohen*
Sasser — *Rudman*
Pryor — *Seymour*
Kohl
Lieberman

JUDICIARY

Phone: 224-5225 — **Room: SD-224**

Majority Chief Counsel: Ron Klain 224-5225 SD-224
Minority Chief Counsel: Terry Wooten 224-9494 SD-148

Civil and criminal judicial proceedings in general; penitentiaries; bankruptcy, mutiny, espionage and counterfeiting; civil liberties; constitutional amendments; apportionment of representatives; government information; immigration and naturalization; interstate compacts in general; claims against the United States; patents, copyrights and trademarks; monopolies and unlawful restraints of trade; holidays and celebrations. Chairman and ranking minority member are members ex officio of all subcommittees of which they are not regular members.

Party Ratio: D 9 — R 7

Joseph R. Biden Jr., Del., chairman — *Strom Thurmond, S.C., ranking member*
Edward M. Kennedy, Mass. — *Orrin G. Hatch, Utah*
Howard M. Metzenbaum, Ohio — *Alan K. Simpson, Wyo.*
Dennis DeConcini, Ariz. — *Charles E. Grassley, Iowa*
Patrick J. Leahy, Vt. — *Arlen Specter, Pa.*
Howell Heflin, Ala. — *Hank Brown, Colo.*
Paul Simon, Ill.
Herb Kohl, Wis.

SUBCOMMITTEES

Antitrust, Monopolies and Business Rights

Phone: 224-5701 — **Room: SH-308**

Metzenbaum, chairman — *Thurmond*
DeConcini — *Specter*
Heflin — *Hatch*
Simon

Constitution

Phone: 224-5573 — **Room: SD-524**

Simon, chairman — *Specter*
Metzenbaum — *Hatch*
DeConcini
Kennedy

Courts and Administrative Practice

Phone: 224-4022 — **Room: SH-223**

Heflin, chairman — *Grassley*
Metzenbaum — *Thurmond*
Kohl

Immigration and Refugee Affairs

Phone: 224-7878 — **Room: SD-520**

Kennedy, chairman — *Simpson*
Simon

Juvenile Justice

Phone: 224-4933 — **Room: SH-305**

Kohl, chairman — *Brown*
Biden

Patents, Copyrights and Trademarks

Phone: 224-8178 — **Room: SH-327**

DeConcini, chairman — *Hatch*
Kennedy — *Simpson*
Leahy — *Grassley*
Heflin

Technology and the Law

Phone: 224-3407 — **Room: SH-815**

Leahy, chairman — *Brown*
Kohl

LABOR AND HUMAN RESOURCES

Phone: 224-5375 **Room: SD-428**

Majority Staff Director & Chief Counsel: Nick Littlefield 224-5465 SD-428
Minority Staff Director: Kristine A. Iverson 224-6770 SD-835

Education, labor, health and public welfare in general; aging; arts and humanities; biomedical research and development; child labor; convict labor; Red Cross; equal employment opportunity; handicapped people; labor standards and statistics; mediation and arbitration of labor disputes; occupational safety and health; private pensions; public health; railway labor and retirement; regulation of foreign laborers; student loans; wages and hours. Chairman and ranking minority member are members ex officio of all subcommittees of which they are not regular members.

Party Ratio: D 9 — R 7

Edward M. Kennedy, Mass., chairman	*Orrin G. Hatch, Utah, ranking member*
Claiborne Pell, R.I.	*Nancy Landon Kassebaum, Kan.*
Howard M. Metzenbaum, Ohio	*James M. Jeffords, Vt.*
Christopher J. Dodd, Conn.	*Daniel R. Coats, Ind.*
Paul Simon, Ill.	*Strom Thurmond, S.C.*
Tom Harkin, Iowa	*Dave Durenberger, Minn.*
Brock Adams, Wash.	*Thad Cochran, Miss.*
Barbara A. Mikulski, Md.	
Jeff Bingaman, N.M.	
Paul Wellstone, Minn.	

SUBCOMMITTEES

Aging

Phone: 224-3239 **Room: SH-404**

Adams, chairman	*Cochran*
Pell	*Durenberger*
Metzenbaum	*Coats*
Dodd	

Children, Families, Drugs and Alcoholism

Phone: 224-5630 **Room: SH-639**

Dodd, chairman	*Coats*
Pell	*Hatch*
Harkin	*Kassebaum*
Adams	*Jeffords*
Mikulski	*Thurmond*
Bingaman	*Durenberger*
Kennedy	
Wellstone	

Disability Policy

Phone: 224-6265 **Room: SH-113**

Harkin, chairman	*Durenberger*
Metzenbaum	*Hatch*
Simon	*Jeffords*
Adams	

Education, Arts and Humanities

Phone: 224-7666 **Room: SD-648**

Pell, chairman	*Kassebaum*
Metzenbaum	*Cochran*
Dodd	*Hatch*
Simon	*Jeffords*
Mikulski	*Thurmond*
Bingaman	*Coats*
Kennedy	
Wellstone	

Employment and Productivity

Phone: 224-5575 **Room: SD-644**

Simon, chairman	*Thurmond*
Harkin	*Durenberger*
Adams	*Kassebaum*
Mikulski	*Coats*
Bingaman	

Labor

Phone: 224-5546 **Room: SH-608**

Metzenbaum, chairman	*Jeffords*
Harkin	*Cochran*
Mikulski	*Thurmond*
Dodd	*Hatch*
Kennedy	
Wellstone	

SELECT POW/MIA AFFAIRS

Phone: 224-2742 **Room: 421 RHOB**

Administrative Assistant: Frances Zwenig 224-2742 SR-421

All messages, petitions, memorials and other matters relating to United States military personnel unaccounted for from military conflicts.

Party Ratio: D 7 — R 6

John Kerry, Mass., chairman	*Robert C. Smith, N.H., vice chairman*
Tom Daschle, S.D.	*John McCain, Ariz.*
Bob Kerrey, Neb.	*Hank Brown, Colo.*
Charles S. Robb, Va.	*Jesse Helms, N.C.*
Harry Reid, Nev.	*Charles E. Grassley, Iowa*
Herb Kohl, Wis.	*Nancy Landon Kassebaum, Kan.*

RULES AND ADMINISTRATION

Phone: 224-6352 **Room: SR-305**

Majority Staff Director: James O. King 224-6352 SR-305
Minority Staff Director: Wayne A. Schley 224-8923 SR-479

Senate administration in general; corrupt practices; qualifications of senators; contested elections; federal elections in general; Government Printing Office; Congressional Record; meetings of Congress and attendance of members; presidential succession; the Capitol, congressional office buildings, the Library of Congress, the Smithsonian Institution and the Botanic Garden.

Party Ratio: D 9 — R 7

Wendell H. Ford, Ky., chairman
Claiborne Pell, R.I.
Robert C. Byrd, W.Va.
Daniel K. Inouye, Hawaii
Dennis DeConcini, Ariz.
Al Gore, Tenn.
Daniel Patrick Moynihan, N.Y.
Christopher J. Dodd, Conn.
Brock Adams, Wash.

Ted Stevens, Alaska, ranking member
Mark O. Hatfield, Ore.
Jesse Helms, N.C.
John W. Warner, Va.
Bob Dole, Kan.
Jake Garn, Utah
Mitch McConnell, Ky.

SELECT ETHICS

Phone: 224-2981 **Room: SH-220**

Staff Director: Wilson Abney 224-2981 SH-220

Studies and investigates standards and conduct of Senate members and employees and may recommend remedial action.

Party Ratio: D 3 — R 3

Terry Sanford, N.C., chairman
Richard H. Bryan, Nev.
David Pryor, Ark.
Jeff Bingaman, N.M.

Warren B. Rudman, N.H., vice chairman
Trent Lott, Miss.
Slade Gorton, Wash.

SELECT INDIAN AFFAIRS

Phone: 224-2251 **Room: SH-838**

Majority Staff Director: Patricia Zell 224-2251 SH-838
Minority Staff Director: Daniel Lewis 224-2251 SH-838

Problems and opportunities of Indians, including Indian land management and trust responsibilities, education, health, special services, loan programs and claims against the United States.

Party Ratio: D 9 — R 7

Daniel K. Inouye, Hawaii, chairman
Dennis DeConcini, Ariz.
Quentin N. Burdick, N.D.
Tom Daschle, S.D.
Kent Conrad, N.D.
Harry Reid, Nev.
Paul Simon, Ill.
Daniel K. Akaka, Hawaii
Paul Wellstone, Minn.

John McCain, Ariz., vice chairman
Frank H. Murkowski, Alaska
Thad Cochran, Miss.
Slade Gorton, Wash.
Pete V. Domenici, N.M.
Nancy Landon Kassebaum, Kan.
Don Nickles, Okla.

SELECT INTELLIGENCE

Phone: 224-1700 **Room: SH-211**

Majority Staff Director: George Tenet 224-1700 SH-211
Minority Staff Director: John Moseman 224-1700 SH-211

Legislative and budgetary authority over the Central Intelligence Agency, the Defense Intelligence Agency, the National Security Agency and intelligence activities of the Federal Bureau of Investigation and other components of the federal intelligence community. The majority leader and minority leader are members ex officio of the committee.

Party Ratio: D 8 — R 7

David L. Boren, Okla., chairman
Sam Nunn, Ga.
Ernest F. Hollings, S.C.
Bill Bradley, N.J.
Alan Cranston, Calif.
Dennis DeConcini, Ariz.
Howard M. Metzenbaum, Ohio
John Glenn, Ohio

Frank H. Murkowski, Alaska, vice chairman
John W. Warner, Va.
Alfonse M. D'Amato, N.Y.
John C. Danforth, Mo.
Warren B. Rudman, N.H.
Slade Gorton, Wash.
John H. Chafee, R.I.

SMALL BUSINESS

Phone: 224-5175 **Room: SR-428A**

Majority Staff Director: John W. Ball 224-5175 SR-428A
Minority Staff Director: Stephen P. Lynch 226-3420 559 FHOB

Problems of small business; Small Business Administration.

Party Ratio: D 10 — R 8

Dale Bumpers, Ark., chairman
Sam Nunn, Ga.
Max Baucus, Mont.
Carl Levin, Mich.
Alan J. Dixon, Ill.
Tom Harkin, Iowa
John Kerry, Mass.
Barbara A. Mikulski, Md.
Joseph I. Lieberman, Conn.
Paul Wellstone, Minn.
Harris L. Wofford Jr., Pa.

Bob Kasten, Wis., ranking member
Larry Pressler, S.D.
Malcolm Wallop, Wyo.
Christopher S. Bond, Mo.
Conrad Burns, Mont.
Ted Stevens, Alaska
Connie Mack, Fla.
John Seymour, Calif.

SUBCOMMITTEES

Competitiveness and Economic Opportunity

Phone: 224-5175 **Room: 428A SR**

Lieberman, chairman
Harkin

Mack

Export Expansion

Phone: 224-5175 **Room: 428A SR**

Mikulski, chairman
Harkin
Lieberman
Bumpers

Pressler
Wallop
Stevens

Government Contracting and Paperwork Reduction

Phone: 224-5175 **Room: 428A SR**

Dixon, chairman
Lieberman
Nunn

Bond
Kasten

Innovation, Technology and Productivity

Phone: 224-5175 **Room: 428A SR**

Levin, chairman
Baucus
Kerry

Stevens
Seymour

Rural Economy and Family Farming

Phone: 224-5175 **Room: 428A SR**

Baucus, chairman
Nunn
Levin
Dixon
Kerry
Bumpers
Wellstone

Kasten
Pressler
Wallop
Bond
Burns
Mack

Urban and Minority-Owned Business Development

Phone: 224-5175 **Room: 428A SR**

Kerry, chairman
Nunn
Mikulski
Wellstone

Burns
Seymour
Mack

SPECIAL AGING

Phone: 224-5364 **Room: SD-G31**

Majority Staff Director: Portia Mittleman 224-5364 SD-G31
Minority Staff Director: Jeff Lewis 224-1467 SH-628

Problems and opportunities of older people including health, income, employment, housing and care and assistance. Reports findings and makes recommendations to the Senate, but cannot report legislation.

Party Ratio: D 10 — R 9

David Pryor, Ark., chairman
John Glenn, Ohio
Bill Bradley, N.J.
Quentin N. Burdick, N.D.
J. Bennett Johnston, La.
John B. Breaux, La.
Richard C. Shelby, Ala.
Harry Reid, Nev.
Bob Graham, Fla.
Herb Kohl, Wis.
Terry Sanford, N.C.

William S. Cohen, Maine
Larry Pressler, S.D.
Charles E. Grassley, Iowa
Alan K. Simpson, Wyo.
James M. Jeffords, Vt.
John McCain, Ariz.
Dave Durenberger, Minn.
Larry E. Craig, Idaho
Conrad Burns, Mont.
Arlen Specter, Pa.
<Vacancy>

VETERANS' AFFAIRS

Phone: 224-9126 **Room: SR-414**

Majority Staff Director: Edward Scott 224-9126 SR-414
Minority Staff Director: Thomas Roberts 224-2074 SH-202

Veterans' measures in general; compensation; armed forces life insurance; national cemeteries; pensions; readjustment benefits; veterans' hospitals, medical care and treatment; vocational rehabilitation and education.

Party Ratio: D 7 — R 5

Alan Cranston, Calif., chairman
Dennis DeConcini, Ariz.
George J. Mitchell, Maine
John D. Rockefeller IV, W.Va.
Bob Graham, Fla.
Daniel K. Akaka, Hawaii
Tom Daschle, S.D.

Arlen Specter, Pa., ranking member
Frank H. Murkowski, Alaska
Alan K. Simpson, Wyo.
Strom Thurmond, S.C.
James M. Jeffords, Vt.

House Committees, 102nd Congress

(As of Nov. 27, 1991)

AGRICULTURE

Phone: 225-2171 **Room: 1301 LHOB**

Majority Staff Director: Dianne Powell 225-2171 1301 LHOB
Minority Staff Director: Dennis Lambert 225-0029 1304 LHOB

Agriculture generally; production, marketing and stabilization of agricultural prices; animal industry and diseases of animals; crop insurance and soil conservation; dairy industry; farm credit and security; forestry in general; human nutrition; home economics; inspection of livestock and meat products; plant industry, soils and agricultural engineering; rural electrification; commodities exchanges; rural development. Chairman and ranking minority member are members ex officio of all subcommittees of which they are not regular members.

Party Ratio: D 27 — R 18

E. "Kika" de la Garza, Texas, chairman
Walter B. Jones, N.C.
George E. Brown Jr., Calif.
Charlie Rose, N.C.
Glenn English, Okla.
Leon E. Panetta, Calif.
Jerry Huckaby, La.
Dan Glickman, Kan.
Charles W. Stenholm, Texas
Harold L. Volkmer, Mo.
Charles Hatcher, Ga.
Robin Tallon, S.C.
Harley O. Staggers Jr., W.Va.
Jim Olin, Va.
Timothy J. Penny, Minn.
Richard Stallings, Idaho
Dave Nagle, Iowa
Jim Jontz, Ind.
Tim Johnson, S.D.
Ben Nighthorse Campbell, Colo.
Mike Espy, Miss.
Bill Sarpalius, Texas
Jill L. Long, Ind.
Gary Condit, Calif.
Collin C. Peterson, Minn.
Calvin Dooley, Calif.
Mike Kopetski, Ore.

Tom Coleman, Mo., ranking member
Ron Marlenee, Mont.
Larry J. Hopkins, Ky.
Pat Roberts, Kan.
Bill Emerson, Mo.
Sid Morrison, Wash.
Steve Gunderson, Wis.
Tom Lewis, Fla.
Bob Smith, Ore.
Larry Combest, Texas
Wally Herger, Calif.
James T. Walsh, N.Y.
Dave Camp, Mich.
Wayne Allard, Colo.
Bill Barrett, Neb.
Jim Nussle, Iowa
John A. Boehner, Ohio
Thomas W. Ewing, Ill.

SUBCOMMITTEES

Conservation, Credit and Rural Development

Phone: 225-0301 **Room: 1430 LHOB**

English, chairman
Staggers
Stallings
Nagle
Sarpalius
Johnson (S.D.)
Huckaby
Glickman
Penny
Espy
Long
Stenholm

Smith (Ore.)
Gunderson
Combest
Allard
Barrett
Nussle
Boehner

Cotton, Rice and Sugar

Phone: 225-1867 **Room: 1336 LHOB**

Huckaby, chairman
Espy
Peterson (Minn.)
Jones (N.C.)
Condit
Hatcher
Tallon
Stallings
Dooley
Rose
Stenholm

Emerson
Lewis (Fla.)
Combest
Herger
Camp
Nussle
Boehner

Department Operations, Research and Foreign Agriculture

Phone: 225-8906 **Room: 1534A LHOB**

Rose, chairman
Brown
Panetta
Jontz
Dooley
Kopetski
Stenholm
Volkmer
Hatcher
Tallon
Campbell (Colo.)
Sarpalius
Huckaby
Glickman

Roberts
Morrison
Gunderson
Herger
Walsh
Allard
Barrett
Boehner
Ewing

Domestic Marketing, Consumer Relations and Nutrition

Phone: 225-1496 **Room: 1301-A LHOB**

Tallon, chairman
Panetta
Staggers
Espy
Hatcher
Dooley

Lewis (Fla.)
Emerson
Herger

Forests, Family Farms and Energy

Phone: 225-1867 **Room: 1336 LHOB**

Volkmer, chairman
Olin
Stallings
Jontz
Panetta

Morrison
Marlenee
Emerson
Smith (Ore.)
Herger

Huckaby
Brown
Kopetski

Livestock, Dairy and Poultry

Phone: 225-1496 **Room: 1301-A LHOB**

Stenholm, chairman
Olin
Campbell (Colo.)
Condit
Peterson (Minn.)
Dooley
Rose
Volkmer
Penny
Nagle
Johnson (S.D.)
Sarpalius
Long

Gunderson
Hopkins
Roberts
Lewis (Fla.)
Smith (Ore.)
Walsh
Allard
Boehner

Peanuts and Tobacco

Phone: 225-1867 **Room: 1336 LHOB**

Hatcher, chairman
Jones (N.C.)
Rose
English
Stenholm

Hopkins
Combest
Gunderson

Wheat, Soybeans and Feed Grains

Phone: 225-0301 **Room: 1430 LHOB**

Glickman, chairman
Penny
Long
English
Nagle
Johnson (S.D.)
Peterson (Minn.)
Volkmer
Sarpalius
Rose
Olin

Marlenee
Roberts
Morrison
Smith (Ore.)
Camp
Barrett
Nussle

APPROPRIATIONS

Phone: 225-2771 **Room: H-218 Capitol**

Majority Staff Director: Frederick G. Mohrman 225-2771 H-218 Capitol
Minority Staff Director: Jim Kulikowski 225-3481 1016 LHOB

Appropriation of revenue for support of the federal government; rescissions of appropriations; transfers of unexpended balances; new spending authority under the Congressional Budget Act. Chairman and ranking minority member are members ex officio of all subcommittees of which they are not regular members.

Party Ratio: D 37 — R 22

Jamie L. Whitten, Miss., chairman
William H. Natcher, Ky.
Neal Smith, Iowa
Sidney R. Yates, Ill.
David R. Obey, Wis.
Edward R. Roybal, Calif.
Louis Stokes, Ohio
Tom Bevill, Ala.
Bill Alexander, Ark.
John P. Murtha, Pa.
Bob Traxler, Mich.
Joseph D. Early, Mass.
Charles Wilson, Texas
Norm Dicks, Wash.
Matthew F. McHugh, N.Y.
William Lehman, Fla.
Martin Olav Sabo, Minn.
Julian C. Dixon, Calif.
Vic Fazio, Calif.
W.G. "Bill" Hefner, N.C.
Les AuCoin, Ore.
Bernard J. Dwyer, N.J.
Steny H. Hoyer, Md.
Bob Carr, Mich.
Robert J. Mrazek, N.Y.
Richard J. Durbin, Ill.
Ronald D. Coleman, Texas
Alan B. Mollohan, W.Va.
Lindsay Thomas, Ga.
Chester G. Atkins, Mass.
Jim Chapman, Texas
Marcy Kaptur, Ohio
Lawrence J. Smith, Fla.
David E. Skaggs, Colo.
David Price, N.C.
Nancy Pelosi, Calif.
Peter J. Visclosky, Ind.

Joseph M. McDade, Pa., ranking member
John T. Myers, Ind.
Clarence E. Miller, Ohio
Lawrence Coughlin, Pa.
C.W. Bill Young, Fla.
Ralph Regula, Ohio
Carl D. Pursell, Mich.
Mickey Edwards, Okla.
Robert L. Livingston, La.
Bill Green, N.Y.
Jerry Lewis, Calif.
John Porter, Ill.
Harold Rogers, Ky.
Joe Skeen, N.M.
Frank R. Wolf, Va.
Bill Lowery, Calif.
Vin Weber, Minn.
Tom DeLay, Texas
Jim Kolbe, Ariz.
Dean A. Gallo, N.J.
Barbara F. Vucanovich, Nev.
Jim Ross Lightfoot, Iowa

SUBCOMMITTEES

Commerce, Justice, State and Judiciary

Phone: 225-3351 **Room: H-309 Capitol**

Smith (Iowa), chairman
Alexander
Early
Carr
Mollohan
Pelosi

Rogers
Regula
Kolbe

Defense

Phone: 225-2847 **Room: H-144 Capitol**

Murtha, chairman
Dicks
Wilson
Hefner
AuCoin
Sabò
Dixon
Dwyer

McDade
Young (Fla.)
Miller (Ohio)
Livingston
Lewis (Calif.)

District of Columbia

Phone: 225-5338 **Room: H-302 Capitol**

Dixon, chairman
Natcher
Stokes
Sabo
AuCoin
Hoyer

Gallo
Regula
DeLay

Energy and Water Development

Phone: 225-3421 **Room: 2362 RHOB**

Bevill, chairman
Fazio
Thomas (Ga.)
Chapman
Skaggs
Dwyer

Myers
Pursell
Gallo

Foreign Operations, Export Financing and Related Programs

Phone: 225-2041 **Room: H-307 Capitol**

Obey, chairman
Yates
McHugh
Lehman (Fla.)
Wilson
Coleman (Texas)
Smith (Fla.)
<Vacancy>

Edwards (Okla.)
Porter
Green
Livingston

Interior

Phone: 225-3081 **Room: B308 RHOB**

Yates, chairman
Murtha
Dicks
AuCoin
Bevill
Atkins

Regula
McDade
Lowery
Skeen

Labor, Health and Human Services, And Education

Phone: 225-3508 **Room: 2358 RHOB**

Natcher, chairman
Smith (Iowa)
Obey
Roybal
Stokes
Early
Hoyer
Mrazek

Pursell
Porter
Young (Fla.)
Weber

Legislative

Phone: 225-5338 **Room: H-302 Capitol**

Fazio, chairman
Mrazek
Smith (Fla.)
Alexander
Murtha
Traxler

Lewis (Calif.)
Porter
Vucanovich

Military Construction

Phone: 225-3047 **Room: B300 RHOB**

Hefner, chairman
Alexander
Thomas (Ga.)
Coleman (Texas)
Bevill
Wilson
Dicks
Fazio

Lowery
Edwards (Okla.)
DeLay
Lightfoot

Rural Development, Agriculture and Related Agencies

Phone: 225-2638 **Room: 2362 RHOB**

Whitten, chairman
Traxler
McHugh
Natcher
Durbin
Kaptur
Price
Smith (Iowa)
Obey

Skeen
Myers
Weber
Vucanovich

Transportation

Phone: 225-2141 **Room: 2358 RHOB**

Lehman (Fla.), chairman
Carr
Durbin
Sabo
Price
<Vacancy>

Coughlin
Wolf
DeLay

Treasury, Postal Service and General Government

Phone: 225-5834 **Room: H-164 Capitol**

Roybal, chairman
Hoyer
Skaggs
Pelosi
Yates
Early

Wolf
Lightfoot
Rogers

Veterans Affairs, Housing and Urban Development, and Independent Agencies

Phone: 225-3241 **Room: H-143 Capitol**

Traxler, chairman
Stokes
Mollohan
Chapman
Atkins
Kaptur

Green
Coughlin
Lowery

Veterans Affairs, Housing and Urban Development, and Independent Agencies

Phone: 225-3241 **Room: H-143 Capitol**

Traxler, chairman
Stokes
Mollohan
Chapman
Atkins
Kaptur

Green
Coughlin
Lowery

ARMED SERVICES

Phone: 225-4151 **Room: 2120 RHOB**

Staff Director: Rudy de Leon 225-4158 2120 RHOB

Common defense generally; Department of Defense; ammunition depots; forts; arsenals; Army, Navy and Air Force reservations and establishments; naval petroleum and oil shale reserves; scientific research and development in support of the armed services; Selective Service System; strategic and critical materials; military applications of nuclear energy; soldiers' and sailors' homes.

Party Ratio: D 33 — R 21

Les Aspin, Wis., chairman
Charles E. Bennett, Fla.
G.V. Montgomery, Miss.
Ronald V. Dellums, Calif.
Patricia Schroeder, Colo.
Beverly B. Byron, Md.
Nicholas Mavroules, Mass.
Earl Hutto, Fla.
Ike Skelton, Mo.
Dave McCurdy, Okla.
Thomas M. Foglietta, Pa.
Dennis M. Hertel, Mich.
Marilyn Lloyd, Tenn.
Norman Sisisky, Va.
Richard Ray, Ga.
John M. Spratt Jr., S.C.
Frank McCloskey, Ind.
Solomon P. Ortiz, Texas
George Darden, Ga.
Albert G. Bustamante, Texas
Barbara Boxer, Calif.
George J. Hochbrueckner, N.Y.
Owen B. Pickett, Va.
H. Martin Lancaster, N.C.
Lane Evans, Ill.
James Bilbray, Nev.
John Tanner, Tenn.
Michael R. McNulty, N.Y.
Glen Browder, Ala.
Gene Taylor, Miss.
Neil Abercrombie, Hawaii
Thomas H. Andrews, Maine
Chet Edwards, Texas

Bill Dickinson, Ala., ranking member
Floyd D. Spence, S.C.
Bob Stump, Ariz.
Larry J. Hopkins, Ky.
Robert W. Davis, Mich.
Duncan Hunter, Calif.
David O'B. Martin, N.Y.
John R. Kasich, Ohio
Herbert H. Bateman, Va.
Ben Blaz, Guam
Andy Ireland, Fla.
James V. Hansen, Utah
Curt Weldon, Pa.
Jon Kyl, Ariz.
Arthur Ravenel Jr., S.C.
Robert K. Dornan, Calif.
Joel Hefley, Colo.
Jim McCrery, La.
Ronald K. Machtley, R.I.
H. James Saxton, N.J.
Randy Cunningham, Calif.
Gary Franks, Conn.

SUBCOMMITTEES

Defense Policy

Phone: 225-4151 **Room: 2120 RHOB**

Aspin, chairman
Skelton
McCurdy
Foglietta
Sisisky
Ray
Spratt
McCloskey
Ortiz
Darden
Lancaster
Evans
McNulty
Browder
Bennett
Dellums
Schroeder
Byron
Mavroules
Hutto

Dickinson
Spence
Stump
Hopkins
Davis
Hunter
Martin
Kasich
Bateman
Blaz
Ireland
Weldon
Kyl
Ravenel
Dornan (Calif.)

Department of Energy Defense Nuclear Facilities

Phone: 225-4151 **Room: 2120 RHOB**

Spratt, chairman
Schroeder
Hertel
Lloyd
Sisisky
Ray
Bustamante
Hochbrueckner
Evans
Bilbray

Kyl
Ireland
Hansen
Spence
Hunter
McCrery

Environmental Restoration

Phone: 225-4151 **Room: 2120 RHOB**

Ray, chairman
Hochbrueckner
Pickett
Lancaster
Abercrombie

Saxton
Cunningham
Hansen

Future Uses of Defense Manufacturing and Technology Resources

Phone: 225-4151 **Room: 2120 RHOB**

Hertel, chairman
Bustamante
Browder
Taylor (Miss.)

Dornan (Calif.)
Franks

Investigations

Phone: 225-2086 **Room: 2343 RHOB**

Mavroules, chairman
Sisisky

Hopkins
Stump

Hertel
Spratt
McCloskey
Darden
Boxer
Evans
Tanner
McNulty

Kyl
Ireland
Hefley
Franks

Military Education

Phone: 225-4256 **Room: 2120 RHOB**

Skelton, chairman
Pickett
McNulty
Browder
Taylor (Miss.)
Edwards (Texas)

Machtley
Blaz
<Vacancy>

Military Installations and Facilities

Phone: 225-7120 **Room: 2119 RHOB**

Schroeder, chairman
Montgomery
McCurdy
Foglietta
Sisisky
Ortiz
Bilbray
Browder
Abercrombie
Edwards (Texas)
Mavroules
Hutto

Martin
Dickinson
Blaz
Spence
Ravenel
Hansen
McCrery
Machtley

Military Personnel and Compensation

Phone: 225-7560 **Room: 2343 RHOB**

Byron, chairman
Montgomery
Skelton
Hertel
Lloyd
Bustamante
Boxer
Hochbrueckner
Pickett
Lancaster

Bateman
Ravenel
Franks
Cunningham
Saxton
McCrery

Morale, Welfare and Recreation (MWR)

Phone: 223-4151 **Room: 2120 RHOB**

Lancaster, chairman
Ortiz
Pickett
Tanner
Hutto

Martin
Bateman
Kasich

North Atlantic Assembly

Phone: 225-4151 **Room: 2120 RHOB**

Sisisky, chairman
Dellums
Schroeder
Ray
Lancaster
Bilbray

Spence
Hefley
Dornan (Calif.)

Procurement and Military Nuclear Systems

Phone: 225-6999 **Room: 2343 RHOB**

Aspin, chairman
Skelton
Lloyd
Sisisky
Ray
Spratt
McCloskey
Bustamante
Evans
Bilbray
Tanner
McNulty
Taylor (Miss.)

Dickinson
Hopkins
Blaz
Ireland
Kasich
Martin
Weldon
Hefley
Saxton

Readiness

Phone: 225-9644 **Room: 2339 RHOB**

Hutto, chairman
Ray
Ortiz
Bustamante
Pickett
Lancaster
Evans
Abercrombie
Bennett

Kasich
Franks
Saxton
Cunningham
Machtley

Research and Development

Phone: 225-5530 **Room: 2117-A RHOB**

Dellums, chairman
McCurdy
Foglietta
Hertel
Darden
Boxer
Hochbrueckner
Browder
Andrews (Maine)
Edwards (Texas)
Bennett
Schroeder
Byron

Davis
Stump
Hunter
Kyl
Dornan (Calif.)
Hansen
McCrery
Cunningham
Blaz

Seapower and Strategic and Critical Materials

Phone: 225-6704 **Room: 2343 RHOB**

Bennett, chairman
Foglietta
Sisisky
Ortiz
Hochbrueckner
Pickett
Bilbray
Taylor (Miss.)

Spence
Hunter
Bateman
Weldon
Blaz
Dornan (Calif.)
Machtley

Andrews (Maine)	
Hutto	

Structure of U.S. Defense Industrial Base

Phone: 225-4151 **Room: 2120 RHOB**

McCurdy, chairman	*Franks*
Sisisky	*Saxton*
Spratt	*Bateman*
Darden	
Tanner	
McNulty	

BANKING, FINANCE AND URBAN AFFAIRS

Phone: 225-4247 **Room: 2129 RHOB**

Majority Clerk and Staff Director: Kelsay Meek 225-7057 2129 RHOB
Minority Staff Director: Tony Cole 225-7502 B301-C RHOB

Banks and banking including deposit insurance and federal monetary policy; money and credit; currency; issuance and redemption of notes; gold and silver; coinage; valuation and revaluation of the dollar; urban development; private and public housing; economic stabilization; defense production; renegotiation; price controls; international finance; financial aid to commerce and industry.

Party Ratio: D 31 — R 20

Henry B. Gonzalez, Texas, chairman	*Chalmers P. Wylie, Ohio, ranking member*
Frank Annunzio, Ill.	*Jim Leach, Iowa*
Stephen L. Neal, N.C.	*Bill McCollum, Fla.*
Carroll Hubbard Jr., Ky.	*Marge Roukema, N.J.*
John J. LaFalce, N.Y.	*Doug Bereuter, Neb.*
Mary Rose Oakar, Ohio	*Tom Ridge, Pa.*
Bruce F. Vento, Minn.	*Toby Roth, Wis.*
Doug Barnard Jr., Ga.	*Al McCandless, Calif.*
Charles E. Schumer, N.Y.	*Richard H. Baker, La.*
Barney Frank, Mass.	*Cliff Stearns, Fla.*
Ben Erdreich, Ala.	*Paul E. Gillmor, Ohio*
Thomas R. Carper, Del.	*Bill Paxon, N.Y.*
Esteban E. Torres, Calif.	*John J. "Jimmy" Duncan Jr., Tenn.*
Gerald D. Kleczka, Wis.	*Tom Campbell, Calif.*
Paul E. Kanjorski, Pa.	*Mel Hancock, Mo.*
Liz J. Patterson, S.C.	*Frank Riggs, Calif.*
Joseph P. Kennedy II, Mass.	*Jim Nussle, Iowa*
Floyd H. Flake, N.Y.	*Dick Armey, Texas*
Kweisi Mfume, Md.	*Craig Thomas, Wyo.*
Peter Hoagland, Neb.	*Sam Johnson, Texas*
Richard E. Neal, Mass.	
Charles Luken, Ohio	
Maxine Waters, Calif.	
Larry LaRocco, Idaho	
Bill Orton, Utah	
Jim Bacchus, Fla.	
James P. Moran Jr., Va.	
John W. Cox Jr., Ill.	
Ted Weiss, N.Y.	
Jim Slattery, Kan.	Bernard Sanders, Vt., Independent
Gary L. Ackerman, N.Y.	

SUBCOMMITTEES

Consumer Affairs and Coinage

Phone: 225-8872 **Room: 604 OHOB**

Torres, chairman	*McCandless*
Gonzalez	*Wylie*
Hubbard	*Baker*
Barnard	*Riggs*
Erdreich	*Armey*
Annunzio	*Thomas (Wyo.)*
Waters	
LaRocco	
Weiss	
<Vacancy>	
<Vacancy>	Sanders (I)

Domestic Monetary Policy

Phone: 226-7315 **Room: 109 FHOB**

Neal (N.C.), chairman	*Roth*
Barnard	*Duncan*
Gonzalez	*Campbell (Calif.)*
Neal (Mass.)	
<Vacancy>	

Economic Stabilization

Phone: 226-7511 **Room: 140 FHOB**

Carper, chairman	*Ridge*
LaFalce	*Paxon*
Oakar	*Hancock*
Vento	*Nussle*
Kanjorski	*Armey*
Patterson	*Thomas (Wyo.)*
Hoagland	
Luken	
Moran	

Financial Institution Supervisory Structure (FISS)

Phone: 225-4101 **Room: 2227 RHOB**

Barnard, chairman	*Wylie*
Hubbard	*Leach*
Neal (N.C.)	*McCollum*
Patterson	*Roukema*
Flake	*McCandless*
LaRocco	*Baker*
Cox (Ill.)	

Financial Institutions Supervision, Regulation and Insurance

Phone: 226-3280 **Room: 212 OHOB**

Annunzio, chairman	*Wylie*
Hubbard	*Leach*
Barnard	*McCollum*

LaFalce	*Roukema*
Vento	*Bereuter*
Schumer	*Roth*
Frank	*Ridge*
Kanjorski	*McCandless*
Neal (N.C.)	*Baker*
Kleczka	*Stearns*
Patterson	*Gillmor*
Kennedy	*Paxon*
Flake	*Duncan*
Mfume	*Campbell (Calif.)*
Hoagland	
Neal (Mass.)	
Luken	
LaRocco	
Orton	
Bacchus	
Moran	
Cox (Ill.)	

General Oversight

Phone: 225-2828 **Room: B304 RHOB**

Hubbard, chairman	*McCollum*
Gonzalez	*McCandless*
Barnard	*Hancock*
Flake	*Riggs*
Annunzio	*Nussle*
Waters	
Ackerman	
<Vacancy>	

Housing and Community Development

Phone: 225-7054 **Room: B303 RHOB**

Gonzalez, chairman	*Roukema*
Oakar	*Wylie*
Vento	*Bereuter*
Schumer	*Ridge*
Frank	*Baker*
Erdreich	*Paxon*
Carper	*Stearns*
Torres	*Gillmor*
Kleczka	*Campbell (Calif.)*
Kanjorski	*Riggs*
Neal (N.C.)	*Armey*
Hubbard	*Thomas (Wyo.)*
Kennedy	*Johnson (Texas)*
Flake	
Mfume	
LaFalce	
Patterson	
Neal (Mass.)	
Waters	
Orton	
Cox (Ill.)	**Sanders (I)**

International Development, Finance, Trade and Monetary Policy

Phone: 226-7515 **Room: 2219 RHOB**

Oakar, chairman	*Leach*
Neal (N.C.)	*Bereuter*
LaFalce	*McCandless*
Torres	*Stearns*
Kleczka	*McCollum*
Kennedy	*Roukema*
Frank	*Gillmor*
Flake	*Duncan*
Neal (Mass.)	*Campbell (Calif.)*
Waters	*Hancock*
LaRocco	
Orton	
Bacchus	
Moran	
Cox (Ill.)	**Sanders (I)**

Policy Research and Insurance

Phone: 225-1271 **Room: 139 FHOB**

Erdreich, chairman	*Bereuter*
Kanjorski	*Roth*
Carper	*Nussle*
Gonzalez	
Luken	

Resolution Trust Corporation

Phone: 225-4247 **Room: 2129 RHOB**

Vento, chairman	*Baker*
LaFalce	*Roukema*
Schumer	*Stearns*
Frank	*Gillmor*
Kanjorski	
Kleczka	
Mfume	
Kennedy	
Orton	
Bacchus	
Moran	

BUDGET

Phone: 226-7200 **Room: 214 OHOB**

Chief of Staff: John Angell 226-7234 222 OHOB
Minority Staff Director: Martha Phillips 226-7270 H2-278 FHOB

Federal budget generally; concurrent budget resolutions; Congressional Budget Office. Chairman and ranking minority member are members ex officio of all task forces of which they are not regular members. The majority leader and the minority leader's designate are ex officio members of all task forces.

Party Ratio: D 23 — R 14

Leon E. Panetta, Calif., chairman	*Bill Gradison, Ohio, ranking member*
Richard A. Gephardt, Mo.	*Alex McMillan, N.C.*
James L. Oberstar, Minn.	*Bill Thomas, Calif.*
Frank J. Guarini, N.J.	*Harold Rogers, Ky.*
Richard J. Durbin, Ill.	*Amo Houghton, N.Y.*
Mike Espy, Miss.	*Jim McCrery, La.*
Dale E. Kildee, Mich.	*John R. Kasich, Ohio*
Anthony C. Beilenson, Calif.	*Helen Delich Bentley, Md.*

Jerry Huckaby, La.
Martin Olav Sabo, Minn.
Bernard J. Dwyer, N.J.
Howard L. Berman, Calif.
Bob Wise, W.Va.
John Bryant, Texas
John M. Spratt Jr., S.C.
Don J. Pease, Ohio
Charles W. Stenholm, Texas
Robert T. Matsui, Calif.
Barney Frank, Mass.
Jim Cooper, Tenn.
Louise M. Slaughter, N.Y.
Lewis F. Payne Jr., Va.
Mike Parker, Miss.

William E. Dannemeyer, Calif.
John Miller, Wash.
Jim Kolbe, Ariz.
Christopher Shays, Conn.
Rick Santorum, Pa.
Bill Paxon, N.Y.

TASK FORCES

Budget Process, Reconciliation and Enforcement

Phone: 226-7200 **Room: 214 OHOB**

Beilenson, chairman
Espy
Dwyer
Sabo
Berman
Spratt
Stenholm
Frank
Payne (Va.)
Parker

Thomas (Calif.)
Rogers
Houghton
Miller (Wash.)
Shays
<Vacancy>

Community Development and Natural Resources

Phone: 226-7200 **Room: 214 OHOB**

Espy, chairman
Dwyer
Wise
Stenholm
Payne (Va.)

Bentley
Santorum

Defense, Foreign Policy and Space

Phone: 226-7200 **Room: 214 OHOB**

Durbin, chairman
Guarini
Beilenson
Huckaby
Berman
Bryant
Spratt
Pease
Matsui
Frank
Cooper
Slaughter

McCrery
Kasich
Bentley
Miller (Wash.)

Economic Policy, Projections and Revenues

Phone: 226-7200 **Room: 214 OHOB**

Kildee, chairman
Durbin
Sabo
Wise
Pease
Matsui
Frank
Parker

Rogers
Houghton
Kasich
Dannemeyer
Shays
Santorum

Human Resources

Phone: 226-7200 **Room: 214 OHOB**

Oberstar, chairman
Durbin
Kildee
Wise
Bryant
Matsui
Cooper

Kasich
Bentley
Kolbe

Urgent Fiscal Issues

Phone: 226-7200 **Room: 214 OHOB**

Guarini, chairman
Oberstar
Huckaby
Spratt
Pease
Cooper
Slaughter

Thomas (Calif.)
McCrery
Dannemeyer
Kolbe
<Vacancy>

DISTRICT OF COLUMBIA

Phone: 225-4457 **Room: 1310 LHOB**

Majority Staff Director: Edward C. Sylvester Jr. 225-4457 1310 LHOB
Minority Staff Director: Dennis Smith 225-7158 1307 LHOB

Municipal affairs of the District of Columbia.

Party Ratio: D 7 — R 4

Ronald V. Dellums, Calif., chairman
Pete Stark, Calif.
Mervyn M. Dymally, Calif.
Alan Wheat, Mo.
Jim McDermott, Wash.
Eleanor Holmes Norton, D.C.
Sander M. Levin, Mich.
<Vacancy>

Thomas J. Bliley Jr., Va., ranking member
Larry Combest, Texas
Dana Rohrabacher, Calif.
Bill Lowery, Calif.

SUBCOMMITTEES

Fiscal Affairs and Health

Phone: 225-4457 **Room: 507 OHOB**

Stark, chairman
Dellums
McDermott
Norton
<Vacancy>

Rohrabacher
Bliley
Combest

Government Operations and Metropolitan Affairs

Phone: 225-4457 **Room: 507 OHOB**

Wheat, chairman
Stark
Dymally
Levin
<Vacancy>

Combest
Bliley
Lowery

Judiciary and Education

Phone: 225-4457 **Room: 441 CHOB**

Dymally, chairman
Stark
Dellums
Wheat
Norton

Lowery
Bliley
Rohrabacher

EDUCATION AND LABOR

Phone: 225-4527 **Room: 2181 RHOB**

Majority Staff Director: Patricia Rissler 225-4527 2181 RHOB
Minority Staff Director: Andrew Hartman 225-6910 2174 RHOB

Education and labor generally; child labor; convict labor; labor standards and statistics; mediation and arbitration of labor disputes; regulation of foreign laborers; school food programs; vocational rehabilitation; wages and hours; welfare of miners; work incentive programs; Indian education; juvenile delinquency; human services programs; Gallaudet College; Howard University. Chairman and ranking minority member are members ex officio of all subcommittees of which they are not regular members.

Party Ratio: D 23 - R 14

William D. Ford, Mich., chairman
Joseph M. Gaydos, Pa.
William L. Clay, Mo.
George Miller, Calif.
Austin J. Murphy, Pa.
Dale E. Kildee, Mich.
Pat Williams, Mont.
Matthew G. Martinez, Calif.
Major R. Owens, N.Y.
Charles A. Hayes, Ill.
Carl C. Perkins, Ky.
Tom Sawyer, Ohio
Donald M. Payne, N.J.
Nita M. Lowey, N.Y.
Jolene Unsoeld, Wash.
Craig Washington, Texas
Jose E. Serrano, N.Y.
Patsy T. Mink, Hawaii
Robert E. Andrews, N.J.
William J. Jefferson, La.
John F. Reed, R.I.
Tim Roemer, Ind.
John Olver, Mass.
Ron de Lugo, V.I.
Jaime B. Fuster, P.R.
Ed Pastor, Ariz.

Bill Goodling, Pa., ranking member
Tom Coleman, Mo.
Tom Petri, Wis.
Marge Roukema, N.J.
Steve Gunderson, Wis.
Dick Armey, Texas
Harris W. Fawell, Ill.
Paul B. Henry, Mich.
Cass Ballenger, N.C.
Susan Molinari, N.Y.
Bill Barrett, Neb.
John A. Boehner, Ohio
Scott L. Klug, Wis.
Mickey Edwards, Okla.
Randy Cunningham, Calif.

SUBCOMMITTEES

Elementary, Secondary and Vocational Education

Phone: 225-4368 **Room: 320 CHOB**

Kildee, chairman
Miller (Calif.)
Williams
Martinez
Perkins
Hayes (Ill.)
Sawyer
Lowey
Unsoeld
Jefferson
Reed
Roemer
Washington
Mink
Fuster
Owens (N.Y.)

Goodling
Klug
Petri
Roukema
Gunderson
Henry
Molinari
Boehner
Edwards (Okla.)

Employment Opportunities

Phone: 225-7594 **Room: 617 OHOB**

Perkins, chairman
Andrews (N.J.)
Olver

Gunderson
Molinari
Henry

Health and Safety

Phone: 225-6876 **Room: B345-A RHOB**

Gaydos, chairman
Andrews (N.J.)
Murphy
Hayes (Ill.)

Henry
Ballenger
Boehner

Human Resources

Phone: 225-1850 **Room: B346-C RHOB**

Martinez, chairman
Kildee
Lowey
de Lugo

Fawell
Coleman (Mo.)
Barrett

Labor Standards

Phone: 225-1927 **Room: B346-A RHOB**

Murphy, chairman
Clay
Perkins
Owens (N.Y.)

Petri
Armey
Fawell

Labor-Management Relations

Phone: 225-5768 **Room: 112 CHOB**

Williams, chairman
Clay
Kildee
Miller (Calif.)
Hayes (Ill.)

Roukema
Armey
Barrett
Boehner
Fawell

Owens (N.Y.)
Sawyer
Serrano
Martinez
Payne (N.J.)
Unsoeld
Washington
Mink
Olver

Ballenger
Petri
Edwards (Okla.)

Postsecondary Education

Phone: 226-3681 **Room: 2451 RHOB**

Ford (Mich.), chairman
Williams
Hayes (Ill.)
Gaydos
Miller (Calif.)
Lowey
Sawyer
Payne (N.J.)
Unsoeld
Washington
Serrano
Mink
Andrews (N.J.)
Jefferson
Reed
Roemer
Kildee

Coleman (Mo.)
Molinari
Klug
Goodling
Petri
Roukema
Gunderson
Henry
Armey
Barrett

Select Education

Phone: 226-7532 **Room: 518 OHOB**

Owens (N.Y.), chairman
Payne (N.J.)
Serrano
Jefferson
Williams

Ballenger
Klug
<Vacancy>

ENERGY AND COMMERCE

Phone: 225-2927 **Room: 2125 RHOB**

Majority Staff Director: Jack Clouth 225-3147 2145 RHOB
Minority Chief Counsel & Staff Director: Margaret Durbin 225-3641 2322 RHOB

Interstate and foreign commerce generally; national energy policy generally; exploration, production, storage, supply, marketing, pricing and regulation of energy resources; nuclear energy; solar energy; energy conservation; generation and marketing of power; inland waterways; railroads and railway labor and retirement; communications generally; securities and exchanges; consumer affairs; travel and tourism; public health and quarantine; health-care facilities; biomedical research and development. Chairman and ranking minority member are members ex officio of all subcommittees of which they are not regular members.

Party Ratio: D 27 — R 16

John D. Dingell, Mich., chairman
James H. Scheuer, N.Y.
Henry A. Waxman, Calif.
Philip R. Sharp, Ind.
Edward J. Markey, Mass.
Al Swift, Wash.
Cardiss Collins, Ill.
Mike Synar, Okla.
W.J. "Billy" Tauzin, La.
Ron Wyden, Ore.
Ralph M. Hall, Texas
Dennis E. Eckart, Ohio
Bill Richardson, N.M.
Jim Slattery, Kan.
Gerry Sikorski, Minn.
John Bryant, Texas
Rick Boucher, Va.
Jim Cooper, Tenn.
Terry L. Bruce, Ill.
J. Roy Rowland, Ga.
Thomas J. Manton, N.Y.
Edolphus Towns, N.Y.
Tom McMillen, Md.
Gerry E. Studds, Mass.
Peter H. Kostmayer, Pa.
Richard H. Lehman, Calif.
Claude Harris, Ala.

Norman F. Lent, N.Y., ranking member
Carlos J. Moorhead, Calif.
Matthew J. Rinaldo, N.J.
William E. Dannemeyer, Calif.
Don Ritter, Pa.
Thomas J. Bliley Jr., Va.
Jack Fields, Texas
Michael G. Oxley, Ohio
Michael Bilirakis, Fla.
Dan Schaefer, Colo.
Joe L. Barton, Texas
Sonny Callahan, Ala.
Alex McMillan, N.C.
Dennis Hastert, Ill.
Clyde C. Holloway, La.
Fred Upton, Mich.

SUBCOMMITTEES

Commerce, Consumer Protection and Competitiveness

Phone: 226-3160 **Room: 151 FHOB**

Collins (Ill.), chairman
Kostmayer
Waxman
Boucher
Cooper
Bruce
Rowland
Manton
Towns
McMillen

McMillan
Oxley
Bilirakis
Barton
Upton

Energy and Power

Phone: 226-2500 **Room: 331 FHOB**

Sharp, chairman
Tauzin
Cooper
Bruce
Towns
McMillen
Studds
Lehman (Calif.)
Harris
Scheuer
Markey
Swift
Synar

Moorhead
Dannemeyer
Oxley
Barton
Callahan
Hastert
Holloway

Health and the Environment

Phone: 225-4952 **Room: 2415 RHOB**

Waxman, chairman
Sikorski
Bruce
Rowland
Towns
Studds
Kostmayer
Scheuer
Synar
Wyden
Hall (Texas)
Richardson
Bryant

Dannemeyer
Bliley
Fields
Bilirakis
McMillan
Hastert
Holloway

Oversight and Investigations

Phone: 225-4441 **Room: 2323 RHOB**

Dingell, chairman
Rowland
Wyden
Eckart
Slattery
Sikorski
Bryant

Bliley
Lent
Schaefer
Upton

Telecommunications and Finance

Phone: 226-2424 **Room: 316 FHOB**

Markey, chairman
Scheuer
Synar
Tauzin
Hall (Texas)
Eckart
Richardson
Slattery
Bryant
Boucher
Cooper
Manton
McMillen
Wyden
Lehman (Calif.)
Harris

Rinaldo
Moorhead
Ritter
Bliley
Fields
Oxley
Bilirakis
Schaefer
Barton

Transportation and Hazardous Materials

Phone: 225-9304 **Room: 324 FHOB**

Swift, chairman
Eckart
Slattery
Sikorski
Boucher
Manton
Sharp
Collins (Ill.)
Tauzin
Richardson

Ritter
Rinaldo
Fields
Schaefer
Callahan

FOREIGN AFFAIRS

Phone: 225-5021 **Room: 2170 RHOB**

Majority Chief of Staff: John J. Brady 225-5021 2170 RHOB
Minority Chief of Staff: John R. Sinclair 225-2170 B360 RHOB

Relations of the United States with foreign nations generally; foreign loans; international conferences and congresses; intervention abroad and declarations of war; diplomatic service; foreign trade; neutrality; protection of Americans abroad; Red Cross; United Nations; international economic policy; export controls including non-proliferation of nuclear technology and hardware; international commodity agreements; trading with the enemy; international financial and monetary organizations.

Party Ratio: D 26 — R 17

Dante B. Fascell, Fla., chairman
Lee H. Hamilton, Ind.
Gus Yatron, Pa.
Stephen J. Solarz, N.Y.
Howard Wolpe, Mich.
Sam Gejdenson, Conn.
Mervyn M. Dymally, Calif.
Tom Lantos, Calif.
Robert G. Torricelli, N.J.
Howard L. Berman, Calif.
Mel Levine, Calif.
Edward F. Feighan, Ohio
Ted Weiss, N.Y.
Gary L. Ackerman, N.Y.
Jaime B. Fuster, P.R.
Wayne Owens, Utah
Harry A. Johnston, Fla.
Eliot L. Engel, N.Y.
Eni F.H. Faleomavaega, Am.Samoa
Gerry E. Studds, Mass.
Austin J. Murphy, Pa.
Peter H. Kostmayer, Pa.
Thomas M. Foglietta, Pa.
Frank McCloskey, Ind.
Tom Sawyer, Ohio
Donald M. Payne, N.J.
Bill Orton, Utah
<Vacancy>

William S. Broomfield, Mich., ranking member
Benjamin A. Gilman, N.Y.
Robert J. Lagomarsino, Calif.
Bill Goodling, Pa.
Jim Leach, Iowa
Toby Roth, Wis.
Olympia J. Snowe, Maine
Henry J. Hyde, Ill.
Doug Bereuter, Neb.
Christopher H. Smith, N.J.
Dan Burton, Ind.
Jan Meyers, Kan.
John Miller, Wash.
Ben Blaz, Guam
Elton Gallegly, Calif.
Amo Houghton, N.Y.
Porter J. Goss, Fla.
Ileana Ros-Lehtinen, Fla.

SUBCOMMITTEES

Africa

Phone: 226-7807 **Room: 816 OHOB**

Dymally, chairman
Wolpe
Fuster
Solarz
Feighan
Payne (N.J.)

Burton
Blaz
Houghton
Roth

Arms Control, International Security and Science

Phone: 225-8926 **Room: 2401-A RHOB**

Fascell, chairman
Berman
Ackerman
Faleomavaega
McCloskey
Sawyer
Foglietta
Hamilton

Broomfield
Hyde
Snowe
Gallegly
Goss

Asian and Pacific Affairs

Phone: 226-7801 **Room: 707 OHOB**

Solarz, chairman
Faleomavaega
Lantos
Torricelli
Ackerman
Foglietta

Leach
Blaz
Lagomarsino
Roth

Europe and the Middle East

Phone: 225-3345 **Room: B359 RHOB**

Hamilton, chairman
Lantos
Levine
Feighan
Ackerman
Owens (Utah)
Johnston
Engel

Gilman
Goodling
Meyers
Gallegly
Leach

Human Rights and International Organizations

Phone: 226-7825 **Room: B358 RHOB**

Yatron, chairman
Owens (Utah)
Weiss
Engel
Hamilton
<Vacancy>

Bereuter
Smith (N.J.)
Hyde
Ros-Lehtinen

International Economic Policy and Trade

Phone: 226-7820 **Room: 702 OHOB**

Gejdenson, chairman
Wolpe
Levine
Feighan
Johnston
Engel
Murphy
Orton

Roth
Miller (Wash.)
Houghton
Bereuter
Blaz

International Narcotics Control

Phone: 225-5021 **Room: 2170 RHOB**

Feighan, chairman
Ackerman, co-chairman
Johnston
Yatron
Payne (N.J.)

Gilman
Meyers
Goss

International Operations

Phone: 225-3424 **Room: 709 OHOB**

Berman, chairman
Weiss
Dymally
Faleomavaega
Lantos
Levine

Snowe
Gilman
Smith (N.J.)
Miller (Wash.)

Western Hemisphere Affairs

Phone: 226-7812 **Room: 705 OHOB**

Torricelli, chairman
Fuster
Solarz
Gejdenson
Weiss
Engel
Studds
Kostmayer
Johnston

Lagomarsino
Goss
Ros-Lehtinen
Burton
Meyers

GOVERNMENT OPERATIONS

Phone: 225-5051 **Room: 2157 RHOB**

Majority Staff Director: Julian Epstein 225-5051 2157 RHOB
Minority Staff Director: Donald W. Upson 225-5074 2153 RHOB

Budget and accounting measures; overall economy and efficiency in government, including federal procurement; executive branch reorganization; general revenue sharing; intergovernmental relations; National Archives. Chairman and ranking minority member are members ex officio of all subcommittees of which they are not regular members.

Party Ratio: D 25 — R 15

John Conyers Jr., Mich., chairman
Cardiss Collins, Ill.
Glenn English, Okla.
Henry A. Waxman, Calif.
Ted Weiss, N.Y.
Mike Synar, Okla.
Stephen L. Neal, N.C.
Doug Barnard Jr., Ga.
Tom Lantos, Calif.
Bob Wise, W.Va.
Barbara Boxer, Calif.
Major R. Owens, N.Y.
Edolphus Towns, N.Y.
Ben Erdreich, Ala.
Gerald D. Kleczka, Wis.
Albert G. Bustamante, Texas
Matthew G. Martinez, Calif.
Donald M. Payne, N.J.
Gary Condit, Calif.
Patsy T. Mink, Hawaii
Ray Thornton, Ark.
Collin C. Peterson, Minn.
Rosa DeLauro, Conn.
Charles Luken, Ohio
John W. Cox Jr., Ill.

Frank Horton, N.Y., ranking member
William F. Clinger, Pa.
Al McCandless, Calif.
Dennis Hastert, Ill.
Jon Kyl, Ariz.
Christopher Shays, Conn.
Steven H. Schiff, N.M.
C. Christopher Cox, Calif.
Craig Thomas, Wyo.
Ileana Ros-Lehtinen, Fla.
Ronald K. Machtley, R.I.
Dick Zimmer, N.J.
Bill Zeliff, N.H.
David L. Hobson, Ohio
Scott L. Klug, Wis.

Bernard Sanders, Vt., Independent

SUBCOMMITTEES

Commerce, Consumer and Monetary Affairs

Phone: 225-4407 **Room: B377 RHOB**

Barnard, chairman
Martinez
Collins (Ill.)
Waxman
Erdreich
Bustamante

Hastert
Machtley
Zimmer
Zeliff

Employment and Housing

Phone: 225-6751 **Room: B349-A RHOB**

Lantos, chairman
Martinez
DeLauro
Luken
<Vacancy>

Ros-Lehtinen
Kyl
Shays

Environment, Energy and Natural Resources

Phone: 225-6427 **Room: B371-B RHOB**

Synar, chairman
Towns
Bustamante
Erdreich
Luken
Cox (Ill.)

Clinger
Hobson
Klug

Government Activities and Transportation

Phone: 225-7920 **Room: B350-A RHOB**

Boxer, chairman
Owens (N.Y.)
English
Kleczka
Condit
Thornton

Cox (Calif.)
Zimmer
Klug

Government Information, Justice and Agriculture

Phone: 225-3741 **Room: B349-C RHOB**

Wise, chairman
Condit
Towns
Mink
Peterson (Minn.)
Cox (Ill.)

McCandless
Schiff
Machtley

Sanders (I)

Human Resources and Intergovernmental Relations

Phone: 225-2548 **Room: B372 RHOB**

Weiss, chairman
Waxman
Payne (N.J.)
Mink
DeLauro

Thomas (Wyo.)
Zeliff
Hobson

Sanders (I)

Legislation and National Security

Phone: 225-5147 **Room: B373 RHOB**

Conyers, chairman
English
Neal (N.C.)
Kleczka
Collins (Ill.)
Thornton
Peterson (Minn.)

Horton
Kyl
Shays
Schiff

HOUSE ADMINISTRATION

Phone: 225-2061 **Room: H-326 Capitol**

Majority Staff Director: Bob Shea 225-2061 H-326 Capitol
Minority Staff Director: Mary Sue Englund 225-8281 H-330 Capitol

House administration generally; contested elections; federal elections generally; corrupt practices; qualifications of members of the House; Congressional Record; the Capitol; Library of Congress; Smithsonian Institution; Botanic Garden. Chairman and ranking minority member are non-voting members ex officio of all subcommittees of which they are not regular members.

Party Ratio: D 15 — R 9

Charlie Rose, N.C., chairman
Frank Annunzio, Ill.
Joseph M. Gaydos, Pa.
Leon E. Panetta, Calif.
Al Swift, Wash.
Mary Rose Oakar, Ohio
William L. Clay, Mo.
Sam Gejdenson, Conn.
Joe Kolter, Pa.
Martin Frost, Texas
Thomas J. Manton, N.Y.
Marty Russo, Ill.
Steny H. Hoyer, Md.
Gerald D. Kleczka, Wis.
Dale E. Kildee, Mich.

Bill Thomas, Calif., ranking member
Bill Dickinson, Ala.
Newt Gingrich, Ga.
Pat Roberts, Kan.
Paul E. Gillmor, Ohio
James T. Walsh, N.Y.
Mickey Edwards, Okla.
Robert L. Livingston, La.
Bill Barrett, Neb.

SUBCOMMITTEES

Accounts

Phone: 226-7540 **Room: 611 OHOB**

Gaydos, chairman
Annunzio
Swift
Oakar
Gejdenson
Manton
Russo

Gillmor
Gingrich
Dickinson
Barrett

Campaign Finance Reform

Phone: 225-2870 **Room: 720 OHOB**

Gejdenson, chairman
Panetta
Frost
Kleczka

Thomas (Calif.)
Edwards (Okla.)
Walsh

Elections

Phone: 226-7616 **Room: 802 OHOB**

Swift, chairman	*Livingston*
Panetta	*Walsh*
Frost	*Gillmor*
Hoyer	
Kildee	

Libraries and Memorials

Phone: 226-2307 **Room: 612 OHOB**

Clay, chairman	*Barrett*
Kolter	*Roberts*
Frost	
Hoyer	

Office Systems

Phone: 225-1608 **Room: 722 OHOB**

Gejdenson, chairman	*Walsh*
Frost	*Dickinson*
Russo	
<Vacancy>	

Personnel and Police

Phone: 226-7614 **Room: 720 OHOB**

Oakar, chairman	*Roberts*
Panetta	*Dickinson*
Kolter	*Livingston*
Manton	
Russo	
Kleczka	

Procurement and Printing

Phone: 225-4658 **Room: 105 CHOB**

Annunzio, chairman	*Edwards (Okla.)*
Gaydos	*Gingrich*
Hoyer	
<Vacancy>	

INTERIOR AND INSULAR AFFAIRS

Phone: 225-2761 **Room: 1324 LHOB**

Majority Staff Director: Daniel P. Beard 225-2761 1324 LHOB
Minority Staff Director: Dan Kish 225-6065 1329 LHOB

Survey; interstate water compacts; irrigation and reclamation; Indian affairs; minerals, mines and mining; petroleum conservation on public lands; regulation of domestic nuclear energy industry, including waste disposal; territorial affairs of the United States. Chairman and ranking minority member are non-voting members ex officio of all subcommittees of which they are not regular members.

Party Ratio: D 26 — R 16

George Miller, Calif., chairman	*Don Young, Alaska, ranking member*
Philip R. Sharp, Ind.	*Robert J. Lagomarsino, Calif.*
Edward J. Markey, Mass.	*Ron Marlenee, Mont.*
Austin J. Murphy, Pa.	*James V. Hansen, Utah*
Nick J. Rahall II, W.Va.	*Barbara F. Vucanovich, Nev.*
Bruce F. Vento, Minn.	*Ben Blaz, Guam*
Pat Williams, Mont.	*John J. Rhodes III, Ariz.*
Beverly B. Byron, Md.	*Elton Gallegly, Calif.*
Ron de Lugo, V.I.	*Bob Smith, Ore.*
Sam Gejdenson, Conn.	*Craig Thomas, Wyo.*
Peter H. Kostmayer, Pa.	*John J. Duncan Jr., Tenn.*
Richard H. Lehman, Calif.	*Dick Schulze, Pa.*
Bill Richardson, N.M.	*Joel Hefley, Colo.*
George Darden, Ga.	*Charles H. Taylor, N.C.*
Jaime B. Fuster, P.R.	*John T. Doolittle, Calif.*
Mel Levine, Calif.	*Wayne Allard, Colo.*
Wayne Owens, Utah	*Richard H. Baker, La.*
John Lewis, Ga.	
Ben Nighthorse Campbell, Colo.	
Peter A. DeFazio, Ore.	
Eni F.H. Faleomavaega, Am.Samoa	
Tim Johnson, S.D.	
Charles E. Schumer, N.Y.	
Jim Jontz, Ind.	
Peter Hoagland, Neb.	
Harry A. Johnston, Fla.	
Larry LaRocco, Idaho	
Neil Abercrombie, Hawaii	
Calvin Dooley, Calif.	

SUBCOMMITTEES

Energy and the Environment

Phone: 226-4085 **Room: 815 OHOB**

Kostmayer, chairman	*Rhodes*
Sharp	*Blaz*
Markey	*Thomas (Wyo.)*
Gejdenson	*Hefley*
Schumer	*Taylor (N.C.)*
Murphy	*Doolittle*
Richardson	*Allard*
Darden	*Baker*
Jontz	
Lehman (Calif.)	
Owens (Utah)	
<Vacancy>	

General Oversight and California Desert Lands

Phone: 225-8331 **Room: 483 FHOB**

Lehman (Calif.), chairman	*Blaz*
Kostmayer	*Duncan*
Levine	*Baker*

Insular and International Affairs

Phone: 225-9297 **Room: 1626 LHOB**

de Lugo, chairman
Fuster
Faleomavaega
Lewis (Ga.)
Darden
Miller (Calif.)

Lagomarsino
Blaz
Gallegly

Mining and Natural Resources

Phone: 226-7761 **Room: 819 OHOB**

Rahall, chairman
Campbell (Colo.)
DeFazio
Jontz

Vucanovich
Thomas (Wyo.)

National Parks and Public Lands

Phone: 226-7736 **Room: 812 OHOB**

Vento, chairman
Murphy
Williams
Byron
Richardson
Darden
Levine
Owens (Utah)
Lewis (Ga.)
Campbell (Colo.)
DeFazio
Johnson (S.D.)
Jontz
Hoagland
Johnston
LaRocco
Markey
Rahall
de Lugo
Fuster
Abercrombie
Dooley

Marlenee
Lagomarsino
Hansen
Vucanovich
Gallegly
Smith (Ore.)
Thomas (Wyo.)
Duncan
Schulze
Hefley
Taylor (N.C.)
Doolittle

Water, Power and Offshore Energy

Phone: 225-6042 **Room: 1328 LHOB**

Miller (Calif.), chairman
Sharp
Vento
Byron
Gejdenson
Lehman (Calif.)
Owens (Utah)
Campbell (Colo.)
DeFazio
Johnson (S.D.)
Hoagland
Johnston
LaRocco
Markey
Abercrombie
Dooley

Hansen
Young (Alaska)
Marlenee
Blaz
Rhodes
Smith (Ore.)
Schulze
Taylor (N.C.)
Doolittle
Allard

JUDICIARY

Phone: 225-3951 **Room: 2138 RHOB**

General Counsel: John Yarowsky 225-3951 2138 RHOB
Minority Chief Counsel: Alan F. Coffey Jr. 225-6906 B351-C RHOB

Civil and criminal judicial proceedings generally; federal courts and judges; bankruptcy, mutiny, espionage and counterfeiting; civil liberties; constitutional amendments; immigration and naturalization; interstate compacts; claims against the United States; apportionment of representatives; meetings of Congress and attendance of members; penitentiaries; patents, copyrights and trademarks; presidential succession; monopolies and unlawful restraints of trade; internal security. Chairman and ranking member are non-voting members ex officio of all subcommittees of which they are not regular members.

Party Ratio: D 21 — R 13

Jack Brooks, Texas, chairman
Don Edwards, Calif.
John Conyers Jr., Mich.
Romano L. Mazzoli, Ky.
William J. Hughes, N.J.
Mike Synar, Okla.
Patricia Schroeder, Colo.
Dan Glickman, Kan.
Barney Frank, Mass.
Charles E. Schumer, N.Y.
Edward F. Feighan, Ohio
Howard L. Berman, Calif.
Rick Boucher, Va.
Harley O. Staggers Jr., W.Va.
John Bryant, Texas
Mel Levine, Calif.
George E. Sangmeister, Ill.
Craig Washington, Texas
Peter Hoagland, Neb.
Mike Kopetski, Ore.
John F. Reed, R.I.

Hamilton Fish Jr., N.Y., ranking member
Carlos J. Moorhead, Calif.
Henry J. Hyde, Ill.
F. James Sensenbrenner Jr., Wis.
Bill McCollum, Fla.
George W. Gekas, Pa.
Howard Coble, N.C.
Lamar Smith, Texas
Craig T. James, Fla.
Tom Campbell, Calif.
Steven H. Schiff, N.M.
Jim Ramstad, Minn.
George F. Allen, Va.

SUBCOMMITTEES

Administrative Law and Governmental Relations

Phone: 225-5741 **Room: B351-A RHOB**

Frank, chairman
Edwards (Calif.)
Mazzoli
Staggers
Reed

Gekas
Schiff
Ramstad

Civil and Constitutional Rights

Phone: 226-7680 **Room: 806 OHOB**

Edwards (Calif.), chairman
Conyers
Schroeder
Washington
Kopetski

Hyde
Coble
McCollum

Crime and Criminal Justice

Phone: 226-2406 **Room: 362 FHOB**

Schumer, chairman
Hughes
Feighan
Bryant
Levine
Sangmeister
Washington
Hoagland

Sensenbrenner
Schiff
Ramstad
McCollum
Gekas

Economic and Commercial Law

Phone: 225-2825 **Room: B353 RHOB**

Brooks, chairman
Edwards (Calif.)
Conyers
Mazzoli
Synar
Glickman
Feighan
Berman
Staggers
Bryant

Fish
Slaughter
Smith (Texas)
James
Campbell (Calif.)
Moorhead
Hyde

Intellectual Property and Judicial Administration

Phone: 225-3926 **Room: 207 CHOB**

Hughes, chairman
Conyers
Synar
Schroeder
Glickman
Frank
Schumer
Boucher
Levine
Sangmeister

Moorhead
Coble
Fish
Sensenbrenner
James
Campbell (Calif.)

International Law, Immigration and Refugees

Phone: 225-5727 **Room: B370-B RHOB**

Mazzoli, chairman
Schumer
Berman
Bryant
Kopetski

McCollum
Smith (Texas)
James
Allen

MERCHANT MARINE AND FISHERIES

Phone: 225-4047 **Room: 1334 LHOB**

Majority Chief Counsel: Edmund B. Welch 225-4047 1334 LHOB
Minority Staff Director: George D. Pence 225-2650 1337 LHOB

Merchant marine generally; oceanography and marine affairs including coastal zone management; Coast Guard; fisheries and wildlife; regulation of common carriers by water and inspection of merchant marine vessels, lights and signals, lifesaving equipment and fire protection; navigation; Panama Canal, Canal Zone and interoceanic canals generally; registration and licensing of vessels; rules and international arrangements to prevent collisions at sea; international fishing agreements; Coast Guard and Merchant Marine academies and state maritime academies. Chairman and ranking minority member are members ex officio of all subcommittees of which they are not regular members.

Party Ratio: D 28 — R 17

Walter B. Jones, N.C., chairman
Gerry E. Studds, Mass.
Carroll Hubbard Jr., Ky.
William J. Hughes, N.J.
Earl Hutto, Fla.
W.J. Tauzin, La.
Thomas M. Foglietta, Pa.
Dennis M. Hertel, Mich.
William O. Lipinski, Ill.
Robert A. Borski, Pa.
Thomas R. Carper, Del.
Robin Tallon, S.C.
Solomon P. Ortiz, Texas
Charles E. Bennett, Fla.
Thomas J. Manton, N.Y.
Owen B. Pickett, Va.
George J. Hochbrueckner, N.Y.
Bob Clement, Tenn.
Stephen J. Solarz, N.Y.
Frank Pallone Jr., N.J.
Greg Laughlin, Texas
Nita M. Lowey, N.Y.
Jolene Unsoeld, Wash.
Gene Taylor, Miss.
Glenn M. Anderson, Calif.
John F. Reed, R.I.
William J. Jefferson, La.
Eni F.H. Faleomavaega, Am.Samoa
H. Martin Lancaster, N.C.

Robert W. Davis, Mich., ranking member
Don Young, Alaska
Norman F. Lent, N.Y.
Jack Fields, Texas
Herbert H. Bateman, Va.
H. James Saxton, N.J.
Helen Delich Bentley, Md.
Howard Coble, N.C.
Curt Weldon, Pa.
Wally Herger, Calif.
James M. Inhofe, Okla.
Porter J. Goss, Fla.
Arthur Ravenel Jr., S.C.
Sonny Callahan, Ala.
Wayne T. Gilchrest, Md.
John T. Doolittle, Calif.
Randy Cunningham, Calif.

SUBCOMMITTEES

Coast Guard and Navigation

Phone: 226-3587 **Room: 547 FHOB**

Tauzin, chairman
Clement
Reed
Hughes
Hutto
Carper
Manton
Pickett
Hochbrueckner
Pallone
Laughlin
Lowey
Taylor (Miss.)
Anderson
Studds
<Vacancy>

Fields
Young (Alaska)
Bateman
Coble
Inhofe
Goss
Callahan
Gilchrest

Fisheries and Wildlife Conservation And the Environment

Phone: 226-3533	**Room: 543 FHOB**
Studds, chairman	*Young (Alaska)*
Hughes	*Saxton*
Hutto	*Coble*
Carper	*Weldon*
Abercrombie	*Herger*
Tallon	*Goss*
Ortiz	*Ravenel*
Manton	*Gilchrest*
Hochbrueckner	*Doolittle*
Solarz	
Pallone	
Unsoeld	
Laughlin	
Lowey	
Anderson	
Reed	
Jefferson	
Faleomavaega	
Tauzin	

Merchant Marine

Phone: 226-2460	**Room: 575 FHOB**
Jones (N.C.), chairman	*Lent*
Hubbard	*Fields*
Borski	*Bateman*
Bennett	*Inhofe*
Pickett	*Ravenel*
Taylor (Miss.)	*Callahan*
Jefferson	*Doolittle*
Studds	*Cunningham*
Hertel	
Tallon	
Ortiz	
Solarz	
Unsoeld	
<Vacancy>	
<Vacancy>	

Oceanography, Great Lakes and Outer Continental Shelf

Phone: 226-3504	**Room: 532 FHOB**
Hertel, chairman	*Bateman*
Clement	*Saxton*
Hughes	*Weldon*
Pallone	*Herger*
Taylor (Miss.)	
Lipinski	
<Vacancy>	
<Vacancy>	

Oversight and Investigations

Phone: 226-3514	**Room: 579 FHOB**
Lipinski, chairman	*Saxton*
Borski	*Cunningham*
<Vacancy>	

POST OFFICE AND CIVIL SERVICE

Phone: 225-4054 **Room: 309 CHOB**

Majority Staff Director: Gail Weiss 225-4054 309 CHOB
Minority Staff Director: Joseph A. Fisher 225-8036 300 CHOB

Postal and federal civil services; census and the collection of statistics generally; Hatch Act; holidays and celebrations.

Party Ratio: D 14 — R 8

William L. Clay, Mo., chairman	*Benjamin A. Gilman, N.Y., ranking member*
Patricia Schroeder, Colo.	*Frank Horton, N.Y.*
Gus Yatron, Pa.	*John T. Myers, Ind.*
Mary Rose Oakar, Ohio	*Don Young, Alaska*
Gerry Sikorski, Minn.	*Dan Burton, Ind.*
Frank McCloskey, Ind.	*Constance A. Morella, Md.*
Gary L. Ackerman, N.Y.	*Tom Ridge, Pa.*
Mervyn M. Dymally, Calif.	*Rod D. Chandler, Wash.*
Tom Sawyer, Ohio	
Paul E. Kanjorski, Pa.	
Charles A. Hayes, Ill.	
Michael R. McNulty, N.Y.	
James P. Moran Jr., Va.	
Eleanor Holmes Norton, D.C.	
Barbara-Rose Collins, Mich.	

SUBCOMMITTEES

Census and Population

Phone: 226-7523	**Room: 608 OHOB**
Sawyer, chairman	*Ridge*
Dymally, vice chairman	*Chandler*
McNulty	

Civil Service

Phone: 225-4025	**Room: 122 CHOB**
Sikorski, chairman	*Morella*
Moran	*Ridge*
Norton	

Compensation and Employee Benefits

Phone: 226-7546	**Room: 515 OHOB**
Ackerman, chairman	*Myers*
Oakar	*Morella*
Schroeder	

Human Resources

Phone: 225-2821 **Room: 603 OHOB**

Kanjorski, chairman
Yatron
Moran

Burton
Horton

Investigations

Phone: 225-6295 **Room: 219 CHOB**

Clay, chairman
McNulty
McCloskey

Chandler
Gilman

Postal Operations and Services

Phone: 225-9124 **Room: 209 CHOB**

McCloskey, chairman
Sikorski
Norton

Horton
Young (Alaska)

Postal Personnel and Modernization

Phone: 226-7520 **Room: 406 CHOB**

Hayes (Ill.), chairman
McNulty
Yatron

Young (Alaska)
Myers

PUBLIC WORKS AND TRANSPORTATION

Phone: 225-4472 **Room: 2165 RHOB**

Majority Staff Director: John Doyle 225-4472 2165 RHOB
Minority Chief Counsel & Staff Director: Jack Schenendorf 225-9446 2163 RHOB

Flood control and improvement of rivers and harbors; construction and maintenance of roads; oil and other pollution of navigable waters; public buildings and grounds; public works for the benefit of navigation including bridges and dams; water power; transportation, except railroads; Botanic Garden; Library of Congress; Smithsonian Institution. Chairman and ranking minority member are members ex officio of all subcommittees of which they are not regular members.

Party Ratio: D 34 — R 21

Robert A. Roe, N.J., chairman
Glenn M. Anderson, Calif.
Norman Y. Mineta, Calif.
James L. Oberstar, Minn.
Henry J. Nowak, N.Y.
Nick J. Rahall II, W.Va.
Douglas Applegate, Ohio
Ron de Lugo, V.I.
Gus Savage, Ill.
Robert A. Borski, Pa.
Joe Kolter, Pa.
Tim Valentine, N.C.
William O. Lipinski, Ill.
James A. Traficant Jr., Ohio
John Lewis, Ga.
Peter A. DeFazio, Ore.
Jimmy Hayes, La.
Bob Clement, Tenn.
Lewis F. Payne Jr., Va.
Jerry F. Costello, Ill.
Frank Pallone Jr., N.J.
Ben Jones, Ga.
Mike Parker, Miss.
Greg Laughlin, Texas
Pete Geren, Texas
George E. Sangmeister, Ill.
Glenn Poshard, Ill.
Dick Swett, N.H.
Bill Brewster, Okla.
Bud Cramer, Ala.
Rosa DeLauro, Conn.
Joan Kelly Horn, Mo.
Barbara-Rose Collins, Mich.
Pete Peterson, Fla.
Eleanor Holmes Norton, D.C.
<Vacancy>

John Paul Hammerschmidt, Ark., ranking member
Bud Shuster, Pa.
William F. Clinger, Pa.
Tom Petri, Wis.
Ron Packard, Calif.
Sherwood Boehlert, N.Y.
Helen Delich Bentley, Md.
James M. Inhofe, Okla.
Cass Ballenger, N.C.
Fred Upton, Mich.
Bill Emerson, Mo.
John J. Duncan Jr., Tenn.
Mel Hancock, Mo.
C. Christopher Cox, Calif.
Susan Molinari, N.Y.
David L. Hobson, Ohio
Frank Riggs, Calif.
Charles H. Taylor, N.C.
Dick Nichols, Kan.
Bill Zeliff, N.H.
Thomas W. Ewing, Ill.

SUBCOMMITTEES

Aviation

Phone: 225-9161 **Room: 2251 RHOB**

Oberstar, chairman
Horn
Collins (Mich.)
Mineta
Nowak
Rahall
de Lugo
Savage
Kolter
Valentine
Lipinski
Traficant
Lewis (Ga.)
DeFazio
Hayes (La.)
Clement
Payne (Va.)
Costello
Parker
Laughlin
Geren
Sangmeister
Poshard
Swett

Clinger
Shuster
Petri
Boehlert
Inhofe
Ballenger
Duncan
Hancock
Cox (Calif.)
Molinari
Hobson
Nichols
<Vacancy>

Economic Development

Phone: 225-6151 **Room: B376 RHOB**

Kolter, chairman
Oberstar
Applegate

Bentley
Boehlert
Inhofe

Savage
Swett
Cramer
DeLauro
Horn
Collins (Mich.)
Nowak
Traficant

Ballenger
Upton
Emerson

Investigations and Oversight

Phone: 225-3274 **Room: 586 FHOB**

Borski, chairman
DeLauro
Peterson (Fla.)
Anderson
Mineta
Hayes (La.)
Laughlin
Brewster
Norton
Oberstar
<Vacancy>
<Vacancy>

Packard
Shuster
Duncan
Hancock
Molinari
Hobson

Public Buildings and Grounds

Phone: 225-9961 **Room: B376 RHOB**

Savage, chairman
Norton
Nowak
Borski
Lipinski
Lewis (Ga.)
Jones (Ga.)
Poshard
Peterson (Fla.)
Oberstar
Kolter

Inhofe
Bentley
Duncan
Cox (Calif.)
<Vacancy>

Surface Transportation

Phone: 225-9989 **Room: B376 RHOB**

Mineta, chairman
Anderson
Rahall
Applegate
de Lugo
Valentine
Lipinski
Traficant
Lewis (Ga.)
Clement
Payne (Va.)
Costello
Pallone
Jones (Ga.)
Parker
Laughlin
Sangmeister
DeFazio
Geren
Poshard
Swett
Brewster
Cramer
Norton
<Vacancy>

Shuster
Clinger
Petri
Packard
Boehlert
Upton
Emerson
Cox (Calif.)
Hobson
Riggs
Taylor (N.C.)
Nichols
Zeliff

Water Resources

Phone: 225-0060 **Room: B370-A RHOB**

Nowak, chairman
Hayes (La.)
DeLauro
Peterson (Fla.)
Anderson
Oberstar
Applegate
Borski
Pallone
Jones (Ga.)
Brewster
Cramer
Horn
Collins (Mich.)
Rahall
Kolter
Clement
Payne (Va.)
Costello
Parker
<Vacancy>
<Vacancy>

Petri
Clinger
Packard
Bentley
Ballenger
Upton
Emerson
Hancock
Molinari
Riggs
Taylor (N.C.)
Zeliff
<Vacancy>

RULES

Phone: 225-9486 **Room: H-312 Capitol**

Majority Staff Director: George Crawford 225-9486 H-312 Capitol
Minority Chief of Staff: Don Wolfensberger 225-9191 H-305 Capitol

Rules and order of business of the House; emergency waivers under the Congressional Budget Act of required reporting date for bills and resolutions authorizing new budget authority; recesses and final adjournments of Congress.

Party Ratio: D 9 — R 4

Joe Moakley, Mass., chairman
Butler Derrick, S.C.
Anthony C. Beilenson, Calif.
Martin Frost, Texas
David E. Bonior, Mich.
Tony P. Hall, Ohio
Alan Wheat, Mo.
Bart Gordon, Tenn.
Louise M. Slaughter, N.Y.

Gerald B.H. Solomon, N.Y., ranking member
James H. Quillen, Tenn.
David Dreier, Calif.
Bob McEwen, Ohio

SUBCOMMITTEES

Legislative Process

Phone: 225-1037 **Room: 1629 LHOB**

Derrick, chairman
Frost
Wheat
Gordon
Moakley

Quillen
McEwen

Rules of the House

Phone: 225-9588 **Room: 1628 LHOB**

Beilenson, chairman
Bonior
Hall (Ohio)
Slaughter
Moakley

Dreier
Solomon

SCIENCE, SPACE AND TECHNOLOGY

Phone: 225-6371 **Room: 2321 RHOB**

Chief of Staff: Dr. Radford Byerly Jr. 225-6375 2320 RHOB
Deputy Chief Staff Director: Dave Clement 225-8772 2320 RHOB

Astronautical research and development, including resources, personnel, equipment and facilities; Bureau of Standards, standardization of weights and measures and the metric system; National Aeronautics and Space Administration; National Aeronautics and Space Council; National Science Foundation; outer space, including exploration and control; science scholarships; scientific research, development and demonstration; federally owned or operated non-military energy laboratories; civil aviation research and development; environmental research and development; energy research, development and demonstration; National Weather Service. Chairman and ranking minority member are members ex officio of all subcommittees of which they are not regular members.

Party Ratio: D 33 — R 20

George E. Brown Jr., Calif., chairman
James H. Scheuer, N.Y.
Marilyn Lloyd, Tenn.
Dan Glickman, Kan.
Harold L. Volkmer, Mo.
Howard Wolpe, Mich.
Ralph M. Hall, Texas
Dave McCurdy, Okla.
Norman Y. Mineta, Calif.
Tim Valentine, N.C.
Robert G. Torricelli, N.J.
Rick Boucher, Va.
Terry L. Bruce, Ill.
Richard Stallings, Idaho
James A. Traficant Jr., Ohio
Henry J. Nowak, N.Y.
Carl C. Perkins, Ky.
Tom McMillen, Md.
Dave Nagle, Iowa
Jimmy Hayes, La.
Jerry F. Costello, Ill.
John Tanner, Tenn.
Glen Browder, Ala.
Pete Geren, Texas
Ray Thornton, Ark.
Jim Bacchus, Fla.
Tim Roemer, Ind.
Bud Cramer, Ala.
Dick Swett, N.H.
Mike Kopetski, Ore.
Joan Kelly Horn, Mo.
John Olver, Mass.
Eliot L. Engel, N.Y.

Robert S. Walker, Pa., ranking member
F. James Sensenbrenner Jr., Wis.
Sherwood Boehlert, N.Y.
Tom Lewis, Fla.
Don Ritter, Pa.
Sid Morrison, Wash.
Ron Packard, Calif.
Paul B. Henry, Mich.
Harris W. Fawell, Ill.
Lamar Smith, Texas
Constance A. Morella, Md.
Dana Rohrabacher, Calif.
Steven H. Schiff, N.M.
Tom Campbell, Calif.
John J. Rhodes III, Ariz.
Joe L. Barton, Texas
Dick Zimmer, N.J.
Wayne T. Gilchrest, Md.
Sam Johnson, Texas
George F. Allen, Va.

SUBCOMMITTEES

Energy

Phone: 225-7858 **Room: 374 RHOB**

Lloyd, chairman
Costello
Hall (Texas)
Bruce
Stallings
Traficant
Cramer
Wolpe
Roemer

Morrison
Fawell
Smith (Texas)
Schiff
Barton

Environment

Phone: 225-6371 **Room: 2321 RHOB**

Scheuer, chairman
Nowak
Swett
Wolpe
Horn
Hall (Texas)
McMillen
Olver

Ritter
Morrison
Morella
Zimmer

Investigations and Oversight

Phone: 225-4494 **Room: 822 OHOB**

Wolpe, chairman
Geren
Nagle
Tanner
Thornton

Boehlert
Sensenbrenner

Science

Phone: 225-7858 **Room: 2320 RHOB**

Boucher, chairman
Bruce
Kopetski
Valentine
Perkins
Nagle
Hayes (La.)
Costello
Browder
Thornton
Roemer
Bacchus
<Vacancy>

Packard
Boehlert
Fawell
Schiff
Campbell (Calif.)
Gilchrest

Space

Phone: 225-8056 **Room: B374 RHOB**

Hall (Texas), chairman
Volkmer
Stallings
Traficant
Perkins
McMillen
Nagle
Hayes (La.)
Tanner
Browder
Geren
Bacchus
Cramer
Scheuer
Mineta
Torricelli
Engel

Sensenbrenner
Lewis (Fla.)
Packard
Rhodes
Henry
Smith (Texas)
Rohrabacher
Zimmer
Johnson (Texas)

Technology and Competitiveness

Phone: 225-9662 **Room: B374 RHOB**

Valentine, chairman
Glickman
Mineta
Torricelli
Thornton
Roemer
Horn
Boucher
Tanner
Bacchus
Swett
Engel
Olver

Lewis (Fla.)
Ritter
Henry
Rohrabacher
Campbell (Calif.)
Gilchrest
Morella

SELECT AGING

Phone: 226-3375 **Room: 712 OHOB**

Majority Staff Director: Richard Veloz 226-3375 712 OHOB
Minority Staff Director: Paul Schlegel 226-3393 606 OHOB

Problems of older Americans including income, housing, health, welfare, employment, education, recreation and participation in family and community life. Studies and reports findings to House, but cannot report legislation. Chairman and ranking minority member are members ex officio of all subcommittees of which they are not regular members.

Party Ratio: D 42 — R 27

Edward R. Roybal, Calif., chairman
Thomas J. Downey, N.Y.
Harold E. Ford, Tenn.
William J. Hughes, N.J.
Marilyn Lloyd, Tenn.
Mary Rose Oakar, Ohio
Beverly B. Byron, Md.
Henry A. Waxman, Calif.
Butler Derrick, S.C.
Bruce F. Vento, Minn.
Barney Frank, Mass.
Tom Lantos, Calif.
Ron Wyden, Ore.
Ike Skelton, Mo.
Dennis M. Hertel, Mich.
Robert A. Borski, Pa.
Ben Erdreich, Ala.
Norman Sisisky, Va.
Bob Wise, W.Va.
Bill Richardson, N.M.
Harold L. Volkmer, Mo.
Bart Gordon, Tenn.
Thomas J. Manton, N.Y.
Richard Stallings, Idaho
Joseph P. Kennedy II, Mass.
Louise M. Slaughter, N.Y.
James Bilbray, Nev.
Jim Jontz, Ind.
Jerry F. Costello, Ill.
Harley O. Staggers Jr., W.Va.
Frank Pallone Jr., N.J.
Jolene Unsoeld, Wash.
Peter A. DeFazio, Ore.
John Lewis, Ga.
Wayne Owens, Utah
Robert A. Roe, N.J.
Gerry E. Studds, Mass.
Neil Abercrombie, Hawaii
Dick Swett, N.H.
Rosa DeLauro, Conn.
<Vacancy>
<Vacancy>

Matthew J. Rinaldo, N.J., ranking member
John Paul Hammerschmidt, Ark.
Ralph Regula, Ohio
Olympia J. Snowe, Maine
Christopher H. Smith, N.J.
Sherwood Boehlert, N.Y.
H. James Saxton, N.J.
Helen Delich Bentley, Md.
Harris W. Fawell, Ill.
Jan Meyers, Kan.
Ben Blaz, Guam
Paul B. Henry, Mich.
Floyd D. Spence, S.C.
Constance A. Morella, Md.
John Porter, Ill.
John J. "Jimmy" Duncan Jr., Tenn.
Cliff Stearns, Fla.
Craig T. James, Fla.
Amo Houghton, N.Y.
Gary Franks, Conn.
David L. Hobson, Ohio
Charles H. Taylor, N.C.
Wayne T. Gilchrest, Md.
Dick Zimmer, N.J.
Dick Nichols, Kan.
Jim Nussle, Iowa
<Vacancy>

SUBCOMMITTEES/TASK FORCES

Health and Long-Term Care

Phone: 226-3381 **Room: 377 FHOB**

Roybal, chairman
Downey
Oakar
Waxman
Derrick
Vento
Frank
Wyden
Skelton
Hertel
Borski
Erdreich
Sisisky
Wise
Richardson
Kennedy
Slaughter (N.Y.)
Owens (Utah)

Regula
Rinaldo
Saxton
Bentley
Henry
Morella
Stearns
James
Hobson
Gilchrest
Zimmer
<Vacancy>

Housing and Consumer Interests

Phone: 226-3344 **Room: 717 OHOB**

Lloyd, chairman
Ford (Tenn.)
Byron
Vento
Gordon
Manton
Bilbray
Costello
Pallone
Unsoeld
Roe
Abercrombie

Smith (N.J.)
Hammerschmidt
Blaz
Porter
Duncan
Taylor (N.C.)
Gilchrest
<Vacancy>

Human Services

Phone: 226-3348 **Room: 715 OHOB**

Downey, chairman
Richardson
Slaughter (N.Y.)
Staggers
Pallone
DeFazio
Lewis (Ga.)
Studds
Abercrombie
Swett
DeLauro

Snowe
Smith (N.J.)
Saxton
Fawell
Blaz
Spence
Duncan
Nussle

Retirement, Income and Employment

Phone: 226-3335 **Room: 714 OHOB**

Hughes, chairman
Ford (Tenn.)
Oakar
Lantos
Wise
Volkmer
Manton
Stallings
Jontz
Costello
DeFazio
Lewis (Ga.)

Boehlert
Meyers
Spence
Porter
Houghton
Franks
Taylor (N.C.)
Nichols

Rural Elderly

Phone: 226-3375 **Room: 712 OHOB**

Derrick, Chairman
Skelton
Wise
Richardson
Volkmer
Sisisky
Stallings
Staggers
DeFazio
Lewis (Ga.)
Swett

Saxton
Snowe
Smith (N.J.)
Bentley
Meyers
Taylor (N.C.)

Social Security and Women

Phone: 226-3375 **Room: 712 OHOB**

Oakar, chairman
Ford (Tenn.)
Lloyd
Waxman
Derrick
Frank
Manton
Slaughter
Owens (Utah)
Roe
Abercrombie
DeLauro

Houghton
Hammerschmidt
Snowe
Nussle

SELECT CHILDREN, YOUTH AND FAMILIES

Phone: 226-7660 **Room: 385 FHOB**

Majority Staff Director: Carol Pizzigati 226-7660 385 FHOB
Minority Staff Director: Danielle Madison 226-7692 384 FHOB

Problems of children, youth and families, including income maintenance, health, nutrition, education, welfare, employment and recreation. Studies and reports findings to House, but cannot report legislation. Chairman and ranking minority member are members ex officio of all task forces.

Party Ratio: D 22 — R 14

Patricia Schroeder, Colo., chairman
George Miller, Calif.
William Lehman, Fla.
Matthew F. McHugh, N.Y.
Ted Weiss, N.Y.
Beryl Anthony Jr., Ark.
Barbara Boxer, Calif.
Sander M. Levin, Mich.
J. Roy Rowland, Ga.
Gerry Sikorski, Minn.
Alan Wheat, Mo.
Matthew G. Martinez, Calif.
Lane Evans, Ill.
Richard J. Durbin, Ill.
David E. Skaggs, Colo.
Bill Sarpalius, Texas
Tim Johnson, S.D.
Barbara-Rose Collins, Mich.
Joan Kelly Horn, Mo.
Jim Bacchus, Fla.
Pete Peterson, Fla.
Bud Cramer, Ala.

Frank R. Wolf, Va., ranking member
Clyde C. Holloway, La.
Curt Weldon, Pa.
Lamar Smith, Texas
James T. Walsh, N.Y.
Ronald K. Machtley, R.I.
Bob McEwen, Ohio
Michael Bilirakis, Fla.
Scott L. Klug, Wis.
Rick Santorum, Pa.
Dave Camp, Mich.
Frank Riggs, Calif.
Bill Barrett, Neb.
Dennis Hastert, Ill.

SELECT HUNGER

Phone: 226-5470 **Room: 505 FHOB**

Majority Staff Director: Martin S. Rendon 226-5470 505 FHOB
Minority Staff Director: Barbara Earman 226-5460 504 FHOB

Comprehensive study and review of hunger and malnutrition, including U.S. development and economic assistance programs; U.S. trade relations with less-developed nations; food production and distribution; agribusiness efforts to further international development; policies of development banks and international development institutions; and food assistance programs in the United States. Review of executive branch recommendations relating to programs affecting hunger and malnutrition, and to recommend legislation or other action with respect to such programs to the appropriate committees of the House. Studies and reports findings to House, but cannot report legislation. Chairman and ranking minority member are members ex officio of all task forces.

Party Ratio: D 20* — R 12

Tony P. Hall, Ohio, chairman
Leon E. Panetta, Calif.
Vic Fazio, Calif.
Peter H. Kostmayer, Pa.
Byron L. Dorgan, N.D.
Bob Carr, Mich.
Timothy J. Penny, Minn.
Gary L. Ackerman, N.Y.
Mike Espy, Miss.
Floyd H. Flake, N.Y.
Liz J. Patterson, S.C.
Albert G. Bustamante, Texas
Michael R. McNulty, N.Y.
Eni F.H. Faleomavaega, Am. Samoa*
Eliot L. Engel, N.Y.
Les AuCoin, Ore.
Alan Wheat, Mo.
Jill L. Long, Ind.
Mike Synar, Okla.
<Vacancy>
<Vacancy>
<Vacancy>

Bill Emerson, Mo., ranking member
Marge Roukema, N.J.
Sid Morrison, Wash.
Benjamin A. Gilman, N.Y.
Bob Smith, Ore.
Doug Bereuter, Neb.
Fred Upton, Mich.
Duncan Hunter, Calif.
Frank R. Wolf, Va.
Christopher H. Smith, N.J.
Wayne T. Gilchrest, Md.
<Vacancy>

* *Party ratios do not include non-voting delegates or resident commissioner.*

TASK FORCES

Domestic

Phone: 226-5470 **Room: 505 FHOB**

Espy, chairman
Panetta
Ackerman
Flake
Patterson
Bustamante
AuCoin
Engel
Synar
Long

Roukema
Morrison
Upton
Gilchrest

International

Phone: 226-5470 **Room: 505 FHOB**

Dorgan, chairman
Fazio
Kostmayer
Carr
Penny
McNulty
Faleomavaega
Wheat
<Vacancy>

Smith (Ore.)
Bereuter
Gilman
Hunter
Wolf
Smith (N.J.)

SELECT INTELLIGENCE

Phone: 225-4121 **Room: H-405 Capitol**

Staff Director: John G. Keliher 225-4121 H-405 Capitol
Minority Counsel: Thomas R. Smeeton 225-4121 H-405 Capitol

Legislative and budgetary authority over the Central Intelligence Agency, the Defense Intelligence Agency, the National Security Agency, intelligence activities of the Federal Bureau of Investigation and other components of the federal intelligence community. House majority leader and minority leader are non-voting members ex officio of the full committee.

Party Ratio: D 12 — R 7

Dave McCurdy, Okla., chairman
Charles Wilson, Texas
Barbara B. Kennelly, Conn.
Dan Glickman, Kan.
Nicholas Mavroules, Mass.
Bill Richardson, N.M.
Stephen J. Solarz, N.Y.
Norm Dicks, Wash.
Ronald V. Dellums, Calif.
David E. Bonior, Mich.
Martin Olav Sabo, Minn.
Wayne Owens, Utah

Bud Shuster, Pa., ranking member
Larry Combest, Texas
Doug Bereuter, Neb.
Robert K. Dornan, Calif.
C.W. Bill Young, Fla.
David O'B. Martin, N.Y.
George W. Gekas, Pa.

SUBCOMMITTEES

Legislation

Phone: 225-7311 **Room: H-405 Capitol**

Kennelly, chairman
Solarz
Dicks
Bonior
Sabo
Owens (Utah)

Gekas
Bereuter
Dornan

Oversight and Evaluation

Phone: 225-5658 **Room: H-405 Capitol**

Wilson, chairman
Mavroules
Bonior
Kennelly
Glickman
Richardson

Combest
Dornan
Shuster

Program and Budget Authorization

Phone: 225-7690 **Room: H-405 Capitol**

McCurdy, chairman
Glickman
Richardson
Solarz
Dicks
Dellums
Sabo
Owens (Utah)

Shuster
Bereuter
Young (Fla.)
Martin

SELECT NARCOTICS ABUSE AND CONTROL

Phone: 226-3040 **Room: 234 FHOB**

Majority Staff Director: Edward Jurith 226-3040 234 FHOB
Minority Staff Director: William S. Smith 225-3779 234 FHOB

Problems of narcotics, drug and polydrug abuse and control, including opium and its derivatives, other narcotic drugs, psychotropics and other controlled substances; trafficking, manufacturing and distribution; treatment, prevention and rehabilitation; narcotics-related violations of tax laws; international treaties and agreements relating to narcotics and drug abuse; role of organized crime in narcotics and drug abuse; abuse and control in the armed forces and in industry; criminal justice system and narcotics and drug law violations and crimes related to drug abuse. Studies and reports findings to House, but cannot report legislation.

Party Ratio: D 22 — R 14

Charles B. Rangel, N.Y., chairman
Jack Brooks, Texas
Pete Stark, Calif.
James H. Scheuer, N.Y.
Cardiss Collins, Ill.
Frank J. Guarini, N.J.
Dante B. Fascell, Fla.
William J. Hughes, N.J.
Mel Levine, Calif.
Solomon P. Ortiz, Texas
Lawrence J. Smith, Fla.
Edolphus Towns, N.Y.
James A. Traficant Jr., Ohio
Kweisi Mfume, Md.
Nita M. Lowey, N.Y.
Donald M. Payne, N.J.
Romano L. Mazzoli, Ky.
Ron de Lugo, V.I.*
George J. Hochbrueckner, N.Y.
Craig Washington, Texas
Robert E. Andrews, N.J.

Lawrence Coughlin, Pa., ranking member
Benjamin A. Gilman, N.Y.
Michael G. Oxley, Ohio
F. James Sensenbrenner Jr., Wis.
Robert K. Dornan, Calif.
Tom Lewis, Fla.
James M. Inhofe, Okla.
Wally Herger, Calif.
Christopher Shays, Conn.
Bill Paxon, N.Y.
William F. Clinger, Pa.
Howard Coble, N.C.
Paul E. Gillmor, Ohio
Jim Ramstad, Minn.

** Party ratios do not include non-voting delegates or resident commissioner.*

SMALL BUSINESS

Phone: 225-5821 **Room: 2361 RHOB**

Majority Staff Director: Don Terry 225-5821 2361 RHOB
Minority Staff Director: Drew Hiatt 225-4038 B343-C RHOB

Assistance to and protection of small business, including financial aid; participation of small business enterprises in federal procurement and government contracts. Chairman and ranking minority member are members ex officio of all subcommittees of which they are not regular members.

Party Ratio: D 27 — R 17

John J. LaFalce, N.Y., chairman
Neal Smith, Iowa
Ike Skelton, Mo.
Romano L. Mazzoli, Ky.
Nicholas Mavroules, Mass.
Charles Hatcher, Ga.
Ron Wyden, Ore.
Dennis E. Eckart, Ohio
Gus Savage, Ill.
Norman Sisisky, Va.
Esteban E. Torres, Calif.
Jim Olin, Va.
Richard Ray, Ga.
John Conyers Jr., Mich.
James Bilbray, Nev.
Kweisi Mfume, Md.
Floyd H. Flake, N.Y.
H. Martin Lancaster, N.C.
Bill Sarpalius, Texas
Richard E. Neal, Mass.
Glenn Poshard, Ill.
Jose E. Serrano, N.Y.
Robert E. Andrews, N.J.
Thomas H. Andrews, Maine
Bill Orton, Utah
Ed Pastor, Ariz.
<Vacancy>

Andy Ireland, Fla., ranking member
Joseph M. McDade, Pa.
William S. Broomfield, Mich.
Jan Meyers, Kan.
Larry Combest, Texas
Richard H. Baker, La.
Joel Hefley, Colo.
Mel Hancock, Mo.
Ronald K. Machtley, R.I.
Jim Ramstad, Minn.
Dave Camp, Mich.
Gary Franks, Conn.
Wayne Allard, Colo.
John A. Boehner, Ohio
Sam Johnson, Texas
Bill Zeliff, N.H.
George F. Allen, Va.

Antitrust, Impact of Deregulation and Ecology

Phone: 225-6026 **Room: B363 RHOB**

Eckart, chairman
Sarpalius
Serrano
Andrews (N.J.)
Mazzoli

Hefley
Allard
Johnson (Texas)

Environment and Employment

Phone: 225-7673 **Room: 568-A FHOB**

Olin, chairman
Torres
Ray
Poshard

Baker
Zeliff

Exports, Tax Policy and Special Problems

Phone: 225-8944 **Room: B363 RHOB**

Sisisky, chairman
Ray
Lancaster
Hatcher
Andrews (Maine)
Orton
Bilbray

Combest
Ramstad
Franks
Boehner

Procurement, Tourism and Rural Development

Phone: 225-9368 **Room: B363 RHOB**

Skelton, chairman
Torres
Bilbray
Poshard
Savage
Lancaster

Hancock
Machtley
Zeliff

Regulation, Business Opportunity and Energy

Phone: 225-7797 **Room: B363 RHOB**

Wyden, chairman
Neal (Mass.)
Flake
Andrews (N.J.)
Dooley
Lancaster
<Vacancy>

Meyers
Broomfield
Camp
Hancock

SBA, the General Economy and Minority Enterprise Development

Phone: 225-5821 **Room: 2361 RHOB**

LaFalce, chairman
Smith (Iowa)
Mazzoli
Mavroules
Savage
Conyers
Mfume
Serrano
Olin

Ireland
McDade
Allard
Camp
Franks
Ramstad

STANDARDS OF OFFICIAL CONDUCT

Phone: 225-7103 **Room: HT-2M Capitol**

Chief Counsel: Bernard Raimo 225-7103 HT-2M Capitol

Measures relating to the Code of Official Conduct; conduct of House members and employees; Ethics in Government Act.

Party Ratio: D 7 — R 7

Louis Stokes, Ohio, chairman
Matthew F. McHugh, N.Y.
Gary L. Ackerman, N.Y.
George "Buddy" Darden, Ga.
Benjamin L. Cardin, Md.
Nancy Pelosi, Calif.
Jim McDermott, Wash.

James V. Hansen, Utah, ranking member
Fred Grandy, Iowa
Nancy L. Johnson, Conn.
Jim Bunning, Ky.
Jon Kyl, Ariz.
Porter J. Goss, Fla.
David L. Hobson, Ohio

VETERANS' AFFAIRS

Phone: 225-3527 **Room: 335 CHOB**

Majority Counsel & Staff Director: Mark G. Fleming 225-3527 335 CHOB
Minority Counsel & Staff Director: Carl Commenator 225-9756 333 CHOB

Veterans measures generally; compensation, vocational rehabilitation and education of veterans; armed forces life insurance; pensions; readjustment benefits; veterans hospitals, medical care and treatment. Chairman and ranking minority member are members ex officio of all subcommittees of which they are not regular members.

Party Ratio: D 21 — R 13

G.V. Montgomery, Miss., chairman
Don Edwards, Calif.
Douglas Applegate, Ohio
Lane Evans, Ill.
Timothy J. Penny, Minn.
Harley O. Staggers Jr., W.Va.
J. Roy Rowland, Ga.
Jim Slattery, Kan.
Claude Harris, Ala.
Joseph P. Kennedy II, Mass.
Liz J. Patterson, S.C.
George E. Sangmeister, Ill.
Ben Jones, Ga.
Jill L. Long, Ind.
Pete Peterson, Fla.
Chet Edwards, Texas
Maxine Waters, Calif.
Bill Brewster, Okla.
Owen B. Pickett, Va.
Pete Geren, Texas
<Vacancy>

Bob Stump, Ariz., ranking member
John Paul Hammerschmidt, Ark.
Chalmers P. Wylie, Ohio
Christopher H. Smith, N.J.
Dan Burton, Ind.
Michael Bilirakis, Fla.
Tom Ridge, Pa.
Craig T. James, Fla.
Cliff Stearns, Fla.
Bill Paxon, N.Y.
Floyd D. Spence, S.C.
Dick Nichols, Kan.
Rick Santorum, Pa.

SUBCOMMITTEES

Compensation, Pension and Insurance

Phone: 225-3569 **Room: 337 CHOB**

Applegate, chairman
Evans
Penny
Rowland
Edwards (Texas)

Stump
Wylie
Spence

Education, Training and Employment

Phone: 225-9166 **Room: 337-A CHOB**

Penny, chairman
Slattery
Patterson
Sangmeister
Geren
<Vacancy>

Smith (N.J.)
Wylie
Santorum
Ridge

Hospitals and Health Care

Phone: 225-9154 **Room: 338 CHOB**

Montgomery, chairman
Rowland
Slattery
Harris
Kennedy
Patterson
Sangmeister
Jones (Ga.)
Long
Edwards (Texas)
Brewster
Applegate

Hammerschmidt
Stump
Smith (N.J.)
Burton
Bilirakis
Ridge
James

Housing and Memorial Affairs

Phone: 225-9164 **Room: 337 CHOB**

Staggers, chairman
Harris
Jones (Ga.)
Brewster
Pickett
<Vacancy>

Burton
Paxon
Nichols
Stearns

Oversight and Investigations

Phone: 225-9044 **Room: 335 CHOB**

Evans, chairman
Edwards (Calif.)
Peterson (Fla.)
Waters
Kennedy
Long

Bilirakis
Stearns
James
Paxon

WAYS AND MEANS

Phone: 225-3625 **Room: 1102 LHOB**

Majority Chief Counsel: Robert J. Leonard 225-3625 1102 LHOB
Minority Chief of Staff: Phil Moseley 225-4021 1106 LHOB

Revenue measures generally; reciprocal trade agreements; customs, collection districts and ports of entry and delivery; bonded debt of the United States; deposit of public moneys; transportation of dutiable goods; tax-exempt foundations and charitable trusts; Social Security. Chairman and ranking minority member are members ex officio of all subcommittees of which they are not regular members.

Party Ratio: D 23 — R 13

Dan Rostenkowski, Ill., chairman
Sam M. Gibbons, Fla.
J.J. Pickle, Texas
Charles B. Rangel, N.Y.
Pete Stark, Calif.
Andrew Jacobs Jr., Ind.
Harold E. Ford, Tenn.
Ed Jenkins, Ga.
Thomas J. Downey, N.Y.
Frank J. Guarini, N.J.
Marty Russo, Ill.
Don J. Pease, Ohio
Robert T. Matsui, Calif.
Beryl Anthony Jr., Ark.
Byron L. Dorgan, N.D.
Barbara B. Kennelly, Conn.
Brian Donnelly, Mass.
William J. Coyne, Pa.
Michael A. Andrews, Texas
Sander M. Levin, Mich.
Jim Moody, Wis.
Benjamin L. Cardin, Md.
Jim McDermott, Wash.

Bill Archer, Texas, ranking member
Guy Vander Jagt, Mich.
Philip M. Crane, Ill.
Dick Schulze, Pa.
Bill Gradison, Ohio
Bill Thomas, Calif.
Raymond J. McGrath, N.Y.
Rod D. Chandler, Wash.
E. Clay Shaw Jr., Fla.
Don Sundquist, Tenn.
Nancy L. Johnson, Conn.
Jim Bunning, Ky.
Fred Grandy, Iowa

SUBCOMMITTEES

Health

Phone: 225-7785 **Room: 1114 LHOB**

Stark, chairman
Russo
Donnelly
Coyne
Levin
Moody
Cardin

Gradison
Chandler
Johnson (Conn.)
McGrath

Human Resources

Phone: 225-1025 **Room: B317 RHOB**

Downey, acting chairman
Ford (Tenn.)
Kennelly
Andrews (Texas)
McDermott
Levin
Moody

Shaw
Johnson (Conn.)
Grandy
Chandler

Oversight

Phone: 225-5525 **Room: 1135 LHOB**

Pickle, chairman
Anthony
Ford (Tenn.)
Rangel
Jacobs
Jenkins
Russo

Schulze
Shaw
Sundquist
Bunning

Select Revenue Measures

Phone: 225-6649 **Room: 1105 LHOB**

Rangel, chairman
Dorgan
Kennelly
Andrews (Texas)
Stark
Donnelly
Coyne

Vander Jagt
Sundquist
Grandy
Chandler

Social Security

Phone: 225-9263 **Room: B316 RHOB**

Jacobs, chairman
Gibbons
Cardin
McDermott
Pickle

Bunning
Crane
Schulze

Trade

Phone: 225-3943 **Room: 1136 LHOB**

Gibbons, chairman
Rostenkowski
Jenkins
Downey
Pease
Guarini
Matsui
Anthony
Dorgan

Crane
Vander Jagt
Schulze
Thomas (Calif.)
McGrath

Pronunciation Guide for Congress

The following is an informal pronunciation guide for some of the most-often-mispronounced names of members of Congress:

SENATE

Daniel K. Akaka, D-Hawaii (ah KAH ka)
John B. Breaux, D-La. (BRO)
Alfonse M. D'Amato, R-N.Y. (dah MAH toe)
Tom Daschle, D-S.D. (DASH el)
Dennis DeConcini, D-Ariz. (dee con SEE nee)
Pete V. Domenici, R-N.M. (da MEN ah chee)
Wyche Fowler Jr., D-Ga. (WHYch)
Daniel K. Inouye, D-Hawaii (in NO ay)
Joseph I. Lieberman, D-Conn. (LEE ber mun)

HOUSE

Les AuCoin, D-Ore. (oh COIN)
Jim Bacchus, D-Fla. (BACK us)
Anthony C. Beilenson, D-Calif. (BEE lin son)
Doug Bereuter, R-Neb. (BEE right er)
Michael Bilirakis, R-Fla. (bill a RACK us)
Ben Blaz, R-Guam (BLAHS)
Sherwood Boehlert, R-N.Y. (BO lert)
John A. Boehner, R-Ohio (BAY ner)
David E. Bonior, D-Mich. (BON yer)
Rick Boucher, D-Va. (BOUGH cher)
Albert G. Bustamante, D-Texas (BOOST uh MAHN tay)
Lawrence Coughlin, R-Pa. (COFF lin)
Peter A. DeFazio, D-Ore. (da FAH zio)
Rosa DeLauro, D-Conn. (da LAUR oh)
Mervyn M. Dymally, D-Calif. (DIE mal ee)
Ben Erdreich, D-Ala. (ER dritch)
Eni F. H. Faleomavaega, D-Am. Samoa (EN ee FALL eh oh mavah ENGA)
Dante B. Fascell, D-Fla. (DON tay fuh SELL)
Harris W. Fawell, R-Ill. (FAY well)
Vic Fazio, D-Calif. (FAY zee o)
Edward F. Feighan, D-Ohio (FEE an)
Thomas M. Foglietta, D-Pa. (fo lee ET ah)
Jaime B. Fuster, Pop. Dem.-P.R. (HI may foo STAIR)
Elton Gallegly, R-Calif. (GAL uh glee)
Sam Gejdenson, D-Conn. (GAY den son)
Frank J. Guarini, D-N.J. (gwar EE nee)
George J. Hochbrueckner, D-N.Y. (HOCK brewk ner)
Amo Houghton, R-N.Y. (AY mo HO tun)
James M. Inhofe, R-Okla. (IN hoff)
John R. Kasich, R-Ohio (KAY sick)
Barbara B. Kennelly, D-Conn. (ka NEL ly)
Gerald D. Kleczka, D-Wis. (KLETCH ka)
Scott L. Klug, R-Wis. (KLOOG)
Jim Kolbe, R-Ariz. (COLE bee)
Mike Kopetski, D-Ore. (ka PET skee)
Robert J. Lagomarsino, R-Calif. (LAH go mar SEE no)
Larry LaRocco, D-Idaho (la ROCK oh)
Greg Laughlin, D-Texas (LAWF lin)
Richard H. Lehman, D-Calif. (LEE mun)
William Lehman, D-Fla. (LAY mun)
Mel Levine, D-Calif. (la VINE)
Nita M. Lowey, D-N.Y. (LOW ee)
Ronald K. Machtley, R-R.I. (MAKE lee)
Ron Marlenee, R-Mont. (MAR la nay)
Nicholas Mavroules, D-Mass. (mah VROOL iss)
Bob McEwen, R-Ohio (ma KEW in)
Kweisi Mfume, D-Md. (kwy E say mm FU may)
Robert J. Mrazek, D-N.Y. (ma RAH zik)
David R. Obey, D-Wis. (O bee)
Frank Pallone Jr., D-N.J. (pa LONE)
Nancy Pelosi, D-Calif. (pel LO see)
Thomas E. Petri, R-Wis. (PEE try)
Glenn Poshard, D-Ill. (pa SHARD)
Arthur Ravenel Jr., R-S.C. (RAV nel)
Ralph Regula, R-Ohio (REG you la)
Dana Rohrabacher, R-Calif. (ROAR ah bach er)
Ileana Ros-Lehtinen, R-Fla. (il ee ANNA ross LAY tin nen)
Marge Roukema, R-N.J. (ROCK ah ma)
George E. Sangmeister, D-Ill. (SANG my stir)
Rick Santorum, R-Pa. (san TORE um)
Bill Sarpalius, D-Texas (sar POLL us)
James H. Scheuer, D-N.Y. (SHOY yur)
Steven H. Schiff, R-N.M. (SHIFF)
Patricia Schroeder, D-Colo. (SHRO dur)
Richard T. Schulze, R-Pa. (SHOOLS)
Jose E. Serrano, D-N.Y. (ho ZAY sa RAH no) (rolled 'R')
W. J. "Billy" Tauzin, D-La. (TOE zan)
Robert G. Torricelli, D-N.J. (tor ah SELL ee)
Jolene Unsoeld, D-Wash. (UN sold)
Guy Vander Jagt, R-Mich. (VAN der jack)
Peter J. Visclosky, D-Ind. (vis KLOSS key)
Barbara F. Vucanovich, R-Nev. (voo CAN oh vitch)
Gus Yatron, D-Pa. (YAT ron)
Bill Zeliff, R-N.H. (ZELL iff)

Senators' Committee Assignments

Adams: Appropriations; Labor & Human Resources; Rules & Administration
Akaka: Energy & Natural Resources; Governmental Affairs; Select Indian Affairs; Veterans' Affairs
Baucus: Agriculture, Nutrition & Forestry; Environment & Public Works; Finance; Joint Taxation; Small Business
Bentsen: Commerce, Science & Transportation; Finance (chairman); Joint Economic; Joint Taxation (vice chairman)
Biden: Foreign Relations; Judiciary (chairman)
Bingaman: Armed Services; Energy & Natural Resources; Joint Economic; Labor & Human Resources; Select Ethics
Bond: Appropriations; Banking, Housing & Urban Affairs; Budget; Small Business
Boren: Agriculture, Nutrition & Forestry; Finance; Select Intelligence (chairman)
Bradley: Energy & Natural Resources; Finance; Select Intelligence; Special Aging
Breaux: Commerce, Science & Transportation; Finance; Special Aging
Brown: Budget; Foreign Relations; Judiciary; POW/MIA Affairs
Bryan: Banking, Housing & Urban Affairs; Commerce, Science & Transportation; Joint Economic; Select Ethics
Bumpers: Appropriations; Energy & Natural Resources; Small Business (chairman)
Burdick: Appropriations; Environment & Public Works (chairman); Select Indian Affairs; Special Aging
Burns: Commerce, Science & Transportation; Energy & Natural Resources; Small Business; Special Aging
Byrd: Appropriations (chairman); Armed Services; Rules & Administration
Chafee: Banking, Housing & Urban Affairs; Environment & Public Works (ranking member); Finance; Select Intelligence
Coats: Armed Services; Labor & Human Resources
Cochran: Agriculture, Nutrition & Forestry; Appropriations; Labor & Human Resources; Select Indian Affairs
Cohen: Armed Services; Governmental Affairs; Special Aging
Conrad: Agriculture, Nutrition & Forestry; Budget; Energy & Natural Resources; Select Indian Affairs
Craig: Agriculture, Nutrition & Forestry; Energy & Natural Resources; Special Aging
Cranston: Banking, Housing & Urban Affairs; Foreign Relations; Select Intelligence; Veterans' Affairs (chairman)
D'Amato: Appropriations; Banking, Housing & Urban Affairs; Select Intelligence
Danforth: Commerce, Science & Transportation (ranking member); Finance; Select Intelligence
Daschle: Agriculture, Nutrition & Forestry; Finance; POW/MIA Affairs; Select Indian Affairs; Veterans' Affairs
DeConcini: Appropriations; Joint Library; Joint Printing; Judiciary; Rules & Administration; Select Indian Affairs; Select Intelligence; Veterans' Affairs
Dixon: Armed Services; Banking, Housing & Urban Affairs; Small Business
Dodd: Banking, Housing & Urban Affairs; Budget; Foreign Relations; Labor & Human Resources; Rules & Administration
Dole: Agriculture, Nutrition & Forestry; Finance; Joint Taxation; Rules & Administration
Domenici: Appropriations; Banking, Housing & Urban Affairs; Budget (ranking member); Energy & Natural Resources; Select Indian Affairs
Durenberger: Environment & Public Works; Finance; Labor & Human Resources; Special Aging
Exon: Armed Services; Budget; Commerce, Science & Transportation
Ford: Commerce, Science & Transportation; Energy & Natural Resources; Joint Printing (vice chairman); Rules & Administration (chairman)
Fowler: Agriculture, Nutrition & Forestry; Appropriations; Budget; Energy & Natural Resources
Garn: Appropriations; Banking, Housing & Urban Affairs (ranking member); Energy & Natural Resources; Rules & Administration
Glenn: Armed Services; Governmental Affairs (chairman); Select Intelligence; Special Aging
Gore: Armed Services; Commerce, Science & Transportation; Joint Economic; Joint Printing; Rules & Administration
Gorton: Appropriations; Commerce, Science & Transportation; Select Ethics; Select Indian Affairs; Select Intelligence
Graham: Banking, Housing & Urban Affairs; Environment & Public Works; Special Aging; Veterans' Affairs
Gramm: Appropriations; Banking, Housing & Urban Affairs; Budget
Grassley: Agriculture, Nutrition & Forestry; Budget; Finance; Judiciary; POW/MIA Affairs; Special Aging
Harkin: Agriculture, Nutrition & Forestry; Appropriations; Labor & Human Resources; Small Business
Hatch: Finance; Judiciary; Labor & Human Resources (ranking member)
Hatfield: Appropriations (ranking member); Energy & Natural Resources; Joint Library; Joint Printing; Rules & Administration
Heflin: Agriculture, Nutrition & Forestry; Judiciary
Helms: Agriculture, Nutrition & Forestry; Foreign Relations (ranking member); POW/MIA Affairs; Rules & Administration
Hollings: Appropriations; Budget; Commerce, Science & Transportation (chairman); Select Intelligence
Inouye: Appropriations; Commerce, Science & Transportation; Rules & Administration; Select Indian Affairs (chairman)
Jeffords: Environment & Public Works; Foreign Relations; Labor & Human Resources; Special Aging; Veterans' Affairs
Johnston: Appropriations; Budget; Energy & Natural Resources (chairman); Special Aging
Kassebaum: Banking, Housing & Urban Affairs; Foreign Relations; Labor & Human Resources; POW/MIA Affairs; Select Indian Affairs
Kasten: Appropriations; Budget; Commerce, Science & Transportation; Small Business (ranking member)
Kennedy: Armed Services; Joint Economic; Judiciary; Labor & Human Resources (chairman)
Kerrey: Agriculture, Nutrition & Forestry; Appropriations; POW/MIA Affairs
Kerry: Banking, Housing & Urban Affairs; Commerce, Science & Transportation; Foreign Relations; POW/MIA Affairs (chairman); Small Business
Kohl: Governmental Affairs; Judiciary; POW/MIA Affairs; Special Aging
Lautenberg: Appropriations; Budget; Environment & Public Works
Leahy: Agriculture, Nutrition & Forestry (chairman); Appropriations; Judiciary
Levin: Armed Services; Governmental Affairs; Small Business
Lieberman: Environment & Public Works; Governmental Affairs; Small Business
Lott: Armed Services; Budget; Commerce, Science & Transportation; Select Ethics
Lugar: Agriculture, Nutrition & Forestry (ranking member); Foreign Relations
Mack: Armed Services; Banking, Housing & Urban Affairs; Joint Economic; Small Business
McCain: Armed Services; Commerce, Science & Transportation; POW/MIA Affairs; Select Indian Affairs (vice chairman); Special Aging
McConnell: Agriculture, Nutrition & Forestry; Foreign Relations; Rules & Administration
Metzenbaum: Environment & Public Works; Judiciary; Labor & Human Resources; Select Intelligence
Mikulski: Appropriations; Labor & Human Resources; Small Business
Mitchell: Environment & Public Works; Finance; Veterans' Affairs
Moynihan: Environment & Public Works; Finance; Foreign Relations; Joint Library; Joint Taxation; Rules & Administration
Murkowski: Energy & Natural Resources; Foreign Relations; Select Indian Affairs; Select Intelligence (vice chairman); Veterans' Affairs
Nickles: Appropriations; Budget; Energy & Natural Resources; Select Indian Affairs

Nunn: Armed Services (chairman); Governmental Affairs; Select Intelligence; Small Business
Packwood: Commerce, Science & Transportation; Finance (ranking member); Joint Taxation
Pell: Foreign Relations (chairman); Joint Library (chairman); Labor & Human Resources; Rules & Administration
Pressler: Commerce, Science & Transportation; Foreign Relations; Small Business; Special Aging
Pryor: Agriculture, Nutrition & Forestry; Finance; Governmental Affairs; Select Ethics; Special Aging (chairman)
Reid: Appropriations; Environment & Public Works; POW/MIA Affairs; Select Indian Affairs; Special Aging
Riegle: Banking, Housing & Urban Affairs (chairman); Budget; Finance
Robb: Commerce, Science & Transportation; Foreign Relations; POW/MIA Affairs
Rockefeller: Commerce, Science & Transportation; Finance; Veterans' Affairs
Roth: Banking, Housing & Urban Affairs; Finance; Governmental Affairs (ranking member); Joint Economic
Rudman: Appropriations; Governmental Affairs; Select Ethics (vice chairman); Select Intelligence
Sanford: Banking, Housing & Urban Affairs; Budget; Foreign Relations; Select Ethics (chairman); Special Aging
Sarbanes: Banking, Housing & Urban Affairs; Foreign Relations; Joint Economic (chairman)
Sasser: Appropriations; Banking, Housing & Urban Affairs; Budget (chairman); Governmental Affairs
Seymour: Agriculture, Nutrition & Forestry; Energy & Natural Resources; Governmental Affairs; Small Business
Shelby: Armed Services; Banking, Housing & Urban Affairs; Energy & Natural Resources; Special Aging
Simon: Budget; Foreign Relations; Judiciary; Labor & Human Resources; Select Indian Affairs
Simpson: Environment & Public Works; Judiciary; Special Aging; Veterans' Affairs
Smith: Armed Services; Environment & Public Works; Joint Economic; POW/MIA Affairs (vice chairman)
Specter: Appropriations; Judiciary; Special Aging; Veterans' Affairs (ranking member)
Stevens: Appropriations; Commerce, Science & Transportation; Governmental Affairs; Joint Library; Joint Printing; Rules & Administration (ranking member); Small Business
Symms: Budget; Environment & Public Works; Finance; Joint Economic
Thurmond: Armed Services; Judiciary (ranking member); Labor & Human Resources; Veterans' Affairs
Wallop: Armed Services; Energy & Natural Resources (ranking member); Small Business
Warner: Armed Services (ranking member); Environment & Public Works; Rules & Administration; Select Intelligence
Wellstone: Energy & Natural Resources; Labor & Human Resources; Select Indian Affairs; Small Business
Wirth: Armed Services; Banking, Housing & Urban Affairs; Budget; Energy & Natural Resources
Wofford: Environment & Public Works; Foreign Relations; Small Business

Representatives' Committee Assignments

Abercrombie: Armed Services; Interior & Insular Affairs; Select Aging
Ackerman: Banking, Finance & Urban Affairs; Foreign Affairs; POW/MIA; Post Office & Civil Service; Select Hunger; Standards of Official Conduct
Alexander: Appropriations
Allard: Agriculture; Interior & Insular Affairs; Small Business
Allen: Judiciary; Science, Space & Technology; Small Business
Anderson: Merchant Marine & Fisheries; Public Works & Transportation
Andrews (Texas): Ways & Means
Andrews (N.J.): Education & Labor; Select Narcotics Abuse & Control; Small Business
Andrews (Maine): Armed Services; Small Business
Annunzio: Banking, Finance & Urban Affairs; House Administration
Anthony: Select Children, Youth & Families; Ways & Means
Applegate: Public Works & Transportation; Veterans' Affairs
Archer: Joint Taxation; Ways & Means (ranking member)
Armey: Banking, Finance & Urban Affairs; Education & Labor; Joint Economic
Aspin: Armed Services (chairman)
Atkins: Appropriations; POW/MIA
AuCoin: Appropriations; Select Hunger
Bacchus: Banking, Finance & Urban Affairs; Science, Space & Technology; Select Children, Youth & Families
Baker: Banking, Finance & Urban Affairs; Interior & Insular Affairs; Small Business
Ballenger: Education & Labor; Public Works & Transportation
Barnard: Banking, Finance & Urban Affairs; Government Operations
Barrett: Agriculture; Education & Labor; House Administration; Joint Library; Select Children, Youth & Families
Barton: Energy & Commerce; Science, Space & Technology
Bateman: Armed Services; Merchant Marine & Fisheries
Beilenson: Budget; Rules
Bennett: Armed Services; Merchant Marine & Fisheries
Bentley: Budget; Merchant Marine & Fisheries; Public Works & Transportation; Select Aging
Bereuter: Banking, Finance & Urban Affairs; Foreign Affairs; Select Hunger; Select Intelligence
Berman: Budget; Foreign Affairs; Judiciary; POW/MIA
Bevill: Appropriations
Bilbray: Armed Services; POW/MIA; Select Aging; Small Business
Bilirakis: Energy & Commerce; POW/MIA; Select Children, Youth & Families; Veterans' Affairs
Blackwell: Merchant Marine & Fisheries; Public Works & Transportation
Blaz: Armed Services; Foreign Affairs; Interior & Insular Affairs; POW/MIA; Select Aging
Bliley: District of Columbia (ranking member); Energy & Commerce
Boehlert: Public Works & Transportation; Science, Space & Technology; Select Aging
Boehner: Agriculture; Education & Labor; Small Business
Bonior: Rules; Select Intelligence
Borski: Merchant Marine & Fisheries; Public Works & Transportation; Select Aging
Boucher: Energy & Commerce; Judiciary; Science, Space & Technology
Boxer: Armed Services; Government Operations; Select Children, Youth & Families
Brewster: Public Works & Transportation; Veterans' Affairs
Brooks: Judiciary (chairman); Select Narcotics Abuse & Control
Broomfield: Foreign Affairs (ranking member); POW/MIA; Small Business
Browder: Armed Services; Science, Space & Technology
Brown: Agriculture; Science, Space & Technology (chairman)
Bruce: Energy & Commerce; Science, Space & Technology
Bryant: Budget; Energy & Commerce; Judiciary
Bunning: Standards of Official Conduct; Ways & Means
Burton: Foreign Affairs; POW/MIA; Post Office & Civil Service; Veterans' Affairs
Bustamante: Armed Services; Government Operations; Select Hunger
Byron: Armed Services; Interior & Insular Affairs; Select Aging
Callahan: Energy & Commerce; Merchant Marine & Fisheries
Camp: Agriculture; Select Children, Youth & Families; Small Business
Campbell (Colo.): Agriculture; Interior & Insular Affairs
Campbell (Calif.): Banking, Finance & Urban Affairs; Judiciary; Science, Space & Technology
Cardin: Standards of Official Conduct; Ways & Means
Carper: Banking, Finance & Urban Affairs; Merchant Marine & Fisheries

Carr: Appropriations; Select Hunger
Chandler: Post Office & Civil Service; Ways & Means
Chapman: Appropriations
Clay: Education & Labor; House Administration; Post Office & Civil Service (chairman)
Clement: Merchant Marine & Fisheries; Public Works & Transportation
Clinger: Government Operations; Public Works & Transportation; Select Narcotics Abuse & Control
Coble: Judiciary; Merchant Marine & Fisheries; Select Narcotics Abuse & Control
Coleman (Texas): Appropriations
Coleman (Mo.): Agriculture (ranking member); Education & Labor
Collins (Mich.): Post Office & Civil Service; Public Works & Transportation; Select Children, Youth & Families
Collins (Ill.): Energy & Commerce; Government Operations; Select Narcotics Abuse & Control
Combest: Agriculture; District of Columbia; Select Intelligence; Small Business
Condit: Agriculture; Government Operations
Conyers: Government Operations (chairman); Judiciary; Small Business
Cooper: Budget; Energy & Commerce
Costello: Public Works & Transportation; Science, Space & Technology; Select Aging
Coughlin: Appropriations; Select Narcotics Abuse & Control (ranking member)
Cox (Calif.): Government Operations; Public Works & Transportation
Cox (Ill.): Banking, Finance & Urban Affairs; Government Operations
Coyne: Ways & Means
Cramer: Public Works & Transportation; Science, Space & Technology; Select Children, Youth & Families
Crane: Ways & Means
Cunningham: Armed Services; Education & Labor; Merchant Marine & Fisheries
Dannemeyer: Budget; Energy & Commerce
Darden: Armed Services; Interior & Insular Affairs; Standards of Official Conduct
Davis: Armed Services; Merchant Marine & Fisheries (ranking member)
de la Garza: Agriculture (chairman)
de Lugo: Education & Labor; Interior & Insular Affairs; Public Works & Transportation; Select Narcotics Abuse & Control
DeFazio: Interior & Insular Affairs; Public Works & Transportation; Select Aging
DeLauro: Government Operations; Public Works & Transportation; Select Aging
DeLay: Appropriations
Dellums: Armed Services; District of Columbia (chairman); Select Intelligence
Derrick: Rules; Select Aging
Dickinson: Armed Services (ranking member); House Administration
Dicks: Appropriations; Select Intelligence
Dingell: Energy & Commerce (chairman)
Dixon: Appropriations
Donnelly: Ways & Means
Dooley: Agriculture; Interior & Insular Affairs
Doolittle: Interior & Insular Affairs; Merchant Marine & Fisheries
Dorgan: Select Hunger; Ways & Means
Dornan: Armed Services; POW/MIA; Select Intelligence; Select Narcotics Abuse & Control
Downey: Select Aging; Ways & Means
Dreier: POW/MIA; Rules
Duncan: Banking, Finance & Urban Affairs; Interior & Insular Affairs; Public Works & Transportation; Select Aging
Durbin: Appropriations; Budget; Select Children, Youth & Families
Dwyer: Appropriations; Budget
Dymally: District of Columbia; Foreign Affairs; Post Office & Civil Service
Early: Appropriations
Eckart: Energy & Commerce; Small Business
Edwards (Texas): Armed Services; Veterans' Affairs
Edwards (Calif.): Judiciary; Veterans' Affairs
Edwards (Okla.): Appropriations; Education & Labor; House Administration
Emerson: Agriculture; Public Works & Transportation; Select Hunger (ranking member)
Engel: Foreign Affairs; POW/MIA; Science, Space & Technology; Select Hunger
English: Agriculture; Government Operations
Erdreich: Banking, Finance & Urban Affairs; Government Operations; Select Aging
Espy: Agriculture; Budget; Select Hunger
Evans: Armed Services; Select Children, Youth & Families; Veterans' Affairs
Ewing: Agriculture; Public Works & Transportation
Faleomavaega: Foreign Affairs; Interior & Insular Affairs; Merchant Marine & Fisheries; POW/MIA; Select Hunger
Fascell: Foreign Affairs (chairman); Select Narcotics Abuse & Control
Fawell: Education & Labor; Science, Space & Technology; Select Aging
Fazio: Appropriations; Select Hunger
Feighan: Foreign Affairs; Judiciary; POW/MIA
Fields: Energy & Commerce; Merchant Marine & Fisheries
Fish: Joint Economic; Judiciary (ranking member)
Flake: Banking, Finance & Urban Affairs; Select Hunger; Small Business
Foglietta: Armed Services; Foreign Affairs; Merchant Marine & Fisheries
Ford (Tenn.): Select Aging; Ways & Means
Ford (Mich.): Education & Labor (chairman)
Frank: Banking, Finance & Urban Affairs; Budget; Judiciary; Select Aging
Franks: Armed Services; Select Aging; Small Business
Frost: House Administration; Rules
Fuster: Education & Labor; Foreign Affairs; Interior & Insular Affairs
Gallegly: Foreign Affairs; Interior & Insular Affairs; POW/MIA
Gallo: Appropriations
Gaydos: Education & Labor; House Administration
Gejdenson: Foreign Affairs; House Administration; Interior & Insular Affairs; Joint Printing; POW/MIA
Gekas: Judiciary; Select Intelligence
Gephardt: Budget
Geren: Public Works & Transportation; Science, Space & Technology; Veterans' Affairs
Gibbons: Joint Taxation; Ways & Means
Gilchrest: Merchant Marine & Fisheries; Science, Space & Technology; Select Aging; Select Hunger
Gillmor: Banking, Finance & Urban Affairs; House Administration; Select Narcotics Abuse & Control
Gilman: Foreign Affairs; POW/MIA (vice-chairman, POW/MIA task force); Post Office & Civil Service (ranking member); Select Hunger; Select Narcotics Abuse & Control
Gingrich: House Administration; Joint Printing
Glickman: Agriculture; Judiciary; Science, Space & Technology; Select Intelligence
Gonzalez: Banking, Finance & Urban Affairs (chairman)
Goodling: Education & Labor (ranking member); Foreign Affairs
Gordon: Rules; Select Aging
Goss: Foreign Affairs; Merchant Marine & Fisheries; Standards of Official Conduct
Gradison: Budget (ranking member); Ways & Means
Grandy: Standards of Official Conduct; Ways & Means
Green: Appropriations
Guarini: Budget; Select Narcotics Abuse & Control; Ways & Means
Gunderson: Agriculture; Education & Labor
Hall (Texas): Energy & Commerce; Science, Space & Technology
Hall (Ohio): Rules; Select Hunger (chairman)
Hamilton: Foreign Affairs; Joint Economic (vice chairman)
Hammerschmidt: Public Works & Transportation (ranking member); Select Aging; Veterans' Affairs

Hancock: Banking, Finance & Urban Affairs; Public Works & Transportation; Small Business
Hansen: Armed Services; Interior & Insular Affairs; Standards of Official Conduct (ranking member)
Harris: Energy & Commerce; Veterans' Affairs
Hastert: Energy & Commerce; Government Operations; Select Children, Youth & Families
Hatcher: Agriculture; Small Business
Hayes (Ill.): Education & Labor; Post Office & Civil Service
Hayes (La.): Public Works & Transportation; Science, Space & Technology
Hefley: Armed Services; Interior & Insular Affairs; Small Business
Hefner: Appropriations
Henry: Education & Labor; Science, Space & Technology; Select Aging
Herger: Agriculture; Merchant Marine & Fisheries; Select Narcotics Abuse & Control
Hertel: Armed Services; Merchant Marine & Fisheries; Select Aging
Hoagland: Banking, Finance & Urban Affairs; Interior & Insular Affairs; Judiciary
Hobson: Government Operations; Public Works & Transportation; Select Aging; Standards of Official Conduct
Hochbrueckner: Armed Services; Merchant Marine & Fisheries; Select Narcotics Abuse & Control
Holloway: Energy & Commerce; Select Children, Youth & Families
Hopkins: Agriculture; Armed Services
Horn: Public Works & Transportation; Science, Space & Technology; Select Children, Youth & Families
Horton: Government Operations (ranking member); Post Office & Civil Service
Houghton: Budget; Foreign Affairs; Select Aging
Hoyer: Appropriations; House Administration
Hubbard: Banking, Finance & Urban Affairs; Merchant Marine & Fisheries
Huckaby: Agriculture; Budget
Hughes: Judiciary; Merchant Marine & Fisheries; Select Aging; Select Narcotics Abuse & Control
Hunter: Armed Services; Select Hunger
Hutto: Armed Services; Merchant Marine & Fisheries
Hyde: Foreign Affairs; Judiciary; POW/MIA
Inhofe: Merchant Marine & Fisheries; Public Works & Transportation; Select Narcotics Abuse & Control
Ireland: Armed Services; Small Business (ranking member)
Jacobs: Ways & Means
James: Judiciary; Select Aging; Veterans' Affairs
Jefferson: Education & Labor; Merchant Marine & Fisheries
Jenkins: Ways & Means
Johnson (Conn.): Standards of Official Conduct; Ways & Means
Johnson (Texas): Banking, Finance & Urban Affairs; Science, Space & Technology; Small Business
Johnson (S.D.): Agriculture; Interior & Insular Affairs; Select Children, Youth & Families
Johnston: Foreign Affairs; Interior & Insular Affairs
Jones (Ga.): Public Works & Transportation; Veterans' Affairs
Jones (N.C.): Agriculture; Merchant Marine & Fisheries (chairman)
Jontz: Agriculture; Interior & Insular Affairs; Select Aging
Kanjorski: Banking, Finance & Urban Affairs; Post Office & Civil Service
Kaptur: Appropriations
Kasich: Armed Services; Budget
Kennedy: Banking, Finance & Urban Affairs; Select Aging; Veterans' Affairs
Kennelly: Select Intelligence; Ways & Means
Kildee: Budget; Education & Labor; House Administration
Kleczka: Banking, Finance & Urban Affairs; Government Operations; House Administration; Joint Printing
Klug: Education & Labor; Government Operations; Select Children, Youth & Families
Kolbe: Appropriations; Budget
Kolter: House Administration; Joint Library; Public Works & Transportation
Kopetski: Agriculture; Judiciary; Science, Space & Technology
Kostmayer: Energy & Commerce; Foreign Affairs; Interior & Insular Affairs; POW/MIA; Select Hunger
Kyl: Armed Services; Government Operations; Standards of Official Conduct
LaFalce: Banking, Finance & Urban Affairs; Small Business (chairman)
Lagomarsino: Foreign Affairs; Interior & Insular Affairs; POW/MIA (chairman, POW/MIA task force)
Lancaster: Armed Services; Merchant Marine & Fisheries; Small Business
Lantos: Foreign Affairs; Government Operations; POW/MIA; Select Aging
LaRocco: Banking, Finance & Urban Affairs; Interior & Insular Affairs
Laughlin: Merchant Marine & Fisheries; Public Works & Transportation
Leach: Banking, Finance & Urban Affairs; Foreign Affairs
Lehman (Calif.): Energy & Commerce; Interior & Insular Affairs
Lehman (Fla.): Appropriations; Select Children, Youth & Families
Lent: Energy & Commerce (ranking member); Merchant Marine & Fisheries; POW/MIA
Levin: District of Columbia; Select Children, Youth & Families; Ways & Means
Levine: Foreign Affairs; Interior & Insular Affairs; Judiciary; Select Narcotics Abuse & Control
Lewis (Calif.): Appropriations
Lewis (Ga.): Interior & Insular Affairs; Public Works & Transportation; Select Aging
Lewis (Fla.): Agriculture; Science, Space & Technology; Select Narcotics Abuse & Control
Lightfoot: Appropriations
Lipinski: Merchant Marine & Fisheries; Public Works & Transportation
Livingston: Appropriations; House Administration
Lloyd: Armed Services; Science, Space & Technology; Select Aging
Long: Agriculture; Select Hunger; Veterans' Affairs
Lowery: Appropriations; District of Columbia
Lowey: Education & Labor; Merchant Marine & Fisheries; Select Narcotics Abuse & Control
Luken: Banking, Finance & Urban Affairs; Government Operations
Machtley: Armed Services; Government Operations; Select Children, Youth & Families; Small Business
Manton: Energy & Commerce; House Administration; Joint Library; Merchant Marine & Fisheries; Select Aging
Markey: Energy & Commerce; Interior & Insular Affairs
Marlenee: Agriculture; Interior & Insular Affairs
Martin: Armed Services; Select Intelligence
Martinez: Education & Labor; Government Operations; Select Children, Youth & Families
Matsui: Budget; Ways & Means
Mavroules: Armed Services; Select Intelligence; Small Business
Mazzoli: Judiciary; Select Narcotics Abuse & Control; Small Business
McCandless: Banking, Finance & Urban Affairs; Government Operations
McCloskey: Armed Services; Foreign Affairs; POW/MIA; Post Office & Civil Service
McCollum: Banking, Finance & Urban Affairs; Judiciary
McCrery: Armed Services; Budget
McCurdy: Armed Services; Science, Space & Technology; Select Intelligence (chairman)
McDade: Appropriations (ranking member); Small Business
McDermott: District of Columbia; Standards of Official Conduct; Ways & Means
McEwen: Rules; Select Children, Youth & Families
McGrath: Ways & Means
McHugh: Appropriations; Select Children, Youth & Families; Standards of Official Conduct
McMillan: Budget; Energy & Commerce
McMillen: Energy & Commerce; Science, Space & Technology
McNulty: Armed Services; Post Office & Civil Service; Select Hunger
Meyers: Foreign Affairs; POW/MIA; Select Aging; Small Business
Mfume: Banking, Finance & Urban Affairs; Joint Economic; Select Narcotics Abuse & Control; Small Business

Miller (Ohio): Appropriations
Miller (Calif.): Education & Labor; Interior & Insular Affairs (chairman); Select Children, Youth & Families
Miller (Wash.): Budget; Foreign Affairs; POW/MIA
Mineta: Public Works & Transportation; Science, Space & Technology
Mink: Education & Labor; Government Operations
Moakley: Rules (chairman)
Molinari: Education & Labor; Public Works & Transportation
Mollohan: Appropriations
Montgomery: Armed Services; Veterans' Affairs (chairman)
Moody: Ways & Means
Moorhead: Energy & Commerce; Judiciary
Moran: Banking, Finance & Urban Affairs; Post Office & Civil Service
Morella: Post Office & Civil Service; Science, Space & Technology; Select Aging
Morrison: Agriculture; Science, Space & Technology; Select Hunger
Mrazek: Appropriations
Murphy: Education & Labor; Foreign Affairs; Interior & Insular Affairs
Murtha: Appropriations
Myers: Appropriations; Post Office & Civil Service
Nagle: Agriculture; Science, Space & Technology
Natcher: Appropriations
Neal (Mass.): Banking, Finance & Urban Affairs; Small Business
Neal (N.C.): Banking, Finance & Urban Affairs; Government Operations
Nichols: Public Works & Transportation; Select Aging; Veterans' Affairs
Norton: District of Columbia; Post Office & Civil Service; Public Works & Transportation
Nowak: Public Works & Transportation; Science, Space & Technology
Nussle: Agriculture; Banking, Finance & Urban Affairs; Select Aging
Oakar: Banking, Finance & Urban Affairs; House Administration; Post Office & Civil Service; Select Aging
Oberstar: Budget; Public Works & Transportation
Obey: Appropriations; Joint Economic
Olin: Agriculture; Small Business
Olver: Education & Labor; Science, Space & Technology
Ortiz: Armed Services; Merchant Marine & Fisheries; Select Narcotics Abuse & Control
Orton: Banking, Finance & Urban Affairs; Foreign Affairs; Small Business
Owens (N.Y.): Education & Labor; Government Operations; POW/MIA
Owens (Utah): Foreign Affairs; Interior & Insular Affairs; Select Aging; Select Intelligence
Oxley: Energy & Commerce; Select Narcotics Abuse & Control
Packard: Public Works & Transportation; Science, Space & Technology
Pallone: Merchant Marine & Fisheries; Public Works & Transportation; Select Aging
Panetta: Agriculture; Budget (chairman); House Administration; Select Hunger
Parker: Budget; Public Works & Transportation
Pastor: Education & Labor; Small Business
Patterson: Banking, Finance & Urban Affairs; Select Hunger; Veterans' Affairs
Paxon: Banking, Finance & Urban Affairs; Budget; Select Narcotics Abuse & Control; Veterans' Affairs
Payne (N.J.): Education & Labor; Foreign Affairs; Government Operations; Select Narcotics Abuse & Control
Payne (Va.): Budget; Public Works & Transportation
Pease: Budget; Ways & Means
Pelosi: Appropriations; Standards of Official Conduct
Penny: Agriculture; Select Hunger; Veterans' Affairs
Perkins: Education & Labor; Science, Space & Technology
Peterson (Minn.): Agriculture; Government Operations
Peterson (Fla.): POW/MIA; Public Works & Transportation; Select Children, Youth & Families; Veterans' Affairs
Petri: Education & Labor; Public Works & Transportation
Pickett: Armed Services; Merchant Marine & Fisheries; Veterans' Affairs
Pickle: Joint Taxation; Ways & Means
Porter: Appropriations; Select Aging
Poshard: Public Works & Transportation; Small Business
Price: Appropriations
Pursell: Appropriations
Quillen: Rules
Rahall: Interior & Insular Affairs; Public Works & Transportation
Ramstad: Judiciary; Select Narcotics Abuse & Control; Small Business
Rangel: Select Narcotics Abuse & Control (chairman); Ways & Means
Ravenel: Armed Services; Merchant Marine & Fisheries
Ray: Armed Services; Small Business
Reed: Education & Labor; Judiciary; Merchant Marine & Fisheries
Regula: Appropriations; Select Aging
Rhodes: Interior & Insular Affairs; Science, Space & Technology
Richardson: Energy & Commerce; Interior & Insular Affairs; POW/MIA; Select Aging; Select Intelligence
Ridge: Banking, Finance & Urban Affairs; POW/MIA; Post Office & Civil Service; Veterans' Affairs
Riggs: Banking, Finance & Urban Affairs; Public Works & Transportation; Select Children, Youth & Families
Rinaldo: Energy & Commerce; Select Aging (ranking member)
Ritter: Energy & Commerce; Science, Space & Technology
Roberts: Agriculture; House Administration; Joint Library; Joint Printing
Roe: Public Works & Transportation (chairman); Select Aging
Roemer: Education & Labor; Science, Space & Technology
Rogers: Appropriations; Budget
Rohrabacher: District of Columbia; Science, Space & Technology
Ros-Lehtinen: Foreign Affairs; Government Operations; POW/MIA
Rose: Agriculture; House Administration (chairman); Joint Library (vice chairman); Joint Printing (chairman)
Rostenkowski: Joint Taxation (chairman); Ways & Means (chairman)
Roth: Banking, Finance & Urban Affairs; Foreign Affairs
Roukema: Banking, Finance & Urban Affairs; Education & Labor; Select Hunger
Rowland: Energy & Commerce; Select Children, Youth & Families; Veterans' Affairs
Roybal: Appropriations; Select Aging (chairman)
Russo: House Administration; Ways & Means
Sabo: Appropriations; Budget; Select Intelligence
Sanders: Banking, Finance & Urban Affairs; Government Operations
Sangmeister: Judiciary; Public Works & Transportation; Veterans' Affairs
Santorum: Budget; Select Children, Youth & Families; Veterans' Affairs
Sarpalius: Agriculture; Select Children, Youth & Families; Small Business
Savage: Public Works & Transportation; Small Business
Sawyer: Education & Labor; Foreign Affairs; Post Office & Civil Service
Saxton: Armed Services; Merchant Marine & Fisheries; Select Aging
Schaefer: Energy & Commerce
Scheuer: Energy & Commerce; Joint Economic; Science, Space & Technology; Select Narcotics Abuse & Control
Schiff: Government Operations; Judiciary; Science, Space & Technology
Schroeder: Armed Services; Judiciary; Post Office & Civil Service; Select Children, Youth & Families (chairman)
Schulze: Interior & Insular Affairs; Ways & Means
Schumer: Banking, Finance & Urban Affairs; Interior & Insular Affairs; Judiciary
Sensenbrenner: Judiciary; Science, Space & Technology; Select Narcotics Abuse & Control
Serrano: Education & Labor; Small Business
Sharp: Energy & Commerce; Interior & Insular Affairs

Shaw: Ways & Means
Shays: Budget; Government Operations; Select Narcotics Abuse & Control
Shuster: Public Works & Transportation; Select Intelligence (ranking member)
Sikorski: Energy & Commerce; Post Office & Civil Service; Select Children, Youth & Families
Sisisky: Armed Services; Select Aging; Small Business
Skaggs: Appropriations; Select Children, Youth & Families
Skeen: Appropriations
Skelton: Armed Services; Select Aging; Small Business
Slattery: Banking, Finance & Urban Affairs; Energy & Commerce; Veterans' Affairs
Slaughter: Budget; Rules; Select Aging
Smith (Ore.): Agriculture; Interior & Insular Affairs; Select Hunger
Smith (N.J.): Foreign Affairs; POW/MIA; Select Aging; Select Hunger; Veterans' Affairs
Smith (Texas): Judiciary; Science, Space & Technology; Select Children, Youth & Families
Smith (Fla.): Appropriations; Select Narcotics Abuse & Control
Smith (Iowa): Appropriations; Small Business
Snowe: Foreign Affairs; Joint Economic; Select Aging
Solarz: Foreign Affairs; Joint Economic; Merchant Marine & Fisheries; POW/MIA (chairman, Subcommittee on Asian & Pacific Affairs); Select Intelligence
Solomon: POW/MIA; Rules (ranking member)
Spence: Armed Services; Select Aging; Veterans' Affairs
Spratt: Armed Services; Budget
Staggers: Agriculture; Judiciary; Select Aging; Veterans' Affairs
Stallings: Agriculture; Science, Space & Technology; Select Aging
Stark: District of Columbia; Joint Economic; Select Narcotics Abuse & Control; Ways & Means
Stearns: Banking, Finance & Urban Affairs; Select Aging; Veterans' Affairs
Stenholm: Agriculture; Budget
Stokes: Appropriations; Standards of Official Conduct (chairman)
Studds: Energy & Commerce; Foreign Affairs; Merchant Marine & Fisheries; POW/MIA; Select Aging
Stump: Armed Services; Veterans' Affairs (ranking member)
Sundquist: Ways & Means
Swett: Public Works & Transportation; Science, Space & Technology; Select Aging
Swift: Energy & Commerce; House Administration
Synar: Energy & Commerce; Government Operations; Judiciary; Select Hunger
Tallon: Agriculture; Merchant Marine & Fisheries
Tanner: Armed Services; Science, Space & Technology
Tauzin: Energy & Commerce; Merchant Marine & Fisheries
Taylor (N.C.): Interior & Insular Affairs; Public Works & Transportation; Select Aging
Taylor (Miss.): Armed Services; Merchant Marine & Fisheries
Thomas (Calif.): Budget; House Administration (ranking member); Ways & Means
Thomas (Wyo.): Banking, Finance & Urban Affairs; Government Operations; Interior & Insular Affairs
Thomas (Ga.): Appropriations
Thornton: Government Operations; Science, Space & Technology
Torres: Banking, Finance & Urban Affairs; Small Business
Torricelli: Foreign Affairs; Science, Space & Technology
Towns: Energy & Commerce; Government Operations; Select Narcotics Abuse & Control
Traficant: Public Works & Transportation; Science, Space & Technology; Select Narcotics Abuse & Control
Traxler: Appropriations
Unsoeld: Education & Labor; Merchant Marine & Fisheries; Select Aging
Upton: Energy & Commerce; Public Works & Transportation; Select Hunger
Valentine: Public Works & Transportation; Science, Space & Technology
Vander Jagt: Joint Taxation; Ways & Means
Vento: Banking, Finance & Urban Affairs; Interior & Insular Affairs; Select Aging
Visclosky: Appropriations
Volkmer: Agriculture; Science, Space & Technology; Select Aging
Vucanovich: Appropriations; Interior & Insular Affairs
Walker: Science, Space & Technology (ranking member)
Walsh: Agriculture; House Administration; Select Children, Youth & Families
Washington: Education & Labor; Judiciary; Select Narcotics Abuse & Control
Waters: Banking, Finance & Urban Affairs; Veterans' Affairs
Waxman: Energy & Commerce; Government Operations; Select Aging
Weber: Appropriations
Weiss: Banking, Finance & Urban Affairs; Foreign Affairs; Government Operations; POW/MIA; Select Children, Youth & Families
Weldon: Armed Services; Merchant Marine & Fisheries; Select Children, Youth & Families
Wheat: District of Columbia; Rules; Select Children, Youth & Families; Select Hunger
Whitten: Appropriations (chairman)
Williams: Education & Labor; Interior & Insular Affairs
Wilson: Appropriations; Select Intelligence
Wise: Budget; Government Operations; Select Aging
Wolf: Appropriations; Select Children, Youth & Families (ranking member); Select Hunger
Wolpe: Foreign Affairs; POW/MIA; Science, Space & Technology
Wyden: Energy & Commerce; Select Aging; Small Business
Wylie: Banking, Finance & Urban Affairs (ranking member); Joint Economic; Veterans' Affairs
Yates: Appropriations
Yatron: Foreign Affairs; POW/MIA; Post Office & Civil Service
Young (Fla.): Appropriations; Select Intelligence
Young (Alaska): Interior & Insular Affairs (ranking member); Merchant Marine & Fisheries; Post Office & Civil Service
Zeliff: Government Operations; Public Works & Transportation; Small Business
Zimmer: Government Operations; Science, Space & Technology; Select Aging

Senators' Phone and Room Directory

(102nd Congress)

Capitol Switchboard: (202) 224-3121

Senate ZIP Code: 20510

SD — Dirksen Building **SH** — Hart Building **SR** — Russell Building

Name, Party, State	Phone	Room
Adams, Brock, D-Wash.	224-2621	SH-513
Akaka, Daniel K., D-Hawaii	224-6361	SH-720
Baucus, Max, D-Mont.	224-2651	SH-706
Bentsen, Lloyd, D-Texas	224-5922	SH-703
Biden, Joseph R. Jr., D-Del.	224-5042	SR-221
Bingaman, Jeff, D-N.M.	224-5521	SH-524
Bond, Christopher S. R-Mo.	224-5721	SR-293
Boren, David L., D-Okla.	224-4721	SR-453
Bradley, Bill, D-N.J.	224-3224	SH-731
Breaux, John, D-La.	224-4623	SH-516
Brown, Hank, R-Colo.	224-5941	SH-717
Bryan, Richard H., D-Nev.	224-6244	SR-364
Bumpers, Dale, D-Ark.	224-4843	SD-229
Burdick, Quentin N., D-N.D.	224-2551	SH-511
Burns, Conrad, R-Mont.	224-2644	SD-183
Byrd, Robert C., D-W.Va.	224-3954	SH-311
Chafee, John H., R-R.I.	224-2921	SD-567
Coats, Daniel R., R-Ind.	224-5623	SR-407
Cochran, Thad, R-Miss.	224-5054	SR-326
Cohen, William S., R-Maine	224-2523	SH-322
Conrad, Kent, D-N.D.	224-2043	SD-724
Craig, Larry E., R-Idaho	244-2752	SH-302
Cranston, Alan, D-Calif.	224-3553	SH-112
D'Amato, Alfonse M., R-N.Y.	224-6542	SH-520
Danforth, John C., R-Mo.	224-6154	SR-249
Daschle, Tom, D-S.D.	224-2321	SH-317
DeConcini, Dennis, D-Ariz.	224-4521	SH-328
Dixon, Alan J., D-Ill.	224-2854	SH-331
Dodd, Christopher J., D-Conn.	224-2823	SR-444
Dole, Bob, R-Kan.	224-6521	SH-141
Domenici, Pete V., R-N.M.	224-6621	SD-434
Durenberger, Dave, R-Minn.	224-3244	SR-154
Exon, Jim, D-Neb.	224-4224	SH-528
Ford, Wendell H., D-Ky.	224-4343	SR-173A
Fowler, Wyche Jr., D-Ga.	224-3643	SR-204
Garn, Jake, R-Utah	224-5444	SD-505
Glenn, John, D-Ohio	224-3353	SH-503
Gore, Al, D-Tenn.	224-4944	SR-393
Gorton, Slade, R-Wash.	224-3441	SH-730
Graham, Bob, D-Fla.	224-3041	SD-241
Gramm, Phil, R-Texas	224-2934	SR-370
Grassley, Charles E., R-Iowa	224-3744	SH-135
Harkin, Tom, D-Iowa	224-3254	SH-531
Hatch, Orrin G., R-Utah	224-5251	SR-135
Hatfield, Mark O., R-Ore.	224-3753	SH-711
Heflin, Howell, D-Ala.	224-4124	SH-728
Helms, Jesse, R-N.C.	224-6342	SD-403
Hollings, Ernest F., D-S.C.	224-6121	SR-125
Inouye, Daniel K., D-Hawaii	224-3934	SH-722
Jeffords, James M., R-Vt.	224-5141	SD-530

Name, Party, State	Phone	Room
Johnston, J. Bennett, D-La.	224-5824	SH-136
Kassebaum, Nancy Landon, R-Kan.	224-4774	SR-302
Kasten, Bob, R-Wis.	224-5323	SH-110
Kennedy, Edward M., D-Mass.	224-4543	SR-315
Kerrey, Bob, D-Neb.	224-6551	SH-316
Kerry, John, D-Mass.	224-2742	SR-421
Kohl, Herb, D-Wis.	224-5653	SH-330
Lautenberg, Frank R., D-N.J.	224-4744	SH-506
Leahy, Patrick J., D-Vt.	224-4242	SR-433
Levin, Carl, D-Mich.	224-6221	SR-459
Lieberman, Joseph I., D-Conn.	224-4041	SH-502
Lott, Trent, R-Miss.	224-6253	SR-487
Lugar, Richard G., R-Ind.	224-4814	SH-306
Mack, Connie, R-Fla.	224-5274	SH-517
McCain, John, R-Ariz.	224-2235	SR-111
McConnell, Mitch, R-Ky.	224-2541	SR-120
Metzenbaum, Howard M., D-Ohio	224-2315	SR-140
Mikulski, Barbara A., D-Md.	224-4654	SH-320
Mitchell, George J., D-Maine	224-5344	SR-176
Moynihan, Daniel Patrick, D-N.Y.	224-4451	SR-464
Murkowski, Frank H., R-Alaska	224-6665	SH-709
Nickles, Don, R-Okla.	224-5754	SH-713
Nunn, Sam, D-Ga.	224-3521	SD-303
Packwood, Bob, R-Ore.	224-5244	SR-259
Pell, Claiborne, D-R.I.	224-4642	SR-335
Pressler, Larry, R-S.D.	224-5842	SH-133
Pryor, David, D-Ark.	224-2353	SR-267
Reid, Harry, D-Nev.	224-3542	SH-324
Riegle, Donald W. Jr., D-Mich.	224-4822	SD-105
Robb, Charles S., D-Va.	224-4024	SR-493
Rockefeller, John D. IV, D-W.Va.	224-6472	SH-109
Roth, William V. Jr., R-Del.	224-2441	SH-104
Rudman, Warren B., R-N.H.	224-3324	SH-530
Sanford, Terry, D-N.C.	224-3154	SH-716
Sarbanes, Paul S., D-Md.	224-4524	SH-309
Sasser, Jim, D-Tenn.	224-3344	SR-363
Seymour, John, R-Calif.	224-3841	SD-367
Shelby, Richard C., D-Ala.	224-5744	SH-313
Simon, Paul, D-Ill.	224-2152	SD-462
Simpson, Alan K., R-Wyo.	224-3424	SD-261
Smith, Robert C., R-N.H.	224-2841	SD-332
Specter, Arlen, R-Pa.	224-4254	SH-303
Stevens, Ted, R-Alaska	224-3004	SH-522
Symms, Steve D., R-Idaho	224-6142	SH-509
Thurmond, Strom, R-S.C.	224-5972	SR-217
Wallop, Malcolm, R-Wyo.	224-6441	SR-237
Warner, John W., R-Va.	224-2023	SR-225
Wellstone, Paul, D-Minn.	224-5641	SH-702
Wirth, Timothy E., D-Colo.	224-5852	SR-380
Wofford, Harris, D-Pa.	224-6324	SR-277

Representatives' Phone and Room Directory

(102nd Congress)

Capitol Switchboard: (202) 224-3121

House ZIP Code: 20515

Three-digit room numbers are in the Cannon Building; four-digit numbers beginning with 1 are in the Longworth Building; four-digit numbers beginning with 2 are in the Rayburn Building.

Name, Party, State	Phone	Room
Abercrombie, Neil, D-Hawaii (1)	225-1440	1440
Ackerman, Gary L., D-N.Y. (7)	225-2601	238
Alexander, Bill, D-Ark. (1)	225-4076	233
Allard, Wayne, R-Colo. (4)	225-4676	513
Allen, George F., R-Va. (7)	225-6561	1407
Anderson, Glenn M., D-Calif. (32)	225-6676	2329
Andrews, Michael A., D-Texas (25)	225-7508	303
Andrews, Robert E., D-N.J. (1)	225-6501	1005
Andrews, Thomas H., D-Maine (1)	225-6116	1724
Annunzio, Frank, D-Ill. (11)	225-6661	2303
Anthony, Beryl Jr., D-Ark. (4)	225-3772	1212
Applegate, Douglas, D-Ohio (18)	225-6265	2183
Archer, Bill, R-Texas (7)	225-2571	1236
Armey, Dick, R-Texas (26)	225-7772	130
Aspin, Les, D-Wis. (1)	225-3031	2336
Atkins, Chester G., D-Mass. (5)	225-3411	123
AuCoin, Les, D-Ore. (1)	225-0855	2159
Bacchus, Jim, D-Fla. (11)	225-3671	431
Baker, Richard H., R-La. (6)	225-3901	404
Ballenger, Cass, R-N.C. (10)	225-2576	328
Barnard, Doug Jr., D-Ga. (10)	225-4101	2227
Barrett, Bill, R-Neb. (3)	225-6435	1607
Barton, Joe L., R-Texas (6)	225-2002	1225
Bateman, Herbert H., R-Va. (1)	225-4261	1030
Beilenson, Anthony C., D-Calif. (23)	225-5911	1025
Bennett, Charles E., D-Fla. (3)	225-2501	2107
Bentley, Helen Delich, R-Md. (2)	225-3061	1610
Bereuter, Doug, R-Neb. (1)	225-4806	2348
Berman, Howard L., D-Calif. (26)	225-4695	137
Bevill, Tom, D-Ala. (4)	225-4876	2302
Bilbray, James, D-Nev. (1)	225-5965	319
Bilirakis, Michael, R-Fla. (9)	225-5755	2432
Blackwell, Lucien E., D-Pa. (2)	225-4001	1725
Blaz, Ben, R-Guam	225-1188	1130
Bliley, Thomas J. Jr., R-Va. (3)	225-2815	2241
Boehlert, Sherwood, R-N.Y. (25)	225-3665	1127
Boehner, John A., R-Ohio (8)	225-6205	1020
Bonior, David E., D-Mich. (12)	225-2106	2242
Borski, Robert A., D-Pa. (3)	225-8251	407
Boucher, Rick, D-Va. (9)	225-3861	405
Boxer, Barbara, D-Calif. (6)	225-5161	307
Brewster, Bill, D-Okla. (3)	225-4565	1404
Brooks, Jack, D-Texas (9)	225-6565	2449
Broomfield, William S., R-Mich. (18)	225-6135	2306
Browder, Glen, D-Ala. (3)	225-3261	1221
Brown, George E. Jr., D-Calif. (36)	225-6161	2300
Bruce, Terry L., D-Ill. (19)	225-5001	419
Bryant, John, D-Texas (5)	225-2231	208
Bunning, Jim, R-Ky. (4)	225-3465	116
Burton, Dan, R-Ind. (6)	225-2276	120
Bustamante, Albert G., D-Texas (23)	225-4511	1113
Byron, Beverly B., D-Md. (6)	225-2721	2430
Callahan, Sonny, R-Ala. (1)	225-4931	1330
Camp, Dave, R-Mich. (10)	225-3561	511
Campbell, Ben Nighthorse, D-Colo. (3)	225-4761	1530
Campbell, Tom, R-Calif. (12)	225-5411	313
Cardin, Benjamin L., D-Md. (3)	225-4016	117
Carper, Thomas R., D-Del. (AL)	225-4165	131
Carr, Bob, D-Mich. (6)	225-4872	2439
Chandler, Rod, R-Wash. (8)	225-7761	223
Chapman, Jim, D-Texas (1)	225-3035	236
Clay, William L., D-Mo. (1)	225-2406	2470
Clement, Bob, D-Tenn. (5)	225-4311	325
Clinger, William F. Jr., R-Pa. (23)	225-5121	2160
Coble, Howard, R-N.C. (6)	225-3065	430
Coleman, Tom, R-Mo. (6)	225-7041	2468
Coleman, Ronald D., D-Texas (16)	225-4831	440
Collins, Barbara-Rose, D-Mich. (13)	225-2261	1541
Collins, Cardiss, D-Ill. (7)	225-5006	2264
Combest, Larry, R-Texas (19)	225-4005	1527
Condit, Gary, D-Calif. (15)	225-6131	1529
Conyers, John Jr., D-Mich. (1)	225-5126	2426
Cooper, Jim, D-Tenn. (4)	225-6831	125
Costello, Jerry F., D-Ill. (21)	225-5661	119
Coughlin, Lawrence, R-Pa. (13)	225-6111	2309
Cox, C. Christopher, R-Calif. (40)	225-5611	412
Cox, John W. Jr., D-Ill. (16)	225-5676	501
Coyne, William J., D-Pa. (14)	225-2301	2455
Cramer, Bud, D-Ala. (5),	2254801	1431
Crane, Philip M., R-Ill. (12)	225-3711	1035
Cunningham, Randy 'Duke', R-Calif. (44)	225-5452	1017
Dannemeyer, William E., R-Calif. (39)	225-4111	2234
Darden, George "Buddy", D-Ga. (7)	225-2931	228
Davis, Robert W., R-Mich. (11)	225-4735	2417
DeFazio, Peter A., D-Ore. (4)	225-6416	1233
de la Garza, E. "Kika", D-Texas (15)	225-2531	1401
DeLauro, Rosa, D-Conn. (3)	225-3661	327
DeLay, Tom, R-Texas (22)	225-5951	308
Dellums, Ronald V., D-Calif. (8)	225-2661	2136
de Lugo, Ron, D-Virgin Islands	225-1790	2238
Derrick, Butler, D-S.C. (3)	225-5301	221
Dickinson, Bill, R-Ala. (2)	225-2901	2406
Dicks, Norm, D-Wash. (6)	225-5916	2429
Dingell, John D., D-Mich. (16)	225-4071	2328
Dixon, Julian C., D-Calif. (28)	225-7084	2400
Donnelly, Brian, D-Mass. (11)	225-3215	2229
Dooley, Calvin, D-Calif. (17)	225-3341	1022
Doolittle, John T., R-Calif. (14)	225-2511	1524
Dorgan, Byron L., D-N.D. (AL)	225-2611	203
Dornan, Robert K., R-Calif. (38)	225-2965	301

Name, Party, State	Phone	Room
Downey, Thomas J., D-N.Y. (2)	225-3335	2232
Dreier, David, R-Calif. (33)	225-2305	411
Duncan, John J. 'Jimmy' Jr., R-Tenn. (2)	225-5435	115
Durbin, Richard J., D-Ill. (20)	225-5271	129
Dwyer, Bernard J., D-N.J. (6)	225-6301	2428
Dymally, Mervyn M., D-Calif. (31)	225-5425	1717
Early, Joseph D., D-Mass. (3)	225-6101	2349
Eckart, Dennis E., D-Ohio (11)	225-6331	1111
Edwards, Chet, D-Texas (11)	225-6105	425
Edwards, Don, D-Calif. (10)	225-3072	2307
Edwards, Mickey, R-Okla. (5)	225-2132	2330
Emerson, Bill, R-Mo. (8)	225-4404	2454
Engel, Eliot L., D-N.Y. (19)	225-2464	1213
English, Glenn, D-Okla. (6)	225-5565	2206
Erdreich, Ben, D-Ala. (6)	225-4921	439
Espy, Mike, D-Miss. (2)	225-5876	332
Evans, Lane, D-Ill. (17)	225-5905	1121
Ewing, Thomas W., R-Ill. (15)	225-2371	1632
Faleomavaega, Eni F. H., D-Am. Samoa	225-8577	413
Fascell, Dante B., D-Fla. (19)	225-4506	2354
Fawell, Harris W., R-Ill. (13)	225-3515	435
Fazio, Vic, D-Calif. (4)	225-5716	2113
Feighan, Edward F., D-Ohio (19)	225-5731	1124
Fields, Jack, R-Texas (8)	225-4901	108
Fish, Hamilton Jr., R-N.Y. (21)	225-5441	2269
Flake, Floyd H., D-N.Y. (6)	225-3461	1034
Foglietta, Thomas M., D-Pa. (1)	225-4731	231
Foley, Thomas S., D-Wash. (5)	225-2006	1201
Ford, Harold E., D-Tenn. (9)	225-3265	2305
Ford, William D., D-Mich. (15)	225-6261	2371
Frank, Barney, D-Mass. (4)	225-5931	2404
Franks, Gary A., FR-Conn. (5)	225-3822	1609
Frost, Martin, D-Texas (24)	225-3605	2459
Fuster, Jaime B., Pop. Dem.-Puerto Rico	225-2615	427
Gallegly, Elton, R-Calif. (21)	225-5811	107
Gallo, Dean A., R-N.J. (11)	225-5034	1318
Gaydos, Joseph M., D-Pa. (20)	225-4631	2186
Gejdenson, Sam, D-Conn. (2)	225-2076	2416
Gekas, George W., R-Pa. (17)	225-4315	1519
Gephardt, Richard A., D-Mo. (3)	225-2671	1432
Geren, Pete, D-Texas (12)	225-5071	1730
Gibbons, Sam, D-Fla. (7)	225-3376	2204
Gilchrest, Wayne T. R-Md. (1)	225-5311	502
Gillmor, Paul E., R-Ohio (5)	225-6405	1203
Gilman, Benjamin A., R-N.Y. (22)	225-3776	2185
Gingrich, Newt, R-Ga. (6)	225-4501	2438
Glickman, Dan, D-Kan. (4)	225-6216	2311
Gonzalez, Henry B., D-Texas (20)	225-3236	2413
Goodling, Bill, R-Pa. (19)	225-5836	2263
Gordon, Bart, D-Tenn. (6)	225-4231	103
Goss, Porter J., R-Fla. (13)	225-2536	224
Gradison, Bill, R-Ohio (2)	225-3164	1125
Grandy, Fred, R-Iowa (6)	225-5476	418
Green, Bill, R-N.Y. (15)	225-2436	2301
Guarini, Frank J., D-N.J. (14)	225-2765	2458
Gunderson, Steve, R-Wis. (3)	225-5506	2235
Hall, Ralph M., D-Texas (4)	225-6673	2236
Hall, Tony P., D-Ohio (3)	225-6465	2162
Hamilton, Lee H., D-Ind. (9)	225-5315	2187
Hammerschmidt, John Paul, R-Ark. (3)	225-4301	2110
Hancock, Melton D. 'Mel', R-Mo. (7)	225-6536	318
Hansen, James V., R-Utah (1)	225-0453	2421
Harris, Claude, D-Ala. (7)	225-2665	1009
Hastert, Dennis, R-Ill. (14)	225-2976	515

Name, Party, State	Phone	Room
Hatcher, Charles, D-Ga. (2)	225-3631	2434
Hayes, Charles A., D-Ill. (1)	225-4372	1131
Hayes, Jimmy, D-La. (7)	225-2031	503
Hefley, Joel, R-Colo. (5)	225-4422	222
Hefner, W. G. "Bill", D-N.C. (8)	225-3715	2161
Henry, Paul B., R-Mich. (5)	225-3831	215
Herger, Wally, R-Calif. (2)	225-3076	1108
Hertel, Dennis M., D-Mich. (14)	225-6276	2442
Hoagland, Peter, D-Neb. (2)	225-4155	1710
Hobson, David L., R-Ohio (7)	225-4324	1338
Hochbrueckner, George J., D-N.Y. (1)	225-3826	124
Holloway, Clyde C., R-La. (8)	225-4926	1206
Hopkins, Larry J., R-Ky. (6)	225-4706	2437
Horn, Joan Kelly, D-Mo. (2)	225-2561	1008
Horton, Frank, R-N.Y. (29)	225-4916	2108
Houghton, Amo, R-N.Y. (34)	225-3161	1216
Hoyer, Steny H., D-Md. (5)	225-4131	1705
Hubbard, Carroll Jr., D-Ky. (1)	225-3115	2268
Huckaby, Jerry, D-La. (5)	225-2376	2182
Hughes, William J., D-N.J. (2)	225-6572	341
Hunter, Duncan, R-Calif. (45)	225-5672	133
Hutto, Earl, D-Fla. (1)	225-4136	2435
Hyde, Henry J., R-Ill. (6)	225-4561	2262
Inhofe, James M., R-Okla. (1)	225-2211	408
Ireland, Andy, D-Fla. (10)	225-5015	2466
Jacobs, Andrew Jr., D-Ind. (10)	225-4011	2313
James, Craig T., R-Fla. (4)	225-4035	1408
Jefferson, William J., D-La. (2)	225-6636	506
Jenkins, Ed, D-Ga. (9)	225-5211	2427
Johnson, Nancy L., R-Conn. (6)	225-4476	227
Johnson, Sam, R-Texas (3)	225-4201	1223
Johnson, Tim, D-S.D. (AL)	225-2801	428
Johnston, Harry A., D-Fla. (14)	225-3001	1028
Jones, Ben, D-Ga. (4)	225-4272	514
Jones, Walter B., D-N.C. (1)	225-3101	241
Jontz, Jim, D-Ind. (5)	225-5037	1317
Kanjorski, Paul E., D-Pa. (11)	225-6511	424
Kaptur, Marcy, D-Ohio (9)	225-4146	1228
Kasich, John R., R-Ohio (12)	225-5355	1133
Kennedy, Joseph P. II, D-Mass. (8)	225-5111	1208
Kennelly, Barbara B., D-Conn. (1)	225-2265	201
Kildee, Dale E., D-Mich. (7)	225-3611	2239
Kleczka, Gerald D., D-Wis. (4)	225-4572	226
Klug, Scott L., R-Wis. (2)	225-2906	1224
Kolbe, Jim, R-Ariz. (5)	225-2542	410
Kolter, Joe, D-Pa. (4)	225-2565	212
Kopetski, Mike, D-Ore. (5)	225-5711	216
Kostmayer, Peter H., D-Pa. (8)	225-4276	2436
Kyl, Jon, R-Ariz. (4)	225-3361	336
LaFalce, John J., D-N.Y. (32)	225-3231	2367
Lagomarsino, Robert J., R-Calif. (19)	225-3601	2332
Lancaster, Martin, D-N.C. (3)	225-3415	1417
Lantos, Tom, D-Calif. (11)	225-3531	1526
LaRocco, Larry, D-Idaho (1)	225-6611	1117
Laughlin, Greg, D-Texas (14)	225-2831	218
Leach, Jim, R-Iowa (1)	225-6576	1514
Lehman, Richard H., D-Calif. (18)	225-4540	1319
Lehman, William, D-Fla. (17)	225-4211	2347
Lent, Norman F., R-N.Y. (4)	225-7896	2408
Levin, Sander M., D-Mich. (17)	225-4961	323
Levine, Mel, D-Calif. (27)	225-6451	2443
Lewis, Jerry, R-Calif. (35)	225-5861	2312
Lewis, John, D-Ga. (5)	225-3801	329
Lewis, Tom, R-Fla. (12)	225-5792	2351

Name, Party, State	Phone	Room
Lightfoot, Jim Ross, R-Iowa (5)	225-3806	1222
Lipinski, William O., D-Ill. (5)	225-5701	1501
Livingston, Robert L., R-La. (1)	225-3015	2368
Lloyd, Marilyn, D-Tenn. (3)	225-3271	2266
Long, Jill L., D-Ind. (4)	225-4436	1513
Lowery, Bill, R-Calif. (41)	225-3201	2433
Lowey, Nita M., D-N.Y. (20)	225-6506	1313
Luken, Charles J., D-Ohio (1)	225-2216	1107
Machtley, Ronald K., R-R.I. (1)	225-4911	132
Manton, Thomas J., D-N.Y. (9)	225-3965	331
Markey, Edward J., D-Mass. (7)	225-2836	2133
Marlenee, Ron, R-Mont. (2)	225-1555	2465
Martin, David O'B., R-N.Y. (26)	225-4611	442
Martinez, Matthew G., D-Calif. (30)	225-5464	2446
Matsui, Robert T., D-Calif. (3)	225-7163	2353
Mavroules, Nicholas, D-Mass. (6)	225-8020	2334
Mazzoli, Romano L., D-Ky. (3)	225-5401	2246
McCandless, Al, R-Calif. (37)	225-5330	2422
McCloskey, Frank, D-Ind. (8)	225-4636	127
McCollum, Bill, R-Fla. (5)	225-2176	2453
McCrery, Jim, R-La. (4)	225-2777	429
McCurdy, Dave, D-Okla. (4)	225-6165	2344
McDade, Joseph M., R-Pa. (10)	225-3731	2370
McDermott, Jim, D-Wash. (7)	225-3106	1707
McEwen, Bob, R-Ohio (6)	225-5705	2431
McGrath, Raymond J., R-N.Y. (5)	225-5516	205
McHugh, Matthew F., D-N.Y. (28)	225-6335	2335
McMillan, J. Alex, R-N.C. (9)	225-1976	401
McMillen, Tom, D-Md. (4)	225-8090	420
McNulty, Michael R., D-N.Y. (23)	225-5076	414
Meyers, Jan, R-Kan. (3)	225-2865	1230
Mfume, Kweisi, D-Md. (7)	225-4741	217
Michel, Robert H., R-Ill. (18)	225-6201	2112
Miller, Clarence E., R-Ohio (10)	225-5131	2308
Miller, George, D-Calif. (7)	225-2095	2228
Miller, John R., R-Wash. (1)	225-6311	322
Mineta, Norman Y., D-Calif. (13)	225-2631	2350
Mink, Patsy T., D-Hawaii (2)	225-4906	2135
Moakley, Joe, D-Mass. (9)	225-8273	235
Molinari, Susan, R-N.Y. (14)	225-3371	315
Mollohan, Alan B., D-W.Va. (1)	225-4172	229
Montgomery, G. V. "Sonny," D-Miss. (3)	225-5031	2184
Moody, Jim, D-Wis. (5)	225-3571	1019
Moorhead, Carlos J., R-Calif. (22)	225-4176	2346
Moran, James P Jr., D-Va. (8)	225-4376	1523
Morella, Constance A., R-Md. (8)	225-5341	1024
Morrison, Sid, R-Wash. (4)	225-5816	1434
Mrazek, Robert J., D-N.Y. (3)	225-5956	306
Murphy, Austin J., D-Pa. (22)	225-4665	2210
Murtha, John P., D-Pa. (12)	225-2065	2423
Myers, John T., R-Ind. (7)	225-5805	2372
Nagle, Dave, D-Iowa (3)	225-3301	214
Natcher, William H., D-Ky. (2)	225-3501	2333
Neal, Richard E., D-Mass. (2)	225-5601	437
Neal, Stephen L., D-N.C. (5)	225-2071	2463
Nichols, Dick, R-Kan. (5)	225-3911	1605
Norton, Eleanor Holmes	225-8050	1631
Nowak, Henry J., D-N.Y. (33)	225-3306	2240
Nussle, Jim, R-Iowa (2)	225-2911	507
Oakar, Mary Rose, D-Ohio (20)	225-5871	2231
Oberstar, James L., D-Minn. (8)	225-6211	2209
Obey, David R., D-Wis. (7)	225-3365	2462
Olin, Jim, D-Va. (6)	225-5431	1410
Olver, John, D-Mass. (1)	225-5335	1116

Name, Party, State	Phone	Room
Ortiz, Solomon P., D-Texas (27)	225-7742	2445
Orton, Bill, D-Utah (3)	225-7751	1723
Owens, Major R., D-N.Y. (12)	225-6231	114
Owens, Wayne, D-Utah (2)	225-3011	1728
Oxley, Michael G., R-Ohio (4)	225-2676	2448
Packard, Ron, R-Calif. (43)	225-3906	434
Pallone, Frank Jr., D-N.J. (3)	225-4671	213
Panetta, Leon E., D-Calif. (16)	225-2861	339
Parker, Mike, D-Miss. (4)	225-5865	1504
Pastor, Ed, D-Ariz. (2)	225-4065	1520
Patterson, Liz J., D-S.C. (4)	225-6030	230
Paxon, Bill, R-N.Y. (31)	225-5265	1314
Payne, Donald M., D-N.J. (10)	225-3436	417
Payne, Lewis F. Jr., D-Va. (5)	255-4711	1118
Pease, Don J., D-Ohio (13)	225-3401	2410
Pelosi, Nancy, D-Calif. (5)	225-4965	109
Penny, Timothy J., D-Minn. (1)	225-2472	436
Perkins, Carl C., D-Ky. (7)	225-4935	1004
Peterson, Collin C., D-Minn. (7)	225-2165	1641
Peterson, Pete, D-Fla. (2)	225-5235	1415
Petri, Thomas E., R-Wis. (6)	225-2476	2245
Pickett, Owen B., D-Va. (2)	225-4215	1204
Pickle, J. J., D-Texas (10)	225-4865	242
Porter, John, R-Ill. (10)	225-4835	1026
Poshard, Glenn, D-Ill. (22)	225-5201	314
Price, David E., D-N.C. (4)	225-1784	1406
Pursell, Carl D., R-Mich. (2)	225-4401	1414
Quillen, James H., R-Tenn. (1)	225-6356	102
Rahall, Nick J. II, D-W.Va. (4)	225-3452	2104
Ramstad, Jim, R-Minn. (3)	225-2871	504
Rangel, Charles B., D-N.Y. (16)	225-4365	2252
Ravenel, Arthur Jr., R-S.C. (1)	225-3176	508
Ray, Richard, D-Ga. (3)	225-5901	225
Reed, John F., D-R.I. (2)	225-2735	1229
Regula, Ralph, R-Ohio (16)	225-3876	2207
Rhodes, John J. III, R-Ariz. (1)	225-2635	326
Richardson, Bill, D-N.M. (3)	225-6190	204
Ridge, Tom, R-Pa. (21)	225-5406	1714
Riggs, Frank, R-Calif. (1)	225-3311	1517
Rinaldo, Matthew J., R-N.J. (7)	225-5361	2469
Ritter, Don, R-Pa. (15)	225-6411	2202
Roberts, Pat, R-Kan. (1)	225-2715	1110
Roe, Robert A., D-N.J. (8)	225-5751	2243
Roemer, Tim, D-Ind. (3)	225-3915	415
Rogers, Harold, R-Ky. (5)	225-4601	343
Rohrabacher, Dana, R-Calif. (42)	225-2415	1039
Ros-Lehtinen, Ileana, R-Fla. (18)	225-3931	416
Rose, Charlie, D-N.C. (7)	225-2731	2230
Rostenkowski, Dan, D-Ill. (8)	225-4061	2111
Roth, Toby, R-Wis. (8)	225-5665	2352
Roukema, Marge, R-N.J. (5)	225-4465	2244
Rowland, J. Roy, D-Ga. (8)	225-6531	423
Roybal, Edward R., D-Calif. (25)	225-6235	2211
Russo, Marty, D-Ill. (30)	225-5736	2233
Sabo, Martin Olav, D-Minn. (5)	225-4755	2201
Sanders, Bernard, I-Vt. (AL)	225-4115	509
Sangmeister, George E., D-Ill. (4)	225-3635	1032
Santorum, Rick, R-Pa. (18)	225-2135	1708
Sarpalius, Bill, D-Texas (13)	225-3706	126
Savage, Gus, D-Ill. (2)	225-0773	2419
Sawyer, Tom, D-Ohio (14)	225-5231	1518
Saxton, H. James, R-N.J. (13)	225-4765	324
Schaefer, Dan, R-Colo. (6)	225-7882	1007
Scheuer, James H., D-N.Y. (8)	225-5471	2221

Name, Party, State	Phone	Room
Schiff, Steven H., R-N.M. (1)	225-6316	1427
Schroeder, Patricia, D-Colo. (1)	225-4431	2208
Schulze, Dick, R-Pa. (5)	225-5761	2267
Schumer, Charles E., D-N.Y. (10)	225-6616	2412
Sensenbrenner, F. James Jr., R-Wis. (9)	225-5101	2444
Serrano, Jose E., D-N.Y. (18)	225-4361	1217
Sharp, Philip R., D-Ind. (2)	225-3021	2217
Shaw, E. Clay Jr., R-Fla. (15)	225-3026	2338
Shays, Christopher, R-Conn. (4)	225-5541	1531
Shuster, Bud, R-Pa. (9)	225-2431	2188
Sikorski, Gerry, D-Minn. (6)	225-2271	403
Sisisky, Norman, D-Va. (4)	225-6365	426
Skaggs, David E., D-Colo. (2)	225-2161	1507
Skeen, Joe, R-N.M. (2)	225-2365	2447
Skelton, Ike, D-Mo. (4)	225-2876	2134
Slattery, Jim, D-Kan. (2)	225-6601	1512
Slaughter, Louise M., D-N.Y. (30)	225-3615	1424
Smith, Bob, R-Ore. (2)	225-6730	118
Smith, Christopher H., R-N.J. (4)	225-3765	2440
Smith, Lamar, R-Texas (21)	225-4236	422
Smith, Lawrence J., D-Fla. (16)	225-7931	113
Smith, Neal, D-Iowa (4)	225-4426	2373
Snowe, Olympia J., R-Maine (2)	225-6306	2464
Solarz, Stephen J., D-N.Y. (13)	225-2361	1536
Solomon, Gerald B. H., R-N.Y. (24)	225-5614	2265
Spence, Floyd, R-S.C. (2)	225-2452	2405
Spratt, John M. Jr., D-S.C. (5)	225-5501	1533
Staggers, Harley O. Jr., D-W.Va. (2)	225-4331	1323
Stallings, Richard, D-Idaho (2)	225-5531	1122
Stark, Pete, D-Calif. (9)	225-5065	239
Stearns, Cliff, R-Fla. (6)	225-5744	1123
Stenholm, Charles W., D-Texas (17)	225-6605	1226
Stokes, Louis, D-Ohio (21)	225-7032	2365
Studds, Gerry E., D-Mass. (10)	225-3111	237
Stump, Bob, R-Ariz. (3)	225-4576	211
Sundquist, Don, R-Tenn. (7)	225-2811	438
Swett, Dick, D-N.H. (2)	225-5206	128
Swift, Al, D-Wash. (2)	225-2605	1502
Synar, Mike, D-Okla. (2)	225-2701	2441
Tallon, Robin, D-S.C. (6)	225-3315	432
Tanner, John, D-Tenn. (8)	225-4714	1232
Tauzin, W. J. "Billy", D-La. (3)	225-4031	2342
Taylor, Charles H., R-N.C. (11)	225-6401	516
Taylor, Gene, D-Miss. (5)	225-5772	1429
Thomas, Bill, R-Calif. (20)	225-2915	2402
Thomas, Craig, R-Wyo. (AL)	225-2311	1721
Thomas, Lindsay, D-Ga. (1)	225-5831	240
Thornton, Ray, D-Ark. (2)	225-2506	1214
Torres, Esteban Edward, D-Calif. (34)	225-5256	1740
Torricelli, Robert G., D-N.J. (9)	225-5061	317
Towns, Edolphus, D-N.Y. (11)	225-5936	1726
Traficant, James A. Jr., D-Ohio (17)	225-5261	312
Traxler, Bob, D-Mich. (8)	225-2806	2366
Unsoeld, Jolene, D-Wash. (3)	225-3536	1508
Upton, Fred, R-Mich (4)	225-3761	1713
Valentine, Tim, D-N.C. (2)	225-4531	1510
Vander Jagt, Guy, R-Mich. (9)	225-3511	2409
Vento, Bruce F., D-Minn. (4)	225-6631	2304
Visclosky, Peter J., D-Ind. (1)	225-2461	330
Volkmer, Harold L., D-Mo. (9)	225-2956	2411
Vucanovich, Barbara F., R-Nev. (2)	225-6155	206
Walker, Robert S., R-Pa. (16)	225-2411	2369
Walsh, James T., R-N.Y. (27)	225-3701	1238
Washington, Craig, D-Texas (18)	225-3816	1711
Waters, Maxine, D-Calif. (29)	225-2201	1207
Waxman, Henry A., D-Calif. (24)	225-3976	2418
Weber, Vin, R-Minn. (2)	225-2331	106
Weiss, Ted, D-N.Y. (17)	225-5635	2467
Weldon, Curt, R-Penn. (7)	225-2011	316
Wheat, Alan, D-Mo. (5)	225-4535	1210
Whitten, Jamie L., D-Miss. (1)	225-4306	2314
Williams, Pat, D-Mont. (1)	225-3211	2457
Wilson, Charles, D-Texas (2)	225-2401	2256
Wise, Bob, D-W.Va. (3)	225-2711	1421
Wolf, Frank R., R-Va. (10)	225-5136	104
Wolpe, Howard, D-Mich. (3)	225-5011	1535
Wyden, Ron, D-Ore. (3)	225-4811	2452
Wylie, Chalmers P., R-Ohio (15)	225-2015	2310
Yates, Sidney R., D-Ill. (9)	225-2111	2109
Yatron, Gus, D-Pa. (6)	225-5546	2205
Young, C. W. Bill, R-Fla. (8)	225-5961	2407
Young, Don, R-Alaska (AL)	225-5765	2331
Zeliff, Bill, R-N.H. (1)	225-5456	512
Zimmer, Dick, R-N.J. (12)	225-5801	510

CAPITOL HILL

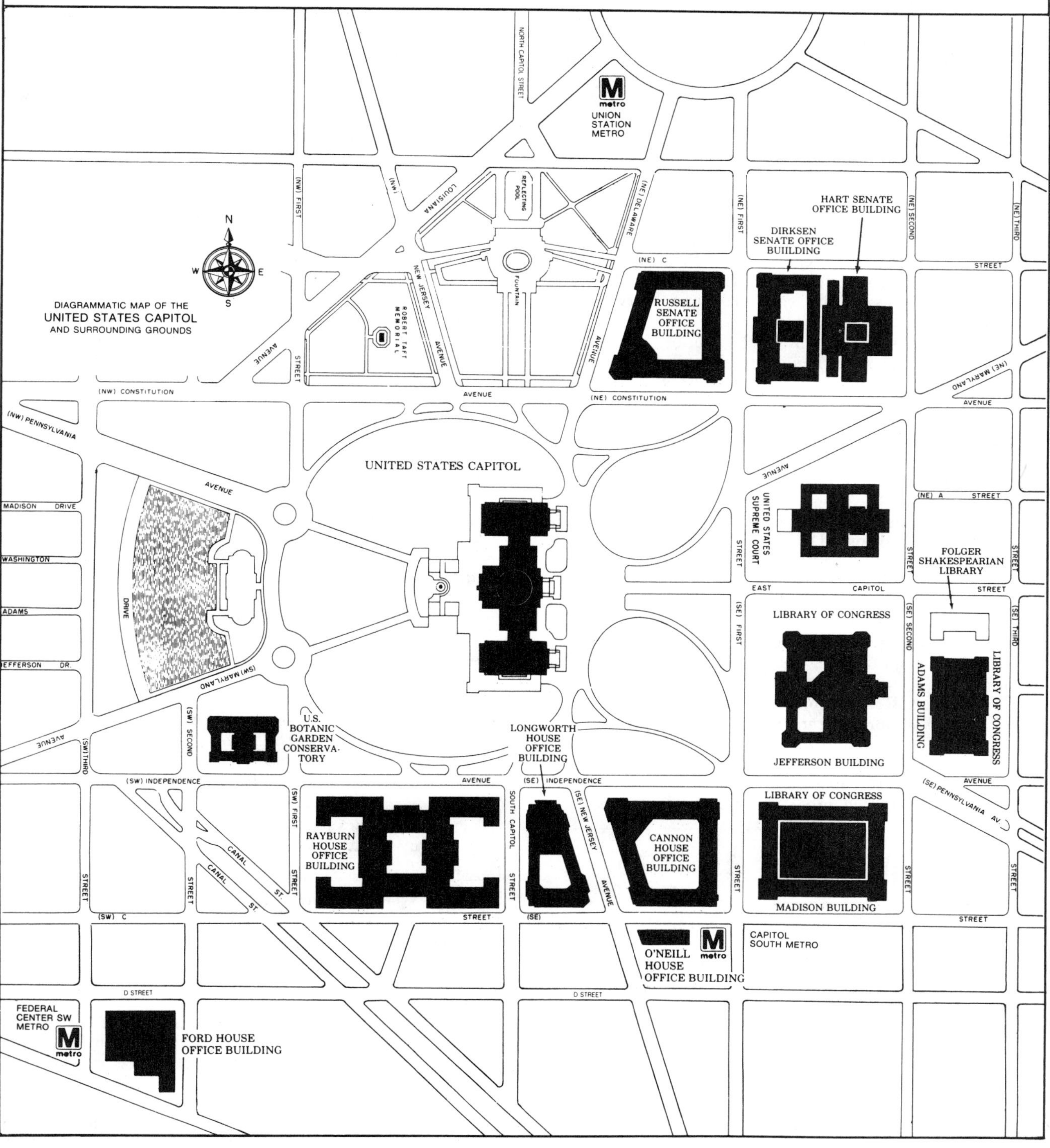

The Legislative Process in Brief

(Parliamentary terms used below are defined in the glossary, p. 77-D)

Introduction of Bills

A House member (including the resident commissioner of Puerto Rico and non-voting delegates of the District of Columbia, Guam, the Virgin Islands and American Samoa) may introduce any one of several types of bills and resolutions by handing it to the clerk of the House or placing it in a box called the hopper.

A senator first gains recognition of the presiding officer to announce the introduction of a bill. If objection is offered by any senator, the introduction of the bill is postponed until the following day.

As the next step in either the House or Senate, the bill is numbered, referred to committee, labeled with the sponsor's name and sent to the Government Printing Office so that copies can be made for subsequent study and action. Senate bills may be jointly sponsored and carry several senators' names.

Until 1978, the House limited the number of members who could cosponsor any one bill; the ceiling was eliminated at the beginning of the 96th Congress.

A bill written in the executive branch and proposed as an administration measure usually is introduced by the chairman of the congressional committee that has jurisdiction over the subject.

Bills—Prefixed with HR in the House, S in the Senate, followed by a number. Used as the form for most legislation, whether general or special, public or private.

Joint Resolutions—Designated H J Res or S J Res. Subject to the same procedure as bills, with the exception of a joint resolution proposing an amendment to the Constitution. The latter must be approved by two-thirds of both houses and is thereupon sent directly to the administrator of general services for submission to the states for ratification instead of being presented to the president for his approval.

Concurrent Resolutions—Designated H Con Res or S Con Res. Used for matters affecting the operations of both houses. These resolutions do not become law.

Resolutions—Designated H Res or S Res. Used for a matter concerning the operation of either house alone and adopted only by the chamber in which it originates.

Committee Action

With few exceptions, bills are referred to the appropriate standing committees. The job of referral formally is the responsibility of the Speaker of the House and the presiding officer of the Senate, but this task usually is carried out on their behalf by the parliamentarians of the House and Senate.

Precedent, statute and the jurisdictional mandates of the committees as set forth in the rules of the House and Senate determine which committees receive what kinds of bills. An exception is the referral of private bills, which are sent to whatever committee is designated by their sponsors. Bills are technically considered "read for the first time" when referred to House committees.

When a bill reaches a committee, it is placed on the committee's calendar. At that time the bill comes under the sharpest congressional focus. Its chances for passage are quickly determined; the great majority of bills falls by the legislative roadside.

Failure of a committee to act on a bill is equivalent to killing it; the measure can be withdrawn from the committee's purview only by a discharge petition signed by a majority of the House membership on House bills or by adoption of a special resolution in the Senate. Discharge attempts rarely succeed.

The first committee action taken on a bill usually is a request for comment on it by interested government agencies. The committee chairman may assign the bill to a subcommittee for study and hearings, or it may be considered by the full committee. Hearings may be public, closed (executive session) or both. After considering a bill, a subcommittee reports to the full committee its recommendations for action and any proposed amendments.

The full committee then votes on its recommendation to the House or Senate. This procedure is called "ordering a bill reported."

Occasionally a committee may order a bill reported unfavorably; most of the time a report, submitted by the committee chairman to the House or Senate, calls for favorable action on the measure since the committee can effectively "kill" a bill by simply not taking any action.

After the bill is reported, the committee chairman instructs the staff to prepare a written report. The report describes the bill's purposes and scope, explains the committee revisions, notes proposed changes in existing law and, usually, includes the views of the executive branch agencies consulted. Often committee members opposing a bill include dissenting views in the report.

Usually, the committee "marks up" or proposes amendments to the bill. If they are substantial and the measure is complicated, the committee may order a "clean bill" introduced, which will embody the proposed amendments. The original bill then is put aside and the clean bill, with a new number, is reported to the floor.

The chamber must approve, alter or reject the committee amendments before the bill itself can be put to a vote.

Floor Action

After a bill is reported back to the house where it originated, it is placed on the calendar.

There are five legislative calendars in the House, issued in one cumulative calendar titled *Calendars of the United States House of Representatives and History of Legislation.* The House calendars are:

The Union Calendar to which are referred bills raising revenues, general appropriations bills and any measures directly or indirectly appropriating money or property. It is the Calendar of the Committee of the Whole House on the State of the Union.

The House Calendar to which are referred bills of public character not raising revenue or appropriating money or property.

The Consent Calendar to which are referred bills of a non-controversial nature that are passed without debate when the Consent Calendar is called on the first and third Mondays of each month.

The Private Calendar to which are referred bills for relief in the nature of claims against the United States or private immigration bills that are passed without debate when the Private Calendar is called the first and third Tuesdays of each month.

The Discharge Calendar to which are referred motions to discharge committees when the necessary signatures are signed to a discharge petition.

There is only one legislative calendar in the Senate and one "executive calendar" for treaties and nominations submitted to the Senate. When the Senate Calendar is called, each senator is limited to five minutes' debate on each bill.

Debate. A bill is brought to debate by varying procedures. If it is a routine measure, it may await the call of the calendar. If it is urgent or important, it can be taken up in the Senate either by unanimous consent or by a majority vote. The majority leader, in consultation with the minority leader and others, schedules the bills that will be taken up for debate.

In the House, precedence is granted if a special rule is obtained from the Rules Committee. A request for a special rule usually is made by the chairman of the committee that favorably reported the bill, supported by the bill's sponsor and other committee members. The request, considered by the Rules Committee in the same way that other committees consider legislative measures, is in the form of a resolution providing for immediate consideration of the bill.

The Rules Committee reports the resolution to the House, where it is debated and voted upon in the same fashion as regular bills. If the Rules Committee should fail to report a rule requested by a committee, there are several ways to bring the bill to the House floor — under suspension of the rules, on Calendar Wednesday or by a discharge motion.

The resolutions providing special rules are important because they specify how long the bill may be debated and whether it may be amended from the floor. If floor amendments are banned, the bill is considered under a "closed rule," which permits only members of the committee that first reported the measure to the House to alter its language, subject to chamber acceptance.

When a bill is debated under an "open rule," amendments may be offered from the floor. Committee amendments always are taken up first but may be changed, like all amendments up to the second degree; that is, an amendment to an amendment to an amendment is not in order.

Duration of debate in the House depends on whether the bill is under discussion by the House proper or before the House when it is sitting as the Committee of the Whole House on the State of the Union.

In the House, the amount of time for debate either is determined by special rule or is allocated with an hour for each member if the measure is under consideration without a rule.

In the Committee of the Whole, the amount of time agreed on for general debate is equally divided between proponents and opponents. At the end of general discussion, the bill is read section by section for amendment. Debate on an amendment is limited to five minutes for each side; this is called the "five-minute rule." In practice, amendments regularly are debated more than 10 minutes, with members gaining the floor by offering pro forma amendments or obtaining unanimous consent to speak longer than five minutes.

Senate debate usually is unlimited. It can be halted only by unanimous consent or by "cloture," which requires a three-fifths majority of the entire Senate or, in the case of a proposed change in the Senate rules, a two-thirds vote.

The House considers almost all important bills within a parliamentary framework known as the Committee of the Whole. It is not a committee as the word usually is understood; it is the full House meeting under another name for the purpose of speeding action on legislation.

Technically, the House sits as the Committee of the Whole when it considers any tax measure or bill dealing with public appropriations. It also can resolve itself into the Committee of the Whole if a member moves to do so and the motion is carried. The Speaker appoints a member to serve as the chairman.

The rules of the House permit the Committee of the Whole to meet when a quorum of 100 members is present on the floor and to amend and act on bills, within certain time limitations. When the Committee of the Whole has acted, it "rises," the Speaker returns as the presiding officer of the House and the member appointed chairman of the Committee of the Whole reports the action of the committee and its recommendations.

The Committee of the Whole cannot pass a bill; it reports the measure to the full House with whatever changes it has approved. The full House then may pass or reject the bill — or, on occasion, recommit the bill to committee. Amendments adopted in the Committee of the Whole may be put to a second vote in the full House.

Votes. Voting on bills may occur repeatedly before they are finally approved or rejected. The House votes on the rule for the bill and on various amendments to the bill. Voting on amendments often is a more illuminating test of a bill's support than is the final tally. Sometimes members approve final passage of bills after vigorously supporting amendments that, if adopted, would scuttle the legislation.

The Senate has three different methods of voting: an untabulated voice vote, a standing vote (called a division) and a recorded roll call to which members answer "yea" or "nay" when their names are called.

The House also employs voice and standing votes, but since January 1973 yeas and nays have been recorded by an electronic voting device, eliminating the need for time-consuming roll calls.

Another method of voting, used in the House only, is the teller vote. Traditionally, members filed up the center aisle past counters; only vote totals were announced. Since 1971, one-fifth of a quorum can demand that the votes of individual members be recorded, thereby forcing them to take a public position on amendments to key bills.

After amendments to a bill have been voted upon, a vote may be taken on a motion to recommit the bill to committee. If carried, this vote removes the bill from the chamber's calendar and is usually a death blow to the bill. If the motion is unsuccessful, the bill then is "read for the third time." An actual reading usually is dispensed with. Until 1965, an opponent of a bill could delay this move by objecting and asking for a full reading of an engrossed (certified in final form) copy of the bill. After the "third reading," the vote on final passage is taken.

The final vote may be followed by a motion to reconsider, and this motion may be followed by a move to lay the motion on the table. Usually, those voting for the bill's passage vote for the tabling motion, thus safeguarding the final passage action. With that, the bill has been formally passed by the chamber. While a motion to reconsider a Senate vote is pending on a bill, the measure cannot be sent to the House.

Action in Second House

After a bill is passed, it is sent to the other chamber. This body may then take one of several steps. It may pass the bill as is — accepting the other chamber's language. It may send the bill to committee for scrutiny or alteration, or reject the entire bill, advising the other house of its actions. Or it simply may ignore the bill submitted while it continues work on its own version of the proposed legislation. Frequently, one chamber may approve a version of a bill that is greatly at variance with the version passed by the other house, and then substitute its contents for the language of the other, retaining only the latter's bill number.

A provision of the Legislative Reorganization Act of 1970 permits a separate House vote on any non-germane amendment added by the Senate to a House-passed bill and requires a majority vote to retain the amendment. Previously, the House was forced to act on the bill as a whole; the only way to defeat the non-germane amendment was to reject the entire bill.

Often, the second chamber makes only minor changes. If these are readily agreed to by the other house, the bill then is sent to the president.

If the opposite chamber significantly alters the bill submitted to it, however, the measure usually is "sent to conference." The chamber that has possession of the "papers" (engrossed bill, engrossed amendments, messages of transmittal) requests a conference and the other chamber must agree to it. If the second house does not agree, the bill dies.

Conference, Final Action

Conference. A conference reconciles the differences between House and Senate versions of a legislative bill. The conferees usually are senior members appointed by the presiding officers of the two houses, from the committees that managed the bills. Under this arrangement the conferees of one house have the duty of trying to maintain their chamber's position in the face of amending actions by the conferees (also referred to as "managers") of the other house.

The number of conferees from each chamber varies, depending upon the length or complexity of the bill involved. A majority vote controls the action of each group; a large representation does not give one chamber a voting advantage over the other.

Theoretically, conferees are not allowed to write new legislation in reconciling the two versions before them, but this curb sometimes is bypassed. Many bills have been put into acceptable compromise form only after new language was provided by the conferees.

The 1970 Reorganization Act attempted to tighten restrictions on conferees by forbidding them to introduce any language on a topic that neither chamber sent to conference or to modify any topic beyond the scope of the differing versions of the bill.

Frequently, the ironing out of difficulties takes days or even weeks. As a conference proceeds, conferees reconcile differences between the versions. Generally, they grant concessions only insofar as they are sure that the chamber they represent will accept the compromises.

Occasionally, uncertainty over how either house will react, or the refusal of a chamber to back down on a disputed amendment, results in an impasse, and the bills die in conference even though each was approved by its sponsoring chamber.

Conferees may go back to their respective chambers for further instructions, when they report certain portions in disagreement. Then the chamber concerned can either "recede and concur" in the amendment of the other house or "insist on its amendment."

When the conferees have reached agreement, they prepare a conference report embodying their recommendations. The report, in document form, must be submitted to each house.

The conference report must be adopted by each house; adoption of the report is approval of the compromise bill. The chamber which asked for a conference yields to the other chamber the opportunity to vote first.

Final Steps. After a bill has been passed by both the House and Senate in identical form, all of the original papers are sent to the enrolling clerk of the chamber in which the bill originated. He then prepares an enrolled bill, which is printed on parchment paper.

When this bill has been certified as correct by the secretary of the Senate or the clerk of the House, depending on which chamber originated the bill, it is signed first (no matter whether it originated in the Senate or House) by the Speaker of the House and then by the president of the Senate. It is next sent to the White House to await action.

If the president approves the bill, he signs it, dates it and usually writes the word "approved" on the document. If he does not sign it within 10 days (Sundays excepted) and Congress is in session, the bill becomes law without his signature. Should Congress adjourn before the 10 days expire, and the president fails to sign the measure, it does not become law. This procedure is called the pocket veto.

A president vetoes a bill by refusing to sign it and, before the 10-day period expires, returning it to Congress with a message stating his reasons. The message is sent to the chamber that originated the bill. If no action is taken on the message, the bill dies.

Congress, however, can attempt to override the veto and enact the bill, "the objections of the president to the contrary notwithstanding." Overriding a veto requires a two-thirds vote of those present, who must number a quorum and vote by roll call.

Debate can precede this vote, with motions permitted to lay the message on the table, postpone action on it or refer it to committee. If the president's veto is overridden in both houses, the bill becomes law. Otherwise, it is dead.

When bills are passed finally and signed, or passed over a veto, they are given law numbers in numerical order as they become law. There are two series of numbers, one for public and one for private laws, starting at the number "1" for each two-year term of Congress. They are then identified by law number and by Congress — for example, Private Law 21, 97th Congress; Public Law 250, 97th Congress (or PL 97-250).

Glossary of Congressional Terms

Act—The term for legislation once it has passed both houses of Congress and has been signed by the president or passed over his veto, thus becoming law. *(See also Veto, Pocket Veto.)*

Also used in parliamentary terminology for a bill that has been passed by one house and engrossed. *(See Engrossed Bill.)*

Adjournment Sine Die—Adjournment without definitely fixing a day for reconvening; literally, "adjournment without a day." Usually used to connote the final adjournment of a session of Congress. A session can continue until noon, Jan. 3, of the following year, when, under the 20th Amendment to the Constitution, it automatically terminates. Both houses must agree to a concurrent resolution for either house to adjourn for more than three days.

Adjournment to a Day Certain—Adjournment under a motion or resolution that fixes the next time of meeting. Under the Constitution, neither house can adjourn for more than three days without the concurrence of the other. A session of Congress is not ended by adjournment to a day certain.

Amendment—A proposal of a member of Congress to alter the language, provisions or stipulations in a bill or in another amendment. An amendment usually is printed, debated and voted upon in the same manner as a bill.

Amendment in the Nature of a Substitute—Usually an amendment that seeks to replace the entire text of a bill. Passage of this type of amendment strikes out everything after the enacting clause and inserts a new version of the bill. An amendment in the nature of a substitute also can refer to an amendment that replaces a large portion of the text of a bill.

Appeal—A member's challenge of a ruling or decision made by the presiding officer of the chamber. In the Senate, the senator appeals to members of the chamber to override the decision. If carried by a majority vote, the appeal nullifies the chair's ruling. In the House, the decision of the Speaker traditionally has been final; seldom are there appeals to the members to reverse the Speaker's stand. To appeal a ruling is considered an attack on the Speaker.

Appropriations Bill—A bill that gives legal authority to spend or obligate money from the Treasury. The Constitution disallows money to be drawn from the Treasury "but in Consequence of Appropriations made by Law."

By congressional custom, an appropriations bill originates in the House, and it is not supposed to be considered by the full House or Senate until a related measure authorizing the funding is enacted. An appropriations bill grants the actual money approved by authorization bills, but not necessarily the full amount permissible under the authorization. The 1985 Gramm-Rudman anti-deficit law stipulated that the House is to pass by June 30 the last regular appropriations bill for the fiscal year starting the following Oct. 1. (There is no such deadline for the Senate.) However, for decades appropriations often have not been final until well after the fiscal year begins, requiring a succession of stopgap bills to continue the government's functions. In addition, much federal spending — about half of all budget authority, notably that for Social Security and interest on the federal debt — does not require annual appropriations; those programs exist under permanent appropriations. *(See also Authorization, Budget Process, Backdoor Spending Authority, Entitlement Program.)*

In addition to general appropriations bills, there are two specialized types. *(See Continuing Resolution, Supplemental Appropriations Bill.)*

Authorization—Basic, substantive legislation that establishes or continues the legal operation of a federal program or agency, either indefinitely or for a specific period of time, or which sanctions a particular type of obligation or expenditure. An authorization normally is a prerequisite for an appropriation or other kind of budget authority. Under the rules of both chambers, the appropriation for a program or agency may not be considered until its authorization has been considered (although this requirement is often waived). An authorization sets the maximum amount of funds that can be given to a program or agency, but sometimes it merely authorizes "such sums as may be necessary." *(See also Backdoor Spending Authority.)*

Backdoor Spending Authority—Budget authority provided in legislation outside the normal appropriations process. The most common forms of backdoor spending are borrowing authority, contract authority, entitlements and loan guarantees that commit the government to payments of principal and interest on loans — such as Guaranteed Student Loans — made by banks or other private lenders. Loan guarantees result in actual outlays only when there is a default by the borrower.

In some cases, such as interest on the public debt, a permanent appropriation is provided that becomes available without further action by Congress.

Bills—Most legislative proposals before Congress are in the form of bills and are designated by HR in the House of Representatives or S in the Senate, according to the house in which they originate, and by a number assigned in the order in which they are introduced during the two-year period of a congressional term. "Public bills" deal with general questions and become public laws if approved by Congress and signed by the president. "Private bills" deal with individual matters such as claims against the government, immigration and naturalization cases or land titles, and become private laws if approved and signed. *(See also Concurrent Resolution, Joint Resolution, Resolution.)*

Bills Introduced—In both the House and Senate, any number of members may join in introducing a single bill or resolution. The first member listed is the sponsor of the bill, and all subsequent members listed are the bill's cosponsors.

Many bills are committee bills and are introduced under the name of the chairman of the committee or subcommittee. All appropriations bills fall into this category. A committee frequently holds hearings on a number of related bills and may agree to one of them or to an entirely new bill. *(See also Report, Clean Bill, By Request.)*

Bills Referred—When introduced, a bill is referred to the committee or committees that have jurisdiction over the subject with which the bill is concerned. Under the standing rules of the House and Senate, bills are referred by the Speaker in the House and by the presiding officer in the Senate. In practice, the House and Senate parliamentarians act for these officials and refer the vast majority of bills.

Borrowing Authority—Statutory authority that permits a federal agency to incur obligations and make payments for specified purposes with borrowed money.

Budget—The document sent to Congress by the president early each year estimating government revenue and expenditures for the ensuing fiscal year.

Budget Act—The common name for the Congressional Budget and Impoundment Control Act of 1974, which established the current budget process and created the Congressional Budget Office. The act also put limits on presidential authority to spend appropriated money. *(See Impoundments, Budget Process.)*

Budget Authority—Authority to enter into obligations that will result in immediate or future outlays involving federal funds. The basic forms of budget authority are appropriations, contract authority and borrowing authority. Budget authority may be classified by (1) the period of availability (one-year, multiple-year or without a time limitation), (2) the timing of congressional action (current or permanent) or (3) the manner of determining the amount available (definite or indefinite).

Budget process — Congress in 1990 overhauled its budget procedures for the third time since it created the congressional budget process in 1974. The 1990 Budget Enforcement Act departed from its predecessor budget laws by holding Congress harmless until fiscal 1994 for budget-deficit increases that it did not explicitly cause.

If the deficit increased because of recession, war or specifically exempted programs, that would no longer trigger the automatic spending cuts ("sequester") threatened by the Gramm-Rudman antideficit law, enacted in 1985 and amended in 1987.

The new budget rules did require, however, that spending programs be hit with a sequester if Congress exceeded pre-agreed caps on discretionary spending (appropriations bills) or violated new "pay-as-you-go" rules for mandatory spending (entitlement programs such as Medicare or food stamps) or tax cuts. *(See also Sequester Order.)*

Discretionary spending was divided into three categories — domestic, defense and international — for fiscal years 1991-93. Each category had a spending cap, and money could not be taken from one category to increase another. For fiscal years 1994-95, the three categories were to be collapsed into a single pot of money with a single cap.

For taxes and entitlements, the pay-as-you-go plan required that new entitlement spending or tax cuts be deficit-neutral. If Congress cut taxes, created a new entitlement program or expanded eligibility or benefits for an existing program, it had to offset the cost or subject entitlement spending programs to a sequester.

The 1990 law made minor changes in the timetable for presidential submission of budgets and for congressional approval of budget resolutions and reconciliation bills, two mechanisms created by the Congressional Budget and Impoundment Control Act of 1974. The president was given until the first Monday in February to submit his proposed budget. Congressional budget resolutions, due by April 15 annually, set guidelines for congressional action on spending and tax measures; they were to be adopted by the House and Senate but not signed by the president and did not have the force of law. Reconciliation bills, due by June 15, made the actual changes in existing law to meet budget resolution goals.

Budget Resolution—A concurrent resolution passed by both houses of Congress, but not requiring the president's signature, setting forth or revising the congressional budget for each of three fiscal years. The budget resolution sets forth various budget totals and functional allocations and may include reconciliation instructions. *(See Functions, Reconciliation.)*

By Request—A phrase used when a senator or representative introduces a bill at the request of an executive agency or private organization but does not necessarily endorse the legislation.

Calendar—An agenda or list of business awaiting possible action by each chamber. The House uses five legislative calendars. *(See Consent, Discharge, House, Private and Union Calendar.)*

In the Senate, all legislative matters reported from committee go on one calendar. They are listed there in the order in which committees report them or the Senate places them on the calendar, but they may be called up out of order by the majority leader, either by obtaining unanimous consent of the Senate or by a motion to call up a bill. The Senate also uses one non-legislative calendar; this is used for treaties and nominations. *(See Executive Calendar.)*

Calendar Wednesday—A procedure in the House, now rarely used, whereby committees, on Wednesdays, may be called in the order in which they appear in Rule X of the House, for the purpose of bringing up any of their bills from either the House or the Union Calendar, except bills that are privileged. General debate is limited to two hours. Bills called up from the Union Calendar are considered in Committee of the Whole. Calendar Wednesday is not observed during the last two weeks of a session and may be dispensed with at other times by a two-thirds vote. This procedure is now routinely is dispensed with by unanimous consent.

Call of the Calendar—Senate bills that are not brought up for debate by a motion, unanimous consent or a unanimous consent agreement are brought before the Senate for action when the calendar listing them is "called." Bills must be called in the order listed. Measures considered by this method usually are non-controversial, and debate on the bill and any proposed amendments is limited to a total of five minutes for each senator.

Chamber—The meeting place for the membership of either the House or the Senate; also the membership of the House or Senate meeting as such.

Clean Bill—Frequently after a committee has finished a major revision of a bill, one of the committee members, usually the chairman, will assemble the changes and what is left of the original bill into a new measure and introduce it as a "clean bill." The revised measure, which is given a new number, then is referred back to the committee, which reports it to the floor for consideration. This often is a timesaver, as committee-recommended changes in a clean bill do not have to be considered and voted on by the chamber. Reporting a clean bill also protects committee amendments that could be subject to points of order concerning germaneness.

Clerk of the House—Chief administrative officer of the House of Representatives, with duties corresponding to those of the secretary of the Senate. *(See also Secretary of the Senate.)*

Cloture—The process by which a filibuster can be ended in the Senate other than by unanimous consent. A motion for cloture can apply to any measure before the Senate, including a proposal to change the chamber's rules. A cloture motion requires the signatures of 16 senators to be introduced. To end a filibuster, the cloture motion must obtain the votes of three-fifths of the entire Senate membership (60 if there are no vacancies), except when the filibuster is against a proposal to amend the standing rules of the Senate and a two-thirds vote of senators present and voting is required. The cloture request is put to a roll call vote one hour after the Senate meets on the second day following introduction of the motion. If approved, cloture limits each senator to one hour of debate. The bill or amendment in question comes to a final vote after 30 hours of consideration (including debate time and the time it takes to conduct roll calls, quorum calls and other procedural motions). *(See Filibuster.)*

Committee—A division of the House or Senate that prepares legislation for action by the parent chamber or makes investigations as directed by the parent chamber.

There are several types of committees. *(See Standing and Select or Special Committees.)* Most standing committees are divided into subcommittees, which study legislation, hold hearings and report bills, with or without amendments, to the full committee. Only the full committee can report legislation for action by the House or Senate.

Committee of the Whole—The working title of what is formally "The Committee of the Whole House [of Representatives] on the State of the Union." The membership is composed of all House members sitting as a committee. Any 100 members who are present on the floor of the chamber to consider legislation comprise a quorum of the committee. Any legislation, however, must first have passed through the regular legislative or Appropriations committee and have been placed on the calendar.

Technically, the Committee of the Whole considers only bills directly or indirectly appropriating money, authorizing appropriations or involving taxes or charges on the public. Because the Committee of the Whole need number only 100 representatives, a quorum is more readily attained, and legislative business is expedited. Before 1971, members' positions were not individually recorded on votes taken in the Committee of the Whole. *(See Teller Vote.)*

When the full House resolves itself into the Committee of the Whole, it replaces the Speaker with a "chairman." A measure is debated and amendments may be proposed, with votes on amendments as needed. *(See Five-Minute Rule.)*

When the committee completes its work on the measure, it dissolves itself by "rising." The Speaker returns, and the chairman of the Committee of the Whole reports to the House that the committee's work has been completed. At this time members may demand a roll call vote on any amendment adopted in the Committee of the Whole. The final vote is on passage of the legislation.

Committee Veto—A requirement added to a few statutes directing that certain policy directives by an executive department or agency be reviewed by certain congressional committees before they are implemented. Under common practice, the government department or agency and the committees involved are expected to reach a consensus before the directives are carried out. *(See also Legislative Veto.)*

Concurrent Resolution—A concurrent resolution, designated H Con Res or S Con Res, must be adopted by both houses, but it is not sent to the president for approval and therefore does not have the force of law. A concurrent resolution, for example, is used to fix the time for adjournment of a Congress. It also is used as the vehicle for expressing the sense of Congress on a foreign policy or domestic issue, and it serves as the vehicle for coordinated decisions on the federal budget under the 1974 Congressional Budget and Impoundment Control Act. *(See also Bills, Joint Resolution, Resolution.)*

Conference—A meeting between the representatives of the House and the Senate to reconcile differences between the two houses on provisions of a bill passed by both chambers. Members of the conference committee are appointed by the Speaker and the presiding officer of the Senate and are called "managers" for their respective chambers. A majority of the managers for each house must reach agreement on the provisions of the bill (often a compromise between the versions of the two chambers) before it can be considered by either chamber in the form of a "conference report." When the conference report goes to the floor, it cannot be amended, and, if it is not approved by both chambers, the bill may go back to conference under certain situations, or a new conference must be convened. Many rules and informal practices govern the conduct of conference committees.

Bills that are passed by both houses with only minor differences need not be sent to conference. Either chamber may "concur" in the other's amendments, completing action on the legislation. Sometimes leaders of the committees of jurisdiction work out an informal compromise instead of having a formal conference. *(See Custody of the Papers.)*

Confirmations—*(See Nominations.)*

Congressional Record—The daily, printed account of proceedings in both the House and Senate chambers, showing substantially verbatim debate, statements and a record of floor action. Highlights of legislative and committee action are embodied in a Daily Digest section of the Record, and members are entitled to have their extraneous remarks printed in an appendix known as "Extension of Remarks." Members may edit and revise remarks made on the floor during debate, and quotations from debate reported by the press are not always found in the Record.

The Congressional Record provides a way to distinguish remarks spoken on the floor of the House and Senate from undelivered speeches. In the Senate, all speeches, articles and other matter that members insert in the Record without actually reading them on the floor are set off by large black dots, or bullets. However, a loophole allows a member to avoid the bulleting if he delivers any portion of the speech in person. In the House, undelivered speeches and other material are printed in a distinctive typeface. *(See also Journal)*

Congressional Terms of Office—Normally begin on Jan. 3 of the year following a general election and are two years for representatives and six years for senators. Representatives elected in special elections are sworn in for the remainder of a term. A person may be appointed to fill a Senate vacancy and serves until a successor is elected; the successor serves until the end of the term applying to the vacant seat.

Consent Calendar—Members of the House may place on this calendar most bills on the Union or House Calendar that are considered to be non-controversial. Bills on the Consent Calendar normally are called on the first and third Mondays of each month. On the first occasion that a bill is called in this manner, consideration may be blocked by the objection of any member. The second time, if there are three objections, the bill is stricken from the Consent Calendar. If fewer than three members object, the bill is given immediate consideration.

A bill on the Consent Calendar may be postponed in another way. A member may ask that the measure be passed over "without prejudice." In that case, no objection is recorded against the bill, and its status on the Consent Calendar remains unchanged. A bill stricken from the Consent Calendar remains on the Union or House Calendar.

Continuing Resolution—A joint resolution, cleared by Congress and signed by the president (when the new fiscal year is about to begin or has begun), to provide new budget authority for federal agencies and programs to continue in operation until the regular appropriations acts are enacted. The continuing resolution usually specifies a maximum rate at which an agency may incur obligations, based on the rate of the prior year, the president's budget request or an appropriations bill passed by either or both houses of Congress but not yet enacted. Continuing resolutions also are called "CRs" or continuing appropriations.

Contract Authority—Budget authority contained in an authorization bill that permits the federal government to enter into contracts or other obligations for future payments from funds not yet appropriated by Congress. The assumption is that funds will be available for payment in a subsequent appropriation act.

Controllable Budget Items—In federal budgeting, this term refers to programs for which the budget authority or outlays during a fiscal year can be controlled without changing existing, substantive law. The concept "relatively uncontrollable under current law" includes outlays for open-ended programs and fixed costs such as interest on the public debt, Social Security benefits, veterans' benefits and outlays to liquidate prior-year obligations. More and more spending for federal programs has become uncontrollable or relatively uncontrollable.

Correcting Recorded Votes—Rules prohibit members from changing their votes after the result has been announced. But, occasionally, hours, days or months after a vote has been taken, a member may announce he was "incorrectly recorded." In the Senate, a request to change one's vote almost always receives unanimous consent. In the House, members are prohibited from changing their votes if tallied by the electronic voting system. If the vote was taken by roll call, a change is permissible if consent is granted.

Cosponsor—*(See Bills Introduced.)*

Current Services Estimates—Estimated budget authority and outlays for federal programs and operations for the forthcoming fiscal year based on continuation of existing levels of service without policy changes. These estimates of budget authority and outlays, accompanied by the underlying economic and policy assumptions upon which they are based, are transmitted by the president to Congress when the budget is submitted.

Custody of the Papers—To reconcile differences between the House and Senate versions of a bill, a conference may be arranged. The chamber with "custody of the papers" — the engrossed bill, engrossed amendments, messages of transmittal — is the only body empowered to request the conference. By custom, the chamber that asks for a conference is the last to act on the conference report once agreement has been reached on the bill by the conferees.

Custody of the papers sometimes is manipulated to ensure that a particular chamber acts either first or last on the conference report.

Deferral—Executive branch action to defer, or delay, the spending of appropriated money. The 1974 Congressional Budget and Impoundment Control Act requires a special message from the president to Congress reporting a proposed deferral of spending. Deferrals may not extend beyond the end of the fiscal year in which the message is transmitted. A federal district court in 1986 struck down the president's authority to defer spending for policy reasons; the ruling was upheld by a federal appeals court in 1987. Congress can prohibit proposed deferrals by enacting a law doing so; most often, cancellations of proposed deferrals are included in appropriations bills. *(See also Rescission.)*

Dilatory Motion—A motion made for the purpose of killing time and preventing action on a bill or amendment. House rules outlaw dilatory motions, but enforcement is largely within the discretion of the Speaker or chairman of the Committee of the Whole. The Senate does not have a rule banning dilatory motions, except under cloture.

Discharge a Committee—Occasionally, attempts are made to relieve a committee from jurisdiction over a measure before it. This is attempted more often in the House than in the Senate, and the procedure rarely is successful.

In the House, if a committee does not report a bill within 30 days after the measure is referred to it, any member may file a discharge motion. Once offered, the motion is treated as a petition needing the signatures of a majority of members (218 if there are no vacancies). After the required signatures have been obtained, there is a delay of seven days. Thereafter, on the second and fourth Mondays of each month, except during the last six days of a session, any member who has signed the petition must be recognized, if he so desires, to move that the committee be discharged. Debate on the motion to discharge is limited to 20 minutes, and, if the motion is carried, consideration of the bill becomes a matter of high privilege.

If a resolution to consider a bill is held up in the Rules Committee for more than seven legislative days, any member may enter a motion to discharge the committee. The motion is handled like any other discharge petition in the House. Occasionally, to expedite non-controversial legislative business, a committee is discharged by unanimous consent of the House, and a petition is not required. *(Senate procedure, see Discharge Resolution.)*

Discharge Calendar—The House calendar to which motions to discharge committees are referred when they have the required number of signatures (218) and are awaiting floor action.

Discharge Petition—*(See Discharge a Committee.)*

Discharge Resolution—In the Senate, a special motion that any senator may introduce to relieve a committee from consideration of a bill before it. The resolution can be called up for Senate approval or disapproval in the same manner as any other Senate business. *(House procedure, see Discharge a Committee.)*

Division of a Question for Voting—A practice that is more common in the Senate but also used in the House whereby a member may demand a division of an amendment or a motion for purposes of voting. Where an amendment or motion can be divided, the individual parts are voted on separately when a member demands a division. This procedure occurs most often during the consideration of conference reports.

Division Vote—*(See Standing Vote.)*

Enacting Clause—Key phrase in bills beginning, "Be it enacted by the Senate and House of Representatives . . ." A successful motion to strike it from legislation kills the measure.

Engrossed Bill—The final copy of a bill as passed by one chamber, with the text as amended by floor action and certified by the clerk of the House or the secretary of the Senate.

Enrolled Bill—The final copy of a bill that has been passed in identical form by both chambers. It is certified by an officer of the house of origin (clerk of the House or secretary of the Senate) and then sent on for the signatures of the House Speaker, the Senate president pro tempore and the president of the United States. An enrolled bill is printed on parchment.

Entitlement Program—A federal program that guarantees a certain level of benefits to persons or other entities who meet requirements set by law, such as Social Security, farm price supports or unemployment benefits. It thus leaves no discretion with Congress on how much money to appropriate, and some entitlements carry permanent appropriations.

Executive Calendar—This is a non-legislative calendar in the Senate on which presidential documents such as treaties and nominations are listed.

Executive Document—A document, usually a treaty, sent to the Senate by the president for consideration or approval. Executive documents are identified for each session of Congress according to the following pattern: Executive A, 97th Congress, 1st Session; Executive B, and so on. They are referred to committee in the same manner as other measures. Unlike legislative documents, however, treaties do not die at the end of a Congress but remain "live" proposals until acted on by the Senate or withdrawn by the president.

Executive Session—A meeting of a Senate or House committee (or occasionally of either chamber) that only its members may attend. Witnesses regularly appear at committee meetings in executive session — for example, Defense Department officials during presentations of classified defense information. Other members of Congress may be invited, but the public and press are not allowed to attend.

Expenditures—The actual spending of money as distinguished from the appropriation of funds. Expenditures are made by the disbursing officers of the administration; appropriations are made only by Congress. The two are rarely identical in any fiscal year. In addition to some current budget authority, expenditures may represent budget authority made available one, two or more years earlier.

Filibuster—A time-delaying tactic associated with the Senate and used by a minority in an effort to prevent a vote on a bill or amendment that probably would pass if voted upon directly. The most common method is to take advantage of the Senate's rules permitting unlimited debate, but other forms of parliamentary maneuvering may be used. The stricter rules of the House make filibusters more difficult, but delaying tactics are employed occasionally through various procedural devices allowed by House rules. *(Senate filibusters, see Cloture.)*

Fiscal Year—Financial operations of the government are carried out in a 12-month fiscal year, beginning on Oct. 1 and ending on Sept. 30. The fiscal year carries the date of the calendar year in which it ends. (From fiscal year 1844 to fiscal year 1976, the fiscal year began July 1 and ended the following June 30.)

Five-Minute Rule—A debate-limiting rule of the House that is invoked when the House sits as the Committee of the Whole. Under the rule, a member offering an amendment is allowed to speak five minutes in its favor, and an opponent of the amendment is allowed to speak five minutes in opposition. Debate is then closed. In practice, amendments regularly are debated more than 10 minutes, with members gaining the floor by offering pro forma amendments or obtaining unanimous consent to speak longer than five minutes. *(See Strike Out the Last Word.)*

Floor Manager—A member who has the task of steering legislation through floor debate and the amendment process to a final vote in the House or the Senate. Floor managers usually are chairmen or ranking members of the committee that reported the bill. Managers are responsible for apportioning the debate time granted supporters of the bill. The ranking minority member of the committee normally apportions time for the minority party's participation in the debate.

Frank—A member's facsimile signature, which is used on envelopes in lieu of stamps, for the member's official outgoing mail. The "franking privilege" is the right to send mail postage-free.

Germane—Pertaining to the subject matter of the measure at hand. All House amendments must be germane to the bill being considered. The Senate requires that amendments be germane when they are proposed to general appropriations bills or to bills being considered once cloture has been adopted or, frequently, when the Senate is proceeding under a unanimous consent agreement placing a time limit on consideration of a bill. The 1974 budget act also requires that amendments to concurrent budget resolutions be germane. In the House, floor debate must be germane, and the first three hours of debate each day in the Senate must be germane to the pending business.

Gramm-Rudman-Hollings Deficit Reduction Act—*(See Budget Process, Sequestration.)*

Grandfather Clause—A provision that exempts persons or other entities already engaged in an activity from rules or legislation affecting that activity. Grandfather clauses sometimes are added to legislation in order to avoid antagonizing groups with established interests in the activities affected.

Hearings—Committee sessions for taking testimony from witnesses. At hearings on legislation, witnesses usually include specialists, government officials and spokespersons for individuals or entities affected by the bill or bills under study. Hearings related to special investigations bring forth a variety of witnesses. Committees sometimes use their subpoena power to summon reluctant witnesses. The public and press may attend open hearings but are barred from closed, or "executive," hearings. The vast majority of hearings are open to the public. *(See Executive Session.)*

Hold-Harmless Clause—A provision added to legislation to ensure that recipients of federal funds do not receive less in a future year than they did in the current year if a new formula for allocating funds authorized in the legislation would result in a reduction to the recipients. This clause has been used most often to soften the impact of sudden reductions in federal grants.

Hopper—Box on House clerk's desk where members deposit bills and resolutions to introduce them. *(See also Bills Introduced.)*

Hour Rule—A provision in the rules of the House that permits one hour of debate time for each member on amendments debated in the House of Representatives sitting as the House. Therefore, the House normally amends bills while sitting as the Committee of the Whole, where the five-minute rule on amendments operates. *(See Committee of the Whole, Five-Minute Rule.)*

House—The House of Representatives, as distinct from the Senate, although each body is a "house" of Congress.

House as in Committee of the Whole—A procedure that can be used to expedite consideration of certain measures such as continuing resolutions and, when there is debate, private bills. The procedure only can be invoked with the unanimous consent of the House or a rule from the Rules Committee and has procedural elements of both the House sitting as the House of Representatives, such as the Speaker presiding and the previous question motion being in order, and the House sitting as the Committee of the Whole, such as the five-minute rule pertaining.

House Calendar—A listing for action by the House of public bills that do not directly or indirectly appropriate money or raise revenue.

Immunity—The constitutional privilege of members of Congress to make verbal statements on the floor and in committee for which they cannot be sued or arrested for slander or libel. Also, freedom from arrest while traveling to or from sessions of Congress or on official business. Members in this status may be arrested only for treason, felonies or a breach of the peace, as defined by congressional manuals.

Joint Committee—A committee composed of a specified number of members of both the House and Senate. A joint committee may be investigative or research-oriented, an example of the latter being the Joint Economic Committee. Others have housekeeping duties such as the joint committees on Printing and on the Library of Congress.

Joint Resolution—A joint resolution, designated H J Res or S J Res, requires the approval of both houses and the signature of the president, just as a bill does, and has the force of law if approved. There is no practical difference between a bill and a joint resolution. A joint resolution generally is used to deal with a limited matter such as a single appropriation.

Joint resolutions also are used to propose amendments to the Constitution. They do not require a presidential signature but become a part of the Constitution when three-fourths of the states have ratified them.

Journal—The official record of the proceedings of the House and Senate. The Journal records the actions taken in each chamber, but, unlike the Congressional Record, it does not include the substantially verbatim report of speeches, debates, statements and the like.

Law—An act of Congress that has been signed by the president or passed over his veto by Congress. Public bills, when signed, become public laws, and are cited by the letters PL and a hyphenated number. The number before the hyphen corresponds to the Congress, and the one or more digits after the hyphen refer to the numerical sequence in which the president signed the bills during that Congress. Private bills, when signed, become private laws. *(See also Pocket Veto, Slip Laws, Statutes at Large, U.S. Code.)*

Legislative Day—The "day" extending from the time either house meets after an adjournment until the time it next adjourns. Because the House normally adjourns from day to day, legislative days and calendar days usually coincide. But in the Senate, a legislative day may, and frequently does, extend over several calendar days. *(See Recess.)*

Legislative Veto—A procedure, held unconstitutional by the Supreme Court, permitting either the House or Senate, or both chambers, to review proposed executive branch regulations or actions and to block or modify those with which they disagreed.

The specifics of the procedure varied, but Congress generally provided for a legislative veto by including in a bill a provision that administrative rules or action taken to implement the law were to go into effect at the end of a designated period of time unless blocked by either or both houses of Congress. Another version of the veto provided for congressional reconsideration and rejection of regulations already in effect.

The Supreme Court in 1983 struck down the legislative veto as an unconstitutional violation of the lawmaking procedure provided in the Constitution.

Loan Guarantees—Loans to third parties for which the federal government in the event of default guarantees, in whole or in part, the repayment of principal or interest to a lender or holder of a security.

Lobby—A group seeking to influence the passage or defeat of legislation. Originally the term referred to persons frequenting the lobbies or corridors of legislative chambers to speak to lawmakers.

The definition of a lobby and the activity of lobbying is a matter of differing interpretation. By some definitions, lobbying is limited to direct attempts to influence lawmakers through personal interviews and persuasion. Under other definitions, lobbying includes attempts at indirect, or "grass-roots," influence, such as persuading members of a group to write or visit their district's representative and state's senators or attempting to create a climate of opinion favorable to a desired legislative goal.

The right to attempt to influence legislation is based on the First Amendment to the Constitution, which says Congress shall make no law abridging the right of the people "to petition the government for a redress of grievances."

Majority Leader—Floor leader for the majority party in each chamber. In the Senate, in consultation with the minority leader and his colleagues, the majority leader directs the legislative schedule for the chamber. He also is his party's spokesperson and chief strategist. In the House, the majority leader is second to the Speaker in the majority party's leadership and serves as his party's legislative strategist.

Majority Whip—In effect, the assistant majority leader, in either the House or Senate. His job is to help marshal majority forces in support of party strategy and legislation.

Manual—The official handbook in each house prescribing in detail its organization, procedures and operations.

Marking Up a Bill—Going through the contents of a piece of legislation in committee or subcommittee to, for example, consider its provisions in large and small portions, act on amendments to provisions and proposed revisions to the language, and insert new sections and phraseology. If the bill is extensively amended, the committee's version may be introduced as a separate bill, with a new number, before being considered by the full House or Senate. *(See Clean Bill.)*

Minority Leader—Floor leader for the minority party in each chamber. *(See also Majority Leader.)*

Minority Whip—Performs duties of whip for the minority party. *(See also Majority Whip.)*

Morning Hour—The time set aside at the beginning of each legislative day for the consideration of regular, routine business. The "hour" is of indefinite duration in the House, where it is rarely used.

In the Senate, it is the first two hours of a session following an adjournment, as distinguished from a recess. The morning hour can be terminated earlier if the morning business has been completed. Business includes such matters as messages from the president, communications from the heads of departments, messages from the House, the presentation of petitions, reports of standing and select committees and the introduction of bills and resolutions. During the first hour of the morning hour in the Senate, no motion to proceed to the consideration of any bill on the calendar is in order except by unanimous consent. During the second hour, motions can be made but must be decided without debate. Senate committees may meet while the Senate conducts morning hour.

Motion—In the House or Senate chamber, a request by a member to institute any one of a wide array of parliamentary actions. He "moves" for a certain procedure, such as the consideration of a measure. The precedence of motions, and whether they are debatable, is set forth in the House and Senate manuals.

Nominations—Presidential appointments to office subject to Senate confirmation. Although most nominations win quick Senate approval, some are controversial and become the topic of hearings and debate. Sometimes senators object to appointees for patronage reasons — for example, when a nomination to a local federal job is made without consulting the senators of the state concerned. In some situations a senator may object that the nominee is "personally obnoxious" to him. Usually other senators join in blocking such appointments out of courtesy to their colleagues. *(See Senatorial Courtesy.)*

One-Minute Speeches—Addresses by House members at the beginning of a legislative day. The speeches may cover any subject but are limited to one minute's duration.

Outlays—Payments made (generally through the issuance of checks or disbursement of cash) to liquidate obligations. Outlays during a fiscal year may be for the payment of obligations incurred in prior years or in the same year.

Override a Veto—If the president disapproves a bill and sends it back to Congress with his objections, Congress may try to override his veto and enact the bill into law. Neither house is required to attempt to override a veto. The override of a veto requires a recorded vote with a two-thirds majority of those present and voting in each chamber. The question put to each house is: "Shall the bill pass, the objections of the president to the contrary notwithstanding?" *(See also Pocket Veto, Veto.)*

Oversight Committee—A congressional committee, or designated subcommittee of a committee, that is charged with general oversight of one or more federal agencies' programs and activities. Usually, the oversight panel for a particular agency also is the authorizing committee for that agency's programs and operations.

Pair—A voluntary, informal arrangement that two lawmakers, usually on opposite sides of an issue, make on recorded votes. In many cases the result is to subtract a vote from each side, with no effect on the outcome. Pairs are not authorized in the rules of either house, are not counted in tabulating the final result and have no official standing. However, members pairing are identified in the Congressional Record, along with their positions on such votes, if known. A member who expects to be absent for a vote can pair with a member who plans to vote, with the latter agreeing to withhold his vote.

There are three types of pairs: 1) A live pair involves a member who is present for a vote and another who is absent. The member in attendance votes and then withdraws the vote, announcing that he has a live pair with colleague "X" and stating how the two members would have voted, one in favor, the other opposed. A live pair may affect the outcome of a closely contested vote, since it subtracts one "yea" or one "nay" from the final tally. A live pair may cover one or several specific issues. 2) A general pair, widely used in the House, does not entail any arrangement between two members and does not affect the vote. Members who expect to be absent notify the clerk that they wish to make a general pair. Each member then is paired with another desiring a pair, and their names are listed in the Congressional Record. The member may or may not be paired with another taking the opposite position, and no indication of how the members would have voted is given. 3) A specific pair is similar to a general pair, except that the opposing stands of the two members are identified and printed in the Record.

Petition—A request or plea sent to one or both chambers from an organization or private citizens' group asking support of particular legislation or favorable consideration of a matter not yet receiving congressional attention. Petitions are referred to appropriate committees.

Pocket Veto—The act of the president in withholding his approval of a bill after Congress has adjourned. When Congress is in session, a bill becomes law without the president's signature if he does not act upon it within 10 days, excluding Sundays, from the time he gets it. But if Congress adjourns sine die within that 10-day period, the bill will die even if the president does not formally veto it.

The Supreme Court in 1986 agreed to decide whether the president can pocket veto a bill during recesses and between sessions of the same Congress or only between Congresses. The justices in 1987 declared the case moot, however, because the bill in question was invalid once the case reached the court. *(See also Veto.)*

Point of Order—An objection raised by a member that the chamber is departing from rules governing its conduct of business. The objector cites the rule violated, the chair sustaining his objection if correctly made. Order is restored by the chair's suspending proceedings of the chamber until it conforms to the prescribed "order of business."

President of the Senate—Under the Constitution, the vice president of the United States presides over the Senate. In his absence, the president pro tempore, or a senator designated by the president pro tempore, presides over the chamber.

President Pro Tempore—The chief officer of the Senate in the absence of the vice president; literally, but loosely, the president for a time. The president pro tempore is elected by his fellow senators, and the recent practice has been to elect the senator of the majority party with the longest period of continuous service.

Previous Question—A motion for the previous question, when carried, has the effect of cutting off all debate, preventing the offering of further amendments and forcing a vote on the pending matter. In the House, the previous question is not permitted in the Committee of the Whole. The motion for the previous question is a debate-limiting device and is not in order in the Senate.

Printed Amendment—A House rule guarantees five minutes of floor debate in support and five minutes in opposition, and no other debate time, on amendments printed in the Congressional Record at least one day prior to the amendment's consideration in the Committee of the Whole. In the Senate, while amendments may be submitted for printing, they have no parliamentary standing or status. An amendment submitted for printing in the Senate, however, may be called up by any senator.

Private Calendar—In the House, private bills dealing with individual matters such as claims against the government, immigration or land titles are put on this calendar. The private calendar must be called on the first Tuesday of each month, and the Speaker may call it on the third Tuesday of each month as well.

When a private bill is before the chamber, two members may block its consideration, which recommits the bill to committee. Backers of a recommitted private bill have recourse. The measure can be put into an "omnibus claims bill" — several private bills rolled into one. As with any bill, no part of an omnibus claims bill may be deleted without a vote. When the private bill goes back to the House floor in this form, it can be deleted from the omnibus bill only by majority vote.

Privileged Questions—The order in which bills, motions and other legislative measures are considered on the floor of the Senate and House is governed by strict priorities. A motion to table, for instance, is more privileged than a motion to recommit. Thus, if a member moves to recommit a bill to committee for further consideration, another member could supersede the first action by moving to table it, and a vote would occur first on the motion to table (or kill) the motion to recommit. A motion to adjourn is considered "of the highest privilege" and would have to be considered before virtually any other motion. *(See also Questions of Privilege.)*

Pro Forma Amendment—*(See Strike Out the Last Word.)*

Public Laws—*(See Law.)*

Questions of Privilege—These are matters affecting members of Congress individually or collectively. Matters affecting the rights, safety, dignity and integrity of proceedings of the House or Senate as a whole are questions of privilege in both chambers.

Questions involving individual members are called questions of "personal privilege." A member rising to ask a question of personal privilege is given precedence over almost all other proceedings. For instance, if a member feels that he has been improperly impugned in comments by another member, he can immediately demand to be heard on the floor on a question of personal privilege. An annotation in the House rules points out that the privilege rests primarily on the Constitution, which gives him a conditional immunity from arrest and an unconditional freedom to speak in the House. *(See also Privileged Questions.)*

Quorum—The number of members whose presence is necessary for the transaction of business. In the Senate and House, it is a majority of the membership. A quorum is 100 in the Committee of the Whole House. If a point of order is made that a quorum is not present, the only business that is in order is either a motion to adjourn or a motion to direct the sergeant-at-arms to request the attendance of absentees.

Readings of Bills—Traditional parliamentary procedure required bills to be read three times before they were passed. This custom is of little modern significance. Normally a bill is considered to have its first reading when it is introduced and printed, by title, in the Congressional Record. In the House, its second reading comes when floor consideration begins. (This is the most likely point at which there is an actual reading of the bill, if there is any.) The second reading in the Senate is supposed to occur on the legislative day after the measure is introduced, but before it is referred to committee. The third reading (again, usually by title) takes place when floor action has been completed on amendments.

Recess—Distinguished from adjournment in that a recess does not end a legislative day and therefore does not interrupt unfinished business. The rules in each house set forth certain matters to be taken up and disposed of at the beginning of each legislative day. The House usually adjourns from day to day. The Senate often recesses, thus meeting on the same legislative day for several calendar days or even weeks at a time.

Recognition—The power of recognition of a member is lodged in the Speaker of the House and the presiding officer of the Senate. The presiding officer names the member to speak first when two or more members simultaneously request recognition.

Recommit to Committee—A motion, made on the floor after a bill has been debated, to return it to the committee that reported it. If approved, recommittal usually is considered a death blow to the bill. In the House, a motion to recommit can be made only by a member opposed to the bill, and, in recognizing a member to make the motion, the Speaker gives preference to members of the minority party over majority-party members.

A motion to recommit may include instructions to the committee to report the bill again with specific amendments or by a certain date. Or the instructions may direct that a particular study be made, with no definite deadline for further action. If the recommittal motion includes instructions to "report the bill back forthwith" and the motion is adopted, floor action on the bill continues; the committee does not actually reconsider the legislation.

Reconciliation—The 1974 budget act provides for a "reconciliation" procedure for bringing existing tax and spending laws into conformity with ceilings enacted in the congressional budget resolution. Under the procedure, Congress instructs designated legislative committees to approve measures adjusting revenues and expenditures by a certain amount. The committees have a deadline by which they must report the legislation, but they have the discretion of deciding what changes are to be made. The recommendations of the various committees are consolidated without change by the Budget committees into an omnibus reconciliation bill, which then must be considered and approved by both houses of Congress. The orders to congressional committees to report recommendations for reconciliation bills are called reconciliation instructions, and they are contained in the budget resolution. Reconciliation instructions are not binding, but Congress must meet annual Gramm-Rudman deficit targets to avoid the automatic spending cuts of sequestration, which means it must also meet the goal of reconciliation. *(See also Budget Resolution, Sequestration.)*

Reconsider a Vote—A motion to reconsider the vote by which an action was taken has, until it is disposed of, the effect of putting the action in abeyance. In the Senate, the motion can be made only by a member who voted on the prevailing side of the original question or by a member who did not vote at all. In the House, it can be made only by a member on the prevailing side.

A common practice in the Senate after close votes on an issue is a motion to reconsider, followed by a motion to table the motion to reconsider. On this motion to table, senators vote as they voted on the original question, which allows the motion to table to prevail, assuming there are no switches. The matter then is finally closed and further motions to reconsider are not entertained. In the House, as a routine precaution, a motion to reconsider usually is made every time a measure is passed. Such a motion almost always is tabled immediately, thus shutting off the possibility of future reconsideration, except by unanimous consent.

Motions to reconsider must be entered in the Senate within the next two days of actual session after the original vote has been taken. In the House, they must be entered either on the same day or on the next succeeding day the House is in session.

Recorded Vote—A vote upon which each member's stand is individually made known. In the Senate, this is accomplished through a roll call of the entire membership, to which each senator on the floor must answer "yea," "nay" or "present." Since January 1973, the House has used an electronic voting system for recorded votes, including yea-and-nay votes formerly taken by roll calls.

When not required by the Constitution, a recorded vote can be obtained on questions in the House on the demand of one-fifth (44 members) of a quorum or one-fourth (25) of a quorum in the Committee of the Whole. *(See Yeas and Nays.)*

Report—Both a verb and a noun as a congressional term. A committee that has been examining a bill referred to it by the parent chamber "reports" its findings and recommendations to the chamber when it completes consideration and returns the measure. The process is called "reporting" a bill.

A "report" is the document setting forth the committee's explanation of its action. Senate and House reports are numbered separately and are designated S Rept or H Rept. When a committee report is not unanimous, the dissenting committee members may file a statement of their views, called minority or dissenting views and referred to as a minority report. Members in disagreement with some provisions of a bill may file additional or supplementary views. Sometimes a bill is reported without a committee recommendation.

Adverse reports occasionally are submitted by legislative committees. However, when a committee is opposed to a bill, it usually fails to report the bill at all. Some laws require that committee reports — favorable or adverse — be made.

Rescission—An item in an appropriations bill rescinding or canceling budget authority previously appropriated but not spent. Also, the repeal of a previous appropriation by Congress at the request of the president to cut spending or because the budget authority no longer is needed. Under the 1974 budget act, however, unless Congress approves a rescission within 45 days of continuous session after receipt of the proposal, the funds must be made available for obligation. *(See also Deferral.)*

Resolution—A "simple" resolution, designated H Res or S Res, deals with matters entirely within the prerogatives of one house or the other. It requires neither passage by the other chamber nor approval by the president, and it does not have the force of law. Most resolutions deal with the rules or procedures of one house. They also are used to express the sentiments of a single house such as condolences to the family of a deceased member or to comment on foreign policy or executive business. A simple resolution is the vehicle for a "rule" from the House Rules Committee. *(See also Concurrent and Joint Resolutions, Rules.)*

Rider—An amendment, usually not germane, that its sponsor hopes to get through more easily by including it in other legislation. Riders become law if the bills embodying them are enacted. Amendments providing legislative directives in appropriations bills are outstanding examples of riders, though technically legislation is banned from appropriations bills.

The House, unlike the Senate, has a strict germaneness rule; thus, riders usually are Senate devices to get legislation enacted quickly or to bypass lengthy House consideration and, possibly, opposition.

Rules—A rule is a standing order governing the conduct of House or Senate business and listed among the permanent rules of either chamber. The rules deal with issues such as duties of officers, the order of business, admission to the floor, parliamentary procedures on handling amendments and voting and jurisdictions of committees.

In the House, a rule also may be a resolution reported by its Rules Committee to govern the handling of a particular bill on the floor. The committee may report a "rule," also called a "special order," in the form of a simple resolution. If the resolution is adopted by the House, the temporary rule becomes as valid as any standing rule and lapses only after action has been completed on the measure to which it pertains. A rule sets the time limit on general debate. It also may waive points of order against provisions of the bill in question such as non-germane language or against certain amendments intended to be proposed to the bill from the floor. It may even forbid all amendments or all amendments except those proposed by the legislative committee that handled the bill. In this instance, it is known as a "closed" rule as opposed to an "open" rule, which puts no limitation on floor amendments, thus leaving the bill completely open to alteration by the adoption of germane amendments.

Secretary of the Senate—Chief administrative officer of the Senate, responsible for overseeing the duties of Senate employees, educating Senate pages, administering oaths, overseeing the registration of lobbyists and handling other tasks necessary for the continuing operation of the Senate. *(See also Clerk of the House.)*

Select or Special Committee—A committee set up for a special purpose and, usually, for a limited time by resolution of either the House or Senate. Most special committees are investigative and lack legislative authority: legislation is not referred to them, and they cannot report bills to their parent chamber. *(See also Standing Committees.)*

Senatorial Courtesy—Sometimes referred to as "the courtesy of the Senate," it is a general practice — with no written rule — applied to consideration of executive nominations. Generally, it means that nominations from a state are not to be confirmed unless they have been approved by the senators of the president's party of that state, with other senators following their colleagues' lead in the attitude they take toward consideration of such nominations. *(See Nominations.)*

Sequester order — Under procedures put in place by the 1985 Gramm-Rudman antideficit law, Congress was threatened with year-end, across-the-board spending cuts known as a sequester if the deficit exceeded a pre-set maximum. The Budget Enforcement Act of 1990 effectively did away with that form of sequester for fiscal years 1991-93, replacing it with a series of targeted "mini-sequesters." *(See also Budget Process.)*

For fiscal 1991-93, discretionary spending in any of the 13 regular appropriations bills that exceeded the cap for its particular category (domestic, defense or international) would trigger a sequester in that category only. For fiscal 1994-95, however, the three categories were collapsed into a single pot of money, which meant that a sequester would affect all discretionary spending. The sequester would take place 15 days after adjournment.

New "pay-as-you-go" rules required that mandatory spending (entitlement programs such as Medicare and food stamps) and tax cuts be deficit-neutral. If Congress cut taxes, expanded existing entitlement programs or created new entitlements, the cost had to be offset. If there was no offset, a sequester of all non-exempt entitlement programs would take place 15 days after Congress adjourns.

Two other types of sequesters affected supplemental appropriations bills. A supplemental that exceeded discretionary spending limits and was enacted before July 1 would trigger a "within-session" sequester within 15 days of enactment. That sequester would require a cutback in spending for the offending category during the current fiscal year.

A supplemental that exceeded the caps and was enacted after June 30 would trigger a "look-back" sequester, which would reduce the cap for the offending category for the next fiscal year by the amount of the excess spending.

Sine Die—*(See Adjournment Sine Die.)*

Slip Laws—The first official publication of a bill that has been enacted and signed into law. Each is published separately in unbound single-sheet or pamphlet form. *(See also Law, Statutes at Large, U.S. Code.)*

Speaker—The presiding officer of the House of Representatives, selected by the caucus of the party to which he belongs and formally elected by the whole House.

Special Session—A session of Congress after it has adjourned sine die, completing its regular session. Special sessions are convened by the president.

Spending Authority—The 1974 budget act defines spending authority as borrowing authority, contract authority and entitlement authority for which budget authority is not provided in advance by appropriation acts.

Sponsor—*(See Bills Introduced.)*

Standing Committees—Committees that are permanently established by House and Senate rules. The standing committees of the House were last reorganized by the committee reorganization of 1974. The last major realignment of Senate committees was in the committee system reorganization of 1977. The standing committees are legislative committees — legislation may be referred to them and they may report bills and resolutions to their parent chambers. *(See also Select or Special Committees.)*

Standing Vote—A non-recorded vote used in both the House and Senate. (A standing vote also is called a division vote.) Members in favor of a proposal stand and are counted by the presiding officer. Then members opposed stand and are counted. There is no record of how individual members voted.

Statutes at Large—A chronological arrangement of the laws enacted in each session of Congress. Though indexed, the laws are not arranged by subject matter, and there is not an indication of how they changed previously enacted laws. *(See also Law, Slip Laws, U.S. Code.)*

Strike From the Record—Remarks made on the House floor may offend some member, who moves that the offending words be "taken down" for the Speaker's cognizance, and then expunged from the debate as published in the Congressional Record.

Strike Out the Last Word—A motion whereby a House member is entitled to speak for five minutes on an amendment then being debated by the chamber. A member gains recognition from the chair by moving to "strike out the last word" of the amendment or section of the bill under consideration. The motion is pro forma, requires no vote and does not change the amendment being debated.

Substitute—A motion, amendment or entire bill introduced in place of the pending legislative business. Passage of a substitute measure kills the original measure by supplanting it. The substitute also may be amended. *(See also Amendment in the Nature of a Substitute.)*

Supplemental Appropriations Bill—Legislation appropriating funds after the regular annual appropriations bill for a federal department or agency has been enacted. A supplemental appropriation provides additional budget authority beyond original estimates for programs or activities, including new programs authorized after the enactment of the regular appropriation act, for which the need for funds is too urgent to be postponed until enactment of the next year's regular appropriation bill.

Suspend the Rules—Often a time-saving procedure for passing bills in the House. The wording of the motion, which may be made by any member recognized by the Speaker, is: "I move to suspend the rules and pass the bill . . ." A favorable vote by two-thirds of those present is required for passage. Debate is limited to 40 minutes and no amendments from the floor are permitted. If a two-thirds favorable vote is not attained, the bill may be considered later under regular procedures. The suspension procedure is in order every Monday and Tuesday and is intended to be reserved for non-controversial bills.

Table a Bill—Motions to table, or to "lay on the table," are used to block or kill amendments or other parliamentary questions. When approved, a tabling motion is considered the final disposition of that issue. One of the most widely used parliamentary procedures, the motion to table is not debatable, and adoption requires a simple majority vote.

In the Senate, however, different language sometimes is used. The motion may be worded to let a bill "lie on the table," perhaps for subsequent "picking up." This motion is more flexible, keeping the bill pending for later action, if desired. Tabling motions on amendments are effective debate-ending devices in the Senate.

Teller Vote—This is a largely moribund House procedure in the Committee of the Whole. Members file past tellers and are counted as for or against a measure, but they are not recorded individually. In the House, tellers are ordered upon demand of one-fifth of a quorum. This is 44 in the House, 20 in the Committee of the Whole.

The House also has a recorded teller vote, now largely supplanted by the electronic voting procedure, under which the votes of each member are made public just as they would be on a recorded vote.

Treaties—Executive proposals — in the form of resolutions of ratification — which must be submitted to the Senate for approval by two-thirds of the senators present. Treaties are normally sent to the Foreign Relations Committee for scrutiny before the Senate takes action. Foreign Relations has jurisdiction over all treaties, regardless of the subject matter. Treaties are read three times and debated on the floor in much the same manner as legislative proposals. After approval by the Senate, treaties are formally ratified by the president.

Trust Funds—Funds collected and used by the federal government for carrying out specific purposes and programs according to terms of a trust agreement or statute such as the Social Security and unemployment compensation trust funds. Such funds are administered by the government in a fiduciary capacity and are not available for the general purposes of the government.

Unanimous Consent—Proceedings of the House or Senate and action on legislation often take place upon the unanimous consent of the chamber, whether or not a rule of the chamber is being violated. Unanimous consent is used to expedite floor action and frequently is used in a routine fashion such as by a senator requesting the unanimous consent of the Senate to have specified members of his staff present on the floor during debate on a specific amendment.

Unanimous Consent Agreement—A device used in the Senate to expedite legislation. Much of the Senate's legislative business, dealing with both minor and controversial issues, is conducted through unanimous consent or unanimous consent agreements. On major legislation, such agreements usually are printed and transmitted to all senators in advance of floor debate. Once agreed to, they are binding on all members unless the Senate, by unanimous consent, agrees to modify them. An agreement may list the order in which various bills are to be considered, specify the length of time bills and contested amendments are to be debated and when they are to be voted upon and, frequently, require that all amendments introduced be germane to the bill under consideration.

In this regard, unanimous consent agreements are similar to the "rules" issued by the House Rules Committee for bills pending in the House.

Union Calendar—Bills that directly or indirectly appropriate money or raise revenue are placed on this House calendar according to the date they are reported from committee.

U.S. Code—A consolidation and codification of the general and permanent laws of the United States arranged by subject under 50 titles, the first six dealing with general or political subjects, and the other 44 alphabetically arranged from agriculture to war. The U.S. Code is updated annually, and a new set of bound volumes is published every six years. *(See also Law, Slip Laws, Statutes at Large.)*

Veto—Disapproval by the president of a bill or joint resolution (other than one proposing an amendment to the Constitution). When Congress is in session, the president must veto a bill within 10 days, excluding Sundays, after he has received it; otherwise, it becomes law without his signature. When the president vetoes a bill, he returns it to the house of origin along with a message stating his objections. *(See also Pocket Veto, Override a Veto.)*

Voice Vote—In either the House or Senate, members answer "aye" or "no" in chorus, and the presiding officer decides the result. The term also is used loosely to indicate action by unanimous consent or without objection.

Whip—*(See Majority and Minority Whip.)*

Without Objection—Used in lieu of a vote on non-controversial motions, amendments or bills that may be passed in either the House or Senate if no member voices an objection.

Yeas and Nays—The Constitution requires that yea-and-nay votes be taken and recorded when requested by one-fifth of the members present. In the House, the Speaker determines whether one-fifth of the members present requested a vote. In the Senate, practice requires only 11 members. The Constitution requires the yeas and nays on a veto override attempt. *(See Recorded Vote.)*

Yielding—When a member has been recognized to speak, no other member may speak unless he obtains permission from the member recognized. This permission is called yielding and usually is requested in the form, "Will the gentleman (or gentlelady) yield to me?" While this activity occasionally is seen in the Senate, the Senate has no rule or practice to parcel out time.

Members' Honoraria Receipts

Financial disclosure forms for 1990 were due May 15, 1991, for members of Congress and made public June 14. They showed the sources of members' incomes, their assets and liabilities, gifts they received, reimbursements for travel expenses from non-governmental groups, and positions they held outside government.

Assets, liabilities and income had to be reported only within broad ranges. Honoraria payments received for activities such as speeches, appearances and articles had to be disclosed in detail.

Members could keep honoraria up to specified limits; amounts over those limits had to be donated to charity.

For 1990, senators could keep $27,337 in honoraria, based on their 1990 salaries.

House members were limited to $26,850 (30 percent of their 1989 salary) in honoraria and other outside earned income. Leaders earned higher salaries and thus could keep more.

Senate

	Total	Amount To Charity	Amount Kept
Alabama			
Howell Heflin (D)	$ 28,150	$ 2,000	$ 26,150
Richard C. Shelby (D)	34,000	7,000	27,000
Alaska			
Frank H. Murkowski (R)	24,800	None	24,800
Ted Stevens (R)	20,000	None	20,000
Arizona			
Dennis DeConcini (D)	None	None	None
John McCain (R)	9,100	9,100	None
Arkansas			
Dale Bumpers (D)	25,800	None	25,800
David Pryor (D)	27,337	None	27,337
California			
Alan Cranston (D)	None	None	None
John Seymour (R)	1,350 [1]	None	1,350
Colorado			
Tim Wirth (D)	2,000	2,100 [2]	None
Hank Brown (R)	28,200	1,200	27,000
Connecticut			
Christopher J. Dodd (D)	None	None	None
Joseph I. Lieberman (D)	None	None	None
Delaware			
Joseph R. Biden Jr. (D)	25,850	None	25,850
William V. Roth Jr. (R)	28,411	1,074	27,337
Florida			
Bob Graham (D)	None	None	None
Connie Mack (R)	24,500	None	24,500
Georgia			
Wyche Fowler Jr. (D)	38,300	12,264	26,036
Sam Nunn (D)	42,045	14,708	27,337
Hawaii			
Daniel K. Akaka (D)	None	None	None
Daniel K. Inouye (D)	13,000	None	13,000
Idaho			
Larry E. Craig (R)	26,750	None	26,750
Steve Symms (R)	39,750	12,413	27,337
Illinois			
Alan J. Dixon (D)	38,950	11,650	27,300
Paul Simon (D)	12,000	None	12,000
Indiana			
Daniel R. Coats (R)	18,380	None	18,380
Richard G. Lugar (R)	41,230	16,518	24,713
Iowa			
Tom Harkin (D)	None	None	None
Charles E. Grassley (R)	13,200	13,200	None

	Total	Amount To Charity	Amount Kept
Kansas			
Bob Dole (R)	$ 78,100	$ 47,700	$ 30,400
Nancy Landon Kassebaum (R)	None	None	None
Kentucky			
Wendell H. Ford (D)	25,300	300	25,000
Mitch McConnell (R)	33,000	5,750	27,250
Louisiana			
John B. Breaux (D)	60,000	32,778	27,222
J. Bennett Johnston (D)	35,500	8,500	27,000
Maine			
George J. Mitchell (D)	40,000	10,000	30,000
William S. Cohen (R)	11,950	None	11,950
Maryland			
Barbara A. Mikulski (D)	13,200	6,500	6,700
Paul S. Sarbanes (D)	21,965	1,000	20,965
Massachusetts			
Edward M. Kennedy (D)	None	None	None
John Kerry (D)	None	None	None
Michigan			
Carl Levin (D)	None	None	None
Donald W. Riegle Jr. (D)	24,000	7,500	16,500
Minnesota			
Paul Wellstone (D)	200	None	200
Dave Durenberger (R)	24,159	None	24,159
Mississippi			
Thad Cochran (R)	35,150	8,000	27,150
Trent Lott (R)	37,300	9,963	27,337
Missouri			
Christopher S. Bond (R)	32,900	9,302	23,598
John C. Danforth (R)	200	None	200
Montana			
Max Baucus (D)	27,000	None	27,000
Conrad Burns (R)	45,400	18,097	27,303
Nebraska			
Jim Exon (D)	None	None	None
Bob Kerrey (D)	None	None	None
Nevada			
Richard H. Bryan (D)	15,000	None	15,000
Harry Reid (D)	None	None	None
New Hampshire			
Warren B. Rudman (R)	27,400	100	27,300
Robert C. Smith (R)	None	None	None
New Jersey			
Bill Bradley (D)	None	None	None
Frank R. Lautenberg (D)	None	None	None

	Total	Amount To Charity	Amount Kept
New Mexico			
Jeff Bingaman (D)	None	None	None
Pete V. Domenici (R)	$ 42,550	$ 17,500	$ 25,050
New York			
Daniel Patrick Moynihan (D)	48,900	22,000	26,900
Alfonse M. D'Amato (R)	37,650	10,325	27,325
North Carolina			
Terry Sanford (D)	None	None	None
Jesse Helms (R)	14,000	None	14,000
North Dakota			
Quentin N. Burdick (D)	None	None	None
Kent Conrad (D)	34,000	7,060	26,940
Ohio			
John Glenn (D)	None	None	None
Howard M. Metzenbaum (D)	10,400	10,400	None
Oklahoma			
David L. Boren (D)	59,600	32,263	27,337
Don Nickles (R)	36,000	8,700	27,300
Oregon			
Mark O. Hatfield (R)	22,600	None	22,600
Bob Packwood (R)	45,000	17,785	27,215
Pennsylvania			
Harris Wofford (D)	None	None	None
Arlen Specter (R)	3,000	None	3,000
Rhode Island			
Claiborne Pell (D)	15,200	15,000	200 [3]
John H. Chafee (R)	40,000	12,972	27,028
South Carolina			
Ernest F. Hollings (D)	82,200	55,212	26,988
Strom Thurmond (R)	12,000	12,000	None

	Total	Amount To Charity	Amount Kept
South Dakota			
Tom Daschle (D)	$ 37,950	$ 10,825	$ 27,125
Larry Pressler (R)	31,000	3,700	27,300
Tennessee			
Al Gore (D)	28,650	1,313	27,337
Jim Sasser (D)	29,350	2,013	27,337
Texas			
Lloyd Bentsen (D)	None	None	None
Phil Gramm (R)	36,400	9,075	27,325
Utah			
Jake Garn (R)	27,500	200	27,300
Orrin G. Hatch (R)	69,900	46,765	23,135
Vermont			
Patrick J. Leahy (D)	31,210	3,905	27,305
James M. Jeffords (R)	18,650	1,750	16,900
Virginia			
Charles S. Robb (D)	None	None	None
John W. Warner (R)	None	None	None
Washington			
Brock Adams (D)	None	None	None
Slade Gorton (R)	30,050	6,750	23,300
West Virginia			
Robert C. Byrd (D)	9,000	None	9,000
John D. Rockefeller IV (D)	None	None	None
Wisconsin			
Herb Kohl (D)	None	None	None
Bob Kasten (R)	38,875	11,800	27,075
Wyoming			
Alan K. Simpson (R)	78,900	51,968	26,932
Malcolm Wallop (R)	31,100	5,900	25,200

NR — No report; granted extension in filing financial disclosure report.

[1] *Honoraria reported as a member of the California Senate; appointed to U.S. Senate in January 1991.*

[2] *Includes $100 of interest earned on money received from honoraria.*

[3] *Given to staff member who helped write article.*

House

	Total	Amount To Charity	Amount Kept
Alabama			
1. Sonny Callahan (R)	$ 10,650	None	$ 10,650
2. Bill Dickinson (R)	26,850	None	26,850
3. Glen Browder (D)	None	None	None
4. Tom Bevill (D)	35,000	8,300	26,700
5. Bud Cramer (D)	None	None	None
6. Ben Erdreich (D)	6,500	6,500	None
7. Claude Harris (D)	None	None	None
Alaska			
AL Don Young (R)	25,900	None	25,900
Arizona			
1. John J. Rhodes III (R)	8,000	None	8,000
2. Morris K. Udall (D)	None	None	None
3. Bob Stump (R)	None	None	None
4. Jon Kyl (R)	2,000	2,000	None
5. Jim Kolbe (R)	None	None	None
Arkansas			
1. Bill Alexander (D)	26,300	None	26,300
2. Ray Thornton (D)	None	None	None
3. John Paul Hammerschmidt (R)	14,500	None	14,500
4. Beryl Anthony Jr. (D)	34,150	7,300	26,850
California			
1. Frank Riggs (R)	None	None	None
2. Wally Herger (R)	8,500	8,500	None
3. Robert T. Matsui (D)	32,600	5,750	26,850
4. Vic Fazio (D)	48,200	21,350	26,850

	Total	Amount To Charity	Amount Kept
5. Nancy Pelosi (D)	$ 2,400	$ 2,400	None
6. Barbara Boxer (D)	8,200	None	8,200
7. George Miller (D)	27,575	725	26,850
8. Ronald V. Dellums (D)	10,700	None	10,700
9. Pete Stark (D)	37,350	10,850	26,500
10. Don Edwards (D)	None	None	None
11. Tom Lantos (D)	25,920	None	25,920
12. Tom Campbell (R)	None	None	None
13. Norman Y. Mineta (D)	44,400	19,650	24,750
14. John T. Doolittle (R)	5,500	None	5,500
15. Gary Condit (D)	None	None	None
16. Leon E. Panetta (D)	25,550	None	25,550
17. Calvin Dooley (D)	None	None	None
18. Richard H. Lehman (D)	28,000	1,150	26,850
19. Robert J. Lagomarsino (R)	None	None	None
20. Bill Thomas (R)	33,025	6,000	27,025
21. Elton Gallegly (R)	3,000	None	3,000
22. Carlos J. Moorhead (R)	17,067	None	17,067
23. Anthony C. Beilenson (D)	None	None	None
24. Henry A. Waxman (D)	70,123	43,463	26,660
25. Edward R. Roybal (D)	2,500	2,500	None
26. Howard L. Berman (D)	13,150	250	12,900
27. Mel Levine (D)	3,450	None	3,450
28. Julian C. Dixon (D)	None	None	None
29. Maxine Waters (D)	9,300	None	9,300
30. Matthew G. Martinez (D)	5,650	None	5,650
31. Mervyn M. Dymally (D)	10,704	None	10,704
32. Glenn M. Anderson (D)	14,800	14,800	None

	Total	Amount To Charity	Amount Kept
33. David Dreier (R)	$ 38,850	$ 12,000	$ 26,850
34. Esteban E. Torres (D)	2,760	None	2,760
35. Jerry Lewis (R)	38,750	10,950	27,800
36. George E. Brown Jr. (D)	15,550	None	15,550
37. Al McCandless (R)	None	None	None
38. Robert K. Dornan (R)	21,419	None	21,419
39. William E. Dannemeyer (R)	4,950	450	4,500
40. C. Christopher Cox (R)	None	None	None
41. Bill Lowery (R)	28,500	1,750	26,750
42. Dana Rohrabacher (R)	3,250	None	3,250
43. Ron Packard (R)	19,300	None	19,300
44. Randy "Duke" Cunningham (R)	12,500	None	12,500
45. Duncan Hunter (R)	1,500	500	1,000
Colorado			
1. Patricia Schroeder (D)	157,697	131,280	26,416
2. David E. Skaggs (D)	2,200	2,200	none
3. Ben Nighthorse Campbell (D)	4.000	None	4,000
4. Wayne Allard (R)	None	None	None
5. Joel Hefley (R)	4,250	None	4,250
6. Dan Schaefer (R)	29,000	2,150	26,850
Connecticut			
1. Barbara B. Kennelly (D)	10,000	10,000	None
2. Sam Gejdenson (D)	11,750	11,750	None
3. Rosa DeLauro (D)	None	None	None
4. Christopher Shays (R)	None	None	None
5. Gary Franks (R)	None	None	None
6. Nancy L. Johnson (R)	None	None	None
Delaware			
AL Thomas R. Carper (D)	None	None	None
Florida			
1. Earl Hutto (D)	7,000	700	6,300
2. Pete Peterson (D)	None	None	None
3. Charles E. Bennett (D)	None	None	None
4. Craig T. James (R)	None	None	None
5. Bill McCollum (R)	21,900	None	21,900
6. Cliff Stearns (R)	None	None	None
7. Sam M. Gibbons (D)	29,907	1,150	28,757
8. C. W. Bill Young (R)	26,000	None	26,000
9. Michael Bilirakis (R)	17,500	16,000	1,500
10. Andy Ireland (R)	None	None	None
11. Jim Bacchus (D)	None	None	None
12. Tom Lewis (R)	13,000	None	13,000
13. Porter J. Goss (R)	None	None	None
14. Harry A. Johnston (D)	None	None	None
15. E. Clay Shaw Jr. (R)	23,500	None	23,500
16. Lawrence J. Smith (D)	14,500	None	14,500
17. William Lehman (D)	2,000	2,000	None
18. Ileana Ros-Lehtinen (R)	None	None	None
19. Dante B. Fascell (D)	None	None	None
Georgia			
1. Lindsay Thomas (D)	14,000	None	14,000
2. Charles Hatcher (D)	26,750	None	26,750
3. Richard Ray (D)	10,700	None	10,700
4. Ben Jones (D)	1,500	None	1,500
5. John Lewis (D)	27,300	500	26,800
6. Newt Gingrich (R)	61,234	34,384	26,850
7. George "Buddy" Darden (D)	13,000	5,000	8,000
8. J. Roy Rowland (D)	30,197	3,347	26,850
9. Ed Jenkins (D)	27,000	2,000	25,000
10. Doug Barnard Jr. (D)	26,250	None	26,250
Hawaii			
1. Neil Abercrombie (D)	None	None	None
2. Patsy T. Mink (D)	2,575	None	2,575
Idaho			
1. Larry LaRocco (D)	None	None	None
2. Richard Stallings (D)	7,800	None	7,800
Illinois			
1. Charles A. Hayes (D)	18,520	None	18,520
2. Gus Savage (D)	6,000	None	6,000
3. Marty Russo (D)	38,000	11,150	26,850
4. George E. Sangmeister (D)	None	None	None
5. William O. Lipinski (D)	9,500	None	9,500
6. Henry J. Hyde (R)	30,625	3,775	26,850

	Total	Amount To Charity	Amount Kept
7. Cardiss Collins (D)	$ 8,500	None	$ 8,500
8. Dan Rostenkowski (D)	310,000	283,150	26,850
9. Sidney R. Yates (D)	None	None	None
10. John Porter (R)	26,800	None	26,800
11. Frank Annunzio (D)	None	None	None
12. Philip M. Crane (R)	34,650	7,800	26,850
13. Harris W. Fawell (R)	12,300	7,300	5,000
14. Dennis Hastert (R)	20,750	None	20,750
15. Vacancy [1]			
16. John W. Cox Jr. (D)	None	None	None
17. Lane Evans (D)	None	None	None
18. Robert H. Michel (R)	56,650	27,650	29,000
19. Terry L. Bruce (D)	23,700	None	23,700
20. Richard J. Durbin (D)	25,100	None	25,100
21. Jerry F. Costello (D)	None	None	None
22. Glenn Poshard (D)	None	None	None
Indiana			
1. Peter J. Visclosky (D)	14,130	None	14,130
2. Philip R. Sharp (D)	2,000	2,000	None
3. Tim Roemer (D)	None	None	None
4. Jill Long (D)	None	None	None
5. Jim Jontz (D)	1,000	1,000	None
6. Dan Burton (R)	18,790	None	18,790
7. John T. Myers (R)	20,800	None	20,800
8. Frank McCloskey (D)	14,500	None	14,500
9. Lee H. Hamilton (D)	44,415	17,565	26,850
10. Andrew Jacobs Jr. (D)	None	None	None
Iowa			
1. Jim Leach (R)	None	None	None
2. Jim Nussle (R)	None	None	None
3. Dave Nagle (D)	None	None	None
4. Neal Smith (D)	None	None	None
5. Jim Ross Lightfoot (R)	1,200	None	1,200
6. Fred Grandy (R)	29,800	3,000	26,800
Kansas			
1. Pat Roberts (R)	23,050	None	23,050
2. Jim Slattery (D)	21,500	None	21,500
3. Jan Meyers (R)	None	None	None
4. Dan Glickman (D)	None	None	None
5. Dick Nichols (R)	None	None	None
Kentucky			
1. Carroll Hubbard Jr. (D)	36,100	9,250	25,850
2. William H. Natcher (D)	None	None	None
3. Romano L. Mazzoli (D)	None	None	None
4. Jim Bunning (R)	20,425	8,615	11,810
5. Harold Rogers (R)	19,500	None	19,500
6. Larry J. Hopkins (R)	33,500	6,675	26,825
7. Carl C. Perkins (D)	19,500	None	19,500
Louisiana			
1. Robert L. Livingston (R)	26,900	50	26,850
2. William J. Jefferson (D)	None	None	None
3. W. J. "Billy" Tauzin (D)	41,500	14,650	26,850
4. Jim McCrery (R)	None	None	None
5. Jerry Huckaby (D)	21,000	None	21,000
6. Richard H. Baker (R)	26,700	None	26,700
7. Jimmy Hayes (D)	24,500	None	24,500
8. Clyde C. Holloway (R)	7,500	None	7,500
Maine			
1. Thomas H. Andrews (D)	None	None	None
2. Olympia J. Snowe (R)	None	None	None
Maryland			
1. Wayne T. Gilchrist (R)	None	None	None
2. Helen Delich Bentley (R)	22,125	None	22,125
3. Benjamin L. Cardin (D)	9,500	9,500	None
4. Tom McMillen (D)	34,800	34,800	None
5. Steny H. Hoyer (D)	None	None	None
6. Beverly B. Byron (D)	18,000	None	18,000
7. Kweisi Mfume (D)	20,600	3,765	16,835
8. Constance A. Morella (R)	None	None	None
Massachusetts			
1. John Olver (D)	None	None	None
2. Richard E. Neal (D)	16,500	None	16,500
3. Joseph D. Early (D)	None	None	None

	Total	Amount To Charity	Amount Kept
4. Barney Frank (D)	$ 4,750	$ 2,500	$ 2,250
5. Chester G. Atkins (D)	400	None	400
6. Nicholas Mavroules (D)	None	None	None
7. Edward J. Markey (D)	None	None	None
8. Joseph P. Kennedy II (D)	None	None	None
9. Joe Moakley (D)	31,000	4,200	26,800
10. Gerry E. Studds (D)	300	None	300
11. Brian Donnelly (D)	21,000	None	21,000
Michigan			
1. John Conyers Jr. (D)	5,000	None	5,000
2. Carl D. Pursell (R)	18,250	None	18,250
3. Howard Wolpe (D)	None	None	None
4. Fred Upton (R)	None	None	None
5. Paul B. Henry (R)	1,000	1,000	None
6. Bob Carr (D)	27,500	1,246	26,254
7. Dale E. Kildee (D)	None	None	None
8. Bob Traxler (D)	26,500	None	26,500
9. Guy Vander Jagt (R)	44,650	17,800	26,850
10. Dave Camp (R)	None	None	None
11. Robert W. Davis (R)	31,500	5,000	26,500
12. David E. Bonior (D)	28,000	1,200	26,800
13. Barbara-Rose Collins (D)	None	None	None
14. Dennis M. Hertel (D)	19,500	1,200	18,300
15. William D. Ford (D)	32,550	6,000	26,550
16. John D. Dingell (D)	39,800	12,950	26,850
17. Sander M. Levin (D)	None	None	None
18. William S. Broomfield (R)	None	None	None
Minnesota			
1. Timothy J. Penny (D)	1,000	1,000	None
2. Vin Weber (R)	30,600	3,750	26,850
3. Jim Ramstad (R)	None	None	None
4. Bruce F. Vento (D)	37,000	10,250	26,750
5. Martin Olav Sabo (D)	27,500	1,000	26,500
6. Gerry Sikorski (D)	28,000	1,150	26,850
7. Collin C. Peterson (D)	1,000	None	1,000
8. James L. Oberstar (D)	36,700	9,850	26,850
Mississippi			
1. Jamie L. Whitten (D)	None	None	None
2. Mike Espy (D)	28,800	2,000	26,800
3. G. V. "Sonny" Montgomery (D)	200	None	200
4. Mike Parker (D)	23,950	None	23,950
5. Gene Taylor (D)	None	None	None
Missouri			
1. William L. Clay (D)	27,000	150	26,850
2. Joan Kelly Horn (D)	None	None	None
3. Richard A. Gephardt (D)	36,000	7,760	28,240
4. Ike Skelton (D)	10,900	None	10,900
5. Alan Wheat (D)	2,000	2,000	None
6. E. Thomas Coleman (R)	27,750	2,000	25,750
7. Mel Hancock (R)	None	None	None
8. Bill Emerson (R)	29,000	2,150	26,850
9. Harold L. Volkmer (D)	19,750	None	19,750
Montana			
1. Pat Williams (D)	26,100	None	26,100
2. Ron Marlenee (R)	27,550	2,250	25,300
Nebraska			
1. Doug Bereuter (R)	2,000	2,000	None
2. Peter Hoagland (D)	None	None	None
3. Bill Barrett (R)	None	None	None
Nevada			
1. James Bilbray (D)	15,500	None	15,500
2. Barbara F. Vucanovich (R)	1,500	None	1,500
New Hampshire			
1. Bill Zeliff (R)	None	None	None
2. Dick Swett (D)	None	None	None
New Jersey			
1. Robert E. Andrews (D)	None	None	None
2. William J. Hughes (D)	None	None	None
3. Frank Pallone Jr. (D)	None	None	None
4. Christopher H. Smith (R)	None	None	None
5. Marge Roukema (R)	5,500	None	5,500
6. Bernard J. Dwyer (D)	None	None	None
7. Matthew J. Rinaldo (R)	47,250	20,403	26,847

	Total	Amount To Charity	Amount Kept
8. Robert A. Roe (D)	$ 31,000	$ 4,650	$ 26,350
9. Robert G. Torricelli (D)	29,750	2,900	26,850
10. Donald M. Payne (D)	8,930	1,000	7,930
11. Dean A. Gallo (R)	3,500	3,500	None
12. Dick Zimmer (R)	None	None	None
13. H. James Saxton (R)	None	None	None
14. Frank J. Guarini (D)	11,250	None	11,250
New Mexico			
1. Steven H. Schiff (R)	None	None	None
2. Joe Skeen (R)	None	None	None
3. Bill Richardson (D)	47,550	21,250	26,300
New York			
1. George J. Hochbrueckner (D)	27,000	2,000	25,000
2. Thomas J. Downey (D)	33,300	6,500	26,800
3. Robert J. Mrazek (D)	22,650	None	22,650
4. Norman F. Lent (R)	62,000	35,150	26,850
5. Raymond J. McGrath (R)	26,750	None	26,750
6. Floyd H. Flake (D)	39,035	22,922	16,113
7. Gary L. Ackerman (D)	32,806	None	32,806
8. James H. Scheuer (D)	6,350	6,350	None
9. Thomas J. Manton (D)	41,650	15,150	26,500
10. Charles E. Schumer (D)	None	None	None
11. Edolphus Towns (D)	32,600	6,950	25,650
12. Major R. Owens (D)	17,680	None	17,680
13. Stephen J. Solarz (D)	36,493	9,643	26,850
14. Susan Molinari (R)	None	None	None
15. Bill Green (R)	3,550	None	3,550
16. Charles B. Rangel (D)	41,950	15,100	26,850
17. Ted Weiss (D)	None	None	None
18. Jose E. Serrano (D)	7,325	None	7,325
19. Eliot L. Engel (D)	13,661	None	13,661
20. Nita M. Lowey (D)	None	None	None
21. Hamilton Fish Jr. (R)	9,000	None	9,000
22. Benjamin A. Gilman (R)	8,000	None	8,000
23. Michael R. McNulty (D)	23,500	None	23,500
24. Gerald B. H. Solomon (R)	25,500	None	25,500
25. Sherwood Boehlert (R)	22,600	150	22,450
26. David O'B. Martin (R)	16,000	None	16,000
27. James T. Walsh (R)	None	None	None
28. Matthew F. McHugh (D)	None	None	None
29. Frank Horton (R)	30,050	3,200	26,850
30. Louise M. Slaughter (D)	None	None	None
31. Bill Paxon (R)	None	None	None
32. John J. LaFalce (D)	93,350	66,545	26,805
33. Henry J. Nowak (D)	23,500	None	23,500
34. Amo Houghton (R)	4,400	3,400	1,000
North Carolina			
1. Walter B. Jones (D)	15,500	None	15,550
2. Tim Valentine (D)	14,750	None	14,750
3. H. Martin Lancaster (D)	17,300	250	17,050
4. David E. Price (D)	1,500	None	1,500
5. Stephen L. Neal (D)	5,000	5,000	None
6. Howard Coble (R)	9,500	1,500	8,000
7. Charlie Rose (D)	33,800	6,950	26,850
8. W. G. "Bill" Hefner (D)	17,250	None	17,250
9. Alex McMillan (R)	8,250	None	8,250
10. Cass Ballenger (R)	7,000	7,000	None
11. Charles H. Taylor (R)	None	None	None
North Dakota			
AL Byron L. Dorgan (D)	30,500	4,020	26,480
Ohio			
1. Charles Luken (D)	None	None	None
2. Bill Gradison (R)	93,600	73,294	20,306
3. Tony P. Hall (D)	26,750	2,500	24,250
4. Michael G. Oxley (R)	29,500	2,650	26,850
5. Paul E. Gillmor (R)	4,000	2,500	1,500
6. Bob McEwen (R)	27,300	450	26,850
7. David L. Hobson (R)	900	None	900
8. John A. Boehner (R)	None	None	None
9. Marcy Kaptur (D)	None	None	None
10. Clarence E. Miller (R)	None	None	None
11. Dennis E. Eckart (D)	500	500	None
12. John R. Kasich (R)	None	None	None
13. Don J. Pease (D)	7,900	2,250	5,650

	Total	Amount To Charity	Amount Kept
14. Tom Sawyer (D)	$ 1,000	$ 1,000	None
15. Chalmers P. Wylie (R)	34,000	7,198	26,802
16. Ralph Regula (R)	5,900	5,900	None
17. James A. Traficant Jr. (D)	19,000	None	19,000
18. Douglas Applegate (D)	None	None	None
19. Edward F. Feighan (D)	27,250	2,000	25,250
20. Mary Rose Oakar (D)	11,500	None	11,500
21. Louis Stokes (D)	28,600	1,750	26,850
Oklahoma			
1. James M. Inhofe (R)	6,500	None	6,500
2. Mike Synar (D)	27,450	2,000	25,450
3. Bill Brewster (D)	1,500	None	1,500
4. Dave McCurdy (D)	25,200	None	25,200
5. Mickey Edwards (R)	26,350	None	26,350
6. Glenn English (D)	30,500	3,650	26,850
Oregon			
1. Les AuCoin (D)	38,750	11,900	26,850
2. Bob Smith (R)	18,850	None	18,850
3. Ron Wyden (D)	26,000	None	26,000
4. Peter A. DeFazio (D)	4,000	None	4,000
5. Mike Kopetski (D)	None	None	None
Pennsylvania			
1. Thomas M. Foglietta (D)	9,250	None	9,250
2. William H. Gray III (D)	75,000	48,500	26,500
3. Robert A. Borski (D)	19,000	None	19,000
4. Joe Kolter (D)	1,500	None	1,500
5. Richard T. Schulze (R)	25,500	None	25,500
6. Gus Yatron (D)	2,000	None	2,000
7. Curt Weldon (R)	11,990	None	11,990
8. Peter H. Kostmayer (D)	None	None	None
9. Bud Shuster (R)	26,850	None	26,850
10. Joseph M. McDade (R)	37,000	10,982	26,018
11. Paul E. Kanjorski (D)	38,000	11,150	26,850
12. John P. Murtha (D)	25,850	None	25,850
13. Lawrence Coughlin (R)	8,250	8,000	250
14. William J. Coyne (D)	7,000	None	7,000
15. Don Ritter (R)	26,750	None	26,750
16. Robert S. Walker (R)	None	None	None
17. George W. Gekas (R)	None	None	None
18. Rick Santorum (R)	None	None	None
19. Bill Goodling (R)	13,200	None	13,200
20. Joseph M. Gaydos (D)	23,500	None	23,500
21. Tom Ridge (R)	13,000	None	13,000
22. Austin J. Murphy (D)	11,000	None	11,000
23. William F. Clinger Jr. (R)	6,800	5,400	1,400
Rhode Island			
1. Ronald K. Machtley (R)	None	None	None
2. John F. Reed (D)	None	None	None
South Carolina			
1. Arthur Ravenel Jr. (R)	None	None	None
2. Floyd D. Spence (R)	None	None	None
3. Butler Derrick (D)	26,800	8,000	18,800
4. Liz J. Patterson (D)	None	None	None
5. John M. Spratt Jr. (D)	None	None	None
6. Robin Tallon (D)	19,500	None	19,500
South Dakota			
AL Tim Johnson (D)	5,300	None	5,300
Tennessee			
1. James H. Quillen (R)	45,000	20,000	25,000
2. John J. "Jimmy" Duncan Jr. (R)	4,000	None	4,000
3. Marilyn Lloyd (D)	5,500	None	5,500
4. Jim Cooper (D)	None	None	None
5. Bob Clement (D)	4,000	None	4,000
6. Bart Gordon (D)	26,500	None	26,500
7. Don Sundquist (R)	29,500	2,750	26,750
8. John Tanner (D)	None	None	None
9. Harold E. Ford (D)	26,500	500	26,000
Texas			
1. Jim Chapman (D)	36,000	9,500	26,500

	Total	Amount To Charity	Amount Kept
2. Charles Wilson (D)	$ 28,575	$ 1,725	$ 26,850
3. Sam Johnson (R)	None	None	None
4. Ralph M. Hall (D)	None	None	None
5. John Bryant (D)	29,850	3,000	26,850
6. Joe L. Barton (R)	27,700	850	26,850
7. Bill Archer (R)	33,500	6,650	26,850
8. Jack Fields (R)	37,600	12,000	25,600
9. Jack Brooks (D)	None	None	None
10. J. J. Pickle (D)	6,000	1,000	5,000
11. Chet Edwards (D)	None	None	None
12. Pete Geren (D)	None	None	None
13. Bill Sarpalius (D)	14,950	200	14,750
14. Greg Laughlin (D)	4,000	None	4,000
15. E. "Kika" de la Garza (D)	36,000	10,150	25,850
16. Ronald D. Coleman (D)	None	None	None
17. Charles W. Stenholm (D)	46,250	19,473	26,777
18. Craig Washington (D)	None	None	None
19. Larry Combest (R)	12,000	None	12,000
20. Henry B. Gonzalez (D)	None	None	None
21. Lamar Smith (R)	None	None	None
22. Tom DeLay (R)	33,050	6,200	26,850
23. Albert G. Bustamante (D)	18,200	None	18,200
24. Martin Frost (D)	23,400	None	23,400
25. Michael A. Andrews (D)	26,750	None	26,750
26. Dick Armey (R)	20,200	None	20,200
27. Solomon P. Ortiz (D)	4,732	None	4,732
Utah			
1. James V. Hansen (R)	24,500	None	24,500
2. Wayne Owens (D)	20,300	2,000	18,300
3. Bill Orton (D)	None	None	None
Vermont			
AL Bernard Sanders (I)	10,273	None	10,273
Virginia			
1. Herbert H. Bateman (R)	2,320	2,320	None
2. Owen B. Pickett (D)	None	None	None
3. Thomas J. Bliley Jr. (R)	29,250	13,800	15,450
4. Norman Sisisky (D)	None	None	None
5. Lewis F. Payne Jr. (D)	None	None	None
6. Jim Olin (D)	None	None	None
7. D. French Slaughter Jr. (R)	None	None	None
8. James P. Moran Jr. (D)	2,000	None	2,000
9. Rick Boucher (D)	None	None	None
10. Frank R. Wolf (R)	None	None	None
Washington			
1. John Miller (R)	450	None	450
2. Al Swift (D)	27,750	900	26,850
3. Jolene Unsoeld (D)	None	None	None
4. Sid Morrison (R)	5,000	5,000	None
5. Thomas S. Foley (D)	30,000	None	30,000
6. Norm Dicks (D)	26,800	None	26,800
7. Jim McDermott (D)	None	None	None
8. Rod Chandler (R)	36,500	9,650	26,850
West Virginia			
1. Alan B. Mollohan (D)	19,000	None	19,000
2. Harley O. Staggers Jr. (D)	4,500	None	4,500
3. Bob Wise (D)	7,000	7,000	None
4. Nick J. Rahall II (D)	32,800	8,000	24,800
Wisconsin			
1. Les Aspin (D)	30,850	4,000	26,850
2. Scott L. Klug (R)	None	None	None
3. Steve Gunderson (R)	24,500	None	24,500
4. Gerald D. Kleczka (D)	16,000	None	16,000
5. Jim Moody (D)	19,850	None	19,850
6. Tom Petri (R)	5,750	5,750	None
7. David R. Obey (D)	25,000	None	25,000
8. Toby Roth (R)	26,000	6,500	19,500
9. F. James Sensenbrenner Jr. (R)	10,750	None	10,750
Wyoming			
AL Craig Thomas (R)	None	None	None

[1] *Edward Madigan, R-Ill., resigned March 8, 1991.*

Appendix E

TEXT

PRESIDENTIAL ADDRESS

Bush Announces War on Iraq, Assures 'We Will Not Fail'

On Jan. 16, President Bush addressed the nation from the Oval Office shortly after the beginning of a multinational military effort to force Iraq to withdraw from Kuwait. Following is the official White House transcript of the address:

PRESIDENT BUSH: Just two hours ago, allied air forces began an attack on military targets in Iraq and Kuwait. These attacks continue as I speak. Ground forces are not engaged.

This conflict started Aug. 2 when the dictator of Iraq invaded a small and helpless neighbor. Kuwait, a member of the Arab League and a member of the United Nations, was crushed, its people brutalized.

Five months ago, Saddam Hussein started this cruel war against Kuwait. Tonight the battle has been joined.

This military action, taken in accord with United Nations resolutions and with the consent of the United States Congress, follows months of constant and virtually endless diplomatic activity on the part of the United Nations, the United States and many, many other countries.

Arab leaders sought what became known as an Arab solution, only to conclude that Saddam Hussein was unwilling to leave Kuwait. Others traveled to Baghdad in a variety of efforts to restore peace and justice.

Our Secretary of State James [A.] Baker [III] held an historic meeting in Geneva, only to be totally rebuffed.

This past weekend, in a last ditch effort, the secretary-general of the United Nations went to the Middle East with peace in his heart — his second such mission. And he came back from Baghdad with no progress at all in getting Saddam Hussein to withdraw from Kuwait.

Now, the 28 countries with forces in the gulf area have exhausted all reasonable efforts to reach a peaceful resolution [and] have no choice but to drive Saddam from Kuwait by force. We will not fail.

As I report to you, air attacks are under way against military targets in Iraq. We are determined to knock out Saddam Hussein's nuclear bomb potential. We will also destroy his chemical weapons facilities. Much of Saddam's artillery and tanks will be destroyed. Our operations are designed to best protect the lives of all the coalition forces by targeting Saddam's vast military arsenal.

Initial reports from Gen. [H. Norman] Schwarzkopf are that our operations are proceeding according to plan. Our objectives are clear: Saddam Hussein's forces will leave Kuwait, the legitimate government of Kuwait will be restored to its rightful place, and Kuwait will once again be free.

Iraq will eventually comply with all relevant United Nations resolutions, and then, when peace is restored, it is our hope that Iraq will live as a peaceful and cooperative member of the family of nations, thus enhancing the security and stability of the gulf.

Some may ask, why act now? Why not wait? The answer is clear. The world could wait no longer. Sanctions, though having some effect, showed no signs of accomplishing their objective. Sanctions were tried for well over five months, and we and our allies concluded that sanctions alone would not force Saddam from Kuwait.

While the world waited, Saddam Hussein systematically raped, pillaged and plundered a tiny nation, no threat to his own. He subjected the people of Kuwait to unspeakable atrocities, and among those maimed and murdered, innocent children.

While the world waited, Saddam sought to add to the chemical weapons arsenal he now possesses an infinitely more dangerous weapon of mass destruction, a nuclear weapon. And while the world waited, while the world talked peace and withdrawal, Saddam Hussein dug in and moved massive forces into Kuwait. While the world waited, while Saddam stalled, more damage was being done to the fragile economies of the Third World, the emerging democracies of Eastern Europe, to the entire world, including to our own economy. The United States, together with the United Nations, exhausted every means at our disposal to bring this crisis to a peaceful end. However, Saddam clearly felt that by stalling and threatening and defying the United Nations, he could weaken the forces arrayed against him. While the world waited, Saddam Hussein met every overture of peace with open contempt. While the world prayed for peace, Saddam prepared for war.

I had hoped that when the United States Congress, in historic debate, took its resolute action, Saddam would realize he could not prevail and would move out of Kuwait in accord with the United Nations resolutions. He did not do that. Instead, he remained intransigent, certain that time was on his side. Saddam was warned over and over again to comply with the will of the United Nations, leave Kuwait or be driven out. Saddam has arrogantly rejected all warnings. Instead he tried to make this a dispute between Iraq and the United States of America. Well, he failed.

Tonight 28 nations, countries from five continents — Europe and Asia, Africa and the Arab League — have forces in the gulf area, standing shoulder to shoulder against Saddam Hussein. These countries had hoped the use of force could be avoided. Regrettably, we now believe that only force will make him leave.

Prior to ordering our forces into battle, I instructed our military commanders to take every necessary step to prevail as quickly as possible and with the greatest degree of protection possible for American and allied servicemen and women.

I've told the American people before that this will not be another Vietnam, and I repeat this here tonight. Our troops will have the best possible support in the entire world, and they will not be asked to fight with one hand tied behind their back.

I'm hopeful that this fighting will not go on for long and that casualties will be held to an absolute minimum. This is an historic moment. We have in this past year made great progress in ending the long era of conflict and cold war. We have before us the opportunity to forge for ourselves and for future generations a new world order, a world where the rule of law, not the law of the jungle, governs the conduct of nations.

When we are successful — and we will be — we have a real chance at this new world order, an order in which a credible United Nations can use its peacekeeping role to fulfill the promise envisioned of the U.N.'s founders. We have no argument with the people of Iraq; indeed, for the innocents caught in this conflict, I pray for their safety. Our goal is not the conquest of Iraq; it is the liberation of Kuwait. It is my hope that somehow the Iraqi people can even now convince their dictator that he must lay down his arms, leave Kuwait and let Iraq itself rejoin the family of peace-loving nations.

Thomas Paine wrote many years ago, "These are the times that try men's souls." Those well-known words are so very true today, but even as planes of the multinational forces attack Iraq, I prefer to think of peace, not war. I am convinced not only that we will prevail, but that out of the horror of combat will come the recognition that no nation can stand against a world united, no nation will be permitted to brutally assault its neighbor.

No president can easily commit our sons and daughters to war. They are the nation's finest. Ours is an all-volunteer force, magnificently trained, highly motivated. The troops know why they're there, and listen to what they say, for they've said it better than any president or prime minister ever could. Listen to Hollywood Huddleston, Marine lance corporal. He says: "Let's free these people so we can go home and be free again."

He's right. The terrible crimes and tortures committed by Saddam's henchmen against the innocent people of Kuwait are an affront to mankind and a challenge to the freedom of all.

Listen to one of our great officers out there, Marine Lt. Gen. Walter Boomer. He said: "There are things worth fighting for. A world in which brutality and lawlessness are allowed to go unchecked isn't the kind of world we're going to want to live in."

Listen to Master Sgt. J. P. Kendall of the 82nd Airborne: "We're here for more than just the price of a gallon of gas. What we're doing is going to chart the future of the world for the next 100 years. It's better to deal with this guy now than five years from now."

And finally we should all sit up and listen to Jackie Jones, an Army lieutenant, when she says: "If we let him get away with this, who knows what's going to be next."

I have called upon Hollywood and Walter and J. P. and Jackie and all their courageous comrades in arms to do what must be done. Tonight, America and the world are deeply grateful to them and to their families. And let me say to everyone listening or watching tonight, when the troops we've sent in finish their work, I am determined to bring them home as soon as possible.

Tonight, as our forces fight, they and their families are in our prayers. May God bless each and every one of them, and the coalition forces at our side in the gulf, and may he continue to bless our nation, the United States of America. ■

GULF WAR

Bush Informs Congress: Diplomacy Has Failed

When Congress on Jan. 12 passed a resolution (H J Res 77 — PL 102-1) authorizing the use of force in the Persian Gulf, it included a requirement that President Bush first certify that efforts to resolve the problem without force had been unsuccessful. Following is the text of Bush's letter and his report to Congress complying with the resolution.

January 16, 1991

Dear Mr. Speaker: (Dear Mr. President:)

Pursuant to Section 2(b) of the Authorization for Use of Military Force Against Iraq Resolution (H J Res 77, PL 102-1), I have concluded that:

1. the United States has used all appropriate diplomatic and other peaceful means to obtain compliance by Iraq with U.N. Security Council Resolutions 660, 661, 662, 664, 665, 666, 667, 669, 670, 674, 677 and 678; and

2. that those efforts have not been and would not be successful in obtaining such compliance.

Enclosed is a report that supports my decision.

Sincerely,
GEORGE BUSH

Attachment

Report for Use in Connection with Section 2(b) of the Joint Congressional Resolution Authorizing the Use of Military Force Against Iraq.

The report that follows is a summary of diplomatic and other peaceful means used in an attempt to obtain compliance by Iraq with the 12 U.N. Security Council resolutions relating to its invasion and occupation of Kuwait.

It is not a definitive rendition of these means, because the administration cannot, of necessity, include at this time all the factual data that would support a complete historical record. This report, therefore, should be considered in light of formal and informal information already provided to the Congress and that which will be provided in the future.

1. Background

For over 5½ months, the international community has sought with unprecedented unity to reverse Iraq's brutal and unprovoked aggression against Kuwait. The United States and the vast majority of governments of the world, working together through the United Nations, have been united both in their determination to compel Iraq's withdrawal from Kuwait and in their strong preference for doing so through peaceful means.

Since Aug. 2, we have sought to build maximum diplomatic and economic pressure against Iraq. Regrettably, Iraq has given no sign whatever that it intends to comply with the will of the international community; nor is there any indication that diplomatic and economic means alone would ever compel Iraq to do so. Instead, Iraq has continued to reject the relevant U.N. Security Council resolutions and refuses to recognize them.

From the beginning of the gulf crisis, the United States has consistently pursued four basic objectives: 1) the immediate, complete and unconditional Iraqi withdrawal from Kuwait; 2) the restoration of the legitimate government of Kuwait; 3) the protection of U.S. citizens abroad; and 4) the security and stability of a region vital to U.S. national security. In pursuit of these objectives, we have sought and obtained action by the U.N. Security Council, resulting in 12 separate resolutions that have been fully consistent with U.S. objectives.

The last of these 12 resolutions, U.N. Security Council Resolution 678 of 29 November 1990, authorizes U.N. member states to use "all necessary means" to implement Resolution 660 and all subsequent relevant resolutions of the Security Council, and to restore international peace and security in the area, unless Iraq fully implements those resolutions on or before Jan. 15, 1991.

The nearly seven week "pause of goodwill" established in U.N. Security Council Resolution 678 has now passed. Iraq has taken no steps whatever to fulfill these requirements.

Iraq has forcefully stated that it considers the Security Council's resolutions invalid and has no intention of complying with them at any time.

Iraqi forces remain in occupation of Kuwait and have been substantially reinforced in recent weeks rather than withdrawn. Iraq has strongly and repeatedly reiterated its annexation of Kuwait and stated its determination that Kuwait will remain permanently a part of Iraq.

The Iraqi closure of diplomatic and consular missions in Kuwait has in no way been rescinded.

In short, the Government of Iraq remains completely intransigent in rejecting the U.N. Security Council's demands — despite the exhaustive use by the United States and the United Nations of all appropriate diplomatic, political and economic measures to persuade or compel Iraq to comply.

This has been a truly international effort. More than two dozen other countries have sent their own military forces to the gulf region, including more than 250,000 troops. They have given or pledged substantial funds and other assistance to us for our operations, including over $8 billion in calendar year 1990 alone. They have taken on the responsibility for assisting those nations that have suffered the most from the effects of international sanctions against Iraq and higher energy prices.

As additional costs are incurred during 1991, we will look to our allies to shoulder their fair share of our military expenses and exceptional economic assistance efforts.

2. Diplomatic and Political Actions

The extensive diplomatic and political efforts undertaken by the United States, other countries, regional organizations including the Arab League and the European Community and the United Nations to persuade or compel Iraq to withdraw from Kuwait have not succeeded.

The U.N. Security Council and General Assembly have overwhelmingly and repeatedly condemned the Iraqi invasion and demanded Iraq's immediate and unconditional withdrawal from Kuwait.

The Security Council has invoked its extraordinary authority under Chapter VII of the U.N. Charter, not only to order comprehensive economic sanctions, but to authorize the use of all other means necessary, including the use of force.

The Security Council has directed other U.N. organizations (e.g., the International Atomic Energy Agency) to take appropriate actions toward the same and within their areas of competence, and they have done so where relevant.

The president, the secretary of State and other U.S. officials have engaged in an exhaustive process of consultation with other governments and international organizations. The secretary of State alone has, since Aug. 2 of last year, held more than 250 meetings with foreign heads of state, foreign ministers and other high foreign officials. He has traveled over 125,000 miles in the course of these contacts.

While this extensive diplomacy has been very successful in maintaining international solidarity in support of our objectives, it has not caused the government of Iraq to withdraw from Kuwait.

Most recently, on Jan. 9, the secretary of State met at length in Geneva with the Iraqi foreign minister, who in 6½ hours of talks demonstrated no readiness whatever to implement the U.N. Security Council resolutions. The Iraqi foreign minister even refused to receive a diplomatic communication from the president intended for Saddam Hussein.

On Jan. 13, the U.N. secretary general was rebuffed by Iraq for a second time, in this case in a direct attempt to persuade Saddam Hussein to withdraw from Kuwait peacefully. Many other heads of state, foreign ministers and private persons have made similar attempts. In short, the international community has in an unprecedented way directed the full scope and vigor of its political and diplomatic means to produce an Iraqi withdrawal.

These exhaustive efforts have produced not the slightest indication of any intention by Saddam Hussein to meet the demands of the international community for immediate and unconditional withdrawal from Kuwait.

For our part, the administration made clear that there could be no reward for aggression lest we undermine prospects for an expanded constructive role for the U.N. Security Council and for a new, more peaceful world order. Attempts to link resolution of Iraq's aggression against Kuwait with other issues were rejected on the grounds that these issues were unrelated to Iraq's aggression and that such efforts would only serve to divert attention from the immediate challenge posed by Iraq.

3. Economic Sanctions

Since Aug. 2 (in the case of the United States) and Aug. 9 (in the case of the Security Council and the other U.N. member states), comprehensive economic sanctions have been imposed on Iraq, prohibiting all trade and financial transactions with Iraq, with the exception of goods for a very limited category of essential humanitarian purposes.

These sanctions have since Aug. 25 been backed by an extensive maritime interception effort involving warships of many states, and since Sept. 25 by rigorous controls on air traffic to and from Iraq. The United States and other countries have engaged in tireless efforts during this period to uncover and defeat attempted evasions of these sanctions around the world, whether by direct attempts to pass through the allied interception cordon or by the use of financial and trade intermediaries.

Our efforts have resulted in a very substantial reduction of the volume of trade to and from Iraq and significant shortages in Iraq's financial resources. The most serious impact on Iraq thus far has been on the financial sector, where hard currency shortages have led Baghdad to take a variety of unusual steps to conserve or obtain foreign exchange.

The sanctions have shut off 97 percent of Iraq's exports and more than 90 percent of its imports and have prevented Baghdad from reaping the proceeds of higher oil prices or its seizure of Kuwaiti oil fields. The departure of foreign workers and the cutoff of imported industrial inputs has caused problems for a variety of industries.

Notwithstanding the substantial economic impact of sanctions to date, and even if sanctions were to continue to be enforced for an additional six to 12 months, economic hardship alone is highly unlikely to compel Saddam to retreat from Kuwait or cause regime-threatening popular discontent in Iraq.

Due to a reduction of domestic consumption, cannibalization of Kuwaiti facilities, smuggling and use of existing stockpiles, the most vital Iraqi industries do not appear to be threatened.

The price of foodstuffs for the Iraqi population has sharply increased and rations have been reduced, but there is still access to sufficient staple foods, and new supplies are being injected from the fall harvest and smuggling.

While we might succeed in substantially reducing the overall Iraqi supply of food and other essential consumer commodities, Saddam Hussein has made clear his willingness to divert such supplies to his military forces, even at the cost of severe deprivation of his civilian population.

Even if the international community were prepared to deprive the Iraqi civilian population of food, there is no reason to believe that this would change Saddam Hussein's policies.

The ability of Iraqi armed forces to defend Kuwait and southern Iraq is unlikely to be eroded substantially over the next six to 12 months even if effective sanctions could be maintained. Iraq's infantry and artillery forces probably would not suffer significantly, since Iraq could maintain the relatively simple Soviet-style weaponry of these forces. Low-technology defensive preparations could also be expanded.

Iraq's armored and mechanized forces would be degraded somewhat, but Iraq has large stocks of spare parts and other supplies that would ameliorate this effect.

Iraqi air forces and air defenses would likely be hit far more severely by continued effective sanctions, but in any case, Iraqi air defense and air forces would play a limited role — in relation to the ground forces — with respect to Iraq's ability to hold Kuwait.

In short, while sanctions might degrade to some extent the operational readiness of some portion of the Iraqi armed forces, it is clear that Iraq would still retain very large and powerful land and air forces, as well as substantial capability to replace ammunition and other essential replacement items.

Delay would also have important military consequences that might make any eventual military action more costly and increase U.S and coalition casualties.

Iraq has already exploited its five-month occupation of Kuwait to increase significantly its ability to resist coalition efforts to restore that country's sovereignty and to increase further its already formidable military capability.

Iraq has increased the size of its forces in the Kuwait theater of operations by 450,000 personnel and has increased the overall size of its armed forces by mobilizing many thousands of combat veterans and reservists.

Additional time has already permitted the Iraqis to extend and reinforce their fortifications along the Saudi border; more time would only make these defenses more formidable. Delay also would give the Iraqis more time to further develop, produce and weaponize weapons of mass destruction, thus making any eventual conflict more destructive and strengthening Iraq's ability to coerce other nations with the threat of mass destruction. Delay may also degrade the readiness of coalition forces.

In short, international sanctions have not caused Iraq to comply with the Jan. 15, 1991, deadline in U.N. Security Council Resolution 678 or to retreat from its insistence that its annexation of Kuwait is permanent.

Even if the world community were to maintain the current high level of success in sanctions enforcement, these economic results would not produce such compliance.

Further, the longer the sanctions continue, the more likely it is that leaks in the sanctions enforcement system will develop, that intermediaries will devise ways to circumvent sanctions, and that Iraq will find means of using its own resources to fill critical shortfalls.

Even more important, if the coalition fails now to carry through on the U.N. Security Council's demands for immediate Iraqi withdrawal from Kuwait, there will be strong pressures and temptations on various countries to ease their enforcement of sanctions and to compromise on demands that Iraq meet existing objectives fully and unconditionally.

In summary, diplomatic and economic pressures have not diminished Iraq's intransigence despite 5½ months of unparalleled international effort, and continued reliance upon them alone could risk achieving the basic objective of bringing about Iraq's complete and unconditional withdrawal from Kuwait. ■

STATE OF THE UNION

Bush Seeks To Inspire Support For His Persian Gulf Mission

On Jan. 29, President Bush delivered his second State of the Union address to a joint session of Congress. Following is the Reuter transcript of the speech as delivered:

PRESIDENT BUSH: Mr. President, Mr. Speaker, members of the United States Congress. I come to this House of the people, to speak to you and all Americans, certain that we stand at a defining hour. Halfway around the world, we are engaged in a great struggle in the skies and on the seas and sands. We know why we're there. We are Americans: part of something larger than ourselves.

For two centuries, we've done the hard work of freedom. And tonight we lead the world in facing down a threat to decency and humanity. What is at stake is more than one small country; it is a big idea: a new world order, where diverse nations are drawn together in common cause to achieve the universal aspirations of mankind: peace and security, freedom and the rule of law. Such is a world worthy of our struggle and worthy of our children's future.

The community of nations has resolutely gathered to condemn and repel lawless aggression. [Iraqi President] Saddam Hussein's unprovoked invasion, his ruthless, systematic rape of a peaceful neighbor, violated everything the community of nations holds dear. The world has said this aggression would not stand — and it will not stand.

Together, we have resisted the trap of appeasement, cynicism and isolation that gives temptation to tyrants. The world has answered Saddam's invasion with 12 United Nations resolutions, starting with a demand for Iraq's immediate and unconditional withdrawal — and backed up by forces from 28 countries of six continents. With few exceptions, the world now stands as one.

The end of the Cold War has been a victory for all humanity. A year and a half ago, in Germany, I said that our goal was a Europe whole and free. Tonight, Germany is united. Europe has become whole and free — and America's leadership was instrumental in making it possible.

Our relationship with the Soviet Union is important, not only to us but to the world. That relationship has helped to shape these and other historic changes. But like many other nations, we have been deeply concerned by the violence in the Baltics, and we have communicated that concern to the Soviet leadership.

The principle that has guided us is simple: Our objective is to help the Baltic peoples achieve their aspirations, not to punish the Soviet Union.

In our recent discussions with the Soviet leadership, we have been given representations, which, if fulfilled, would result in the withdrawal of some Soviet forces, a reopening of dialogue with the republics and a move away from violence. We will watch carefully as the situation develops. And we will maintain our contact with the Soviet leadership to encourage continued commitment to democratization and reform.

Victory Over Tyranny

If it is possible, I want to continue to build a lasting basis for U.S.-Soviet cooperation, for a more peaceful future for all mankind. The triumph of democratic ideas in Eastern Europe and Latin America — and the continuing struggle for freedom elsewhere all around the world — all confirm the wisdom of our nation's founders. Tonight, we work to achieve another victory, a victory over tyranny and savage aggression.

We in this union enter the last decade of the 20th century thankful for our blessings, steadfast in our purpose, aware of our difficulties and responsive to our duties at home and around the world.

For two centuries, America has served the world as an inspiring example of freedom and democracy. For generations, America has led the struggle to preserve and extend the blessings of liberty. And today, in a rapidly changing world, American leadership is indispensable. Americans know that leadership brings burdens and sacrifices.

But we also [know] why the hopes of humanity turn to us.

We are Americans: We have a unique responsibility to do the hard work of freedom. And when we do — freedom works.

The conviction and courage we see in the Persian Gulf today is simply the American character in action. The indomitable spirit that is contributing to this victory for world peace and justice is the same spirit that gives us the power and the potential to meet our toughest challenges at home.

We are resolute and resourceful. If we can selflessly confront the evil for the sake of good in a land so far away, then surely we can make this land all that it should be.

If anyone tells you that America's best days are behind her, they're looking the wrong way.

An Appeal for Renewal

Tonight, I come before this House and the American people with an appeal for renewal. This is not merely a call for new government initiatives, it is a call for new initiative in government, in our communities and from every American to prepare for the next American century.

America has always led by example. So who among us will set the example? Which of our citizens will lead us in this American century? Everyone who steps forward today to get one addict off drugs, to convince one troubled teenager not to give up on life, to comfort one AIDS patient, to help one hungry child.

We have within our reach the promise of a renewed America. We can find meaning and reward by serving some higher purpose than ourselves — a shining purpose, the illumination of a thousand points of light. And it is expressed by all who know the irresistible force of a child's hand, of a friend who stands by you and stays there, a volunteer's generous gesture, an idea that is simply right.

The problems before us may be different, but the key to solving them remains the same: It is the individual — the individual — who steps forward. And the state of our union is the union of each of us, one to the other; the sum of our friendships, marriages, families and communities.

We all have something to give. So if you know how to read, find someone who can't. If you've got a hammer, find a nail. If you're not hungry, not lonely, not in trouble — seek out someone who is.

Join the community of conscience. Do the hard work of freedom. And that will define the state of our union.

Since the birth of our nation, "We, the people" has been the source of our strength. What government can do alone is limited, but the potential of the American people knows no limits.

We are a nation of rock-solid realism and clear-eyed idealism. We are Americans: We are the nation that believes in the future; we are the nation that can shape the future.

And we've begun to do just that — by strengthening the power and choice of individuals and families.

Together, these last two years, we've put dollars for child care directly in the hands of parents, instead of bureaucracies. Unshackled the potential of Americans with disabilities. Applied the creativity of the marketplace in the service of the environment, for clean air. And made home ownership possible for more Americans.

The strength of a democracy is not in bureaucracy, it is in the people and their communities. In everything we do, let us unleash the potential of our most precious resource — our citizens, our citizens themselves. We must return to families, communities, counties, cities, states and institutions of every kind the power to chart their own destiny, and the freedom and opportunity provided by strong economic growth. And that's what America is all about.

I know, tonight, in some regions of our country, people are in genuine economic distress. And I hear them.

'My Heart Is Aching'

Earlier this month, Kathy Blackwell of Massachusetts wrote me about what can happen when the economy slows down, saying, "My heart is aching, and I think that you should know: Your people out here are hurting badly."

I understand. And I'm not unrealistic about the future. But there are reasons to be optimistic about our economy.

First, we don't have to fight double-digit inflation. Second, most industries won't have to make big cuts in production, because they don't have big inventories piled up. And, third, our exports are running solid and strong. In fact, American businesses are exporting at a record rate.

So let's put these times in perspective. Together, since 1981, we've created almost 20 million jobs, cut inflation in half and cut interest rates in half.

And, yes, the largest peacetime economic expansion in history has been temporarily interrupted. But our economy is still over twice as large as our closest competitor.

We will get this recession behind us and return to growth soon.

We will get on our way to a new record of expansion and achieve the competitive strength that will carry us into the next American century.

We should focus our efforts today on encouraging economic growth, investing in the future, and giving power and opportunity to the individual.

We must begin with control of federal spending.

And that's why I'm submitting a budget that holds the growth in spending to less than the rate of inflation. And that's why, amid all the sound and fury of last year's budget debate, we put into law new enforceable spending caps so that future spending debates will mean a battle of ideas, not a bidding war.

Though controversial, the budget agreement finally put the government on a pay-as-you-go plan — and cut the growth of debt by nearly $500 billion. And that frees funds for saving and job-creating investment.

Now, let's do more. My budget again includes tax-free family savings accounts; penalty-free withdrawals from IRA's for first-time home buyers; and, to increase jobs and growth, a reduced tax for long-term capital gains.

I know there are differences among us about the impact and the effects of a capital gains incentive. So tonight I am asking the congressional leaders and the Federal Reserve to cooperate with us in a study, led by Chairman Alan Greenspan, to sort out our technical differences so that we can avoid a return to unproductive partisan bickering.

But just as our efforts will bring economic growth now and in the future, they must also be matched by long-term investments for the next American century.

Investment in the Future

And that requires a forward-looking plan of action — and that's exactly what we will be sending to the Congress. We have prepared a detailed series of proposals that include:

A budget that promotes investment in America's future — in children, education, infrastructure, space and high technology.

Legislation to achieve excellence in education — building on the partnership forged with the 50 governors at the Education Summit, enabling parents to choose their children's schools and helping to make America No. 1 in math and science.

A blueprint for a new national highway system, a critical investment in our transportation infrastructure.

A research and development agenda that includes record levels of federal investment and a permanent tax credit to strengthen private R&D and to create jobs.

A comprehensive national energy strategy that calls for energy conservation and efficiency, increased development and greater use of alternative fuels.

A banking reform plan to bring America's financial system into the 21st century so that our banks remain safe and secure and can continue to make job-creating loans for our factories, businesses and home buyers. You know, I do think there has been too much pessimism. Sound banks should be making sound loans, now — and interest rates should be lower, now.

In addition to these proposals, we must recognize that our economic strength depends upon being competitive in world markets. We must continue to expand American exports. A successful Uruguay Round of world trade negotiations will create more real jobs and more real growth — for all nations. You and I know that if the playing field is level, America's workers and farmers can outwork and outproduce anyone, any time, anywhere.

And with a Mexican free trade agreement and our Enterprise for the Americas Initiative, we can help our partners strengthen their economies and move toward a free trade zone throughout this entire hemisphere.

The budget also includes a plan of action right here at home to put more power and opportunity in the hands of the individual. And that means new incentives to create jobs in our inner cities by encouraging investment through enterprise zones. It also means tenant control and ownership of public housing. Freedom and the power to choose should not be the privilege of wealth. They are the birthright of every American.

Civil rights are also crucial to protecting equal opportunity.

Every one of us has a responsibility to speak out against racism, bigotry and hate.

We will continue our vigorous enforcement of existing statutes, and I will once again press the Congress to strengthen the laws against employment discrimination without resorting to the use of unfair preferences.

We're determined to protect another fundamental civil right — freedom from crime and the fear that stalks our cities. The attorney general will soon convene a crime summit of our nation's law enforcement officials. And to help us support them, we need tough crime-control legislation, and we need it now.

And as we fight crime, we will fully implement our national strategy for combating drug abuse. Recent data show we are making progress, but much remains to be done. We will not rest until the day of the dealer is over forever.

Good health care is every American's right and every American's responsibility. And so we are proposing an aggressive program of new prevention initiatives — for infants, for children, for adults and for the elderly — to promote a healthier America and to help keep costs from spiraling.

Eliminating PACs

It's time to give people more choice in government by reviving the ideal of the citizen politician who comes not to stay but to serve. And one of the reasons there is so much support for term limitations is that the American people are increasingly concerned about big-money influence in politics. So we must look beyond the next election to the next generation. And the time has come to put the national interest above the special interest and totally eliminate political action committees [PACs].

And that would truly put more competition in elections and more power in the hands of individuals. And where power cannot be put directly in the hands of the individual, it should be moved closer to the people — away from Washington. The federal government too often treats government programs as if they are of Washington, by Washington and for Washington. Once established, federal programs seem to become immortal. It's time for a more dynamic program life cycle: Some programs should increase, some should decrease, some should be terminated, and some should be consolidated and turned over to the states.

My budget includes a list of programs for potential turnover totaling more than $20 billion. Working with Congress and the governors, I propose we select at least $15 billion in such programs and turn them over to the states in a single consolidated grant, fully funded, for flexible management by the states.

The value of this turnover approach is straightforward. It allows the federal government to reduce overhead. It allows states to manage more flexibly and more efficiently. It moves power and decision-making closer to the people. And it re-enforces a theme of this administration: appreciation and encouragement of the innovative power of "states as laboratories."

This nation was founded by leaders who understood that power belongs in the hands of people. And they planned for the future. And so must we, here and all around the world. As Americans, we know there are times when we must step forward and accept our responsibility to lead the world away from the dark chaos of dictators toward the brighter promise of a better day. Almost 50 years ago we began a long struggle against aggressive totalitarianism. Now we face another defining hour for America and the world.

There is no one more devoted, more committed to the hard work of freedom, than every soldier and sailor, every Marine, airman, and Coast Guardsman, every man and woman now serving in the Persian Gulf.

[Bush interrupted by extended applause.]

What a wonderful fitting tribute to them. Each of them has volunteered, volunteered to provide for this nation's defense — and now they bravely struggle, to earn for America, for the world, and for future generations a just and lasting peace.

Our commitment to them must be the equal of their commitment to their country. They are truly America's finest.

War in the Gulf

The war in the gulf is not a war we wanted. We worked hard to avoid war. For more than five months we, along with the Arab League, the European Community, and the United Nations, tried every diplomatic avenue. U.N. Secretary General Perez de Cuellar; Presidents [Mikhail S.] Gorbachev [of the Soviet Union], [François] Mitterrand [of France], [Turgut] Ozal [of Turkey], [Hosni] Mubarak [of Egypt], and [Chadli] Benjedid [of Algeria]; Kings Fahd [of Saudi Arabia] and Hassan [of Morocco]; Prime Ministers [John] Major [of Britain] and [Giulio] Andreotti [of Italy] — just to name a few — all worked for a solution. But time and again, Saddam Hussein flatly rejected the path of diplomacy and peace. The world well knows how this conflict began and when: It began on Aug. 2nd, when Saddam invaded and sacked a small, defenseless neighbor. And I am certain of how it will end. So that peace can prevail, we will prevail.

Tonight, I am pleased to report that we are on course. Iraq's capacity to sustain war is being destroyed. Our investment, our training, our planning — all are paying off. Time will not be Saddam's salvation. Our purpose in the Persian Gulf remains constant: to drive Iraq out of Kuwait, to restore Kuwait's legitimate government and to ensure the stability and security of this critical region. Let me make clear what I mean by the region's stability and security. We do not seek the destruction of Iraq, its culture or its people. Rather, we seek an Iraq that uses its great resources not to destroy, not to serve the ambitions of a tyrant, but to build a better life for itself and its neighbors. We seek a Persian Gulf where conflict is no longer the rule, where the strong are neither tempted nor able to intimidate the weak.

Most Americans know instinctively why we are in the gulf. They know we had to stop Saddam now, not later. They know that this brutal dictator will do anything, will use any weapon, will commit any outrage, no matter how many innocents must suffer. They know we must make sure that control of the world's oil resources does not fall into his hands, only to finance further aggression. They know that we need to build a new, enduring peace — based not on arms races and confrontation, but on shared principles and the rule of law. And we all realize that our responsibility to be the catalyst for peace in the region does not end with the successful conclusion of this war.

Democracy brings the undeniable value of thoughtful dissent — and we have heard some dissenting voices here at home — some, a handful, reckless; most responsible. But the fact that all voices have the right to speak out is one of the reasons we've been united in purpose and principle for 200 years.

A Strong Defense

Our progress in this great struggle is the result of years of vigilance and a steadfast commitment to a strong defense. Now, with remarkable technological advances like the Patriot missile, we can defend against ballistic missile attacks aimed at innocent civilians.

Looking forward, I have directed that the SDI [strategic defense initiative] program be refocused on providing protection from limited ballistic missile strikes — whatever their source.

Let us pursue an SDI program that can deal with any future threat to the United States, to our forces overseas, and to our friends and allies. The quality of American technology, thanks to the American worker, has enabled us to successfully deal with difficult military conditions and help minimize precious loss of life. We have given our men and women the very best. And they deserve it.

We all have a special place in our hearts for the families of our men and women serving in the gulf. They are represented here tonight by Mrs. Norman Schwarzkopf.

We are all very grateful to Gen. [H. Norman] Schwarzkopf [commander of U.S. troops in the Persian Gulf] and to all those serving with him. And I might also recognize one who came with Mrs. Schwarzkopf, Alma Powell, wife of the distinguished chairman of the Joint Chiefs.

And to the families, let me say our forces in the gulf will not stay there one day longer than is necessary to complete their mission.

The courage and success of the R.A.F. [Royal Air Force] pilots — of the Kuwaiti, Saudi, French, the Canadians, the Italians, the pilots of Qatar and Bahrain — all are proof that for the first time since World War II, the international community is united. The leadership of the United Nations, once only a hoped-for ideal, is now confirming its founders' vision.

And I am heartened that we are not being asked to bear alone the financial burden of this struggle. Last year, our friends and allies provided the bulk of the economic costs of Desert Shield, and now, having received commitments of over $40 billion for the first three months of 1991, I am confident they will do no less as we move through Desert Storm.

The Dictator of Iraq

But the world has to wonder what the dictator of Iraq is thinking. If he thinks that by targeting innocent civilians in Israel and Saudi Arabia, that he will gain advantage, he is dead wrong.

And if he thinks that he will advance his cause through tragic and despicable environmental terrorism — he is dead wrong.

And if he thinks that by abusing the coalition prisoners of war, he will benefit — he is dead wrong.

We will succeed in the gulf. And when we do, the world community will have sent an enduring warning to any dictator or despot, present or future, who contemplates outlaw aggression. The world can therefore seize this opportunity to fulfill the long-held promise of a new world order — where brutality will go unrewarded and aggression will meet collective resistance.

Yes, the United States bears a major share of leadership in this effort. Among the nations of the world, only the United States of America has had both the moral standing and the means to back it up. We are the only nation on this Earth that could assemble the forces of peace. This is the burden of leadership — and the strength that has made America the beacon of freedom in a searching world. This nation has never found glory in war. Our people have never wanted to abandon the blessings of home and work for distant lands and deadly conflict. If we fight in anger, it is only because we have to fight at all. And all of us yearn for a world where we will never have to fight again.

Each of us will measure, within ourselves, the value of this great struggle. Any cost in lives, any cost, is beyond our power to measure. But the cost of closing our eyes to aggression is beyond mankind's power to imagine. This we do know: Our cause is just, our cause is moral, our cause is right.

Let future generations understand the burden and the blessings of freedom. Let them say, we stood where duty required us to stand. Let them know that together, we affirmed America and the world as a community of conscience.

The winds of change are with us now. The forces of freedom are together and united. And we move toward the next century more confident than ever that we have the will at home and abroad to do what must be done — the hard work of freedom.

May God bless the United States of America. Thank you very, very much. ■

PRESIDENTIAL ADDRESS

Bush Calls on Postwar Congress For Reform and Renewal

President Bush was invited by Democratic leaders to speak to a joint session of Congress on March 6 about the allied victory in the Persian Gulf War. Following is the Reuter transcript of that speech:

PRESIDENT BUSH: Five short weeks ago I came to this House to speak to you about the state of the union. We met then in time of war. Tonight, we meet in a world blessed by the promise of peace.

From the moment Operation Desert Storm commenced on January 16th until the time the guns fell silent at midnight one week ago, this nation has watched its sons and daughters with pride, watched over them with prayer.

As commander in chief, I can report to you: Our armed forces fought with honor and valor. And as president, I can report to the nation: Aggression is defeated; the war is over.

This is a victory for every country in the coalition, for the United Nations. A victory for unprecedented international cooperation and diplomacy, so well led by our Secretary of State James A. Baker III. It is a victory for the rule of law and for what is right.

Desert Storm's success belongs to the team that so ably leads our armed forces, our secretary of Defense and our chairman of the Joint Chiefs: Dick Cheney and Gen. Colin L. Powell Jr..

And while you're standing — this military victory also belongs to the one the British call the "Man of the Match," the tower of calm at the eye of Desert Storm, Gen. H. Norman Schwarzkopf.

And let us, recognizing this was a coalition effort, let us not forget Saudi Gen. Khalid, or Britain's Gen. de la Billiere, or Gen. Roquejoffre of France, and all the others whose leadership played such a vital role. And, most importantly, most importantly of all, those who served in the field.

I thank the members of this Congress: Support here for our troops in battle was overwhelming. And above all, I thank those whose unfailing love and support sustained our courageous men and women: I thank the American people.

Tonight, I come to this House to speak about the world, the world after war.

The recent challenge could not have been clearer. Saddam Hussein was the villain, Kuwait the victim. To the aid of this small country came nations from North America and Europe, from Asia, South America, from Africa and the Arab world — all united against aggression.

Our uncommon coalition must now work in common purpose to forge a future that should never again be held hostage to the darker side of human nature.

Tonight in Iraq, Saddam walks amidst ruin. His war machine is crushed. His ability to threaten mass destruction is itself destroyed. His people have been lied to, denied the truth. And when his defeated legions come home, all Iraqis will see and feel the havoc he has wrought. And this I promise you: For all that Saddam has done to his own people, to the Kuwaitis and to the entire world, Saddam and those around him are accountable.

All of us grieve for the victims of war, for the people of Kuwait and the suffering that scars the soul of that proud nation. We grieve for all our fallen soldiers and their families, for all the innocents caught up in this conflict. And, yes, we grieve for the people of Iraq, a people who have never been our enemy. My hope is that one day we will once again welcome them as friends into the community of nations.

Our commitment to peace in the Middle East does not end with the liberation of Kuwait. So tonight let me outline four key challenges to be met:

First, we must work together to create shared security arrangements in the region. Our friends and allies in the Middle East recognize that they will bear the bulk of the responsibility for regional security. But we want them to know that just as we stood with them to repel aggression, so now America stands ready to work with them to secure the peace.

This does not mean stationing U.S. ground forces on the Arabian peninsula, but it does mean American participation in joint exercises involving both air and ground forces. It means maintaining a capable U.S. naval presence in the region, just as we have for over 40 years. Let it be clear: Our vital national interests depend on a stable and secure gulf.

Second, we must act to control the proliferation of weapons of mass destruction and the missiles used to deliver them. It would be tragic if the nations of the Middle East and Persian Gulf were now, in the wake of war, to embark on a new arms race. Iraq requires special vigilance. Until Iraq convinces the world of its peaceful intentions, that its leaders will not use new revenues to rearm and rebuild its menacing war machine, Iraq must not have access to the instruments of war.

And, third, we must work to create new opportunities for peace and stability in the Middle East. On the night I announced Operation Desert Storm, I expressed my hope that out of the horrors of war might come new momentum for peace. We have learned in the modern age [that] geography cannot guarantee security, and security does not come from military power alone.

All of us know the depth of bitterness that has made the dispute between Israel and its neighbors so painful and intractable. Yet in the conflict just concluded, Israel and many of the Arab states have for the first time found themselves confronting the same aggressor. By now it should be plain to all parties that peacemaking in the Middle East requires compromise. At the same time, peace brings real benefits to everyone. We must do all that we can to close the gap between Israel and the Arab states, and between Israelis and Palestinians. The tactics of terror lead absolutely nowhere. There can be no substitute for diplomacy.

A comprehensive peace must be grounded in United Nations Security Council Resolutions 242 and 338 and the principle of territory for peace. This principle must be elaborated to provide for Israel's security and recognition, and at the same time for legitimate Palestinian political rights. Anything else would fail the twin tests of fairness and security. The time has come to put an end to Arab-Israeli conflict.

The war with Iraq is over. The quest for solutions to the problems in Lebanon, in the Arab-Israeli dispute and in the gulf must go forward with new vigor and determination. And I guarantee you: No one will work harder for a stable peace in the region than we will.

Fourth, we must foster economic development for the sake of peace and progress. The Persian Gulf and Middle East form a region rich in natural resources, with a wealth of untapped human potential. Resources once squandered on military might must be redirected to more peaceful ends. We are already addressing the immediate economic consequences of Iraq's aggression. Now, the challenge is to reach higher, to foster economic freedom and prosperity for all people of the region.

By meeting these four challenges, we can build a framework for peace. I have asked Secretary of State Baker to go to the Middle East to begin the process. He will go to listen, to probe, to offer suggestions, to advance the search for peace and stability. I have also asked him to raise the plight of the hostages held in Lebanon. We have not forgotten them, and we will not forget them.

To all the challenges that confront this region of the world, there is no single solution, no solely American answer. But we can make a difference. America will work tirelessly as a catalyst for positive change.

But we cannot lead a new world abroad if, at home, it's politics as usual on American defense and diplomacy. It's time to turn away from the temptation to protect unneeded weapons systems and obsolete bases.

It's time to put an end to micro-management of foreign- and security-assistance programs, micro-management that humiliates our friends and allies, and hamstrings our diplomacy.

It's time to rise above the parochial and the pork barrel to do what is necessary, what's right and what will enable this nation to play the leadership role required of us.

The consequences of the conflict in the gulf reach far beyond the confines of the Middle East. Twice before in this century, an entire world was convulsed by war. Twice this century, out of the horrors of war, hope emerged for enduring peace. Twice before, those hopes proved to be a distant dream, beyond the grasp of man.

Until now, the world we've known has been a world divided, a world of barbed wire and concrete block, conflict and Cold War.

Now, we can see a new world coming into view. A world in which there is the very real prospect of a new world order. In the words of Winston Churchill: "a world order in which the principles of justice and fair play protect the weak against the strong." A world where the United Nations, freed from Cold War stalemate, is poised to fulfill the historic vision of its founders. A world in which freedom and respect for human rights find a home among all nations.

The gulf war put this new world to its first test. And, my fellow Americans, we passed that test.

For the sake of our principles, for the sake of the Kuwaiti people, we stood our ground. Because the world would not look the other way, Ambassador Al-Sabah, tonight Kuwait is free.

Tonight, as our troops begin to come home, let us recognize that the hard work of freedom still calls us forward. We've learned the hard lessons of history. The victory over Iraq was not waged as a war to end all wars. Even the new world order cannot guarantee an era of perpetual peace. But enduring peace must be our mission.

Our success in the gulf will shape not only the new world order we seek but our mission here at home.

In the war just ended, there were clear-cut objectives, timetables and, above all, an overriding imperative to achieve results. We must bring that same sense of self-discipline, that same sense of urgency, to the way we meet challenges here at home.

In my State of the Union address and in my budget, I defined a comprehensive agenda to prepare for the next American century.

Our first priority is to get this economy rolling again. The fear and uncertainty caused by the gulf crisis were understandable. But now that the war is over, oil prices are down, interest rates are down, and confidence is rightly coming back. Americans can move forward to lend, spend, and invest in this, the strongest economy on earth.

We must also enact the legislation that is key to building a better America. For example, in 1990, we enacted an historic Clean Air Act. And now we've proposed a national energy strategy. We passed a child-care bill that put power in the hands of parents. And today we're ready to do the same thing with our schools, and expand choice in education. We passed a crime bill that made a useful start in fighting crime and drugs. This year we're sending to Congress our comprehensive crime package to finish the job. We passed the landmark Americans with Disabilities Act. And now we've sent forward our civil rights bill. We also passed the aviation bill. This year we've sent up our new highway bill.

And these are just a few of our pending proposals for reform and renewal.

So tonight I call on Congress to move forward aggressively on our domestic front. Let's begin with two initiatives we should be able to agree on quickly: transportation and crime. And then let's build on success with those and enact the rest of our agenda. If our forces could win the ground war in 100 hours, then surely the Congress can pass this legislation in 100 days.

Let that be a promise we make tonight to the American people.

When I spoke in this House about the state of our union, I asked all of you: If we can selflessly confront evil for the sake of good in a land so far away, then surely we can make this land all that it should be. In the time since then, the brave men and women of Desert Storm accomplished more than even they may realize. They set out to confront an enemy abroad and in the process, they transformed a nation at home.

Think of the way they went about their mission: with confidence and quiet pride. Think about their sense of duty, about all they taught us about our values, about ourselves.

We hear so often about our young people in turmoil, how our children fall short, how our schools fail us, how American products and American workers are second-class. Well, don't you believe it. The America we saw in Desert Storm was first-class talent.

And they did it using America's state-of-the-art technology. We saw the excellence embodied in the Patriot missile and the patriots who made it work.

And we saw soldiers who know about honor and bravery and duty and country and the world-shaking power of these simple words.

There is something noble and majestic about the pride, about the patriotism, that we feel tonight.

So to everyone here and everyone watching at home, think about the men and women of Desert Storm. Let us honor them with our gratitude. Let us comfort the families of the fallen and remember each precious life lost.

Let us learn from them as well. Let us honor those who have served us by serving others.

Let us honor them as individuals — men and women of every race, all creeds and colors — by setting the face of this nation against discrimination, bigotry and hate. Eliminate them.

I'm sure many of you saw on television the unforgettable scene of four terrified Iraqi soldiers surrendering. They emerged from their bunker broken, tears streaming from their eyes, fearing the worst. And then there was an American soldier. Remember what he said? He said: "It's okay, you're all right now, you're all right now."

That scene says a lot about America, a lot about who we are. Americans are a caring people. We are a good people, a generous people. Let us always be caring and good and generous in all we do.

Soon, very soon, our troops will begin the march we've all been waiting for: their march home. And I have directed Secretary Cheney to begin the immediate return of American combat units from the gulf.

Less than two hours from now, the first plane-load of American soldiers will lift off from Saudi Arabia headed for the U.S.A.

That plane will carry men and women of the 24th Mechanized Infantry Division bound for Ft. Stewart, Ga. This is just the beginning of a steady flow of American troops coming home.

Let their return remind us that all those who have gone before are linked with us in the long line of freedom's march.

Americans have always tried to serve, to sacrifice nobly for what we believe to be right.

Tonight, I ask every community in this country to make this coming Fourth of July a day of special celebration for our returning troops. They may have missed Thanksgiving and Christmas, but I can tell you this: For them and for their families, we can make this a holiday they'll never forget.

In a very real sense, this victory belongs to them: to the privates and the pilots, to the sergeants and the supply officers, to the men and women in the machines, and the men and women who made them work. It belongs to the regulars, to the reserves, to the National Guard. This victory belongs to the finest fighting force this nation has ever known in its history.

We went halfway around the world to do what is moral and just and right. We fought hard, and, with others, we won the war. We lifted the yoke of aggression and tyranny from a small country that many Americans had never even heard of, and we ask nothing in return.

We're coming home now — proud, confident, heads high. There is much we must do at home and abroad. And we will do it. We are Americans.

May God bless this great nation, the United States of America. Thank you all very, very much. ■

PRESIDENTIAL ADDRESS

Bush Unveils Education Plan In Speech at White House

President Bush released his education proposals April 18 in a speech at the White House. Following are excerpts from the Reuter transcript of his remarks *(Story, p. 983):*

PRESIDENT BUSH: . . . Across this country people have started to transform the American school. They know that the time for talk is over; their slogan is: Don't dither, just do it. And let's push the reform effort forward, use each experiment, each advance, to build for the next American century: new schools for a new world.

As a first step in this strategy, we must challenge not only the methods and the means that we've used in the past but also the yardsticks that we've used to measure our progress. Let's stop trying to measure progress in terms of money spent. We spend 33 percent more per pupil in 1991 than we did in 1981. Thirty-three percent more in real, constant dollars. And I don't think there's a person anywhere who would say, anywhere in the country, who would say that we've seen a 33 percent improvement in our schools' performance. And dollar bills don't educate students; education depends on committed communities determined to be places where learning will flourish; committed teachers, free from the non-educational burdens; committed parents, determined to support excellence; committed students, excited about school and learning. To those who want to see real improvement in American education, I say there will be no renaissance without revolution. We who would be revolutionaries must accept responsibilities for our schools.

Until now, we've treated education like a manufacturing process, assuming that if the gauges seemed right, if we had good pay scales, the right pupil-teacher ratios, good students would just pop out of our schools.

It's time to turn things around, to focus on students, to set standards for our schools, and let teachers and principals figure out how best to meet them.

We've made a good beginning by setting the nation's sights on six ambitious national education goals and setting for our target the year 2000. Our goals have been forged in partnership with the nation's governors. . . . And those who have taken the leadership are well known to everyone in this room.

And for those who need a refresher course — there may be a quiz later on — let me list those goals right now. By 2000 we've got to, first, ensure that every child starts school ready to learn. The second one: raise the high school graduation rate to 90 percent. The third one: ensure that each student leaving the fourth, eighth and 12th grades can demonstrate competence in core subjects.

Four: make our students first in the world in math and science achievement. Fifth: ensure that every American adult is literate and has the skills necessary to compete in a global economy and exercise the rights and responsibilities of citizenship. And six: liberate every American school from drugs and violence.

Ambitious Strategy

Our strategy to meet these noble national goals is founded in common sense and common values. It's ambitious, and yet with hard work, it's within our reach. And I can outline our strategy in one paragraph, and here it is:

For today's students, we must make existing schools better and more accountable. For tomorrow's students, the next generation, we must create a new generation of American schools. For all of us — for the adults who think our school days are over — we've got to become a nation of students, recognize that learning is a lifelong process. And finally, outside our schools, we must cultivate communities where learning can happen. That's our strategy.

People who want Washington to solve our educational problems are missing the point. We can lend appropriate help through such programs as Head Start, but what happens here in Washington won't matter half as much as what happens in each school, each local community and, yes, in each home.

Still, the federal government will serve as a catalyst for change in several important ways. Working closely with the governors, we will define new world-class standards for schools, teachers, and students in the five core subjects: math and science, English, history and geography.

We will develop voluntary — let me repeat it — we will develop voluntary national tests for fourth, eighth and 12th graders in the five core subjects. These achievement tests will tell parents and educators, politicians and employers just how well our schools are doing. I am determined to have the first of these tests for our fourth graders in place by the time that school starts in September of 1993. And for high school seniors, let's add another incentive, a distinction sure to attract the attention of colleges and companies in every community across the country: a presidential citation to students who excel on the 12th grade test.

We can encourage educational excellence by encouraging parental choice. The concept of choice draws its fundamental strength from the principle at the very heart of the democratic idea. Every adult American has a right to vote, right to decide where to work, where to live; it's time parents were free to choose the schools that their children attend. This approach will create the competitive climate that stimulates excellence in our private and parochial schools as well.

But the centerpiece of our national education strategy is not a program, is not a test, it's a new challenge to reinvent, to reinvent American education, to design new American schools for the year 2000 and beyond. And the idea is simple but powerful: Put America's special genius for invention to work for America's schools. I will challenge communities to become what we will call America 2000 communities. Governors will honor communities with this designation if the communities embrace the national education goals; create local strategies for reaching these goals; devise report cards for measuring progress; and agree to encourage and support one of the new generation of America's schools.

We must also foster educational innovation. I'm delighted to announce today that America's business leaders, under the chairmanship of Paul O'Neil, will create the new American Schools Development Corporation, a private sector research and development fund of at least $150 million to generate innovation in education. This fund offers an open-end challenge to the dreamers and the doers eager to reinvent, eager to reinvigorate our schools.

With the results of this R&D in hand, I will urge Congress to provide $1 million in start-up funds for each of the 535 new American schools. At least one in every congressional district and to have them up and running by 1996. The new American schools must be more than rooms full of children seated at computers. If we mean to prepare our children for life, classrooms also must cultivate values and good character. Give real meaning to right and wrong.

We ask only two things of these architects of our new American schools: That their students meet the new national standards for the five course subjects and that, outside of the costs of the initial research and development, the schools operate on a budget comparable to conventional schools.

The architects of the new American schools should break the mold, build for the next century, reinvent, literally start from scratch and reinvent the American school. No question should be offlimits, no answers automatically assumed. We're not after one single solution for every school; we're interested in finding every way to make schools better. . . . Our challenge amounts to nothing less than a revolution in American education — a battle for our future. . . . ■

TRADE

Bush Defends Fast Track In Letter to Members

Following is the text of a letter sent by President Bush on May 1 to House Majority Leader Richard A. Gephardt, D-Mo.; House Ways and Means Chairman Dan Rostenkowski, D-Ill.; and Senate Finance Chairman Lloyd Bentsen, D-Texas, urging an extension of fast-track procedures, which prevent Congress from amending trade agreements submitted for approval. A similar letter was sent to all members of Congress. (Story, p. 1120)

Through the better part of this century, successive Congresses and administrations — Republican and Democratic — have worked to open markets and expand American exports. This partnership has resulted in unparalleled growth in world trade and huge economic benefits for the United States. Opening foreign markets means economic growth and jobs for all Americans.

Historically, the fast-track procedures established by the Congress have served us well. On March 1, I requested an extension of fast track so that we could continue to realize increased economic growth and the other benefits of expanded trade. The fast track in no way limits the ability of Congress to review any agreement negotiated, including the Uruguay Round or a North American Free Trade Agreement (NAFTA). If Congress is not satisfied, it retains the unqualified right to reject whatever is negotiated. But refusing to extend the fast track would end negotiations before they have even begun and relinquish a critical opportunity for future economic growth.

Initiatives to open markets will enhance the global competitiveness of the United States and create new opportunities for American workers, American exports and American economic growth. The Uruguay Round offers a vital opportunity to eliminate barriers to our goods, investments, services and ideas. A NAFTA offers a historic opportunity to bring together the energies and talents of three great nations, already bound by strong ties of family, business and culture. [Canadian] Prime Minister [Brian] Mulroney and [Mexican] President [Carlos] Salinas [de Gortari] are both leaders of great vision. They believe, as do I, that a NAFTA would enhance the well-being of our peoples. They are ready to move forward with us in this unprecedented enterprise.

In seeking to expand our economic growth, I am committed to achieving a balance that recognizes the need to preserve the environment, protect worker safety and facilitate adjustment. In your letter of March 7, you conveyed a number of important congressional concerns about free trade with Mexico. At my direction, [U.S. Trade Representative] [Carla A.] Hills and my Economic Policy Council have undertaken an intensive review of our NAFTA objectives and strategy to ensure thorough consideration of the economic, labor and environmental issues raised by you and your colleagues. The administration's response is presented in the attached report. Let me emphasize the following:

First, you have my personal commitment to close bipartisan cooperation in the negotiations and beyond. And you have my personal assurance that we will take the time necessary to conclude agreements in which both the Congress and the administration can take pride.

Second, while economic studies show that a free-trade agreement would create jobs and promote growth in the United States, I know there is concern about adjustment in some sectors. These concerns will be addressed through provisions in the NAFTA designed to ease the transition for import-sensitive industries.

In addition, my administration is committed to working with the Congress to ensure that there is adequate assistance and effective retraining for dislocated workers.

Third, based on my discussions with President Salinas, I am convinced that he is firmly committed to strengthened environmental protection, and that there is strong support for this objective among the Mexican people. Because economic growth can and should be supported by enhanced environmental protection, we will develop and implement an expanded program of environmental cooperation in parallel with the free-trade talks.

Fourth, President Salinas has also made it clear to me that his objective in pursuing free trade is to better the lives of Mexican working people. Mexico has strong laws regulating labor standards and worker rights. Beyond what Mexico is already doing, we will work through new initiatives to expand U.S.-Mexico labor cooperation.

Thus, our efforts toward economic integration will be complemented by expanded programs of cooperation on labor and the environment. The catalyst for these efforts is the promise of economic growth that a NAFTA can provide, and the key to these efforts is the extension of unencumbered fast-track procedures.

There are great challenges ahead. The world is changing dramatically as nations move toward democracy and free markets. The United States must continue to open new markets and lead in technological innovation, confident that America can and will prevail in this new and emerging world. By working together, we can negotiate good trade agreements that assure a strong and healthy America as we prepare to meet the challenges of the next century.

Sincerely,
George Bush ■

TRADE

President Addresses Mexico Concerns

On May 1, President Bush spoke to the Society of American Business Editors and Writers. The following excerpts from the Reuter transcript include remarks on the status of trade talks with Mexico.

While economic studies show that a free-trade agreement would produce jobs in the United States, as well as greater exports and output, I know that there's a concern, not just on Capitol Hill, but in many of the labor halls around this country, about job loss. And our negotiators will address these concerns in provisions of the North American Free Trade Agreement.

We will ensure an adequate transition period for workers in import-sensitive industries. We will work with Congress to see that dislocated workers receive proper assistance and retraining. I believe we have the answers to the questions that are being raised by the labor unions and by some on Capitol Hill. At the same time, it is worth noting that the agreement will create high-wage, high-skill manufacturing jobs in the machinery, computer, telecommunications and electronic industries.

As Mexico develops further, it will need even more of these high-tech goods and services. Those goods and services are more likely to come from the United States than from anyone else in the world.

And, secondly, President [Carlos] Salinas [de Gortari] and the Mexican people have no interest in allowing their country to become a pollution haven for U.S. companies, because economic growth goes hand in hand with environmental protection. We will expand environmental cooperation programs parallel to the free-trade talks....

And finally, President Salinas has also made it clear that this agreement will improve opportunities for Mexican working people. Mexico has strong laws regulating labor standards and workers' rights. Beyond those, we will also begin new initiatives to expand labor cooperation between our two countries. None of these things can happen though, none of this can happen if we cannot bargain in good faith.... ■

PRESIDENTIAL ADDRESS

Bush Says China MFN Status Will Be Catalyst for Change

During a commencement address at Yale University on May 27, President Bush announced that he was extending most-favored-nation (MFN) trade status to the People's Republic of China. Following are excerpts of the Reuter transcript of his remarks:

... Today, this dynamic region [East Asia] plays an important role in the world economy. And as it has grown more prosperous, it has also grown more free, driven forward by the engine of economic growth and trade, especially with the United States. South Korea and Taiwan have shed their once-authoritarian rule in favor of democracy and freer trade.

This same approach guides our policy toward the People's Republic of China, home to fully one-fifth of the world's people. China can — easily can — affect the stability of the Asian Pacific region and therefore affect the entire world's peace and prosperity. The Chinese play a central role in working to resolve the conflict in Cambodia, to relax tensions on the Korean peninsula.

China has a voice now in the multinational organizations, and its votes in the United Nations Security Council against Iraq's brutal aggression helped us forge the broad coalition that brought us victory in the gulf.

And so when we find opportunities to cooperate with China, we will explore them. When problems arise with China's behavior, we will take appropriate action.

After the tragedy of Tiananmen [Square], the United States was the first nation to condemn the use of violence against the peacefully demonstrating people of Beijing. We were the first to guarantee the rights of Chinese students studying on campuses across the country, including here at Yale.

The United States was the first nation to impose sanctions, and we are now the last — alone among the Western democracies — to keep those original sanctions in place. At every high-level meeting with the Chinese government, U.S. officials reiterate our position on human rights violations.

Unfair trade is also high on our agenda. Just last month we cited China under the trade rules of the Special 301 for pirating U.S. copyrights and patents. And for the sake of national security, we will ban technology and equipment to any Chinese company found to violate rules outlawing transfer of missile technology.

We will continue to advance — to advance our interests and ideals for free and fair trade, for broader democratization, for respect, for human rights throughout China. And let me be clear — as a member of the United Nations, China is bound by the U.N. Declaration of Human Rights. We will hold China to the obligations that it has freely accepted.

And, finally, we continue urging China to exercise restraint in its weapons exports. Our recent experience with Iraq proves how dangerous the deadly trade can be, and very soon, I will announce significant new steps that we can take to control arms exports to the entire Middle East.

"We will continue to advance our interests and ideals for free and fair trade, for broader democratization, for respect, for human rights throughout China."

—President Bush

Every nation must play a part in this effort, and that's why we urge the Chinese government to abide by the letter and spirit of international agreements on missile technology controls and to do what 141 other nations have already done — sign the nuclear nonproliferation treaty.

And this is one way that the United States can be a catalyst for positive change.

This week I will employ another, by proposing formally that MFN trade status continue for China. This policy has generated considerable controversy. Some critics have said revoke MFN or endanger it with sweeping conditions — to censor China, cut our ties and isolate them. We are told this is a principled policy, a moral thing to do. This advice is not new, it's not wise, it is not in the best interest of our country, the United States, and in the end, in spite of noble and best intentions, it is not moral.

First, MFN is special. It's not a favor. It is the ordinary basis of trade worldwide. Second, MFN is a means to bring the influence of the outside world to bear on China. Critics who attack MFN today act as if the point is to punish China — as if hurting China's economy will somehow help the cause of privatization and human rights.

The real point is to pursue a policy that has the best chance of changing Chinese behavior. And if we withdrew MFN or imposed conditions that would make trade impossible, we would punish South China, in particular Guandong Province, the very region where free-market reforms and the challenge to central authority are the strongest.

Right now, there's an estimated 2 million Chinese who are working and proving that privatization can work all in South China. Withdraw MFN and their jobs would be in jeopardy. In addition, endangering MFN would deal a body blow to Hong Kong, the bastion of freedom and free trade in the Far East.

But the most compelling reason to renew MFN and remain engaged in China is not economic; it's not strategic but moral. It is right to export the ideals of freedom and democracy to China. It is right to encourage Chinese students to come to the United States and for talented American students to go to China. It is wrong to isolate China if we hope to influence China.

For two decades after the communists seized power in 1949, the Western world followed a policy of isolation toward China. This period proved to be among the most brutal episodes in Chinese history, a nightmare of anguish, death and suffering that will scar the soul of China for decades to come.

So it comes down to the strength of our belief in the power of the democratic idea. If we pursue a policy that cultivates contacts with the Chinese people, promotes commerce to our benefit, we can help create a climate for democratic change. No nation on earth has discovered a way to import the world's goods and services while stopping foreign ideas at the border. Just as the democratic idea has transformed nations on every continent, so, too, change will inevitably come to China.

This nation's foreign policy has always been more than simply an expression of American interests. It's an extension of American ideals. This moral dimension of American policy requires us to remain active, engaged in the world. Many times that means trying to chart a moral course through a world of lesser evils. And that's the real world; not black and white, very few moral absolutes, enormous potential for error and embarrassment, but all are part of the risks that we willingly take to advance the American ideal.

Many times in the past 40 years, people

have encouraged us to adopt a policy of righteous isolationism, but we remained engaged. We cannot advance principles if we curl up into a defensive ball. We cannot transform a world if we hide from its unpleasant realities. We can advance our cherished ideals only by extending our hand, showing our best side, sticking patiently to our values, even if we risk rejection.

Look at the way American encouragement and the American example, the power of the American example, is paying off in Taiwan and Korea. We will have no leverage; we will not be able to advance our cause or resist repression if we pull back and declare that China is simply too impure a place for us. We want to promote positive change in the world through the force of our example, not simply profess our purity. We want to advance the cause of freedom, not just snub nations that aren't yet wholly free. . . .

* * *

Soon after Bush's comments, Senate Majority Leader George J. Mitchell, D-Maine, said the president's comments were "without any moral or logical basis" and added that "Congress will do all it can to reverse this most unwise Bush policy." Congress can block MFN status for China if a majority of both chambers votes to do so, but it would take a two-thirds majority to overcome a veto.

During a meeting with reporters May 28 in Kennebunkport, Maine, Bush was asked about reaction to his announcement. Following are excerpts from the Reuter transcript of his remarks:

Q: Have you set any conditions on MFN?

BUSH: We're not talking conditions. I want it done the way I talked about and that's the way it should be done; it's only right that it be done that way. I recognize I've got a hard sell from some congressmen who did not listen to what I said before they were ready with their rebuttals. But that's all right. I can understand that. I can understand their anxiety about human rights.

All I want them to do is understand mine and then understand that the way to move forward is to, is to continue contacts and to continue supporting those elements in the Chinese society that are already changing and have changed. And I referred to Gwandong Province in South China yesterday.

So I — and I also noted — this I should have said in my speech — that one of the, one of the mothers of one of the leading dissidents came to this country and was quoted in the newspapers as saying things were improving there, and she was permitted to come here, and she was out front. Now, yesterday, I noticed they quoted — I forget — I believe it was on television, it might have been in the papers — one of the Yale students saying I didn't understand. But they might well have quoted the guy that walked across the platform, stopped, went out of his way — that wasn't easy to do — and said thank you for what you're doing for the students.

So there's difference of opinion. We found that many of the student groups before supported our position on MFN. And so we've got a selling job, though, because I don't think I've made that point clearly enough yet. But just as we started uphill on M — on fair trade, free-trade agreement — we're starting perhaps a little behind on this, but I think I can explain it. I understand it. I'm strongly for it, and I know what I'm suggesting is in the best interest of the United States — not just China — in the best interest of our country. So I've got to — I've got to get out and make that as clear as I possibly can.

Q: Sen. Mitchell sounded like he's going to give you a pretty good fight.

P: Well, he's already indicated that, but I'd like to talk to George, and I'd like to reason with him. I'd like him to understand exactly what will happen to Hong Kong, for example. I know that a lot of the leaders in other countries will be weighing in, just as they did on the free-trade agreement. The British, particularly, are concerned, and I've already talked to the prime minister about that. If we cut off MFN, what happens to Hong Kong? I talked to [Canadian Prime Minister] Brian Mulroney. And I, I hate to quote these leaders without asking their permission. But in this case I have no qualms saying that Mulroney will come back and say extension of MFN is in the interests of the free world as well as in China's interest. So I think when I sit down with Mitchell — I understand his position and I understand the politics of all of this also — but for me this transcends politics. Hey, the easy cop-out, the easy election-year politics would be to go the other way.

But that's not good foreign policy.

Q: Well, is Mitchell making a political issue out of this?

P: Well, listen carefully. My view is I want to reason with him and see that he doesn't.

Q: Can you reason with him?

P: Oh, yes. Yes, I have a good relationship with him.

Q: But you're not ruling out —

P: He's the leader of the Democratic Party, pretty much — [Democratic National Party Chairman] Ron Brown maybe — but Mitchell, Jesse Jackson, a handful of others. But he's got to stand up there and say what he thinks and rally his troops. But I want to get him to rally around what's good for the United States in this instance and leave the politics aside. I think the good politics are probably on the other side of this issue. But I know I'm right on it, and therefore I'm going to fight for it, as I did and as we did — I shouldn't put this personally — on the fast track.

We started — and all of you know this — with some big uphill odds on it, and we came through because [U.S. Trade Representative Carla A.] Hills and others, [Secretary of Commerce Robert A.] Mosbacher and so many others, were very persuasive, and we'll have the same approach to this question. But I have no argument with George Mitchell to start with; I mean, he takes a position the minute I finish speaking — but that's politics. Now we sit down and talk about the issue, and if I can convince him, fine. And it's not just Mitchell; we got people in our own party that are out there jumping around you still. So I'm not aiming the partisan shot at him. I just happened to hear what he had to say. . . .

Q: Are the Democrats desperate for an issue?

P: Well, I don't know — you'd have to ask them.

Q: Do you think it might be necessary in the end to accept some sort of conditions in order to save MFN at all, and are you willing to —

P: I'm not thinking about that; I'm thinking about winning it on the merits — what's best for the foreign policy of the United States, and what's best for the foreign policies of the Western countries — and what's best for China. And I think the answer is to continue MFN as is. So I'm not into the concession business or sitting down and trading at this juncture. And I know we start off a little behind here, but — I may have jumped the gun on getting it out a week or so ago. I did it because I feel so certain that what I'm proposing is good foreign policy, and I think we've got a good record, our administration, on foreign policy. And so we will, you know, go down that path.

Q: [On the Soviet Union,] what about this business of possibly a Western aid package in exchange for economic reforms in Moscow?

P: Well, again, we have made clear that we want these reforms to continue. But when you're dealing with equality and respect with sovereign nations, you don't try to dictate terms. You don't always put it in "You do this or else you won't get that, you do this and we'll give you that." Clearly it's a two-way street and we want to see things done. But you've got to deal with respect with these people. When you have differences, make clear what they are. But the way you phrased that question, I'm not sure is the way I would approach this. But they know that we want to see reforms continue, and they know, if we're convinced of that, that good things will happen. But I stop short of, you know, "You do 3B, AB and C, and we'll do D, E and F."

Q: Are you going to give them the [agricultural credits?]

P: Well, that's one of the matters that we'll be discussing . . . . The Soviets make the point — and I think with some justification — that they have never failed to pay on ag credits, never failed to pay back. And I think they look at me now and say what's the president doing? We have never failed on this. And I'm —

Q: Sounds like you're going to give it to them.

P: Well, and I'm looking at it in terms of overall reforms and wanting to see the credits, if granted, be help, not just alleviate hunger but be used perhaps to help in their whole agricultural system. And that's why we sent the team over there. And before I get into that, I want to sit down and talk to our returning specialists, who are good and who were well-received there. ■

PRESIDENTIAL ADDRESS

Bush Talks of Government Role, Criticizes Congress' Inaction

Members do not pass transportation, crime bills by 100-day mark set by president

In an address on the White House lawn June 12, President Bush spoke to about 1,000 guests, including leaders of businesses and veterans groups, education associations and volunteer organizations, about his frustration with Congress and his philosophy of the role of government. Following are excerpts of the Reuter transcript of his remarks:

Ninety-eight days ago I asked the Congress to tackle the urgent problems on the home front with that same energy that we dedicated to tackling the crisis on the battle front. And I spelled out my domestic priorities, setting out, I'll admit, an ambitious agenda founded upon enhancing economic growth, investing in our future and increasing opportunity for all Americans. And I sent to the Congress literally hundreds of recommendations for legislative change. And then I specifically asked that Congress pass just two laws in a hundred days — a comprehensive anticrime bill and a transportation bill. Now, you've heard a lot about that lately, but this kind of challenge is not new. Presidents as different as [Lyndon B.] Johnson and [Gerald R.] Ford have a history of encouraging the Congress to meet a deadline. In fact, Lyndon Johnson, in his State of the Union Address in January of 1964, challenged the Congress to act on at least eight broad domestic issues, all within five months.

And I thought a hundred days was fairly reasonable. And I was not asking the Congress to deliver hot pizza in less than 30 minutes.

That would be revolutionary for the Congress. I only asked for two pieces of legislation in a hundred days. And it's now clear that neither will be on my desk by Friday — and, look, I'm disappointed, but frankly I'm not surprised. And tonight I'd like to put this all — try to put it in some perspective. I haven't asked you here to sit through a litany of programs and policies. We have a long list of legislative priorities already before the Congress, awaiting congressional action. And I won't repeat that list here tonight. But, rather, I'd like to do something different and describe to you how I personally see the shared strength and promise of America.

It is hard for the American people to understand, frankly, why a bill to fight crime cannot be acted on in a hundred days or why Congress can't pass a highway bill in a hundred days. But, look, if it can't be done, if a hundred days isn't enough, let me just ask this rhetorical question: How many days are? These are important issues, and there are many, many others. And most Americans believe fear of crime and violence threatens our most basic freedoms and denies us opportunity. And they also believe we must invest in our future to provide an infrastructure for those who come along after us.

And so they don't understand — the American people don't understand the complications and the inaction and the bickering, particularly when so many do understand what it takes to solve problems in their own neighborhoods — commitment, compassion and courage.

I cannot fully explain this inaction to the American people. As I said, I'm disappointed but not surprised. But I can say this as a partial consolation: America's problem-solving does not begin or end with the Congress nor with the White House.

Yes, it would help if Congress would do what the people are asking of them. And I'll keep working with the Congress — my hand remains extended. But we cannot let Congress discourage or deter us from meeting our responsibilities.

... Conventional wisdom in our day once held that all solutions were in the hands of government: call in the best and the brightest and hand over the keys to the national treasury; bigger government was better government; compassion was measured in dollars and cents, progress by price tag. We tried that course. As we ended the '70s, our economy strangling on inflation, soaring interest rates and unemployment — America turned away from government as "the answer."

So conventional wisdom then turned to the genius of the free market, and we began a decade of exceptional economic growth and created 20 million new jobs. And yet, let's face it, many of our streets are still not safe, our schools have lost their edge and millions, millions, still trudge the path of poverty. There is more to be done, and the marketplace alone can't solve all our problems.

Is the harsh lesson that there must always be those who are left behind? America must have but one answer, and that answer is no. There is a better way, one that combines our efforts — those of a government properly defined, the marketplace properly understood and services to others properly engaged. This is the only way, all three of these, to an America whole and good.

It requires all three forces of our national life. First, it requires the power of the free market; second, a competent, compassionate government; and, third, the ethic of serving others, including what I call "the points of light." These three powerful forces create the conditions for communities to be whole and free, and it's time we harnessed all three of them.... Transforming America requires not only the power of the free market but also a dynamic government. To be the enlightened instrument of the people — the government of Jefferson and Lincoln and Roosevelt — and the embodiment of their vision, it must truly be a force for good.

I believe in this kind of government, a government of compassion and competence. And I believe in backing it up with action. Here tonight, for example, is Mrs. Lauren Jackson-Floyd, one of the first Head Start graduates. And now she teaches preschoolers in that same marvelous program. Her success is why we expanded Head Start by almost three quarters of a billion dollars. And last year I signed our child-care bill to expand parents' choices in caring for their children.

And we fought for a Clean Air Act that puts the free market in the service of the environment, and we won that one. And the Americans with Disabilities Act — the most important civil rights bill in decades — has brought new dignity and opportunity to our nation's disabled. Disability leaders like Justin Dart and Evan Kemp were right here, right on this platform, when I signed it. And they are with us tonight.

[Housing and Urban Development Secretary] Jack [F.] Kemp and I stood with Ramona Younger, Jack, across the river in Charles Houston Community Center over there in Alexandria. And if the Congress enacts our HOPE Initiative, these public housing tenants can become America's newest homeowners.

Dewey Stokes here, president of the Fraternal Order of Police, wants to help make our neighborhoods safer, and that's why he supports our crime bill. And if we get a civil rights bill — and I want one like the one I sent to the Congress — we will take an important step against discrimination in the workplace.

This is not big government — this is good government....

The Congress can refer our proposals to its committees, tie itself up with debate and produce complicated and sometimes expensive and sometimes unworkable legislation.

But in the end, we and [Congress] must carry forward the magic of America — we must carry forward what is good and reach out and embrace what is best. And we must do the hard work of freedom. You see, I know you have. And I know you will.

Through you, our country can become an America whole and good. For that our country is grateful, and because of that our country — the greatest and freest on the face of the earth — will prevail. Thank you all very, very much. ■

TREATY

Bush, Gorbachev Salute Treaty As New Foundation of Peace

On July 31, President Bush and Soviet President Mikhail S. Gorbachev signed the strategic arms reduction treaty (START) in the Kremlin's St. Vladimir's Hall. Following is the Reuter transcript of their remarks:

PRESIDENT GORBACHEV: (through interpreter): In a few moments, President Bush and I will put our signatures under the treaty on the reduction of strategic offensive arms.

This completes many years of efforts that required hard work and patience on the part of government leaders, diplomats and military officials. They required will, courage and the rejection of outdated perceptions of each other. They required trust.

This is also a beginning, the beginning of voluntary reduction of the nuclear arsenals of the U.S.S.R. and the United States, a process with unprecedented scope and objectives. It is an event of global significance that we, imparting to the dismantling of the infrastructure of fear that has ruled the world, and momentum which is so powerful that it will be hard to stop.

In both countries we face the complex process of the ratification of the new treaty. There will be critics. Here in Moscow some will point to our unilateral concessions, while in Washington there will be talk about concessions made to the Soviet Union.

Some will say the new treaty does not really fulfill the promise of a peace dividend, since considerable resources will be required to destroy the missiles. And if the missiles are not destroyed, critics will say they are obsolete and must be replaced with new ones. And that will be even more expensive.

Sharp criticism is to be expected also from those who want to see faster and more ambitious steps toward abolishing nuclear weapons. In other words, the treaty will have to be defended. I'm sure we have achieved the best that is now possible, and that is required to continue progress. Tremendous work has been done, and unique experience has been gained of cooperating in this enormously complex area.

It is important that there is a growing realization of the absurdity of armament, now that the world has started to move toward an era of economic interdependence and that the information revolution is making the indivisibility of the world ever more evident.

But the policy-makers have to bear in mind that as we move toward that era we will have to make new immense efforts to remove the dangers inherited from the past and newly emerging dangers. To overcome various physical, intellectual and psychological obstacles, normal human thinking will have to replace the kind of militarized political thinking that has taken root in the minds of men. That will take time.

A new conceptual foundation of security will be of great help. Doctrines of all fighting must be abandoned in favor of concepts of preventing war. Plans calling for a crushing defeat of the perceived enemy must be replaced with joint projects of strategic stability and defense sufficiency.

The document before us marks a moral achievement and a major breakthrough in our country's thinking and behavior.

Our next goal is to make full use of this breakthrough to make disarmament an irreversible process. So as we give credit to what has been achieved, let us express our appreciation to those who have contributed to this treaty their talent and their intellectual and numerous resources, and let us get down to work again for the sake of our own and global security.

The treaty stands as "a monument to . . . U.S. and Soviet negotiators, for their tireless efforts to carve out common ground from a thicket of contentious issues."

—President Bush

Mr. President, we can congratulate each other. We can congratulate the Soviet and American people and the world community on the conclusion of this agreement. Thank you.

PRESIDENT BUSH: Thank you, Mr. President.

To President Gorbachev and to members of the Soviet government and all the honored guests here, may I salute you. The treaty that we sign today is most — is a most complicated one. The most complicated contract governing the most serious of concerns. Its 700 pages stand as a monument to several generations of U.S. and Soviet negotiators, for their tireless efforts to carve out common ground from a thicket of contentious issues, and it represents a major step forward for our mutual security and the cause of world peace.

And may I, too, thank everybody who worked on this treaty, military and State Department, arms control negotiators, really on both sides, and I would like to say that many are here today, some like my predecessor, President Reagan, is not here, but I think all of us realize that there are many who are not in this room that deserve an awful lot of credit on both the Soviet side and the United States' side.

The START treaty vindicates an approach to arms control that guided us for almost a decade: the belief that we could do more than merely halt the growth of our nuclear arsenals. We could seek more than limits on the number of arms. In our talks we sought stabilizing reductions in our strategic arsenals.

START makes that a reality. In a historic first for arms control we will actually reduce U.S. and Soviet strategic nuclear arsenals. But reductions alone are not enough. So START requires even deeper cuts of the most dangerous and destabilizing weapons.

The agreement itself is exceedingly complex. But the central idea at the heart of this treaty can be put simply: Stabilizing reductions in our strategic nuclear forces reduce the risk of war.

But these promises to reduce arms levels cannot automatically guarantee success. Just as important are the treaty's monitoring mechanisms, so that we know that the commitments made are being translated into real security. In this area, START builds on the experience of earlier agreements but goes far beyond them in provisions to ensure that we can verify this treaty effectively.

Mr. President, in the warming relations between our nations, this treaty stands as both cause and consequence. Many times during the START talks, reaching agreement seemed all but impossible.

In the end, the progress that we made in the past year's time, progress in easing tensions and ending the Cold War, change the atmosphere at the negotiating table and pave the way for START's success.

Neither side won unilateral advantage over the other. Both sides committed themselves instead to achieving a strong effective treaty and securing the mutual stability that a good agreement would provide.

Mr. President, by reducing arms, we reverse a half-century of steadily growing strategic arsenals. But more than that, we take a significant step forward in dispelling a half-century of mistrust. By building trust, we pave a path to peace.

We sign the START treaty as testament to the new relationship emerging between our two countries and the promise of further progress toward lasting peace.

Thank you very much. ■

NOMINATION HEARINGS

Thomas Spars With Committee Over Natural Law, Abortion

Judge Clarence Thomas began his testimony Sept. 10 before the Senate Judiciary Committee to be associate justice of the U.S. Supreme Court. Following are excerpts of the Reuter transcript of the proceedings held Sept. 10 and 11. (Story, p. 2619)

THOMAS: Mr. Chairman, Sen. [Strom] Thurmond, members of the committee: I am humbled and honored to have been nominated by President Bush to be an associate justice of the Supreme Court of the United States. I would like to thank the committee, especially you, Chairman [Joseph R.] Biden [Jr.] , for your extraordinary fairness throughout this process, and I would like to thank each of you and so many of your colleagues here in the Senate for taking the time to visit with me.

There are not enough words to express my deep gratitude and appreciation to Sen. [John C.] Danforth, who gave me my first job out of Yale Law School. I have never forgotten the terms of his offer to me: more work for less pay than anyone in the country could offer. Believe me, he delivered on his promise, especially the less pay.

I appreciate his wise counsel and his example over the years, and his tireless efforts on my behalf during the confirmation process.

And I would like to thank Sens. [Christopher S.] Bond, [Sam] Nunn, [Wyche] Fowler [Jr.] , [John W.] Warner, and [Charles S.] Robb, for taking the time to introduce me today.

Much has been written about my family and me over the past 10 weeks. Through all that has happened throughout our lives and through all adversity, we have grown closer, and our love for each other has grown stronger and deeper. I hope these hearings will help to show more clearly who this person Clarence Thomas is and what really makes me tick.

My earliest memories, as alluded to earlier, are those of Pin Point, Ga., a life far removed in space and time from this room, this day and this moment. As kids, we caught minnows in the creeks, fiddler crabs in the marshes; we played with plovers and skipped shells across the water. It was a world so vastly different from all this.

In 1955, my brother and I went to live with my mother in Savannah. We lived in one room in a tenement. We shared a kitchen with other tenants, and we had a common bathroom in the back yard which was unworkable and unusable. It was hard, but it was all we had and all there was.

Our mother only earned $20 every two weeks as a maid, not enough to take care of us. So she arranged for us to live with our grandparents later in 1955. Imagine, if you will, two little boys with all their belongings in two grocery bags. Our grandparents were two great and wonderful people who loved us dearly. I wish they were sitting here today. Sitting here so they could see that all their efforts, their hard work were not in vain, and so that they could see that hard work and strong values can make for a better life.

I am grateful that my mother and my sister could be here. Unfortunately, my brother could not be.

I attended segregated parochial schools and later attended a seminary near Savannah. The nuns gave us hope and belief in ourselves when society didn't. They reinforced the importance of religious beliefs in our personal lives. Sister Mary Virgilius, my eighth-grade teacher, and the other nuns were unyielding in their expectations that we use all of our talents, no matter what the rest of the world said or did.

After high school, I left Savannah and attended Immaculate Conception Seminary, then Holy Cross College. I attended Yale Law School. Yale had opened its doors, its heart, its conscience to recruit and admit minority students. I benefited from this effort.

My career is as has been delineated today. I was an assistant attorney general in the state of Missouri. I was an attorney in the corporate law department of Monsanto Co. I joined Sen. Danforth's staff here in the Senate, was an assistant secretary in the Department of Education, chairman of EEOC [Equal Employment Oppurtunity Commission], and since 1990 a judge on the U.S. Court of Appeals for the District of Columbia Circuit.

But for the efforts of so many others who have gone before me, I would not be here today. It would be unimaginable. Only by standing on their shoulders could I be here. At each turn in my life, each obstacle confronted, each fork in the road, someone came along to help.

I remember, for example, in 1974 after I completed law school I had no money, no place to live. Mrs. Margaret Bush Wilson, who would later become chairperson of the NAACP, allowed me to live at her house. She provided me not only with room and board, but advice, counsel and guidance.

As I left her house that summer, I asked her, "How much do I owe you?" Her response was, "Just along the way, help someone who is in your position." I have tried to live by my promise to her to do just that, to help others.

So many others gave their lives, their blood, their talents. But for them, I would not be here. Justice [Thurgood] Marshall, whose seat I have been nominated to fill, is one of those who had the courage and the intellect. He is one of the great architects of the legal battles to open doors that seemed so hopelessly and permanently sealed, and to knock down barriers that seemed so insurmountable to those of us in the Pin Point, Georgias of the world.

The civil rights movement, [the] Rev. Martin Luther King and the SCLC [Southern Christian Leadership Conference], Roy Wilkins and the NAACP, Whitney Young and the Urban League, Fannie Lou Hamer, Rosa Parks and Dorothy Hite, they changed society and made it reach out and affirmatively help. I have benefited greatly from their efforts. But for them, there would have been no road to travel.

My grandparents always said there would be more opportunities for us. I can still hear my grandfather, "Y'all goin' have mo' of a chance than me," and he was right. He felt that if others sacrificed and created opportunities for us, we had an obligation to work hard, to be decent citizens, to be fair and good people, and he was right.

You see, Mr. Chairman, my grandparents grew up and lived their lives in an era of blatant segregation and overt discrimination. Their sense of fairness was molded in a crucible of unfairness. I watched as my grandfather was called "boy." I watched as my grandmother suffered the indignity of being denied the use of a bathroom. But through it all they remained fair, decent, good people. Fair in spite of the terrible contradictions in our country.

They were hard-working, productive people who always gave back to others. They gave produce from the farm, fuel oil from the fuel-oil truck. They bought groceries for those who were without, and they never lost sight of the promise of a better tomorrow. I follow in their footsteps, and I have always tried to give back.

Over the years I have grown and matured. I have learned to listen carefully, carefully to other points of views and to others, to think through problems recognizing that there are no easy answers to difficult problems, to think deeply about those who will be affected by the decisions that I make and the decisions made by others. But I have always carried in my heart the world, the life, the people, the values of my youth, the values of my grandparents and my neighbors, the values of people who believed so very deeply in this country in spite of all the contradictions.

It is my hope that when these hearings are completed that this committee will conclude that I am an honest, decent, fair person. I believe that the obligations and responsibilities of a judge, in essence, involve just such basic values. A judge must be fair and impartial. A judge must not bring to his job, to the court, the baggage of preconceived notions, of ideology, and certainly not an agenda. And the judge must get the decision right. Because when all is said and done, the little guy, the average person, the people of Pin Point, the real people of America will be affected not only by what we as judges do, but by the way we do our jobs.

If confirmed by the Senate, I pledge that I will preserve and protect our Constitution and carry with me the values of my heritage: fairness, integrity, open-mindedness, honesty and hard work.

Thoughts on Natural Law

JUDICIARY COMMITTEE CHAIRMAN BIDEN, D-DEL.: And, as I said at the outset, there is good natural law, if you will, and bad natural law in terms of informing the Constitution, and there is a whole new school of thought in America that would like very much to use natural law to lower the protections for individuals in the zone of personal privacy — and I will speak to those later — and who want to heighten the protection for businesses and corporations.

Now, one of those people is a Professor Macedo, a fine, first-class scholar at Harvard University. Another is Mr. Epstein, a professor at the University of Chicago. And, in the speech you gave in 1987 to the Pacific Research Institute, you said, and I quote: "I find attractive the arguments of scholars such as Stephen Macedo, who defend an activist Supreme Court that would — not could, would — strike down laws restricting property rights."

My question is a very simple one, Judge. What exactly do you find attractive about the arguments of Professor Macedo and other scholars like him?

THOMAS: Senator, again, it has been quite some time since I have read Professor Macedo and others. That was, I believe, 1987 or 1988. My interest in the whole area was as a political philosophy. My interest was in reassessing and demonstrating a sense that we understood what our Founding Fathers were thinking when they used phrases such as "all men are created equal," and what that meant for our form of government.

I found Macedo interesting and his arguments interesting, as I remembered. Again, it has been quite some time. But I don't believe that in my writings I have indicated that we should have an activist Supreme Court or that we should have any form of activism on the Supreme Court. Again, I found his arguments interesting, and I was not talking particularly of natural law, Mr. Chairman, in the context of adjudication.

BIDEN: I am not quite sure I understand your answer, Judge. You indicated that you find the arguments — not interesting — attractive, and you explicitly say one of the things you find attractive — I am quoting from you: "I find attractive the arguments of scholars such as Stephen Macedo, who defend an activist Supreme Court that would strike down laws resisting property rights."

Now, it would seem to me what you were talking about is you find attractive the fact that they are activists and they would like to strike down existing laws that impact on restricting the use of property rights because, you know, that is what they write about.

THOMAS: Well, let me clarify something. I think it is important, Mr. Chairman.

BIDEN: Please.

THOMAS: As I indicated, I believe, or attempted to allude to in my confirmation to the Court of Appeals, I don't see a role for the use of natural law in constitutional adjudication. My interest in exploring natural law and natural rights was purely in the context of political theory. I was interested in that. There were debates that I had with individuals, and I pursued that on a part-time basis. I was an agency chairman.

BIDEN: Well, Judge, in preparing for these hearings, some suggested that might be your answer. So I went back through some of your writings and speeches to see if I misread them. And, quite frankly, I find it hard to square your speeches, which I will discuss with you in a minute, with what you are telling me today.

Just let me read some of your quotes. In a speech before the Federalist Society at the University of Virginia, in a variation of that speech that you published in the Harvard Journal of Law and Policy, you praised the first Justice [John] Harlan's opinion in *Plessy v. Ferguson,* and you said: "Implicit reliance on political first principles was implicit rather than explicit, as is generally appropriate for the Court's opinions. He gives us a foundation for interpreting not only cases involving race, but the entire Constitution in the scheme of protecting rights." You went on to say, "Harlan's opinion provides one of our best examples of natural law and higher law jurisprudence."

Then you say, "The higher law background of the American government, whether explicitly appealed to or not, provides the only firm basis for a just and wise constitutional decision."

Judge, what I would like to know is, I find it hard to understand how you can say what you are now saying, that natural law was only a — you were only talking about the philosophy in a general philosophic sense, and not how it informed or impacted upon constitutional interpretation.

THOMAS: Well, let me attempt to clarify. That, in fact, though, was my approach. I was interested in the political theory standpoint. I was not interested in constitutional adjudication. I was not at the time adjudicating cases. But with respect to the background, I think that we can both agree that the founders of our country, or at least some of the drafters of our Constitution and our declaration, believed in natural rights. And my point was simply that in understanding overall our constitutional government, that it was important that we understood how they believed — or what they believed in natural law or natural rights.

BIDEN: For what purpose, Judge?

THOMAS: My purpose was this, in looking at this entire area: The question for me was from a political theory standpoint. You and I are sitting here in Washington, D.C., with Abraham Lincoln or with Frederick Douglass, and from a theory, how do we get out of slavery? There is no constitutional amendment. There is no provision in the Constitution. But by what theory? Repeatedly Lincoln referred to the notion that all men are created equal. And that was my attraction to, or beginning of my attraction to, this approach. But I did not — I would maintain that I did not feel that natural rights or natural law has a basis or has a use in constitutional adjudication.

My interest in this area started with the notion, with a simple question: How do you end slavery? By what theory do you end slavery? After you end slavery, by what theory do you protect the right of someone who was a former slave or someone like my grandfather, for example, to enjoy the fruits of his or her labor?

At no point did I — or do I — believe that the approach of natural law or that natural rights has a role in constitutional adjudication. I attempted to make that plain or to allude to that in my confirmation to the Court of Appeals. And I think that that is the position that I take here.

Rights of Women

BIDEN: Now, Judge, in your view, does the liberty clause of the 14th Amendment protect the right of women to decide for themselves in certain instances whether or not to terminate pregnancy?

THOMAS: Senator, first of all, let me look at that in the context other than with natural law principles.

BIDEN: Let's forget about natural law for a minute.

THOMAS: My view is that there is a right to privacy in the 14th Amendment.

BIDEN: Well, Judge, does that right to privacy in the liberty clause of the 14th Amendment protect the right of a woman to decide for herself in certain instances whether or not to terminate a pregnancy?

THOMAS: Senator, I think that the Supreme Court has made clear that the issue of marital privacy is protected, that the State cannot infringe on that without a compelling interest, and the Supreme Court, of course, in the case of *Roe v. Wade* has found an interest in the woman's right to — as a fundamental interest — a woman's right to terminate a pregnancy. I do not think that at this time that I could maintain my impartiality as a member of the judiciary and comment on that specific case.

BIDEN: Well, let's try it another way, Judge. I don't want to ask you to comment specifically on Roe there. What I am trying to get at, there are two schools of thought out there. There is a gentleman like Professor Michael Moore of the University of Pennsylvania and Mr. Louis Lehrman of the Heritage

Foundation who both think natural law philosophy informs their view, and they conclude one who strongly supports a woman's right and the other one who strongly opposes a woman's right to terminate a pregnancy.

Then there are those who say that, no, this should be left strictly to the legislative bodies, not for the courts to interpret, and they fall into the school of thought represented by John Hart Healy and former Judge Robert H. Bork, for example, who say the court has nothing to do with that.

Now, let me ask you this: Where does the decision lie? Does it lie with the court? For example, you quote, with admiration, Mr. Lehrman's article. Mr. Lehrman's article was on natural law and — I forget the exact title here. Let me find it. "Natural Law and the Right to Life." And you say when you are speaking at a gathering that you think that that is a superb application of natural law. You say, "It is a splendid example of applying natural law."

Now, what did you mean by that?

THOMAS: Well, let me go back to, I guess, my first comment to you when we were discussing natural law — I think that is important — and then come back to the question of the due process analysis.

The speech that I was giving there was before the Heritage Foundation. Again, as I indicated earlier, my interest was civil rights and slavery. What I was attempting to do in the beginning of that speech was to make clear to a conservative audience that blacks who were Republicans — and the issues that affected blacks — were being addressed and being dealt with by conservatives in what I considered a less-than-acceptable manner.

... The second point that I wanted to make to them was that they had, based on what I thought was an appropriate approach, they had an obligation just as conservatives to be more open and more aggressive on civil rights enforcement. What I thought would be the best way to approach that would be using the underlying concept of our Constitution that we were all created equal.

I felt that conservatives would be skeptical about the notion of natural law. I was using that as the underlying approach. I felt that they would be conservative and that they would not — or be skeptical about that concept. I was speaking in the Lou Lehrman Auditorium of the Heritage Foundation. I thought that if I demonstrated that one of their own accepted at least the concept of natural rights, that they would be more apt to accept that concept as an underlying principle for being more aggressive on civil rights. My whole interest was civil rights enforcement.

Privacy Decisions

BIDEN: Well, Judge, let me conclude this round by saying that — picking up that context, that you were a part of the Reagan administration. In 1986, as a member of the administration, you were part of what has been referred to here, the administration's Working Group on the Family.

This group put out what I think can only be characterized as a controversial report. And you sign that report, which recommends more state regulation of the family than is now allowed under the law. That report concludes that the Supreme Court's privacy decisions for the last 20 years are fatally flawed and should be corrected.

Judge, did you read this report before it was released?

THOMAS: Well, let me explain to you how working groups work in the domestic policy context — or the way that they worked in the [Reagan] administration. Normally what would happen is that there would be a number of informal meetings. At those meetings, you would express your — there would be some discussion around the table. My interest was in low-income families. I transmitted — after several meetings — transmitted to the head of that working group, my views on the low-income family and the need to address the problems of low-income families in the report.

The report, as it normally works in these working groups in domestic policy, the report is not finalized, nor is it a team effort in drafting. You are submitted your document. That document is then, as far as I know, it may be sent around or may not be sent around. But there is no signature required on those.

BIDEN: Did you ever read the report, Judge?

THOMAS: The section that I read was on the family. I was only interested in whether they included my comments on the low-income family.....

BIDEN: Well, let me conclude. This is the last thing I will ask you. This report, which is only 67 pages long, of which your report is part of — and I acknowledge your suggesting, telling us that you did not read the report before or after, and your part was only a small part of this. But in this report, take my word for it, it says that one of these fatally flawed decisions — and they explicitly pick out one — is *Moore v. City of East Cleveland*, where the city of East Cleveland said a grandmother raising two grandchildren who are cousins and not brothers is violating the zoning law and therefore has to do one of two things: move out of the neighborhood or tell one of her grandchildren to leave.

As you know, that case, I believe, was appealed to the Supreme Court, that grandmother, and the court said, "Hey, no, she has an absolute right of privacy to be able to have two of those grandchildren, even though they are cousins, to live with her and no zoning law can tell her otherwise."

Now, this report says, explicitly it says, that the city of East Cleveland and other cities should be able to pass such laws if they want and they should be upheld. And if we can't get them upheld, then we should change the court. That is what this report says. And they say that the cities and states should be able to establish norms of a traditional family.

If you will give me the benefit of the doubt that I am telling you the truth and accurately characterizing the report on that point, do you agree with what I suggested to you is the conclusion of that report in the section you have not read?

THOMAS: I have heard recently that that was the conclusion, but I would like to make a point there. I think — and I think the Supreme Court's rulings in the privacy area support — that the notion of family is one of the most personal and most private relationships that we have in our country. If I had, of course, known that that section was in the report before it became final, of course I would have expressed my concerns.

Marbury v. Madison

THURMOND, R-S.C.: ... Judge Thomas, *Marbury v. Madison* is a famous Supreme Court decision. It provides the basis of the Supreme Court's authority to interpret the Constitution and issue decisions which are binding on both the executive and legislative branches. Would you briefly discuss your views on this authority?

THOMAS: Senator, I think it is important to recognize — and we all do recognize — that *Marbury v. Madison* is the underpinning of our current judicial system, that the courts do decide and do the cases in the constitutional area, and it is certainly an approach that we have grown accustomed to and around which our institutions, our legal institutions, have grown.

THURMOND: Judge Thomas, the 10th Amendment to the Constitution provides that all powers are reserved to the states or the people if not specifically delegated to the federal government. What is your general view about the proper relationship between the federal and state governments, and do you believe that there has been an substantial increase in federal authority over the last few decades?

THOMAS: Senator, I think that it is clear that our country has grown and expanded in very important ways. Through the commerce clause, for example, there has been growth in the national scope of our government. Through the 14th Amendment, there has been application of our Bill of Rights, or portions, to the state governments. Through the growth in communications and travel, of course, we are more nationalized than we were in the past.

I think what the Court has attempted to do is to preserve in a way as best it possibly could, the autonomy of the state governments, but at the same time recognize the growth and expansion and the natural growth and expansion of our national government.

Sex Discrimination

SEN. EDWARD M. KENNEDY, D-MASS.: ... Let me move to another subject area, and this is referring to an article about you in the Atlantic Monthly in 1987. You said that hiring disparities could be due to cultural differences between men and women. This is the article "A Question of Fairness," by Juan Williams.

That article states that you said that it

could be that women are generally unprepared to do certain kinds of work by their own choice, it could be that women choose to have babies instead of going to medical school. Do you still think that that explains the underrepresentation of women in so many jobs in our economy today?

THOMAS: I think, and I think it is important to state this unequivocally, and I have said this unequivocally in speech after speech. There is discrimination. There is sex discrimination in our society. My only point in discussing statistics is that I don't think any of us can say that we have all the answers as to why there are statistical disparities. For example, if I sit here and I were to look at the statistics in this city, say with the example of number of blacks, I couldn't — and compare the number of blacks that are on that side of the table, for example. I cannot automatically conclude that that is a result of discrimination. There could be other reasons that should be explored that aren't necessarily discriminatory reasons.

I am not justifying discrimination, nor would I shy away from it. But when we use statistics, I think that we need to be careful with those disparities.

KENNEDY: Very little I could differ with you on the comment. But I was really driving at a different point, and that is whether you consider [that] women are generally unprepared to do certain kinds of work by their own choice; it could be that women choose babies instead of going to medical school.

Let me just move on to your comments about Thomas Sowell, an author whose work you respect and many — whose ideas you have stated that you agree with. Mr. Sowell wrote a book called the "Civil Rights Rhetoric: A Reality." You reviewed that book for the Lincoln Review in 1988 as part of a review of the works of Thomas Sowell, and in particular you praised Mr. Sowell's discussion, Chapter 5 of his book, entitled "A Special Case of Women," and you called it a much needed anecdote to cliches about women's earnings and professional status.

Mr. Sowell explains that women are paid 59 percent of what men receive for the same work by saying that women are typically not educated as often in such highly paid fields as mathematics, science and engineering, nor attracted to physically taxing and well-paid fields, such as construction work, lumberjacking and coal mining, and the like.

As a matter of fact, there were no women employed in the coal mine industry in 1973. In 1980, after the federal government had begun an effort to enforce anti-discrimination laws, 3,300 women were working in coal mines.

Does that surprise you at all?

THOMAS: If there is discrimination, it doesn't surprise me. There were lots of places I think in our society. You know, I used to when I — I can remember in my own classrooms looking around and realizing that seven or eight of the top 10 students in my classroom in grammar school were the smartest students and wondering at that age: If eight of the 10 of them are the brightest, then why aren't there women doctors and why aren't there women lawyers?

But the point that I was making with respect to Professor Sowell again is a statistical one. There is a difference between the problem that, say, a 16-year-old or 18-year-old minority kid, female, in this city or in Savannah or across the country, who is about to — who has dropped out of high school — there is a difference between the problems of that child or that student than there is for someone who has a Ph.D. or someone who has a college degree.

And I thought that it would be more appropriate, again referring back to the programs that you talked about, that we talked about earlier, in looking at how to solve these problems that you disaggregate the problems and you be more specific instead of lumping it all into one set of statistics.

Woman's Right To Choose

REP. HOWARD M. METZENBAUM, D-OHIO: . . . Your statement yesterday in support of the right to privacy does not tell us anything about whether you believe that the Constitution protects a woman's right to choose to terminate her pregnancy. I fear that you, like other nominees before the committee, could assure us that you support a fundamental right to privacy but could also decline to find that a woman's right to choose is protected by the Constitution. If that happens soon, there could be nowhere for many women to go for a safe and legal abortion.

I must ask you to tell us here and now whether you believe that the Constitution protects a woman's right to choose to terminate her pregnancy, and I am not asking you as to how you would vote in connection with any case before the court.

THOMAS: . . . I am afraid, though, on your final question, Senator, that it is important for any of us who are judges, in areas that are very deeply contested, in areas where I think we all understand and are sensitive to both sides of a very difficult debate, that for a judge — and as I said yesterday, for us who are judges, we have to look ourselves in the mirror and say, Are we impartial or will we be perceived to be impartial? I think that to take a position would undermine my ability to be impartial, and I have attempted to avoid that in all areas of my life after I became a judge. And I think it is important.

I can assure you — and I know, I understand your concern that people come here and they might tell you A and then do B. But I have no agenda. I have tried to wrestle with every difficult case that has come before me. I don't have an ideology to take to the court to do all sorts of things. I am there to take the cases that come before me and to do the fairest, most open-minded, decent job that I can as a judge. And I am afraid that to begin to answer questions about what my specific position is in these contested areas would greatly — or leave the impression that I prejudged this issue.

METZENBAUM: Having said that, Judge, I will just repeat the question. Do you believe — I am not asking you to prejudge the case. I am just asking you whether you believe that the Constitution protects a woman's right to choose to terminate her pregnancy.

THOMAS: Senator, as I noted yesterday, and I think we all feel strongly in this country about our privacy — I do — I believe the Constitution protects the right to privacy. And I have no reason or agenda to prejudge the issue or to predispose to rule one way or the other on the issue of abortion, which is a difficult issue.

METZENBAUM: I am not asking you to prejudge it. Just as you can respond — and I will get into some of the questions to which you responded yesterday, both from Sens. Thurmond, Hatch and Biden about matters that might come before the court. You certainly can express an opinion as to whether or not you believe that a woman has a right to choose to terminate her pregnancy without indicating how you expect to vote in any particular case. And I am asking you to do that.

THOMAS: Senator, I think to do that would seriously compromise my ability to sit on a case of that importance and involving that important issue.

METZENBAUM: Let us proceed. Judge Thomas, in 1990, I chaired a committee hearing on the Freedom of Choice Act, where we heard from women who were maimed by back-alley abortionists. Prior to the *Roe* decision, only wealthy women could be sure of having access to safe abortions. Poor [and] middle-class women were forced to unsafe back alleys, if they needed an abortion. It was a very heart-rending hearing.

Frankly, I am terrified that if we turn the clock back on legal abortion services, women will once again be forced to resort to brutal and illegal abortions, the kinds of abortions where coat hangers are substitutes for surgical instruments.

The consequences of Roe's demise are so horrifying to me and to millions of American women and men that I want to ask you once again, of appealing to your sense of compassion, whether or not you believe the Constitution protects a woman's right to an abortion.

THOMAS: Senator, the prospect — and I guess as a kid we heard the hushed whispers about illegal abortions and individuals performing them in less than safe environments, but they were whispers. It would, of course, if a woman is subjected to the agony of an environment like that, on a personal level, certainly, I am very, very pained by that. I think any of us would be. I would not want to see people subjected to torture of that nature.

I think it is important to me, though, on the issue, the question that you asked me, as difficult as it is for me to anticipate or to want to see that kind of illegal activity, I think it would undermine my ability to sit in an impartial way on an important case like that.

Conversion on Natural Law?

SEN. ALAN K. SIMPSON, R-WYO.: . . . I might ask you, then, to set the record straight: Is it accurate to say that on the day of Sept. 10, 1991, was that the day on which Clarence Thomas "changed" his views or had a conversion or sprinted from his previous record on natural law? Or were those the views you explained so well and ones that you have held for some period of time?

THOMAS: Senator, I have been consistent on this issue of natural law. As I indicated, my interest in the area resulted from an interest in finding a common theme and finding a theme that could rekindle and strengthen enforcement of civil rights, and ask the basic or answer a basic question of how do you get rid of slavery, how do you end it.

Our founders, the drafters of the 13th, 14th Amendments, abolitionists, believed in natural law, but they reduced it to positive law. The positive law is our Constitution. And when we look at constitutional adjudication, we look to that document. We may want to know, and I think it is important at times to understand, what the drafters believed they were doing as a part of our history and tradition in some of the provisions such as the liberty component of the due process clause of the 14th Amendment. But we don't make an independent search or an independent reference to some notion or a notion of natural law.

That is the point that I tried to make, and there was no follow-up question, as I remember it, at my confirmation to the Court of Appeals. But that has been a consistent point. We look at natural law beliefs of the founders as a background to our Constitution.

SIMPSON: Have you seen anything come up at this hearing thus far that is really anything different, much different than what happened when we confirmed you for the Circuit Court, other than the fact that you have remained absolutely silent as those out there decided to distort these issues?

THOMAS: Well, I think the one difference, Senator, of course is that I am a sitting federal judge now. When I came before this committee the last time, I was a policy-maker. I was someone who had taken policy positions, and those questions and concerns were raised of me as chairman of EEOC.

Today I am a sitting federal judge, and I find myself in a much different posture. It is a different role. I have no occasion to make policy speeches, have no occasion to speculate about policy in our government or to be a part of that policy debate. And I believe at my last confirmation, much of that debate or those debates were explored in the hearings.

Today I have refrained from it, from those debates, primarily because, as I have said before, engaging in such policy debate, particularly in public, I think undermines the impartiality of a federal judge. Taking strong positions on issues that are of some controversy in our society when there are viewpoints on both sides undermines your ability.

My Dallas Cowboys, for example, played the Redskins on Monday night, and I am totally convinced that every referee in those games is a Redskins fan. But none would admit to it.

I think that in something as simple as that, even though we have strong views about who should win, something as simple as that, we would want to feel that the referees — and judges are, to a large extent, referees — are fair and impartial, even when we don't agree with the calls.

The Equal Protection Clause

SEN. DENNIS DeCONCINI, D-ARIZ.: Judge Thomas, I would like to pursue the equal protection clause, the 14th Amendment and how it relates to discrimination. As you so well know, but for purposes of clarity, the 14th Amendment prohibits a state from depriving a person of life, liberty or property, without due process of law or equal protection of those laws.

The equal protection clause provides the primary constitutional protection against laws that discriminate on the basis of gender. And as we also know from previous hearings, there are three tests. There is the rational relationship test, which is the most lenient of those tests. There is the intermediate scrutiny test or a heightened test, which has been used in gender cases. And then there is the scrutiny test, which has been used in race and national origin.

Judge Thomas, there has been much discussion already regarding reliance on natural law. Unfortunately, natural law has been invoked historically, or maybe it is fortunate, depending on how you define it, but it goes back a long time that my staff was able to dig out.

For example, in 1873, in the *Bradwell v. Illinois* case, the Supreme Court denied a woman a license to practice law, arguing the following: "Civil law, as well as nature herself, has always recognized a wide difference in the respective spheres and destinies of man and woman. The natural and proper delicacy which belong to the female sex evidently unfits it for many of the occupations of civil life. The paramount destiny and mission of women is to fulfill the noble and benign office of wife and mother. This is the law of the Creator."

Now, I know you went on with Sen. Kennedy at some length about your position on natural law, which I did review this morning, and I welcome some clarification that you have given. But with the Bradwell case, we see that those justices applied natural law.

I know that you stated that your duty would be to uphold the Constitution and not a natural law philosophy, but I would like to just clarify for the record, do you disagree with the justices' decisions that were held back in 1873 in the *Bradwell* case?

THOMAS: Senator, I do.

DeCONCINI: Thank you. That is really all I want to know, because I want to be very clear, based on your statements to Sen. Kennedy, that you do not have any lingering thoughts that stare decisis, or what have you, dating back to a clear case where natural law was used poses any problems to you.

THOMAS: No.

DeCONCINI: Thank you.

When you were nominated, Judge Thomas, to the Court of Appeals, I submitted written questions, because of time constraints and other things that prohibited me from coming to those hearings at any length and waiting my turn to ask you questions, to comment on the Court's approach to the Equal Protection Clause. We also discussed this before these hearings when you were in to see me, and I told you I would address you with some questions and some thought on that.

In response to my written questions, your partial response was, "Though I do not have a fully developed constitutional philosophy, I have no personal reservations about applying the three standards as an appellate court judge in cases which might come before me."

Now that you have been on the court for 18 months and may soon be making decisions on important equal protection cases on the highest court of the land, let me ask you if you have developed a constitutional philosophy regarding the court's three-tier approach to the equal protection cases.

THOMAS: Senator, I have no reason and had no reason to question or to disagree with the three-tier approach. Of course, the rational basis test being the least structured or least strict of the tests, the heightened scrutiny test, which has been used in the area of gender and alienage and legitimacy, and the strict scrutiny test, which has been used in the area of fundamental rights and race, Senator, I think that those tests attempt in our society to demonstrate the concern that we have for classifications that could infringe on fundamental rights, and I believe that underlying, when we move away just from the legalese — and I do accept this structure of the three-tier test — when we move away from it, at bottom what we are talking about is are we going to allow people to be treated in arbitrary ways, either because of their gender or because of their race, are we going to defer to classifications based on gender or race, and what the court is attempting to do in an important way is to say no, we are going to look at those classifications.

DeCONCINI: Thank you, Judge Thomas. That is helpful, and I guess it goes without saying, but I am going to say it anyway, you have no agenda or hidden belief or anything else regarding the present position that the Supreme Court has taken with these three tiers on equal protection as they relate to gender or any other minority or class that it may be applied to.

THOMAS: Senator, I think it is important for judges not to have agendas or to have strong ideology or ideological views. That is baggage, I think, that you take to the court or you take as a judge.

It is important for us, and I believe one

of the justices, whose name I cannot recall right now, spoke about having to strip down, like a runner, to eliminate agendas, to eliminate ideologies, and when one becomes a judge, it is an amazing process, because that is precisely what you start doing. You start putting the speeches away, you start putting the policy statements away. You begin to decline forming opinions in important areas that could come before your court, because you want to be stripped down like a runner. So, I have no agenda, Senator.

Hispanic Concerns

DeCONCINI: Judge Thomas, I want to go into some areas that deal with Hispanic concerns. As a former chairman of the Equal Employment Opportunity Commission, you were responsible [for] — and I am sure you are familiar with — the 1983 charge study — you weren't responsible, but I am sure you are familiar with it, or I hope you are — titled "Analysis of the EEOC Service by Hispanics in the United States," which was conducted by the EEOC-appointed task force. That task force concluded that the needs of Hispanics were not being adequately addressed by the EEOC.

At the time, the task force indicated a need to improve EEOC's record of investigations of Hispanic charges and to increase outreach and education efforts within the Hispanic community.

Now, as the commissioner, what programs did you initiate to improve the accessibility of the EEOC within the Hispanic community?

THOMAS: Senator, when I arrived at EEOC, one of the first concerns among many — believe me, there were many — with which I met was that EEOC was underserving the Hispanic community; for example, in Los Angeles and certainly in your home state.

There were a number of hearings, some of which I participated in, across the country in various major cities discussing the problem and what the probable or possible responses could be. A number of the, I think, concerns were that the national origin charges were low. The problem there, of course, is that not all of the charges which we received from Hispanic employees or Hispanic-Americans are national origin charges. They go across the line. They can involve age; they can involve gender discrimination also.

A number of the things that we did included opening offices in predominantly Hispanic communities — satellite offices. That was a part of our expanded presence program. I made sure that we developed public service announcements that were bilingual. I installed a 1-800 number at EEOC so that the agency could be accessible. We developed posters that were bilingual. We took all of our documents, our brochures, and translated them into Spanish.

The effort was to make sure that we reached out, that we included, and also in areas where we had — there was a significant Hispanic population — we made every effort to see to it that the top managers and the investigators spoke Spanish. Again, the effort, the overall effort was to reach out, and that was consistent with the recommendations.

I might also add that during the major part of my tenure, two of our five commissioners were also Hispanic. So there was considerable interest on my part, on their part, and, indeed, the commission's part, in being of greater service to Hispanic-Americans.

DeCONCINI: Judge, an interim result of a study conducted by the National Council of La Raza indicates that since the 1983 task force study, the situation at EEOC with regard to Hispanics has not improved. While the Hispanic population in the United States has grown in the last decade from 6 percent of the total U.S. population in 1980 to over 9 percent of the total population today, the percentage of the EEOC total charge caseloads filed by Hispanics was only 4.15 percent.

Given your efforts to improve the EEOC record with regard to Hispanics since 1983, how do you account for the disproportionate[ly] small number of charges filed by Hispanics?

THOMAS: Again, Senator, I have and had the very same concern that we were underserving — or that EEOC during my tenure and when I arrived there — was underserving the Hispanic community. I don't know how the numbers were arrived at. To my knowledge, the agency does not keep data in areas that do not involve national origin charges by national origin. So I don't know, for example, whether we are looking at numbers reflecting only the national origin charges as opposed to other areas.

I can say this: That we made every effort during my tenure to change the commission's accessibility to Hispanic-Americans, to individuals across this country. That was the purpose for our expanded presence program, for our satellite offices, for our educational programs, all of which were started during my tenure. Our outreach efforts were all designed so that we are not sitting in our offices waiting for people to come in, but we actually go to them.

Sometimes it is frustrating because they don't all work, but it certainly was not because of a lack of trying.

Right to Life

SEN. PATRICK J. LEAHY, D-VT.: Well, let me make sure that I understand. Is it your testimony here today and yesterday that you do not endorse the Lewis Lehrman article to the extent that it argues under the natural law principles of the Declaration of Independence, a fetus has an inalienable right to life in the moment of conception? Is that your testimony?

THOMAS: I do not — my testimony is that, with respect to those issues, the issues involved or implicated in the issue of abortion, I do not believe that Mr. Lehrman's application of natural law is appropriate.

LEAHY: Had you read that article before you praised it?

THOMAS: I think I skimmed it, Senator. My interest, again, was in the fact that he used the notion or the concept of natural law, and my idea was to import that notion to something that I was very interested in.

LEAHY: When you gave the speech, which was in 1987, as I recall the testimony, did you understand that the consequences of Mr. Lehrman's position was not that just that *Roe v. Wade* should be overturned, but that abortion, even in cases of rape and incest, should be banned in every state of the Union? Did you understand that to be the position that he was taking in that article?

THOMAS: Senator, until recently, in reflecting on it, I did not know, I could not recall the entire content of that article until I read recent articles about it. Again, my interest was very, very limited....

LEAHY: Well, let's just go, then, to Mr. Lehrman's positions. Under his theory of natural law, that would criminalize every abortion in this country. Do you understand that to be his position? I am not asking whether it is yours, but do you understand that to be his position in that article?

THOMAS: Again, I would have to reread the article, Senator. I understand the criticisms that you have of the article, but my point to you here today, as well as in other questioning concerning this article, is that I did not adopt or import anything more from this article than the use of this one notion of natural law....

LEAHY: Judge, you were in law school at the time *Roe v. Wade* was decided. That was 17 or 18 years ago. I would assume — well, let me back up this way. You would accept, would you not, that in the last generation *Roe v. Wade* is certainly one of the more important cases to be decided by the U.S. Supreme Court?

THOMAS: I would accept that it has certainly been one of the more important, as well as one that has been one of the more highly publicized and debated cases.

LEAHY: So, I would assume that it would be safe to assume that when that came down, you were in law school, recent case law is oft discussed, that *Roe v. Wade* would have been discussed in the law school while you were there?

THOMAS: The case that I remember being discussed most during my early part of law school was I believe in my small group with Thomas Emerson, may have been Griswold, since he argued that, and we may have touched on *Roe v. Wade* at some point and debated that, but let me add one point to that.

Because I was a married student and I worked, I did not spend a lot of time around the law school doing what the other students enjoyed so much, and that is debating all the current cases and all of the slip opinions. My schedule was such that I went to classes and generally went to work and went home.

LEAHY: Judge Thomas, I was a married law student who also worked, but I also found at least between classes that we did discuss some of the law, and I am sure you are not suggesting that there wasn't any discussion at any time of *Roe v. Wade*?

THOMAS: Senator, I cannot remember personally engaging in those discussions. ■

NOMINATION HEARINGS

Thomas, Hill Make Statements As Panel Begins Hearings

Nominee, former employee give different recollections of the time they spent working together

On Oct. 11, the Senate Judiciary Committee convened hearings into allegations of sexual harassment against Clarence Thomas, President Bush's nominee to be an associate justice of the Supreme Court. Following are excerpts from the Reuter transcript: (Story, p. 2948):

COMMITTEE CHAIRMAN SEN. JOSEPH R. BIDEN JR.: We are here today to hold open hearings on Professor Anita Hill's allegations concerning Judge Thomas. This committee's handling of her charges has been criticized....

Some have asked: How could you have the United States Senate vote on Judge Thomas' nomination and leave senators in the dark about Professor Hill's charges?

To this I answer: How can you expect us to have forced Professor Hill against her will into the blinding light which you see here today?

But I'm deeply sorry that our actions in this respect have been seen by many across this country as a sign that this committee does not take the charge of sexual harassment seriously. We emphatically do.

Sexual harassment of working women is an issue of national concern. But that said, let me make clear that this is not — I emphasize: this is not — a hearing about the extent and nature of sexual harassment in America. That question is for a different sort of meeting, of this or any other committee.

This is a hearing convened for a specific purpose: to air specific allegations against one specific individual, allegations which may be true or may not be true.

Whichever may be the case, this hearing has not been convened to investigate the widespread problem, and it is indisputably widespread, the widespread problem of sexual harassment in this country.

* * *

Perhaps 14 men sitting here today cannot understand these things fully. I know there are many people watching today who suspect we never will understand. But fairness means doing our best to understand, no matter what we do or do not believe about the specific charges, that we are going to listen as closely as we can to these charges.

Fairness also means that Judge Thomas must be given a full and fair opportunity to confront these charges against him, to respond fully, to tell his side of the story, to be given the benefit of the doubt.

SEN. STROM THURMOND, R-S.C., ranking member: Both Judge Thomas and Professor Hill find themselves in the unenviable position of having to discuss very personal matters in a very public forum.

I want to assure them at the outset that they will be dealt with fairly. This will be an exceedingly uncomfortable process for us all, but a great deal hangs in the balance, and our duty is clear: We must find the truth.

* * *

In conclusion I want to comment briefly about the allegations that have been raised by Professor Hill. The alleged harassment she describes took place some 10 years ago. During that time, she continued to initiate contact with Judge Thomas, in an apparently friendly manner. In addition, Professor Hill chose to publicize her allegations the day before the full Senate would have voted to confirm Judge Thomas.

While I fully intend to maintain an open mind during today's testimony, I must say that the timing of these statements raises a tremendous number of questions which must be dealt with. And I can assure all the witnesses that we shall be unstinting in our effort to ascertain the truth.

Judge Clarence Thomas appeared first before the Senate Judiciary Committee and read a statement as the hearings began.

CLARENCE THOMAS: As excruciatingly difficult as the last two weeks have been, I welcome the opportunity to clear my name today. No one other than my wife and Sen. [John C.] Danforth [R-Mo.], to whom I read this statement at 6:30 a.m., has seen or heard the statement. No handlers, no advisers.

The first I learned of the allegations by Professor Anita Hill was on Sept. 25, 1991, when the FBI came to my home to investigate her allegations. When informed by the FBI agent of the nature of the allegations and the person making them, I was shocked, surprised, hurt and enormously saddened. I have not been the same since that day.

For almost a decade, my responsibilities included enforcing the rights of victims of sexual harassment. As a boss, as a friend and as a human being, I was proud that I have never had such an allegation leveled against me, even as I sought to promote women and minorities into non-traditional jobs.

In addition, several of my friends who are women have confided in me about the horror of harassment, on the job or elsewhere. I thought I really understood the anguish, the fears, the doubts, the seriousness of the matter. But since Sept. 25, I have suffered immensely as these very serious charges were leveled against me. I have been racking my brains and eating my insides out trying to think of what I could have said or done to Anita Hill to lead her to allege that I was interested in her in more than a professional way and that I talked with her about pornographic or X-rated films.

Contrary to some press reports, I categorically denied all of the allegations and denied that I ever attempted to date Anita Hill when first interviewed by the FBI. I strongly reaffirm that denial.

Let me describe my relationship with Anita Hill. In 1981, after I went to the Department of Education as an assistant secretary in the Office of Civil Rights, one of my closest friends from both college and law schools, Gil Hardy, brought Anita Hill to my attention. As I remember, he indicated that she was dissatisfied with her law firm and wanted to work in government. Based primarily, if not solely, on Gil's recommendation, I hired Anita Hill.

During my tenure at the Department of Education, Anita Hill was an attorney-adviser who worked directly with me. She worked on special projects as well as day-to-day matters. As I recall, she was one of two professionals working directly with me at the time. As a result, we worked closely on numerous matters.

I recalled being pleased with her work product and the professional, but cordial, relationship which we enjoyed at work. I also recall engaging in discussions about politics and current events.

Upon my nomination to become chairman of the Equal Employment Opportunity Commission [EEOC], Anita Hill, to the best of my recollection, assisted me in the nomination and confirmation process. After my confirmation, she and Diane Holt, then my secretary, joined me at EEOC.

I do not recall that there was any question or doubt that she would become a special assistant to me at EEOC, although as a career employee, she retained the option of remaining at the Department of Education.

At EEOC our relationship was more distant, and our contacts less frequent, as a result of the increased size of my personal staff and the dramatic increase and diversity of my day-to-day responsibilities.

Upon reflection, I recall that she seemed to have had some difficulty adjusting to this change in her role. In any case, our relationship remained both cordial and professional. At no time did I become aware, either directly or indirectly, that she felt I had said or done anything to change the cordial nature of our relationship.

I detected nothing from her, or from my staff, or from Gil Hardy, our mutual friend, with whom I maintained regular contact.

I am certain that had any statement or conduct on my part been brought to my attention, I would remember it clearly because of the nature and seriousness of such conduct, as well as my adamant opposition to sex discrimination and sexual harassment.

But there were no such statements.

Hill's Teaching Job

In the spring of 1983, Mr. Charles Coffey contacted me to speak at the law school at Oral Roberts University in Tulsa, Okla. Anita Hill, who is from Oklahoma, accompanied me on that trip. It was not unusual that individuals on my staff would travel with me occasionally.

Anita Hill accompanied me on that trip primarily because this was an opportunity to combine business and a visit to her home.

As I recall, during our visit at Oral Roberts University, Mr. Coffey mentioned to me the possibility of approaching Anita Hill to join the faculty at Oral Roberts University Law School.

I encouraged him to do so and noted to him, as I recall, that Anita Hill would do well in teaching. I recommended her highly, and she eventually was offered a teaching position.

Although I did not see Anita Hill often after she left EEOC, I did see her on one or two subsequent visits to Tulsa [Okla.] and on one visit, I believe she drove me to the airport.

I also occasionally received telephone calls from her. She would speak directly with me or with my secretary, Diane Holt. Since Anita Hill and Diane Holt had been with me at the Department of Education, they were fairly close personally, and I believe they occasionally socialized together.

I would also hear about her through Linda Jackson, then Linda Lambert, whom both Anita Hill and I met at the Department of Education, and I would hear of her from my friend Gil.

Throughout the time that Anita Hill worked with me, I treated her as I treated my other special assistants. I tried to treat them all cordially, professionally and respectfully. And I tried to support them in their endeavors and be interested in and supportive of their success. I had no reason or basis to believe my relationship with Anita Hill was anything but this way until the FBI visited me a little more than two weeks ago.

I find it particularly troubling that she never raised any hint that she was uncomfortable with me. She did not raise or mention it when considering moving with me to EEOC from the Department of Education. And she never raised it with me when she left EEOC and was moving on in her life. And to my fullest knowledge, she did not speak to any other women working with or around me who would feel comfortable enough to raise it with me, especially Diane Holt, to whom she seemed closest on my personal staff. Nor did she raise it with mutual friends such as Linda Jackson and Gil Hardy.

Cordial Relationship

This is a person I have helped at every turn in the road since we met. She seemed to appreciate the continued cordial relationship we had since day one. She sought my advice and counsel, as did virtually all of the members of my personal staff.

During my tenure in the executive branch, as a manager, as a policy-maker and as a person, I have adamantly condemned sex harassment. There is no member of this committee or this Senate who feels stronger about sex harassment than I do. As a manager, I made every effort to take swift and decisive action when sex harassment raised or reared its ugly head.

The fact that I feel so very strongly about sex harassment and spoke loudly about it at EEOC has made these allegations doubly hard on me. I cannot imagine anything that I said or did to Anita Hill that could have been mistaken for sexual harassment. But with that said, if there is anything that I have said that has been misconstrued by Anita Hill or anyone else to be sexual harassment, then I can say that I am so very sorry, and I wish I had known. If I did know, I would have stopped immediately, and I would not, as I've done over the past two weeks, had to tear away at myself trying to think of what I could possibly have done.

But I have not said or done the things that Anita Hill has alleged. God has gotten me through the days since Sept. 25, and he is my judge.

Mr. Chairman, something has happened to me in the dark days that have followed since the FBI agents informed me about these allegations. And the days have grown darker as this very serious, very explosive and very sensitive allegation, or these sensitive allegations were selectively leaked in a distorted way to the media over the past weekend.

As if the confidential allegations themselves were not enough, this apparently calculated public disclosure has caused me, my family and my friends enormous pain and great harm.

I have never, in all my life, felt such hurt, such pain, such agony.

My family and I have been done a grave and irreparable injustice. During the past two weeks, I lost the belief that if I did my best all would work out. I called upon the strength that helped me get here from Pin Point[, Ga.] And it was all sapped out of me.

It was sapped out of me because Anita Hill was a person I considered a friend, whom I admired and thought I had treated fairly and with the utmost respect.

Perhaps I could have been — better weathered this if it was from someone else. But here was someone I truly felt I had done my best with.

Though I am, by no means, a perfect person — no means — I have not done what she has alleged. And I still don't know what I could possibly have done to cause her to make these allegations.

When I stood next to the president in Kennebunkport, [Maine,] being nominated to the Supreme Court of the United States, that was a high honor. But as I sit here before you, 103 days later, that honor has been crushed.

From the very beginning, charges were leveled against me from the shadows — charges of drug abuse, anti-Semitism, wife beating, drug use by family members, that I was a quota appointment, confirmation conversion and much, much more. And now, this.

'Enough is Enough'

I have complied with the rules. I responded to a document request that produced over 30,000 pages of documents. And I have testified for five full days under oath.

I have endured this ordeal for 103 days. Reporters sneaking into my garage to examine books that I read. Reporters and interest groups swarming over divorce papers, looking for dirt. Unnamed people starting preposterous and damaging rumors. Calls all over the country specifically requesting dirt.

This is not American. This is Kafkaesque. It has got to stop. It must stop for the benefit of future nominees and our country. Enough is enough.

I am not going to allow myself to be further humiliated in order to be confirmed. I am here specifically to respond to allegations of sex harassment in the workplace. I am not here to be further humiliated by this committee or anyone else, or to put my private life on display for prurient interests or other reasons.

I will not allow this committee or anyone else to probe into my private life.

This is not what America is all about. To ask me to do that would be to ask me to go beyond fundamental fairness.

Yesterday, I called my mother. She was confined to her bed, unable to work and unable to stop crying. Enough is enough.

Mr. Chairman, in my 43 years on this earth, I have been able with the help of others and with the help of God to defy poverty, avoid prison, overcome segregation, bigotry, racism and obtain one of the finest educations available in this country.

But I have not been able to overcome this process. This is worse than any obstacle or anything that I have ever faced. Throughout my life I have been energized by the expectation and the hope that in this country I would be treated fairly in all endeavors. When there was segregation, I hoped there would be fairness one day, or someday. When there was bigotry and prejudice, I hoped that there would be tolerance and understanding — someday.

Mr. Chairman, I am proud of my life. Proud of what I have done and what I've accomplished, proud of my family. And this process, this process, is trying to destroy it all.

No job is worth what I've been through — no job. No horror in my life has been so debilitating. Confirm me if you want. Don't confirm me if you are so led. But let this process end. Let me and my family regain our lives.

Too High a Price

I never asked to be nominated. It was an honor. Little did I know the price, but it is too high.

I enjoy and appreciate my current position, and I am comfortable with the prospect of returning to my work as a judge on the U.S. Court of Appeals for the D.C. Circuit and to my friends there. Each of these positions is public service, and I have given at the office.

I want my life and my family's life back, and I want them returned expeditiously.

I have experienced the exhilaration of new heights from the moment I was called to Kennebunkport by the president to have lunch, and he nominated me. That was the high point. At that time I was told, eye to eye, that, Clarence, you made it this far on merit; the rest is going to be politics. And it surely has been.

There have been other highs. The outpouring of support from my friends of longstanding, a bonding like I have never experienced with my old boss, Sen. Danforth. The wonderful support of those who have worked with me. There have been prayers said for my family and me by people I know and people I will never meet, prayers that were heard, and that sustained not only me but also my wife and my entire family.

Instead of understanding and appreciating the great honor bestowed upon me, I find myself here today defending my name, my integrity, because somehow select portions of confidential documents dealing with this matter were leaked to the public.

Mr. Chairman, I am a victim of this process. My name has been harmed. My integrity has been harmed. My character has been harmed. My family has been harmed. My friends have been harmed. There is nothing this committee, this body or this country can do to give me my good name back. Nothing.

I will not provide the rope for my own lynching or for further humiliation. I am not going to engage in discussions, nor will I submit to roving questions, of what goes on in the most intimate parts of my private life or the sanctity of my bedroom. These are the most intimate parts of my privacy, and they will remain just that: private.

Law Professor Anita Hill addressed the committee after Thomas' statement.

ANITA HILL: My name is Anita F. Hill, and I am a professor of law at the University of Oklahoma. I was born on a farm in Okmulgee County, Okla., in 1956. I am the youngest of 13 children.

I had my early education in Okmulgee County. My father, Albert Hill, is a farmer in that area. My mother's name is Irma Hill. She is also a farmer and a housewife.

My childhood was one of a lot of hard work and not much money, but it was one of solid family affection as represented by my parents. I was reared in a religious atmosphere in the Baptist faith, and I have been a member of the Antioch Baptist Church in Tulsa, Okla., since 1983. It is a very warm part of my life at the present time.

For my undergraduate work, I went to Oklahoma State University and graduated from there in 1977. . . . I graduated from the university with academic honors and proceeded to the Yale Law School, where I received my J.D. degree in 1980.

Upon graduation from law school, I became a practicing lawyer with the Washington, D.C., firm of Wald, Hardraker & Ross. In 1981, I was introduced to now-Judge Thomas by a mutual friend.

Judge Thomas told me that he was anticipating a political appointment, and he asked if I would be interested in working with him.

He was in fact appointed as assistant secretary of Education for civil rights. After he was, after he had taken that post, he asked if I would become his assistant, and I accepted that position.

In my early period there, I had two major projects. The first was an article I wrote for Judge Thomas' signature on the education of minority students. The second was the organization of a seminar on high-risk students, which was abandoned because Judge Thomas transferred to the EEOC, where he became the chairman of that office.

During this period at the Department of Education my working relationship with Judge Thomas was positive. I had a good deal of responsibility and independence. I thought he respected my work and that he trusted my judgment.

Alleged Harassment

After approximately three months of working there, he asked me to go out socially with him. What happened next, and telling the world about it, are the two most difficult things — experiences of my life.

It is only after a great deal of agonizing consideration and sleepless — number of — great number of sleepless nights that I am able to talk of these unpleasant matters to anyone but my close friends.

I declined the invitation to go out socially with him and explained to him that I thought it would jeopardize at — what at the time I considered to be a very good working relationship. I had a normal social life with other men outside the office. I believe then, as now, that having a social relationship with a person who was supervising my work would be ill-advised. I was very uncomfortable with the idea and told him so.

I thought that by saying no and explaining my reasons, my employer would abandon his social suggestions. However, to my regret, in the following few weeks, he continued to ask me out on several occasions.

He pressed me to justify my reasons for saying no to him. These incidents took place in his office or mine. They were in the form of private conversations, which not — would not have been overheard by anyone else.

My working relationship became even more strained when Judge Thomas began to use work situations to discuss sex. On these occasions he would call me into his office for a course on education issues and projects, or he might suggest that because of the time pressures of his schedule we go to lunch to a government cafeteria.

After a brief discussion of work, he would turn the conversation to a discussion of sexual matters. His conversations were very vivid. He spoke about acts that he had seen in pornographic films involving such matters as women having sex with animals and films showing group sex or rape scenes.

He talked about pornographic materials depicting individuals with large penises or large breasts involving various sex acts. On several occasions, Thomas told me graphically of his own sexual prowess.

Because I was extremely uncomfortable talking about sex with him at all, and particularly in such a graphic way, I told him that I did not want to talk about this subject. I would also try to change the subject to education matters or to non-sexual personal matters, such as his background or his beliefs.

My efforts to change the subject were rarely successful.

Throughout the period of these conversations, he also from time to time asked me for social engagements. My reaction to these conversations was to avoid them by eliminating opportunities for us to engage in extended conversations.

This was difficult because, at the time, I was his only assistant at the office of education — or Office for Civil Rights. During the latter part of my time at the Department of Education, the social pressures, and any conversation of his offensive behavior, ended. I began both to believe and hope that our working relationship could be a proper, cordial and professional one.

Changing Jobs Together

When Judge Thomas was made chair of the EEOC, I needed to face the question of whether to go with him. I was asked to do so, and I did.

The work itself was interesting, and at that time it appeared that the sexual overtures which had so troubled me had ended.

I also faced the realistic fact that I had no alternative job. While I might have gone back to private practice, perhaps in my old firm or at another, I was dedicated to civil rights work, and my first choice was to be in that field. Moreover, at that time, the Department of Education itself was a dubious venture. President [Ronald] Reagan was seeking to abolish the entire department.

For my first months at the EEOC where I continued to be an assistant to Judge Thomas, there were no sexual conversations or overtures. However, during the fall and winter of 1982, these began again. The comments were random and ranged from pressing me about why I didn't go out with him to remarks about my personal appearance. I remember his saying that some day I would have to tell him the real reason that I wouldn't go out with him.

He began to show displeasure in his tone and voice and his demeanor and his continued pressure for an explanation. He commented on what I was wearing in terms of whether it made me more or less sexually attractive. The incidents occurred in his inner office at the EEOC.

One of the oddest episodes I remember was an occasion in which Thomas was drinking a Coke in his office. He got up from the table at which we were working, went over to his desk to get the Coke, looked at the can and asked, "Who has put pubic hair on my Coke?"

On other occasions, he referred to the size of his own penis as being larger than normal, and he also spoke on some occasions of the pleasures he had given to women with oral sex. At this point, late 1982, I began to feel severe stress on the job. I began to be concerned that Clarence Thomas might take out his anger with me by degrading me or not giving me important assignments. I also thought that he might find an excuse for dismissing me. In January of 1983, I began looking for another job. I was handicapped because I feared that if he found out, he might make it difficult for me to find other employment, and I might be dismissed from the job I had. Another factor that made my search more difficult was that there was a period — this was during a period — of a hiring freeze in the government.

In February 1983 I was hospitalized for five days on an emergency basis for acute stomach pain, which I attributed to stress on the job. Once out of the hospital I became more committed to find other employment and sought further to minimize my contact with Thomas. This became easier when Allison Duncan became office director, because most of my work was then funneled through her, and I had contact with Clarence Thomas mostly in staff meetings.

In the spring of 1983, an opportunity to teach at Oral Roberts University opened up. I participated in a seminar, taught an afternoon session in a seminar at Oral Roberts University. The dean of the university saw me teaching and inquired as to whether I would be interested in further pursuing a career in teaching beginning at Oral Roberts University. I agreed to take the job, in large part because of my desire to escape the pressures I felt at the EEOC due to Judge Thomas.

When I informed him that I was leaving in July, I recall that his response was that now I would no longer have an excuse for not going out with him. I told him that I still preferred not to do so. At some time after that meeting, he asked if he could take me to dinner at the end of the term. When I declined, he assured me that the dinner was a professional courtesy only and not a social invitation. I reluctantly agreed to accept that invitation but only if it was at the very end of a working day.

On, as I recall, the last day of my employment at the EEOC in the summer of 1983, I did have dinner with Clarence Thomas. We went directly from work to a restaurant near the office. We talked about the work I had done, both at Education and at the EEOC. He told me that he was pleased with all of it except for an article and speech that I had done for him while we were at the Office for Civil Rights. Finally he made a comment that I will vividly remember. He said that if I ever told anyone of his behavior that it would ruin his career. This was not an apology, nor was it an explanation. That was his last remark about the possibility of our going out or reference to his behavior.

Continued Contacts

In July of 1983 I left the Washington, D.C., area, and I've had minimal contacts with Judge Clarence Thomas since. I am of course aware from the press that some questions have been raised about conversations I had with Judge Clarence Thomas after I left the EEOC. From 1983 until today, I have seen Judge Thomas only twice. On one occasion I needed to get a reference from him, and on another, he made a public appearance in Tulsa. On one occasion he called me at home, and we had an inconsequential conversation. On one occasion he called me without reaching me, and I returned the call without reaching him, and nothing came of it.

I have, on at least three occasions, been asked to act as a conduit to him for others. I knew his secretary, Diane Holt. We had worked together at both EEOC and Education. There were occasions on which I spoke to her, and on some of these occasions, undoubtedly, I passed on some casual comment to then-Chairman Thomas.

There were a series of calls in the first three months of 1985 occasioned by a group in Tulsa, which wished to have a civil rights conference. They wanted Judge Thomas to be the speaker and enlisted my assistance for this purpose. I did call in January and February, to no effect, and finally suggested to the person directly involved, Susan Cahall, that she put the matter into her own hands and call directly. She did so in March of 1985.

In connection with that March invitation, Miss Cahall wanted conference materials for the seminar, and some research was needed. I was asked to try to get the information and did attempt to do so. There was another call about possible conference in July of 1985.

In August of 1987 I was in Washington, D.C., and I did call Diane Holt. In the course of this conversation, she asked me how long I was going to be in town, and I told her. It is recorded in the message as Aug. 15. It was in fact Aug. 20. She told me about Judge Thomas' marriage, and I did say congratulate him.

It is only after a great deal of agonizing consideration that I am able to talk of these unpleasant matters to anyone except my closest friends. As I've said before, these last few days have been very trying and very hard for me, and it hasn't just been the last few days this week.

It has actually been over a month now that I have been under the strain of this issue.

Telling the world is the most difficult experience of my life, but it is very close to having to live through the experience that occasioned this meeting. I may have used poor judgment early on in my relationship with this issue. I was aware, however, that telling at any point in my career could adversely affect my future career, and I did not want, early on, to burn all the bridges to the EEOC.

As I said, I may have used poor judgment. Perhaps I should have taken angry or even militant steps, both when I was in the agency or after I left it. But I must confess to the world that the course that I took seemed the better, as well as the easier, approach.

I declined any comment to newspapers, but later, when Senate staff asked me about these matters, I felt I had a duty to report. I have no personal vendetta against Clarence Thomas. I seek only to provide the committee with information which it may regard as relevant.

It would have been more comfortable to remain silent. It took no initiative to inform anyone — I took no initiative to inform anyone. But when I was asked by a representative of this committee to report my experience, I felt that I had to tell the truth. I could not keep silent. ■

NOMINATION HEARINGS

Gates Counters Criticism On Iran-Contra Actions

Following are excerpts of the Reuters transcripts from the Senate Intelligence Committee hearings on the confirmation of Robert M. Gates to be director of central intelligence, beginning with Gates' opening statement Sept. 16. (Story, p. 2698)

GATES: I welcome these confirmation hearings to address the many issues that I know you will raise....

I have been in public service for 25 years. I arrived in Washington 25 years ago this summer, with everything I owned in the back of a 1965 Mustang and no money. The Mustang is long gone, sold before it became a collector's item, and I still have no money.

But I am enriched by a wonderful and patient wife, and two great kids. I believe I still have the idealism that I brought with me from Kansas a quarter-century ago: a deep conviction in the greatness of this country, in the uniqueness and wonder of its constitution and in its mission as a force for good in the world.

My decision to commit my life to national service springs from these beliefs.

I also have still the values that I brought with me from Kansas: family, hard work, candor and truthfulness, integrity, obeying the law and a basic optimism about life.

During these 25 years I have worked for six presidents, Republicans and Democrats alike. I served four of them in the National Security Council. I've served eight directors of the CIA. I have worked closely and harmoniously with this committee and its House of Representatives counterpart for more than 10 years as CIA's deputy director for intelligence, chairman of the National Intelligence Council, deputy director of central intelligence, acting director of central intelligence and deputy national security adviser.

I have appeared before this committee more than 50 times during that period, so we are not strangers to one another. In short, I do not come before this committee as a new face, but rather as a nominee with a long track record.

I anticipate that the committee will want to examine both that record as well as my view of the future course of CIA and U.S. intelligence. I think all of the opening statements point to that.

The committees, appropriately, have been looking at the future of U.S. intelligence, its structure and mission in the aftermath of the Cold War, and now most recently, after the revolution in the Soviet Union. Who would have thought that just five years ago we would stand where we are today? Certainly not the intelligence analyst sitting before you. Talk about humbling experiences.

The old verities that have guided this country's national security policy for 45 years and thus its intelligence service have disappeared in an historical instant. Communism is dead or dying. A number of longstanding regional conflicts are coming to an end. The Cold War is over. The Communist Party lies mortally wounded in the Soviet Union, wounded by its own hand. And the forces of real reform are at last ascendant in the Soviet Union.

Still, as ever, there are challenges, concerns and risks. The collapse of the Soviet and Russian empire offers the promise of democracy and economic transformation, but it also contains the seeds of grave instability, chaos and civil war, in a country possessing nearly 30,000 nuclear warheads, the most powerful of which are still aimed at us.

We cannot yet divert our attention from the Soviet Union, but clearly our priorities and our concerns have changed.

Meanwhile, a growing number of nations have, or are developing, nuclear, chemical and biological weapons, together with the ballistic missile technologies to deliver them. Some of our allies in that long Cold War are now at times serious adversaries in that global marketplace.

Political instability in the Third World spawns conflict, famine and chaos, challenging us politically, economically, sometimes militarily, and always morally.

International narcotics cartels not only feed growing global demand but increasingly have the capability to buy governments and rule countries.

Regional conflict and its terrorist stepchildren, as in the Middle East, remain a reality despite our best efforts.

I have been deeply engaged in dealing with all of these problems. I have been by the president's side when we prevented a coup attempt in the Philippines; liberated Panama; defeated Iraq's aggression against Kuwait; saw the Berlin Wall go down and led the effort to unify Germany and NATO; fostered the Polish roundtable agreement; completed the CFE [the Conventional Forces in Europe Treaty] and START [Strategic Arms Reduction Treaty] agreements; and played a role in the success of the democratic forces during the recent Soviet coup attempt.

The president and the Congress know that just as some threats have diminished, other dangers remain or have altered shape, just as new challenges and problems have emerged.

The death of Soviet communism has vastly diminished the danger of global war, but the world remains a very rough neighborhood. Our nation's leaders, at both ends of Pennsylvania Avenue, have no wish to walk these streets blindfolded.

We approach the close of the most violent century in man's history. Two world wars, a long and hostile peace punctuated by protracted, bloody regional wars, the destruction of ancient empires and the defeat of two inhuman ideologies — communism and Nazism — have set in motion vast political, social and economic forces long frozen by totalitarianism and its legacy.

The path to a new and brighter day is finally apparent but will require still American leadership, strength and vision; the willingness to act against those who would prey on the weak; and skillful navigation around the many obstacles that can thwart progress or send newly free but fragile democracies hurtling back into the darkness.

The role of intelligence is to help the president, his senior advisers and the Congress understand and deal with these changing realities. The challenge, then, to CIA and to U.S. intelligence is to adapt to this changing world, not just in places like the Soviet Union and Europe but to the very idea of change, the idea that for years to come, change and uncertainty will dominate international life; that the unthinkable and the not-even-thought-about will be commonplace.

For us in intelligence to adapt to such a changing world will require unprecedentedly close collaboration of the president and his advisers, the intelligence community and the Congress.

If confirmed, I look forward to a close partnership with this committee in this remarkably challenging and stimulating process.

Normally a nominee would be circumspect about specific ideas for change. However my nomination comes at a time when this committee is deeply engaged in looking at the future of U.S. intelligence and has, as this morning's statements made apparent, considerable interest in my views about the future and what I would do, if confirmed, to help guide CIA and its sister agencies toward the 21st century.

I believe Director [William H.] Webster's emphasis on flexibility is central to being responsive in a time of radical change and unpredictability.

What follows are my ideas on where we ought to go from here.

First, this remarkable moment in history affords us a not-to-be-missed opportunity to reassess the role, mission, priorities and structure of American intelligence in the aftermath of the Cold War. This should not be done off the cuff.

If confirmed, I will recommend that the president launch, with the direct involvement of his most senior security advisers, a major effort to determine the intelligence needs of the United States for the next decade or more, to the year 2005.

He should then, in my view, charge the DCI [director of central intelligence] to identify what the intelligence community must do to meet those needs. The two Intelligence committees should have the opportunity to participate even before these proposals come before the Congress.

At a time of revolutionary change abroad and governmentwide fiscal constraints at home, U.S. intelligence cannot remain fundamentally unaffected. Accordingly, we, the executive branch and Congress, must reach agreement on mission and priorities. Once these are determined, we can then logically address structure and budget.

Adm. Bob Inman, as deputy DCI, managed a similar process for the intelligence buildup during the first half of the 1980s. It is time to follow up that effort with an even bolder, much more far-reaching effort.

This effort ought to be completed by the end of the year, in time to influence the next budget cycle.

There are other problems and innovations that must be addressed as we change to cope with a changing and different world. The intelligence budget should be considered by the president, his senior advisers and the Congress, within, but independently of, the defense budget.

We must dramatically expand our clandestine human intelligence collection effort. At the same time, we must consider the implications for our covert action capabilities of a dramatic decline in Soviet aggressiveness and disruptive activities in the Third World.

We must remedy the gap between 21st century collection systems and a 19th century system for informing policy-makers.

We publish too much intelligence of questionable relevance to policy-makers. Less and better should be the rule.

CIA's relationship to and support for the U.S. military must be approved. The process by which the information needs of policy-makers are translated into intelligence requirements must be strengthened.

The relationship between our national and tactical intelligence programs must be dramatically improved.

Finally, the intelligence community, and CIA in particular, must build on the openness Director Webster has encouraged to develop better popular understanding [of] and support for U.S. intelligence activities.

President [John F.] Kennedy once said that CIA successes remain a secret while its failures are trumpeted. However, things have gotten out of hand when the most outrageous allegations against the agency are taken seriously; when the honor and integrity of thousands of patriotic public servants are suspect merely by virtue of where they work.

The CIA and its people deserve better. But changing perceptions first requires greater openness by the agency.

I can elaborate on these proposals I've just made and others that I have in mind. But my point is clear: CIA and U.S. intelligence must change and be seen to change or confront irrelevance and growing sentiment for their dismantlement.

I look forward to tackling this challenge with you.

Contrary to popular perceptions of an adversary relationship, Congress has long been a strong supporter of a vital and effective U.S. intelligence service. It was the congressional Intelligence committees that launched the rebuilding of U.S. intelligence capabilities in 1979, and their support helped sustain the rebuilding in following years.

This congressional support, not surprisingly, is valued in the intelligence community. But the community also recognizes and values the role of Congress in making intelligence accountable and in ensuring that it operates within the law and in a manner consistent with American values.

Access to our assessments by Congress — Republicans, Democrats, liberals, conservatives, moderates — helps assure our objectivity and independence.

We know that many Americans are uneasy about CIA and U.S. intelligence activities. They understand the need for information, and even on occasion for covert action, but they are uncomfortable with secrecy. And therein lies the value of congressional oversight: the reassurance to Americans that the laws are being obeyed and that there is accountability. This then puts a special responsibility on intelligence agencies to be truthful, straightforward, candid and forthcoming in dealings with Congress.

For more than 10 years, I have had a strong and positive relationship with this committee. I understand and respect its role and that of its House counterpart as surrogates for both the rest of the Congress and the American people. Consequently, a relationship of trust and confidence between the intelligence community and the two intelligence committees is of vital interest and importance.

Accordingly, I commit to you that, should I be confirmed, whatever differences may develop from time to time between the Intelligence committees and the executive branch generally or CIA in particular, I would resign rather than jeopardize that relationship of trust and confidence.

Mr. Chairman, that completes my formally prepared statement. Because of the great interest that this committee has and the centrality of Iran-contra to these proceedings, I wanted to add some additional personal thoughts on this subject at the end that I wrote down last night.

I've just referred to a commitment about trust and confidence. I don't make that commitment lightly. It is a direct outgrowth of watching the constant crises, primarily over covert action, in CIA-congressional relations between 1981 and 1986, culminating in Iran-contra.

I suspect few people have reflected more than I have on the Iran-contra affair: what went wrong, why CIA played by rules not of its own making and what might have been done to prevent or at least stop this tragic affair. CIA has already paid a fearful price and learned costly lessons.

But today, I want to speak about the misjudgments I made and the lessons I learned. First, in retrospect, I should have taken more seriously after the 1st of October, 1986, the possibility of impropriety or even wrongdoing in the government and pursued this possibility more aggressively. I should have pressed the issue of a possible diversion more strenuously with Director [William J.] Casey and with Adm. [John M.] Poindexter. I should have done more.

Instead, I contented myself with taking the information I had received to Casey and Poindexter, as well as to CIA's general counsel, and then did not follow up after returning from overseas.

Second, I should have been more skeptical about what I was told. I should have asked more questions, and I should have been less satisfied with the answers I received, especially from Director Casey.

Third, I should have pressed harder for reversing the provision in the January finding prohibiting informing the Congress.

At the same time, I believe that the actions I did take were well-intentioned and honest. While differences naturally exist in recalling the details of conversations and meetings at a remove or a distance of months or sometimes even years, the record is clear that I opposed the Iran initiative, I urged notification of Congress, I acted to ensure CIA's compliance with the law. And when for the first time problems were brought to me, I informed Director Casey, consulted CIA's general counsel and followed the counsel's recommendations.

Even before the Iran initiative became public, I urged full public disclosure. After it became public, I pressed for full disclosure to the Congress. I ensured full CIA cooperation with multiple investigations, and I began trying to rebuild that relationship of trust and confidence between CIA and the Congress.

Clearly, if I could relive October 1986, perhaps part of November, I would do certain things differently and I believe better. And indeed, my actions as acting director for more than five months and as Director Webster's deputy for nearly two years demonstrate that I learned the lessons of Iran-contra. During that period, from Dec. 15, 1986, to spring of 1989, there was not a single crisis of confidence between CIA and the Congress, in stark contrast to the preceding six years.

Nor will there be such a crisis under my stewardship if I am confirmed. You will not find a nominee for director of central intelligence more aware of and sensitive to the lessons of that time or more understanding of the importance of a good faith relationship with the Congress.

Thank you, Mr. Chairman.

* * *

COMMITTEE CHAIRMAN DAVID L. BOREN, D-OKLA.: Before I get into the questions that I had planned to ask you, let me turn to what you had said in your remarks at the end of your statement this morning.

You said: "Second, I should have been more skeptical about what I was told, I should have asked more questions, and I should have been less satisfied with the answers I received, especially from Director Casey."

When you look back on it, could you identify for us those areas where you think you should have been more skeptical, and what additional questions do you think that you should have asked that you didn't ask?

GATES: Mr. Chairman, I think of two examples that I had in mind when I wrote that portion of those remarks.

The first was following the lunch on Oct. 9, 1986, which Director Casey had with Col. [Oliver L.] North, and which I'm — which I joined. I've testified before that at the very end of that lunch, and at the end of a discussion of the [crash and capture in Nicaragua of the] Hassenfus aircraft, in which I had sought assurance that — although I'd already gotten it from our directorate of operations, I double-checked with Col. North just to try and cross every "t" and dot every "i" that he wasn't aware through his contacts with the private benefactors of any CIA connection with anything that they might be up to.

And in connection with that discussion, at the very end of the luncheon as I was getting up to leave, Col. North made, as I've referred to before, a comment with respect to — a cryptic remark about Swiss bank accounts and the contras. I walked on out of the room and a few minutes later went back into Mr. Casey's office and said, you know, that just puzzled me, and I wonder if there's something that we should be concerned about there. Is there some problem or something we should pursue?

And Mr. Casey basically said, well, I didn't pick up on what he said, or I didn't catch it; there's nothing to it, don't worry about it. And I let it go.

And in retrospect that's the first instance where I believe if I had the opportunity to do it over again, I would have pressed him harder and said, well, now, no, let's think about this. Maybe there's a real problem here.

The second example is after the director and I met with Adm. Poindexter and gave him Mr. [Charles] Allen's memorandum of 14 October 1986. We met with him on the 15th and gave him that memorandum. And during that meeting, Mr. Casey had advised him to have the White House counsel review the entire Iran initiative, make sure everything was OK, much as I had asked our CIA counsel to review it, and also to think about making it public, that it ought to be made public.

And I should have at that point drawn Adm. Poindexter's attention to the specific reference in the Allen memorandum to the possibility that if Mr. [Manucher] Ghorbanifar wasn't paid his money, one of the allegations he might make against the United States was that the money was going to other projects of the United States and the government of Israel. I did not push him on that....

BOREN: Let me go back over some questions I have in regard to your knowledge of the diversion of funds from the arms sales to the contras — and I think it's important that we look into these questions thoroughly. It's not my desire to try to go over unnecessary ground, but I think it's our responsibility to look back very specifically at some of the questions that have already been asked you and at your answers and to follow up on them.

The most important development in the unraveling of the Iran-contra affair, of course, came at the news conference of the attorney general on Nov. 25, 1986, when he explained that a document had been found that showed that the proceeds from the U.S. arms sales to Iran had indeed been used to assist the Nicaraguan resistance. This occurred during a period of time when U.S. assistance to the contras, other than intelligence-sharing and communications assistance, was prohibited by law....

Mr. Gates, you testified that the first time you recall hearing about a possible diversion of funds from the Iran arms sales to the Nicaraguan contras was on Oct. 1, 1986, when Mr. Charles Allen, the national intelligence officer for counterterrorism, brought his concerns to you, is that correct?

GATES: That is correct.

BOREN: You testified about this matter at your DCI confirmation hearing in February of 1987. The Iran-contra investigation was just getting under way. Now we have the results of that investigation, and one thing that has emerged from that investigation was an interview with the CIA deputy director for intelligence, Mr. Richard Kerr. Mr. Kerr is now the acting director of the agency. We will be hearing from him in the course of these hearings.

He did not testify under oath in 1987, but we received his sworn testimony in closed session last Wednesday. Mr. Kerr testified in late August of 1986 that Charlie Allen came to him with his concerns about a possible diversion, and he testified that he — Mr. Kerr — then discussed those concerns with you. This could have been at least a month, he said, before Mr. Allen brought his concerns to you on Oct. 1, 1986.

Do you have any recollection of Mr. Kerr's discussing the diversion with you prior to your meeting with Charlie Allen when he discussed it with you on Oct. 1, 1986?

GATES: No, sir, I do not.... I think it's important, in placing this in context — and, again, I'm reconstructing at this point the kind of relationship that Mr. Kerr and I had at that time. He had served as my deputy when I was DDI, deputy director for intelligence, and I had certainly supported his promotion to that position when I became deputy director of central intelligence.

Mr. Kerr and I talked many times virtually every day. We would have hall conversations, we would have many informal conversations.

And I believe that Mr. Kerr has testified that on this occasion when he talked to me that he had briefed me on several items and that he did not dwell on this item in particular. He briefly went over it, he indicated, I gather from the testimony, that he did so very quickly. And he did indicate that I told him to keep him informed, and he also acknowledges that he never came back to me.

So, as I say, I have no recollection of that conversation, and frankly, given the circumstances in which he describes that it took place, that doesn't surprise me.

BOREN: So again not only do you not recall the conversation, you can't think of any other time in which Mr. Kerr returned to you with any additional information in the sense of reporting back to you about these concerns?

GATES: That is correct.

BOREN: ... But if Mr. Kerr did indeed have some conversation with you about it, either for the way in which the conversation occurred, whether it included several other subjects, or the circumstances in which it occurred, it did not register with you that this serious accusation was being made?

GATES: No, sir, and to the degree that I was concerned — as I say, Mr. Kerr has said I asked him to keep me informed.

* * *

BOREN: It's obvious from your statement to us this morning that for a long time you have given some thought about the implications, the question of how much Director Casey might have known about the diversion.... And you've been thinking to yourself about how much Mr. Casey knew about the diversion, when he may have known it.

He's not here for us to ask him directly. If Oliver North told Alan Fiers [former chief of the CIA's Central American Task Force] about the diversion, as he now admits, and as Col. North has testified that he had told Mr. Casey about the diversion, and if you now believe that Director Casey may have known about the diversion, and you say, your statement this morning, you should have been less satisfied with the answers you received, especially from Director Casey, why do you think that he didn't tell you about the diversion, if indeed he did know about it?

GATES: Well, with the caveat that at least I don't know, and I don't think anyone does, I think that he must have — he would have done it in order to shield CIA as an institution from the activity. There was a lot of testimony during the Iran-contra hearings, during the summer of 1987, about cutting CIA out, about misrepresentations to CIA by various people involved, protecting the institution and so on; that if the presumption of the question is correct, then it seems to me that that's as good an answer I can come up with as to his motive.

BOREN: He did know about the diversion and clearly indicated that he never told you, is that correct?

GATES: That is correct.

BOREN: Is this a painful thing for you to contemplate, the possibility that he did withhold this information from you?

GATES: Yes.

CIA's Future

SEN. SAM NUNN, D-GA.: Mr. Gates, I want to shift your thinking a little bit from the past to the future, particularly relating to your statement in your prepared statement, where you state and cite the need for a remedy to the gap between the 21st century collections systems and the 19th century system for informing policy-makers.

I found that to be not only intriguing, but I think very important when we look to the future.

As I understand it, as director for intelligence for several years, you were in charge of intelligence assessments, and intelligence assessments are the primary vehicle through which policy-makers are informed.

So you have a unique perspective on this.

What is it that is lacking now in informing policy-makers, and what is it you would do to improve that, because after all intelligence is to no avail if policy-makers do not have access to it and understand it in a timely fashion?

GATES: Senator, what I had in mind in my statement this morning is that we have spent a great deal of money, billions and billions of dollars on collection systems, particularly technical collection systems that can deliver information to us in real time, or near real time.

Then too often our analytical components will look at that information and sit on it overnight to print it in the president's daily brief or the National Intelligence Daily the next morning.

So in a system where we've spent perhaps tens of billions of dollars to get the information quickly, other than in crisis situations we then wait and deliver the information pretty much the same way it was delivered by the War Department a century ago, and that is by the written word on the succeeding day, like the daily newspaper.

It seems to me that this is an area where in the, in the new age, we need to be more supportive of the policy-maker and his needs throughout the day, and what I have in mind is a proposal that I made and that failed in the mid-1980s, that would provide electronic intelligence to the policy-maker, where the several score most-senior policy-makers in the government would have monitors where, throughout the day, the intelligence would be updated for them on situations all around the world and where it would be integrated so that there could be maps and photographs, and so on.

So that not just when it's convenient to the agency or the intelligence organizations, that is, developed overnight or the preceding day, the policy-maker, at his convenience during the course of the day could receive continually updated information.

I think that we have not, frankly, taken sufficiently into account in the intelligence business the implications of the arrival on the scene of CNN and other 24-hour-a-day news broadcasting systems, and as a result I think much of our current intelligence is in fact old news by the time that it reaches many of the policy-makers.

There are other areas where I think that support from intelligence is inadequate.

I think that many of these problems are continuing problems, they are problems that have been around for a long time.

There is a sense that assessments are often not sharp enough, that the policy-maker has to wade through too much prose to get to the bottom line, a sense that alternative views are not sufficiently spelled out, that there is too much of a presumption of a right answer and a wrong answer, when in fact the policy-maker may be better informed by simply knowing better how to think about a problem than an answer in a situation where there may be no answer.

So these are two areas where I think, where I think that improvements can be obtained, and my specific reference this morning was to the one where I think we need to take a new look at the way we provide current intelligence support for policy-makers.

Reporting to Congress

SEN. JOHN W. WARNER, R-VA.: ... I'd like to turn [to] this issue of presidential approval and reporting on covert actions, and we come to that famous phrase, which is in Section 503(c)(3): "Whenever a finding is not reported pursuant to paragraph 1 of this section, the president shall fully inform the Intelligence committees in a timely fashion."

What is your general understanding and what would you hope to pursue as a policy as a definition of timely fashion?

GATES: Sen. Warner, the standard practice for CIA is to notify the two Intelligence committees within 48 hours of the president's signature of a finding. I think that that constitutes timely notice. If there were a non-notification, if the president decided not to notify the two committees, then, as I indicated to Sen. Nunn, I would consider timely notice or that period to be a few days.

WARNER: A few days. And so we're not getting into the area of weeks or months or anything like that in your judgment?

GATES: No, sir.

'Cooking the Books'

WARNER: Now, you understand [the term] "cooking the books," which means that as you gather the intelligence in the field, and then to come back towards the assessment, and finally there's one or two individuals that compact it, synthesize it in such a way that it moves on up to the final echelon, and from there distributed to the president and throughout government.

As I understand it, there's going to be some witnesses that are going to come in and point their finger, frankly, at your record, and say you're guilty of politicization of intelligence and cooking the books.

And I'd like to have you now lay a foundation for what you understand those terms to be and how you would refute such allegations.

GATES: I look forward to the opportunity to respond to those allegations, Senator. This is an area that I have grappled with throughout my career. When I was a young analyst, I was absolutely convinced that the refusal to accept my analysis was politically motivated by the people on the seventh floor at the agency.

At the other end of the spectrum, as a policy-maker, I have been absolutely convinced at times that the CIA and the intelligence community went out of their way to stick their thumb in the eye of the policy-maker and make them look stupid....

My perception is that — or my view is that we have a perceptions problem, and we have reality. And I think the perception of the question of cooking the books depends on where you sit. I think that most policy-makers believe that the agency does — let me rephrase that. I think some policy-makers believe that the agency occasionally does have a slant, but it's the agency's own slant in the view of the policy-maker, not an idea of supporting the policy. Quite the contrary. That the agency is publishing intelligence designed to weaken the policy.

I think that — I had many discussions about this with Secretary [of State George P.] Shultz, and he was very concerned about our work on the Philippines and Angola and the Soviet Union where he felt that we had our own agenda.

If you're a young analyst or a junior analyst and your work comes back, and it's got criticisms written all over it, or somebody says this isn't germane, or this doesn't address the question, it's a lot easier to assume that the people on the seventh floor rejected it because it was politically motivated, or their rejection was politically motivated, than perhaps their work didn't meet the standard required.

The reality is that year in and year out, the agency publishes time and time and time again intelligence that challenges the policy-maker and challenges the policies of any administration that is in power at the time. During the Reagan administration was published papers saying that Soviet defense spending — the rate of growth in Soviet defense spending — was going down. And if you think it was fun to publish that when [Secretary of Defense Caspar W.] Weinberger was sitting over in the Pentagon, I think you'll appreciate the situation.

Or just to take one other example, involving Secretary Shultz, the estimate that we did on Lebanon in 1983, where the first sentence of the estimate was, "The prospect for the achievement of American objectives is very bleak."

So, Senator, I think that the reality — let me just make one other comment — the reality is that I think intelligence does an honest job of reporting what it truly believes, but the belief that there is a problem is important enough that it requires constant attention. And that's why we repeatedly have the inspector general look at these problems or these allegations, why we've welcomed those occasions when the Hill has looked into it, and it's one of the reasons why, as I indicated in my opening statement, one of the surest protections for the objectivity of CIA's work is that virtually all of it comes up here to the Hill to anywhere from two to eight committees.

Confirmation Conversion

SEN. HOWARD M. METZENBAUM, D-OHIO: Mr. Gates, as you know, I've been attending two hearings, this one and the [Supreme Court nominee Clarence] Thomas hearing. In the Thomas hearing, Mr. Thomas takes the position that what he said in yesteryear is not his view as of today. In your case, you made three self-critical statements in your opening remarks regarding Iran-contra, remarks that pretty much indicated that if you had [it] to do over again, it would have been done differently — a different approach than Judge Thomas', but in a sense, to use a term used by another member of the Judiciary Committee, almost a confirmation conversion.

You said that you should have taken more seriously after Oct. 1, 1986, the possibility of a diversion and that you should have done more in response to such concerns; secondly, that you should have been more skeptical of what you were told, including what you were told by CIA Director Bill Casey; and, third, that you should have pressed harder for notification to Congress.

Now, all of us welcome those remarks and we also understand how hard it is for anybody to make them in the glare of public attention. We still have a duty, however, to fully understand your activities during that period, and in particular to look at what you have told this and other committees in the past, for that record may tell us much about how you will act in the future. At a minimum, that record must inform our own concerns regarding your nomination; it regards concerns which you can then address.

* * *

METZENBAUM: Mr. Gates, you're a seasoned intelligence officer with decades of experience.

It's come out that not only did your boss, Mr. Casey, know about the secret resupply efforts carried out during the two-year period they were restricted, but your immediate subordinate, Clair [E.] George, CIA deputy director of operations, also allegedly knew; Alan [D.] Fiers [Jr.], CIA chief of the Latin American task force, knew. And Mr. Fiers said he told his immediate superior, Mr. [Jay K.] Gruner , the CIA chief of the Latin American division, as well.

Now, that would make everybody up and down the line with anything to do with Central America knowing that the contras were getting U.S. support illegally all along. . . .

The question really is, how could a man with your experience and position have not been aware or knowledgeable of the fact that the contras were getting illegal military support from the U.S., especially when agency officials working for you knew this was going on? And how could you have helped the contras if you didn't take steps to find out what they had and what they needed?

GATES: Senator, when I became deputy director of central intelligence in April 1986, we were less than — well, some 30 days away from Senate approval of the new program for the contras. The House approved it 30 days after that. So within 60 or 90 days of my becoming deputy director of central intelligence, the Congress had approved a new official program of support for the contras.

As deputy director for intelligence, I had no direct knowledge or need to know, nor did anyone come to me with information about the private benefactor effort in support of the contras. I arrived on the scene contemplating this new legislation, and my attention was focused wholly on the future, to the degree that I was involved with it at all. And I was along the lines that I described earlier.

You'll find a remarkable consistency in all those memoranda that I did of meetings with Secretary Shultz and Deputy Secretary [John C.] Whitehead and Secretary Weinberger and Adm. Poindexter, and so on, about the nature of the problems that were discussed.

In no case did those involve conversations about the private benefactor effort in any detail or in any way that would be improper or inappropriate. And no one came to me with the view that there was anything improper or illegal going on or even the suspicion of that. Again, the focus was completely on the future.

Violation of U.S. Policy

METZENBAUM: You gave written testimony to this committee that you saw a scenario paper from the National Security Council in February 1986, which laid out a schedule for the exchange of arms for hostages.

You have described the scenario which predicted the Ayatollah Khomeini would be dead by May of that year as laughable. That was the quality of the intelligence operation that had been taken out of your agency's control. Yet you allowed it to go forward.

At the same time, you, in your words, "lost touch with the project" as you became involved with the confirmation process to become deputy director of central intelligence. Now, the foreign policy implications of an arms for hostages swap with Iran were staggering. The plan being implemented was doomed to be a fiasco.

The question is, how could you put your personal agenda over your obvious obligations as a professional to put a halt to this violation of U.S. policy?

And let me point out that I'm not making an accusation or a statement that you did what I just said — put your personal agenda over your obligations. I am referring to previous testimony — previous statements of yours — either in the questionnaire or at some other point — that that was the reason that you didn't give more attention to the subject.

GATES: Sen. Metzenbaum, the president of the United States made the decision to sell arms for hostages. He may have made that decision in the context of larger objectives and an opening to Iran and so on and so forth. But that was his decision. It was a policy decision.

It was a policy decision that was protested by the secretary of State and the secretary of Defense and the acting director of central intelligence. Again, it was a policy decision. The president decided to go forward.

It seems to me that it is not the role of CIA to question the policy decision. We should have questioned how our part of that operation was carried out and the fact that it was in violation of all the procedures and approaches that we normally would take in one of these covert actions.

In that area, I think we were negligent as an agency. But I would say as a policy matter it was not up to me . . . to question the policy decision that the president had made.

Relationship to the President

JOHN C. DANFORTH, R-MO.: OK. You are very close to President Bush. You've worked in the White House now for some time. He is a person who has served in the job for which you've been nominated. He is a person who is very knowledgeable about foreign affairs.

At first blush it would appear to be a great advantage to have a director of central intelligence who has a close working familiarity with the president of the United

States. I suppose that those who are concerned, particularly about politicization, could be fearful that maybe close has its advantages, but it also has its disadvantages.

You've said that in your working with the president he wants analysis with the bark off, he wants objectivity. Do you believe that as director of central intelligence you would be in any way co-opted by virtue of your past relationship with the president?

GATES: No, sir, I don't. I've written in some ways this is in microcosm a problem that is broader for intelligence and policy. And that is the basic question that has been with the agency from its founding — of how close does the intelligence agency get to the policy-maker.

One part of that view is that you remain at a distance, and that a distance is the best place from which you can protect your objectivity and your integrity and so forth.

Speaking a little pejoratively, those are the circumstances under which you basically throw the intelligence that you think you ought to be doing over the transom and hope that it bears some faint resemblance to something that somebody in the policy community may be interested in.

But the likelihood of being able to actually provide intelligence that is of value in the day-to-day decision-making is remote if the intelligence community is itself remote from the policy community.

I have the other view. My view has been all along, from the very beginning of my career, and perhaps it's due to the fact that I've served on the NSC, that the intelligence community has to be right next to the policy-maker, that he has to be at his elbow, that he has to understand what is on his mind, he has to understand what his future concerns are, he has to understand what his agenda is, he has to understand some of the initiatives that he's thinking of taking, he has to be willing to ask the policy-maker what he's working on, or what came out of his last conversation with a world leader, so that the intelligence can be made relevant so that the director or the office director or whatever level with a corresponding policy officer can go back and give guidance to the analyst.

These are the questions that they're asking. This is what's of interest to them. This is when the briefing book closes. The president is going to take this trip. These are the kinds of issues that are going to be addressed.

I think that having a director who has a close personal relationship with the president offers a unique opportunity for the intelligence community to provide relevant intelligence and sharper intelligence to the policy process and, frankly, also to the Congress.

DANFORTH: Let me just ask one more question, Mr. Gates, and it's the reverse of the prior one, not so much how you deal with people up the chain, but how you deal with people down the chain.

In one of the newspaper articles, I think it was a New York Times article this past week, some unknown person said that you were capable of intimidation. In receiving your own information, how do you deal with people who are down the line from you? Is the CIA going to be under your directorship, is it simply going to be a rationalization for Bob Gates' basic view of the world? How do you guard yourself against maybe not being open to what the thoughts and what the advice and analysis is of people who are working in the agency?

GATES: Well, Senator, I would concede that I am probably not the easiest person in the world to work for. I am fairly demanding, and I am probably at times more direct than I might be in terms of people s egos.

But fundamental to my approach to analysis — and it begins with the article that I wrote in 1973 — is my belief that the policy-maker must be exposed to alternative points of view; that all points of view have to be heard, and they have to be presented.

And I, on this, give you one example that happened that I was reminded of just the other day by the former director of Soviet analysis, and it concerned the question of the possibility of unilateral Soviet cuts. This was two or three years ago, maybe three years ago. And I was testifying before this committee, and expressing my view that I didn't think it would happen. And then Mr. McCacken came in, was late to the hearing, and I invited him to come to the table and express his view and the Office of Soviet Analysis view, which was precisely the opposite, that they thought that the Soviets would offer some unilateral cuts.

They were right, and I was wrong. But I have always believed in alternative analysis. I believe that if you look at the record of intelligence failures over the last 20 years, in virtually every instance, it is because there was a single outcome forecast; it is going to be X or Y or Z, instead of telling the policy-maker, look, we really don't know how this is going to come out. Here are the possibilities, and here is our best estimate.

One of the major initiatives that I had when I was deputy director for intelligence was getting CIA analysts out of the building and talking to other experts outside of CIA, outside of the U.S. government, specifically telling them to go talk to people that they knew disagreed with them.

That's my view of how the intelligence business ought to be run, and it's my view on how I ought to do my own work.

We're going to end up talking here about some papers at some point, particularly with respect to the attempt at the assassination of the pope. It was in connection with that paper that I then ordered one of the offices to write an attack on the paper that we had just published, and then asked the product evaluation staff to go back and review the entire record of how we'd done on that problem.

So the way I would characterize myself is as a person who has strong views, but I am open to different interpretations, and I also recognize, and am willing to acknowledge, when I have been wrong.

Lessons Learned

SEN. BILL BRADLEY, D-N.J.: Yesterday, you were rather disarming in admitting error, when you said that you should have taken more seriously the possibility of impropriety or even wrongdoing, when you said you [should] have been more skeptical, when you said you should have pressed harder.

And I'm just curious now, five years later, as you reflect on those failures, tell me what — why do you think they occurred? In other words, what part of you didn't assert itself?

GATES: I think that I was too cautious in approaching the clandestine service, Senator, and also in deferring to Mr. Casey's special relationship with the clandestine service. Having grown up in a different culture, in the analytical culture, knowing that there were some strains, and perhaps even a measure of mistrust of me in the clandestine service, I paid attention to other aspects of the work, and did not press these issues.

I think that one of the — I think the salient lesson that I learned out of Iran-contra was that other parts of the intelligence community can cause controversy, but it seems like the clandestine service is the only part that can cause real trouble. And therefore, that what I described as the unique relationship between previous DCIs and the clandestine service — in fact on reflection — I think is an understanding of what I just described on the part of those directors, and the need to pay special attention to the clandestine service.

The Role of the DCI

BRADLEY: OK, I'd like to move, if I could, to the role of the DCI.

Do you agree that the DCI and CIA should not publicize one-sided views of strategic issues?

GATES: Yes, sir.

BRADLEY: Do you agree that the DCI and CIA should not publicize, or should not participate as advocates in policy debates?

GATES: Yes, sir.

BRADLEY: So you agree with President Bush, who was former DCI, in enjoining the DCI and CIA from even appearing to take sides in policy debates?

GATES: Yes, sir.

BRADLEY: If that is all true, what I'd like you to do is to explain the speech you made to the World Affairs Council in Northern California on Nov. 25, 1986, which was a real piece of advocacy for SDI [Strategic Defense Initiative].

And I'd like to focus in particular on the basis for some of the things you said in that.

In the speech it is true, isn't it, that you publicly predicted a Soviet ground-based laser device would be tested in the 1980s at high energy levels that would show the feasibility of ballistic missile defense?

GATES: I assume you have the text in front of you, so I'll agree.

BRADLEY: You say, we expect the Soviets to test the feasibility of ground-based lasers for defense against ballistic missiles by the late 1980s and could begin testing components for a large-scale deployment system in the 1990s.

So the question is, were you wrong? Did any such tests take place in the 1980s?

GATES: I don't know the answer to that, Senator. I'd have to check. I gather from the nature of your question that it probably didn't, but I'd have to check to make sure.

BRADLEY: Well, take my word.

Could you tell me that the — your kind of unqualified prediction here, was that based on a full reading of all of the intelligence information available to you? Were there any uncertainties that you glossed over?

GATES: Senator, it's worth taking just a moment, I think, to describe how I developed these speeches, because I assume that you're going to have some other questions about them.

My speeches would begin by gathering information from the intelligence product. I would gather intelligence assessments, current intelligence and so on, and then from that develop a speech which I would then share — I would share the draft with various analysts and managers in the agency to get their views and see whether I was in the ballpark.

The particular speech that you're talking about on the Soviet SDI program, Soviet air defense and strategic defense program, I drew from a DIA [Defense Intelligence Agency] white paper, an unclassified DIA paper on Soviet SDI and strategic defense from the current issue of Soviet Military Power, and from a white paper prepared by a CIA analyst in the office of scientific and weapons research.

I didn't make that stuff up. I guarantee you, I wouldn't know a ground-based laser from a shoeshine box. So that material was drawn presumably from one of those papers.

BRADLEY: But it was a very strong case of advocacy for a billion-billion-billions dollars of defense expenditures.

GATES: What I was trying to do in that speech, Senator, was outline what I believed to be the comprehensive nature of the Soviet strategic defense program; the degree to which they had spent themselves many tens of billions of dollars on strategic defense in a situation that left them potentially with a strategic advantage over the United States, because they had a strategic defense, however flawed, and we had none.

BRADLEY: My point is really not to debate SDI but to ask you why you chose to emphasize the more alarming aspects of the intelligence information as opposed to the more reassuring aspects of the intelligence information.

There were embodied in the intelligence information a lot of reassuring aspects that would not lead one to the conclusion that you drew and that you spoke publicly about the need to build SDI in the United States or about Soviet development.

And so my question to you is: Why did you choose to strike the more alarming pose as opposed to the more reassuring pose? And was it that you just felt very strongly about this? Or was it that [you] were essentially trying to support an administration's policy view?

GATES: I was not intentionally trying to support the administration's specific policy. The SDI idea was more than three years old by that time.

What I was trying to do was highlight an area of Soviet advantage that I thought had not received sufficient attention prior to that time.

I may have erred on the side of focusing on the concerns. But it was a speech that as I say was shared with a number of analysts in the agency before I gave it.

BRADLEY: So would you today say that you think that was a mistake to have done?

GATES: Senator, one area where I have changed my views since we last had a dialogue on this subject in February '87 has to do with speeches by the DCI, substantive speeches.

I believe that occasionally those speeches have value. I think that the speech that either Adm. Inman or John McMahon gave in the early '80s about technology transfer was an important contribution. I think that the speech that Judge Webster gave about proliferation was important.

But by and large, I think that the DCI should avoid giving substantive speeches, particularly those where there is a risk of the speech being misinterpreted as advocacy of a policy. I think that the DCI should speak publicly, but I think he should speak about intelligence issues and try and inform the American people.

This is an area where I frankly have changed my view and believe that substantive speeches should be given sparingly.

BRADLEY: So you wouldn't do that again?

GATES: No, sir, I don't think I would.

Predicting Changes

BRADLEY: OK. Another area of real importance in the world, of course, in the new world, is China, and I recall an exchange we had back in 1986 in the committee, when I think Defense Secretary Weinberger, and I think [then-Assistant Secretary of State] Roz Ridgway, and Gen. Peretz and Parutz and a number of other people were testifying, you were testifying.

And we were talking about the Soviet Union.

And I basically asked you, well, you know, let's throw conventional wisdom aside. Can you imagine any kind of significant change in the Soviet Union? What kind of intelligence data, what kind of work should the intelligence community be doing to equip policy-makers with the information that they might need if that event took place.

And in 1986 you responded: "Quite frankly, I am without any hint that such fundamental change is going on. My resources do not permit me the luxury of sort of just idly speculating on what a different kind of Soviet Union might look like."

Now, you know, a lot of water is under the bridge; things have happened.

Here is another communist nation, China. Will you be idly speculating with China? Will you be trying to think through what happens there?

Or what have you learned from your kind of reticence to entertain the unthinkable at a time when conventional wisdom said it was unthinkable, and then finding that it became reality?

GATES: Senator, I think I did not take until 1991 to pick up on your suggestion, and I think that we did go out subsequently, perhaps not immediately, and begin talking about different kinds of futures for the Soviet Union.

I think that a couple of papers were in fact commissioned along those lines. Clearly I think that we've all learned some important lessons from the events of the last three or four years in terms of thinking the unthinkable, and clearly we need to be thinking about alternative futures for China as well, and I think that that work should be under way if it is not already under way.

BRADLEY: Well, my question to you is: What would you do differently, now, to catch that kind of change in China, that you did not do to catch that kind of change in the Soviet Union?

GATES: Part of the problem is being able to measure broad popular sentiment and overall conditions in a country that is fundamentally a difficult place in which to travel or to gather information or to talk to people.

Now I know lots of travelers go to China, lots of travelers went to the Soviet Union, but it certainly is an environment in which people are afraid to talk and often afraid to be candid.

I think more can be done through expanded human intelligence collection.

I think part of what can be done is simply to ensure that people are thinking about these problems, that they are sitting down and trying to identify, here are what the different alternative paths may be historically for this country, and here are the indications of what we might see if the country were moving in one or another of those paths, and those indications would then perhaps provide a guide for collection.

And I think we did some of that on the Soviet Union, almost certainly not enough.

BRADLEY: So more broad path analysis?

GATES: Yes, sir, and I think also more human intelligence collection.

BRADLEY: If I could, on the issue of economic intelligence, do you think that we should do more economic intelligence?

GATES: I think that economic intelligence, Senator, is something where we need to proceed with some care.

I know that there's a lot of concern about doing industrial espionage, if you will, and I frankly don't think that U.S. intelligence should be engaged in that.

I think that [there] are two areas where we should do economic intelligence. One is in gathering and reporting information where other countries are not playing by the international rules, where they are colluding with their industry in ways that disadvantage U.S. industry unfairly.

In other words, collecting and reporting information that will help our policy- makers level the playing field in a policy sense.

The second area where I think we ought to be aggressive and even more aggressive than we are is in responding to the actions of foreign intelligence services directed against U.S. companies and U.S. technology.

We know that foreign intelligence services plant moles in our high-tech companies; we know that they rifle briefcases of our businessmen who travel in their countries; we know that they collect information on what we're doing.

And I think that CIA and the FBI, working together, should have a very aggressive program against it.

So those are the two areas where I think we need to be more aggressive in economic intelligence.

BRADLEY: If I could, other than former communist countries, how many countries do you have evidence of such espionage against U.S. businessmen?

GATES: I will check, but I can think of two, right off the top of my head.

BRADLEY: OK. I think that's right.

Now let me ask you, when you're talking about economic espionage, you're not talking about the service being used to ferret our commercial secrets for the benefit of American companies?

GATES: No, sir, I don't think that's an appropriate role. In fact a case officer once told me, he said: "I'm not afraid to risk my life for the United States, but I won't do it for" — and he mentioned the U.S. company.

BRADLEY: That makes two of us, Mr. Gates.

Iran-Contra Again

SEN. WARREN B. RUDMAN, R-N.H.: I want to, for the record, refer to Iran-contra Exhibit JMP-28, which is on the White House stationery of Jan. 17, 1986.

I might say parenthetically I hope that some day I will never have to talk about this subject again, but I guess it just keeps coming up; it's almost like a typhus epidemic in that anybody within five miles of the germ either died, is infected or is barely able to survive. And so I guess we're back in that mode again.

The Jan. 17 White House exhibit I have in front of me was a memorandum for the president of the United States, then Ronald Reagan, from his national security adviser, John Poindexter. It's very instructive in reading that to read the last paragraph. The rest of it is in the record, but that paragraph is instructive as to the discussion you had with the senator from Ohio.

It said the following — and I would point out this time you were the deputy director for intelligence — am I correct?

GATES: Yes, sir.

RUDMAN: That is a very esteemed position, but it is hardly the final policy leadership of the CIA, is that correct?

GATES: Yes, sir.

> **"I want to speak about the misjudgments I made.... I should have been more skeptical.... I should have asked more questions, and I should have been less satisfied with the answers."**
>
> **—Robert M. Gates**

RUDMAN: Here was Adm. Poindexter's memorandum to the president, which the president initialed. "You have discussed the general outlines of the Israeli plan with secretaries Shultz and Weinberger, Attorney General Meese and Director Casey. The secretaries do not recommend you proceed with this plan. Attorney General Meese and Director Casey believe the short-term and long-term objectives of the plan warrant the policy risks involved and recommend you approve the attached finding.

"Because of the extreme sensitivity of this project, it is recommended that you exercise your statutory prerogatives ... " — which you referred to in your answer to the senator from Ohio — "that you exercise your statutory prerogatives to withhold notification of the finding of the congressional oversight committees until such time that you" — the president — "deem it to be appropriate."

Do you recall that?

GATES: Yes, sir.

RUDMAN: In the finding itself, in the operative clause, it says the following: "I hereby find . . . " — this is the president of the United States speaking — "I hereby find that the following operation in a foreign country, including all support necessary to such operation, is important to the national security of the United States, and, due to its extreme sensitivity and security risks, I determine it is essential to limit prior notice, and direct the director of Central Intelligence to refrain from reporting this finding to the Congress, as provided in Section 501 of the National Security Act of 1947, as amended, until I otherwise direct."

Do you recall that?

GATES: Yes, sir.

RUDMAN: And you were familiar with that at the time of the appearance discussed in your prior testimony.

GATES: Yes, sir.

RUDMAN: Do you feel that as a deputy director of intelligence or as the deputy director of intelligence, that you at that point were free to violate that restriction laid on the agency by the president of the United States?

GATES: No, sir.

RUDMAN: Now, to carry it a step further, what you have said to us in testimony is that were you to find yourself in that position, you would — and I'd like you to finish the sentence.

GATES: I characterized that if I had found myself asked the specific question in April 1986, confronted with the directive from the president, I would in effect seek to seek time to go back and say that I had been confronted with this situation, that I had to respond to the committee, and that the only possibilities were either to tell them about the finding or to go back and tell them that I had been directed by the president not to answer the question. But I would have sought guidance in that way, and I would have come back to the committee immediately. I'm assuming it would have been the very next day.

RUDMAN: I think that it is stretching reality to accuse you of misrepresentation of your views about notification when in fact you were operating under that kind of directive from the president himself.

As a matter of fact, Mr. Gates — you correct me if I'm wrong — but there is still a dispute between this committee and this president, who was not involved in that finding, as to the whole constitutional question of notification and the 48-hour rule, am I correct?

GATES: Yes, sir.

Limits on Testimony?

BOREN: The statement of the government in the Fiers plea bargain agreement states, in essence, that on Oct. 9, 1986, Clair George ordered Alan Fiers to limit his testimony to the Senate Foreign Relations Committee in order to, quote, "not turn the spotlight on activities of the NSC staff."

At 6:30 p.m. on that afternoon of Oct. 9, the day before the testimony is to be given, Director Casey's schedule shows that he met with you, Clair George, Alan Fiers and your congressional affairs officer, David Greze, to discuss the testimony of the following day.

Do you recall that meeting?

GATES: No, sir. I do not.

BOREN: Do you recall whether there was any direction at all, either at that meeting, or at any other time by Mr. Casey or any suggestion by Clair George that the testimony should be limited in order to not turn the spotlight on the administration?

GATES: I have no recollection of any such thing, Mr. Chairman.

BOREN: As far as you can remember, that phrase was not used in your presence in regard to the Fiers testimony?

GATES: No, sir, and I believe that if it had been I would remember. ■

PRESIDENTIAL ADDRESS

Bush Wants Leak Investigated, New Confirmation Process

On Oct. 24, President Bush offered his suggestions for revising the Senate's confirmation process. Following is the Reuter transcript of his remarks:

PRESIDENT BUSH: . . . When Congress considers issues, no one minds a tough and honest discussion. We expect it. And by the same token we want and expect our free press to look beneath events, take account of people's motives and ask tough questions, rather than numbly repeating partisan propaganda or baseless rumor.

We demand integrity in public behavior and discourse. And when we don't get it, we react.

The recent hearings on Judge [Clarence] Thomas stirred a kind of anger. The American people saw some of the seamier sides of Washington life. They saw proceedings that degenerated into target practice against good men and women. Ronnie Perry of Brunswick, Ga., wrote me a letter. I don't know him. Here's what it said. "It is my fear that good, honest, moral men and women in this country will no longer subject themselves to the ridicule that Judge Thomas had to face." And likewise Anita [F.] Hill's backers might wonder how anyone might be expected to come forward in the future if public officials cannot maintain proper confidentiality such as the confidentiality promised to Professor Hill.

I want to digress though, in fairness, to read from page 3 of the hearings on the committee in the Judiciary. Because Sen. [Joseph R.] Biden [Jr., D-Del.], in my judgment, tried. Here's what he said at the very opening of these hearings.

"Second, while I have less discretion than a judge in a trial to bar inappropriate or embarrassing questions, all of the witnesses should know that they have a right to ask that the committee go into closed session." He cites a rule here, Rule 265, "to go into a closed session if a question requires an answer that is a clear invasion to the right to privacy. The committee will take very seriously the request of any witness to answer particularly embarrassing questions as they view whether or not it is embarrassing to answer those questions in private."

So I think — I salute the chairman for those words that went unheeded as the process unfolded.

The bruising hearings showed what happens when political factions let agendas overwhelm personal decency. Some people have tried to drag public debate to a new low, searching openly for dirt. Any dirt, without regard to people's rights to privacy. Sometimes without concern for the facts.

While crusading pressure groups talk about their favorite issues, they forget that human beings sit there beneath the glare of the spotlight, vulnerable to assault from all quarters. The piranha tactics of smearing the individual and ignoring the issue serve no public purpose. They aim to destroy lives and wreck reputations.

The dramatic hearings and the theatrics outside the hearing rooms captivated the attention of the American public all right. Millions upon millions of Americans watched the hearings with a combination of curiosity, suspense, and I submit to you all, disgust.

The nation was stunned and repulsed by the spectacle. The scenes from the Senate bore little resemblance to the tidy legislative process that we all studied in school and that we described to our children, now me, to our grandchildren: X-rated statements, cross-examinations, pushed aside the soaps and Saturday cartoons — and the process seemed unreal, more like a satire than like the government in which all of you, and which I, take so much pride, more like a burlesque show than a civics class.

The hearings also showed that politicians must contend with a host of different forces and influences. The public saw the congressional staffers everywhere, saw outside pressure groups exhorting and twisting and the staffs ever-present everywhere.

I worry that the hearings sent our people this kind of false message: If you want to make a difference, don't enter public service; join a special interest group, and that way, whether it's the right, left — join a special interest group and that way you can fight as hard as you want or as dirty as you want without any responsibility for the results.

I served in Congress, I have great respect for Congress. I know the incredible pressure and difficulty of working there. But public faith in Congress is absolutely vital for our form of government. I think we can all work together to help strengthen its image and build greater public support. Members of Congress criticize the executive branch all the time — and that's fine — often constructively. And I offer these suggestions, then, in a spirit of constructive criticism.

First, given the outrageous nature of the leaks and the Senate's announced intention of going after them, the Senate must determine who leaked the information and turned what should have been a confidential investigation into what many people who wrote me described as a circus and a travesty.

Special Prosecutor

Here's a proposal that I support. The Senate should appoint immediately a special counsel to find out who leaked what and for what reasons. The public cares very much about this case — in my view, they will for a long, long time. And the investigation ought to focus just on this case. And the special counsel should receive unfettered access to all relevant records and witnesses, and should have subpoena power to get to the truth. The Senate ought to set a clear goal for finishing up the investigation. I suggest Jan. 3, when it returns for a new session. Frankly, the American people just will not understand it if the Senate fails to bring the leaker or leakers to justice. Second, we must promote more tolerant, less viciously partisan debate. I've heard complaints that the White House does not consult sufficiently with Congress in matters of these nominations.

Frankly I have tried to consult with Congress on many issues. And we have worked hard to cooperate with Congress. And we welcome closer consultation. Let me just get that out on the table.

I don't want to put any nominee through a public meat grinder. And I always welcome advice, especially in cases that might prove controversial. Much of what I have to say today has been sharpened by discussion with members of Congress. But let me make it clear, I will not give a group of senators veto power over a nominee before the Senate has conducted hearings and held a confirmation vote.

I will not surrender presidential authority or powers any more than Congress will surrender its power. In any event, no one ought to accept the charge of insufficient consultation as an excuse for this unforgivable leak.

Third, the hearings focused attention on the problem of sexual harassment in the workplace. We have taken additional steps at the White House as recently as yesterday to address the problem. We will ensure that employees of the Executive Office of the President are aware of the problem and appreciate fully our strong commitment to building a workplace free of harassment.

And on March 1, our administration submitted a civil rights bill that contains specific provisions to strengthen penalties against sexual harassment and encourage compliance with the law. That was back on March 1. Congress will act soon, I hope by passing my civil rights bill, and at the very least, I hope Congress will pass the portions on which we have reached agreement.

But legislation alone can't solve the problem of sexual harassment in the workplace.

Sexual harassment is ugly behavior. Together we must eradicate prejudices — not just through laws, but through simple respect for other human beings. In the end laws can punish prejudice, but they cannot alone any way produce enlightenment. Only we can do that, by acting on our convictions.

Changing the Process

The Thomas hearings also raise concerns about the confirmation process generally. And let me offer several specific recommendations for reforming the process. First, shorten the time lapse between nominations and confirmations, shorten it to six weeks. It takes four times as long to secure a vote today, four times as long as it did just 30 years ago during the presidency of John [F.] Kennedy. It took the Senate an average of 63 days to confirm our appointments set up in 1989; 65 days for the group nominated in 1990. We now have a large group of people waiting for the Senate to vote on their nominations, and they've been waiting an average of 80 days.

At the beginning of this week, more than 190 nominations remained pending before the Senate. A few examples. I nominated Bob Clark, Robert Clark, for appointment as comptroller of the currency on Jan. 23, more than nine months ago. I nominated Larry Lindsey for a seat on the Federal Reserve Board on Feb. 28. In times of economic concern, we need the service of these people. And if members of the Senate don't like my nominees, then they should vote against them. But they should not stall progress by resorting to the old, and in my view obsolete, technique of placing a hold on nominations. Once again, this isn't Republican or Democrat; it is institutional.

We in the White House certainly must do our part. We will redouble our efforts to ensure that nominees complete all the required paperwork promptly and will respond promptly to requests for further important information. I've asked our Office of the White House Counsel and Office of Government Ethics to see that our regulations and clearance procedures do not, however, discourage public service. I am committed to an ethical administration. But we must ensure that our rules have not become so detailed and so onerous as to scare good honest people away from public service.

And, second, we will work with committees in Congress to ensure the confidentiality of information. I have ordered that the FBI reports be carried directly to committee chairmen and any members designated by the chairmen. The members will read the reports immediately in the presence of the agent, and then return them. No FBI reports will stay on Capitol Hill.

And, furthermore, members only will have access to these reports. Staffs will not have access to these reports. This preserves confidentiality. In my view it protects nominees, it protects potential witnesses against the nominees and it protects the members of Congress.

Third, Congress should establish a mechanism for investigating congressional leaks — thoroughly, professionally, promptly. And I've met this week with several leaders from the Senate from both parties, and they agree that we must prevent future leaks and establish a suitable mechanism for investigating them swiftly, bringing culprits to justice.

There is no excuse for leaks that wreck lives and needlessly destroy reputations. The law already prohibits such leaks from the executive branch, and again we intend to enforce that law rigorously. I know it's not easy; I've been there. I saw it when I was director of central intelligence, when we dealt with national security. I've seen frustrating leaks in the White House that have nothing to do with character assassination or national security, simply relate to policy matters. I know it's not a simple matter here. But we've got to do better, both the executive and the legislative branch.

And, fourth, Congress ought to follow the same laws that it imposes on everyone else.

More than a dozen laws apply to the executive branch but not to Congress. Most of these laws apply to everyone in America except members of Congress. Congress does not have to comply with the Equal Pay Act of 1963; it does not have to follow Title VII of the Civil Rights Act of 1964, a title that prohibits sexual harassment and discrimination on the basis of race, color, sex, religion and national origin; it doesn't have to obey the provisions of the Americans with Disabilities Act of 1990; the Age Discrimination in Employment Act.

I would wager that the American people do not know that Congress has exempted itself from the sexual harassment laws private employers and the executive branch must obey. And they have. We've heard choruses of criticism against the evils of sexual harassment, and we've received good suggestions about how to become more vigilant about this insidious crime.

But these lessons should not be wasted on the men and women who drafted the law.

For, you see, when Congress exempts itself from the very laws that it writes for others, it strikes at its own reputation and shatters public confidence in government. These exemptions encourage special interest groups to press then for reckless regulations, knowing that Congress might adopt such laws if it won't feel the sting of these laws.

This practice creates the appearance and reality of a privileged class of rulers who stand above the law.

Our founders thought it preposterous to suggest that such behavior would ever take place in America.

We did a little research. Federalist Paper No. 57 asserts that elected officials — and here's the exact language — "can make no law which will not have in full operation on themselves and their friends as well as on the great mass of society." The writer of that paper also noted ominously: "If this spirit shall ever be so far debased as to tolerate a law not obligatory on the legislature as well as on the people, the people will be prepared to tolerate anything but liberty."

The people have begun to speak now. And today I call upon the Congress to take a simple step toward increasing public confidence: submit to the laws it imposes on others, including strict enforcement provisions — not just ethics committees' jurisdiction — and do so by the year's end.

There's a lot of just plain people up there on the Hill trying to make a living, and people who work for Congress ought to have the same rights and legal remedies as those who work for anyone else.

But Congress also must submit to the law that is imposed on the executive branch, and this includes the Privacy Act which prohibits inappropriate leaks by executive agencies, Title VI of the Ethics in Government Act of 1978, the independent counsel law.

And all of us should demonstrate our commitment to clean and effective government.

From the very start of my administration, I made it absolutely clear that I expect my appointees to follow strict standards of propriety so the American people would have full and increasing confidence in our ability and integrity.

I established a commission on federal ethics law reform in January of 1989. I pushed for initiatives that resulted in the Ethics Reform Act of 1989. I signed an executive order in April '89 setting forth the principles of ethical government service.

And I charged the Office of Government Ethics with issuing a single comprehensive and clear set of objective, reasonable and enforceable standards. Those standards will be ready soon — they're out now for review.

And in the executive departments in the White House, we do strive to set and meet high standards of public service. I'll never be happy; we can always do better in the executive branch, in the departments and in the White House. And I pledge to the American people that I'm not here to point fingers: I will continue to see that we do a better job of all of this in the executive branch of the government — and I'm going to keep on trying. But all I'm doing here is inviting the Congress to do the same.

Sometimes we protest too much, and we reform too little. And so now is the time to act.

And, finally — going on too long here, but I'm wound up on this subject, I really feel strongly about this. Finally, we all must remember that our business is to do the public's business.

That becomes increasingly difficult for a Congress that contains more than 300 committees and subcommittees and makes use of nearly 40,000 workers.

It becomes increasingly difficult for a Congress that answers to no one with respect to its budget, its staff, its perks — even the enforcement of its own rules. ■

COMMITTEE FINDINGS

Four of 'Keating Five' Escape Punishment

Sen. Dennis DeConcini, D-Ariz.

From the Ethics Committee:

While aggressive conduct by senators in dealing with regulatory agencies is sometimes appropriate and necessary, the committee concludes that Sen. DeConcini's aggressive conduct with the regulators was inappropriate. The committee further concludes that the actions of Sen. DeConcini after the April 9, 1987, meeting where he learned of the criminal referral, were not improper in and of themselves.

While the committee concludes that Sen. DeConcini has violated no law of the United States or specific rule of the Senate, it emphasizes that it does not condone his conduct. The committee has concluded that the totality of the evidence shows that Sen. DeConcini's conduct gave the appearance of being improper and was certainly attended with insensitivity and poor judgment. However, the committee finds that his conduct did not reach a level requiring institutional action.

From Sen. DeConcini:

I am relieved that this long and difficult ordeal is over and that the Ethics Committee has concluded that no further action as to me is warranted. From the very beginning I have maintained that I broke no law or Senate rule, and this decision by the Ethics Committee confirms that. The committee also affirms that my actions did not cause the eventual failure of Lincoln Savings.

In its decision, the committee questions my judgment in being aggressive, but the committee also pointed out that "aggressive conduct by senators in dealing with regulatory agencies is sometimes appropriate and necessary."

Aggressiveness has been my hallmark in standing up for Arizona constituents when they are mistreated.... As the committee effectively acknowledges, in early 1987 I had strong reason to believe that a major Arizona company was being treated unfairly by the federal government. I further had reason to believe that 2,000 Arizona jobs were unfairly at stake. Certainly, had I known in 1987 what I know today I would not have taken the actions I did.

Sen. John Glenn, D-Ohio

From the Ethics Committee:

The committee concludes that Sen. Glenn, although believing that the Lincoln matter was in the process of resolution, exercised poor judgment in arranging a luncheon meeting between Mr. Keating and Speaker [Jim] Wright [D-Texas] in January 1988, some eight months after Sen. Glenn learned of the criminal referral. There is disputed evidence as to whether Lincoln's problems with the Federal Home Loan Bank Board were discussed at that meeting. The evidence indicates that Sen. Glenn's participation did not go beyond serving as host. The committee further concludes that Sen. Glenn's actions were not improper or attended with gross negligence and did not reach the level requiring institutional action against him.

From Sen. Glenn:

After spending almost one and a half years investigating this case from top to bottom, the Senate Ethics Committee today confirmed what I have said from the very beginning; namely, that in the case of Lincoln Savings, my conduct was proper and ethical in every respect....

Although the committee was very clear on the subject of my innocence, for some reason, it felt compelled to offer an opinion regarding my judgment. Now I am the first to admit that I am human and that my judgment may not always be perfect. But in this instance, I think some are sure to ask whether the committe's judgment was the result of old-fashioned horse sense or old-fashioned horse-trading....

I've said it before, and now the Senate Ethics Committee has said it again: John Glenn does not peddle influence, period.

Sen. John McCain, R-Ariz.

From the Ethics Committee:

The committee concludes that Sen. McCain exercised poor judgment in intervening with the regulators. The committee concludes that Sen. McCain's actions were not improper nor attended with gross negligence and did not reach the level of requiring institutional action against him. The committee finds that Sen. McCain took no further action after the April 9, 1987, meeting when he learned of the criminal referral.

The committee reaffirms its prior decision that it does not have jurisdiction to determine the issues of disclosure or reimbursement pertaining to flights provided by American Continental Corp. while Sen. McCain was a member of the House of Representatives. The committee did consider the effect of such on his state of mind and judgment in taking steps to assist Lincoln Savings & Loan Association.

From. Sen. McCain:

I am, of course, relieved that I have been exonerated. To quote the committee, "no improper conduct." It is an affirmation of the findings of the special counsel [Robert S. Bennett]. I believe that the people of Arizona will accept this verdict, and I will maintain their full trust and confidence. Again, I'm very relieved that this chapter is closed, and I will be able to continue to focus on being a good representative of the people of my state.

Sen. Donald W. Riegle Jr., D-Mich.

From the Ethics Committee:

The committee finds that Sen. Riegle took steps to assist Lincoln Savings & Loan Association with its regulatory problems at a time that Charles Keating was raising substantial campaign funds for Sen. Riegle. During the course of the hearings, possible conflicts arose concerning actions on the part of Sen. Riegle that caused the committee concern, but the committee finds that the evidence indicates no deliberate intent to deceive. ...

While the committee concludes that Sen. Riegle has violated no law of the United States or specific rule of the Senate, it emphasizes that it does not condone his conduct. The committee has concluded that the totality of the evidence shows that Sen. Riegle's conduct gave the appearance of being improper and was certainly attended with insensitivity and poor judgment. However, the committee finds that his conduct did not reach a level requiring institutional action.

From Sen. Riegle:

I believe the committee's findings are fair and constructive. While I'm gratified to be cleared, cleared of any wrongdoing, I accept the committee's view that an appearance of a conflict of interest was created by the proximity of legal campaign contributions to otherwise proper conduct.

With the benefit of hindsight, the events of early 1987 in this case did lend themselves to the appearance of a conflict of interest. When I first saw this three years ago, in 1988, based on news accounts, I acted upon it at that time, and I returned the campaign contributions in question.

I certainly regret and accept responsibility for this appearance problem, even though no conflict or wrongful conduct ever actually occurred.

Unhappily, appearance problems of this kind are part of our current system of campaign financing, as the committee indicated, and every senator is vulnerable to this until the system is changed. ■

COMMITTEE FINDINGS

Cranston Responds To Ethics Reprimand

Following the presentation of the Ethics Committee report on the Senate floor Nov. 20, Sen. Alan Cranston, D-Calif., rose to present his defense.

I rise with deep remorse in my heart to accept the reprimand of the committee. I deeply regret the pain all this has caused my family, my friends, my supporters, my constituents.

I'm proud of my 23-year record in the Senate. Most of all, of my accomplishments in the cause of peace and for our nation's veterans and their families, and their survivors.

I'm proud of what I accomplished for the environment, the protection I've won for so many of California's wild rivers, for so much of its wilderness and seascapes. I'm proud of what I've accomplished for equal rights and equal opportunity and equal justice and for affording housing and rapid transit. I'm not proud of this moment.

My intentions were proper in all I did. As were the intentions of the four other senators who were involved, Sens. [John] Glenn [D-Ohio], [Dennis] DeConcini [D-Ariz.], [John] McCain [R-Ariz.], and [Donald W.] Riegle [Jr., D-Mich.]. The committee acknowledges that. But in retrospect, I grant that I should not have solicited and received, even though it was on behalf of others, charitable donations close in time to official actions.

That conduct came in time to reflect upon me and hence upon the Senate, this body that I love and revere. And for that, I apologize.

So yes, I accept the committee reprimand. Let me make plain, however, that while I accept the ultimate conclusion of the committee, there is documentary and other irrebuttable evidence that contradicts some of the committee's specific findings.

Mr. President, I ask unanimous consent that two documents relevant to that point appear in the record at the conclusion of my remarks....

Mr. President, up to the very last moment of the committee's long, long deliberations, and they were very long, I considered waging an all-out battle against its verdict. If the committee had called for any action by the full Senate against me, I would have fought it tooth and nail, with the help of the man who sits beside me, Professor Alan Dershowitz, one of our nation's leading defenders of human rights.

Let me tell you why I would have done so. First I ask each of you, I ask everyone to note that the committee found and acknowledged the following: that nothing I did violated any law or specific Senate rule; that I acted without corrupt intent; that no evidence was presented to the committee, no evidence, that I ever agreed to help Charles [H.] Keating [Jr.] in return for a contribution; that none of the contributions constituted a personal gift to me; and that I did not receive or intend to receive any personal benefit from any of the funds I raised.

The committee found and acknowledged that all my actions regarding Lincoln Savings and Loan were legal and proper and violated no law or Senate rule; that the money I raised was appropriate in that respect; the committee found and acknowledged that I had substantial reasons relating to the jobs and financial security of thousands of my constituents for intervening with federal officials on behalf of Lincoln; that I had information which raised legitimate questions about the regulation of Lincoln, Sen. [Warren B.] Rudman [R-N.H.], I had that information before I attended those meetings. Lincoln was vouched for by two of the eight of the big eight accounting firms, Arthur Young and Arthur Andersen. And by Alan Greenspan, now chairman of the Federal Reserve Board, a man with tremendous impact upon the economy of our entire nation. Alan Greenspan told me that Lincoln was well managed and viable for the foreseeable future.

The committee found and acknowledged in its earlier Feb. 27 resolution that my contacts and the contacts of the other so-called Keating Five senators, with regulators, regarding Lincoln, did not cause the eventual failure of Lincoln and did not cause the eventual failure of the thrift industry in general.

The committee found and acknowledged in its Feb. 27 resolution that my attendance and the attendance of the other Keating Five senators, at two meetings with the regulators violated no law or Senate rule. It was those two meetings, my colleagues, that started this long and painful saga. Yet the committee found and acknowledged that I attended one of those meetings for approximately one minute. The record shows that all I said at the other meeting was that I shared the concerns of the other senators. It was at that meeting.

The record shows that all I did at the other meeting was to ask why an audit of Lincoln was taking so long. It was the longest audit ever, the end apparently was never in sight, and the only other thing I did at that meeting was agree with Sen. Glenn that if Mr. Keating had broken any law he should be prosecuted. But if he hadn't broken any law, the regulators should get off his back.

Thus it is clear, Mr. President, my colleagues, whoever else is observing this, it is clear that I have not been reprimanded for doing anything improper for Mr. Keating. I have been reprimanded because there was or appeared to be a proximity in time between legitimate, charitable donations that I accepted for bona fide charities, and legitimate official actions that I took.

Question of Linkage

There has been no charge that there was any other connection between the donations and the actions. And it's been acknowledged today on the floor that I did not take any action, there was no evidence that I did, because of any contribution.

The record is replete with evidence that there was no other connection of any sort. The record shows, too, that my official actions were not only proper, but were de minimis in nature. They were all routine status inquiries, or requests that somebody sue somebody, or requests that various proposed sales of Lincoln be carefully considered.

It is not unusual for me and for many of you to work with great diligence for constituents. Let me give you an example of another time I did so.

Back in the '70s another large corporation, Lockheed, was facing bankruptcy. The livelihoods of many thousands of my constituents and their families were at risk, as was the case with Lincoln.

I devoted far more time and effort and made many more phone calls about Lockheed than I ever did about Lincoln, as I successfully fought to obtain a government guaranteed loan for Lockheed.

Lockheed was not a supporter of my campaign or causes. Lockheed had supported and raised money for my opponent in the previous election.

I sought the charitable donations in question because of my zeal in a cause that relates to the very foundation of our democracy, voter participation. The deplorable decline in the number of citizens who vote puts the essence and vitality of our democracy at risk. My long and deep dedication to this cause stems from what I witnessed and lived under in Hitler Germany, Mussolini Italy, and in communist countries where citizen participation was forbidden.

Since my motives and actions were well intentioned and honest, I recognize now that I failed to anticipate that raising these funds could be looked upon as improper.

And that's what we're now talking about, appearance.

I failed in that respect for a couple of reasons. First, most of the donations went for nationwide, nonpartisan registration drives conducted by organizations which were approved by IRS [Internal Revenue Service] for tax deductibility, and in which I held no position, and whose use of the money was not under my control.

Second, these donations were made after my 1986 re-election for registration drives conducted all across the country in 1987 and 1988. Obviously they could not benefit my 1986 campaign.

'Norms of Behavior'

In retrospect, nonetheless, I now realize that what I did looked improper. But I differ and I differ very, very deeply with the committee statement in the resolution that my conduct "violated established norms of behavior in the Senate." If I had chosen to fight, I would have challenged that statement even more forcefully than I now will.

There are no such established norms of behavior in the Senate. There is no precedent and there is no rule establishing that it is unethical for a senator to engage in legitimate constituent service on behalf of a constituent because it was close in time to a lawful contribution to the senator's campaign or to a charity that the senator supports.

In its consideration of this case, the committee acknowledges that it has referred to sources for ethical guidance which may be largely unknown. It also acknowledges that there are no "written guidelines in the Senate" in several relevant areas.

[Supreme Court] Justice [Hugo] Black once referred to a tyrant king who wrote his laws in a hand so fine and placed them so high and so far from view that his subjects could not read them. That is the essence of tyranny. The essence of due process is to have laws written in advance so all can know them.

I have stated repeatedly that my actions were not fundamentally different from the actions of many other senators. My statements fell on deaf ears, perhaps because I was undergoing treatment for cancer and unable to present my case strongly at a crucial stage of the committee's proceedings.

Whatever the reason, I was left with no alterative except to see if I could prove that I am far from being the only senator to do what I have done. I found abundant evidence that I could do so. The evidence is available in various studies, reports and documents, all in the public domain.

I was prepared, on the advice of Professor Dershowitz, to demonstrate to the Senate and to the nation, through example after example of comparable conduct, that my behavior did not violate established norms. But instead of using examples, I will now simply summarize what I found.

At least two-thirds of you, my colleagues in the Senate, are involved with charities or foundations. Some are institutions set up by a senator or by his or her friends, admirers and contributors, which bear the senator's name or advance causes related to the senator's legislative efforts. In many cases the senator raises funds for the institution or permits others to raise the funds in his or her name.

The contributors include a great many individuals and corporations that have a direct interest in matters before the Senate and government agencies. More than a few of these contributors have benefited from actions taken by the senator involved, sometimes close in time to a contribution. Many of the contributions are immense. $750,000, one contribution. $500,000. $250,000. $200,000. There are many $100,000 contributions. The totals run into many millions.

In many instances there are overlapping campaign contributions, PAC [political action committee] contributions and honorary payments to senators from the individuals, special interests, corporations, and their officers and directors, who contribute to the senator's causes.

I tell you this, my colleagues, for several reasons.

First, and most importantly to me, to demonstrate that I did not violate any established norm of Senate behavior.

Second, to warn any one of you who plays any part, direct or indirect, in fundraising for a charity, or a foundation, or whatever, that you are in jeopardy if you ever do anything, at any time, to help a contributor to that charity, no matter how worthy the cause, no matter how proper the need for help, no matter how proper the help you render.

I stand before you as an example of that jeopardy.

Third, to suggest that reform is needed to protect you and to protect the Senate. I doubt that anything less will do than a ban on charitable fundraising by senators, or in their names.

If you engage in such fundraising, sooner or later, some of those who help you will want your help. If they have a legitimate need, you'll be hard put to refuse their request, simply because they responded to your request. And then you're headed for trouble.

On the other hand, how can you not help them?

Political Contributions

Let me turn to the matter of political contributions. The committee stated on Feb. 27, quote: "It is a fact of life that candidates for the Senate must solicit and receive assistance in their campaigns, including the raising of campaign funds." Unquote. Of course we all know that.

Raising these funds can often lead, as we also know, to charges of wrongdoing. It is now more likely than ever to lead to charges of wrongdoing, because the Ethics Committee has enunciated formally a new principle. That it is improper for a senator to engage in legitimate constituent service on behalf of a contributor close in time to a lawful contribution to a senator's campaign or PAC.

It seems to me, and it seems to my attorney, Alan Dershowitz, that the committee has applied this new principle to me in ex post facto fashion.

But this point really has less to do with me than it does with most of you.

My fundraising for my campaigns is over since I decided not to run again, and my political fundraising was not a major issue with the Ethics Committee. I received less in such political contributions than the other Keating Five senators, in one case 80 percent less.

Congress — the House and our Senate — are the branch of government, is the branch of government closest to the people. We represent the people; we must serve the proper interest of the people who support us and elect us. If we don't, our constituents won't get the help they need and deserve and we won't be re-elected.

I ask you this. Think about this question. How can you rationally refuse to give legal and proper help at any time to someone who seems to have a reasonable grievance because he or she has contributed to your campaign? Can you only help people who haven't contributed or can you only help people who haven't contributed lately? How lately? Unless you refrain from helping people who might contribute in the future, how far in the future?

A majority of senators feel it necessary to raise money all the time. Campaigns now go on for six years. Constituents, whether contributors or non-contributors, seek help all the time. Inevitably, contributions and actions sometimes overlap timewise.

How many of you, how many of you, after really thinking about it, could rise and declare you've never, ever helped or agreed to help a contributor close in time to the solicitation or receipt of a contribution? I don't believe any of you could say never. I'm sure you don't really know at any time exactly who has contributed and who hasn't and how much and when. But all a political opponent, a reporter or anyone else has to do to find out is to look at your contribution report at the Federal Election Commission and match it with what appears in the Congressional Record and the committee records about your official acts, speeches, motions, amendments, votes, and then to make you look bad, charge improper conduct.

I assure you that the examples I could use are plentiful. The present system makes it virtually impossible, virtually impossible for a senator to avoid what some will assert is a conflict of interest. There is no Senate rule stating when you can and when you can't help a contributor. I don't see how one could be formulated.

The Supreme Court, in a wise ruling in 1964, that I wish applied to Senate rules as well as to statutes, observed that "a statute which either forbids or requires the doing of an act in terms so vague that men of common intelligence must necessarily guess at its meaning and differ as to its application violates the first essential of due process law."

I believe the only remedy is to get money out of politics. Therein lies salvation for you, for the Senate, and most of all, for the American people, who are the ultimate losers until we end the role money plays or seems to play in our decision-making and end the business of senators and would-be senators having to spend more and more of their time chasing the money needed to fund a successful campaign. That means public financing. Nothing less will suffice.

Let us end the practice, a practice we engage in here, unfortunately, let us end the practice of considering campaign reform on the basis of what will help or hurt Republicans, Democrats, incumbents and challengers. That way everybody loses. Let's enact a campaign reform measure that will benefit the Senate, our country and all the people. If we don't, what happened to me and the other Keating Five senators can happen to any one of you.

I'm particularly troubled by one other aspect of the resolution, and you should be, too. I differ with the suggestion that the way I handled so-called access differs from the established norm in the Senate.

How many of you could stand up and declare you've never ever decided to see or take a call from someone whose name you recognize, be it a friend, a prominent leader in your state or the nation, a volunteer in your campaigns, or a contributor, while asking your staff to tend to someone you don't recognize? I doubt that any of you could honestly do so.

Furthermore, you know and I know that the Democratic Senatorial Campaign Committee, the [National] Republican Senatorial Campaign [*sic*] Committee and the White House stage events where lobbyists and other individuals who pay [$]10,000, [$]15,000, or even $100,000 a year can mingle with the president, the vice president, Cabinet members and senators. The more people contribute, the more exclusive and intimate the event they may attend. That's access.

And events are not the only time and place these generous contributors get access. So let me ask: Since I have been singled out for a reprimand on access today, who among you can be sure you will not be singled out for a reprimand on access tomorrow?

Here but for the grace of God stand you.

There is only one way out: Get money out of politics. Enact public financing and enact it now.

The Ethics Committee

There's another reform I urge upon you. Before any of you who haven't yet endured this experience land before the Ethics Committee, it should be restructured.

I recognize that the committee labored under particularly difficult circumstances in my case, but its role is difficult in all cases and difficult most of all for the senators who are hailed before it.

Today there is no real due process in the Senate for senators.

We are not afforded constitutional rights that are available to all other citizens.

So long as ethics charges are dealt with by senators, our fellow senators, we are about as far away as we could possibly be from a jury that comes from anonymity and returns to anonymity when its work is done.

Unlike a sequestered jury, the senators on the Ethics Committee read the press. They are public figures whose decisions will be weighed by their constituents. They've been buffeted in my case by vicious and inaccurate leaks that violated the rules, by press pressures, by perceived public pressures, and by mood swings in the public and within the Senate, especially in the wake of the Thomas-Hill affair and the matter of bounced checks over on the House side.

And apparently the committee was deadlocked along partisan lines for months.

It's been suggested that the committee should be revamped so its members would consist not of sitting senators, but instead, of former senators, former judges, and outstanding laymen. I endorse that concept, until and unless something wiser is proposed.

One more suggestion or warning. Beware of special counsels who transmogrify into special prosecutors.

And one final point. Now that the Keating Five are finally leaving center stage, perhaps we should turn to the neglected causes and culprits in the S&L crisis.

This case has distracted attention from the central role of two successive administrations whose ideology and policies led not to the failure of one institution, but to the decimation of the entire thrift industry, and contributions from S&L officials and PACs to the campaigns that brought these administrations to power were notably generous, far beyond any sum received by any of the Keating Five.

There's a certain irony in the fact that I stand before you a few days before Thanksgiving. At least and at least I am thankful that this long ordeal is finally coming to an end.

For those of you who may feel that I should pay for my conduct, let me assure you I have paid. In terms of dollars, legal fees for myself and others for whom I feel a sense of responsibility approach $1 million.

I am deeply grateful to Alan Dershowitz for pitching in pro bono with his wisdom and skill in these last days. I'm deeply grateful to Sen. Harry Reid [D-Nev.] for his invaluable advice and help when I didn't have an attorney and when I did.

I'm also more grateful than I can say to the people of California who have so often honored me with their votes and who have always let me fight for my beliefs, even when they weren't sure they agreed.

What I have paid as a result of this whole episode, of course, goes far beyond money. The thing that is hardest is what it has done to my reputation and to the trust Californians have placed in me, things I value above all else.

I pledge to the people of California my best efforts for them in the 13 months left of my time in the Senate.

I hope — I hope very deeply — as time passes, that I will be remembered for my commitment to California's promise, and my loyalty, in good times and bad, to great progressive principles.

Surely I have not done everything right but I hope that when my public life is weighed in the balance, it will not be found wanting.

These two years have taken much from me. The greatest cost is the anguish and uncertainty felt by my family and others who have stood with us. May none of you, may none of you ever have to battle cancer and something like this at the same time in your lives. ■

PEACE CONFERENCE

Fairness, Security, 5-Year Plan Tops Bush's Mideast List

On Oct. 30, President Bush addressed the Middle East Peace Conference in Madrid, Spain. Following is the Reuter transcript of his remarks:

PRESIDENT BUSH: Let me begin by thanking the government of Spain for hosting this historic gathering. With short notice, the Spanish people and their leaders stepped forward to make available this magnificent setting. And let us hope that this conference of Madrid will mark the beginning of a new chapter in the history of the Middle East.

I also want to express at the outset my pleasure at the presence of our fellow co-sponsor, President [Mikhail S.] Gorbachev. At a time of momentous challenges at home, President Gorbachev and his senior associates have demonstrated their intent to engage the Soviet Union as a force for positive change in the Middle East. And this sends a powerful signal to all those who long for peace.

We come to Madrid on a mission of hope, to begin work on a just, lasting and comprehensive settlement to the conflict in the Middle East.

We come here to seek peace for part of the world that in the long memory of man has known far too much hatred, anguish and war. I can think of no endeavor more worthy or more necessary. Our objective must be clear and straightforward. It is not simply to end the state of war in the Middle East and replace it with a state of non-belligerency. This is not enough. This would not last. Rather we seek peace, real peace. And by real peace I mean treaties, security, diplomatic relations, economic relations, trade, investment, cultural exchange, even tourism.

What we seek is a Middle East where vast resources are no longer devoted to armaments. A Middle East where young people no longer have to dedicate and all too often give their lives to combat. A Middle East no longer victimized by fear and terror. A Middle East where normal men and woman lead normal lives.

Hope Vs. History

Let no one mistake the magnitude of this challenge. The struggle we seek to end has a long and painful history. Every life lost, every outrage, every act of violence, is etched deep in the hearts and history of the people of this region.

There is a history that weighs heavily against hope, and yet history need not be man's master.

I expect that some will say that what I'm suggesting is impossible. But think back. Who back in 1945 would have thought that France and Germany, bitter rivals for nearly a century, would become allies in the aftermath of World War II? And who, two years ago, would have predicted that the Berlin Wall would come down? And who in the early 1960s would have believed that the Cold War would come to a peaceful end, replaced by cooperation, exemplified by the fact that the United States and the Soviet Union are here today, not as rivals, but as partners, as Prime Minister [Felipe] González pointed out.

> **"We come here to seek peace for part of the world that in the long memory of man has known far too much hatred, anguish and war. I can think of no endeavor more worthy or more necessary."**
>
> **—President Bush**

Peace is Possible

No, peace in the Middle East need not be a dream. Peace is possible. The Egyptian-Israeli peace treaty is striking proof that former adversaries can make and sustain peace. And moreover, parties in the Middle East have respected agreements, not only in the Sinai, but on the Golan Heights as well.

The fact that we are all gathered here today for the first time attests to a new potential for peace. Each of us has taken an important step toward real peace by meeting here in Madrid.

All the formulas on paper, all the pious declarations in the world won't bring peace if there is not a practical mechanism for moving ahead.

Peace will only come as the result of direct negotiations, compromise, give-and-take. Peace cannot be imposed from the outside by the United States or anyone else. And while we will continue to do everything possible to help the parties overcome obstacles, peace must come from within.

We come here to Madrid as realists. We don't expect peace to be negotiated in a day or a week or a month or even a year. It will take time. Indeed, it should take time: time for parties so long at war to learn to talk to one another, to listen to one another; time to heal old wounds and build trust.

In this quest, time need not be the enemy of progress. What we envision is a process of direct negotiations proceeding along two tracks: one between Israel and the Arab states, the other between Israel and the Palestinians. Negotiations are to be conducted on the basis of U.N. Security Council resolutions 242 and 338. The real work will not happen here in this — in the plenary sessions, but in direct, bilateral negotiations.

This conference cannot impose a settlement on the participants or veto agreements. And just as important, the conference can only be reconvened with the consent of every participant.

Progress is in the hands of the parties who must live with the consequences. Soon after the bilateral talks commence, parties will convene as well to organize multilateral negotiations. These will focus on issues that cross national boundaries and are common to the region: arms control, water, refugee concerns, economic development.

Progress in these four is not intended as a substitute for what must be decided in the bilateral talks. To the contrary, progress in the multilateral issues can help create an atmosphere in which long-standing bilateral disputes can more easily be settled.

For Israel and the Palestinians, a framework already exists for diplomacy. Negotiations will be conducted in phases, beginning with talks on interim self-government arrangements.

We aim to reach agreement within one year, and once agreed, interim self-government arrangements will last for five years. Beginning the third year, negotiations will commence on permanent status.

No one can say with any precision what the end result will be. In our view, something must be developed, something acceptable to Israel, the Palestinians and Jordan that gives the Palestinian people meaningful control over their own lives and fate and provides for the acceptance and security of Israel.

Israeli-Palestinian Compromise

We can all appreciate that both Israelis and Palestinians are worried about compromise, worried about compromising even the smallest point for fear it becomes a precedent for what really matters.

But no one should avoid compromise on interim arrangements for a simple reason: Nothing agreed to now will prejudice permanent status negotiations. To the contrary, these subsequent negotiations will be determined on their own merits.

Peace cannot depend upon promises alone. Real peace, lasting peace, must be based upon security for all states and people, including Israel. For too long, the Israeli people have lived in fear surrounded by an unaccepting Arab world. And now is the ideal moment for the Arab world to demonstrate that attitudes have changed, that the Arab world is willing to live in peace with Israel and make allowances for Israel's reasonable security needs.

We know that peace must also be based on fairness. In the absence of fairness, there will be no legitimacy, no stability. And this applies above all to the Palestinian people, many of whom have known turmoil and frustration above all else.

Israel now has an opportunity to demonstrate that it is willing to enter into a new relationship with its Palestinian neighbors, one predicated upon mutual respect and cooperation. Throughout the Middle East we seek a stable and enduring settlement. We've not defined what this means. Indeed, I make these points with no map showing where the final borders are to be drawn. And nevertheless, we believe that territorial compromise is essential for peace. Boundaries should reflect the quality of both security and political arrangements, and the United States is prepared to accept whatever the parties themselves find acceptable.

What we seek, as I said on March 6th, is a solution that meets the twin tests of fairness and security.

Focus on a Vision

I know, I expect we all know, that these negotiations will not be easy. I know too that these negotiations will not be smooth. There will be disagreement and criticism. Setbacks. Who knows, possibly interruptions. Negotiation and compromise are always painful. Success will escape us if we focus solely upon what is being given up. We must fix our vision on what real peace would bring. Peace, after all, means not just avoiding war and the costs of preparing for it. The Middle East is blessed with great resources, physical, financial and, yes, above all, human. And new opportunities are within reach, if we only have the vision to embrace them.

To succeed, we must recognize that peace is in the interest of all parties — war, the absolute advantage of none. The alternative to peace in the Middle East is a future of violence and waste and tragedy.

In any future wars lurk the dangers of weapons of mass destruction. As we learned in the gulf war, modern arsenals make it possible to attack urban areas, to put the lives of innocent men, women and children at risk, to transform city streets, schools, children's playgrounds, into battlefields.

Today we can decide to take a different path to the future, to avoid conflict. And I call upon all parties to avoid unilateral acts, be they words or deeds, that would invite retaliation, or worse yet, prejudice or even threaten the process itself.

I call upon all parties to consider taking measures that will bolster mutual confidence and trust, steps that signal a sincere commitment to reconciliation.

U.S. Guarantees

I want to say something about the role of the United States of America. We played an active role in making this conference possible. And both the secretary of State, Jim Baker, and I will play an active role in helping the process succeed.

Toward this end we've provided written assurances to Israel, to Syria, to Jordan, Lebanon and the Palestinians, and in the spirit of openness and honesty, we will brief all parties on assurances that we have provided to the others.

We're prepared to extend guarantees, provide technology and support, if that is what peace requires. And we will call upon our friends and allies in Europe and in Asia to join with us in providing resources so that peace and prosperity go hand in hand.

Seize the Moment

Outsiders can assist, but in the end, it is up to the peoples and the governments of the Middle East to shape the future of the Middle East. It is their opportunity and it is their responsibility to do all that they can to take advantage of this gathering, this historic gathering, and what it symbolizes and what it promises.

No one should assume that the opportunity before us to make peace will remain if we fail to seize the moment.

Ironically, this is an opportunity born of war, the destruction of past wars, the fear of future wars. The time has come to put an end to war. The time has come to choose peace.

And speaking for the American people, I want to reaffirm that the United States is prepared to facilitate the search for peace, to be a catalyst as we have been in the past, and as we've been very recently.

We seek only one thing, and this we seek not for ourselves, but for the peoples of the area, and particularly the children: that this and future generations of the Middle East may know the meaning and blessing of peace.

We have seen too many generations of children whose haunted eyes show only fear. Too many funerals for the brothers and sisters — the mothers and fathers who died too soon. Too much hatred, too little love.

And if we cannot summon the courage to lay down the past for ourselves, let us resolve to do it for the children.

May God bless and guide the work of this conference and may this conference set us on the path of peace.

Thank you. ■

Opening Positions

THE ISRAELIS

Israel's Prime Minister Yitzhak Shamir addressed the Middle East conference on Oct. 31. This is an excerpt from the Reuter transcript:

I stand before you today in yet another quest for peace, not only on behalf of the State of Israel, but in the name of the entire Jewish people, that has maintained an unbreakable bond with the Land of Israel for almost 4,000 years. . . .

It will be regrettable if the talks focus primarily and exclusively on territory. It is the quickest way to an impasse. What we need, first and foremost, is the building of confidence, the removal of the danger of confrontation and the development of relations in as many spheres as possible. . . .

We submit that the best venue for the talks is in our region, in close proximity to the decision-makers, not in a foreign land. We invite our partners to this process to come to Israel for the first round of talks. On our part, we are ready to go to Jordan, to Lebanon and to Syria. . . .

We must learn to live without war, without bloodshed. Judaism has given the world not only the belief in one God, but the idea that all men and women are created in God's image. There is no greater sin than to ravage this image by shedding blood.

THE PALESTINIANS

Haidar Abdul-Shafi, head of the Palestinian delegation, was among Arab representatives who addressed the conference on Oct. 31. An excerpt:

For too long the Palestinian people have gone unheeded, silenced and denied — our identity negated by political expediency, our rightful struggle against injustice maligned, and our present existence subsumed by the past tragedy of another people. . . .

We come here wrenched from our sisters and brothers in exile to stand before you as the Palestinians under occupation, although we maintain that each of us represents the rights and interest of the whole. We have been denied the right to publicly acknowledge our loyalty to our leadership and system of government, but allegiance and loyalty cannot be censored. . . .

Israel must demonstrate its willingness to negotiate in good faith by immediately halting all settlement activity and land confiscation while implementing meaningful confidence-building measures. . . .

In the words of Chairman [Yasir] Arafat in 1989 before the U.N. General Assembly: "Let not the olive branch fall from my hands." Let not the olive branch fall from the hands of the Palestinian people. ■

CQ

HOUSE ROLL-CALL VOTES

HOUSE VOTES 2, 3, 4, 5, 6, 7, 8, 9

2. Election of Speaker. Nominees for Speaker of the House of Representatives for the 102nd Congress were Thomas S. Foley, D-Wash., Speaker since June 1989, and Robert H. Michel, R-Ill., the minority leader since 1981. Foley elected 262-165: R 0-165; D 261-0 (ND 178-0, SD 83-0); I 1-0, Jan. 3, 1991. A "Y" on the chart represents a vote for Foley, an "N" a vote for Michel. A "+" on the chart means the member announced for Foley.

3. H Res 5. Rules of the House. Frost, D-Texas, motion to order the previous question (thus ending debate and the possibility of amendment) on the resolution to adopt the rules of the 101st Congress for the 102nd, except for 19 changes approved by the Democratic Caucus on Dec. 4, 1990, including an amendment to require that any House legislation involving direct spending or revenues include a binding Congressional Budget Office estimate through 1995 for the purposes of "pay-as-you-go" sequestration. Motion agreed to 250-162: R 0-161; D 249-1 (ND 169-1, SD 80-0); I 1-0, Jan. 3, 1991. A "nay" was a vote supporting the president's position.

4. H Res 5. Rules of the House. Michel, R-Ill., motion to commit the resolution to adopt the rules of the 101st Congress for the 102nd with 19 changes to a select committee made up of the majority leader and the minority leader, with instructions to report the resolution back to the House after deleting the provision that requires any House legislation involving direct spending or revenues to include a binding Congressional Budget Office estimate. Motion rejected 160-256: R 160-0; D 0-255 (ND 0-173, SD 0-82); I 0-1, Jan. 3, 1991. A "yea" was a vote supporting the president's position.

5. H Res 5. Rules of the House/Adoption. Adoption of the resolution to adopt the rules of the 101st Congress for the 102nd, except for 19 changes approved by the Democratic Caucus on Dec. 4, 1990. Adopted 242-160: R 0-160; D 241-0 (ND 163-0, SD 78-0); 1-0, Jan. 3, 1991. A "nay" was a vote supporting the president's position.

6. Procedural Motion. Edwards, R-Okla., motion to approve the House Journal of Friday, Jan. 11. Motion agreed to 286-92: R 73-87; D 212-5 (ND 142-5, SD 70-0); I 1-0, Jan. 12, 1991.

7. H Con Res 32. Congressional Authorization for Offensive Action Against Iraq/Adoption. Adoption of the concurrent resolution to express the sense of Congress that the Constitution vests the power to declare war in Congress, and the president must gain congressional approval before any offensive military action can be taken against Iraq. Adopted 302-131: R 41-126; D 260-5 (ND 179-1, SD 81-4); I 1-0, Jan. 12, 1991. A "nay" was a vote supporting the president's position.

8. H Con Res 33. Sanctions Against Iraq/Adoption. Adoption of the concurrent resolution to express the sense of Congress that the wisest course of action is the continued use of international sanctions and diplomatic efforts to pressure Iraq to withdraw from Kuwait. The resolution declares that the president must obtain congressional approval before undertaking any offensive action against Iraq. Rejected 183-250: R 3-164; D 179-86 (ND 146-34, SD 33-52); I-1-0, Jan. 12, 1991. A "nay" was a vote supporting the president's position.

9. H J Res 77. Use of Force Against Iraq/Passage. Passage of the joint resolution to authorize the use of military force if Iraq has not withdrawn from Kuwait and complied with U.N. Security Council resolutions by Jan. 15. The resolution authorizes the use of force and the expenditure of funds under the War Powers act and requires the president to report to Congress every 60 days on the efforts to obtain Iraqi compliance. Passed 250-183: R 164-3; D 86-179 (ND 33-147, SD 53-32); I 0-1, Jan. 12, 1991. A "yea" was a vote supporting the president's position.

†: Bob Carr, D-Mich.; Jim Chapman, D-Texas; Paul E. Gillmor, R-Ohio; and Frank J. Guarini, D-N.J., had not been sworn in as of Jan. 4.

KEY

- Y Voted for (yea).
- # Paired for.
- \+ Announced for.
- N Voted against (nay).
- X Paired against.
- \- Announced against.
- P Voted "present."
- C Voted "present" to avoid possible conflict of interest.
- ? Did not vote or otherwise make a position known.

Democrats ***Republicans***
Independent

	2	3	4	5	6	7	8	9
ALABAMA								
1 ***Callahan***	N	N	Y	N	Y	N	N	Y
2 ***Dickinson***	N	N	Y	N	N	N	N	Y
3 Browder	Y	Y	N	Y	Y	Y	N	Y
4 Bevill	Y	Y	N	Y	Y	Y	N	Y
5 Cramer	Y	Y	N	Y	Y	Y	N	Y
6 Erdreich	Y	Y	N	Y	Y	Y	N	Y
7 Harris	Y	Y	N	Y	Y	Y	N	Y
ALASKA								
AL ***Young***	N	N	Y	N	N	N	N	Y
ARIZONA								
1 ***Rhodes***	N	N	Y	N	N	N	N	Y
2 Udall	Y	Y	N	Y	?	?	?	?
3 ***Stump***	N	N	Y	N	N	N	N	Y
4 ***Kyl***	N	N	Y	N	N	N	N	Y
5 ***Kolbe***	N	N	Y	N	N	N	N	Y
ARKANSAS								
1 Alexander	Y	Y	N	Y	Y	Y	Y	N
2 Thornton	Y	Y	N	Y	?	Y	N	Y
3 ***Hammerschmidt***	N	N	Y	N	Y	Y	N	Y
4 Anthony	Y	Y	N	Y	Y	Y	Y	N
CALIFORNIA								
1 ***Riggs***	N	N	Y	N	N	N	Y	N
2 ***Herger***	N	N	Y	N	N	N	N	Y
3 Matsui	Y	Y	N	Y	Y	Y	Y	N
4 Fazio	Y	Y	N	Y	Y	Y	Y	N
5 Pelosi	Y	Y	N	Y	Y	Y	Y	N
6 Boxer	Y	Y	N	Y	Y	Y	Y	N
7 Miller	Y	Y	N	Y	Y	Y	Y	N
8 Dellums	Y	Y	N	Y	Y	Y	Y	N
9 Stark	Y	Y	N	Y	?	Y	Y	N
10 Edwards	Y	Y	N	Y	Y	Y	Y	N
11 Lantos	Y	Y	N	Y	Y	Y	N	Y
12 ***Campbell***	N	N	Y	N	N	N	N	Y
13 Mineta	Y	Y	N	Y	Y	Y	Y	N
14 ***Doolittle***	N	N	Y	N	N	N	N	Y
15 Condit	Y	Y	N	Y	?	Y	N	Y
16 Panetta	Y	Y	N	Y	Y	Y	Y	N
17 Dooley	Y	Y	N	Y	Y	Y	Y	N
18 Lehman	Y	Y	N	Y	Y	Y	N	Y
19 ***Lagomarsino***	N	N	Y	N	N	N	N	Y
20 ***Thomas***	N	N	Y	N	N	N	N	Y
21 ***Gallegly***	N	N	Y	N	N	N	N	Y
22 ***Moorhead***	N	N	Y	N	N	N	N	Y
23 Beilenson	Y	Y	N	Y	?	Y	Y	N
24 Waxman	Y	Y	N	Y	?	Y	Y	N
25 Roybal	Y	Y	N	Y	Y	Y	Y	N
26 Berman	Y	Y	N	Y	Y	Y	N	Y
27 Levine	Y	?	?	?	Y	Y	N	Y
28 Dixon	Y	Y	N	Y	?	Y	Y	N
29 Waters	Y	Y	N	Y	?	Y	Y	N
30 Martinez	Y	Y	N	Y	?	Y	Y	N
31 Dymally	Y	?	?	?	?	+	+	-
32 Anderson	Y	Y	N	Y	Y	Y	N	Y
33 ***Dreier***	N	N	Y	N	Y	N	N	Y
34 Torres	Y	Y	N	Y	?	Y	Y	N
35 ***Lewis***	N	N	Y	N	N	N	N	Y
36 Brown	Y	Y	N	?	Y	Y	Y	N
37 ***McCandless***	N	N	Y	N	N	N	N	Y
38 ***Dornan***	N	N	Y	N	N	N	N	Y
39 ***Dannemeyer***	N	N	Y	N	N	N	N	Y
40 ***Cox***	N	N	Y	N	?	N	N	Y
41 ***Lowery***	N	N	Y	N	N	N	N	Y
42 ***Rohrabacher***	N	N	Y	N	N	N	N	Y
43 ***Packard***	N	N	Y	N	Y	N	N	Y
44 ***Cunningham***	N	N	Y	N	Y	N	N	Y
45 ***Hunter***	N	N	Y	N	N	N	N	Y
COLORADO								
1 Schroeder	Y	Y	N	Y	N	Y	Y	N
2 Skaggs	Y	Y	N	Y	Y	Y	Y	N
3 Campbell	Y	Y	N	Y	Y	Y	N	Y
4 ***Allard***	N	N	Y	N	N	N	N	Y
5 ***Hefley***	N	N	Y	N	N	N	N	Y
6 ***Schaefer***	N	N	Y	N	N	N	N	Y
CONNECTICUT								
1 Kennelly	Y	Y	N	Y	Y	Y	Y	N
2 Gejdenson	Y	Y	N	Y	Y	Y	Y	N
3 DeLauro	Y	Y	N	Y	Y	Y	Y	N
4 ***Shays***	N	N	Y	N	N	Y	N	Y
5 ***Franks***	N	N	Y	N	Y	N	N	Y
6 ***Johnson***	N	N	Y	N	Y	Y	N	Y
DELAWARE								
AL Carper	Y	Y	N	Y	?	Y	N	Y
FLORIDA								
1 Hutto	Y	Y	N	Y	?	Y	N	Y
2 Peterson	Y	Y	N	Y	Y	Y	Y	N
3 Bennett	Y	Y	N	Y	Y	Y	Y	N
4 ***James***	N	N	Y	N	N	N	N	Y
5 ***McCollum***	N	N	Y	N	Y	N	N	Y
6 ***Stearns***	N	N	Y	N	N	N	N	Y
7 Gibbons	Y	Y	N	Y	Y	Y	Y	N
8 ***Young***	N	N	Y	N	N	Y	N	Y
9 ***Bilirakis***	N	N	Y	N	Y	N	N	Y
10 ***Ireland***	N	N	Y	N	N	N	N	Y
11 Bacchus	Y	Y	N	Y	Y	Y	N	Y
12 ***Lewis***	N	N	Y	N	N	N	N	Y
13 ***Goss***	N	N	Y	N	N	N	N	Y
14 Johnston	Y	Y	N	Y	Y	Y	Y	N
15 ***Shaw***	N	N	Y	N	Y	N	N	Y
16 Smith	Y	Y	N	Y	Y	Y	Y	N
17 Lehman	Y	Y	N	Y	Y	Y	Y	N
18 ***Ros-Lehtinen***	N	N	Y	N	N	N	N	Y
19 Fascell	Y	Y	N	Y	Y	Y	N	Y
GEORGIA								
1 Thomas	Y	Y	N	Y	Y	Y	N	Y
2 Hatcher	Y	Y	N	Y	Y	N	N	Y
3 Ray	Y	Y	N	Y	?	N	N	Y
4 Jones	Y	Y	N	Y	Y	Y	N	Y
5 Lewis	Y	Y	N	?	Y	Y	Y	N
6 ***Gingrich***	N	N	Y	N	N	N	N	Y
7 Darden	Y	Y	N	Y	Y	Y	N	Y
8 Rowland	Y	Y	N	Y	Y	Y	N	Y
9 Jenkins	Y	Y	N	Y	Y	Y	Y	N
10 Barnard	Y	Y	N	Y	Y	Y	N	Y
HAWAII								
1 Abercrombie	Y	Y	N	Y	Y	Y	Y	N
2 Mink	Y	Y	N	Y	Y	Y	Y	N
IDAHO								
1 LaRocco	Y	Y	N	Y	Y	Y	Y	N
2 Stallings	Y	Y	N	Y	Y	Y	Y	N
ILLINOIS								
1 Hayes	Y	Y	N	Y	N	Y	Y	N
2 Savage	Y	?	?	?	?	Y	Y	N
3 Russo	Y	Y	N	Y	Y	Y	Y	N
4 Sangmeister	Y	Y	N	Y	Y	Y	Y	N
5 Lipinski	Y	?	N	Y	Y	Y	Y	N
6 ***Hyde***	N	N	Y	N	N	N	N	Y
7 Collins	Y	Y	N	Y	Y	Y	Y	N
8 Rostenkowski	Y	Y	N	Y	?	Y	N	Y
9 Yates	Y	Y	N	Y	Y	Y	Y	N
10 ***Porter***	N	N	Y	N	Y	Y	N	Y
11 Annunzio	Y	Y	N	Y	Y	Y	Y	N
12 ***Crane***	N	N	Y	N	?	N	N	Y
13 ***Fawell***	N	N	Y	N	N	Y	N	Y
14 ***Hastert***	N	N	Y	N	N	N	N	Y
15 Madigan	N	N	Y	N	Y	N	N	Y
16 Cox	Y	Y	N	Y	Y	Y	Y	N
17 Evans	Y	Y	N	Y	Y	Y	Y	N
18 ***Michel***	P	N	Y	N	Y	N	N	Y
19 Bruce	Y	Y	N	Y	Y	Y	Y	N
20 Durbin	Y	Y	N	Y	Y	Y	Y	N
21 Costello	Y	Y	N	Y	Y	Y	Y	N
22 Poshard	Y	Y	N	Y	Y	Y	Y	N
INDIANA								
1 Visclosky	Y	Y	N	Y	Y	Y	Y	N
2 Sharp	Y	Y	N	Y	Y	Y	Y	N
3 Roemer	Y	Y	N	Y	Y	Y	Y	N

ND Northern Democrats SD Southern Democrats

	2	3	4	5	6	7	8	9
4 Long	Y	Y	N	Y	Y	Y	Y	N
5 Jontz	Y	Y	N	Y	Y	Y	Y	N
6 ***Burton***	N	N	Y	N	N	N	N	Y
7 ***Myers***	N	N	Y	N	Y	N	N	Y
8 McCloskey	Y	Y	N	Y	?	Y	Y	N
9 Hamilton	Y	Y	N	Y	Y	Y	Y	N
10 Jacobs	Y	N	N	Y	Y	Y	Y	N
IOWA								
1 ***Leach***	N	N	Y	N	N	Y	N	Y
2 ***Nussle***	N	N	Y	N	N	N	N	Y
3 Nagle	Y	Y	N	Y	Y	Y	Y	N
4 Smith	Y	Y	N	Y	Y	N	N	N
5 ***Lightfoot***	N	N	Y	N	N	N	N	Y
6 ***Grandy***	N	N	Y	N	Y	N	N	Y
KANSAS								
1 ***Roberts***	N	N	Y	N	?	N	N	Y
2 Slattery	Y	Y	N	Y	?	Y	N	Y
3 ***Meyers***	N	N	Y	N	Y	Y	N	Y
4 Glickman	Y	Y	N	Y	Y	Y	N	Y
5 ***Nichols***	N	N	Y	N	Y	N	N	Y
KENTUCKY								
1 Hubbard	Y	Y	N	Y	Y	Y	N	Y
2 Natcher	Y	Y	N	Y	Y	Y	Y	N
3 Mazzoli	Y	Y	N	Y	Y	Y	Y	N
4 ***Bunning***	N	N	Y	N	N	N	N	Y
5 ***Rogers***	N	N	Y	N	N	N	N	Y
6 ***Hopkins***	N	N	?	N	N	N	N	Y
7 Perkins	Y	Y	N	Y	Y	Y	Y	N
LOUISIANA								
1 ***Livingston***	N	N	Y	N	Y	N	N	Y
2 Jefferson	Y	?	N	?	Y	Y	Y	N
3 Tauzin	Y	Y	N	Y	?	Y	N	Y
4 ***McCrery***	N	N	Y	N	Y	N	N	Y
5 Huckaby	Y	Y	N	Y	Y	Y	N	Y
6 ***Baker***	N	N	Y	N	N	N	N	Y
7 Hayes	Y	Y	N	Y	?	Y	N	Y
8 ***Holloway***	N	N	Y	N	N	N	N	Y
MAINE								
1 Andrews	Y	Y	N	Y	Y	Y	Y	N
2 ***Snowe***	N	?	?	?	Y	Y	N	Y
MARYLAND								
1 ***Gilchrest***	N	N	Y	N	N	Y	N	Y
2 ***Bentley***	N	N	Y	N	N	Y	N	Y
3 Cardin	Y	Y	N	Y	Y	Y	Y	N
4 McMillen	Y	Y	N	Y	Y	Y	N	Y
5 Hoyer	Y	Y	N	Y	Y	Y	Y	N
6 Byron	Y	Y	N	Y	Y	Y	N	Y
7 Mfume	Y	Y	N	?	Y	Y	Y	N
8 ***Morella***	N	N	Y	N	N	Y	Y	N
MASSACHUSETTS								
1 Conte	N	N	Y	N	Y	Y	Y	N
2 Neal	Y	Y	N	?	Y	Y	Y	N
3 Early	Y	Y	N	Y	Y	Y	Y	N
4 Frank	Y	Y	N	Y	Y	Y	Y	N
5 Atkins	Y	Y	N	Y	Y	Y	Y	N
6 Mavroules	Y	Y	N	Y	Y	Y	Y	N
7 Markey	Y	Y	N	Y	Y	Y	Y	N
8 Kennedy	Y	Y	N	Y	Y	Y	Y	N
9 Moakley	Y	Y	N	Y	?	Y	Y	N
10 Studds	Y	Y	N	Y	Y	Y	Y	N
11 Donnelly	Y	Y	N	Y	?	Y	Y	N
MICHIGAN								
1 Conyers	Y	Y	N	Y	?	Y	Y	N
2 ***Pursell***	N	N	Y	N	Y	N	N	Y
3 Wolpe	Y	Y	N	Y	Y	Y	Y	N
4 ***Upton***	N	N	Y	N	N	Y	N	Y
5 ***Henry***	N	N	Y	N	Y	Y	N	Y
6 Carr †	?				Y	Y	Y	N
7 Kildee	Y	Y	N	Y	Y	Y	Y	N
8 Traxler	Y	Y	N	Y	Y	Y	Y	N
9 ***Vander Jagt***	N	N	Y	N	?	N	N	Y
10 ***Camp***	N	N	Y	N	N	N	N	Y
11 ***Davis***	N	?	?	?	Y	N	N	Y
12 Bonior	Y	Y	N	Y	Y	Y	Y	N
13 Collins	Y	Y	N	?	?	Y	Y	N
14 Hertel	Y	Y	N	Y	Y	Y	Y	N
15 Ford	Y	Y	N	Y	?	Y	Y	N
16 Dingell	Y	Y	N	Y	Y	Y	N	Y
17 Levin	Y	Y	N	Y	Y	Y	Y	N
18 ***Broomfield***	N	N	Y	N	Y	N	N	Y
MINNESOTA								
1 Penny	Y	Y	N	Y	?	Y	Y	N
2 ***Weber***	N	N	Y	N	N	N	N	Y
3 ***Ramstad***	N	N	Y	N	Y	Y	N	Y
4 Vento	Y	Y	N	Y	?	Y	Y	N
5 Sabo	Y	Y	N	Y	Y	Y	Y	N
6 Sikorski	Y	?	?	?	N	Y	Y	N
7 Peterson	Y	Y	N	Y	Y	Y	Y	N
8 Oberstar	Y	Y	N	Y	Y	Y	Y	N
MISSISSIPPI								
1 Whitten	Y	Y	N	Y	Y	Y	N	Y
2 Espy	Y	Y	N	?	Y	Y	Y	N
3 Montgomery	Y	Y	N	Y	Y	N	N	Y
4 Parker	Y	Y	N	Y	Y	Y	N	Y
5 Taylor	Y	Y	N	Y	Y	Y	Y	N
MISSOURI								
1 Clay	Y	Y	N	?	N	Y	Y	N
2 Horn	Y	Y	N	Y	Y	Y	Y	N
3 Gephardt	Y	Y	N	Y	Y	Y	Y	N
4 Skelton	Y	Y	N	Y	Y	Y	N	Y
5 Wheat	Y	Y	N	Y	Y	Y	Y	N
6 ***Coleman***	N	N	Y	N	Y	Y	N	Y
7 ***Hancock***	N	N	Y	N	?	N	N	Y
8 ***Emerson***	N	N	Y	N	Y	Y	N	Y
9 Volkmer	Y	Y	N	Y	Y	Y	N	Y
MONTANA								
1 Williams	Y	Y	N	Y	Y	Y	Y	N
2 ***Marlenee***	N	N	Y	N	N	N	N	Y
NEBRASKA								
1 ***Bereuter***	N	N	Y	N	Y	Y	N	Y
2 Hoagland	Y	Y	N	Y	?	Y	N	Y
3 ***Barrett***	N	N	Y	N	N	N	N	Y
NEVADA								
1 Bilbray	Y	Y	N	Y	?	Y	N	Y
2 ***Vucanovich***	N	N	Y	N	N	N	N	Y
NEW HAMPSHIRE								
1 ***Zeliff***	N	N	Y	N	N	N	N	Y
2 Swett	Y	?	N	Y	Y	Y	N	Y
NEW JERSEY								
1 Andrews	Y	Y	N	Y	Y	Y	N	N
2 Hughes	Y	Y	N	Y	Y	Y	N	Y
3 Pallone	Y	?	N	Y	Y	Y	N	Y
4 ***Smith***	N	N	Y	N	Y	N	N	Y
5 ***Roukema***	N	N	Y	N	N	Y	N	Y
6 Dwyer	Y	Y	N	?	Y	Y	Y	N
7 ***Rinaldo***	N	N	Y	N	Y	Y	N	Y
8 Roe	Y	Y	N	Y	Y	Y	Y	N
9 Torricelli	Y	Y	N	Y	Y	Y	N	Y
10 Payne	Y	Y	N	Y	Y	Y	Y	N
11 ***Gallo***	N	N	Y	N	Y	N	N	Y
12 ***Zimmer***	N	N	Y	N	N	Y	N	Y
13 ***Saxton***	N	N	Y	N	N	N	N	Y
14 Guarini †	?				Y	Y	Y	N
NEW MEXICO								
1 ***Schiff***	N	N	Y	N	Y	N	N	Y
2 ***Skeen***	N	N	Y	N	Y	N	N	Y
3 Richardson	Y	Y	N	Y	Y	Y	Y	N
NEW YORK								
1 Hochbrueckner	Y	?	?	?	Y	Y	Y	N
2 Downey	Y	Y	N	Y	Y	Y	Y	N
3 Mrazek	Y	Y	N	?	Y	Y	Y	N
4 ***Lent***	N	N	Y	N	Y	N	N	Y
5 ***McGrath***	N	N	Y	N	N	Y	N	Y
6 Flake	Y	Y	N	?	?	Y	Y	N
7 Ackerman	Y	Y	N	Y	Y	Y	N	Y
8 Scheuer	Y	Y	N	Y	Y	Y	Y	N
9 Manton	Y	Y	N	Y	?	Y	Y	N
10 Schumer	Y	Y	N	Y	Y	Y	Y	N
11 Towns	Y	Y	N	?	Y	Y	Y	N
12 Owens	Y	Y	N	?	?	Y	Y	N
13 Solarz	Y	Y	N	Y	Y	Y	N	Y
14 ***Molinari***	N	N	Y	N	N	N	N	Y
15 ***Green***	N	N	Y	N	Y	Y	N	Y
16 Rangel	Y	Y	N	?	Y	Y	Y	N
17 Weiss	Y	Y	N	Y	?	Y	Y	N
18 Serrano	Y	Y	N	Y	Y	Y	Y	N
19 Engel	Y	Y	N	Y	Y	Y	N	Y
20 Lowey	Y	Y	N	Y	Y	Y	Y	N
21 ***Fish***	N	N	Y	N	Y	N	N	Y
22 ***Gilman***	N	N	Y	N	Y	N	N	Y
23 McNulty	Y	Y	N	Y	Y	Y	Y	Y
24 ***Solomon***	N	N	Y	N	N	N	N	Y
25 ***Boehlert***	N	N	Y	N	N	Y	N	Y
26 ***Martin***	N	N	Y	N	N	N	N	Y
27 ***Walsh***	N	N	Y	N	Y	Y	N	Y
28 McHugh	Y	Y	N	Y	?	Y	Y	N
29 ***Horton***	N	N	Y	N	Y	N	N	Y
30 Slaughter	Y	Y	N	Y	Y	Y	Y	N
31 ***Paxon***	N	N	Y	N	N	N	N	Y
32 LaFalce	Y	Y	N	Y	Y	Y	Y	N
33 Nowak	Y	Y	N	Y	Y	Y	Y	N
34 ***Houghton***	N	N	Y	N	Y	N	N	Y
NORTH CAROLINA								
1 Jones	Y	Y	N	Y	?	Y	N	Y
2 Valentine	Y	Y	N	Y	?	Y	N	Y
3 Lancaster	Y	Y	N	Y	Y	Y	N	Y
4 Price	+	Y	N	Y	Y	Y	Y	N
5 Neal	Y	Y	?	Y	Y	Y	Y	N
6 ***Coble***	N	N	Y	N	N	Y	N	Y
7 Rose	Y	Y	N	Y	Y	Y	Y	N
8 Hefner	Y	Y	N	Y	Y	Y	Y	N
9 ***McMillan***	N	N	Y	N	Y	N	N	Y
10 ***Ballenger***	N	-	+	-	N	N	N	Y
11 ***Taylor***	N	N	Y	N	N	N	N	Y
NORTH DAKOTA								
AL Dorgan	Y	Y	N	Y	Y	Y	Y	N
OHIO								
1 Luken	Y	Y	N	Y	Y	Y	N	Y
2 ***Gradison***	N	N	Y	N	Y	N	N	Y
3 Hall	Y	Y	N	Y	Y	Y	Y	N
4 ***Oxley***	N	N	Y	N	Y	N	N	Y
5 ***Gillmor*** †	?				Y	N	N	Y
6 ***McEwen***	N	N	Y	N	Y	N	N	Y
7 ***Hobson***	N	N	Y	N	N	Y	N	Y
8 ***Boehner***	N	N	Y	N	Y	N	N	Y
9 Kaptur	Y	Y	N	Y	Y	Y	Y	N
10 ***Miller***	N	N	Y	N	N	N	N	Y
11 Eckart	Y	Y	N	Y	Y	Y	Y	N
12 ***Kasich***	N	N	?	N	Y	N	N	Y
13 Pease	Y	Y	N	Y	?	Y	Y	N
14 Sawyer	Y	Y	N	Y	Y	Y	Y	N
15 ***Wylie***	N	N	Y	N	Y	N	N	Y
16 ***Regula***	N	N	Y	N	N	Y	N	Y
17 Traficant	Y	Y	N	Y	Y	Y	Y	N
18 Applegate	Y	Y	N	Y	Y	Y	Y	N
19 Feighan	Y	Y	N	Y	?	Y	Y	N
20 Oakar	Y	Y	N	Y	Y	Y	Y	N
21 Stokes	Y	Y	N	Y	Y	Y	Y	N
OKLAHOMA								
1 ***Inhofe***	N	?	Y	N	N	N	N	Y
2 Synar	Y	Y	N	Y	Y	Y	Y	N
3 Brewster	Y	Y	N	Y	Y	Y	N	Y
4 McCurdy	Y	Y	N	Y	Y	Y	N	Y
5 ***Edwards***	N	N	Y	N	Y	N	N	Y
6 English	Y	Y	N	Y	Y	Y	Y	N
OREGON								
1 AuCoin	Y	Y	N	Y	?	Y	Y	N
2 ***Smith***	N	N	Y	?	N	N	N	Y
3 Wyden	Y	Y	N	Y	Y	Y	Y	N
4 DeFazio	Y	Y	N	Y	Y	Y	Y	N
5 Kopetski	Y	Y	N	Y	Y	Y	Y	N
PENNSYLVANIA								
1 Foglietta	Y	Y	N	Y	Y	Y	Y	N
2 Gray	Y	Y	N	Y	Y	Y	Y	N
3 Borski	Y	Y	N	Y	Y	Y	N	Y
4 Kolter	Y	Y	N	Y	Y	Y	Y	N
5 ***Schulze***	N	N	Y	N	Y	N	N	Y
6 Yatron	Y	Y	N	Y	Y	Y	Y	N
7 ***Weldon***	N	N	Y	N	N	Y	N	Y
8 Kostmayer	Y	Y	N	Y	Y	Y	Y	N
9 ***Shuster***	N	N	Y	N	Y	N	N	Y
10 ***McDade***	N	N	Y	N	Y	Y	N	Y
11 Kanjorski	Y	Y	N	Y	Y	Y	Y	N
12 Murtha	Y	Y	N	Y	Y	Y	N	Y
13 ***Coughlin***	N	N	Y	N	N	N	N	Y
14 Coyne	Y	Y	N	Y	?	Y	Y	N
15 ***Ritter***	N	N	Y	N	?	N	N	Y
16 ***Walker***	N	N	Y	N	N	N	N	Y
17 ***Gekas***	N	N	Y	N	N	N	N	Y
18 ***Santorum***	N	N	Y	N	N	Y	N	Y
19 ***Goodling***	N	N	Y	N	N	Y	N	Y
20 Gaydos	Y	Y	N	Y	Y	Y	Y	N
21 ***Ridge***	N	N	Y	N	?	Y	N	Y
22 Murphy	?	Y	N	Y	N	Y	Y	N
23 ***Clinger***	N	N	Y	N	Y	N	N	Y
RHODE ISLAND								
1 ***Machtley***	N	N	Y	N	N	Y	N	Y
2 Reed	Y	Y	N	Y	Y	Y	Y	N
SOUTH CAROLINA								
1 ***Ravenel***	N	N	Y	N	Y	N	N	Y
2 ***Spence***	N	N	Y	N	Y	N	N	Y
3 Derrick	Y	Y	N	Y	Y	Y	N	Y
4 Patterson	Y	Y	N	Y	Y	Y	N	Y
5 Spratt	Y	Y	N	Y	?	Y	N	Y
6 Tallon	Y	Y	N	Y	Y	Y	N	Y
SOUTH DAKOTA								
AL Johnson	Y	Y	N	Y	Y	Y	Y	N
TENNESSEE								
1 ***Quillen***	N	N	Y	N	Y	N	N	Y
2 ***Duncan***	N	N	Y	N	Y	Y	N	Y
3 Lloyd	Y	Y	N	Y	?	Y	N	Y
4 Cooper	Y	Y	N	Y	Y	Y	N	Y
5 Clement	Y	Y	N	Y	?	Y	N	Y
6 Gordon	Y	Y	N	Y	Y	Y	Y	Y
7 ***Sundquist***	N	N	Y	N	N	N	N	Y
8 Tanner	Y	Y	N	Y	Y	Y	N	Y
9 Ford	Y	Y	N	Y	?	Y	Y	N
TEXAS								
1 Chapman †	?				?	Y	N	Y
2 Wilson	Y	Y	N	Y	Y	Y	N	Y
3 ***Bartlett***	N	N	Y	N	Y	N	N	Y
4 Hall	Y	Y	N	Y	Y	Y	N	Y
5 Bryant	Y	Y	N	Y	Y	Y	Y	N
6 ***Barton***	N	N	Y	N	Y	N	N	Y
7 ***Archer***	N	N	Y	?	Y	N	N	Y
8 ***Fields***	N	N	Y	N	Y	N	N	Y
9 Brooks	Y	Y	N	Y	Y	Y	N	Y
10 Pickle	Y	Y	N	Y	Y	N	Y	N
11 Edwards	Y	Y	N	Y	Y	Y	N	Y
12 Geren	Y	Y	N	Y	Y	Y	N	Y
13 Sarpalius	Y	Y	N	Y	Y	Y	N	Y
14 Laughlin	Y	Y	N	Y	Y	Y	N	Y
15 de la Garza	Y	Y	N	Y	Y	Y	Y	Y
16 Coleman	Y	Y	N	Y	?	Y	Y	N
17 Stenholm	Y	Y	N	Y	Y	Y	N	Y
18 Washington	Y	Y	N	?	?	Y	Y	N
19 ***Combest***	N	N	Y	N	Y	N	N	Y
20 Gonzalez	Y	Y	N	Y	Y	Y	N	N
21 ***Smith***	N	?	?	?	N	N	N	Y
22 ***DeLay***	N	N	Y	N	Y	N	N	Y
23 Bustamante	Y	?	N	Y	Y	Y	Y	N
24 Frost	Y	Y	N	Y	Y	Y	N	Y
25 Andrews	Y	?	N	Y	Y	Y	N	Y
26 ***Armey***	N	N	Y	N	N	N	N	Y
27 Ortiz	Y	Y	N	Y	?	Y	N	Y
UTAH								
1 ***Hansen***	N	N	Y	N	Y	N	N	Y
2 Owens	Y	Y	N	Y	Y	Y	Y	N
3 Orton	Y	Y	N	Y	Y	Y	N	Y
VERMONT								
AL Sanders	Y	Y	N	Y	Y	Y	Y	N
VIRGINIA								
1 ***Bateman***	N	N	Y	N	Y	N	N	Y
2 Pickett	Y	Y	N	?	Y	Y	N	Y
3 ***Bliley***	N	N	Y	N	Y	N	N	Y
4 Sisisky	Y	Y	N	Y	Y	Y	N	Y
5 Payne	Y	Y	N	Y	Y	Y	N	Y
6 Olin	Y	Y	N	Y	Y	Y	Y	N
7 ***Slaughter***	N	N	Y	N	Y	N	N	Y
8 Moran	Y	?	?	?	Y	Y	Y	N
9 Boucher	Y	Y	N	Y	Y	Y	Y	N
10 ***Wolf***	N	N	Y	N	N	N	N	Y
WASHINGTON								
1 ***Miller***	N	N	Y	N	N	Y	N	Y
2 Swift	Y	Y	N	Y	Y	Y	Y	N
3 Unsoeld	Y	Y	N	Y	Y	Y	Y	N
4 ***Morrison***	N	N	Y	N	Y	N	N	Y
5 Foley	P					Y	Y	N
6 Dicks	Y	Y	N	Y	?	Y	Y	N
7 McDermott	Y	Y	N	Y	Y	Y	Y	N
8 ***Chandler***	N	N	Y	N	N	N	N	Y
WEST VIRGINIA								
1 Mollohan	Y	Y	N	Y	Y	Y	N	Y
2 Staggers	Y	Y	N	Y	Y	Y	Y	N
3 Wise	Y	Y	N	Y	Y	Y	Y	N
4 Rahall	Y	Y	N	Y	Y	Y	N	Y
WISCONSIN								
1 Aspin	Y	?	?	Y	Y	Y	N	Y
2 ***Klug***	N	N	Y	N	Y	Y	N	Y
3 ***Gunderson***	N	N	Y	N	Y	N	N	Y
4 Kleczka	Y	Y	N	Y	Y	Y	Y	N
5 Moody	Y	Y	N	Y	Y	Y	Y	N
6 ***Petri***	N	N	Y	N	Y	N	N	Y
7 Obey	Y	Y	N	Y	Y	Y	Y	N
8 ***Roth***	N	N	Y	N	Y	Y	N	Y
9 ***Sensenbrenner***	N	N	Y	N	N	Y	N	Y
WYOMING								
AL ***Thomas***	N	N	Y	N	N	N	N	Y

Southern states - Ala., Ark., Fla., Ga., Ky., La., Miss., N.C., Okla., S.C., Tenn., Texas, Va.
Omitted votes are quorum calls, which CQ does not include in its vote charts.

HOUSE VOTES 10, 11, 12, 13, 14, 15, 16, 17

10. S Con Res 2. U.S. Forces in the Gulf. Gephardt, D-Mo., motion to suspend the rules and adopt the concurrent resolution to express the sense of Congress commending and supporting the efforts of the president in the Persian Gulf and stating unequivocal support for the members of the armed forces. Motion agreed to 399-6: R 156-0; D 243-5 (ND 162-4, SD 81-1); I 0-1, Jan. 18, 1991. A two-thirds majority of those present and voting (270 in this case) is required for passage under suspension of the rules.

11. H Con Res 41. Condemn Iraqi Attacks on Israel/ Adoption. Fascell, D-Fla., motion to suspend the rules and adopt the concurrent resolution to condemn the unprovoked attack by Iraq on Israel. Motion agreed to 416-0: R 164-0; D 251-0 (ND 171-0, SD 80-0); I 1-0, Jan. 23, 1991. A two-thirds majority of those present and voting (277 in this case) is required for passage under suspension of the rules.

12. H Con Res 48. Condemn Iraqi Treatment of POWs/ Adoption. Byron, D-Md., motion to suspend the rules and adopt the concurrent resolution to condemn the abuse by Iraq of allied prisoners of war (POWs). Motion agreed to 418-0: R 164-0; D 253-0 (ND 172-0, SD 81-0); I 1-0, Jan. 23, 1991. A two-thirds majority of those present and voting (279 in this case) is required for passage under suspension of the rules.

13. HR 4. IRS Extension for Troops in the Gulf/Passage. Rostenkowski, D-Ill., motion to suspend the rules and pass the bill to provide all personnel involved in Operations Desert Shield and Desert Storm with a six-month extension after their service in the gulf has ended to file federal tax returns. Motion agreed to 415-0: R 164-0; D 250-0 (ND 170-0, SD 80-0); I 1-0, Jan. 23, 1991. A two-thirds majority of those present and voting (277 in this case) is required for passage under suspension of the rules.

14. HR 3. Veterans Compensation Amendments/Passage. Montgomery, D-Miss., motion to suspend the rules and pass the bill to authorize retroactive to Jan. 1, 1991, a 5.4 percent cost of living adjustment for veterans with service-connected disabilities. Motion agreed to 421-0: R 165-0; D 255-0 (ND 173-0, SD 82-0); I 1-0, Jan. 23, 1991. A two-thirds majority of those present and voting (281 in this case) is required for passage under suspension of the rules. A "yea" was a vote supporting the president's position.

15. H Con Res 40. Condemn Soviet Force in the Baltics/ Adoption. Fascell, D-Fla., motion to suspend the rules and adopt the concurrent resolution to condemn the recent violence by Soviet forces in Lithuania and Latvia. Motion agreed to 417-0: R 165-0; D 251-0 (ND 171-0, SD 80-0); I 1-0, Jan. 23, 1991. A two-thirds majority of those present and voting (278 in this case) is required for passage under suspension of the rules.

16. HR 556. Agent Orange Act/Passage. Montgomery, D-Miss., motion to suspend the rules and pass the bill to provide permanent disability benefits for veterans who suffer certain conditions due to exposure to Agent Orange. The bill also would require examining additional permanent disability benefits based on a study to be done by the National Academy of Sciences. Motion agreed to 412-0: R 160-0; D 251-0 (ND 169-0, SD 82-0); I 1-0, Jan. 29, 1991. A two-thirds majority of those present and voting (275 in this case) is required for passage under suspension of the rules. A "yea" was a vote supporting the president's position.

17. HR 555. Soldiers' and Sailors' Civil Relief Amendments/Passage. Montgomery, D-Miss., motion to suspend the rules and pass the bill to reinstate immediately automatic health insurance for people in the armed forces called up for active duty, to suspend tenant evictions, to suspend civil actions until July 1, 1991, and to suspend professional liability insurance for them. Motion agreed to 414-0: R 161-0; D 252-0 (ND 170-0, SD 82-0); I 1-0, Jan. 29, 1991. A two-thirds majority of those present and voting (276 in this case) is required for passage under suspension of the rules. A "yea" was a vote supporting the president's position.

KEY

- Y Voted for (yea).
- # Paired for.
- + Announced for.
- N Voted against (nay).
- X Paired against.
- \- Announced against.
- P Voted "present."
- C Voted "present" to avoid possible conflict of interest.
- ? Did not vote or otherwise make a position known.

Democrats ***Republicans***
Independent

	10	11	12	13	14	15	16	17
ALABAMA								
1 ***Callahan***	Y	Y	Y	Y	Y	Y	Y	Y
2 ***Dickinson***	Y	Y	Y	Y	Y	Y	Y	Y
3 Browder	Y	Y	Y	Y	Y	Y	Y	Y
4 Bevill	Y	Y	Y	Y	Y	Y	Y	Y
5 Cramer	Y	+	+	Y	Y	Y	Y	Y
6 Erdreich	Y	Y	Y	Y	Y	Y	Y	Y
7 Harris	Y	Y	Y	Y	Y	Y	Y	Y
ALASKA								
AL ***Young***	Y	Y	Y	Y	Y	Y	Y	Y
ARIZONA								
1 ***Rhodes***	Y	Y	Y	Y	Y	Y	Y	Y
2 Udall	?	?	?	?	?	?	?	?
3 ***Stump***	Y	Y	Y	Y	Y	Y	Y	Y
4 ***Kyl***	Y	Y	Y	Y	Y	Y	Y	Y
5 ***Kolbe***	Y	Y	Y	Y	Y	Y	?	?
ARKANSAS								
1 Alexander	Y	Y	Y	Y	Y	Y	Y	Y
2 Thornton	Y	Y	Y	Y	Y	Y	Y	Y
3 ***Hammerschmidt***	Y	Y	Y	Y	Y	Y	Y	Y
4 Anthony	Y	Y	Y	Y	Y	Y	Y	Y
CALIFORNIA								
1 ***Riggs***	Y	Y	Y	Y	Y	Y	Y	Y
2 ***Herger***	Y	Y	Y	Y	Y	Y	Y	Y
3 Matsui	Y	?	?	?	?	?	Y	Y
4 Fazio	Y	Y	Y	Y	Y	Y	Y	Y
5 Pelosi	Y	Y	Y	Y	Y	Y	Y	Y
6 Boxer	Y	Y	Y	Y	Y	Y	Y	Y
7 Miller	Y	Y	Y	Y	Y	Y	Y	Y
8 Dellums	P	Y	Y	Y	Y	Y	Y	Y
9 Stark	Y	Y	Y	Y	Y	Y	Y	Y
10 Edwards	Y	Y	Y	Y	Y	Y	Y	Y
11 Lantos	Y	Y	Y	Y	Y	Y	?	?
12 ***Campbell***	Y	Y	Y	Y	Y	Y	Y	Y
13 Mineta	Y	Y	Y	Y	Y	Y	Y	Y
14 ***Doolittle***	Y	Y	Y	Y	Y	Y	Y	Y
15 Condit	Y	Y	Y	Y	Y	Y	Y	Y
16 Panetta	Y	Y	Y	Y	Y	Y	Y	Y
17 Dooley	Y	Y	Y	Y	Y	Y	Y	Y
18 Lehman	Y	Y	Y	Y	Y	Y	Y	?
19 ***Lagomarsino***	Y	Y	Y	Y	Y	Y	Y	Y
20 ***Thomas***	?	Y	Y	Y	Y	Y	Y	Y
21 ***Gallegly***	Y	Y	Y	Y	Y	Y	Y	Y
22 ***Moorhead***	Y	Y	Y	Y	Y	Y	Y	Y
23 Beilenson	Y	Y	Y	Y	Y	Y	Y	Y
24 Waxman	Y	Y	Y	Y	Y	Y	Y	Y
25 Roybal	Y	?	?	?	?	?	Y	Y
26 Berman	Y	Y	Y	Y	Y	?	Y	Y
27 Levine	?	?	?	?	?	?	Y	Y
28 Dixon	#	Y	Y	Y	Y	Y	Y	Y
29 Waters	N	Y	Y	Y	Y	Y	Y	Y
30 Martinez	?	Y	Y	Y	Y	Y	Y	Y
31 Dymally	N	+	+	+	+	+	Y	Y
32 Anderson	Y	Y	Y	Y	Y	Y	Y	Y
33 ***Dreier***	Y	Y	Y	Y	Y	Y	Y	Y
34 Torres	Y	+	+	+	+	+	+	+
35 ***Lewis***	Y	Y	Y	Y	Y	Y	Y	Y
36 Brown	Y	Y	Y	Y	Y	Y	Y	Y
37 ***McCandless***	Y	Y	Y	+	Y	Y	Y	Y
38 ***Dornan***	Y	Y	Y	Y	Y	Y	?	?
39 ***Dannemeyer***	Y	Y	Y	Y	Y	Y	Y	Y
40 ***Cox***	Y	Y	Y	Y	Y	Y	Y	Y
41 ***Lowery***	Y	Y	Y	Y	Y	Y	Y	Y
42 ***Rohrabacher***	Y	Y	Y	Y	Y	Y	Y	Y
43 ***Packard***	Y	Y	Y	Y	Y	Y	Y	Y
44 ***Cunningham***	Y	Y	Y	Y	Y	Y	Y	Y
45 ***Hunter***	Y	Y	Y	Y	Y	Y	Y	Y
COLORADO								
1 Schroeder	Y	Y	Y	Y	Y	Y	+	Y
2 Skaggs	Y	Y	Y	Y	Y	Y	Y	Y
3 Campbell	Y	?	?	?	?	?	Y	Y
4 ***Allard***	Y	Y	Y	Y	Y	Y	Y	Y
5 ***Hefley***	?	Y	Y	Y	Y	Y	Y	Y
6 ***Schaefer***	Y	Y	Y	Y	Y	Y	Y	Y
CONNECTICUT								
1 Kennelly	Y	Y	Y	Y	Y	Y	Y	Y
2 Gejdenson	Y	Y	Y	Y	Y	Y	Y	Y
3 DeLauro	Y	Y	Y	Y	Y	Y	Y	Y
4 ***Shays***	Y	Y	Y	Y	Y	Y	Y	Y
5 ***Franks***	Y	Y	Y	Y	Y	Y	+	+
6 ***Johnson***	Y	Y	Y	Y	Y	Y	Y	Y
DELAWARE								
AL Carper	Y	Y	Y	Y	Y	Y	Y	Y
FLORIDA								
1 Hutto	Y	Y	Y	Y	Y	Y	Y	Y
2 Peterson	Y	Y	Y	Y	Y	Y	Y	Y
3 Bennett	Y	Y	Y	Y	Y	Y	Y	Y
4 ***James***	Y	Y	Y	Y	Y	Y	Y	Y
5 ***McCollum***	Y	Y	Y	Y	Y	Y	Y	Y
6 ***Stearns***	Y	Y	Y	Y	Y	Y	Y	Y
7 Gibbons	Y	Y	Y	Y	Y	Y	Y	Y
8 ***Young***	Y	Y	Y	Y	Y	Y	Y	Y
9 ***Bilirakis***	Y	Y	Y	Y	Y	Y	Y	Y
10 ***Ireland***	Y	Y	Y	Y	Y	Y	Y	Y
11 Bacchus	Y	Y	Y	Y	Y	Y	Y	Y
12 ***Lewis***	Y	Y	Y	Y	Y	Y	Y	Y
13 ***Goss***	Y	Y	Y	Y	Y	Y	Y	Y
14 Johnston	Y	Y	Y	Y	Y	Y	Y	Y
15 ***Shaw***	Y	Y	Y	Y	Y	Y	Y	Y
16 Smith	Y	Y	Y	Y	Y	Y	Y	Y
17 Lehman	Y	Y	Y	Y	Y	Y	Y	Y
18 ***Ros-Lehtinen***	Y	Y	Y	Y	Y	Y	Y	Y
19 Fascell	Y	Y	Y	Y	Y	Y	Y	Y
GEORGIA								
1 Thomas	Y	Y	Y	Y	Y	Y	Y	Y
2 Hatcher	Y	Y	Y	Y	Y	Y	Y	Y
3 Ray	Y	Y	Y	Y	Y	Y	Y	Y
4 Jones	Y	Y	Y	Y	Y	Y	Y	Y
5 Lewis	Y	Y	Y	Y	Y	Y	Y	Y
6 ***Gingrich***	Y	Y	Y	Y	Y	Y	Y	Y
7 Darden	Y	Y	Y	Y	Y	Y	Y	Y
8 Rowland	Y	Y	Y	Y	Y	Y	Y	Y
9 Jenkins	Y	Y	Y	Y	Y	Y	Y	Y
10 Barnard	Y	Y	Y	Y	Y	Y	?	?
HAWAII								
1 Abercrombie	Y	Y	Y	Y	Y	Y	Y	Y
2 Mink	Y	Y	Y	Y	Y	Y	?	?
IDAHO								
1 LaRocco	Y	Y	Y	Y	Y	Y	Y	Y
2 Stallings	Y	Y	Y	Y	Y	Y	Y	Y
ILLINOIS								
1 Hayes	N	Y	Y	Y	Y	Y	Y	Y
2 Savage	N	Y	Y	Y	Y	Y	Y	Y
3 Russo	Y	Y	Y	Y	Y	Y	Y	Y
4 Sangmeister	Y	Y	Y	Y	Y	Y	Y	Y
5 Lipinski	Y	Y	Y	Y	Y	Y	Y	Y
6 ***Hyde***	Y	Y	Y	Y	Y	Y	Y	Y
7 Collins	P	Y	Y	Y	Y	Y	Y	Y
8 Rostenkowski	?	Y	Y	Y	Y	Y	?	?
9 Yates	Y	Y	Y	Y	Y	Y	Y	Y
10 ***Porter***	Y	Y	Y	Y	Y	Y	Y	Y
11 Annunzio	Y	Y	Y	Y	Y	Y	Y	Y
12 ***Crane***	?	Y	Y	Y	Y	Y	Y	Y
13 ***Fawell***	Y	Y	Y	Y	Y	Y	Y	Y
14 ***Hastert***	Y	Y	Y	Y	Y	Y	Y	Y
15 ***Madigan***	Y	Y	Y	Y	Y	Y	Y	Y
16 Cox	Y	Y	Y	Y	Y	Y	Y	Y
17 Evans	Y	Y	Y	Y	Y	Y	Y	Y
18 ***Michel***	Y	Y	Y	Y	Y	Y	Y	Y
19 Bruce	Y	Y	Y	Y	Y	Y	Y	Y
20 Durbin	Y	Y	Y	Y	Y	Y	Y	Y
21 Costello	Y	Y	Y	Y	Y	Y	Y	Y
22 Poshard	Y	Y	Y	Y	Y	Y	Y	Y
INDIANA								
1 Visclosky	Y	Y	Y	Y	Y	Y	Y	Y
2 Sharp	Y	Y	Y	Y	Y	Y	Y	Y
3 Roemer	Y	Y	Y	Y	Y	Y	Y	Y

ND Northern Democrats SD Southern Democrats

	10	11	12	13	14	15	16	17
4 Long	Y	Y	Y	Y	Y	Y	Y	Y
5 Jontz	Y	Y	Y	Y	Y	Y	Y	Y
6 **Burton**	?	Y	Y	Y	Y	Y	Y	Y
7 **Myers**	?	Y	Y	Y	Y	Y	Y	Y
8 McCloskey	Y	Y	Y	?	Y	Y	Y	Y
9 Hamilton	Y	Y	Y	Y	Y	Y	Y	Y
10 Jacobs	?	Y	Y	?	Y	Y	Y	Y
IOWA								
1 **Leach**	Y	?	?	Y	Y	Y	Y	Y
2 **Nussle**	Y	Y	Y	Y	Y	Y	Y	Y
3 Nagle	Y	Y	Y	Y	Y	Y	Y	Y
4 Smith	Y	Y	Y	Y	Y	Y	?	?
5 **Lightfoot**	Y	Y	Y	Y	Y	Y	Y	Y
6 **Grandy**	Y	Y	Y	Y	Y	Y	Y	Y
KANSAS								
1 **Roberts**	Y	Y	Y	Y	Y	Y	Y	Y
2 Slattery	Y	Y	Y	Y	Y	Y	Y	Y
3 **Meyers**	Y	Y	Y	Y	Y	Y	Y	Y
4 Glickman	Y	Y	Y	Y	Y	Y	Y	Y
5 **Nichols**	Y	Y	Y	Y	Y	Y	Y	Y
KENTUCKY								
1 Hubbard	Y	Y	Y	Y	Y	Y	Y	Y
2 Natcher	Y	Y	Y	Y	Y	Y	Y	Y
3 Mazzoli	Y	Y	Y	Y	Y	Y	Y	Y
4 **Bunning**	Y	Y	Y	Y	Y	Y	Y	Y
5 **Rogers**	Y	Y	Y	Y	Y	Y	Y	Y
6 **Hopkins**	Y	Y	Y	Y	Y	Y	Y	Y
7 Perkins	Y	Y	Y	Y	Y	Y	Y	Y
LOUISIANA								
1 **Livingston**	Y	Y	Y	Y	Y	Y	Y	Y
2 Jefferson	Y	Y	Y	Y	Y	Y	Y	Y
3 Tauzin	Y	Y	Y	Y	Y	Y	+	+
4 **McCrery**	Y	Y	Y	Y	Y	Y	Y	Y
5 Huckaby	Y	Y	Y	Y	Y	Y	Y	Y
6 **Baker**	Y	Y	Y	Y	Y	Y	Y	Y
7 Hayes	Y	+	?	+	+	+	Y	Y
8 **Holloway**	Y	Y	Y	Y	Y	Y	Y	Y
MAINE								
1 Andrews	Y	Y	Y	Y	Y	Y	Y	Y
2 **Snowe**	?	?	?	?	?	?	?	?
MARYLAND								
1 **Gilchrest**	Y	Y	Y	Y	Y	Y	Y	Y
2 **Bentley**	Y	Y	Y	Y	Y	Y	Y	Y
3 Cardin	Y	Y	Y	Y	Y	Y	?	Y
4 McMillen	Y	Y	Y	Y	Y	Y	Y	Y
5 Hoyer	Y	Y	Y	Y	Y	Y	Y	Y
6 Byron	Y	Y	Y	Y	Y	Y	Y	Y
7 Mfume	Y	Y	Y	Y	Y	Y	Y	Y
8 **Morella**	Y	Y	Y	Y	Y	Y	Y	Y
MASSACHUSETTS								
1 **Conte**	Y	Y	Y	Y	Y	Y	Y	Y
2 Neal	Y	Y	Y	Y	Y	Y	Y	Y
3 Early	Y	Y	Y	Y	Y	Y	Y	Y
4 Frank	Y	Y	Y	Y	Y	Y	Y	Y
5 Atkins	Y	Y	Y	Y	Y	Y	Y	Y
6 Mavroules	Y	Y	Y	Y	Y	Y	Y	Y
7 Markey	Y	Y	Y	Y	Y	Y	Y	Y
8 Kennedy	Y	Y	Y	Y	Y	Y	Y	Y
9 Moakley	Y	Y	Y	Y	Y	Y	Y	Y
10 Studds	Y	Y	Y	Y	Y	Y	Y	Y
11 Donnelly	Y	Y	Y	Y	Y	Y	Y	Y
MICHIGAN								
1 Conyers	Y	Y	Y	Y	Y	Y	Y	Y
2 **Pursell**	Y	Y	Y	Y	Y	Y	Y	Y
3 Wolpe	Y	Y	Y	Y	Y	Y	Y	Y
4 **Upton**	Y	Y	Y	Y	Y	Y	Y	Y
5 **Henry**	Y	Y	Y	Y	Y	Y	Y	Y
6 Carr	Y	+	Y	Y	Y	Y	Y	Y
7 Kildee	Y	Y	Y	Y	Y	Y	Y	Y
8 Traxler	Y	Y	Y	Y	Y	Y	Y	Y
9 **Vander Jagt**	Y	Y	Y	Y	Y	Y	Y	Y
10 **Camp**	Y	Y	Y	Y	Y	Y	Y	Y
11 **Davis**	?	Y	Y	Y	Y	Y	Y	Y
12 Bonior	Y	Y	Y	Y	Y	Y	Y	Y
13 Collins	Y	Y	Y	Y	Y	Y	Y	Y
14 Hertel	Y	Y	Y	Y	Y	Y	Y	Y
15 Ford	Y	Y	Y	Y	Y	Y	Y	Y
16 Dingell	Y	Y	Y	Y	Y	Y	?	?
17 Levin	Y	Y	Y	Y	Y	Y	Y	Y
18 **Broomfield**	Y	Y	Y	Y	Y	Y	Y	Y
MINNESOTA								
1 Penny	Y	Y	Y	Y	Y	Y	Y	Y
2 **Weber**	Y	Y	Y	Y	Y	Y	Y	Y
3 **Ramstad**	Y	Y	Y	Y	Y	Y	Y	Y
4 Vento	Y	Y	Y	Y	Y	Y	Y	Y

	10	11	12	13	14	15	16	17
5 Sabo	Y	Y	Y	Y	Y	Y	Y	Y
6 Sikorski	Y	Y	Y	Y	Y	Y	Y	Y
7 Peterson	Y	Y	Y	Y	Y	Y	Y	Y
8 Oberstar	Y	Y	Y	Y	Y	Y	Y	Y
MISSISSIPPI								
1 Whitten	Y	Y	Y	Y	Y	Y	Y	Y
2 Espy	Y	Y	Y	Y	Y	Y	Y	Y
3 Montgomery	Y	Y	Y	Y	Y	Y	Y	Y
4 Parker	Y	Y	Y	Y	Y	Y	Y	Y
5 Taylor	Y	Y	Y	Y	Y	Y	Y	Y
MISSOURI								
1 Clay	X	Y	Y	Y	Y	Y	Y	Y
2 Horn	Y	Y	Y	Y	Y	Y	Y	Y
3 Gephardt	Y	Y	Y	Y	Y	Y	Y	Y
4 Skelton	Y	Y	Y	Y	Y	Y	Y	Y
5 Wheat	Y	Y	Y	Y	Y	Y	Y	Y
6 **Coleman**	Y	Y	Y	Y	Y	Y	Y	Y
7 **Hancock**	Y	Y	Y	Y	Y	Y	Y	Y
8 **Emerson**	Y	Y	Y	Y	Y	Y	Y	Y
9 Volkmer	Y	Y	Y	Y	Y	Y	Y	Y
MONTANA								
1 Williams	Y	Y	Y	Y	Y	Y	Y	Y
2 **Marlenee**	?	Y	Y	Y	Y	Y	Y	Y
NEBRASKA								
1 **Bereuter**	Y	Y	Y	Y	Y	Y	Y	Y
2 Hoagland	Y	Y	Y	Y	Y	Y	Y	Y
3 **Barrett**	Y	Y	Y	Y	Y	Y	Y	Y
NEVADA								
1 Bilbray	Y	Y	Y	Y	Y	Y	Y	Y
2 **Vucanovich**	Y	Y	Y	Y	Y	Y	Y	Y
NEW HAMPSHIRE								
1 **Zeliff**	Y	Y	Y	Y	Y	Y	Y	Y
2 Swett	Y	Y	Y	Y	Y	Y	Y	Y
NEW JERSEY								
1 Andrews	Y	Y	Y	Y	Y	Y	Y	Y
2 Hughes	Y	Y	Y	Y	Y	Y	Y	Y
3 Pallone	Y	Y	Y	Y	Y	Y	Y	Y
4 **Smith**	Y	Y	Y	Y	Y	Y	Y	Y
5 **Roukema**	Y	Y	Y	Y	Y	Y	Y	Y
6 Dwyer	Y	Y	Y	Y	Y	Y	Y	Y
7 **Rinaldo**	Y	Y	Y	Y	Y	Y	Y	Y
8 Roe	Y	Y	Y	Y	Y	Y	Y	Y
9 Torricelli	Y	Y	Y	Y	Y	Y	Y	Y
10 Payne	P	Y	Y	Y	Y	Y	Y	Y
11 **Gallo**	Y	Y	Y	Y	Y	Y	Y	Y
12 **Zimmer**	Y	Y	Y	Y	Y	Y	Y	Y
13 **Saxton**	Y	Y	Y	Y	Y	Y	Y	Y
14 Guarini	Y	Y	Y	Y	Y	Y	Y	Y
NEW MEXICO								
1 **Schiff**	Y	Y	Y	Y	Y	Y	Y	Y
2 **Skeen**	Y	Y	Y	Y	Y	Y	Y	Y
3 Richardson	Y	Y	Y	Y	Y	Y	Y	Y
NEW YORK								
1 Hochbrueckner	Y	Y	Y	Y	Y	Y	Y	Y
2 Downey	Y	Y	Y	Y	Y	Y	Y	Y
3 Mrazek	?	?	Y	Y	Y	Y	?	?
4 **Lent**	Y	Y	Y	Y	Y	Y	Y	Y
5 **McGrath**	Y	Y	Y	Y	Y	Y	Y	Y
6 Flake	Y	Y	Y	Y	Y	Y	Y	Y
7 Ackerman	Y	Y	Y	Y	Y	Y	Y	Y
8 Scheuer	Y	Y	Y	Y	Y	Y	Y	Y
9 Manton	Y	Y	Y	Y	Y	Y	Y	Y
10 Schumer	Y	Y	Y	Y	Y	Y	Y	Y
11 Towns	P	Y	Y	Y	Y	Y	Y	Y
12 Owens	P	Y	Y	Y	Y	Y	Y	Y
13 Solarz	Y	Y	Y	Y	Y	Y	Y	Y
14 **Molinari**	Y	Y	Y	Y	Y	Y	Y	Y
15 **Green**	Y	Y	Y	Y	Y	Y	Y	Y
16 Rangel	Y	Y	Y	Y	Y	Y	Y	Y
17 Weiss	?	?	?	?	?	?	?	?
18 Serrano	Y	Y	Y	Y	Y	Y	Y	Y
19 Engel	Y	Y	Y	Y	Y	Y	Y	Y
20 Lowey	Y	Y	Y	Y	Y	Y	Y	Y
21 **Fish**	?	Y	Y	Y	Y	Y	Y	Y
22 **Gilman**	Y	Y	Y	Y	Y	Y	Y	Y
23 McNulty	Y	Y	Y	Y	Y	Y	Y	Y
24 **Solomon**	Y	Y	Y	Y	Y	Y	Y	Y
25 **Boehlert**	Y	Y	Y	Y	Y	Y	Y	Y
26 **Martin**	Y	Y	Y	Y	Y	Y	Y	Y
27 **Walsh**	Y	Y	Y	Y	Y	Y	Y	Y
28 McHugh	Y	Y	Y	Y	Y	Y	Y	Y
29 **Horton**	Y	Y	Y	Y	Y	Y	Y	Y
30 Slaughter	Y	Y	Y	Y	Y	Y	Y	Y
31 **Paxon**	Y	Y	Y	Y	Y	Y	Y	Y

	10	11	12	13	14	15	16	17
32 LaFalce	Y	Y	Y	Y	Y	Y	Y	Y
33 Nowak	Y	Y	Y	Y	Y	Y	Y	Y
34 **Houghton**	Y	Y	Y	Y	Y	Y	Y	Y
NORTH CAROLINA								
1 Jones	Y	Y	Y	Y	Y	Y	Y	Y
2 Valentine	Y	Y	Y	Y	Y	Y	Y	Y
3 Lancaster	Y	Y	Y	Y	Y	Y	Y	Y
4 Price	Y	Y	Y	Y	Y	Y	Y	Y
5 Neal	Y	Y	Y	Y	Y	Y	Y	Y
6 **Coble**	?	Y	Y	Y	Y	Y	Y	Y
7 Rose	Y	Y	Y	Y	Y	Y	Y	Y
8 Hefner	Y	Y	Y	Y	Y	Y	Y	Y
9 **McMillan**	Y	Y	Y	Y	Y	Y	Y	Y
10 **Ballenger**	Y	Y	Y	Y	Y	Y	Y	Y
11 **Taylor**	Y	Y	Y	Y	Y	Y	Y	Y
NORTH DAKOTA								
AL Dorgan	Y	Y	Y	Y	Y	Y	Y	Y
OHIO								
1 Luken	Y	Y	Y	Y	Y	Y	Y	Y
2 **Gradison**	Y	Y	Y	Y	Y	Y	Y	Y
3 Hall	Y	Y	Y	Y	Y	Y	Y	Y
4 **Oxley**	Y	Y	Y	Y	Y	Y	Y	Y
5 **Gillmor**	Y	Y	Y	Y	Y	Y	Y	Y
6 **McEwen**	Y	?	?	?	?	?	Y	Y
7 **Hobson**	Y	Y	Y	Y	Y	Y	Y	Y
8 **Boehner**	Y	Y	Y	Y	Y	Y	?	Y
9 Kaptur	Y	Y	Y	Y	Y	Y	Y	Y
10 **Miller**	Y	Y	Y	Y	Y	Y	Y	Y
11 Eckart	Y	Y	Y	Y	Y	+	Y	Y
12 **Kasich**	Y	Y	Y	Y	Y	Y	Y	Y
13 Pease	Y	Y	Y	Y	Y	Y	Y	Y
14 Sawyer	Y	Y	Y	Y	Y	Y	Y	Y
15 **Wylie**	Y	Y	Y	Y	Y	Y	Y	Y
16 **Regula**	Y	Y	Y	Y	Y	Y	Y	Y
17 Traficant	Y	Y	Y	Y	Y	Y	Y	Y
18 Applegate	?	Y	Y	Y	Y	Y	Y	Y
19 Feighan	Y	Y	Y	Y	Y	Y	Y	Y
20 Oakar	Y	Y	Y	Y	Y	Y	Y	Y
21 Stokes	Y	Y	Y	Y	Y	Y	Y	Y
OKLAHOMA								
1 **Inhofe**	Y	Y	Y	Y	Y	Y	Y	Y
2 Synar	Y	Y	Y	Y	Y	+	Y	Y
3 Brewster	Y	Y	Y	Y	Y	Y	Y	Y
4 McCurdy	Y	Y	Y	Y	Y	Y	Y	Y
5 **Edwards**	Y	Y	Y	Y	Y	Y	Y	Y
6 English	Y	Y	Y	Y	Y	Y	Y	Y
OREGON								
1 AuCoin	Y	Y	Y	Y	Y	Y	Y	Y
2 **Smith**	Y	Y	Y	Y	Y	Y	Y	Y
3 Wyden	Y	Y	Y	Y	Y	Y	Y	Y
4 DeFazio	Y	Y	Y	Y	Y	Y	Y	Y
5 Kopetski	Y	Y	Y	Y	Y	Y	Y	Y
PENNSYLVANIA								
1 Foglietta	Y	Y	Y	Y	Y	Y	Y	Y
2 Gray	Y	Y	Y	Y	Y	Y	Y	Y
3 Borski	Y	Y	Y	Y	Y	Y	Y	Y
4 Kolter	Y	Y	Y	Y	Y	Y	Y	Y
5 **Schulze**	Y	Y	Y	Y	Y	Y	Y	Y
6 Yatron	Y	Y	Y	Y	Y	Y	Y	Y
7 **Weldon**	Y	Y	Y	Y	Y	Y	Y	Y
8 Kostmayer	Y	Y	Y	Y	Y	Y	Y	Y
9 **Shuster**	Y	Y	Y	Y	Y	Y	Y	Y
10 **McDade**	Y	Y	Y	Y	Y	Y	Y	Y
11 Kanjorski	Y	Y	Y	Y	Y	Y	Y	Y
12 Murtha	Y	Y	Y	Y	Y	Y	Y	Y
13 **Coughlin**	Y	Y	Y	Y	Y	Y	Y	Y
14 Coyne	Y	Y	Y	Y	Y	Y	Y	Y
15 **Ritter**	Y	Y	Y	Y	Y	Y	Y	Y
16 **Walker**	Y	Y	Y	Y	Y	Y	Y	Y
17 **Gekas**	Y	Y	Y	Y	Y	Y	Y	Y
18 **Santorum**	Y	Y	Y	Y	Y	Y	Y	Y
19 **Goodling**	Y	Y	Y	Y	Y	Y	Y	Y
20 Gaydos	Y	Y	Y	Y	Y	Y	Y	Y
21 **Ridge**	Y	Y	Y	Y	Y	Y	Y	Y
22 Murphy	?	Y	?	Y	Y	Y	Y	Y
23 **Clinger**	Y	Y	Y	Y	Y	Y	Y	Y
RHODE ISLAND								
1 **Machtley**	Y	Y	Y	Y	Y	Y	Y	Y
2 Reed	Y	Y	Y	Y	Y	Y	Y	Y
SOUTH CAROLINA								
1 **Ravenel**	Y	Y	Y	Y	Y	Y	Y	Y
2 **Spence**	Y	Y	Y	Y	Y	Y	Y	Y
3 Derrick	Y	Y	Y	Y	Y	Y	Y	Y
4 Patterson	Y	Y	Y	Y	Y	Y	Y	Y
5 Spratt	Y	Y	Y	Y	Y	Y	Y	Y
6 Tallon	Y	Y	Y	Y	Y	Y	Y	Y

	10	11	12	13	14	15	16	17
SOUTH DAKOTA								
AL Johnson	Y	Y	Y	Y	Y	Y	Y	Y
TENNESSEE								
1 **Quillen**	Y	Y	Y	Y	Y	Y	Y	Y
2 **Duncan**	Y	Y	Y	Y	Y	Y	Y	Y
3 Lloyd	Y	Y	Y	Y	Y	Y	Y	Y
4 Cooper	Y	Y	Y	Y	Y	Y	Y	Y
5 Clement	#	Y	Y	Y	Y	Y	Y	Y
6 Gordon	Y	Y	Y	Y	Y	?	Y	Y
7 **Sundquist**	?	Y	Y	Y	Y	Y	Y	Y
8 Tanner	Y	Y	Y	Y	Y	Y	Y	Y
9 Ford	?	?	?	?	?	?	Y	Y
TEXAS								
1 Chapman	Y	Y	Y	Y	Y	Y	Y	Y
2 Wilson	Y	Y	Y	Y	Y	Y	?	?
3 **Bartlett**	Y	Y	Y	Y	Y	Y	Y	Y
4 Hall	Y	Y	Y	Y	Y	Y	Y	Y
5 Bryant	Y	Y	Y	Y	Y	Y	Y	Y
6 **Barton**	Y	Y	Y	Y	Y	Y	Y	Y
7 **Archer**	Y	Y	Y	Y	Y	Y	Y	Y
8 **Fields**	Y	Y	Y	Y	Y	Y	?	?
9 Brooks	Y	Y	Y	Y	Y	Y	Y	Y
10 Pickle	Y	Y	Y	Y	Y	Y	Y	Y
11 Edwards	Y	Y	Y	Y	Y	Y	Y	Y
12 Geren	Y	Y	Y	Y	Y	Y	Y	Y
13 Sarpalius	Y	Y	Y	Y	Y	Y	Y	Y
14 Laughlin	Y	Y	Y	Y	Y	Y	Y	Y
15 de la Garza	Y	?	?	?	?	?	Y	Y
16 Coleman	Y	Y	Y	Y	Y	Y	Y	Y
17 Stenholm	Y	Y	Y	Y	Y	Y	Y	Y
18 Washington	N	?	Y	Y	Y	Y	Y	Y
19 **Combest**	Y	Y	Y	Y	Y	Y	Y	Y
20 Gonzalez	P	Y	Y	Y	Y	Y	Y	Y
21 **Smith**	Y	Y	Y	Y	Y	Y	Y	Y
22 **DeLay**	Y	Y	Y	Y	Y	Y	Y	Y
23 Bustamante	Y	Y	Y	Y	Y	Y	Y	Y
24 Frost	Y	Y	Y	Y	Y	Y	Y	Y
25 Andrews	Y	Y	Y	Y	Y	Y	Y	Y
26 **Armey**	Y	Y	Y	Y	Y	Y	Y	Y
27 Ortiz	Y	Y	Y	Y	Y	Y	Y	Y
UTAH								
1 **Hansen**	Y	Y	Y	Y	Y	Y	Y	Y
2 Owens	Y	Y	Y	Y	Y	Y	Y	Y
3 Orton	Y	Y	Y	Y	Y	Y	Y	Y
VERMONT								
AL Sanders	N	Y	Y	Y	Y	Y	Y	Y
VIRGINIA								
1 **Bateman**	Y	Y	Y	Y	Y	Y	Y	Y
2 Pickett	Y	Y	Y	Y	Y	Y	Y	Y
3 **Bliley**	Y	Y	Y	Y	Y	Y	Y	Y
4 Sisisky	Y	Y	Y	Y	Y	Y	Y	Y
5 Payne	Y	Y	Y	?	Y	Y	Y	Y
6 Olin	Y	Y	Y	?	Y	Y	Y	Y
7 **Slaughter**	Y	Y	Y	Y	Y	Y	Y	Y
8 Moran	Y	Y	Y	Y	Y	Y	Y	Y
9 Boucher	Y	Y	Y	Y	Y	Y	Y	Y
10 **Wolf**	Y	Y	Y	Y	Y	Y	Y	Y
WASHINGTON								
1 **Miller**	Y	Y	Y	Y	Y	Y	Y	Y
2 Swift	Y	Y	Y	Y	Y	Y	Y	Y
3 Unsoeld	Y	Y	Y	Y	Y	Y	Y	Y
4 **Morrison**	?	Y	Y	Y	Y	Y	Y	Y
5 Foley	Y							
6 Dicks	Y	Y	Y	Y	Y	Y	Y	Y
7 McDermott	Y	Y	Y	Y	Y	Y	Y	Y
8 **Chandler**	Y	Y	Y	Y	Y	Y	Y	Y
WEST VIRGINIA								
1 Mollohan	Y	Y	Y	Y	Y	Y	Y	Y
2 Staggers	Y	Y	Y	Y	Y	Y	Y	Y
3 Wise	Y	Y	Y	+	Y	Y	+	+
4 Rahall	Y	Y	Y	Y	Y	Y	Y	Y
WISCONSIN								
1 Aspin	Y	Y	Y	Y	Y	Y	Y	Y
2 **Klug**	Y	Y	Y	Y	Y	Y	Y	Y
3 **Gunderson**	Y	Y	Y	Y	Y	Y	Y	Y
4 Kleczka	Y	Y	Y	Y	Y	Y	Y	Y
5 Moody	Y	Y	Y	Y	Y	Y	Y	Y
6 **Petri**	Y	Y	Y	Y	Y	Y	Y	Y
7 Obey	Y	Y	Y	Y	Y	Y	Y	Y
8 **Roth**	Y	Y	Y	Y	Y	Y	Y	Y
9 **Sensenbrenner**	Y	Y	Y	Y	Y	Y	Y	Y
WYOMING								
AL **Thomas**	Y	Y	Y	Y	Y	Y	+	+

Southern states - Ala., Ark., Fla., Ga., Ky., La., Miss., N.C., Okla., S.C., Tenn., Texas, Va.
Omitted votes are quorum calls, which CQ does not include in its vote charts.

HOUSE VOTES 18, 19, 20, 21, 22, 23, 24, 25

18. HR 598. VA Physician and Dentist Compensation Act/Passage. Montgomery, D-Miss., motion to suspend the rules and pass the bill to increase salary levels of Veterans Affairs (VA) physicians and dentists, enhancing the VA's ability to recruit and retain such professionals. Motion agreed to 399-0: R 163-0; D 235-0 (ND 156-0, SD 79-0); I 1-0, Jan. 30, 1991. A two-thirds majority of those present and voting (266 in this case) is required for passage under suspension of the rules. A "nay" was a vote supporting the president's position.

19. HR 180. Veterans' Education Amendments/Passage. Montgomery, D-Miss., motion to suspend the rules and pass the bill to extend through 1994 eligibility for employment and training benefits under Vietnam War-era programs. Motion agreed to 402-0: R 157-0; D 244-0 (ND 165-0, SD 79-0); I 1-0, Feb. 5, 1991. A two-thirds majority of those present and voting (268 in this case) is required for passage under suspension of the rules.

20. HR 154. Pershing Hall Transfer/Passage. Montgomery, D-Miss., motion to suspend the rules and pass the bill to transfer custody and control of the Pershing Hall memorial in Paris, France, from the American Legion to the Veterans' Affairs Department. Motion agreed to 405-0: R 160-0; D 244-0 (ND 164-0, SD 80-0); I 1-0, Feb. 5, 1991. A two-thirds majority of those present and voting (270 in this case) is required for passage under suspension of the rules.

21. HR 232. Veterans' Housing Amendments/Passage. Montgomery, D-Miss., motion to suspend the rules and pass the bill to modify certain existing veterans' housing programs. Motion agreed to 411-0: R 162-0; D 248-0 (ND 170-0, SD 78-0); I 1-0, Feb. 6, 1991. A two-thirds majority of those present and voting (274 in this case) is required for passage under suspension of the rules.

22. H Con Res 44. Flag Display/Adoption. Brooks, D-Texas, motion to suspend the rules and adopt the concurrent resolution to call on the American people to display the American flag in support of the U.S. troops in the Persian Gulf. Motion agreed to 409-0: R 158-0; D 250-0 (ND 169-0, SD 81-0); I 1-0, Feb. 20, 1991. A two-thirds majority of those present and voting (273 in this case) is required for passage under suspension of the rules.

23. HR 586. Desert Storm Cost Reports/Passage. Aspin, D-Wis., motion to suspend the rules and pass the bill to require the administration to submit within two weeks of enactment reports on the 1990 cost of military operations in the Persian Gulf region and the contributions by U.S. allies, with monthly updates of 1991 figures. Motion agreed to 393-1: R 149-1; D 243-0 (ND 169-0, SD 74-0); I 1-0, Feb. 21, 1991. A two-thirds majority of those present and voting (263 in this case) is required for passage under suspension of the rules. *(Story, p. 479)*

24. H Res 19. Persian Gulf Crisis Inquiry. Fascell, D-Fla., motion to table (kill) the resolution directing the administration to submit to Congress extensive documents dealing with U.S. military and political commitments in the Persian Gulf region. Motion agreed to 390-0: R 150-0; D 239-0 (ND 165-0, SD 74-0); I 1-0, Feb. 21, 1991. *(Story, p. 479)*

25. S J Res 55. Portuguese Relations Anniversary/Passage. Hamilton, D-Ind., motion to suspend the rules and pass the joint resolution to commemorate the 200th anniversary of the establishment of diplomatic relations between the United States and Portugal. Motion agreed to 411-0: R 158-0; D 252-0 (ND 173-0, SD 79-0); I 1-0, Feb. 27, 1991. A two-thirds majority of those present and voting (274 in this case) is required for passage under suspension of the rules.

† *Rep. Silvio O. Conte, R-Mass., died Feb. 8, 1991. Vote 21 was the last vote for which he was eligible.*

KEY

- Y Voted for (yea).
- # Paired for.
- + Announced for.
- N Voted against (nay).
- X Paired against.
- \- Announced against.
- P Voted "present."
- C Voted "present" to avoid possible conflict of interest.
- ? Did not vote or otherwise make a position known.

Democrats ***Republicans***
Independent

	18	19	20	21	22	23	24	25
ALABAMA								
1 ***Callahan***	Y	Y	Y	Y	Y	Y	Y	Y
2 ***Dickinson***	Y	Y	Y	Y	Y	Y	Y	Y
3 Browder	Y	Y	Y	Y	Y	Y	Y	Y
4 Bevill	Y	Y	Y	Y	Y	Y	?	Y
5 Cramer	Y	Y	Y	Y	Y	Y	Y	Y
6 Erdreich	Y	Y	Y	Y	Y	Y	Y	Y
7 Harris	Y	Y	Y	Y	Y	Y	Y	Y
ALASKA								
AL ***Young***	Y	?	?	Y	Y	Y	Y	Y
ARIZONA								
1 ***Rhodes***	Y	Y	Y	Y	Y	Y	Y	?
2 Udall	?	?	?	?	?	?	?	?
3 ***Stump***	Y	Y	Y	Y	Y	N	Y	Y
4 ***Kyl***	Y	Y	Y	Y	Y	Y	Y	Y
5 ***Kolbe***	Y	Y	Y	Y	Y	Y	Y	Y
ARKANSAS								
1 Alexander	Y	Y	Y	Y	Y	Y	Y	Y
2 Thornton	Y	Y	Y	Y	Y	Y	Y	Y
3 ***Hammerschmidt***	Y	Y	Y	Y	Y	Y	Y	Y
4 Anthony	?	?	?	?	Y	Y	Y	Y
CALIFORNIA								
1 ***Riggs***	Y	Y	Y	Y	Y	Y	Y	Y
2 ***Herger***	Y	Y	Y	Y	Y	Y	Y	Y
3 Matsui	Y	Y	Y	Y	Y	Y	Y	Y
4 Fazio	Y	Y	Y	Y	Y	Y	Y	Y
5 Pelosi	+	Y	Y	Y	Y	Y	Y	Y
6 Boxer	?	Y	Y	Y	Y	Y	Y	Y
7 Miller	Y	Y	Y	Y	Y	Y	Y	Y
8 Dellums	?	Y	Y	Y	Y	Y	?	Y
9 Stark	Y	Y	Y	Y	Y	Y	Y	Y
10 Edwards	?	Y	Y	Y	Y	Y	Y	Y
11 Lantos	Y	Y	Y	Y	Y	Y	Y	Y
12 ***Campbell***	Y	Y	Y	Y	Y	Y	Y	?
13 Mineta	Y	Y	Y	Y	Y	Y	Y	Y
14 ***Doolittle***	Y	Y	Y	Y	Y	Y	Y	Y
15 Condit	+	Y	Y	Y	Y	Y	Y	Y
16 Panetta	Y	Y	Y	Y	Y	Y	Y	Y
17 Dooley	Y	Y	Y	Y	Y	Y	Y	Y
18 Lehman	Y	Y	Y	Y	Y	?	?	Y
19 ***Lagomarsino***	Y	Y	Y	Y	Y	Y	Y	Y
20 ***Thomas***	Y	Y	Y	Y	Y	?	?	Y
21 ***Gallegly***	Y	Y	Y	Y	Y	Y	?	Y
22 ***Moorhead***	Y	Y	Y	Y	Y	Y	Y	Y
23 Beilenson	Y	Y	Y	Y	Y	Y	Y	Y
24 Waxman	Y	Y	Y	Y	Y	Y	Y	Y
25 Roybal	Y	Y	Y	Y	?	Y	Y	Y
26 Berman	Y	Y	Y	Y	Y	Y	Y	?
27 Levine	Y	?	?	?	Y	Y	Y	?
28 Dixon	Y	Y	Y	Y	Y	Y	Y	Y
29 Waters	Y	Y	Y	Y	Y	?	?	Y
30 Martinez	Y	Y	Y	Y	Y	Y	Y	Y
31 Dymally	Y	+	+	+	Y	?	?	Y
32 Anderson	Y	Y	Y	Y	Y	Y	Y	Y
33 ***Dreier***	Y	Y	Y	Y	?	?	?	Y
34 Torres	Y	Y	Y	Y	+	+	+	Y
35 ***Lewis***	Y	Y	Y	Y	Y	Y	Y	Y
36 Brown	Y	Y	Y	Y	Y	?	?	Y
37 ***McCandless***	Y	Y	Y	Y	Y	Y	Y	Y
38 ***Dornan***	Y	Y	Y	Y	?	?	?	Y
39 ***Dannemeyer***	Y	Y	Y	Y	Y	Y	Y	Y
40 ***Cox***	Y	Y	Y	Y	Y	Y	Y	Y
41 ***Lowery***	Y	Y	Y	Y	Y	Y	Y	?
42 ***Rohrabacher***	Y	Y	Y	Y	Y	Y	Y	Y
43 ***Packard***	Y	Y	Y	Y	Y	Y	Y	Y
44 ***Cunningham***	Y	Y	Y	Y	Y	Y	Y	Y
45 ***Hunter***	Y	Y	Y	Y	Y	?	Y	Y
COLORADO								
1 Schroeder	Y	Y	Y	Y	Y	Y	Y	Y
2 Skaggs	Y	Y	Y	Y	Y	Y	?	Y
3 Campbell	Y	Y	Y	Y	Y	Y	Y	Y
4 ***Allard***	Y	?	Y	Y	Y	Y	Y	Y
5 ***Hefley***	Y	Y	Y	Y	Y	Y	Y	Y
6 ***Schaefer***	Y	Y	Y	Y	Y	Y	Y	Y
CONNECTICUT								
1 Kennelly	Y	Y	Y	Y	Y	Y	Y	Y
2 Gejdenson	?	Y	Y	Y	Y	Y	Y	Y
3 DeLauro	Y	Y	Y	Y	Y	Y	Y	Y
4 ***Shays***	Y	Y	Y	Y	Y	Y	Y	Y
5 ***Franks***	Y	Y	Y	Y	Y	Y	Y	Y
6 ***Johnson***	Y	?	Y	Y	Y	Y	Y	Y
DELAWARE								
AL Carper	Y	Y	Y	Y	Y	Y	Y	Y
FLORIDA								
1 Hutto	Y	Y	Y	Y	Y	Y	Y	Y
2 Peterson	Y	Y	Y	Y	Y	Y	Y	Y
3 Bennett	Y	Y	Y	Y	Y	Y	Y	Y
4 ***James***	Y	Y	Y	Y	Y	Y	Y	Y
5 ***McCollum***	Y	Y	Y	Y	Y	Y	Y	Y
6 ***Stearns***	Y	Y	Y	Y	Y	Y	Y	Y
7 Gibbons	Y	Y	Y	Y	Y	Y	Y	Y
8 ***Young***	Y	Y	Y	Y	Y	Y	Y	Y
9 ***Bilirakis***	Y	+	?	Y	Y	Y	Y	Y
10 ***Ireland***	Y	?	?	?	Y	Y	Y	Y
11 Bacchus	Y	Y	Y	Y	Y	Y	Y	Y
12 ***Lewis***	Y	Y	Y	+	Y	Y	Y	Y
13 ***Goss***	Y	Y	Y	Y	Y	Y	Y	Y
14 Johnston	Y	Y	Y	Y	Y	Y	Y	Y
15 ***Shaw***	Y	Y	Y	Y	Y	Y	Y	Y
16 Smith	Y	Y	Y	?	Y	Y	Y	?
17 Lehman	Y	Y	Y	Y	Y	Y	Y	Y
18 ***Ros-Lehtinen***	Y	Y	Y	Y	Y	Y	Y	Y
19 Fascell	Y	Y	Y	Y	Y	Y	Y	Y
GEORGIA								
1 Thomas	Y	Y	Y	Y	Y	Y	Y	Y
2 Hatcher	Y	?	Y	Y	Y	Y	Y	Y
3 Ray	Y	Y	Y	Y	Y	Y	Y	?
4 Jones	Y	Y	Y	Y	Y	Y	Y	Y
5 Lewis	Y	Y	Y	Y	Y	Y	Y	Y
6 ***Gingrich***	Y	Y	Y	Y	Y	Y	?	Y
7 Darden	Y	Y	Y	Y	Y	Y	Y	Y
8 Rowland	Y	Y	Y	Y	Y	Y	Y	Y
9 Jenkins	Y	Y	Y	Y	Y	Y	Y	Y
10 Barnard	Y	Y	Y	Y	Y	?	?	Y
HAWAII								
1 Abercrombie	Y	Y	Y	Y	Y	Y	Y	Y
2 Mink	Y	Y	Y	Y	Y	Y	Y	Y
IDAHO								
1 LaRocco	Y	Y	Y	Y	Y	Y	Y	Y
2 Stallings	Y	Y	Y	Y	Y	Y	Y	Y
ILLINOIS								
1 Hayes	Y	Y	Y	Y	Y	Y	Y	Y
2 Savage	Y	Y	Y	?	Y	Y	Y	Y
3 Russo	Y	?	?	Y	Y	Y	Y	Y
4 Sangmeister	Y	Y	Y	Y	Y	Y	Y	Y
5 Lipinski	Y	Y	Y	Y	Y	Y	Y	Y
6 ***Hyde***	Y	Y	Y	Y	Y	Y	Y	Y
7 Collins	Y	Y	Y	Y	Y	Y	Y	Y
8 Rostenkowski	?	?	?	?	?	?	?	?
9 Yates	?	Y	Y	Y	Y	Y	Y	Y
10 ***Porter***	+	Y	Y	Y	Y	Y	Y	Y
11 Annunzio	Y	Y	Y	Y	Y	Y	Y	Y
12 ***Crane***	?	Y	Y	Y	Y	Y	Y	Y
13 ***Fawell***	Y	Y	Y	Y	Y	Y	Y	Y
14 ***Hastert***	Y	Y	Y	Y	Y	Y	Y	Y
15 ***Madigan***	Y	Y	Y	Y	?	Y	Y	Y
16 Cox	Y	Y	Y	Y	Y	Y	Y	Y
17 Evans	Y	Y	Y	Y	Y	Y	Y	Y
18 ***Michel***	Y	Y	Y	Y	Y	Y	Y	Y
19 Bruce	Y	Y	Y	Y	Y	Y	Y	Y
20 Durbin	Y	+	+	Y	Y	Y	Y	Y
21 Costello	Y	Y	Y	Y	Y	Y	Y	Y
22 Poshard	Y	Y	Y	Y	Y	Y	Y	Y
INDIANA								
1 Visclosky	Y	Y	Y	Y	Y	Y	Y	Y
2 Sharp	Y	Y	Y	Y	Y	Y	Y	?
3 Roemer	Y	Y	Y	Y	Y	Y	Y	Y

ND Northern Democrats SD Southern Democrats

	18	19	20	21	22	23	24	25
4 Long	Y	Y	Y	Y	Y	Y	Y	Y
5 Jontz	Y	Y	Y	Y	Y	Y	Y	Y
6 ***Burton***	Y	Y	Y	Y	Y	Y	Y	Y
7 ***Myers***	Y	Y	Y	Y	Y	Y	Y	Y
8 McCloskey	Y	+	+	Y	Y	Y	Y	Y
9 Hamilton	Y	Y	Y	Y	Y	Y	Y	Y
10 Jacobs	Y	?	?	Y	Y	Y	Y	Y
IOWA								
1 ***Leach***	Y	Y	Y	Y	Y	Y	Y	?
2 ***Nussle***	Y	Y	Y	Y	Y	Y	Y	Y
3 Nagle	Y	Y	Y	Y	Y	Y	Y	Y
4 Smith	?	?	?	?	Y	Y	Y	Y
5 ***Lightfoot***	Y	Y	Y	Y	Y	Y	Y	Y
6 ***Grandy***	Y	Y	Y	Y	Y	Y	Y	Y
KANSAS								
1 ***Roberts***	Y	Y	Y	Y	Y	?	?	Y
2 Slattery	Y	Y	Y	Y	Y	Y	Y	Y
3 ***Meyers***	Y	Y	Y	Y	Y	Y	Y	Y
4 Glickman	Y	Y	Y	Y	Y	Y	Y	Y
5 ***Nichols***	Y	Y	Y	Y	Y	Y	Y	Y
KENTUCKY								
1 Hubbard	Y	Y	Y	Y	Y	Y	Y	Y
2 Natcher	Y	Y	Y	Y	Y	Y	Y	Y
3 Mazzoli	Y	Y	Y	Y	Y	Y	Y	Y
4 ***Bunning***	Y	Y	Y	Y	Y	Y	Y	Y
5 ***Rogers***	Y	Y	Y	Y	Y	Y	Y	Y
6 ***Hopkins***	Y	Y	Y	Y	Y	Y	Y	Y
7 Perkins	Y	Y	Y	Y	Y	Y	Y	Y
LOUISIANA								
1 ***Livingston***	Y	Y	Y	Y	Y	Y	Y	Y
2 Jefferson	Y	Y	Y	Y	Y	?	?	Y
3 Tauzin	+	Y	Y	Y	Y	Y	Y	?
4 ***McCrery***	Y	Y	Y	Y	Y	Y	Y	Y
5 Huckaby	Y	Y	Y	Y	Y	?	?	Y
6 ***Baker***	Y	Y	Y	Y	Y	Y	Y	Y
7 Hayes	Y	Y	Y	Y	?	?	?	Y
8 ***Holloway***	Y	Y	Y	Y	Y	Y	Y	Y
MAINE								
1 Andrews	?	Y	Y	Y	Y	Y	Y	Y
2 ***Snowe***	?	Y	Y	Y	Y	Y	Y	Y
MARYLAND								
1 ***Gilchrest***	Y	Y	Y	Y	Y	Y	Y	Y
2 ***Bentley***	Y	Y	Y	Y	Y	Y	Y	Y
3 Cardin	Y	Y	Y	Y	Y	Y	Y	Y
4 McMillen	Y	Y	Y	Y	Y	Y	Y	Y
5 Hoyer	Y	Y	Y	Y	Y	Y	Y	Y
6 Byron	Y	Y	Y	Y	Y	Y	Y	Y
7 Mfume	Y	Y	Y	Y	Y	Y	Y	Y
8 ***Morella***	Y	Y	Y	Y	Y	Y	Y	Y
MASSACHUSETTS								
1 ***Conte*** †	Y	?	?	?				
2 Neal	Y	Y	Y	Y	Y	Y	Y	Y
3 Early	Y	Y	Y	?	Y	Y	Y	Y
4 Frank	Y	Y	Y	Y	+	Y	Y	Y
5 Atkins	Y	Y	Y	Y	Y	Y	Y	Y
6 Mavroules	Y	Y	Y	Y	?	?	?	Y
7 Markey	Y	?	?	Y	?	Y	Y	Y
8 Kennedy	?	Y	Y	?	Y	Y	Y	Y
9 Moakley	Y	Y	Y	Y	Y	Y	Y	Y
10 Studds	Y	Y	Y	Y	Y	Y	?	Y
11 Donnelly	?	?	?	?	Y	Y	Y	?
MICHIGAN								
1 Conyers	Y	Y	Y	Y	Y	Y	Y	Y
2 ***Pursell***	Y	Y	Y	Y	Y	Y	Y	Y
3 Wolpe	?	Y	Y	Y	Y	Y	Y	Y
4 ***Upton***	Y	Y	Y	Y	Y	Y	Y	Y
5 ***Henry***	Y	Y	Y	Y	Y	Y	Y	Y
6 Carr	Y	Y	Y	Y	Y	Y	Y	Y
7 Kildee	Y	Y	Y	Y	Y	Y	Y	Y
8 Traxler	Y	Y	Y	Y	Y	?	?	Y
9 ***Vander Jagt***	Y	Y	Y	Y	Y	Y	Y	Y
10 ***Camp***	Y	Y	Y	Y	Y	Y	Y	Y
11 ***Davis***	Y	Y	Y	Y	Y	Y	Y	Y
12 Bonior	Y	Y	Y	Y	Y	Y	Y	Y
13 Collins	Y	Y	Y	Y	Y	Y	Y	Y
14 Hertel	Y	Y	Y	Y	Y	Y	Y	Y
15 Ford	Y	Y	Y	Y	?	Y	Y	Y
16 Dingell	Y	Y	Y	Y	Y	Y	Y	Y
17 Levin	Y	Y	Y	Y	Y	Y	Y	Y
18 ***Broomfield***	Y	Y	Y	Y	Y	Y	Y	Y
MINNESOTA								
1 Penny	Y	Y	Y	Y	Y	Y	Y	Y
2 ***Weber***	Y	Y	Y	Y	Y	Y	Y	Y
3 ***Ramstad***	Y	Y	Y	Y	Y	Y	Y	Y
4 Vento	Y	Y	Y	Y	Y	Y	Y	Y
5 Sabo	Y	Y	Y	Y	Y	Y	Y	Y
6 Sikorski	Y	Y	Y	Y	Y	Y	Y	Y
7 Peterson	Y	+	+	Y	Y	Y	Y	Y
8 Oberstar	Y	Y	Y	Y	Y	Y	Y	Y
MISSISSIPPI								
1 Whitten	Y	Y	Y	Y	Y	?	?	Y
2 Espy	Y	Y	Y	Y	Y	Y	Y	Y
3 Montgomery	Y	Y	Y	Y	Y	Y	Y	Y
4 Parker	Y	Y	Y	Y	Y	Y	Y	Y
5 Taylor	Y	Y	Y	Y	Y	Y	Y	Y
MISSOURI								
1 Clay	Y	Y	Y	Y	Y	Y	Y	Y
2 Horn	Y	Y	Y	Y	Y	Y	Y	Y
3 Gephardt	Y	Y	Y	Y	Y	Y	Y	Y
4 Skelton	Y	Y	Y	Y	Y	Y	Y	Y
5 Wheat	Y	Y	?	Y	?	Y	Y	Y
6 ***Coleman***	Y	Y	Y	Y	Y	Y	Y	Y
7 ***Hancock***	Y	Y	Y	Y	Y	Y	Y	Y
8 ***Emerson***	Y	Y	Y	Y	Y	Y	Y	Y
9 Volkmer	Y	Y	Y	Y	Y	Y	Y	Y
MONTANA								
1 Williams	Y	Y	Y	Y	Y	Y	Y	Y
2 ***Marlenee***	Y	Y	Y	Y	Y	?	?	Y
NEBRASKA								
1 ***Bereuter***	Y	Y	Y	Y	Y	Y	Y	Y
2 Hoagland	Y	Y	Y	Y	Y	Y	Y	Y
3 ***Barrett***	Y	Y	Y	Y	Y	Y	Y	Y
NEVADA								
1 Bilbray	Y	Y	Y	Y	Y	Y	Y	Y
2 ***Vucanovich***	Y	Y	Y	Y	Y	Y	Y	Y
NEW HAMPSHIRE								
1 ***Zeliff***	Y	Y	Y	Y	Y	Y	Y	Y
2 Swett	Y	Y	Y	Y	Y	Y	Y	Y
NEW JERSEY								
1 Andrews	Y	Y	Y	Y	Y	Y	Y	Y
2 Hughes	Y	Y	Y	Y	Y	Y	Y	Y
3 Pallone	Y	Y	Y	Y	Y	Y	Y	Y
4 ***Smith***	Y	Y	Y	Y	Y	Y	Y	Y
5 ***Roukema***	Y	Y	Y	Y	Y	Y	Y	Y
6 Dwyer	Y	Y	Y	Y	Y	Y	Y	Y
7 ***Rinaldo***	Y	Y	Y	Y	Y	Y	Y	Y
8 Roe	Y	Y	Y	Y	Y	Y	Y	Y
9 Torricelli	Y	Y	Y	Y	Y	Y	Y	Y
10 Payne	Y	Y	Y	Y	Y	Y	Y	Y
11 ***Gallo***	Y	Y	Y	Y	Y	Y	Y	Y
12 ***Zimmer***	Y	Y	Y	Y	Y	+	Y	Y
13 ***Saxton***	Y	Y	Y	Y	Y	Y	Y	Y
14 Guarini	Y	Y	Y	Y	Y	Y	Y	Y
NEW MEXICO								
1 ***Schiff***	Y	Y	Y	Y	Y	Y	Y	Y
2 ***Skeen***	Y	Y	Y	Y	Y	Y	Y	Y
3 Richardson	Y	Y	Y	Y	Y	Y	Y	Y
NEW YORK								
1 Hochbrueckner	Y	Y	Y	Y	Y	Y	Y	Y
2 Downey	Y	Y	Y	Y	Y	Y	Y	Y
3 Mrazek	?	?	?	Y	Y	Y	Y	Y
4 ***Lent***	Y	Y	Y	Y	Y	?	?	Y
5 ***McGrath***	Y	Y	Y	Y	Y	Y	Y	Y
6 Flake	Y	Y	Y	Y	Y	Y	Y	?
7 Ackerman	?	Y	Y	Y	?	?	?	Y
8 Scheuer	Y	Y	Y	Y	Y	Y	Y	Y
9 Manton	Y	Y	Y	Y	Y	Y	Y	Y
10 Schumer	Y	Y	Y	Y	Y	Y	Y	Y
11 Towns	Y	Y	Y	Y	Y	Y	Y	Y
12 Owens	Y	Y	Y	Y	Y	Y	Y	Y
13 Solarz	Y	Y	Y	Y	?	?	?	Y
14 ***Molinari***	Y	Y	Y	Y	Y	Y	Y	Y
15 ***Green***	Y	Y	Y	Y	Y	Y	Y	Y
16 Rangel	Y	Y	Y	Y	Y	Y	Y	Y
17 Weiss	?	?	?	?	?	?	?	Y
18 Serrano	Y	Y	Y	Y	Y	Y	Y	Y
19 Engel	Y	Y	Y	Y	Y	Y	Y	Y
20 Lowey	+	Y	Y	Y	Y	Y	Y	Y
21 ***Fish***	Y	Y	Y	Y	Y	Y	Y	Y
22 ***Gilman***	Y	Y	Y	Y	Y	Y	Y	+
23 McNulty	Y	Y	Y	Y	Y	Y	Y	Y
24 ***Solomon***	Y	Y	Y	Y	Y	Y	Y	Y
25 ***Boehlert***	Y	Y	Y	Y	Y	Y	Y	Y
26 ***Martin***	Y	Y	Y	Y	Y	Y	Y	?
27 ***Walsh***	Y	Y	Y	Y	Y	Y	Y	Y
28 McHugh	Y	Y	Y	Y	Y	Y	Y	Y
29 ***Horton***	Y	Y	Y	Y	Y	Y	Y	Y
30 Slaughter	Y	Y	Y	Y	Y	Y	Y	Y
31 ***Paxon***	Y	Y	Y	Y	Y	Y	Y	Y
32 LaFalce	Y	Y	Y	Y	Y	Y	Y	Y
33 Nowak	Y	Y	Y	Y	Y	Y	Y	Y
34 ***Houghton***	Y	Y	Y	Y	Y	Y	Y	Y
NORTH CAROLINA								
1 Jones	Y	Y	Y	Y	Y	Y	Y	Y
2 Valentine	Y	Y	Y	Y	Y	Y	Y	Y
3 Lancaster	Y	Y	Y	Y	?	Y	Y	Y
4 Price	Y	Y	Y	Y	Y	Y	Y	Y
5 Neal	Y	Y	Y	Y	Y	Y	Y	Y
6 ***Coble***	Y	Y	Y	Y	Y	Y	Y	Y
7 Rose	Y	Y	Y	Y	Y	Y	Y	Y
8 Hefner	?	Y	Y	Y	Y	Y	Y	Y
9 ***McMillan***	Y	Y	Y	Y	Y	Y	Y	Y
10 ***Ballenger***	Y	Y	Y	Y	Y	Y	Y	Y
11 ***Taylor***	Y	Y	Y	Y	Y	Y	Y	Y
NORTH DAKOTA								
AL Dorgan	Y	Y	Y	Y	Y	Y	Y	Y
OHIO								
1 Luken	Y	Y	Y	Y	Y	Y	Y	Y
2 ***Gradison***	Y	Y	Y	Y	Y	Y	Y	Y
3 Hall	Y	Y	Y	Y	Y	Y	Y	Y
4 ***Oxley***	Y	?	?	Y	Y	Y	Y	Y
5 ***Gillmor***	Y	Y	Y	Y	Y	Y	Y	Y
6 ***McEwen***	Y	Y	Y	Y	Y	Y	Y	Y
7 ***Hobson***	Y	Y	Y	Y	Y	Y	Y	Y
8 ***Boehner***	Y	Y	Y	Y	Y	Y	Y	Y
9 Kaptur	Y	Y	Y	Y	Y	Y	Y	Y
10 ***Miller***	Y	Y	Y	?	?	?	?	?
11 Eckart	Y	Y	Y	Y	Y	Y	Y	?
12 ***Kasich***	Y	Y	Y	Y	Y	Y	Y	Y
13 Pease	Y	Y	Y	Y	Y	Y	Y	Y
14 Sawyer	Y	Y	Y	Y	Y	Y	Y	Y
15 ***Wylie***	Y	Y	Y	Y	Y	Y	Y	Y
16 ***Regula***	Y	Y	Y	Y	Y	Y	Y	Y
17 Traficant	Y	Y	Y	Y	Y	Y	Y	Y
18 Applegate	Y	Y	Y	Y	Y	Y	Y	Y
19 Feighan	Y	Y	Y	Y	Y	Y	Y	Y
20 Oakar	Y	Y	Y	Y	Y	Y	Y	Y
21 Stokes	Y	Y	Y	Y	Y	Y	Y	Y
OKLAHOMA								
1 ***Inhofe***	Y	Y	Y	Y	Y	Y	Y	Y
2 Synar	+	Y	Y	Y	Y	Y	Y	Y
3 Brewster	Y	Y	Y	Y	Y	Y	Y	?
4 McCurdy	?	?	?	Y	Y	Y	Y	Y
5 ***Edwards***	Y	?	?	Y	Y	Y	Y	Y
6 English	Y	Y	Y	Y	Y	Y	Y	Y
OREGON								
1 AuCoin	Y	?	?	Y	Y	Y	Y	Y
2 ***Smith***	Y	Y	Y	Y	Y	Y	Y	Y
3 Wyden	Y	Y	Y	Y	Y	Y	Y	Y
4 DeFazio	Y	Y	Y	Y	Y	Y	Y	Y
5 Kopetski	Y	Y	Y	Y	Y	Y	Y	Y
PENNSYLVANIA								
1 Foglietta	?	Y	Y	Y	Y	Y	Y	Y
2 Gray	Y	Y	Y	Y	Y	Y	Y	Y
3 Borski	Y	Y	Y	Y	Y	Y	Y	Y
4 Kolter	Y	Y	Y	Y	Y	Y	Y	Y
5 ***Schulze***	?	Y	Y	Y	Y	?	?	Y
6 Yatron	Y	Y	Y	Y	Y	Y	Y	Y
7 ***Weldon***	Y	Y	Y	Y	Y	Y	Y	Y
8 Kostmayer	Y	Y	Y	Y	Y	Y	?	Y
9 ***Shuster***	Y	Y	Y	Y	Y	Y	Y	Y
10 ***McDade***	Y	?	?	?	Y	Y	Y	Y
11 Kanjorski	Y	Y	Y	Y	Y	Y	Y	Y
12 Murtha	Y	Y	Y	Y	Y	Y	Y	Y
13 ***Coughlin***	Y	Y	Y	Y	Y	Y	Y	Y
14 Coyne	Y	Y	Y	Y	Y	Y	Y	Y
15 ***Ritter***	Y	Y	Y	Y	Y	Y	Y	Y
16 ***Walker***	Y	Y	Y	Y	Y	Y	Y	Y
17 ***Gekas***	Y	Y	Y	Y	Y	Y	Y	Y
18 ***Santorum***	Y	Y	Y	Y	Y	Y	Y	Y
19 ***Goodling***	Y	Y	Y	Y	Y	Y	Y	Y
20 Gaydos	?	Y	Y	Y	Y	Y	Y	Y
21 ***Ridge***	Y	Y	Y	Y	?	?	?	Y
22 Murphy	Y	Y	Y	Y	Y	Y	Y	Y
23 ***Clinger***	Y	Y	Y	Y	Y	Y	Y	Y
RHODE ISLAND								
1 ***Machtley***	Y	Y	Y	Y	Y	Y	Y	Y
2 Reed	Y	Y	Y	Y	Y	Y	Y	Y
SOUTH CAROLINA								
1 ***Ravenel***	Y	Y	Y	Y	Y	Y	Y	Y
2 ***Spence***	Y	Y	Y	Y	Y	Y	Y	Y
3 Derrick	Y	Y	Y	Y	Y	Y	Y	Y
4 Patterson	Y	Y	Y	Y	Y	Y	Y	Y
5 Spratt	Y	Y	Y	Y	Y	Y	Y	Y
6 Tallon	Y	Y	Y	Y	Y	Y	Y	Y
SOUTH DAKOTA								
AL Johnson	Y	Y	Y	Y	Y	Y	Y	Y
TENNESSEE								
1 ***Quillen***	Y	Y	Y	Y	Y	Y	Y	Y
2 ***Duncan***	Y	Y	Y	Y	?	?	?	Y
3 Lloyd	?	Y	Y	Y	Y	Y	Y	Y
4 Cooper	Y	Y	Y	Y	Y	Y	Y	Y
5 Clement	Y	Y	Y	Y	Y	Y	Y	Y
6 Gordon	Y	Y	Y	?	Y	Y	Y	Y
7 ***Sundquist***	Y	Y	Y	Y	Y	?	?	Y
8 Tanner	Y	?	?	Y	Y	Y	Y	Y
9 Ford	Y	?	?	?	Y	?	?	?
TEXAS								
1 Chapman	Y	Y	Y	Y	Y	Y	Y	Y
2 Wilson	Y	Y	Y	Y	?	?	Y	?
3 ***Bartlett***	Y	Y	Y	Y	?	?	?	?
4 Hall	Y	Y	Y	Y	Y	Y	Y	Y
5 Bryant	Y	Y	Y	Y	Y	Y	Y	Y
6 ***Barton***	Y	Y	Y	Y	?	?	?	Y
7 ***Archer***	Y	Y	Y	Y	Y	Y	Y	Y
8 ***Fields***	Y	Y	Y	Y	Y	?	?	Y
9 Brooks	Y	Y	Y	Y	Y	Y	Y	Y
10 Pickle	Y	Y	Y	Y	Y	Y	Y	Y
11 Edwards	Y	Y	Y	+	Y	Y	Y	Y
12 Geren	Y	Y	Y	Y	Y	Y	Y	Y
13 Sarpalius	Y	Y	Y	Y	Y	Y	Y	Y
14 Laughlin	Y	?	?	Y	Y	Y	Y	Y
15 de la Garza	Y	Y	Y	?	Y	?	?	Y
16 Coleman	Y	Y	Y	Y	Y	Y	Y	Y
17 Stenholm	Y	Y	Y	Y	Y	Y	Y	Y
18 Washington	Y	Y	Y	Y	Y	?	?	Y
19 ***Combest***	Y	Y	Y	Y	Y	Y	Y	Y
20 Gonzalez	Y	Y	Y	Y	Y	Y	Y	Y
21 ***Smith***	Y	Y	Y	Y	Y	Y	Y	Y
22 ***DeLay***	Y	Y	Y	Y	Y	Y	Y	Y
23 Bustamante	Y	Y	Y	?	?	?	?	Y
24 Frost	Y	Y	Y	Y	Y	Y	Y	Y
25 Andrews	Y	Y	Y	Y	Y	Y	Y	Y
26 ***Armey***	Y	Y	Y	Y	Y	Y	Y	Y
27 Ortiz	Y	Y	Y	Y	Y	?	?	Y
UTAH								
1 ***Hansen***	Y	Y	Y	Y	Y	Y	Y	Y
2 Owens	?	Y	Y	?	Y	Y	Y	Y
3 Orton	Y	Y	Y	Y	Y	Y	Y	Y
VERMONT								
AL *Sanders*	Y	Y	Y	Y	Y	Y	Y	Y
VIRGINIA								
1 ***Bateman***	Y	Y	Y	Y	Y	Y	Y	Y
2 Pickett	Y	Y	Y	Y	Y	Y	Y	Y
3 ***Bliley***	Y	Y	Y	Y	Y	Y	Y	Y
4 Sisisky	Y	Y	Y	Y	Y	Y	Y	Y
5 Payne	Y	Y	Y	Y	Y	Y	Y	Y
6 Olin	Y	Y	Y	Y	Y	Y	Y	Y
7 ***Slaughter***	Y	Y	Y	Y	Y	Y	Y	Y
8 Moran	Y	Y	Y	Y	Y	Y	Y	Y
9 Boucher	Y	Y	Y	Y	Y	Y	Y	Y
10 ***Wolf***	Y	Y	Y	Y	Y	Y	Y	Y
WASHINGTON								
1 ***Miller***	Y	Y	Y	Y	Y	Y	Y	Y
2 Swift	Y	Y	Y	Y	Y	Y	Y	Y
3 Unsoeld	?	Y	Y	Y	Y	Y	Y	Y
4 ***Morrison***	Y	Y	Y	Y	Y	Y	Y	Y
5 Foley								
6 Dicks	Y	Y	Y	Y	Y	Y	Y	Y
7 McDermott	+	Y	Y	Y	Y	Y	Y	Y
8 ***Chandler***	Y	Y	Y	Y	Y	Y	Y	Y
WEST VIRGINIA								
1 Mollohan	Y	Y	Y	Y	Y	Y	Y	Y
2 Staggers	?	Y	Y	Y	Y	Y	Y	Y
3 Wise	Y	Y	Y	Y	Y	Y	Y	Y
4 Rahall	+	+	+	Y	Y	Y	Y	Y
WISCONSIN								
1 Aspin	Y	Y	Y	Y	Y	Y	Y	Y
2 ***Klug***	Y	Y	Y	Y	Y	Y	Y	Y
3 ***Gunderson***	Y	?	Y	Y	Y	Y	Y	Y
4 Kleczka	Y	Y	Y	Y	Y	Y	Y	Y
5 Moody	Y	Y	Y	Y	Y	Y	Y	Y
6 ***Petri***	Y	Y	Y	Y	Y	Y	Y	Y
7 Obey	Y	Y	Y	Y	Y	Y	Y	Y
8 ***Roth***	Y	Y	Y	Y	Y	Y	Y	Y
9 ***Sensenbrenner***	Y	Y	Y	Y	Y	Y	Y	Y
WYOMING								
AL ***Thomas***	Y	Y	Y	Y	Y	Y	Y	Y

Southern states - Ala., Ark., Fla., Ga., Ky., La., Miss., N.C., Okla., S.C., Tenn., Texas, Va.
Omitted votes are quorum calls, which CQ does not include in its vote charts.

HOUSE VOTES 26, 27, 28, 29, 30, 32, 33, 34

26. H Res 88. Cuban Human Rights Violations/Adoption. Adoption of the resolution to condemn Cuba's human rights violations and commend the United Nations Human Rights Commission for its attention to the human rights situation in Cuba. Adopted 404-1: R 156-0; D 247-1 (ND 169-1, SD 78-0); I 1-0, Feb. 28, 1991.

27. HR 707. CFTC Reauthorization/Passage. De la Garza, D-Texas, motion to suspend the rules and pass the bill to reauthorize the Commodity Futures Trading Commission (CFTC) at $48.5 million in fiscal 1992 and $53 million in fiscal 1993. Motion agreed to 395-27: R 154-10; D 240-17 (ND 163-13, SD 77-4); I 1-0, March 5, 1991. A two-thirds majority of those present and voting (282 in this case) is required for passage under suspension of the rules. A "yea" was a vote supporting the president's position.

28. H Res 95. Desert Storm Commendation/Adoption. Fascell, D-Fla., motion to suspend the rules and adopt the resolution to acclaim the president for his decisive leadership in the Persian Gulf and express the highest commendation for the U.S. troops and members of the coalition participating in Operation Desert Storm. Motion agreed to 410-8: R 164-0; D 246-7 (ND 166-6, SD 80-1); I 0-1, March 5, 1991. A two-thirds majority of those present and voting (279 in this case) is required for passage under suspension of the rules.

29. HR 991. Defense Production Act/ Passage. Carper, D-Del., motion to suspend the rules and pass the bill to reauthorize the Defense Production Act through Sept. 30, 1991, and retroactive to Oct. 20, 1990. The bill would authorize $50 million for programs to ensure adequate domestic capacity to produce goods necessary for national defense. Motion agreed to 416-0: R 161-0; D 254-0 (ND 173-0, SD 81-0), I 1-0, March 6, 1991. A two-thirds majority of those present and voting (278 in this case) is required for passage under suspension of the rules. A "yea" was a vote supporting the president's position.

30. HR 1281. Fiscal 1991 Supplemental Appropriations/ Israel Aid. Valentine, D-N.C., amendment to eliminate the $650 million in aid earmarked for Israel to offset costs associated with the Persian Gulf conflict. Rejected 24-397: R 11-151; D 13-245 (ND 6-168, SD 7-77); I 0-1, March 7, 1991. A "nay" was a vote supporting the president's position.

32. HR 1281. Fiscal 1991 Supplemental Appropriations/ Navy Funds. Burton, R-Ind., amendment to strike the provision directing the Navy to begin spending $405 million in fiscal 1991 funds for the Service Life Extension Program for the aircraft carrier USS *Kennedy* at the Philadelphia Naval Shipyard. Rejected 105-315: R 91-71; D 14-243 (ND 9-164, SD 5-79); I 0-1, March 7, 1991.

33. HR 1281. Fiscal 1991 Supplemental Appropriations/ Housing. Kolbe, R-Ariz., en bloc amendment to provide $500 million for the HOME program (home investment partnerships), $165 million for the HOPE (Homeownership and Opportunity for People Everywhere) program, and $122 million for the Shelter Plus Care program by transferring $942 million from the construction of new public housing and housing programs scheduled for termination in fiscal 1992. Rejected 177-240: R 154-6; D 23-233 (ND 11-164, SD 12-69); I 0-1, March 7, 1991. A "yea" was a vote supporting the president's position.

34. HR 1281. Fiscal 1991 Supplemental Appropriations/ Construction Help. Stenholm, D-Texas, amendment to strike provisions from the bill that prohibit the Labor Department from expending funds to implement regulations that permit the expanded use of helpers on federally funded construction projects. Rejected 173-244: R 135-25; D 38-218 (ND 2-172, SD 36-46); I 0-1, March 7, 1991. A "yea" was a vote supporting the president's position.

KEY

- Y Voted for (yea).
- # Paired for.
- \+ Announced for.
- N Voted against (nay).
- X Paired against.
- \- Announced against.
- P Voted "present."
- C Voted "present" to avoid possible conflict of interest.
- ? Did not vote or otherwise make a position known.

Democrats ***Republicans***
Independent

	26	27	28	29	30	32	33	34
ALABAMA								
1 ***Callahan***	Y	Y	Y	Y	N	Y	Y	Y
2 ***Dickinson***	Y	?	?	Y	N	Y	Y	Y
3 Browder	Y	Y	Y	Y	N	N	N	N
4 Bevill	Y	Y	Y	Y	N	N	N	N
5 Cramer	Y	Y	Y	Y	N	N	N	N
6 Erdreich	Y	Y	Y	Y	N	N	N	N
7 Harris	Y	Y	Y	Y	N	N	N	N
ALASKA								
AL ***Young***	Y	N	Y	Y	N	N	Y	N
ARIZONA								
1 ***Rhodes***	Y	Y	Y	Y	N	Y	Y	Y
2 Udall	?	?	?	?	?	?	?	?
3 ***Stump***	Y	Y	Y	Y	Y	Y	Y	Y
4 ***Kyl***	Y	Y	Y	Y	N	Y	Y	Y
5 ***Kolbe***	Y	Y	Y	Y	N	N	Y	Y
ARKANSAS								
1 Alexander	Y	Y	Y	Y	N	N	N	N
2 Thornton	?	Y	Y	Y	N	N	N	N
3 ***Hammerschmidt***	Y	Y	Y	Y	N	N	N	Y
4 Anthony	?	Y	Y	Y	N	N	N	Y
CALIFORNIA								
1 ***Riggs***	Y	Y	Y	Y	N	?	Y	Y
2 ***Herger***	Y	Y	Y	Y	N	Y	Y	Y
3 Matsui	?	Y	Y	Y	N	N	N	N
4 Fazio	Y	Y	Y	Y	N	N	N	N
5 Pelosi	Y	Y	Y	Y	N	N	N	N
6 Boxer	Y	Y	Y	Y	N	N	N	N
7 Miller	Y	Y	Y	Y	N	N	N	N
8 Dellums	Y	Y	N	Y	N	N	N	N
9 Stark	Y	Y	Y	Y	N	N	N	N
10 Edwards	Y	Y	Y	Y	N	N	N	N
11 Lantos	Y	Y	Y	Y	N	N	N	N
12 ***Campbell***	?	Y	Y	?	N	Y	Y	Y
13 Mineta	Y	Y	Y	Y	N	N	N	N
14 ***Doolittle***	Y	Y	Y	Y	N	N	Y	Y
15 Condit	Y	Y	Y	Y	N	Y	N	N
16 Panetta	Y	Y	Y	Y	N	N	N	N
17 Dooley	Y	Y	Y	Y	N	N	N	N
18 Lehman	Y	Y	Y	Y	N	N	N	N
19 ***Lagomarsino***	Y	Y	Y	?	N	Y	Y	Y
20 ***Thomas***	Y	Y	Y	Y	N	N	Y	Y
21 ***Gallegly***	Y	Y	Y	Y	N	Y	Y	Y
22 ***Moorhead***	Y	Y	Y	Y	N	N	Y	Y
23 Beilenson	Y	N	Y	Y	N	N	N	Y
24 Waxman	Y	Y	Y	Y	N	N	N	N
25 Roybal	Y	Y	Y	Y	N	N	?	?
26 Berman	Y	N	Y	Y	N	N	N	N
27 Levine	?	?	?	?	?	?	?	?
28 Dixon	Y	Y	Y	Y	N	N	N	N
29 Waters	Y	Y	N	Y	N	N	N	N
30 Martinez	Y	Y	Y	?	N	Y	Y	N
31 Dymally	?	Y	?	Y	Y	N	N	N
32 Anderson	Y	Y	Y	Y	N	N	N	N
33 ***Dreier***	Y	Y	Y	Y	N	Y	Y	Y
34 Torres	Y	Y	Y	Y	N	N	N	N
35 ***Lewis***	Y	Y	Y	Y	N	N	Y	Y
36 Brown	Y	Y	Y	Y	N	N	N	N
37 ***McCandless***	Y	Y	Y	Y	N	Y	Y	Y
38 ***Dornan***	Y	Y	Y	Y	N	N	Y	Y
39 ***Dannemeyer***	Y	Y	Y	Y	N	Y	Y	Y
40 ***Cox***	Y	Y	Y	Y	N	Y	Y	Y
41 ***Lowery***	Y	Y	Y	Y	N	N	Y	Y
42 ***Rohrabacher***	Y	Y	Y	Y	N	Y	Y	Y
43 ***Packard***	Y	Y	Y	Y	N	N	Y	Y
44 ***Cunningham***	?	Y	Y	Y	N	N	Y	Y
45 ***Hunter***	Y	Y	Y	Y	?	N	Y	Y
COLORADO								
1 Schroeder	Y	Y	Y	Y	N	N	N	N
2 Skaggs	Y	Y	Y	Y	N	N	N	N
3 Campbell	Y	Y	Y	Y	N	N	N	N
4 ***Allard***	Y	Y	Y	Y	N	Y	Y	Y
5 ***Hefley***	Y	Y	Y	Y	N	Y	Y	Y
6 ***Schaefer***	Y	Y	Y	Y	N	Y	Y	Y
CONNECTICUT								
1 Kennelly	Y	Y	Y	Y	N	N	N	N
2 Gejdenson	Y	N	Y	Y	N	N	N	N
3 DeLauro	Y	Y	Y	+	N	N	N	N
4 ***Shays***	Y	Y	Y	Y	N	Y	Y	N
5 ***Franks***	Y	Y	Y	Y	N	N	Y	Y
6 ***Johnson***	Y	Y	Y	Y	N	N	Y	Y
DELAWARE								
AL Carper	Y	Y	Y	Y	N	N	N	N
FLORIDA								
1 Hutto	Y	Y	Y	Y	N	N	N	Y
2 Peterson	Y	Y	Y	Y	N	N	N	N
3 Bennett	Y	Y	Y	Y	N	N	N	N
4 ***James***	Y	Y	Y	Y	N	Y	Y	Y
5 ***McCollum***	Y	Y	Y	Y	N	Y	Y	Y
6 ***Stearns***	Y	Y	Y	Y	N	Y	Y	Y
7 Gibbons	Y	Y	Y	Y	N	N	N	N
8 ***Young***	Y	Y	Y	Y	N	N	Y	Y
9 ***Bilirakis***	Y	Y	Y	Y	N	Y	Y	Y
10 ***Ireland***	Y	Y	Y	Y	N	N	#	#
11 Bacchus	Y	Y	Y	Y	N	N	N	N
12 ***Lewis***	Y	Y	Y	Y	N	Y	Y	Y
13 ***Goss***	Y	Y	Y	Y	N	Y	Y	Y
14 Johnston	Y	Y	Y	Y	N	N	N	N
15 ***Shaw***	Y	Y	Y	Y	N	Y	Y	Y
16 Smith	Y	Y	Y	Y	N	N	N	N
17 Lehman	Y	Y	Y	Y	N	N	N	N
18 ***Ros-Lehtinen***	Y	Y	Y	Y	N	Y	Y	Y
19 Fascell	Y	Y	Y	Y	N	N	N	N
GEORGIA								
1 Thomas	Y	Y	Y	Y	N	N	N	Y
2 Hatcher	?	Y	Y	Y	N	N	N	Y
3 Ray	Y	Y	Y	Y	N	N	N	Y
4 Jones	Y	Y	Y	Y	N	N	N	N
5 Lewis	Y	Y	Y	Y	N	N	N	N
6 ***Gingrich***	Y	Y	Y	Y	N	N	Y	Y
7 Darden	Y	Y	Y	Y	N	N	N	Y
8 Rowland	Y	Y	Y	Y	N	N	N	Y
9 Jenkins	Y	Y	Y	Y	N	N	N	Y
10 Barnard	Y	Y	Y	Y	N	N	Y	Y
HAWAII								
1 Abercrombie	Y	Y	Y	Y	N	N	N	N
2 Mink	Y	Y	Y	Y	N	N	N	N
IDAHO								
1 LaRocco	Y	Y	Y	Y	N	N	N	N
2 Stallings	Y	Y	Y	Y	N	N	Y	N
ILLINOIS								
1 Hayes	Y	Y	N	Y	Y	N	N	N
2 Savage	N	Y	N	Y	Y	N	N	N
3 Russo	Y	Y	Y	Y	N	N	N	N
4 Sangmeister	Y	?	?	?	?	?	?	?
5 Lipinski	Y	Y	Y	Y	N	N	Y	N
6 ***Hyde***	Y	Y	Y	Y	N	Y	Y	Y
7 Collins	Y	Y	Y	Y	N	N	N	N
8 Rostenkowski	Y	Y	Y	Y	N	N	N	N
9 Yates	Y	N	Y	Y	N	N	N	N
10 ***Porter***	?	Y	Y	Y	N	Y	Y	Y
11 Annunzio	?	Y	Y	Y	N	N	Y	N
12 ***Crane***	Y	Y	Y	Y	N	Y	?	?
13 ***Fawell***	Y	Y	Y	Y	N	Y	Y	Y
14 ***Hastert***	Y	Y	Y	Y	N	Y	Y	Y
15 Madigan	Y	Y	Y	Y	?	?	?	Y
16 Cox	Y	Y	Y	Y	N	N	N	N
17 Evans	Y	Y	Y	Y	N	N	N	N
18 ***Michel***	Y	Y	Y	Y	N	N	?	?
19 Bruce	Y	Y	Y	Y	N	N	N	N
20 Durbin	Y	Y	Y	Y	N	N	N	N
21 Costello	Y	Y	Y	Y	N	N	N	N
22 Poshard	Y	Y	Y	Y	N	N	N	N
INDIANA								
1 Visclosky	Y	N	Y	Y	N	Y	N	N
2 Sharp	Y	Y	Y	Y	N	Y	N	N
3 Roemer	Y	Y	Y	Y	N	N	N	N

ND Northern Democrats SD Southern Democrats

Member	26	27	28	29	30	32	33	34
4 Long	Y	Y	Y	Y	N	N	N	N
5 Jontz	Y	Y	Y	Y	N	N	N	N
6 ***Burton***	Y	Y	Y	Y	N	Y	Y	N
7 ***Myers***	Y	Y	Y	Y	N	N	Y	Y
8 McCloskey	Y	Y	Y	Y	N	N	N	N
9 Hamilton	Y	Y	Y	Y	N	N	N	N
10 Jacobs	Y	Y	Y	Y	N	Y	N	N
IOWA								
1 ***Leach***	Y	N	Y	Y	N	Y	Y	Y
2 ***Nussle***	Y	Y	Y	Y	N	Y	Y	Y
3 Nagle	Y	Y	Y	Y	N	N	N	N
4 Smith	Y	Y	Y	Y	N	N	N	N
5 ***Lightfoot***	Y	Y	Y	Y	N	N	Y	Y
6 ***Grandy***	Y	Y	Y	Y	N	Y	Y	Y
KANSAS								
1 ***Roberts***	Y	Y	Y	Y	Y	Y	Y	Y
2 Slattery	Y	Y	Y	Y	N	Y	Y	N
3 ***Meyers***	Y	Y	Y	Y	N	Y	Y	Y
4 Glickman	Y	Y	Y	Y	N	Y	N	N
5 ***Nichols***	Y	Y	Y	Y	N	N	Y	Y
KENTUCKY								
1 Hubbard	Y	Y	Y	Y	Y	Y	N	N
2 Natcher	Y	Y	Y	Y	N	N	N	N
3 Mazzoli	Y	Y	Y	Y	N	N	N	N
4 ***Bunning***	?	Y	Y	Y	N	Y	Y	Y
5 ***Rogers***	Y	Y	Y	Y	N	Y	Y	Y
6 ***Hopkins***	Y	Y	Y	Y	N	Y	Y	Y
7 Perkins	Y	Y	Y	Y	Y	N	N	N
LOUISIANA								
1 ***Livingston***	Y	N	Y	Y	N	N	Y	Y
2 Jefferson	?	Y	Y	?	N	N	N	N
3 Tauzin	Y	N	Y	Y	N	N	Y	Y
4 ***McCrery***	Y	N	Y	Y	N	N	Y	Y
5 Huckaby	Y	N	Y	Y	N	N	Y	Y
6 ***Baker***	Y	Y	Y	Y	N	Y	Y	Y
7 Hayes	Y	N	Y	Y	N	N	Y	Y
8 ***Holloway***	Y	Y	Y	Y	N	Y	Y	Y
MAINE								
1 Andrews	?	Y	Y	Y	-	N	N	N
2 ***Snowe***	Y	Y	Y	Y	N	N	Y	Y
MARYLAND								
1 ***Gilchrest***	Y	Y	Y	Y	N	N	Y	Y
2 ***Bentley***	Y	N	Y	Y	N	N	Y	Y
3 Cardin	Y	Y	Y	Y	N	N	N	N
4 McMillen	Y	Y	Y	Y	N	N	N	N
5 Hoyer	Y	Y	Y	Y	N	N	N	N
6 Byron	Y	Y	Y	Y	N	N	N	Y
7 Mfume	Y	Y	Y	Y	N	N	N	N
8 ***Morella***	Y	Y	Y	Y	N	Y	N	Y
MASSACHUSETTS								
1 Vacancy								
2 Neal	Y	Y	Y	Y	N	N	N	N
3 Early	Y	Y	Y	Y	N	Y	Y	N
4 Frank	Y	Y	Y	Y	N	N	N	N
5 Atkins	?	Y	Y	Y	N	N	N	N
6 Mavroules	Y	Y	Y	Y	N	N	N	N
7 Markey	Y	Y	Y	Y	N	N	N	N
8 Kennedy	Y	Y	Y	Y	N	N	N	N
9 Moakley	Y	Y	Y	Y	N	N	N	N
10 Studds	Y	Y	Y	Y	N	N	N	N
11 Donnelly	?	?	?	?	?	?	?	?
MICHIGAN								
1 Conyers	Y	Y	N	Y	N	N	N	N
2 ***Pursell***	?	Y	Y	Y	N	N	Y	Y
3 Wolpe	Y	Y	Y	Y	N	N	N	N
4 ***Upton***	Y	Y	Y	Y	N	Y	Y	Y
5 ***Henry***	Y	Y	Y	Y	N	N	Y	Y
6 Carr	Y	Y	Y	Y	N	N	N	N
7 Kildee	Y	Y	Y	Y	N	N	N	N
8 Traxler	Y	N	Y	Y	N	N	N	N
9 ***Vander Jagt***	Y	Y	Y	Y	N	Y	Y	Y
10 ***Camp***	Y	Y	Y	Y	N	Y	Y	Y
11 ***Davis***	Y	Y	Y	Y	N	N	Y	N
12 Bonior	Y	Y	Y	Y	N	N	N	N
13 Collins	Y	Y	Y	Y	N	N	N	N
14 Hertel	Y	Y	Y	Y	N	N	N	N
15 Ford	Y	Y	Y	Y	N	N	N	N
16 Dingell	Y	Y	Y	?	N	?	N	N
17 Levin	Y	Y	Y	Y	N	N	N	N
18 ***Broomfield***	Y	Y	Y	Y	N	Y	Y	Y
MINNESOTA								
1 Penny	Y	Y	Y	Y	N	N	Y	N
2 ***Weber***	?	Y	Y	Y	N	N	Y	Y
3 ***Ramstad***	Y	Y	Y	Y	N	Y	Y	Y
4 Vento	Y	Y	Y	Y	N	N	N	N
5 Sabo	Y	Y	Y	Y	N	N	N	N
6 Sikorski	Y	Y	Y	Y	N	N	N	N
7 Peterson	Y	Y	Y	Y	N	N	N	N
8 Oberstar	Y	Y	Y	Y	N	N	N	N
MISSISSIPPI								
1 Whitten	Y	Y	Y	Y	N	N	N	Y
2 Espy	Y	Y	Y	Y	N	N	N	N
3 Montgomery	Y	Y	Y	Y	N	N	N	Y
4 Parker	Y	Y	Y	Y	N	N	N	Y
5 Taylor	Y	Y	Y	Y	Y	N	N	Y
MISSOURI								
1 Clay	Y	Y	Y	Y	N	N	N	N
2 Horn	Y	Y	Y	Y	N	N	N	N
3 Gephardt	Y	Y	Y	Y	N	N	N	N
4 Skelton	Y	Y	Y	Y	N	N	N	N
5 Wheat	Y	Y	Y	Y	N	N	N	N
6 ***Coleman***	Y	Y	Y	Y	N	N	Y	Y
7 ***Hancock***	Y	Y	Y	Y	Y	Y	Y	Y
8 ***Emerson***	Y	Y	Y	Y	N	N	Y	Y
9 Volkmer	Y	Y	Y	Y	N	N	N	N
MONTANA								
1 Williams	Y	Y	Y	Y	Y	N	N	N
2 ***Marlenee***	Y	Y	Y	Y	N	Y	Y	Y
NEBRASKA								
1 ***Bereuter***	Y	Y	Y	Y	N	Y	Y	Y
2 Hoagland	Y	Y	Y	Y	N	N	N	N
3 ***Barrett***	Y	Y	Y	Y	N	Y	Y	Y
NEVADA								
1 Bilbray	Y	Y	Y	Y	N	N	N	N
2 ***Vucanovich***	Y	Y	Y	Y	N	N	Y	Y
NEW HAMPSHIRE								
1 ***Zeliff***	Y	Y	Y	Y	N	N	Y	Y
2 Swett	Y	Y	Y	Y	N	N	Y	N
NEW JERSEY								
1 Andrews	Y	Y	Y	Y	N	N	Y	N
2 Hughes	Y	Y	Y	Y	N	N	N	N
3 Pallone	Y	Y	Y	Y	N	N	Y	N
4 ***Smith***	Y	Y	Y	Y	N	N	Y	N
5 ***Roukema***	Y	Y	Y	Y	N	Y	N	N
6 Dwyer	Y	Y	Y	Y	N	N	N	N
7 ***Rinaldo***	Y	Y	Y	Y	N	N	Y	N
8 Roe	Y	Y	Y	Y	N	N	N	N
9 Torricelli	Y	Y	Y	Y	N	N	N	N
10 Payne	Y	Y	P	Y	N	N	N	N
11 ***Gallo***	Y	Y	Y	Y	N	N	Y	N
12 ***Zimmer***	Y	Y	Y	Y	N	Y	Y	Y
13 ***Saxton***	Y	Y	Y	Y	N	N	Y	N
14 Guarini	Y	Y	Y	Y	N	N	N	N
NEW MEXICO								
1 ***Schiff***	Y	Y	Y	Y	N	N	Y	Y
2 ***Skeen***	Y	Y	Y	Y	N	N	Y	Y
3 Richardson	Y	Y	Y	Y	N	N	N	N
NEW YORK								
1 Hochbrueckner	Y	Y	Y	Y	N	N	N	N
2 Downey	Y	Y	Y	Y	N	N	N	N
3 Mrazek	Y	Y	Y	Y	N	N	N	?
4 ***Lent***	Y	Y	Y	Y	N	N	Y	N
5 ***McGrath***	Y	Y	Y	Y	N	N	Y	N
6 Flake	?	Y	Y	Y	N	N	N	N
7 Ackerman	Y	Y	Y	Y	N	?	N	N
8 Scheuer	Y	N	Y	Y	N	N	N	N
9 Manton	Y	Y	Y	Y	N	N	N	N
10 Schumer	Y	Y	Y	Y	N	N	N	N
11 Towns	Y	Y	N	Y	N	N	N	N
12 Owens	Y	Y	P	Y	N	N	N	N
13 Solarz	Y	Y	Y	Y	N	N	N	N
14 ***Molinari***	Y	Y	Y	Y	N	N	Y	Y
15 ***Green***	Y	N	Y	Y	N	N	N	N
16 Rangel	Y	Y	Y	Y	N	N	N	N
17 Weiss	Y	N	P	Y	N	?	X	N
18 Serrano	Y	?	?	Y	N	N	N	N
19 Engel	Y	Y	Y	Y	N	N	N	N
20 Lowey	Y	Y	Y	Y	N	N	N	N
21 ***Fish***	Y	Y	Y	Y	N	N	N	N
22 ***Gilman***	+	Y	Y	Y	N	Y	Y	N
23 McNulty	Y	Y	Y	Y	N	N	N	N
24 ***Solomon***	Y	Y	Y	Y	N	N	Y	?
25 ***Boehlert***	Y	Y	Y	Y	N	N	Y	N
26 ***Martin***	Y	Y	Y	Y	N	Y	Y	Y
27 ***Walsh***	Y	Y	Y	Y	N	Y	Y	N
28 McHugh	Y	N	Y	Y	N	N	N	N
29 ***Horton***	Y	Y	Y	?	N	N	Y	N
30 Slaughter	Y	Y	Y	Y	N	N	N	N
31 ***Paxon***	Y	Y	Y	Y	N	Y	Y	Y
32 LaFalce	Y	Y	Y	Y	N	N	N	N
33 Nowak	Y	Y	Y	Y	N	N	N	N
34 ***Houghton***	?	Y	Y	Y	N	N	Y	N
NORTH CAROLINA								
1 Jones	Y	Y	Y	Y	N	N	N	Y
2 Valentine	Y	Y	Y	Y	Y	N	N	Y
3 Lancaster	Y	Y	Y	Y	N	N	N	Y
4 Price	Y	Y	Y	Y	N	N	N	Y
5 Neal	Y	Y	Y	Y	N	N	N	Y
6 ***Coble***	Y	Y	Y	Y	N	N	Y	Y
7 Rose	Y	Y	Y	Y	N	N	N	Y
8 Hefner	Y	Y	Y	Y	N	N	N	Y
9 ***McMillan***	Y	Y	Y	Y	N	Y	Y	Y
10 ***Ballenger***	Y	Y	Y	Y	N	Y	Y	Y
11 ***Taylor***	Y	Y	Y	Y	N	Y	Y	Y
NORTH DAKOTA								
AL Dorgan	Y	Y	Y	Y	N	N	N	N
OHIO								
1 Luken	?	Y	Y	Y	N	Y	N	N
2 ***Gradison***	Y	N	Y	Y	Y	Y	Y	Y
3 Hall	Y	Y	Y	Y	N	N	N	N
4 ***Oxley***	Y	Y	Y	Y	N	Y	Y	Y
5 ***Gillmor***	Y	N	Y	?	N	Y	Y	Y
6 ***McEwen***	Y	Y	Y	Y	N	Y	Y	Y
7 ***Hobson***	Y	Y	Y	Y	N	Y	Y	Y
8 ***Boehner***	Y	Y	Y	Y	N	Y	Y	Y
9 Kaptur	Y	Y	Y	Y	N	N	N	N
10 ***Miller***	?	?	?	?	?	?	?	?
11 Eckart	?	N	Y	Y	N	N	N	N
12 ***Kasich***	Y	Y	Y	Y	N	Y	Y	Y
13 Pease	Y	N	Y	Y	N	N	N	N
14 Sawyer	Y	Y	Y	Y	N	N	N	N
15 ***Wylie***	Y	Y	Y	Y	N	Y	Y	Y
16 ***Regula***	Y	Y	Y	Y	N	N	Y	N
17 Traficant	Y	Y	Y	Y	Y	N	N	N
18 Applegate	Y	Y	Y	Y	N	N	N	N
19 Feighan	Y	Y	Y	Y	N	N	N	N
20 Oakar	Y	Y	Y	Y	N	N	N	N
21 Stokes	Y	Y	Y	Y	N	N	N	N
OKLAHOMA								
1 ***Inhofe***	Y	Y	Y	Y	N	Y	Y	Y
2 Synar	Y	Y	Y	Y	N	N	N	N
3 Brewster	Y	Y	Y	Y	N	N	N	N
4 McCurdy	Y	Y	Y	Y	N	N	Y	Y
5 ***Edwards***	Y	Y	Y	Y	N	N	Y	Y
6 English	Y	Y	Y	Y	N	N	Y	N
OREGON								
1 AuCoin	Y	Y	Y	Y	N	N	N	N
2 ***Smith***	Y	Y	Y	Y	N	Y	Y	Y
3 Wyden	Y	N	Y	Y	N	N	N	N
4 DeFazio	Y	Y	Y	Y	N	N	N	N
5 Kopetski	Y	Y	Y	Y	N	N	N	N
PENNSYLVANIA								
1 Foglietta	Y	Y	Y	Y	N	N	N	N
2 Gray	Y	Y	Y	Y	N	N	N	N
3 Borski	Y	Y	Y	Y	N	N	N	N
4 Kolter	Y	Y	Y	Y	?	N	N	N
5 ***Schulze***	Y	Y	Y	Y	N	N	Y	Y
6 Yatron	Y	Y	Y	Y	N	N	N	N
7 ***Weldon***	Y	Y	Y	Y	N	N	Y	N
8 Kostmayer	Y	Y	Y	Y	N	N	N	N
9 ***Shuster***	Y	Y	Y	Y	N	N	Y	Y
10 ***McDade***	Y	Y	Y	Y	N	N	Y	?
11 Kanjorski	Y	Y	Y	Y	N	N	N	N
12 Murtha	Y	Y	Y	Y	N	N	N	N
13 ***Coughlin***	Y	Y	Y	Y	N	N	Y	N
14 Coyne	Y	Y	Y	Y	N	N	N	N
15 ***Ritter***	Y	Y	Y	Y	N	Y	Y	Y
16 ***Walker***	Y	Y	Y	Y	Y	Y	Y	Y
17 ***Gekas***	Y	Y	Y	Y	N	Y	Y	Y
18 ***Santorum***	Y	Y	Y	Y	N	N	Y	N
19 ***Goodling***	Y	Y	Y	Y	?	Y	Y	Y
20 Gaydos	Y	Y	Y	Y	N	N	N	N
21 ***Ridge***	Y	Y	Y	Y	N	N	Y	N
22 Murphy	Y	Y	Y	Y	N	?	Y	?
23 ***Clinger***	Y	Y	Y	Y	N	N	Y	Y
RHODE ISLAND								
1 ***Machtley***	Y	Y	Y	Y	N	N	Y	N
2 Reed	Y	Y	Y	Y	N	N	N	N
SOUTH CAROLINA								
1 ***Ravenel***	Y	Y	Y	Y	N	N	Y	Y
2 ***Spence***	Y	Y	Y	Y	N	Y	Y	Y
3 Derrick	Y	Y	Y	Y	N	N	N	Y
4 Patterson	Y	Y	Y	Y	N	N	Y	Y
5 Spratt	Y	Y	Y	Y	N	N	N	N
6 Tallon	Y	Y	Y	Y	N	N	N	N
SOUTH DAKOTA								
AL Johnson	Y	Y	Y	Y	N	N	N	N
TENNESSEE								
1 ***Quillen***	Y	Y	Y	Y	N	N	N	Y
2 ***Duncan***	Y	N	Y	Y	N	Y	Y	Y
3 Lloyd	Y	Y	Y	Y	N	N	?	N
4 Cooper	Y	Y	Y	Y	N	Y	N	Y
5 Clement	Y	Y	Y	Y	N	N	Y	N
6 Gordon	Y	Y	Y	Y	N	N	N	N
7 ***Sundquist***	Y	Y	Y	Y	N	Y	Y	Y
8 Tanner	Y	Y	Y	Y	N	N	N	Y
9 Ford	Y	Y	Y	?	N	N	?	?
TEXAS								
1 Chapman	Y	Y	Y	Y	N	N	N	Y
2 Wilson	?	?	?	?	?	?	?	?
3 ***Bartlett***	?	Y	Y	Y	N	?	Y	Y
4 Hall	Y	Y	Y	Y	N	N	Y	Y
5 Bryant	Y	Y	Y	Y	Y	N	N	N
6 ***Barton***	Y	Y	Y	Y	N	Y	Y	Y
7 ***Archer***	Y	Y	Y	Y	N	Y	Y	Y
8 ***Fields***	Y	Y	Y	Y	N	Y	Y	Y
9 Brooks	Y	Y	Y	Y	N	N	N	N
10 Pickle	Y	Y	Y	Y	N	N	N	Y
11 Edwards	Y	Y	Y	Y	N	N	N	N
12 Geren	Y	Y	Y	Y	N	N	N	Y
13 Sarpalius	Y	?	?	Y	N	N	N	N
14 Laughlin	Y	?	?	Y	N	N	N	N
15 de la Garza	?	Y	Y	Y	N	N	N	Y
16 Coleman	Y	Y	Y	Y	N	N	N	N
17 Stenholm	Y	Y	Y	Y	Y	Y	Y	Y
18 Washington	?	Y	N	Y	Y	Y	N	N
19 ***Combest***	Y	Y	Y	Y	Y	Y	Y	Y
20 Gonzalez	Y	P	P	Y	N	N	N	N
21 ***Smith***	Y	Y	Y	Y	N	N	Y	Y
22 ***DeLay***	Y	Y	Y	Y	Y	N	Y	Y
23 Bustamante	Y	Y	Y	Y	N	N	N	N
24 Frost	Y	Y	Y	Y	N	N	N	N
25 Andrews	Y	Y	Y	Y	N	N	N	Y
26 ***Armey***	Y	Y	Y	Y	Y	Y	Y	Y
27 Ortiz	Y	Y	Y	Y	N	N	?	X
UTAH								
1 ***Hansen***	Y	Y	Y	Y	Y	Y	Y	Y
2 Owens	Y	Y	Y	Y	N	N	N	N
3 Orton	Y	Y	Y	Y	N	N	N	N
VERMONT								
AL *Sanders*	Y	Y	N	Y	N	N	N	N
VIRGINIA								
1 ***Bateman***	Y	Y	Y	Y	N	Y	Y	Y
2 Pickett	Y	Y	Y	Y	N	N	N	N
3 ***Bliley***	Y	Y	Y	Y	N	N	Y	Y
4 Sisisky	Y	Y	Y	Y	N	N	Y	N
5 Payne	Y	Y	Y	Y	N	N	Y	Y
6 Olin	Y	Y	Y	Y	N	N	N	N
7 ***Slaughter***	Y	Y	Y	Y	N	N	Y	Y
8 Moran	Y	N	Y	Y	N	N	Y	N
9 Boucher	Y	Y	Y	?	N	N	N	N
10 ***Wolf***	Y	Y	Y	Y	N	N	Y	Y
WASHINGTON								
1 ***Miller***	Y	Y	Y	Y	N	Y	Y	Y
2 Swift	Y	Y	Y	Y	N	N	N	N
3 Unsoeld	Y	Y	Y	Y	N	N	N	N
4 ***Morrison***	Y	Y	Y	Y	N	N	Y	N
5 Foley								
6 Dicks	Y	Y	Y	Y	N	N	N	N
7 McDermott	Y	Y	Y	Y	-	N	N	N
8 ***Chandler***	Y	Y	Y	Y	N	N	Y	Y
WEST VIRGINIA								
1 Mollohan	Y	Y	Y	Y	N	N	N	N
2 Staggers	Y	Y	Y	Y	N	N	N	N
3 Wise	Y	Y	Y	Y	N	N	N	N
4 Rahall	Y	Y	Y	Y	N	N	N	N
WISCONSIN								
1 Aspin	Y	Y	Y	?	N	N	N	N
2 ***Klug***	Y	Y	Y	Y	N	N	Y	Y
3 ***Gunderson***	Y	Y	Y	Y	N	Y	Y	Y
4 Kleczka	Y	Y	Y	Y	Y	N	N	N
5 Moody	Y	Y	Y	Y	N	N	N	N
6 ***Petri***	Y	Y	Y	Y	Y	Y	Y	Y
7 Obey	Y	N	Y	Y	N	N	N	N
8 ***Roth***	Y	Y	Y	Y	N	Y	Y	Y
9 ***Sensenbrenner***	Y	N	Y	Y	Y	Y	?	Y
WYOMING								
AL ***Thomas***	Y	Y	Y	Y	N	Y	Y	Y

Southern states - Ala., Ark., Fla., Ga., Ky., La., Miss., N.C., Okla., S.C., Tenn., Texas, Va.
Omitted votes are quorum calls, which CQ does not include in its vote charts.

HOUSE VOTES 35, 36, 37, 38, 39, 40, 41, 42

35. HR 1281. Fiscal 1991 Supplemental Appropriations/ Passage. Passage of the bill to provide $4,136,377,100 in new budget authority in fiscal 1991 for various government agencies. The administration requested $2,852,884,000. Passed 365-43: R 121-3.54; D 243-9 (ND 165-5, SD 78-4); I 1-0, March 7, 1991.

36. HR 1282. Desert Storm Supplemental Appropriations/Passage. Passage of the bill to provide $42,588,372,000 in new budget authority for Persian Gulf operations. It provided for up to $15 billion in U.S. funds and $42.6 billion in contributions that foreign nations have pledged. Passed 380-19: R 149-1; D 230-18 (ND 152-15, SD 78-3.5); I 1-0, March 7, 1991. A "yea" was a vote supporting the president's position.

37. H Con Res 45. Holocaust Memorial Ceremonies/ Adoption. Frost, D-Texas, motion to suspend the rules and adopt the concurrent resolution to permit using the Capitol rotunda on April 11, 1991, and April 30, 1992, to commemorate Holocaust victims. Motion agreed to 389-0: R 151-0; D 238-0 (ND 160-0, SD 78-0); March 12, 1991. A two-thirds majority of those present and voting (260 in this case) was required for passage under suspension of the rules.

38. HR 1315. RTC Financing/Rule. Adoption of the rule (H Res 105) to provide for House floor consideration of the bill to provide $30 billion to the Resolution Trust Corporation to cover failed thrift losses in fiscal 1991. The rule provided for considering three substitute amendments, of which the last approved would be deemed the only substitute approved. Adopted 272-146: R 109-52; D 163-93 (ND 102-74, SD 61-19); I 0-1, March 12, 1991.

39. HR 1315. RTC Financing/Pay-As-You-Go Alternative. Slattery, D-Kan., substitute amendment to authorize, subject to appropriation, $30 billion for the Resolution Trust Corporation to cover fiscal 1991 thrift losses and require that requests for more money for the RTC be accompanied by a spending plan. The substitute would authorize $20 billion immediately and the final $10 billion on receipt from the president of a detailed plan on how future financing for thrift losses would be provided. Rejected 186-237: R 6-155; D 179-82 (ND 132-46, SD 47-3.56); I 1-0, March 12, 1991. A "nay" was a vote supporting the president's position.

40. HR 1315. RTC Financing/Management Reforms Alternative. Wylie, R-Ohio, substitute amendment to provide the Resolution Trust Corporation $30 billion to cover fiscal 1991 thrift losses; require that requests for more money for the RTC be accompanied by a spending plan; reduce the time institutions remain in conservatorship to no more than nine months; review its organizational structure and standardize its contracting procedures; and take other actions to achieve management enhancement goals. Rejected 190-235: R 151-11; D 39-223 (ND 13-165, SD 26-58); I 0-1, March 12, 1991. A "yea" was a vote supporting the president's position.

41. HR 1315. RTC Financing/Substitute. Gonzalez, D-Texas, substitute amendment to provide to the Resolution Trust Corporation (RTC) $30 billion to cover thrift losses in fiscal 1991; require that requests for additional money for the RTC be accompanied by a detailed spending plan; require the RTC to use the least costly means of resolving insolvent thrifts; expand the RTC's affordable housing program; require the RTC to avoid displacing tenants from single-family properties; and establish an overall goal of awarding 25 percent of RTC contracts to companies owned and controlled by minorities and women. Rejected 121-3.503: R 2-160; D 118-143 (ND 95-82, SD 23-61); I 1-0, March 12, 1991. A "nay" was a vote supporting the president's position.

42. HR 1315. RTC Financing/Passage. Passage of the bill to provide $30 billion to the Resolution Trust Corporation to cover fiscal 1991 losses of failed thrifts; also requires that requests for more money for the RTC be accompanied by a spending plan. Rejected 201-220: R 120-42; D 81-177 (ND 44-132, SD 37-45); I 0-1, March 12, 1991. A "yea" was a vote supporting the president's position.

[1] *Rep. Edward Madigan, R-Ill., resigned March 8, 1991, to become secretary of Agriculture. The last vote for which he was eligible was 36.*

[2] *Rep. Steve Bartlett, R-Texas, resigned March 11, 1991, to run for mayor of Dallas. The last vote for which he was eligible was 36.*

KEY

- Y Voted for (yea).
- # Paired for.
- + Announced for.
- N Voted against (nay).
- X Paired against.
- \- Announced against.
- P Voted "present."
- C Voted "present" to avoid possible conflict of interest.
- ? Did not vote or otherwise make a position known.

Democrats ***Republicans***
Independent

	35	36	37	38	39	40	41	42
ALABAMA								
1 ***Callahan***	?	?	Y	Y	N	Y	N	Y
2 ***Dickinson***	N	Y	?	Y	N	Y	N	Y
3 Browder	Y	Y	Y	Y	Y	N	N	N
4 Bevill	Y	Y	?	Y	N	N	N	N
5 Cramer	Y	Y	Y	Y	Y	N	N	N
6 Erdreich	Y	Y	Y	Y	Y	Y	N	Y
7 Harris	Y	Y	Y	Y	Y	N	N	N
ALASKA								
AL ***Young***	Y	Y	Y	Y	N	Y	N	Y
ARIZONA								
1 ***Rhodes***	Y	Y	Y	Y	N	Y	N	Y
2 Udall	?	?	?	?	?	?	?	?
3 ***Stump***	N	Y	Y	N	N	Y	N	Y
4 ***Kyl***	Y	Y	Y	Y	N	Y	N	Y
5 ***Kolbe***	N	Y	Y	Y	N	Y	N	Y
ARKANSAS								
1 Alexander	Y	Y	Y	?	Y	N	Y	Y
2 Thornton	Y	Y	Y	Y	N	N	N	N
3 ***Hammerschmidt***	Y	Y	?	?	?	?	?	?
4 Anthony	Y	Y	Y	Y	N	Y	N	Y
CALIFORNIA								
1 ***Riggs***	Y	Y	Y	Y	N	Y	N	Y
2 ***Herger***	Y	Y	Y	Y	N	N	N	N
3 Matsui	Y	Y	Y	Y	N	N	?	?
4 Fazio	Y	Y	Y	Y	N	N	Y	Y
5 Pelosi	Y	Y	Y	Y	Y	N	Y	N
6 Boxer	Y	Y	?	Y	Y	N	Y	N
7 Miller	Y	Y	Y	N	Y	N	Y	N
8 Dellums	N	N	Y	Y	Y	N	Y	N
9 Stark	Y	Y	?	?	Y	N	Y	N
10 Edwards	Y	Y	Y	Y	Y	N	Y	Y
11 Lantos	Y	Y	Y	Y	N	N	N	N
12 ***Campbell***	Y	Y	Y	Y	Y	Y	N	Y
13 Mineta	Y	Y	Y	Y	Y	N	Y	Y
14 ***Doolittle***	Y	Y	Y	Y	N	Y	N	Y
15 Condit	Y	Y	Y	Y	N	N	N	N
16 Panetta	N	Y	Y	Y	N	Y	N	Y
17 Dooley	Y	Y	Y	Y	Y	N	N	N
18 Lehman	Y	Y	Y	Y	Y	N	N	Y
19 ***Lagomarsino***	Y	Y	Y	Y	N	Y	N	Y
20 ***Thomas***	Y	Y	Y	Y	N	Y	N	Y
21 ***Gallegly***	Y	Y	Y	Y	N	Y	N	Y
22 ***Moorhead***	N	Y	Y	N	N	Y	N	Y
23 Beilenson	Y	Y	Y	Y	Y	N	Y	Y
24 Waxman	Y	Y	Y	Y	N	N	Y	Y
25 Roybal	?	?	Y	Y	Y	N	Y	N
26 Berman	Y	Y	?	Y	Y	N	Y	Y
27 Levine	?	?	Y	Y	N	Y	Y	Y
28 Dixon	Y	?	Y	N	Y	N	Y	N
29 Waters	Y	N	?	Y	Y	N	Y	N
30 Martinez	Y	Y	Y	Y	Y	Y	N	N
31 Dymally	?	?	?	N	Y	N	Y	N
32 Anderson	Y	Y	Y	Y	Y	N	Y	Y
33 ***Dreier***	Y	?	Y	Y	N	Y	N	Y
34 Torres	Y	Y	Y	Y	Y	N	Y	N
35 ***Lewis***	Y	Y	Y	Y	N	Y	N	Y
36 Brown	Y	Y	Y	Y	Y	N	Y	N
37 ***McCandless***	Y	Y	Y	Y	N	Y	N	Y
38 ***Dornan***	Y	Y	Y	N	N	Y	N	Y
39 ***Dannemeyer***	N	Y	Y	N	N	Y	N	Y
40 ***Cox***	Y	Y	Y	N	N	N	N	N
41 ***Lowery***	Y	Y	Y	Y	N	Y	N	Y
42 ***Rohrabacher***	Y	Y	Y	N	N	N	N	N
43 ***Packard***	Y	Y	Y	N	N	Y	N	N
44 ***Cunningham***	Y	Y	Y	Y	N	Y	N	N
45 ***Hunter***	Y	Y	?	?	N	Y	N	Y
COLORADO								
1 Schroeder	Y	Y	Y	Y	Y	N	Y	N
2 Skaggs	Y	Y	Y	Y	N	N	N	Y
3 Campbell	Y	Y	Y	N	Y	N	N	N
4 ***Allard***	N	Y	Y	N	N	Y	N	N
5 ***Hefley***	N	Y	Y	N	N	Y	N	N
6 ***Schaefer***	Y	Y	Y	Y	N	Y	N	N
CONNECTICUT								
1 Kennelly	Y	Y	Y	Y	N	N	N	N
2 Gejdenson	Y	Y	Y	N	Y	N	Y	N
3 DeLauro	Y	Y	Y	N	N	N	N	N
4 ***Shays***	Y	Y	Y	Y	N	Y	N	Y
5 ***Franks***	Y	Y	Y	Y	N	Y	N	Y
6 ***Johnson***	Y	?	Y	N	N	Y	N	Y
DELAWARE								
AL Carper	Y	Y	Y	Y	Y	Y	Y	Y
FLORIDA								
1 Hutto	Y	Y	Y	N	N	Y	N	N
2 Peterson	Y	Y	Y	N	Y	N	N	N
3 Bennett	Y	Y	Y	Y	N	N	N	N
4 ***James***	Y	Y	Y	N	N	Y	N	N
5 ***McCollum***	Y	Y	Y	Y	N	Y	N	Y
6 ***Stearns***	Y	Y	Y	Y	Y	Y	N	N
7 Gibbons	Y	Y	Y	Y	Y	N	N	N
8 ***Young***	Y	Y	Y	Y	N	Y	N	N
9 ***Bilirakis***	Y	Y	Y	Y	N	Y	N	Y
10 ***Ireland***	#	?	Y	Y	N	Y	N	Y
11 Bacchus	Y	Y	Y	N	Y	N	N	N
12 ***Lewis***	N	Y	Y	N	N	N	N	N
13 ***Goss***	Y	Y	Y	Y	N	Y	N	Y
14 Johnston	Y	Y	Y	Y	N	Y	N	Y
15 ***Shaw***	Y	Y	Y	Y	N	Y	N	Y
16 Smith	Y	Y	Y	Y	Y	N	Y	Y
17 Lehman	Y	Y	Y	Y	N	N	Y	Y
18 ***Ros-Lehtinen***	Y	Y	Y	Y	N	Y	Y	Y
19 Fascell	Y	Y	Y	Y	Y	N	Y	Y
GEORGIA								
1 Thomas	Y	Y	Y	Y	N	Y	N	Y
2 Hatcher	Y	Y	Y	Y	N	Y	N	Y
3 Ray	Y	Y	Y	Y	Y	Y	N	Y
4 Jones	Y	Y	Y	Y	Y	N	N	N
5 Lewis	Y	N	Y	N	Y	N	Y	N
6 ***Gingrich***	Y	Y	?	Y	N	Y	N	Y
7 Darden	Y	Y	Y	Y	N	Y	N	Y
8 Rowland	Y	Y	Y	Y	N	Y	N	Y
9 Jenkins	Y	Y	Y	Y	N	Y	N	Y
10 Barnard	Y	Y	?	Y	N	Y	N	Y
HAWAII								
1 Abercrombie	Y	Y	Y	Y	Y	N	N	N
2 Mink	Y	Y	Y	N	Y	N	Y	N
IDAHO								
1 LaRocco	Y	Y	Y	Y	Y	N	Y	N
2 Stallings	Y	Y	Y	Y	Y	Y	N	N
ILLINOIS								
1 Hayes	Y	N	Y	N	Y	N	Y	N
2 Savage	N	N	Y	N	Y	N	Y	N
3 Russo	N	Y	Y	N	N	N	N	N
4 Sangmeister	?	?	Y	N	Y	N	N	N
5 Lipinski	Y	Y	Y	N	Y	N	N	N
6 ***Hyde***	Y	Y	Y	Y	N	Y	N	Y
7 Collins	Y	N	Y	N	Y	N	Y	N
8 Rostenkowski	Y	Y	Y	Y	N	N	N	Y
9 Yates	Y	Y	Y	Y	Y	N	Y	N
10 ***Porter***	+	+	Y	N	N	Y	N	Y
11 Annunzio	Y	Y	Y	N	Y	N	N	N
12 ***Crane***	?	?	Y	N	N	Y	N	N
13 ***Fawell***	Y	Y	Y	Y	N	Y	N	Y
14 ***Hastert***	Y	Y	Y	Y	N	Y	N	Y
15 ***Madigan***	?	?						
16 Cox	Y	Y	+	Y	Y	N	Y	Y
17 Evans	Y	Y	Y	N	Y	N	N	N
18 ***Michel***	Y	Y	Y	Y	N	Y	N	Y
19 Bruce	Y	Y	Y	N	Y	N	N	N
20 Durbin	?	Y	Y	N	Y	N	N	Y
21 Costello	Y	Y	Y	N	Y	N	N	N
22 Poshard	Y	Y	Y	N	N	N	N	N
INDIANA								
1 Visclosky	Y	Y	Y	Y	Y	N	N	N
2 Sharp	Y	Y	Y	N	Y	N	N	N
3 Roemer	Y	Y	Y	N	N	N	N	N

ND Northern Democrats SD Southern Democrats

	35	36	37	38	39	40	41	42
4 Long	Y	Y	Y	N	Y	N	N	N
5 Jontz	Y	Y	Y	N	Y	N	Y	N
6 ***Burton***	N	Y	Y	N	N	Y	N	Y
7 ***Myers***	Y	Y	Y	Y	N	Y	N	Y
8 McCloskey	Y	Y	Y	N	Y	N	N	N
9 Hamilton	Y	Y	Y	N	Y	N	N	Y
10 Jacobs	Y	Y	Y	N	Y	N	Y	N
IOWA								
1 ***Leach***	Y	Y	Y	Y	N	Y	N	Y
2 ***Nussle***	N	N	Y	N	N	N	N	N
3 Nagle	Y	Y	?	N	Y	N	N	N
4 Smith	Y	Y	Y	N	N	N	N	Y
5 ***Lightfoot***	Y	Y	Y	Y	N	Y	N	Y
6 ***Grandy***	N	Y	Y	Y	N	Y	N	Y
KANSAS								
1 ***Roberts***	N	Y	Y	Y	N	Y	N	Y
2 Slattery	Y	Y	Y	Y	Y	N	N	N
3 ***Meyers***	Y	Y	Y	Y	N	Y	N	Y
4 Glickman	Y	Y	Y	N	Y	N	N	N
5 ***Nichols***	Y	Y	Y	Y	N	Y	N	Y
KENTUCKY								
1 Hubbard	N	Y	Y	Y	Y	N	Y	Y
2 Natcher	Y	Y	Y	Y	N	N	Y	N
3 Mazzoli	Y	Y	Y	Y	Y	N	Y	N
4 ***Bunning***	N	Y	Y	Y	N	Y	N	Y
5 ***Rogers***	Y	Y	Y	Y	N	Y	N	N
6 ***Hopkins***	Y	Y	Y	N	N	Y	N	N
7 Perkins	Y	Y	Y	N	N	N	N	N
LOUISIANA								
1 ***Livingston***	Y	Y	Y	Y	N	Y	N	Y
2 Jefferson	Y	Y	Y	?	?	?	Y	N
3 Tauzin	Y	Y	Y	N	N	N	N	N
4 ***McCrery***	?	?	Y	Y	N	Y	N	Y
5 Huckaby	N	Y	Y	N	N	Y	N	Y
6 ***Baker***	?	?	Y	Y	N	Y	N	Y
7 Hayes	N	Y	Y	Y	N	Y	N	P
8 ***Holloway***	Y	Y	Y	N	N	Y	N	Y
MAINE								
1 Andrews	Y	Y	Y	Y	Y	N	N	N
2 ***Snowe***	Y	Y	Y	N	N	Y	N	Y
MARYLAND								
1 ***Gilchrest***	Y	Y	Y	Y	N	Y	N	Y
2 ***Bentley***	Y	Y	Y	N	N	Y	N	N
3 Cardin	Y	Y	Y	Y	Y	N	N	Y
4 McMillen	Y	Y	Y	Y	Y	Y	N	N
5 Hoyer	Y	Y	Y	Y	Y	N	Y	Y
6 Byron	Y	Y	Y	N	N	Y	N	Y
7 Mfume	Y	N	?	Y	Y	N	Y	N
8 ***Morella***	Y	Y	Y	Y	N	Y	N	Y
MASSACHUSETTS								
1 Vacancy								
2 Neal	Y	Y	Y	Y	Y	N	Y	N
3 Early	Y	Y	Y	Y	Y	N	Y	N
4 Frank	Y	Y	Y	Y	N	N	Y	N
5 Atkins	Y	Y	Y	Y	Y	N	Y	N
6 Mavroules	Y	Y	Y	Y	Y	N	Y	N
7 Markey	Y	Y	Y	Y	Y	N	Y	N
8 Kennedy	Y	Y	Y	Y	Y	N	Y	N
9 Moakley	Y	?	Y	Y	Y	N	Y	N
10 Studds	Y	Y	Y	Y	Y	N	Y	N
11 Donnelly	?	?	Y	Y	Y	N	Y	N
MICHIGAN								
1 Conyers	Y	N	Y	N	Y	N	N	N
2 ***Pursell***	X	?	Y	N	N	Y	N	N
3 Wolpe	Y	Y	Y	N	Y	N	Y	N
4 ***Upton***	N	Y	Y	N	N	Y	N	N
5 ***Henry***	X	?	Y	N	N	Y	N	N
6 Carr	Y	Y	Y	N	Y	N	N	N
7 Kildee	Y	Y	Y	N	Y	N	N	N
8 Traxler	Y	Y	?	Y	N	N	Y	Y
9 ***Vander Jagt***	Y	Y	Y	Y	N	Y	N	Y
10 ***Camp***	Y	Y	Y	N	N	Y	N	N
11 ***Davis***	Y	Y	Y	N	N	Y	N	Y
12 Bonior	Y	Y	Y	Y	N	N	Y	Y
13 Collins	Y	Y	Y	Y	Y	N	Y	N
14 Hertel	Y	Y	Y	N	Y	N	N	N
15 Ford	Y	Y	Y	N	Y	N	N	N
16 Dingell	Y	Y	Y	Y	Y	N	Y	Y
17 Levin	Y	Y	Y	N	N	N	Y	Y
18 ***Broomfield***	Y	Y	Y	Y	N	Y	N	Y
MINNESOTA								
1 Penny	N	Y	Y	Y	Y	Y	N	N
2 ***Weber***	Y	Y	Y	Y	N	Y	N	Y
3 ***Ramstad***	Y	Y	Y	N	N	Y	N	N
4 Vento	Y	Y	Y	N	Y	N	Y	Y

	35	36	37	38	39	40	41	42
5 Sabo	Y	Y	Y	Y	N	N	Y	Y
6 Sikorski	Y	Y	+	N	Y	N	Y	N
7 Peterson	Y	Y	?	Y	Y	N	N	N
8 Oberstar	Y	Y	Y	N	Y	N	Y	N
MISSISSIPPI								
1 Whitten	Y	Y	Y	Y	N	N	N	N
2 Espy	Y	Y	Y	N	N	N	Y	N
3 Montgomery	Y	Y	Y	Y	N	Y	N	Y
4 Parker	Y	?	Y	Y	N	Y	N	Y
5 Taylor	Y	Y	Y	N	N	N	N	N
MISSOURI								
1 Clay	Y	N	Y	N	Y	N	Y	N
2 Horn	Y	Y	+	Y	Y	N	Y	N
3 Gephardt	Y	Y	Y	Y	Y	N	Y	Y
4 Skelton	Y	Y	Y	N	N	N	N	N
5 Wheat	Y	Y	Y	Y	N	N	Y	N
6 ***Coleman***	Y	Y	Y	Y	N	Y	N	Y
7 ***Hancock***	N	Y	Y	N	N	Y	N	Y
8 ***Emerson***	Y	Y	Y	Y	N	Y	N	Y
9 Volkmer	Y	Y	?	Y	Y	N	N	N
MONTANA								
1 Williams	Y	?	Y	Y	N	N	N	N
2 ***Marlenee***	Y	Y	?	N	N	N	N	N
NEBRASKA								
1 ***Bereuter***	Y	Y	Y	Y	N	Y	N	Y
2 Hoagland	Y	Y	Y	Y	N	Y	Y	Y
3 ***Barrett***	Y	Y	Y	Y	N	Y	N	Y
NEVADA								
1 Bilbray	Y	Y	Y	N	Y	N	N	N
2 ***Vucanovich***	Y	Y	Y	N	N	Y	N	Y
NEW HAMPSHIRE								
1 ***Zeliff***	Y	Y	Y	Y	N	Y	N	Y
2 Swett	Y	Y	Y	Y	N	Y	N	Y
NEW JERSEY								
1 Andrews	Y	Y	Y	N	N	N	N	N
2 Hughes	Y	Y	Y	N	Y	N	N	Y
3 Pallone	Y	Y	Y	Y	N	N	N	N
4 ***Smith***	Y	Y	Y	Y	N	Y	N	Y
5 ***Roukema***	Y	Y	Y	Y	N	Y	N	Y
6 Dwyer	?	?	Y	Y	Y	Y	Y	Y
7 ***Rinaldo***	Y	Y	Y	N	N	Y	N	Y
8 Roe	Y	Y	Y	N	Y	N	Y	N
9 Torricelli	Y	?	?	Y	Y	N	N	N
10 Payne	Y	N	Y	N	Y	N	Y	N
11 ***Gallo***	Y	Y	Y	Y	N	Y	N	Y
12 ***Zimmer***	Y	Y	Y	Y	N	Y	N	Y
13 ***Saxton***	Y	Y	Y	Y	N	Y	N	Y
14 Guarini	Y	Y	Y	N	N	N	N	N
NEW MEXICO								
1 ***Schiff***	Y	Y	Y	Y	N	Y	N	Y
2 ***Skeen***	Y	Y	Y	Y	N	Y	N	Y
3 Richardson	Y	Y	Y	Y	Y	N	N	N
NEW YORK								
1 Hochbrueckner	Y	Y	Y	Y	Y	N	Y	N
2 Downey	Y	Y	Y	Y	Y	N	Y	N
3 Mrazek	?	?	?	?	?	?	?	?
4 ***Lent***	Y	Y	Y	Y	N	Y	N	Y
5 ***McGrath***	Y	Y	Y	N	N	N	N	N
6 Flake	Y	N	?	?	?	?	?	?
7 Ackerman	Y	Y	Y	Y	Y	N	Y	N
8 Scheuer	Y	Y	Y	N	Y	N	Y	N
9 Manton	Y	Y	Y	Y	N	N	Y	N
10 Schumer	Y	Y	Y	Y	N	Y	Y	Y
11 Towns	Y	N	Y	N	Y	N	Y	N
12 Owens	Y	N	Y	N	Y	N	Y	N
13 Solarz	Y	Y	Y	Y	N	N	Y	N
14 ***Molinari***	Y	Y	Y	Y	N	Y	N	Y
15 ***Green***	Y	Y	Y	N	N	Y	Y	Y
16 Rangel	Y	N	Y	N	Y	N	Y	N
17 Weiss	#	Y	Y	Y	N	N	Y	N
18 Serrano	Y	N	Y	Y	Y	N	Y	N
19 Engel	Y	Y	?	Y	Y	N	Y	N
20 Lowey	Y	Y	Y	Y	Y	N	N	N
21 ***Fish***	Y	Y	?	N	N	Y	N	Y
22 ***Gilman***	Y	Y	Y	N	N	Y	N	Y
23 McNulty	Y	Y	Y	Y	Y	N	N	N
24 ***Solomon***	Y	Y	Y	Y	N	Y	N	Y
25 ***Boehlert***	Y	Y	Y	N	N	Y	N	Y
26 ***Martin***	Y	?	Y	Y	N	Y	N	Y
27 ***Walsh***	Y	Y	Y	Y	N	Y	N	Y
28 McHugh	Y	Y	Y	N	Y	N	N	Y
29 ***Horton***	Y	Y	?	N	N	Y	N	Y
30 Slaughter	Y	Y	Y	Y	Y	N	N	N
31 ***Paxon***	Y	Y	Y	N	N	Y	N	Y

	35	36	37	38	39	40	41	42
32 LaFalce	Y	Y	Y	N	Y	N	N	N
33 Nowak	Y	Y	Y	N	Y	N	N	N
34 ***Houghton***	N	Y	?	N	N	Y	N	Y
NORTH CAROLINA								
1 Jones	Y	Y	Y	Y	Y	Y	N	N
2 Valentine	Y	Y	Y	N	Y	N	N	N
3 Lancaster	Y	Y	Y	Y	Y	Y	Y	N
4 Price	Y	Y	Y	Y	Y	Y	N	Y
5 Neal	Y	Y	Y	N	Y	N	N	N
6 ***Coble***	N	Y	Y	Y	N	Y	N	N
7 Rose	Y	Y	Y	Y	Y	N	N	Y
8 Hefner	Y	Y	?	N	Y	N	N	N
9 ***McMillan***	Y	Y	Y	Y	N	Y	N	Y
10 ***Ballenger***	N	Y	Y	Y	N	Y	N	Y
11 ***Taylor***	Y	Y	Y	Y	N	Y	N	Y
NORTH DAKOTA								
AL Dorgan	Y	Y	?	?	Y	N	N	N
OHIO								
1 Luken	Y	Y	Y	Y	Y	N	Y	N
2 ***Gradison***	?	?	Y	Y	N	Y	N	Y
3 Hall	Y	Y	Y	Y	Y	N	N	?
4 ***Oxley***	N	Y	Y	Y	N	Y	N	Y
5 ***Gillmor***	Y	Y	Y	Y	N	Y	N	Y
6 ***McEwen***	Y	Y	Y	Y	N	Y	N	Y
7 ***Hobson***	Y	Y	Y	Y	N	Y	N	Y
8 ***Boehner***	Y	Y	Y	Y	N	Y	N	Y
9 Kaptur	Y	Y	Y	N	Y	N	N	N
10 ***Miller***	?	?	?	?	?	?	?	?
11 Eckart	Y	Y	Y	N	Y	N	N	N
12 ***Kasich***	Y	Y	Y	N	Y	Y	N	N
13 Pease	Y	Y	Y	Y	Y	N	N	Y
14 Sawyer	Y	Y	Y	N	Y	N	N	N
15 ***Wylie***	Y	Y	Y	Y	N	Y	N	Y
16 ***Regula***	Y	Y	Y	Y	N	Y	N	Y
17 Traficant	Y	Y	Y	N	N	N	N	N
18 Applegate	Y	Y	Y	N	N	N	N	N
19 Feighan	Y	Y	Y	Y	Y	N	Y	N
20 Oakar	Y	Y	Y	Y	Y	N	Y	N
21 Stokes	Y	N	Y	N	Y	N	Y	N
OKLAHOMA								
1 ***Inhofe***	Y	Y	Y	Y	N	Y	N	N
2 Synar	Y	Y	Y	Y	Y	N	N	N
3 Brewster	Y	Y	Y	N	Y	N	N	N
4 McCurdy	Y	Y	Y	Y	Y	N	N	N
5 ***Edwards***	Y	Y	Y	Y	N	Y	N	Y
6 English	Y	Y	?	Y	Y	N	N	N
OREGON								
1 AuCoin	Y	Y	Y	Y	Y	N	N	Y
2 ***Smith***	N	Y	Y	Y	N	Y	N	N
3 Wyden	Y	Y	Y	Y	N	N	N	N
4 DeFazio	Y	Y	Y	N	N	N	N	N
5 Kopetski	Y	Y	Y	Y	N	N	Y	Y
PENNSYLVANIA								
1 Foglietta	Y	Y	Y	N	Y	N	Y	N
2 Gray	Y	Y	Y	Y	Y	N	Y	N
3 Borski	Y	Y	Y	N	Y	N	Y	N
4 Kolter	Y	Y	Y	N	Y	N	N	N
5 ***Schulze***	Y	Y	Y	Y	N	Y	N	N
6 Yatron	Y	Y	Y	Y	Y	N	N	N
7 ***Weldon***	Y	Y	Y	Y	N	Y	N	N
8 Kostmayer	Y	Y	Y	Y	Y	N	Y	Y
9 ***Shuster***	N	Y	Y	Y	N	Y	N	N
10 ***McDade***	Y	Y	Y	Y	N	Y	N	Y
11 Kanjorski	Y	Y	Y	N	Y	N	N	N
12 Murtha	Y	Y	Y	Y	N	N	N	Y
13 ***Coughlin***	Y	Y	Y	N	N	Y	N	Y
14 Coyne	Y	Y	Y	Y	Y	N	Y	N
15 ***Ritter***	Y	Y	Y	N	N	Y	N	Y
16 ***Walker***	N	Y	Y	Y	N	Y	N	Y
17 ***Gekas***	Y	Y	Y	Y	N	Y	N	Y
18 ***Santorum***	N	Y	Y	N	N	Y	N	N
19 ***Goodling***	N	Y	Y	Y	-	Y	N	Y
20 Gaydos	Y	Y	Y	N	Y	N	N	N
21 ***Ridge***	Y	Y	Y	N	Y	Y	N	N
22 Murphy	?	?	Y	Y	Y	N	N	N
23 ***Clinger***	Y	Y	?	N	N	Y	N	Y
RHODE ISLAND								
1 ***Machtley***	Y	Y	Y	N	N	Y	N	N
2 Reed	Y	Y	Y	Y	N	N	N	N
SOUTH CAROLINA								
1 ***Ravenel***	Y	Y	Y	Y	Y	Y	N	N
2 ***Spence***	Y	Y	Y	Y	N	Y	N	N
3 Derrick	Y	Y	Y	Y	Y	N	N	Y
4 Patterson	Y	Y	Y	N	Y	N	N	N
5 Spratt	Y	Y	Y	Y	Y	N	N	Y
6 Tallon	Y	Y	Y	N	Y	N	N	N

	35	36	37	38	39	40	41	42
SOUTH DAKOTA								
AL Johnson	Y	Y	Y	Y	Y	Y	N	N
TENNESSEE								
1 ***Quillen***	Y	?	Y	Y	N	Y	N	N
2 ***Duncan***	N	Y	Y	N	N	N	N	N
3 Lloyd	Y	Y	Y	Y	N	Y	N	N
4 Cooper	Y	Y	Y	Y	Y	Y	N	Y
5 Clement	Y	Y	Y	Y	Y	N	N	N
6 Gordon	Y	Y	Y	Y	Y	N	N	N
7 ***Sundquist***	Y	Y	Y	Y	N	Y	N	Y
8 Tanner	Y	Y	?	?	?	N	N	N
9 Ford	?	?	Y	N	Y	N	Y	N
TEXAS								
1 Chapman	Y	Y	Y	Y	Y	N	N	Y
2 Wilson	?	?	?	?	Y	N	?	?
3 ***Bartlett*** [1]	Y	Y						
4 Hall	Y	Y	Y	N	Y	N	N	?
5 Bryant	Y	Y	Y	N	Y	N	Y	N
6 ***Barton***	N	Y	Y	Y	N	Y	N	Y
7 ***Archer***	N	Y	?	Y	N	Y	N	Y
8 ***Fields***	Y	Y	?	Y	N	Y	N	Y
9 Brooks	Y	Y	Y	Y	Y	N	Y	Y
10 Pickle	Y	Y	Y	Y	N	N	Y	Y
11 Edwards	Y	Y	Y	Y	N	N	N	Y
12 Geren	Y	Y	Y	Y	Y	Y	N	Y
13 Sarpalius	Y	Y	Y	Y	N	N	N	Y
14 Laughlin	Y	Y	Y	Y	Y	N	N	N
15 de la Garza	Y	Y	Y	Y	N	N	Y	N
16 Coleman	Y	Y	Y	Y	Y	N	Y	N
17 Stenholm	N	Y	Y	Y	N	Y	N	Y
18 Washington	Y	N	Y	?	Y	N	Y	N
19 ***Combest***	N	Y	Y	Y	N	Y	N	Y
20 Gonzalez	Y	N	Y	Y	N	N	Y	N
21 ***Smith***	Y	Y	Y	Y	N	Y	N	Y
22 ***DeLay***	Y	?	Y	Y	N	Y	N	Y
23 Bustamante	Y	Y	Y	Y	N	N	N	N
24 Frost	Y	Y	Y	Y	Y	N	Y	Y
25 Andrews	Y	Y	Y	Y	Y	N	N	N
26 ***Armey***	N	Y	Y	Y	N	Y	N	Y
27 Ortiz	?	?	Y	Y	N	N	Y	N
UTAH								
1 ***Hansen***	N	Y	Y	Y	N	Y	N	Y
2 Owens	Y	Y	Y	Y	Y	N	Y	Y
3 Orton	Y	Y	Y	Y	Y	N	Y	Y
VERMONT								
AL *Sanders*	Y	Y	?	N	Y	N	Y	N
VIRGINIA								
1 ***Bateman***	Y	Y	?	Y	N	Y	N	Y
2 Pickett	Y	Y	?	Y	N	N	N	Y
3 ***Bliley***	Y	Y	Y	Y	N	Y	N	Y
4 Sisisky	Y	Y	Y	Y	N	Y	N	Y
5 Payne	Y	Y	Y	Y	N	Y	N	Y
6 Olin	Y	Y	Y	Y	Y	Y	N	Y
7 ***Slaughter***	Y	Y	Y	Y	N	Y	N	Y
8 Moran	Y	Y	Y	N	Y	N	Y	Y
9 Boucher	Y	Y	Y	Y	N	Y	Y	Y
10 ***Wolf***	Y	Y	Y	Y	N	Y	N	Y
WASHINGTON								
1 ***Miller***	Y	Y	Y	N	Y	Y	N	Y
2 Swift	Y	Y	Y	N	Y	N	Y	N
3 Unsoeld	Y	Y	Y	Y	Y	N	Y	Y
4 ***Morrison***	Y	Y	Y	Y	N	Y	N	Y
5 Foley								
6 Dicks	Y	Y	Y	Y	N	N	N	Y
7 McDermott	Y	Y	Y	Y	Y	N	Y	Y
8 ***Chandler***	Y	Y	Y	Y	N	Y	N	Y
WEST VIRGINIA								
1 Mollohan	Y	Y	N	N	N	N	N	N
2 Staggers	Y	?	Y	N	Y	N	Y	N
3 Wise	Y	Y	?	Y	N	N	N	N
4 Rahall	Y	Y	Y	N	N	N	N	N
WISCONSIN								
1 Aspin	Y	Y	Y	N	N	N	Y	N
2 ***Klug***	Y	Y	Y	N	N	Y	N	Y
3 ***Gunderson***	Y	Y	Y	N	N	Y	N	Y
4 Kleczka	Y	Y	Y	Y	Y	N	Y	N
5 Moody	Y	Y	?	N	Y	N	Y	N
6 ***Petri***	N	Y	Y	N	N	N	N	N
7 Obey	Y	Y	Y	N	N	N	N	N
8 ***Roth***	N	Y	Y	N	N	N	N	N
9 ***Sensenbrenner***	N	Y	Y	N	N	N	N	N
WYOMING								
AL ***Thomas***	N	Y	Y	Y	N	Y	N	Y

Southern states - Ala., Ark., Fla., Ga., Ky., La., Miss., N.C., Okla., S.C., Tenn., Texas, Va.
Omitted votes are quorum calls, which CQ does not include in its vote charts.

HOUSE VOTES 43, 44, 45, 46, 47, 48, 49, 50

43. Procedural Motion. Schiff, R-N.M., motion to approve the House Journal of Tuesday, March 12. Motion agreed to 292-98: R 58-93; D 234-5 (ND 157-5, SD 77-0); March 13, 1991.

44. HR 1175. Fiscal 1991 Defense Supplemental Authorization/Rule. Adoption of the rule (H Res 111) to provide for House floor consideration of the bill to authorize $15 billion in appropriations from the Desert Shield Working Capital Account and the appropriations of funds credited to the Defense Cooperation Account, consisting of allied contributions; authorize an increase in troop levels; require reports on Persian Gulf conflict costs; and authorize changes in military personnel and veterans' benefits. Adopted 247-171: R 0-159; D 246-12 (ND 169-6, SD 77-6); I 1-0, March 13, 1991.

45. HR 1175. Fiscal 1991 Defense Supplemental Authorization/Budget. Panetta, D-Calif., amendment to remove the designation of the military personnel and veterans' benefits as emergency spending. The effect of the motion would be to subject those benefits to the pay-as-you-go requirements of the Budget Enforcement Act of 1990 (PL 101-508). Rejected 175-248: R 115-47; D 60-200 (ND 45-133, SD 15-67); I 0-1, March 13, 1991. A "yea" was a vote supporting the president's position.

46. HR 1175. Fiscal 1991 Defense Supplemental Authorization/Budget. Michel, R-Ill., amendment to guarantee that the veterans' benefits authorized by this bill be provided in a manner consistent with the Budget Enforcement Act of 1990 (PL 101-508). Rejected 165-260: R 156-6; D 9-253 (ND 6-172, SD 3-81); I 0-1, March 13, 1991.

47. HR 1175. Fiscal 1991 Defense Supplemental Authorization/Strategic Defense. Cox, R-Calif., motion to recommit to the Armed Services Committee the bill to authorize supplemental defense programs for fiscal 1991, with instructions to report it back to the House with provisions stating it is the sense of the Congress that the administration should negotiate an agreement with the Soviet Union that would allow the research, development, testing and deployment of defenses against ballistic missiles of all ranges. Rejected 145-281: R 138-24; D 7-256 (ND 0-178, SD 7-78); I 0-1, March 13, 1991.

48. HR 1175. Fiscal 1991 Defense Supplemental Authorization/Passage. Passage of the bill to authorize $15 billion to be appropriated from the Desert Shield Working Capital Account and to authorize the appropriation of funds credited to the Defense Cooperation Account, consisting of allied contributions; authorize an increase in troop levels; and authorize $1.4 billion in changes in military personnel and veterans' benefits programs over five years. Passed 398-25: R 145-17; D 252-8 (ND 169-6, SD 83-2); I 1-0, March 13, 1991. A "nay" was a vote supporting the president's position.

49. S 419. RTC Financing/Rule. Derrick, D-S.C., motion to consider the rule (H Res 112) to provide for House floor consideration of the bill to authorize and appropriate $30 billion to the Resolution Trust Corporation (RTC) to cover losses of failed thrifts in fiscal 1991. Motion agreed to 327-78: R 140-13; D 187-64 (ND 113-59, SD 74-5); I 0-1, March 13, 1991. A two-thirds majority of those present and voting (270 in this case) is required to consider a rule that has not laid over for more than 24 hours.

50. S 419. RTC Financing/Compromise Substitute. Gonzalez, D-Texas, substitute amendment to authorize and appropriate $30 billion to the Resolution Trust Corporation (RTC) to cover losses of failed thrifts in fiscal 1991; require future requests for additional funding from the RTC to be accompanied by a detailed financial plan; expand the RTC's affordable housing program; take actions to achieve management enhancement goals; and to require the RTC to report on steps taken to award contracts to companies owned and controlled by minorities and women. Adopted 213-197: R 118-39; D 95-157 (ND 58-113, SD 37-44); I 0-1, March 13, 1991. A "yea" was a vote supporting the president's position.

KEY

Y Voted for (yea).
Paired for.
+ Announced for.
N Voted against (nay).
X Paired against.
- Announced against.
P Voted "present."
C Voted "present" to avoid possible conflict of interest.
? Did not vote or otherwise make a position known.

Democrats ***Republicans***
Independent

	43	44	45	46	47	48	49	50
ALABAMA								
1 ***Callahan***	Y	N	N	Y	Y	Y	Y	Y
2 ***Dickinson***	N	N	N	Y	Y	Y	Y	Y
3 Browder	Y	Y	N	N	N	Y	Y	N
4 Bevill	Y	Y	N	N	N	Y	Y	N
5 Cramer	Y	Y	N	N	N	Y	Y	N
6 Erdreich	Y	Y	N	N	N	Y	Y	N
7 Harris	Y	Y	N	N	N	Y	Y	N
ALASKA								
AL ***Young***	N	N	N	N	Y	Y	N	Y
ARIZONA								
1 ***Rhodes***	N	N	Y	Y	Y	Y	Y	Y
2 Udall	?	?	?	?	?	?	?	?
3 ***Stump***	N	N	Y	Y	Y	N	Y	N
4 ***Kyl***	N	N	Y	Y	Y	Y	Y	Y
5 ***Kolbe***	N	N	Y	Y	Y	Y	Y	Y
ARKANSAS								
1 Alexander	Y	Y	N	N	N	Y	Y	N
2 Thornton	Y	Y	N	N	N	Y	Y	N
3 ***Hammerschmidt***	?	?	?	?	?	?	?	?
4 Anthony	Y	Y	N	N	N	Y	Y	Y
CALIFORNIA								
1 ***Riggs***	Y	N	Y	Y	N	Y	Y	Y
2 ***Herger***	N	N	Y	Y	Y	Y	Y	N
3 Matsui	Y	Y	N	N	N	Y	Y	N
4 Fazio	Y	Y	N	N	N	Y	Y	Y
5 Pelosi	Y	Y	Y	N	N	Y	?	Y
6 Boxer	Y	Y	N	N	N	Y	N	?
7 Miller	Y	Y	Y	N	N	Y	Y	N
8 Dellums	?	Y	Y	N	N	N	N	N
9 Stark	Y	Y	Y	N	N	Y	Y	N
10 Edwards	Y	Y	N	N	N	Y	Y	Y
11 Lantos	Y	Y	N	N	N	Y	Y	Y
12 ***Campbell***	N	N	Y	Y	Y	Y	Y	Y
13 Mineta	Y	Y	N	N	N	Y	Y	Y
14 ***Doolittle***	N	N	Y	Y	Y	Y	Y	Y
15 Condit	Y	Y	N	N	N	Y	Y	N
16 Panetta	Y	Y	Y	N	N	Y	Y	Y
17 Dooley	Y	Y	N	N	N	Y	Y	N
18 Lehman	Y	Y	N	N	N	Y	Y	Y
19 ***Lagomarsino***	N	N	N	Y	Y	Y	Y	Y
20 ***Thomas***	N	N	Y	Y	Y	N	Y	Y
21 ***Gallegly***	N	N	N	Y	Y	Y	Y	Y
22 ***Moorhead***	N	N	Y	Y	Y	Y	Y	Y
23 Beilenson	Y	Y	Y	N	N	N	Y	Y
24 Waxman	Y	Y	N	N	N	Y	Y	Y
25 Roybal	Y	Y	N	N	N	Y	N	Y
26 Berman	Y	Y	Y	N	N	Y	Y	Y
27 Levine	?	?	?	?	?	?	?	?
28 Dixon	Y	Y	N	N	N	Y	Y	N
29 Waters	?	Y	N	N	N	Y	N	N
30 Martinez	Y	Y	N	N	N	Y	?	?
31 Dymally	?	Y	N	?	N	Y	?	?
32 Anderson	Y	Y	Y	N	N	Y	N	Y
33 ***Dreier***	Y	N	Y	Y	Y	Y	Y	Y
34 Torres	+	Y	N	N	N	Y	N	N
35 ***Lewis***	N	N	Y	Y	Y	Y	Y	Y
36 Brown	Y	Y	N	N	N	Y	Y	Y
37 ***McCandless***	N	N	Y	Y	Y	Y	Y	Y
38 ***Dornan***	?	N	N	Y	Y	Y	Y	N
39 ***Dannemeyer***	N	N	Y	Y	Y	Y	Y	Y
40 ***Cox***	?	N	Y	Y	Y	N	?	N
41 ***Lowery***	N	N	N	Y	Y	Y	Y	Y
42 ***Rohrabacher***	N	N	Y	Y	Y	Y	Y	N
43 ***Packard***	Y	N	Y	Y	Y	Y	N	N
44 ***Cunningham***	Y	N	N	Y	Y	Y	Y	Y
45 ***Hunter***	?	N	Y	Y	Y	Y	Y	Y
COLORADO								
1 Schroeder	N	Y	N	N	N	Y	N	N
2 Skaggs	Y	Y	Y	N	N	Y	Y	Y
3 Campbell	Y	N	N	N	N	Y	?	N
4 ***Allard***	N	N	Y	Y	Y	Y	Y	N
5 ***Hefley***	N	N	Y	Y	Y	Y	N	N
6 ***Schaefer***	N	N	N	Y	Y	Y	Y	N
CONNECTICUT								
1 Kennelly	Y	Y	Y	N	N	Y	Y	N
2 Gejdenson	Y	Y	N	N	N	Y	Y	N
3 DeLauro	Y	Y	N	N	N	Y	Y	N
4 ***Shays***	N	N	Y	Y	N	Y	Y	Y
5 ***Franks***	Y	N	Y	Y	Y	Y	Y	Y
6 ***Johnson***	Y	N	Y	Y	Y	Y	Y	Y
DELAWARE								
AL Carper	Y	N	Y	N	N	Y	Y	Y
FLORIDA								
1 Hutto	Y	Y	N	N	Y	Y	Y	N
2 Peterson	Y	Y	N	N	N	Y	Y	N
3 Bennett	Y	Y	N	N	N	Y	Y	N
4 ***James***	N	N	N	Y	Y	Y	Y	N
5 ***McCollum***	N	N	Y	Y	Y	Y	Y	Y
6 ***Stearns***	N	N	Y	Y	Y	Y	Y	Y
7 Gibbons	Y	Y	Y	N	N	Y	Y	Y
8 ***Young***	Y	N	Y	Y	Y	Y	Y	N
9 ***Bilirakis***	N	N	N	N	Y	Y	Y	Y
10 ***Ireland***	?	N	Y	Y	Y	Y	Y	Y
11 Bacchus	Y	Y	N	N	N	Y	N	N
12 ***Lewis***	N	N	Y	Y	Y	Y	Y	N
13 ***Goss***	N	N	N	Y	Y	Y	Y	Y
14 Johnston	Y	Y	Y	N	N	Y	Y	Y
15 ***Shaw***	Y	N	Y	Y	Y	Y	Y	Y
16 Smith	Y	Y	N	N	N	Y	Y	Y
17 Lehman	Y	Y	N	N	N	Y	Y	Y
18 ***Ros-Lehtinen***	N	N	Y	Y	Y	Y	Y	Y
19 Fascell	Y	Y	N	N	N	Y	Y	Y
GEORGIA								
1 Thomas	Y	Y	N	N	N	Y	Y	Y
2 Hatcher	Y	Y	N	N	N	Y	?	Y
3 Ray	Y	Y	Y	N	N	Y	Y	Y
4 Jones	Y	Y	N	N	N	Y	Y	N
5 Lewis	Y	Y	N	N	N	Y	Y	N
6 ***Gingrich***	Y	N	Y	Y	Y	Y	Y	Y
7 Darden	Y	Y	N	N	N	Y	Y	Y
8 Rowland	Y	Y	N	N	N	Y	Y	Y
9 Jenkins	Y	Y	N	N	N	Y	Y	Y
10 Barnard	Y	Y	N	N	N	Y	Y	Y
HAWAII								
1 Abercrombie	Y	Y	N	N	N	Y	N	N
2 Mink	Y	Y	N	N	N	Y	Y	N
IDAHO								
1 LaRocco	Y	Y	Y	N	N	Y	Y	Y
2 Stallings	Y	Y	Y	N	N	Y	Y	Y
ILLINOIS								
1 Hayes	Y	Y	N	N	N	Y	N	N
2 Savage	?	Y	N	N	N	Y	N	N
3 Russo	Y	Y	Y	N	N	Y	N	N
4 Sangmeister	Y	Y	N	N	N	Y	Y	N
5 Lipinski	Y	Y	N	N	N	Y	Y	N
6 ***Hyde***	N	N	Y	Y	Y	Y	Y	Y
7 Collins	Y	Y	N	N	N	Y	N	N
8 Rostenkowski	Y	Y	Y	N	N	Y	Y	Y
9 Yates	Y	Y	Y	N	N	Y	N	N
10 ***Porter***	N	N	Y	Y	Y	Y	Y	Y
11 Annunzio	Y	Y	N	N	N	Y	N	N
12 ***Crane***	?	N	Y	Y	Y	Y	N	N
13 ***Fawell***	Y	N	Y	Y	Y	Y	Y	Y
14 ***Hastert***	N	N	Y	Y	Y	Y	Y	Y
15 Vacancy								
16 Cox	Y	Y	Y	Y	N	Y	N	Y
17 Evans	Y	Y	N	N	N	Y	N	N
18 ***Michel***	N	N	Y	Y	Y	N	Y	Y
19 Bruce	Y	Y	N	N	N	Y	Y	N
20 Durbin	Y	Y	N	N	N	Y	Y	Y
21 Costello	Y	Y	N	N	N	Y	N	N
22 Poshard	Y	Y	N	N	N	Y	N	N
INDIANA								
1 Visclosky	Y	N	Y	N	N	N	Y	N
2 Sharp	Y	Y	N	N	N	Y	Y	?
3 Roemer	Y	Y	N	N	N	Y	Y	N

ND Northern Democrats SD Southern Democrats

	43	44	45	46	47	48	49	50
4 Long	Y	Y	N	N	N	Y	Y	N
5 Jontz	Y	Y	N	N	N	Y	N	N
6 ***Burton***	N	N	Y	Y	Y	Y	Y	Y
7 ***Myers***	Y	N	N	N	Y	Y	?	Y
8 McCloskey	Y	Y	N	N	N	Y	N	N
9 Hamilton	Y	Y	N	Y	N	Y	Y	Y
10 Jacobs	N	Y	Y	N	N	Y	Y	N
IOWA								
1 ***Leach***	N	N	Y	Y	N	Y	Y	Y
2 ***Nussle***	N	N	Y	Y	Y	N	N	N
3 Nagle	Y	Y	N	N	N	Y	Y	N
4 Smith	Y	Y	N	N	N	Y	Y	Y
5 ***Lightfoot***	N	N	Y	Y	Y	Y	Y	Y
6 ***Grandy***	N	N	Y	Y	Y	N	Y	Y
KANSAS								
1 ***Roberts***	N	N	Y	Y	N	Y	Y	Y
2 Slattery	Y	Y	Y	N	N	Y	Y	N
3 ***Meyers***	Y	N	Y	Y	N	Y	Y	Y
4 Glickman	Y	Y	N	N	?	?	?	?
5 ***Nichols***	Y	N	N	Y	Y	Y	Y	Y
KENTUCKY								
1 Hubbard	Y	N	N	N	N	Y	Y	N
2 Natcher	Y	Y	N	N	N	Y	Y	N
3 Mazzoli	Y	Y	Y	N	N	Y	Y	N
4 ***Bunning***	N	N	N	Y	Y	Y	Y	Y
5 ***Rogers***	N	N	N	Y	Y	Y	Y	N
6 ***Hopkins***	N	N	N	Y	Y	Y	Y	N
7 Perkins	Y	Y	N	N	N	Y	Y	N
LOUISIANA								
1 ***Livingston***	Y	N	Y	Y	Y	Y	Y	Y
2 Jefferson	?	Y	?	N	N	Y	?	Y
3 Tauzin	Y	N	N	N	Y	Y	Y	N
4 ***McCrery***	N	N	Y	Y	Y	N	Y	Y
5 Huckaby	Y	Y	N	N	Y	Y	?	?
6 ***Baker***	N	N	N	Y	Y	Y	Y	Y
7 Hayes	Y	Y	N	N	Y	Y	Y	Y
8 ***Holloway***	N	N	N	N	Y	Y	Y	Y
MAINE								
1 Andrews	Y	Y	N	N	N	Y	N	N
2 ***Snowe***	Y	N	N	Y	N	Y	Y	Y
MARYLAND								
1 ***Gilchrest***	N	N	Y	Y	Y	Y	Y	Y
2 ***Bentley***	N	N	N	Y	N	Y	?	?
3 Cardin	Y	Y	Y	N	N	Y	Y	Y
4 McMillen	Y	Y	N	N	N	Y	Y	Y
5 Hoyer	Y	Y	Y	N	N	Y	Y	Y
6 Byron	Y	Y	N	N	N	Y	Y	N
7 Mfume	?	Y	N	N	N	Y	N	N
8 ***Morella***	N	N	Y	Y	N	Y	Y	Y
MASSACHUSETTS								
1 Vacancy								
2 Neal	Y	Y	N	N	N	Y	Y	N
3 Early	?	?	Y	N	N	Y	?	?
4 Frank	Y	Y	N	N	N	Y	Y	Y
5 Atkins	Y	Y	N	N	N	Y	Y	N
6 Mavroules	Y	Y	N	N	N	Y	Y	N
7 Markey	Y	Y	N	N	N	Y	Y	Y
8 Kennedy	?	Y	N	N	N	Y	N	N
9 Moakley	Y	Y	N	N	N	Y	Y	Y
10 Studds	Y	Y	Y	N	N	Y	Y	N
11 Donnelly	Y	Y	N	N	N	Y	Y	N
MICHIGAN								
1 Conyers	Y	?	Y	N	N	N	N	N
2 ***Pursell***	?	N	Y	Y	Y	Y	Y	N
3 Wolpe	Y	Y	Y	N	N	Y	N	N
4 ***Upton***	N	N	Y	Y	Y	Y	Y	N
5 ***Henry***	N	N	Y	Y	N	N	N	N
6 Carr	Y	Y	N	N	N	Y	N	N
7 Kildee	Y	Y	N	N	N	Y	N	N
8 Traxler	Y	Y	N	N	N	Y	Y	Y
9 ***Vander Jagt***	Y	?	Y	Y	Y	Y	Y	Y
10 ***Camp***	N	N	Y	Y	Y	Y	Y	N
11 ***Davis***	Y	N	N	Y	Y	Y	Y	Y
12 Bonior	Y	Y	N	N	N	?	Y	Y
13 Collins	?	Y	N	N	N	Y	N	N
14 Hertel	Y	Y	N	N	N	Y	N	N
15 Ford	?	Y	N	N	N	Y	N	N
16 Dingell	Y	Y	N	N	N	Y	Y	Y
17 Levin	Y	Y	N	N	N	Y	Y	Y
18 ***Broomfield***	Y	N	Y	Y	Y	Y	Y	Y
MINNESOTA								
1 Penny	Y	N	Y	N	N	N	N	N
2 ***Weber***	Y	N	Y	Y	Y	Y	Y	Y
3 ***Ramstad***	N	N	Y	Y	Y	Y	Y	N
4 Vento	Y	Y	N	N	N	Y	Y	Y

	43	44	45	46	47	48	49	50
5 Sabo	Y	Y	Y	N	N	Y	Y	Y
6 Sikorski	N	Y	N	N	N	Y	Y	N
7 Peterson	Y	Y	N	N	N	Y	Y	N
8 Oberstar	Y	Y	N	N	N	Y	Y	Y
MISSISSIPPI								
1 Whitten	Y	Y	N	N	N	Y	Y	N
2 Espy	Y	Y	N	N	N	Y	Y	N
3 Montgomery	Y	Y	N	N	N	Y	Y	Y
4 Parker	Y	Y	N	N	N	Y	Y	Y
5 Taylor	Y	Y	N	N	N	Y	Y	N
MISSOURI								
1 Clay	N	Y	N	N	N	Y	N	N
2 Horn	Y	Y	N	N	N	Y	Y	N
3 Gephardt	Y	Y	N	N	N	Y	Y	Y
4 Skelton	Y	Y	N	N	N	Y	Y	N
5 Wheat	Y	Y	N	N	N	Y	Y	N
6 ***Coleman***	N	N	N	Y	Y	Y	Y	Y
7 ***Hancock***	N	N	Y	Y	Y	N	Y	?
8 ***Emerson***	Y	N	N	Y	Y	Y	Y	N
9 Volkmer	Y	Y	N	N	N	Y	Y	N
MONTANA								
1 Williams	Y	Y	N	N	N	Y	N	N
2 ***Marlenee***	?	N	N	N	N	Y	N	N
NEBRASKA								
1 ***Bereuter***	Y	N	Y	Y	Y	Y	Y	Y
2 Hoagland	Y	Y	Y	N	N	Y	Y	Y
3 ***Barrett***	Y	N	Y	Y	Y	Y	Y	Y
NEVADA								
1 Bilbray	Y	Y	N	N	N	Y	Y	N
2 ***Vucanovich***	N	N	Y	Y	Y	Y	Y	Y
NEW HAMPSHIRE								
1 ***Zeliff***	Y	N	Y	Y	N	Y	Y	Y
2 Swett	Y	Y	Y	N	N	Y	Y	Y
NEW JERSEY								
1 Andrews	Y	Y	Y	Y	N	Y	N	N
2 Hughes	Y	Y	Y	N	N	Y	N	N
3 Pallone	Y	Y	N	Y	N	Y	Y	N
4 ***Smith***	Y	N	N	Y	Y	Y	Y	Y
5 ***Roukema***	N	N	Y	Y	N	Y	Y	Y
6 Dwyer	Y	Y	N	N	N	Y	Y	Y
7 ***Rinaldo***	Y	N	N	Y	Y	Y	Y	N
8 Roe	Y	Y	N	N	N	Y	Y	N
9 Torricelli	Y	Y	Y	N	N	Y	Y	N
10 Payne	Y	Y	N	N	N	Y	N	N
11 ***Gallo***	N	N	Y	Y	Y	Y	Y	Y
12 ***Zimmer***	N	N	Y	Y	Y	Y	Y	Y
13 ***Saxton***	N	N	N	Y	Y	Y	Y	Y
14 Guarini	Y	N	Y	N	N	Y	Y	N
NEW MEXICO								
1 ***Schiff***	Y	N	Y	Y	Y	Y	Y	Y
2 ***Skeen***	Y	N	Y	Y	Y	Y	Y	Y
3 Richardson	Y	Y	N	N	N	Y	Y	N
NEW YORK								
1 Hochbrueckner	?	?	?	N	N	Y	Y	N
2 Downey	Y	Y	N	N	N	Y	Y	N
3 Mrazek	?	?	N	N	N	Y	Y	N
4 ***Lent***	Y	N	N	Y	Y	Y	Y	Y
5 ***McGrath***	Y	N	N	Y	Y	Y	N	N
6 Flake	?	#	Y	N	N	Y	N	N
7 Ackerman	Y	Y	N	N	N	Y	N	N
8 Scheuer	Y	Y	N	N	N	Y	N	N
9 Manton	Y	Y	N	N	N	Y	N	N
10 Schumer	Y	Y	N	N	N	Y	Y	Y
11 Towns	Y	Y	N	N	N	N	N	N
12 Owens	Y	Y	N	N	N	Y	N	N
13 Solarz	Y	Y	N	N	N	Y	Y	Y
14 ***Molinari***	N	N	N	Y	Y	Y	Y	Y
15 ***Green***	Y	N	Y	Y	N	Y	Y	Y
16 Rangel	Y	Y	N	N	N	Y	N	N
17 Weiss	Y	Y	N	N	N	Y	N	N
18 Serrano	Y	Y	N	N	N	Y	N	N
19 Engel	Y	Y	N	N	N	Y	N	N
20 Lowey	Y	Y	N	N	N	Y	N	N
21 ***Fish***	Y	N	Y	Y	Y	Y	?	?
22 ***Gilman***	Y	N	N	Y	Y	Y	Y	Y
23 McNulty	Y	Y	N	N	N	Y	Y	N
24 ***Solomon***	N	N	Y	Y	Y	Y	Y	Y
25 ***Boehlert***	N	N	N	Y	N	Y	Y	Y
26 ***Martin***	N	N	N	Y	Y	Y	Y	Y
27 ***Walsh***	Y	N	N	Y	N	Y	Y	Y
28 McHugh	Y	Y	N	N	N	Y	Y	Y
29 ***Horton***	Y	N	N	Y	N	Y	Y	Y
30 Slaughter	Y	Y	N	N	N	Y	Y	N
31 ***Paxon***	N	N	Y	Y	Y	Y	Y	Y

	43	44	45	46	47	48	49	50
32 LaFalce	Y	Y	N	N	N	Y	Y	N
33 Nowak	Y	Y	N	N	N	Y	Y	N
34 ***Houghton***	Y	N	Y	Y	Y	N	Y	Y
NORTH CAROLINA								
1 Jones	Y	Y	N	N	N	Y	N	N
2 Valentine	Y	N	Y	Y	Y	N	N	N
3 Lancaster	Y	Y	N	N	N	Y	Y	N
4 Price	Y	Y	N	N	N	Y	Y	Y
5 Neal	?	N	N	Y	N	Y	Y	N
6 ***Coble***	N	N	Y	Y	Y	Y	Y	N
7 Rose	Y	Y	N	N	N	Y	?	N
8 Hefner	?	Y	N	N	N	Y	Y	N
9 ***McMillan***	N	N	Y	Y	Y	Y	Y	Y
10 ***Ballenger***	N	N	Y	Y	Y	N	Y	Y
11 ***Taylor***	Y	N	Y	Y	Y	Y	Y	Y
NORTH DAKOTA								
AL Dorgan	Y	Y	N	N	N	Y	?	N
OHIO								
1 Luken	Y	Y	Y	N	N	Y	N	N
2 ***Gradison***	Y	N	Y	Y	Y	N	Y	Y
3 Hall	Y	Y	Y	N	N	Y	Y	N
4 ***Oxley***	N	N	Y	Y	Y	Y	Y	Y
5 ***Gillmor***	Y	N	Y	Y	N	Y	?	Y
6 ***McEwen***	Y	N	Y	Y	Y	Y	Y	Y
7 ***Hobson***	Y	N	Y	Y	Y	Y	Y	Y
8 ***Boehner***	N	N	Y	Y	Y	N	Y	Y
9 Kaptur	Y	Y	N	N	N	Y	Y	N
10 ***Miller***	?	?	?	?	?	?	?	?
11 Eckart	Y	Y	N	N	N	Y	N	N
12 ***Kasich***	?	N	Y	Y	Y	Y	Y	Y
13 Pease	Y	Y	Y	Y	N	Y	Y	Y
14 Sawyer	?	Y	N	N	N	Y	N	Y
15 ***Wylie***	Y	N	Y	Y	Y	Y	Y	Y
16 ***Regula***	N	N	N	Y	N	Y	Y	Y
17 Traficant	Y	Y	N	N	N	Y	Y	N
18 Applegate	?	N	N	N	N	Y	N	N
19 Feighan	Y	Y	N	N	N	Y	Y	-
20 Oakar	Y	Y	N	N	N	Y	Y	Y
21 Stokes	Y	Y	N	N	N	Y	N	N
OKLAHOMA								
1 ***Inhofe***	N	N	N	Y	Y	Y	Y	N
2 Synar	Y	Y	Y	N	N	Y	Y	N
3 Brewster	Y	Y	N	N	N	Y	Y	N
4 McCurdy	Y	Y	Y	N	N	Y	Y	N
5 ***Edwards***	N	N	Y	Y	Y	Y	?	Y
6 English	Y	Y	N	N	N	Y	Y	N
OREGON								
1 AuCoin	Y	Y	N	N	N	Y	Y	N
2 ***Smith***	N	N	Y	Y	Y	Y	Y	N
3 Wyden	Y	Y	N	N	N	Y	Y	N
4 DeFazio	Y	Y	N	N	N	Y	N	N
5 Kopetski	Y	Y	Y	N	N	Y	Y	Y
PENNSYLVANIA								
1 Foglietta	Y	Y	N	N	N	Y	N	Y
2 Gray	?	Y	N	N	N	Y	Y	N
3 Borski	Y	Y	N	N	N	Y	Y	Y
4 Kolter	Y	Y	N	N	N	Y	N	N
5 ***Schulze***	Y	N	Y	Y	Y	Y	Y	N
6 Yatron	Y	Y	N	N	N	Y	Y	N
7 ***Weldon***	Y	N	Y	Y	Y	Y	?	?
8 Kostmayer	Y	Y	Y	N	N	Y	Y	Y
9 ***Shuster***	Y	N	Y	Y	Y	Y	Y	N
10 ***McDade***	N	N	Y	Y	Y	Y	Y	Y
11 Kanjorski	Y	Y	N	N	N	Y	N	N
12 Murtha	Y	Y	N	N	N	?	Y	Y
13 ***Coughlin***	N	N	Y	Y	N	Y	?	Y
14 Coyne	Y	Y	Y	N	N	Y	Y	Y
15 ***Ritter***	Y	N	N	Y	Y	Y	Y	Y
16 ***Walker***	N	N	Y	Y	Y	N	Y	Y
17 ***Gekas***	N	N	Y	Y	Y	Y	Y	Y
18 ***Santorum***	N	N	Y	Y	Y	Y	Y	Y
19 ***Goodling***	N	N	Y	Y	Y	Y	Y	Y
20 Gaydos	Y	Y	N	N	N	Y	N	N
21 ***Ridge***	N	N	Y	Y	N	Y	N	Y
22 Murphy	N	Y	N	N	N	Y	Y	N
23 ***Clinger***	Y	N	Y	Y	N	Y	Y	Y
RHODE ISLAND								
1 ***Machtley***	N	N	N	Y	N	Y	N	N
2 Reed	Y	Y	N	N	N	Y	Y	N
SOUTH CAROLINA								
1 ***Ravenel***	Y	N	Y	Y	Y	Y	Y	N
2 ***Spence***	Y	N	N	Y	Y	Y	Y	N
3 Derrick	Y	Y	Y	Y	Y	Y	Y	Y
4 Patterson	Y	Y	N	N	N	Y	Y	N
5 Spratt	Y	?	?	?	N	Y	Y	Y
6 Tallon	Y	Y	N	N	N	Y	N	N

	43	44	45	46	47	48	49	50
SOUTH DAKOTA								
AL Johnson	Y	Y	N	N	N	Y	Y	Y
TENNESSEE								
1 ***Quillen***	N	X	N	N	Y	Y	?	N
2 ***Duncan***	Y	N	Y	Y	Y	Y	N	N
3 Lloyd	Y	Y	N	N	N	Y	Y	N
4 Cooper	Y	Y	Y	N	N	Y	Y	Y
5 Clement	Y	Y	N	N	N	Y	Y	N
6 Gordon	Y	Y	Y	N	N	Y	Y	Y
7 ***Sundquist***	N	N	Y	Y	Y	Y	Y	Y
8 Tanner	Y	Y	N	N	N	Y	Y	N
9 Ford	Y	Y	N	N	N	Y	N	N
TEXAS								
1 Chapman	?	Y	N	N	N	Y	Y	?
2 Wilson	?	?	?	N	N	Y	?	?
3 Vacancy								
4 Hall	Y	Y	N	N	Y	Y	Y	N
5 Bryant	Y	Y	N	N	N	Y	Y	N
6 ***Barton***	?	N	Y	Y	Y	Y	Y	Y
7 ***Archer***	?	?	Y	Y	Y	Y	Y	Y
8 ***Fields***	?	N	N	Y	Y	Y	Y	Y
9 Brooks	Y	Y	N	N	N	Y	Y	Y
10 Pickle	Y	Y	N	N	N	Y	Y	Y
11 Edwards	Y	Y	N	N	N	Y	Y	Y
12 Geren	?	Y	N	N	N	Y	Y	?
13 Sarpalius	Y	Y	N	N	N	Y	Y	Y
14 Laughlin	Y	Y	N	N	N	Y	Y	Y
15 de la Garza	Y	Y	N	N	N	Y	Y	N
16 Coleman	Y	Y	N	N	N	Y	Y	N
17 Stenholm	Y	N	Y	N	N	N	Y	Y
18 Washington	?	Y	N	N	N	Y	?	N
19 ***Combest***	Y	N	N	Y	Y	Y	Y	Y
20 Gonzalez	Y	Y	N	N	N	Y	Y	Y
21 ***Smith***	Y	N	Y	Y	Y	Y	Y	Y
22 ***DeLay***	N	N	Y	Y	Y	N	Y	Y
23 Bustamante	Y	Y	N	N	N	Y	Y	N
24 Frost	Y	Y	N	N	N	Y	Y	Y
25 Andrews	Y	Y	Y	N	N	Y	Y	Y
26 ***Armey***	N	N	Y	Y	Y	Y	Y	Y
27 Ortiz	Y	Y	N	N	N	Y	Y	N
UTAH								
1 ***Hansen***	Y	N	Y	Y	Y	Y	Y	Y
2 Owens	Y	Y	Y	N	N	Y	Y	Y
3 Orton	?	Y	Y	Y	N	Y	Y	Y
VERMONT								
AL *Sanders*	?	Y	N	N	N	Y	N	N
VIRGINIA								
1 ***Bateman***	Y	N	N	Y	Y	Y	Y	Y
2 Pickett	Y	Y	N	N	N	Y	Y	Y
3 ***Bliley***	N	N	Y	Y	Y	Y	Y	Y
4 Sisisky	Y	Y	N	N	N	Y	Y	Y
5 Payne	Y	Y	Y	N	N	Y	Y	Y
6 Olin	Y	N	Y	N	N	Y	Y	Y
7 ***Slaughter***	N	N	Y	Y	Y	Y	Y	Y
8 Moran	+	Y	Y	N	N	Y	Y	Y
9 Boucher	Y	Y	N	N	N	Y	Y	Y
10 ***Wolf***	N	N	Y	Y	Y	Y	Y	Y
WASHINGTON								
1 ***Miller***	N	N	Y	Y	Y	Y	Y	Y
2 Swift	Y	Y	Y	N	N	Y	Y	Y
3 Unsoeld	Y	Y	N	N	N	Y	Y	Y
4 ***Morrison***	Y	N	Y	Y	Y	Y	Y	?
5 Foley								
6 Dicks	Y	Y	N	N	N	Y	Y	?
7 McDermott	Y	Y	Y	N	N	Y	Y	Y
8 ***Chandler***	N	N	Y	Y	Y	Y	Y	Y
WEST VIRGINIA								
1 Mollohan	Y	Y	N	N	N	Y	Y	N
2 Staggers	Y	Y	N	N	N	Y	Y	N
3 Wise	Y	Y	N	N	N	Y	Y	N
4 Rahall	Y	Y	N	N	N	Y	Y	N
WISCONSIN								
1 Aspin	Y	Y	N	N	N	Y	Y	Y
2 ***Klug***	Y	N	Y	Y	N	N	Y	Y
3 ***Gunderson***	Y	N	Y	Y	Y	Y	Y	Y
4 Kleczka	Y	Y	N	N	N	+	Y	N
5 Moody	Y	Y	N	N	N	Y	N	N
6 ***Petri***	Y	N	N	Y	N	Y	N	N
7 Obey	Y	Y	N	N	N	Y	N	N
8 ***Roth***	N	N	N	Y	Y	Y	Y	N
9 ***Sensenbrenner***	N	N	Y	Y	Y	N	N	N
WYOMING								
AL ***Thomas***	N	N	Y	Y	Y	Y	Y	Y

Southern states - Ala., Ark., Fla., Ga., Ky., La., Miss., N.C., Okla., S.C., Tenn., Texas, Va.
Omitted votes are quorum calls, which CQ does not include in its vote charts.

HOUSE VOTES 51, 52, 53, 54, 55, 56, 57, 58

51. S 419. RTC Financing/Passage. Passage of the bill to authorize and appropriate $30 billion to the Resolution Trust Corporation (RTC) to cover losses of failed thrifts in fiscal 1991; require future requests for additional funding from the RTC to be accompanied by a detailed financial plan; expand the RTC's affordable housing program; take actions to achieve management enhancement goals; and require the RTC to report on steps taken to award contracts to companies owned and controlled by minorities and women. Passed 192-181: R 103-39; D 89-141 (ND 54-100, SD 35-41); I 0-1, March 13, 1991. A "yea" was a vote supporting the president's position.

52. H Res 92. House Committee Funding Resolution. Gaydos, D-Pa., motion to order the previous question (thus ending debate and the possibility of amendment) on the adoption of the committee substitute amendment to authorize $60.8 million for the 25 House standing and select committees and House Information Systems during the first session of the 102nd Congress. Motion agreed to 345-76: R 86-76; D 259-0 (ND 175-0, SD 84-0); I 0-0, March 20, 1991.

53. H Res 92. House Committee Funding Resolution/Adoption. Adoption of the resolution to authorize $60.8 million for the 25 House standing and select committees and House Information Systems during the first session of the 102nd Congress. Adopted 363-58: R 106-56; D 256-2 (ND 175-0, SD 81-2); I 1-0, March 20, 1991.

54. Procedural Motion. Frank, D-Mass., motion to approve the House Journal of Wednesday, March 20, 1991. Motion agreed to 280-101: R 53-98; D 227-3 (ND 152-3, SD 75-0); I 0-0, March 21, 1991.

55. HR 355. Reclamation Drought Assistance/Passage. Passage of the bill to authorize $30 million for emergency spending to help relieve the drought conditions in California and other Western states. The bill also would authorize $12 million for work at California's Shasta Dam. Passed 387-23: R 139-20; D 247-3 (ND 168-2, SD 79-1); I 1-0, March 21, 1991.

56. S 419. RTC Financing/Conference Report. Adoption of the conference report (thus clearing the measure for the president) to provide $30 billion to the Resolution Trust Corporation (RTC) to cover losses of failed thrifts in fiscal 1991; require that future requests for additional funding be accompanied by a spending plan; expand the RTC's affordable housing program; and require the RTC to report on steps taken to award contracts to companies owned and controlled by minorities. Adopted 225-188: R 119-40; D 106-147 (ND 63-110, SD 43-37); I 0-1, March 21, 1991. A "yea" was a vote supporting the president's position.

57. HR 1282. Desert Storm Supplemental Appropriations/Conference Meetings Closed to the Public. Whitten, D-Miss., motion to close to the public the conference committee meeting on the bill to appropriate funds to pay for the incremental costs of the Persian Gulf War, when classified national security information is under consideration. Motion agreed to 402-0: R 159-0; D 243-0 (ND 167-0, SD 76-0); I 0-0, March 21, 1991.

58. S 725. Fiscal 1991 Defense Supplemental Authorization/Passage. Passage of the compromise bill (thus clearing the measure for the president) to authorize the Defense Department to draw on an unlimited amount of foreign contributions to pay for the incremental costs of Operation Desert Shield/Storm and to authorize $15 billion in U.S. funds if sufficient foreign funds have not yet been received. The bill also would authorize an increase in troop levels and authorize $400 million for military personnel benefits and $255 million for veterans' education benefits in fiscal 1992-93 to be funded from foreign contributions. Passed 396-4: R 157-1; D 238-3 (ND 159-2, SD 79-1); I 1-0, March 21, 1991. A "yea" was a vote supporting the president's position.

KEY

- Y Voted for (yea).
- # Paired for.
- + Announced for.
- N Voted against (nay).
- X Paired against.
- \- Announced against.
- P Voted "present."
- C Voted "present" to avoid possible conflict of interest.
- ? Did not vote or otherwise make a position known.

Democrats ***Republicans***
Independent

	51	52	53	54	55	56	57	58
ALABAMA								
1 ***Callahan***	N	Y	Y	N	N	N	Y	Y
2 ***Dickinson***	Y	Y	Y	N	Y	?	Y	Y
3 Browder	N	Y	Y	Y	Y	N	Y	Y
4 Bevill	N	Y	Y	Y	Y	N	Y	Y
5 Cramer	N	Y	Y	Y	Y	N	Y	Y
6 Erdreich	N	Y	Y	Y	Y	N	Y	Y
7 Harris	N	Y	Y	Y	Y	N	Y	Y
ALASKA								
AL ***Young***	?	Y	Y	?	Y	N	Y	Y
ARIZONA								
1 ***Rhodes***	Y	Y	Y	N	Y	Y	Y	Y
2 Udall	?	?	?	?	?	?	?	?
3 ***Stump***	N	N	N	N	Y	N	Y	Y
4 ***Kyl***	Y	N	Y	N	Y	Y	Y	Y
5 ***Kolbe***	Y	Y	Y	N	Y	Y	Y	Y
ARKANSAS								
1 Alexander	N	Y	Y	Y	Y	Y	Y	Y
2 Thornton	N	Y	Y	?	Y	N	Y	Y
3 ***Hammerschmidt***	?	Y	Y	Y	Y	Y	Y	Y
4 Anthony	Y	Y	Y	Y	Y	Y	Y	Y
CALIFORNIA								
1 ***Riggs***	Y	N	N	N	Y	Y	Y	Y
2 ***Herger***	N	N	N	N	Y	N	Y	Y
3 Matsui	N	Y	Y	Y	Y	N	Y	Y
4 Fazio	Y	Y	Y	Y	Y	Y	Y	Y
5 Pelosi	Y	Y	Y	Y	Y	Y	Y	Y
6 Boxer	X	Y	Y	Y	Y	N	Y	Y
7 Miller	N	Y	Y	Y	Y	N	?	Y
8 Dellums	N	Y	Y	Y	Y	N	Y	?
9 Stark	N	Y	Y	Y	Y	N	Y	Y
10 Edwards	?	Y	Y	Y	Y	Y	Y	Y
11 Lantos	Y	Y	Y	Y	Y	Y	Y	Y
12 ***Campbell***	Y	Y	N	N	Y	Y	Y	Y
13 Mineta	Y	Y	Y	Y	Y	Y	Y	Y
14 ***Doolittle***	Y	Y	Y	N	Y	Y	Y	Y
15 Condit	-	Y	Y	Y	Y	N	Y	Y
16 Panetta	Y	Y	Y	Y	Y	Y	Y	Y
17 Dooley	N	Y	Y	Y	Y	N	Y	Y
18 Lehman	Y	Y	Y	Y	Y	Y	Y	Y
19 ***Lagomarsino***	Y	Y	Y	N	Y	Y	Y	Y
20 ***Thomas***	?	Y	Y	N	Y	Y	Y	Y
21 ***Gallegly***	Y	Y	Y	N	Y	Y	Y	Y
22 ***Moorhead***	Y	N	N	N	Y	Y	Y	Y
23 Beilenson	Y	Y	Y	Y	Y	Y	Y	Y
24 Waxman	Y	Y	Y	Y	Y	Y	Y	Y
25 Roybal	Y	Y	Y	Y	Y	Y	Y	Y
26 Berman	Y	Y	Y	Y	Y	Y	Y	Y
27 Levine	#	?	?	?	?	?	?	?
28 Dixon	?	Y	Y	Y	Y	N	Y	Y
29 Waters	N	Y	Y	?	Y	N	Y	Y
30 Martinez	?	Y	Y	Y	Y	Y	Y	Y
31 Dymally	X	Y	?	?	Y	N	?	?
32 Anderson	Y	Y	Y	Y	Y	Y	Y	Y
33 ***Dreier***	Y	N	N	Y	Y	Y	Y	Y
34 Torres	N	Y	Y	Y	Y	Y	Y	Y
35 ***Lewis***	Y	Y	Y	N	Y	Y	Y	Y
36 Brown	Y	Y	Y	Y	Y	Y	Y	Y
37 ***McCandless***	Y	Y	Y	N	Y	Y	Y	Y
38 ***Dornan***	?	N	N	Y	Y	Y	Y	Y
39 ***Dannemeyer***	Y	N	N	N	Y	Y	Y	Y
40 ***Cox***	N	N	N	?	Y	N	Y	Y
41 ***Lowery***	Y	Y	Y	N	Y	Y	Y	Y
42 ***Rohrabacher***	N	N	N	N	Y	N	Y	Y
43 ***Packard***	N	N	Y	Y	Y	N	Y	Y
44 ***Cunningham***	Y	N	N	Y	Y	Y	Y	Y
45 ***Hunter***	Y	N	N	?	Y	Y	?	Y
COLORADO								
1 Schroeder	N	Y	Y	N	Y	N	Y	Y
2 Skaggs	Y	Y	Y	Y	Y	Y	Y	Y
3 Campbell	?	Y	Y	Y	Y	N	Y	Y
4 ***Allard***	N	N	N	N	Y	N	Y	Y
5 ***Hefley***	N	N	N	N	Y	N	Y	Y
6 ***Schaefer***	N	Y	Y	Y	Y	N	Y	?
CONNECTICUT								
1 Kennelly	N	Y	Y	?	Y	N	Y	Y
2 Gejdenson	N	Y	Y	Y	Y	N	Y	Y
3 DeLauro	N	Y	Y	Y	Y	N	Y	Y
4 ***Shays***	Y	N	N	N	Y	Y	Y	Y
5 ***Franks***	Y	N	Y	N	Y	Y	Y	Y
6 ***Johnson***	Y	N	Y	Y	Y	Y	Y	Y
DELAWARE								
AL Carper	Y	Y	Y	Y	Y	Y	Y	Y
FLORIDA								
1 Hutto	N	Y	Y	Y	Y	N	Y	Y
2 Peterson	N	Y	Y	Y	Y	N	Y	Y
3 Bennett	N	Y	Y	Y	Y	N	Y	Y
4 ***James***	N	N	N	N	Y	N	Y	Y
5 ***McCollum***	Y	Y	Y	Y	Y	Y	Y	Y
6 ***Stearns***	N	N	N	N	N	N	Y	Y
7 Gibbons	Y	Y	Y	Y	Y	Y	Y	Y
8 ***Young***	N	Y	Y	N	Y	N	Y	Y
9 ***Bilirakis***	Y	Y	Y	N	Y	Y	Y	Y
10 ***Ireland***	Y	Y	Y	N	Y	Y	Y	Y
11 Bacchus	N	Y	Y	Y	Y	N	Y	Y
12 ***Lewis***	N	+	+	-	+	-	+	+
13 ***Goss***	Y	Y	Y	N	Y	Y	Y	Y
14 Johnston	Y	Y	Y	Y	Y	Y	Y	Y
15 ***Shaw***	Y	Y	Y	Y	Y	Y	Y	Y
16 Smith	Y	Y	Y	?	?	+	Y	Y
17 Lehman	Y	Y	Y	Y	Y	Y	Y	Y
18 ***Ros-Lehtinen***	Y	Y	Y	N	Y	Y	Y	Y
19 Fascell	Y	Y	Y	?	Y	Y	Y	Y
GEORGIA								
1 Thomas	Y	Y	Y	Y	Y	Y	Y	Y
2 Hatcher	Y	Y	Y	Y	Y	Y	Y	Y
3 Ray	Y	Y	Y	Y	Y	Y	Y	Y
4 Jones	N	Y	Y	Y	Y	N	?	Y
5 Lewis	N	Y	Y	Y	Y	N	Y	Y
6 ***Gingrich***	Y	Y	Y	N	Y	Y	Y	Y
7 Darden	Y	Y	Y	Y	Y	Y	Y	Y
8 Rowland	Y	Y	Y	Y	Y	Y	Y	Y
9 Jenkins	Y	Y	Y	Y	Y	Y	Y	Y
10 Barnard	Y	Y	Y	?	Y	Y	Y	Y
HAWAII								
1 Abercrombie	N	Y	Y	Y	Y	N	?	Y
2 Mink	N	Y	Y	Y	Y	N	Y	Y
IDAHO								
1 LaRocco	Y	Y	Y	Y	Y	Y	Y	Y
2 Stallings	Y	?	?	?	?	#	?	?
ILLINOIS								
1 Hayes	N	Y	Y	Y	Y	N	Y	Y
2 Savage	N	Y	Y	?	Y	N	Y	N
3 Russo	N	Y	Y	Y	Y	N	Y	Y
4 Sangmeister	N	Y	Y	Y	Y	N	Y	Y
5 Lipinski	N	Y	Y	Y	Y	N	Y	Y
6 ***Hyde***	Y	N	Y	N	Y	Y	Y	?
7 Collins	N	Y	Y	Y	Y	N	Y	Y
8 Rostenkowski	Y	Y	Y	Y	Y	Y	Y	Y
9 Yates	?	Y	Y	Y	Y	N	Y	Y
10 ***Porter***	Y	N	Y	Y	Y	Y	Y	Y
11 Annunzio	N	Y	Y	Y	Y	N	Y	Y
12 ***Crane***	N	N	N	N	N	N	Y	Y
13 ***Fawell***	Y	N	N	Y	N	Y	Y	Y
14 ***Hastert***	Y	Y	Y	N	Y	Y	Y	Y
15 Vacancy								
16 Cox	Y	Y	Y	Y	Y	Y	Y	Y
17 Evans	N	Y	Y	Y	Y	N	Y	Y
18 ***Michel***	Y	Y	Y	N	Y	Y	Y	Y
19 Bruce	N	Y	Y	Y	Y	N	Y	Y
20 Durbin	?	Y	Y	Y	Y	Y	Y	Y
21 Costello	N	Y	Y	Y	Y	N	Y	Y
22 Poshard	N	Y	Y	Y	Y	N	Y	Y
INDIANA								
1 Visclosky	N	Y	Y	Y	Y	N	Y	Y
2 Sharp	?	Y	Y	Y	Y	N	Y	Y
3 Roemer	N	Y	Y	Y	Y	N	Y	Y

ND Northern Democrats SD Southern Democrats

	51	52	53	54	55	56	57	58
4 Long	N	Y	Y	Y	Y	N	Y	Y
5 Jontz	?	Y	Y	Y	Y	N	Y	Y
6 ***Burton***	?	N	N	N	Y	Y	Y	Y
7 ***Myers***	Y	N	Y	Y	Y	Y	Y	Y
8 McCloskey	N	Y	Y	Y	Y	N	?	Y
9 Hamilton	Y	Y	Y	Y	Y	Y	Y	Y
10 Jacobs	?	?	?	?	?	?	?	?
IOWA								
1 ***Leach***	Y	N	N	N	Y	Y	Y	Y
2 ***Nussle***	N	N	N	N	N	N	Y	N
3 Nagle	N	Y	Y	Y	Y	N	Y	Y
4 Smith	Y	Y	Y	Y	Y	Y	Y	Y
5 ***Lightfoot***	Y	Y	Y	N	Y	Y	Y	Y
6 ***Grandy***	Y	Y	Y	N	Y	Y	Y	Y
KANSAS								
1 ***Roberts***	Y	Y	Y	N	Y	Y	Y	Y
2 Slattery	N	Y	Y	Y	Y	N	Y	Y
3 ***Meyers***	Y	N	Y	N	Y	Y	Y	Y
4 Glickman	?	Y	Y	Y	Y	N	Y	Y
5 ***Nichols***	Y	N	N	Y	Y	Y	Y	Y
KENTUCKY								
1 Hubbard	N	Y	Y	Y	Y	N	Y	Y
2 Natcher	N	Y	Y	Y	Y	Y	Y	Y
3 Mazzoli	N	Y	Y	Y	Y	N	Y	Y
4 ***Bunning***	Y	N	N	N	Y	Y	Y	Y
5 ***Rogers***	N	Y	Y	N	Y	N	Y	Y
6 ***Hopkins***	N	N	N	N	Y	N	Y	Y
7 Perkins	N	Y	Y	Y	Y	N	Y	Y
LOUISIANA								
1 ***Livingston***	Y	Y	Y	Y	Y	Y	Y	Y
2 Jefferson	N	Y	Y	?	?	?	Y	Y
3 Tauzin	N	Y	Y	Y	Y	N	Y	Y
4 ***McCrery***	Y	N	Y	Y	Y	Y	Y	Y
5 Huckaby	?	Y	Y	Y	Y	Y	Y	Y
6 ***Baker***	Y	Y	Y	N	Y	Y	Y	Y
7 Hayes	N	Y	Y	Y	Y	N	?	Y
8 ***Holloway***	Y	N	N	N	Y	Y	Y	Y
MAINE								
1 Andrews	N	Y	Y	Y	Y	N	Y	Y
2 ***Snowe***	Y	N	N	Y	Y	Y	Y	Y
MARYLAND								
1 ***Gilchrest***	Y	N	Y	N	Y	Y	Y	Y
2 ***Bentley***	?	Y	Y	?	Y	?	Y	Y
3 Cardin	Y	Y	Y	Y	Y	Y	Y	Y
4 McMillen	Y	Y	Y	Y	Y	Y	Y	Y
5 Hoyer	Y	Y	Y	Y	Y	Y	Y	Y
6 Byron	N	Y	Y	Y	Y	N	Y	Y
7 Mfume	N	Y	Y	?	Y	N	Y	Y
8 ***Morella***	Y	Y	Y	Y	Y	Y	Y	Y
MASSACHUSETTS								
1 Vacancy								
2 Neal	N	Y	Y	Y	Y	N	Y	?
3 Early	?	Y	Y	Y	Y	N	Y	Y
4 Frank	Y	Y	Y	Y	Y	Y	Y	?
5 Atkins	N	Y	Y	Y	Y	Y	Y	Y
6 Mavroules	N	Y	Y	Y	Y	Y	Y	Y
7 Markey	Y	Y	Y	Y	Y	Y	Y	Y
8 Kennedy	N	Y	Y	Y	Y	N	Y	Y
9 Moakley	Y	Y	Y	Y	Y	Y	Y	Y
10 Studds	?	Y	Y	Y	Y	N	Y	Y
11 Donnelly	N	Y	Y	Y	Y	N	Y	Y
MICHIGAN								
1 Conyers	N	Y	Y	Y	?	N	Y	Y
2 ***Pursell***	N	N	N	N	Y	N	Y	Y
3 Wolpe	N	Y	Y	Y	Y	N	Y	Y
4 ***Upton***	N	N	N	N	Y	N	Y	Y
5 ***Henry***	N	N	N	N	N	N	Y	Y
6 Carr	N	Y	Y	Y	Y	N	Y	?
7 Kildee	N	Y	Y	Y	Y	N	Y	Y
8 Traxler	Y	Y	Y	Y	Y	Y	Y	Y
9 ***Vander Jagt***	?	Y	Y	?	Y	Y	Y	Y
10 ***Camp***	N	N	N	N	Y	N	Y	Y
11 ***Davis***	?	Y	Y	Y	Y	Y	Y	Y
12 Bonior	Y	Y	Y	?	Y	Y	Y	Y
13 Collins	N	Y	Y	?	Y	N	Y	Y
14 Hertel	N	Y	Y	Y	Y	N	Y	Y
15 Ford	N	Y	Y	?	Y	N	Y	Y
16 Dingell	Y	Y	Y	Y	Y	Y	Y	Y
17 Levin	Y	Y	Y	Y	Y	Y	Y	Y
18 ***Broomfield***	?	Y	Y	Y	Y	Y	Y	Y
MINNESOTA								
1 Penny	N	Y	Y	Y	N	N	Y	Y
2 ***Weber***	?	N	N	N	Y	Y	Y	Y
3 ***Ramstad***	N	N	N	N	N	N	Y	Y
4 Vento	Y	Y	Y	Y	Y	Y	Y	Y

	51	52	53	54	55	56	57	58
5 Sabo	Y	Y	Y	Y	Y	Y	Y	Y
6 Sikorski	N	Y	Y	N	Y	N	Y	Y
7 Peterson	N	Y	Y	Y	Y	N	Y	Y
8 Oberstar	Y	Y	Y	Y	Y	Y	Y	Y
MISSISSIPPI								
1 Whitten	N	Y	Y	Y	Y	N	Y	Y
2 Espy	N	Y	Y	Y	Y	N	Y	Y
3 Montgomery	Y	Y	Y	Y	Y	Y	Y	Y
4 Parker	Y	Y	N	Y	Y	Y	Y	Y
5 Taylor	N	Y	Y	Y	Y	N	Y	Y
MISSOURI								
1 Clay	N	Y	Y	N	Y	N	Y	Y
2 Horn	N	Y	Y	Y	Y	Y	Y	Y
3 Gephardt	Y	Y	Y	?	Y	Y	Y	Y
4 Skelton	Y	Y	Y	Y	Y	Y	Y	Y
5 Wheat	N	Y	Y	Y	Y	N	Y	Y
6 ***Coleman***	Y	Y	Y	N	Y	?	Y	Y
7 ***Hancock***	Y	N	N	N	N	Y	Y	Y
8 ***Emerson***	Y	Y	Y	Y	Y	Y	Y	Y
9 Volkmer	Y	Y	Y	Y	Y	Y	Y	?
MONTANA								
1 Williams	?	Y	Y	Y	Y	N	Y	Y
2 ***Marlenee***	N	Y	Y	N	Y	N	Y	Y
NEBRASKA								
1 ***Bereuter***	Y	Y	Y	N	Y	Y	Y	Y
2 Hoagland	Y	Y	Y	Y	Y	Y	Y	Y
3 ***Barrett***	Y	Y	Y	N	Y	Y	Y	Y
NEVADA								
1 Bilbray	N	Y	Y	?	Y	N	Y	?
2 ***Vucanovich***	Y	Y	Y	?	Y	Y	Y	Y
NEW HAMPSHIRE								
1 ***Zeliff***	Y	N	N	Y	N	Y	Y	Y
2 Swett	Y	Y	Y	Y	Y	Y	Y	Y
NEW JERSEY								
1 Andrews	N	Y	Y	Y	N	N	Y	Y
2 Hughes	N	Y	Y	Y	Y	N	Y	?
3 Pallone	N	Y	Y	Y	Y	N	Y	Y
4 ***Smith***	Y	Y	Y	?	Y	Y	Y	?
5 ***Roukema***	Y	Y	Y	N	Y	Y	?	Y
6 Dwyer	N	Y	Y	Y	Y	Y	Y	Y
7 ***Rinaldo***	N	Y	Y	Y	Y	N	Y	Y
8 Roe	N	Y	Y	Y	?	-	Y	Y
9 Torricelli	N	Y	Y	Y	Y	N	Y	Y
10 Payne	N	Y	Y	Y	Y	N	Y	Y
11 ***Gallo***	Y	Y	Y	N	Y	Y	Y	Y
12 ***Zimmer***	Y	N	N	N	Y	Y	Y	Y
13 ***Saxton***	Y	Y	Y	N	Y	Y	Y	Y
14 Guarini	N	Y	Y	Y	?	N	Y	Y
NEW MEXICO								
1 ***Schiff***	Y	Y	Y	Y	Y	Y	Y	Y
2 ***Skeen***	Y	Y	Y	Y	Y	Y	Y	Y
3 Richardson	N	Y	Y	Y	Y	N	Y	Y
NEW YORK								
1 Hochbrueckner	N	Y	Y	Y	Y	N	Y	Y
2 Downey	N	Y	Y	Y	Y	N	Y	Y
3 Mrazek	N	Y	Y	?	Y	N	Y	Y
4 ***Lent***	?	Y	Y	?	Y	Y	Y	Y
5 ***McGrath***	N	Y	Y	Y	Y	N	?	Y
6 Flake	?	Y	Y	?	?	?	?	?
7 Ackerman	N	Y	Y	Y	?	?	?	?
8 Scheuer	N	Y	Y	Y	Y	N	Y	Y
9 Manton	?	Y	Y	?	?	?	?	?
10 Schumer	Y	Y	Y	Y	Y	Y	Y	Y
11 Towns	N	Y	Y	?	Y	N	Y	Y
12 Owens	N	Y	Y	Y	Y	N	Y	N
13 Solarz	Y	Y	Y	Y	Y	Y	Y	Y
14 ***Molinari***	Y	N	Y	N	Y	Y	Y	Y
15 ***Green***	Y	N	Y	Y	Y	Y	Y	Y
16 Rangel	N	Y	Y	?	Y	N	Y	Y
17 Weiss	N	Y	Y	?	Y	N	Y	Y
18 Serrano	N	Y	Y	?	Y	N	Y	Y
19 Engel	N	Y	Y	Y	Y	N	Y	Y
20 Lowey	?	Y	Y	?	Y	N	Y	Y
21 ***Fish***	?	Y	Y	Y	Y	Y	Y	Y
22 ***Gilman***	Y	Y	Y	Y	Y	Y	Y	Y
23 McNulty	?	Y	Y	Y	Y	N	Y	Y
24 ***Solomon***	N	Y	Y	N	N	N	Y	Y
25 ***Boehlert***	Y	Y	Y	N	Y	Y	Y	Y
26 ***Martin***	Y	Y	Y	N	Y	Y	Y	Y
27 ***Walsh***	Y	Y	Y	Y	Y	Y	Y	Y
28 McHugh	Y	Y	Y	?	Y	Y	Y	Y
29 ***Horton***	Y	Y	Y	Y	Y	Y	Y	Y
30 Slaughter	N	Y	Y	Y	Y	N	Y	?
31 ***Paxon***	Y	Y	Y	?	Y	Y	Y	Y

	51	52	53	54	55	56	57	58
32 LaFalce	N	Y	Y	Y	Y	N	?	?
33 Nowak	?	Y	Y	Y	Y	N	Y	Y
34 ***Houghton***	Y	Y	Y	Y	Y	Y	Y	Y
NORTH CAROLINA								
1 Jones	N	Y	Y	Y	Y	Y	Y	Y
2 Valentine	?	Y	Y	Y	Y	N	Y	Y
3 Lancaster	N	Y	Y	Y	Y	N	Y	Y
4 Price	Y	Y	Y	Y	Y	Y	Y	Y
5 Neal	N	Y	Y	Y	Y	N	Y	Y
6 ***Coble***	N	N	N	N	Y	N	Y	Y
7 Rose	Y	Y	Y	Y	Y	N	Y	Y
8 Hefner	N	Y	Y	Y	Y	N	Y	Y
9 ***McMillan***	Y	Y	Y	N	Y	Y	Y	Y
10 ***Ballenger***	Y	N	N	N	Y	Y	Y	Y
11 ***Taylor***	Y	N	N	N	Y	Y	Y	Y
NORTH DAKOTA								
AL Dorgan	N	Y	Y	Y	Y	N	Y	Y
OHIO								
1 Luken	N	Y	Y	Y	Y	N	Y	Y
2 ***Gradison***	?	N	Y	Y	Y	Y	Y	Y
3 Hall	?	Y	Y	Y	Y	N	Y	Y
4 ***Oxley***	Y	Y	Y	Y	Y	Y	Y	Y
5 ***Gillmor***	Y	Y	Y	?	Y	Y	Y	Y
6 ***McEwen***	Y	N	N	Y	Y	Y	Y	Y
7 ***Hobson***	Y	N	Y	Y	Y	Y	Y	Y
8 ***Boehner***	Y	N	N	N	Y	Y	Y	Y
9 Kaptur	N	Y	Y	Y	Y	N	Y	+
10 ***Miller***	?	?	?	?	?	?	?	?
11 Eckart	N	Y	Y	Y	Y	N	Y	Y
12 ***Kasich***	Y	N	Y	Y	Y	Y	Y	Y
13 Pease	Y	Y	Y	Y	Y	Y	?	Y
14 Sawyer	Y	Y	Y	Y	Y	Y	Y	Y
15 ***Wylie***	Y	Y	Y	Y	Y	Y	Y	Y
16 ***Regula***	Y	N	Y	N	Y	Y	Y	Y
17 Traficant	N	Y	Y	Y	Y	N	Y	Y
18 Applegate	N	Y	Y	Y	Y	N	Y	Y
19 Feighan	N	Y	Y	Y	Y	N	Y	Y
20 Oakar	Y	Y	Y	Y	Y	Y	Y	+
21 Stokes	N	Y	Y	?	Y	N	Y	Y
OKLAHOMA								
1 ***Inhofe***	N	N	N	N	Y	N	Y	Y
2 Synar	N	Y	Y	Y	Y	N	Y	Y
3 Brewster	N	Y	Y	Y	Y	N	Y	Y
4 McCurdy	N	Y	Y	Y	Y	N	Y	Y
5 ***Edwards***	Y	Y	Y	?	?	Y	Y	Y
6 English	?	Y	Y	Y	Y	N	Y	Y
OREGON								
1 AuCoin	N	Y	Y	Y	Y	N	Y	Y
2 ***Smith***	N	Y	N	N	Y	N	Y	Y
3 Wyden	N	Y	Y	Y	Y	N	Y	Y
4 DeFazio	N	Y	Y	Y	Y	N	Y	Y
5 Kopetski	Y	Y	Y	Y	Y	Y	Y	Y
PENNSYLVANIA								
1 Foglietta	N	Y	Y	Y	Y	N	Y	Y
2 Gray	N	Y	Y	Y	?	N	Y	Y
3 Borski	Y	Y	Y	Y	Y	Y	Y	Y
4 Kolter	N	Y	Y	Y	Y	N	Y	Y
5 ***Schulze***	N	Y	Y	Y	Y	N	Y	Y
6 Yatron	N	Y	Y	Y	Y	N	Y	Y
7 ***Weldon***	?	Y	Y	N	Y	N	Y	Y
8 Kostmayer	?	Y	Y	Y	Y	Y	Y	Y
9 ***Shuster***	N	N	Y	Y	Y	N	Y	Y
10 ***McDade***	Y	Y	Y	N	Y	Y	Y	Y
11 Kanjorski	N	Y	Y	Y	Y	N	Y	Y
12 Murtha	Y	Y	Y	Y	Y	Y	Y	Y
13 ***Coughlin***	Y	Y	Y	N	Y	Y	Y	Y
14 Coyne	?	Y	Y	Y	Y	Y	Y	Y
15 ***Ritter***	Y	N	Y	Y	Y	Y	Y	Y
16 ***Walker***	Y	N	Y	N	N	Y	Y	Y
17 ***Gekas***	Y	N	N	N	Y	Y	Y	?
18 ***Santorum***	Y	N	N	N	N	Y	Y	Y
19 ***Goodling***	Y	Y	Y	N	+	Y	Y	Y
20 Gaydos	?	Y	Y	Y	Y	N	Y	Y
21 ***Ridge***	Y	Y	Y	N	N	Y	Y	Y
22 Murphy	N	Y	Y	?	Y	N	?	?
23 ***Clinger***	Y	N	Y	Y	Y	Y	Y	Y
RHODE ISLAND								
1 ***Machtley***	N	Y	Y	N	Y	N	Y	Y
2 Reed	N	Y	Y	Y	Y	N	Y	Y
SOUTH CAROLINA								
1 ***Ravenel***	N	N	N	Y	Y	N	Y	Y
2 ***Spence***	N	Y	Y	Y	Y	N	Y	Y
3 Derrick	Y	Y	Y	Y	Y	Y	Y	Y
4 Patterson	N	Y	Y	Y	N	N	Y	Y
5 Spratt	Y	Y	Y	Y	Y	Y	Y	Y
6 Tallon	N	Y	Y	Y	Y	N	Y	Y

	51	52	53	54	55	56	57	58
SOUTH DAKOTA								
AL Johnson	N	Y	Y	Y	Y	N	Y	Y
TENNESSEE								
1 ***Quillen***	N	Y	Y	Y	Y	N	Y	Y
2 ***Duncan***	N	N	N	N	N	N	Y	Y
3 Lloyd	N	Y	Y	Y	?	X	?	?
4 Cooper	Y	Y	Y	Y	Y	Y	Y	Y
5 Clement	N	Y	Y	Y	Y	N	Y	Y
6 Gordon	?	Y	Y	Y	Y	Y	Y	Y
7 ***Sundquist***	Y	Y	Y	N	Y	Y	Y	Y
8 Tanner	N	Y	Y	Y	?	?	?	?
9 Ford	Y	Y	Y	?	Y	N	Y	Y
TEXAS								
1 Chapman	N	Y	Y	Y	Y	N	?	Y
2 Wilson	?	Y	Y	Y	Y	Y	Y	Y
3 Vacancy								
4 Hall	N	Y	Y	Y	Y	N	Y	Y
5 Bryant	N	Y	Y	Y	Y	N	Y	Y
6 ***Barton***	Y	Y	Y	Y	Y	Y	Y	Y
7 ***Archer***	?	N	N	Y	N	Y	Y	Y
8 ***Fields***	Y	N	Y	N	N	Y	Y	Y
9 Brooks	?	Y	Y	?	Y	Y	Y	Y
10 Pickle	?	Y	Y	Y	Y	Y	Y	Y
11 Edwards	Y	Y	Y	Y	Y	Y	Y	Y
12 Geren	#	Y	Y	Y	Y	Y	Y	Y
13 Sarpalius	Y	Y	Y	Y	Y	Y	Y	Y
14 Laughlin	Y	Y	Y	Y	Y	Y	Y	Y
15 de la Garza	N	Y	Y	Y	Y	Y	?	?
16 Coleman	Y	Y	Y	Y	Y	Y	Y	Y
17 Stenholm	Y	Y	Y	Y	Y	Y	?	?
18 Washington	N	Y	Y	?	Y	N	?	Y
19 ***Combest***	?	Y	N	Y	Y	Y	Y	Y
20 Gonzalez	Y	Y	Y	Y	Y	Y	Y	N
21 ***Smith***	Y	Y	Y	N	Y	Y	Y	Y
22 ***DeLay***	Y	N	N	N	?	Y	Y	Y
23 Bustamante	Y	?	?	?	?	?	?	?
24 Frost	Y	Y	Y	?	Y	Y	Y	Y
25 Andrews	Y	Y	Y	Y	Y	Y	Y	Y
26 ***Armey***	Y	N	N	N	N	Y	Y	Y
27 Ortiz	N	Y	Y	Y	Y	Y	Y	Y
UTAH								
1 ***Hansen***	?	Y	Y	Y	Y	Y	Y	Y
2 Owens	Y	Y	Y	Y	Y	Y	Y	Y
3 Orton	Y	Y	Y	Y	Y	Y	Y	Y
VERMONT								
AL *Sanders*	N	?	Y	?	Y	N	?	Y
VIRGINIA								
1 ***Bateman***	Y	Y	Y	Y	Y	Y	Y	Y
2 Pickett	Y	Y	?	Y	Y	Y	Y	Y
3 ***Bliley***	Y	Y	Y	N	Y	Y	Y	Y
4 Sisisky	Y	Y	Y	Y	Y	Y	Y	Y
5 Payne	Y	Y	N	Y	Y	Y	Y	Y
6 Olin	?	Y	Y	Y	Y	Y	Y	Y
7 ***Slaughter***	Y	Y	Y	Y	Y	Y	Y	Y
8 Moran	Y	Y	Y	Y	Y	Y	Y	Y
9 Boucher	Y	Y	Y	Y	Y	Y	Y	Y
10 ***Wolf***	?	Y	Y	N	Y	Y	Y	Y
WASHINGTON								
1 ***Miller***	Y	N	N	N	N	Y	Y	Y
2 Swift	Y	Y	Y	Y	Y	Y	Y	Y
3 Unsoeld	Y	Y	Y	Y	Y	Y	Y	Y
4 ***Morrison***	?	Y	Y	Y	Y	Y	Y	Y
5 Foley	Y							
6 Dicks	+	Y	Y	Y	Y	Y	Y	Y
7 McDermott	Y	Y	Y	Y	Y	Y	Y	Y
8 ***Chandler***	Y	Y	Y	N	Y	Y	Y	Y
WEST VIRGINIA								
1 Mollohan	N	Y	Y	?	Y	N	Y	Y
2 Staggers	N	Y	Y	Y	Y	N	Y	Y
3 Wise	N	Y	Y	Y	Y	N	Y	Y
4 Rahall	N	Y	Y	Y	Y	N	Y	Y
WISCONSIN								
1 Aspin	Y	Y	Y	Y	Y	Y	Y	Y
2 ***Klug***	Y	N	N	N	Y	Y	Y	Y
3 ***Gunderson***	?	N	Y	Y	Y	Y	Y	Y
4 Kleczka	N	?	?	Y	Y	N	Y	Y
5 Moody	N	Y	Y	Y	Y	N	Y	Y
6 ***Petri***	N	N	N	Y	N	N	Y	Y
7 Obey	N	?	Y	Y	Y	N	Y	Y
8 ***Roth***	N	N	N	N	Y	N	Y	Y
9 ***Sensenbrenner***	N	N	N	N	N	N	Y	Y
WYOMING								
AL ***Thomas***	?	N	Y	N	Y	Y	Y	Y

Southern states - Ala., Ark., Fla., Ga., Ky., La., Miss., N.C., Okla., S.C., Tenn., Texas, Va.
Omitted votes are quorum calls, which CQ does not include in its vote charts.

HOUSE VOTES 59, 60, 61, 62, 63, 64, 65, 66

59. HR 1281. Fiscal 1991 Supplemental Appropriations/ Budget. McDade, R-Pa., motion to instruct the House conferees on the fiscal 1991 supplemental appropriation bill to insist that the conferees not violate budget totals agreed to in the Budget Enforcement Act of 1990 (PL 101-508). Motion agreed to 398-2: R 156-0; D 241-2 (ND 162-2, SD 79-0); I 1-0, March 21, 1991.

60. HR 1281. Fiscal 1991 Supplemental Appropriations/ Strike Navy Funds. Burton, R-Ind., motion to recommit to conference the bill to provide supplemental appropriations in fiscal 1991, with instructions to report it back to the House including the Senate amendment that strikes provisions directing the Navy to begin spending funds for the Service Life Extension Program for the aircraft carrier USS *Kennedy* at the Philadelphia Naval Shipyard. Rejected 91-295: R 85-67; D 6-227 (ND 2-156, SD 4-71); I 0-1, March 22, 1991.

61. HR 1281. Fiscal 1991 Supplemental Appropriations/ Conference Report. Adoption of the conference report to provide $5,441,058,100 in new budget authority in fiscal 1991 for various government agencies and programs, including $1.5 billion for food stamps, $150 million for unemployment insurance administration, $623 million for Rocky Flats environmental cleanup and plutonium production, $30 million in drought relief, $100 million for the District of Columbia, $650 million in aid to Israel, and $200 million in aid to Turkey. The bill also would provide $655 million for military and veterans' benefits in fiscal 1991-95. The administration requested $4,376,212,000. Adopted 340-48: R 124-28; D 215-20 (ND 146-14, SD 69-6); I 1-0, March 22, 1991.

62. HR 1282. Desert Storm Supplemental Appropriation/ Conference Report. Adoption of the conference report to provide $42,625,822,000 in new budget authority for the incremental costs of the Persian Gulf War. The bill would provide that up to $15 billion in U.S. funds can be obligated, if there are no more funds available from allied contributions in the Defense Cooperation Account. Adopted 379-11: R 152-1; D 226-10 (ND 153-8, SD 73-2); I 1-0, March 22, 1991.

63. S 534. Gold Medal for Gen. H. Norman Schwarzkopf/Passage. Torres, D-Calif., motion to suspend the rules and pass the bill to award a Congressional Gold Medal to Gen. H. Norman Schwarzkopf in recognition of his service in Operation Desert Storm. Motion agreed to 405-0: R 154-0; D 250-0 (ND 169-0, SD 81-0); I 1-0, April 11, 1991. A two-thirds majority of those present and voting (270 in this case) is required for passage under suspension of the rules.

64. S 565. Gold Medal for Gen. Colin L. Powell Jr./Passage. Torres, D-Calif., motion to suspend the rules and pass the bill to award a Congressional Gold Medal to Gen. Colin L. Powell Jr. in recognition of his service during the U.S. military response to the Iraqi invasion of Kuwait. Motion agreed to 400-0: R 153-0; D 247-0 (ND 168-0, SD 79-0); April 11, 1991. A two-thirds majority of those present and voting (267 in this case) is required for passage under suspension of the rules.

65. HR 1047. Veterans' Benefits Improvement Act/ Passage. Montgomery, D-Miss., motion to suspend the rules and pass the bill to make improvements to several aspects of the compensation, pension and life insurance programs administered by the Department of Veterans Affairs. Motion agreed to 399-3: R 150-3; D 248-0 (ND 170-0, SD 78-0); I 1-0, April 11, 1991. A two-thirds majority of those present and voting (268 in this case) is required for passage under suspension of the rules.

66. H Con Res 121. Fiscal 1992 Budget Resolution/Rule. Adoption of the rule (H Res 123) to provide for House floor consideration of the concurrent resolution to set forth the congressional budget for the government for fiscal 1992-96. Adopted 392-9: R 149-8; D 243-0 (ND 164-0, SD 79-0); I 0-1, April 16, 1991.

KEY

Y Voted for (yea).
Paired for.
+ Announced for.
N Voted against (nay).
X Paired against.
- Announced against.
P Voted "present."
C Voted "present" to avoid possible conflict of interest.
? Did not vote or otherwise make a position known.

Democrats ***Republicans***
Independent

	59	60	61	62	63	64	65	66
ALABAMA								
1 ***Callahan***	Y	Y	N	Y	Y	Y	Y	Y
2 ***Dickinson***	Y	Y	Y	Y	Y	Y	Y	Y
3 Browder	Y	N	Y	Y	Y	Y	Y	Y
4 Bevill	Y	N	Y	Y	?	?	?	?
5 Cramer	Y	N	Y	Y	Y	?	Y	Y
6 Erdreich	Y	N	Y	Y	Y	Y	Y	Y
7 Harris	Y	N	Y	Y	Y	Y	Y	Y
ALASKA								
AL ***Young***	Y	N	Y	Y	Y	Y	Y	Y
ARIZONA								
1 ***Rhodes***	Y	Y	Y	Y	Y	Y	Y	Y
2 Udall	?	?	?	?	?	?	?	?
3 ***Stump***	Y	Y	N	Y	Y	Y	Y	N
4 ***Kyl***	Y	Y	Y	Y	Y	Y	Y	Y
5 ***Kolbe***	Y	N	Y	Y	?	?	?	Y
ARKANSAS								
1 Alexander	Y	N	Y	Y	Y	Y	Y	Y
2 Thornton	Y	N	Y	Y	Y	Y	Y	Y
3 ***Hammerschmidt***	Y	N	Y	Y	Y	Y	Y	Y
4 Anthony	Y	N	Y	Y	Y	Y	Y	Y
CALIFORNIA								
1 ***Riggs***	Y	Y	Y	Y	Y	Y	Y	Y
2 ***Herger***	Y	Y	Y	Y	Y	Y	Y	Y
3 Matsui	Y	?	?	?	Y	Y	Y	Y
4 Fazio	Y	N	Y	Y	Y	Y	Y	Y
5 Pelosi	Y	N	Y	Y	Y	Y	Y	Y
6 Boxer	?	X	?	?	Y	Y	Y	Y
7 Miller	Y	N	N	Y	Y	Y	Y	?
8 Dellums	?	N	N	N	Y	Y	Y	Y
9 Stark	Y	N	N	Y	Y	Y	Y	Y
10 Edwards	Y	N	Y	Y	Y	Y	Y	Y
11 Lantos	Y	N	Y	Y	Y	Y	Y	Y
12 ***Campbell***	Y	Y	Y	Y	Y	Y	Y	Y
13 Mineta	Y	N	Y	Y	Y	Y	Y	Y
14 ***Doolittle***	Y	Y	Y	Y	Y	Y	Y	Y
15 Condit	Y	N	Y	Y	Y	Y	Y	Y
16 Panetta	Y	N	N	Y	Y	Y	Y	Y
17 Dooley	Y	N	Y	Y	Y	Y	Y	Y
18 Lehman	Y	N	N	Y	Y	Y	Y	Y
19 ***Lagomarsino***	Y	N	Y	Y	Y	Y	Y	Y
20 ***Thomas***	Y	Y	Y	Y	Y	Y	Y	Y
21 ***Gallegly***	Y	Y	Y	Y	Y	Y	Y	Y
22 ***Moorhead***	Y	Y	N	Y	Y	Y	Y	Y
23 Beilenson	Y	?	Y	Y	Y	Y	Y	Y
24 Waxman	Y	?	?	?	Y	Y	Y	Y
25 Roybal	Y	N	Y	Y	Y	Y	Y	Y
26 Berman	?	N	Y	Y	Y	Y	Y	?
27 Levine	?	?	?	?	?	?	?	Y
28 Dixon	Y	N	Y	Y	+	+	+	Y
29 Waters	Y	N	Y	N	Y	Y	Y	Y
30 Martinez	Y	N	Y	?	Y	Y	Y	?
31 Dymally	Y	N	N	N	?	?	?	?
32 Anderson	Y	N	Y	Y	Y	Y	Y	Y
33 ***Dreier***	Y	Y	N	Y	?	?	?	Y
34 Torres	Y	N	Y	Y	Y	Y	Y	Y
35 ***Lewis***	Y	N	Y	Y	Y	Y	Y	Y
36 Brown	Y	N	Y	Y	Y	Y	Y	Y
37 ***McCandless***	Y	Y	Y	Y	Y	Y	Y	Y
38 ***Dornan***	Y	Y	Y	Y	?	?	?	?
39 ***Dannemeyer***	Y	?	?	?	Y	Y	Y	Y
40 ***Cox***	?	Y	Y	Y	Y	Y	Y	Y
41 ***Lowery***	Y	N	Y	Y	Y	Y	Y	Y
42 ***Rohrabacher***	Y	Y	Y	Y	Y	Y	Y	Y
43 ***Packard***	Y	N	Y	Y	Y	Y	Y	Y
44 ***Cunningham***	Y	N	Y	Y	Y	Y	Y	Y
45 ***Hunter***	Y	N	Y	Y	?	?	?	Y
COLORADO								
1 Schroeder	Y	N	N	Y	Y	Y	Y	Y
2 Skaggs	Y	N	Y	Y	Y	Y	Y	Y
3 Campbell	Y	N	Y	Y	Y	Y	Y	Y
4 ***Allard***	Y	Y	N	Y	Y	Y	Y	Y
5 ***Hefley***	Y	Y	N	Y	Y	Y	Y	N
6 ***Schaefer***	?	N	Y	Y	Y	Y	Y	Y
CONNECTICUT								
1 Kennelly	Y	N	Y	Y	Y	Y	Y	Y
2 Gejdenson	Y	N	Y	Y	Y	Y	Y	Y
3 DeLauro	Y	N	Y	Y	Y	Y	Y	Y
4 ***Shays***	Y	Y	Y	Y	Y	Y	Y	Y
5 ***Franks***	Y	N	Y	Y	Y	Y	Y	Y
6 ***Johnson***	Y	N	Y	Y	Y	Y	Y	Y
DELAWARE								
AL Carper	Y	N	Y	Y	Y	Y	Y	Y
FLORIDA								
1 Hutto	Y	N	Y	Y	Y	Y	Y	Y
2 Peterson	Y	N	Y	Y	Y	Y	Y	Y
3 Bennett	Y	N	Y	Y	Y	Y	Y	Y
4 ***James***	Y	Y	Y	Y	Y	Y	Y	Y
5 ***McCollum***	Y	?	?	?	Y	Y	Y	Y
6 ***Stearns***	Y	Y	Y	Y	Y	Y	Y	Y
7 Gibbons	Y	N	Y	Y	Y	Y	Y	?
8 ***Young***	Y	N	Y	Y	Y	Y	Y	?
9 ***Bilirakis***	Y	N	Y	Y	Y	Y	Y	Y
10 ***Ireland***	Y	N	Y	Y	Y	Y	Y	Y
11 Bacchus	Y	N	Y	Y	Y	Y	Y	Y
12 ***Lewis***	+	#	X	+	Y	Y	Y	Y
13 ***Goss***	Y	Y	Y	Y	Y	Y	Y	Y
14 Johnston	Y	?	?	?	Y	Y	Y	Y
15 ***Shaw***	Y	Y	Y	Y	Y	Y	Y	Y
16 Smith	Y	N	Y	Y	Y	Y	Y	Y
17 Lehman	Y	N	Y	Y	?	?	?	?
18 ***Ros-Lehtinen***	Y	Y	Y	Y	Y	Y	Y	Y
19 Fascell	Y	N	Y	Y	Y	Y	Y	Y
GEORGIA								
1 Thomas	Y	N	Y	Y	Y	Y	Y	Y
2 Hatcher	Y	?	?	?	Y	Y	Y	Y
3 Ray	Y	?	X	?	Y	Y	Y	Y
4 Jones	Y	N	Y	Y	Y	Y	Y	Y
5 Lewis	Y	N	Y	Y	Y	Y	Y	Y
6 ***Gingrich***	Y	?	?	?	Y	Y	Y	Y
7 Darden	Y	N	Y	Y	Y	Y	Y	Y
8 Rowland	Y	N	Y	Y	Y	Y	Y	Y
9 Jenkins	Y	?	?	?	Y	Y	Y	Y
10 Barnard	Y	X	?	?	Y	Y	Y	?
HAWAII								
1 Abercrombie	Y	N	Y	Y	Y	Y	Y	Y
2 Mink	Y	N	Y	Y	Y	Y	Y	Y
IDAHO								
1 LaRocco	Y	N	Y	Y	Y	Y	Y	Y
2 Stallings	?	?	?	?	Y	Y	Y	Y
ILLINOIS								
1 Hayes	Y	N	Y	N	Y	Y	Y	Y
2 Savage	Y	N	N	N	P	P	Y	Y
3 Russo	Y	N	N	Y	Y	Y	Y	Y
4 Sangmeister	Y	N	Y	Y	Y	Y	Y	Y
5 Lipinski	Y	N	Y	Y	Y	Y	Y	Y
6 ***Hyde***	?	Y	Y	Y	Y	Y	Y	Y
7 Collins	Y	N	Y	N	?	?	?	Y
8 Rostenkowski	Y	?	?	?	Y	Y	Y	Y
9 Yates	N	N	Y	Y	Y	Y	Y	?
10 ***Porter***	Y	Y	Y	Y	Y	Y	Y	Y
11 Annunzio	Y	N	Y	Y	Y	Y	Y	Y
12 ***Crane***	Y	Y	N	Y	Y	Y	Y	N
13 ***Fawell***	Y	Y	N	Y	Y	Y	Y	N
14 ***Hastert***	Y	Y	Y	Y	+	+	?	Y
15 Vacancy								
16 Cox	Y	N	Y	Y	Y	Y	Y	Y
17 Evans	Y	N	Y	Y	Y	Y	Y	Y
18 ***Michel***	Y	N	Y	Y	Y	Y	N	Y
19 Bruce	Y	N	Y	Y	Y	Y	Y	Y
20 Durbin	Y	N	Y	Y	Y	Y	Y	Y
21 Costello	Y	N	Y	Y	Y	Y	Y	Y
22 Poshard	Y	N	Y	Y	Y	Y	Y	Y
INDIANA								
1 Visclosky	Y	N	Y	Y	Y	Y	Y	Y
2 Sharp	Y	?	?	Y	Y	Y	Y	Y
3 Roemer	Y	N	Y	Y	Y	Y	Y	Y

ND Northern Democrats SD Southern Democrats

	59	60	61	62	63	64	65	66
4 Long	Y	N	Y	Y	Y	Y	Y	Y
5 Jontz	Y	N	Y	Y	Y	Y	Y	?
6 ***Burton***	Y	Y	Y	Y	Y	Y	Y	Y
7 ***Myers***	Y	N	Y	Y	?	?	?	?
8 McCloskey	Y	N	Y	Y	Y	Y	Y	Y
9 Hamilton	Y	N	Y	Y	Y	Y	Y	Y
10 Jacobs	?	?	?	?	Y	Y	Y	Y
IOWA								
1 ***Leach***	Y	Y	Y	Y	Y	Y	Y	Y
2 ***Nussle***	Y	Y	N	N	Y	Y	N	Y
3 Nagle	Y	N	Y	Y	Y	Y	Y	?
4 Smith	Y	N	Y	Y	Y	Y	Y	Y
5 ***Lightfoot***	Y	N	Y	Y	Y	Y	Y	Y
6 ***Grandy***	Y	Y	N	Y	Y	Y	Y	Y
KANSAS								
1 ***Roberts***	Y	N	Y	Y	Y	Y	Y	Y
2 Slattery	Y	N	Y	Y	Y	Y	Y	Y
3 ***Meyers***	Y	Y	Y	Y	Y	Y	Y	Y
4 Glickman	Y	N	Y	Y	Y	Y	Y	Y
5 ***Nichols***	Y	Y	Y	Y	Y	Y	Y	Y
KENTUCKY								
1 Hubbard	Y	N	N	Y	Y	Y	Y	Y
2 Natcher	Y	N	Y	Y	Y	Y	Y	Y
3 Mazzoli	Y	N	Y	Y	Y	Y	Y	Y
4 ***Bunning***	Y	Y	N	Y	Y	Y	Y	Y
5 ***Rogers***	Y	N	Y	Y	Y	Y	Y	Y
6 ***Hopkins***	Y	Y	Y	Y	Y	Y	Y	Y
7 Perkins	Y	N	Y	Y	Y	Y	Y	Y
LOUISIANA								
1 ***Livingston***	Y	N	Y	Y	Y	Y	Y	Y
2 Jefferson	Y	N	Y	Y	Y	Y	Y	Y
3 Tauzin	Y	N	Y	Y	Y	Y	Y	Y
4 ***McCrery***	Y	N	Y	Y	Y	Y	Y	Y
5 Huckaby	Y	N	N	Y	Y	Y	Y	Y
6 ***Baker***	Y	Y	Y	Y	Y	Y	Y	Y
7 Hayes	Y	N	N	Y	Y	Y	Y	Y
8 ***Holloway***	Y	Y	Y	Y	Y	Y	Y	Y
MAINE								
1 Andrews	Y	N	Y	Y	Y	Y	Y	Y
2 ***Snowe***	Y	N	Y	Y	Y	Y	Y	Y
MARYLAND								
1 ***Gilchrest***	Y	Y	Y	Y	Y	Y	Y	Y
2 ***Bentley***	Y	N	Y	Y	Y	Y	Y	Y
3 Cardin	Y	N	Y	Y	Y	Y	Y	Y
4 McMillen	Y	N	Y	Y	Y	Y	Y	Y
5 Hoyer	Y	N	Y	Y	Y	Y	Y	Y
6 Byron	Y	N	Y	Y	Y	Y	Y	Y
7 Mfume	Y	-	+	Y	Y	Y	Y	Y
8 ***Morella***	Y	N	Y	Y	Y	Y	Y	Y
MASSACHUSETTS								
1 Vacancy								
2 Neal	?	N	Y	Y	Y	Y	Y	Y
3 Early	Y	N	Y	Y	Y	Y	Y	Y
4 Frank	?	N	Y	Y	Y	Y	Y	Y
5 Atkins	Y	N	Y	Y	Y	Y	Y	Y
6 Mavroules	Y	N	Y	Y	Y	Y	Y	?
7 Markey	Y	N	Y	Y	Y	Y	Y	Y
8 Kennedy	Y	N	Y	Y	Y	Y	Y	Y
9 Moakley	Y	N	Y	Y	Y	Y	Y	Y
10 Studds	Y	N	Y	Y	Y	Y	Y	Y
11 Donnelly	Y	N	Y	Y	Y	Y	Y	Y
MICHIGAN								
1 Conyers	Y	?	Y	N	Y	Y	?	?
2 ***Pursell***	Y	N	Y	Y	Y	Y	Y	Y
3 Wolpe	Y	N	Y	Y	Y	Y	Y	Y
4 ***Upton***	Y	Y	N	Y	Y	Y	Y	Y
5 ***Henry***	Y	Y	Y	Y	Y	Y	Y	Y
6 Carr	?	N	Y	Y	Y	Y	Y	Y
7 Kildee	Y	N	Y	Y	Y	Y	Y	Y
8 Traxler	Y	N	Y	Y	Y	Y	Y	?
9 ***Vander Jagt***	Y	Y	Y	Y	Y	Y	Y	Y
10 ***Camp***	Y	Y	Y	Y	Y	Y	Y	Y
11 ***Davis***	Y	N	Y	Y	Y	Y	Y	Y
12 Bonior	Y	N	Y	Y	Y	Y	Y	Y
13 Collins	Y	N	Y	Y	Y	Y	Y	Y
14 Hertel	Y	N	Y	Y	Y	Y	Y	Y
15 Ford	Y	N	Y	Y	Y	Y	Y	Y
16 Dingell	Y	?	?	?	Y	Y	Y	Y
17 Levin	Y	N	Y	Y	Y	Y	Y	Y
18 ***Broomfield***	Y	Y	Y	Y	Y	Y	Y	Y
MINNESOTA								
1 Penny	Y	N	N	Y	Y	Y	Y	Y
2 ***Weber***	Y	N	Y	Y	Y	Y	Y	Y
3 ***Ramstad***	Y	Y	Y	Y	Y	Y	Y	Y
4 Vento	Y	N	Y	Y	Y	Y	Y	Y

	59	60	61	62	63	64	65	66
5 Sabo	Y	N	Y	Y	Y	Y	Y	Y
6 Sikorski	Y	N	Y	Y	Y	Y	Y	Y
7 Peterson	Y	N	N	Y	Y	Y	Y	Y
8 Oberstar	Y	N	Y	Y	Y	Y	Y	Y
MISSISSIPPI								
1 Whitten	Y	N	Y	Y	Y	Y	Y	Y
2 Espy	Y	N	Y	Y	Y	Y	Y	Y
3 Montgomery	Y	N	Y	Y	Y	Y	Y	Y
4 Parker	Y	N	Y	Y	Y	Y	Y	Y
5 Taylor	Y	N	Y	Y	Y	Y	Y	Y
MISSOURI								
1 Clay	Y	?	?	?	Y	Y	Y	Y
2 Horn	Y	N	Y	Y	Y	Y	Y	Y
3 Gephardt	Y	N	Y	Y	Y	Y	Y	Y
4 Skelton	Y	N	Y	Y	Y	Y	Y	Y
5 Wheat	Y	N	Y	Y	Y	Y	Y	Y
6 ***Coleman***	Y	N	Y	Y	Y	Y	Y	Y
7 ***Hancock***	Y	Y	N	Y	Y	Y	Y	N
8 ***Emerson***	Y	N	Y	Y	Y	Y	Y	Y
9 Volkmer	Y	N	Y	Y	+	+	+	Y
MONTANA								
1 Williams	Y	N	Y	Y	+	+	+	Y
2 ***Marlenee***	?	#	?	?	?	?	?	Y
NEBRASKA								
1 ***Bereuter***	Y	Y	Y	Y	Y	Y	Y	Y
2 Hoagland	Y	N	Y	Y	Y	Y	Y	Y
3 ***Barrett***	Y	Y	Y	Y	Y	Y	Y	Y
NEVADA								
1 Bilbray	Y	N	Y	Y	Y	Y	Y	Y
2 ***Vucanovich***	Y	N	Y	Y	Y	Y	Y	Y
NEW HAMPSHIRE								
1 ***Zeliff***	Y	Y	Y	Y	Y	Y	Y	N
2 Swett	Y	N	Y	Y	Y	Y	Y	Y
NEW JERSEY								
1 Andrews	Y	N	Y	Y	Y	Y	Y	Y
2 Hughes	?	N	N	Y	Y	Y	Y	?
3 Pallone	Y	N	N	Y	Y	Y	Y	Y
4 ***Smith***	?	N	Y	Y	Y	Y	Y	Y
5 ***Roukema***	Y	Y	Y	Y	Y	Y	Y	Y
6 Dwyer	Y	?	#	?	?	?	?	?
7 ***Rinaldo***	Y	N	Y	Y	Y	Y	Y	Y
8 Roe	Y	N	Y	Y	Y	Y	Y	Y
9 Torricelli	Y	?	?	?	Y	Y	Y	Y
10 Payne	Y	N	Y	Y	Y	Y	Y	Y
11 ***Gallo***	Y	N	Y	Y	Y	Y	Y	Y
12 ***Zimmer***	Y	Y	Y	Y	Y	Y	Y	Y
13 ***Saxton***	Y	N	Y	Y	Y	Y	Y	Y
14 Guarini	Y	Y	Y	Y	Y	?	Y	Y
NEW MEXICO								
1 ***Schiff***	Y	N	Y	Y	Y	Y	Y	Y
2 ***Skeen***	Y	N	Y	Y	Y	Y	Y	Y
3 Richardson	Y	N	Y	Y	Y	Y	Y	Y
NEW YORK								
1 Hochbrueckner	Y	N	Y	Y	Y	Y	Y	Y
2 Downey	Y	N	Y	Y	Y	Y	Y	Y
3 Mrazek	Y	N	Y	Y	Y	Y	Y	?
4 ***Lent***	Y	?	?	?	Y	Y	Y	Y
5 ***McGrath***	Y	N	Y	Y	Y	Y	Y	Y
6 Flake	?	?	?	?	Y	Y	Y	Y
7 Ackerman	?	?	?	?	Y	Y	Y	Y
8 Scheuer	Y	N	Y	Y	?	?	?	Y
9 Manton	?	?	?	?	Y	Y	Y	Y
10 Schumer	Y	N	Y	Y	Y	Y	Y	Y
11 Towns	Y	N	Y	Y	Y	Y	Y	Y
12 Owens	Y	N	Y	N	Y	Y	Y	?
13 Solarz	Y	N	Y	Y	?	?	?	Y
14 ***Molinari***	Y	N	Y	Y	Y	Y	Y	Y
15 ***Green***	Y	N	Y	Y	Y	Y	Y	Y
16 Rangel	Y	N	Y	Y	Y	Y	Y	Y
17 Weiss	Y	N	Y	Y	Y	Y	Y	Y
18 Serrano	Y	N	Y	Y	Y	Y	Y	Y
19 Engel	Y	N	Y	Y	Y	Y	Y	Y
20 Lowey	Y	N	Y	Y	Y	Y	Y	Y
21 ***Fish***	Y	N	Y	Y	Y	Y	Y	Y
22 ***Gilman***	Y	N	Y	Y	Y	Y	Y	Y
23 McNulty	Y	N	Y	Y	Y	Y	Y	Y
24 ***Solomon***	Y	Y	N	Y	Y	Y	Y	Y
25 ***Boehlert***	Y	N	Y	Y	Y	Y	Y	Y
26 ***Martin***	Y	Y	Y	Y	Y	Y	Y	?
27 ***Walsh***	Y	N	Y	Y	+	+	Y	Y
28 McHugh	Y	N	Y	Y	Y	Y	Y	Y
29 ***Horton***	Y	N	Y	Y	Y	Y	Y	Y
30 Slaughter	Y	N	Y	Y	Y	Y	Y	Y
31 ***Paxon***	Y	N	Y	Y	Y	Y	Y	Y

	59	60	61	62	63	64	65	66
32 LaFalce	?	?	?	?	Y	Y	Y	Y
33 Nowak	Y	N	Y	Y	Y	Y	Y	Y
34 ***Houghton***	Y	Y	N	Y	Y	Y	Y	?
NORTH CAROLINA								
1 Jones	Y	N	Y	?	Y	Y	Y	Y
2 Valentine	Y	Y	N	Y	Y	Y	Y	Y
3 Lancaster	Y	N	Y	Y	Y	Y	Y	Y
4 Price	Y	N	Y	Y	Y	Y	Y	Y
5 Neal	Y	N	Y	Y	Y	Y	Y	Y
6 ***Coble***	Y	Y	Y	Y	Y	Y	Y	Y
7 Rose	Y	N	Y	Y	Y	Y	Y	Y
8 Hefner	Y	N	Y	Y	Y	Y	Y	Y
9 ***McMillan***	Y	Y	Y	Y	Y	Y	Y	Y
10 ***Ballenger***	Y	Y	N	Y	Y	Y	Y	N
11 ***Taylor***	Y	Y	Y	Y	Y	Y	Y	Y
NORTH DAKOTA								
AL Dorgan	Y	N	N	Y	Y	Y	Y	Y
OHIO								
1 Luken	Y	N	Y	Y	Y	Y	Y	Y
2 ***Gradison***	Y	Y	N	Y	Y	Y	N	Y
3 Hall	Y	N	Y	Y	Y	Y	Y	Y
4 ***Oxley***	Y	N	Y	Y	Y	Y	Y	Y
5 ***Gillmor***	Y	Y	Y	Y	Y	Y	Y	Y
6 ***McEwen***	Y	Y	Y	Y	Y	Y	Y	Y
7 ***Hobson***	Y	Y	Y	Y	Y	Y	Y	Y
8 ***Boehner***	Y	N	Y	Y	Y	Y	Y	Y
9 Kaptur	Y	N	Y	Y	Y	Y	Y	Y
10 ***Miller***	?	?	?	?	Y	Y	Y	Y
11 Eckart	Y	N	Y	Y	Y	Y	Y	Y
12 ***Kasich***	Y	Y	Y	Y	Y	Y	Y	Y
13 Pease	Y	Y	Y	Y	Y	Y	Y	Y
14 Sawyer	Y	N	Y	Y	Y	Y	Y	Y
15 ***Wylie***	Y	Y	Y	Y	Y	Y	Y	Y
16 ***Regula***	Y	N	Y	Y	Y	Y	Y	Y
17 Traficant	Y	N	Y	Y	Y	Y	Y	Y
18 Applegate	Y	N	Y	Y	Y	Y	Y	Y
19 Feighan	Y	N	Y	Y	Y	Y	Y	Y
20 Oakar	Y	N	Y	Y	Y	Y	Y	Y
21 Stokes	Y	N	Y	Y	Y	Y	Y	Y
OKLAHOMA								
1 ***Inhofe***	Y	N	Y	Y	Y	Y	Y	Y
2 Synar	Y	N	Y	Y	Y	Y	Y	Y
3 Brewster	Y	N	Y	Y	Y	Y	Y	Y
4 McCurdy	?	N	Y	Y	Y	Y	?	Y
5 ***Edwards***	Y	N	Y	Y	?	?	?	Y
6 English	Y	N	Y	Y	Y	Y	Y	Y
OREGON								
1 AuCoin	Y	?	?	?	Y	Y	Y	Y
2 ***Smith***	Y	Y	N	Y	Y	Y	Y	Y
3 Wyden	Y	N	Y	Y	Y	Y	Y	Y
4 DeFazio	Y	N	Y	Y	Y	Y	Y	Y
5 Kopetski	Y	N	Y	Y	Y	Y	Y	Y
PENNSYLVANIA								
1 Foglietta	Y	N	Y	Y	Y	Y	Y	Y
2 Gray	Y	N	Y	Y	?	?	Y	Y
3 Borski	Y	N	Y	Y	Y	Y	Y	Y
4 Kolter	Y	N	Y	Y	Y	Y	Y	Y
5 ***Schulze***	Y	N	Y	Y	Y	Y	Y	Y
6 Yatron	Y	N	Y	Y	Y	Y	Y	Y
7 ***Weldon***	Y	N	Y	Y	Y	Y	Y	?
8 Kostmayer	Y	N	Y	Y	Y	Y	Y	Y
9 ***Shuster***	?	N	Y	Y	Y	Y	Y	Y
10 ***McDade***	Y	N	Y	Y	Y	Y	Y	Y
11 Kanjorski	Y	N	Y	Y	Y	Y	Y	Y
12 Murtha	Y	N	Y	Y	Y	Y	Y	Y
13 ***Coughlin***	Y	N	Y	Y	Y	Y	Y	Y
14 Coyne	Y	N	Y	Y	Y	Y	Y	Y
15 ***Ritter***	Y	N	?	Y	Y	Y	Y	Y
16 ***Walker***	Y	Y	N	Y	?	?	?	Y
17 ***Gekas***	Y	N	Y	Y	Y	Y	Y	Y
18 ***Santorum***	Y	N	Y	Y	Y	Y	Y	Y
19 ***Goodling***	Y	N	Y	Y	Y	Y	Y	Y
20 Gaydos	Y	N	Y	Y	Y	Y	Y	Y
21 ***Ridge***	Y	?	?	?	Y	Y	Y	Y
22 Murphy	?	N	Y	Y	Y	Y	Y	Y
23 ***Clinger***	Y	?	?	?	Y	Y	Y	Y
RHODE ISLAND								
1 ***Machtley***	Y	N	Y	Y	Y	Y	Y	Y
2 Reed	Y	?	+	+	Y	Y	Y	Y
SOUTH CAROLINA								
1 ***Ravenel***	Y	N	Y	Y	Y	Y	Y	Y
2 ***Spence***	Y	Y	Y	Y	Y	Y	Y	Y
3 Derrick	Y	N	Y	Y	Y	Y	Y	?
4 Patterson	Y	Y	Y	Y	Y	Y	Y	Y
5 Spratt	Y	N	Y	Y	Y	Y	Y	Y
6 Tallon	Y	N	Y	Y	Y	Y	Y	Y

	59	60	61	62	63	64	65	66
SOUTH DAKOTA								
AL Johnson	Y	N	Y	Y	Y	Y	Y	Y
TENNESSEE								
1 ***Quillen***	Y	N	Y	Y	Y	Y	Y	Y
2 ***Duncan***	Y	Y	N	Y	Y	Y	Y	N
3 Lloyd	?	?	#	?	Y	Y	Y	Y
4 Cooper	Y	N	Y	Y	Y	Y	Y	Y
5 Clement	Y	N	Y	Y	Y	Y	Y	Y
6 Gordon	Y	N	Y	Y	Y	Y	Y	Y
7 ***Sundquist***	Y	Y	Y	Y	Y	Y	Y	Y
8 Tanner	?	?	?	Y	Y	Y	Y	Y
9 Ford	Y	?	?	?	Y	Y	Y	?
TEXAS								
1 Chapman	Y	N	Y	Y	Y	Y	Y	Y
2 Wilson	Y	N	Y	Y	Y	?	?	Y
3 Vacancy								
4 Hall	Y	Y	N	Y	Y	Y	Y	Y
5 Bryant	Y	N	Y	Y	Y	Y	Y	Y
6 ***Barton***	Y	Y	N	Y	Y	?	?	Y
7 ***Archer***	Y	Y	N	Y	Y	Y	Y	Y
8 ***Fields***	Y	Y	Y	Y	Y	Y	Y	Y
9 Brooks	Y	N	Y	Y	Y	Y	Y	Y
10 Pickle	Y	N	Y	Y	Y	Y	Y	Y
11 Edwards	Y	N	Y	Y	Y	Y	Y	Y
12 Geren	Y	N	Y	Y	+	+	+	Y
13 Sarpalius	Y	N	Y	Y	Y	Y	Y	Y
14 Laughlin	Y	N	Y	Y	Y	Y	Y	Y
15 de la Garza	?	N	Y	Y	?	?	?	Y
16 Coleman	Y	N	Y	Y	Y	Y	Y	Y
17 Stenholm	?	?	?	?	Y	Y	Y	Y
18 Washington	Y	Y	Y	N	Y	Y	Y	Y
19 ***Combest***	Y	Y	N	Y	Y	Y	Y	Y
20 Gonzalez	Y	N	N	N	Y	Y	Y	Y
21 ***Smith***	Y	?	?	?	Y	Y	Y	Y
22 ***DeLay***	Y	?	N	Y	Y	Y	Y	Y
23 Bustamante	?	?	?	?	Y	Y	Y	Y
24 Frost	Y	N	Y	Y	Y	Y	?	Y
25 Andrews	Y	N	Y	Y	Y	Y	Y	Y
26 ***Armey***	Y	?	?	?	Y	Y	Y	Y
27 Ortiz	Y	N	Y	Y	Y	Y	Y	Y
UTAH								
1 ***Hansen***	Y	Y	N	Y	Y	Y	Y	Y
2 Owens	Y	N	Y	Y	Y	Y	Y	Y
3 Orton	Y	N	Y	Y	Y	Y	Y	Y
VERMONT								
AL *Sanders*	Y	N	Y	Y	Y	+	Y	N
VIRGINIA								
1 ***Bateman***	Y	Y	Y	Y	Y	Y	Y	Y
2 Pickett	Y	N	Y	Y	Y	Y	Y	Y
3 ***Bliley***	Y	Y	Y	Y	Y	Y	Y	Y
4 Sisisky	Y	N	Y	Y	Y	Y	Y	Y
5 Payne	Y	N	Y	Y	Y	Y	Y	Y
6 Olin	Y	N	Y	Y	Y	Y	Y	Y
7 ***Slaughter***	Y	Y	Y	Y	Y	Y	Y	Y
8 Moran	Y	N	Y	Y	Y	Y	Y	Y
9 Boucher	Y	N	Y	Y	Y	Y	Y	Y
10 ***Wolf***	Y	N	Y	Y	Y	Y	Y	Y
WASHINGTON								
1 ***Miller***	Y	Y	Y	Y	Y	Y	Y	Y
2 Swift	Y	N	Y	Y	Y	Y	Y	Y
3 Unsoeld	Y	N	Y	Y	Y	Y	Y	Y
4 ***Morrison***	Y	N	Y	Y	Y	Y	Y	Y
5 Foley								
6 Dicks	?	N	Y	Y	Y	Y	Y	?
7 McDermott	Y	N	Y	Y	Y	Y	Y	Y
8 ***Chandler***	Y	Y	Y	Y	Y	Y	?	Y
WEST VIRGINIA								
1 Mollohan	Y	N	Y	Y	Y	Y	Y	Y
2 Staggers	Y	N	Y	Y	Y	Y	Y	Y
3 Wise	Y	N	Y	Y	Y	Y	Y	Y
4 Rahall	Y	N	Y	Y	Y	Y	Y	Y
WISCONSIN								
1 Aspin	Y	?	?	?	Y	Y	Y	Y
2 ***Klug***	Y	Y	Y	Y	Y	Y	Y	?
3 ***Gunderson***	Y	N	Y	Y	Y	Y	Y	Y
4 Kleczka	Y	N	Y	Y	Y	Y	Y	Y
5 Moody	Y	N	Y	Y	Y	Y	Y	?
6 ***Petri***	Y	Y	N	Y	Y	Y	Y	Y
7 Obey	N	N	Y	Y	Y	Y	Y	Y
8 ***Roth***	Y	Y	N	Y	Y	Y	Y	Y
9 ***Sensenbrenner***	Y	Y	N	Y	Y	Y	Y	Y
WYOMING								
AL ***Thomas***	Y	N	Y	Y	Y	Y	Y	Y

Southern states - Ala., Ark., Fla., Ga., Ky., La., Miss., N.C., Okla., S.C., Tenn., Texas, Va.
Omitted votes are quorum calls, which CQ does not include in its vote charts.

HOUSE VOTES 67, 68, 69, 70, 71, 72, 73, 74

67. H Con Res 121. Fiscal 1992 Budget Resolution/ Education Increases. Ford, D-Mich., amendment to increase the budget authority target for education, training, employment and social services by $400 million and the outlay target by $200 million, permitting additional funding for Head Start, Chapter 1 Compensatory Education, student financial aid, vocational and adult education, and Job Corps. Adopted 261-158: R 39-122; D 221-36 (ND 155-19, SD 66-17); I 1-0, April 17, 1991.

68. H Con Res 121. Fiscal 1992 Budget Resolution/ Growth Ceilings. Dannemeyer, R-Calif., substitute amendment to hold domestic discretionary spending at fiscal 1990 levels with certain adjustments for inflation, resulting in outlays that were about $18 billion lower than the domestic cap set in the Budget Enforcement Act of 1990 (PL 101-508). Rejected 79-332: R 78-83; D 1-248 (ND 0-169, SD 1-79); I 0-1, April 17, 1991.

69. H Con Res 121. Fiscal 1992 Budget Resolution/ Medicare Cuts. Kasich, R-Ohio, substitute amendment to hold domestic discretionary spending at the fiscal 1990 baseline or the president's request, whichever is lower, resulting in domestic discretionary outlays that were about $7.5 billion lower than the cap set in the Budget Enforcement Act of 1990 (PL 101-508); cut entitlement programs by $6.4 billion in fiscal 1992 and $48.6 billion over five years, including cuts in Medicare, totaling $27.2 billion over five years; and increase revenues by $3.1 billion. Rejected 114-303: R 105-56; D 9-246 (ND 4-168, SD 5-78); I 0-1, April 17, 1991.

70. H Con Res 121. Fiscal 1992 Budget Resolution/ Spending Caps. Gradison, R-Ohio, substitute amendment to incorporate the president's budget by setting domestic, international and defense spending at the caps set in the Budget Enforcement Act of 1990 (PL 101-508); cut entitlements by $6.3 billion in fiscal 1992 and $46.6 billion over five years, including Medicare cuts of $25.2 billion over five years; and increase revenues by $3 billion in fiscal 1992 by cutting the capital gains tax rate and extending the Medicare payroll tax to some state and local employees. A "yea" was a vote supporting the president's position. Rejected 89-335: R 89-74; D 0-260 (ND 0-176, SD 0-84); I 0-1, April 17, 1991.

71. H Con Res 121. Fiscal 1992 Budget Resolution/ Adoption. Adoption of the resolution to set binding budget levels for the fiscal year ending Sept. 30, 1992: budget authority, $1.590 trillion; outlays, $1.459 trillion; revenues, $1.169 trillion; deficit, $289.6 billion. The resolution conforms with the specific spending ceilings for defense, international affairs, and domestic discretionary programs set in the Budget Enforcement Act of 1990 (PL 101-508). Adopted 261-163: R 18-145; D 243-17 (ND 164-12, SD 79-5); I 0-1, April 17, 1991.

72. H J Res 222. Railroad Labor Dispute/Passage. Passage of the joint resolution to provide for a settlement of the railroad labor-management disputes between certain railroads represented by the National Carriers Conference Committee of the National Railway Labor conference and certain employees on strike. Passed 400-5: R 156-0; D 243-5 (ND 163-3, SD 80-2); I 1-0, April 17, 1991. A "yea" was a vote supporting the president's position.

73. Procedural Motion. Fields, R-Texas, motion to approve the House Journal of Tuesday, April 30. Motion agreed to 288-106: R 51-102; D 236-4 (ND 162-4, SD 74-0); I 1-0, May 1, 1991.

74. HR 1236. National Flood Insurance/CBO Cost Estimate. Gradison, R-Ohio, amendment to strike the section of the bill making the Congressional Budget Office estimate of the bill's net effect on federal outlays binding for the purposes of pay-as-you-go sequestration. The Budget Enforcement Act had made the Office of Management and Budget the official scorekeeper. Rejected 160-248: R 157-0; D 3-247 (ND 1-170, SD 2-77); I 0-1, May 1, 1991. A "yea" was a vote supporting the president's position.

KEY

Y Voted for (yea).
Paired for.
+ Announced for.
N Voted against (nay).
X Paired against.
- Announced against.
P Voted "present."
C Voted "present" to avoid possible conflict of interest.
? Did not vote or otherwise make a position known.

Democrats ***Republicans***
Independent

	67	68	69	70	71	72	73	74
ALABAMA								
1 ***Callahan***	N	Y	Y	N	N	Y	N	Y
2 ***Dickinson***	N	N	Y	Y	N	Y	N	Y
3 Browder	Y	N	N	N	Y	Y	Y	N
4 Bevill	N	?	N	N	Y	Y	?	?
5 Cramer	Y	N	N	N	Y	Y	Y	N
6 Erdreich	Y	N	N	N	Y	Y	Y	N
7 Harris	Y	N	N	N	Y	Y	Y	N
ALASKA								
AL ***Young***	N	N	N	Y	N	?	N	Y
ARIZONA								
1 ***Rhodes***	N	Y	Y	Y	N	Y	N	?
2 Udall	?	?	?	?	?	?	?	?
3 ***Stump***	N	Y	Y	N	N	Y	N	Y
4 ***Kyl***	N	Y	Y	N	N	Y	N	Y
5 ***Kolbe***	N	N	Y	Y	N	Y	N	Y
ARKANSAS								
1 Alexander	Y	?	N	N	Y	Y	?	N
2 Thornton	Y	N	N	N	Y	Y	Y	N
3 ***Hammerschmidt***	N	Y	Y	Y	N	Y	Y	Y
4 Anthony	Y	N	N	N	Y	Y	Y	N
CALIFORNIA								
1 ***Riggs***	N	N	Y	N	N	Y	N	Y
2 ***Herger***	N	Y	Y	N	N	Y	N	Y
3 Matsui	Y	N	N	N	Y	Y	Y	N
4 Fazio	Y	N	N	N	Y	Y	Y	N
5 Pelosi	N	N	N	N	Y	Y	Y	N
6 Boxer	Y	N	N	N	Y	Y	Y	N
7 Miller	Y	N	N	N	Y	Y	Y	?
8 Dellums	Y	N	N	N	Y	Y	Y	N
9 Stark	Y	N	N	N	Y	Y	Y	N
10 Edwards	Y	N	N	N	Y	N	Y	N
11 Lantos	Y	N	N	N	Y	Y	Y	N
12 ***Campbell***	N	N	N	N	N	Y	N	Y
13 Mineta	Y	N	N	N	Y	Y	Y	N
14 ***Doolittle***	N	Y	N	N	N	Y	N	Y
15 Condit	Y	N	Y	N	Y	Y	Y	N
16 Panetta	Y	N	N	N	Y	Y	Y	N
17 Dooley	Y	N	N	N	Y	Y	Y	N
18 Lehman	Y	N	N	N	Y	Y	Y	N
19 ***Lagomarsino***	N	N	Y	Y	N	Y	N	Y
20 ***Thomas***	N	N	Y	Y	N	Y	N	Y
21 ***Gallegly***	N	N	Y	Y	N	Y	N	Y
22 ***Moorhead***	N	Y	Y	Y	N	Y	N	?
23 Beilenson	N	N	N	N	Y	Y	Y	N
24 Waxman	Y	N	N	N	Y	?	?	N
25 Roybal	Y	N	N	N	Y	Y	Y	N
26 Berman	Y	N	N	N	Y	?	Y	N
27 Levine	Y	?	?	?	?	?	Y	N
28 Dixon	Y	N	N	N	Y	Y	Y	N
29 Waters	Y	N	N	N	Y	Y	Y	N
30 Martinez	Y	N	N	N	Y	Y	Y	N
31 Dymally	#	?	?	?	?	?	Y	X
32 Anderson	Y	N	N	N	Y	Y	Y	N
33 ***Dreier***	N	Y	Y	N	N	Y	Y	Y
34 Torres	Y	N	N	N	Y	Y	Y	N
35 ***Lewis***	N	N	Y	Y	N	Y	N	Y
36 Brown	Y	N	N	N	Y	Y	Y	N
37 ***McCandless***	N	N	Y	N	N	Y	N	Y
38 ***Dornan***	X	#	#	?	X	?	?	#
39 ***Dannemeyer***	N	Y	Y	N	N	Y	N	Y
40 ***Cox***	N	Y	N	N	N	Y	N	Y
41 ***Lowery***	N	Y	Y	Y	N	Y	N	Y
42 ***Rohrabacher***	N	Y	Y	N	N	Y	N	Y
43 ***Packard***	N	Y	Y	N	N	Y	Y	Y
44 ***Cunningham***	N	Y	Y	N	N	Y	Y	Y
45 ***Hunter***	N	Y	Y	Y	N	Y	N	Y
COLORADO								
1 Schroeder	Y	N	N	N	Y	Y	N	N
2 Skaggs	Y	N	N	N	Y	Y	Y	N
3 Campbell	Y	N	N	N	Y	Y	Y	N
4 ***Allard***	Y	Y	Y	N	N	Y	N	Y
5 ***Hefley***	N	Y	N	N	N	Y	N	Y
6 ***Schaefer***	Y	Y	Y	N	N	Y	N	Y
CONNECTICUT								
1 Kennelly	Y	?	N	N	Y	Y	Y	N
2 Gejdenson	Y	N	N	N	Y	Y	Y	N
3 DeLauro	Y	N	N	N	Y	Y	Y	N
4 ***Shays***	Y	Y	Y	N	Y	Y	N	Y
5 ***Franks***	N	Y	Y	Y	N	Y	N	Y
6 ***Johnson***	Y	N	N	N	N	Y	Y	Y
DELAWARE								
AL Carper	Y	N	N	N	Y	Y	Y	N
FLORIDA								
1 Hutto	N	N	N	N	Y	Y	Y	N
2 Peterson	Y	N	N	N	Y	Y	Y	N
3 Bennett	Y	N	Y	N	Y	Y	Y	N
4 ***James***	N	Y	Y	N	N	Y	N	Y
5 ***McCollum***	N	N	Y	Y	N	Y	?	?
6 ***Stearns***	N	Y	N	N	N	Y	N	Y
7 Gibbons	Y	N	N	N	Y	Y	Y	N
8 ***Young***	N	Y	N	Y	N	Y	Y	Y
9 ***Bilirakis***	Y	N	N	N	N	Y	N	Y
10 ***Ireland***	N	Y	Y	Y	N	Y	N	Y
11 Bacchus	Y	N	N	N	Y	Y	Y	N
12 ***Lewis***	N	Y	Y	Y	N	Y	N	Y
13 ***Goss***	N	Y	Y	Y	N	Y	N	Y
14 Johnston	Y	N	N	N	Y	Y	Y	N
15 ***Shaw***	N	N	Y	Y	N	Y	Y	Y
16 Smith	Y	N	N	N	Y	Y	?	?
17 Lehman	X	?	?	?	?	?	?	X
18 ***Ros-Lehtinen***	N	N	N	N	N	Y	N	Y
19 Fascell	Y	N	N	N	Y	Y	Y	N
GEORGIA								
1 Thomas	Y	N	N	N	Y	Y	?	Y
2 Hatcher	Y	N	N	N	Y	Y	Y	N
3 Ray	N	N	N	N	Y	Y	Y	N
4 Jones	N	N	N	N	Y	Y	Y	N
5 Lewis	Y	N	N	N	Y	Y	Y	N
6 ***Gingrich***	Y	Y	Y	Y	N	Y	N	Y
7 Darden	Y	N	N	N	Y	Y	Y	N
8 Rowland	Y	N	N	N	Y	Y	Y	N
9 Jenkins	Y	N	N	N	Y	Y	Y	N
10 Barnard	N	N	N	N	Y	Y	Y	N
HAWAII								
1 Abercrombie	Y	N	N	N	Y	Y	Y	N
2 Mink	Y	N	N	N	Y	Y	Y	N
IDAHO								
1 LaRocco	Y	N	N	N	Y	Y	Y	N
2 Stallings	Y	N	N	N	Y	Y	Y	N
ILLINOIS								
1 Hayes	Y	N	N	N	Y	Y	Y	N
2 Savage	Y	N	N	N	Y	Y	Y	?
3 Russo	Y	N	N	N	Y	Y	Y	N
4 Sangmeister	Y	N	N	N	Y	Y	Y	N
5 Lipinski	N	N	N	N	Y	Y	Y	N
6 ***Hyde***	N	N	N	Y	N	Y	N	Y
7 Collins	Y	N	N	N	Y	Y	?	N
8 Rostenkowski	Y	N	N	N	Y	Y	Y	N
9 Yates	?	?	?	?	?	?	Y	N
10 ***Porter***	N	Y	Y	Y	N	Y	N	Y
11 Annunzio	Y	N	N	N	Y	Y	Y	N
12 ***Crane***	N	Y	Y	Y	N	Y	N	Y
13 ***Fawell***	Y	Y	Y	N	N	Y	N	Y
14 ***Hastert***	N	Y	Y	Y	N	Y	N	Y
15 Vacancy								
16 Cox	Y	N	N	N	Y	Y	Y	N
17 Evans	Y	N	N	N	Y	Y	Y	N
18 ***Michel***	N	N	Y	Y	N	Y	N	Y
19 Bruce	Y	N	N	N	Y	Y	Y	N
20 Durbin	Y	N	N	N	Y	Y	Y	N
21 Costello	Y	N	N	N	Y	Y	Y	N
22 Poshard	Y	N	N	N	Y	Y	Y	N
INDIANA								
1 Visclosky	Y	N	N	N	N	Y	Y	N
2 Sharp	Y	N	N	N	Y	?	Y	N
3 Roemer	Y	N	N	N	N	Y	Y	N

ND Northern Democrats SD Southern Democrats

Member	67	68	69	70	71	72	73	74
4 Long	N	N	N	N	Y	Y	Y	N
5 Jontz	Y	N	N	N	Y	Y	Y	N
6 ***Burton***	N	Y	Y	N	N	Y	N	Y
7 ***Myers***	N	N	Y	Y	N	Y	Y	Y
8 McCloskey	Y	N	N	N	Y	Y	?	N
9 Hamilton	Y	N	N	N	Y	Y	Y	Y
10 Jacobs	Y	N	N	N	N	Y	N	N
IOWA								
1 ***Leach***	Y	N	N	N	N	Y	N	Y
2 ***Nussle***	N	N	N	N	N	Y	N	Y
3 Nagle	Y	N	N	N	Y	Y	Y	N
4 Smith	N	N	N	N	N	Y	Y	N
5 ***Lightfoot***	N	Y	Y	N	N	Y	N	Y
6 ***Grandy***	N	Y	Y	Y	N	Y	N	Y
KANSAS								
1 ***Roberts***	N	N	N	N	N	Y	N	Y
2 Slattery	Y	N	Y	N	Y	Y	Y	N
3 ***Meyers***	N	N	N	N	Y	Y	?	Y
4 Glickman	Y	N	N	N	Y	Y	Y	N
5 ***Nichols***	N	Y	Y	N	N	Y	Y	Y
KENTUCKY								
1 Hubbard	Y	N	N	N	Y	Y	?	?
2 Natcher	Y	N	N	N	Y	Y	Y	N
3 Mazzoli	N	N	N	N	Y	Y	Y	N
4 ***Bunning***	N	Y	Y	N	N	Y	N	Y
5 ***Rogers***	N	N	N	Y	N	Y	N	Y
6 ***Hopkins***	N	Y	N	N	N	Y	?	?
7 Perkins	Y	N	N	N	Y	N	Y	N
LOUISIANA								
1 ***Livingston***	N	N	Y	Y	N	Y	?	Y
2 Jefferson	Y	N	N	N	Y	Y	?	N
3 Tauzin	Y	N	N	N	Y	Y	?	N
4 ***McCrery***	N	N	N	Y	Y	Y	N	Y
5 Huckaby	Y	N	N	N	Y	Y	Y	N
6 ***Baker***	N	N	Y	Y	N	Y	N	Y
7 Hayes	Y	N	N	N	Y	Y	Y	N
8 ***Holloway***	N	Y	Y	Y	N	Y	N	Y
MAINE								
1 Andrews	Y	N	N	N	Y	Y	Y	N
2 ***Snowe***	Y	N	N	N	Y	Y	Y	Y
MARYLAND								
1 ***Gilchrest***	N	Y	Y	Y	N	Y	N	Y
2 ***Bentley***	Y	N	N	N	N	Y	N	Y
3 Cardin	N	N	N	N	Y	Y	Y	N
4 McMillen	N	N	N	N	Y	Y	Y	N
5 Hoyer	Y	N	N	N	Y	Y	?	N
6 Byron	N	N	N	N	Y	Y	Y	N
7 Mfume	Y	N	N	N	Y	Y	Y	N
8 ***Morella***	Y	N	N	N	Y	Y	N	Y
MASSACHUSETTS								
1 Vacancy								
2 Neal	Y	N	N	N	Y	Y	Y	N
3 Early	Y	N	N	N	Y	Y	Y	N
4 Frank	Y	N	N	N	Y	Y	Y	N
5 Atkins	Y	N	N	N	Y	Y	Y	N
6 Mavroules	Y	N	N	N	Y	Y	?	N
7 Markey	Y	N	N	N	Y	?	Y	N
8 Kennedy	Y	N	N	N	Y	Y	Y	N
9 Moakley	Y	N	N	N	Y	Y	Y	N
10 Studds	Y	N	N	N	Y	Y	Y	N
11 Donnelly	Y	N	N	N	Y	Y	Y	N
MICHIGAN								
1 Conyers	Y	N	N	N	Y	Y	Y	N
2 ***Pursell***	Y	Y	Y	Y	N	Y	Y	Y
3 Wolpe	Y	N	N	N	Y	Y	Y	N
4 ***Upton***	Y	Y	Y	Y	Y	Y	N	Y
5 ***Henry***	Y	N	N	Y	N	Y	N	Y
6 Carr	Y	N	N	N	N	Y	Y	?
7 Kildee	Y	N	N	N	Y	Y	Y	N
8 Traxler	N	N	N	N	Y	Y	Y	N
9 ***Vander Jagt***	Y	N	Y	Y	N	?	?	Y
10 ***Camp***	N	N	Y	N	N	Y	N	Y
11 ***Davis***	Y	N	N	N	Y	Y	?	Y
12 Bonior	Y	N	N	N	Y	Y	Y	N
13 Collins	Y	N	N	N	Y	Y	Y	N
14 Hertel	Y	N	N	N	Y	Y	Y	N
15 Ford	Y	N	N	N	Y	Y	Y	N
16 Dingell	Y	N	N	N	Y	Y	?	N
17 Levin	Y	N	N	N	Y	Y	Y	N
18 ***Broomfield***	Y	Y	Y	Y	N	Y	Y	Y
MINNESOTA								
1 Penny	Y	N	Y	N	Y	Y	Y	N
2 ***Weber***	Y	Y	Y	Y	N	?	N	Y
3 ***Ramstad***	Y	N	Y	Y	N	Y	N	Y
4 Vento	Y	N	N	N	Y	Y	Y	N
5 Sabo	N	N	N	N	Y	Y	Y	N
6 Sikorski	Y	N	N	N	Y	Y	N	N
7 Peterson	?	N	N	N	Y	Y	?	N
8 Oberstar	Y	N	N	N	Y	Y	Y	N
MISSISSIPPI								
1 Whitten	N	N	N	N	Y	Y	Y	N
2 Espy	Y	N	N	N	Y	Y	Y	N
3 Montgomery	N	N	N	N	Y	Y	Y	N
4 Parker	N	N	Y	N	Y	Y	Y	N
5 Taylor	Y	Y	Y	N	N	Y	Y	N
MISSOURI								
1 Clay	Y	N	N	N	Y	Y	?	?
2 Horn	Y	N	N	N	Y	Y	Y	N
3 Gephardt	Y	?	N	N	Y	Y	Y	N
4 Skelton	N	N	N	N	Y	Y	Y	?
5 Wheat	Y	N	N	N	Y	Y	Y	N
6 ***Coleman***	Y	N	N	Y	N	Y	N	Y
7 ***Hancock***	N	Y	Y	N	N	Y	N	Y
8 ***Emerson***	N	Y	N	N	N	Y	Y	Y
9 Volkmer	Y	?	N	N	Y	Y	Y	N
MONTANA								
1 Williams	Y	N	N	N	Y	Y	Y	N
2 ***Marlenee***	?	?	?	N	N	Y	N	Y
NEBRASKA								
1 ***Bereuter***	N	N	Y	Y	N	Y	N	Y
2 Hoagland	Y	N	N	N	Y	Y	Y	N
3 ***Barrett***	N	N	N	N	N	Y	?	Y
NEVADA								
1 Bilbray	Y	N	N	N	Y	Y	Y	N
2 ***Vucanovich***	N	Y	N	Y	N	Y	N	Y
NEW HAMPSHIRE								
1 ***Zeliff***	N	N	Y	N	N	Y	N	Y
2 Swett	N	N	N	N	N	Y	Y	N
NEW JERSEY								
1 Andrews	Y	N	N	N	N	Y	?	N
2 Hughes	?	X	?	?	#	?	Y	N
3 Pallone	Y	N	N	N	N	Y	Y	N
4 ***Smith***	N	N	N	N	Y	Y	Y	Y
5 ***Roukema***	?	?	X	N	Y	Y	N	Y
6 Dwyer	Y	N	N	N	Y	Y	Y	N
7 ***Rinaldo***	N	N	N	N	Y	Y	Y	Y
8 Roe	N	N	N	N	Y	Y	Y	N
9 Torricelli	N	N	N	N	Y	Y	Y	N
10 Payne	Y	N	N	N	Y	Y	Y	N
11 ***Gallo***	N	N	Y	Y	N	Y	?	#
12 ***Zimmer***	N	Y	Y	N	N	Y	N	?
13 ***Saxton***	N	N	N	N	N	Y	N	Y
14 Guarini	Y	N	N	N	Y	Y	Y	N
NEW MEXICO								
1 ***Schiff***	N	N	N	N	N	Y	Y	Y
2 ***Skeen***	N	N	N	N	N	Y	Y	Y
3 Richardson	Y	N	N	N	Y	Y	Y	N
NEW YORK								
1 Hochbrueckner	Y	N	N	N	Y	Y	Y	N
2 Downey	Y	N	N	N	Y	Y	Y	N
3 Mrazek	Y	N	N	N	Y	Y	Y	N
4 ***Lent***	N	N	Y	Y	N	Y	Y	Y
5 ***McGrath***	Y	N	N	N	N	Y	Y	Y
6 Flake	Y	N	N	N	Y	?	Y	N
7 Ackerman	Y	N	N	N	Y	Y	Y	?
8 Scheuer	Y	N	N	N	Y	Y	Y	N
9 Manton	Y	N	N	N	Y	Y	Y	N
10 Schumer	Y	N	N	N	Y	Y	Y	N
11 Towns	?	?	?	N	Y	Y	Y	N
12 Owens	Y	N	N	N	Y	Y	Y	N
13 Solarz	Y	N	N	N	Y	?	Y	N
14 ***Molinari***	N	N	N	N	N	?	N	Y
15 ***Green***	N	N	N	N	N	Y	Y	Y
16 Rangel	Y	N	N	N	Y	Y	Y	N
17 Weiss	Y	N	N	N	Y	Y	Y	N
18 Serrano	Y	N	N	N	Y	Y	Y	N
19 Engel	Y	N	N	N	Y	Y	Y	N
20 Lowey	Y	N	N	N	Y	Y	?	N
21 ***Fish***	Y	N	N	Y	Y	Y	Y	Y
22 ***Gilman***	Y	N	N	N	Y	Y	Y	Y
23 McNulty	Y	N	N	N	Y	Y	Y	N
24 ***Solomon***	Y	Y	Y	Y	N	Y	Y	Y
25 ***Boehlert***	Y	N	N	N	Y	Y	N	Y
26 ***Martin***	Y	N	Y	N	N	?	Y	Y
27 ***Walsh***	Y	N	Y	Y	N	Y	Y	Y
28 McHugh	Y	N	N	N	Y	Y	Y	N
29 ***Horton***	Y	N	N	N	Y	Y	Y	Y
30 Slaughter	Y	N	N	N	Y	Y	Y	N
31 ***Paxon***	N	N	N	N	N	Y	N	Y
32 LaFalce	Y	N	N	N	Y	Y	Y	N
33 Nowak	N	N	N	N	Y	Y	Y	N
34 ***Houghton***	N	Y	Y	Y	N	Y	Y	Y
NORTH CAROLINA								
1 Jones	Y	N	N	N	Y	Y	Y	N
2 Valentine	N	N	Y	N	Y	Y	Y	N
3 Lancaster	Y	N	N	N	Y	Y	Y	N
4 Price	Y	N	N	N	Y	Y	Y	N
5 Neal	Y	N	N	N	Y	Y	Y	N
6 ***Coble***	N	Y	Y	Y	N	Y	N	Y
7 Rose	Y	?	N	N	Y	Y	Y	N
8 Hefner	Y	N	N	N	Y	Y	Y	N
9 ***McMillan***	N	N	Y	Y	N	Y	N	Y
10 ***Ballenger***	N	Y	Y	N	N	Y	N	Y
11 ***Taylor***	Y	Y	Y	Y	N	Y	N	Y
NORTH DAKOTA								
AL Dorgan	Y	N	N	N	N	Y	Y	N
OHIO								
1 Luken	Y	N	N	N	Y	Y	Y	N
2 ***Gradison***	N	N	N	Y	N	Y	Y	Y
3 Hall	Y	N	N	N	Y	?	Y	N
4 ***Oxley***	N	Y	Y	Y	N	Y	N	Y
5 ***Gillmor***	N	N	Y	Y	N	Y	Y	Y
6 ***McEwen***	N	Y	Y	Y	N	Y	Y	Y
7 ***Hobson***	N	N	Y	Y	N	Y	Y	Y
8 ***Boehner***	N	N	Y	N	N	Y	N	Y
9 Kaptur	Y	N	N	N	Y	Y	Y	N
10 ***Miller***	N	Y	Y	Y	N	?	N	Y
11 Eckart	Y	N	N	N	Y	Y	Y	N
12 ***Kasich***	N	N	Y	Y	N	Y	Y	Y
13 Pease	N	N	N	N	Y	Y	Y	N
14 Sawyer	Y	N	N	N	Y	Y	Y	N
15 ***Wylie***	N	N	Y	Y	Y	Y	Y	Y
16 ***Regula***	N	N	N	Y	Y	Y	N	Y
17 Traficant	Y	N	N	N	Y	Y	Y	N
18 Applegate	N	N	N	N	N	Y	Y	N
19 Feighan	Y	N	N	N	Y	Y	Y	N
20 Oakar	Y	N	N	N	Y	Y	Y	N
21 Stokes	Y	N	N	N	Y	Y	?	?
OKLAHOMA								
1 ***Inhofe***	N	Y	Y	N	N	Y	N	Y
2 Synar	Y	N	N	N	Y	Y	Y	N
3 Brewster	Y	N	N	N	Y	Y	Y	N
4 McCurdy	Y	N	N	N	Y	Y	?	N
5 ***Edwards***	Y	Y	Y	Y	N	Y	N	Y
6 English	N	N	N	N	N	Y	Y	N
OREGON								
1 AuCoin	Y	N	N	N	Y	Y	?	N
2 ***Smith***	N	N	N	N	N	Y	N	Y
3 Wyden	Y	N	N	N	Y	Y	Y	N
4 DeFazio	Y	N	N	N	Y	N	Y	N
5 Kopetski	Y	-	N	N	Y	Y	Y	N
PENNSYLVANIA								
1 Foglietta	Y	N	N	N	Y	Y	Y	N
2 Gray	Y	N	?	N	Y	Y	Y	?
3 Borski	Y	N	N	N	Y	Y	Y	N
4 Kolter	N	N	N	N	Y	Y	Y	N
5 ***Schulze***	N	Y	Y	Y	N	Y	Y	Y
6 Yatron	Y	N	N	N	Y	Y	Y	N
7 ***Weldon***	Y	N	Y	N	N	Y	?	Y
8 Kostmayer	#	-	-	N	Y	Y	Y	N
9 ***Shuster***	N	Y	Y	Y	N	Y	Y	Y
10 ***McDade***	Y	N	N	Y	N	?	N	Y
11 Kanjorski	Y	N	N	N	Y	Y	Y	N
12 Murtha	Y	N	N	N	Y	Y	Y	N
13 ***Coughlin***	Y	N	N	Y	N	Y	N	Y
14 Coyne	Y	N	N	N	Y	Y	Y	N
15 ***Ritter***	N	Y	Y	Y	N	Y	Y	Y
16 ***Walker***	N	Y	Y	Y	N	Y	N	Y
17 ***Gekas***	N	Y	Y	Y	N	Y	N	Y
18 ***Santorum***	N	N	Y	N	N	Y	N	Y
19 ***Goodling***	Y	N	N	N	N	Y	N	Y
20 Gaydos	Y	N	N	N	Y	Y	Y	N
21 ***Ridge***	N	N	Y	Y	N	Y	N	Y
22 Murphy	Y	N	N	N	Y	?	N	N
23 ***Clinger***	N	N	N	Y	N	Y	Y	Y
RHODE ISLAND								
1 ***Machtley***	Y	N	N	N	N	Y	?	Y
2 Reed	Y	N	N	N	Y	Y	Y	N
SOUTH CAROLINA								
1 ***Ravenel***	N	Y	Y	N	N	Y	Y	Y
2 ***Spence***	N	Y	Y	Y	N	Y	Y	Y
3 Derrick	Y	N	N	N	Y	Y	Y	N
4 Patterson	N	N	N	N	Y	Y	Y	N
5 Spratt	Y	N	N	N	Y	Y	Y	N
6 Tallon	N	N	N	N	Y	Y	Y	N
SOUTH DAKOTA								
AL Johnson	Y	N	N	N	Y	Y	Y	N
TENNESSEE								
1 ***Quillen***	N	Y	Y	Y	N	Y	Y	Y
2 ***Duncan***	Y	Y	Y	N	N	Y	N	Y
3 Lloyd	Y	N	N	N	Y	Y	Y	N
4 Cooper	Y	N	Y	N	Y	Y	Y	N
5 Clement	Y	N	N	N	Y	Y	Y	N
6 Gordon	Y	N	N	N	Y	Y	Y	N
7 ***Sundquist***	N	N	Y	Y	N	Y	N	Y
8 Tanner	N	N	N	N	Y	Y	Y	N
9 Ford	Y	N	N	N	Y	?	Y	N
TEXAS								
1 Chapman	Y	N	N	N	N	Y	Y	N
2 Wilson	Y	N	N	N	Y	Y	?	N
3 Vacancy								
4 Hall	Y	N	N	N	N	Y	Y	Y
5 Bryant	?	?	?	N	Y	?	Y	N
6 ***Barton***	N	N	N	Y	N	Y	Y	Y
7 ***Archer***	N	N	Y	Y	N	Y	Y	Y
8 ***Fields***	N	Y	Y	N	N	Y	N	Y
9 Brooks	Y	N	N	N	Y	Y	Y	?
10 Pickle	Y	N	N	N	Y	Y	Y	N
11 Edwards	Y	N	N	N	Y	Y	Y	N
12 Geren	Y	N	N	N	Y	Y	Y	N
13 Sarpalius	N	N	N	N	N	Y	Y	N
14 Laughlin	N	N	N	N	Y	Y	Y	N
15 de la Garza	Y	N	N	N	Y	Y	Y	N
16 Coleman	Y	N	N	N	Y	Y	Y	N
17 Stenholm	N	N	N	N	Y	Y	Y	N
18 Washington	Y	N	N	N	Y	Y	?	?
19 ***Combest***	N	Y	N	N	N	Y	Y	Y
20 Gonzalez	Y	N	N	N	Y	N	Y	N
21 ***Smith***	N	N	N	Y	N	Y	N	Y
22 ***DeLay***	N	Y	Y	N	N	Y	N	Y
23 Bustamante	Y	N	N	N	Y	Y	Y	N
24 Frost	Y	N	N	N	Y	Y	Y	N
25 Andrews	Y	N	N	N	Y	Y	Y	N
26 ***Armey***	N	Y	Y	Y	N	Y	N	Y
27 Ortiz	Y	N	N	N	Y	Y	Y	N
UTAH								
1 ***Hansen***	N	Y	Y	N	N	Y	Y	Y
2 Owens	Y	N	N	N	N	Y	Y	N
3 Orton	N	N	N	N	N	Y	P	N
VERMONT								
AL *Sanders*	Y	N	N	N	N	Y	Y	N
VIRGINIA								
1 ***Bateman***	N	N	Y	Y	N	Y	Y	Y
2 Pickett	Y	N	N	N	Y	Y	Y	N
3 ***Bliley***	N	Y	Y	Y	N	Y	N	Y
4 Sisisky	Y	N	N	N	Y	Y	Y	N
5 Payne	Y	N	N	N	Y	Y	Y	N
6 Olin	Y	N	N	N	Y	Y	Y	N
7 ***Slaughter***	N	Y	N	Y	N	Y	N	Y
8 Moran	Y	N	N	N	Y	Y	Y	N
9 Boucher	Y	N	N	N	Y	Y	Y	N
10 ***Wolf***	N	N	N	Y	N	Y	N	Y
WASHINGTON								
1 ***Miller***	N	N	Y	Y	N	Y	N	Y
2 Swift	Y	N	N	N	Y	Y	Y	N
3 Unsoeld	Y	N	N	N	Y	Y	Y	N
4 ***Morrison***	N	N	N	N	Y	Y	Y	Y
5 Foley								
6 Dicks	Y	N	N	N	Y	Y	Y	N
7 McDermott	Y	N	N	N	Y	+	Y	N
8 ***Chandler***	N	N	N	Y	N	Y	N	Y
WEST VIRGINIA								
1 Mollohan	Y	N	N	N	Y	Y	Y	N
2 Staggers	Y	N	N	N	Y	Y	Y	N
3 Wise	Y	N	N	N	Y	Y	Y	N
4 Rahall	Y	N	N	N	Y	Y	Y	N
WISCONSIN								
1 Aspin	Y	?	?	N	Y	?	?	N
2 ***Klug***	Y	N	Y	Y	N	Y	Y	Y
3 ***Gunderson***	Y	N	Y	Y	Y	Y	Y	Y
4 Kleczka	Y	N	N	N	Y	Y	Y	N
5 Moody	Y	N	Y	N	Y	N	Y	N
6 ***Petri***	Y	Y	Y	Y	N	Y	Y	Y
7 Obey	Y	N	N	N	Y	Y	Y	N
8 ***Roth***	N	Y	N	Y	N	Y	Y	Y
9 ***Sensenbrenner***	N	Y	Y	N	N	Y	N	Y
WYOMING								
AL ***Thomas***	N	Y	Y	Y	N	Y	Y	Y

Southern states - Ala., Ark., Fla., Ga., Ky., La., Miss., N.C., Okla., S.C., Tenn., Texas, Va.
Omitted votes are quorum calls, which CQ does not include in its vote charts.

HOUSE VOTES 75, 76, 77, 78, 79, 81, 82, 83

75. HR 1236. National Flood Insurance/Passage. Passage of the bill to increase financial penalties against banks that do not require mortgage loan applicants to buy flood insurance for property in designated flood areas; to establish a flood mitigation program to reduce the risks of flooding and erosion hazards by providing flood mitigation grants; to establish a community rating system by which insurance premiums may be reduced to encourage communities to go beyond current flood plain management measures; and to establish a program to reduce coastal erosion hazards. Passed 388-18: R 139-18; D 248-0 (ND 169-0, SD 79-0); I 1-0, May 1, 1991.

76. HR 1988. Fiscal 1992-94 NASA Authorization/Passage. Passage of the bill to authorize $14.9 billion in fiscal 1992, $10.8 billion in fiscal 1993 and $11 billion in fiscal 1994 for the programs of the National Aeronautics and Space Administration (NASA), bringing authorizations for NASA to $15.3 billion in fiscal 1992, $16.6 billion in fiscal 1993 and $17.2 billion in fiscal 1994. Passed 361-36: R 143-6; D 217-30 (ND 139-28, SD 78-2); I 1-0, May 2, 1991.

77. Procedural Motion. Russo, D-Ill., motion to approve the House Journal of Tuesday, May 7. Motion agreed to 295-103: R 60-99; D 235-4 (ND 156-4, SD 79-0); I 0-0, May 8, 1991.

78. HR 479. National Historic Trails/Passage. Vento, D-Minn., motion to suspend the rules and pass the bill to designate the 5,700 mile California National Historic Trail and the 1,900 mile Pony Express National Historic Trail as parts of the National Trails System. Motion agreed to 409-0: R 156-0; D 252-0 (ND 171-0, SD 81-0); I 1-0, May 8, 1991. A two-thirds majority of those present and voting (273 in this case) is required for passage under suspension of the rules.

79. HR 7. Handgun Waiting Period/Rule. Adoption of the rule (H Res 144) to provide for House floor consideration of the bill to require a seven-day waiting period for handgun purchases. Adopted 405-16: R 152-11; D 252-5 (ND 170-4, SD 82-1); I 1-0, May 8, 1991.

81. HR 7. Handgun Waiting Period/Dealer Hot Line. Staggers, D-W.Va., substitute amendment to require the Justice Department to establish a national hot line that licensed dealers must use to determine whether the prospective buyer is prohibited by law from buying a handgun. If the hot line is unable to provide an immediate response, the purchase could be completed after 24 hours. Rejected 193-234: R 107-56; D 85-178 (ND 38-141, SD 47-37); I 1-0, May 8, 1991.

82. HR 7. Handgun Waiting Period/Recommittal Motion. McCollum, R-Fla., motion to recommit to the House Judiciary Committee the bill to require a seven-day waiting period for handgun purchases, with instruction not to report the bill back until it has conducted a thorough study in the context of the nation's crime problem and the president's message on violent crime of March 12, 1991. Motion rejected 162-265: R 115-48; D 46-217 (ND 19-160, SD 27-57); I 1-0, May 8, 1991.

83. HR 7. Handgun Waiting Period/Passage. Passage of the bill to require a seven-day waiting period for handgun purchases, allowing local law enforcement authorities to check the background of prospective buyers to determine whether they have a criminal record. The waiting period requirement would end when a national computer system for instant checks began. Passed 239-186: R 60-102; D 179-83 (ND 138-41, SD 41-42); I 0-1, May 8, 1991.

[1] *Rep. Morris K. Udall, D-Ariz., resigned May 4, 1991, because of health problems. The last vote he was eligible for was 76.*

KEY

Y Voted for (yea).
\# Paired for.
\+ Announced for.
N Voted against (nay).
X Paired against.
\- Announced against.
P Voted "present."
C Voted "present" to avoid possible conflict of interest.
? Did not vote or otherwise make a position known.

Democrats ***Republicans***
Independent

	75	76	77	78	79	81	82	83
ALABAMA								
1 ***Callahan***	Y	Y	Y	Y	Y	Y	Y	N
2 ***Dickinson***	Y	Y	N	Y	Y	Y	Y	N
3 Browder	Y	Y	Y	Y	Y	Y	Y	N
4 Bevill	?	Y	Y	Y	Y	Y	Y	N
5 Cramer	Y	Y	Y	Y	Y	Y	Y	N
6 Erdreich	Y	Y	Y	Y	Y	Y	Y	N
7 Harris	Y	Y	Y	Y	Y	Y	Y	N
ALASKA								
AL ***Young***	Y	Y	N	Y	Y	Y	Y	N
ARIZONA								
1 ***Rhodes***	?	Y	N	Y	Y	Y	Y	N
2 Udall [1]	?	?						
3 ***Stump***	N	N	N	Y	Y	Y	Y	N
4 ***Kyl***	Y	Y	N	Y	Y	Y	Y	N
5 ***Kolbe***	Y	Y	N	Y	Y	Y	Y	N
ARKANSAS								
1 Alexander	Y	Y	Y	?	Y	Y	N	N
2 Thornton	Y	Y	Y	Y	Y	Y	N	N
3 ***Hammerschmidt***	Y	Y	Y	Y	Y	Y	Y	N
4 Anthony	Y	Y	Y	Y	Y	N	N	Y
CALIFORNIA								
1 ***Riggs***	Y	Y	N	Y	Y	N	Y	Y
2 ***Herger***	Y	Y	N	Y	Y	Y	Y	N
3 Matsui	Y	Y	Y	Y	Y	N	N	Y
4 Fazio	Y	Y	Y	Y	Y	N	N	Y
5 Pelosi	Y	Y	Y	Y	Y	N	N	Y
6 Boxer	Y	X	Y	Y	Y	N	N	Y
7 Miller	?	N	Y	Y	Y	N	N	Y
8 Dellums	Y	N	?	Y	Y	N	N	Y
9 Stark	Y	?	Y	Y	Y	N	N	Y
10 Edwards	Y	Y	Y	Y	Y	N	N	Y
11 Lantos	Y	Y	Y	Y	Y	N	N	Y
12 ***Campbell***	Y	Y	N	Y	Y	N	N	Y
13 Mineta	Y	Y	Y	Y	Y	N	N	Y
14 ***Doolittle***	Y	Y	N	Y	Y	Y	Y	N
15 Condit	Y	Y	Y	Y	?	Y	N	N
16 Panetta	Y	?	Y	Y	Y	N	N	Y
17 Dooley	Y	Y	Y	Y	?	N	N	Y
18 Lehman	Y	Y	Y	?	Y	N	N	Y
19 ***Lagomarsino***	Y	Y	N	Y	Y	Y	Y	Y
20 ***Thomas***	N	Y	N	Y	Y	Y	Y	Y
21 ***Gallegly***	Y	Y	N	Y	N	Y	Y	Y
22 ***Moorhead***	?	Y	N	Y	Y	Y	Y	N
23 Beilenson	Y	N	Y	Y	Y	N	N	Y
24 Waxman	Y	Y	Y	Y	Y	N	N	Y
25 Roybal	Y	?	?	?	?	?	?	?
26 Berman	Y	Y	Y	Y	Y	N	N	Y
27 Levine	Y	?	Y	Y	Y	N	N	Y
28 Dixon	Y	Y	?	Y	Y	N	N	Y
29 Waters	Y	?	Y	Y	Y	N	N	Y
30 Martinez	Y	Y	Y	Y	Y	N	N	Y
31 Dymally	?	?	Y	Y	Y	N	N	Y
32 Anderson	Y	Y	Y	Y	Y	N	N	Y
33 ***Dreier***	Y	Y	?	Y	Y	Y	Y	N
34 Torres	Y	Y	Y	Y	Y	N	N	Y
35 ***Lewis***	Y	Y	N	Y	Y	Y	Y	N
36 Brown	Y	Y	?	Y	Y	N	N	Y
37 ***McCandless***	Y	Y	N	Y	Y	Y	Y	N
38 ***Dornan***	?	Y	Y	Y	N	Y	Y	Y
39 ***Dannemeyer***	N	Y	N	Y	N	Y	Y	N
40 ***Cox***	Y	Y	N	Y	N	N	Y	N
41 ***Lowery***	Y	Y	N	Y	Y	Y	Y	Y
42 ***Rohrabacher***	Y	Y	N	Y	N	Y	Y	N
43 ***Packard***	Y	Y	N	Y	Y	Y	Y	Y
44 ***Cunningham***	Y	Y	N	Y	Y	Y	Y	N
45 ***Hunter***	N	Y	N	Y	Y	Y	Y	N
COLORADO								
1 Schroeder	Y	Y	N	Y	Y	N	N	Y
2 Skaggs	Y	Y	Y	Y	Y	N	N	Y
3 Campbell	Y	Y	Y	Y	Y	Y	Y	N
4 ***Allard***	Y	Y	N	Y	Y	Y	Y	N
5 ***Hefley***	Y	Y	N	Y	Y	Y	Y	N
6 ***Schaefer***	Y	Y	N	Y	Y	Y	Y	N
CONNECTICUT								
1 Kennelly	Y	Y	?	Y	Y	N	N	Y
2 Gejdenson	Y	Y	Y	Y	Y	N	N	Y
3 DeLauro	Y	Y	Y	Y	Y	N	N	Y
4 ***Shays***	Y	Y	N	Y	Y	N	N	Y
5 ***Franks***	Y	Y	N	Y	Y	Y	Y	N
6 ***Johnson***	Y	Y	Y	Y	Y	N	Y	Y
DELAWARE								
AL Carper	Y	Y	Y	Y	Y	N	Y	Y
FLORIDA								
1 Hutto	Y	Y	Y	Y	Y	Y	Y	Y
2 Peterson	Y	Y	Y	Y	Y	N	N	N
3 Bennett	Y	Y	Y	Y	Y	N	N	Y
4 ***James***	Y	Y	N	Y	Y	N	N	Y
5 ***McCollum***	?	Y	Y	Y	Y	Y	Y	N
6 ***Stearns***	Y	Y	N	Y	Y	Y	Y	Y
7 Gibbons	Y	Y	Y	Y	Y	N	N	Y
8 ***Young***	Y	Y	Y	Y	Y	N	N	Y
9 ***Bilirakis***	Y	Y	N	Y	Y	N	Y	Y
10 ***Ireland***	Y	?	N	Y	Y	Y	Y	N
11 Bacchus	Y	Y	Y	Y	Y	N	N	Y
12 ***Lewis***	Y	Y	N	Y	Y	Y	Y	N
13 ***Goss***	Y	Y	N	Y	Y	N	N	Y
14 Johnston	Y	N	Y	Y	Y	N	N	Y
15 ***Shaw***	Y	?	Y	Y	Y	Y	Y	N
16 Smith	?	Y	Y	Y	Y	N	N	Y
17 Lehman	?	#	?	?	?	?	?	?
18 ***Ros-Lehtinen***	Y	Y	?	?	Y	N	N	Y
19 Fascell	Y	Y	Y	Y	Y	N	N	Y
GEORGIA								
1 Thomas	Y	Y	Y	Y	Y	Y	N	N
2 Hatcher	Y	Y	Y	Y	Y	N	N	Y
3 Ray	Y	Y	?	Y	Y	N	N	N
4 Jones	Y	Y	Y	Y	Y	N	N	Y
5 Lewis	Y	Y	Y	Y	Y	N	N	Y
6 ***Gingrich***	Y	?	N	?	Y	Y	Y	N
7 Darden	Y	Y	Y	Y	Y	N	N	Y
8 Rowland	Y	Y	Y	Y	Y	Y	N	Y
9 Jenkins	Y	Y	Y	Y	Y	Y	N	N
10 Barnard	Y	Y	Y	Y	Y	N	N	N
HAWAII								
1 Abercrombie	Y	Y	Y	Y	Y	N	N	Y
2 Mink	Y	Y	Y	Y	Y	N	N	Y
IDAHO								
1 LaRocco	Y	Y	Y	Y	Y	Y	N	N
2 Stallings	Y	Y	?	Y	Y	Y	Y	N
ILLINOIS								
1 Hayes	Y	N	Y	Y	Y	N	N	Y
2 Savage	?	N	Y	Y	Y	N	N	Y
3 Russo	Y	N	Y	Y	Y	N	N	Y
4 Sangmeister	Y	Y	Y	Y	Y	N	N	Y
5 Lipinski	Y	Y	Y	Y	Y	N	N	Y
6 ***Hyde***	Y	Y	N	Y	Y	N	N	Y
7 Collins	Y	Y	Y	Y	Y	N	N	Y
8 Rostenkowski	Y	Y	Y	Y	Y	N	N	Y
9 Yates	Y	N	Y	Y	Y	N	N	Y
10 ***Porter***	N	Y	Y	Y	Y	N	N	Y
11 Annunzio	Y	Y	Y	Y	Y	N	N	Y
12 ***Crane***	N	Y	N	Y	N	Y	Y	N
13 ***Fawell***	Y	Y	N	Y	Y	N	N	Y
14 ***Hastert***	Y	Y	N	Y	Y	Y	Y	N
15 Vacancy								
16 Cox	Y	Y	Y	Y	Y	N	N	Y
17 Evans	Y	Y	?	Y	Y	N	N	Y
18 ***Michel***	Y	?	N	Y	Y	Y	Y	?
19 Bruce	Y	Y	Y	Y	Y	Y	Y	N
20 Durbin	Y	N	Y	Y	Y	N	N	Y
21 Costello	Y	Y	Y	Y	Y	Y	Y	N
22 Poshard	Y	Y	Y	Y	Y	Y	Y	N
INDIANA								
1 Visclosky	Y	N	Y	Y	Y	N	N	Y
2 Sharp	Y	Y	Y	Y	Y	N	N	Y
3 Roemer	Y	N	Y	Y	Y	N	N	Y

ND Northern Democrats SD Southern Democrats

	75	76	77	78	79	81	82	83
4 Long	Y	Y	Y	Y	Y	Y	N	N
5 Jontz	Y	Y	Y	Y	Y	Y	Y	N
6 ***Burton***	N	Y	N	Y	Y	Y	Y	N
7 ***Myers***	Y	?	Y	Y	Y	Y	Y	N
8 McCloskey	Y	Y	Y	Y	Y	N	N	Y
9 Hamilton	Y	Y	Y	Y	Y	N	N	Y
10 Jacobs	Y	N	N	Y	Y	N	N	Y
IOWA								
1 ***Leach***	Y	Y	N	Y	Y	N	N	Y
2 ***Nussle***	Y	N	N	Y	Y	N	Y	N
3 Nagle	Y	Y	Y	Y	Y	Y	N	N
4 Smith	Y	Y	Y	Y	Y	N	N	N
5 ***Lightfoot***	Y	Y	N	Y	Y	Y	Y	N
6 ***Grandy***	Y	Y	N	Y	Y	N	Y	N
KANSAS								
1 ***Roberts***	Y	Y	N	Y	Y	Y	Y	N
2 Slattery	Y	Y	?	+	-	Y	N	N
3 ***Meyers***	Y	Y	N	Y	Y	N	N	Y
4 Glickman	Y	Y	Y	Y	Y	N	N	Y
5 ***Nichols***	Y	Y	Y	Y	Y	Y	Y	N
KENTUCKY								
1 Hubbard	?	?	Y	Y	N	Y	Y	Y
2 Natcher	Y	Y	Y	Y	Y	Y	N	N
3 Mazzoli	Y	+	Y	Y	Y	N	N	Y
4 ***Bunning***	Y	Y	N	Y	Y	Y	Y	N
5 ***Rogers***	Y	Y	N	Y	Y	Y	Y	N
6 ***Hopkins***	?	?	N	Y	Y	Y	Y	N
7 Perkins	Y	Y	Y	Y	Y	Y	Y	N
LOUISIANA								
1 ***Livingston***	Y	Y	Y	Y	Y	Y	Y	N
2 Jefferson	Y	Y	Y	Y	Y	N	N	Y
3 Tauzin	Y	Y	Y	Y	Y	Y	Y	N
4 ***McCrery***	Y	Y	Y	Y	Y	Y	Y	N
5 Huckaby	Y	Y	Y	Y	Y	Y	Y	N
6 ***Baker***	Y	Y	?	?	Y	Y	Y	N
7 Hayes	Y	Y	Y	Y	Y	Y	Y	N
8 ***Holloway***	Y	?	N	Y	Y	Y	Y	N
MAINE								
1 Andrews	?	N	Y	Y	Y	N	N	Y
2 ***Snowe***	Y	Y	Y	Y	Y	Y	Y	N
MARYLAND								
1 ***Gilchrest***	Y	Y	N	Y	Y	N	N	Y
2 ***Bentley***	Y	Y	N	Y	Y	N	N	Y
3 Cardin	Y	Y	Y	Y	N	N	N	Y
4 McMillen	Y	Y	Y	Y	Y	N	N	Y
5 Hoyer	Y	Y	Y	Y	Y	N	N	Y
6 Byron	Y	Y	Y	Y	Y	Y	Y	N
7 Mfume	Y	Y	Y	Y	Y	N	N	Y
8 ***Morella***	Y	Y	Y	Y	Y	N	N	Y
MASSACHUSETTS								
1 Vacancy								
2 Neal	Y	N	Y	Y	Y	N	N	Y
3 Early	Y	Y	Y	Y	Y	N	N	Y
4 Frank	Y	N	Y	Y	Y	N	N	Y
5 Atkins	Y	Y	Y	Y	Y	N	N	Y
6 Mavroules	Y	Y	Y	Y	Y	N	N	Y
7 Markey	Y	Y	Y	Y	Y	N	N	Y
8 Kennedy	Y	Y	Y	Y	Y	N	N	Y
9 Moakley	Y	Y	Y	Y	Y	N	N	Y
10 Studds	Y	N	Y	Y	Y	N	N	Y
11 Donnelly	Y	N	Y	Y	Y	N	N	Y
MICHIGAN								
1 Conyers	Y	N	Y	Y	Y	N	N	Y
2 ***Pursell***	Y	Y	Y	Y	Y	N	N	Y
3 Wolpe	Y	Y	Y	Y	Y	N	N	Y
4 ***Upton***	Y	Y	N	Y	N	N	N	Y
5 ***Henry***	Y	Y	N	Y	Y	N	N	Y
6 Carr	?	Y	Y	Y	Y	Y	N	N
7 Kildee	Y	Y	Y	Y	Y	N	N	Y
8 Traxler	Y	Y	Y	Y	Y	Y	N	N
9 ***Vander Jagt***	Y	Y	Y	Y	Y	Y	Y	N
10 ***Camp***	Y	Y	N	Y	Y	Y	Y	N
11 ***Davis***	Y	Y	Y	Y	Y	Y	Y	N
12 Bonior	Y	Y	Y	Y	Y	N	N	Y
13 Collins	Y	Y	Y	Y	N	N	N	Y
14 Hertel	Y	N	Y	Y	Y	N	N	Y
15 Ford	Y	Y	?	?	Y	N	N	Y
16 Dingell	Y	Y	Y	Y	Y	Y	N	N
17 Levin	Y	Y	Y	Y	Y	N	N	Y
18 ***Broomfield***	Y	Y	Y	Y	Y	N	N	Y
MINNESOTA								
1 Penny	Y	N	Y	Y	Y	N	N	N
2 ***Weber***	Y	Y	N	Y	Y	Y	Y	N
3 ***Ramstad***	Y	Y	N	Y	Y	Y	Y	N
4 Vento	Y	Y	Y	Y	Y	N	N	Y

	75	76	77	78	79	81	82	83
5 Sabo	Y	Y	Y	Y	Y	N	N	Y
6 Sikorski	Y	N	N	Y	Y	N	N	Y
7 Peterson	Y	Y	Y	Y	Y	Y	Y	N
8 Oberstar	Y	?	Y	Y	Y	Y	Y	N
MISSISSIPPI								
1 Whitten	Y	Y	Y	Y	Y	Y	Y	?
2 Espy	Y	Y	Y	Y	Y	Y	Y	N
3 Montgomery	Y	Y	Y	Y	Y	Y	Y	N
4 Parker	Y	Y	Y	Y	Y	Y	Y	N
5 Taylor	Y	Y	Y	Y	Y	Y	Y	N
MISSOURI								
1 Clay	?	?	?	Y	Y	N	N	Y
2 Horn	Y	Y	Y	Y	Y	N	N	Y
3 Gephardt	?	Y	?	Y	Y	N	N	Y
4 Skelton	?	Y	Y	Y	Y	Y	N	N
5 Wheat	Y	Y	Y	Y	Y	N	N	Y
6 ***Coleman***	Y	?	Y	Y	Y	N	N	Y
7 ***Hancock***	N	N	N	Y	N	Y	Y	N
8 ***Emerson***	Y	Y	Y	Y	Y	Y	Y	N
9 Volkmer	Y	Y	Y	Y	Y	Y	N	N
MONTANA								
1 Williams	Y	N	?	Y	N	Y	N	N
2 ***Marlenee***	Y	Y	N	Y	Y	Y	Y	N
NEBRASKA								
1 ***Bereuter***	Y	Y	N	Y	Y	Y	Y	N
2 Hoagland	Y	Y	Y	Y	Y	N	N	Y
3 ***Barrett***	Y	Y	N	Y	Y	Y	Y	N
NEVADA								
1 Bilbray	Y	Y	Y	Y	Y	Y	N	N
2 ***Vucanovich***	N	?	N	Y	Y	Y	Y	N
NEW HAMPSHIRE								
1 ***Zeliff***	N	Y	Y	Y	Y	Y	Y	N
2 Swett	Y	Y	Y	Y	Y	Y	Y	Y
NEW JERSEY								
1 Andrews	Y	Y	Y	Y	Y	N	N	Y
2 Hughes	Y	Y	Y	Y	Y	N	N	Y
3 Pallone	Y	Y	Y	Y	Y	N	N	Y
4 ***Smith***	Y	Y	Y	Y	Y	N	N	Y
5 ***Roukema***	Y	N	N	Y	Y	N	N	Y
6 Dwyer	Y	Y	Y	Y	Y	N	N	Y
7 ***Rinaldo***	Y	Y	Y	Y	Y	N	N	Y
8 Roe	Y	Y	Y	Y	Y	N	N	Y
9 Torricelli	Y	Y	Y	Y	Y	N	N	Y
10 Payne	Y	N	Y	Y	Y	N	N	Y
11 ***Gallo***	?	?	Y	Y	Y	N	N	Y
12 ***Zimmer***	?	Y	N	Y	Y	Y	Y	N
13 ***Saxton***	Y	Y	N	Y	Y	N	N	Y
14 Guarini	Y	Y	Y	Y	Y	N	N	Y
NEW MEXICO								
1 ***Schiff***	Y	Y	Y	Y	Y	N	Y	N
2 ***Skeen***	Y	Y	Y	Y	Y	Y	Y	N
3 Richardson	Y	Y	Y	Y	Y	Y	N	N
NEW YORK								
1 Hochbrueckner	Y	Y	Y	Y	Y	N	N	Y
2 Downey	Y	Y	Y	Y	Y	N	N	Y
3 Mrazek	Y	Y	Y	Y	Y	N	N	Y
4 ***Lent***	Y	Y	Y	Y	Y	N	N	Y
5 ***McGrath***	Y	Y	Y	Y	Y	N	N	Y
6 Flake	Y	Y	Y	Y	Y	N	N	Y
7 Ackerman	?	?	Y	Y	Y	N	N	Y
8 Scheuer	Y	Y	?	Y	Y	N	N	Y
9 Manton	Y	Y	Y	Y	Y	N	N	Y
10 Schumer	Y	Y	Y	Y	Y	N	N	Y
11 Towns	Y	Y	?	Y	Y	N	N	Y
12 Owens	Y	N	Y	Y	Y	N	N	Y
13 Solarz	Y	Y	Y	?	Y	N	N	Y
14 ***Molinari***	Y	Y	N	Y	Y	N	N	Y
15 ***Green***	Y	Y	Y	Y	Y	N	N	Y
16 Rangel	Y	Y	?	?	Y	N	N	Y
17 Weiss	Y	N	Y	Y	Y	N	N	Y
18 Serrano	Y	Y	Y	Y	Y	N	N	Y
19 Engel	Y	Y	Y	?	?	N	N	Y
20 Lowey	Y	Y	Y	Y	Y	N	N	Y
21 ***Fish***	Y	Y	Y	Y	Y	N	N	Y
22 ***Gilman***	Y	Y	Y	Y	Y	N	N	Y
23 McNulty	Y	Y	Y	Y	Y	N	N	Y
24 ***Solomon***	Y	Y	Y	Y	Y	Y	Y	N
25 ***Boehlert***	Y	Y	N	Y	Y	N	N	Y
26 ***Martin***	Y	Y	?	?	?	?	?	?
27 ***Walsh***	Y	Y	Y	Y	Y	N	N	Y
28 McHugh	Y	Y	Y	Y	Y	N	N	Y
29 ***Horton***	Y	Y	Y	Y	Y	Y	Y	N
30 Slaughter	Y	Y	Y	Y	Y	N	N	Y
31 ***Paxon***	Y	Y	N	Y	Y	Y	Y	N

	75	76	77	78	79	81	82	83
32 LaFalce	Y	Y	Y	Y	Y	N	N	Y
33 Nowak	Y	Y	Y	Y	Y	N	N	Y
34 ***Houghton***	Y	?	Y	Y	Y	Y	Y	N
NORTH CAROLINA								
1 Jones	Y	Y	Y	Y	Y	Y	N	Y
2 Valentine	Y	Y	?	Y	Y	N	N	Y
3 Lancaster	Y	Y	Y	Y	Y	Y	N	Y
4 Price	Y	Y	Y	Y	Y	N	N	Y
5 Neal	Y	N	?	?	Y	Y	N	Y
6 ***Coble***	Y	Y	N	Y	Y	Y	Y	N
7 Rose	Y	?	Y	Y	Y	N	N	Y
8 Hefner	Y	Y	Y	Y	Y	Y	N	Y
9 ***McMillan***	Y	Y	Y	Y	Y	N	N	Y
10 ***Ballenger***	Y	Y	N	Y	Y	Y	Y	N
11 ***Taylor***	N	Y	N	Y	Y	Y	Y	N
NORTH DAKOTA								
AL Dorgan	Y	Y	Y	Y	Y	Y	N	N
OHIO								
1 Luken	Y	N	Y	Y	Y	N	N	Y
2 ***Gradison***	Y	Y	Y	Y	Y	N	N	Y
3 Hall	Y	Y	Y	Y	Y	N	N	Y
4 ***Oxley***	Y	?	Y	Y	Y	N	N	Y
5 ***Gillmor***	Y	Y	Y	Y	Y	Y	Y	N
6 ***McEwen***	Y	Y	Y	Y	Y	Y	Y	N
7 ***Hobson***	Y	Y	N	Y	Y	Y	Y	N
8 ***Boehner***	Y	Y	N	Y	Y	Y	Y	N
9 Kaptur	Y	Y	Y	Y	Y	N	N	Y
10 ***Miller***	Y	?	N	Y	Y	Y	Y	N
11 Eckart	Y	Y	Y	Y	Y	N	N	Y
12 ***Kasich***	Y	Y	Y	Y	Y	Y	Y	N
13 Pease	Y	Y	Y	Y	Y	N	N	Y
14 Sawyer	Y	Y	Y	Y	Y	N	N	Y
15 ***Wylie***	Y	Y	Y	Y	Y	N	N	Y
16 ***Regula***	Y	Y	N	Y	Y	N	N	Y
17 Traficant	Y	Y	Y	Y	Y	N	N	Y
18 Applegate	Y	Y	Y	Y	Y	Y	Y	N
19 Feighan	Y	Y	Y	Y	Y	N	N	Y
20 Oakar	Y	Y	Y	Y	Y	N	N	Y
21 Stokes	?	?	Y	Y	Y	N	N	Y
OKLAHOMA								
1 ***Inhofe***	Y	Y	N	Y	Y	Y	Y	N
2 Synar	Y	Y	Y	Y	Y	N	N	Y
3 Brewster	Y	Y	Y	Y	Y	Y	N	N
4 McCurdy	Y	Y	Y	Y	Y	N	N	Y
5 ***Edwards***	Y	?	N	?	Y	Y	Y	N
6 English	Y	Y	Y	Y	Y	Y	Y	N
OREGON								
1 AuCoin	Y	Y	?	?	Y	N	N	Y
2 ***Smith***	Y	Y	N	Y	Y	Y	Y	N
3 Wyden	Y	Y	Y	Y	Y	N	N	Y
4 DeFazio	Y	N	Y	Y	Y	Y	N	N
5 Kopetski	Y	Y	Y	Y	Y	Y	N	N
PENNSYLVANIA								
1 Foglietta	Y	Y	Y	Y	Y	N	N	Y
2 Gray	?	?	Y	Y	?	N	N	Y
3 Borski	Y	Y	Y	Y	Y	N	N	Y
4 Kolter	Y	Y	Y	?	Y	Y	Y	N
5 ***Schulze***	Y	Y	Y	Y	Y	Y	Y	N
6 Yatron	Y	Y	Y	Y	Y	Y	Y	N
7 ***Weldon***	Y	Y	Y	Y	Y	N	N	Y
8 Kostmayer	Y	Y	Y	Y	Y	N	N	Y
9 ***Shuster***	Y	Y	Y	Y	Y	Y	Y	N
10 ***McDade***	Y	Y	N	Y	Y	N	Y	Y
11 Kanjorski	Y	Y	?	Y	Y	Y	Y	N
12 Murtha	Y	Y	Y	Y	Y	Y	N	N
13 ***Coughlin***	Y	Y	?	Y	Y	N	N	Y
14 Coyne	Y	Y	Y	Y	Y	N	N	Y
15 ***Ritter***	Y	Y	Y	Y	Y	Y	Y	N
16 ***Walker***	N	Y	N	Y	Y	Y	Y	N
17 ***Gekas***	Y	Y	N	Y	Y	Y	Y	N
18 ***Santorum***	Y	Y	N	Y	Y	Y	Y	N
19 ***Goodling***	Y	Y	N	Y	N	N	Y	Y
20 Gaydos	Y	Y	?	Y	Y	Y	Y	Y
21 ***Ridge***	Y	Y	N	Y	Y	Y	N	N
22 Murphy	Y	?	N	Y	Y	N	N	N
23 ***Clinger***	Y	Y	N	Y	Y	Y	Y	N
RHODE ISLAND								
1 ***Machtley***	Y	Y	N	Y	Y	N	N	Y
2 Reed	Y	Y	Y	Y	Y	N	N	Y
SOUTH CAROLINA								
1 ***Ravenel***	Y	Y	Y	Y	Y	Y	Y	N
2 ***Spence***	Y	Y	Y	Y	Y	Y	Y	N
3 Derrick	Y	Y	Y	Y	Y	N	N	Y
4 Patterson	Y	Y	Y	Y	Y	Y	N	N
5 Spratt	Y	Y	Y	Y	Y	N	N	Y
6 Tallon	Y	Y	Y	Y	Y	Y	Y	N

	75	76	77	78	79	81	82	83
SOUTH DAKOTA								
AL Johnson	Y	Y	Y	Y	Y	Y	Y	N
TENNESSEE								
1 ***Quillen***	Y	N	Y	Y	Y	Y	Y	N
2 ***Duncan***	N	N	N	Y	N	Y	Y	N
3 Lloyd	Y	Y	Y	Y	Y	N	N	Y
4 Cooper	Y	Y	Y	Y	Y	N	N	Y
5 Clement	Y	Y	Y	Y	Y	N	N	Y
6 Gordon	Y	Y	Y	Y	Y	N	N	Y
7 ***Sundquist***	Y	Y	N	Y	Y	Y	Y	N
8 Tanner	Y	Y	Y	Y	Y	Y	Y	N
9 Ford	Y	Y	Y	?	Y	N	N	Y
TEXAS								
1 Chapman	Y	Y	Y	Y	Y	N	N	Y
2 Wilson	Y	Y	Y	Y	Y	Y	Y	N
3 Vacancy								
4 Hall	Y	Y	Y	Y	Y	Y	N	N
5 Bryant	Y	Y	Y	Y	Y	N	N	Y
6 ***Barton***	Y	Y	Y	Y	Y	Y	Y	N
7 ***Archer***	Y	Y	Y	Y	Y	Y	Y	N
8 ***Fields***	Y	Y	N	Y	Y	Y	Y	N
9 Brooks	?	Y	Y	Y	Y	Y	N	N
10 Pickle	Y	Y	Y	Y	Y	N	N	Y
11 Edwards	Y	Y	Y	Y	Y	Y	N	N
12 Geren	Y	Y	Y	Y	Y	Y	Y	N
13 Sarpalius	Y	Y	Y	Y	Y	Y	N	N
14 Laughlin	Y	Y	Y	Y	Y	Y	Y	N
15 de la Garza	Y	Y	Y	Y	Y	Y	N	N
16 Coleman	Y	Y	Y	Y	Y	Y	Y	N
17 Stenholm	Y	Y	Y	Y	Y	N	N	Y
18 Washington	?	?	?	Y	?	N	N	Y
19 ***Combest***	Y	Y	Y	Y	Y	Y	Y	N
20 Gonzalez	Y	Y	Y	Y	Y	N	N	Y
21 ***Smith***	N	Y	N	Y	Y	Y	Y	N
22 ***DeLay***	Y	Y	N	?	Y	Y	Y	N
23 Bustamante	Y	Y	?	Y	Y	Y	N	N
24 Frost	Y	Y	Y	Y	Y	N	N	Y
25 Andrews	Y	Y	Y	Y	Y	N	N	Y
26 ***Armey***	N	Y	N	Y	Y	Y	Y	N
27 Ortiz	Y	Y	Y	Y	Y	Y	N	N
UTAH								
1 ***Hansen***	N	Y	Y	Y	Y	Y	Y	N
2 Owens	Y	Y	Y	Y	Y	N	N	Y
3 Orton	Y	Y	Y	Y	Y	N	N	N
VERMONT								
AL *Sanders*	Y	Y	?	Y	Y	Y	Y	N
VIRGINIA								
1 ***Bateman***	Y	Y	Y	Y	Y	N	N	Y
2 Pickett	Y	Y	Y	Y	Y	Y	Y	N
3 ***Bliley***	Y	Y	N	Y	Y	Y	Y	N
4 Sisisky	Y	Y	Y	Y	Y	Y	Y	N
5 Payne	Y	Y	Y	Y	Y	Y	Y	N
6 Olin	Y	Y	Y	Y	Y	Y	N	N
7 ***Slaughter***	Y	Y	Y	Y	Y	Y	Y	Y
8 Moran	Y	Y	Y	Y	Y	N	N	Y
9 Boucher	Y	Y	Y	Y	Y	Y	Y	N
10 ***Wolf***	Y	Y	N	Y	Y	N	N	Y
WASHINGTON								
1 ***Miller***	Y	Y	N	Y	Y	N	N	Y
2 Swift	Y	Y	?	Y	Y	N	N	Y
3 Unsoeld	Y	N	Y	Y	Y	Y	N	N
4 ***Morrison***	Y	Y	Y	Y	Y	N	N	Y
5 Foley								
6 Dicks	Y	Y	Y	Y	Y	N	N	Y
7 McDermott	Y	Y	Y	Y	Y	N	N	Y
8 ***Chandler***	Y	Y	N	Y	Y	N	N	Y
WEST VIRGINIA								
1 Mollohan	Y	Y	?	Y	Y	Y	N	N
2 Staggers	Y	Y	Y	Y	Y	Y	N	N
3 Wise	Y	Y	Y	Y	Y	Y	N	N
4 Rahall	Y	Y	Y	Y	Y	Y	Y	N
WISCONSIN								
1 Aspin	Y	Y	Y	Y	Y	N	N	Y
2 ***Klug***	Y	Y	Y	?	Y	N	N	Y
3 ***Gunderson***	Y	Y	Y	Y	Y	Y	Y	N
4 Kleczka	Y	Y	Y	Y	Y	N	N	Y
5 Moody	Y	Y	Y	Y	Y	N	N	Y
6 ***Petri***	N	Y	Y	Y	N	Y	Y	N
7 Obey	Y	N	Y	Y	N	N	Y	N
8 ***Roth***	Y	Y	Y	?	Y	Y	Y	N
9 ***Sensenbrenner***	N	Y	N	Y	Y	N	N	Y
WYOMING								
AL ***Thomas***	Y	?	N	Y	Y	Y	Y	N

Southern states - Ala., Ark., Fla., Ga., Ky., La., Miss., N.C., Okla., S.C., Tenn., Texas, Va.
Omitted votes are quorum calls, which CQ does not include in its vote charts.

HOUSE VOTES 84, 85, 87, 88, 89, 90, 91, 92

84. HR 2251. Gulf War Refugee Supplemental Appropriations/Passage. Passage of the bill to appropriate $572 million in fiscal 1991, consisting of $235.5 million in humanitarian aid to Iraqi refugees and international peacekeeping operations, $320.5 million for the incremental costs of the Defense Department's humanitarian relief operations, and $16 million for military service organizations providing financial aid to the families of U.S. servicemen. Passed 384-25: R 138-15; D 245-10 (ND 168-6, SD 77-4); I 1-0, May 9, 1991.

85. H Con Res 121. Fiscal 1992 Budget Resolution/Previous Question. Gradison, R-Ohio, motion to order the previous question (thus ending debate and the possibility of amendment) on the Gradison motion to instruct House conferees to agree to the Senate provision requiring that entitlement increases be offset by spending cuts, not tax increases. Rejected 132-284: R 131-29; D 1-254 (ND 1-175, SD 0-79); I 0-1, May 9, 1991. (Panetta, D-Calif., offered a substitute amendment to the Gradison motion, to require that any pay-as-you-go legislation not harm working families and Medicare beneficiaries, and adhere to the Budget Enforcement Act of 1990 (PL 101-508). The Panetta substitute was adopted by voice vote; the Gradison motion, as amended, was adopted by voice vote.) *(Story, p. 1183)*

87. S 248. Niobrara River Designation/Remove Areas. Barrett, R-Neb., substitute amendment to eliminate the designation of certain segments of the Niobrara River as components of the National Wild and Scenic River System and require a three-year study for possible future designation of such segments of the river. Rejected 109-293: R 93-63; D 16-229 (ND 7-164, SD 9-65); I 0-1, May 14, 1991.

88. S 248. Niobrara River Designation/Owner Consent. Young, R-Alaska, amendment to require the consent of the owner before the Department of Interior may acquire land or land interests within designated river corridors unless the department finds that the land has changed substantially and acquisition of lands is necessary to assure integrity within the Wild and Scenic Rivers Act. Rejected 124-283: R 100-59; D 24-223 (ND 12-160, SD 12-63); I 0-1, May 14, 1991.

89. S 248. Niobrara River Designation/Passage. Passage of the bill to authorize such sums as necessary to designate segments of the Niobrara River in Nebraska and the Missouri River along the Nebraska-South Dakota border as components of the Wild and Scenic Rivers System. Passed 333-71: R 91-66; D 241-5 (ND 169-1, SD 72-4); I 1-0, May 14, 1991. A "nay" was a vote supporting the president's position.

90. HR 1415. Fiscal 1992-93 State Department Authorization/Security Alternative. Berman, D-Calif., amendment to the Snowe, R-Maine, en bloc amendments, to authorize $130 million in fiscal 1992 for construction at the bug-riddled U.S. Embassy in Moscow. The amendment would also strike the language reported from committee, that would replace the top two floors of the embassy with four secure floors, and insert language to allow the administration to develop and report to Congress a plan that meets security needs. The Snowe amendment would require the State Department to tear down the embassy and rebuild it with all U.S. materials and labor. Adopted 223-185: R 6-155; D 216-30 (ND 156-12, SD 60-18); I 1-0, May 15, 1991. (Subsequently, the Snowe amendment, as amended, was adopted by voice vote.) A "yea" was a vote supporting the president's position.

91. HR 1415. Fiscal 1992-93 State Department Authorization/Restore Snowe Language. Upton, R-Mich., substitute amendment to the Snowe, R-Maine, amendment, as amended, to restore the Snowe language, which directed the State Department to tear down and rebuild the U.S. Embassy in Moscow, and require the secretary of State to seek reimbursement from the Soviet Union for the full costs incurred by the United States in reconstruction of the U.S. Embassy in Moscow. Rejected 196-207: R 153-5; D 43-201 (ND 21-143, SD 22-58); I 0-1, May 15, 1991.

92. HR 1415. Fiscal 1992-93 State Department Authorization/Soviet Reimbursement. Upton, R-Mich., amendment to the Snowe, R-Maine, amendment, as amended, to require the secretary of State to seek reimbursement from the Soviet Union for U.S. costs resulting from the Soviet bugging of the U.S. Embassy in Moscow. Adopted 414-0: R 160-0; D 253-0 (ND 172-0, SD 81-0); I 1-0, May 15, 1991. (Subsequently, the Snowe amendment, as amended, was adopted by voice vote.)

KEY

Y Voted for (yea).
\# Paired for.
+ Announced for.
N Voted against (nay).
X Paired against.
\- Announced against.
P Voted "present."
C Voted "present" to avoid possible conflict of interest.
? Did not vote or otherwise make a position known.

Democrats ***Republicans***
Independent

	84	85	87	88	89	90	91	92
ALABAMA								
1 ***Callahan***	Y	Y	Y	Y	Y	N	Y	Y
2 ***Dickinson***	Y	Y	?	?	?	Y	Y	Y
3 Browder	Y	N	N	N	Y	Y	N	Y
4 Bevill	Y	?	Y	N	Y	Y	N	Y
5 Cramer	Y	N	N	N	Y	?	N	Y
6 Erdreich	Y	N	N	N	Y	N	Y	Y
7 Harris	Y	N	N	N	Y	N	Y	Y
ALASKA								
AL ***Young***	Y	N	Y	Y	N	N	Y	Y
ARIZONA								
1 ***Rhodes***	Y	Y	Y	Y	N	N	Y	Y
2 Vacancy								
3 ***Stump***	N	Y	Y	Y	N	N	Y	Y
4 ***Kyl***	Y	Y	Y	Y	N	N	Y	Y
5 ***Kolbe***	Y	Y	Y	Y	Y	Y	N	Y
ARKANSAS								
1 Alexander	Y	N	?	?	?	?	?	Y
2 Thornton	Y	N	N	N	Y	N	N	Y
3 ***Hammerschmidt***	Y	N	Y	Y	N	N	Y	Y
4 Anthony	Y	N	?	?	?	Y	N	Y
CALIFORNIA								
1 ***Riggs***	Y	Y	Y	Y	N	N	Y	Y
2 ***Herger***	Y	Y	Y	Y	N	N	Y	Y
3 Matsui	?	?	N	?	?	Y	N	Y
4 Fazio	Y	N	N	N	Y	Y	N	Y
5 Pelosi	Y	N	N	N	Y	Y	?	Y
6 Boxer	Y	N	?	?	?	?	?	?
7 Miller	Y	N	N	N	Y	Y	N	Y
8 Dellums	Y	N	N	N	Y	Y	N	Y
9 Stark	Y	N	N	N	Y	Y	N	Y
10 Edwards	Y	N	N	N	Y	Y	N	Y
11 Lantos	Y	N	N	N	Y	Y	N	Y
12 ***Campbell***	Y	Y	N	N	Y	N	Y	Y
13 Mineta	Y	N	N	N	Y	Y	N	Y
14 ***Doolittle***	Y	Y	Y	Y	N	N	Y	Y
15 Condit	Y	N	N	N	Y	Y	N	Y
16 Panetta	Y	N	N	Y	Y	Y	?	Y
17 Dooley	Y	N	N	N	Y	Y	N	Y
18 Lehman	Y	N	?	?	?	Y	N	Y
19 ***Lagomarsino***	Y	Y	Y	Y	N	N	Y	Y
20 ***Thomas***	Y	Y	N	N	Y	N	Y	Y
21 ***Gallegly***	Y	Y	Y	Y	N	N	Y	Y
22 ***Moorhead***	Y	Y	N	Y	Y	N	Y	Y
23 Beilenson	Y	N	N	N	Y	?	?	Y
24 Waxman	Y	N	N	N	Y	Y	N	Y
25 Roybal	?	?	N	N	Y	Y	N	Y
26 Berman	Y	N	N	N	Y	Y	N	Y
27 Levine	Y	N	?	?	?	?	?	?
28 Dixon	Y	N	N	N	Y	Y	N	Y
29 Waters	Y	N	N	N	?	Y	?	Y
30 Martinez	Y	N	N	Y	Y	?	?	?
31 Dymally	Y	N	?	N	Y	Y	N	Y
32 Anderson	Y	N	Y	N	Y	Y	N	Y
33 ***Dreier***	Y	Y	N	N	Y	N	Y	Y
34 Torres	Y	N	N	N	Y	+	N	Y
35 ***Lewis***	Y	Y	Y	Y	Y	N	?	?
36 Brown	Y	N	N	N	Y	Y	N	Y
37 ***McCandless***	Y	Y	Y	Y	N	N	Y	Y
38 ***Dornan***	Y	Y	Y	Y	N	N	Y	?
39 ***Dannemeyer***	N	Y	Y	Y	N	N	Y	Y
40 ***Cox***	Y	Y	N	N	Y	N	Y	Y
41 ***Lowery***	Y	Y	Y	Y	Y	N	Y	Y
42 ***Rohrabacher***	N	N	Y	Y	N	N	Y	Y
43 ***Packard***	Y	N	Y	Y	N	N	Y	Y
44 ***Cunningham***	Y	Y	Y	Y	Y	N	Y	Y
45 ***Hunter***	Y	Y	Y	Y	N	N	Y	Y
COLORADO								
1 Schroeder	Y	N	N	N	Y	Y	N	Y
2 Skaggs	Y	N	N	N	Y	Y	N	Y
3 Campbell	Y	N	Y	N	Y	Y	N	Y
4 ***Allard***	Y	Y	Y	Y	N	N	Y	Y
5 ***Hefley***	Y	Y	Y	Y	Y	N	Y	Y
6 ***Schaefer***	Y	Y	Y	Y	N	N	Y	Y
CONNECTICUT								
1 Kennelly	Y	N	N	N	Y	Y	N	Y
2 Gejdenson	Y	N	N	N	Y	Y	N	Y
3 DeLauro	Y	N	N	N	Y	Y	N	Y
4 ***Shays***	Y	Y	N	N	Y	N	Y	Y
5 ***Franks***	Y	Y	Y	Y	N	N	Y	Y
6 ***Johnson***	Y	Y	Y	N	Y	Y	Y	Y
DELAWARE								
AL Carper	Y	N	N	N	Y	Y	Y	Y
FLORIDA								
1 Hutto	Y	N	N	N	Y	Y	Y	Y
2 Peterson	Y	N	N	N	Y	Y	N	Y
3 Bennett	Y	N	N	N	Y	N	Y	Y
4 ***James***	Y	Y	N	N	Y	N	Y	Y
5 ***McCollum***	Y	Y	N	N	Y	N	Y	Y
6 ***Stearns***	N	Y	Y	Y	Y	N	Y	Y
7 Gibbons	Y	N	N	N	Y	Y	N	Y
8 ***Young***	Y	Y	N	N	Y	N	Y	Y
9 ***Bilirakis***	N	Y	N	N	Y	N	Y	Y
10 ***Ireland***	Y	Y	N	N	Y	N	Y	Y
11 Bacchus	+	?	N	N	Y	Y	N	Y
12 ***Lewis***	Y	Y	N	N	Y	N	Y	Y
13 ***Goss***	Y	Y	N	N	Y	N	Y	Y
14 Johnston	Y	N	N	N	Y	Y	N	Y
15 ***Shaw***	Y	N	Y	Y	Y	N	Y	Y
16 Smith	Y	N	N	N	Y	Y	N	Y
17 Lehman	?	?	X	?	?	#	X	?
18 ***Ros-Lehtinen***	Y	Y	N	N	Y	N	Y	Y
19 Fascell	Y	N	N	N	Y	Y	N	Y
GEORGIA								
1 Thomas	Y	N	N	N	Y	Y	N	Y
2 Hatcher	Y	N	?	?	?	?	?	?
3 Ray	N	N	N	N	Y	Y	N	Y
4 Jones	Y	N	N	N	Y	N	Y	Y
5 Lewis	Y	N	N	N	Y	Y	N	Y
6 ***Gingrich***	Y	Y	Y	Y	Y	N	Y	Y
7 Darden	Y	N	N	N	Y	Y	N	Y
8 Rowland	Y	N	N	N	Y	Y	N	Y
9 Jenkins	Y	N	N	N	Y	N	N	Y
10 Barnard	Y	X	N	N	Y	N	N	Y
HAWAII								
1 Abercrombie	Y	N	N	N	Y	Y	N	Y
2 Mink	Y	N	N	N	Y	Y	N	Y
IDAHO								
1 LaRocco	Y	N	N	N	Y	Y	N	Y
2 Stallings	Y	N	N	Y	Y	Y	N	Y
ILLINOIS								
1 Hayes	N	N	N	N	Y	Y	N	Y
2 Savage	N	N	N	N	Y	Y	N	Y
3 Russo	Y	N	N	N	Y	Y	N	Y
4 Sangmeister	Y	N	N	N	Y	N	Y	Y
5 Lipinski	Y	N	N	N	Y	N	Y	Y
6 ***Hyde***	Y	Y	Y	Y	N	N	Y	Y
7 Collins	Y	N	?	N	?	Y	N	Y
8 Rostenkowski	Y	N	N	N	Y	Y	N	Y
9 Yates	Y	N	N	N	Y	Y	N	Y
10 ***Porter***	Y	Y	N	N	Y	N	Y	Y
11 Annunzio	Y	N	N	N	Y	Y	N	Y
12 ***Crane***	?	Y	Y	Y	N	N	Y	Y
13 ***Fawell***	Y	Y	N	N	Y	N	Y	Y
14 ***Hastert***	Y	Y	Y	Y	Y	N	Y	Y
15 Vacancy								
16 Cox	Y	N	N	?	Y	Y	N	Y
17 Evans	Y	N	N	N	Y	N	Y	Y
18 ***Michel***	Y	Y	Y	Y	N	N	Y	Y
19 Bruce	Y	N	N	N	Y	Y	N	Y
20 Durbin	Y	N	N	N	Y	Y	N	Y
21 Costello	Y	N	N	Y	Y	Y	N	Y
22 Poshard	Y	N	N	Y	Y	Y	N	Y
INDIANA								
1 Visclosky	N	N	Y	N	Y	Y	N	Y
2 Sharp	Y	N	N	N	Y	Y	N	Y
3 Roemer	Y	N	N	N	Y	Y	N	Y

ND Northern Democrats SD Southern Democrats

	84	85	87	88	89	90	91	92
4 Long	Y	N	N	N	Y	Y	N	Y
5 Jontz	Y	N	N	N	Y	Y	N	Y
6 ***Burton***	Y	Y	Y	Y	N	N	Y	Y
7 ***Myers***	Y	N	Y	Y	N	N	N	Y
8 McCloskey	Y	N	N	N	Y	Y	N	Y
9 Hamilton	Y	N	N	N	Y	Y	N	Y
10 Jacobs	Y	N	N	N	Y	Y	Y	Y
IOWA								
1 ***Leach***	Y	Y	N	N	Y	N	Y	Y
2 ***Nussle***	N	Y	Y	Y	N	N	Y	Y
3 Nagle	Y	N	N	N	Y	Y	N	Y
4 Smith	Y	N	N	Y	Y	?	?	?
5 ***Lightfoot***	Y	N	Y	Y	N	N	Y	Y
6 ***Grandy***	Y	Y	Y	Y	N	N	Y	Y
KANSAS								
1 ***Roberts***	Y	Y	Y	Y	N	N	?	Y
2 Slattery	Y	N	N	N	Y	Y	Y	Y
3 ***Meyers***	Y	Y	N	N	Y	N	Y	Y
4 Glickman	Y	N	N	Y	Y	Y	Y	Y
5 ***Nichols***	?	Y	Y	Y	N	N	Y	Y
KENTUCKY								
1 Hubbard	Y	N	N	N	Y	N	Y	Y
2 Natcher	Y	N	N	N	Y	Y	N	Y
3 Mazzoli	Y	N	N	N	Y	Y	N	Y
4 ***Bunning***	Y	Y	Y	Y	N	N	Y	Y
5 ***Rogers***	Y	N	Y	Y	N	Y	N	Y
6 ***Hopkins***	?	?	?	?	?	?	?	?
7 Perkins	Y	N	N	N	Y	Y	N	Y
LOUISIANA								
1 ***Livingston***	Y	Y	Y	Y	N	N	Y	Y
2 Jefferson	?	?	N	N	Y	Y	N	Y
3 Tauzin	Y	N	Y	Y	Y	N	Y	Y
4 ***McCrery***	Y	Y	?	?	?	N	Y	Y
5 Huckaby	Y	N	N	N	Y	Y	N	Y
6 ***Baker***	Y	Y	Y	Y	N	N	Y	Y
7 Hayes	Y	N	N	Y	Y	N	Y	Y
8 ***Holloway***	?	?	?	?	?	N	Y	Y
MAINE								
1 Andrews	Y	N	N	N	Y	Y	N	Y
2 ***Snowe***	Y	Y	N	N	Y	N	Y	Y
MARYLAND								
1 ***Gilchrest***	Y	Y	N	Y	Y	N	Y	Y
2 ***Bentley***	Y	Y	Y	Y	N	N	Y	Y
3 Cardin	Y	N	?	N	Y	Y	N	Y
4 McMillen	Y	N	N	N	Y	Y	N	Y
5 Hoyer	Y	N	N	N	Y	Y	N	Y
6 Byron	Y	N	N	N	Y	Y	N	Y
7 Mfume	Y	N	?	N	Y	Y	N	Y
8 ***Morella***	+	N	N	N	Y	N	Y	Y
MASSACHUSETTS								
1 Vacancy								
2 Neal	+	N	N	N	Y	Y	N	Y
3 Early	N	N	N	Y	Y	Y	N	Y
4 Frank	Y	N	N	N	Y	Y	N	Y
5 Atkins	Y	N	N	N	Y	Y	N	Y
6 Mavroules	Y	N	N	N	Y	Y	N	Y
7 Markey	Y	N	N	?	?	Y	N	Y
8 Kennedy	Y	N	N	N	Y	Y	N	Y
9 Moakley	Y	N	N	N	Y	Y	N	Y
10 Studds	Y	N	N	N	Y	Y	N	Y
11 Donnelly	N	N	N	N	Y	Y	N	Y
MICHIGAN								
1 Conyers	Y	N	N	N	Y	Y	N	Y
2 ***Pursell***	Y	Y	N	N	Y	N	Y	Y
3 Wolpe	Y	N	N	N	Y	Y	N	Y
4 ***Upton***	Y	N	N	N	Y	N	Y	Y
5 ***Henry***	Y	Y	N	N	Y	N	Y	Y
6 Carr	Y	N	N	N	Y	Y	Y	Y
7 Kildee	Y	N	N	N	Y	Y	N	Y
8 Traxler	Y	N	N	N	Y	Y	N	Y
9 ***Vander Jagt***	Y	Y	Y	N	Y	N	Y	Y
10 ***Camp***	Y	Y	Y	Y	Y	N	Y	Y
11 ***Davis***	?	Y	Y	Y	N	N	Y	Y
12 Bonior	Y	N	N	N	Y	Y	N	Y
13 Collins	Y	N	N	N	Y	N	N	Y
14 Hertel	Y	N	N	N	Y	Y	N	Y
15 Ford	Y	N	N	N	Y	Y	?	Y
16 Dingell	Y	N	N	N	Y	?	?	Y
17 Levin	Y	N	N	N	Y	Y	N	Y
18 ***Broomfield***	Y	Y	N	N	Y	X	#	Y
MINNESOTA								
1 Penny	Y	N	N	Y	Y	Y	Y	Y
2 ***Weber***	Y	Y	Y	Y	Y	N	Y	Y
3 ***Ramstad***	Y	Y	N	N	Y	N	Y	Y
4 Vento	Y	N	N	N	Y	Y	N	Y

	84	85	87	88	89	90	91	92
5 Sabo	Y	N	N	N	Y	Y	N	Y
6 Sikorski	Y	N	N	N	Y	Y	N	Y
7 Peterson	Y	N	N	N	Y	Y	N	Y
8 Oberstar	Y	N	N	N	Y	Y	N	Y
MISSISSIPPI								
1 Whitten	Y	N	N	N	Y	Y	N	Y
2 Espy	Y	N	N	Y	Y	N	Y	Y
3 Montgomery	Y	N	Y	Y	Y	Y	N	Y
4 Parker	Y	N	Y	Y	Y	N	Y	Y
5 Taylor	Y	N	N	Y	Y	Y	Y	Y
MISSOURI								
1 Clay	Y	N	N	N	Y	Y	N	Y
2 Horn	Y	N	N	N	Y	Y	N	Y
3 Gephardt	Y	N	N	N	Y	Y	N	Y
4 Skelton	Y	N	Y	N	Y	Y	N	Y
5 Wheat	Y	N	N	N	Y	Y	N	Y
6 ***Coleman***	Y	Y	Y	Y	Y	N	Y	Y
7 ***Hancock***	N	Y	Y	Y	?	N	Y	Y
8 ***Emerson***	Y	N	Y	Y	N	N	Y	Y
9 Volkmer	Y	N	Y	N	Y	Y	N	Y
MONTANA								
1 Williams	Y	N	N	N	Y	N	Y	Y
2 ***Marlenee***	?	#	#	Y	N	?	Y	Y
NEBRASKA								
1 ***Bereuter***	Y	Y	N	N	Y	N	Y	Y
2 Hoagland	Y	N	N	N	Y	Y	N	Y
3 ***Barrett***	Y	Y	Y	Y	N	N	?	Y
NEVADA								
1 Bilbray	Y	N	N	N	Y	Y	N	Y
2 ***Vucanovich***	?	Y	Y	Y	N	N	?	Y
NEW HAMPSHIRE								
1 ***Zeliff***	N	Y	Y	Y	N	N	Y	Y
2 Swett	Y	N	N	N	Y	Y	N	Y
NEW JERSEY								
1 Andrews	Y	N	N	N	Y	Y	N	Y
2 Hughes	Y	N	N	N	Y	Y	N	Y
3 Pallone	Y	N	N	N	Y	Y	Y	Y
4 ***Smith***	Y	N	N	N	Y	N	Y	Y
5 ***Roukema***	Y	N	N	N	Y	N	Y	Y
6 Dwyer	Y	N	N	N	Y	Y	N	Y
7 ***Rinaldo***	Y	Y	N	N	Y	N	Y	Y
8 Roe	Y	N	N	N	Y	Y	N	Y
9 Torricelli	Y	N	N	N	Y	Y	Y	Y
10 Payne	Y	N	N	N	Y	Y	N	Y
11 ***Gallo***	Y	Y	N	N	Y	N	Y	Y
12 ***Zimmer***	Y	Y	N	N	Y	N	Y	Y
13 ***Saxton***	Y	Y	N	N	Y	N	Y	Y
14 Guarini	Y	N	N	N	Y	Y	Y	Y
NEW MEXICO								
1 ***Schiff***	Y	Y	Y	N	Y	N	Y	Y
2 ***Skeen***	Y	Y	Y	Y	Y	N	Y	Y
3 Richardson	Y	N	N	N	Y	Y	N	Y
NEW YORK								
1 Hochbrueckner	Y	N	N	N	Y	Y	N	Y
2 Downey	Y	N	N	N	Y	Y	N	Y
3 Mrazek	?	?	?	?	?	Y	N	Y
4 ***Lent***	Y	N	Y	Y	Y	N	Y	Y
5 ***McGrath***	?	N	N	N	Y	N	Y	Y
6 Flake	Y	N	N	N	Y	Y	N	Y
7 Ackerman	Y	N	N	N	Y	Y	N	Y
8 Scheuer	Y	N	N	N	?	?	N	Y
9 Manton	Y	N	N	N	Y	Y	N	Y
10 Schumer	Y	N	N	N	Y	Y	N	Y
11 Towns	Y	N	N	N	Y	Y	N	Y
12 Owens	Y	N	N	N	Y	Y	N	Y
13 Solarz	Y	N	N	N	Y	Y	N	Y
14 ***Molinari***	Y	N	Y	Y	Y	N	Y	Y
15 ***Green***	Y	N	N	N	Y	N	Y	Y
16 Rangel	Y	N	N	N	Y	Y	N	Y
17 Weiss	Y	N	N	N	Y	Y	N	Y
18 Serrano	Y	N	N	N	Y	Y	N	Y
19 Engel	Y	N	N	N	Y	Y	N	Y
20 Lowey	Y	N	N	N	Y	Y	N	Y
21 ***Fish***	Y	Y	N	N	Y	N	Y	Y
22 ***Gilman***	Y	N	N	N	Y	N	Y	Y
23 McNulty	Y	N	N	N	Y	Y	N	Y
24 ***Solomon***	Y	Y	Y	Y	?	N	Y	Y
25 ***Boehlert***	Y	N	N	N	Y	N	Y	Y
26 ***Martin***	?	?	Y	Y	N	N	Y	Y
27 ***Walsh***	Y	Y	N	N	Y	N	Y	Y
28 McHugh	Y	N	N	N	Y	Y	N	Y
29 ***Horton***	Y	N	N	N	Y	N	Y	Y
30 Slaughter	Y	N	N	N	Y	Y	?	?
31 ***Paxon***	Y	Y	N	Y	Y	N	Y	Y

	84	85	87	88	89	90	91	92
32 LaFalce	Y	N	N	N	Y	Y	N	Y
33 Nowak	Y	N	N	N	Y	Y	N	Y
34 ***Houghton***	Y	Y	Y	Y	Y	N	Y	Y
NORTH CAROLINA								
1 Jones	Y	N	N	Y	Y	Y	Y	Y
2 Valentine	Y	N	N	N	Y	Y	N	Y
3 Lancaster	Y	N	N	N	Y	Y	N	Y
4 Price	Y	N	N	N	Y	Y	N	Y
5 Neal	?	?	N	N	Y	Y	Y	Y
6 ***Coble***	Y	Y	N	Y	Y	N	Y	Y
7 Rose	Y	N	N	N	Y	?	?	Y
8 Hefner	Y	N	N	N	Y	Y	N	Y
9 ***McMillan***	Y	Y	N	N	Y	N	Y	Y
10 ***Ballenger***	Y	Y	Y	Y	N	N	Y	Y
11 ***Taylor***	Y	N	Y	Y	N	N	Y	Y
NORTH DAKOTA								
AL Dorgan	Y	N	Y	Y	Y	Y	N	Y
OHIO								
1 Luken	Y	Y	N	N	Y	Y	Y	Y
2 ***Gradison***	Y	Y	Y	N	Y	N	Y	Y
3 Hall	Y	N	N	N	Y	Y	N	Y
4 ***Oxley***	Y	Y	Y	Y	N	N	Y	Y
5 ***Gillmor***	Y	Y	N	Y	Y	N	Y	Y
6 ***McEwen***	Y	Y	Y	Y	N	N	Y	Y
7 ***Hobson***	Y	N	Y	Y	Y	N	Y	Y
8 ***Boehner***	Y	Y	Y	Y	N	N	Y	Y
9 Kaptur	Y	N	?	?	?	Y	N	Y
10 ***Miller***	N	Y	?	Y	N	N	Y	Y
11 Eckart	Y	N	N	N	Y	N	N	Y
12 ***Kasich***	Y	Y	N	Y	Y	N	Y	Y
13 Pease	Y	N	N	N	Y	Y	N	Y
14 Sawyer	Y	N	N	N	Y	Y	N	Y
15 ***Wylie***	Y	Y	N	N	Y	N	Y	?
16 ***Regula***	Y	Y	N	N	Y	Y	N	Y
17 Traficant	N	N	N	N	Y	N	Y	Y
18 Applegate	Y	N	N	N	Y	N	Y	Y
19 Feighan	Y	N	N	N	Y	Y	N	Y
20 Oakar	Y	N	N	N	Y	?	?	Y
21 Stokes	Y	N	N	N	Y	Y	N	Y
OKLAHOMA								
1 ***Inhofe***	Y	Y	Y	Y	N	N	Y	Y
2 Synar	Y	N	N	N	Y	Y	N	Y
3 Brewster	Y	N	N	N	Y	Y	N	Y
4 McCurdy	Y	N	N	N	Y	Y	N	Y
5 ***Edwards***	Y	Y	Y	Y	N	N	Y	Y
6 English	Y	N	Y	N	Y	N	Y	Y
OREGON								
1 AuCoin	Y	N	N	N	Y	Y	N	Y
2 ***Smith***	Y	Y	Y	Y	N	N	Y	Y
3 Wyden	Y	N	N	N	Y	Y	N	Y
4 DeFazio	Y	N	N	N	Y	Y	N	Y
5 Kopetski	Y	N	N	N	Y	Y	N	Y
PENNSYLVANIA								
1 Foglietta	Y	N	N	N	Y	Y	N	Y
2 Gray	Y	N	N	N	Y	Y	?	?
3 Borski	Y	N	N	N	Y	Y	N	Y
4 Kolter	Y	N	N	N	Y	?	?	?
5 ***Schulze***	Y	N	Y	Y	N	N	Y	Y
6 Yatron	Y	N	N	N	Y	N	Y	Y
7 ***Weldon***	Y	Y	N	N	Y	N	Y	Y
8 Kostmayer	Y	N	N	N	Y	Y	N	Y
9 ***Shuster***	Y	N	Y	Y	N	N	Y	Y
10 ***McDade***	Y	Y	N	Y	Y	N	Y	Y
11 Kanjorski	Y	N	N	N	Y	N	Y	Y
12 Murtha	Y	N	N	N	Y	?	?	Y
13 ***Coughlin***	Y	Y	N	N	Y	N	Y	Y
14 Coyne	Y	N	N	N	Y	Y	N	Y
15 ***Ritter***	Y	N	N	Y	Y	N	Y	Y
16 ***Walker***	N	Y	Y	Y	N	N	Y	Y
17 ***Gekas***	Y	N	Y	Y	N	N	Y	Y
18 ***Santorum***	Y	Y	Y	N	Y	N	Y	Y
19 ***Goodling***	Y	Y	Y	Y	N	N	Y	Y
20 Gaydos	Y	N	N	N	Y	N	Y	Y
21 ***Ridge***	Y	N	?	Y	N	N	Y	Y
22 Murphy	Y	N	N	Y	Y	Y	Y	Y
23 ***Clinger***	Y	N	Y	N	Y	N	Y	Y
RHODE ISLAND								
1 ***Machtley***	Y	Y	N	Y	Y	N	Y	Y
2 Reed	Y	N	N	N	Y	Y	N	Y
SOUTH CAROLINA								
1 ***Ravenel***	Y	Y	N	N	Y	N	Y	Y
2 ***Spence***	Y	Y	N	N	Y	N	Y	Y
3 Derrick	Y	N	N	N	Y	?	?	?
4 Patterson	Y	N	N	N	Y	Y	N	Y
5 Spratt	Y	N	N	N	Y	Y	N	Y
6 Tallon	Y	N	N	N	Y	Y	Y	Y

	84	85	87	88	89	90	91	92
SOUTH DAKOTA								
AL Johnson	Y	N	N	N	Y	Y	N	Y
TENNESSEE								
1 ***Quillen***	Y	Y	Y	Y	N	N	Y	Y
2 ***Duncan***	N	Y	Y	Y	N	N	Y	Y
3 Lloyd	Y	N	N	N	Y	N	Y	Y
4 Cooper	Y	N	N	N	Y	N	Y	Y
5 Clement	Y	N	N	N	Y	Y	N	Y
6 Gordon	Y	N	N	N	Y	Y	N	Y
7 ***Sundquist***	Y	Y	N	Y	Y	N	Y	Y
8 Tanner	Y	N	N	N	Y	N	Y	Y
9 Ford	Y	N	?	?	Y	Y	N	Y
TEXAS								
1 Chapman	Y	N	?	?	?	Y	N	?
2 Wilson	Y	N	N	N	Y	N	Y	Y
3 Vacancy								
4 Hall	N	N	Y	Y	N	Y	Y	Y
5 Bryant	Y	N	N	N	Y	?	N	Y
6 ***Barton***	N	Y	#	#	X	N	Y	Y
7 ***Archer***	Y	Y	Y	Y	N	N	Y	Y
8 ***Fields***	Y	Y	Y	Y	N	N	Y	Y
9 Brooks	Y	N	N	N	Y	Y	N	Y
10 Pickle	Y	N	?	?	?	Y	N	Y
11 Edwards	Y	N	N	N	Y	Y	N	Y
12 Geren	N	N	X	X	#	Y	Y	Y
13 Sarpalius	Y	N	N	Y	Y	Y	N	Y
14 Laughlin	Y	N	N	N	Y	Y	N	Y
15 de la Garza	Y	N	N	N	Y	Y	N	Y
16 Coleman	Y	N	N	N	Y	Y	N	Y
17 Stenholm	N	N	Y	Y	N	Y	N	Y
18 Washington	Y	N	?	N	Y	Y	N	Y
19 ***Combest***	N	Y	Y	Y	Y	N	Y	Y
20 Gonzalez	Y	N	Y	Y	N	Y	N	Y
21 ***Smith***	Y	Y	N	N	Y	N	Y	Y
22 ***DeLay***	Y	Y	Y	Y	N	N	Y	Y
23 Bustamante	Y	N	?	?	?	Y	N	Y
24 Frost	Y	N	?	?	?	Y	N	Y
25 Andrews	Y	N	N	N	Y	Y	N	Y
26 ***Armey***	Y	Y	Y	Y	N	N	Y	Y
27 Ortiz	Y	N	N	N	Y	Y	N	Y
UTAH								
1 ***Hansen***	Y	Y	Y	Y	N	N	Y	Y
2 Owens	Y	N	N	N	Y	Y	N	Y
3 Orton	Y	?	Y	Y	Y	Y	N	Y
VERMONT								
AL *Sanders*	Y	N	N	N	Y	Y	N	Y
VIRGINIA								
1 ***Bateman***	Y	N	Y	Y	N	N	Y	Y
2 Pickett	Y	N	N	N	Y	Y	N	Y
3 ***Bliley***	Y	Y	Y	Y	Y	N	Y	Y
4 Sisisky	Y	N	N	N	Y	Y	N	Y
5 Payne	Y	N	N	Y	Y	Y	N	Y
6 Olin	Y	N	Y	N	N	N	Y	Y
7 ***Slaughter***	Y	Y	Y	Y	N	N	Y	Y
8 Moran	Y	N	N	N	Y	Y	N	Y
9 Boucher	Y	N	N	N	Y	Y	N	Y
10 ***Wolf***	Y	Y	Y	Y	Y	N	Y	Y
WASHINGTON								
1 ***Miller***	?	Y	N	N	Y	N	Y	Y
2 Swift	Y	N	N	N	N	Y	N	Y
3 Unsoeld	Y	N	N	N	Y	Y	N	Y
4 ***Morrison***	Y	Y	N	N	Y	N	Y	Y
5 Foley								
6 Dicks	Y	N	N	N	Y	Y	N	Y
7 McDermott	?	N	N	N	Y	Y	N	Y
8 ***Chandler***	Y	Y	N	N	Y	N	Y	Y
WEST VIRGINIA								
1 Mollohan	Y	N	N	N	Y	Y	Y	Y
2 Staggers	Y	N	N	N	Y	Y	N	Y
3 Wise	Y	N	N	N	Y	Y	N	Y
4 Rahall	Y	N	N	N	Y	Y	N	Y
WISCONSIN								
1 Aspin	Y	N	N	N	Y	Y	N	Y
2 ***Klug***	Y	Y	Y	N	Y	N	Y	Y
3 ***Gunderson***	Y	Y	N	N	Y	N	Y	Y
4 Kleczka	?	N	N	N	Y	Y	N	Y
5 Moody	Y	N	N	N	Y	?	?	?
6 ***Petri***	Y	Y	N	N	Y	Y	N	Y
7 Obey	Y	N	N	N	Y	Y	N	Y
8 ***Roth***	Y	N	Y	Y	Y	N	Y	Y
9 ***Sensenbrenner***	N	Y	N	N	Y	N	Y	Y
WYOMING								
AL ***Thomas***	N	Y	Y	Y	N	N	Y	Y

Southern states - Ala., Ark., Fla., Ga., Ky., La., Miss., N.C., Okla., S.C., Tenn., Texas, Va.
Omitted votes are quorum calls, which CQ does not include in its vote charts.

HOUSE VOTES 93, 94, 95, 96, 97, 98, 99, 100

93. HR 1415. Fiscal 1992-93 State Department Authorization/Drug Testing. Solomon, R-N.Y., amendment to require random drug testing of all State Department employees. Rejected 145-265: R 118-42; D 27-222 (ND 6-165, SD 21-57); I 0-1, May 15, 1991.

94. HR 1415. Fiscal 1992-93 State Department Authorization/National Endowment for Democracy. Kanjorski, D-Pa., amendment to reduce the authorization for the National Endowment for Democracy from $30 million to $16 million. Rejected 189-224: R 55-106; D 133-118 (ND 87-84, SD 46-34); I 1-0, May 15, 1991.

95. HR 1415. Fiscal 1992-93 State Department Authorization/Reduce Funding. Walker, R-Pa., amendment to cap spending authorized under the bill at 2.4 percent more than the fiscal 1991 level, reducing the total authorization in the bill from $5.606 billion to $5.022 billion. Rejected 155-248: R 110-50; D 45-197 (ND 21-143, SD 24-54); I 0-1), May 15, 1991.

96. HR 2100. Fiscal 1992 Defense Authorization/Rule. Adoption of the rule (H Res 156) to provide for House floor consideration of the bill to authorize appropriations for the Defense Department and defense-related programs in fiscal 1992. Adopted 260-56: R 82-51; D 177-5 (ND 124-2, SD 53-3); I 1-0, May 20, 1991.

97. HR 2100. Fiscal 1992 Defense Authorization/SDI. Dellums, D-Calif., amendment to terminate the Strategic Defense Initiative program and permit only a basic SDI research program funded at $1.1 billion. Rejected 118-266: R 2-149; D 115-117 (ND 104-55, SD 11-62); I 1-0, May 20, 1991. A "nay" was a vote supporting the president's position.

98. HR 2100. Fiscal 1992 Defense Authorization/Seawolf. Gejdenson, D-Conn., amendment to provide that the contract for the third nuclear attack Seawolf SSN-21 submarine be awarded by a competitive bid and require the Navy to submit to Congress a report describing its basis for selecting a contractor and its acquisition strategy for the Seawolf program. Adopted 235-157: R 88-65; D 146-92 (ND 123-37, SD 23-55); I 1-0, May 20, 1991.

99. HR 2100. Fiscal 1992 Defense Authorization/Administration Request. Michel, R-Ill., substitute amendment to substitute the administration's defense request for the committee's. The amendment would increase Strategic Defense Initiative funding by $1.7 billion to $5.2 billion; terminate the remanufacture of Navy F-14 fighters; authorize $3.2 billion for procurement for four new B-2 stealth bombers and start-up costs for seven more; eliminate funds for the V-22 Osprey; authorize $124 million in procurement funds for the M-1 tank and no funds for upgrading older M-1 tanks; and authorize selected reserve troop cuts of 67,496. Rejected 127-287: R 122-37; D 5-249 (ND 3-169, SD 2-80); I 0-1, May 21, 1991. A "yea" was a vote supporting the president's position.

100. HR 2100. Fiscal 1992 Defense Authorization/Reduce Troops in Europe. Schroeder, D-Colo., amendment to express the sense of Congress that the United States should work with its allies to adapt NATO to the post-Cold War era by lowering the number of U.S. troops in Europe to less than 100,000 by fiscal 1995. Adopted 260-163: R 37-124; D 222-39 (ND 166-11, SD 56-28); I 1-0, May 21, 1991.

KEY

- Y Voted for (yea).
- # Paired for.
- + Announced for.
- N Voted against (nay).
- X Paired against.
- - Announced against.
- P Voted "present."
- C Voted "present" to avoid possible conflict of interest.
- ? Did not vote or otherwise make a position known.

Democrats ***Republicans***
Independent

	93	94	95	96	97	98	99	100
ALABAMA								
1 ***Callahan***	Y	N	Y	Y	N	N	Y	Y
2 ***Dickinson***	Y	Y	Y	Y	N	N	Y	N
3 Browder	N	Y	N	Y	N	N	N	Y
4 Bevill	N	Y	N	Y	N	N	N	N
5 Cramer	N	Y	N	Y	N	N	N	Y
6 Erdreich	N	Y	Y	Y	N	N	N	Y
7 Harris	N	Y	N	Y	N	N	N	Y
ALASKA								
AL ***Young***	N	N	Y	N	N	N	?	N
ARIZONA								
1 ***Rhodes***	Y	N	N	N	N	N	Y	N
2 Vacancy								
3 ***Stump***	Y	Y	Y	N	N	N	Y	N
4 ***Kyl***	Y	N	Y	N	N	Y	Y	N
5 ***Kolbe***	Y	N	N	N	N	Y	Y	N
ARKANSAS								
1 Alexander	N	N	N	?	?	?	Y	Y
2 Thornton	N	N	N	Y	N	N	N	Y
3 ***Hammerschmidt***	Y	Y	Y	Y	N	N	Y	N
4 Anthony	N	N	?	?	?	N	?	Y
CALIFORNIA								
1 ***Riggs***	Y	N	Y	Y	N	Y	Y	N
2 ***Herger***	Y	N	Y	N	N	N	Y	N
3 Matsui	N	N	?	Y	Y	Y	N	Y
4 Fazio	N	N	N	Y	N	N	N	Y
5 Pelosi	N	N	N	?	Y	Y	N	Y
6 Boxer	?	?	?	Y	Y	Y	N	Y
7 Miller	N	Y	N	Y	Y	Y	N	Y
8 Dellums	N	Y	N	Y	Y	Y	N	Y
9 Stark	N	Y	?	Y	Y	Y	N	Y
10 Edwards	N	N	N	Y	Y	Y	N	Y
11 Lantos	?	?	?	Y	N	Y	N	Y
12 ***Campbell***	N	Y	Y	+	+	-	Y	N
13 Mineta	?	N	N	Y	Y	Y	N	Y
14 ***Doolittle***	Y	N	Y	+	X	X	Y	N
15 Condit	Y	Y	Y	?	Y	Y	?	Y
16 Panetta	N	Y	N	Y	Y	Y	N	Y
17 Dooley	N	Y	N	?	N	Y	N	N
18 Lehman	N	Y	N	?	?	Y	N	Y
19 ***Lagomarsino***	Y	N	Y	N	N	N	Y	N
20 ***Thomas***	Y	N	Y	N	N	N	Y	N
21 ***Gallegly***	Y	N	Y	-	N	Y	Y	N
22 ***Moorhead***	Y	N	Y	Y	N	Y	Y	N
23 Beilenson	N	Y	N	Y	Y	Y	N	Y
24 Waxman	N	N	N	Y	Y	Y	N	Y
25 Roybal	N	N	N	Y	?	?	N	Y
26 Berman	N	N	N	?	Y	Y	-	Y
27 Levine	?	?	?	?	Y	Y	N	Y
28 Dixon	N	N	N	?	?	?	N	Y
29 Waters	N	Y	N	Y	Y	Y	N	Y
30 Martinez	N	N	N	?	?	N	N	Y
31 Dymally	N	N	N	Y	Y	Y	N	Y
32 Anderson	Y	N	N	?	?	?	Y	Y
33 ***Dreier***	Y	N	Y	Y	N	Y	Y	N
34 Torres	N	N	N	+	+	+	Y	Y
35 ***Lewis***	Y	N	Y	Y	N	Y	Y	N
36 Brown	N	N	?	?	N	?	N	Y
37 ***McCandless***	Y	Y	Y	Y	N	N	Y	N
38 ***Dornan***	Y	N	Y	N	N	N	Y	N
39 ***Dannemeyer***	Y	Y	Y	N	N	Y	Y	Y
40 ***Cox***	Y	N	Y	N	N	Y	Y	N
41 ***Lowery***	Y	N	N	?	N	Y	Y	N
42 ***Rohrabacher***	Y	N	Y	N	N	Y	Y	Y
43 ***Packard***	Y	N	Y	N	N	Y	Y	N
44 ***Cunningham***	Y	N	Y	Y	N	Y	Y	N
45 ***Hunter***	Y	N	Y	N	N	N	Y	N
COLORADO								
1 Schroeder	N	Y	N	Y	Y	Y	N	Y
2 Skaggs	N	N	N	Y	Y	N	N	Y
3 Campbell	N	N	N	?	?	?	Y	Y
4 ***Allard***	Y	N	Y	N	N	Y	Y	N
5 ***Hefley***	Y	Y	Y	N	N	N	Y	Y
6 ***Schaefer***	Y	Y	Y	N	N	N	Y	N
CONNECTICUT								
1 Kennelly	N	Y	N	Y	N	Y	N	Y
2 Gejdenson	N	N	N	Y	Y	Y	N	Y
3 DeLauro	N	N	N	Y	Y	Y	N	Y
4 ***Shays***	Y	Y	N	Y	Y	Y	N	Y
5 ***Franks***	Y	Y	Y	N	N	Y	Y	N
6 ***Johnson***	N	N	N	?	N	Y	Y	Y
DELAWARE								
AL Carper	N	N	N	Y	Y	N	N	Y
FLORIDA								
1 Hutto	Y	Y	Y	Y	N	N	N	N
2 Peterson	N	N	N	Y	N	Y	N	Y
3 Bennett	Y	Y	Y	Y	N	N	N	Y
4 ***James***	Y	Y	Y	Y	N	N	N	N
5 ***McCollum***	Y	N	Y	?	N	N	Y	N
6 ***Stearns***	Y	Y	+	N	N	Y	Y	N
7 Gibbons	?	?	?	Y	N	N	N	N
8 ***Young***	Y	Y	Y	Y	N	Y	Y	N
9 ***Bilirakis***	Y	Y	Y	Y	N	Y	Y	N
10 ***Ireland***	Y	N	Y	Y	N	N	Y	N
11 Bacchus	N	N	N	?	N	Y	N	Y
12 ***Lewis***	Y	Y	Y	Y	N	Y	Y	N
13 ***Goss***	Y	N	Y	N	N	Y	Y	N
14 Johnston	N	N	N	Y	Y	N	N	Y
15 ***Shaw***	Y	N	Y	N	N	N	Y	N
16 Smith	N	?	?	?	Y	N	N	Y
17 Lehman	?	?	?	?	#	?	?	?
18 ***Ros-Lehtinen***	Y	N	N	N	N	Y	Y	N
19 Fascell	N	N	N	Y	N	N	N	N
GEORGIA								
1 Thomas	N	Y	N	Y	N	N	N	N
2 Hatcher	?	?	?	Y	N	N	N	Y
3 Ray	N	Y	Y	Y	N	N	N	N
4 Jones	N	Y	N	Y	N	Y	N	Y
5 Lewis	N	Y	N	?	?	Y	N	Y
6 ***Gingrich***	Y	N	N	?	N	Y	Y	N
7 Darden	N	N	N	Y	N	N	N	Y
8 Rowland	N	Y	Y	?	N	N	N	Y
9 Jenkins	N	Y	Y	Y	N	N	N	Y
10 Barnard	N	Y	Y	Y	N	N	N	N
HAWAII								
1 Abercrombie	N	Y	N	Y	Y	Y	N	Y
2 Mink	N	N	N	?	Y	Y	N	Y
IDAHO								
1 LaRocco	N	Y	N	?	?	Y	-	Y
2 Stallings	N	Y	N	N	N	N	N	Y
ILLINOIS								
1 Hayes	N	Y	N	Y	Y	N	N	Y
2 Savage	N	Y	Y	?	Y	Y	N	Y
3 Russo	N	Y	Y	Y	Y	Y	N	Y
4 Sangmeister	N	Y	Y	Y	Y	Y	N	Y
5 Lipinski	N	?	?	Y	N	Y	N	Y
6 ***Hyde***	N	N	N	?	N	Y	Y	N
7 Collins	N	Y	N	?	Y	Y	N	Y
8 Rostenkowski	N	Y	N	Y	N	N	N	Y
9 Yates	N	Y	N	Y	Y	Y	N	Y
10 ***Porter***	N	N	N	?	N	Y	Y	Y
11 Annunzio	?	Y	N	Y	N	Y	N	Y
12 ***Crane***	Y	Y	Y	?	?	Y	Y	Y
13 ***Fawell***	Y	N	Y	Y	N	Y	Y	N
14 ***Hastert***	Y	N	Y	?	N	N	Y	N
15 Vacancy								
16 Cox	N	Y	N	Y	Y	Y	N	Y
17 Evans	N	Y	N	N	Y	Y	N	Y
18 ***Michel***	Y	N	N	Y	N	N	Y	N
19 Bruce	N	Y	N	Y	Y	Y	N	Y
20 Durbin	N	Y	N	Y	Y	Y	N	Y
21 Costello	N	Y	Y	Y	N	Y	N	Y
22 Poshard	N	Y	Y	Y	Y	Y	N	Y
INDIANA								
1 Visclosky	N	Y	N	Y	N	Y	N	Y
2 Sharp	N	Y	N	+	-	+	N	Y
3 Roemer	N	Y	N	Y	N	Y	N	Y

ND Northern Democrats SD Southern Democrats

	93	94	95	96	97	98	99	100
4 Long	N	Y	Y	Y	Y	Y	N	Y
5 Jontz	N	Y	Y	Y	Y	Y	N	Y
6 ***Burton***	Y	N	Y	N	N	N	Y	N
7 ***Myers***	N	N	N	?	N	N	N	N
8 McCloskey	N	Y	N	Y	N	N	N	Y
9 Hamilton	N	Y	N	Y	N	Y	N	Y
10 Jacobs	N	Y	Y	Y	Y	Y	N	Y
IOWA								
1 ***Leach***	N	N	N	Y	Y	Y	N	Y
2 ***Nussle***	Y	Y	Y	Y	N	Y	N	Y
3 Nagle	N	Y	N	?	?	Y	N	Y
4 Smith	?	?	?	Y	N	Y	N	Y
5 ***Lightfoot***	Y	Y	Y	Y	N	Y	Y	Y
6 ***Grandy***	N	Y	Y	Y	N	Y	Y	Y
KANSAS								
1 ***Roberts***	Y	Y	Y	Y	N	N	Y	N
2 Slattery	N	Y	Y	Y	N	N	N	N
3 ***Meyers***	Y	N	N	Y	N	Y	Y	N
4 Glickman	N	Y	N	Y	N	Y	N	Y
5 ***Nichols***	Y	N	Y	Y	N	Y	Y	N
KENTUCKY								
1 Hubbard	Y	Y	Y	?	?	?	N	N
2 Natcher	N	Y	Y	Y	N	N	N	Y
3 Mazzoli	N	Y	N	Y	N	N	N	Y
4 ***Bunning***	Y	N	Y	N	N	N	Y	N
5 ***Rogers***	Y	N	N	+	-	-	#	-
6 ***Hopkins***	?	?	?	?	?	?	?	?
7 Perkins	N	Y	N	Y	Y	N	N	Y
LOUISIANA								
1 ***Livingston***	N	N	N	Y	N	N	Y	N
2 Jefferson	?	Y	N	Y	Y	Y	N	Y
3 Tauzin	Y	N	Y	?	N	Y	N	Y
4 ***McCrery***	Y	N	N	Y	N	N	Y	N
5 Huckaby	N	N	N	Y	N	Y	Y	Y
6 ***Baker***	Y	N	N	Y	N	Y	Y	N
7 Hayes	Y	N	N	Y	N	Y	N	Y
8 ***Holloway***	Y	N	Y	N	N	N	Y	Y
MAINE								
1 Andrews	N	Y	N	Y	Y	?	N	Y
2 ***Snowe***	N	Y	Y	Y	N	N	N	N
MARYLAND								
1 ***Gilchrest***	N	N	Y	Y	N	N	Y	Y
2 ***Bentley***	N	N	Y	Y	N	?	Y	N
3 Cardin	N	N	N	?	N	N	N	Y
4 McMillen	N	N	N	Y	N	N	N	Y
5 Hoyer	N	N	N	?	N	N	N	Y
6 Byron	N	Y	Y	+	N	N	N	N
7 Mfume	N	Y	N	+	Y	Y	N	Y
8 ***Morella***	N	N	N	Y	N	Y	N	Y
MASSACHUSETTS								
1 Vacancy								
2 Neal	N	N	N	Y	Y	Y	N	Y
3 Early	Y	Y	N	Y	Y	Y	N	Y
4 Frank	N	Y	N	Y	Y	Y	N	Y
5 Atkins	N	N	N	Y	Y	Y	N	Y
6 Mavroules	N	N	N	Y	Y	N	N	Y
7 Markey	N	N	N	Y	Y	Y	N	Y
8 Kennedy	N	Y	N	Y	Y	Y	N	Y
9 Moakley	N	N	N	?	Y	Y	X	Y
10 Studds	N	Y	N	?	?	?	N	Y
11 Donnelly	Y	Y	N	Y	Y	Y	N	Y
MICHIGAN								
1 Conyers	N	Y	N	?	?	?	N	Y
2 ***Pursell***	Y	Y	Y	Y	N	Y	N	Y
3 Wolpe	N	N	N	Y	Y	Y	N	Y
4 ***Upton***	Y	Y	Y	N	N	Y	Y	Y
5 ***Henry***	Y	Y	Y	Y	N	Y	N	Y
6 Carr	N	Y	N	?	N	Y	N	Y
7 Kildee	N	N	N	Y	Y	Y	N	Y
8 Traxler	?	N	N	Y	Y	?	N	Y
9 ***Vander Jagt***	Y	N	N	?	N	Y	Y	N
10 ***Camp***	Y	Y	Y	Y	N	Y	N	N
11 ***Davis***	N	N	Y	Y	N	N	Y	N
12 Bonior	N	N	N	Y	Y	Y	N	Y
13 Collins	-	N	N	Y	Y	Y	N	Y
14 Hertel	N	N	N	?	Y	N	N	Y
15 Ford	N	Y	N	Y	Y	Y	N	Y
16 Dingell	N	?	?	Y	N	N	N	Y
17 Levin	N	N	N	Y	Y	Y	N	Y
18 ***Broomfield***	N	N	N	Y	N	Y	Y	N
MINNESOTA								
1 Penny	N	Y	N	Y	N	Y	N	Y
2 ***Weber***	N	N	N	N	N	N	Y	N
3 ***Ramstad***	Y	Y	Y	Y	N	Y	Y	N
4 Vento	N	Y	N	Y	Y	Y	N	Y

	93	94	95	96	97	98	99	100
5 Sabo	N	N	N	Y	Y	Y	N	Y
6 Sikorski	N	N	N	Y	Y	Y	N	Y
7 Peterson	N	N	N	Y	Y	Y	N	Y
8 Oberstar	N	N	N	?	Y	Y	N	Y
MISSISSIPPI								
1 Whitten	N	Y	Y	?	?	?	N	Y
2 Espy	N	Y	N	?	Y	N	N	Y
3 Montgomery	Y	Y	Y	Y	N	N	N	N
4 Parker	Y	Y	Y	?	?	N	N	N
5 Taylor	Y	Y	Y	N	N	N	-	N
MISSOURI								
1 Clay	N	Y	?	Y	Y	N	N	Y
2 Horn	N	N	N	Y	N	Y	N	Y
3 Gephardt	N	N	N	Y	Y	?	N	Y
4 Skelton	N	Y	Y	Y	N	N	N	N
5 Wheat	N	Y	N	Y	Y	Y	N	Y
6 ***Coleman***	N	N	N	N	?	?	Y	N
7 ***Hancock***	Y	Y	Y	N	N	N	Y	N
8 ***Emerson***	Y	Y	Y	N	N	N	N	Y
9 Volkmer	N	N	Y	?	N	Y	N	Y
MONTANA								
1 Williams	N	Y	N	?	Y	Y	N	Y
2 ***Marlenee***	Y	N	Y	?	N	N	Y	N
NEBRASKA								
1 ***Bereuter***	N	N	N	N	N	Y	Y	N
2 Hoagland	N	N	N	Y	N	N	N	Y
3 ***Barrett***	Y	N	N	Y	N	Y	Y	N
NEVADA								
1 Bilbray	Y	Y	N	Y	N	N	N	Y
2 ***Vucanovich***	Y	Y	Y	N	N	N	Y	N
NEW HAMPSHIRE								
1 ***Zeliff***	Y	Y	Y	N	N	Y	Y	N
2 Swett	N	Y	N	Y	N	Y	N	Y
NEW JERSEY								
1 Andrews	N	Y	N	Y	N	N	N	N
2 Hughes	N	Y	N	Y	N	Y	N	N
3 Pallone	N	N	Y	Y	N	N	N	N
4 ***Smith***	Y	N	N	?	N	N	N	N
5 ***Roukema***	Y	Y	N	?	N	Y	N	Y
6 Dwyer	N	N	?	Y	N	Y	N	Y
7 ***Rinaldo***	N	Y	Y	Y	N	N	N	N
8 Roe	N	Y	N	Y	N	Y	N	Y
9 Torricelli	N	Y	N	?	N	Y	N	N
10 Payne	N	Y	N	?	?	?	N	Y
11 ***Gallo***	N	N	N	?	N	Y	N	N
12 ***Zimmer***	Y	Y	Y	Y	N	Y	N	Y
13 ***Saxton***	N	N	N	Y	N	Y	N	N
14 Guarini	N	Y	N	?	N	Y	N	Y
NEW MEXICO								
1 ***Schiff***	N	N	N	Y	N	Y	Y	N
2 ***Skeen***	Y	Y	N	Y	N	N	Y	N
3 Richardson	N	N	N	Y	N	N	N	Y
NEW YORK								
1 Hochbrueckner	N	N	N	Y	N	N	N	Y
2 Downey	N	N	N	Y	Y	Y	N	Y
3 Mrazek	N	?	?	?	Y	Y	N	Y
4 ***Lent***	?	?	?	?	?	?	N	N
5 ***McGrath***	N	Y	N	Y	N	Y	N	N
6 Flake	N	N	N	?	Y	Y	N	Y
7 Ackerman	N	N	N	Y	Y	Y	N	Y
8 Scheuer	N	N	N	Y	Y	Y	N	Y
9 Manton	N	N	N	Y	N	Y	N	Y
10 Schumer	N	N	N	Y	Y	Y	N	Y
11 Towns	N	N	N	?	Y	Y	N	Y
12 Owens	N	N	N	Y	Y	Y	N	Y
13 Solarz	N	N	N	?	Y	Y	N	Y
14 ***Molinari***	Y	N	N	Y	N	Y	Y	N
15 ***Green***	N	N	N	Y	N	Y	N	Y
16 Rangel	N	N	N	?	#	#	X	Y
17 Weiss	N	N	N	Y	Y	Y	N	Y
18 Serrano	N	Y	N	Y	Y	Y	N	Y
19 Engel	N	N	N	?	Y	Y	N	Y
20 Lowey	N	N	N	?	Y	Y	N	Y
21 ***Fish***	N	N	?	Y	N	Y	Y	N
22 ***Gilman***	N	N	N	Y	N	Y	N	N
23 McNulty	N	N	N	Y	N	N	N	Y
24 ***Solomon***	Y	N	Y	Y	N	Y	Y	N
25 ***Boehlert***	N	N	N	Y	N	Y	Y	Y
26 ***Martin***	Y	N	N	Y	N	N	Y	N
27 ***Walsh***	N	N	Y	Y	N	Y	Y	N
28 McHugh	N	N	N	Y	Y	Y	N	Y
29 ***Horton***	N	N	N	Y	N	Y	N	Y
30 Slaughter	N	N	N	?	Y	Y	N	Y
31 ***Paxon***	Y	N	N	Y	N	Y	Y	N

	93	94	95	96	97	98	99	100
32 LaFalce	N	N	N	Y	Y	Y	N	Y
33 Nowak	N	N	N	Y	N	Y	N	Y
34 ***Houghton***	N	N	N	Y	N	Y	Y	N
NORTH CAROLINA								
1 Jones	N	Y	N	Y	N	N	N	Y
2 Valentine	Y	Y	Y	?	N	N	N	N
3 Lancaster	Y	N	Y	?	N	N	N	N
4 Price	N	N	N	?	N	N	N	Y
5 Neal	N	N	Y	?	?	?	N	N
6 ***Coble***	Y	Y	Y	N	N	N	N	N
7 Rose	N	N	N	Y	Y	N	N	Y
8 Hefner	N	Y	N	Y	N	N	N	Y
9 ***McMillan***	Y	N	N	Y	N	N	Y	N
10 ***Ballenger***	Y	N	Y	N	N	N	Y	N
11 ***Taylor***	Y	N	Y	N	N	N	N	N
NORTH DAKOTA								
AL Dorgan	N	Y	Y	Y	Y	Y	N	Y
OHIO								
1 Luken	N	Y	Y	Y	N	Y	N	Y
2 ***Gradison***	Y	Y	N	Y	N	N	?	?
3 Hall	N	Y	N	Y	Y	Y	N	Y
4 ***Oxley***	N	N	Y	N	N	Y	N	N
5 ***Gillmor***	N	N	Y	?	N	Y	Y	N
6 ***McEwen***	Y	N	Y	N	N	Y	Y	N
7 ***Hobson***	Y	N	Y	Y	N	Y	Y	N
8 ***Boehner***	Y	N	Y	Y	N	Y	Y	N
9 Kaptur	N	Y	Y	?	N	Y	N	Y
10 ***Miller***	Y	Y	Y	Y	N	N	Y	Y
11 Eckart	N	Y	N	Y	Y	Y	N	Y
12 ***Kasich***	Y	N	Y	Y	N	N	N	N
13 Pease	N	Y	N	Y	Y	Y	N	Y
14 Sawyer	N	N	N	Y	Y	Y	N	Y
15 ***Wylie***	?	N	Y	Y	N	N	Y	N
16 ***Regula***	Y	N	Y	Y	N	Y	N	Y
17 Traficant	N	Y	Y	Y	Y	Y	N	Y
18 Applegate	Y	Y	Y	?	?	Y	N	Y
19 Feighan	N	N	N	Y	Y	Y	N	Y
20 Oakar	N	N	N	Y	Y	Y	N	Y
21 Stokes	N	N	N	?	Y	Y	N	Y
OKLAHOMA								
1 ***Inhofe***	Y	N	Y	N	N	N	Y	N
2 Synar	N	Y	N	Y	Y	Y	N	Y
3 Brewster	N	Y	N	?	?	N	N	N
4 McCurdy	N	N	N	Y	N	N	N	N
5 ***Edwards***	Y	N	Y	Y	N	N	Y	N
6 English	Y	Y	Y	Y	N	N	N	Y
OREGON								
1 AuCoin	N	N	?	Y	Y	Y	N	Y
2 ***Smith***	Y	N	Y	Y	N	N	Y	N
3 Wyden	N	Y	N	Y	Y	Y	N	Y
4 DeFazio	N	Y	?	Y	Y	Y	?	Y
5 Kopetski	N	N	N	Y	Y	Y	N	Y
PENNSYLVANIA								
1 Foglietta	N	N	N	Y	Y	N	N	?
2 Gray	N	Y	N	?	?	?	?	?
3 Borski	N	N	N	Y	N	N	N	Y
4 Kolter	N	Y	N	?	?	?	N	Y
5 ***Schulze***	Y	N	Y	Y	N	N	Y	N
6 Yatron	N	N	N	?	?	?	N	Y
7 ***Weldon***	Y	N	Y	N	N	N	N	N
8 Kostmayer	N	N	N	?	Y	Y	N	Y
9 ***Shuster***	Y	Y	Y	?	N	N	Y	N
10 ***McDade***	N	N	N	Y	N	Y	Y	N
11 Kanjorski	N	Y	N	Y	N	N	N	Y
12 Murtha	N	N	N	Y	N	Y	N	N
13 ***Coughlin***	Y	N	N	Y	N	Y	Y	N
14 Coyne	N	N	N	?	?	?	N	Y
15 ***Ritter***	Y	N	Y	N	N	Y	Y	Y
16 ***Walker***	Y	Y	Y	N	N	Y	Y	N
17 ***Gekas***	Y	Y	Y	N	N	N	Y	N
18 ***Santorum***	Y	Y	Y	N	N	Y	N	Y
19 ***Goodling***	?	Y	Y	Y	N	Y	N	N
20 Gaydos	N	Y	N	Y	N	N	N	Y
21 ***Ridge***	N	N	Y	?	?	?	N	N
22 Murphy	N	Y	N	?	?	?	?	?
23 ***Clinger***	N	N	Y	Y	N	Y	Y	N
RHODE ISLAND								
1 ***Machtley***	N	N	Y	Y	N	Y	N	N
2 Reed	N	Y	N	Y	Y	Y	N	Y
SOUTH CAROLINA								
1 ***Ravenel***	Y	N	N	Y	N	Y	N	Y
2 ***Spence***	Y	N	Y	Y	N	Y	Y	N
3 Derrick	Y	Y	N	Y	N	N	N	Y
4 Patterson	Y	Y	Y	Y	N	Y	N	Y
5 Spratt	?	N	N	N	N	Y	N	Y
6 Tallon	Y	N	Y	?	N	Y	N	Y

	93	94	95	96	97	98	99	100
SOUTH DAKOTA								
AL Johnson	N	Y	Y	Y	N	Y	N	Y
TENNESSEE								
1 ***Quillen***	Y	N	Y	?	N	N	N	Y
2 ***Duncan***	Y	?	Y	Y	?	Y	Y	N
3 Lloyd	Y	Y	N	Y	N	N	N	N
4 Cooper	N	Y	N	Y	N	Y	N	N
5 Clement	N	Y	N	?	N	N	N	Y
6 Gordon	N	Y	N	Y	N	Y	N	Y
7 ***Sundquist***	Y	Y	N	?	?	N	Y	N
8 Tanner	N	Y	N	Y	N	N	N	N
9 Ford	?	N	?	Y	Y	?	N	Y
TEXAS								
1 Chapman	N	N	N	?	?	Y	N	Y
2 Wilson	N	N	N	?	?	?	N	N
3 Vacancy								
4 Hall	Y	N	Y	Y	N	N	N	Y
5 Bryant	N	N	N	?	Y	N	N	Y
6 ***Barton***	Y	N	Y	?	X	?	N	N
7 ***Archer***	Y	Y	Y	N	N	N	Y	N
8 ***Fields***	Y	Y	Y	?	N	N	Y	N
9 Brooks	N	N	N	?	N	Y	N	Y
10 Pickle	N	N	N	Y	N	N	N	Y
11 Edwards	N	N	N	?	N	N	N	Y
12 Geren	Y	Y	Y	Y	N	Y	N	N
13 Sarpalius	Y	N	N	Y	N	Y	N	Y
14 Laughlin	Y	N	Y	Y	N	Y	N	N
15 de la Garza	?	N	N	Y	N	N	N	Y
16 Coleman	N	N	N	?	N	Y	N	Y
17 Stenholm	Y	Y	N	Y	N	N	N	N
18 Washington	N	Y	N	?	?	Y	N	Y
19 ***Combest***	Y	Y	Y	Y	N	N	Y	N
20 Gonzalez	N	Y	N	Y	Y	N	N	Y
21 ***Smith***	Y	N	Y	Y	N	Y	Y	N
22 ***DeLay***	Y	N	Y	N	N	Y	Y	N
23 Bustamante	N	N	N	?	N	N	N	Y
24 Frost	N	?	?	Y	N	Y	N	Y
25 Andrews	N	N	N	?	N	Y	N	N
26 ***Armey***	Y	N	Y	N	N	N	Y	N
27 Ortiz	N	N	N	Y	N	N	N	N
UTAH								
1 ***Hansen***	Y	N	Y	N	N	Y	Y	N
2 Owens	N	N	N	?	?	?	N	Y
3 Orton	N	N	N	Y	N	Y	N	Y
VERMONT								
AL *Sanders*	N	Y	N	Y	Y	Y	N	Y
VIRGINIA								
1 ***Bateman***	N	Y	N	Y	N	N	Y	N
2 Pickett	N	Y	N	Y	N	N	N	N
3 ***Bliley***	Y	Y	Y	Y	N	N	Y	N
4 Sisisky	N	Y	N	Y	N	N	N	N
5 Payne	Y	Y	N	Y	N	N	N	Y
6 Olin	N	Y	Y	N	N	N	N	N
7 ***Slaughter***	Y	Y	N	Y	N	N	Y	N
8 Moran	N	N	N	Y	N	N	N	Y
9 Boucher	N	Y	N	?	Y	N	N	Y
10 ***Wolf***	N	N	N	Y	N	N	Y	Y
WASHINGTON								
1 ***Miller***	N	N	N	N	N	Y	Y	Y
2 Swift	N	Y	Y	Y	Y	Y	N	Y
3 Unsoeld	N	Y	N	Y	Y	Y	N	Y
4 ***Morrison***	N	N	N	N	N	N	Y	Y
5 Foley								
6 Dicks	N	N	N	Y	N	N	N	N
7 McDermott	N	N	N	?	Y	Y	N	Y
8 ***Chandler***	Y	Y	Y	Y	N	Y	Y	Y
WEST VIRGINIA								
1 Mollohan	N	N	N	?	N	N	N	N
2 Staggers	N	Y	N	Y	N	N	N	Y
3 Wise	N	N	N	Y	N	Y	N	Y
4 Rahall	N	Y	N	Y	Y	N	N	Y
WISCONSIN								
1 Aspin	N	?	?	Y	N	N	N	Y
2 ***Klug***	Y	Y	Y	?	?	?	N	N
3 ***Gunderson***	N	N	Y	Y	N	?	Y	Y
4 Kleczka	N	N	N	Y	Y	N	N	Y
5 Moody	?	?	?	?	Y	N	N	Y
6 ***Petri***	N	Y	Y	?	N	Y	Y	N
7 Obey	N	Y	N	Y	Y	N	N	Y
8 ***Roth***	Y	Y	Y	?	N	Y	#	Y
9 ***Sensenbrenner***	Y	Y	Y	N	N	Y	N	Y
WYOMING								
AL ***Thomas***	Y	N	Y	?	?	Y	Y	N

Southern states - Ala., Ark., Fla., Ga., Ky., La., Miss., N.C., Okla., S.C., Tenn., Texas, Va.
Omitted votes are quorum calls, which CQ does not include in its vote charts.

HOUSE VOTES 101, 102, 103, 104, 105, 106, 107, 108

101. HR 2100. Fiscal 1992 Defense Authorization/Cuts. Frank, D-Mass., amendment to cut $8 billion from the bill's total authorization by the withdrawal of U.S. forces from Europe, Japan or South Korea. The reduction could be offset if there were an increase in support from a host nation of an equal amount. The amendment also would require reports on steps being taken to close overseas military installations. Rejected 167-255: R 9-151; D 157-104 (ND 137-40, SD 20-64); I 1-0, May 21, 1991. A "nay" was a vote supporting the president's position.

102. HR 2100. Fiscal 1992 Defense Authorization/Cost Sharing. Dorgan, D-N.D., amendment to require the president to seek defense cost-sharing agreements with nations in which the United States has bilateral or multilateral defense agreements and establish an allies mutual defense payments account. Adopted 357-58: R 103-56; D 253-2 (ND 171-1, SD 82-1); I 1-0, May 21, 1991.

103. HR 2100. Fiscal 1992 Defense Authorization/Reduce Troops in South Korea. Mrazek, D-N.Y., amendment to reduce the current troop level of 43,000 U.S. troops in South Korea by placing a permanent ceiling of 30,000 troops by fiscal 1994, of which not more than 20,000 may be members of the Army. The president could waive the ceiling in the event of an armed attack or an emergency. Rejected 143-275: R 8-151; D 134-124 (ND 112-63, SD 22-61); I 1-0, May 21, 1991. A "nay" was a vote supporting the president's position.

104. Procedural Motion. Nussle, R-Iowa, motion to approve the House Journal of Tuesday, May 21. Motion agreed to 284-105: R 49-100; D 235-5 (ND 156-4, SD 79-1); I 0-0, May 22, 1991.

105. HR 2100. Fiscal 1992 Defense Authorization/Tactical Missile. Hunter, R-Calif., amendment to require the new tactical missile defense program to have the capability of defending against all ballistic missiles being deployed and developed by certain nations; have a capability at least equal to the Soviet SA-12 system with upgrades; have a high probability of intercepting and destroying chemical, biological, nuclear, and conventional warheads; and have the capability of destroying multiple threats of the Chinese CSS-2 class missile. Rejected 161-265: R 150-14; D 11-250 (ND 5-173, SD 6-77); I 0-1, May 22, 1991.

106. HR 2100. Fiscal 1992 Defense Authorization/ICBM. Frank, D-Mass., amendment to terminate the small intercontinental ballistic missile (ICBM) program, Midgetman missile program, by cutting the $549 million authorized for continued research and development of the program. Rejected 109-317: R 28-136; D 80-181 (ND 74-104, SD 6-77); I 1-0, May 22, 1991. A "nay" was a vote supporting the president's position.

107. HR 2100. Fiscal 1992 Defense Authorization/Drug Testing. Solomon, R-N.Y., amendment to require the Department of Defense to establish and implement a program to test all its employees for the illegal use of drugs. Rejected 157-269: R 124-40; D 33-228 (ND 11-167, SD 22-61); I 0-1, May 22, 1991.

108. HR 2100. Fiscal 1992 Defense Authorization/Drug Testing of New Employees. Solomon, R-N.Y., amendment to require the Department of Defense to test all prospective employees for the illegal use of drugs. Rejected 197-231: R 137-27; D 60-203 (ND 21-158, SD 39-45); I 0-1, May 22, 1991.

** Rep. Sam Johnson, R-Texas, was sworn in May 22, 1991. The first vote for which he was eligible was vote 105.*

KEY

Y Voted for (yea).
\# Paired for.
\+ Announced for.
N Voted against (nay).
X Paired against.
\- Announced against.
P Voted "present."
C Voted "present" to avoid possible conflict of interest.
? Did not vote or otherwise make a position known.

Democrats ***Republicans***
Independent

	101	102	103	104	105	106	107	108
ALABAMA								
1 ***Callahan***	N	N	N	Y	Y	N	Y	Y
2 ***Dickinson***	N	N	N	N	Y	Y	Y	Y
3 Browder	N	Y	N	Y	?	?	?	Y
4 Bevill	N	Y	N	Y	N	N	N	Y
5 Cramer	N	Y	N	Y	N	N	N	Y
6 Erdreich	N	Y	N	Y	N	N	N	Y
7 Harris	N	Y	N	Y	N	N	N	Y
ALASKA								
AL ***Young***	N	Y	N	N	Y	N	N	Y
ARIZONA								
1 ***Rhodes***	N	N	N	N	Y	Y	Y	Y
2 Vacancy								
3 ***Stump***	N	N	N	N	Y	N	Y	Y
4 ***Kyl***	N	N	N	N	Y	N	Y	Y
5 ***Kolbe***	N	N	N	N	N	N	Y	Y
ARKANSAS								
1 Alexander	Y	Y	N	Y	Y	N	N	N
2 Thornton	N	Y	N	Y	N	N	N	N
3 ***Hammerschmidt***	N	N	N	Y	Y	N	Y	Y
4 Anthony	Y	Y	N	Y	N	N	N	N
CALIFORNIA								
1 ***Riggs***	N	Y	N	?	Y	N	Y	Y
2 ***Herger***	N	Y	N	N	Y	Y	Y	Y
3 Matsui	Y	Y	Y	Y	N	N	N	N
4 Fazio	N	Y	N	Y	N	N	N	N
5 Pelosi	Y	+	Y	Y	N	Y	N	N
6 Boxer	Y	Y	Y	Y	N	Y	N	N
7 Miller	Y	Y	Y	Y	N	Y	N	N
8 Dellums	Y	Y	Y	Y	N	Y	N	N
9 Stark	Y	Y	Y	Y	N	Y	N	N
10 Edwards	Y	Y	Y	?	N	Y	N	N
11 Lantos	Y	Y	N	Y	N	N	N	N
12 ***Campbell***	N	Y	N	N	Y	Y	N	N
13 Mineta	Y	Y	Y	Y	N	Y	N	N
14 ***Doolittle***	N	N	N	Y	Y	N	Y	Y
15 Condit	N	Y	Y	Y	N	N	Y	Y
16 Panetta	Y	Y	N	Y	N	N	N	N
17 Dooley	Y	Y	N	Y	N	N	N	N
18 Lehman	Y	Y	Y	Y	N	N	N	N
19 ***Lagomarsino***	N	Y	N	N	Y	N	Y	Y
20 ***Thomas***	N	Y	N	N	Y	N	Y	N
21 ***Gallegly***	N	Y	N	N	Y	N	Y	Y
22 ***Moorhead***	N	Y	N	N	Y	N	Y	Y
23 Beilenson	Y	Y	Y	Y	N	Y	N	N
24 Waxman	Y	Y	N	Y	N	N	N	N
25 Roybal	Y	Y	Y	?	N	Y	N	N
26 Berman	Y	Y	N	?	N	N	N	N
27 Levine	N	Y	N	Y	N	N	N	N
28 Dixon	Y	Y	Y	Y	N	N	N	N
29 Waters	Y	Y	Y	Y	N	Y	N	N
30 Martinez	N	Y	Y	Y	N	N	N	N
31 Dymally	Y	Y	Y	Y	N	Y	N	N
32 Anderson	Y	Y	Y	Y	N	N	N	N
33 ***Dreier***	N	Y	N	Y	Y	N	Y	Y
34 Torres	Y	Y	Y	Y	N	Y	N	N
35 ***Lewis***	N	N	N	N	Y	N	Y	Y
36 Brown	Y	Y	N	Y	N	N	N	N
37 ***McCandless***	N	N	N	N	Y	N	Y	Y
38 ***Dornan***	N	Y	N	Y	Y	N	Y	Y
39 ***Dannemeyer***	N	Y	N	N	Y	N	Y	Y
40 ***Cox***	N	Y	N	Y	Y	N	Y	Y
41 ***Lowery***	N	Y	N	?	Y	N	Y	Y
42 ***Rohrabacher***	Y	Y	Y	N	Y	Y	Y	Y
43 ***Packard***	N	N	N	N	Y	N	Y	Y
44 ***Cunningham***	N	Y	N	Y	Y	N	Y	Y
45 ***Hunter***	N	Y	N	N	Y	N	Y	Y
COLORADO								
1 Schroeder	Y	Y	Y	N	N	Y	N	N
2 Skaggs	Y	N	N	Y	N	N	N	N
3 Campbell	Y	Y	N	Y	N	N	N	N
4 ***Allard***	N	Y	N	N	Y	N	Y	Y
5 ***Hefley***	N	Y	Y	N	Y	N	Y	Y
6 ***Schaefer***	N	Y	N	N	Y	N	Y	Y
CONNECTICUT								
1 Kennelly	Y	Y	N	Y	N	Y	N	N
2 Gejdenson	Y	Y	Y	?	N	Y	N	N
3 DeLauro	Y	Y	Y	Y	N	N	N	N
4 ***Shays***	Y	Y	N	N	N	Y	Y	Y
5 ***Franks***	N	N	N	N	Y	N	Y	Y
6 ***Johnson***	N	Y	N	Y	Y	Y	Y	N
DELAWARE								
AL Carper	N	Y	Y	Y	N	Y	N	Y
FLORIDA								
1 Hutto	N	Y	N	Y	Y	N	Y	Y
2 Peterson	N	Y	N	Y	N	N	N	N
3 Bennett	Y	Y	N	Y	N	N	Y	Y
4 ***James***	N	Y	N	N	Y	N	Y	Y
5 ***McCollum***	N	Y	N	N	Y	N	Y	Y
6 ***Stearns***	N	Y	N	N	Y	N	Y	Y
7 Gibbons	N	Y	N	Y	N	N	Y	Y
8 ***Young***	N	Y	N	N	Y	N	Y	Y
9 ***Bilirakis***	N	Y	N	N	Y	Y	Y	Y
10 ***Ireland***	N	N	N	N	Y	N	Y	Y
11 Bacchus	N	Y	N	Y	N	N	N	N
12 ***Lewis***	N	Y	N	N	Y	N	Y	Y
13 ***Goss***	N	N	N	N	Y	N	Y	Y
14 Johnston	Y	Y	Y	Y	N	Y	N	N
15 ***Shaw***	N	Y	N	Y	Y	N	Y	Y
16 Smith	Y	Y	Y	Y	N	N	N	N
17 Lehman	?	?	?	?	?	?	?	?
18 ***Ros-Lehtinen***	N	Y	N	N	Y	N	Y	Y
19 Fascell	N	Y	N	Y	N	N	N	N
GEORGIA								
1 Thomas	N	Y	N	Y	N	N	N	N
2 Hatcher	N	Y	N	Y	N	N	N	N
3 Ray	N	Y	N	Y	N	N	N	N
4 Jones	N	Y	Y	Y	N	N	N	N
5 Lewis	Y	Y	Y	Y	N	Y	N	N
6 ***Gingrich***	N	N	N	N	Y	N	Y	Y
7 Darden	N	Y	N	Y	N	N	N	N
8 Rowland	N	Y	N	Y	N	N	N	N
9 Jenkins	N	Y	N	Y	N	N	N	N
10 Barnard	N	Y	N	Y	N	N	N	N
HAWAII								
1 Abercrombie	Y	Y	Y	Y	N	Y	N	N
2 Mink	Y	Y	Y	Y	N	Y	N	N
IDAHO								
1 LaRocco	N	Y	N	Y	N	N	N	N
2 Stallings	N	Y	N	Y	N	N	Y	N
ILLINOIS								
1 Hayes	Y	Y	Y	Y	N	Y	N	N
2 Savage	Y	?	Y	?	N	Y	N	N
3 Russo	Y	Y	Y	Y	N	Y	N	N
4 Sangmeister	Y	Y	Y	Y	N	Y	N	Y
5 Lipinski	Y	Y	Y	Y	Y	N	N	Y
6 ***Hyde***	N	N	N	N	Y	N	Y	Y
7 Collins	Y	Y	Y	Y	N	Y	N	N
8 Rostenkowski	N	Y	Y	Y	N	Y	Y	N
9 Yates	Y	Y	Y	Y	N	Y	N	N
10 ***Porter***	N	N	Y	N	Y	N	N	Y
11 Annunzio	N	Y	Y	Y	N	N	N	N
12 ***Crane***	N	N	Y	N	Y	N	Y	Y
13 ***Fawell***	N	Y	N	N	Y	N	Y	Y
14 ***Hastert***	N	N	N	N	Y	N	Y	Y
15 Vacancy								
16 Cox	Y	Y	Y	Y	N	Y	N	N
17 Evans	Y	Y	Y	Y	N	Y	N	N
18 ***Michel***	N	N	N	N	Y	N	Y	Y
19 Bruce	Y	Y	Y	Y	N	N	N	N
20 Durbin	Y	Y	Y	Y	N	Y	N	N
21 Costello	N	Y	Y	Y	N	N	N	Y
22 Poshard	Y	Y	Y	Y	N	Y	N	Y
INDIANA								
1 Visclosky	N	Y	N	Y	N	N	N	N
2 Sharp	Y	Y	N	Y	N	N	N	N
3 Roemer	N	Y	N	Y	N	N	N	Y

ND Northern Democrats SD Southern Democrats

	101	102	103	104	105	106	107	108
4 Long	Y	Y	N	Y	N	N	N	N
5 Jontz	Y	Y	Y	Y	N	N	N	N
6 ***Burton***	N	N	N	N	Y	N	Y	Y
7 ***Myers***	N	N	N	Y	N	N	N	N
8 McCloskey	Y	Y	N	Y	N	N	N	N
9 Hamilton	N	Y	N	Y	N	N	N	N
10 Jacobs	Y	Y	Y	N	N	N	N	N
IOWA								
1 ***Leach***	Y	Y	N	N	N	Y	N	N
2 ***Nussle***	Y	Y	N	N	Y	Y	Y	Y
3 Nagle	Y	Y	Y	Y	N	N	N	N
4 Smith	N	Y	N	Y	N	N	N	N
5 ***Lightfoot***	N	N	N	?	Y	N	Y	Y
6 ***Grandy***	Y	Y	N	N	Y	Y	N	N
KANSAS								
1 ***Roberts***	N	Y	N	N	N	N	Y	Y
2 Slattery	N	Y	N	Y	N	Y	N	N
3 ***Meyers***	N	Y	N	N	N	N	Y	Y
4 Glickman	N	Y	N	Y	N	N	Y	Y
5 ***Nichols***	N	Y	N	?	Y	N	Y	Y
KENTUCKY								
1 Hubbard	N	Y	Y	Y	N	N	Y	Y
2 Natcher	N	Y	Y	Y	N	N	N	N
3 Mazzoli	N	Y	N	Y	N	N	N	N
4 ***Bunning***	N	N	N	N	Y	N	Y	Y
5 ***Rogers***	-	+	-	?	Y	N	Y	Y
6 ***Hopkins***	?	?	?	?	?	?	?	?
7 Perkins	Y	Y	Y	Y	N	N	N	N
LOUISIANA								
1 ***Livingston***	N	N	N	?	Y	N	N	Y
2 Jefferson	Y	Y	?	Y	N	N	N	Y
3 Tauzin	N	Y	N	Y	N	N	Y	Y
4 ***McCrery***	N	N	N	N	Y	N	Y	Y
5 Huckaby	N	Y	N	Y	Y	N	N	Y
6 ***Baker***	N	N	N	N	Y	N	N	Y
7 Hayes	Y	Y	Y	Y	Y	N	Y	Y
8 ***Holloway***	N	?	?	?	Y	N	Y	Y
MAINE								
1 Andrews	Y	Y	Y	Y	N	Y	N	N
2 ***Snowe***	N	Y	N	Y	Y	N	N	N
MARYLAND								
1 ***Gilchrest***	N	Y	N	N	Y	N	Y	Y
2 ***Bentley***	N	Y	N	N	Y	N	N	Y
3 Cardin	Y	Y	Y	Y	N	N	N	N
4 McMillen	N	Y	Y	Y	N	N	N	N
5 Hoyer	N	Y	N	Y	N	N	N	N
6 Byron	N	N	Y	N	Y	N	N	N
7 Mfume	Y	Y	Y	Y	N	Y	N	N
8 ***Morella***	N	Y	N	Y	N	Y	N	N
MASSACHUSETTS								
1 Vacancy								
2 Neal	Y	Y	Y	Y	N	N	N	N
3 Early	Y	Y	Y	Y	N	Y	Y	Y
4 Frank	Y	Y	Y	?	N	Y	N	N
5 Atkins	Y	Y	Y	?	N	Y	N	N
6 Mavroules	N	Y	N	?	N	N	N	N
7 Markey	Y	Y	Y	Y	N	Y	N	N
8 Kennedy	Y	Y	Y	Y	N	N	N	N
9 Moakley	Y	Y	N	Y	N	Y	N	N
10 Studds	Y	Y	Y	Y	N	Y	N	N
11 Donnelly	Y	Y	Y	Y	N	Y	Y	N
MICHIGAN								
1 Conyers	Y	Y	Y	Y	N	N	N	N
2 ***Pursell***	N	Y	N	?	Y	N	Y	Y
3 Wolpe	Y	Y	Y	Y	N	Y	N	N
4 ***Upton***	N	Y	N	N	Y	Y	Y	Y
5 ***Henry***	N	Y	N	N	Y	Y	Y	Y
6 Carr	Y	Y	N	Y	N	N	Y	N
7 Kildee	Y	Y	Y	Y	N	Y	N	N
8 Traxler	Y	Y	Y	Y	N	Y	N	N
9 ***Vander Jagt***	N	Y	N	Y	Y	N	Y	Y
10 ***Camp***	N	Y	N	N	Y	N	Y	Y
11 ***Davis***	N	Y	N	Y	Y	N	N	N
12 Bonior	Y	Y	Y	Y	N	Y	N	N
13 Collins	Y	Y	Y	Y	N	Y	N	N
14 Hertel	Y	Y	Y	Y	N	Y	N	N
15 Ford	Y	Y	Y	?	?	?	?	?
16 Dingell	Y	Y	Y	Y	N	Y	N	N
17 Levin	Y	Y	N	Y	N	Y	N	N
18 ***Broomfield***	N	Y	N	Y	Y	N	Y	Y
MINNESOTA								
1 Penny	N	Y	Y	Y	N	N	N	N
2 ***Weber***	N	Y	N	N	Y	Y	N	Y
3 ***Ramstad***	N	Y	N	N	Y	N	Y	Y
4 Vento	Y	Y	Y	Y	N	Y	N	N

	101	102	103	104	105	106	107	108
5 Sabo	N	Y	Y	Y	N	N	N	N
6 Sikorski	Y	Y	Y	N	N	Y	N	N
7 Peterson	N	Y	N	Y	N	N	N	N
8 Oberstar	Y	Y	Y	Y	N	Y	N	N
MISSISSIPPI								
1 Whitten	N	Y	Y	Y	N	N	N	N
2 Espy	N	Y	Y	Y	N	N	N	N
3 Montgomery	N	Y	N	Y	N	N	N	Y
4 Parker	N	Y	N	Y	N	N	N	Y
5 Taylor	N	Y	N	Y	N	N	Y	Y
MISSOURI								
1 Clay	Y	Y	Y	N	N	Y	N	N
2 Horn	Y	Y	N	Y	N	N	N	N
3 Gephardt	Y	?	?	Y	N	N	N	N
4 Skelton	N	Y	N	Y	N	N	N	N
5 Wheat	Y	Y	Y	Y	N	Y	N	N
6 ***Coleman***	N	Y	N	Y	Y	N	Y	Y
7 ***Hancock***	N	N	N	N	Y	N	Y	Y
8 ***Emerson***	N	Y	N	Y	Y	N	Y	Y
9 Volkmer	N	Y	N	Y	N	N	N	N
MONTANA								
1 Williams	Y	Y	Y	Y	N	N	N	N
2 ***Marlenee***	N	N	N	N	Y	N	Y	Y
NEBRASKA								
1 ***Bereuter***	N	Y	Y	N	Y	N	Y	Y
2 Hoagland	N	Y	N	Y	N	N	N	N
3 ***Barrett***	-	N	N	N	Y	N	Y	Y
NEVADA								
1 Bilbray	N	Y	N	Y	N	N	N	N
2 ***Vucanovich***	N	N	N	?	Y	N	Y	Y
NEW HAMPSHIRE								
1 ***Zeliff***	N	Y	N	N	Y	N	Y	Y
2 Swett	Y	Y	N	?	N	N	N	N
NEW JERSEY								
1 Andrews	N	Y	N	Y	N	N	N	Y
2 Hughes	Y	Y	N	Y	N	N	N	N
3 Pallone	N	Y	N	Y	N	N	N	Y
4 ***Smith***	N	Y	N	Y	Y	Y	Y	Y
5 ***Roukema***	N	Y	N	N	N	N	Y	Y
6 Dwyer	Y	Y	N	Y	N	N	N	N
7 ***Rinaldo***	N	Y	N	Y	Y	N	N	Y
8 Roe	Y	Y	N	?	N	N	N	N
9 Torricelli	Y	?	?	Y	N	N	N	Y
10 Payne	Y	Y	Y	Y	N	Y	N	N
11 ***Gallo***	N	Y	N	N	Y	N	N	Y
12 ***Zimmer***	N	Y	N	N	Y	N	Y	Y
13 ***Saxton***	N	Y	N	N	Y	N	N	Y
14 Guarini	N	Y	Y	Y	Y	Y	N	Y
NEW MEXICO								
1 ***Schiff***	N	Y	N	Y	Y	Y	N	Y
2 ***Skeen***	N	Y	N	Y	Y	N	Y	Y
3 Richardson	N	Y	N	Y	N	N	N	N
NEW YORK								
1 Hochbrueckner	Y	Y	Y	Y	N	Y	N	N
2 Downey	Y	Y	Y	Y	N	N	N	N
3 Mrazek	Y	Y	Y	Y	N	Y	N	N
4 ***Lent***	N	N	N	Y	Y	N	N	Y
5 ***McGrath***	N	Y	N	Y	Y	Y	N	N
6 Flake	Y	Y	Y	Y	N	Y	N	N
7 Ackerman	Y	Y	N	Y	N	N	N	N
8 Scheuer	Y	Y	Y	Y	N	Y	N	N
9 Manton	N	Y	N	Y	N	N	N	N
10 Schumer	Y	Y	Y	Y	N	N	N	N
11 Towns	Y	Y	Y	Y	N	Y	N	N
12 Owens	Y	?	Y	Y	N	Y	N	N
13 Solarz	N	Y	N	Y	N	N	N	N
14 ***Molinari***	N	N	N	N	Y	Y	Y	Y
15 ***Green***	Y	Y	N	Y	N	N	N	N
16 Rangel	Y	Y	Y	?	N	Y	N	N
17 Weiss	Y	Y	Y	Y	N	Y	N	N
18 Serrano	Y	Y	Y	?	?	?	?	N
19 Engel	Y	Y	Y	Y	N	N	N	N
20 Lowey	Y	Y	N	Y	N	Y	N	N
21 ***Fish***	N	Y	N	Y	Y	N	N	N
22 ***Gilman***	N	N	N	Y	Y	N	N	N
23 McNulty	Y	Y	Y	Y	N	N	N	N
24 ***Solomon***	N	N	N	N	Y	N	Y	Y
25 ***Boehlert***	N	Y	N	N	N	N	N	N
26 ***Martin***	N	N	N	N	Y	N	N	Y
27 ***Walsh***	N	N	N	Y	Y	Y	Y	Y
28 McHugh	N	Y	N	?	N	N	N	N
29 ***Horton***	N	Y	N	Y	Y	N	N	N
30 Slaughter	Y	Y	Y	Y	N	Y	N	N
31 ***Paxon***	N	Y	N	N	Y	N	Y	Y

	101	102	103	104	105	106	107	108
32 LaFalce	Y	Y	N	Y	N	N	N	N
33 Nowak	Y	Y	Y	Y	N	N	N	N
34 ***Houghton***	N	N	N	Y	N	N	N	N
NORTH CAROLINA								
1 Jones	N	Y	N	Y	Y	N	N	N
2 Valentine	N	Y	N	Y	N	N	Y	Y
3 Lancaster	N	Y	N	Y	N	N	Y	Y
4 Price	N	Y	N	Y	N	N	N	N
5 Neal	N	Y	N	Y	N	N	N	Y
6 ***Coble***	N	Y	N	N	Y	N	Y	Y
7 Rose	N	Y	N	Y	N	N	N	N
8 Hefner	N	Y	N	Y	N	N	N	Y
9 ***McMillan***	N	Y	N	N	Y	N	Y	Y
10 ***Ballenger***	N	Y	N	N	Y	N	Y	Y
11 ***Taylor***	N	Y	N	?	Y	N	Y	Y
NORTH DAKOTA								
AL Dorgan	Y	Y	Y	Y	N	Y	N	N
OHIO								
1 Luken	N	Y	N	Y	N	N	N	Y
2 ***Gradison***	?	?	?	Y	Y	N	Y	Y
3 Hall	Y	Y	Y	Y	N	N	N	N
4 ***Oxley***	N	N	N	N	Y	N	N	Y
5 ***Gillmor***	N	Y	N	Y	Y	N	N	N
6 ***McEwen***	N	N	N	Y	Y	N	Y	Y
7 ***Hobson***	N	Y	N	Y	Y	N	Y	Y
8 ***Boehner***	N	Y	N	N	Y	N	Y	Y
9 Kaptur	Y	Y	N	?	N	N	N	N
10 ***Miller***	Y	Y	Y	N	Y	N	Y	Y
11 Eckart	Y	Y	Y	Y	N	Y	N	N
12 ***Kasich***	N	Y	N	Y	Y	N	Y	Y
13 Pease	N	Y	N	Y	N	N	N	N
14 Sawyer	Y	Y	N	Y	N	N	N	N
15 ***Wylie***	N	Y	N	Y	Y	N	Y	Y
16 ***Regula***	N	Y	N	N	Y	N	Y	Y
17 Traficant	Y	Y	Y	Y	Y	Y	N	N
18 Applegate	Y	Y	Y	Y	Y	N	Y	Y
19 Feighan	Y	Y	N	Y	N	N	N	N
20 Oakar	Y	Y	N	Y	N	N	N	N
21 Stokes	Y	Y	Y	Y	N	Y	N	N
OKLAHOMA								
1 ***Inhofe***	N	N	N	N	Y	N	Y	Y
2 Synar	Y	Y	Y	Y	N	N	N	N
3 Brewster	N	Y	N	N	N	N	Y	Y
4 McCurdy	N	Y	N	Y	N	N	N	Y
5 ***Edwards***	N	Y	N	N	Y	N	N	Y
6 English	N	Y	N	Y	N	N	Y	Y
OREGON								
1 AuCoin	Y	Y	Y	Y	N	N	N	N
2 ***Smith***	N	N	N	N	Y	N	N	Y
3 Wyden	Y	Y	Y	Y	N	Y	N	N
4 DeFazio	Y	Y	Y	Y	N	Y	N	Y
5 Kopetski	Y	Y	N	Y	N	N	N	Y
PENNSYLVANIA								
1 Foglietta	?	?	?	Y	N	N	N	N
2 Gray	?	?	?	Y	N	N	N	N
3 Borski	Y	Y	Y	Y	N	N	N	N
4 Kolter	Y	Y	Y	?	N	N	Y	Y
5 ***Schulze***	N	Y	N	Y	Y	N	Y	Y
6 Yatron	Y	Y	Y	Y	N	N	Y	Y
7 ***Weldon***	N	Y	N	N	Y	Y	Y	Y
8 Kostmayer	Y	Y	Y	Y	N	N	N	N
9 ***Shuster***	N	N	N	Y	Y	N	Y	Y
10 ***McDade***	N	N	N	N	Y	N	N	N
11 Kanjorski	Y	Y	Y	Y	N	N	N	N
12 Murtha	N	Y	N	Y	N	N	N	N
13 ***Coughlin***	N	Y	N	N	N	N	Y	Y
14 Coyne	Y	Y	N	Y	N	Y	N	N
15 ***Ritter***	N	Y	N	Y	Y	Y	Y	Y
16 ***Walker***	N	N	N	N	Y	Y	Y	Y
17 ***Gekas***	N	N	N	N	Y	N	Y	Y
18 ***Santorum***	N	Y	N	N	Y	N	Y	Y
19 ***Goodling***	N	N	N	?	N	N	Y	Y
20 Gaydos	Y	Y	Y	?	N	N	N	N
21 ***Ridge***	N	Y	N	N	Y	N	N	N
22 Murphy	?	?	?	P	N	N	Y	Y
23 ***Clinger***	N	Y	N	Y	Y	N	N	N
RHODE ISLAND								
1 ***Machtley***	N	N	N	N	Y	Y	N	N
2 Reed	Y	Y	N	Y	N	Y	N	N
SOUTH CAROLINA								
1 ***Ravenel***	N	Y	N	?	Y	N	Y	Y
2 ***Spence***	N	Y	N	Y	Y	N	Y	Y
3 Derrick	Y	Y	Y	Y	N	N	N	Y
4 Patterson	N	Y	N	Y	N	N	Y	Y
5 Spratt	N	Y	N	Y	N	N	N	Y
6 Tallon	N	Y	N	?	N	N	Y	Y

	101	102	103	104	105	106	107	108
SOUTH DAKOTA								
AL Johnson	Y	Y	Y	Y	Y	N	N	N
TENNESSEE								
1 ***Quillen***	N	N	N	N	N	N	Y	Y
2 ***Duncan***	Y	Y	Y	N	Y	Y	Y	Y
3 Lloyd	N	Y	N	Y	N	N	Y	Y
4 Cooper	N	N	N	Y	N	N	N	N
5 Clement	N	Y	N	Y	N	N	N	N
6 Gordon	Y	Y	Y	Y	N	N	N	N
7 ***Sundquist***	N	N	N	?	Y	N	Y	Y
8 Tanner	N	Y	N	Y	N	N	N	N
9 Ford	Y	?	Y	Y	N	Y	N	N
TEXAS								
1 Chapman	N	Y	N	Y	N	N	N	Y
2 Wilson	N	Y	Y	?	Y	N	Y	Y
3 ***Johnson***[1]					Y	N	Y	Y
4 Hall	N	Y	N	Y	N	N	Y	Y
5 Bryant	Y	Y	Y	Y	N	Y	N	N
6 ***Barton***	N	Y	?	Y	Y	N	Y	Y
7 ***Archer***	N	Y	N	Y	Y	N	Y	Y
8 ***Fields***	N	Y	N	N	Y	N	Y	Y
9 Brooks	N	Y	N	Y	N	N	N	N
10 Pickle	N	Y	Y	Y	N	N	N	N
11 Edwards	N	Y	N	P	N	N	N	N
12 Geren	N	Y	N	Y	N	N	Y	Y
13 Sarpalius	Y	Y	N	Y	N	N	Y	Y
14 Laughlin	N	Y	N	Y	N	N	Y	Y
15 de la Garza	Y	Y	N	Y	N	N	Y	N
16 Coleman	N	Y	N	Y	N	N	N	Y
17 Stenholm	N	Y	N	Y	N	N	Y	Y
18 Washington	Y	Y	Y	?	N	Y	N	N
19 ***Combest***	N	N	N	Y	Y	N	Y	Y
20 Gonzalez	N	Y	Y	Y	N	N	N	N
21 ***Smith***	N	N	N	N	Y	N	Y	Y
22 ***DeLay***	N	N	N	N	Y	N	Y	Y
23 Bustamante	Y	Y	N	Y	N	N	N	N
24 Frost	N	Y	N	Y	N	N	N	N
25 Andrews	N	Y	Y	Y	N	N	N	Y
26 ***Armey***	N	Y	N	N	Y	N	Y	Y
27 Ortiz	N	Y	N	Y	N	N	N	Y
UTAH								
1 ***Hansen***	N	N	N	N	Y	N	Y	Y
2 Owens	Y	Y	Y	Y	N	N	N	N
3 Orton	Y	Y	N	Y	N	N	N	Y
VERMONT								
AL *Sanders*	Y	Y	Y	?	N	Y	N	N
VIRGINIA								
1 ***Bateman***	N	N	N	Y	Y	N	N	N
2 Pickett	N	Y	N	Y	N	N	N	N
3 ***Bliley***	N	N	N	N	Y	N	Y	Y
4 Sisisky	N	Y	N	Y	N	N	N	N
5 Payne	N	Y	N	Y	N	N	Y	Y
6 Olin	N	Y	N	Y	N	N	N	N
7 ***Slaughter***	N	Y	N	N	Y	N	Y	Y
8 Moran	Y	Y	Y	Y	N	Y	N	N
9 Boucher	Y	Y	Y	Y	N	N	N	N
10 ***Wolf***	N	Y	N	N	Y	N	N	N
WASHINGTON								
1 ***Miller***	N	Y	N	?	Y	N	N	N
2 Swift	Y	Y	Y	Y	N	N	N	N
3 Unsoeld	Y	Y	Y	Y	N	Y	N	N
4 ***Morrison***	N	Y	N	Y	Y	N	N	N
5 Foley								
6 Dicks	N	Y	N	Y	N	N	N	N
7 McDermott	Y	Y	Y	Y	N	Y	N	N
8 ***Chandler***	N	?	N	N	Y	N	Y	Y
WEST VIRGINIA								
1 Mollohan	N	Y	N	Y	N	N	N	N
2 Staggers	Y	Y	N	Y	N	N	N	N
3 Wise	Y	Y	N	Y	N	N	N	N
4 Rahall	Y	Y	Y	Y	N	N	N	N
WISCONSIN								
1 Aspin	N	Y	N	Y	N	N	N	N
2 ***Klug***	N	Y	N	Y	Y	N	Y	Y
3 ***Gunderson***	N	Y	N	Y	Y	N	N	N
4 Kleczka	Y	Y	Y	Y	N	N	N	N
5 Moody	Y	Y	Y	?	N	Y	N	N
6 ***Petri***	N	Y	N	Y	Y	Y	N	N
7 Obey	Y	Y	Y	?	N	N	N	N
8 ***Roth***	Y	Y	Y	Y	Y	N	Y	Y
9 ***Sensenbrenner***	N	Y	N	N	Y	Y	Y	Y
WYOMING								
AL ***Thomas***	N	Y	N	N	Y	Y	Y	Y

Southern states - Ala., Ark., Fla., Ga., Ky., La., Miss., N.C., Okla., S.C., Tenn., Texas, Va.
Omitted votes are quorum calls, which CQ does not include in its vote charts.

HOUSE VOTES 109, 110, 111, 112, 113, 114, 115, 116

109. HR 2100. Fiscal 1992 Defense Authorization/ Abortion. AuCoin, D-Ore., amendment to provide servicemen and their dependents stationed overseas with reproductive health services, including privately paid abortions, at military hospitals. Adopted 220-208: R 35-129; D 184-79 (ND 129-51, SD 55-28); 1-0, May 22, 1991. A "nay" was a vote supporting the president's position.

110. HR 2100. Fiscal 1992 Defense Authorization/ Passage. Passage of the bill to authorize appropriations of $291 billion for the Defense Department and defense-related programs for fiscal 1992. The bill would terminate new production of the B-2 Stealth bomber and funding for early deployment of SDI programs as well as remove the prohibition against women flying combat missions. Passed 268-161: R 26-138; D 242-22 (ND 160-20, SD 82-2); I 0-1, May 22, 1991. A "nay" was a vote supporting the president's position.

111. H Con Res 121. Fiscal 1992 Budget Resolution/Rule. Adoption of the rule (H Res 157) to waive all points of order against and provide for House floor consideration of the conference report on the resolution to set binding budget levels for the fiscal year ending Sept. 30, 1992: budget authority, $1.590 trillion; outlays, $1.448 trillion; revenues, $1.169.2 trillion; deficit, $278.8 billion. Adopted 257-164: R 0-164; D 256-0 (ND 174-0, SD 82-0); I 1-0, May 22, 1991.

112. H Con Res 121. Fiscal 1992 Budget Resolution/ Conference Report. Adoption of the conference report on the resolution to set binding budget levels for the fiscal year ending Sept. 30, 1992: budget authority, $1.59 trillion; outlays, $1.448 trillion; revenues, $1.169 trillion; deficit, $278.8 billion. The conference report conforms with the spending caps for defense, international and domestic discretionary spending and with the pay-as-you-go requirements established by the Budget Enforcement Act of 1990 (PL 101-508). Adopted 239-181: R 8-155; D 231-25 (ND 154-19, SD 77-6); I 0-1, May 22, 1991.

113. HR 2251. Gulf War Refugee Supplemental Appropriations/Conference Report. Adoption of the conference report to appropriate $572 million in fiscal 1991, consisting of $235.5 million in humanitarian aid to Iraqi refugees and international peacekeeping operation, $320.5 million for the incremental costs of the Defense Department's humanitarian relief operations, and $16 million for military service organizations providing financial aid to U.S. military personnel and their families. Adopted 387-33: R 143-18; D 243-15 (ND 166-10, SD 77-5); I 1-0, May 22, 1991.

114. H Res 101 & H Res 146. Fast-Track Resolutions/ Rule. Adoption of the rule (H Res 158) to provide for House floor consideration of the resolution to disapprove a two-year extension of fast-track procedures that would require legislation implementing trade agreements to be considered within 60 days of introduction under limited debate and with no amendments permitted. Adopted 274-148: R 144-17; D 129-131 (ND 73-105, SD 56-26); I 1-0, May 23, 1991.

115. H Res 101. Disapproval of Fast-Track Procedures/ Adoption. Adoption of the resolution to disapprove the president's request to extend for two more years fast-track procedures that would require legislation implementing trade agreements to be considered within 60 days of introduction under limited debate and with no amendments permitted. Rejected 192-231: R 21-140; D 170-91 (ND 128-50, SD 42-41); I 1-0, May 23, 1991. A "nay" was a vote supporting the president's position.

116. H Res 146. Grant Fast-Track Procedures/Adoption. Adoption of the resolution to express the sense of the House that fast-track procedures should be extended and that a variety of objectives should be achieved in trade agreements negotiated by the United States. Adopted 329-85: R 156-4; D 173-80 (ND 105-67, SD 68-13); I 0-1, May 23, 1991.

KEY

- Y Voted for (yea).
- # Paired for.
- + Announced for.
- N Voted against (nay).
- X Paired against.
- - Announced against.
- P Voted "present."
- C Voted "present" to avoid possible conflict of interest.
- ? Did not vote or otherwise make a position known.

Democrats ***Republicans***
Independent

	109	110	111	112	113	114	115	116
ALABAMA								
1 ***Callahan***	N	N	N	N	Y	Y	N	Y
2 ***Dickinson***	N	N	N	N	Y	Y	N	Y
3 Browder	N	Y	Y	Y	Y	?	#	X
4 Bevill	N	Y	Y	Y	Y	Y	Y	Y
5 Cramer	Y	Y	Y	Y	Y	N	Y	Y
6 Erdreich	Y	Y	Y	Y	Y	N	Y	Y
7 Harris	N	Y	Y	Y	Y	N	Y	Y
ALASKA								
AL ***Young***	N	N	N	N	Y	Y	N	Y
ARIZONA								
1 ***Rhodes***	N	N	N	N	Y	Y	N	Y
2 Vacancy								
3 ***Stump***	N	N	N	N	N	Y	N	Y
4 ***Kyl***	N	N	N	N	Y	Y	N	Y
5 ***Kolbe***	Y	N	N	N	Y	Y	N	Y
ARKANSAS								
1 Alexander	Y	Y	Y	+	Y	N	Y	N
2 Thornton	N	Y	Y	Y	Y	Y	N	Y
3 ***Hammerschmidt***	N	N	N	N	Y	Y	N	Y
4 Anthony	Y	Y	Y	Y	Y	Y	N	Y
CALIFORNIA								
1 ***Riggs***	Y	N	N	N	Y	Y	N	Y
2 ***Herger***	N	N	N	N	Y	Y	N	Y
3 Matsui	Y	Y	Y	Y	Y	Y	N	?
4 Fazio	Y	Y	Y	Y	Y	Y	N	Y
5 Pelosi	Y	Y	Y	Y	Y	N	N	Y
6 Boxer	Y	Y	Y	Y	Y	N	Y	Y
7 Miller	Y	Y	Y	Y	Y	N	Y	N
8 Dellums	Y	N	Y	Y	Y	N	Y	N
9 Stark	Y	Y	Y	Y	Y	N	Y	N
10 Edwards	Y	N	Y	Y	Y	N	Y	N
11 Lantos	Y	Y	Y	Y	Y	Y	Y	Y
12 ***Campbell***	Y	N	N	N	Y	Y	N	Y
13 Mineta	Y	Y	Y	Y	Y	N	Y	Y
14 ***Doolittle***	N	N	N	N	Y	Y	N	Y
15 Condit	Y	Y	Y	N	Y	Y	Y	Y
16 Panetta	Y	Y	Y	Y	Y	N	N	Y
17 Dooley	Y	Y	Y	Y	Y	Y	N	Y
18 Lehman	Y	Y	Y	Y	Y	N	Y	Y
19 ***Lagomarsino***	N	N	N	N	Y	Y	N	Y
20 ***Thomas***	Y	N	N	N	Y	Y	N	Y
21 ***Gallegly***	N	N	N	N	Y	Y	N	Y
22 ***Moorhead***	N	N	N	N	N	Y	N	Y
23 Beilenson	Y	Y	Y	Y	Y	Y	N	Y
24 Waxman	Y	Y	Y	Y	Y	Y	Y	?
25 Roybal	Y	N	Y	Y	Y	Y	N	Y
26 Berman	Y	Y	Y	Y	Y	Y	N	Y
27 Levine	Y	Y	Y	Y	Y	Y	?	?
28 Dixon	Y	Y	Y	Y	Y	Y	Y	Y
29 Waters	Y	N	Y	?	Y	N	Y	N
30 Martinez	N	Y	?	Y	Y	Y	Y	?
31 Dymally	Y	Y	Y	Y	Y	N	Y	N
32 Anderson	Y	Y	Y	Y	Y	Y	N	Y
33 ***Dreier***	N	N	N	N	Y	Y	N	Y
34 Torres	Y	Y	Y	Y	Y	N	Y	N
35 ***Lewis***	N	N	N	N	Y	Y	N	Y
36 Brown	Y	Y	Y	N	Y	N	Y	Y
37 ***McCandless***	N	N	N	N	Y	Y	N	Y
38 ***Dornan***	N	N	N	N	Y	Y	X	Y
39 ***Dannemeyer***	N	N	N	N	N	Y	N	Y
40 ***Cox***	N	N	N	N	Y	Y	N	Y
41 ***Lowery***	N	N	N	N	Y	Y	N	Y
42 ***Rohrabacher***	N	N	N	N	N	Y	N	Y
43 ***Packard***	N	N	N	N	Y	Y	N	Y
44 ***Cunningham***	N	N	N	N	Y	Y	N	Y
45 ***Hunter***	N	N	N	N	Y	N	Y	Y
COLORADO								
1 Schroeder	Y	Y	Y	Y	Y	Y	N	Y
2 Skaggs	Y	Y	Y	Y	Y	N	N	Y
3 Campbell	Y	Y	Y	N	Y	Y	Y	Y
4 ***Allard***	N	N	N	N	Y	Y	N	Y
5 ***Hefley***	N	N	N	N	Y	Y	N	Y
6 ***Schaefer***	N	N	N	N	Y	Y	N	Y
CONNECTICUT								
1 Kennelly	Y	Y	Y	Y	Y	Y	N	Y
2 Gejdenson	Y	Y	Y	Y	Y	Y	Y	N
3 DeLauro	Y	Y	Y	Y	Y	N	Y	Y
4 ***Shays***	Y	Y	N	Y	Y	Y	N	Y
5 ***Franks***	Y	N	N	N	Y	Y	N	Y
6 ***Johnson***	Y	Y	N	N	Y	Y	N	Y
DELAWARE								
AL Carper	Y	Y	Y	Y	Y	Y	N	Y
FLORIDA								
1 Hutto	N	Y	Y	Y	Y	Y	N	Y
2 Peterson	Y	Y	Y	Y	Y	N	Y	Y
3 Bennett	Y	Y	Y	Y	Y	Y	N	Y
4 ***James***	N	Y	N	N	Y	Y	N	Y
5 ***McCollum***	N	N	N	N	?	?	X	?
6 ***Stearns***	N	N	N	N	N	Y	Y	Y
7 Gibbons	Y	Y	Y	Y	Y	Y	N	Y
8 ***Young***	N	N	N	N	Y	?	N	Y
9 ***Bilirakis***	N	N	N	N	N	Y	N	Y
10 ***Ireland***	N	N	N	N	Y	N	N	Y
11 Bacchus	Y	Y	Y	Y	Y	Y	N	Y
12 ***Lewis***	N	N	N	N	Y	Y	N	Y
13 ***Goss***	N	N	N	N	Y	N	N	Y
14 Johnston	Y	Y	Y	Y	Y	Y	Y	N
15 ***Shaw***	N	N	N	N	Y	Y	N	Y
16 Smith	Y	Y	Y	Y	Y	N	Y	Y
17 Lehman	?	?	?	?	?	?	?	?
18 ***Ros-Lehtinen***	N	N	N	N	Y	Y	N	Y
19 Fascell	Y	Y	Y	Y	Y	Y	N	Y
GEORGIA								
1 Thomas	Y	Y	Y	Y	Y	Y	Y	Y
2 Hatcher	?	Y	Y	Y	Y	?	Y	Y
3 Ray	N	Y	Y	Y	N	Y	Y	N
4 Jones	Y	Y	Y	Y	Y	N	Y	Y
5 Lewis	Y	N	Y	Y	Y	N	Y	N
6 ***Gingrich***	N	N	N	N	Y	Y	N	Y
7 Darden	Y	Y	Y	Y	Y	Y	Y	Y
8 Rowland	Y	Y	Y	Y	Y	Y	Y	Y
9 Jenkins	N	Y	Y	Y	Y	Y	Y	Y
10 Barnard	N	Y	Y	Y	Y	Y	Y	Y
HAWAII								
1 Abercrombie	Y	Y	Y	Y	Y	N	Y	N
2 Mink	Y	Y	Y	Y	Y	Y	Y	Y
IDAHO								
1 LaRocco	Y	Y	Y	Y	Y	Y	N	Y
2 Stallings	N	Y	Y	Y	Y	Y	Y	N
ILLINOIS								
1 Hayes	Y	N	Y	Y	N	N	Y	N
2 Savage	Y	N	Y	Y	N	N	Y	N
3 Russo	N	Y	Y	Y	Y	Y	Y	N
4 Sangmeister	N	Y	Y	Y	Y	N	Y	N
5 Lipinski	N	Y	Y	Y	Y	Y	Y	N
6 ***Hyde***	N	N	N	N	Y	Y	N	Y
7 Collins	Y	N	Y	Y	Y	N	Y	N
8 Rostenkowski	N	Y	Y	Y	Y	Y	N	Y
9 Yates	Y	Y	Y	N	Y	N	Y	N
10 ***Porter***	Y	Y	N	N	Y	N	N	Y
11 Annunzio	N	Y	Y	Y	Y	Y	Y	N
12 ***Crane***	N	N	N	N	N	Y	N	Y
13 ***Fawell***	Y	N	N	N	Y	Y	N	Y
14 ***Hastert***	N	N	N	N	Y	Y	N	Y
15 Vacancy								
16 Cox	Y	Y	Y	Y	Y	Y	N	Y
17 Evans	Y	Y	Y	Y	Y	N	Y	N
18 ***Michel***	N	N	N	N	Y	Y	N	Y
19 Bruce	N	Y	Y	Y	Y	N	Y	Y
20 Durbin	Y	Y	Y	Y	Y	Y	Y	N
21 Costello	N	Y	Y	Y	Y	N	Y	N
22 Poshard	N	Y	Y	Y	Y	N	Y	N
INDIANA								
1 Visclosky	Y	Y	Y	N	N	N	Y	N
2 Sharp	Y	Y	Y	Y	Y	N	N	Y
3 Roemer	N	Y	Y	N	Y	N	Y	Y

ND Northern Democrats SD Southern Democrats

	109	110	111	112	113	114	115	116
4 Long	Y	Y	Y	Y	Y	N	Y	Y
5 Jontz	Y	Y	Y	Y	Y	N	Y	N
6 ***Burton***	N	N	N	N	Y	N	N	Y
7 ***Myers***	N	N	N	N	Y	Y	N	Y
8 McCloskey	Y	Y	Y	Y	Y	N	Y	Y
9 Hamilton	Y	Y	Y	Y	Y	Y	N	Y
10 Jacobs	Y	Y	Y	N	N	N	Y	N
IOWA								
1 ***Leach***	Y	N	N	N	Y	Y	N	Y
2 ***Nussle***	N	N	N	N	N	Y	N	Y
3 Nagle	Y	Y	Y	Y	Y	N	Y	Y
4 Smith	Y	Y	Y	N	Y	Y	N	Y
5 ***Lightfoot***	N	N	N	N	Y	Y	N	Y
6 ***Grandy***	N	N	N	N	Y	Y	N	Y
KANSAS								
1 ***Roberts***	N	N	N	N	Y	Y	N	Y
2 Slattery	Y	Y	Y	N	Y	Y	N	Y
3 ***Meyers***	Y	N	N	N	Y	N	Y	Y
4 Glickman	Y	Y	Y	Y	Y	Y	Y	Y
5 ***Nichols***	Y	N	N	N	Y	Y	N	Y
KENTUCKY								
1 Hubbard	Y	Y	Y	N	Y	Y	N	Y
2 Natcher	N	Y	Y	Y	Y	Y	Y	Y
3 Mazzoli	N	Y	Y	Y	Y	Y	N	Y
4 ***Bunning***	N	N	N	N	Y	Y	N	?
5 ***Rogers***	N	N	N	N	Y	N	N	Y
6 ***Hopkins***	?	?	?	?	?	?	?	?
7 Perkins	N	Y	Y	Y	Y	N	Y	N
LOUISIANA								
1 ***Livingston***	N	N	N	N	Y	Y	N	Y
2 Jefferson	Y	Y	?	Y	Y	N	N	Y
3 Tauzin	N	Y	Y	Y	Y	N	N	Y
4 ***McCrery***	N	N	N	Y	Y	Y	N	Y
5 Huckaby	N	Y	Y	Y	Y	Y	N	Y
6 ***Baker***	N	N	N	N	Y	Y	N	Y
7 Hayes	N	Y	Y	Y	Y	Y	Y	Y
8 ***Holloway***	N	N	N	N	Y	N	Y	Y
MAINE								
1 Andrews	Y	Y	Y	Y	Y	N	Y	N
2 ***Snowe***	Y	Y	N	N	Y	Y	Y	N
MARYLAND								
1 ***Gilchrest***	Y	N	N	N	Y	Y	N	Y
2 ***Bentley***	N	N	N	N	Y	N	Y	N
3 Cardin	Y	Y	Y	Y	Y	Y	N	Y
4 McMillen	Y	Y	Y	Y	Y	Y	N	Y
5 Hoyer	Y	Y	Y	Y	Y	N	N	Y
6 Byron	N	Y	Y	Y	Y	Y	N	Y
7 Mfume	Y	N	Y	Y	Y	N	Y	N
8 ***Morella***	Y	Y	N	Y	+	Y	N	Y
MASSACHUSETTS								
1 Vacancy								
2 Neal	N	Y	?	Y	Y	N	Y	N
3 Early	N	Y	Y	Y	N	N	Y	N
4 Frank	Y	Y	Y	Y	Y	N	Y	N
5 Atkins	Y	Y	Y	Y	Y	Y	N	Y
6 Mavroules	N	Y	?	Y	Y	N	Y	N
7 Markey	Y	Y	Y	?	?	Y	Y	Y
8 Kennedy	Y	Y	Y	Y	Y	N	Y	Y
9 Moakley	N	Y	?	Y	Y	Y	Y	Y
10 Studds	Y	Y	Y	Y	Y	N	Y	N
11 Donnelly	N	Y	Y	Y	N	N	N	Y
MICHIGAN								
1 Conyers	Y	Y	Y	Y	Y	N	Y	N
2 ***Pursell***	N	N	N	N	Y	Y	N	?
3 Wolpe	Y	Y	Y	Y	Y	N	Y	Y
4 ***Upton***	N	Y	N	N	Y	Y	N	Y
5 ***Henry***	N	Y	N	N	Y	N	N	Y
6 Carr	Y	Y	Y	N	Y	Y	N	Y
7 Kildee	N	Y	Y	Y	Y	N	Y	N
8 Traxler	N	Y	Y	Y	Y	N	Y	Y
9 ***Vander Jagt***	N	N	N	N	Y	Y	N	Y
10 ***Camp***	N	Y	N	N	Y	Y	N	Y
11 ***Davis***	N	N	N	Y	Y	Y	N	Y
12 Bonior	N	Y	Y	Y	Y	Y	Y	Y
13 Collins	Y	N	Y	+	Y	N	Y	N
14 Hertel	N	Y	Y	Y	Y	N	Y	N
15 Ford	Y	Y	Y	Y	Y	Y	Y	N
16 Dingell	Y	Y	?	Y	Y	Y	Y	N
17 Levin	Y	Y	Y	Y	Y	N	Y	N
18 ***Broomfield***	N	N	N	N	Y	Y	N	Y
MINNESOTA								
1 Penny	N	Y	Y	Y	N	Y	N	Y
2 ***Weber***	N	N	N	N	Y	Y	N	Y
3 ***Ramstad***	Y	N	N	N	Y	Y	N	Y
4 Vento	Y	Y	Y	Y	Y	N	Y	Y

	109	110	111	112	113	114	115	116
5 Sabo	Y	Y	Y	Y	Y	N	Y	Y
6 Sikorski	Y	Y	Y	Y	Y	N	Y	N
7 Peterson	N	Y	Y	Y	Y	N	Y	N
8 Oberstar	N	Y	Y	Y	Y	N	Y	N
MISSISSIPPI								
1 Whitten	N	Y	Y	Y	Y	Y	Y	Y
2 Espy	Y	Y	Y	Y	Y	N	N	Y
3 Montgomery	N	Y	Y	Y	Y	Y	N	?
4 Parker	N	Y	Y	Y	Y	Y	N	N
5 Taylor	N	Y	Y	N	Y	N	Y	N
MISSOURI								
1 Clay	Y	N	Y	Y	Y	N	Y	N
2 Horn	Y	Y	Y	Y	Y	Y	Y	Y
3 Gephardt	Y	Y	Y	Y	Y	Y	N	Y
4 Skelton	N	Y	?	?	?	?	N	Y
5 Wheat	Y	Y	Y	Y	Y	Y	Y	Y
6 ***Coleman***	N	N	N	N	Y	Y	N	Y
7 ***Hancock***	N	N	N	N	N	Y	N	Y
8 ***Emerson***	N	N	N	N	Y	Y	N	Y
9 Volkmer	N	N	Y	Y	Y	N	Y	N
MONTANA								
1 Williams	Y	Y	Y	N	N	?	#	#
2 ***Marlenee***	N	N	N	N	Y	Y	Y	Y
NEBRASKA								
1 ***Bereuter***	N	N	N	N	Y	Y	N	Y
2 Hoagland	Y	Y	Y	Y	Y	N	Y	Y
3 ***Barrett***	N	N	N	N	Y	Y	N	Y
NEVADA								
1 Bilbray	N	Y	Y	Y	Y	N	Y	Y
2 ***Vucanovich***	N	N	N	N	Y	Y	-	Y
NEW HAMPSHIRE								
1 ***Zeliff***	Y	N	N	N	Y	Y	N	Y
2 Swett	Y	Y	Y	N	Y	N	Y	Y
NEW JERSEY								
1 Andrews	Y	Y	Y	N	Y	N	Y	Y
2 Hughes	Y	Y	Y	N	Y	N	N	Y
3 Pallone	Y	Y	Y	N	Y	N	Y	N
4 ***Smith***	N	N	N	N	Y	Y	Y	Y
5 ***Roukema***	Y	Y	N	Y	Y	N	N	Y
6 Dwyer	N	Y	Y	Y	Y	N	Y	?
7 ***Rinaldo***	N	N	N	N	Y	Y	N	Y
8 Roe	N	Y	Y	Y	Y	N	Y	N
9 Torricelli	Y	Y	Y	Y	Y	Y	N	Y
10 Payne	Y	N	Y	Y	Y	N	Y	N
11 ***Gallo***	Y	N	N	N	Y	Y	N	Y
12 ***Zimmer***	Y	N	N	N	Y	Y	N	Y
13 ***Saxton***	N	N	N	N	Y	Y	N	Y
14 Guarini	Y	Y	Y	Y	Y	Y	N	Y
NEW MEXICO								
1 ***Schiff***	Y	N	N	N	Y	Y	N	Y
2 ***Skeen***	N	N	N	N	Y	Y	N	Y
3 Richardson	Y	Y	Y	Y	Y	Y	N	Y
NEW YORK								
1 Hochbrueckner	Y	Y	Y	Y	Y	Y	Y	Y
2 Downey	Y	Y	Y	Y	Y	Y	N	Y
3 Mrazek	Y	Y	Y	Y	Y	Y	N	Y
4 ***Lent***	N	Y	N	N	Y	Y	N	Y
5 ***McGrath***	N	Y	N	N	Y	?	N	Y
6 Flake	Y	Y	Y	Y	Y	N	Y	Y
7 Ackerman	Y	Y	Y	Y	Y	N	Y	N
8 Scheuer	Y	Y	Y	Y	Y	N	Y	N
9 Manton	N	Y	Y	Y	Y	N	Y	Y
10 Schumer	Y	Y	Y	Y	Y	Y	N	Y
11 Towns	Y	N	Y	Y	Y	N	Y	X
12 Owens	Y	N	Y	#	Y	N	Y	N
13 Solarz	Y	Y	Y	Y	Y	Y	N	Y
14 ***Molinari***	Y	N	N	N	Y	Y	N	Y
15 ***Green***	Y	Y	N	N	Y	Y	N	Y
16 Rangel	Y	N	Y	Y	Y	N	Y	N
17 Weiss	Y	Y	Y	Y	Y	N	Y	Y
18 Serrano	Y	N	Y	Y	Y	Y	Y	N
19 Engel	Y	Y	Y	Y	Y	N	Y	Y
20 Lowey	Y	Y	Y	Y	?	N	Y	Y
21 ***Fish***	N	N	N	N	Y	Y	N	Y
22 ***Gilman***	Y	Y	N	Y	Y	Y	Y	N
23 McNulty	N	Y	Y	Y	Y	Y	Y	Y
24 ***Solomon***	N	N	N	N	Y	Y	Y	Y
25 ***Boehlert***	Y	N	N	Y	Y	Y	N	Y
26 ***Martin***	N	N	N	N	Y	Y	N	Y
27 ***Walsh***	N	N	N	N	Y	Y	N	Y
28 McHugh	Y	Y	Y	Y	Y	N	N	Y
29 ***Horton***	Y	Y	N	Y	Y	Y	N	Y
30 Slaughter	Y	Y	Y	Y	Y	Y	Y	Y
31 ***Paxon***	N	N	N	N	Y	Y	N	Y

	109	110	111	112	113	114	115	116
32 LaFalce	N	Y	Y	Y	Y	N	Y	N
33 Nowak	N	Y	Y	Y	Y	N	Y	N
34 ***Houghton***	Y	N	N	N	Y	Y	N	Y
NORTH CAROLINA								
1 Jones	Y	Y	Y	Y	Y	Y	Y	Y
2 Valentine	Y	Y	Y	Y	N	Y	Y	Y
3 Lancaster	Y	Y	Y	Y	Y	N	Y	Y
4 Price	Y	Y	Y	Y	Y	Y	N	Y
5 Neal	Y	Y	Y	Y	Y	N	Y	Y
6 ***Coble***	N	N	N	N	N	N	Y	Y
7 Rose	N	Y	Y	Y	?	Y	Y	N
8 Hefner	Y	Y	Y	Y	Y	Y	Y	Y
9 ***McMillan***	N	N	N	N	Y	Y	N	Y
10 ***Ballenger***	N	N	N	N	+	Y	Y	Y
11 ***Taylor***	N	N	N	N	Y	N	Y	Y
NORTH DAKOTA								
AL Dorgan	N	Y	Y	N	Y	Y	Y	N
OHIO								
1 Luken	N	Y	Y	Y	Y	N	N	Y
2 ***Gradison***	N	N	N	N	Y	Y	N	?
3 Hall	N	Y	Y	Y	Y	Y	N	Y
4 ***Oxley***	N	Y	N	N	Y	Y	N	Y
5 ***Gillmor***	N	N	N	N	Y	Y	N	Y
6 ***McEwen***	N	N	N	N	Y	Y	N	Y
7 ***Hobson***	N	N	N	N	Y	Y	N	Y
8 ***Boehner***	N	N	N	N	Y	Y	N	Y
9 Kaptur	N	Y	Y	Y	Y	Y	Y	N
10 ***Miller***	N	N	N	N	Y	Y	Y	Y
11 Eckart	Y	Y	Y	Y	Y	Y	Y	Y
12 ***Kasich***	N	Y	N	N	Y	Y	N	Y
13 Pease	Y	Y	Y	Y	Y	N	Y	N
14 Sawyer	Y	Y	Y	?	?	N	N	Y
15 ***Wylie***	N	N	N	N	Y	Y	N	Y
16 ***Regula***	N	Y	N	N	Y	N	N	Y
17 Traficant	Y	N	Y	Y	N	N	Y	N
18 Applegate	N	N	Y	N	Y	N	Y	Y
19 Feighan	Y	Y	Y	Y	Y	N	Y	Y
20 Oakar	N	Y	Y	Y	Y	N	Y	N
21 Stokes	Y	N	Y	Y	Y	N	Y	N
OKLAHOMA								
1 ***Inhofe***	N	N	N	N	Y	Y	N	Y
2 Synar	Y	Y	Y	Y	Y	Y	N	#
3 Brewster	Y	Y	Y	Y	Y	N	Y	Y
4 McCurdy	Y	Y	Y	Y	Y	Y	N	Y
5 ***Edwards***	N	N	N	N	Y	Y	N	Y
6 English	N	Y	Y	N	Y	N	Y	Y
OREGON								
1 AuCoin	Y	Y	Y	Y	Y	N	Y	Y
2 ***Smith***	N	N	N	N	Y	Y	N	Y
3 Wyden	Y	Y	Y	Y	Y	Y	N	Y
4 DeFazio	Y	Y	Y	Y	Y	N	Y	Y
5 Kopetski	Y	Y	Y	Y	Y	Y	N	Y
PENNSYLVANIA								
1 Foglietta	Y	Y	Y	Y	Y	Y	Y	Y
2 Gray	Y	Y	Y	?	Y	Y	Y	Y
3 Borski	N	Y	Y	Y	Y	N	Y	Y
4 Kolter	N	Y	Y	Y	N	N	Y	Y
5 ***Schulze***	N	N	N	N	Y	Y	N	Y
6 Yatron	N	Y	Y	Y	Y	N	Y	N
7 ***Weldon***	N	Y	N	N	Y	N	N	Y
8 Kostmayer	Y	Y	Y	Y	Y	Y	N	Y
9 ***Shuster***	N	N	N	N	Y	Y	Y	Y
10 ***McDade***	N	N	N	N	Y	N	Y	Y
11 Kanjorski	N	Y	Y	Y	Y	N	Y	Y
12 Murtha	N	Y	Y	Y	Y	Y	Y	N
13 ***Coughlin***	Y	Y	N	N	Y	Y	N	Y
14 Coyne	Y	Y	Y	Y	Y	Y	N	Y
15 ***Ritter***	N	N	N	N	Y	Y	N	Y
16 ***Walker***	N	N	N	N	N	Y	N	Y
17 ***Gekas***	N	N	N	N	N	Y	N	Y
18 ***Santorum***	N	N	N	N	Y	Y	N	Y
19 ***Goodling***	N	N	N	N	Y	Y	Y	Y
20 Gaydos	N	Y	Y	Y	Y	N	Y	?
21 ***Ridge***	Y	Y	N	N	Y	Y	N	Y
22 Murphy	N	Y	Y	Y	Y	N	Y	Y
23 ***Clinger***	N	N	N	N	Y	Y	N	Y
RHODE ISLAND								
1 ***Machtley***	Y	Y	N	N	Y	Y	N	Y
2 Reed	Y	Y	Y	Y	Y	Y	Y	Y
SOUTH CAROLINA								
1 ***Ravenel***	N	Y	N	N	Y	Y	Y	Y
2 ***Spence***	N	N	N	N	Y	N	Y	Y
3 Derrick	Y	Y	Y	Y	Y	Y	Y	Y
4 Patterson	Y	Y	Y	Y	Y	Y	Y	Y
5 Spratt	Y	Y	Y	Y	Y	N	Y	Y
6 Tallon	N	Y	Y	Y	Y	N	Y	Y

	109	110	111	112	113	114	115	116
SOUTH DAKOTA								
AL Johnson	Y	Y	Y	Y	Y	Y	Y	N
TENNESSEE								
1 ***Quillen***	N	N	N	N	Y	Y	Y	N
2 ***Duncan***	N	Y	N	N	N	Y	Y	Y
3 Lloyd	N	Y	Y	Y	Y	N	Y	N
4 Cooper	Y	Y	Y	Y	Y	Y	N	Y
5 Clement	Y	Y	Y	Y	Y	Y	N	Y
6 Gordon	Y	Y	Y	Y	Y	Y	N	Y
7 ***Sundquist***	N	N	N	N	Y	Y	N	Y
8 Tanner	Y	Y	Y	Y	Y	Y	N	Y
9 Ford	Y	Y	?	Y	Y	N	Y	N
TEXAS								
1 Chapman	Y	Y	Y	Y	Y	Y	N	Y
2 Wilson	Y	Y	Y	Y	Y	Y	N	Y
3 ***Johnson***	N	N	N	N	Y	Y	N	Y
4 Hall	N	Y	Y	N	N	Y	N	Y
5 Bryant	Y	Y	Y	N	Y	N	N	Y
6 ***Barton***	N	Y	N	N	N	Y	N	Y
7 ***Archer***	N	N	N	N	Y	Y	N	Y
8 ***Fields***	N	N	N	N	Y	Y	N	Y
9 Brooks	Y	Y	Y	Y	Y	Y	Y	N
10 Pickle	Y	Y	Y	Y	Y	Y	N	Y
11 Edwards	Y	Y	Y	Y	Y	Y	N	Y
12 Geren	Y	Y	Y	Y	N	Y	N	Y
13 Sarpalius	N	Y	Y	N	Y	Y	N	Y
14 Laughlin	N	Y	Y	Y	Y	Y	N	Y
15 de la Garza	N	Y	Y	Y	Y	Y	N	Y
16 Coleman	Y	Y	Y	Y	Y	Y	N	Y
17 Stenholm	N	Y	Y	Y	N	Y	N	Y
18 Washington	Y	N	Y	Y	Y	N	Y	N
19 ***Combest***	N	N	N	N	N	Y	N	Y
20 Gonzalez	Y	Y	Y	Y	Y	N	Y	N
21 ***Smith***	N	N	N	X	Y	Y	N	Y
22 ***DeLay***	N	N	N	N	Y	Y	N	Y
23 Bustamante	Y	Y	Y	Y	Y	Y	N	Y
24 Frost	Y	Y	Y	Y	Y	Y	Y	Y
25 Andrews	Y	Y	Y	Y	Y	Y	N	Y
26 ***Armey***	N	N	N	N	Y	Y	N	Y
27 Ortiz	N	Y	Y	Y	Y	Y	N	Y
UTAH								
1 ***Hansen***	N	N	N	N	Y	Y	N	Y
2 Owens	Y	Y	Y	N	Y	Y	N	Y
3 Orton	N	N	Y	N	Y	N	N	Y
VERMONT								
AL *Sanders*	Y	N	Y	N	Y	Y	Y	N
VIRGINIA								
1 ***Bateman***	N	N	N	N	Y	Y	N	Y
2 Pickett	Y	Y	Y	Y	?	Y	N	Y
3 ***Bliley***	N	N	N	N	Y	Y	N	Y
4 Sisisky	Y	Y	Y	Y	Y	N	Y	Y
5 Payne	Y	Y	Y	Y	Y	Y	Y	Y
6 Olin	Y	Y	Y	Y	Y	Y	N	Y
7 ***Slaughter***	N	N	N	N	Y	Y	N	Y
8 Moran	Y	Y	Y	Y	Y	N	N	Y
9 Boucher	Y	Y	Y	Y	Y	Y	N	Y
10 ***Wolf***	N	N	N	N	Y	Y	N	Y
WASHINGTON								
1 ***Miller***	Y	N	N	N	Y	Y	N	Y
2 Swift	Y	Y	Y	Y	Y	Y	N	Y
3 Unsoeld	Y	Y	Y	Y	Y	N	Y	Y
4 ***Morrison***	Y	N	N	N	Y	Y	N	Y
5 Foley								
6 Dicks	Y	Y	Y	Y	Y	Y	N	Y
7 McDermott	Y	Y	Y	Y	Y	Y	N	Y
8 ***Chandler***	Y	N	N	N	Y	Y	N	Y
WEST VIRGINIA								
1 Mollohan	N	Y	Y	Y	Y	N	Y	Y
2 Staggers	N	Y	Y	Y	Y	N	Y	Y
3 Wise	Y	Y	Y	Y	Y	N	Y	Y
4 Rahall	N	Y	Y	Y	Y	N	Y	N
WISCONSIN								
1 Aspin	Y	Y	Y	Y	Y	Y	Y	N
2 ***Klug***	Y	N	N	N	Y	Y	N	Y
3 ***Gunderson***	Y	Y	N	N	Y	Y	N	Y
4 Kleczka	N	Y	Y	Y	Y	N	Y	N
5 Moody	Y	Y	Y	Y	Y	N	Y	N
6 ***Petri***	N	N	N	N	Y	Y	N	Y
7 Obey	Y	Y	Y	Y	Y	N	Y	Y
8 ***Roth***	N	N	N	N	N	Y	N	Y
9 ***Sensenbrenner***	N	N	N	N	N	Y	N	Y
WYOMING								
AL ***Thomas***	N	N	N	N	N	Y	N	Y

Southern states - Ala., Ark., Fla., Ga., Ky., La., Miss., N.C., Okla., S.C., Tenn., Texas, Va.
Omitted votes are quorum calls, which CQ does not include in its vote charts.

HOUSE VOTES 117, 118, 119, 120, 121, 122, 123, 124

117. HR 2427. Fiscal 1992 Energy and Water Appropriations/Superconducting Super Collider. Slattery, D-Kan., amendment to eliminate all funding for the superconducting super collider, $434 million, by reducing the bill's funding level for general science and research activities by $390 million and transferring $43.5 million to the construction of an injector for the "Tevatron" particle accelerator at the Fermi National Accelerator Laboratory in Illinois. Rejected 165-251: R 58-101; D 106-150 (ND 86-87, SD 20-63); I 1-0, May 29, 1991. A "nay" was a vote supporting the president's position.

118. HR 2427. Fiscal 1992 Energy and Water Appropriations/Discretionary Programs. Dannemeyer, R-Calif., amendment to limit overall growth in the bill to 2.4 percent above the fiscal 1991 outlay level by cutting 0.5 percent or about $107 million from discretionary programs in the bill. Rejected 92-320: R 76-83; D 16-236 (ND 10-160, SD 6-76); I 0-1, May 29, 1991.

119. HR 2427. Fiscal 1992 Energy and Water Appropriations/Passage. Passage of the bill to provide $21,494,999,000 in new budget authority in fiscal 1992 for energy, water and nuclear weapons programs. The administration requested $21,609,828,000. Passed 392-24: R 140-19; D 252-4 (ND 172-2, SD 80-2); I 0-1, May 29, 1991.

120. HR 2426. Fiscal 1992 Military Construction Appropriations/Rule. Adoption of the rule (H Res 159) to waive certain points of order against and provide for House floor consideration of the bill to provide $8,483,006,000 in new budget authority in fiscal 1992 for military construction and family housing. Adopted 390-4: R 143-4; D 247-0 (ND 168-0, SD 79-0); May 30, 1991.

121. HR 2426. Fiscal 1992 Military Construction Appropriations/Passage. Passage of the bill to provide $8,483,006,000 in new budget authority in fiscal 1992 for military construction and family housing. The president requested $8,563,030,000. Passed 392-18: R 143-15; D 248-3 (ND 167-3, SD 81-0); I 1-0, May 30, 1991.

122. HR 1642. Palo Alto Battlefield Historic Site/Passage. Vento, D-Minn., motion to suspend the rules and pass the bill to authorize the Interior Department to enlarge the Palo Alto Battlefield National Historic Site in Texas by approximately 3,400 acres, commemorating the first major battle of the Mexican-American War. Motion agreed to 323-8: R 123-8; D 200-0 (ND 137-0, SD 63-0); June 3, 1991. A two-thirds majority of those present and voting (221 in this case) is required for passage under suspension of the rules.

123. HR 2042. Federal Fire Prevention and Control Act/Passage. Boucher, D-Va., motion to suspend the rules and pass the bill to authorize $79.6 million for fiscal 1992-94 for programs of the U.S. Fire Administration to help reduce fatalities, injuries and damage caused by fires. Motion agreed to 326-5: R 126-5; D 200-0 (ND 137-0, SD 63-0); June 3, 1991. A two-thirds majority of those present and voting (221 in this case) is required for passage under suspension of the rules.

124. S 483. Taconic Mountains Protection/Passage. De la Garza, D-Texas, motion to suspend the rules and pass the bill to authorize the Agriculture Department to expand the boundaries of the Green Mountain National Forest in Vermont to include 185,000 acres of the Taconic Mountain Range to protect the undeveloped forestland from conversion to non-forest uses. Motion agreed to 316-15: R 116-15; D 200-0 (ND 137-0, SD 63-0); June 3, 1991. A two-thirds majority of those present and voting (221 in this case) is required for passage under suspension of the rules.

KEY

Y Voted for (yea).
\# Paired for.
\+ Announced for.
N Voted against (nay).
X Paired against.
\- Announced against.
P Voted "present."
C Voted "present" to avoid possible conflict of interest.
? Did not vote or otherwise make a position known.

Democrats ***Republicans***
Independent

	117	118	119	120	121	122	123	124
ALABAMA								
1 ***Callahan***	N	N	Y	Y	Y	?	?	?
2 ***Dickinson***	Y	Y	Y	?	Y	?	?	?
3 Browder	N	N	Y	Y	Y	Y	Y	Y
4 Bevill	N	N	Y	Y	Y	Y	Y	Y
5 Cramer	N	N	Y	Y	Y	Y	Y	Y
6 Erdreich	N	N	Y	Y	Y	Y	Y	Y
7 Harris	N	N	Y	Y	Y	Y	Y	Y
ALASKA								
AL ***Young***	N	N	Y	Y	Y	Y	Y	Y
ARIZONA								
1 ***Rhodes***	N	N	Y	Y	Y	Y	Y	Y
2 Vacancy								
3 ***Stump***	N	Y	N	Y	N	N	N	N
4 ***Kyl***	N	Y	Y	Y	Y	Y	Y	Y
5 ***Kolbe***	Y	N	Y	Y	Y	Y	Y	Y
ARKANSAS								
1 Alexander	N	N	Y	Y	Y	?	?	?
2 Thornton	N	N	Y	Y	Y	?	?	?
3 ***Hammerschmidt***	N	Y	Y	Y	Y	Y	Y	N
4 Anthony	N	N	Y	Y	Y	Y	Y	Y
CALIFORNIA								
1 ***Riggs***	N	Y	Y	+	Y	Y	Y	Y
2 ***Herger***	Y	N	Y	Y	Y	Y	Y	Y
3 Matsui	N	N	Y	Y	Y	Y	Y	Y
4 Fazio	N	N	Y	Y	Y	Y	Y	Y
5 Pelosi	N	N	Y	Y	Y	Y	Y	Y
6 Boxer	Y	N	Y	Y	Y	?	?	?
7 Miller	Y	N	Y	Y	Y	Y	Y	Y
8 Dellums	N	N	Y	Y	?	Y	Y	Y
9 Stark	Y	N	Y	Y	Y	Y	Y	Y
10 Edwards	N	N	Y	Y	Y	Y	Y	Y
11 Lantos	Y	N	Y	Y	Y	Y	Y	Y
12 ***Campbell***	Y	Y	N	Y	N	?	?	?
13 Mineta	N	N	Y	Y	Y	Y	Y	Y
14 ***Doolittle***	N	Y	Y	Y	Y	Y	Y	N
15 Condit	N	Y	Y	Y	Y	Y	Y	Y
16 Panetta	N	N	Y	Y	Y	?	?	?
17 Dooley	Y	N	Y	?	?	Y	Y	Y
18 Lehman	N	N	Y	Y	Y	?	?	?
19 ***Lagomarsino***	N	N	Y	Y	Y	Y	Y	Y
20 ***Thomas***	N	Y	Y	Y	Y	Y	Y	Y
21 ***Gallegly***	N	N	Y	Y	Y	+	+	+
22 ***Moorhead***	Y	Y	Y	Y	N	Y	Y	Y
23 Beilenson	Y	N	Y	Y	Y	Y	Y	Y
24 Waxman	N	N	Y	Y	Y	?	?	?
25 Roybal	N	N	Y	Y	Y	Y	Y	Y
26 Berman	N	N	Y	Y	Y	Y	Y	Y
27 Levine	N	N	Y	?	?	?	?	?
28 Dixon	N	N	Y	Y	Y	Y	Y	Y
29 Waters	Y	?	Y	?	N	Y	Y	Y
30 Martinez	N	N	Y	Y	Y	Y	Y	Y
31 Dymally	N	N	Y	?	Y	Y	Y	Y
32 Anderson	N	N	Y	Y	Y	Y	Y	Y
33 ***Dreier***	N	Y	N	Y	N	Y	Y	Y
34 Torres	N	N	Y	Y	Y	+	+	+
35 ***Lewis***	N	N	Y	Y	Y	Y	Y	Y
36 Brown	N	N	Y	Y	Y	Y	Y	Y
37 ***McCandless***	N	N	Y	Y	Y	?	?	?
38 ***Dornan***	N	Y	Y	Y	N	Y	Y	N
39 ***Dannemeyer***	N	Y	Y	N	Y	N	N	N
40 ***Cox***	N	Y	Y	Y	Y	Y	Y	Y
41 ***Lowery***	N	N	Y	Y	Y	Y	Y	Y
42 ***Rohrabacher***	Y	Y	Y	Y	Y	N	Y	N
43 ***Packard***	N	Y	Y	Y	Y	Y	Y	Y
44 ***Cunningham***	N	N	Y	Y	Y	Y	Y	Y
45 ***Hunter***	N	Y	Y	Y	Y	Y	Y	Y
COLORADO								
1 Schroeder	Y	N	Y	Y	Y	Y	Y	Y
2 Skaggs	N	N	Y	Y	Y	Y	Y	Y
3 Campbell	Y	N	Y	Y	Y	?	?	?
4 ***Allard***	N	N	Y	Y	Y	Y	Y	Y
5 ***Hefley***	Y	Y	N	Y	Y	?	?	?
6 ***Schaefer***	Y	N	Y	Y	Y	Y	Y	Y
CONNECTICUT								
1 Kennelly	N	N	Y	Y	Y	Y	Y	Y
2 Gejdenson	Y	N	Y	Y	Y	+	+	+
3 DeLauro	N	N	Y	Y	Y	Y	Y	Y
4 ***Shays***	Y	Y	N	Y	Y	Y	Y	Y
5 ***Franks***	N	N	Y	Y	Y	Y	Y	Y
6 ***Johnson***	Y	N	Y	Y	Y	Y	Y	Y
DELAWARE								
AL Carper	N	N	Y	Y	Y	Y	Y	Y
FLORIDA								
1 Hutto	N	Y	Y	Y	Y	?	?	?
2 Peterson	Y	N	Y	Y	Y	Y	Y	Y
3 Bennett	Y	Y	Y	Y	Y	Y	Y	Y
4 ***James***	Y	N	Y	?	Y	?	?	?
5 ***McCollum***	N	Y	Y	Y	Y	Y	Y	Y
6 ***Stearns***	N	Y	Y	Y	N	Y	Y	N
7 Gibbons	N	N	Y	Y	Y	Y	Y	Y
8 ***Young***	N	N	Y	Y	Y	Y	Y	Y
9 ***Bilirakis***	Y	Y	Y	?	Y	Y	Y	Y
10 ***Ireland***	N	Y	Y	Y	Y	?	?	?
11 Bacchus	?	?	+	?	Y	Y	Y	Y
12 ***Lewis***	N	Y	Y	Y	Y	+	+	+
13 ***Goss***	N	N	Y	Y	N	Y	Y	Y
14 Johnston	Y	Y	N	Y	Y	?	?	?
15 ***Shaw***	N	N	Y	Y	Y	Y	Y	Y
16 Smith	N	N	Y	Y	Y	Y	Y	Y
17 Lehman	N	-	+	Y	Y	?	?	?
18 ***Ros-Lehtinen***	Y	N	Y	Y	Y	Y	Y	Y
19 Fascell	N	N	Y	Y	Y	Y	Y	Y
GEORGIA								
1 Thomas	N	N	Y	Y	Y	Y	Y	Y
2 Hatcher	N	N	Y	Y	Y	?	?	?
3 Ray	N	N	Y	Y	Y	?	?	?
4 Jones	Y	N	Y	Y	Y	?	?	?
5 Lewis	Y	N	Y	Y	Y	Y	Y	Y
6 ***Gingrich***	N	Y	Y	Y	Y	?	?	?
7 Darden	N	N	Y	Y	Y	Y	Y	Y
8 Rowland	N	N	Y	Y	Y	Y	Y	Y
9 Jenkins	N	N	Y	Y	Y	?	?	?
10 Barnard	N	N	Y	?	?	Y	Y	Y
HAWAII								
1 Abercrombie	N	N	Y	Y	Y	Y	Y	Y
2 Mink	N	N	Y	Y	Y	Y	Y	Y
IDAHO								
1 LaRocco	N	N	Y	Y	Y	Y	Y	Y
2 Stallings	N	N	Y	Y	Y	Y	Y	Y
ILLINOIS								
1 Hayes	Y	N	Y	Y	N	Y	Y	Y
2 Savage	N	N	Y	Y	N	?	?	?
3 Russo	Y	N	Y	Y	Y	Y	Y	Y
4 Sangmeister	Y	N	Y	Y	Y	?	?	?
5 Lipinski	Y	N	Y	Y	Y	?	?	?
6 ***Hyde***	N	N	Y	Y	Y	Y	Y	Y
7 Collins	Y	N	Y	Y	Y	Y	Y	Y
8 Rostenkowski	Y	N	Y	Y	Y	Y	Y	Y
9 Yates	N	N	Y	Y	Y	Y	Y	Y
10 ***Porter***	Y	N	Y	Y	Y	Y	Y	Y
11 Annunzio	N	N	Y	Y	Y	Y	Y	Y
12 ***Crane***	?	?	?	N	N	N	N	N
13 ***Fawell***	N	Y	Y	Y	N	Y	Y	Y
14 ***Hastert***	N	N	Y	Y	Y	Y	Y	Y
15 Vacancy								
16 Cox	Y	N	Y	Y	Y	Y	Y	Y
17 Evans	Y	N	Y	Y	Y	Y	Y	Y
18 ***Michel***	N	N	Y	?	Y	Y	Y	Y
19 Bruce	N	Y	Y	Y	Y	Y	Y	Y
20 Durbin	Y	N	Y	Y	Y	Y	Y	Y
21 Costello	N	N	Y	Y	Y	Y	Y	Y
22 Poshard	Y	N	Y	Y	Y	?	?	?
INDIANA								
1 Visclosky	Y	N	Y	Y	Y	Y	Y	Y
2 Sharp	Y	Y	Y	Y	Y	Y	Y	Y
3 Roemer	N	Y	Y	Y	Y	Y	Y	Y

ND Northern Democrats SD Southern Democrats

	117	118	119	120	121	122	123	124
4 Long	Y	N	Y	Y	Y	Y	Y	Y
5 Jontz	Y	Y	Y	Y	Y	Y	Y	Y
6 ***Burton***	Y	Y	N	Y	Y	?	?	?
7 ***Myers***	N	N	Y	Y	Y	Y	Y	Y
8 McCloskey	N	N	Y	Y	Y	Y	Y	Y
9 Hamilton	Y	Y	Y	Y	Y	Y	Y	Y
10 Jacobs	Y	Y	N	Y	Y	?	?	?
IOWA								
1 ***Leach***	Y	N	Y	Y	Y	Y	Y	Y
2 ***Nussle***	N	Y	N	Y	N	?	?	?
3 Nagle	N	N	Y	Y	Y	Y	Y	Y
4 Smith	N	N	Y	Y	Y	Y	Y	Y
5 ***Lightfoot***	N	N	Y	Y	Y	Y	Y	Y
6 ***Grandy***	Y	N	Y	Y	Y	Y	Y	Y
KANSAS								
1 ***Roberts***	N	Y	Y	Y	Y	Y	Y	Y
2 Slattery	Y	N	N	Y	Y	Y	Y	Y
3 ***Meyers***	Y	Y	Y	Y	Y	Y	Y	Y
4 Glickman	Y	Y	Y	Y	Y	Y	Y	Y
5 ***Nichols***	N	Y	Y	Y	Y	Y	Y	Y
KENTUCKY								
1 Hubbard	N	N	Y	Y	Y	Y	Y	Y
2 Natcher	N	N	Y	Y	Y	Y	Y	Y
3 Mazzoli	N	N	Y	Y	Y	Y	Y	Y
4 ***Bunning***	Y	Y	Y	Y	Y	Y	Y	Y
5 ***Rogers***	N	N	Y	Y	Y	Y	Y	Y
6 ***Hopkins***	?	?	?	?	?	Y	Y	Y
7 Perkins	N	N	Y	Y	Y	Y	Y	Y
LOUISIANA								
1 ***Livingston***	N	N	Y	Y	+	?	?	?
2 Jefferson	N	N	Y	?	?	?	?	?
3 Tauzin	N	N	Y	Y	Y	Y	Y	Y
4 ***McCrery***	N	N	Y	?	Y	?	?	?
5 Huckaby	N	N	N	Y	Y	Y	Y	Y
6 ***Baker***	N	N	Y	Y	Y	?	?	?
7 Hayes	N	N	Y	Y	Y	Y	Y	Y
8 ***Holloway***	N	Y	Y	Y	Y	?	?	?
MAINE								
1 Andrews	Y	N	Y	Y	Y	Y	Y	Y
2 ***Snowe***	Y	Y	Y	Y	Y	?	?	?
MARYLAND								
1 ***Gilchrest***	N	Y	Y	Y	Y	Y	Y	Y
2 ***Bentley***	N	Y	Y	Y	Y	Y	Y	Y
3 Cardin	N	N	Y	Y	Y	Y	Y	Y
4 McMillen	N	N	Y	Y	Y	Y	Y	Y
5 Hoyer	N	N	Y	Y	Y	Y	Y	Y
6 Byron	N	N	Y	Y	Y	Y	Y	Y
7 Mfume	Y	N	Y	Y	Y	Y	Y	Y
8 ***Morella***	Y	N	Y	Y	Y	Y	Y	Y
MASSACHUSETTS								
1 Vacancy								
2 Neal	Y	N	Y	Y	Y	?	?	?
3 Early	Y	N	Y	Y	Y	Y	Y	Y
4 Frank	Y	N	Y	Y	Y	Y	Y	Y
5 Atkins	Y	N	Y	Y	Y	Y	Y	Y
6 Mavroules	N	N	Y	Y	Y	Y	Y	Y
7 Markey	Y	N	Y	Y	Y	Y	Y	Y
8 Kennedy	N	N	Y	Y	Y	?	?	?
9 Moakley	N	N	Y	Y	Y	Y	Y	Y
10 Studds	Y	N	Y	Y	Y	Y	Y	Y
11 Donnelly	Y	N	Y	Y	Y	Y	Y	Y
MICHIGAN								
1 Conyers	Y	N	Y	Y	Y	Y	Y	Y
2 ***Pursell***	N	N	Y	Y	Y	Y	Y	Y
3 Wolpe	Y	N	Y	Y	Y	Y	Y	Y
4 ***Upton***	Y	Y	Y	N	Y	Y	Y	Y
5 ***Henry***	Y	Y	N	Y	N	Y	Y	Y
6 Carr	N	N	Y	Y	Y	Y	Y	Y
7 Kildee	N	N	Y	Y	Y	Y	Y	Y
8 Traxler	Y	N	Y	Y	Y	Y	Y	Y
9 ***Vander Jagt***	Y	Y	Y	Y	Y	Y	Y	Y
10 ***Camp***	Y	Y	Y	Y	Y	+	+	+
11 ***Davis***	Y	N	Y	?	?	Y	Y	Y
12 Bonior	?	N	Y	Y	Y	Y	Y	Y
13 Collins	Y	N	Y	Y	Y	Y	Y	Y
14 Hertel	Y	N	Y	Y	Y	Y	Y	Y
15 Ford	Y	N	Y	Y	Y	Y	Y	Y
16 Dingell	Y	N	Y	Y	Y	Y	Y	Y
17 Levin	Y	N	Y	Y	Y	Y	Y	Y
18 ***Broomfield***	Y	Y	Y	Y	Y	Y	Y	Y
MINNESOTA								
1 Penny	Y	Y	Y	Y	Y	Y	Y	Y
2 ***Weber***	N	N	Y	?	Y	Y	Y	Y
3 ***Ramstad***	#	#	X	Y	Y	Y	Y	Y
4 Vento	Y	N	Y	Y	Y	Y	Y	Y

	117	118	119	120	121	122	123	124
5 Sabo	Y	N	Y	Y	Y	Y	Y	Y
6 Sikorski	Y	N	Y	Y	Y	?	Y	Y
7 Peterson	Y	N	Y	Y	Y	Y	Y	Y
8 Oberstar	Y	N	Y	?	?	Y	Y	Y
MISSISSIPPI								
1 Whitten	N	N	Y	Y	Y	Y	Y	Y
2 Espy	Y	N	Y	Y	Y	?	?	?
3 Montgomery	N	N	Y	Y	Y	Y	Y	Y
4 Parker	Y	N	Y	Y	Y	Y	Y	Y
5 Taylor	N	N	Y	Y	Y	Y	Y	Y
MISSOURI								
1 Clay	N	N	Y	Y	Y	?	?	?
2 Horn	Y	N	Y	Y	Y	Y	Y	Y
3 Gephardt	N	N	Y	Y	Y	?	?	?
4 Skelton	N	?	Y	Y	Y	Y	Y	Y
5 Wheat	N	N	Y	Y	Y	Y	Y	Y
6 ***Coleman***	N	N	Y	Y	Y	Y	Y	Y
7 ***Hancock***	Y	Y	N	N	N	N	N	N
8 ***Emerson***	N	N	Y	Y	Y	Y	Y	Y
9 Volkmer	N	N	Y	Y	Y	?	?	?
MONTANA								
1 Williams	Y	N	Y	Y	Y	?	?	?
2 ***Marlenee***	?	?	?	?	?	?	?	?
NEBRASKA								
1 ***Bereuter***	Y	N	Y	Y	Y	Y	Y	Y
2 Hoagland	Y	N	Y	Y	Y	Y	Y	Y
3 ***Barrett***	N	Y	Y	Y	Y	Y	Y	Y
NEVADA								
1 Bilbray	Y	N	Y	Y	Y	Y	Y	Y
2 ***Vucanovich***	N	N	Y	Y	Y	Y	Y	Y
NEW HAMPSHIRE								
1 ***Zeliff***	Y	Y	Y	Y	Y	Y	Y	Y
2 Swett	Y	N	Y	Y	Y	?	?	?
NEW JERSEY								
1 Andrews	N	N	Y	Y	Y	Y	Y	Y
2 Hughes	N	N	Y	Y	Y	Y	Y	Y
3 Pallone	Y	N	Y	Y	Y	Y	Y	Y
4 ***Smith***	N	N	Y	Y	Y	Y	Y	Y
5 ***Roukema***	Y	N	Y	Y	Y	Y	Y	Y
6 Dwyer	N	N	Y	Y	Y	Y	?	?
7 ***Rinaldo***	N	N	Y	Y	Y	Y	Y	Y
8 Roe	N	N	Y	Y	Y	Y	Y	Y
9 Torricelli	N	N	Y	Y	Y	Y	Y	Y
10 Payne	Y	N	Y	Y	Y	Y	Y	Y
11 ***Gallo***	N	N	Y	Y	Y	Y	Y	Y
12 ***Zimmer***	Y	N	Y	Y	Y	Y	Y	Y
13 ***Saxton***	N	N	Y	Y	Y	Y	Y	Y
14 Guarini	N	N	Y	Y	Y	Y	Y	Y
NEW MEXICO								
1 ***Schiff***	N	N	Y	Y	Y	Y	Y	Y
2 ***Skeen***	N	N	Y	Y	Y	Y	Y	Y
3 Richardson	N	N	Y	Y	Y	Y	Y	Y
NEW YORK								
1 Hochbrueckner	N	N	Y	Y	Y	?	?	?
2 Downey	N	N	Y	Y	Y	?	?	?
3 Mrazek	?	?	?	?	Y	?	?	?
4 ***Lent***	N	N	Y	Y	Y	Y	Y	Y
5 ***McGrath***	N	N	Y	Y	Y	Y	Y	Y
6 Flake	Y	N	Y	?	Y	Y	Y	Y
7 Ackerman	?	?	?	?	?	?	?	?
8 Scheuer	Y	?	Y	Y	Y	?	?	?
9 Manton	N	N	Y	Y	Y	Y	Y	Y
10 Schumer	N	N	Y	Y	Y	Y	Y	Y
11 Towns	N	N	Y	Y	Y	?	?	?
12 Owens	Y	N	Y	Y	Y	?	?	?
13 Solarz	Y	N	Y	Y	Y	Y	Y	Y
14 ***Molinari***	N	N	Y	Y	Y	Y	Y	Y
15 ***Green***	N	N	Y	Y	Y	?	?	?
16 Rangel	N	X	Y	Y	Y	Y	Y	Y
17 Weiss	Y	N	Y	Y	?	Y	Y	Y
18 Serrano	N	N	Y	Y	Y	?	?	?
19 Engel	?	X	?	?	?	Y	Y	Y
20 Lowey	Y	N	Y	Y	Y	?	?	?
21 ***Fish***	Y	N	Y	Y	Y	Y	Y	Y
22 ***Gilman***	Y	N	Y	Y	Y	Y	Y	Y
23 McNulty	N	N	Y	Y	Y	Y	Y	Y
24 ***Solomon***	Y	Y	N	Y	Y	Y	Y	Y
25 ***Boehlert***	Y	Y	Y	Y	Y	?	?	?
26 ***Martin***	Y	Y	Y	Y	Y	?	?	?
27 ***Walsh***	N	Y	Y	Y	Y	Y	Y	Y
28 McHugh	N	N	Y	Y	Y	?	?	?
29 ***Horton***	?	?	?	?	?	Y	Y	Y
30 Slaughter	Y	N	Y	Y	Y	Y	Y	Y
31 ***Paxon***	Y	Y	Y	Y	Y	Y	Y	Y

	117	118	119	120	121	122	123	124
32 LaFalce	Y	N	Y	Y	Y	?	?	?
33 Nowak	Y	N	Y	Y	Y	Y	Y	Y
34 ***Houghton***	N	N	Y	?	?	Y	Y	Y
NORTH CAROLINA								
1 Jones	N	N	Y	Y	Y	Y	Y	Y
2 Valentine	Y	N	Y	Y	Y	Y	Y	Y
3 Lancaster	Y	N	Y	Y	Y	?	?	?
4 Price	N	N	Y	Y	Y	?	?	?
5 Neal	Y	N	Y	Y	Y	Y	Y	Y
6 ***Coble***	Y	Y	N	Y	Y	N	Y	N
7 Rose	N	N	Y	Y	Y	Y	Y	Y
8 Hefner	N	N	Y	Y	Y	Y	Y	Y
9 ***McMillan***	N	N	Y	Y	Y	?	?	?
10 ***Ballenger***	N	Y	N	Y	Y	+	+	+
11 ***Taylor***	N	Y	Y	Y	Y	Y	Y	N
NORTH DAKOTA								
AL Dorgan	Y	N	Y	Y	Y	?	?	?
OHIO								
1 Luken	N	N	Y	Y	Y	?	?	?
2 ***Gradison***	Y	Y	Y	Y	Y	?	?	?
3 Hall	Y	N	Y	Y	Y	Y	Y	Y
4 ***Oxley***	N	N	Y	Y	Y	?	?	?
5 ***Gillmor***	Y	N	Y	Y	Y	Y	Y	Y
6 ***McEwen***	N	Y	Y	Y	Y	Y	Y	Y
7 ***Hobson***	N	Y	Y	Y	Y	Y	Y	Y
8 ***Boehner***	N	N	Y	Y	Y	?	?	?
9 Kaptur	N	N	Y	Y	Y	Y	Y	Y
10 ***Miller***	N	Y	Y	Y	Y	Y	Y	Y
11 Eckart	Y	N	Y	Y	Y	Y	Y	Y
12 ***Kasich***	N	Y	Y	?	Y	Y	Y	Y
13 Pease	N	N	Y	Y	Y	Y	Y	Y
14 Sawyer	Y	N	Y	Y	Y	Y	Y	Y
15 ***Wylie***	N	N	Y	Y	Y	Y	Y	Y
16 ***Regula***	Y	N	Y	Y	Y	Y	Y	Y
17 Traficant	N	N	Y	Y	Y	Y	Y	Y
18 Applegate	N	N	Y	Y	Y	Y	Y	Y
19 Feighan	Y	N	Y	Y	Y	?	?	?
20 Oakar	N	N	Y	Y	Y	Y	Y	Y
21 Stokes	N	N	Y	Y	Y	Y	Y	Y
OKLAHOMA								
1 ***Inhofe***	N	Y	Y	Y	Y	?	?	?
2 Synar	Y	N	Y	Y	Y	Y	Y	Y
3 Brewster	N	N	Y	Y	Y	Y	Y	Y
4 McCurdy	Y	N	Y	Y	Y	Y	Y	Y
5 ***Edwards***	N	N	Y	?	Y	Y	Y	Y
6 English	N	N	Y	Y	Y	Y	Y	Y
OREGON								
1 AuCoin	?	?	?	?	?	Y	Y	Y
2 ***Smith***	N	N	Y	Y	Y	Y	Y	Y
3 Wyden	Y	N	Y	Y	Y	Y	Y	Y
4 DeFazio	Y	N	Y	Y	Y	Y	Y	Y
5 Kopetski	N	N	Y	Y	Y	Y	Y	Y
PENNSYLVANIA								
1 Foglietta	N	N	Y	Y	Y	?	?	?
2 Gray	N	N	Y	Y	Y	?	?	?
3 Borski	N	N	Y	Y	Y	Y	Y	Y
4 Kolter	N	N	Y	Y	Y	Y	Y	Y
5 ***Schulze***	Y	Y	Y	Y	Y	Y	Y	Y
6 Yatron	N	N	Y	Y	Y	Y	Y	Y
7 ***Weldon***	Y	Y	Y	Y	Y	Y	Y	Y
8 Kostmayer	Y	N	Y	Y	Y	Y	Y	Y
9 ***Shuster***	Y	Y	Y	Y	Y	Y	Y	Y
10 ***McDade***	N	N	Y	Y	Y	Y	Y	Y
11 Kanjorski	Y	N	Y	Y	Y	Y	Y	Y
12 Murtha	N	N	Y	Y	Y	Y	Y	Y
13 ***Coughlin***	Y	N	Y	?	Y	Y	Y	Y
14 Coyne	N	N	Y	Y	Y	Y	Y	Y
15 ***Ritter***	Y	Y	N	Y	Y	Y	Y	Y
16 ***Walker***	N	Y	N	Y	Y	Y	Y	N
17 ***Gekas***	N	Y	Y	Y	Y	Y	Y	Y
18 ***Santorum***	Y	Y	Y	Y	Y	+	+	+
19 ***Goodling***	Y	N	Y	?	Y	+	+	+
20 Gaydos	N	N	Y	Y	Y	Y	Y	Y
21 ***Ridge***	Y	Y	Y	Y	Y	Y	Y	Y
22 Murphy	Y	Y	Y	Y	Y	Y	Y	Y
23 ***Clinger***	N	N	Y	Y	Y	Y	Y	Y
RHODE ISLAND								
1 ***Machtley***	Y	N	Y	Y	Y	Y	Y	Y
2 Reed	Y	N	Y	Y	Y	Y	Y	Y
SOUTH CAROLINA								
1 ***Ravenel***	Y	Y	Y	Y	Y	?	?	?
2 ***Spence***	N	Y	Y	Y	Y	Y	Y	Y
3 Derrick	Y	N	Y	Y	Y	Y	Y	Y
4 Patterson	Y	Y	Y	Y	Y	?	?	?
5 Spratt	Y	N	Y	Y	Y	?	?	?
6 Tallon	Y	Y	Y	?	Y	Y	Y	Y

	117	118	119	120	121	122	123	124
SOUTH DAKOTA								
AL Johnson	Y	N	Y	Y	Y	Y	Y	Y
TENNESSEE								
1 ***Quillen***	N	N	Y	Y	Y	?	?	?
2 ***Duncan***	Y	Y	N	Y	N	N	N	Y
3 Lloyd	N	N	Y	Y	Y	Y	Y	Y
4 Cooper	N	Y	Y	Y	Y	Y	Y	Y
5 Clement	Y	N	Y	Y	Y	Y	Y	Y
6 Gordon	Y	N	Y	Y	Y	?	?	?
7 ***Sundquist***	Y	N	Y	Y	Y	Y	Y	Y
8 Tanner	N	N	Y	Y	Y	Y	Y	Y
9 Ford	N	N	Y	Y	Y	?	?	?
TEXAS								
1 Chapman	N	N	Y	Y	Y	Y	Y	Y
2 Wilson	N	N	Y	?	?	Y	Y	Y
3 ***Johnson***	N	Y	Y	Y	Y	Y	Y	Y
4 Hall	N	N	Y	Y	Y	Y	Y	Y
5 Bryant	N	N	Y	Y	Y	Y	Y	Y
6 ***Barton***	N	N	Y	Y	Y	Y	Y	N
7 ***Archer***	N	Y	N	Y	Y	Y	Y	Y
8 ***Fields***	N	N	Y	?	Y	+	+	+
9 Brooks	N	N	Y	?	Y	Y	Y	Y
10 Pickle	N	N	Y	Y	Y	?	?	?
11 Edwards	N	N	Y	Y	Y	Y	Y	Y
12 Geren	N	N	Y	Y	Y	Y	Y	Y
13 Sarpalius	N	N	Y	Y	Y	Y	Y	Y
14 Laughlin	N	N	Y	Y	Y	Y	Y	Y
15 de la Garza	?	?	?	Y	Y	Y	Y	Y
16 Coleman	N	N	Y	Y	Y	Y	Y	Y
17 Stenholm	N	N	Y	Y	Y	?	?	?
18 Washington	N	N	Y	Y	Y	?	?	?
19 ***Combest***	N	N	Y	Y	Y	Y	Y	Y
20 Gonzalez	N	N	Y	Y	Y	Y	Y	Y
21 ***Smith***	N	Y	Y	Y	Y	Y	Y	Y
22 ***DeLay***	N	N	Y	Y	Y	Y	Y	N
23 Bustamante	N	N	Y	Y	?	Y	Y	Y
24 Frost	N	N	Y	Y	Y	?	?	?
25 Andrews	N	N	Y	Y	Y	+	?	?
26 ***Armey***	N	Y	Y	Y	Y	?	?	?
27 Ortiz	N	N	Y	Y	Y	Y	Y	Y
UTAH								
1 ***Hansen***	N	N	Y	Y	Y	Y	Y	Y
2 Owens	N	N	Y	?	?	Y	Y	Y
3 Orton	N	N	Y	Y	Y	?	?	?
VERMONT								
AL *Sanders*	Y	N	N	?	Y	+	+	+
VIRGINIA								
1 ***Bateman***	N	N	Y	Y	Y	Y	Y	Y
2 Pickett	N	N	Y	Y	Y	Y	Y	Y
3 ***Bliley***	N	N	Y	Y	Y	Y	Y	Y
4 Sisisky	Y	N	Y	Y	Y	Y	Y	Y
5 Payne	N	N	Y	Y	Y	Y	Y	Y
6 Olin	N	N	Y	Y	Y	Y	Y	Y
7 ***Slaughter***	N	N	Y	Y	Y	Y	Y	Y
8 Moran	Y	N	Y	Y	Y	Y	Y	Y
9 Boucher	N	N	Y	Y	Y	Y	Y	Y
10 ***Wolf***	N	N	Y	Y	Y	Y	Y	Y
WASHINGTON								
1 ***Miller***	N	Y	Y	Y	Y	Y	Y	Y
2 Swift	Y	N	Y	Y	Y	Y	Y	Y
3 Unsoeld	Y	N	Y	Y	Y	Y	Y	Y
4 ***Morrison***	N	N	Y	Y	Y	Y	Y	Y
5 Foley								
6 Dicks	N	N	Y	Y	Y	?	?	?
7 McDermott	Y	N	Y	Y	Y	?	?	?
8 ***Chandler***	X	#	#	?	?	Y	Y	Y
WEST VIRGINIA								
1 Mollohan	N	N	Y	Y	Y	Y	Y	Y
2 Staggers	?	?	?	Y	Y	Y	Y	Y
3 Wise	Y	N	Y	Y	Y	?	?	?
4 Rahall	N	N	Y	Y	Y	Y	Y	Y
WISCONSIN								
1 Aspin	?	?	?	?	?	?	?	?
2 ***Klug***	N	N	Y	Y	Y	Y	Y	Y
3 ***Gunderson***	N	N	Y	Y	Y	Y	Y	Y
4 Kleczka	Y	N	Y	Y	Y	Y	Y	Y
5 Moody	Y	N	Y	Y	Y	?	?	?
6 ***Petri***	Y	Y	N	Y	N	Y	Y	Y
7 Obey	Y	N	Y	Y	Y	Y	Y	Y
8 ***Roth***	Y	Y	N	Y	Y	Y	Y	Y
9 ***Sensenbrenner***	Y	Y	N	Y	N	N	Y	N
WYOMING								
AL ***Thomas***	Y	N	Y	Y	Y	Y	Y	Y

Southern states - Ala., Ark., Fla., Ga., Ky., La., Miss., N.C., Okla., S.C., Tenn., Texas, Va.
Omitted votes are quorum calls, which CQ does not include in its vote charts.

125. HR 1. Civil Rights Act of 1991. Wheat, D-Mo., motion to order the previous question (thus ending debate and the possibility of amendment) on the rule (H Res 162) to provide for House floor consideration of the bill to reverse or modify a series of Supreme Court rulings that narrowed the reach and remedies of job discrimination laws and to authorize compensatory and punitive damages for victims of discrimination based on sex, religion or disability. Motion agreed to 259-165: R 0-164; D 258-1 (ND 175-1, SD 83-0); I 1-0; June 4, 1991.

126. HR 1. Civil Rights Act of 1991/Rule. Adoption of the rule (H Res 162) to provide for House floor consideration of the bill to reverse or modify a series of Supreme Court rulings that narrowed the reach and remedies of job discrimination laws and to authorize compensatory and punitive damages for victims of discrimination based on sex, religion or disability. Motion agreed to 247-175: R 6-159; D 240-16 (ND 163-11, SD 77-5); I 1-0, June 4, 1991.

127. HR 1. Civil Rights Act of 1991/Unlimited Punitive Damages. Towns, D-N.Y., substitute amendment to provide for unlimited punitive damages for discrimination based on sex, religion or disability as opposed to the $150,000 cap provided for in the Brooks, D-Texas, substitute. Rejected 152-277: R 6-159; D 145-118 (ND 122-58, SD 23-60); I 1-0, June 4, 1991. A "nay" was a vote supporting the president's position.

128. HR 1. Civil Rights Act of 1991/Administration's Substitute. Michel, R-Ill., to substitute the administration's civil rights bill. The substitute would remove compensatory and punitive damages for job discrimination based on sex, religion or disability but allow up to $150,000 for cases involving harassment; define "business necessity" as a practice that has a manifest relationship to the employment or that serves a legitimate employment goal; allow intentional discrimination when it is only a contributing factor; allow challenges to consent decrees; ban the use of race-based adjustments to hiring-test scores; and make other changes. Rejected 162-266: R 146-19; D 16-246 (ND 0-179, SD 16-67); I 0-1; June 4, 1991. A "yea" was a vote supporting the president's position.

129. Procedural Motion. Nagle, D-Iowa, motion to approve the House Journal of Tuesday, June 4. Motion agreed to 282-116: R 46-109; D 236-7 (ND 158-6, SD 78-1), June 5, 1991.

130. HR 1. Civil Rights Act of 1991/Punitive Damages Cap. Brooks, D-Texas, substitute amendment to place a cap of $150,000 on punitive damages for victims of intentional job discrimination on the basis of sex, religion or disability, or the amount of compensatory damages, whichever is greater; define "business necessity" as a practice that must bear a significant manifest relationship to the requirements for effective job performance; ban the use of race-based adjustments to hiring-test scores; include a provision explicitly prohibiting the use of quotas; and for other purposes. Adopted 264-166: R 22-143; D 241-23 (ND 170-10, SD 71-13); I 1-0; June 5, 1991.

131. HR 1. Civil Rights Act of 1991/Passage. Passage of the bill to reverse or modify a series of Supreme Court rulings that narrowed the reach and remedies of job discrimination laws and to authorize compensatory and punitive damages for victims of discrimination based on sex, religion or disability. Passed 273-158: R 22-143; D 250-15 (ND 177-4, SD 73-11); I 1-0; June 5, 1991. A "nay" was a vote supporting the president's position.

132. HR 2506. Fiscal 1992 Legislative Branch Appropriations/Bar on Transfer of Unspent Funds. Santorum, R-Pa., en bloc amendments to prohibit the Appropriations Committee from shifting unspent funds between various accounts. Santorum said the purpose was to have unspent money revert to the Treasury, thereby reducing the deficit. Rejected 150-276: R 127-38; D 23-237 (ND 13-165, SD 10-72); I 0-1; June 5, 1991.

KEY

- Y Voted for (yea).
- # Paired for.
- + Announced for.
- N Voted against (nay).
- X Paired against.
- - Announced against.
- P Voted "present."
- C Voted "present" to avoid possible conflict of interest.
- ? Did not vote or otherwise make a position known.

Democrats ***Republicans***
Independent

	125	126	127	128	129	130	131	132
ALABAMA								
1 ***Callahan***	N	N	N	Y	N	N	N	Y
2 ***Dickinson***	N	N	N	Y	?	N	N	Y
3 Browder	Y	Y	N	N	Y	Y	Y	Y
4 Bevill	Y	Y	N	N	Y	Y	Y	N
5 Cramer	Y	Y	N	N	Y	Y	Y	N
6 Erdreich	Y	Y	N	N	Y	Y	Y	Y
7 Harris	Y	Y	N	N	Y	Y	Y	N
ALASKA								
AL ***Young***	N	N	N	Y	N	N	N	N
ARIZONA								
1 ***Rhodes***	N	N	N	Y	N	N	N	Y
2 Vacancy								
3 ***Stump***	N	N	N	Y	N	N	N	Y
4 ***Kyl***	N	N	N	Y	N	N	N	Y
5 ***Kolbe***	N	N	N	Y	N	N	N	N
ARKANSAS								
1 Alexander	Y	Y	N	N	Y	Y	Y	N
2 Thornton	Y	Y	Y	N	Y	Y	Y	N
3 ***Hammerschmidt***	N	N	N	Y	Y	N	N	N
4 Anthony	Y	Y	N	N	Y	Y	Y	N
CALIFORNIA								
1 ***Riggs***	N	N	N	Y	?	N	N	Y
2 ***Herger***	N	N	N	Y	N	N	N	Y
3 Matsui	Y	Y	Y	N	Y	Y	Y	N
4 Fazio	Y	Y	Y	N	Y	Y	Y	N
5 Pelosi	Y	?	Y	N	Y	Y	Y	N
6 Boxer	Y	Y	Y	N	?	N	Y	N
7 Miller	Y	?	Y	N	Y	Y	Y	N
8 Dellums	Y	Y	Y	N	Y	N	Y	N
9 Stark	Y	Y	Y	?	Y	Y	Y	N
10 Edwards	Y	Y	Y	N	N	Y	Y	N
11 Lantos	Y	Y	Y	N	Y	Y	Y	N
12 ***Campbell***	N	N	Y	Y	N	Y	Y	Y
13 Mineta	Y	Y	Y	N	Y	Y	Y	N
14 ***Doolittle***	N	N	N	N	N	N	N	Y
15 Condit	Y	Y	Y	N	Y	Y	Y	Y
16 Panetta	Y	Y	Y	N	Y	Y	Y	N
17 Dooley	Y	Y	N	N	Y	Y	Y	N
18 Lehman	Y	Y	N	N	Y	Y	Y	N
19 ***Lagomarsino***	N	N	N	Y	N	N	N	Y
20 ***Thomas***	N	N	N	Y	N	N	N	N
21 ***Gallegly***	N	N	N	Y	N	N	N	Y
22 ***Moorhead***	N	N	N	Y	N	N	N	Y
23 Beilenson	Y	Y	N	N	Y	Y	Y	N
24 Waxman	Y	Y	Y	N	Y	Y	Y	N
25 Roybal	Y	Y	Y	N	Y	Y	Y	N
26 Berman	Y	Y	Y	N	Y	Y	Y	N
27 Levine	Y	Y	Y	N	Y	Y	Y	N
28 Dixon	Y	Y	Y	N	?	Y	Y	N
29 Waters	?	?	Y	N	?	Y	Y	N
30 Martinez	Y	Y	Y	N	Y	Y	Y	?
31 Dymally	Y	Y	Y	N	Y	Y	Y	N
32 Anderson	Y	Y	Y	N	Y	Y	Y	N
33 ***Dreier***	N	N	N	Y	Y	N	N	Y
34 Torres	Y	Y	Y	N	Y	Y	Y	N
35 ***Lewis***	N	N	N	Y	N	N	N	N
36 Brown	Y	Y	Y	N	?	Y	Y	N
37 ***McCandless***	N	N	N	Y	N	N	N	Y
38 ***Dornan***	N	N	N	Y	?	N	N	Y
39 ***Dannemeyer***	N	N	N	Y	N	N	N	Y
40 ***Cox***	N	N	N	Y	Y	N	N	Y
41 ***Lowery***	N	N	N	Y	N	N	N	N
42 ***Rohrabacher***	N	N	N	Y	N	N	N	Y
43 ***Packard***	N	N	N	Y	N	N	N	Y
44 ***Cunningham***	N	N	N	Y	N	N	N	Y
45 ***Hunter***	?	N	N	Y	?	N	N	Y
COLORADO								
1 Schroeder	Y	N	Y	N	N	N	Y	N
2 Skaggs	Y	Y	N	N	Y	Y	Y	N
3 Campbell	Y	N	Y	N	Y	Y	Y	N
4 ***Allard***	N	N	N	N	N	N	N	Y
5 ***Hefley***	N	N	N	Y	N	N	N	Y
6 ***Schaefer***	N	N	N	Y	N	N	N	Y
CONNECTICUT								
1 Kennelly	Y	Y	Y	N	Y	Y	Y	N
2 Gejdenson	Y	Y	Y	N	Y	Y	Y	N
3 DeLauro	Y	Y	Y	N	Y	Y	Y	N
4 ***Shays***	N	N	N	N	N	Y	Y	Y
5 ***Franks***	N	N	N	Y	N	N	N	Y
6 ***Johnson***	N	N	N	Y	Y	N	N	Y
DELAWARE								
AL Carper	Y	Y	N	N	Y	Y	Y	N
FLORIDA								
1 Hutto	Y	Y	N	N	Y	N	N	Y
2 Peterson	Y	Y	Y	N	+	Y	Y	N
3 Bennett	Y	Y	N	N	Y	Y	Y	N
4 ***James***	N	N	N	Y	N	N	N	Y
5 ***McCollum***	N	N	N	Y	N	N	N	Y
6 ***Stearns***	N	N	N	Y	N	N	N	Y
7 Gibbons	Y	Y	Y	Y	Y	Y	Y	N
8 ***Young***	N	N	Y	Y	N	N	N	Y
9 ***Bilirakis***	N	Y	N	Y	N	N	N	Y
10 ***Ireland***	N	N	N	Y	?	N	N	Y
11 Bacchus	Y	Y	N	N	Y	Y	Y	N
12 ***Lewis***	N	N	N	Y	N	N	N	Y
13 ***Goss***	N	N	N	Y	N	N	N	Y
14 Johnston	Y	Y	Y	N	Y	Y	Y	N
15 ***Shaw***	N	N	N	Y	Y	N	N	Y
16 Smith	Y	Y	Y	N	Y	Y	Y	N
17 Lehman	?	?	?	?	?	Y	Y	?
18 ***Ros-Lehtinen***	N	N	N	Y	N	Y	Y	Y
19 Fascell	Y	Y	Y	N	Y	Y	Y	N
GEORGIA								
1 Thomas	Y	Y	N	Y	Y	Y	Y	N
2 Hatcher	Y	Y	N	Y	Y	Y	Y	N
3 Ray	Y	N	N	Y	Y	Y	Y	N
4 Jones	Y	Y	N	N	Y	Y	Y	N
5 Lewis	Y	Y	Y	N	Y	Y	Y	N
6 ***Gingrich***	N	N	N	Y	N	N	N	Y
7 Darden	Y	Y	N	N	Y	N	N	N
8 Rowland	Y	Y	N	Y	Y	Y	Y	N
9 Jenkins	Y	Y	N	Y	Y	N	N	N
10 Barnard	Y	Y	N	Y	N	N	N	N
HAWAII								
1 Abercrombie	Y	Y	Y	N	?	Y	Y	N
2 Mink	Y	N	Y	N	Y	N	Y	N
IDAHO								
1 LaRocco	Y	Y	N	N	Y	Y	Y	N
2 Stallings	Y	Y	N	N	Y	Y	Y	N
ILLINOIS								
1 Hayes	Y	Y	Y	N	Y	Y	Y	N
2 Savage	Y	Y	Y	N	Y	N	Y	N
3 Russo	Y	Y	N	N	Y	N	N	Y
4 Sangmeister	Y	Y	N	N	Y	Y	Y	N
5 Lipinski	Y	Y	N	N	Y	N	N	N
6 ***Hyde***	N	N	N	Y	N	N	N	Y
7 Collins	Y	Y	Y	N	Y	Y	Y	N
8 Rostenkowski	Y	Y	N	N	Y	Y	Y	N
9 Yates	Y	Y	Y	N	Y	Y	Y	N
10 ***Porter***	N	N	N	Y	Y	N	N	N
11 Annunzio	Y	Y	N	N	Y	N	N	N
12 ***Crane***	N	N	N	Y	?	N	N	Y
13 ***Fawell***	N	N	N	Y	Y	N	N	Y
14 ***Hastert***	N	N	N	Y	N	N	N	Y
15 Vacancy								
16 Cox	Y	Y	N	N	Y	Y	Y	N
17 Evans	Y	Y	Y	N	Y	Y	Y	N
18 ***Michel***	N	N	N	Y	N	N	N	Y
19 Bruce	Y	Y	Y	N	Y	Y	Y	Y
20 Durbin	Y	Y	Y	N	Y	Y	Y	N
21 Costello	Y	Y	N	N	Y	Y	Y	Y
22 Poshard	Y	Y	N	N	Y	Y	Y	Y
INDIANA								
1 Visclosky	Y	Y	N	N	Y	Y	Y	N
2 Sharp	Y	Y	Y	N	Y	Y	Y	Y
3 Roemer	Y	Y	N	N	Y	Y	Y	Y

ND Northern Democrats SD Southern Democrats

	125	126	127	128	129	130	131	132
4 Long	Y	Y	N	N	Y	Y	Y	N
5 Jontz	Y	Y	Y	N	Y	Y	Y	N
6 ***Burton***	N	N	N	Y	N	N	N	Y
7 ***Myers***	N	N	N	Y	Y	N	N	N
8 McCloskey	Y	Y	Y	N	Y	Y	Y	N
9 Hamilton	Y	Y	N	N	Y	Y	Y	N
10 Jacobs	N	Y	N	N	N	Y	Y	Y
IOWA								
1 ***Leach***	N	N	N	N	N	Y	Y	Y
2 ***Nussle***	N	N	N	Y	N	N	N	Y
3 Nagle	Y	Y	Y	N	Y	Y	Y	N
4 Smith	Y	Y	N	N	Y	Y	Y	N
5 ***Lightfoot***	N	N	N	Y	N	N	N	Y
6 ***Grandy***	N	N	N	Y	N	N	N	Y
KANSAS								
1 ***Roberts***	N	N	N	Y	N	N	N	Y
2 Slattery	Y	Y	N	N	Y	Y	Y	N
3 ***Meyers***	N	N	N	Y	N	N	N	Y
4 Glickman	Y	Y	N	N	?	Y	Y	N
5 ***Nichols***	N	N	N	Y	Y	N	N	Y
KENTUCKY								
1 Hubbard	Y	Y	N	N	Y	Y	Y	N
2 Natcher	Y	Y	N	N	Y	Y	Y	N
3 Mazzoli	Y	Y	N	N	Y	Y	Y	N
4 ***Bunning***	N	N	N	Y	N	N	N	Y
5 ***Rogers***	N	N	N	Y	N	N	N	N
6 ***Hopkins***	N	N	N	Y	N	N	N	Y
7 Perkins	Y	Y	Y	N	Y	Y	Y	N
LOUISIANA								
1 ***Livingston***	N	N	N	Y	Y	N	N	Y
2 Jefferson	Y	Y	Y	N	Y	Y	Y	N
3 Tauzin	Y	Y	N	Y	Y	N	Y	N
4 ***McCrery***	N	N	N	Y	?	N	N	Y
5 Huckaby	Y	Y	N	Y	Y	N	N	N
6 ***Baker***	N	N	N	Y	N	N	N	Y
7 Hayes	Y	Y	Y	Y	Y	N	N	N
8 ***Holloway***	N	N	N	N	N	N	N	Y
MAINE								
1 Andrews	Y	Y	Y	N	Y	Y	Y	N
2 ***Snowe***	N	N	N	N	Y	Y	Y	Y
MARYLAND								
1 ***Gilchrest***	N	N	N	Y	N	N	N	Y
2 ***Bentley***	N	N	N	Y	N	N	N	N
3 Cardin	Y	Y	Y	N	Y	Y	Y	N
4 McMillen	Y	Y	N	N	Y	Y	Y	N
5 Hoyer	Y	Y	Y	N	Y	Y	Y	N
6 Byron	Y	N	N	N	Y	Y	Y	N
7 Mfume	Y	Y	Y	N	Y	Y	Y	N
8 ***Morella***	N	N	Y	N	Y	Y	Y	N
MASSACHUSETTS								
1 Vacancy								
2 Neal	Y	Y	Y	N	Y	Y	Y	N
3 Early	Y	Y	Y	N	Y	Y	Y	N
4 Frank	Y	Y	Y	N	Y	Y	Y	N
5 Atkins	Y	Y	Y	N	Y	Y	Y	N
6 Mavroules	Y	Y	Y	N	Y	Y	Y	N
7 Markey	Y	Y	Y	N	Y	Y	Y	N
8 Kennedy	Y	Y	Y	N	Y	Y	Y	N
9 Moakley	Y	Y	Y	N	Y	Y	Y	N
10 Studds	Y	Y	Y	N	Y	Y	Y	N
11 Donnelly	Y	Y	Y	N	Y	Y	Y	N
MICHIGAN								
1 Conyers	Y	Y	Y	N	Y	Y	Y	N
2 ***Pursell***	N	N	N	Y	Y	N	N	N
3 Wolpe	Y	Y	Y	N	Y	Y	Y	N
4 ***Upton***	N	N	N	Y	N	N	N	Y
5 ***Henry***	N	N	N	N	N	Y	Y	Y
6 Carr	Y	Y	N	N	Y	Y	Y	N
7 Kildee	Y	Y	Y	N	Y	Y	Y	N
8 Traxler	Y	Y	Y	N	Y	Y	Y	N
9 ***Vander Jagt***	N	N	N	Y	N	N	N	Y
10 ***Camp***	N	N	N	Y	N	N	N	Y
11 ***Davis***	N	N	N	Y	Y	Y	Y	N
12 Bonior	Y	Y	Y	N	Y	Y	Y	N
13 Collins	Y	Y	Y	N	Y	Y	Y	N
14 Hertel	Y	Y	Y	N	Y	Y	Y	N
15 Ford	Y	Y	Y	N	Y	Y	Y	N
16 Dingell	Y	Y	N	N	Y	Y	Y	N
17 Levin	Y	Y	Y	N	Y	Y	Y	N
18 ***Broomfield***	N	N	N	Y	Y	N	N	Y
MINNESOTA								
1 Penny	Y	Y	N	N	Y	Y	Y	N
2 ***Weber***	N	N	N	Y	N	N	N	Y
3 ***Ramstad***	N	N	N	Y	N	N	N	Y
4 Vento	Y	Y	Y	N	Y	Y	Y	N
5 Sabo	Y	Y	Y	N	Y	Y	Y	?
6 Sikorski	Y	Y	Y	N	N	Y	Y	N
7 Peterson	Y	Y	N	N	Y	Y	Y	N
8 Oberstar	Y	Y	Y	N	Y	Y	Y	N
MISSISSIPPI								
1 Whitten	Y	Y	N	N	Y	Y	Y	N
2 Espy	Y	Y	Y	N	Y	Y	Y	N
3 Montgomery	Y	Y	N	Y	Y	N	N	N
4 Parker	Y	N	N	Y	Y	N	N	Y
5 Taylor	Y	Y	N	Y	Y	N	N	Y
MISSOURI								
1 Clay	Y	Y	Y	N	N	Y	Y	N
2 Horn	Y	Y	Y	N	Y	Y	Y	Y
3 Gephardt	Y	Y	Y	N	Y	Y	Y	N
4 Skelton	Y	Y	N	N	Y	Y	Y	N
5 Wheat	Y	Y	Y	N	Y	N	Y	N
6 ***Coleman***	N	N	N	Y	N	N	N	N
7 ***Hancock***	N	N	N	Y	N	N	N	Y
8 ***Emerson***	N	N	N	Y	Y	N	N	Y
9 Volkmer	Y	Y	N	N	Y	Y	Y	N
MONTANA								
1 Williams	Y	N	Y	N	Y	Y	Y	N
2 ***Marlenee***	N	N	N	N	N	N	N	N
NEBRASKA								
1 ***Bereuter***	N	N	N	Y	N	N	N	Y
2 Hoagland	Y	Y	N	N	Y	Y	Y	N
3 ***Barrett***	N	N	N	Y	N	N	N	N
NEVADA								
1 Bilbray	Y	N	N	N	Y	Y	Y	N
2 ***Vucanovich***	N	N	N	Y	N	N	N	N
NEW HAMPSHIRE								
1 ***Zeliff***	N	N	N	Y	?	N	N	Y
2 Swett	Y	Y	N	N	Y	Y	Y	N
NEW JERSEY								
1 Andrews	?	?	Y	N	Y	Y	Y	N
2 Hughes	Y	N	N	N	Y	Y	Y	N
3 Pallone	Y	Y	Y	N	Y	Y	Y	Y
4 ***Smith***	N	N	N	Y	Y	N	N	Y
5 ***Roukema***	N	N	N	Y	N	N	N	N
6 Dwyer	Y	Y	Y	N	Y	Y	Y	N
7 ***Rinaldo***	N	N	N	N	Y	Y	Y	Y
8 Roe	Y	Y	Y	N	Y	Y	Y	N
9 Torricelli	Y	Y	Y	N	Y	Y	Y	N
10 Payne	Y	Y	Y	N	Y	Y	Y	N
11 ***Gallo***	N	N	N	Y	N	N	N	N
12 ***Zimmer***	N	N	N	Y	N	Y	Y	Y
13 ***Saxton***	N	N	N	Y	N	N	N	N
14 Guarini	Y	Y	N	N	Y	Y	Y	N
NEW MEXICO								
1 ***Schiff***	N	N	Y	Y	Y	Y	Y	Y
2 ***Skeen***	N	N	N	Y	Y	N	N	N
3 Richardson	Y	Y	Y	N	Y	Y	Y	N
NEW YORK								
1 Hochbrueckner	Y	Y	N	N	Y	Y	Y	N
2 Downey	Y	Y	N	N	Y	Y	Y	N
3 Mrazek	Y	Y	Y	N	?	Y	Y	N
4 ***Lent***	N	N	N	Y	Y	N	N	N
5 ***McGrath***	N	N	N	Y	N	N	N	Y
6 Flake	Y	Y	Y	N	Y	Y	Y	N
7 Ackerman	Y	Y	Y	N	Y	Y	Y	N
8 Scheuer	Y	Y	Y	N	Y	Y	Y	N
9 Manton	Y	Y	Y	N	Y	Y	Y	N
10 Schumer	Y	Y	N	N	Y	Y	Y	N
11 Towns	Y	Y	Y	N	Y	Y	Y	N
12 Owens	Y	Y	Y	N	Y	Y	Y	N
13 Solarz	Y	Y	N	N	Y	Y	Y	N
14 ***Molinari***	N	N	N	Y	N	N	N	Y
15 ***Green***	N	Y	Y	N	Y	Y	Y	Y
16 Rangel	Y	Y	Y	N	Y	Y	Y	N
17 Weiss	Y	Y	Y	N	?	Y	Y	N
18 Serrano	Y	Y	Y	N	Y	Y	Y	N
19 Engel	Y	Y	N	N	Y	Y	Y	N
20 Lowey	Y	Y	Y	N	Y	Y	Y	N
21 ***Fish***	N	Y	N	N	Y	Y	Y	N
22 ***Gilman***	N	Y	N	N	Y	Y	Y	N
23 McNulty	Y	Y	N	N	Y	Y	Y	N
24 ***Solomon***	N	N	N	Y	N	N	N	Y
25 ***Boehlert***	N	Y	N	N	N	Y	Y	N
26 ***Martin***	N	N	N	Y	N	N	N	N
27 ***Walsh***	N	N	N	N	Y	Y	Y	Y
28 McHugh	Y	Y	Y	N	?	Y	Y	N
29 ***Horton***	N	Y	N	N	Y	Y	Y	N
30 Slaughter	Y	Y	Y	N	Y	Y	Y	N
31 ***Paxon***	N	N	N	Y	N	N	N	Y
32 LaFalce	Y	Y	N	N	?	Y	Y	N
33 Nowak	Y	Y	Y	N	Y	Y	Y	N
34 ***Houghton***	N	N	N	N	Y	Y	Y	N
NORTH CAROLINA								
1 Jones	Y	Y	N	N	Y	Y	Y	N
2 Valentine	Y	N	N	Y	?	Y	Y	Y
3 Lancaster	Y	Y	N	Y	Y	Y	Y	N
4 Price	Y	Y	N	N	Y	Y	Y	N
5 Neal	Y	Y	N	N	?	Y	Y	N
6 ***Coble***	N	N	N	Y	N	N	N	Y
7 Rose	Y	Y	Y	N	Y	Y	Y	N
8 Hefner	Y	Y	N	N	Y	Y	Y	N
9 ***McMillan***	N	N	N	Y	N	N	N	Y
10 ***Ballenger***	N	N	N	Y	N	N	N	Y
11 ***Taylor***	N	N	N	Y	P	N	N	Y
NORTH DAKOTA								
AL Dorgan	Y	Y	N	N	Y	Y	Y	N
OHIO								
1 Luken	Y	Y	N	N	Y	Y	Y	Y
2 ***Gradison***	N	N	N	Y	N	N	N	Y
3 Hall	Y	Y	N	N	Y	Y	Y	N
4 ***Oxley***	N	N	N	Y	N	N	N	Y
5 ***Gillmor***	N	N	N	Y	Y	N	N	Y
6 ***McEwen***	N	N	N	Y	Y	N	N	Y
7 ***Hobson***	N	N	N	Y	N	Y	Y	Y
8 ***Boehner***	N	N	N	Y	N	N	N	Y
9 Kaptur	Y	N	Y	N	Y	Y	Y	N
10 ***Miller***	N	N	N	Y	N	N	N	Y
11 Eckart	Y	Y	N	N	Y	Y	Y	N
12 ***Kasich***	N	N	N	Y	Y	N	N	Y
13 Pease	Y	Y	N	N	Y	Y	Y	N
14 Sawyer	Y	Y	Y	N	Y	Y	Y	N
15 ***Wylie***	N	N	N	Y	Y	N	N	Y
16 ***Regula***	N	N	N	Y	N	N	N	N
17 Traficant	Y	Y	Y	N	Y	Y	Y	N
18 Applegate	Y	Y	N	N	Y	Y	Y	N
19 Feighan	Y	Y	Y	N	Y	Y	Y	N
20 Oakar	Y	N	Y	N	Y	Y	Y	N
21 Stokes	Y	Y	Y	N	Y	Y	Y	N
OKLAHOMA								
1 ***Inhofe***	N	N	N	Y	N	N	N	Y
2 Synar	Y	Y	Y	N	Y	Y	Y	N
3 Brewster	Y	Y	N	N	Y	Y	Y	N
4 McCurdy	Y	Y	N	N	Y	Y	Y	N
5 ***Edwards***	N	N	N	Y	?	N	N	Y
6 English	Y	Y	N	N	Y	Y	Y	N
OREGON								
1 AuCoin	Y	Y	Y	N	Y	Y	Y	N
2 ***Smith***	N	N	N	Y	N	N	N	Y
3 Wyden	Y	Y	Y	N	Y	Y	Y	N
4 DeFazio	Y	Y	Y	N	Y	Y	Y	N
5 Kopetski	Y	Y	Y	N	Y	Y	Y	N
PENNSYLVANIA								
1 Foglietta	?	?	Y	N	Y	Y	Y	N
2 Gray	Y	Y	Y	N	Y	Y	Y	N
3 Borski	Y	Y	N	N	Y	Y	Y	N
4 Kolter	Y	Y	Y	N	Y	Y	Y	N
5 ***Schulze***	N	N	N	Y	Y	Y	Y	Y
6 Yatron	Y	Y	N	N	?	Y	Y	Y
7 ***Weldon***	N	N	N	Y	N	N	N	Y
8 Kostmayer	Y	N	Y	N	Y	Y	Y	N
9 ***Shuster***	N	N	N	Y	Y	N	N	Y
10 ***McDade***	N	N	N	Y	N	N	N	N
11 Kanjorski	Y	Y	N	N	?	Y	Y	N
12 Murtha	Y	Y	Y	N	Y	Y	Y	N
13 ***Coughlin***	N	N	N	Y	N	N	N	N
14 Coyne	Y	Y	Y	N	Y	Y	Y	N
15 ***Ritter***	N	N	N	Y	Y	N	N	Y
16 ***Walker***	N	N	N	Y	N	N	N	Y
17 ***Gekas***	N	N	N	Y	N	N	N	Y
18 ***Santorum***	N	N	N	Y	N	N	N	Y
19 ***Goodling***	N	N	N	Y	N	N	N	Y
20 Gaydos	Y	Y	Y	N	Y	Y	Y	N
21 ***Ridge***	N	N	N	Y	N	N	N	Y
22 Murphy	Y	Y	N	N	N	Y	Y	Y
23 ***Clinger***	N	N	N	Y	Y	N	N	Y
RHODE ISLAND								
1 ***Machtley***	N	N	N	Y	N	Y	Y	Y
2 Reed	Y	Y	Y	N	Y	Y	Y	N
SOUTH CAROLINA								
1 ***Ravenel***	N	N	N	Y	Y	N	N	Y
2 ***Spence***	N	N	N	Y	Y	N	N	Y
3 Derrick	Y	?	N	N	Y	Y	Y	N
4 Patterson	Y	Y	N	N	Y	Y	Y	Y
5 Spratt	Y	Y	N	N	Y	Y	Y	N
6 Tallon	Y	Y	N	N	Y	Y	Y	N
SOUTH DAKOTA								
AL Johnson	Y	Y	Y	N	Y	Y	Y	N
TENNESSEE								
1 ***Quillen***	N	N	N	Y	N	N	N	N
2 ***Duncan***	N	N	N	Y	N	N	N	Y
3 Lloyd	Y	Y	N	N	Y	Y	Y	N
4 Cooper	Y	Y	N	N	Y	Y	Y	N
5 Clement	Y	Y	N	N	Y	Y	Y	N
6 Gordon	Y	Y	N	N	Y	Y	Y	N
7 ***Sundquist***	N	N	N	Y	N	N	N	Y
8 Tanner	Y	Y	N	N	Y	Y	Y	N
9 Ford	Y	Y	Y	N	Y	Y	Y	?
TEXAS								
1 Chapman	Y	Y	N	N	Y	Y	Y	N
2 Wilson	Y	Y	N	N	Y	Y	Y	N
3 ***Johnson***	N	N	N	Y	N	N	N	Y
4 Hall	Y	N	N	N	Y	N	N	Y
5 Bryant	Y	Y	Y	N	Y	Y	Y	N
6 ***Barton***	N	N	Y	Y	Y	N	N	N
7 ***Archer***	N	N	N	Y	N	N	N	Y
8 ***Fields***	N	N	N	Y	N	N	N	Y
9 Brooks	Y	Y	Y	N	Y	Y	Y	N
10 Pickle	Y	Y	N	N	Y	Y	Y	N
11 Edwards	Y	Y	N	N	Y	Y	Y	N
12 Geren	Y	Y	N	N	Y	Y	Y	Y
13 Sarpalius	Y	Y	N	N	Y	Y	Y	N
14 Laughlin	Y	Y	N	N	Y	Y	Y	N
15 de la Garza	Y	Y	Y	N	Y	Y	Y	N
16 Coleman	Y	Y	Y	N	Y	Y	Y	N
17 Stenholm	Y	N	N	N	Y	N	N	N
18 Washington	Y	Y	Y	N	Y	N	Y	N
19 ***Combest***	N	N	N	Y	Y	N	N	Y
20 Gonzalez	Y	Y	Y	N	Y	Y	Y	N
21 ***Smith***	N	N	N	Y	N	N	N	Y
22 ***DeLay***	N	N	N	N	N	N	N	Y
23 Bustamante	Y	Y	Y	N	Y	Y	Y	N
24 Frost	Y	Y	Y	N	Y	Y	Y	N
25 Andrews	Y	Y	N	N	Y	Y	Y	N
26 ***Armey***	N	N	N	Y	N	N	N	Y
27 Ortiz	Y	Y	N	N	Y	Y	Y	N
UTAH								
1 ***Hansen***	N	N	N	Y	N	N	N	Y
2 Owens	Y	Y	N	N	Y	Y	Y	N
3 Orton	Y	N	N	N	Y	N	N	N
VERMONT								
AL *Sanders*	Y	Y	Y	N	?	Y	Y	N
VIRGINIA								
1 ***Bateman***	N	N	N	Y	Y	N	N	N
2 Pickett	Y	Y	N	Y	Y	Y	Y	N
3 ***Bliley***	N	N	N	Y	N	N	N	N
4 Sisisky	?	?	?	?	?	+	?	?
5 Payne	Y	Y	N	N	Y	Y	Y	Y
6 Olin	Y	Y	N	N	Y	Y	Y	N
7 ***Slaughter***	N	N	N	Y	N	N	N	N
8 Moran	Y	Y	Y	N	Y	Y	Y	N
9 Boucher	Y	Y	N	N	?	Y	Y	N
10 ***Wolf***	N	N	N	Y	N	N	N	Y
WASHINGTON								
1 ***Miller***	N	N	N	Y	N	N	N	Y
2 Swift	Y	Y	Y	N	Y	Y	Y	N
3 Unsoeld	Y	Y	Y	N	Y	Y	Y	N
4 ***Morrison***	N	N	N	Y	Y	N	N	N
5 Foley							Y	
6 Dicks	Y	Y	Y	N	Y	Y	Y	N
7 McDermott	Y	Y	Y	N	?	Y	Y	N
8 ***Chandler***	N	N	N	Y	N	N	N	Y
WEST VIRGINIA								
1 Mollohan	Y	Y	N	N	?	Y	Y	N
2 Staggers	Y	Y	Y	N	?	Y	Y	N
3 Wise	Y	Y	N	N	Y	Y	Y	N
4 Rahall	Y	Y	Y	N	Y	Y	Y	N
WISCONSIN								
1 Aspin	Y	Y	Y	N	?	Y	Y	N
2 ***Klug***	N	N	N	N	Y	Y	Y	Y
3 ***Gunderson***	N	N	N	Y	Y	N	N	N
4 Kleczka	Y	Y	Y	N	Y	Y	Y	N
5 Moody	?	?	Y	N	Y	Y	Y	N
6 ***Petri***	N	N	N	Y	Y	N	N	Y
7 Obey	Y	Y	N	N	Y	Y	Y	N
8 ***Roth***	N	N	N	Y	N	N	N	Y
9 ***Sensenbrenner***	N	N	N	Y	N	N	N	Y
WYOMING								
AL ***Thomas***	N	N	N	Y	N	N	N	Y

Southern states - Ala., Ark., Fla., Ga., Ky., La., Miss., N.C., Okla., S.C., Tenn., Texas, Va.
Omitted votes are quorum calls, which CQ does not include in its vote charts.

HOUSE VOTES 133, 135, 136, 137, 138, 140, 141, 142

133. HR 2506. Fiscal 1992 Legislative Branch Appropriations/Reduce House Mail Costs. Penny, D-Minn., amendment to cut $21 million from the $80 million appropriation for House official mail costs, bringing it to the fiscal 1991 level of $59 million. Rejected 198-227: R 142-22; D 55-205 (ND 28-151, SD 27-54); I 1-0; June 5, 1991.

135. HR 2506. Fiscal 1992 Legislative Branch Appropriations/Limit Growth. Hefley, R-Colo., amendment to limit overall growth in the bill to 2.4 percent above the fiscal 1991 level by cutting 1.4 percent or about $21.4 million. Rejected 171-255: R 138-26; D 33-228 (ND 15-164, SD 18-64); I 0-1; June 5, 1991.

136. HR 2506. Fiscal 1992 Legislative Branch Appropriations/Reduce General Accounting Office Account. Cox, R-Calif., amendment to reduce the General Accounting Office account from $441 million to $333 million. Rejected 130-294: R 128-37; D 2-256 (ND 1-176, SD 1-80); I 0-1; June 5, 1991.

137. HR 2506. Fiscal 1992 Legislative Branch Appropriations/Passage. Passage of the bill to provide $1,805,378,000 in new budget authority for the operations of Congress and legislative branch agencies in fiscal 1992. The Senate is expected to add about $500 million for their expenses. The agencies covered by the bill requested $2,093,691,000. Passed 308-110: R 59-104; D 248-6 (ND 170-4, SD 78-2); I 1-0; June 5, 1991.

138. HR 2519. Fiscal 1992 VA and HUD Appropriations/Rule. Adoption of the rule (H Res 166) to waive certain points of order against and provide for House floor consideration of the bill to provide $80,926,578,000 in new budget authority for the Department of Housing and Urban Development (HUD), the Department of Veterans Affairs (VA) and independent agencies in fiscal 1992. Adopted 404-14: R 150-14; D 253-0 (ND 173-0, SD 80-0); I 1-0; June 6, 1991.

140. HR 2519. Fiscal 1992 VA and HUD Appropriations/Block Transfer to Space Station. Smith, D-Fla., amendment to the Chapman, D-Texas, en bloc amendments to eliminate the transfer in the Chapman amendment of $217 million from HUD public housing operation subsidies to the space station *Freedom*. Rejected 122-296: R 12-153; D 109-143 (ND 91-78, SD 18-65); I 1-0; June 6, 1991. A "nay" was a vote supporting the president's position.

141. HR 2519. Fiscal 1992 VA and HUD Appropriations/Restore Space Station Funding. Chapman, D-Texas, en bloc amendments to provide $1.9 billion for the space station *Freedom*, restoring its funding to the fiscal 1991 level, and to offset the increase by holding all NASA programs to fiscal 1991 levels — a decrease of $1.7 billion — and by cutting $217 million from Housing and Urban Development public housing operating subsidies that would not be available until the last 10 days of fiscal 1992. Adopted 240-173: R 133-27; D 107-145 (ND 55-114, SD 52-31); I 0-1, June 6, 1991. A "yea" was a vote supporting the president's position.

142. HR 2519. Fiscal 1992 VA and HUD Appropriations/HOPE. Kolbe, R-Ariz., en bloc amendments to provide $151 million for Housing and Urban Development's HOPE I home ownership program to help public housing tenants purchase housing units and offset the increase by cutting $151 million from HUD's Flexible Subsidy Program, whose appropriation of $203 million exceeds its authorization by $151 million in the bill. Adopted 216-183: R 151-5; D 65-177 (ND 31-133, SD 34-44); I 0-1; June 6, 1991.

KEY

- Y Voted for (yea).
- # Paired for.
- + Announced for.
- N Voted against (nay).
- X Paired against.
- \- Announced against.
- P Voted "present."
- C Voted "present" to avoid possible conflict of interest.
- ? Did not vote or otherwise make a position known.

Democrats ***Republicans***
Independent

	133	135	136	137	138	140	141	142
ALABAMA								
1 ***Callahan***	Y	?	Y	N	Y	N	Y	Y
2 ***Dickinson***	Y	Y	Y	Y	Y	N	Y	Y
3 Browder	Y	N	N	Y	Y	N	Y	N
4 Bevill	N	N	N	?	Y	N	Y	Y
5 Cramer	N	N	N	Y	Y	N	Y	N
6 Erdreich	Y	Y	N	N	Y	N	Y	N
7 Harris	Y	N	N	Y	Y	N	Y	N
ALASKA								
AL ***Young***	N	N	N	Y	Y	N	Y	Y
ARIZONA								
1 ***Rhodes***	Y	Y	Y	N	Y	N	Y	Y
2 Vacancy								
3 ***Stump***	Y	Y	Y	N	N	N	Y	Y
4 ***Kyl***	Y	Y	Y	N	Y	N	Y	Y
5 ***Kolbe***	Y	Y	Y	N	Y	N	N	Y
ARKANSAS								
1 Alexander	N	N	N	Y	Y	N	N	N
2 Thornton	N	N	N	Y	Y	N	Y	N
3 ***Hammerschmidt***	N	Y	N	N	Y	N	Y	Y
4 Anthony	N	N	N	Y	?	N	N	?
CALIFORNIA								
1 ***Riggs***	Y	Y	Y	N	Y	N	Y	Y
2 ***Herger***	Y	Y	Y	N	N	N	Y	Y
3 Matsui	N	N	?	?	Y	N	Y	N
4 Fazio	N	N	N	Y	Y	N	Y	N
5 Pelosi	N	N	N	Y	Y	+	N	-
6 Boxer	N	N	N	Y	Y	Y	N	?
7 Miller	N	N	N	Y	Y	Y	N	?
8 Dellums	N	N	N	Y	Y	Y	N	N
9 Stark	N	N	N	Y	Y	Y	N	N
10 Edwards	N	N	N	Y	Y	Y	Y	N
11 Lantos	N	N	N	Y	Y	N	Y	Y
12 ***Campbell***	Y	Y	Y	N	Y	Y	Y	?
13 Mineta	N	N	N	Y	Y	Y	Y	N
14 ***Doolittle***	Y	Y	Y	Y	Y	N	Y	Y
15 Condit	Y	Y	N	Y	Y	Y	N	Y
16 Panetta	N	N	N	Y	Y	Y	N	Y
17 Dooley	N	N	N	Y	Y	Y	Y	N
18 Lehman	N	N	N	Y	Y	Y	Y	N
19 ***Lagomarsino***	Y	Y	Y	N	Y	N	Y	Y
20 ***Thomas***	Y	Y	Y	Y	Y	N	Y	Y
21 ***Gallegly***	Y	Y	Y	N	Y	N	Y	Y
22 ***Moorhead***	Y	Y	Y	N	Y	N	Y	Y
23 Beilenson	N	N	N	Y	Y	Y	N	N
24 Waxman	N	N	N	Y	Y	Y	N	N
25 Roybal	N	N	N	Y	Y	N	N	N
26 Berman	N	N	N	Y	Y	Y	N	N
27 Levine	N	N	N	Y	?	N	Y	N
28 Dixon	N	N	N	Y	Y	N	Y	N
29 Waters	N	N	N	Y	Y	Y	N	N
30 Martinez	N	N	N	Y	Y	?	?	?
31 Dymally	N	N	N	Y	Y	?	#	X
32 Anderson	N	N	N	Y	Y	N	Y	N
33 ***Dreier***	Y	Y	Y	N	Y	N	Y	Y
34 Torres	N	N	N	Y	Y	Y	Y	N
35 ***Lewis***	N	N	N	Y	Y	N	Y	Y
36 Brown	N	N	N	Y	Y	N	Y	N
37 ***McCandless***	Y	Y	Y	N	Y	N	Y	Y
38 ***Dornan***	Y	Y	Y	N	Y	N	Y	Y
39 ***Dannemeyer***	Y	Y	Y	N	N	N	Y	Y
40 ***Cox***	Y	Y	Y	N	N	N	Y	Y
41 ***Lowery***	Y	N	Y	Y	Y	N	Y	Y
42 ***Rohrabacher***	Y	Y	Y	N	Y	N	Y	Y
43 ***Packard***	Y	Y	Y	N	Y	N	Y	Y
44 ***Cunningham***	Y	Y	Y	Y	Y	N	Y	Y
45 ***Hunter***	Y	Y	Y	N	?	N	Y	Y
COLORADO								
1 Schroeder	N	Y	N	Y	Y	Y	N	Y
2 Skaggs	N	N	N	Y	Y	N	N	N
3 Campbell	Y	N	Y	Y	Y	?	?	?
4 ***Allard***	Y	Y	Y	N	N	N	Y	Y
5 ***Hefley***	Y	Y	Y	N	N	N	Y	Y
6 ***Schaefer***	Y	Y	N	N	Y	N	Y	Y
CONNECTICUT								
1 Kennelly	N	N	N	Y	Y	Y	Y	Y
2 Gejdenson	N	N	N	Y	Y	Y	Y	N
3 DeLauro	N	N	N	Y	Y	Y	N	N
4 ***Shays***	Y	Y	N	N	Y	Y	N	Y
5 ***Franks***	Y	Y	Y	N	Y	N	Y	Y
6 ***Johnson***	Y	Y	Y	N	Y	N	Y	Y
DELAWARE								
AL Carper	N	N	N	Y	Y	Y	N	Y
FLORIDA								
1 Hutto	Y	Y	N	Y	Y	N	Y	Y
2 Peterson	N	N	N	Y	Y	N	Y	N
3 Bennett	Y	Y	Y	Y	Y	Y	Y	N
4 ***James***	Y	Y	Y	N	Y	N	Y	Y
5 ***McCollum***	Y	Y	Y	N	Y	N	Y	Y
6 ***Stearns***	Y	Y	Y	N	Y	N	Y	Y
7 Gibbons	N	N	N	Y	Y	N	Y	N
8 ***Young***	Y	N	N	Y	Y	N	Y	Y
9 ***Bilirakis***	Y	Y	Y	N	Y	N	Y	Y
10 ***Ireland***	Y	Y	N	N	Y	N	Y	Y
11 Bacchus	N	N	N	Y	Y	N	Y	N
12 ***Lewis***	Y	Y	N	N	Y	N	Y	Y
13 ***Goss***	Y	Y	Y	N	Y	N	Y	Y
14 Johnston	Y	N	N	Y	Y	Y	N	N
15 ***Shaw***	Y	Y	Y	N	Y	N	Y	Y
16 Smith	N	N	N	Y	Y	Y	N	N
17 Lehman	?	?	?	?	Y	N	N	?
18 ***Ros-Lehtinen***	Y	Y	Y	Y	Y	Y	N	Y
19 Fascell	N	N	N	Y	Y	Y	Y	N
GEORGIA								
1 Thomas	?	?	?	?	?	N	Y	N
2 Hatcher	N	N	N	Y	Y	N	N	N
3 Ray	Y	N	N	Y	Y	N	N	Y
4 Jones	Y	N	N	Y	Y	N	N	N
5 Lewis	N	N	N	Y	Y	Y	N	N
6 ***Gingrich***	Y	Y	Y	?	Y	N	Y	Y
7 Darden	N	N	N	Y	Y	N	Y	N
8 Rowland	N	N	N	Y	Y	N	N	N
9 Jenkins	N	N	N	Y	Y	N	Y	?
10 Barnard	N	N	N	Y	Y	N	Y	N
HAWAII								
1 Abercrombie	N	N	N	Y	Y	Y	N	N
2 Mink	N	N	N	Y	Y	Y	N	N
IDAHO								
1 LaRocco	N	N	N	Y	Y	N	Y	N
2 Stallings	N	N	N	Y	Y	N	Y	Y
ILLINOIS								
1 Hayes	N	N	N	Y	Y	Y	N	N
2 Savage	N	N	N	Y	?	Y	N	N
3 Russo	N	N	N	Y	Y	Y	N	N
4 Sangmeister	N	N	N	Y	Y	N	N	N
5 Lipinski	N	N	N	Y	Y	N	Y	Y
6 ***Hyde***	Y	N	Y	Y	Y	N	Y	Y
7 Collins	?	?	?	?	?	Y	N	N
8 Rostenkowski	N	N	N	Y	Y	N	N	Y
9 Yates	N	N	N	Y	Y	N	N	N
10 ***Porter***	Y	Y	Y	Y	Y	N	Y	Y
11 Annunzio	N	N	N	Y	Y	N	Y	N
12 ***Crane***	Y	Y	Y	N	N	N	Y	Y
13 ***Fawell***	Y	Y	Y	N	Y	N	Y	Y
14 ***Hastert***	Y	Y	Y	Y	Y	N	Y	?
15 Vacancy								
16 Cox	N	N	N	Y	Y	Y	N	N
17 Evans	N	N	N	Y	Y	Y	N	N
18 ***Michel***	Y	Y	N	Y	Y	N	Y	Y
19 Bruce	N	N	N	Y	Y	N	N	N
20 Durbin	N	N	N	Y	Y	Y	N	N
21 Costello	N	N	N	Y	Y	N	N	N
22 Poshard	Y	Y	N	Y	Y	Y	N	N
INDIANA								
1 Visclosky	N	N	N	Y	Y	N	N	N
2 Sharp	Y	Y	N	?	Y	N	N	Y
3 Roemer	Y	N	N	Y	Y	N	N	Y

ND Northern Democrats SD Southern Democrats

	133	135	136	137	138	140	141	142
4 Long	Y	Y	N	Y	Y	Y	Y	N
5 Jontz	Y	N	N	Y	Y	N	N	N
6 ***Burton***	Y	Y	Y	N	N	N	Y	Y
7 ***Myers***	N	Y	Y	Y	Y	N	Y	Y
8 McCloskey	N	N	N	Y	Y	Y	N	N
9 Hamilton	Y	Y	N	Y	Y	N	N	N
10 Jacobs	Y	Y	N	N	Y	N	N	N
IOWA								
1 ***Leach***	Y	Y	Y	N	Y	N	N	Y
2 ***Nussle***	Y	Y	Y	N	Y	N	N	Y
3 Nagle	N	N	N	Y	Y	N	N	N
4 Smith	N	N	N	Y	Y	N	N	N
5 ***Lightfoot***	Y	N	Y	N	Y	N	Y	Y
6 ***Grandy***	Y	Y	Y	N	Y	N	N	Y
KANSAS								
1 ***Roberts***	Y	Y	Y	N	Y	N	Y	Y
2 Slattery	Y	Y	N	N	Y	N	Y	N
3 ***Meyers***	Y	Y	N	N	Y	N	Y	N
4 Glickman	Y	Y	N	N	Y	N	Y	Y
5 ***Nichols***	Y	Y	Y	N	Y	N	Y	Y
KENTUCKY								
1 Hubbard	Y	Y	N	Y	Y	N	Y	Y
2 Natcher	N	N	N	Y	Y	N	N	N
3 Mazzoli	N	N	N	Y	Y	Y	N	N
4 ***Bunning***	Y	Y	Y	N	Y	N	N	Y
5 ***Rogers***	Y	Y	Y	Y	Y	N	Y	Y
6 ***Hopkins***	Y	Y	Y	N	Y	N	Y	Y
7 Perkins	N	N	N	Y	Y	N	Y	N
LOUISIANA								
1 ***Livingston***	Y	N	Y	Y	Y	N	Y	?
2 Jefferson	N	N	N	Y	Y	Y	Y	Y
3 Tauzin	Y	Y	N	Y	Y	N	Y	Y
4 ***McCrery***	Y	Y	Y	Y	Y	N	Y	Y
5 Huckaby	Y	N	N	Y	Y	N	?	Y
6 ***Baker***	Y	Y	Y	Y	Y	N	Y	Y
7 Hayes	Y	N	N	Y	Y	N	Y	Y
8 ***Holloway***	Y	Y	Y	N	Y	N	Y	Y
MAINE								
1 Andrews	N	N	N	Y	Y	Y	N	N
2 ***Snowe***	Y	Y	N	N	Y	Y	Y	Y
MARYLAND								
1 ***Gilchrest***	Y	Y	Y	N	Y	N	Y	Y
2 ***Bentley***	Y	Y	Y	Y	Y	N	Y	Y
3 Cardin	N	N	N	Y	Y	Y	Y	N
4 McMillen	N	N	N	Y	Y	N	Y	Y
5 Hoyer	N	N	N	Y	Y	N	N	N
6 Byron	Y	Y	N	?	Y	N	Y	N
7 Mfume	Y	N	N	Y	?	Y	N	N
8 ***Morella***	Y	N	N	Y	Y	N	Y	N
MASSACHUSETTS								
1 Vacancy								
2 Neal	N	N	N	Y	Y	Y	Y	N
3 Early	Y	N	N	Y	Y	Y	N	N
4 Frank	Y	N	N	Y	Y	Y	N	N
5 Atkins	N	N	N	Y	Y	Y	N	N
6 Mavroules	N	N	N	Y	?	Y	N	N
7 Markey	N	N	N	Y	Y	Y	N	N
8 Kennedy	N	N	N	Y	Y	Y	N	N
9 Moakley	N	N	N	Y	Y	Y	N	N
10 Studds	N	N	N	Y	Y	Y	N	N
11 Donnelly	N	N	N	Y	Y	Y	N	Y
MICHIGAN								
1 Conyers	N	N	N	Y	Y	Y	N	N
2 ***Pursell***	Y	Y	Y	N	Y	N	N	Y
3 Wolpe	N	N	N	Y	Y	N	N	N
4 ***Upton***	Y	Y	Y	N	N	N	N	Y
5 ***Henry***	Y	Y	Y	N	Y	N	N	Y
6 Carr	N	N	N	Y	Y	N	N	N
7 Kildee	N	N	N	Y	Y	N	N	N
8 Traxler	N	N	N	Y	Y	N	N	N
9 ***Vander Jagt***	Y	Y	Y	N	Y	N	Y	Y
10 ***Camp***	Y	Y	Y	N	Y	N	N	Y
11 ***Davis***	N	N	N	Y	Y	N	Y	Y
12 Bonior	N	N	N	Y	Y	N	N	N
13 Collins	N	N	N	Y	Y	Y	N	N
14 Hertel	N	N	N	Y	Y	N	N	N
15 Ford	N	N	N	Y	Y	N	N	N
16 Dingell	N	N	N	Y	Y	N	N	N
17 Levin	N	N	N	Y	Y	Y	N	N
18 ***Broomfield***	Y	Y	Y	N	Y	N	Y	Y
MINNESOTA								
1 Penny	Y	N	N	Y	Y	N	N	Y
2 ***Weber***	Y	Y	Y	N	Y	N	Y	Y
3 ***Ramstad***	Y	Y	Y	N	Y	N	N	Y
4 Vento	N	N	N	Y	Y	?	X	?

	133	135	136	137	138	140	141	142
5 Sabo	N	N	N	Y	Y	N	N	N
6 Sikorski	N	N	N	Y	Y	Y	N	N
7 Peterson	N	N	N	Y	Y	N	N	N
8 Oberstar	N	N	N	Y	Y	N	N	N
MISSISSIPPI								
1 Whitten	N	N	N	Y	Y	N	N	N
2 Espy	N	N	N	Y	Y	N	N	Y
3 Montgomery	Y	Y	N	Y	Y	N	N	Y
4 Parker	Y	Y	N	Y	Y	N	N	Y
5 Taylor	Y	Y	N	Y	Y	N	Y	Y
MISSOURI								
1 Clay	N	N	N	Y	Y	Y	N	N
2 Horn	Y	N	N	Y	Y	N	Y	N
3 Gephardt	N	N	?	?	Y	Y	Y	N
4 Skelton	N	N	N	Y	Y	N	N	Y
5 Wheat	N	N	N	Y	Y	Y	N	N
6 ***Coleman***	N	Y	Y	Y	Y	N	Y	Y
7 ***Hancock***	Y	Y	Y	N	N	N	Y	Y
8 ***Emerson***	Y	Y	Y	N	Y	N	Y	Y
9 Volkmer	N	Y	N	Y	Y	N	Y	Y
MONTANA								
1 Williams	N	N	N	Y	Y	?	?	?
2 ***Marlenee***	Y	Y	Y	Y	Y	N	Y	Y
NEBRASKA								
1 ***Bereuter***	Y	Y	Y	N	Y	Y	N	Y
2 Hoagland	N	N	N	Y	Y	Y	N	N
3 ***Barrett***	Y	Y	Y	N	Y	N	Y	Y
NEVADA								
1 Bilbray	N	N	N	Y	?	N	?	?
2 ***Vucanovich***	Y	N	Y	Y	N	N	Y	Y
NEW HAMPSHIRE								
1 ***Zeliff***	Y	Y	Y	N	Y	N	Y	Y
2 Swett	Y	Y	N	Y	Y	N	Y	Y
NEW JERSEY								
1 Andrews	N	N	N	Y	Y	N	Y	Y
2 Hughes	Y	N	N	Y	Y	Y	N	N
3 Pallone	Y	Y	N	N	Y	Y	Y	Y
4 ***Smith***	Y	N	Y	Y	Y	Y	Y	Y
5 ***Roukema***	N	N	Y	Y	N	Y	N	N
6 Dwyer	N	N	N	Y	Y	Y	N	N
7 ***Rinaldo***	Y	N	Y	Y	Y	N	Y	Y
8 Roe	N	N	N	Y	Y	N	Y	N
9 Torricelli	N	N	N	?	Y	N	Y	N
10 Payne	N	N	N	Y	Y	Y	N	N
11 ***Gallo***	N	N	N	Y	Y	N	?	?
12 ***Zimmer***	Y	Y	Y	N	Y	N	N	Y
13 ***Saxton***	Y	N	Y	N	Y	N	Y	Y
14 Guarini	N	N	N	Y	Y	Y	N	N
NEW MEXICO								
1 ***Schiff***	N	Y	Y	Y	Y	N	Y	Y
2 ***Skeen***	N	N	Y	Y	Y	N	Y	Y
3 Richardson	N	N	N	Y	Y	N	Y	N
NEW YORK								
1 Hochbrueckner	N	N	N	Y	Y	Y	Y	Y
2 Downey	N	N	N	Y	Y	Y	Y	N
3 Mrazek	N	N	N	Y	Y	?	?	?
4 ***Lent***	N	N	N	Y	Y	N	Y	Y
5 ***McGrath***	N	N	Y	Y	Y	N	Y	Y
6 Flake	N	N	N	Y	Y	Y	N	N
7 Ackerman	N	N	N	Y	Y	?	X	?
8 Scheuer	N	N	N	Y	Y	Y	N	N
9 Manton	N	N	N	Y	Y	N	N	?
10 Schumer	N	N	N	Y	Y	Y	N	N
11 Towns	N	N	N	Y	Y	N	N	N
12 Owens	N	N	N	Y	Y	Y	N	N
13 Solarz	N	N	N	Y	Y	Y	N	N
14 ***Molinari***	Y	Y	Y	N	Y	N	N	Y
15 ***Green***	N	N	N	Y	Y	Y	N	N
16 Rangel	N	N	N	Y	Y	Y	N	N
17 Weiss	N	N	N	Y	Y	Y	N	N
18 Serrano	N	N	N	Y	Y	Y	N	N
19 Engel	N	N	N	Y	Y	Y	N	N
20 Lowey	N	N	N	Y	Y	Y	N	N
21 ***Fish***	N	N	N	?	Y	Y	N	N
22 ***Gilman***	N	Y	N	Y	Y	Y	N	Y
23 McNulty	N	N	N	Y	Y	N	N	N
24 ***Solomon***	Y	Y	Y	N	Y	N	#	Y
25 ***Boehlert***	N	Y	N	Y	Y	N	Y	Y
26 ***Martin***	Y	Y	Y	Y	Y	N	?	?
27 ***Walsh***	Y	Y	Y	Y	Y	N	Y	Y
28 McHugh	N	N	N	Y	Y	N	N	N
29 ***Horton***	N	N	N	Y	Y	N	Y	Y
30 Slaughter	N	N	N	Y	Y	N	-	-
31 ***Paxon***	Y	Y	Y	N	Y	N	N	Y

	133	135	136	137	138	140	141	142
32 LaFalce	N	N	N	Y	Y	Y	N	N
33 Nowak	Y	N	N	Y	Y	N	N	Y
34 ***Houghton***	Y	Y	Y	Y	Y	N	Y	Y
NORTH CAROLINA								
1 Jones	N	N	N	Y	Y	N	Y	Y
2 Valentine	N	N	N	Y	Y	N	Y	Y
3 Lancaster	N	N	N	Y	Y	Y	N	Y
4 Price	N	N	N	Y	Y	Y	N	N
5 Neal	N	Y	N	Y	?	N	N	N
6 ***Coble***	Y	Y	Y	N	N	Y	N	Y
7 Rose	N	N	N	Y	Y	Y	N	?
8 Hefner	N	N	N	Y	Y	Y	N	N
9 ***McMillan***	Y	Y	N	Y	Y	N	N	Y
10 ***Ballenger***	Y	Y	N	N	Y	N	Y	Y
11 ***Taylor***	Y	Y	Y	N	Y	N	Y	Y
NORTH DAKOTA								
AL Dorgan	Y	N	N	Y	Y	Y	N	N
OHIO								
1 Luken	Y	Y	N	Y	Y	N	N	Y
2 ***Gradison***	Y	Y	Y	N	Y	N	Y	Y
3 Hall	N	N	N	Y	Y	N	Y	Y
4 ***Oxley***	Y	Y	N	Y	Y	N	Y	Y
5 ***Gillmor***	N	N	Y	Y	Y	N	Y	Y
6 ***McEwen***	Y	Y	Y	N	Y	N	Y	Y
7 ***Hobson***	Y	Y	N	N	Y	N	Y	Y
8 ***Boehner***	Y	Y	Y	N	Y	N	Y	Y
9 Kaptur	N	N	N	Y	Y	N	N	N
10 ***Miller***	Y	Y	Y	Y	Y	N	Y	Y
11 Eckart	N	Y	N	Y	Y	Y	Y	Y
12 ***Kasich***	Y	Y	N	N	Y	N	Y	Y
13 Pease	N	N	N	Y	Y	Y	Y	N
14 Sawyer	N	N	N	Y	Y	Y	Y	N
15 ***Wylie***	Y	Y	Y	N	Y	N	Y	Y
16 ***Regula***	Y	Y	Y	Y	Y	N	Y	Y
17 Traficant	N	N	N	Y	Y	N	Y	N
18 Applegate	N	N	N	Y	Y	N	Y	Y
19 Feighan	N	N	N	Y	Y	Y	Y	Y
20 Oakar	N	N	N	Y	Y	Y	Y	N
21 Stokes	N	N	N	Y	Y	Y	N	N
OKLAHOMA								
1 ***Inhofe***	Y	Y	Y	N	Y	N	Y	Y
2 Synar	N	N	N	Y	Y	N	N	N
3 Brewster	N	N	N	Y	Y	N	Y	Y
4 McCurdy	N	N	N	Y	Y	N	Y	?
5 ***Edwards***	Y	Y	Y	N	Y	N	Y	Y
6 English	Y	N	N	Y	Y	N	Y	Y
OREGON								
1 AuCoin	Y	N	N	Y	Y	?	N	N
2 ***Smith***	Y	Y	Y	N	Y	N	Y	Y
3 Wyden	N	N	N	Y	Y	N	N	N
4 DeFazio	N	N	N	Y	Y	Y	Y	Y
5 Kopetski	N	N	N	Y	Y	N	Y	N
PENNSYLVANIA								
1 Foglietta	N	N	N	Y	Y	Y	N	N
2 Gray	N	N	N	Y	Y	?	N	?
3 Borski	N	N	N	Y	Y	?	?	?
4 Kolter	N	N	N	Y	Y	N	Y	N
5 ***Schulze***	Y	Y	Y	Y	Y	N	Y	Y
6 Yatron	Y	N	N	Y	Y	N	Y	N
7 ***Weldon***	Y	Y	Y	N	Y	N	Y	Y
8 Kostmayer	N	N	N	Y	Y	Y	?	?
9 ***Shuster***	Y	Y	Y	N	Y	N	?	?
10 ***McDade***	Y	Y	N	Y	Y	N	Y	Y
11 Kanjorski	N	N	N	Y	Y	N	N	N
12 Murtha	N	N	N	Y	Y	N	N	N
13 ***Coughlin***	Y	N	N	Y	Y	N	N	Y
14 Coyne	N	N	N	Y	Y	Y	N	N
15 ***Ritter***	Y	Y	N	N	Y	N	Y	Y
16 ***Walker***	Y	Y	Y	N	Y	N	Y	Y
17 ***Gekas***	Y	Y	Y	N	Y	N	Y	Y
18 ***Santorum***	Y	Y	Y	N	Y	N	Y	Y
19 ***Goodling***	?	Y	Y	Y	Y	N	Y	Y
20 Gaydos	N	N	N	Y	Y	N	Y	N
21 ***Ridge***	Y	Y	N	Y	Y	N	Y	?
22 Murphy	Y	N	N	Y	Y	N	N	N
23 ***Clinger***	N	Y	N	Y	Y	N	Y	Y
RHODE ISLAND								
1 ***Machtley***	Y	Y	Y	Y	Y	N	Y	Y
2 Reed	N	N	N	Y	Y	Y	N	N
SOUTH CAROLINA								
1 ***Ravenel***	Y	Y	N	N	Y	N	N	Y
2 ***Spence***	Y	Y	Y	N	Y	N	Y	Y
3 Derrick	N	N	N	Y	Y	N	N	N
4 Patterson	Y	N	N	Y	Y	Y	N	N
5 Spratt	N	N	N	Y	Y	Y	N	N
6 Tallon	Y	N	N	Y	Y	N	Y	Y

	133	135	136	137	138	140	141	142
SOUTH DAKOTA								
AL Johnson	Y	N	N	Y	Y	Y	N	Y
TENNESSEE								
1 ***Quillen***	N	N	Y	Y	Y	N	Y	#
2 ***Duncan***	Y	Y	Y	N	Y	N	N	Y
3 Lloyd	Y	Y	N	Y	Y	N	Y	N
4 Cooper	N	Y	N	Y	Y	N	Y	Y
5 Clement	N	N	N	Y	Y	N	N	Y
6 Gordon	N	N	N	Y	Y	N	Y	N
7 ***Sundquist***	Y	Y	Y	N	Y	N	Y	Y
8 Tanner	N	N	N	Y	Y	N	Y	Y
9 Ford	N	N	?	?	Y	?	N	Y
TEXAS								
1 Chapman	N	N	N	Y	Y	N	Y	N
2 Wilson	N	N	N	Y	Y	N	Y	Y
3 ***Johnson***	Y	Y	Y	Y	Y	N	Y	Y
4 Hall	Y	Y	N	Y	Y	N	Y	Y
5 Bryant	N	N	N	Y	Y	N	Y	N
6 ***Barton***	Y	Y	Y	N	Y	N	Y	Y
7 ***Archer***	Y	Y	Y	N	Y	N	Y	Y
8 ***Fields***	Y	Y	N	N	Y	N	Y	Y
9 Brooks	?	N	N	Y	Y	N	Y	N
10 Pickle	N	N	N	Y	Y	N	Y	Y
11 Edwards	N	N	N	Y	Y	N	Y	Y
12 Geren	Y	Y	N	Y	Y	N	Y	Y
13 Sarpalius	Y	Y	N	N	Y	N	Y	Y
14 Laughlin	Y	Y	N	Y	Y	N	Y	Y
15 de la Garza	Y	N	N	Y	Y	N	Y	N
16 Coleman	N	N	N	Y	Y	N	Y	N
17 Stenholm	Y	Y	N	Y	Y	N	Y	Y
18 Washington	N	N	N	Y	Y	Y	N	Y
19 ***Combest***	Y	Y	Y	N	Y	N	Y	Y
20 Gonzalez	N	N	N	Y	Y	Y	N	N
21 ***Smith***	Y	Y	Y	N	Y	N	Y	Y
22 ***DeLay***	Y	Y	Y	N	Y	N	Y	Y
23 Bustamante	N	N	N	Y	Y	N	Y	N
24 Frost	N	N	N	Y	Y	N	Y	N
25 Andrews	Y	N	N	Y	Y	N	Y	Y
26 ***Armey***	Y	Y	Y	N	Y	N	Y	Y
27 Ortiz	N	N	N	Y	Y	N	Y	Y
UTAH								
1 ***Hansen***	Y	Y	Y	N	Y	N	Y	Y
2 Owens	N	N	N	Y	Y	Y	N	N
3 Orton	Y	N	N	Y	Y	Y	N	N
VERMONT								
AL *Sanders*	Y	N	N	Y	Y	Y	N	N
VIRGINIA								
1 ***Bateman***	Y	Y	N	Y	Y	N	Y	Y
2 Pickett	N	Y	N	Y	Y	N	Y	N
3 ***Bliley***	Y	Y	N	Y	Y	N	Y	Y
4 Sisisky	?	?	?	?	?	?	?	?
5 Payne	Y	N	N	Y	Y	Y	N	Y
6 Olin	N	N	N	Y	?	Y	N	N
7 ***Slaughter***	N	Y	Y	N	Y	N	Y	Y
8 Moran	N	N	N	Y	Y	Y	Y	N
9 Boucher	N	N	N	Y	Y	N	Y	?
10 ***Wolf***	Y	Y	N	Y	Y	N	Y	Y
WASHINGTON								
1 ***Miller***	Y	Y	Y	N	Y	N	+	+
2 Swift	N	N	N	Y	Y	Y	Y	N
3 Unsoeld	N	N	N	Y	Y	N	N	N
4 ***Morrison***	N	N	N	Y	Y	N	Y	Y
5 Foley								
6 Dicks	N	N	N	Y	Y	Y	Y	N
7 McDermott	N	N	N	Y	Y	N	N	N
8 ***Chandler***	Y	Y	Y	Y	Y	N	Y	Y
WEST VIRGINIA								
1 Mollohan	N	N	N	Y	Y	N	Y	N
2 Staggers	N	N	N	Y	Y	Y	N	Y
3 Wise	N	N	N	Y	?	N	Y	N
4 Rahall	N	N	N	Y	Y	N	Y	N
WISCONSIN								
1 Aspin	N	N	N	Y	Y	Y	Y	Y
2 ***Klug***	Y	Y	Y	N	Y	N	Y	Y
3 ***Gunderson***	Y	N	Y	Y	Y	N	Y	Y
4 Kleczka	N	N	N	Y	Y	Y	N	N
5 Moody	N	N	N	Y	Y	Y	N	N
6 ***Petri***	Y	Y	Y	N	N	N	Y	Y
7 Obey	N	N	N	Y	Y	Y	N	N
8 ***Roth***	Y	Y	N	N	Y	N	N	Y
9 ***Sensenbrenner***	Y	Y	Y	N	Y	N	Y	Y
WYOMING								
AL ***Thomas***	Y	Y	Y	N	Y	N	Y	Y

Southern states - Ala., Ark., Fla., Ga., Ky., La., Miss., N.C., Okla., S.C., Tenn., Texas, Va.
Omitted votes are quorum calls, which CQ does not include in its vote charts.

HOUSE VOTES 143, 144, 145, 146, 147, 148, 149, 150

143. HR 2519. Fiscal 1992 VA and HUD Appropriations/Passage. Passage of the bill to provide $80,926,578,000 in new budget authority in fiscal 1992 for the Department of Housing and Urban Development, the Department of Veterans Affairs, the Environmental Protection Agency, NASA, the National Science Foundation and various other agencies. The administration requested $82,134,184,000. Passed 363-39: R 142-16; D 220-23 (ND 141-21, SD 79-2); I 1-0; June 6, 1991.

144. HR 2521. Fiscal 1992 Defense Appropriations/MX Missile Rail Garrison. Frank, D-Mass., amendment to cut the $260 million in the bill for research and development of the MX missile rail garrison. Rejected 155-229: R 14-138; D 140-91 (ND 122-37, SD 18-54); I 1-0, June 7, 1991. A "nay" was a vote supporting the president's position.

145. HR 2521. Fiscal 1992 Defense Appropriations/Passage. Passage of the bill to provide $270,565,792,000 in new budget authority for the Department of Defense for military personnel, operations and maintenance, procurement, and research and development in fiscal 1992. The administration requested $270,945,322,000. Passed 273-105: R 76-74; D 197-30 (ND 130-27, SD 67-3); I 0-1, June 7, 1991. A "nay" was a vote supporting the president's position.

146. HR 2038. Fiscal 1992 Intelligence Authorization/Drug Testing. Solomon, R-N.Y., amendment to require random drug testing of intelligence agency employees. Rejected 169-234: R 128-21; D 41-212 (ND 17-153, SD 24-59); I 0-1, June 11, 1991.

147. HR 26. Money-Laundering Enforcement/Passage. Annunzio, D-Ill., motion to suspend the rules and pass the bill to give federal regulators more tools to crack down on banks and bank officers involved in money-laundering schemes, impose fines on institutions that are negligent in filing currency-transaction reports, direct the Treasury Department to study the feasibility of removing $50 and $100 bills from circulation, and for other purposes. Motion agreed to 406-0: R 152-0; D 253-0 (ND 171-0, SD 82-0); I 1-0, June 11, 1991. A two-thirds majority of those present and voting (271 in this case) is required for passage under suspension of the rules.

148. HR 2508. Fiscal 1992-93 Foreign Aid Authorization/United Nations Population Fund. Kostmayer, D-Pa., amendment to the Smith, R-N.J., amendment, to preserve the $20 million in funding for the United Nations population fund (UNFPA), which supports family-planning programs in many countries. The Smith amendment would have removed the funding on the grounds that the UNFPA operates in China, which uses forced abortions and involuntary sterilization as means of family planning. Adopted 234-188: R 40-121; D 193-67 (ND 134-41, SD 59-26); I 1-0), June 12, 1991. A "nay" was a vote supporting the president's position.

149. HR 2508. Fiscal 1992-93 Foreign Aid Authorization/Mexico City Policy. Berman, D-Calif., amendment to the Smith, R-N.J., amendment, to overturn the administration's Mexico City policy, which prohibits the Agency for International Development from funding foreign non-governmental organizations that provide abortions or abortion counseling. The Smith amendment would have reinstated the Mexico City policy. Adopted 222-200: R 35-126; D 186-74 (ND 129-48, SD 57-26); I 1-0, June 12, 1991. A "nay" was a vote supporting the president's position.

150. HR 2508. Fiscal 1992-93 Foreign Aid Authorization/Agricultural Products. Bereuter, R-Neb., amendment to strike the cargo-preference and cash-purchase requirements in the bill and to require U.S. foreign-aid recipients to encourage importers to buy U.S. agricultural products. Rejected 175-246: R 96-64; D 79-181 (ND 50-128, SD 29-53); I 0-1, June 12, 1991. A "yea" was a vote supporting the president's position.

KEY

- Y Voted for (yea).
- # Paired for.
- + Announced for.
- N Voted against (nay).
- X Paired against.
- \- Announced against.
- P Voted "present."
- C Voted "present" to avoid possible conflict of interest.
- ? Did not vote or otherwise make a position known.

Democrats ***Republicans*** *Independent*

	143	144	145	146	147	148	149	150
ALABAMA								
1 ***Callahan***	Y	N	Y	Y	Y	N	N	N
2 ***Dickinson***	Y	N	Y	Y	?	Y	Y	Y
3 Browder	Y	N	Y	Y	Y	N	Y	N
4 Bevill	Y	N	Y	Y	Y	N	N	N
5 Cramer	Y	N	Y	Y	Y	Y	Y	N
6 Erdreich	Y	N	Y	Y	Y	Y	Y	N
7 Harris	Y	N	Y	Y	Y	N	N	N
ALASKA								
AL ***Young***	Y	N	Y	Y	Y	N	N	N
ARIZONA								
1 ***Rhodes***	Y	N	N	Y	Y	N	N	Y
2 Vacancy								
3 ***Stump***	N	N	N	Y	Y	N	N	Y
4 ***Kyl***	Y	N	N	Y	Y	N	N	Y
5 ***Kolbe***	Y	N	N	Y	Y	Y	Y	Y
ARKANSAS								
1 Alexander	Y	N	?	N	Y	Y	Y	Y
2 Thornton	Y	?	?	N	Y	Y	N	N
3 ***Hammerschmidt***	Y	N	N	Y	Y	N	N	Y
4 Anthony	Y	Y	Y	N	Y	Y	?	Y
CALIFORNIA								
1 ***Riggs***	Y	N	N	Y	Y	Y	N	Y
2 ***Herger***	Y	N	N	Y	Y	N	N	N
3 Matsui	Y	Y	Y	N	Y	Y	Y	N
4 Fazio	Y	X	#	N	Y	Y	Y	N
5 Pelosi	+	+	+	N	Y	Y	Y	N
6 Boxer	?	?	?	N	Y	Y	Y	N
7 Miller	?	?	?	N	Y	Y	Y	N
8 Dellums	Y	Y	N	N	Y	Y	Y	N
9 Stark	N	Y	N	N	Y	Y	Y	N
10 Edwards	Y	Y	N	N	Y	Y	Y	N
11 Lantos	Y	Y	Y	N	Y	Y	Y	N
12 ***Campbell***	?	?	?	?	?	Y	Y	Y
13 Mineta	Y	Y	Y	N	Y	Y	Y	N
14 ***Doolittle***	Y	N	N	Y	Y	N	N	Y
15 Condit	Y	Y	Y	?	?	Y	Y	N
16 Panetta	Y	Y	Y	N	Y	Y	Y	Y
17 Dooley	Y	Y	Y	N	Y	Y	Y	Y
18 Lehman	Y	Y	Y	N	Y	Y	Y	N
19 ***Lagomarsino***	Y	N	N	Y	Y	N	N	Y
20 ***Thomas***	Y	N	Y	Y	Y	Y	Y	Y
21 ***Gallegly***	Y	N	N	Y	Y	N	N	Y
22 ***Moorhead***	N	N	N	Y	Y	N	N	Y
23 Beilenson	N	Y	N	N	Y	Y	Y	Y
24 Waxman	Y	Y	Y	N	Y	Y	Y	Y
25 Roybal	Y	Y	N	N	Y	Y	Y	N
26 Berman	Y	Y	Y	N	Y	Y	Y	Y
27 Levine	Y	Y	Y	N	Y	Y	Y	N
28 Dixon	Y	N	Y	N	Y	Y	Y	N
29 Waters	Y	Y	N	N	Y	Y	Y	N
30 Martinez	?	?	?	N	Y	Y	Y	N
31 Dymally	?	X	#	X	?	?	Y	N
32 Anderson	Y	Y	Y	N	Y	Y	Y	N
33 ***Dreier***	N	N	N	Y	Y	N	N	Y
34 Torres	Y	Y	Y	N	Y	Y	Y	N
35 ***Lewis***	Y	N	Y	Y	Y	N	N	N
36 Brown	Y	N	Y	N	Y	Y	Y	N
37 ***McCandless***	Y	N	N	Y	Y	Y	N	Y
38 ***Dornan***	Y	N	X	Y	Y	N	N	Y
39 ***Dannemeyer***	N	+	-	Y	Y	N	N	Y
40 ***Cox***	N	N	N	Y	Y	N	N	Y
41 ***Lowery***	Y	N	Y	Y	Y	N	N	N
42 ***Rohrabacher***	Y	Y	N	Y	Y	N	N	Y
43 ***Packard***	Y	N	N	Y	Y	N	N	Y
44 ***Cunningham***	Y	N	Y	Y	Y	N	N	N
45 ***Hunter***	Y	N	N	Y	Y	N	N	N
COLORADO								
1 Schroeder	N	Y	N	N	Y	Y	Y	N
2 Skaggs	Y	Y	Y	N	Y	Y	Y	N
3 Campbell	?	?	?	N	Y	Y	Y	N
4 ***Allard***	Y	N	N	Y	Y	N	N	Y
5 ***Hefley***	Y	N	N	Y	Y	N	N	N
6 ***Schaefer***	Y	N	N	Y	Y	N	N	N
CONNECTICUT								
1 Kennelly	Y	Y	Y	N	Y	Y	Y	N
2 Gejdenson	Y	Y	Y	N	Y	Y	Y	N
3 DeLauro	Y	Y	Y	N	Y	Y	Y	N
4 ***Shays***	Y	Y	Y	Y	Y	Y	Y	N
5 ***Franks***	Y	N	N	+	+	Y	Y	N
6 ***Johnson***	Y	Y	Y	Y	Y	Y	Y	Y
DELAWARE								
AL Carper	Y	N	Y	N	Y	Y	Y	N
FLORIDA								
1 Hutto	Y	N	Y	Y	Y	N	N	N
2 Peterson	Y	N	Y	N	Y	Y	Y	Y
3 Bennett	Y	N	Y	Y	Y	N	N	N
4 ***James***	Y	N	Y	Y	Y	N	N	N
5 ***McCollum***	Y	?	?	Y	Y	N	N	N
6 ***Stearns***	Y	N	N	Y	Y	N	N	N
7 Gibbons	Y	N	Y	Y	Y	Y	Y	Y
8 ***Young***	Y	X	#	Y	Y	N	N	Y
9 ***Bilirakis***	Y	N	Y	Y	Y	N	N	N
10 ***Ireland***	Y	N	Y	Y	Y	N	N	Y
11 Bacchus	Y	N	Y	N	Y	Y	Y	N
12 ***Lewis***	Y	N	N	Y	Y	N	N	Y
13 ***Goss***	Y	N	N	Y	Y	N	N	N
14 Johnston	Y	Y	Y	N	Y	Y	Y	N
15 ***Shaw***	Y	?	?	Y	Y	N	N	N
16 Smith	Y	Y	Y	?	?	Y	Y	N
17 Lehman	?	#	?	N	Y	Y	Y	Y
18 ***Ros-Lehtinen***	Y	N	Y	Y	Y	N	N	N
19 Fascell	Y	N	Y	N	Y	Y	Y	N
GEORGIA								
1 Thomas	Y	N	Y	N	Y	Y	Y	Y
2 Hatcher	Y	N	Y	N	Y	Y	Y	Y
3 Ray	Y	N	Y	N	Y	N	N	Y
4 Jones	Y	Y	Y	N	Y	Y	Y	N
5 Lewis	Y	?	X	N	Y	Y	Y	N
6 ***Gingrich***	Y	N	Y	?	Y	N	N	N
7 Darden	Y	N	Y	N	Y	Y	Y	N
8 Rowland	Y	N	Y	N	Y	Y	Y	Y
9 Jenkins	Y	?	?	N	Y	Y	Y	N
10 Barnard	Y	N	Y	N	Y	N	N	Y
HAWAII								
1 Abercrombie	Y	Y	Y	?	Y	Y	Y	N
2 Mink	Y	Y	Y	N	Y	Y	Y	N
IDAHO								
1 LaRocco	Y	N	Y	N	Y	Y	Y	Y
2 Stallings	Y	N	Y	N	Y	N	N	Y
ILLINOIS								
1 Hayes	Y	Y	N	N	Y	Y	Y	N
2 Savage	Y	Y	N	N	Y	Y	Y	N
3 Russo	N	Y	N	N	Y	N	N	N
4 Sangmeister	Y	#	?	N	Y	Y	N	Y
5 Lipinski	Y	?	?	N	Y	N	N	Y
6 ***Hyde***	Y	N	Y	Y	Y	N	N	Y
7 Collins	Y	Y	N	N	Y	Y	Y	N
8 Rostenkowski	?	?	?	?	?	?	?	?
9 Yates	?	Y	N	?	?	?	?	?
10 ***Porter***	Y	Y	Y	N	Y	Y	Y	Y
11 Annunzio	N	Y	Y	N	Y	N	N	Y
12 ***Crane***	N	N	N	Y	Y	N	N	Y
13 ***Fawell***	N	N	N	Y	Y	Y	Y	Y
14 ***Hastert***	?	?	?	Y	Y	N	N	Y
15 Vacancy								
16 Cox	Y	Y	Y	N	Y	Y	Y	Y
17 Evans	Y	Y	Y	N	Y	Y	Y	N
18 ***Michel***	Y	N	Y	?	Y	N	N	Y
19 Bruce	Y	N	Y	N	Y	N	N	N
20 Durbin	Y	Y	?	N	Y	Y	Y	Y
21 Costello	Y	N	Y	N	Y	N	N	Y
22 Poshard	Y	N	Y	N	Y	N	N	Y
INDIANA								
1 Visclosky	Y	Y	Y	N	Y	Y	Y	Y
2 Sharp	Y	Y	Y	N	Y	Y	Y	Y
3 Roemer	N	Y	Y	Y	Y	N	N	Y

ND Northern Democrats SD Southern Democrats

	143	144	145	146	147	148	149	150
4 Long	Y	Y	Y	N	Y	Y	Y	Y
5 Jontz	Y	Y	Y	N	Y	Y	Y	Y
6 ***Burton***	Y	N	N	Y	Y	N	N	Y
7 ***Myers***	Y	N	?	N	Y	N	N	Y
8 McCloskey	Y	Y	Y	N	Y	Y	Y	Y
9 Hamilton	Y	Y	Y	N	Y	Y	Y	Y
10 Jacobs	N	Y	Y	N	Y	Y	Y	Y
IOWA								
1 ***Leach***	Y	Y	N	Y	Y	Y	Y	Y
2 ***Nussle***	N	Y	N	Y	Y	N	N	Y
3 Nagle	N	Y	Y	N	Y	Y	Y	N
4 Smith	Y	?	?	N	Y	Y	Y	?
5 ***Lightfoot***	Y	N	Y	Y	Y	N	N	Y
6 ***Grandy***	Y	N	N	N	Y	N	N	Y
KANSAS								
1 ***Roberts***	Y	Y	N	Y	Y	N	N	Y
2 Slattery	Y	N	Y	Y	Y	Y	N	Y
3 ***Meyers***	Y	N	N	Y	Y	Y	Y	Y
4 Glickman	Y	Y	Y	Y	Y	Y	Y	Y
5 ***Nichols***	Y	N	N	Y	Y	Y	Y	Y
KENTUCKY								
1 Hubbard	N	Y	Y	Y	Y	Y	Y	N
2 Natcher	Y	N	Y	N	Y	N	N	N
3 Mazzoli	Y	N	Y	N	Y	N	N	Y
4 ***Bunning***	N	N	N	Y	Y	N	N	Y
5 ***Rogers***	Y	N	Y	Y	Y	N	N	Y
6 ***Hopkins***	Y	N	N	?	?	?	?	?
7 Perkins	Y	Y	Y	N	Y	N	N	N
LOUISIANA								
1 ***Livingston***	Y	N	Y	N	Y	N	N	N
2 Jefferson	Y	N	N	N	Y	Y	Y	N
3 Tauzin	Y	N	Y	Y	Y	N	N	N
4 ***McCrery***	Y	N	Y	Y	Y	N	N	Y
5 Huckaby	Y	N	Y	N	Y	N	N	Y
6 ***Baker***	Y	N	N	Y	Y	N	N	N
7 Hayes	Y	N	?	Y	Y	N	N	N
8 ***Holloway***	Y	N	Y	Y	Y	N	N	N
MAINE								
1 Andrews	Y	Y	Y	N	Y	Y	Y	N
2 ***Snowe***	Y	N	N	Y	Y	Y	Y	N
MARYLAND								
1 ***Gilchrest***	Y	N	Y	Y	Y	Y	Y	Y
2 ***Bentley***	Y	N	Y	Y	Y	Y	N	N
3 Cardin	Y	Y	Y	N	Y	Y	Y	N
4 McMillen	Y	N	Y	N	Y	Y	Y	N
5 Hoyer	Y	N	Y	N	Y	Y	Y	N
6 Byron	Y	N	Y	Y	Y	N	N	N
7 Mfume	Y	Y	N	N	Y	Y	Y	N
8 ***Morella***	Y	#	Y	N	Y	Y	Y	N
MASSACHUSETTS								
1 Vacancy								
2 Neal	Y	Y	Y	N	Y	N	N	N
3 Early	N	Y	Y	N	Y	N	N	N
4 Frank	Y	Y	Y	N	Y	Y	Y	Y
5 Atkins	Y	Y	Y	N	Y	Y	Y	Y
6 Mavroules	Y	Y	Y	N	Y	N	N	N
7 Markey	Y	Y	Y	?	Y	Y	Y	N
8 Kennedy	Y	Y	Y	N	Y	Y	Y	N
9 Moakley	Y	Y	Y	N	Y	N	N	N
10 Studds	Y	Y	Y	N	Y	Y	Y	N
11 Donnelly	N	?	Y	N	Y	N	N	N
MICHIGAN								
1 Conyers	Y	Y	Y	N	Y	Y	Y	N
2 ***Pursell***	Y	N	?	Y	Y	N	Y	Y
3 Wolpe	Y	Y	Y	N	Y	Y	Y	N
4 ***Upton***	Y	N	Y	Y	Y	Y	Y	Y
5 ***Henry***	N	N	N	Y	Y	N	N	Y
6 Carr	Y	Y	Y	N	Y	Y	Y	Y
7 Kildee	Y	Y	Y	N	Y	N	N	N
8 Traxler	Y	Y	?	N	Y	N	N	Y
9 ***Vander Jagt***	Y	N	N	?	?	N	N	N
10 ***Camp***	Y	N	Y	Y	Y	N	N	Y
11 ***Davis***	Y	N	?	N	Y	X	X	?
12 Bonior	Y	Y	Y	N	Y	Y	N	N
13 Collins	Y	Y	Y	N	Y	Y	Y	N
14 Hertel	Y	Y	Y	N	Y	Y	N	N
15 Ford	Y	Y	Y	N	Y	Y	Y	N
16 Dingell	Y	N	Y	X	Y	?	Y	N
17 Levin	Y	Y	Y	N	Y	Y	Y	N
18 ***Broomfield***	Y	N	N	Y	Y	N	N	Y
MINNESOTA								
1 Penny	Y	Y	Y	Y	Y	Y	N	Y
2 ***Weber***	Y	N	Y	N	Y	N	N	Y
3 ***Ramstad***	Y	N	Y	Y	Y	N	N	Y
4 Vento	?	#	?	N	Y	Y	Y	Y

	143	144	145	146	147	148	149	150
5 Sabo	Y	Y	Y	N	Y	Y	Y	Y
6 Sikorski	Y	Y	Y	N	Y	Y	Y	Y
7 Peterson	N	Y	Y	N	Y	N	N	Y
8 Oberstar	N	Y	N	N	Y	N	N	Y
MISSISSIPPI								
1 Whitten	Y	N	Y	N	Y	N	N	N
2 Espy	Y	N	Y	N	Y	Y	Y	Y
3 Montgomery	Y	N	Y	Y	Y	N	N	Y
4 Parker	Y	N	Y	N	Y	N	N	Y
5 Taylor	Y	N	Y	Y	Y	N	N	N
MISSOURI								
1 Clay	Y	?	?	N	Y	Y	Y	N
2 Horn	Y	Y	Y	N	Y	Y	Y	N
3 Gephardt	Y	Y	Y	N	Y	Y	Y	N
4 Skelton	Y	N	Y	Y	Y	N	N	Y
5 Wheat	Y	Y	Y	N	Y	Y	Y	N
6 ***Coleman***	Y	N	N	Y	Y	N	N	Y
7 ***Hancock***	N	N	N	Y	Y	N	N	Y
8 ***Emerson***	Y	N	N	Y	Y	N	N	Y
9 Volkmer	Y	Y	Y	N	Y	N	N	Y
MONTANA								
1 Williams	+	?	#	N	Y	Y	Y	Y
2 ***Marlenee***	Y	N	Y	#	?	N	N	N
NEBRASKA								
1 ***Bereuter***	Y	N	N	Y	Y	N	N	Y
2 Hoagland	Y	N	Y	N	Y	Y	Y	N
3 ***Barrett***	Y	N	N	Y	Y	N	N	Y
NEVADA								
1 Bilbray	?	N	Y	N	Y	N	N	N
2 ***Vucanovich***	Y	N	Y	Y	Y	N	N	Y
NEW HAMPSHIRE								
1 ***Zeliff***	Y	N	Y	Y	Y	Y	N	Y
2 Swett	?	N	Y	N	Y	N	N	N
NEW JERSEY								
1 Andrews	Y	N	Y	N	Y	Y	Y	N
2 Hughes	N	Y	Y	N	Y	Y	Y	N
3 Pallone	N	N	Y	N	Y	Y	Y	N
4 ***Smith***	Y	Y	Y	Y	Y	N	N	N
5 ***Roukema***	Y	Y	Y	#	?	#	#	?
6 Dwyer	Y	N	Y	N	Y	Y	Y	N
7 ***Rinaldo***	Y	N	Y	?	Y	N	N	N
8 Roe	Y	N	Y	?	Y	N	N	N
9 Torricelli	Y	?	?	Y	Y	Y	Y	N
10 Payne	Y	Y	N	N	Y	Y	Y	N
11 ***Gallo***	?	N	Y	N	Y	Y	Y	N
12 ***Zimmer***	Y	N	N	Y	Y	Y	Y	N
13 ***Saxton***	Y	N	Y	Y	Y	N	N	N
14 Guarini	N	N	Y	X	?	Y	Y	N
NEW MEXICO								
1 ***Schiff***	Y	N	N	N	Y	Y	Y	N
2 ***Skeen***	Y	N	Y	Y	Y	N	N	Y
3 Richardson	Y	N	Y	N	Y	Y	Y	N
NEW YORK								
1 Hochbrueckner	Y	N	Y	N	Y	Y	N	N
2 Downey	Y	Y	Y	N	Y	Y	Y	N
3 Mrazek	?	?	?	N	?	Y	Y	N
4 ***Lent***	Y	?	?	?	Y	N	N	N
5 ***McGrath***	Y	N	Y	N	Y	N	N	N
6 Flake	Y	Y	Y	N	Y	Y	Y	N
7 Ackerman	?	?	?	X	?	Y	Y	N
8 Scheuer	Y	Y	Y	N	Y	Y	Y	N
9 Manton	Y	Y	Y	N	Y	N	N	N
10 Schumer	Y	Y	Y	N	Y	Y	Y	N
11 Towns	?	#	X	N	Y	Y	Y	N
12 Owens	Y	Y	N	N	Y	Y	Y	N
13 Solarz	Y	Y	Y	N	?	Y	Y	N
14 ***Molinari***	Y	N	N	#	Y	Y	Y	N
15 ***Green***	Y	Y	Y	N	Y	Y	Y	N
16 Rangel	Y	Y	N	N	Y	Y	Y	N
17 Weiss	N	Y	N	N	Y	Y	Y	N
18 Serrano	Y	Y	N	N	Y	Y	Y	N
19 Engel	Y	Y	Y	N	Y	Y	Y	N
20 Lowey	Y	Y	Y	N	Y	Y	Y	N
21 ***Fish***	Y	N	Y	Y	Y	Y	Y	N
22 ***Gilman***	Y	N	Y	Y	Y	Y	Y	N
23 McNulty	Y	N	Y	N	Y	N	N	N
24 ***Solomon***	Y	N	N	Y	Y	N	N	N
25 ***Boehlert***	Y	N	Y	N	Y	Y	Y	N
26 ***Martin***	?	N	N	Y	Y	?	?	?
27 ***Walsh***	Y	N	Y	N	Y	N	N	N
28 McHugh	Y	N	Y	N	Y	Y	Y	Y
29 ***Horton***	Y	Y	Y	N	Y	Y	Y	N
30 Slaughter	+	Y	N	N	Y	Y	Y	N
31 ***Paxon***	Y	N	N	Y	Y	N	N	Y

	143	144	145	146	147	148	149	150
32 LaFalce	Y	Y	Y	N	Y	N	N	Y
33 Nowak	Y	Y	Y	N	Y	N	N	N
34 ***Houghton***	Y	N	Y	?	?	Y	Y	Y
NORTH CAROLINA								
1 Jones	Y	N	Y	N	Y	Y	Y	N
2 Valentine	Y	N	Y	Y	Y	Y	Y	N
3 Lancaster	Y	N	Y	N	Y	Y	Y	N
4 Price	Y	Y	Y	N	Y	Y	Y	N
5 Neal	Y	Y	Y	N	?	Y	Y	N
6 ***Coble***	Y	N	Y	Y	Y	N	N	N
7 Rose	?	?	?	N	Y	Y	Y	N
8 Hefner	Y	N	Y	N	Y	Y	Y	N
9 ***McMillan***	Y	N	Y	Y	Y	N	N	N
10 ***Ballenger***	Y	N	N	Y	Y	N	N	Y
11 ***Taylor***	Y	N	Y	Y	Y	N	N	N
NORTH DAKOTA								
AL Dorgan	Y	Y	Y	N	Y	N	N	Y
OHIO								
1 Luken	Y	N	Y	Y	Y	N	N	N
2 ***Gradison***	Y	N	Y	Y	Y	N	N	Y
3 Hall	Y	Y	Y	Y	Y	N	N	Y
4 ***Oxley***	Y	N	Y	Y	Y	N	N	Y
5 ***Gillmor***	Y	N	Y	N	Y	N	N	Y
6 ***McEwen***	N	N	N	Y	Y	N	N	Y
7 ***Hobson***	Y	N	Y	Y	Y	Y	Y	Y
8 ***Boehner***	Y	?	N	Y	Y	N	N	Y
9 Kaptur	N	Y	Y	N	Y	Y	Y	Y
10 ***Miller***	Y	N	N	Y	Y	N	N	Y
11 Eckart	Y	Y	N	N	Y	Y	Y	Y
12 ***Kasich***	Y	N	Y	Y	Y	N	N	Y
13 Pease	N	Y	N	N	Y	Y	Y	Y
14 Sawyer	Y	Y	Y	N	Y	Y	Y	N
15 ***Wylie***	Y	N	N	?	?	N	N	Y
16 ***Regula***	Y	N	Y	Y	Y	N	N	Y
17 Traficant	Y	Y	Y	Y	Y	Y	Y	N
18 Applegate	Y	Y	Y	Y	Y	N	N	N
19 Feighan	Y	Y	Y	N	Y	Y	Y	N
20 Oakar	Y	Y	Y	N	Y	Y	Y	Y
21 Stokes	Y	Y	N	N	Y	Y	Y	N
OKLAHOMA								
1 ***Inhofe***	Y	N	N	Y	Y	N	N	Y
2 Synar	Y	Y	Y	N	Y	Y	Y	Y
3 Brewster	Y	N	Y	Y	Y	Y	Y	N
4 McCurdy	Y	N	Y	N	Y	Y	Y	?
5 ***Edwards***	Y	N	Y	Y	Y	N	N	Y
6 English	Y	N	Y	Y	Y	N	N	Y
OREGON								
1 AuCoin	Y	Y	N	N	?	Y	Y	N
2 ***Smith***	Y	N	N	Y	Y	N	N	Y
3 Wyden	Y	Y	N	N	Y	Y	Y	N
4 DeFazio	Y	#	+	N	Y	Y	Y	N
5 Kopetski	Y	Y	Y	N	Y	Y	Y	N
PENNSYLVANIA								
1 Foglietta	Y	Y	Y	N	Y	Y	Y	N
2 Gray	Y	Y	Y	N	Y	Y	Y	N
3 Borski	?	Y	Y	N	Y	N	N	N
4 Kolter	Y	N	Y	Y	Y	?	N	N
5 ***Schulze***	Y	N	Y	Y	Y	N	N	N
6 Yatron	Y	N	Y	Y	Y	N	N	N
7 ***Weldon***	Y	N	Y	Y	Y	N	N	N
8 Kostmayer	?	Y	Y	N	Y	Y	Y	N
9 ***Shuster***	?	N	Y	Y	Y	N	N	N
10 ***McDade***	Y	N	Y	N	Y	N	N	?
11 Kanjorski	Y	N	Y	N	Y	N	N	N
12 Murtha	Y	N	Y	N	Y	N	N	N
13 ***Coughlin***	Y	N	Y	Y	?	Y	Y	N
14 Coyne	Y	N	Y	N	Y	Y	Y	N
15 ***Ritter***	Y	N	N	?	?	N	N	N
16 ***Walker***	Y	N	N	Y	Y	N	N	Y
17 ***Gekas***	Y	N	N	Y	Y	Y	N	Y
18 ***Santorum***	Y	N	N	Y	Y	N	N	N
19 ***Goodling***	Y	N	Y	Y	Y	N	N	Y
20 Gaydos	Y	N	Y	Y	Y	N	N	N
21 ***Ridge***	Y	N	Y	N	Y	Y	Y	N
22 Murphy	Y	Y	Y	Y	Y	N	Y	N
23 ***Clinger***	Y	N	Y	Y	Y	N	N	N
RHODE ISLAND								
1 ***Machtley***	Y	N	Y	N	Y	Y	Y	N
2 Reed	Y	Y	Y	N	Y	Y	Y	N
SOUTH CAROLINA								
1 ***Ravenel***	Y	N	Y	Y	Y	Y	Y	N
2 ***Spence***	Y	N	Y	Y	Y	N	N	N
3 Derrick	Y	Y	Y	N	Y	Y	Y	N
4 Patterson	Y	N	Y	Y	Y	Y	Y	N
5 Spratt	Y	N	Y	N	Y	Y	Y	N
6 Tallon	Y	N	N	Y	Y	N	N	N

	143	144	145	146	147	148	149	150
SOUTH DAKOTA								
AL Johnson	Y	Y	Y	N	Y	Y	Y	Y
TENNESSEE								
1 ***Quillen***	?	X	X	Y	Y	N	N	N
2 ***Duncan***	N	N	Y	Y	Y	N	N	N
3 Lloyd	Y	N	Y	Y	Y	Y	?	N
4 Cooper	Y	N	Y	N	Y	Y	Y	Y
5 Clement	Y	Y	Y	N	Y	Y	N	Y
6 Gordon	Y	N	Y	N	Y	Y	Y	N
7 ***Sundquist***	Y	-	+	Y	Y	N	N	N
8 Tanner	Y	Y	Y	N	Y	Y	Y	Y
9 Ford	Y	N	Y	?	?	Y	Y	?
TEXAS								
1 Chapman	Y	?	?	N	Y	N	Y	N
2 Wilson	Y	N	Y	N	Y	Y	Y	N
3 ***Johnson***	Y	N	Y	Y	Y	N	N	Y
4 Hall	Y	N	Y	Y	Y	N	N	Y
5 Bryant	Y	Y	Y	N	Y	Y	Y	N
6 ***Barton***	Y	N	Y	Y	Y	N	N	Y
7 ***Archer***	Y	N	N	Y	Y	N	N	Y
8 ***Fields***	Y	N	N	Y	Y	N	N	N
9 Brooks	Y	Y	Y	N	Y	Y	Y	N
10 Pickle	Y	N	Y	N	Y	Y	Y	Y
11 Edwards	Y	N	Y	N	Y	Y	Y	N
12 Geren	Y	N	Y	Y	Y	Y	Y	N
13 Sarpalius	Y	N	Y	Y	Y	N	N	Y
14 Laughlin	Y	N	Y	N	Y	N	N	N
15 de la Garza	Y	?	?	N	Y	N	N	Y
16 Coleman	Y	N	Y	N	Y	Y	Y	N
17 Stenholm	Y	N	Y	Y	Y	N	N	Y
18 Washington	Y	Y	N	N	Y	Y	Y	N
19 ***Combest***	Y	N	N	Y	Y	N	N	Y
20 Gonzalez	Y	Y	Y	N	Y	Y	Y	N
21 ***Smith***	Y	N	N	Y	Y	Y	N	Y
22 ***DeLay***	Y	N	N	#	?	N	N	Y
23 Bustamante	Y	?	?	N	Y	Y	Y	N
24 Frost	Y	?	?	N	Y	Y	Y	N
25 Andrews	Y	X	?	N	Y	Y	Y	N
26 ***Armey***	N	N	N	Y	Y	N	N	Y
27 Ortiz	Y	N	Y	N	Y	N	N	N
UTAH								
1 ***Hansen***	Y	N	N	Y	Y	N	N	Y
2 Owens	Y	Y	Y	N	Y	Y	Y	N
3 Orton	N	?	X	Y	Y	N	N	N
VERMONT								
AL *Sanders*	Y	Y	N	N	Y	Y	Y	N
VIRGINIA								
1 ***Bateman***	Y	N	Y	Y	Y	N	N	N
2 Pickett	Y	N	Y	N	Y	Y	Y	N
3 ***Bliley***	Y	N	Y	Y	Y	N	N	N
4 Sisisky	?	?	?	N	Y	Y	Y	N
5 Payne	Y	?	?	Y	Y	Y	Y	Y
6 Olin	N	Y	Y	N	Y	Y	Y	Y
7 ***Slaughter***	Y	N	N	Y	Y	N	N	Y
8 Moran	Y	Y	Y	N	Y	Y	Y	Y
9 Boucher	?	?	?	N	Y	Y	Y	Y
10 ***Wolf***	Y	N	Y	N	Y	N	N	Y
WASHINGTON								
1 ***Miller***	+	+	+	Y	Y	Y	Y	N
2 Swift	Y	Y	Y	N	Y	Y	Y	N
3 Unsoeld	Y	Y	N	N	Y	Y	Y	N
4 ***Morrison***	Y	N	Y	N	Y	Y	Y	Y
5 Foley								
6 Dicks	Y	N	Y	N	Y	Y	Y	N
7 McDermott	Y	Y	Y	N	Y	Y	Y	N
8 ***Chandler***	Y	?	#	Y	Y	Y	N	Y
WEST VIRGINIA								
1 Mollohan	Y	N	Y	N	Y	N	N	N
2 Staggers	Y	Y	Y	N	Y	N	N	N
3 Wise	Y	N	Y	N	Y	Y	Y	N
4 Rahall	Y	Y	N	N	Y	N	N	N
WISCONSIN								
1 Aspin	Y	N	Y	N	Y	Y	?	Y
2 ***Klug***	Y	N	Y	Y	Y	Y	Y	Y
3 ***Gunderson***	Y	N	Y	?	?	N	N	Y
4 Kleczka	Y	Y	Y	N	Y	Y	Y	Y
5 Moody	N	Y	?	N	Y	Y	Y	Y
6 ***Petri***	N	Y	N	N	Y	N	N	Y
7 Obey	N	Y	Y	N	Y	N	N	Y
8 ***Roth***	Y	N	Y	Y	Y	N	N	Y
9 ***Sensenbrenner***	N	Y	N	Y	Y	N	N	Y
WYOMING								
AL ***Thomas***	Y	N	N	Y	Y	N	N	Y

Southern states - Ala., Ark., Fla., Ga., Ky., La., Miss., N.C., Okla., S.C., Tenn., Texas, Va.
Omitted votes are quorum calls, which CQ does not include in its vote charts.

HOUSE VOTES 151, 152, 153, 154, 155, 156, 157, 158

151. HR 2508. Fiscal 1992-93 Foreign Aid Authorization/Pakistan. Hyde, R-Ill., en bloc amendment to eliminate the law that prohibits U.S. foreign aid to Pakistan unless the president certifies annually that Pakistan does not have a nuclear explosive device. Rejected 151-252: R 116-37; D 35-214 (ND 11-159, SD 24-55); I 0-1, June 12, 1991. A "yea" was a vote supporting the president's position.

152. HR 2608. Fiscal 1992 Commerce, Justice, State and Judiciary Appropriations/Growth Limits. Armey, R-Texas, amendment to limit overall growth in the bill to 2.4 percent above the fiscal 1991 level by cutting discretionary programs in the bill by 8.16 percent. Rejected 122-295: R 106-55; D 16-239 (ND 10-162, SD 6-77); I 0-1, June 13, 1991.

153. HR 2608. Fiscal 1992 Commerce, Justice, State and Judiciary Appropriations/Recommittal Motion. Burton, R-Ind., motion to recommit to the House Appropriations Committee the bill to provide $20.9 billion in fiscal 1992 for Commerce, Justice and State departments, with instructions to report it back to the House after striking the $936,000 to fund a fish farm lab in Arkansas and a semitropical research facility in Florida. Motion rejected 151-267: R 138-23; D 13-243 (ND 9-165, SD 4-78); I 0-1, June 13, 1991.

154. HR 2608. Fiscal 1992 Commerce, Justice, State and Judiciary Appropriations/Passage. Passage of the bill to provide $20,974,683,000 in new budget authority in fiscal 1992 for the Departments of Commerce, Justice and State, the Judiciary and related agencies. The administration requested $22,342,064,000. Passed 338-80: R 90-70; D 247-10 (ND 165-9, SD 82-1); I 1-0, June 13, 1991.

155. HR 2508. Fiscal 1992-93 Foreign Aid Authorization/India. Lagomarsino, R-Calif., amendment to prohibit U.S. aid to India unless the president certifies that India does not possess a nuclear explosive device and that the proposed assistance will reduce the risk that India will possess a nuclear device. Before being adopted, the Lagomarsino amendment was modified by a Kostmayer, D-Pa., amendment to take into account that India has already detonated a nuclear device and therefore require presidential certification that India is not developing additional nuclear weapons. Adopted 242-141: R 115-35; D 126-106 (ND 70-85, SD 56-21); I 1-0, June 13, 1991. A "nay" was a vote supporting the president's position.

156. Procedural Motion. Fazio, D-Calif., motion to approve the House Journal of Monday, June 17. Motion agreed to 281-102: R 46-95; D 235-7 (ND 158-7, SD 77-0); June 18, 1991.

157. HR 2622. Fiscal 1992 Treasury-Postal Appropriations/Previous Question. Slaughter, D-N.Y., motion to order the previous question (thus ending debate and the possibility of amendment) on the rule (H Res 176) to waive certain points of order against and provide for House floor consideration of the bill to provide $19.7 billion in new budget authority for the Treasury Department, the Postal Service and other related agencies in fiscal 1992. Motion agreed to 252-162: R 0-157; D 251-5 (ND 171-3, SD 80-2); I 1-0; June 18, 1991.

158. HR 2622. Fiscal 1992 Treasury-Postal Appropriations/Rule. Adoption of the rule (H Res 176) to waive certain points of order against and provide for House floor consideration of the bill to provide $19.7 billion in new budget authority for the Treasury Department, the Postal Service and other related agencies in fiscal 1992. Adopted 253-163: R 0-158; D 252-5 (ND 170-4, SD 82-1); I 1-0; June 18, 1991.

† *Rep. John Olver, D-Mass., was sworn in June 18, 1991. The first vote for which he was eligible was vote 157. Olver replaces Silvio O. Conte, R-Mass., who died Feb. 8, 1991. The last vote for which Conte was eligible was vote 21.*

KEY

Y Voted for (yea).
Paired for.
\+ Announced for.
N Voted against (nay).
X Paired against.
\- Announced against.
P Voted "present."
C Voted "present" to avoid possible conflict of interest.
? Did not vote or otherwise make a position known.

Democrats ***Republicans***
Independent

	151	152	153	154	155	156	157	158
ALABAMA								
1 ***Callahan***	Y	Y	Y	Y	Y	N	N	N
2 ***Dickinson***	Y	Y	N	N	Y	N	N	N
3 Browder	N	N	N	Y	Y	Y	Y	Y
4 Bevill	N	N	N	Y	Y	Y	Y	Y
5 Cramer	N	N	N	Y	Y	Y	Y	Y
6 Erdreich	N	Y	N	Y	Y	Y	Y	Y
7 Harris	N	N	N	Y	Y	Y	Y	Y
ALASKA								
AL ***Young***	Y	N	N	Y	Y	N	N	N
ARIZONA								
1 ***Rhodes***	Y	Y	Y	N	Y	N	N	N
2 Vacancy								
3 ***Stump***	Y	Y	Y	N	Y	N	N	N
4 ***Kyl***	Y	Y	Y	N	Y	N	N	N
5 ***Kolbe***	Y	N	Y	Y	N	N	N	N
ARKANSAS								
1 Alexander	Y	N	N	Y	Y	Y	Y	Y
2 Thornton	Y	N	N	Y	Y	Y	Y	Y
3 ***Hammerschmidt***	Y	Y	N	Y	Y	Y	N	N
4 Anthony	Y	N	N	Y	Y	Y	Y	Y
CALIFORNIA								
1 ***Riggs***	N	Y	Y	N	Y	N	N	N
2 ***Herger***	Y	Y	Y	N	Y	N	N	N
3 Matsui	N	N	N	Y	?	?	Y	Y
4 Fazio	N	N	N	Y	Y	Y	Y	Y
5 Pelosi	N	N	N	Y	?	Y	Y	Y
6 Boxer	?	N	N	Y	N	Y	Y	Y
7 Miller	N	N	N	Y	X	Y	Y	Y
8 Dellums	N	N	N	Y	N	Y	Y	Y
9 Stark	N	N	N	Y	Y	Y	Y	Y
10 Edwards	N	N	N	Y	N	Y	Y	Y
11 Lantos	N	N	N	Y	N	Y	Y	Y
12 ***Campbell***	?	Y	Y	N	N	N	N	N
13 Mineta	?	N	N	Y	N	Y	Y	Y
14 ***Doolittle***	Y	Y	Y	N	Y	N	N	N
15 Condit	N	Y	N	Y	Y	Y	Y	Y
16 Panetta	N	N	N	Y	?	Y	Y	Y
17 Dooley	N	N	N	Y	Y	Y	Y	Y
18 Lehman	Y	?	N	Y	Y	Y	Y	Y
19 ***Lagomarsino***	Y	Y	Y	N	Y	N	N	N
20 ***Thomas***	Y	Y	Y	Y	Y	N	N	N
21 ***Gallegly***	Y	Y	Y	N	?	N	N	N
22 ***Moorhead***	Y	Y	Y	N	Y	N	N	N
23 Beilenson	N	N	N	Y	N	Y	Y	Y
24 Waxman	N	N	N	Y	N	Y	Y	Y
25 Roybal	N	N	N	Y	N	Y	Y	Y
26 Berman	N	N	N	Y	X	Y	Y	Y
27 Levine	N	N	N	Y	N	?	?	?
28 Dixon	N	N	N	Y	N	Y	Y	Y
29 Waters	N	?	N	Y	N	Y	Y	Y
30 Martinez	N	N	N	Y	Y	Y	?	Y
31 Dymally	N	N	N	Y	N	Y	Y	?
32 Anderson	N	N	N	Y	N	Y	Y	Y
33 ***Dreier***	Y	Y	Y	N	Y	Y	N	N
34 Torres	N	N	N	Y	N	Y	Y	Y
35 ***Lewis***	Y	N	Y	Y	Y	N	N	N
36 Brown	N	N	N	Y	Y	Y	Y	Y
37 ***McCandless***	N	Y	Y	N	?	N	N	N
38 ***Dornan***	Y	Y	Y	N	N	Y	N	N
39 ***Dannemeyer***	N	Y	Y	N	Y	N	N	N
40 ***Cox***	N	Y	Y	N	N	N	N	N
41 ***Lowery***	Y	N	Y	Y	Y	N	N	N
42 ***Rohrabacher***	Y	Y	Y	N	Y	N	N	N
43 ***Packard***	Y	Y	Y	N	Y	N	N	N
44 ***Cunningham***	Y	Y	Y	Y	Y	N	N	N
45 ***Hunter***	Y	Y	Y	N	Y	?	N	N
COLORADO								
1 Schroeder	N	Y	N	N	Y	N	Y	Y
2 Skaggs	N	N	N	Y	Y	Y	Y	Y
3 Campbell	Y	N	N	Y	Y	N	Y	Y
4 ***Allard***	Y	Y	Y	N	N	N	N	N
5 ***Hefley***	N	Y	Y	N	Y	N	N	N
6 ***Schaefer***	Y	Y	Y	N	?	N	N	N
CONNECTICUT								
1 Kennelly	N	N	N	Y	N	Y	Y	Y
2 Gejdenson	N	N	N	Y	N	Y	Y	Y
3 DeLauro	N	N	N	Y	-	Y	Y	Y
4 ***Shays***	N	Y	Y	N	N	N	N	N
5 ***Franks***	N	Y	Y	N	Y	N	N	N
6 ***Johnson***	N	N	Y	Y	Y	Y	N	N
DELAWARE								
AL Carper	N	N	Y	Y	Y	Y	Y	Y
FLORIDA								
1 Hutto	N	N	N	Y	Y	Y	Y	Y
2 Peterson	N	N	N	Y	Y	Y	Y	Y
3 Bennett	N	Y	N	Y	Y	Y	Y	Y
4 ***James***	N	Y	Y	Y	Y	N	N	N
5 ***McCollum***	N	N	N	Y	N	Y	N	N
6 ***Stearns***	N	Y	Y	Y	Y	?	N	N
7 Gibbons	N	N	N	Y	N	Y	Y	Y
8 ***Young***	?	N	N	Y	Y	Y	N	N
9 ***Bilirakis***	N	Y	N	Y	N	N	N	N
10 ***Ireland***	Y	N	N	Y	Y	N	N	N
11 Bacchus	N	N	N	Y	N	Y	Y	Y
12 ***Lewis***	Y	Y	N	N	Y	N	N	N
13 ***Goss***	Y	Y	Y	Y	Y	N	N	N
14 Johnston	N	N	N	Y	?	Y	Y	Y
15 ***Shaw***	Y	N	N	Y	Y	?	N	N
16 Smith	N	N	N	Y	N	Y	Y	Y
17 Lehman	?	N	N	Y	?	?	Y	Y
18 ***Ros-Lehtinen***	N	N	N	Y	Y	N	N	N
19 Fascell	N	N	N	Y	N	Y	Y	Y
GEORGIA								
1 Thomas	N	N	N	Y	Y	Y	Y	Y
2 Hatcher	N	N	N	Y	?	Y	Y	Y
3 Ray	N	N	N	Y	Y	Y	N	N
4 Jones	N	N	N	Y	N	Y	Y	Y
5 Lewis	N	N	N	Y	N	Y	Y	Y
6 ***Gingrich***	Y	N	Y	Y	N	N	N	N
7 Darden	N	N	N	Y	N	Y	Y	Y
8 Rowland	Y	N	N	Y	Y	Y	Y	Y
9 Jenkins	Y	N	N	Y	Y	?	Y	Y
10 Barnard	Y	N	N	Y	#	Y	N	Y
HAWAII								
1 Abercrombie	N	N	N	Y	Y	Y	Y	Y
2 Mink	N	N	N	Y	N	Y	Y	Y
IDAHO								
1 LaRocco	N	N	N	Y	?	Y	Y	Y
2 Stallings	N	N	N	Y	N	Y	Y	Y
ILLINOIS								
1 Hayes	N	N	N	Y	N	Y	Y	Y
2 Savage	N	?	N	Y	N	Y	Y	Y
3 Russo	N	N	N	Y	Y	Y	Y	Y
4 Sangmeister	Y	N	N	Y	Y	Y	Y	Y
5 Lipinski	Y	N	N	Y	Y	Y	Y	Y
6 ***Hyde***	Y	N	Y	Y	N	Y	N	N
7 Collins	N	N	N	Y	N	Y	Y	Y
8 Rostenkowski	?	?	?	?	?	Y	Y	Y
9 Yates	?	?	?	?	?	Y	Y	Y
10 ***Porter***	N	Y	Y	Y	Y	?	N	N
11 Annunzio	N	N	N	Y	Y	Y	Y	Y
12 ***Crane***	Y	Y	Y	N	Y	N	N	N
13 ***Fawell***	Y	Y	Y	N	Y	N	N	N
14 ***Hastert***	Y	Y	Y	Y	N	N	N	N
15 Vacancy								
16 Cox	N	N	N	Y	Y	Y	Y	Y
17 Evans	N	N	N	Y	Y	Y	Y	Y
18 ***Michel***	Y	N	Y	Y	Y	Y	N	N
19 Bruce	N	N	N	Y	Y	Y	Y	Y
20 Durbin	N	N	N	Y	Y	Y	Y	Y
21 Costello	N	N	N	Y	Y	Y	Y	Y
22 Poshard	N	N	N	Y	Y	Y	Y	Y
INDIANA								
1 Visclosky	N	N	N	Y	Y	Y	Y	Y
2 Sharp	?	N	Y	Y	Y	?	Y	N
3 Roemer	N	N	N	Y	Y	Y	Y	Y

ND Northern Democrats SD Southern Democrats

	151	152	153	154	155	156	157	158
4 Long	N	N	N	Y	N	Y	Y	Y
5 Jontz	N	N	N	Y	N	Y	Y	Y
6 ***Burton***	Y	Y	Y	N	Y	N	N	N
7 ***Myers***	Y	N	N	Y	Y	Y	N	N
8 McCloskey	N	N	N	Y	N	Y	Y	Y
9 Hamilton	N	Y	Y	Y	N	Y	Y	Y
10 Jacobs	N	Y	Y	N	Y	N	N	N
IOWA								
1 ***Leach***	N	Y	Y	Y	N	?	N	N
2 ***Nussle***	Y	Y	Y	N	N	N	N	N
3 Nagle	N	N	N	Y	N	Y	Y	Y
4 Smith	N	N	N	Y	?	Y	Y	Y
5 ***Lightfoot***	Y	N	N	Y	N	N	N	N
6 ***Grandy***	N	N	Y	Y	Y	N	N	N
KANSAS								
1 ***Roberts***	Y	Y	Y	N	Y	N	N	N
2 Slattery	N	Y	N	N	Y	Y	Y	Y
3 ***Meyers***	N	Y	Y	N	+	N	N	N
4 Glickman	N	Y	Y	N	Y	Y	Y	Y
5 ***Nichols***	Y	Y	Y	N	Y	Y	N	N
KENTUCKY								
1 Hubbard	Y	Y	N	N	Y	?	?	?
2 Natcher	N	N	N	Y	N	Y	Y	Y
3 Mazzoli	N	N	N	Y	N	Y	Y	Y
4 ***Bunning***	Y	Y	Y	N	Y	N	N	N
5 ***Rogers***	Y	N	Y	Y	Y	N	N	N
6 ***Hopkins***	?	?	?	?	?	?	?	?
7 Perkins	N	N	N	Y	Y	Y	Y	Y
LOUISIANA								
1 ***Livingston***	Y	N	N	Y	Y	Y	N	N
2 Jefferson	N	N	N	Y	?	?	Y	Y
3 Tauzin	Y	N	N	Y	Y	Y	Y	Y
4 ***McCrery***	Y	N	N	Y	N	Y	N	N
5 Huckaby	Y	N	N	Y	Y	Y	Y	Y
6 ***Baker***	Y	Y	Y	N	Y	N	N	N
7 Hayes	Y	N	N	Y	Y	Y	Y	Y
8 ***Holloway***	Y	Y	Y	N	Y	N	N	N
MAINE								
1 Andrews	N	N	N	Y	Y	Y	Y	Y
2 ***Snowe***	N	Y	Y	Y	Y	Y	N	N
MARYLAND								
1 ***Gilchrest***	Y	Y	Y	N	N	N	N	N
2 ***Bentley***	Y	Y	Y	N	N	N	N	N
3 Cardin	N	N	N	Y	N	Y	Y	Y
4 McMillen	N	N	N	Y	N	Y	Y	Y
5 Hoyer	N	N	N	Y	Y	Y	Y	Y
6 Byron	Y	N	N	Y	N	Y	Y	Y
7 Mfume	N	N	N	Y	Y	Y	Y	Y
8 ***Morella***	N	N	N	Y	Y	Y	N	N
MASSACHUSETTS								
1 Olver †							Y	Y
2 Neal	N	N	N	Y	N	Y	Y	Y
3 Early	N	N	N	Y	?	Y	Y	Y
4 Frank	N	N	N	Y	Y	Y	Y	Y
5 Atkins	N	N	N	Y	N	Y	Y	Y
6 Mavroules	N	N	N	Y	?	Y	Y	Y
7 Markey	N	N	N	Y	Y	Y	Y	Y
8 Kennedy	N	N	N	Y	N	Y	Y	Y
9 Moakley	N	X	?	?	?	Y	Y	Y
10 Studds	?	N	N	Y	Y	Y	Y	Y
11 Donnelly	N	N	N	Y	?	Y	Y	Y
MICHIGAN								
1 Conyers	N	N	N	Y	N	Y	Y	Y
2 ***Pursell***	Y	Y	Y	Y	?	?	N	N
3 Wolpe	N	N	N	Y	N	Y	Y	Y
4 ***Upton***	N	Y	Y	Y	Y	N	N	N
5 ***Henry***	Y	Y	Y	N	Y	N	N	N
6 Carr	N	N	N	Y	Y	Y	Y	Y
7 Kildee	N	N	N	Y	Y	Y	Y	Y
8 Traxler	N	N	N	Y	?	Y	Y	Y
9 ***Vander Jagt***	Y	Y	Y	Y	Y	Y	N	N
10 ***Camp***	N	Y	Y	Y	Y	N	N	N
11 ***Davis***	Y	?	Y	Y	Y	Y	N	N
12 Bonior	N	N	N	Y	N	Y	Y	Y
13 Collins	N	N	N	Y	N	Y	Y	Y
14 Hertel	N	N	N	Y	N	Y	Y	Y
15 Ford	N	N	N	Y	Y	Y	Y	Y
16 Dingell	N	N	N	Y	Y	?	Y	Y
17 Levin	N	N	N	Y	N	Y	Y	Y
18 ***Broomfield***	Y	N	Y	Y	N	Y	N	N
MINNESOTA								
1 Penny	N	Y	Y	N	Y	Y	Y	Y
2 ***Weber***	Y	Y	Y	Y	Y	N	N	N
3 ***Ramstad***	N	Y	Y	N	Y	?	N	N
4 Vento	N	N	N	Y	N	Y	Y	Y

	151	152	153	154	155	156	157	158
5 Sabo	N	N	N	Y	N	Y	Y	Y
6 Sikorski	N	N	N	Y	N	N	Y	Y
7 Peterson	N	N	N	Y	N	Y	Y	Y
8 Oberstar	N	N	N	Y	N	Y	Y	Y
MISSISSIPPI								
1 Whitten	N	N	N	Y	N	Y	Y	Y
2 Espy	N	N	N	Y	Y	Y	Y	Y
3 Montgomery	Y	N	N	Y	Y	Y	Y	Y
4 Parker	N	Y	N	Y	Y	Y	Y	Y
5 Taylor	N	N	Y	Y	N	Y	Y	Y
MISSOURI								
1 Clay	N	N	N	?	?	N	Y	Y
2 Horn	N	N	N	Y	Y	Y	Y	Y
3 Gephardt	?	N	N	Y	?	Y	Y	Y
4 Skelton	Y	N	N	Y	Y	Y	Y	Y
5 Wheat	N	N	N	Y	N	Y	Y	Y
6 ***Coleman***	Y	Y	Y	Y	Y	N	N	N
7 ***Hancock***	Y	Y	Y	N	Y	N	N	N
8 ***Emerson***	Y	N	N	Y	Y	Y	N	N
9 Volkmer	Y	N	N	Y	Y	Y	Y	Y
MONTANA								
1 Williams	N	N	N	Y	Y	Y	Y	Y
2 ***Marlenee***	N	Y	Y	N	?	N	N	N
NEBRASKA								
1 ***Bereuter***	Y	N	Y	Y	N	N	N	N
2 Hoagland	N	N	N	Y	N	Y	Y	Y
3 ***Barrett***	Y	Y	Y	Y	Y	N	N	N
NEVADA								
1 Bilbray	N	N	N	Y	N	?	?	?
2 ***Vucanovich***	Y	Y	Y	Y	N	N	N	N
NEW HAMPSHIRE								
1 ***Zeliff***	Y	Y	Y	N	Y	N	N	N
2 Swett	N	Y	Y	N	Y	Y	Y	Y
NEW JERSEY								
1 Andrews	N	N	N	Y	Y	Y	Y	Y
2 Hughes	N	N	N	Y	Y	Y	Y	Y
3 Pallone	N	Y	N	N	N	Y	Y	Y
4 ***Smith***	N	Y	N	Y	Y	Y	N	N
5 ***Roukema***	?	#	?	?	?	?	?	?
6 Dwyer	N	N	N	Y	N	Y	Y	Y
7 ***Rinaldo***	N	N	Y	Y	Y	Y	N	N
8 Roe	?	N	N	Y	N	Y	Y	Y
9 Torricelli	Y	N	N	Y	Y	Y	Y	Y
10 Payne	N	N	N	Y	N	Y	Y	Y
11 ***Gallo***	Y	N	Y	Y	N	N	N	N
12 ***Zimmer***	Y	Y	Y	N	Y	N	N	N
13 ***Saxton***	Y	Y	Y	Y	Y	N	N	N
14 Guarini	N	N	N	Y	Y	Y	Y	Y
NEW MEXICO								
1 ***Schiff***	Y	N	Y	Y	Y	Y	N	N
2 ***Skeen***	Y	N	Y	Y	Y	Y	N	N
3 Richardson	N	N	N	Y	Y	Y	Y	Y
NEW YORK								
1 Hochbrueckner	N	N	N	Y	N	Y	Y	Y
2 Downey	N	N	N	Y	N	Y	Y	Y
3 Mrazek	N	N	N	Y	N	?	?	?
4 ***Lent***	Y	N	Y	Y	Y	Y	N	N
5 ***McGrath***	N	N	Y	Y	N	?	N	N
6 Flake	N	N	N	Y	N	Y	Y	Y
7 Ackerman	N	N	N	Y	N	Y	Y	Y
8 Scheuer	N	N	N	Y	N	Y	Y	Y
9 Manton	N	N	N	Y	N	Y	Y	Y
10 Schumer	N	N	N	Y	Y	Y	Y	Y
11 Towns	N	N	N	Y	N	Y	Y	Y
12 Owens	N	N	N	Y	N	Y	Y	Y
13 Solarz	N	N	N	Y	N	Y	Y	Y
14 ***Molinari***	Y	N	Y	Y	N	N	N	N
15 ***Green***	N	N	N	?	?	Y	N	N
16 Rangel	N	N	N	Y	N	Y	Y	Y
17 Weiss	N	N	N	Y	N	Y	Y	Y
18 Serrano	N	N	?	?	Y	?	?	?
19 Engel	N	N	N	Y	N	Y	Y	Y
20 Lowey	N	N	N	Y	N	Y	Y	Y
21 ***Fish***	Y	N	Y	Y	N	Y	N	N
22 ***Gilman***	Y	N	Y	Y	N	Y	N	N
23 McNulty	N	N	N	Y	N	Y	Y	Y
24 ***Solomon***	Y	Y	Y	N	Y	N	N	N
25 ***Boehlert***	N	N	N	Y	N	N	N	N
26 ***Martin***	?	N	Y	Y	Y	?	N	N
27 ***Walsh***	Y	N	Y	Y	N	Y	N	N
28 McHugh	N	N	N	Y	N	Y	Y	Y
29 ***Horton***	?	N	N	Y	N	Y	N	N
30 Slaughter	N	N	Y	Y	Y	Y	Y	Y
31 ***Paxon***	Y	Y	Y	Y	Y	N	N	N

	151	152	153	154	155	156	157	158
32 LaFalce	N	N	N	Y	Y	Y	Y	Y
33 Nowak	N	N	N	Y	Y	?	Y	Y
34 ***Houghton***	Y	N	?	#	?	Y	N	N
NORTH CAROLINA								
1 Jones	?	N	N	Y	Y	Y	Y	Y
2 Valentine	?	N	Y	Y	Y	Y	Y	Y
3 Lancaster	N	N	N	Y	Y	Y	Y	Y
4 Price	N	N	N	Y	Y	Y	Y	Y
5 Neal	N	Y	?	Y	Y	Y	Y	Y
6 ***Coble***	Y	Y	Y	N	Y	N	N	N
7 Rose	N	N	N	Y	?	Y	Y	Y
8 Hefner	N	N	N	Y	Y	Y	Y	Y
9 ***McMillan***	Y	Y	Y	Y	Y	N	N	N
10 ***Ballenger***	+	Y	Y	N	Y	N	N	N
11 ***Taylor***	Y	Y	Y	N	Y	P	N	N
NORTH DAKOTA								
AL Dorgan	N	N	Y	N	N	Y	Y	Y
OHIO								
1 Luken	N	Y	N	N	Y	Y	Y	Y
2 ***Gradison***	Y	Y	Y	Y	Y	Y	N	N
3 Hall	N	N	N	Y	N	Y	Y	Y
4 ***Oxley***	?	Y	Y	N	Y	Y	N	N
5 ***Gillmor***	Y	N	Y	Y	Y	Y	N	N
6 ***McEwen***	Y	Y	Y	N	N	?	N	N
7 ***Hobson***	Y	Y	Y	Y	N	Y	N	N
8 ***Boehner***	Y	Y	Y	Y	Y	N	N	N
9 Kaptur	N	N	N	Y	Y	?	Y	Y
10 ***Miller***	Y	Y	Y	N	Y	N	N	N
11 Eckart	N	N	N	Y	N	Y	Y	Y
12 ***Kasich***	N	Y	Y	N	Y	Y	N	N
13 Pease	N	N	N	Y	N	Y	Y	Y
14 Sawyer	N	N	N	Y	N	Y	Y	Y
15 ***Wylie***	Y	Y	Y	Y	Y	Y	N	N
16 ***Regula***	Y	N	Y	Y	Y	N	N	N
17 Traficant	N	N	N	Y	Y	Y	N	N
18 Applegate	Y	N	N	Y	Y	Y	N	N
19 Feighan	N	N	N	Y	N	Y	Y	Y
20 Oakar	N	N	N	Y	Y	Y	Y	Y
21 Stokes	N	N	N	Y	N	N	Y	Y
OKLAHOMA								
1 ***Inhofe***	N	Y	Y	N	Y	N	N	N
2 Synar	N	N	?	?	?	Y	Y	Y
3 Brewster	Y	N	N	Y	Y	?	Y	Y
4 McCurdy	N	N	N	Y	Y	Y	Y	Y
5 ***Edwards***	N	Y	Y	Y	Y	N	N	N
6 English	N	N	N	Y	Y	?	Y	Y
OREGON								
1 AuCoin	N	N	N	Y	N	?	?	?
2 ***Smith***	?	Y	Y	Y	Y	N	N	N
3 Wyden	N	N	N	Y	?	Y	Y	Y
4 DeFazio	N	N	N	Y	?	Y	Y	Y
5 Kopetski	N	N	N	Y	N	Y	Y	Y
PENNSYLVANIA								
1 Foglietta	N	N	N	Y	N	?	Y	Y
2 Gray	N	N	N	Y	N	?	Y	Y
3 Borski	N	N	N	Y	Y	Y	Y	Y
4 Kolter	?	N	N	Y	Y	Y	Y	Y
5 ***Schulze***	Y	Y	Y	Y	Y	Y	N	N
6 Yatron	N	N	N	Y	Y	Y	Y	Y
7 ***Weldon***	N	Y	Y	Y	Y	N	N	N
8 Kostmayer	N	N	N	Y	Y	?	Y	Y
9 ***Shuster***	?	Y	Y	N	Y	Y	N	N
10 ***McDade***	?	N	N	Y	?	?	?	?
11 Kanjorski	Y	N	N	Y	Y	Y	Y	Y
12 Murtha	?	N	N	Y	N	Y	Y	Y
13 ***Coughlin***	Y	N	Y	Y	Y	?	N	N
14 Coyne	N	N	N	Y	N	Y	Y	Y
15 ***Ritter***	Y	N	Y	Y	Y	Y	N	N
16 ***Walker***	Y	Y	Y	N	Y	N	N	N
17 ***Gekas***	Y	Y	Y	Y	Y	N	N	N
18 ***Santorum***	Y	Y	Y	N	Y	N	N	N
19 ***Goodling***	-	N	N	Y	Y	N	N	N
20 Gaydos	Y	?	?	?	?	?	Y	Y
21 ***Ridge***	Y	N	N	Y	Y	N	N	N
22 Murphy	N	N	N	Y	?	N	Y	Y
23 ***Clinger***	N	N	Y	N	?	?	?	?
RHODE ISLAND								
1 ***Machtley***	N	N	Y	Y	N	?	N	N
2 Reed	N	N	N	Y	Y	Y	Y	Y
SOUTH CAROLINA								
1 ***Ravenel***	Y	Y	Y	Y	Y	N	N	N
2 ***Spence***	Y	Y	Y	Y	Y	?	?	?
3 Derrick	Y	N	N	Y	N	Y	Y	Y
4 Patterson	N	N	N	Y	Y	Y	Y	Y
5 Spratt	N	N	N	Y	Y	Y	Y	Y
6 Tallon	Y	N	Y	Y	Y	Y	Y	Y

	151	152	153	154	155	156	157	158
SOUTH DAKOTA								
AL Johnson	N	N	N	Y	N	Y	Y	Y
TENNESSEE								
1 ***Quillen***	Y	#	?	X	#	Y	N	N
2 ***Duncan***	Y	Y	Y	N	Y	Y	N	N
3 Lloyd	Y	N	N	Y	Y	?	?	?
4 Cooper	N	Y	N	Y	N	Y	Y	Y
5 Clement	N	N	N	Y	N	Y	Y	Y
6 Gordon	N	N	N	Y	Y	Y	Y	Y
7 ***Sundquist***	Y	Y	Y	N	Y	N	N	N
8 Tanner	N	N	N	Y	Y	Y	Y	Y
9 Ford	N	N	N	Y	N	Y	Y	Y
TEXAS								
1 Chapman	?	N	N	Y	Y	Y	?	Y
2 Wilson	Y	N	N	Y	Y	Y	Y	Y
3 ***Johnson***	Y	Y	Y	N	N	Y	?	N
4 Hall	Y	N	N	Y	Y	Y	Y	Y
5 Bryant	N	N	N	Y	Y	Y	Y	Y
6 ***Barton***	Y	Y	Y	N	Y	Y	N	N
7 ***Archer***	Y	Y	Y	N	Y	?	N	N
8 ***Fields***	Y	Y	Y	N	Y	?	N	N
9 Brooks	N	N	N	Y	Y	?	Y	Y
10 Pickle	Y	N	N	Y	Y	Y	Y	Y
11 Edwards	N	N	N	Y	Y	Y	Y	Y
12 Geren	Y	N	N	Y	Y	Y	Y	Y
13 Sarpalius	N	N	N	Y	Y	Y	Y	Y
14 Laughlin	Y	N	N	Y	Y	Y	Y	Y
15 de la Garza	N	N	N	Y	Y	Y	Y	Y
16 Coleman	N	?	?	?	?	Y	Y	Y
17 Stenholm	Y	N	N	Y	Y	Y	Y	Y
18 Washington	N	?	N	Y	N	Y	Y	Y
19 ***Combest***	Y	Y	Y	N	Y	Y	N	N
20 Gonzalez	N	N	N	Y	N	Y	Y	Y
21 ***Smith***	Y	N	Y	Y	Y	?	?	?
22 ***DeLay***	Y	Y	Y	Y	Y	N	N	N
23 Bustamante	?	N	N	Y	Y	Y	Y	Y
24 Frost	N	N	N	Y	Y	Y	Y	Y
25 Andrews	Y	N	Y	Y	Y	Y	Y	Y
26 ***Armey***	Y	Y	Y	N	Y	N	N	N
27 Ortiz	Y	N	N	Y	Y	Y	Y	Y
UTAH								
1 ***Hansen***	Y	Y	Y	N	?	N	N	N
2 Owens	N	N	N	Y	N	Y	Y	Y
3 Orton	N	N	N	Y	?	Y	Y	Y
VERMONT								
AL *Sanders*	N	N	N	Y	Y	?	Y	Y
VIRGINIA								
1 ***Bateman***	Y	N	Y	Y	N	?	N	N
2 Pickett	N	N	N	Y	N	Y	Y	Y
3 ***Bliley***	Y	Y	Y	Y	Y	N	N	N
4 Sisisky	N	N	N	Y	N	Y	Y	Y
5 Payne	N	N	N	Y	Y	Y	Y	Y
6 Olin	?	N	N	Y	N	Y	Y	Y
7 ***Slaughter***	Y	Y	Y	Y	Y	Y	N	N
8 Moran	Y	N	N	Y	Y	Y	Y	Y
9 Boucher	N	N	N	Y	N	Y	Y	Y
10 ***Wolf***	Y	N	Y	Y	Y	N	N	N
WASHINGTON								
1 ***Miller***	N	N	Y	Y	Y	N	N	N
2 Swift	N	N	N	Y	Y	Y	Y	Y
3 Unsoeld	N	N	N	Y	?	Y	Y	Y
4 ***Morrison***	N	N	N	Y	N	?	N	N
5 Foley								
6 Dicks	N	N	N	Y	N	Y	Y	Y
7 McDermott	N	N	N	Y	N	Y	Y	Y
8 ***Chandler***	Y	N	Y	Y	Y	?	?	?
WEST VIRGINIA								
1 Mollohan	N	N	N	Y	Y	?	?	?
2 Staggers	N	N	N	Y	Y	Y	Y	Y
3 Wise	N	N	N	Y	?	Y	Y	Y
4 Rahall	N	N	N	Y	-	Y	Y	Y
WISCONSIN								
1 Aspin	N	N	N	Y	N	Y	Y	Y
2 ***Klug***	Y	Y	Y	N	N	Y	N	N
3 ***Gunderson***	Y	N	Y	Y	Y	N	N	N
4 Kleczka	N	X	?	Y	Y	Y	Y	Y
5 Moody	N	N	N	Y	Y	Y	Y	Y
6 ***Petri***	N	Y	Y	N	Y	Y	N	N
7 Obey	N	N	N	Y	N	Y	Y	Y
8 ***Roth***	Y	Y	Y	N	Y	N	N	N
9 ***Sensenbrenner***	N	Y	Y	N	Y	N	N	N
WYOMING								
AL ***Thomas***	Y	Y	Y	N	?	N	N	N

Southern states - Ala., Ark., Fla., Ga., Ky., La., Miss., N.C., Okla., S.C., Tenn., Texas, Va.
Omitted votes are quorum calls, which CQ does not include in its vote charts.

HOUSE VOTES 159, 160, 161, 162, 163, 164, 165, 166

159. HR 2622. Fiscal 1992 Treasury-Postal Appropriations/Tax Examination. Obey, D-Wis., amendment to provide that any funds in excess of the amount used in fiscal 1991 for the information reporting program of the Internal Revenue Service shall be used for examination of the tax returns of high-income and high-asset taxpayers. Adopted 411-1: R 157-1; D 253-0 (ND 171-0, SD 82-0); I 1-0; June 18, 1991.

160. HR 2622. Fiscal 1992 Treasury-Postal Appropriations/Internal Revenue Service Transfers. Roybal, D-Calif., amendment to prohibit the transfer of funds in excess of 4 percent between the accounts of the Internal Revenue Service. Adopted 411-0: R 158-0; D 252-0 (ND 169-0, SD 83-0); I 1-0; June 18, 1991.

161. HR 2622. Fiscal 1992 Treasury-Postal Appropriations/Secret Service. Roybal, D-Calif., amendment to appropriate $475,423,000 for the necessary expenses of the United States Secret Service, including purchasing and hiring passenger motor vehicles and hiring aircraft, of which no more than $12,500 could be used for official reception and representation expenses. Adopted 412-0: R 160-0; D 251-0 (ND 169-0, SD 82-0); I 1-0; June 18, 1991.

162. HR 2622. Fiscal 1992 Treasury-Postal Appropriations/Vice President's Residence. Roybal, D-Calif., amendment to appropriate $324,000 for the care, maintenance and improvement of the official residence of the vice president and hiring passenger motor vehicles, of which no more than $90,000 could be used for official entertainment expenses of the vice president. Adopted 397-15: R 160-0; D 236-15 (ND 158-11, SD 78-4); I 1-0; June 18, 1991.

163. HR 2622. Fiscal 1992 Treasury-Postal Appropriations/Chief Financial Officers. Conyers, D-Mich., amendment to strike the provisions in the bill that prohibit the use of funds for the implementation of the Chief Financial Officers Act of 1990. Adopted 341-52: R 153-0; D 187-52 (ND 135-29, SD 52-23); I 1-0, June 18, 1991.

164. HR 2622. Fiscal 1992 Treasury-Postal Appropriations/Passage. Passage of the bill to provide new budget authority for the Treasury Department, the U.S. Postal Service, the Executive Office of the President, and certain independent agencies for fiscal 1992. Before House floor consideration the committee recommended $19,747,595,000 in new budget authority. The administration requested $19,988,560,000. Passed 349-48: R 109-44; D 239-4 (ND 160-3, SD 79-1); I 1-0, June 18, 1991.

165. Procedural Motion. Russo, D-Ill., motion to approve the House Journal of Tuesday, June 18. Motion agreed to 291-110: R 47-104; D 243-6 (ND 166-5, SD 77-1); I 1-0, June 19, 1991.

166. HR 2508. Fiscal 1992-93 Foreign Aid Authorization/Grant Defense Equipment to States. McCollum, R-Fla., amendment to the Taylor, D-Miss., amendment, to allow the president to waive the requirement in the Taylor amendment to grant non-lethal excess defense construction equipment to state governments if the president determines it is in the national interest or is needed for humanitarian purposes. Rejected 150-267: R 145-15; D 5-251 (ND 4-170, SD 1-81); 0-1, June 19, 1991. (Subsequently, the Taylor amendment was adopted by voice vote.)

KEY

- Y Voted for (yea).
- # Paired for.
- + Announced for.
- N Voted against (nay).
- X Paired against.
- \- Announced against.
- P Voted "present."
- C Voted "present" to avoid possible conflict of interest.
- ? Did not vote or otherwise make a position known.

Democrats ***Republicans***
Independent

	159	160	161	162	163	164	165	166
ALABAMA								
1 ***Callahan***	Y	Y	Y	Y	Y	Y	Y	Y
2 ***Dickinson***	Y	Y	Y	Y	Y	N	N	Y
3 Browder	Y	Y	Y	Y	Y	Y	Y	N
4 Bevill	Y	Y	Y	Y	N	Y	Y	N
5 Cramer	Y	Y	Y	Y	Y	Y	Y	N
6 Erdreich	Y	Y	Y	Y	Y	Y	Y	N
7 Harris	Y	Y	Y	Y	Y	Y	Y	N
ALASKA								
AL ***Young***	Y	Y	Y	Y	?	?	?	Y
ARIZONA								
1 ***Rhodes***	Y	Y	Y	Y	Y	Y	N	Y
2 Vacancy								
3 ***Stump***	Y	Y	Y	Y	Y	N	N	Y
4 ***Kyl***	Y	Y	Y	Y	Y	N	N	Y
5 ***Kolbe***	Y	Y	Y	Y	Y	Y	N	Y
ARKANSAS								
1 Alexander	Y	Y	Y	Y	N	Y	Y	N
2 Thornton	Y	Y	Y	Y	N	Y	Y	N
3 ***Hammerschmidt***	Y	Y	Y	Y	Y	Y	Y	Y
4 Anthony	Y	Y	Y	Y	Y	Y	Y	N
CALIFORNIA								
1 ***Riggs***	Y	Y	Y	Y	Y	Y	N	Y
2 ***Herger***	Y	Y	Y	Y	Y	Y	N	Y
3 Matsui	Y	?	Y	Y	?	?	Y	N
4 Fazio	Y	Y	Y	?	N	Y	Y	N
5 Pelosi	Y	Y	Y	Y	N	Y	Y	N
6 Boxer	Y	Y	Y	Y	Y	Y	Y	N
7 Miller	Y	Y	Y	Y	Y	Y	Y	N
8 Dellums	Y	Y	Y	Y	Y	Y	Y	N
9 Stark	Y	Y	Y	Y	Y	Y	Y	N
10 Edwards	Y	Y	Y	Y	Y	Y	Y	N
11 Lantos	Y	Y	Y	Y	Y	Y	Y	N
12 ***Campbell***	Y	Y	Y	Y	Y	Y	N	Y
13 Mineta	Y	Y	Y	Y	Y	Y	Y	N
14 ***Doolittle***	Y	Y	Y	Y	Y	N	N	Y
15 Condit	Y	Y	Y	Y	Y	Y	?	?
16 Panetta	Y	Y	Y	Y	Y	Y	Y	N
17 Dooley	Y	Y	Y	Y	Y	Y	Y	N
18 Lehman	Y	Y	Y	Y	Y	Y	Y	N
19 ***Lagomarsino***	Y	Y	Y	Y	Y	N	N	Y
20 ***Thomas***	Y	Y	Y	Y	Y	Y	N	Y
21 ***Gallegly***	Y	Y	Y	Y	Y	N	?	Y
22 ***Moorhead***	Y	Y	Y	Y	Y	N	N	Y
23 Beilenson	Y	Y	Y	Y	Y	Y	Y	N
24 Waxman	Y	Y	Y	Y	Y	Y	Y	N
25 Roybal	Y	Y	Y	Y	N	Y	Y	N
26 Berman	Y	Y	Y	Y	Y	?	Y	N
27 Levine	?	?	?	?	?	?	?	?
28 Dixon	Y	Y	Y	Y	?	Y	Y	N
29 Waters	Y	Y	Y	N	Y	Y	Y	N
30 Martinez	Y	Y	Y	Y	Y	Y	Y	N
31 Dymally	?	Y	Y	Y	Y	Y	Y	N
32 Anderson	Y	Y	Y	Y	Y	Y	Y	N
33 ***Dreier***	Y	Y	Y	Y	Y	N	N	Y
34 Torres	Y	Y	Y	Y	Y	+	Y	N
35 ***Lewis***	Y	Y	Y	Y	Y	Y	?	Y
36 Brown	Y	Y	Y	Y	Y	Y	Y	N
37 ***McCandless***	Y	Y	Y	Y	Y	Y	N	Y
38 ***Dornan***	Y	Y	Y	Y	Y	N	N	Y
39 ***Dannemeyer***	Y	Y	Y	Y	Y	N	N	Y
40 ***Cox***	Y	Y	Y	Y	Y	N	Y	Y
41 ***Lowery***	Y	Y	Y	Y	Y	Y	N	?
42 ***Rohrabacher***	Y	Y	Y	Y	Y	N	N	Y
43 ***Packard***	Y	Y	Y	Y	Y	N	N	Y
44 ***Cunningham***	Y	Y	Y	Y	Y	Y	N	Y
45 ***Hunter***	Y	Y	Y	Y	Y	N	?	Y
COLORADO								
1 Schroeder	Y	Y	Y	N	Y	Y	N	N
2 Skaggs	Y	Y	Y	Y	N	Y	Y	N
3 Campbell	Y	Y	Y	Y	Y	Y	Y	Y
4 ***Allard***	Y	Y	Y	Y	Y	Y	N	Y
5 ***Hefley***	Y	Y	Y	Y	Y	N	N	Y
6 ***Schaefer***	Y	Y	Y	Y	Y	N	N	Y
CONNECTICUT								
1 Kennelly	Y	Y	Y	Y	Y	Y	Y	N
2 Gejdenson	Y	Y	Y	Y	Y	Y	Y	N
3 DeLauro	Y	Y	Y	Y	Y	Y	Y	N
4 ***Shays***	Y	Y	Y	Y	Y	N	N	Y
5 ***Franks***	Y	Y	Y	Y	Y	Y	N	Y
6 ***Johnson***	Y	Y	Y	Y	Y	Y	Y	Y
DELAWARE								
AL Carper	Y	Y	Y	Y	Y	Y	Y	N
FLORIDA								
1 Hutto	Y	Y	Y	Y	Y	Y	Y	N
2 Peterson	Y	Y	Y	Y	?	Y	Y	N
3 Bennett	Y	Y	Y	N	Y	Y	Y	N
4 ***James***	Y	Y	Y	Y	Y	Y	N	Y
5 ***McCollum***	Y	Y	Y	Y	Y	Y	N	Y
6 ***Stearns***	Y	Y	Y	Y	Y	Y	N	Y
7 Gibbons	Y	Y	Y	Y	Y	Y	Y	Y
8 ***Young***	Y	Y	Y	Y	Y	Y	N	Y
9 ***Bilirakis***	Y	Y	Y	Y	Y	Y	N	N
10 ***Ireland***	Y	Y	Y	Y	?	?	N	Y
11 Bacchus	Y	Y	Y	Y	Y	Y	Y	N
12 ***Lewis***	Y	Y	Y	Y	Y	N	N	Y
13 ***Goss***	Y	Y	Y	Y	Y	N	N	Y
14 Johnston	Y	Y	Y	Y	Y	Y	Y	N
15 ***Shaw***	Y	Y	Y	Y	Y	Y	Y	Y
16 Smith	Y	Y	Y	Y	?	Y	Y	N
17 Lehman	Y	Y	Y	?	?	?	Y	N
18 ***Ros-Lehtinen***	Y	Y	Y	Y	Y	Y	N	Y
19 Fascell	Y	Y	Y	Y	N	Y	Y	N
GEORGIA								
1 Thomas	Y	Y	Y	Y	N	Y	Y	N
2 Hatcher	Y	Y	Y	Y	Y	Y	?	N
3 Ray	Y	Y	Y	Y	Y	Y	Y	N
4 Jones	Y	Y	Y	Y	Y	Y	N	N
5 Lewis	Y	Y	Y	Y	Y	Y	Y	N
6 ***Gingrich***	Y	Y	Y	Y	Y	Y	?	Y
7 Darden	Y	Y	Y	Y	Y	Y	Y	N
8 Rowland	Y	Y	Y	Y	Y	Y	Y	N
9 Jenkins	Y	Y	Y	Y	Y	Y	Y	N
10 Barnard	Y	Y	Y	Y	Y	Y	Y	N
HAWAII								
1 Abercrombie	Y	Y	Y	Y	N	Y	Y	N
2 Mink	Y	Y	Y	Y	Y	Y	Y	N
IDAHO								
1 LaRocco	Y	Y	Y	Y	Y	Y	Y	N
2 Stallings	Y	Y	Y	Y	Y	Y	Y	N
ILLINOIS								
1 Hayes	Y	Y	Y	Y	Y	Y	Y	N
2 Savage	Y	Y	Y	N	Y	Y	?	N
3 Russo	Y	Y	Y	Y	Y	Y	Y	N
4 Sangmeister	Y	Y	Y	Y	Y	Y	Y	N
5 Lipinski	Y	Y	Y	Y	Y	Y	Y	N
6 ***Hyde***	Y	Y	Y	Y	Y	Y	Y	Y
7 Collins	Y	Y	Y	Y	Y	Y	Y	N
8 Rostenkowski	Y	Y	Y	Y	Y	Y	Y	N
9 Yates	Y	Y	Y	Y	?	?	Y	N
10 ***Porter***	Y	Y	Y	Y	Y	Y	Y	Y
11 Annunzio	Y	Y	Y	Y	Y	Y	Y	N
12 ***Crane***	N	Y	Y	Y	Y	N	N	Y
13 ***Fawell***	Y	Y	Y	Y	Y	Y	N	Y
14 ***Hastert***	Y	Y	Y	Y	Y	Y	N	Y
15 Vacancy								
16 Cox	Y	Y	Y	Y	Y	Y	Y	N
17 Evans	Y	Y	Y	Y	Y	Y	Y	N
18 ***Michel***	Y	Y	Y	Y	Y	Y	?	Y
19 Bruce	Y	Y	Y	Y	Y	Y	Y	N
20 Durbin	Y	Y	Y	Y	N	Y	Y	N
21 Costello	Y	Y	Y	Y	Y	Y	Y	N
22 Poshard	Y	Y	Y	Y	Y	Y	Y	N
INDIANA								
1 Visclosky	Y	Y	Y	Y	N	Y	Y	N
2 Sharp	Y	Y	Y	Y	Y	Y	Y	N
3 Roemer	Y	Y	Y	Y	Y	Y	Y	N

ND Northern Democrats SD Southern Democrats

	159	160	161	162	163	164	165	166
4 Long	Y	Y	Y	Y	Y	Y	Y	N
5 Jontz	Y	Y	Y	Y	N	Y	Y	N
6 ***Burton***	Y	Y	Y	Y	Y	N	N	Y
7 ***Myers***	Y	Y	Y	Y	Y	Y	Y	Y
8 McCloskey	Y	Y	Y	Y	N	Y	Y	N
9 Hamilton	Y	Y	Y	Y	Y	Y	Y	N
10 Jacobs	Y	Y	Y	N	Y	N	N	N
IOWA								
1 ***Leach***	Y	Y	Y	Y	Y	Y	N	Y
2 ***Nussle***	Y	Y	Y	Y	Y	Y	N	Y
3 Nagle	Y	?	Y	Y	N	Y	Y	N
4 Smith	Y	Y	Y	N	N	Y	Y	N
5 ***Lightfoot***	Y	Y	Y	Y	Y	Y	N	Y
6 ***Grandy***	Y	Y	Y	Y	Y	Y	N	Y
KANSAS								
1 ***Roberts***	Y	?	Y	Y	Y	N	N	Y
2 Slattery	Y	Y	?	Y	Y	N	Y	N
3 ***Meyers***	Y	Y	Y	Y	Y	Y	N	Y
4 Glickman	Y	Y	Y	Y	Y	Y	Y	N
5 ***Nichols***	Y	Y	Y	Y	Y	Y	Y	Y
KENTUCKY								
1 Hubbard	?	?	?	?	?	?	Y	N
2 Natcher	Y	Y	Y	Y	N	Y	Y	N
3 Mazzoli	Y	Y	Y	Y	Y	Y	Y	N
4 ***Bunning***	Y	Y	Y	Y	Y	N	N	Y
5 ***Rogers***	Y	Y	Y	Y	?	?	N	Y
6 ***Hopkins***	?	?	?	?	?	?	?	?
7 Perkins	Y	Y	Y	Y	N	Y	Y	N
LOUISIANA								
1 ***Livingston***	Y	Y	Y	Y	Y	Y	Y	Y
2 Jefferson	Y	Y	Y	Y	N	Y	?	N
3 Tauzin	Y	Y	Y	Y	Y	Y	Y	N
4 ***McCrery***	Y	Y	Y	Y	Y	Y	N	Y
5 Huckaby	Y	Y	Y	Y	Y	Y	Y	N
6 ***Baker***	Y	Y	Y	Y	Y	Y	N	Y
7 Hayes	Y	Y	Y	Y	Y	Y	Y	N
8 ***Holloway***	Y	Y	Y	Y	Y	Y	Y	N
MAINE								
1 Andrews	Y	Y	Y	Y	Y	Y	Y	N
2 ***Snowe***	Y	Y	Y	Y	Y	Y	Y	Y
MARYLAND								
1 ***Gilchrest***	Y	Y	Y	Y	?	?	?	Y
2 ***Bentley***	Y	Y	?	Y	Y	Y	N	N
3 Cardin	Y	Y	Y	Y	Y	Y	Y	N
4 McMillen	Y	Y	Y	Y	Y	Y	Y	N
5 Hoyer	Y	Y	Y	Y	N	Y	Y	N
6 Byron	Y	Y	Y	Y	Y	Y	Y	N
7 Mfume	Y	Y	Y	Y	Y	Y	Y	N
8 ***Morella***	Y	Y	Y	Y	Y	Y	Y	Y
MASSACHUSETTS								
1 Olver	Y	Y	Y	Y	Y	Y	Y	N
2 Neal	Y	Y	Y	Y	Y	Y	Y	N
3 Early	Y	Y	Y	Y	N	Y	Y	N
4 Frank	Y	Y	Y	Y	Y	Y	Y	N
5 Atkins	Y	Y	Y	Y	N	Y	Y	N
6 Mavroules	Y	Y	Y	Y	Y	Y	Y	N
7 Markey	Y	Y	Y	Y	Y	Y	Y	N
8 Kennedy	Y	Y	Y	Y	Y	Y	Y	N
9 Moakley	Y	Y	Y	Y	Y	Y	Y	N
10 Studds	Y	Y	Y	Y	Y	Y	Y	N
11 Donnelly	Y	Y	Y	Y	Y	Y	Y	N
MICHIGAN								
1 Conyers	Y	Y	Y	Y	Y	Y	?	?
2 ***Pursell***	Y	?	Y	Y	Y	Y	Y	?
3 Wolpe	Y	Y	Y	Y	Y	Y	Y	N
4 ***Upton***	Y	Y	Y	Y	Y	Y	N	Y
5 ***Henry***	Y	Y	Y	Y	Y	N	N	Y
6 Carr	Y	Y	Y	Y	N	Y	Y	N
7 Kildee	Y	Y	Y	Y	Y	Y	Y	N
8 Traxler	Y	Y	Y	N	N	Y	Y	N
9 ***Vander Jagt***	Y	Y	Y	Y	Y	Y	?	Y
10 ***Camp***	Y	Y	Y	Y	Y	Y	N	Y
11 ***Davis***	Y	Y	Y	Y	Y	Y	Y	Y
12 Bonior	Y	Y	Y	Y	Y	Y	Y	N
13 Collins	Y	Y	Y	Y	Y	Y	Y	N
14 Hertel	Y	Y	?	Y	Y	Y	Y	N
15 Ford	Y	Y	Y	Y	Y	Y	Y	Y
16 Dingell	Y	Y	Y	Y	?	?	Y	N
17 Levin	Y	Y	Y	Y	Y	Y	Y	N
18 ***Broomfield***	Y	Y	Y	Y	Y	Y	Y	Y
MINNESOTA								
1 Penny	Y	Y	Y	N	Y	Y	Y	N
2 ***Weber***	Y	Y	Y	Y	Y	Y	?	Y
3 ***Ramstad***	Y	Y	Y	Y	Y	Y	N	Y
4 Vento	Y	Y	Y	Y	Y	Y	Y	N

	159	160	161	162	163	164	165	166
5 Sabo	Y	Y	Y	Y	N	Y	Y	N
6 Sikorski	Y	Y	Y	Y	Y	Y	N	N
7 Peterson	Y	Y	Y	Y	Y	Y	Y	N
8 Oberstar	?	?	?	?	?	?	?	?
MISSISSIPPI								
1 Whitten	Y	Y	Y	Y	N	Y	Y	N
2 Espy	Y	Y	Y	Y	N	Y	Y	N
3 Montgomery	Y	Y	Y	Y	N	Y	Y	N
4 Parker	Y	Y	Y	Y	N	Y	Y	N
5 Taylor	Y	Y	Y	N	N	Y	Y	N
MISSOURI								
1 Clay	Y	Y	Y	?	?	?	N	N
2 Horn	Y	Y	Y	Y	Y	Y	Y	N
3 Gephardt	Y	Y	Y	Y	Y	Y	?	N
4 Skelton	Y	Y	Y	Y	Y	Y	Y	N
5 Wheat	Y	Y	Y	Y	Y	Y	Y	N
6 ***Coleman***	Y	Y	Y	Y	Y	Y	N	Y
7 ***Hancock***	Y	Y	Y	Y	Y	N	N	Y
8 ***Emerson***	Y	Y	Y	Y	Y	Y	Y	N
9 Volkmer	Y	Y	Y	Y	Y	Y	Y	N
MONTANA								
1 Williams	Y	Y	Y	N	?	?	Y	N
2 ***Marlenee***	Y	Y	Y	Y	Y	N	N	Y
NEBRASKA								
1 ***Bereuter***	Y	Y	Y	Y	Y	Y	N	Y
2 Hoagland	Y	Y	Y	Y	Y	Y	Y	N
3 ***Barrett***	Y	Y	Y	Y	Y	Y	N	Y
NEVADA								
1 Bilbray	?	?	?	?	?	?	Y	N
2 ***Vucanovich***	Y	Y	Y	Y	Y	Y	N	Y
NEW HAMPSHIRE								
1 ***Zeliff***	Y	Y	Y	Y	Y	Y	N	Y
2 Swett	Y	Y	Y	Y	Y	Y	Y	N
NEW JERSEY								
1 Andrews	Y	Y	Y	Y	N	Y	Y	Y
2 Hughes	Y	Y	Y	Y	Y	Y	Y	N
3 Pallone	Y	Y	Y	Y	Y	N	Y	N
4 ***Smith***	Y	Y	Y	Y	Y	Y	Y	Y
5 ***Roukema***	?	?	Y	Y	Y	Y	N	Y
6 Dwyer	?	?	?	?	?	?	Y	N
7 ***Rinaldo***	Y	Y	Y	Y	Y	Y	Y	Y
8 Roe	Y	Y	Y	Y	Y	Y	Y	N
9 Torricelli	Y	Y	Y	Y	Y	Y	Y	N
10 Payne	Y	Y	Y	Y	Y	Y	Y	N
11 ***Gallo***	Y	Y	Y	Y	Y	Y	N	Y
12 ***Zimmer***	Y	Y	Y	Y	Y	N	N	Y
13 ***Saxton***	Y	Y	Y	Y	Y	Y	N	Y
14 Guarini	Y	Y	Y	Y	Y	Y	Y	N
NEW MEXICO								
1 ***Schiff***	Y	Y	Y	Y	Y	Y	Y	Y
2 ***Skeen***	Y	Y	Y	Y	Y	Y	Y	Y
3 Richardson	Y	Y	Y	Y	Y	Y	Y	N
NEW YORK								
1 Hochbrueckner	Y	Y	Y	Y	Y	Y	Y	N
2 Downey	Y	Y	Y	Y	Y	Y	Y	N
3 Mrazek	?	?	?	?	?	?	?	?
4 ***Lent***	Y	Y	Y	Y	Y	Y	Y	Y
5 ***McGrath***	?	Y	Y	Y	Y	Y	Y	Y
6 Flake	Y	Y	Y	Y	Y	Y	Y	N
7 Ackerman	Y	Y	Y	Y	Y	Y	Y	N
8 Scheuer	Y	Y	Y	Y	Y	Y	Y	N
9 Manton	Y	Y	Y	Y	Y	Y	Y	N
10 Schumer	Y	Y	Y	+	+	+	?	?
11 Towns	Y	Y	Y	Y	Y	Y	Y	N
12 Owens	Y	Y	Y	Y	Y	Y	Y	N
13 Solarz	Y	Y	Y	Y	Y	Y	Y	Y
14 ***Molinari***	Y	Y	Y	Y	?	?	N	Y
15 ***Green***	Y	Y	Y	Y	Y	Y	Y	Y
16 Rangel	Y	Y	Y	Y	Y	Y	Y	N
17 Weiss	Y	Y	+	Y	Y	Y	Y	N
18 Serrano	?	?	?	?	?	?	?	?
19 Engel	Y	?	Y	Y	Y	Y	Y	N
20 Lowey	Y	Y	Y	Y	N	Y	Y	N
21 ***Fish***	Y	Y	Y	Y	Y	Y	Y	Y
22 ***Gilman***	Y	Y	Y	Y	Y	Y	Y	Y
23 McNulty	Y	Y	Y	Y	Y	Y	Y	N
24 ***Solomon***	Y	Y	Y	Y	Y	Y	N	N
25 ***Boehlert***	Y	Y	Y	Y	Y	Y	N	Y
26 ***Martin***	Y	Y	Y	Y	?	?	N	Y
27 ***Walsh***	Y	Y	Y	Y	Y	Y	Y	Y
28 McHugh	Y	Y	Y	Y	N	Y	Y	N
29 ***Horton***	Y	Y	Y	Y	Y	Y	Y	Y
30 Slaughter	Y	Y	Y	Y	Y	Y	Y	N
31 ***Paxon***	Y	Y	Y	Y	?	?	N	Y

	159	160	161	162	163	164	165	166
32 LaFalce	?	Y	Y	Y	Y	Y	Y	N
33 Nowak	Y	Y	Y	Y	Y	Y	Y	N
34 ***Houghton***	Y	Y	Y	Y	Y	Y	Y	Y
NORTH CAROLINA								
1 Jones	Y	Y	Y	Y	?	?	Y	N
2 Valentine	Y	Y	Y	Y	Y	Y	Y	N
3 Lancaster	Y	Y	Y	Y	Y	Y	?	N
4 Price	Y	Y	Y	Y	N	Y	Y	N
5 Neal	Y	Y	?	Y	?	N	Y	N
6 ***Coble***	Y	Y	Y	Y	Y	Y	N	Y
7 Rose	Y	Y	Y	Y	Y	Y	?	?
8 Hefner	Y	Y	Y	Y	N	Y	Y	N
9 ***McMillan***	Y	Y	Y	Y	Y	Y	N	Y
10 ***Ballenger***	Y	Y	Y	Y	Y	Y	N	Y
11 ***Taylor***	Y	Y	Y	Y	Y	Y	P	Y
NORTH DAKOTA								
AL Dorgan	Y	Y	Y	Y	Y	Y	Y	N
OHIO								
1 Luken	Y	Y	Y	Y	Y	Y	Y	N
2 ***Gradison***	Y	Y	Y	Y	Y	Y	Y	Y
3 Hall	Y	Y	Y	Y	Y	Y	Y	N
4 ***Oxley***	Y	Y	Y	Y	Y	N	Y	Y
5 ***Gillmor***	Y	Y	Y	Y	Y	Y	Y	Y
6 ***McEwen***	Y	Y	Y	Y	Y	N	Y	Y
7 ***Hobson***	Y	Y	Y	Y	Y	Y	N	Y
8 ***Boehner***	Y	Y	Y	Y	Y	Y	N	Y
9 Kaptur	Y	Y	?	Y	N	Y	Y	N
10 ***Miller***	Y	Y	Y	Y	Y	N	N	Y
11 Eckart	Y	Y	Y	Y	Y	Y	Y	N
12 ***Kasich***	Y	Y	Y	Y	Y	N	Y	N
13 Pease	Y	Y	Y	Y	Y	Y	Y	N
14 Sawyer	Y	Y	Y	Y	Y	Y	Y	N
15 ***Wylie***	Y	Y	Y	?	Y	Y	Y	Y
16 ***Regula***	Y	Y	Y	Y	Y	Y	N	N
17 Traficant	Y	Y	Y	N	Y	Y	Y	N
18 Applegate	Y	Y	Y	N	Y	Y	Y	N
19 Feighan	Y	Y	Y	Y	Y	Y	Y	N
20 Oakar	Y	Y	Y	Y	Y	Y	Y	N
21 Stokes	Y	Y	Y	Y	Y	Y	Y	N
OKLAHOMA								
1 ***Inhofe***	Y	Y	Y	Y	Y	Y	N	Y
2 Synar	Y	Y	Y	Y	Y	Y	Y	N
3 Brewster	Y	Y	Y	Y	Y	Y	Y	N
4 McCurdy	Y	Y	Y	Y	Y	Y	Y	N
5 ***Edwards***	Y	Y	Y	Y	Y	Y	?	Y
6 English	Y	Y	Y	Y	Y	Y	Y	N
OREGON								
1 AuCoin	?	?	?	?	?	?	Y	N
2 ***Smith***	Y	Y	Y	Y	Y	Y	N	Y
3 Wyden	Y	Y	Y	Y	Y	Y	Y	N
4 DeFazio	Y	?	Y	Y	N	Y	Y	N
5 Kopetski	Y	Y	Y	Y	N	Y	Y	N
PENNSYLVANIA								
1 Foglietta	Y	Y	Y	Y	Y	Y	Y	N
2 Gray	?	?	?	?	?	?	Y	N
3 Borski	Y	Y	Y	Y	Y	Y	Y	N
4 Kolter	Y	Y	Y	Y	N	Y	Y	N
5 ***Schulze***	Y	Y	Y	Y	Y	Y	Y	Y
6 Yatron	Y	Y	Y	Y	Y	Y	Y	N
7 ***Weldon***	Y	Y	Y	Y	+	+	-	+
8 Kostmayer	Y	Y	Y	Y	Y	Y	Y	N
9 ***Shuster***	Y	Y	Y	Y	Y	N	Y	Y
10 ***McDade***	?	?	?	?	?	?	N	Y
11 Kanjorski	Y	Y	Y	Y	Y	Y	Y	N
12 Murtha	Y	Y	Y	Y	N	Y	Y	N
13 ***Coughlin***	Y	Y	Y	Y	Y	Y	N	Y
14 Coyne	Y	Y	Y	Y	N	Y	Y	N
15 ***Ritter***	Y	Y	Y	Y	Y	Y	Y	N
16 ***Walker***	Y	Y	Y	Y	Y	N	N	Y
17 ***Gekas***	Y	Y	Y	Y	Y	N	N	Y
18 ***Santorum***	Y	Y	Y	Y	Y	N	N	Y
19 ***Goodling***	Y	Y	Y	Y	Y	Y	N	Y
20 Gaydos	Y	Y	Y	Y	?	?	Y	N
21 ***Ridge***	Y	Y	Y	Y	Y	Y	N	N
22 Murphy	Y	Y	Y	N	Y	Y	N	N
23 ***Clinger***	?	Y	Y	Y	Y	Y	N	Y
RHODE ISLAND								
1 ***Machtley***	Y	Y	Y	Y	Y	Y	N	N
2 Reed	Y	Y	Y	Y	Y	Y	Y	N
SOUTH CAROLINA								
1 ***Ravenel***	Y	Y	Y	Y	Y	Y	Y	Y
2 ***Spence***	?	?	?	?	?	?	?	?
3 Derrick	?	Y	Y	Y	Y	Y	Y	N
4 Patterson	Y	Y	Y	Y	Y	Y	Y	N
5 Spratt	Y	Y	Y	Y	Y	Y	Y	N
6 Tallon	Y	Y	Y	Y	Y	Y	Y	N

	159	160	161	162	163	164	165	166
SOUTH DAKOTA								
AL Johnson	Y	Y	Y	Y	Y	Y	Y	N
TENNESSEE								
1 ***Quillen***	Y	Y	Y	Y	Y	Y	N	N
2 ***Duncan***	Y	Y	Y	Y	Y	Y	N	N
3 Lloyd	?	?	?	?	?	?	?	?
4 Cooper	Y	Y	Y	Y	Y	Y	Y	N
5 Clement	Y	Y	Y	Y	Y	Y	Y	N
6 Gordon	Y	Y	Y	Y	?	?	Y	N
7 ***Sundquist***	Y	Y	Y	Y	Y	Y	N	Y
8 Tanner	Y	Y	Y	Y	Y	Y	Y	N
9 Ford	Y	Y	Y	Y	Y	Y	?	N
TEXAS								
1 Chapman	Y	Y	Y	Y	N	Y	Y	N
2 Wilson	Y	Y	Y	Y	Y	Y	?	N
3 ***Johnson***	Y	Y	Y	Y	Y	Y	Y	Y
4 Hall	Y	Y	Y	Y	Y	Y	Y	N
5 Bryant	Y	Y	Y	Y	N	Y	Y	N
6 ***Barton***	Y	Y	Y	Y	Y	N	Y	Y
7 ***Archer***	Y	Y	Y	Y	Y	N	Y	Y
8 ***Fields***	Y	Y	Y	Y	Y	N	N	Y
9 Brooks	Y	Y	Y	Y	N	Y	Y	N
10 Pickle	Y	Y	Y	Y	N	Y	Y	N
11 Edwards	Y	Y	Y	Y	N	Y	Y	N
12 Geren	Y	Y	Y	Y	Y	Y	Y	N
13 Sarpalius	Y	Y	Y	N	Y	Y	Y	N
14 Laughlin	Y	Y	Y	Y	N	Y	Y	N
15 de la Garza	Y	Y	Y	Y	Y	Y	Y	N
16 Coleman	Y	Y	Y	Y	N	Y	Y	N
17 Stenholm	Y	Y	Y	N	Y	Y	Y	N
18 Washington	Y	Y	Y	Y	Y	Y	Y	N
19 ***Combest***	Y	Y	Y	Y	Y	N	Y	Y
20 Gonzalez	Y	Y	Y	Y	Y	Y	Y	N
21 ***Smith***	?	?	?	?	?	?	N	Y
22 ***DeLay***	Y	Y	Y	Y	Y	Y	N	Y
23 Bustamante	Y	Y	Y	Y	Y	Y	Y	N
24 Frost	Y	Y	Y	Y	Y	Y	Y	?
25 Andrews	Y	Y	Y	Y	Y	Y	Y	N
26 ***Armey***	Y	Y	Y	Y	Y	N	N	Y
27 Ortiz	Y	Y	Y	Y	N	Y	Y	N
UTAH								
1 ***Hansen***	Y	Y	Y	Y	Y	N	N	N
2 Owens	Y	Y	Y	Y	Y	Y	Y	N
3 Orton	Y	Y	Y	Y	?	?	Y	N
VERMONT								
AL *Sanders*	Y	Y	Y	Y	Y	Y	Y	N
VIRGINIA								
1 ***Bateman***	Y	Y	Y	Y	Y	Y	Y	Y
2 Pickett	Y	Y	Y	Y	Y	Y	Y	N
3 ***Bliley***	Y	Y	Y	Y	Y	Y	N	Y
4 Sisisky	Y	Y	Y	Y	Y	Y	Y	N
5 Payne	Y	Y	Y	Y	Y	Y	Y	N
6 Olin	Y	Y	Y	Y	Y	Y	Y	N
7 ***Slaughter***	Y	Y	Y	Y	Y	Y	N	Y
8 Moran	Y	Y	Y	Y	+	Y	Y	N
9 Boucher	Y	Y	Y	Y	?	?	Y	N
10 ***Wolf***	Y	Y	Y	Y	Y	Y	N	Y
WASHINGTON								
1 ***Miller***	Y	Y	Y	Y	Y	Y	N	Y
2 Swift	Y	Y	Y	Y	Y	Y	Y	N
3 Unsoeld	Y	Y	Y	Y	Y	Y	Y	N
4 ***Morrison***	Y	Y	Y	Y	Y	Y	Y	N
5 Foley								
6 Dicks	Y	Y	Y	Y	N	Y	Y	N
7 McDermott	Y	Y	Y	Y	Y	Y	Y	N
8 ***Chandler***	Y	Y	Y	Y	Y	Y	N	Y
WEST VIRGINIA								
1 Mollohan	Y	Y	Y	Y	N	Y	Y	N
2 Staggers	Y	Y	Y	Y	Y	Y	Y	N
3 Wise	Y	Y	Y	?	Y	Y	?	N
4 Rahall	Y	Y	Y	Y	Y	Y	Y	N
WISCONSIN								
1 Aspin	Y	Y	Y	Y	Y	Y	Y	N
2 ***Klug***	Y	Y	Y	Y	Y	Y	Y	Y
3 ***Gunderson***	Y	Y	Y	Y	Y	Y	N	Y
4 Kleczka	Y	Y	Y	Y	Y	Y	Y	N
5 Moody	Y	Y	Y	Y	Y	Y	Y	N
6 ***Petri***	Y	Y	Y	Y	Y	N	Y	N
7 Obey	Y	Y	Y	Y	N	Y	Y	N
8 ***Roth***	Y	Y	Y	Y	Y	N	N	Y
9 ***Sensenbrenner***	Y	Y	Y	Y	Y	N	N	Y
WYOMING								
AL ***Thomas***	Y	Y	Y	Y	Y	Y	N	Y

Southern states - Ala., Ark., Fla., Ga., Ky., La., Miss., N.C., Okla., S.C., Tenn., Texas, Va.
Omitted votes are quorum calls, which CQ does not include in its vote charts.

HOUSE VOTES 167, 168, 169, 170, 171, 172, 173, 174

167. HR 2508. Fiscal 1992-93 Foreign Aid Authorization/Unused Funds. Roth, R-Wis., amendment to cancel authority to obligate foreign aid funds that have remained unused after three years except for long-term construction projects and for unforeseen delays in projects. Adopted 216-203: R 134-27; D 82-175 (ND 46-129, SD 36-46); I 0-1, June 19, 1991. A "nay" was a vote supporting the president's position.

168. HR 2508. Fiscal 1992-93 Foreign Aid Authorization/Jordan Aid. Cunningham, R-Calif., amendment to the Burton, R-Ind., amendment, to allow the president to waive the prohibition against aid to Jordan in fiscal 1992 contained in the Burton amendment, if the president certifies that such aid is in the national interest. Adopted 315-105: R 100-61; D 215-44 (ND 158-19, SD 57-25); I 0-0, June 19, 1991. A "yea" was a vote supporting the president's position.

169. HR 2508. Fiscal 1992-93 Foreign Aid Authorization/Jordan Aid-Additional Year. Hamilton, D-Ind., amendment to the Volkmer, D-Mo., substitute amendment to the Burton, R-Ind., amendment, to allow the president to waive the prohibition against aid to Jordan for the additional year that the Volkmer substitute would add to the Burton amendment if the president certifies that such aid is in the national interest. Adopted 289-135: R 78-84; D 210-51 (ND 151-27, SD 59-24); I 1-0, June 19, 1991. (Subsequently, the Volkmer amendment as amended was adopted by voice vote.) A "yea" was a vote for the president's position.

170. HR 2508. Fiscal 1992-93 Foreign Aid Authorization/Jordan Aid-Israel. Miller, R-Wash., amendment to the Volkmer, D-Mo., substitute amendment to the Burton, R-Ind., amendment to also prohibit aid to Jordan, unless Jordan recognizes Israel's right to exist and enters into negotiations with Israel. Adopted 410-8: R 158-1; D 251-7 (ND 171-5, SD 80-2); I 1-0, June 19, 1991. (Subsequently, the Volkmer amendment as amended was adopted by voice vote.) A "nay" was a vote for the president's position.

171. HR 2508. Fiscal 1992-93 Foreign Aid Authorization/Jordan Aid-Fiscal 1992-93. Burton, R-Ind., amendment, as amended, to prohibit aid to Jordan for fiscal 1992-93, unless the president certifies that such aid is in the national interest and Jordan recognizes Israel's right to exist and enters into negotiations with Israel. Adopted 410-4: R 160-0; D 249-4 (ND 169-3, SD 80-1); I 1-0, June 19, 1991. A "nay" was a vote for the president's position.

172. HR 2508. Fiscal 1992-93 Foreign Aid Authorization/Saddam Hussein. Kasich, R-Ohio, amendment to express the belief of Congress that the United States should increase efforts to bring Saddam Hussein to trial for war crimes. Adopted 421-1: R 162-0; D 258-1 (ND 175-1, SD 83-0); I 1-0, June 19, 1991. (Before being adopted, the amendment was amended by a Hamilton, D-Ind., amendment to state that the United States should seek meetings with the United Nations to establish a means of trying Saddam.)

173. HR 2508. Fiscal 1992-93 Foreign Aid Authorization/Israel. Bryant, D-Texas, amendment to withhold $82.5 million of the amount earmarked for Israel in fiscal 1992 from the Economic Support Fund, unless the president certifies that the Israeli government has demonstrated that it is not investing in new and expanded settlements in the West Bank and Gaza Strip. Rejected 44-378: R 10-151; D 33-227 (ND 23-153, SD 10-74); I 1-0, June 19, 1991.

174. HR 2508. Fiscal 1992-93 Foreign Aid Authorization/Yugoslavia. Kleczka, D-Wis., amendment to strike the sense of Congress language that the people of Kosovo province in Yugoslavia should be allowed to have free and fair elections because of the language's specific reference to one side in the ethnic conflict. Adopted 289-127: R 73-88; D 215-39 (ND 142-32, SD 73-7); I 1-0, June 19, 1991.

KEY

- Y Voted for (yea).
- # Paired for.
- + Announced for.
- N Voted against (nay).
- X Paired against.
- - Announced against.
- P Voted "present."
- C Voted "present" to avoid possible conflict of interest.
- ? Did not vote or otherwise make a position known.

Democrats ***Republicans***
Independent

	167	168	169	170	171	172	173	174
ALABAMA								
1 ***Callahan***	Y	N	N	Y	Y	Y	N	Y
2 ***Dickinson***	Y	Y	N	Y	Y	Y	Y	Y
3 Browder	Y	N	N	Y	Y	Y	N	Y
4 Bevill	Y	N	N	Y	Y	Y	N	Y
5 Cramer	Y	N	N	Y	Y	Y	N	Y
6 Erdreich	Y	N	N	Y	Y	Y	N	Y
7 Harris	Y	N	N	Y	Y	Y	N	Y
ALASKA								
AL ***Young***	Y	Y	Y	Y	Y	Y	N	Y
ARIZONA								
1 ***Rhodes***	Y	Y	Y	Y	Y	Y	N	N
2 Vacancy								
3 ***Stump***	Y	N	N	Y	Y	Y	Y	Y
4 ***Kyl***	Y	N	N	Y	Y	Y	N	N
5 ***Kolbe***	Y	Y	Y	Y	Y	Y	N	Y
ARKANSAS								
1 Alexander	N	Y	Y	Y	?	Y	N	Y
2 Thornton	N	Y	Y	Y	Y	Y	N	Y
3 ***Hammerschmidt***	Y	Y	N	Y	Y	Y	N	N
4 Anthony	Y	Y	Y	Y	Y	Y	N	Y
CALIFORNIA								
1 ***Riggs***	Y	Y	Y	Y	Y	Y	Y	N
2 ***Herger***	Y	Y	N	Y	Y	Y	N	N
3 Matsui	N	Y	Y	Y	Y	Y	N	Y
4 Fazio	N	Y	Y	Y	Y	Y	N	Y
5 Pelosi	N	Y	Y	Y	Y	Y	N	Y
6 Boxer	N	Y	Y	Y	Y	Y	N	Y
7 Miller	N	Y	Y	Y	Y	Y	N	Y
8 Dellums	N	Y	Y	Y	Y	Y	Y	Y
9 Stark	?	Y	Y	Y	Y	Y	N	N
10 Edwards	N	Y	Y	Y	Y	Y	N	Y
11 Lantos	N	Y	Y	Y	Y	Y	N	N
12 ***Campbell***	Y	Y	Y	Y	Y	Y	N	N
13 Mineta	N	Y	Y	Y	Y	Y	N	Y
14 ***Doolittle***	Y	N	N	Y	Y	Y	N	N
15 Condit	Y	N	N	Y	Y	Y	N	Y
16 Panetta	N	Y	Y	Y	Y	Y	N	Y
17 Dooley	Y	Y	Y	Y	Y	Y	N	Y
18 Lehman	N	Y	Y	Y	Y	Y	N	Y
19 ***Lagomarsino***	N	Y	Y	Y	Y	Y	N	N
20 ***Thomas***	Y	Y	N	Y	Y	Y	N	N
21 ***Gallegly***	Y	N	N	Y	Y	Y	N	N
22 ***Moorhead***	Y	Y	Y	Y	Y	Y	N	N
23 Beilenson	N	Y	Y	Y	Y	Y	N	Y
24 Waxman	N	Y	Y	Y	?	Y	N	?
25 Roybal	N	Y	Y	Y	Y	Y	N	Y
26 Berman	N	Y	Y	Y	Y	Y	N	Y
27 Levine	?	?	?	?	?	?	?	?
28 Dixon	N	Y	Y	Y	Y	Y	N	Y
29 Waters	N	Y	N	N	Y	Y	Y	Y
30 Martinez	N	Y	Y	Y	Y	Y	N	Y
31 Dymally	N	Y	Y	Y	Y	Y	Y	Y
32 Anderson	N	Y	Y	Y	Y	Y	N	N
33 ***Dreier***	Y	Y	Y	Y	Y	Y	N	N
34 Torres	N	Y	Y	Y	Y	Y	N	Y
35 ***Lewis***	N	Y	Y	Y	Y	Y	N	N
36 Brown	N	Y	Y	Y	Y	Y	N	Y
37 ***McCandless***	Y	Y	Y	Y	Y	Y	N	N
38 ***Dornan***	Y	Y	N	Y	Y	Y	N	Y
39 ***Dannemeyer***	Y	Y	N	Y	Y	Y	N	Y
40 ***Cox***	Y	N	N	Y	Y	Y	N	N
41 ***Lowery***	Y	Y	Y	Y	Y	Y	N	N
42 ***Rohrabacher***	Y	N	N	Y	Y	Y	Y	N
43 ***Packard***	Y	Y	Y	Y	Y	Y	N	Y
44 ***Cunningham***	Y	Y	Y	Y	Y	Y	N	Y
45 ***Hunter***	Y	Y	Y	Y	Y	Y	N	Y
COLORADO								
1 Schroeder	Y	N	N	Y	Y	Y	N	Y
2 Skaggs	N	Y	Y	?	Y	Y	N	Y
3 Campbell	N	Y	Y	Y	Y	Y	N	Y
4 ***Allard***	Y	Y	N	Y	Y	Y	N	Y
5 ***Hefley***	Y	N	N	Y	Y	Y	N	N
6 ***Schaefer***	Y	N	N	Y	Y	Y	N	Y
CONNECTICUT								
1 Kennelly	N	Y	Y	Y	Y	Y	N	Y
2 Gejdenson	N	Y	Y	Y	Y	Y	N	Y
3 DeLauro	N	Y	Y	Y	Y	Y	N	Y
4 ***Shays***	Y	Y	Y	Y	Y	Y	N	N
5 ***Franks***	Y	Y	Y	Y	Y	Y	N	N
6 ***Johnson***	N	Y	Y	Y	Y	Y	N	N
DELAWARE								
AL Carper	N	Y	Y	Y	Y	Y	Y	Y
FLORIDA								
1 Hutto	Y	Y	Y	Y	Y	Y	N	Y
2 Peterson	N	Y	Y	Y	Y	Y	N	Y
3 Bennett	N	Y	Y	Y	Y	Y	Y	Y
4 ***James***	Y	N	N	Y	Y	Y	N	Y
5 ***McCollum***	Y	N	N	Y	Y	Y	N	N
6 ***Stearns***	Y	N	N	Y	Y	Y	N	N
7 Gibbons	N	Y	Y	Y	Y	Y	N	?
8 ***Young***	N	Y	N	Y	Y	Y	N	N
9 ***Bilirakis***	Y	Y	Y	Y	Y	Y	N	Y
10 ***Ireland***	Y	Y	Y	Y	Y	Y	N	N
11 Bacchus	N	N	N	Y	Y	Y	N	Y
12 ***Lewis***	Y	N	N	Y	Y	Y	N	N
13 ***Goss***	N	Y	Y	Y	Y	Y	N	N
14 Johnston	N	Y	Y	Y	Y	Y	N	Y
15 ***Shaw***	Y	Y	Y	Y	Y	Y	N	N
16 Smith	N	Y	Y	Y	Y	Y	N	Y
17 Lehman	N	Y	Y	Y	Y	Y	N	?
18 ***Ros-Lehtinen***	N	N	N	Y	Y	Y	N	N
19 Fascell	N	Y	Y	Y	Y	Y	N	N
GEORGIA								
1 Thomas	N	Y	Y	Y	Y	Y	N	Y
2 Hatcher	N	Y	Y	Y	Y	Y	N	Y
3 Ray	Y	Y	Y	Y	Y	Y	Y	Y
4 Jones	N	N	N	Y	Y	Y	N	N
5 Lewis	N	Y	Y	Y	Y	Y	N	Y
6 ***Gingrich***	Y	Y	N	Y	Y	Y	N	N
7 Darden	N	Y	Y	Y	Y	Y	N	Y
8 Rowland	N	Y	Y	Y	Y	Y	N	Y
9 Jenkins	N	Y	Y	Y	Y	Y	N	Y
10 Barnard	N	Y	Y	Y	Y	Y	N	Y
HAWAII								
1 Abercrombie	N	Y	Y	Y	Y	Y	Y	Y
2 Mink	N	Y	Y	Y	Y	Y	N	Y
IDAHO								
1 LaRocco	Y	Y	Y	Y	Y	Y	N	Y
2 Stallings	N	N	N	Y	Y	Y	N	Y
ILLINOIS								
1 Hayes	N	Y	Y	Y	Y	Y	Y	Y
2 Savage	Y	N	N	N	N	N	Y	Y
3 Russo	Y	Y	Y	Y	Y	Y	N	Y
4 Sangmeister	Y	N	N	Y	Y	Y	N	Y
5 Lipinski	N	Y	Y	Y	Y	Y	Y	N
6 ***Hyde***	Y	Y	Y	Y	Y	Y	N	N
7 Collins	N	Y	Y	Y	Y	Y	N	Y
8 Rostenkowski	N	Y	Y	Y	Y	Y	N	Y
9 Yates	N	Y	Y	Y	Y	Y	N	Y
10 ***Porter***	Y	Y	Y	Y	Y	Y	N	N
11 Annunzio	N	Y	Y	Y	Y	Y	N	Y
12 ***Crane***	Y	N	N	Y	Y	Y	N	Y
13 ***Fawell***	Y	Y	Y	Y	Y	?	?	?
14 ***Hastert***	Y	N	Y	Y	Y	Y	N	N
15 Vacancy								
16 Cox	Y	Y	N	Y	Y	Y	N	Y
17 Evans	Y	N	N	Y	Y	Y	N	Y
18 ***Michel***	N	Y	Y	?	?	Y	N	N
19 Bruce	N	Y	Y	Y	Y	Y	N	Y
20 Durbin	Y	Y	Y	Y	Y	Y	N	Y
21 Costello	Y	N	N	Y	Y	Y	N	Y
22 Poshard	Y	N	N	Y	Y	Y	Y	Y
INDIANA								
1 Visclosky	N	Y	Y	Y	Y	Y	N	Y
2 Sharp	Y	Y	Y	Y	Y	Y	N	Y
3 Roemer	Y	Y	N	Y	Y	Y	N	Y

ND Northern Democrats SD Southern Democrats

	167	168	169	170	171	172	173	174
4 Long	Y	Y	Y	Y	Y	Y	Y	Y
5 Jontz	Y	Y	Y	Y	Y	Y	N	Y
6 ***Burton***	Y	N	N	Y	Y	Y	N	Y
7 ***Myers***	Y	Y	N	Y	Y	Y	N	Y
8 McCloskey	N	Y	Y	Y	Y	Y	Y	Y
9 Hamilton	N	Y	Y	Y	Y	Y	N	Y
10 Jacobs	Y	N	N	Y	Y	Y	N	Y
IOWA								
1 ***Leach***	N	Y	Y	Y	Y	Y	N	N
2 ***Nussle***	Y	Y	Y	Y	Y	Y	N	Y
3 Nagle	N	Y	Y	Y	Y	Y	N	Y
4 Smith	N	Y	Y	Y	Y	Y	N	Y
5 ***Lightfoot***	Y	N	N	Y	Y	Y	N	Y
6 ***Grandy***	Y	Y	N	Y	Y	Y	N	Y
KANSAS								
1 ***Roberts***	Y	Y	Y	Y	Y	Y	N	N
2 Slattery	Y	Y	Y	Y	Y	Y	N	N
3 ***Meyers***	N	Y	Y	Y	Y	Y	N	N
4 Glickman	Y	Y	Y	Y	Y	Y	N	N
5 ***Nichols***	Y	Y	Y	Y	Y	Y	N	N
KENTUCKY								
1 Hubbard	Y	N	N	Y	Y	Y	Y	Y
2 Natcher	N	N	N	Y	Y	Y	N	Y
3 Mazzoli	N	N	N	Y	Y	Y	Y	Y
4 ***Bunning***	Y	N	N	Y	Y	Y	N	N
5 ***Rogers***	Y	Y	Y	Y	Y	Y	N	N
6 ***Hopkins***	?	?	?	?	?	?	?	?
7 Perkins	Y	N	N	Y	Y	Y	N	Y
LOUISIANA								
1 ***Livingston***	Y	Y	Y	?	Y	Y	N	N
2 Jefferson	N	Y	Y	Y	Y	Y	N	Y
3 Tauzin	Y	N	N	Y	Y	Y	N	Y
4 ***McCrery***	N	Y	Y	Y	Y	Y	N	Y
5 Huckaby	Y	Y	?	Y	Y	Y	N	?
6 ***Baker***	Y	Y	Y	?	Y	Y	N	N
7 Hayes	Y	Y	Y	Y	Y	Y	N	Y
8 ***Holloway***	Y	Y	N	Y	Y	Y	N	Y
MAINE								
1 Andrews	N	Y	Y	Y	Y	Y	N	Y
2 ***Snowe***	N	Y	Y	Y	Y	Y	N	N
MARYLAND								
1 ***Gilchrest***	Y	Y	Y	N	Y	Y	N	Y
2 ***Bentley***	Y	N	N	Y	Y	Y	N	Y
3 Cardin	N	Y	Y	Y	Y	Y	N	Y
4 McMillen	N	Y	Y	Y	Y	Y	N	Y
5 Hoyer	N	Y	Y	Y	Y	Y	N	N
6 Byron	Y	Y	Y	Y	Y	Y	N	Y
7 Mfume	N	Y	Y	Y	Y	Y	N	Y
8 ***Morella***	Y	Y	Y	Y	Y	Y	N	Y
MASSACHUSETTS								
1 Olver	N	Y	Y	Y	Y	Y	N	Y
2 Neal	N	Y	N	Y	Y	Y	N	Y
3 Early	Y	N	N	Y	Y	Y	N	Y
4 Frank	N	Y	Y	Y	Y	Y	N	N
5 Atkins	N	Y	Y	Y	Y	Y	N	Y
6 Mavroules	N	Y	Y	Y	?	Y	N	Y
7 Markey	N	Y	Y	Y	Y	Y	N	Y
8 Kennedy	N	Y	Y	Y	Y	Y	N	N
9 Moakley	N	Y	Y	Y	Y	Y	N	Y
10 Studds	N	Y	Y	Y	Y	Y	N	Y
11 Donnelly	N	N	N	Y	Y	Y	N	Y
MICHIGAN								
1 Conyers	N	Y	Y	Y	Y	Y	Y	Y
2 ***Pursell***	?	Y	Y	Y	Y	Y	N	N
3 Wolpe	N	Y	Y	Y	Y	Y	N	Y
4 ***Upton***	Y	N	N	Y	Y	Y	N	N
5 ***Henry***	Y	N	N	Y	Y	Y	N	N
6 Carr	N	Y	Y	Y	Y	Y	N	Y
7 Kildee	N	Y	Y	Y	Y	Y	N	Y
8 Traxler	N	Y	Y	Y	Y	Y	N	?
9 ***Vander Jagt***	Y	N	N	Y	Y	Y	N	Y
10 ***Camp***	Y	Y	Y	Y	Y	Y	N	N
11 ***Davis***	Y	Y	Y	Y	Y	Y	N	Y
12 Bonior	N	Y	Y	Y	Y	Y	Y	N
13 Collins	N	Y	Y	Y	Y	Y	N	Y
14 Hertel	N	Y	Y	Y	Y	Y	N	Y
15 Ford	N	Y	Y	Y	Y	Y	Y	Y
16 Dingell	N	Y	Y	Y	Y	Y	Y	N
17 Levin	N	Y	Y	Y	Y	Y	N	Y
18 ***Broomfield***	N	Y	Y	Y	Y	Y	N	N
MINNESOTA								
1 Penny	N	Y	Y	Y	Y	Y	Y	Y
2 ***Weber***	Y	N	N	Y	Y	Y	N	N
3 ***Ramstad***	Y	N	N	Y	Y	Y	N	N
4 Vento	N	Y	Y	Y	Y	Y	Y	Y
5 Sabo	N	Y	Y	Y	Y	Y	N	Y
6 Sikorski	N	Y	Y	Y	Y	Y	N	Y
7 Peterson	Y	Y	Y	Y	Y	Y	N	Y
8 Oberstar	?	?	?	?	?	?	?	?
MISSISSIPPI								
1 Whitten	N	N	N	Y	Y	Y	N	Y
2 Espy	N	Y	Y	Y	Y	Y	N	Y
3 Montgomery	Y	Y	Y	Y	Y	Y	Y	Y
4 Parker	Y	Y	Y	Y	Y	Y	N	N
5 Taylor	Y	N	Y	Y	Y	Y	Y	Y
MISSOURI								
1 Clay	N	Y	Y	Y	Y	Y	N	Y
2 Horn	Y	Y	Y	Y	Y	Y	N	Y
3 Gephardt	N	Y	Y	Y	Y	Y	N	Y
4 Skelton	N	N	N	Y	Y	Y	N	Y
5 Wheat	N	Y	Y	Y	Y	Y	N	Y
6 ***Coleman***	Y	Y	Y	Y	Y	Y	N	N
7 ***Hancock***	Y	N	N	Y	Y	Y	N	N
8 ***Emerson***	Y	N	N	Y	Y	Y	N	Y
9 Volkmer	Y	N	N	Y	Y	Y	N	Y
MONTANA								
1 Williams	Y	Y	Y	Y	Y	Y	N	Y
2 ***Marlenee***	Y	Y	N	Y	Y	Y	N	Y
NEBRASKA								
1 ***Bereuter***	N	Y	Y	Y	Y	Y	N	Y
2 Hoagland	N	Y	Y	Y	Y	Y	N	N
3 ***Barrett***	Y	?	Y	Y	Y	Y	N	N
NEVADA								
1 Bilbray	N	Y	Y	Y	Y	Y	N	Y
2 ***Vucanovich***	Y	Y	N	Y	Y	Y	N	Y
NEW HAMPSHIRE								
1 ***Zeliff***	Y	Y	Y	Y	Y	Y	N	N
2 Swett	N	Y	N	Y	Y	Y	N	N
NEW JERSEY								
1 Andrews	Y	Y	Y	Y	Y	Y	N	N
2 Hughes	Y	Y	N	Y	Y	Y	N	Y
3 Pallone	Y	Y	Y	Y	Y	Y	N	Y
4 ***Smith***	Y	Y	Y	Y	Y	Y	N	N
5 ***Roukema***	Y	Y	Y	Y	Y	Y	N	N
6 Dwyer	Y	Y	Y	Y	Y	Y	N	Y
7 ***Rinaldo***	Y	Y	N	Y	Y	Y	N	Y
8 Roe	N	Y	Y	Y	Y	Y	N	Y
9 Torricelli	N	Y	Y	Y	Y	?	?	?
10 Payne	N	Y	Y	?	Y	Y	N	Y
11 ***Gallo***	Y	Y	Y	Y	Y	Y	N	N
12 ***Zimmer***	Y	N	N	Y	Y	Y	N	N
13 ***Saxton***	Y	N	N	Y	Y	Y	N	N
14 Guarini	Y	Y	Y	Y	Y	Y	N	Y
NEW MEXICO								
1 ***Schiff***	Y	Y	Y	Y	Y	Y	N	Y
2 ***Skeen***	Y	Y	Y	Y	Y	Y	N	Y
3 Richardson	N	Y	Y	Y	Y	Y	N	Y
NEW YORK								
1 Hochbrueckner	N	Y	Y	Y	Y	Y	N	Y
2 Downey	N	Y	Y	Y	Y	Y	N	Y
3 Mrazek	?	Y	Y	Y	Y	Y	N	Y
4 ***Lent***	N	N	N	Y	Y	Y	N	Y
5 ***McGrath***	N	N	N	Y	Y	Y	N	Y
6 Flake	N	Y	Y	Y	Y	Y	N	N
7 Ackerman	N	Y	Y	Y	Y	Y	N	N
8 Scheuer	N	Y	Y	Y	Y	Y	N	Y
9 Manton	N	Y	Y	Y	Y	Y	N	N
10 Schumer	?	?	Y	Y	Y	Y	N	N
11 Towns	N	Y	Y	Y	?	Y	N	N
12 Owens	N	Y	Y	Y	Y	Y	N	?
13 Solarz	N	Y	Y	Y	Y	Y	N	N
14 ***Molinari***	N	N	N	Y	Y	Y	N	N
15 ***Green***	N	N	N	Y	Y	Y	N	N
16 Rangel	N	Y	Y	Y	Y	Y	N	Y
17 Weiss	N	Y	Y	Y	Y	Y	N	N
18 Serrano	?	?	?	?	?	?	?	?
19 Engel	N	Y	Y	Y	Y	Y	N	N
20 Lowey	N	Y	Y	Y	Y	Y	N	Y
21 ***Fish***	N	Y	Y	Y	Y	Y	N	N
22 ***Gilman***	N	Y	Y	Y	Y	Y	N	N
23 McNulty	N	Y	Y	Y	Y	Y	N	N
24 ***Solomon***	Y	N	N	Y	Y	Y	Y	Y
25 ***Boehlert***	N	Y	Y	?	Y	Y	N	Y
26 ***Martin***	Y	Y	Y	Y	Y	Y	N	Y
27 ***Walsh***	Y	Y	Y	Y	Y	Y	N	Y
28 McHugh	N	Y	Y	Y	Y	Y	N	Y
29 ***Horton***	N	Y	Y	Y	Y	Y	N	N
30 Slaughter	N	Y	Y	Y	Y	Y	N	Y
31 ***Paxon***	Y	N	N	Y	Y	Y	N	N
32 LaFalce	N	Y	Y	Y	Y	Y	N	Y
33 Nowak	N	Y	Y	Y	Y	Y	N	Y
34 ***Houghton***	Y	Y	Y	Y	Y	Y	N	N
NORTH CAROLINA								
1 Jones	N	Y	Y	Y	?	Y	N	Y
2 Valentine	Y	Y	N	?	Y	Y	N	?
3 Lancaster	Y	Y	Y	Y	Y	Y	N	N
4 Price	N	Y	Y	Y	Y	Y	N	N
5 Neal	Y	Y	Y	Y	Y	Y	N	Y
6 ***Coble***	Y	N	N	Y	Y	Y	N	N
7 Rose	?	?	Y	Y	Y	Y	N	Y
8 Hefner	Y	Y	N	Y	Y	Y	N	Y
9 ***McMillan***	Y	Y	N	Y	Y	Y	Y	Y
10 ***Ballenger***	Y	N	N	Y	Y	Y	N	N
11 ***Taylor***	Y	Y	Y	Y	Y	Y	N	Y
NORTH DAKOTA								
AL Dorgan	Y	N	N	Y	Y	Y	N	Y
OHIO								
1 Luken	N	Y	Y	Y	Y	Y	N	Y
2 ***Gradison***	Y	Y	Y	Y	Y	Y	N	Y
3 Hall	N	Y	Y	Y	?	Y	N	N
4 ***Oxley***	Y	N	N	Y	Y	Y	N	Y
5 ***Gillmor***	Y	Y	Y	Y	Y	Y	N	N
6 ***McEwen***	Y	N	N	Y	?	Y	N	Y
7 ***Hobson***	Y	Y	N	Y	Y	Y	N	Y
8 ***Boehner***	Y	Y	N	Y	Y	Y	N	N
9 Kaptur	Y	Y	Y	Y	Y	Y	N	Y
10 ***Miller***	Y	Y	N	Y	Y	Y	Y	N
11 Eckart	Y	N	N	Y	Y	Y	N	Y
12 ***Kasich***	Y	N	N	Y	Y	Y	N	Y
13 Pease	N	Y	Y	Y	Y	Y	Y	Y
14 Sawyer	N	Y	Y	Y	Y	Y	N	Y
15 ***Wylie***	Y	N	N	Y	Y	Y	N	N
16 ***Regula***	Y	Y	N	Y	Y	Y	N	N
17 Traficant	Y	N	N	Y	Y	Y	Y	Y
18 Applegate	Y	N	N	N	Y	Y	N	Y
19 Feighan	N	Y	Y	Y	Y	Y	N	Y
20 Oakar	N	Y	Y	Y	Y	Y	Y	Y
21 Stokes	N	Y	Y	Y	Y	Y	N	Y
OKLAHOMA								
1 ***Inhofe***	Y	N	N	Y	Y	Y	N	N
2 Synar	N	Y	Y	Y	Y	Y	N	Y
3 Brewster	Y	Y	Y	Y	Y	Y	N	Y
4 McCurdy	Y	?	Y	Y	Y	Y	N	Y
5 ***Edwards***	Y	N	N	Y	Y	Y	N	N
6 English	Y	N	N	Y	Y	Y	N	Y
OREGON								
1 AuCoin	N	N	N	Y	Y	Y	N	Y
2 ***Smith***	Y	Y	Y	Y	?	Y	N	Y
3 Wyden	N	Y	Y	Y	Y	Y	N	Y
4 DeFazio	Y	Y	Y	Y	Y	Y	Y	Y
5 Kopetski	Y	Y	Y	Y	Y	Y	N	Y
PENNSYLVANIA								
1 Foglietta	N	Y	Y	Y	Y	Y	N	Y
2 Gray	N	Y	Y	Y	?	?	?	Y
3 Borski	N	Y	Y	Y	Y	Y	N	Y
4 Kolter	Y	Y	N	Y	Y	Y	N	N
5 ***Schulze***	Y	Y	Y	Y	Y	Y	N	Y
6 Yatron	N	Y	Y	Y	Y	Y	N	N
7 ***Weldon***	+	-	-	Y	Y	Y	N	Y
8 Kostmayer	N	Y	Y	Y	Y	Y	N	Y
9 ***Shuster***	Y	N	N	Y	Y	Y	N	Y
10 ***McDade***	Y	Y	Y	Y	Y	Y	N	N
11 Kanjorski	Y	Y	Y	Y	Y	Y	N	N
12 Murtha	Y	Y	Y	Y	Y	Y	N	N
13 ***Coughlin***	N	Y	Y	Y	Y	Y	N	Y
14 Coyne	N	Y	Y	Y	Y	Y	N	Y
15 ***Ritter***	Y	N	N	Y	Y	Y	N	N
16 ***Walker***	Y	N	N	Y	Y	Y	N	N
17 ***Gekas***	Y	Y	N	Y	Y	Y	N	Y
18 ***Santorum***	Y	N	N	Y	Y	Y	N	N
19 ***Goodling***	Y	Y	Y	Y	Y	Y	N	Y
20 Gaydos	Y	Y	N	Y	Y	Y	N	N
21 ***Ridge***	Y	N	N	Y	Y	Y	N	Y
22 Murphy	Y	Y	Y	Y	Y	Y	Y	Y
23 ***Clinger***	Y	Y	Y	Y	Y	Y	N	Y
RHODE ISLAND								
1 ***Machtley***	Y	N	N	Y	Y	Y	N	Y
2 Reed	N	Y	Y	Y	Y	Y	N	Y
SOUTH CAROLINA								
1 ***Ravenel***	N	Y	Y	Y	Y	Y	N	Y
2 ***Spence***	?	?	?	?	?	?	?	?
3 Derrick	N	Y	Y	Y	Y	Y	N	Y
4 Patterson	Y	N	N	Y	Y	Y	N	Y
5 Spratt	N	Y	Y	Y	Y	Y	N	Y
6 Tallon	N	N	N	Y	Y	Y	N	Y
SOUTH DAKOTA								
AL Johnson	Y	N	N	Y	Y	Y	N	Y
TENNESSEE								
1 ***Quillen***	Y	Y	N	Y	Y	Y	N	Y
2 ***Duncan***	Y	N	N	Y	Y	Y	N	N
3 Lloyd	?	?	?	?	?	?	?	?
4 Cooper	N	Y	Y	Y	Y	Y	N	Y
5 Clement	N	Y	Y	Y	Y	Y	N	Y
6 Gordon	N	Y	Y	Y	Y	Y	N	Y
7 ***Sundquist***	Y	N	N	Y	Y	Y	N	Y
8 Tanner	Y	N	N	Y	Y	Y	N	N
9 Ford	N	Y	Y	?	Y	Y	N	Y
TEXAS								
1 Chapman	Y	Y	Y	Y	Y	Y	N	Y
2 Wilson	N	Y	Y	Y	Y	Y	N	Y
3 ***Johnson***	Y	Y	Y	Y	Y	Y	N	Y
4 Hall	Y	Y	Y	Y	Y	Y	N	Y
5 Bryant	N	N	N	Y	Y	Y	Y	Y
6 ***Barton***	Y	N	N	Y	Y	Y	N	Y
7 ***Archer***	Y	Y	Y	Y	Y	Y	N	N
8 ***Fields***	Y	Y	N	Y	Y	Y	N	N
9 Brooks	Y	N	Y	Y	Y	Y	N	Y
10 Pickle	N	N	N	Y	Y	Y	N	Y
11 Edwards	N	N	N	Y	Y	Y	N	Y
12 Geren	Y	N	N	Y	Y	Y	N	N
13 Sarpalius	Y	N	Y	Y	Y	Y	N	Y
14 Laughlin	Y	Y	Y	Y	Y	Y	N	Y
15 de la Garza	N	Y	Y	Y	Y	Y	N	Y
16 Coleman	N	Y	Y	Y	Y	Y	N	Y
17 Stenholm	Y	Y	Y	Y	Y	Y	N	Y
18 Washington	N	N	N	N	N	Y	Y	Y
19 ***Combest***	Y	N	N	Y	Y	Y	N	N
20 Gonzalez	N	Y	Y	N	P	P	N	Y
21 ***Smith***	Y	Y	Y	Y	Y	Y	N	N
22 ***DeLay***	Y	N	N	Y	Y	Y	N	Y
23 Bustamante	N	Y	Y	Y	Y	Y	N	Y
24 Frost	?	Y	Y	Y	Y	Y	N	Y
25 Andrews	Y	Y	Y	Y	Y	Y	N	Y
26 ***Armey***	Y	Y	N	Y	Y	Y	N	N
27 Ortiz	Y	Y	Y	Y	Y	Y	N	Y
UTAH								
1 ***Hansen***	Y	N	N	Y	Y	Y	Y	Y
2 Owens	N	Y	Y	N	N	Y	N	N
3 Orton	N	Y	Y	Y	N	Y	N	N
VERMONT								
AL *Sanders*	N	?	Y	Y	Y	Y	Y	Y
VIRGINIA								
1 ***Bateman***	Y	Y	Y	Y	Y	Y	P	P
2 Pickett	Y	Y	Y	Y	Y	Y	N	Y
3 ***Bliley***	Y	Y	Y	Y	Y	Y	N	Y
4 Sisisky	Y	Y	Y	Y	Y	Y	N	Y
5 Payne	N	Y	Y	Y	Y	Y	N	Y
6 Olin	N	Y	Y	Y	Y	Y	N	Y
7 ***Slaughter***	Y	Y	Y	Y	Y	Y	N	Y
8 Moran	N	Y	Y	Y	Y	Y	Y	Y
9 Boucher	N	Y	Y	Y	Y	Y	Y	Y
10 ***Wolf***	N	Y	Y	Y	Y	Y	N	Y
WASHINGTON								
1 ***Miller***	N	N	N	Y	Y	Y	N	N
2 Swift	N	Y	Y	Y	Y	Y	N	Y
3 Unsoeld	N	Y	Y	Y	Y	Y	N	Y
4 ***Morrison***	N	Y	Y	Y	Y	Y	N	Y
5 Foley								
6 Dicks	N	Y	Y	Y	Y	Y	N	N
7 McDermott	N	Y	Y	Y	Y	Y	N	Y
8 ***Chandler***	N	Y	Y	Y	Y	Y	N	N
WEST VIRGINIA								
1 Mollohan	Y	Y	Y	Y	Y	Y	N	Y
2 Staggers	N	Y	Y	Y	Y	Y	N	Y
3 Wise	N	Y	Y	Y	Y	Y	N	Y
4 Rahall	Y	Y	Y	N	P	Y	Y	Y
WISCONSIN								
1 Aspin	Y	Y	Y	Y	Y	Y	N	Y
2 ***Klug***	Y	Y	Y	Y	Y	Y	N	Y
3 ***Gunderson***	Y	N	N	Y	Y	Y	N	Y
4 Kleczka	N	Y	Y	Y	Y	Y	N	Y
5 Moody	N	Y	Y	Y	Y	Y	N	Y
6 ***Petri***	Y	N	N	Y	Y	Y	Y	Y
7 Obey	N	Y	Y	Y	Y	Y	N	Y
8 ***Roth***	Y	N	N	Y	Y	Y	Y	N
9 ***Sensenbrenner***	Y	N	N	Y	Y	Y	N	N
WYOMING								
AL ***Thomas***	Y	N	N	Y	Y	Y	N	Y

Southern states - Ala., Ark., Fla., Ga., Ky., La., Miss., N.C., Okla., S.C., Tenn., Texas, Va.
Omitted votes are quorum calls, which CQ does not include in its vote charts.

HOUSE VOTES 175, 176, 177, 178, 179, 180, 181, 182

175. HR 2508. Fiscal 1992-93 Foreign Aid Authorization/ Soviet Union. Johnston, D-Fla., amendment to the Kyl, R-Ariz., amendment to express the sense of Congress that the Soviet Union continue to progress toward a free society and a free market economy. Rejected 130-286: R 2-157; D 127-129 (ND 100-73, SD 27-56); I 1-0, June 19, 1991.

176. HR 2508. Fiscal 1992-93 Foreign Aid Authorization/ Soviet Human Rights. Kyl, R-Ariz., amendment to prohibit aid to the Soviet Union unless the president certifies that the Soviet government has improved human rights and met other conditions. Adopted 374-41: R 159-1; D 215-39 (ND 137-33, SD 78-6); I 0-1, June 19, 1991. (Before being adopted, the Kyl amendment was amended by a Durbin, D-Ill., amendment to include requirements that the Soviet government return control of government buildings seized in the Baltics and to provide for the equitable distribution of assets in the Republics and a McCollum, R-Fla., amendment to require the Soviet Union to include Afghanistan and Vietnam as countries to which they must scale back military aid.) A "nay" is a vote supporting the president's position.

177. HR 2508. Fiscal 1992-93 Foreign Aid Authorization/ Soviet Union-Cuba. McCollum, R-Fla., amendment to prohibit aid to the Soviet Union unless that country stops giving military aid to Cuba. Adopted 386-29: R 158-1; D 228-27 (ND 149-22, SD 79-5); I 0-1, June 19, 1991.

178. HR 2508. Fiscal 1992-93 Foreign Aid Authorization/ India Human Rights. Feighan, D-Ohio, amendment to the Burton, R-Ind., amendment, to express the concern of Congress about human rights abuses by Indian security forces in Punjab and Kashmir and to call upon the Indian government to take actions to promote adherence to human rights standards. The Burton amendment would have terminated all developmental aid to India if the president determined the Indian government was preventing human rights groups from monitoring conditions in that country. Adopted 271-144: R 70-87; D 201-56 (ND 143-31, SD 58-25); I 0-1, June 19, 1991. (Subsequently, the Burton amendment, as amended, was adopted by voice vote.)

179. HR 2508. Fiscal 1992-93 Foreign Aid Authorization/ India Human Rights. Burton, R-Ind., amendment to cut over two years $100 million of the aid to India, if human rights groups are not allowed into the country. Rejected 182-229: R 110-46; D 72-182 (ND 35-137, SD 37-45); I 0-1, June 19, 1991.

180. HR 2621. Fiscal 1992 Foreign Operations Appropriations/Rule. Adoption of the rule (H Res 177) to provide for House floor consideration of the bill to provide $15,347,153,994 in new budget authority for foreign military and economic assistance and export financing in fiscal 1992. Adopted 264-135: R 24-127; D 239-8 (ND 162-5, SD 77-3); I 1-0, June 19, 1991.

181. HR 2621. Fiscal 1992 Foreign Operations Appropriations/Passage. Passage of the bill to provide $15,196,532,000 in new budget authority for foreign military and economic assistance and export financing in fiscal 1992. The administration requested $27,626,542,022. Passed 301-102: R 103-52; D 197-50 (ND 142-25, SD 55-25); I 1-0, June 19, 1991.

182. HR 2508. Fiscal 1992-93 Foreign Aid Authorization/South Africa. Dymally, D-Calif., amendment to the Burton, R-Ind., amendment, to prohibit aid to the South African Communist Party and to require the president to ensure that recipients of aid in South Africa "do not have" democratic processes in place for selecting leaders and do not have a record of human rights violation. Rejected 16-399: R 0-158; D 16-240 (ND 10-165, SD 6-75); I 0-1, June 20, 1991. (Dymally, acknowledging a drafting error, subsequently offered an amendment to require the president to ensure that recipients of aid "do have" democratic processes in place for selecting leaders and do not have a record of human rights violations, which was adopted by voice vote.)

KEY

- Y Voted for (yea).
- # Paired for.
- + Announced for.
- N Voted against (nay).
- X Paired against.
- \- Announced against.
- P Voted "present."
- C Voted "present" to avoid possible conflict of interest.
- ? Did not vote or otherwise make a position known.

Democrats ***Republicans***
Independent

	175	176	177	178	179	180	181	182
ALABAMA								
1 ***Callahan***	N	Y	Y	N	Y	N	Y	N
2 ***Dickinson***	N	Y	Y	N	Y	N	N	N
3 Browder	N	Y	Y	N	Y	Y	Y	N
4 Bevill	N	Y	Y	N	Y	Y	Y	N
5 Cramer	N	Y	Y	N	Y	Y	Y	N
6 Erdreich	N	Y	Y	N	Y	Y	Y	N
7 Harris	N	Y	Y	N	Y	Y	Y	N
ALASKA								
AL ***Young***	N	Y	Y	N	Y	Y	Y	N
ARIZONA								
1 ***Rhodes***	N	Y	Y	N	Y	N	Y	N
2 Vacancy								
3 ***Stump***	N	Y	Y	N	Y	N	N	N
4 ***Kyl***	N	Y	Y	N	Y	N	Y	N
5 ***Kolbe***	N	Y	Y	Y	Y	N	Y	N
ARKANSAS								
1 Alexander	N	N	Y	Y	N	Y	Y	N
2 Thornton	Y	Y	Y	Y	N	Y	Y	N
3 ***Hammerschmidt***	?	?	?	?	?	X	?	?
4 Anthony	N	Y	Y	Y	N	Y	N	Y
CALIFORNIA								
1 ***Riggs***	N	Y	Y	N	Y	N	Y	N
2 ***Herger***	N	Y	Y	N	Y	N	N	N
3 Matsui	Y	Y	Y	Y	N	Y	Y	N
4 Fazio	Y	Y	Y	N	Y	Y	Y	N
5 Pelosi	Y	Y	Y	Y	N	Y	Y	N
6 Boxer	N	Y	Y	Y	N	Y	Y	N
7 Miller	Y	N	Y	N	Y	Y	Y	N
8 Dellums	Y	N	N	Y	N	Y	Y	N
9 Stark	N	Y	Y	N	N	Y	Y	N
10 Edwards	N	Y	Y	N	Y	Y	Y	N
11 Lantos	Y	Y	Y	Y	N	Y	Y	N
12 ***Campbell***	N	Y	Y	Y	?	?	?	N
13 Mineta	Y	Y	Y	Y	?	Y	Y	N
14 ***Doolittle***	N	Y	Y	N	Y	N	Y	N
15 Condit	N	Y	Y	N	Y	Y	N	N
16 Panetta	Y	N	Y	Y	N	Y	Y	N
17 Dooley	N	Y	Y	N	Y	Y	Y	N
18 Lehman	Y	Y	Y	Y	Y	Y	Y	N
19 ***Lagomarsino***	N	Y	Y	Y	N	N	N	N
20 ***Thomas***	N	Y	Y	Y	N	N	Y	N
21 ***Gallegly***	N	Y	Y	N	Y	N	N	N
22 ***Moorhead***	N	Y	Y	N	Y	N	N	N
23 Beilenson	Y	N	Y	Y	N	Y	+	N
24 Waxman	Y	?	Y	Y	N	Y	Y	N
25 Roybal	Y	N	N	Y	N	Y	Y	N
26 Berman	Y	N	Y	Y	N	Y	Y	N
27 Levine	?	?	?	?	X	?	?	?
28 Dixon	Y	N	Y	N	N	Y	Y	Y
29 Waters	N	Y	N	Y	N	Y	Y	N
30 Martinez	Y	?	?	?	?	?	?	?
31 Dymally	Y	N	N	Y	N	Y	Y	Y
32 Anderson	N	Y	Y	Y	N	Y	Y	N
33 ***Dreier***	N	Y	Y	N	Y	N	N	N
34 Torres	N	Y	N	N	N	Y	Y	N
35 ***Lewis***	N	Y	Y	Y	N	N	Y	N
36 Brown	Y	Y	Y	Y	N	?	?	N
37 ***McCandless***	N	Y	Y	Y	N	N	N	N
38 ***Dornan***	N	Y	Y	N	Y	N	Y	N
39 ***Dannemeyer***	N	Y	Y	N	Y	N	N	N
40 ***Cox***	N	Y	Y	N	Y	N	Y	N
41 ***Lowery***	N	Y	Y	N	Y	?	Y	N
42 ***Rohrabacher***	N	Y	Y	N	Y	N	Y	N
43 ***Packard***	N	Y	Y	N	Y	N	N	N
44 ***Cunningham***	N	Y	Y	N	Y	N	Y	N
45 ***Hunter***	N	Y	Y	N	Y	N	Y	N
COLORADO								
1 Schroeder	Y	Y	Y	Y	N	Y	Y	N
2 Skaggs	Y	N	Y	?	?	Y	Y	N
3 Campbell	N	Y	N	Y	N	Y	Y	N
4 ***Allard***	N	Y	Y	Y	Y	N	Y	N
5 ***Hefley***	N	Y	Y	Y	Y	N	N	N
6 ***Schaefer***	N	Y	Y	N	Y	N	Y	N
CONNECTICUT								
1 Kennelly	Y	Y	Y	Y	N	Y	Y	N
2 Gejdenson	Y	Y	Y	Y	N	Y	Y	N
3 DeLauro	N	Y	Y	Y	N	Y	Y	N
4 ***Shays***	N	Y	Y	Y	N	N	Y	N
5 ***Franks***	N	Y	Y	N	Y	N	Y	N
6 ***Johnson***	Y	Y	Y	Y	N	N	Y	N
DELAWARE								
AL Carper	Y	Y	Y	Y	N	Y	Y	N
FLORIDA								
1 Hutto	N	Y	Y	Y	N	Y	N	N
2 Peterson	N	Y	Y	Y	N	Y	Y	N
3 Bennett	N	Y	Y	Y	Y	Y	N	N
4 ***James***	N	Y	Y	N	Y	N	N	N
5 ***McCollum***	N	Y	Y	Y	N	N	Y	N
6 ***Stearns***	N	Y	Y	Y	Y	N	N	N
7 Gibbons	Y	Y	Y	Y	N	Y	Y	N
8 ***Young***	N	Y	Y	N	Y	N	N	N
9 ***Bilirakis***	N	Y	Y	N	Y	N	Y	N
10 ***Ireland***	N	Y	Y	N	Y	N	N	N
11 Bacchus	N	Y	Y	N	N	Y	Y	N
12 ***Lewis***	N	Y	Y	N	Y	N	N	N
13 ***Goss***	N	Y	Y	N	Y	N	N	N
14 Johnston	Y	Y	Y	Y	N	Y	Y	Y
15 ***Shaw***	N	Y	Y	Y	N	N	Y	N
16 Smith	Y	Y	Y	Y	N	Y	Y	N
17 Lehman	?	Y	Y	Y	?	Y	?	N
18 ***Ros-Lehtinen***	N	Y	Y	N	Y	N	Y	N
19 Fascell	Y	Y	Y	Y	N	Y	Y	Y
GEORGIA								
1 Thomas	N	Y	Y	N	N	Y	?	N
2 Hatcher	N	Y	Y	Y	N	Y	Y	N
3 Ray	Y	Y	Y	Y	Y	Y	N	N
4 Jones	N	Y	Y	Y	N	Y	Y	N
5 Lewis	Y	N	N	Y	N	Y	Y	N
6 ***Gingrich***	N	Y	?	?	?	N	Y	N
7 Darden	N	Y	Y	Y	N	Y	Y	N
8 Rowland	N	Y	Y	Y	Y	Y	Y	N
9 Jenkins	N	Y	Y	Y	Y	Y	N	N
10 Barnard	N	Y	Y	Y	N	Y	N	N
HAWAII								
1 Abercrombie	N	N	N	N	Y	Y	Y	Y
2 Mink	Y	N	Y	Y	N	Y	Y	N
IDAHO								
1 LaRocco	Y	Y	Y	Y	N	Y	Y	N
2 Stallings	N	Y	Y	Y	N	Y	Y	N
ILLINOIS								
1 Hayes	Y	N	N	Y	N	Y	Y	N
2 Savage	N	N	N	Y	N	Y	N	N
3 Russo	N	Y	Y	Y	N	Y	N	N
4 Sangmeister	Y	Y	Y	Y	Y	Y	N	N
5 Lipinski	N	Y	Y	N	Y	Y	Y	N
6 ***Hyde***	N	Y	Y	Y	N	N	N	N
7 Collins	N	Y	Y	Y	N	Y	Y	N
8 Rostenkowski	N	Y	Y	Y	N	Y	Y	N
9 Yates	N	N	N	Y	N	Y	#	N
10 ***Porter***	N	Y	Y	Y	Y	N	Y	N
11 Annunzio	N	Y	Y	Y	N	Y	Y	N
12 ***Crane***	N	Y	Y	N	Y	N	N	N
13 ***Fawell***	?	?	?	?	?	?	?	?
14 ***Hastert***	N	Y	Y	Y	N	N	Y	N
15 Vacancy								
16 Cox	N	Y	Y	N	N	Y	Y	N
17 Evans	N	Y	Y	Y	N	Y	Y	N
18 ***Michel***	N	Y	Y	Y	Y	Y	Y	N
19 Bruce	N	Y	Y	Y	N	Y	Y	N
20 Durbin	N	Y	Y	Y	N	Y	Y	N
21 Costello	N	Y	Y	Y	Y	Y	N	N
22 Poshard	N	Y	Y	Y	Y	Y	N	N
INDIANA								
1 Visclosky	N	Y	Y	Y	N	Y	Y	N
2 Sharp	Y	Y	Y	Y	N	Y	Y	N
3 Roemer	N	Y	Y	N	Y	Y	N	N

ND Northern Democrats SD Southern Democrats

	175	176	177	178	179	180	181	182
4 Long	N	Y	Y	Y	N	Y	N	N
5 Jontz	Y	Y	Y	Y	N	Y	N	N
6 ***Burton***	N	Y	Y	N	Y	N	Y	N
7 ***Myers***	N	Y	Y	N	Y	Y	N	N
8 McCloskey	Y	Y	Y	Y	?	?	Y	N
9 Hamilton	Y	N	Y	Y	N	Y	Y	N
10 Jacobs	Y	Y	Y	N	Y	Y	N	N
IOWA								
1 ***Leach***	N	Y	Y	Y	Y	N	Y	N
2 ***Nussle***	N	Y	Y	Y	Y	N	N	N
3 Nagle	N	N	N	Y	N	Y	Y	N
4 Smith	Y	N	N	Y	N	Y	Y	N
5 ***Lightfoot***	N	Y	Y	Y	Y	N	Y	N
6 ***Grandy***	N	Y	Y	Y	N	N	Y	N
KANSAS								
1 ***Roberts***	N	Y	Y	Y	Y	N	N	N
2 Slattery	N	Y	Y	Y	Y	Y	N	N
3 ***Meyers***	N	Y	Y	N	Y	Y	Y	N
4 Glickman	Y	Y	Y	N	Y	Y	Y	N
5 ***Nichols***	N	Y	Y	Y	Y	N	Y	N
KENTUCKY								
1 Hubbard	N	Y	Y	Y	Y	N	N	N
2 Natcher	N	Y	Y	Y	N	Y	Y	N
3 Mazzoli	Y	Y	Y	Y	N	Y	N	N
4 ***Bunning***	N	Y	Y	N	Y	N	N	N
5 ***Rogers***	N	Y	Y	N	Y	N	N	N
6 ***Hopkins***	?	?	?	?	?	?	?	?
7 Perkins	N	Y	Y	Y	N	Y	N	N
LOUISIANA								
1 ***Livingston***	N	Y	Y	Y	Y	N	Y	N
2 Jefferson	N	Y	Y	Y	N	Y	Y	N
3 Tauzin	N	Y	Y	N	Y	Y	N	N
4 ***McCrery***	N	Y	Y	Y	N	N	Y	N
5 Huckaby	N	Y	Y	?	?	?	?	?
6 ***Baker***	N	Y	Y	N	Y	N	Y	N
7 Hayes	N	Y	Y	Y	Y	Y	N	N
8 ***Holloway***	N	Y	Y	N	Y	N	Y	N
MAINE								
1 Andrews	Y	Y	Y	N	Y	Y	Y	N
2 ***Snowe***	N	Y	Y	Y	N	Y	Y	N
MARYLAND								
1 ***Gilchrest***	N	Y	Y	Y	N	N	Y	N
2 ***Bentley***	N	Y	Y	Y	N	?	Y	N
3 Cardin	N	Y	Y	Y	N	Y	Y	N
4 McMillen	N	Y	Y	Y	N	Y	Y	N
5 Hoyer	Y	Y	Y	Y	N	Y	Y	N
6 Byron	N	Y	Y	Y	N	Y	Y	N
7 Mfume	Y	Y	N	Y	N	Y	+	N
8 ***Morella***	N	Y	Y	Y	N	Y	Y	N
MASSACHUSETTS								
1 Olver	Y	Y	Y	Y	N	Y	Y	N
2 Neal	N	Y	Y	Y	N	Y	Y	N
3 Early	N	Y	Y	N	Y	N	N	N
4 Frank	N	Y	Y	Y	N	Y	Y	Y
5 Atkins	Y	Y	Y	Y	N	Y	Y	N
6 Mavroules	N	Y	Y	Y	N	Y	Y	N
7 Markey	Y	Y	Y	Y	N	Y	Y	N
8 Kennedy	Y	Y	Y	Y	N	Y	Y	N
9 Moakley	Y	Y	Y	Y	N	Y	Y	N
10 Studds	Y	Y	Y	Y	N	Y	Y	N
11 Donnelly	N	Y	Y	N	Y	Y	N	N
MICHIGAN								
1 Conyers	Y	?	?	Y	N	Y	Y	N
2 ***Pursell***	N	Y	Y	Y	?	N	N	N
3 Wolpe	Y	N	Y	Y	N	Y	Y	N
4 ***Upton***	N	Y	Y	N	Y	N	Y	N
5 ***Henry***	N	Y	Y	N	Y	N	N	N
6 Carr	N	Y	Y	Y	Y	Y	?	?
7 Kildee	Y	N	Y	Y	N	Y	Y	N
8 Traxler	N	Y	Y	Y	Y	Y	Y	N
9 ***Vander Jagt***	N	Y	Y	N	Y	N	Y	N
10 ***Camp***	N	Y	Y	N	Y	N	Y	N
11 ***Davis***	N	Y	Y	N	Y	N	Y	N
12 Bonior	Y	Y	Y	Y	N	Y	Y	N
13 Collins	N	Y	N	Y	N	Y	Y	N
14 Hertel	N	Y	Y	Y	N	Y	Y	N
15 Ford	Y	Y	Y	Y	N	Y	Y	N
16 Dingell	N	Y	?	Y	Y	Y	Y	N
17 Levin	Y	Y	Y	Y	N	Y	Y	N
18 ***Broomfield***	N	Y	Y	Y	N	N	Y	N
MINNESOTA								
1 Penny	Y	Y	Y	Y	N	Y	Y	N
2 ***Weber***	N	Y	Y	N	Y	Y	Y	N
3 ***Ramstad***	N	Y	Y	N	Y	N	Y	N
4 Vento	Y	Y	Y	Y	N	Y	Y	N

	175	176	177	178	179	180	181	182
5 Sabo	Y	Y	Y	Y	N	Y	Y	N
6 Sikorski	N	Y	Y	N	Y	Y	Y	N
7 Peterson	Y	Y	Y	Y	N	Y	Y	N
8 Oberstar	?	?	?	?	?	#	?	?
MISSISSIPPI								
1 Whitten	N	Y	Y	Y	N	Y	Y	N
2 Espy	Y	Y	N	N	N	?	Y	Y
3 Montgomery	N	Y	Y	N	Y	Y	N	N
4 Parker	N	Y	Y	N	Y	Y	N	N
5 Taylor	N	Y	Y	N	Y	Y	N	N
MISSOURI								
1 Clay	Y	N	N	N	N	?	Y	N
2 Horn	N	Y	Y	Y	N	Y	Y	N
3 Gephardt	Y	Y	Y	Y	N	Y	Y	N
4 Skelton	N	Y	Y	Y	N	Y	Y	N
5 Wheat	Y	N	N	N	Y	Y	Y	Y
6 ***Coleman***	N	Y	Y	Y	Y	N	Y	N
7 ***Hancock***	N	Y	Y	N	Y	N	N	N
8 ***Emerson***	N	Y	Y	N	Y	N	Y	N
9 Volkmer	N	Y	Y	Y	N	Y	N	N
MONTANA								
1 Williams	Y	N	Y	Y	N	N	N	N
2 ***Marlenee***	N	Y	Y	N	Y	N	N	N
NEBRASKA								
1 ***Bereuter***	N	Y	Y	Y	N	N	Y	N
2 Hoagland	Y	Y	Y	Y	N	Y	Y	N
3 ***Barrett***	N	Y	Y	N	Y	N	N	N
NEVADA								
1 Bilbray	N	Y	Y	Y	N	Y	Y	N
2 ***Vucanovich***	N	Y	Y	N	Y	?	?	N
NEW HAMPSHIRE								
1 ***Zeliff***	N	Y	Y	N	Y	N	Y	N
2 Swett	N	Y	Y	Y	N	Y	Y	N
NEW JERSEY								
1 Andrews	Y	Y	Y	Y	N	Y	Y	Y
2 Hughes	N	Y	Y	Y	N	Y	N	N
3 Pallone	N	Y	Y	Y	N	Y	Y	N
4 ***Smith***	N	Y	Y	Y	N	N	N	N
5 ***Roukema***	N	Y	Y	Y	N	Y	Y	N
6 Dwyer	Y	Y	Y	Y	N	Y	Y	N
7 ***Rinaldo***	N	Y	Y	Y	N	N	Y	N
8 Roe	?	Y	Y	Y	N	Y	Y	N
9 Torricelli	?	?	?	?	?	?	?	N
10 Payne	Y	N	N	Y	N	Y	Y	N
11 ***Gallo***	N	Y	Y	Y	Y	Y	Y	N
12 ***Zimmer***	N	Y	Y	Y	N	N	Y	N
13 ***Saxton***	N	Y	Y	Y	Y	N	Y	N
14 Guarini	N	Y	Y	Y	N	Y	Y	N
NEW MEXICO								
1 ***Schiff***	N	Y	Y	N	N	N	Y	N
2 ***Skeen***	N	Y	Y	N	Y	Y	Y	N
3 Richardson	Y	Y	Y	Y	N	Y	Y	N
NEW YORK								
1 Hochbrueckner	Y	Y	Y	Y	N	Y	Y	N
2 Downey	Y	Y	Y	Y	N	Y	Y	N
3 Mrazek	Y	Y	Y	Y	N	Y	Y	N
4 ***Lent***	N	Y	Y	Y	N	N	Y	N
5 ***McGrath***	N	Y	Y	Y	N	Y	Y	N
6 Flake	Y	N	Y	Y	N	Y	Y	N
7 Ackerman	Y	Y	Y	Y	N	Y	Y	N
8 Scheuer	Y	Y	Y	Y	N	Y	Y	N
9 Manton	Y	Y	Y	Y	N	Y	Y	N
10 Schumer	N	Y	Y	N	Y	Y	Y	N
11 Towns	Y	Y	?	Y	N	Y	Y	N
12 Owens	?	N	N	Y	N	Y	Y	N
13 Solarz	Y	Y	Y	Y	N	Y	Y	N
14 ***Molinari***	N	Y	Y	N	Y	N	Y	N
15 ***Green***	N	Y	Y	Y	N	Y	Y	N
16 Rangel	Y	Y	N	Y	N	Y	Y	Y
17 Weiss	Y	N	Y	Y	N	Y	Y	N
18 Serrano	?	?	?	?	?	#	#	?
19 Engel	N	Y	Y	Y	N	Y	Y	N
20 Lowey	N	Y	Y	Y	N	Y	Y	N
21 ***Fish***	N	Y	Y	Y	N	Y	Y	N
22 ***Gilman***	N	Y	Y	Y	N	Y	Y	N
23 McNulty	Y	Y	Y	Y	N	Y	Y	N
24 ***Solomon***	N	Y	Y	N	Y	N	N	N
25 ***Boehlert***	N	Y	Y	Y	N	Y	Y	N
26 ***Martin***	?	Y	Y	?	Y	?	?	?
27 ***Walsh***	N	Y	Y	Y	N	N	N	?
28 McHugh	Y	N	Y	Y	N	Y	Y	N
29 ***Horton***	N	Y	Y	Y	N	Y	Y	N
30 Slaughter	N	Y	Y	Y	N	Y	Y	N
31 ***Paxon***	N	Y	Y	N	Y	N	Y	N

	175	176	177	178	179	180	181	182
32 LaFalce	Y	Y	Y	N	Y	?	Y	N
33 Nowak	Y	Y	Y	N	Y	?	Y	N
34 ***Houghton***	Y	N	N	Y	N	Y	Y	N
NORTH CAROLINA								
1 Jones	N	Y	Y	Y	Y	Y	Y	N
2 Valentine	N	Y	Y	N	Y	Y	N	N
3 Lancaster	N	Y	Y	Y	N	Y	Y	N
4 Price	Y	Y	Y	Y	N	Y	Y	N
5 Neal	N	Y	Y	Y	Y	Y	N	N
6 ***Coble***	N	Y	Y	N	Y	N	Y	N
7 Rose	Y	Y	Y	Y	N	Y	Y	N
8 Hefner	N	Y	Y	N	Y	Y	N	N
9 ***McMillan***	N	Y	Y	Y	Y	N	Y	N
10 ***Ballenger***	N	Y	Y	N	Y	-	+	N
11 ***Taylor***	N	Y	Y	N	Y	N	Y	N
NORTH DAKOTA								
AL Dorgan	N	Y	Y	Y	N	Y	Y	N
OHIO								
1 Luken	N	Y	Y	Y	Y	Y	+	N
2 ***Gradison***	N	Y	Y	Y	N	N	Y	N
3 Hall	Y	Y	Y	Y	N	Y	Y	N
4 ***Oxley***	N	Y	Y	Y	Y	N	Y	N
5 ***Gillmor***	N	Y	Y	N	Y	N	Y	N
6 ***McEwen***	N	Y	Y	N	Y	N	N	N
7 ***Hobson***	N	Y	Y	Y	N	N	Y	N
8 ***Boehner***	N	Y	Y	N	Y	N	Y	N
9 Kaptur	Y	Y	Y	Y	N	Y	Y	N
10 ***Miller***	N	Y	Y	N	Y	Y	N	N
11 Eckart	N	+	Y	Y	N	Y	Y	N
12 ***Kasich***	N	Y	Y	N	Y	Y	Y	N
13 Pease	Y	Y	Y	Y	N	Y	N	N
14 Sawyer	Y	Y	Y	Y	N	Y	Y	N
15 ***Wylie***	N	Y	Y	N	Y	N	N	N
16 ***Regula***	N	Y	Y	N	Y	Y	Y	N
17 Traficant	N	Y	Y	N	Y	N	N	N
18 Applegate	N	Y	Y	N	Y	Y	N	N
19 Feighan	N	Y	?	Y	N	Y	Y	N
20 Oakar	N	?	Y	Y	N	Y	Y	N
21 Stokes	Y	Y	N	Y	N	Y	Y	N
OKLAHOMA								
1 ***Inhofe***	N	Y	Y	N	Y	N	Y	N
2 Synar	Y	Y	Y	Y	N	Y	Y	N
3 Brewster	N	Y	Y	N	Y	Y	Y	N
4 McCurdy	N	Y	Y	N	Y	Y	Y	N
5 ***Edwards***	N	Y	Y	N	Y	N	Y	N
6 English	N	Y	Y	Y	Y	Y	N	N
OREGON								
1 AuCoin	N	Y	Y	Y	N	N	Y	N
2 ***Smith***	N	Y	Y	N	Y	N	N	N
3 Wyden	N	Y	Y	Y	N	Y	Y	N
4 DeFazio	N	Y	Y	N	Y	?	N	N
5 Kopetski	Y	N	Y	Y	N	N	Y	N
PENNSYLVANIA								
1 Foglietta	Y	N	Y	Y	N	Y	Y	N
2 Gray	?	?	?	?	?	?	?	?
3 Borski	Y	Y	Y	Y	N	Y	Y	N
4 Kolter	Y	Y	Y	N	Y	Y	?	N
5 ***Schulze***	N	Y	Y	N	Y	Y	Y	N
6 Yatron	Y	Y	Y	Y	N	Y	Y	N
7 ***Weldon***	N	Y	Y	N	Y	N	Y	N
8 Kostmayer	Y	N	N	N	N	Y	Y	N
9 ***Shuster***	N	Y	Y	N	Y	N	N	N
10 ***McDade***	N	Y	Y	Y	N	N	Y	N
11 Kanjorski	N	Y	Y	Y	N	Y	Y	N
12 Murtha	N	Y	Y	Y	N	Y	Y	N
13 ***Coughlin***	N	Y	Y	Y	Y	N	Y	N
14 Coyne	Y	Y	Y	Y	N	Y	Y	N
15 ***Ritter***	N	Y	Y	Y	N	N	Y	N
16 ***Walker***	N	Y	Y	N	Y	N	N	N
17 ***Gekas***	N	Y	Y	N	Y	?	Y	N
18 ***Santorum***	N	Y	Y	Y	N	N	Y	N
19 ***Goodling***	N	Y	Y	Y	N	-	-	N
20 Gaydos	N	Y	Y	N	Y	Y	N	N
21 ***Ridge***	N	Y	Y	Y	Y	N	Y	N
22 Murphy	Y	Y	Y	Y	Y	Y	N	N
23 ***Clinger***	N	Y	Y	Y	N	N	N	N
RHODE ISLAND								
1 ***Machtley***	N	Y	Y	N	Y	Y	Y	N
2 Reed	N	Y	Y	Y	N	Y	Y	N
SOUTH CAROLINA								
1 ***Ravenel***	N	Y	Y	N	Y	Y	Y	N
2 ***Spence***	?	?	?	?	?	?	X	?
3 Derrick	Y	Y	Y	Y	N	Y	Y	N
4 Patterson	N	Y	Y	N	Y	Y	N	N
5 Spratt	Y	Y	Y	Y	N	?	Y	N
6 Tallon	N	Y	Y	N	Y	Y	Y	N

	175	176	177	178	179	180	181	182
SOUTH DAKOTA								
AL Johnson	N	Y	Y	Y	N	Y	Y	N
TENNESSEE								
1 ***Quillen***	N	Y	Y	N	Y	Y	N	N
2 ***Duncan***	N	Y	Y	Y	Y	N	N	N
3 Lloyd	?	?	?	?	?	?	?	?
4 Cooper	N	Y	Y	Y	N	Y	Y	N
5 Clement	N	Y	Y	Y	Y	Y	Y	N
6 Gordon	Y	Y	Y	N	N	Y	Y	N
7 ***Sundquist***	N	Y	Y	N	Y	N	Y	N
8 Tanner	N	Y	Y	N	Y	Y	N	N
9 Ford	Y	Y	Y	Y	Y	Y	?	N
TEXAS								
1 Chapman	N	Y	Y	N	Y	Y	Y	N
2 Wilson	N	Y	Y	N	Y	Y	N	N
3 ***Johnson***	N	Y	Y	Y	Y	N	N	N
4 Hall	N	Y	Y	N	Y	N	N	N
5 Bryant	N	Y	Y	Y	N	N	N	N
6 ***Barton***	N	Y	Y	N	Y	N	N	N
7 ***Archer***	N	Y	Y	Y	Y	N	N	N
8 ***Fields***	N	Y	Y	N	Y	N	N	N
9 Brooks	N	Y	Y	Y	Y	Y	Y	?
10 Pickle	N	Y	Y	Y	N	Y	Y	N
11 Edwards	N	Y	Y	Y	Y	Y	Y	N
12 Geren	N	Y	Y	N	Y	Y	Y	N
13 Sarpalius	N	Y	Y	Y	N	Y	N	N
14 Laughlin	N	Y	Y	N	Y	Y	Y	N
15 de la Garza	Y	Y	Y	Y	N	Y	Y	N
16 Coleman	Y	Y	Y	Y	N	Y	Y	N
17 Stenholm	N	Y	Y	Y	Y	Y	Y	N
18 Washington	Y	N	N	Y	N	Y	Y	Y
19 ***Combest***	N	Y	Y	Y	N	N	N	N
20 Gonzalez	Y	N	N	Y	N	Y	N	N
21 ***Smith***	N	Y	Y	Y	Y	N	Y	N
22 ***DeLay***	?	?	?	?	#	X	X	?
23 Bustamante	Y	Y	Y	Y	N	Y	Y	N
24 Frost	Y	Y	Y	Y	Y	?	Y	N
25 Andrews	N	Y	Y	Y	Y	Y	Y	N
26 ***Armey***	N	Y	Y	N	Y	N	N	N
27 Ortiz	Y	Y	Y	Y	N	Y	Y	?
UTAH								
1 ***Hansen***	N	Y	Y	Y	Y	N	N	N
2 Owens	Y	N	Y	Y	N	Y	Y	N
3 Orton	Y	Y	Y	Y	N	Y	Y	N
VERMONT								
AL *Sanders*	Y	N	N	N	N	Y	Y	N
VIRGINIA								
1 ***Bateman***	N	Y	Y	P	P	N	Y	N
2 Pickett	N	Y	Y	Y	N	Y	Y	N
3 ***Bliley***	N	Y	Y	N	Y	N	Y	N
4 Sisisky	N	Y	Y	Y	N	Y	Y	N
5 Payne	Y	Y	Y	Y	N	Y	Y	N
6 Olin	Y	N	Y	Y	N	Y	Y	N
7 ***Slaughter***	N	Y	Y	N	Y	N	N	N
8 Moran	N	N	N	N	Y	Y	Y	N
9 Boucher	Y	Y	Y	Y	N	Y	Y	Y
10 ***Wolf***	N	Y	Y	N	N	N	Y	N
WASHINGTON								
1 ***Miller***	N	Y	Y	N	Y	N	Y	N
2 Swift	Y	Y	Y	Y	N	Y	?	Y
3 Unsoeld	Y	Y	Y	N	N	Y	Y	N
4 ***Morrison***	N	Y	Y	Y	N	Y	Y	N
5 Foley								
6 Dicks	Y	Y	Y	Y	N	?	Y	N
7 McDermott	Y	Y	Y	Y	N	Y	Y	N
8 ***Chandler***	N	Y	Y	Y	N	N	Y	N
WEST VIRGINIA								
1 Mollohan	Y	Y	Y	Y	Y	Y	N	N
2 Staggers	Y	Y	Y	Y	N	Y	N	N
3 Wise	?	?	Y	Y	N	Y	Y	Y
4 Rahall	N	Y	Y	Y	N	?	N	Y
WISCONSIN								
1 Aspin	Y	N	Y	Y	N	Y	Y	N
2 ***Klug***	N	Y	Y	Y	N	?	Y	N
3 ***Gunderson***	N	Y	Y	Y	N	N	Y	N
4 Kleczka	N	Y	Y	Y	N	Y	Y	N
5 Moody	Y	Y	Y	N	Y	Y	Y	N
6 ***Petri***	N	Y	Y	Y	N	N	N	N
7 Obey	Y	N	N	Y	N	Y	Y	N
8 ***Roth***	N	Y	Y	N	Y	N	N	N
9 ***Sensenbrenner***	N	Y	Y	N	Y	N	N	N
WYOMING								
AL ***Thomas***	N	Y	Y	N	Y	N	Y	N

Southern states - Ala., Ark., Fla., Ga., Ky., La., Miss., N.C., Okla., S.C., Tenn., Texas, Va.
Omitted votes are quorum calls, which CQ does not include in its vote charts.

HOUSE VOTES 183, 184, 185, 186, 187, 188, 190, 191

183. HR 2508. Fiscal 1992-93 Foreign Aid Authorization/South Africa. Walker, R-Pa., substitute amendment to the Burton, R-Ind., amendment, to prohibit aid to the South African Communist Party and to any organization or association affiliated with a communist party and to require the president to ensure that recipients of aid have democratic processes in place for selecting leaders and do not have a record of human rights abuses. Adopted 279-134: R 152-5; D 127-128 (ND 64-110, SD 63-18); I 0-1, June 20, 1991. (The Burton amendment as amended was subsequently adopted by voice vote.)

184. HR 2508. Fiscal 1992-93 Foreign Aid Authorization/Horn of Africa. Bereuter, R-Neb., amendment to provide expanded relief, rehabilitation and food assistance, enhanced peace efforts and grass-roots-based development aid to Ethiopia, Somalia, Sudan, Djibouti and the Horn of Africa. Adopted 410-0: R 156-0; D 253-0 (ND 172-0, SD 81-0); I 1-0, June 20, 1991.

185. HR 2508. Fiscal 1992-93 Foreign Aid Authorization/Passage. Passage of the bill to authorize $12.4 billion in fiscal 1992 and $13 billion in fiscal 1993 for foreign economic and military assistance. Passed 274-138: R 77-80; D 196-58 (ND 146-28, SD 50-30); I 1-0, June 20, 1991. A "nay" was a vote supporting the president's position.

186. HR 429. Reclamation Projects Authorization/Trinity River Fishery. Riggs, R-Calif., amendment to increase the water supply to the Trinity River Fishery in California from the Shasta Reservoir through 1996. Adopted 300-95: R 77-74; D 222-21 (ND 157-12, SD 65-9); I 1-0, June 20, 1991.

187. HR 429. Reclamation Projects Authorization/Passage. Passage of the bill to authorize funds for various water projects; limit the eligibility for federally subsidized irrigation water; provide for fish and wildlife restoration; amend federal reclamation law; authorize the Bureau of Reclamation to study, build, or sell various water and hydroelectric power projects; and for other purposes. Passed 360-24: R 123-21; D 236-3 (ND 162-3, SD 74-0); I 1-0, June 20, 1991. A "nay" was a vote supporting the president's position.

188. HR 2686. Fiscal 1992 Interior Appropriations/Rule. Adoption of the rule (H Res 179) to waive certain points of order against and provide for House floor consideration of the bill to provide $12,717,527,000 in new budget authority for the Interior Department and related agencies in fiscal 1992. Adopted 200-168: R 2-141; D 197-27 (ND 135-15, SD 62-12); I 1-0, June 24, 1991.

190. HR 2686. Fiscal 1992 Interior Appropriations/Chicago Public Library. Burton, R-Ind., amendment to cut the $2 million for restoring the Chicago Public Library. Rejected 104-318: R 95-67; D 9-250 (ND 8-168, SD 1-82); I 0-1, June 25, 1991.

191. HR 2686. Fiscal 1992 Interior Appropriations/Gateway Park. Burton, R-Ind., amendment to cut the $3.65 million for the construction of the Gateway Park associated with the Illinois and Michigan Canal National Heritage Corridor. Rejected 92-323: R 83-81; D 9-241 (ND 6-170, SD 3-71); I 0-1, June 25, 1991.

KEY

Y Voted for (yea).
Paired for.
+ Announced for.
N Voted against (nay).
X Paired against.
- Announced against.
P Voted "present."
C Voted "present" to avoid possible conflict of interest.
? Did not vote or otherwise make a position known.

Democrats ***Republicans***
Independent

	183	184	185	186	187	188	190	191
ALABAMA								
1 ***Callahan***	Y	Y	Y	N	Y	N	Y	N
2 ***Dickinson***	Y	Y	N	N	Y	N	Y	N
3 Browder	Y	Y	Y	Y	Y	Y	N	N
4 Bevill	Y	Y	Y	Y	Y	Y	N	N
5 Cramer	Y	Y	Y	N	Y	Y	N	N
6 Erdreich	Y	Y	Y	Y	Y	Y	N	N
7 Harris	Y	Y	Y	Y	Y	Y	N	N
ALASKA								
AL ***Young***	Y	Y	Y	N	Y	N	Y	N
ARIZONA								
1 ***Rhodes***	Y	Y	N	N	Y	N	+	+
2 Vacancy								
3 ***Stump***	Y	Y	N	N	N	N	Y	Y
4 ***Kyl***	Y	Y	Y	N	Y	N	Y	N
5 ***Kolbe***	Y	Y	Y	N	Y	N	Y	N
ARKANSAS								
1 Alexander	N	Y	N	Y	?	Y	N	?
2 Thornton	N	Y	Y	Y	Y	Y	N	N
3 ***Hammerschmidt***	?	?	X	?	?	N	N	N
4 Anthony	Y	Y	N	Y	Y	Y	N	N
CALIFORNIA								
1 ***Riggs***	Y	Y	Y	Y	Y	N	Y	Y
2 ***Herger***	Y	Y	N	N	N	N	Y	N
3 Matsui	N	Y	Y	N	Y	Y	N	N
4 Fazio	N	Y	Y	N	Y	Y	N	N
5 Pelosi	N	Y	Y	Y	Y	Y	N	N
6 Boxer	N	Y	Y	Y	Y	?	N	N
7 Miller	N	Y	Y	Y	Y	Y	N	N
8 Dellums	N	Y	Y	Y	Y	Y	N	N
9 Stark	N	Y	N	Y	Y	Y	N	N
10 Edwards	N	Y	Y	Y	Y	Y	N	N
11 Lantos	N	Y	Y	Y	Y	Y	N	N
12 ***Campbell***	Y	Y	Y	Y	Y	?	Y	Y
13 Mineta	N	Y	Y	Y	Y	Y	N	N
14 ***Doolittle***	Y	Y	Y	N	Y	N	Y	Y
15 Condit	Y	Y	N	N	Y	N	N	N
16 Panetta	Y	Y	N	Y	Y	Y	N	N
17 Dooley	N	Y	Y	N	Y	N	N	N
18 Lehman	Y	Y	Y	N	Y	N	N	N
19 ***Lagomarsino***	Y	Y	N	Y	Y	N	N	N
20 ***Thomas***	Y	Y	N	N	Y	N	N	N
21 ***Gallegly***	Y	Y	N	Y	Y	N	Y	Y
22 ***Moorhead***	Y	Y	N	Y	Y	N	Y	Y
23 Beilenson	N	Y	Y	?	?	?	N	N
24 Waxman	N	Y	Y	Y	Y	?	N	N
25 Roybal	N	Y	Y	Y	Y	Y	N	N
26 Berman	N	Y	Y	Y	Y	Y	N	N
27 Levine	?	?	?	?	?	?	?	?
28 Dixon	N	Y	Y	N	Y	Y	N	N
29 Waters	N	Y	Y	Y	Y	Y	N	N
30 Martinez	?	?	?	?	?	?	N	N
31 Dymally	N	Y	Y	Y	Y	#	N	N
32 Anderson	N	Y	Y	Y	Y	Y	N	N
33 ***Dreier***	Y	Y	N	N	Y	N	Y	Y
34 Torres	N	Y	Y	Y	Y	+	N	N
35 ***Lewis***	Y	Y	Y	Y	Y	N	N	N
36 Brown	N	Y	Y	Y	Y	Y	N	N
37 ***McCandless***	Y	Y	N	N	Y	N	Y	N
38 ***Dornan***	Y	Y	N	N	Y	N	Y	Y
39 ***Dannemeyer***	Y	Y	N	N	Y	-	Y	Y
40 ***Cox***	Y	Y	Y	N	Y	?	Y	Y
41 ***Lowery***	Y	Y	Y	Y	Y	N	N	N
42 ***Rohrabacher***	Y	Y	Y	N	N	N	Y	Y
43 ***Packard***	Y	Y	N	N	Y	X	Y	Y
44 ***Cunningham***	Y	Y	Y	Y	Y	N	Y	N
45 ***Hunter***	Y	Y	N	N	Y	N	Y	Y
COLORADO								
1 Schroeder	N	Y	Y	Y	Y	Y	?	N
2 Skaggs	N	Y	Y	Y	Y	Y	N	N
3 Campbell	Y	Y	Y	Y	Y	N	N	N
4 ***Allard***	Y	Y	Y	N	Y	N	Y	Y
5 ***Hefley***	Y	Y	N	N	Y	N	Y	N
6 ***Schaefer***	Y	Y	Y	N	Y	N	N	N
CONNECTICUT								
1 Kennelly	N	Y	Y	Y	Y	Y	N	N
2 Gejdenson	N	Y	Y	Y	Y	Y	N	N
3 DeLauro	N	Y	Y	Y	Y	Y	N	N
4 ***Shays***	Y	Y	Y	Y	N	N	N	Y
5 ***Franks***	Y	Y	Y	Y	Y	N	N	N
6 ***Johnson***	Y	Y	Y	Y	Y	N	N	N
DELAWARE								
AL Carper	Y	Y	Y	Y	Y	Y	N	N
FLORIDA								
1 Hutto	Y	Y	N	Y	?	Y	N	N
2 Peterson	Y	Y	Y	Y	Y	N	N	N
3 Bennett	Y	Y	Y	Y	Y	Y	N	N
4 ***James***	Y	Y	N	Y	Y	N	Y	Y
5 ***McCollum***	Y	Y	Y	Y	Y	N	Y	Y
6 ***Stearns***	Y	Y	N	Y	Y	?	Y	Y
7 Gibbons	Y	Y	Y	Y	Y	Y	N	N
8 ***Young***	Y	Y	N	Y	Y	N	N	N
9 ***Bilirakis***	Y	Y	N	Y	Y	N	Y	Y
10 ***Ireland***	Y	Y	N	Y	Y	N	N	Y
11 Bacchus	N	Y	Y	N	Y	Y	N	?
12 ***Lewis***	Y	Y	N	Y	Y	N	Y	Y
13 ***Goss***	Y	Y	N	Y	N	N	N	N
14 Johnston	Y	Y	Y	Y	Y	Y	Y	Y
15 ***Shaw***	Y	Y	Y	N	Y	N	N	N
16 Smith	N	Y	Y	Y	Y	?	N	N
17 Lehman	N	Y	Y	?	Y	Y	N	N
18 ***Ros-Lehtinen***	Y	Y	Y	Y	Y	N	Y	Y
19 Fascell	N	Y	Y	Y	Y	Y	N	N
GEORGIA								
1 Thomas	Y	Y	Y	Y	Y	Y	N	N
2 Hatcher	Y	Y	Y	?	?	Y	N	?
3 Ray	Y	Y	N	Y	Y	Y	N	N
4 Jones	N	Y	Y	Y	Y	Y	N	N
5 Lewis	N	Y	Y	Y	Y	Y	N	N
6 ***Gingrich***	Y	Y	Y	N	Y	N	Y	Y
7 Darden	Y	Y	N	Y	Y	Y	N	N
8 Rowland	Y	Y	Y	Y	Y	Y	N	N
9 Jenkins	Y	Y	N	Y	Y	?	N	N
10 Barnard	Y	Y	N	Y	Y	Y	N	N
HAWAII								
1 Abercrombie	N	Y	Y	Y	Y	?	?	N
2 Mink	N	Y	Y	Y	Y	Y	N	N
IDAHO								
1 LaRocco	Y	Y	Y	N	Y	N	N	N
2 Stallings	Y	Y	Y	N	Y	N	Y	N
ILLINOIS								
1 Hayes	N	Y	Y	Y	Y	Y	N	N
2 Savage	N	Y	N	Y	Y	N	N	N
3 Russo	Y	Y	N	Y	Y	?	N	N
4 Sangmeister	Y	Y	N	Y	Y	Y	N	N
5 Lipinski	Y	Y	Y	Y	Y	Y	N	N
6 ***Hyde***	Y	Y	N	N	Y	N	N	Y
7 Collins	N	Y	Y	Y	Y	?	N	N
8 Rostenkowski	N	Y	Y	Y	Y	Y	N	N
9 Yates	N	Y	Y	Y	Y	Y	N	N
10 ***Porter***	Y	Y	Y	Y	Y	N	N	N
11 Annunzio	Y	Y	Y	Y	Y	Y	N	N
12 ***Crane***	Y	Y	N	N	N	N	Y	Y
13 ***Fawell***	?	?	?	?	?	N	Y	Y
14 ***Hastert***	Y	Y	N	N	Y	N	N	N
15 Vacancy								
16 Cox	N	Y	Y	Y	Y	Y	N	N
17 Evans	N	Y	Y	Y	Y	Y	N	N
18 ***Michel***	Y	Y	N	N	Y	N	N	N
19 Bruce	Y	Y	Y	Y	Y	Y	N	N
20 Durbin	Y	Y	Y	Y	Y	Y	N	N
21 Costello	Y	Y	N	Y	#	Y	N	N
22 Poshard	Y	Y	N	Y	Y	Y	N	N
INDIANA								
1 Visclosky	Y	Y	Y	Y	Y	Y	N	N
2 Sharp	N	Y	Y	Y	Y	Y	N	N
3 Roemer	Y	Y	N	Y	Y	Y	N	N

ND Northern Democrats SD Southern Democrats

	183	184	185	186	187	188	190	191
4 Long	N	Y	N	Y	Y	Y	N	N
5 Jontz	N	Y	N	Y	Y	Y	N	N
6 ***Burton***	Y	Y	Y	N	N	N	Y	Y
7 ***Myers***	Y	Y	N	N	Y	N	N	N
8 McCloskey	N	Y	Y	Y	Y	Y	N	N
9 Hamilton	Y	Y	Y	Y	Y	Y	Y	Y
10 Jacobs	Y	Y	N	Y	N	N	N	N
IOWA								
1 ***Leach***	N	Y	Y	Y	Y	N	Y	Y
2 ***Nussle***	Y	Y	N	N	N	N	Y	Y
3 Nagle	Y	Y	Y	Y	Y	N	N	N
4 Smith	N	Y	Y	Y	Y	N	N	N
5 ***Lightfoot***	Y	Y	Y	N	Y	N	N	N
6 ***Grandy***	N	Y	N	N	Y	N	N	N
KANSAS								
1 ***Roberts***	Y	Y	N	N	N	N	Y	Y
2 Slattery	Y	Y	Y	Y	Y	Y	N	N
3 ***Meyers***	Y	Y	Y	Y	Y	N	Y	Y
4 Glickman	Y	Y	Y	Y	Y	Y	Y	N
5 ***Nichols***	Y	Y	Y	N	Y	N	Y	Y
KENTUCKY								
1 Hubbard	Y	Y	N	Y	Y	N	N	N
2 Natcher	N	Y	Y	Y	Y	Y	N	N
3 Mazzoli	Y	Y	N	Y	Y	Y	N	N
4 ***Bunning***	Y	Y	N	N	Y	N	Y	Y
5 ***Rogers***	Y	Y	N	N	?	N	N	N
6 ***Hopkins***	?	?	?	?	?	?	?	Y
7 Perkins	Y	Y	N	N	Y	Y	N	N
LOUISIANA								
1 ***Livingston***	Y	?	N	N	Y	N	N	N
2 Jefferson	N	Y	Y	?	Y	Y	N	N
3 Tauzin	Y	Y	N	Y	Y	?	N	?
4 ***McCrery***	Y	Y	Y	N	Y	N	Y	N
5 Huckaby	?	?	?	?	?	Y	N	N
6 ***Baker***	Y	Y	Y	N	Y	N	Y	Y
7 Hayes	Y	Y	N	Y	Y	Y	N	?
8 ***Holloway***	Y	Y	N	N	Y	?	Y	Y
MAINE								
1 Andrews	N	Y	Y	Y	Y	Y	N	N
2 ***Snowe***	Y	Y	Y	Y	Y	N	N	N
MARYLAND								
1 ***Gilchrest***	Y	Y	Y	Y	Y	N	Y	Y
2 ***Bentley***	Y	Y	Y	Y	Y	N	Y	Y
3 Cardin	N	Y	Y	Y	Y	Y	N	N
4 McMillen	Y	Y	Y	Y	Y	Y	Y	Y
5 Hoyer	N	Y	Y	Y	Y	Y	N	N
6 Byron	Y	Y	Y	Y	Y	Y	Y	?
7 Mfume	N	?	Y	Y	Y	?	N	N
8 ***Morella***	N	Y	Y	Y	?	N	Y	Y
MASSACHUSETTS								
1 Olver	N	Y	Y	Y	Y	Y	N	N
2 Neal	N	Y	Y	Y	Y	?	N	N
3 Early	Y	Y	N	Y	Y	Y	N	N
4 Frank	N	Y	Y	Y	Y	Y	N	N
5 Atkins	N	Y	Y	Y	Y	Y	N	N
6 Mavroules	Y	Y	Y	?	?	?	N	N
7 Markey	N	Y	Y	Y	Y	Y	N	N
8 Kennedy	N	Y	Y	Y	?	N	Y	N
9 Moakley	N	Y	Y	Y	Y	Y	N	N
10 Studds	N	Y	Y	Y	Y	Y	N	N
11 Donnelly	N	Y	N	Y	Y	Y	N	N
MICHIGAN								
1 Conyers	?	Y	Y	Y	Y	Y	N	N
2 ***Pursell***	Y	Y	N	?	?	N	N	Y
3 Wolpe	N	Y	Y	Y	Y	Y	N	N
4 ***Upton***	Y	Y	N	Y	Y	N	Y	Y
5 ***Henry***	Y	Y	N	Y	Y	N	N	N
6 Carr	?	?	#	?	?	Y	N	N
7 Kildee	N	Y	Y	Y	Y	Y	N	N
8 Traxler	Y	Y	Y	Y	Y	Y	N	N
9 ***Vander Jagt***	Y	Y	N	Y	Y	N	N	N
10 ***Camp***	Y	Y	Y	N	Y	N	Y	Y
11 ***Davis***	Y	Y	Y	Y	?	?	N	N
12 Bonior	N	Y	Y	Y	Y	Y	N	N
13 Collins	N	Y	Y	Y	Y	Y	N	N
14 Hertel	N	Y	Y	Y	Y	Y	N	N
15 Ford	N	Y	Y	Y	Y	Y	N	N
16 Dingell	N	Y	Y	Y	Y	Y	N	N
17 Levin	N	Y	Y	Y	Y	Y	N	N
18 ***Broomfield***	Y	Y	N	Y	Y	N	Y	Y
MINNESOTA								
1 Penny	Y	Y	Y	N	N	N	Y	Y
2 ***Weber***	Y	Y	Y	Y	Y	?	Y	Y
3 ***Ramstad***	Y	Y	Y	Y	Y	N	Y	Y
4 Vento	N	Y	Y	Y	Y	Y	N	N

	183	184	185	186	187	188	190	191
5 Sabo	N	Y	Y	Y	?	Y	N	N
6 Sikorski	N	Y	Y	Y	Y	Y	N	N
7 Peterson	Y	Y	Y	Y	Y	?	N	N
8 Oberstar	?	?	#	?	?	?	N	N
MISSISSIPPI								
1 Whitten	N	Y	N	Y	Y	Y	N	N
2 Espy	N	Y	Y	N	Y	?	N	N
3 Montgomery	Y	Y	N	Y	Y	Y	N	N
4 Parker	Y	Y	N	Y	Y	?	N	N
5 Taylor	Y	Y	N	Y	Y	N	N	Y
MISSOURI								
1 Clay	N	Y	Y	?	?	?	N	N
2 Horn	Y	Y	Y	Y	Y	Y	N	N
3 Gephardt	N	Y	Y	Y	Y	?	N	N
4 Skelton	Y	Y	Y	Y	Y	Y	N	N
5 Wheat	N	Y	Y	Y	Y	Y	N	N
6 ***Coleman***	Y	Y	Y	?	?	N	N	N
7 ***Hancock***	Y	Y	N	N	N	N	Y	Y
8 ***Emerson***	Y	Y	Y	N	Y	N	N	N
9 Volkmer	Y	Y	N	Y	Y	Y	N	N
MONTANA								
1 Williams	Y	Y	N	Y	N	N	N	N
2 ***Marlenee***	Y	Y	N	N	N	N	N	Y
NEBRASKA								
1 ***Bereuter***	Y	Y	N	Y	Y	N	N	N
2 Hoagland	N	Y	Y	Y	Y	Y	N	N
3 ***Barrett***	Y	Y	N	N	Y	N	Y	Y
NEVADA								
1 Bilbray	Y	Y	Y	Y	Y	Y	N	N
2 ***Vucanovich***	Y	Y	N	N	Y	N	N	N
NEW HAMPSHIRE								
1 ***Zeliff***	Y	Y	Y	Y	N	N	Y	Y
2 Swett	Y	Y	Y	N	Y	Y	N	Y
NEW JERSEY								
1 Andrews	N	Y	Y	Y	Y	Y	N	N
2 Hughes	Y	Y	N	Y	Y	Y	N	N
3 Pallone	N	Y	Y	Y	Y	Y	Y	N
4 ***Smith***	Y	Y	N	Y	Y	N	Y	N
5 ***Roukema***	Y	Y	Y	Y	Y	N	Y	N
6 Dwyer	Y	Y	Y	Y	Y	Y	N	N
7 ***Rinaldo***	Y	Y	N	Y	Y	N	Y	N
8 Roe	Y	Y	Y	Y	Y	Y	N	N
9 Torricelli	Y	?	Y	Y	?	Y	N	N
10 Payne	N	Y	Y	Y	Y	?	N	N
11 ***Gallo***	Y	Y	Y	Y	?	?	N	N
12 ***Zimmer***	Y	Y	Y	Y	Y	N	Y	Y
13 ***Saxton***	Y	Y	Y	Y	Y	N	Y	Y
14 Guarini	Y	Y	Y	Y	Y	#	N	N
NEW MEXICO								
1 ***Schiff***	Y	Y	Y	Y	Y	N	Y	N
2 ***Skeen***	Y	Y	Y	N	Y	N	N	N
3 Richardson	Y	Y	Y	Y	Y	Y	N	N
NEW YORK								
1 Hochbrueckner	N	Y	Y	Y	Y	Y	N	N
2 Downey	N	Y	Y	Y	Y	Y	N	N
3 Mrazek	N	Y	Y	Y	Y	Y	N	N
4 ***Lent***	Y	Y	N	Y	Y	?	N	N
5 ***McGrath***	Y	Y	Y	Y	Y	N	N	N
6 Flake	N	Y	Y	Y	Y	Y	N	N
7 Ackerman	N	Y	Y	Y	Y	Y	N	N
8 Scheuer	N	Y	Y	Y	Y	Y	N	N
9 Manton	N	Y	Y	Y	?	Y	N	N
10 Schumer	N	Y	Y	Y	Y	?	N	N
11 Towns	N	Y	Y	Y	Y	?	N	N
12 Owens	N	Y	Y	Y	Y	?	N	N
13 Solarz	N	Y	Y	Y	Y	Y	N	N
14 ***Molinari***	Y	Y	Y	Y	Y	N	N	N
15 ***Green***	N	Y	Y	Y	Y	Y	N	N
16 Rangel	N	Y	Y	Y	Y	Y	N	N
17 Weiss	N	Y	Y	Y	Y	Y	N	N
18 Serrano	?	?	#	#	?	?	N	N
19 Engel	Y	Y	Y	Y	Y	Y	N	N
20 Lowey	N	Y	Y	Y	Y	Y	N	N
21 ***Fish***	Y	Y	Y	?	Y	N	N	N
22 ***Gilman***	Y	Y	Y	Y	Y	N	N	N
23 McNulty	N	Y	Y	Y	Y	Y	N	N
24 ***Solomon***	Y	Y	N	N	N	N	Y	Y
25 ***Boehlert***	Y	Y	Y	Y	Y	N	N	N
26 ***Martin***	?	?	?	?	?	N	Y	N
27 ***Walsh***	?	?	?	?	?	N	N	N
28 McHugh	Y	Y	Y	Y	Y	Y	N	N
29 ***Horton***	Y	Y	Y	Y	Y	N	?	N
30 Slaughter	Y	Y	Y	Y	Y	Y	N	N
31 ***Paxon***	Y	Y	Y	Y	Y	?	Y	Y

	183	184	185	186	187	188	190	191
32 LaFalce	Y	Y	Y	Y	Y	Y	N	N
33 Nowak	N	Y	Y	Y	Y	Y	N	N
34 ***Houghton***	N	Y	N	Y	?	N	N	N
NORTH CAROLINA								
1 Jones	Y	Y	Y	Y	Y	Y	N	N
2 Valentine	Y	Y	N	Y	Y	Y	N	N
3 Lancaster	Y	Y	Y	Y	Y	#	N	?
4 Price	Y	Y	Y	Y	Y	Y	N	N
5 Neal	Y	Y	N	Y	Y	Y	N	N
6 ***Coble***	Y	Y	Y	N	Y	?	Y	Y
7 Rose	N	Y	Y	Y	Y	Y	N	N
8 Hefner	Y	Y	N	Y	Y	Y	N	N
9 ***McMillan***	Y	Y	Y	Y	Y	N	N	N
10 ***Ballenger***	Y	Y	Y	N	Y	N	Y	Y
11 ***Taylor***	Y	Y	Y	N	N	N	Y	Y
NORTH DAKOTA								
AL Dorgan	Y	Y	Y	Y	Y	N	N	N
OHIO								
1 Luken	Y	Y	Y	N	Y	Y	Y	Y
2 ***Gradison***	Y	Y	Y	Y	?	?	Y	Y
3 Hall	Y	Y	Y	?	Y	Y	N	N
4 ***Oxley***	Y	Y	N	N	Y	N	Y	Y
5 ***Gillmor***	Y	Y	Y	N	Y	?	N	N
6 ***McEwen***	Y	Y	N	N	Y	N	Y	Y
7 ***Hobson***	Y	Y	N	Y	Y	N	N	N
8 ***Boehner***	Y	Y	Y	Y	Y	N	Y	N
9 Kaptur	Y	Y	Y	Y	Y	Y	N	N
10 ***Miller***	Y	Y	N	N	Y	N	N	Y
11 Eckart	N	Y	Y	Y	Y	Y	N	N
12 ***Kasich***	Y	Y	Y	N	Y	N	Y	Y
13 Pease	N	Y	N	Y	Y	Y	N	Y
14 Sawyer	N	Y	Y	Y	Y	Y	N	N
15 ***Wylie***	Y	Y	N	Y	Y	N	N	N
16 ***Regula***	Y	Y	N	Y	?	N	N	N
17 Traficant	Y	Y	N	Y	Y	P	N	N
18 Applegate	Y	Y	N	Y	Y	Y	N	N
19 Feighan	N	Y	Y	Y	Y	Y	N	N
20 Oakar	N	Y	Y	Y	Y	?	N	N
21 Stokes	N	Y	Y	Y	Y	?	N	N
OKLAHOMA								
1 ***Inhofe***	Y	Y	Y	N	Y	N	Y	Y
2 Synar	N	Y	Y	Y	Y	Y	N	N
3 Brewster	Y	Y	Y	N	Y	N	N	N
4 McCurdy	Y	Y	Y	Y	Y	Y	N	N
5 ***Edwards***	Y	Y	N	Y	?	N	N	N
6 English	Y	Y	N	Y	Y	N	N	N
OREGON								
1 AuCoin	N	Y	Y	Y	Y	N	N	N
2 ***Smith***	Y	Y	N	N	N	N	Y	N
3 Wyden	N	Y	Y	Y	Y	Y	N	N
4 DeFazio	Y	?	N	Y	Y	N	N	N
5 Kopetski	N	Y	Y	Y	Y	?	N	N
PENNSYLVANIA								
1 Foglietta	N	Y	Y	Y	Y	Y	N	N
2 Gray	?	?	?	?	?	Y	N	N
3 Borski	N	Y	Y	Y	Y	Y	N	N
4 Kolter	Y	Y	N	N	Y	Y	N	N
5 ***Schulze***	Y	Y	N	?	?	N	Y	Y
6 Yatron	N	Y	Y	Y	Y	Y	N	N
7 ***Weldon***	Y	Y	N	Y	Y	N	Y	Y
8 Kostmayer	N	Y	Y	Y	Y	Y	N	N
9 ***Shuster***	Y	Y	N	N	Y	N	Y	Y
10 ***McDade***	Y	Y	Y	Y	Y	N	N	N
11 Kanjorski	Y	Y	N	Y	Y	Y	N	N
12 Murtha	N	Y	Y	Y	Y	Y	N	N
13 ***Coughlin***	Y	Y	?	N	Y	N	N	N
14 Coyne	N	Y	Y	Y	Y	?	N	N
15 ***Ritter***	Y	Y	Y	Y	Y	N	N	N
16 ***Walker***	Y	Y	N	N	Y	N	Y	Y
17 ***Gekas***	Y	Y	Y	N	Y	?	Y	Y
18 ***Santorum***	Y	Y	Y	Y	N	N	Y	Y
19 ***Goodling***	Y	Y	N	Y	Y	N	N	N
20 Gaydos	Y	Y	N	?	?	Y	N	N
21 ***Ridge***	Y	Y	Y	Y	Y	?	Y	N
22 Murphy	Y	Y	Y	Y	Y	?	N	N
23 ***Clinger***	Y	Y	N	N	Y	Y	N	Y
RHODE ISLAND								
1 ***Machtley***	?	Y	Y	Y	Y	?	N	N
2 Reed	N	Y	Y	Y	Y	Y	N	N
SOUTH CAROLINA								
1 ***Ravenel***	Y	Y	Y	Y	Y	N	N	N
2 ***Spence***	?	?	X	?	?	N	N	N
3 Derrick	Y	Y	N	?	Y	Y	N	N
4 Patterson	Y	Y	N	Y	Y	Y	N	N
5 Spratt	Y	Y	Y	Y	Y	Y	N	N
6 Tallon	Y	Y	Y	Y	Y	N	N	N

	183	184	185	186	187	188	190	191
SOUTH DAKOTA								
AL Johnson	Y	Y	Y	Y	Y	N	N	N
TENNESSEE								
1 ***Quillen***	Y	Y	N	X	?	N	N	N
2 ***Duncan***	Y	Y	N	Y	N	N	Y	Y
3 Lloyd	?	?	?	?	?	Y	?	?
4 Cooper	Y	Y	Y	Y	Y	Y	N	?
5 Clement	Y	Y	Y	Y	Y	Y	N	N
6 Gordon	Y	Y	Y	Y	Y	Y	N	N
7 ***Sundquist***	Y	?	Y	N	Y	N	N	N
8 Tanner	Y	Y	N	N	Y	Y	N	N
9 Ford	N	Y	Y	Y	Y	?	N	N
TEXAS								
1 Chapman	Y	Y	N	Y	Y	Y	?	?
2 Wilson	Y	Y	N	?	Y	Y	N	N
3 ***Johnson***	Y	Y	N	Y	Y	N	Y	Y
4 Hall	Y	Y	N	N	Y	N	N	N
5 Bryant	Y	Y	N	Y	Y	Y	N	N
6 ***Barton***	Y	Y	N	?	?	N	Y	Y
7 ***Archer***	Y	Y	N	N	N	N	Y	Y
8 ***Fields***	Y	Y	N	N	Y	N	Y	Y
9 Brooks	?	?	?	?	?	Y	N	N
10 Pickle	Y	Y	Y	Y	Y	?	N	N
11 Edwards	Y	Y	Y	Y	Y	N	N	N
12 Geren	Y	Y	Y	N	?	Y	N	?
13 Sarpalius	Y	Y	N	Y	Y	Y	N	N
14 Laughlin	Y	Y	Y	Y	Y	N	N	N
15 de la Garza	Y	Y	Y	?	?	N	N	N
16 Coleman	Y	Y	Y	Y	Y	Y	N	N
17 Stenholm	Y	Y	Y	N	Y	N	N	Y
18 Washington	N	Y	?	?	?	?	N	N
19 ***Combest***	Y	Y	N	N	Y	N	Y	Y
20 Gonzalez	N	Y	Y	Y	Y	Y	N	N
21 ***Smith***	Y	Y	Y	?	Y	N	Y	Y
22 ***DeLay***	#	?	X	X	X	?	Y	N
23 Bustamante	N	Y	Y	Y	?	Y	N	N
24 Frost	Y	Y	Y	Y	Y	?	N	N
25 Andrews	Y	Y	Y	Y	Y	Y	N	N
26 ***Armey***	Y	Y	N	Y	N	N	Y	Y
27 Ortiz	X	?	?	#	?	Y	N	?
UTAH								
1 ***Hansen***	Y	Y	N	N	Y	N	Y	Y
2 Owens	Y	Y	Y	?	Y	X	?	?
3 Orton	Y	Y	N	Y	Y	X	?	?
VERMONT								
AL *Sanders*	N	Y	Y	Y	Y	Y	N	N
VIRGINIA								
1 ***Bateman***	Y	Y	N	N	Y	N	N	N
2 Pickett	Y	Y	N	Y	Y	Y	N	N
3 ***Bliley***	Y	Y	Y	N	Y	?	Y	N
4 Sisisky	Y	Y	Y	Y	Y	Y	N	N
5 Payne	Y	Y	Y	Y	Y	?	N	N
6 Olin	Y	Y	Y	Y	Y	N	N	N
7 ***Slaughter***	Y	Y	N	Y	Y	N	Y	N
8 Moran	Y	Y	Y	Y	Y	Y	N	N
9 Boucher	Y	Y	N	Y	Y	Y	N	N
10 ***Wolf***	Y	Y	N	Y	Y	N	N	N
WASHINGTON								
1 ***Miller***	Y	Y	Y	Y	Y	N	N	Y
2 Swift	N	Y	Y	Y	Y	Y	N	N
3 Unsoeld	N	Y	Y	Y	Y	Y	N	N
4 ***Morrison***	Y	Y	N	N	Y	N	N	N
5 Foley								
6 Dicks	Y	Y	Y	Y	?	Y	N	N
7 McDermott	N	Y	Y	Y	Y	Y	N	N
8 ***Chandler***	Y	Y	Y	N	Y	?	N	N
WEST VIRGINIA								
1 Mollohan	Y	Y	N	Y	Y	Y	N	N
2 Staggers	N	Y	N	Y	Y	Y	N	N
3 Wise	N	Y	Y	Y	Y	Y	N	N
4 Rahall	N	Y	N	Y	Y	Y	N	N
WISCONSIN								
1 Aspin	Y	Y	?	Y	Y	Y	N	N
2 ***Klug***	Y	Y	Y	Y	Y	?	Y	Y
3 ***Gunderson***	Y	Y	N	Y	Y	N	N	N
4 Kleczka	N	Y	Y	Y	Y	Y	N	?
5 Moody	Y	Y	Y	Y	Y	Y	N	N
6 ***Petri***	Y	Y	N	Y	N	N	Y	Y
7 Obey	Y	Y	Y	Y	Y	Y	N	N
8 ***Roth***	Y	Y	N	N	Y	N	N	Y
9 ***Sensenbrenner***	Y	Y	N	Y	N	N	Y	Y
WYOMING								
AL ***Thomas***	Y	Y	Y	N	Y	N	N	N

Southern states - Ala., Ark., Fla., Ga., Ky., La., Miss., N.C., Okla., S.C., Tenn., Texas, Va.
Omitted votes are quorum calls, which CQ does not include in its vote charts.

HOUSE VOTES 192, 193, 194, 195, 196, 197, 198, 199

192. HR 2686. Fiscal 1992 Interior Appropriations/Eliminate Funds for National Endowment for the Arts. Crane, R-Ill., amendment to eliminate $178 million or all of the funding for the National Endowment for the Arts. Rejected 66-361: R 54-110; D 12-250 (ND 2-175, SD 10-75); I 0-1, June 25, 1991.

193. HR 2686. Fiscal 1992 Interior Appropriations/Cut Funds for National Endowment for the Arts. Stearns, R-Fla., amendment to cut funding for the National Endowment for the Arts by about 5 percent or $7.4 million. Rejected 196-228: R 124-38; D 72-189 (ND 25-151, SD 47-38); I 0-1, June 25, 1991.

194. HR 2686. Fiscal 1992 Interior Appropriations/Grazing Fees. Synar, D-Okla., amendment to increase over four years the domestic livestock grazing fee on public lands administered by the Bureau of Land Management from $1.97 to $8.70 per animal unit month or to fair market value, whichever is higher by fiscal 1995. Adopted 232-192: R 47-114; D 184-78 (ND 140-38, SD 44-40); I 1-0, June 25, 1991. A "nay" was a vote supporting the president's position.

195. HR 2686. Fiscal 1992 Interior Appropriations/Discretionary Accounts. Upton, R-Mich., amendment to provide for an across-the-board cut of 1.67 percent in all discretionary accounts in the bill, reducing spending in the bill by $213 million. The $213 million is the amount that is projected to be needed for the firefighting accounts of the Interior and Agriculture departments and that will have to be funded through an emergency designation and thus break the spending caps from the Budget Enforcement Act of 1990 (PL 101-508). Rejected 169-249: R 127-31; D 42-217 (ND 21-155, SD 21-62); I 0-1, June 25, 1991.

196. HR 2686. Fiscal 1992 Interior Appropriations/Passage. Passage of the bill to provide $12,717,527,000 in new budget authority for the Department of the Interior and related agencies for fiscal 1992. The administration requested $11,595,927,000. Passed 345-76: R 92-66; D 252-10 (ND 171-6, SD 81-4); I 1-0, June 25, 1991.

197. HR 2699. Fiscal 1992 D.C. Appropriations/Reduce Payment. Rohrabacher, R-Calif., amendment to reduce the federal payment to the District of Columbia from $630.5 million to $611.3 million to limit overall growth to 2.4 percent over the fiscal 1991 level. Rejected 153-270: R 114-45; D 39-224 (ND 20-159, SD 19-65); I 0-1, June 26, 1991.

198. HR 2699. Fiscal 1992 D.C. Appropriations/Passage. Passage of the bill to provide $699,797,000 in federal funds for the District of Columbia and to approve spending of $3,894,193,946 in funds raised from local taxes for the District of Columbia in fiscal 1992. The bill provides for $630.5 million in a federal payment to the District. The administration requested $682,570,000 in federal funds and to approve spending of $3,879,866,946 in funds raised from local taxes. The bill would prohibit the use of federal funds for abortions but would allow the District to use locally raised taxes for abortions. Passed 300-123: R 54-105; D 245-18 (ND 169-9, SD 76-9); I 1-0, June 26, 1991. A "nay" was a vote supporting the president's position.

199. HR 2707. Fiscal 1992 Labor, HHS and Education Appropriations/Discretionary Accounts. Walker, R-Pa., amendment to provide an across-the-board cut of 5.9 percent in all accounts in the bill to limit overall growth in the bill to 2.4 percent over the fiscal 1991 level. Rejected 55-366: R 54-104; D 1-261 (ND 0-179, SD 1-82); I 0-1, June 26, 1991.

KEY

Y Voted for (yea).
Paired for.
\+ Announced for.
N Voted against (nay).
X Paired against.
\- Announced against.
P Voted "present."
C Voted "present" to avoid possible conflict of interest.
? Did not vote or otherwise make a position known.

Democrats ***Republicans***
Independent

	192	193	194	195	196	197	198	199
ALABAMA								
1 ***Callahan***	Y	Y	N	Y	Y	?	N	N
2 ***Dickinson***	N	Y	N	Y	Y	Y	N	N
3 Browder	N	Y	N	N	Y	N	Y	N
4 Bevill	N	Y	N	N	Y	N	Y	N
5 Cramer	N	Y	N	N	Y	N	Y	N
6 Erdreich	N	Y	Y	N	Y	N	Y	N
7 Harris	N	Y	N	N	Y	?	Y	N
ALASKA								
AL ***Young***	N	Y	N	N	Y	N	N	N
ARIZONA								
1 ***Rhodes***	-	+	-	+	+	+	-	+
2 Vacancy								
3 ***Stump***	Y	Y	N	Y	N	Y	N	Y
4 ***Kyl***	Y	Y	N	Y	N	Y	N	Y
5 ***Kolbe***	N	Y	N	N	N	Y	Y	N
ARKANSAS								
1 Alexander	N	N	N	N	Y	N	Y	N
2 Thornton	N	N	?	N	Y	N	Y	N
3 ***Hammerschmidt***	N	Y	N	Y	Y	Y	Y	N
4 Anthony	N	N	N	N	Y	N	Y	N
CALIFORNIA								
1 ***Riggs***	N	Y	N	Y	Y	Y	Y	Y
2 ***Herger***	Y	Y	N	Y	N	Y	N	Y
3 Matsui	?	N	Y	N	Y	N	Y	N
4 Fazio	N	N	Y	N	Y	N	Y	N
5 Pelosi	N	N	Y	N	Y	N	Y	N
6 Boxer	N	N	Y	N	Y	N	Y	N
7 Miller	N	N	Y	N	Y	N	Y	N
8 Dellums	N	N	Y	N	Y	N	Y	N
9 Stark	N	N	Y	?	Y	N	Y	N
10 Edwards	N	N	Y	N	Y	N	Y	N
11 Lantos	N	N	Y	N	Y	N	Y	N
12 ***Campbell***	Y	Y	Y	Y	Y	Y	Y	Y
13 Mineta	N	N	Y	?	Y	N	Y	N
14 ***Doolittle***	Y	Y	N	Y	N	Y	N	Y
15 Condit	Y	Y	N	Y	N	N	N	N
16 Panetta	N	N	N	N	Y	N	Y	N
17 Dooley	N	Y	N	N	Y	N	Y	N
18 Lehman	N	N	N	N	Y	N	Y	N
19 ***Lagomarsino***	N	Y	N	Y	Y	Y	N	N
20 ***Thomas***	N	Y	N	Y	Y	Y	Y	N
21 ***Gallegly***	N	Y	N	Y	Y	Y	N	N
22 ***Moorhead***	Y	Y	N	Y	N	Y	N	Y
23 Beilenson	N	N	Y	N	Y	N	Y	N
24 Waxman	N	N	Y	?	?	N	Y	N
25 Roybal	N	N	Y	N	Y	N	Y	N
26 Berman	N	N	Y	N	Y	N	Y	N
27 Levine	?	?	?	?	?	N	Y	N
28 Dixon	N	N	Y	N	Y	N	Y	N
29 Waters	N	N	Y	N	Y	N	Y	N
30 Martinez	N	N	N	N	Y	N	Y	N
31 Dymally	N	N	N	N	Y	N	Y	?
32 Anderson	N	N	Y	N	Y	N	Y	N
33 ***Dreier***	Y	Y	Y	Y	N	Y	N	Y
34 Torres	N	N	Y	N	Y	N	Y	N
35 ***Lewis***	N	N	N	N	Y	N	Y	N
36 Brown	N	N	Y	N	Y	N	Y	N
37 ***McCandless***	Y	Y	N	Y	Y	Y	N	Y
38 ***Dornan***	Y	Y	N	Y	N	Y	N	Y
39 ***Dannemeyer***	Y	Y	N	Y	N	Y	N	Y
40 ***Cox***	Y	Y	Y	Y	-	Y	N	Y
41 ***Lowery***	N	N	N	N	Y	N	Y	N
42 ***Rohrabacher***	Y	Y	Y	Y	N	Y	N	Y
43 ***Packard***	Y	Y	N	Y	N	Y	N	Y
44 ***Cunningham***	N	N	N	Y	N	Y	N	N
45 ***Hunter***	Y	Y	N	Y	N	Y	N	Y
COLORADO								
1 Schroeder	N	N	Y	N	Y	N	Y	N
2 Skaggs	N	N	Y	N	Y	N	Y	N
3 Campbell	N	Y	N	N	Y	Y	N	N
4 ***Allard***	N	Y	N	Y	N	Y	N	Y
5 ***Hefley***	Y	Y	N	Y	N	Y	N	Y
6 ***Schaefer***	N	Y	N	Y	N	Y	N	N
CONNECTICUT								
1 Kennelly	N	N	Y	N	Y	N	Y	N
2 Gejdenson	N	N	Y	N	Y	N	Y	N
3 DeLauro	N	N	Y	N	Y	N	Y	N
4 ***Shays***	N	Y	Y	Y	Y	N	Y	N
5 ***Franks***	N	Y	N	Y	Y	N	Y	N
6 ***Johnson***	N	N	Y	N	Y	N	Y	N
DELAWARE								
AL Carper	N	Y	Y	Y	Y	N	Y	N
FLORIDA								
1 Hutto	Y	Y	N	Y	Y	Y	N	N
2 Peterson	N	N	N	Y	Y	N	Y	N
3 Bennett	Y	Y	Y	N	Y	Y	Y	Y
4 ***James***	Y	Y	Y	Y	Y	Y	N	N
5 ***McCollum***	N	Y	N	Y	Y	Y	N	N
6 ***Stearns***	Y	Y	N	Y	Y	Y	N	N
7 Gibbons	N	N	Y	N	Y	N	Y	N
8 ***Young***	N	Y	?	?	?	N	Y	N
9 ***Bilirakis***	Y	Y	N	Y	N	Y	N	N
10 ***Ireland***	N	Y	Y	Y	?	Y	N	N
11 Bacchus	N	N	Y	N	Y	N	Y	N
12 ***Lewis***	N	Y	N	Y	Y	Y	N	N
13 ***Goss***	N	Y	Y	Y	Y	Y	N	N
14 Johnston	N	N	Y	N	Y	N	Y	N
15 ***Shaw***	N	Y	N	Y	Y	Y	N	N
16 Smith	N	N	Y	N	Y	N	Y	N
17 Lehman	N	N	Y	N	Y	N	Y	?
18 ***Ros-Lehtinen***	N	Y	Y	Y	Y	Y	N	N
19 Fascell	N	N	Y	N	Y	N	Y	N
GEORGIA								
1 Thomas	N	Y	N	N	Y	N	Y	N
2 Hatcher	N	N	N	N	Y	N	Y	N
3 Ray	N	N	N	N	Y	N	Y	N
4 Jones	N	N	Y	N	Y	N	Y	N
5 Lewis	N	N	Y	N	Y	N	Y	N
6 ***Gingrich***	Y	Y	N	Y	N	N	Y	?
7 Darden	N	N	Y	N	Y	N	Y	N
8 Rowland	N	Y	Y	N	Y	N	Y	N
9 Jenkins	N	Y	Y	N	Y	N	Y	N
10 Barnard	N	N	Y	Y	Y	N	Y	N
HAWAII								
1 Abercrombie	N	N	Y	N	Y	N	Y	N
2 Mink	N	N	Y	N	Y	N	Y	N
IDAHO								
1 LaRocco	N	N	N	N	Y	Y	Y	N
2 Stallings	N	Y	N	N	Y	N	N	N
ILLINOIS								
1 Hayes	N	N	Y	N	Y	N	Y	N
2 Savage	N	?	Y	N	?	N	Y	N
3 Russo	N	N	Y	N	Y	N	Y	N
4 Sangmeister	N	N	Y	N	Y	N	Y	N
5 Lipinski	N	Y	Y	N	Y	Y	Y	N
6 ***Hyde***	Y	Y	N	Y	Y	Y	N	N
7 Collins	N	N	Y	N	Y	N	Y	N
8 Rostenkowski	N	N	Y	N	Y	N	Y	N
9 Yates	N	N	Y	N	Y	N	Y	N
10 ***Porter***	N	Y	?	Y	Y	Y	N	N
11 Annunzio	N	N	Y	N	Y	N	Y	N
12 ***Crane***	Y	Y	Y	Y	N	Y	N	Y
13 ***Fawell***	N	Y	Y	Y	N	Y	N	Y
14 ***Hastert***	N	Y	N	Y	?	Y	N	N
15 Vacancy								
16 Cox	N	N	Y	N	Y	N	Y	N
17 Evans	N	N	Y	N	Y	N	Y	N
18 ***Michel***	N	Y	N	Y	Y	?	?	N
19 Bruce	N	N	Y	N	Y	N	Y	N
20 Durbin	N	N	Y	N	Y	N	Y	N
21 Costello	N	Y	Y	N	Y	N	Y	N
22 Poshard	N	Y	Y	N	Y	N	Y	N
INDIANA								
1 Visclosky	N	N	Y	N	Y	N	Y	N
2 Sharp	N	N	Y	N	Y	N	Y	N
3 Roemer	N	Y	Y	Y	Y	Y	Y	N

ND Northern Democrats SD Southern Democrats

	192	193	194	195	196	197	198	199
4 Long	N	Y	N	Y	Y	N	Y	N
5 Jontz	N	N	Y	N	Y	N	Y	N
6 ***Burton***	Y	Y	N	Y	N	Y	N	Y
7 ***Myers***	N	Y	N	N	Y	N	N	N
8 McCloskey	N	N	Y	N	Y	N	Y	N
9 Hamilton	N	Y	Y	Y	Y	N	Y	N
10 Jacobs	N	Y	Y	Y	N	N	Y	N
IOWA								
1 ***Leach***	N	N	N	Y	Y	Y	N	N
2 ***Nussle***	N	Y	N	Y	N	Y	N	N
3 Nagle	N	N	N	N	Y	N	Y	N
4 Smith	N	N	N	N	Y	N	Y	N
5 ***Lightfoot***	Y	Y	N	N	Y	Y	N	N
6 ***Grandy***	N	N	N	Y	Y	Y	N	N
KANSAS								
1 ***Roberts***	N	Y	N	Y	N	Y	N	Y
2 Slattery	N	N	Y	N	Y	N	Y	N
3 ***Meyers***	N	Y	Y	Y	Y	N	Y	N
4 Glickman	N	N	Y	Y	Y	Y	Y	N
5 ***Nichols***	Y	Y	N	Y	N	Y	N	Y
KENTUCKY								
1 Hubbard	N	Y	N	Y	Y	N	Y	N
2 Natcher	N	Y	N	N	Y	N	Y	N
3 Mazzoli	N	N	Y	N	Y	N	Y	N
4 ***Bunning***	Y	Y	N	Y	N	Y	N	Y
5 ***Rogers***	N	Y	N	N	Y	Y	N	N
6 ***Hopkins***	N	Y	N	Y	Y	?	?	?
7 Perkins	N	N	N	N	Y	N	Y	N
LOUISIANA								
1 ***Livingston***	Y	Y	N	?	?	Y	N	N
2 Jefferson	N	N	Y	N	Y	N	Y	N
3 Tauzin	N	Y	Y	Y	Y	Y	Y	N
4 ***McCrery***	N	Y	Y	Y	N	Y	?	N
5 Huckaby	N	Y	Y	Y	Y	Y	N	N
6 ***Baker***	Y	Y	N	?	?	Y	X	Y
7 Hayes	Y	Y	Y	Y	Y	Y	N	N
8 ***Holloway***	Y	Y	N	?	N	Y	N	Y
MAINE								
1 Andrews	N	N	Y	N	Y	N	Y	N
2 ***Snowe***	N	Y	Y	N	Y	Y	Y	N
MARYLAND								
1 ***Gilchrest***	N	Y	N	Y	Y	N	Y	N
2 ***Bentley***	N	Y	N	Y	Y	Y	N	N
3 Cardin	N	N	Y	N	Y	N	Y	N
4 McMillen	N	N	Y	Y	Y	N	Y	N
5 Hoyer	N	N	Y	N	Y	N	Y	N
6 Byron	N	Y	Y	Y	Y	Y	Y	N
7 Mfume	N	N	Y	Y	Y	N	Y	N
8 ***Morella***	N	N	Y	Y	Y	N	Y	N
MASSACHUSETTS								
1 Olver	N	N	Y	N	Y	N	Y	N
2 Neal	N	N	Y	N	Y	N	Y	N
3 Early	N	N	Y	N	Y	?	?	N
4 Frank	N	N	Y	N	Y	N	Y	N
5 Atkins	N	N	Y	N	Y	N	Y	N
6 Mavroules	N	N	Y	N	Y	N	Y	N
7 Markey	N	N	Y	N	Y	N	Y	N
8 Kennedy	N	N	Y	N	Y	N	Y	N
9 Moakley	N	N	Y	N	Y	N	Y	N
10 Studds	N	N	Y	N	Y	N	Y	N
11 Donnelly	N	Y	Y	N	Y	N	Y	N
MICHIGAN								
1 Conyers	N	N	Y	N	Y	N	Y	N
2 ***Pursell***	N	Y	?	?	Y	Y	Y	N
3 Wolpe	N	N	Y	N	Y	N	Y	N
4 ***Upton***	N	Y	Y	Y	N	Y	N	N
5 ***Henry***	N	Y	Y	Y	N	Y	N	N
6 Carr	N	N	N	N	Y	N	Y	N
7 Kildee	N	N	Y	N	Y	N	Y	N
8 Traxler	N	N	Y	N	Y	Y	Y	N
9 ***Vander Jagt***	N	?	N	Y	Y	Y	N	N
10 ***Camp***	N	Y	N	Y	N	Y	N	N
11 ***Davis***	N	Y	N	N	Y	N	N	N
12 Bonior	N	N	Y	N	Y	N	Y	N
13 Collins	N	N	N	N	Y	N	Y	N
14 Hertel	N	N	Y	N	Y	N	Y	N
15 Ford	N	N	Y	N	Y	N	Y	N
16 Dingell	N	N	Y	N	Y	N	Y	N
17 Levin	N	N	Y	N	Y	N	Y	N
18 ***Broomfield***	N	N	N	Y	N	Y	N	N
MINNESOTA								
1 Penny	N	N	N	Y	N	Y	Y	N
2 ***Weber***	N	Y	N	Y	Y	Y	N	N
3 ***Ramstad***	N	N	Y	Y	Y	Y	N	N
4 Vento	N	N	Y	N	Y	N	Y	N

	192	193	194	195	196	197	198	199
5 Sabo	N	N	Y	N	Y	N	Y	N
6 Sikorski	N	N	Y	N	Y	N	Y	N
7 Peterson	N	N	N	N	Y	Y	Y	N
8 Oberstar	N	N	N	N	Y	N	Y	N
MISSISSIPPI								
1 Whitten	N	N	N	N	Y	N	Y	N
2 Espy	N	N	N	N	Y	N	Y	N
3 Montgomery	N	Y	N	Y	Y	N	Y	N
4 Parker	Y	Y	N	Y	Y	N	Y	N
5 Taylor	Y	Y	N	Y	N	Y	N	N
MISSOURI								
1 Clay	N	N	Y	N	Y	N	Y	N
2 Horn	N	Y	Y	Y	Y	N	Y	N
3 Gephardt	N	N	Y	N	Y	N	Y	N
4 Skelton	N	Y	N	Y	N	Y	N	N
5 Wheat	N	N	Y	N	Y	N	Y	N
6 ***Coleman***	N	N	N	Y	Y	Y	N	N
7 ***Hancock***	Y	Y	N	Y	N	Y	N	Y
8 ***Emerson***	N	Y	N	Y	N	N	N	N
9 Volkmer	N	Y	N	N	Y	Y	N	N
MONTANA								
1 Williams	N	N	N	N	Y	N	Y	N
2 ***Marlenee***	Y	Y	N	N	N	Y	N	Y
NEBRASKA								
1 ***Bereuter***	N	N	N	N	Y	Y	N	N
2 Hoagland	N	Y	Y	Y	Y	N	Y	N
3 ***Barrett***	N	Y	N	Y	N	Y	N	N
NEVADA								
1 Bilbray	N	N	N	N	Y	N	Y	N
2 ***Vucanovich***	Y	Y	N	N	N	Y	N	N
NEW HAMPSHIRE								
1 ***Zeliff***	N	N	Y	Y	N	Y	N	Y
2 Swett	N	N	Y	Y	Y	Y	Y	N
NEW JERSEY								
1 Andrews	N	N	N	Y	N	N	Y	N
2 Hughes	N	Y	Y	Y	Y	Y	Y	N
3 Pallone	N	N	Y	N	Y	Y	N	N
4 ***Smith***	N	Y	Y	Y	Y	N	N	N
5 ***Roukema***	N	Y	Y	Y	Y	Y	N	N
6 Dwyer	N	N	Y	N	Y	N	Y	N
7 ***Rinaldo***	N	Y	Y	?	Y	Y	N	N
8 Roe	N	N	N	N	Y	N	Y	N
9 Torricelli	N	N	Y	N	Y	N	Y	N
10 Payne	N	N	Y	N	Y	N	Y	N
11 ***Gallo***	N	N	Y	N	Y	Y	N	N
12 ***Zimmer***	N	Y	Y	Y	Y	Y	N	N
13 ***Saxton***	N	Y	Y	Y	Y	Y	N	N
14 Guarini	N	Y	Y	N	Y	N	Y	N
NEW MEXICO								
1 ***Schiff***	N	N	N	N	Y	N	Y	N
2 ***Skeen***	N	N	N	N	N	N	Y	N
3 Richardson	N	N	N	N	Y	N	Y	N
NEW YORK								
1 Hochbrueckner	N	N	Y	N	Y	N	Y	N
2 Downey	N	N	Y	N	Y	N	Y	N
3 Mrazek	N	N	Y	N	Y	N	Y	N
4 ***Lent***	N	N	N	N	Y	Y	Y	N
5 ***McGrath***	N	N	Y	N	Y	N	N	N
6 Flake	N	N	N	N	Y	N	Y	N
7 Ackerman	N	N	Y	N	Y	?	#	N
8 Scheuer	N	N	Y	N	Y	N	Y	N
9 Manton	N	N	Y	N	Y	N	Y	N
10 Schumer	N	N	Y	N	Y	N	Y	N
11 Towns	N	N	Y	N	Y	N	Y	N
12 Owens	N	N	Y	N	Y	N	Y	N
13 Solarz	N	N	Y	N	Y	N	Y	N
14 ***Molinari***	N	N	N	Y	Y	N	Y	N
15 ***Green***	N	N	Y	N	Y	N	Y	N
16 Rangel	N	N	Y	N	Y	N	Y	N
17 Weiss	N	N	Y	N	Y	N	Y	N
18 Serrano	N	N	Y	N	Y	N	Y	N
19 Engel	N	N	Y	N	Y	N	Y	N
20 Lowey	N	N	Y	N	Y	N	Y	N
21 ***Fish***	N	N	Y	N	Y	N	Y	N
22 ***Gilman***	N	N	Y	N	Y	N	Y	N
23 McNulty	N	N	Y	N	Y	N	Y	N
24 ***Solomon***	Y	Y	Y	Y	N	Y	N	N
25 ***Boehlert***	N	N	Y	Y	Y	N	Y	N
26 ***Martin***	N	Y	N	Y	N	?	Y	N
27 ***Walsh***	N	N	N	Y	Y	Y	Y	N
28 McHugh	N	N	Y	N	Y	N	Y	N
29 ***Horton***	N	N	N	N	Y	N	Y	N
30 Slaughter	N	N	Y	N	Y	N	Y	N
31 ***Paxon***	N	Y	N	Y	N	Y	N	N

	192	193	194	195	196	197	198	199
32 LaFalce	N	N	Y	N	Y	N	N	N
33 Nowak	N	N	Y	N	Y	N	Y	N
34 ***Houghton***	N	N	N	N	Y	N	Y	?
NORTH CAROLINA								
1 Jones	N	N	N	N	Y	N	Y	N
2 Valentine	N	Y	Y	N	Y	Y	Y	N
3 Lancaster	N	Y	Y	N	Y	N	Y	N
4 Price	N	N	Y	N	Y	N	Y	N
5 Neal	N	Y	Y	Y	Y	Y	Y	N
6 ***Coble***	N	Y	N	Y	N	Y	N	Y
7 Rose	N	N	N	N	Y	N	Y	N
8 Hefner	N	Y	Y	N	Y	N	Y	N
9 ***McMillan***	N	Y	N	Y	N	N	Y	N
10 ***Ballenger***	N	Y	N	Y	N	Y	Y	Y
11 ***Taylor***	N	Y	N	Y	Y	Y	N	N
NORTH DAKOTA								
AL Dorgan	N	Y	N	N	Y	Y	Y	N
OHIO								
1 Luken	Y	Y	Y	Y	Y	Y	N	N
2 ***Gradison***	N	Y	Y	Y	N	N	Y	N
3 Hall	N	N	Y	Y	Y	Y	Y	N
4 ***Oxley***	N	Y	N	Y	Y	N	Y	Y
5 ***Gillmor***	N	Y	N	Y	Y	Y	N	Y
6 ***McEwen***	Y	Y	N	Y	Y	Y	N	Y
7 ***Hobson***	N	Y	N	Y	Y	N	Y	Y
8 ***Boehner***	Y	Y	N	Y	N	Y	N	Y
9 Kaptur	N	N	Y	N	Y	N	Y	N
10 ***Miller***	Y	Y	Y	Y	Y	Y	N	Y
11 Eckart	N	N	Y	N	Y	N	Y	N
12 ***Kasich***	N	Y	Y	Y	N	Y	N	Y
13 Pease	N	N	Y	N	Y	N	Y	N
14 Sawyer	N	N	Y	N	Y	N	Y	N
15 ***Wylie***	N	Y	N	Y	Y	Y	N	N
16 ***Regula***	N	N	N	N	Y	N	Y	N
17 Traficant	N	Y	N	N	Y	N	Y	N
18 Applegate	N	N	Y	Y	Y	Y	Y	N
19 Feighan	N	N	Y	N	Y	N	Y	N
20 Oakar	N	N	Y	N	Y	N	Y	N
21 Stokes	N	N	Y	N	Y	N	Y	N
OKLAHOMA								
1 ***Inhofe***	Y	Y	N	Y	N	Y	Y	Y
2 Synar	N	N	Y	N	Y	N	Y	N
3 Brewster	N	Y	N	N	Y	N	Y	N
4 McCurdy	N	Y	Y	Y	Y	N	Y	N
5 ***Edwards***	N	Y	N	Y	Y	Y	N	N
6 English	N	Y	N	Y	Y	Y	N	N
OREGON								
1 AuCoin	N	N	N	N	Y	N	Y	N
2 ***Smith***	N	N	N	Y	N	Y	N	N
3 Wyden	N	N	Y	N	Y	N	Y	N
4 DeFazio	N	N	N	N	Y	N	Y	N
5 Kopetski	N	N	N	N	Y	N	Y	N
PENNSYLVANIA								
1 Foglietta	N	N	Y	N	Y	N	Y	N
2 Gray	N	?	?	?	?	N	Y	N
3 Borski	N	N	Y	N	Y	N	Y	N
4 Kolter	N	Y	?	N	Y	N	Y	?
5 ***Schulze***	N	Y	N	N	Y	Y	N	N
6 Yatron	N	N	Y	N	Y	N	Y	N
7 ***Weldon***	N	Y	Y	Y	Y	Y	Y	?
8 Kostmayer	N	N	Y	N	Y	N	Y	N
9 ***Shuster***	Y	Y	N	Y	Y	Y	N	Y
10 ***McDade***	N	N	N	N	Y	N	Y	N
11 Kanjorski	N	N	Y	N	Y	N	Y	N
12 Murtha	N	N	N	N	Y	N	Y	N
13 ***Coughlin***	N	Y	N	N	Y	N	Y	N
14 Coyne	N	N	Y	N	Y	N	Y	N
15 ***Ritter***	N	Y	Y	Y	Y	Y	N	N
16 ***Walker***	Y	Y	Y	Y	N	Y	N	Y
17 ***Gekas***	Y	Y	N	Y	N	N	Y	N
18 ***Santorum***	N	Y	N	Y	N	Y	N	Y
19 ***Goodling***	N	Y	N	Y	Y	N	Y	N
20 Gaydos	N	N	N	N	Y	N	Y	N
21 ***Ridge***	N	N	N	Y	Y	N	Y	?
22 Murphy	N	N	Y	N	Y	Y	N	N
23 ***Clinger***	N	N	Y	Y	Y	Y	N	N
RHODE ISLAND								
1 ***Machtley***	N	N	Y	Y	Y	Y	Y	N
2 Reed	N	N	N	N	Y	N	Y	N
SOUTH CAROLINA								
1 ***Ravenel***	N	N	Y	Y	Y	Y	Y	N
2 ***Spence***	N	Y	N	Y	Y	Y	N	N
3 Derrick	N	N	Y	N	Y	N	Y	N
4 Patterson	N	Y	Y	Y	Y	Y	N	N
5 Spratt	N	Y	Y	N	Y	N	Y	N
6 Tallon	N	Y	N	N	Y	N	Y	N

	192	193	194	195	196	197	198	199
SOUTH DAKOTA								
AL Johnson	N	N	N	N	Y	Y	Y	N
TENNESSEE								
1 ***Quillen***	Y	Y	N	Y	Y	Y	N	N
2 ***Duncan***	Y	Y	N	Y	N	Y	N	Y
3 Lloyd	N	Y	Y	N	Y	N	Y	N
4 Cooper	N	Y	Y	Y	Y	N	Y	N
5 Clement	N	Y	Y	Y	Y	Y	N	N
6 Gordon	N	Y	Y	N	Y	N	Y	N
7 ***Sundquist***	N	Y	N	Y	N	?	?	?
8 Tanner	Y	Y	Y	N	Y	N	Y	N
9 Ford	N	N	Y	Y	Y	N	Y	N
TEXAS								
1 Chapman	N	Y	N	N	Y	N	Y	N
2 Wilson	N	Y	Y	N	Y	Y	Y	N
3 ***Johnson***	Y	Y	N	Y	N	Y	N	Y
4 Hall	Y	Y	N	N	Y	Y	Y	N
5 Bryant	N	N	Y	N	Y	N	Y	N
6 ***Barton***	Y	Y	N	Y	N	Y	N	Y
7 ***Archer***	Y	Y	Y	Y	N	Y	N	Y
8 ***Fields***	Y	Y	N	Y	N	Y	N	Y
9 Brooks	N	N	Y	N	Y	Y	Y	N
10 Pickle	N	N	N	N	Y	N	Y	N
11 Edwards	N	Y	N	N	Y	Y	Y	N
12 Geren	N	Y	N	Y	Y	Y	Y	N
13 Sarpalius	Y	Y	N	?	N	Y	N	N
14 Laughlin	Y	Y	N	Y	Y	Y	N	N
15 de la Garza	N	Y	N	N	Y	N	Y	N
16 Coleman	N	N	N	N	Y	N	Y	N
17 Stenholm	Y	Y	N	Y	N	N	Y	N
18 Washington	N	N	Y	N	Y	N	Y	N
19 ***Combest***	N	Y	N	Y	N	Y	N	Y
20 Gonzalez	N	N	N	N	Y	N	Y	N
21 ***Smith***	Y	Y	Y	Y	N	Y	N	N
22 ***DeLay***	Y	Y	Y	Y	N	Y	N	Y
23 Bustamante	N	N	N	?	Y	N	Y	N
24 Frost	N	N	N	N	Y	N	Y	N
25 Andrews	N	Y	Y	N	Y	Y	Y	N
26 ***Armey***	Y	Y	N	Y	N	Y	N	Y
27 Ortiz	N	Y	N	N	Y	N	Y	N
UTAH								
1 ***Hansen***	Y	Y	N	Y	Y	Y	N	Y
2 Owens	?	?	N	N	Y	N	Y	N
3 Orton	?	Y	N	Y	N	Y	Y	N
VERMONT								
AL *Sanders*	N	N	Y	N	Y	N	Y	N
VIRGINIA								
1 ***Bateman***	N	?	N	Y	Y	N	Y	N
2 Pickett	N	Y	Y	N	Y	N	Y	N
3 ***Bliley***	N	Y	N	Y	Y	N	Y	N
4 Sisisky	N	Y	Y	N	Y	N	Y	N
5 Payne	N	Y	Y	Y	N	N	Y	N
6 Olin	N	N	N	N	Y	N	Y	N
7 ***Slaughter***	Y	Y	N	Y	Y	N	N	Y
8 Moran	N	N	N	N	Y	N	Y	-
9 Boucher	N	N	Y	N	Y	N	Y	N
10 ***Wolf***	N	Y	N	Y	Y	N	Y	N
WASHINGTON								
1 ***Miller***	N	N	Y	Y	Y	N	Y	N
2 Swift	N	?	N	N	Y	N	?	N
3 Unsoeld	N	N	Y	N	Y	N	Y	N
4 ***Morrison***	N	N	N	N	Y	N	Y	N
5 Foley								
6 Dicks	N	N	Y	N	Y	N	Y	N
7 McDermott	N	N	Y	N	Y	N	Y	N
8 ***Chandler***	N	N	N	N	Y	N	Y	N
WEST VIRGINIA								
1 Mollohan	N	N	N	N	Y	N	Y	N
2 Staggers	N	N	N	N	Y	N	Y	N
3 Wise	N	N	Y	N	Y	N	Y	N
4 Rahall	N	N	Y	N	Y	N	Y	N
WISCONSIN								
1 Aspin	N	N	Y	N	Y	N	Y	N
2 ***Klug***	N	N	N	Y	Y	N	Y	N
3 ***Gunderson***	N	N	N	N	Y	Y	Y	N
4 Kleczka	N	N	Y	N	Y	N	Y	N
5 Moody	N	N	Y	N	Y	N	Y	N
6 ***Petri***	Y	Y	Y	Y	N	Y	N	Y
7 Obey	N	N	Y	N	Y	N	Y	N
8 ***Roth***	Y	Y	N	N	N	Y	N	N
9 ***Sensenbrenner***	Y	Y	Y	Y	N	Y	N	Y
WYOMING								
AL ***Thomas***	N	Y	N	Y	N	Y	N	Y

Southern states - Ala., Ark., Fla., Ga., Ky., La., Miss., N.C., Okla., S.C., Tenn., Texas, Va.
Omitted votes are quorum calls, which CQ does not include in its vote charts.

HOUSE VOTES 200, 201, 202, 203, 204, 205, 206, 207

200. HR 2707. Fiscal 1992 Labor, HHS and Education Appropriations/Passage. Passage of the bill to provide $203,993,247,000 in new budget authority for the Departments of Labor, Education, and Health and Human Services and related agencies, $176 billion in fiscal 1992, $28 billion in fiscal 1993, and $253 million in fiscal 1994. The administration requested $200,611,414,000. The bill prohibits the use of funds to implement the administration's rules, which prohibit family planning projects that receive federal funds from providing information about abortions. Passed 353-74: R 95-66; D 257-8 (ND 177-3, SD 80-5); I 1-0, June 26, 1991.

201. HR 2698. Fiscal 1992 Agriculture Appropriations/Passage. Passage of the bill to provide $52,570,051,000 in new budget authority for Agriculture, Rural Development, Food and Drug Administration and related agencies in fiscal 1992. The administration requested $52,579,946,000. Passed 368-48: R 120-41; D 247-7 (ND 167-7, SD 80-0); I 1-0, June 26, 1991.

202. Procedural Motion. Doolittle, R-Calif., motion to approve the House Journal of Tuesday, July 9. Motion agreed to 292-103: R 52-100; D 240-3 (ND 162-2, SD 78-1), July 10, 1991.

203. H J Res 263. Disapproval of MFN for China/Passage. Passage of the joint resolution to disapprove President Bush's waiver of the Jackson-Vanik amendment to the 1974 trade act with respect to China. Jackson-Vanik bars most-favored-nation trade status to communist countries that do not allow free emigration. Passed 223-204: R 51-112; D 171-92 (ND 119-60, SD 53-32); I 1-0, July 10, 1991. A "nay" was a vote supporting the president's position.

204. HR 2212. Conditional MFN for China in 1992/Recommittal Motion. Archer, R-Texas, motion to recommit HR 2212 to the Ways and Means Committee with instructions to report it back to the House, incorporating a substitute bill that would require the president to report on and take into account similar conditions in the bill but give the president wide discretion to decide whether to continue MFN for China in 1992. Motion rejected 118-308: R 94-69; D 24-238 (ND 13-166, SD 11-72); I 0-1, July 10, 1991.

205. HR 2212. Conditional MFN for China in 1992/Passage. Passage of the bill to prohibit the president from waiving the Jackson-Vanik amendment to the 1974 trade act with respect to China in 1992 unless he certifies that China has released and accounted for all prisoners from the Tiananmen Square demonstrations, ended the practice of coercive abortions, stopped assisting other nations in acquiring nuclear weapons, stopped the export of goods made with forced labor, ended human rights violations, and met other conditions. Jackson-Vanik bars most-favored-nation trade status to communist countries that do not allow free emigration. Passed 313-112: R 82-81; D 230-31 (ND 161-17, SD 69-14); I 1-0, July 10, 1991. A "nay" was a vote supporting the president's position.

206. HR 1989. American Technology Pre-Eminence Act/Technology Loans. Walker, R-Pa., amendment to strike provisions to establish a $10 million fund for loans to small and medium-size firms to study or develop advanced technology practices. Rejected 172-246: R 160-2; D 12-243 (ND 7-165, SD 5-78); I 0-1, July 16, 1991. A "yea" was a vote supporting the president's position.

207. HR 1989. American Technology Pre-Eminence Act/Passage. Passage of the bill to authorize $289.7 million in fiscal 1991 and $347.5 million in fiscal 1992 for federal programs intended to help U.S. high-technology firms compete in world markets. Passed 296-122: R 42-120; D 253-2 (ND 170-2, SD 83-0); I 1-0, July 16, 1991. A "nay" was a vote supporting the president's position.

[1] *Rep. Thomas W. Ewing, R-Ill., was sworn in July 10, 1991. The first vote for which he was eligible was vote 203. Ewing replaced Edward Madigan, R-Ill., who resigned to become Agriculture secretary on March 8, 1991. The last vote for which Madigan was eligible was vote 36.*

KEY

Y Voted for (yea).
\# Paired for.
\+ Announced for.
N Voted against (nay).
X Paired against.
\- Announced against.
P Voted "present."
C Voted "present" to avoid possible conflict of interest.
? Did not vote or otherwise make a position known.

Democrats ***Republicans***
Independent

	200	201	202	203	204	205	206	207
ALABAMA								
1 ***Callahan***	Y	Y	Y	N	Y	N	Y	N
2 ***Dickinson***	Y	Y	N	Y	N	Y	Y	N
3 Browder	Y	Y	Y	Y	N	Y	N	Y
4 Bevill	Y	Y	Y	Y	N	Y	N	Y
5 Cramer	Y	Y	Y	Y	N	Y	N	Y
6 Erdreich	Y	Y	Y	Y	N	Y	N	Y
7 Harris	Y	Y	Y	Y	N	Y	N	Y
ALASKA								
AL ***Young***	Y	Y	N	N	Y	N	N	Y
ARIZONA								
1 ***Rhodes***	-	-	N	N	Y	N	Y	N
2 Vacancy								
3 ***Stump***	N	N	N	N	Y	N	Y	N
4 ***Kyl***	N	N	N	Y	N	Y	Y	N
5 ***Kolbe***	Y	Y	Y	N	Y	N	Y	N
ARKANSAS								
1 Alexander	Y	Y	Y	N	Y	N	N	Y
2 Thornton	Y	Y	Y	Y	N	Y	N	Y
3 ***Hammerschmidt***	Y	Y	Y	N	Y	N	Y	Y
4 Anthony	Y	Y	Y	Y	N	Y	N	Y
CALIFORNIA								
1 ***Riggs***	Y	Y	N	Y	N	Y	Y	Y
2 ***Herger***	N	Y	N	Y	N	Y	Y	N
3 Matsui	Y	Y	Y	N	Y	N	?	?
4 Fazio	Y	Y	Y	N	N	Y	N	Y
5 Pelosi	Y	Y	Y	Y	N	Y	N	Y
6 Boxer	Y	Y	Y	Y	N	Y	N	Y
7 Miller	Y	Y	Y	Y	N	Y	N	Y
8 Dellums	Y	Y	Y	Y	N	Y	N	Y
9 Stark	Y	Y	Y	Y	N	Y	N	Y
10 Edwards	Y	Y	Y	Y	N	Y	N	Y
11 Lantos	Y	Y	Y	Y	N	Y	N	Y
12 ***Campbell***	Y	N	N	N	Y	N	Y	Y
13 Mineta	Y	Y	Y	Y	N	Y	N	Y
14 ***Doolittle***	N	Y	N	Y	N	Y	Y	N
15 Condit	Y	Y	Y	Y	N	Y	N	Y
16 Panetta	Y	Y	Y	Y	N	Y	N	Y
17 Dooley	Y	Y	Y	N	N	Y	N	Y
18 Lehman	Y	Y	Y	Y	N	Y	N	Y
19 ***Lagomarsino***	N	N	N	N	N	Y	Y	N
20 ***Thomas***	N	Y	N	N	Y	N	Y	N
21 ***Gallegly***	N	N	N	N	N	Y	Y	N
22 ***Moorhead***	N	N	Y	Y	N	Y	Y	N
23 Beilenson	Y	N	Y	N	N	Y	N	Y
24 Waxman	Y	Y	?	Y	N	Y	N	Y
25 Roybal	Y	Y	Y	Y	N	Y	N	Y
26 Berman	Y	Y	Y	Y	N	Y	N	Y
27 Levine	Y	Y	Y	Y	N	Y	?	Y
28 Dixon	Y	Y	Y	Y	N	Y	N	?
29 Waters	Y	Y	Y	Y	N	Y	N	Y
30 Martinez	Y	Y	?	Y	N	Y	N	Y
31 Dymally	Y	Y	Y	N	N	Y	N	Y
32 Anderson	Y	Y	Y	N	N	N	N	Y
33 ***Dreier***	N	N	Y	N	Y	N	Y	N
34 Torres	Y	Y	Y	N	N	N	N	Y
35 ***Lewis***	Y	Y	N	N	Y	N	Y	Y
36 Brown	Y	Y	Y	N	N	N	N	Y
37 ***McCandless***	N	Y	N	Y	Y	N	Y	N
38 ***Dornan***	N	N	?	Y	Y	Y	Y	N
39 ***Dannemeyer***	N	N	N	Y	Y	Y	Y	N
40 ***Cox***	N	N	Y	Y	N	Y	Y	N
41 ***Lowery***	Y	Y	?	N	Y	N	Y	N
42 ***Rohrabacher***	N	N	N	Y	N	Y	Y	N
43 ***Packard***	N	N	Y	N	Y	N	Y	N
44 ***Cunningham***	Y	N	N	N	N	Y	Y	N
45 ***Hunter***	N	N	N	Y	?	#	Y	N
COLORADO								
1 Schroeder	Y	N	N	Y	N	Y	N	Y
2 Skaggs	Y	Y	Y	N	N	Y	N	Y
3 Campbell	Y	Y	Y	Y	N	Y	N	Y
4 ***Allard***	N	Y	N	N	Y	N	Y	N
5 ***Hefley***	N	N	N	Y	N	Y	Y	N
6 ***Schaefer***	Y	Y	N	N	Y	Y	Y	N
CONNECTICUT								
1 Kennelly	Y	Y	Y	N	N	Y	N	Y
2 Gejdenson	Y	Y	Y	Y	N	Y	N	Y
3 DeLauro	Y	Y	Y	N	N	Y	N	Y
4 ***Shays***	Y	N	N	N	Y	N	Y	Y
5 ***Franks***	Y	Y	N	N	Y	N	Y	N
6 ***Johnson***	Y	Y	Y	N	Y	N	Y	Y
DELAWARE								
AL Carper	Y	Y	Y	Y	N	Y	N	Y
FLORIDA								
1 Hutto	N	Y	Y	Y	N	Y	N	Y
2 Peterson	Y	Y	Y	N	N	Y	N	Y
3 Bennett	N	Y	Y	Y	N	Y	Y	Y
4 ***James***	Y	Y	N	Y	N	Y	Y	N
5 ***McCollum***	N	N	N	N	N	Y	Y	N
6 ***Stearns***	Y	Y	?	Y	N	Y	Y	N
7 Gibbons	Y	Y	Y	N	N	Y	N	Y
8 ***Young***	Y	Y	?	N	Y	N	Y	N
9 ***Bilirakis***	Y	Y	N	N	Y	N	Y	N
10 ***Ireland***	N	Y	N	N	N	N	Y	N
11 Bacchus	Y	Y	Y	N	N	Y	N	Y
12 ***Lewis***	Y	Y	N	Y	N	Y	Y	Y
13 ***Goss***	Y	N	N	N	N	N	Y	N
14 Johnston	Y	Y	Y	N	Y	N	N	Y
15 ***Shaw***	Y	N	Y	N	Y	N	Y	N
16 Smith	Y	?	Y	Y	N	Y	N	Y
17 Lehman	Y	Y	?	N	N	Y	N	Y
18 ***Ros-Lehtinen***	Y	Y	N	Y	N	Y	Y	N
19 Fascell	Y	Y	Y	N	N	Y	N	Y
GEORGIA								
1 Thomas	Y	Y	Y	Y	N	Y	N	Y
2 Hatcher	Y	Y	Y	Y	N	Y	?	Y
3 Ray	Y	Y	Y	Y	N	Y	Y	Y
4 Jones	Y	?	Y	Y	N	Y	N	Y
5 Lewis	Y	Y	Y	Y	N	Y	N	Y
6 ***Gingrich***	Y	Y	N	N	N	Y	Y	N
7 Darden	Y	Y	Y	N	N	Y	N	Y
8 Rowland	Y	Y	Y	N	N	Y	N	Y
9 Jenkins	Y	Y	Y	Y	N	Y	N	Y
10 Barnard	Y	Y	Y	Y	N	Y	Y	Y
HAWAII								
1 Abercrombie	Y	Y	Y	Y	N	Y	N	?
2 Mink	Y	Y	?	Y	N	Y	N	Y
IDAHO								
1 LaRocco	Y	Y	Y	N	N	Y	N	Y
2 Stallings	Y	Y	Y	N	N	Y	N	Y
ILLINOIS								
1 Hayes	Y	Y	?	Y	N	Y	N	Y
2 Savage	Y	Y	?	N	N	Y	N	Y
3 Russo	Y	N	Y	Y	N	Y	N	Y
4 Sangmeister	Y	Y	Y	N	N	Y	N	Y
5 Lipinski	N	Y	?	Y	N	Y	N	Y
6 ***Hyde***	N	Y	N	N	Y	Y	Y	N
7 Collins	Y	Y	Y	Y	N	Y	N	Y
8 Rostenkowski	Y	Y	Y	N	N	Y	N	Y
9 Yates	Y	Y	Y	Y	N	Y	N	Y
10 ***Porter***	Y	Y	Y	Y	N	Y	Y	N
11 Annunzio	Y	Y	Y	Y	N	Y	N	Y
12 ***Crane***	N	N	N	N	Y	N	Y	N
13 ***Fawell***	N	N	N	N	Y	N	Y	N
14 ***Hastert***	Y	Y	N	N	Y	N	Y	N
15 ***Ewing*** [1]				N	Y	N	Y	N
16 Cox	Y	Y	Y	N	N	Y	N	Y
17 Evans	Y	Y	Y	Y	N	Y	N	Y
18 ***Michel***	N	Y	N	N	Y	N	Y	N
19 Bruce	Y	Y	Y	Y	N	Y	N	Y
20 Durbin	Y	Y	Y	Y	N	Y	N	Y
21 Costello	Y	Y	Y	Y	N	Y	N	Y
22 Poshard	Y	Y	Y	Y	N	Y	N	Y
INDIANA								
1 Visclosky	Y	Y	Y	Y	N	Y	N	Y
2 Sharp	Y	Y	Y	N	N	Y	N	Y
3 Roemer	Y	Y	Y	N	Y	N	N	Y

ND Northern Democrats SD Southern Democrats

	200	201	202	203	204	205	206	207
4 Long	Y	Y	Y	N	N	Y	N	Y
5 Jontz	Y	Y	Y	N	N	Y	N	Y
6 ***Burton***	N	N	N	Y	N	Y	Y	N
7 ***Myers***	Y	Y	Y	N	Y	N	Y	N
8 McCloskey	Y	Y	Y	N	N	Y	N	Y
9 Hamilton	Y	Y	Y	N	Y	N	Y	Y
10 Jacobs	Y	N	?	?	?	X	Y	N
IOWA								
1 ***Leach***	Y	Y	N	N	Y	N	Y	N
2 ***Nussle***	N	Y	Y	N	Y	N	Y	N
3 Nagle	Y	Y	Y	N	N	Y	N	Y
4 Smith	Y	Y	Y	N	?	?	N	Y
5 ***Lightfoot***	N	Y	N	N	Y	N	Y	N
6 ***Grandy***	Y	Y	N	N	Y	N	Y	N
KANSAS								
1 ***Roberts***	N	Y	N	N	Y	N	Y	N
2 Slattery	Y	Y	Y	N	N	Y	N	Y
3 ***Meyers***	Y	Y	N	N	Y	N	Y	Y
4 Glickman	Y	Y	Y	N	N	N	N	Y
5 ***Nichols***	N	Y	?	N	Y	N	Y	N
KENTUCKY								
1 Hubbard	Y	Y	Y	Y	N	Y	Y	Y
2 Natcher	Y	Y	Y	Y	N	N	N	Y
3 Mazzoli	Y	Y	Y	N	N	Y	N	Y
4 ***Bunning***	N	N	N	Y	N	Y	Y	N
5 ***Rogers***	Y	Y	N	Y	N	Y	Y	Y
6 ***Hopkins***	?	?	?	?	?	?	?	?
7 Perkins	Y	Y	Y	Y	N	Y	N	Y
LOUISIANA								
1 ***Livingston***	N	Y	Y	N	Y	N	Y	N
2 Jefferson	Y	Y	Y	Y	N	Y	N	Y
3 Tauzin	N	Y	Y	Y	N	N	N	Y
4 ***McCrery***	Y	Y	Y	N	Y	N	Y	N
5 Huckaby	Y	Y	Y	N	N	N	Y	Y
6 ***Baker***	Y	Y	N	N	Y	N	Y	N
7 Hayes	Y	?	Y	Y	N	N	N	Y
8 ***Holloway***	N	Y	N	N	Y	N	?	?
MAINE								
1 Andrews	Y	Y	Y	Y	N	Y	N	Y
2 ***Snowe***	Y	Y	Y	Y	N	Y	Y	Y
MARYLAND								
1 ***Gilchrest***	Y	Y	N	N	Y	Y	Y	Y
2 ***Bentley***	Y	Y	N	N	N	Y	N	Y
3 Cardin	Y	Y	Y	Y	N	Y	N	Y
4 McMillen	Y	Y	Y	N	N	Y	N	Y
5 Hoyer	Y	Y	Y	Y	N	Y	N	Y
6 Byron	Y	Y	Y	N	N	Y	Y	Y
7 Mfume	Y	Y	Y	Y	N	Y	N	Y
8 ***Morella***	Y	Y	Y	Y	N	Y	Y	Y
MASSACHUSETTS								
1 Olver	Y	Y	Y	Y	N	Y	N	Y
2 Neal	Y	Y	Y	Y	N	Y	N	Y
3 Early	Y	Y	Y	Y	N	Y	?	?
4 Frank	Y	Y	Y	Y	N	Y	N	Y
5 Atkins	Y	Y	?	Y	N	Y	N	Y
6 Mavroules	Y	Y	Y	Y	N	Y	N	Y
7 Markey	Y	Y	Y	Y	N	Y	N	Y
8 Kennedy	Y	Y	Y	Y	N	Y	N	Y
9 Moakley	Y	Y	Y	Y	N	Y	N	Y
10 Studds	Y	Y	Y	Y	N	Y	N	Y
11 Donnelly	Y	Y	Y	Y	N	Y	N	Y
MICHIGAN								
1 Conyers	Y	Y	Y	Y	N	Y	N	Y
2 ***Pursell***	Y	Y	Y	N	Y	Y	Y	Y
3 Wolpe	Y	Y	Y	Y	N	Y	N	Y
4 ***Upton***	Y	Y	N	N	N	Y	Y	Y
5 ***Henry***	N	N	N	N	N	Y	Y	Y
6 Carr	Y	Y	Y	N	N	Y	Y	Y
7 Kildee	Y	Y	Y	Y	N	Y	N	Y
8 Traxler	Y	?	Y	Y	N	Y	N	Y
9 ***Vander Jagt***	Y	Y	Y	N	Y	N	Y	N
10 ***Camp***	Y	Y	N	N	Y	N	Y	Y
11 ***Davis***	Y	Y	Y	N	Y	N	Y	Y
12 Bonior	Y	Y	Y	Y	N	Y	N	Y
13 Collins	Y	?	Y	Y	N	Y	N	Y
14 Hertel	Y	Y	Y	Y	N	Y	N	Y
15 Ford	Y	Y	Y	Y	N	Y	N	Y
16 Dingell	Y	Y	Y	N	N	Y	N	Y
17 Levin	Y	Y	Y	Y	N	Y	N	Y
18 ***Broomfield***	Y	N	Y	N	Y	Y	Y	Y
MINNESOTA								
1 Penny	Y	Y	Y	N	N	Y	Y	N
2 ***Weber***	Y	Y	N	N	Y	N	Y	N
3 ***Ramstad***	Y	Y	N	N	N	Y	Y	Y
4 Vento	Y	Y	Y	Y	N	Y	N	Y

	200	201	202	203	204	205	206	207
5 Sabo	Y	Y	Y	Y	N	Y	N	Y
6 Sikorski	Y	Y	Y	Y	N	Y	N	Y
7 Peterson	Y	Y	Y	N	N	N	N	Y
8 Oberstar	Y	Y	Y	Y	N	Y	N	Y
MISSISSIPPI								
1 Whitten	Y	Y	Y	Y	?	?	N	Y
2 Espy	Y	Y	Y	Y	N	Y	N	Y
3 Montgomery	Y	Y	Y	N	Y	N	N	Y
4 Parker	Y	Y	?	Y	N	Y	N	Y
5 Taylor	Y	Y	Y	Y	N	N	N	Y
MISSOURI								
1 Clay	Y	?	?	Y	N	Y	N	Y
2 Horn	Y	Y	Y	Y	N	Y	N	Y
3 Gephardt	Y	Y	Y	Y	N	Y	N	Y
4 Skelton	Y	Y	Y	N	Y	Y	N	Y
5 Wheat	Y	Y	Y	Y	N	Y	N	Y
6 ***Coleman***	Y	Y	N	N	Y	N	Y	Y
7 ***Hancock***	N	N	N	Y	N	Y	Y	N
8 ***Emerson***	Y	Y	Y	N	N	Y	Y	Y
9 Volkmer	Y	Y	Y	N	Y	Y	N	Y
MONTANA								
1 Williams	Y	Y	Y	N	Y	N	?	?
2 ***Marlenee***	N	Y	N	N	Y	N	Y	N
NEBRASKA								
1 ***Bereuter***	Y	Y	N	N	Y	N	Y	N
2 Hoagland	Y	Y	Y	N	N	N	N	Y
3 ***Barrett***	N	Y	N	N	Y	N	Y	N
NEVADA								
1 Bilbray	Y	Y	Y	Y	N	Y	N	Y
2 ***Vucanovich***	Y	Y	N	N	Y	N	Y	N
NEW HAMPSHIRE								
1 ***Zeliff***	N	N	N	N	N	Y	Y	N
2 Swett	Y	Y	Y	N	N	Y	N	Y
NEW JERSEY								
1 Andrews	Y	Y	?	Y	N	Y	N	Y
2 Hughes	Y	Y	Y	Y	N	Y	N	Y
3 Pallone	N	N	Y	Y	N	Y	N	Y
4 ***Smith***	N	Y	Y	Y	N	Y	Y	Y
5 ***Roukema***	Y	N	N	N	N	Y	Y	N
6 Dwyer	Y	Y	Y	Y	N	Y	N	Y
7 ***Rinaldo***	Y	Y	Y	N	Y	N	Y	N
8 Roe	N	Y	Y	N	Y	Y	N	Y
9 Torricelli	Y	Y	?	Y	N	Y	N	Y
10 Payne	Y	Y	Y	Y	N	Y	N	Y
11 ***Gallo***	Y	Y	N	N	N	Y	Y	N
12 ***Zimmer***	Y	N	N	N	Y	N	Y	N
13 ***Saxton***	Y	Y	N	N	N	Y	Y	N
14 Guarini	Y	Y	Y	N	Y	N	N	Y
NEW MEXICO								
1 ***Schiff***	Y	Y	Y	N	N	Y	Y	Y
2 ***Skeen***	Y	Y	Y	N	Y	N	Y	Y
3 Richardson	Y	Y	Y	Y	N	Y	N	Y
NEW YORK								
1 Hochbrueckner	Y	Y	Y	Y	N	Y	N	Y
2 Downey	Y	Y	Y	Y	N	Y	N	Y
3 Mrazek	?	?	Y	Y	N	Y	N	Y
4 ***Lent***	Y	Y	Y	N	Y	N	Y	N
5 ***McGrath***	N	Y	N	Y	N	Y	Y	N
6 Flake	Y	Y	Y	Y	N	Y	N	Y
7 Ackerman	Y	Y	Y	Y	N	Y	N	Y
8 Scheuer	Y	Y	Y	Y	Y	Y	N	Y
9 Manton	Y	Y	Y	Y	N	Y	?	?
10 Schumer	Y	Y	Y	Y	N	Y	N	Y
11 Towns	Y	?	Y	Y	N	Y	N	Y
12 Owens	Y	Y	?	Y	N	Y	N	Y
13 Solarz	Y	Y	Y	N	Y	Y	N	Y
14 ***Molinari***	Y	Y	?	Y	N	Y	Y	N
15 ***Green***	Y	Y	Y	N	N	Y	Y	Y
16 Rangel	Y	Y	Y	Y	N	Y	N	Y
17 Weiss	Y	Y	Y	Y	N	Y	-	+
18 Serrano	Y	Y	Y	?	N	Y	N	Y
19 Engel	Y	Y	Y	Y	N	Y	N	Y
20 Lowey	Y	Y	Y	Y	N	Y	N	Y
21 ***Fish***	Y	Y	Y	Y	Y	Y	Y	Y
22 ***Gilman***	Y	Y	Y	Y	N	Y	Y	Y
23 McNulty	Y	Y	Y	Y	N	Y	N	Y
24 ***Solomon***	?	?	?	Y	N	Y	Y	N
25 ***Boehlert***	Y	Y	N	N	N	Y	Y	Y
26 ***Martin***	Y	Y	N	N	Y	N	Y	N
27 ***Walsh***	Y	Y	Y	N	N	Y	Y	N
28 McHugh	Y	Y	Y	Y	N	Y	N	Y
29 ***Horton***	Y	Y	Y	N	N	Y	Y	Y
30 Slaughter	Y	Y	Y	Y	N	Y	N	Y
31 ***Paxon***	N	Y	?	Y	Y	N	Y	N

	200	201	202	203	204	205	206	207
32 LaFalce	Y	Y	?	Y	N	Y	N	Y
33 Nowak	Y	Y	?	Y	N	Y	N	Y
34 ***Houghton***	Y	Y	Y	N	Y	N	Y	N
NORTH CAROLINA								
1 Jones	Y	Y	Y	Y	N	Y	N	Y
2 Valentine	Y	Y	Y	Y	N	Y	N	Y
3 Lancaster	Y	Y	Y	N	N	Y	N	Y
4 Price	Y	Y	Y	Y	N	Y	N	Y
5 Neal	Y	Y	Y	Y	N	Y	Y	Y
6 ***Coble***	Y	Y	N	Y	Y	Y	Y	N
7 Rose	Y	Y	Y	Y	N	Y	N	?
8 Hefner	Y	Y	Y	Y	N	Y	N	Y
9 ***McMillan***	N	Y	N	Y	Y	Y	Y	N
10 ***Ballenger***	N	Y	N	Y	Y	Y	Y	N
11 ***Taylor***	Y	Y	N	N	Y	Y	Y	N
NORTH DAKOTA								
AL Dorgan	Y	Y	Y	N	N	Y	N	Y
OHIO								
1 Luken	Y	N	Y	N	Y	N	N	Y
2 ***Gradison***	N	Y	Y	N	Y	N	Y	N
3 Hall	Y	Y	Y	Y	N	Y	N	Y
4 ***Oxley***	Y	Y	N	N	Y	N	Y	N
5 ***Gillmor***	Y	Y	Y	N	Y	N	Y	Y
6 ***McEwen***	N	Y	Y	Y	N	Y	Y	N
7 ***Hobson***	Y	Y	N	N	Y	Y	Y	N
8 ***Boehner***	N	Y	N	N	Y	N	Y	N
9 Kaptur	Y	Y	Y	N	N	Y	N	Y
10 ***Miller***	N	Y	N	N	Y	N	Y	N
11 Eckart	Y	Y	Y	Y	N	Y	N	Y
12 ***Kasich***	Y	Y	Y	Y	N	Y	Y	N
13 Pease	Y	N	Y	N	N	Y	N	Y
14 Sawyer	Y	Y	Y	Y	N	Y	N	Y
15 ***Wylie***	Y	Y	Y	Y	Y	N	Y	N
16 ***Regula***	Y	Y	N	N	Y	Y	Y	N
17 Traficant	Y	Y	Y	Y	N	Y	N	Y
18 Applegate	Y	Y	Y	Y	N	N	Y	Y
19 Feighan	Y	Y	Y	N	N	Y	N	Y
20 Oakar	Y	Y	Y	Y	N	Y	N	Y
21 Stokes	Y	Y	Y	Y	N	Y	N	Y
OKLAHOMA								
1 ***Inhofe***	N	Y	?	?	?	?	?	?
2 Synar	Y	Y	Y	Y	N	Y	N	Y
3 Brewster	Y	Y	Y	N	N	Y	N	Y
4 McCurdy	Y	Y	?	Y	N	Y	N	Y
5 ***Edwards***	N	Y	N	Y	N	Y	Y	N
6 English	Y	Y	Y	N	Y	Y	N	Y
OREGON								
1 AuCoin	Y	Y	Y	N	N	?	N	Y
2 ***Smith***	N	Y	N	N	Y	N	Y	N
3 Wyden	Y	Y	Y	N	N	N	N	Y
4 DeFazio	Y	Y	Y	Y	N	Y	N	Y
5 Kopetski	Y	Y	Y	N	Y	N	N	Y
PENNSYLVANIA								
1 Foglietta	Y	Y	Y	Y	N	Y	N	Y
2 Gray	Y	?	?	?	N	Y	?	?
3 Borski	Y	Y	Y	Y	N	Y	N	Y
4 Kolter	Y	Y	Y	Y	N	Y	N	Y
5 ***Schulze***	Y	Y	Y	Y	N	Y	Y	N
6 Yatron	Y	Y	Y	Y	N	Y	?	?
7 ***Weldon***	Y	N	?	Y	N	Y	Y	Y
8 Kostmayer	Y	Y	Y	Y	N	Y	N	Y
9 ***Shuster***	N	Y	Y	Y	N	Y	Y	N
10 ***McDade***	Y	Y	?	N	Y	N	Y	Y
11 Kanjorski	Y	Y	Y	Y	N	Y	N	Y
12 Murtha	Y	Y	Y	N	N	N	N	Y
13 ***Coughlin***	Y	Y	N	N	Y	Y	Y	Y
14 Coyne	Y	Y	?	N	N	Y	N	Y
15 ***Ritter***	Y	Y	Y	Y	N	Y	Y	Y
16 ***Walker***	N	N	N	Y	N	Y	Y	N
17 ***Gekas***	Y	N	N	N	Y	N	Y	N
18 ***Santorum***	N	N	N	N	N	Y	Y	N
19 ***Goodling***	Y	Y	N	N	N	Y	Y	N
20 Gaydos	Y	Y	?	Y	N	Y	N	Y
21 ***Ridge***	Y	Y	N	Y	N	Y	Y	Y
22 Murphy	Y	Y	N	N	N	Y	Y	Y
23 ***Clinger***	Y	Y	Y	N	Y	N	Y	N
RHODE ISLAND								
1 ***Machtley***	Y	Y	N	N	Y	Y	Y	Y
2 Reed	Y	Y	Y	N	N	Y	N	Y
SOUTH CAROLINA								
1 ***Ravenel***	Y	Y	Y	Y	N	Y	Y	Y
2 ***Spence***	N	Y	Y	N	N	Y	Y	N
3 Derrick	Y	Y	Y	Y	N	Y	N	Y
4 Patterson	Y	Y	Y	Y	N	Y	N	Y
5 Spratt	Y	Y	Y	Y	N	Y	N	Y
6 Tallon	Y	Y	Y	Y	N	Y	N	Y

	200	201	202	203	204	205	206	207
SOUTH DAKOTA								
AL Johnson	Y	Y	Y	N	Y	N	N	Y
TENNESSEE								
1 ***Quillen***	N	Y	N	Y	Y	N	Y	N
2 ***Duncan***	Y	N	N	Y	N	Y	Y	N
3 Lloyd	Y	?	?	Y	N	Y	N	Y
4 Cooper	Y	Y	?	N	N	Y	N	Y
5 Clement	Y	Y	Y	N	N	Y	N	Y
6 Gordon	Y	Y	Y	Y	N	Y	N	Y
7 ***Sundquist***	?	?	N	N	Y	N	Y	N
8 Tanner	Y	Y	Y	N	N	Y	N	Y
9 Ford	Y	?	Y	Y	N	Y	N	Y
TEXAS								
1 Chapman	Y	Y	Y	N	N	Y	N	Y
2 Wilson	Y	Y	Y	Y	N	Y	?	?
3 ***Johnson***	N	N	Y	N	Y	N	Y	N
4 Hall	N	Y	Y	N	Y	N	N	Y
5 Bryant	Y	Y	Y	Y	N	Y	N	Y
6 ***Barton***	N	Y	?	Y	N	Y	?	?
7 ***Archer***	N	N	Y	N	Y	N	Y	N
8 ***Fields***	N	Y	N	N	Y	N	Y	N
9 Brooks	Y	Y	Y	N	Y	Y	N	Y
10 Pickle	Y	Y	Y	N	Y	Y	N	Y
11 Edwards	Y	Y	Y	Y	N	Y	N	Y
12 Geren	Y	Y	Y	N	Y	N	N	Y
13 Sarpalius	N	Y	Y	N	Y	N	N	Y
14 Laughlin	Y	Y	Y	N	Y	N	N	Y
15 de la Garza	Y	Y	?	N	?	?	N	Y
16 Coleman	Y	Y	Y	Y	N	Y	N	Y
17 Stenholm	Y	Y	Y	N	Y	N	N	Y
18 Washington	Y	Y	Y	Y	N	Y	N	Y
19 ***Combest***	N	Y	Y	N	Y	N	Y	N
20 Gonzalez	Y	Y	Y	Y	N	N	N	Y
21 ***Smith***	Y	Y	N	Y	N	Y	Y	N
22 ***DeLay***	N	Y	N	?	Y	Y	Y	N
23 Bustamante	Y	Y	Y	Y	N	Y	N	Y
24 Frost	Y	Y	Y	Y	N	Y	N	Y
25 Andrews	Y	Y	Y	N	N	Y	N	Y
26 ***Armey***	N	N	N	N	Y	N	Y	N
27 Ortiz	Y	Y	Y	N	N	Y	N	Y
UTAH								
1 ***Hansen***	N	N	N	N	Y	N	Y	N
2 Owens	Y	Y	Y	Y	N	Y	?	Y
3 Orton	Y	Y	Y	N	N	Y	N	Y
VERMONT								
AL *Sanders*	Y	Y	?	Y	N	Y	N	Y
VIRGINIA								
1 ***Bateman***	Y	Y	Y	N	N	N	Y	N
2 Pickett	Y	Y	Y	N	N	N	N	Y
3 ***Bliley***	Y	Y	N	N	N	N	Y	N
4 Sisisky	Y	Y	N	Y	N	Y	N	Y
5 Payne	Y	Y	Y	N	N	Y	N	Y
6 Olin	Y	Y	Y	Y	N	Y	N	Y
7 ***Slaughter***	Y	Y	Y	N	Y	N	Y	N
8 Moran	Y	Y	Y	Y	N	Y	N	Y
9 Boucher	Y	Y	Y	N	N	Y	N	Y
10 ***Wolf***	Y	Y	N	Y	N	Y	Y	Y
WASHINGTON								
1 ***Miller***	Y	Y	N	N	N	Y	Y	N
2 Swift	Y	Y	Y	N	N	Y	N	Y
3 Unsoeld	Y	Y	Y	Y	N	Y	N	Y
4 ***Morrison***	Y	Y	Y	N	Y	N	Y	Y
5 Foley								
6 Dicks	Y	Y	Y	N	N	Y	N	Y
7 McDermott	Y	Y	Y	N	N	Y	N	Y
8 ***Chandler***	Y	Y	N	N	Y	N	Y	Y
WEST VIRGINIA								
1 Mollohan	Y	Y	Y	Y	N	Y	N	Y
2 Staggers	Y	Y	Y	Y	N	Y	N	Y
3 Wise	Y	Y	Y	Y	N	Y	N	Y
4 Rahall	Y	Y	Y	Y	N	Y	N	Y
WISCONSIN								
1 Aspin	Y	?	Y	N	N	Y	N	Y
2 ***Klug***	Y	Y	Y	N	N	Y	Y	N
3 ***Gunderson***	Y	Y	Y	N	N	Y	Y	N
4 Kleczka	Y	Y	Y	Y	N	Y	N	Y
5 Moody	Y	Y	Y	N	N	Y	N	Y
6 ***Petri***	N	N	Y	N	Y	N	Y	N
7 Obey	Y	Y	Y	Y	N	Y	N	Y
8 ***Roth***	N	N	N	N	Y	N	Y	N
9 ***Sensenbrenner***	N	N	N	Y	N	Y	Y	N
WYOMING								
AL ***Thomas***	N	Y	N	N	Y	N	Y	N

Southern states - Ala., Ark., Fla., Ga., Ky., La., Miss., N.C., Okla., S.C., Tenn., Texas, Va.
Omitted votes are quorum calls, which CQ does not include in its vote charts.

HOUSE VOTES 208, 209, 210, 211, 212, 213, 214, 215

208. Procedural Motion. Moakley, D-Mass., motion to adjourn. Motion agreed to 186-75: R 23-74; D 163-1 (ND 104-1, SD 59-0), July 16, 1991.

209. HR 5. Striker Replacement. Moakley, D-Mass., motion to order the previous question (thus ending debate and the possibility of amendment) on the rule (H Res 195) to provide for House floor consideration of the bill to prohibit hiring permanent replacements for striking workers, if the strike was by union-represented employees. Motion agreed to 262-157: R 6-156; D 255-1 (ND 173-1, SD 82-0); I 1-0, July 17, 1991.

210. HR 5. Striker Replacement/Rule. Adoption of the rule (H Res 195) to provide for House floor consideration of the bill to prohibit hiring permanent replacements for striking workers, if the strike was by union-represented employees. Adopted 265-153: R 13-149; D 251-4 (ND 170-2, SD 81-2); I 1-0, July 17, 1991.

211. HR 5. Striker Replacement/Limit on Prohibition. Goodling, R-Pa., substitute amendment to the Peterson, D-Fla., substitute amendment, to limit the prohibition on hiring permanent replacements for striking union workers to the first eight weeks of a strike, after which an employer would be free to hire permanent replacements. The bill would indefinitely prohibit employers from hiring permanent replacements. Rejected 28-399: R 27-138; D 1-260 (ND 0-176, SD 1-84); I 0-1, July 17, 1991.

212. HR 5. Striker Replacement/Limit to Union Workplaces. Peterson, D-Fla., substitute amendment to clarify that the bill does not apply to non-union workplaces and only covers recognized or certified union workplaces. Under the amendment, strikers are protected only if a majority of the employees have filed for recognition with the National Labor Relations Board at least 30 days before a strike. Adopted 252-174: R 17-148; D 234-26 (ND 176-0, SD 58-26); I 1-0, July 17, 1991.

213. HR 5. Striker Replacement/Passage. Passage of the bill to prohibit employers from hiring permanent replacements for workers striking over economic issues, if the strike was by union-represented employees. Passed 247-182: R 16-149; D 230-33 (ND 178-0, SD 52-33); I 1-0, July 17, 1991. A "nay" was a vote supporting the president's position.

214. HR 1776. Fiscal 1992 Coast Guard Authorization/Recreational Boat Fees. Davis, R-Mich., amendment to express the sense of Congress that the annual fee collected by the Coast Guard on recreational boats should be repealed. Adopted 412-6: R 160-2; D 251-4 (ND 169-4, SD 82-0); I 1-0, July 18, 1991. (Before being adopted the Davis amendment was amended by a Panetta, D-Calif., amendment to state that if the repeal takes place, the costs must be offset with pay-as-you-go legislation.)

215. HR 1776. Fiscal 1992 Coast Guard Authorization/Drug Testing Employees. Solomon, R-N.Y., amendment to require the Coast Guard to establish a program for random drug testing of its civilian employees. Rejected 177-240: R 131-31; D 46-208 (ND 17-156, SD 29-52); I 0-1, July 18, 1991.

KEY

Y Voted for (yea).
\# Paired for.
\+ Announced for.
N Voted against (nay).
X Paired against.
\- Announced against.
P Voted "present."
C Voted "present" to avoid possible conflict of interest.
? Did not vote or otherwise make a position known.

Democrats ***Republicans***
Independent

	208	209	210	211	212	213	214	215
ALABAMA								
1 ***Callahan***	N	N	N	Y	N	N	Y	Y
2 ***Dickinson***	?	N	N	N	N	N	Y	Y
3 Browder	Y	Y	Y	N	Y	Y	Y	Y
4 Bevill	Y	Y	Y	N	Y	Y	Y	Y
5 Cramer	Y	Y	Y	N	Y	Y	Y	Y
6 Erdreich	?	Y	Y	N	Y	Y	Y	Y
7 Harris	Y	Y	Y	N	Y	Y	Y	Y
ALASKA								
AL ***Young***	?	Y	Y	Y	Y	Y	Y	N
ARIZONA								
1 ***Rhodes***	N	N	N	N	N	N	Y	Y
2 Vacancy								
3 ***Stump***	N	N	N	N	N	N	Y	Y
4 ***Kyl***	N	N	N	N	N	N	Y	Y
5 ***Kolbe***	N	N	N	N	N	N	Y	Y
ARKANSAS								
1 Alexander	Y	Y	Y	N	Y	Y	Y	?
2 Thornton	Y	Y	Y	N	Y	Y	Y	N
3 ***Hammerschmidt***	N	N	N	N	N	N	Y	Y
4 Anthony	?	Y	Y	N	N	N	Y	N
CALIFORNIA								
1 ***Riggs***	N	N	N	N	N	N	Y	Y
2 ***Herger***	N	N	N	N	N	N	Y	Y
3 Matsui	?	?	?	?	?	?	?	?
4 Fazio	Y	Y	Y	N	Y	Y	Y	N
5 Pelosi	Y	Y	Y	N	Y	Y	Y	N
6 Boxer	Y	Y	Y	N	Y	Y	?	?
7 Miller	Y	Y	Y	N	Y	Y	Y	N
8 Dellums	?	Y	Y	N	Y	Y	Y	N
9 Stark	?	Y	?	N	Y	Y	Y	N
10 Edwards	?	Y	Y	N	Y	Y	Y	N
11 Lantos	Y	Y	Y	N	Y	Y	Y	N
12 ***Campbell***	N	N	N	N	N	N	Y	N
13 Mineta	Y	Y	Y	N	Y	Y	Y	N
14 ***Doolittle***	?	N	N	N	N	N	Y	Y
15 Condit	Y	Y	Y	N	Y	Y	Y	Y
16 Panetta	Y	Y	Y	N	Y	Y	Y	N
17 Dooley	Y	Y	Y	N	Y	Y	Y	N
18 Lehman	?	Y	Y	N	Y	Y	Y	N
19 ***Lagomarsino***	N	N	N	N	N	N	Y	Y
20 ***Thomas***	?	N	N	N	N	N	Y	Y
21 ***Gallegly***	N	N	N	N	N	N	Y	Y
22 ***Moorhead***	?	N	N	N	N	N	Y	Y
23 Beilenson	Y	Y	Y	N	Y	Y	N	N
24 Waxman	Y	Y	Y	N	Y	Y	Y	N
25 Roybal	?	Y	Y	N	Y	Y	Y	N
26 Berman	?	Y	Y	N	Y	Y	Y	N
27 Levine	Y	Y	Y	N	Y	Y	Y	N
28 Dixon	?	?	?	N	Y	Y	Y	Y
29 Waters	?	Y	Y	N	Y	Y	Y	N
30 Martinez	?	Y	Y	N	Y	Y	Y	N
31 Dymally	?	Y	Y	N	Y	Y	Y	N
32 Anderson	Y	Y	Y	N	Y	Y	Y	N
33 ***Dreier***	N	N	N	N	N	N	Y	Y
34 Torres	+	Y	Y	N	Y	Y	Y	N
35 ***Lewis***	N	N	N	N	N	N	Y	Y
36 Brown	Y	Y	Y	N	Y	Y	Y	N
37 ***McCandless***	?	N	N	N	N	N	Y	Y
38 ***Dornan***	?	N	N	N	N	N	Y	Y
39 ***Dannemeyer***	?	N	N	N	N	N	Y	Y
40 ***Cox***	Y	N	N	N	N	N	Y	Y
41 ***Lowery***	N	?	X	N	N	N	Y	Y
42 ***Rohrabacher***	?	N	N	N	N	N	Y	Y
43 ***Packard***	?	N	N	N	N	N	Y	Y
44 ***Cunningham***	Y	N	N	N	N	N	Y	Y
45 ***Hunter***	N	N	N	N	N	N	Y	Y
COLORADO								
1 Schroeder	?	Y	Y	N	Y	Y	Y	N
2 Skaggs	Y	Y	Y	N	Y	Y	Y	N
3 Campbell	?	Y	Y	N	Y	Y	Y	N
4 ***Allard***	N	N	N	N	N	N	Y	Y
5 ***Hefley***	?	N	N	N	N	N	Y	Y
6 ***Schaefer***	N	N	N	N	N	N	Y	Y
CONNECTICUT								
1 Kennelly	Y	Y	Y	N	Y	Y	Y	N
2 Gejdenson	Y	Y	Y	N	Y	Y	Y	N
3 DeLauro	Y	Y	Y	N	Y	Y	Y	N
4 ***Shays***	N	N	N	Y	N	N	Y	Y
5 ***Franks***	N	N	N	N	N	N	Y	Y
6 ***Johnson***	N	N	N	Y	N	N	Y	N
DELAWARE								
AL Carper	?	Y	Y	N	Y	Y	Y	N
FLORIDA								
1 Hutto	?	Y	Y	N	N	N	Y	Y
2 Peterson	Y	Y	Y	N	Y	Y	Y	N
3 Bennett	Y	Y	Y	N	Y	Y	Y	Y
4 ***James***	N	N	N	N	N	N	?	#
5 ***McCollum***	?	N	N	N	N	N	Y	Y
6 ***Stearns***	N	N	N	N	N	N	Y	Y
7 Gibbons	?	Y	Y	N	N	N	?	Y
8 ***Young***	?	N	N	N	N	N	Y	Y
9 ***Bilirakis***	N	N	N	N	N	N	Y	Y
10 ***Ireland***	N	N	N	N	N	N	Y	Y
11 Bacchus	Y	Y	Y	N	Y	Y	Y	N
12 ***Lewis***	N	N	N	N	N	N	Y	Y
13 ***Goss***	N	N	N	N	N	N	Y	Y
14 Johnston	Y	Y	Y	N	Y	Y	Y	N
15 ***Shaw***	?	N	N	N	N	N	Y	Y
16 Smith	?	Y	Y	N	Y	Y	Y	N
17 Lehman	?	Y	Y	N	Y	Y	Y	N
18 ***Ros-Lehtinen***	N	N	N	N	N	N	Y	Y
19 Fascell	Y	Y	Y	N	Y	Y	Y	N
GEORGIA								
1 Thomas	Y	Y	Y	N	N	N	Y	N
2 Hatcher	Y	Y	Y	N	N	N	Y	N
3 Ray	Y	Y	N	N	N	N	Y	N
4 Jones	Y	Y	Y	N	Y	Y	Y	N
5 Lewis	?	Y	Y	N	Y	Y	Y	N
6 ***Gingrich***	N	N	N	N	N	N	Y	Y
7 Darden	?	Y	Y	N	Y	Y	Y	N
8 Rowland	Y	Y	Y	N	N	N	Y	N
9 Jenkins	?	Y	Y	N	N	N	Y	N
10 Barnard	?	Y	Y	N	N	N	Y	Y
HAWAII								
1 Abercrombie	?	Y	Y	N	Y	Y	Y	N
2 Mink	Y	Y	Y	N	Y	Y	Y	N
IDAHO								
1 LaRocco	Y	Y	Y	N	Y	Y	Y	N
2 Stallings	Y	Y	Y	N	Y	Y	Y	N
ILLINOIS								
1 Hayes	Y	Y	Y	N	Y	Y	N	N
2 Savage	?	Y	Y	N	Y	Y	?	N
3 Russo	Y	Y	Y	N	Y	Y	Y	N
4 Sangmeister	Y	Y	Y	N	Y	Y	Y	N
5 Lipinski	?	Y	Y	N	Y	Y	Y	N
6 ***Hyde***	?	N	N	N	N	N	Y	Y
7 Collins	?	Y	Y	N	Y	Y	Y	N
8 Rostenkowski	Y	Y	Y	N	Y	Y	Y	N
9 Yates	?	Y	Y	N	Y	Y	N	N
10 ***Porter***	?	N	N	N	N	N	Y	N
11 Annunzio	?	Y	Y	N	Y	Y	Y	Y
12 ***Crane***	N	N	N	N	N	N	Y	Y
13 ***Fawell***	N	N	N	N	N	N	Y	Y
14 ***Hastert***	N	N	N	N	N	N	Y	Y
15 ***Ewing***	N	N	N	N	N	N	Y	Y
16 Cox	Y	Y	Y	N	Y	Y	?	?
17 Evans	?	Y	Y	N	Y	Y	Y	N
18 ***Michel***	?	?	?	?	?	?	Y	Y
19 Bruce	Y	Y	Y	N	Y	Y	Y	N
20 Durbin	Y	Y	Y	N	Y	Y	Y	N
21 Costello	Y	Y	Y	N	Y	Y	Y	N
22 Poshard	Y	Y	Y	N	Y	Y	Y	N
INDIANA								
1 Visclosky	N	Y	Y	N	Y	Y	Y	N
2 Sharp	?	Y	Y	N	?	Y	Y	N
3 Roemer	Y	Y	Y	N	Y	Y	Y	Y

ND Northern Democrats SD Southern Democrats

	208	209	210	211	212	213	214	215
4 Long	Y	Y	N	N	Y	Y	Y	N
5 Jontz	Y	Y	Y	N	Y	Y	Y	N
6 ***Burton***	N	N	N	N	N	N	Y	Y
7 ***Myers***	N	N	N	N	N	N	Y	Y
8 McCloskey	Y	Y	Y	N	Y	Y	Y	N
9 Hamilton	Y	Y	Y	N	Y	Y	Y	N
10 Jacobs	Y	N	N	N	Y	Y	Y	N
IOWA								
1 ***Leach***	N	N	N	N	N	N	Y	N
2 ***Nussle***	N	N	N	N	N	N	Y	Y
3 Nagle	Y	Y	Y	N	Y	Y	Y	?
4 Smith	Y	Y	Y	N	Y	Y	Y	N
5 ***Lightfoot***	?	N	N	N	N	N	Y	Y
6 ***Grandy***	Y	N	N	Y	N	N	Y	N
KANSAS								
1 ***Roberts***	?	N	N	N	N	N	Y	Y
2 Slattery	?	Y	Y	N	Y	Y	Y	N
3 ***Meyers***	N	N	N	Y	N	N	Y	Y
4 Glickman	?	Y	Y	N	Y	Y	Y	Y
5 ***Nichols***	Y	N	N	N	N	N	Y	Y
KENTUCKY								
1 Hubbard	Y	Y	Y	N	Y	Y	Y	Y
2 Natcher	Y	Y	Y	N	Y	Y	Y	N
3 Mazzoli	Y	Y	Y	Y	Y	Y	Y	N
4 ***Bunning***	?	N	N	N	N	N	Y	Y
5 ***Rogers***	?	N	N	N	N	N	Y	Y
6 ***Hopkins***	?	N	N	N	N	N	?	?
7 Perkins	Y	Y	Y	N	Y	Y	Y	N
LOUISIANA								
1 ***Livingston***	?	N	N	N	N	N	Y	N
2 Jefferson	Y	?	?	N	Y	Y	Y	N
3 Tauzin	Y	Y	Y	N	N	N	Y	Y
4 ***McCrery***	Y	N	N	N	N	N	Y	Y
5 Huckaby	?	Y	Y	N	N	N	Y	N
6 ***Baker***	?	N	N	N	N	N	Y	Y
7 Hayes	?	Y	Y	N	Y	Y	Y	Y
8 ***Holloway***	?	N	N	N	N	N	Y	Y
MAINE								
1 Andrews	Y	Y	?	N	Y	Y	Y	N
2 ***Snowe***	Y	N	N	Y	N	N	Y	N
MARYLAND								
1 ***Gilchrest***	?	N	N	N	N	N	Y	Y
2 ***Bentley***	N	N	N	Y	Y	Y	Y	Y
3 Cardin	Y	Y	Y	N	Y	Y	Y	N
4 McMillen	Y	Y	Y	N	Y	Y	Y	N
5 Hoyer	Y	Y	Y	N	Y	Y	Y	N
6 Byron	Y	Y	Y	N	Y	Y	Y	Y
7 Mfume	Y	Y	Y	N	Y	Y	Y	N
8 ***Morella***	Y	N	N	N	Y	N	Y	N
MASSACHUSETTS								
1 Olver	?	Y	Y	N	Y	Y	Y	N
2 Neal	?	Y	Y	N	Y	Y	Y	Y
3 Early	?	Y	Y	N	Y	Y	Y	Y
4 Frank	?	Y	Y	N	Y	Y	Y	N
5 Atkins	Y	?	Y	N	Y	Y	Y	N
6 Mavroules	?	Y	Y	N	Y	Y	Y	N
7 Markey	?	Y	Y	N	Y	Y	Y	N
8 Kennedy	?	?	?	N	Y	Y	Y	N
9 Moakley	Y	Y	Y	N	Y	Y	Y	N
10 Studds	?	Y	Y	N	Y	Y	Y	N
11 Donnelly	Y	Y	Y	N	Y	Y	Y	Y
MICHIGAN								
1 Conyers	?	Y	Y	N	Y	Y	Y	N
2 ***Pursell***	?	N	N	Y	N	N	Y	?
3 Wolpe	Y	Y	Y	N	Y	Y	Y	N
4 ***Upton***	N	N	N	N	N	N	Y	Y
5 ***Henry***	?	N	N	Y	N	N	Y	Y
6 Carr	Y	Y	Y	N	Y	Y	Y	N
7 Kildee	Y	Y	Y	N	Y	Y	Y	N
8 Traxler	?	Y	Y	N	Y	Y	Y	N
9 ***Vander Jagt***	?	N	N	N	N	N	Y	Y
10 ***Camp***	Y	N	N	N	N	N	Y	Y
11 ***Davis***	?	Y	Y	N	Y	Y	Y	N
12 Bonior	Y	Y	Y	N	Y	Y	Y	N
13 Collins	Y	Y	Y	N	Y	Y	Y	N
14 Hertel	?	Y	Y	N	Y	Y	Y	N
15 Ford	Y	Y	Y	N	Y	Y	Y	N
16 Dingell	Y	Y	Y	N	Y	Y	Y	N
17 Levin	Y	Y	Y	N	Y	Y	Y	N
18 ***Broomfield***	?	N	N	N	N	N	Y	Y
MINNESOTA								
1 Penny	Y	Y	Y	N	Y	Y	Y	N
2 ***Weber***	?	N	N	N	N	N	Y	N
3 ***Ramstad***	N	N	N	N	N	N	Y	Y
4 Vento	?	Y	Y	N	Y	Y	Y	N

	208	209	210	211	212	213	214	215
5 Sabo	?	Y	Y	N	Y	Y	Y	N
6 Sikorski	Y	Y	Y	N	Y	Y	Y	N
7 Peterson	Y	Y	Y	N	Y	Y	Y	N
8 Oberstar	?	Y	Y	N	Y	Y	Y	N
MISSISSIPPI								
1 Whitten	?	Y	Y	N	N	N	Y	Y
2 Espy	?	Y	Y	N	Y	Y	Y	N
3 Montgomery	Y	Y	Y	N	N	N	Y	Y
4 Parker	Y	Y	Y	N	Y	Y	Y	Y
5 Taylor	Y	Y	Y	N	N	N	Y	Y
MISSOURI								
1 Clay	?	Y	Y	N	Y	Y	Y	N
2 Horn	Y	Y	Y	N	Y	Y	Y	N
3 Gephardt	Y	Y	Y	N	Y	Y	Y	N
4 Skelton	?	Y	Y	N	Y	Y	Y	N
5 Wheat	?	Y	Y	N	Y	Y	Y	N
6 ***Coleman***	?	N	N	Y	N	N	Y	Y
7 ***Hancock***	?	N	N	N	N	N	Y	Y
8 ***Emerson***	?	N	N	N	N	N	Y	Y
9 Volkmer	?	Y	Y	N	Y	Y	Y	N
MONTANA								
1 Williams	?	Y	?	N	Y	Y	Y	N
2 ***Marlenee***	N	N	N	N	N	N	?	Y
NEBRASKA								
1 ***Bereuter***	N	N	N	N	N	N	Y	Y
2 Hoagland	Y	Y	Y	N	Y	Y	Y	N
3 ***Barrett***	?	N	N	N	N	N	Y	Y
NEVADA								
1 Bilbray	Y	Y	Y	N	Y	Y	Y	N
2 ***Vucanovich***	?	N	N	N	N	N	Y	Y
NEW HAMPSHIRE								
1 ***Zeliff***	Y	N	N	N	N	N	Y	Y
2 Swett	Y	Y	Y	N	Y	Y	Y	N
NEW JERSEY								
1 Andrews	Y	Y	Y	N	Y	Y	Y	N
2 Hughes	Y	Y	Y	N	Y	Y	Y	N
3 Pallone	?	Y	Y	N	Y	Y	Y	N
4 ***Smith***	Y	Y	Y	N	Y	Y	Y	Y
5 ***Roukema***	?	N	N	Y	N	N	Y	Y
6 Dwyer	?	Y	Y	N	Y	Y	Y	N
7 ***Rinaldo***	?	Y	Y	N	Y	Y	Y	Y
8 Roe	Y	Y	Y	N	Y	Y	Y	N
9 Torricelli	Y	Y	Y	N	Y	Y	Y	Y
10 Payne	Y	Y	Y	N	Y	Y	Y	N
11 ***Gallo***	N	N	N	N	N	N	Y	N
12 ***Zimmer***	?	N	N	N	N	N	Y	Y
13 ***Saxton***	N	?	?	N	N	N	Y	Y
14 Guarini	Y	Y	Y	N	Y	Y	Y	N
NEW MEXICO								
1 ***Schiff***	N	N	N	Y	N	N	?	?
2 ***Skeen***	?	N	N	N	N	N	Y	Y
3 Richardson	?	Y	Y	N	Y	Y	Y	N
NEW YORK								
1 Hochbrueckner	Y	Y	Y	N	Y	Y	Y	N
2 Downey	?	Y	Y	N	Y	Y	Y	N
3 Mrazek	Y	Y	Y	N	Y	Y	Y	N
4 ***Lent***	?	N	N	N	N	N	Y	Y
5 ***McGrath***	Y	Y	Y	N	Y	Y	Y	N
6 Flake	?	Y	Y	N	Y	Y	Y	N
7 Ackerman	Y	Y	Y	N	Y	Y	Y	N
8 Scheuer	?	Y	Y	N	Y	Y	Y	N
9 Manton	?	Y	Y	N	Y	Y	Y	N
10 Schumer	Y	Y	Y	N	Y	Y	Y	N
11 Towns	Y	Y	Y	N	Y	Y	Y	N
12 Owens	?	Y	Y	N	Y	Y	Y	N
13 Solarz	Y	Y	Y	N	Y	Y	Y	N
14 ***Molinari***	?	N	N	N	N	N	Y	Y
15 ***Green***	N	N	N	N	Y	Y	N	N
16 Rangel	?	Y	Y	N	Y	Y	Y	N
17 Weiss	+	+	+	-	+	+	+	-
18 Serrano	Y	Y	Y	N	Y	Y	Y	N
19 Engel	Y	Y	Y	N	Y	Y	Y	N
20 Lowey	Y	Y	Y	N	Y	Y	Y	N
21 ***Fish***	?	N	Y	N	Y	Y	Y	N
22 ***Gilman***	N	N	Y	N	Y	Y	Y	N
23 McNulty	Y	Y	Y	N	Y	Y	Y	N
24 ***Solomon***	?	N	N	N	N	Y	Y	Y
25 ***Boehlert***	Y	N	Y	N	Y	Y	Y	N
26 ***Martin***	?	N	N	N	N	N	Y	Y
27 ***Walsh***	N	N	N	Y	N	N	Y	Y
28 McHugh	?	Y	Y	N	Y	Y	Y	N
29 ***Horton***	?	N	Y	N	Y	Y	Y	N
30 Slaughter	?	Y	Y	N	Y	Y	Y	N
31 ***Paxon***	?	N	N	N	N	N	Y	Y

	208	209	210	211	212	213	214	215
32 LaFalce	Y	Y	Y	N	Y	Y	Y	N
33 Nowak	?	Y	Y	N	Y	Y	Y	N
34 ***Houghton***	Y	N	N	Y	N	N	Y	N
NORTH CAROLINA								
1 Jones	Y	Y	Y	N	Y	Y	Y	N
2 Valentine	?	Y	Y	N	N	N	Y	Y
3 Lancaster	Y	Y	Y	N	N	N	Y	N
4 Price	Y	Y	Y	N	Y	Y	Y	N
5 Neal	?	Y	Y	N	Y	N	Y	N
6 ***Coble***	?	N	N	N	N	N	Y	Y
7 Rose	?	?	?	N	Y	Y	Y	N
8 Hefner	?	Y	Y	N	Y	Y	Y	N
9 ***McMillan***	N	N	N	N	N	N	Y	Y
10 ***Ballenger***	?	N	N	N	N	N	Y	Y
11 ***Taylor***	Y	N	N	N	N	N	Y	Y
NORTH DAKOTA								
AL Dorgan	?	Y	Y	N	Y	Y	Y	N
OHIO								
1 Luken	Y	Y	Y	N	Y	Y	Y	Y
2 ***Gradison***	?	N	N	N	N	N	Y	Y
3 Hall	?	Y	Y	N	Y	Y	Y	N
4 ***Oxley***	?	N	N	N	N	N	Y	N
5 ***Gillmor***	N	N	N	N	N	N	Y	N
6 ***McEwen***	Y	N	N	N	N	N	Y	Y
7 ***Hobson***	N	N	N	Y	N	N	Y	Y
8 ***Boehner***	N	N	N	N	N	N	Y	Y
9 Kaptur	Y	Y	Y	N	Y	Y	Y	N
10 ***Miller***	N	N	Y	Y	N	Y	Y	Y
11 Eckart	Y	Y	Y	N	Y	Y	Y	N
12 ***Kasich***	Y	N	N	N	N	N	Y	Y
13 Pease	?	Y	Y	N	Y	Y	Y	N
14 Sawyer	?	Y	Y	N	Y	Y	Y	N
15 ***Wylie***	N	N	N	N	N	N	Y	Y
16 ***Regula***	N	N	Y	Y	Y	Y	Y	Y
17 Traficant	Y	Y	Y	N	Y	Y	Y	Y
18 Applegate	?	Y	Y	N	Y	Y	Y	Y
19 Feighan	?	Y	Y	N	Y	Y	Y	N
20 Oakar	Y	Y	Y	N	Y	Y	Y	N
21 Stokes	Y	Y	Y	N	Y	Y	Y	N
OKLAHOMA								
1 ***Inhofe***	?	N	N	N	N	N	Y	Y
2 Synar	?	Y	Y	N	Y	Y	Y	N
3 Brewster	Y	Y	Y	N	N	N	Y	Y
4 McCurdy	?	Y	Y	N	Y	N	?	N
5 ***Edwards***	N	N	N	N	N	N	Y	Y
6 English	Y	Y	Y	N	N	N	Y	Y
OREGON								
1 AuCoin	?	Y	Y	N	Y	Y	Y	N
2 ***Smith***	N	N	N	N	N	N	Y	Y
3 Wyden	Y	Y	Y	N	Y	Y	Y	N
4 DeFazio	Y	Y	Y	N	Y	Y	Y	N
5 Kopetski	Y	Y	Y	N	Y	Y	Y	N
PENNSYLVANIA								
1 Foglietta	Y	Y	Y	N	Y	Y	Y	N
2 Gray	?	Y	Y	?	Y	Y	?	?
3 Borski	Y	Y	Y	N	Y	Y	Y	N
4 Kolter	?	Y	Y	N	Y	Y	Y	Y
5 ***Schulze***	Y	N	N	N	N	N	Y	Y
6 Yatron	?	?	?	?	?	?	?	?
7 ***Weldon***	N	N	N	Y	Y	Y	Y	Y
8 Kostmayer	Y	Y	Y	N	Y	Y	N	N
9 ***Shuster***	N	N	N	N	N	N	Y	Y
10 ***McDade***	?	N	Y	N	Y	Y	Y	N
11 Kanjorski	Y	Y	Y	N	Y	Y	Y	N
12 Murtha	?	Y	Y	N	Y	Y	Y	N
13 ***Coughlin***	?	?	?	N	N	N	N	Y
14 Coyne	Y	Y	Y	N	Y	Y	Y	N
15 ***Ritter***	N	N	N	Y	N	N	Y	Y
16 ***Walker***	N	N	N	N	N	N	Y	Y
17 ***Gekas***	?	N	N	N	N	N	Y	Y
18 ***Santorum***	N	N	N	N	Y	Y	Y	Y
19 ***Goodling***	?	N	N	Y	N	N	Y	Y
20 Gaydos	?	Y	Y	N	Y	Y	Y	Y
21 ***Ridge***	?	N	N	N	N	N	Y	N
22 Murphy	?	Y	Y	N	Y	Y	Y	Y
23 ***Clinger***	Y	N	N	Y	N	N	Y	N
RHODE ISLAND								
1 ***Machtley***	?	N	N	Y	N	N	Y	N
2 Reed	?	Y	Y	N	Y	Y	Y	N
SOUTH CAROLINA								
1 ***Ravenel***	?	N	N	N	N	N	Y	Y
2 ***Spence***	N	N	N	N	N	N	Y	Y
3 Derrick	Y	Y	Y	N	Y	N	Y	N
4 Patterson	Y	Y	Y	N	Y	N	Y	Y
5 Spratt	Y	Y	Y	N	Y	N	Y	N
6 Tallon	Y	Y	Y	N	Y	N	Y	Y

	208	209	210	211	212	213	214	215
SOUTH DAKOTA								
AL Johnson	Y	Y	Y	N	Y	Y	Y	N
TENNESSEE								
1 ***Quillen***	Y	N	N	N	N	N	Y	Y
2 ***Duncan***	Y	N	N	Y	N	N	Y	Y
3 Lloyd	Y	Y	N	N	Y	Y	Y	Y
4 Cooper	Y	Y	Y	N	N	N	Y	N
5 Clement	Y	Y	Y	N	Y	Y	Y	N
6 Gordon	Y	Y	Y	N	Y	Y	Y	N
7 ***Sundquist***	N	N	N	N	N	N	Y	Y
8 Tanner	Y	Y	Y	N	Y	Y	Y	Y
9 Ford	Y	Y	Y	N	Y	Y	Y	N
TEXAS								
1 Chapman	Y	Y	Y	N	Y	Y	Y	N
2 Wilson	?	Y	Y	N	Y	Y	Y	Y
3 ***Johnson***	Y	N	N	N	N	N	Y	Y
4 Hall	Y	Y	Y	N	N	N	Y	Y
5 Bryant	?	Y	Y	N	Y	Y	Y	N
6 ***Barton***	N	N	N	N	N	N	Y	Y
7 ***Archer***	?	N	N	N	N	N	Y	Y
8 ***Fields***	?	N	N	N	N	N	Y	Y
9 Brooks	?	Y	Y	N	Y	Y	Y	N
10 Pickle	Y	Y	Y	N	Y	N	Y	N
11 Edwards	Y	Y	Y	N	Y	Y	Y	N
12 Geren	Y	?	Y	N	N	N	Y	Y
13 Sarpalius	Y	Y	Y	N	Y	Y	Y	Y
14 Laughlin	Y	Y	Y	N	Y	Y	Y	?
15 de la Garza	Y	Y	Y	N	Y	Y	Y	N
16 Coleman	Y	Y	Y	N	Y	Y	Y	N
17 Stenholm	Y	Y	Y	N	N	N	Y	Y
18 Washington	?	Y	Y	N	Y	Y	Y	N
19 ***Combest***	?	N	N	N	N	N	Y	Y
20 Gonzalez	Y	Y	Y	N	Y	Y	Y	N
21 ***Smith***	N	N	N	N	N	N	Y	Y
22 ***DeLay***	N	N	N	N	N	N	Y	Y
23 Bustamante	Y	Y	Y	N	Y	Y	Y	?
24 Frost	?	Y	Y	N	Y	Y	Y	N
25 Andrews	Y	Y	Y	N	Y	Y	Y	N
26 ***Armey***	?	N	N	N	N	N	Y	Y
27 Ortiz	Y	Y	Y	N	N	N	Y	N
UTAH								
1 ***Hansen***	?	N	N	N	N	N	Y	Y
2 Owens	?	Y	Y	N	Y	Y	Y	N
3 Orton	Y	Y	Y	N	Y	Y	Y	N
VERMONT								
AL *Sanders*	?	Y	Y	N	Y	Y	Y	N
VIRGINIA								
1 ***Bateman***	N	N	N	N	N	N	Y	N
2 Pickett	Y	Y	Y	N	N	N	Y	N
3 ***Bliley***	?	N	N	N	N	N	Y	Y
4 Sisisky	?	Y	Y	N	N	N	Y	N
5 Payne	Y	Y	Y	N	N	N	Y	Y
6 Olin	Y	Y	Y	N	Y	Y	Y	N
7 ***Slaughter***	Y	N	N	N	N	N	Y	Y
8 Moran	Y	Y	Y	N	Y	Y	+	X
9 Boucher	Y	Y	Y	N	?	Y	Y	N
10 ***Wolf***	?	N	N	N	N	N	Y	N
WASHINGTON								
1 ***Miller***	N	N	N	N	N	N	Y	N
2 Swift	Y	Y	Y	N	Y	Y	Y	N
3 Unsoeld	Y	Y	Y	N	Y	Y	Y	N
4 ***Morrison***	Y	N	N	N	N	N	Y	N
5 Foley							Y	
6 Dicks	?	Y	Y	N	Y	Y	Y	N
7 McDermott	Y	Y	Y	N	Y	Y	Y	N
8 ***Chandler***	N	N	N	Y	N	N	Y	Y
WEST VIRGINIA								
1 Mollohan	?	Y	Y	N	Y	Y	Y	N
2 Staggers	?	Y	Y	N	Y	Y	Y	N
3 Wise	Y	Y	Y	N	Y	Y	Y	N
4 Rahall	Y	Y	Y	N	Y	Y	Y	N
WISCONSIN								
1 Aspin	?	Y	Y	N	Y	Y	Y	N
2 ***Klug***	N	N	N	Y	N	N	Y	Y
3 ***Gunderson***	N	N	N	Y	N	N	Y	N
4 Kleczka	?	+	#	-	+	+	+	-
5 Moody	Y	Y	Y	N	Y	Y	Y	Y
6 ***Petri***	?	Y	Y	N	Y	N	Y	N
7 Obey	Y	Y	Y	N	Y	Y	Y	N
8 ***Roth***	?	N	N	N	N	N	Y	Y
9 ***Sensenbrenner***	N	N	N	N	N	N	Y	Y
WYOMING								
AL ***Thomas***	N	N	N	N	N	N	Y	Y

Southern states - Ala., Ark., Fla., Ga., Ky., La., Miss., N.C., Okla., S.C., Tenn., Texas, Va.
Omitted votes are quorum calls, which CQ does not include in its vote charts.

HOUSE VOTES 216, 217, 218, 220, 221, 223, 224, 225

216. HR 1776. Fiscal 1992 Coast Guard Authorization/Drug Testing Applicants. Solomon, R-N.Y., amendment to require the Coast Guard to establish a program for random drug testing of applicants for civilian employment. Rejected 204-213: R 136-26; D 68-186 (ND 27-145, SD 41-41); I 0-1, July 18, 1991.

217. Procedural Motion. Marlenee, R-Mont., motion to approve the House Journal of Monday, July 22. Motion agreed to 274-104: R 48-99; D 225-5 (ND 151-5, SD 74-0); I 1-0, July 23, 1991.

218. HR 1096. Bureau of Land Management Authorization/Grazing Fees. Regula, R-Ohio, substitute amendment to the Synar, D-Okla., amendment to set fees for grazing livestock on federal lands at fair market value starting during the 1992 grazing season with a limit of 33 percent on increases or decreases in any given year. Adopted 254-165: R 63-98; D 190-67 (ND 148-26, SD 42-41); I 1-0, July 23, 1991.

220. HR 2942. Fiscal 1992 Transportation Appropriations/Increase Caps. Penny, D-Minn., en bloc amendment to hold increases for five administration accounts of the Department of Transportation to 9 percent over fiscal 1991 by cutting about $2 million. Rejected 84-339: R 37-127; D 46-212 (ND 29-146, SD 17-66), July 24, 1991.

221. HR 2942. Fiscal 1992 Transportation Appropriations/Demonstration Projects. Fawell, R-Ill., en bloc amendment to cut $243 million from the bill by eliminating 63 demonstration projects. Rejected 61-365: R 58-105; D 2-260 (ND 2-176, SD 0-84); I 1-0, July 24, 1991.

223. HR 2942. Fiscal 1992 Transportation Appropriations/Discretionary Outlays. Zeliff, R-N.H., amendment to provide for an across-the-board cut of 9.89 percent in budget authority for all discretionary accounts in the bill, limiting the overall growth of outlays to 0.36 percent from the fiscal 1991 level. Rejected 64-362: R 59-105; D 5-256 (ND 5-173, SD 0-83); I 0-1, July 24, 1991.

224. HR 2942. Fiscal 1992 Transportation Appropriations/Passage. Passage of the bill to provide $34,413,452,569 for the Department of Transportation and related agencies in fiscal 1992. The administration requested $33,381,198,569. Passed 379-47: R 120-42; D 258-5 (ND 174-5, SD 84-0); I 1-0, July 24, 1991.

225. HR 2893. Agricultural Disaster Assistance/Passage. De la Garza, D-Texas, motion to suspend the rules and pass the bill to extend through 1991 a disaster assistance program for crop producers that was authorized in the 1990 farm bill (PL 101-624). Motion agreed to 328-67: R 90-63; D 237-4 (ND 159-4, SD 78-0); I 1-0, July 25, 1991. A two-thirds majority of those present and voting (264 in this case) is required for passage under suspension of the rules.

KEY

- Y Voted for (yea).
- # Paired for.
- + Announced for.
- N Voted against (nay).
- X Paired against.
- - Announced against.
- P Voted "present."
- C Voted "present" to avoid possible conflict of interest.
- ? Did not vote or otherwise make a position known.

Democrats ***Republicans***
Independent

	216	217	218	220	221	223	224	225
ALABAMA								
1 ***Callahan***	Y	?	?	N	N	N	Y	Y
2 ***Dickinson***	Y	N	N	N	N	N	Y	N
3 Browder	Y	Y	N	N	N	N	Y	Y
4 Bevill	Y	Y	N	N	N	N	Y	Y
5 Cramer	Y	Y	N	N	N	N	Y	Y
6 Erdreich	Y	Y	Y	N	N	N	Y	Y
7 Harris	Y	Y	N	N	N	N	Y	Y
ALASKA								
AL ***Young***	N	?	N	N	N	N	Y	?
ARIZONA								
1 ***Rhodes***	Y	N	N	N	Y	Y	N	N
2 Vacancy								
3 ***Stump***	Y	N	N	Y	Y	Y	N	N
4 ***Kyl***	Y	N	N	N	Y	Y	N	N
5 ***Kolbe***	Y	N	N	Y	N	Y	Y	N
ARKANSAS								
1 Alexander	?	Y	N	N	N	N	Y	Y
2 Thornton	N	Y	N	N	N	N	Y	Y
3 ***Hammerschmidt***	Y	Y	N	N	N	N	Y	Y
4 Anthony	N	Y	N	N	N	N	Y	?
CALIFORNIA								
1 ***Riggs***	Y	N	N	Y	N	N	Y	?
2 ***Herger***	Y	N	N	Y	Y	Y	N	Y
3 Matsui	?	?	?	N	N	N	Y	Y
4 Fazio	N	Y	Y	N	N	N	Y	Y
5 Pelosi	N	?	Y	N	N	N	Y	Y
6 Boxer	?	Y	Y	N	N	N	Y	Y
7 Miller	N	Y	Y	N	N	N	Y	Y
8 Dellums	N	?	Y	N	N	N	Y	?
9 Stark	N	Y	Y	N	N	N	Y	Y
10 Edwards	N	Y	Y	N	N	N	Y	Y
11 Lantos	N	Y	Y	N	N	N	Y	Y
12 ***Campbell***	N	N	N	N	Y	Y	N	?
13 Mineta	N	Y	Y	N	N	N	Y	Y
14 ***Doolittle***	Y	N	N	N	Y	Y	N	Y
15 Condit	Y	?	N	Y	N	Y	Y	Y
16 Panetta	N	Y	N	Y	N	N	Y	Y
17 Dooley	N	Y	N	N	N	N	Y	Y
18 Lehman	N	Y	N	N	N	N	Y	Y
19 ***Lagomarsino***	Y	N	N	?	?	?	?	Y
20 ***Thomas***	N	?	X	N	N	N	Y	Y
21 ***Gallegly***	Y	N	N	N	Y	Y	Y	Y
22 ***Moorhead***	Y	N	N	N	Y	N	N	N
23 Beilenson	N	Y	Y	N	N	N	Y	?
24 Waxman	N	Y	Y	N	N	N	Y	Y
25 Roybal	N	Y	Y	N	N	N	Y	Y
26 Berman	N	Y	Y	N	N	N	Y	Y
27 Levine	N	?	Y	N	N	N	Y	Y
28 Dixon	N	Y	Y	N	N	N	Y	?
29 Waters	N	Y	Y	Y	N	N	Y	?
30 Martinez	N	Y	Y	N	N	N	Y	Y
31 Dymally	N	Y	Y	N	N	N	Y	Y
32 Anderson	N	Y	Y	N	N	N	Y	Y
33 ***Dreier***	Y	Y	N	N	Y	Y	N	N
34 Torres	N	Y	Y	N	N	N	Y	Y
35 ***Lewis***	Y	Y	N	N	N	N	Y	N
36 Brown	N	Y	Y	N	N	N	Y	Y
37 ***McCandless***	Y	N	N	Y	N	N	Y	Y
38 ***Dornan***	Y	N	N	N	Y	N	Y	?
39 ***Dannemeyer***	Y	N	Y	Y	Y	Y	N	N
40 ***Cox***	Y	N	Y	N	Y	Y	Y	N
41 ***Lowery***	Y	?	?	N	N	N	Y	?
42 ***Rohrabacher***	Y	N	Y	N	Y	Y	N	N
43 ***Packard***	Y	Y	N	N	N	N	Y	Y
44 ***Cunningham***	Y	N	N	N	N	Y	N	Y
45 ***Hunter***	Y	N	N	N	Y	Y	N	Y
COLORADO								
1 Schroeder	N	N	Y	N	N	N	Y	Y
2 Skaggs	N	Y	N	N	N	N	Y	Y
3 Campbell	N	Y	N	N	N	N	Y	Y
4 ***Allard***	Y	N	N	N	Y	Y	N	Y
5 ***Hefley***	Y	N	N	Y	Y	Y	N	N
6 ***Schaefer***	Y	N	N	N	N	N	Y	N
CONNECTICUT								
1 Kennelly	N	Y	Y	N	N	N	Y	Y
2 Gejdenson	N	?	Y	N	N	N	Y	Y
3 DeLauro	N	Y	Y	N	N	N	Y	Y
4 ***Shays***	Y	N	Y	N	N	Y	Y	N
5 ***Franks***	Y	?	Y	N	N	N	Y	N
6 ***Johnson***	N	Y	Y	N	N	N	Y	N
DELAWARE								
AL Carper	N	Y	Y	Y	N	N	Y	N
FLORIDA								
1 Hutto	Y	Y	N	Y	N	N	Y	Y
2 Peterson	N	Y	N	Y	N	N	Y	Y
3 Bennett	Y	Y	Y	Y	N	N	Y	Y
4 ***James***	?	N	Y	N	N	N	Y	Y
5 ***McCollum***	Y	Y	N	N	N	N	Y	N
6 ***Stearns***	Y	?	Y	Y	Y	Y	N	Y
7 Gibbons	Y	Y	Y	N	N	N	Y	Y
8 ***Young***	Y	N	N	N	N	N	Y	Y
9 ***Bilirakis***	Y	N	N	N	N	N	Y	Y
10 ***Ireland***	Y	?	Y	N	N	N	Y	N
11 Bacchus	N	Y	Y	N	N	N	Y	Y
12 ***Lewis***	Y	N	Y	N	N	N	Y	Y
13 ***Goss***	Y	N	Y	N	Y	N	N	N
14 Johnston	N	?	Y	N	N	N	Y	Y
15 ***Shaw***	Y	?	N	N	N	N	Y	N
16 Smith	Y	Y	Y	N	N	N	Y	Y
17 Lehman	N	?	Y	N	N	N	Y	Y
18 ***Ros-Lehtinen***	Y	Y	Y	N	N	N	Y	N
19 Fascell	N	Y	Y	N	N	N	Y	Y
GEORGIA								
1 Thomas	N	Y	N	N	N	N	Y	Y
2 Hatcher	N	Y	N	N	N	N	Y	Y
3 Ray	N	Y	N	Y	N	N	Y	Y
4 Jones	Y	Y	Y	N	N	N	Y	Y
5 Lewis	N	Y	Y	N	N	N	Y	Y
6 ***Gingrich***	Y	N	N	N	N	N	Y	Y
7 Darden	N	Y	Y	N	N	N	Y	Y
8 Rowland	N	Y	Y	N	N	N	Y	Y
9 Jenkins	N	?	Y	N	N	N	Y	Y
10 Barnard	Y	?	Y	N	N	N	Y	Y
HAWAII								
1 Abercrombie	N	Y	Y	N	N	N	Y	Y
2 Mink	N	Y	Y	N	N	N	Y	Y
IDAHO								
1 LaRocco	N	Y	N	Y	N	N	Y	Y
2 Stallings	N	Y	N	Y	N	N	Y	Y
ILLINOIS								
1 Hayes	N	Y	Y	N	N	N	Y	Y
2 Savage	N	Y	Y	N	N	N	Y	?
3 Russo	N	Y	Y	N	N	N	Y	Y
4 Sangmeister	Y	Y	Y	N	N	N	Y	Y
5 Lipinski	Y	Y	Y	N	N	N	Y	Y
6 ***Hyde***	Y	?	Y	N	Y	Y	N	N
7 Collins	N	Y	Y	N	N	N	Y	Y
8 Rostenkowski	N	Y	Y	N	N	N	Y	Y
9 Yates	N	Y	Y	N	N	N	Y	Y
10 ***Porter***	Y	N	Y	Y	N	Y	Y	N
11 Annunzio	N	Y	Y	N	N	N	Y	Y
12 ***Crane***	Y	N	N	Y	Y	Y	N	N
13 ***Fawell***	Y	N	Y	Y	Y	Y	N	N
14 ***Hastert***	Y	N	N	N	Y	Y	Y	Y
15 ***Ewing***	Y	N	N	N	Y	Y	Y	Y
16 Cox	?	Y	Y	N	N	N	Y	Y
17 Evans	N	Y	Y	N	N	N	Y	Y
18 ***Michel***	Y	N	N	N	Y	N	Y	Y
19 Bruce	N	Y	Y	N	N	N	Y	Y
20 Durbin	N	Y	Y	N	N	N	Y	Y
21 Costello	Y	Y	Y	N	N	N	Y	Y
22 Poshard	Y	Y	Y	N	N	N	Y	Y
INDIANA								
1 Visclosky	N	Y	Y	N	N	N	Y	Y
2 Sharp	N	Y	Y	?	N	N	Y	Y
3 Roemer	Y	Y	Y	Y	N	N	Y	Y

ND Northern Democrats SD Southern Democrats

	216	217	218	220	221	223	224	225
4 Long	Y	Y	N	N	N	N	Y	Y
5 Jontz	N	Y	Y	N	N	N	Y	Y
6 ***Burton***	Y	N	N	N	Y	Y	N	N
7 ***Myers***	N	Y	N	N	N	N	Y	Y
8 McCloskey	N	Y	Y	N	N	N	Y	Y
9 Hamilton	N	Y	Y	Y	N	N	Y	Y
10 Jacobs	N	N	N	Y	N	Y	N	Y
IOWA								
1 ***Leach***	N	N	N	N	Y	N	Y	Y
2 ***Nussle***	Y	N	N	N	N	Y	N	Y
3 Nagle	?	Y	Y	N	N	N	Y	Y
4 Smith	N	?	Y	N	N	N	Y	Y
5 ***Lightfoot***	Y	N	N	N	N	N	Y	Y
6 ***Grandy***	N	N	N	N	N	Y	Y	Y
KANSAS								
1 ***Roberts***	Y	N	N	N	Y	Y	N	Y
2 Slattery	Y	Y	Y	Y	N	N	Y	Y
3 ***Meyers***	Y	N	Y	Y	N	N	Y	Y
4 Glickman	Y	Y	Y	N	N	N	Y	Y
5 ***Nichols***	Y	Y	N	N	N	N	Y	Y
KENTUCKY								
1 Hubbard	Y	Y	N	N	N	N	Y	Y
2 Natcher	N	Y	N	N	N	N	Y	Y
3 Mazzoli	N	Y	Y	N	N	N	Y	Y
4 ***Bunning***	Y	N	N	N	Y	Y	N	Y
5 ***Rogers***	Y	N	N	N	N	N	Y	Y
6 ***Hopkins***	?	?	?	?	?	?	?	?
7 Perkins	N	Y	N	N	N	N	Y	Y
LOUISIANA								
1 ***Livingston***	Y	Y	N	N	N	N	Y	?
2 Jefferson	N	?	Y	N	N	N	Y	?
3 Tauzin	Y	Y	Y	N	N	N	Y	Y
4 ***McCrery***	Y	Y	Y	N	N	N	Y	?
5 Huckaby	Y	Y	Y	Y	N	N	Y	Y
6 ***Baker***	N	N	N	N	N	N	N	Y
7 Hayes	Y	Y	Y	N	N	N	Y	Y
8 ***Holloway***	Y	?	N	Y	Y	Y	N	?
MAINE								
1 Andrews	N	Y	Y	N	N	N	Y	Y
2 ***Snowe***	N	Y	Y	Y	N	N	Y	Y
MARYLAND								
1 ***Gilchrest***	Y	N	N	N	Y	Y	Y	?
2 ***Bentley***	Y	N	N	N	N	N	Y	N
3 Cardin	N	Y	Y	N	N	N	Y	Y
4 McMillen	N	Y	Y	N	N	N	Y	Y
5 Hoyer	N	Y	Y	N	N	N	Y	Y
6 Byron	Y	Y	Y	Y	N	N	Y	Y
7 Mfume	N	Y	N	N	N	N	Y	Y
8 ***Morella***	N	N	Y	N	N	N	Y	N
MASSACHUSETTS								
1 Olver	N	Y	Y	N	N	N	Y	?
2 Neal	Y	?	Y	N	N	N	Y	Y
3 Early	Y	Y	Y	Y	N	N	Y	Y
4 Frank	N	Y	Y	N	N	N	Y	Y
5 Atkins	N	Y	Y	N	N	N	Y	Y
6 Mavroules	N	?	Y	N	N	N	Y	Y
7 Markey	N	Y	Y	N	N	N	Y	Y
8 Kennedy	N	Y	Y	N	N	N	Y	Y
9 Moakley	N	Y	Y	N	N	N	Y	Y
10 Studds	N	Y	Y	N	N	N	Y	Y
11 Donnelly	Y	?	Y	N	N	N	Y	N
MICHIGAN								
1 Conyers	N	Y	Y	N	N	N	Y	Y
2 ***Pursell***	?	Y	N	N	N	N	Y	Y
3 Wolpe	N	Y	Y	N	N	N	Y	Y
4 ***Upton***	Y	N	Y	Y	N	N	Y	Y
5 ***Henry***	Y	N	Y	N	N	N	N	Y
6 Carr	N	Y	N	N	N	N	Y	Y
7 Kildee	N	Y	Y	N	N	N	Y	Y
8 Traxler	N	Y	Y	N	N	N	Y	Y
9 ***Vander Jagt***	Y	?	Y	N	N	N	Y	?
10 ***Camp***	Y	N	N	Y	N	N	Y	Y
11 ***Davis***	N	Y	N	N	N	N	Y	Y
12 Bonior	N	?	Y	N	N	N	Y	Y
13 Collins	N	Y	Y	N	N	N	Y	Y
14 Hertel	N	Y	Y	N	N	N	N	Y
15 Ford	N	Y	Y	N	N	N	Y	Y
16 Dingell	N	?	Y	N	N	N	Y	Y
17 Levin	N	Y	Y	N	N	N	Y	Y
18 ***Broomfield***	Y	Y	Y	Y	N	N	Y	Y
MINNESOTA								
1 Penny	N	Y	Y	Y	Y	Y	N	N
2 ***Weber***	Y	?	N	N	N	Y	Y	?
3 ***Ramstad***	Y	N	Y	Y	N	Y	Y	N
4 Vento	N	Y	Y	N	N	N	Y	N

	216	217	218	220	221	223	224	225
5 Sabo	N	Y	Y	N	N	N	Y	Y
6 Sikorski	N	N	Y	N	N	N	Y	Y
7 Peterson	N	Y	N	Y	N	N	Y	Y
8 Oberstar	N	?	Y	N	N	N	Y	Y
MISSISSIPPI								
1 Whitten	Y	Y	N	N	N	N	Y	Y
2 Espy	N	Y	N	N	N	N	Y	Y
3 Montgomery	Y	Y	N	N	N	N	Y	Y
4 Parker	Y	Y	N	Y	N	N	Y	Y
5 Taylor	Y	Y	N	Y	N	N	Y	Y
MISSOURI								
1 Clay	N	N	Y	N	N	N	Y	Y
2 Horn	N	Y	Y	N	N	N	Y	Y
3 Gephardt	N	Y	Y	N	N	N	Y	Y
4 Skelton	Y	Y	Y	Y	N	N	Y	Y
5 Wheat	N	Y	Y	N	N	N	Y	Y
6 ***Coleman***	Y	N	N	N	N	N	Y	Y
7 ***Hancock***	Y	N	N	Y	Y	Y	N	N
8 ***Emerson***	Y	Y	N	N	?	N	Y	Y
9 Volkmer	Y	Y	Y	Y	N	N	Y	Y
MONTANA								
1 Williams	N	Y	N	Y	N	?	Y	Y
2 ***Marlenee***	Y	N	N	N	N	N	Y	Y
NEBRASKA								
1 ***Bereuter***	Y	N	Y	N	N	N	Y	Y
2 Hoagland	N	Y	Y	N	N	N	Y	?
3 ***Barrett***	Y	N	N	N	N	Y	Y	Y
NEVADA								
1 Bilbray	N	Y	N	N	N	N	Y	Y
2 ***Vucanovich***	Y	N	N	N	N	N	Y	N
NEW HAMPSHIRE								
1 ***Zeliff***	Y	N	N	N	Y	Y	N	N
2 Swett	N	Y	Y	Y	N	Y	Y	Y
NEW JERSEY								
1 Andrews	Y	Y	-	Y	N	N	Y	Y
2 Hughes	N	Y	Y	Y	N	N	Y	Y
3 Pallone	N	Y	Y	N	N	N	Y	Y
4 ***Smith***	Y	Y	Y	N	N	N	Y	Y
5 ***Roukema***	N	N	Y	N	N	N	Y	N
6 Dwyer	N	Y	Y	N	N	N	Y	Y
7 ***Rinaldo***	Y	Y	Y	N	N	N	Y	Y
8 Roe	N	Y	Y	N	N	N	Y	Y
9 Torricelli	Y	?	Y	N	N	N	Y	Y
10 Payne	N	?	Y	N	N	N	Y	Y
11 ***Gallo***	Y	N	Y	N	N	N	Y	N
12 ***Zimmer***	Y	N	Y	Y	Y	Y	N	N
13 ***Saxton***	Y	N	Y	N	Y	N	Y	Y
14 Guarini	Y	Y	Y	N	N	N	Y	Y
NEW MEXICO								
1 ***Schiff***	?	?	N	Y	Y	N	Y	?
2 ***Skeen***	Y	Y	N	N	N	N	Y	Y
3 Richardson	N	Y	N	N	N	N	Y	Y
NEW YORK								
1 Hochbrueckner	N	Y	Y	N	N	N	Y	Y
2 Downey	N	Y	Y	N	N	N	Y	Y
3 Mrazek	N	?	Y	N	N	N	Y	?
4 ***Lent***	Y	Y	N	N	N	N	Y	Y
5 ***McGrath***	N	N	Y	N	N	N	Y	Y
6 Flake	N	Y	Y	?	N	N	Y	?
7 Ackerman	N	?	#	N	N	N	Y	Y
8 Scheuer	N	Y	Y	N	N	N	Y	Y
9 Manton	N	Y	Y	N	N	N	Y	Y
10 Schumer	N	Y	Y	Y	N	N	Y	Y
11 Towns	N	Y	Y	N	N	N	Y	Y
12 Owens	N	Y	Y	N	N	N	Y	Y
13 Solarz	N	Y	Y	N	N	N	Y	Y
14 ***Molinari***	Y	N	N	N	N	N	Y	Y
15 ***Green***	N	?	Y	N	N	N	Y	N
16 Rangel	N	Y	Y	N	N	N	Y	Y
17 Weiss	-	+	+	-	-	-	+	+
18 Serrano	N	Y	Y	N	N	N	Y	Y
19 Engel	N	?	Y	N	N	N	Y	Y
20 Lowey	N	Y	Y	N	N	N	Y	Y
21 ***Fish***	N	Y	Y	N	N	N	?	Y
22 ***Gilman***	Y	Y	Y	N	N	N	Y	Y
23 McNulty	N	Y	Y	N	N	N	Y	Y
24 ***Solomon***	Y	N	N	N	Y	Y	?	Y
25 ***Boehlert***	N	N	Y	N	N	N	Y	Y
26 ***Martin***	Y	N	N	N	N	N	Y	Y
27 ***Walsh***	Y	Y	N	N	N	N	Y	Y
28 McHugh	N	Y	Y	N	N	N	Y	?
29 ***Horton***	N	Y	Y	N	N	N	Y	Y
30 Slaughter	N	?	Y	N	N	N	Y	Y
31 ***Paxon***	Y	N	N	N	Y	N	Y	Y

	216	217	218	220	221	223	224	225
32 LaFalce	N	Y	Y	N	N	N	Y	Y
33 Nowak	N	Y	Y	N	N	N	Y	Y
34 ***Houghton***	N	Y	N	N	N	N	Y	Y
NORTH CAROLINA								
1 Jones	N	Y	N	N	N	N	Y	Y
2 Valentine	Y	Y	Y	N	N	N	Y	Y
3 Lancaster	N	Y	Y	N	N	N	Y	Y
4 Price	N	?	Y	N	N	N	Y	Y
5 Neal	N	Y	Y	?	N	N	Y	Y
6 ***Coble***	Y	N	N	N	Y	Y	N	N
7 Rose	Y	Y	N	N	N	N	Y	Y
8 Hefner	Y	Y	Y	N	N	N	Y	?
9 ***McMillan***	Y	Y	Y	N	N	N	Y	N
10 ***Ballenger***	Y	N	N	N	Y	N	N	N
11 ***Taylor***	Y	N	N	N	Y	Y	N	N
NORTH DAKOTA								
AL Dorgan	N	Y	N	Y	N	N	N	Y
OHIO								
1 Luken	Y	Y	Y	Y	Y	Y	N	Y
2 ***Gradison***	Y	Y	Y	N	Y	Y	Y	N
3 Hall	N	Y	Y	Y	N	N	Y	?
4 ***Oxley***	Y	Y	Y	N	N	N	Y	Y
5 ***Gillmor***	N	Y	Y	N	N	N	Y	Y
6 ***McEwen***	Y	Y	Y	N	N	N	Y	Y
7 ***Hobson***	Y	N	Y	N	N	N	Y	Y
8 ***Boehner***	Y	N	N	Y	Y	Y	N	N
9 Kaptur	N	Y	Y	N	N	N	Y	Y
10 ***Miller***	Y	N	Y	N	N	Y	Y	N
11 Eckart	N	Y	Y	Y	N	N	Y	Y
12 ***Kasich***	Y	?	Y	Y	Y	Y	Y	Y
13 Pease	?	Y	Y	Y	N	N	Y	Y
14 Sawyer	N	Y	Y	N	N	N	Y	Y
15 ***Wylie***	Y	Y	N	N	N	N	Y	N
16 ***Regula***	Y	N	Y	N	N	N	Y	Y
17 Traficant	Y	Y	Y	N	N	N	Y	Y
18 Applegate	Y	Y	Y	N	N	N	Y	Y
19 Feighan	N	Y	Y	Y	N	N	Y	Y
20 Oakar	N	?	Y	N	N	N	Y	Y
21 Stokes	N	Y	Y	?	?	N	Y	Y
OKLAHOMA								
1 ***Inhofe***	Y	N	N	N	Y	N	Y	N
2 Synar	N	Y	Y	Y	N	N	Y	Y
3 Brewster	Y	Y	N	N	N	N	Y	Y
4 McCurdy	Y	Y	Y	Y	N	N	Y	?
5 ***Edwards***	Y	N	N	Y	N	Y	Y	Y
6 English	Y	Y	N	Y	N	N	Y	Y
OREGON								
1 AuCoin	N	Y	N	N	N	N	Y	?
2 ***Smith***	Y	N	N	N	N	N	Y	Y
3 Wyden	N	Y	N	N	N	N	Y	Y
4 DeFazio	N	Y	N	N	N	N	Y	Y
5 Kopetski	N	Y	N	N	N	N	Y	Y
PENNSYLVANIA								
1 Foglietta	N	Y	Y	N	N	N	Y	Y
2 Gray	?	?	Y	N	N	N	Y	?
3 Borski	N	Y	Y	N	N	N	Y	Y
4 Kolter	Y	?	?	?	N	N	Y	Y
5 ***Schulze***	Y	Y	N	N	N	N	Y	Y
6 Yatron	?	?	?	?	?	?	?	?
7 ***Weldon***	Y	N	Y	N	N	Y	Y	N
8 Kostmayer	N	Y	Y	N	N	N	Y	Y
9 ***Shuster***	Y	Y	Y	N	N	N	Y	Y
10 ***McDade***	N	N	Y	N	N	N	Y	Y
11 Kanjorski	N	Y	Y	N	N	N	Y	Y
12 Murtha	N	Y	N	N	N	N	Y	Y
13 ***Coughlin***	Y	N	Y	N	N	N	Y	N
14 Coyne	N	Y	Y	N	N	N	Y	Y
15 ***Ritter***	Y	Y	Y	N	N	N	Y	N
16 ***Walker***	Y	N	Y	N	N	Y	Y	N
17 ***Gekas***	Y	N	N	N	N	N	N	N
18 ***Santorum***	Y	N	Y	N	N	N	Y	N
19 ***Goodling***	Y	N	Y	N	Y	Y	Y	Y
20 Gaydos	Y	Y	Y	N	N	N	Y	Y
21 ***Ridge***	N	N	Y	N	N	N	Y	Y
22 Murphy	Y	N	Y	N	N	N	Y	Y
23 ***Clinger***	Y	Y	Y	N	N	N	Y	Y
RHODE ISLAND								
1 ***Machtley***	Y	N	N	N	N	Y	Y	Y
2 Reed	N	Y	Y	N	N	N	Y	Y
SOUTH CAROLINA								
1 ***Ravenel***	Y	Y	Y	N	N	N	Y	Y
2 ***Spence***	Y	Y	N	Y	N	N	Y	Y
3 Derrick	N	Y	Y	N	N	N	Y	Y
4 Patterson	Y	Y	Y	Y	N	N	Y	Y
5 Spratt	Y	Y	Y	N	N	N	Y	Y
6 Tallon	Y	Y	Y	N	N	N	Y	Y

	216	217	218	220	221	223	224	225
SOUTH DAKOTA								
AL Johnson	N	Y	N	N	N	N	Y	Y
TENNESSEE								
1 ***Quillen***	N	Y	N	N	N	N	Y	Y
2 ***Duncan***	Y	Y	Y	Y	Y	Y	N	N
3 Lloyd	Y	Y	Y	N	N	?	Y	Y
4 Cooper	N	Y	Y	Y	N	N	Y	Y
5 Clement	N	Y	N	N	N	N	Y	Y
6 Gordon	N	Y	Y	N	N	N	Y	Y
7 ***Sundquist***	Y	?	Y	N	N	Y	Y	N
8 Tanner	Y	Y	N	N	N	N	Y	Y
9 Ford	N	?	?	N	N	N	Y	Y
TEXAS								
1 Chapman	Y	Y	N	N	N	N	Y	?
2 Wilson	Y	?	Y	N	N	N	Y	?
3 ***Johnson***	Y	?	N	N	N	Y	Y	N
4 Hall	Y	Y	N	Y	N	N	Y	Y
5 Bryant	N	Y	Y	Y	N	N	Y	Y
6 ***Barton***	Y	Y	N	N	Y	Y	N	N
7 ***Archer***	Y	Y	Y	Y	Y	Y	N	N
8 ***Fields***	Y	N	N	Y	Y	Y	Y	N
9 Brooks	Y	?	Y	N	N	N	Y	Y
10 Pickle	N	Y	N	N	N	N	Y	Y
11 Edwards	N	Y	N	N	N	N	Y	Y
12 Geren	Y	Y	N	N	N	N	Y	Y
13 Sarpalius	Y	Y	N	?	?	?	?	Y
14 Laughlin	?	Y	N	N	N	N	Y	Y
15 de la Garza	N	Y	N	N	N	N	Y	Y
16 Coleman	Y	Y	N	N	N	N	Y	Y
17 Stenholm	Y	?	N	Y	N	N	Y	Y
18 Washington	N	?	?	N	N	N	Y	?
19 ***Combest***	Y	Y	N	N	N	N	N	Y
20 Gonzalez	N	Y	N	N	N	N	Y	Y
21 ***Smith***	Y	N	Y	N	Y	N	Y	N
22 ***DeLay***	Y	N	N	N	N	N	Y	N
23 Bustamante	?	Y	N	N	N	N	Y	Y
24 Frost	N	Y	N	N	N	N	Y	Y
25 Andrews	Y	Y	Y	Y	N	N	Y	Y
26 ***Armey***	Y	N	N	Y	Y	Y	N	N
27 Ortiz	Y	Y	N	N	N	N	Y	Y
UTAH								
1 ***Hansen***	Y	N	N	Y	N	N	Y	Y
2 Owens	N	Y	N	N	N	N	Y	Y
3 Orton	Y	Y	N	N	N	N	Y	?
VERMONT								
AL *Sanders*	N	Y	Y	Y	Y	N	Y	Y
VIRGINIA								
1 ***Bateman***	N	Y	N	N	N	N	Y	Y
2 Pickett	N	Y	Y	N	N	N	Y	Y
3 ***Bliley***	Y	N	N	N	N	N	Y	N
4 Sisisky	N	Y	Y	N	N	N	Y	Y
5 Payne	Y	Y	Y	N	N	N	Y	Y
6 Olin	N	Y	N	N	N	N	Y	Y
7 ***Slaughter***	Y	N	N	N	N	N	Y	Y
8 Moran	N	Y	Y	N	N	N	Y	Y
9 Boucher	N	Y	Y	N	N	N	Y	Y
10 ***Wolf***	N	N	N	N	N	N	Y	N
WASHINGTON								
1 ***Miller***	N	?	?	Y	N	N	Y	Y
2 Swift	N	?	?	N	N	N	Y	Y
3 Unsoeld	N	Y	Y	N	N	N	Y	Y
4 ***Morrison***	Y	Y	N	N	N	N	Y	Y
5 Foley								
6 Dicks	N	Y	Y	N	N	N	Y	Y
7 McDermott	N	Y	Y	N	N	N	Y	Y
8 ***Chandler***	Y	N	N	Y	N	N	Y	Y
WEST VIRGINIA								
1 Mollohan	N	Y	N	N	N	N	Y	?
2 Staggers	N	Y	N	Y	N	N	Y	Y
3 Wise	N	Y	Y	N	N	N	Y	Y
4 Rahall	N	Y	Y	N	N	N	Y	Y
WISCONSIN								
1 Aspin	Y	Y	Y	N	N	N	Y	Y
2 ***Klug***	Y	Y	Y	Y	Y	Y	Y	Y
3 ***Gunderson***	N	Y	N	Y	N	N	Y	Y
4 Kleczka	-	Y	Y	N	N	N	Y	Y
5 Moody	Y	Y	Y	Y	N	N	Y	?
6 ***Petri***	Y	Y	Y	Y	Y	Y	N	Y
7 Obey	N	Y	Y	N	N	N	Y	Y
8 ***Roth***	Y	Y	N	N	N	Y	N	Y
9 ***Sensenbrenner***	Y	N	Y	Y	Y	Y	N	N
WYOMING								
AL ***Thomas***	Y	N	N	Y	Y	Y	Y	Y

Southern states - Ala., Ark., Fla., Ga., Ky., La., Miss., N.C., Okla., S.C., Tenn., Texas, Va.
Omitted votes are quorum calls, which CQ does not include in its vote charts.

HOUSE VOTES 226, 227, 228, 229, 230, 231, 232, 233

226. HR 2507. National Institutes of Health Reauthorization/Adolescents Study. Schroeder, D-Colo., amendment to earmark $3 million for each of the fiscal years 1992-94 to conduct a study for the purpose of gathering information on the health and well-being of adolescents in the United States. Adopted 271-142: R 33-123; D 237-19 (ND 168-7, SD 69-12); I 1-0, July 25, 1991.

227. HR 2507. National Institutes of Health Reauthorization/Human Sexual Surveys. Waxman, D-Calif., substitute amendment to the Dannemeyer, R-Calif., amendment to require that surveys regarding human sexual behavior conducted or supported through the National Institutes of Health be in accordance with peer and ethical review board procedures and that such surveys will assist in reducing the incidence of sexually transmitted and infectious diseases or improve reproductive health. The Dannemeyer amendment would have prohibited all surveys of human sexual behavior. Adopted 283-137: R 45-115; D 237-22 (ND 165-12, SD 72-10); I 1-0, July 25, 1991. (Subsequently, the Dannemeyer amendment as amended was adopted by voice vote.)

228. HR 2507. National Institutes of Health Reauthorization/Limit Authorization. Dannemeyer, R-Calif., amendment to limit the increase in the National Institutes of Health authorization for each year for fiscal 1992-96 to 2.4 percent of the previous year. Rejected 132-283: R 108-52; D 24-230 (ND 9-163, SD 15-67); I 0-1, July 25, 1991.

229. HR 2507. National Institutes of Health Reauthorization/Passage. Passage of the bill to reauthorize the National Cancer Institute and the National Heart, Lung and Blood Institute and other programs of the National Institutes of Health. The bill would also overturn the administration's ban on research using tissue from aborted fetuses. Passed 274-144: R 40-119; D 233-25 (ND 159-16, SD 74-9); I 1-0, July 25, 1991. A "nay" was a vote supporting the president's position.

230. H J Res 313. Overseas Base Closings/Rule. Adoption of the rule (H Res 206) to provide for House floor consideration of the joint resolution to require the Defense Department and the Defense Base Closure and Realignment Commission to make recommendations for the closure and realignment of U.S. military installations overseas in 1993 and 1995. Adopted 262-161: R 2-160; D 259-1 (ND 177-1, SD 82-0); I 1-0, July 30, 1991.

231. H J Res 313. Overseas Base Closings/Passage. Passage of the joint resolution to require the Defense Department and the Defense Base Closure and Realignment Commission to make recommendations for the closure and realignment of U.S. military installations overseas in 1993 and 1995. Passed 412-14: R 150-14; D 261-0 (ND 178-0, SD 83-0); I 1-0, July 30, 1991. A "nay" was a vote supporting the president's position.

232. H J Res 308. Base Closure and Realignment Disapproval/Passage. Passage of the joint resolution to disapprove the Defense Base Closure and Realignment Commission's list of military bases for closure or realignment. Rejected 60-364: R 14-150; D 46-213 (ND 37-139, SD 9-74); I 0-1, July 30, 1991. A "nay" was a vote supporting the president's position.

233. Procedural Motion. Frank, D-Mass., motion to adjourn. Motion agreed to 109-72: R 1-72; D 108-0 (ND 83-0, SD 25-0), July 30, 1991.

KEY

Y Voted for (yea).
\# Paired for.
\+ Announced for.
N Voted against (nay).
X Paired against.
\- Announced against.
P Voted "present."
C Voted "present" to avoid possible conflict of interest.
? Did not vote or otherwise make a position known.

Democrats ***Republicans***
Independent

	226	227	228	229	230	231	232	233
ALABAMA								
1 ***Callahan***	N	N	Y	N	N	Y	N	N
2 ***Dickinson***	N	Y	N	N	N	Y	N	?
3 Browder	Y	Y	N	Y	Y	Y	N	?
4 Bevill	Y	Y	N	Y	Y	Y	N	?
5 Cramer	Y	Y	N	Y	Y	Y	N	Y
6 Erdreich	Y	Y	N	Y	Y	Y	N	?
7 Harris	Y	Y	N	Y	Y	Y	N	?
ALASKA								
AL ***Young***	?	N	N	N	N	Y	N	?
ARIZONA								
1 ***Rhodes***	N	N	Y	N	N	Y	Y	N
2 Vacancy								
3 ***Stump***	N	N	Y	N	N	Y	N	N
4 ***Kyl***	N	N	Y	N	N	Y	N	N
5 ***Kolbe***	Y	Y	Y	Y	N	N	N	?
ARKANSAS								
1 Alexander	Y	Y	N	Y	Y	Y	Y	?
2 Thornton	Y	Y	N	Y	Y	Y	Y	?
3 ***Hammerschmidt***	N	N	Y	Y	N	Y	N	N
4 Anthony	Y	Y	N	Y	Y	Y	N	?
CALIFORNIA								
1 ***Riggs***	Y	N	Y	Y	N	Y	N	N
2 ***Herger***	N	N	Y	N	N	Y	N	?
3 Matsui	Y	Y	N	Y	Y	Y	N	?
4 Fazio	Y	Y	N	Y	Y	Y	N	Y
5 Pelosi	+	Y	N	Y	Y	Y	N	Y
6 Boxer	Y	Y	N	Y	Y	Y	N	Y
7 Miller	Y	Y	N	Y	Y	Y	N	Y
8 Dellums	Y	Y	N	Y	Y	Y	N	?
9 Stark	Y	Y	N	Y	Y	Y	N	Y
10 Edwards	Y	Y	N	Y	Y	Y	?	Y
11 Lantos	Y	Y	N	Y	Y	Y	N	?
12 ***Campbell***	?	?	?	?	?	?	?	?
13 Mineta	Y	Y	N	Y	Y	Y	N	Y
14 ***Doolittle***	N	N	Y	N	N	Y	N	?
15 Condit	N	N	Y	Y	Y	Y	Y	Y
16 Panetta	Y	Y	N	Y	Y	Y	Y	Y
17 Dooley	Y	Y	N	Y	Y	Y	N	Y
18 Lehman	Y	Y	N	Y	Y	Y	N	?
19 ***Lagomarsino***	N	N	Y	N	N	Y	N	N
20 ***Thomas***	N	N	Y	Y	N	Y	N	?
21 ***Gallegly***	N	N	Y	N	N	Y	N	?
22 ***Moorhead***	N	N	Y	N	N	Y	N	?
23 Beilenson	Y	Y	N	Y	Y	Y	N	?
24 Waxman	Y	Y	N	Y	Y	Y	?	?
25 Roybal	Y	Y	N	Y	Y	Y	N	?
26 Berman	Y	Y	N	Y	Y	Y	N	?
27 Levine	Y	Y	N	Y	Y	Y	N	Y
28 Dixon	Y	Y	N	Y	Y	Y	N	Y
29 Waters	Y	Y	N	Y	?	Y	N	Y
30 Martinez	Y	Y	N	Y	Y	Y	N	?
31 Dymally	Y	Y	N	Y	Y	Y	N	?
32 Anderson	Y	Y	N	Y	Y	Y	N	Y
33 ***Dreier***	N	N	Y	N	N	Y	N	N
34 Torres	Y	Y	N	Y	Y	Y	N	Y
35 ***Lewis***	N	Y	N	N	N	N	N	N
36 Brown	Y	Y	N	Y	Y	Y	N	Y
37 ***McCandless***	N	N	Y	N	N	Y	N	N
38 ***Dornan***	N	N	Y	N	N	Y	N	?
39 ***Dannemeyer***	N	N	Y	N	N	Y	N	?
40 ***Cox***	N	N	Y	N	N	Y	N	N
41 ***Lowery***	N	N	N	N	N	N	N	N
42 ***Rohrabacher***	N	N	Y	N	N	Y	N	?
43 ***Packard***	N	N	Y	N	N	Y	N	?
44 ***Cunningham***	N	N	Y	N	N	Y	N	N
45 ***Hunter***	?	N	Y	N	N	Y	N	?
COLORADO								
1 Schroeder	Y	Y	N	Y	Y	Y	Y	?
2 Skaggs	Y	Y	N	Y	Y	Y	N	Y
3 Campbell	Y	Y	N	Y	Y	Y	Y	?
4 ***Allard***	N	N	Y	N	N	Y	N	N
5 ***Hefley***	N	N	Y	N	N	Y	N	?
6 ***Schaefer***	N	N	Y	N	N	Y	N	?
CONNECTICUT								
1 Kennelly	Y	Y	N	Y	Y	Y	Y	Y
2 Gejdenson	Y	Y	N	Y	Y	Y	Y	Y
3 DeLauro	Y	Y	N	Y	Y	Y	Y	Y
4 ***Shays***	Y	Y	N	Y	N	Y	N	N
5 ***Franks***	Y	N	Y	Y	N	Y	N	N
6 ***Johnson***	Y	Y	N	Y	?	Y	N	N
DELAWARE								
AL Carper	Y	Y	N	Y	Y	Y	N	?
FLORIDA								
1 Hutto	N	N	Y	N	Y	Y	N	?
2 Peterson	Y	Y	N	Y	Y	Y	N	Y
3 Bennett	Y	Y	Y	Y	Y	Y	N	Y
4 ***James***	N	N	N	N	N	Y	N	N
5 ***McCollum***	N	N	N	N	N	Y	N	?
6 ***Stearns***	N	N	N	N	N	Y	N	N
7 Gibbons	Y	Y	N	Y	Y	Y	N	?
8 ***Young***	N	N	N	N	N	N	N	?
9 ***Bilirakis***	Y	Y	Y	N	N	Y	N	?
10 ***Ireland***	Y	N	Y	N	N	Y	N	?
11 Bacchus	Y	Y	N	Y	Y	Y	N	Y
12 ***Lewis***	N	N	Y	N	N	Y	N	?
13 ***Goss***	N	N	Y	N	N	N	N	N
14 Johnston	Y	Y	N	Y	Y	Y	N	?
15 ***Shaw***	N	N	Y	N	N	Y	N	?
16 Smith	Y	Y	N	Y	Y	Y	N	Y
17 Lehman	Y	?	?	Y	Y	Y	N	?
18 ***Ros-Lehtinen***	N	N	N	N	N	Y	N	N
19 Fascell	Y	Y	N	Y	Y	Y	N	Y
GEORGIA								
1 Thomas	Y	Y	N	Y	Y	Y	N	?
2 Hatcher	Y	Y	N	Y	Y	Y	N	?
3 Ray	Y	Y	N	N	Y	Y	N	?
4 Jones	Y	Y	N	Y	Y	Y	N	?
5 Lewis	Y	Y	N	Y	Y	Y	N	Y
6 ***Gingrich***	N	N	Y	N	N	Y	N	N
7 Darden	Y	Y	N	Y	Y	Y	N	?
8 Rowland	Y	Y	N	Y	Y	Y	N	Y
9 Jenkins	Y	Y	N	Y	Y	Y	N	?
10 Barnard	Y	Y	N	Y	Y	Y	N	?
HAWAII								
1 Abercrombie	Y	Y	N	Y	Y	Y	N	?
2 Mink	Y	Y	N	Y	Y	Y	N	Y
IDAHO								
1 LaRocco	Y	Y	Y	Y	Y	Y	N	Y
2 Stallings	Y	Y	Y	N	Y	Y	N	?
ILLINOIS								
1 Hayes	Y	Y	N	Y	Y	Y	N	?
2 Savage	Y	Y	N	Y	Y	?	N	Y
3 Russo	Y	Y	N	Y	Y	Y	N	Y
4 Sangmeister	Y	Y	N	Y	Y	Y	N	?
5 Lipinski	Y	Y	N	Y	Y	Y	N	?
6 ***Hyde***	N	N	Y	N	N	N	N	?
7 Collins	Y	Y	N	Y	Y	Y	N	?
8 Rostenkowski	Y	Y	N	Y	Y	Y	N	?
9 Yates	Y	Y	N	Y	Y	Y	N	?
10 ***Porter***	Y	Y	N	Y	N	Y	N	?
11 Annunzio	Y	Y	N	Y	Y	Y	N	Y
12 ***Crane***	N	N	Y	N	N	N	N	?
13 ***Fawell***	N	Y	Y	Y	N	Y	N	N
14 ***Hastert***	N	N	Y	N	N	Y	N	N
15 ***Ewing***	N	N	Y	N	N	Y	N	N
16 Cox	Y	Y	N	Y	Y	Y	N	?
17 Evans	Y	Y	N	Y	Y	Y	Y	Y
18 ***Michel***	N	N	Y	N	N	Y	N	N
19 Bruce	Y	Y	N	Y	Y	Y	Y	Y
20 Durbin	Y	Y	N	Y	Y	Y	Y	?
21 Costello	Y	Y	N	Y	Y	Y	Y	?
22 Poshard	Y	Y	N	Y	Y	Y	N	?
INDIANA								
1 Visclosky	Y	Y	N	Y	Y	Y	N	?
2 Sharp	Y	Y	N	Y	Y	Y	N	?
3 Roemer	Y	Y	Y	N	Y	Y	-	Y

ND Northern Democrats SD Southern Democrats

	226	227	228	229	230	231	232	233
4 Long	Y	Y	Y	Y	Y	Y	N	?
5 Jontz	Y	Y	N	Y	Y	Y	Y	Y
6 ***Burton***	N	N	Y	N	N	Y	Y	?
7 ***Myers***	N	N	N	N	Y	Y	Y	?
8 McCloskey	Y	Y	N	Y	Y	Y	Y	?
9 Hamilton	Y	Y	N	Y	Y	Y	N	?
10 Jacobs	Y	Y	Y	Y	N	Y	Y	?
IOWA								
1 ***Leach***	Y	Y	N	Y	N	Y	N	?
2 ***Nussle***	Y	Y	Y	N	N	Y	N	?
3 Nagle	Y	Y	N	Y	Y	Y	N	Y
4 Smith	Y	Y	N	Y	Y	Y	N	Y
5 ***Lightfoot***	N	N	Y	N	N	Y	N	?
6 ***Grandy***	Y	Y	Y	N	N	Y	N	?
KANSAS								
1 ***Roberts***	N	N	Y	N	X	Y	N	?
2 Slattery	Y	Y	N	Y	Y	Y	N	Y
3 ***Meyers***	N	Y	N	Y	N	Y	N	N
4 Glickman	Y	Y	N	Y	Y	Y	N	Y
5 ***Nichols***	N	Y	Y	N	N	Y	N	N
KENTUCKY								
1 Hubbard	Y	Y	Y	Y	Y	Y	N	Y
2 Natcher	Y	Y	N	Y	Y	Y	Y	Y
3 Mazzoli	Y	Y	N	Y	Y	Y	N	?
4 ***Bunning***	N	N	Y	N	N	Y	N	?
5 ***Rogers***	N	N	Y	N	N	Y	N	N
6 ***Hopkins***	?	?	?	?	?	?	?	?
7 Perkins	Y	Y	N	Y	Y	Y	Y	?
LOUISIANA								
1 ***Livingston***	?	N	Y	N	N	Y	N	?
2 Jefferson	Y	Y	N	Y	Y	Y	N	?
3 Tauzin	Y	Y	Y	N	Y	Y	N	?
4 ***McCrery***	?	?	?	?	N	Y	N	?
5 Huckaby	N	Y	Y	Y	Y	Y	Y	?
6 ***Baker***	N	N	Y	N	N	Y	N	?
7 Hayes	?	Y	Y	N	Y	Y	Y	?
8 ***Holloway***	?	?	?	?	N	Y	Y	N
MAINE								
1 Andrews	Y	Y	N	Y	Y	Y	N	?
2 ***Snowe***	Y	N	N	Y	Y	Y	Y	N
MARYLAND								
1 ***Gilchrest***	Y	Y	N	Y	N	Y	N	N
2 ***Bentley***	N	Y	N	Y	N	Y	Y	?
3 Cardin	Y	Y	N	Y	Y	Y	N	Y
4 McMillen	Y	Y	N	Y	Y	Y	Y	?
5 Hoyer	Y	Y	N	Y	Y	Y	N	Y
6 Byron	N	N	N	Y	Y	Y	N	Y
7 Mfume	Y	Y	N	Y	Y	Y	N	Y
8 ***Morella***	Y	Y	N	Y	N	Y	N	N
MASSACHUSETTS								
1 Olver	Y	Y	N	Y	Y	Y	N	Y
2 Neal	Y	Y	N	Y	Y	Y	Y	Y
3 Early	N	Y	N	Y	Y	Y	Y	?
4 Frank	Y	Y	N	Y	Y	Y	N	Y
5 Atkins	Y	Y	N	Y	Y	Y	Y	Y
6 Mavroules	N	Y	N	Y	Y	Y	N	?
7 Markey	Y	Y	N	Y	Y	Y	N	Y
8 Kennedy	Y	Y	N	Y	Y	Y	Y	Y
9 Moakley	N	Y	N	Y	Y	Y	N	?
10 Studds	Y	Y	N	Y	Y	Y	N	?
11 Donnelly	N	N	N	Y	Y	Y	Y	Y
MICHIGAN								
1 Conyers	Y	Y	N	Y	Y	Y	N	?
2 ***Pursell***	N	Y	Y	Y	N	Y	N	?
3 Wolpe	Y	Y	N	Y	Y	Y	N	?
4 ***Upton***	N	N	N	Y	N	Y	N	?
5 ***Henry***	N	N	N	N	N	Y	N	?
6 Carr	Y	Y	N	Y	Y	Y	N	?
7 Kildee	Y	Y	N	Y	Y	Y	N	Y
8 Traxler	Y	Y	N	Y	Y	Y	Y	?
9 ***Vander Jagt***	N	N	N	N	N	Y	N	?
10 ***Camp***	N	N	N	N	N	Y	Y	N
11 ***Davis***	Y	Y	N	N	N	Y	Y	?
12 Bonior	Y	Y	N	Y	Y	Y	N	Y
13 Collins	Y	Y	N	Y	Y	Y	N	?
14 Hertel	Y	Y	N	Y	Y	Y	Y	?
15 Ford	Y	Y	N	Y	Y	Y	N	?
16 Dingell	Y	Y	?	Y	Y	Y	N	Y
17 Levin	Y	Y	N	Y	Y	Y	N	?
18 ***Broomfield***	N	N	N	N	N	Y	N	?
MINNESOTA								
1 Penny	Y	N	N	N	Y	Y	N	?
2 ***Weber***	N	N	Y	N	N	Y	N	?
3 ***Ramstad***	N	N	Y	N	N	Y	N	?
4 Vento	Y	Y	N	Y	Y	Y	N	?

	226	227	228	229	230	231	232	233
5 Sabo	Y	Y	N	Y	Y	Y	N	?
6 Sikorski	Y	Y	N	Y	Y	Y	N	Y
7 Peterson	Y	N	N	Y	Y	Y	N	Y
8 Oberstar	Y	Y	N	Y	?	?	?	?
MISSISSIPPI								
1 Whitten	Y	Y	N	Y	Y	Y	N	?
2 Espy	Y	Y	N	Y	Y	Y	N	?
3 Montgomery	N	N	Y	N	Y	Y	N	?
4 Parker	N	N	Y	N	Y	Y	N	?
5 Taylor	N	N	Y	N	Y	Y	N	Y
MISSOURI								
1 Clay	Y	Y	?	Y	Y	Y	N	?
2 Horn	Y	Y	N	Y	Y	Y	N	Y
3 Gephardt	Y	Y	N	Y	Y	Y	N	?
4 Skelton	Y	N	Y	N	Y	Y	N	Y
5 Wheat	Y	Y	N	Y	Y	Y	N	?
6 ***Coleman***	N	Y	N	N	N	Y	N	N
7 ***Hancock***	N	N	Y	N	N	N	N	N
8 ***Emerson***	N	N	Y	N	N	Y	Y	?
9 Volkmer	Y	N	Y	N	Y	Y	N	?
MONTANA								
1 Williams	Y	Y	N	Y	Y	Y	N	?
2 ***Marlenee***	N	N	Y	N	N	Y	N	?
NEBRASKA								
1 ***Bereuter***	Y	Y	Y	N	N	Y	N	?
2 Hoagland	Y	Y	N	Y	Y	Y	N	?
3 ***Barrett***	N	Y	Y	N	N	Y	N	?
NEVADA								
1 Bilbray	Y	Y	N	Y	Y	Y	N	Y
2 ***Vucanovich***	N	N	Y	N	N	Y	N	N
NEW HAMPSHIRE								
1 ***Zeliff***	Y	Y	Y	N	N	Y	N	N
2 Swett	Y	Y	N	Y	Y	Y	Y	Y
NEW JERSEY								
1 Andrews	Y	Y	N	Y	Y	Y	Y	?
2 Hughes	Y	Y	N	Y	Y	Y	Y	?
3 Pallone	Y	Y	N	Y	Y	Y	Y	Y
4 ***Smith***	N	N	N	N	N	Y	N	?
5 ***Roukema***	N	N	N	Y	N	Y	N	N
6 Dwyer	Y	Y	N	Y	Y	Y	N	?
7 ***Rinaldo***	N	N	N	N	N	Y	N	?
8 Roe	Y	Y	N	N	Y	Y	N	Y
9 Torricelli	Y	Y	N	Y	Y	Y	N	?
10 Payne	Y	Y	N	Y	Y	Y	N	?
11 ***Gallo***	N	Y	N	Y	N	Y	N	N
12 ***Zimmer***	N	Y	Y	N	Y	Y	N	N
13 ***Saxton***	N	N	N	N	N	Y	N	N
14 Guarini	Y	Y	N	Y	Y	Y	N	Y
NEW MEXICO								
1 ***Schiff***	Y	Y	N	Y	N	Y	N	N
2 ***Skeen***	N	N	Y	Y	N	Y	N	?
3 Richardson	Y	Y	N	Y	Y	Y	N	?
NEW YORK								
1 Hochbrueckner	Y	Y	N	Y	Y	Y	N	?
2 Downey	Y	Y	N	Y	Y	Y	N	?
3 Mrazek	Y	Y	N	#	Y	Y	N	?
4 ***Lent***	N	N	N	N	N	Y	N	?
5 ***McGrath***	N	N	N	N	N	Y	N	N
6 Flake	Y	Y	N	Y	Y	Y	N	Y
7 Ackerman	Y	Y	N	Y	Y	Y	N	Y
8 Scheuer	Y	Y	?	Y	Y	Y	N	Y
9 Manton	Y	Y	N	Y	Y	Y	N	?
10 Schumer	Y	Y	N	Y	Y	Y	N	Y
11 Towns	Y	Y	N	Y	Y	Y	N	?
12 Owens	Y	Y	N	Y	Y	Y	Y	Y
13 Solarz	Y	Y	N	Y	Y	Y	N	?
14 ***Molinari***	N	Y	N	Y	N	Y	N	?
15 ***Green***	Y	Y	N	Y	N	Y	N	N
16 Rangel	Y	Y	N	Y	Y	Y	N	Y
17 Weiss	+	+	-	+	Y	Y	N	Y
18 Serrano	Y	Y	N	Y	Y	Y	N	?
19 Engel	Y	Y	N	Y	Y	Y	N	Y
20 Lowey	Y	Y	N	Y	Y	Y	N	Y
21 ***Fish***	Y	Y	Y	N	N	Y	N	?
22 ***Gilman***	Y	Y	N	Y	N	Y	N	N
23 McNulty	Y	Y	N	Y	Y	Y	N	Y
24 ***Solomon***	N	N	Y	N	N	Y	N	N
25 ***Boehlert***	Y	Y	N	Y	N	Y	N	N
26 ***Martin***	N	Y	N	Y	N	Y	N	?
27 ***Walsh***	?	N	N	N	N	Y	N	N
28 McHugh	Y	Y	N	Y	Y	Y	N	?
29 ***Horton***	Y	Y	N	Y	N	Y	N	?
30 Slaughter	Y	Y	N	Y	Y	Y	N	Y
31 ***Paxon***	N	N	N	N	N	Y	N	?

	226	227	228	229	230	231	232	233
32 LaFalce	Y	Y	N	Y	Y	Y	N	?
33 Nowak	Y	Y	N	Y	Y	Y	N	?
34 ***Houghton***	N	Y	Y	Y	N	Y	N	?
NORTH CAROLINA								
1 Jones	Y	Y	N	Y	Y	Y	N	?
2 Valentine	Y	Y	N	Y	Y	Y	N	?
3 Lancaster	Y	Y	N	Y	Y	Y	N	Y
4 Price	Y	Y	N	Y	Y	Y	N	Y
5 Neal	Y	Y	Y	Y	Y	Y	N	?
6 ***Coble***	N	N	Y	N	N	Y	N	N
7 Rose	Y	Y	N	Y	Y	Y	N	?
8 Hefner	?	?	?	?	?	?	?	?
9 ***McMillan***	N	Y	Y	N	N	Y	N	?
10 ***Ballenger***	N	N	Y	N	N	N	N	N
11 ***Taylor***	N	N	Y	N	N	Y	N	N
NORTH DAKOTA								
AL Dorgan	?	Y	N	Y	Y	Y	N	?
OHIO								
1 Luken	N	N	Y	N	Y	Y	N	Y
2 ***Gradison***	N	N	Y	N	N	Y	N	?
3 Hall	Y	Y	N	N	Y	Y	N	?
4 ***Oxley***	N	N	Y	N	N	Y	N	?
5 ***Gillmor***	N	Y	Y	N	N	Y	N	?
6 ***McEwen***	N	N	Y	N	N	Y	N	N
7 ***Hobson***	Y	N	Y	Y	N	Y	N	N
8 ***Boehner***	N	N	Y	N	N	Y	N	N
9 Kaptur	Y	Y	N	Y	Y	Y	N	Y
10 ***Miller***	N	N	Y	N	N	Y	N	N
11 Eckart	Y	Y	N	Y	Y	Y	N	Y
12 ***Kasich***	Y	N	Y	N	N	Y	N	?
13 Pease	Y	Y	?	Y	Y	Y	N	?
14 Sawyer	Y	Y	N	Y	Y	Y	N	?
15 ***Wylie***	N	N	Y	N	N	Y	N	N
16 ***Regula***	N	N	Y	N	N	Y	N	?
17 Traficant	Y	Y	N	Y	Y	Y	Y	?
18 Applegate	Y	N	N	N	Y	Y	N	?
19 Feighan	Y	Y	N	Y	Y	Y	N	?
20 Oakar	Y	Y	N	Y	Y	Y	N	?
21 Stokes	Y	Y	N	Y	Y	Y	N	Y
OKLAHOMA								
1 ***Inhofe***	N	N	Y	N	N	Y	N	N
2 Synar	Y	Y	N	Y	Y	Y	N	?
3 Brewster	Y	Y	N	Y	Y	Y	N	?
4 McCurdy	Y	Y	N	Y	Y	Y	N	Y
5 ***Edwards***	N	N	Y	N	N	Y	N	N
6 English	Y	Y	N	Y	Y	Y	N	?
OREGON								
1 AuCoin	Y	Y	N	Y	Y	Y	N	Y
2 ***Smith***	N	N	Y	N	N	Y	N	?
3 Wyden	Y	Y	N	Y	Y	Y	N	Y
4 DeFazio	Y	Y	N	Y	Y	Y	N	?
5 Kopetski	Y	Y	N	Y	Y	Y	N	?
PENNSYLVANIA								
1 Foglietta	Y	Y	N	Y	Y	Y	Y	?
2 Gray	Y	Y	N	Y	Y	Y	Y	?
3 Borski	Y	Y	N	Y	Y	Y	Y	Y
4 Kolter	Y	Y	N	N	Y	Y	Y	Y
5 ***Schulze***	N	Y	Y	Y	N	Y	N	?
6 Yatron	?	?	?	?	?	?	?	?
7 ***Weldon***	?	N	Y	N	N	Y	Y	?
8 Kostmayer	Y	Y	N	Y	Y	Y	Y	Y
9 ***Shuster***	N	N	Y	N	N	Y	Y	N
10 ***McDade***	N	Y	N	N	N	Y	Y	?
11 Kanjorski	Y	Y	N	N	Y	Y	N	Y
12 Murtha	Y	Y	N	N	Y	Y	Y	?
13 ***Coughlin***	Y	Y	N	N	N	Y	Y	?
14 Coyne	Y	Y	N	Y	Y	Y	Y	Y
15 ***Ritter***	N	N	Y	N	N	Y	N	?
16 ***Walker***	N	N	Y	N	N	Y	N	N
17 ***Gekas***	N	N	N	Y	N	Y	N	?
18 ***Santorum***	N	N	Y	N	N	Y	N	N
19 ***Goodling***	N	N	N	N	N	N	N	N
20 Gaydos	Y	Y	?	?	Y	Y	Y	?
21 ***Ridge***	N	N	Y	N	Y	Y	Y	?
22 Murphy	Y	N	N	N	Y	Y	Y	?
23 ***Clinger***	N	Y	Y	N	N	Y	N	?
RHODE ISLAND								
1 ***Machtley***	Y	Y	N	?	N	Y	N	?
2 Reed	Y	Y	N	Y	Y	Y	N	Y
SOUTH CAROLINA								
1 ***Ravenel***	Y	Y	Y	Y	N	Y	N	?
2 ***Spence***	Y	N	Y	Y	N	Y	N	?
3 Derrick	Y	Y	N	Y	Y	Y	N	?
4 Patterson	Y	Y	N	Y	Y	Y	N	?
5 Spratt	Y	Y	N	Y	Y	Y	N	?
6 Tallon	Y	N	N	N	Y	Y	Y	?

	226	227	228	229	230	231	232	233
SOUTH DAKOTA								
AL Johnson	Y	Y	N	Y	Y	Y	N	?
TENNESSEE								
1 ***Quillen***	N	X	?	X	N	N	N	Y
2 ***Duncan***	N	N	Y	N	N	Y	N	N
3 Lloyd	N	N	N	Y	Y	Y	N	?
4 Cooper	Y	Y	Y	Y	Y	Y	N	Y
5 Clement	Y	Y	N	Y	Y	Y	N	Y
6 Gordon	Y	Y	N	Y	Y	Y	N	Y
7 ***Sundquist***	?	?	?	?	N	Y	N	N
8 Tanner	Y	N	N	Y	Y	Y	N	Y
9 Ford	Y	Y	N	Y	?	Y	N	Y
TEXAS								
1 Chapman	Y	Y	Y	Y	Y	Y	N	?
2 Wilson	?	?	?	?	Y	Y	N	?
3 ***Johnson***	N	N	Y	N	N	Y	N	?
4 Hall	N	N	N	N	Y	Y	N	?
5 Bryant	Y	Y	N	Y	Y	Y	N	?
6 ***Barton***	N	N	Y	N	N	Y	N	N
7 ***Archer***	N	N	Y	N	N	Y	N	?
8 ***Fields***	N	N	Y	N	N	Y	N	?
9 Brooks	Y	Y	N	Y	Y	Y	N	?
10 Pickle	Y	Y	N	Y	Y	Y	N	?
11 Edwards	Y	Y	N	Y	Y	Y	N	Y
12 Geren	N	Y	Y	Y	Y	Y	Y	?
13 Sarpalius	N	N	Y	Y	Y	Y	N	Y
14 Laughlin	N	N	N	Y	Y	Y	N	?
15 de la Garza	Y	Y	N	Y	Y	Y	N	Y
16 Coleman	Y	Y	N	Y	Y	Y	N	Y
17 Stenholm	N	Y	N	Y	Y	Y	N	?
18 Washington	Y	Y	N	Y	Y	Y	N	?
19 ***Combest***	Y	N	Y	N	N	Y	N	?
20 Gonzalez	Y	Y	N	Y	Y	Y	N	Y
21 ***Smith***	N	N	Y	Y	N	Y	N	?
22 ***DeLay***	N	N	Y	N	N	N	N	?
23 Bustamante	Y	Y	N	Y	#	?	?	?
24 Frost	?	Y	N	Y	Y	Y	Y	?
25 Andrews	Y	Y	Y	Y	Y	Y	N	?
26 ***Armey***	N	N	Y	N	N	N	N	?
27 Ortiz	Y	Y	N	Y	Y	Y	N	?
UTAH								
1 ***Hansen***	N	N	Y	N	N	Y	N	?
2 Owens	Y	Y	N	Y	Y	Y	N	?
3 Orton	?	?	?	X	Y	Y	N	?
VERMONT								
AL *Sanders*	Y	Y	N	Y	Y	Y	N	?
VIRGINIA								
1 ***Bateman***	N	N	Y	N	N	Y	N	?
2 Pickett	N	Y	N	Y	Y	Y	N	?
3 ***Bliley***	N	N	Y	N	N	Y	N	N
4 Sisisky	Y	Y	N	Y	Y	Y	N	?
5 Payne	Y	Y	N	Y	Y	Y	N	?
6 Olin	Y	Y	N	Y	Y	Y	N	?
7 ***Slaughter***	N	N	Y	N	N	Y	N	?
8 Moran	Y	Y	N	Y	Y	Y	N	Y
9 Boucher	Y	Y	N	Y	Y	Y	N	?
10 ***Wolf***	N	N	N	N	N	Y	N	?
WASHINGTON								
1 ***Miller***	Y	Y	Y	Y	N	Y	N	?
2 Swift	Y	Y	N	Y	Y	Y	N	Y
3 Unsoeld	Y	Y	N	Y	Y	Y	N	?
4 ***Morrison***	Y	Y	N	Y	N	Y	N	N
5 Foley								
6 Dicks	Y	Y	N	Y	Y	Y	N	?
7 McDermott	Y	Y	N	Y	Y	Y	N	Y
8 ***Chandler***	Y	Y	N	Y	N	Y	N	N
WEST VIRGINIA								
1 Mollohan	Y	N	N	N	Y	Y	N	?
2 Staggers	Y	Y	N	N	Y	Y	N	?
3 Wise	Y	Y	N	Y	Y	Y	N	?
4 Rahall	Y	N	N	N	Y	Y	N	Y
WISCONSIN								
1 Aspin	Y	Y	N	Y	Y	Y	N	Y
2 ***Klug***	N	Y	N	Y	N	Y	N	N
3 ***Gunderson***	N	N	N	N	N	Y	N	N
4 Kleczka	Y	Y	N	Y	Y	Y	N	?
5 Moody	?	#	?	#	Y	Y	N	?
6 ***Petri***	N	N	Y	N	N	N	N	?
7 Obey	Y	Y	N	Y	Y	Y	N	?
8 ***Roth***	N	N	Y	N	N	Y	N	?
9 ***Sensenbrenner***	N	N	Y	N	N	Y	N	?
WYOMING								
AL ***Thomas***	N	N	Y	N	N	Y	N	N

Southern states - Ala., Ark., Fla., Ga., Ky., La., Miss., N.C., Okla., S.C., Tenn., Texas, Va.
Omitted votes are quorum calls, which CQ does not include in its vote charts.

HOUSE VOTES 234, 235, 236, 237, 238, 239, 240, 241

234. Procedural Motion. Walsh, R-N.Y., motion to approve the House Journal of Tuesday, July 30. Motion agreed to 280-132: R 36-126; D 243-6 (ND 162-6, SD 81-0); I 1-0, July 31, 1991.

235. Procedural Motion. Gingrich, R-Ga., motion to adjourn. Motion rejected 129-295: R 129-33; D 0-261 (ND 0-179, SD 0-82); I 0-1, July 31, 1991.

236. HR 1455. Fiscal 1991 Intelligence Authorization. McCurdy, D-Okla., motion to order the previous question (thus limiting debate and possibility of amendment) on the adoption of the conference report to authorize a classified level of funding for U.S. intelligence agencies and other government intelligence activities in fiscal 1991. Motion agreed to 422-0: R 164-0; D 258-0 (ND 175-0, SD 83-0), July 31, 1991.

237. HR 1455. Fiscal 1991 Intelligence Authorization/Conference Report. Adoption of the conference report to authorize a classified level of funding for U.S. intelligence agencies and other government intelligence activities and impose new requirements for reporting covert actions to Congress in fiscal 1991. Adopted 419-4: R 163-0; D 256-3 (ND 173-3, SD 83-0); I 0-1, July 31, 1991.

238. HR 1455. Fiscal 1991 Intelligence Authorization. Kennelly, D-Conn., motion to table (kill) the motion to reconsider the vote by which the House adopted the conference report to authorize a classified level of funding for U.S. intelligence agencies and other government intelligence activities in fiscal 1991. Motion agreed to 425-3: R 162-3; D 262-0 (ND 179-0, SD 83-0); I 1-0), July 31, 1991.

239. HR 3029. 1990 Farm Bill Technical Amendments/Passage. de la Garza, D-Texas, motion to suspend the rules and pass the bill to make technical and clarifying amendments to the 1990 farm bill (PL 101-624). Motion agreed to 417-5: R 159-4; D 257-1 (ND 174-1, SD 83-0); I 1-0, July 31, 1991. A two-thirds majority of those present and voting (282 in this case) is required for passage under suspension of the rules.

240. HR 3029. 1990 Farm Bill Technical Amendments. de la Garza, D-Texas, motion to table (kill) the motion to reconsider the vote by which the House suspended the rules and passed the bill to make technical and clarifying amendments to the 1990 farm bill (PL 101-624). Motion agreed to 422-4: R 161-4; D 260-0 (ND 178-0, SD 82-0); I 1-0, July 31, 1991.

241. HR 1107. Persian Gulf Silver Medals/Passage. Torres, D-Calif., motion to suspend the rules and pass the bill to establish a silver congressional commemorative medal for members of the U.S. armed forces who served in the combat zone during the Persian Gulf conflict. Motion agreed to 381-37: R 131-33; D 249-4 (ND 171-3, SD 78-1); I 1-0, July 31, 1991. A two-thirds majority of those present and voting (279 in this case) is required for passage under suspension of the rules.

KEY

Y Voted for (yea).
\# Paired for.
\+ Announced for.
N Voted against (nay).
X Paired against.
\- Announced against.
P Voted "present."
C Voted "present" to avoid possible conflict of interest.
? Did not vote or otherwise make a position known.

Democrats ***Republicans***
Independent

	234	235	236	237	238	239	240	241
ALABAMA								
1 ***Callahan***	N	N	Y	Y	Y	Y	Y	Y
2 ***Dickinson***	N	N	Y	Y	Y	Y	Y	N
3 Browder	Y	N	Y	Y	Y	Y	Y	Y
4 Bevill	Y	N	Y	Y	Y	Y	Y	Y
5 Cramer	Y	N	Y	Y	Y	Y	Y	Y
6 Erdreich	Y	N	Y	Y	Y	Y	Y	Y
7 Harris	Y	N	Y	Y	Y	Y	Y	Y
ALASKA								
AL ***Young***	N	Y	Y	Y	Y	Y	Y	Y
ARIZONA								
1 ***Rhodes***	N	Y	Y	Y	Y	Y	Y	Y
2 Vacancy								
3 ***Stump***	N	Y	Y	Y	Y	N	N	N
4 ***Kyl***	N	Y	Y	Y	Y	Y	Y	Y
5 ***Kolbe***	N	Y	Y	Y	Y	Y	Y	Y
ARKANSAS								
1 Alexander	Y	N	Y	Y	Y	Y	Y	Y
2 Thornton	Y	N	Y	Y	Y	Y	Y	Y
3 ***Hammerschmidt***	Y	N	Y	Y	Y	Y	Y	Y
4 Anthony	Y	N	Y	Y	Y	Y	Y	Y
CALIFORNIA								
1 ***Riggs***	N	Y	Y	Y	Y	Y	Y	Y
2 ***Herger***	N	Y	Y	Y	Y	Y	Y	Y
3 Matsui	?	N	Y	Y	Y	Y	Y	Y
4 Fazio	Y	N	Y	Y	Y	Y	Y	Y
5 Pelosi	Y	N	Y	Y	Y	Y	Y	Y
6 Boxer	Y	N	?	?	Y	Y	Y	Y
7 Miller	Y	N	Y	Y	Y	Y	Y	Y
8 Dellums	Y	N	Y	Y	Y	Y	Y	Y
9 Stark	Y	N	Y	Y	Y	Y	Y	Y
10 Edwards	Y	N	Y	Y	Y	Y	Y	Y
11 Lantos	Y	N	Y	Y	Y	Y	Y	Y
12 ***Campbell***	N	Y	Y	Y	Y	Y	Y	Y
13 Mineta	Y	N	Y	Y	Y	Y	Y	Y
14 ***Doolittle***	N	Y	Y	Y	N	Y	Y	Y
15 Condit	Y	N	Y	Y	Y	Y	Y	Y
16 Panetta	Y	N	Y	Y	Y	Y	Y	Y
17 Dooley	Y	N	Y	Y	Y	Y	Y	Y
18 Lehman	Y	N	Y	Y	Y	Y	Y	Y
19 ***Lagomarsino***	N	Y	Y	Y	Y	Y	Y	Y
20 ***Thomas***	N	Y	Y	Y	Y	Y	Y	Y
21 ***Gallegly***	P	Y	Y	Y	Y	Y	Y	Y
22 ***Moorhead***	N	Y	Y	Y	Y	Y	Y	Y
23 Beilenson	Y	N	Y	Y	Y	Y	Y	N
24 Waxman	Y	N	Y	Y	Y	Y	Y	?
25 Roybal	Y	N	Y	Y	Y	Y	Y	Y
26 Berman	Y	N	Y	Y	Y	Y	Y	?
27 Levine	Y	N	Y	Y	Y	Y	Y	Y
28 Dixon	Y	N	Y	Y	Y	Y	Y	?
29 Waters	Y	N	Y	N	Y	?	Y	Y
30 Martinez	?	N	Y	Y	Y	Y	Y	Y
31 Dymally	?	N	Y	N	Y	Y	Y	N
32 Anderson	Y	N	Y	Y	Y	Y	Y	Y
33 ***Dreier***	Y	Y	Y	Y	Y	Y	Y	N
34 Torres	Y	N	Y	Y	Y	Y	Y	Y
35 ***Lewis***	N	Y	Y	Y	Y	Y	Y	N
36 Brown	Y	N	Y	Y	Y	Y	Y	Y
37 ***McCandless***	N	Y	Y	Y	Y	Y	Y	Y
38 ***Dornan***	N	Y	?	Y	Y	Y	Y	Y
39 ***Dannemeyer***	N	Y	Y	Y	Y	Y	Y	Y
40 ***Cox***	?	?	Y	Y	Y	Y	Y	Y
41 ***Lowery***	N	Y	Y	Y	Y	Y	Y	Y
42 ***Rohrabacher***	N	Y	Y	Y	N	Y	Y	Y
43 ***Packard***	N	N	Y	Y	Y	Y	Y	Y
44 ***Cunningham***	N	Y	Y	Y	Y	Y	Y	Y
45 ***Hunter***	N	Y	Y	Y	Y	Y	Y	Y
COLORADO								
1 Schroeder	N	N	Y	Y	Y	Y	Y	Y
2 Skaggs	Y	N	Y	Y	Y	Y	Y	Y
3 Campbell	Y	N	Y	Y	Y	Y	Y	Y
4 ***Allard***	N	Y	Y	Y	Y	Y	Y	Y
5 ***Hefley***	N	Y	Y	Y	Y	Y	Y	Y
6 ***Schaefer***	N	Y	Y	Y	Y	Y	Y	Y
CONNECTICUT								
1 Kennelly	Y	N	Y	Y	Y	Y	Y	Y
2 Gejdenson	Y	N	Y	Y	Y	Y	Y	Y
3 DeLauro	Y	N	Y	Y	Y	Y	Y	Y
4 ***Shays***	N	Y	Y	Y	Y	Y	Y	Y
5 ***Franks***	N	Y	Y	Y	Y	Y	Y	Y
6 ***Johnson***	Y	Y	Y	Y	Y	Y	Y	Y
DELAWARE								
AL Carper	Y	N	Y	Y	Y	Y	Y	Y
FLORIDA								
1 Hutto	Y	N	Y	Y	Y	Y	Y	Y
2 Peterson	Y	N	Y	Y	Y	Y	Y	N
3 Bennett	Y	N	Y	Y	Y	Y	Y	Y
4 ***James***	N	N	Y	Y	Y	Y	Y	Y
5 ***McCollum***	Y	N	Y	Y	Y	Y	Y	Y
6 ***Stearns***	N	Y	Y	Y	Y	Y	Y	N
7 Gibbons	Y	N	Y	Y	Y	Y	Y	Y
8 ***Young***	N	Y	Y	Y	Y	Y	Y	Y
9 ***Bilirakis***	N	Y	Y	Y	Y	Y	Y	Y
10 ***Ireland***	N	Y	Y	Y	Y	Y	Y	N
11 Bacchus	Y	N	Y	Y	Y	Y	?	Y
12 ***Lewis***	N	Y	Y	Y	Y	Y	Y	Y
13 ***Goss***	N	Y	Y	Y	Y	Y	Y	N
14 Johnston	Y	N	Y	Y	Y	Y	Y	?
15 ***Shaw***	N	N	Y	Y	Y	Y	Y	Y
16 Smith	Y	N	Y	Y	Y	Y	Y	Y
17 Lehman	Y	N	Y	Y	Y	Y	Y	?
18 ***Ros-Lehtinen***	N	N	Y	Y	Y	Y	Y	N
19 Fascell	Y	N	Y	Y	Y	Y	Y	Y
GEORGIA								
1 Thomas	Y	N	Y	Y	Y	Y	Y	Y
2 Hatcher	Y	N	Y	Y	Y	Y	Y	Y
3 Ray	Y	N	Y	Y	Y	Y	Y	Y
4 Jones	Y	N	Y	Y	Y	Y	Y	Y
5 Lewis	Y	N	Y	Y	Y	Y	Y	Y
6 ***Gingrich***	N	Y	Y	Y	Y	?	Y	N
7 Darden	Y	N	Y	Y	Y	Y	Y	Y
8 Rowland	Y	N	Y	Y	Y	Y	Y	Y
9 Jenkins	Y	N	Y	Y	Y	Y	Y	Y
10 Barnard	Y	N	Y	Y	Y	Y	Y	Y
HAWAII								
1 Abercrombie	Y	N	Y	Y	Y	Y	Y	Y
2 Mink	Y	N	Y	Y	Y	Y	Y	Y
IDAHO								
1 LaRocco	Y	N	Y	Y	Y	Y	Y	Y
2 Stallings	Y	N	Y	Y	Y	Y	Y	Y
ILLINOIS								
1 Hayes	Y	N	Y	Y	Y	Y	Y	Y
2 Savage	?	N	Y	N	Y	Y	Y	P
3 Russo	Y	N	Y	Y	Y	Y	Y	Y
4 Sangmeister	Y	N	Y	Y	Y	Y	Y	Y
5 Lipinski	Y	N	Y	Y	Y	Y	Y	Y
6 ***Hyde***	N	Y	Y	Y	Y	Y	Y	N
7 Collins	Y	N	Y	Y	Y	Y	Y	Y
8 Rostenkowski	Y	N	Y	Y	Y	Y	Y	Y
9 Yates	Y	N	Y	Y	Y	N	Y	N
10 ***Porter***	N	Y	Y	Y	Y	Y	Y	Y
11 Annunzio	Y	N	Y	Y	Y	Y	Y	Y
12 ***Crane***	N	Y	Y	Y	Y	N	N	N
13 ***Fawell***	N	Y	Y	Y	Y	Y	Y	?
14 ***Hastert***	N	Y	Y	Y	Y	Y	Y	Y
15 ***Ewing***	N	N	Y	Y	Y	Y	Y	Y
16 Cox	Y	N	Y	Y	Y	Y	Y	Y
17 Evans	Y	N	Y	Y	Y	Y	Y	Y
18 ***Michel***	N	Y	Y	Y	Y	Y	Y	N
19 Bruce	Y	N	Y	Y	Y	Y	Y	Y
20 Durbin	Y	N	Y	Y	Y	Y	Y	Y
21 Costello	Y	N	Y	Y	Y	Y	Y	Y
22 Poshard	Y	N	Y	Y	Y	Y	Y	Y
INDIANA								
1 Visclosky	Y	N	Y	Y	Y	Y	Y	Y
2 Sharp	Y	N	Y	Y	Y	Y	Y	Y
3 Roemer	Y	N	Y	Y	Y	Y	Y	Y

ND Northern Democrats SD Southern Democrats

	234	235	236	237	238	239	240	241
4 Long	Y	N	Y	Y	Y	Y	Y	Y
5 Jontz	Y	N	Y	Y	Y	Y	Y	Y
6 ***Burton***	?	Y	Y	Y	Y	Y	Y	Y
7 ***Myers***	Y	N	Y	Y	Y	Y	Y	Y
8 McCloskey	Y	N	?	Y	Y	Y	Y	Y
9 Hamilton	Y	N	Y	Y	Y	Y	Y	Y
10 Jacobs	N	N	?	Y	Y	Y	Y	Y
IOWA								
1 ***Leach***	N	Y	Y	Y	Y	Y	Y	Y
2 ***Nussle***	N	Y	Y	Y	Y	Y	Y	Y
3 Nagle	Y	N	Y	Y	Y	Y	Y	Y
4 Smith	Y	N	Y	Y	Y	Y	Y	Y
5 ***Lightfoot***	N	Y	Y	Y	Y	Y	Y	Y
6 ***Grandy***	N	N	Y	Y	Y	Y	Y	N
KANSAS								
1 ***Roberts***	N	Y	Y	Y	Y	Y	Y	Y
2 Slattery	Y	N	Y	Y	Y	Y	Y	Y
3 ***Meyers***	N	Y	Y	Y	Y	Y	Y	Y
4 Glickman	Y	N	Y	Y	Y	Y	Y	Y
5 ***Nichols***	Y	Y	Y	Y	Y	Y	Y	Y
KENTUCKY								
1 Hubbard	Y	N	Y	Y	Y	Y	Y	Y
2 Natcher	Y	N	Y	Y	Y	Y	Y	Y
3 Mazzoli	Y	N	Y	Y	Y	Y	Y	Y
4 ***Bunning***	N	Y	Y	Y	Y	Y	Y	N
5 ***Rogers***	N	Y	Y	Y	Y	Y	Y	Y
6 ***Hopkins***	?	?	?	?	?	?	?	?
7 Perkins	Y	N	Y	Y	Y	Y	Y	Y
LOUISIANA								
1 ***Livingston***	Y	N	Y	Y	Y	Y	Y	N
2 Jefferson	Y	N	Y	Y	Y	Y	Y	Y
3 Tauzin	Y	N	Y	Y	Y	Y	Y	Y
4 ***McCrery***	N	N	Y	Y	Y	Y	Y	Y
5 Huckaby	Y	N	Y	Y	Y	Y	Y	Y
6 ***Baker***	N	N	Y	Y	Y	Y	Y	Y
7 Hayes	Y	?	Y	Y	Y	Y	Y	Y
8 ***Holloway***	N	Y	Y	Y	Y	Y	Y	Y
MAINE								
1 Andrews	Y	N	Y	Y	Y	Y	Y	Y
2 ***Snowe***	Y	Y	Y	Y	Y	Y	Y	Y
MARYLAND								
1 ***Gilchrest***	N	Y	Y	Y	Y	Y	Y	Y
2 ***Bentley***	N	Y	Y	Y	Y	Y	Y	Y
3 Cardin	Y	N	Y	Y	Y	Y	Y	Y
4 McMillen	Y	N	Y	Y	Y	Y	Y	Y
5 Hoyer	Y	N	Y	Y	Y	Y	Y	Y
6 Byron	Y	N	Y	Y	Y	Y	Y	Y
7 Mfume	?	N	Y	Y	Y	Y	Y	Y
8 ***Morella***	N	Y	Y	Y	Y	Y	Y	Y
MASSACHUSETTS								
1 Olver	Y	N	Y	Y	Y	Y	Y	Y
2 Neal	Y	N	Y	Y	Y	Y	Y	Y
3 Early	Y	N	Y	Y	Y	Y	Y	Y
4 Frank	Y	N	Y	Y	Y	Y	Y	Y
5 Atkins	Y	N	Y	Y	Y	Y	Y	Y
6 Mavroules	Y	N	Y	Y	Y	Y	Y	Y
7 Markey	Y	N	Y	Y	Y	Y	Y	Y
8 Kennedy	Y	N	Y	Y	Y	Y	Y	Y
9 Moakley	?	N	Y	Y	Y	Y	Y	Y
10 Studds	Y	N	Y	Y	Y	Y	Y	Y
11 Donnelly	Y	N	Y	Y	Y	Y	Y	Y
MICHIGAN								
1 Conyers	Y	N	Y	Y	Y	Y	Y	Y
2 ***Pursell***	Y	Y	Y	Y	Y	Y	Y	Y
3 Wolpe	Y	N	Y	Y	Y	Y	Y	Y
4 ***Upton***	N	Y	Y	Y	Y	Y	Y	Y
5 ***Henry***	N	Y	Y	Y	Y	Y	Y	Y
6 Carr	Y	N	Y	Y	Y	?	Y	Y
7 Kildee	Y	N	Y	Y	Y	Y	Y	Y
8 Traxler	Y	N	Y	Y	Y	Y	?	Y
9 ***Vander Jagt***	N	Y	Y	Y	Y	Y	Y	Y
10 ***Camp***	N	Y	Y	Y	Y	Y	Y	Y
11 ***Davis***	N	N	Y	Y	Y	Y	Y	Y
12 Bonior	Y	N	Y	Y	Y	Y	Y	Y
13 Collins	?	N	Y	Y	Y	Y	Y	Y
14 Hertel	Y	N	Y	Y	Y	Y	Y	Y
15 Ford	Y	N	Y	Y	Y	Y	Y	Y
16 Dingell	Y	N	Y	Y	Y	?	Y	Y
17 Levin	Y	N	Y	Y	Y	Y	Y	Y
18 ***Broomfield***	Y	Y	Y	Y	Y	Y	Y	Y
MINNESOTA								
1 Penny	Y	N	Y	Y	Y	Y	Y	Y
2 ***Weber***	N	Y	Y	Y	Y	Y	Y	Y
3 ***Ramstad***	N	Y	Y	Y	Y	Y	Y	Y
4 Vento	Y	N	Y	Y	Y	Y	Y	Y

	234	235	236	237	238	239	240	241
5 Sabo	Y	N	Y	Y	Y	Y	Y	Y
6 Sikorski	N	N	Y	Y	Y	Y	Y	Y
7 Peterson	Y	N	Y	Y	Y	Y	Y	Y
8 Oberstar	Y	N	Y	Y	Y	Y	Y	Y
MISSISSIPPI								
1 Whitten	Y	N	Y	Y	Y	Y	Y	Y
2 Espy	Y	N	Y	Y	Y	Y	Y	Y
3 Montgomery	Y	N	Y	Y	Y	Y	Y	Y
4 Parker	Y	N	Y	Y	Y	Y	Y	Y
5 Taylor	Y	N	Y	Y	Y	Y	Y	Y
MISSOURI								
1 Clay	N	N	Y	Y	Y	Y	Y	Y
2 Horn	Y	N	Y	Y	Y	Y	Y	Y
3 Gephardt	Y	N	Y	Y	Y	Y	Y	Y
4 Skelton	Y	N	Y	Y	Y	Y	Y	Y
5 Wheat	Y	N	Y	Y	Y	Y	Y	Y
6 ***Coleman***	N	N	Y	Y	Y	Y	Y	Y
7 ***Hancock***	N	Y	Y	Y	Y	N	N	N
8 ***Emerson***	N	Y	Y	Y	Y	Y	Y	Y
9 Volkmer	N	N	Y	Y	Y	Y	Y	Y
MONTANA								
1 Williams	?	N	Y	Y	Y	Y	Y	Y
2 ***Marlenee***	N	Y	Y	Y	Y	Y	Y	Y
NEBRASKA								
1 ***Bereuter***	N	Y	Y	Y	Y	Y	Y	Y
2 Hoagland	Y	N	Y	Y	Y	Y	Y	Y
3 ***Barrett***	N	Y	Y	Y	Y	Y	Y	Y
NEVADA								
1 Bilbray	Y	N	Y	Y	Y	Y	Y	Y
2 ***Vucanovich***	N	Y	Y	Y	Y	Y	Y	Y
NEW HAMPSHIRE								
1 ***Zeliff***	N	Y	Y	Y	Y	Y	Y	N
2 Swett	Y	N	Y	Y	Y	?	Y	Y
NEW JERSEY								
1 Andrews	Y	N	Y	Y	Y	Y	Y	Y
2 Hughes	Y	N	Y	Y	Y	Y	Y	Y
3 Pallone	Y	N	Y	Y	Y	Y	Y	Y
4 ***Smith***	N	Y	Y	Y	Y	Y	Y	Y
5 ***Roukema***	N	Y	Y	Y	Y	Y	Y	Y
6 Dwyer	Y	N	Y	Y	Y	Y	Y	Y
7 ***Rinaldo***	Y	N	Y	Y	Y	Y	Y	Y
8 Roe	Y	N	Y	Y	Y	Y	Y	Y
9 Torricelli	Y	N	Y	Y	Y	Y	Y	Y
10 Payne	Y	N	Y	Y	Y	Y	Y	Y
11 ***Gallo***	N	Y	Y	Y	Y	Y	Y	Y
12 ***Zimmer***	N	Y	Y	Y	Y	Y	Y	Y
13 ***Saxton***	N	Y	Y	Y	Y	Y	Y	Y
14 Guarini	Y	N	Y	Y	Y	Y	Y	Y
NEW MEXICO								
1 ***Schiff***	Y	Y	Y	Y	Y	Y	Y	Y
2 ***Skeen***	Y	Y	Y	Y	Y	Y	Y	Y
3 Richardson	Y	N	Y	Y	Y	Y	Y	Y
NEW YORK								
1 Hochbrueckner	Y	N	Y	Y	Y	Y	Y	Y
2 Downey	Y	N	Y	Y	Y	Y	Y	Y
3 Mrazek	Y	N	Y	?	Y	Y	Y	Y
4 ***Lent***	Y	Y	Y	Y	Y	?	Y	Y
5 ***McGrath***	N	N	Y	Y	Y	Y	Y	Y
6 Flake	Y	N	Y	Y	Y	Y	Y	Y
7 Ackerman	Y	N	Y	Y	Y	Y	Y	Y
8 Scheuer	Y	N	Y	Y	Y	Y	Y	Y
9 Manton	Y	N	Y	Y	Y	Y	Y	Y
10 Schumer	Y	N	Y	Y	Y	Y	Y	Y
11 Towns	Y	N	Y	Y	Y	Y	Y	Y
12 Owens	?	N	Y	Y	Y	Y	Y	Y
13 Solarz	Y	N	Y	Y	Y	Y	Y	Y
14 ***Molinari***	N	Y	Y	Y	Y	Y	Y	Y
15 ***Green***	Y	N	Y	?	Y	Y	Y	N
16 Rangel	Y	N	Y	Y	Y	Y	Y	Y
17 Weiss	Y	N	Y	Y	Y	Y	Y	Y
18 Serrano	Y	N	Y	Y	Y	Y	Y	Y
19 Engel	Y	N	Y	Y	Y	Y	Y	Y
20 Lowey	Y	N	Y	Y	Y	Y	Y	Y
21 ***Fish***	Y	N	Y	Y	Y	Y	Y	Y
22 ***Gilman***	Y	N	Y	Y	Y	Y	Y	Y
23 McNulty	Y	N	Y	Y	Y	Y	Y	Y
24 ***Solomon***	N	Y	Y	Y	Y	Y	Y	Y
25 ***Boehlert***	N	N	Y	Y	Y	Y	Y	Y
26 ***Martin***	N	Y	Y	Y	Y	Y	Y	Y
27 ***Walsh***	N	Y	Y	Y	Y	Y	Y	Y
28 McHugh	Y	N	Y	Y	Y	Y	Y	Y
29 ***Horton***	Y	?	Y	Y	Y	Y	Y	Y
30 Slaughter	Y	N	Y	Y	Y	Y	Y	Y
31 ***Paxon***	N	Y	Y	Y	Y	Y	Y	Y

	234	235	236	237	238	239	240	241
32 LaFalce	Y	N	Y	Y	Y	Y	Y	Y
33 Nowak	Y	N	Y	Y	Y	Y	Y	Y
34 ***Houghton***	Y	N	Y	Y	Y	Y	Y	N
NORTH CAROLINA								
1 Jones	Y	N	Y	Y	Y	Y	Y	Y
2 Valentine	Y	N	Y	Y	Y	Y	Y	Y
3 Lancaster	Y	N	Y	Y	Y	Y	Y	Y
4 Price	Y	N	Y	Y	Y	Y	Y	Y
5 Neal	Y	N	Y	Y	Y	Y	Y	Y
6 ***Coble***	N	Y	Y	Y	Y	Y	Y	Y
7 Rose	Y	N	Y	Y	Y	Y	Y	Y
8 Hefner	?	?	?	?	?	?	?	?
9 ***McMillan***	Y	?	Y	Y	Y	Y	Y	Y
10 ***Ballenger***	N	Y	Y	Y	Y	Y	Y	N
11 ***Taylor***	N	Y	Y	Y	Y	Y	Y	Y
NORTH DAKOTA								
AL Dorgan	Y	N	Y	Y	Y	Y	Y	Y
OHIO								
1 Luken	Y	N	Y	Y	Y	Y	Y	Y
2 ***Gradison***	N	Y	Y	Y	Y	Y	Y	Y
3 Hall	Y	N	Y	Y	Y	Y	Y	Y
4 ***Oxley***	N	N	Y	Y	Y	Y	Y	Y
5 ***Gillmor***	Y	Y	Y	Y	Y	Y	Y	Y
6 ***McEwen***	Y	Y	Y	Y	Y	Y	Y	Y
7 ***Hobson***	N	Y	Y	Y	Y	Y	Y	Y
8 ***Boehner***	N	Y	Y	Y	Y	Y	Y	N
9 Kaptur	Y	N	Y	Y	Y	Y	Y	Y
10 ***Miller***	N	Y	Y	Y	Y	Y	Y	Y
11 Eckart	Y	N	Y	Y	Y	Y	Y	Y
12 ***Kasich***	Y	Y	Y	Y	Y	Y	Y	Y
13 Pease	Y	N	Y	Y	Y	Y	Y	Y
14 Sawyer	Y	N	Y	Y	Y	Y	Y	Y
15 ***Wylie***	Y	Y	Y	Y	Y	Y	Y	N
16 ***Regula***	N	N	Y	Y	Y	Y	Y	Y
17 Traficant	Y	N	Y	Y	Y	Y	Y	Y
18 Applegate	Y	N	Y	Y	Y	Y	Y	Y
19 Feighan	?	?	?	?	?	?	?	?
20 Oakar	Y	N	Y	Y	Y	Y	Y	Y
21 Stokes	Y	N	Y	Y	Y	Y	Y	Y
OKLAHOMA								
1 ***Inhofe***	N	Y	Y	Y	Y	Y	Y	Y
2 Synar	Y	N	Y	Y	Y	Y	Y	Y
3 Brewster	Y	N	Y	Y	Y	Y	Y	Y
4 McCurdy	Y	N	Y	Y	Y	Y	Y	Y
5 ***Edwards***	N	Y	Y	Y	Y	Y	Y	Y
6 English	Y	N	Y	Y	Y	Y	Y	Y
OREGON								
1 AuCoin	Y	N	Y	Y	Y	Y	Y	Y
2 ***Smith***	N	Y	Y	Y	Y	Y	Y	Y
3 Wyden	Y	N	Y	Y	Y	Y	Y	Y
4 DeFazio	Y	N	Y	Y	Y	Y	Y	Y
5 Kopetski	Y	N	Y	Y	Y	Y	Y	Y
PENNSYLVANIA								
1 Foglietta	Y	N	Y	Y	Y	Y	Y	Y
2 Gray	?	N	?	?	Y	Y	Y	?
3 Borski	Y	N	Y	Y	Y	Y	Y	Y
4 Kolter	Y	N	Y	Y	Y	Y	Y	Y
5 ***Schulze***	Y	Y	Y	Y	Y	Y	Y	Y
6 Yatron	?	?	?	?	?	?	?	?
7 ***Weldon***	N	N	Y	Y	Y	Y	Y	Y
8 Kostmayer	Y	N	Y	Y	Y	Y	Y	Y
9 ***Shuster***	Y	N	Y	Y	Y	Y	Y	Y
10 ***McDade***	N	N	Y	Y	Y	Y	Y	Y
11 Kanjorski	Y	N	Y	Y	Y	Y	Y	Y
12 Murtha	Y	N	Y	Y	Y	Y	Y	Y
13 ***Coughlin***	N	Y	Y	?	Y	Y	Y	Y
14 Coyne	Y	N	Y	Y	Y	Y	Y	Y
15 ***Ritter***	Y	Y	Y	Y	Y	Y	Y	Y
16 ***Walker***	N	Y	Y	Y	Y	Y	Y	N
17 ***Gekas***	N	Y	Y	Y	Y	Y	Y	N
18 ***Santorum***	N	Y	Y	Y	Y	Y	Y	Y
19 ***Goodling***	N	Y	Y	Y	Y	Y	Y	Y
20 Gaydos	?	N	Y	Y	Y	Y	Y	Y
21 ***Ridge***	N	Y	Y	Y	Y	Y	Y	Y
22 Murphy	N	N	Y	Y	Y	Y	Y	Y
23 ***Clinger***	Y	N	Y	Y	Y	Y	Y	Y
RHODE ISLAND								
1 ***Machtley***	N	Y	Y	Y	Y	Y	Y	Y
2 Reed	Y	N	Y	Y	Y	Y	Y	Y
SOUTH CAROLINA								
1 ***Ravenel***	Y	N	Y	Y	Y	Y	Y	Y
2 ***Spence***	N	Y	Y	Y	Y	Y	Y	Y
3 Derrick	Y	N	Y	Y	Y	Y	Y	Y
4 Patterson	Y	N	Y	Y	Y	Y	Y	Y
5 Spratt	Y	N	Y	Y	Y	Y	Y	Y
6 Tallon	Y	N	Y	Y	Y	Y	Y	Y

	234	235	236	237	238	239	240	241
SOUTH DAKOTA								
AL Johnson	Y	N	Y	Y	Y	Y	Y	Y
TENNESSEE								
1 ***Quillen***	N	Y	Y	Y	Y	Y	Y	Y
2 ***Duncan***	N	Y	Y	Y	Y	Y	Y	Y
3 Lloyd	Y	N	Y	Y	Y	Y	Y	Y
4 Cooper	Y	N	Y	Y	Y	Y	Y	Y
5 Clement	Y	N	Y	Y	Y	Y	Y	Y
6 Gordon	Y	N	Y	Y	Y	Y	Y	Y
7 ***Sundquist***	N	Y	Y	Y	Y	Y	Y	Y
8 Tanner	Y	N	Y	Y	Y	Y	Y	Y
9 Ford	Y	N	Y	Y	Y	Y	Y	?
TEXAS								
1 Chapman	Y	N	Y	Y	Y	Y	Y	Y
2 Wilson	?	N	Y	Y	Y	Y	Y	Y
3 ***Johnson***	Y	Y	Y	Y	Y	Y	Y	N
4 Hall	Y	N	Y	Y	Y	Y	Y	Y
5 Bryant	Y	N	Y	Y	Y	Y	Y	Y
6 ***Barton***	N	Y	Y	Y	Y	Y	Y	N
7 ***Archer***	Y	Y	Y	Y	Y	Y	Y	N
8 ***Fields***	N	Y	Y	Y	Y	Y	Y	N
9 Brooks	Y	N	Y	Y	Y	Y	Y	Y
10 Pickle	Y	N	Y	Y	Y	Y	Y	Y
11 Edwards	Y	N	Y	Y	Y	Y	Y	Y
12 Geren	Y	N	Y	Y	Y	Y	Y	Y
13 Sarpalius	Y	N	Y	Y	Y	Y	Y	Y
14 Laughlin	Y	N	Y	Y	Y	Y	Y	Y
15 de la Garza	Y	N	Y	Y	Y	Y	Y	Y
16 Coleman	Y	N	Y	Y	Y	Y	Y	Y
17 Stenholm	Y	N	Y	Y	Y	Y	Y	Y
18 Washington	?	N	Y	Y	Y	Y	Y	?
19 ***Combest***	Y	N	Y	Y	Y	Y	Y	Y
20 Gonzalez	Y	N	Y	Y	Y	Y	Y	Y
21 ***Smith***	N	Y	Y	Y	Y	Y	Y	Y
22 ***DeLay***	N	Y	Y	Y	N	Y	Y	N
23 Bustamante	?	?	?	?	?	?	?	?
24 Frost	Y	N	Y	Y	Y	Y	Y	Y
25 Andrews	Y	N	Y	Y	Y	Y	Y	Y
26 ***Armey***	N	Y	Y	Y	Y	N	N	N
27 Ortiz	Y	N	Y	Y	Y	Y	Y	Y
UTAH								
1 ***Hansen***	N	Y	Y	Y	Y	Y	Y	Y
2 Owens	Y	N	Y	Y	Y	Y	Y	Y
3 Orton	Y	N	Y	Y	Y	Y	Y	Y
VERMONT								
AL *Sanders*	Y	N	?	N	Y	Y	Y	Y
VIRGINIA								
1 ***Bateman***	N	Y	Y	Y	Y	Y	Y	N
2 Pickett	Y	N	Y	Y	Y	Y	Y	Y
3 ***Bliley***	N	Y	Y	Y	Y	Y	Y	Y
4 Sisisky	Y	N	Y	Y	Y	Y	Y	Y
5 Payne	Y	N	Y	Y	Y	Y	Y	Y
6 Olin	Y	N	Y	Y	Y	Y	Y	Y
7 ***Slaughter***	N	Y	Y	Y	Y	Y	Y	Y
8 Moran	Y	N	Y	Y	Y	Y	Y	Y
9 Boucher	Y	N	Y	Y	Y	Y	Y	Y
10 ***Wolf***	N	Y	Y	Y	Y	Y	Y	Y
WASHINGTON								
1 ***Miller***	N	Y	Y	Y	Y	Y	Y	Y
2 Swift	Y	N	Y	Y	Y	Y	Y	Y
3 Unsoeld	Y	N	Y	Y	Y	Y	Y	Y
4 ***Morrison***	Y	N	Y	Y	Y	Y	Y	Y
5 Foley								
6 Dicks	Y	N	Y	Y	Y	Y	Y	Y
7 McDermott	Y	N	Y	Y	Y	Y	Y	Y
8 ***Chandler***	N	Y	Y	Y	Y	Y	Y	N
WEST VIRGINIA								
1 Mollohan	Y	N	Y	Y	Y	Y	Y	Y
2 Staggers	Y	N	Y	Y	Y	Y	Y	Y
3 Wise	Y	N	Y	Y	Y	Y	Y	Y
4 Rahall	Y	N	Y	Y	Y	Y	Y	Y
WISCONSIN								
1 Aspin	Y	N	Y	Y	Y	Y	Y	Y
2 ***Klug***	Y	Y	Y	Y	Y	Y	Y	Y
3 ***Gunderson***	Y	Y	Y	Y	Y	Y	Y	Y
4 Kleczka	Y	N	Y	Y	Y	Y	Y	Y
5 Moody	Y	N	Y	Y	Y	Y	Y	Y
6 ***Petri***	Y	N	Y	Y	Y	Y	Y	Y
7 Obey	Y	N	Y	Y	Y	Y	Y	Y
8 ***Roth***	N	Y	Y	Y	Y	Y	Y	N
9 ***Sensenbrenner***	N	Y	Y	Y	Y	Y	Y	Y
WYOMING								
AL ***Thomas***	N	Y	Y	Y	Y	Y	Y	Y

Southern states - Ala., Ark., Fla., Ga., Ky., La., Miss., N.C., Okla., S.C., Tenn., Texas, Va.
Omitted votes are quorum calls, which CQ does not include in its vote charts.

HOUSE VOTES 242, 243, 244, 245, 246, 247, 248, 249

242. HR 1107. Persian Gulf Silver Medals. Kostmayer, D-Pa., motion to table (kill) the motion to reconsider the vote by which the House suspended the rules and passed the bill to establish a silver congressional commemorative medal for members of the U.S. armed forces who served in the combat zone during the Persian Gulf conflict. Motion agreed to 408-15: R 149-15; D 258-0 (ND 179-0, SD 79-0); I 1-0, July 31, 1991.

243. HR 500. Christopher Columbus 500th Anniversary/Passage. Torres, D-Calif., motion to suspend the rules and pass the bill to require the secretary of the Treasury to mint coins to commemorate the 500th anniversary of the discovery of America by Christopher Columbus and to establish the Christopher Columbus Fellowship Foundation. Motion agreed to 408-2: R 160-2; D 248-0 (ND 171-0, SD 77-0), July 31, 1991. A two-thirds majority of those present and voting (274 in this case) is required for passage under suspension of the rules.

244. HR 500. Christopher Columbus 500th Anniversary. Kostmayer, D-Pa., motion table (kill) the motion to reconsider the vote by which the House suspended the rules and passed the bill to require the secretary of the Treasury to mint coins to commemorate the 500th anniversary of the discovery of America by Christopher Columbus and to establish the Christopher Columbus Fellowship Foundation. Motion agreed to 418-0: R 163-0; D 255-0 (ND 177-0, SD 78-0), July 31, 1991.

245. HR 2427. Fiscal 1992 Energy and Water Appropriations/Conference Report. Adoption of the conference report to provide $20,812,710,000 in new budget authority in fiscal 1992 for energy, water and nuclear weapons programs. The administration requested $21,874,500,000. Adopted 393-32: R 142-23; D 251-8 (ND 171-6, SD 80-2); I 0-1, July 31, 1991.

246. H Con Res 191. Adjournment Resolution. Adoption of the concurrent resolution to allow the House to adjourn on Aug. 2, 3, 4, or 5 until Sept. 11. Adopted 406-16: R 150-14; D 255-2 (ND 174-2, SD 81-0); I 1-0, July 31, 1991.

247. H Con Res 191. Adjournment Resolution. Kostmayer, D-Pa., motion to table (kill) the Slaughter, D-N.Y, motion to reconsider the vote by which the House adopted the concurrent resolution to allow the House to adjourn on Aug. 2, 3, 4, or 5 until Sept. 11. Motion agreed to 391-22: R 143-22; D 247-0 (ND 171-0, SD 76-0); I 1-0, July 31, 1991.

248. Procedural Motion. Gephardt, D-Mo., motion to adjourn. Motion agreed to 342-70: R 94-68; D 247-2 (ND 170-2, SD 77-0); I 1-0, July 31, 1991.

249. HR 2427. Fiscal 1992 Energy and Water Appropriations/Water Projects. Bevill, D-Ala., motion to recede and concur in the amendment of the Senate with an amendment to fund unauthorized water projects. Motion agreed to 338-80: R 96-67; D 241-13 (ND 163-11, SD 78-2); I 1-0, Aug. 1, 1991.

KEY

- Y Voted for (yea).
- # Paired for.
- + Announced for.
- N Voted against (nay).
- X Paired against.
- - Announced against.
- P Voted "present."
- C Voted "present" to avoid possible conflict of interest.
- ? Did not vote or otherwise make a position known.

Democrats ***Republicans***
Independent

	242	243	244	245	246	247	248	249
ALABAMA								
1 ***Callahan***	Y	Y	Y	Y	Y	Y	Y	Y
2 ***Dickinson***	Y	Y	Y	Y	Y	Y	Y	Y
3 Browder	Y	Y	Y	Y	Y	Y	Y	Y
4 Bevill	Y	Y	Y	Y	Y	Y	Y	Y
5 Cramer	Y	Y	Y	Y	Y	Y	Y	Y
6 Erdreich	Y	Y	Y	Y	Y	Y	Y	Y
7 Harris	Y	Y	Y	Y	Y	Y	Y	Y
ALASKA								
AL ***Young***	Y	Y	Y	Y	Y	Y	Y	Y
ARIZONA								
1 ***Rhodes***	Y	Y	Y	Y	Y	Y	N	Y
2 Vacancy								
3 ***Stump***	N	Y	Y	N	Y	N	N	N
4 ***Kyl***	Y	Y	Y	Y	Y	N	N	Y
5 ***Kolbe***	Y	Y	Y	Y	Y	Y	Y	Y
ARKANSAS								
1 Alexander	Y	Y	Y	Y	Y	Y	Y	Y
2 Thornton	Y	Y	Y	Y	Y	Y	Y	Y
3 ***Hammerschmidt***	Y	Y	Y	Y	Y	Y	Y	Y
4 Anthony	Y	Y	?	Y	Y	Y	Y	Y
CALIFORNIA								
1 ***Riggs***	Y	Y	Y	Y	Y	Y	N	N
2 ***Herger***	Y	Y	Y	Y	Y	Y	?	Y
3 Matsui	Y	Y	Y	Y	Y	Y	Y	?
4 Fazio	Y	Y	Y	Y	Y	Y	Y	Y
5 Pelosi	Y	Y	Y	Y	Y	Y	Y	Y
6 Boxer	Y	Y	Y	Y	Y	Y	Y	Y
7 Miller	Y	Y	Y	Y	Y	Y	Y	Y
8 Dellums	Y	Y	Y	Y	Y	Y	Y	Y
9 Stark	Y	Y	Y	Y	Y	Y	Y	Y
10 Edwards	Y	Y	Y	Y	Y	Y	Y	Y
11 Lantos	Y	Y	Y	Y	?	Y	Y	Y
12 ***Campbell***	Y	Y	Y	N	Y	Y	Y	N
13 Mineta	Y	Y	Y	Y	Y	Y	Y	Y
14 ***Doolittle***	N	Y	Y	Y	Y	N	N	N
15 Condit	Y	Y	Y	Y	Y	Y	Y	Y
16 Panetta	Y	Y	Y	Y	Y	Y	Y	Y
17 Dooley	Y	Y	Y	Y	Y	Y	Y	Y
18 Lehman	Y	Y	Y	Y	Y	Y	Y	Y
19 ***Lagomarsino***	Y	Y	Y	Y	Y	Y	N	Y
20 ***Thomas***	Y	Y	Y	Y	Y	Y	N	Y
21 ***Gallegly***	Y	Y	Y	Y	Y	Y	N	Y
22 ***Moorhead***	Y	Y	Y	N	Y	Y	Y	N
23 Beilenson	Y	?	Y	Y	Y	Y	Y	Y
24 Waxman	Y	Y	Y	?	Y	Y	Y	Y
25 Roybal	Y	Y	Y	Y	Y	Y	Y	Y
26 Berman	Y	Y	Y	Y	?	?	Y	Y
27 Levine	Y	Y	Y	Y	Y	Y	Y	N
28 Dixon	Y	Y	Y	Y	Y	Y	Y	Y
29 Waters	Y	Y	Y	Y	Y	Y	Y	N
30 Martinez	Y	Y	Y	Y	Y	Y	?	Y
31 Dymally	Y	Y	Y	Y	Y	Y	Y	Y
32 Anderson	Y	Y	Y	Y	Y	Y	Y	Y
33 ***Dreier***	Y	Y	Y	N	Y	Y	Y	N
34 Torres	Y	Y	Y	Y	Y	?	Y	Y
35 ***Lewis***	Y	Y	?	Y	Y	N	Y	Y
36 Brown	Y	Y	Y	Y	Y	Y	Y	Y
37 ***McCandless***	Y	Y	Y	Y	Y	Y	Y	Y
38 ***Dornan***	Y	Y	Y	Y	Y	Y	N	N
39 ***Dannemeyer***	Y	Y	Y	Y	Y	Y	N	N
40 ***Cox***	Y	Y	Y	Y	N	Y	N	N
41 ***Lowery***	Y	Y	Y	Y	Y	Y	Y	Y
42 ***Rohrabacher***	Y	Y	Y	Y	Y	N	Y	N
43 ***Packard***	Y	Y	Y	Y	Y	Y	Y	Y
44 ***Cunningham***	Y	Y	Y	Y	Y	Y	N	N
45 ***Hunter***	Y	Y	Y	Y	Y	N	N	N
COLORADO								
1 Schroeder	Y	Y	Y	N	Y	Y	Y	N
2 Skaggs	Y	Y	Y	Y	Y	Y	Y	Y
3 Campbell	Y	Y	Y	Y	Y	Y	Y	?
4 ***Allard***	Y	Y	Y	Y	Y	Y	Y	Y
5 ***Hefley***	Y	Y	Y	N	N	Y	Y	N
6 ***Schaefer***	N	Y	Y	Y	Y	Y	Y	Y
CONNECTICUT								
1 Kennelly	Y	Y	Y	Y	Y	Y	Y	Y
2 Gejdenson	Y	Y	Y	Y	Y	Y	Y	Y
3 DeLauro	Y	+	Y	Y	Y	Y	Y	Y
4 ***Shays***	Y	Y	Y	N	Y	Y	Y	N
5 ***Franks***	Y	Y	Y	Y	Y	Y	N	N
6 ***Johnson***	?	Y	Y	Y	Y	Y	Y	Y
DELAWARE								
AL Carper	Y	Y	?	Y	Y	?	?	Y
FLORIDA								
1 Hutto	Y	Y	Y	Y	Y	Y	Y	Y
2 Peterson	Y	Y	Y	Y	Y	Y	Y	Y
3 Bennett	Y	Y	Y	Y	Y	Y	Y	Y
4 ***James***	Y	Y	Y	Y	Y	Y	Y	Y
5 ***McCollum***	Y	Y	Y	Y	Y	Y	N	N
6 ***Stearns***	Y	Y	Y	Y	Y	Y	Y	N
7 Gibbons	Y	Y	Y	Y	Y	Y	Y	Y
8 ***Young***	Y	Y	Y	Y	Y	Y	N	Y
9 ***Bilirakis***	Y	Y	Y	Y	Y	Y	N	N
10 ***Ireland***	Y	Y	Y	Y	Y	Y	Y	Y
11 Bacchus	Y	Y	Y	Y	Y	Y	Y	Y
12 ***Lewis***	Y	Y	Y	Y	Y	Y	N	N
13 ***Goss***	Y	Y	Y	Y	Y	Y	N	Y
14 Johnston	?	?	Y	N	Y	Y	Y	Y
15 ***Shaw***	Y	Y	Y	Y	Y	Y	Y	Y
16 Smith	Y	Y	Y	Y	Y	Y	Y	Y
17 Lehman	?	?	?	Y	Y	Y	Y	Y
18 ***Ros-Lehtinen***	N	Y	Y	Y	Y	Y	N	Y
19 Fascell	Y	Y	Y	Y	Y	Y	Y	?
GEORGIA								
1 Thomas	Y	Y	Y	Y	Y	Y	Y	Y
2 Hatcher	Y	Y	Y	Y	Y	?	Y	Y
3 Ray	Y	Y	Y	Y	Y	Y	Y	Y
4 Jones	Y	Y	Y	Y	Y	Y	Y	Y
5 Lewis	Y	Y	Y	Y	Y	Y	Y	Y
6 ***Gingrich***	Y	Y	Y	Y	Y	Y	N	N
7 Darden	Y	Y	Y	Y	Y	Y	Y	Y
8 Rowland	Y	Y	Y	Y	Y	Y	Y	Y
9 Jenkins	Y	Y	Y	Y	Y	Y	Y	Y
10 Barnard	Y	Y	Y	Y	Y	Y	Y	Y
HAWAII								
1 Abercrombie	Y	?	Y	Y	Y	Y	Y	Y
2 Mink	Y	Y	Y	Y	Y	Y	Y	Y
IDAHO								
1 LaRocco	Y	Y	Y	Y	Y	Y	Y	Y
2 Stallings	Y	Y	Y	Y	Y	Y	Y	Y
ILLINOIS								
1 Hayes	Y	Y	Y	Y	Y	Y	Y	Y
2 Savage	Y	Y	Y	Y	Y	Y	Y	Y
3 Russo	Y	Y	Y	Y	Y	Y	Y	Y
4 Sangmeister	Y	Y	Y	Y	Y	Y	Y	Y
5 Lipinski	Y	Y	Y	Y	Y	Y	Y	Y
6 ***Hyde***	Y	Y	Y	Y	Y	Y	Y	N
7 Collins	Y	Y	Y	Y	Y	Y	Y	Y
8 Rostenkowski	Y	Y	Y	Y	Y	Y	Y	Y
9 Yates	Y	Y	Y	Y	Y	?	?	Y
10 ***Porter***	Y	?	Y	Y	Y	Y	N	Y
11 Annunzio	Y	Y	Y	Y	Y	Y	Y	Y
12 ***Crane***	N	Y	Y	N	N	Y	Y	N
13 ***Fawell***	Y	Y	Y	Y	Y	Y	Y	Y
14 ***Hastert***	Y	Y	Y	Y	Y	Y	Y	Y
15 ***Ewing***	Y	Y	Y	Y	Y	Y	Y	Y
16 Cox	Y	Y	Y	Y	Y	Y	Y	Y
17 Evans	Y	Y	Y	Y	Y	Y	Y	Y
18 ***Michel***	Y	Y	Y	Y	Y	Y	Y	Y
19 Bruce	Y	Y	Y	Y	Y	Y	Y	Y
20 Durbin	Y	Y	Y	Y	Y	Y	Y	Y
21 Costello	Y	Y	Y	Y	Y	Y	Y	Y
22 Poshard	Y	Y	Y	Y	Y	Y	Y	Y
INDIANA								
1 Visclosky	Y	Y	Y	Y	Y	Y	Y	Y
2 Sharp	Y	Y	Y	Y	Y	Y	Y	N
3 Roemer	Y	Y	Y	Y	Y	Y	Y	N

ND Northern Democrats SD Southern Democrats

	242	243	244	245	246	247	248	249
4 Long	Y	Y	Y	Y	Y	Y	Y	Y
5 Jontz	Y	Y	Y	Y	Y	Y	Y	N
6 ***Burton***	N	Y	Y	N	Y	Y	N	N
7 ***Myers***	Y	Y	Y	Y	Y	Y	Y	Y
8 McCloskey	Y	Y	Y	Y	Y	Y	Y	Y
9 Hamilton	Y	Y	Y	Y	Y	Y	Y	Y
10 Jacobs	Y	Y	Y	Y	Y	Y	N	N
IOWA								
1 ***Leach***	Y	Y	Y	Y	Y	Y	N	Y
2 ***Nussle***	Y	Y	Y	N	N	N	Y	N
3 Nagle	Y	Y	Y	Y	Y	Y	Y	Y
4 Smith	Y	Y	Y	Y	Y	Y	Y	Y
5 ***Lightfoot***	Y	N	Y	Y	Y	Y	Y	Y
6 ***Grandy***	N	Y	Y	Y	N	Y	Y	Y
KANSAS								
1 ***Roberts***	Y	Y	Y	Y	Y	Y	Y	Y
2 Slattery	Y	Y	Y	N	Y	Y	Y	N
3 ***Meyers***	N	Y	Y	Y	Y	Y	N	Y
4 Glickman	Y	Y	Y	N	Y	Y	Y	N
5 ***Nichols***	Y	Y	Y	Y	Y	Y	Y	Y
KENTUCKY								
1 Hubbard	Y	Y	Y	Y	Y	Y	Y	Y
2 Natcher	Y	Y	Y	Y	Y	Y	Y	Y
3 Mazzoli	Y	Y	Y	Y	Y	Y	Y	Y
4 ***Bunning***	N	Y	Y	Y	Y	Y	N	N
5 ***Rogers***	Y	Y	Y	Y	Y	Y	N	Y
6 ***Hopkins***	?	?	?	?	?	?	?	?
7 Perkins	Y	Y	Y	Y	Y	Y	Y	Y
LOUISIANA								
1 ***Livingston***	N	Y	Y	Y	Y	Y	Y	Y
2 Jefferson	Y	Y	Y	Y	Y	Y	Y	Y
3 Tauzin	?	?	?	?	?	?	?	Y
4 ***McCrery***	Y	Y	Y	Y	Y	Y	Y	Y
5 Huckaby	Y	?	Y	Y	Y	Y	Y	Y
6 ***Baker***	Y	Y	Y	Y	Y	Y	Y	Y
7 Hayes	Y	Y	Y	Y	Y	?	?	Y
8 ***Holloway***	Y	Y	Y	Y	N	N	N	Y
MAINE								
1 Andrews	Y	Y	Y	Y	Y	Y	Y	Y
2 ***Snowe***	Y	Y	Y	Y	Y	Y	Y	N
MARYLAND								
1 ***Gilchrest***	Y	Y	?	Y	Y	N	N	Y
2 ***Bentley***	Y	Y	Y	Y	Y	Y	N	Y
3 Cardin	Y	Y	Y	Y	Y	Y	Y	Y
4 McMillen	Y	Y	Y	Y	Y	Y	Y	Y
5 Hoyer	Y	Y	Y	Y	Y	Y	Y	Y
6 Byron	Y	?	Y	Y	Y	Y	Y	Y
7 Mfume	Y	Y	Y	Y	Y	Y	Y	Y
8 ***Morella***	Y	Y	Y	Y	Y	Y	Y	Y
MASSACHUSETTS								
1 Olver	Y	Y	Y	Y	Y	Y	Y	Y
2 Neal	Y	Y	Y	Y	Y	Y	Y	Y
3 Early	Y	Y	Y	Y	Y	Y	Y	Y
4 Frank	Y	Y	Y	Y	Y	?	Y	Y
5 Atkins	Y	Y	Y	Y	Y	Y	Y	Y
6 Mavroules	Y	Y	Y	Y	Y	Y	Y	Y
7 Markey	Y	Y	Y	Y	Y	Y	Y	Y
8 Kennedy	Y	Y	Y	Y	Y	Y	Y	Y
9 Moakley	Y	Y	Y	Y	Y	Y	Y	Y
10 Studds	Y	Y	Y	Y	Y	Y	Y	Y
11 Donnelly	Y	Y	Y	Y	Y	Y	Y	Y
MICHIGAN								
1 Conyers	Y	?	Y	Y	Y	?	Y	Y
2 ***Pursell***	Y	Y	Y	Y	N	N	N	Y
3 Wolpe	Y	Y	Y	N	Y	Y	Y	Y
4 ***Upton***	Y	Y	Y	Y	Y	Y	Y	N
5 ***Henry***	Y	Y	Y	N	N	N	N	N
6 Carr	Y	Y	Y	Y	Y	Y	Y	Y
7 Kildee	Y	Y	Y	Y	Y	Y	Y	Y
8 Traxler	Y	Y	Y	Y	Y	Y	Y	Y
9 ***Vander Jagt***	Y	Y	Y	Y	Y	Y	N	Y
10 ***Camp***	Y	Y	Y	Y	Y	Y	N	N
11 ***Davis***	Y	Y	Y	Y	Y	Y	Y	Y
12 Bonior	Y	Y	Y	Y	Y	Y	Y	Y
13 Collins	Y	Y	Y	Y	Y	Y	Y	Y
14 Hertel	Y	Y	Y	Y	Y	Y	Y	Y
15 Ford	Y	Y	Y	Y	Y	Y	Y	Y
16 Dingell	Y	Y	Y	Y	Y	Y	Y	Y
17 Levin	Y	Y	Y	Y	Y	Y	Y	Y
18 ***Broomfield***	Y	Y	Y	N	Y	Y	N	N
MINNESOTA								
1 Penny	Y	Y	Y	N	N	Y	Y	N
2 ***Weber***	Y	Y	Y	Y	Y	Y	N	N
3 ***Ramstad***	Y	Y	Y	Y	Y	Y	Y	N
4 Vento	Y	Y	Y	Y	Y	Y	Y	Y

	242	243	244	245	246	247	248	249
5 Sabo	Y	Y	Y	Y	Y	Y	Y	Y
6 Sikorski	Y	Y	Y	Y	Y	Y	Y	N
7 Peterson	Y	Y	Y	Y	Y	Y	Y	Y
8 Oberstar	Y	Y	Y	Y	Y	Y	Y	Y
MISSISSIPPI								
1 Whitten	Y	Y	Y	Y	Y	Y	Y	Y
2 Espy	Y	Y	Y	Y	Y	Y	Y	Y
3 Montgomery	Y	Y	Y	Y	Y	Y	Y	Y
4 Parker	Y	Y	Y	Y	Y	Y	Y	Y
5 Taylor	Y	Y	Y	Y	Y	Y	Y	Y
MISSOURI								
1 Clay	Y	Y	Y	Y	Y	Y	Y	Y
2 Horn	Y	Y	Y	Y	Y	Y	Y	Y
3 Gephardt	Y	Y	Y	Y	Y	Y	Y	?
4 Skelton	Y	?	Y	Y	Y	Y	Y	Y
5 Wheat	Y	Y	Y	Y	Y	Y	Y	Y
6 ***Coleman***	Y	Y	Y	Y	Y	Y	N	N
7 ***Hancock***	N	Y	Y	N	Y	Y	N	N
8 ***Emerson***	Y	Y	Y	Y	Y	Y	N	Y
9 Volkmer	Y	Y	Y	Y	Y	Y	Y	Y
MONTANA								
1 Williams	Y	Y	Y	Y	Y	Y	N	Y
2 ***Marlenee***	Y	Y	Y	Y	Y	Y	Y	Y
NEBRASKA								
1 ***Bereuter***	Y	Y	Y	Y	Y	Y	Y	Y
2 Hoagland	Y	Y	Y	Y	Y	Y	Y	Y
3 ***Barrett***	Y	Y	Y	Y	Y	Y	Y	Y
NEVADA								
1 Bilbray	Y	Y	Y	Y	Y	Y	Y	Y
2 ***Vucanovich***	Y	Y	Y	Y	Y	Y	Y	?
NEW HAMPSHIRE								
1 ***Zeliff***	Y	Y	Y	Y	Y	Y	N	N
2 Swett	Y	Y	Y	Y	Y	Y	Y	Y
NEW JERSEY								
1 Andrews	Y	Y	Y	Y	Y	Y	Y	Y
2 Hughes	Y	Y	Y	Y	Y	Y	Y	Y
3 Pallone	Y	Y	Y	Y	Y	Y	Y	Y
4 ***Smith***	Y	Y	Y	Y	Y	Y	Y	Y
5 ***Roukema***	Y	Y	Y	Y	Y	Y	Y	N
6 Dwyer	Y	Y	Y	Y	Y	Y	Y	Y
7 ***Rinaldo***	Y	Y	Y	Y	Y	Y	Y	Y
8 Roe	Y	Y	Y	Y	Y	Y	Y	Y
9 Torricelli	Y	Y	Y	Y	Y	Y	Y	Y
10 Payne	Y	Y	Y	Y	Y	Y	Y	Y
11 ***Gallo***	Y	Y	Y	Y	Y	Y	Y	Y
12 ***Zimmer***	Y	Y	Y	Y	Y	Y	Y	N
13 ***Saxton***	Y	Y	Y	Y	Y	Y	Y	Y
14 Guarini	Y	Y	Y	Y	Y	Y	Y	?
NEW MEXICO								
1 ***Schiff***	Y	Y	Y	Y	Y	Y	Y	Y
2 ***Skeen***	Y	Y	Y	Y	Y	N	Y	Y
3 Richardson	Y	Y	Y	Y	Y	Y	Y	Y
NEW YORK								
1 Hochbrueckner	Y	?	Y	Y	Y	Y	Y	Y
2 Downey	Y	Y	?	Y	Y	Y	Y	Y
3 Mrazek	Y	Y	Y	Y	Y	Y	Y	Y
4 ***Lent***	Y	Y	Y	Y	Y	Y	Y	Y
5 ***McGrath***	Y	Y	Y	Y	Y	Y	Y	Y
6 Flake	Y	Y	Y	Y	Y	Y	Y	Y
7 Ackerman	Y	Y	Y	Y	Y	Y	Y	Y
8 Scheuer	Y	Y	Y	Y	Y	Y	Y	Y
9 Manton	Y	Y	Y	Y	Y	Y	Y	Y
10 Schumer	Y	Y	Y	Y	Y	Y	Y	Y
11 Towns	Y	Y	Y	Y	Y	Y	Y	Y
12 Owens	Y	Y	Y	Y	Y	Y	Y	Y
13 Solarz	Y	Y	Y	Y	Y	Y	Y	Y
14 ***Molinari***	Y	Y	Y	Y	Y	Y	Y	Y
15 ***Green***	Y	Y	Y	Y	Y	Y	Y	Y
16 Rangel	Y	Y	Y	Y	Y	Y	Y	Y
17 Weiss	Y	Y	Y	Y	Y	Y	Y	Y
18 Serrano	Y	Y	Y	Y	Y	Y	Y	Y
19 Engel	Y	Y	Y	Y	Y	Y	Y	Y
20 Lowey	Y	Y	Y	Y	Y	Y	Y	Y
21 ***Fish***	Y	Y	Y	Y	Y	Y	Y	Y
22 ***Gilman***	Y	Y	Y	Y	Y	Y	N	Y
23 McNulty	Y	Y	Y	Y	Y	Y	Y	Y
24 ***Solomon***	Y	Y	Y	N	Y	N	N	N
25 ***Boehlert***	Y	Y	Y	Y	Y	Y	Y	Y
26 ***Martin***	Y	Y	Y	Y	Y	Y	N	Y
27 ***Walsh***	Y	Y	Y	Y	Y	Y	Y	Y
28 McHugh	Y	Y	Y	Y	Y	Y	Y	Y
29 ***Horton***	Y	Y	Y	Y	Y	Y	?	Y
30 Slaughter	Y	Y	Y	Y	Y	Y	Y	Y
31 ***Paxon***	Y	Y	Y	Y	Y	Y	Y	N

	242	243	244	245	246	247	248	249
32 LaFalce	Y	Y	Y	Y	Y	Y	Y	Y
33 Nowak	Y	Y	Y	Y	Y	?	?	Y
34 ***Houghton***	Y	Y	Y	Y	Y	Y	Y	Y
NORTH CAROLINA								
1 Jones	Y	Y	Y	Y	Y	Y	Y	Y
2 Valentine	Y	Y	?	Y	Y	Y	?	Y
3 Lancaster	Y	Y	Y	Y	Y	Y	Y	Y
4 Price	Y	Y	Y	Y	Y	Y	Y	Y
5 Neal	?	Y	Y	Y	Y	Y	Y	N
6 ***Coble***	Y	Y	Y	N	Y	Y	N	N
7 Rose	Y	Y	Y	Y	Y	Y	Y	Y
8 Hefner	?	?	?	?	?	?	?	?
9 ***McMillan***	Y	Y	Y	Y	Y	Y	N	Y
10 ***Ballenger***	Y	Y	Y	N	Y	N	N	N
11 ***Taylor***	Y	Y	Y	Y	Y	Y	N	N
NORTH DAKOTA								
AL Dorgan	Y	Y	Y	Y	Y	Y	Y	Y
OHIO								
1 Luken	Y	Y	Y	Y	Y	Y	Y	Y
2 ***Gradison***	Y	Y	Y	Y	Y	Y	Y	Y
3 Hall	Y	Y	Y	Y	Y	Y	Y	Y
4 ***Oxley***	Y	Y	Y	Y	Y	Y	Y	N
5 ***Gillmor***	Y	Y	Y	Y	Y	Y	Y	Y
6 ***McEwen***	Y	Y	Y	Y	?	Y	Y	N
7 ***Hobson***	Y	Y	Y	Y	Y	Y	Y	N
8 ***Boehner***	Y	Y	Y	Y	Y	Y	N	N
9 Kaptur	Y	Y	Y	Y	Y	Y	?	?
10 ***Miller***	Y	Y	Y	Y	Y	Y	N	Y
11 Eckart	Y	Y	Y	N	Y	Y	Y	Y
12 ***Kasich***	Y	Y	Y	Y	Y	Y	Y	N
13 Pease	Y	Y	Y	Y	Y	Y	Y	Y
14 Sawyer	Y	Y	Y	Y	Y	Y	Y	Y
15 ***Wylie***	Y	Y	Y	Y	Y	Y	Y	Y
16 ***Regula***	Y	Y	Y	Y	Y	Y	Y	Y
17 Traficant	Y	Y	Y	Y	Y	Y	Y	Y
18 Applegate	Y	Y	Y	Y	Y	Y	Y	Y
19 Feighan	?	?	?	?	?	?	?	Y
20 Oakar	Y	Y	Y	Y	Y	Y	Y	Y
21 Stokes	Y	Y	Y	Y	Y	Y	Y	Y
OKLAHOMA								
1 ***Inhofe***	Y	Y	Y	Y	Y	Y	N	N
2 Synar	Y	Y	Y	Y	Y	Y	Y	Y
3 Brewster	Y	Y	Y	Y	Y	Y	Y	Y
4 McCurdy	Y	Y	Y	Y	Y	?	Y	Y
5 ***Edwards***	Y	Y	Y	Y	Y	Y	N	Y
6 English	Y	Y	Y	Y	Y	Y	Y	Y
OREGON								
1 AuCoin	Y	Y	Y	Y	Y	Y	Y	Y
2 ***Smith***	Y	Y	Y	Y	Y	Y	Y	Y
3 Wyden	Y	Y	Y	Y	Y	Y	Y	Y
4 DeFazio	Y	Y	Y	Y	Y	Y	Y	Y
5 Kopetski	Y	Y	Y	Y	Y	Y	Y	Y
PENNSYLVANIA								
1 Foglietta	Y	Y	Y	Y	Y	Y	Y	Y
2 Gray	Y	Y	Y	Y	Y	?	?	Y
3 Borski	Y	Y	Y	Y	Y	Y	Y	?
4 Kolter	Y	Y	Y	Y	Y	Y	Y	Y
5 ***Schulze***	Y	Y	Y	Y	Y	Y	Y	Y
6 Yatron	?	?	?	?	?	?	?	?
7 ***Weldon***	Y	Y	Y	Y	Y	Y	N	N
8 Kostmayer	Y	Y	Y	Y	Y	Y	Y	Y
9 ***Shuster***	Y	Y	Y	Y	Y	Y	Y	Y
10 ***McDade***	Y	Y	Y	Y	Y	Y	Y	?
11 Kanjorski	Y	Y	Y	Y	Y	Y	Y	Y
12 Murtha	Y	Y	Y	Y	Y	Y	?	Y
13 ***Coughlin***	Y	Y	Y	Y	Y	Y	N	Y
14 Coyne	Y	Y	Y	Y	Y	Y	Y	Y
15 ***Ritter***	Y	Y	Y	N	Y	Y	Y	N
16 ***Walker***	N	Y	Y	N	Y	N	N	N
17 ***Gekas***	N	Y	Y	Y	Y	N	N	N
18 ***Santorum***	Y	Y	Y	N	Y	Y	N	N
19 ***Goodling***	Y	Y	Y	Y	Y	N	?	N
20 Gaydos	Y	Y	Y	Y	Y	Y	Y	Y
21 ***Ridge***	Y	?	Y	Y	N	Y	N	Y
22 Murphy	Y	Y	Y	Y	?	Y	Y	Y
23 ***Clinger***	Y	Y	Y	Y	Y	Y	Y	Y
RHODE ISLAND								
1 ***Machtley***	Y	Y	Y	Y	Y	Y	Y	Y
2 Reed	Y	Y	Y	Y	Y	Y	Y	Y
SOUTH CAROLINA								
1 ***Ravenel***	Y	Y	Y	Y	Y	Y	Y	Y
2 ***Spence***	Y	Y	Y	Y	Y	Y	Y	Y
3 Derrick	Y	Y	Y	Y	Y	Y	Y	Y
4 Patterson	Y	Y	Y	N	Y	Y	Y	N
5 Spratt	Y	Y	Y	Y	Y	Y	Y	Y
6 Tallon	Y	Y	Y	Y	Y	Y	Y	Y

	242	243	244	245	246	247	248	249
SOUTH DAKOTA								
AL Johnson	Y	Y	Y	Y	Y	Y	Y	Y
TENNESSEE								
1 ***Quillen***	Y	Y	Y	Y	Y	N	Y	Y
2 ***Duncan***	Y	Y	Y	N	Y	Y	N	N
3 Lloyd	Y	Y	Y	Y	Y	Y	Y	Y
4 Cooper	Y	Y	Y	Y	Y	Y	Y	Y
5 Clement	Y	Y	Y	Y	Y	?	?	?
6 Gordon	Y	Y	Y	Y	Y	Y	Y	Y
7 ***Sundquist***	Y	Y	Y	Y	Y	Y	Y	Y
8 Tanner	Y	Y	Y	Y	Y	Y	Y	Y
9 Ford	Y	Y	Y	Y	?	Y	Y	Y
TEXAS								
1 Chapman	Y	?	Y	Y	Y	Y	Y	Y
2 Wilson	Y	Y	Y	Y	Y	Y	Y	Y
3 ***Johnson***	Y	Y	Y	Y	Y	Y	Y	N
4 Hall	Y	Y	Y	Y	Y	Y	Y	Y
5 Bryant	Y	Y	Y	Y	Y	Y	Y	Y
6 ***Barton***	Y	Y	Y	Y	Y	Y	N	Y
7 ***Archer***	Y	Y	Y	N	Y	Y	Y	N
8 ***Fields***	Y	Y	Y	Y	Y	Y	N	N
9 Brooks	Y	Y	Y	Y	Y	Y	Y	Y
10 Pickle	Y	Y	Y	Y	Y	Y	Y	Y
11 Edwards	Y	Y	Y	Y	Y	Y	Y	Y
12 Geren	Y	Y	Y	Y	Y	Y	Y	Y
13 Sarpalius	Y	Y	Y	Y	Y	Y	Y	Y
14 Laughlin	Y	Y	Y	Y	Y	Y	Y	Y
15 de la Garza	Y	Y	Y	Y	Y	Y	Y	Y
16 Coleman	Y	Y	?	Y	Y	Y	Y	Y
17 Stenholm	Y	Y	Y	Y	Y	Y	Y	Y
18 Washington	Y	Y	Y	Y	Y	?	?	Y
19 ***Combest***	Y	Y	Y	Y	Y	Y	Y	Y
20 Gonzalez	Y	Y	Y	Y	Y	Y	Y	Y
21 ***Smith***	Y	Y	Y	Y	Y	Y	Y	N
22 ***DeLay***	N	Y	Y	Y	Y	Y	N	Y
23 Bustamante	?	?	?	?	?	?	?	?
24 Frost	Y	Y	Y	Y	Y	Y	Y	Y
25 Andrews	Y	Y	Y	Y	Y	Y	Y	Y
26 ***Armey***	N	Y	Y	N	Y	Y	N	N
27 Ortiz	Y	Y	Y	Y	Y	Y	Y	?
UTAH								
1 ***Hansen***	Y	Y	Y	Y	Y	Y	Y	Y
2 Owens	Y	Y	Y	Y	Y	Y	Y	Y
3 Orton	Y	Y	Y	Y	N	Y	Y	Y
VERMONT								
AL *Sanders*	Y	?	?	N	Y	Y	Y	Y
VIRGINIA								
1 ***Bateman***	Y	?	Y	Y	Y	Y	Y	Y
2 Pickett	Y	Y	Y	Y	Y	Y	Y	Y
3 ***Bliley***	Y	Y	Y	Y	Y	Y	N	Y
4 Sisisky	Y	Y	Y	Y	Y	Y	Y	Y
5 Payne	Y	Y	Y	Y	Y	Y	Y	Y
6 Olin	Y	Y	Y	Y	Y	?	?	Y
7 ***Slaughter***	Y	Y	Y	Y	Y	Y	Y	N
8 Moran	Y	Y	Y	Y	Y	Y	Y	Y
9 Boucher	Y	?	Y	Y	Y	Y	Y	Y
10 ***Wolf***	Y	Y	Y	Y	Y	Y	N	Y
WASHINGTON								
1 ***Miller***	Y	Y	Y	Y	Y	Y	Y	N
2 Swift	Y	Y	Y	Y	Y	Y	Y	Y
3 Unsoeld	Y	?	Y	?	Y	Y	Y	Y
4 ***Morrison***	Y	Y	Y	Y	Y	Y	Y	Y
5 Foley								
6 Dicks	Y	Y	Y	Y	Y	Y	Y	Y
7 McDermott	Y	Y	Y	Y	Y	Y	Y	Y
8 ***Chandler***	Y	Y	Y	Y	Y	Y	N	Y
WEST VIRGINIA								
1 Mollohan	Y	Y	Y	Y	Y	Y	Y	Y
2 Staggers	Y	Y	Y	Y	Y	Y	Y	Y
3 Wise	Y	Y	Y	Y	Y	Y	Y	Y
4 Rahall	Y	Y	Y	Y	Y	Y	Y	Y
WISCONSIN								
1 Aspin	Y	Y	Y	Y	Y	Y	Y	Y
2 ***Klug***	Y	Y	Y	Y	N	N	N	N
3 ***Gunderson***	Y	N	Y	Y	N	N	Y	Y
4 Kleczka	Y	Y	Y	Y	Y	Y	Y	Y
5 Moody	Y	Y	Y	Y	Y	Y	Y	Y
6 ***Petri***	Y	Y	Y	N	N	N	N	N
7 Obey	Y	Y	Y	Y	Y	Y	Y	Y
8 ***Roth***	Y	Y	Y	Y	N	Y	N	N
9 ***Sensenbrenner***	Y	Y	Y	N	N	N	N	N
WYOMING								
AL ***Thomas***	Y	Y	Y	Y	Y	Y	Y	Y

Southern states - Ala., Ark., Fla., Ga., Ky., La., Miss., N.C., Okla., S.C., Tenn., Texas, Va.
Omitted votes are quorum calls, which CQ does not include in its vote charts.

HOUSE VOTES 250, 251, 253, 254, 256, 257, 258, 259

250. HR 14. Flight Attendant Duty Time/Passage. Passage of the bill to require the Department of Transportation to issue regulations that limit the amount of time airline attendants can be required to work. Passed 228-195: R 29-134; D 198-61 (ND 162-14, SD 36-47); I 1-0, Aug. 1, 1991. A "nay" was a vote supporting the president's position.

251. HR 2699. Fiscal 1992 D.C. Appropriations/Conference Report. Adoption of the conference report to provide $699,850,000 in federal funds for the District of Columbia and to approve spending $3,895,771,946 in funds raised from local taxes for the District of Columbia in fiscal 1992. The bill provides for a $630.5 million federal payment to the District. The administration requested $682,570,000 in federal funds and approval of $3,879,866,946 in funds raised from local taxes. The bill would prohibit the use of federal funds for abortions but would allow the District to use locally raised taxes for abortions. Adopted 239-180: R 39-122; D 199-58 (ND 137-38, SD 62-20); I 1-0, Aug. 1, 1991. A "nay" was a vote supporting the president's position.

253. HR 3201. Extended Unemployment Benefits/Passage. Passage of the bill to provide an estimated $5.3 billion in temporary unemployment benefits for workers who have exhausted regular benefits until July 4, 1992. The bill requires the president to declare an emergency for the bill to take effect. Passed 375-45: R 118-44; D 256-1 (ND 174-1, SD 82-0); I 1-0, Aug. 2, 1991. A "nay" was a vote supporting the president's position.

254. Procedural Motion. Riggs, R-Calif., motion to approve the House Journal of Wednesday, Sept. 11. Motion agreed to 277-94: R 56-90; D 220-4 (ND 147-4, SD 73-0); I 1-0, Sept. 12, 1991.

256. HR 2967. Older Americans Reauthorization/Social Security Earnings Test. Hastert, R-Ill., amendment to express the sense of Congress that the 1993 White House Conference on Aging should consider the impact of the Social Security earnings test on older workers. Adopted 383-0: R 147-0; D 235-0 (ND 160-0, SD 75-0); I 1-0, Sept. 12, 1991.

257. HR 2967. Older Americans Reauthorization/Passage. Passage of the bill to reauthorize for four years through fiscal 1995 the Older Americans Act of 1965, which covers federal meals, transportation and employment aid programs for the elderly poor. Passed 385-0: R 148-0; D 236-0 (ND 159-0, SD 77-0); I 1-0, Sept. 12, 1991.

258. Procedural Motion. Walker, R-Pa., motion to approve the House Journal of Thursday, Sept. 12. Motion agreed to 211-87: R 33-84; D 178-3 (ND 121-3, SD 57-0), Sept. 16, 1991.

259. HR 3040. Unemployment Benefits Extension. Bonior, D-Mich., motion to order the previous question (thus ending debate and the possibility of amendment) on the rule (H Res 221) to provide for House floor consideration of the bill to permanently extend unemployment benefits to long-term unemployed workers for up to 20 additional weeks at an estimated cost of $6.3 billion through fiscal 1996. The bill automatically declares the benefits as emergency spending and would not require a presidential declaration to be exempt from the spending requirements of last year's budget agreement. Motion agreed to 214-141: R 0-137; D 213-4 (ND 146-4, SD 67-0); I 1-0, Sept. 16, 1991.

† Rep. William H. Gray III resigned Sept. 4, 1991, to become the president of the United Negro College Fund. The last vote he was eligible for was vote 253.

KEY

- Y Voted for (yea).
- # Paired for.
- + Announced for.
- N Voted against (nay).
- X Paired against.
- \- Announced against.
- P Voted "present."
- C Voted "present" to avoid possible conflict of interest.
- ? Did not vote or otherwise make a position known.

Democrats ***Republicans***
Independent

	250	251	253	254	256	257	258	259
ALABAMA								
1 ***Callahan***	N	N	Y	Y	Y	Y	Y	N
2 ***Dickinson***	N	Y	Y	N	Y	Y	N	N
3 Browder	N	Y	Y	Y	Y	Y	Y	Y
4 Bevill	N	N	Y	Y	Y	Y	Y	Y
5 Cramer	N	Y	Y	Y	Y	Y	Y	Y
6 Erdreich	N	Y	Y	Y	Y	Y	Y	Y
7 Harris	N	Y	Y	Y	Y	Y	Y	Y
ALASKA								
AL ***Young***	Y	N	Y	N	Y	Y	N	N
ARIZONA								
1 ***Rhodes***	N	N	Y	N	Y	Y	N	N
2 Vacancy								
3 ***Stump***	N	N	N	N	Y	Y	N	N
4 ***Kyl***	N	N	Y	N	Y	Y	N	N
5 ***Kolbe***	N	Y	Y	N	Y	Y	N	N
ARKANSAS								
1 Alexander	Y	Y	Y	Y	Y	Y	?	?
2 Thornton	Y	Y	Y	Y	Y	Y	Y	Y
3 ***Hammerschmidt***	Y	N	Y	Y	Y	Y	Y	N
4 Anthony	N	Y	Y	Y	Y	Y	Y	Y
CALIFORNIA								
1 ***Riggs***	N	Y	Y	N	Y	Y	?	?
2 ***Herger***	N	N	Y	?	?	?	?	?
3 Matsui	?	?	?	Y	Y	Y	Y	Y
4 Fazio	Y	Y	Y	?	?	?	?	#
5 Pelosi	Y	Y	Y	Y	Y	Y	Y	Y
6 Boxer	Y	Y	Y	Y	Y	Y	Y	Y
7 Miller	Y	Y	Y	?	Y	Y	?	?
8 Dellums	Y	Y	Y	Y	Y	Y	Y	Y
9 Stark	Y	Y	Y	?	?	?	?	Y
10 Edwards	Y	Y	Y	Y	Y	Y	Y	Y
11 Lantos	Y	Y	Y	Y	Y	Y	?	?
12 ***Campbell***	N	Y	N	N	Y	Y	?	?
13 Mineta	Y	Y	Y	Y	Y	Y	?	Y
14 ***Doolittle***	N	N	Y	?	?	?	?	X
15 Condit	Y	Y	Y	Y	Y	?	?	Y
16 Panetta	Y	Y	Y	Y	Y	Y	Y	Y
17 Dooley	Y	Y	Y	Y	Y	Y	Y	Y
18 Lehman	Y	Y	?	?	?	?	Y	Y
19 ***Lagomarsino***	N	N	Y	N	Y	Y	N	N
20 ***Thomas***	N	Y	Y	?	?	?	?	X
21 ***Gallegly***	N	N	Y	?	+	+	N	N
22 ***Moorhead***	N	N	N	N	Y	Y	N	N
23 Beilenson	Y	Y	Y	Y	Y	Y	Y	Y
24 Waxman	Y	Y	Y	Y	Y	Y	Y	Y
25 Roybal	Y	Y	Y	Y	Y	Y	?	?
26 Berman	Y	Y	Y	?	?	?	?	#
27 Levine	Y	Y	Y	?	?	?	Y	Y
28 Dixon	Y	Y	Y	?	Y	Y	Y	Y
29 Waters	Y	Y	Y	?	?	Y	?	Y
30 Martinez	Y	?	?	Y	Y	Y	?	?
31 Dymally	Y	Y	Y	?	Y	?	Y	Y
32 Anderson	Y	Y	Y	Y	Y	Y	Y	Y
33 ***Dreier***	N	N	N	?	?	?	N	N
34 Torres	Y	Y	Y	Y	Y	Y	Y	Y
35 ***Lewis***	N	Y	N	?	?	?	?	?
36 Brown	Y	Y	Y	Y	Y	Y	?	?
37 ***McCandless***	N	N	N	N	Y	Y	N	N
38 ***Dornan***	N	N	N	N	Y	Y	?	N
39 ***Dannemeyer***	N	N	N	-	+	+	N	N
40 ***Cox***	N	N	N	N	Y	Y	N	N
41 ***Lowery***	N	N	Y	?	?	?	?	?
42 ***Rohrabacher***	N	N	N	N	Y	Y	N	N
43 ***Packard***	N	N	N	Y	Y	Y	?	X
44 ***Cunningham***	N	N	Y	-	Y	Y	N	N
45 ***Hunter***	N	N	N	?	?	?	?	?
COLORADO								
1 Schroeder	Y	Y	Y	N	Y	Y	N	Y
2 Skaggs	Y	Y	Y	Y	Y	Y	Y	Y
3 Campbell	Y	Y	Y	Y	Y	Y	?	Y
4 ***Allard***	N	N	N	N	Y	Y	N	N
5 ***Hefley***	N	N	Y	N	Y	Y	N	N
6 ***Schaefer***	Y	N	Y	N	Y	Y	N	N
CONNECTICUT								
1 Kennelly	Y	Y	Y	Y	Y	Y	Y	Y
2 Gejdenson	Y	Y	Y	Y	Y	Y	Y	Y
3 DeLauro	Y	Y	Y	Y	Y	Y	Y	Y
4 ***Shays***	N	Y	Y	N	Y	Y	N	N
5 ***Franks***	N	Y	Y	N	Y	Y	N	N
6 ***Johnson***	Y	Y	Y	Y	Y	+	Y	N
DELAWARE								
AL Carper	Y	Y	Y	Y	Y	Y	Y	Y
FLORIDA								
1 Hutto	N	N	Y	Y	Y	Y	?	?
2 Peterson	N	Y	Y	Y	Y	Y	Y	Y
3 Bennett	Y	Y	Y	Y	Y	Y	Y	Y
4 ***James***	N	N	Y	N	Y	Y	N	N
5 ***McCollum***	N	N	Y	N	Y	Y	?	X
6 ***Stearns***	N	N	Y	N	Y	Y	N	N
7 Gibbons	N	Y	Y	Y	?	?	Y	Y
8 ***Young***	N	N	Y	Y	Y	Y	?	N
9 ***Bilirakis***	N	N	Y	N	Y	Y	N	N
10 ***Ireland***	N	N	N	?	?	?	N	N
11 Bacchus	Y	Y	Y	Y	Y	Y	Y	Y
12 ***Lewis***	N	N	Y	N	Y	Y	N	N
13 ***Goss***	N	N	N	N	Y	Y	N	N
14 Johnston	Y	Y	Y	Y	Y	Y	Y	Y
15 ***Shaw***	N	N	N	Y	Y	Y	Y	N
16 Smith	Y	Y	Y	Y	Y	Y	Y	Y
17 Lehman	Y	Y	Y	?	?	?	?	?
18 ***Ros-Lehtinen***	N	N	Y	N	Y	Y	N	N
19 Fascell	Y	Y	Y	Y	?	Y	Y	Y
GEORGIA								
1 Thomas	N	Y	Y	Y	Y	Y	?	?
2 Hatcher	N	Y	Y	?	?	?	?	?
3 Ray	N	N	Y	?	?	?	?	Y
4 Jones	N	Y	Y	Y	Y	Y	Y	Y
5 Lewis	N	Y	Y	Y	Y	Y	Y	Y
6 ***Gingrich***	N	N	Y	N	Y	Y	N	N
7 Darden	N	Y	Y	Y	Y	Y	Y	Y
8 Rowland	N	Y	Y	Y	Y	Y	?	?
9 Jenkins	N	Y	Y	Y	?	Y	?	?
10 Barnard	N	Y	?	Y	Y	Y	?	?
HAWAII								
1 Abercrombie	Y	Y	Y	Y	Y	Y	Y	Y
2 Mink	Y	Y	Y	Y	Y	Y	Y	Y
IDAHO								
1 LaRocco	Y	Y	Y	Y	Y	Y	Y	Y
2 Stallings	Y	N	Y	Y	Y	Y	?	?
ILLINOIS								
1 Hayes	Y	Y	Y	Y	Y	Y	Y	Y
2 Savage	Y	Y	Y	?	Y	Y	Y	Y
3 Russo	Y	N	Y	Y	Y	Y	Y	Y
4 Sangmeister	Y	N	Y	Y	Y	Y	Y	Y
5 Lipinski	Y	N	Y	Y	Y	?	Y	Y
6 ***Hyde***	N	N	Y	?	Y	Y	N	N
7 Collins	Y	Y	Y	Y	Y	Y	Y	Y
8 Rostenkowski	N	N	Y	Y	Y	Y	Y	Y
9 Yates	Y	Y	Y	Y	Y	Y	Y	Y
10 ***Porter***	N	N	N	Y	Y	Y	?	N
11 Annunzio	Y	N	Y	Y	Y	Y	Y	Y
12 ***Crane***	N	N	N	?	?	?	?	N
13 ***Fawell***	N	Y	N	N	Y	Y	N	N
14 ***Hastert***	N	N	Y	N	Y	Y	?	?
15 ***Ewing***	N	N	Y	N	Y	Y	N	N
16 Cox	Y	Y	Y	Y	Y	Y	Y	Y
17 Evans	Y	Y	Y	Y	Y	Y	Y	Y
18 ***Michel***	N	N	Y	Y	Y	Y	N	N
19 Bruce	Y	N	Y	Y	Y	Y	Y	Y
20 Durbin	Y	Y	Y	Y	Y	Y	Y	Y
21 Costello	Y	N	Y	Y	Y	Y	Y	Y
22 Poshard	Y	N	Y	Y	Y	Y	Y	Y
INDIANA								
1 Visclosky	Y	Y	Y	Y	Y	Y	Y	Y
2 Sharp	Y	Y	Y	Y	Y	Y	Y	Y
3 Roemer	N	N	Y	Y	Y	Y	Y	Y

ND Northern Democrats SD Southern Democrats

	250	251	253	254	256	257	258	259
4 Long	Y	Y	Y	Y	Y	Y	Y	Y
5 Jontz	Y	Y	Y	Y	Y	Y	Y	Y
6 **Burton**	N	N	N	N	Y	Y	N	N
7 **Myers**	N	N	Y	Y	Y	Y	Y	N
8 McCloskey	Y	Y	Y	Y	Y	Y	?	?
9 Hamilton	N	Y	Y	Y	Y	Y	Y	N
10 Jacobs	Y	Y	Y	N	Y	Y	N	N
IOWA								
1 **Leach**	N	N	Y	N	Y	Y	N	N
2 **Nussle**	N	N	N	N	Y	Y	N	N
3 Nagle	Y	Y	Y	?	Y	Y	Y	Y
4 Smith	Y	Y	Y	Y	Y	Y	Y	Y
5 **Lightfoot**	N	N	Y	N	Y	Y	N	N
6 **Grandy**	N	N	Y	N	Y	Y	N	N
KANSAS								
1 **Roberts**	N	N	Y	N	Y	Y	?	N
2 Slattery	Y	N	Y	Y	Y	Y	Y	Y
3 **Meyers**	Y	Y	Y	Y	Y	Y	N	N
4 Glickman	N	N	Y	Y	Y	Y	Y	Y
5 **Nichols**	N	N	Y	Y	Y	Y	?	N
KENTUCKY								
1 Hubbard	Y	Y	Y	Y	Y	Y	Y	Y
2 Natcher	Y	Y	Y	Y	Y	Y	Y	Y
3 Mazzoli	Y	N	Y	Y	Y	Y	Y	Y
4 **Bunning**	N	N	Y	N	Y	Y	N	N
5 **Rogers**	N	N	Y	N	Y	Y	N	N
6 **Hopkins**	?	?	?	?	?	?	?	?
7 Perkins	Y	N	Y	Y	Y	Y	Y	Y
LOUISIANA								
1 **Livingston**	N	N	N	N	Y	Y	Y	N
2 Jefferson	Y	Y	Y	Y	Y	Y	Y	Y
3 Tauzin	N	N	Y	Y	Y	Y	?	Y
4 **McCrery**	N	N	?	Y	Y	Y	?	?
5 Huckaby	N	N	Y	Y	Y	Y	Y	Y
6 **Baker**	N	N	N	N	Y	Y	N	N
7 Hayes	N	N	Y	Y	?	?	Y	Y
8 **Holloway**	?	?	?	?	?	?	?	?
MAINE								
1 Andrews	Y	Y	Y	Y	Y	Y	Y	Y
2 **Snowe**	Y	Y	Y	Y	Y	Y	Y	N
MARYLAND								
1 **Gilchrest**	N	Y	Y	N	Y	Y	N	N
2 **Bentley**	N	N	Y	N	Y	Y	N	N
3 Cardin	Y	Y	Y	Y	Y	Y	Y	Y
4 McMillen	Y	Y	Y	Y	Y	Y	Y	N
5 Hoyer	Y	Y	Y	Y	Y	Y	?	Y
6 Byron	N	N	Y	Y	Y	Y	?	Y
7 Mfume	Y	Y	Y	Y	?	?	?	Y
8 **Morella**	Y	Y	Y	Y	Y	Y	?	N
MASSACHUSETTS								
1 Olver	Y	Y	Y	Y	Y	Y	?	Y
2 Neal	Y	Y	Y	Y	Y	?	Y	Y
3 Early	Y	Y	Y	Y	Y	Y	Y	Y
4 Frank	N	Y	Y	Y	Y	Y	Y	Y
5 Atkins	Y	Y	Y	Y	Y	Y	?	Y
6 Mavroules	Y	N	Y	Y	Y	Y	?	?
7 Markey	Y	Y	Y	?	Y	?	Y	Y
8 Kennedy	Y	Y	Y	Y	Y	Y	?	Y
9 Moakley	Y	Y	Y	Y	Y	Y	Y	Y
10 Studds	Y	Y	Y	Y	Y	Y	Y	Y
11 Donnelly	Y	N	Y	Y	Y	Y	Y	Y
MICHIGAN								
1 Conyers	Y	Y	Y	?	Y	Y	?	?
2 **Pursell**	N	N	Y	N	Y	Y	?	?
3 Wolpe	Y	Y	Y	Y	Y	Y	Y	Y
4 **Upton**	N	N	Y	N	Y	Y	N	N
5 **Henry**	N	N	Y	N	Y	Y	N	N
6 Carr	N	Y	Y	Y	Y	Y	?	?
7 Kildee	Y	N	Y	Y	Y	Y	Y	Y
8 Traxler	Y	Y	?	Y	Y	Y	?	Y
9 **Vander Jagt**	N	N	Y	Y	Y	Y	Y	N
10 **Camp**	N	N	Y	N	Y	Y	N	N
11 **Davis**	Y	N	Y	Y	?	?	Y	N
12 Bonior	Y	Y	Y	Y	Y	Y	Y	Y
13 Collins	Y	Y	Y	?	Y	Y	Y	Y
14 Hertel	Y	Y	Y	Y	Y	Y	?	Y
15 Ford	Y	Y	Y	?	Y	Y	?	?
16 Dingell	Y	Y	Y	Y	Y	Y	Y	Y
17 Levin	Y	Y	Y	Y	Y	Y	Y	Y
18 **Broomfield**	N	N	N	Y	Y	Y	N	N
MINNESOTA								
1 Penny	N	N	N	Y	Y	Y	Y	Y
2 **Weber**	N	N	Y	Y	Y	Y	N	N
3 **Ramstad**	Y	N	N	N	Y	Y	N	N
4 Vento	Y	Y	Y	Y	Y	Y	Y	Y

	250	251	253	254	256	257	258	259
5 Sabo	Y	Y	Y	Y	Y	Y	?	?
6 Sikorski	Y	Y	Y	N	Y	Y	N	Y
7 Peterson	Y	N	Y	Y	Y	Y	Y	Y
8 Oberstar	Y	N	Y	Y	Y	Y	Y	Y
MISSISSIPPI								
1 Whitten	Y	Y	Y	Y	Y	Y	?	?
2 Espy	N	Y	Y	Y	Y	Y	?	?
3 Montgomery	N	N	Y	Y	Y	Y	Y	Y
4 Parker	N	N	Y	Y	Y	Y	Y	Y
5 Taylor	N	N	Y	Y	Y	Y	Y	Y
MISSOURI								
1 Clay	Y	Y	Y	N	Y	Y	?	?
2 Horn	Y	Y	Y	Y	Y	Y	Y	Y
3 Gephardt	Y	Y	Y	Y	?	?	Y	Y
4 Skelton	Y	N	Y	Y	Y	Y	Y	Y
5 Wheat	Y	Y	Y	Y	Y	Y	Y	Y
6 **Coleman**	Y	N	Y	N	Y	Y	N	N
7 **Hancock**	N	N	N	N	Y	Y	N	N
8 **Emerson**	Y	N	Y	?	Y	Y	Y	N
9 Volkmer	Y	N	Y	Y	Y	Y	Y	Y
MONTANA								
1 Williams	Y	Y	Y	Y	Y	Y	?	?
2 **Marlenee**	N	N	Y	?	?	?	?	?
NEBRASKA								
1 **Bereuter**	N	N	Y	N	Y	Y	N	N
2 Hoagland	N	Y	Y	Y	Y	Y	Y	Y
3 **Barrett**	N	N	N	N	Y	Y	N	N
NEVADA								
1 Bilbray	Y	Y	Y	Y	Y	Y	Y	Y
2 **Vucanovich**	N	N	N	N	Y	Y	N	N
NEW HAMPSHIRE								
1 **Zeliff**	N	N	N	N	Y	Y	?	X
2 Swett	Y	N	Y	Y	Y	Y	Y	Y
NEW JERSEY								
1 Andrews	Y	Y	Y	?	Y	Y	Y	N
2 Hughes	Y	N	Y	Y	Y	Y	Y	Y
3 Pallone	Y	Y	Y	Y	Y	Y	Y	Y
4 **Smith**	Y	N	Y	Y	Y	Y	?	N
5 **Roukema**	Y	Y	Y	N	Y	Y	?	N
6 Dwyer	Y	Y	Y	Y	Y	Y	Y	Y
7 **Rinaldo**	Y	N	Y	Y	Y	Y	Y	N
8 Roe	Y	Y	Y	?	Y	Y	Y	Y
9 Torricelli	Y	Y	Y	Y	Y	Y	Y	Y
10 Payne	Y	Y	Y	P	?	?	Y	Y
11 **Gallo**	N	Y	Y	N	Y	Y	N	N
12 **Zimmer**	N	Y	Y	N	Y	Y	?	N
13 **Saxton**	N	N	Y	N	Y	Y	?	?
14 Guarini	?	Y	Y	Y	Y	Y	?	Y
NEW MEXICO								
1 **Schiff**	N	Y	Y	Y	Y	Y	?	N
2 **Skeen**	N	Y	Y	Y	Y	Y	N	N
3 Richardson	Y	Y	Y	Y	Y	Y	Y	Y
NEW YORK								
1 Hochbrueckner	Y	N	Y	Y	Y	Y	Y	Y
2 Downey	Y	Y	Y	Y	Y	Y	Y	Y
3 Mrazek	Y	?	Y	Y	?	Y	Y	?
4 **Lent**	N	N	Y	?	?	Y	Y	N
5 **McGrath**	Y	X	Y	Y	Y	Y	?	?
6 Flake	Y	Y	Y	Y	Y	Y	Y	Y
7 Ackerman	Y	Y	Y	Y	Y	Y	?	?
8 Scheuer	Y	Y	Y	Y	Y	Y	Y	Y
9 Manton	Y	Y	Y	Y	Y	Y	Y	Y
10 Schumer	Y	Y	Y	Y	Y	Y	Y	Y
11 Towns	Y	Y	Y	?	?	?	?	?
12 Owens	Y	Y	Y	?	?	Y	?	Y
13 Solarz	Y	Y	Y	Y	Y	Y	Y	Y
14 **Molinari**	Y	Y	Y	N	Y	Y	N	N
15 **Green**	Y	Y	Y	Y	Y	Y	Y	N
16 Rangel	Y	Y	Y	Y	?	?	?	Y
17 Weiss	Y	Y	Y	Y	Y	Y	+	+
18 Serrano	Y	Y	Y	?	?	?	Y	Y
19 Engel	Y	Y	Y	?	Y	Y	?	Y
20 Lowey	Y	Y	Y	Y	Y	Y	?	Y
21 **Fish**	N	N	Y	Y	Y	Y	Y	N
22 **Gilman**	Y	Y	Y	Y	Y	Y	Y	N
23 McNulty	Y	Y	Y	Y	Y	Y	Y	Y
24 **Solomon**	N	N	Y	N	Y	Y	N	N
25 **Boehlert**	Y	Y	Y	N	Y	Y	N	N
26 **Martin**	N	Y	Y	Y	Y	Y	?	?
27 **Walsh**	Y	N	Y	Y	Y	Y	Y	N
28 McHugh	Y	Y	Y	Y	Y	Y	?	?
29 **Horton**	Y	Y	Y	Y	Y	Y	?	N
30 Slaughter	Y	Y	Y	Y	Y	Y	Y	Y
31 **Paxon**	N	N	Y	N	Y	Y	N	N

	250	251	253	254	256	257	258	259
32 LaFalce	Y	N	Y	Y	Y	Y	Y	Y
33 Nowak	Y	N	Y	?	Y	Y	Y	Y
34 **Houghton**	Y	Y	Y	?	Y	Y	?	?
NORTH CAROLINA								
1 Jones	Y	Y	Y	?	?	?	?	?
2 Valentine	N	Y	Y	Y	Y	Y	?	Y
3 Lancaster	N	Y	Y	Y	Y	Y	Y	Y
4 Price	Y	Y	Y	Y	Y	Y	Y	Y
5 Neal	N	Y	Y	Y	Y	Y	?	Y
6 **Coble**	N	N	Y	N	Y	Y	N	N
7 Rose	Y	Y	Y	Y	Y	Y	Y	Y
8 Hefner	?	?	?	Y	Y	Y	Y	Y
9 **McMillan**	N	N	Y	Y	Y	Y	Y	N
10 **Ballenger**	N	N	Y	N	Y	Y	N	N
11 **Taylor**	N	N	Y	N	Y	Y	N	N
NORTH DAKOTA								
AL Dorgan	N	Y	Y	Y	Y	Y	Y	Y
OHIO								
1 Luken	N	N	Y	Y	Y	Y	Y	Y
2 **Gradison**	N	Y	N	Y	Y	Y	N	N
3 Hall	Y	Y	Y	Y	Y	Y	Y	Y
4 **Oxley**	N	N	Y	Y	Y	Y	Y	N
5 **Gillmor**	N	N	Y	?	Y	Y	Y	N
6 **McEwen**	N	N	Y	Y	Y	Y	?	?
7 **Hobson**	N	Y	Y	N	Y	Y	N	N
8 **Boehner**	N	N	N	N	Y	Y	N	N
9 Kaptur	?	#	Y	Y	Y	?	Y	Y
10 **Miller**	N	N	Y	N	Y	Y	N	N
11 Eckart	Y	Y	Y	Y	Y	Y	Y	Y
12 **Kasich**	N	N	Y	Y	Y	Y	?	N
13 Pease	Y	Y	Y	Y	Y	Y	Y	Y
14 Sawyer	Y	Y	Y	Y	Y	Y	?	Y
15 **Wylie**	N	N	Y	Y	Y	Y	Y	N
16 **Regula**	Y	Y	Y	N	Y	Y	N	N
17 Traficant	Y	Y	Y	Y	Y	Y	Y	Y
18 Applegate	Y	N	Y	Y	Y	Y	?	?
19 Feighan	Y	Y	Y	Y	Y	Y	?	Y
20 Oakar	Y	Y	Y	Y	Y	Y	?	Y
21 Stokes	Y	Y	Y	?	Y	Y	Y	Y
OKLAHOMA								
1 **Inhofe**	N	N	Y	N	Y	Y	N	N
2 Synar	N	Y	Y	Y	Y	Y	Y	Y
3 Brewster	Y	Y	Y	?	Y	Y	?	Y
4 McCurdy	N	Y	Y	Y	Y	Y	Y	Y
5 **Edwards**	N	X	Y	Y	Y	Y	N	N
6 English	N	N	Y	Y	Y	Y	Y	Y
OREGON								
1 AuCoin	Y	Y	Y	Y	Y	Y	Y	Y
2 **Smith**	N	N	Y	N	Y	Y	N	N
3 Wyden	Y	Y	Y	Y	Y	Y	Y	Y
4 DeFazio	Y	Y	Y	?	Y	Y	Y	Y
5 Kopetski	Y	Y	Y	Y	Y	Y	+	+
PENNSYLVANIA								
1 Foglietta	Y	Y	Y	Y	Y	Y	Y	Y
2 Gray†	N	Y	?					
3 Borski	?	?	Y	Y	Y	Y	?	Y
4 Kolter	Y	N	Y	?	?	?	?	Y
5 **Schulze**	N	N	N	Y	Y	Y	?	?
6 Yatron	?	?	?	?	?	?	?	?
7 **Weldon**	N	N	Y	N	Y	Y	N	N
8 Kostmayer	Y	Y	Y	Y	Y	Y	+	+
9 **Shuster**	N	N	Y	Y	Y	Y	Y	N
10 **McDade**	?	?	Y	Y	Y	Y	?	?
11 Kanjorski	Y	N	Y	Y	Y	Y	?	?
12 Murtha	Y	N	Y	Y	?	?	Y	Y
13 **Coughlin**	N	Y	Y	N	?	?	?	N
14 Coyne	Y	Y	Y	Y	Y	Y	Y	Y
15 **Ritter**	N	N	Y	Y	Y	Y	?	N
16 **Walker**	N	N	N	N	Y	Y	N	N
17 **Gekas**	N	Y	Y	N	Y	Y	?	N
18 **Santorum**	Y	N	Y	N	Y	Y	N	N
19 **Goodling**	N	N	Y	N	Y	Y	?	N
20 Gaydos	Y	N	Y	Y	Y	Y	?	?
21 **Ridge**	Y	Y	Y	N	Y	Y	?	Y
22 Murphy	Y	N	Y	?	?	?	?	Y
23 **Clinger**	Y	N	Y	Y	Y	Y	Y	N
RHODE ISLAND								
1 **Machtley**	Y	Y	Y	N	Y	Y	?	N
2 Reed	Y	Y	Y	Y	Y	Y	Y	Y
SOUTH CAROLINA								
1 **Ravenel**	N	N	Y	Y	Y	Y	?	N
2 **Spence**	N	N	Y	Y	?	Y	?	?
3 Derrick	Y	Y	Y	Y	Y	Y	Y	Y
4 Patterson	N	N	Y	Y	Y	Y	Y	Y
5 Spratt	N	Y	Y	Y	Y	Y	Y	Y
6 Tallon	N	N	Y	Y	Y	Y	Y	Y

	250	251	253	254	256	257	258	259
SOUTH DAKOTA								
AL Johnson	Y	N	Y	Y	Y	Y	Y	Y
TENNESSEE								
1 **Quillen**	N	N	Y	Y	?	?	Y	N
2 **Duncan**	N	N	N	Y	Y	Y	Y	N
3 Lloyd	N	N	Y	Y	Y	Y	?	Y
4 Cooper	Y	Y	Y	?	Y	Y	Y	Y
5 Clement	Y	N	Y	Y	Y	Y	Y	Y
6 Gordon	Y	Y	Y	Y	Y	Y	Y	Y
7 **Sundquist**	N	N	?	N	Y	Y	?	?
8 Tanner	N	Y	Y	Y	Y	Y	Y	Y
9 Ford	Y	Y	Y	Y	Y	Y	Y	Y
TEXAS								
1 Chapman	N	Y	Y	?	Y	Y	?	Y
2 Wilson	N	Y	Y	Y	Y	Y	?	?
3 **Johnson**	N	N	N	Y	Y	Y	?	N
4 Hall	N	N	Y	Y	Y	Y	Y	Y
5 Bryant	Y	Y	Y	Y	Y	Y	?	?
6 **Barton**	N	N	N	Y	Y	Y	Y	N
7 **Archer**	N	N	N	Y	Y	Y	Y	N
8 **Fields**	N	N	N	N	Y	Y	N	N
9 Brooks	Y	Y	Y	Y	Y	Y	Y	Y
10 Pickle	Y	Y	Y	?	?	?	?	?
11 Edwards	N	Y	?	Y	Y	Y	Y	Y
12 Geren	N	Y	Y	Y	Y	Y	Y	Y
13 Sarpalius	N	?	Y	Y	Y	Y	?	Y
14 Laughlin	Y	N	Y	?	?	?	Y	Y
15 de la Garza	Y	Y	Y	Y	Y	Y	?	?
16 Coleman	Y	Y	Y	Y	Y	Y	Y	Y
17 Stenholm	N	N	Y	Y	Y	Y	Y	Y
18 Washington	Y	Y	Y	?	Y	Y	?	#
19 **Combest**	N	N	N	Y	Y	Y	Y	N
20 Gonzalez	Y	Y	Y	Y	Y	Y	Y	Y
21 **Smith**	N	N	Y	N	Y	Y	N	N
22 **DeLay**	N	N	N	N	Y	Y	?	?
23 Bustamante	?	#	Y	Y	Y	Y	?	?
24 Frost	Y	Y	Y	Y	Y	Y	Y	Y
25 Andrews	N	Y	Y	Y	Y	Y	Y	Y
26 **Armey**	N	N	N	N	Y	Y	N	N
27 Ortiz	Y	Y	Y	?	Y	Y	Y	Y
UTAH								
1 **Hansen**	N	N	N	N	Y	Y	N	N
2 Owens	N	Y	Y	Y	Y	Y	Y	Y
3 Orton	N	N	Y	Y	Y	Y	Y	Y
VERMONT								
AL *Sanders*	Y	Y	Y	Y	Y	Y	?	Y
VIRGINIA								
1 **Bateman**	N	Y	Y	Y	Y	Y	Y	N
2 Pickett	N	N	Y	Y	Y	Y	Y	Y
3 **Bliley**	N	Y	Y	N	Y	Y	N	N
4 Sisisky	N	Y	Y	Y	Y	Y	Y	Y
5 Payne	Y	Y	Y	Y	Y	Y	?	Y
6 Olin	N	Y	Y	Y	Y	Y	?	Y
7 **Slaughter**	N	N	Y	Y	Y	Y	N	N
8 Moran	Y	Y	Y	?	Y	Y	Y	Y
9 Boucher	Y	Y	Y	Y	Y	Y	Y	?
10 **Wolf**	N	N	Y	N	Y	Y	N	N
WASHINGTON								
1 **Miller**	Y	Y	Y	N	Y	Y	?	?
2 Swift	Y	Y	Y	Y	Y	Y	Y	Y
3 Unsoeld	Y	Y	Y	Y	Y	Y	Y	Y
4 **Morrison**	N	Y	Y	Y	Y	Y	Y	N
5 Foley								
6 Dicks	Y	Y	Y	?	?	?	?	Y
7 McDermott	Y	Y	Y	Y	Y	Y	Y	Y
8 **Chandler**	N	Y	Y	N	Y	Y	N	N
WEST VIRGINIA								
1 Mollohan	Y	N	Y	Y	Y	Y	?	Y
2 Staggers	Y	N	Y	Y	Y	Y	Y	Y
3 Wise	Y	Y	Y	Y	Y	Y	?	Y
4 Rahall	Y	N	Y	Y	Y	Y	?	#
WISCONSIN								
1 Aspin	Y	Y	Y	Y	Y	Y	Y	Y
2 **Klug**	N	Y	Y	Y	Y	Y	Y	N
3 **Gunderson**	Y	N	Y	Y	Y	Y	Y	N
4 Kleczka	Y	Y	Y	Y	Y	Y	?	#
5 Moody	Y	Y	Y	Y	Y	Y	?	?
6 **Petri**	N	N	N	Y	Y	Y	Y	N
7 Obey	Y	Y	Y	Y	Y	Y	Y	Y
8 **Roth**	N	N	Y	Y	Y	Y	Y	N
9 **Sensenbrenner**	N	N	N	N	Y	Y	N	N
WYOMING								
AL **Thomas**	N	N	Y	N	Y	Y	N	N

Southern states - Ala., Ark., Fla., Ga., Ky., La., Miss., N.C., Okla., S.C., Tenn., Texas, Va.
Omitted votes are quorum calls, which CQ does not include in its vote charts.

HOUSE VOTES 260, 261, 262, 264, 265, 266, 267, 268

260. HR 3040. Unemployment Benefits Extension/Rule. Adoption of the rule (H Res 221) to provide for House floor consideration of the bill to permanently extend unemployment benefits to long-term unemployed workers for up to 20 additional weeks at an estimated cost of $6.3 billion through fiscal 1996. The bill automatically declares the benefits as emergency spending and would not require a presidential declaration to be exempt from the spending requirements of last year's budget agreement. Adopted 230-128: R 13-124; D 216-4 (ND 151-1, SD 65-3); I 1-0, Sept. 16, 1991.

261. HR 2100. Fiscal 1992 Defense Authorization. Dickinson, R-Ala., motion to order the previous question (thus ending debate and the possibility of amendment) on the Dickinson motion to instruct the House conferees on the fiscal 1992 defense authorization bill to insist on the House position to make permanent certain changes in benefits for military personnel who served in Operation Desert Shield/Storm. Motion agreed to 220-145: R 136-4; D 84-140 (ND 30-124, SD 54-16); I 0-1, Sept. 16, 1991.

262. HR 2100. Fiscal 1992 Defense Authorization/Close Conference. Aspin, D-Wis., motion to close to the public the conference on the fiscal 1992 defense authorization bill, when classified national security information is under consideration. Motion agreed to 363-0: R 139-0; D 223-0 (ND 153-0, SD 70-0); I 1-0, Sept. 16, 1991.

264. HR 3040. Unemployment Benefits Extension/Employer Contribution. Rostenkowski, D-Ill., amendment to replace the bill's provisions that automatically declare the extended benefits as emergency spending with provisions that would raise the wage base subject to the federal unemployment tax for certain employers to pay for the extended benefits, if the president does not declare the benefits an emergency. Rejected 65-341: R 5-151; D 59-190 (ND 49-122, SD 10-68); I 1-0, Sept. 17, 1991. A "nay" was a vote supporting the president's position.

265. HR 3040. Unemployment Benefits Extension/Educational Workers. Separate vote at the request of Gingrich, R-Ga., on the Rostenkowski, D-Ill., en bloc amendment to strike provisions that would allow states to pay unemployment benefits to non-professional workers of educational institutions between academic terms. Rejected 84-324: R 31-125; D 53-198 (ND 34-139, SD 19-59); I 0-1, Sept. 17, 1991.

266. HR 3040. Unemployment Benefits Extension/Recommittal Motion. Archer, R-Texas, motion to recommit the bill to the Ways and Means Committee with instruction to report it back to the House with provisions that give the president until the end of 1991 to decide whether to declare the spending for the extended benefits in the bill as emergency spending. Rejected 129-279: R 122-34; D 7-244 (ND 0-173, SD 7-71); I 0-1, Sept. 17, 1991.

267. HR 3040. Unemployment Benefits Extension/Passage. Passage of the bill to permanently extend unemployment benefits to long-term unemployed workers for up to 20 additional weeks at an estimated cost of $6.3 billion through fiscal 1996. The bill automatically declares the benefits to be emergency spending and would not require a presidential declaration to be exempt from the spending requirements of the 1990 budget agreement. Passed 283-125: R 48-107; D 234-18 (ND 172-2, SD 62-16); I 1-0, Sept. 17, 1991. A "nay" was a vote supporting the president's position.

268. HR 3291. Fiscal 1991 D.C. Appropriations/George Washington University. Dixon, D-Calif., motion to disagree to Senate amendments that commit $50 million over four years of the District of Columbia's budget allocation to the George Washington University Medical Center to pay for improvements of the facility. Motion agreed to 405-0: R 152-0; D 252-0 (ND 173-0, SD 79-0); I 1-0, Sept. 17, 1991.

KEY

Y Voted for (yea).
Paired for.
+ Announced for.
N Voted against (nay).
X Paired against.
- Announced against.
P Voted "present."
C Voted "present" to avoid possible conflict of interest.
? Did not vote or otherwise make a position known.

Democrats ***Republicans***
Independent

	260	261	262	264	265	266	267	268
ALABAMA								
1 ***Callahan***	N	Y	Y	N	N	Y	N	Y
2 ***Dickinson***	N	Y	Y	N	Y	Y	N	?
3 Browder	Y	Y	Y	N	N	N	Y	Y
4 Bevill	Y	Y	Y	N	N	N	Y	Y
5 Cramer	Y	Y	Y	N	N	N	Y	Y
6 Erdreich	Y	Y	Y	N	N	N	Y	Y
7 Harris	Y	Y	Y	N	N	N	Y	Y
ALASKA								
AL ***Young***	N	Y	Y	N	N	Y	Y	Y
ARIZONA								
1 ***Rhodes***	N	?	?	N	N	Y	N	Y
2 Vacancy								
3 ***Stump***	N	Y	Y	N	N	Y	N	Y
4 ***Kyl***	N	Y	Y	N	N	Y	N	Y
5 ***Kolbe***	N	Y	Y	N	N	Y	N	Y
ARKANSAS								
1 Alexander	Y	N	Y	?	?	?	?	Y
2 Thornton	Y	N	Y	N	N	N	Y	Y
3 ***Hammerschmidt***	N	Y	Y	N	N	Y	N	Y
4 Anthony	Y	N	Y	N	Y	N	Y	Y
CALIFORNIA								
1 ***Riggs***	?	?	?	N	N	Y	N	Y
2 ***Herger***	?	?	?	?	?	?	?	?
3 Matsui	Y	N	Y	Y	N	N	Y	Y
4 Fazio	#	?	?	Y	N	N	Y	Y
5 Pelosi	Y	N	Y	Y	N	N	Y	Y
6 Boxer	Y	N	Y	N	N	N	Y	Y
7 Miller	?	?	?	N	N	N	Y	Y
8 Dellums	Y	N	Y	N	N	N	Y	Y
9 Stark	Y	N	Y	N	N	N	Y	Y
10 Edwards	Y	N	Y	Y	N	N	Y	Y
11 Lantos	?	?	?	?	?	?	#	X
12 ***Campbell***	?	?	?	N	N	Y	N	Y
13 Mineta	Y	N	Y	N	N	N	Y	Y
14 ***Doolittle***	X	?	?	?	?	?	X	#
15 Condit	Y	N	Y	N	N	N	Y	Y
16 Panetta	Y	N	Y	Y	N	N	Y	Y
17 Dooley	Y	Y	Y	N	N	N	Y	Y
18 Lehman	Y	N	Y	N	N	N	Y	Y
19 ***Lagomarsino***	N	Y	Y	N	N	Y	N	Y
20 ***Thomas***	X	?	?	?	?	?	X	?
21 ***Gallegly***	N	Y	Y	N	N	Y	N	Y
22 ***Moorhead***	N	Y	Y	N	N	Y	N	Y
23 Beilenson	Y	N	Y	Y	Y	N	Y	Y
24 Waxman	Y	N	Y	Y	N	N	Y	Y
25 Roybal	?	?	?	Y	N	N	Y	Y
26 Berman	#	?	?	?	?	?	?	?
27 Levine	Y	?	?	?	?	?	?	?
28 Dixon	Y	N	Y	Y	N	N	Y	Y
29 Waters	Y	N	Y	N	N	N	Y	Y
30 Martinez	?	?	?	Y	N	N	Y	Y
31 Dymally	Y	?	?	?	?	?	?	?
32 Anderson	Y	Y	Y	N	Y	N	Y	Y
33 ***Dreier***	N	Y	Y	N	N	Y	N	Y
34 Torres	Y	N	Y	N	N	N	Y	Y
35 ***Lewis***	?	?	?	?	?	?	X	#
36 Brown	Y	N	Y	N	N	N	Y	Y
37 ***McCandless***	N	Y	Y	N	Y	Y	N	Y
38 ***Dornan***	N	Y	Y	N	N	Y	N	Y
39 ***Dannemeyer***	N	Y	Y	N	N	Y	N	Y
40 ***Cox***	N	Y	Y	N	N	Y	N	Y
41 ***Lowery***	?	?	?	N	N	Y	N	?
42 ***Rohrabacher***	N	Y	Y	N	N	Y	N	Y
43 ***Packard***	X	?	?	N	N	Y	N	Y
44 ***Cunningham***	N	Y	Y	N	N	Y	N	Y
45 ***Hunter***	?	?	?	?	?	?	?	?
COLORADO								
1 Schroeder	Y	N	Y	N	N	N	Y	Y
2 Skaggs	Y	N	Y	N	Y	N	Y	Y
3 Campbell	Y	Y	Y	N	N	N	Y	Y
4 ***Allard***	N	Y	Y	N	N	Y	N	Y
5 ***Hefley***	N	Y	Y	N	N	Y	N	Y
6 ***Schaefer***	N	Y	Y	N	N	Y	N	Y
CONNECTICUT								
1 Kennelly	Y	Y	Y	Y	N	N	Y	Y
2 Gejdenson	Y	N	Y	N	N	N	Y	Y
3 DeLauro	Y	Y	Y	N	N	N	Y	Y
4 ***Shays***	N	N	Y	N	Y	Y	N	Y
5 ***Franks***	N	Y	Y	N	Y	Y	Y	Y
6 ***Johnson***	N	Y	Y	N	Y	Y	Y	Y
DELAWARE								
AL Carper	Y	Y	Y	Y	Y	N	Y	Y
FLORIDA								
1 Hutto	?	?	?	N	Y	Y	N	Y
2 Peterson	Y	Y	Y	N	N	N	Y	Y
3 Bennett	Y	Y	Y	Y	N	N	Y	Y
4 ***James***	N	Y	Y	N	N	Y	N	Y
5 ***McCollum***	X	?	?	N	N	Y	N	Y
6 ***Stearns***	N	Y	Y	N	N	Y	Y	Y
7 Gibbons	Y	N	Y	Y	Y	N	Y	Y
8 ***Young***	N	Y	Y	N	N	Y	Y	Y
9 ***Bilirakis***	N	Y	Y	N	Y	Y	N	Y
10 ***Ireland***	N	Y	Y	N	N	Y	N	Y
11 Bacchus	Y	Y	Y	N	N	N	Y	Y
12 ***Lewis***	N	Y	Y	N	N	Y	Y	Y
13 ***Goss***	N	Y	Y	N	N	Y	N	Y
14 Johnston	Y	N	Y	?	?	?	?	?
15 ***Shaw***	N	Y	Y	N	Y	Y	N	Y
16 Smith	Y	N	Y	N	Y	N	Y	Y
17 Lehman	?	?	?	?	?	?	?	?
18 ***Ros-Lehtinen***	N	Y	Y	N	N	Y	Y	Y
19 Fascell	Y	Y	Y	N	N	N	Y	Y
GEORGIA								
1 Thomas	?	Y	Y	N	N	N	Y	Y
2 Hatcher	?	?	?	N	N	N	Y	Y
3 Ray	Y	Y	Y	N	Y	N	N	Y
4 Jones	Y	N	Y	N	N	N	Y	Y
5 Lewis	Y	N	Y	Y	Y	N	Y	Y
6 ***Gingrich***	N	Y	Y	N	N	Y	N	Y
7 Darden	Y	Y	Y	N	N	N	Y	Y
8 Rowland	?	?	?	?	?	?	#	X
9 Jenkins	?	?	?	N	N	N	Y	Y
10 Barnard	?	Y	Y	N	N	N	N	Y
HAWAII								
1 Abercrombie	Y	N	Y	Y	Y	N	Y	Y
2 Mink	Y	N	Y	N	N	N	Y	Y
IDAHO								
1 LaRocco	Y	N	Y	N	N	N	Y	Y
2 Stallings	?	?	?	N	N	N	Y	Y
ILLINOIS								
1 Hayes	Y	N	Y	N	N	N	Y	Y
2 Savage	Y	N	Y	N	N	N	Y	Y
3 Russo	Y	N	Y	N	N	N	Y	Y
4 Sangmeister	Y	N	Y	N	N	N	Y	Y
5 Lipinski	Y	Y	Y	Y	Y	N	Y	Y
6 ***Hyde***	N	Y	Y	N	N	Y	N	Y
7 Collins	Y	N	Y	N	N	N	Y	Y
8 Rostenkowski	Y	N	Y	Y	Y	N	Y	Y
9 Yates	Y	N	Y	N	N	N	Y	Y
10 ***Porter***	N	Y	Y	N	Y	Y	N	Y
11 Annunzio	Y	N	Y	N	N	N	Y	Y
12 ***Crane***	N	Y	Y	N	Y	Y	N	Y
13 ***Fawell***	N	Y	Y	N	N	Y	N	Y
14 ***Hastert***	?	Y	Y	N	Y	Y	N	Y
15 ***Ewing***	N	Y	Y	N	N	Y	N	Y
16 Cox	Y	N	Y	N	N	N	Y	Y
17 Evans	Y	N	Y	N	N	N	Y	Y
18 ***Michel***	N	Y	Y	N	N	Y	N	Y
19 Bruce	Y	N	Y	N	N	N	Y	Y
20 Durbin	Y	N	Y	N	N	N	Y	Y
21 Costello	Y	Y	Y	N	N	N	Y	Y
22 Poshard	Y	N	Y	N	N	N	Y	Y
INDIANA								
1 Visclosky	Y	N	Y	Y	N	N	Y	Y
2 Sharp	Y	?	?	N	N	N	Y	Y
3 Roemer	Y	Y	Y	N	N	N	Y	Y

ND Northern Democrats SD Southern Democrats

	260	261	262	264	265	266	267	268
4 Long	Y	N	Y	N	N	N	Y	Y
5 Jontz	Y	N	Y	Y	N	N	Y	Y
6 ***Burton***	N	Y	Y	N	N	Y	N	Y
7 ***Myers***	N	Y	Y	N	N	Y	N	Y
8 McCloskey	?	N	Y	Y	N	N	Y	Y
9 Hamilton	Y	N	Y	Y	N	N	Y	Y
10 Jacobs	Y	N	Y	N	N	N	Y	Y
IOWA								
1 ***Leach***	N	Y	Y	N	Y	Y	Y	Y
2 ***Nussle***	N	Y	Y	N	N	Y	N	Y
3 Nagle	Y	N	Y	N	N	N	Y	Y
4 Smith	Y	N	Y	N	N	N	Y	Y
5 ***Lightfoot***	N	Y	Y	N	N	Y	N	Y
6 ***Grandy***	N	Y	Y	N	Y	Y	N	Y
KANSAS								
1 ***Roberts***	N	Y	Y	N	N	Y	N	Y
2 Slattery	Y	N	Y	N	N	N	Y	Y
3 ***Meyers***	N	Y	Y	N	Y	Y	N	Y
4 Glickman	Y	N	Y	N	N	N	Y	Y
5 ***Nichols***	N	Y	Y	N	N	Y	N	Y
KENTUCKY								
1 Hubbard	Y	Y	Y	N	N	N	Y	Y
2 Natcher	Y	Y	Y	N	N	N	Y	Y
3 Mazzoli	Y	Y	Y	Y	N	N	Y	Y
4 ***Bunning***	N	Y	Y	N	N	Y	N	Y
5 ***Rogers***	N	Y	Y	N	N	N	Y	Y
6 ***Hopkins***	?	?	?	?	?	?	?	?
7 Perkins	Y	N	Y	N	N	N	Y	Y
LOUISIANA								
1 ***Livingston***	N	Y	Y	N	N	Y	N	Y
2 Jefferson	Y	Y	Y	Y	N	N	Y	Y
3 Tauzin	N	Y	Y	N	N	N	Y	Y
4 ***McCrery***	?	?	?	N	N	Y	N	Y
5 Huckaby	Y	Y	Y	N	N	N	Y	Y
6 ***Baker***	N	Y	Y	N	N	Y	N	Y
7 Hayes	Y	Y	Y	N	N	N	N	Y
8 ***Holloway***	?	?	?	?	?	?	?	?
MAINE								
1 Andrews	Y	N	Y	N	N	N	Y	Y
2 ***Snowe***	Y	Y	Y	N	N	N	Y	Y
MARYLAND								
1 ***Gilchrest***	N	Y	Y	N	N	N	Y	Y
2 ***Bentley***	Y	Y	Y	N	N	N	Y	Y
3 Cardin	Y	N	Y	N	Y	N	Y	Y
4 McMillen	Y	Y	Y	N	Y	N	Y	Y
5 Hoyer	Y	N	Y	N	Y	N	Y	Y
6 Byron	Y	Y	Y	N	N	N	Y	Y
7 Mfume	Y	N	Y	N	N	N	Y	Y
8 ***Morella***	N	N	Y	N	Y	N	Y	Y
MASSACHUSETTS								
1 Olver	Y	N	Y	N	N	N	Y	Y
2 Neal	Y	N	Y	N	N	N	Y	Y
3 Early	Y	N	Y	Y	N	N	Y	Y
4 Frank	Y	N	Y	N	N	N	Y	Y
5 Atkins	Y	N	Y	N	N	N	Y	Y
6 Mavroules	?	?	?	N	N	N	Y	Y
7 Markey	Y	N	Y	N	N	N	Y	Y
8 Kennedy	Y	N	Y	N	N	N	Y	Y
9 Moakley	Y	N	Y	N	N	N	Y	Y
10 Studds	Y	N	Y	N	N	N	Y	Y
11 Donnelly	Y	N	Y	N	N	N	Y	Y
MICHIGAN								
1 Conyers	?	?	?	N	N	N	Y	Y
2 ***Pursell***	?	?	?	N	Y	N	Y	Y
3 Wolpe	Y	N	Y	N	N	N	Y	Y
4 ***Upton***	N	Y	Y	N	Y	N	Y	Y
5 ***Henry***	N	Y	Y	N	Y	N	Y	Y
6 Carr	?	?	?	N	N	N	Y	Y
7 Kildee	Y	N	Y	Y	N	N	Y	Y
8 Traxler	Y	N	Y	Y	Y	N	Y	Y
9 ***Vander Jagt***	N	Y	Y	N	Y	Y	N	Y
10 ***Camp***	?	Y	Y	N	N	N	Y	Y
11 ***Davis***	Y	Y	Y	N	N	N	Y	Y
12 Bonior	Y	N	Y	N	Y	N	Y	Y
13 Collins	Y	N	Y	N	N	N	Y	Y
14 Hertel	Y	Y	Y	N	N	N	Y	Y
15 Ford	?	?	?	+	N	N	Y	Y
16 Dingell	Y	N	Y	P	Y	N	Y	Y
17 Levin	Y	N	Y	N	Y	N	Y	Y
18 ***Broomfield***	N	Y	Y	N	N	Y	N	Y
MINNESOTA								
1 Penny	Y	?	?	Y	Y	N	N	Y
2 ***Weber***	N	Y	Y	N	N	Y	N	Y
3 ***Ramstad***	N	Y	Y	N	Y	Y	N	Y
4 Vento	Y	N	Y	Y	N	N	Y	Y

	260	261	262	264	265	266	267	268
5 Sabo	?	?	?	Y	N	N	Y	Y
6 Sikorski	Y	N	Y	N	N	N	Y	Y
7 Peterson	Y	N	Y	N	Y	N	Y	Y
8 Oberstar	Y	N	Y	N	Y	N	Y	Y
MISSISSIPPI								
1 Whitten	?	?	?	N	N	N	Y	Y
2 Espy	?	N	Y	N	N	N	Y	Y
3 Montgomery	Y	Y	Y	N	Y	Y	N	Y
4 Parker	Y	Y	Y	N	Y	Y	N	Y
5 Taylor	Y	Y	Y	N	N	Y	N	Y
MISSOURI								
1 Clay	?	?	?	N	N	N	Y	Y
2 Horn	Y	N	Y	N	N	N	Y	Y
3 Gephardt	Y	N	Y	Y	N	N	Y	Y
4 Skelton	Y	Y	Y	N	N	N	Y	Y
5 Wheat	Y	N	Y	Y	N	N	Y	Y
6 ***Coleman***	N	Y	Y	N	N	Y	N	Y
7 ***Hancock***	N	Y	Y	N	N	Y	N	Y
8 ***Emerson***	N	Y	Y	N	N	N	Y	Y
9 Volkmer	Y	Y	Y	N	N	N	Y	Y
MONTANA								
1 Williams	?	?	?	N	N	N	Y	Y
2 ***Marlenee***	?	?	?	?	?	?	?	?
NEBRASKA								
1 ***Bereuter***	N	Y	Y	N	Y	Y	N	Y
2 Hoagland	Y	N	Y	Y	Y	N	Y	Y
3 ***Barrett***	N	Y	Y	N	N	Y	N	Y
NEVADA								
1 Bilbray	Y	Y	Y	N	N	N	Y	Y
2 ***Vucanovich***	N	Y	Y	N	N	Y	N	Y
NEW HAMPSHIRE								
1 ***Zeliff***	X	Y	Y	N	N	Y	N	Y
2 Swett	Y	Y	Y	N	N	N	Y	Y
NEW JERSEY								
1 Andrews	N	Y	Y	N	Y	N	Y	Y
2 Hughes	Y	N	Y	N	N	N	Y	Y
3 Pallone	Y	Y	Y	N	N	N	Y	Y
4 ***Smith***	Y	?	?	N	N	N	Y	Y
5 ***Roukema***	N	N	Y	N	N	N	Y	Y
6 Dwyer	Y	N	Y	N	N	N	Y	Y
7 ***Rinaldo***	Y	Y	Y	N	N	N	Y	Y
8 Roe	Y	N	Y	N	N	N	Y	Y
9 Torricelli	Y	N	Y	N	N	N	Y	Y
10 Payne	Y	N	Y	N	N	N	Y	Y
11 ***Gallo***	N	Y	Y	N	N	Y	Y	Y
12 ***Zimmer***	N	Y	Y	N	Y	Y	Y	Y
13 ***Saxton***	?	?	?	?	?	?	?	?
14 Guarini	?	N	Y	Y	Y	N	Y	Y
NEW MEXICO								
1 ***Schiff***	N	Y	Y	N	N	Y	N	Y
2 ***Skeen***	N	Y	Y	N	N	Y	N	Y
3 Richardson	Y	Y	Y	N	N	N	Y	Y
NEW YORK								
1 Hochbrueckner	Y	Y	Y	N	N	N	Y	Y
2 Downey	Y	N	Y	Y	N	N	Y	Y
3 Mrazek	?	?	?	Y	Y	?	Y	Y
4 ***Lent***	N	Y	Y	N	N	Y	N	Y
5 ***McGrath***	?	?	?	Y	N	N	Y	Y
6 Flake	Y	N	Y	N	N	N	Y	Y
7 Ackerman	?	?	?	N	N	N	Y	Y
8 Scheuer	Y	N	Y	Y	Y	N	Y	Y
9 Manton	Y	N	Y	N	N	N	Y	Y
10 Schumer	Y	N	?	N	N	N	Y	Y
11 Towns	?	N	Y	N	N	N	Y	?
12 Owens	Y	N	Y	?	?	N	Y	Y
13 Solarz	Y	Y	Y	Y	N	N	Y	Y
14 ***Molinari***	N	Y	Y	N	N	N	Y	Y
15 ***Green***	Y	N	Y	Y	N	Y	N	Y
16 Rangel	Y	N	Y	N	N	N	Y	Y
17 Weiss	+	N	Y	Y	N	N	Y	Y
18 Serrano	Y	N	Y	Y	N	N	Y	Y
19 Engel	Y	N	Y	N	N	N	Y	Y
20 Lowey	Y	N	Y	N	N	N	Y	Y
21 ***Fish***	Y	Y	Y	N	N	N	Y	Y
22 ***Gilman***	Y	Y	Y	N	N	N	Y	Y
23 McNulty	Y	Y	Y	N	N	N	Y	Y
24 ***Solomon***	N	Y	Y	N	N	Y	N	Y
25 ***Boehlert***	N	Y	Y	N	N	N	Y	Y
26 ***Martin***	?	?	?	N	N	N	Y	Y
27 ***Walsh***	Y	Y	Y	N	N	Y	Y	Y
28 McHugh	Y	N	Y	Y	N	N	Y	Y
29 ***Horton***	Y	Y	Y	N	N	N	Y	Y
30 Slaughter	Y	N	Y	N	N	N	Y	Y
31 ***Paxon***	N	Y	Y	N	N	N	Y	Y

	260	261	262	264	265	266	267	268
32 LaFalce	Y	N	Y	N	Y	N	Y	Y
33 Nowak	Y	N	Y	N	Y	N	Y	Y
34 ***Houghton***	?	?	?	N	Y	Y	Y	Y
NORTH CAROLINA								
1 Jones	?	?	?	?	?	?	?	?
2 Valentine	Y	Y	Y	N	N	N	N	Y
3 Lancaster	Y	Y	Y	N	N	N	Y	Y
4 Price	Y	N	Y	N	N	N	Y	Y
5 Neal	Y	Y	Y	N	N	N	Y	Y
6 ***Coble***	N	Y	Y	N	N	Y	N	Y
7 Rose	Y	N	Y	N	N	N	Y	Y
8 Hefner	Y	Y	Y	N	N	N	Y	Y
9 ***McMillan***	N	Y	Y	N	N	Y	N	Y
10 ***Ballenger***	N	Y	Y	N	N	Y	N	Y
11 ***Taylor***	N	Y	Y	N	N	Y	N	Y
NORTH DAKOTA								
AL Dorgan	Y	N	Y	N	N	N	Y	Y
OHIO								
1 Luken	Y	Y	Y	N	N	N	Y	Y
2 ***Gradison***	N	?	?	N	N	Y	N	Y
3 Hall	Y	Y	Y	N	N	N	Y	Y
4 ***Oxley***	N	Y	Y	N	N	Y	N	Y
5 ***Gillmor***	N	Y	Y	N	N	N	Y	Y
6 ***McEwen***	?	?	?	N	N	Y	N	Y
7 ***Hobson***	N	Y	Y	N	N	Y	N	Y
8 ***Boehner***	N	Y	Y	N	N	Y	N	Y
9 Kaptur	Y	N	Y	N	N	N	Y	Y
10 ***Miller***	N	Y	Y	N	N	Y	N	Y
11 Eckart	Y	N	Y	N	N	N	Y	Y
12 ***Kasich***	N	Y	Y	N	N	Y	N	Y
13 Pease	Y	N	Y	Y	Y	N	Y	Y
14 Sawyer	Y	N	Y	N	N	N	Y	Y
15 ***Wylie***	N	Y	Y	N	N	Y	N	Y
16 ***Regula***	N	Y	Y	N	N	N	Y	Y
17 Traficant	Y	N	Y	N	N	N	Y	Y
18 Applegate	?	N	Y	N	N	N	Y	Y
19 Feighan	Y	N	Y	N	N	N	Y	Y
20 Oakar	Y	N	Y	N	N	N	Y	Y
21 Stokes	Y	N	Y	N	N	N	Y	Y
OKLAHOMA								
1 ***Inhofe***	N	Y	Y	N	N	Y	N	Y
2 Synar	Y	N	Y	N	N	N	Y	Y
3 Brewster	Y	Y	Y	N	N	N	N	Y
4 McCurdy	Y	Y	Y	N	N	N	Y	Y
5 ***Edwards***	N	Y	?	N	N	Y	?	?
6 English	Y	Y	Y	N	N	N	Y	Y
OREGON								
1 AuCoin	Y	N	Y	N	N	N	Y	Y
2 ***Smith***	N	Y	Y	N	N	N	Y	Y
3 Wyden	Y	N	Y	N	N	N	Y	Y
4 DeFazio	Y	N	Y	N	N	N	Y	Y
5 Kopetski	+	+	+	Y	Y	N	Y	Y
PENNSYLVANIA								
1 Foglietta	Y	Y	Y	Y	Y	N	Y	Y
2 Vacancy								
3 Borski	Y	N	Y	Y	N	N	Y	Y
4 Kolter	Y	N	Y	N	N	N	Y	Y
5 ***Schulze***	?	?	?	N	N	Y	N	Y
6 Yatron	?	?	?	?	?	?	?	?
7 ***Weldon***	N	Y	Y	N	Y	N	Y	Y
8 Kostmayer	Y	N	Y	Y	N	N	Y	Y
9 ***Shuster***	N	Y	Y	N	N	N	Y	Y
10 ***McDade***	?	?	?	N	N	N	Y	Y
11 Kanjorski	Y	N	Y	Y	Y	N	Y	Y
12 Murtha	Y	Y	Y	N	N	N	Y	Y
13 ***Coughlin***	N	Y	Y	N	N	Y	Y	Y
14 Coyne	Y	N	Y	Y	Y	N	Y	Y
15 ***Ritter***	Y	Y	Y	N	N	N	Y	Y
16 ***Walker***	N	Y	Y	N	N	Y	N	Y
17 ***Gekas***	N	Y	Y	N	N	Y	Y	Y
18 ***Santorum***	N	Y	Y	N	N	Y	N	Y
19 ***Goodling***	N	Y	Y	Y	Y	Y	N	Y
20 Gaydos	?	?	?	N	N	N	Y	Y
21 ***Ridge***	N	Y	Y	N	N	N	Y	Y
22 Murphy	Y	Y	Y	N	Y	N	Y	Y
23 ***Clinger***	N	Y	Y	N	N	N	Y	Y
RHODE ISLAND								
1 ***Machtley***	Y	Y	Y	N	N	N	Y	Y
2 Reed	Y	N	Y	N	N	N	Y	Y
SOUTH CAROLINA								
1 ***Ravenel***	Y	Y	Y	N	N	N	Y	Y
2 ***Spence***	?	Y	Y	N	N	Y	N	Y
3 Derrick	Y	?	?	N	Y	N	Y	Y
4 Patterson	Y	Y	Y	N	N	N	Y	Y
5 Spratt	Y	Y	Y	N	Y	N	Y	Y
6 Tallon	Y	Y	Y	N	N	N	Y	Y

	260	261	262	264	265	266	267	268
SOUTH DAKOTA								
AL Johnson	Y	N	Y	N	N	N	Y	Y
TENNESSEE								
1 ***Quillen***	N	Y	Y	N	N	Y	N	Y
2 ***Duncan***	N	Y	Y	N	N	Y	N	Y
3 Lloyd	N	Y	Y	?	?	?	?	?
4 Cooper	Y	Y	Y	Y	Y	N	N	Y
5 Clement	Y	Y	Y	N	N	N	Y	Y
6 Gordon	Y	Y	Y	N	N	N	Y	Y
7 ***Sundquist***	?	Y	Y	N	Y	Y	N	?
8 Tanner	Y	Y	Y	N	N	N	N	Y
9 Ford	Y	N	Y	N	N	N	Y	Y
TEXAS								
1 Chapman	Y	Y	Y	N	N	N	Y	Y
2 Wilson	?	?	?	N	N	N	Y	Y
3 ***Johnson***	N	Y	Y	N	N	Y	N	Y
4 Hall	N	Y	Y	N	N	Y	N	Y
5 Bryant	?	?	?	N	Y	N	Y	Y
6 ***Barton***	N	Y	Y	N	N	Y	N	Y
7 ***Archer***	N	Y	Y	N	Y	Y	N	Y
8 ***Fields***	N	Y	Y	N	N	Y	N	Y
9 Brooks	Y	N	Y	N	N	N	Y	Y
10 Pickle	?	?	?	?	?	?	?	?
11 Edwards	Y	Y	Y	N	N	N	Y	Y
12 Geren	Y	Y	Y	N	Y	N	Y	Y
13 Sarpalius	Y	Y	Y	N	N	Y	N	Y
14 Laughlin	Y	Y	Y	N	Y	Y	N	Y
15 de la Garza	?	?	?	N	N	N	Y	Y
16 Coleman	Y	Y	Y	N	Y	N	Y	Y
17 Stenholm	Y	Y	Y	N	Y	N	N	Y
18 Washington	#	?	?	Y	N	N	Y	Y
19 ***Combest***	N	Y	Y	N	Y	Y	N	Y
20 Gonzalez	Y	Y	Y	Y	Y	N	Y	Y
21 ***Smith***	N	Y	Y	N	N	Y	N	Y
22 ***DeLay***	?	?	?	N	N	Y	N	Y
23 Bustamante	?	?	?	N	N	N	Y	Y
24 Frost	Y	Y	Y	N	N	N	Y	Y
25 Andrews	Y	Y	Y	N	Y	N	Y	Y
26 ***Armey***	N	Y	Y	N	N	Y	N	Y
27 Ortiz	Y	Y	Y	N	N	N	Y	Y
UTAH								
1 ***Hansen***	N	Y	Y	N	N	Y	N	Y
2 Owens	Y	N	Y	N	Y	N	Y	Y
3 Orton	Y	Y	Y	Y	Y	N	N	Y
VERMONT								
AL *Sanders*	Y	N	Y	Y	N	N	Y	Y
VIRGINIA								
1 ***Bateman***	N	Y	Y	N	Y	Y	N	Y
2 Pickett	Y	Y	Y	Y	N	N	Y	Y
3 ***Bliley***	N	Y	Y	N	N	Y	N	Y
4 Sisisky	Y	Y	Y	N	N	N	Y	Y
5 Payne	Y	Y	Y	N	N	N	Y	Y
6 Olin	Y	Y	Y	Y	N	N	N	Y
7 ***Slaughter***	N	Y	Y	?	?	?	?	?
8 Moran	Y	N	Y	N	Y	N	Y	Y
9 Boucher	?	?	?	N	N	N	Y	Y
10 ***Wolf***	N	Y	Y	N	N	Y	N	Y
WASHINGTON								
1 ***Miller***	?	Y	Y	N	Y	Y	N	Y
2 Swift	Y	N	Y	Y	N	N	Y	Y
3 Unsoeld	?	N	Y	Y	N	N	Y	Y
4 ***Morrison***	N	Y	Y	N	N	Y	N	Y
5 Foley								
6 Dicks	Y	Y	Y	N	N	N	Y	Y
7 McDermott	Y	N	Y	Y	Y	N	Y	Y
8 ***Chandler***	N	Y	Y	N	Y	Y	N	Y
WEST VIRGINIA								
1 Mollohan	Y	Y	Y	N	N	N	Y	Y
2 Staggers	Y	N	Y	N	N	N	Y	Y
3 Wise	Y	N	Y	N	N	N	Y	Y
4 Rahall	#	?	?	?	?	?	#	?
WISCONSIN								
1 Aspin	Y	N	Y	Y	Y	N	Y	Y
2 ***Klug***	N	Y	Y	N	Y	Y	N	Y
3 ***Gunderson***	N	Y	Y	N	N	N	Y	Y
4 Kleczka	#	?	?	Y	N	N	Y	Y
5 Moody	?	?	?	N	N	N	Y	Y
6 ***Petri***	N	Y	Y	Y	N	Y	N	Y
7 Obey	Y	N	Y	N	N	N	Y	Y
8 ***Roth***	N	Y	Y	Y	N	Y	N	Y
9 ***Sensenbrenner***	N	Y	Y	N	N	Y	N	Y
WYOMING								
AL ***Thomas***	N	Y	Y	N	N	Y	N	Y

Southern states - Ala., Ark., Fla., Ga., Ky., La., Miss., N.C., Okla., S.C., Tenn., Texas, Va.
Omitted votes are quorum calls, which CQ does not include in its vote charts.

HOUSE VOTES 269, 270, 271, 272, 273, 274, 275, 277

269. Procedural Motion. Zimmer, R-N.J., motion to approve the House Journal of Monday, Sept. 23. Motion agreed to 287-107: R 49-102; D 238-5 (ND 155-5, SD 83-0); I 0-0, Sept. 24, 1991.

270. HR 2707. Fiscal 1992 Labor, HHS and Education Appropriations/Student Loan Costs. Pursell, R-Mich., motion to order the previous question (thus ending debate and the possibility of amendment) on the Pursell motion to instruct the House conferees to insist on the House provisions for student loan administrative costs. Motion agreed to 262-154: R 26-135; D 235-19 (ND 162-9, SD 73-10); I 1-0, Sept. 24, 1991. (The Pursell motion to instruct was subsequently adopted by voice vote.)

271. HR 2622. Fiscal 1992 Treasury-Postal Appropriations/Child Pornography. Wolf, R-Va., motion to instruct the House conferees to insist on the Senate amendment to mandate prison terms for selling child pornography. Motion agreed to 414-0: R 159-0; D 254-0 (ND 172-0, SD 82-0); I 1-0, Sept. 24, 1991.

272. HR 2686. Fiscal 1992 Interior Appropriations/Lower Income Weatherization Program. Green, R-N.Y., motion to order the previous question (thus ending debate and the possibility of amendment) on the Green motion to instruct the House conferees to disagree with the Senate amendment to reduce funding for the lower income weatherization program at the Department of Energy. Motion agreed to 213-204: R 20-141; D 192-63 (ND 151-23, SD 41-40); I 1-0, Sept. 24, 1991. (The Green motion to instruct was subsequently adopted by voice vote.)

273. HR 2942. Fiscal 1992 Transportation Appropriations/Drug and Alcohol Testing. Coughlin, R-Pa., motion to instruct the House conferees to agree to the Senate amendment to require mandatory drug and alcohol testing of transportation workers in safety-related jobs. Motion agreed to 413-5: R 161-0; D 251-5 (ND 170-4, SD 81-1); I 1-0, Sept. 24, 1991.

274. H Con Res 199. Commendation of the People of the Soviet Union. Hamilton, D-Ind., motion to suspend the rules and pass the concurrent resolution to commend the people of the Soviet Union and their democratically elected leaders for their continuing courage and commitment to freedom. Motion agreed to 409-0: R 160-0; D 249-0 (ND 169-0, SD 80-0); I 0-0, Sept. 24, 1991. A two-thirds majority vote of those present and voting (273 in this case) is required for passage under suspension of the rules.

275. HR 2900. Government-Sponsored Housing Enterprises Rule. Adoption of the rule (H Res 226) to provide for House floor consideration of the bill to improve the supervision and regulation with respect to the financial safety and soundness of the Federal National Mortgage Association, the Federal Home Loan Mortgage Corporation and the Federal Home Loan Bank System. Adopted 405-0: R 152-0; D 252-0 (ND 170-0, SD 82-0); I 1-

277. HR 2900. Government-Sponsored Housing Enterprises Capital Standards. Leach, R-Iowa, en bloc amendment to increase the capital standards established by the bill for the Federal National Mortgage Association and Federal Home Loan Mortgage Corporation and allow the Office of Secondary Market Examination and Oversight greater discretion in establishing certain capital standards. Rejected 119-298: R 69-91; D 50-206 (ND 42-132, SD 8-74); I 0-1, Sept. 25, 1991.

KEY

Y Voted for (yea).
\# Paired for.
\+ Announced for.
N Voted against (nay).
X Paired against.
\- Announced against.
P Voted "present."
C Voted "present" to avoid possible conflict of interest.
? Did not vote or otherwise make a position known.

Democrats ***Republicans***
Independent

	269	270	271	272	273	274	275	277
ALABAMA								
1 ***Callahan***	?	?	?	?	?	?	?	?
2 ***Dickinson***	N	Y	Y	N	Y	Y	Y	Y
3 Browder	Y	Y	Y	N	Y	Y	Y	N
4 Bevill	Y	Y	Y	N	Y	Y	Y	N
5 Cramer	Y	Y	Y	N	Y	Y	Y	N
6 Erdreich	Y	Y	Y	N	Y	Y	Y	N
7 Harris	Y	Y	Y	N	Y	Y	Y	N
ALASKA								
AL ***Young***	N	N	Y	N	Y	Y	Y	N
ARIZONA								
1 ***Rhodes***	N	N	Y	N	Y	Y	Y	Y
2 Vacancy								
3 ***Stump***	N	N	Y	N	Y	Y	Y	Y
4 ***Kyl***	N	N	Y	N	Y	Y	Y	Y
5 ***Kolbe***	N	Y	Y	Y	Y	Y	Y	Y
ARKANSAS								
1 Alexander	Y	Y	Y	Y	Y	Y	Y	N
2 Thornton	Y	Y	Y	Y	Y	Y	Y	N
3 ***Hammerschmidt***	Y	N	Y	N	Y	Y	Y	N
4 Anthony	Y	Y	Y	?	Y	Y	Y	N
CALIFORNIA								
1 ***Riggs***	N	N	Y	N	Y	Y	Y	N
2 ***Herger***	N	N	Y	N	Y	Y	Y	Y
3 Matsui	Y	Y	Y	Y	Y	Y	Y	N
4 Fazio	Y	Y	Y	Y	Y	Y	Y	N
5 Pelosi	Y	Y	Y	Y	Y	Y	Y	N
6 Boxer	?	?	?	?	?	?	?	?
7 Miller	Y	Y	Y	Y	Y	Y	Y	Y
8 Dellums	Y	Y	Y	Y	Y	Y	Y	N
9 Stark	Y	Y	Y	Y	Y	Y	Y	N
10 Edwards	Y	Y	Y	Y	Y	Y	Y	N
11 Lantos	Y	Y	Y	Y	Y	Y	Y	Y
12 ***Campbell***	N	N	Y	Y	Y	Y	Y	N
13 Mineta	Y	Y	Y	Y	Y	Y	Y	N
14 ***Doolittle***	N	N	Y	N	Y	Y	Y	N
15 Condit	Y	Y	Y	N	Y	Y	Y	N
16 Panetta	Y	Y	Y	Y	Y	Y	Y	Y
17 Dooley	Y	Y	Y	Y	Y	Y	Y	N
18 Lehman	Y	Y	Y	Y	Y	Y	Y	N
19 ***Lagomarsino***	N	N	Y	N	Y	Y	Y	Y
20 ***Thomas***	N	Y	Y	N	Y	Y	Y	Y
21 ***Gallegly***	N	N	Y	N	Y	Y	Y	Y
22 ***Moorhead***	N	N	Y	N	Y	Y	Y	N
23 Beilenson	Y	Y	Y	Y	Y	Y	Y	Y
24 Waxman	Y	Y	?	Y	Y	?	Y	Y
25 Roybal	Y	Y	Y	Y	Y	Y	Y	N
26 Berman	Y	Y	Y	Y	Y	?	Y	N
27 Levine	?	?	?	?	?	?	?	?
28 Dixon	?	?	Y	Y	Y	Y	Y	N
29 Waters	Y	Y	Y	Y	Y	Y	Y	Y
30 Martinez	?	Y	Y	Y	Y	Y	Y	N
31 Dymally	?	?	Y	Y	Y	?	?	N
32 Anderson	Y	Y	Y	Y	Y	Y	Y	N
33 ***Dreier***	Y	N	Y	N	Y	Y	Y	N
34 Torres	Y	Y	Y	Y	Y	Y	Y	N
35 ***Lewis***	N	N	Y	N	Y	Y	?	Y
36 Brown	?	?	Y	Y	Y	Y	Y	N
37 ***McCandless***	N	N	Y	N	Y	Y	Y	N
38 ***Dornan***	N	N	Y	N	Y	Y	Y	Y
39 ***Dannemeyer***	N	N	Y	N	Y	Y	Y	Y
40 ***Cox***	N	N	Y	N	Y	Y	Y	N
41 ***Lowery***	N	N	Y	N	Y	Y	Y	N
42 ***Rohrabacher***	N	N	Y	N	Y	Y	Y	N
43 ***Packard***	Y	N	Y	N	Y	Y	Y	Y
44 ***Cunningham***	N	N	Y	N	Y	Y	Y	N
45 ***Hunter***	?	N	Y	N	Y	Y	?	N
COLORADO								
1 Schroeder	N	Y	Y	Y	Y	Y	Y	Y
2 Skaggs	Y	Y	Y	Y	Y	Y	Y	Y
3 Campbell	Y	Y	Y	N	Y	Y	Y	N
4 ***Allard***	N	N	Y	N	Y	Y	Y	N
5 ***Hefley***	N	N	Y	N	Y	Y	Y	Y
6 ***Schaefer***	N	N	Y	N	Y	Y	Y	N
CONNECTICUT								
1 Kennelly	Y	Y	Y	Y	Y	Y	Y	Y
2 Gejdenson	Y	Y	Y	Y	Y	Y	Y	N
3 DeLauro	Y	Y	Y	Y	Y	Y	Y	N
4 ***Shays***	N	Y	Y	Y	Y	Y	Y	Y
5 ***Franks***	N	N	Y	N	Y	Y	Y	N
6 ***Johnson***	Y	N	Y	Y	Y	Y	Y	N
DELAWARE								
AL Carper	Y	Y	Y	N	Y	Y	?	N
FLORIDA								
1 Hutto	Y	N	Y	N	Y	Y	Y	N
2 Peterson	Y	Y	Y	Y	Y	Y	Y	N
3 Bennett	Y	Y	Y	Y	Y	Y	Y	N
4 ***James***	N	N	Y	N	Y	Y	Y	N
5 ***McCollum***	Y	N	Y	N	Y	Y	?	N
6 ***Stearns***	N	N	Y	N	Y	Y	Y	N
7 Gibbons	Y	Y	Y	N	Y	Y	Y	N
8 ***Young***	Y	N	Y	N	Y	Y	Y	N
9 ***Bilirakis***	N	Y	Y	N	Y	Y	Y	N
10 ***Ireland***	N	N	Y	N	Y	Y	?	N
11 Bacchus	Y	Y	Y	Y	Y	Y	Y	Y
12 ***Lewis***	N	N	Y	N	Y	Y	Y	N
13 ***Goss***	N	N	Y	N	Y	Y	Y	N
14 Johnston	Y	Y	Y	Y	Y	Y	Y	N
15 ***Shaw***	Y	N	?	?	Y	Y	Y	Y
16 Smith	Y	Y	Y	Y	Y	?	Y	?
17 Lehman	Y	Y	Y	Y	N	Y	Y	Y
18 ***Ros-Lehtinen***	N	N	Y	N	Y	Y	Y	N
19 Fascell	Y	Y	Y	Y	?	?	Y	N
GEORGIA								
1 Thomas	Y	Y	Y	N	Y	Y	Y	N
2 Hatcher	Y	?	Y	Y	Y	Y	Y	N
3 Ray	Y	N	Y	N	Y	Y	Y	N
4 Jones	Y	Y	Y	Y	Y	Y	Y	N
5 Lewis	Y	Y	Y	Y	Y	Y	Y	N
6 ***Gingrich***	N	N	Y	N	Y	Y	?	Y
7 Darden	Y	Y	Y	Y	Y	Y	Y	N
8 Rowland	Y	Y	Y	N	Y	Y	Y	N
9 Jenkins	Y	Y	Y	N	Y	Y	Y	N
10 Barnard	Y	Y	Y	N	Y	Y	Y	N
HAWAII								
1 Abercrombie	Y	Y	Y	Y	Y	Y	Y	N
2 Mink	Y	Y	Y	Y	Y	Y	Y	Y
IDAHO								
1 LaRocco	Y	Y	Y	Y	Y	Y	Y	N
2 Stallings	Y	N	Y	N	Y	Y	Y	N
ILLINOIS								
1 Hayes	Y	Y	Y	Y	Y	Y	Y	N
2 Savage	Y	Y	Y	Y	Y	Y	Y	N
3 Russo	Y	Y	Y	Y	Y	Y	Y	Y
4 Sangmeister	Y	Y	Y	Y	Y	Y	Y	Y
5 Lipinski	Y	Y	Y	Y	Y	Y	?	Y
6 ***Hyde***	?	?	?	?	?	?	Y	Y
7 Collins	Y	Y	Y	Y	Y	Y	Y	N
8 Rostenkowski	Y	Y	Y	Y	Y	Y	Y	N
9 Yates	Y	Y	Y	Y	Y	Y	Y	Y
10 ***Porter***	Y	N	Y	N	Y	Y	Y	Y
11 Annunzio	Y	Y	Y	Y	Y	Y	Y	N
12 ***Crane***	N	N	Y	N	Y	Y	Y	Y
13 ***Fawell***	N	N	Y	N	Y	Y	Y	Y
14 ***Hastert***	N	N	Y	N	Y	Y	Y	Y
15 ***Ewing***	N	N	Y	N	Y	Y	Y	N
16 Cox	Y	Y	Y	Y	Y	Y	Y	Y
17 Evans	Y	Y	Y	Y	Y	Y	Y	Y
18 ***Michel***	?	N	Y	N	Y	Y	?	N
19 Bruce	Y	Y	Y	N	Y	Y	Y	N
20 Durbin	Y	Y	Y	Y	Y	Y	Y	N
21 Costello	Y	Y	Y	N	Y	Y	Y	N
22 Poshard	Y	Y	Y	N	Y	Y	Y	N
INDIANA								
1 Visclosky	Y	Y	Y	Y	Y	Y	Y	Y
2 Sharp	Y	Y	Y	Y	Y	Y	Y	Y
3 Roemer	Y	Y	Y	N	Y	Y	Y	Y

ND Northern Democrats SD Southern Democrats

	269	270	271	272	273	274	275	277
4 Long	Y	Y	Y	Y	Y	Y	Y	N
5 Jontz	Y	Y	Y	Y	Y	Y	Y	N
6 ***Burton***	N	N	Y	N	Y	Y	Y	N
7 ***Myers***	Y	Y	Y	N	Y	Y	?	N
8 McCloskey	Y	Y	?	Y	Y	Y	Y	N
9 Hamilton	Y	Y	Y	N	Y	Y	Y	N
10 Jacobs	N	N	Y	N	N	Y	Y	N
IOWA								
1 ***Leach***	N	Y	Y	Y	Y	Y	Y	Y
2 ***Nussle***	N	N	Y	Y	Y	Y	Y	Y
3 Nagle	Y	Y	Y	?	Y	Y	Y	N
4 Smith	Y	Y	Y	Y	Y	Y	Y	Y
5 ***Lightfoot***	N	N	Y	N	Y	Y	Y	Y
6 ***Grandy***	N	N	Y	Y	Y	Y	Y	Y
KANSAS								
1 ***Roberts***	N	N	Y	N	Y	Y	Y	N
2 Slattery	Y	Y	Y	N	Y	Y	Y	N
3 ***Meyers***	N	Y	Y	N	Y	Y	Y	Y
4 Glickman	Y	Y	Y	N	Y	Y	Y	Y
5 ***Nichols***	Y	N	Y	N	Y	Y	Y	N
KENTUCKY								
1 Hubbard	Y	Y	Y	N	Y	Y	Y	N
2 Natcher	Y	Y	Y	Y	Y	Y	Y	N
3 Mazzoli	Y	Y	Y	Y	Y	Y	Y	N
4 ***Bunning***	N	N	Y	N	Y	Y	Y	N
5 ***Rogers***	N	Y	Y	N	Y	Y	Y	N
6 ***Hopkins***	?	?	?	?	?	?	?	?
7 Perkins	Y	Y	Y	Y	Y	Y	Y	N
LOUISIANA								
1 ***Livingston***	Y	N	Y	N	Y	Y	Y	N
2 Jefferson	Y	Y	Y	Y	Y	Y	Y	?
3 Tauzin	Y	N	Y	N	Y	Y	Y	N
4 ***McCrery***	N	N	Y	N	Y	Y	Y	N
5 Huckaby	Y	N	Y	N	Y	Y	Y	N
6 ***Baker***	N	N	Y	N	Y	Y	Y	N
7 Hayes	Y	N	Y	N	Y	Y	Y	N
8 ***Holloway***	?	N	Y	N	Y	Y	?	?
MAINE								
1 Andrews	Y	Y	Y	Y	Y	Y	Y	N
2 ***Snowe***	Y	Y	Y	N	Y	Y	Y	N
MARYLAND								
1 ***Gilchrest***	N	N	Y	N	Y	Y	Y	N
2 ***Bentley***	?	?	?	N	Y	Y	Y	N
3 Cardin	?	Y	Y	Y	Y	Y	Y	Y
4 McMillen	?	Y	Y	N	Y	Y	Y	N
5 Hoyer	?	Y	Y	Y	Y	Y	Y	N
6 Byron	?	N	Y	N	Y	Y	Y	N
7 Mfume	?	Y	Y	Y	Y	Y	Y	Y
8 ***Morella***	N	Y	Y	Y	Y	Y	Y	N
MASSACHUSETTS								
1 Olver	Y	Y	Y	Y	Y	Y	Y	N
2 Neal	Y	Y	Y	Y	Y	Y	Y	N
3 Early	Y	Y	Y	Y	Y	Y	Y	Y
4 Frank	Y	Y	Y	Y	Y	Y	Y	N
5 Atkins	Y	Y	Y	Y	Y	Y	Y	N
6 Mavroules	Y	Y	Y	Y	Y	Y	Y	N
7 Markey	Y	Y	Y	Y	Y	Y	Y	N
8 Kennedy	Y	Y	Y	Y	Y	Y	Y	Y
9 Moakley	Y	Y	Y	Y	Y	Y	Y	N
10 Studds	Y	Y	Y	Y	Y	Y	Y	Y
11 Donnelly	Y	Y	Y	Y	Y	Y	Y	N
MICHIGAN								
1 Conyers	Y	Y	Y	Y	?	Y	Y	N
2 ***Pursell***	Y	Y	Y	N	Y	?	?	Y
3 Wolpe	Y	Y	Y	Y	Y	Y	Y	N
4 ***Upton***	N	N	Y	N	Y	Y	Y	Y
5 ***Henry***	N	N	Y	N	Y	Y	Y	Y
6 Carr	Y	Y	Y	Y	Y	Y	Y	N
7 Kildee	Y	Y	Y	Y	Y	Y	Y	N
8 Traxler	Y	Y	Y	Y	Y	Y	Y	N
9 ***Vander Jagt***	Y	N	Y	N	Y	Y	?	Y
10 ***Camp***	N	N	Y	N	Y	Y	Y	Y
11 ***Davis***	Y	N	Y	N	Y	Y	Y	N
12 Bonior	Y	Y	Y	Y	Y	Y	Y	N
13 Collins	Y	Y	Y	Y	Y	Y	Y	N
14 Hertel	Y	Y	Y	Y	Y	Y	Y	N
15 Ford	?	Y	Y	Y	Y	Y	?	N
16 Dingell	Y	Y	Y	Y	N	Y	Y	Y
17 Levin	Y	Y	Y	Y	Y	Y	Y	N
18 ***Broomfield***	N	N	Y	N	?	?	Y	Y
MINNESOTA								
1 Penny	Y	Y	Y	N	Y	Y	Y	Y
2 ***Weber***	N	N	Y	N	Y	Y	?	N
3 ***Ramstad***	N	N	Y	Y	Y	Y	Y	N
4 Vento	Y	Y	Y	Y	Y	Y	Y	N

	269	270	271	272	273	274	275	277
5 Sabo	Y	Y	Y	Y	N	Y	Y	N
6 Sikorski	N	Y	Y	Y	Y	Y	Y	N
7 Peterson	Y	Y	Y	Y	Y	Y	Y	Y
8 Oberstar	Y	Y	Y	Y	N	Y	Y	N
MISSISSIPPI								
1 Whitten	Y	Y	Y	Y	Y	Y	Y	N
2 Espy	Y	Y	Y	Y	Y	Y	Y	N
3 Montgomery	Y	Y	Y	N	Y	Y	Y	N
4 Parker	Y	Y	Y	N	Y	Y	Y	N
5 Taylor	Y	N	Y	N	Y	Y	Y	N
MISSOURI								
1 Clay	N	Y	Y	Y	Y	Y	Y	N
2 Horn	Y	Y	Y	Y	Y	Y	Y	N
3 Gephardt	?	Y	Y	Y	Y	Y	Y	N
4 Skelton	Y	Y	Y	N	Y	Y	Y	N
5 Wheat	Y	Y	Y	Y	Y	Y	Y	N
6 ***Coleman***	N	N	Y	N	Y	Y	Y	Y
7 ***Hancock***	N	N	Y	N	Y	Y	Y	Y
8 ***Emerson***	Y	N	Y	N	Y	Y	Y	N
9 Volkmer	Y	N	Y	N	Y	Y	Y	N
MONTANA								
1 Williams	Y	Y	Y	Y	Y	Y	Y	N
2 ***Marlenee***	?	N	Y	N	Y	Y	Y	N
NEBRASKA								
1 ***Bereuter***	N	N	Y	N	Y	Y	Y	Y
2 Hoagland	Y	Y	Y	Y	Y	Y	Y	N
3 ***Barrett***	N	N	Y	N	Y	Y	Y	Y
NEVADA								
1 Bilbray	Y	Y	Y	Y	Y	Y	Y	N
2 ***Vucanovich***	N	N	Y	N	Y	Y	Y	Y
NEW HAMPSHIRE								
1 ***Zeliff***	N	N	Y	N	Y	Y	Y	N
2 Swett	Y	Y	Y	Y	Y	Y	Y	Y
NEW JERSEY								
1 Andrews	Y	Y	Y	Y	Y	Y	Y	Y
2 Hughes	Y	Y	Y	Y	Y	Y	Y	Y
3 Pallone	Y	Y	Y	Y	Y	Y	Y	Y
4 ***Smith***	Y	N	?	N	Y	Y	Y	Y
5 ***Roukema***	N	N	Y	N	Y	Y	Y	N
6 Dwyer	Y	Y	Y	Y	Y	Y	Y	N
7 ***Rinaldo***	Y	N	Y	N	Y	Y	Y	N
8 Roe	Y	Y	Y	Y	Y	Y	Y	N
9 Torricelli	Y	Y	Y	Y	Y	Y	Y	?
10 Payne	Y	Y	Y	Y	Y	Y	Y	N
11 ***Gallo***	?	Y	Y	N	Y	Y	Y	N
12 ***Zimmer***	N	N	Y	N	Y	Y	Y	N
13 ***Saxton***	?	N	Y	N	Y	Y	Y	N
14 Guarini	Y	Y	Y	Y	Y	?	?	?
NEW MEXICO								
1 ***Schiff***	Y	N	Y	N	Y	Y	Y	N
2 ***Skeen***	Y	N	Y	N	Y	Y	Y	N
3 Richardson	Y	Y	Y	Y	Y	Y	Y	N
NEW YORK								
1 Hochbrueckner	Y	Y	Y	Y	Y	Y	Y	N
2 Downey	Y	Y	Y	Y	Y	Y	Y	N
3 Mrazek	?	?	?	?	?	?	Y	N
4 ***Lent***	Y	N	Y	N	Y	Y	Y	N
5 ***McGrath***	Y	N	Y	N	Y	Y	Y	?
6 Flake	Y	Y	Y	Y	Y	Y	Y	N
7 Ackerman	Y	Y	Y	Y	Y	?	Y	N
8 Scheuer	Y	Y	Y	Y	Y	Y	Y	N
9 Manton	Y	Y	Y	Y	Y	Y	Y	N
10 Schumer	Y	Y	Y	Y	Y	Y	Y	N
11 Towns	?	Y	Y	Y	Y	Y	Y	N
12 Owens	Y	Y	Y	Y	Y	Y	Y	N
13 Solarz	Y	Y	Y	Y	Y	Y	Y	N
14 ***Molinari***	N	Y	Y	Y	Y	Y	Y	N
15 ***Green***	Y	Y	Y	Y	Y	Y	Y	N
16 Rangel	Y	Y	Y	Y	Y	Y	?	N
17 Weiss	Y	Y	Y	Y	Y	Y	Y	N
18 Serrano	Y	Y	Y	Y	Y	Y	Y	N
19 Engel	Y	Y	Y	Y	Y	Y	Y	N
20 Lowey	Y	Y	Y	Y	Y	Y	Y	N
21 ***Fish***	Y	N	Y	Y	Y	Y	Y	Y
22 ***Gilman***	Y	Y	Y	Y	Y	Y	Y	N
23 McNulty	Y	Y	Y	N	Y	Y	Y	N
24 ***Solomon***	N	N	Y	N	Y	Y	Y	Y
25 ***Boehlert***	N	Y	Y	Y	Y	Y	Y	N
26 ***Martin***	N	Y	Y	N	Y	Y	Y	N
27 ***Walsh***	Y	N	Y	N	Y	Y	Y	N
28 McHugh	Y	Y	Y	Y	Y	Y	Y	N
29 ***Horton***	Y	Y	Y	Y	Y	Y	Y	N
30 Slaughter	Y	Y	Y	Y	Y	Y	Y	N
31 ***Paxon***	N	N	Y	N	Y	Y	Y	N

	269	270	271	272	273	274	275	277
32 LaFalce	Y	Y	Y	Y	Y	Y	Y	N
33 Nowak	Y	Y	Y	Y	Y	Y	Y	N
34 ***Houghton***	Y	Y	Y	Y	Y	Y	Y	N
NORTH CAROLINA								
1 Jones	Y	Y	Y	Y	Y	Y	Y	N
2 Valentine	Y	Y	Y	?	Y	Y	Y	N
3 Lancaster	Y	Y	Y	N	Y	Y	Y	N
4 Price	Y	Y	Y	Y	Y	Y	Y	N
5 Neal	Y	Y	Y	Y	Y	Y	Y	N
6 ***Coble***	N	N	Y	N	Y	Y	Y	N
7 Rose	Y	Y	Y	Y	Y	Y	Y	N
8 Hefner	Y	Y	?	N	Y	Y	Y	N
9 ***McMillan***	N	N	Y	N	Y	Y	Y	N
10 ***Ballenger***	N	N	Y	N	Y	Y	Y	Y
11 ***Taylor***	N	N	Y	N	Y	Y	Y	N
NORTH DAKOTA								
AL Dorgan	Y	Y	Y	Y	Y	Y	Y	Y
OHIO								
1 Luken	Y	N	Y	N	Y	Y	Y	N
2 ***Gradison***	Y	Y	Y	N	Y	Y	Y	Y
3 Hall	Y	Y	Y	N	Y	Y	Y	N
4 ***Oxley***	N	N	Y	N	Y	Y	Y	N
5 ***Gillmor***	Y	Y	Y	N	Y	Y	Y	N
6 ***McEwen***	Y	N	Y	N	Y	Y	Y	N
7 ***Hobson***	N	N	Y	N	Y	Y	Y	Y
8 ***Boehner***	N	N	Y	N	Y	Y	Y	N
9 Kaptur	Y	Y	Y	Y	Y	Y	Y	N
10 ***Miller***	N	N	Y	N	Y	Y	Y	Y
11 Eckart	Y	Y	Y	Y	Y	Y	Y	N
12 ***Kasich***	Y	N	Y	N	Y	Y	Y	N
13 Pease	Y	Y	Y	Y	Y	Y	Y	Y
14 Sawyer	Y	Y	Y	Y	Y	Y	Y	N
15 ***Wylie***	Y	N	Y	N	Y	Y	Y	N
16 ***Regula***	N	N	Y	N	Y	Y	Y	Y
17 Traficant	Y	Y	Y	Y	Y	Y	Y	N
18 Applegate	Y	N	Y	N	Y	Y	Y	N
19 Feighan	Y	Y	Y	Y	Y	Y	Y	N
20 Oakar	Y	Y	Y	Y	Y	Y	Y	N
21 Stokes	?	?	?	?	?	?	?	?
OKLAHOMA								
1 ***Inhofe***	N	N	Y	N	Y	Y	Y	Y
2 Synar	Y	Y	Y	Y	Y	Y	Y	N
3 Brewster	Y	Y	Y	N	Y	Y	Y	N
4 McCurdy	Y	Y	Y	Y	Y	Y	Y	N
5 ***Edwards***	?	N	Y	N	Y	Y	?	N
6 English	Y	Y	Y	N	Y	Y	Y	Y
OREGON								
1 AuCoin	?	Y	Y	Y	Y	Y	Y	N
2 ***Smith***	N	N	Y	N	Y	Y	Y	N
3 Wyden	Y	Y	Y	Y	Y	Y	Y	Y
4 DeFazio	Y	Y	Y	Y	Y	Y	Y	?
5 Kopetski	Y	Y	Y	Y	Y	Y	Y	N
PENNSYLVANIA								
1 Foglietta	?	Y	Y	Y	Y	Y	Y	N
2 Vacancy								
3 Borski	Y	Y	Y	Y	Y	Y	Y	N
4 Kolter	Y	Y	Y	Y	Y	Y	Y	N
5 ***Schulze***	Y	N	Y	N	Y	Y	Y	N
6 Yatron	Y	Y	Y	Y	Y	Y	Y	N
7 ***Weldon***	N	N	Y	N	Y	Y	Y	N
8 Kostmayer	Y	Y	Y	Y	Y	Y	Y	Y
9 ***Shuster***	Y	N	Y	N	Y	Y	Y	N
10 ***McDade***	N	Y	Y	Y	Y	Y	Y	Y
11 Kanjorski	Y	Y	Y	Y	Y	Y	Y	N
12 Murtha	Y	Y	Y	Y	Y	Y	Y	N
13 ***Coughlin***	N	N	Y	Y	Y	Y	Y	N
14 Coyne	?	Y	Y	Y	Y	Y	Y	N
15 ***Ritter***	Y	N	Y	N	Y	Y	Y	Y
16 ***Walker***	N	N	Y	N	Y	Y	Y	Y
17 ***Gekas***	N	Y	Y	N	Y	Y	Y	Y
18 ***Santorum***	N	N	Y	N	Y	Y	Y	Y
19 ***Goodling***	N	Y	Y	N	Y	Y	Y	N
20 Gaydos	Y	Y	?	Y	Y	Y	Y	N
21 ***Ridge***	?	N	Y	N	Y	Y	Y	N
22 Murphy	N	Y	Y	Y	Y	Y	Y	Y
23 ***Clinger***	Y	N	Y	N	Y	Y	Y	Y
RHODE ISLAND								
1 ***Machtley***	N	Y	Y	Y	Y	Y	Y	N
2 Reed	Y	Y	Y	Y	Y	Y	Y	N
SOUTH CAROLINA								
1 ***Ravenel***	Y	N	Y	N	Y	Y	Y	N
2 ***Spence***	Y	N	Y	N	Y	Y	Y	N
3 Derrick	Y	Y	Y	Y	Y	Y	Y	N
4 Patterson	Y	Y	Y	N	Y	Y	Y	N
5 Spratt	Y	Y	Y	N	Y	Y	Y	N
6 Tallon	Y	N	Y	N	Y	Y	?	?

	269	270	271	272	273	274	275	277
SOUTH DAKOTA								
AL Johnson	Y	Y	Y	N	Y	Y	Y	Y
TENNESSEE								
1 ***Quillen***	Y	N	Y	N	Y	Y	Y	N
2 ***Duncan***	N	N	Y	N	Y	Y	Y	Y
3 Lloyd	?	N	Y	N	Y	Y	Y	N
4 Cooper	Y	Y	Y	Y	Y	Y	Y	N
5 Clement	Y	Y	Y	N	Y	Y	Y	N
6 Gordon	Y	Y	Y	Y	Y	Y	Y	N
7 ***Sundquist***	N	N	Y	N	Y	Y	Y	Y
8 Tanner	Y	Y	Y	N	Y	Y	Y	Y
9 Ford	?	?	?	?	?	?	?	N
TEXAS								
1 Chapman	Y	Y	Y	N	Y	Y	Y	N
2 Wilson	Y	Y	Y	N	Y	Y	?	N
3 ***Johnson***	Y	N	Y	N	Y	Y	Y	N
4 Hall	Y	N	Y	N	Y	Y	Y	N
5 Bryant	Y	Y	Y	Y	Y	Y	Y	N
6 ***Barton***	Y	N	Y	N	Y	Y	Y	Y
7 ***Archer***	Y	N	Y	N	Y	Y	Y	Y
8 ***Fields***	N	N	Y	N	Y	Y	Y	Y
9 Brooks	Y	Y	Y	Y	Y	Y	Y	N
10 Pickle	Y	Y	Y	Y	Y	Y	Y	Y
11 Edwards	Y	Y	Y	N	Y	Y	Y	N
12 Geren	Y	Y	Y	Y	Y	Y	Y	N
13 Sarpalius	Y	N	Y	N	Y	Y	Y	N
14 Laughlin	Y	Y	Y	Y	Y	Y	Y	N
15 de la Garza	Y	Y	?	Y	Y	Y	Y	N
16 Coleman	Y	Y	Y	Y	Y	Y	Y	Y
17 Stenholm	Y	Y	Y	N	Y	Y	Y	N
18 Washington	Y	Y	Y	?	?	?	Y	N
19 ***Combest***	Y	N	Y	N	Y	Y	Y	Y
20 Gonzalez	Y	Y	Y	Y	Y	Y	Y	N
21 ***Smith***	N	N	Y	N	Y	Y	Y	Y
22 ***DeLay***	N	N	Y	N	Y	Y	Y	Y
23 Bustamante	Y	Y	Y	Y	Y	Y	Y	N
24 Frost	Y	Y	Y	Y	Y	Y	Y	N
25 Andrews	Y	Y	Y	N	Y	Y	Y	Y
26 ***Armey***	N	N	Y	N	Y	Y	Y	Y
27 Ortiz	Y	Y	Y	N	Y	Y	Y	N
UTAH								
1 ***Hansen***	N	N	Y	N	Y	Y	Y	?
2 Owens	Y	N	Y	Y	Y	Y	Y	N
3 Orton	Y	N	Y	N	Y	Y	Y	Y
VERMONT								
AL *Sanders*	?	Y	Y	Y	Y	?	Y	N
VIRGINIA								
1 ***Bateman***	Y	N	Y	N	Y	Y	Y	N
2 Pickett	Y	Y	Y	N	Y	Y	Y	N
3 ***Bliley***	N	N	Y	N	Y	Y	Y	N
4 Sisisky	Y	Y	Y	N	Y	Y	Y	N
5 Payne	Y	Y	Y	N	Y	Y	Y	N
6 Olin	Y	Y	Y	Y	Y	Y	Y	N
7 ***Slaughter***	?	?	?	?	?	?	?	?
8 Moran	Y	Y	Y	Y	Y	+	Y	N
9 Boucher	Y	Y	Y	Y	Y	Y	Y	N
10 ***Wolf***	N	N	Y	N	Y	Y	Y	N
WASHINGTON								
1 ***Miller***	N	N	Y	Y	Y	Y	Y	Y
2 Swift	Y	Y	Y	Y	Y	Y	Y	N
3 Unsoeld	Y	Y	Y	Y	Y	Y	Y	N
4 ***Morrison***	?	N	Y	Y	Y	Y	Y	Y
5 Foley								
6 Dicks	Y	Y	Y	Y	Y	Y	Y	N
7 McDermott	Y	Y	Y	Y	Y	Y	Y	N
8 ***Chandler***	N	N	Y	N	Y	Y	Y	Y
WEST VIRGINIA								
1 Mollohan	Y	N	Y	Y	Y	Y	Y	N
2 Staggers	?	?	?	?	?	?	Y	N
3 Wise	Y	Y	Y	Y	Y	Y	?	N
4 Rahall	Y	?	Y	Y	Y	Y	Y	N
WISCONSIN								
1 Aspin	Y	Y	Y	Y	Y	Y	Y	N
2 ***Klug***	Y	N	Y	N	Y	Y	Y	Y
3 ***Gunderson***	Y	N	Y	N	Y	Y	Y	N
4 Kleczka	Y	Y	Y	Y	Y	?	Y	Y
5 Moody	Y	Y	Y	Y	Y	Y	Y	N
6 ***Petri***	Y	N	Y	N	Y	Y	Y	Y
7 Obey	Y	Y	Y	Y	Y	Y	Y	Y
8 ***Roth***	Y	N	Y	N	Y	Y	Y	Y
9 ***Sensenbrenner***	N	N	Y	N	Y	Y	Y	Y
WYOMING								
AL ***Thomas***	?	N	Y	N	Y	Y	Y	N

Southern states - Ala., Ark., Fla., Ga., Ky., La., Miss., N.C., Okla., S.C., Tenn., Texas, Va.
Omitted votes are quorum calls, which CQ does not include in its vote charts.

HOUSE VOTES 278, 279, 280, 281, 282, 283, 284, 285

278. HR 2900. Government-Sponsored Housing Enterprises/Passage. Passage of the bill to improve the supervision and regulation with respect to the financial safety and soundness of the Federal National Mortgage Association, the Federal Home Loan Mortgage Corporation, and the Federal Home Loan Bank System. Passed 412-8: R 156-4; D 255-4 (ND 172-4, SD 83-0); I 1-0, Sept. 25, 1991.

279. S 1722. Unemployment Benefits Extension/Rule. Bonior, D-Mich., motion to order the previous question (thus limiting debate and the possibility of amendment) on the adoption of the rule (H Res 227) to provide for House floor consideration of the bill to provide extended unemployment benefits to long-term unemployed workers. The rule struck all after the enacting clause and replaced the Senate language with the text of HR 3040 as passed by the House on Sept. 17 except for several tax-related provisions. Motion agreed to 257-163: R 0-160; D 256-3 (ND 174-2, SD 82-1); I 1-0, Sept. 25, 1991.

280. S 1722. Unemployment Benefits Extension/Passage. Passage of the bill to permanently extend unemployment benefits to long-term unemployed workers for up to 20 additional weeks at an estimated cost of $6.3 billion through fiscal 1996. The bill automatically declares the benefits to be emergency spending and would not require a presidential declaration to be exempt from the spending requirements of the 1990 budget agreement. Passed 294-127: R 50-109; D 243-18 (ND 174-2, SD 69-16); I 1-0, Sept. 25, 1991. (After passage, the House insisted on its amendments and requested a conference with the Senate.) A "nay" was a vote supporting the president's position.

281. HR 1426. Lumbee Tribe Recognition/Deadline for Review. Rhodes, R-Ariz., substitute amendment to, instead of granting federal recognition for the Lumbee Tribe, establish a deadline for a review of the tribe's petition. Rejected 159-251: R 146-11; D 13-239 (ND 5-164, SD 8-75); I 0-1, Sept. 26, 1991.

282. HR 1426. Lumbee Tribe Recognition/Passage. Passage of the bill to extend federal recognition to the Lumbee Tribe of Cheraw Indians of North Carolina, which would make the tribe eligible for social programs and protection under federal Indian laws. Passed 263-154: R 24-136; D 238-18 (ND 165-8, SD 73-10); I 1-0, Sept. 26, 1991. A "nay" was a vote supporting the president's position.

283. Procedural Motion. Kennelly, D-Conn., motion to approve the House Journal of Monday, Sept. 30. Motion agreed to 282-108: R 47-105; D 235-3 (ND 159-3, SD 76-0); I 0-0, Oct. 1, 1991.

284. S 1722. Unemployment Benefits Extension/Rule. Adoption of the rule (H Res 230) to provide for House floor consideration of the conference report to provide an estimated $6.4 billion for up to 20 additional weeks of unemployment benefits based on a state's average total unemployment rate. Adopted 270-147: R 14-147; D 255-0 (ND 174-0, SD 81-0); I 1-0, Oct. 1, 1991.

285. S 1722. Unemployment Benefits Extension/Conference Report. Adoption of the conference report (thus clearing it for the president) to provide an estimated $6.4 billion for up to 20 additional weeks of unemployment benefits based on a state's average total unemployment rate. The benefits would temporarily be extended from Oct. 6, 1991, through July 4, 1992. The conference report designates the spending as an emergency and would not require a presidential declaration to be exempt from the spending limits of last year's budget agreement. Adopted 300-118: R 55-107; D 244-11 (ND 173-1, SD 71-10); I 1-0, Oct. 1, 1991. A "nay" was a vote supporting the president's position.

KEY

- Y Voted for (yea).
- # Paired for.
- + Announced for.
- N Voted against (nay).
- X Paired against.
- \- Announced against.
- P Voted "present."
- C Voted "present" to avoid possible conflict of interest.
- ? Did not vote or otherwise make a position known.

Democrats ***Republicans***
Independent

	278	279	280	281	282	283	284	285
ALABAMA								
1 ***Callahan***	?	?	?	?	?	Y	N	N
2 ***Dickinson***	Y	N	N	N	N	N	N	N
3 Browder	Y	Y	Y	N	Y	Y	Y	Y
4 Bevill	Y	Y	Y	N	Y	Y	Y	Y
5 Cramer	Y	Y	Y	N	Y	Y	Y	Y
6 Erdreich	Y	Y	Y	N	Y	Y	Y	Y
7 Harris	Y	Y	Y	N	Y	Y	Y	Y
ALASKA								
AL ***Young***	Y	N	Y	Y	Y	N	N	Y
ARIZONA								
1 ***Rhodes***	Y	N	N	Y	N	N	N	N
2 Vacancy								
3 ***Stump***	Y	N	N	Y	N	N	N	N
4 ***Kyl***	Y	N	N	Y	N	N	N	N
5 ***Kolbe***	Y	N	N	Y	N	N	N	N
ARKANSAS								
1 Alexander	Y	Y	Y	N	Y	Y	Y	Y
2 Thornton	Y	Y	Y	N	Y	?	Y	Y
3 ***Hammerschmidt***	Y	N	N	Y	N	Y	N	N
4 Anthony	Y	Y	Y	N	Y	Y	Y	Y
CALIFORNIA								
1 ***Riggs***	Y	N	N	Y	N	N	N	Y
2 ***Herger***	Y	N	Y	Y	N	N	Y	Y
3 Matsui	Y	Y	Y	N	Y	Y	Y	Y
4 Fazio	Y	Y	Y	N	Y	Y	Y	Y
5 Pelosi	Y	Y	Y	N	Y	Y	Y	Y
6 Boxer	?	?	?	?	?	Y	Y	Y
7 Miller	N	Y	Y	N	Y	Y	Y	Y
8 Dellums	Y	Y	Y	N	Y	?	Y	Y
9 Stark	Y	Y	Y	?	?	Y	Y	Y
10 Edwards	Y	Y	Y	N	Y	Y	Y	Y
11 Lantos	Y	Y	Y	N	Y	Y	Y	Y
12 ***Campbell***	Y	N	N	Y	N	N	N	N
13 Mineta	Y	Y	Y	N	Y	Y	Y	Y
14 ***Doolittle***	Y	N	N	Y	N	N	N	N
15 Condit	Y	Y	Y	N	Y	Y	Y	Y
16 Panetta	Y	Y	Y	N	Y	Y	Y	Y
17 Dooley	Y	Y	Y	N	Y	?	Y	Y
18 Lehman	Y	Y	Y	N	Y	Y	Y	Y
19 ***Lagomarsino***	Y	N	N	Y	N	N	N	N
20 ***Thomas***	Y	N	N	Y	N	N	N	N
21 ***Gallegly***	Y	N	N	Y	N	N	N	N
22 ***Moorhead***	Y	N	N	Y	N	N	N	N
23 Beilenson	Y	Y	Y	N	Y	Y	Y	Y
24 Waxman	Y	Y	Y	N	Y	Y	Y	Y
25 Roybal	Y	Y	Y	?	?	Y	Y	Y
26 Berman	Y	Y	Y	N	Y	Y	Y	Y
27 Levine	?	Y	Y	?	?	Y	Y	Y
28 Dixon	Y	Y	Y	N	Y	Y	Y	Y
29 Waters	Y	Y	Y	?	Y	+	+	+
30 Martinez	Y	Y	Y	N	Y	Y	Y	Y
31 Dymally	Y	Y	Y	N	Y	?	?	?
32 Anderson	Y	Y	Y	N	Y	Y	Y	Y
33 ***Dreier***	Y	N	N	Y	N	Y	N	N
34 Torres	Y	Y	Y	N	Y	Y	Y	Y
35 ***Lewis***	Y	N	N	Y	N	N	N	N
36 Brown	Y	Y	Y	N	Y	Y	Y	Y
37 ***McCandless***	Y	N	N	Y	N	N	N	N
38 ***Dornan***	Y	N	N	Y	N	N	N	N
39 ***Dannemeyer***	Y	N	N	Y	N	N	N	N
40 ***Cox***	Y	N	N	Y	N	N	N	N
41 ***Lowery***	Y	N	N	Y	N	N	N	N
42 ***Rohrabacher***	Y	N	N	Y	N	N	N	N
43 ***Packard***	Y	N	N	Y	N	Y	N	N
44 ***Cunningham***	Y	N	N	Y	N	N	N	N
45 ***Hunter***	Y	N	N	N	N	N	N	N
COLORADO								
1 Schroeder	Y	Y	Y	N	Y	N	Y	Y
2 Skaggs	Y	Y	Y	N	Y	Y	Y	Y
3 Campbell	Y	Y	Y	N	Y	Y	Y	Y
4 ***Allard***	Y	N	N	Y	N	N	X	N
5 ***Hefley***	Y	N	N	Y	N	N	N	N
6 ***Schaefer***	Y	N	N	Y	N	N	N	N
CONNECTICUT								
1 Kennelly	N	Y	Y	N	Y	Y	Y	Y
2 Gejdenson	Y	Y	Y	N	Y	Y	Y	Y
3 DeLauro	Y	Y	Y	N	Y	Y	Y	Y
4 ***Shays***	Y	N	N	Y	N	N	N	N
5 ***Franks***	Y	N	Y	Y	N	N	N	Y
6 ***Johnson***	Y	N	Y	Y	N	Y	N	Y
DELAWARE								
AL Carper	Y	Y	Y	N	Y	Y	Y	Y
FLORIDA								
1 Hutto	Y	Y	N	N	Y	Y	Y	N
2 Peterson	Y	Y	Y	N	Y	Y	Y	Y
3 Bennett	Y	Y	Y	N	Y	Y	Y	Y
4 ***James***	Y	N	N	Y	N	N	N	N
5 ***McCollum***	Y	N	N	Y	N	Y	N	N
6 ***Stearns***	Y	N	Y	Y	N	N	N	Y
7 Gibbons	Y	Y	Y	N	Y	Y	Y	Y
8 ***Young***	Y	N	N	Y	N	N	N	Y
9 ***Bilirakis***	Y	N	N	Y	N	N	N	N
10 ***Ireland***	Y	N	N	Y	N	N	N	N
11 Bacchus	Y	Y	Y	N	Y	Y	Y	Y
12 ***Lewis***	Y	N	Y	Y	N	N	N	Y
13 ***Goss***	Y	N	N	Y	N	N	N	N
14 Johnston	Y	Y	Y	N	Y	Y	Y	Y
15 ***Shaw***	Y	N	N	Y	N	Y	N	N
16 Smith	Y	Y	Y	N	Y	Y	Y	Y
17 Lehman	Y	Y	Y	?	?	?	Y	Y
18 ***Ros-Lehtinen***	Y	N	Y	Y	N	N	N	Y
19 Fascell	Y	Y	Y	N	Y	Y	Y	Y
GEORGIA								
1 Thomas	Y	Y	Y	N	Y	Y	Y	Y
2 Hatcher	Y	Y	Y	N	Y	Y	Y	Y
3 Ray	Y	Y	N	N	Y	Y	Y	Y
4 Jones	Y	Y	Y	N	Y	Y	Y	Y
5 Lewis	Y	Y	Y	N	Y	Y	Y	Y
6 ***Gingrich***	Y	N	N	Y	N	N	N	N
7 Darden	Y	Y	Y	N	Y	Y	Y	Y
8 Rowland	Y	Y	N	N	Y	Y	Y	Y
9 Jenkins	Y	Y	Y	N	Y	Y	Y	Y
10 Barnard	Y	Y	N	N	Y	Y	Y	N
HAWAII								
1 Abercrombie	Y	Y	Y	N	Y	Y	Y	Y
2 Mink	Y	Y	Y	N	Y	Y	Y	Y
IDAHO								
1 LaRocco	Y	Y	Y	N	Y	Y	Y	Y
2 Stallings	Y	Y	Y	N	Y	Y	Y	Y
ILLINOIS								
1 Hayes	Y	Y	Y	N	Y	Y	Y	Y
2 Savage	Y	Y	Y	N	Y	?	Y	Y
3 Russo	Y	Y	Y	N	Y	Y	Y	Y
4 Sangmeister	Y	Y	Y	N	Y	Y	Y	Y
5 Lipinski	Y	Y	Y	?	Y	Y	Y	Y
6 ***Hyde***	Y	N	N	?	?	N	N	N
7 Collins	Y	Y	Y	N	Y	Y	Y	Y
8 Rostenkowski	Y	Y	Y	?	?	Y	Y	Y
9 Yates	Y	Y	Y	N	Y	Y	Y	Y
10 ***Porter***	Y	N	N	Y	N	Y	N	N
11 Annunzio	Y	Y	Y	N	Y	Y	Y	Y
12 ***Crane***	N	N	N	Y	N	?	X	?
13 ***Fawell***	Y	N	N	Y	N	N	N	N
14 ***Hastert***	Y	N	N	?	N	N	N	N
15 ***Ewing***	Y	N	N	?	N	N	N	N
16 Cox	Y	Y	Y	N	Y	Y	Y	Y
17 Evans	Y	Y	Y	N	Y	Y	Y	Y
18 ***Michel***	Y	N	N	Y	N	N	N	N
19 Bruce	Y	Y	Y	N	Y	Y	Y	Y
20 Durbin	Y	Y	Y	N	Y	Y	Y	Y
21 Costello	Y	Y	Y	N	Y	Y	Y	Y
22 Poshard	Y	Y	Y	N	Y	Y	Y	Y
INDIANA								
1 Visclosky	Y	Y	Y	N	Y	Y	Y	Y
2 Sharp	Y	Y	?	N	Y	Y	Y	Y
3 Roemer	Y	Y	Y	N	Y	Y	Y	Y

ND Northern Democrats SD Southern Democrats

	278	279	280	281	282	283	284	285
4 Long	Y	Y	Y	N	Y	Y	Y	Y
5 Jontz	Y	Y	Y	N	Y	Y	Y	Y
6 ***Burton***	Y	N	N	Y	Y	?	N	N
7 ***Myers***	Y	N	N	Y	Y	?	?	?
8 McCloskey	Y	Y	Y	N	Y	?	#	?
9 Hamilton	Y	N	Y	N	Y	Y	Y	Y
10 Jacobs	Y	N	Y	N	Y	?	Y	Y
IOWA								
1 ***Leach***	N	N	Y	Y	Y	N	N	Y
2 ***Nussle***	Y	N	N	Y	N	N	N	N
3 Nagle	Y	Y	Y	N	Y	Y	Y	Y
4 Smith	Y	Y	Y	N	Y	Y	Y	Y
5 ***Lightfoot***	Y	N	N	Y	N	N	N	N
6 ***Grandy***	Y	N	N	Y	N	N	N	N
KANSAS								
1 ***Roberts***	Y	N	N	Y	N	N	N	N
2 Slattery	Y	Y	Y	N	Y	Y	Y	Y
3 ***Meyers***	Y	N	N	Y	N	N	N	N
4 Glickman	Y	Y	Y	N	Y	Y	Y	Y
5 ***Nichols***	Y	N	N	Y	N	Y	N	N
KENTUCKY								
1 Hubbard	Y	Y	Y	N	Y	Y	Y	Y
2 Natcher	Y	Y	Y	N	Y	Y	Y	Y
3 Mazzoli	Y	Y	Y	N	Y	Y	Y	Y
4 ***Bunning***	Y	N	N	Y	N	N	N	N
5 ***Rogers***	Y	N	Y	Y	N	N	N	Y
6 ***Hopkins***	?	?	?	?	?	?	?	?
7 Perkins	Y	Y	Y	N	Y	Y	Y	Y
LOUISIANA								
1 ***Livingston***	Y	N	N	Y	N	Y	N	N
2 Jefferson	Y	Y	Y	N	Y	?	Y	Y
3 Tauzin	Y	Y	Y	N	Y	Y	Y	Y
4 ***McCrery***	Y	N	N	Y	N	N	N	N
5 Huckaby	Y	Y	Y	N	Y	Y	Y	Y
6 ***Baker***	Y	N	X	Y	N	N	N	N
7 Hayes	Y	Y	N	N	Y	Y	Y	N
8 ***Holloway***	?	?	?	?	?	?	?	?
MAINE								
1 Andrews	Y	Y	Y	N	Y	Y	Y	Y
2 ***Snowe***	Y	N	Y	N	Y	Y	Y	Y
MARYLAND								
1 ***Gilchrest***	Y	N	Y	Y	N	N	N	Y
2 ***Bentley***	Y	N	Y	Y	N	N	N	Y
3 Cardin	Y	Y	Y	N	Y	Y	Y	Y
4 McMillen	Y	Y	Y	N	Y	Y	Y	Y
5 Hoyer	Y	Y	Y	N	Y	Y	Y	Y
6 Byron	Y	Y	Y	N	Y	Y	Y	Y
7 Mfume	Y	Y	Y	N	Y	Y	Y	Y
8 ***Morella***	Y	N	Y	Y	N	N	N	Y
MASSACHUSETTS								
1 Olver	Y	Y	Y	N	Y	Y	Y	Y
2 Neal	Y	Y	Y	N	Y	Y	Y	Y
3 Early	Y	Y	Y	N	Y	Y	Y	Y
4 Frank	Y	Y	Y	N	Y	Y	Y	Y
5 Atkins	Y	Y	Y	N	Y	Y	Y	Y
6 Mavroules	Y	Y	Y	N	Y	Y	Y	Y
7 Markey	Y	Y	Y	N	Y	Y	Y	Y
8 Kennedy	Y	Y	Y	N	Y	Y	Y	Y
9 Moakley	Y	Y	Y	N	Y	Y	Y	Y
10 Studds	Y	Y	Y	N	Y	Y	Y	Y
11 Donnelly	Y	Y	Y	N	Y	Y	Y	Y
MICHIGAN								
1 Conyers	Y	Y	Y	N	Y	Y	Y	Y
2 ***Pursell***	Y	N	Y	?	?	N	N	Y
3 Wolpe	Y	Y	Y	N	Y	Y	Y	Y
4 ***Upton***	Y	N	Y	Y	Y	N	N	Y
5 ***Henry***	Y	N	Y	Y	N	N	Y	Y
6 Carr	Y	Y	Y	?	Y	Y	Y	Y
7 Kildee	Y	Y	Y	N	Y	Y	Y	Y
8 Traxler	Y	Y	Y	?	Y	Y	Y	Y
9 ***Vander Jagt***	Y	N	N	Y	N	Y	N	N
10 ***Camp***	Y	N	Y	Y	N	N	N	Y
11 ***Davis***	Y	N	Y	N	Y	Y	Y	Y
12 Bonior	Y	Y	Y	N	Y	Y	Y	Y
13 Collins	Y	Y	Y	N	Y	Y	Y	Y
14 Hertel	Y	Y	Y	N	Y	Y	Y	Y
15 Ford	Y	?	Y	N	Y	?	Y	Y
16 Dingell	Y	Y	Y	N	Y	Y	Y	Y
17 Levin	Y	Y	Y	N	Y	Y	Y	Y
18 ***Broomfield***	Y	N	N	Y	N	Y	N	N
MINNESOTA								
1 Penny	N	Y	N	Y	N	Y	Y	N
2 ***Weber***	Y	N	N	Y	N	?	N	N
3 ***Ramstad***	Y	N	N	Y	N	N	N	N
4 Vento	Y	Y	Y	N	Y	Y	Y	Y

	278	279	280	281	282	283	284	285
5 Sabo	Y	Y	Y	N	Y	Y	Y	Y
6 Sikorski	Y	Y	Y	N	Y	N	Y	Y
7 Peterson	Y	Y	Y	Y	N	Y	Y	Y
8 Oberstar	Y	Y	Y	N	Y	Y	Y	Y
MISSISSIPPI								
1 Whitten	Y	Y	Y	N	Y	Y	Y	Y
2 Espy	Y	Y	Y	N	Y	Y	Y	Y
3 Montgomery	Y	Y	N	Y	N	Y	Y	N
4 Parker	?	?	N	Y	N	Y	Y	N
5 Taylor	Y	N	N	N	N	Y	Y	N
MISSOURI								
1 Clay	Y	Y	Y	N	Y	Y	Y	Y
2 Horn	Y	Y	Y	N	Y	Y	Y	Y
3 Gephardt	Y	Y	Y	N	Y	?	Y	Y
4 Skelton	Y	Y	Y	N	Y	Y	Y	Y
5 Wheat	Y	Y	Y	N	Y	Y	Y	Y
6 ***Coleman***	Y	N	Y	Y	N	N	N	N
7 ***Hancock***	Y	N	N	Y	N	?	N	N
8 ***Emerson***	Y	N	Y	Y	N	Y	N	Y
9 Volkmer	Y	Y	Y	N	Y	Y	Y	Y
MONTANA								
1 Williams	Y	Y	Y	N	Y	Y	Y	Y
2 ***Marlenee***	Y	N	N	Y	N	N	N	Y
NEBRASKA								
1 ***Bereuter***	Y	N	N	Y	Y	N	N	N
2 Hoagland	Y	Y	Y	N	Y	Y	Y	Y
3 ***Barrett***	Y	N	N	Y	N	N	N	N
NEVADA								
1 Bilbray	Y	Y	Y	N	Y	Y	Y	Y
2 ***Vucanovich***	Y	N	N	Y	N	N	N	N
NEW HAMPSHIRE								
1 ***Zeliff***	Y	N	N	Y	N	?	N	N
2 Swett	Y	Y	Y	N	Y	Y	Y	Y
NEW JERSEY								
1 Andrews	Y	Y	Y	N	Y	Y	Y	Y
2 Hughes	Y	Y	Y	N	N	Y	Y	Y
3 Pallone	Y	Y	Y	N	Y	Y	Y	Y
4 ***Smith***	Y	N	Y	Y	N	Y	N	Y
5 ***Roukema***	Y	N	Y	Y	N	N	Y	Y
6 Dwyer	Y	Y	Y	N	Y	Y	Y	Y
7 ***Rinaldo***	Y	N	Y	Y	N	Y	Y	Y
8 Roe	Y	Y	Y	N	Y	Y	Y	Y
9 Torricelli	Y	Y	Y	N	Y	?	Y	Y
10 Payne	Y	Y	Y	N	Y	?	Y	Y
11 ***Gallo***	Y	N	Y	Y	N	N	N	Y
12 ***Zimmer***	Y	N	Y	Y	N	N	N	Y
13 ***Saxton***	Y	N	Y	Y	N	N	N	Y
14 Guarini	?	?	?	N	N	?	Y	Y
NEW MEXICO								
1 ***Schiff***	Y	N	N	Y	N	Y	N	N
2 ***Skeen***	Y	N	N	Y	N	Y	N	N
3 Richardson	Y	Y	Y	N	Y	Y	Y	Y
NEW YORK								
1 Hochbrueckner	Y	Y	Y	N	Y	Y	Y	Y
2 Downey	Y	Y	Y	N	Y	Y	Y	Y
3 Mrazek	Y	Y	Y	?	Y	Y	Y	Y
4 ***Lent***	Y	N	N	Y	N	Y	N	Y
5 ***McGrath***	?	?	#	N	Y	Y	Y	Y
6 Flake	Y	Y	Y	?	?	Y	Y	Y
7 Ackerman	Y	Y	Y	N	Y	Y	Y	Y
8 Scheuer	Y	Y	Y	N	Y	Y	Y	Y
9 Manton	Y	Y	Y	N	Y	Y	Y	Y
10 Schumer	Y	Y	Y	N	Y	Y	Y	Y
11 Towns	Y	Y	Y	N	Y	Y	Y	Y
12 Owens	Y	Y	Y	N	Y	?	Y	Y
13 Solarz	Y	Y	Y	N	?	Y	Y	Y
14 ***Molinari***	Y	N	Y	Y	N	N	N	Y
15 ***Green***	Y	N	N	Y	N	Y	N	N
16 Rangel	Y	Y	Y	N	Y	?	#	?
17 Weiss	Y	Y	Y	N	Y	+	Y	Y
18 Serrano	Y	Y	Y	N	Y	Y	?	Y
19 Engel	Y	Y	Y	N	Y	Y	Y	+
20 Lowey	Y	Y	Y	N	Y	Y	Y	Y
21 ***Fish***	Y	N	Y	Y	Y	Y	N	Y
22 ***Gilman***	Y	N	Y	Y	Y	Y	N	Y
23 McNulty	Y	Y	Y	N	Y	Y	Y	Y
24 ***Solomon***	Y	N	N	Y	N	N	N	N
25 ***Boehlert***	Y	N	Y	Y	N	N	Y	Y
26 ***Martin***	Y	N	Y	Y	N	Y	Y	Y
27 ***Walsh***	Y	N	Y	Y	N	Y	N	Y
28 McHugh	Y	Y	Y	N	Y	Y	Y	Y
29 ***Horton***	Y	N	Y	Y	N	Y	Y	Y
30 Slaughter	Y	Y	Y	N	Y	Y	Y	Y
31 ***Paxon***	Y	N	Y	Y	N	N	N	Y

	278	279	280	281	282	283	284	285
32 LaFalce	Y	Y	Y	N	Y	Y	Y	Y
33 Nowak	Y	Y	Y	N	Y	Y	Y	Y
34 ***Houghton***	Y	N	Y	Y	N	Y	N	Y
NORTH CAROLINA								
1 Jones	Y	Y	Y	N	Y	Y	Y	Y
2 Valentine	Y	Y	N	N	Y	Y	Y	N
3 Lancaster	Y	Y	Y	N	Y	Y	Y	Y
4 Price	Y	Y	Y	N	Y	Y	Y	Y
5 Neal	Y	Y	Y	N	Y	Y	Y	Y
6 ***Coble***	?	N	N	N	Y	N	N	N
7 Rose	Y	Y	Y	N	Y	Y	Y	Y
8 Hefner	Y	Y	Y	N	Y	Y	Y	Y
9 ***McMillan***	Y	N	N	Y	N	N	N	N
10 ***Ballenger***	Y	N	N	Y	N	N	N	N
11 ***Taylor***	Y	N	N	Y	N	N	N	N
NORTH DAKOTA								
AL Dorgan	N	Y	Y	N	N	Y	Y	Y
OHIO								
1 Luken	Y	Y	Y	N	Y	Y	Y	Y
2 ***Gradison***	Y	N	N	Y	N	Y	N	N
3 Hall	Y	Y	Y	N	Y	Y	Y	Y
4 ***Oxley***	Y	N	N	Y	N	Y	N	N
5 ***Gillmor***	Y	N	Y	Y	N	Y	N	N
6 ***McEwen***	Y	N	N	Y	N	Y	N	N
7 ***Hobson***	Y	N	N	Y	N	N	N	N
8 ***Boehner***	Y	N	N	Y	N	N	N	N
9 Kaptur	Y	Y	Y	N	Y	?	?	?
10 ***Miller***	Y	N	N	Y	N	N	N	N
11 Eckart	Y	Y	Y	N	Y	?	Y	Y
12 ***Kasich***	Y	N	N	Y	N	Y	N	N
13 Pease	Y	Y	Y	N	Y	Y	Y	Y
14 Sawyer	Y	Y	Y	N	Y	Y	Y	Y
15 ***Wylie***	Y	N	N	Y	N	?	N	N
16 ***Regula***	Y	N	Y	Y	N	Y	Y	Y
17 Traficant	Y	Y	Y	N	Y	Y	Y	Y
18 Applegate	Y	Y	Y	N	Y	Y	Y	Y
19 Feighan	Y	Y	Y	N	Y	Y	Y	Y
20 Oakar	Y	Y	Y	N	Y	Y	Y	Y
21 Stokes	?	#	#	N	Y	Y	Y	Y
OKLAHOMA								
1 ***Inhofe***	Y	N	N	Y	N	N	N	N
2 Synar	Y	Y	Y	Y	N	Y	Y	Y
3 Brewster	Y	Y	N	Y	N	Y	Y	Y
4 McCurdy	Y	Y	Y	Y	N	Y	Y	Y
5 ***Edwards***	Y	N	N	Y	N	N	N	N
6 English	Y	Y	Y	Y	N	?	Y	Y
OREGON								
1 AuCoin	Y	Y	Y	N	Y	?	Y	Y
2 ***Smith***	Y	N	Y	Y	N	?	N	Y
3 Wyden	Y	Y	Y	N	Y	Y	Y	Y
4 DeFazio	Y	Y	Y	N	Y	Y	Y	Y
5 Kopetski	Y	Y	Y	N	Y	Y	Y	Y
PENNSYLVANIA								
1 Foglietta	Y	Y	Y	N	Y	Y	Y	Y
2 Vacancy								
3 Borski	Y	Y	Y	N	Y	Y	Y	Y
4 Kolter	Y	Y	Y	N	Y	Y	Y	Y
5 ***Schulze***	Y	N	N	Y	N	Y	N	N
6 Yatron	Y	Y	Y	N	Y	Y	Y	Y
7 ***Weldon***	Y	N	Y	Y	N	N	N	Y
8 Kostmayer	Y	Y	Y	N	Y	Y	Y	Y
9 ***Shuster***	Y	N	Y	Y	N	Y	N	Y
10 ***McDade***	Y	N	Y	Y	Y	N	Y	Y
11 Kanjorski	Y	Y	Y	N	Y	Y	Y	Y
12 Murtha	Y	Y	Y	N	Y	Y	Y	Y
13 ***Coughlin***	Y	N	Y	Y	N	N	N	Y
14 Coyne	Y	Y	Y	N	Y	Y	Y	Y
15 ***Ritter***	Y	N	Y	Y	N	?	N	Y
16 ***Walker***	N	N	N	Y	N	N	N	N
17 ***Gekas***	Y	N	Y	Y	Y	N	N	Y
18 ***Santorum***	Y	N	N	Y	N	N	N	N
19 ***Goodling***	Y	N	Y	Y	N	N	N	Y
20 Gaydos	Y	Y	Y	N	Y	Y	Y	Y
21 ***Ridge***	Y	N	Y	Y	Y	?	N	Y
22 Murphy	Y	Y	Y	N	Y	N	Y	Y
23 ***Clinger***	Y	N	Y	Y	N	Y	N	Y
RHODE ISLAND								
1 ***Machtley***	Y	N	Y	Y	N	N	Y	Y
2 Reed	Y	Y	Y	N	Y	Y	Y	Y
SOUTH CAROLINA								
1 ***Ravenel***	Y	N	N	Y	N	Y	Y	Y
2 ***Spence***	Y	N	N	N	Y	Y	N	N
3 Derrick	Y	Y	Y	N	Y	?	?	?
4 Patterson	Y	Y	Y	N	Y	Y	Y	Y
5 Spratt	Y	Y	Y	N	Y	Y	Y	Y
6 Tallon	?	Y	Y	N	Y	Y	Y	Y

	278	279	280	281	282	283	284	285
SOUTH DAKOTA								
AL Johnson	Y	Y	Y	Y	N	Y	Y	Y
TENNESSEE								
1 ***Quillen***	Y	N	N	N	Y	Y	N	N
2 ***Duncan***	Y	N	N	Y	N	N	N	N
3 Lloyd	Y	Y	Y	N	Y	Y	Y	Y
4 Cooper	Y	Y	N	N	Y	Y	Y	Y
5 Clement	Y	Y	Y	N	Y	Y	Y	Y
6 Gordon	Y	Y	Y	N	Y	Y	Y	Y
7 ***Sundquist***	Y	N	N	?	Y	N	N	N
8 Tanner	Y	Y	N	?	?	Y	Y	Y
9 Ford	Y	Y	Y	N	Y	?	?	?
TEXAS								
1 Chapman	Y	Y	Y	N	Y	Y	Y	Y
2 Wilson	Y	Y	Y	N	Y	Y	Y	Y
3 ***Johnson***	Y	X	N	Y	N	Y	N	N
4 Hall	Y	Y	N	Y	Y	Y	Y	Y
5 Bryant	Y	Y	Y	N	Y	Y	Y	Y
6 ***Barton***	Y	N	N	Y	N	N	N	N
7 ***Archer***	Y	N	N	Y	N	Y	N	N
8 ***Fields***	Y	N	N	Y	N	N	N	N
9 Brooks	Y	Y	Y	N	Y	Y	Y	Y
10 Pickle	Y	?	Y	N	Y	Y	Y	Y
11 Edwards	Y	Y	Y	N	Y	Y	Y	Y
12 Geren	Y	Y	Y	Y	N	Y	Y	Y
13 Sarpalius	Y	Y	N	Y	Y	Y	Y	N
14 Laughlin	Y	Y	Y	N	Y	Y	Y	Y
15 de la Garza	Y	Y	Y	N	Y	Y	Y	Y
16 Coleman	Y	Y	Y	N	Y	Y	Y	Y
17 Stenholm	Y	Y	N	N	N	?	Y	N
18 Washington	Y	Y	Y	N	Y	Y	Y	Y
19 ***Combest***	Y	N	N	Y	N	Y	N	N
20 Gonzalez	Y	Y	Y	N	N	Y	Y	Y
21 ***Smith***	Y	N	N	Y	N	N	N	N
22 ***DeLay***	Y	N	N	Y	N	N	N	N
23 Bustamante	Y	Y	Y	N	Y	Y	Y	Y
24 Frost	Y	Y	Y	N	Y	Y	Y	Y
25 Andrews	Y	Y	Y	N	Y	Y	Y	Y
26 ***Armey***	Y	N	N	Y	N	N	N	N
27 Ortiz	Y	Y	Y	N	Y	Y	Y	Y
UTAH								
1 ***Hansen***	Y	N	N	Y	N	N	N	N
2 Owens	Y	Y	Y	N	Y	Y	Y	Y
3 Orton	Y	Y	N	Y	N	Y	Y	Y
VERMONT								
AL *Sanders*	Y	Y	Y	N	Y	?	Y	Y
VIRGINIA								
1 ***Bateman***	Y	N	X	Y	N	Y	N	N
2 Pickett	Y	Y	Y	N	Y	Y	Y	Y
3 ***Bliley***	Y	N	N	N	Y	N	N	N
4 Sisisky	Y	Y	Y	N	Y	Y	Y	Y
5 Payne	Y	Y	Y	N	Y	?	?	?
6 Olin	Y	Y	N	N	Y	?	?	?
7 ***Slaughter***	?	?	?	?	?	?	N	N
8 Moran	Y	Y	Y	N	Y	Y	Y	Y
9 Boucher	Y	Y	Y	N	Y	Y	Y	Y
10 ***Wolf***	Y	N	N	Y	N	N	N	N
WASHINGTON								
1 ***Miller***	Y	N	N	Y	N	N	N	N
2 Swift	Y	Y	Y	Y	N	Y	Y	Y
3 Unsoeld	Y	Y	Y	N	Y	Y	Y	Y
4 ***Morrison***	Y	N	N	Y	N	Y	N	Y
5 Foley								
6 Dicks	Y	Y	Y	N	Y	Y	Y	Y
7 McDermott	Y	Y	Y	N	Y	Y	Y	Y
8 ***Chandler***	Y	N	N	Y	N	N	N	N
WEST VIRGINIA								
1 Mollohan	Y	Y	Y	N	Y	Y	Y	Y
2 Staggers	Y	Y	Y	N	Y	Y	Y	Y
3 Wise	Y	Y	Y	N	Y	Y	Y	Y
4 Rahall	Y	Y	Y	N	Y	Y	Y	Y
WISCONSIN								
1 Aspin	Y	Y	Y	N	Y	Y	Y	Y
2 ***Klug***	Y	N	N	Y	Y	?	N	N
3 ***Gunderson***	Y	N	Y	Y	Y	Y	N	Y
4 Kleczka	Y	Y	Y	N	Y	Y	Y	Y
5 Moody	Y	Y	Y	N	Y	Y	Y	Y
6 ***Petri***	Y	N	N	Y	N	Y	N	N
7 Obey	Y	Y	Y	N	Y	Y	Y	Y
8 ***Roth***	Y	N	N	Y	N	Y	N	N
9 ***Sensenbrenner***	N	N	N	Y	N	N	N	N
WYOMING								
AL ***Thomas***	Y	N	N	Y	N	N	N	N

Southern states - Ala., Ark., Fla., Ga., Ky., La., Miss., N.C., Okla., S.C., Tenn., Texas, Va.
Omitted votes are quorum calls, which CQ does not include in its vote charts.

HOUSE VOTES 286, 287, 288, 289, 290, 291, 292, 293

286. HR 2519. Fiscal 1992 VA and HUD Appropriations/ Conference Report. Adoption of the conference report to provide $80,941,044,000 in new budget authority in fiscal 1992 for the Department of Housing and Urban Development, the Department of Veterans Affairs, the Environmental Protection Agency, NASA, the National Science Foundation and various other agencies. The administration requested $82,230,434,000. Adopted 390-30: R 141-19; D 248-11 (ND 165-11, SD 83-0); I 1-0, Oct. 2, 1991.

287. HR 2519. Fiscal 1992 VA and HUD Appropriations/ Laboratory Standards. Montgomery, D-Miss, motion to concur in the Senate amendment to require the Department of Veterans Affairs to establish standards for clinical laboratories consistent with private laboratories. Motion agreed to 390-24: R 152-4; D 237-20 (ND 158-18, SD 79-2); I 1-0, Oct. 2, 1991.

288. HR 3039. Defense Production Act/Passage. Passage of the bill to reauthorize the Defense Production Act of 1950 for fiscal 1992-94 to provide the president the authority to ensure that the United States maintains the ability to produce material critical to national defense. Passed 419-3: R 159-2; D 259-1 (ND 176-1, SD 83-0); I 1-0, Oct. 2, 1991.

289. Procedural Motion. Dixon, D-Calif., motion to approve the House Journal of Wednesday, Oct. 2. Motion agreed to 282-115: R 47-110; D 235-5 (ND 156-5, SD 79-0); I 0-0, Oct. 3, 1991.

290. HR 2608. Fiscal 1992 Commerce, Justice, State Appropriations/FBI Complex. Smith, D-Iowa, motion to recede and concur to a Senate amendment with an amendment to provide $48 million to initiate development and acquisition of a new FBI automated fingerprinting identification complex in West Virginia. Motion agreed to 252-162: R 49-111; D 203-51 (ND 131-40, SD 72-11); I 0-0, Oct. 3, 1991.

291. HR 2608. Fiscal 1992 Commerce, Justice, State Appropriations/Office of Textiles and Apparel. Smith, D-Iowa, motion to recede and concur to a Senate amendment with an amendment to provide $15.2 million for the Office of Textiles and Apparel, including $3.3 million for a grant to the Tailored Clothing Technology Corporation, $8 million for a grant to the National Textile Center University Research Consortium, and $3 million for a new material center in Ames, Iowa. Motion agreed to 300-111: R 66-96; D 234-15 (ND 155-13, SD 79-2); I 0-0, Oct. 3, 1991.

292. HR 2608. Fiscal 1992 Commerce, Justice, State Appropriations/Small Business Administration. Smith, D-Iowa, motion to recede and concur to a Senate amendment with an amendment to provide $236 million for the Small Business Administration, including $60.5 million for grants to small business development centers throughout the country. Motion agreed to 310-106: R 80-82; D 230-24 (ND 151-22, SD 79-2); I 0-0, Oct. 3, 1991.

293. HR 2608. Fiscal 1992 Commerce, Justice, State Appropriations/Moscow Embassy. Smith, D-Iowa, motion to recede and concur to a Senate amendment with an amendment to provide $100 million for construction of an entirely new and secure chancery for the U.S. Embassy in Moscow, leaving undecided what to do with the unfinished bug-riddled building. The House had provided $130 million for the administration to choose a plan for the embassy and report back. The Senate provided for $130 million for a teardown-reconstruction option. Motion rejected 175-231: R 13-148; D 162-83 (ND 110-56, SD 52-27); I 0-0, Oct. 3, 1991. (The House subsequently adopted by voice vote an amendment to provide $100 million for the administration to choose a plan and report back.)

* *Ed Pastor, D-Ariz., was sworn in Oct. 3, 1991. The first vote for which he was eligible was vote 290. Pastor replaces Morris K. Udall, D-Ariz., who resigned May 4, 1991, for health reasons. The last vote for which Udall was eligible was vote 76.*

KEY

Y Voted for (yea).
\# Paired for.
\+ Announced for.
N Voted against (nay).
X Paired against.
\- Announced against.
P Voted "present."
C Voted "present" to avoid possible conflict of interest.
? Did not vote or otherwise make a position known.

Democrats ***Republicans***
Independent

	286	287	288	289	290	291	292	293
ALABAMA								
1 ***Callahan***	Y	Y	Y	Y	Y	Y	Y	Y
2 ***Dickinson***	Y	Y	Y	N	N	Y	Y	Y
3 Browder	Y	Y	Y	Y	Y	Y	Y	Y
4 Bevill	Y	Y	Y	Y	Y	Y	Y	Y
5 Cramer	Y	Y	Y	Y	Y	Y	Y	N
6 Erdreich	Y	Y	Y	Y	Y	Y	Y	N
7 Harris	Y	Y	Y	Y	Y	Y	Y	N
ALASKA								
AL ***Young***	Y	Y	Y	N	N	Y	Y	N
ARIZONA								
1 ***Rhodes***	Y	Y	Y	N	N	N	N	N
2 Pastor					Y	Y	Y	Y
3 ***Stump***	N	Y	Y	N	N	N	N	N
4 ***Kyl***	N	Y	Y	N	N	N	N	N
5 ***Kolbe***	Y	?	Y	N	Y	Y	Y	N
ARKANSAS								
1 Alexander	Y	Y	Y	Y	Y	Y	Y	Y
2 Thornton	Y	Y	Y	Y	Y	Y	Y	Y
3 ***Hammerschmidt***	Y	Y	Y	Y	Y	N	Y	Y
4 Anthony	Y	Y	Y	Y	Y	Y	Y	Y
CALIFORNIA								
1 ***Riggs***	Y	Y	Y	N	N	Y	Y	N
2 ***Herger***	Y	Y	Y	N	N	N	N	N
3 Matsui	Y	Y	Y	Y	Y	Y	Y	Y
4 Fazio	Y	Y	Y	Y	Y	Y	Y	Y
5 Pelosi	Y	Y	Y	?	Y	Y	Y	Y
6 Boxer	Y	Y	Y	Y	Y	?	Y	Y
7 Miller	Y	Y	Y	Y	Y	Y	Y	N
8 Dellums	Y	Y	Y	Y	N	Y	Y	?
9 Stark	Y	Y	Y	?	Y	Y	Y	N
10 Edwards	Y	Y	Y	Y	Y	Y	Y	Y
11 Lantos	Y	Y	Y	Y	Y	Y	Y	N
12 ***Campbell***	Y	Y	Y	N	N	N	N	N
13 Mineta	Y	Y	Y	Y	Y	Y	Y	Y
14 ***Doolittle***	Y	Y	Y	N	N	N	N	N
15 Condit	Y	Y	Y	Y	N	N	N	Y
16 Panetta	Y	N	Y	Y	Y	Y	Y	N
17 Dooley	Y	Y	Y	Y	N	Y	Y	N
18 Lehman	Y	Y	Y	Y	Y	Y	Y	N
19 ***Lagomarsino***	Y	Y	Y	N	Y	N	Y	N
20 ***Thomas***	Y	Y	Y	N	Y	Y	?	N
21 ***Gallegly***	Y	Y	Y	N	Y	N	N	N
22 ***Moorhead***	N	Y	Y	N	N	N	N	N
23 Beilenson	N	N	Y	?	N	Y	N	Y
24 Waxman	Y	N	Y	Y	Y	Y	Y	Y
25 Roybal	Y	Y	Y	Y	Y	Y	Y	Y
26 Berman	Y	Y	Y	?	?	?	?	#
27 Levine	Y	?	Y	Y	Y	?	?	?
28 Dixon	Y	Y	Y	Y	Y	Y	Y	Y
29 Waters	?	N	Y	?	N	Y	Y	N
30 Martinez	Y	Y	Y	?	Y	Y	Y	?
31 Dymally	Y	Y	Y	?	?	?	?	?
32 Anderson	Y	Y	Y	Y	Y	Y	Y	Y
33 ***Dreier***	N	Y	Y	Y	N	N	N	N
34 Torres	Y	Y	Y	Y	Y	Y	Y	Y
35 ***Lewis***	Y	Y	Y	N	Y	Y	Y	N
36 Brown	Y	Y	Y	Y	Y	Y	Y	Y
37 ***McCandless***	Y	Y	Y	N	N	N	N	N
38 ***Dornan***	Y	Y	Y	N	N	N	N	N
39 ***Dannemeyer***	N	Y	Y	N	N	N	N	N
40 ***Cox***	N	Y	Y	N	N	N	N	N
41 ***Lowery***	Y	Y	Y	?	Y	Y	N	N
42 ***Rohrabacher***	N	Y	Y	N	N	N	N	N
43 ***Packard***	N	Y	Y	Y	N	N	N	N
44 ***Cunningham***	Y	Y	Y	N	N	Y	N	N
45 ***Hunter***	Y	Y	Y	?	N	Y	N	N
COLORADO								
1 Schroeder	Y	Y	Y	N	N	Y	N	N
2 Skaggs	Y	N	Y	Y	Y	Y	Y	Y
3 Campbell	Y	Y	Y	Y	Y	Y	Y	Y
4 ***Allard***	Y	Y	Y	N	N	N	N	N
5 ***Hefley***	Y	Y	Y	N	N	N	N	N
6 ***Schaefer***	Y	Y	Y	N	N	N	N	N
CONNECTICUT								
1 Kennelly	Y	Y	Y	Y	Y	Y	Y	Y
2 Gejdenson	Y	Y	Y	Y	Y	Y	Y	Y
3 DeLauro	Y	Y	Y	Y	N	Y	Y	N
4 ***Shays***	Y	Y	Y	N	N	N	N	N
5 ***Franks***	Y	Y	Y	N	N	N	N	N
6 ***Johnson***	Y	Y	Y	Y	Y	Y	Y	Y
DELAWARE								
AL Carper	Y	Y	Y	?	N	N	N	N
FLORIDA								
1 Hutto	Y	Y	Y	Y	Y	Y	Y	Y
2 Peterson	Y	Y	Y	Y	N	Y	Y	N
3 Bennett	Y	Y	Y	Y	Y	N	N	N
4 ***James***	Y	Y	Y	N	N	N	Y	N
5 ***McCollum***	Y	Y	Y	N	Y	N	N	N
6 ***Stearns***	Y	Y	Y	N	N	N	N	N
7 Gibbons	Y	Y	Y	Y	Y	Y	Y	Y
8 ***Young***	Y	Y	Y	N	Y	Y	Y	N
9 ***Bilirakis***	Y	Y	Y	N	N	N	Y	N
10 ***Ireland***	Y	Y	Y	N	N	N	Y	N
11 Bacchus	Y	Y	Y	Y	N	Y	Y	Y
12 ***Lewis***	Y	Y	Y	N	N	N	N	N
13 ***Goss***	Y	Y	Y	N	N	N	Y	N
14 Johnston	Y	Y	Y	Y	Y	Y	Y	Y
15 ***Shaw***	Y	Y	Y	Y	Y	N	N	N
16 Smith	Y	Y	Y	Y	Y	Y	Y	Y
17 Lehman	Y	N	Y	?	Y	Y	Y	?
18 ***Ros-Lehtinen***	Y	Y	Y	N	Y	N	N	N
19 Fascell	Y	Y	Y	Y	Y	Y	Y	Y
GEORGIA								
1 Thomas	Y	Y	Y	Y	Y	Y	Y	Y
2 Hatcher	Y	?	Y	Y	Y	Y	Y	Y
3 Ray	Y	Y	Y	Y	N	Y	Y	Y
4 Jones	Y	Y	Y	Y	Y	Y	Y	N
5 Lewis	Y	Y	Y	Y	N	Y	Y	Y
6 ***Gingrich***	Y	Y	Y	N	N	Y	Y	N
7 Darden	Y	Y	Y	Y	Y	Y	Y	Y
8 Rowland	Y	Y	Y	Y	Y	Y	Y	N
9 Jenkins	Y	Y	Y	Y	Y	Y	Y	Y
10 Barnard	Y	Y	Y	Y	Y	Y	Y	Y
HAWAII								
1 Abercrombie	Y	Y	Y	Y	Y	Y	Y	Y
2 Mink	Y	Y	Y	Y	Y	Y	Y	Y
IDAHO								
1 LaRocco	+	Y	Y	Y	N	Y	Y	N
2 Stallings	Y	Y	Y	Y	N	Y	Y	N
ILLINOIS								
1 Hayes	Y	Y	Y	Y	N	Y	Y	N
2 Savage	Y	Y	Y	Y	N	Y	Y	N
3 Russo	Y	Y	Y	Y	Y	Y	Y	N
4 Sangmeister	Y	Y	Y	Y	Y	Y	Y	N
5 Lipinski	Y	Y	Y	Y	Y	Y	Y	N
6 ***Hyde***	Y	Y	Y	N	N	N	N	N
7 Collins	Y	Y	Y	Y	N	Y	Y	N
8 Rostenkowski	Y	Y	Y	?	?	?	?	?
9 Yates	Y	N	Y	Y	Y	Y	Y	N
10 ***Porter***	Y	Y	Y	Y	Y	N	N	N
11 Annunzio	Y	Y	Y	Y	Y	Y	Y	Y
12 ***Crane***	N	Y	Y	N	N	N	N	N
13 ***Fawell***	N	Y	N	N	Y	N	N	N
14 ***Hastert***	Y	Y	Y	N	N	N	N	N
15 ***Ewing***	Y	Y	Y	Y	N	N	N	N
16 Cox	Y	Y	Y	Y	N	Y	Y	N
17 Evans	Y	Y	Y	Y	Y	Y	Y	N
18 ***Michel***	Y	Y	Y	N	?	Y	Y	Y
19 Bruce	Y	Y	Y	Y	Y	Y	Y	N
20 Durbin	Y	Y	Y	Y	Y	Y	Y	N
21 Costello	Y	Y	Y	Y	Y	Y	Y	N
22 Poshard	Y	Y	Y	Y	Y	Y	Y	N
INDIANA								
1 Visclosky	Y	N	Y	Y	Y	Y	Y	Y
2 Sharp	Y	Y	Y	Y	N	N	N	Y
3 Roemer	N	Y	Y	Y	N	N	Y	N

ND Northern Democrats SD Southern Democrats

	286	287	288	289	290	291	292	293
4 Long	Y	Y	Y	Y	Y	Y	Y	Y
5 Jontz	Y	Y	Y	Y	Y	Y	Y	N
6 ***Burton***	N	Y	Y	N	N	N	N	N
7 ***Myers***	Y	Y	Y	Y	Y	Y	Y	Y
8 McCloskey	Y	Y	Y	?	Y	Y	Y	Y
9 Hamilton	Y	Y	Y	Y	N	Y	N	Y
10 Jacobs	N	Y	Y	N	N	N	N	N
IOWA								
1 ***Leach***	Y	Y	Y	N	N	Y	N	N
2 ***Nussle***	Y	Y	Y	N	N	Y	Y	N
3 Nagle	Y	Y	Y	?	X	+	Y	Y
4 Smith	Y	?	Y	Y	Y	Y	Y	Y
5 ***Lightfoot***	Y	N	Y	N	Y	Y	Y	N
6 ***Grandy***	Y	Y	Y	N	N	Y	Y	N
KANSAS								
1 ***Roberts***	Y	Y	Y	N	N	?	N	N
2 Slattery	Y	Y	Y	?	Y	Y	N	N
3 ***Meyers***	Y	Y	Y	N	N	N	Y	N
4 Glickman	Y	Y	Y	Y	N	Y	N	N
5 ***Nichols***	Y	Y	Y	Y	N	N	N	N
KENTUCKY								
1 Hubbard	Y	Y	Y	Y	Y	Y	Y	N
2 Natcher	Y	Y	Y	Y	Y	Y	Y	Y
3 Mazzoli	Y	Y	Y	Y	Y	Y	Y	Y
4 ***Bunning***	Y	Y	Y	N	N	N	Y	N
5 ***Rogers***	Y	Y	Y	N	Y	Y	Y	N
6 ***Hopkins***	?	?	?	?	?	?	?	?
7 Perkins	Y	Y	Y	Y	Y	Y	Y	Y
LOUISIANA								
1 ***Livingston***	Y	Y	Y	Y	Y	Y	Y	N
2 Jefferson	Y	Y	Y	Y	Y	Y	Y	Y
3 Tauzin	Y	Y	Y	Y	Y	?	Y	N
4 ***McCrery***	Y	Y	Y	N	N	Y	N	N
5 Huckaby	Y	Y	Y	Y	Y	N	N	N
6 ***Baker***	Y	Y	Y	N	N	N	N	N
7 Hayes	Y	Y	Y	Y	Y	Y	Y	N
8 ***Holloway***	?	?	?	?	?	?	?	?
MAINE								
1 Andrews	Y	Y	Y	Y	N	Y	Y	N
2 ***Snowe***	Y	Y	Y	Y	N	Y	Y	N
MARYLAND								
1 ***Gilchrest***	Y	Y	Y	N	N	N	N	N
2 ***Bentley***	Y	Y	Y	N	N	Y	N	N
3 Cardin	Y	Y	Y	Y	Y	Y	Y	Y
4 McMillen	Y	Y	Y	Y	Y	Y	Y	Y
5 Hoyer	Y	Y	Y	?	Y	Y	Y	Y
6 Byron	Y	Y	Y	Y	Y	Y	N	N
7 Mfume	Y	N	Y	Y	N	N	N	N
8 ***Morella***	Y	Y	Y	N	N	N	Y	N
MASSACHUSETTS								
1 Olver	Y	Y	Y	Y	Y	Y	Y	Y
2 Neal	Y	Y	Y	Y	Y	Y	Y	Y
3 Early	Y	N	Y	Y	Y	Y	Y	Y
4 Frank	Y	Y	Y	Y	N	Y	Y	Y
5 Atkins	Y	N	Y	Y	Y	Y	Y	Y
6 Mavroules	Y	Y	Y	Y	Y	Y	Y	Y
7 Markey	Y	Y	Y	?	Y	Y	Y	Y
8 Kennedy	Y	N	Y	Y	Y	Y	Y	Y
9 Moakley	Y	Y	Y	Y	Y	Y	Y	Y
10 Studds	Y	Y	Y	Y	N	Y	Y	Y
11 Donnelly	Y	Y	Y	Y	Y	Y	Y	Y
MICHIGAN								
1 Conyers	Y	Y	Y	Y	N	Y	Y	Y
2 ***Pursell***	Y	?	Y	Y	N	Y	Y	N
3 Wolpe	Y	Y	Y	Y	Y	Y	Y	Y
4 ***Upton***	Y	Y	Y	N	N	N	Y	N
5 ***Henry***	Y	Y	Y	N	N	Y	Y	N
6 Carr	Y	N	Y	Y	Y	Y	Y	Y
7 Kildee	Y	Y	Y	Y	Y	Y	Y	Y
8 Traxler	Y	N	Y	Y	Y	Y	Y	Y
9 ***Vander Jagt***	Y	Y	Y	Y	N	N	Y	N
10 ***Camp***	Y	Y	Y	N	N	N	Y	N
11 ***Davis***	Y	Y	Y	Y	N	Y	Y	Y
12 Bonior	Y	Y	Y	Y	Y	Y	Y	Y
13 Collins	Y	Y	Y	Y	Y	Y	Y	N
14 Hertel	Y	Y	Y	Y	Y	Y	Y	N
15 Ford	Y	Y	Y	Y	?	?	Y	Y
16 Dingell	Y	Y	Y	Y	N	N	N	?
17 Levin	Y	Y	Y	Y	Y	Y	Y	N
18 ***Broomfield***	Y	Y	Y	P	N	Y	N	N
MINNESOTA								
1 Penny	N	Y	N	Y	N	N	N	N
2 ***Weber***	Y	Y	Y	N	N	Y	Y	N
3 ***Ramstad***	Y	Y	Y	N	N	N	N	N
4 Vento	Y	Y	Y	Y	Y	Y	Y	Y

	286	287	288	289	290	291	292	293
5 Sabo	Y	N	Y	Y	Y	Y	Y	Y
6 Sikorski	Y	Y	Y	N	Y	Y	Y	N
7 Peterson	Y	Y	Y	Y	N	Y	N	N
8 Oberstar	Y	Y	Y	Y	Y	Y	Y	Y
MISSISSIPPI								
1 Whitten	Y	Y	Y	Y	Y	Y	Y	Y
2 Espy	Y	Y	Y	Y	Y	Y	Y	Y
3 Montgomery	Y	Y	Y	Y	Y	Y	Y	Y
4 Parker	Y	Y	Y	Y	Y	Y	Y	Y
5 Taylor	Y	Y	Y	Y	Y	Y	Y	N
MISSOURI								
1 Clay	Y	Y	Y	N	N	Y	Y	Y
2 Horn	Y	Y	Y	Y	Y	Y	Y	Y
3 Gephardt	Y	Y	Y	Y	Y	Y	Y	Y
4 Skelton	Y	Y	Y	Y	Y	Y	Y	Y
5 Wheat	Y	Y	Y	Y	Y	Y	Y	Y
6 ***Coleman***	Y	Y	Y	N	N	Y	N	N
7 ***Hancock***	N	Y	Y	N	N	N	N	N
8 ***Emerson***	Y	Y	Y	Y	Y	Y	Y	N
9 Volkmer	Y	Y	Y	Y	Y	Y	Y	Y
MONTANA								
1 Williams	Y	Y	Y	Y	Y	Y	Y	Y
2 ***Marlenee***	Y	Y	Y	N	Y	N	Y	N
NEBRASKA								
1 ***Bereuter***	Y	Y	Y	N	Y	Y	Y	Y
2 Hoagland	Y	Y	Y	Y	Y	Y	Y	Y
3 ***Barrett***	Y	Y	Y	N	N	N	N	N
NEVADA								
1 Bilbray	Y	Y	Y	Y	Y	Y	Y	Y
2 ***Vucanovich***	Y	Y	Y	?	Y	Y	Y	N
NEW HAMPSHIRE								
1 ***Zeliff***	Y	Y	Y	N	N	N	Y	N
2 Swett	Y	Y	Y	Y	N	Y	Y	N
NEW JERSEY								
1 Andrews	Y	Y	Y	Y	N	N	N	N
2 Hughes	N	Y	Y	Y	Y	Y	Y	Y
3 Pallone	N	Y	Y	Y	N	N	N	N
4 ***Smith***	Y	Y	Y	Y	N	N	N	N
5 ***Roukema***	Y	Y	Y	N	N	Y	Y	N
6 Dwyer	Y	Y	Y	Y	Y	?	Y	Y
7 ***Rinaldo***	Y	Y	Y	Y	N	Y	Y	Y
8 Roe	Y	Y	Y	Y	Y	Y	Y	Y
9 Torricelli	Y	Y	Y	Y	Y	Y	Y	Y
10 Payne	Y	Y	Y	Y	Y	Y	Y	Y
11 ***Gallo***	Y	Y	Y	N	N	N	Y	N
12 ***Zimmer***	Y	Y	Y	N	N	N	N	N
13 ***Saxton***	Y	Y	Y	N	N	N	N	N
14 Guarini	Y	Y	Y	Y	N	Y	Y	Y
NEW MEXICO								
1 ***Schiff***	Y	Y	Y	Y	Y	Y	Y	N
2 ***Skeen***	Y	Y	Y	Y	Y	Y	Y	N
3 Richardson	Y	Y	Y	Y	Y	Y	Y	Y
NEW YORK								
1 Hochbrueckner	Y	Y	Y	Y	Y	Y	Y	Y
2 Downey	Y	Y	?	Y	Y	Y	Y	N
3 Mrazek	?	?	?	?	?	?	?	?
4 ***Lent***	Y	Y	Y	Y	?	Y	N	N
5 ***McGrath***	Y	Y	Y	Y	Y	Y	Y	?
6 Flake	Y	Y	Y	Y	Y	Y	Y	N
7 Ackerman	Y	Y	Y	Y	Y	Y	Y	Y
8 Scheuer	Y	N	Y	Y	Y	Y	Y	Y
9 Manton	Y	Y	Y	Y	Y	Y	Y	Y
10 Schumer	Y	Y	Y	Y	Y	Y	Y	Y
11 Towns	Y	Y	Y	Y	Y	Y	Y	N
12 Owens	Y	Y	Y	Y	Y	Y	Y	N
13 Solarz	Y	Y	Y	Y	Y	Y	Y	Y
14 ***Molinari***	Y	Y	Y	N	N	Y	Y	N
15 ***Green***	Y	N	Y	Y	Y	Y	Y	N
16 Rangel	Y	Y	Y	Y	Y	Y	Y	Y
17 Weiss	Y	N	Y	Y	Y	Y	Y	Y
18 Serrano	Y	Y	Y	Y	N	Y	Y	Y
19 Engel	Y	Y	Y	Y	Y	Y	Y	Y
20 Lowey	Y	Y	Y	Y	Y	Y	Y	Y
21 ***Fish***	Y	Y	Y	Y	Y	Y	Y	N
22 ***Gilman***	Y	Y	Y	Y	Y	Y	Y	N
23 McNulty	Y	Y	Y	Y	Y	Y	Y	Y
24 ***Solomon***	Y	Y	Y	N	N	N	N	N
25 ***Boehlert***	Y	Y	Y	N	N	Y	Y	N
26 ***Martin***	Y	Y	Y	N	Y	Y	Y	N
27 ***Walsh***	Y	Y	Y	N	N	N	Y	N
28 McHugh	Y	Y	Y	Y	Y	Y	Y	Y
29 ***Horton***	Y	Y	Y	Y	Y	Y	Y	N
30 Slaughter	Y	Y	Y	?	?	?	?	?
31 ***Paxon***	Y	Y	Y	N	N	N	Y	N

	286	287	288	289	290	291	292	293
32 LaFalce	Y	Y	Y	Y	Y	Y	Y	?
33 Nowak	Y	Y	Y	Y	Y	Y	Y	Y
34 ***Houghton***	Y	Y	Y	Y	Y	Y	Y	N
NORTH CAROLINA								
1 Jones	Y	Y	Y	Y	Y	Y	Y	Y
2 Valentine	Y	Y	Y	Y	Y	Y	Y	Y
3 Lancaster	Y	Y	Y	Y	Y	Y	Y	Y
4 Price	Y	Y	Y	Y	Y	Y	Y	Y
5 Neal	?	?	Y	Y	Y	Y	Y	Y
6 ***Coble***	Y	Y	Y	N	N	Y	N	N
7 Rose	Y	Y	Y	Y	Y	Y	?	?
8 Hefner	Y	Y	Y	Y	Y	Y	Y	Y
9 ***McMillan***	Y	Y	Y	N	N	Y	Y	N
10 ***Ballenger***	Y	Y	Y	N	N	Y	N	N
11 ***Taylor***	Y	Y	Y	N	N	Y	N	N
NORTH DAKOTA								
AL Dorgan	Y	Y	Y	Y	N	Y	N	N
OHIO								
1 Luken	N	Y	Y	Y	N	N	N	N
2 ***Gradison***	Y	N	Y	Y	N	N	N	N
3 Hall	Y	Y	Y	Y	Y	Y	Y	N
4 ***Oxley***	Y	Y	Y	N	N	N	N	N
5 ***Gillmor***	Y	Y	Y	Y	Y	N	Y	N
6 ***McEwen***	N	Y	Y	N	N	Y	N	N
7 ***Hobson***	Y	Y	Y	N	Y	N	N	N
8 ***Boehner***	Y	Y	Y	N	N	N	N	N
9 Kaptur	?	?	?	?	?	?	?	?
10 ***Miller***	Y	Y	Y	N	Y	N	N	Y
11 Eckart	Y	Y	Y	Y	Y	Y	Y	N
12 ***Kasich***	Y	Y	Y	Y	N	N	N	N
13 Pease	N	Y	Y	?	?	?	N	Y
14 Sawyer	Y	Y	Y	Y	Y	Y	Y	Y
15 ***Wylie***	Y	Y	Y	Y	N	N	N	N
16 ***Regula***	Y	Y	Y	N	Y	Y	Y	Y
17 Traficant	Y	Y	Y	Y	Y	Y	Y	N
18 Applegate	Y	Y	Y	Y	Y	Y	Y	N
19 Feighan	Y	Y	Y	Y	Y	Y	Y	Y
20 Oakar	Y	Y	Y	Y	Y	Y	Y	Y
21 Stokes	Y	N	Y	Y	N	Y	Y	Y
OKLAHOMA								
1 ***Inhofe***	Y	Y	Y	N	N	N	N	N
2 Synar	Y	Y	Y	Y	Y	Y	Y	Y
3 Brewster	Y	Y	Y	Y	Y	Y	Y	Y
4 McCurdy	Y	Y	Y	Y	Y	Y	?	N
5 ***Edwards***	?	Y	Y	N	Y	N	Y	N
6 English	Y	Y	Y	Y	Y	Y	Y	N
OREGON								
1 AuCoin	Y	Y	Y	Y	Y	Y	Y	Y
2 ***Smith***	Y	Y	Y	N	N	Y	Y	N
3 Wyden	Y	Y	Y	Y	Y	Y	Y	Y
4 DeFazio	Y	Y	Y	Y	Y	Y	Y	Y
5 Kopetski	Y	Y	Y	Y	Y	Y	Y	Y
PENNSYLVANIA								
1 Foglietta	Y	Y	Y	Y	Y	Y	Y	Y
2 Vacancy								
3 Borski	Y	Y	Y	Y	Y	Y	Y	Y
4 Kolter	Y	Y	Y	Y	Y	Y	Y	?
5 ***Schulze***	Y	Y	Y	Y	N	Y	Y	N
6 Yatron	Y	Y	Y	Y	Y	Y	Y	Y
7 ***Weldon***	Y	Y	Y	N	Y	N	N	N
8 Kostmayer	Y	Y	Y	Y	Y	Y	Y	Y
9 ***Shuster***	Y	Y	Y	Y	Y	N	Y	N
10 ***McDade***	Y	Y	Y	N	Y	Y	Y	N
11 Kanjorski	Y	Y	Y	Y	Y	Y	Y	Y
12 Murtha	Y	Y	Y	Y	Y	Y	Y	Y
13 ***Coughlin***	Y	Y	Y	N	Y	Y	Y	N
14 Coyne	Y	Y	Y	Y	Y	Y	Y	Y
15 ***Ritter***	Y	Y	Y	Y	N	Y	Y	N
16 ***Walker***	Y	Y	Y	?	N	N	N	N
17 ***Gekas***	Y	Y	Y	N	Y	Y	Y	Y
18 ***Santorum***	?	?	?	N	N	N	N	N
19 ***Goodling***	Y	Y	Y	N	N	N	Y	N
20 Gaydos	Y	Y	Y	Y	Y	Y	Y	?
21 ***Ridge***	?	?	Y	N	?	N	N	N
22 Murphy	N	Y	Y	N	Y	N	N	N
23 ***Clinger***	Y	Y	Y	Y	Y	Y	Y	N
RHODE ISLAND								
1 ***Machtley***	Y	Y	Y	N	N	N	Y	N
2 Reed	Y	Y	Y	Y	N	Y	Y	N
SOUTH CAROLINA								
1 ***Ravenel***	Y	Y	Y	Y	Y	Y	Y	N
2 ***Spence***	Y	Y	Y	Y	Y	Y	Y	N
3 Derrick	Y	Y	Y	Y	Y	Y	Y	Y
4 Patterson	Y	Y	Y	Y	N	Y	Y	N
5 Spratt	Y	Y	Y	Y	Y	Y	Y	Y
6 Tallon	Y	Y	Y	Y	Y	Y	Y	Y

	286	287	288	289	290	291	292	293
SOUTH DAKOTA								
AL Johnson	Y	Y	Y	Y	N	Y	N	N
TENNESSEE								
1 ***Quillen***	Y	Y	Y	Y	N	Y	Y	X
2 ***Duncan***	N	Y	Y	N	Y	N	N	N
3 Lloyd	Y	Y	Y	?	Y	Y	Y	N
4 Cooper	Y	Y	Y	Y	Y	Y	Y	Y
5 Clement	Y	?	?	Y	Y	Y	Y	N
6 Gordon	Y	Y	Y	Y	Y	Y	Y	Y
7 ***Sundquist***	Y	?	?	?	Y	Y	N	N
8 Tanner	Y	Y	Y	Y	Y	Y	Y	Y
9 Ford	?	?	?	?	?	?	?	?
TEXAS								
1 Chapman	Y	N	Y	Y	Y	Y	Y	Y
2 Wilson	Y	Y	Y	?	Y	Y	Y	N
3 ***Johnson***	Y	Y	Y	Y	N	N	N	N
4 Hall	Y	Y	Y	Y	Y	Y	Y	N
5 Bryant	Y	Y	Y	Y	Y	Y	Y	Y
6 ***Barton***	Y	Y	Y	N	N	N	N	N
7 ***Archer***	N	Y	Y	Y	N	N	N	N
8 ***Fields***	Y	Y	Y	N	N	N	N	N
9 Brooks	Y	Y	Y	Y	Y	Y	Y	Y
10 Pickle	Y	Y	Y	Y	Y	Y	Y	Y
11 Edwards	Y	Y	Y	Y	Y	?	Y	Y
12 Geren	Y	Y	Y	Y	N	Y	Y	N
13 Sarpalius	Y	Y	Y	Y	Y	Y	Y	?
14 Laughlin	Y	Y	Y	Y	Y	Y	Y	Y
15 de la Garza	Y	Y	Y	?	Y	Y	Y	Y
16 Coleman	Y	Y	Y	Y	Y	Y	Y	Y
17 Stenholm	Y	Y	Y	Y	Y	Y	Y	N
18 Washington	Y	Y	Y	Y	N	Y	Y	?
19 ***Combest***	Y	Y	Y	Y	Y	N	N	N
20 Gonzalez	Y	Y	Y	Y	Y	Y	Y	Y
21 ***Smith***	Y	Y	Y	N	N	N	N	N
22 ***DeLay***	N	Y	Y	N	N	N	N	N
23 Bustamante	Y	Y	Y	Y	Y	Y	Y	Y
24 Frost	Y	Y	Y	?	?	?	?	?
25 Andrews	Y	Y	Y	Y	N	N	Y	N
26 ***Armey***	N	Y	N	N	N	N	N	N
27 Ortiz	Y	Y	Y	Y	Y	Y	Y	Y
UTAH								
1 ***Hansen***	Y	Y	Y	N	N	N	Y	N
2 Owens	Y	Y	Y	Y	Y	Y	Y	Y
3 Orton	N	Y	Y	Y	N	N	N	N
VERMONT								
AL *Sanders*	Y	Y	Y	?	?	?	?	?
VIRGINIA								
1 ***Bateman***	Y	Y	Y	Y	Y	Y	Y	N
2 Pickett	Y	Y	Y	Y	Y	Y	Y	Y
3 ***Bliley***	Y	Y	Y	N	N	N	Y	N
4 Sisisky	Y	Y	Y	Y	Y	Y	Y	N
5 Payne	Y	Y	Y	Y	N	Y	Y	N
6 Olin	Y	Y	Y	Y	Y	Y	Y	N
7 ***Slaughter***	?	?	?	?	?	?	?	?
8 Moran	Y	Y	Y	Y	N	Y	Y	N
9 Boucher	Y	Y	Y	Y	Y	Y	Y	Y
10 ***Wolf***	Y	Y	Y	N	N	Y	Y	N
WASHINGTON								
1 ***Miller***	Y	Y	Y	N	N	N	N	N
2 Swift	Y	Y	Y	Y	Y	Y	Y	Y
3 Unsoeld	Y	Y	Y	Y	Y	Y	Y	Y
4 ***Morrison***	Y	Y	Y	Y	N	N	Y	N
5 Foley								
6 Dicks	Y	Y	Y	Y	Y	Y	Y	Y
7 McDermott	Y	N	Y	Y	Y	Y	Y	Y
8 ***Chandler***	Y	?	Y	N	N	N	N	N
WEST VIRGINIA								
1 Mollohan	Y	Y	Y	Y	Y	Y	Y	Y
2 Staggers	Y	Y	Y	?	#	?	?	?
3 Wise	Y	Y	Y	Y	Y	Y	Y	Y
4 Rahall	Y	Y	Y	Y	Y	Y	Y	Y
WISCONSIN								
1 Aspin	Y	Y	Y	Y	Y	Y	Y	Y
2 ***Klug***	Y	Y	Y	Y	N	N	Y	Y
3 ***Gunderson***	Y	Y	Y	Y	N	N	Y	N
4 Kleczka	Y	Y	Y	Y	Y	Y	Y	Y
5 Moody	Y	Y	Y	Y	N	Y	Y	?
6 ***Petri***	N	?	Y	Y	N	N	Y	N
7 Obey	N	Y	Y	Y	Y	Y	Y	Y
8 ***Roth***	Y	Y	Y	N	N	N	Y	N
9 ***Sensenbrenner***	N	Y	Y	N	N	N	N	N
WYOMING								
AL ***Thomas***	Y	N	Y	Y	N	N	N	N

Southern states - Ala., Ark., Fla., Ga., Ky., La., Miss., N.C., Okla., S.C., Tenn., Texas, Va.
Omitted votes are quorum calls, which CQ does not include in its vote charts.

HOUSE VOTES 294, 295, 296, 297, 298, 299, 300, 301

294. H Res 236. House Members Bank Closure/Adoption. Adoption of the resolution to instruct the sergeant-at-arms to close the House Bank as soon as possible but no later than Dec. 31, 1991. The resolution would also instruct the House ethics committee to examine a General Accounting Office audit to determine if there were significant, substantial and repeated abuses by individual members. Adopted 390-8: R 155-2; D 235-6 (ND 160-3, SD 75-3); I 0-0, Oct. 3, 1991.

295. Procedural Motion. Sensenbrenner, R-Wis., motion to table (kill) the chair's motion to allow DeLauro, D-Conn., to proceed in order after the chair ruled that DeLauro's one-minute speech was out of order and that her words should be taken down for referring to the action of the Senate in regard to the vote on the confirmation of Clarence Thomas to be an associate justice of the Supreme Court. Under House procedures, once a member's words are taken down, they are not allowed to speak on the House floor for the remainder of the day unless a motion to allow the member to proceed in order is agreed to. Motion rejected 142-257: R 142-10; D 0-246 (ND 0-166, SD 0-80); I 0-1, Oct. 8, 1991.

296. Procedural Motion. Chair's motion to allow DeLauro, D-Conn., to proceed in order after the chair ruled that DeLauro's one-minute speech was out of order and that her words should be taken down for referring to the action of the Senate in regard to the vote on the confirmation of Clarence Thomas to be an associate justice of the Supreme Court. Under House procedures, once a member's words are taken down, they are not allowed to speak on the House floor for the remainder of the day unless a motion to allow the member to proceed in order is agreed to. Motion agreed to 260-145: R 12-144; D 247-1 (ND 168-1, SD 79-0); I 1-0, Oct. 8, 1991.

297. S 1722. Unemployment Benefits Extension/Delay in Transmittal to President. Gephardt, D-Mo., motion to table (kill) the resolution (239) that resolves that the Speaker shall appoint a bipartisan committee to determine whether there has been unreasonable delay in transmitting to the president the enrolled bill of S 1722, providing extended unemployment benefits. Motion agreed to 253-156: R 0-156; D 252-0 (ND 171-0, SD 81-0); I 1-0, Oct. 8, 1991.

298. HR 3033. Job Training Partnership Act/Passage. Perkins, D-Ky., motion to suspend the rules and pass the bill to make changes to the Job Training Partnership Act of 1982, which is aimed at retraining economically disadvantaged individuals who are unprepared to compete in the labor market. Motion agreed to 420-6: R 157-6; D 262-0 (ND 180-0, SD 82-0); I 1-0, Oct. 9, 1991. A two-thirds majority of those present and voting (284 in this case) is required for passage under suspension of the rules.

299. HR 2942. Fiscal 1992 Transportation Appropriations/Conference Report. Adoption of the conference report to provide $35,153,872,569 in new budget authority in fiscal 1992 for the Department of Transportation and related agencies. The administration requested $33,381,198,569. Adopted 374-49: R 121-41; D 252-8 (ND 169-8, SD 83-0); I 1-0, Oct. 9, 1991.

300. HR 2942. Fiscal 1992 Transportation Appropriations/Demonstration Projects. Lehman, D-Fla., motion to recede and concur to a Senate amendment with an amendment to provide $249.1 million for 89 highway demonstration projects throughout the country. Motion agreed to 330-96: R 89-75; D 241-20 (ND 169-10, SD 72-10); I 0-1, Oct. 9, 1991.

301. HR 2942. Fiscal 1992 Transportation Appropriations/Appalachian Highway Improvements. Lehman, D-Fla., motion to recede and concur to a Senate amendment with an amendment to provide $148.5 million to improve Corridor G of the Appalachian Highway System in southern West Virginia. Motion agreed to 238-186: R 27-136; D 211-49 (ND 152-26, SD 59-23); I 0-1, Oct. 9, 1991.

KEY

- Y Voted for (yea).
- # Paired for.
- \+ Announced for.
- N Voted against (nay).
- X Paired against.
- \- Announced against.
- P Voted "present."
- C Voted "present" to avoid possible conflict of interest.
- ? Did not vote or otherwise make a position known.

Democrats ***Republicans***
Independent

	294	295	296	297	298	299	300	301
ALABAMA								
1 ***Callahan***	Y	Y	N	N	Y	Y	Y	N
2 ***Dickinson***	Y	Y	N	N	Y	Y	Y	N
3 Browder	Y	N	Y	Y	Y	Y	Y	Y
4 Bevill	Y	N	Y	Y	Y	Y	Y	Y
5 Cramer	Y	N	Y	Y	Y	Y	Y	N
6 Erdreich	Y	N	Y	Y	Y	Y	Y	Y
7 Harris	Y	N	Y	Y	Y	Y	Y	Y
ALASKA								
AL ***Young***	Y	Y	N	N	Y	Y	Y	Y
ARIZONA								
1 ***Rhodes***	Y	Y	N	N	Y	N	N	N
2 Pastor	Y	N	Y	Y	Y	Y	Y	Y
3 ***Stump***	Y	Y	N	N	N	N	N	N
4 ***Kyl***	Y	Y	N	N	Y	N	N	N
5 ***Kolbe***	Y	Y	N	N	Y	Y	N	N
ARKANSAS								
1 Alexander	Y	N	Y	Y	Y	Y	Y	Y
2 Thornton	Y	N	Y	Y	Y	Y	Y	Y
3 ***Hammerschmidt***	Y	Y	N	N	Y	Y	Y	N
4 Anthony	Y	N	?	Y	Y	Y	Y	Y
CALIFORNIA								
1 ***Riggs***	Y	?	P	N	Y	Y	Y	N
2 ***Herger***	Y	Y	N	N	Y	N	N	N
3 Matsui	Y	N	Y	Y	Y	Y	Y	Y
4 Fazio	Y	N	Y	Y	Y	Y	Y	Y
5 Pelosi	Y	?	?	Y	Y	Y	Y	Y
6 Boxer	Y	N	Y	Y	Y	Y	Y	Y
7 Miller	Y	N	Y	Y	Y	Y	Y	Y
8 Dellums	Y	N	Y	Y	Y	Y	Y	Y
9 Stark	Y	N	?	Y	Y	Y	Y	Y
10 Edwards	Y	N	Y	Y	Y	Y	Y	Y
11 Lantos	Y	N	Y	Y	Y	Y	Y	Y
12 ***Campbell***	Y	Y	N	N	Y	N	N	N
13 Mineta	Y	N	Y	Y	Y	Y	Y	Y
14 ***Doolittle***	Y	Y	N	N	Y	N	N	N
15 Condit	Y	N	Y	Y	Y	Y	N	N
16 Panetta	Y	N	Y	Y	Y	Y	Y	N
17 Dooley	Y	N	Y	Y	Y	Y	Y	N
18 Lehman	Y	N	Y	Y	Y	Y	Y	Y
19 ***Lagomarsino***	Y	Y	N	N	Y	Y	Y	N
20 ***Thomas***	Y	Y	N	N	Y	Y	Y	N
21 ***Gallegly***	Y	Y	N	N	Y	Y	Y	N
22 ***Moorhead***	?	Y	N	N	Y	Y	N	N
23 Beilenson	Y	N	Y	Y	Y	Y	Y	N
24 Waxman	Y	N	Y	Y	Y	Y	Y	Y
25 Roybal	N	N	Y	Y	Y	Y	Y	Y
26 Berman	?	N	Y	Y	Y	Y	Y	Y
27 Levine	?	?	?	?	Y	Y	Y	Y
28 Dixon	?	N	Y	Y	Y	Y	Y	Y
29 Waters	Y	N	Y	Y	Y	Y	Y	Y
30 Martinez	?	N	Y	Y	Y	Y	Y	Y
31 Dymally	?	?	Y	Y	Y	?	Y	Y
32 Anderson	Y	N	Y	Y	Y	Y	Y	Y
33 ***Dreier***	Y	?	N	N	Y	N	N	N
34 Torres	Y	N	Y	Y	Y	Y	Y	Y
35 ***Lewis***	Y	Y	N	N	Y	Y	Y	Y
36 Brown	Y	N	Y	Y	Y	Y	Y	Y
37 ***McCandless***	Y	Y	N	N	Y	?	Y	N
38 ***Dornan***	Y	Y	N	N	Y	Y	N	N
39 ***Dannemeyer***	Y	Y	N	N	N	N	N	N
40 ***Cox***	Y	Y	N	N	Y	Y	N	N
41 ***Lowery***	Y	Y	N	N	Y	Y	Y	Y
42 ***Rohrabacher***	Y	Y	N	N	Y	N	N	N
43 ***Packard***	Y	Y	N	N	Y	Y	Y	N
44 ***Cunningham***	Y	Y	N	N	Y	Y	N	N
45 ***Hunter***	Y	?	?	?	Y	Y	N	N
COLORADO								
1 Schroeder	Y	N	Y	Y	Y	Y	Y	N
2 Skaggs	Y	N	Y	Y	Y	Y	Y	Y
3 Campbell	Y	N	Y	Y	Y	Y	Y	Y
4 ***Allard***	Y	Y	N	N	Y	Y	N	N
5 ***Hefley***	Y	Y	N	N	Y	N	N	N
6 ***Schaefer***	Y	Y	N	N	Y	Y	N	N
CONNECTICUT								
1 Kennelly	Y	N	Y	Y	Y	Y	Y	Y
2 Gejdenson	Y	N	Y	Y	Y	Y	Y	Y
3 DeLauro	Y	N	Y	Y	Y	Y	Y	Y
4 ***Shays***	Y	N	Y	N	Y	N	N	N
5 ***Franks***	Y	Y	N	N	Y	N	N	N
6 ***Johnson***	Y	N	Y	N	Y	Y	N	N
DELAWARE								
AL Carper	Y	N	Y	Y	Y	Y	N	N
FLORIDA								
1 Hutto	Y	N	Y	Y	Y	Y	Y	N
2 Peterson	Y	N	Y	Y	Y	Y	Y	N
3 Bennett	Y	N	Y	Y	Y	Y	Y	Y
4 ***James***	Y	Y	N	N	Y	N	Y	N
5 ***McCollum***	Y	Y	N	N	Y	Y	N	N
6 ***Stearns***	Y	Y	N	N	Y	N	N	N
7 Gibbons	Y	N	Y	Y	Y	Y	Y	Y
8 ***Young***	Y	Y	N	N	Y	Y	N	N
9 ***Bilirakis***	Y	?	?	?	Y	Y	Y	N
10 ***Ireland***	?	Y	N	N	Y	Y	N	N
11 Bacchus	Y	N	Y	Y	Y	Y	Y	Y
12 ***Lewis***	Y	Y	N	N	Y	Y	Y	N
13 ***Goss***	Y	Y	N	N	Y	N	N	N
14 Johnston	Y	N	Y	Y	Y	Y	Y	Y
15 ***Shaw***	Y	Y	N	N	Y	Y	Y	Y
16 Smith	Y	?	?	?	Y	Y	Y	Y
17 Lehman	?	?	?	?	Y	Y	Y	Y
18 ***Ros-Lehtinen***	Y	?	?	?	Y	Y	Y	N
19 Fascell	Y	N	Y	Y	Y	Y	Y	Y
GEORGIA								
1 Thomas	Y	N	Y	Y	Y	Y	Y	Y
2 Hatcher	?	N	Y	Y	Y	Y	Y	Y
3 Ray	Y	N	Y	Y	Y	Y	N	N
4 Jones	N	N	Y	Y	Y	Y	Y	Y
5 Lewis	Y	N	Y	Y	Y	Y	Y	Y
6 ***Gingrich***	Y	Y	N	N	Y	?	N	N
7 Darden	Y	N	Y	Y	Y	Y	Y	Y
8 Rowland	Y	N	Y	Y	Y	Y	Y	Y
9 Jenkins	Y	N	Y	Y	Y	Y	Y	Y
10 Barnard	?	N	Y	Y	?	?	?	?
HAWAII								
1 Abercrombie	Y	N	Y	Y	Y	Y	Y	Y
2 Mink	Y	N	Y	Y	Y	Y	Y	Y
IDAHO								
1 LaRocco	Y	N	Y	Y	Y	Y	Y	Y
2 Stallings	Y	N	Y	Y	Y	Y	Y	Y
ILLINOIS								
1 Hayes	Y	N	Y	Y	Y	Y	Y	Y
2 Savage	N	?	?	?	Y	Y	Y	Y
3 Russo	Y	N	Y	Y	Y	Y	Y	Y
4 Sangmeister	Y	N	Y	Y	Y	Y	Y	Y
5 Lipinski	Y	N	Y	Y	Y	Y	Y	Y
6 ***Hyde***	Y	Y	N	N	Y	Y	N	N
7 Collins	Y	?	?	?	?	?	?	?
8 Rostenkowski	?	N	Y	Y	Y	Y	Y	Y
9 Yates	Y	N	Y	Y	Y	Y	Y	Y
10 ***Porter***	Y	Y	N	N	Y	Y	N	N
11 Annunzio	Y	N	Y	Y	Y	Y	Y	Y
12 ***Crane***	Y	Y	N	N	N	N	N	N
13 ***Fawell***	Y	Y	N	N	Y	N	N	N
14 ***Hastert***	Y	?	?	?	Y	N	N	N
15 ***Ewing***	Y	?	?	?	Y	Y	N	N
16 Cox	Y	N	Y	Y	Y	Y	Y	Y
17 Evans	Y	N	Y	Y	Y	Y	Y	Y
18 ***Michel***	Y	Y	N	N	Y	Y	Y	N
19 Bruce	Y	-	+	+	Y	N	Y	Y
20 Durbin	Y	-	+	+	Y	Y	Y	Y
21 Costello	Y	N	Y	Y	Y	Y	Y	Y
22 Poshard	Y	-	+	+	Y	Y	Y	Y
INDIANA								
1 Visclosky	Y	N	Y	Y	Y	Y	Y	Y
2 Sharp	Y	N	Y	Y	Y	Y	Y	Y
3 Roemer	Y	N	Y	Y	Y	Y	Y	N

ND Northern Democrats SD Southern Democrats

	294	295	296	297	298	299	300	301
4 Long	Y	N	Y	Y	Y	Y	Y	Y
5 Jontz	Y	N	Y	Y	Y	Y	Y	Y
6 ***Burton***	Y	Y	N	N	Y	N	N	N
7 ***Myers***	Y	Y	N	N	Y	Y	Y	Y
8 McCloskey	Y	N	Y	Y	Y	Y	Y	Y
9 Hamilton	Y	N	Y	Y	Y	Y	Y	Y
10 Jacobs	Y	N	Y	Y	Y	N	Y	N
IOWA								
1 ***Leach***	Y	N	Y	N	Y	Y	Y	N
2 ***Nussle***	Y	N	Y	?	Y	N	Y	N
3 Nagle	Y	N	Y	Y	Y	Y	Y	Y
4 Smith	Y	N	Y	Y	Y	Y	Y	Y
5 ***Lightfoot***	Y	Y	N	N	Y	Y	Y	Y
6 ***Grandy***	Y	Y	N	N	Y	Y	Y	N
KANSAS								
1 ***Roberts***	Y	Y	N	N	Y	N	N	N
2 Slattery	Y	N	Y	Y	Y	Y	Y	N
3 ***Meyers***	+	Y	Y	N	Y	Y	Y	N
4 Glickman	Y	N	Y	Y	Y	Y	Y	N
5 ***Nichols***	Y	Y	N	N	Y	Y	Y	N
KENTUCKY								
1 Hubbard	Y	N	Y	Y	Y	Y	Y	Y
2 Natcher	Y	N	Y	Y	Y	Y	Y	Y
3 Mazzoli	Y	N	Y	Y	Y	Y	Y	Y
4 ***Bunning***	Y	Y	N	N	Y	N	N	N
5 ***Rogers***	Y	Y	N	N	Y	Y	Y	Y
6 ***Hopkins***	?	?	?	?	?	?	?	?
7 Perkins	Y	N	Y	Y	Y	Y	Y	Y
LOUISIANA								
1 ***Livingston***	Y	Y	N	N	Y	Y	Y	N
2 Jefferson	Y	N	Y	Y	Y	Y	Y	Y
3 Tauzin	Y	N	Y	Y	Y	Y	Y	N
4 ***McCrery***	Y	Y	N	N	Y	Y	Y	N
5 Huckaby	Y	N	Y	Y	Y	Y	N	N
6 ***Baker***	Y	Y	N	N	Y	Y	N	N
7 Hayes	Y	N	Y	Y	Y	Y	Y	Y
8 ***Holloway***	?	?	?	?	?	?	?	?
MAINE								
1 Andrews	Y	N	Y	Y	Y	Y	Y	N
2 ***Snowe***	Y	N	Y	N	Y	Y	Y	N
MARYLAND								
1 ***Gilchrest***	Y	Y	N	N	Y	Y	N	N
2 ***Bentley***	Y	Y	N	N	Y	Y	Y	N
3 Cardin	Y	N	Y	Y	Y	Y	Y	Y
4 McMillen	Y	N	Y	Y	Y	Y	Y	Y
5 Hoyer	Y	N	Y	Y	Y	Y	Y	Y
6 Byron	Y	N	Y	Y	Y	Y	Y	Y
7 Mfume	Y	N	Y	Y	Y	Y	Y	N
8 ***Morella***	Y	?	Y	N	Y	Y	Y	N
MASSACHUSETTS								
1 Olver	Y	N	Y	Y	Y	Y	Y	Y
2 Neal	Y	N	Y	Y	Y	Y	Y	Y
3 Early	?	N	Y	Y	Y	Y	Y	Y
4 Frank	Y	N	Y	Y	Y	Y	Y	Y
5 Atkins	Y	N	Y	Y	Y	Y	Y	Y
6 Mavroules	Y	N	Y	Y	Y	Y	Y	Y
7 Markey	Y	N	Y	Y	Y	Y	Y	Y
8 Kennedy	Y	N	Y	Y	Y	Y	Y	Y
9 Moakley	Y	N	Y	Y	Y	Y	Y	Y
10 Studds	Y	N	Y	Y	Y	Y	Y	Y
11 Donnelly	Y	N	Y	Y	Y	Y	Y	Y
MICHIGAN								
1 Conyers	Y	N	Y	Y	Y	Y	Y	Y
2 ***Pursell***	Y	Y	N	N	Y	Y	Y	N
3 Wolpe	Y	N	Y	Y	Y	Y	Y	Y
4 ***Upton***	Y	Y	N	N	Y	Y	Y	N
5 ***Henry***	Y	Y	N	N	Y	Y	Y	N
6 ***Carr***	Y	N	Y	Y	Y	Y	Y	Y
7 Kildee	Y	N	Y	Y	Y	Y	Y	Y
8 Traxler	Y	N	Y	Y	Y	Y	Y	Y
9 ***Vander Jagt***	Y	Y	N	N	Y	Y	Y	N
10 ***Camp***	Y	Y	N	N	Y	Y	Y	N
11 ***Davis***	Y	Y	N	N	Y	Y	Y	N
12 Bonior	Y	N	Y	Y	Y	Y	Y	Y
13 Collins	Y	N	Y	Y	Y	Y	Y	Y
14 Hertel	Y	N	Y	Y	Y	Y	Y	Y
15 Ford	Y	?	Y	Y	Y	Y	Y	Y
16 Dingell	Y	N	Y	Y	Y	Y	Y	Y
17 Levin	Y	N	Y	Y	Y	Y	Y	Y
18 ***Broomfield***	Y	Y	N	N	Y	Y	Y	?
MINNESOTA								
1 Penny	Y	N	Y	Y	Y	N	N	N
2 ***Weber***	Y	Y	N	N	Y	Y	Y	N
3 ***Ramstad***	Y	Y	N	N	Y	Y	N	N
4 Vento	Y	N	Y	Y	Y	Y	Y	Y

	294	295	296	297	298	299	300	301
5 Sabo	Y	N	Y	Y	Y	Y	Y	Y
6 Sikorski	Y	N	Y	Y	Y	Y	Y	Y
7 Peterson	Y	N	Y	Y	Y	Y	N	N
8 Oberstar	Y	N	Y	Y	Y	Y	Y	Y
MISSISSIPPI								
1 Whitten	Y	N	Y	Y	Y	Y	Y	Y
2 Espy	Y	N	Y	Y	Y	Y	Y	Y
3 Montgomery	Y	N	Y	Y	Y	Y	Y	Y
4 Parker	Y	N	Y	Y	Y	Y	Y	N
5 Taylor	Y	N	Y	Y	Y	Y	N	N
MISSOURI								
1 Clay	Y	N	Y	Y	Y	Y	Y	Y
2 Horn	Y	N	Y	Y	Y	Y	Y	Y
3 Gephardt	Y	N	Y	Y	Y	Y	Y	Y
4 Skelton	Y	N	Y	Y	Y	Y	N	Y
5 Wheat	Y	N	Y	Y	Y	Y	Y	Y
6 ***Coleman***	Y	Y	N	N	Y	Y	N	N
7 ***Hancock***	Y	Y	N	N	Y	N	N	N
8 ***Emerson***	Y	Y	N	N	Y	Y	Y	N
9 Volkmer	Y	N	Y	Y	Y	Y	Y	Y
MONTANA								
1 Williams	Y	N	N	Y	Y	Y	N	Y
2 ***Marlenee***	Y	Y	N	N	Y	Y	Y	Y
NEBRASKA								
1 ***Bereuter***	Y	Y	N	N	Y	Y	Y	Y
2 Hoagland	Y	N	Y	Y	Y	Y	Y	Y
3 ***Barrett***	Y	Y	N	N	Y	Y	Y	N
NEVADA								
1 Bilbray	Y	N	Y	Y	Y	Y	Y	Y
2 ***Vucanovich***	Y	Y	N	N	Y	Y	Y	N
NEW HAMPSHIRE								
1 ***Zeliff***	Y	Y	N	N	Y	N	N	N
2 Swett	Y	N	Y	Y	Y	Y	Y	N
NEW JERSEY								
1 Andrews	Y	N	Y	Y	Y	Y	N	N
2 Hughes	Y	N	Y	Y	Y	Y	Y	N
3 Pallone	Y	N	Y	Y	Y	N	Y	N
4 ***Smith***	Y	Y	N	N	Y	Y	Y	N
5 ***Roukema***	Y	N	Y	N	Y	Y	Y	N
6 Dwyer	Y	N	Y	Y	Y	Y	?	?
7 ***Rinaldo***	?	Y	N	N	Y	Y	Y	N
8 Roe	Y	N	Y	Y	Y	Y	Y	N
9 Torricelli	?	?	?	Y	Y	Y	Y	Y
10 Payne	Y	N	Y	Y	Y	Y	Y	Y
11 ***Gallo***	Y	Y	N	N	Y	Y	Y	N
12 ***Zimmer***	Y	Y	N	N	Y	N	N	N
13 ***Saxton***	Y	Y	N	N	Y	Y	Y	N
14 Guarini	Y	N	Y	Y	Y	Y	Y	Y
NEW MEXICO								
1 ***Schiff***	Y	Y	N	N	Y	Y	Y	N
2 ***Skeen***	Y	Y	N	N	Y	Y	Y	Y
3 Richardson	Y	N	Y	Y	Y	Y	Y	Y
NEW YORK								
1 Hochbrueckner	Y	N	Y	Y	Y	Y	Y	Y
2 Downey	Y	N	Y	Y	Y	Y	Y	Y
3 Mrazek	?	?	?	?	Y	Y	Y	Y
4 ***Lent***	Y	Y	N	N	Y	Y	Y	N
5 ***McGrath***	Y	Y	N	N	Y	Y	Y	Y
6 Flake	Y	N	Y	Y	Y	Y	Y	Y
7 Ackerman	Y	N	Y	Y	Y	Y	Y	Y
8 Scheuer	Y	N	Y	Y	Y	Y	Y	Y
9 Manton	Y	N	Y	Y	Y	Y	Y	Y
10 Schumer	Y	N	Y	Y	Y	Y	Y	Y
11 Towns	N	N	Y	Y	Y	?	Y	Y
12 Owens	?	?	?	?	Y	Y	Y	Y
13 Solarz	Y	N	Y	Y	Y	Y	Y	Y
14 ***Molinari***	Y	N	Y	N	Y	Y	Y	N
15 ***Green***	Y	N	Y	N	Y	Y	Y	Y
16 Rangel	Y	N	Y	Y	Y	Y	Y	?
17 Weiss	Y	N	Y	Y	Y	Y	Y	Y
18 Serrano	Y	N	Y	Y	Y	Y	Y	Y
19 Engel	Y	?	Y	Y	Y	Y	Y	Y
20 Lowey	Y	N	Y	Y	Y	Y	Y	Y
21 ***Fish***	Y	Y	N	N	Y	Y	Y	N
22 ***Gilman***	Y	N	Y	N	Y	Y	Y	N
23 McNulty	Y	N	Y	Y	Y	Y	Y	Y
24 ***Solomon***	Y	Y	N	N	Y	N	N	N
25 ***Boehlert***	Y	Y	N	N	Y	Y	Y	N
26 ***Martin***	Y	?	N	N	Y	Y	Y	N
27 ***Walsh***	Y	Y	N	N	Y	Y	Y	N
28 McHugh	Y	N	Y	Y	Y	Y	Y	Y
29 ***Horton***	Y	Y	N	N	Y	Y	Y	Y
30 Slaughter	?	N	Y	Y	Y	Y	Y	Y
31 ***Paxon***	Y	Y	N	N	Y	Y	N	N

	294	295	296	297	298	299	300	301
32 LaFalce	?	N	Y	Y	Y	Y	Y	Y
33 Nowak	Y	N	Y	Y	Y	Y	Y	Y
34 ***Houghton***	Y	Y	N	N	Y	Y	Y	Y
NORTH CAROLINA								
1 Jones	Y	N	Y	Y	Y	Y	Y	Y
2 Valentine	Y	N	?	Y	Y	Y	Y	N
3 Lancaster	Y	?	?	Y	Y	Y	Y	Y
4 Price	Y	N	Y	Y	Y	Y	Y	Y
5 Neal	Y	N	Y	Y	Y	Y	N	N
6 ***Coble***	Y	Y	N	N	Y	N	N	N
7 Rose	?	N	Y	Y	Y	Y	?	Y
8 Hefner	Y	N	Y	Y	?	Y	Y	Y
9 ***McMillan***	Y	Y	N	N	Y	Y	Y	N
10 ***Ballenger***	Y	Y	N	N	Y	N	N	N
11 ***Taylor***	Y	Y	N	N	Y	N	N	N
NORTH DAKOTA								
AL Dorgan	Y	N	Y	Y	Y	N	Y	N
OHIO								
1 Luken	Y	N	Y	Y	Y	N	N	N
2 ***Gradison***	Y	Y	N	N	Y	Y	N	N
3 Hall	Y	N	Y	Y	Y	Y	Y	Y
4 ***Oxley***	Y	Y	N	N	Y	Y	N	N
5 ***Gillmor***	Y	Y	N	N	Y	Y	Y	Y
6 ***McEwen***	Y	Y	N	N	Y	N	Y	Y
7 ***Hobson***	Y	Y	N	N	Y	Y	Y	N
8 ***Boehner***	N	Y	N	N	Y	N	N	N
9 Kaptur	?	N	Y	Y	Y	Y	Y	Y
10 ***Miller***	Y	Y	N	?	Y	Y	N	N
11 Eckart	Y	N	Y	?	Y	Y	Y	N
12 ***Kasich***	Y	Y	N	N	Y	Y	N	N
13 Pease	?	N	Y	Y	Y	N	N	N
14 Sawyer	Y	N	Y	Y	Y	Y	Y	Y
15 ***Wylie***	Y	Y	N	N	Y	Y	N	N
16 ***Regula***	Y	Y	N	N	Y	Y	Y	Y
17 Traficant	Y	N	Y	Y	Y	Y	Y	Y
18 Applegate	?	N	Y	Y	Y	Y	Y	Y
19 Feighan	Y	N	Y	Y	Y	Y	Y	Y
20 Oakar	Y	?	Y	Y	Y	Y	Y	Y
21 Stokes	Y	N	Y	Y	Y	Y	Y	Y
OKLAHOMA								
1 ***Inhofe***	?	Y	N	N	Y	Y	N	N
2 Synar	Y	N	Y	Y	Y	Y	Y	N
3 Brewster	Y	N	Y	Y	Y	Y	Y	N
4 McCurdy	Y	N	Y	Y	Y	Y	N	N
5 ***Edwards***	Y	P	P	N	Y	Y	Y	N
6 English	Y	N	Y	Y	Y	Y	N	N
OREGON								
1 AuCoin	Y	N	Y	Y	Y	Y	Y	Y
2 ***Smith***	Y	Y	N	N	Y	Y	Y	N
3 Wyden	Y	N	Y	Y	Y	Y	Y	N
4 DeFazio	Y	N	Y	Y	Y	Y	Y	Y
5 Kopetski	Y	N	Y	Y	Y	Y	Y	Y
PENNSYLVANIA								
1 Foglietta	Y	N	Y	Y	Y	Y	Y	Y
2 Vacancy								
3 Borski	Y	N	Y	Y	Y	Y	Y	Y
4 Kolter	?	N	Y	Y	Y	Y	Y	Y
5 ***Schulze***	Y	Y	N	N	Y	Y	Y	N
6 Yatron	Y	N	Y	Y	Y	Y	Y	Y
7 ***Weldon***	Y	Y	N	N	Y	Y	N	N
8 Kostmayer	Y	N	Y	Y	Y	Y	Y	Y
9 ***Shuster***	Y	Y	N	N	Y	Y	Y	Y
10 ***McDade***	Y	Y	N	N	Y	Y	Y	Y
11 Kanjorski	Y	N	Y	Y	Y	Y	Y	Y
12 Murtha	Y	N	Y	Y	Y	Y	Y	Y
13 ***Coughlin***	Y	Y	N	N	Y	Y	Y	Y
14 Coyne	Y	N	Y	Y	Y	Y	Y	Y
15 ***Ritter***	Y	Y	N	N	Y	Y	Y	N
16 ***Walker***	Y	Y	N	N	N	N	N	N
17 ***Gekas***	Y	Y	N	N	+	N	N	N
18 ***Santorum***	Y	Y	N	N	Y	Y	N	N
19 ***Goodling***	Y	Y	N	N	Y	Y	N	N
20 Gaydos	?	N	Y	Y	Y	Y	Y	Y
21 ***Ridge***	Y	?	N	N	Y	Y	Y	Y
22 Murphy	Y	N	Y	Y	Y	Y	Y	Y
23 ***Clinger***	Y	Y	N	N	Y	Y	Y	Y
RHODE ISLAND								
1 ***Machtley***	Y	N	N	N	Y	Y	N	N
2 Reed	Y	N	Y	Y	Y	Y	Y	N
SOUTH CAROLINA								
1 ***Ravenel***	Y	Y	N	N	Y	Y	Y	Y
2 ***Spence***	Y	Y	N	N	Y	Y	Y	Y
3 Derrick	Y	N	Y	Y	Y	Y	Y	N
4 Patterson	Y	N	Y	Y	Y	Y	Y	Y
5 Spratt	Y	N	Y	Y	Y	Y	Y	Y
6 Tallon	Y	N	Y	Y	Y	Y	N	N

	294	295	296	297	298	299	300	301
SOUTH DAKOTA								
AL Johnson	Y	N	Y	Y	Y	Y	Y	Y
TENNESSEE								
1 ***Quillen***	?	Y	N	N	Y	Y	Y	Y
2 ***Duncan***	Y	Y	N	N	Y	N	N	N
3 Lloyd	Y	?	?	?	?	Y	Y	Y
4 Cooper	Y	N	Y	Y	Y	Y	N	N
5 Clement	Y	N	Y	Y	Y	Y	Y	Y
6 Gordon	Y	N	Y	Y	Y	Y	Y	Y
7 ***Sundquist***	Y	Y	N	N	Y	Y	Y	N
8 Tanner	Y	N	Y	Y	Y	Y	Y	N
9 Ford	?	N	Y	Y	Y	Y	Y	Y
TEXAS								
1 Chapman	Y	N	Y	Y	Y	Y	Y	Y
2 Wilson	Y	N	Y	?	Y	Y	Y	?
3 ***Johnson***	Y	Y	N	N	Y	Y	N	N
4 Hall	Y	N	Y	Y	Y	Y	Y	N
5 Bryant	Y	N	Y	Y	Y	Y	Y	Y
6 ***Barton***	Y	Y	N	N	Y	N	N	N
7 ***Archer***	Y	Y	N	N	Y	N	N	N
8 ***Fields***	Y	Y	N	N	Y	Y	N	N
9 Brooks	Y	N	Y	Y	Y	Y	Y	Y
10 Pickle	Y	N	Y	Y	Y	Y	Y	Y
11 Edwards	Y	N	Y	Y	Y	Y	Y	Y
12 Geren	Y	N	Y	Y	Y	Y	Y	Y
13 Sarpalius	?	N	Y	Y	Y	Y	Y	N
14 Laughlin	Y	?	Y	Y	Y	Y	Y	Y
15 de la Garza	Y	N	Y	Y	Y	Y	Y	Y
16 Coleman	Y	N	Y	Y	Y	Y	Y	Y
17 Stenholm	Y	N	Y	Y	Y	Y	N	N
18 Washington	N	N	Y	Y	?	?	?	?
19 ***Combest***	Y	Y	N	N	Y	N	N	N
20 Gonzalez	N	N	Y	Y	Y	Y	Y	Y
21 ***Smith***	Y	Y	N	N	Y	Y	N	N
22 ***DeLay***	N	Y	N	N	N	Y	Y	N
23 Bustamante	Y	N	Y	Y	Y	Y	Y	Y
24 Frost	?	N	Y	Y	Y	Y	Y	Y
25 Andrews	Y	N	Y	Y	Y	Y	N	N
26 ***Armey***	Y	Y	N	N	Y	N	N	N
27 Ortiz	Y	N	Y	Y	Y	Y	Y	Y
UTAH								
1 ***Hansen***	Y	Y	N	N	Y	Y	Y	N
2 Owens	Y	N	Y	Y	Y	Y	Y	Y
3 Orton	Y	N	Y	Y	Y	Y	Y	N
VERMONT								
AL *Sanders*	?	N	Y	Y	Y	Y	N	N
VIRGINIA								
1 ***Bateman***	Y	Y	N	N	Y	Y	Y	Y
2 Pickett	Y	N	Y	Y	Y	Y	Y	Y
3 ***Bliley***	Y	Y	N	N	Y	Y	Y	N
4 Sisisky	Y	N	Y	Y	Y	Y	Y	Y
5 Payne	Y	N	Y	Y	Y	Y	Y	Y
6 Olin	Y	N	Y	Y	Y	Y	Y	Y
7 ***Slaughter***	?	?	?	?	Y	Y	Y	N
8 Moran	Y	N	Y	Y	Y	Y	Y	N
9 Boucher	Y	N	Y	Y	Y	Y	Y	Y
10 ***Wolf***	Y	Y	N	N	Y	Y	Y	N
WASHINGTON								
1 ***Miller***	Y	Y	N	N	Y	Y	Y	N
2 Swift	Y	N	Y	Y	Y	Y	Y	Y
3 Unsoeld	Y	N	Y	Y	Y	Y	Y	Y
4 ***Morrison***	Y	Y	N	N	Y	Y	Y	N
5 Foley	Y							
6 Dicks	Y	N	Y	Y	Y	?	Y	Y
7 McDermott	Y	N	Y	Y	Y	Y	Y	Y
8 ***Chandler***	Y	Y	N	N	Y	Y	Y	N
WEST VIRGINIA								
1 Mollohan	Y	N	Y	Y	Y	Y	Y	Y
2 Staggers	?	N	Y	Y	Y	Y	Y	Y
3 Wise	Y	N	Y	Y	Y	Y	Y	Y
4 Rahall	Y	N	Y	Y	Y	Y	Y	Y
WISCONSIN								
1 Aspin	Y	N	Y	Y	Y	Y	Y	Y
2 ***Klug***	Y	Y	N	N	Y	Y	N	N
3 ***Gunderson***	Y	Y	N	N	Y	Y	N	N
4 Kleczka	Y	N	Y	Y	Y	Y	Y	Y
5 Moody	?	?	?	?	Y	N	N	N
6 ***Petri***	Y	Y	N	N	Y	N	N	N
7 Obey	Y	N	Y	Y	Y	Y	Y	Y
8 ***Roth***	Y	Y	N	N	Y	Y	N	N
9 ***Sensenbrenner***	Y	Y	N	N	N	N	N	N
WYOMING								
AL ***Thomas***	Y	Y	N	N	Y	N	N	N

Southern states - Ala., Ark., Fla., Ga., Ky., La., Miss., N.C., Okla., S.C., Tenn., Texas, Va.
Omitted votes are quorum calls, which CQ does not include in its vote charts.

HOUSE VOTES 302, 303, 304, 305, 306, 307, 308, 309

302. HR 1470. Vertical Price Fixing/Rule. Adoption of the rule (H Res 241) to provide for House floor consideration of the bill to amend the Sherman Antitrust Act of 1890 to tighten the ban on vertical price fixing, which occurs when a manufacturer conspires with a retailer to force a competing merchant to charge at least a certain price for goods or face a cutoff of supplies. The bill would lower the standard of evidence needed to get a resale price maintenance case to a jury trial. Adopted 412-0: R 161-0; D 251-0 (ND 174-0, SD 77-0), Oct. 10, 1991.

303. HR 1470. Vertical Price Fixing/Conspiracy Factor. Fish, R-N.Y., amendment to require a plaintiff to show evidence that a conspiracy to fix prices was the major rather than a substantial contributing factor in the termination of a contract in order to receive a jury trial. Rejected 196-218: R 148-13; D 48-204 (ND 13-162, SD 35-42); I 0-1, Oct. 10, 1991.

304. HR 1470. Vertical Price Fixing/Market Power. Campbell, R-Calif., amendment to allow as a defense against price-fixing actions that the manufacturer is so small in the relevant market as to lack market power. Adopted 218-195: R 156-6; D 62-188 (ND 27-148, SD 35-40); I 0-1, Oct. 10, 1991.

305. HR 2369. Flint Hills Prairie National Monument/Funding. Nichols, R-Kan., amendment to prohibit the national tall grass prairie monument in Kansas from being funded until there is no federal budget deficit. Rejected 153-249: R 135-20; D 18-228 (ND 4-162, SD 14-66); I 0-1, Oct. 15, 1991.

306. HR 2369. Flint Hills Prairie National Monument/Passage. Passage of the Glickman, D-Kan., bill to authorize the National Park Service to acquire land in the Flint Hills region of Kansas to establish a federal tall grass prairie preserve. Passed 284-121: R 46-110; D 237-11 (ND 164-4, SD 73-7); I 1-0, Oct. 15, 1991. A "nay" was a vote supporting the president's position.

307. HR 2521. Fiscal 1992 Defense Appropriations/Close Conference. Murtha, D-Pa., motion to close the conference on the bill to appropriate funds in fiscal 1992 for the Defense Department during consideration of classified national security matters. Motion agreed to 422-0: R 159-0; D 262-0 (ND 178-0, SD 84-0); I 1-0, Oct. 16, 1991.

308. HR 2686. Fiscal 1992 Interior Appropriations/National Endowment of the Arts. Yates, D-Ill., motion to table (kill) the Dannemeyer, R-Calif., motion to instruct conferees to insist on the Senate amendment to prohibit the National Endowment for the Arts from funding projects that depict or describe, in a patently offensive way, sexual or excretory activities or organs. Motion rejected 181-243: R 15-145; D 165-98 (ND 136-43, SD 29-55); I 1-0, Oct. 16, 1991.

309. HR 2686. Fiscal 1992 Interior Appropriations/National Endowment of the Arts. Dannemeyer, R-Calif., motion to instruct conferees to insist on the Senate amendment to prohibit the National Endowment for the Arts from funding projects that depict or describe, in a patently offensive way, sexual or excretory activities or organs. Motion agreed to 286-135: R 146-13; D 140-121 (ND 73-106, SD 67-15); I 0-1, Oct. 16, 1991.

KEY

- Y Voted for (yea).
- # Paired for.
- + Announced for.
- N Voted against (nay).
- X Paired against.
- \- Announced against.
- P Voted "present."
- C Voted "present" to avoid possible conflict of interest.
- ? Did not vote or otherwise make a position known.

Democrats ***Republicans***
Independent

	302	303	304	305	306	307	308	309
ALABAMA								
1 ***Callahan***	Y	Y	Y	?	?	?	?	?
2 ***Dickinson***	Y	Y	Y	Y	N	Y	N	Y
3 Browder	Y	Y	Y	N	Y	Y	N	Y
4 Bevill	Y	Y	N	?	?	Y	N	Y
5 Cramer	Y	Y	Y	N	Y	Y	N	Y
6 Erdreich	Y	Y	N	N	Y	Y	N	Y
7 Harris	Y	Y	N	N	Y	Y	N	Y
ALASKA								
AL ***Young***	Y	Y	Y	Y	N	Y	N	Y
ARIZONA								
1 ***Rhodes***	Y	Y	Y	Y	N	Y	N	Y
2 Pastor	Y	N	N	N	Y	Y	Y	N
3 ***Stump***	Y	Y	Y	Y	N	Y	N	Y
4 ***Kyl***	Y	Y	Y	Y	N	Y	N	Y
5 ***Kolbe***	Y	Y	Y	Y	N	Y	N	Y
ARKANSAS								
1 Alexander	?	N	Y	N	Y	Y	Y	Y
2 Thornton	Y	Y	Y	?	?	Y	N	Y
3 ***Hammerschmidt***	Y	Y	Y	Y	N	Y	N	Y
4 Anthony	Y	Y	Y	N	Y	Y	Y	Y
CALIFORNIA								
1 ***Riggs***	Y	Y	Y	Y	N	Y	N	Y
2 ***Herger***	Y	Y	Y	#	N	Y	N	Y
3 Matsui	Y	N	N	N	Y	Y	Y	N
4 Fazio	Y	N	N	N	Y	Y	Y	N
5 Pelosi	Y	N	N	N	Y	Y	Y	N
6 Boxer	?	?	?	?	?	?	Y	N
7 Miller	Y	N	N	N	Y	Y	Y	N
8 Dellums	Y	N	N	X	#	Y	Y	N
9 Stark	Y	N	N	N	Y	Y	Y	N
10 Edwards	Y	N	N	N	Y	Y	Y	N
11 Lantos	Y	N	N	N	Y	Y	Y	Y
12 ***Campbell***	Y	Y	Y	Y	Y	Y	N	N
13 Mineta	Y	N	N	?	+	Y	Y	N
14 ***Doolittle***	Y	Y	Y	Y	N	Y	N	Y
15 Condit	Y	Y	Y	Y	Y	Y	N	Y
16 Panetta	Y	N	N	N	Y	Y	Y	N
17 Dooley	Y	N	Y	N	Y	Y	N	Y
18 Lehman	Y	N	Y	N	Y	Y	Y	Y
19 ***Lagomarsino***	Y	Y	Y	Y	N	Y	N	Y
20 ***Thomas***	Y	Y	Y	Y	N	Y	N	Y
21 ***Gallegly***	Y	Y	Y	Y	N	Y	N	Y
22 ***Moorhead***	Y	Y	Y	Y	N	Y	N	Y
23 Beilenson	Y	N	N	N	Y	Y	Y	N
24 Waxman	Y	N	N	N	Y	Y	Y	N
25 Roybal	Y	N	N	N	Y	Y	?	N
26 Berman	Y	N	N	?	?	Y	Y	N
27 Levine	Y	N	N	?	?	Y	Y	N
28 Dixon	Y	N	N	N	Y	Y	Y	N
29 Waters	Y	N	N	N	Y	Y	Y	N
30 Martinez	Y	N	N	N	Y	Y	Y	N
31 Dymally	Y	N	N	?	?	Y	Y	N
32 Anderson	Y	N	N	N	Y	Y	Y	N
33 ***Dreier***	Y	Y	Y	Y	Y	Y	N	Y
34 Torres	?	N	N	N	Y	Y	Y	N
35 ***Lewis***	Y	Y	Y	?	X	?	?	?
36 Brown	Y	N	N	?	?	Y	Y	N
37 ***McCandless***	Y	Y	Y	N	N	Y	N	Y
38 ***Dornan***	Y	Y	Y	Y	Y	Y	N	Y
39 ***Dannemeyer***	Y	Y	Y	Y	N	Y	N	Y
40 ***Cox***	Y	Y	Y	Y	Y	Y	N	Y
41 ***Lowery***	Y	Y	Y	Y	N	Y	N	Y
42 ***Rohrabacher***	Y	Y	Y	Y	N	Y	N	Y
43 ***Packard***	Y	Y	Y	Y	N	Y	N	Y
44 ***Cunningham***	Y	Y	Y	Y	N	Y	N	Y
45 ***Hunter***	Y	Y	Y	Y	N	Y	N	Y
COLORADO								
1 Schroeder	Y	N	N	N	Y	Y	Y	N
2 Skaggs	Y	N	N	N	Y	Y	Y	N
3 Campbell	Y	Y	Y	Y	Y	Y	Y	Y
4 ***Allard***	Y	Y	Y	Y	N	Y	N	Y
5 ***Hefley***	Y	Y	Y	Y	N	Y	N	Y
6 ***Schaefer***	Y	Y	Y	Y	N	Y	N	Y
CONNECTICUT								
1 Kennelly	Y	N	N	N	Y	Y	Y	Y
2 Gejdenson	Y	N	N	N	Y	Y	Y	N
3 DeLauro	Y	N	N	N	Y	Y	Y	N
4 ***Shays***	Y	Y	Y	Y	Y	Y	N	Y
5 ***Franks***	Y	Y	Y	Y	N	Y	N	Y
6 ***Johnson***	Y	Y	Y	Y	N	Y	Y	Y
DELAWARE								
AL Carper	Y	N	Y	N	Y	Y	N	Y
FLORIDA								
1 Hutto	Y	Y	Y	N	Y	Y	N	Y
2 Peterson	Y	Y	Y	N	Y	Y	N	Y
3 Bennett	Y	N	N	N	Y	Y	N	Y
4 ***James***	Y	Y	Y	Y	Y	Y	N	Y
5 ***McCollum***	?	Y	Y	Y	N	Y	N	Y
6 ***Stearns***	Y	Y	Y	Y	N	Y	N	Y
7 Gibbons	Y	N	N	N	Y	Y	N	Y
8 ***Young***	Y	Y	Y	Y	N	Y	N	Y
9 ***Bilirakis***	Y	Y	Y	Y	N	Y	N	Y
10 ***Ireland***	Y	Y	Y	Y	N	Y	N	Y
11 Bacchus	Y	?	?	N	Y	Y	Y	N
12 ***Lewis***	Y	Y	Y	Y	N	Y	N	Y
13 ***Goss***	Y	Y	Y	Y	N	Y	N	Y
14 Johnston	Y	N	N	N	Y	Y	Y	N
15 ***Shaw***	Y	Y	Y	Y	Y	Y	N	Y
16 Smith	?	?	X	N	Y	Y	Y	N
17 Lehman	Y	N	N	?	?	Y	Y	N
18 ***Ros-Lehtinen***	Y	Y	Y	Y	Y	Y	N	Y
19 Fascell	Y	N	N	N	Y	Y	Y	N
GEORGIA								
1 Thomas	Y	N	Y	N	Y	Y	N	Y
2 Hatcher	?	N	N	N	Y	Y	Y	?
3 Ray	Y	Y	Y	N	Y	Y	N	Y
4 Jones	Y	N	N	N	Y	Y	Y	N
5 Lewis	Y	N	N	N	Y	Y	Y	N
6 ***Gingrich***	Y	Y	Y	Y	Y	Y	N	Y
7 Darden	Y	Y	N	N	Y	Y	N	Y
8 Rowland	Y	Y	Y	N	Y	Y	N	Y
9 Jenkins	Y	N	?	N	Y	Y	N	Y
10 Barnard	?	?	?	N	Y	Y	N	Y
HAWAII								
1 Abercrombie	Y	N	N	N	Y	Y	Y	N
2 Mink	Y	N	N	N	Y	Y	Y	N
IDAHO								
1 LaRocco	Y	N	Y	N	Y	Y	Y	N
2 Stallings	Y	Y	Y	N	Y	Y	N	Y
ILLINOIS								
1 Hayes	Y	N	N	N	Y	Y	Y	N
2 Savage	?	?	?	N	Y	?	?	?
3 Russo	Y	N	N	N	Y	?	Y	Y
4 Sangmeister	Y	N	N	N	Y	Y	N	Y
5 Lipinski	Y	N	N	N	Y	Y	N	Y
6 ***Hyde***	Y	N	N	Y	N	Y	N	Y
7 Collins	Y	N	N	N	Y	Y	Y	N
8 Rostenkowski	Y	N	N	N	Y	Y	Y	Y
9 Yates	Y	N	N	N	Y	Y	Y	N
10 ***Porter***	Y	N	N	-	+	Y	N	Y
11 Annunzio	Y	N	N	N	Y	Y	N	Y
12 ***Crane***	Y	Y	Y	?	?	Y	N	?
13 ***Fawell***	Y	Y	Y	N	Y	Y	N	Y
14 ***Hastert***	Y	Y	Y	Y	N	Y	N	Y
15 ***Ewing***	Y	?	Y	Y	N	Y	N	Y
16 Cox	Y	N	N	N	Y	Y	Y	N
17 Evans	Y	N	N	N	Y	Y	Y	N
18 ***Michel***	Y	Y	Y	Y	N	?	N	Y
19 Bruce	Y	N	N	N	Y	Y	N	Y
20 Durbin	Y	N	N	N	Y	Y	Y	N
21 Costello	Y	N	N	N	N	Y	N	Y
22 Poshard	Y	N	N	N	Y	Y	N	Y
INDIANA								
1 Visclosky	Y	N	Y	N	Y	Y	Y	Y
2 Sharp	Y	N	N	N	Y	Y	N	Y
3 Roemer	Y	Y	Y	N	Y	Y	N	Y

ND Northern Democrats SD Southern Democrats

	302	303	304	305	306	307	308	309
4 Long	Y	Y	Y	N	Y	Y	N	Y
5 Jontz	Y	N	N	N	Y	Y	Y	Y
6 ***Burton***	Y	Y	Y	Y	N	Y	N	Y
7 ***Myers***	Y	Y	Y	Y	N	Y	N	Y
8 McCloskey	Y	N	N	N	Y	Y	N	Y
9 Hamilton	Y	N	Y	N	Y	Y	N	Y
10 Jacobs	Y	N	N	N	Y	Y	N	Y
IOWA								
1 ***Leach***	Y	N	Y	Y	Y	Y	Y	N
2 ***Nussle***	Y	Y	Y	Y	N	Y	Y	Y
3 Nagle	?	N	N	?	Y	Y	Y	N
4 Smith	Y	N	N	N	Y	Y	Y	N
5 ***Lightfoot***	Y	Y	Y	Y	N	Y	N	Y
6 ***Grandy***	Y	Y	Y	Y	N	Y	Y	N
KANSAS								
1 ***Roberts***	Y	Y	Y	Y	N	Y	N	Y
2 Slattery	Y	N	N	N	Y	Y	N	Y
3 ***Meyers***	Y	N	Y	N	Y	Y	N	Y
4 Glickman	Y	N	N	N	Y	Y	N	Y
5 ***Nichols***	Y	Y	Y	Y	N	Y	N	Y
KENTUCKY								
1 Hubbard	Y	Y	Y	N	Y	Y	N	Y
2 Natcher	Y	N	N	N	Y	Y	Y	Y
3 Mazzoli	Y	N	N	N	Y	Y	Y	N
4 ***Bunning***	Y	Y	Y	Y	N	Y	N	Y
5 ***Rogers***	Y	Y	Y	Y	N	Y	N	Y
6 ***Hopkins***	?	?	?	?	?	?	?	?
7 Perkins	Y	N	N	N	Y	Y	Y	Y
LOUISIANA								
1 ***Livingston***	Y	Y	Y	Y	N	Y	N	Y
2 Jefferson	Y	N	N	N	Y	Y	Y	N
3 Tauzin	Y	Y	Y	N	Y	Y	N	Y
4 ***McCrery***	Y	Y	Y	Y	N	Y	N	Y
5 Huckaby	Y	?	?	N	Y	Y	N	Y
6 ***Baker***	Y	Y	Y	Y	N	Y	N	Y
7 Hayes	Y	?	#	Y	Y	Y	N	Y
8 ***Holloway***	?	?	?	?	?	?	?	?
MAINE								
1 Andrews	Y	N	N	N	Y	Y	Y	N
2 ***Snowe***	Y	Y	Y	Y	Y	Y	N	Y
MARYLAND								
1 ***Gilchrest***	Y	Y	Y	N	Y	Y	N	Y
2 ***Bentley***	Y	N	N	Y	N	Y	N	Y
3 Cardin	Y	N	N	N	Y	Y	Y	N
4 McMillen	Y	N	Y	N	Y	Y	N	Y
5 Hoyer	Y	X	N	N	Y	Y	Y	N
6 Byron	Y	Y	Y	N	Y	Y	N	Y
7 Mfume	Y	N	N	N	Y	Y	Y	N
8 ***Morella***	Y	Y	Y	N	Y	Y	Y	N
MASSACHUSETTS								
1 Olver	Y	N	N	N	Y	Y	Y	N
2 Neal	Y	N	N	N	Y	Y	Y	Y
3 Early	Y	N	N	N	Y	Y	Y	Y
4 Frank	Y	N	N	N	Y	Y	Y	N
5 Atkins	Y	N	N	N	Y	Y	Y	N
6 Mavroules	Y	N	N	N	Y	Y	Y	Y
7 Markey	Y	N	N	N	Y	Y	Y	N
8 Kennedy	Y	N	N	N	Y	Y	Y	Y
9 Moakley	Y	N	N	N	Y	Y	Y	Y
10 Studds	Y	N	N	N	Y	Y	Y	N
11 Donnelly	Y	N	N	N	Y	Y	N	Y
MICHIGAN								
1 Conyers	Y	N	N	N	Y	Y	Y	N
2 ***Pursell***	Y	Y	Y	Y	Y	Y	N	Y
3 Wolpe	Y	N	N	N	Y	Y	Y	N
4 ***Upton***	Y	Y	Y	Y	Y	Y	N	Y
5 ***Henry***	Y	Y	Y	Y	Y	Y	N	Y
6 Carr	Y	N	N	N	Y	Y	Y	N
7 Kildee	Y	N	N	N	Y	Y	Y	N
8 Traxler	Y	N	N	N	Y	Y	Y	Y
9 ***Vander Jagt***	Y	Y	Y	Y	N	Y	N	Y
10 ***Camp***	Y	Y	Y	Y	N	Y	N	Y
11 ***Davis***	Y	Y	Y	Y	Y	Y	N	Y
12 Bonior	Y	N	N	N	Y	Y	Y	N
13 Collins	Y	N	N	N	Y	Y	Y	N
14 Hertel	Y	N	N	N	Y	Y	Y	N
15 Ford	?	?	?	?	?	Y	Y	N
16 Dingell	Y	N	N	N	Y	Y	Y	N
17 Levin	Y	N	N	N	Y	Y	Y	N
18 ***Broomfield***	?	#	?	Y	Y	Y	N	Y
MINNESOTA								
1 Penny	Y	Y	Y	N	Y	Y	N	Y
2 ***Weber***	Y	Y	Y	Y	N	Y	N	Y
3 ***Ramstad***	Y	Y	Y	Y	Y	Y	N	Y
4 Vento	Y	N	N	N	Y	Y	Y	N

	302	303	304	305	306	307	308	309
5 Sabo	Y	N	N	N	Y	Y	Y	N
6 Sikorski	Y	N	N	N	Y	Y	Y	N
7 Peterson	Y	N	Y	N	Y	Y	N	Y
8 Oberstar	Y	N	N	N	Y	Y	Y	N
MISSISSIPPI								
1 Whitten	Y	N	N	N	Y	Y	N	Y
2 Espy	Y	Y	Y	N	Y	Y	Y	Y
3 Montgomery	Y	Y	Y	Y	Y	Y	N	Y
4 Parker	Y	Y	Y	Y	Y	Y	N	Y
5 Taylor	Y	Y	Y	Y	N	Y	N	Y
MISSOURI								
1 Clay	Y	N	N	N	Y	Y	Y	N
2 Horn	Y	Y	Y	N	Y	Y	Y	Y
3 Gephardt	Y	N	N	N	Y	Y	Y	Y
4 Skelton	Y	N	Y	N	Y	Y	N	Y
5 Wheat	Y	N	N	N	Y	Y	Y	Y
6 ***Coleman***	Y	Y	Y	Y	N	Y	N	N
7 ***Hancock***	Y	Y	Y	Y	N	Y	N	Y
8 ***Emerson***	Y	Y	Y	Y	N	Y	N	Y
9 Volkmer	Y	N	Y	N	Y	Y	N	Y
MONTANA								
1 Williams	Y	N	Y	N	Y	Y	Y	N
2 ***Marlenee***	Y	Y	Y	?	?	Y	N	Y
NEBRASKA								
1 ***Bereuter***	Y	Y	Y	N	Y	Y	N	Y
2 Hoagland	Y	N	N	N	Y	Y	N	Y
3 ***Barrett***	Y	Y	Y	Y	N	Y	N	Y
NEVADA								
1 Bilbray	Y	N	N	N	Y	Y	N	Y
2 ***Vucanovich***	Y	Y	Y	#	X	Y	N	Y
NEW HAMPSHIRE								
1 ***Zeliff***	Y	Y	Y	Y	N	Y	N	Y
2 Swett	Y	N	N	N	Y	Y	N	Y
NEW JERSEY								
1 Andrews	Y	N	N	N	Y	Y	Y	N
2 Hughes	Y	N	N	N	Y	Y	Y	N
3 Pallone	Y	N	N	N	Y	Y	N	Y
4 ***Smith***	Y	Y	Y	N	Y	Y	N	Y
5 ***Roukema***	Y	Y	Y	Y	Y	Y	N	Y
6 Dwyer	Y	N	N	N	Y	Y	Y	Y
7 ***Rinaldo***	Y	N	N	N	Y	Y	N	Y
8 Roe	Y	N	N	?	N	Y	Y	Y
9 Torricelli	Y	N	N	N	Y	Y	Y	Y
10 Payne	Y	N	N	N	Y	Y	Y	N
11 ***Gallo***	Y	Y	Y	Y	N	Y	N	Y
12 ***Zimmer***	Y	Y	Y	N	Y	Y	N	Y
13 ***Saxton***	Y	Y	Y	N	Y	Y	N	Y
14 Guarini	Y	N	N	N	Y	Y	N	Y
NEW MEXICO								
1 ***Schiff***	Y	Y	Y	Y	N	Y	N	Y
2 ***Skeen***	Y	Y	Y	Y	N	Y	N	Y
3 Richardson	Y	N	N	N	Y	Y	Y	N
NEW YORK								
1 Hochbrueckner	Y	N	N	N	Y	Y	N	Y
2 Downey	Y	N	N	N	Y	Y	Y	N
3 Mrazek	?	?	?	?	?	Y	Y	N
4 ***Lent***	Y	N	Y	Y	N	Y	N	Y
5 ***McGrath***	Y	N	Y	N	Y	Y	N	Y
6 Flake	Y	N	N	?	?	Y	Y	N
7 Ackerman	Y	N	N	N	Y	Y	Y	N
8 Scheuer	Y	N	N	N	Y	Y	Y	N
9 Manton	Y	N	N	N	Y	Y	Y	N
10 Schumer	Y	N	N	N	Y	Y	Y	N
11 Towns	Y	N	N	N	Y	Y	Y	N
12 Owens	Y	N	N	?	?	Y	Y	N
13 Solarz	Y	?	N	N	Y	Y	Y	N
14 ***Molinari***	Y	N	Y	Y	N	Y	N	Y
15 ***Green***	Y	Y	Y	N	Y	Y	Y	N
16 Rangel	Y	N	N	N	Y	Y	Y	N
17 Weiss	Y	N	N	N	Y	Y	Y	N
18 Serrano	Y	N	N	N	Y	Y	Y	N
19 Engel	Y	N	N	Y	Y	Y	Y	N
20 Lowey	Y	Y	N	N	Y	Y	Y	N
21 ***Fish***	Y	Y	Y	Y	Y	Y	Y	N
22 ***Gilman***	Y	N	N	N	N	Y	Y	N
23 McNulty	Y	N	N	N	Y	Y	Y	Y
24 ***Solomon***	Y	Y	Y	Y	N	Y	N	Y
25 ***Boehlert***	Y	Y	Y	N	Y	Y	Y	N
26 ***Martin***	Y	Y	Y	Y	N	Y	N	Y
27 ***Walsh***	Y	Y	Y	N	Y	Y	N	Y
28 McHugh	Y	Y	N	N	Y	Y	Y	N
29 ***Horton***	Y	Y	N	N	Y	Y	Y	N
30 Slaughter	Y	Y	N	N	Y	Y	Y	N
31 ***Paxon***	Y	Y	Y	Y	N	Y	N	Y

	302	303	304	305	306	307	308	309
32 LaFalce	Y	N	N	N	Y	Y	Y	N
33 Nowak	Y	N	N	N	Y	Y	Y	N
34 ***Houghton***	Y	Y	Y	N	N	Y	Y	N
NORTH CAROLINA								
1 Jones	Y	N	N	N	Y	Y	Y	Y
2 Valentine	Y	Y	Y	N	Y	Y	N	Y
3 Lancaster	Y	N	N	N	Y	Y	N	Y
4 Price	Y	N	N	N	Y	Y	N	Y
5 Neal	?	Y	Y	N	Y	Y	N	Y
6 ***Coble***	Y	Y	Y	Y	N	Y	N	Y
7 Rose	Y	N	N	N	Y	Y	N	Y
8 Hefner	Y	N	N	N	Y	Y	N	Y
9 ***McMillan***	Y	Y	Y	Y	N	Y	N	Y
10 ***Ballenger***	Y	Y	Y	Y	N	Y	N	Y
11 ***Taylor***	Y	Y	Y	Y	N	Y	N	Y
NORTH DAKOTA								
AL Dorgan	Y	N	Y	Y	N	Y	N	Y
OHIO								
1 Luken	Y	N	Y	N	Y	Y	N	Y
2 ***Gradison***	Y	Y	Y	Y	N	Y	N	Y
3 Hall	Y	N	N	N	Y	Y	Y	Y
4 ***Oxley***	Y	Y	Y	Y	N	Y	N	Y
5 ***Gillmor***	Y	Y	Y	Y	Y	Y	N	Y
6 ***McEwen***	Y	Y	Y	Y	N	Y	N	Y
7 ***Hobson***	Y	Y	Y	Y	N	Y	N	Y
8 ***Boehner***	Y	Y	Y	Y	N	Y	N	Y
9 Kaptur	?	N	N	N	Y	Y	Y	Y
10 ***Miller***	Y	Y	Y	Y	N	Y	N	Y
11 Eckart	Y	N	N	N	Y	Y	Y	N
12 ***Kasich***	Y	Y	Y	Y	N	Y	N	Y
13 Pease	Y	N	N	N	Y	Y	Y	N
14 Sawyer	Y	N	N	N	Y	Y	Y	N
15 ***Wylie***	Y	Y	Y	Y	N	Y	N	Y
16 ***Regula***	Y	Y	Y	Y	N	Y	N	Y
17 Traficant	Y	N	N	N	Y	Y	N	Y
18 Applegate	Y	N	N	N	Y	Y	N	Y
19 Feighan	Y	N	N	?	?	Y	Y	N
20 Oakar	Y	N	N	N	Y	Y	Y	N
21 Stokes	Y	N	?	N	Y	Y	Y	N
OKLAHOMA								
1 ***Inhofe***	Y	Y	Y	Y	N	Y	N	Y
2 Synar	Y	N	N	N	Y	Y	Y	N
3 Brewster	?	Y	Y	Y	N	Y	N	Y
4 McCurdy	Y	N	N	N	Y	Y	N	Y
5 ***Edwards***	Y	Y	Y	Y	N	?	?	?
6 English	Y	Y	Y	Y	Y	Y	N	Y
OREGON								
1 AuCoin	Y	N	N	N	Y	Y	Y	N
2 ***Smith***	Y	Y	Y	Y	N	Y	N	Y
3 Wyden	Y	N	N	N	Y	Y	Y	N
4 DeFazio	Y	N	N	N	Y	Y	Y	N
5 Kopetski	Y	N	N	N	Y	Y	Y	N
PENNSYLVANIA								
1 Foglietta	Y	N	?	N	Y	Y	Y	N
2 Vacancy								
3 Borski	Y	N	N	N	Y	Y	Y	Y
4 Kolter	Y	N	Y	N	Y	Y	Y	Y
5 ***Schulze***	Y	Y	Y	Y	N	Y	N	Y
6 Yatron	Y	N	N	N	Y	Y	N	Y
7 ***Weldon***	Y	Y	Y	Y	Y	Y	N	Y
8 Kostmayer	Y	N	N	N	Y	Y	Y	N
9 ***Shuster***	Y	Y	Y	Y	N	Y	N	Y
10 ***McDade***	Y	N	N	Y	Y	Y	Y	Y
11 Kanjorski	Y	N	N	N	Y	Y	Y	Y
12 Murtha	Y	N	N	N	Y	Y	Y	N
13 ***Coughlin***	Y	Y	Y	Y	Y	Y	N	Y
14 Coyne	Y	N	N	N	Y	Y	Y	N
15 ***Ritter***	Y	Y	Y	N	Y	Y	N	Y
16 ***Walker***	Y	Y	Y	Y	N	Y	N	Y
17 ***Gekas***	Y	Y	Y	Y	N	Y	N	Y
18 ***Santorum***	Y	Y	Y	Y	N	Y	N	Y
19 ***Goodling***	Y	Y	Y	Y	N	Y	N	Y
20 Gaydos	Y	N	N	N	Y	Y	Y	Y
21 ***Ridge***	Y	N	Y	N	Y	Y	N	Y
22 Murphy	Y	N	Y	N	Y	Y	N	Y
23 ***Clinger***	Y	Y	Y	Y	Y	Y	Y	N
RHODE ISLAND								
1 ***Machtley***	Y	N	Y	Y	Y	Y	Y	N
2 Reed	Y	N	N	N	Y	Y	Y	N
SOUTH CAROLINA								
1 ***Ravenel***	Y	Y	Y	N	Y	Y	N	Y
2 ***Spence***	Y	Y	Y	Y	N	Y	N	Y
3 Derrick	Y	Y	Y	N	Y	Y	Y	N
4 Patterson	Y	Y	Y	Y	Y	Y	N	Y
5 Spratt	Y	Y	N	N	Y	Y	N	Y
6 Tallon	Y	Y	Y	N	Y	Y	N	Y

	302	303	304	305	306	307	308	309
SOUTH DAKOTA								
AL Johnson	Y	N	Y	N	Y	Y	N	Y
TENNESSEE								
1 ***Quillen***	Y	Y	Y	Y	N	Y	N	Y
2 ***Duncan***	Y	Y	Y	Y	N	Y	N	Y
3 Lloyd	Y	Y	Y	Y	N	Y	N	Y
4 Cooper	Y	N	N	N	Y	Y	Y	Y
5 Clement	Y	N	N	N	Y	Y	N	Y
6 Gordon	Y	N	N	N	Y	Y	Y	Y
7 ***Sundquist***	Y	Y	Y	Y	N	Y	N	Y
8 Tanner	Y	Y	Y	Y	N	Y	N	Y
9 Ford	Y	N	?	X	#	?	Y	N
TEXAS								
1 Chapman	Y	?	?	?	?	Y	N	Y
2 Wilson	?	?	?	N	Y	Y	N	Y
3 ***Johnson***	Y	Y	Y	Y	N	Y	N	Y
4 Hall	Y	N	Y	Y	N	Y	N	Y
5 Bryant	Y	N	N	N	Y	Y	N	Y
6 ***Barton***	Y	Y	Y	?	?	Y	N	Y
7 ***Archer***	Y	Y	Y	Y	Y	Y	N	Y
8 ***Fields***	Y	Y	Y	Y	N	Y	N	Y
9 Brooks	Y	N	N	N	Y	Y	N	Y
10 Pickle	Y	N	N	N	Y	Y	Y	Y
11 Edwards	Y	N	N	N	Y	Y	N	Y
12 Geren	Y	N	Y	N	Y	Y	N	Y
13 Sarpalius	Y	Y	Y	Y	Y	Y	N	Y
14 Laughlin	Y	N	Y	N	Y	Y	N	Y
15 de la Garza	Y	N	N	Y	Y	Y	?	?
16 Coleman	Y	N	N	N	Y	Y	Y	Y
17 Stenholm	Y	Y	Y	Y	Y	Y	N	Y
18 Washington	?	?	?	N	Y	Y	Y	N
19 ***Combest***	Y	Y	Y	Y	N	Y	N	Y
20 Gonzalez	Y	N	N	N	Y	Y	Y	N
21 ***Smith***	Y	Y	Y	Y	N	Y	N	Y
22 ***DeLay***	Y	Y	Y	Y	N	Y	N	Y
23 Bustamante	Y	N	N	N	Y	Y	Y	Y
24 Frost	Y	N	N	N	Y	Y	N	Y
25 Andrews	Y	N	N	N	Y	Y	N	Y
26 ***Armey***	Y	Y	Y	Y	N	Y	N	Y
27 Ortiz	Y	N	N	N	Y	Y	N	Y
UTAH								
1 ***Hansen***	Y	Y	Y	Y	N	Y	N	Y
2 Owens	Y	N	Y	?	?	Y	Y	N
3 Orton	Y	Y	Y	Y	N	Y	N	Y
VERMONT								
AL *Sanders*	?	N	N	N	Y	Y	Y	N
VIRGINIA								
1 ***Bateman***	Y	Y	Y	Y	N	Y	N	Y
2 Pickett	Y	N	N	Y	N	Y	N	?
3 ***Bliley***	Y	Y	Y	Y	N	Y	N	Y
4 Sisisky	Y	Y	Y	N	Y	Y	N	Y
5 Payne	Y	Y	Y	N	Y	Y	N	Y
6 Olin	Y	Y	Y	Y	N	Y	Y	Y
7 ***Slaughter***	?	?	?	?	?	?	?	?
8 Moran	Y	Y	Y	N	N	Y	Y	N
9 Boucher	Y	N	N	N	Y	Y	Y	Y
10 ***Wolf***	Y	Y	Y	Y	N	Y	N	Y
WASHINGTON								
1 ***Miller***	Y	Y	Y	Y	N	Y	N	Y
2 Swift	Y	N	N	N	Y	Y	Y	N
3 Unsoeld	Y	N	N	N	Y	Y	Y	N
4 ***Morrison***	Y	Y	Y	Y	Y	Y	N	Y
5 Foley								
6 Dicks	Y	N	N	N	Y	Y	Y	Y
7 McDermott	Y	N	N	N	Y	Y	Y	N
8 ***Chandler***	Y	Y	Y	Y	N	Y	N	Y
WEST VIRGINIA								
1 Mollohan	Y	Y	N	N	Y	Y	N	Y
2 Staggers	Y	N	N	N	Y	Y	Y	Y
3 Wise	Y	N	N	N	Y	Y	Y	Y
4 Rahall	Y	N	N	N	Y	Y	N	Y
WISCONSIN								
1 Aspin	Y	N	N	N	Y	Y	Y	N
2 ***Klug***	Y	Y	Y	Y	N	Y	Y	Y
3 ***Gunderson***	Y	Y	Y	Y	Y	Y	N	Y
4 Kleczka	Y	N	N	N	Y	Y	N	Y
5 Moody	Y	N	N	N	Y	Y	N	Y
6 ***Petri***	Y	Y	Y	Y	Y	Y	N	Y
7 Obey	Y	N	N	N	Y	Y	Y	?
8 ***Roth***	Y	Y	Y	Y	N	Y	N	Y
9 ***Sensenbrenner***	Y	Y	Y	Y	N	Y	N	Y
WYOMING								
AL ***Thomas***	Y	Y	Y	Y	N	Y	N	Y

Southern states - Ala., Ark., Fla., Ga., Ky., La., Miss., N.C., Okla., S.C., Tenn., Texas, Va.
Omitted votes are quorum calls, which CQ does not include in its vote charts.

HOUSE VOTES 310, 311, 312, 313, 314, 315, 316, 317

310. HR 3371. Omnibus Crime Bill/Rule. Adoption of the rule (H Res 247) to provide for House floor consideration of the bill to expand the death penalty to about 50 additional crimes, reform habeas corpus procedures, ban 13 types of semiautomatic assault weapons, codify the "good faith" exception to the exclusionary rule, authorize $1.1 billion for law enforcement measures and for other purposes. Adopted 233-193: R 0-160; D 232-33 (ND 169-11, SD 63-22); I 1-0, Oct. 16, 1991.

311. HR 3371. Omnibus Crime Bill/Death Penalty Replacement. Staggers, D-W.Va., en bloc amendment to provide mandatory life imprisonment without parole in all places where the bill imposes the death penalty and to require restitution of no less than half of offender's earnings to the victim's family. Rejected 101-322: R 5-156; D 95-166 (ND 89-88, SD 6-78); I 1-0, Oct. 16, 1991.

312. HR 3371. Omnibus Crime Bill/Death Penalty for Drug Kingpins. Hughes, D-N.J., amendment to strike the bill's provisions that provide for the death penalty for drug kingpins convicted of selling large quantities of drugs, where no death resulted. Rejected 106-317: R 4-157; D 101-160 (ND 92-85, SD 9-75); I 1-0, Oct. 16, 1991. A "nay" was a vote supporting the president's position.

313. HR 3371. Omnibus Crime Bill/Death Penalty. Gekas, R-Pa., en bloc amendment to allow the jury in capital cases to impose the death penalty where there has been a reckless disregard for life. The amendment also removes the requirement that the jury be told that it does not have to impose the death penalty and allows the prosecution to seek the death penalty anytime before sentencing. Adopted 213-206: R 150-10; D 63-195 (ND 28-147, SD 35-48); I 0-1, Oct. 16, 1991. (Before adoption, the Gekas amendment was modified by a Brooks, D-Texas, amendment to provide for adequate competent counsel in federal death penalty cases and federal habeas corpus appeals.) A "yea" was a vote supporting the president's position.

314. HR 2686. Fiscal 1992 Interior Appropriations/National Endowment for the Arts. Dannemeyer, R-Calif., motion to instruct conferees to insist on the Senate amendment to prohibit the National Endowment for the Arts from funding projects that depict or describe, in a patently offensive way, sexual or excretory activities or organs. Motion agreed to 287-133: R 149-13; D 138-119 (ND 70-103, SD 68-16); I 0-1, Oct. 17, 1991.

315. HR 2686. Fiscal 1992 Interior Appropriations/New Conferees. Derrick, D-S.C., motion to table (kill) the Dannemeyer, R-Calif., motion to discharge the managers of the fiscal 1992 Interior Appropriations conference and appoint new conferees. Motion agreed to 286-136: R 33-129; D 253-7 (ND 173-2, SD 80-5); I 0-0, Oct. 17, 1991.

316. HR 3371. Omnibus Crime Bill/Habeas Corpus. Hyde, R-Ill., amendment to prohibit federal habeas corpus appeals in cases that had a "full and fair" hearing at the state level; require all habeas corpus appeals to be filed within one year of exhausting state appeals; limit death row prisoners to one federal habeas corpus petition that must be filed within six months of exhausting appeals; and set time limits for consideration of habeas corpus petitions. Rejected 208-218: R 153-9; D 55-208 (ND 19-161, SD 36-47); I 0-1, Oct. 17, 1991. A "yea" was a vote supporting the president's position.

317. HR 3371. Omnibus Crime Bill/En Bloc Amendments. Brooks, D-Texas, en bloc amendments incorporating 26 individual amendments made in order by the rule. Adopted 216-207: R 0-161; D 215-46 (ND 161-16, SD 54-30); I 1-0, Oct. 17, 1991.

KEY

- Y Voted for (yea).
- # Paired for.
- + Announced for.
- N Voted against (nay).
- X Paired against.
- - Announced against.
- P Voted "present."
- C Voted "present" to avoid possible conflict of interest.
- ? Did not vote or otherwise make a position known.

Democrats ***Republicans***
Independent

	310	311	312	313	314	315	316	317
ALABAMA								
1 ***Callahan***	?	?	?	?	?	?	?	?
2 ***Dickinson***	N	N	N	Y	Y	N	Y	N
3 Browder	N	N	N	Y	Y	Y	Y	N
4 Bevill	N	N	N	Y	Y	Y	Y	N
5 Cramer	N	N	N	Y	Y	Y	Y	N
6 Erdreich	N	N	N	Y	Y	Y	Y	N
7 Harris	N	N	N	Y	Y	Y	Y	N
ALASKA								
AL ***Young***	N	N	N	Y	Y	Y	Y	N
ARIZONA								
1 ***Rhodes***	N	N	N	Y	Y	Y	Y	N
2 Pastor	Y	N	N	N	N	Y	N	Y
3 ***Stump***	N	N	N	Y	Y	N	Y	N
4 ***Kyl***	N	N	N	Y	Y	Y	Y	N
5 ***Kolbe***	N	N	N	Y	Y	Y	Y	N
ARKANSAS								
1 Alexander	Y	N	N	Y	Y	Y	N	Y
2 Thornton	Y	N	N	N	?	Y	N	Y
3 ***Hammerschmidt***	N	N	N	Y	Y	N	Y	?
4 Anthony	Y	N	N	N	Y	Y	N	Y
CALIFORNIA								
1 ***Riggs***	N	N	N	Y	Y	N	Y	N
2 ***Herger***	N	N	N	Y	Y	N	Y	N
3 Matsui	Y	N	N	N	N	Y	N	Y
4 Fazio	Y	Y	?	N	N	Y	N	Y
5 Pelosi	Y	Y	Y	N	N	Y	N	Y
6 Boxer	Y	N	N	N	N	Y	N	Y
7 Miller	Y	Y	Y	N	N	Y	N	Y
8 Dellums	Y	Y	Y	N	N	Y	N	Y
9 Stark	Y	Y	Y	N	N	Y	N	Y
10 Edwards	Y	Y	Y	N	N	Y	N	Y
11 Lantos	Y	N	N	N	Y	Y	N	Y
12 ***Campbell***	N	N	N	Y	N	N	Y	N
13 Mineta	Y	Y	Y	N	N	Y	N	Y
14 ***Doolittle***	N	N	N	Y	Y	N	Y	N
15 Condit	N	N	N	Y	Y	Y	Y	N
16 Panetta	Y	N	N	N	N	Y	N	Y
17 Dooley	Y	N	N	N	Y	Y	Y	Y
18 Lehman	Y	N	N	N	N	Y	Y	Y
19 ***Lagomarsino***	N	N	N	Y	Y	N	Y	N
20 ***Thomas***	N	N	N	Y	Y	N	Y	N
21 ***Gallegly***	N	N	N	Y	Y	N	Y	N
22 ***Moorhead***	N	N	N	Y	Y	N	Y	N
23 Beilenson	Y	N	N	N	N	Y	N	Y
24 Waxman	Y	#	?	X	?	?	?	?
25 Roybal	Y	Y	Y	N	N	Y	N	Y
26 Berman	Y	Y	Y	N	N	Y	N	?
27 Levine	Y	N	Y	N	N	Y	N	?
28 Dixon	Y	Y	Y	N	N	Y	N	Y
29 Waters	Y	Y	Y	N	?	Y	N	Y
30 Martinez	Y	N	N	Y	Y	Y	Y	?
31 Dymally	Y	?	?	?	N	Y	N	Y
32 Anderson	Y	N	N	N	Y	Y	N	Y
33 ***Dreier***	N	N	N	Y	Y	N	Y	N
34 Torres	Y	N	N	N	N	Y	N	Y
35 ***Lewis***	?	X	N	Y	Y	Y	Y	N
36 Brown	Y	Y	N	N	N	Y	Y	Y
37 ***McCandless***	N	N	N	Y	Y	N	Y	N
38 ***Dornan***	N	N	N	Y	Y	N	Y	N
39 ***Dannemeyer***	N	N	N	Y	Y	N	Y	N
40 ***Cox***	N	N	N	Y	Y	N	Y	N
41 ***Lowery***	N	N	N	Y	Y	Y	Y	N
42 ***Rohrabacher***	N	N	N	Y	Y	N	Y	N
43 ***Packard***	N	N	N	Y	Y	N	Y	N
44 ***Cunningham***	N	N	N	Y	Y	N	Y	N
45 ***Hunter***	N	N	N	Y	Y	N	Y	N
COLORADO								
1 Schroeder	N	N	Y	N	N	Y	N	Y
2 Skaggs	Y	Y	Y	N	N	Y	N	Y
3 Campbell	N	N	N	Y	Y	Y	Y	Y
4 ***Allard***	N	N	N	Y	Y	Y	Y	N
5 ***Hefley***	N	N	N	Y	Y	N	Y	N
6 ***Schaefer***	N	N	N	Y	Y	N	Y	N
CONNECTICUT								
1 Kennelly	Y	N	Y	N	Y	Y	N	Y
2 Gejdenson	Y	Y	Y	N	N	Y	N	Y
3 DeLauro	Y	N	N	N	N	Y	N	Y
4 ***Shays***	N	Y	N	N	Y	N	Y	N
5 ***Franks***	N	N	N	Y	Y	N	Y	N
6 ***Johnson***	N	N	N	N	Y	Y	N	N
DELAWARE								
AL Carper	Y	N	N	N	Y	Y	N	Y
FLORIDA								
1 Hutto	N	N	N	Y	Y	Y	Y	N
2 Peterson	Y	N	N	Y	Y	Y	N	Y
3 Bennett	N	N	N	N	Y	Y	N	N
4 ***James***	N	N	N	Y	Y	N	Y	N
5 ***McCollum***	N	N	N	Y	Y	N	Y	N
6 ***Stearns***	N	N	N	Y	Y	N	Y	N
7 Gibbons	Y	N	N	Y	Y	Y	N	Y
8 ***Young***	N	N	N	Y	Y	N	Y	N
9 ***Bilirakis***	N	N	N	Y	Y	N	Y	N
10 ***Ireland***	N	N	N	Y	Y	N	Y	N
11 Bacchus	Y	N	N	Y	N	Y	N	Y
12 ***Lewis***	N	N	N	Y	Y	N	Y	N
13 ***Goss***	N	N	N	Y	Y	N	Y	N
14 Johnston	Y	N	N	N	N	Y	N	Y
15 ***Shaw***	N	N	N	Y	Y	N	Y	N
16 Smith	Y	N	Y	N	N	Y	N	Y
17 Lehman	Y	Y	Y	N	N	Y	N	Y
18 ***Ros-Lehtinen***	N	N	N	Y	Y	N	Y	N
19 Fascell	Y	N	N	N	N	Y	N	Y
GEORGIA								
1 Thomas	N	N	N	Y	Y	Y	Y	Y
2 Hatcher	Y	N	N	N	N	Y	Y	N
3 Ray	N	N	N	Y	Y	Y	Y	Y
4 Jones	Y	N	Y	N	N	Y	N	N
5 Lewis	Y	Y	Y	N	N	Y	N	Y
6 ***Gingrich***	N	N	N	Y	Y	N	Y	N
7 Darden	Y	N	N	N	Y	Y	Y	Y
8 Rowland	Y	N	N	Y	Y	Y	Y	Y
9 Jenkins	Y	N	N	N	Y	Y	N	Y
10 Barnard	Y	N	N	N	Y	Y	Y	N
HAWAII								
1 Abercrombie	Y	Y	Y	N	N	Y	N	Y
2 Mink	Y	Y	Y	N	N	Y	N	Y
IDAHO								
1 LaRocco	Y	N	N	N	N	Y	N	Y
2 Stallings	Y	N	N	Y	Y	?	N	Y
ILLINOIS								
1 Hayes	Y	Y	N	N	N	Y	N	Y
2 Savage	?	?	?	?	N	Y	N	Y
3 Russo	Y	N	N	N	Y	Y	N	Y
4 Sangmeister	N	N	N	N	Y	?	N	Y
5 Lipinski	Y	N	N	N	Y	Y	Y	N
6 ***Hyde***	N	N	N	Y	Y	N	Y	N
7 Collins	Y	Y	Y	N	N	Y	N	Y
8 Rostenkowski	Y	N	N	N	Y	Y	N	Y
9 Yates	Y	Y	Y	N	N	Y	N	Y
10 ***Porter***	N	N	N	Y	Y	N	Y	N
11 Annunzio	Y	N	N	N	Y	Y	N	Y
12 ***Crane***	N	N	N	Y	Y	N	Y	N
13 ***Fawell***	N	N	N	Y	Y	N	Y	N
14 ***Hastert***	N	N	N	Y	Y	N	Y	N
15 ***Ewing***	N	N	N	Y	Y	N	Y	N
16 Cox	Y	Y	Y	N	N	Y	N	Y
17 Evans	Y	Y	Y	N	N	Y	N	Y
18 ***Michel***	N	N	N	Y	Y	N	Y	N
19 Bruce	Y	N	N	Y	Y	Y	N	Y
20 Durbin	N	N	N	N	N	Y	N	Y
21 Costello	N	N	N	N	Y	Y	N	N
22 Poshard	Y	N	N	Y	Y	Y	N	Y
INDIANA								
1 Visclosky	Y	Y	Y	N	Y	Y	N	Y
2 Sharp	Y	Y	Y	N	Y	Y	N	Y
3 Roemer	Y	N	N	N	Y	Y	Y	Y

ND Northern Democrats SD Southern Democrats

	310	311	312	313	314	315	316	317
4 Long	Y	N	N	N	Y	Y	N	Y
5 Jontz	Y	Y	N	N	Y	Y	N	Y
6 ***Burton***	N	N	N	Y	Y	N	Y	N
7 ***Myers***	N	N	N	Y	Y	Y	Y	N
8 McCloskey	Y	Y	Y	N	Y	Y	N	Y
9 Hamilton	Y	Y	Y	N	Y	Y	N	Y
10 Jacobs	Y	Y	Y	N	Y	Y	N	Y
IOWA								
1 ***Leach***	N	N	N	N	N	Y	N	N
2 ***Nussle***	N	N	N	Y	Y	N	Y	N
3 Nagle	Y	Y	Y	N	N	Y	N	N
4 Smith	Y	Y	Y	N	N	Y	N	Y
5 ***Lightfoot***	N	N	N	Y	Y	Y	Y	N
6 ***Grandy***	N	N	N	Y	N	Y	Y	N
KANSAS								
1 ***Roberts***	N	N	N	#	Y	N	Y	N
2 Slattery	Y	N	N	N	Y	Y	N	Y
3 ***Meyers***	N	N	N	Y	Y	N	Y	N
4 Glickman	Y	N	Y	N	Y	Y	N	Y
5 ***Nichols***	N	N	N	Y	Y	N	Y	N
KENTUCKY								
1 Hubbard	Y	N	N	Y	Y	Y	Y	N
2 Natcher	Y	N	N	N	Y	Y	Y	Y
3 Mazzoli	Y	N	N	N	N	Y	N	Y
4 ***Bunning***	N	N	N	Y	Y	N	Y	N
5 ***Rogers***	N	N	N	Y	Y	N	Y	N
6 ***Hopkins***	?	?	?	?	?	?	?	?
7 Perkins	Y	N	N	N	Y	N	N	Y
LOUISIANA								
1 ***Livingston***	N	N	N	Y	Y	N	Y	N
2 Jefferson	Y	Y	N	N	N	Y	N	Y
3 Tauzin	N	N	N	Y	Y	Y	Y	N
4 ***McCrery***	N	N	N	Y	Y	N	Y	N
5 Huckaby	N	N	N	Y	Y	Y	?	?
6 ***Baker***	N	N	N	Y	Y	N	Y	N
7 Hayes	N	N	N	Y	Y	Y	Y	N
8 ***Holloway***	?	?	?	?	?	?	?	?
MAINE								
1 Andrews	Y	Y	Y	N	N	Y	N	N
2 ***Snowe***	N	N	N	Y	Y	N	Y	N
MARYLAND								
1 ***Gilchrest***	N	N	N	Y	Y	N	N	N
2 ***Bentley***	N	N	N	Y	Y	N	Y	N
3 Cardin	Y	N	Y	N	N	Y	N	Y
4 McMillen	Y	N	N	N	Y	Y	N	Y
5 Hoyer	Y	Y	Y	N	N	Y	N	Y
6 Byron	N	N	N	Y	Y	Y	N	N
7 Mfume	Y	Y	Y	N	N	Y	N	Y
8 ***Morella***	N	N	N	N	N	Y	N	N
MASSACHUSETTS								
1 Olver	Y	Y	Y	N	N	Y	N	Y
2 Neal	Y	Y	Y	N	Y	Y	N	Y
3 Early	Y	N	N	Y	N	Y	N	Y
4 Frank	Y	Y	Y	N	N	Y	N	Y
5 Atkins	Y	N	N	N	N	Y	N	Y
6 Mavroules	Y	N	N	N	Y	Y	N	Y
7 Markey	Y	Y	Y	N	N	Y	N	Y
8 Kennedy	Y	N	N	N	Y	Y	N	Y
9 Moakley	Y	N	N	N	?	Y	N	Y
10 Studds	Y	Y	Y	N	N	Y	N	Y
11 Donnelly	Y	N	N	Y	Y	Y	N	Y
MICHIGAN								
1 Conyers	Y	Y	Y	N	N	Y	N	Y
2 ***Pursell***	N	N	N	Y	Y	Y	Y	N
3 Wolpe	Y	Y	Y	N	N	Y	N	Y
4 ***Upton***	N	N	N	Y	Y	N	Y	N
5 ***Henry***	N	N	N	Y	Y	N	Y	N
6 Carr	N	?	N	N	?	Y	N	Y
7 Kildee	Y	Y	Y	N	N	Y	N	Y
8 Traxler	Y	N	N	N	Y	Y	N	Y
9 ***Vander Jagt***	N	N	N	Y	Y	N	Y	N
10 ***Camp***	N	N	N	Y	Y	N	Y	N
11 ***Davis***	N	N	N	Y	Y	Y	Y	N
12 Bonior	Y	Y	Y	N	?	Y	N	Y
13 Collins	Y	Y	Y	N	N	Y	N	Y
14 Hertel	Y	Y	Y	N	N	Y	N	Y
15 Ford	Y	Y	Y	N	N	Y	N	Y
16 Dingell	Y	N	N	N	Y	Y	N	Y
17 Levin	Y	Y	Y	N	N	Y	N	Y
18 ***Broomfield***	N	N	N	Y	Y	N	Y	N
MINNESOTA								
1 Penny	Y	Y	Y	N	Y	Y	N	N
2 ***Weber***	N	Y	Y	N	Y	N	Y	N
3 ***Ramstad***	N	N	N	Y	Y	N	Y	N
4 Vento	Y	Y	Y	N	N	Y	N	Y

	310	311	312	313	314	315	316	317
5 Sabo	Y	Y	Y	N	N	Y	N	Y
6 Sikorski	Y	N	N	N	N	Y	N	Y
7 Peterson	Y	Y	Y	N	Y	Y	N	Y
8 Oberstar	Y	Y	Y	N	N	Y	N	Y
MISSISSIPPI								
1 Whitten	Y	N	?	?	Y	Y	N	Y
2 Espy	Y	N	N	Y	Y	Y	N	Y
3 Montgomery	N	N	N	Y	Y	Y	Y	N
4 Parker	N	N	N	Y	Y	Y	Y	N
5 Taylor	N	N	N	Y	Y	N	Y	N
MISSOURI								
1 Clay	Y	Y	Y	N	N	Y	N	Y
2 Horn	Y	N	N	N	N	Y	N	Y
3 Gephardt	Y	N	N	N	?	Y	N	Y
4 Skelton	Y	N	N	Y	Y	Y	Y	N
5 Wheat	Y	Y	Y	N	N	Y	N	Y
6 ***Coleman***	N	N	N	Y	Y	Y	Y	N
7 ***Hancock***	N	N	N	Y	Y	N	Y	N
8 ***Emerson***	N	N	N	Y	Y	N	Y	N
9 Volkmer	Y	N	N	Y	Y	Y	Y	Y
MONTANA								
1 Williams	Y	N	N	N	N	Y	N	Y
2 ***Marlenee***	N	N	N	Y	Y	N	Y	N
NEBRASKA								
1 ***Bereuter***	N	N	N	Y	Y	N	Y	N
2 Hoagland	Y	N	N	N	Y	Y	N	Y
3 ***Barrett***	N	N	N	Y	Y	N	Y	N
NEVADA								
1 Bilbray	Y	N	N	Y	Y	Y	N	N
2 ***Vucanovich***	N	N	N	Y	Y	Y	Y	N
NEW HAMPSHIRE								
1 ***Zeliff***	N	N	N	Y	Y	N	Y	N
2 Swett	Y	N	N	Y	Y	Y	N	N
NEW JERSEY								
1 Andrews	Y	N	Y	Y	N	Y	Y	Y
2 Hughes	N	N	Y	N	N	Y	N	Y
3 Pallone	Y	N	N	Y	Y	Y	N	Y
4 ***Smith***	N	Y	Y	N	Y	N	Y	N
5 ***Roukema***	N	N	N	N	Y	N	Y	N
6 Dwyer	Y	N	N	N	Y	Y	N	Y
7 ***Rinaldo***	N	N	N	Y	Y	N	Y	N
8 Roe	Y	N	N	N	Y	Y	N	Y
9 Torricelli	Y	N	N	N	Y	Y	N	N
10 Payne	Y	Y	Y	N	N	Y	N	Y
11 ***Gallo***	N	N	N	Y	Y	Y	Y	N
12 ***Zimmer***	N	N	N	Y	Y	N	Y	N
13 ***Saxton***	N	N	N	Y	Y	N	Y	N
14 Guarini	Y	N	N	Y	Y	Y	N	Y
NEW MEXICO								
1 ***Schiff***	N	N	N	Y	Y	N	N	N
2 ***Skeen***	N	N	N	Y	N	Y	Y	N
3 Richardson	Y	N	N	Y	N	Y	N	Y
NEW YORK								
1 Hochbrueckner	Y	Y	N	N	Y	Y	N	Y
2 Downey	Y	Y	Y	N	N	Y	N	Y
3 Mrazek	Y	Y	Y	N	N	?	N	Y
4 ***Lent***	N	N	N	Y	Y	N	Y	N
5 ***McGrath***	N	N	N	Y	Y	N	Y	N
6 Flake	Y	Y	Y	N	N	Y	N	Y
7 Ackerman	Y	Y	Y	N	N	Y	N	Y
8 Scheuer	Y	Y	Y	N	N	Y	N	Y
9 Manton	Y	N	N	Y	Y	Y	N	Y
10 Schumer	Y	N	N	N	N	Y	N	Y
11 Towns	Y	Y	Y	?	?	?	N	Y
12 Owens	Y	Y	Y	N	N	Y	N	Y
13 Solarz	Y	N	Y	N	N	Y	N	Y
14 ***Molinari***	N	N	N	Y	Y	N	Y	N
15 ***Green***	N	N	Y	N	N	Y	N	N
16 Rangel	Y	Y	Y	N	N	Y	N	Y
17 Weiss	Y	Y	Y	N	N	Y	N	Y
18 Serrano	Y	Y	Y	N	N	Y	N	Y
19 Engel	Y	Y	Y	N	N	Y	N	Y
20 Lowey	Y	Y	Y	N	N	Y	N	Y
21 ***Fish***	N	N	N	N	N	Y	N	N
22 ***Gilman***	N	N	N	Y	N	Y	N	N
23 McNulty	Y	Y	Y	N	Y	Y	N	Y
24 ***Solomon***	N	N	N	Y	Y	N	Y	N
25 ***Boehlert***	N	N	N	Y	N	Y	Y	N
26 ***Martin***	N	N	N	Y	Y	N	Y	N
27 ***Walsh***	N	N	N	Y	Y	Y	Y	N
28 McHugh	Y	Y	Y	N	N	Y	N	Y
29 ***Horton***	N	N	N	Y	N	Y	N	N
30 Slaughter	Y	Y	N	N	N	Y	N	Y
31 ***Paxon***	N	N	N	Y	Y	N	Y	N

	310	311	312	313	314	315	316	317
32 LaFalce	Y	Y	Y	N	N	Y	N	Y
33 Nowak	Y	N	N	N	N	Y	N	Y
34 ***Houghton***	N	N	N	Y	N	Y	Y	N
NORTH CAROLINA								
1 Jones	Y	N	N	?	Y	Y	N	Y
2 Valentine	Y	N	N	Y	Y	Y	Y	N
3 Lancaster	Y	N	N	Y	Y	Y	N	Y
4 Price	Y	N	N	N	Y	Y	N	Y
5 Neal	Y	?	N	N	Y	Y	Y	N
6 ***Coble***	N	N	N	Y	Y	N	Y	N
7 Rose	Y	N	N	N	Y	Y	N	Y
8 Hefner	Y	N	N	N	Y	Y	N	Y
9 ***McMillan***	N	N	N	Y	Y	N	Y	N
10 ***Ballenger***	N	N	N	Y	Y	N	Y	N
11 ***Taylor***	N	N	N	Y	Y	N	Y	N
NORTH DAKOTA								
AL Dorgan	Y	Y	Y	N	Y	Y	N	Y
OHIO								
1 Luken	Y	N	N	Y	Y	Y	N	Y
2 ***Gradison***	N	N	N	Y	Y	N	Y	N
3 Hall	Y	N	N	N	Y	Y	N	Y
4 ***Oxley***	N	N	N	Y	Y	N	Y	N
5 ***Gillmor***	N	N	N	Y	Y	N	Y	N
6 ***McEwen***	N	N	N	Y	Y	N	Y	N
7 ***Hobson***	N	N	N	Y	Y	N	Y	N
8 ***Boehner***	N	N	N	Y	Y	N	Y	N
9 Kaptur	Y	N	N	N	Y	Y	N	Y
10 ***Miller***	N	N	N	Y	Y	N	Y	N
11 Eckart	Y	N	N	N	N	Y	N	Y
12 ***Kasich***	N	N	N	Y	Y	N	Y	N
13 Pease	Y	N	Y	N	N	Y	N	Y
14 Sawyer	Y	Y	Y	N	N	Y	N	Y
15 ***Wylie***	N	N	N	Y	Y	N	Y	N
16 ***Regula***	N	N	N	Y	Y	N	Y	N
17 Traficant	N	N	N	Y	Y	Y	N	Y
18 Applegate	Y	N	N	Y	?	N	Y	N
19 Feighan	Y	Y	Y	N	N	Y	N	Y
20 Oakar	Y	N	N	N	N	Y	N	Y
21 Stokes	Y	Y	Y	N	N	N	N	Y
OKLAHOMA								
1 ***Inhofe***	N	N	N	Y	Y	N	Y	N
2 Synar	Y	N	Y	N	N	Y	N	Y
3 Brewster	Y	N	N	N	Y	Y	Y	N
4 McCurdy	Y	N	N	N	Y	Y	?	N
5 ***Edwards***	N	N	N	Y	?	?	Y	N
6 English	Y	N	N	Y	Y	Y	Y	N
OREGON								
1 AuCoin	Y	Y	Y	N	N	Y	N	Y
2 ***Smith***	N	N	N	Y	Y	N	Y	N
3 Wyden	Y	N	N	Y	N	Y	N	Y
4 DeFazio	Y	Y	N	N	N	Y	N	Y
5 Kopetski	Y	Y	Y	N	N	Y	N	Y
PENNSYLVANIA								
1 Foglietta	Y	Y	Y	N	N	Y	N	Y
2 Vacancy								
3 Borski	Y	N	N	Y	Y	Y	Y	Y
4 Kolter	Y	N	N	Y	Y	Y	Y	Y
5 ***Schulze***	N	N	N	Y	Y	N	Y	N
6 Yatron	Y	N	N	Y	Y	Y	Y	Y
7 ***Weldon***	N	N	N	Y	Y	N	Y	N
8 Kostmayer	Y	Y	Y	N	N	Y	N	Y
9 ***Shuster***	N	N	N	Y	Y	N	Y	N
10 ***McDade***	N	N	N	Y	Y	Y	Y	N
11 Kanjorski	Y	N	N	N	Y	Y	N	N
12 Murtha	Y	N	N	N	N	?	Y	Y
13 ***Coughlin***	N	N	N	Y	Y	Y	Y	N
14 Coyne	Y	N	Y	N	N	Y	N	Y
15 ***Ritter***	N	N	N	Y	Y	N	Y	N
16 ***Walker***	N	N	N	Y	Y	N	Y	N
17 ***Gekas***	N	N	N	Y	Y	N	Y	N
18 ***Santorum***	N	N	N	Y	Y	N	Y	N
19 ***Goodling***	?	Y	P	P	Y	N	P	N
20 Gaydos	Y	N	N	Y	Y	Y	Y	N
21 ***Ridge***	N	N	N	Y	Y	N	Y	N
22 Murphy	N	N	N	?	Y	Y	Y	N
23 ***Clinger***	N	N	N	Y	N	Y	Y	N
RHODE ISLAND								
1 ***Machtley***	N	N	N	Y	N	N	Y	N
2 Reed	Y	N	N	N	N	Y	N	Y
SOUTH CAROLINA								
1 ***Ravenel***	N	N	N	Y	Y	N	Y	N
2 ***Spence***	N	N	N	Y	Y	N	Y	N
3 Derrick	Y	N	N	N	N	Y	N	Y
4 Patterson	N	N	N	Y	Y	Y	N	N
5 Spratt	Y	N	N	N	Y	Y	N	Y
6 Tallon	N	N	N	Y	Y	Y	Y	N

	310	311	312	313	314	315	316	317
SOUTH DAKOTA								
AL Johnson	Y	N	N	N	Y	Y	N	Y
TENNESSEE								
1 ***Quillen***	N	N	N	Y	Y	Y	Y	N
2 ***Duncan***	N	N	N	Y	Y	N	Y	N
3 Lloyd	N	N	N	Y	Y	Y	Y	N
4 Cooper	Y	N	N	Y	Y	Y	N	Y
5 Clement	Y	N	N	N	Y	Y	N	N
6 Gordon	Y	N	N	N	Y	Y	N	Y
7 ***Sundquist***	N	N	N	Y	Y	N	Y	N
8 Tanner	Y	N	N	Y	Y	Y	N	N
9 Ford	Y	Y	Y	N	N	Y	N	Y
TEXAS								
1 Chapman	Y	N	N	N	Y	Y	Y	Y
2 Wilson	Y	N	N	N	Y	Y	N	Y
3 ***Johnson***	N	N	N	Y	Y	N	Y	N
4 Hall	N	N	N	Y	Y	N	Y	N
5 Bryant	Y	N	N	N	Y	Y	N	Y
6 ***Barton***	N	N	N	Y	Y	N	Y	N
7 ***Archer***	N	N	N	Y	Y	N	Y	N
8 ***Fields***	N	N	N	Y	Y	N	Y	N
9 Brooks	Y	N	N	N	Y	Y	N	Y
10 Pickle	Y	N	N	N	Y	Y	N	Y
11 Edwards	Y	N	N	N	Y	Y	Y	Y
12 Geren	N	N	N	Y	Y	Y	Y	Y
13 Sarpalius	Y	N	N	Y	Y	N	Y	N
14 Laughlin	Y	N	N	N	Y	N	N	Y
15 de la Garza	Y	N	N	N	Y	Y	N	Y
16 Coleman	Y	N	N	N	Y	Y	N	Y
17 Stenholm	N	N	N	Y	Y	Y	Y	N
18 Washington	Y	Y	Y	N	N	Y	N	Y
19 ***Combest***	N	N	N	Y	Y	N	Y	N
20 Gonzalez	Y	N	Y	N	N	Y	N	Y
21 ***Smith***	N	N	N	Y	Y	N	Y	N
22 ***DeLay***	N	N	N	Y	Y	N	Y	N
23 Bustamante	Y	N	N	N	Y	Y	N	Y
24 Frost	Y	N	N	Y	Y	Y	N	Y
25 Andrews	N	N	N	Y	Y	Y	Y	Y
26 ***Armey***	N	N	N	Y	Y	N	Y	N
27 Ortiz	Y	N	N	N	Y	Y	N	Y
UTAH								
1 ***Hansen***	N	N	N	Y	Y	N	Y	N
2 Owens	Y	N	Y	N	N	Y	N	Y
3 Orton	Y	N	N	N	Y	Y	Y	N
VERMONT								
AL *Sanders*	Y	Y	Y	N	N	?	N	Y
VIRGINIA								
1 ***Bateman***	N	N	N	Y	Y	N	Y	N
2 Pickett	Y	N	N	N	Y	Y	Y	Y
3 ***Bliley***	N	N	N	Y	Y	N	Y	N
4 Sisisky	Y	N	N	N	Y	Y	Y	N
5 Payne	Y	N	N	N	Y	Y	Y	Y
6 Olin	Y	Y	N	N	Y	Y	N	Y
7 ***Slaughter***	?	?	?	?	Y	N	Y	?
8 Moran	Y	N	N	N	N	Y	Y	Y
9 Boucher	Y	N	N	N	Y	Y	N	Y
10 ***Wolf***	N	N	N	Y	Y	N	Y	N
WASHINGTON								
1 ***Miller***	N	N	N	Y	Y	Y	Y	N
2 Swift	Y	Y	Y	N	N	Y	N	Y
3 Unsoeld	Y	Y	Y	N	N	Y	N	Y
4 ***Morrison***	N	N	N	Y	Y	Y	Y	N
5 Foley								
6 Dicks	Y	N	N	N	Y	Y	N	Y
7 McDermott	Y	Y	Y	N	N	Y	N	Y
8 ***Chandler***	N	N	N	Y	Y	N	Y	N
WEST VIRGINIA								
1 Mollohan	Y	Y	Y	N	Y	Y	N	Y
2 Staggers	Y	Y	Y	N	Y	Y	N	Y
3 Wise	Y	Y	Y	N	Y	Y	N	Y
4 Rahall	Y	Y	N	N	Y	Y	N	Y
WISCONSIN								
1 Aspin	Y	N	N	Y	N	Y	N	Y
2 ***Klug***	N	Y	Y	N	Y	N	Y	N
3 ***Gunderson***	N	N	N	Y	Y	N	Y	N
4 Kleczka	Y	Y	Y	N	Y	Y	N	Y
5 Moody	Y	Y	Y	?	Y	Y	N	Y
6 ***Petri***	N	N	N	Y	Y	N	Y	N
7 Obey	Y	Y	Y	N	N	Y	N	Y
8 ***Roth***	N	N	N	Y	Y	N	Y	N
9 ***Sensenbrenner***	N	N	N	Y	Y	N	Y	N
WYOMING								
AL ***Thomas***	N	N	N	Y	Y	Y	Y	N

Southern states - Ala., Ark., Fla., Ga., Ky., La., Miss., N.C., Okla., S.C., Tenn., Texas, Va.
Omitted votes are quorum calls, which CQ does not include in its vote charts.

318. HR 3371. Omnibus Crime Bill/Assault Weapons. Volkmer, D-Mo., amendment to strike the provisions that prohibit the ownership or sale of 13 types of semi-automatic assault weapons. The amendment would also delete provisions that make it illegal to own or sell ammunition clips of more than seven rounds. Adopted 247-177: R 133-29; D 114-147 (ND 53-124, SD 61-23); I 0-1, Oct. 17, 1991.

319. HR 3371. Omnibus Crime Bill/Federal Funds for Habeas Corpus. Hyde, R-Ill., amendment to allow states to use federal funds for prosecutors to respond to death row habeas corpus appeals and require that an amount equal to the federal funding that helps death row prisoners pursue such appeals be available for prosecutors. Adopted 281-137: R 158-2; D 123-134 (ND 62-111, SD 61-23); I 0-1, Oct. 17, 1991.

320. HR 3371. Omnibus Crime Bill/Search and Seizure. McCollum, R-Fla., amendment to codify the "good faith" exception to the exclusionary rule that allows evidence seized without a warrant but under an objectively reasonable belief that the search was in conformity with the Fourth Amendment to be used against a defendant. Adopted 247-165: R 156-3; D 91-161 (ND 38-132, SD 53-29); I 0-1, Oct. 17, 1991. A "yea" was a vote supporting the president's position.

321. HR 3371. Omnibus Crime Bill/Bureau of Justice Assistance Formula Grants. Schiff, R-N.M., amendment to change the permanent extension of the 25 percent state match for Bureau of Justice Assistance formula grants in the bill to a one-year extension and require a 50 percent state match after 1992. Rejected 129-286: R 125-33; D 4-252 (ND 2-172, SD 2-80); I 0-1, Oct. 22, 1991.

322. HR 3371. Omnibus Crime Bill/Race-Based Sentencing. McCollum, R-Fla., amendment to replace the provisions that would allow minorities to challenge a death sentence as discriminatory if statistics show a disproportionate number of their race being condemned to die, with provisions that would prohibit considering race in determining a defendant's sentence and using statistics to invalidate a sentence. Adopted 223-191: R 150-6; D 73-184 (ND 26-149, SD 47-35); I 0-1, Oct. 22, 1991. A "yea" was a vote supporting the president's position.

323. HR 3371. Omnibus Crime Bill/'Drug-Free Zones'. Clement, D-Tenn., amendment to establish "drug-free zones" around truck stops and highway rest areas. Adopted 371-48: R 158-0; D 213-47 (ND 139-38, SD 74-9); I 0-1, Oct. 22, 1991.

324. HR 3371. Omnibus Crime Bill/Race-Based Sentencing. Hyde, R-Ill., amendment to strike the provisions that allow death row prisoners to raise certain race-bias claims in habeas corpus appeals. Adopted 238-180: R 151-8; D 87-171 (ND 33-144, SD 54-27); I 0-1, Oct. 22, 1991. A "yea" was a vote supporting the president's position.

325. HR 3371. Omnibus Crime Bill/Police Corps Program. McCurdy, D-Okla., amendment to establish a Police Corps program that provides a federal college scholarship of up to $10,000 per year in return for a four-year commitment to serve in a state or local police force. Adopted 369-51: R 129-32; D 239-19 (ND 159-18, SD 80-1); I 1-0, Oct. 22, 1991.

KEY

- Y Voted for (yea).
- # Paired for.
- + Announced for.
- N Voted against (nay).
- X Paired against.
- - Announced against.
- P Voted "present."
- C Voted "present" to avoid possible conflict of interest.
- ? Did not vote or otherwise make a position known.

Democrats ***Republicans***
Independent

	318	319	320	321	322	323	324	325
ALABAMA								
1 ***Callahan***	?	?	?	?	?	?	?	?
2 ***Dickinson***	Y	Y	Y	N	Y	Y	Y	Y
3 Browder	Y	Y	Y	N	Y	Y	Y	Y
4 Bevill	Y	Y	Y	N	Y	Y	Y	Y
5 Cramer	Y	Y	Y	N	Y	Y	Y	Y
6 Erdreich	Y	Y	Y	N	Y	Y	Y	Y
7 Harris	Y	Y	Y	N	Y	Y	Y	Y
ALASKA								
AL ***Young***	Y	Y	Y	Y	Y	Y	Y	Y
ARIZONA								
1 ***Rhodes***	Y	Y	Y	Y	Y	Y	Y	Y
2 Pastor	N	Y	N	N	N	Y	N	Y
3 ***Stump***	Y	Y	Y	Y	Y	Y	Y	N
4 ***Kyl***	Y	Y	Y	Y	Y	Y	Y	Y
5 ***Kolbe***	Y	Y	Y	Y	Y	Y	Y	N
ARKANSAS								
1 Alexander	Y	Y	Y	N	N	Y	N	Y
2 Thornton	Y	Y	Y	N	N	Y	N	Y
3 ***Hammerschmidt***	Y	Y	Y	N	Y	Y	Y	Y
4 Anthony	N	Y	Y	N	Y	Y	N	Y
CALIFORNIA								
1 ***Riggs***	Y	Y	Y	Y	Y	Y	Y	Y
2 ***Herger***	Y	Y	Y	Y	Y	Y	Y	Y
3 Matsui	N	?	?	N	N	Y	N	Y
4 Fazio	N	N	N	N	N	N	N	Y
5 Pelosi	N	N	N	N	N	N	N	Y
6 Boxer	N	N	?	N	N	Y	N	Y
7 Miller	N	N	N	?	N	Y	N	N
8 Dellums	N	N	N	X	X	?	X	?
9 Stark	N	?	?	N	N	Y	N	Y
10 Edwards	N	N	N	N	N	N	N	N
11 Lantos	N	N	N	N	N	Y	N	Y
12 ***Campbell***	N	Y	Y	Y	Y	Y	Y	Y
13 Mineta	N	N	N	N	N	Y	N	Y
14 ***Doolittle***	Y	Y	Y	Y	Y	Y	Y	Y
15 Condit	Y	Y	Y	N	Y	Y	Y	Y
16 Panetta	N	Y	N	N	N	Y	Y	Y
17 Dooley	N	Y	Y	N	Y	Y	Y	N
18 Lehman	N	Y	N	N	Y	Y	Y	Y
19 ***Lagomarsino***	Y	Y	Y	Y	Y	Y	Y	Y
20 ***Thomas***	Y	Y	Y	Y	Y	Y	Y	Y
21 ***Gallegly***	Y	Y	Y	Y	Y	Y	Y	Y
22 ***Moorhead***	Y	Y	Y	Y	?	?	?	?
23 Beilenson	N	N	N	N	N	N	N	N
24 Waxman	X	?	?	N	N	N	N	Y
25 Roybal	N	N	N	N	N	N	N	Y
26 Berman	N	N	N	N	N	Y	N	Y
27 Levine	X	?	?	N	N	Y	N	Y
28 Dixon	N	N	N	N	N	N	N	Y
29 Waters	N	N	N	?	X	?	X	?
30 Martinez	?	?	?	N	N	Y	N	Y
31 Dymally	N	N	N	N	N	N	N	Y
32 Anderson	N	N	N	N	N	Y	N	Y
33 ***Dreier***	Y	Y	Y	Y	Y	Y	Y	N
34 Torres	N	N	N	N	N	Y	N	Y
35 ***Lewis***	Y	Y	Y	Y	Y	Y	Y	Y
36 Brown	N	N	N	N	Y	Y	Y	Y
37 ***McCandless***	Y	Y	Y	N	Y	Y	Y	Y
38 ***Dornan***	Y	Y	Y	Y	Y	Y	Y	Y
39 ***Dannemeyer***	Y	?	+	Y	Y	Y	Y	N
40 ***Cox***	Y	Y	Y	Y	Y	Y	Y	N
41 ***Lowery***	Y	Y	Y	Y	Y	Y	Y	Y
42 ***Rohrabacher***	Y	Y	Y	Y	Y	Y	Y	N
43 ***Packard***	Y	Y	Y	Y	Y	Y	Y	Y
44 ***Cunningham***	Y	Y	Y	Y	Y	Y	Y	Y
45 ***Hunter***	Y	Y	Y	Y	Y	Y	Y	Y
COLORADO								
1 Schroeder	N	N	N	N	N	Y	N	Y
2 Skaggs	N	N	N	N	N	N	N	Y
3 Campbell	Y	N	Y	N	N	Y	Y	Y
4 ***Allard***	Y	Y	Y	Y	Y	Y	Y	N
5 ***Hefley***	Y	Y	Y	Y	Y	Y	Y	Y
6 ***Schaefer***	Y	Y	Y	Y	Y	Y	Y	Y
CONNECTICUT								
1 Kennelly	N	N	N	N	N	Y	N	Y
2 Gejdenson	N	Y	N	N	N	Y	N	Y
3 DeLauro	N	Y	N	N	N	Y	N	Y
4 ***Shays***	N	Y	Y	N	N	Y	N	Y
5 ***Franks***	Y	Y	Y	Y	Y	Y	Y	Y
6 ***Johnson***	N	N	Y	N	Y	Y	Y	Y
DELAWARE								
AL Carper	N	Y	Y	N	N	Y	Y	Y
FLORIDA								
1 Hutto	Y	Y	Y	N	Y	Y	Y	Y
2 Peterson	Y	Y	Y	N	N	Y	Y	Y
3 Bennett	N	N	Y	N	Y	Y	N	Y
4 ***James***	Y	Y	Y	Y	Y	Y	N	Y
5 ***McCollum***	Y	Y	Y	Y	Y	Y	Y	Y
6 ***Stearns***	Y	Y	Y	Y	Y	Y	Y	N
7 Gibbons	N	N	N	N	N	Y	N	Y
8 ***Young***	N	Y	Y	Y	Y	Y	N	Y
9 ***Bilirakis***	Y	Y	Y	Y	#	?	#	?
10 ***Ireland***	Y	Y	Y	Y	Y	Y	Y	Y
11 Bacchus	N	Y	Y	N	Y	Y	Y	Y
12 ***Lewis***	Y	Y	Y	Y	Y	Y	Y	Y
13 ***Goss***	Y	Y	Y	Y	Y	Y	Y	Y
14 Johnston	N	Y	N	Y	N	Y	N	Y
15 ***Shaw***	Y	Y	Y	Y	Y	Y	Y	Y
16 Smith	N	N	Y	N	N	Y	Y	Y
17 Lehman	N	N	N	N	N	N	N	Y
18 ***Ros-Lehtinen***	N	Y	Y	N	Y	Y	Y	Y
19 Fascell	N	N	N	N	N	N	N	Y
GEORGIA								
1 Thomas	Y	Y	Y	N	Y	Y	Y	Y
2 Hatcher	Y	Y	Y	N	Y	Y	Y	Y
3 Ray	Y	Y	Y	N	Y	Y	Y	Y
4 Jones	Y	Y	N	N	N	Y	N	Y
5 Lewis	N	N	N	N	N	N	?	?
6 ***Gingrich***	Y	Y	Y	Y	Y	Y	Y	Y
7 Darden	Y	Y	Y	N	Y	Y	Y	Y
8 Rowland	Y	Y	Y	N	Y	Y	Y	Y
9 Jenkins	Y	Y	Y	N	Y	Y	Y	Y
10 Barnard	Y	Y	Y	N	Y	Y	Y	Y
HAWAII								
1 Abercrombie	N	N	N	N	N	Y	N	Y
2 Mink	N	N	N	N	N	Y	N	Y
IDAHO								
1 LaRocco	Y	Y	Y	N	N	Y	Y	Y
2 Stallings	Y	Y	Y	N	N	Y	Y	Y
ILLINOIS								
1 Hayes	N	N	N	N	N	N	N	Y
2 Savage	N	N	N	N	N	N	N	N
3 Russo	N	N	N	N	Y	Y	Y	Y
4 Sangmeister	N	N	N	N	Y	Y	Y	Y
5 Lipinski	N	Y	N	N	Y	Y	Y	Y
6 ***Hyde***	Y	Y	Y	Y	Y	Y	Y	Y
7 Collins	N	N	N	?	?	?	?	?
8 Rostenkowski	N	N	N	N	Y	Y	N	Y
9 Yates	N	N	N	N	N	N	N	Y
10 ***Porter***	N	Y	Y	Y	Y	Y	Y	N
11 Annunzio	N	N	N	N	N	Y	Y	Y
12 ***Crane***	Y	Y	Y	Y	Y	Y	Y	N
13 ***Fawell***	N	Y	Y	Y	Y	Y	Y	N
14 ***Hastert***	Y	Y	Y	Y	Y	Y	Y	Y
15 ***Ewing***	Y	Y	Y	N	Y	Y	Y	N
16 Cox	N	N	N	N	N	Y	N	Y
17 Evans	N	N	N	N	N	Y	N	Y
18 ***Michel***	Y	Y	Y	Y	Y	Y	Y	Y
19 Bruce	Y	N	N	N	N	Y	N	Y
20 Durbin	N	N	N	N	N	Y	N	Y
21 Costello	Y	Y	N	N	N	Y	N	Y
22 Poshard	Y	N	N	N	N	Y	N	Y
INDIANA								
1 Visclosky	N	N	N	N	N	Y	N	Y
2 Sharp	Y	N	Y	N	N	Y	N	Y
3 Roemer	Y	Y	Y	N	Y	Y	Y	Y

ND Northern Democrats SD Southern Democrats

	318	319	320	321	322	323	324	325
4 Long	Y	Y	Y	N	N	Y	N	Y
5 Jontz	Y	N	N	N	N	Y	N	Y
6 ***Burton***	Y	Y	Y	Y	Y	Y	Y	N
7 ***Myers***	Y	Y	Y	Y	Y	Y	Y	Y
8 McCloskey	N	N	N	N	N	Y	N	Y
9 Hamilton	Y	N	Y	N	N	Y	N	Y
10 Jacobs	Y	N	Y	N	N	N	N	Y
IOWA								
1 ***Leach***	N	Y	Y	Y	Y	Y	Y	Y
2 ***Nussle***	Y	Y	Y	Y	Y	Y	Y	Y
3 Nagle	Y	N	N	N	N	Y	N	Y
4 Smith	Y	N	N	N	N	Y	N	Y
5 ***Lightfoot***	Y	Y	Y	Y	Y	Y	Y	Y
6 ***Grandy***	Y	Y	Y	Y	Y	Y	Y	N
KANSAS								
1 ***Roberts***	Y	Y	Y	Y	Y	Y	Y	N
2 Slattery	Y	Y	N	N	N	Y	N	Y
3 ***Meyers***	N	Y	Y	Y	Y	Y	Y	Y
4 Glickman	N	Y	N	N	N	Y	Y	N
5 ***Nichols***	Y	Y	Y	Y	Y	Y	Y	Y
KENTUCKY								
1 Hubbard	Y	Y	Y	N	Y	Y	Y	Y
2 Natcher	Y	N	N	N	N	Y	N	Y
3 Mazzoli	N	N	Y	N	N	Y	N	Y
4 ***Bunning***	Y	Y	Y	Y	Y	Y	Y	Y
5 ***Rogers***	Y	Y	Y	N	Y	Y	Y	Y
6 ***Hopkins***	?	?	?	?	?	?	?	?
7 Perkins	Y	N	N	N	N	Y	N	Y
LOUISIANA								
1 ***Livingston***	Y	Y	Y	Y	Y	Y	Y	Y
2 Jefferson	N	Y	N	N	N	Y	N	Y
3 Tauzin	Y	Y	Y	N	Y	Y	Y	Y
4 ***McCrery***	Y	Y	Y	N	Y	Y	Y	Y
5 Huckaby	#	?	?	N	Y	Y	Y	Y
6 ***Baker***	Y	Y	Y	#	#	?	#	Y
7 Hayes	Y	Y	Y	N	Y	Y	Y	Y
8 ***Holloway***	#	?	?	Y	Y	Y	Y	Y
MAINE								
1 Andrews	N	N	N	N	N	N	N	Y
2 ***Snowe***	Y	Y	Y	N	Y	Y	Y	Y
MARYLAND								
1 ***Gilchrest***	Y	Y	Y	Y	Y	Y	Y	Y
2 ***Bentley***	Y	Y	Y	Y	Y	Y	Y	Y
3 Cardin	N	N	N	N	N	Y	N	Y
4 McMillen	Y	Y	N	N	N	Y	N	Y
5 Hoyer	N	N	N	N	N	Y	N	Y
6 Byron	Y	Y	Y	N	Y	Y	Y	Y
7 Mfume	N	N	N	N	N	Y	N	Y
8 ***Morella***	N	Y	N	N	N	Y	N	Y
MASSACHUSETTS								
1 Olver	N	Y	N	N	N	Y	N	Y
2 Neal	N	Y	N	N	N	Y	N	Y
3 Early	N	Y	N	N	Y	N	N	Y
4 Frank	N	Y	Y	N	N	Y	N	Y
5 Atkins	N	Y	N	N	N	Y	N	Y
6 Mavroules	N	Y	N	N	N	Y	N	Y
7 Markey	N	Y	N	N	N	Y	N	Y
8 Kennedy	N	Y	N	N	N	Y	N	Y
9 Moakley	N	Y	N	N	N	Y	N	Y
10 Studds	N	Y	N	N	N	Y	N	Y
11 Donnelly	N	Y	N	N	N	Y	N	Y
MICHIGAN								
1 Conyers	N	N	N	N	N	N	N	N
2 ***Pursell***	N	Y	Y	N	?	Y	Y	Y
3 Wolpe	N	N	N	N	N	Y	N	Y
4 ***Upton***	Y	Y	Y	N	Y	Y	Y	Y
5 ***Henry***	N	Y	Y	N	Y	Y	Y	Y
6 Carr	Y	?	?	N	N	Y	N	Y
7 Kildee	N	N	N	N	N	Y	N	Y
8 Traxler	Y	Y	?	N	N	Y	N	Y
9 ***Vander Jagt***	Y	?	?	Y	Y	Y	Y	Y
10 ***Camp***	Y	Y	Y	Y	Y	Y	Y	Y
11 ***Davis***	Y	Y	Y	Y	Y	Y	Y	Y
12 Bonior	N	N	N	N	N	Y	N	Y
13 Collins	N	N	N	N	N	N	N	Y
14 Hertel	N	N	N	N	N	Y	N	Y
15 Ford	Y	?	?	N	N	N	N	Y
16 Dingell	Y	Y	N	N	N	Y	N	N
17 Levin	N	N	N	N	N	Y	N	Y
18 ***Broomfield***	N	Y	Y	N	Y	Y	Y	Y
MINNESOTA								
1 Penny	Y	Y	Y	N	N	N	N	Y
2 ***Weber***	Y	Y	Y	Y	Y	Y	Y	Y
3 ***Ramstad***	Y	Y	Y	Y	Y	Y	Y	Y
4 Vento	N	Y	N	N	N	N	N	Y

	318	319	320	321	322	323	324	325
5 Sabo	N	N	N	N	N	N	N	Y
6 Sikorski	N	N	N	N	N	Y	N	Y
7 Peterson	Y	Y	Y	N	N	Y	N	Y
8 Oberstar	Y	N	N	N	N	Y	N	Y
MISSISSIPPI								
1 Whitten	Y	Y	?	N	Y	Y	P	Y
2 Espy	Y	N	N	?	?	?	N	Y
3 Montgomery	Y	Y	Y	N	Y	Y	Y	Y
4 Parker	Y	Y	Y	N	Y	Y	Y	Y
5 Taylor	Y	Y	Y	Y	Y	Y	Y	Y
MISSOURI								
1 Clay	-	N	N	N	N	N	N	Y
2 Horn	N	Y	N	N	N	Y	N	Y
3 Gephardt	Y	N	N	N	N	Y	N	Y
4 Skelton	Y	Y	Y	N	Y	Y	Y	Y
5 Wheat	N	N	N	N	N	N	N	Y
6 ***Coleman***	Y	Y	Y	Y	Y	Y	Y	Y
7 ***Hancock***	Y	Y	Y	Y	Y	Y	Y	N
8 ***Emerson***	Y	Y	Y	Y	Y	Y	Y	Y
9 Volkmer	Y	Y	Y	N	Y	Y	Y	Y
MONTANA								
1 Williams	Y	N	N	N	N	Y	N	Y
2 ***Marlenee***	Y	Y	Y	N	Y	Y	Y	Y
NEBRASKA								
1 ***Bereuter***	N	Y	Y	Y	Y	Y	Y	Y
2 Hoagland	N	N	N	N	Y	Y	N	Y
3 ***Barrett***	Y	Y	Y	Y	Y	Y	Y	Y
NEVADA								
1 Bilbray	Y	Y	Y	N	Y	Y	Y	Y
2 ***Vucanovich***	Y	Y	Y	Y	Y	Y	Y	Y
NEW HAMPSHIRE								
1 ***Zeliff***	Y	Y	Y	Y	Y	Y	Y	N
2 Swett	Y	Y	Y	N	Y	Y	Y	Y
NEW JERSEY								
1 Andrews	N	Y	Y	N	N	Y	N	Y
2 Hughes	N	N	N	N	N	N	N	N
3 Pallone	Y	Y	Y	N	N	Y	N	Y
4 ***Smith***	N	Y	Y	N	Y	Y	Y	Y
5 ***Roukema***	N	Y	Y	Y	Y	Y	Y	Y
6 Dwyer	N	N	Y	N	N	Y	N	Y
7 ***Rinaldo***	N	Y	Y	N	Y	Y	Y	Y
8 Roe	N	N	N	N	N	Y	N	Y
9 Torricelli	N	N	N	N	N	Y	Y	Y
10 Payne	N	N	N	N	N	N	N	Y
11 ***Gallo***	Y	Y	Y	Y	Y	Y	Y	Y
12 ***Zimmer***	Y	Y	Y	Y	Y	Y	Y	N
13 ***Saxton***	Y	Y	Y	N	Y	Y	Y	Y
14 Guarini	N	N	Y	N	N	Y	N	Y
NEW MEXICO								
1 ***Schiff***	Y	Y	Y	Y	Y	Y	Y	Y
2 ***Skeen***	Y	Y	Y	Y	Y	Y	Y	Y
3 Richardson	Y	Y	Y	N	Y	Y	Y	Y
NEW YORK								
1 Hochbrueckner	N	N	N	N	N	Y	N	Y
2 Downey	N	N	N	N	N	Y	N	Y
3 Mrazek	N	N	?	?	?	?	?	?
4 ***Lent***	N	Y	Y	Y	Y	Y	Y	Y
5 ***McGrath***	N	Y	Y	Y	Y	Y	Y	Y
6 Flake	N	N	N	N	N	Y	N	Y
7 Ackerman	N	N	N	N	N	N	N	Y
8 Scheuer	N	N	N	N	N	N	N	Y
9 Manton	N	N	N	N	N	Y	N	Y
10 Schumer	N	N	N	N	N	N	N	N
11 Towns	N	N	N	?	X	N	N	Y
12 Owens	N	N	N	N	N	Y	N	Y
13 Solarz	N	N	N	N	N	Y	N	Y
14 ***Molinari***	Y	Y	Y	N	Y	Y	Y	Y
15 ***Green***	N	N	Y	N	N	Y	N	Y
16 Rangel	N	N	N	N	N	Y	N	Y
17 Weiss	N	N	N	-	-	N	N	Y
18 Serrano	N	N	N	N	N	N	N	Y
19 Engel	N	N	N	N	N	Y	N	Y
20 Lowey	N	N	N	N	N	Y	N	Y
21 ***Fish***	Y	Y	Y	Y	N	Y	N	N
22 ***Gilman***	Y	Y	Y	N	N	Y	N	Y
23 McNulty	N	N	N	N	N	Y	N	Y
24 ***Solomon***	Y	Y	Y	Y	Y	Y	Y	Y
25 ***Boehlert***	Y	Y	Y	N	Y	Y	Y	Y
26 ***Martin***	Y	Y	Y	Y	Y	Y	Y	Y
27 ***Walsh***	Y	Y	Y	Y	Y	Y	Y	Y
28 McHugh	N	N	N	N	N	N	N	Y
29 ***Horton***	Y	Y	N	N	N	Y	N	Y
30 Slaughter	N	N	N	N	N	Y	N	Y
31 ***Paxon***	Y	Y	Y	N	Y	Y	Y	Y

	318	319	320	321	322	323	324	325
32 LaFalce	N	N	N	N	N	N	N	Y
33 Nowak	N	Y	N	N	N	Y	N	Y
34 ***Houghton***	Y	Y	Y	?	Y	Y	Y	Y
NORTH CAROLINA								
1 Jones	Y	N	Y	N	Y	Y	Y	Y
2 Valentine	Y	Y	Y	N	Y	Y	Y	Y
3 Lancaster	Y	Y	Y	N	Y	Y	Y	Y
4 Price	N	Y	Y	N	Y	Y	Y	Y
5 Neal	Y	Y	N	N	Y	Y	Y	Y
6 ***Coble***	Y	Y	Y	Y	Y	Y	Y	N
7 Rose	Y	N	N	N	N	Y	N	Y
8 Hefner	Y	Y	Y	N	Y	Y	Y	Y
9 ***McMillan***	Y	Y	Y	Y	Y	Y	Y	Y
10 ***Ballenger***	Y	Y	Y	Y	Y	Y	Y	N
11 ***Taylor***	Y	Y	N	Y	Y	Y	Y	N
NORTH DAKOTA								
AL Dorgan	Y	N	N	N	N	Y	N	Y
OHIO								
1 Luken	N	Y	Y	N	Y	Y	Y	Y
2 ***Gradison***	N	Y	Y	Y	Y	Y	Y	N
3 Hall	N	N	N	N	N	Y	N	Y
4 ***Oxley***	Y	Y	Y	Y	Y	Y	Y	N
5 ***Gillmor***	Y	Y	Y	Y	Y	Y	Y	Y
6 ***McEwen***	Y	Y	Y	Y	Y	Y	Y	Y
7 ***Hobson***	Y	Y	Y	Y	Y	Y	Y	Y
8 ***Boehner***	Y	Y	Y	Y	Y	Y	Y	Y
9 Kaptur	N	N	Y	N	N	Y	N	Y
10 ***Miller***	Y	Y	Y	Y	Y	Y	Y	N
11 Eckart	N	N	N	N	N	Y	N	Y
12 ***Kasich***	Y	Y	Y	Y	Y	Y	Y	Y
13 Pease	N	N	N	N	N	Y	N	N
14 Sawyer	N	N	N	N	N	Y	N	N
15 ***Wylie***	N	Y	Y	Y	Y	Y	Y	Y
16 ***Regula***	Y	Y	Y	N	Y	Y	Y	Y
17 Traficant	N	Y	Y	N	N	Y	N	N
18 Applegate	Y	Y	Y	N	Y	Y	Y	Y
19 Feighan	N	N	N	N	N	Y	N	N
20 Oakar	N	N	N	N	N	Y	N	Y
21 Stokes	N	N	N	N	N	N	N	Y
OKLAHOMA								
1 ***Inhofe***	Y	Y	Y	Y	Y	Y	Y	Y
2 Synar	N	N	N	N	N	N	N	N
3 Brewster	Y	Y	Y	N	Y	Y	Y	Y
4 McCurdy	Y	Y	Y	N	Y	Y	Y	Y
5 ***Edwards***	Y	Y	Y	Y	Y	Y	Y	Y
6 English	Y	Y	Y	N	N	Y	Y	Y
OREGON								
1 AuCoin	N	Y	N	N	N	Y	N	Y
2 ***Smith***	Y	Y	Y	N	Y	Y	Y	Y
3 Wyden	N	Y	Y	N	N	Y	N	Y
4 DeFazio	Y	N	N	N	N	Y	N	Y
5 Kopetski	Y	N	N	N	N	N	N	N
PENNSYLVANIA								
1 Foglietta	N	N	N	N	N	Y	N	Y
2 Vacancy								
3 Borski	N	Y	Y	N	Y	Y	Y	Y
4 Kolter	Y	Y	Y	N	Y	Y	Y	Y
5 ***Schulze***	Y	Y	Y	Y	Y	Y	Y	Y
6 Yatron	Y	Y	Y	N	N	Y	Y	Y
7 ***Weldon***	Y	Y	Y	Y	Y	Y	Y	Y
8 Kostmayer	Y	Y	N	N	N	Y	N	Y
9 ***Shuster***	Y	Y	Y	Y	Y	Y	Y	Y
10 ***McDade***	N	Y	Y	Y	Y	Y	Y	Y
11 Kanjorski	Y	Y	Y	N	Y	Y	Y	Y
12 Murtha	Y	Y	Y	N	N	Y	Y	Y
13 ***Coughlin***	N	Y	Y	Y	Y	Y	Y	Y
14 Coyne	N	N	N	N	N	N	N	Y
15 ***Ritter***	Y	Y	Y	Y	Y	Y	Y	Y
16 ***Walker***	Y	Y	Y	Y	Y	Y	Y	Y
17 ***Gekas***	Y	Y	Y	Y	Y	Y	Y	Y
18 ***Santorum***	Y	Y	Y	?	Y	Y	Y	Y
19 ***Goodling***	Y	Y	P	Y	P	Y	P	Y
20 Gaydos	Y	?	?	N	N	Y	Y	Y
21 ***Ridge***	Y	Y	Y	N	Y	Y	Y	Y
22 Murphy	Y	Y	N	Y	Y	Y	Y	Y
23 ***Clinger***	Y	Y	Y	Y	Y	Y	Y	Y
RHODE ISLAND								
1 ***Machtley***	N	Y	Y	N	Y	Y	Y	N
2 Reed	N	Y	Y	N	N	Y	N	N
SOUTH CAROLINA								
1 ***Ravenel***	Y	Y	Y	Y	Y	Y	Y	Y
2 ***Spence***	Y	Y	Y	Y	Y	Y	Y	Y
3 Derrick	N	Y	N	N	N	Y	N	Y
4 Patterson	N	Y	Y	N	N	Y	Y	Y
5 Spratt	Y	Y	N	N	N	Y	N	Y
6 Tallon	Y	Y	Y	N	N	Y	N	Y

	318	319	320	321	322	323	324	325
SOUTH DAKOTA								
AL Johnson	Y	Y	Y	N	Y	Y	N	Y
TENNESSEE								
1 ***Quillen***	Y	Y	Y	Y	Y	Y	Y	Y
2 ***Duncan***	Y	Y	Y	Y	Y	Y	Y	N
3 Lloyd	Y	Y	Y	-	Y	Y	Y	Y
4 Cooper	Y	N	Y	N	N	Y	Y	Y
5 Clement	Y	Y	Y	N	Y	Y	Y	Y
6 Gordon	Y	Y	Y	N	N	Y	Y	Y
7 ***Sundquist***	Y	Y	Y	N	Y	Y	Y	Y
8 Tanner	Y	Y	N	N	Y	Y	Y	Y
9 Ford	N	N	N	?	?	?	?	?
TEXAS								
1 Chapman	Y	Y	Y	N	?	Y	Y	Y
2 Wilson	Y	Y	N	N	Y	Y	Y	Y
3 ***Johnson***	Y	Y	Y	Y	Y	Y	Y	N
4 Hall	Y	Y	Y	N	Y	Y	Y	Y
5 Bryant	N	N	N	N	N	Y	N	Y
6 ***Barton***	Y	Y	Y	Y	Y	Y	Y	Y
7 ***Archer***	Y	Y	Y	Y	Y	Y	Y	Y
8 ***Fields***	Y	Y	Y	?	?	?	Y	Y
9 Brooks	Y	N	N	N	N	N	?	?
10 Pickle	N	Y	Y	N	Y	N	N	Y
11 Edwards	N	Y	Y	N	Y	Y	Y	Y
12 Geren	Y	Y	Y	N	Y	Y	Y	Y
13 Sarpalius	Y	Y	Y	N	Y	Y	Y	Y
14 Laughlin	Y	N	Y	N	Y	Y	Y	Y
15 de la Garza	Y	Y	N	N	N	Y	Y	Y
16 Coleman	Y	Y	N	N	N	Y	N	Y
17 Stenholm	Y	Y	Y	N	Y	Y	Y	Y
18 Washington	N	N	N	N	N	N	N	?
19 ***Combest***	Y	Y	Y	Y	Y	Y	Y	Y
20 Gonzalez	N	N	N	N	N	N	N	Y
21 ***Smith***	Y	Y	Y	Y	Y	Y	Y	Y
22 ***DeLay***	Y	Y	Y	Y	Y	Y	Y	N
23 Bustamante	Y	N	?	N	N	Y	N	Y
24 Frost	N	Y	N	N	N	Y	N	Y
25 Andrews	Y	Y	Y	N	Y	Y	Y	Y
26 ***Armey***	Y	Y	Y	Y	Y	Y	Y	N
27 Ortiz	Y	Y	N	N	N	Y	N	Y
UTAH								
1 ***Hansen***	Y	Y	Y	N	Y	Y	Y	Y
2 Owens	Y	N	N	N	N	Y	Y	Y
3 Orton	Y	Y	N	N	Y	Y	Y	Y
VERMONT								
AL *Sanders*	N	N	N	N	N	N	N	Y
VIRGINIA								
1 ***Bateman***	N	Y	Y	Y	Y	Y	Y	Y
2 Pickett	Y	Y	N	N	N	Y	Y	Y
3 ***Bliley***	Y	Y	Y	Y	Y	Y	Y	Y
4 Sisisky	Y	Y	Y	N	N	Y	Y	Y
5 Payne	Y	Y	Y	N	Y	Y	Y	Y
6 Olin	Y	N	N	N	Y	N	Y	Y
7 ***Slaughter***	?	?	?	?	?	?	?	?
8 Moran	N	Y	Y	N	N	Y	Y	Y
9 Boucher	Y	N	N	N	N	Y	N	Y
10 ***Wolf***	N	Y	Y	N	Y	Y	Y	Y
WASHINGTON								
1 ***Miller***	N	Y	Y	Y	Y	Y	Y	Y
2 Swift	N	N	N	N	N	Y	N	Y
3 Unsoeld	Y	N	N	N	N	N	N	Y
4 ***Morrison***	N	Y	Y	Y	Y	Y	Y	Y
5 Foley								
6 Dicks	N	N	Y	N	Y	N	N	Y
7 McDermott	N	N	N	N	N	N	N	Y
8 ***Chandler***	Y	Y	Y	?	#	?	Y	Y
WEST VIRGINIA								
1 Mollohan	Y	N	N	N	N	Y	N	Y
2 Staggers	Y	N	N	N	N	Y	N	N
3 Wise	Y	N	N	N	N	Y	N	Y
4 Rahall	Y	Y	Y	N	N	Y	N	Y
WISCONSIN								
1 Aspin	N	Y	Y	N	Y	Y	Y	Y
2 ***Klug***	Y	Y	Y	Y	Y	Y	Y	Y
3 ***Gunderson***	Y	Y	Y	N	Y	Y	Y	Y
4 Kleczka	N	Y	N	N	N	Y	N	Y
5 Moody	N	N	N	N	N	Y	N	Y
6 ***Petri***	Y	Y	Y	Y	Y	Y	Y	N
7 Obey	Y	N	N	N	N	Y	N	N
8 ***Roth***	Y	Y	Y	Y	Y	Y	Y	Y
9 ***Sensenbrenner***	Y	Y	Y	Y	Y	Y	Y	N
WYOMING								
AL ***Thomas***	Y	Y	Y	Y	Y	Y	Y	Y

Southern states - Ala., Ark., Fla., Ga., Ky., La., Miss., N.C., Okla., S.C., Tenn., Texas, Va.
Omitted votes are quorum calls, which CQ does not include in its vote charts.

HOUSE VOTES 326, 327, 328, 329, 330, 331, 332, 333

326. HR 3371. Omnibus Crime Bill/Recommittal Motion. Hyde, R-Ill., motion to recommit the bill to the Judiciary Committee, with instructions to report it back to the House after replacing the habeas corpus reform in the bill with alternative habeas corpus reform that codifies the Powell Commission findings by creating an optional system under which states could limit the time within which prisoners must file habeas corpus petitions and limit the filing of successive petitions. Rejected 201-221: R 158-5; D 43-215 (ND 13-163, SD 30-52); I 0-1, Oct. 22, 1991. A "yea" was a vote supporting the president's position.

327. HR 3371. Omnibus Crime Bill/Passage. Passage of the bill to expand the death penalty to about 50 additional crimes, reform habeas corpus procedures, codify the "good faith" exception to the exclusionary rule, authorize $1.1 billion for law enforcement measures and for other purposes. 305-118: R 94-68; D 211-49 (ND 135-42, SD 76-7); I 0-1, Oct. 22, 1991.

328. HR 2032. Nez Perce National Historical Park/Passage. Vento, D-Minn., motion to suspend the rules and pass the bill to make additions to the Nez Perce National Historical Park in Idaho, Montana, Oregon, Washington and Wyoming. Motion agreed to 402-21: R 141-21; D 260-0 (ND 177-0, SD 83-0); I 1-0, Oct. 22, 1991. A two-thirds majority of those present and voting (282 in this case) is required for passage under suspension of the rules.

329. H Con Res 197. U.N. Disaster and Humanitarian Relief/Adoption. Yatron, D-Pa., motion to suspend the rules and pass the resolution to urge the secretary-general of the United Nations to develop plans to make the United Nations more effective in responding to international disasters. Motion agreed to 422-1: R 162-0; D 259-1 (ND 177-0, SD 82-1); I 1-0, Oct. 22, 1991. A two-thirds majority of those present and voting (282 in this case) is required for passage under suspension of the rules.

330. H Res 116. Convention on Discrimination Against Women/Adoption. Yatron, D-Pa., motion to suspend the rules and pass the resolution to urge the president to promptly complete the review of the Women's Human Rights Convention and submit it to the Senate for its advice and consent to ratification. Motion agreed to 374-48: R 114-48; D 259-0 (ND 177-0, SD 82-0); I 1-0, Oct. 22, 1991. A two-thirds majority of those present and voting (282 in this case) is required for passage under suspension of the rules.

331. HR 2950. Surface Transportation Reauthorization. Wheat, D-Mo., motion to order the previous question (thus limiting debate and the possibility of amendment) on the rule (H Res 252) to provide for House floor consideration of the bill to authorize $151 billion for highway and mass transit programs in fiscal 1992-97 and extend the current gasoline tax through fiscal 1999. Motion agreed to 319-104: R 61-100; D 257-4 (ND 176-3, SD 81-1); I 1-0, Oct. 23, 1991.

332. HR 2950. Surface Transportation Reauthorization/Rule. Adoption of the rule (H Res 252) to provide for House floor consideration of the bill to authorize $151 billion for highway and mass transit programs in fiscal 1992-97 and extend through fiscal 1999 half of the nickel added to the federal gasoline tax in 1990. Adopted 323-102: R 66-97; D 257-4 (ND 174-4, SD 83-0); I 0-1, Oct. 23, 1991.

333. HR 2950. Surface Transportation Reauthorization. Moakley, D-Mass., motion to table (kill) the Wheat, D-Mo., motion to reconsider the vote by which the House adopted the rule (H Res 252) to provide for House floor consideration of the bill to authorize $151 billion for highway and mass transit programs in fiscal 1992-97 and extend the current gas tax through fiscal 1999. Motion agreed to 319-89: R 69-88; D 249-1 (ND 171-1, SD 78-0); I 1-0, Oct. 23, 1991.

KEY

- Y Voted for (yea).
- # Paired for.
- + Announced for.
- N Voted against (nay).
- X Paired against.
- \- Announced against.
- P Voted "present."
- C Voted "present" to avoid possible conflict of interest.
- ? Did not vote or otherwise make a position known.

Democrats ***Republicans***
Independent

	326	327	328	329	330	331	332	333
ALABAMA								
1 ***Callahan***	?	?	?	?	?	?	Y	Y
2 ***Dickinson***	Y	N	Y	Y	Y	Y	Y	Y
3 Browder	Y	Y	Y	Y	Y	Y	Y	Y
4 Bevill	Y	Y	Y	Y	?	Y	Y	Y
5 Cramer	Y	Y	Y	Y	Y	Y	Y	Y
6 Erdreich	Y	Y	Y	Y	Y	Y	Y	Y
7 Harris	Y	Y	Y	Y	Y	Y	Y	Y
ALASKA								
AL ***Young***	Y	Y	Y	Y	Y	Y	Y	Y
ARIZONA								
1 ***Rhodes***	Y	N	Y	Y	Y	N	N	N
2 Pastor	N	Y	Y	Y	Y	Y	Y	Y
3 ***Stump***	Y	N	N	Y	N	N	N	N
4 ***Kyl***	Y	Y	Y	Y	Y	N	N	N
5 ***Kolbe***	Y	N	Y	Y	Y	N	N	N
ARKANSAS								
1 Alexander	N	Y	Y	Y	Y	Y	Y	Y
2 Thornton	N	Y	Y	Y	Y	Y	Y	Y
3 ***Hammerschmidt***	Y	N	N	Y	N	Y	Y	Y
4 Anthony	N	Y	Y	Y	Y	Y	Y	?
CALIFORNIA								
1 ***Riggs***	Y	N	N	Y	Y	Y	Y	Y
2 ***Herger***	Y	N	N	Y	N	N	N	?
3 Matsui	N	Y	Y	Y	Y	Y	Y	Y
4 Fazio	N	Y	Y	Y	Y	Y	Y	Y
5 Pelosi	N	N	Y	Y	Y	Y	Y	Y
6 Boxer	N	Y	Y	Y	Y	Y	Y	Y
7 Miller	N	Y	Y	Y	Y	Y	Y	Y
8 Dellums	?	?	?	?	?	Y	Y	Y
9 Stark	N	Y	Y	Y	Y	Y	Y	Y
10 Edwards	N	N	Y	Y	Y	Y	Y	Y
11 Lantos	N	Y	Y	Y	Y	Y	Y	Y
12 ***Campbell***	Y	Y	Y	Y	Y	N	N	N
13 Mineta	N	Y	Y	Y	Y	Y	Y	Y
14 ***Doolittle***	Y	N	Y	Y	N	N	N	?
15 Condit	Y	Y	Y	Y	Y	Y	Y	Y
16 Panetta	N	Y	Y	Y	Y	Y	Y	Y
17 Dooley	Y	Y	Y	Y	Y	Y	Y	Y
18 Lehman	Y	Y	Y	Y	Y	Y	Y	Y
19 ***Lagomarsino***	Y	Y	Y	Y	N	N	N	N
20 ***Thomas***	Y	Y	Y	Y	Y	N	Y	N
21 ***Gallegly***	Y	Y	Y	Y	Y	N	N	N
22 ***Moorhead***	Y	N	Y	Y	Y	N	N	N
23 Beilenson	N	N	Y	Y	Y	Y	Y	Y
24 Waxman	N	N	Y	Y	Y	Y	Y	Y
25 Roybal	N	N	Y	Y	Y	Y	Y	Y
26 Berman	N	Y	Y	Y	Y	Y	Y	Y
27 Levine	N	Y	Y	Y	Y	Y	Y	Y
28 Dixon	N	N	Y	Y	Y	Y	Y	Y
29 Waters	?	?	?	?	?	?	?	?
30 Martinez	?	Y	Y	Y	Y	?	N	N
31 Dymally	N	N	Y	Y	Y	Y	Y	Y
32 Anderson	N	Y	Y	Y	Y	Y	Y	Y
33 ***Dreier***	Y	N	Y	Y	Y	N	N	N
34 Torres	N	Y	Y	Y	Y	Y	?	Y
35 ***Lewis***	Y	Y	Y	Y	Y	Y	Y	N
36 Brown	N	Y	Y	Y	Y	Y	Y	?
37 ***McCandless***	Y	Y	Y	Y	Y	N	Y	N
38 ***Dornan***	Y	N	Y	Y	N	N	N	N
39 ***Dannemeyer***	Y	N	N	Y	Y	N	N	N
40 ***Cox***	Y	N	Y	Y	Y	N	N	N
41 ***Lowery***	Y	N	Y	Y	N	Y	Y	Y
42 ***Rohrabacher***	Y	N	N	Y	N	N	N	N
43 ***Packard***	Y	N	Y	Y	N	Y	Y	?
44 ***Cunningham***	Y	N	Y	Y	N	N	N	N
45 ***Hunter***	Y	N	Y	Y	N	N	N	N
COLORADO								
1 Schroeder	N	Y	Y	Y	Y	N	N	Y
2 Skaggs	N	N	Y	Y	Y	Y	Y	Y
3 Campbell	N	Y	Y	Y	Y	Y	Y	Y
4 ***Allard***	Y	N	Y	Y	Y	N	N	N
5 ***Hefley***	Y	N	Y	Y	Y	N	N	N
6 ***Schaefer***	Y	N	Y	Y	Y	Y	N	N
CONNECTICUT								
1 Kennelly	N	Y	Y	Y	Y	Y	Y	Y
2 Gejdenson	N	Y	Y	Y	Y	Y	Y	Y
3 DeLauro	N	Y	Y	Y	Y	Y	Y	Y
4 ***Shays***	Y	Y	Y	Y	Y	N	N	N
5 ***Franks***	Y	Y	Y	Y	Y	N	N	N
6 ***Johnson***	Y	Y	Y	Y	Y	Y	Y	Y
DELAWARE								
AL Carper	Y	Y	Y	Y	Y	Y	Y	Y
FLORIDA								
1 Hutto	Y	Y	Y	Y	Y	Y	Y	Y
2 Peterson	N	Y	Y	Y	Y	Y	Y	Y
3 Bennett	N	Y	Y	Y	Y	Y	Y	Y
4 ***James***	Y	Y	Y	Y	N	N	N	N
5 ***McCollum***	Y	N	Y	Y	Y	Y	N	N
6 ***Stearns***	Y	Y	N	Y	N	N	N	N
7 Gibbons	N	Y	Y	Y	Y	Y	Y	Y
8 ***Young***	Y	N	Y	Y	Y	Y	N	Y
9 ***Bilirakis***	Y	Y	Y	Y	Y	N	N	Y
10 ***Ireland***	Y	Y	Y	Y	Y	N	N	N
11 Bacchus	N	Y	Y	Y	Y	Y	Y	Y
12 ***Lewis***	Y	Y	Y	Y	Y	Y	Y	Y
13 ***Goss***	Y	Y	Y	Y	Y	N	N	N
14 Johnston	N	Y	Y	Y	Y	Y	Y	Y
15 ***Shaw***	Y	Y	Y	Y	Y	?	Y	Y
16 Smith	N	Y	Y	Y	Y	Y	Y	Y
17 Lehman	N	N	Y	Y	Y	Y	Y	Y
18 ***Ros-Lehtinen***	Y	Y	Y	Y	N	N	N	N
19 Fascell	N	Y	Y	Y	Y	Y	Y	Y
GEORGIA								
1 Thomas	Y	Y	Y	Y	Y	Y	Y	Y
2 Hatcher	N	Y	Y	Y	Y	Y	Y	?
3 Ray	Y	Y	Y	Y	Y	Y	Y	Y
4 Jones	N	Y	Y	Y	Y	Y	Y	Y
5 Lewis	X	?	?	?	?	Y	Y	Y
6 ***Gingrich***	Y	N	Y	Y	N	N	N	N
7 Darden	#	?	?	?	?	Y	Y	Y
8 Rowland	Y	Y	Y	Y	Y	Y	Y	Y
9 Jenkins	N	Y	Y	Y	Y	Y	Y	Y
10 Barnard	Y	Y	Y	Y	Y	Y	Y	Y
HAWAII								
1 Abercrombie	N	Y	Y	Y	Y	Y	Y	Y
2 Mink	N	Y	Y	Y	Y	N	Y	Y
IDAHO								
1 LaRocco	N	Y	Y	Y	Y	Y	Y	Y
2 Stallings	N	Y	Y	Y	Y	Y	Y	?
ILLINOIS								
1 Hayes	N	N	Y	Y	Y	Y	Y	Y
2 Savage	N	N	Y	Y	Y	Y	Y	Y
3 Russo	N	Y	Y	Y	Y	Y	Y	Y
4 Sangmeister	N	Y	Y	Y	Y	Y	Y	Y
5 Lipinski	Y	Y	Y	Y	Y	Y	Y	Y
6 ***Hyde***	Y	N	Y	Y	N	N	Y	Y
7 Collins	?	?	?	?	?	Y	Y	Y
8 Rostenkowski	N	Y	Y	Y	Y	Y	Y	Y
9 Yates	N	N	Y	Y	Y	Y	Y	Y
10 ***Porter***	Y	Y	Y	Y	Y	N	N	N
11 Annunzio	N	Y	Y	Y	Y	Y	Y	Y
12 ***Crane***	Y	N	N	Y	N	N	N	N
13 ***Fawell***	Y	Y	Y	Y	Y	N	N	N
14 ***Hastert***	Y	N	Y	Y	N	Y	Y	Y
15 ***Ewing***	Y	N	Y	Y	N	Y	Y	Y
16 Cox	N	Y	Y	Y	Y	Y	Y	Y
17 Evans	N	Y	Y	Y	Y	Y	N	Y
18 ***Michel***	Y	Y	Y	Y	N	?	?	?
19 Bruce	N	Y	Y	Y	Y	Y	Y	Y
20 Durbin	N	Y	Y	Y	Y	Y	Y	Y
21 Costello	N	Y	Y	Y	Y	Y	Y	Y
22 Poshard	N	Y	Y	Y	Y	Y	Y	Y
INDIANA								
1 Visclosky	N	Y	Y	Y	Y	Y	Y	Y
2 Sharp	N	Y	Y	Y	Y	Y	Y	Y
3 Roemer	N	Y	Y	Y	Y	Y	Y	Y

ND Northern Democrats SD Southern Democrats

	326	327	328	329	330	331	332	333
4 Long	N	Y	Y	Y	Y	Y	Y	Y
5 Jontz	N	Y	Y	Y	Y	Y	Y	Y
6 **Burton**	Y	N	N	Y	N	N	N	N
7 **Myers**	Y	Y	Y	Y	Y	Y	Y	Y
8 McCloskey	N	Y	Y	Y	Y	Y	Y	Y
9 Hamilton	N	Y	Y	Y	Y	Y	Y	Y
10 Jacobs	N	Y	Y	Y	Y	N	N	Y
IOWA								
1 **Leach**	Y	Y	Y	Y	Y	Y	Y	Y
2 **Nussle**	Y	N	Y	Y	Y	Y	Y	Y
3 Nagle	N	N	Y	Y	Y	Y	Y	Y
4 Smith	N	N	Y	Y	Y	Y	Y	Y
5 **Lightfoot**	Y	N	Y	Y	N	N	N	Y
6 **Grandy**	Y	Y	Y	Y	Y	Y	Y	Y
KANSAS								
1 **Roberts**	Y	Y	Y	Y	Y	N	N	N
2 Slattery	N	Y	Y	Y	Y	Y	Y	Y
3 **Meyers**	Y	Y	Y	Y	Y	N	N	N
4 Glickman	N	Y	Y	Y	Y	Y	Y	Y
5 **Nichols**	Y	N	Y	Y	Y	Y	Y	Y
KENTUCKY								
1 Hubbard	Y	Y	Y	Y	Y	Y	Y	Y
2 Natcher	N	Y	Y	Y	Y	Y	Y	Y
3 Mazzoli	N	Y	Y	Y	Y	Y	Y	Y
4 **Bunning**	Y	Y	Y	Y	N	N	N	N
5 **Rogers**	Y	Y	Y	Y	Y	Y	Y	Y
6 **Hopkins**	?	?	?	?	?	?	?	?
7 Perkins	N	Y	Y	Y	Y	Y	Y	Y
LOUISIANA								
1 **Livingston**	Y	N	Y	Y	N	N	N	N
2 Jefferson	N	Y	Y	Y	Y	?	Y	Y
3 Tauzin	Y	Y	Y	Y	Y	Y	Y	?
4 **McCrery**	Y	N	Y	Y	Y	N	Y	Y
5 Huckaby	Y	Y	Y	Y	Y	Y	Y	Y
6 **Baker**	Y	N	Y	Y	Y	N	N	N
7 Hayes	Y	Y	Y	Y	Y	Y	Y	Y
8 **Holloway**	Y	N	N	Y	N	N	N	N
MAINE								
1 Andrews	Y	N	Y	Y	Y	Y	Y	Y
2 **Snowe**	Y	N	Y	Y	Y	N	N	N
MARYLAND								
1 **Gilchrest**	Y	Y	Y	Y	Y	N	N	N
2 **Bentley**	Y	Y	Y	Y	Y	Y	Y	Y
3 Cardin	N	Y	Y	Y	Y	Y	Y	Y
4 McMillen	N	Y	Y	Y	Y	Y	Y	Y
5 Hoyer	N	Y	Y	Y	Y	Y	Y	Y
6 Byron	N	Y	Y	Y	Y	Y	Y	Y
7 Mfume	N	N	Y	Y	Y	Y	Y	Y
8 **Morella**	N	Y	Y	Y	Y	Y	Y	Y
MASSACHUSETTS								
1 Olver	N	N	Y	Y	Y	Y	Y	Y
2 Neal	N	Y	Y	Y	Y	Y	Y	Y
3 Early	N	Y	Y	Y	Y	Y	Y	Y
4 Frank	N	Y	Y	Y	Y	Y	Y	Y
5 Atkins	N	Y	Y	Y	Y	Y	Y	Y
6 Mavroules	N	Y	Y	Y	Y	Y	Y	Y
7 Markey	N	Y	Y	Y	Y	Y	Y	Y
8 Kennedy	N	Y	Y	Y	Y	Y	Y	Y
9 Moakley	N	Y	Y	Y	Y	Y	Y	Y
10 Studds	N	Y	Y	Y	Y	Y	Y	Y
11 Donnelly	N	Y	Y	Y	Y	Y	Y	Y
MICHIGAN								
1 Conyers	N	N	Y	Y	Y	Y	Y	Y
2 **Pursell**	Y	Y	Y	Y	Y	Y	Y	Y
3 Wolpe	N	Y	Y	Y	Y	Y	Y	Y
4 **Upton**	Y	Y	Y	Y	Y	Y	Y	Y
5 **Henry**	Y	Y	Y	Y	N	Y	Y	Y
6 Carr	N	Y	Y	Y	Y	Y	Y	Y
7 Kildee	N	N	Y	Y	Y	Y	Y	Y
8 Traxler	N	Y	Y	Y	Y	Y	Y	?
9 **Vander Jagt**	Y	N	Y	Y	Y	Y	Y	Y
10 **Camp**	Y	Y	Y	Y	N	N	N	N
11 **Davis**	Y	N	Y	Y	Y	Y	Y	?
12 Bonior	N	Y	Y	Y	Y	Y	Y	Y
13 Collins	N	N	Y	Y	Y	Y	Y	Y
14 Hertel	N	Y	Y	Y	Y	Y	Y	?
15 Ford	N	N	Y	Y	Y	Y	Y	Y
16 Dingell	N	Y	Y	Y	Y	Y	Y	Y
17 Levin	N	Y	Y	Y	Y	Y	Y	Y
18 **Broomfield**	Y	Y	Y	Y	Y	N	N	N
MINNESOTA								
1 Penny	N	N	Y	Y	Y	Y	Y	Y
2 **Weber**	Y	Y	Y	Y	N	N	N	N
3 **Ramstad**	Y	Y	Y	Y	Y	N	N	N
4 Vento	N	N	Y	Y	Y	Y	Y	Y

	326	327	328	329	330	331	332	333
5 Sabo	N	N	Y	Y	Y	Y	Y	Y
6 Sikorski	N	Y	Y	Y	Y	Y	Y	Y
7 Peterson	N	Y	Y	Y	Y	Y	Y	Y
8 Oberstar	N	N	Y	Y	Y	Y	Y	Y
MISSISSIPPI								
1 Whitten	N	Y	Y	Y	Y	Y	Y	Y
2 Espy	N	Y	Y	Y	Y	Y	Y	Y
3 Montgomery	Y	Y	Y	Y	Y	Y	Y	Y
4 Parker	Y	Y	Y	Y	Y	Y	Y	Y
5 Taylor	Y	Y	Y	N	Y	Y	Y	Y
MISSOURI								
1 Clay	N	N	Y	Y	Y	Y	Y	Y
2 Horn	N	Y	Y	Y	Y	Y	Y	Y
3 Gephardt	N	Y	Y	Y	Y	Y	Y	Y
4 Skelton	Y	Y	Y	Y	Y	Y	Y	Y
5 Wheat	N	N	Y	Y	Y	Y	Y	Y
6 **Coleman**	Y	Y	Y	Y	Y	N	N	Y
7 **Hancock**	Y	N	N	Y	N	N	N	N
8 **Emerson**	Y	Y	Y	Y	Y	Y	Y	Y
9 Volkmer	Y	Y	Y	Y	Y	Y	Y	Y
MONTANA								
1 Williams	N	N	Y	Y	Y	Y	Y	Y
2 **Marlenee**	Y	N	Y	Y	N	N	N	N
NEBRASKA								
1 **Bereuter**	Y	Y	Y	Y	Y	Y	Y	Y
2 Hoagland	N	Y	Y	Y	Y	Y	Y	Y
3 **Barrett**	Y	Y	Y	Y	Y	N	N	N
NEVADA								
1 Bilbray	N	Y	Y	Y	Y	Y	Y	Y
2 **Vucanovich**	Y	N	Y	Y	N	N	N	N
NEW HAMPSHIRE								
1 **Zeliff**	Y	N	Y	Y	Y	N	N	N
2 Swett	N	Y	Y	Y	Y	Y	Y	?
NEW JERSEY								
1 Andrews	N	Y	Y	Y	Y	Y	Y	Y
2 Hughes	N	Y	Y	Y	Y	Y	Y	Y
3 Pallone	N	Y	Y	Y	Y	Y	Y	Y
4 **Smith**	Y	Y	Y	Y	N	Y	Y	Y
5 **Roukema**	Y	Y	Y	Y	Y	N	Y	Y
6 Dwyer	N	Y	Y	Y	Y	Y	Y	Y
7 **Rinaldo**	Y	Y	Y	Y	Y	Y	Y	Y
8 Roe	N	Y	Y	Y	Y	Y	Y	Y
9 Torricelli	N	Y	Y	Y	Y	Y	Y	Y
10 Payne	N	N	Y	Y	Y	Y	Y	Y
11 **Gallo**	Y	Y	Y	Y	Y	Y	Y	Y
12 **Zimmer**	Y	Y	Y	Y	Y	N	N	N
13 **Saxton**	Y	Y	Y	Y	Y	N	N	N
14 Guarini	N	Y	Y	Y	Y	Y	Y	Y
NEW MEXICO								
1 **Schiff**	Y	Y	Y	Y	Y	N	N	N
2 **Skeen**	Y	Y	Y	Y	Y	N	N	Y
3 Richardson	N	Y	Y	Y	Y	Y	Y	Y
NEW YORK								
1 Hochbrueckner	N	Y	Y	Y	Y	Y	Y	Y
2 Downey	N	Y	Y	Y	Y	Y	?	Y
3 Mrazek	?	?	?	?	?	?	Y	Y
4 **Lent**	Y	Y	Y	Y	Y	Y	Y	N
5 **McGrath**	Y	Y	Y	Y	Y	Y	Y	Y
6 Flake	N	N	Y	Y	Y	Y	Y	Y
7 Ackerman	N	Y	Y	Y	Y	Y	Y	Y
8 Scheuer	N	Y	Y	Y	Y	Y	Y	Y
9 Manton	N	Y	Y	Y	Y	Y	Y	Y
10 Schumer	N	Y	Y	Y	Y	Y	Y	Y
11 Towns	N	Y	Y	Y	Y	Y	Y	Y
12 Owens	N	N	Y	Y	Y	Y	Y	Y
13 Solarz	N	Y	Y	Y	Y	Y	Y	Y
14 **Molinari**	Y	Y	Y	Y	Y	Y	Y	Y
15 **Green**	N	Y	Y	Y	Y	Y	Y	Y
16 Rangel	N	N	Y	Y	Y	Y	Y	Y
17 Weiss	N	N	Y	Y	Y	Y	Y	Y
18 Serrano	N	N	Y	Y	Y	Y	Y	Y
19 Engel	N	Y	Y	Y	Y	Y	Y	Y
20 Lowey	N	Y	Y	Y	Y	Y	Y	Y
21 **Fish**	N	Y	Y	Y	Y	Y	Y	Y
22 **Gilman**	N	Y	Y	Y	Y	Y	Y	Y
23 McNulty	N	Y	Y	Y	Y	Y	Y	Y
24 **Solomon**	Y	Y	Y	Y	N	N	N	N
25 **Boehlert**	Y	Y	Y	Y	Y	Y	Y	Y
26 **Martin**	Y	Y	Y	Y	Y	N	N	?
27 **Walsh**	Y	Y	Y	Y	Y	N	N	N
28 McHugh	N	N	Y	Y	Y	Y	Y	Y
29 **Horton**	N	Y	Y	Y	Y	Y	Y	Y
30 Slaughter	N	Y	Y	Y	Y	Y	Y	Y
31 **Paxon**	Y	N	Y	Y	N	N	N	N

	326	327	328	329	330	331	332	333
32 LaFalce	N	Y	Y	Y	Y	Y	Y	Y
33 Nowak	N	Y	Y	Y	Y	Y	Y	Y
34 **Houghton**	Y	Y	Y	Y	Y	Y	Y	Y
NORTH CAROLINA								
1 Jones	N	Y	Y	Y	Y	Y	Y	Y
2 Valentine	Y	Y	Y	Y	Y	Y	Y	Y
3 Lancaster	N	Y	Y	Y	Y	Y	Y	Y
4 Price	N	Y	Y	Y	Y	Y	Y	Y
5 Neal	Y	Y	Y	Y	Y	?	?	?
6 **Coble**	Y	N	N	Y	N	N	N	N
7 Rose	N	Y	Y	Y	Y	N	Y	Y
8 Hefner	N	Y	Y	Y	Y	Y	Y	Y
9 **McMillan**	Y	Y	Y	Y	Y	N	N	N
10 **Ballenger**	Y	N	+	+	+	N	N	N
11 **Taylor**	Y	N	N	Y	N	Y	N	N
NORTH DAKOTA								
AL Dorgan	N	Y	Y	Y	Y	Y	Y	Y
OHIO								
1 Luken	N	Y	Y	Y	Y	Y	Y	Y
2 **Gradison**	Y	N	Y	Y	Y	N	N	N
3 Hall	N	Y	Y	Y	Y	Y	Y	Y
4 **Oxley**	Y	Y	Y	Y	Y	Y	Y	Y
5 **Gillmor**	Y	Y	Y	Y	Y	N	Y	?
6 **McEwen**	Y	N	N	Y	N	N	N	N
7 **Hobson**	Y	Y	Y	Y	Y	Y	Y	Y
8 **Boehner**	Y	N	Y	Y	Y	N	N	N
9 Kaptur	N	Y	Y	Y	Y	Y	Y	Y
10 **Miller**	Y	Y	Y	Y	N	N	N	N
11 Eckart	N	Y	Y	Y	Y	Y	Y	?
12 **Kasich**	Y	Y	Y	Y	Y	N	Y	N
13 Pease	N	N	Y	Y	Y	Y	Y	Y
14 Sawyer	N	Y	Y	Y	Y	Y	Y	Y
15 **Wylie**	Y	Y	Y	Y	Y	Y	Y	Y
16 **Regula**	Y	Y	Y	Y	Y	Y	Y	Y
17 Traficant	N	Y	Y	Y	Y	Y	Y	Y
18 Applegate	Y	Y	Y	Y	Y	Y	Y	Y
19 Feighan	N	Y	Y	Y	Y	Y	Y	Y
20 Oakar	N	Y	Y	Y	Y	Y	Y	Y
21 Stokes	N	N	Y	Y	Y	Y	Y	Y
OKLAHOMA								
1 **Inhofe**	Y	Y	Y	Y	N	Y	Y	Y
2 Synar	N	Y	Y	Y	Y	Y	Y	Y
3 Brewster	N	Y	Y	Y	Y	Y	Y	Y
4 McCurdy	Y	Y	Y	Y	Y	Y	Y	Y
5 **Edwards**	Y	Y	Y	Y	Y	N	N	N
6 English	Y	Y	Y	Y	Y	Y	Y	Y
OREGON								
1 AuCoin	N	Y	Y	Y	Y	Y	Y	Y
2 **Smith**	Y	Y	Y	Y	Y	N	N	N
3 Wyden	N	Y	Y	Y	Y	Y	Y	Y
4 DeFazio	N	Y	Y	Y	Y	Y	Y	Y
5 Kopetski	N	Y	Y	Y	Y	Y	Y	Y
PENNSYLVANIA								
1 Foglietta	N	Y	Y	Y	Y	Y	Y	Y
2 Vacancy								
3 Borski	Y	Y	Y	Y	Y	Y	Y	Y
4 Kolter	Y	Y	Y	Y	Y	Y	Y	Y
5 **Schulze**	Y	N	Y	Y	Y	Y	Y	Y
6 Yatron	Y	Y	Y	Y	Y	Y	Y	Y
7 **Weldon**	Y	Y	Y	Y	Y	N	N	N
8 Kostmayer	N	Y	Y	Y	Y	Y	Y	Y
9 **Shuster**	Y	N	Y	Y	Y	Y	Y	Y
10 **McDade**	Y	Y	Y	Y	Y	Y	Y	Y
11 Kanjorski	N	Y	Y	Y	Y	Y	Y	Y
12 Murtha	N	Y	Y	Y	Y	Y	Y	Y
13 **Coughlin**	Y	Y	Y	Y	Y	Y	Y	Y
14 Coyne	N	Y	Y	Y	Y	Y	Y	Y
15 **Ritter**	Y	Y	Y	Y	Y	Y	Y	Y
16 **Walker**	Y	N	N	Y	N	N	N	N
17 **Gekas**	Y	Y	Y	Y	N	Y	Y	Y
18 **Santorum**	Y	Y	Y	Y	N	Y	Y	Y
19 **Goodling**	Y	P	Y	Y	Y	Y	Y	Y
20 Gaydos	N	Y	Y	Y	Y	Y	Y	Y
21 **Ridge**	Y	Y	Y	Y	Y	Y	Y	Y
22 Murphy	Y	Y	Y	Y	Y	Y	Y	Y
23 **Clinger**	Y	N	Y	Y	Y	Y	Y	Y
RHODE ISLAND								
1 **Machtley**	Y	Y	Y	Y	Y	N	Y	Y
2 Reed	N	Y	Y	Y	Y	Y	Y	Y
SOUTH CAROLINA								
1 **Ravenel**	Y	Y	Y	Y	Y	N	N	Y
2 **Spence**	Y	Y	Y	Y	Y	N	N	N
3 Derrick	N	Y	Y	Y	Y	Y	Y	Y
4 Patterson	N	Y	Y	Y	Y	Y	Y	Y
5 Spratt	N	Y	Y	Y	Y	Y	Y	Y
6 Tallon	N	Y	Y	Y	Y	Y	Y	Y

	326	327	328	329	330	331	332	333
SOUTH DAKOTA								
AL Johnson	N	Y	Y	Y	Y	Y	Y	Y
TENNESSEE								
1 **Quillen**	Y	Y	Y	Y	Y	Y	Y	Y
2 **Duncan**	Y	Y	N	Y	Y	N	N	N
3 Lloyd	Y	Y	Y	Y	Y	Y	Y	Y
4 Cooper	N	Y	Y	Y	Y	Y	Y	Y
5 Clement	N	Y	Y	Y	Y	Y	Y	Y
6 Gordon	N	Y	Y	Y	Y	Y	Y	?
7 **Sundquist**	Y	Y	Y	Y	Y	N	N	Y
8 Tanner	N	Y	Y	Y	Y	Y	Y	Y
9 Ford	N	Y	Y	Y	Y	Y	Y	Y
TEXAS								
1 Chapman	N	Y	Y	Y	Y	Y	Y	?
2 Wilson	N	Y	Y	Y	Y	Y	Y	Y
3 **Johnson**	Y	N	Y	Y	N	N	N	N
4 Hall	Y	Y	Y	Y	Y	Y	Y	Y
5 Bryant	N	Y	Y	Y	Y	Y	Y	Y
6 **Barton**	Y	N	Y	Y	Y	N	N	N
7 **Archer**	Y	N	N	Y	N	N	N	N
8 **Fields**	Y	N	Y	Y	Y	N	N	N
9 Brooks	N	Y	Y	Y	Y	Y	Y	Y
10 Pickle	N	Y	Y	Y	Y	Y	Y	Y
11 Edwards	N	Y	Y	Y	Y	Y	Y	Y
12 Geren	Y	Y	Y	Y	Y	Y	Y	Y
13 Sarpalius	Y	N	Y	Y	Y	Y	Y	Y
14 Laughlin	N	Y	Y	Y	Y	Y	Y	Y
15 de la Garza	N	Y	Y	Y	Y	Y	Y	Y
16 Coleman	N	Y	Y	Y	Y	Y	Y	Y
17 Stenholm	Y	Y	Y	Y	Y	Y	Y	Y
18 Washington	?	N	Y	Y	Y	?	?	?
19 **Combest**	Y	N	Y	Y	Y	N	N	N
20 Gonzalez	N	N	Y	Y	Y	Y	Y	Y
21 **Smith**	Y	N	Y	Y	Y	N	N	N
22 **DeLay**	Y	N	N	Y	N	N	N	N
23 Bustamante	N	Y	Y	Y	Y	Y	Y	Y
24 Frost	N	Y	Y	Y	Y	Y	Y	Y
25 Andrews	N	Y	Y	Y	Y	Y	Y	Y
26 **Armey**	Y	N	N	Y	N	N	N	N
27 Ortiz	Y	Y	Y	Y	Y	Y	Y	Y
UTAH								
1 **Hansen**	Y	Y	N	Y	N	N	N	N
2 Owens	N	Y	Y	Y	Y	Y	Y	?
3 Orton	N	Y	Y	Y	Y	Y	Y	?
VERMONT								
AL *Sanders*	N	N	Y	Y	Y	Y	N	Y
VIRGINIA								
1 **Bateman**	Y	Y	Y	Y	Y	Y	Y	Y
2 Pickett	N	N	Y	Y	Y	Y	Y	Y
3 **Bliley**	Y	Y	Y	Y	Y	N	N	N
4 Sisisky	Y	Y	Y	Y	Y	Y	Y	Y
5 Payne	Y	Y	Y	Y	Y	Y	Y	Y
6 Olin	N	N	Y	Y	Y	Y	Y	Y
7 **Slaughter**	?	?	?	?	?	?	?	?
8 Moran	Y	N	Y	Y	Y	Y	Y	Y
9 Boucher	N	Y	Y	Y	Y	Y	Y	Y
10 **Wolf**	Y	Y	Y	Y	Y	N	N	N
WASHINGTON								
1 **Miller**	Y	Y	Y	Y	Y	Y	N	Y
2 Swift	N	N	Y	Y	Y	Y	Y	Y
3 Unsoeld	N	N	Y	Y	Y	Y	Y	Y
4 **Morrison**	Y	N	Y	Y	Y	N	N	Y
5 Foley								
6 Dicks	N	Y	Y	Y	Y	Y	Y	Y
7 McDermott	N	Y	Y	Y	Y	Y	Y	Y
8 **Chandler**	Y	N	Y	Y	Y	N	N	N
WEST VIRGINIA								
1 Mollohan	N	N	Y	Y	Y	Y	Y	Y
2 Staggers	N	N	Y	Y	Y	Y	Y	Y
3 Wise	N	N	Y	Y	Y	Y	Y	Y
4 Rahall	N	Y	Y	Y	Y	Y	Y	Y
WISCONSIN								
1 Aspin	N	Y	Y	Y	Y	Y	Y	Y
2 **Klug**	Y	Y	Y	Y	Y	N	N	N
3 **Gunderson**	Y	Y	Y	Y	Y	N	N	Y
4 Kleczka	N	Y	Y	Y	Y	Y	Y	Y
5 Moody	N	Y	Y	Y	Y	Y	Y	Y
6 **Petri**	Y	N	Y	Y	Y	Y	Y	Y
7 Obey	N	N	Y	Y	Y	Y	Y	Y
8 **Roth**	Y	N	Y	Y	Y	N	N	Y
9 **Sensenbrenner**	Y	N	N	Y	Y	N	N	N
WYOMING								
AL **Thomas**	Y	N	Y	Y	N	N	N	N

Southern states - Ala., Ark., Fla., Ga., Ky., La., Miss., N.C., Okla., S.C., Tenn., Texas, Va.
Omitted votes are quorum calls, which CQ does not include in its vote charts.

HOUSE VOTES 334, 335, 336, 337, 338, 339, 340, 341

334. Procedural Motion. Burton, R-Ind., motion to adjourn. Motion rejected 30-385: R 29-131; D 1-253 (ND 1-176, SD 0-77); I 0-1, Oct. 23, 1991.

335. HR 2950. Surface Transportation Reauthorization/State-Awarded Contracts. Norton, D-D.C., en bloc amendment to require that when states award contracts with federal highway funds that 10 percent of the funds go to minority-owned businesses and 5 percent to women-owned businesses rather than the 10 percent that is currently required by law to be split between the two groups. Rejected 133-295: R 2-161; D 130-134 (ND 105-75, SD 25-59); I 1-0, Oct. 23, 1991.

336. HR 2950. Surface Transportation Reauthorization/Warranty Clause. Beilenson, D-Calif., amendment to allow state highway departments to include a warranty or guaranty clause in contracts for materials and workmanship regarding the construction of federal-aid highway projects. Adopted 400-26: R 145-18; D 254-8 (ND 178-1, SD 76-7); I 1-0, Oct. 23, 1991.

337. HR 2950. Surface Transportation Reauthorization/Office of Intermodalism. Walker, R-Pa., amendment to eliminate the $11.5 million authorization to establish an Office of Intermodalism within the Department of Transportation for the promotion of an intermodal system that integrates different types of transportation. Rejected 69-348: R 67-93; D 2-254 (ND 1-175, SD 1-79); I 0-1, Oct. 23, 1991.

338. HR 2950. Surface Transportation Reauthorization/Passage. Passage of the bill to authorize $151 billion for highway and mass transit programs in fiscal 1992-97 and extend through fiscal 1999 half of the nickel added to the federal gasoline tax in 1990. Passed 343-83: R 101-61; D 241-22 (ND 160-20, SD 81-2); I 1-0, Oct. 23, 1991. A "nay" was a vote supporting the president's position.

339. HR 2038. Fiscal 1992 Intelligence Authorization/CIA Consolidation. Shuster, R-Pa., motion to instruct the House conferees to insist that no final decision regarding the consolidation of CIA facilities in Virginia and West Virginia be made prior to approval and implementation of written procedures on acquisition of real estate. Motion agreed to 388-32: R 157-2; D 230-30 (ND 156-21, SD 74-9); I 1-0, Oct. 24, 1991.

340. H J Res 360. Fiscal 1992 Continuing Resolution/Passage. Passage of the joint resolution to provide continuing appropriations through Nov. 14 for nine fiscal 1992 appropriations bills not yet enacted into law. The foreign operations bill would be extended through March 31, 1992. Passed 288-126: R 55-102; D 232-24 (ND 156-18, SD 76-6); I 1-0, Oct. 24, 1991.

341. HR 2686. Fiscal 1992 Interior Appropriations/Recommittal Motion. Lowery, R-Calif., motion to recommit the conference report with instruction to accept the Senate provision that would prohibit the use of funds by the National Endowment for the Arts to promote, disseminate or produce materials that depict or describe, in a patently offensive way, sexual or excretory activities or organs. Motion rejected 205-214: R 128-32; D 77-181 (ND 30-147, SD 47-34); I 0-1, Oct. 24, 1991.

KEY

- Y Voted for (yea).
- # Paired for.
- + Announced for.
- N Voted against (nay).
- X Paired against.
- \- Announced against.
- P Voted "present."
- C Voted "present" to avoid possible conflict of interest.
- ? Did not vote or otherwise make a position known.

Democrats ***Republicans***
Independent

	334	335	336	337	338	339	340	341
ALABAMA								
1 ***Callahan***	N	N	Y	N	Y	Y	N	Y
2 ***Dickinson***	N	N	Y	?	?	?	?	?
3 Browder	N	N	Y	N	Y	Y	Y	N
4 Bevill	N	Y	Y	N	Y	N	Y	N
5 Cramer	N	N	Y	N	Y	Y	Y	N
6 Erdreich	?	N	Y	N	Y	Y	Y	N
7 Harris	N	N	Y	N	Y	Y	Y	N
ALASKA								
AL ***Young***	Y	N	Y	N	Y	Y	Y	N
ARIZONA								
1 ***Rhodes***	N	N	Y	N	N	Y	N	N
2 Pastor	N	Y	Y	N	Y	Y	Y	N
3 ***Stump***	Y	N	Y	Y	N	Y	N	Y
4 ***Kyl***	N	N	Y	Y	N	Y	N	N
5 ***Kolbe***	N	N	Y	N	Y	Y	N	N
ARKANSAS								
1 Alexander	N	Y	Y	N	Y	N	Y	N
2 Thornton	N	N	N	N	Y	Y	Y	Y
3 ***Hammerschmidt***	N	N	Y	N	Y	Y	N	Y
4 Anthony	N	N	Y	N	Y	Y	Y	N
CALIFORNIA								
1 ***Riggs***	N	N	Y	N	Y	Y	N	Y
2 ***Herger***	Y	N	Y	Y	N	Y	N	Y
3 Matsui	N	Y	Y	N	Y	?	?	?
4 Fazio	N	Y	Y	N	Y	Y	Y	N
5 Pelosi	N	Y	Y	N	Y	Y	Y	N
6 Boxer	N	Y	Y	N	Y	Y	Y	X
7 Miller	N	Y	Y	N	Y	Y	Y	N
8 Dellums	N	Y	Y	N	Y	Y	Y	N
9 Stark	N	Y	Y	?	Y	Y	Y	N
10 Edwards	N	Y	Y	N	Y	Y	?	N
11 Lantos	N	Y	Y	N	Y	Y	Y	N
12 ***Campbell***	Y	N	Y	N	N	Y	Y	N
13 Mineta	N	Y	N	N	Y	Y	Y	N
14 ***Doolittle***	Y	N	Y	Y	N	Y	N	Y
15 Condit	N	N	Y	Y	N	Y	N	Y
16 Panetta	N	Y	Y	N	Y	Y	Y	N
17 Dooley	N	N	Y	N	Y	Y	Y	N
18 Lehman	N	N	Y	N	Y	Y	Y	N
19 ***Lagomarsino***	N	N	Y	N	Y	Y	N	Y
20 ***Thomas***	N	N	Y	N	Y	Y	N	Y
21 ***Gallegly***	N	N	Y	N	Y	Y	N	Y
22 ***Moorhead***	N	N	Y	N	N	Y	N	Y
23 Beilenson	N	Y	Y	N	Y	Y	Y	N
24 Waxman	N	N	Y	N	N	Y	Y	N
25 Roybal	N	N	Y	N	Y	Y	Y	N
26 Berman	N	Y	Y	N	Y	Y	Y	N
27 Levine	N	Y	Y	N	Y	Y	Y	N
28 Dixon	N	Y	Y	N	Y	Y	Y	N
29 Waters	?	?	?	?	?	Y	Y	N
30 Martinez	N	Y	Y	N	Y	?	?	N
31 Dymally	N	Y	Y	N	Y	Y	Y	N
32 Anderson	N	Y	Y	N	Y	Y	Y	N
33 ***Dreier***	N	N	Y	Y	N	Y	N	Y
34 Torres	N	Y	Y	N	Y	Y	Y	N
35 ***Lewis***	N	N	Y	N	Y	Y	N	N
36 Brown	?	N	Y	N	Y	Y	Y	N
37 ***McCandless***	N	N	Y	Y	N	Y	N	Y
38 ***Dornan***	Y	N	Y	Y	Y	Y	N	Y
39 ***Dannemeyer***	Y	N	Y	Y	N	Y	?	+
40 ***Cox***	Y	N	Y	Y	N	?	?	#
41 ***Lowery***	N	N	Y	N	Y	Y	?	Y
42 ***Rohrabacher***	Y	N	Y	Y	Y	Y	N	Y
43 ***Packard***	N	N	N	N	Y	Y	N	Y
44 ***Cunningham***	Y	N	Y	N	Y	Y	N	Y
45 ***Hunter***	Y	N	N	Y	N	Y	N	Y
COLORADO								
1 Schroeder	N	N	Y	N	N	Y	N	N
2 Skaggs	N	N	Y	N	N	Y	Y	N
3 Campbell	N	Y	Y	N	N	Y	Y	N
4 ***Allard***	Y	N	Y	N	N	Y	N	Y
5 ***Hefley***	N	N	Y	Y	N	Y	N	Y
6 ***Schaefer***	N	N	N	N	N	Y	N	Y
CONNECTICUT								
1 Kennelly	N	Y	Y	N	Y	Y	Y	N
2 Gejdenson	N	N	Y	N	Y	Y	Y	N
3 DeLauro	N	N	Y	N	Y	Y	Y	N
4 ***Shays***	N	N	Y	N	N	Y	N	Y
5 ***Franks***	Y	N	Y	Y	N	Y	N	Y
6 ***Johnson***	N	N	Y	N	Y	Y	N	N
DELAWARE								
AL Carper	N	N	Y	N	Y	Y	Y	?
FLORIDA								
1 Hutto	N	N	Y	N	Y	Y	Y	Y
2 Peterson	N	N	Y	N	Y	Y	Y	Y
3 Bennett	N	Y	Y	N	Y	Y	N	Y
4 ***James***	N	N	Y	Y	N	Y	Y	Y
5 ***McCollum***	N	N	Y	N	Y	Y	N	Y
6 ***Stearns***	Y	N	Y	Y	N	Y	N	Y
7 Gibbons	N	Y	Y	N	Y	Y	?	Y
8 ***Young***	N	N	Y	Y	N	Y	Y	Y
9 ***Bilirakis***	N	N	Y	Y	N	Y	N	Y
10 ***Ireland***	N	N	Y	Y	N	Y	N	Y
11 Bacchus	N	Y	Y	N	Y	Y	Y	N
12 ***Lewis***	N	N	Y	Y	N	Y	N	Y
13 ***Goss***	N	N	Y	Y	N	Y	N	Y
14 Johnston	N	N	Y	N	Y	Y	Y	N
15 ***Shaw***	N	N	Y	N	Y	Y	Y	Y
16 Smith	N	Y	Y	N	Y	Y	Y	N
17 Lehman	N	Y	Y	?	Y	Y	Y	N
18 ***Ros-Lehtinen***	Y	Y	Y	Y	N	Y	Y	Y
19 Fascell	N	Y	Y	N	Y	N	Y	N
GEORGIA								
1 Thomas	N	N	Y	N	Y	Y	Y	N
2 Hatcher	?	N	Y	N	Y	Y	Y	N
3 Ray	N	N	N	N	Y	Y	Y	Y
4 Jones	N	Y	Y	N	Y	Y	Y	N
5 Lewis	N	Y	Y	N	Y	Y	Y	N
6 ***Gingrich***	N	N	Y	?	Y	Y	N	Y
7 Darden	N	N	Y	N	Y	Y	Y	Y
8 Rowland	N	N	Y	N	Y	Y	Y	Y
9 Jenkins	N	N	Y	N	Y	Y	Y	?
10 Barnard	N	N	Y	N	Y	Y	Y	Y
HAWAII								
1 Abercrombie	N	Y	Y	N	Y	Y	Y	N
2 Mink	N	Y	Y	N	Y	Y	Y	N
IDAHO								
1 LaRocco	N	N	Y	N	Y	Y	Y	N
2 Stallings	N	N	Y	N	Y	Y	Y	N
ILLINOIS								
1 Hayes	N	Y	Y	N	Y	Y	Y	N
2 Savage	N	Y	Y	N	Y	?	?	?
3 Russo	N	N	Y	N	Y	Y	Y	Y
4 Sangmeister	N	N	Y	N	Y	Y	N	Y
5 Lipinski	N	N	Y	N	Y	Y	Y	Y
6 ***Hyde***	Y	N	Y	Y	Y	Y	Y	Y
7 Collins	N	Y	Y	N	Y	Y	Y	N
8 Rostenkowski	N	N	Y	N	Y	Y	Y	N
9 Yates	N	Y	Y	N	Y	Y	Y	N
10 ***Porter***	N	N	Y	Y	N	Y	N	Y
11 Annunzio	N	Y	Y	N	Y	Y	Y	N
12 ***Crane***	Y	N	Y	Y	N	Y	N	Y
13 ***Fawell***	Y	N	Y	Y	N	Y	N	Y
14 ***Hastert***	N	N	Y	N	Y	Y	Y	Y
15 ***Ewing***	N	N	Y	N	Y	Y	Y	Y
16 Cox	N	Y	Y	N	Y	Y	Y	N
17 Evans	N	Y	Y	N	Y	Y	Y	N
18 ***Michel***	?	N	Y	Y	Y	Y	Y	Y
19 Bruce	N	N	Y	N	Y	Y	N	Y
20 Durbin	N	N	Y	N	Y	Y	Y	N
21 Costello	N	Y	Y	N	Y	Y	N	Y
22 Poshard	N	N	Y	N	Y	Y	N	Y
INDIANA								
1 Visclosky	N	Y	Y	N	Y	Y	Y	N
2 Sharp	N	N	Y	N	Y	Y	Y	N
3 Roemer	N	N	Y	N	N	Y	Y	N

ND Northern Democrats SD Southern Democrats

	334	335	336	337	338	339	340	341
4 Long	N	N	Y	N	N	Y	Y	Y
5 Jontz	N	N	Y	N	Y	Y	Y	N
6 ***Burton***	Y	N	Y	Y	N	Y	N	Y
7 ***Myers***	N	N	Y	N	Y	Y	Y	Y
8 McCloskey	N	N	Y	N	Y	Y	Y	N
9 Hamilton	N	N	Y	N	Y	Y	Y	Y
10 Jacobs	Y	Y	Y	N	Y	Y	N	Y
IOWA								
1 ***Leach***	N	N	Y	N	Y	Y	Y	N
2 ***Nussle***	N	N	N	Y	Y	Y	N	Y
3 Nagle	N	Y	Y	N	Y	Y	Y	N
4 Smith	N	N	Y	N	Y	N	Y	N
5 ***Lightfoot***	N	N	Y	N	Y	Y	Y	N
6 ***Grandy***	N	N	N	N	Y	Y	N	N
KANSAS								
1 ***Roberts***	N	N	Y	Y	N	?	N	Y
2 Slattery	N	N	Y	N	Y	Y	N	N
3 ***Meyers***	N	N	Y	Y	Y	Y	N	Y
4 Glickman	N	N	Y	N	Y	Y	Y	Y
5 ***Nichols***	N	N	Y	N	Y	Y	N	Y
KENTUCKY								
1 Hubbard	N	N	Y	N	Y	N	N	Y
2 Natcher	N	Y	Y	N	Y	Y	N	N
3 Mazzoli	N	N	Y	N	Y	Y	Y	N
4 ***Bunning***	N	N	N	Y	N	Y	N	Y
5 ***Rogers***	N	N	Y	N	Y	Y	N	Y
6 ***Hopkins***	?	?	?	?	?	?	?	?
7 Perkins	N	Y	Y	N	Y	N	Y	N
LOUISIANA								
1 ***Livingston***	Y	N	Y	N	N	Y	Y	Y
2 Jefferson	N	Y	Y	N	Y	Y	Y	N
3 Tauzin	N	N	Y	N	Y	Y	Y	Y
4 ***McCrery***	N	N	N	N	Y	Y	Y	Y
5 Huckaby	N	N	Y	N	N	Y	Y	Y
6 ***Baker***	N	N	N	N	N	Y	N	Y
7 Hayes	N	N	N	N	Y	Y	Y	Y
8 ***Holloway***	Y	N	Y	Y	N	Y	N	Y
MAINE								
1 Andrews	N	Y	Y	N	N	Y	Y	N
2 ***Snowe***	N	N	Y	Y	N	Y	N	Y
MARYLAND								
1 ***Gilchrest***	Y	N	N	Y	N	Y	Y	Y
2 ***Bentley***	N	N	N	N	Y	Y	N	Y
3 Cardin	N	Y	Y	N	Y	Y	Y	N
4 McMillen	N	Y	Y	N	N	Y	Y	Y
5 Hoyer	N	Y	Y	N	Y	Y	Y	N
6 Byron	N	N	Y	N	Y	Y	Y	Y
7 Mfume	N	Y	Y	N	Y	Y	Y	N
8 ***Morella***	N	N	Y	N	Y	Y	+	N
MASSACHUSETTS								
1 Olver	N	Y	Y	N	Y	Y	Y	N
2 Neal	N	N	Y	N	Y	N	Y	N
3 Early	N	N	Y	N	N	N	Y	Y
4 Frank	N	Y	?	?	Y	N	Y	N
5 Atkins	N	N	Y	N	Y	N	Y	N
6 Mavroules	N	N	Y	N	Y	Y	Y	N
7 Markey	N	Y	Y	N	Y	Y	Y	N
8 Kennedy	N	Y	Y	N	Y	Y	Y	N
9 Moakley	N	Y	Y	N	Y	Y	Y	N
10 Studds	N	Y	Y	N	Y	Y	Y	N
11 Donnelly	N	N	Y	N	Y	N	N	Y
MICHIGAN								
1 Conyers	N	Y	Y	N	Y	Y	Y	N
2 ***Pursell***	N	N	Y	N	Y	Y	N	Y
3 Wolpe	N	Y	Y	N	Y	Y	Y	N
4 ***Upton***	N	N	Y	N	Y	Y	N	Y
5 ***Henry***	N	N	Y	N	Y	Y	N	Y
6 Carr	N	N	Y	N	N	Y	Y	N
7 Kildee	N	Y	Y	N	Y	Y	Y	N
8 Traxler	N	N	Y	N	Y	N	Y	N
9 ***Vander Jagt***	N	N	Y	N	Y	Y	Y	Y
10 ***Camp***	N	N	Y	Y	N	Y	N	Y
11 ***Davis***	?	N	Y	Y	Y	N	Y	N
12 Bonior	?	Y	Y	N	Y	?	Y	N
13 Collins	N	Y	Y	N	Y	Y	Y	N
14 Hertel	N	N	Y	N	N	Y	N	N
15 Ford	N	Y	Y	N	Y	N	Y	N
16 Dingell	N	N	Y	N	Y	Y	Y	N
17 Levin	N	Y	Y	N	Y	Y	Y	N
18 ***Broomfield***	N	N	Y	Y	Y	Y	N	Y
MINNESOTA								
1 Penny	N	N	Y	N	N	Y	N	Y
2 ***Weber***	Y	N	Y	N	Y	Y	N	Y
3 ***Ramstad***	N	N	Y	Y	Y	Y	N	Y
4 Vento	N	Y	Y	N	Y	Y	Y	N

	334	335	336	337	338	339	340	341
5 Sabo	N	Y	Y	N	Y	Y	Y	N
6 Sikorski	N	Y	Y	N	Y	Y	Y	N
7 Peterson	N	N	Y	N	N	Y	Y	Y
8 Oberstar	N	Y	Y	N	Y	Y	Y	N
MISSISSIPPI								
1 Whitten	N	Y	Y	N	Y	N	Y	Y
2 Espy	N	Y	Y	N	Y	Y	Y	N
3 Montgomery	N	N	Y	N	Y	Y	Y	Y
4 Parker	N	N	Y	N	Y	Y	Y	Y
5 Taylor	N	N	Y	N	Y	Y	Y	Y
MISSOURI								
1 Clay	N	Y	Y	N	Y	Y	Y	N
2 Horn	N	N	Y	N	Y	Y	+	N
3 Gephardt	N	Y	Y	N	Y	N	Y	N
4 Skelton	N	N	Y	N	Y	Y	Y	Y
5 Wheat	N	Y	Y	N	Y	Y	Y	N
6 ***Coleman***	N	N	Y	N	Y	Y	Y	N
7 ***Hancock***	Y	N	Y	Y	N	Y	N	Y
8 ***Emerson***	N	N	Y	N	Y	Y	Y	Y
9 Volkmer	N	N	Y	N	Y	Y	Y	N
MONTANA								
1 Williams	N	N	Y	N	N	Y	Y	N
2 ***Marlenee***	Y	N	Y	Y	N	Y	N	Y
NEBRASKA								
1 ***Bereuter***	N	N	Y	N	Y	Y	N	N
2 Hoagland	N	N	Y	N	Y	Y	Y	Y
3 ***Barrett***	N	N	Y	N	Y	Y	N	Y
NEVADA								
1 Bilbray	N	N	Y	N	Y	Y	Y	N
2 ***Vucanovich***	N	N	N	N	Y	Y	Y	N
NEW HAMPSHIRE								
1 ***Zeliff***	N	N	Y	Y	N	Y	N	Y
2 Swett	N	N	Y	N	Y	Y	Y	Y
NEW JERSEY								
1 Andrews	N	Y	Y	N	N	Y	Y	N
2 Hughes	N	N	Y	N	Y	Y	Y	N
3 Pallone	N	Y	Y	N	N	Y	N	Y
4 ***Smith***	N	N	Y	N	Y	Y	Y	Y
5 ***Roukema***	N	N	Y	N	Y	Y	Y	Y
6 Dwyer	N	Y	Y	N	Y	Y	Y	N
7 ***Rinaldo***	N	N	Y	N	Y	Y	Y	Y
8 Roe	N	Y	Y	N	Y	Y	Y	N
9 Torricelli	N	Y	Y	N	Y	Y	Y	N
10 Payne	N	Y	Y	N	Y	Y	Y	N
11 ***Gallo***	N	N	Y	N	Y	Y	Y	Y
12 ***Zimmer***	N	N	Y	Y	N	Y	N	Y
13 ***Saxton***	N	N	Y	N	Y	Y	Y	Y
14 Guarini	N	N	Y	N	Y	Y	Y	Y
NEW MEXICO								
1 ***Schiff***	N	N	Y	N	Y	Y	Y	N
2 ***Skeen***	N	N	Y	N	Y	Y	Y	N
3 Richardson	N	Y	Y	N	Y	N	Y	N
NEW YORK								
1 Hochbrueckner	N	Y	Y	N	Y	Y	Y	Y
2 Downey	N	Y	Y	N	Y	Y	Y	N
3 Mrazek	N	Y	Y	N	Y	Y	Y	N
4 ***Lent***	?	N	Y	N	Y	Y	Y	Y
5 ***McGrath***	N	N	Y	N	Y	?	Y	Y
6 Flake	N	Y	Y	N	Y	Y	#	N
7 Ackerman	N	Y	Y	N	Y	Y	Y	N
8 Scheuer	N	Y	Y	N	Y	N	Y	N
9 Manton	N	Y	Y	N	Y	Y	Y	N
10 Schumer	N	Y	Y	N	Y	Y	Y	N
11 Towns	N	Y	Y	N	Y	N	Y	N
12 Owens	N	Y	Y	N	Y	Y	Y	N
13 Solarz	N	Y	Y	N	Y	Y	Y	N
14 ***Molinari***	N	N	Y	N	Y	Y	Y	Y
15 ***Green***	N	N	Y	N	Y	Y	Y	N
16 Rangel	N	Y	Y	N	Y	Y	Y	N
17 Weiss	N	Y	Y	N	Y	Y	Y	N
18 Serrano	N	Y	Y	N	Y	Y	Y	N
19 Engel	N	Y	Y	N	Y	Y	Y	N
20 Lowey	N	Y	Y	N	Y	Y	Y	N
21 ***Fish***	N	N	Y	N	Y	Y	Y	N
22 ***Gilman***	N	N	Y	N	Y	Y	Y	N
23 McNulty	N	Y	Y	N	Y	Y	Y	Y
24 ***Solomon***	N	N	Y	Y	N	Y	N	Y
25 ***Boehlert***	N	N	Y	N	Y	Y	Y	N
26 ***Martin***	N	N	Y	N	N	Y	N	Y
27 ***Walsh***	N	N	Y	Y	Y	Y	N	Y
28 McHugh	N	N	Y	N	Y	Y	Y	N
29 ***Horton***	N	N	Y	N	Y	Y	Y	N
30 Slaughter	N	N	Y	N	Y	Y	Y	N
31 ***Paxon***	N	N	Y	Y	N	Y	N	Y

	334	335	336	337	338	339	340	341
32 LaFalce	N	N	Y	N	Y	Y	Y	N
33 Nowak	N	Y	Y	N	Y	Y	Y	N
34 ***Houghton***	N	N	Y	N	Y	Y	Y	N
NORTH CAROLINA								
1 Jones	N	N	?	?	?	Y	Y	N
2 Valentine	?	N	Y	N	Y	Y	Y	Y
3 Lancaster	N	N	N	N	Y	Y	Y	Y
4 Price	N	N	Y	N	Y	Y	Y	Y
5 Neal	?	?	?	?	?	?	?	?
6 ***Coble***	N	N	Y	Y	N	Y	N	Y
7 Rose	N	N	Y	N	Y	Y	Y	Y
8 Hefner	N	N	Y	N	Y	Y	Y	Y
9 ***McMillan***	N	N	Y	N	Y	Y	Y	Y
10 ***Ballenger***	N	N	Y	Y	N	Y	N	Y
11 ***Taylor***	N	N	Y	Y	N	Y	N	Y
NORTH DAKOTA								
AL Dorgan	N	N	Y	N	Y	Y	N	N
OHIO								
1 Luken	N	N	Y	N	N	Y	Y	Y
2 ***Gradison***	N	N	Y	N	N	Y	Y	Y
3 Hall	N	Y	Y	N	Y	Y	Y	Y
4 ***Oxley***	N	N	N	Y	Y	Y	X	Y
5 ***Gillmor***	?	N	Y	N	Y	Y	N	Y
6 ***McEwen***	N	N	Y	Y	Y	Y	N	Y
7 ***Hobson***	N	N	Y	N	Y	Y	N	Y
8 ***Boehner***	N	N	Y	N	N	Y	N	Y
9 Kaptur	N	N	Y	N	Y	Y	Y	N
10 ***Miller***	N	N	Y	Y	Y	Y	Y	Y
11 Eckart	?	Y	Y	N	Y	Y	Y	N
12 ***Kasich***	N	N	Y	Y	N	Y	N	Y
13 Pease	N	N	Y	N	Y	Y	N	N
14 Sawyer	N	Y	Y	N	Y	Y	Y	N
15 ***Wylie***	N	N	Y	N	Y	Y	N	Y
16 ***Regula***	N	N	Y	N	Y	N	Y	Y
17 Traficant	N	Y	Y	N	Y	N	N	Y
18 Applegate	N	N	Y	N	Y	N	N	Y
19 Feighan	N	Y	Y	N	Y	Y	Y	N
20 Oakar	N	N	Y	N	Y	Y	Y	N
21 Stokes	N	Y	Y	N	Y	Y	Y	N
OKLAHOMA								
1 ***Inhofe***	N	N	Y	N	Y	Y	N	Y
2 Synar	N	N	Y	N	Y	Y	Y	Y
3 Brewster	N	N	N	?	Y	Y	Y	Y
4 McCurdy	N	N	Y	N	Y	Y	Y	Y
5 ***Edwards***	N	N	Y	Y	Y	Y	Y	N
6 English	N	N	Y	N	Y	Y	N	Y
OREGON								
1 AuCoin	N	Y	Y	N	Y	Y	Y	N
2 ***Smith***	N	N	N	N	Y	Y	N	Y
3 Wyden	N	Y	Y	N	Y	Y	Y	N
4 DeFazio	N	Y	Y	?	Y	Y	Y	N
5 Kopetski	N	Y	Y	N	Y	Y	Y	N
PENNSYLVANIA								
1 Foglietta	N	Y	Y	N	Y	Y	Y	N
2 Vacancy								
3 Borski	N	Y	Y	N	Y	Y	Y	N
4 Kolter	N	N	Y	N	Y	Y	Y	N
5 ***Schulze***	N	N	Y	N	Y	?	?	?
6 Yatron	N	N	Y	N	Y	N	Y	N
7 ***Weldon***	N	?	?	?	?	Y	N	Y
8 Kostmayer	N	N	Y	N	Y	Y	Y	N
9 ***Shuster***	N	N	Y	N	Y	Y	N	Y
10 ***McDade***	N	N	Y	N	Y	Y	Y	N
11 Kanjorski	N	N	Y	N	Y	N	Y	N
12 Murtha	N	N	Y	N	Y	Y	Y	N
13 ***Coughlin***	N	N	Y	N	Y	Y	Y	N
14 Coyne	N	Y	Y	N	Y	Y	Y	N
15 ***Ritter***	N	N	Y	N	Y	Y	N	Y
16 ***Walker***	N	N	Y	Y	N	Y	N	Y
17 ***Gekas***	N	N	Y	N	Y	Y	N	Y
18 ***Santorum***	N	N	Y	N	Y	Y	N	Y
19 ***Goodling***	N	N	Y	?	Y	Y	Y	Y
20 Gaydos	N	N	Y	N	Y	Y	Y	N
21 ***Ridge***	N	N	Y	N	Y	Y	N	Y
22 Murphy	N	N	Y	N	Y	N	Y	N
23 ***Clinger***	N	N	Y	N	Y	Y	N	N
RHODE ISLAND								
1 ***Machtley***	N	N	Y	N	N	Y	Y	N
2 Reed	N	N	Y	N	Y	Y	Y	N
SOUTH CAROLINA								
1 ***Ravenel***	N	N	Y	Y	Y	Y	Y	Y
2 ***Spence***	N	N	Y	N	Y	Y	Y	Y
3 Derrick	N	N	Y	N	Y	Y	Y	N
4 Patterson	N	N	Y	N	Y	Y	Y	Y
5 Spratt	N	N	Y	?	Y	Y	Y	Y
6 Tallon	N	N	Y	N	Y	Y	Y	Y

	334	335	336	337	338	339	340	341
SOUTH DAKOTA								
AL Johnson	N	N	Y	N	Y	Y	Y	Y
TENNESSEE								
1 ***Quillen***	N	N	N	N	Y	Y	N	Y
2 ***Duncan***	N	N	Y	Y	Y	Y	N	Y
3 Lloyd	N	N	Y	N	Y	Y	Y	Y
4 Cooper	N	N	Y	N	Y	Y	Y	Y
5 Clement	N	N	Y	N	Y	Y	Y	Y
6 Gordon	?	N	Y	N	Y	Y	Y	N
7 ***Sundquist***	N	N	Y	N	Y	Y	N	Y
8 Tanner	N	N	Y	N	Y	Y	Y	Y
9 Ford	N	Y	Y	N	Y	Y	Y	N
TEXAS								
1 Chapman	?	N	Y	N	Y	Y	Y	Y
2 Wilson	N	N	Y	N	Y	Y	Y	Y
3 ***Johnson***	N	N	N	Y	N	Y	N	Y
4 Hall	N	N	Y	N	Y	N	N	Y
5 Bryant	N	N	Y	N	Y	Y	Y	N
6 ***Barton***	N	N	Y	Y	N	Y	N	Y
7 ***Archer***	N	N	Y	Y	N	Y	N	Y
8 ***Fields***	N	N	N	Y	N	Y	N	Y
9 Brooks	?	N	Y	N	Y	Y	Y	N
10 Pickle	N	Y	Y	N	Y	N	Y	N
11 Edwards	N	N	Y	N	Y	Y	Y	Y
12 Geren	N	N	N	N	Y	Y	Y	Y
13 Sarpalius	N	N	Y	N	Y	Y	Y	Y
14 Laughlin	N	N	Y	N	Y	Y	Y	Y
15 de la Garza	N	Y	Y	N	Y	Y	Y	N
16 Coleman	N	Y	Y	N	Y	Y	Y	N
17 Stenholm	N	N	Y	Y	Y	Y	Y	Y
18 Washington	?	Y	Y	N	Y	?	Y	N
19 ***Combest***	N	N	Y	N	Y	Y	N	Y
20 Gonzalez	N	Y	Y	N	Y	Y	N	N
21 ***Smith***	Y	N	Y	Y	N	Y	Y	Y
22 ***DeLay***	Y	N	N	Y	N	Y	N	Y
23 Bustamante	N	Y	Y	N	Y	Y	Y	N
24 Frost	N	Y	Y	N	Y	Y	Y	N
25 Andrews	N	N	Y	N	N	Y	Y	Y
26 ***Armey***	N	N	Y	Y	N	Y	N	Y
27 Ortiz	N	Y	Y	N	Y	Y	Y	Y
UTAH								
1 ***Hansen***	N	N	Y	N	N	Y	N	N
2 Owens	N	Y	Y	N	N	Y	Y	N
3 Orton	N	N	Y	N	N	Y	Y	N
VERMONT								
AL *Sanders*	N	Y	Y	N	Y	Y	Y	N
VIRGINIA								
1 ***Bateman***	N	N	Y	N	Y	Y	Y	Y
2 Pickett	N	N	Y	N	Y	Y	N	Y
3 ***Bliley***	N	N	Y	Y	Y	Y	Y	Y
4 Sisisky	N	N	Y	N	Y	Y	Y	Y
5 Payne	N	N	N	N	Y	Y	Y	Y
6 Olin	N	N	Y	N	Y	Y	Y	Y
7 ***Slaughter***	?	?	?	?	?	?	?	?
8 Moran	N	Y	Y	N	Y	Y	?	?
9 Boucher	N	N	Y	N	Y	Y	Y	?
10 ***Wolf***	N	N	Y	N	Y	Y	Y	Y
WASHINGTON								
1 ***Miller***	N	N	Y	N	Y	Y	N	N
2 Swift	N	Y	Y	N	Y	Y	?	N
3 Unsoeld	N	Y	Y	N	Y	Y	Y	N
4 ***Morrison***	N	N	Y	N	Y	Y	Y	Y
5 Foley								
6 Dicks	N	N	Y	N	Y	Y	Y	N
7 McDermott	N	Y	Y	N	Y	Y	Y	N
8 ***Chandler***	N	N	Y	N	Y	Y	Y	Y
WEST VIRGINIA								
1 Mollohan	N	N	Y	N	Y	N	Y	N
2 Staggers	N	Y	Y	N	Y	N	Y	Y
3 Wise	N	N	Y	N	Y	N	Y	N
4 Rahall	N	Y	Y	N	Y	N	N	N
WISCONSIN								
1 Aspin	N	N	Y	?	Y	Y	Y	N
2 ***Klug***	Y	N	Y	N	Y	Y	Y	N
3 ***Gunderson***	N	N	N	Y	Y	Y	N	Y
4 Kleczka	N	N	Y	N	Y	Y	Y	N
5 Moody	N	N	Y	N	Y	Y	N	N
6 ***Petri***	N	N	Y	N	Y	Y	N	Y
7 Obey	N	N	Y	N	Y	Y	Y	N
8 ***Roth***	N	Y	Y	Y	Y	Y	N	Y
9 ***Sensenbrenner***	N	N	Y	Y	Y	Y	N	Y
WYOMING								
AL ***Thomas***	Y	N	Y	N	N	Y	N	N

Southern states - Ala., Ark., Fla., Ga., Ky., La., Miss., N.C., Okla., S.C., Tenn., Texas, Va.
Omitted votes are quorum calls, which CQ does not include in its vote charts.

HOUSE VOTES 342, 343, 344, 345, 346, 347, 348, 349

342. HR 2686. Fiscal 1992 Interior Appropriations/Conference Report. Adoption of the conference report to provide $12,623,563,000 in new budget authority for the Department of the Interior and related agencies for fiscal 1992. The administration requested $12,312,266,000. Adopted 310-104: R 85-71; D 224-33 (ND 164-13, SD 60-20); I 1-0, Oct. 24, 1991.

343. HR 2686. Fiscal 1992 Interior Appropriations/Rehabilitate Gormley Stadium. Yates, D-Ill., motion to recede and concur in the Senate amendment to provide $1 million to rehabilitate the Tad Gormley Stadium in New Orleans for the 1994 Track and Field Olympics. Motion agreed to 243-164: R 53-104; D 189-60 (ND 127-42, SD 62-18); I 1-0, Oct. 24, 1991.

344. HR 2686. Fiscal 1992 Interior Appropriations/Hardwood Training. Yates, D-Ill., motion to recede and concur in the Senate amendment to provide a grant of $4.5 million to Mercer County, W.Va., for a hardwood training and flexible manufacturing center. Motion rejected 178-224: R 20-136; D 158-87 (ND 106-59, SD 52-28); I 0-1, Oct. 24, 1991.

345. HR 2686. Fiscal 1992 Interior Appropriations/Alaska Park Plan. Yates, D-Ill., motion to recede and concur in the Senate amendment with an amendment to prohibit the 62 acres proposed for the Native Heritage Park from being included in 4,325 acres to be released from the restrictions of a bicentennial park master development plan in the Campbell Tract in Anchorage, Alaska. Motion agreed to 213-135: R 149-2; D 64-132 (ND 43-102, SD 21-30); I 0-1, Oct. 24, 1991.

346. HR 3543. Fiscal 1992 Supplemental Appropriations. Slaughter, D-N.Y., motion to order the previous question (thus limiting debate and the possibility of amendment) on the rule (H Res 256) to provide for House floor consideration of the bill to provide $5,761,200,000 for various emergency spending in fiscal 1992. Motion agreed to 254-164: R 0-162; D 253-2 (ND 173-1, SD 80-1); I 1-0, Oct. 29, 1991.

347. HR 3543. Fiscal 1992 Supplemental Appropriations/Head Start. Schroeder, D-Colo., amendment to provide additional funds for: the Head Start preschool program ($1.2 billion), the Women, Infants and Children nutrition program ($100 million) and the childhood immunization program ($90 million). Adopted 243-180: R 30-134; D 212-46 (ND 158-18, SD 54-28); I 1-0, Oct. 29, 1991.

348. HR 3543. Fiscal 1992 Supplemental Appropriations/Wetlands. Gilchrest, R-Md., amendment to provide $500,000 for a National Academy of Sciences study of the science and methodology of wetlands definition and delineation. Rejected 181-241: R 34-129; D 146-112 (ND 125-50, SD 21-62); I 1-0, Oct. 29, 1991.

349. HR 3543. Fiscal 1992 Supplemental Appropriations/House of Representatives. Barton, R-Texas, amendment to provide an additional $50,000 in internal spending for the House of Representatives. Barton had tried in two earlier amendments to have the money earmarked for mandatory drug testing of House members, but those riders were defeated on points of order on the grounds that they were legislation on an appropriations bill. Adopted 226-190: R 145-17; D 81-172 (ND 40-131, SD 41-41); I 0-1, Oct. 29, 1991.

KEY

Y Voted for (yea).
\# Paired for.
\+ Announced for.
N Voted against (nay).
X Paired against.
\- Announced against.
P Voted "present."
C Voted "present" to avoid possible conflict of interest.
? Did not vote or otherwise make a position known.

Democrats ***Republicans***
Independent

	342	343	344	345	346	347	348	349
ALABAMA								
1 ***Callahan***	N	Y	N	Y	N	N	N	Y
2 ***Dickinson***	?	?	?	?	N	N	N	Y
3 Browder	Y	Y	Y	?	Y	Y	N	Y
4 Bevill	Y	Y	Y	N	Y	Y	N	Y
5 Cramer	Y	Y	Y	N	Y	Y	N	Y
6 Erdreich	N	Y	N	Y	Y	Y	Y	Y
7 Harris	N	Y	Y	?	Y	Y	N	Y
ALASKA								
AL ***Young***	Y	?	Y	Y	N	N	N	Y
ARIZONA								
1 ***Rhodes***	Y	N	N	Y	N	N	N	Y
2 Pastor	Y	Y	Y	N	Y	Y	Y	Y
3 ***Stump***	N	N	N	Y	N	N	N	Y
4 ***Kyl***	Y	N	N	Y	N	N	N	Y
5 ***Kolbe***	Y	N	N	Y	N	N	N	Y
ARKANSAS								
1 Alexander	Y	Y	Y	Y	Y	Y	N	N
2 Thornton	Y	Y	Y	N	Y	Y	N	N
3 ***Hammerschmidt***	Y	Y	N	Y	N	N	N	Y
4 Anthony	Y	Y	Y	Y	Y	Y	N	N
CALIFORNIA								
1 ***Riggs***	Y	N	N	Y	N	Y	Y	Y
2 ***Herger***	N	N	Y	Y	N	N	N	Y
3 Matsui	?	?	?	?	?	?	?	?
4 Fazio	Y	Y	Y	Y	Y	Y	N	N
5 Pelosi	Y	Y	Y	N	Y	Y	Y	N
6 Boxer	?	?	?	?	?	?	?	?
7 Miller	N	Y	Y	N	Y	Y	Y	N
8 Dellums	Y	Y	Y	N	Y	Y	Y	N
9 Stark	Y	?	?	?	Y	Y	Y	?
10 Edwards	Y	Y	Y	Y	Y	Y	Y	N
11 Lantos	Y	Y	N	N	Y	Y	Y	N
12 ***Campbell***	Y	N	N	Y	N	N	N	Y
13 Mineta	Y	Y	Y	N	Y	Y	Y	N
14 ***Doolittle***	N	N	N	Y	N	N	N	Y
15 Condit	N	N	N	?	Y	Y	N	Y
16 Panetta	Y	Y	Y	N	Y	N	N	N
17 Dooley	Y	Y	N	N	Y	Y	N	N
18 Lehman	Y	Y	Y	?	?	Y	Y	N
19 ***Lagomarsino***	N	N	N	Y	N	N	Y	Y
20 ***Thomas***	Y	Y	N	Y	N	N	N	Y
21 ***Gallegly***	N	N	N	?	N	N	N	Y
22 ***Moorhead***	N	N	N	Y	N	N	N	Y
23 Beilenson	Y	N	N	N	Y	N	Y	N
24 Waxman	Y	N	Y	N	Y	Y	Y	N
25 Roybal	Y	Y	Y	N	Y	Y	Y	N
26 Berman	Y	N	Y	N	Y	Y	Y	N
27 Levine	Y	Y	?	?	Y	Y	?	?
28 Dixon	Y	Y	Y	N	Y	Y	N	N
29 Waters	Y	Y	Y	N	Y	Y	Y	N
30 Martinez	Y	Y	Y	Y	Y	Y	N	N
31 Dymally	Y	Y	Y	N	Y	Y	Y	N
32 Anderson	Y	Y	Y	Y	Y	Y	Y	Y
33 ***Dreier***	N	N	N	Y	N	N	N	Y
34 Torres	Y	Y	Y	N	Y	Y	Y	N
35 ***Lewis***	Y	Y	N	Y	N	N	N	Y
36 Brown	Y	Y	Y	Y	Y	Y	Y	Y
37 ***McCandless***	Y	N	N	Y	N	N	N	Y
38 ***Dornan***	N	N	N	Y	N	N	N	Y
39 ***Dannemeyer***	-	-	-	+	N	N	N	Y
40 ***Cox***	X	X	?	?	N	N	N	Y
41 ***Lowery***	N	Y	N	Y	N	N	N	Y
42 ***Rohrabacher***	N	N	N	Y	N	N	N	Y
43 ***Packard***	N	N	N	Y	N	N	N	Y
44 ***Cunningham***	N	Y	N	Y	N	N	N	Y
45 ***Hunter***	N	Y	N	Y	N	N	N	Y
COLORADO								
1 Schroeder	N	N	N	N	Y	Y	Y	N
2 Skaggs	Y	N	N	N	Y	N	N	N
3 Campbell	Y	Y	Y	N	Y	Y	N	Y
4 ***Allard***	Y	N	N	Y	N	N	N	Y
5 ***Hefley***	N	N	N	Y	?	N	N	N
6 ***Schaefer***	N	N	N	Y	N	N	N	Y
CONNECTICUT								
1 Kennelly	Y	Y	Y	N	Y	Y	Y	Y
2 Gejdenson	Y	Y	N	N	Y	Y	Y	N
3 DeLauro	Y	Y	N	N	Y	Y	Y	N
4 ***Shays***	Y	N	N	Y	N	N	N	N
5 ***Franks***	Y	Y	N	Y	N	N	N	Y
6 ***Johnson***	Y	Y	Y	Y	N	N	Y	N
DELAWARE								
AL Carper	Y	N	Y	Y	Y	N	N	Y
FLORIDA								
1 Hutto	Y	Y	N	?	Y	N	N	Y
2 Peterson	Y	Y	N	N	Y	Y	N	N
3 Bennett	Y	Y	Y	N	Y	Y	Y	Y
4 ***James***	Y	N	N	Y	N	Y	N	Y
5 ***McCollum***	Y	N	N	Y	N	N	N	Y
6 ***Stearns***	Y	N	N	Y	N	N	N	Y
7 Gibbons	Y	Y	N	N	Y	Y	Y	Y
8 ***Young***	Y	N	N	Y	N	Y	N	Y
9 ***Bilirakis***	Y	N	N	Y	N	Y	Y	Y
10 ***Ireland***	N	N	N	Y	N	N	N	Y
11 Bacchus	Y	N	N	N	Y	Y	Y	N
12 ***Lewis***	Y	N	N	Y	N	N	N	Y
13 ***Goss***	Y	N	N	Y	N	N	Y	Y
14 Johnston	Y	Y	N	N	Y	N	N	N
15 ***Shaw***	Y	Y	N	Y	N	N	N	Y
16 Smith	Y	Y	N	?	Y	Y	Y	N
17 Lehman	Y	Y	Y	Y	Y	Y	Y	N
18 ***Ros-Lehtinen***	Y	N	N	Y	N	Y	Y	Y
19 Fascell	Y	Y	Y	N	Y	Y	Y	N
GEORGIA								
1 Thomas	Y	Y	Y	Y	Y	Y	N	N
2 Hatcher	Y	?	?	?	Y	Y	N	N
3 Ray	Y	N	N	?	Y	N	N	N
4 Jones	Y	Y	Y	N	?	?	?	N
5 Lewis	Y	Y	Y	N	Y	Y	Y	N
6 ***Gingrich***	N	Y	?	?	N	N	N	Y
7 Darden	Y	Y	Y	?	Y	Y	N	N
8 Rowland	Y	Y	Y	?	Y	Y	N	?
9 Jenkins	?	?	?	?	Y	Y	N	N
10 Barnard	N	Y	N	?	Y	Y	N	N
HAWAII								
1 Abercrombie	Y	Y	Y	N	Y	Y	Y	N
2 Mink	Y	Y	Y	N	Y	Y	Y	N
IDAHO								
1 LaRocco	Y	N	N	N	Y	N	N	N
2 Stallings	Y	Y	Y	Y	Y	Y	Y	Y
ILLINOIS								
1 Hayes	Y	Y	Y	N	Y	Y	Y	N
2 Savage	?	?	?	?	Y	Y	Y	?
3 Russo	N	Y	N	?	Y	Y	Y	N
4 Sangmeister	Y	Y	N	N	Y	Y	Y	Y
5 Lipinski	N	Y	N	?	Y	Y	N	Y
6 ***Hyde***	N	N	N	Y	N	N	N	Y
7 Collins	Y	Y	Y	N	Y	Y	Y	N
8 Rostenkowski	Y	Y	Y	Y	Y	N	N	N
9 Yates	Y	Y	Y	Y	Y	Y	Y	N
10 ***Porter***	Y	N	N	Y	N	N	N	N
11 Annunzio	Y	Y	Y	N	Y	Y	N	Y
12 ***Crane***	N	N	N	Y	N	N	N	Y
13 ***Fawell***	N	N	N	N	N	N	N	Y
14 ***Hastert***	N	N	N	Y	N	N	N	Y
15 ***Ewing***	Y	N	N	Y	N	N	N	N
16 Cox	Y	Y	Y	N	Y	Y	Y	N
17 Evans	Y	Y	Y	N	Y	Y	Y	N
18 ***Michel***	Y	Y	N	Y	N	N	N	?
19 Bruce	Y	Y	Y	N	Y	Y	N	Y
20 Durbin	Y	Y	Y	N	Y	Y	N	N
21 Costello	N	Y	N	N	Y	Y	N	Y
22 Poshard	Y	Y	Y	N	Y	Y	N	Y
INDIANA								
1 Visclosky	Y	Y	N	Y	Y	N	N	N
2 Sharp	Y	N	N	?	Y	Y	N	N
3 Roemer	Y	Y	N	N	Y	Y	N	Y

ND Northern Democrats SD Southern Democrats

	342	343	344	345	346	347	348	349
4 Long	Y	N	N	N	Y	Y	N	N
5 Jontz	Y	N	Y	N	Y	Y	Y	N
6 ***Burton***	N	N	N	Y	N	N	N	Y
7 ***Myers***	Y	Y	Y	Y	N	N	N	Y
8 McCloskey	Y	Y	Y	N	Y	Y	N	N
9 Hamilton	Y	N	N	N	Y	Y	N	N
10 Jacobs	N	N	N	?	N	Y	Y	N
IOWA								
1 ***Leach***	?	?	?	?	N	Y	N	Y
2 ***Nussle***	N	N	N	Y	N	N	N	Y
3 Nagle	Y	Y	Y	N	Y	Y	Y	N
4 Smith	Y	Y	Y	Y	Y	Y	N	N
5 ***Lightfoot***	Y	Y	N	Y	N	N	N	Y
6 ***Grandy***	Y	N	N	Y	N	Y	N	Y
KANSAS								
1 ***Roberts***	N	N	N	Y	N	N	N	Y
2 Slattery	Y	N	Y	N	Y	Y	Y	N
3 ***Meyers***	Y	N	N	Y	N	N	Y	Y
4 Glickman	Y	Y	N	N	?	?	?	?
5 ***Nichols***	N	N	N	Y	N	N	N	Y
KENTUCKY								
1 Hubbard	N	N	Y	?	Y	Y	N	Y
2 Natcher	Y	Y	Y	Y	Y	Y	N	Y
3 Mazzoli	Y	Y	N	Y	Y	Y	Y	Y
4 ***Bunning***	N	N	N	Y	N	N	N	Y
5 ***Rogers***	Y	Y	N	Y	N	N	N	Y
6 ***Hopkins***	?	?	?	?	?	?	?	?
7 Perkins	Y	Y	Y	Y	Y	Y	N	N
LOUISIANA								
1 ***Livingston***	Y	Y	Y	Y	N	N	N	Y
2 Jefferson	Y	Y	Y	N	Y	Y	Y	N
3 Tauzin	N	Y	N	?	N	N	N	Y
4 ***McCrery***	N	Y	N	Y	N	N	N	Y
5 Huckaby	N	Y	Y	?	Y	N	N	Y
6 ***Baker***	N	Y	N	Y	N	N	N	Y
7 Hayes	Y	Y	Y	?	Y	N	N	Y
8 ***Holloway***	N	Y	N	Y	N	N	N	Y
MAINE								
1 Andrews	Y	N	N	N	Y	Y	Y	N
2 ***Snowe***	Y	N	N	Y	N	Y	Y	Y
MARYLAND								
1 ***Gilchrest***	Y	Y	N	Y	N	N	Y	Y
2 ***Bentley***	Y	Y	Y	Y	N	N	Y	Y
3 Cardin	Y	Y	N	N	Y	N	Y	N
4 McMillen	Y	Y	N	N	Y	Y	Y	Y
5 Hoyer	Y	Y	Y	Y	Y	Y	Y	N
6 Byron	Y	N	N	?	Y	Y	Y	Y
7 Mfume	Y	N	N	N	Y	Y	Y	N
8 ***Morella***	Y	N	N	Y	N	Y	Y	N
MASSACHUSETTS								
1 Olver	Y	Y	Y	N	Y	Y	Y	N
2 Neal	Y	?	?	?	Y	Y	Y	Y
3 Early	Y	Y	Y	?	Y	Y	N	Y
4 Frank	Y	?	?	?	Y	Y	Y	N
5 Atkins	Y	Y	Y	Y	Y	Y	Y	N
6 Mavroules	Y	Y	Y	Y	Y	Y	Y	Y
7 Markey	Y	Y	Y	N	Y	Y	Y	N
8 Kennedy	Y	Y	Y	N	Y	Y	Y	N
9 Moakley	Y	Y	Y	N	Y	Y	Y	N
10 Studds	Y	Y	Y	N	Y	Y	Y	N
11 Donnelly	Y	Y	Y	Y	Y	Y	Y	N
MICHIGAN								
1 Conyers	Y	Y	N	?	Y	Y	Y	N
2 ***Pursell***	Y	N	N	Y	N	N	N	Y
3 Wolpe	Y	N	N	N	Y	Y	Y	N
4 ***Upton***	N	N	N	Y	N	N	N	Y
5 ***Henry***	N	N	N	Y	N	N	N	Y
6 Carr	Y	N	N	Y	Y	Y	Y	N
7 Kildee	Y	Y	Y	N	Y	Y	Y	N
8 Traxler	Y	Y	Y	Y	Y	Y	Y	N
9 ***Vander Jagt***	N	Y	N	Y	N	N	N	Y
10 ***Camp***	N	N	N	Y	N	N	N	Y
11 ***Davis***	Y	Y	Y	?	N	Y	N	Y
12 Bonior	Y	Y	Y	N	Y	Y	Y	N
13 Collins	Y	Y	Y	N	Y	Y	Y	N
14 Hertel	Y	N	Y	N	Y	Y	Y	N
15 Ford	N	N	Y	N	Y	Y	Y	N
16 Dingell	Y	N	N	Y	Y	Y	Y	N
17 Levin	Y	Y	N	N	Y	Y	N	N
18 ***Broomfield***	N	N	N	Y	N	N	N	Y
MINNESOTA								
1 Penny	N	N	N	?	Y	N	N	N
2 ***Weber***	N	Y	N	?	N	N	N	Y
3 ***Ramstad***	Y	N	N	Y	N	Y	N	Y
4 Vento	Y	N	Y	N	Y	Y	Y	N

	342	343	344	345	346	347	348	349
5 Sabo	Y	Y	Y	Y	Y	P	Y	N
6 Sikorski	Y	Y	N	N	Y	Y	Y	N
7 Peterson	Y	N	N	N	Y	Y	N	Y
8 Oberstar	Y	Y	Y	Y	Y	Y	Y	N
MISSISSIPPI								
1 Whitten	N	Y	Y	Y	Y	N	N	N
2 Espy	Y	Y	Y	N	Y	Y	N	N
3 Montgomery	N	Y	Y	?	Y	N	N	Y
4 Parker	Y	N	N	?	Y	N	N	Y
5 Taylor	N	N	Y	?	Y	N	N	Y
MISSOURI								
1 Clay	Y	Y	Y	?	Y	Y	Y	N
2 Horn	Y	Y	Y	N	Y	Y	Y	N
3 Gephardt	Y	Y	Y	N	Y	Y	N	N
4 Skelton	N	Y	N	?	Y	Y	N	Y
5 Wheat	Y	Y	Y	N	Y	Y	Y	N
6 ***Coleman***	Y	N	N	Y	N	N	N	Y
7 ***Hancock***	N	N	N	Y	N	N	N	Y
8 ***Emerson***	N	Y	Y	N	Y	N	Y	Y
9 Volkmer	Y	N	Y	Y	Y	Y	N	Y
MONTANA								
1 Williams	Y	?	N	N	Y	Y	N	?
2 ***Marlenee***	Y	Y	N	Y	N	N	N	Y
NEBRASKA								
1 ***Bereuter***	Y	Y	Y	Y	N	N	N	N
2 Hoagland	Y	Y	N	N	Y	N	Y	Y
3 ***Barrett***	N	N	N	Y	N	N	N	Y
NEVADA								
1 Bilbray	Y	Y	N	N	Y	Y	Y	Y
2 ***Vucanovich***	Y	N	N	Y	N	N	N	Y
NEW HAMPSHIRE								
1 ***Zeliff***	N	N	N	Y	N	N	N	Y
2 Swett	Y	N	N	N	Y	N	N	N
NEW JERSEY								
1 Andrews	N	Y	N	N	Y	Y	Y	Y
2 Hughes	Y	N	N	Y	Y	N	Y	N
3 Pallone	Y	N	N	+	Y	Y	Y	Y
4 ***Smith***	N	Y	N	Y	N	Y	Y	Y
5 ***Roukema***	N	N	N	Y	N	N	Y	Y
6 Dwyer	Y	Y	Y	N	Y	Y	Y	Y
7 ***Rinaldo***	Y	N	N	Y	N	Y	Y	Y
8 Roe	Y	Y	Y	Y	Y	Y	Y	?
9 Torricelli	Y	Y	N	?	Y	Y	Y	N
10 Payne	Y	Y	Y	N	Y	Y	Y	N
11 ***Gallo***	Y	N	N	Y	N	N	N	Y
12 ***Zimmer***	Y	N	N	Y	N	N	Y	Y
13 ***Saxton***	Y	N	N	Y	N	N	Y	Y
14 Guarini	Y	Y	N	Y	Y	N	Y	N
NEW MEXICO								
1 ***Schiff***	Y	N	N	Y	?	N	N	Y
2 ***Skeen***	Y	Y	Y	Y	N	N	N	Y
3 Richardson	Y	Y	Y	N	Y	Y	Y	Y
NEW YORK								
1 Hochbrueckner	Y	Y	Y	N	Y	Y	Y	N
2 Downey	Y	Y	Y	?	Y	Y	Y	N
3 Mrazek	Y	Y	Y	N	?	?	?	?
4 ***Lent***	Y	Y	N	Y	N	N	N	Y
5 ***McGrath***	Y	N	N	Y	N	Y	Y	Y
6 Flake	Y	Y	Y	N	Y	Y	Y	N
7 Ackerman	Y	Y	N	N	Y	Y	Y	N
8 Scheuer	Y	Y	N	N	?	Y	Y	N
9 Manton	Y	Y	Y	?	Y	Y	Y	N
10 Schumer	Y	Y	Y	N	Y	Y	Y	N
11 Towns	Y	Y	N	N	Y	Y	Y	N
12 Owens	Y	Y	Y	N	Y	Y	Y	N
13 Solarz	Y	N	Y	N	Y	Y	Y	N
14 ***Molinari***	Y	Y	N	Y	N	Y	Y	Y
15 ***Green***	Y	Y	Y	Y	N	Y	Y	N
16 Rangel	Y	Y	?	?	Y	Y	Y	N
17 Weiss	Y	Y	Y	Y	Y	Y	Y	N
18 Serrano	Y	?	?	?	Y	Y	Y	N
19 Engel	Y	Y	N	N	Y	Y	Y	N
20 Lowey	Y	Y	N	N	Y	Y	Y	N
21 ***Fish***	Y	Y	N	Y	N	N	Y	N
22 ***Gilman***	Y	Y	N	Y	N	Y	Y	Y
23 McNulty	Y	Y	Y	N	Y	Y	Y	Y
24 ***Solomon***	N	N	N	Y	N	N	N	Y
25 ***Boehlert***	Y	Y	N	Y	N	Y	Y	N
26 ***Martin***	N	N	N	Y	N	N	N	Y
27 ***Walsh***	Y	Y	N	Y	N	Y	Y	Y
28 McHugh	Y	N	N	Y	Y	Y	Y	N
29 ***Horton***	?	Y	Y	Y	N	Y	N	N
30 Slaughter	Y	Y	Y	N	Y	Y	Y	N
31 ***Paxon***	N	N	N	Y	N	N	N	Y

	342	343	344	345	346	347	348	349
32 LaFalce	Y	Y	Y	Y	Y	Y	N	N
33 Nowak	Y	Y	Y	Y	Y	Y	Y	N
34 ***Houghton***	Y	N	N	Y	N	N	Y	N
NORTH CAROLINA								
1 Jones	Y	Y	Y	Y	Y	Y	N	Y
2 Valentine	Y	N	N	?	Y	N	N	Y
3 Lancaster	Y	Y	Y	?	Y	N	N	Y
4 Price	Y	Y	Y	Y	Y	Y	N	N
5 Neal	?	?	?	?	Y	Y	Y	N
6 ***Coble***	N	N	N	Y	N	N	N	Y
7 Rose	Y	Y	Y	N	Y	Y	N	N
8 Hefner	Y	Y	Y	Y	Y	Y	N	N
9 ***McMillan***	Y	N	N	Y	N	N	N	Y
10 ***Ballenger***	N	N	N	Y	N	N	N	Y
11 ***Taylor***	N	N	N	Y	N	N	N	Y
NORTH DAKOTA								
AL Dorgan	Y	N	N	N	Y	Y	N	N
OHIO								
1 Luken	N	N	N	?	Y	N	N	N
2 ***Gradison***	Y	Y	Y	Y	N	N	N	Y
3 Hall	Y	Y	Y	N	Y	Y	Y	Y
4 ***Oxley***	N	Y	N	Y	N	N	N	N
5 ***Gillmor***	Y	Y	Y	Y	N	Y	Y	Y
6 ***McEwen***	N	N	N	Y	N	N	N	Y
7 ***Hobson***	Y	N	N	Y	N	N	Y	Y
8 ***Boehner***	N	N	N	Y	N	N	N	Y
9 Kaptur	Y	N	N	N	Y	Y	N	N
10 ***Miller***	N	N	N	Y	N	N	Y	Y
11 Eckart	Y	Y	Y	N	Y	Y	Y	N
12 ***Kasich***	Y	N	N	Y	N	Y	N	Y
13 Pease	Y	N	N	Y	Y	N	N	N
14 Sawyer	Y	Y	Y	Y	Y	Y	Y	N
15 ***Wylie***	N	N	N	Y	N	N	N	Y
16 ***Regula***	Y	Y	Y	Y	N	N	N	Y
17 Traficant	N	N	Y	N	Y	Y	N	Y
18 Applegate	Y	Y	Y	Y	Y	Y	N	Y
19 Feighan	Y	Y	Y	?	Y	Y	Y	N
20 Oakar	Y	Y	Y	N	Y	Y	Y	Y
21 Stokes	Y	Y	Y	Y	Y	Y	Y	N
OKLAHOMA								
1 ***Inhofe***	N	N	N	Y	N	N	N	Y
2 Synar	N	N	N	N	Y	Y	Y	N
3 Brewster	Y	Y	N	?	Y	N	N	Y
4 McCurdy	Y	N	N	Y	N	N	N	N
5 ***Edwards***	Y	Y	N	Y	N	N	N	Y
6 English	Y	N	Y	N	Y	N	N	Y
OREGON								
1 AuCoin	Y	?	?	?	Y	Y	Y	N
2 ***Smith***	Y	Y	N	Y	N	N	N	Y
3 Wyden	Y	N	?	?	Y	Y	Y	N
4 DeFazio	Y	Y	Y	N	Y	Y	Y	N
5 Kopetski	Y	Y	Y	N	Y	Y	Y	N
PENNSYLVANIA								
1 Foglietta	Y	Y	Y	N	Y	Y	Y	N
2 Vacancy								
3 Borski	Y	Y	Y	Y	Y	Y	Y	N
4 Kolter	Y	Y	Y	?	Y	Y	Y	Y
5 ***Schulze***	?	?	?	?	N	N	N	Y
6 Yatron	Y	?	?	?	Y	Y	Y	Y
7 ***Weldon***	Y	N	N	Y	N	N	Y	Y
8 Kostmayer	Y	Y	Y	N	Y	Y	Y	N
9 ***Shuster***	N	N	N	Y	N	N	N	Y
10 ***McDade***	Y	Y	Y	Y	N	N	N	Y
11 Kanjorski	Y	Y	Y	Y	Y	Y	Y	N
12 Murtha	Y	Y	Y	Y	Y	N	N	N
13 ***Coughlin***	Y	Y	Y	Y	N	N	Y	Y
14 Coyne	Y	Y	Y	Y	Y	Y	Y	N
15 ***Ritter***	Y	N	N	Y	N	N	N	Y
16 ***Walker***	N	N	N	Y	N	N	N	Y
17 ***Gekas***	N	N	N	Y	N	N	N	Y
18 ***Santorum***	N	N	N	Y	N	Y	N	Y
19 ***Goodling***	Y	N	N	Y	N	N	N	N
20 Gaydos	Y	?	?	?	Y	Y	N	Y
21 ***Ridge***	Y	N	N	Y	N	N	N	N
22 Murphy	Y	Y	Y	Y	Y	Y	Y	N
23 ***Clinger***	Y	Y	N	Y	N	N	N	Y
RHODE ISLAND								
1 ***Machtley***	Y	N	N	Y	N	Y	Y	Y
2 Reed	Y	N	N	N	Y	Y	Y	N
SOUTH CAROLINA								
1 ***Ravenel***	Y	Y	N	?	N	Y	Y	Y
2 ***Spence***	Y	Y	N	Y	N	N	Y	Y
3 Derrick	Y	Y	N	Y	Y	Y	N	N
4 Patterson	N	N	N	?	Y	N	N	Y
5 Spratt	Y	N	N	N	Y	N	Y	Y
6 Tallon	N	Y	Y	N	Y	Y	Y	Y

	342	343	344	345	346	347	348	349
SOUTH DAKOTA								
AL Johnson	Y	N	N	N	Y	Y	N	N
TENNESSEE								
1 ***Quillen***	#	#	?	?	N	N	N	Y
2 ***Duncan***	N	N	N	?	N	N	N	Y
3 Lloyd	Y	N	N	?	Y	Y	N	Y
4 Cooper	N	N	N	N	?	N	N	Y
5 Clement	Y	Y	Y	Y	Y	Y	N	Y
6 Gordon	Y	Y	Y	N	Y	Y	N	Y
7 ***Sundquist***	N	N	N	Y	N	N	N	Y
8 Tanner	N	Y	Y	Y	?	?	?	?
9 Ford	Y	Y	Y	?	?	?	Y	N
TEXAS								
1 Chapman	Y	Y	Y	Y	Y	N	N	Y
2 Wilson	?	N	N	N	Y	N	N	Y
3 ***Johnson***	N	N	N	Y	N	N	N	Y
4 Hall	N	Y	Y	Y	Y	Y	N	?
5 Bryant	Y	Y	Y	N	Y	Y	Y	N
6 ***Barton***	N	Y	N	Y	N	N	N	Y
7 ***Archer***	N	N	N	Y	N	N	N	Y
8 ***Fields***	N	N	N	Y	N	N	N	Y
9 Brooks	Y	Y	Y	N	Y	Y	N	N
10 Pickle	Y	Y	Y	Y	Y	Y	N	N
11 Edwards	Y	Y	Y	N	Y	Y	N	Y
12 Geren	N	Y	N	?	Y	N	N	Y
13 Sarpalius	N	N	Y	N	Y	Y	N	Y
14 Laughlin	N	N	N	?	Y	N	N	Y
15 de la Garza	Y	Y	Y	?	Y	Y	Y	Y
16 Coleman	Y	Y	Y	N	Y	Y	N	N
17 Stenholm	N	N	N	?	Y	N	N	Y
18 Washington	Y	Y	Y	N	Y	Y	Y	N
19 ***Combest***	N	N	N	Y	N	N	N	Y
20 Gonzalez	Y	Y	Y	N	Y	Y	Y	N
21 ***Smith***	Y	N	N	Y	N	N	Y	Y
22 ***DeLay***	N	N	N	Y	N	N	N	Y
23 Bustamante	Y	Y	Y	?	Y	Y	Y	N
24 Frost	Y	?	?	?	Y	Y	Y	N
25 Andrews	Y	Y	Y	N	Y	N	N	Y
26 ***Armey***	N	N	N	Y	N	N	N	Y
27 Ortiz	?	Y	Y	Y	Y	Y	N	N
UTAH								
1 ***Hansen***	Y	N	?	?	N	N	N	Y
2 Owens	Y	Y	?	?	Y	Y	Y	Y
3 Orton	Y	N	N	?	Y	N	N	Y
VERMONT								
AL *Sanders*	Y	Y	N	N	Y	Y	Y	N
VIRGINIA								
1 ***Bateman***	?	Y	Y	Y	N	N	N	Y
2 Pickett	N	N	N	Y	Y	N	N	N
3 ***Bliley***	N	Y	N	Y	N	N	?	?
4 Sisisky	Y	Y	N	Y	Y	N	N	Y
5 Payne	Y	Y	N	?	Y	N	N	Y
6 Olin	Y	Y	Y	?	Y	N	N	N
7 ***Slaughter***	?	?	?	?	?	?	?	?
8 Moran	?	?	?	?	Y	Y	Y	Y
9 Boucher	Y	Y	Y	?	Y	Y	N	N
10 ***Wolf***	Y	N	N	Y	N	N	N	Y
WASHINGTON								
1 ***Miller***	Y	N	N	Y	N	N	Y	Y
2 Swift	Y	Y	Y	Y	Y	Y	N	N
3 Unsoeld	Y	Y	Y	Y	Y	Y	Y	N
4 ***Morrison***	Y	Y	Y	Y	N	Y	N	Y
5 Foley								
6 Dicks	?	Y	?	?	Y	Y	?	N
7 McDermott	Y	Y	N	N	Y	Y	Y	N
8 ***Chandler***	Y	N	N	Y	N	N	N	Y
WEST VIRGINIA								
1 Mollohan	Y	Y	Y	Y	Y	Y	Y	N
2 Staggers	Y	N	Y	Y	Y	Y	N	Y
3 Wise	Y	N	Y	N	?	Y	N	N
4 Rahall	Y	Y	Y	N	Y	Y	Y	N
WISCONSIN								
1 Aspin	Y	Y	N	N	Y	Y	N	N
2 ***Klug***	Y	Y	Y	Y	N	Y	N	Y
3 ***Gunderson***	Y	N	N	Y	N	Y	N	N
4 Kleczka	Y	Y	Y	N	Y	Y	Y	N
5 Moody	Y	?	?	?	Y	Y	Y	N
6 ***Petri***	N	N	N	N	N	N	N	Y
7 Obey	Y	Y	Y	Y	Y	Y	Y	?
8 ***Roth***	N	N	N	Y	N	Y	N	Y
9 ***Sensenbrenner***	N	N	N	Y	N	N	N	N
WYOMING								
AL ***Thomas***	Y	N	N	Y	N	N	N	Y

Southern states - Ala., Ark., Fla., Ga., Ky., La., Miss., N.C., Okla., S.C., Tenn., Texas, Va.
Omitted votes are quorum calls, which CQ does not include in its vote charts.

HOUSE VOTES 350, 351, 352, 353, 354, 355, 356, 357

350. HR 3543. Fiscal 1992 Supplemental Appropriations/Voter Registration Lists Project. Boehner, R-Ohio, amendment to provide $1 to the House Administration Committee to cancel the contract with Aristotle Industries for the CD-Rom Voter Registration Lists project. Rejected 182-231: R 155-4; D 27-226 (ND 16-156, SD 11-70); I 0-1, Oct. 29, 1991.

351. HR 3543. Fiscal 1992 Supplemental Appropriations/Recommittal Motion. McDade, R-Pa., motion to recommit the bill to the Appropriations Committee with instructions to report it back after striking provisions that direct the Treasury to transfer to the Presidential Election Campaign Fund an amount estimated to be collected from the taxpayer checkoff during fiscal 1992 to ensure that funds will be available to pay matching funds for presidential candidates during the primaries. The motion would also direct the committee to include offsets to assure that the bill would comply with the domestic discretionary spending caps of last year's budget agreement and not result in a sequestration. Motion rejected 180-232: R 159-0; D 21-231 (ND 8-163, SD 13-68); I 0-1, Oct. 29, 1991.

352. HR 3543. Fiscal 1992 Supplemental Appropriations/Passage. Passage of the bill to provide $7,486,250,000 for various emergencies in fiscal 1992, including $3.3 billion for the cleanup costs of Operation Desert Storm, $1.75 billion for payments to farmers and ranchers and $943 million for the Federal Emergency Management Agency to help communities recover from natural disasters. All spending in the bill is designated as emergency and thus exempt from the discretionary spending limits of last year's budget agreement. Passed 252-162: R 29-131; D 222-31 (ND 155-16, SD 67-15); I 1-0, Oct. 29, 1991.

353. HR 2508. Fiscal 1992-93 Foreign Aid Authorization/Rule. Adoption of the rule (H Res 232) to waive all points of order against and provide for House floor consideration of the conference report to authorize $25 billion in fiscal 1992-93 for foreign economic and military assistance. Adopted 227-191: R 12-148; D 215-42 (ND 157-19, SD 58-23); I 0-1, Oct. 30, 1991.

354. HR 2508. Fiscal 1992-93 Foreign Aid Authorization/Conference Report. Adoption of the conference report to authorize $25 billion in fiscal 1992-93 for foreign economic and military assistance. The conference report would overturn the administration's Mexico City Policy, provide funds to the United Nations Population Fund and require cargo preferences. Rejected 159-262: R 28-134; D 131-127 (ND 105-73, SD 26-54); I 0-1, Oct. 30, 1991. A "nay" was a vote supporting the president's position.

355. HR 3489. Export Administration Act/Technology. Hunter, R-Calif., amendment to give authority to the secretary of Defense to review the sale of any goods or technology under the 1979 Export Administration Act and make a recommendation to disapprove the sale within 20 days if he determines it would be detrimental to U.S. national security. Rejected 189-217: R 131-27; D 58-189 (ND 33-134, SD 25-55); I 0-1, Oct. 30, 1991.

356. HR 3489. Export Administration Act/Munitions Control List. Kyl, R-Ariz., amendment to prohibit items from being included on both the commodity control list and the munitions control list and to require the president to conduct a case by case review of items that are on the U.S. munitions list and not on the international munitions list. Adopted 223-180: R 144-13; D 79-166 (ND 38-130, SD 41-36); I 0-1, Oct. 30, 1991.

357. HR 3489. Export Administration Act/Munitions Control List. Hunter, R-Calif., amendment to give the secretary of Defense authority to determine whether to add or remove items from the munitions control list along with the secretary of Commerce. If the two secretaries fail to agree, the president would make the final determination. Rejected 135-270: R 99-59; D 36-210 (ND 18-149, SD 18-61); I 0-1, Oct. 30, 1991.

KEY

- Y Voted for (yea).
- # Paired for.
- + Announced for.
- N Voted against (nay).
- X Paired against.
- - Announced against.
- P Voted "present."
- C Voted "present" to avoid possible conflict of interest.
- ? Did not vote or otherwise make a position known.

Democrats ***Republicans***
Independent

	350	351	352	353	354	355	356	357
ALABAMA								
1 ***Callahan***	Y	Y	Y	N	N	Y	Y	Y
2 ***Dickinson***	Y	Y	N	N	N	Y	Y	Y
3 Browder	N	N	Y	Y	N	N	Y	N
4 Bevill	N	N	Y	Y	N	N	Y	N
5 Cramer	N	N	Y	Y	N	N	N	N
6 Erdreich	N	N	Y	N	N	N	N	N
7 Harris	N	N	Y	N	N	N	N	N
ALASKA								
AL ***Young***	Y	Y	Y	?	Y	Y	?	N
ARIZONA								
1 ***Rhodes***	Y	Y	N	N	N	Y	Y	Y
2 Pastor	N	N	Y	Y	Y	N	N	N
3 ***Stump***	Y	Y	N	N	N	Y	Y	Y
4 ***Kyl***	Y	Y	N	N	N	Y	Y	Y
5 ***Kolbe***	Y	Y	N	N	Y	N	Y	N
ARKANSAS								
1 Alexander	N	N	Y	Y	N	N	N	N
2 Thornton	N	N	Y	Y	N	N	N	N
3 ***Hammerschmidt***	Y	Y	N	N	N	Y	Y	N
4 Anthony	N	N	Y	N	N	N	N	N
CALIFORNIA								
1 ***Riggs***	Y	Y	N	N	Y	Y	Y	Y
2 ***Herger***	Y	Y	?	?	N	Y	Y	Y
3 Matsui	?	?	?	?	?	N	N	N
4 Fazio	N	N	Y	Y	Y	N	N	N
5 Pelosi	N	N	Y	Y	Y	N	N	?
6 Boxer	?	?	?	?	?	?	?	?
7 Miller	N	N	Y	Y	N	N	N	N
8 Dellums	N	N	Y	Y	Y	N	Y	N
9 Stark	N	N	Y	Y	N	N	N	N
10 Edwards	N	N	Y	Y	Y	N	?	?
11 Lantos	N	N	Y	Y	Y	N	N	N
12 ***Campbell***	Y	Y	N	N	Y	N	Y	N
13 Mineta	N	N	Y	Y	Y	N	N	N
14 ***Doolittle***	Y	Y	N	N	N	Y	Y	Y
15 Condit	N	N	Y	N	N	N	Y	Y
16 Panetta	N	N	Y	Y	Y	N	N	Y
17 Dooley	N	N	Y	Y	N	N	N	N
18 Lehman	N	N	Y	Y	N	N	N	N
19 ***Lagomarsino***	Y	Y	N	N	N	Y	Y	Y
20 ***Thomas***	N	Y	N	N	N	Y	Y	Y
21 ***Gallegly***	Y	Y	N	N	N	Y	Y	Y
22 ***Moorhead***	Y	Y	N	N	N	Y	Y	Y
23 Beilenson	N	N	N	Y	Y	Y	Y	Y
24 Waxman	N	N	Y	Y	Y	Y	Y	Y
25 Roybal	N	N	Y	Y	Y	N	N	N
26 Berman	N	N	Y	Y	Y	N	N	N
27 Levine	?	?	?	Y	Y	N	N	N
28 Dixon	N	N	Y	Y	Y	N	N	N
29 Waters	N	N	Y	Y	N	N	N	N
30 Martinez	N	N	Y	Y	Y	?	?	N
31 Dymally	N	N	Y	Y	Y	N	N	N
32 Anderson	N	N	Y	Y	N	N	N	N
33 ***Dreier***	Y	Y	N	N	N	Y	Y	Y
34 Torres	N	N	Y	Y	Y	N	N	N
35 ***Lewis***	Y	Y	N	N	N	Y	Y	Y
36 Brown	N	N	Y	Y	Y	?	?	?
37 ***McCandless***	Y	Y	N	N	N	Y	Y	Y
38 ***Dornan***	Y	Y	N	N	N	Y	Y	Y
39 ***Dannemeyer***	Y	Y	N	N	N	Y	Y	Y
40 ***Cox***	Y	Y	N	N	N	Y	Y	Y
41 ***Lowery***	Y	Y	N	N	N	Y	Y	Y
42 ***Rohrabacher***	Y	Y	N	N	N	Y	Y	Y
43 ***Packard***	Y	Y	N	N	N	Y	Y	Y
44 ***Cunningham***	Y	Y	N	N	N	Y	Y	Y
45 ***Hunter***	Y	Y	N	N	N	Y	Y	Y
COLORADO								
1 Schroeder	N	N	Y	Y	Y	Y	N	N
2 Skaggs	N	N	Y	Y	Y	N	N	N
3 Campbell	N	N	Y	Y	N	N	Y	N
4 ***Allard***	Y	Y	N	N	N	N	Y	N
5 ***Hefley***	Y	Y	N	N	N	Y	Y	Y
6 ***Schaefer***	Y	Y	N	N	N	Y	Y	Y
CONNECTICUT								
1 Kennelly	N	N	Y	Y	Y	N	N	N
2 Gejdenson	N	N	Y	Y	Y	N	N	N
3 DeLauro	N	N	Y	Y	Y	N	N	N
4 ***Shays***	Y	Y	N	N	Y	N	Y	N
5 ***Franks***	Y	Y	N	N	N	Y	Y	N
6 ***Johnson***	Y	Y	N	N	Y	N	Y	N
DELAWARE								
AL Carper	Y	N	N	Y	Y	N	N	N
FLORIDA								
1 Hutto	Y	Y	N	N	N	Y	Y	Y
2 Peterson	N	N	Y	Y	Y	N	N	N
3 Bennett	N	N	Y	Y	N	Y	Y	Y
4 ***James***	Y	Y	N	N	N	Y	Y	Y
5 ***McCollum***	Y	Y	N	N	N	Y	Y	Y
6 ***Stearns***	Y	Y	N	N	N	Y	Y	Y
7 Gibbons	N	N	Y	Y	Y	N	N	N
8 ***Young***	Y	Y	N	N	N	Y	Y	Y
9 ***Bilirakis***	Y	Y	N	N	N	Y	Y	Y
10 ***Ireland***	Y	Y	N	N	N	Y	?	Y
11 Bacchus	N	N	Y	Y	Y	Y	N	Y
12 ***Lewis***	Y	Y	N	N	N	Y	Y	Y
13 ***Goss***	Y	Y	N	N	N	Y	Y	Y
14 Johnston	N	N	Y	Y	Y	N	N	N
15 ***Shaw***	Y	Y	N	N	N	Y	Y	Y
16 Smith	N	N	Y	Y	Y	N	Y	N
17 Lehman	N	N	Y	Y	Y	?	?	N
18 ***Ros-Lehtinen***	Y	Y	Y	N	N	Y	Y	Y
19 Fascell	N	N	Y	Y	Y	N	N	N
GEORGIA								
1 Thomas	N	N	Y	Y	N	Y	Y	Y
2 Hatcher	N	N	Y	Y	N	N	N	N
3 Ray	Y	Y	Y	N	N	N	Y	N
4 Jones	N	N	Y	Y	Y	Y	N	N
5 Lewis	N	N	Y	Y	Y	N	N	N
6 ***Gingrich***	Y	Y	N	N	N	Y	Y	Y
7 Darden	N	N	Y	Y	N	Y	Y	Y
8 Rowland	?	?	?	?	?	?	?	?
9 Jenkins	N	N	Y	N	N	Y	?	N
10 Barnard	N	N	Y	N	N	Y	Y	Y
HAWAII								
1 Abercrombie	N	N	Y	Y	Y	Y	N	N
2 Mink	Y	N	Y	Y	Y	N	N	N
IDAHO								
1 LaRocco	N	N	Y	Y	N	N	N	N
2 Stallings	N	N	Y	Y	N	N	Y	N
ILLINOIS								
1 Hayes	N	N	Y	Y	N	N	N	N
2 Savage	?	?	?	N	N	N	?	?
3 Russo	N	N	Y	Y	N	N	N	N
4 Sangmeister	N	N	Y	Y	N	N	Y	Y
5 Lipinski	N	N	Y	Y	N	Y	Y	Y
6 ***Hyde***	Y	Y	N	N	N	Y	Y	Y
7 Collins	N	N	Y	Y	N	N	N	N
8 Rostenkowski	N	N	Y	Y	Y	N	N	?
9 Yates	N	N	Y	Y	Y	N	N	N
10 ***Porter***	Y	Y	N	P	Y	Y	Y	N
11 Annunzio	N	N	Y	Y	N	N	N	N
12 ***Crane***	Y	Y	N	N	N	Y	Y	Y
13 ***Fawell***	Y	Y	N	N	N	Y	Y	Y
14 ***Hastert***	Y	Y	N	N	N	Y	Y	Y
15 ***Ewing***	Y	Y	Y	Y	N	Y	Y	Y
16 Cox	N	N	Y	Y	Y	Y	Y	N
17 Evans	Y	N	Y	Y	Y	Y	Y	Y
18 ***Michel***	?	?	?	N	N	Y	Y	Y
19 Bruce	N	N	Y	N	N	Y	N	N
20 Durbin	N	N	Y	Y	N	N	N	N
21 Costello	N	N	Y	N	N	Y	Y	Y
22 Poshard	Y	N	Y	N	N	Y	N	N
INDIANA								
1 Visclosky	N	N	Y	Y	Y	N	N	N
2 Sharp	Y	N	Y	Y	N	N	Y	N
3 Roemer	N	N	Y	Y	N	N	Y	N

ND Northern Democrats SD Southern Democrats

	350	351	352	353	354	355	356	357
4 Long	Y	N	Y	Y	N	N	Y	N
5 Jontz	N	N	Y	N	N	N	N	N
6 ***Burton***	Y	Y	N	N	N	Y	Y	Y
7 ***Myers***	Y	Y	Y	N	N	Y	Y	Y
8 McCloskey	N	N	Y	Y	N	N	Y	N
9 Hamilton	Y	N	Y	Y	Y	N	Y	N
10 Jacobs	Y	N	N	N	N	N	N	N
IOWA								
1 ***Leach***	?	?	N	N	N	N	N	N
2 ***Nussle***	Y	Y	N	N	N	Y	Y	N
3 Nagle	N	N	Y	Y	Y	N	N	N
4 Smith	N	N	Y	Y	Y	N	N	N
5 ***Lightfoot***	Y	Y	N	N	N	Y	Y	Y
6 ***Grandy***	Y	Y	N	N	N	N	Y	N
KANSAS								
1 ***Roberts***	Y	Y	N	N	N	Y	Y	N
2 Slattery	N	Y	N	N	N	N	Y	Y
3 ***Meyers***	Y	Y	N	Y	Y	N	Y	N
4 Glickman	?	?	?	?	#	?	?	?
5 ***Nichols***	Y	Y	N	N	N	Y	Y	N
KENTUCKY								
1 Hubbard	N	N	Y	N	N	Y	Y	N
2 Natcher	N	N	Y	Y	N	N	N	N
3 Mazzoli	N	N	Y	Y	N	N	N	N
4 ***Bunning***	Y	Y	N	N	N	Y	Y	Y
5 ***Rogers***	Y	Y	Y	N	N	Y	Y	Y
6 ***Hopkins***	?	?	?	?	?	?	?	?
7 Perkins	N	N	Y	Y	N	N	N	N
LOUISIANA								
1 ***Livingston***	Y	Y	N	N	N	Y	Y	Y
2 Jefferson	N	N	Y	?	#	?	?	?
3 Tauzin	Y	Y	Y	N	N	Y	Y	Y
4 ***McCrery***	Y	Y	N	N	N	Y	Y	Y
5 Huckaby	N	N	Y	N	N	N	Y	N
6 ***Baker***	Y	Y	N	N	N	Y	Y	Y
7 Hayes	N	N	Y	Y	N	N	Y	N
8 ***Holloway***	Y	Y	N	N	N	Y	Y	Y
MAINE								
1 Andrews	N	N	Y	Y	Y	Y	Y	Y
2 ***Snowe***	Y	Y	Y	Y	Y	Y	Y	Y
MARYLAND								
1 ***Gilchrest***	Y	Y	N	N	Y	Y	Y	N
2 ***Bentley***	Y	Y	Y	N	N	Y	Y	Y
3 Cardin	Y	N	N	Y	Y	N	N	N
4 McMillen	N	N	Y	Y	Y	N	N	N
5 Hoyer	N	N	Y	Y	Y	N	N	N
6 Byron	Y	Y	N	Y	N	Y	Y	Y
7 Mfume	N	N	Y	Y	N	N	N	N
8 ***Morella***	Y	Y	Y	Y	Y	N	N	N
MASSACHUSETTS								
1 Olver	N	N	Y	Y	Y	N	N	N
2 Neal	N	N	Y	Y	N	N	N	N
3 Early	N	N	Y	N	N	N	N	N
4 Frank	N	N	Y	Y	Y	N	N	N
5 Atkins	N	N	Y	Y	Y	N	N	N
6 Mavroules	N	N	Y	Y	N	N	N	N
7 Markey	N	N	Y	Y	Y	N	N	N
8 Kennedy	N	N	Y	Y	Y	Y	N	N
9 Moakley	N	N	Y	Y	N	N	N	N
10 Studds	N	N	Y	Y	Y	N	N	N
11 Donnelly	N	N	Y	N	N	N	N	N
MICHIGAN								
1 Conyers	N	N	Y	Y	N	N	N	N
2 ***Pursell***	Y	Y	N	N	N	Y	Y	N
3 Wolpe	N	N	Y	Y	Y	N	N	N
4 ***Upton***	Y	Y	N	N	N	Y	Y	N
5 ***Henry***	Y	Y	N	N	N	N	N	N
6 Carr	N	N	Y	N	Y	Y	N	N
7 Kildee	N	N	Y	Y	N	Y	Y	N
8 Traxler	N	N	Y	Y	N	?	?	?
9 ***Vander Jagt***	Y	Y	Y	N	N	Y	Y	Y
10 ***Camp***	Y	Y	Y	N	N	Y	Y	N
11 ***Davis***	Y	Y	Y	N	N	?	Y	Y
12 Bonior	N	N	Y	Y	Y	N	N	N
13 Collins	N	N	Y	Y	N	N	N	N
14 Hertel	N	N	Y	Y	Y	N	N	N
15 Ford	N	N	Y	N	N	N	N	N
16 Dingell	N	N	Y	?	Y	N	N	N
17 Levin	N	N	Y	Y	Y	N	N	N
18 ***Broomfield***	Y	Y	N	N	N	Y	Y	Y
MINNESOTA								
1 Penny	N	Y	N	Y	Y	N	N	N
2 ***Weber***	Y	Y	Y	N	N	N	N	?
3 ***Ramstad***	Y	Y	N	N	N	N	N	N
4 Vento	N	N	Y	Y	Y	N	N	N
5 Sabo	N	N	Y	Y	Y	N	N	N
6 Sikorski	N	N	Y	Y	Y	N	N	N
7 Peterson	N	Y	Y	Y	N	Y	Y	Y
8 Oberstar	N	N	N	Y	N	N	N	N
MISSISSIPPI								
1 Whitten	N	N	Y	Y	N	N	N	N
2 Espy	N	N	Y	Y	N	N	N	N
3 Montgomery	N	Y	N	Y	N	N	Y	?
4 Parker	N	Y	N	Y	N	Y	Y	N
5 Taylor	N	Y	N	N	N	Y	Y	Y
MISSOURI								
1 Clay	N	N	Y	Y	N	N	N	N
2 Horn	N	N	Y	Y	N	N	N	N
3 Gephardt	N	N	Y	Y	Y	?	N	N
4 Skelton	N	N	Y	N	N	Y	Y	N
5 Wheat	N	N	Y	Y	Y	N	N	N
6 ***Coleman***	Y	Y	Y	N	N	Y	Y	Y
7 ***Hancock***	Y	Y	N	N	N	Y	Y	Y
8 ***Emerson***	Y	Y	Y	N	N	Y	Y	Y
9 Volkmer	N	N	Y	N	N	N	Y	N
MONTANA								
1 Williams	?	?	?	Y	N	?	?	?
2 ***Marlenee***	Y	Y	N	N	N	Y	Y	Y
NEBRASKA								
1 ***Bereuter***	Y	Y	Y	N	N	N	Y	N
2 Hoagland	N	N	Y	Y	Y	Y	Y	Y
3 ***Barrett***	Y	Y	Y	N	N	Y	Y	N
NEVADA								
1 Bilbray	N	N	Y	Y	N	N	Y	N
2 ***Vucanovich***	Y	Y	N	N	N	Y	Y	Y
NEW HAMPSHIRE								
1 ***Zeliff***	Y	Y	N	N	N	Y	Y	N
2 Swett	N	N	Y	Y	Y	N	N	N
NEW JERSEY								
1 Andrews	N	N	Y	Y	Y	Y	Y	N
2 Hughes	N	N	N	N	N	Y	Y	N
3 Pallone	N	N	N	Y	Y	Y	Y	Y
4 ***Smith***	Y	Y	N	N	N	Y	Y	N
5 ***Roukema***	Y	Y	N	N	Y	N	N	N
6 Dwyer	?	N	Y	Y	Y	N	?	N
7 ***Rinaldo***	Y	Y	N	N	N	Y	Y	N
8 Roe	?	?	?	Y	N	N	N	N
9 Torricelli	N	N	Y	Y	Y	Y	N	Y
10 Payne	N	N	Y	Y	Y	N	N	N
11 ***Gallo***	Y	Y	N	Y	Y	Y	Y	N
12 ***Zimmer***	Y	Y	N	N	Y	Y	Y	N
13 ***Saxton***	Y	Y	N	Y	Y	Y	Y	N
14 Guarini	N	N	N	Y	N	N	N	N
NEW MEXICO								
1 ***Schiff***	Y	Y	N	N	Y	Y	Y	Y
2 ***Skeen***	Y	Y	N	N	Y	Y	Y	Y
3 Richardson	N	N	Y	Y	Y	N	N	N
NEW YORK								
1 Hochbrueckner	N	N	Y	Y	Y	Y	Y	Y
2 Downey	N	N	Y	Y	Y	N	N	N
3 Mrazek	?	?	?	Y	Y	?	?	?
4 ***Lent***	Y	Y	N	N	N	?	?	?
5 ***McGrath***	N	Y	N	N	?	N	Y	N
6 Flake	N	N	Y	Y	Y	N	N	N
7 Ackerman	N	?	?	Y	Y	?	N	N
8 Scheuer	N	N	Y	Y	Y	?	?	?
9 Manton	N	?	?	Y	N	N	N	N
10 Schumer	N	N	Y	Y	Y	?	?	?
11 Towns	N	N	Y	Y	Y	N	N	N
12 Owens	N	N	Y	N	Y	N	N	N
13 Solarz	N	N	Y	Y	Y	N	N	N
14 ***Molinari***	Y	Y	N	N	Y	Y	Y	Y
15 ***Green***	N	Y	N	Y	Y	N	N	N
16 Rangel	N	N	Y	Y	Y	?	N	N
17 Weiss	N	N	Y	Y	Y	N	N	N
18 Serrano	N	N	Y	Y	Y	N	N	N
19 Engel	N	N	Y	Y	Y	N	N	N
20 Lowey	N	N	Y	Y	Y	N	N	N
21 ***Fish***	?	?	N	N	Y	N	N	N
22 ***Gilman***	Y	Y	Y	Y	Y	Y	Y	Y
23 McNulty	N	N	Y	Y	Y	N	Y	N
24 ***Solomon***	Y	Y	N	N	N	Y	Y	Y
25 ***Boehlert***	Y	Y	Y	Y	Y	N	N	N
26 ***Martin***	Y	Y	N	N	N	Y	Y	Y
27 ***Walsh***	Y	Y	N	N	N	Y	N	N
28 McHugh	Y	N	Y	Y	Y	N	N	N
29 ***Horton***	N	Y	Y	Y	N	N	Y	N
30 Slaughter	N	N	Y	Y	N	N	N	N
31 ***Paxon***	Y	Y	Y	N	N	Y	Y	Y
32 LaFalce	N	N	Y	Y	N	N	N	N
33 Nowak	N	N	Y	Y	N	N	N	N
34 ***Houghton***	Y	Y	N	Y	Y	N	N	N
NORTH CAROLINA								
1 Jones	N	N	Y	N	N	N	Y	N
2 Valentine	N	Y	N	N	N	N	?	N
3 Lancaster	N	N	N	Y	Y	N	Y	Y
4 Price	N	N	Y	Y	Y	N	N	N
5 Neal	Y	N	Y	N	N	Y	Y	N
6 ***Coble***	Y	Y	Y	N	N	Y	?	Y
7 Rose	N	N	Y	Y	Y	N	N	N
8 Hefner	N	N	Y	N	N	N	N	N
9 ***McMillan***	Y	Y	N	N	N	Y	Y	Y
10 ***Ballenger***	Y	Y	N	N	N	Y	Y	Y
11 ***Taylor***	Y	Y	N	N	N	Y	Y	Y
NORTH DAKOTA								
AL Dorgan	N	Y	Y	Y	N	Y	Y	?
OHIO								
1 Luken	N	Y	N	Y	N	N	N	N
2 ***Gradison***	Y	Y	N	N	N	Y	Y	Y
3 Hall	N	N	Y	Y	Y	N	Y	N
4 ***Oxley***	Y	Y	N	N	N	Y	Y	Y
5 ***Gillmor***	Y	Y	Y	N	N	Y	Y	N
6 ***McEwen***	Y	Y	N	N	N	Y	Y	Y
7 ***Hobson***	Y	Y	N	N	N	Y	Y	Y
8 ***Boehner***	Y	Y	N	N	N	Y	Y	Y
9 Kaptur	N	N	Y	N	N	Y	N	Y
10 ***Miller***	Y	Y	N	N	N	Y	Y	Y
11 Eckart	N	N	Y	Y	Y	?	N	N
12 ***Kasich***	Y	Y	N	N	N	Y	Y	Y
13 Pease	Y	N	N	Y	N	N	N	N
14 Sawyer	N	N	N	Y	Y	?	N	N
15 ***Wylie***	Y	Y	N	N	N	Y	Y	Y
16 ***Regula***	Y	Y	N	N	N	Y	Y	N
17 Traficant	Y	N	Y	N	N	Y	N	N
18 Applegate	Y	N	Y	Y	N	Y	Y	N
19 Feighan	N	N	Y	Y	Y	N	N	N
20 Oakar	N	N	Y	Y	Y	N	N	N
21 Stokes	N	N	Y	?	Y	N	N	N
OKLAHOMA								
1 ***Inhofe***	Y	Y	N	N	N	Y	Y	Y
2 Synar	N	N	Y	Y	Y	N	N	N
3 Brewster	N	N	Y	Y	Y	N	N	N
4 McCurdy	N	N	N	Y	Y	N	N	N
5 ***Edwards***	Y	Y	N	?	?	Y	Y	Y
6 English	Y	N	Y	N	N	N	Y	N
OREGON								
1 AuCoin	N	N	Y	Y	Y	N	N	N
2 ***Smith***	Y	Y	N	N	N	Y	Y	N
3 Wyden	N	N	Y	Y	Y	N	N	N
4 DeFazio	N	N	Y	Y	N	N	N	N
5 Kopetski	N	N	Y	Y	Y	N	N	N
PENNSYLVANIA								
1 Foglietta	N	N	Y	Y	Y	N	N	N
2 Vacancy								
3 Borski	N	N	Y	Y	Y	N	N	N
4 Kolter	N	N	Y	N	N	N	Y	N
5 ***Schulze***	?	?	?	N	N	Y	Y	?
6 Yatron	N	N	Y	Y	Y	N	Y	N
7 ***Weldon***	Y	Y	N	N	N	Y	Y	Y
8 Kostmayer	Y	Y	Y	Y	Y	N	N	N
9 ***Shuster***	Y	Y	N	N	N	?	?	?
10 ***McDade***	Y	Y	N	N	N	Y	?	?
11 Kanjorski	N	N	Y	Y	N	N	N	N
12 Murtha	N	N	Y	N	Y	N	N	N
13 ***Coughlin***	Y	Y	N	N	N	N	Y	N
14 Coyne	N	N	Y	Y	Y	N	N	N
15 ***Ritter***	Y	Y	N	N	N	Y	Y	Y
16 ***Walker***	Y	Y	N	N	N	Y	Y	Y
17 ***Gekas***	Y	Y	N	N	N	Y	Y	Y
18 ***Santorum***	Y	Y	N	N	N	Y	Y	N
19 ***Goodling***	Y	Y	N	N	N	+	+	+
20 Gaydos	N	N	Y	Y	N	Y	Y	N
21 ***Ridge***	Y	Y	N	N	N	Y	Y	N
22 Murphy	N	N	Y	Y	N	N	N	?
23 ***Clinger***	Y	Y	N	N	N	N	Y	N
RHODE ISLAND								
1 ***Machtley***	Y	Y	Y	N	Y	Y	Y	Y
2 Reed	Y	N	Y	Y	Y	N	N	N
SOUTH CAROLINA								
1 ***Ravenel***	Y	Y	Y	Y	Y	Y	Y	N
2 ***Spence***	Y	Y	N	N	N	Y	Y	Y
3 Derrick	N	N	Y	Y	N	N	N	N
4 Patterson	Y	Y	N	Y	N	Y	Y	Y
5 Spratt	N	N	Y	Y	N	N	Y	N
6 Tallon	N	N	Y	N	N	Y	N	Y
SOUTH DAKOTA								
AL Johnson	N	N	Y	Y	Y	Y	N	N
TENNESSEE								
1 ***Quillen***	Y	Y	N	N	N	Y	Y	N
2 ***Duncan***	Y	Y	N	N	N	Y	Y	Y
3 Lloyd	N	Y	N	N	X	?	?	?
4 Cooper	Y	N	Y	N	N	N	Y	N
5 Clement	N	N	Y	Y	N	Y	Y	N
6 Gordon	N	N	Y	Y	Y	N	N	N
7 ***Sundquist***	Y	Y	N	N	N	Y	Y	N
8 Tanner	?	?	?	?	X	?	?	?
9 Ford	N	N	Y	Y	N	N	?	N
TEXAS								
1 Chapman	N	N	Y	Y	N	N	Y	N
2 Wilson	N	N	Y	N	N	Y	Y	Y
3 ***Johnson***	Y	Y	N	N	N	Y	Y	Y
4 Hall	?	?	?	?	?	Y	Y	Y
5 Bryant	N	N	Y	N	N	N	Y	N
6 ***Barton***	Y	Y	N	N	N	Y	Y	Y
7 ***Archer***	Y	Y	N	N	N	Y	Y	N
8 ***Fields***	Y	Y	N	N	N	+	Y	N
9 Brooks	N	N	Y	Y	N	N	N	N
10 Pickle	N	N	Y	Y	Y	N	Y	N
11 Edwards	N	N	Y	Y	N	Y	Y	Y
12 Geren	Y	Y	N	Y	N	N	Y	N
13 Sarpalius	N	N	Y	Y	N	Y	Y	?
14 Laughlin	N	Y	N	Y	N	Y	Y	Y
15 de la Garza	N	N	Y	Y	Y	N	Y	N
16 Coleman	N	N	Y	Y	N	N	N	N
17 Stenholm	Y	Y	N	N	N	Y	Y	Y
18 Washington	N	N	Y	Y	N	N	N	N
19 ***Combest***	Y	Y	Y	N	N	Y	Y	Y
20 Gonzalez	N	N	Y	Y	Y	N	N	N
21 ***Smith***	Y	Y	N	N	Y	?	Y	Y
22 ***DeLay***	Y	Y	N	N	N	Y	Y	N
23 Bustamante	N	N	Y	Y	Y	N	N	N
24 Frost	N	N	Y	Y	Y	N	Y	N
25 Andrews	Y	N	N	Y	Y	N	Y	N
26 ***Armey***	Y	Y	N	N	N	Y	Y	Y
27 Ortiz	N	N	Y	Y	N	N	N	N
UTAH								
1 ***Hansen***	Y	Y	N	N	N	Y	Y	Y
2 Owens	N	N	Y	Y	Y	N	N	N
3 Orton	N	Y	N	Y	N	N	N	N
VERMONT								
AL *Sanders*	N	N	Y	N	N	N	N	N
VIRGINIA								
1 ***Bateman***	Y	Y	N	N	N	Y	Y	Y
2 Pickett	N	N	N	N	N	Y	Y	N
3 ***Bliley***	?	?	?	N	N	Y	Y	Y
4 Sisisky	N	Y	Y	Y	Y	Y	Y	Y
5 Payne	N	N	N	Y	Y	Y	Y	Y
6 Olin	Y	N	Y	Y	Y	N	Y	N
7 ***Slaughter***	?	?	?	?	?	?	?	?
8 Moran	-	-	Y	Y	Y	N	N	N
9 Boucher	N	N	Y	Y	N	N	N	N
10 ***Wolf***	Y	Y	N	N	N	Y	Y	Y
WASHINGTON								
1 ***Miller***	Y	Y	N	N	Y	N	N	N
2 Swift	N	N	Y	Y	Y	N	N	N
3 Unsoeld	N	N	Y	Y	Y	N	N	N
4 ***Morrison***	Y	Y	Y	N	N	N	Y	N
5 Foley								
6 Dicks	N	N	Y	Y	Y	N	N	N
7 McDermott	N	N	Y	Y	Y	N	N	N
8 ***Chandler***	Y	Y	Y	N	Y	Y	Y	N
WEST VIRGINIA								
1 Mollohan	N	N	Y	Y	N	Y	N	N
2 Staggers	N	N	Y	Y	N	N	Y	N
3 Wise	N	N	Y	Y	Y	N	N	N
4 Rahall	N	N	Y	N	N	N	N	N
WISCONSIN								
1 Aspin	N	N	Y	Y	Y	Y	Y	Y
2 ***Klug***	Y	Y	N	N	N	Y	Y	N
3 ***Gunderson***	Y	Y	N	N	N	N	Y	N
4 Kleczka	N	N	Y	Y	N	N	?	N
5 Moody	N	N	N	Y	Y	Y	N	N
6 ***Petri***	Y	Y	N	N	N	N	N	N
7 Obey	N	N	Y	Y	N	N	N	N
8 ***Roth***	Y	Y	N	N	N	N	Y	N
9 ***Sensenbrenner***	Y	Y	N	N	N	Y	Y	N
WYOMING								
AL ***Thomas***	Y	Y	N	N	N	Y	Y	Y

Southern states - Ala., Ark., Fla., Ga., Ky., La., Miss., N.C., Okla., S.C., Tenn., Texas, Va.
Omitted votes are quorum calls, which CQ does not include in its vote charts.

HOUSE VOTES 358, 359, 361, 362, 363, 364, 365, 366

358. HR 6. Banking Reform. Adoption of the resolution (H Res 266) to provide for House floor consideration of the bill to restructure the banking industry, overhaul the federal bank deposit insurance system and allow the Federal Deposit Insurance Corporation to borrow $30 billion to cover bank failures. Adopted 210-208: R 8-153; D 202-54 (ND 149-26, SD 53-28); I 0-1, Oct. 31, 1991.

359. HR 2454. Generic Drug Enforcement Act/Passage. Waxman, D-Calif., motion to suspend the rules and pass the bill to give the Food and Drug Administration authority to take action against companies and individuals who have abused the generic-drug approval process. Motion agreed to 413-0: R 159-0; D 253-0 (ND 174-0, SD 79-0); I 1-0, Oct. 31, 1991. A two-thirds majority of those present and voting (276 in this case) is required for passage under suspension of the rules.

361. HR 6. Banking Reform/Core Banking System. Schumer, D-N.Y., amendment to create a core banking system, in which banks with federal deposit insurance would be limited in the amount they could lend any single person and in the amount of interest they could pay depositors. Rejected 106-312: R 4-157; D 101-155 (ND 86-90, SD 15-65); I 1-0, Oct. 31, 1991.

362. HR 6. Banking Reform/New Activities. Barnard, D-Ga., amendment to strike Title IV of the bill, which would allow banks to affiliate with securities firms, limit the financial transactions and information-sharing between affiliated banks and securities firms and allow federally chartered banks to conduct certain securities and insurance activities. Rejected 200-216: R 130-28; D 70-187 (ND 39-138, SD 31-49); I 0-1, Oct. 31, 1991.

363. HR 6. Banking Reform/Failed Banks. Rinaldo, R-N.J., amendment to allow commercial companies to buy failed or failing banks. Rejected 137-272: R 105-51; D 32-220 (ND 21-151, SD 11-69); I 0-1, Oct. 31, 1991.

364. HR 6. Banking Reform/Strike Enacting Clause. Michel, R-Ill., motion to rise and report the bill back with the enacting clause stricken. Striking the enacting clause could have killed the bill or caused it to be sent back to committee for revision. Motion rejected 158-243: R 156-0; D 2-242 (ND 1-167, SD 1-75); I 0-1, Nov. 1, 1991. A "yea" was a vote supporting the president's position.

365. HR 6. Banking Reform/'Non-Bank Banks'. Frank, D-Mass., amendment to repeal the 7 percent asset growth cap for "non-bank banks," whose continued existence had been grandfathered since 1987. Rejected 104-290: R 55-95; D 49-194 (ND 45-122, SD 4-72); I 0-1, Nov. 1, 1991.

366. HR 6. Banking Reform/Community Reinvestment. Kennedy, D-Mass., amendment to require banks and regulators to take steps to prevent discriminatory lending practices and require banks that engage in interstate banking to show a record of reinvesting in the communities they serve. Rejected 152-241: R 18-135; D 133-106 (ND 107-58, SD 26-48); I 1-0, Nov. 1, 1991.

KEY

Y Voted for (yea).
Paired for.
+ Announced for.
N Voted against (nay).
X Paired against.
- Announced against.
P Voted "present."
C Voted "present" to avoid possible conflict of interest.
? Did not vote or otherwise make a position known.

Democrats ***Republicans***
Independent

	358	359	361	362	363	364	365	366
ALABAMA								
1 ***Callahan***	N	Y	N	Y	Y	Y	N	N
2 ***Dickinson***	N	Y	N	Y	Y	Y	N	N
3 Browder	N	Y	N	N	N	N	N	N
4 Bevill	Y	Y	N	N	N	N	N	N
5 Cramer	N	Y	N	N	N	N	N	N
6 Erdreich	N	Y	N	Y	Y	N	N	N
7 Harris	Y	Y	N	N	N	N	N	N
ALASKA								
AL ***Young***	N	Y	N	Y	Y	Y	Y	N
ARIZONA								
1 ***Rhodes***	N	Y	N	Y	Y	Y	N	N
2 Pastor	Y	Y	N	N	N	N	N	Y
3 ***Stump***	N	Y	N	Y	Y	Y	N	N
4 ***Kyl***	N	Y	N	Y	Y	Y	N	N
5 ***Kolbe***	N	Y	N	Y	Y	Y	Y	N
ARKANSAS								
1 Alexander	N	Y	N	N	N	N	N	N
2 Thornton	N	Y	N	N	N	N	N	N
3 ***Hammerschmidt***	N	Y	N	N	N	Y	N	N
4 Anthony	N	Y	N	N	N	N	N	N
CALIFORNIA								
1 ***Riggs***	N	Y	N	Y	Y	Y	Y	N
2 ***Herger***	N	Y	N	N	N	Y	?	N
3 Matsui	Y	Y	N	Y	N	N	N	N
4 Fazio	Y	Y	N	Y	N	N	Y	Y
5 Pelosi	Y	Y	Y	N	N	N	Y	#
6 Boxer	?	?	?	?	?	?	?	?
7 Miller	Y	Y	Y	N	N	N	N	Y
8 Dellums	Y	Y	Y	N	N	N	N	Y
9 Stark	Y	Y	Y	N	N	N	N	Y
10 Edwards	Y	Y	Y	N	N	N	Y	Y
11 Lantos	Y	Y	N	N	N	N	N	Y
12 ***Campbell***	?	?	?	?	?	Y	Y	N
13 Mineta	Y	Y	Y	N	N	X	?	#
14 ***Doolittle***	N	Y	N	Y	Y	Y	Y	N
15 Condit	N	Y	Y	Y	N	N	N	Y
16 Panetta	Y	Y	Y	N	N	N	N	Y
17 Dooley	Y	Y	N	Y	Y	N	Y	N
18 Lehman	N	Y	Y	N	N	N	N	N
19 ***Lagomarsino***	N	Y	N	Y	Y	Y	N	N
20 ***Thomas***	N	Y	N	Y	Y	Y	Y	N
21 ***Gallegly***	N	Y	N	Y	Y	Y	N	N
22 ***Moorhead***	N	Y	N	Y	Y	Y	N	N
23 Beilenson	Y	Y	Y	N	N	N	Y	Y
24 Waxman	Y	Y	Y	N	N	N	N	Y
25 Roybal	Y	Y	Y	N	N	N	N	Y
26 Berman	Y	Y	Y	N	N	N	Y	Y
27 Levine	Y	Y	Y	N	N	N	?	?
28 Dixon	Y	Y	N	N	N	N	Y	Y
29 Waters	Y	Y	Y	N	N	N	N	Y
30 Martinez	Y	Y	N	N	N	N	N	N
31 Dymally	Y	Y	?	?	?	X	#	?
32 Anderson	Y	Y	N	Y	N	N	N	N
33 ***Dreier***	N	Y	N	Y	Y	Y	Y	N
34 Torres	Y	Y	N	N	N	N	N	Y
35 ***Lewis***	N	Y	N	Y	Y	Y	N	N
36 Brown	?	?	?	?	?	X	?	?
37 ***McCandless***	N	Y	N	Y	Y	Y	Y	N
38 ***Dornan***	N	Y	N	Y	Y	Y	N	N
39 ***Dannemeyer***	N	Y	N	+	+	+	+	-
40 ***Cox***	N	Y	N	Y	Y	Y	Y	N
41 ***Lowery***	N	Y	N	Y	Y	Y	?	N
42 ***Rohrabacher***	N	Y	Y	Y	Y	Y	Y	N
43 ***Packard***	N	Y	N	Y	Y	Y	N	N
44 ***Cunningham***	N	Y	N	Y	Y	Y	N	N
45 ***Hunter***	N	Y	N	Y	N	Y	N	Y
COLORADO								
1 Schroeder	Y	Y	Y	N	Y	N	Y	Y
2 Skaggs	Y	Y	N	Y	N	N	Y	N
3 Campbell	N	Y	N	N	Y	N	N	?
4 ***Allard***	N	Y	N	Y	Y	Y	Y	N
5 ***Hefley***	N	Y	N	Y	Y	Y	Y	N
6 ***Schaefer***	N	Y	N	Y	N	Y	N	N
CONNECTICUT								
1 Kennelly	Y	Y	Y	N	N	N	Y	Y
2 Gejdenson	Y	Y	Y	N	N	N	Y	Y
3 DeLauro	Y	Y	N	N	N	N	N	Y
4 ***Shays***	Y	Y	N	Y	N	Y	N	Y
5 ***Franks***	N	Y	N	Y	Y	Y	N	Y
6 ***Johnson***	Y	Y	N	Y	N	Y	N	N
DELAWARE								
AL Carper	N	?	N	Y	Y	Y	Y	Y
FLORIDA								
1 Hutto	N	Y	N	Y	N	N	N	N
2 Peterson	Y	Y	N	Y	N	N	N	N
3 Bennett	N	Y	Y	N	N	N	N	Y
4 ***James***	N	Y	N	N	N	Y	N	N
5 ***McCollum***	N	Y	N	Y	Y	Y	N	X
6 ***Stearns***	N	Y	N	N	Y	Y	N	N
7 Gibbons	Y	Y	N	N	N	N	N	N
8 ***Young***	N	Y	N	Y	?	Y	Y	N
9 ***Bilirakis***	?	?	?	?	?	?	?	?
10 ***Ireland***	N	Y	N	Y	Y	?	?	?
11 Bacchus	Y	Y	Y	Y	N	N	N	Y
12 ***Lewis***	N	Y	N	Y	Y	Y	N	N
13 ***Goss***	N	Y	N	Y	Y	Y	Y	N
14 Johnston	Y	Y	N	Y	Y	X	?	X
15 ***Shaw***	N	Y	N	Y	Y	Y	N	N
16 Smith	Y	Y	Y	N	N	N	N	Y
17 Lehman	Y	Y	Y	N	N	N	N	Y
18 ***Ros-Lehtinen***	N	Y	N	Y	N	Y	?	?
19 Fascell	Y	Y	N	N	N	N	N	Y
GEORGIA								
1 Thomas	N	Y	N	Y	N	N	N	N
2 Hatcher	Y	Y	N	N	N	N	N	N
3 Ray	Y	Y	N	Y	N	N	N	N
4 Jones	N	Y	N	N	N	N	N	Y
5 Lewis	Y	Y	Y	N	N	N	N	Y
6 ***Gingrich***	N	Y	N	Y	Y	Y	N	Y
7 Darden	Y	Y	N	Y	N	N	N	N
8 Rowland	?	?	?	?	?	?	?	?
9 Jenkins	N	Y	N	Y	N	N	N	N
10 Barnard	Y	Y	N	Y	Y	Y	Y	?
HAWAII								
1 Abercrombie	Y	Y	N	N	N	N	N	Y
2 Mink	Y	Y	Y	N	N	?	N	Y
IDAHO								
1 LaRocco	Y	Y	N	Y	Y	N	Y	N
2 Stallings	N	Y	N	Y	N	N	N	N
ILLINOIS								
1 Hayes	Y	Y	Y	N	N	N	N	Y
2 Savage	?	?	?	?	?	?	?	?
3 Russo	Y	Y	Y	N	N	N	N	N
4 Sangmeister	N	Y	Y	N	N	?	?	#
5 Lipinski	N	Y	Y	N	Y	N	N	N
6 ***Hyde***	N	Y	N	Y	Y	Y	N	N
7 Collins	Y	Y	Y	N	N	N	N	Y
8 Rostenkowski	Y	Y	Y	N	N	N	N	N
9 Yates	Y	Y	Y	N	N	N	N	Y
10 ***Porter***	N	Y	N	Y	N	Y	N	N
11 Annunzio	Y	Y	Y	N	N	N	N	N
12 ***Crane***	N	Y	N	Y	Y	Y	Y	N
13 ***Fawell***	N	Y	N	Y	N	Y	N	N
14 ***Hastert***	N	Y	N	Y	Y	Y	Y	N
15 ***Ewing***	N	Y	N	Y	N	Y	N	N
16 Cox	Y	Y	Y	Y	N	N	N	Y
17 Evans	Y	Y	N	N	N	N	N	Y
18 ***Michel***	Y	Y	N	Y	?	Y	N	?
19 Bruce	Y	Y	N	N	N	N	N	N
20 Durbin	Y	Y	Y	N	N	N	N	Y
21 Costello	N	Y	N	N	N	N	N	Y
22 Poshard	N	Y	Y	N	N	N	N	N
INDIANA								
1 Visclosky	Y	Y	Y	N	N	N	N	Y
2 Sharp	Y	Y	N	N	?	N	N	N
3 Roemer	Y	Y	N	Y	N	N	N	N

ND Northern Democrats SD Southern Democrats

	358	359	361	362	363	364	365	366
4 Long	Y	Y	N	N	N	N	N	N
5 Jontz	Y	Y	Y	N	N	N	N	Y
6 ***Burton***	N	Y	N	N	N	#	N	N
7 ***Myers***	N	Y	N	Y	Y	Y	N	N
8 McCloskey	Y	Y	Y	N	N	N	N	N
9 Hamilton	Y	Y	N	Y	N	N	N	N
10 Jacobs	N	Y	N	N	N	N	N	Y
IOWA								
1 ***Leach***	Y	Y	N	Y	N	Y	N	N
2 ***Nussle***	N	Y	N	Y	N	Y	N	N
3 Nagle	Y	Y	N	N	N	N	N	N
4 Smith	Y	Y	N	Y	N	N	N	N
5 ***Lightfoot***	N	Y	N	Y	N	Y	N	N
6 ***Grandy***	N	Y	N	Y	N	Y	N	N
KANSAS								
1 ***Roberts***	N	Y	N	Y	N	Y	N	N
2 Slattery	Y	Y	Y	N	N	N	N	N
3 ***Meyers***	Y	Y	N	Y	N	Y	N	N
4 Glickman	Y	Y	Y	N	Y	N	N	N
5 ***Nichols***	N	Y	N	Y	N	Y	N	N
KENTUCKY								
1 Hubbard	N	Y	N	Y	N	N	N	Y
2 Natcher	Y	Y	N	Y	N	N	N	N
3 Mazzoli	Y	Y	Y	N	N	N	N	Y
4 ***Bunning***	?	?	?	?	?	Y	Y	N
5 ***Rogers***	N	Y	N	Y	N	Y	N	N
6 ***Hopkins***	?	?	?	?	?	?	?	?
7 Perkins	Y	Y	N	N	N	N	N	Y
LOUISIANA								
1 ***Livingston***	N	Y	N	Y	Y	Y	N	N
2 Jefferson	Y	Y	Y	N	N	N	N	Y
3 Tauzin	Y	Y	N	N	N	N	N	N
4 ***McCrery***	N	Y	N	N	Y	Y	N	N
5 Huckaby	Y	Y	N	Y	N	N	N	N
6 ***Baker***	N	Y	N	Y	Y	Y	?	?
7 Hayes	Y	Y	N	N	N	N	N	?
8 ***Holloway***	N	Y	N	N	Y	Y	Y	N
MAINE								
1 Andrews	Y	Y	Y	N	N	N	N	Y
2 ***Snowe***	N	Y	N	Y	Y	Y	Y	N
MARYLAND								
1 ***Gilchrest***	N	Y	N	N	N	Y	N	N
2 ***Bentley***	N	Y	N	N	N	Y	N	N
3 Cardin	Y	Y	Y	Y	N	N	N	N
4 McMillen	N	Y	N	N	N	N	N	N
5 Hoyer	Y	Y	Y	Y	N	N	N	Y
6 Byron	Y	Y	N	Y	N	N	N	N
7 Mfume	Y	Y	Y	N	N	N	Y	Y
8 ***Morella***	N	Y	N	Y	N	Y	Y	N
MASSACHUSETTS								
1 Olver	Y	Y	Y	N	N	N	Y	Y
2 Neal	Y	Y	Y	N	N	N	Y	Y
3 Early	Y	Y	N	N	N	N	Y	Y
4 Frank	Y	Y	N	Y	Y	N	Y	Y
5 Atkins	Y	Y	N	N	Y	N	Y	Y
6 Mavroules	Y	Y	N	Y	N	N	Y	?
7 Markey	Y	Y	Y	N	N	N	N	Y
8 Kennedy	Y	Y	Y	N	N	N	N	Y
9 Moakley	Y	Y	N	N	N	N	Y	Y
10 Studds	Y	Y	Y	N	N	N	Y	Y
11 Donnelly	Y	Y	Y	N	N	N	Y	Y
MICHIGAN								
1 Conyers	Y	Y	Y	N	?	N	N	Y
2 ***Pursell***	N	?	N	Y	N	Y	Y	N
3 Wolpe	Y	Y	Y	N	N	N	N	Y
4 ***Upton***	N	Y	N	Y	Y	Y	Y	Y
5 ***Henry***	N	Y	N	Y	N	Y	N	N
6 Carr	Y	Y	N	N	N	N	N	N
7 Kildee	Y	Y	Y	N	N	N	N	Y
8 Traxler	Y	Y	N	N	N	N	?	?
9 ***Vander Jagt***	N	Y	N	Y	Y	Y	Y	N
10 ***Camp***	N	Y	N	Y	N	Y	N	N
11 ***Davis***	N	Y	N	Y	N	#	?	?
12 Bonior	Y	Y	Y	N	N	N	N	Y
13 Collins	Y	Y	Y	N	N	N	N	Y
14 Hertel	Y	Y	Y	N	?	N	N	Y
15 Ford	?	?	Y	N	N	N	N	Y
16 Dingell	Y	Y	N	N	N	N	N	Y
17 Levin	Y	Y	N	N	N	N	N	Y
18 ***Broomfield***	N	Y	N	Y	Y	Y	Y	N
MINNESOTA								
1 Penny	Y	Y	N	N	N	N	N	N
2 ***Weber***	N	Y	N	Y	N	Y	N	N
3 ***Ramstad***	N	Y	N	Y	N	Y	N	N
4 Vento	Y	Y	N	N	N	N	N	Y

	358	359	361	362	363	364	365	366
5 Sabo	?	Y	N	N	N	N	N	Y
6 Sikorski	Y	Y	N	N	N	N	N	Y
7 Peterson	Y	Y	N	Y	N	N	N	N
8 Oberstar	Y	Y	N	N	N	?	?	?
MISSISSIPPI								
1 Whitten	Y	?	?	?	?	?	?	N
2 Espy	Y	Y	N	N	N	N	N	Y
3 Montgomery	Y	Y	N	N	N	N	N	N
4 Parker	Y	Y	N	N	N	N	N	N
5 Taylor	N	Y	Y	N	N	N	N	N
MISSOURI								
1 Clay	Y	Y	Y	N	N	N	N	Y
2 Horn	Y	Y	Y	N	N	N	N	Y
3 Gephardt	Y	Y	Y	N	N	N	N	Y
4 Skelton	N	Y	N	Y	Y	N	N	N
5 Wheat	Y	Y	Y	N	N	N	N	Y
6 ***Coleman***	N	Y	N	Y	N	Y	N	N
7 ***Hancock***	N	Y	N	N	Y	Y	N	N
8 ***Emerson***	N	Y	N	Y	Y	Y	N	N
9 Volkmer	Y	Y	N	N	N	N	N	N
MONTANA								
1 Williams	Y	Y	N	N	N	N	N	Y
2 ***Marlenee***	N	Y	N	#	?	#	?	X
NEBRASKA								
1 ***Bereuter***	N	Y	N	Y	N	Y	N	N
2 Hoagland	Y	Y	N	Y	Y	N	Y	N
3 ***Barrett***	N	Y	N	Y	N	Y	N	N
NEVADA								
1 Bilbray	Y	Y	N	N	N	N	N	N
2 ***Vucanovich***	N	Y	N	Y	Y	Y	N	N
NEW HAMPSHIRE								
1 ***Zeliff***	N	Y	N	Y	Y	Y	Y	N
2 Swett	Y	Y	N	Y	N	N	Y	N
NEW JERSEY								
1 Andrews	Y	Y	N	Y	N	N	N	N
2 Hughes	N	Y	Y	Y	Y	N	Y	N
3 Pallone	Y	Y	Y	N	N	N	N	Y
4 ***Smith***	N	Y	N	N	Y	Y	Y	N
5 ***Roukema***	N	Y	Y	N	N	Y	N	N
6 Dwyer	Y	Y	Y	N	N	N	X	?
7 ***Rinaldo***	N	Y	N	Y	Y	Y	Y	N
8 Roe	Y	Y	N	Y	Y	N	N	Y
9 Torricelli	Y	Y	Y	N	N	N	N	Y
10 Payne	?	?	Y	N	N	N	N	Y
11 ***Gallo***	N	Y	N	Y	Y	Y	N	N
12 ***Zimmer***	N	Y	Y	Y	Y	Y	Y	N
13 ***Saxton***	Y	Y	N	N	N	Y	Y	N
14 Guarini	Y	Y	?	N	N	N	N	N
NEW MEXICO								
1 ***Schiff***	N	Y	N	Y	Y	Y	Y	N
2 ***Skeen***	N	Y	N	Y	N	Y	N	N
3 Richardson	Y	Y	N	N	N	N	N	Y
NEW YORK								
1 Hochbrueckner	Y	Y	Y	N	N	N	N	Y
2 Downey	Y	Y	Y	N	N	N	N	Y
3 Mrazek	Y	Y	N	N	N	N	N	Y
4 ***Lent***	N	Y	N	Y	Y	Y	Y	N
5 ***McGrath***	N	Y	N	C	Y	Y	C	N
6 Flake	Y	Y	N	Y	N	N	Y	Y
7 Ackerman	Y	Y	Y	N	N	N	Y	Y
8 Scheuer	Y	Y	N	N	N	N	Y	Y
9 Manton	Y	Y	N	N	N	N	N	Y
10 Schumer	Y	Y	Y	N	Y	N	Y	Y
11 Towns	Y	Y	N	N	N	?	?	Y
12 Owens	N	Y	Y	N	N	N	N	Y
13 Solarz	Y	?	N	N	N	N	N	Y
14 ***Molinari***	N	Y	N	Y	Y	Y	N	N
15 ***Green***	N	Y	N	Y	Y	Y	Y	Y
16 Rangel	Y	Y	Y	N	N	N	Y	Y
17 Weiss	Y	Y	Y	N	-	N	Y	Y
18 Serrano	Y	Y	Y	N	N	N	N	Y
19 Engel	Y	Y	Y	Y	N	N	N	Y
20 Lowey	Y	Y	Y	N	Y	N	N	Y
21 ***Fish***	N	Y	N	N	N	Y	N	N
22 ***Gilman***	N	Y	N	Y	Y	Y	N	N
23 McNulty	Y	Y	N	N	N	N	N	Y
24 ***Solomon***	N	Y	N	N	Y	Y	N	N
25 ***Boehlert***	N	Y	N	Y	N	Y	N	Y
26 ***Martin***	N	Y	N	Y	Y	Y	N	N
27 ***Walsh***	N	Y	N	N	Y	Y	Y	Y
28 McHugh	Y	Y	N	Y	N	N	Y	N
29 ***Horton***	N	Y	N	Y	N	Y	?	Y
30 Slaughter	Y	Y	N	Y	N	N	N	Y
31 ***Paxon***	N	Y	N	N	Y	Y	N	N

	358	359	361	362	363	364	365	366
32 LaFalce	Y	Y	N	N	Y	N	Y	Y
33 Nowak	Y	Y	N	Y	N	N	Y	Y
34 ***Houghton***	Y	Y	N	Y	Y	Y	Y	N
NORTH CAROLINA								
1 Jones	Y	Y	N	N	N	N	N	N
2 Valentine	N	Y	N	N	Y	N	N	N
3 Lancaster	N	Y	N	N	N	N	N	N
4 Price	N	Y	N	Y	N	N	N	N
5 Neal	N	Y	N	Y	Y	?	?	?
6 ***Coble***	N	Y	N	Y	Y	Y	N	N
7 Rose	?	?	N	Y	N	N	N	N
8 Hefner	N	Y	N	Y	N	N	N	N
9 ***McMillan***	N	Y	N	Y	Y	Y	Y	N
10 ***Ballenger***	N	Y	N	Y	Y	Y	Y	N
11 ***Taylor***	N	Y	N	Y	Y	Y	Y	N
NORTH DAKOTA								
AL Dorgan	Y	Y	Y	N	N	N	N	N
OHIO								
1 Luken	Y	Y	N	N	N	N	N	N
2 ***Gradison***	N	Y	N	Y	Y	Y	Y	N
3 Hall	Y	Y	Y	Y	N	N	N	N
4 ***Oxley***	N	Y	N	Y	Y	Y	Y	N
5 ***Gillmor***	N	Y	N	N	N	Y	N	N
6 ***McEwen***	N	Y	N	Y	Y	Y	N	N
7 ***Hobson***	N	Y	N	Y	Y	Y	N	N
8 ***Boehner***	N	Y	N	Y	Y	Y	Y	N
9 Kaptur	N	Y	Y	N	?	N	N	?
10 ***Miller***	N	Y	N	Y	Y	Y	N	N
11 Eckart	N	Y	Y	N	N	N	N	Y
12 ***Kasich***	N	Y	N	Y	Y	Y	Y	Y
13 Pease	Y	Y	N	N	N	N	N	N
14 Sawyer	Y	Y	N	N	N	N	N	N
15 ***Wylie***	N	Y	N	Y	Y	Y	Y	N
16 ***Regula***	N	Y	Y	N	N	Y	N	N
17 Traficant	N	Y	Y	N	N	N	Y	Y
18 Applegate	N	Y	N	N	N	N	N	N
19 Feighan	Y	Y	N	N	N	N	N	Y
20 Oakar	Y	Y	N	N	Y	N	Y	Y
21 Stokes	Y	Y	Y	N	N	N	?	Y
OKLAHOMA								
1 ***Inhofe***	N	Y	N	N	Y	Y	N	N
2 Synar	Y	Y	N	N	N	N	N	Y
3 Brewster	Y	?	N	N	N	N	N	N
4 McCurdy	N	Y	N	N	N	?	?	?
5 ***Edwards***	N	Y	N	Y	N	Y	N	N
6 English	N	Y	N	Y	N	N	N	N
OREGON								
1 AuCoin	Y	Y	Y	Y	N	N	N	Y
2 ***Smith***	N	Y	N	Y	Y	Y	N	N
3 Wyden	Y	Y	Y	N	N	N	N	Y
4 DeFazio	Y	Y	Y	Y	N	N	N	Y
5 Kopetski	Y	Y	N	Y	N	N	Y	N
PENNSYLVANIA								
1 Foglietta	Y	Y	Y	N	N	N	Y	Y
2 Vacancy								
3 Borski	Y	Y	Y	N	N	N	N	Y
4 Kolter	N	Y	N	N	N	N	N	N
5 ***Schulze***	N	Y	N	Y	N	Y	Y	N
6 Yatron	N	Y	N	N	Y	N	Y	Y
7 ***Weldon***	N	Y	N	N	Y	Y	Y	Y
8 Kostmayer	Y	Y	N	N	N	N	N	Y
9 ***Shuster***	N	Y	N	Y	N	Y	N	N
10 ***McDade***	N	Y	N	Y	N	Y	N	N
11 Kanjorski	Y	Y	N	N	N	N	N	N
12 Murtha	Y	Y	N	N	N	?	?	?
13 ***Coughlin***	N	Y	N	Y	Y	Y	Y	N
14 Coyne	Y	Y	Y	N	N	N	Y	Y
15 ***Ritter***	N	Y	N	Y	Y	Y	Y	Y
16 ***Walker***	N	Y	N	Y	?	Y	N	Y
17 ***Gekas***	N	?	N	Y	Y	Y	Y	Y
18 ***Santorum***	N	Y	N	Y	Y	Y	N	N
19 ***Goodling***	N	Y	N	Y	Y	Y	Y	N
20 Gaydos	N	Y	N	N	N	?	?	?
21 ***Ridge***	N	Y	N	Y	Y	Y	N	N
22 Murphy	N	Y	N	N	N	N	Y	N
23 ***Clinger***	Y	Y	N	Y	Y	Y	N	N
RHODE ISLAND								
1 ***Machtley***	N	Y	N	Y	Y	Y	Y	N
2 Reed	Y	Y	N	N	N	N	N	Y
SOUTH CAROLINA								
1 ***Ravenel***	N	Y	N	Y	Y	Y	N	N
2 ***Spence***	N	Y	N	Y	Y	Y	N	N
3 Derrick	Y	Y	N	N	N	N	N	N
4 Patterson	N	Y	N	N	Y	N	N	N
5 Spratt	Y	Y	N	Y	N	N	N	N
6 Tallon	N	Y	N	Y	Y	N	N	Y

	358	359	361	362	363	364	365	366
SOUTH DAKOTA								
AL Johnson	Y	Y	Y	Y	Y	N	N	N
TENNESSEE								
1 ***Quillen***	N	Y	N	N	N	Y	N	N
2 ***Duncan***	N	Y	N	N	N	Y	N	N
3 Lloyd	?	?	?	X	?	N	N	N
4 Cooper	Y	Y	C	C	C	C	C	C
5 Clement	Y	Y	N	Y	N	N	N	N
6 Gordon	Y	Y	N	N	N	N	N	N
7 ***Sundquist***	N	Y	N	N	N	Y	N	N
8 Tanner	?	?	?	?	?	?	?	?
9 Ford	Y	Y	N	Y	N	N	Y	Y
TEXAS								
1 Chapman	Y	Y	N	N	Y	N	N	N
2 Wilson	N	Y	N	N	Y	N	N	N
3 ***Johnson***	N	Y	N	Y	Y	Y	N	?
4 Hall	N	Y	Y	N	N	N	N	N
5 Bryant	Y	Y	Y	N	N	?	?	?
6 ***Barton***	N	Y	N	N	Y	Y	Y	Y
7 ***Archer***	N	Y	N	Y	Y	Y	?	N
8 ***Fields***	N	Y	N	Y	Y	Y	N	N
9 Brooks	Y	Y	N	N	N	?	?	?
10 Pickle	Y	Y	N	Y	N	N	N	Y
11 Edwards	Y	Y	N	N	N	N	N	Y
12 Geren	Y	Y	N	Y	N	N	N	N
13 Sarpalius	Y	Y	N	N	N	N	N	N
14 Laughlin	Y	Y	N	Y	N	N	N	N
15 de la Garza	Y	Y	N	Y	N	N	N	Y
16 Coleman	N	Y	N	Y	N	N	N	Y
17 Stenholm	Y	Y	Y	N	N	N	N	N
18 Washington	Y	Y	Y	N	N	N	N	Y
19 ***Combest***	N	Y	N	N	N	Y	N	N
20 Gonzalez	Y	Y	Y	N	N	N	N	Y
21 ***Smith***	N	Y	N	Y	Y	Y	N	N
22 ***DeLay***	N	Y	N	Y	Y	#	?	N
23 Bustamante	Y	Y	N	N	N	N	N	?
24 Frost	Y	Y	N	Y	N	N	Y	Y
25 Andrews	Y	Y	N	N	Y	N	N	Y
26 ***Armey***	N	Y	N	Y	Y	Y	Y	N
27 Ortiz	Y	Y	N	N	N	N	N	Y
UTAH								
1 ***Hansen***	N	Y	N	Y	Y	Y	N	N
2 Owens	Y	Y	Y	N	Y	N	N	N
3 Orton	Y	Y	N	Y	Y	N	N	N
VERMONT								
AL *Sanders*	N	Y	Y	N	N	N	N	Y
VIRGINIA								
1 ***Bateman***	N	Y	N	Y	Y	Y	N	N
2 Pickett	N	Y	N	Y	N	N	N	N
3 ***Bliley***	N	Y	N	Y	Y	Y	Y	N
4 Sisisky	Y	Y	N	Y	N	N	N	Y
5 Payne	N	Y	N	Y	N	N	N	N
6 Olin	N	Y	N	Y	N	N	N	N
7 ***Slaughter***	?	?	?	?	?	?	?	?
8 Moran	Y	Y	Y	N	Y	N	Y	Y
9 Boucher	Y	Y	N	N	N	N	N	N
10 ***Wolf***	N	Y	N	Y	N	Y	N	N
WASHINGTON								
1 ***Miller***	N	Y	N	Y	Y	?	?	?
2 Swift	Y	Y	N	N	N	?	N	N
3 Unsoeld	Y	Y	N	N	N	N	N	N
4 ***Morrison***	N	Y	N	Y	Y	Y	N	N
5 Foley								
6 Dicks	Y	Y	N	N	N	?	N	Y
7 McDermott	Y	Y	Y	N	N	N	N	Y
8 ***Chandler***	N	Y	N	Y	Y	Y	N	N
WEST VIRGINIA								
1 Mollohan	N	Y	N	Y	N	N	N	N
2 Staggers	Y	Y	N	Y	N	N	N	N
3 Wise	Y	Y	N	N	N	N	N	N
4 Rahall	N	Y	N	N	N	N	N	N
WISCONSIN								
1 Aspin	Y	Y	N	Y	N	N	Y	Y
2 ***Klug***	N	Y	N	N	Y	Y	N	N
3 ***Gunderson***	N	Y	N	Y	N	Y	N	Y
4 Kleczka	N	Y	N	N	N	N	N	Y
5 Moody	N	Y	N	N	N	N	Y	Y
6 ***Petri***	N	Y	N	Y	N	Y	Y	Y
7 Obey	Y	Y	N	N	N	N	N	N
8 ***Roth***	N	Y	N	Y	Y	Y	Y	N
9 ***Sensenbrenner***	N	Y	N	Y	Y	Y	Y	Y
WYOMING								
AL ***Thomas***	N	Y	N	Y	Y	Y	N	N

Southern states - Ala., Ark., Fla., Ga., Ky., La., Miss., N.C., Okla., S.C., Tenn., Texas, Va.
Omitted votes are quorum calls, which CQ does not include in its vote charts.

HOUSE VOTES 367, 368, 369, 370, 371, 372, 373, 374

367. HR 6. Banking Reform/'Opt-Out' Interstate Branching. Vento, D-Minn., amendment to allow banks to open branch offices across state lines, unless a state votes to "opt out" of interstate branching within three years. Adopted 366-4: R 144-1; D 221-3 (ND 149-1, SD 72-2); I 1-0, Nov. 4, 1991.

368. HR 6. Banking Reform/'Opt-In' Interstate Branching. Richardson, D-N.M., amendment to allow banks to open branches across state lines in a particular state, only if the state votes to "opt in" by passing a law allowing interstate branching. Rejected 142-250: R 41-112; D 100-138 (ND 64-98, SD 36-40); I 1-0, Nov. 4, 1991. A "nay" was a vote supporting the president's position.

369. HR 6. Banking Reform/Interstate Branching. Sanders, I-Vt., amendment to strike Title III of the bill, which would allow banks to open branch offices across state lines. Rejected 20-374: R 4-151; D 15-223 (ND 10-155, SD 5-68); I 1-0, Nov. 4, 1991. A "nay" was a vote supporting the president's position.

370. HR 6. Banking Reform/Bank Fees. Waters, R-Calif., amendment to freeze for two years bank fees for depositors with average daily balances below $1,000. Rejected 70-336: R 0-157; D 69-179 (ND 64-107, SD 5-72); I 1-0, Nov. 4, 1991.

371. HR 6. Banking Reform/Reduced Premiums. Gradison, R-Ohio, amendment to strike the provisions of the bill that would reduce deposit insurance premiums for banks with low-cost checking accounts for low-income people and premiums for banks that provide increased assistance and lending to communities with high rates of poverty and unemployment. Rejected 204-205: R 113-45; D 91-159 (ND 55-117, SD 36-42); I 0-1, Nov. 4, 1991.

372. HR 6. Banking Reform/Deposit Insurance Coverage. Wylie, R-Ohio, amendment to roll back deposit insurance coverage to one account of $100,000 per individual for each bank plus a second $100,000 for a retirement account. Rejected 153-264: R 56-103; D 97-160 (ND 84-93, SD 13-67); I 0-1, Nov. 4, 1991.

373. HR 6. Banking Reform/Charitable Exemptions. Towns, D-N.Y., amendment to exempt charitable organizations from the $100,000 federal deposit insurance limit per bank account and provide them with unlimited deposit insurance. Rejected 63-350: R 0-159; D 63-190 (ND 55-120, SD 8-70); I 0-1, Nov. 4, 1991.

374. HR 6. Banking Reform/Recommittal Motion. Wylie, R-Ohio, motion to recommit the bill to the Banking Committee with instructions to report it back with an amendment that deletes Title IV of the bill, which would allow banks to affiliate with securities firms and limit the financial transactions and information-sharing between affiliated banks and securities firms. The motion included language to roll back provisions of state law that permit banks in limited cases to sell insurance across state lines. Rejected 160-253: R 149-10; D 11-242 (ND 3-170, SD 8-72); I 0-1, Nov. 4, 1991. A "yea" was a vote supporting the president's position.

KEY

Y Voted for (yea).
\# Paired for.
\+ Announced for.
N Voted against (nay).
X Paired against.
\- Announced against.
P Voted "present."
C Voted "present" to avoid possible conflict of interest.
? Did not vote or otherwise make a position known.

Democrats ***Republicans***
Independent

	367	368	369	370	371	372	373	374
ALABAMA								
1 ***Callahan***	Y	N	N	N	Y	N	N	Y
2 ***Dickinson***	?	N	N	N	Y	Y	N	Y
3 Browder	Y	Y	N	N	N	N	N	N
4 Bevill	Y	Y	N	N	N	N	N	N
5 Cramer	Y	Y	N	N	N	N	N	N
6 Erdreich	Y	N	N	N	N	N	N	Y
7 Harris	Y	Y	N	N	N	N	N	N
ALASKA								
AL ***Young***	Y	N	N	N	Y	N	N	Y
ARIZONA								
1 ***Rhodes***	Y	N	N	N	Y	Y	N	Y
2 Pastor	Y	Y	N	Y	N	N	N	N
3 ***Stump***	Y	N	N	N	Y	N	N	Y
4 ***Kyl***	Y	N	N	N	Y	N	N	Y
5 ***Kolbe***	Y	N	N	N	Y	Y	N	Y
ARKANSAS								
1 Alexander	?	?	N	N	Y	N	N	N
2 Thornton	Y	Y	N	N	Y	N	N	N
3 ***Hammerschmidt***	Y	N	N	N	Y	N	N	Y
4 Anthony	Y	N	N	N	Y	N	N	N
CALIFORNIA								
1 ***Riggs***	Y	N	N	N	N	N	N	Y
2 ***Herger***	N	Y	N	N	Y	Y	N	N
3 Matsui	Y	Y	N	Y	N	Y	N	N
4 Fazio	Y	N	N	Y	N	N	Y	N
5 Pelosi	?	?	?	?	?	N	Y	N
6 Boxer	Y	Y	N	Y	N	Y	Y	N
7 Miller	Y	N	N	N	Y	N	N	N
8 Dellums	Y	Y	Y	Y	N	Y	Y	N
9 Stark	Y	N	N	Y	N	Y	Y	N
10 Edwards	Y	N	N	Y	N	Y	N	N
11 Lantos	?	?	?	?	?	N	N	N
12 ***Campbell***	Y	N	N	N	Y	N	N	Y
13 Mineta	Y	N	N	Y	N	Y	Y	N
14 ***Doolittle***	Y	N	N	N	N	N	N	Y
15 Condit	Y	N	N	N	Y	N	N	N
16 Panetta	Y	N	N	N	Y	N	N	N
17 Dooley	Y	N	N	N	Y	N	N	N
18 Lehman	Y	N	N	N	Y	Y	N	N
19 ***Lagomarsino***	Y	N	N	N	N	N	N	Y
20 ***Thomas***	?	X	?	X	#	?	?	?
21 ***Gallegly***	Y	N	N	N	N	N	N	Y
22 ***Moorhead***	Y	N	N	N	Y	N	N	Y
23 Beilenson	Y	N	N	N	Y	Y	N	N
24 Waxman	Y	N	N	Y	N	Y	Y	N
25 Roybal	Y	N	N	Y	N	Y	Y	N
26 Berman	Y	N	N	N	N	N	Y	N
27 Levine	?	?	?	?	?	N	Y	N
28 Dixon	?	?	?	?	?	?	?	?
29 Waters	Y	N	N	Y	N	Y	Y	N
30 Martinez	Y	?	N	?	Y	N	N	N
31 Dymally	?	?	?	X	X	Y	Y	N
32 Anderson	Y	N	N	N	Y	N	N	N
33 ***Dreier***	Y	N	N	N	Y	Y	N	Y
34 Torres	Y	Y	N	Y	N	Y	Y	N
35 ***Lewis***	Y	N	N	N	Y	N	N	Y
36 Brown	Y	N	N	Y	N	N	Y	N
37 ***McCandless***	Y	N	N	N	Y	Y	N	Y
38 ***Dornan***	Y	N	N	N	Y	N	N	Y
39 ***Dannemeyer***	+	-	-	-	+	+	-	+
40 ***Cox***	Y	N	N	N	Y	Y	N	Y
41 ***Lowery***	?	N	N	N	Y	Y	N	Y
42 ***Rohrabacher***	Y	N	N	N	Y	Y	N	Y
43 ***Packard***	Y	N	N	N	Y	Y	N	Y
44 ***Cunningham***	Y	N	N	N	Y	N	N	Y
45 ***Hunter***	Y	N	N	N	Y	Y	N	Y
COLORADO								
1 Schroeder	Y	Y	N	Y	N	Y	N	N
2 Skaggs	Y	N	N	N	Y	Y	N	N
3 Campbell	?	?	?	?	?	?	?	?
4 ***Allard***	Y	Y	N	N	Y	N	N	Y
5 ***Hefley***	Y	Y	N	N	Y	Y	N	Y
6 ***Schaefer***	Y	Y	N	N	Y	N	N	Y
CONNECTICUT								
1 Kennelly	Y	N	N	N	N	N	N	N
2 Gejdenson	Y	N	N	N	Y	Y	Y	N
3 DeLauro	Y	N	N	N	N	N	N	N
4 ***Shays***	Y	N	N	N	N	Y	N	Y
5 ***Franks***	Y	N	N	N	Y	Y	N	Y
6 ***Johnson***	Y	N	N	N	N	Y	N	Y
DELAWARE								
AL Carper	Y	N	N	Y	N	Y	N	N
FLORIDA								
1 Hutto	Y	Y	N	N	Y	N	N	N
2 Peterson	Y	N	N	N	N	N	N	N
3 Bennett	Y	Y	Y	N	Y	Y	N	N
4 ***James***	Y	N	N	N	Y	N	N	Y
5 ***McCollum***	?	N	N	N	Y	Y	N	Y
6 ***Stearns***	Y	N	N	N	Y	Y	N	Y
7 Gibbons	Y	N	N	N	Y	N	N	N
8 ***Young***	Y	N	N	N	Y	N	N	Y
9 ***Bilirakis***	?	Y	N	N	Y	N	N	Y
10 ***Ireland***	Y	Y	N	N	Y	N	N	Y
11 Bacchus	Y	Y	N	N	N	N	N	N
12 ***Lewis***	Y	N	N	N	Y	N	N	Y
13 ***Goss***	Y	Y	N	N	Y	N	N	Y
14 Johnston	N	N	N	N	?	N	N	N
15 ***Shaw***	Y	Y	N	N	Y	N	N	Y
16 Smith	Y	N	N	N	N	Y	?	?
17 Lehman	Y	N	N	Y	N	Y	N	N
18 ***Ros-Lehtinen***	?	?	N	N	N	N	N	Y
19 Fascell	Y	N	N	N	N	Y	N	N
GEORGIA								
1 Thomas	Y	Y	N	N	N	N	N	N
2 Hatcher	?	?	?	?	N	N	N	N
3 Ray	?	?	?	?	N	N	N	N
4 Jones	Y	Y	N	N	Y	N	Y	N
5 Lewis	Y	Y	N	Y	N	N	Y	N
6 ***Gingrich***	?	?	?	N	N	Y	N	Y
7 Darden	Y	Y	N	N	N	N	N	N
8 Rowland	Y	Y	N	N	N	N	N	N
9 Jenkins	Y	N	N	N	Y	Y	N	N
10 Barnard	Y	N	N	N	N	N	N	Y
HAWAII								
1 Abercrombie	Y	Y	N	Y	N	Y	Y	N
2 Mink	?	?	?	?	?	Y	N	N
IDAHO								
1 LaRocco	Y	N	N	N	Y	N	N	N
2 Stallings	?	#	N	N	Y	N	N	N
ILLINOIS								
1 Hayes	Y	Y	N	Y	N	Y	Y	N
2 Savage	?	N	N	Y	N	Y	Y	N
3 Russo	Y	Y	N	N	Y	Y	N	N
4 Sangmeister	Y	Y	N	N	N	N	?	?
5 Lipinski	Y	Y	N	N	Y	Y	N	N
6 ***Hyde***	?	N	N	N	Y	N	N	Y
7 Collins	Y	Y	N	Y	N	Y	Y	N
8 Rostenkowski	Y	Y	N	N	N	N	N	N
9 Yates	Y	N	Y	Y	N	Y	N	N
10 ***Porter***	Y	Y	N	N	Y	N	N	Y
11 Annunzio	Y	Y	N	Y	N	N	Y	N
12 ***Crane***	Y	Y	N	N	Y	Y	N	Y
13 ***Fawell***	Y	N	N	N	Y	Y	N	Y
14 ***Hastert***	Y	N	N	N	Y	N	N	Y
15 ***Ewing***	Y	Y	N	N	N	N	N	Y
16 Cox	Y	N	N	N	N	N	N	N
17 Evans	Y	Y	Y	Y	N	Y	Y	N
18 ***Michel***	?	?	?	?	?	?	?	?
19 Bruce	Y	Y	N	N	N	N	N	N
20 Durbin	Y	Y	N	N	N	Y	N	N
21 Costello	Y	Y	N	N	Y	N	N	N
22 Poshard	Y	Y	Y	N	Y	N	N	N
INDIANA								
1 Visclosky	Y	N	N	N	N	Y	N	N
2 Sharp	Y	N	N	N	N	N	N	N
3 Roemer	Y	N	N	N	N	N	N	N

ND Northern Democrats SD Southern Democrats

	367	368	369	370	371	372	373	374
4 Long	Y	Y	N	N	N	N	N	N
5 Jontz	Y	Y	Y	N	N	N	Y	N
6 ***Burton***	Y	Y	N	N	Y	N	N	Y
7 ***Myers***	Y	Y	Y	N	Y	N	N	Y
8 McCloskey	Y	N	N	N	N	Y	N	N
9 Hamilton	Y	N	N	N	Y	N	N	Y
10 Jacobs	Y	N	N	N	Y	N	N	N
IOWA								
1 ***Leach***	Y	N	N	N	Y	Y	N	N
2 ***Nussle***	Y	N	N	N	N	N	N	Y
3 Nagle	Y	Y	?	N	Y	N	Y	N
4 Smith	Y	N	N	N	Y	N	N	N
5 ***Lightfoot***	Y	N	N	N	Y	N	N	Y
6 ***Grandy***	Y	N	N	N	N	N	N	Y
KANSAS								
1 ***Roberts***	Y	Y	N	N	Y	N	N	Y
2 Slattery	Y	Y	N	N	N	Y	N	N
3 ***Meyers***	Y	Y	N	N	Y	Y	N	Y
4 Glickman	Y	Y	N	N	N	N	N	N
5 ***Nichols***	Y	Y	N	N	N	N	N	Y
KENTUCKY								
1 Hubbard	Y	Y	Y	N	N	N	N	Y
2 Natcher	Y	Y	N	N	N	N	N	N
3 Mazzoli	Y	Y	N	N	Y	N	N	N
4 ***Bunning***	Y	Y	N	N	Y	N	N	Y
5 ***Rogers***	Y	Y	Y	N	N	N	N	Y
6 ***Hopkins***	?	?	?	?	?	?	?	?
7 Perkins	Y	Y	Y	N	N	N	Y	N
LOUISIANA								
1 ***Livingston***	Y	N	N	N	N	Y	N	Y
2 Jefferson	Y	Y	N	Y	N	N	Y	N
3 Tauzin	Y	N	N	N	N	N	N	N
4 ***McCrery***	Y	N	N	N	Y	N	N	Y
5 Huckaby	Y	N	N	N	Y	N	N	N
6 ***Baker***	Y	N	N	N	N	N	N	Y
7 Hayes	Y	N	N	N	Y	N	N	N
8 ***Holloway***	?	?	?	N	N	N	N	Y
MAINE								
1 Andrews	Y	Y	N	Y	N	N	N	N
2 ***Snowe***	Y	N	N	N	Y	N	N	Y
MARYLAND								
1 ***Gilchrest***	Y	N	N	N	N	N	N	Y
2 ***Bentley***	?	?	N	N	Y	Y	N	N
3 Cardin	Y	N	N	N	Y	Y	N	N
4 McMillen	Y	N	N	N	Y	N	N	N
5 Hoyer	Y	N	N	N	N	Y	N	N
6 Byron	?	N	N	N	Y	N	N	N
7 Mfume	Y	Y	N	Y	N	Y	Y	N
8 ***Morella***	Y	Y	N	N	Y	Y	N	Y
MASSACHUSETTS								
1 Olver	Y	Y	N	Y	N	Y	N	N
2 Neal	?	N	N	Y	N	N	N	N
3 Early	Y	N	N	Y	N	Y	N	N
4 Frank	Y	N	N	N	N	Y	N	N
5 Atkins	Y	N	N	Y	N	Y	N	N
6 Mavroules	Y	N	N	N	N	Y	N	N
7 Markey	Y	N	N	Y	N	Y	N	N
8 Kennedy	Y	N	N	Y	N	N	Y	N
9 Moakley	Y	N	N	Y	N	Y	N	N
10 Studds	?	?	?	Y	N	Y	N	N
11 Donnelly	Y	N	N	Y	N	Y	N	N
MICHIGAN								
1 Conyers	Y	Y	Y	Y	N	Y	Y	N
2 ***Pursell***	Y	N	N	N	Y	N	N	Y
3 Wolpe	?	#	?	N	N	Y	N	N
4 ***Upton***	Y	Y	N	N	N	N	N	Y
5 ***Henry***	Y	N	N	N	Y	N	N	Y
6 Carr	Y	N	N	N	Y	N	N	N
7 Kildee	Y	Y	N	N	N	Y	N	N
8 Traxler	?	?	N	N	N	Y	N	N
9 ***Vander Jagt***	Y	Y	N	N	Y	N	N	Y
10 ***Camp***	Y	Y	N	N	Y	N	N	Y
11 ***Davis***	Y	Y	N	N	Y	N	N	Y
12 Bonior	Y	Y	N	Y	N	Y	Y	N
13 Collins	Y	N	N	Y	N	N	Y	N
14 Hertel	Y	N	N	Y	N	N	Y	N
15 Ford	?	?	?	N	N	Y	N	N
16 Dingell	Y	Y	N	N	N	N	N	N
17 Levin	Y	N	N	N	Y	N	N	N
18 ***Broomfield***	Y	N	N	N	Y	N	N	Y
MINNESOTA								
1 Penny	Y	Y	N	N	Y	Y	N	N
2 ***Weber***	Y	Y	N	N	Y	N	N	Y
3 ***Ramstad***	Y	N	N	N	Y	N	N	Y
4 Vento	Y	N	N	Y	N	Y	N	N

	367	368	369	370	371	372	373	374
5 Sabo	Y	N	N	N	N	Y	N	N
6 Sikorski	?	Y	N	N	N	Y	N	N
7 Peterson	?	Y	N	N	Y	N	N	N
8 Oberstar	Y	Y	N	N	Y	N	N	N
MISSISSIPPI								
1 Whitten	Y	N	N	N	?	N	N	N
2 Espy	Y	Y	N	Y	N	N	Y	N
3 Montgomery	Y	Y	Y	N	Y	N	N	N
4 Parker	Y	Y	Y	N	Y	N	N	N
5 Taylor	+	+	-	-	Y	N	N	N
MISSOURI								
1 Clay	?	Y	N	Y	N	Y	Y	N
2 Horn	Y	N	N	N	N	N	N	N
3 Gephardt	?	N	N	N	N	Y	N	N
4 Skelton	Y	Y	N	N	Y	N	N	N
5 Wheat	Y	Y	N	Y	N	N	Y	N
6 ***Coleman***	Y	Y	N	N	Y	N	N	Y
7 ***Hancock***	Y	N	N	N	Y	N	N	Y
8 ***Emerson***	Y	Y	N	N	Y	N	N	Y
9 Volkmer	Y	Y	Y	N	Y	N	N	N
MONTANA								
1 Williams	Y	N	N	N	N	N	N	N
2 ***Marlenee***	?	#	?	?	?	N	N	Y
NEBRASKA								
1 ***Bereuter***	Y	N	N	N	Y	N	N	Y
2 Hoagland	Y	N	N	N	Y	N	N	Y
3 ***Barrett***	Y	N	N	N	Y	N	N	Y
NEVADA								
1 Bilbray	Y	N	N	N	Y	N	Y	N
2 ***Vucanovich***	Y	N	N	N	Y	N	N	Y
NEW HAMPSHIRE								
1 ***Zeliff***	Y	N	N	N	Y	N	N	Y
2 Swett	Y	N	N	N	N	N	N	N
NEW JERSEY								
1 Andrews	Y	N	N	N	Y	N	Y	N
2 Hughes	Y	Y	N	N	Y	Y	N	N
3 Pallone	Y	Y	N	Y	Y	N	N	N
4 ***Smith***	Y	N	N	N	N	N	N	Y
5 ***Roukema***	Y	N	N	N	Y	N	N	N
6 Dwyer	?	?	?	?	?	?	?	?
7 ***Rinaldo***	Y	N	N	N	Y	N	N	Y
8 Roe	Y	N	N	N	N	N	N	N
9 Torricelli	Y	N	N	Y	Y	Y	N	N
10 Payne	?	?	?	Y	N	Y	Y	N
11 ***Gallo***	Y	N	N	N	Y	N	N	Y
12 ***Zimmer***	Y	N	N	N	Y	Y	N	N
13 ***Saxton***	Y	N	N	N	Y	N	N	Y
14 Guarini	?	X	N	N	Y	Y	N	N
NEW MEXICO								
1 ***Schiff***	Y	Y	N	N	N	N	N	Y
2 ***Skeen***	Y	Y	N	N	N	N	N	Y
3 Richardson	Y	Y	Y	N	N	N	N	N
NEW YORK								
1 Hochbrueckner	Y	N	N	N	N	Y	N	N
2 Downey	Y	N	N	N	N	Y	N	N
3 Mrazek	?	?	?	?	?	?	?	?
4 ***Lent***	Y	N	N	N	Y	Y	N	Y
5 ***McGrath***	Y	N	N	N	Y	Y	N	N
6 Flake	Y	N	N	Y	N	N	Y	N
7 Ackerman	Y	N	N	Y	N	N	Y	N
8 Scheuer	Y	N	N	N	N	Y	Y	N
9 Manton	?	N	N	N	N	N	Y	N
10 Schumer	Y	N	N	N	N	Y	N	N
11 Towns	?	Y	N	Y	N	Y	Y	N
12 Owens	Y	N	Y	Y	N	Y	Y	N
13 Solarz	Y	N	N	N	N	N	N	N
14 ***Molinari***	?	X	?	?	Y	Y	N	Y
15 ***Green***	?	?	?	?	#	?	?	?
16 Rangel	?	N	N	Y	N	Y	Y	N
17 Weiss	Y	N	N	Y	N	Y	Y	N
18 Serrano	Y	Y	N	Y	N	N	Y	N
19 Engel	?	N	N	Y	N	Y	Y	N
20 Lowey	-	N	N	N	N	N	Y	N
21 ***Fish***	Y	N	N	N	N	N	N	N
22 ***Gilman***	Y	N	N	N	N	N	N	Y
23 McNulty	Y	N	N	N	N	Y	N	N
24 ***Solomon***	Y	Y	N	N	Y	Y	N	Y
25 ***Boehlert***	Y	N	N	N	N	N	N	Y
26 ***Martin***	Y	N	N	N	Y	Y	N	Y
27 ***Walsh***	Y	N	N	N	Y	Y	N	N
28 McHugh	?	?	N	N	N	N	N	N
29 ***Horton***	Y	N	N	N	N	N	N	Y
30 Slaughter	Y	N	N	Y	N	N	N	N
31 ***Paxon***	Y	N	N	N	Y	N	N	Y

	367	368	369	370	371	372	373	374
32 LaFalce	N	N	N	N	N	N	N	N
33 Nowak	Y	N	?	Y	Y	Y	N	N
34 ***Houghton***	Y	N	N	N	Y	Y	N	Y
NORTH CAROLINA								
1 Jones	Y	Y	N	N	N	N	N	N
2 Valentine	Y	N	?	N	Y	Y	N	N
3 Lancaster	Y	N	N	N	Y	N	N	N
4 Price	Y	N	N	N	N	Y	N	N
5 Neal	Y	N	N	N	N	N	N	Y
6 ***Coble***	Y	N	N	N	Y	N	N	Y
7 Rose	?	?	?	N	N	N	N	N
8 Hefner	Y	N	N	N	Y	N	N	N
9 ***McMillan***	Y	N	N	N	Y	N	N	Y
10 ***Ballenger***	Y	N	N	N	Y	Y	N	Y
11 ***Taylor***	Y	N	N	N	N	N	N	Y
NORTH DAKOTA								
AL Dorgan	Y	Y	Y	N	Y	N	N	N
OHIO								
1 Luken	Y	N	N	N	N	N	N	N
2 ***Gradison***	Y	N	N	N	Y	Y	N	Y
3 Hall	Y	N	N	N	N	N	Y	N
4 ***Oxley***	Y	N	N	N	Y	Y	N	Y
5 ***Gillmor***	Y	Y	N	N	Y	N	N	Y
6 ***McEwen***	Y	N	N	N	X	?	?	?
7 ***Hobson***	Y	N	N	N	N	N	N	Y
8 ***Boehner***	Y	N	N	N	Y	N	N	Y
9 Kaptur	Y	Y	N	Y	N	Y	Y	N
10 ***Miller***	Y	N	Y	N	Y	Y	N	Y
11 Eckart	Y	Y	N	N	N	N	N	N
12 ***Kasich***	Y	N	N	N	N	Y	N	Y
13 Pease	?	N	N	N	Y	Y	N	N
14 Sawyer	Y	N	N	N	Y	N	N	N
15 ***Wylie***	Y	N	N	N	N	Y	N	Y
16 ***Regula***	Y	N	N	N	Y	N	N	Y
17 Traficant	Y	Y	N	Y	N	Y	Y	N
18 Applegate	Y	Y	N	N	Y	N	N	N
19 Feighan	Y	N	N	N	N	N	N	N
20 Oakar	Y	N	N	Y	N	N	Y	N
21 Stokes	Y	Y	N	Y	N	Y	Y	N
OKLAHOMA								
1 ***Inhofe***	Y	N	N	N	Y	N	N	Y
2 Synar	Y	Y	N	N	N	N	N	N
3 Brewster	Y	N	N	N	N	N	N	N
4 McCurdy	Y	N	N	N	N	N	?	N
5 ***Edwards***	Y	Y	N	N	N	N	N	N
6 English	Y	Y	N	N	N	N	N	N
OREGON								
1 AuCoin	Y	N	N	Y	N	Y	N	N
2 ***Smith***	Y	N	N	N	Y	N	N	Y
3 Wyden	Y	N	N	Y	N	N	N	N
4 DeFazio	Y	N	N	Y	N	Y	N	N
5 Kopetski	Y	N	N	N	Y	N	N	N
PENNSYLVANIA								
1 Foglietta	Y	N	N	Y	N	Y	?	?
2 Vacancy								
3 Borski	?	?	?	N	N	N	N	N
4 Kolter	Y	N	N	N	N	N	N	N
5 ***Schulze***	Y	Y	N	N	Y	Y	N	Y
6 Yatron	Y	Y	N	N	Y	N	N	N
7 ***Weldon***	?	Y	N	N	N	Y	N	Y
8 Kostmayer	Y	N	N	Y	N	Y	N	N
9 ***Shuster***	Y	N	N	N	N	Y	N	Y
10 ***McDade***	Y	N	N	N	N	N	N	Y
11 Kanjorski	Y	N	N	N	Y	Y	N	N
12 Murtha	Y	N	N	N	N	N	N	N
13 ***Coughlin***	Y	N	N	N	Y	N	N	Y
14 Coyne	Y	N	N	Y	N	Y	Y	N
15 ***Ritter***	?	N	N	N	N	Y	N	Y
16 ***Walker***	Y	N	N	N	N	N	N	Y
17 ***Gekas***	Y	N	N	N	Y	Y	N	Y
18 ***Santorum***	Y	N	N	N	N	Y	N	Y
19 ***Goodling***	Y	N	N	N	N	Y	N	Y
20 Gaydos	Y	Y	N	N	Y	N	N	N
21 ***Ridge***	Y	N	N	N	N	N	N	Y
22 Murphy	Y	Y	N	N	Y	Y	Y	?
23 ***Clinger***	Y	N	N	N	Y	Y	N	Y
RHODE ISLAND								
1 ***Machtley***	Y	N	N	N	Y	N	N	Y
2 Reed	Y	N	N	N	N	Y	N	N
SOUTH CAROLINA								
1 ***Ravenel***	Y	N	N	N	N	N	N	Y
2 ***Spence***	Y	N	N	N	Y	N	N	Y
3 Derrick	Y	N	N	N	Y	Y	N	N
4 Patterson	Y	N	N	N	Y	N	N	N
5 Spratt	Y	N	N	N	N	N	N	Y
6 Tallon	Y	N	N	N	N	N	N	Y

	367	368	369	370	371	372	373	374
SOUTH DAKOTA								
AL Johnson	Y	Y	N	N	Y	N	N	N
TENNESSEE								
1 ***Quillen***	Y	Y	N	N	Y	N	N	Y
2 ***Duncan***	Y	Y	Y	N	N	N	N	Y
3 Lloyd	Y	Y	?	N	N	N	N	N
4 Cooper	C	C	C	C	C	C	C	C
5 Clement	Y	Y	N	N	Y	N	N	Y
6 Gordon	Y	N	N	N	Y	N	N	N
7 ***Sundquist***	?	?	?	?	Y	N	N	Y
8 Tanner	Y	Y	N	N	Y	N	N	N
9 Ford	?	?	?	?	?	?	?	?
TEXAS								
1 Chapman	?	?	?	?	?	?	?	?
2 Wilson	Y	Y	N	N	Y	N	N	N
3 ***Johnson***	Y	N	N	N	Y	Y	N	Y
4 Hall	Y	N	N	N	Y	N	N	Y
5 Bryant	?	?	?	?	?	?	?	?
6 ***Barton***	Y	Y	N	N	Y	N	N	N
7 ***Archer***	Y	N	N	N	Y	N	N	Y
8 ***Fields***	Y	N	N	N	Y	N	N	Y
9 Brooks	Y	Y	N	N	C	C	C	N
10 Pickle	Y	N	N	N	Y	N	N	N
11 Edwards	Y	Y	?	N	Y	N	N	N
12 Geren	Y	Y	N	N	Y	N	N	N
13 Sarpalius	N	Y	N	N	Y	N	N	N
14 Laughlin	?	N	N	N	Y	N	N	N
15 de la Garza	Y	Y	N	N	N	N	N	N
16 Coleman	Y	N	N	N	N	Y	N	N
17 Stenholm	Y	Y	N	N	Y	N	N	N
18 Washington	Y	Y	?	?	N	Y	Y	N
19 ***Combest***	Y	N	N	N	Y	N	N	Y
20 Gonzalez	Y	N	N	Y	N	Y	Y	N
21 ***Smith***	?	N	N	N	Y	N	N	Y
22 ***DeLay***	Y	N	N	N	Y	Y	N	Y
23 Bustamante	Y	N	N	N	N	N	N	N
24 Frost	Y	N	N	N	N	N	N	N
25 Andrews	Y	N	N	N	N	N	N	N
26 ***Armey***	Y	N	N	N	Y	Y	N	Y
27 Ortiz	?	Y	N	N	N	N	N	N
UTAH								
1 ***Hansen***	Y	N	N	N	Y	N	N	Y
2 Owens	Y	N	N	N	Y	N	N	N
3 Orton	Y	N	N	N	N	N	N	N
VERMONT								
AL *Sanders*	Y	Y	Y	Y	N	N	N	N
VIRGINIA								
1 ***Bateman***	Y	N	N	N	Y	N	N	Y
2 Pickett	Y	N	N	N	Y	N	N	N
3 ***Bliley***	Y	N	N	N	N	Y	N	Y
4 Sisisky	Y	N	N	N	Y	N	N	N
5 Payne	Y	N	N	N	Y	Y	N	N
6 Olin	Y	N	N	N	Y	Y	N	N
7 ***Slaughter***	?	?	?	?	?	?	?	?
8 Moran	Y	N	N	N	N	N	Y	N
9 Boucher	Y	N	N	N	Y	N	N	N
10 ***Wolf***	Y	N	N	N	N	Y	N	Y
WASHINGTON								
1 ***Miller***	Y	N	N	N	N	Y	N	Y
2 Swift	Y	Y	N	N	N	N	N	N
3 Unsoeld	Y	Y	N	N	N	Y	N	N
4 ***Morrison***	Y	N	N	N	N	N	N	Y
5 Foley								
6 Dicks	Y	Y	N	N	Y	N	N	N
7 McDermott	Y	N	N	Y	N	Y	Y	N
8 ***Chandler***	Y	Y	N	N	Y	N	N	Y
WEST VIRGINIA								
1 Mollohan	Y	Y	N	N	Y	N	N	N
2 Staggers	Y	N	N	N	N	Y	N	N
3 Wise	Y	Y	N	N	N	N	N	N
4 Rahall	Y	Y	N	N	Y	N	Y	N
WISCONSIN								
1 Aspin	Y	Y	N	N	Y	N	N	Y
2 ***Klug***	Y	Y	N	N	Y	N	N	Y
3 ***Gunderson***	Y	Y	N	N	Y	N	N	Y
4 Kleczka	Y	N	N	N	Y	Y	N	N
5 Moody	Y	Y	N	N	N	N	Y	?
6 ***Petri***	Y	Y	N	N	Y	Y	N	Y
7 Obey	Y	Y	N	N	Y	N	N	N
8 ***Roth***	Y	N	N	N	N	N	N	Y
9 ***Sensenbrenner***	Y	Y	N	N	Y	Y	N	Y
WYOMING								
AL ***Thomas***	Y	N	N	N	Y	N	N	Y

Southern states - Ala., Ark., Fla., Ga., Ky., La., Miss., N.C., Okla., S.C., Tenn., Texas, Va.
Omitted votes are quorum calls, which CQ does not include in its vote charts.

HOUSE VOTES 375, 376, 377, 378, 379, 380, 381, 382

375. HR 6. Banking Reform/Passage. Passage of the bill to restructure the banking industry, overhaul the federal bank deposit insurance system and allow the Federal Deposit Insurance Corporation to borrow $30 billion to cover losses in failed banks. Rejected 89-324: R 6-153; D 83-170 (ND 69-105, SD 14-65); I 0-1, Nov. 4, 1991. A "nay" was a vote supporting the president's position.

376. Procedural Motion. Bonior, D-Mich., motion to approve the House Journal of Tuesday, Nov. 5. Motion agreed to 278-107: R 45-102; D 232-5 (ND 155-5, SD 77-0); I 1-0, Nov. 6, 1991.

377. H Res 268. Term Limits. Gephardt, D-Mo., motion to table (kill) the resolution stating that the House had taken no position on the constitutionality of term limits for members of Congress and that the House clerk should notify the Florida Supreme Court that the House regrets the assistance of the House legal counsel in drafting a brief contesting the constitutionality of term limits. Motion agreed to 265-160: R 6-157; D 258-3 (ND 174-3, SD 84-0); I 1-0, Nov. 6, 1991.

378. HR 3350. Civil Rights Commission Reauthorization/Passage. Brooks, D-Texas, motion to suspend the rules and agree to the Senate amendment to the bill (thus clearing the measure for the president) to reauthorize the Civil Rights Commission for fiscal 1992-94. Motion agreed to 420-7: R 157-7; D 262-0 (ND 178-0, SD 84-0); I 1-0, Nov. 6, 1991. A two-thirds majority of those present and voting (285 in this case) is required for passage under suspension of the rules.

379. HR 3298. Farm Credit Bank Safety and Soundness Act/Passage. De la Garza, D-Texas, motion to suspend the rules and pass the bill to improve the financial safety and soundness of farm credit banks by tightening regulation. Motion rejected 221-203: R 74-89; D 146-114 (ND 97-80, SD 49-34); I 1-0, Nov. 6, 1991. A two-thirds majority of those present and voting (283 in this case) is required for passage under suspension of the rules.

380. HR 2707. Fiscal 1992 Labor, HHS and Education Appropriations/Conference Report. Adoption of the conference report to provide $204,919,763,000 in new budget authority for the Departments of Labor, Health and Human Services, and Education and related agencies, $176,796,071,000 in fiscal 1992, $27,848,692,000 in fiscal 1993, and $275,000,000 in fiscal 1994. The administration requested $200,611,414,000. The bill would block enforcing the administration rule, known as the "gag rule," barring abortion counseling in federally funded family planning clinics. The measure also includes more than $4 billion worth of delayed obligations, funds that will not be available until the end of fiscal year 1992 or early in fiscal year 1993. Adopted 272-156: R 51-113; D 220-43 (ND 152-27, SD 68-16); I 1-0, Nov. 6, 1991. A "nay" was a vote supporting the president's position.

381. HR 2707. Fiscal 1992 Labor, HHS and Education Appropriations/Summer Youth Employment Programs. Natcher, D-Ky., motion to recede and concur in the Senate amendment with an amendment to change the availability of $187 million for summer youth employment programs to Oct. 1, 1992, instead of July 1, 1992, as originally proposed in both the House and Senate bills. The amendment also includes $73 million for Job Corps rehabilitations. Motion agreed to 250-175: R 26-138; D 223-37 (ND 161-16, SD 62-21); I 1-0, Nov. 6, 1991.

382. HR 2707. Fiscal 1992 Labor, HHS and Education Appropriations/Healthy Start Program. Natcher, D-Ky., motion to recede and concur in the Senate amendment with an amendment to provide $125 million in delayed obligations, funds that will not become available until the last day of the fiscal year, for the Healthy Start Program, of which $25 million is designated for the Healthy Start infant mortality program. Motion agreed to 253-168: R 29-132; D 223-36 (ND 163-14, SD 60-22); I 1-0, Nov. 6, 1991.

[1] *Rep. D. French Slaughter Jr. resigned Nov. 5, 1991, for health reasons. The last vote for which he was eligible was 375.*

KEY

- Y Voted for (yea).
- # Paired for.
- + Announced for.
- N Voted against (nay).
- X Paired against.
- - Announced against.
- P Voted "present."
- C Voted "present" to avoid possible conflict of interest.
- ? Did not vote or otherwise make a position known.

Democrats ***Republicans*** *Independent*

	375	376	377	378	379	380	381	382
ALABAMA								
1 ***Callahan***	N	Y	N	Y	N	N	N	N
2 ***Dickinson***	N	?	N	Y	N	Y	N	N
3 Browder	N	Y	Y	Y	N	Y	Y	Y
4 Bevill	N	Y	Y	Y	N	Y	Y	Y
5 Cramer	N	Y	Y	Y	N	Y	Y	Y
6 Erdreich	N	Y	Y	Y	N	Y	Y	Y
7 Harris	N	Y	Y	Y	N	Y	Y	Y
ALASKA								
AL ***Young***	N	N	N	Y	Y	N	N	Y
ARIZONA								
1 ***Rhodes***	N	N	N	Y	N	N	N	N
2 Pastor	N	Y	Y	Y	Y	Y	Y	Y
3 ***Stump***	N	N	N	N	N	N	N	N
4 ***Kyl***	N	N	N	Y	N	N	N	N
5 ***Kolbe***	N	N	N	Y	N	N	N	N
ARKANSAS								
1 Alexander	N	?	Y	Y	Y	Y	Y	Y
2 Thornton	N	Y	Y	Y	Y	Y	Y	Y
3 ***Hammerschmidt***	N	Y	Y	Y	Y	N	N	N
4 Anthony	N	Y	Y	Y	N	Y	Y	Y
CALIFORNIA								
1 ***Riggs***	N	N	N	Y	Y	N	N	N
2 ***Herger***	N	N	N	N	Y	N	N	N
3 Matsui	Y	Y	Y	Y	Y	Y	Y	Y
4 Fazio	Y	?	Y	Y	N	Y	Y	Y
5 Pelosi	Y	Y	Y	Y	N	Y	Y	Y
6 Boxer	N	Y	Y	Y	N	Y	Y	Y
7 Miller	N	Y	Y	Y	Y	Y	Y	Y
8 Dellums	N	Y	Y	Y	N	Y	Y	Y
9 Stark	N	Y	Y	Y	N	Y	Y	Y
10 Edwards	Y	Y	Y	Y	N	Y	Y	Y
11 Lantos	N	Y	Y	Y	N	Y	Y	Y
12 ***Campbell***	N	N	N	Y	N	Y	N	N
13 Mineta	N	Y	Y	Y	N	Y	Y	Y
14 ***Doolittle***	N	N	N	Y	N	N	N	N
15 Condit	N	Y	Y	Y	Y	Y	N	N
16 Panetta	Y	Y	Y	Y	Y	Y	N	N
17 Dooley	N	Y	Y	Y	Y	Y	Y	Y
18 Lehman	Y	Y	Y	Y	Y	Y	Y	Y
19 ***Lagomarsino***	N	N	N	Y	Y	N	N	N
20 ***Thomas***	?	N	N	Y	Y	Y	N	N
21 ***Gallegly***	N	N	N	Y	N	N	N	N
22 ***Moorhead***	N	N	N	Y	N	N	N	N
23 Beilenson	Y	Y	Y	Y	N	Y	N	N
24 Waxman	Y	Y	Y	Y	N	Y	Y	Y
25 Roybal	Y	Y	Y	Y	?	Y	Y	Y
26 Berman	Y	Y	Y	Y	N	Y	Y	Y
27 Levine	N	Y	Y	Y	N	Y	Y	Y
28 Dixon	?	?	Y	Y	Y	Y	Y	Y
29 Waters	N	Y	?	Y	N	Y	Y	Y
30 Martinez	N	?	?	?	?	?	?	?
31 Dymally	Y	Y	?	?	?	Y	Y	Y
32 Anderson	N	Y	Y	Y	Y	Y	Y	Y
33 ***Dreier***	N	Y	N	Y	N	N	N	N
34 Torres	Y	Y	Y	Y	Y	Y	Y	Y
35 ***Lewis***	N	N	N	Y	N	N	Y	Y
36 Brown	N	Y	Y	Y	Y	Y	Y	Y
37 ***McCandless***	N	N	N	Y	N	N	N	N
38 ***Dornan***	N	N	N	Y	?	N	N	N
39 ***Dannemeyer***	-	N	N	Y	N	N	N	N
40 ***Cox***	N	N	N	Y	N	N	N	N
41 ***Lowery***	N	?	N	Y	N	N	N	N
42 ***Rohrabacher***	N	N	N	Y	N	N	N	N
43 ***Packard***	N	Y	N	Y	N	N	N	N
44 ***Cunningham***	N	N	N	Y	N	N	N	N
45 ***Hunter***	N	N	N	Y	N	N	N	N
COLORADO								
1 Schroeder	Y	N	Y	Y	N	Y	Y	Y
2 Skaggs	N	Y	Y	Y	Y	Y	N	Y
3 Campbell	?	Y	Y	Y	Y	Y	Y	Y
4 ***Allard***	N	N	N	Y	Y	N	N	N
5 ***Hefley***	N	?	N	Y	Y	N	N	N
6 ***Schaefer***	N	N	N	Y	N	N	N	N
CONNECTICUT								
1 Kennelly	Y	Y	Y	Y	N	Y	Y	Y
2 Gejdenson	N	Y	Y	Y	Y	Y	Y	Y
3 DeLauro	Y	Y	Y	Y	N	Y	Y	Y
4 ***Shays***	N	N	N	Y	N	Y	N	N
5 ***Franks***	N	N	N	Y	N	Y	N	N
6 ***Johnson***	N	?	N	Y	N	Y	N	N
DELAWARE								
AL Carper	N	Y	Y	Y	N	Y	N	N
FLORIDA								
1 Hutto	N	Y	Y	Y	Y	N	N	N
2 Peterson	N	Y	Y	Y	N	Y	Y	Y
3 Bennett	N	Y	Y	Y	Y	N	Y	N
4 ***James***	N	?	N	Y	Y	N	N	N
5 ***McCollum***	N	N	N	Y	N	N	N	N
6 ***Stearns***	N	N	N	Y	Y	N	N	N
7 Gibbons	Y	Y	Y	Y	Y	Y	Y	Y
8 ***Young***	N	Y	N	Y	N	N	N	N
9 ***Bilirakis***	N	N	N	Y	N	N	N	N
10 ***Ireland***	N	N	N	Y	N	N	N	N
11 Bacchus	N	Y	Y	Y	N	Y	Y	Y
12 ***Lewis***	N	N	N	Y	Y	N	N	N
13 ***Goss***	N	N	N	Y	N	N	N	N
14 Johnston	Y	Y	Y	Y	N	Y	Y	Y
15 ***Shaw***	N	Y	N	Y	N	N	N	N
16 Smith	#	Y	Y	Y	Y	Y	Y	?
17 Lehman	Y	Y	Y	Y	N	Y	Y	Y
18 ***Ros-Lehtinen***	N	N	N	Y	Y	N	N	N
19 Fascell	Y	Y	Y	Y	N	Y	Y	Y
GEORGIA								
1 Thomas	N	Y	Y	Y	Y	Y	Y	Y
2 Hatcher	N	Y	Y	Y	Y	Y	Y	Y
3 Ray	N	?	Y	Y	Y	N	N	N
4 Jones	Y	Y	Y	Y	Y	Y	Y	Y
5 Lewis	Y	Y	Y	Y	Y	Y	Y	Y
6 ***Gingrich***	N	?	N	Y	N	N	N	N
7 Darden	N	Y	Y	Y	Y	Y	Y	Y
8 Rowland	N	Y	Y	Y	N	Y	N	N
9 Jenkins	N	Y	Y	Y	N	Y	Y	Y
10 Barnard	N	Y	Y	Y	Y	N	N	N
HAWAII								
1 Abercrombie	Y	Y	Y	Y	Y	Y	Y	Y
2 Mink	Y	Y	Y	Y	Y	Y	Y	Y
IDAHO								
1 LaRocco	N	Y	Y	Y	Y	Y	Y	Y
2 Stallings	N	Y	Y	Y	Y	N	Y	Y
ILLINOIS								
1 Hayes	Y	Y	Y	Y	Y	Y	Y	Y
2 Savage	N	Y	Y	Y	Y	Y	Y	Y
3 Russo	N	Y	Y	Y	N	Y	Y	Y
4 Sangmeister	?	?	?	?	?	?	?	?
5 Lipinski	N	?	Y	Y	N	N	Y	Y
6 ***Hyde***	N	?	Y	Y	N	N	N	N
7 Collins	Y	Y	Y	Y	Y	Y	Y	Y
8 Rostenkowski	N	Y	Y	Y	N	Y	?	?
9 Yates	Y	Y	Y	Y	N	Y	Y	Y
10 ***Porter***	N	Y	N	Y	N	Y	N	N
11 Annunzio	Y	Y	Y	Y	Y	N	Y	Y
12 ***Crane***	N	N	N	N	N	N	N	N
13 ***Fawell***	N	N	N	Y	N	Y	N	N
14 ***Hastert***	N	N	N	Y	Y	N	N	N
15 ***Ewing***	N	Y	N	Y	Y	N	N	N
16 Cox	N	Y	Y	Y	Y	Y	Y	Y
17 Evans	N	Y	Y	Y	Y	Y	Y	Y
18 ***Michel***	?	N	N	Y	N	N	N	N
19 Bruce	Y	Y	Y	Y	Y	Y	Y	Y
20 Durbin	N	Y	Y	Y	Y	Y	Y	Y
21 Costello	N	Y	Y	Y	Y	N	Y	Y
22 Poshard	N	Y	Y	Y	Y	N	Y	Y
INDIANA								
1 Visclosky	N	Y	Y	Y	N	Y	Y	Y
2 Sharp	N	Y	Y	Y	N	Y	Y	Y
3 Roemer	N	Y	Y	Y	Y	Y	Y	Y

ND Northern Democrats SD Southern Democrats

	375	376	377	378	379	380	381	382
4 Long	N	Y	Y	Y	Y	Y	Y	Y
5 Jontz	N	Y	Y	Y	Y	Y	Y	Y
6 ***Burton***	N	N	N	Y	Y	N	N	N
7 ***Myers***	N	Y	N	Y	N	Y	Y	?
8 McCloskey	N	Y	Y	Y	Y	Y	Y	Y
9 Hamilton	N	Y	Y	Y	Y	Y	Y	Y
10 Jacobs	Y	N	Y	Y	N	Y	Y	Y
IOWA								
1 ***Leach***	Y	N	N	Y	N	Y	N	N
2 ***Nussle***	N	N	N	Y	Y	N	N	N
3 Nagle	N	Y	Y	Y	Y	Y	Y	Y
4 Smith	N	Y	Y	Y	N	Y	Y	Y
5 ***Lightfoot***	N	N	N	Y	Y	N	N	N
6 ***Grandy***	N	N	N	Y	Y	Y	N	N
KANSAS								
1 ***Roberts***	N	N	N	Y	Y	N	N	N
2 Slattery	Y	Y	Y	Y	Y	Y	N	N
3 ***Meyers***	N	?	N	Y	Y	N	Y	N
4 Glickman	Y	Y	Y	Y	Y	Y	N	N
5 ***Nichols***	N	Y	N	Y	Y	N	N	N
KENTUCKY								
1 Hubbard	N	Y	Y	Y	Y	Y	Y	Y
2 Natcher	N	Y	Y	Y	N	Y	Y	Y
3 Mazzoli	N	Y	Y	Y	Y	N	Y	Y
4 ***Bunning***	N	N	N	Y	Y	N	N	N
5 ***Rogers***	N	?	N	Y	Y	N	Y	N
6 ***Hopkins***	?	?	?	?	?	?	?	?
7 Perkins	N	Y	Y	Y	Y	Y	Y	Y
LOUISIANA								
1 ***Livingston***	N	Y	N	Y	N	N	N	Y
2 Jefferson	N	Y	Y	Y	N	Y	Y	Y
3 Tauzin	N	Y	Y	Y	N	N	N	N
4 ***McCrery***	N	?	N	Y	N	N	N	N
5 Huckaby	N	Y	Y	Y	N	N	N	N
6 ***Baker***	N	N	N	Y	N	N	N	N
7 Hayes	N	Y	?	?	?	?	?	?
8 ***Holloway***	N	N	N	Y	N	N	N	N
MAINE								
1 Andrews	N	Y	Y	Y	N	Y	Y	Y
2 ***Snowe***	N	Y	N	Y	N	Y	N	N
MARYLAND								
1 ***Gilchrest***	N	N	N	Y	Y	Y	N	N
2 ***Bentley***	N	N	N	Y	Y	Y	N	N
3 Cardin	N	Y	Y	Y	Y	Y	Y	Y
4 McMillen	N	Y	Y	Y	Y	Y	Y	Y
5 Hoyer	Y	Y	Y	Y	N	Y	Y	Y
6 Byron	N	Y	Y	Y	Y	Y	Y	Y
7 Mfume	N	?	Y	Y	Y	Y	Y	Y
8 ***Morella***	N	?	N	Y	N	Y	Y	Y
MASSACHUSETTS								
1 Olver	Y	Y	Y	Y	N	Y	Y	Y
2 Neal	Y	Y	Y	Y	N	Y	Y	Y
3 Early	Y	Y	Y	Y	N	Y	Y	Y
4 Frank	N	Y	Y	Y	N	Y	Y	Y
5 Atkins	Y	Y	Y	Y	N	Y	Y	Y
6 Mavroules	Y	Y	Y	Y	N	N	Y	Y
7 Markey	Y	Y	Y	Y	N	Y	Y	Y
8 Kennedy	N	Y	Y	Y	N	Y	Y	Y
9 Moakley	Y	Y	Y	Y	N	N	Y	Y
10 Studds	Y	Y	N	Y	N	Y	Y	Y
11 Donnelly	Y	Y	Y	Y	N	N	Y	Y
MICHIGAN								
1 Conyers	N	Y	Y	Y	Y	Y	Y	Y
2 ***Pursell***	N	Y	N	Y	Y	Y	N	N
3 Wolpe	Y	Y	Y	Y	N	Y	Y	Y
4 ***Upton***	N	N	N	Y	Y	Y	N	N
5 ***Henry***	N	N	N	Y	N	N	N	N
6 Carr	N	?	Y	Y	Y	Y	Y	Y
7 Kildee	Y	Y	Y	Y	Y	Y	Y	Y
8 Traxler	Y	Y	Y	Y	N	Y	Y	Y
9 ***Vander Jagt***	N	?	N	Y	Y	N	N	N
10 ***Camp***	N	N	N	Y	Y	N	N	N
11 ***Davis***	N	?	?	Y	Y	N	Y	N
12 Bonior	Y	Y	Y	Y	Y	Y	Y	Y
13 Collins	Y	Y	Y	Y	Y	Y	Y	Y
14 Hertel	Y	Y	Y	Y	Y	Y	Y	Y
15 Ford	N	?	Y	Y	Y	Y	Y	Y
16 Dingell	Y	Y	Y	Y	Y	Y	Y	Y
17 Levin	Y	Y	Y	Y	Y	Y	Y	Y
18 ***Broomfield***	N	Y	N	Y	N	N	N	N
MINNESOTA								
1 Penny	Y	Y	Y	Y	Y	Y	N	N
2 ***Weber***	N	N	N	Y	Y	N	N	N
3 ***Ramstad***	N	N	N	Y	Y	Y	N	N
4 Vento	Y	Y	Y	Y	Y	Y	Y	Y

	375	376	377	378	379	380	381	382
5 Sabo	Y	Y	Y	Y	Y	Y	Y	Y
6 Sikorski	Y	N	Y	Y	Y	Y	Y	Y
7 Peterson	N	Y	Y	Y	Y	N	Y	Y
8 Oberstar	N	Y	Y	Y	Y	Y	Y	?
MISSISSIPPI								
1 Whitten	N	Y	Y	Y	N	Y	Y	Y
2 Espy	N	Y	Y	Y	N	Y	Y	Y
3 Montgomery	N	Y	Y	Y	N	N	Y	Y
4 Parker	N	?	Y	Y	N	N	N	N
5 Taylor	N	Y	Y	Y	N	N	N	N
MISSOURI								
1 Clay	N	N	Y	Y	N	Y	Y	Y
2 Horn	N	Y	Y	Y	N	Y	Y	Y
3 Gephardt	Y	Y	Y	Y	Y	Y	Y	Y
4 Skelton	N	Y	Y	Y	Y	Y	N	N
5 Wheat	N	Y	Y	Y	N	Y	Y	Y
6 ***Coleman***	N	Y	N	Y	Y	Y	N	N
7 ***Hancock***	N	N	N	N	N	N	N	N
8 ***Emerson***	N	Y	N	Y	Y	N	Y	Y
9 Volkmer	N	Y	Y	Y	Y	N	Y	Y
MONTANA								
1 Williams	N	Y	Y	Y	Y	Y	Y	Y
2 ***Marlenee***	N	N	N	Y	Y	N	N	N
NEBRASKA								
1 ***Bereuter***	N	N	N	Y	N	Y	N	N
2 Hoagland	N	Y	Y	Y	Y	Y	N	N
3 ***Barrett***	N	N	N	Y	Y	N	N	N
NEVADA								
1 Bilbray	N	Y	Y	Y	Y	Y	N	Y
2 ***Vucanovich***	N	N	N	Y	N	N	N	Y
NEW HAMPSHIRE								
1 ***Zeliff***	N	N	N	Y	N	Y	N	N
2 Swett	N	Y	N	Y	N	Y	Y	Y
NEW JERSEY								
1 Andrews	N	Y	Y	Y	N	Y	Y	Y
2 Hughes	N	Y	Y	Y	N	Y	N	N
3 Pallone	N	Y	N	Y	N	Y	N	N
4 ***Smith***	N	Y	N	Y	N	N	Y	Y
5 ***Roukema***	Y	N	N	Y	N	Y	N	?
6 Dwyer	?	Y	Y	Y	N	Y	Y	Y
7 ***Rinaldo***	N	Y	N	Y	N	N	Y	Y
8 Roe	N	Y	Y	Y	N	N	Y	Y
9 Torricelli	N	?	Y	Y	N	Y	Y	Y
10 Payne	N	?	Y	Y	N	Y	Y	Y
11 ***Gallo***	N	?	N	Y	N	Y	Y	Y
12 ***Zimmer***	N	N	N	Y	N	Y	N	N
13 ***Saxton***	N	N	N	Y	N	N	N	N
14 Guarini	N	?	Y	Y	N	Y	Y	Y
NEW MEXICO								
1 ***Schiff***	N	Y	N	Y	Y	Y	Y	Y
2 ***Skeen***	N	Y	N	Y	Y	Y	Y	Y
3 Richardson	N	Y	Y	Y	Y	Y	Y	Y
NEW YORK								
1 Hochbrueckner	Y	Y	Y	Y	N	Y	Y	Y
2 Downey	Y	Y	Y	Y	Y	Y	Y	Y
3 Mrazek	?	Y	Y	Y	N	Y	Y	Y
4 ***Lent***	N	Y	N	Y	Y	N	N	Y
5 ***McGrath***	N	Y	N	Y	N	N	Y	Y
6 Flake	N	Y	Y	Y	N	Y	Y	Y
7 Ackerman	N	Y	Y	Y	N	Y	Y	Y
8 Scheuer	Y	Y	Y	Y	N	Y	Y	Y
9 Manton	Y	?	Y	Y	N	N	Y	Y
10 Schumer	Y	Y	Y	Y	N	Y	Y	Y
11 Towns	Y	?	Y	Y	N	Y	Y	Y
12 Owens	N	?	Y	Y	Y	Y	Y	Y
13 Solarz	Y	Y	Y	Y	Y	Y	Y	Y
14 ***Molinari***	N	N	N	Y	N	Y	N	N
15 ***Green***	?	Y	N	Y	N	Y	Y	Y
16 Rangel	N	Y	Y	Y	Y	Y	Y	Y
17 Weiss	Y	+	Y	Y	N	Y	Y	Y
18 Serrano	N	?	Y	Y	N	Y	Y	Y
19 Engel	N	?	Y	Y	Y	Y	Y	Y
20 Lowey	Y	?	Y	Y	Y	Y	Y	Y
21 ***Fish***	N	Y	N	Y	N	Y	N	?
22 ***Gilman***	N	Y	N	Y	N	Y	Y	Y
23 McNulty	N	Y	Y	Y	Y	Y	Y	Y
24 ***Solomon***	N	N	N	Y	N	N	N	N
25 ***Boehlert***	N	N	N	Y	Y	Y	Y	Y
26 ***Martin***	N	N	N	Y	N	Y	N	N
27 ***Walsh***	Y	N	N	Y	Y	N	Y	Y
28 McHugh	N	Y	Y	Y	Y	Y	Y	Y
29 ***Horton***	N	Y	Y	Y	Y	Y	Y	Y
30 Slaughter	N	Y	Y	Y	Y	Y	Y	Y
31 ***Paxon***	N	N	N	Y	N	N	N	N

	375	376	377	378	379	380	381	382
32 LaFalce	N	?	Y	Y	N	N	Y	Y
33 Nowak	N	Y	Y	Y	N	N	Y	Y
34 ***Houghton***	N	Y	N	Y	N	Y	Y	Y
NORTH CAROLINA								
1 Jones	N	?	Y	Y	Y	Y	Y	Y
2 Valentine	N	Y	Y	Y	N	Y	N	N
3 Lancaster	Y	Y	Y	Y	Y	Y	N	N
4 Price	N	Y	Y	Y	N	Y	Y	Y
5 Neal	N	Y	Y	Y	N	Y	Y	Y
6 ***Coble***	N	N	N	Y	N	N	N	N
7 Rose	N	Y	Y	Y	Y	Y	Y	Y
8 Hefner	N	Y	Y	Y	N	Y	Y	Y
9 ***McMillan***	N	N	N	Y	N	N	N	N
10 ***Ballenger***	N	N	N	Y	N	N	N	N
11 ***Taylor***	N	N	N	Y	Y	N	N	N
NORTH DAKOTA								
AL Dorgan	N	Y	Y	Y	Y	Y	N	N
OHIO								
1 Luken	Y	Y	Y	Y	Y	N	N	N
2 ***Gradison***	N	Y	N	Y	N	N	Y	N
3 Hall	N	?	Y	Y	Y	N	Y	Y
4 ***Oxley***	N	N	N	Y	Y	N	N	N
5 ***Gillmor***	N	Y	N	Y	Y	N	N	Y
6 ***McEwen***	?	N	N	Y	Y	N	N	N
7 ***Hobson***	N	N	N	Y	Y	Y	N	N
8 ***Boehner***	N	N	N	Y	Y	N	N	N
9 Kaptur	N	Y	Y	Y	Y	Y	Y	Y
10 ***Miller***	N	N	N	Y	N	N	N	N
11 Eckart	Y	Y	Y	Y	N	Y	Y	Y
12 ***Kasich***	N	?	N	Y	N	N	N	N
13 Pease	Y	Y	Y	Y	N	Y	Y	Y
14 Sawyer	Y	Y	Y	Y	N	Y	Y	Y
15 ***Wylie***	N	Y	N	Y	N	N	N	N
16 ***Regula***	N	N	N	Y	N	Y	Y	Y
17 Traficant	N	Y	Y	Y	Y	Y	Y	Y
18 Applegate	N	Y	Y	Y	N	N	Y	Y
19 Feighan	N	Y	Y	Y	N	Y	Y	Y
20 Oakar	Y	Y	Y	Y	Y	Y	Y	Y
21 Stokes	N	Y	Y	Y	N	Y	Y	Y
OKLAHOMA								
1 ***Inhofe***	N	N	N	Y	N	N	N	N
2 Synar	Y	Y	Y	Y	Y	Y	Y	Y
3 Brewster	N	Y	Y	Y	Y	Y	Y	Y
4 McCurdy	N	Y	Y	Y	Y	Y	N	N
5 ***Edwards***	N	?	Y	Y	Y	N	N	N
6 English	N	Y	Y	Y	Y	Y	N	N
OREGON								
1 AuCoin	N	Y	Y	Y	N	Y	Y	Y
2 ***Smith***	N	N	N	Y	Y	N	N	N
3 Wyden	Y	Y	Y	Y	Y	Y	Y	Y
4 DeFazio	N	Y	Y	Y	Y	Y	Y	Y
5 Kopetski	N	Y	Y	Y	Y	Y	Y	Y
PENNSYLVANIA								
1 Foglietta	?	?	Y	Y	N	Y	Y	Y
2 Vacancy								
3 Borski	Y	Y	Y	Y	N	N	Y	Y
4 Kolter	N	Y	Y	Y	Y	N	Y	Y
5 ***Schulze***	N	Y	N	Y	Y	N	N	N
6 Yatron	N	Y	Y	Y	N	N	Y	Y
7 ***Weldon***	N	?	N	Y	Y	Y	Y	Y
8 Kostmayer	Y	Y	Y	Y	N	Y	N	N
9 ***Shuster***	N	Y	N	Y	N	N	N	N
10 ***McDade***	N	N	Y	Y	Y	N	Y	Y
11 Kanjorski	N	Y	Y	Y	N	N	Y	Y
12 Murtha	N	Y	Y	Y	Y	Y	Y	Y
13 ***Coughlin***	N	N	N	Y	Y	Y	N	N
14 Coyne	Y	Y	Y	Y	Y	Y	Y	Y
15 ***Ritter***	N	Y	N	Y	Y	N	N	N
16 ***Walker***	N	N	N	Y	N	N	N	N
17 ***Gekas***	Y	N	N	Y	N	Y	N	Y
18 ***Santorum***	N	N	N	Y	N	N	N	N
19 ***Goodling***	N	N	N	Y	Y	Y	Y	Y
20 Gaydos	N	Y	Y	Y	N	N	Y	Y
21 ***Ridge***	N	N	N	Y	Y	Y	N	N
22 Murphy	X	N	Y	Y	Y	N	?	Y
23 ***Clinger***	N	Y	N	Y	Y	Y	Y	N
RHODE ISLAND								
1 ***Machtley***	Y	N	N	Y	N	Y	Y	Y
2 Reed	Y	Y	Y	Y	N	Y	Y	Y
SOUTH CAROLINA								
1 ***Ravenel***	N	Y	N	Y	Y	Y	N	N
2 ***Spence***	N	N	N	Y	Y	N	N	N
3 Derrick	N	Y	Y	Y	N	Y	Y	Y
4 Patterson	N	Y	Y	Y	N	Y	N	N
5 Spratt	N	Y	Y	Y	Y	Y	Y	Y
6 Tallon	N	Y	Y	Y	Y	N	Y	Y

	375	376	377	378	379	380	381	382
SOUTH DAKOTA								
AL Johnson	N	Y	Y	Y	Y	Y	Y	Y
TENNESSEE								
1 ***Quillen***	N	Y	N	Y	Y	N	N	Y
2 ***Duncan***	N	N	N	Y	Y	N	N	N
3 Lloyd	N	Y	Y	Y	Y	Y	Y	Y
4 Cooper	C	Y	Y	Y	N	Y	N	N
5 Clement	N	Y	Y	Y	N	Y	Y	Y
6 Gordon	N	Y	Y	Y	N	Y	Y	Y
7 ***Sundquist***	N	N	N	Y	Y	N	N	N
8 Tanner	N	Y	Y	Y	N	Y	Y	Y
9 Ford	?	?	Y	Y	Y	Y	Y	Y
TEXAS								
1 Chapman	?	Y	Y	Y	Y	Y	Y	Y
2 Wilson	N	?	Y	Y	?	Y	Y	Y
3 ***Johnson***	N	Y	N	Y	Y	N	N	N
4 Hall	N	Y	Y	Y	Y	N	N	N
5 Bryant	?	?	Y	Y	Y	Y	Y	Y
6 ***Barton***	N	N	N	Y	Y	N	N	N
7 ***Archer***	N	Y	N	Y	N	N	N	N
8 ***Fields***	N	N	N	Y	Y	N	N	N
9 Brooks	C	Y	Y	Y	Y	Y	Y	Y
10 Pickle	Y	Y	Y	Y	Y	Y	N	N
11 Edwards	N	Y	Y	Y	Y	Y	Y	Y
12 Geren	N	Y	Y	Y	Y	Y	N	N
13 Sarpalius	N	Y	Y	Y	Y	N	Y	Y
14 Laughlin	N	Y	Y	Y	Y	Y	N	N
15 de la Garza	N	Y	Y	Y	Y	N	Y	Y
16 Coleman	N	Y	Y	Y	Y	Y	Y	Y
17 Stenholm	N	Y	Y	Y	Y	N	N	N
18 Washington	N	Y	Y	Y	Y	Y	Y	Y
19 ***Combest***	N	Y	N	Y	Y	N	N	N
20 Gonzalez	Y	Y	Y	Y	N	Y	Y	Y
21 ***Smith***	N	N	N	Y	Y	Y	N	N
22 ***DeLay***	N	N	N	N	N	N	N	N
23 Bustamante	N	Y	Y	Y	Y	Y	Y	Y
24 Frost	Y	?	Y	Y	Y	Y	?	?
25 Andrews	N	Y	Y	Y	Y	Y	Y	Y
26 ***Armey***	N	N	N	N	N	N	N	N
27 Ortiz	Y	Y	Y	Y	Y	N	Y	Y
UTAH								
1 ***Hansen***	N	Y	N	Y	N	N	N	N
2 Owens	N	Y	Y	Y	Y	Y	Y	Y
3 Orton	N	Y	Y	Y	Y	N	Y	Y
VERMONT								
AL *Sanders*	N	Y	Y	Y	Y	Y	Y	Y
VIRGINIA								
1 ***Bateman***	N	Y	N	Y	Y	N	N	N
2 Pickett	N	Y	Y	Y	Y	Y	Y	Y
3 ***Bliley***	N	N	N	Y	N	N	N	N
4 Sisisky	N	Y	Y	Y	Y	Y	N	N
5 Payne	N	Y	Y	Y	Y	Y	N	N
6 Olin	N	Y	Y	Y	Y	Y	Y	Y
7 ***Slaughter***[1]	?							
8 Moran	Y	Y	Y	Y	N	Y	Y	Y
9 Boucher	Y	Y	Y	Y	Y	Y	Y	Y
10 ***Wolf***	N	N	N	Y	N	N	N	N
WASHINGTON								
1 ***Miller***	N	N	N	Y	N	Y	N	N
2 Swift	N	Y	Y	Y	Y	Y	Y	Y
3 Unsoeld	N	Y	Y	Y	Y	Y	Y	Y
4 ***Morrison***	N	Y	Y	Y	Y	Y	Y	Y
5 Foley								
6 Dicks	N	Y	Y	Y	N	Y	Y	Y
7 McDermott	N	Y	Y	Y	Y	Y	Y	Y
8 ***Chandler***	N	N	N	Y	Y	Y	N	N
WEST VIRGINIA								
1 Mollohan	N	Y	Y	Y	Y	N	Y	Y
2 Staggers	N	Y	Y	Y	Y	N	Y	Y
3 Wise	N	Y	Y	Y	N	Y	Y	Y
4 Rahall	N	Y	Y	Y	Y	N	Y	Y
WISCONSIN								
1 Aspin	N	Y	Y	Y	Y	Y	Y	Y
2 ***Klug***	N	?	N	Y	Y	Y	N	N
3 ***Gunderson***	N	Y	N	Y	Y	Y	N	N
4 Kleczka	Y	Y	Y	Y	Y	Y	Y	Y
5 Moody	Y	Y	Y	Y	N	Y	Y	Y
6 ***Petri***	N	Y	N	Y	N	N	N	N
7 Obey	N	Y	Y	Y	Y	Y	Y	Y
8 ***Roth***	N	Y	N	Y	Y	N	N	N
9 ***Sensenbrenner***	N	N	N	N	N	N	N	N
WYOMING								
AL ***Thomas***	N	N	N	Y	Y	N	N	N

Southern states - Ala., Ark., Fla., Ga., Ky., La., Miss., N.C., Okla., S.C., Tenn., Texas, Va.
Omitted votes are quorum calls, which CQ does not include in its vote charts.

HOUSE VOTES 383, 384, 385, 386, 387, 388, 389, 390

383. HR 2707. Fiscal 1992 Labor, HHS and Education Appropriations/Delayed Obligations. Natcher, D-Ky., motion to recede and concur en bloc with 15 Senate amendments to provide more than $4 billion in delayed obligations for various programs. By delaying the funds until the end of the fiscal year, appropriators are able to provide higher funding for programs by pushing the scoring for the higher amounts into the next fiscal year and thus staying within their spending limits for the particular year. Motion agreed to 234-188: R 31-132; D 202-56 (ND 153-24, SD 49-32); I 1-0, Nov. 6, 1991.

384. HR 2950. Surface Transportation Reauthorization. Hammerschmidt, R-Ark., motion to instruct the House conferees to insist on the House position for funding the National Highway System. Motion agreed to 394-3: R 157-2; D 236-1 (ND 161-1, SD 75-0); I 1-0, Nov. 6, 1991.

385. S 1745. Civil Rights Act of 1991/Rule. Adoption of the rule (H Res 270) to provide for House floor consideration of the bill to make it easier for workers to sue for employment discrimination, allow victims of sex bias to collect damages, and permit women and religious minorities to win compensatory and punitive damages for intentional discrimination, mainly by reversing several recent Supreme Court decisions and by expanding Title VII of the 1964 Civil Rights Act. Adopted 327-93: R 100-62; D 226-31 (ND 153-23, SD 73-8); I 1-0, Nov. 7, 1991.

386. S 1745. Civil Rights Act of 1991/Passage. Passage of the bill (thus clearing the measure for the president) to make it easier for workers to sue for employment discrimination, allow victims of sex bias to collect damages, and permit women and religious minorities to win compensatory and punitive damages for intentional discrimination, mainly by reversing several recent Supreme Court decisions and by expanding Title VII of the 1964 Civil Rights Act. Passed 381-38: R 128-33; D 252-5 (ND 172-4, SD 80-1); I 1-0, Nov. 7, 1991. A "yea" was a vote supporting the president's position.

387. Procedural Motion. DeLay, R-Texas, motion to approve the House Journal of Friday, Nov. 8. Motion agreed to 247-98: R 43-94; D 204-4 (ND 138-4, SD 66-0), Nov. 12, 1991.

388. Procedural Motion. Gephardt, D-Mo., motion to approve the House Journal of Tuesday, Nov. 12. Motion agreed to 296-121: R 45-115; D 250-6 (ND 171-6, SD 79-0); I 1-0, Nov. 13, 1991.

389. HR 2. Family and Medical Leave Act/Rule. Adoption of the rule (H Res 275) to provide for House floor consideration of the bill to require employers with 50 or more employees to provide up to 12 weeks of unpaid leave a year for a serious illness, to care for a new child, or to care for a seriously ill child, spouse or parent. Adopted 269-156: R 11-151; D 257-5 (ND 175-3, SD 82-2); I 1-0, Nov. 13, 1991.

390. HR 2. Family and Medical Leave Act/Preferential Hiring Rights. Stenholm, D-Texas, substitute amendment to allow parents of young children to take up to six years of unpaid leave and workers caring for an ill family member to take up to two years of unpaid leave and still have preferential hiring rights. Rejected 138-291: R 107-56; D 31-234 (ND 7-174, SD 24-60); I 0-1, Nov. 13, 1991.

[1] *Lucien Blackwell, D-Pa., was sworn in Nov. 13, 1991. The first vote for which he was eligible was vote 389.*

[2] *George F. Allen, R-Va., was sworn in Nov. 12, 1991. The first vote for which he was eligible was vote 388.*

KEY

- Y Voted for (yea).
- # Paired for.
- + Announced for.
- N Voted against (nay).
- X Paired against.
- \- Announced against.
- P Voted "present."
- C Voted "present" to avoid possible conflict of interest.
- ? Did not vote or otherwise make a position known.

Democrats ***Republicans*** *Independent*

	383	384	385	386	387	388	389	390
ALABAMA								
1 ***Callahan***	N	Y	N	N	Y	Y	N	Y
2 ***Dickinson***	N	Y	Y	N	?	N	N	N
3 Browder	N	?	Y	Y	Y	Y	Y	Y
4 Bevill	Y	Y	Y	Y	Y	Y	Y	N
5 Cramer	N	Y	Y	Y	Y	Y	Y	Y
6 Erdreich	N	Y	Y	Y	Y	Y	Y	N
7 Harris	N	Y	Y	Y	Y	Y	Y	Y
ALASKA								
AL ***Young***	Y	Y	Y	Y	?	?	?	?
ARIZONA								
1 ***Rhodes***	N	Y	Y	Y	N	N	N	Y
2 Pastor	Y	Y	Y	Y	?	Y	Y	N
3 ***Stump***	N	Y	N	N	N	N	N	Y
4 ***Kyl***	N	Y	N	Y	N	N	N	N
5 ***Kolbe***	N	Y	Y	Y	N	N	N	Y
ARKANSAS								
1 Alexander	Y	Y	Y	Y	?	Y	Y	N
2 Thornton	Y	Y	Y	Y	Y	Y	Y	N
3 ***Hammerschmidt***	N	Y	N	N	?	Y	N	Y
4 Anthony	Y	?	?	+	?	Y	Y	N
CALIFORNIA								
1 ***Riggs***	N	Y	N	Y	?	N	N	Y
2 ***Herger***	N	Y	N	N	N	N	N	Y
3 Matsui	Y	Y	N	Y	Y	Y	Y	N
4 Fazio	Y	Y	Y	Y	Y	Y	Y	N
5 Pelosi	Y	Y	Y	Y	?	Y	Y	N
6 Boxer	Y	Y	?	?	Y	Y	Y	N
7 Miller	Y	Y	N	Y	Y	?	Y	N
8 Dellums	Y	Y	N	Y	Y	Y	Y	N
9 Stark	Y	Y	Y	Y	?	Y	Y	N
10 Edwards	Y	Y	Y	Y	Y	Y	Y	N
11 Lantos	Y	Y	Y	Y	Y	Y	Y	N
12 ***Campbell***	N	Y	Y	Y	N	N	N	Y
13 Mineta	Y	Y	N	Y	Y	Y	Y	N
14 ***Doolittle***	N	Y	N	N	N	N	N	Y
15 Condit	N	Y	Y	Y	?	Y	Y	Y
16 Panetta	N	Y	Y	Y	Y	Y	Y	N
17 Dooley	Y	Y	Y	Y	Y	Y	Y	N
18 Lehman	Y	Y	Y	Y	?	Y	Y	N
19 ***Lagomarsino***	N	Y	Y	Y	N	N	N	Y
20 ***Thomas***	N	Y	N	Y	N	N	N	N
21 ***Gallegly***	N	Y	Y	Y	N	N	N	Y
22 ***Moorhead***	N	Y	Y	Y	N	N	N	Y
23 Beilenson	N	Y	Y	Y	Y	Y	Y	N
24 Waxman	Y	Y	N	Y	Y	Y	Y	N
25 Roybal	Y	Y	Y	Y	Y	Y	Y	N
26 Berman	Y	Y	N	Y	?	Y	Y	N
27 Levine	Y	Y	?	?	?	Y	Y	N
28 Dixon	Y	Y	Y	Y	Y	Y	Y	N
29 Waters	Y	Y	Y	Y	?	Y	Y	N
30 Martinez	?	?	Y	Y	?	Y	Y	N
31 Dymally	Y	Y	Y	Y	Y	Y	Y	N
32 Anderson	Y	Y	N	Y	?	Y	Y	N
33 ***Dreier***	N	Y	N	Y	Y	Y	N	Y
34 Torres	Y	Y	Y	Y	?	Y	Y	N
35 ***Lewis***	Y	Y	N	Y	N	N	N	Y
36 Brown	Y	Y	Y	Y	?	Y	Y	N
37 ***McCandless***	N	Y	N	Y	N	N	N	Y
38 ***Dornan***	N	Y	N	Y	Y	N	N	Y
39 ***Dannemeyer***	N	Y	N	-	-	N	N	Y
40 ***Cox***	N	Y	N	Y	N	N	N	N
41 ***Lowery***	N	Y	Y	Y	?	N	N	Y
42 ***Rohrabacher***	N	Y	N	N	N	N	N	Y
43 ***Packard***	N	Y	N	Y	Y	Y	N	N
44 ***Cunningham***	N	Y	Y	Y	N	N	N	Y
45 ***Hunter***	N	Y	Y	Y	?	N	N	Y
COLORADO								
1 Schroeder	Y	Y	N	Y	?	N	Y	N
2 Skaggs	Y	?	Y	Y	Y	Y	Y	N
3 Campbell	Y	Y	Y	Y	Y	Y	N	Y
4 ***Allard***	N	Y	N	N	N	N	N	Y
5 ***Hefley***	N	Y	N	N	N	N	N	Y
6 ***Schaefer***	N	Y	N	Y	N	N	N	N
CONNECTICUT								
1 Kennelly	Y	Y	Y	Y	Y	Y	Y	N
2 Gejdenson	Y	Y	Y	Y	Y	Y	Y	N
3 DeLauro	Y	Y	Y	Y	?	Y	Y	N
4 ***Shays***	N	Y	Y	Y	N	N	N	N
5 ***Franks***	N	Y	Y	Y	N	N	N	Y
6 ***Johnson***	N	Y	Y	Y	Y	Y	N	N
DELAWARE								
AL Carper	N	Y	Y	Y	Y	Y	Y	N
FLORIDA								
1 Hutto	N	Y	Y	Y	Y	Y	Y	Y
2 Peterson	Y	Y	Y	Y	?	Y	Y	N
3 Bennett	N	Y	N	Y	Y	Y	Y	N
4 ***James***	N	Y	Y	Y	N	N	N	N
5 ***McCollum***	N	Y	Y	Y	?	?	N	Y
6 ***Stearns***	N	Y	N	N	N	N	N	Y
7 Gibbons	Y	Y	Y	Y	?	Y	Y	N
8 ***Young***	Y	Y	Y	Y	?	N	N	N
9 ***Bilirakis***	N	Y	Y	Y	N	N	N	Y
10 ***Ireland***	N	?	Y	Y	N	N	N	Y
11 Bacchus	N	Y	Y	Y	Y	Y	Y	N
12 ***Lewis***	N	Y	N	Y	N	N	N	Y
13 ***Goss***	N	Y	N	Y	N	N	N	Y
14 Johnston	N	Y	Y	Y	?	Y	Y	N
15 ***Shaw***	N	Y	Y	Y	?	Y	N	Y
16 Smith	?	?	?	?	?	Y	Y	N
17 Lehman	Y	?	Y	Y	Y	Y	Y	N
18 ***Ros-Lehtinen***	N	Y	Y	Y	N	N	N	N
19 Fascell	Y	?	Y	Y	Y	Y	Y	N
GEORGIA								
1 Thomas	Y	Y	Y	Y	Y	Y	Y	N
2 Hatcher	Y	Y	Y	Y	?	?	?	?
3 Ray	N	Y	Y	Y	?	Y	Y	Y
4 Jones	Y	Y	Y	Y	?	Y	Y	N
5 Lewis	Y	Y	Y	Y	Y	Y	Y	N
6 ***Gingrich***	N	Y	Y	Y	N	N	N	Y
7 Darden	Y	Y	Y	Y	Y	Y	Y	N
8 Rowland	N	Y	Y	Y	Y	Y	Y	Y
9 Jenkins	Y	Y	Y	Y	Y	Y	Y	N
10 Barnard	N	?	Y	Y	Y	Y	Y	Y
HAWAII								
1 Abercrombie	Y	Y	N	N	Y	Y	Y	N
2 Mink	Y	Y	N	N	Y	Y	Y	N
IDAHO								
1 LaRocco	Y	Y	Y	Y	Y	Y	Y	N
2 Stallings	Y	Y	Y	Y	Y	Y	?	N
ILLINOIS								
1 Hayes	Y	Y	Y	Y	Y	Y	Y	N
2 Savage	Y	Y	N	Y	Y	Y	Y	N
3 Russo	N	Y	Y	N	?	Y	Y	N
4 Sangmeister	?	?	?	?	?	Y	Y	N
5 Lipinski	N	Y	N	N	?	Y	Y	N
6 ***Hyde***	N	Y	Y	Y	N	Y	N	N
7 Collins	Y	Y	Y	Y	?	Y	Y	N
8 Rostenkowski	?	?	Y	Y	Y	Y	Y	N
9 Yates	Y	?	Y	Y	Y	Y	Y	N
10 ***Porter***	N	Y	Y	Y	?	Y	N	Y
11 Annunzio	Y	Y	Y	Y	Y	Y	Y	N
12 ***Crane***	N	Y	N	N	N	N	N	Y
13 ***Fawell***	N	Y	Y	Y	?	N	N	Y
14 ***Hastert***	N	Y	N	Y	N	N	N	Y
15 ***Ewing***	N	Y	Y	Y	Y	N	N	N
16 Cox	Y	Y	Y	Y	Y	Y	Y	N
17 Evans	Y	Y	N	Y	Y	Y	Y	N
18 ***Michel***	N	Y	Y	Y	N	N	N	Y
19 Bruce	Y	Y	Y	Y	Y	Y	Y	N
20 Durbin	Y	Y	Y	Y	Y	Y	Y	N
21 Costello	N	Y	Y	Y	Y	Y	Y	N
22 Poshard	Y	Y	Y	Y	Y	Y	Y	N
INDIANA								
1 Visclosky	Y	Y	Y	Y	Y	Y	Y	N
2 Sharp	Y	?	Y	Y	Y	Y	Y	N
3 Roemer	N	Y	Y	Y	Y	Y	Y	N

ND Northern Democrats SD Southern Democrats

	383	384	385	386	387	388	389	390
4 Long	N	Y	Y	Y	Y	Y	Y	N
5 Jontz	Y	Y	Y	Y	Y	Y	Y	N
6 ***Burton***	N	Y	N	Y	N	N	N	N
7 ***Myers***	Y	Y	Y	Y	Y	Y	N	Y
8 McCloskey	Y	Y	Y	Y	Y	Y	Y	N
9 Hamilton	Y	Y	Y	Y	Y	Y	Y	N
10 Jacobs	Y	Y	Y	Y	N	N	Y	N
IOWA								
1 ***Leach***	N	Y	Y	Y	N	N	Y	N
2 ***Nussle***	N	Y	Y	Y	N	N	N	Y
3 Nagle	Y	Y	N	Y	Y	Y	Y	Y
4 Smith	Y	Y	Y	Y	Y	Y	Y	N
5 ***Lightfoot***	N	Y	Y	Y	?	N	N	Y
6 ***Grandy***	N	Y	Y	Y	N	Y	N	N
KANSAS								
1 ***Roberts***	N	Y	N	N	N	N	N	Y
2 Slattery	N	Y	Y	Y	Y	Y	Y	N
3 ***Meyers***	N	Y	Y	Y	N	N	N	Y
4 Glickman	N	Y	Y	Y	Y	Y	Y	N
5 ***Nichols***	N	Y	N	N	Y	Y	N	N
KENTUCKY								
1 Hubbard	Y	Y	Y	Y	Y	Y	Y	N
2 Natcher	Y	Y	Y	Y	Y	Y	Y	N
3 Mazzoli	Y	Y	Y	Y	Y	Y	Y	N
4 ***Bunning***	N	Y	N	?	N	N	N	Y
5 ***Rogers***	Y	Y	N	Y	N	N	N	Y
6 ***Hopkins***	?	?	?	?	N	N	N	Y
7 Perkins	Y	Y	Y	Y	Y	Y	Y	N
LOUISIANA								
1 ***Livingston***	Y	Y	N	N	Y	Y	N	Y
2 Jefferson	Y	Y	Y	Y	?	Y	Y	N
3 Tauzin	N	Y	Y	Y	Y	Y	Y	Y
4 ***McCrery***	N	Y	Y	Y	N	N	N	Y
5 Huckaby	N	Y	Y	Y	Y	?	Y	N
6 ***Baker***	N	Y	N	N	N	N	N	Y
7 Hayes	?	?	?	?	Y	Y	Y	Y
8 ***Holloway***	N	Y	N	N	N	N	N	N
MAINE								
1 Andrews	Y	Y	Y	Y	Y	Y	Y	N
2 ***Snowe***	Y	Y	N	Y	Y	Y	N	N
MARYLAND								
1 ***Gilchrest***	Y	Y	Y	Y	N	N	N	Y
2 ***Bentley***	N	Y	N	Y	N	N	N	Y
3 Cardin	Y	Y	Y	Y	Y	Y	Y	N
4 McMillen	Y	Y	N	Y	Y	Y	Y	N
5 Hoyer	Y	Y	Y	Y	?	Y	Y	N
6 Byron	Y	Y	Y	Y	?	Y	Y	Y
7 Mfume	Y	Y	Y	Y	Y	Y	Y	N
8 ***Morella***	Y	Y	N	Y	N	N	N	N
MASSACHUSETTS								
1 Olver	Y	Y	Y	Y	Y	Y	Y	N
2 Neal	Y	Y	Y	Y	Y	Y	Y	N
3 Early	Y	Y	N	Y	Y	Y	Y	N
4 Frank	Y	?	Y	Y	Y	Y	Y	N
5 Atkins	Y	Y	Y	Y	Y	Y	Y	N
6 Mavroules	Y	?	Y	Y	Y	Y	Y	N
7 Markey	Y	Y	Y	Y	Y	Y	Y	N
8 Kennedy	N	Y	Y	Y	Y	Y	Y	N
9 Moakley	Y	Y	Y	Y	Y	Y	Y	N
10 Studds	Y	?	Y	Y	Y	Y	Y	N
11 Donnelly	Y	Y	Y	Y	Y	Y	Y	N
MICHIGAN								
1 Conyers	Y	Y	N	Y	?	Y	Y	N
2 ***Pursell***	N	Y	Y	Y	Y	Y	N	Y
3 Wolpe	Y	Y	Y	Y	Y	Y	Y	N
4 ***Upton***	N	Y	N	Y	N	N	N	Y
5 ***Henry***	N	Y	Y	Y	N	N	N	Y
6 Carr	Y	Y	Y	Y	Y	Y	N	Y
7 Kildee	Y	Y	Y	Y	Y	Y	Y	N
8 Traxler	Y	Y	Y	Y	Y	Y	Y	N
9 ***Vander Jagt***	N	Y	N	N	Y	Y	N	Y
10 ***Camp***	N	Y	Y	Y	N	N	N	Y
11 ***Davis***	Y	?	Y	Y	Y	N	Y	N
12 Bonior	Y	Y	Y	Y	Y	Y	Y	N
13 Collins	Y	Y	Y	Y	Y	Y	Y	N
14 Hertel	Y	Y	Y	Y	?	?	Y	N
15 Ford	Y	Y	Y	Y	Y	Y	Y	N
16 Dingell	Y	Y	Y	Y	Y	?	?	N
17 Levin	Y	Y	Y	Y	Y	Y	Y	N
18 ***Broomfield***	N	Y	Y	Y	Y	Y	N	Y
MINNESOTA								
1 Penny	N	N	Y	Y	Y	Y	Y	N
2 ***Weber***	N	Y	Y	Y	?	N	N	Y
3 ***Ramstad***	N	Y	Y	Y	N	N	N	N
4 Vento	Y	Y	Y	Y	Y	Y	Y	N

	383	384	385	386	387	388	389	390
5 Sabo	Y	Y	Y	Y	?	Y	Y	N
6 Sikorski	Y	Y	N	Y	N	N	Y	N
7 Peterson	Y	Y	Y	Y	?	Y	Y	N
8 Oberstar	?	?	?	?	Y	Y	Y	N
MISSISSIPPI								
1 Whitten	Y	Y	Y	Y	Y	Y	Y	N
2 Espy	Y	Y	Y	Y	Y	?	Y	N
3 Montgomery	N	Y	Y	Y	Y	Y	Y	Y
4 Parker	N	Y	Y	Y	Y	Y	Y	Y
5 Taylor	N	Y	Y	Y	Y	Y	Y	Y
MISSOURI								
1 Clay	Y	?	Y	Y	N	N	Y	N
2 Horn	Y	Y	Y	Y	Y	Y	Y	N
3 Gephardt	Y	?	Y	Y	Y	Y	Y	N
4 Skelton	N	Y	Y	Y	Y	Y	Y	N
5 Wheat	Y	Y	Y	Y	Y	Y	Y	N
6 ***Coleman***	N	Y	Y	Y	N	N	N	Y
7 ***Hancock***	N	Y	N	N	N	N	N	Y
8 ***Emerson***	Y	Y	Y	Y	Y	?	N	Y
9 Volkmer	Y	Y	Y	Y	Y	Y	Y	N
MONTANA								
1 Williams	Y	Y	Y	Y	Y	Y	N	N
2 ***Marlenee***	N	Y	N	N	?	N	N	Y
NEBRASKA								
1 ***Bereuter***	N	Y	Y	Y	N	N	N	N
2 Hoagland	N	Y	Y	Y	Y	Y	Y	N
3 ***Barrett***	N	Y	Y	Y	N	N	N	Y
NEVADA								
1 Bilbray	Y	?	Y	Y	Y	Y	Y	N
2 ***Vucanovich***	Y	Y	Y	Y	N	N	N	Y
NEW HAMPSHIRE								
1 ***Zeliff***	N	Y	N	N	N	N	N	N
2 Swett	N	Y	Y	Y	Y	Y	Y	N
NEW JERSEY								
1 Andrews	Y	Y	Y	Y	Y	Y	Y	N
2 Hughes	N	Y	Y	Y	Y	Y	Y	N
3 Pallone	N	Y	Y	Y	Y	Y	Y	N
4 ***Smith***	Y	Y	Y	Y	Y	Y	N	N
5 ***Roukema***	N	Y	Y	Y	?	N	N	N
6 Dwyer	Y	?	Y	Y	Y	Y	Y	N
7 ***Rinaldo***	Y	Y	Y	Y	Y	Y	Y	N
8 Roe	Y	Y	Y	Y	Y	Y	Y	N
9 Torricelli	Y	Y	Y	Y	?	Y	Y	N
10 Payne	Y	?	N	Y	Y	Y	Y	N
11 ***Gallo***	Y	Y	Y	Y	?	N	N	Y
12 ***Zimmer***	N	Y	N	Y	N	N	N	N
13 ***Saxton***	N	Y	Y	Y	N	N	N	Y
14 Guarini	Y	?	Y	Y	Y	Y	Y	N
NEW MEXICO								
1 ***Schiff***	Y	Y	Y	Y	?	Y	N	N
2 ***Skeen***	Y	Y	Y	Y	Y	Y	N	N
3 Richardson	Y	Y	Y	Y	Y	Y	Y	N
NEW YORK								
1 Hochbrueckner	Y	Y	Y	Y	Y	Y	Y	N
2 Downey	Y	Y	Y	Y	Y	Y	Y	N
3 Mrazek	Y	Y	Y	Y	?	Y	Y	?
4 ***Lent***	Y	?	Y	Y	?	Y	N	N
5 ***McGrath***	Y	Y	Y	Y	Y	Y	Y	N
6 Flake	Y	Y	Y	Y	?	?	Y	N
7 Ackerman	Y	Y	Y	Y	Y	Y	Y	N
8 Scheuer	Y	Y	Y	Y	?	Y	Y	N
9 Manton	Y	Y	Y	Y	Y	Y	Y	N
10 Schumer	Y	Y	Y	Y	?	Y	Y	N
11 Towns	Y	Y	Y	Y	Y	N	Y	N
12 Owens	Y	Y	Y	Y	?	Y	Y	N
13 Solarz	Y	Y	Y	Y	Y	Y	Y	N
14 ***Molinari***	Y	Y	N	Y	N	N	N	N
15 ***Green***	Y	N	Y	Y	Y	Y	Y	N
16 Rangel	Y	Y	Y	Y	?	Y	Y	N
17 Weiss	Y	Y	+	+	Y	Y	Y	N
18 Serrano	Y	Y	Y	Y	Y	Y	Y	N
19 Engel	Y	Y	Y	Y	Y	Y	Y	N
20 Lowey	Y	Y	Y	Y	Y	Y	Y	N
21 ***Fish***	?	?	Y	Y	Y	Y	N	N
22 ***Gilman***	Y	Y	Y	Y	Y	Y	Y	N
23 McNulty	Y	Y	Y	Y	Y	Y	Y	N
24 ***Solomon***	N	Y	N	Y	N	N	N	Y
25 ***Boehlert***	Y	Y	Y	Y	N	N	Y	N
26 ***Martin***	N	Y	N	Y	?	N	N	N
27 ***Walsh***	Y	Y	Y	Y	Y	N	N	Y
28 McHugh	Y	Y	Y	Y	Y	Y	Y	N
29 ***Horton***	Y	?	Y	Y	Y	Y	Y	N
30 Slaughter	Y	Y	Y	Y	Y	Y	Y	N
31 ***Paxon***	N	Y	N	Y	N	N	N	Y

	383	384	385	386	387	388	389	390
32 LaFalce	Y	Y	Y	Y	Y	Y	Y	N
33 Nowak	Y	Y	Y	Y	Y	Y	Y	N
34 ***Houghton***	Y	Y	Y	Y	Y	?	N	Y
NORTH CAROLINA								
1 Jones	Y	Y	Y	Y	?	?	Y	N
2 Valentine	N	Y	N	Y	Y	Y	Y	N
3 Lancaster	N	Y	Y	Y	Y	Y	N	Y
4 Price	Y	Y	Y	Y	?	Y	Y	N
5 Neal	N	Y	Y	Y	Y	Y	Y	Y
6 ***Coble***	N	Y	N	Y	?	N	N	Y
7 Rose	Y	Y	Y	Y	Y	Y	Y	N
8 Hefner	Y	Y	Y	Y	Y	Y	Y	N
9 ***McMillan***	N	Y	Y	Y	N	N	N	Y
10 ***Ballenger***	N	Y	N	Y	N	N	N	N
11 ***Taylor***	N	Y	N	Y	N	N	N	Y
NORTH DAKOTA								
AL Dorgan	N	-	Y	Y	N	Y	Y	N
OHIO								
1 Luken	N	Y	Y	Y	Y	Y	Y	Y
2 ***Gradison***	N	N	?	?	?	N	N	Y
3 Hall	Y	Y	Y	Y	Y	Y	Y	N
4 ***Oxley***	N	Y	Y	N	Y	Y	N	Y
5 ***Gillmor***	N	Y	Y	Y	Y	Y	?	N
6 ***McEwen***	N	Y	?	N	N	N	N	Y
7 ***Hobson***	N	Y	Y	Y	N	N	N	Y
8 ***Boehner***	N	Y	N	N	N	N	N	N
9 Kaptur	Y	Y	Y	Y	Y	Y	?	N
10 ***Miller***	N	Y	Y	Y	N	N	N	Y
11 Eckart	Y	Y	Y	Y	Y	Y	Y	N
12 ***Kasich***	N	Y	Y	Y	Y	Y	N	Y
13 Pease	Y	Y	Y	Y	Y	Y	Y	N
14 Sawyer	Y	Y	Y	Y	?	Y	Y	N
15 ***Wylie***	N	Y	Y	Y	?	Y	N	Y
16 ***Regula***	N	Y	Y	Y	N	N	N	N
17 Traficant	Y	Y	Y	Y	Y	Y	Y	N
18 Applegate	Y	Y	Y	Y	Y	Y	Y	N
19 Feighan	Y	Y	Y	Y	Y	Y	Y	N
20 Oakar	Y	Y	N	Y	?	Y	Y	N
21 Stokes	Y	Y	Y	Y	Y	Y	Y	N
OKLAHOMA								
1 ***Inhofe***	N	Y	N	N	N	N	N	Y
2 Synar	Y	Y	Y	Y	Y	Y	Y	N
3 Brewster	Y	Y	Y	Y	?	Y	Y	Y
4 McCurdy	N	Y	Y	Y	Y	Y	Y	N
5 ***Edwards***	N	Y	Y	Y	Y	N	N	Y
6 English	N	Y	Y	Y	Y	Y	Y	N
OREGON								
1 AuCoin	Y	Y	Y	Y	Y	Y	?	N
2 ***Smith***	N	Y	Y	Y	N	N	N	Y
3 Wyden	Y	Y	Y	Y	Y	Y	Y	N
4 DeFazio	Y	Y	Y	Y	?	Y	Y	N
5 Kopetski	Y	Y	Y	Y	Y	Y	Y	N
PENNSYLVANIA								
1 Foglietta	Y	Y	N	Y	Y	Y	Y	N
2 Blackwell [1]							Y	N
3 Borski	Y	Y	Y	Y	Y	Y	Y	N
4 Kolter	Y	Y	Y	Y	Y	Y	Y	N
5 ***Schulze***	N	Y	Y	Y	?	?	?	?
6 Yatron	Y	Y	Y	Y	Y	Y	Y	N
7 ***Weldon***	N	Y	Y	Y	N	N	N	N
8 Kostmayer	N	Y	Y	Y	Y	Y	Y	N
9 ***Shuster***	N	Y	N	N	Y	Y	N	Y
10 ***McDade***	Y	Y	Y	Y	N	N	Y	N
11 Kanjorski	Y	Y	Y	Y	Y	Y	Y	N
12 Murtha	Y	Y	Y	Y	Y	Y	Y	N
13 ***Coughlin***	N	Y	Y	Y	N	N	N	Y
14 Coyne	Y	Y	Y	Y	?	Y	Y	N
15 ***Ritter***	N	Y	Y	Y	?	Y	N	Y
16 ***Walker***	N	Y	Y	Y	N	N	N	Y
17 ***Gekas***	Y	Y	Y	Y	N	N	N	Y
18 ***Santorum***	N	Y	N	Y	N	N	N	Y
19 ***Goodling***	Y	Y	Y	Y	?	N	Y	N
20 Gaydos	Y	Y	Y	Y	?	Y	Y	N
21 ***Ridge***	N	Y	Y	Y	N	N	N	Y
22 Murphy	Y	?	Y	Y	?	N	Y	N
23 ***Clinger***	N	Y	Y	Y	Y	Y	N	Y
RHODE ISLAND								
1 ***Machtley***	N	Y	Y	Y	?	N	N	N
2 Reed	N	Y	Y	Y	Y	Y	Y	N
SOUTH CAROLINA								
1 ***Ravenel***	N	Y	Y	Y	Y	Y	Y	N
2 ***Spence***	N	Y	N	Y	N	Y	N	N
3 Derrick	Y	Y	Y	Y	Y	Y	Y	N
4 Patterson	N	Y	Y	Y	?	Y	Y	N
5 Spratt	Y	Y	Y	Y	Y	Y	Y	N
6 Tallon	Y	Y	Y	Y	Y	Y	Y	N

	383	384	385	386	387	388	389	390
SOUTH DAKOTA								
AL Johnson	Y	Y	Y	Y	Y	Y	Y	N
TENNESSEE								
1 ***Quillen***	Y	Y	Y	Y	Y	Y	N	Y
2 ***Duncan***	N	Y	Y	Y	Y	N	N	Y
3 Lloyd	N	Y	Y	Y	?	?	Y	Y
4 Cooper	N	Y	Y	Y	?	Y	Y	Y
5 Clement	Y	Y	Y	Y	Y	Y	Y	N
6 Gordon	Y	Y	Y	Y	Y	Y	Y	N
7 ***Sundquist***	N	Y	Y	Y	N	N	N	Y
8 Tanner	Y	Y	Y	Y	Y	Y	Y	Y
9 Ford	Y	Y	Y	Y	Y	Y	Y	N
TEXAS								
1 Chapman	Y	Y	Y	Y	Y	Y	Y	N
2 Wilson	Y	Y	Y	Y	?	Y	Y	N
3 ***Johnson***	N	Y	Y	Y	Y	Y	N	N
4 Hall	N	Y	N	Y	Y	Y	N	Y
5 Bryant	Y	Y	N	Y	Y	Y	Y	N
6 ***Barton***	N	Y	Y	Y	N	N	N	Y
7 ***Archer***	N	Y	N	N	Y	Y	N	Y
8 ***Fields***	N	Y	N	N	N	N	N	Y
9 Brooks	Y	Y	Y	Y	Y	Y	Y	N
10 Pickle	N	Y	Y	Y	Y	Y	Y	N
11 Edwards	Y	Y	Y	Y	Y	Y	Y	Y
12 Geren	N	Y	Y	Y	Y	Y	Y	N
13 Sarpalius	Y	?	Y	Y	Y	Y	Y	Y
14 Laughlin	N	Y	Y	Y	?	Y	Y	Y
15 de la Garza	Y	Y	Y	Y	Y	Y	Y	N
16 Coleman	Y	Y	N	Y	Y	Y	Y	N
17 Stenholm	N	Y	Y	Y	Y	Y	Y	Y
18 Washington	Y	Y	N	Y	Y	?	Y	N
19 ***Combest***	N	Y	N	N	Y	Y	N	Y
20 Gonzalez	Y	Y	N	N	Y	Y	Y	N
21 ***Smith***	N	Y	Y	Y	N	N	N	Y
22 ***DeLay***	N	Y	N	N	N	N	N	Y
23 Bustamante	Y	Y	Y	Y	Y	Y	Y	N
24 Frost	?	?	Y	Y	Y	Y	Y	N
25 Andrews	Y	Y	Y	Y	Y	Y	Y	N
26 ***Armey***	N	Y	N	N	N	N	N	N
27 Ortiz	Y	Y	Y	Y	Y	Y	Y	N
UTAH								
1 ***Hansen***	N	Y	Y	Y	Y	Y	N	Y
2 Owens	Y	?	Y	Y	Y	Y	Y	N
3 Orton	N	Y	Y	Y	Y	Y	Y	Y
VERMONT								
AL *Sanders*	Y	Y	Y	Y	?	Y	Y	N
VIRGINIA								
1 ***Bateman***	N	Y	N	N	Y	?	?	?
2 Pickett	Y	Y	Y	Y	Y	Y	Y	N
3 ***Bliley***	N	Y	N	N	N	N	N	Y
4 Sisisky	N	Y	Y	Y	Y	Y	Y	N
5 Payne	N	Y	Y	Y	Y	Y	Y	Y
6 Olin	N	?	?	?	?	Y	Y	N
7 ***Allen*** [2]						Y	N	N
8 Moran	Y	Y	N	Y	Y	Y	Y	N
9 Boucher	?	Y	Y	Y	Y	Y	Y	N
10 ***Wolf***	N	Y	Y	Y	N	N	N	Y
WASHINGTON								
1 ***Miller***	N	Y	Y	Y	N	N	N	N
2 Swift	Y	Y	Y	Y	Y	Y	Y	N
3 Unsoeld	Y	Y	Y	Y	Y	Y	Y	N
4 ***Morrison***	Y	Y	Y	Y	Y	Y	N	N
5 Foley								
6 Dicks	Y	Y	Y	Y	Y	Y	Y	N
7 McDermott	Y	Y	N	Y	Y	Y	Y	N
8 ***Chandler***	N	Y	Y	Y	?	N	N	Y
WEST VIRGINIA								
1 Mollohan	Y	Y	Y	Y	Y	Y	Y	N
2 Staggers	Y	Y	Y	Y	?	Y	Y	N
3 Wise	Y	Y	Y	Y	?	Y	Y	N
4 Rahall	Y	Y	Y	Y	Y	Y	Y	N
WISCONSIN								
1 Aspin	Y	Y	Y	Y	Y	Y	Y	N
2 ***Klug***	N	Y	N	Y	Y	Y	N	N
3 ***Gunderson***	N	Y	Y	Y	Y	Y	N	Y
4 Kleczka	Y	Y	Y	Y	Y	Y	Y	N
5 Moody	N	Y	N	Y	Y	Y	Y	N
6 ***Petri***	N	Y	Y	Y	N	Y	N	Y
7 Obey	Y	Y	Y	Y	Y	Y	Y	N
8 ***Roth***	N	Y	Y	Y	N	N	N	Y
9 ***Sensenbrenner***	N	Y	N	N	N	N	N	Y
WYOMING								
AL ***Thomas***	N	Y	Y	Y	Y	N	N	N

Southern states - Ala., Ark., Fla., Ga., Ky., La., Miss., N.C., Okla., S.C., Tenn., Texas, Va.
Omitted votes are quorum calls, which CQ does not include in its vote charts.

HOUSE VOTES 391, 392, 393, 394, 395, 396, 398, 399

391. HR 2. Family and Medical Leave Act/Substitute. Gordon, D-Tenn., substitute amendment to amendment to raise the number of hours an employee must work in order to be eligible for up to 12 weeks of unpaid leave from 1,000 to 1,250 a year, require employees to provide 30 days' notice in non-emergency cases before taking leave, as opposed to "reasonable notice" as provided in the bill, among other changes. Adopted 287-143: R 48-115; D 238-28 (ND 175-7, SD 63-21); I 1-0, Nov. 13, 1991.

392. HR 2. Family and Medical Leave Act/Recommittal Motion. Goodling, R-Pa., motion to recommit the bill to the Education and Labor Committee with instructions to report it back providing eight weeks of unpaid leave for the birth or adoption of a child. Motion rejected 119-312: R 103-61; D 16-250 (ND 5-177, SD 11-73); I 0-1, Nov. 13, 1991.

393. HR 2. Family and Medical Leave Act/Passage. Passage of the bill to require employers with 50 or more employees to provide up to 12 weeks of unpaid leave a year for a serious illness, the birth or adoption of a child, or to care for a seriously ill child, spouse or parent. Passed 253-177: R 35-129; D 217-48 (ND 169-12, SD 48-36); I 1-0, Nov. 13, 1991. A "nay" was a vote supporting the president's position.

394. HR 2094. Banking Reform/Rule. Adoption of the rule (H Res 277) to provide for House floor consideration of the bill to allow the Federal Deposit Insurance Corporation to borrow up to $30 billion to cover losses of failed banks, initiate regulatory reforms to strengthen federal supervision of banks, and take other measures to reduce risks to the bank insurance fund. Adopted 305-112: R 111-48; D 194-63 (ND 123-53, SD 71-10); I 0-1, Nov. 13, 1991.

395. HR 3575. Unemployment Benefits Extension/Rule. Adoption of the rule (H Res 280) to provide for House floor consideration of the compromise bill to provide an estimated $5.2 billion for six, 13 or 20 weeks of extended unemployment benefits. The increased spending caused by the bill would be offset by a number of tax changes. Adopted 391-37: R 126-37; D 264-0 (ND 180-0, SD 84-0); I 1-0, Nov. 14, 1991.

396. HR 3575. Unemployment Benefits Extension/Passage. Passage of the compromise bill to provide an estimated $5.2 billion for six, 13 or 20 weeks of extended unemployment benefits. The increased spending caused by the bill would be offset by a number of tax changes. Passed 396-30: R 135-26; D 260-4 (ND 181-1, SD 79-3); I 1-0, Nov. 14, 1991. A "yea" was a vote supporting the president's position.

398. HR 2094. Banking Reform/Interstate Branching. Wylie, R-Ohio, amendment to allow banks that meet minimum capital requirements to open branch offices across state lines, unless a state votes to "opt out" of interstate branching within three years; prohibit the interstate sale of insurance by banks, unless authorized by the recipient state; prohibit regulators from allowing banks to engage in certain real estate activities; and for other purposes. Adopted 210-208: R 111-47; D 99-160 (ND 67-113, SD 32-47); I 0-1, Nov. 14, 1991. A "yea" was a vote supporting the president's position.

399. HR 2094. Banking Reform/Passage. Passage of the bill to allow the Federal Deposit Insurance Corporation to borrow up to $30 billion to cover losses of failed banks; take measures to reduce risks to the bank insurance fund; allow banks that meet minimum capital requirements to open branch offices across state lines, unless a state votes to "opt out" of interstate branching within three years; prohibit the interstate sale of insurance by banks, unless authorized by the recipient state; prohibit regulators from allowing banks to engage in certain real estate activities; and for other purposes. Rejected 191-227: R 114-45; D 77-181 (ND 43-137, SD 34-44); I 0-1, Nov. 14, 1991. A "yea" was a vote supporting the president's position.

KEY

Y Voted for (yea).
Paired for.
+ Announced for.
N Voted against (nay).
X Paired against.
- Announced against.
P Voted "present."
C Voted "present" to avoid possible conflict of interest.
? Did not vote or otherwise make a position known.

Democrats ***Republicans***
Independent

	391	392	393	394	395	396	398	399
ALABAMA								
1 ***Callahan***	N	Y	N	N	Y	Y	Y	N
2 ***Dickinson***	N	Y	N	N	Y	Y	Y	N
3 Browder	Y	N	N	Y	Y	Y	N	N
4 Bevill	Y	N	Y	Y	Y	Y	N	N
5 Cramer	Y	N	N	Y	Y	Y	N	N
6 Erdreich	Y	N	Y	N	Y	Y	N	N
7 Harris	N	N	N	N	Y	Y	N	N
ALASKA								
AL ***Young***	?	?	?	?	?	?	?	?
ARIZONA								
1 ***Rhodes***	N	Y	N	N	Y	Y	Y	Y
2 Pastor	Y	N	Y	Y	Y	Y	Y	Y
3 ***Stump***	N	Y	N	N	N	N	N	N
4 ***Kyl***	N	N	N	N	Y	Y	N	Y
5 ***Kolbe***	N	Y	N	N	Y	Y	?	?
ARKANSAS								
1 Alexander	Y	N	Y	Y	Y	Y	N	N
2 Thornton	Y	N	Y	Y	Y	Y	N	N
3 ***Hammerschmidt***	N	N	N	Y	Y	Y	N	N
4 Anthony	Y	N	Y	Y	Y	Y	Y	N
CALIFORNIA								
1 ***Riggs***	N	Y	N	Y	Y	Y	Y	Y
2 ***Herger***	N	Y	N	?	Y	Y	N	N
3 Matsui	Y	N	Y	Y	Y	Y	Y	N
4 Fazio	Y	N	Y	Y	Y	Y	Y	Y
5 Pelosi	Y	N	Y	Y	Y	Y	N	Y
6 Boxer	Y	N	Y	?	Y	Y	N	N
7 Miller	Y	N	Y	?	Y	Y	N	N
8 Dellums	Y	N	Y	N	Y	Y	N	N
9 Stark	Y	N	Y	Y	Y	Y	N	N
10 Edwards	Y	N	Y	Y	Y	Y	N	Y
11 Lantos	Y	N	Y	Y	Y	Y	N	N
12 ***Campbell***	Y	Y	Y	?	?	?	?	?
13 Mineta	Y	N	Y	Y	Y	Y	Y	Y
14 ***Doolittle***	N	N	N	Y	N	N	Y	N
15 Condit	Y	N	Y	Y	Y	Y	Y	N
16 Panetta	Y	N	Y	Y	Y	Y	N	N
17 Dooley	Y	N	Y	Y	Y	Y	Y	Y
18 Lehman	Y	N	Y	N	Y	Y	Y	N
19 ***Lagomarsino***	N	N	N	Y	Y	Y	Y	Y
20 ***Thomas***	Y	Y	N	Y	Y	Y	Y	Y
21 ***Gallegly***	N	N	N	Y	Y	N	Y	Y
22 ***Moorhead***	N	Y	N	Y	Y	Y	Y	Y
23 Beilenson	Y	N	Y	N	Y	Y	N	N
24 Waxman	Y	N	Y	Y	Y	Y	N	N
25 Roybal	Y	N	Y	Y	Y	Y	Y	Y
26 Berman	Y	N	Y	Y	Y	Y	Y	Y
27 Levine	Y	N	Y	N	Y	Y	N	N
28 Dixon	Y	N	Y	Y	Y	Y	Y	Y
29 Waters	Y	N	Y	N	Y	Y	N	N
30 Martinez	Y	N	Y	Y	Y	Y	Y	N
31 Dymally	Y	N	Y	?	Y	Y	Y	Y
32 Anderson	Y	N	Y	N	Y	Y	N	Y
33 ***Dreier***	N	Y	N	Y	Y	Y	Y	Y
34 Torres	Y	N	Y	Y	Y	Y	Y	Y
35 ***Lewis***	N	Y	N	Y	Y	Y	Y	Y
36 Brown	Y	N	Y	Y	?	Y	Y	Y
37 ***McCandless***	N	Y	N	N	N	Y	Y	Y
38 ***Dornan***	N	Y	N	N	N	Y	Y	Y
39 ***Dannemeyer***	N	N	N	N	N	N	N	N
40 ***Cox***	N	Y	N	Y	Y	Y	Y	Y
41 ***Lowery***	N	Y	N	Y	Y	Y	Y	Y
42 ***Rohrabacher***	N	Y	N	Y	N	Y	Y	N
43 ***Packard***	N	Y	N	Y	Y	Y	Y	Y
44 ***Cunningham***	N	Y	N	Y	Y	Y	Y	Y
45 ***Hunter***	Y	Y	N	Y	Y	Y	Y	Y
COLORADO								
1 Schroeder	Y	N	Y	N	Y	Y	N	N
2 Skaggs	Y	N	Y	Y	Y	Y	N	N
3 Campbell	Y	N	Y	Y	Y	Y	N	Y
4 ***Allard***	N	Y	N	N	N	N	Y	Y
5 ***Hefley***	N	N	N	N	N	Y	N	N
6 ***Schaefer***	N	Y	N	N	N	N	N	Y
CONNECTICUT								
1 Kennelly	Y	N	Y	N	Y	Y	Y	Y
2 Gejdenson	Y	N	Y	Y	Y	Y	Y	N
3 DeLauro	Y	N	Y	Y	Y	Y	Y	Y
4 ***Shays***	Y	N	Y	Y	Y	Y	Y	Y
5 ***Franks***	N	Y	N	N	Y	Y	Y	Y
6 ***Johnson***	Y	N	Y	Y	Y	Y	Y	Y
DELAWARE								
AL Carper	Y	N	Y	N	Y	Y	N	N
FLORIDA								
1 Hutto	N	Y	N	Y	Y	Y	N	N
2 Peterson	Y	N	Y	Y	Y	Y	N	N
3 Bennett	Y	N	Y	Y	Y	Y	N	N
4 ***James***	Y	N	Y	N	Y	Y	Y	Y
5 ***McCollum***	N	N	N	Y	Y	Y	Y	Y
6 ***Stearns***	N	Y	N	Y	Y	Y	Y	Y
7 Gibbons	Y	N	Y	Y	Y	Y	Y	Y
8 ***Young***	Y	N	N	Y	Y	Y	Y	Y
9 ***Bilirakis***	Y	N	N	Y	Y	Y	Y	Y
10 ***Ireland***	N	N	N	Y	Y	Y	Y	Y
11 Bacchus	Y	N	Y	Y	Y	Y	N	N
12 ***Lewis***	N	N	N	Y	Y	Y	Y	Y
13 ***Goss***	N	N	N	Y	Y	Y	Y	Y
14 Johnston	Y	N	Y	Y	Y	Y	Y	Y
15 ***Shaw***	Y	N	N	Y	Y	Y	Y	Y
16 Smith	Y	N	Y	Y	Y	Y	Y	Y
17 Lehman	Y	N	Y	Y	Y	Y	N	?
18 ***Ros-Lehtinen***	Y	N	Y	Y	Y	Y	Y	Y
19 Fascell	Y	N	Y	Y	Y	Y	N	Y
GEORGIA								
1 Thomas	Y	N	N	Y	Y	Y	N	N
2 Hatcher	?	?	?	?	?	?	?	?
3 Ray	Y	N	N	N	Y	Y	N	N
4 Jones	N	Y	N	N	Y	Y	N	N
5 Lewis	Y	N	Y	Y	Y	Y	Y	Y
6 ***Gingrich***	N	Y	N	Y	Y	Y	Y	Y
7 Darden	Y	Y	N	Y	Y	Y	N	N
8 Rowland	Y	Y	N	N	Y	Y	N	N
9 Jenkins	Y	N	Y	Y	Y	?	?	?
10 Barnard	Y	N	N	N	Y	Y	N	N
HAWAII								
1 Abercrombie	Y	N	Y	Y	Y	Y	N	N
2 Mink	Y	N	Y	Y	Y	Y	N	N
IDAHO								
1 LaRocco	N	N	N	Y	Y	Y	N	N
2 Stallings	N	N	N	Y	Y	Y	Y	N
ILLINOIS								
1 Hayes	Y	N	Y	N	Y	Y	N	N
2 Savage	Y	N	Y	Y	Y	Y	N	N
3 Russo	Y	N	Y	Y	Y	Y	N	N
4 Sangmeister	Y	N	Y	Y	Y	Y	Y	N
5 Lipinski	Y	N	Y	Y	Y	Y	Y	Y
6 ***Hyde***	Y	N	Y	Y	Y	Y	Y	Y
7 Collins	Y	N	Y	N	Y	Y	N	N
8 Rostenkowski	Y	N	Y	Y	Y	Y	?	?
9 Yates	Y	N	Y	N	Y	Y	N	N
10 ***Porter***	N	Y	N	Y	Y	Y	Y	Y
11 Annunzio	Y	N	Y	Y	Y	Y	Y	N
12 ***Crane***	N	Y	N	N	N	N	Y	N
13 ***Fawell***	N	Y	N	N	N	Y	N	Y
14 ***Hastert***	N	N	N	Y	Y	Y	Y	N
15 ***Ewing***	N	Y	N	Y	Y	Y	N	Y
16 Cox	Y	N	Y	Y	Y	Y	N	N
17 Evans	Y	N	Y	N	Y	Y	N	N
18 ***Michel***	N	Y	N	Y	Y	Y	Y	Y
19 Bruce	Y	N	Y	N	Y	Y	Y	N
20 Durbin	Y	N	Y	Y	Y	Y	Y	N
21 Costello	Y	N	Y	N	Y	Y	Y	N
22 Poshard	Y	N	Y	N	Y	Y	N	N
INDIANA								
1 Visclosky	Y	N	Y	Y	Y	Y	N	N
2 Sharp	Y	N	Y	Y	Y	Y	N	N
3 Roemer	Y	N	Y	Y	Y	Y	N	N

ND Northern Democrats SD Southern Democrats

	391	392	393	394	395	396	398	399
4 Long	Y	N	Y	Y	Y	N	N	N
5 Jontz	Y	N	Y	?	Y	Y	N	N
6 ***Burton***	N	Y	N	Y	N	N	Y	Y
7 ***Myers***	N	Y	N	Y	Y	Y	N	Y
8 McCloskey	Y	N	Y	Y	Y	Y	Y	N
9 Hamilton	N	N	N	Y	Y	Y	N	N
10 Jacobs	Y	N	Y	N	Y	Y	N	N
IOWA								
1 ***Leach***	Y	N	Y	Y	Y	Y	Y	Y
2 ***Nussle***	N	Y	N	Y	Y	Y	Y	Y
3 Nagle	Y	Y	Y	N	Y	Y	N	N
4 Smith	Y	N	Y	Y	Y	Y	N	N
5 ***Lightfoot***	N	Y	N	Y	N	N	N	N
6 ***Grandy***	N	N	N	Y	Y	Y	Y	Y
KANSAS								
1 ***Roberts***	N	N	N	N	Y	Y	N	N
2 Slattery	Y	Y	N	N	Y	Y	Y	N
3 ***Meyers***	Y	Y	N	Y	Y	Y	N	Y
4 Glickman	Y	Y	N	Y	Y	Y	Y	N
5 ***Nichols***	N	N	N	Y	Y	N	N	N
KENTUCKY								
1 Hubbard	Y	N	Y	N	Y	Y	N	N
2 Natcher	Y	N	Y	Y	Y	Y	N	N
3 Mazzoli	Y	N	Y	Y	Y	Y	N	N
4 ***Bunning***	N	N	N	N	N	Y	N	N
5 ***Rogers***	Y	Y	N	N	Y	Y	N	N
6 ***Hopkins***	N	Y	N	N	N	Y	N	N
7 Perkins	Y	N	Y	Y	Y	Y	N	N
LOUISIANA								
1 ***Livingston***	Y	Y	N	N	Y	N	Y	Y
2 Jefferson	Y	N	Y	Y	Y	Y	?	?
3 Tauzin	Y	Y	N	Y	Y	Y	Y	N
4 ***McCrery***	N	Y	N	Y	Y	Y	Y	Y
5 Huckaby	N	N	N	Y	Y	Y	N	Y
6 ***Baker***	N	Y	N	Y	N	N	N	Y
7 Hayes	Y	Y	N	Y	Y	N	Y	Y
8 ***Holloway***	N	Y	N	N	N	N	N	N
MAINE								
1 Andrews	Y	N	Y	N	Y	Y	N	N
2 ***Snowe***	Y	N	Y	N	Y	Y	N	Y
MARYLAND								
1 ***Gilchrest***	N	Y	N	N	Y	Y	Y	Y
2 ***Bentley***	N	Y	N	N	Y	Y	Y	N
3 Cardin	Y	N	Y	Y	Y	Y	N	Y
4 McMillen	Y	N	Y	Y	Y	Y	Y	N
5 Hoyer	Y	N	Y	Y	Y	Y	N	Y
6 Byron	N	N	N	Y	Y	Y	N	N
7 Mfume	Y	N	Y	N	Y	Y	N	N
8 ***Morella***	Y	N	Y	N	Y	Y	+	Y
MASSACHUSETTS								
1 Olver	Y	N	Y	Y	Y	Y	N	N
2 Neal	Y	N	Y	Y	Y	Y	Y	Y
3 Early	Y	N	Y	N	Y	Y	Y	Y
4 Frank	Y	N	Y	Y	Y	Y	Y	Y
5 Atkins	Y	N	Y	Y	Y	Y	Y	N
6 Mavroules	Y	N	Y	Y	Y	Y	Y	Y
7 Markey	Y	N	Y	N	Y	Y	N	N
8 Kennedy	Y	N	Y	N	Y	Y	N	N
9 Moakley	Y	N	Y	Y	Y	Y	Y	Y
10 Studds	Y	N	Y	Y	Y	Y	N	N
11 Donnelly	Y	N	Y	Y	Y	Y	Y	N
MICHIGAN								
1 Conyers	Y	N	Y	Y	Y	Y	N	N
2 ***Pursell***	N	N	N	Y	Y	Y	Y	Y
3 Wolpe	Y	N	Y	N	Y	Y	N	N
4 ***Upton***	N	Y	N	N	Y	Y	Y	Y
5 ***Henry***	N	Y	N	N	Y	Y	Y	N
6 Carr	Y	Y	N	N	Y	Y	N	N
7 Kildee	Y	N	Y	Y	Y	Y	N	N
8 Traxler	Y	N	Y	Y	Y	Y	N	N
9 ***Vander Jagt***	N	Y	N	Y	N	Y	Y	Y
10 ***Camp***	N	Y	N	Y	Y	Y	Y	Y
11 ***Davis***	Y	N	Y	Y	Y	Y	Y	Y
12 Bonior	Y	N	Y	Y	Y	Y	Y	Y
13 Collins	Y	N	Y	N	Y	Y	N	N
14 Hertel	Y	N	Y	N	Y	Y	N	N
15 Ford	Y	N	Y	N	Y	Y	N	N
16 Dingell	Y	N	Y	N	Y	Y	N	N
17 Levin	Y	N	Y	Y	Y	Y	N	N
18 ***Broomfield***	N	Y	N	Y	Y	Y	Y	Y
MINNESOTA								
1 Penny	Y	Y	N	Y	Y	Y	N	Y
2 ***Weber***	N	Y	N	Y	N	N	Y	N
3 ***Ramstad***	Y	N	Y	N	Y	Y	Y	Y
4 Vento	Y	N	Y	N	Y	Y	N	N

	391	392	393	394	395	396	398	399
5 Sabo	Y	N	Y	N	Y	Y	N	N
6 Sikorski	Y	N	Y	N	Y	Y	N	N
7 Peterson	Y	N	Y	Y	Y	Y	N	N
8 Oberstar	Y	N	Y	N	Y	Y	N	N
MISSISSIPPI								
1 Whitten	N	N	N	Y	Y	Y	N	N
2 Espy	Y	N	Y	Y	Y	Y	N	N
3 Montgomery	N	N	N	Y	Y	Y	N	N
4 Parker	N	N	N	Y	Y	Y	N	N
5 Taylor	Y	Y	N	N	Y	Y	N	N
MISSOURI								
1 Clay	Y	N	Y	N	Y	Y	N	N
2 Horn	Y	N	Y	Y	Y	Y	Y	Y
3 Gephardt	Y	N	Y	Y	Y	Y	Y	Y
4 Skelton	N	N	N	N	Y	Y	N	N
5 Wheat	Y	N	Y	Y	Y	Y	N	N
6 ***Coleman***	Y	N	N	Y	Y	Y	Y	Y
7 ***Hancock***	N	Y	N	N	N	Y	N	N
8 ***Emerson***	N	Y	N	N	Y	Y	Y	N
9 Volkmer	Y	N	Y	N	Y	Y	N	N
MONTANA								
1 Williams	Y	N	Y	Y	Y	Y	N	N
2 ***Marlenee***	N	Y	N	N	N	Y	N	N
NEBRASKA								
1 ***Bereuter***	N	Y	N	N	Y	Y	N	N
2 Hoagland	Y	N	Y	Y	Y	Y	Y	Y
3 ***Barrett***	N	Y	N	Y	Y	N	N	N
NEVADA								
1 Bilbray	Y	N	Y	Y	Y	Y	Y	Y
2 ***Vucanovich***	N	Y	N	Y	Y	Y	N	Y
NEW HAMPSHIRE								
1 ***Zeliff***	N	Y	N	N	Y	Y	Y	Y
2 Swett	Y	N	Y	Y	Y	Y	Y	Y
NEW JERSEY								
1 Andrews	Y	N	Y	Y	Y	Y	Y	N
2 Hughes	Y	N	Y	N	Y	Y	N	N
3 Pallone	Y	N	Y	Y	Y	Y	Y	N
4 ***Smith***	Y	N	Y	Y	Y	Y	Y	Y
5 ***Roukema***	Y	N	Y	Y	Y	Y	Y	N
6 Dwyer	Y	N	Y	Y	Y	Y	Y	Y
7 ***Rinaldo***	Y	N	Y	Y	Y	Y	Y	Y
8 Roe	Y	N	Y	Y	Y	Y	N	N
9 Torricelli	Y	N	Y	Y	Y	Y	Y	N
10 Payne	Y	N	Y	Y	Y	Y	Y	N
11 ***Gallo***	N	Y	N	Y	Y	Y	Y	Y
12 ***Zimmer***	Y	N	Y	N	Y	Y	Y	N
13 ***Saxton***	N	Y	N	Y	Y	Y	Y	Y
14 Guarini	Y	N	Y	Y	Y	Y	N	N
NEW MEXICO								
1 ***Schiff***	Y	N	N	N	Y	Y	N	N
2 ***Skeen***	N	Y	N	N	Y	Y	N	N
3 Richardson	Y	N	Y	N	Y	Y	N	N
NEW YORK								
1 Hochbrueckner	Y	N	Y	Y	Y	Y	N	N
2 Downey	Y	N	Y	Y	Y	Y	N	N
3 Mrazek	Y	N	Y	?	?	Y	N	N
4 ***Lent***	N	Y	N	Y	Y	Y	Y	Y
5 ***McGrath***	Y	N	Y	Y	Y	Y	Y	Y
6 Flake	Y	N	Y	Y	Y	Y	Y	N
7 Ackerman	Y	N	Y	Y	Y	Y	N	N
8 Scheuer	Y	N	Y	Y	Y	Y	N	N
9 Manton	Y	N	Y	Y	Y	Y	Y	N
10 Schumer	Y	N	Y	Y	Y	Y	N	N
11 Towns	Y	N	Y	Y	Y	Y	N	N
12 Owens	Y	N	Y	N	Y	Y	N	N
13 Solarz	Y	N	Y	Y	Y	Y	N	N
14 ***Molinari***	Y	N	Y	Y	Y	Y	?	?
15 ***Green***	Y	N	Y	Y	Y	Y	N	N
16 Rangel	Y	N	Y	Y	Y	Y	N	N
17 Weiss	Y	N	Y	Y	Y	Y	N	N
18 Serrano	Y	N	Y	Y	Y	Y	Y	N
19 Engel	Y	N	Y	Y	Y	Y	Y	N
20 Lowey	Y	N	Y	Y	Y	Y	Y	N
21 ***Fish***	Y	N	Y	Y	Y	Y	Y	Y
22 ***Gilman***	Y	N	Y	Y	Y	Y	Y	Y
23 McNulty	Y	N	Y	Y	Y	Y	Y	N
24 ***Solomon***	Y	Y	Y	Y	Y	Y	Y	Y
25 ***Boehlert***	Y	N	Y	Y	Y	Y	Y	Y
26 ***Martin***	Y	N	Y	Y	Y	Y	Y	Y
27 ***Walsh***	N	Y	N	Y	Y	Y	Y	Y
28 McHugh	Y	N	Y	Y	Y	Y	N	N
29 ***Horton***	Y	N	Y	?	Y	Y	N	N
30 Slaughter	Y	N	Y	Y	Y	Y	N	N
31 ***Paxon***	N	Y	N	Y	Y	?	?	?

	391	392	393	394	395	396	398	399
32 LaFalce	Y	N	Y	Y	Y	Y	N	N
33 Nowak	Y	N	Y	Y	Y	Y	N	N
34 ***Houghton***	N	Y	N	N	Y	Y	N	N
NORTH CAROLINA								
1 Jones	Y	N	Y	Y	Y	Y	N	N
2 Valentine	N	N	N	Y	Y	N	Y	Y
3 Lancaster	Y	N	N	Y	Y	Y	Y	Y
4 Price	Y	N	Y	Y	Y	Y	Y	Y
5 Neal	Y	N	N	Y	Y	Y	Y	Y
6 ***Coble***	N	Y	N	Y	N	Y	Y	Y
7 Rose	Y	N	Y	Y	Y	Y	Y	Y
8 Hefner	Y	N	Y	Y	Y	Y	Y	Y
9 ***McMillan***	N	Y	N	Y	Y	Y	Y	Y
10 ***Ballenger***	N	Y	N	Y	Y	Y	Y	Y
11 ***Taylor***	N	Y	N	N	N	Y	Y	Y
NORTH DAKOTA								
AL Dorgan	Y	N	Y	N	Y	Y	N	N
OHIO								
1 Luken	N	N	N	Y	Y	Y	Y	N
2 ***Gradison***	N	N	N	Y	Y	Y	Y	Y
3 Hall	Y	N	Y	Y	Y	Y	N	N
4 ***Oxley***	N	Y	N	Y	Y	Y	Y	Y
5 ***Gillmor***	Y	N	Y	Y	Y	Y	Y	Y
6 ***McEwen***	N	Y	N	Y	N	Y	N	Y
7 ***Hobson***	N	Y	N	Y	Y	Y	Y	Y
8 ***Boehner***	N	N	N	Y	Y	Y	Y	Y
9 Kaptur	Y	N	Y	Y	Y	Y	N	N
10 ***Miller***	Y	Y	N	Y	Y	Y	N	Y
11 Eckart	Y	N	Y	N	Y	Y	N	N
12 ***Kasich***	N	Y	N	Y	Y	Y	Y	Y
13 Pease	Y	N	Y	Y	Y	Y	Y	Y
14 Sawyer	Y	N	Y	Y	Y	Y	Y	Y
15 ***Wylie***	N	Y	N	Y	Y	Y	Y	Y
16 ***Regula***	Y	N	Y	Y	Y	Y	Y	Y
17 Traficant	Y	N	Y	Y	Y	Y	N	N
18 Applegate	Y	N	Y	Y	Y	Y	N	N
19 Feighan	Y	N	Y	Y	Y	Y	Y	Y
20 Oakar	Y	N	Y	?	Y	Y	Y	Y
21 Stokes	Y	N	Y	N	Y	Y	N	N
OKLAHOMA								
1 ***Inhofe***	N	Y	N	Y	N	N	Y	N
2 Synar	Y	N	Y	N	Y	Y	N	Y
3 Brewster	Y	N	N	Y	Y	Y	N	N
4 McCurdy	Y	N	Y	Y	Y	Y	N	N
5 ***Edwards***	Y	Y	N	Y	Y	Y	N	N
6 English	Y	N	Y	Y	Y	Y	N	N
OREGON								
1 AuCoin	Y	N	Y	N	Y	Y	Y	N
2 ***Smith***	N	Y	N	N	Y	Y	N	N
3 Wyden	Y	N	Y	N	Y	Y	Y	N
4 DeFazio	Y	N	Y	N	Y	Y	Y	N
5 Kopetski	Y	N	Y	Y	Y	Y	N	Y
PENNSYLVANIA								
1 Foglietta	Y	N	Y	Y	Y	Y	N	N
2 Blackwell	Y	N	Y	Y	Y	Y	N	N
3 Borski	Y	N	Y	Y	Y	Y	N	N
4 Kolter	Y	N	Y	Y	Y	Y	N	N
5 ***Schulze***	?	?	?	?	?	?	?	?
6 Yatron	Y	N	Y	Y	Y	Y	Y	N
7 ***Weldon***	Y	N	Y	Y	Y	Y	Y	Y
8 Kostmayer	Y	N	Y	Y	Y	Y	N	Y
9 ***Shuster***	N	Y	N	Y	Y	Y	Y	Y
10 ***McDade***	Y	N	Y	Y	Y	Y	Y	Y
11 Kanjorski	Y	N	Y	N	Y	Y	Y	N
12 Murtha	Y	N	Y	Y	Y	Y	N	N
13 ***Coughlin***	Y	N	Y	Y	Y	Y	Y	Y
14 Coyne	Y	N	Y	Y	Y	Y	N	N
15 ***Ritter***	N	N	N	Y	Y	Y	Y	Y
16 ***Walker***	N	Y	N	Y	Y	Y	Y	Y
17 ***Gekas***	N	Y	N	N	Y	Y	Y	Y
18 ***Santorum***	N	Y	N	Y	Y	Y	Y	Y
19 ***Goodling***	N	Y	N	Y	Y	Y	Y	Y
20 Gaydos	Y	N	Y	Y	Y	Y	N	N
21 ***Ridge***	N	Y	N	Y	N	Y	Y	N
22 Murphy	Y	N	Y	Y	Y	Y	N	N
23 ***Clinger***	N	Y	N	Y	Y	Y	Y	Y
RHODE ISLAND								
1 ***Machtley***	Y	N	Y	Y	Y	Y	Y	Y
2 Reed	Y	N	Y	Y	Y	Y	Y	Y
SOUTH CAROLINA								
1 ***Ravenel***	Y	N	Y	Y	Y	Y	Y	Y
2 ***Spence***	Y	Y	N	Y	Y	Y	Y	Y
3 Derrick	N	N	N	Y	Y	Y	Y	Y
4 Patterson	N	N	N	Y	Y	Y	Y	Y
5 Spratt	Y	N	Y	Y	Y	Y	Y	Y
6 Tallon	Y	N	Y	Y	Y	Y	Y	Y

	391	392	393	394	395	396	398	399
SOUTH DAKOTA								
AL Johnson	Y	N	Y	N	Y	Y	Y	Y
TENNESSEE								
1 ***Quillen***	N	Y	N	Y	Y	Y	Y	Y
2 ***Duncan***	N	Y	N	Y	N	N	Y	Y
3 Lloyd	N	Y	N	Y	Y	?	?	?
4 Cooper	N	Y	N	C	Y	Y	C	C
5 Clement	Y	N	Y	Y	Y	Y	Y	Y
6 Gordon	Y	N	Y	Y	Y	Y	Y	Y
7 ***Sundquist***	N	Y	N	Y	Y	Y	Y	Y
8 Tanner	N	Y	N	Y	Y	Y	Y	Y
9 Ford	Y	N	Y	Y	Y	Y	Y	Y
TEXAS								
1 Chapman	Y	N	Y	Y	Y	Y	N	N
2 Wilson	Y	N	Y	Y	Y	Y	Y	Y
3 ***Johnson***	N	Y	N	?	N	N	Y	Y
4 Hall	N	N	N	Y	Y	Y	Y	Y
5 Bryant	Y	N	Y	?	Y	Y	N	N
6 ***Barton***	N	N	N	Y	N	N	N	Y
7 ***Archer***	N	Y	N	Y	N	N	Y	Y
8 ***Fields***	N	Y	N	Y	Y	Y	Y	Y
9 Brooks	Y	N	Y	Y	Y	Y	C	C
10 Pickle	Y	N	Y	Y	Y	Y	Y	Y
11 Edwards	Y	N	N	Y	Y	Y	N	N
12 Geren	N	N	N	Y	Y	Y	Y	Y
13 Sarpalius	N	N	N	Y	Y	Y	N	N
14 Laughlin	N	N	N	Y	Y	Y	N	N
15 de la Garza	Y	N	Y	Y	Y	Y	Y	N
16 Coleman	Y	N	Y	Y	Y	Y	N	Y
17 Stenholm	N	N	N	Y	Y	N	N	Y
18 Washington	Y	N	Y	Y	Y	Y	N	N
19 ***Combest***	N	N	N	Y	N	N	N	N
20 Gonzalez	Y	N	Y	Y	Y	Y	Y	Y
21 ***Smith***	Y	N	Y	N	N	Y	N	Y
22 ***DeLay***	N	Y	N	?	N	N	Y	N
23 Bustamante	Y	N	Y	Y	Y	Y	N	N
24 Frost	Y	N	Y	Y	Y	Y	Y	Y
25 Andrews	Y	N	Y	Y	Y	Y	Y	Y
26 ***Armey***	N	Y	N	Y	N	N	Y	N
27 Ortiz	Y	N	Y	Y	Y	Y	N	N
UTAH								
1 ***Hansen***	N	Y	N	Y	Y	N	Y	Y
2 Owens	Y	N	Y	N	Y	Y	Y	N
3 Orton	Y	N	N	N	Y	Y	N	Y
VERMONT								
AL *Sanders*	Y	N	Y	N	Y	Y	N	N
VIRGINIA								
1 ***Bateman***	?	N	N	Y	Y	Y	N	Y
2 Pickett	N	N	N	Y	Y	Y	Y	Y
3 ***Bliley***	N	Y	N	Y	Y	Y	Y	Y
4 Sisisky	Y	N	N	Y	Y	Y	Y	Y
5 Payne	N	N	N	Y	Y	Y	N	N
6 Olin	N	Y	N	?	Y	Y	N	N
7 ***Allen***	N	Y	N	N	N	Y	N	N
8 Moran	Y	N	Y	Y	Y	Y	Y	Y
9 Boucher	Y	N	Y	Y	Y	Y	N	N
10 ***Wolf***	N	Y	N	Y	Y	Y	Y	Y
WASHINGTON								
1 ***Miller***	Y	N	Y	Y	Y	Y	N	Y
2 Swift	Y	N	Y	Y	Y	Y	N	N
3 Unsoeld	Y	N	Y	Y	Y	Y	N	N
4 ***Morrison***	Y	N	Y	N	Y	Y	N	Y
5 Foley								
6 Dicks	Y	N	?	Y	Y	Y	Y	Y
7 McDermott	Y	N	Y	Y	Y	Y	N	N
8 ***Chandler***	N	Y	N	Y	Y	Y	N	Y
WEST VIRGINIA								
1 Mollohan	Y	N	Y	Y	Y	Y	N	N
2 Staggers	Y	N	Y	Y	Y	Y	N	N
3 Wise	Y	N	Y	N	Y	Y	N	N
4 Rahall	Y	N	Y	Y	Y	Y	N	N
WISCONSIN								
1 Aspin	N	N	N	Y	Y	Y	N	N
2 ***Klug***	Y	N	Y	N	Y	Y	N	Y
3 ***Gunderson***	Y	Y	N	Y	Y	Y	N	N
4 Kleczka	Y	N	Y	Y	Y	Y	N	Y
5 Moody	Y	N	Y	N	Y	Y	?	?
6 ***Petri***	N	Y	N	N	N	N	N	N
7 Obey	Y	N	Y	N	Y	Y	N	N
8 ***Roth***	N	Y	N	N	Y	Y	N	N
9 ***Sensenbrenner***	N	Y	N	N	N	N	N	N
WYOMING								
AL ***Thomas***	N	Y	N	Y	Y	?	?	?

Southern states - Ala., Ark., Fla., Ga., Ky., La., Miss., N.C., Okla., S.C., Tenn., Texas, Va.
Omitted votes are quorum calls, which CQ does not include in its vote charts.

HOUSE VOTES 400, 401, 403, 404, 405, 406, 407, 408

400. HR 2100. Fiscal 1992 Defense Authorization/Conference Report. Adoption of the conference report to authorize $290.8 billion for defense programs in fiscal 1992. The measure authorizes $4.36 billion for the B-2 bomber but halts most new production of the bomber and authorizes $4.15 billion for the Strategic Defense Initiative. Adopted 329-82: R 122-35; D 207-46 (ND 129-43, SD 78-3); I 0-1, Nov. 18, 1991.

401. HR 355. Bureau of Reclamation Drought Assistance/Senate Amendments. Miller, D-Calif., motion to suspend the rules and adopt the resolution (H Res 282) to take from the Speaker's table the bill HR 355 and concur in the Senate amendments with an amendment. The bill provides for emergency drought assistance and for changes in the Central Utah Project. Motion rejected 245-164: R 57-100; D 187-64 (ND 142-28, SD 45-36); I 1-0, Nov. 18, 1991. A two-thirds majority of those present and voting (273 in this case) is required for passage under suspension of the rules.

403. HR 2707. Fiscal 1992 Labor, HHS, and Education Appropriations/Passage. Passage, over President Bush's Nov. 19 veto, of the bill to provide $204,919,763,000 in new budget authority for the Departments of Labor, Health and Human Services, and Education and related agencies. The measure would block enforcement of the administration rule, known as the "gag rule," barring abortion counseling in federally funded family planning clinics. Rejected 276-156: R 53-113; D 222-43 (ND 155-26, SD 67-17); I 1-0, Nov. 19, 1991. A two-thirds majority of those present and voting (288 in this case) of both chambers is required to override a veto. A "nay" was a vote supporting the president's position.

404. HR 3595. Medicaid Moratorium/Rule. Adoption of the rule (H Res 283) to provide for House floor consideration of the bill to block the administration rules that prohibit states from using voluntary contributions, provider-specific taxes and intergovernmental transfers to finance their share of Medicaid programs. Adopted 382-41: R 127-38; D 254-3 (ND 170-3, SD 84-0); I 1-0, Nov. 19, 1991.

405. HR 3595. Medicaid Moratorium/Strike Congressional Budget Office Estimates. Gradison, R-Ohio, amendment to strike the provisions of the bill that assure that the Congressional Budget Office estimates, instead of the estimates of the Office of Management and Budget, will be used for the purposes of the pay-as-you-go requirements of the Balanced Budget and Emergency Deficit Control Act. Rejected 156-262: R 148-15; D 8-246 (ND 7-164, SD 1-82); I 0-1, Nov. 19, 1991. A "yea" was a vote supporting the president's position.

406. HR 3595. Medicaid Moratorium/Recommittal Motion. Lent, R-N.Y., motion to recommit the bill to the Energy and Commerce Committee, with instructions to report back to the House by the end of the session a bill, which, while taking into account the overall impact on Medicaid recipients, would eliminate the abuse by states of voluntary contributions. Motion rejected 117-302: R 112-52; D 5-249 (ND 5-166, SD 0-83); I 0-1, Nov. 19, 1991.

407. HR 3595. Medicaid Moratorium/Passage. Passage of the bill to block the administration rules that prohibit states from using voluntary contributions, provider-specific taxes and intergovernmental transfers to finance their share of Medicaid. Passed 348-71: R 101-63; D 246-8 (ND 164-7, SD 82-1); I 1-0, Nov. 19, 1991. A "nay" was a vote supporting the president's position.

408. HR 2521. Fiscal 1992 Defense Appropriations/Rule. Adoption of the rule (H Res 286) to waive all points of order against and provide for House floor consideration of the conference report to provide $269,911,240,000 in new budget authority for the Department of Defense in fiscal 1992. The administration requested $270,936,322,000. Adopted 359-59: R 102-58; D 256-1 (ND 172-1, SD 84-0); I 1-0, Nov. 20, 1991.

KEY

Y Voted for (yea).
Paired for.
\+ Announced for.
N Voted against (nay).
X Paired against.
\- Announced against.
P Voted "present."
C Voted "present" to avoid possible conflict of interest.
? Did not vote or otherwise make a position known.

Democrats ***Republicans*** *Independent*

	400	401	403	404	405	406	407	408
ALABAMA								
1 ***Callahan***	Y	N	N	Y	N	N	Y	Y
2 ***Dickinson***	Y	N	N	Y	Y	N	Y	?
3 Browder	Y	Y	Y	Y	N	N	Y	Y
4 Bevill	Y	Y	Y	Y	N	N	Y	Y
5 Cramer	Y	N	Y	Y	N	N	Y	Y
6 Erdreich	Y	Y	Y	Y	N	N	Y	Y
7 Harris	Y	Y	Y	Y	N	N	Y	Y
ALASKA								
AL ***Young***	Y	N	N	N	?	?	?	Y
ARIZONA								
1 ***Rhodes***	Y	Y	N	Y	Y	Y	Y	N
2 Pastor	Y	Y	Y	Y	N	N	Y	?
3 ***Stump***	N	N	N	N	Y	Y	N	N
4 ***Kyl***	Y	Y	N	Y	Y	Y	N	N
5 ***Kolbe***	Y	Y	Y	Y	Y	Y	Y	Y
ARKANSAS								
1 Alexander	N	Y	Y	Y	N	N	Y	Y
2 Thornton	Y	Y	Y	Y	N	N	Y	Y
3 ***Hammerschmidt***	Y	N	N	Y	Y	Y	Y	Y
4 Anthony	Y	Y	Y	Y	N	N	Y	Y
CALIFORNIA								
1 ***Riggs***	N	P	Y	Y	Y	Y	Y	Y
2 ***Herger***	Y	N	N	N	Y	Y	N	N
3 Matsui	Y	N	Y	Y	N	N	Y	Y
4 Fazio	Y	N	Y	?	?	?	?	Y
5 Pelosi	N	Y	Y	Y	N	N	Y	Y
6 Boxer	N	Y	Y	Y	N	N	Y	Y
7 Miller	N	Y	Y	Y	N	N	Y	Y
8 Dellums	N	Y	Y	Y	N	N	Y	Y
9 Stark	Y	Y	Y	Y	?	?	Y	Y
10 Edwards	N	Y	Y	Y	N	N	Y	Y
11 Lantos	Y	Y	Y	Y	N	N	Y	Y
12 ***Campbell***	?	?	Y	Y	Y	Y	N	Y
13 Mineta	Y	Y	Y	Y	N	N	Y	Y
14 ***Doolittle***	Y	N	N	Y	Y	Y	N	N
15 Condit	Y	N	Y	Y	N	N	Y	Y
16 Panetta	Y	Y	Y	Y	N	N	Y	Y
17 Dooley	Y	N	Y	Y	N	N	Y	Y
18 Lehman	Y	N	Y	Y	N	N	Y	Y
19 ***Lagomarsino***	Y	N	N	N	Y	Y	Y	N
20 ***Thomas***	N	N	Y	Y	Y	Y	Y	N
21 ***Gallegly***	Y	N	N	N	Y	Y	Y	N
22 ***Moorhead***	N	N	N	Y	Y	Y	N	N
23 Beilenson	N	Y	Y	Y	N	N	N	Y
24 Waxman	Y	Y	Y	Y	N	N	Y	Y
25 Roybal	N	Y	Y	Y	N	N	Y	Y
26 Berman	Y	Y	Y	Y	N	N	Y	Y
27 Levine	?	?	?	?	?	?	?	Y
28 Dixon	?	?	Y	Y	N	N	Y	Y
29 Waters	N	Y	Y	Y	N	N	Y	Y
30 Martinez	Y	N	Y	Y	N	N	Y	Y
31 Dymally	Y	Y	Y	Y	N	N	Y	Y
32 Anderson	Y	Y	Y	Y	N	N	Y	Y
33 ***Dreier***	Y	N	N	Y	Y	Y	N	Y
34 Torres	Y	Y	Y	Y	N	N	Y	Y
35 ***Lewis***	?	?	N	Y	Y	Y	Y	Y
36 Brown	Y	Y	Y	Y	N	N	Y	Y
37 ***McCandless***	Y	N	N	Y	Y	Y	Y	Y
38 ***Dornan***	N	N	N	Y	Y	Y	N	N
39 ***Dannemeyer***	N	N	N	N	Y	Y	N	N
40 ***Cox***	N	N	N	Y	Y	Y	N	N
41 ***Lowery***	Y	N	N	Y	Y	Y	Y	N
42 ***Rohrabacher***	Y	N	N	N	Y	Y	N	N
43 ***Packard***	N	N	N	Y	Y	Y	N	N
44 ***Cunningham***	N	N	N	Y	Y	N	Y	Y
45 ***Hunter***	N	N	N	N	Y	Y	Y	N
COLORADO								
1 Schroeder	N	Y	Y	Y	N	N	Y	Y
2 Skaggs	N	Y	Y	Y	N	N	Y	Y
3 Campbell	Y	Y	Y	Y	N	N	Y	Y
4 ***Allard***	Y	N	N	N	Y	Y	N	N
5 ***Hefley***	Y	N	N	Y	Y	N	Y	N
6 ***Schaefer***	Y	N	N	N	Y	Y	Y	N
CONNECTICUT								
1 Kennelly	Y	Y	Y	Y	N	N	Y	Y
2 Gejdenson	Y	Y	Y	Y	N	N	Y	Y
3 DeLauro	Y	Y	Y	Y	N	N	Y	Y
4 ***Shays***	N	Y	Y	Y	Y	Y	N	N
5 ***Franks***	Y	N	Y	Y	Y	Y	Y	Y
6 ***Johnson***	Y	Y	Y	Y	Y	Y	N	Y
DELAWARE								
AL Carper	Y	Y	Y	Y	N	N	Y	Y
FLORIDA								
1 Hutto	Y	Y	N	Y	N	N	Y	Y
2 Peterson	Y	N	Y	Y	N	N	Y	Y
3 Bennett	Y	Y	N	Y	N	N	Y	Y
4 ***James***	Y	Y	N	Y	Y	Y	Y	N
5 ***McCollum***	Y	N	N	Y	Y	Y	N	Y
6 ***Stearns***	Y	N	N	Y	Y	Y	Y	N
7 Gibbons	Y	Y	Y	Y	N	N	Y	Y
8 ***Young***	Y	N	N	Y	Y	Y	Y	Y
9 ***Bilirakis***	?	?	N	Y	Y	Y	N	N
10 ***Ireland***	Y	Y	N	?	Y	Y	Y	N
11 Bacchus	Y	N	Y	Y	N	N	Y	Y
12 ***Lewis***	Y	N	N	Y	Y	Y	N	N
13 ***Goss***	Y	Y	N	Y	Y	Y	N	N
14 Johnston	Y	Y	Y	Y	N	N	Y	Y
15 ***Shaw***	Y	N	N	Y	Y	Y	N	?
16 Smith	N	Y	Y	Y	N	N	Y	Y
17 Lehman	Y	Y	Y	Y	N	N	Y	Y
18 ***Ros-Lehtinen***	Y	Y	N	Y	Y	Y	Y	N
19 Fascell	Y	Y	Y	Y	N	N	Y	Y
GEORGIA								
1 Thomas	Y	Y	Y	Y	N	N	Y	Y
2 Hatcher	?	?	?	?	?	?	?	?
3 Ray	Y	Y	N	Y	N	N	Y	Y
4 Jones	Y	Y	Y	Y	N	N	Y	Y
5 Lewis	Y	Y	Y	Y	N	N	Y	Y
6 ***Gingrich***	Y	N	N	Y	?	Y	Y	Y
7 Darden	Y	Y	Y	Y	N	N	Y	Y
8 Rowland	Y	Y	Y	Y	N	N	Y	Y
9 Jenkins	Y	Y	Y	Y	N	N	Y	Y
10 Barnard	Y	N	N	Y	N	N	Y	Y
HAWAII								
1 Abercrombie	Y	Y	Y	Y	N	N	Y	Y
2 Mink	Y	Y	Y	Y	N	N	Y	Y
IDAHO								
1 LaRocco	Y	Y	+	Y	N	N	Y	Y
2 Stallings	Y	Y	N	Y	N	N	Y	Y
ILLINOIS								
1 Hayes	N	Y	Y	Y	N	N	Y	Y
2 Savage	N	Y	Y	Y	N	N	Y	?
3 Russo	N	Y	Y	Y	N	N	Y	Y
4 Sangmeister	Y	Y	Y	Y	N	N	Y	Y
5 Lipinski	Y	Y	N	Y	N	N	Y	Y
6 ***Hyde***	Y	N	N	Y	Y	Y	Y	Y
7 Collins	N	Y	Y	Y	N	N	Y	Y
8 Rostenkowski	Y	Y	Y	Y	N	N	Y	Y
9 Yates	N	Y	Y	Y	N	N	Y	Y
10 ***Porter***	Y	Y	Y	Y	Y	Y	Y	Y
11 Annunzio	Y	Y	N	Y	N	N	Y	Y
12 ***Crane***	N	Y	N	N	Y	Y	N	N
13 ***Fawell***	N	Y	Y	Y	Y	Y	N	Y
14 ***Hastert***	Y	N	N	Y	Y	Y	Y	N
15 ***Ewing***	Y	N	N	Y	Y	Y	Y	Y
16 Cox	Y	Y	Y	Y	N	N	Y	Y
17 Evans	Y	Y	Y	Y	N	N	Y	Y
18 ***Michel***	Y	N	N	N	Y	Y	N	Y
19 Bruce	Y	Y	Y	Y	N	N	Y	Y
20 Durbin	Y	Y	Y	Y	N	N	Y	Y
21 Costello	Y	Y	N	Y	N	N	Y	Y
22 Poshard	Y	Y	N	Y	N	N	Y	Y
INDIANA								
1 Visclosky	Y	Y	Y	Y	Y	N	Y	Y
2 Sharp	Y	Y	Y	Y	N	N	Y	Y
3 Roemer	Y	Y	Y	Y	N	N	Y	Y

ND Northern Democrats SD Southern Democrats

	400	401	403	404	405	406	407	408
4 Long	Y	Y	Y	Y	N	N	Y	Y
5 Jontz	Y	Y	Y	Y	N	N	Y	Y
6 ***Burton***	N	N	N	N	Y	Y	N	N
7 ***Myers***	Y	N	Y	Y	Y	Y	Y	Y
8 McCloskey	Y	Y	Y	Y	N	N	Y	Y
9 Hamilton	Y	Y	Y	Y	Y	N	N	Y
10 Jacobs	Y	Y	Y	Y	N	N	Y	Y
IOWA								
1 ***Leach***	N	Y	Y	Y	Y	Y	N	N
2 ***Nussle***	N	N	N	Y	Y	Y	N	N
3 Nagle	Y	Y	Y	Y	N	N	Y	Y
4 Smith	Y	Y	Y	N	N	Y	N	Y
5 ***Lightfoot***	Y	N	N	N	Y	Y	N	N
6 ***Grandy***	Y	N	Y	N	Y	Y	N	Y
KANSAS								
1 ***Roberts***	Y	N	N	Y	Y	Y	N	N
2 Slattery	Y	N	Y	Y	N	N	Y	Y
3 ***Meyers***	Y	Y	Y	Y	Y	Y	N	Y
4 Glickman	Y	Y	Y	Y	N	N	Y	Y
5 ***Nichols***	Y	N	N	Y	Y	Y	N	N
KENTUCKY								
1 Hubbard	Y	N	Y	Y	N	N	Y	Y
2 Natcher	Y	Y	Y	Y	N	N	Y	Y
3 Mazzoli	Y	Y	N	Y	N	N	Y	Y
4 ***Bunning***	Y	N	N	Y	Y	Y	Y	N
5 ***Rogers***	Y	N	N	Y	Y	N	Y	Y
6 ***Hopkins***	Y	N	N	Y	Y	Y	Y	Y
7 Perkins	Y	N	Y	Y	N	N	Y	Y
LOUISIANA								
1 ***Livingston***	Y	N	N	N	Y	Y	N	Y
2 Jefferson	Y	N	Y	Y	N	N	Y	Y
3 Tauzin	Y	N	N	Y	N	N	Y	Y
4 ***McCrery***	Y	N	N	Y	Y	Y	N	?
5 Huckaby	Y	N	N	Y	N	N	Y	Y
6 ***Baker***	?	?	N	N	Y	Y	N	Y
7 Hayes	Y	N	N	Y	?	?	?	Y
8 ***Holloway***	Y	N	N	N	Y	Y	N	N
MAINE								
1 Andrews	Y	Y	Y	Y	N	N	Y	Y
2 ***Snowe***	Y	Y	Y	Y	N	N	Y	Y
MARYLAND								
1 ***Gilchrest***	Y	Y	Y	Y	Y	Y	Y	Y
2 ***Bentley***	Y	N	Y	Y	Y	N	Y	Y
3 Cardin	Y	Y	Y	Y	N	N	Y	Y
4 McMillen	Y	Y	Y	Y	N	N	Y	Y
5 Hoyer	Y	N	Y	Y	N	N	Y	Y
6 Byron	Y	Y	Y	Y	N	N	Y	Y
7 Mfume	N	Y	Y	Y	N	N	Y	Y
8 ***Morella***	N	Y	Y	Y	Y	N	Y	?
MASSACHUSETTS								
1 Olver	Y	Y	Y	Y	N	N	Y	Y
2 Neal	Y	Y	Y	Y	N	N	Y	Y
3 Early	Y	Y	Y	Y	N	N	Y	Y
4 Frank	Y	Y	Y	?	?	?	?	Y
5 Atkins	Y	Y	Y	Y	N	N	Y	Y
6 Mavroules	Y	N	N	Y	N	N	Y	Y
7 Markey	Y	Y	Y	Y	N	N	Y	Y
8 Kennedy	?	?	Y	Y	N	N	Y	Y
9 Moakley	Y	Y	Y	Y	N	N	Y	Y
10 Studds	N	Y	Y	Y	N	N	Y	Y
11 Donnelly	Y	Y	N	Y	N	N	Y	Y
MICHIGAN								
1 Conyers	N	Y	Y	Y	N	N	Y	Y
2 ***Pursell***	N	N	Y	Y	Y	N	Y	Y
3 Wolpe	Y	Y	Y	Y	N	N	Y	Y
4 ***Upton***	Y	Y	Y	N	Y	N	Y	N
5 ***Henry***	Y	N	N	Y	Y	N	Y	N
6 Carr	Y	N	Y	?	N	N	Y	Y
7 Kildee	Y	Y	N	Y	N	N	Y	Y
8 Traxler	Y	Y	Y	Y	?	?	?	?
9 ***Vander Jagt***	Y	N	N	Y	Y	N	Y	Y
10 ***Camp***	Y	N	N	Y	Y	N	Y	Y
11 ***Davis***	Y	N	N	Y	N	N	Y	Y
12 Bonior	Y	Y	Y	Y	N	N	Y	?
13 Collins	N	Y	Y	Y	N	N	Y	Y
14 Hertel	Y	Y	Y	Y	N	N	Y	Y
15 Ford	N	Y	Y	Y	N	N	Y	Y
16 Dingell	Y	N	Y	Y	N	N	Y	Y
17 Levin	Y	Y	Y	Y	N	N	Y	Y
18 ***Broomfield***	Y	Y	N	Y	Y	N	Y	Y
MINNESOTA								
1 Penny	Y	N	Y	N	Y	Y	N	Y
2 ***Weber***	N	N	N	N	Y	N	Y	Y
3 ***Ramstad***	Y	Y	Y	Y	Y	N	Y	Y
4 Vento	N	Y	Y	Y	N	N	Y	Y
5 Sabo	Y	Y	Y	Y	N	N	Y	Y
6 Sikorski	N	Y	Y	Y	N	N	Y	Y
7 Peterson	Y	N	N	Y	N	N	Y	Y
8 Oberstar	N	Y	N	Y	N	N	Y	Y
MISSISSIPPI								
1 Whitten	Y	Y	Y	Y	N	N	Y	Y
2 Espy	Y	N	Y	Y	N	N	Y	Y
3 Montgomery	Y	N	N	Y	N	N	Y	Y
4 Parker	Y	N	N	Y	N	N	Y	Y
5 Taylor	Y	N	N	Y	N	N	Y	Y
MISSOURI								
1 Clay	N	Y	Y	Y	N	N	Y	Y
2 Horn	Y	Y	Y	Y	N	N	Y	Y
3 Gephardt	Y	Y	Y	Y	N	N	Y	Y
4 Skelton	Y	N	Y	Y	N	N	Y	Y
5 Wheat	N	Y	Y	Y	N	N	Y	Y
6 ***Coleman***	Y	N	Y	Y	Y	N	Y	Y
7 ***Hancock***	?	?	N	N	Y	Y	N	N
8 ***Emerson***	Y	N	N	Y	N	N	Y	Y
9 Volkmer	Y	N	N	Y	N	N	Y	Y
MONTANA								
1 Williams	Y	N	Y	Y	N	Y	N	Y
2 ***Marlenee***	Y	N	N	Y	N	Y	N	N
NEBRASKA								
1 ***Bereuter***	Y	N	Y	Y	Y	Y	N	Y
2 Hoagland	Y	Y	Y	Y	N	N	Y	Y
3 ***Barrett***	Y	N	N	N	Y	Y	N	Y
NEVADA								
1 Bilbray	Y	N	Y	Y	N	N	Y	Y
2 ***Vucanovich***	Y	N	N	N	Y	N	Y	N
NEW HAMPSHIRE								
1 ***Zeliff***	N	N	Y	Y	Y	Y	N	N
2 Swett	Y	N	Y	Y	N	N	Y	Y
NEW JERSEY								
1 Andrews	Y	N	Y	Y	N	N	Y	?
2 Hughes	N	Y	Y	Y	N	N	Y	Y
3 Pallone	Y	Y	Y	Y	Y	N	Y	Y
4 ***Smith***	Y	Y	N	Y	Y	N	Y	Y
5 ***Roukema***	Y	Y	Y	Y	Y	N	Y	Y
6 Dwyer	Y	Y	Y	Y	N	N	Y	Y
7 ***Rinaldo***	Y	Y	N	Y	N	N	Y	Y
8 Roe	Y	Y	N	Y	N	N	Y	Y
9 Torricelli	Y	Y	Y	Y	N	N	Y	Y
10 Payne	N	Y	Y	Y	N	N	Y	Y
11 ***Gallo***	Y	Y	Y	Y	Y	N	Y	Y
12 ***Zimmer***	N	Y	Y	Y	Y	Y	N	N
13 ***Saxton***	Y	Y	N	Y	Y	N	Y	Y
14 Guarini	N	Y	Y	Y	N	N	Y	Y
NEW MEXICO								
1 ***Schiff***	Y	Y	Y	N	Y	Y	Y	N
2 ***Skeen***	Y	Y	Y	Y	Y	Y	Y	Y
3 Richardson	Y	Y	Y	Y	N	N	Y	Y
NEW YORK								
1 Hochbrueckner	Y	Y	Y	Y	N	N	Y	Y
2 Downey	Y	Y	Y	Y	N	N	Y	Y
3 Mrazek	?	?	Y	?	?	?	?	?
4 ***Lent***	N	Y	N	N	Y	Y	N	Y
5 ***McGrath***	N	N	Y	N	Y	N	Y	Y
6 Flake	N	N	Y	Y	?	?	?	Y
7 Ackerman	?	?	Y	?	?	?	?	Y
8 Scheuer	N	Y	Y	?	?	?	?	Y
9 Manton	Y	Y	N	?	?	?	?	Y
10 Schumer	Y	?	Y	Y	N	N	Y	Y
11 Towns	?	?	Y	Y	N	N	Y	?
12 Owens	?	?	Y	Y	N	N	Y	Y
13 Solarz	Y	Y	Y	Y	N	N	Y	Y
14 ***Molinari***	Y	N	Y	Y	Y	N	Y	Y
15 ***Green***	N	Y	Y	Y	Y	N	Y	Y
16 Rangel	N	Y	Y	Y	N	N	Y	Y
17 Weiss	N	Y	Y	Y	N	N	Y	Y
18 Serrano	N	Y	Y	Y	N	N	Y	Y
19 Engel	Y	Y	Y	Y	N	N	Y	Y
20 Lowey	Y	Y	Y	Y	N	N	Y	Y
21 ***Fish***	Y	N	Y	Y	?	?	?	Y
22 ***Gilman***	Y	Y	Y	Y	N	N	Y	Y
23 McNulty	Y	Y	Y	Y	N	N	Y	Y
24 ***Solomon***	Y	Y	N	Y	Y	Y	N	Y
25 ***Boehlert***	Y	Y	Y	Y	N	N	Y	Y
26 ***Martin***	Y	N	Y	Y	Y	N	Y	Y
27 ***Walsh***	Y	Y	N	Y	Y	Y	Y	Y
28 McHugh	Y	Y	Y	Y	N	N	Y	Y
29 ***Horton***	?	?	Y	Y	N	N	Y	Y
30 Slaughter	Y	Y	Y	Y	N	N	Y	Y
31 ***Paxon***	Y	N	N	Y	Y	Y	Y	Y
32 LaFalce	Y	Y	N	Y	N	N	Y	Y
33 Nowak	Y	Y	N	Y	N	N	Y	Y
34 ***Houghton***	Y	N	Y	Y	Y	Y	Y	Y
NORTH CAROLINA								
1 Jones	Y	N	Y	Y	N	N	Y	Y
2 Valentine	Y	N	Y	Y	N	N	Y	Y
3 Lancaster	Y	N	Y	Y	N	N	Y	Y
4 Price	Y	Y	Y	Y	N	N	Y	Y
5 Neal	?	?	Y	Y	N	N	Y	Y
6 ***Coble***	N	N	N	Y	Y	Y	N	Y
7 Rose	Y	Y	Y	Y	N	N	Y	Y
8 Hefner	Y	Y	Y	Y	N	N	Y	Y
9 ***McMillan***	Y	N	N	Y	Y	Y	N	Y
10 ***Ballenger***	Y	N	N	N	Y	Y	N	N
11 ***Taylor***	N	N	N	Y	Y	Y	N	N
NORTH DAKOTA								
AL Dorgan	Y	Y	Y	N	Y	Y	N	N
OHIO								
1 Luken	?	?	N	Y	N	N	Y	Y
2 ***Gradison***	Y	N	Y	Y	Y	Y	N	Y
3 Hall	Y	Y	N	Y	N	N	Y	?
4 ***Oxley***	Y	N	N	Y	Y	N	Y	Y
5 ***Gillmor***	Y	N	N	Y	Y	N	Y	Y
6 ***McEwen***	Y	Y	N	Y	Y	N	Y	Y
7 ***Hobson***	Y	Y	Y	Y	Y	N	Y	Y
8 ***Boehner***	Y	N	N	Y	Y	Y	Y	Y
9 Kaptur	Y	Y	Y	Y	N	N	Y	Y
10 ***Miller***	Y	N	N	Y	Y	Y	Y	Y
11 Eckart	Y	Y	Y	Y	N	N	Y	Y
12 ***Kasich***	Y	N	N	Y	Y	Y	N	Y
13 Pease	?	?	Y	Y	N	N	N	Y
14 Sawyer	Y	Y	Y	Y	N	N	Y	Y
15 ***Wylie***	Y	N	N	Y	Y	Y	Y	Y
16 ***Regula***	Y	N	Y	Y	Y	N	Y	Y
17 Traficant	N	N	Y	Y	N	N	Y	Y
18 Applegate	Y	N	N	Y	N	N	Y	Y
19 Feighan	Y	Y	Y	Y	N	N	Y	Y
20 Oakar	Y	Y	Y	Y	N	N	Y	Y
21 Stokes	N	Y	Y	Y	N	N	Y	Y
OKLAHOMA								
1 ***Inhofe***	Y	N	N	N	Y	Y	Y	Y
2 Synar	Y	Y	Y	Y	N	N	Y	Y
3 Brewster	Y	N	Y	Y	N	N	Y	Y
4 McCurdy	?	?	Y	Y	N	N	Y	Y
5 ***Edwards***	Y	N	N	Y	Y	N	Y	N
6 English	Y	N	Y	Y	N	N	Y	Y
OREGON								
1 AuCoin	?	?	Y	?	?	?	?	Y
2 ***Smith***	Y	N	N	N	Y	Y	N	Y
3 Wyden	Y	Y	Y	Y	N	N	Y	Y
4 DeFazio	N	Y	Y	Y	N	N	Y	Y
5 Kopetski	Y	N	Y	Y	N	N	Y	Y
PENNSYLVANIA								
1 Foglietta	Y	Y	Y	Y	N	N	Y	Y
2 Blackwell	Y	Y	Y	Y	N	N	Y	Y
3 Borski	Y	Y	N	Y	N	N	Y	Y
4 Kolter	Y	N	N	Y	N	N	Y	Y
5 ***Schulze***	Y	N	N	Y	Y	Y	N	Y
6 Yatron	Y	Y	N	Y	N	N	Y	Y
7 ***Weldon***	Y	Y	N	Y	Y	N	Y	Y
8 Kostmayer	N	Y	Y	Y	N	N	Y	Y
9 ***Shuster***	N	N	N	N	Y	Y	N	Y
10 ***McDade***	Y	N	N	Y	Y	N	Y	Y
11 Kanjorski	Y	Y	N	Y	N	N	Y	Y
12 Murtha	Y	Y	Y	Y	N	N	Y	Y
13 ***Coughlin***	Y	N	Y	Y	Y	Y	Y	Y
14 Coyne	Y	Y	Y	Y	N	N	Y	Y
15 ***Ritter***	?	Y	N	Y	Y	Y	Y	N
16 ***Walker***	N	N	N	N	Y	Y	N	N
17 ***Gekas***	Y	N	Y	N	N	N	Y	N
18 ***Santorum***	Y	N	N	Y	Y	Y	Y	Y
19 ***Goodling***	Y	Y	Y	Y	Y	Y	Y	Y
20 Gaydos	Y	Y	Y	Y	N	N	Y	Y
21 ***Ridge***	Y	Y	Y	Y	Y	N	Y	Y
22 Murphy	Y	Y	N	Y	N	N	Y	Y
23 ***Clinger***	Y	Y	Y	Y	N	Y	Y	Y
RHODE ISLAND								
1 ***Machtley***	Y	Y	Y	Y	Y	Y	Y	Y
2 Reed	Y	Y	Y	Y	N	N	Y	Y
SOUTH CAROLINA								
1 ***Ravenel***	Y	Y	Y	Y	Y	N	Y	Y
2 ***Spence***	Y	N	N	Y	Y	N	Y	Y
3 Derrick	Y	Y	Y	Y	N	N	Y	Y
4 Patterson	Y	Y	Y	Y	N	N	Y	Y
5 Spratt	Y	Y	Y	Y	N	N	Y	Y
6 Tallon	Y	Y	N	Y	N	N	Y	Y
SOUTH DAKOTA								
AL Johnson	Y	Y	Y	Y	Y	Y	Y	Y
TENNESSEE								
1 ***Quillen***	?	?	N	Y	N	N	Y	Y
2 ***Duncan***	N	N	N	Y	Y	Y	Y	N
3 Lloyd	Y	N	Y	Y	N	N	Y	Y
4 Cooper	Y	Y	Y	Y	N	N	Y	Y
5 Clement	Y	N	Y	Y	N	N	Y	Y
6 Gordon	Y	Y	Y	Y	N	N	Y	Y
7 ***Sundquist***	Y	N	N	Y	N	N	Y	Y
8 Tanner	Y	N	Y	Y	N	N	Y	Y
9 Ford	?	?	Y	Y	N	N	Y	Y
TEXAS								
1 Chapman	Y	N	Y	Y	N	N	Y	Y
2 Wilson	Y	Y	Y	Y	N	N	Y	Y
3 ***Johnson***	N	N	N	Y	Y	Y	Y	Y
4 Hall	Y	N	N	Y	N	N	Y	Y
5 Bryant	Y	Y	Y	Y	N	N	Y	Y
6 ***Barton***	Y	Y	N	Y	N	N	Y	Y
7 ***Archer***	Y	Y	N	Y	Y	Y	Y	?
8 ***Fields***	Y	Y	N	Y	N	N	Y	N
9 Brooks	Y	Y	Y	Y	N	N	Y	Y
10 Pickle	Y	Y	Y	Y	N	N	Y	Y
11 Edwards	Y	N	Y	Y	N	N	Y	Y
12 Geren	Y	N	Y	Y	N	N	Y	Y
13 Sarpalius	Y	Y	N	Y	N	N	Y	Y
14 Laughlin	Y	N	Y	Y	N	N	Y	Y
15 de la Garza	Y	Y	N	Y	N	N	Y	Y
16 Coleman	Y	Y	Y	Y	N	N	Y	Y
17 Stenholm	Y	N	N	Y	N	N	Y	Y
18 Washington	N	N	Y	Y	N	N	Y	Y
19 ***Combest***	N	Y	N	Y	Y	N	Y	Y
20 Gonzalez	Y	Y	Y	Y	N	N	Y	Y
21 ***Smith***	Y	N	Y	Y	Y	N	Y	Y
22 ***DeLay***	Y	Y	N	Y	Y	Y	Y	N
23 Bustamante	Y	Y	Y	Y	N	N	Y	Y
24 Frost	Y	Y	Y	Y	N	N	Y	Y
25 Andrews	Y	Y	Y	Y	N	N	Y	Y
26 ***Armey***	Y	Y	N	N	Y	Y	N	Y
27 Ortiz	Y	N	N	Y	N	N	Y	Y
UTAH								
1 ***Hansen***	N	Y	N	N	Y	Y	Y	N
2 Owens	N	Y	Y	Y	N	N	Y	Y
3 Orton	N	Y	N	Y	Y	N	Y	Y
VERMONT								
AL *Sanders*	N	Y	Y	Y	N	N	Y	Y
VIRGINIA								
1 ***Bateman***	Y	N	N	Y	Y	Y	N	Y
2 Pickett	Y	N	Y	Y	N	N	Y	Y
3 ***Bliley***	Y	N	N	Y	Y	Y	N	Y
4 Sisisky	Y	Y	Y	Y	N	N	Y	Y
5 Payne	Y	N	Y	Y	N	N	Y	Y
6 Olin	Y	N	Y	Y	Y	N	N	Y
7 ***Allen***	Y	N	Y	Y	Y	Y	N	Y
8 Moran	Y	N	Y	Y	N	N	Y	Y
9 Boucher	Y	N	Y	Y	N	N	Y	Y
10 ***Wolf***	Y	Y	N	Y	Y	N	Y	Y
WASHINGTON								
1 ***Miller***	Y	Y	Y	Y	Y	Y	N	Y
2 Swift	Y	N	Y	Y	N	N	Y	Y
3 Unsoeld	N	Y	Y	Y	N	N	?	?
4 ***Morrison***	Y	N	Y	Y	Y	Y	Y	Y
5 Foley			Y					
6 Dicks	Y	N	Y	Y	N	N	Y	Y
7 McDermott	N	Y	Y	Y	N	N	Y	Y
8 ***Chandler***	Y	N	Y	N	Y	Y	Y	Y
WEST VIRGINIA								
1 Mollohan	Y	Y	N	Y	N	N	Y	Y
2 Staggers	Y	N	N	Y	N	N	Y	Y
3 Wise	Y	N	Y	Y	N	N	Y	Y
4 Rahall	Y	Y	Y	Y	N	N	Y	Y
WISCONSIN								
1 Aspin	Y	Y	Y	Y	N	N	Y	Y
2 ***Klug***	+	?	Y	Y	Y	N	N	Y
3 ***Gunderson***	Y	N	Y	Y	Y	Y	N	?
4 Kleczka	Y	Y	Y	Y	N	N	Y	Y
5 Moody	N	?	Y	Y	N	N	Y	Y
6 ***Petri***	N	Y	N	N	Y	Y	N	N
7 Obey	N	Y	Y	Y	N	N	Y	Y
8 ***Roth***	N	Y	N	N	Y	Y	N	N
9 ***Sensenbrenner***	N	Y	N	N	Y	Y	N	N
WYOMING								
AL ***Thomas***	Y	Y	N	N	Y	Y	Y	Y

Southern states - Ala., Ark., Fla., Ga., Ky., La., Miss., N.C., Okla., S.C., Tenn., Texas, Va.
Omitted votes are quorum calls, which CQ does not include in its vote charts.

HOUSE VOTES 409, 410, 411, 412, 413, 414, 415, 416

409. H Con Res 226. Commend Middle East Peace Process Participants/Passage. Owens, D-Utah, motion to suspend the rules and pass the concurrent resolution to commend the Middle East Peace Conference participants. Motion agreed to 426-0: R 163-0; D 262-0 (ND 180-0, SD 82-0); I 1-0, Nov. 20, 1991. A two-thirds majority of those present and voting (284 in this case) is required for passage under suspension of the rules.

410. H J Res 346. MFN for the Soviet Union/Passage. Rostenkowski, D-Ill., motion to suspend the rules and pass the joint resolution to approve the extension of non-discriminatory treatment, most-favored-nation (MFN) trading status, with respect to the products of the Soviet Union. Motion agreed to 350-78: R 113-53; D 236-25 (ND 168-11, SD 68-14); I 1-0, Nov. 20, 1991. A two-thirds majority of those present and voting (286 in this case) is required for passage under suspension of the rules. A "yea" was a vote supporting the president's position.

411. HR 1724. MFN for Hungary and Unemployment Benefits/Passage. Rostenkowski, D-Ill., motion to suspend the rules and adopt the resolution (H Res 287) to take the bill (HR 1724) to provide most-favored-nation (MFN) trading status for Czechoslovakia and Hungary from the Speaker's table and agree to the Senate amendment with an amendment. The Senate amendment modifies the Extended Unemployment Benefits bill (HR 3575) signed into law to provide a two-tier system with states receiving 13 or 20 weeks of extended benefits. The House amendment incorporated several trade measures as well as a bill that would impose import sanctions to curb proliferation of chemical weapons. Motion agreed to 407-21: R 146-20; D 260-1 (ND 179-0, SD 81-1); I 1-0, Nov. 20, 1991. A two-thirds majority of those present and voting (286 in this case) is required for passage under suspension of the rules. A "yea" was a vote supporting the president's position.

412. HR 1724. Hungary MFN and Unemployment Benefits/Andean Nations. Crane, R-Ill., motion to instruct House conferees to insist on the House provisions to combat illegal drug imports by providing trade incentives to Andean nations to stimulate alternatives to drug exports. Motion agreed to 416-0: R 157-0; D 258-0 (ND 177-0, SD 81-0); I 1-0, Nov. 21, 1991.

413. HR 3371. Crime Bill/Mandatory Minimum Sentences and Death Penalty. Sensenbrenner, R-Wis., motion to instruct the House conferees to accept the Senate provisions providing for mandatory minimum sentences and the possibility of the death penalty for individuals who use a firearm while committing a crime. Motion rejected 155-271: R 127-38; D 28-232 (ND 7-169, SD 21-63); I 0-1, Nov. 21, 1991.

414. HR 3768. Banking Reform/Recommittal Motion. Armey, R-Texas, motion to recommit the bill to the House Banking Committee, with instructions to report it back to the House with an amendment to roll back deposit insurance coverage to one account of $100,000 per individual for each bank plus a second $100,000 for a retirement account. Motion rejected 74-355: R 49-116; D 25-238 (ND 23-157, SD 2-81); I 0-1, Nov. 21, 1991.

415. HR 3768. Banking Reform/Passage. Passage of the bill to allow the Federal Deposit Insurance Corporation to borrow $30 billion to cover losses of failed banks and strengthen the regulation and supervision of the insured depository institutions. Passed 344-84: R 135-29; D 209-54 (ND 135-45, SD 74-9); I 0-1, Nov. 21, 1991. A "yea" was a vote supporting the president's position.

416. HR 3839. Fiscal 1992 Labor, HHS and Education Appropriations/Recommittal Motion. Kolbe, R-Ariz., motion to recommit the bill to the Appropriations Committee with instructions to report it back to the House after reducing the "excessive" use of delayed spending obligations in the bill. Motion rejected 148-276: R 120-42; D 28-233 (ND 17-162, SD 11-71); I 0-1, Nov. 22, 1991.

KEY

- Y Voted for (yea).
- # Paired for.
- \+ Announced for.
- N Voted against (nay).
- X Paired against.
- \- Announced against.
- P Voted "present."
- C Voted "present" to avoid possible conflict of interest.
- ? Did not vote or otherwise make a position known.

Democrats ***Republicans***
Independent

	409	410	411	412	413	414	415	416
ALABAMA								
1 ***Callahan***	Y	N	Y	Y	Y	N	Y	N
2 ***Dickinson***	Y	N	Y	Y	N	N	Y	Y
3 Browder	Y	Y	Y	Y	N	N	Y	N
4 Bevill	Y	Y	Y	Y	N	N	Y	N
5 Cramer	Y	N	Y	Y	N	N	Y	N
6 Erdreich	Y	N	Y	Y	N	N	Y	N
7 Harris	Y	Y	Y	Y	N	N	Y	N
ALASKA								
AL ***Young***	Y	Y	Y	Y	Y	N	Y	N
ARIZONA								
1 ***Rhodes***	Y	N	Y	Y	Y	N	Y	Y
2 Pastor	Y	Y	Y	Y	N	N	Y	Y
3 ***Stump***	Y	N	N	Y	Y	N	N	Y
4 ***Kyl***	Y	N	Y	Y	Y	N	Y	Y
5 ***Kolbe***	Y	Y	Y	Y	Y	Y	Y	Y
ARKANSAS								
1 Alexander	?	Y	Y	Y	N	N	Y	N
2 Thornton	Y	Y	Y	Y	N	N	Y	N
3 ***Hammerschmidt***	Y	Y	Y	Y	Y	N	Y	N
4 Anthony	Y	Y	Y	Y	N	N	Y	N
CALIFORNIA								
1 ***Riggs***	Y	Y	Y	Y	Y	N	Y	Y
2 ***Herger***	Y	N	Y	Y	Y	Y	N	Y
3 Matsui	Y	Y	Y	Y	N	N	Y	N
4 Fazio	Y	Y	Y	Y	N	N	Y	N
5 Pelosi	Y	Y	Y	Y	N	N	Y	N
6 Boxer	Y	Y	Y	Y	N	N	Y	N
7 Miller	Y	Y	Y	Y	N	Y	N	N
8 Dellums	Y	Y	Y	Y	N	N	Y	N
9 Stark	Y	Y	Y	Y	N	Y	Y	N
10 Edwards	Y	Y	Y	Y	N	N	Y	N
11 Lantos	Y	Y	Y	Y	N	N	Y	N
12 ***Campbell***	Y	Y	Y	Y	Y	N	Y	Y
13 Mineta	Y	Y	Y	Y	N	N	Y	N
14 ***Doolittle***	Y	N	N	Y	Y	N	X	?
15 Condit	Y	N	Y	Y	N	N	N	Y
16 Panetta	Y	Y	Y	Y	N	N	Y	Y
17 Dooley	Y	Y	Y	Y	N	N	Y	N
18 Lehman	Y	Y	Y	Y	N	N	Y	N
19 ***Lagomarsino***	Y	Y	Y	Y	Y	N	Y	Y
20 ***Thomas***	Y	Y	Y	Y	Y	Y	Y	Y
21 ***Gallegly***	Y	N	Y	Y	Y	N	Y	Y
22 ***Moorhead***	Y	N	Y	Y	Y	N	Y	Y
23 Beilenson	Y	Y	Y	Y	N	Y	Y	Y
24 Waxman	Y	Y	Y	?	?	?	#	N
25 Roybal	Y	Y	Y	Y	N	N	Y	N
26 Berman	Y	Y	Y	Y	N	N	Y	N
27 Levine	Y	Y	Y	Y	N	N	N	N
28 Dixon	Y	Y	Y	Y	N	N	Y	N
29 Waters	Y	?	Y	Y	N	N	N	N
30 Martinez	Y	Y	Y	Y	N	N	Y	N
31 Dymally	Y	Y	Y	Y	N	N	Y	N
32 Anderson	Y	Y	Y	Y	N	N	Y	N
33 ***Dreier***	Y	N	Y	Y	Y	Y	Y	Y
34 Torres	Y	Y	Y	Y	N	N	Y	N
35 ***Lewis***	Y	Y	Y	?	Y	Y	Y	Y
36 Brown	Y	Y	Y	Y	N	N	Y	N
37 ***McCandless***	Y	N	Y	Y	Y	Y	Y	Y
38 ***Dornan***	Y	N	Y	Y	Y	Y	Y	Y
39 ***Dannemeyer***	Y	N	N	Y	Y	Y	N	Y
40 ***Cox***	Y	N	Y	Y	N	Y	Y	Y
41 ***Lowery***	Y	Y	Y	Y	Y	N	Y	Y
42 ***Rohrabacher***	Y	N	Y	Y	N	Y	N	Y
43 ***Packard***	Y	N	Y	Y	Y	N	Y	Y
44 ***Cunningham***	Y	N	Y	Y	Y	N	N	Y
45 ***Hunter***	Y	N	N	?	Y	N	N	Y
COLORADO								
1 Schroeder	Y	Y	Y	Y	N	N	Y	N
2 Skaggs	Y	Y	Y	Y	N	Y	Y	N
3 Campbell	Y	Y	Y	Y	N	N	Y	N
4 ***Allard***	Y	Y	Y	Y	Y	N	Y	Y
5 ***Hefley***	Y	Y	Y	Y	Y	Y	Y	Y
6 ***Schaefer***	Y	N	Y	Y	Y	N	Y	Y
CONNECTICUT								
1 Kennelly	Y	Y	Y	Y	N	N	Y	N
2 Gejdenson	Y	Y	Y	Y	N	N	Y	N
3 DeLauro	Y	Y	Y	Y	N	N	Y	N
4 ***Shays***	Y	Y	Y	Y	N	Y	Y	Y
5 ***Franks***	?	Y	Y	?	Y	N	Y	Y
6 ***Johnson***	Y	Y	Y	Y	N	N	Y	Y
DELAWARE								
AL Carper	Y	Y	Y	Y	N	Y	Y	Y
FLORIDA								
1 Hutto	Y	Y	Y	Y	N	N	Y	Y
2 Peterson	Y	Y	Y	Y	N	N	Y	N
3 Bennett	Y	N	Y	Y	N	Y	Y	Y
4 ***James***	Y	N	Y	Y	N	N	Y	Y
5 ***McCollum***	Y	N	Y	Y	N	Y	Y	Y
6 ***Stearns***	Y	N	N	Y	N	Y	Y	Y
7 Gibbons	Y	Y	Y	Y	Y	N	Y	N
8 ***Young***	Y	N	Y	Y	Y	N	Y	N
9 ***Bilirakis***	Y	Y	Y	Y	Y	N	Y	N
10 ***Ireland***	Y	Y	Y	Y	Y	N	Y	Y
11 Bacchus	Y	Y	Y	Y	N	N	N	N
12 ***Lewis***	Y	N	Y	Y	Y	N	Y	Y
13 ***Goss***	Y	N	Y	Y	Y	N	Y	Y
14 Johnston	Y	Y	Y	Y	N	N	Y	N
15 ***Shaw***	Y	Y	Y	Y	Y	N	Y	Y
16 Smith	Y	Y	Y	Y	N	N	Y	N
17 Lehman	?	Y	Y	Y	N	N	Y	N
18 ***Ros-Lehtinen***	Y	N	Y	Y	N	N	Y	Y
19 Fascell	Y	Y	Y	Y	N	N	Y	N
GEORGIA								
1 Thomas	Y	Y	Y	Y	N	N	Y	N
2 Hatcher	?	?	?	?	N	N	Y	N
3 Ray	Y	Y	Y	Y	N	N	Y	N
4 Jones	Y	Y	Y	Y	N	N	Y	N
5 Lewis	Y	+	+	Y	N	N	Y	N
6 ***Gingrich***	Y	Y	Y	Y	Y	Y	Y	Y
7 Darden	Y	Y	Y	Y	N	N	Y	N
8 Rowland	Y	Y	Y	Y	N	N	Y	N
9 Jenkins	Y	Y	Y	Y	N	N	Y	N
10 Barnard	Y	Y	Y	Y	N	N	Y	N
HAWAII								
1 Abercrombie	Y	Y	Y	Y	N	N	Y	N
2 Mink	Y	Y	Y	Y	N	N	Y	N
IDAHO								
1 LaRocco	Y	Y	Y	Y	N	N	Y	N
2 Stallings	Y	Y	Y	Y	N	N	Y	N
ILLINOIS								
1 Hayes	Y	Y	Y	Y	N	N	N	N
2 Savage	Y	Y	Y	Y	N	N	N	N
3 Russo	Y	N	Y	Y	N	Y	N	N
4 Sangmeister	Y	Y	Y	Y	N	N	N	N
5 Lipinski	Y	N	Y	Y	N	Y	N	N
6 ***Hyde***	Y	Y	Y	Y	N	N	Y	N
7 Collins	Y	Y	Y	Y	N	N	Y	N
8 Rostenkowski	Y	Y	Y	Y	N	N	Y	N
9 Yates	Y	Y	Y	Y	N	Y	Y	N
10 ***Porter***	Y	N	Y	Y	N	N	Y	Y
11 Annunzio	Y	Y	Y	Y	N	N	Y	N
12 ***Crane***	Y	N	N	Y	Y	Y	N	?
13 ***Fawell***	Y	Y	Y	Y	?	?	?	Y
14 ***Hastert***	Y	Y	Y	Y	Y	N	Y	Y
15 ***Ewing***	Y	Y	Y	Y	Y	N	Y	N
16 Cox	Y	Y	Y	Y	N	N	Y	N
17 Evans	Y	Y	Y	Y	N	N	N	N
18 ***Michel***	Y	Y	Y	Y	N	N	Y	Y
19 Bruce	Y	Y	Y	Y	N	N	N	N
20 Durbin	Y	Y	Y	Y	N	Y	N	N
21 Costello	Y	Y	Y	Y	Y	N	N	N
22 Poshard	Y	Y	Y	Y	N	N	N	N
INDIANA								
1 Visclosky	Y	Y	Y	Y	N	N	N	N
2 Sharp	Y	Y	Y	Y	N	N	Y	N
3 Roemer	Y	Y	Y	Y	N	N	N	N

ND Northern Democrats SD Southern Democrats

Member	409	410	411	412	413	414	415	416
4 Long	Y	Y	Y	Y	N	N	Y	N
5 Jontz	Y	Y	Y	Y	N	N	N	N
6 ***Burton***	Y	N	N	Y	Y	Y	N	Y
7 ***Myers***	Y	N	Y	Y	Y	N	Y	?
8 McCloskey	Y	Y	Y	Y	N	N	Y	N
9 Hamilton	Y	Y	Y	Y	N	N	Y	N
10 Jacobs	Y	Y	Y	Y	N	N	Y	N
IOWA								
1 ***Leach***	Y	Y	Y	?	N	Y	Y	Y
2 ***Nussle***	Y	Y	Y	Y	Y	N	Y	Y
3 Nagle	Y	Y	Y	Y	?	N	Y	N
4 Smith	Y	Y	Y	Y	N	N	Y	N
5 ***Lightfoot***	Y	Y	Y	Y	Y	N	Y	Y
6 ***Grandy***	Y	Y	Y	Y	Y	N	Y	Y
KANSAS								
1 ***Roberts***	Y	Y	Y	Y	Y	N	Y	Y
2 Slattery	Y	Y	Y	Y	N	N	Y	Y
3 ***Meyers***	Y	Y	Y	Y	N	N	Y	Y
4 Glickman	Y	Y	Y	Y	N	N	Y	Y
5 ***Nichols***	Y	Y	Y	Y	Y	N	Y	Y
KENTUCKY								
1 Hubbard	Y	N	Y	Y	Y	N	Y	N
2 Natcher	Y	Y	Y	Y	N	N	Y	N
3 Mazzoli	Y	Y	Y	Y	N	N	Y	N
4 ***Bunning***	Y	N	Y	Y	Y	N	Y	Y
5 ***Rogers***	Y	Y	Y	Y	Y	N	Y	N
6 ***Hopkins***	Y	N	Y	Y	Y	N	Y	Y
7 Perkins	Y	Y	Y	Y	N	N	N	N
LOUISIANA								
1 ***Livingston***	Y	Y	Y	Y	N	Y	Y	N
2 Jefferson	Y	Y	Y	Y	N	N	Y	N
3 Tauzin	Y	Y	Y	Y	Y	N	Y	Y
4 ***McCrery***	Y	Y	Y	Y	Y	N	Y	Y
5 Huckaby	Y	Y	Y	Y	Y	N	Y	Y
6 ***Baker***	Y	Y	Y	Y	Y	N	Y	Y
7 Hayes	Y	Y	Y	Y	N	N	N	N
8 ***Holloway***	Y	N	Y	Y	Y	N	Y	Y
MAINE								
1 Andrews	Y	Y	Y	Y	N	N	N	N
2 ***Snowe***	Y	N	Y	Y	Y	N	Y	N
MARYLAND								
1 ***Gilchrest***	Y	Y	Y	Y	Y	N	Y	Y
2 ***Bentley***	Y	N	Y	Y	N	Y	N	Y
3 Cardin	Y	Y	Y	Y	N	N	Y	N
4 McMillen	Y	Y	Y	Y	N	N	Y	N
5 Hoyer	Y	Y	Y	Y	N	N	Y	N
6 Byron	Y	Y	Y	Y	Y	N	Y	N
7 Mfume	Y	Y	Y	Y	N	N	Y	N
8 ***Morella***	Y	Y	Y	Y	N	Y	Y	N
MASSACHUSETTS								
1 Olver	Y	Y	Y	Y	N	N	Y	N
2 Neal	Y	Y	Y	Y	N	N	Y	N
3 Early	Y	N	Y	?	N	N	Y	N
4 Frank	Y	Y	Y	Y	N	Y	Y	N
5 Atkins	Y	Y	Y	Y	N	N	Y	N
6 Mavroules	Y	Y	Y	Y	N	N	Y	N
7 Markey	Y	Y	Y	Y	N	N	Y	N
8 Kennedy	Y	Y	Y	Y	N	N	Y	Y
9 Moakley	Y	Y	Y	Y	N	N	Y	N
10 Studds	Y	Y	Y	Y	N	Y	Y	N
11 Donnelly	Y	Y	Y	Y	N	N	Y	N
MICHIGAN								
1 Conyers	Y	Y	Y	Y	N	N	Y	N
2 ***Pursell***	Y	Y	Y	Y	N	N	Y	Y
3 Wolpe	Y	Y	Y	Y	N	N	Y	N
4 ***Upton***	Y	Y	Y	Y	Y	N	N	Y
5 ***Henry***	?	Y	Y	Y	N	N	N	Y
6 Carr	Y	Y	Y	Y	N	N	N	N
7 Kildee	Y	Y	Y	Y	N	Y	Y	N
8 Traxler	Y	Y	Y	Y	N	N	Y	N
9 ***Vander Jagt***	Y	Y	Y	Y	Y	N	Y	N
10 ***Camp***	Y	Y	Y	Y	N	N	Y	Y
11 ***Davis***	Y	N	Y	Y	Y	N	Y	N
12 Bonior	Y	Y	Y	Y	N	N	Y	N
13 Collins	Y	Y	Y	Y	N	N	N	N
14 Hertel	Y	Y	Y	Y	N	N	N	N
15 Ford	Y	Y	Y	Y	N	N	Y	N
16 Dingell	Y	Y	Y	Y	N	N	Y	N
17 Levin	Y	Y	Y	Y	N	N	Y	N
18 ***Broomfield***	Y	Y	Y	Y	N	N	Y	N
MINNESOTA								
1 Penny	Y	Y	Y	Y	N	Y	Y	Y
2 ***Weber***	Y	N	Y	Y	Y	N	N	Y
3 ***Ramstad***	Y	N	Y	Y	Y	N	Y	Y
4 Vento	Y	Y	Y	Y	N	N	Y	N
5 Sabo	Y	Y	Y	Y	N	N	Y	N
6 Sikorski	Y	Y	Y	Y	N	Y	N	N
7 Peterson	Y	Y	Y	Y	N	N	Y	N
8 Oberstar	Y	Y	Y	?	N	N	Y	N
MISSISSIPPI								
1 Whitten	Y	Y	Y	Y	N	N	Y	N
2 Espy	Y	Y	Y	Y	Y	N	Y	N
3 Montgomery	Y	Y	Y	Y	Y	N	Y	N
4 Parker	Y	N	Y	Y	N	N	Y	N
5 Taylor	Y	N	N	Y	Y	N	N	N
MISSOURI								
1 Clay	Y	Y	Y	Y	N	N	Y	N
2 Horn	Y	Y	Y	Y	N	N	Y	N
3 Gephardt	Y	Y	Y	Y	N	N	Y	N
4 Skelton	Y	Y	Y	?	?	N	Y	N
5 Wheat	Y	Y	Y	Y	N	N	Y	N
6 ***Coleman***	Y	Y	Y	Y	N	N	Y	Y
7 ***Hancock***	Y	N	N	Y	Y	N	Y	Y
8 ***Emerson***	Y	Y	Y	Y	Y	N	Y	N
9 Volkmer	Y	Y	Y	Y	N	N	Y	N
MONTANA								
1 Williams	Y	Y	Y	Y	Y	N	N	N
2 ***Marlenee***	Y	Y	Y	Y	Y	N	N	Y
NEBRASKA								
1 ***Bereuter***	Y	Y	Y	Y	Y	N	Y	Y
2 Hoagland	Y	Y	Y	Y	N	N	Y	Y
3 ***Barrett***	Y	Y	Y	Y	Y	N	Y	Y
NEVADA								
1 Bilbray	Y	Y	Y	Y	Y	N	Y	N
2 ***Vucanovich***	Y	N	Y	Y	Y	N	N	Y
NEW HAMPSHIRE								
1 ***Zeliff***	Y	Y	Y	Y	Y	N	N	Y
2 Swett	Y	Y	Y	Y	N	N	Y	N
NEW JERSEY								
1 Andrews	Y	N	Y	Y	N	N	N	N
2 Hughes	Y	Y	Y	Y	N	N	N	Y
3 Pallone	Y	N	Y	Y	N	N	N	Y
4 ***Smith***	Y	Y	Y	Y	Y	N	Y	N
5 ***Roukema***	Y	Y	Y	Y	N	N	Y	N
6 Dwyer	Y	Y	Y	Y	N	N	N	N
7 ***Rinaldo***	Y	Y	Y	Y	Y	N	Y	N
8 Roe	Y	Y	Y	Y	?	N	Y	-
9 Torricelli	Y	Y	Y	Y	N	N	Y	N
10 Payne	Y	Y	Y	Y	N	N	Y	N
11 ***Gallo***	Y	Y	Y	Y	N	N	Y	Y
12 ***Zimmer***	Y	Y	Y	Y	Y	Y	N	Y
13 ***Saxton***	Y	Y	Y	Y	Y	N	Y	Y
14 Guarini	Y	Y	Y	Y	N	N	N	N
NEW MEXICO								
1 ***Schiff***	Y	Y	Y	Y	Y	N	Y	Y
2 ***Skeen***	Y	Y	Y	Y	Y	N	Y	N
3 Richardson	Y	Y	Y	Y	N	N	N	N
NEW YORK								
1 Hochbrueckner	Y	Y	Y	Y	N	N	Y	N
2 Downey	Y	Y	Y	Y	N	N	Y	N
3 Mrazek	?	?	?	?	?	?	?	?
4 ***Lent***	?	Y	Y	Y	Y	Y	Y	N
5 ***McGrath***	Y	Y	Y	Y	Y	Y	Y	N
6 Flake	Y	Y	Y	Y	N	N	Y	N
7 Ackerman	Y	Y	Y	Y	N	N	Y	N
8 Scheuer	Y	Y	Y	Y	N	Y	Y	N
9 Manton	Y	Y	Y	Y	Y	N	Y	N
10 Schumer	Y	N	Y	Y	N	Y	Y	N
11 Towns	?	?	?	Y	N	N	N	?
12 Owens	Y	Y	Y	Y	N	N	N	N
13 Solarz	Y	Y	Y	Y	N	N	Y	N
14 ***Molinari***	Y	Y	Y	?	Y	Y	Y	N
15 ***Green***	Y	Y	Y	Y	N	Y	Y	N
16 Rangel	Y	Y	Y	Y	N	N	Y	N
17 Weiss	Y	Y	Y	Y	N	Y	Y	N
18 Serrano	Y	Y	Y	Y	N	N	N	N
19 Engel	Y	Y	Y	Y	N	N	Y	N
20 Lowey	Y	Y	Y	Y	N	N	Y	N
21 ***Fish***	Y	Y	Y	?	N	N	Y	N
22 ***Gilman***	Y	Y	Y	Y	Y	N	Y	N
23 McNulty	Y	N	Y	Y	N	N	N	N
24 ***Solomon***	Y	N	Y	Y	Y	Y	N	Y
25 ***Boehlert***	Y	Y	Y	Y	N	N	Y	N
26 ***Martin***	Y	Y	Y	Y	Y	N	Y	N
27 ***Walsh***	Y	Y	Y	Y	Y	Y	Y	N
28 McHugh	Y	Y	?	Y	N	N	Y	N
29 ***Horton***	Y	Y	Y	Y	N	N	Y	N
30 Slaughter	Y	Y	Y	Y	N	N	Y	N
31 ***Paxon***	Y	N	Y	Y	Y	N	Y	Y
32 LaFalce	Y	Y	Y	Y	N	N	Y	N
33 Nowak	Y	Y	Y	Y	N	N	Y	N
34 ***Houghton***	Y	Y	Y	Y	Y	Y	Y	Y
NORTH CAROLINA								
1 Jones	Y	Y	Y	Y	N	N	Y	N
2 Valentine	Y	N	Y	Y	Y	N	Y	N
3 Lancaster	Y	Y	Y	Y	N	N	Y	Y
4 Price	Y	Y	Y	Y	N	N	Y	N
5 Neal	Y	N	Y	Y	N	N	Y	?
6 ***Coble***	Y	N	Y	Y	Y	N	Y	Y
7 Rose	Y	Y	Y	Y	N	N	Y	N
8 Hefner	Y	Y	Y	Y	N	N	Y	N
9 ***McMillan***	Y	Y	Y	Y	Y	N	Y	Y
10 ***Ballenger***	Y	Y	Y	Y	Y	Y	Y	Y
11 ***Taylor***	Y	Y	Y	Y	Y	Y	Y	Y
NORTH DAKOTA								
AL Dorgan	Y	Y	Y	Y	N	N	N	Y
OHIO								
1 Luken	Y	Y	Y	Y	N	N	Y	Y
2 ***Gradison***	Y	Y	Y	Y	Y	N	Y	Y
3 Hall	Y	Y	Y	Y	N	N	Y	N
4 ***Oxley***	Y	Y	Y	Y	N	N	Y	Y
5 ***Gillmor***	Y	N	Y	Y	N	N	Y	Y
6 ***McEwen***	Y	N	Y	Y	Y	Y	Y	Y
7 ***Hobson***	Y	Y	Y	Y	Y	N	Y	Y
8 ***Boehner***	Y	Y	Y	?	Y	N	Y	Y
9 Kaptur	Y	Y	Y	Y	N	N	N	N
10 ***Miller***	Y	Y	Y	Y	Y	Y	Y	Y
11 Eckart	Y	Y	Y	Y	N	N	Y	N
12 ***Kasich***	Y	Y	Y	Y	Y	Y	Y	Y
13 Pease	Y	Y	Y	Y	N	N	Y	Y
14 Sawyer	Y	Y	Y	Y	N	N	Y	N
15 ***Wylie***	Y	Y	Y	Y	Y	Y	Y	N
16 ***Regula***	Y	Y	Y	Y	Y	N	Y	Y
17 Traficant	Y	N	Y	Y	Y	N	N	N
18 Applegate	Y	N	Y	Y	Y	N	Y	N
19 Feighan	Y	Y	Y	Y	N	N	Y	N
20 Oakar	Y	Y	Y	Y	N	N	Y	N
21 Stokes	Y	Y	Y	Y	N	N	Y	N
OKLAHOMA								
1 ***Inhofe***	Y	N	Y	Y	Y	N	Y	Y
2 Synar	Y	Y	Y	Y	N	N	Y	N
3 Brewster	Y	Y	Y	Y	Y	N	Y	N
4 McCurdy	Y	Y	Y	Y	N	N	Y	Y
5 ***Edwards***	Y	N	Y	Y	Y	N	Y	?
6 English	Y	N	Y	Y	Y	N	N	Y
OREGON								
1 AuCoin	Y	Y	Y	Y	N	N	N	N
2 ***Smith***	Y	Y	Y	Y	Y	N	Y	Y
3 Wyden	Y	Y	Y	Y	N	N	Y	N
4 DeFazio	Y	Y	Y	Y	N	Y	N	N
5 Kopetski	Y	Y	Y	Y	N	N	Y	N
PENNSYLVANIA								
1 Foglietta	Y	Y	Y	Y	N	N	Y	N
2 Blackwell	Y	Y	Y	Y	N	N	N	N
3 Borski	Y	Y	Y	Y	N	N	Y	N
4 Kolter	Y	Y	Y	Y	N	N	N	N
5 ***Schulze***	Y	Y	N	Y	Y	N	N	Y
6 Yatron	Y	Y	Y	Y	N	N	Y	N
7 ***Weldon***	Y	Y	N	Y	Y	Y	N	Y
8 Kostmayer	Y	Y	Y	Y	N	N	Y	Y
9 ***Shuster***	Y	Y	Y	Y	Y	N	Y	Y
10 ***McDade***	Y	Y	Y	Y	N	N	Y	N
11 Kanjorski	Y	Y	Y	Y	N	Y	N	N
12 Murtha	Y	Y	Y	Y	N	N	Y	N
13 ***Coughlin***	Y	Y	N	Y	N	N	Y	N
14 Coyne	Y	Y	Y	Y	N	N	Y	N
15 ***Ritter***	Y	Y	Y	Y	N	Y	N	Y
16 ***Walker***	Y	N	N	Y	Y	Y	N	Y
17 ***Gekas***	Y	Y	Y	Y	Y	N	Y	N
18 ***Santorum***	Y	Y	N	Y	Y	Y	N	Y
19 ***Goodling***	Y	Y	Y	+	Y	Y	Y	N
20 Gaydos	Y	Y	Y	Y	N	N	N	N
21 ***Ridge***	Y	Y	Y	Y	Y	Y	N	N
22 Murphy	Y	Y	Y	Y	N	N	Y	N
23 ***Clinger***	Y	Y	Y	Y	Y	N	Y	N
RHODE ISLAND								
1 ***Machtley***	Y	Y	Y	Y	Y	N	Y	N
2 Reed	Y	Y	Y	Y	N	N	Y	N
SOUTH CAROLINA								
1 ***Ravenel***	Y	Y	Y	Y	Y	N	Y	N
2 ***Spence***	Y	Y	Y	Y	Y	N	Y	Y
3 Derrick	Y	Y	Y	Y	N	N	Y	N
4 Patterson	Y	N	Y	Y	N	N	Y	Y
5 Spratt	Y	Y	Y	Y	N	N	Y	N
6 Tallon	Y	Y	Y	Y	Y	N	N	N
SOUTH DAKOTA								
AL Johnson	Y	Y	Y	Y	N	Y	Y	N
TENNESSEE								
1 ***Quillen***	Y	N	N	Y	N	N	Y	N
2 ***Duncan***	Y	N	Y	Y	N	N	Y	Y
3 Lloyd	Y	N	Y	Y	Y	N	Y	N
4 Cooper	Y	Y	Y	Y	N	C	C	N
5 Clement	Y	Y	Y	Y	N	N	Y	N
6 Gordon	Y	Y	Y	Y	N	N	Y	N
7 ***Sundquist***	Y	Y	Y	Y	N	N	Y	Y
8 Tanner	Y	Y	Y	Y	N	N	Y	N
9 Ford	Y	?	?	Y	N	N	Y	N
TEXAS								
1 Chapman	Y	N	Y	Y	Y	N	N	N
2 Wilson	Y	Y	Y	Y	N	N	Y	N
3 ***Johnson***	Y	Y	N	Y	Y	Y	Y	Y
4 Hall	Y	N	Y	Y	Y	N	Y	N
5 Bryant	Y	Y	Y	Y	N	N	Y	N
6 ***Barton***	Y	Y	Y	Y	Y	N	Y	Y
7 ***Archer***	Y	Y	N	Y	Y	Y	Y	Y
8 ***Fields***	Y	Y	N	Y	Y	N	Y	Y
9 Brooks	Y	Y	Y	?	?	?	?	?
10 Pickle	Y	Y	Y	Y	Y	N	Y	N
11 Edwards	Y	Y	Y	Y	Y	N	Y	N
12 Geren	Y	N	Y	Y	Y	N	Y	Y
13 Sarpalius	Y	Y	Y	Y	Y	N	Y	N
14 Laughlin	Y	Y	Y	Y	N	N	N	N
15 de la Garza	Y	Y	Y	Y	N	N	Y	N
16 Coleman	Y	Y	Y	Y	N	N	N	N
17 Stenholm	Y	Y	Y	Y	Y	N	Y	Y
18 Washington	Y	Y	Y	?	N	N	Y	N
19 ***Combest***	Y	Y	N	Y	Y	N	Y	Y
20 Gonzalez	Y	Y	Y	Y	N	N	Y	N
21 ***Smith***	Y	Y	Y	Y	Y	N	Y	Y
22 ***DeLay***	Y	N	N	Y	Y	Y	N	Y
23 Bustamante	Y	Y	Y	Y	N	N	Y	N
24 Frost	Y	Y	Y	Y	N	N	Y	N
25 Andrews	Y	Y	Y	Y	Y	N	Y	N
26 ***Armey***	Y	Y	N	Y	Y	Y	N	Y
27 Ortiz	Y	Y	Y	Y	N	N	Y	N
UTAH								
1 ***Hansen***	Y	Y	Y	Y	Y	N	Y	Y
2 Owens	Y	Y	Y	Y	N	N	Y	N
3 Orton	Y	Y	Y	Y	N	N	Y	Y
VERMONT								
AL *Sanders*	Y	Y	Y	Y	N	N	N	N
VIRGINIA								
1 ***Bateman***	Y	Y	Y	Y	N	N	Y	N
2 Pickett	Y	Y	Y	Y	N	N	Y	N
3 ***Bliley***	Y	Y	Y	Y	Y	N	Y	Y
4 Sisisky	Y	Y	Y	?	N	N	Y	N
5 Payne	Y	Y	Y	Y	N	N	Y	Y
6 Olin	Y	Y	Y	Y	N	Y	Y	N
7 ***Allen***	Y	N	Y	Y	Y	N	Y	Y
8 Moran	Y	Y	Y	Y	Y	N	Y	N
9 Boucher	Y	Y	Y	Y	N	N	Y	?
10 ***Wolf***	Y	N	Y	Y	Y	Y	Y	Y
WASHINGTON								
1 ***Miller***	Y	Y	Y	Y	Y	Y	Y	Y
2 Swift	Y	Y	Y	Y	N	N	Y	N
3 Unsoeld	Y	Y	Y	Y	N	Y	Y	N
4 ***Morrison***	Y	Y	Y	Y	Y	N	Y	N
5 Foley								
6 Dicks	Y	Y	Y	Y	?	N	Y	N
7 McDermott	Y	Y	Y	Y	N	N	Y	N
8 ***Chandler***	Y	Y	Y	Y	Y	N	Y	Y
WEST VIRGINIA								
1 Mollohan	Y	Y	Y	Y	N	N	Y	N
2 Staggers	Y	N	Y	Y	N	N	Y	N
3 Wise	Y	Y	Y	Y	N	N	Y	N
4 Rahall	Y	Y	Y	Y	N	N	N	N
WISCONSIN								
1 Aspin	Y	Y	Y	Y	N	N	Y	N
2 ***Klug***	Y	Y	Y	Y	Y	N	Y	Y
3 ***Gunderson***	Y	Y	Y	?	N	N	N	N
4 Kleczka	Y	Y	Y	Y	N	N	Y	N
5 Moody	Y	Y	Y	Y	N	N	N	N
6 ***Petri***	Y	Y	Y	Y	Y	Y	N	Y
7 Obey	Y	Y	Y	Y	N	N	N	N
8 ***Roth***	Y	Y	Y	Y	Y	N	N	Y
9 ***Sensenbrenner***	Y	Y	Y	Y	Y	Y	N	Y
WYOMING								
AL ***Thomas***	Y	Y	Y	Y	Y	N	Y	Y

Southern states - Ala., Ark., Fla., Ga., Ky., La., Miss., N.C., Okla., S.C., Tenn., Texas, Va.
Omitted votes are quorum calls, which CQ does not include in its vote charts.

HOUSE VOTES 417, 418, 419, 420, 421, 422, 423, 424

417. HR 3839. Fiscal 1992 Labor, HHS and Education Appropriations/Passage. Passage of the bill to provide $204,919,763,000 in new budget authority for the Departments of Labor, Health and Human Services, and Education and related agencies: $176,796,071,000 in fiscal 1992, $27,848,692,000 in fiscal 1993, and $275,000,000 in fiscal 1994. The administration requested $200,611,414,000. The bill is identical to HR 2707, vetoed by President Bush on Nov. 19, except that it does not include the provision that would have blocked enforcement of the administration rules barring abortion counseling in federally funded family planning clinics, known as the "gag rule." Passed 364-58: R 105-56; D 258-2 (ND 178-1, SD 80-1); I 1-0, Nov. 22, 1991. A "yea" was a vote supporting the president's position.

418. HR 2929. California Desert Protection/Previous Question. Beilenson, D-Calif., motion to order the previous question (thus limiting debate and the possibility of amendment) on adoption of the rule (H Res 279) to provide for House floor consideration of the bill that would designate more than 8 million acres as wilderness. Motion agreed to 256-160: R 2-159; D 253-1 (ND 171-1, SD 82-0); I 1-0, Nov. 22, 1991.

419. HR 2929. California Desert Protection/Rule. Adoption of the rule (H Res 279) to provide for House floor consideration of the bill to designate 73 wilderness areas in the desert region of California for management by the Bureau of Land Management among other changes. In all, the bill would designate more than 8 million acres as wilderness. Adopted 269-135: R 19-135; D 249-0 (ND 170-0, SD 79-0); I 1-0, Nov. 22, 1991.

420. HR 2929. California Desert Protection/Substitute. Lewis, R-Calif., substitute amendment to designate 2.3 million acres in 62 areas as wilderness instead of the more than 8 million acres in 73 areas designated by the bill. Rejected 150-241: R 121-30; D 29-210 (ND 6-155, SD 23-55); I 0-1, Nov. 22, 1991. A "yea" was a vote supporting the president's position.

421. H Res 294. Expedited Consideration of Certain Bills/Adoption. Adoption of the resolution to allow expedited consideration of certain bills by waiving the requirement for a two-thirds vote that is needed in order to consider a bill the same day it is reported from the Rules Committee, allow the Speaker to declare recess at any time, and allow the Speaker to entertain motions to suspend the rules with one hour's notice. The resolution would be effective through Wednesday, Nov. 27. Adopted 214-127: R 0-127; D 213-0 (ND 143-0, SD 70-0); I 1-0, Nov. 23, 1991.

422. S 543. Banking Reform/Adoption. Adoption of the resolution (H Res 298) to expedite a conference with the Senate on the banking bill by taking from the Speaker's table the Senate-passed banking bill, S 543, and striking all after the enacting clause and inserting the House-passed banking bill, HR 3768, and requesting a conference. Adopted 215-91: R 25-90; D 189-1 (ND 129-0, SD 60-1); I 1-0, Nov. 23, 1991.

423. S 543. Banking Reform/House Preference. Wylie, R-Ohio, motion to instruct the House conferees on the banking reform bill to insist on the House's narrow banking bill that would provide the Federal Deposit Insurance Corporation with authority to borrow up to $30 billion to cover losses of failed banks and not include the more controversial provisions in the Senate bill. Motion agreed to 398-3: R 155-3; D 242-0 (ND 165-0, SD 77-0); I 1-0, Nov. 25, 1991.

424. HR 3750. Campaign Finance. Adoption of the resolution (H Res 299) to provide for House floor consideration of the bill to limit spending in House campaigns to $600,000 and provide up to $200,000 in public matching funds to House candidates who agree to abide by the limits. Regardless of agreeing to the voluntary spending limits, all House candidates would be limited to $200,000 in contributions from political action committees or for contributions of more than $200. Adopted 246-180: R 0-164; D 245-16 (ND 164-14, SD 81-2); I 1-0, Nov. 25, 1991.

KEY

- Y Voted for (yea).
- # Paired for.
- + Announced for.
- N Voted against (nay).
- X Paired against.
- \- Announced against.
- P Voted "present."
- C Voted "present" to avoid possible conflict of interest.
- ? Did not vote or otherwise make a position known.

Democrats ***Republicans*** *Independent*

	417	418	419	420	421	422	423	424
ALABAMA								
1 ***Callahan***	Y	N	N	Y	?	?	Y	N
2 ***Dickinson***	Y	N	N	Y	N	?	Y	N
3 Browder	Y	Y	Y	N	Y	Y	Y	Y
4 Bevill	Y	Y	Y	N	Y	Y	Y	Y
5 Cramer	Y	Y	Y	N	Y	Y	Y	Y
6 Erdreich	Y	Y	Y	N	?	?	Y	Y
7 Harris	Y	Y	Y	N	?	?	Y	Y
ALASKA								
AL ***Young***	Y	N	N	Y	N	Y	Y	N
ARIZONA								
1 ***Rhodes***	N	N	N	Y	N	N	Y	N
2 Pastor	Y	Y	Y	N	Y	Y	Y	Y
3 ***Stump***	N	N	N	Y	N	N	Y	N
4 ***Kyl***	N	N	N	Y	N	N	Y	N
5 ***Kolbe***	N	N	N	Y	N	N	Y	N
ARKANSAS								
1 Alexander	Y	Y	Y	?	Y	?	?	Y
2 Thornton	Y	Y	Y	N	Y	?	Y	Y
3 ***Hammerschmidt***	Y	N	N	Y	N	N	Y	N
4 Anthony	Y	Y	Y	Y	Y	Y	Y	N
CALIFORNIA								
1 ***Riggs***	N	N	N	Y	N	N	Y	N
2 ***Herger***	N	N	N	Y	N	N	Y	N
3 Matsui	Y	Y	Y	N	Y	Y	Y	Y
4 Fazio	Y	Y	Y	N	Y	Y	Y	Y
5 Pelosi	Y	Y	Y	N	Y	Y	Y	Y
6 Boxer	Y	Y	Y	N	?	?	Y	Y
7 Miller	Y	Y	Y	N	Y	Y	Y	Y
8 Dellums	Y	Y	Y	N	?	?	Y	Y
9 Stark	Y	Y	Y	N	Y	Y	Y	Y
10 Edwards	Y	Y	Y	N	Y	?	Y	Y
11 Lantos	Y	Y	Y	N	?	?	Y	Y
12 ***Campbell***	Y	N	N	N	N	N	Y	N
13 Mineta	Y	Y	Y	N	Y	Y	Y	Y
14 ***Doolittle***	?	X	X	?	N	N	Y	N
15 Condit	Y	Y	Y	Y	Y	Y	Y	Y
16 Panetta	Y	Y	Y	N	Y	Y	Y	Y
17 Dooley	Y	Y	Y	N	Y	Y	Y	Y
18 Lehman	Y	Y	Y	N	Y	?	Y	Y
19 ***Lagomarsino***	N	N	N	Y	N	N	Y	N
20 ***Thomas***	Y	N	N	Y	N	?	Y	N
21 ***Gallegly***	N	N	N	Y	?	?	Y	N
22 ***Moorhead***	N	N	N	Y	N	N	Y	N
23 Beilenson	Y	Y	Y	N	Y	Y	Y	N
24 Waxman	Y	Y	Y	?	?	?	Y	Y
25 Roybal	Y	Y	Y	N	Y	Y	Y	N
26 Berman	Y	Y	Y	N	?	?	Y	Y
27 Levine	Y	Y	Y	N	?	?	Y	Y
28 Dixon	Y	Y	Y	?	Y	?	Y	Y
29 Waters	Y	Y	Y	N	Y	Y	Y	Y
30 Martinez	Y	Y	Y	Y	Y	Y	Y	Y
31 Dymally	Y	Y	Y	N	Y	Y	Y	Y
32 Anderson	Y	N	Y	Y	Y	Y	Y	Y
33 ***Dreier***	N	N	N	Y	N	Y	Y	N
34 Torres	Y	Y	Y	N	Y	Y	Y	Y
35 ***Lewis***	Y	N	N	Y	N	N	Y	N
36 Brown	Y	Y	Y	N	Y	Y	Y	Y
37 ***McCandless***	N	N	N	Y	N	Y	Y	N
38 ***Dornan***	N	N	N	Y	?	?	Y	N
39 ***Dannemeyer***	N	N	N	Y	N	N	Y	N
40 ***Cox***	N	N	N	Y	N	N	Y	N
41 ***Lowery***	Y	N	N	Y	N	?	Y	N
42 ***Rohrabacher***	N	N	?	Y	N	N	Y	N
43 ***Packard***	N	N	N	Y	N	N	Y	N
44 ***Cunningham***	Y	N	N	Y	?	?	Y	N
45 ***Hunter***	Y	N	N	Y	?	?	Y	N
COLORADO								
1 Schroeder	Y	Y	Y	N	Y	Y	Y	Y
2 Skaggs	Y	Y	Y	N	Y	Y	Y	Y
3 Campbell	Y	Y	Y	N	Y	Y	Y	Y
4 ***Allard***	N	N	N	Y	N	N	Y	N
5 ***Hefley***	N	N	N	Y	N	?	Y	N
6 ***Schaefer***	N	N	N	Y	N	?	Y	N
CONNECTICUT								
1 Kennelly	Y	Y	Y	N	Y	Y	Y	Y
2 Gejdenson	Y	Y	Y	N	Y	Y	Y	Y
3 DeLauro	Y	Y	Y	N	Y	Y	Y	Y
4 ***Shays***	Y	N	N	N	N	Y	Y	N
5 ***Franks***	Y	N	N	Y	N	N	Y	N
6 ***Johnson***	?	N	N	Y	N	Y	Y	N
DELAWARE								
AL Carper	Y	Y	Y	N	Y	Y	Y	N
FLORIDA								
1 Hutto	Y	Y	Y	Y	?	?	?	Y
2 Peterson	Y	Y	Y	Y	Y	Y	Y	Y
3 Bennett	N	Y	Y	N	Y	Y	Y	Y
4 ***James***	Y	N	N	N	N	N	Y	N
5 ***McCollum***	N	N	N	N	N	N	Y	N
6 ***Stearns***	Y	N	N	Y	N	N	Y	N
7 Gibbons	Y	Y	Y	N	Y	Y	Y	Y
8 ***Young***	Y	N	Y	?	N	N	Y	N
9 ***Bilirakis***	Y	N	N	Y	N	Y	Y	N
10 ***Ireland***	Y	N	N	?	?	?	Y	?
11 Bacchus	Y	Y	Y	N	Y	Y	Y	Y
12 ***Lewis***	N	N	N	N	N	?	Y	N
13 ***Goss***	Y	N	N	N	N	N	Y	N
14 Johnston	Y	Y	?	?	?	?	Y	Y
15 ***Shaw***	N	N	N	Y	?	?	?	N
16 Smith	Y	Y	Y	N	?	?	Y	Y
17 Lehman	Y	Y	Y	N	Y	Y	Y	Y
18 ***Ros-Lehtinen***	Y	N	N	N	?	?	Y	N
19 Fascell	Y	Y	Y	N	Y	Y	Y	Y
GEORGIA								
1 Thomas	Y	Y	Y	N	Y	Y	Y	Y
2 Hatcher	Y	Y	Y	N	Y	Y	?	N
3 Ray	Y	Y	Y	Y	Y	Y	?	?
4 Jones	Y	Y	Y	N	Y	Y	Y	Y
5 Lewis	Y	Y	Y	N	Y	Y	Y	Y
6 ***Gingrich***	Y	N	N	Y	N	N	Y	N
7 Darden	Y	Y	Y	N	Y	Y	Y	Y
8 Rowland	Y	Y	Y	N	Y	Y	Y	Y
9 Jenkins	Y	Y	Y	N	Y	Y	Y	Y
10 Barnard	Y	Y	Y	N	Y	Y	Y	Y
HAWAII								
1 Abercrombie	Y	Y	Y	N	Y	?	Y	Y
2 Mink	Y	Y	Y	N	Y	Y	Y	Y
IDAHO								
1 LaRocco	Y	Y	Y	N	Y	Y	Y	Y
2 Stallings	Y	Y	Y	N	Y	Y	Y	Y
ILLINOIS								
1 Hayes	Y	?	Y	N	Y	Y	Y	Y
2 Savage	Y	Y	Y	N	Y	?	?	N
3 Russo	Y	Y	Y	?	?	?	?	Y
4 Sangmeister	Y	Y	Y	N	Y	Y	Y	Y
5 Lipinski	Y	Y	Y	?	?	?	Y	Y
6 ***Hyde***	Y	N	N	Y	N	N	Y	N
7 Collins	Y	Y	Y	N	Y	?	?	Y
8 Rostenkowski	Y	Y	Y	N	Y	Y	?	Y
9 Yates	Y	Y	Y	?	Y	Y	Y	Y
10 ***Porter***	Y	N	Y	N	N	?	Y	N
11 Annunzio	Y	Y	Y	N	Y	Y	Y	Y
12 ***Crane***	?	?	?	?	?	?	?	N
13 ***Fawell***	N	N	N	N	?	?	Y	N
14 ***Hastert***	Y	N	N	Y	N	N	Y	N
15 ***Ewing***	Y	N	N	Y	N	Y	Y	N
16 Cox	Y	Y	Y	N	Y	Y	Y	Y
17 Evans	Y	Y	Y	N	Y	Y	Y	Y
18 ***Michel***	Y	N	N	?	N	Y	Y	N
19 Bruce	Y	Y	Y	N	Y	Y	Y	Y
20 Durbin	Y	Y	Y	N	Y	Y	Y	Y
21 Costello	Y	Y	Y	N	?	?	Y	Y
22 Poshard	Y	Y	Y	N	Y	Y	Y	Y
INDIANA								
1 Visclosky	Y	Y	Y	N	Y	Y	Y	Y
2 Sharp	Y	?	?	N	?	?	?	N
3 Roemer	Y	Y	Y	N	Y	Y	Y	Y

ND Northern Democrats SD Southern Democrats

	417	418	419	420	421	422	423	424
4 Long	Y	Y	Y	N	Y	Y	Y	Y
5 Jontz	Y	Y	Y	N	Y	Y	Y	Y
6 ***Burton***	N	N	N	Y	N	N	N	N
7 ***Myers***	?	?	?	?	?	?	Y	N
8 McCloskey	Y	Y	Y	N	Y	Y	Y	Y
9 Hamilton	Y	Y	Y	N	Y	Y	Y	Y
10 Jacobs	Y	Y	Y	N	?	?	Y	N
IOWA								
1 ***Leach***	Y	N	Y	N	?	?	Y	N
2 ***Nussle***	N	N	N	Y	N	N	Y	N
3 Nagle	Y	Y	?	N	Y	Y	Y	N
4 Smith	Y	?	?	?	?	?	Y	Y
5 ***Lightfoot***	N	N	N	Y	N	N	Y	N
6 ***Grandy***	Y	N	N	Y	N	N	Y	N
KANSAS								
1 ***Roberts***	N	N	N	Y	N	N	Y	N
2 Slattery	Y	?	Y	N	Y	?	Y	N
3 ***Meyers***	Y	N	N	Y	N	Y	Y	N
4 Glickman	Y	Y	Y	N	Y	Y	Y	Y
5 ***Nichols***	N	N	N	Y	N	N	Y	N
KENTUCKY								
1 Hubbard	Y	Y	Y	Y	Y	Y	Y	Y
2 Natcher	Y	Y	Y	N	Y	Y	Y	Y
3 Mazzoli	Y	Y	Y	N	Y	Y	Y	Y
4 ***Bunning***	N	N	N	Y	N	N	Y	N
5 ***Rogers***	Y	N	N	Y	N	?	Y	N
6 ***Hopkins***	Y	N	?	Y	?	?	Y	N
7 Perkins	Y	Y	Y	N	Y	Y	Y	Y
LOUISIANA								
1 ***Livingston***	Y	N	N	Y	N	N	Y	N
2 Jefferson	Y	Y	Y	N	?	?	Y	Y
3 Tauzin	Y	Y	?	Y	Y	?	Y	Y
4 ***McCrery***	Y	N	N	Y	N	?	Y	N
5 Huckaby	Y	Y	?	N	Y	Y	Y	Y
6 ***Baker***	Y	N	N	?	?	?	Y	N
7 Hayes	Y	Y	Y	Y	Y	Y	Y	Y
8 ***Holloway***	N	N	N	Y	?	?	Y	N
MAINE								
1 Andrews	Y	Y	Y	N	Y	Y	Y	Y
2 ***Snowe***	Y	N	N	N	N	N	Y	N
MARYLAND								
1 ***Gilchrest***	Y	N	N	N	N	N	Y	N
2 ***Bentley***	Y	N	N	Y	N	N	Y	N
3 Cardin	Y	Y	Y	N	Y	?	?	Y
4 McMillen	Y	Y	Y	N	Y	?	Y	Y
5 Hoyer	Y	Y	Y	N	Y	?	Y	Y
6 Byron	Y	Y	Y	N	Y	Y	Y	Y
7 Mfume	Y	Y	Y	N	?	?	?	N
8 ***Morella***	Y	N	Y	N	N	Y	Y	N
MASSACHUSETTS								
1 Olver	Y	Y	Y	N	?	?	Y	Y
2 Neal	Y	Y	Y	?	?	?	Y	Y
3 Early	Y	Y	Y	N	?	?	Y	Y
4 Frank	Y	Y	Y	N	Y	Y	Y	Y
5 Atkins	Y	Y	Y	N	?	?	Y	Y
6 Mavroules	Y	Y	Y	N	?	?	Y	Y
7 Markey	Y	Y	Y	N	Y	Y	Y	Y
8 Kennedy	Y	Y	Y	N	?	?	Y	Y
9 Moakley	Y	Y	Y	N	Y	Y	Y	Y
10 Studds	Y	Y	Y	N	Y	Y	Y	Y
11 Donnelly	Y	Y	Y	N	?	?	Y	Y
MICHIGAN								
1 Conyers	Y	Y	Y	N	Y	Y	Y	Y
2 ***Pursell***	Y	N	N	?	N	?	Y	N
3 Wolpe	Y	Y	Y	N	?	?	?	Y
4 ***Upton***	Y	N	N	Y	?	?	Y	N
5 ***Henry***	Y	N	N	Y	?	?	Y	N
6 Carr	Y	?	?	N	Y	Y	Y	N
7 Kildee	Y	Y	Y	N	Y	Y	Y	Y
8 Traxler	Y	Y	Y	?	Y	Y	Y	Y
9 ***Vander Jagt***	Y	N	N	Y	N	N	Y	N
10 ***Camp***	Y	N	N	Y	N	N	Y	N
11 ***Davis***	Y	N	N	Y	N	N	Y	N
12 Bonior	Y	Y	Y	N	Y	Y	Y	Y
13 Collins	Y	Y	Y	N	Y	Y	Y	Y
14 Hertel	Y	Y	Y	N	Y	Y	?	Y
15 Ford	Y	Y	Y	N	Y	Y	Y	Y
16 Dingell	Y	Y	Y	Y	Y	Y	Y	Y
17 Levin	Y	Y	Y	N	Y	Y	Y	Y
18 ***Broomfield***	Y	N	N	?	?	?	Y	N
MINNESOTA								
1 Penny	Y	Y	Y	Y	Y	Y	Y	Y
2 ***Weber***	Y	N	N	Y	N	N	?	N
3 ***Ramstad***	Y	N	N	N	N	N	Y	N
4 Vento	Y	Y	Y	N	Y	Y	Y	Y

	417	418	419	420	421	422	423	424
5 Sabo	Y	Y	Y	N	Y	Y	Y	Y
6 Sikorski	Y	Y	Y	N	Y	Y	?	Y
7 Peterson	Y	Y	Y	N	Y	Y	Y	Y
8 Oberstar	Y	Y	Y	N	Y	Y	?	Y
MISSISSIPPI								
1 Whitten	Y	Y	Y	N	Y	Y	Y	Y
2 Espy	Y	Y	Y	Y	?	Y	Y	Y
3 Montgomery	Y	Y	Y	Y	Y	Y	Y	Y
4 Parker	Y	Y	Y	Y	Y	Y	?	Y
5 Taylor	Y	Y	Y	Y	Y	Y	Y	Y
MISSOURI								
1 Clay	Y	Y	?	?	?	?	?	Y
2 Horn	Y	Y	Y	N	Y	Y	Y	Y
3 Gephardt	Y	Y	Y	N	Y	Y	Y	Y
4 Skelton	Y	Y	Y	Y	Y	Y	Y	Y
5 Wheat	Y	Y	Y	N	Y	Y	Y	Y
6 ***Coleman***	Y	N	N	Y	?	?	Y	N
7 ***Hancock***	N	N	N	Y	N	N	Y	N
8 ***Emerson***	Y	N	N	Y	N	Y	Y	N
9 Volkmer	Y	Y	Y	N	Y	Y	Y	Y
MONTANA								
1 Williams	Y	Y	Y	N	Y	?	Y	Y
2 ***Marlenee***	Y	N	?	Y	?	?	Y	N
NEBRASKA								
1 ***Bereuter***	Y	N	N	Y	N	Y	Y	N
2 Hoagland	Y	Y	Y	N	Y	Y	Y	Y
3 ***Barrett***	Y	N	N	Y	N	N	Y	N
NEVADA								
1 Bilbray	Y	Y	Y	N	Y	Y	Y	Y
2 ***Vucanovich***	Y	N	N	Y	N	N	Y	N
NEW HAMPSHIRE								
1 ***Zeliff***	Y	N	N	Y	?	?	Y	N
2 Swett	Y	Y	Y	N	?	?	Y	Y
NEW JERSEY								
1 Andrews	Y	Y	?	?	Y	Y	Y	Y
2 Hughes	Y	Y	Y	N	Y	Y	Y	N
3 Pallone	N	Y	Y	N	Y	Y	Y	Y
4 ***Smith***	Y	N	Y	N	N	Y	Y	N
5 ***Roukema***	Y	N	Y	N	?	?	Y	N
6 Dwyer	Y	Y	Y	N	?	?	Y	Y
7 ***Rinaldo***	Y	N	Y	N	N	Y	Y	N
8 Roe	+	Y	Y	?	Y	Y	Y	Y
9 Torricelli	Y	#	#	X	?	?	Y	N
10 Payne	Y	Y	Y	N	Y	Y	?	Y
11 ***Gallo***	Y	N	Y	N	N	N	Y	N
12 ***Zimmer***	N	N	Y	N	N	N	Y	N
13 ***Saxton***	Y	N	Y	N	N	N	Y	N
14 Guarini	Y	Y	Y	N	Y	Y	Y	Y
NEW MEXICO								
1 ***Schiff***	Y	N	N	Y	N	Y	Y	N
2 ***Skeen***	Y	N	N	Y	N	Y	Y	N
3 Richardson	Y	Y	Y	N	Y	Y	Y	Y
NEW YORK								
1 Hochbrueckner	Y	Y	Y	N	Y	Y	Y	Y
2 Downey	Y	Y	Y	N	Y	Y	Y	Y
3 Mrazek	?	?	?	?	?	?	?	?
4 ***Lent***	Y	N	N	Y	N	N	Y	N
5 ***McGrath***	Y	N	Y	N	N	Y	Y	N
6 Flake	Y	Y	Y	N	Y	Y	Y	Y
7 Ackerman	Y	Y	Y	N	?	?	Y	Y
8 Scheuer	Y	Y	Y	?	Y	Y	Y	Y
9 Manton	Y	Y	?	N	Y	Y	Y	Y
10 Schumer	Y	Y	Y	N	?	?	Y	Y
11 Towns	?	?	?	?	?	?	?	?
12 Owens	Y	Y	Y	N	?	?	Y	Y
13 Solarz	Y	Y	Y	N	Y	Y	Y	Y
14 ***Molinari***	Y	N	N	Y	N	N	Y	N
15 ***Green***	Y	N	Y	N	N	Y	Y	N
16 Rangel	Y	Y	Y	N	Y	Y	Y	Y
17 Weiss	Y	Y	Y	N	Y	Y	Y	Y
18 Serrano	Y	Y	Y	N	Y	Y	Y	Y
19 Engel	Y	Y	Y	N	Y	Y	?	Y
20 Lowey	Y	Y	Y	N	Y	Y	Y	Y
21 ***Fish***	Y	N	N	N	N	?	Y	N
22 ***Gilman***	Y	N	N	N	N	Y	Y	N
23 McNulty	Y	Y	Y	N	Y	Y	Y	Y
24 ***Solomon***	N	N	?	?	N	?	N	N
25 ***Boehlert***	Y	N	Y	N	N	Y	Y	N
26 ***Martin***	Y	N	?	Y	N	N	Y	N
27 ***Walsh***	Y	N	N	Y	N	N	Y	N
28 McHugh	Y	Y	Y	N	Y	Y	Y	Y
29 ***Horton***	Y	N	Y	Y	N	Y	?	N
30 Slaughter	Y	Y	Y	N	Y	Y	Y	Y
31 ***Paxon***	Y	N	N	Y	N	N	Y	N

	417	418	419	420	421	422	423	424
32 LaFalce	Y	Y	Y	N	Y	Y	Y	Y
33 Nowak	Y	Y	Y	N	Y	Y	Y	Y
34 ***Houghton***	Y	N	N	Y	?	?	Y	N
NORTH CAROLINA								
1 Jones	Y	Y	Y	Y	Y	Y	Y	Y
2 Valentine	Y	Y	Y	N	Y	Y	Y	Y
3 Lancaster	Y	Y	Y	N	Y	Y	Y	Y
4 Price	Y	Y	Y	N	?	?	Y	Y
5 Neal	?	Y	Y	N	?	Y	Y	Y
6 ***Coble***	N	N	N	Y	?	?	Y	N
7 Rose	Y	Y	Y	N	Y	Y	Y	Y
8 Hefner	Y	Y	Y	N	Y	Y	Y	Y
9 ***McMillan***	N	N	N	Y	N	Y	Y	N
10 ***Ballenger***	N	N	N	Y	N	-	Y	N
11 ***Taylor***	Y	N	N	Y	?	?	Y	N
NORTH DAKOTA								
AL Dorgan	Y	Y	Y	?	Y	Y	Y	Y
OHIO								
1 Luken	Y	Y	Y	N	?	?	Y	Y
2 ***Gradison***	Y	N	N	Y	N	N	Y	N
3 Hall	Y	Y	Y	N	Y	Y	Y	Y
4 ***Oxley***	N	N	N	Y	N	N	?	N
5 ***Gillmor***	Y	N	N	Y	N	N	Y	N
6 ***McEwen***	N	N	N	Y	N	N	Y	N
7 ***Hobson***	Y	N	N	Y	N	N	Y	N
8 ***Boehner***	N	N	N	Y	N	N	Y	N
9 Kaptur	Y	Y	Y	N	Y	Y	Y	Y
10 ***Miller***	N	N	Y	Y	N	N	Y	N
11 Eckart	Y	Y	Y	N	Y	Y	Y	Y
12 ***Kasich***	Y	N	N	Y	N	N	Y	N
13 Pease	Y	Y	Y	N	Y	Y	Y	Y
14 Sawyer	Y	Y	Y	N	Y	Y	Y	Y
15 ***Wylie***	Y	N	N	?	?	?	Y	N
16 ***Regula***	Y	N	N	Y	N	N	Y	N
17 Traficant	Y	Y	Y	N	Y	Y	Y	Y
18 Applegate	Y	Y	Y	N	Y	Y	Y	Y
19 Feighan	Y	Y	Y	N	?	?	Y	Y
20 Oakar	Y	Y	Y	N	Y	?	Y	Y
21 Stokes	Y	Y	Y	N	?	?	?	?
OKLAHOMA								
1 ***Inhofe***	N	N	N	Y	N	N	Y	N
2 Synar	Y	Y	Y	N	+	+	Y	Y
3 Brewster	Y	Y	Y	Y	Y	?	Y	Y
4 McCurdy	Y	Y	Y	N	Y	?	Y	Y
5 ***Edwards***	?	N	N	Y	?	N	Y	N
6 English	Y	Y	Y	N	Y	Y	Y	Y
OREGON								
1 AuCoin	Y	Y	Y	N	Y	Y	Y	Y
2 ***Smith***	Y	N	N	Y	N	N	Y	N
3 Wyden	Y	Y	Y	N	Y	Y	Y	Y
4 DeFazio	Y	Y	Y	N	Y	?	Y	Y
5 Kopetski	Y	Y	Y	N	Y	Y	Y	Y
PENNSYLVANIA								
1 Foglietta	Y	Y	Y	N	Y	Y	?	?
2 Blackwell	Y	Y	Y	N	Y	Y	Y	Y
3 Borski	Y	Y	Y	N	Y	Y	Y	Y
4 Kolter	Y	Y	Y	?	Y	Y	Y	Y
5 ***Schulze***	Y	N	N	Y	?	?	Y	N
6 Yatron	Y	?	?	?	?	?	Y	Y
7 ***Weldon***	Y	N	?	Y	N	N	?	N
8 Kostmayer	Y	Y	Y	N	Y	Y	Y	Y
9 ***Shuster***	N	N	N	Y	N	N	Y	N
10 ***McDade***	Y	N	?	?	N	N	Y	N
11 Kanjorski	Y	Y	Y	N	Y	Y	Y	Y
12 Murtha	Y	Y	Y	N	Y	Y	Y	Y
13 ***Coughlin***	Y	N	N	Y	N	N	Y	N
14 Coyne	Y	Y	Y	N	Y	?	Y	Y
15 ***Ritter***	Y	N	N	N	N	N	Y	N
16 ***Walker***	N	N	N	Y	N	N	Y	N
17 ***Gekas***	Y	N	N	Y	N	N	Y	N
18 ***Santorum***	N	N	N	Y	N	N	Y	N
19 ***Goodling***	Y	N	N	Y	?	?	Y	N
20 Gaydos	Y	?	?	?	?	?	Y	Y
21 ***Ridge***	Y	N	N	Y	?	N	Y	N
22 Murphy	Y	Y	Y	?	?	?	Y	Y
23 ***Clinger***	Y	Y	Y	Y	N	N	Y	N
RHODE ISLAND								
1 ***Machtley***	Y	N	Y	N	N	Y	Y	N
2 Reed	Y	Y	Y	N	Y	Y	Y	Y
SOUTH CAROLINA								
1 ***Ravenel***	Y	Y	Y	N	N	N	Y	N
2 ***Spence***	Y	N	N	Y	N	N	Y	N
3 Derrick	Y	Y	Y	N	Y	Y	Y	Y
4 Patterson	Y	Y	Y	N	Y	Y	Y	Y
5 Spratt	Y	Y	Y	N	Y	Y	Y	Y
6 Tallon	Y	Y	Y	N	?	?	Y	Y

	417	418	419	420	421	422	423	424
SOUTH DAKOTA								
AL Johnson	Y	Y	Y	N	Y	Y	Y	Y
TENNESSEE								
1 ***Quillen***	N	?	?	#	?	?	N	N
2 ***Duncan***	Y	N	N	Y	N	?	Y	N
3 Lloyd	Y	?	?	?	Y	Y	Y	Y
4 Cooper	Y	Y	Y	N	Y	C	C	Y
5 Clement	Y	Y	Y	?	Y	Y	Y	Y
6 Gordon	Y	Y	Y	N	Y	Y	Y	Y
7 ***Sundquist***	Y	N	N	Y	?	?	?	N
8 Tanner	Y	Y	Y	Y	Y	Y	Y	Y
9 Ford	Y	Y	Y	N	Y	N	?	?
TEXAS								
1 Chapman	Y	Y	Y	Y	Y	?	Y	Y
2 Wilson	Y	Y	Y	N	Y	Y	?	Y
3 ***Johnson***	N	N	N	Y	?	?	Y	N
4 Hall	Y	Y	Y	Y	Y	Y	Y	Y
5 Bryant	Y	Y	Y	N	Y	Y	Y	Y
6 ***Barton***	N	N	Y	Y	?	?	Y	N
7 ***Archer***	N	N	N	Y	?	?	Y	N
8 ***Fields***	N	N	N	Y	N	N	Y	?
9 Brooks	?	?	?	?	Y	Y	Y	Y
10 Pickle	Y	Y	Y	N	Y	Y	Y	Y
11 Edwards	?	Y	Y	N	Y	?	Y	Y
12 Geren	Y	Y	Y	Y	Y	?	Y	Y
13 Sarpalius	Y	Y	Y	Y	Y	Y	Y	Y
14 Laughlin	Y	Y	Y	?	?	?	Y	Y
15 de la Garza	Y	?	?	?	?	?	Y	Y
16 Coleman	Y	Y	Y	N	Y	Y	Y	Y
17 Stenholm	Y	Y	Y	Y	Y	?	Y	Y
18 Washington	Y	Y	Y	N	Y	?	Y	Y
19 ***Combest***	N	N	N	Y	N	Y	Y	N
20 Gonzalez	Y	Y	Y	N	Y	Y	Y	Y
21 ***Smith***	Y	N	N	Y	N	N	?	N
22 ***DeLay***	N	N	N	Y	N	N	Y	N
23 Bustamante	Y	Y	Y	Y	Y	Y	Y	Y
24 Frost	Y	Y	Y	N	Y	Y	Y	Y
25 Andrews	Y	Y	Y	N	Y	Y	Y	Y
26 ***Armey***	N	N	N	Y	N	N	Y	N
27 Ortiz	Y	Y	Y	N	Y	Y	Y	Y
UTAH								
1 ***Hansen***	N	N	N	Y	N	N	Y	N
2 Owens	Y	Y	Y	N	Y	Y	Y	Y
3 Orton	Y	Y	Y	N	Y	Y	Y	Y
VERMONT								
AL *Sanders*	Y	Y	Y	N	Y	Y	Y	Y
VIRGINIA								
1 ***Bateman***	Y	N	N	Y	N	Y	Y	N
2 Pickett	Y	Y	Y	Y	?	?	Y	Y
3 ***Bliley***	Y	N	N	Y	N	N	Y	N
4 Sisisky	Y	Y	Y	Y	Y	Y	Y	Y
5 Payne	Y	Y	Y	N	?	?	Y	Y
6 Olin	Y	Y	Y	Y	Y	Y	Y	Y
7 ***Allen***	Y	N	N	Y	N	N	Y	N
8 Moran	Y	Y	Y	N	Y	Y	Y	Y
9 Boucher	?	Y	Y	N	Y	Y	Y	Y
10 ***Wolf***	Y	N	N	Y	N	N	Y	N
WASHINGTON								
1 ***Miller***	Y	N	N	N	N	N	Y	N
2 Swift	Y	Y	Y	N	Y	Y	Y	Y
3 Unsoeld	Y	Y	Y	N	?	?	Y	Y
4 ***Morrison***	Y	?	?	?	?	?	Y	N
5 Foley								
6 Dicks	Y	Y	Y	N	Y	Y	Y	Y
7 McDermott	Y	Y	Y	N	Y	Y	Y	Y
8 ***Chandler***	Y	N	N	Y	?	?	Y	N
WEST VIRGINIA								
1 Mollohan	Y	Y	Y	N	Y	Y	Y	Y
2 Staggers	Y	Y	Y	N	Y	Y	Y	Y
3 Wise	Y	Y	Y	N	?	?	Y	Y
4 Rahall	Y	Y	Y	N	Y	Y	Y	Y
WISCONSIN								
1 Aspin	Y	Y	Y	?	?	?	Y	Y
2 ***Klug***	Y	N	N	Y	N	N	Y	N
3 ***Gunderson***	Y	N	N	Y	N	N	Y	N
4 Kleczka	Y	Y	Y	N	Y	Y	Y	Y
5 Moody	Y	Y	Y	N	Y	Y	Y	N
6 ***Petri***	N	N	N	N	N	N	Y	N
7 Obey	Y	Y	Y	N	Y	Y	Y	N
8 ***Roth***	Y	N	N	?	?	?	Y	N
9 ***Sensenbrenner***	N	N	N	Y	?	?	Y	N
WYOMING								
AL ***Thomas***	N	N	N	Y	N	N	Y	N

Southern states - Ala., Ark., Fla., Ga., Ky., La., Miss., N.C., Okla., S.C., Tenn., Texas, Va.
Omitted votes are quorum calls, which CQ does not include in its vote charts.

425. HR 3750. Campaign Finance/Substitute. Michel, R-Ill., substitute amendment to require the majority of individual campaign contributions to come from within the congressional district, cut the amount political action committees can give from $5,000 to $1,000 and require all money used in federal elections to be subject to federal election law. Rejected 165-265: R 163-3; D 2-261 (ND 1-179, SD 1-82); I 0-1, Nov. 25, 1991.

426. HR 3750. Campaign Finance/Recommittal Motion. Thomas, R-Calif., motion to recommit to the House Administration Committee (thus killing) the bill to limit spending in House campaigns by providing voluntary spending limits, encourage candidates to raise small donations, restrict the amount candidates can take from political action committees and in large contributions, and close certain campaign finance loopholes. Motion rejected 155-270: R 155-6; D 0-263 (ND 0-180, SD 0-83); I 0-1, Nov. 25, 1991.

427. HR 3750. Campaign Finance/Passage. Passage of the bill to provide lower mail costs and up to $200,000 in public matching funds for the first $200 of individual contributions for House candidates who have raised more than $60,000 in individual contributions of less than $200 and agreed to a voluntary spending limit of $600,000. Regardless of agreeing to the voluntary spending limits, all House candidates would be limited to $200,000 in contributions from political action committees. Passed 273-156: R 21-144; D 251-12 (ND 176-4, SD 75-8); I 1-0, Nov. 25, 1991. A "nay" was a vote supporting the president's position.

428. Procedural Motion. Derrick, D-S.C., motion to approve the House Journal of Monday, Nov. 25. Motion agreed to 283-112: R 44-106; D 239-6 (ND 161-6, SD 78-0); I 0-0, Nov. 26, 1991.

429. HR 2929. California Desert Protection/Hunting. Marlenee, R-Mont., amendment to permit hunting on all lands within the Mojave National Monument in accordance with federal and state laws. Adopted 235-193: R 136-28; D 99-164 (ND 43-135, SD 56-29); I 0-1, Nov. 26, 1991.

430. HR 2929. California Desert Protection/Prohibit Condemnation Procedures. Delay, R-Texas, amendment to allow the secretary of Interior to only acquire land for wilderness, national park or monument-designation purposes of the bill from willing sellers, thus prohibiting the use of condemnation procedures to acquire land. Rejected 143-289: R 119-46; D 24-242 (ND 13-168, SD 11-74); I 0-1, Nov. 26, 1991.

431. HR 2929. California Desert Protection/Water Rights. Allard, R-Colo., amendment to express that the provisions reserving water rights for the United States to sufficiently fulfill the purposes of each of the wilderness areas designated in the bill does not include water rights to the Colorado River. Rejected 155-274: R 135-30; D 20-243 (ND 12-169, SD 8-74); I 0-1, Nov. 26, 1991.

432. HR 2929. California Desert Protection/Economic Impact. Dannemeyer, R-Calif., amendment to make the designation of land as wilderness, a national park or monument contingent upon an economic impact analysis that finds the environmental benefits of each land designation outweighs the economic costs of each designation. The amendment would also require the secretary of the Interior to pay any person who incurs an economic loss as a result of the bill the amount of the loss. Rejected 110-316: R 103-60; D 7-255 (ND 2-177, SD 5-78); I 0-1, Nov. 26, 1991.

KEY

Y Voted for (yea).
\# Paired for.
\+ Announced for.
N Voted against (nay).
X Paired against.
\- Announced against.
P Voted "present."
C Voted "present" to avoid possible conflict of interest.
? Did not vote or otherwise make a position known.

Democrats ***Republicans***
Independent

	425	426	427	428	429	430	431	432
ALABAMA								
1 ***Callahan***	Y	Y	N	Y	Y	Y	Y	Y
2 ***Dickinson***	Y	Y	N	?	Y	Y	Y	Y
3 Browder	N	N	Y	Y	Y	N	N	N
4 Bevill	N	N	Y	Y	Y	N	N	N
5 Cramer	N	N	Y	Y	Y	N	N	N
6 Erdreich	N	N	Y	Y	Y	N	N	N
7 Harris	N	N	Y	Y	Y	N	N	N
ALASKA								
AL ***Young***	Y	Y	N	?	Y	Y	Y	Y
ARIZONA								
1 ***Rhodes***	Y	Y	N	Y	Y	Y	Y	Y
2 Pastor	N	N	Y	Y	Y	N	Y	N
3 ***Stump***	Y	Y	N	N	Y	Y	Y	Y
4 ***Kyl***	Y	Y	N	N	Y	Y	Y	Y
5 ***Kolbe***	Y	Y	N	N	Y	Y	Y	Y
ARKANSAS								
1 Alexander	N	N	N	?	Y	N	N	N
2 Thornton	N	N	Y	Y	N	N	N	N
3 ***Hammerschmidt***	Y	Y	N	?	Y	Y	?	Y
4 Anthony	N	N	N	?	Y	Y	N	N
CALIFORNIA								
1 ***Riggs***	Y	Y	N	N	N	N	Y	?
2 ***Herger***	Y	Y	N	N	Y	Y	Y	Y
3 Matsui	N	N	Y	Y	N	N	N	N
4 Fazio	N	N	Y	Y	N	N	N	N
5 Pelosi	N	N	Y	?	N	N	N	N
6 Boxer	N	N	Y	?	N	N	N	N
7 Miller	N	N	Y	Y	N	N	N	N
8 Dellums	N	N	Y	Y	N	N	N	N
9 Stark	N	N	Y	Y	N	N	N	N
10 Edwards	N	N	Y	Y	N	N	N	N
11 Lantos	N	N	Y	Y	N	N	N	N
12 ***Campbell***	Y	Y	N	N	N	N	N	N
13 Mineta	N	N	Y	Y	N	N	N	N
14 ***Doolittle***	Y	Y	N	N	Y	Y	Y	Y
15 Condit	N	N	Y	Y	Y	N	N	N
16 Panetta	N	N	Y	Y	N	Y	N	N
17 Dooley	N	N	Y	Y	N	N	N	N
18 Lehman	N	N	Y	Y	N	N	N	N
19 ***Lagomarsino***	Y	Y	N	N	Y	Y	N	Y
20 ***Thomas***	Y	Y	N	N	Y	Y	Y	Y
21 ***Gallegly***	Y	Y	N	N	Y	Y	N	Y
22 ***Moorhead***	Y	Y	N	N	Y	Y	Y	Y
23 Beilenson	N	N	Y	?	N	N	N	N
24 Waxman	N	N	Y	Y	N	N	N	N
25 Roybal	N	N	Y	Y	N	N	N	N
26 Berman	N	N	Y	Y	N	N	N	N
27 Levine	N	N	Y	Y	N	N	N	N
28 Dixon	N	N	Y	?	N	N	N	N
29 Waters	N	N	Y	?	N	N	N	N
30 Martinez	N	N	Y	Y	Y	N	N	N
31 Dymally	N	N	Y	Y	N	N	N	N
32 Anderson	N	N	Y	Y	Y	Y	N	Y
33 ***Dreier***	Y	Y	N	Y	Y	Y	Y	Y
34 Torres	N	N	Y	Y	N	N	N	N
35 ***Lewis***	Y	Y	N	N	Y	Y	Y	Y
36 Brown	N	N	Y	Y	N	N	N	N
37 ***McCandless***	Y	Y	N	N	Y	Y	Y	Y
38 ***Dornan***	Y	Y	N	?	Y	Y	Y	Y
39 ***Dannemeyer***	Y	Y	N	N	Y	Y	Y	Y
40 ***Cox***	Y	Y	N	N	Y	Y	Y	Y
41 ***Lowery***	Y	Y	N	?	#	?	Y	Y
42 ***Rohrabacher***	Y	Y	N	N	Y	Y	Y	Y
43 ***Packard***	Y	Y	N	Y	Y	Y	Y	Y
44 ***Cunningham***	Y	Y	N	N	Y	Y	Y	Y
45 ***Hunter***	Y	Y	N	N	Y	Y	Y	Y
COLORADO								
1 Schroeder	N	N	Y	N	N	N	N	N
2 Skaggs	N	N	Y	Y	N	N	N	N
3 Campbell	N	N	N	Y	Y	N	Y	N
4 ***Allard***	Y	Y	N	N	Y	Y	Y	Y
5 ***Hefley***	N	Y	N	N	Y	Y	Y	Y
6 ***Schaefer***	Y	Y	N	N	Y	Y	Y	Y
CONNECTICUT								
1 Kennelly	N	N	Y	Y	N	N	N	N
2 Gejdenson	N	N	Y	Y	N	N	N	N
3 DeLauro	N	N	Y	Y	N	N	N	N
4 ***Shays***	Y	N	Y	N	N	N	N	N
5 ***Franks***	Y	Y	N	N	Y	Y	Y	Y
6 ***Johnson***	Y	Y	N	Y	Y	N	N	N
DELAWARE								
AL Carper	N	N	Y	Y	Y	N	N	N
FLORIDA								
1 Hutto	N	N	Y	Y	Y	Y	N	N
2 Peterson	N	N	Y	Y	Y	N	N	N
3 Bennett	N	N	N	Y	N	N	N	N
4 ***James***	Y	Y	Y	N	N	N	Y	N
5 ***McCollum***	Y	Y	N	Y	Y	N	Y	N
6 ***Stearns***	Y	Y	N	N	Y	N	Y	Y
7 Gibbons	N	N	Y	Y	N	N	N	N
8 ***Young***	Y	Y	Y	N	Y	Y	Y	Y
9 ***Bilirakis***	Y	Y	Y	N	N	Y	Y	Y
10 ***Ireland***	Y	Y	N	?	Y	Y	Y	N
11 Bacchus	N	N	Y	Y	N	N	N	N
12 ***Lewis***	Y	Y	N	N	N	Y	Y	Y
13 ***Goss***	Y	Y	N	N	N	N	Y	N
14 Johnston	N	N	Y	Y	N	N	?	N
15 ***Shaw***	Y	Y	N	?	Y	Y	Y	Y
16 Smith	N	N	Y	Y	N	N	N	N
17 Lehman	N	N	Y	Y	N	N	N	N
18 ***Ros-Lehtinen***	Y	Y	N	N	N	N	N	N
19 Fascell	N	N	Y	Y	N	N	N	N
GEORGIA								
1 Thomas	N	N	Y	Y	Y	N	N	N
2 Hatcher	N	N	Y	Y	Y	N	N	N
3 Ray	?	?	?	Y	Y	N	N	N
4 Jones	N	N	Y	Y	N	N	N	N
5 Lewis	N	N	Y	Y	N	N	N	N
6 ***Gingrich***	Y	?	N	N	Y	Y	Y	N
7 Darden	N	N	Y	Y	Y	N	N	N
8 Rowland	N	N	Y	Y	Y	N	N	N
9 Jenkins	N	N	Y	Y	Y	N	N	N
10 Barnard	N	N	Y	Y	Y	N	N	N
HAWAII								
1 Abercrombie	N	N	Y	Y	N	N	N	N
2 Mink	N	N	Y	Y	N	N	N	N
IDAHO								
1 LaRocco	N	N	Y	Y	Y	N	Y	N
2 Stallings	N	N	Y	Y	Y	Y	Y	N
ILLINOIS								
1 Hayes	N	N	Y	Y	N	N	N	N
2 Savage	N	N	Y	Y	N	N	N	N
3 Russo	N	N	Y	Y	N	N	N	N
4 Sangmeister	N	N	Y	Y	N	N	N	N
5 Lipinski	N	N	Y	Y	N	N	N	N
6 ***Hyde***	Y	Y	N	N	Y	Y	Y	Y
7 Collins	N	N	Y	?	N	N	N	N
8 Rostenkowski	N	N	Y	Y	N	N	N	N
9 Yates	N	N	Y	Y	N	N	N	N
10 ***Porter***	Y	Y	N	N	N	N	Y	N
11 Annunzio	N	N	Y	Y	N	N	N	N
12 ***Crane***	Y	Y	N	?	Y	Y	Y	Y
13 ***Fawell***	Y	Y	N	Y	N	N	Y	N
14 ***Hastert***	Y	Y	N	N	Y	Y	Y	N
15 ***Ewing***	Y	Y	N	Y	Y	Y	Y	Y
16 Cox	N	N	Y	Y	N	N	N	N
17 Evans	N	N	Y	Y	N	N	N	N
18 ***Michel***	Y	?	N	N	Y	Y	Y	Y
19 Bruce	N	N	Y	Y	Y	Y	N	N
20 Durbin	N	N	Y	Y	N	N	N	N
21 Costello	N	N	Y	Y	Y	Y	N	N
22 Poshard	Y	N	Y	Y	Y	Y	N	N
INDIANA								
1 Visclosky	N	N	Y	Y	N	N	N	N
2 Sharp	N	N	Y	Y	N	N	N	N
3 Roemer	N	N	Y	Y	Y	N	N	N

ND Northern Democrats SD Southern Democrats

	425	426	427	428	429	430	431	432
4 Long	N	N	Y	Y	N	N	N	N
5 Jontz	N	N	Y	Y	N	N	N	N
6 ***Burton***	Y	Y	N	N	Y	Y	Y	Y
7 ***Myers***	Y	Y	N	Y	Y	Y	Y	Y
8 McCloskey	N	N	Y	Y	N	N	N	N
9 Hamilton	N	N	Y	Y	N	N	N	N
10 Jacobs	N	N	Y	N	N	N	N	N
IOWA								
1 ***Leach***	Y	Y	Y	N	Y	Y	N	N
2 ***Nussle***	Y	Y	N	N	Y	Y	Y	N
3 Nagle	N	N	N	Y	Y	N	N	N
4 Smith	N	N	Y	Y	Y	Y	N	N
5 ***Lightfoot***	Y	Y	N	N	Y	Y	Y	Y
6 ***Grandy***	Y	Y	N	N	Y	Y	Y	Y
KANSAS								
1 ***Roberts***	Y	Y	N	N	Y	Y	Y	Y
2 Slattery	N	N	Y	Y	Y	N	N	N
3 ***Meyers***	Y	Y	N	N	N	N	Y	N
4 Glickman	N	N	Y	Y	Y	N	N	N
5 ***Nichols***	Y	Y	N	Y	Y	Y	Y	Y
KENTUCKY								
1 Hubbard	N	N	Y	Y	Y	N	N	N
2 Natcher	N	N	Y	Y	N	N	N	N
3 Mazzoli	N	N	Y	Y	N	N	N	N
4 ***Bunning***	Y	Y	N	N	Y	Y	Y	Y
5 ***Rogers***	Y	Y	N	N	Y	Y	Y	Y
6 ***Hopkins***	Y	Y	N	N	Y	Y	Y	Y
7 Perkins	N	N	N	Y	Y	N	N	N
LOUISIANA								
1 ***Livingston***	Y	?	N	N	Y	Y	Y	Y
2 Jefferson	N	N	Y	Y	Y	N	N	N
3 Tauzin	N	N	Y	Y	Y	Y	Y	Y
4 ***McCrery***	Y	Y	N	?	Y	Y	Y	N
5 Huckaby	N	N	Y	Y	Y	N	N	N
6 ***Baker***	Y	Y	N	N	Y	Y	Y	Y
7 Hayes	N	N	Y	Y	Y	Y	Y	Y
8 ***Holloway***	Y	?	N	N	Y	Y	Y	Y
MAINE								
1 Andrews	N	N	Y	Y	N	N	N	N
2 ***Snowe***	Y	Y	Y	Y	Y	Y	N	N
MARYLAND								
1 ***Gilchrest***	Y	Y	N	N	Y	Y	N	N
2 ***Bentley***	Y	Y	N	N	Y	Y	Y	Y
3 Cardin	N	N	Y	Y	N	N	N	N
4 McMillen	N	N	Y	Y	N	N	N	N
5 Hoyer	N	N	Y	Y	N	N	N	N
6 Byron	N	N	Y	?	?	Y	N	Y
7 Mfume	N	N	Y	Y	N	N	N	N
8 ***Morella***	Y	N	Y	?	N	N	N	N
MASSACHUSETTS								
1 Olver	N	N	Y	Y	N	N	N	N
2 Neal	N	N	Y	Y	N	N	N	N
3 Early	N	N	Y	Y	N	N	Y	N
4 Frank	N	N	Y	Y	N	N	N	N
5 Atkins	N	N	Y	Y	N	N	N	N
6 Mavroules	N	N	Y	Y	N	N	N	N
7 Markey	N	N	Y	?	N	N	N	N
8 Kennedy	N	N	Y	Y	N	N	N	N
9 Moakley	N	N	Y	Y	N	N	N	N
10 Studds	N	N	Y	Y	N	N	N	N
11 Donnelly	N	N	Y	Y	N	N	N	N
MICHIGAN								
1 Conyers	N	N	Y	Y	N	N	N	N
2 ***Pursell***	Y	Y	N	Y	Y	Y	Y	Y
3 Wolpe	N	N	Y	Y	N	N	N	N
4 ***Upton***	Y	Y	N	N	Y	N	Y	N
5 ***Henry***	Y	Y	N	N	N	Y	N	N
6 Carr	N	N	N	Y	Y	N	N	N
7 Kildee	N	N	Y	Y	N	N	N	N
8 Traxler	N	N	Y	Y	Y	N	N	N
9 ***Vander Jagt***	Y	Y	N	Y	Y	N	Y	Y
10 ***Camp***	Y	Y	N	N	Y	N	Y	N
11 ***Davis***	Y	Y	N	?	Y	Y	Y	Y
12 Bonior	N	N	Y	Y	N	N	N	N
13 Collins	N	N	Y	Y	N	N	N	N
14 Hertel	N	N	Y	Y	N	N	N	N
15 Ford	N	N	Y	?	?	N	N	N
16 Dingell	N	N	Y	Y	Y	N	N	N
17 Levin	N	N	Y	Y	N	N	N	N
18 ***Broomfield***	Y	Y	N	Y	Y	Y	Y	Y
MINNESOTA								
1 Penny	N	N	Y	Y	Y	Y	N	N
2 ***Weber***	Y	Y	N	?	Y	N	Y	N
3 ***Ramstad***	Y	Y	N	N	Y	N	Y	N
4 Vento	N	N	Y	Y	N	N	N	N

	425	426	427	428	429	430	431	432
5 Sabo	N	N	Y	Y	N	N	N	N
6 Sikorski	N	N	Y	N	Y	N	N	N
7 Peterson	N	N	Y	Y	Y	Y	N	N
8 Oberstar	N	N	Y	?	N	N	N	N
MISSISSIPPI								
1 Whitten	N	N	Y	Y	N	N	N	?
2 Espy	N	N	Y	Y	Y	N	N	N
3 Montgomery	N	N	Y	Y	Y	N	N	N
4 Parker	N	N	Y	Y	Y	N	N	N
5 Taylor	Y	N	Y	Y	Y	Y	N	N
MISSOURI								
1 Clay	N	N	Y	N	N	N	N	N
2 Horn	N	N	Y	Y	N	N	N	N
3 Gephardt	N	N	Y	Y	N	N	N	N
4 Skelton	N	N	Y	Y	Y	N	Y	N
5 Wheat	N	N	Y	Y	N	N	N	N
6 ***Coleman***	Y	Y	N	N	Y	Y	Y	Y
7 ***Hancock***	Y	Y	N	N	Y	Y	Y	Y
8 ***Emerson***	Y	Y	N	Y	Y	Y	Y	Y
9 Volkmer	N	N	Y	Y	Y	N	Y	N
MONTANA								
1 Williams	N	N	Y	Y	Y	N	Y	N
2 ***Marlenee***	Y	Y	Y	N	Y	Y	Y	Y
NEBRASKA								
1 ***Bereuter***	Y	Y	N	N	N	N	Y	N
2 Hoagland	N	N	Y	Y	N	N	N	N
3 ***Barrett***	Y	Y	N	N	Y	Y	Y	Y
NEVADA								
1 Bilbray	N	N	Y	Y	Y	N	N	N
2 ***Vucanovich***	Y	Y	N	N	Y	Y	Y	Y
NEW HAMPSHIRE								
1 ***Zeliff***	Y	Y	N	N	Y	N	Y	N
2 Swett	N	N	Y	Y	N	N	N	N
NEW JERSEY								
1 Andrews	N	N	Y	Y	N	N	N	N
2 Hughes	N	N	Y	Y	N	N	N	?
3 Pallone	N	N	Y	Y	N	N	N	N
4 ***Smith***	Y	Y	Y	?	Y	N	N	N
5 ***Roukema***	Y	Y	N	N	N	N	N	N
6 Dwyer	N	N	Y	Y	N	N	N	N
7 ***Rinaldo***	Y	Y	Y	Y	N	N	N	N
8 Roe	N	N	Y	Y	N	?	?	N
9 Torricelli	N	N	Y	Y	N	N	N	N
10 Payne	N	N	Y	Y	N	N	N	N
11 ***Gallo***	Y	Y	N	N	Y	Y	Y	N
12 ***Zimmer***	Y	Y	N	N	N	N	Y	N
13 ***Saxton***	Y	Y	N	N	Y	N	N	N
14 Guarini	N	N	Y	Y	N	N	N	N
NEW MEXICO								
1 ***Schiff***	Y	Y	N	Y	Y	N	Y	N
2 ***Skeen***	Y	Y	N	Y	Y	Y	Y	Y
3 Richardson	N	N	Y	Y	N	N	N	N
NEW YORK								
1 Hochbrueckner	N	N	Y	Y	N	N	N	N
2 Downey	N	N	Y	Y	N	N	N	N
3 Mrazek	?	?	?	?	N	N	N	?
4 ***Lent***	Y	Y	N	Y	Y	N	N	Y
5 ***McGrath***	Y	Y	N	Y	N	N	N	N
6 Flake	N	N	Y	Y	N	N	N	N
7 Ackerman	N	N	Y	Y	N	N	N	N
8 Scheuer	N	N	Y	?	N	N	N	N
9 Manton	N	N	Y	Y	N	N	N	N
10 Schumer	N	N	Y	Y	N	N	N	N
11 Towns	N	N	Y	?	X	N	N	N
12 Owens	N	N	Y	Y	N	N	N	N
13 Solarz	N	N	Y	Y	N	N	N	N
14 ***Molinari***	Y	Y	N	N	N	Y	Y	N
15 ***Green***	Y	N	Y	Y	N	N	N	N
16 Rangel	N	N	Y	Y	N	N	N	N
17 Weiss	N	N	Y	Y	N	N	N	N
18 Serrano	N	N	Y	Y	N	N	N	N
19 Engel	N	N	Y	Y	N	N	N	N
20 Lowey	N	N	Y	Y	N	N	N	N
21 ***Fish***	Y	Y	Y	Y	N	N	N	N
22 ***Gilman***	Y	N	Y	Y	N	N	N	Y
23 McNulty	N	N	Y	Y	Y	N	N	N
24 ***Solomon***	Y	Y	N	N	Y	Y	Y	Y
25 ***Boehlert***	Y	N	Y	N	N	N	N	N
26 ***Martin***	Y	Y	N	Y	Y	Y	Y	Y
27 ***Walsh***	Y	Y	N	Y	Y	Y	N	N
28 McHugh	N	N	Y	Y	N	N	N	N
29 ***Horton***	N	N	Y	Y	N	N	N	N
30 Slaughter	N	N	Y	Y	N	N	N	N
31 ***Paxon***	Y	Y	N	N	Y	Y	Y	Y

	425	426	427	428	429	430	431	432
32 LaFalce	N	N	Y	Y	N	N	N	N
33 Nowak	N	N	Y	Y	N	N	N	N
34 ***Houghton***	Y	Y	N	Y	Y	Y	Y	Y
NORTH CAROLINA								
1 Jones	N	N	Y	Y	N	N	N	N
2 Valentine	N	N	Y	Y	Y	N	N	N
3 Lancaster	N	N	Y	Y	Y	N	N	N
4 Price	N	N	Y	Y	N	N	N	N
5 Neal	N	N	Y	Y	Y	N	N	N
6 ***Coble***	Y	Y	N	N	Y	Y	Y	Y
7 Rose	N	N	Y	?	N	N	N	N
8 Hefner	N	N	Y	Y	Y	N	N	N
9 ***McMillan***	Y	Y	N	N	Y	Y	Y	Y
10 ***Ballenger***	Y	Y	N	N	Y	Y	Y	Y
11 ***Taylor***	Y	Y	N	N	Y	Y	Y	Y
NORTH DAKOTA								
AL Dorgan	N	N	Y	Y	Y	Y	N	N
OHIO								
1 Luken	N	N	Y	Y	N	N	N	N
2 ***Gradison***	Y	Y	N	Y	Y	N	Y	N
3 Hall	N	N	Y	Y	N	N	N	N
4 ***Oxley***	Y	Y	N	N	Y	Y	Y	Y
5 ***Gillmor***	Y	Y	N	Y	Y	Y	Y	N
6 ***McEwen***	Y	Y	N	Y	Y	Y	Y	Y
7 ***Hobson***	Y	Y	N	N	Y	Y	Y	N
8 ***Boehner***	Y	Y	N	N	Y	Y	Y	Y
9 Kaptur	N	N	Y	Y	N	N	N	N
10 ***Miller***	Y	Y	N	N	Y	Y	Y	Y
11 Eckart	N	N	Y	?	N	N	N	N
12 ***Kasich***	Y	Y	N	Y	Y	Y	Y	N
13 Pease	N	N	Y	Y	N	N	N	N
14 Sawyer	N	N	Y	Y	N	N	N	N
15 ***Wylie***	Y	Y	N	Y	N	Y	Y	N
16 ***Regula***	Y	Y	N	N	Y	Y	Y	N
17 Traficant	N	N	Y	Y	N	N	N	N
18 Applegate	N	N	Y	Y	Y	Y	N	N
19 Feighan	N	N	Y	Y	N	N	N	N
20 Oakar	N	N	Y	Y	N	N	N	N
21 Stokes	N	N	Y	Y	N	N	N	N
OKLAHOMA								
1 ***Inhofe***	Y	Y	N	N	Y	Y	Y	Y
2 Synar	N	N	Y	Y	N	N	N	N
3 Brewster	N	N	Y	Y	Y	N	N	N
4 McCurdy	N	N	Y	Y	Y	N	N	N
5 ***Edwards***	Y	Y	N	N	?	Y	Y	Y
6 English	N	N	Y	Y	Y	N	N	N
OREGON								
1 AuCoin	N	N	Y	Y	N	N	N	N
2 ***Smith***	Y	Y	N	N	Y	Y	Y	Y
3 Wyden	N	N	Y	Y	Y	N	N	N
4 DeFazio	N	N	Y	Y	Y	N	N	N
5 Kopetski	N	N	Y	Y	Y	N	N	N
PENNSYLVANIA								
1 Foglietta	N	N	Y	Y	N	N	N	N
2 Blackwell	N	N	Y	Y	N	N	N	N
3 Borski	N	N	Y	Y	N	N	N	N
4 Kolter	N	N	Y	Y	Y	Y	N	N
5 ***Schulze***	Y	Y	N	Y	Y	Y	Y	Y
6 Yatron	N	N	Y	Y	Y	N	N	N
7 ***Weldon***	Y	Y	Y	N	Y	N	N	N
8 Kostmayer	N	N	Y	Y	N	N	N	N
9 ***Shuster***	Y	?	?	Y	Y	Y	Y	Y
10 ***McDade***	Y	Y	N	N	Y	N	Y	N
11 Kanjorski	N	N	Y	N	N	N	N	N
12 Murtha	N	N	Y	Y	N	N	N	N
13 ***Coughlin***	Y	Y	N	N	Y	N	N	N
14 Coyne	N	N	Y	Y	N	N	N	N
15 ***Ritter***	Y	Y	N	?	Y	Y	N	N
16 ***Walker***	Y	Y	N	N	Y	Y	Y	Y
17 ***Gekas***	Y	Y	N	N	Y	Y	Y	Y
18 ***Santorum***	Y	Y	N	N	Y	Y	Y	N
19 ***Goodling***	Y	Y	N	N	Y	Y	Y	N
20 Gaydos	N	N	N	Y	Y	N	N	N
21 ***Ridge***	Y	Y	N	?	N	Y	N	?
22 Murphy	N	N	Y	N	Y	N	N	N
23 ***Clinger***	Y	Y	N	Y	Y	Y	Y	Y
RHODE ISLAND								
1 ***Machtley***	Y	Y	N	N	N	N	N	N
2 Reed	N	N	Y	Y	?	N	N	N
SOUTH CAROLINA								
1 ***Ravenel***	Y	Y	Y	Y	N	N	N	N
2 ***Spence***	Y	Y	N	N	Y	Y	Y	Y
3 Derrick	N	N	Y	Y	Y	N	N	N
4 Patterson	N	N	Y	Y	Y	N	N	N
5 Spratt	N	N	Y	Y	Y	N	N	N
6 Tallon	N	N	Y	?	Y	Y	N	N

	425	426	427	428	429	430	431	432
SOUTH DAKOTA								
AL Johnson	N	N	Y	Y	N	N	N	N
TENNESSEE								
1 ***Quillen***	Y	Y	N	Y	Y	Y	Y	N
2 ***Duncan***	Y	Y	Y	N	Y	Y	Y	Y
3 Lloyd	N	N	Y	Y	Y	N	N	N
4 Cooper	N	N	Y	Y	N	N	N	N
5 Clement	N	N	Y	Y	N	N	N	N
6 Gordon	N	N	Y	Y	Y	N	N	N
7 ***Sundquist***	Y	Y	N	N	Y	Y	Y	Y
8 Tanner	N	N	Y	Y	Y	N	N	N
9 Ford	?	?	?	?	N	N	N	N
TEXAS								
1 Chapman	N	N	Y	?	Y	Y	N	N
2 Wilson	N	N	Y	?	Y	N	?	?
3 ***Johnson***	Y	Y	N	N	Y	Y	Y	Y
4 Hall	N	N	N	Y	Y	Y	Y	Y
5 Bryant	N	N	Y	Y	Y	N	N	N
6 ***Barton***	Y	Y	N	N	Y	Y	Y	Y
7 ***Archer***	Y	Y	N	Y	Y	Y	Y	Y
8 ***Fields***	Y	Y	N	N	Y	Y	Y	Y
9 Brooks	N	N	Y	Y	Y	N	N	N
10 Pickle	N	N	Y	Y	Y	N	Y	N
11 Edwards	N	N	Y	Y	Y	N	N	N
12 Geren	N	N	Y	Y	Y	N	N	N
13 Sarpalius	N	N	N	Y	Y	N	N	N
14 Laughlin	N	N	Y	Y	Y	Y	Y	N
15 de la Garza	N	N	Y	Y	N	N	N	N
16 Coleman	N	N	Y	Y	N	N	N	N
17 Stenholm	N	N	Y	Y	Y	Y	Y	Y
18 Washington	N	N	Y	Y	N	N	?	N
19 ***Combest***	Y	Y	N	Y	Y	Y	Y	Y
20 Gonzalez	N	N	Y	Y	N	N	N	N
21 ***Smith***	Y	Y	N	N	Y	Y	Y	?
22 ***DeLay***	N	Y	N	N	Y	Y	Y	Y
23 Bustamante	N	N	Y	Y	N	N	N	N
24 Frost	N	N	Y	Y	Y	N	N	N
25 Andrews	N	N	Y	Y	N	N	N	N
26 ***Armey***	Y	Y	N	N	Y	Y	Y	Y
27 Ortiz	N	N	Y	Y	Y	Y	N	N
UTAH								
1 ***Hansen***	Y	Y	N	N	Y	Y	Y	Y
2 Owens	N	N	Y	Y	Y	N	Y	N
3 Orton	N	N	Y	Y	Y	Y	Y	N
VERMONT								
AL *Sanders*	N	N	Y	?	N	N	N	N
VIRGINIA								
1 ***Bateman***	Y	Y	N	Y	Y	N	Y	Y
2 Pickett	N	N	N	Y	Y	N	N	N
3 ***Bliley***	Y	Y	N	N	Y	Y	Y	Y
4 Sisisky	N	N	N	Y	Y	N	Y	Y
5 Payne	N	N	Y	Y	Y	N	N	N
6 Olin	N	N	Y	Y	Y	N	N	N
7 ***Allen***	Y	Y	N	N	Y	Y	Y	Y
8 Moran	N	N	Y	Y	N	N	Y	N
9 Boucher	N	N	Y	Y	N	N	N	N
10 ***Wolf***	Y	Y	N	N	Y	N	Y	Y
WASHINGTON								
1 ***Miller***	Y	Y	Y	?	N	N	Y	N
2 Swift	N	N	Y	Y	N	N	Y	N
3 Unsoeld	N	N	Y	Y	Y	N	N	N
4 ***Morrison***	Y	N	Y	Y	Y	Y	Y	N
5 Foley								
6 Dicks	N	N	Y	Y	N	N	N	N
7 McDermott	N	N	Y	Y	N	N	N	N
8 ***Chandler***	Y	Y	N	N	Y	Y	Y	Y
WEST VIRGINIA								
1 Mollohan	N	N	Y	Y	Y	N	N	N
2 Staggers	N	N	Y	Y	Y	N	N	N
3 Wise	N	N	Y	Y	Y	N	N	N
4 Rahall	N	N	Y	Y	Y	N	N	N
WISCONSIN								
1 Aspin	N	N	Y	?	N	N	N	N
2 ***Klug***	Y	Y	Y	Y	Y	N	Y	N
3 ***Gunderson***	Y	Y	N	Y	Y	N	Y	N
4 Kleczka	N	N	Y	Y	N	N	N	N
5 Moody	?	-	+	Y	N	N	N	N
6 ***Petri***	Y	Y	Y	Y	Y	Y	N	N
7 Obey	N	N	Y	Y	N	N	N	?
8 ***Roth***	Y	Y	N	N	Y	N	N	Y
9 ***Sensenbrenner***	Y	Y	N	N	Y	Y	Y	Y
WYOMING								
AL ***Thomas***	Y	Y	N	N	Y	Y	Y	Y

Southern states - Ala., Ark., Fla., Ga., Ky., La., Miss., N.C., Okla., S.C., Tenn., Texas, Va.
Omitted votes are quorum calls, which CQ does not include in its vote charts.

HOUSE VOTES 433, 434, 435, 436, 437, 438, 439, 440

433. HR 2929. California Desert Protection/Budget Deficit. Nichols, R-Kan., amendment to prohibit the bill from taking effect until the fiscal year after the first fiscal year there is no federal budget deficit. Rejected 133-292: R 117-47; D 16-244 (ND 4-175, SD 12-69); I 0-1, Nov. 26, 1991.

434. HR 2929. California Desert Protection/Land Disposal. DeLay, R-Texas, amendment to require that when the secretary of Interior acquires non-federal land under the bill, a quantity of federal land equal in value be disposed of within one year. Rejected 49-379: R 45-120; D 4-258 (ND 0-177, SD 4-81); I 0-1), Nov. 26, 1991.

435. HR 2929. California Desert Protection/Passage. Passage of the bill to designate 73 wilderness areas in the desert region of California for management by the Bureau of Land Management, among other changes. In all, the bill would designate more than 8 million acres as wilderness. Passed 297-136: R 45-120; D 251-16 (ND 178-4, SD 73-12); I 1-0, Nov. 26, 1991. A "nay" was a vote supporting the president's position.

436. HR 2212. MFN for China/Conference Report. Adoption of the conference report to allow the president to renew the extension of non-discriminatory treatment for the products of China, most-favored-nation (MFN) trading status, only if the Chinese government releases non-violent Tiananmen Square demonstrators, does not sell missiles to Syria or Iran, and makes significant progress in human rights, its nuclear proliferation policy and certain trade practices. Adopted 409-21: R 151-14; D 257-7 (ND 174-5, SD 83-2); I 1-0, Nov. 26, 1991. A "nay" was a vote supporting the president's position.

437. H J Res 157. Fiscal 1992 Supplemental Appropriations/Rule. Adoption of the rule (H Res 309) to waive all points of order against and provide for House floor consideration of the conference report to provide $6.9 billion for various emergencies in fiscal 1992, including $4.1 billion for the cleanup costs of Operation Desert Shield/Desert Storm and $2.7 billion for emergency domestic disaster relief programs. Adopted 242-175: R 66-95; D 176-79 (ND 106-70, SD 70-9); I 0-1, Nov. 27, 1991.

438. H J Res 157. Fiscal 1992 Supplemental Appropriations/Conference Report. Adoption of the conference report to provide $6.9 billion for various emergencies in fiscal 1992, including $4.1 billion for the cleanup costs of Operation Desert Shield/Desert Storm and $2.7 billion for emergency domestic disaster relief programs. The conference agreement authorizes the Defense Department to transfer $400 million to help the Soviet Union dismantle its nuclear weapons and $100 million to transport humanitarian aid to the Soviet Union. All funds in the bill are designated as emergency and thus exempt from the budget spending caps. Adopted 303-114: R 100-62; D 202-52 (ND 132-42, SD 70-10); I 1-0, Nov. 27, 1991.

439. HR 3909. Extend Expiring Tax Provisions/Passage. Rostenkowski, D-Ill., motion to suspend the rules and pass the bill to extend from Dec. 31 through June 30, 1992, 12 expiring tax provisions that offer about $3.2 billion in incentives for low-income housing, education, research and development, health care and to improve the availability of mortgages. The estimated loss in revenue to the Treasury would be offset by an acceleration in payments of estimated taxes by corporations with income of more than $1 million. Motion agreed to 420-0: R 163-0; D 256-0 (ND 175-0, SD 81-0); I 1-0, Nov. 27, 1991. A two-thirds majority of those present and voting (280 in this case) is required for passage under suspension of the rules.

440. HR 2950. Surface Transportation Reauthorization/-Conference Report. Adoption of the conference report to provide $151 billion for highway and mass transit programs for the six years through fiscal 1997, which would give states greater flexibility to decide how their transportation funds are spent. Adopted 372-47: R 130-33; D 241-14 (ND 163-10, SD 78-4); I 1-0, Nov. 27, 1991.

KEY

- Y Voted for (yea).
- # Paired for.
- + Announced for.
- N Voted against (nay).
- X Paired against.
- - Announced against.
- P Voted "present."
- C Voted "present" to avoid possible conflict of interest.
- ? Did not vote or otherwise make a position known.

Democrats ***Republicans***
Independent

	433	434	435	436	437	438	439	440
ALABAMA								
1 ***Callahan***	Y	N	N	Y	N	N	Y	Y
2 ***Dickinson***	Y	N	N	Y	?	?	?	?
3 Browder	N	N	Y	Y	Y	Y	Y	Y
4 Bevill	N	N	Y	Y	Y	Y	Y	Y
5 Cramer	N	N	Y	Y	Y	Y	Y	Y
6 Erdreich	N	N	Y	Y	Y	N	Y	Y
7 Harris	N	N	Y	Y	Y	Y	Y	Y
ALASKA								
AL ***Young***	Y	Y	N	Y	N	Y	Y	Y
ARIZONA								
1 ***Rhodes***	Y	Y	N	Y	N	N	Y	N
2 Pastor	N	N	Y	Y	Y	N	Y	+
3 ***Stump***	Y	Y	N	Y	N	N	Y	N
4 ***Kyl***	Y	Y	N	Y	Y	Y	Y	N
5 ***Kolbe***	Y	Y	N	N	N	N	Y	Y
ARKANSAS								
1 Alexander	N	N	Y	Y	Y	Y	Y	Y
2 Thornton	N	N	Y	Y	Y	Y	Y	Y
3 ***Hammerschmidt***	Y	N	N	Y	N	Y	Y	Y
4 Anthony	?	N	Y	Y	Y	Y	Y	Y
CALIFORNIA								
1 ***Riggs***	Y	N	N	Y	?	Y	Y	Y
2 ***Herger***	Y	Y	N	Y	N	N	Y	N
3 Matsui	N	N	Y	N	N	Y	Y	Y
4 Fazio	N	N	Y	Y	Y	Y	Y	Y
5 Pelosi	?	N	Y	Y	N	Y	Y	Y
6 Boxer	N	N	Y	Y	N	Y	Y	Y
7 Miller	N	N	Y	Y	N	Y	Y	Y
8 Dellums	N	N	Y	Y	N	Y	Y	Y
9 Stark	N	N	Y	Y	N	N	Y	Y
10 Edwards	N	N	Y	Y	N	N	Y	Y
11 Lantos	N	N	Y	Y	Y	Y	Y	Y
12 ***Campbell***	N	N	Y	N	N	N	Y	N
13 Mineta	N	N	Y	Y	N	Y	Y	Y
14 ***Doolittle***	Y	Y	N	Y	N	N	Y	N
15 Condit	N	N	Y	Y	Y	Y	Y	N
16 Panetta	N	N	Y	Y	Y	Y	Y	Y
17 Dooley	N	N	Y	Y	Y	Y	Y	Y
18 Lehman	N	N	Y	Y	Y	?	Y	Y
19 ***Lagomarsino***	N	N	N	Y	Y	Y	Y	Y
20 ***Thomas***	Y	N	N	Y	?	?	?	?
21 ***Gallegly***	Y	N	N	Y	N	Y	Y	Y
22 ***Moorhead***	Y	N	N	Y	Y	N	Y	Y
23 Beilenson	N	N	Y	Y	Y	Y	Y	Y
24 Waxman	N	N	Y	Y	Y	Y	Y	?
25 Roybal	N	N	Y	Y	Y	Y	Y	Y
26 Berman	N	N	Y	Y	N	Y	Y	Y
27 Levine	N	N	Y	Y	N	Y	Y	Y
28 Dixon	N	N	Y	Y	Y	Y	Y	Y
29 Waters	N	N	Y	Y	N	N	Y	Y
30 Martinez	N	N	Y	?	N	Y	Y	Y
31 Dymally	N	?	Y	Y	?	?	?	?
32 Anderson	Y	N	N	Y	Y	Y	Y	Y
33 ***Dreier***	Y	N	N	Y	N	N	Y	N
34 Torres	N	N	Y	Y	Y	Y	Y	Y
35 ***Lewis***	Y	N	N	Y	Y	Y	Y	Y
36 Brown	N	N	Y	Y	Y	Y	Y	Y
37 ***McCandless***	Y	Y	N	N	N	N	Y	Y
38 ***Dornan***	Y	N	N	Y	N	N	Y	Y
39 ***Dannemeyer***	Y	Y	N	Y	N	N	Y	N
40 ***Cox***	Y	N	N	Y	N	N	Y	N
41 ***Lowery***	Y	N	N	Y	Y	Y	Y	Y
42 ***Rohrabacher***	Y	Y	N	Y	N	Y	Y	N
43 ***Packard***	Y	Y	N	Y	N	N	Y	Y
44 ***Cunningham***	Y	N	N	Y	N	N	Y	Y
45 ***Hunter***	Y	Y	N	Y	N	N	Y	Y
COLORADO								
1 Schroeder	N	N	Y	Y	N	N	Y	Y
2 Skaggs	N	N	Y	Y	Y	Y	Y	Y
3 Campbell	N	N	Y	Y	Y	N	Y	Y
4 ***Allard***	Y	N	N	Y	N	Y	Y	N
5 ***Hefley***	Y	N	N	Y	N	N	Y	N
6 ***Schaefer***	Y	N	N	Y	N	N	Y	N
CONNECTICUT								
1 Kennelly	N	N	Y	Y	Y	Y	Y	Y
2 Gejdenson	N	N	Y	Y	N	N	Y	Y
3 DeLauro	N	N	Y	Y	Y	Y	Y	Y
4 ***Shays***	N	N	Y	N	N	N	Y	Y
5 ***Franks***	Y	N	N	Y	N	N	Y	N
6 ***Johnson***	N	N	Y	N	Y	Y	Y	Y
DELAWARE								
AL Carper	N	N	Y	Y	N	N	Y	Y
FLORIDA								
1 Hutto	Y	N	N	Y	N	N	Y	Y
2 Peterson	N	N	Y	Y	Y	Y	Y	Y
3 Bennett	N	N	Y	Y	Y	Y	Y	N
4 ***James***	Y	N	Y	Y	N	N	Y	N
5 ***McCollum***	N	N	Y	Y	N	N	Y	Y
6 ***Stearns***	Y	N	N	Y	N	N	Y	Y
7 Gibbons	N	N	Y	Y	Y	Y	Y	Y
8 ***Young***	N	N	N	Y	Y	Y	Y	Y
9 ***Bilirakis***	Y	N	N	Y	N	N	Y	Y
10 ***Ireland***	Y	N	N	Y	N	N	Y	Y
11 Bacchus	N	N	Y	Y	Y	Y	Y	N
12 ***Lewis***	Y	N	Y	N	N	N	Y	Y
13 ***Goss***	Y	N	Y	Y	N	N	Y	N
14 Johnston	N	N	Y	Y	Y	Y	Y	Y
15 ***Shaw***	N	N	Y	Y	N	N	Y	Y
16 Smith	N	N	Y	Y	Y	Y	Y	Y
17 Lehman	N	N	Y	Y	?	Y	?	?
18 ***Ros-Lehtinen***	Y	N	Y	Y	N	N	Y	N
19 Fascell	N	N	Y	Y	Y	Y	Y	Y
GEORGIA								
1 Thomas	N	N	Y	Y	Y	Y	Y	Y
2 Hatcher	N	N	Y	Y	Y	Y	Y	Y
3 Ray	Y	N	N	Y	Y	N	Y	N
4 Jones	N	N	Y	Y	Y	Y	Y	Y
5 Lewis	N	N	Y	Y	Y	Y	Y	Y
6 ***Gingrich***	Y	N	N	Y	N	Y	Y	Y
7 Darden	N	N	Y	Y	Y	Y	Y	Y
8 Rowland	N	N	Y	Y	Y	Y	Y	Y
9 Jenkins	N	N	Y	Y	Y	Y	Y	Y
10 Barnard	N	N	Y	Y	Y	Y	Y	Y
HAWAII								
1 Abercrombie	N	N	Y	Y	N	N	Y	Y
2 Mink	N	N	Y	Y	N	Y	Y	Y
IDAHO								
1 LaRocco	N	N	Y	?	Y	Y	Y	Y
2 Stallings	N	N	N	Y	Y	Y	Y	Y
ILLINOIS								
1 Hayes	N	N	Y	Y	N	N	Y	Y
2 Savage	N	N	Y	Y	N	N	Y	Y
3 Russo	N	N	Y	Y	N	Y	Y	Y
4 Sangmeister	N	N	Y	Y	Y	Y	Y	Y
5 Lipinski	N	N	Y	Y	Y	Y	Y	Y
6 ***Hyde***	Y	N	N	Y	Y	Y	Y	Y
7 Collins	N	N	Y	Y	N	?	?	?
8 Rostenkowski	N	N	Y	Y	Y	Y	Y	Y
9 Yates	N	N	Y	Y	?	?	?	?
10 ***Porter***	Y	N	Y	Y	N	N	Y	Y
11 Annunzio	N	N	Y	Y	N	Y	Y	Y
12 ***Crane***	Y	Y	N	N	N	N	Y	N
13 ***Fawell***	N	N	Y	N	N	N	Y	N
14 ***Hastert***	Y	N	N	Y	N	Y	Y	Y
15 ***Ewing***	Y	N	N	Y	Y	Y	Y	Y
16 Cox	N	N	Y	Y	N	Y	Y	Y
17 Evans	N	N	Y	Y	Y	Y	Y	Y
18 ***Michel***	Y	N	N	Y	Y	Y	Y	Y
19 Bruce	N	N	Y	Y	Y	Y	Y	Y
20 Durbin	N	N	Y	Y	N	Y	Y	Y
21 Costello	N	N	Y	Y	N	Y	Y	Y
22 Poshard	N	N	Y	Y	N	Y	Y	Y
INDIANA								
1 Visclosky	N	N	Y	Y	Y	Y	Y	Y
2 Sharp	N	N	Y	Y	N	Y	Y	Y
3 Roemer	N	N	Y	N	N	N	Y	N

ND Northern Democrats SD Southern Democrats

	433	434	435	436	437	438	439	440
4 Long	N	N	Y	Y	Y	Y	Y	N
5 Jontz	N	N	Y	Y	Y	Y	Y	Y
6 ***Burton***	Y	Y	N	Y	Y	N	Y	N
7 ***Myers***	Y	Y	N	N	Y	Y	Y	Y
8 McCloskey	N	N	Y	Y	Y	Y	Y	Y
9 Hamilton	N	N	Y	Y	Y	Y	Y	Y
10 Jacobs	N	N	Y	Y	N	N	Y	N
IOWA								
1 ***Leach***	N	N	Y	Y	N	Y	Y	Y
2 ***Nussle***	Y	N	N	N	N	N	Y	Y
3 Nagle	N	?	Y	Y	Y	Y	Y	Y
4 Smith	N	N	Y	Y	Y	Y	Y	Y
5 ***Lightfoot***	Y	Y	N	Y	Y	Y	Y	Y
6 ***Grandy***	Y	Y	N	N	N	Y	Y	Y
KANSAS								
1 ***Roberts***	Y	N	N	Y	N	Y	Y	Y
2 Slattery	N	N	Y	Y	Y	N	Y	Y
3 ***Meyers***	N	N	Y	Y	Y	Y	Y	Y
4 Glickman	N	N	Y	Y	Y	Y	Y	Y
5 ***Nichols***	Y	Y	N	Y	N	Y	Y	Y
KENTUCKY								
1 Hubbard	N	N	N	Y	Y	Y	Y	Y
2 Natcher	N	N	Y	Y	Y	Y	Y	Y
3 Mazzoli	N	N	Y	Y	Y	Y	Y	Y
4 ***Bunning***	Y	N	N	Y	N	Y	Y	Y
5 ***Rogers***	Y	N	N	Y	Y	Y	Y	Y
6 ***Hopkins***	Y	N	N	Y	N	Y	Y	Y
7 Perkins	N	N	Y	Y	Y	Y	Y	Y
LOUISIANA								
1 ***Livingston***	Y	Y	N	Y	Y	Y	Y	Y
2 Jefferson	N	N	Y	Y	Y	Y	Y	Y
3 Tauzin	Y	Y	N	Y	Y	Y	Y	Y
4 ***McCrery***	Y	N	N	Y	Y	Y	Y	Y
5 Huckaby	N	N	Y	Y	Y	Y	Y	Y
6 ***Baker***	Y	N	N	Y	N	Y	Y	Y
7 Hayes	Y	Y	N	Y	Y	Y	Y	Y
8 ***Holloway***	Y	Y	N	Y	N	Y	Y	Y
MAINE								
1 Andrews	N	N	Y	Y	N	Y	Y	Y
2 ***Snowe***	N	N	Y	Y	N	Y	Y	Y
MARYLAND								
1 ***Gilchrest***	N	N	Y	Y	N	Y	Y	Y
2 ***Bentley***	Y	N	N	Y	Y	Y	Y	Y
3 Cardin	N	N	Y	Y	Y	Y	Y	Y
4 McMillen	N	N	Y	Y	Y	Y	Y	Y
5 Hoyer	N	N	Y	Y	Y	Y	Y	Y
6 Byron	N	N	Y	Y	Y	Y	Y	Y
7 Mfume	N	N	Y	Y	N	N	Y	Y
8 ***Morella***	N	N	Y	Y	Y	Y	Y	Y
MASSACHUSETTS								
1 Olver	N	N	Y	Y	Y	Y	Y	Y
2 Neal	N	N	Y	Y	Y	Y	Y	N
3 Early	N	N	Y	Y	N	N	Y	N
4 Frank	N	N	Y	Y	Y	Y	Y	Y
5 Atkins	N	N	Y	Y	N	?	?	Y
6 Mavroules	N	N	Y	Y	Y	Y	Y	Y
7 Markey	N	N	Y	Y	N	Y	Y	Y
8 Kennedy	N	N	Y	Y	N	N	Y	Y
9 Moakley	N	N	Y	Y	Y	Y	Y	Y
10 Studds	N	N	Y	Y	Y	Y	Y	Y
11 Donnelly	N	N	Y	Y	Y	Y	Y	Y
MICHIGAN								
1 Conyers	N	N	Y	Y	N	N	Y	Y
2 ***Pursell***	N	N	Y	Y	Y	N	Y	Y
3 Wolpe	N	N	Y	Y	Y	Y	Y	Y
4 ***Upton***	N	N	Y	Y	N	Y	Y	Y
5 ***Henry***	N	N	Y	Y	N	N	Y	Y
6 Carr	N	N	Y	Y	Y	Y	Y	Y
7 Kildee	N	N	Y	Y	N	Y	Y	Y
8 Traxler	N	N	Y	Y	?	?	?	?
9 ***Vander Jagt***	Y	N	N	Y	Y	Y	?	Y
10 ***Camp***	Y	N	N	Y	N	Y	Y	Y
11 ***Davis***	Y	N	N	?	N	Y	Y	Y
12 Bonior	N	N	Y	Y	Y	Y	Y	Y
13 Collins	N	N	Y	Y	N	N	Y	Y
14 Hertel	N	N	Y	Y	Y	N	Y	?
15 Ford	N	N	Y	Y	Y	Y	Y	Y
16 Dingell	N	N	Y	Y	Y	Y	Y	Y
17 Levin	N	N	Y	Y	Y	Y	Y	Y
18 ***Broomfield***	Y	N	N	Y	Y	Y	Y	Y
MINNESOTA								
1 Penny	N	N	Y	Y	N	N	Y	N
2 ***Weber***	N	N	Y	Y	Y	Y	Y	Y
3 ***Ramstad***	Y	N	Y	Y	N	N	Y	Y
4 Vento	N	N	Y	Y	N	Y	Y	Y

	433	434	435	436	437	438	439	440
5 Sabo	N	N	Y	Y	Y	Y	Y	Y
6 Sikorski	N	N	Y	Y	Y	Y	Y	Y
7 Peterson	N	N	Y	Y	Y	Y	Y	Y
8 Oberstar	N	N	Y	Y	Y	Y	Y	Y
MISSISSIPPI								
1 Whitten	N	N	Y	Y	Y	Y	Y	Y
2 Espy	N	N	Y	Y	Y	Y	Y	Y
3 Montgomery	Y	N	N	Y	Y	Y	Y	Y
4 Parker	Y	N	N	Y	Y	Y	Y	Y
5 Taylor	Y	N	Y	N	Y	Y	Y	Y
MISSOURI								
1 Clay	N	N	Y	Y	N	N	Y	Y
2 Horn	N	N	Y	Y	Y	Y	Y	Y
3 Gephardt	N	?	Y	Y	Y	Y	Y	Y
4 Skelton	Y	N	N	Y	Y	Y	Y	Y
5 Wheat	N	N	Y	Y	Y	Y	Y	Y
6 ***Coleman***	Y	N	N	Y	Y	Y	Y	Y
7 ***Hancock***	Y	Y	N	Y	N	N	Y	N
8 ***Emerson***	Y	Y	N	Y	Y	Y	Y	Y
9 Volkmer	N	N	Y	Y	Y	Y	Y	Y
MONTANA								
1 Williams	?	N	Y	Y	N	Y	Y	Y
2 ***Marlenee***	Y	Y	N	Y	Y	Y	Y	?
NEBRASKA								
1 ***Bereuter***	N	N	N	Y	Y	Y	Y	Y
2 Hoagland	N	N	Y	Y	Y	Y	Y	Y
3 ***Barrett***	Y	N	N	Y	Y	Y	Y	Y
NEVADA								
1 Bilbray	N	N	Y	Y	Y	Y	Y	Y
2 ***Vucanovich***	Y	Y	N	N	Y	Y	Y	Y
NEW HAMPSHIRE								
1 ***Zeliff***	N	N	N	Y	N	N	Y	Y
2 Swett	N	N	Y	Y	N	N	Y	Y
NEW JERSEY								
1 Andrews	N	N	Y	Y	N	N	Y	N
2 Hughes	N	N	Y	Y	N	N	Y	Y
3 Pallone	N	N	Y	Y	Y	N	Y	N
4 ***Smith***	N	N	Y	Y	Y	Y	Y	Y
5 ***Roukema***	N	N	Y	Y	Y	Y	Y	Y
6 Dwyer	N	N	Y	Y	Y	Y	Y	Y
7 ***Rinaldo***	N	N	Y	Y	Y	N	Y	Y
8 Roe	N	N	Y	Y	Y	Y	Y	Y
9 Torricelli	N	N	Y	Y	Y	Y	Y	Y
10 Payne	N	N	Y	Y	Y	Y	Y	Y
11 ***Gallo***	N	N	Y	Y	Y	Y	Y	Y
12 ***Zimmer***	N	Y	Y	Y	N	N	Y	N
13 ***Saxton***	N	N	Y	Y	?	?	Y	Y
14 Guarini	N	N	Y	Y	Y	N	Y	Y
NEW MEXICO								
1 ***Schiff***	N	N	Y	Y	N	Y	Y	Y
2 ***Skeen***	Y	Y	N	Y	Y	Y	Y	Y
3 Richardson	N	N	Y	Y	Y	Y	Y	Y
NEW YORK								
1 Hochbrueckner	N	N	Y	Y	Y	Y	Y	Y
2 Downey	N	N	Y	Y	Y	Y	Y	Y
3 Mrazek	N	N	Y	Y	Y	Y	Y	Y
4 ***Lent***	Y	N	N	Y	Y	Y	Y	Y
5 ***McGrath***	N	N	Y	Y	Y	Y	Y	Y
6 Flake	N	N	Y	Y	+	+	+	Y
7 Ackerman	N	N	Y	Y	N	Y	Y	Y
8 Scheuer	N	N	Y	Y	N	Y	Y	Y
9 Manton	N	N	Y	Y	Y	Y	Y	Y
10 Schumer	N	N	Y	Y	N	N	Y	Y
11 Towns	N	N	Y	Y	?	?	?	?
12 Owens	N	N	Y	Y	N	N	Y	?
13 Solarz	N	N	Y	Y	Y	Y	Y	Y
14 ***Molinari***	Y	N	N	Y	N	Y	Y	Y
15 ***Green***	N	N	Y	Y	Y	Y	Y	Y
16 Rangel	N	?	Y	Y	N	N	Y	Y
17 Weiss	N	N	Y	Y	N	N	Y	Y
18 Serrano	N	N	Y	Y	N	Y	Y	Y
19 Engel	N	N	Y	Y	Y	Y	Y	Y
20 Lowey	N	N	Y	Y	N	Y	Y	Y
21 ***Fish***	N	N	Y	Y	Y	Y	Y	Y
22 ***Gilman***	-	N	Y	Y	Y	N	Y	Y
23 McNulty	N	N	Y	Y	Y	Y	Y	Y
24 ***Solomon***	Y	N	N	Y	N	N	Y	N
25 ***Boehlert***	N	N	Y	Y	Y	Y	Y	Y
26 ***Martin***	Y	N	N	Y	Y	Y	Y	Y
27 ***Walsh***	N	N	Y	Y	Y	Y	Y	Y
28 McHugh	N	N	Y	Y	Y	Y	Y	Y
29 ***Horton***	N	N	N	Y	Y	Y	Y	Y
30 Slaughter	N	N	Y	Y	Y	Y	Y	Y
31 ***Paxon***	Y	N	N	Y	N	Y	Y	Y

	433	434	435	436	437	438	439	440
32 LaFalce	N	N	Y	Y	N	Y	Y	Y
33 Nowak	N	N	Y	Y	Y	Y	Y	Y
34 ***Houghton***	N	N	N	Y	Y	Y	Y	Y
NORTH CAROLINA								
1 Jones	N	N	Y	Y	Y	Y	Y	Y
2 Valentine	N	N	Y	Y	N	N	Y	Y
3 Lancaster	N	N	Y	Y	Y	Y	Y	Y
4 Price	N	N	Y	Y	Y	Y	Y	Y
5 Neal	N	N	Y	Y	N	Y	Y	Y
6 ***Coble***	Y	Y	N	Y	N	Y	Y	N
7 Rose	N	N	Y	Y	?	?	?	Y
8 Hefner	N	N	Y	Y	Y	Y	Y	Y
9 ***McMillan***	Y	N	N	Y	Y	Y	Y	Y
10 ***Ballenger***	Y	Y	N	Y	-	+	Y	N
11 ***Taylor***	Y	Y	N	Y	N	Y	Y	N
NORTH DAKOTA								
AL Dorgan	N	N	Y	Y	N	Y	Y	Y
OHIO								
1 Luken	N	N	Y	Y	Y	N	Y	Y
2 ***Gradison***	N	N	N	Y	Y	Y	Y	Y
3 Hall	N	N	Y	Y	?	Y	Y	Y
4 ***Oxley***	Y	N	N	Y	Y	Y	Y	Y
5 ***Gillmor***	N	N	N	Y	N	Y	Y	Y
6 ***McEwen***	Y	Y	N	Y	N	N	Y	Y
7 ***Hobson***	Y	N	N	Y	N	Y	Y	Y
8 ***Boehner***	Y	N	N	Y	Y	Y	Y	N
9 Kaptur	N	N	Y	Y	Y	Y	Y	Y
10 ***Miller***	Y	Y	N	Y	Y	Y	Y	Y
11 Eckart	N	N	Y	Y	Y	Y	Y	Y
12 ***Kasich***	Y	N	N	Y	N	Y	Y	Y
13 Pease	N	N	Y	Y	Y	N	Y	Y
14 Sawyer	N	N	Y	Y	Y	Y	Y	Y
15 ***Wylie***	Y	N	N	Y	Y	Y	Y	Y
16 ***Regula***	Y	N	N	Y	Y	Y	Y	Y
17 Traficant	N	N	Y	N	N	N	Y	Y
18 Applegate	Y	N	Y	Y	Y	N	Y	Y
19 Feighan	N	N	Y	Y	N	Y	Y	Y
20 Oakar	N	N	Y	Y	N	N	Y	Y
21 Stokes	N	N	Y	Y	N	Y	Y	Y
OKLAHOMA								
1 ***Inhofe***	Y	Y	N	Y	N	N	Y	Y
2 Synar	N	N	Y	Y	Y	Y	Y	Y
3 Brewster	Y	N	N	Y	Y	Y	Y	Y
4 McCurdy	N	N	Y	Y	Y	Y	Y	Y
5 ***Edwards***	Y	Y	N	Y	N	Y	Y	Y
6 English	N	N	Y	Y	Y	Y	Y	Y
OREGON								
1 AuCoin	N	N	Y	Y	N	N	Y	Y
2 ***Smith***	Y	Y	N	Y	Y	Y	Y	Y
3 Wyden	N	N	Y	N	N	Y	Y	Y
4 DeFazio	N	N	Y	Y	N	N	Y	Y
5 Kopetski	N	N	Y	N	Y	Y	Y	Y
PENNSYLVANIA								
1 Foglietta	N	N	Y	Y	N	N	Y	Y
2 Blackwell	N	N	Y	Y	N	N	Y	Y
3 Borski	N	N	Y	Y	Y	Y	Y	Y
4 Kolter	N	N	Y	Y	N	Y	Y	Y
5 ***Schulze***	Y	N	N	Y	N	Y	Y	Y
6 Yatron	N	N	Y	Y	Y	Y	Y	Y
7 ***Weldon***	N	N	Y	Y	N	N	Y	Y
8 Kostmayer	N	N	Y	Y	Y	Y	Y	Y
9 ***Shuster***	Y	N	N	Y	N	N	Y	Y
10 ***McDade***	Y	N	N	Y	Y	Y	Y	Y
11 Kanjorski	N	N	Y	Y	Y	Y	Y	Y
12 Murtha	N	N	Y	Y	Y	Y	Y	Y
13 ***Coughlin***	N	N	Y	Y	Y	Y	Y	Y
14 Coyne	N	N	Y	Y	Y	Y	Y	Y
15 ***Ritter***	Y	N	Y	Y	N	N	Y	Y
16 ***Walker***	Y	N	N	Y	N	N	Y	N
17 ***Gekas***	Y	Y	N	Y	N	Y	Y	Y
18 ***Santorum***	N	N	Y	Y	N	N	Y	Y
19 ***Goodling***	Y	N	N	Y	Y	Y	Y	Y
20 Gaydos	N	N	Y	Y	Y	Y	Y	Y
21 ***Ridge***	?	?	?	Y	N	Y	Y	Y
22 Murphy	Y	N	Y	P	N	Y	Y	Y
23 ***Clinger***	Y	N	N	Y	Y	Y	Y	Y
RHODE ISLAND								
1 ***Machtley***	N	N	Y	Y	Y	Y	Y	Y
2 Reed	N	N	Y	Y	Y	Y	Y	Y
SOUTH CAROLINA								
1 ***Ravenel***	N	N	Y	Y	Y	Y	Y	Y
2 ***Spence***	Y	N	N	Y	N	Y	Y	Y
3 Derrick	?	N	Y	Y	Y	Y	Y	Y
4 Patterson	N	N	Y	Y	N	Y	Y	Y
5 Spratt	N	N	Y	Y	Y	Y	Y	Y
6 Tallon	N	N	Y	Y	Y	Y	Y	Y

	433	434	435	436	437	438	439	440
SOUTH DAKOTA								
AL Johnson	N	N	Y	Y	Y	Y	Y	Y
TENNESSEE								
1 ***Quillen***	Y	N	N	Y	Y	Y	Y	Y
2 ***Duncan***	Y	Y	N	Y	N	N	Y	Y
3 Lloyd	?	N	Y	Y	N	N	Y	Y
4 Cooper	N	N	Y	Y	Y	Y	Y	Y
5 Clement	N	N	Y	Y	Y	Y	Y	Y
6 Gordon	N	N	Y	Y	Y	Y	Y	Y
7 ***Sundquist***	Y	N	N	Y	Y	Y	Y	Y
8 Tanner	N	N	Y	Y	Y	Y	Y	Y
9 Ford	N	N	Y	Y	N	N	Y	Y
TEXAS								
1 Chapman	N	N	N	Y	Y	Y	Y	Y
2 Wilson	N	N	Y	Y	Y	Y	Y	Y
3 ***Johnson***	Y	Y	N	Y	N	N	Y	N
4 Hall	Y	Y	N	Y	Y	Y	Y	Y
5 Bryant	N	N	Y	Y	N	Y	Y	Y
6 ***Barton***	Y	Y	N	Y	N	N	Y	Y
7 ***Archer***	Y	Y	N	N	N	N	Y	N
8 ***Fields***	Y	Y	N	Y	N	N	Y	Y
9 Brooks	N	N	Y	Y	Y	Y	Y	Y
10 Pickle	N	N	Y	Y	Y	?	Y	Y
11 Edwards	N	N	Y	Y	Y	Y	Y	Y
12 Geren	Y	N	Y	Y	Y	N	Y	Y
13 Sarpalius	N	N	Y	Y	?	?	Y	Y
14 Laughlin	N	N	N	Y	Y	N	Y	Y
15 de la Garza	N	N	Y	Y	Y	Y	Y	Y
16 Coleman	N	N	Y	Y	Y	Y	Y	Y
17 Stenholm	Y	N	N	Y	N	N	Y	Y
18 Washington	?	N	Y	Y	N	N	Y	N
19 ***Combest***	Y	Y	N	Y	N	Y	Y	Y
20 Gonzalez	N	N	Y	Y	Y	Y	Y	Y
21 ***Smith***	Y	Y	N	Y	N	Y	Y	Y
22 ***DeLay***	Y	Y	N	Y	Y	Y	Y	N
23 Bustamante	N	N	Y	Y	Y	Y	Y	Y
24 Frost	N	N	Y	Y	Y	Y	Y	Y
25 Andrews	N	N	Y	Y	Y	Y	Y	Y
26 ***Armey***	Y	Y	N	N	N	N	Y	N
27 Ortiz	N	N	Y	Y	?	?	?	?
UTAH								
1 ***Hansen***	Y	N	N	Y	N	N	Y	N
2 Owens	N	N	Y	Y	Y	Y	Y	N
3 Orton	N	N	N	Y	Y	N	Y	Y
VERMONT								
AL *Sanders*	N	N	Y	Y	N	Y	Y	Y
VIRGINIA								
1 ***Bateman***	N	N	N	Y	Y	Y	Y	Y
2 Pickett	N	N	Y	N	+	+	+	+
3 ***Bliley***	N	N	N	Y	N	N	Y	Y
4 Sisisky	Y	N	Y	Y	Y	Y	Y	Y
5 Payne	N	Y	Y	Y	Y	Y	Y	Y
6 Olin	N	N	Y	Y	Y	Y	Y	Y
7 ***Allen***	Y	N	N	Y	N	Y	Y	Y
8 Moran	N	N	Y	Y	Y	Y	Y	Y
9 Boucher	N	N	Y	Y	?	Y	Y	Y
10 ***Wolf***	N	N	N	Y	Y	Y	Y	Y
WASHINGTON								
1 ***Miller***	N	N	Y	Y	Y	Y	Y	Y
2 Swift	N	N	Y	Y	Y	Y	Y	Y
3 Unsoeld	N	N	Y	Y	N	Y	Y	Y
4 ***Morrison***	N	N	Y	Y	Y	Y	Y	Y
5 Foley								
6 Dicks	N	N	Y	Y	Y	Y	Y	Y
7 McDermott	N	N	Y	Y	N	Y	Y	Y
8 ***Chandler***	Y	N	N	Y	Y	Y	Y	Y
WEST VIRGINIA								
1 Mollohan	N	N	Y	Y	Y	Y	Y	Y
2 Staggers	N	N	Y	Y	N	Y	Y	Y
3 Wise	?	N	Y	Y	Y	Y	Y	Y
4 Rahall	N	N	Y	Y	Y	N	Y	Y
WISCONSIN								
1 Aspin	N	N	Y	Y	Y	Y	Y	Y
2 ***Klug***	N	N	Y	Y	N	Y	Y	Y
3 ***Gunderson***	N	N	Y	Y	N	N	Y	Y
4 Kleczka	N	?	Y	Y	Y	Y	Y	Y
5 Moody	N	N	Y	Y	N	Y	Y	Y
6 ***Petri***	Y	N	Y	Y	N	N	Y	Y
7 Obey	N	N	Y	Y	Y	Y	Y	Y
8 ***Roth***	Y	N	N	Y	Y	Y	Y	Y
9 ***Sensenbrenner***	Y	N	N	Y	N	N	Y	Y
WYOMING								
AL ***Thomas***	Y	Y	N	Y	N	N	Y	Y

Southern states - Ala., Ark., Fla., Ga., Ky., La., Miss., N.C., Okla., S.C., Tenn., Texas, Va.
Omitted votes are quorum calls, which CQ does not include in its vote charts.

HOUSE VOTES 441, 442, 443, 444

441. HR 3371. Crime Bill/Rule. Adoption of the rule (H Res 301) to waive all points of order against and provide for House floor consideration of the conference report to mandate a five-day waiting period and a background check for handgun purchases; authorize $3 billion for federal, state and local law enforcement; codify the "good faith" exception to the exclusionary rule; extend the federal death penalty to more than 50 crimes; require federal death row habeas corpus appeals to be filed within one year from when their direct appeals were exhausted; and limit such appeals to cases in which the petitioner could not have discovered relevant facts or in which state officials acted unconstitutionally and the information is sufficient to undermine the prisoner's guilt. Adopted 232-160: R 5-148; D 227-11 (ND 155-5, SD 72-6); I 0-1, Nov. 27, 1991.

442. HR 3371. Crime Bill/Recommittal Motion. Hyde, R-Ill., motion to recommit the conference report to the conference committee with instructions to the House managers to insist on certain House provisions, including restitution of crime victims, HIV testing of sex offenders, the exclusionary rule, the Equal Justice Act, the death penalty, the seven-day waiting period for handgun purchases and others. The motion would also instruct the House conferees to insist on the Senate provisions for habeas corpus proceedings in federal death penalty cases and terrorism and public corruption cases. Motion rejected 174-237: R 152-4; D 22-232 (ND 8-166, SD 14-66); I 0-1, Nov. 27, 1991.

443. HR 3371. Crime Bill/Conference Report. Adoption of the conference report to mandate a five-day waiting period and a background check for handgun purchases; authorize $3 billion for federal, state and local law enforcement; codify the "good faith" exception to the exclusionary rule; extend the federal death penalty to 50 crimes; require federal death row habeas corpus appeals to be filed within one year from the date on which their direct appeals were exhausted; and limit such appeals to cases where the petitioner could not have discovered relevant facts or in which state officials acted unconstitutionally and the information is sufficient to undermine the prisoner's guilt. Adopted 205-203: R 6-149; D 199-53 (ND 136-37, SD 63-16); I 0-1, Nov. 27, 1991. A "nay" was a vote supporting the president's position.

444. HR 3435. RTC Funding. Derrick, D-S.C., motion to order the previous question (thus limiting debate and the possibility of amendment) on the rule (H Res 320) to waive all points of order against and provide for House floor consideration of the bill to provide additional taxpayer money to the Resolution Trust Corporation (RTC) and to restructure the RTC. Republicans tried to defeat the previous question, which would have allowed them to try to amend the rule to allow a floor amendment to attach an economic growth package to the bill. Motion agreed to 248-144: R 4-143; D 243-1 (ND 166-1, SD 77-0); I 1-0, Nov. 27, 1991.

KEY

Y Voted for (yea).
Paired for.
+ Announced for.
N Voted against (nay).
X Paired against.
- Announced against.
P Voted "present."
C Voted "present" to avoid possible conflict of interest.
? Did not vote or otherwise make a position known.

Democrats ***Republicans***
Independent

	441	442	443	444
ALABAMA				
1 ***Callahan***	N	Y	N	?
2 ***Dickinson***	?	?	?	?
3 Browder	Y	Y	N	Y
4 Bevill	Y	?	?	?
5 Cramer	Y	Y	N	Y
6 Erdreich	Y	Y	N	Y
7 Harris	N	Y	N	Y
ALASKA				
AL ***Young***	N	Y	N	N
ARIZONA				
1 ***Rhodes***	N	Y	N	?
2 Pastor	Y	N	Y	Y
3 ***Stump***	N	Y	N	N
4 ***Kyl***	N	Y	N	N
5 ***Kolbe***	N	Y	N	N
ARKANSAS				
1 Alexander	Y	N	Y	Y
2 Thornton	Y	N	Y	Y
3 ***Hammerschmidt***	N	Y	N	N
4 Anthony	Y	N	Y	Y
CALIFORNIA				
1 ***Riggs***	N	Y	N	N
2 ***Herger***	N	Y	N	N
3 Matsui	?	N	Y	?
4 Fazio	Y	N	Y	Y
5 Pelosi	Y	N	Y	?
6 Boxer	Y	N	Y	Y
7 Miller	Y	N	Y	Y
8 Dellums	Y	N	N	Y
9 Stark	?	N	Y	Y
10 Edwards	Y	N	Y	Y
11 Lantos	Y	N	Y	Y
12 ***Campbell***	?	?	?	?
13 Mineta	Y	N	Y	Y
14 ***Doolittle***	N	Y	N	N
15 Condit	Y	Y	N	?
16 Panetta	Y	N	Y	Y
17 Dooley	Y	N	Y	Y
18 Lehman	?	N	Y	Y
19 ***Lagomarsino***	N	Y	N	N
20 ***Thomas***	?	Y	N	N
21 ***Gallegly***	N	Y	N	N
22 ***Moorhead***	N	Y	N	N
23 Beilenson	Y	N	Y	Y
24 Waxman	?	?	#	?
25 Roybal	Y	N	?	Y
26 Berman	Y	N	Y	Y
27 Levine	Y	N	Y	Y
28 Dixon	?	N	N	Y
29 Waters	Y	N	N	Y
30 Martinez	Y	N	Y	Y
31 Dymally	?	N	N	?
32 Anderson	Y	N	Y	Y
33 ***Dreier***	N	Y	N	N
34 Torres	Y	N	Y	Y
35 ***Lewis***	N	Y	N	N
36 Brown	?	?	#	?
37 ***McCandless***	N	Y	N	N
38 ***Dornan***	N	Y	N	N
39 ***Dannemeyer***	N	Y	N	N
40 ***Cox***	N	Y	N	N
41 ***Lowery***	N	Y	N	N
42 ***Rohrabacher***	N	Y	N	N
43 ***Packard***	N	Y	N	N
44 ***Cunningham***	N	Y	N	N
45 ***Hunter***	N	Y	N	N
COLORADO				
1 Schroeder	Y	N	Y	Y
2 Skaggs	Y	N	Y	Y
3 Campbell	N	N	N	Y
4 ***Allard***	N	Y	N	N
5 ***Hefley***	N	Y	N	?
6 ***Schaefer***	N	Y	N	N
CONNECTICUT				
1 Kennelly	Y	N	Y	Y
2 Gejdenson	Y	N	Y	Y
3 DeLauro	Y	N	Y	Y
4 ***Shays***	N	Y	N	N
5 ***Franks***	N	Y	N	N
6 ***Johnson***	N	Y	N	N
DELAWARE				
AL Carper	Y	N	Y	Y
FLORIDA				
1 Hutto	N	Y	N	Y
2 Peterson	Y	N	Y	Y
3 Bennett	Y	N	Y	Y
4 ***James***	N	Y	N	N
5 ***McCollum***	N	Y	N	N
6 ***Stearns***	N	Y	N	N
7 Gibbons	Y	N	Y	Y
8 ***Young***	N	Y	N	N
9 ***Bilirakis***	N	Y	N	N
10 ***Ireland***	N	Y	N	N
11 Bacchus	Y	N	Y	Y
12 ***Lewis***	N	Y	N	N
13 ***Goss***	N	Y	N	N
14 Johnston	Y	N	Y	Y
15 ***Shaw***	?	?	X	?
16 Smith	Y	N	Y	Y
17 Lehman	Y	Y	Y	Y
18 ***Ros-Lehtinen***	N	Y	N	N
19 Fascell	Y	N	Y	Y
GEORGIA				
1 Thomas	Y	N	Y	Y
2 Hatcher	Y	N	Y	Y
3 Ray	Y	N	Y	Y
4 Jones	?	N	Y	Y
5 Lewis	Y	N	Y	Y
6 ***Gingrich***	N	Y	N	N
7 Darden	Y	N	Y	Y
8 Rowland	Y	N	Y	Y
9 Jenkins	Y	N	Y	Y
10 Barnard	Y	N	Y	Y
HAWAII				
1 Abercrombie	Y	N	Y	Y
2 Mink	Y	N	Y	Y
IDAHO				
1 LaRocco	Y	N	N	Y
2 Stallings	Y	N	N	Y
ILLINOIS				
1 Hayes	Y	N	Y	Y
2 Savage	N	N	N	Y
3 Russo	Y	N	Y	Y
4 Sangmeister	Y	N	Y	Y
5 Lipinski	Y	N	Y	Y
6 ***Hyde***	N	Y	N	N
7 Collins	?	?	X	?
8 Rostenkowski	Y	N	Y	Y
9 Yates	?	N	N	Y
10 ***Porter***	N	Y	N	N
11 Annunzio	Y	N	Y	Y
12 ***Crane***	N	Y	N	N
13 ***Fawell***	N	Y	N	N
14 ***Hastert***	N	Y	N	N
15 ***Ewing***	N	Y	N	N
16 Cox	Y	N	Y	Y
17 Evans	Y	N	Y	Y
18 ***Michel***	N	Y	N	N
19 Bruce	Y	N	Y	Y
20 Durbin	Y	N	Y	Y
21 Costello	Y	N	Y	Y
22 Poshard	Y	N	Y	Y
INDIANA				
1 Visclosky	Y	N	Y	Y
2 Sharp	Y	N	Y	Y
3 Roemer	Y	N	N	Y

ND Northern Democrats SD Southern Democrats

	441	442	443	444
4 Long	Y	N	Y	Y
5 Jontz	Y	N	Y	Y
6 ***Burton***	N	Y	N	N
7 ***Myers***	N	Y	N	N
8 McCloskey	Y	N	Y	Y
9 Hamilton	Y	N	Y	Y
10 Jacobs	Y	N	Y	N
IOWA				
1 ***Leach***	N	Y	N	N
2 ***Nussle***	N	Y	N	N
3 Nagle	?	N	N	Y
4 Smith	Y	N	Y	?
5 ***Lightfoot***	N	Y	N	N
6 ***Grandy***	N	Y	N	N
KANSAS				
1 ***Roberts***	N	Y	N	N
2 Slattery	Y	N	Y	Y
3 ***Meyers***	N	Y	N	N
4 Glickman	Y	N	Y	Y
5 ***Nichols***	N	Y	N	N
KENTUCKY				
1 Hubbard	Y	N	Y	Y
2 Natcher	Y	N	Y	Y
3 Mazzoli	Y	N	Y	+
4 ***Bunning***	N	Y	N	N
5 ***Rogers***	N	Y	N	N
6 ***Hopkins***	N	Y	N	N
7 Perkins	Y	N	N	Y
LOUISIANA				
1 ***Livingston***	N	Y	N	N
2 Jefferson	Y	N	Y	Y
3 Tauzin	Y	Y	N	Y
4 ***McCrery***	N	Y	N	N
5 Huckaby	N	Y	N	Y
6 ***Baker***	?	Y	N	?
7 Hayes	Y	N	N	Y
8 ***Holloway***	N	Y	N	N
MAINE				
1 Andrews	Y	N	N	Y
2 ***Snowe***	N	Y	N	N
MARYLAND				
1 ***Gilchrest***	N	Y	N	N
2 ***Bentley***	N	Y	N	N
3 Cardin	Y	N	Y	Y
4 McMillen	Y	N	Y	Y
5 Hoyer	Y	N	Y	Y
6 Byron	Y	Y	N	Y
7 Mfume	Y	N	N	Y
8 ***Morella***	Y	N	Y	Y
MASSACHUSETTS				
1 Olver	Y	N	Y	Y
2 Neal	Y	N	Y	Y
3 Early	Y	N	Y	Y
4 Frank	?	N	Y	Y
5 Atkins	Y	N	Y	Y
6 Mavroules	Y	N	Y	Y
7 Markey	Y	N	Y	Y
8 Kennedy	Y	N	Y	Y
9 Moakley	Y	N	Y	Y
10 Studds	Y	N	Y	Y
11 Donnelly	Y	N	Y	?
MICHIGAN				
1 Conyers	Y	N	Y	Y
2 ***Pursell***	N	Y	N	N
3 Wolpe	Y	N	Y	Y
4 ***Upton***	N	Y	N	N
5 ***Henry***	N	N	Y	N
6 Carr	Y	N	Y	Y
7 Kildee	Y	N	N	Y
8 Traxler	?	?	Y	Y
9 ***Vander Jagt***	N	Y	N	N
10 ***Camp***	N	Y	N	N
11 ***Davis***	N	Y	N	?
12 Bonior	Y	N	Y	Y
13 Collins	Y	N	Y	?
14 Hertel	?	N	Y	Y
15 Ford	N	N	Y	Y
16 Dingell	Y	N	Y	?
17 Levin	Y	N	Y	Y
18 ***Broomfield***	?	?	?	N
MINNESOTA				
1 Penny	Y	N	Y	Y
2 ***Weber***	N	Y	N	N
3 ***Ramstad***	Y	Y	Y	N
4 Vento	Y	N	N	Y

	441	442	443	444
5 Sabo	Y	N	?	Y
6 Sikorski	Y	N	Y	Y
7 Peterson	?	?	?	?
8 Oberstar	Y	N	N	Y
MISSISSIPPI				
1 Whitten	Y	N	Y	Y
2 Espy	Y	N	Y	Y
3 Montgomery	N	?	?	?
4 Parker	N	Y	N	Y
5 Taylor	Y	Y	N	Y
MISSOURI				
1 Clay	N	N	N	Y
2 Horn	Y	N	Y	Y
3 Gephardt	Y	N	Y	Y
4 Skelton	Y	Y	N	Y
5 Wheat	Y	N	Y	Y
6 ***Coleman***	N	Y	N	N
7 ***Hancock***	N	Y	N	N
8 ***Emerson***	N	Y	N	N
9 Volkmer	N	Y	N	Y
MONTANA				
1 Williams	?	Y	N	Y
2 ***Marlenee***	?	?	X	?
NEBRASKA				
1 ***Bereuter***	N	Y	N	N
2 Hoagland	Y	N	Y	Y
3 ***Barrett***	N	Y	N	N
NEVADA				
1 Bilbray	Y	N	Y	Y
2 ***Vucanovich***	N	Y	N	N
NEW HAMPSHIRE				
1 ***Zeliff***	N	Y	N	N
2 Swett	Y	N	Y	Y
NEW JERSEY				
1 Andrews	Y	N	Y	Y
2 Hughes	Y	N	Y	Y
3 Pallone	Y	Y	Y	Y
4 ***Smith***	N	Y	N	N
5 ***Roukema***	N	Y	N	Y
6 Dwyer	Y	N	?	?
7 ***Rinaldo***	N	Y	N	N
8 Roe	?	-	+	Y
9 Torricelli	Y	N	Y	Y
10 Payne	Y	N	N	Y
11 ***Gallo***	N	Y	N	N
12 ***Zimmer***	N	Y	N	N
13 ***Saxton***	N	Y	N	N
14 Guarini	Y	N	Y	Y
NEW MEXICO				
1 ***Schiff***	N	Y	N	N
2 ***Skeen***	N	Y	N	N
3 Richardson	Y	N	Y	Y
NEW YORK				
1 Hochbrueckner	Y	N	Y	Y
2 Downey	Y	N	Y	Y
3 Mrazek	Y	N	Y	Y
4 ***Lent***	N	Y	N	?
5 ***McGrath***	N	Y	N	N
6 Flake	Y	N	N	Y
7 Ackerman	Y	N	Y	Y
8 Scheuer	Y	N	Y	Y
9 Manton	Y	N	Y	Y
10 Schumer	Y	N	Y	Y
11 Towns	?	N	N	Y
12 Owens	?	?	N	Y
13 Solarz	Y	N	Y	Y
14 ***Molinari***	N	Y	N	N
15 ***Green***	Y	N	Y	N
16 Rangel	Y	N	N	Y
17 Weiss	Y	N	N	?
18 Serrano	Y	N	N	Y
19 Engel	Y	N	Y	Y
20 Lowey	Y	N	Y	Y
21 ***Fish***	?	?	?	?
22 ***Gilman***	Y	Y	Y	N
23 McNulty	Y	N	Y	Y
24 ***Solomon***	N	Y	N	N
25 ***Boehlert***	N	Y	N	N
26 ***Martin***	N	Y	N	N
27 ***Walsh***	N	Y	N	Y
28 McHugh	Y	N	Y	Y
29 ***Horton***	N	N	Y	N
30 Slaughter	Y	N	Y	Y
31 ***Paxon***	N	Y	N	N

	441	442	443	444
32 LaFalce	Y	N	Y	Y
33 Nowak	Y	N	Y	Y
34 ***Houghton***	N	Y	N	Y
NORTH CAROLINA				
1 Jones	Y	N	Y	Y
2 Valentine	Y	N	Y	Y
3 Lancaster	Y	N	Y	?
4 Price	Y	N	Y	Y
5 Neal	Y	N	Y	Y
6 ***Coble***	N	Y	N	?
7 Rose	Y	N	Y	Y
8 Hefner	Y	N	Y	Y
9 ***McMillan***	Y	Y	N	N
10 ***Ballenger***	N	Y	N	-
11 ***Taylor***	N	Y	N	N
NORTH DAKOTA				
AL Dorgan	Y	N	Y	Y
OHIO				
1 Luken	Y	N	Y	Y
2 ***Gradison***	?	Y	N	N
3 Hall	Y	N	Y	Y
4 ***Oxley***	N	Y	N	N
5 ***Gillmor***	N	Y	N	N
6 ***McEwen***	N	Y	N	N
7 ***Hobson***	N	Y	N	N
8 ***Boehner***	N	Y	N	N
9 Kaptur	Y	N	Y	Y
10 ***Miller***	N	Y	N	N
11 Eckart	Y	N	Y	Y
12 ***Kasich***	N	Y	N	N
13 Pease	Y	N	N	Y
14 Sawyer	Y	N	Y	Y
15 ***Wylie***	N	Y	N	N
16 ***Regula***	N	Y	N	N
17 Traficant	Y	N	N	Y
18 Applegate	?	Y	Y	Y
19 Feighan	Y	N	Y	Y
20 Oakar	Y	N	Y	Y
21 Stokes	Y	N	N	Y
OKLAHOMA				
1 ***Inhofe***	N	Y	N	?
2 Synar	Y	N	Y	Y
3 Brewster	Y	N	Y	Y
4 McCurdy	Y	N	Y	Y
5 ***Edwards***	N	Y	N	N
6 English	Y	Y	N	Y
OREGON				
1 AuCoin	Y	N	Y	?
2 ***Smith***	N	Y	N	N
3 Wyden	Y	N	Y	Y
4 DeFazio	Y	N	Y	Y
5 Kopetski	Y	N	Y	Y
PENNSYLVANIA				
1 Foglietta	Y	N	Y	Y
2 Blackwell	Y	N	N	Y
3 Borski	Y	N	Y	Y
4 Kolter	Y	N	N	Y
5 ***Schulze***	N	Y	N	?
6 Yatron	Y	N	N	Y
7 ***Weldon***	N	Y	N	N
8 Kostmayer	Y	N	Y	Y
9 ***Shuster***	?	?	?	?
10 ***McDade***	N	Y	N	N
11 Kanjorski	Y	N	Y	Y
12 Murtha	Y	N	Y	Y
13 ***Coughlin***	N	Y	N	N
14 Coyne	Y	N	Y	Y
15 ***Ritter***	N	Y	N	?
16 ***Walker***	N	Y	N	N
17 ***Gekas***	N	Y	N	N
18 ***Santorum***	N	Y	N	N
19 ***Goodling***	P	P	P	N
20 Gaydos	?	N	N	Y
21 ***Ridge***	N	Y	N	N
22 Murphy	Y	N	Y	Y
23 ***Clinger***	N	Y	N	N
RHODE ISLAND				
1 ***Machtley***	N	Y	N	N
2 Reed	Y	N	Y	Y
SOUTH CAROLINA				
1 ***Ravenel***	N	Y	N	N
2 ***Spence***	N	Y	N	N
3 Derrick	Y	N	Y	Y
4 Patterson	Y	N	Y	Y
5 Spratt	Y	N	Y	Y
6 Tallon	Y	N	N	Y

	441	442	443	444
SOUTH DAKOTA				
AL Johnson	Y	N	Y	Y
TENNESSEE				
1 ***Quillen***	?	Y	?	?
2 ***Duncan***	N	Y	N	N
3 Lloyd	Y	N	Y	Y
4 Cooper	Y	N	Y	Y
5 Clement	Y	N	Y	Y
6 Gordon	Y	N	Y	Y
7 ***Sundquist***	N	Y	N	N
8 Tanner	Y	N	Y	Y
9 Ford	Y	N	Y	Y
TEXAS				
1 Chapman	?	N	Y	Y
2 Wilson	Y	N	Y	Y
3 ***Johnson***	N	Y	N	N
4 Hall	Y	Y	Y	Y
5 Bryant	Y	N	Y	?
6 ***Barton***	N	?	?	N
7 ***Archer***	N	Y	N	N
8 ***Fields***	N	Y	N	N
9 Brooks	Y	N	Y	Y
10 Pickle	Y	N	Y	Y
11 Edwards	Y	N	Y	Y
12 Geren	Y	N	Y	Y
13 Sarpalius	Y	N	N	Y
14 Laughlin	Y	N	Y	Y
15 de la Garza	?	?	?	?
16 Coleman	Y	N	Y	Y
17 Stenholm	Y	Y	Y	Y
18 Washington	?	N	?	Y
19 ***Combest***	N	Y	N	N
20 Gonzalez	Y	N	Y	Y
21 ***Smith***	N	Y	N	N
22 ***DeLay***	N	Y	N	N
23 Bustamante	Y	N	Y	Y
24 Frost	Y	N	Y	Y
25 Andrews	Y	N	N	Y
26 ***Armey***	N	Y	N	N
27 Ortiz	?	?	#	?
UTAH				
1 ***Hansen***	?	?	?	?
2 Owens	Y	N	Y	Y
3 Orton	Y	Y	N	Y
VERMONT				
AL *Sanders*	N	N	N	Y
VIRGINIA				
1 ***Bateman***	N	Y	N	N
2 Pickett	+	-	+	+
3 ***Bliley***	N	Y	N	N
4 Sisisky	Y	N	Y	Y
5 Payne	Y	N	Y	Y
6 Olin	Y	N	Y	Y
7 ***Allen***	N	Y	N	N
8 Moran	N	Y	N	Y
9 Boucher	?	N	Y	Y
10 ***Wolf***	N	Y	N	N
WASHINGTON				
1 ***Miller***	N	Y	N	N
2 Swift	Y	N	Y	Y
3 Unsoeld	Y	N	Y	Y
4 ***Morrison***	N	Y	N	N
5 Foley			Y	
6 Dicks	Y	N	Y	Y
7 McDermott	Y	N	Y	Y
8 ***Chandler***	N	Y	N	N
WEST VIRGINIA				
1 Mollohan	Y	N	Y	Y
2 Staggers	Y	N	?	Y
3 Wise	Y	N	Y	Y
4 Rahall	Y	N	Y	Y
WISCONSIN				
1 Aspin	?	?	?	Y
2 ***Klug***	N	Y	N	N
3 ***Gunderson***	N	Y	N	N
4 Kleczka	?	N	Y	Y
5 Moody	Y	N	Y	Y
6 ***Petri***	N	Y	N	N
7 Obey	Y	N	Y	Y
8 ***Roth***	N	Y	N	N
9 ***Sensenbrenner***	N	Y	N	N
WYOMING				
AL ***Thomas***	N	Y	N	N

Southern states - Ala., Ark., Fla., Ga., Ky., La., Miss., N.C., Okla., S.C., Tenn., Texas, Va.
Omitted votes are quorum calls, which CQ does not include in its vote charts.

CQ

Appendix S

SENATE ROLL-CALL VOTES

SENATE VOTES 1, 2, 3, 4, 5, 6, 7, 8

	1	2	3	4	5	6	7	8
ALABAMA								
Heflin	N	Y	Y	Y	Y	Y	Y	Y
Shelby	N	Y	Y	Y	Y	Y	Y	Y
ALASKA								
Murkowski	N	Y	Y	Y	Y	Y	Y	Y
Stevens	N	Y	Y	Y	Y	Y	Y	Y
ARIZONA								
DeConcini	Y	N	Y	Y	Y	Y	Y	Y
McCain	N	Y	Y	Y	Y	Y	Y	Y
ARKANSAS								
Bumpers	Y	N	Y	Y	Y	Y	Y	Y
Pryor	Y	N	Y	Y	Y	Y	Y	Y
CALIFORNIA								
Cranston	+	-	?	?	?	?	?	?
Seymour	N	Y	Y	Y	Y	Y	Y	Y
COLORADO								
Wirth	Y	N	Y	Y	Y	Y	Y	Y
Brown	N	Y	Y	Y	Y	Y	Y	Y
CONNECTICUT								
Dodd	Y	N	Y	Y	Y	Y	Y	Y
Lieberman	N	Y	Y	Y	Y	Y	Y	Y
DELAWARE								
Biden	Y	N	Y	Y	Y	Y	Y	Y
Roth	N	Y	Y	Y	Y	Y	Y	Y
FLORIDA								
Graham	N	Y	Y	Y	Y	Y	Y	Y
Mack	N	Y	Y	Y	Y	Y	Y	Y
GEORGIA								
Fowler	Y	N	Y	Y	Y	Y	Y	Y
Nunn	Y	N	Y	Y	Y	Y	Y	Y
HAWAII								
Akaka	Y	N	Y	Y	Y	Y	Y	Y
Inouye	Y	N	Y	Y	Y	Y	Y	Y
IDAHO								
Craig	N	Y	Y	Y	Y	Y	Y	Y
Symms	N	Y	Y	Y	Y	Y	Y	Y
ILLINOIS								
Dixon	Y	N	Y	Y	Y	Y	Y	Y
Simon	Y	N	Y	Y	Y	Y	Y	Y
INDIANA								
Coats	N	Y	Y	Y	Y	Y	Y	Y
Lugar	N	Y	Y	Y	Y	Y	Y	Y
IOWA								
Harkin	Y	N	Y	Y	Y	Y	Y	Y
Grassley	Y	N	Y	Y	Y	Y	Y	Y
KANSAS								
Dole	N	Y	Y	Y	Y	Y	Y	Y
Kassebaum	N	Y	Y	Y	Y	Y	Y	Y
KENTUCKY								
Ford	Y	N	Y	Y	Y	Y	Y	Y
McConnell	N	Y	Y	Y	Y	Y	Y	Y
LOUISIANA								
Breaux	N	Y	Y	Y	Y	Y	Y	Y
Johnston	N	Y	Y	Y	Y	Y	Y	Y
MAINE								
Mitchell	Y	N	Y	Y	Y	Y	Y	Y
Cohen	N	Y	Y	Y	Y	Y	Y	Y
MARYLAND								
Mikulski	Y	N	Y	Y	Y	Y	Y	Y
Sarbanes	Y	N	Y	Y	Y	Y	Y	Y
MASSACHUSETTS								
Kennedy	Y	N	Y	Y	Y	Y	Y	Y
Kerry	Y	N	Y	Y	Y	Y	Y	Y
MICHIGAN								
Levin	Y	N	Y	Y	Y	Y	Y	Y
Riegle	Y	N	Y	Y	Y	Y	Y	Y
MINNESOTA								
Wellstone	Y	N	Y	Y	Y	Y	Y	Y
Durenberger	N	Y	Y	Y	Y	Y	Y	Y
MISSISSIPPI								
Cochran	N	Y	Y	Y	Y	Y	Y	Y
Lott	N	Y	Y	Y	Y	Y	Y	Y
MISSOURI								
Bond	N	Y	Y	Y	Y	Y	Y	Y
Danforth	N	Y	Y	Y	Y	Y	Y	Y
MONTANA								
Baucus	Y	N	Y	Y	Y	Y	Y	Y
Burns	N	Y	Y	Y	Y	Y	Y	Y
NEBRASKA								
Exon	Y	N	Y	Y	Y	Y	Y	Y
Kerrey	Y	N	Y	Y	Y	Y	Y	Y
NEVADA								
Bryan	N	Y	Y	Y	Y	Y	Y	Y
Reid	N	Y	Y	Y	Y	Y	Y	Y
NEW HAMPSHIRE								
Rudman	N	Y	Y	Y	Y	Y	Y	Y
Smith	N	Y	Y	Y	Y	Y	Y	Y
NEW JERSEY								
Bradley	Y	N	Y	Y	Y	Y	Y	Y
Lautenberg	Y	N	Y	Y	Y	Y	Y	Y
NEW MEXICO								
Bingaman	Y	N	Y	Y	Y	Y	Y	Y
Domenici	N	Y	Y	Y	Y	Y	Y	Y
NEW YORK								
Moynihan	Y	N	Y	Y	Y	Y	Y	Y
D'Amato	N	Y	Y	Y	Y	Y	Y	Y
NORTH CAROLINA								
Sanford	Y	N	Y	Y	Y	Y	Y	Y
Helms	N	Y	Y	Y	Y	Y	Y	Y
NORTH DAKOTA								
Burdick	Y	N	Y	Y	Y	Y	Y	Y
Conrad	Y	N	Y	Y	Y	Y	Y	Y
OHIO								
Glenn	Y	N	?	Y	Y	Y	Y	Y
Metzenbaum	Y	N	Y	Y	Y	Y	Y	Y
OKLAHOMA								
Boren	Y	N	Y	Y	Y	Y	Y	Y
Nickles	N	Y	Y	Y	Y	Y	Y	Y
OREGON								
Hatfield	N	N	Y	Y	Y	Y	Y	Y
Packwood	N	Y	Y	Y	Y	Y	Y	Y
PENNSYLVANIA								
Heinz	N	Y	Y	Y	Y	Y	Y	Y
Specter	N	Y	Y	Y	Y	Y	Y	Y
RHODE ISLAND								
Pell	Y	N	Y	Y	Y	Y	Y	Y
Chafee	N	Y	Y	Y	Y	Y	Y	Y
SOUTH CAROLINA								
Hollings	Y	N	Y	Y	Y	Y	Y	Y
Thurmond	N	Y	Y	Y	Y	Y	Y	Y
SOUTH DAKOTA								
Daschle	Y	N	Y	Y	Y	Y	Y	Y
Pressler	N	Y	Y	Y	Y	Y	Y	Y
TENNESSEE								
Gore	N	Y	Y	Y	Y	Y	Y	Y
Sasser	Y	N	Y	Y	Y	Y	Y	Y
TEXAS								
Bentsen	Y	N	Y	Y	Y	Y	Y	Y
Gramm	N	Y	Y	Y	Y	Y	Y	Y
UTAH								
Garn	N	Y	Y	Y	Y	Y	Y	Y
Hatch	N	Y	Y	Y	Y	Y	Y	Y
VERMONT								
Leahy	Y	N	Y	Y	Y	Y	Y	Y
Jeffords	N	Y	Y	Y	Y	Y	Y	Y
VIRGINIA								
Robb	N	Y	Y	Y	Y	Y	Y	Y
Warner	N	Y	Y	Y	Y	Y	Y	Y
WASHINGTON								
Adams	Y	N	Y	Y	Y	Y	Y	Y
Gorton	N	Y	Y	Y	Y	Y	Y	Y
WEST VIRGINIA								
Byrd	Y	N	Y	Y	Y	Y	Y	Y
Rockefeller	Y	N	Y	Y	Y	Y	Y	Y
WISCONSIN								
Kohl	Y	N	Y	Y	Y	Y	Y	Y
Kasten	N	Y	Y	Y	Y	Y	Y	Y
WYOMING								
Simpson	N	Y	Y	Y	Y	Y	Y	Y
Wallop	N	Y	Y	Y	Y	Y	Y	Y

KEY

- Y Voted for (yea).
- # Paired for.
- + Announced for.
- N Voted against (nay).
- X Paired against.
- \- Announced against.
- P Voted "present."
- C Voted "present" to avoid possible conflict of interest.
- ? Did not vote or otherwise make a position known.

Democrats ***Republicans***

ND Northern Democrats SD Southern Democrats

Southern states - Ala., Ark., Fla., Ga., Ky., La., Miss., N.C., Okla., S.C., Tenn., Texas, Va.

1. S J Res 1. Sanctions Against Iraq/Adoption. Passage of the joint resolution to express the sense of Congress that the wisest course of action at this time is to continue international sanctions and diplomatic efforts to pressure Iraq to withdraw from Kuwait. The resolution declares that the president must obtain congressional approval before undertaking an offensive action against Iraq. Rejected 46-53: R 1-43; D 45-10 (ND 35-3, SD 10-7), Jan. 12, 1991. A "nay" was a vote supporting the president's position.

2. S J Res 2. Use of Force Against Iraq/Passage. Passage of the joint resolution to authorize the use of military force if Iraq has not withdrawn from Kuwait and complied with U.N. Security Council resolutions by Jan. 15. The resolution authorizes the use of force and the expenditure of funds under the War Powers act and requires the president to report to Congress every 60 days on the efforts to obtain Iraqi compliance with the U.N. resolutions. Passed 52-47: R 42-2; D 10-45 (ND 3-35, SD 7-10), Jan. 12, 1991. (Subsequently, the Senate passed an identical House resolution, H J Res 77, thus clearing the joint resolution for the president.) A "yea" was a vote supporting the president's position.

3. S Con Res 2. U.S. Forces in the Gulf/Adoption. Adoption of the concurrent resolution to express the sense of Congress commending and supporting the efforts and leadership of the president in the Persian Gulf and stating unequivocal support for the members of the armed forces carrying out missions in the Persian Gulf. Adopted 98-0: R 44-0; D 54-0 (ND 37-0, SD 17-0), Jan. 17, 1991.

4. HR 4. IRS Extension for Troops in the Gulf/Passage. Passage of the bill (thus clearing the measure for the president) to provide all soldiers and support personnel involved in Operation Desert Shield and Desert Storm with a six-month extension after their service in the gulf has ended to file federal tax returns. The bill also requires the Internal Revenue Service to pay interest on any tax refunds due between April 15 and the date the individual files, provided the person files within the six-month deadline. Passed 99-0: R 44-0; D 55-0 (ND 38-0, SD 17-0), Jan. 24, 1991.

5. HR 3. Veterans Compensation Amendments/Passage. Passage of the bill (thus clearing the measure for the president) to authorize retroactive to Jan. 1, 1991, a 5.4 percent cost of living adjustment for veterans with service-connected disabilities and for families of veterans who died from service-connected causes. Passed 99-0: R 44-0; D 55-0 (ND 38-0, SD 17-0), Jan. 24, 1991. A "yea" was a vote supporting the president's position.

6. S Con Res 6. Condemn Soviet Force in the Baltics/Adoption. Adoption of the concurrent resolution to condemn Soviet violence against the people and democratic governments of Lithuania, Latvia and Estonia. Adopted 99-0: R 44-0; D 55-0 (ND 38-0, SD 17-0), Jan. 24, 1991.

7. S Con Res 5. Condemn Iraqi Treatment of POWs/Adoption. Adoption of the concurrent resolution to condemn Iraq for not treating prisoners of war in conformity with the Third Geneva Convention. Adopted 99-0: R 44-0; D 55-0 (ND 38-0, SD 17-0), Jan. 24, 1991.

8. S Con Res 4. Condemn Iraqi Attacks on Israel/Adoption. Adoption of the concurrent resolution to condemn the unprovoked attack by Iraq on Israel. Adopted 99-0: R 44-0; D 55-0 (ND 38-0, SD 17-0), Jan. 24, 1991.

	9	10	11	12	13	14	15	16
ALABAMA								
Heflin	Y	N	Y	N	N	?	?	N
Shelby	Y	N	Y	N	N	Y	Y	N
ALASKA								
Murkowski	Y	N	Y	N	N	Y	N	N
Stevens	Y	N	Y	N	N	Y	N	N
ARIZONA								
DeConcini	Y	N	Y	N	N	Y	N	Y
McCain	Y	N	Y	N	N	Y	N	N
ARKANSAS								
Bumpers	Y	N	?	N	N	Y	Y	Y
Pryor	Y	N	Y	N	N	Y	Y	Y
CALIFORNIA								
Cranston	?	?	?	?	?	?	?	?
Seymour	Y	N	Y	N	N	Y	N	N
COLORADO								
Wirth	Y	N	Y	N	N	Y	Y	Y
Brown	Y	N	Y	N	N	Y	N	?
CONNECTICUT								
Dodd	Y	N	Y	N	N	Y	Y	N
Lieberman	Y	N	Y	N	N	Y	N	N
DELAWARE								
Biden	Y	N	Y	N	N	Y	N	N
Roth	Y	N	Y	N	N	Y	Y	Y
FLORIDA								
Graham	Y	N	Y	N	N	Y	N	N
Mack	Y	N	Y	N	N	Y	N	N
GEORGIA								
Fowler	Y	N	Y	N	N	Y	Y	N
Nunn	Y	N	+	N	N	Y	N	N
HAWAII								
Akaka	Y	N	Y	Y	Y	Y	Y	Y
Inouye	Y	N	Y	?	?	?	?	N
IDAHO								
Craig	Y	N	Y	N	N	Y	N	N
Symms	Y	N	Y	N	N	Y	N	N
ILLINOIS								
Dixon	Y	N	Y	N	N	Y	N	N
Simon	Y	N	Y	Y	Y	Y	N	Y
INDIANA								
Coats	Y	N	Y	N	N	Y	Y	Y
Lugar	Y	N	Y	N	N	Y	Y	Y
IOWA								
Harkin	Y	Y	Y	Y	Y	Y	Y	Y
Grassley	Y	N	Y	N	N	Y	Y	Y
KANSAS								
Dole	Y	N	Y	N	N	Y	N	Y
Kassebaum	Y	N	Y	N	Y	Y	N	Y
KENTUCKY								
Ford	Y	N	Y	N	N	Y	N	Y
McConnell	Y	N	Y	N	N	Y	N	N
LOUISIANA								
Breaux	Y	N	Y	N	N	Y	N	N
Johnston	Y	N	Y	N	N	Y	N	Y
MAINE								
Mitchell	Y	N	Y	Y	Y	Y	N	Y
Cohen	Y	N	Y	Y	Y	Y	N	N
MARYLAND								
Mikulski	Y	N	Y	N	N	Y	Y	Y
Sarbanes	Y	N	Y	Y	N	Y	Y	Y
MASSACHUSETTS								
Kennedy	Y	N	Y	Y	Y	Y	N	N
Kerry	Y	N	Y	Y	Y	Y	Y	N
MICHIGAN								
Levin	Y	N	Y	Y	Y	Y	N	Y
Riegle	Y	N	Y	N	N	Y	Y	Y
MINNESOTA								
Wellstone	Y	Y	Y	Y	Y	Y	Y	Y
Durenberger	Y	N	Y	Y	Y	Y	Y	N
MISSISSIPPI								
Cochran	Y	N	Y	N	N	Y	N	N
Lott	Y	N	Y	N	N	Y	N	N
MISSOURI								
Bond	Y	N	Y	N	N	Y	N	N
Danforth	Y	N	Y	Y	Y	?	?	N
MONTANA								
Baucus	Y	N	Y	N	N	Y	N	Y
Burns	Y	N	Y	N	N	Y	N	N
NEBRASKA								
Exon	Y	N	Y	N	N	?	Y	N
Kerrey	Y	N	Y	N	N	Y	Y	Y
NEVADA								
Bryan	Y	N	Y	N	N	Y	N	Y
Reid	Y	N	Y	N	N	Y	N	Y
NEW HAMPSHIRE								
Rudman	Y	N	Y	N	N	Y	N	Y
Smith	Y	N	Y	N	N	Y	N	N
NEW JERSEY								
Bradley	Y	N	Y	N	N	?	?	Y
Lautenberg	Y	N	Y	Y	Y	Y	Y	Y
NEW MEXICO								
Bingaman	Y	N	Y	N	N	Y	N	?
Domenici	Y	N	Y	?	?	?	?	N
NEW YORK								
Moynihan	Y	N	Y	Y	Y	Y	N	Y
D'Amato	Y	N	Y	N	N	Y	Y	N
NORTH CAROLINA								
Sanford	Y	N	Y	Y	Y	?	?	Y
Helms	Y	N	Y	N	N	Y	N	N
NORTH DAKOTA								
Burdick	Y	N	Y	Y	Y	Y	Y	Y
Conrad	Y	N	Y	N	N	Y	Y	N
OHIO								
Glenn	Y	N	Y	Y	Y	Y	N	Y
Metzenbaum	Y	N	Y	Y	Y	Y	Y	Y
OKLAHOMA								
Boren	Y	N	Y	N	N	Y	Y	Y
Nickles	Y	N	Y	N	N	Y	N	Y
OREGON								
Hatfield	Y	N	+	Y	Y	Y	Y	Y
Packwood	Y	N	Y	N	N	Y	Y	Y
PENNSYLVANIA								
Heinz	Y	N	Y	N	N	Y	Y	Y
Specter	Y	N	Y	N	N	Y	Y	N
RHODE ISLAND								
Pell	Y	N	Y	Y	Y	Y	Y	N
Chafee	Y	N	Y	Y	Y	Y	N	N
SOUTH CAROLINA								
Hollings	Y	N	Y	N	N	Y	Y	N
Thurmond	Y	N	Y	N	N	Y	N	N
SOUTH DAKOTA								
Daschle	Y	N	Y	N	N	Y	Y	Y
Pressler	Y	N	Y	N	N	Y	Y	N
TENNESSEE								
Gore	Y	N	Y	Y	N	Y	N	Y
Sasser	Y	N	Y	Y	N	Y	Y	Y
TEXAS								
Bentsen	Y	N	?	N	N	Y	N	Y
Gramm	Y	N	Y	N	N	?	?	N
UTAH								
Garn	Y	N	Y	N	N	Y	N	?
Hatch	Y	N	Y	N	N	Y	N	N
VERMONT								
Leahy	Y	N	Y	Y	Y	Y	N	Y
Jeffords	Y	N	Y	N	N	Y	N	?
VIRGINIA								
Robb	Y	N	Y	N	N	Y	N	N
Warner	Y	N	Y	N	N	Y	N	N
WASHINGTON								
Adams	Y	N	Y	N	N	Y	Y	Y
Gorton	Y	N	Y	N	N	Y	N	Y
WEST VIRGINIA								
Byrd	Y	N	Y	N	N	Y	Y	Y
Rockefeller	Y	N	Y	N	N	Y	Y	Y
WISCONSIN								
Kohl	Y	N	Y	Y	Y	Y	N	Y
Kasten	Y	N	Y	N	N	Y	N	N
WYOMING								
Simpson	Y	N	Y	N	N	Y	N	N
Wallop	Y	N	+	N	N	Y	N	N

KEY

Y Voted for (yea).
Paired for.
+ Announced for.
N Voted against (nay).
X Paired against.
- Announced against.
P Voted "present."
C Voted "present" to avoid possible conflict of interest.
? Did not vote or otherwise make a position known.

Democrats *Republicans*

ND Northern Democrats SD Southern Democrats

Southern states - Ala., Ark., Fla., Ga., Ky., La., Miss., N.C., Okla., S.C., Tenn., Texas, Va.

9. HR 556. Agent Orange Act/Passage. Passage of the bill (thus clearing the measure for the president) to provide permanent disability benefits for veterans who suffer certain conditions due to exposure to Agent Orange. The bill would also require the Veterans Affairs Department to decide whether permanent disability benefits should be given to veterans suffering from other diseases associated with Agent Orange, based on a study to be performed by the National Academy of Sciences. Passed 99-0: R 44-0; D 55-0 (ND 38-0, SD 17-0), Jan. 30, 1991. A "yea" was a vote supporting the president's position.

10. S J Res 44. Recession Resolution to Suspend Gramm-Rudman/Passage. Passage of the joint resolution to suspend spending caps and pay-as-you-go restrictions for 1991 and 1992. The Balanced Budget and Emergency Deficit Control Act, as amended last year, compels the majority leader to introduce such a resolution after notification of a government projection that the nation is in a recession. Rejected 2-97: R 0-44; D 2-53 (ND 2-36, SD 0-17), Jan. 31, 1991. A "nay" was a vote supporting the president's position.

11. Martin Nomination. Confirmation of President Bush's nomination of Lynn Martin of Illinois to be secretary of Labor. Confirmed 94-0: R 42-0; D 52-0 (ND 38-0, SD 14-0), Feb. 7, 1991. A "yea" was a vote supporting the president's position.

12. S 320. Export Administration Reauthorization/Death Penalty for Terrorists. Hatfield, R-Ore., amendment to the Specter, R-Pa., amendment, to substitute a mandatory term of life imprisonment for the death penalty for terrorists who murder people in the United States or U.S. citizens abroad. Rejected 25-72: R 5-38; D 20-34 (ND 17-20, SD 3-14), Feb. 20, 1991.

13. S 320. Export Administration Reauthorization/Death Penalty for Terrorists. Metzenbaum, D-Ohio, motion to table (kill) the Specter, R-Pa., amendment to establish procedures for imposing the death penalty on terrorists who murder people in the United States or U.S. citizens abroad. Motion rejected 23-74: R 6-37; D 17-37 (ND 16-21, SD 1-16), Feb. 20, 1991. (Subsequently, the Specter amendment was adopted by voice vote.)

14. S 320. Export Administration Reauthorization/-Parents in Combat. Glenn, D-Ohio, amendment to express the sense of the Senate that the secretary of Defense should prescribe uniform regulations to give appropriate consideration to the requests of single parents or families in which both parents are members of the armed forces to be transferred out of the imminent danger areas of Operation Desert Storm. Adopted 91-0: R 41-0; D 50-0 (ND 35-0, SD 15-0), Feb. 20, 1991.

15. S 320. Export Administration Reauthorization/-Parents in Combat. Heinz, R-Pa., amendment to express the sense of the Senate that the secretary of Defense at the request of an individual should arrange for prompt and appropriate reassignment of one parent, in cases in which both parents, or a single parent, is in the imminent danger area of Operation Desert Storm, unless such reassignment would have a negative impact on safety, mission capability, or the combat effectiveness of the unit. Rejected 38-54: R 11-30; D 27-24 (ND 20-16, SD 7-8), Feb. 20, 1991. A "nay" was a vote supporting the president's position.

16. S 347. Defense Production Act/Military Sales. Sarbanes, D-Md., motion to table (kill) the Dodd, D-Conn., amendment to permit the Export-Import Bank to finance military sales through loan guarantees to NATO countries, Japan, Israel, Australia and New Zealand. Motion agreed to 48-47: R 12-29; D 36-18 (ND 27-10, SD 9-8), Feb. 21, 1991.

KEY

- Y Voted for (yea).
- # Paired for.
- + Announced for.
- N Voted against (nay).
- X Paired against.
- \- Announced against.
- P Voted "present."
- C Voted "present" to avoid possible conflict of interest.
- ? Did not vote or otherwise make a position known.

Democrats *Republicans*

	17	18	19	20	21	22	23	24
ALABAMA								
Heflin	Y	Y	Y	Y	Y	Y	Y	Y
Shelby	Y	Y	Y	Y	N	N	N	Y
ALASKA								
Murkowski	N	N	N	N	Y	Y	Y	Y
Stevens	Y	Y	Y	Y	Y	Y	Y	Y
ARIZONA								
DeConcini	Y	Y	Y	Y	Y	N	N	Y
McCain	?	?	?	?	Y	Y	Y	Y
ARKANSAS								
Bumpers	N	Y	Y	Y	Y	N	Y	Y
Pryor	Y	Y	Y	Y	Y	N	Y	Y
CALIFORNIA								
Cranston	?	?	?	?	Y	Y	?	Y
Seymour	?	?	?	?	Y	Y	Y	Y
COLORADO								
Wirth	Y	N	Y	N	N	Y	N	Y
Brown	N	N	N	N	N	Y	N	Y
CONNECTICUT								
Dodd	Y	Y	Y	Y	N	Y	Y	Y
Lieberman	Y	Y	Y	Y	N	Y	Y	Y
DELAWARE								
Biden	Y	Y	Y	Y	?	Y	Y	Y
Roth	N	N	N	Y	Y	Y	Y	Y
FLORIDA								
Graham	Y	Y	Y	Y	Y	Y	N	Y
Mack	N	N	N	N	Y	Y	Y	Y
GEORGIA								
Fowler	Y	Y	Y	Y	Y	N	N	Y
Nunn	Y	Y	Y	Y	Y	Y	N	Y
HAWAII								
Akaka	Y	Y	Y	Y	N	N	N	Y
Inouye	Y	Y	Y	Y	Y	Y	Y	Y
IDAHO								
Craig	N	N	N	N	Y	Y	Y	Y
Symms	N	N	N	?	Y	Y	Y	Y
ILLINOIS								
Dixon	N	Y	Y	Y	Y	Y	Y	Y
Simon	Y	Y	Y	Y	N	N	N	Y
INDIANA								
Coats	N	N	N	N	Y	Y	Y	Y
Lugar	N	N	N	Y	Y	Y	Y	Y
IOWA								
Harkin	Y	Y	Y	Y	N	Y	Y	Y
Grassley	N	N	N	N	N	Y	Y	Y
KANSAS								
Dole	N	N	N	Y	Y	Y	Y	Y
Kassebaum	Y	N	N	Y	Y	Y	Y	Y
KENTUCKY								
Ford	Y	Y	Y	Y	Y	N	N	Y
McConnell	Y	N	N	Y	Y	Y	Y	Y
LOUISIANA								
Breaux	Y	Y	Y	Y	Y	Y	Y	Y
Johnston	Y	Y	Y	Y	Y	Y	Y	Y
MAINE								
Mitchell	Y	Y	Y	Y	Y	Y	Y	Y
Cohen	N	N	N	Y	Y	Y	Y	Y
MARYLAND								
Mikulski	Y	Y	Y	Y	N	N	N	Y
Sarbanes	Y	Y	Y	Y	Y	Y	Y	Y
MASSACHUSETTS								
Kennedy	Y	Y	Y	Y	Y	Y	Y	Y
Kerry	Y	Y	Y	Y	N	N	N	Y
MICHIGAN								
Levin	Y	Y	Y	Y	N	Y	Y	Y
Riegle	Y	Y	Y	Y	Y	Y	Y	Y
MINNESOTA								
Wellstone	?	?	?	?	N	N	Y	Y
Durenberger	N	N	N	Y	Y	Y	Y	Y
MISSISSIPPI								
Cochran	N	N	N	Y	Y	Y	Y	Y
Lott	N	N	N	N	Y	Y	Y	Y
MISSOURI								
Bond	N	N	N	N	Y	Y	Y	Y
Danforth	N	N	N	Y	Y	Y	Y	Y
MONTANA								
Baucus	Y	Y	Y	Y	N	N	Y	Y
Burns	N	N	N	N	Y	Y	Y	Y
NEBRASKA								
Exon	Y	Y	Y	Y	Y	N	Y	Y
Kerrey	Y	Y	Y	Y	Y	N	Y	Y
NEVADA								
Bryan	Y	Y	Y	Y	Y	N	N	Y
Reid	Y	Y	Y	Y	Y	N	Y	Y
NEW HAMPSHIRE								
Rudman	N	Y	N	Y	Y	N	Y	Y
Smith	N	N	N	N	Y	Y	Y	Y
NEW JERSEY								
Bradley	N	N	N	Y	N	N	N	Y
Lautenberg	N	N	N	Y	N	N	N	Y
NEW MEXICO								
Bingaman	Y	Y	Y	Y	Y	N	Y	Y
Domenici	N	N	N	Y	Y	Y	Y	Y
NEW YORK								
Moynihan	Y	Y	Y	Y	Y	N	Y	Y
D'Amato	N	N	N	N	Y	Y	Y	Y
NORTH CAROLINA								
Sanford	Y	Y	Y	Y	N	N	Y	Y
Helms	N	N	N	N	Y	Y	Y	Y
NORTH DAKOTA								
Burdick	Y	Y	Y	Y	Y	N	N	Y
Conrad	N	Y	N	N	N	N	N	Y
OHIO								
Glenn	N	N	Y	Y	N	N	Y	Y
Metzenbaum	Y	Y	Y	Y	N	N	Y	Y
OKLAHOMA								
Boren	Y	Y	Y	Y	Y	N	Y	Y
Nickles	N	N	N	N	Y	N	Y	Y
OREGON								
Hatfield	Y	Y	Y	Y	Y	Y	Y	Y
Packwood	Y	Y	Y	?	Y	Y	Y	Y
PENNSYLVANIA								
Heinz	N	N	N	Y	Y	Y	Y	Y
Specter	N	N	N	Y	N	Y	Y	Y
RHODE ISLAND								
Pell	Y	Y	Y	Y	Y	N	Y	Y
Chafee	N	N	N	N	Y	Y	Y	Y
SOUTH CAROLINA								
Hollings	Y	Y	Y	Y	N	N	Y	Y
Thurmond	N	N	N	Y	Y	Y	Y	+
SOUTH DAKOTA								
Daschle	Y	Y	Y	Y	N	N	N	Y
Pressler	N	N	N	N	Y	Y	Y	Y
TENNESSEE								
Gore	Y	Y	Y	Y	Y	Y	Y	Y
Sasser	Y	Y	Y	Y	Y	Y	Y	Y
TEXAS								
Bentsen	Y	Y	Y	Y	Y	Y	Y	Y
Gramm	N	N	N	N	Y	Y	Y	Y
UTAH								
Garn	N	N	N	Y	Y	Y	Y	Y
Hatch	N	Y	N	Y	Y	Y	Y	Y
VERMONT								
Leahy	Y	Y	Y	Y	N	N	Y	Y
Jeffords	Y	Y	N	Y	N	Y	Y	Y
VIRGINIA								
Robb	Y	Y	Y	Y	N	N	Y	Y
Warner	Y	Y	Y	Y	Y	Y	Y	Y
WASHINGTON								
Adams	Y	Y	Y	Y	N	N	N	Y
Gorton	N	N	N	Y	Y	Y	Y	Y
WEST VIRGINIA								
Byrd	Y	Y	Y	Y	Y	N	Y	Y
Rockefeller	Y	Y	Y	Y	Y	N	Y	Y
WISCONSIN								
Kohl	Y	N	Y	N	N	N	Y	Y
Kasten	N	N	N	N	Y	Y	Y	Y
WYOMING								
Simpson	N	N	N	N	Y	Y	Y	Y
Wallop	N	N	N	N	Y	Y	Y	Y

ND Northern Democrats SD Southern Democrats

Southern states - Ala., Ark., Fla., Ga., Ky., La., Miss., N.C., Okla., S.C., Tenn., Texas, Va.

17. S Res 62. 1991-92 Committee Funding/Foreign Relations. Ford, D-Ky., motion to table (kill) the Helms, R-N.C., amendment to cut the $703,000 increase in the Foreign Relations Committee budget for the next two years. Motion agreed to 55-41: R 7-35; D 48-6 (ND 32-5, SD 16-1), Feb. 28, 1991.

18. S Res 62. 1991-92 Committee Funding/Limits. Ford, D-Ky., motion to table (kill) the Brown, R-Colo., substitute amendment to limit all increases in committee funding levels to 4.1 percent. Motion agreed 56-40: R 7-35; D 49-5 (ND 32-5, SD 17-0), Feb. 28, 1991.

19. S Res 62. 1991-92 Committee Funding/Staffing. Ford, D-Ky., motion to table (kill) the Chafee, R-R.I., amendment to limit the number of committee staff on each committee to the 1990 authorized levels, unless a committee with more than 100 staff members reduces its staff by a number equal to the number of new staff members. The amendment would also give the Committee on Rules and Administration the power to reduce the committees with more than 100 staff positions to accommodate the requests of smaller committees. Motion agreed to 55-41: R 4-38; D 51-3 (ND 34-3, SD 17-0), Feb. 28, 1991.

20. S Res 62. 1991-92 Committee Funding/Adoption. Adoption of the resolution to provide $113.9 million for the operations of the 19 Senate committees through Feb. 28, 1993. Motion agreed to 72-22: R 21-19; D 51-3 (ND 34-3, SD 17-0), Feb. 28, 1991.

21. S 419. RTC Funding/Tax Offsets. Riegle, D-Mich., motion to table (kill) the Harkin, D-Iowa, amendment to reduce from $30 billion to $15 billion the level of financing provided in the bill to the Resolution Trust Corporation to cover fiscal 1991 losses in failed thrifts and to require the president to submit with any financing requests tax proposals to offset such requests. Motion agreed to 71-28: R 40-4; D 31-24 (ND 18-20, SD 13-4), March 6, 1991. A "yea" was a vote supporting the president's position.

22. S 419. RTC Funding/Restructuring. Riegle, D-Mich., motion to table (kill) the Kerrey, D-Neb., amendment to replace the dual managing board structure of the Resolution Trust Corporation, which includes an oversight board and a board of directors, with a single board of governors. Motion agreed to 63-37: R 42-2; D 21-35 (ND 13-26, SD 8-9), March 6, 1991. A "yea" was a vote supporting the president's position.

23. S 419. RTC Funding/Matching Funds. Riegle, D-Mich., motion to table (kill) the Graham, D-Fla., amendment to provide $15 billion to the Resolution Trust Corporation in fiscal 1991 to cover losses in failed thrifts and to make available an additional $15 billion for fiscal 1991 on a dollar-for-dollar basis for cash dividends the RTC gets from the sale of assets in receivership. Motion agreed to 80-19: R 43-1; D 37-18 (ND 25-13, SD 12-5), March 6, 1991. A "yea" was a vote supporting the president's position.

24. Madigan Nomination. Confirmation of President Bush's nomination of Edward Madigan of Illinois to be secretary of Agriculture. Confirmed 99-0: R 43-0; D 56-0 (ND 39-0, SD 17-0), March 7, 1991. A "yea" was a vote supporting the president's position.

	25	26	27	28	29	30	31	32
ALABAMA								
Heflin	Y	N	Y	N	Y	Y	Y	N
Shelby	N	N	Y	N	Y	Y	Y	N
ALASKA								
Murkowski	Y	Y	Y	N	Y	Y	Y	N
Stevens	Y	N	Y	N	Y	Y	Y	N
ARIZONA								
DeConcini	N	N	Y	N	Y	Y	Y	N
McCain	Y	Y	Y	N	Y	Y	Y	N
ARKANSAS								
Bumpers	Y	N	Y	N	Y	Y	Y	Y
Pryor	N	N	Y	N	Y	Y	Y	Y
CALIFORNIA								
Cranston	Y	Y	Y	N	Y	Y	Y	Y
Seymour	Y	Y	Y	N	Y	Y	Y	N
COLORADO								
Wirth	N	Y	Y	N	Y	Y	Y	N
Brown	N	Y	Y	N	Y	Y	Y	N
CONNECTICUT								
Dodd	Y	N	Y	N	Y	Y	Y	Y
Lieberman	Y	Y	Y	N	Y	Y	Y	Y
DELAWARE								
Biden	Y	Y	Y	N	Y	Y	Y	N
Roth	Y	Y	Y	N	Y	Y	Y	N
FLORIDA								
Graham	N	?	?	?	?	?	Y	N
Mack	Y	Y	Y	N	Y	Y	Y	N
GEORGIA								
Fowler	Y	Y	Y	N	Y	Y	Y	Y
Nunn	Y	Y	Y	N	Y	Y	Y	N
HAWAII								
Akaka	N	Y	Y	N	Y	Y	Y	Y
Inouye	Y	Y	Y	N	Y	Y	Y	Y
IDAHO								
Craig	N	Y	Y	N	Y	Y	Y	N
Symms	Y	Y	Y	N	Y	Y	Y	N
ILLINOIS								
Dixon	Y	N	Y	N	Y	Y	Y	N
Simon	Y	N	Y	N	Y	Y	Y	Y
INDIANA								
Coats	Y	Y	Y	N	Y	Y	Y	N
Lugar	Y	Y	Y	N	Y	Y	Y	N
IOWA								
Harkin	N	N	Y	N	Y	Y	Y	Y
Grassley	Y	N	Y	N	Y	Y	Y	Y
KANSAS								
Dole	Y	Y	Y	N	Y	Y	Y	N
Kassebaum	Y	Y	Y	N	Y	Y	Y	N
KENTUCKY								
Ford	Y	Y	Y	N	Y	Y	Y	Y
McConnell	Y	N	Y	N	Y	Y	Y	Y
LOUISIANA								
Breaux	Y	N	Y	N	Y	Y	Y	Y
Johnston	Y	Y	Y	N	Y	Y	Y	Y
MAINE								
Mitchell	Y	Y	Y	N	Y	Y	Y	Y
Cohen	Y	Y	Y	N	Y	Y	Y	Y
MARYLAND								
Mikulski	Y	N	Y	N	Y	Y	Y	Y
Sarbanes	Y	N	Y	N	Y	Y	Y	Y
MASSACHUSETTS								
Kennedy	Y	Y	Y	N	Y	Y	Y	Y
Kerry	N	N	Y	N	Y	Y	Y	Y
MICHIGAN								
Levin	Y	N	Y	N	Y	Y	Y	Y
Riegle	Y	N	Y	N	Y	Y	Y	Y
MINNESOTA								
Wellstone	N	N	Y	N	Y	Y	Y	Y
Durenberger	Y	Y	Y	N	Y	Y	Y	Y
MISSISSIPPI								
Cochran	Y	Y	Y	N	Y	Y	Y	Y
Lott	Y	Y	Y	N	Y	Y	Y	Y
MISSOURI								
Bond	Y	Y	Y	N	Y	Y	Y	Y
Danforth	Y	Y	Y	N	Y	Y	Y	Y
MONTANA								
Baucus	N	N	Y	N	Y	Y	Y	Y
Burns	N	Y	Y	N	Y	Y	Y	N
NEBRASKA								
Exon	N	Y	Y	N	Y	Y	Y	Y
Kerrey	N	Y	Y	N	Y	Y	Y	Y
NEVADA								
Bryan	Y	Y	Y	N	Y	Y	Y	Y
Reid	Y	N	Y	N	Y	Y	Y	N
NEW HAMPSHIRE								
Rudman	Y	Y	Y	N	Y	Y	Y	Y
Smith	N	Y	Y	N	Y	Y	Y	N
NEW JERSEY								
Bradley	N	Y	Y	N	Y	Y	?	N
Lautenberg	N	N	Y	N	Y	Y	Y	N
NEW MEXICO								
Bingaman	Y	?	?	N	Y	Y	Y	Y
Domenici	Y	?	Y	N	Y	Y	Y	N
NEW YORK								
Moynihan	Y	Y	Y	N	Y	Y	Y	Y
D'Amato	Y	N	Y	N	Y	Y	Y	Y
NORTH CAROLINA								
Sanford	N	N	Y	N	Y	Y	Y	Y
Helms	N	N	Y	N	Y	Y	Y	N
NORTH DAKOTA								
Burdick	Y	N	Y	N	Y	Y	Y	Y
Conrad	N	N	Y	N	Y	Y	Y	Y
OHIO								
Glenn	Y	Y	Y	N	Y	Y	Y	N
Metzenbaum	Y	N	Y	N	Y	Y	Y	N
OKLAHOMA								
Boren	Y	Y	Y	N	Y	Y	Y	Y
Nickles	Y	Y	Y	N	Y	Y	Y	N
OREGON								
Hatfield	Y	N	Y	N	Y	N	N	N
Packwood	Y	Y	Y	N	Y	Y	Y	N
PENNSYLVANIA								
Heinz	Y	Y	Y	N	Y	Y	Y	Y
Specter	N	N	Y	N	Y	Y	Y	Y
RHODE ISLAND								
Pell	Y	Y	Y	N	Y	Y	Y	Y
Chafee	Y	Y	Y	N	Y	Y	Y	N
SOUTH CAROLINA								
Hollings	N	N	Y	N	Y	Y	Y	Y
Thurmond	+	Y	Y	N	Y	Y	Y	Y
SOUTH DAKOTA								
Daschle	N	N	Y	N	Y	Y	Y	Y
Pressler	Y	N	Y	N	Y	Y	Y	Y
TENNESSEE								
Gore	Y	Y	Y	N	Y	Y	Y	Y
Sasser	Y	N	Y	N	Y	Y	Y	Y
TEXAS								
Bentsen	Y	Y	Y	N	Y	Y	Y	Y
Gramm	Y	Y	Y	N	Y	Y	Y	N
UTAH								
Garn	Y	Y	Y	N	Y	Y	Y	N
Hatch	Y	Y	Y	N	Y	Y	Y	N
VERMONT								
Leahy	N	N	Y	N	Y	Y	Y	Y
Jeffords	Y	?	?	?	?	?	Y	Y
VIRGINIA								
Robb	Y	Y	Y	N	Y	Y	Y	Y
Warner	Y	Y	Y	N	Y	Y	Y	N
WASHINGTON								
Adams	N	N	Y	N	Y	Y	Y	Y
Gorton	Y	Y	Y	N	Y	Y	Y	Y
WEST VIRGINIA								
Byrd	N	Y	Y	N	Y	Y	Y	Y
Rockefeller	N	Y	Y	N	Y	Y	Y	Y
WISCONSIN								
Kohl	N	N	Y	N	Y	Y	Y	Y
Kasten	N	N	Y	N	Y	Y	Y	Y
WYOMING								
Simpson	Y	Y	Y	N	Y	Y	Y	N
Wallop	Y	Y	Y	N	Y	Y	Y	N

KEY

- Y Voted for (yea).
- # Paired for.
- + Announced for.
- N Voted against (nay).
- X Paired against.
- \- Announced against.
- P Voted "present."
- C Voted "present" to avoid possible conflict of interest.
- ? Did not vote or otherwise make a position known.

Democrats ***Republicans***

ND Northern Democrats SD Southern Democrats

Southern states - Ala., Ark., Fla., Ga., Ky., La., Miss., N.C., Okla., S.C., Tenn., Texas, Va.

25. S 419. RTC Funding/Passage. Passage of the bill to provide the Resolution Trust Corporation (RTC) with $30 billion in financing to cover losses in failed thrifts through fiscal 1991; require the RTC to provide Congress with financial operating plans and schedules of projected insolvencies; require the RTC to provide audit and financial statements within six months of the end of the fiscal year; and clarify the personal civil liability of the RTC's officers and directors. Passed 69-30: R 36-7; D 33-23 (ND 21-18, SD 12-5), March 7, 1991. A "yea" was a vote supporting the president's position.

26. S 578. Fiscal 1991 Supplemental Defense Authorization/Small Business Loans. Glenn, D-Ohio, motion to table (kill) the Bumpers, D-Ark., amendment to authorize temporary deferral of Small Business Administration loan repayments for military personnel serving in the Persian Gulf and to authorize disaster loans for military personnel whose businesses suffered as a result of their service in the gulf. Motion agreed to 58-38: R 33-9; D 25-29 (ND 17-21, SD 8-8), March 14, 1991.

27. S Res 76. War Crimes Resolution. Adoption of the resolution to express the sense of the Senate that the president confer with other nations to establish an international court to try Iraqi President Saddam Hussein and other Iraqis on charges of war crimes. Adopted 97-0: R 43-0; D 54-0 (ND 38-0, SD 16-0), March 14, 1991.

28. S 578. Fiscal 1991 Supplemental Defense Authorization/Iraq Reconstruction. McCain, R-Ariz., motion to table (kill) the Helms, R-N.C., amendment to prohibit U.S. funds from being expended for the purpose of reconstructing Iraq. Rejected 0-98: R 0-43; D 0-55 (ND 0-39, SD 0-16), March 14, 1991. (Subsequently, the Helms amendment, as amended by the Mitchell, D-Maine, amendment, was adopted by voice vote (See vote 29).

29. S 578. Fiscal 1991 Supplemental Defense Authorization/Iraq Reconstruction. Mitchell, D-Maine, amendment to the Helms, R-N.C., amendment to express the sense of the Senate that no U.S. funds be expended for the purposes of reconstructing Iraq while Saddam Hussein remains in power. Adopted 98-0: R 43-0; D 55-0 (ND 39-0, SD 16-0), March 14, 1991.

30. S 578. Fiscal 1991 Supplemental Defense Authorization. Passage of the bill to authorize $15 billion to be appropriated from the Desert Shield Working Capital Account and to authorize the appropriation of funds credited to the Defense Cooperation Account, consisting of allied contributions; authorize an increase in troop levels; and authorize $500 million in military personnel and veterans' benefits over five years. Passed 97-1: R 42-1; D 55-0 (ND 39-0, SD 16-0), March 14, 1991. A "yea" was a vote supporting the president's position.

31. HR 1282. Desert Storm Supplemental Appropriations/Passage. Passage of the bill to provide $42,625,822,000 in new budget authority to pay for Persian Gulf operations. It would provide for up to $15 billion in U.S. funds and $42.6 billion in contributions that foreign nations have pledged. The bill prohibits the president from transferring equipment from Operation Desert Storm to other Middle East countries without congressional authorization. Passed: 98-1: R 43-1; D 55-0 (ND 38-0, SD 17-0), March 19, 1991.

32. HR 1281. Fiscal 1991 Supplemental Appropriations/Dairy. Leahy, D-Vt., amendment to the committee amendment to provide assistance to dairy farmers by increasing the fluid milk price through Dec. 31, 1991, to a level not less than the price in August 1990. Adopted 60-40: R 17-27; D 43-13 (ND 30-9, SD 13-4), March 19, 1991. A "nay" was a vote supporting the president's position.

	33	34	35	36	37	38	39	40
ALABAMA								
Heflin	N	Y	N	Y	Y	Y	N	Y
Shelby	Y	N	N	N	Y	Y	N	Y
ALASKA								
Murkowski	Y	N	N	N	N	N	Y	Y
Stevens	Y	N	N	Y	N	N	Y	Y
ARIZONA								
DeConcini	N	Y	N	N	Y	Y	Y	Y
McCain	Y	N	Y	N	N	N	N	Y
ARKANSAS								
Bumpers	N	Y	N	N	Y	Y	N	Y
Pryor	N	Y	N	N	Y	Y	Y	Y
CALIFORNIA								
Cranston	N	Y	N	Y	Y	Y	Y	Y
Seymour	Y	N	Y	N	N	N	N	Y
COLORADO								
Wirth	N	Y	N	Y	Y	Y	N	Y
Brown	N	N	Y	N	N	N	N	N
CONNECTICUT								
Dodd	Y	N	N	N	Y	Y	Y	Y
Lieberman	Y	N	N	N	Y	Y	Y	Y
DELAWARE								
Biden	N	Y	N	N	Y	Y	Y	Y
Roth	Y	N	Y	Y	N	N	N	N
FLORIDA								
Graham	N	Y	N	N	Y	Y	N	Y
Mack	Y	N	Y	N	N	N	N	Y
GEORGIA								
Fowler	N	Y	N	Y	Y	Y	N	Y
Nunn	N	Y	Y	Y	Y	Y	N	Y
HAWAII								
Akaka	N	Y	N	N	Y	Y	Y	Y
Inouye	N	Y	N	N	Y	Y	Y	Y
IDAHO								
Craig	Y	N	Y	Y	N	N	N	Y
Symms	Y	N	Y	Y	N	N	N	Y
ILLINOIS								
Dixon	N	Y	N	N	Y	Y	N	Y
Simon	N	Y	N	N	Y	Y	N	Y
INDIANA								
Coats	Y	N	Y	N	N	N	N	Y
Lugar	Y	N	Y	Y	N	N	N	N
IOWA								
Harkin	N	Y	N	N	Y	Y	Y	Y
Grassley	Y	N	Y	N	N	N	N	Y
KANSAS								
Dole	Y	N	Y	Y	N	N	Y	Y
Kassebaum	Y	N	Y	Y	N	N	Y	N
KENTUCKY								
Ford	N	Y	N	N	Y	Y	Y	Y
McConnell	Y	N	Y	Y	N	N	N	Y
LOUISIANA								
Breaux	N	Y	N	N	Y	Y	N	Y
Johnston	N	Y	N	N	Y	Y	Y	Y
MAINE								
Mitchell	N	Y	N	Y	Y	Y	N	Y
Cohen	N	N	Y	Y	N	N	N	Y
MARYLAND								
Mikulski	N	Y	N	N	Y	Y	Y	Y
Sarbanes	N	Y	N	N	Y	Y	Y	Y
MASSACHUSETTS								
Kennedy	N	Y	N	N	Y	Y	Y	Y
Kerry	N	Y	N	N	Y	Y	Y	Y
MICHIGAN								
Levin	N	Y	N	N	Y	Y	Y	Y
Riegle	N	Y	N	N	Y	Y	N	Y
MINNESOTA								
Wellstone	N	Y	N	N	Y	Y	N	Y
Durenberger	Y	N	N	Y	N	N	N	Y
MISSISSIPPI								
Cochran	Y	N	Y	Y	N	Y	N	Y
Lott	Y	N	Y	N	N	N	N	Y
MISSOURI								
Bond	N	N	Y	Y	N	N	Y	Y
Danforth	N	N	Y	Y	N	N	N	Y
MONTANA								
Baucus	N	Y	N	N	Y	Y	Y	Y
Burns	Y	N	Y	Y	N	N	N	Y
NEBRASKA								
Exon	N	Y	N	Y	Y	Y	N	Y
Kerrey	N	Y	N	Y	Y	Y	N	Y
NEVADA								
Bryan	N	Y	N	N	Y	Y	N	Y
Reid	N	Y	N	N	Y	Y	Y	Y
NEW HAMPSHIRE								
Rudman	Y	N	Y	Y	N	N	Y	Y
Smith	Y	N	Y	N	N	N	N	N
NEW JERSEY								
Bradley	N	Y	N	N	Y	Y	Y	Y
Lautenberg	N	Y	N	N	Y	Y	Y	Y
NEW MEXICO								
Bingaman	N	Y	N	Y	Y	Y	N	Y
Domenici	Y	N	Y	Y	N	N	Y	Y
NEW YORK								
Moynihan	Y	N	N	N	Y	Y	Y	Y
D'Amato	Y	N	N	N	N	N	Y	Y
NORTH CAROLINA								
Sanford	N	Y	N	Y	Y	Y	N	Y
Helms	Y	N	Y	N	N	N	N	N
NORTH DAKOTA								
Burdick	N	Y	N	N	Y	Y	N	Y
Conrad	N	Y	N	N	Y	Y	N	Y
OHIO								
Glenn	N	Y	N	N	Y	Y	N	Y
Metzenbaum	N	Y	N	N	Y	Y	N	Y
OKLAHOMA								
Boren	Y	N	Y	N	Y	Y	N	Y
Nickles	Y	N	Y	N	N	N	N	N
OREGON								
Hatfield	N	Y	N	Y	Y	N	Y	Y
Packwood	N	N	N	Y	N	N	Y	Y
PENNSYLVANIA								
Heinz	N	N	N	Y	N	Y	Y	Y
Specter	Y	N	N	Y	Y	Y	Y	Y
RHODE ISLAND								
Pell	N	Y	N	Y	Y	Y	N	Y
Chafee	N	N	N	Y	Y	N	Y	Y
SOUTH CAROLINA								
Hollings	N	Y	N	N	Y	Y	N	Y
Thurmond	Y	N	Y	Y	N	N	N	Y
SOUTH DAKOTA								
Daschle	N	Y	N	N	Y	Y	N	Y
Pressler	Y	N	Y	N	N	N	Y	Y
TENNESSEE								
Gore	N	Y	N	Y	Y	Y	N	Y
Sasser	N	Y	N	N	Y	Y	N	Y
TEXAS								
Bentsen	N	Y	N	N	Y	Y	N	Y
Gramm	Y	N	Y	N	N	N	N	Y
UTAH								
Garn	Y	N	Y	Y	N	N	Y	Y
Hatch	Y	N	Y	Y	N	N	Y	Y
VERMONT								
Leahy	N	Y	N	N	Y	Y	Y	Y
Jeffords	N	N	Y	Y	Y	Y	Y	Y
VIRGINIA								
Robb	N	Y	N	Y	Y	Y	N	Y
Warner	Y	N	Y	Y	N	N	N	Y
WASHINGTON								
Adams	N	Y	N	N	Y	Y	Y	Y
Gorton	Y	N	Y	Y	N	N	N	Y
WEST VIRGINIA								
Byrd	N	Y	N	Y	Y	Y	Y	Y
Rockefeller	N	Y	N	N	Y	Y	Y	Y
WISCONSIN								
Kohl	N	Y	N	N	Y	Y	N	Y
Kasten	Y	N	Y	N	N	Y	Y	Y
WYOMING								
Simpson	Y	N	Y	Y	N	N	Y	Y
Wallop	Y	N	Y	Y	N	N	N	N

KEY

Y Voted for (yea).
\# Paired for.
\+ Announced for.
N Voted against (nay).
X Paired against.
\- Announced against.
P Voted "present."
C Voted "present" to avoid possible conflict of interest.
? Did not vote or otherwise make a position known.

Democrats *Republicans*

ND Northern Democrats SD Southern Democrats

Southern states - Ala., Ark., Fla., Ga., Ky., La., Miss., N.C., Okla., S.C., Tenn., Texas, Va.

33. HR 1281. Fiscal 1991 Supplemental Appropriations/Housing. D'Amato, R-N.Y., amendment to provide $500 million for the Home Investment Partnerships (HOME) program, $165 million for the Homeownership and Opportunity for People Everywhere (HOPE) program and $122 million for the Shelter Plus Care program, by reducing fiscal 1991 funding for public housing programs. Rejected 40-60: R 35-9; D 5-51 (ND 3-36, SD 2-15), March 19, 1991. A "yea" was a vote supporting the president's position.

34. HR 1281. Fiscal 1991 Supplemental Appropriations/Housing. Mikulski, D-Md., motion to table (kill) the D'Amato, R-N.Y., amendment to use excess funds carried over from 1990 to provide $165 million for the Homeownership and Opportunity for People Everywhere (HOPE) program and $122 million for the Shelter Plus Care program. Motion agreed to 52-48: R 1-43; D 51-5 (ND 36-3, SD 15-2), March 19, 1991. A "nay" was a vote supporting the president's position.

35. HR 1281. Fiscal 1991 Supplemental Appropriations/Construction Help. Nickles, R-Okla., amendment to strike the provisions from the bill that prohibit the Labor Department from expending funds to implement regulations that permit the expanded use of helpers on federally funded construction projects. Rejected 37-63: R 35-9; D 2-54 (ND 0-39, SD 2-15), March 20, 1991. A "yea" was a vote supporting the president's position.

36. HR 1281. Fiscal 1991 Supplemental Appropriations/Jordan. Dole, R-Kan., motion to table (kill) the Nickles, R-Okla., amendment to repeal all economic and military aid to Jordan in response to its support for Iraq in the Persian Gulf War. The amendment would permit economic aid to be resumed, if the president certifies that Jordan has taken steps to advance the Mideast peace process. Rejected 43-57: R 29-15; D 14-42 (ND 8-31, SD 6-11), March 20, 1991. (Subsequently, the Nickles amendment was adopted by voice vote). A "yea" was a vote supporting the president's position.

37. HR 1281. Fiscal 1991 Supplemental Appropriations/Teaching Standards Authorization. Judgment of the Senate whether the committee amendment to eliminate the requirement of an authorization before an appropriation for the National Board for Professional Teaching Standards was germane. Ruled germane 60-40: R 4-40; D 56-0 (ND 39-0, SD 17-0), March 20, 1991.

38. HR 1281. Fiscal 1991 Supplemental Appropriations/Teaching Standards Authorization Nullification. Harkin, D-Iowa, motion to table (kill) the Helms, R-N.C., amendment to nullify the provision to eliminate the requirement that there be an authorization before an appropriation for the National Board for Professional Teaching Standards. Motion agreed to 61-39: R 5-39; D 56-0 (ND 39-0, SD 17-0), March 20, 1991.

39. HR 1281. Fiscal 1991 Supplemental Appropriations/Navy Funds. Specter, R-Pa., motion to table (kill) the Coats, R-Ind., amendment to strike the provision directing the Navy to begin spending funds in fiscal 1991 for the Service Life Extension Program for the aircraft carrier USS *Kennedy* at the Philadelphia Naval Shipyard. Rejected 44-56: R 19-25; D 25-31 (ND 22-17, SD 3-14), March 20, 1991. (Subsequently, the Coats amendment was adopted by voice vote.)

40. HR 1281. Fiscal 1991 Supplemental Appropriations/Passage. Passage of the bill to provide $5,237,031,100 in new budget authority in fiscal 1991 for various programs, including $1.5 billion for the Food Stamp program, $1.2 billion in benefits for veterans and active-duty troops, $650 million for economic aid to Israel, $200 million for economic aid to Turkey, and $100 million for the District of Columbia. The administration requested $3,702,884,000. Passed 92-8: R 36-8; D 56-0 (ND 39-0, SD 17-0), March 20, 1991.

	41	42	43	44	45	46	47	48
ALABAMA								
Heflin	Y	Y	N	Y	Y	Y	Y	N
Shelby	Y	Y	N	Y	Y	Y	Y	N
ALASKA								
Murkowski	Y	Y	Y	N	Y	Y	N	N
Stevens	Y	Y	Y	N	N	Y	Y	N
ARIZONA								
DeConcini	Y	Y	N	Y	Y	Y	N	N
McCain	Y	Y	N	Y	Y	Y	N	N
ARKANSAS								
Bumpers	Y	Y	N	Y	Y	Y	Y	N
Pryor	N	?	?	?	?	?	?	?
CALIFORNIA								
Cranston	Y	Y	N	Y	Y	N	Y	N
Seymour	Y	Y	N	Y	Y	N	Y	N
COLORADO								
Wirth	Y	Y	Y	N	N	N	Y	N
Brown	Y	Y	N	N	N	Y	N	N
CONNECTICUT								
Dodd	Y	Y	Y	N	Y	N	Y	N
Lieberman	Y	Y	Y	N	Y	N	Y	N
DELAWARE								
Biden	Y	Y	N	Y	Y	N	N	N
Roth	Y	Y	Y	N	Y	Y	N	N
FLORIDA								
Graham	Y	Y	Y	N	Y	Y	Y	N
Mack	Y	Y	N	Y	Y	N	N	N
GEORGIA								
Fowler	Y	Y	N	Y	Y	N	N	N
Nunn	Y	Y	N	Y	Y	N	N	N
HAWAII								
Akaka	Y	Y	N	Y	Y	N	Y	N
Inouye	Y	Y	N	Y	Y	N	Y	N
IDAHO								
Craig	Y	Y	N	Y	Y	N	N	N
Symms	Y	Y	N	Y	Y	N	N	N
ILLINOIS								
Dixon	Y	Y	N	Y	Y	Y	N	N
Simon	N	Y	N	Y	Y	Y	Y	N
INDIANA								
Coats	Y	Y	N	Y	Y	Y	N	N
Lugar	Y	Y	N	Y	Y	Y	N	?
IOWA								
Harkin	Y	Y	N	Y	Y	N	Y	N
Grassley	Y	Y	N	Y	Y	Y	N	N
KANSAS								
Dole	Y	Y	N	Y	Y	Y	Y	N
Kassebaum	Y	Y	Y	N	Y	Y	N	N
KENTUCKY								
Ford	N	Y	N	Y	Y	Y	N	N
McConnell	Y	Y	N	Y	Y	Y	N	N
LOUISIANA								
Breaux	Y	Y	N	Y	Y	Y	Y	N
Johnston	Y	Y	N	Y	Y	Y	Y	N
MAINE								
Mitchell	Y	Y	Y	N	Y	N	Y	N
Cohen	Y	Y	N	N	Y	Y	Y	N
MARYLAND								
Mikulski	Y	Y	Y	N	Y	Y	Y	N
Sarbanes	N	Y	Y	N	Y	N	Y	N
MASSACHUSETTS								
Kennedy	N	Y	Y	N	Y	N	Y	N
Kerry	Y	Y	Y	N	Y	N	Y	N
MICHIGAN								
Levin	Y	Y	Y	N	Y	Y	Y	N
Riegle	Y	Y	Y	N	Y	N	Y	N
MINNESOTA								
Wellstone	N	Y	N	Y	Y	N	Y	N
Durenberger	Y	Y	N	Y	Y	Y	Y	N
MISSISSIPPI								
Cochran	Y	Y	N	Y	Y	Y	Y	N
Lott	Y	Y	N	Y	Y	Y	N	N
MISSOURI								
Bond	Y	Y	Y	N	Y	Y	Y	N
Danforth	Y	Y	Y	N	Y	Y	Y	N
MONTANA								
Baucus	Y	Y	N	N	Y	Y	Y	N
Burns	Y	Y	N	Y	Y	Y	N	N
NEBRASKA								
Exon	Y	Y	N	Y	Y	N	Y	N
Kerrey	Y	Y	N	Y	Y	N	Y	N
NEVADA								
Bryan	Y	Y	N	N	Y	N	Y	N
Reid	Y	Y	N	Y	Y	N	Y	N
NEW HAMPSHIRE								
Rudman	Y	Y	Y	N	N	Y	Y	N
Smith	Y	Y	N	Y	N	Y	N	N
NEW JERSEY								
Bradley	Y	Y	Y	N	Y	Y	Y	N
Lautenberg	Y	Y	Y	N	Y	Y	Y	N
NEW MEXICO								
Bingaman	N	Y	N	N	Y	Y	Y	N
Domenici	Y	Y	Y	N	N	Y	Y	N
NEW YORK								
Moynihan	Y	Y	Y	N	N	N	Y	N
D'Amato	Y	Y	N	N	Y	Y	N	N
NORTH CAROLINA								
Sanford	Y	Y	Y	N	Y	N	Y	N
Helms	Y	Y	N	Y	Y	N	N	N
NORTH DAKOTA								
Burdick	Y	Y	N	Y	Y	Y	Y	N
Conrad	Y	Y	N	Y	Y	Y	N	N
OHIO								
Glenn	Y	Y	N	Y	Y	Y	Y	N
Metzenbaum	N	Y	Y	N	Y	N	Y	N
OKLAHOMA								
Boren	Y	Y	N	Y	Y	N	N	N
Nickles	Y	Y	N	Y	Y	N	N	N
OREGON								
Hatfield	Y	Y	N	N	Y	Y	Y	N
Packwood	Y	Y	Y	Y	Y	Y	Y	N
PENNSYLVANIA								
Heinz †	Y							
Specter	Y	Y	Y	N	Y	Y	N	N
RHODE ISLAND								
Pell	Y	Y	N	N	Y	N	Y	N
Chafee	Y	Y	Y	N	Y	Y	Y	N
SOUTH CAROLINA								
Hollings	Y	Y	N	N	Y	N	N	N
Thurmond	Y	Y	N	Y	Y	Y	N	N
SOUTH DAKOTA								
Daschle	N	Y	N	Y	Y	Y	N	N
Pressler	Y	Y	N	Y	Y	Y	N	N
TENNESSEE								
Gore	N	Y	N	N	Y	N	Y	N
Sasser	N	Y	Y	Y	Y	Y	Y	N
TEXAS								
Bentsen	Y	Y	N	Y	Y	Y	Y	N
Gramm	Y	Y	N	Y	Y	Y	N	N
UTAH								
Garn	Y	Y	Y	N	N	Y	?	?
Hatch	Y	Y	Y	Y	Y	N	N	N
VERMONT								
Leahy	Y	Y	N	Y	Y	N	N	N
Jeffords	Y	Y	N	Y	Y	Y	Y	N
VIRGINIA								
Robb	Y	Y	N	Y	Y	Y	N	N
Warner	Y	Y	N	Y	Y	Y	Y	N
WASHINGTON								
Adams	N	Y	Y	N	Y	N	Y	N
Gorton	Y	Y	Y	N	Y	Y	Y	N
WEST VIRGINIA								
Byrd	Y	Y	N	N	Y	Y	Y	N
Rockefeller	Y	Y	Y	N	Y	Y	Y	N
WISCONSIN								
Kohl	Y	Y	N	Y	Y	Y	N	N
Kasten	Y	Y	N	Y	Y	N	Y	N
WYOMING								
Simpson	Y	Y	N	Y	Y	Y	Y	N
Wallop	Y	Y	N	Y	Y	N	N	-

KEY

- Y Voted for (yea).
- # Paired for.
- + Announced for.
- N Voted against (nay).
- X Paired against.
- - Announced against.
- P Voted "present."
- C Voted "present" to avoid possible conflict of interest.
- ? Did not vote or otherwise make a position known.

Democrats ***Republicans***

ND Northern Democrats SD Southern Democrats Southern states - Ala., Ark., Fla., Ga., Ky., La., Miss., N.C., Okla., S.C., Tenn., Texas, Va.

41. Martinez Nomination. Confirmation of President Bush's nomination of former Florida Gov. Bob Martinez to be director of National Drug Control Policy. Confirmed 88-12: R 44-0; D 44-12 (ND 31-8, SD 13-4), March 21, 1991. A "yea" was a vote supporting the president's position.

42. S 207. CFTC Reauthorization/Bank Deposits. Bond, R-Mo., amendment to the committee amendment, to exclude bank deposits that might also be deemed to be futures contracts from regulation by the Commodity Futures Trading Commission (CFTC). Adopted 98-0: R 43-0; D 55-0 (ND 39-0, SD 16-0), April 18, 1991.

43. S 207. CFTC Reauthorization/Hybrid Instruments. Bond, R-Mo., amendment to the committee amendment, to ensure that hybrid financial instruments incorporating elements of stocks and futures contracts could be traded under the jurisdiction of both the Commodity Futures Trading Commission and the Securities Exchange Commission. Rejected 33-65: R 14-29; D 19-36 (ND 16-23, SD 3-13), April 18, 1991.

44. S 207. CFTC Reauthorization/Intermarket Coordination. Leahy, D-Vt., motion to table (kill) the Wirth, D-Colo., amendment to the committee amendment, to require the Securities Exchange Commission and the Commodity Futures Trading Commission to develop regulations in consultation with each other and the secretary of the Treasury, and the chairman of the Federal Reserve Board to strengthen the stability of domestic equity markets through coordinated "circuit breaker" mechanisms and other means. Motion agreed to 57-41: R 27-16; D 30-25 (ND 18-21, SD 12-4), April 18, 1991.

45. HR 707. CFTC Reauthorization/Passage. Passage of the bill to reauthorize the Commodity Futures Trading Commission for five years, rising from $48.3 million in fiscal 1992 to $71.9 million in fiscal 1996. (Before passage, the text of S 207 was substituted for the text of HR 707, a similar bill passed by the House.) Passed 90-8: R 37-6; D 53-2 (ND 37-2, SD 16-0), April 18, 1991. A "yea" was a vote supporting the president's position.

46. S Con Res 29. Fiscal 1992 Budget Resolution/Social Security. Domenici, R-N.M., motion to table (kill) the Moynihan, D-N.Y., amendment to make room in the budget resolution for a proposal to cut the Social Security payroll tax and finance Social Security on a pay-as-you-go basis. A "yea" was a vote supporting the president's position. Motion agreed to 60-38: R 34-9; D 26-29 (ND 16-23, SD 10-6), April 24, 1991.

47. S Con Res 29. Fiscal 1992 Budget Resolution/Freeze. Sasser, D-Tenn., motion to table (kill) the Grassley, R-Iowa, substitute amendment to freeze budget authority and outlays for all fiscal 1992 discretionary spending at fiscal 1991 levels, reducing outlays by $8.2 billion in fiscal 1992 and $22.4 billion in fiscal 1992-96. Motion agreed to 60-37: R 18-24; D 42-13 (ND 32-7, SD 10-6), April 24, 1991.

48. S Con Res 29. Fiscal 1992 Budget Resolution/Campaign Finance. McConnell, R-Ky., motion to table (kill) the McConnell amendment to transfer fiscal 1992 funds from the presidential election campaign fund to federal child-nutrition programs. Motion rejected 0-95: R 0-40; D 0-55 (ND 0-39, SD 0-16), April 25, 1991. (Subsequently, The McConnell amendment was withdrawn and a Kerry, D-Mass., amendment to the McConnell amendment was rendered moot.)

† Sen. John Heinz, R-Pa., died April 4, 1991, in a plane crash. The last vote for which he was eligible was 41.

	49	50	51	52	53	54	55	56
ALABAMA								
Heflin	N	N	N	Y	N	N	N	Y
Shelby	N	N	N	Y	Y	Y	N	Y
ALASKA								
Murkowski	N	N	N	N	Y	Y	N	Y
Stevens	N	N	N	N	N	N	N	Y
ARIZONA								
DeConcini	N	N	Y	Y	Y	Y	N	Y
McCain	N	N	N	N	N	N	N	Y
ARKANSAS								
Bumpers	N	N	N	Y	Y	Y	N	Y
Pryor	?	?	?	?	?	?	?	?
CALIFORNIA								
Cranston	Y	Y	Y	Y	Y	Y	N	Y
Seymour	N	N	N	Y	N	N	N	Y
COLORADO								
Wirth	Y	Y	Y	N	Y	Y	N	Y
Brown	N	N	Y	N	Y	Y	N	Y
CONNECTICUT								
Dodd	N	N	N	N	Y	Y	N	Y
Lieberman	N	N	N	N	Y	Y	N	+
DELAWARE								
Biden	Y	Y	Y	N	Y	Y	N	Y
Roth	N	N	Y	N	N	N	N	Y
FLORIDA								
Graham	N	N	N	Y	Y	Y	N	Y
Mack	N	N	N	Y	N	N	N	Y
GEORGIA								
Fowler	N	N	N	Y	Y	Y	N	Y
Nunn	N	N	N	Y	Y	Y	N	Y
HAWAII								
Akaka	N	N	N	Y	Y	Y	N	Y
Inouye	N	N	N	Y	Y	Y	N	Y
IDAHO								
Craig	N	N	N	Y	N	N	N	Y
Symms	N	N	N	Y	N	N	N	Y
ILLINOIS								
Dixon	N	N	N	Y	N	N	N	Y
Simon	Y	Y	Y	Y	Y	Y	N	Y
INDIANA								
Coats	N	N	N	N	N	N	N	Y
Lugar	?	?	?	?	N	N	N	Y
IOWA								
Harkin	Y	Y	Y	Y	Y	Y	Y	Y
Grassley	N	Y	Y	Y	Y	N	N	Y
KANSAS								
Dole	N	N	N	Y	N	N	N	Y
Kassebaum	N	N	N	Y	N	Y	N	Y
KENTUCKY								
Ford	N	N	N	Y	Y	Y	N	Y
McConnell	N	N	N	N	N	N	N	Y
LOUISIANA								
Breaux	N	N	N	Y	Y	Y	N	Y
Johnston	N	N	N	Y	N	N	N	Y
MAINE								
Mitchell	N	Y	Y	Y	Y	Y	N	Y
Cohen	N	N	N	N	Y	Y	N	Y
MARYLAND								
Mikulski	N	N	N	Y	N	N	N	Y
Sarbanes	Y	N	Y	N	Y	Y	Y	Y
MASSACHUSETTS								
Kennedy	Y	Y	Y	N	Y	Y	N	Y
Kerry	Y	N	N	N	Y	Y	N	Y
MICHIGAN								
Levin	N	N	Y	N	Y	Y	N	Y
Riegle	Y	Y	Y	Y	Y	Y	Y	Y
MINNESOTA								
Wellstone	Y	Y	Y	Y	Y	Y	Y	Y
Durenberger	N	N	N	Y	N	N	N	Y
MISSISSIPPI								
Cochran	N	N	N	Y	N	N	N	Y
Lott	N	N	N	Y	N	N	N	Y
MISSOURI								
Bond	N	N	N	Y	N	N	?	Y
Danforth	N	N	N	N	N	N	N	?
MONTANA								
Baucus	Y	Y	Y	Y	Y	Y	N	Y
Burns	N	N	N	Y	N	N	N	Y
NEBRASKA								
Exon	N	N	N	Y	Y	Y	N	Y
Kerrey	N	N	N	Y	Y	Y	N	Y
NEVADA								
Bryan	N	N	N	N	Y	Y	N	Y
Reid	N	N	N	N	Y	Y	N	Y
NEW HAMPSHIRE								
Rudman	N	N	N	N	Y	Y	N	Y
Smith	N	N	N	N	N	N	N	Y
NEW JERSEY								
Bradley	Y	Y	Y	N	Y	Y	N	Y
Lautenberg	Y	N	Y	N	Y	Y	N	Y
NEW MEXICO								
Bingaman	N	N	N	Y	Y	Y	N	Y
Domenici	N	N	N	Y	N	Y	N	Y
NEW YORK								
Moynihan	N	N	N	N	Y	Y	N	Y
D'Amato	N	N	N	N	Y	Y	N	Y
NORTH CAROLINA								
Sanford	N	N	N	Y	Y	Y	N	Y
Helms	N	N	N	N	N	N	N	Y
NORTH DAKOTA								
Burdick	Y	Y	Y	Y	Y	Y	N	Y
Conrad	Y	Y	Y	Y	Y	Y	N	Y
OHIO								
Glenn	N	N	N	N	Y	Y	N	Y
Metzenbaum	Y	Y	Y	N	Y	Y	N	Y
OKLAHOMA								
Boren	N	N	N	Y	N	N	N	Y
Nickles	N	N	N	N	N	N	N	Y
OREGON								
Hatfield	Y	Y	Y	N	Y	Y	N	Y
Packwood	N	N	N	N	Y	N	N	Y
PENNSYLVANIA								
Wofford †							N	Y
Specter	N	N	N	N	Y	Y	N	Y
RHODE ISLAND								
Pell	Y	Y	Y	N	Y	Y	Y	Y
Chafee	N	N	N	N	N	Y	N	Y
SOUTH CAROLINA								
Hollings	N	N	N	N	Y	Y	N	Y
Thurmond	N	N	N	Y	N	N	N	Y
SOUTH DAKOTA								
Daschle	Y	Y	Y	Y	Y	Y	N	Y
Pressler	N	N	N	Y	N	N	N	Y
TENNESSEE								
Gore	N	N	N	Y	Y	Y	N	Y
Sasser	N	Y	Y	Y	Y	Y	N	Y
TEXAS								
Bentsen	N	N	N	Y	Y	Y	N	Y
Gramm	N	N	N	Y	N	N	N	Y
UTAH								
Garn	?	?	?	?	N	N	?	Y
Hatch	N	N	N	N	N	N	N	Y
VERMONT								
Leahy	N	Y	+	Y	Y	Y	N	Y
Jeffords	N	Y	Y	Y	Y	Y	N	Y
VIRGINIA								
Robb	N	N	N	Y	Y	Y	N	Y
Warner	N	N	N	Y	N	Y	N	Y
WASHINGTON								
Adams	Y	Y	Y	Y	Y	Y	N	Y
Gorton	N	N	N	N	Y	Y	N	Y
WEST VIRGINIA								
Byrd	N	Y	Y	Y	Y	Y	N	Y
Rockefeller	Y	Y	Y	Y	Y	Y	N	Y
WISCONSIN								
Kohl	Y	Y	Y	Y	Y	Y	N	Y
Kasten	N	N	N	N	N	N	N	Y
WYOMING								
Simpson	N	N	N	Y	N	N	N	Y
Wallop	-	-	-	+	N	N	N	Y

KEY

- Y Voted for (yea).
- # Paired for.
- + Announced for.
- N Voted against (nay).
- X Paired against.
- - Announced against.
- P Voted "present."
- C Voted "present" to avoid possible conflict of interest.
- ? Did not vote or otherwise make a position known.

Democrats *Republicans*

ND Northern Democrats SD Southern Democrats

Southern states - Ala., Ark., Fla., Ga., Ky., La., Miss., N.C., Okla., S.C., Tenn., Texas, Va.

49. S Con Res 29. Fiscal 1992 Budget Resolution/Defense Transfer. Bradley, D-N.J., motion to waive the Budget Act with respect to the Sasser, D-Tenn., point of order, which stated that the Bradley amendment to cut defense spending by 2 percent over the next five years and to transfer the funds to domestic programs and deficit reduction would violate a Budget Act prohibition against transferring money between defense and domestic spending. Motion rejected 22-73: R 1-39; D 21-34 (ND 21-18, SD 0-16), April 25, 1991. A three-fifths majority (60) of the total Senate is required to waive the Budget Act. (The Bradley amendment subsequently fell on the Sasser point of order.)

50. S Con Res 29. Fiscal 1992 Budget Resolution/2 Percent Defense Cut. Simon, D-Ill., amendment to provide for a 2 percent cut in defense spending. Rejected 25-70: R 3-37; D 22-33 (ND 21-18, SD 1-15), April 25, 1991.

51. S Con Res 29. Fiscal 1992 Budget Resolution/1 Percent Defense Cut. Simon, D-Ill., amendment to provide for a 1 percent cut in defense spending. Rejected 30-64: R 5-35; D 25-29 (ND 24-14, SD 1-15), April 25, 1991.

52. S Con Res 29. Fiscal 1992 Budget Resolution/Honey Price Support. Daschle, D-S.D., motion to table (kill) the Brown, R-Colo., amendment to eliminate the honey price support program. Motion agreed to 57-38: R 19-21; D 38-17 (ND 23-16, SD 15-1), April 25, 1991.

53. S 429. Vertical Price Fixing. Ford, D-Ky., motion to invoke cloture (thus limiting debate) on the motion to proceed to the bill to amend the Sherman Antitrust Act of 1890 to tighten the ban on vertical price fixing, which occurs when a manufacturer conspires with a retailer to force a competing merchant to charge at least a certain price for goods or face a cutoff of supplies. Motion agreed to 61-37: R 11-32; D 50-5 (ND 37-2, SD 13-3), May 7, 1991. A three-fifths majority vote (60) of the total Senate is required to invoke cloture.

54. S 429. Vertical Price Fixing. Mitchell, D-Maine, motion to invoke cloture (thus limiting debate) on the bill to amend the Sherman Antitrust Act of 1890 to tighten the ban on vertical price fixing, which occurs when a manufacturer conspires with a retailer to force a competing merchant to charge at least a certain price for goods or face a cutoff of supplies. Motion agreed to 63-35: R 13-30; D 50-5 (ND 37-2, SD 13-3), May 8, 1991. A three-fifths majority vote (60) of the total Senate is required to invoke cloture.

55. S J Res 137. Recession Resolution To Suspend Gramm-Rudman/Passage. Passage of the joint resolution to suspend spending caps and pay-as-you-go restrictions for 1991 and 1992. The Balanced Budget and Emergency Deficit Control Act, as amended in 1990, compels the majority leader to introduce such a resolution after a government projection that the nation is in recession. Rejected 5-92: R 0-41; D 5-51 (ND 5-35, SD 0-16), May 9, 1991. A "nay" was a vote supporting the president's position.

56. Treaty Doc Ex. EE, 96-1. Convention on Standards of Training, Certification and Watchkeeping for Seafarers. Adoption of the resolution of ratification of the treaty to establish standards of training, certification and watchkeeping for seafarers to ensure the quality of personnel on seagoing merchant ships. Adopted 97-0: 42-0; D 55-0 (ND 39-0, SD 16-0), May 14, 1991. A two-thirds majority of those present and voting (65 in this case) is required for adoption of resolutions of ratification. A "yea" was a vote supporting the president's position.

† Harris Wofford, D-Pa., was sworn in May 9, 1991. The first vote for which he was eligible was vote 55.

	57	58	59	60	61	62	63	64
ALABAMA								
Heflin	Y	Y	Y	Y	Y	Y	N	N
Shelby	Y	Y	Y	Y	Y	Y	N	Y
ALASKA								
Murkowski	Y	Y	Y	Y	Y	Y	N	N
Stevens	Y	Y	Y	Y	Y	Y	N	?
ARIZONA								
DeConcini	Y	Y	Y	N	Y	N	Y	N
McCain	Y	Y	Y	Y	Y	N	N	N
ARKANSAS								
Bumpers	Y	Y	Y	N	Y	Y	Y	?
Pryor	?	?	?	?	?	?	?	?
CALIFORNIA								
Cranston	Y	Y	Y	N	Y	Y	N	N
Seymour	Y	Y	Y	Y	Y	Y	N	?
COLORADO								
Wirth	Y	Y	Y	N	Y	Y	?	?
Brown	Y	Y	Y	Y	N	Y	N	Y
CONNECTICUT								
Dodd	Y	Y	Y	N	Y	N	Y	Y
Lieberman	+	+	+	-	+	N	Y	Y
DELAWARE								
Biden	Y	Y	Y	N	Y	Y	?	?
Roth	Y	Y	Y	Y	N	Y	N	N
FLORIDA								
Graham	Y	Y	Y	N	Y	N	Y	Y
Mack	Y	Y	Y	Y	Y	N	N	?
GEORGIA								
Fowler	Y	Y	Y	N	Y	Y	Y	Y
Nunn	Y	Y	Y	N	Y	Y	Y	Y
HAWAII								
Akaka	Y	Y	Y	N	Y	Y	Y	Y
Inouye	Y	Y	Y	N	Y	N	Y	Y
IDAHO								
Craig	Y	Y	Y	Y	N	Y	N	N
Symms	Y	Y	Y	Y	N	Y	N	?
ILLINOIS								
Dixon	Y	Y	Y	N	Y	Y	Y	N
Simon	Y	Y	Y	N	Y	Y	Y	Y
INDIANA								
Coats	Y	Y	Y	Y	Y	Y	N	N
Lugar	Y	Y	Y	N	Y	Y	N	N
IOWA								
Harkin	Y	Y	Y	N	Y	Y	Y	Y
Grassley	Y	Y	Y	Y	Y	Y	N	N
KANSAS								
Dole	Y	Y	Y	Y	Y	Y	N	N
Kassebaum	Y	Y	Y	Y	Y	Y	?	Y
KENTUCKY								
Ford	Y	Y	Y	?	?	Y	Y	Y
McConnell	Y	Y	Y	Y	Y	Y	N	N
LOUISIANA								
Breaux	Y	Y	Y	N	Y	Y	Y	?
Johnston	Y	Y	Y	N	Y	N	N	Y
MAINE								
Mitchell	Y	Y	Y	N	Y	Y	Y	Y
Cohen	Y	Y	Y	Y	Y	N	N	N
MARYLAND								
Mikulski	Y	Y	Y	N	Y	N	Y	Y
Sarbanes	Y	Y	Y	N	Y	N	Y	Y
MASSACHUSETTS								
Kennedy	Y	Y	Y	N	Y	Y	Y	N
Kerry	Y	Y	Y	N	Y	Y	Y	Y
MICHIGAN								
Levin	Y	Y	Y	N	Y	Y	Y	Y
Riegle	Y	Y	Y	N	Y	N	Y	Y
MINNESOTA								
Wellstone	Y	Y	Y	N	Y	Y	Y	Y
Durenberger	Y	Y	Y	N	Y	Y	?	?
MISSISSIPPI								
Cochran	Y	Y	Y	Y	Y	Y	N	N
Lott	Y	Y	Y	Y	Y	Y	N	N
MISSOURI								
Bond	Y	Y	Y	Y	Y	Y	N	N
Danforth	?	?	?	?	?	?	?	?
MONTANA								
Baucus	Y	Y	Y	N	Y	Y	Y	Y
Burns	Y	Y	Y	Y	Y	Y	N	N
NEBRASKA								
Exon	Y	Y	Y	N	Y	Y	Y	Y
Kerrey	Y	Y	Y	N	Y	Y	Y	Y
NEVADA								
Bryan	Y	Y	Y	N	Y	N	Y	Y
Reid	Y	Y	Y	N	Y	N	Y	Y
NEW HAMPSHIRE								
Rudman	Y	Y	Y	Y	Y	N	N	N
Smith	Y	Y	Y	Y	N	N	N	N
NEW JERSEY								
Bradley	Y	Y	Y	N	Y	N	Y	Y
Lautenberg	Y	Y	Y	N	Y	N	Y	Y
NEW MEXICO								
Bingaman	Y	Y	Y	N	Y	N	Y	Y
Domenici	Y	Y	Y	Y	Y	Y	N	N
NEW YORK								
Moynihan	Y	Y	Y	N	Y	Y	Y	?
D'Amato	Y	Y	Y	Y	Y	N	N	N
NORTH CAROLINA								
Sanford	Y	Y	Y	N	Y	Y	Y	Y
Helms	Y	Y	Y	Y	N	N	N	N
NORTH DAKOTA								
Burdick	Y	Y	Y	N	Y	Y	Y	Y
Conrad	Y	Y	Y	N	Y	Y	Y	Y
OHIO								
Glenn	Y	Y	Y	N	Y	N	Y	N
Metzenbaum	Y	Y	Y	N	Y	N	Y	N
OKLAHOMA								
Boren	Y	Y	Y	N	Y	Y	Y	N
Nickles	Y	Y	Y	Y	N	Y	N	?
OREGON								
Hatfield	Y	Y	Y	N	Y	Y	N	N
Packwood	Y	Y	Y	N	Y	Y	N	N
PENNSYLVANIA								
Wofford	Y	Y	Y	N	Y	Y	Y	Y
Specter	Y	Y	Y	Y	Y	Y	N	N
RHODE ISLAND								
Pell	Y	Y	Y	N	Y	Y	Y	Y
Chafee	Y	Y	Y	N	Y	Y	N	N
SOUTH CAROLINA								
Hollings	Y	Y	Y	N	Y	Y	Y	Y
Thurmond	Y	Y	Y	Y	N	Y	N	N
SOUTH DAKOTA								
Daschle	Y	Y	Y	N	Y	Y	Y	Y
Pressler	Y	Y	Y	Y	Y	Y	N	N
TENNESSEE								
Gore	Y	Y	Y	N	Y	Y	Y	Y
Sasser	Y	Y	Y	N	Y	Y	Y	Y
TEXAS								
Bentsen	Y	Y	Y	N	Y	Y	Y	Y
Gramm	Y	Y	Y	Y	Y	Y	N	N
UTAH								
Garn	Y	Y	Y	Y	Y	Y	N	N
Hatch	Y	Y	Y	Y	Y	Y	N	N
VERMONT								
Leahy	Y	Y	Y	N	Y	N	Y	Y
Jeffords	Y	Y	Y	N	Y	Y	N	N
VIRGINIA								
Robb	Y	Y	Y	N	Y	N	Y	Y
Warner	Y	Y	Y	Y	Y	Y	N	N
WASHINGTON								
Adams	Y	Y	Y	N	Y	Y	Y	Y
Gorton	Y	Y	Y	Y	Y	Y	N	N
WEST VIRGINIA								
Byrd	Y	Y	Y	N	Y	N	Y	N
Rockefeller	Y	Y	Y	N	Y	N	Y	Y
WISCONSIN								
Kohl	Y	Y	Y	N	Y	Y	Y	Y
Kasten	Y	Y	Y	Y	Y	Y	N	N
WYOMING								
Simpson	Y	Y	Y	Y	Y	Y	N	N
Wallop	Y	Y	Y	Y	N	N	N	N

KEY

Y Voted for (yea).
\# Paired for.
\+ Announced for.
N Voted against (nay).
X Paired against.
\- Announced against.
P Voted "present."
C Voted "present" to avoid possible conflict of interest.
? Did not vote or otherwise make a position known.

Democrats ***Republicans***

ND Northern Democrats SD Southern Democrats

Southern states - Ala., Ark., Fla., Ga., Ky., La., Miss., N.C., Okla., S.C., Tenn., Texas, Va.

57. Treaty Doc 101-7. Convention for the Prevention of Pollution From Ships. Adoption of the resolution of ratification of the treaty to control pollution from ships by establishing regulations for the transport and packaging of harmful substances. Adopted 97-0: 42-0; D 55-0 (ND 39-0, SD 16-0), May 14, 1991. A two-thirds majority of those present and voting (65 in this case) is required for adoption of resolutions of ratification. A "yea" was a vote supporting the president's position.

58. Treaty Doc 102-2. Safety of Life at Sea and Load Line Conventions. Adoption of the resolution of ratification of the treaty to eliminate the duplication of inspections that were previously required under the Convention for Safety of Life at Sea, which contains standards and procedures relating to vessel safety, and the Convention on Load Lines, which establishes uniform principles governing the loading of ships. The treaty would provide that a ship can be inspected by the same inspector for compliance with both conventions during one visit. Adopted 97-0: 42-0; D 55-0 (ND 39-0, SD 16-0), May 14, 1991. A two-thirds majority of those present and voting (65 in this case) is required for adoption of resolutions of ratification. A "yea" was a vote supporting the president's position.

59. Treaty Doc EX. K, 88-1. Convention Concerning the Abolition of Forced Labor. Adoption of the resolution of ratification of the treaty to promote the elimination of forced and compulsory labor. Adopted 97-0: 42-0; D 55-0 (ND 39-0, SD 16-0), May 14, 1991. A two-thirds majority of those present and voting (65 in this case) is required for adoption of resolutions of ratification. A "yea" was a vote supporting the president's position.

60. S 100. Central American Democracy and Development Act/Free Market Policies. Helms, R-N.C., amendment to require that any U.S. economic assistance to Latin America would be used to promote certain free market policies. Rejected 38-58: R 36-6; D 2-52 (ND 0-39, SD 2-13), May 14, 1991.

61. S 100. Central American Democracy and Development Act/Passage. Passage of the bill to encourage and support the Central American countries to build democratic governments; resolve armed conflict and restore peace; promote and protect human rights; expand economic opportunity through sustained development; and improve living conditions. Passed 87-9: R 33-9; D 54-0 (ND 39-0, SD 15-0), May 14, 1991.

62. S Res 117. Agricultural Export Credits for the Soviet Union. Adoption of the resolution to express the sense of the Senate that the administration should provide $1.5 billion in agricultural credits to the Soviet Union if the Soviet Union can provide assurances that the credits will be repaid, will help the Soviet people and will not be used for political purposes. Adopted 70-28: R 34-8; D 36-20 (ND 23-17, SD 13-3), May 15, 1991.

63. S 3. Campaign Finance Reform/Tax Deductions. Boren, D-Okla., amendment to the Boren substitute amendment, to express the sense of the Senate that legislation that would reform Senate campaigns should be funded by removing tax deductions for political action committees and lobbyists, and not be funded by tax increases for taxpayers, spending cuts of existing federal programs, or increasing the deficit. Adopted 50-44: R 0-40; D 50-4 (ND 37-1, SD 13-3), May 16, 1991.

64. S 3. Campaign Finance/Presidential Debates. Graham, D-Fla., amendment to the Boren, D-Okla., substitute amendment, to require presidential candidates to participate in four debates and vice presidential candidates to participate in one debate to be eligible for public campaign financing during the general election. Adopted 44-43: R 2-34; D 42-9 (ND 30-7, SD 12-2), May 17, 1991.

	65	66	67	68	69	70	71	72
ALABAMA								
Heflin	Y	N	Y	N	Y	Y	Y	Y
Shelby	Y	N	N	N	Y	Y	Y	Y
ALASKA								
Murkowski	Y	Y	N	Y	N	N	N	N
Stevens	N	N	N	Y	N	N	N	Y
ARIZONA								
DeConcini	Y	N	N	N	Y	Y	Y	Y
McCain	Y	Y	N	Y	N	N	N	N
ARKANSAS								
Bumpers	Y	N	N	N	Y	Y	Y	Y
Pryor	?	?	?	?	?	?	?	?
CALIFORNIA								
Cranston	Y	N	N	N	Y	Y	Y	Y
Seymour	Y	Y	N	Y	N	N	N	N
COLORADO								
Wirth	Y	N	N	N	Y	Y	N	Y
Brown	Y	N	N	Y	N	N	N	N
CONNECTICUT								
Dodd	Y	N	Y	N	Y	Y	Y	Y
Lieberman	Y	Y	N	N	Y	Y	Y	Y
DELAWARE								
Biden	?	?	?	N	Y	Y	Y	N
Roth	N	N	N	Y	Y	N	N	Y
FLORIDA								
Graham	Y	N	Y	N	Y	Y	Y	Y
Mack	N	N	N	Y	N	N	N	N
GEORGIA								
Fowler	Y	Y	Y	N	Y	Y	Y	N
Nunn	Y	N	Y	N	Y	Y	Y	Y
HAWAII								
Akaka	Y	Y	Y	N	Y	Y	Y	Y
Inouye	N	?	?	N	Y	Y	Y	Y
IDAHO								
Craig	N	Y	N	Y	N	N	N	N
Symms	?	?	?	Y	N	N	N	N
ILLINOIS								
Dixon	Y	N	N	N	Y	Y	Y	Y
Simon	Y	Y	Y	N	Y	Y	Y	Y
INDIANA								
Coats	N	Y	N	Y	N	N	N	Y
Lugar	N	N	N	Y	Y	N	Y	Y
IOWA								
Harkin	Y	Y	Y	N	Y	Y	Y	Y
Grassley	Y	Y	Y	Y	N	N	N	N
KANSAS								
Dole	N	N	N	Y	N	N	N	N
Kassebaum	Y	N	N	Y	Y	N	N	N
KENTUCKY								
Ford	Y	N	N	N	Y	Y	Y	Y
McConnell	N	Y	N	Y	N	N	N	N
LOUISIANA								
Breaux	Y	N	N	N	Y	N	Y	Y
Johnston	Y	Y	N	N	Y	Y	Y	Y
MAINE								
Mitchell	Y	Y	N	N	Y	Y	Y	Y
Cohen	N	Y	N	Y	Y	N	N	N
MARYLAND								
Mikulski	Y	Y	N	N	Y	Y	Y	Y
Sarbanes	Y	Y	Y	N	Y	Y	Y	Y
MASSACHUSETTS								
Kennedy	Y	N	Y	N	Y	Y	Y	Y
Kerry	Y	Y	Y	N	Y	Y	Y	Y
MICHIGAN								
Levin	Y	N	Y	N	Y	Y	Y	Y
Riegle	Y	Y	Y	N	Y	Y	Y	Y
MINNESOTA								
Wellstone	Y	Y	Y	N	Y	Y	Y	N
Durenberger	Y	Y	N	Y	Y	N	Y	N
MISSISSIPPI								
Cochran	N	Y	N	Y	N	N	N	N
Lott	N	Y	N	Y	N	N	N	N
MISSOURI								
Bond	Y	Y	N	Y	N	N	N	N
Danforth	N	N	N	Y	Y	N	Y	Y
MONTANA								
Baucus	Y	Y	Y	N	Y	Y	Y	Y
Burns	N	Y	Y	Y	N	N	N	N
NEBRASKA								
Exon	Y	N	Y	N	Y	Y	Y	N
Kerrey	Y	Y	N	N	Y	Y	Y	Y
NEVADA								
Bryan	Y	N	Y	N	Y	Y	Y	Y
Reid	Y	N	Y	N	Y	Y	Y	Y
NEW HAMPSHIRE								
Rudman	N	N	Y	Y	Y	N	N	N
Smith	N	N	N	Y	N	N	N	N
NEW JERSEY								
Bradley	Y	Y	N	N	Y	Y	Y	Y
Lautenberg	Y	N	N	N	Y	Y	Y	N
NEW MEXICO								
Bingaman	Y	N	Y	N	Y	Y	Y	Y
Domenici	N	Y	N	Y	N	N	N	N
NEW YORK								
Moynihan	Y	Y	Y	N	Y	Y	Y	Y
D'Amato	Y	Y	N	Y	N	N	N	N
NORTH CAROLINA								
Sanford	Y	N	N	N	Y	Y	Y	Y
Helms	?	?	?	?	?	?	?	?
NORTH DAKOTA								
Burdick	Y	N	Y	N	Y	Y	Y	Y
Conrad	Y	Y	N	N	Y	Y	Y	Y
OHIO								
Glenn	Y	N	N	N	Y	Y	Y	Y
Metzenbaum	Y	N	Y	N	Y	Y	Y	Y
OKLAHOMA								
Boren	Y	N	Y	N	Y	Y	Y	Y
Nickles	Y	N	N	Y	N	N	Y	N
OREGON								
Hatfield	Y	Y	N	Y	Y	N	Y	N
Packwood	Y	Y	N	Y	Y	N	N	N
PENNSYLVANIA								
Wofford	Y	Y	N	N	Y	Y	Y	Y
Specter	Y	Y	N	Y	Y	N	N	N
RHODE ISLAND								
Pell	Y	N	Y	N	Y	Y	Y	N
Chafee	N	Y	N	Y	Y	N	N	N
SOUTH CAROLINA								
Hollings	Y	N	Y	N	Y	N	Y	Y
Thurmond	Y	Y	N	Y	N	N	N	N
SOUTH DAKOTA								
Daschle	Y	Y	N	N	Y	Y	Y	Y
Pressler	Y	Y	N	Y	N	N	N	N
TENNESSEE								
Gore	Y	N	Y	N	Y	Y	Y	Y
Sasser	Y	Y	Y	N	Y	Y	Y	Y
TEXAS								
Bentsen	Y	N	Y	N	Y	Y	Y	Y
Gramm	N	N	N	Y	N	N	N	Y
UTAH								
Garn	N	Y	N	Y	N	N	N	Y
Hatch	N	Y	N	Y	N	N	N	N
VERMONT								
Leahy	Y	Y	N	N	Y	Y	Y	Y
Jeffords	N	Y	Y	Y	Y	N	N	Y
VIRGINIA								
Robb	Y	N	N	N	Y	Y	Y	Y
Warner	Y	Y	N	Y	N	N	N	N
WASHINGTON								
Adams	Y	N	N	N	Y	Y	Y	Y
Gorton	N	Y	N	Y	N	N	N	N
WEST VIRGINIA								
Byrd	Y	N	Y	N	Y	Y	Y	Y
Rockefeller	Y	N	Y	N	Y	Y	Y	Y
WISCONSIN								
Kohl	Y	N	Y	N	Y	Y	Y	N
Kasten	Y	Y	N	Y	N	N	N	N
WYOMING								
Simpson	Y	Y	N	Y	N	N	N	N
Wallop	N	N	N	Y	N	N	N	N

KEY

Y Voted for (yea).
\# Paired for.
\+ Announced for.
N Voted against (nay).
X Paired against.
\- Announced against.
P Voted "present."
C Voted "present" to avoid possible conflict of interest.
? Did not vote or otherwise make a position known.

Democrats ***Republicans***

ND Northern Democrats SD Southern Democrats

Southern states - Ala., Ark., Fla., Ga., Ky., La., Miss., N.C., Okla., S.C., Tenn., Texas, Va.

65. S 3. Campaign Finance/Honoraria Ban. Dodd, D-Conn., amendment to the Boren, D-Okla., substitute amendment, to bar senators from accepting honoraria, limit all outside earned income to 15 percent of a senator's salary, prohibit senators from maintaining a fiduciary relationship with a corporation or partnership, and restrict charitable contributions made in behalf of a senator. Adopted 72-24: R 18-23; D 54-1 (ND 38-1, SD 16-0), May 21, 1991.

66. S 3. Campaign Finance/Limit on Unearned Income. Moynihan, D-N.Y., amendment to the Boren, D-Okla., substitute amendment, to limit the amount a senator may receive in unearned income to 15 percent of each senator's salary. The Dodd amendment (vote 65) only limited earned income. Adopted 49-46: R 28-13; D 21-33 (ND 18-20, SD 3-13), May 21, 1991.

67. S 3. Campaign Finance/Political Action Committees. Bentsen, D-Texas, motion to table (kill) the Breaux, D-La., substitute amendment to the Bentsen amendment to the Boren, D-Okla., substitute amendment, to codify current regulations on political action committees (PACs) that bar foreign nationals from operating or contributing to PACs. The Bentsen amendment would have barred companies with majority foreign ownership from operating a political action committee. Motion rejected 35-60: R 4-37; D 31-23 (ND 22-16, SD 9-7), May 21, 1991. (Subsequently, the Breaux amendment was adopted by voice vote, and the Bentsen amendment as amended by the Breaux amendment was adopted by voice vote.)

68. S 3. Campaign Finance/Elimination of Public Financing. McConnell, R-Ky., amendment to the Boren, D-Okla., substitute amendment, to eliminate all the public financing and spending limit provisions from the bill. Rejected 42-56: R 42-0; D 0-56 (ND 0-40, SD 0-16), May 22, 1991.

69. S 3. Campaign Finance/Limit Terms. Boren, D-Okla., motion to table (kill) the Brown, R-Colo., amendment to the McConnell, R-Ky., amendment, to limit terms of successful Senate candidates to two consecutive terms if they received public financing. Motion agreed to 68-30: R 12-30; D 56-0 (ND 40-0, SD 16-0), May 22, 1991.

70. S 3. Campaign Finance/Ad Disclosure. Boren, D-Okla., motion to table (kill) the McConnell, R-Ky., amendment to the Boren substitute amendment, to require that political ads paid for with public financing contain a sentence stating that the ad was paid for with taxpayer funds. Motion agreed to 54-44: R 0-42; D 54-2 (ND 40-0, SD 14-2), May 22, 1991.

71. S 3. Campaign Finance/Spending Limit. Boren, D-Okla., motion to table (kill) the Cochran, R-Miss., amendment to the Boren substitute amendment, to establish a general election spending limit for challengers at 150 percent of the limit for incumbent senators. Motion agreed to 60-38: R 5-37; D 55-1 (ND 39-1, SD 16-0), May 22, 1991.

72. S 3. Campaign Finance/Revert Funds to Treasury. Boren, D-Okla., motion to table (kill) the McCain, R-Ariz., amendment to the Boren substitute amendment, to require candidates to give any leftover funds at the end of a campaign to the Treasury. Motion agreed to 57-41: R 8-34; D 49-7 (ND 34-6, SD 15-1), May 22, 1991.

	73	74	75	76	77	78	79	80
ALABAMA								
Heflin	Y	N	Y	Y	Y	Y	Y	Y
Shelby	Y	N	N	Y	Y	Y	Y	Y
ALASKA								
Murkowski	N	N	N	N	N	N	N	N
Stevens	N	N	N	N	Y	N	Y	N
ARIZONA								
DeConcini	Y	Y	N	Y	Y	Y	Y	Y
McCain	N	N	N	N	Y	N	N	N
ARKANSAS								
Bumpers	Y	Y	Y	Y	Y	Y	Y	Y
Pryor	?	?	?	?	?	?	?	?
CALIFORNIA								
Cranston	Y	Y	Y	Y	Y	Y	Y	?
Seymour	N	N	N	N	N	N	N	N
COLORADO								
Wirth	Y	Y	Y	Y	Y	Y	Y	Y
Brown	N	N	N	N	Y	N	N	Y
CONNECTICUT								
Dodd	Y	Y	Y	Y	Y	Y	Y	Y
Lieberman	Y	Y	Y	Y	Y	Y	Y	Y
DELAWARE								
Biden	Y	Y	Y	Y	Y	Y	Y	Y
Roth	N	N	N	N	N	Y	N	N
FLORIDA								
Graham	Y	N	Y	Y	Y	Y	Y	Y
Mack	N	N	N	N	Y	N	N	N
GEORGIA								
Fowler	Y	Y	Y	Y	Y	Y	Y	Y
Nunn	Y	N	Y	Y	Y	Y	Y	Y
HAWAII								
Akaka	Y	Y	Y	Y	Y	Y	Y	Y
Inouye	Y	Y	Y	Y	Y	Y	Y	Y
IDAHO								
Craig	N	N	N	N	Y	N	N	N
Symms	N	N	N	N	Y	N	N	N
ILLINOIS								
Dixon	Y	N	Y	Y	Y	Y	Y	Y
Simon	Y	Y	Y	Y	Y	Y	Y	Y
INDIANA								
Coats	N	N	N	N	Y	N	N	N
Lugar	N	N	N	N	N	N	N	Y
IOWA								
Harkin	Y	Y	Y	Y	Y	Y	Y	Y
Grassley	N	N	N	N	N	N	N	N
KANSAS								
Dole	N	N	N	N	N	N	N	N
Kassebaum	N	N	Y	N	N	N	N	N
KENTUCKY								
Ford	Y	N	Y	Y	Y	Y	Y	Y
McConnell	N	N	N	N	N	N	N	N
LOUISIANA								
Breaux	Y	N	Y	Y	Y	Y	Y	Y
Johnston	Y	N	Y	Y	Y	Y	Y	Y
MAINE								
Mitchell	Y	Y	Y	Y	Y	Y	Y	Y
Cohen	Y	N	Y	N	N	Y	N	N
MARYLAND								
Mikulski	Y	Y	Y	Y	Y	Y	Y	Y
Sarbanes	Y	Y	Y	Y	Y	Y	Y	Y
MASSACHUSETTS								
Kennedy	Y	Y	Y	Y	Y	Y	Y	Y
Kerry	Y	Y	N	Y	Y	Y	Y	Y
MICHIGAN								
Levin	Y	N	Y	Y	Y	N	Y	Y
Riegle	Y	Y	Y	Y	Y	Y	Y	Y
MINNESOTA								
Wellstone	Y	Y	Y	Y	Y	Y	Y	Y
Durenberger	N	N	Y	N	Y	Y	N	N
MISSISSIPPI								
Cochran	N	N	N	N	N	N	N	N
Lott	N	N	N	N	N	Y	N	N
MISSOURI								
Bond	N	N	N	N	Y	N	N	N
Danforth	N	N	Y	N	Y	N	N	N
MONTANA								
Baucus	Y	Y	Y	Y	Y	Y	Y	Y
Burns	N	N	N	N	Y	N	N	N
NEBRASKA								
Exon	Y	N	Y	Y	Y	N	Y	Y
Kerrey	Y	N	Y	Y	Y	N	Y	Y
NEVADA								
Bryan	Y	N	Y	Y	Y	N	Y	Y
Reid	Y	?	Y	Y	Y	N	Y	Y
NEW HAMPSHIRE								
Rudman	N	N	N	N	N	Y	N	N
Smith	N	N	N	N	N	N	N	N
NEW JERSEY								
Bradley	Y	Y	N	Y	Y	Y	Y	Y
Lautenberg	Y	Y	Y	Y	Y	Y	Y	Y
NEW MEXICO								
Bingaman	Y	Y	Y	Y	Y	Y	Y	Y
Domenici	N	N	N	N	Y	N	N	N
NEW YORK								
Moynihan	Y	Y	Y	Y	Y	Y	Y	Y
D'Amato	N	N	N	N	Y	N	N	N
NORTH CAROLINA								
Sanford	Y	Y	Y	Y	Y	Y	Y	Y
Helms	?	?	?	?	?	?	?	?
NORTH DAKOTA								
Burdick	Y	Y	Y	Y	Y	Y	Y	Y
Conrad	Y	Y	N	Y	Y	N	Y	Y
OHIO								
Glenn	Y	Y	Y	Y	Y	Y	Y	Y
Metzenbaum	Y	Y	Y	Y	Y	Y	Y	Y
OKLAHOMA								
Boren	Y	Y	Y	Y	Y	Y	N	Y
Nickles	N	N	N	N	Y	N	N	N
OREGON								
Hatfield	N	N	Y	N	Y	N	N	N
Packwood	N	N	Y	N	Y	N	Y	N
PENNSYLVANIA								
Wofford	Y	Y	Y	Y	Y	Y	Y	Y
Specter	Y	N	N	N	Y	N	N	N
RHODE ISLAND								
Pell	Y	Y	Y	Y	Y	Y	Y	Y
Chafee	Y	N	Y	N	N	N	N	N
SOUTH CAROLINA								
Hollings	Y	N	N	N	Y	N	Y	Y
Thurmond	N	N	N	N	N	N	N	N
SOUTH DAKOTA								
Daschle	Y	Y	Y	Y	Y	Y	Y	Y
Pressler	N	N	N	N	N	N	N	N
TENNESSEE								
Gore	Y	Y	Y	Y	Y	Y	Y	Y
Sasser	Y	Y	Y	Y	Y	Y	Y	Y
TEXAS								
Bentsen	Y	Y	Y	Y	Y	Y	Y	Y
Gramm	N	N	N	N	Y	N	N	N
UTAH								
Garn	N	N	N	N	N	N	N	N
Hatch	N	N	N	N	N	N	N	N
VERMONT								
Leahy	Y	Y	Y	Y	Y	Y	Y	Y
Jeffords	N	N	Y	N	Y	N	Y	N
VIRGINIA								
Robb	Y	N	Y	Y	Y	Y	Y	Y
Warner	N	N	N	N	Y	N	N	N
WASHINGTON								
Adams	Y	Y	Y	Y	Y	Y	Y	Y
Gorton	N	N	N	N	Y	N	N	N
WEST VIRGINIA								
Byrd	Y	Y	Y	Y	Y	Y	Y	Y
Rockefeller	Y	N	Y	Y	Y	Y	Y	Y
WISCONSIN								
Kohl	Y	N	N	Y	Y	Y	N	Y
Kasten	Y	N	N	N	Y	N	N	N
WYOMING								
Simpson	N	N	N	N	N	N	N	N
Wallop	N	N	N	N	Y	N	N	N

KEY

Y Voted for (yea).
\# Paired for.
\+ Announced for.
N Voted against (nay).
X Paired against.
\- Announced against.
P Voted "present."
C Voted "present" to avoid possible conflict of interest.
? Did not vote or otherwise make a position known.

Democrats *Republicans*

ND Northern Democrats SD Southern Democrats

Southern states - Ala., Ark., Fla., Ga., Ky., La., Miss., N.C., Okla., S.C., Tenn., Texas, Va.

73. S 3. Campaign Finance/Repeal Public Financing. Boren, D-Okla., motion to table (kill) the McConnell, R-Ky., amendment to the Boren substitute amendment, to repeal public financing and spending limits in presidential elections and the preferential mailing rate for political parties. Motion agreed to 60-38: R 4-38; D 56-0 (ND 40-0, SD 16-0), May 22, 1991.

74. S 3. Campaign Finance/Spending Limit Formula. Kerry, D-Mass., amendment to set public financing of Senate campaigns at 90 percent of the general-election spending limits. Rejected 39-58: R 0-42; D 39-16 (ND 32-7, SD 7-9), May 22, 1991.

75. H Con Res 121. Fiscal 1992 Budget Resolution/Conference Report. Adoption of the conference report on the resolution to set binding budget levels for the fiscal year ending Sept. 30, 1992: budget authority, $1.59 trillion; outlays, $1.448 trillion; revenues, $1.169 trillion; deficit, $278.8 billion. The conference report conforms with the spending caps for defense, international, domestic discretionary spending, and the pay-as-you-go requirements established by the Budget Enforcement Act of 1990 (PL 101-508). Adopted 57-41: R 8-34; D 49-7 (ND 35-5, SD 14-2), May 22, 1991.

76. S 3. Campaign Finance/Eliminate Public Financing. Boren, D-Okla., motion to table (kill) the Nickles, R-Okla., amendment to the Boren substitute amendment, to eliminate all public financing for Senate campaigns but leave the voluntary spending limits in the bill. Motion agreed to 55-43: R 0-42; D 55-1 (ND 40-0, SD 15-1), May 22, 1991.

77. S 3. Campaign Finance/Free Television Time. Boren, D-Okla., motion to table (kill) the Roth, R-Del., amendment to the Boren substitute amendment, to strike all public funding and spending limits and establish free television time for Senate candidates in the last 45 days of a campaign. Motion agreed to 79-19: R 23-19; D 56-0 (ND 40-0, SD 16-0), May 23, 1991.

78. S 3. Campaign Finance/Eliminate Broadcast Subsidy. Boren, D-Okla., motion to table (kill) the Nickles, R-Okla., amendment to the Boren substitute amendment, to eliminate the 50 percent subsidy to candidates from the broadcast industry. Motion agreed to 54-44: R 5-37; D 49-7 (ND 34-6, SD 15-1), May 23, 1991.

79. S 3. Campaign Finance/Union Disclosure. Mitchell, D-Maine motion to table (kill) the Hatch, R-Utah, amendment to the Boren substitute amendment, to require labor unions to file a written report disclosing the amount and for what purpose union dues or fees were spent on direct or indirect political activities. Motion agreed to 57-41: R 3-39; D 54-2 (ND 39-1, SD 15-1), May 23, 1991.

80. S 3. Campaign Finance/Matching Funds. Boren, D-Okla., motion to table (kill) the Dole, R-Kan., amendment to the Boren substitute amendment, to allow political party committees to give challengers "seed money" in the early stages of their campaigns against incumbents. The party matching funds would be limited to $150,000 for House challengers and $250,000 for Senate challengers. Motion agreed to 57-40: R 2-40; D 55-0 (ND 39-0, SD 16-0), May 23, 1991.

	81	82	83	84	85	86	87	88
ALABAMA								
Heflin	Y	Y	Y	Y	Y	Y	Y	Y
Shelby	Y	Y	N	Y	N	Y	Y	Y
ALASKA								
Murkowski	N	N	N	N	N	N	Y	N
Stevens	N	N	N	N	N	N	Y	Y
ARIZONA								
DeConcini	Y	Y	Y	Y	Y	N	Y	Y
McCain	N	N	N	N	Y	N	Y	N
ARKANSAS								
Bumpers	Y	Y	Y	Y	Y	Y	Y	Y
Pryor	?	?	?	?	?	?	?	?
CALIFORNIA								
Cranston	?	Y	Y	Y	Y	X	Y	Y
Seymour	N	N	N	N	N	N	Y	N
COLORADO								
Wirth	Y	Y	Y	Y	Y	N	?	?
Brown	N	N	N	N	N	N	Y	N
CONNECTICUT								
Dodd	Y	Y	Y	Y	Y	Y	Y	Y
Lieberman	Y	Y	Y	Y	Y	N	Y	Y
DELAWARE								
Biden	Y	Y	Y	Y	Y	N	Y	Y
Roth	N	N	N	N	N	N	Y	N
FLORIDA								
Graham	Y	Y	Y	Y	Y	N	Y	Y
Mack	N	N	N	N	N	Y	Y	N
GEORGIA								
Fowler	Y	Y	Y	N	Y	#	Y	Y
Nunn	Y	Y	Y	Y	Y	N	Y	Y
HAWAII								
Akaka	Y	Y	Y	Y	Y	Y	Y	Y
Inouye	Y	Y	Y	Y	Y	Y	Y	Y
IDAHO								
Craig	N	N	N	N	N	N	Y	N
Symms	N	N	N	N	N	N	Y	N
ILLINOIS								
Dixon	Y	Y	Y	Y	Y	Y	Y	Y
Simon	Y	Y	Y	Y	Y	Y	N	Y
INDIANA								
Coats	N	N	N	N	N	N	Y	N
Lugar	N	N	N	N	N	N	Y	N
IOWA								
Harkin	Y	Y	Y	Y	Y	Y	Y	?
Grassley	N	N	N	N	N	N	Y	N
KANSAS								
Dole	N	N	N	N	N	N	Y	N
Kassebaum	N	N	N	N	N	N	Y	Y
KENTUCKY								
Ford	Y	Y	Y	Y	Y	Y	Y	Y
McConnell	N	N	N	N	N	N	Y	N
LOUISIANA								
Breaux	Y	Y	Y	Y	N	N	Y	Y
Johnston	Y	Y	Y	Y	N	Y	Y	Y
MAINE								
Mitchell	Y	Y	Y	Y	Y	N	Y	Y
Cohen	N	N	N	N	Y	Y	Y	Y
MARYLAND								
Mikulski	Y	Y	Y	Y	Y	Y	Y	Y
Sarbanes	Y	Y	Y	Y	Y	Y	Y	Y
MASSACHUSETTS								
Kennedy	Y	Y	Y	Y	Y	N	Y	Y
Kerry	Y	Y	Y	Y	Y	N	Y	Y
MICHIGAN								
Levin	Y	Y	Y	Y	Y	Y	Y	Y
Riegle	Y	Y	Y	Y	Y	Y	Y	Y
MINNESOTA								
Wellstone	Y	Y	Y	Y	Y	Y	N	Y
Durenberger	N	N	N	N	Y	N	Y	N
MISSISSIPPI								
Cochran	N	N	N	N	N	N	Y	N
Lott	N	N	N	N	N	X	Y	Y
MISSOURI								
Bond	N	N	N	N	N	N	Y	N
Danforth	N	N	N	N	N	N	Y	Y
MONTANA								
Baucus	Y	Y	Y	Y	Y	N	Y	Y
Burns	N	N	N	N	N	N	Y	Y
NEBRASKA								
Exon	Y	N	Y	Y	Y	Y	Y	Y
Kerrey	Y	N	Y	Y	Y	N	Y	N
NEVADA								
Bryan	Y	N	Y	Y	Y	N	Y	Y
Reid	Y	Y	Y	Y	Y	Y	Y	Y
NEW HAMPSHIRE								
Rudman	N	N	N	N	N	N	Y	N
Smith	N	N	N	N	N	N	Y	N
NEW JERSEY								
Bradley	Y	Y	Y	Y	Y	N	Y	N
Lautenberg	Y	Y	Y	Y	Y	N	Y	Y
NEW MEXICO								
Bingaman	Y	Y	Y	Y	Y	N	N	Y
Domenici	N	N	N	N	N	N	Y	N
NEW YORK								
Moynihan	Y	Y	Y	Y	Y	Y	Y	Y
D'Amato	N	N	N	N	N	N	Y	N
NORTH CAROLINA								
Sanford	Y	Y	Y	Y	Y	Y	Y	Y
Helms	?	?	?	?	?	#	Y	Y
NORTH DAKOTA								
Burdick	Y	Y	Y	Y	N	Y	Y	Y
Conrad	Y	Y	N	Y	Y	Y	Y	Y
OHIO								
Glenn	Y	Y	Y	Y	Y	Y	Y	Y
Metzenbaum	Y	Y	Y	Y	Y	Y	Y	Y
OKLAHOMA								
Boren	Y	Y	Y	Y	Y	N	Y	Y
Nickles	N	N	N	N	N	N	Y	N
OREGON								
Hatfield	Y	N	N	N	N	N	Y	N
Packwood	N	N	N	N	N	N	Y	N
PENNSYLVANIA								
Wofford	Y	Y	Y	Y	Y	Y	Y	Y
Specter	N	N	N	N	N	Y	Y	Y
RHODE ISLAND								
Pell	Y	Y	Y	Y	Y	N	N	Y
Chafee	N	N	N	N	N	N	N	?
SOUTH CAROLINA								
Hollings	Y	Y	N	N	N	Y	Y	Y
Thurmond	N	N	N	N	N	Y	Y	Y
SOUTH DAKOTA								
Daschle	Y	Y	Y	Y	Y	Y	Y	Y
Pressler	N	N	N	N	Y	N	Y	N
TENNESSEE								
Gore	Y	Y	Y	Y	Y	N	Y	Y
Sasser	Y	Y	Y	Y	Y	Y	Y	Y
TEXAS								
Bentsen	Y	Y	Y	Y	Y	N	Y	Y
Gramm	N	N	N	N	N	N	Y	N
UTAH								
Garn	N	N	N	N	N	N	Y	N
Hatch	N	N	N	N	N	N	Y	N
VERMONT								
Leahy	Y	Y	Y	Y	Y	Y	Y	Y
Jeffords	N	N	N	N	Y	Y	N	Y
VIRGINIA								
Robb	Y	Y	Y	Y	Y	N	Y	Y
Warner	N	N	N	N	N	N	Y	N
WASHINGTON								
Adams	Y	Y	Y	Y	Y	Y	Y	Y
Gorton	N	N	N	N	N	N	Y	Y
WEST VIRGINIA								
Byrd	Y	Y	Y	Y	Y	Y	Y	Y
Rockefeller	Y	Y	Y	Y	Y	N	Y	Y
WISCONSIN								
Kohl	Y	Y	Y	Y	Y	N	Y	Y
Kasten	N	N	N	N	N	N	Y	Y
WYOMING								
Simpson	N	N	N	N	N	N	Y	N
Wallop	N	N	N	N	N	N	Y	N

KEY

- Y Voted for (yea).
- # Paired for.
- + Announced for.
- N Voted against (nay).
- X Paired against.
- - Announced against.
- P Voted "present."
- C Voted "present" to avoid possible conflict of interest.
- ? Did not vote or otherwise make a position known.

Democrats *Republicans*

ND Northern Democrats SD Southern Democrats

Southern states - Ala., Ark., Fla., Ga., Ky., La., Miss., N.C., Okla., S.C., Tenn., Texas, Va.

81. S 3. Campaign Finance/Tax-Exempt Status. Boren, D-Okla., motion to table (kill) the McConnell, R-Ky., amendment to the Boren substitute amendment, to deny tax-exempt status to organizations participating in campaigns. Motion agreed to 56-41: R 1-41; D 55-0 (ND 39-0, SD 16-0), May 23, 1991.

82. S 3. Campaign Finance/Party Conventions. Boren, D-Okla., motion to table (kill) the McConnell, R-Ky., amendment to the Boren substitute amendment, to repeal public financing of party conventions. Motion agreed to 53-45: R 0-42; D 53-3 (ND 37-3, SD 16-0), May 23, 1991.

83. S 3. Campaign Finance/Public Financing. Boren, D-Okla., motion to table (kill) the McConnell, R-Ky., amendment to the Boren substitute amendment, to prohibit public financing of Senate campaigns until the Federal budget is balanced. Motion agreed to 53-45: R 0-42; D 53-3 (ND 39-1, SD 14-2), May 23, 1991.

84. S 3. Campaign Finance/Disclosure Reports. Boren, D-Okla., motion to table (kill) the Gramm, R-Texas, amendment to the Boren substitute amendment, to require organizations that intend to make an expenditure of $5,000 or more on political activities, to file a written report disclosing the intended expenditure at least 10 days in advance. Motion agreed to 54-44: R 0-42; D 54-2 (ND 40-0, SD 14-2), May 23, 1991.

85. S 3. Campaign Finance/Passage. Passage of the bill to revise federal laws governing the financing of federal campaigns by providing for a voluntary system of spending limits for elections that gives candidates public subsidies as an incentive to participate. Motion agreed to 56-42: R 5-37; D 51-5 (ND 39-1, SD 12-4), May 23, 1991. A "nay" was a vote supporting the president's position.

86. S Res 78. Disapproval of Fast-Track Procedures/Adoption. Adoption of the resolution to disapprove the president's request to extend for two years fast-track procedures that would require legislation implementing trade agreements to be considered within 60 days of introduction under limited debate and with no amendments permitted. Rejected 36-59: R 5-36; D 31-23 (ND 23-16, SD 8-7), May 24, 1991. A "nay" was a vote supporting the president's position.

87. S 173. Telecommunications Equipment Manufacturing Competition Act/Desert Storm Parade Representation. D'Amato, R-N.Y., amendment to express the sense of the Senate that any country that has repeatedly provided support for international acts of terrorism should not be represented in any form at the Desert Storm victory parade to be held in Washington, D.C., on June 8, 1991. The amendment was directed at opposing any Syrian presence in the parade. Adopted 92-6: R 41-2; D 51-4 (ND 35-4, SD 16-0), June 5, 1991.

88. S 173. Telecommunications Equipment Manufacturing Competition Act/Remove Domestic Content. Hollings, D-S.C., motion to table (kill) the Gramm, R-Texas, amendment to remove the domestic content and local manufacturing requirements in the bill. Motion agreed to 64-32: R 12-30; D 52-2 (ND 36-2, SD 16-0), June 5, 1991. A "nay" was a vote supporting the president's position.

	89	90	91	92	93	94	95	96
ALABAMA								
Heflin	Y	Y	N	N	N	N	Y	Y
Shelby	Y	Y	N	N	N	N	Y	Y
ALASKA								
Murkowski	Y	Y	N	N	Y	Y	Y	N
Stevens	Y	Y	N	Y	Y	Y	Y	N
ARIZONA								
DeConcini	Y	Y	N	Y	N	N	?	?
McCain	Y	N	N	N	Y	N	Y	Y
ARKANSAS								
Bumpers	Y	Y	N	N	Y	N	Y	Y
Pryor	?	?	?	?	?	?	?	?
CALIFORNIA								
Cranston	N	Y	Y	N	N	Y	Y	N
Seymour	N	N	N	N	Y	N	Y	Y
COLORADO								
Wirth	?	N	Y	N	N	N	Y	N
Brown	Y	Y	N	N	Y	N	Y	N
CONNECTICUT								
Dodd	N	N	Y	N	N	Y	Y	N
Lieberman	N	N	Y	Y	Y	Y	Y	N
DELAWARE								
Biden	N	N	Y	N	Y	Y	Y	N
Roth	Y	N	N	N	Y	Y	N	N
FLORIDA								
Graham	Y	N	Y	N	Y	N	N	Y
Mack	Y	Y	N	Y	Y	N	N	Y
GEORGIA								
Fowler	Y	Y	N	N	N	N	Y	Y
Nunn	Y	Y	N	N	N	Y	Y	Y
HAWAII								
Akaka	N	N	Y	N	N	N	Y	N
Inouye	N	Y	Y	N	Y	N	Y	N
IDAHO								
Craig	Y	Y	N	Y	Y	Y	Y	N
Symms	Y	Y	N	Y	Y	Y	Y	N
ILLINOIS								
Dixon	N	Y	N	N	N	N	N	Y
Simon	N	Y	Y	N	N	Y	N	Y
INDIANA								
Coats	Y	Y	N	Y	Y	Y	Y	Y
Lugar	Y	Y	N	N	Y	Y	Y	Y
IOWA								
Harkin	?	N	Y	Y	Y	Y	Y	N
Grassley	Y	Y	N	Y	Y	Y	Y	N
KANSAS								
Dole	N	Y	N	N	Y	N	Y	N
Kassebaum	Y	Y	N	N	Y	Y	Y	N
KENTUCKY								
Ford	Y	Y	N	N	N	N	Y	Y
McConnell	Y	N	N	N	Y	Y	Y	Y
LOUISIANA								
Breaux	Y	Y	N	N	N	Y	Y	Y
Johnston	Y	Y	N	N	N	Y	Y	Y
MAINE								
Mitchell	Y	N	Y	N	Y	Y	Y	N
Cohen	Y	N	Y	Y	Y	Y	Y	N
MARYLAND								
Mikulski	Y	Y	Y	N	Y	Y	Y	N
Sarbanes	Y	N	Y	N	Y	Y	Y	N
MASSACHUSETTS								
Kennedy	+	N	Y	N	Y	Y	Y	N
Kerry	Y	N	Y	N	Y	Y	Y	N
MICHIGAN								
Levin	Y	Y	Y	Y	N	Y	Y	Y
Riegle	Y	Y	Y	Y	N	N	Y	Y
MINNESOTA								
Wellstone	Y	Y	Y	N	Y	Y	Y	N
Durenberger	Y	N	N	-	Y	Y	Y	N
MISSISSIPPI								
Cochran	Y	Y	N	Y	Y	Y	Y	Y
Lott	Y	Y	N	Y	Y	Y	Y	Y
MISSOURI								
Bond	N	Y	N	N	Y	N	Y	Y
Danforth	Y	N	Y	N	Y	Y	Y	Y
MONTANA								
Baucus	Y	N	Y	N	Y	Y	Y	N
Burns	Y	Y	N	N	Y	Y	Y	N
NEBRASKA								
Exon	Y	Y	N	N	Y	N	Y	N
Kerrey	Y	N	Y	N	Y	N	Y	N
NEVADA								
Bryan	Y	Y	Y	Y	Y	N	Y	N
Reid	Y	Y	Y	Y	Y	N	Y	N
NEW HAMPSHIRE								
Rudman	Y	N	Y	N	Y	Y	N	N
Smith	Y	N	N	N	Y	Y	N	N
NEW JERSEY								
Bradley	N	N	Y	N	Y	Y	Y	N
Lautenberg	N	N	Y	N	Y	Y	Y	N
NEW MEXICO								
Bingaman	Y	Y	Y	N	Y	N	Y	N
Domenici	Y	Y	N	N	Y	N	Y	N
NEW YORK								
Moynihan	N	N	Y	Y	Y	Y	Y	N
D'Amato	Y	Y	N	Y	Y	Y	Y	N
NORTH CAROLINA								
Sanford	Y	Y	Y	N	Y	N	Y	Y
Helms	Y	Y	N	N	Y	Y	Y	Y
NORTH DAKOTA								
Burdick	Y	Y	N	N	Y	Y	Y	N
Conrad	Y	Y	N	Y	N	Y	Y	N
OHIO								
Glenn	N	N	Y	N	N	N	Y	Y
Metzenbaum	N	N	Y	N	N	Y	Y	Y
OKLAHOMA								
Boren	Y	Y	N	Y	N	N	Y	Y
Nickles	N	Y	N	Y	Y	Y	Y	Y
OREGON								
Hatfield	N	N	N	N	Y	N	Y	Y
Packwood	Y	Y	N	N	Y	N	Y	Y
PENNSYLVANIA								
Wofford	N	N	Y	Y	N	Y	Y	N
Specter	N	Y	N	Y	Y	Y	Y	N
RHODE ISLAND								
Pell	Y	N	Y	N	Y	Y	Y	N
Chafee	?	N	Y	N	Y	Y	N	N
SOUTH CAROLINA								
Hollings	Y	N	N	Y	N	Y	Y	Y
Thurmond	Y	Y	N	N	Y	Y	Y	Y
SOUTH DAKOTA								
Daschle	Y	Y	N	Y	Y	N	Y	N
Pressler	N	Y	N	Y	Y	N	Y	N
TENNESSEE								
Gore	Y	Y	Y	N	Y	N	Y	Y
Sasser	N	Y	Y	N	N	N	Y	Y
TEXAS								
Bentsen	Y	N	N	N	N	Y	Y	Y
Gramm	N	Y	N	N	Y	Y	Y	Y
UTAH								
Garn	Y	Y	N	N	Y	Y	Y	N
Hatch	Y	Y	N	N	Y	Y	Y	N
VERMONT								
Leahy	Y	N	Y	Y	Y	Y	Y	N
Jeffords	Y	N	N	Y	Y	Y	N	N
VIRGINIA								
Robb	Y	N	Y	N	N	N	Y	Y
Warner	Y	N	N	N	Y	N	Y	Y
WASHINGTON								
Adams	Y	Y	Y	N	Y	Y	Y	N
Gorton	Y	N	N	N	Y	Y	Y	N
WEST VIRGINIA								
Byrd	Y	Y	Y	N	Y	Y	Y	N
Rockefeller	Y	N	Y	N	Y	Y	Y	N
WISCONSIN								
Kohl	Y	Y	Y	N	N	Y	Y	Y
Kasten	Y	Y	Y	Y	Y	Y	Y	Y
WYOMING								
Simpson	Y	Y	N	N	Y	N	Y	N
Wallop	N	Y	N	N	+	+	Y	N

KEY

- Y Voted for (yea).
- # Paired for.
- + Announced for.
- N Voted against (nay).
- X Paired against.
- \- Announced against.
- P Voted "present."
- C Voted "present" to avoid possible conflict of interest.
- ? Did not vote or otherwise make a position known.

Democrats ***Republicans***

ND Northern Democrats SD Southern Democrats

Southern states - Ala., Ark., Fla., Ga., Ky., La., Miss., N.C., Okla., S.C., Tenn., Texas, Va.

89. S 173. Telecommunications Equipment Manufacturing Competition Act/Passage. Passage of the bill to allow the seven regional Bell telephone operating companies to engage in the design, research and manufacture of telecommunications equipment. Passed 71-24: R 33-9; D 38-15 (ND 23-14, SD 15-1), June 5, 1991. A "nay" was a vote supporting the president's position.

90. S 1204. Surface Transportation Reauthorization/Billboards. Reid, D-Nev., amendment to strike the section of the bill that would place a moratorium on all new billboards along federally subsidized highways and allow states to remove existing billboards from private property without giving cash compensation to the owners of such property. Adopted 60-39: R 29-14; D 31-25 (ND 19-21, SD 12-4), June 12, 1991.

91. S 1204. Surface Transportation Reauthorization/Private Property. Mitchell, D-Maine, motion to table (kill) the Symms, R-Idaho, amendment to ensure that no agency regulations would take effect until they were certified by the attorney general to be in compliance with procedures that assess the impact and attempt to minimize the taking of private property in the course of federal regulatory activity. Rejected 44-55: R 5-38; D 39-17 (ND 34-6, SD 5-11), June 12, 1991. (Subsequently, the Symms amendment was adopted by voice vote.)

92. S 1204. Surface Transportation Reauthorization/Budget Act Waiver. Specter, R-Pa., motion to waive the 1974 budget act with respect to the Sasser, D-Tenn., point of order, which stated that the Specter amendment to take the Highway Trust Fund off-budget would violate Section 306 of the budget act. Motion rejected 29-69: R 15-27; D 14-42 (ND 12-28, SD 2-14), June 12, 1991. A three-fifths majority (60) of the total Senate is required to waive the budget act. (The Specter amendment subsequently fell on the Sasser point of order.)

93. S 1204. Surface Transportation Reauthorization/Highway Numbering. Moynihan, D-N.Y., motion to table (kill) the Dixon, D-Ill., amendment to give the secretary of Transportation the authority to establish a commission to number interstate highways when bordering states fail to agree to the number designation of an interstate highway. Motion agreed to 72-26: R 42-0; D 30-26 (ND 26-14, SD 4-12), June 13, 1991.

94. S 1204. Surface Transportation Reauthorization/Interstate Maintenance Funds. Moynihan, D-N.Y., motion to table (kill) the Reid, D-Nev., amendment to give states discretion to use interstate maintenance funds for the construction of additional lanes on interstates to lower concentrations of air pollution to levels required by the Clean Air Act. Motion agreed to 62-36: R 30-12; D 32-24 (ND 27-13, 5-11), June 13, 1991.

95. S 1204. Surface Transportation Reauthorization/Fund Accounts. Byrd, D-W.Va., amendment to the Byrd amendment, to take the $8.2 billion that the budget resolution shifted to transportation programs from other domestic programs over 5 years and divide the money into two equal accounts. Adopted 89-9: R 37-6; D 52-3 (ND 37-2, SD 15-1), June 18, 1991.

96. S 1204. Surface Transportation Reauthorization/Minimum Allocation Formula. Graham, D-Fla., amendment to increase the minimum allocation from the Highway Trust Fund to 90 percent of what a state pays into the fund and establish a new minimum allocation formula based on the number of lane miles, diesel fuel consumption, and vehicle miles traveled in rural and urban areas. Rejected 41-57: R 18-25; D 23-32 (ND 7-32, SD 16-0), June 18, 1991. A "yea" was a vote supporting the president's position.

	97	98	99	100	101	102	103	104
ALABAMA								
Heflin	N	Y	N	N	N	Y	N	Y
Shelby	N	Y	N	N	Y	Y	Y	Y
ALASKA								
Murkowski	Y	N	Y	Y	Y	Y	Y	Y
Stevens	Y	N	Y	Y	Y	Y	Y	Y
ARIZONA								
DeConcini	?	?	?	?	?	+	-	Y
McCain	N	N	Y	Y	Y	Y	Y	Y
ARKANSAS								
Bumpers	N	Y	Y	N	Y	Y	N	N
Pryor	?	?	?	?	?	?	?	?
CALIFORNIA								
Cranston	Y	N	Y	Y	Y	N	N	N
Seymour	N	N	Y	N	Y	Y	Y	Y
COLORADO								
Wirth	Y	N	Y	Y	Y	N	N	N
Brown	Y	N	Y	Y	Y	Y	Y	Y
CONNECTICUT								
Dodd	Y	Y	Y	Y	Y	N	N	N
Lieberman	Y	Y	Y	Y	Y	Y	N	Y
DELAWARE								
Biden	Y	N	Y	Y	Y	N	N	N
Roth	Y	N	Y	Y	N	Y	Y	Y
FLORIDA								
Graham	N	N	N	N	N	Y	N	N
Mack	N	N	N	N	N	Y	Y	Y
GEORGIA								
Fowler	Y	N	N	N	Y	Y	N	N
Nunn	?	N	N	N	Y	Y	N	N
HAWAII								
Akaka	Y	N	Y	Y	Y	N	N	N
Inouye	Y	Y	Y	Y	Y	N	N	N
IDAHO								
Craig	Y	Y	Y	Y	Y	Y	Y	Y
Symms	Y	Y	Y	Y	Y	Y	Y	Y
ILLINOIS								
Dixon	Y	Y	Y	Y	Y	Y	N	Y
Simon	Y	Y	Y	Y	Y	N	N	N
INDIANA								
Coats	N	Y	Y	N	Y	Y	Y	Y
Lugar	N	Y	Y	N	Y	Y	Y	Y
IOWA								
Harkin	Y	Y	Y	Y	Y	N	N	N
Grassley	N	Y	Y	Y	Y	Y	Y	Y
KANSAS								
Dole	N	N	Y	Y	Y	Y	Y	Y
Kassebaum	N	Y	Y	Y	Y	Y	Y	Y
KENTUCKY								
Ford	N	Y	Y	N	Y	Y	N	Y
McConnell	N	Y	Y	N	Y	Y	Y	Y
LOUISIANA								
Breaux	N	Y	Y	Y	Y	Y	N	Y
Johnston	N	Y	Y	Y	Y	Y	N	Y
MAINE								
Mitchell	Y	N	Y	Y	Y	N	N	N
Cohen	N	Y	Y	N	Y	N	Y	N
MARYLAND								
Mikulski	Y	Y	Y	Y	Y	N	N	N
Sarbanes	Y	N	Y	Y	Y	N	N	N
MASSACHUSETTS								
Kennedy	Y	Y	Y	Y	Y	N	N	N
Kerry	Y	Y	Y	Y	Y	N	N	N
MICHIGAN								
Levin	N	Y	Y	Y	Y	N	N	N
Riegle	N	Y	Y	Y	Y	N	N	N
MINNESOTA								
Wellstone	Y	Y	Y	Y	Y	?	?	N
Durenberger	Y	Y	Y	Y	Y	N	N	N
MISSISSIPPI								
Cochran	N	N	Y	Y	Y	Y	Y	Y
Lott	N	N	Y	Y	Y	Y	Y	Y
MISSOURI								
Bond	N	Y	Y	N	N	Y	Y	Y
Danforth	N	Y	Y	N	Y	N	Y	Y
MONTANA								
Baucus	Y	Y	Y	Y	Y	Y	N	N
Burns	N	Y	Y	Y	Y	Y	Y	Y
NEBRASKA								
Exon	Y	Y	Y	Y	Y	Y	N	Y
Kerrey	Y	Y	Y	Y	Y	N	N	N
NEVADA								
Bryan	N	N	Y	N	Y	Y	N	N
Reid	Y	N	Y	N	Y	N	N	Y
NEW HAMPSHIRE								
Rudman	Y	N	Y	Y	Y	Y	N	N
Smith	Y	N	Y	Y	Y	Y	Y	?
NEW JERSEY								
Bradley	Y	Y	Y	Y	Y	N	N	N
Lautenberg	Y	Y	Y	Y	Y	N	N	N
NEW MEXICO								
Bingaman	N	N	Y	N	Y	Y	N	N
Domenici	Y	Y	Y	Y	Y	Y	Y	Y
NEW YORK								
Moynihan	Y	Y	Y	Y	Y	N	N	N
D'Amato	Y	Y	Y	Y	Y	Y	Y	Y
NORTH CAROLINA								
Sanford	Y	N	N	N	Y	N	N	N
Helms	N	N	N	N	Y	Y	Y	Y
NORTH DAKOTA								
Burdick	Y	Y	Y	Y	Y	N	N	N
Conrad	N	Y	Y	Y	Y	N	N	N
OHIO								
Glenn	N	Y	N	Y	Y	N	N	N
Metzenbaum	N	Y	N	Y	Y	N	N	N
OKLAHOMA								
Boren	N	Y	Y	Y	Y	N	N	N
Nickles	Y	Y	N	Y	Y	Y	Y	Y
OREGON								
Hatfield	N	Y	Y	Y	Y	N	Y	N
Packwood	N	Y	Y	N	Y	N	Y	N
PENNSYLVANIA								
Wofford	N	Y	Y	Y	Y	Y	N	N
Specter	N	Y	Y	Y	Y	Y	Y	N
RHODE ISLAND								
Pell	Y	Y	Y	Y	Y	N	N	N
Chafee	Y	Y	Y	Y	Y	N	N	N
SOUTH CAROLINA								
Hollings	N	N	N	N	Y	Y	Y	Y
Thurmond	N	N	N	N	Y	Y	Y	Y
SOUTH DAKOTA								
Daschle	N	Y	Y	Y	Y	N	N	N
Pressler	Y	Y	Y	Y	Y	Y	Y	Y
TENNESSEE								
Gore	N	Y	Y	Y	Y	N	N	N
Sasser	N	Y	Y	Y	Y	N	N	N
TEXAS								
Bentsen	Y	N	Y	Y	Y	Y	N	N
Gramm	Y	N	N	Y	Y	Y	Y	Y
UTAH								
Garn	Y	N	Y	Y	Y	Y	Y	?
Hatch	N	N	Y	Y	Y	Y	Y	Y
VERMONT								
Leahy	Y	Y	Y	Y	Y	N	N	N
Jeffords	Y	Y	Y	Y	Y	N	N	N
VIRGINIA								
Robb	N	N	N	N	Y	Y	N	N
Warner	N	N	Y	N	Y	Y	Y	Y
WASHINGTON								
Adams	Y	Y	Y	Y	Y	N	N	N
Gorton	Y	N	Y	Y	Y	Y	Y	N
WEST VIRGINIA								
Byrd	Y	Y	Y	Y	Y	Y	N	N
Rockefeller	Y	Y	Y	Y	Y	N	N	N
WISCONSIN								
Kohl	Y	Y	N	Y	N	N	N	N
Kasten	N	Y	N	N	N	Y	Y	Y
WYOMING								
Simpson	Y	Y	Y	Y	Y	+	+	Y
Wallop	Y	Y	Y	Y	Y	Y	Y	Y

KEY

- Y Voted for (yea).
- # Paired for.
- + Announced for.
- N Voted against (nay).
- X Paired against.
- - Announced against.
- P Voted "present."
- C Voted "present" to avoid possible conflict of interest.
- ? Did not vote or otherwise make a position known.

Democrats *Republicans*

ND Northern Democrats SD Southern Democrats

Southern states - Ala., Ark., Fla., Ga., Ky., La., Miss., N.C., Okla., S.C., Tenn., Texas, Va.

97. S 1204. Surface Transportation Reauthorization/Interstate Maintenance. Moynihan, D-N.Y., motion to table (kill) the Lott, R-Miss., amendment to retain the current 90 percent federal share for Interstate maintenance and 80 percent for bridge projects. Motion agreed to 53-44: R 20-23; D 33-21 (ND 30-9, SD 3-12), June 19, 1991.

98. S 1204. Surface Transportation Reauthorization/Use of Census Data. Symms, R-Idaho, motion to table (kill) the Mack, R-Fla., amendment to require the use of 1990 census data as part of the formula to calculate the apportionment of funds to states. Motion agreed to 63-35: R 24-19; D 39-16 (ND 30-9, SD 9-7), June 19, 1991.

99. S 1204. Surface Transportation Reauthorization/Highway Trust Fund. Moynihan, D-N.Y., motion to table (kill) the Graham, D-Fla., amendment to ensure that states receive minimum payments from the surpluses in the Highway Trust Fund. Motion agreed to 81-17: R 37-6; D 44-11 (ND 36-3, SD 8-8), June 19, 1991.

100. S 1204. Surface Transportation Reauthorization/Maintenance Funds. Moynihan, D-N.Y., motion to table (kill) the Graham, D-Fla., amendment to allow maintenance funds to be used for capacity enhancement programs on the Interstate Highway System at an 80-20 federal/state ratio rather than the 75-25 ratio in the bill. Motion agreed to 72-26: R 30-13; D 42-13 (ND 36-3, SD 6-10), June 19, 1991.

101. S 1204. Surface Transportation Reauthorization/Passage. Passage of the bill to authorize $123 billion over the next five years for the nation's surface transportation programs. The bill would give states more flexibility to decide how their federal transportation dollars are spent by allocating $37.2 billion to spend as they see fit. The bill also would require states to spend 17.5 percent of their surface transportation funds on a national highway system. Passed 91-7: R 39-4; D 52-3 (ND 38-1, SD 14-2), June 19, 1991.

102. S 1241. Crime Bill/Minority Discrimination. Mitchell, D-Maine, for Graham, D-Fla., amendment to strike the provisions that would allow minorities to challenge a death sentence as discriminatory if statistics show a disproportionate number of their race being condemned to die. Adopted 55-41: R 35-7; D 20-34 (ND 8-30, SD 12-4), June 20, 1991. A "yea" was a vote supporting the president's position.

103. S 1241. Crime Bill/ Substitute President's Crime Bill. Thurmond, R-S.C., amendment to substitute the president's crime bill. The amendment would allow the death penalty for more than 40 crimes, including the operation of a major drug enterprise; expand consideration of aggravating factors in imposing the death penalty; significantly cut back on habeas corpus petitions; extend the "good faith" exception to warrantless searches; and remove the provision to require a background check over seven days before someone could purchase a handgun. Rejected 40-56: R 38-4; D 2-52 (ND 0-38, SD 2-14), June 20, 1991. A "yea" was a vote supporting the president's position.

104. S 1241. Crime Bill/Search and Seizure. Thurmond, R-S.C., amendment to codify the "good faith" exception to the exclusionary rule that allows evidence seized without a warrant but under an objectively reasonable belief that the search was in conformity with the Fourth Amendment to be used against a defendant. Rejected 43-54: R 32-9; D 11-45 (ND 5-35, SD 6-10), June 25, 1991. A "yea" was a vote supporting the president's position.

	105	106	107	108	109	110	111	112
ALABAMA								
Heflin	N	N	N	Y	N	Y	Y	N
Shelby	Y	N	N	Y	Y	Y	Y	Y
ALASKA								
Murkowski	N	N	N	Y	Y	N	Y	Y
Stevens	N	N	N	Y	Y	N	Y	Y
ARIZONA								
DeConcini	N	N	N	Y	Y	Y	Y	Y
McCain	N	N	N	Y	Y	Y	Y	Y
ARKANSAS								
Bumpers	N	N	N	Y	Y	Y	N	Y
Pryor	?	?	?	?	?	?	?	?
CALIFORNIA								
Cranston	N	Y	Y	N	N	Y	N	N
Seymour	Y	N	N	Y	Y	N	Y	Y
COLORADO								
Wirth	N	N	N	N	Y	Y	N	Y
Brown	Y	N	N	Y	Y	N	Y	Y
CONNECTICUT								
Dodd	N	N	N	N	Y	Y	N	Y
Lieberman	N	N	N	Y	Y	Y	N	Y
DELAWARE								
Biden	N	Y	N	N	N	Y	N	Y
Roth	Y	N	N	Y	Y	Y	Y	Y
FLORIDA								
Graham	N	N	N	N	Y	Y	N	Y
Mack	N	N	N	Y	Y	N	Y	Y
GEORGIA								
Fowler	N	N	Y	Y	Y	Y	N	Y
Nunn	N	N	N	Y	Y	Y	Y	Y
HAWAII								
Akaka	N	Y	Y	N	N	Y	N	Y
Inouye	N	Y	Y	N	N	Y	N	Y
IDAHO								
Craig	Y	N	N	Y	Y	N	Y	Y
Symms	Y	N	N	Y	Y	N	Y	Y
ILLINOIS								
Dixon	N	N	N	Y	Y	Y	Y	Y
Simon	N	Y	Y	N	N	Y	N	N
INDIANA								
Coats	Y	N	N	Y	Y	N	Y	Y
Lugar	Y	N	N	Y	Y	N	Y	Y
IOWA								
Harkin	N	Y	Y	N	N	Y	N	Y
Grassley	Y	N	N	Y	Y	N	Y	Y
KANSAS								
Dole	Y	N	N	Y	Y	N	Y	Y
Kassebaum	N	N	N	Y	Y	Y	Y	Y
KENTUCKY								
Ford	N	N	N	Y	Y	Y	Y	Y
McConnell	Y	N	N	Y	Y	N	Y	Y
LOUISIANA								
Breaux	N	N	N	Y	Y	Y	Y	Y
Johnston	N	N	N	Y	Y	Y	Y	Y
MAINE								
Mitchell	N	Y	Y	N	N	Y	N	Y
Cohen	N	Y	Y	Y	N	Y	N	N
MARYLAND								
Mikulski	N	Y	N	N	Y	Y	N	Y
Sarbanes	N	Y	Y	N	N	Y	N	Y
MASSACHUSETTS								
Kennedy	N	Y	Y	N	N	Y	N	Y
Kerry	N	Y	Y	N	N	Y	N	Y
MICHIGAN								
Levin	N	Y	Y	N	N	Y	N	Y
Riegle	N	N	N	N	Y	Y	Y	Y
MINNESOTA								
Wellstone	N	Y	Y	N	N	Y	N	Y
Durenberger	N	Y	Y	Y	N	Y	N	Y
MISSISSIPPI								
Cochran	N	N	N	Y	Y	N	Y	Y
Lott	Y	N	N	Y	Y	N	Y	Y
MISSOURI								
Bond	Y	N	N	Y	Y	Y	Y	N
Danforth	N	Y	Y	Y	N	Y	N	Y
MONTANA								
Baucus	Y	N	N	N	Y	Y	Y	Y
Burns	Y	N	N	Y	Y	N	Y	N
NEBRASKA								
Exon	N	N	N	N	Y	Y	Y	Y
Kerrey	N	N	N	N	Y	Y	Y	Y
NEVADA								
Bryan	N	N	N	N	Y	Y	Y	Y
Reid	N	N	N	Y	Y	Y	Y	Y
NEW HAMPSHIRE								
Rudman	Y	N	N	Y	N	Y	Y	N
Smith	Y	N	N	Y	Y	N	Y	Y
NEW JERSEY								
Bradley	N	N	N	N	Y	Y	Y	Y
Lautenberg	N	Y	Y	N	N	Y	N	Y
NEW MEXICO								
Bingaman	N	N	N	N	N	Y	N	N
Domenici	N	N	N	Y	Y	N	Y	Y
NEW YORK								
Moynihan	N	Y	Y	N	N	Y	N	Y
D'Amato	N	N	N	Y	Y	Y	Y	Y
NORTH CAROLINA								
Sanford	N	Y	N	N	Y	Y	N	Y
Helms	Y	N	N	Y	Y	N	Y	Y
NORTH DAKOTA								
Burdick	N	Y	Y	N	N	Y	N	Y
Conrad	N	N	N	N	N	Y	N	Y
OHIO								
Glenn	N	Y	Y	N	N	Y	N	Y
Metzenbaum	N	Y	Y	N	N	Y	N	N
OKLAHOMA								
Boren	N	N	N	Y	Y	Y	Y	Y
Nickles	Y	N	N	Y	Y	Y	Y	Y
OREGON								
Hatfield	N	Y	Y	Y	N	Y	N	Y
Packwood	N	N	N	Y	Y	Y	N	Y
PENNSYLVANIA								
Wofford	N	Y	N	N	Y	Y	Y	Y
Specter	Y	N	N	Y	Y	Y	Y	Y
RHODE ISLAND								
Pell	N	Y	Y	N	N	Y	N	Y
Chafee	N	Y	Y	Y	N	Y	N	Y
SOUTH CAROLINA								
Hollings	Y	N	N	Y	Y	N	Y	Y
Thurmond	Y	N	N	Y	Y	N	Y	Y
SOUTH DAKOTA								
Daschle	N	Y	N	N	Y	Y	Y	Y
Pressler	Y	N	N	Y	Y	N	Y	Y
TENNESSEE								
Gore	N	Y	N	N	N	Y	Y	Y
Sasser	N	Y	N	N	N	Y	Y	Y
TEXAS								
Bentsen	N	N	N	Y	Y	Y	N	Y
Gramm	Y	N	N	Y	Y	N	Y	Y
UTAH								
Garn	?	?	?	?	?	N	Y	Y
Hatch	Y	N	N	Y	Y	N	Y	Y
VERMONT								
Leahy	N	Y	Y	N	N	Y	N	Y
Jeffords	N	N	N	Y	N	Y	N	N
VIRGINIA								
Robb	N	N	N	N	Y	Y	Y	Y
Warner	Y	N	N	Y	Y	N	Y	Y
WASHINGTON								
Adams	N	N	N	N	Y	Y	N	Y
Gorton	Y	N	N	Y	N	Y	Y	N
WEST VIRGINIA								
Byrd	N	N	N	Y	Y	Y	Y	Y
Rockefeller	N	N	N	N	Y	Y	Y	Y
WISCONSIN								
Kohl	N	N	Y	N	N	Y	N	Y
Kasten	N	N	N	Y	Y	N	Y	Y
WYOMING								
Simpson	Y	N	N	Y	Y	N	Y	Y
Wallop	Y	N	N	Y	Y	N	Y	Y

ND Northern Democrats SD Southern Democrats

Southern states - Ala., Ark., Fla., Ga., Ky., La., Miss., N.C., Okla., S.C., Tenn., Texas, Va.

KEY

- Y Voted for (yea).
- # Paired for.
- + Announced for.
- N Voted against (nay).
- X Paired against.
- - Announced against.
- P Voted "present."
- C Voted "present" to avoid possible conflict of interest.
- ? Did not vote or otherwise make a position known.

Democrats *Republicans*

105. S 1241. Crime Bill/Indian Tribes. Thurmond, R-S.C., amendment to the Inouye, D-Hawaii, amendment, to limit the provisions in the Inouye amendment, which allow Indian tribes to choose whether to have the death penalty for crimes committed within their jurisdictions, to states in which there is no death penalty. Rejected 29-69: R 26-16; D 3-53 (ND 1-39, SD 2-14), June 25, 1991. (The Inouye amendment was subsequently adopted by voice vote.)

106. S 1241. Crime Bill/Drug Cases. Biden, D-Del., amendment to provide that the maximum penalty for drug cases shall be life in prison without release, unless there is an intentional killing, and then the maximum penalty shall be death. Rejected 30-68: R 5-37; D 25-31 (ND 22-18, SD 3-13), June 25, 1991. A "nay" was a vote supporting the president's position.

107. S 1241. Crime Bill/Replace Death Penalty. Simon, D-Ill., amendment to substitute where the bill would impose the death penalty a mandatory life imprisonment term without the possibility of release. Rejected 25-73: R 5-37; D 20-36 (ND 19-21, SD 1-15), June 25, 1991. A "nay" was a vote supporting the president's position.

108. S 1241. Crime Bill/Habeas Corpus. Hatch, R-Utah, amendment to the Mitchell, D-Maine, amendment for Graham, D-Fla., to limit the ability of death-row prisoners to file federal habeas corpus petitions by requiring prisoners to file petitions within six months of exhausting their state appeals, restricting the grounds for challenges to their sentences, and allowing federal courts to dismiss petitions if a court decides the prisoner has had a "full and fair hearing at the state level." Adopted 58-40: R 42-0; D 16-40 (ND 5-35, SD 11-5), June 26, 1991. (The Graham amendment as amended was subsequently adopted by voice vote.) A "yea" was a vote supporting the president's position.

109. S 1241. Crime Bill/Federal Death Penalty. D'Amato, R-N.Y., amendment to allow for federal jurisdiction to impose the death penalty for homicides committed with a gun if they were committed in the course of a federal crime or the firearm involved had been moved across state or national borders. Adopted 65-33: R 34-8; D 31-25 (ND 18-22, SD 13-3), June 26, 1991.

110. S 1241. Crime Bill/Preferential Treatment. Mitchell, D-Maine, motion to table (kill) the Helms, R-N.C., amendment to the Symms, R-Idaho, amendment, to prohibit federal agencies and courts from interpreting Title VII of the Civil Rights Act of 1964 to permit an employer to grant preferential treatment in employment to any group or individual on account of race, religion, sex or national origin. Motion agreed to 71-28: R 16-27; D 55-1 (ND 40-0, SD 15-1), June 26, 1991.

111. S 1241. Crime Bill/District of Columbia. Symms, R-Idaho, amendment to mandate a 20-year prison term and allow for the death penalty for drug-related homicides in the District of Columbia. Adopted 60-39: R 36-7; D 24-32 (ND 13-27, SD 11-5), June 26, 1991.

112. S 1241. Crime Bill/Prison Terms for Firearm Use. D'Amato, R-N.Y., amendment to provide for mandatory prison terms for the possession or use of a firearm during any drug-related or violent crime committed under state jurisdiction. Adopted 88-11: R 37-6; D 51-5 (ND 36-4, SD 15-1), June 27, 1991.

	113	114	115	116	117	118	119	120
ALABAMA								
Heflin	Y	N	N	Y	Y	N	Y	N
Shelby	Y	N	N	Y	N	N	Y	N
ALASKA								
Murkowski	Y	N	N	?	Y	Y	Y	N
Stevens	Y	N	N	N	Y	Y	Y	N
ARIZONA								
DeConcini	N	Y	N	Y	N	N	Y	Y
McCain	Y	N	N	N	Y	Y	Y	N
ARKANSAS								
Bumpers	N	Y	Y	?	Y	N	Y	Y
Pryor	?	?	?	?	?	?	?	?
CALIFORNIA								
Cranston	N	Y	Y	?	?	N	N	Y
Seymour	Y	N	Y	N	Y	Y	Y	N
COLORADO								
Wirth	N	Y	Y	Y	N	N	N	Y
Brown	Y	N	N	N	Y	Y	N	N
CONNECTICUT								
Dodd	N	Y	Y	Y	N	N	N	Y
Lieberman	N	Y	Y	Y	N	N	N	Y
DELAWARE								
Biden	N	Y	Y	Y	N	N	N	Y
Roth	N	N	Y	?	Y	Y	N	N
FLORIDA								
Graham	N	Y	Y	Y	Y	N	N	Y
Mack	Y	N	N	N	Y	Y	Y	N
GEORGIA								
Fowler	N	Y	Y	Y	Y	N	N	Y
Nunn	N	Y	Y	Y	Y	N	N	Y
HAWAII								
Akaka	N	Y	Y	Y	N	N	N	Y
Inouye	N	Y	Y	Y	N	N	?	Y
IDAHO								
Craig	Y	N	N	N	Y	Y	Y	N
Symms	Y	N	N	N	Y	Y	Y	N
ILLINOIS								
Dixon	N	Y	Y	Y	N	N	N	Y
Simon	N	Y	Y	Y	N	N	N	Y
INDIANA								
Coats	Y	N	Y	N	Y	Y	Y	N
Lugar	Y	N	Y	N	Y	Y	Y	N

	113	114	115	116	117	118	119	120
IOWA								
Harkin	N	Y	Y	?	?	N	N	Y
Grassley	Y	N	N	N	Y	Y	Y	N
KANSAS								
Dole	Y	N	Y	N	Y	Y	Y	Y
Kassebaum	N	N	Y	N	Y	Y	Y	Y
KENTUCKY								
Ford	N	N	Y	Y	Y	N	Y	Y
McConnell	Y	N	N	N	Y	N	Y	N
LOUISIANA								
Breaux	Y	N	N	Y	Y	N	Y	N
Johnston	Y	N	N	Y	N	N	Y	N
MAINE								
Mitchell	N	Y	Y	Y	Y	N	N	Y
Cohen	Y	N	Y	N	Y	Y	N	N
MARYLAND								
Mikulski	N	Y	Y	Y	N	N	N	Y
Sarbanes	N	Y	Y	Y	N	N	N	Y
MASSACHUSETTS								
Kennedy	N	Y	Y	Y	N	N	N	Y
Kerry	N	Y	Y	Y	N	N	N	Y
MICHIGAN								
Levin	N	N	Y	Y	N	N	N	Y
Riegle	N	Y	Y	Y	N	N	N	Y
MINNESOTA								
Wellstone	N	N	Y	Y	N	N	N	N
Durenberger	Y	Y	Y	N	Y	Y	Y	Y
MISSISSIPPI								
Cochran	Y	N	N	N	Y	Y	Y	N
Lott	Y	N	N	N	Y	Y	Y	N
MISSOURI								
Bond	Y	N	N	N	Y	Y	Y	N
Danforth	N	N	N	N	Y	Y	Y	N
MONTANA								
Baucus	Y	N	N	Y	N	N	N	N
Burns	Y	N	N	-	Y	Y	Y	N
NEBRASKA								
Exon	N	N	Y	Y	Y	N	N	Y
Kerrey	N	Y	Y	?	Y	N	N	Y
NEVADA								
Bryan	Y	N	Y	Y	Y	N	Y	Y
Reid	Y	N	Y	Y	N	N	Y	Y

	113	114	115	116	117	118	119	120
NEW HAMPSHIRE								
Rudman	Y	N	Y	N	Y	Y	Y	N
Smith	Y	N	N	N	Y	Y	Y	N
NEW JERSEY								
Bradley	N	Y	Y	Y	N	N	N	Y
Lautenberg	N	Y	Y	N	N	N	N	Y
NEW MEXICO								
Bingaman	N	N	Y	Y	N	N	Y	Y
Domenici	Y	N	Y	N	N	Y	Y	N
NEW YORK								
Moynihan	N	Y	Y	N	N	N	Y	Y
D'Amato	Y	N	Y	N	Y	Y	Y	N
NORTH CAROLINA								
Sanford	N	Y	Y	Y	N	N	N	Y
Helms	Y	N	N	N	Y	Y	Y	N
NORTH DAKOTA								
Burdick	N	Y	Y	+	-	N	Y	Y
Conrad	Y	N	Y	Y	N	N	Y	N
OHIO								
Glenn	N	Y	Y	Y	N	N	N	Y
Metzenbaum	N	N	Y	Y	N	N	N	Y
OKLAHOMA								
Boren	N	N	Y	Y	N	N	N	Y
Nickles	Y	N	N	N	Y	Y	Y	N
OREGON								
Hatfield	N	N	Y	N	Y	Y	Y	Y
Packwood	N	N	Y	N	Y	Y	Y	N
PENNSYLVANIA								
Wofford	N	Y	Y	Y	N	N	N	Y
Specter	Y	N	N	N	Y	Y	Y	N
RHODE ISLAND								
Pell	N	Y	Y	Y	N	N	N	Y
Chafee	N	Y	Y	?	?	Y	Y	Y
SOUTH CAROLINA								
Hollings	Y	Y	N	Y	Y	Y	Y	Y
Thurmond	Y	N	Y	N	Y	Y	Y	Y
SOUTH DAKOTA								
Daschle	N	Y	Y	Y	N	N	N	Y
Pressler	Y	N	N	N	Y	Y	Y	N
TENNESSEE								
Gore	N	Y	Y	Y	N	N	N	Y
Sasser	N	N	Y	Y	N	N	Y	Y

KEY

Y Voted for (yea).
Paired for.
+ Announced for.
N Voted against (nay).
X Paired against.
- Announced against.
P Voted "present."
C Voted "present" to avoid possible conflict of interest.
? Did not vote or otherwise make a position known.

Democrats *Republicans*

	113	114	115	116	117	118	119	120
TEXAS								
Bentsen	?	Y	Y	Y	N	N	Y	Y
Gramm	Y	N	N	N	Y	Y	Y	N
UTAH								
Garn	Y	N	N	?	Y	Y	Y	N
Hatch	Y	N	N	N	Y	Y	Y	N
VERMONT								
Leahy	N	Y	N	Y	Y	Y	N	Y
Jeffords	N	Y	Y	?	?	?	?	Y
VIRGINIA								
Robb	N	Y	Y	Y	Y	N	N	Y
Warner	N	N	Y	N	Y	Y	Y	N
WASHINGTON								
Adams	N	Y	Y	Y	N	N	N	Y
Gorton	Y	N	Y	N	Y	Y	N	N
WEST VIRGINIA								
Byrd	N	N	Y	Y	Y	N	Y	Y
Rockefeller	N	N	Y	Y	N	N	N	Y
WISCONSIN								
Kohl	N	Y	Y	Y	N	N	N	Y
Kasten	Y	N	Y	N	Y	Y	N	N
WYOMING								
Simpson	Y	N	N	N	Y	Y	Y	N
Wallop	Y	N	N	N	Y	Y	Y	N

ND Northern Democrats SD Southern Democrats Southern states - Ala., Ark., Fla., Ga., Ky., La., Miss., N.C., Okla., S.C., Tenn., Texas, Va.

113. S 1241. Crime Bill/Replace Handgun Bill. Stevens, R-Alaska, amendment to replace the bill's provisions that require a background check over seven days before someone could purchase a handgun with provisions that require states within two years of the date of enactment of the bill to establish a system to provide an instant background check. Rejected 44-54: R 35-8; D 9-46 (ND 4-36, SD 5-10), June 28, 1991 (in the session that began, and the Congressional Record dated, June 27).

114. S 1241. Crime Bill/Cloture. Mitchell, D-Maine, motion to invoke cloture (thus limiting debate) on the bill to impose a waiting period for handgun purchases, broaden the federal death penalty to about 50 crimes, restrict death row inmate appeals and allow prosecutors under certain circumstances to use illegally seized evidence. Motion rejected 41-58: R 3-40; D 38-18 (ND 29-11, SD 9-7), June 28, 1991. A three-fifths majority vote (60) of the total Senate is required to invoke cloture.

115. S 1241. Crime Bill/Handgun Waiting Period. Dole, R-Kan., amendment to require a waiting period of five business days before handgun purchases, during which time a mandatory background check of the prospective handgun buyers would be conducted, and to require the attorney general within six months of enactment to select a system and computer software for a National Instant Check system that within five years would be able to provide a record of criminal activity. Adopted 67-32: R 19-24; D 48-8 (ND 37-3, SD 11-5), June 28, 1991.

116. S 1241. Crime Bill/State and Local Grants. Biden, D-Del., motion to table (kill) the Rudman, R-N.H., amendment to authorize $2.2 billion in fiscal 1992 and such sums as necessary through fiscal 1995 for grants to state and local law enforcement agencies for programs authorized in the bill. Motion agreed to 49-39: R 0-37; D 49-2 (ND 34-2, SD 15-0), July 8, 1991.

117. S 1241. Crime Bill/Literacy Program. Thurmond, R-S.C., amendment to the Bingaman, D-N.M., amendment, to allow states the discretion to establish a mandatory literacy program for prisoners rather than require them to do so, as the Bingaman amendment would. Adopted 55-39: R 40-1; D 15-38 (ND 6-31, SD 9-7), July 9, 1991. (The Bingaman amendment, as amended, was subsequently adopted by voice voice.)

118. S 1241. Crime Bill/Police Officers' Bill of Rights. Thurmond, R-S.C., amendment to make voluntary the adoption of the Police Officers' Bill of Rights by states and to strike provisions in the bill to allow off-duty police officers to engage in political activity. Rejected 43-55: R 41-1; D 2-54 (ND 1-39, SD 1-15), July 9, 1991.

119. HR 2427. Fiscal 1992 Energy and Water Appropriations/Accounts Transfer. Johnston, D-La., motion to table (kill) the Glenn, D-Ohio, amendment to transfer $118 million from the Department of Energy's weapons activities account to the department's Office of Environmental Restorations and Waste Management account. Motion agreed to 54-43: R 37-5; D 17-38 (ND 8-31, SD 9-7), July 9, 1991.

120. S 1241. Crime Bill/Cloture. Mitchell, D-Maine, motion to invoke cloture (thus limiting debate) on the bill to impose a waiting period for handgun purchases, broaden the federal death penalty to about 50 crimes, restrict death row inmate appeals, authorize $3.3 billion for law enforcement and prisons, and for other purposes. Motion rejected 56-43: R 7-36; D 49-7 (ND 37-3, SD 12-4), July 10, 1991. A three-fifths majority vote (60) of the total Senate is required to invoke cloture.

SENATE VOTES 121, 122, 123, 124, 125, 126, 127, 128

	121	122	123	124	125	126	127	128
ALABAMA								
Heflin	Y	Y	N	Y	Y	Y	Y	Y
Shelby	Y	Y	N	Y	Y	Y	Y	N
ALASKA								
Murkowski	Y	Y	N	Y	N	Y	Y	Y
Stevens	Y	Y	N	Y	N	Y	Y	N
ARIZONA								
DeConcini	N	Y	Y	Y	Y	Y	Y	Y
McCain	Y	Y	N	Y	N	Y	Y	Y
ARKANSAS								
Bumpers	N	Y	Y	Y	Y	Y	Y	N
Pryor	?	?	?	?	?	?	?	?
CALIFORNIA								
Cranston	N	Y	Y	Y	N	Y	Y	N
Seymour	Y	Y	Y	Y	Y	Y	Y	N
COLORADO								
Wirth	N	Y	Y	Y	Y	N	Y	N
Brown	Y	N	Y	Y	Y	Y	N	N
CONNECTICUT								
Dodd	Y	Y	Y	Y	Y	Y	Y	N
Lieberman	Y	Y	Y	Y	Y	Y	Y	N
DELAWARE								
Biden	N	Y	Y	Y	Y	?	?	N
Roth	Y	Y	Y	Y	Y	Y	N	N
FLORIDA								
Graham	Y	Y	Y	Y	Y	Y	Y	N
Mack	Y	Y	N	Y	Y	Y	N	Y
GEORGIA								
Fowler	N	Y	Y	Y	Y	N	Y	N
Nunn	Y	Y	Y	Y	Y	N	Y	N
HAWAII								
Akaka	Y	Y	Y	Y	Y	N	Y	N
Inouye	Y	Y	Y	Y	Y	Y	Y	N
IDAHO								
Craig	Y	Y	N	Y	N	Y	N	Y
Symms	Y	Y	N	Y	N	Y	N	Y
ILLINOIS								
Dixon	Y	Y	Y	Y	Y	N	Y	N
Simon	Y	Y	Y	Y	N	N	Y	N
INDIANA								
Coats	N	Y	N	Y	Y	Y	N	Y
Lugar	N	Y	N	Y	Y	Y	Y	Y
IOWA								
Harkin	N	Y	Y	Y	Y	?	?	N
Grassley	Y	Y	N	Y	Y	Y	N	Y
KANSAS								
Dole	Y	Y	Y	Y	Y	Y	N	Y
Kassebaum	N	Y	Y	Y	Y	Y	Y	N
KENTUCKY								
Ford	Y	Y	Y	Y	Y	Y	Y	Y
McConnell	Y	Y	Y	Y	Y	Y	Y	Y
LOUISIANA								
Breaux	Y	Y	N	Y	N	Y	Y	Y
Johnston	Y	Y	N	Y	N	Y	Y	Y
MAINE								
Mitchell	N	Y	Y	Y	Y	Y	Y	N
Cohen	N	Y	Y	Y	Y	Y	Y	N
MARYLAND								
Mikulski	Y	Y	Y	Y	Y	Y	Y	N
Sarbanes	Y	Y	Y	Y	Y	Y	Y	N
MASSACHUSETTS								
Kennedy	N	Y	Y	Y	N	Y	Y	N
Kerry	N	Y	Y	Y	Y	Y	Y	N
MICHIGAN								
Levin	N	Y	Y	Y	Y	Y	Y	N
Riegle	N	Y	Y	Y	Y	Y	Y	N
MINNESOTA								
Wellstone	N	Y	N	Y	N	N	Y	N
Durenberger	Y	Y	Y	Y	N	Y	Y	Y
MISSISSIPPI								
Cochran	Y	Y	Y	Y	Y	Y	N	Y
Lott	Y	Y	N	Y	Y	Y	N	Y
MISSOURI								
Bond	N	Y	?	Y	N	Y	N	N
Danforth	Y	Y	N	Y	Y	Y	Y	Y
MONTANA								
Baucus	Y	Y	N	Y	Y	Y	Y	N
Burns	N	Y	N	Y	N	Y	N	Y
NEBRASKA								
Exon	N	Y	Y	Y	Y	N	Y	Y
Kerrey	N	Y	Y	Y	Y	Y	Y	N
NEVADA								
Bryan	N	Y	Y	Y	Y	Y	Y	N
Reid	Y	Y	Y	Y	Y	Y	Y	Y
NEW HAMPSHIRE								
Rudman	Y	Y	Y	Y	Y	Y	N	N
Smith	N	N	N	Y	N	Y	N	Y
NEW JERSEY								
Bradley	N	Y	Y	Y	+	Y	Y	N
Lautenberg	N	Y	Y	Y	Y	Y	Y	N
NEW MEXICO								
Bingaman	Y	Y	Y	Y	Y	Y	Y	N
Domenici	Y	Y	Y	Y	Y	Y	Y	Y
NEW YORK								
Moynihan	Y	Y	Y	Y	N	N	Y	N
D'Amato	Y	Y	Y	Y	Y	?	?	Y
NORTH CAROLINA								
Sanford	N	Y	Y	Y	Y	Y	Y	N
Helms	Y	N	N	Y	N	Y	N	Y
NORTH DAKOTA								
Burdick	Y	Y	Y	Y	N	Y	Y	N
Conrad	N	Y	Y	Y	Y	N	Y	N
OHIO								
Glenn	Y	Y	Y	Y	Y	N	Y	N
Metzenbaum	N	Y	Y	Y	N	N	Y	N
OKLAHOMA								
Boren	Y	Y	Y	Y	Y	Y	Y	Y
Nickles	Y	Y	N	Y	Y	?	?	Y
OREGON								
Hatfield	Y	Y	Y	Y	N	Y	Y	N
Packwood	Y	Y	Y	Y	Y	Y	Y	N
PENNSYLVANIA								
Wofford	Y	Y	Y	Y	Y	Y	Y	N
Specter	Y	Y	Y	?	?	Y	Y	N
RHODE ISLAND								
Pell	Y	Y	Y	Y	Y	N	Y	N
Chafee	N	Y	Y	Y	Y	Y	Y	N
SOUTH CAROLINA								
Hollings	N	Y	Y	Y	Y	Y	Y	N
Thurmond	Y	Y	Y	Y	Y	Y	Y	Y
SOUTH DAKOTA								
Daschle	Y	Y	Y	Y	Y	Y	Y	N
Pressler	Y	Y	N	Y	N	Y	N	Y
TENNESSEE								
Gore	N	Y	Y	Y	Y	N	Y	N
Sasser	N	Y	Y	Y	Y	Y	Y	N
TEXAS								
Bentsen	Y	Y	Y	Y	Y	Y	Y	N
Gramm	Y	Y	N	Y	Y	Y	N	Y
UTAH								
Garn	Y	Y	N	Y	N	Y	N	Y
Hatch	Y	Y	N	Y	N	Y	N	Y
VERMONT								
Leahy	N	Y	Y	Y	N	Y	Y	N
Jeffords	N	Y	Y	Y	Y	Y	Y	N
VIRGINIA								
Robb	Y	Y	Y	Y	Y	N	Y	N
Warner	Y	Y	N	Y	Y	Y	Y	N
WASHINGTON								
Adams	N	Y	Y	Y	Y	Y	Y	N
Gorton	Y	Y	Y	Y	Y	Y	Y	N
WEST VIRGINIA								
Byrd	Y	Y	Y	Y	Y	Y	Y	N
Rockefeller	Y	Y	Y	Y	Y	?	?	N
WISCONSIN								
Kohl	N	Y	Y	Y	Y	N	Y	N
Kasten	Y	Y	Y	Y	Y	Y	N	Y
WYOMING								
Simpson	N	Y	Y	Y	N	Y	N	N
Wallop	Y	Y	N	Y	N	Y	N	Y

KEY

- Y Voted for (yea).
- # Paired for.
- + Announced for.
- N Voted against (nay).
- X Paired against.
- - Announced against.
- P Voted "present."
- C Voted "present" to avoid possible conflict of interest.
- ? Did not vote or otherwise make a position known.

Democrats *Republicans*

ND Northern Democrats SD Southern Democrats Southern states - A a., Ark., Fla., Ga., Ky., La., Miss., N.C., Okla., S.C., Tenn., Texas, Va.

121. HR 2427. Fiscal 1992 Energy and Water Appropriations/Superconducting Super Collider. Johnston, D-La., motion to table (kill) the Bumpers, D-Ark., amendment to eliminate all funding for the superconducting super collider by reducing the bill's funding level for the General Science and Research Activities account by $508,700,000. Motion agreed to 62-37: R 33-10; D 29-27 (ND 19-21, SD 10-6), July 10, 1991. A "yea" was a vote supporting the president's position.

122. HR 2427. Fiscal 1992 Energy and Water Appropriations/Passage. Passage of the bill to provide $21,984,482,000 in new budget authority for energy, water and nuclear weapons programs. The administration requested $21,609,828,000. Passed 96-3: R 40-3; D 56-0 (ND 40-0, SD 16-0), July 10, 1991.

123. S 1241. Crime Bill/Cloture. Mitchell, D-Maine, motion to invoke cloture (thus limiting debate) on the bill to impose a waiting period for handgun purchases, broaden the federal death penalty to about 50 crimes, restrict death row inmate appeals, authorize $3.3 billion for law enforcement and prisons, and for other purposes. Motion agreed to 71-27: R 21-21; D 50-6 (ND 38-2, SD 12-4), July 10, 1991. A three-fifths majority vote (60) of the total Senate is required to invoke cloture.

124. HR 2622. Fiscal 1992 Treasury-Postal Appropriations/Postal Subsidies. DeConcini, D-Ariz., amendment to the Appropriations Committee amendment, to remove the third-class mail subsidy for the larger mail flats to try to adequately fund revenue that has been forgone for certain preferred mailers, such as nonprofit organizations, and to encourage organizations to use smaller mail items that can be processed by machine at less cost to the Postal Service. The amendment would maintain postal rates for rural newspapers, organizations for the blind and all subsidized mailings that use letter-sized envelopes. Adopted 98-0: R 42-0; D 56-0 (ND 40-0, SD 16-0), July 11, 1991.

125. S 1241. Crime Bill/Passage. Passage of the bill to impose a waiting period for handguns, ban nine classifications of assault weapons, broaden the federal death penalty to 51 crimes, restrict death row inmate appeals, authorize funds to hire 10,000 new local law enforcement officers, and for other purposes. Passed 71-26: R 26-16; D 45-10 (ND 31-8, SD 14-2), July 11, 1991.

126. HR 2622. Fiscal 1992 Treasury-Postal Appropriations/Increase Internal Revenue Service Account. DeConcini, D-Ariz., motion to table (kill) the Kohl, D-Wis., amendment to reduce the account for the operation and maintenance of the U.S. Customs Service's air and marine interdiction programs by $48,500,000 and increase the Internal Revenue Service's tax law enforcement account by $29,639,000. Motion agreed to 78-16: R 41-0; D 37-16 (ND 25-12, SD 12-4), July 15, 1991.

127. HR 2622. Fiscal 1992 Treasury-Postal Appropriations/Portsmouth Naval Shipyard. Cohen, R-Maine, motion to table (kill) the Smith, R-N.H., amendment to prohibit the withholding of about $8.8 million a year in Maine state income tax from 4,000 New Hampshire residents who work at the Portsmouth Naval Shipyard until the boundary dispute as to whether the shipyard is in Maine or New Hampshire is resolved. Motion agreed to 72-22: R 19-22; D 53-0 (ND 37-0, SD 16-0), July 15, 1991.

128. S 323. Title X Pregnancy Counseling/Prohibit Pregnancy Counseling. Durenberger, R-Minn., amendment to the Chafee, R-R.I., substitute, to prohibit entities that receive Title X funding from providing counsel to pregnant women and require such entities to refer pregnant women for prenatal care by furnishing them with a list of health-care providers. The list may include health-care providers that provide abortion but not as a principal means of business. Rejected 35-64: R 27-16; D 8-48 (ND 3-37, SD 5-11), July 16, 1991. A "yea" was a vote supporting the president's position.

SENATE VOTES 129, 130, 131, 132, 133, 134, 135, 136

	129	130	131	132	133	134	135	136
ALABAMA								
Heflin	N	N	Y	N	N	Y	Y	Y
Shelby	N	Y	Y	N	N	Y	Y	Y
ALASKA								
Murkowski	N	N	Y	N	Y	N	Y	Y
Stevens	N	Y	Y	N	Y	N	Y	Y
ARIZONA								
DeConcini	N	N	Y	Y	N	Y	Y	N
McCain	N	N	Y	N	N	N	Y	Y
ARKANSAS								
Bumpers	N	Y	N	Y	N	Y	Y	Y
Pryor	?	?	?	?	#	?	?	?
CALIFORNIA								
Cranston	N	Y	N	N	Y	Y	Y	N
Seymour	N	N	Y	N	N	N	Y	Y
COLORADO								
Wirth	N	Y	N	N	Y	Y	Y	Y
Brown	N	N	Y	N	N	N	Y	Y
CONNECTICUT								
Dodd	N	Y	N	N	N	Y	Y	Y
Lieberman	N	Y	N	N	Y	Y	Y	Y
DELAWARE								
Biden	N	Y	N	Y	Y	Y	Y	Y
Roth	N	N	Y	N	Y	N	Y	Y
FLORIDA								
Graham	N	Y	N	N	N	Y	Y	Y
Mack	N	N	Y	N	N	N	Y	Y
GEORGIA								
Fowler	N	Y	N	Y	N	Y	Y	Y
Nunn	N	N	Y	Y	Y	Y	Y	Y
HAWAII								
Akaka	N	Y	N	N	Y	Y	Y	N
Inouye	N	Y	N	N	Y	Y	Y	N
IDAHO								
Craig	N	N	Y	N	Y	N	Y	Y
Symms	N	N	Y	N	Y	N	Y	Y
ILLINOIS								
Dixon	N	N	Y	Y	N	?	Y	Y
Simon	N	Y	N	Y	Y	Y	Y	Y
INDIANA								
Coats	N	N	Y	N	N	N	Y	Y
Lugar	Y	N	Y	N	Y	N	Y	N
IOWA								
Harkin	N	Y	N	Y	Y	Y	Y	Y
Grassley	N	N	Y	N	N	N	Y	Y
KANSAS								
Dole	Y	N	Y	N	Y	N	Y	Y
Kassebaum	N	Y	Y	N	Y	N	Y	N
KENTUCKY								
Ford	N	N	Y	N	X	Y	Y	Y
McConnell	N	N	Y	N	N	N	Y	Y
LOUISIANA								
Breaux	N	N	Y	Y	Y	Y	Y	Y
Johnston	N	N	Y	Y	Y	Y	Y	Y
MAINE								
Mitchell	N	Y	N	Y	Y	Y	Y	N
Cohen	N	Y	N	Y	N	N	Y	Y
MARYLAND								
Mikulski	N	Y	N	N	N	Y	Y	N
Sarbanes	N	Y	N	N	Y	Y	Y	Y
MASSACHUSETTS								
Kennedy	N	Y	N	Y	Y	Y	Y	N
Kerry	N	Y	N	Y	N	Y	Y	Y
MICHIGAN								
Levin	N	Y	N	Y	N	Y	Y	Y
Riegle	N	Y	N	N	N	Y	Y	Y
MINNESOTA								
Wellstone	N	Y	N	Y	N	Y	Y	N
Durenberger	N	N	Y	N	Y	Y	Y	N
MISSISSIPPI								
Cochran	Y	N	Y	N	Y	N	Y	Y
Lott	Y	N	Y	N	Y	N	Y	Y
MISSOURI								
Bond	Y	N	Y	N	N	N	Y	Y
Danforth	Y	N	Y	N	Y	N	Y	Y
MONTANA								
Baucus	N	Y	N	Y	Y	Y	Y	Y
Burns	N	N	Y	N	Y	N	Y	Y
NEBRASKA								
Exon	N	N	Y	Y	Y	Y	Y	Y
Kerrey	N	Y	N	N	Y	Y	Y	Y
NEVADA								
Bryan	N	Y	N	Y	N	Y	Y	Y
Reid	N	N	Y	N	N	Y	Y	Y
NEW HAMPSHIRE								
Rudman	N	N	Y	N	Y	N	Y	Y
Smith	N	N	Y	N	Y	N	Y	Y
NEW JERSEY								
Bradley	N	Y	N	Y	N	Y	Y	Y
Lautenberg	N	Y	N	Y	N	Y	Y	Y
NEW MEXICO								
Bingaman	N	Y	N	N	Y	Y	Y	Y
Domenici	Y	N	Y	N	Y	N	Y	Y
NEW YORK								
Moynihan	N	Y	N	Y	Y	Y	Y	Y
D'Amato	Y	N	Y	N	N	N	Y	Y
NORTH CAROLINA								
Sanford	N	Y	N	Y	N	Y	Y	Y
Helms	N	N	Y	N	N	N	Y	Y
NORTH DAKOTA								
Burdick	N	Y	N	Y	Y	Y	Y	Y
Conrad	Y	N	Y	Y	N	Y	Y	Y
OHIO								
Glenn	N	Y	N	N	N	Y	Y	Y
Metzenbaum	N	Y	N	Y	Y	Y	Y	Y
OKLAHOMA								
Boren	Y	N	Y	N	Y	Y	Y	Y
Nickles	N	N	Y	N	N	N	Y	Y
OREGON								
Hatfield	N	N	Y	N	Y	Y	Y	N
Packwood	N	Y	N	N	N	N	Y	Y
PENNSYLVANIA								
Wofford	N	Y	N	N	N	Y	Y	Y
Specter	N	Y	N	Y	N	N	Y	Y
RHODE ISLAND								
Pell	N	Y	N	Y	Y	Y	Y	Y
Chafee	N	Y	N	Y	Y	N	Y	N
SOUTH CAROLINA								
Hollings	N	Y	N	Y	N	Y	Y	Y
Thurmond	Y	N	Y	N	Y	N	Y	Y
SOUTH DAKOTA								
Daschle	N	Y	N	Y	N	Y	Y	Y
Pressler	Y	N	Y	N	N	N	Y	Y
TENNESSEE								
Gore	N	Y	N	N	N	Y	Y	N
Sasser	N	Y	N	Y	N	Y	Y	Y
TEXAS								
Bentsen	N	Y	N	N	Y	Y	Y	Y
Gramm	N	N	Y	N	N	N	Y	Y
UTAH								
Garn	N	N	Y	N	Y	N	Y	Y
Hatch	N	N	Y	N	N	N	Y	Y
VERMONT								
Leahy	N	Y	N	Y	Y	Y	Y	N
Jeffords	N	Y	N	N	Y	N	Y	N
VIRGINIA								
Robb	N	Y	N	N	Y	Y	Y	Y
Warner	N	Y	Y	N	Y	N	Y	Y
WASHINGTON								
Adams	N	Y	N	N	N	Y	Y	Y
Gorton	N	N	Y	N	Y	N	Y	N
WEST VIRGINIA								
Byrd	N	Y	Y	N	Y	Y	Y	Y
Rockefeller	N	Y	N	Y	Y	Y	Y	N
WISCONSIN								
Kohl	N	Y	Y	Y	N	Y	Y	Y
Kasten	Y	N	Y	N	N	N	Y	Y
WYOMING								
Simpson	N	Y	Y	N	Y	N	Y	Y
Wallop	Y	N	Y	N	Y	N	Y	Y

KEY

- Y Voted for (yea).
- # Paired for.
- + Announced for.
- N Voted against (nay).
- X Paired against.
- - Announced against.
- P Voted "present."
- C Voted "present" to avoid possible conflict of interest.
- ? Did not vote or otherwise make a position known.

Democrats ***Republicans***

ND Northern Democrats SD Southern Democrats

Southern states - Ala., Ark., Fla., Ga., Ky., La., Miss., N.C., Okla., S.C., Tenn., Texas, Va.

129. S 323. Title X Pregnancy Counseling/Prohibit Abortion Advocacy. Cochran, R-Miss., amendment to the Chafee, R-R.I., substitute amendment, to allow entities that receive Title X funding to provide upon request abortion information. The Cochran amendment would also prohibit projects that receive federal funds from using their own funds to encourage or promote abortion. Rejected 14-85: R 12-31; D 2-54 (ND 1-39, SD 1-15), July 16, 1991.

130. S 323. Title X Pregnancy Counseling/Parental Consent. Mitchell, D-Maine, amendment to require entities that receive Title X funding to obtain consent from a parent, grandparent, adult sibling, aunt or uncle for a minor to have an abortion. If the consent is not forthcoming, the attending physician could give parents or guardians 48 hours' notice before the abortion. The amendment also contains court or clergy bypass provisions. Adopted 54-45: R 9-34; D 45-11 (ND 35-5, SD 10-6), July 16, 1991.

131. S 323. Title X Pregnancy Counseling/Abortions for Minors. Coats, R-Ind., amendment to prohibit entities that receive Title X funding from performing an abortion for a minor under the age of 18 unless a parent or guardian has been given 48 hours' notice, the life of the minor is endangered, the pregnancy is the result of parental incest, or the minor has been subjected to sexual abuse, child abuse, or child neglect by a parent or guardian. Adopted 52-47: R 38-5; D 14-42 (ND 7-33, SD 7-9), July 16, 1991.

132. HR 2519. Fiscal 1992 VA-HUD Appropriations/Space Station. Bumpers, D-Ark., amendment to reduce funding for the space station from $2 billion to $100 million and transfer $182 million to other federal science programs, $431 million to veterans' programs, and about $1.3 billion to deficit reduction. Rejected 35-64: R 3-40; D 32-24 (ND 24-16, SD 8-8), July 17, 1991. A "nay" was a vote supporting the president's position.

133. HR 2506. Fiscal 1992 Legislative Branch Appropriations/Pay Raise. Byrd, D-W.Va., amendment to raise senators' pay from $101,900 to $125,100, ban senators' honoraria and limit outside earned income to 15 percent of a senator's base pay. Adopted 53-45: R 25-18; D 28-27 (ND 22-18, SD 6-9), July 17, 1991.

134. S 250. National Motor-Voter Registration Act/Cloture. Motion to invoke cloture (thus limiting debate) on the motion to proceed to the bill to require states to permit voter registration simultaneously with applying for a driver's license. Motion rejected 57-41: R 2-41; D 55-0 (ND 39-0, SD 16-0), July 18, 1991. A three-fifths majority vote (60) of the total Senate is required to invoke cloture.

135. HR 2622. Fiscal 1992 Treasury-Postal Appropriations/Child Pornography. Helms, R-N.C., amendment to mandate prison terms for selling child pornography. Adopted 99-0: R 43-0; D 56-0 (ND 40-0, SD 16-0), July 18, 1991.

136. HR 2622. Fiscal 1992 Treasury-Postal Appropriations/AIDS. Helms, R-N.C., amendment to provide for a $10,000 fine and a prison term of not less than 10 years for health-care providers who knowingly have the AIDS virus and perform invasive medical procedures without notifying the patient. Adopted 81-18: R 36-7; D 45-11 (ND 30-10, SD 15-1), July 18, 1991.

	137	138	139	140	141	142	143	144
ALABAMA								
Heflin	Y	Y	Y	Y	N	Y	Y	Y
Shelby	Y	Y	Y	Y	Y	N	Y	Y
ALASKA								
Murkowski	Y	Y	N	N	?	N	?	Y
Stevens	Y	Y	N	N	N	N	Y	Y
ARIZONA								
DeConcini	Y	Y	Y	Y	Y	Y	Y	N
McCain	Y	Y	Y	N	N	N	Y	Y
ARKANSAS								
Bumpers	Y	Y	Y	Y	Y	Y	Y	Y
Pryor	?	?	?	?	?	?	?	?
CALIFORNIA								
Cranston	Y	Y	Y	Y	Y	Y	Y	Y
Seymour	Y	Y	N	N	N	N	Y	Y
COLORADO								
Wirth	Y	Y	Y	Y	Y	Y	Y	Y
Brown	Y	N	Y	N	N	N	Y	Y
CONNECTICUT								
Dodd	Y	Y	Y	Y	Y	Y	Y	Y
Lieberman	Y	Y	Y	Y	Y	Y	Y	Y
DELAWARE								
Biden	Y	Y	Y	Y	Y	Y	Y	Y
Roth	Y	N	N	N	?	N	Y	Y
FLORIDA								
Graham	Y	Y	Y	Y	Y	Y	Y	Y
Mack	Y	Y	N	N	Y	Y	N	Y
GEORGIA								
Fowler	Y	Y	Y	Y	?	Y	Y	Y
Nunn	Y	Y	Y	Y	Y	Y	Y	Y
HAWAII								
Akaka	Y	Y	Y	Y	Y	Y	Y	Y
Inouye	Y	Y	Y	Y	Y	Y	Y	Y
IDAHO								
Craig	Y	N	N	N	N	N	N	N
Symms	Y	N	N	N	N	N	N	N
ILLINOIS								
Dixon	Y	N	Y	Y	Y	Y	N	Y
Simon	Y	Y	Y	Y	Y	Y	Y	Y
INDIANA								
Coats	Y	N	N	N	N	N	Y	Y
Lugar	Y	Y	N	N	N	N	Y	Y
IOWA								
Harkin	Y	Y	Y	Y	Y	Y	Y	Y
Grassley	Y	Y	N	N	N	N	Y	Y
KANSAS								
Dole	Y	Y	N	N	N	N	Y	N
Kassebaum	Y	Y	N	N	N	N	Y	Y
KENTUCKY								
Ford	Y	Y	Y	Y	Y	Y	Y	Y
McConnell	Y	Y	N	N	N	N	Y	Y
LOUISIANA								
Breaux	Y	Y	Y	Y	Y	N	Y	Y
Johnston	Y	Y	Y	Y	N	N	Y	Y
MAINE								
Mitchell	Y	Y	Y	Y	Y	Y	Y	Y
Cohen	Y	Y	N	N	N	N	Y	Y
MARYLAND								
Mikulski	Y	Y	Y	Y	Y	Y	Y	Y
Sarbanes	Y	Y	Y	Y	Y	Y	Y	Y
MASSACHUSETTS								
Kennedy	Y	Y	Y	Y	Y	Y	Y	Y
Kerry	Y	Y	Y	Y	Y	Y	Y	Y
MICHIGAN								
Levin	Y	Y	Y	Y	Y	Y	Y	Y
Riegle	Y	Y	Y	Y	Y	Y	Y	Y
MINNESOTA								
Wellstone	Y	Y	Y	Y	Y	Y	Y	Y
Durenberger	Y	Y	N	Y	?	N	N	Y
MISSISSIPPI								
Cochran	Y	Y	N	N	N	N	Y	Y
Lott	Y	Y	N	N	N	N	N	Y
MISSOURI								
Bond	Y	Y	N	N	N	N	Y	Y
Danforth	Y	Y	N	N	N	N	Y	Y
MONTANA								
Baucus	Y	Y	Y	Y	Y	N	Y	Y
Burns	Y	Y	N	N	N	N	Y	Y
NEBRASKA								
Exon	Y	Y	Y	Y	Y	N	Y	Y
Kerrey	Y	Y	Y	Y	Y	Y	?	Y
NEVADA								
Bryan	Y	Y	Y	Y	Y	Y	Y	Y
Reid	Y	Y	Y	Y	Y	Y	Y	Y
NEW HAMPSHIRE								
Rudman	Y	Y	N	N	N	N	Y	Y
Smith	Y	N	?	N	Y	Y	N	N
NEW JERSEY								
Bradley	Y	Y	Y	Y	?	Y	Y	Y
Lautenberg	Y	Y	Y	Y	Y	Y	Y	Y
NEW MEXICO								
Bingaman	Y	Y	Y	Y	Y	Y	Y	Y
Domenici	Y	Y	N	N	N	N	Y	Y
NEW YORK								
Moynihan	Y	Y	Y	Y	Y	Y	Y	Y
D'Amato	Y	Y	N	N	Y	Y	Y	Y
NORTH CAROLINA								
Sanford	Y	Y	?	Y	Y	Y	Y	Y
Helms	Y	Y	N	N	Y	Y	N	N
NORTH DAKOTA								
Burdick	Y	Y	Y	Y	Y	N	Y	Y
Conrad	Y	Y	Y	Y	Y	N	Y	Y
OHIO								
Glenn	Y	Y	Y	Y	Y	Y	Y	Y
Metzenbaum	Y	Y	Y	Y	Y	Y	Y	Y
OKLAHOMA								
Boren	Y	Y	Y	Y	Y	Y	Y	N
Nickles	Y	Y	N	N	N	N	Y	N
OREGON								
Hatfield	Y	Y	N	Y	N	N	Y	Y
Packwood	Y	Y	N	N	N	N	Y	Y
PENNSYLVANIA								
Wofford	Y	Y	Y	Y	Y	Y	Y	Y
Specter	Y	Y	N	N	N	N	Y	Y
RHODE ISLAND								
Pell	Y	Y	Y	Y	Y	Y	Y	Y
Chafee	Y	Y	N	N	N	N	Y	Y
SOUTH CAROLINA								
Hollings	Y	Y	Y	Y	Y	Y	Y	N
Thurmond	Y	Y	N	N	N	N	Y	Y
SOUTH DAKOTA								
Daschle	Y	Y	Y	Y	?	Y	Y	Y
Pressler	Y	Y	N	N	?	N	Y	Y
TENNESSEE								
Gore	Y	Y	Y	Y	Y	Y	Y	Y
Sasser	Y	Y	Y	Y	Y	Y	Y	Y
TEXAS								
Bentsen	Y	Y	Y	Y	Y	Y	Y	Y
Gramm	Y	Y	N	N	N	N	N	Y
UTAH								
Garn	Y	Y	N	N	?	Y	Y	N
Hatch	Y	Y	N	N	N	N	Y	Y
VERMONT								
Leahy	Y	Y	Y	Y	Y	Y	Y	N
Jeffords	Y	Y	N	Y	?	N	Y	Y
VIRGINIA								
Robb	Y	Y	Y	Y	Y	Y	Y	Y
Warner	Y	Y	N	N	N	N	Y	Y
WASHINGTON								
Adams	Y	Y	Y	Y	Y	Y	Y	Y
Gorton	Y	Y	N	N	N	N	Y	Y
WEST VIRGINIA								
Byrd	Y	Y	Y	Y	Y	Y	Y	Y
Rockefeller	Y	Y	Y	Y	Y	Y	Y	Y
WISCONSIN								
Kohl	Y	Y	Y	Y	Y	Y	Y	Y
Kasten	Y	N	N	N	N	N	Y	Y
WYOMING								
Simpson	Y	Y	N	N	N	N	Y	Y
Wallop	Y	Y	N	N	N	Y	N	N

KEY

- Y Voted for (yea).
- # Paired for.
- + Announced for.
- N Voted against (nay).
- X Paired against.
- \- Announced against.
- P Voted "present."
- C Voted "present" to avoid possible conflict of interest.
- ? Did not vote or otherwise make a position known.

Democrats ***Republicans***

ND Northern Democrats SD Southern Democrats

Southern states - Ala., Ark., Fla., Ga., Ky., La., Miss., N.C., Okla., S.C., Tenn., Texas, Va.

137. HR 2622. Fiscal 1992 Treasury-Postal Appropriations/Centers for Disease Control Guidelines. Dole, R-Kan., amendment to require states within one year to adopt the guidelines issued by the Centers for Disease Control for preventing the transmission of the human immunodeficiency virus (HIV) by health-care professionals to patients during invasive medical procedures. Adopted 99-0: R 43-0; D 56-0 (ND 40-0, SD 16-0), July 18, 1991.

138. HR 2622. Fiscal 1992 Treasury-Postal Appropriations/Passage. Passage of the bill to provide $19,581,993,750 in new budget authority for the Treasury Department, the U.S. Postal Service, the Executive Office of the President, and certain independent agencies for fiscal 1992. The administration requested $19,522,037,000. The House bill provides for $19,630,702,000. Passed 91-8: R 36-7; D 55-1 (ND 39-1, SD 16-0), July 18, 1991.

139. HR 2519. Fiscal 1992 VA and HUD Appropriations/Cloture. Motion to invoke cloture on the Wirth, D-Colo., amendment to require that all of the examination reports of the failed savings and loans resolved in the 1988 Resolution Trust Corporation deals be made public. Motion rejected 57-40: R 2-40; D 55-0 (ND 40-0, SD 15-0), July 18, 1991. A three-fifths majority vote (60) of the total Senate is required to invoke cloture.

140. S 250. National Motor-Voter Registration Act/Cloture. Motion to invoke cloture (thus limiting debate) on the motion to proceed to the bill to require states to permit voter registration simultaneously with applying for a driver's license. Motion rejected 59-40: R 3-40; D 56-0 (ND 40-0, SD 16-0), July 18, 1991. A three-fifths majority vote (60) of the total Senate is required to invoke cloture.

141. S 1367. Conditional MFN for China in 1992/Restrictions. Bingaman, D-N.M., amendment to add to the bill's findings that the United States has failed to use existing laws and other means to respond to China's human rights violations, weapons proliferation and unfair trade practices. In addition to the other provisions for renewal of most-favored-nation trade status, the amendment would add the requirement that China cease unfair trade practices. Adopted 55-35: R 4-33; D 51-2 (ND 38-0, SD 13-2), July 22, 1991.

142. HR 2212. Conditional MFN for China in 1992/Passage. Passage of the bill to prohibit the president from granting most-favored-nation status to China for the 12-month period beginning July 3, 1992, unless he reports that China has accounted for and released all political prisoners, made progress in human rights, among other conditions. Passed 55-44: R 6-37; D 49-7 (ND 36-4, SD 13-3), July 23, 1991. (Before passage of HR 2212, the Senate inserted the text of S 1367.) A "nay" vote was in support of the president's position.

143. S 1435. Fiscal 1992-93 Foreign Aid Authorization/Cloture. Mitchell, D-Maine, motion to invoke cloture (thus limiting debate) on the motion to proceed to the bill to authorize $14.04 billion in fiscal 1992 for foreign economic and military assistance. Motion agreed to 87-10: R 33-9; D 54-1 (ND 38-1, SD 16-0), July 24, 1991. A three-fifths majority vote (60) of the total Senate is required to invoke cloture.

144. S 1435. Fiscal 1992-93 Foreign Aid Authorization/Transfer to Education and Law Enforcement Agencies. McConnell, R-Ky., motion to table (kill) the Helms, R-N.C., amendment to reduce all programs in the bill by 10 percent and transfer the savings to state block grants for elementary and secondary education and law enforcement services. Motion agreed to 87-12: R 35-8; D 52-4 (ND 38-2, SD 14-2), July 24, 1991.

	145	146	147	148	149	150	151	152
ALABAMA								
Heflin	Y	Y	Y	Y	N	N	N	N
Shelby	Y	Y	Y	Y	N	N	Y	N
ALASKA								
Murkowski	Y	Y	Y	Y	N	N	Y	Y
Stevens	Y	Y	Y	Y	N	N	Y	Y
ARIZONA								
DeConcini	Y	Y	Y	N	Y	Y	Y	N
McCain	Y	N	Y	Y	Y	N	N	N
ARKANSAS								
Bumpers	Y	N	Y	N	Y	Y	Y	N
Pryor	?	?	?	?	?	?	?	?
CALIFORNIA								
Cranston	N	Y	Y	N	N	Y	Y	N
Seymour	Y	Y	Y	Y	N	N	Y	N
COLORADO								
Wirth	Y	Y	Y	N	Y	Y	Y	N
Brown	Y	N	Y	Y	Y	N	Y	Y
CONNECTICUT								
Dodd	Y	Y	Y	N	N	Y	Y	N
Lieberman	Y	Y	Y	N	N	Y	Y	N
DELAWARE								
Biden	Y	Y	Y	N	N	Y	Y	N
Roth	Y	N	Y	Y	N	N	Y	Y
FLORIDA								
Graham	Y	Y	Y	Y	N	N	Y	N
Mack	Y	Y	Y	Y	Y	N	N	N
GEORGIA								
Fowler	Y	N	Y	N	Y	Y	Y	N
Nunn	Y	Y	Y	Y	Y	N	Y	?
HAWAII								
Akaka	Y	Y	Y	N	N	Y	Y	N
Inouye	Y	Y	Y	N	N	Y	Y	N
IDAHO								
Craig	Y	N	Y	Y	Y	N	N	Y
Symms	Y	N	Y	Y	Y	N	N	Y
ILLINOIS								
Dixon	Y	N	Y	N	Y	Y	Y	N
Simon	Y	N	Y	N	N	Y	Y	N
INDIANA								
Coats	Y	N	Y	Y	Y	N	N	N
Lugar	Y	N	Y	Y	N	N	N	Y
IOWA								
Harkin	Y	Y	Y	N	?	?	?	?
Grassley	Y	N	Y	N	Y	N	N	N
KANSAS								
Dole	Y	N	Y	Y	N	N	N	Y
Kassebaum	Y	N	Y	N	N	Y	Y	Y
KENTUCKY								
Ford	Y	Y	Y	N	N	Y	N	N
McConnell	Y	N	Y	Y	N	N	N	Y
LOUISIANA								
Breaux	Y	Y	Y	N	N	N	N	Y
Johnston	Y	Y	Y	N	N	Y	N	N
MAINE								
Mitchell	Y	Y	Y	N	N	Y	Y	N
Cohen	Y	Y	Y	Y	N	N	Y	Y
MARYLAND								
Mikulski	Y	Y	Y	N	N	Y	Y	N
Sarbanes	Y	Y	Y	N	N	Y	Y	N
MASSACHUSETTS								
Kennedy	Y	Y	Y	N	N	Y	Y	N
Kerry	Y	Y	Y	N	N	Y	Y	N
MICHIGAN								
Levin	Y	N	Y	N	N	Y	Y	N
Riegle	Y	N	Y	N	N	Y	Y	N
MINNESOTA								
Wellstone	Y	N	Y	N	N	Y	Y	N
Durenberger	Y	N	Y	Y	N	N	N	Y
MISSISSIPPI								
Cochran	Y	Y	Y	Y	?	?	?	Y
Lott	Y	Y	Y	Y	Y	N	N	Y
MISSOURI								
Bond	Y	?	Y	Y	N	N	N	Y
Danforth	Y	N	Y	Y	N	N	N	Y
MONTANA								
Baucus	Y	N	Y	N	N	Y	Y	N
Burns	Y	N	Y	Y	N	N	N	Y
NEBRASKA								
Exon	Y	Y	Y	N	Y	Y	Y	Y
Kerrey	Y	Y	Y	N	Y	Y	Y	Y
NEVADA								
Bryan	Y	Y	Y	N	N	Y	Y	N
Reid	Y	Y	Y	N	N	Y	N	N
NEW HAMPSHIRE								
Rudman	Y	N	Y	Y	N	N	Y	Y
Smith	Y	N	Y	Y	Y	N	N	Y
NEW JERSEY								
Bradley	Y	Y	Y	N	N	Y	Y	N
Lautenberg	Y	N	Y	N	N	Y	Y	N
NEW MEXICO								
Bingaman	Y	Y	Y	N	N	Y	Y	N
Domenici	Y	N	Y	Y	N	N	N	Y
NEW YORK								
Moynihan	Y	Y	Y	N	N	Y	Y	N
D'Amato	Y	Y	Y	Y	N	N	Y	N
NORTH CAROLINA								
Sanford	Y	Y	Y	N	N	Y	Y	N
Helms	Y	N	Y	Y	Y	N	N	Y
NORTH DAKOTA								
Burdick	Y	Y	Y	N	N	Y	Y	N
Conrad	Y	Y	Y	N	Y	Y	Y	N
OHIO								
Glenn	Y	N	Y	N	N	Y	Y	?
Metzenbaum	Y	N	Y	N	Y	Y	Y	N
OKLAHOMA								
Boren	Y	N	Y	N	N	Y	N	Y
Nickles	Y	N	Y	Y	Y	N	N	N
OREGON								
Hatfield	Y	Y	Y	N	N	Y	Y	Y
Packwood	Y	Y	Y	Y	N	N	Y	Y
PENNSYLVANIA								
Wofford	Y	Y	Y	N	N	Y	Y	N
Specter	Y	Y	Y	N	N	Y	Y	N
RHODE ISLAND								
Pell	Y	Y	Y	N	N	Y	Y	N
Chafee	Y	?	Y	Y	N	N	Y	Y
SOUTH CAROLINA								
Hollings	Y	Y	Y	N	N	Y	Y	N
Thurmond	Y	N	Y	Y	Y	N	N	Y
SOUTH DAKOTA								
Daschle	Y	Y	Y	N	N	Y	Y	N
Pressler	Y	N	Y	Y	Y	N	N	N
TENNESSEE								
Gore	Y	Y	Y	N	N	Y	Y	Y
Sasser	Y	Y	Y	N	N	Y	Y	N
TEXAS								
Bentsen	Y	Y	Y	N	?	?	?	Y
Gramm	Y	N	Y	Y	Y	N	N	Y
UTAH								
Garn	Y	N	Y	Y	N	N	N	Y
Hatch	Y	N	Y	Y	Y	N	N	Y
VERMONT								
Leahy	Y	Y	Y	N	Y	Y	Y	N
Jeffords	Y	N	Y	N	N	Y	Y	Y
VIRGINIA								
Robb	Y	Y	Y	Y	N	N	Y	N
Warner	Y	Y	Y	Y	Y	N	N	N
WASHINGTON								
Adams	Y	Y	Y	N	N	Y	Y	N
Gorton	Y	N	Y	Y	N	N	N	Y
WEST VIRGINIA								
Byrd	Y	Y	Y	N	Y	Y	Y	N
Rockefeller	Y	Y	Y	N	N	Y	Y	N
WISCONSIN								
Kohl	Y	N	Y	N	Y	Y	Y	N
Kasten	Y	N	Y	Y	Y	N	N	Y
WYOMING								
Simpson	Y	N	Y	Y	N	N	Y	Y
Wallop	Y	N	Y	Y	Y	N	N	Y

KEY

- Y Voted for (yea).
- # Paired for.
- \+ Announced for.
- N Voted against (nay).
- X Paired against.
- \- Announced against.
- P Voted "present."
- C Voted "present" to avoid possible conflict of interest.
- ? Did not vote or otherwise make a position known.

Democrats ***Republicans***

ND Northern Democrats SD Southern Democrats Southern states - Ala., Ark., Fla., Ga., Ky., La., Miss., N.C., Okla., S.C., Tenn., Texas, Va.

145. S 1435. Fiscal 1992-93 Foreign Aid Authorization/Soviet Union Certification. Helms, R-N.C., amendment to prohibit the Soviet Union from receiving funds in the bill unless the president certifies that the Soviet Union has ceased all direct or indirect military or economic assistance to Cuba. Adopted 98-1: R 43-0; D 55-1 (ND 39-1, SD 16-0), July 24, 1991.

146. S 1435. Fiscal 1992-93 Foreign Aid Authorization/Cargo Preference and Cash Purchase Requirements. Sarbanes, D-Md., motion to table (kill) the Dixon, D-Ill., amendment to strike the cargo preference and cash purchase requirements in the bill. Motion agreed to 55-42: R 12-29; D 43-13 (ND 30-10, SD 13-3), July 24, 1991. A "nay" vote was in support of the president's position.

147. S 1435. Fiscal 1992-93 Foreign Aid Authorization/"Tied-Aid." Boren, D-Okla., amendment to the Lieberman, D-Conn., amendment, to increase the level of "tied-aid." The amendment would reduce the level of direct cash transfers to countries and require them to spend U.S. foreign aid on roads, dams and other capital projects built and designed by U.S. companies. Adopted 99-0: R 43-0; D 56-0 (ND 40-0, SD 16-0), July 25, 1991. A "nay" was a vote supporting the president's position.

148. S 1435. Fiscal 1992-93 Foreign Aid Authorization/El Salvador. Dole, R-Kan., motion to table (kill) the Dodd, D-Conn., amendment to limit military aid to El Salvador to $85 million in fiscal 1992 and prohibit military aid, if the president determines El Salvador has declined to participate in good-faith negotiations, rejected an active role of the United Nations in a settlement, is not conducting a thorough investigation into the murder of the Jesuit priests, or is assassinating or abducting civilian non-combatants. Motion rejected 43-56: R 38-5; D 5-51 (ND 0-40, SD 5-11), July 25, 1991. A "yea" was a vote supporting the president's position.

149. S 1435. Fiscal 1992-93 Foreign Aid Authorization/International Monetary Fund. Brown, R-Colo., amendment to strike from the bill U.S. contributions to the International Monetary Fund of $12 billion. Rejected 31-65: R 18-24; D 13-41 (ND 10-29, SD 3-12), July 25, 1991. A "nay" was a vote supporting the president' s position.

150. S 1435. Fiscal 1992-93 Foreign Aid Authorization/Cloture. Motion to invoke cloture (thus limiting debate) on the Dodd, D-Conn., amendment to limit military aid to El Salvador to $85 million in fiscal 1992 and prohibit military aid, if the president determines El Salvador has not met specified conditions. Rejected 52-44: R 4-38; D 48-6 (ND 39-0, SD 9-6), July 25, 1991. A three-fifths majority vote (60) of the total Senate is required to invoke cloture.

151. S 1435. Fiscal 1992-93 Foreign Aid Authorization/Cloture. Motion to invoke cloture (thus limiting debate) on the Simon, D-Ill., amendment to authorize $20 million to be used for the U.N. Population Fund Activities (UNFPA) with the stipulation that if any UNPFA funds go to China, the entire $20 million will be returned to the United States. Motion agreed to 63-33: R 15-27; D 48-6 (ND 38-1, SD 10-5), July 25, 1991. A three-fifths majority vote (60) of the total Senate is required to invoke cloture.

152. S 1435. Fiscal 1992-93 Foreign Aid Authorization/Middle East Arms Sales. McConnell, R-Ky., motion to table (kill) the Biden, D-Del., amendment to condition arms sales to the Middle East on presidential certification that the recipient country is already a democracy or is making progress toward establishing institutions that embody democratic ideals. Motion rejected 39-57: R 33-10; D 6-47 (ND 2-36, SD 4-11), July 26, 1991. A "yea" was a vote supporting the president's position.

	153	154	155	156	157	158	159	160
ALABAMA								
Heflin	Y	Y	N	Y	Y	Y	N	Y
Shelby	Y	Y	N	Y	Y	Y	N	Y
ALASKA								
Murkowski	Y	Y	N	N	Y	Y	Y	Y
Stevens	N	Y	N	N	Y	Y	Y	Y
ARIZONA								
DeConcini	Y	N	N	N	N	Y	N	Y
McCain	Y	Y	N	N	Y	Y	Y	Y
ARKANSAS								
Bumpers	N	Y	N	Y	Y	Y	N	Y
Pryor	?	?	?	?	?	?	?	?
CALIFORNIA								
Cranston	Y	N	Y	Y	Y	Y	Y	Y
Seymour	Y	Y	N	N	Y	Y	Y	Y
COLORADO								
Wirth	?	N	N	Y	Y	Y	Y	Y
Brown	Y	Y	N	N	Y	Y	Y	N
CONNECTICUT								
Dodd	Y	N	N	Y	Y	Y	Y	Y
Lieberman	Y	N	N	Y	Y	Y	Y	Y
DELAWARE								
Biden	Y	N	N	Y	Y	Y	Y	Y
Roth	N	Y	N	N	Y	Y	Y	N
FLORIDA								
Graham	Y	N	N	Y	Y	Y	Y	Y
Mack	Y	Y	N	N	Y	Y	Y	Y
GEORGIA								
Fowler	Y	N	Y	Y	Y	Y	Y	Y
Nunn	?	N	N	Y	Y	Y	Y	Y
HAWAII								
Akaka	Y	N	N	Y	Y	Y	Y	Y
Inouye	Y	Y	N	Y	Y	Y	Y	Y
IDAHO								
Craig	N	Y	N	N	N	Y	Y	Y
Symms	N	Y	N	N	N	Y	Y	Y
ILLINOIS								
Dixon	Y	N	N	Y	N	Y	N	Y
Simon	Y	Y	Y	Y	Y	Y	Y	Y
INDIANA								
Coats	Y	Y	N	N	Y	Y	Y	Y
Lugar	Y	Y	N	N	Y	Y	Y	Y
IOWA								
Harkin	?	N	N	Y	Y	Y	Y	Y
Grassley	Y	Y	N	N	Y	Y	Y	Y
KANSAS								
Dole	N	Y	N	N	Y	Y	N	Y
Kassebaum	Y	Y	N	N	Y	Y	Y	Y
KENTUCKY								
Ford	Y	N	N	Y	Y	Y	N	Y
McConnell	Y	Y	N	N	Y	Y	Y	Y
LOUISIANA								
Breaux	Y	Y	Y	Y	Y	Y	Y	Y
Johnston	Y	N	N	Y	Y	Y	N	Y
MAINE								
Mitchell	Y	N	N	Y	Y	Y	Y	Y
Cohen	Y	Y	N	Y	Y	Y	Y	Y
MARYLAND								
Mikulski	Y	N	N	Y	Y	Y	Y	Y
Sarbanes	Y	N	Y	Y	Y	Y	Y	Y
MASSACHUSETTS								
Kennedy	Y	N	Y	Y	Y	Y	?	Y
Kerry	Y	Y	Y	Y	Y	Y	Y	Y
MICHIGAN								
Levin	Y	N	N	Y	Y	Y	Y	Y
Riegle	Y	N	N	Y	Y	Y	Y	Y
MINNESOTA								
Wellstone	Y	N	Y	Y	Y	Y	N	Y
Durenberger	N	Y	Y	Y	Y	Y	Y	Y
MISSISSIPPI								
Cochran	Y	Y	N	N	Y	Y	N	Y
Lott	?	Y	N	N	N	Y	N	Y
MISSOURI								
Bond	Y	Y	N	N	Y	Y	Y	Y
Danforth	Y	Y	N	Y	Y	Y	Y	Y
MONTANA								
Baucus	Y	N	N	Y	Y	Y	N	Y
Burns	Y	Y	N	N	N	Y	N	Y
NEBRASKA								
Exon	Y	N	N	N	Y	Y	N	Y
Kerrey	Y	N	N	N	Y	Y	N	Y
NEVADA								
Bryan	Y	Y	Y	Y	Y	Y	Y	Y
Reid	Y	N	Y	Y	Y	Y	Y	Y
NEW HAMPSHIRE								
Rudman	N	Y	N	N	Y	Y	Y	N
Smith	N	Y	N	N	N	Y	Y	N
NEW JERSEY								
Bradley	Y	N	Y	Y	Y	Y	Y	Y
Lautenberg	Y	N	N	Y	Y	Y	Y	Y
NEW MEXICO								
Bingaman	?	N	N	Y	Y	Y	Y	Y
Domenici	Y	Y	N	N	Y	Y	Y	Y
NEW YORK								
Moynihan	Y	N	Y	Y	Y	Y	Y	Y
D'Amato	Y	Y	N	Y	Y	Y	Y	Y
NORTH CAROLINA								
Sanford	Y	N	Y	Y	Y	Y	N	Y
Helms	N	Y	N	N	N	N	Y	Y
NORTH DAKOTA								
Burdick	Y	N	Y	Y	Y	Y	N	Y
Conrad	N	N	N	N	N	Y	N	Y
OHIO								
Glenn	Y	Y	Y	Y	Y	Y	Y	Y
Metzenbaum	?	N	N	Y	Y	Y	Y	Y
OKLAHOMA								
Boren	Y	Y	N	Y	Y	Y	Y	Y
Nickles	?	?	?	?	?	?	Y	Y
OREGON								
Hatfield	Y	Y	Y	N	Y	Y	Y	Y
Packwood	Y	Y	Y	N	Y	Y	Y	Y
PENNSYLVANIA								
Wofford	Y	N	Y	Y	Y	Y	Y	Y
Specter	Y	Y	N	N	Y	Y	Y	Y
RHODE ISLAND								
Pell	Y	N	Y	Y	Y	Y	Y	N
Chafee	Y	Y	N	N	Y	Y	Y	Y
SOUTH CAROLINA								
Hollings	N	Y	N	N	Y	Y	Y	Y
Thurmond	Y	Y	N	N	Y	Y	Y	Y
SOUTH DAKOTA								
Daschle	Y	N	N	Y	Y	Y	N	Y
Pressler	Y	Y	N	N	Y	Y	N	Y
TENNESSEE								
Gore	Y	N	Y	Y	Y	Y	Y	Y
Sasser	Y	N	N	Y	Y	Y	Y	Y
TEXAS								
Bentsen	Y	Y	N	Y	Y	Y	Y	Y
Gramm	N	Y	N	N	Y	Y	Y	Y
UTAH								
Garn	N	Y	N	N	Y	Y	Y	N
Hatch	N	+	-	+	+	+	Y	Y
VERMONT								
Leahy	Y	N	N	Y	Y	Y	Y	Y
Jeffords	Y	Y	Y	Y	Y	Y	Y	Y
VIRGINIA								
Robb	Y	Y	Y	Y	Y	Y	Y	Y
Warner	Y	Y	N	Y	Y	Y	N	Y
WASHINGTON								
Adams	Y	N	Y	Y	Y	Y	Y	Y
Gorton	Y	Y	N	N	Y	Y	Y	Y
WEST VIRGINIA								
Byrd	N	N	Y	Y	N	Y	N	Y
Rockefeller	Y	Y	N	Y	Y	Y	Y	Y
WISCONSIN								
Kohl	Y	N	N	Y	Y	Y	Y	Y
Kasten	N	Y	N	N	Y	Y	Y	Y
WYOMING								
Simpson	Y	Y	N	N	Y	Y	Y	Y
Wallop	N	Y	N	N	N	Y	Y	N

KEY

Y Voted for (yea).
\# Paired for.
\+ Announced for.
N Voted against (nay).
X Paired against.
\- Announced against.
P Voted "present."
C Voted "present" to avoid possible conflict of interest.
? Did not vote or otherwise make a position known.

Democrats *Republicans*

ND Northern Democrats SD Southern Democrats

Southern states - Ala., Ark., Fla., Ga., Ky., La., Miss., N.C., Okla., S.C., Tenn., Texas, Va.

153. HR 2508. Fiscal 1992-93 Foreign Aid Authorization/Passage. Passage of the bill to authorize $14.04 billion in fiscal 1992 for foreign economic and military assistance. Passed 74-18: R 27-14; D 47-4 (ND 34-2, SD 13-2), July 26, 1991. (Before passage, the text of S 1435, as amended, was substituted in lieu of the House language. A "nay" was a vote supporting the president's position.

154. S 1433. Fiscal 1992-93 State Department Authorization/Worldnet. Kerry, D-Mass., motion to table (kill) the Wofford, D-Pa., amendment to prohibit funding for the Worldnet television program by reducing the U.S. Information Agency's salaries and expense account by $22,718,000. Worldnet television broadcasts the position of the United States throughout the world. Motion agreed to 55-42: R 41-0; D 14-42 (ND 6-34, SD 8-8), July 29, 1991. A "yea" was a vote supporting the president's position.

155. S 1433. Fiscal 1992-93 State Department Authorization/U.S. Staffing. Kerry, D-Mass., motion to table (kill) the Pressler, R-S.D., amendment to encourage the employment of U.S. citizens by certain international organizations by withholding funds to pay arrearages for assessed contributions from prior years, unless the secretary of State certifies that an organization has met certain criteria. Motion rejected 25-72: R 4-37; D 21-35 (ND 16-24, SD 5-11), July 29, 1991. (Subsequently, the Pressler amendment was adopted by voice vote.)

156. S 1433. Fiscal 1992-93 State Department Authorization/Protection Services. Kerry, D-Mass., motion to table (kill) the Helms, R-N.C., amendment to strike the provisions that would allow the U.S. Secret Service to protect persons visiting an international organization and allow state and local governments to submit claims for reimbursement of expenses incurred after Jan. 1, 1989, in helping to provide for the protection of such persons. Motion agreed to 57-40: R 6-35; D 51-5 (ND 36-4, SD 15-1), July 29, 1991.

157. HR 1415. Fiscal 1992-93 State Department Authorization/Passage. Passage of the bill to authorize $6 billion in fiscal 1992 and $5.5 billion in fiscal 1993 for the State Department, the U.S. Information Agency, the Board for International Broadcasting and related programs. Passed 86-11: R 34-7; D 52-4 (ND 36-4, SD 16-0), July 29, 1991. (Before final passage, the Senate struck the all after the enacting clause of HR 1415 and inserted the text of S 1433.)

158. S 1554. Unemployment Benefits Extension/Cloture. Mitchell, D-Maine, motion to invoke cloture (thus limiting debate) on the motion to proceed to the bill to provide $6 billion to the states to extend the number of weeks an unemployed worker could receive insurance benefits. The bill would call on the president to classify the spending as an emergency, which would exempt the spending from budgetary caps. Motion agreed to 96-1: R 40-1; D 56-0 (ND 40-0, SD 16-0), July 29, 1991. A three-fifths majority vote (60) of the total Senate is required to invoke cloture.

159. HR 2698. Fiscal 1992 Agriculture Appropriations/Wetlands. Leahy, D-Vt., amendment to the committee amendment to preserve 1990 farm bill language that allowed the secretary of Agriculture to enter into pacts that established perpetual easements with annual and lump-sum payments to landowners to preserve and restore wetlands for 30 years or the maximum duration under state law. Adopted 76-22: R 37-6; D 39-16 (ND 29-10, SD 10-6), July 30, 1991.

160. HR 2698. Fiscal 1992 Agriculture Appropriations/Passage. Passage of the bill to provide $53,120,030,000 in new budget authority for Agriculture, Rural Development, Food and Drug Administration, and related agencies' programs in fiscal 1992. The administration requested $52,579,946,000. The House-passed bill provided for $52,570,051,000. Passed 92-7: R 37-6; D 55-1 (ND 39-1, SD 16-0), July 30, 1991.

SENATE VOTES 161, 162, 163, 164, 165, 166, 167, 168

	161	162	163	164	165	166	167	168
ALABAMA								
Heflin	N	N	Y	Y	Y	N	Y	N
Shelby	N	N	Y	Y	Y	Y	Y	N
ALASKA								
Murkowski	N	N	N	N	Y	Y	N	N
Stevens	Y	N	Y	N	Y	Y	N	N
ARIZONA								
DeConcini	N	N	Y	N	Y	Y	N	Y
McCain	N	N	Y	N	Y	Y	Y	N
ARKANSAS								
Bumpers	N	N	Y	Y	Y	Y	Y	Y
Pryor	?	?	?	?	?	?	?	?
CALIFORNIA								
Cranston	Y	Y	Y	N	Y	Y	N	Y
Seymour	N	N	N	N	Y	Y	N	N
COLORADO								
Wirth	Y	Y	Y	Y	Y	Y	N	N
Brown	N	N	N	N	N	Y	N	N
CONNECTICUT								
Dodd	N	Y	Y	Y	Y	Y	N	N
Lieberman	N	Y	Y	Y	Y	Y	N	N
DELAWARE								
Biden	Y	Y	Y	Y	Y	Y	N	Y
Roth	N	N	N	N	N	Y	N	N
FLORIDA								
Graham	N	N	Y	Y	Y	Y	N	Y
Mack	N	N	N	N	Y	Y	N	N
GEORGIA								
Fowler	N	N	Y	Y	Y	Y	Y	Y
Nunn	N	N	Y	Y	Y	Y	Y	N
HAWAII								
Akaka	Y	Y	Y	Y	Y	Y	N	Y
Inouye	Y	Y	Y	Y	Y	Y	Y	N
IDAHO								
Craig	N	N	N	N	N	Y	Y	N
Symms	N	N	N	N	N	Y	Y	N
ILLINOIS								
Dixon	N	N	Y	Y	N	Y	N	N
Simon	Y	Y	Y	Y	Y	Y	N	Y
INDIANA								
Coats	N	N	N	N	Y	Y	N	N
Lugar	Y	N	Y	N	Y	Y	N	N
IOWA								
Harkin	Y	Y	Y	Y	Y	Y	N	Y
Grassley	N	N	N	N	Y	Y	N	N
KANSAS								
Dole	N	N	N	N	Y	Y	N	N
Kassebaum	Y	Y	Y	N	Y	Y	N	Y
KENTUCKY								
Ford	N	N	Y	Y	Y	Y	N	N
McConnell	N	N	N	N	Y	Y	N	N
LOUISIANA								
Breaux	N	N	Y	Y	Y	Y	Y	N
Johnston	N	N	Y	Y	Y	Y	Y	Y
MAINE								
Mitchell	Y	Y	Y	Y	Y	Y	N	Y
Cohen	N	Y	Y	Y	Y	Y	N	N
MARYLAND								
Mikulski	N	Y	Y	Y	Y	Y	N	Y
Sarbanes	Y	Y	Y	Y	Y	Y	N	Y
MASSACHUSETTS								
Kennedy	Y	Y	Y	Y	Y	Y	N	Y
Kerry	Y	Y	Y	Y	Y	Y	N	Y
MICHIGAN								
Levin	N	Y	Y	Y	Y	Y	N	Y
Riegle	N	N	Y	Y	Y	Y	N	Y
MINNESOTA								
Wellstone	?	Y	Y	Y	Y	Y	N	Y
Durenberger	Y	Y	Y	N	Y	Y	N	N
MISSISSIPPI								
Cochran	Y	N	Y	N	Y	Y	N	N
Lott	N	N	N	N	N	Y	Y	N
MISSOURI								
Bond	N	N	N	N	Y	Y	Y	N
Danforth	Y	N	Y	N	Y	Y	N	N
MONTANA								
Baucus	N	Y	Y	Y	Y	Y	N	N
Burns	N	N	N	N	N	Y	Y	N
NEBRASKA								
Exon	N	N	Y	Y	Y	Y	N	N
Kerrey	N	Y	Y	Y	Y	Y	N	Y
NEVADA								
Bryan	N	N	Y	Y	Y	Y	Y	Y
Reid	N	N	Y	Y	Y	Y	N	Y
NEW HAMPSHIRE								
Rudman	N	N	Y	Y	Y	Y	Y	N
Smith	N	N	N	N	N	Y	Y	N
NEW JERSEY								
Bradley	Y	Y	Y	Y	Y	Y	N	Y
Lautenberg	Y	Y	Y	Y	Y	Y	N	Y
NEW MEXICO								
Bingaman	Y	Y	Y	N	Y	Y	N	N
Domenici	N	N	Y	N	Y	Y	N	N
NEW YORK								
Moynihan	Y	Y	Y	Y	N	Y	Y	Y
D'Amato	N	N	Y	N	Y	Y	N	N
NORTH CAROLINA								
Sanford	Y	Y	Y	Y	Y	Y	Y	Y
Helms	N	N	N	N	N	Y	Y	N
NORTH DAKOTA								
Burdick	N	Y	Y	Y	Y	Y	N	N
Conrad	Y	N	Y	N	Y	Y	Y	N
OHIO								
Glenn	Y	N	Y	Y	Y	Y	Y	Y
Metzenbaum	Y	Y	Y	Y	Y	Y	N	Y
OKLAHOMA								
Boren	N	N	Y	N	Y	Y	Y	N
Nickles	N	N	N	N	Y	Y	N	N
OREGON								
Hatfield	Y	Y	Y	Y	Y	Y	N	Y
Packwood	N	N	Y	Y	Y	Y	N	N
PENNSYLVANIA								
Wofford	Y	Y	Y	Y	Y	Y	N	Y
Specter	Y	Y	Y	N	Y	Y	N	N
RHODE ISLAND								
Pell	Y	Y	Y	Y	Y	Y	N	Y
Chafee	Y	Y	Y	N	Y	Y	N	Y
SOUTH CAROLINA								
Hollings	N	N	Y	Y	Y	Y	Y	N
Thurmond	N	N	N	N	Y	Y	Y	N
SOUTH DAKOTA								
Daschle	Y	Y	Y	Y	N	Y	N	Y
Pressler	N	N	N	N	Y	Y	N	N
TENNESSEE								
Gore	Y	Y	Y	Y	Y	Y	N	Y
Sasser	N	Y	Y	Y	Y	Y	N	Y
TEXAS								
Bentsen	N	N	Y	Y	Y	N	N	N
Gramm	N	N	N	N	Y	Y	Y	N
UTAH								
Garn	N	N	N	N	Y	Y	Y	N
Hatch	N	Y	N	N	Y	Y	N	N
VERMONT								
Leahy	Y	Y	Y	Y	Y	Y	N	Y
Jeffords	Y	Y	Y	N	Y	Y	N	Y
VIRGINIA								
Robb	Y	Y	Y	Y	Y	Y	N	N
Warner	N	N	N	N	Y	Y	Y	N
WASHINGTON								
Adams	Y	Y	Y	Y	Y	Y	N	Y
Gorton	N	Y	Y	N	Y	Y	N	N
WEST VIRGINIA								
Byrd	N	N	Y	Y	Y	N	Y	N
Rockefeller	Y	Y	Y	Y	Y	Y	N	Y
WISCONSIN								
Kohl	N	Y	Y	Y	Y	Y	N	N
Kasten	N	N	N	N	Y	Y	N	N
WYOMING								
Simpson	N	N	N	N	Y	Y	N	N
Wallop	Y	N	N	N	N	Y	Y	N

KEY

- Y Voted for (yea).
- # Paired for.
- \+ Announced for.
- N Voted against (nay).
- X Paired against.
- \- Announced against.
- P Voted "present."
- C Voted "present" to avoid possible conflict of interest.
- ? Did not vote or otherwise make a position known.

Democrats *Republicans*

ND Northern Democrats SD Southern Democrats

Southern states - Ala., Ark., Fla., Ga., Ky., La., Miss., N.C., Okla., S.C., Tenn., Texas, Va.

161. HR 2608. Fiscal 1992 Commerce, Justice, State Appropriations/Pell Grants. Pell, D-R.I., motion to table (kill) the Helms, R-N.C., amendment to prohibit state or federal prisoners from receiving Pell grants. Motion rejected 38-60: R 11-32; D 27-28 (ND 24-15, SD 3-13), July 30, 1991. (The Helms amendment was subsequently adopted by voice vote.)

162. HR 2608. Fiscal 1992 Commerce, Justice, State Appropriations/HIV Testing. Kennedy, D-Mass., motion to table (kill) the Helms, R-N.C., amendment to allow health-care professionals to test patients for human immunodeficiency virus (HIV) before invasive medical procedures except in emergencies. The test results would be confidential, and a person violating the confidentiality would be fined $10,000 or face a prison term of not more than one year. States without regulations to protect health-care workers from HIV after one year would be ineligible to receive federal funds under the Public Health Service Act. Motion rejected 44-55: R 9-34; D 35-21 (ND 31-9, SD 4-12), July 30, 1991. (The Helms amendment was subsequently adopted by voice vote.)

163. HR 2608. Fiscal 1992 Commerce, Justice, State Appropriations/Legal Services Corporation. Hollings, D-S.C., motion to table (kill) the Gramm, R-Texas, amendment to cut the Legal Services Corporation by $48.41 million and transfer the funds to the FBI. Motion agreed to 73-26: R 17-26; D 56-0 (ND 40-0, SD 16-0), July 31, 1991.

164. HR 2608. Fiscal 1992 Commerce, Justice, State Appropriations/Border Patrol Program. Hollings, D-S.C., motion to table (kill) the Seymour, R-Calif., amendment to provide an across-the-board cut of $40 million from all discretionary spending in salaries and expense accounts in the bill and transfer the funds to the Border Patrol program. Motion agreed to 56-43: R 4-39; D 52-4 (ND 37-3, SD 15-1), July 31, 1991.

165. HR 2608. Fiscal 1992 Commerce, Justice, State Appropriations/Passage. Passage of the bill to provide $22,123,488,000 in new budget authority for the Departments of Commerce, Justice and State, the judiciary, and related agencies in fiscal 1992. The administration requested $22,342,064,000. The House-passed bill provided for $20,974,822,000. Passed 86-13: R 34-9; D 52-4 (ND 36-4, SD 16-0), July 31, 1991.

166. S 1507. Fiscal 1992-93 Defense Authorization/Women in Combat. Glenn, D-Ohio, amendment to require the Commission on the Assignment of Women in the Armed Forces to conduct comprehensive research and analyses on the potential for women in combat. The secretary of Defense in consultation with the commission would be able to waive prohibitions against women in combat pilot positions in order to conduct test assignments. Adopted 96-3: R 43-0; D 53-3 (ND 39-1, SD 14-2), July 31, 1991.

167. S 1507. Fiscal 1992-93 Defense Authorization/-Women in Combat Pilot Positions. Glenn, D-Ohio, motion to table (kill) the Roth, R-Del., amendment to repeal the 1948 law that prohibits women from flying in combat pilot positions. Motion rejected 30-69: R 14-29; D 16-40 (ND 6-34, SD 10-6), July 31, 1991. (The Roth amendment was subsequently adopted by voice vote.)

168. S 1507. Fiscal 1992-93 Defense Authorization/-Strategic Defense Initiative. Gore, D-Tenn., amendment to eliminate the provisions in the committee bill that would allow for multiple missile interceptor sites and deployment of space-based missile sensors prohibited by the 1972 anti-ballistic missile treaty. The amendment would keep the Strategic Defense Initiative in the research and development stage. Rejected 39-60: R 4-39; D 35-21 (ND 28-12, SD 7-9), July 31, 1991. A "nay" was a vote supporting the president's position.

	169	170	171	172	173	174	175	176
ALABAMA								
Heflin	N	Y	Y	Y	N	N	N	Y
Shelby	N	Y	Y	Y	N	N	N	Y
ALASKA								
Murkowski	N	Y	Y	Y	N	N	Y	Y
Stevens	N	Y	Y	Y	N	N	?	?
ARIZONA								
DeConcini	Y	Y	N	N	Y	Y	N	N
McCain	N	Y	Y	Y	N	Y	N	Y
ARKANSAS								
Bumpers	Y	Y	N	N	Y	Y	N	N
Pryor	?	?	?	?	#	?	?	?
CALIFORNIA								
Cranston	Y	Y	?	?	Y	Y	Y	N
Seymour	N	Y	Y	Y	N	N	Y	Y
COLORADO								
Wirth	Y	Y	Y	Y	Y	Y	N	N
Brown	N	Y	Y	Y	N	N	N	Y
CONNECTICUT								
Dodd	Y	Y	Y	Y	N	N	N	N
Lieberman	Y	Y	N	Y	Y	Y	N	N
DELAWARE								
Biden	Y	Y	N	N	Y	Y	?	N
Roth	N	Y	Y	Y	N	Y	N	N
FLORIDA								
Graham	Y	Y	Y	N	Y	Y	Y	Y
Mack	N	Y	Y	Y	N	N	Y	Y
GEORGIA								
Fowler	Y	Y	N	Y	Y	N	N	Y
Nunn	N	Y	Y	Y	N	N	N	Y
HAWAII								
Akaka	N	Y	N	N	Y	N	N	N
Inouye	N	Y	Y	Y	N	N	N	N
IDAHO								
Craig	N	Y	Y	Y	N	N	N	Y
Symms	N	Y	Y	Y	N	N	N	Y
ILLINOIS								
Dixon	N	Y	Y	Y	N	N	Y	N
Simon	Y	Y	N	N	Y	Y	Y	N
INDIANA								
Coats	N	Y	Y	Y	N	N	N	Y
Lugar	N	Y	Y	Y	N	N	N	Y
IOWA								
Harkin	Y	Y	N	N	Y	Y	Y	N
Grassley	N	Y	Y	Y	Y	Y	Y	Y
KANSAS								
Dole	N	Y	Y	Y	N	N	Y	Y
Kassebaum	N	Y	Y	N	Y	N	N	Y
KENTUCKY								
Ford	N	Y	Y	Y	Y	N	N	N
McConnell	N	Y	Y	Y	N	N	N	Y
LOUISIANA								
Breaux	Y	Y	N	Y	N	N	N	Y
Johnston	Y	Y	N	N	Y	N	N	N
MAINE								
Mitchell	Y	Y	N	N	Y	Y	N	N
Cohen	N	Y	Y	Y	N	Y	N	Y
MARYLAND								
Mikulski	Y	Y	N	N	Y	Y	N	N
Sarbanes	Y	Y	N	N	Y	Y	Y	Y
MASSACHUSETTS								
Kennedy	Y	Y	N	N	Y	Y	N	N
Kerry	Y	Y	N	N	Y	Y	N	N
MICHIGAN								
Levin	Y	Y	N	N	Y	N	N	N
Riegle	Y	Y	N	N	Y	Y	N	N
MINNESOTA								
Wellstone	Y	Y	N	N	Y	Y	N	N
Durenberger	N	Y	Y	Y	N	N	Y	Y
MISSISSIPPI								
Cochran	N	Y	Y	Y	N	N	Y	Y
Lott	N	Y	Y	Y	N	N	N	Y
MISSOURI								
Bond	N	Y	Y	Y	N	N	Y	Y
Danforth	N	Y	Y	Y	N	N	Y	Y
MONTANA								
Baucus	Y	Y	Y	Y	Y	Y	N	N
Burns	N	Y	Y	Y	N	N	N	Y
NEBRASKA								
Exon	N	Y	Y	Y	N	N	N	N
Kerrey	Y	Y	N	Y	Y	Y	N	N
NEVADA								
Bryan	Y	Y	Y	Y	Y	N	N	N
Reid	Y	Y	N	Y	Y	Y	N	N
NEW HAMPSHIRE								
Rudman	N	Y	Y	Y	N	N	N	Y
Smith	N	Y	Y	Y	N	N	Y	Y
NEW JERSEY								
Bradley	Y	Y	N	N	Y	Y	N	N
Lautenberg	Y	Y	N	N	Y	Y	N	N
NEW MEXICO								
Bingaman	Y	Y	Y	Y	N	N	N	N
Domenici	N	Y	Y	Y	N	N	N	Y
NEW YORK								
Moynihan	Y	Y	N	N	Y	Y	Y	N
D'Amato	N	Y	Y	Y	N	N	N	Y
NORTH CAROLINA								
Sanford	Y	Y	N	N	Y	N	N	N
Helms	N	Y	Y	Y	N	N	N	Y
NORTH DAKOTA								
Burdick	Y	Y	Y	Y	X	Y	N	N
Conrad	Y	Y	Y	Y	N	Y	N	N
OHIO								
Glenn	N	Y	N	N	Y	Y	Y	N
Metzenbaum	Y	Y	N	N	Y	Y	Y	N
OKLAHOMA								
Boren	N	Y	Y	Y	Y	N	Y	N
Nickles	N	Y	Y	Y	N	N	N	Y
OREGON								
Hatfield	N	Y	N	N	Y	Y	N	N
Packwood	N	Y	Y	Y	N	Y	N	N
PENNSYLVANIA								
Wofford	Y	Y	Y	N	Y	Y	N	N
Specter	N	Y	Y	Y	N	N	N	Y
RHODE ISLAND								
Pell	Y	Y	N	N	Y	Y	Y	N
Chafee	Y	Y	N	N	Y	N	Y	Y
SOUTH CAROLINA								
Hollings	N	Y	Y	Y	N	Y	N	Y
Thurmond	N	Y	Y	Y	N	N	N	Y
SOUTH DAKOTA								
Daschle	Y	Y	N	N	Y	Y	N	N
Pressler	N	Y	Y	Y	N	N	Y	Y
TENNESSEE								
Gore	Y	Y	N	N	Y	N	N	Y
Sasser	Y	Y	N	N	Y	Y	N	Y
TEXAS								
Bentsen	N	Y	Y	Y	N	N	N	N
Gramm	N	Y	Y	Y	N	N	N	Y
UTAH								
Garn	N	Y	Y	Y	N	N	N	Y
Hatch	N	Y	Y	Y	N	N	N	Y
VERMONT								
Leahy	N	Y	N	N	Y	Y	N	N
Jeffords	Y	Y	N	N	Y	Y	Y	Y
VIRGINIA								
Robb	N	Y	Y	Y	N	N	Y	N
Warner	N	Y	Y	Y	N	N	Y	Y
WASHINGTON								
Adams	Y	Y	N	N	Y	Y	N	N
Gorton	N	Y	Y	Y	N	N	Y	Y
WEST VIRGINIA								
Byrd	N	Y	N	Y	N	N	N	Y
Rockefeller	Y	Y	N	N	Y	Y	N	Y
WISCONSIN								
Kohl	Y	Y	N	Y	Y	Y	N	N
Kasten	N	Y	Y	Y	N	N	Y	Y
WYOMING								
Simpson	N	Y	Y	Y	N	N	Y	Y
Wallop	N	Y	Y	Y	N	N	Y	Y

KEY

- Y Voted for (yea).
- # Paired for.
- + Announced for.
- N Voted against (nay).
- X Paired against.
- \- Announced against.
- P Voted "present."
- C Voted "present" to avoid possible conflict of interest.
- ? Did not vote or otherwise make a position known.

Democrats *Republicans*

ND Northern Democrats SD Southern Democrats

Southern states - Ala., Ark., Fla., Ga., Ky., La., Miss., N.C., Okla., S.C., Tenn., Texas, Va.

169. S 1507. Fiscal 1992-93 Defense Authorization/-Strategic Stability. Bingaman, D-N.M., amendment to state that it is the goal of the United States to maintain strategic stability with the Soviet Union while deploying an anti-ballistic missile system with one or more ground-based sites and space-based sensors. The amendment would clarify that current actions by the U.S. are treaty compliant, and the U.S. would deploy at only one site and additional sites as the result of a mutual agreement. Rejected 43-56: R 2-41; D 41-15 (ND 33-7, SD 8-8), July 31, 1991. A "nay" was a vote supporting the president's position.

170. S 1507. Fiscal 1992-93 Defense Authorization/ABM Treaty. Levin, D-Mich., amendment to state that nothing in the bill's provisions for an anti-missile system is in violation of the 1972 U.S.-Soviet anti-ballistic missile (ABM) treaty. Adopted 99-0: R 43-0; D 56-0 (ND 40-0, SD 16-0), Aug. 1, 1991.

171. S 1507. Fiscal 1992-93 Defense Authorization/Transfer Strategic Defense Initiative Funding. Nunn, D-Ga., motion to table (kill) the Harkin, D-Iowa, amendment to cut $1.4 billion of the $4.6 billion authorized for the Strategic Defense Initiative and prohibit any funding for the spaced-based interceptors program. Motion agreed to 60-38: R 40-3; D 20-35 (ND 11-28, SD 9-7), Aug. 1, 1991. A "yea" was a vote supporting the president's position.

172. S 1507. Fiscal 1992-93 Defense Authorization/North Dakota Deployment. Nunn, D-Ga., motion to table (kill) the Harkin, D-Iowa, amendment to prohibit the deployment of the ground-based anti-ballistic missile system at Grand Forks, N.D., in 1996, as proposed in the bill. Motion agreed to 64-34: R 39-4; D 25-30 (ND 15-24, SD 10-6), Aug. 1, 1991. A "yea" was a vote supporting the president's position.

173. S 1507. Fiscal 1992-93 Defense Authorization/-Strategic Defense Initiative. Bumpers, D-Ark., amendment to cut $1 billion of the $4.6 billion authorized for the Strategic Defense Initiative and transfer the savings to reducing the deficit. Rejected 46-52: R 5-38; D 41-14 (ND 32-7, SD 9-7), Aug. 1, 1991. A "nay" was a vote supporting the president's position.

174. S 1507. Fiscal 1992-93 Defense Authorization/B-2 Bomber. Leahy, D-Vt., amendment to eliminate the bill's provision allowing for producing four B-2 bombers, stopping production at the 15 planes already funded. The amendment would change the scope of the B-2 program to end production of the bomber but allow for research and development, testing, and evaluation. Rejected 42-57: R 7-36; D 35-21 (ND 31-9, SD 4-12), Aug. 1, 1991. A "nay" was a vote supporting the president's position.

175. S 1507. Fiscal 1992-93 Defense Authorization/-Transfer of Closed Military Bases. Glenn, D-Ohio, motion to table (kill) the Breaux, D-La., amendment to require the Defense Department to make available for transfer free of charge closed military bases to local communities. Motion rejected 30-67: R 18-24; D 12-43 (ND 9-30, SD 3-13), Aug. 2, 1991. (The Breaux amendment subsequently was adopted by voice vote.)

176. S 1507. Fiscal 1992-93 Defense Authorization/-SRAM-T Nuclear Missile Program. Thurmond, R-S.C., motion to table (kill) the Exon, D-Neb., amendment to terminate the short-range attack missile tactical (SRAM-T) nuclear missile program. Motion agreed to 51-47: R 39-3; D 12-44 (ND 3-37, SD 9-7), Aug. 2, 1991. A "yea" was a vote supporting the president's position.

	177	178	179	180	181	182	183	184
ALABAMA								
Heflin	N	Y	Y	Y	Y	N	Y	Y
Shelby	Y	Y	Y	Y	N	N	Y	Y
ALASKA								
Murkowski	N	Y	Y	Y	N	N	Y	Y
Stevens	?	Y	Y	Y	N	N	Y	Y
ARIZONA								
DeConcini	Y	Y	Y	N	N	?	Y	Y
McCain	N	Y	Y	Y	N	N	Y	Y
ARKANSAS								
Bumpers	Y	Y	Y	N	N	N	Y	Y
Pryor	?	?	?	?	?	N	Y	Y
CALIFORNIA								
Cranston	Y	Y	N	N	N	?	Y	Y
Seymour	Y	Y	Y	Y	N	N	Y	Y
COLORADO								
Wirth	Y	Y	N	N	N	Y	Y	Y
Brown	Y	Y	Y	Y	N	N	N	N
CONNECTICUT								
Dodd	Y	Y	N	N	N	N	Y	Y
Lieberman	Y	Y	N	N	N	N	Y	Y
DELAWARE								
Biden	Y	Y	N	N	N	Y	Y	Y
Roth	N	Y	N	Y	N	?	N	Y
FLORIDA								
Graham	Y	Y	N	Y	N	N	Y	Y
Mack	N	Y	N	Y	Y	N	N	Y
GEORGIA								
Fowler	Y	Y	Y	Y	N	N	Y	Y
Nunn	Y	Y	Y	Y	N	N	N	Y
HAWAII								
Akaka	Y	Y	N	N	N	Y	Y	Y
Inouye	Y	Y	Y	Y	N	N	Y	Y
IDAHO								
Craig	N	Y	Y	Y	Y	N	N	Y
Symms	N	Y	Y	Y	Y	N	N	Y
ILLINOIS								
Dixon	Y	Y	Y	Y	N	N	N	Y
Simon	Y	Y	N	N	N	Y	Y	Y
INDIANA								
Coats	N	Y	Y	Y	Y	N	Y	Y
Lugar	N	Y	N	Y	Y	N	Y	Y
IOWA								
Harkin	Y	Y	N	N	N	Y	Y	Y
Grassley	N	Y	Y	Y	N	N	Y	Y
KANSAS								
Dole	N	Y	Y	Y	Y	N	N	Y
Kassebaum	Y	Y	Y	N	Y	N	N	Y
KENTUCKY								
Ford	N	Y	Y	N	N	N	Y	Y
McConnell	N	Y	Y	Y	Y	N	Y	Y
LOUISIANA								
Breaux	N	Y	Y	Y	N	N	N	Y
Johnston	N	Y	Y	N	N	N	Y	Y
MAINE								
Mitchell	Y	Y	N	N	N	Y	Y	Y
Cohen	Y	Y	Y	Y	Y	N	Y	Y
MARYLAND								
Mikulski	Y	Y	N	N	N	N	Y	Y
Sarbanes	Y	Y	N	N	N	Y	Y	Y
MASSACHUSETTS								
Kennedy	Y	Y	N	N	Y	Y	Y	Y
Kerry	Y	Y	Y	N	N	Y	Y	Y
MICHIGAN								
Levin	Y	Y	Y	N	N	N	Y	Y
Riegle	Y	Y	N	N	N	Y	Y	Y
MINNESOTA								
Wellstone	Y	N	N	N	N	Y	Y	Y
Durenberger	N	Y	N	N	N	N	Y	Y
MISSISSIPPI								
Cochran	N	Y	Y	Y	Y	N	Y	Y
Lott	N	Y	?	?	?	N	N	Y
MISSOURI								
Bond	N	Y	Y	Y	Y	N	Y	Y
Danforth	N	Y	Y	Y	Y	N	N	Y
MONTANA								
Baucus	Y	Y	N	N	N	Y	Y	Y
Burns	N	Y	Y	Y	N	N	Y	Y
NEBRASKA								
Exon	N	Y	Y	N	Y	N	Y	Y
Kerrey	Y	Y	Y	N	N	N	Y	Y
NEVADA								
Bryan	Y	Y	Y	N	N	N	Y	Y
Reid	N	Y	N	Y	N	N	Y	Y
NEW HAMPSHIRE								
Rudman	N	Y	Y	Y	Y	N	Y	Y
Smith	N	Y	Y	Y	N	N	Y	Y
NEW JERSEY								
Bradley	Y	Y	N	?	?	Y	Y	Y
Lautenberg	Y	Y	N	N	N	Y	Y	Y
NEW MEXICO								
Bingaman	Y	Y	N	N	Y	N	Y	Y
Domenici	N	Y	Y	Y	Y	N	N	Y
NEW YORK								
Moynihan	Y	Y	N	N	N	N	Y	Y
D'Amato	N	Y	Y	Y	N	N	Y	Y
NORTH CAROLINA								
Sanford	Y	Y	Y	N	N	N	Y	Y
Helms	N	Y	Y	Y	N	N	N	Y
NORTH DAKOTA								
Burdick	Y	Y	N	Y	N	Y	Y	Y
Conrad	Y	Y	N	N	N	Y	Y	Y
OHIO								
Glenn	Y	Y	N	N	Y	N	Y	Y
Metzenbaum	Y	Y	N	N	N	Y	Y	Y
OKLAHOMA								
Boren	N	Y	N	N	Y	N	Y	Y
Nickles	N	Y	Y	Y	Y	N	N	Y
OREGON								
Hatfield	N	N	N	N	Y	Y	Y	Y
Packwood	Y	Y	Y	Y	N	Y	Y	Y
PENNSYLVANIA								
Wofford	Y	Y	Y	N	N	Y	Y	Y
Specter	Y	Y	Y	Y	?	Y	Y	Y
RHODE ISLAND								
Pell	Y	Y	N	N	Y	Y	Y	Y
Chafee	Y	Y	N	N	Y	N	Y	Y
SOUTH CAROLINA								
Hollings	Y	Y	Y	N	Y	Y	Y	Y
Thurmond	N	Y	Y	Y	+	N	N	Y
SOUTH DAKOTA								
Daschle	Y	Y	N	N	?	Y	Y	Y
Pressler	N	Y	N	Y	N	N	Y	Y
TENNESSEE								
Gore	Y	Y	N	Y	N	N	Y	Y
Sasser	Y	Y	Y	N	N	N	Y	Y
TEXAS								
Bentsen	Y	Y	Y	Y	Y	N	Y	Y
Gramm	N	Y	Y	Y	Y	N	N	Y
UTAH								
Garn	N	Y	N	Y	Y	N	N	Y
Hatch	N	Y	N	Y	Y	N	Y	Y
VERMONT								
Leahy	Y	Y	N	N	N	Y	Y	Y
Jeffords	Y	Y	N	N	N	N	Y	Y
VIRGINIA								
Robb	Y	Y	Y	N	N	N	Y	Y
Warner	N	Y	Y	Y	Y	N	Y	Y
WASHINGTON								
Adams	Y	Y	N	N	N	Y	Y	Y
Gorton	Y	Y	Y	Y	Y	N	Y	Y
WEST VIRGINIA								
Byrd	Y	Y	Y	N	Y	N	N	Y
Rockefeller	Y	Y	N	N	N	Y	Y	Y
WISCONSIN								
Kohl	Y	Y	Y	N	N	Y	N	Y
Kasten	N	Y	Y	Y	N	N	Y	Y
WYOMING								
Simpson	N	Y	N	Y	Y	N	Y	Y
Wallop	N	Y	Y	Y	Y	N	N	Y

KEY

- Y Voted for (yea).
- # Paired for.
- \+ Announced for.
- N Voted against (nay).
- X Paired against.
- \- Announced against.
- P Voted "present."
- C Voted "present" to avoid possible conflict of interest.
- ? Did not vote or otherwise make a position known.

Democrats *Republicans*

ND Northern Democrats SD Southern Democrats

Southern states - Ala., Ark., Fla., Ga., Ky., La., Miss., N.C., Okla., S.C., Tenn., Texas, Va.

177. S 1507. Fiscal 1992-93 Defense Authorization/ Cloture. Motion to invoke cloture (thus limiting debate) on the Wirth, D-Colo., amendment to allow military personnel and their dependents stationed overseas to obtain privately paid abortions in U.S. military hospitals. Motion rejected 58-40: R 9-33; D 49-7 (ND 38-2, SD 11-5), Aug. 2, 1991. A three-fifths majority vote (60) of the total Senate was required to invoke cloture. A "nay" was a vote supporting the president's position.

178. S 1507. Fiscal 1992-93 Defense Authorization/ Iraq's Nuclear Weapons. Dole, R-Kan., amendment to express the sense of Congress to support the use of all necessary means to achieve the goals of U.N. Resolution 687, which requires that Iraq place all of its nuclear weapons in control of the International Atomic Energy Agency and destroy all of its chemical and biological weapons. Adopted 97-2: R 42-1; D 55-1 (ND 39-1, SD 16-0), Aug. 2, 1991.

179. S 1507. Fiscal 1992-93 Defense Authorization/ Tobacco Products. Ford, D-Ky., motion to table (kill) the Bingaman, D-N.M., amendment to require tobacco products sold at military stores in the United States and abroad to be sold at competitive prices. Motion agreed to 55-43: R 31-11; D 24-32 (ND 11-29, SD 13-3), Aug. 2, 1991.

180. S 1507. Fiscal 1992-93 Defense Authorization/MX Train. Thurmond, R-S.C., motion to table (kill) the Exon, D-Neb., amendment to cut $225 million in funds to build one operational model rail garrison MX train. Motion agreed to 49-48: R 37-5; D 12-43 (ND 4-35, SD 8-8), Aug. 2, 1991.

181. S 1507. Fiscal 1992-93 Defense Authorization/ POW/MIA Flag Display. Warner, R-Va., motion to table (kill) the Reid, D-Nev., amendment to require the display of the POW/MIA flag at federal buildings and the National Vietnam Veterans Memorial until the fullest possible accounting has been made of all prisoners of war or people missing in action in Southeast Asia. Motion rejected 34-60: R 24-16; D 10-44 (ND 6-32, SD 4-12), Aug. 2, 1991. (The Reid amendment was adopted by voice vote.)

182. HR 2707. Fiscal 1992 Labor, HHS and Education Appropriations/Budget Waiver. Harkin, D-Iowa, motion to waive the Budget Act with respect to the Harkin amendment to the committee amendment, to rescind $3.148 billion in budget authority from unobligated balances in Defense Department accounts from fiscal 1988-91 and transfer the $3.148 billion in budget authority to domestic programs. Motion rejected 28-69: R 3-39; D 25-30 (ND 24-14, SD 1-16), Sept. 10, 1991. A three-fifths majority (60) of the Senate was required to waive the Budget Act. A "nay" was a vote supporting the president's position.

183. HR 2707. Fiscal 1992 Labor, HHS and Education Appropriations/New Budget Authority. Harkin, D-Iowa, amendment to provide new budget authority of $310 million in education and child health programs and $200 million for the Low Income Home Energy Assistance Program. The amendment would defer outlay spending from the programs until Sept. 30, 1992. Adopted 79-21: R 27-16; D 52-5 (ND 37-3, SD 15-2), Sept. 11, 1991.

184. HR 2707. Fiscal 1992 Labor, HHS and Education Appropriations/Occupational Safety and Health Administration Rules. Dole, R-Kan., amendment to require the Occupational Safety and Health Administration to issue final rules on bloodborne diseases by Dec. 1, 1991. Adopted 99-1: R 42-1; D 57-0 (ND 40-0, SD 17-0), Sept. 11, 1991.

	185	186	187	188	189	190	191	192
ALABAMA								
Heflin	Y	Y	N	N	N	N	Y	Y
Shelby	Y	Y	N	N	Y	N	Y	Y
ALASKA								
Murkowski	Y	Y	Y	N	Y	N	Y	Y
Stevens	N	Y	Y	N	Y	N	Y	Y
ARIZONA								
DeConcini	Y	Y	N	Y	Y	Y	Y	Y
McCain	Y	Y	Y	N	N	Y	Y	N
ARKANSAS								
Bumpers	N	Y	N	N	Y	N	N	Y
Pryor	N	Y	N	N	Y	N	N	Y
CALIFORNIA								
Cranston	N	N	N	Y	Y	N	N	Y
Seymour	N	Y	Y	N	Y	Y	?	?
COLORADO								
Wirth	N	Y	N	Y	Y	N	Y	?
Brown	Y	Y	Y	N	N	Y	Y	Y
CONNECTICUT								
Dodd	N	Y	N	Y	Y	N	?	Y
Lieberman	N	Y	N	Y	Y	Y	N	Y
DELAWARE								
Biden	N	Y	N	N	Y	N	N	Y
Roth	Y	Y	Y	N	N	Y	N	Y
FLORIDA								
Graham	N	Y	N	N	Y	N	-	Y
Mack	Y	Y	Y	N	N	Y	Y	Y
GEORGIA								
Fowler	N	Y	N	Y	N	Y	N	Y
Nunn	Y	Y	N	Y	Y	N	?	Y
HAWAII								
Akaka	N	Y	N	Y	Y	N	N	Y
Inouye	N	Y	N	Y	Y	N	Y	Y
IDAHO								
Craig	Y	Y	Y	N	N	Y	Y	N
Symms	Y	Y	Y	N	N	Y	Y	N
ILLINOIS								
Dixon	Y	Y	N	N	N	N	N	Y
Simon	N	Y	N	Y	Y	N	N	Y
INDIANA								
Coats	Y	Y	Y	N	N	Y	N	Y
Lugar	Y	Y	Y	N	N	Y	N	Y
IOWA								
Harkin	N	Y	N	Y	Y	N	?	?
Grassley	Y	Y	Y	N	Y	Y	Y	N
KANSAS								
Dole	Y	Y	Y	N	Y	Y	Y	Y
Kassebaum	N	Y	N	N	Y	Y	N	Y
KENTUCKY								
Ford	Y	Y	Y	N	Y	N	Y	Y
McConnell	Y	Y	Y	N	Y	Y	Y	Y
LOUISIANA								
Breaux	Y	Y	N	N	Y	N	N	Y
Johnston	Y	Y	N	N	Y	N	N	Y
MAINE								
Mitchell	N	Y	N	Y	Y	N	N	Y
Cohen	N	Y	N	Y	Y	Y	N	Y
MARYLAND								
Mikulski	N	Y	N	Y	Y	N	N	Y
Sarbanes	N	Y	N	Y	Y	N	N	Y
MASSACHUSETTS								
Kennedy	N	N	N	Y	Y	N	N	Y
Kerry	N	Y	N	Y	Y	N	N	Y
MICHIGAN								
Levin	N	Y	N	Y	Y	N	N	Y
Riegle	N	Y	N	Y	Y	N	N	Y
MINNESOTA								
Wellstone	N	Y	N	Y	Y	N	N	Y
Durenberger	Y	Y	N	N	Y	Y	Y	Y
MISSISSIPPI								
Cochran	Y	Y	Y	N	Y	Y	Y	Y
Lott	Y	Y	Y	N	Y	Y	Y	Y
MISSOURI								
Bond	Y	Y	N	N	N	Y	?	?
Danforth	Y	Y	N	N	Y	N	Y	Y
MONTANA								
Baucus	N	Y	N	N	Y	N	Y	Y
Burns	Y	Y	Y	N	Y	N	Y	Y
NEBRASKA								
Exon	Y	Y	N	N	N	N	N	Y
Kerrey	N	Y	N	N	Y	N	N	?
NEVADA								
Bryan	N	Y	N	N	Y	N	Y	Y
Reid	Y	Y	N	N	Y	N	Y	Y
NEW HAMPSHIRE								
Rudman	N	Y	N	N	Y	Y	Y	Y
Smith	Y	Y	Y	N	N	Y	Y	N
NEW JERSEY								
Bradley	N	N	N	Y	Y	N	N	Y
Lautenberg	N	N	N	Y	Y	N	N	Y
NEW MEXICO								
Bingaman	N	Y	N	Y	Y	Y	Y	Y
Domenici	Y	Y	Y	N	Y	N	Y	Y
NEW YORK								
Moynihan	N	Y	N	Y	Y	N	N	Y
D'Amato	Y	Y	Y	N	Y	Y	Y	Y
NORTH CAROLINA								
Sanford	N	Y	N	Y	Y	N	N	Y
Helms	Y	Y	Y	N	N	-	Y	N
NORTH DAKOTA								
Burdick	N	Y	N	Y	Y	N	N	Y
Conrad	Y	Y	N	N	N	N	Y	Y
OHIO								
Glenn	N	Y	N	Y	Y	N	N	?
Metzenbaum	N	N	N	Y	Y	N	N	Y
OKLAHOMA								
Boren	Y	Y	N	N	Y	N	N	Y
Nickles	Y	Y	Y	N	N	N	Y	Y
OREGON								
Hatfield	Y	Y	N	N	Y	N	Y	Y
Packwood	N	N	N	N	Y	N	Y	?
PENNSYLVANIA								
Wofford	N	Y	N	Y	Y	N	N	Y
Specter	N	Y	N	N	Y	Y	Y	Y
RHODE ISLAND								
Pell	N	Y	N	Y	Y	Y	N	Y
Chafee	N	Y	N	Y	Y	Y	Y	Y
SOUTH CAROLINA								
Hollings	N	Y	Y	N	Y	N	N	Y
Thurmond	Y	Y	Y	N	N	Y	Y	Y
SOUTH DAKOTA								
Daschle	N	Y	N	N	Y	N	N	Y
Pressler	Y	Y	Y	N	Y	Y	N	Y
TENNESSEE								
Gore	N	Y	N	Y	Y	Y	Y	Y
Sasser	N	Y	N	N	Y	N	N	Y
TEXAS								
Bentsen	Y	Y	Y	Y	Y	N	N	Y
Gramm	Y	Y	Y	N	N	N	?	Y
UTAH								
Garn	Y	Y	Y	N	N	N	Y	Y
Hatch	Y	Y	Y	N	N	N	Y	Y
VERMONT								
Leahy	N	Y	N	Y	Y	Y	N	Y
Jeffords	N	N	N	N	Y	Y	N	Y
VIRGINIA								
Robb	N	Y	N	N	Y	N	N	Y
Warner	N	Y	N	N	Y	N	Y	Y
WASHINGTON								
Adams	N	N	N	Y	Y	N	N	Y
Gorton	N	Y	N	N	Y	Y	Y	Y
WEST VIRGINIA								
Byrd	Y	Y	N	N	Y	N	Y	Y
Rockefeller	N	Y	N	N	Y	N	N	Y
WISCONSIN								
Kohl	N	Y	N	N	Y	N	N	Y
Kasten	Y	Y	Y	N	N	Y	Y	Y
WYOMING								
Simpson	N	Y	Y	N	Y	N	Y	?
Wallop	Y	Y	Y	N	N	N	Y	Y

KEY

- Y Voted for (yea).
- # Paired for.
- \+ Announced for.
- N Voted against (nay).
- X Paired against.
- \- Announced against.
- P Voted "present."
- C Voted "present" to avoid possible conflict of interest.
- ? Did not vote or otherwise make a position known.

Democrats *Republicans*

ND Northern Democrats SD Southern Democrats

Southern states - Ala., Ark., Fla., Ga., Ky., La., Miss., N.C., Okla., S.C., Tenn., Texas, Va.

185. HR 2707. Fiscal 1992 Labor, HHS and Education Appropriations/Parental Consent for Abortions. Nickles, R-Okla., amendment to require organizations that receive funding under Title X of the Public Health Service Act to notify at least one parent or legal guardian 48 hours before performing an abortion on a minor. Rejected 45-55: R 31-12; D 14-43 (ND 6-34, SD 8-9), Sept. 11, 1991.

186. HR 2707. Fiscal 1992 Labor, HHS and Education Appropriations/Parental Consent and Title X Facilities. Kassebaum, R-Kan., amendment to prohibit organizations that receive funding under Title X of the Public Health Service Act from allowing their facilities to be used for an abortion on a minor. Adopted 92-8: R 41-2, D 51-6 (ND 34-6, SD 17-0), Sept. 11, 1991.

187. HR 2707. Fiscal 1992 Labor, HHS and Education Appropriations/Preferential Treatment. Judgment of the Senate whether the Helms, R-N.C., amendment to prohibit employers from granting preferential treatment was germane. Ruled non-germane 33-67: R 30-13; D 3-54 (ND 0-40, SD 3-14), Sept. 11, 1991.

188. HR 2707. Fiscal 1992 Labor, HHS and Education Appropriations/Sex Survey Funding. Moynihan, D-N.Y., motion to table (kill) the Helms, R-N.C., amendment to transfer the $10 million provided to the National Institutes of Health for conducting a survey of adult sexual behavior to the Adolescent Family Life Program. Motion rejected 34-66: R 2-41; D 32-25 (ND 28-12, SD 4-13), Sept. 12, 1991. (The Helms amendment was adopted by voice vote.)

189. HR 2707. Fiscal 1992 Labor, HHS and Education Appropriations/Passage. Passage of the bill to provide new budget authority for the Departments of Labor, Health and Human Services, and Education and related agencies in fiscal 1992-94. Passed 78-22: R 25-18; D 53-4 (ND 37-3, SD 16-1), Sept. 12, 1991.

190. HR 2686. Fiscal 1992 Interior Appropriations/Budget Waiver. McCain, R-Ariz., motion to waive the Budget Act with respect to consideration of the McCain amendment on the Grand Canyon National Park. Motion rejected 34-65: R 28-14; D 6-51 (ND 5-35, SD 1-16), Sept. 13, 1991. A three-fifths majority (60) of the total Senate is required to waive the Budget Act. (Subsequently, the chair ruled that the amendment did not violate Section 401 of the Budget Act, and the amendment was rejected by voice vote.)

191. HR 2686. Fiscal 1992 Interior Appropriations/Mining Patents. Reid, D-Nev., motion to table (kill) the Bumpers, D-Ark., amendment to prohibit the use of funds for one year to accept or process applications for mining patents under the 1872 Mining Act. Motion agreed to 47-46: R 33-7; D 14-39 (ND 9-29, SD 5-10), Sept. 13, 1991. A "yea" was a vote supporting the president's position.

192. Treaty Doc 101-22. Maritime Boundary With the Soviet Union. Adoption of the resolution of ratification of the treaty to define the maritime boundary between the United States and the Soviet Union. Adopted 86-6: R 33-6; D 53-0 (ND 36-0, SD 17-0), Sept. 16, 1991. A two-thirds majority of those present and voting (62 in this case) is required for adoption of resolutions of ratification.

	193	194	195	196	197	198	199	200
ALABAMA								
Heflin	Y	Y	Y	N	Y	N	Y	Y
Shelby	Y	Y	Y	N	Y	N	N	Y
ALASKA								
Murkowski	Y	Y	Y	Y	Y	N	N	Y
Stevens	Y	Y	Y	N	Y	N	N	Y
ARIZONA								
DeConcini	Y	Y	Y	N	N	N	Y	Y
McCain	Y	Y	Y	Y	Y	N	N	Y
ARKANSAS								
Bumpers	Y	Y	N	N	Y	N	Y	Y
Pryor	Y	Y	Y	N	Y	N	Y	Y
CALIFORNIA								
Cranston	Y	Y	N	N	N	Y	Y	Y
Seymour	Y	Y	Y	?	?	?	?	+
COLORADO								
Wirth	Y	Y	Y	N	N	Y	Y	Y
Brown	N	Y	Y	Y	Y	N	N	Y
CONNECTICUT								
Dodd	Y	Y	Y	N	Y	N	Y	Y
Lieberman	Y	Y	N	N	N	N	Y	Y
DELAWARE								
Biden	N	Y	N	N	N	N	Y	Y
Roth	N	N	Y	Y	Y	N	N	N
FLORIDA								
Graham	Y	Y	N	N	Y	N	Y	Y
Mack	?	?	?	Y	Y	N	N	Y
GEORGIA								
Fowler	Y	Y	N	N	Y	N	Y	Y
Nunn	Y	Y	N	N	Y	N	Y	Y
HAWAII								
Akaka	Y	Y	N	N	N	N	Y	Y
Inouye	?	?	?	N	Y	N	Y	Y
IDAHO								
Craig	N	Y	Y	Y	Y	N	N	Y
Symms	N	Y	Y	Y	Y	N	N	Y
ILLINOIS								
Dixon	Y	Y	N	N	Y	N	Y	Y
Simon	Y	Y	N	N	Y	N	Y	Y
INDIANA								
Coats	N	Y	Y	Y	Y	N	N	Y
Lugar	N	Y	Y	N	Y	N	N	Y
IOWA								
Harkin	Y	Y	Y	?	?	?	?	?
Grassley	Y	Y	Y	Y	Y	N	N	Y
KANSAS								
Dole	N	Y	Y	Y	Y	N	N	Y
Kassebaum	Y	Y	Y	Y	N	N	N	Y
KENTUCKY								
Ford	Y	Y	Y	Y	Y	N	Y	Y
McConnell	Y	Y	Y	Y	Y	N	N	Y
LOUISIANA								
Breaux	Y	Y	Y	?	Y	N	Y	Y
Johnston	Y	Y	Y	N	Y	N	Y	Y
MAINE								
Mitchell	Y	Y	N	N	N	N	Y	Y
Cohen	Y	Y	N	N	Y	N	N	Y
MARYLAND								
Mikulski	Y	Y	N	N	Y	N	Y	Y
Sarbanes	Y	Y	N	N	N	Y	Y	Y
MASSACHUSETTS								
Kennedy	Y	Y	N	N	N	N	Y	Y
Kerry	Y	Y	N	N	N	N	Y	Y
MICHIGAN								
Levin	Y	Y	N	N	N	N	Y	Y
Riegle	Y	Y	N	N	N	Y	Y	Y
MINNESOTA								
Wellstone	Y	Y	N	N	N	Y	Y	Y
Durenberger	Y	Y	Y	N	N	N	N	Y
MISSISSIPPI								
Cochran	Y	Y	Y	N	Y	N	N	Y
Lott	Y	Y	Y	Y	Y	N	N	Y
MISSOURI								
Bond	Y	Y	Y	Y	Y	N	N	Y
Danforth	Y	Y	Y	N	N	N	N	Y
MONTANA								
Baucus	Y	Y	Y	N	Y	N	Y	Y
Burns	Y	Y	Y	N	Y	N	N	Y
NEBRASKA								
Exon	Y	Y	Y	N	Y	N	Y	Y
Kerrey	Y	Y	Y	N	Y	N	Y	Y
NEVADA								
Bryan	Y	Y	Y	N	Y	N	Y	Y
Reid	Y	Y	Y	N	Y	N	Y	Y
NEW HAMPSHIRE								
Rudman	Y	Y	N	Y	Y	N	N	Y
Smith	N	N	N	Y	Y	N	N	N
NEW JERSEY								
Bradley	Y	Y	N	N	N	N	Y	Y
Lautenberg	Y	Y	N	N	N	N	Y	Y
NEW MEXICO								
Bingaman	Y	Y	Y	N	Y	N	Y	Y
Domenici	Y	Y	Y	N	Y	N	N	Y
NEW YORK								
Moynihan	Y	Y	N	N	N	Y	Y	Y
D'Amato	Y	Y	Y	N	Y	N	N	Y
NORTH CAROLINA								
Sanford	Y	Y	Y	N	Y	N	Y	Y
Helms	N	N	Y	Y	Y	N	N	N
NORTH DAKOTA								
Burdick	Y	Y	Y	N	Y	N	Y	Y
Conrad	Y	Y	Y	N	Y	N	Y	Y
OHIO								
Glenn	Y	Y	N	N	Y	N	Y	Y
Metzenbaum	Y	Y	N	N	N	N	Y	Y
OKLAHOMA								
Boren	Y	Y	Y	N	Y	N	Y	Y
Nickles	Y	Y	Y	Y	Y	N	N	Y
OREGON								
Hatfield	Y	Y	Y	N	Y	N	N	Y
Packwood	Y	Y	Y	?	?	?	?	?
PENNSYLVANIA								
Wofford	Y	Y	N	N	N	N	Y	Y
Specter	N	Y	Y	Y	Y	N	N	Y
RHODE ISLAND								
Pell	Y	Y	N	N	N	Y	Y	Y
Chafee	Y	Y	N	N	N	N	N	Y
SOUTH CAROLINA								
Hollings	Y	Y	N	Y	Y	N	Y	Y
Thurmond	Y	Y	Y	Y	Y	N	N	Y
SOUTH DAKOTA								
Daschle	Y	Y	Y	N	Y	N	Y	Y
Pressler	N	Y	Y	Y	Y	N	N	Y
TENNESSEE								
Gore	Y	Y	N	N	N	N	Y	Y
Sasser	Y	Y	N	N	Y	N	Y	Y
TEXAS								
Bentsen	Y	Y	Y	N	Y	N	Y	Y
Gramm	N	Y	Y	Y	Y	N	N	Y
UTAH								
Garn	Y	Y	Y	?	?	?	?	?
Hatch	Y	Y	Y	-	Y	N	N	Y
VERMONT								
Leahy	Y	Y	N	N	N	N	Y	Y
Jeffords	Y	Y	N	N	N	N	N	Y
VIRGINIA								
Robb	Y	Y	N	N	Y	N	Y	Y
Warner	Y	Y	N	N	Y	N	N	Y
WASHINGTON								
Adams	Y	Y	Y	N	N	Y	Y	Y
Gorton	Y	Y	Y	Y	Y	N	N	Y
WEST VIRGINIA								
Byrd	Y	Y	Y	Y	Y	N	Y	Y
Rockefeller	Y	Y	Y	N	N	N	Y	Y
WISCONSIN								
Kohl	Y	Y	N	N	Y	N	Y	Y
Kasten	Y	Y	N	N	Y	N	N	Y
WYOMING								
Simpson	Y	Y	Y	N	Y	N	N	Y
Wallop	N	Y	Y	Y	Y	N	N	Y

KEY

- Y Voted for (yea).
- # Paired for.
- \+ Announced for.
- N Voted against (nay).
- X Paired against.
- \- Announced against.
- P Voted "present."
- C Voted "present" to avoid possible conflict of interest.
- ? Did not vote or otherwise make a position known.

Democrats *Republicans*

ND Northern Democrats SD Southern Democrats

Southern states - Ala., Ark., Fla., Ga., Ky., La., Miss., N.C., Okla., S.C., Tenn., Texas, Va.

193. HR 2942. Fiscal 1992 Transportation Appropriations/Demonstration Project Cuts. D'Amato, R-N.Y., motion to table (kill) the Smith, R-N.H., amendment to cut $387.5 million for unauthorized demonstration projects in the bill and redistribute the $387 million to states. Motion agreed to 84-14: R 29-13; D 55-1 (ND 38-1, SD 17-0), Sept. 17, 1991.

194. HR 2942. Fiscal 1992 Transportation Appropriations/Passage. Passage of the bill to provide $14,439,382,569 in new budget authority for the Department of Transportation and related agencies in fiscal 1992. The House bill provided for $14,169,377,569. The administration requested $15,110,123,569. Passed 95-3: R 39-3; D 56-0 (ND 39-0, SD 17-0), Sept. 17, 1991.

195. HR 2686. Fiscal 1992 Interior Appropriations/Grazing Fees. Domenici, R-N.M., motion to table (kill) the Jeffords, R-Vt., amendment to increase grazing fees on Forest Service and Bureau of Land Management Lands. Motion agreed to 60-38: R 35-7; D 25-31 (ND 16-23, SD 9-8), Sept. 17, 1991.

196. HR 2686. Fiscal 1992 Interior Appropriations/National Endowment for the Arts Cuts. Kassebaum, R-Kan., amendment to cut 10 percent of the $145,583,000 provided to the National Endowment for the Arts. Rejected 27-67: R 24-15; D 3-52 (ND 1-38, SD 2-14), Sept. 19, 1991.

197. HR 2686. Fiscal 1992 Interior Appropriations/National Endowment for the Arts Prohibitions. Helms, R-N.C., amendment to the committee amendment, to prohibit the National Endowment for the Arts from funding projects that depict or describe, in a patently offensive way, sexual or excretory activities or organs. Adopted 68-28: R 35-5; D 33-23 (ND 17-22, SD 16-1), Sept. 19, 1991.

198. S J Res 186. Recession Resolution to Suspend the Budget Rules/Passage. Passage of the joint resolution to suspend the spending caps and pay-as-you-go restrictions of the Balanced Budget and Emergency Deficit Control Act as amended in 1990 (PL 101-508). Budget rules require the Senate to vote to suspend the rules if actual gross national product growth is less than 1 percent or forecasted growth is negative for two consecutive quarters. Rejected 8-88: R 0-40; D 8-48 (ND 8-31, SD 0-17), Sept. 19, 1991. A "nay" was a vote supporting the president's position.

199. HR 2686. Fiscal 1992 Interior Appropriations/Cloture. Byrd, D-W.Va., motion to invoke cloture (thus limiting debate) on the Sanford, D-N.C., amendment to provide Swain County, N.C., with $16 million to provide for a complete settlement of all claims against the federal government and the Tennessee Valley Authority (TVA) for not completing a road to replace a road that was flooded by construction of a TVA dam to create the Fontana Reservoir in 1943. Motion rejected 55-41: R 0-40; D 55-1 (ND 39-0, SD 16-1), Sept. 19, 1991. A three-fifths majority vote (60) of the total Senate is required to invoke cloture. (Subsequently, under a previous order the amendment was withdrawn.)

200. HR 2686. Fiscal 1992 Interior Appropriations/Passage. Passage of the bill to provide $12,678,693,000 in new budget authority for the Department of the Interior and related agencies for fiscal 1992. The House bill provided for $12,717,527,000. The administration requested $11,595,927,000. Passed 93-3: R 37-3: D 56-0 (ND 39-0, SD 17-0), Sept. 19, 1991.

	201	202	203	204	205	206	207	208
ALABAMA								
Heflin	Y	N	N	N	Y	Y	Y	N
Shelby	Y	N	N	Y	Y	Y	Y	N
ALASKA								
Murkowski	N	Y	N	Y	N	Y	Y	N
Stevens	N	Y	N	Y	N	Y	Y	N
ARIZONA								
DeConcini	Y	N	Y	N	Y	N	N	Y
McCain	N	Y	N	Y	N	N	Y	N
ARKANSAS								
Bumpers	Y	N	Y	N	Y	N	N	Y
Pryor	Y	N	N	N	Y	N	N	Y
CALIFORNIA								
Cranston	Y	N	Y	N	Y	N	N	Y
Seymour	N	Y	N	Y	Y	Y	Y	N
COLORADO								
Wirth	Y	N	N	N	Y	N	N	Y
Brown	N	Y	N	Y	N	Y	Y	N
CONNECTICUT								
Dodd	Y	N	N	N	Y	Y	Y	Y
Lieberman	Y	N	Y	N	Y	N	N	Y
DELAWARE								
Biden	Y	N	Y	N	Y	N	N	Y
Roth	N	Y	N	Y	N	N	Y	N
FLORIDA								
Graham	Y	N	Y	N	Y	N	N	Y
Mack	N	Y	N	Y	N	Y	Y	N
GEORGIA								
Fowler	Y	N	Y	N	Y	Y	N	Y
Nunn	Y	N	Y	N	Y	Y	Y	N
HAWAII								
Akaka	Y	N	Y	N	Y	Y	N	Y
Inouye	Y	N	Y	N	Y	Y	Y	N
IDAHO								
Craig	N	Y	N	Y	N	Y	Y	N
Symms	N	Y	N	Y	N	Y	Y	N
ILLINOIS								
Dixon	Y	N	N	N	Y	Y	Y	Y
Simon	Y	N	N	N	Y	N	N	Y
INDIANA								
Coats	N	Y	N	Y	N	Y	Y	Y
Lugar	N	Y	N	Y	N	Y	Y	N
IOWA								
Harkin	?	?	?	?	?	N	N	Y
Grassley	N	Y	N	Y	N	N	N	N
KANSAS								
Dole	N	Y	N	Y	N	Y	Y	N
Kassebaum	N	N	N	N	N	Y	N	Y
KENTUCKY								
Ford	Y	N	Y	N	Y	N	N	Y
McConnell	N	Y	N	Y	N	Y	Y	N
LOUISIANA								
Breaux	Y	N	Y	N	Y	N	N	Y
Johnston	Y	N	Y	N	Y	N	N	Y
MAINE								
Mitchell	Y	N	Y	N	Y	N	N	Y
Cohen	N	Y	N	Y	Y	N	Y	Y
MARYLAND								
Mikulski	Y	N	N	N	Y	N	N	Y
Sarbanes	Y	N	Y	N	Y	N	N	Y
MASSACHUSETTS								
Kennedy	Y	N	Y	N	Y	N	N	Y
Kerry	Y	N	Y	N	Y	N	N	Y
MICHIGAN								
Levin	Y	N	N	N	Y	Y	N	Y
Riegle	Y	N	N	N	Y	N	N	Y
MINNESOTA								
Wellstone	Y	N	Y	N	Y	N	N	Y
Durenberger	N	Y	N	N	Y	Y	Y	Y
MISSISSIPPI								
Cochran	N	Y	N	Y	N	Y	Y	N
Lott	N	Y	N	Y	N	Y	Y	Y
MISSOURI								
Bond	N	Y	N	Y	Y	Y	Y	Y
Danforth	N	Y	Y	N	Y	Y	Y	Y
MONTANA								
Baucus	Y	N	Y	N	Y	N	N	Y
Burns	N	Y	N	Y	Y	Y	Y	N
NEBRASKA								
Exon	Y	N	N	N	Y	Y	Y	Y
Kerrey	Y	N	Y	N	Y	?	?	Y
NEVADA								
Bryan	Y	N	Y	N	Y	N	N	Y
Reid	Y	N	Y	N	Y	N	N	Y
NEW HAMPSHIRE								
Rudman	N	N	N	N	N	Y	Y	N
Smith	N	Y	N	Y	N	Y	Y	N
NEW JERSEY								
Bradley	Y	N	Y	N	Y	N	N	Y
Lautenberg	Y	N	N	N	Y	N	N	Y
NEW MEXICO								
Bingaman	Y	N	N	N	Y	Y	Y	Y
Domenici	N	Y	N	N	N	Y	Y	Y
NEW YORK								
Moynihan	Y	N	Y	N	Y	N	N	Y
D'Amato	N	Y	N	Y	Y	Y	Y	Y
NORTH CAROLINA								
Sanford	Y	N	Y	N	Y	N	N	Y
Helms	N	Y	N	Y	N	Y	Y	N
NORTH DAKOTA								
Burdick	Y	N	Y	N	Y	N	Y	N
Conrad	Y	N	Y	N	Y	N	N	Y
OHIO								
Glenn	Y	N	N	N	Y	N	N	Y
Metzenbaum	Y	N	N	N	Y	N	N	Y
OKLAHOMA								
Boren	Y	N	Y	N	Y	Y	N	Y
Nickles	N	Y	N	Y	N	Y	Y	N
OREGON								
Hatfield	N	Y	N	Y	Y	N	N	Y
Packwood	Y	Y	Y	Y	Y	N	Y	Y
PENNSYLVANIA								
Wofford	Y	N	N	N	Y	N	N	Y
Specter	N	Y	N	Y	Y	Y	Y	Y
RHODE ISLAND								
Pell	Y	N	Y	N	Y	N	N	Y
Chafee	N	N	N	N	Y	Y	N	Y
SOUTH CAROLINA								
Hollings	Y	N	Y	N	Y	N	Y	Y
Thurmond	N	Y	N	Y	N	Y	Y	N
SOUTH DAKOTA								
Daschle	Y	N	Y	N	Y	N	N	Y
Pressler	N	Y	N	Y	N	Y	Y	N
TENNESSEE								
Gore	Y	N	Y	N	Y	Y	N	N
Sasser	Y	N	Y	N	Y	N	N	Y
TEXAS								
Bentsen	Y	N	Y	N	Y	Y	Y	Y
Gramm	N	Y	N	Y	N	Y	Y	N
UTAH								
Garn	N	Y	N	Y	N	Y	Y	N
Hatch	N	Y	N	Y	N	Y	Y	N
VERMONT								
Leahy	Y	N	N	N	Y	N	N	Y
Jeffords	N	N	N	N	Y	N	N	Y
VIRGINIA								
Robb	Y	N	Y	N	Y	Y	Y	Y
Warner	N	Y	N	Y	N	Y	Y	N
WASHINGTON								
Adams	Y	N	Y	N	Y	N	N	Y
Gorton	N	Y	N	Y	N	Y	Y	Y
WEST VIRGINIA								
Byrd	Y	N	Y	N	Y	N	N	Y
Rockefeller	Y	N	Y	N	Y	N	N	Y
WISCONSIN								
Kohl	Y	N	N	N	Y	N	N	Y
Kasten	N	Y	N	Y	Y	Y	Y	Y
WYOMING								
Simpson	N	Y	N	Y	N	Y	Y	N
Wallop	N	Y	N	Y	N	Y	Y	N

KEY

- Y Voted for (yea).
- \# Paired for.
- \+ Announced for.
- N Voted against (nay).
- X Paired against.
- \- Announced against.
- P Voted "present."
- C Voted "present" to avoid possible conflict of interest.
- ? Did not vote or otherwise make a position known.

Democrats *Republicans*

ND Northern Democrats SD Southern Democrats

Southern states - Ala., Ark., Fla., Ga., Ky., La., Miss., N.C., Okla., S.C., Tenn., Texas, Va.

201. S 1722. Unemployment Benefits Extension/Alternative Measure. Bentsen, D-Texas, motion to table (kill) the Dole, R-Kan., amendment to provide up to 10 weeks of additional unemployment benefits and allow the president to finance extended unemployment benefits through either declaring the additional spending an emergency or through financing the benefits by the auction of frequencies on the electromagnetic spectrum and student loan reform. Motion agreed to 57-42: R 1-42; D 56-0 (ND 39-0, SD 17-0), Sept. 24, 1991. A "nay" was a vote supporting the president's position.

202. S 1722. Unemployment Benefits Extension/Capital Gains. Gramm, R-Texas, motion to table (kill) the Mitchell, D-Maine, point of order against the Gramm amendment to index capital gains and cut the capital gains tax rate from 28 percent to 19.6 percent for assets held more than three years. Motion rejected 39-60: R 39-4; D 0-56 (ND 0-39, SD 0-17), Sept. 24, 1991. (Subsequently, the Mitchell point of order, that the Gramm amendment violated the Constitution by originating a revenue bill in the Senate, was sustained and the amendment was ruled out of order.)

203. S 1722. Unemployment Benefits Extension/Price of Coffee. Packwood, R-Ore., motion to table (kill) the Brown, R-Colo., amendment to express the sense of the Senate that the United States should not be a party to any agreement that would raise the price of coffee for the American consumer. Motion rejected 40-59: R 2-41; D 38-18 (ND 24-15, SD 14-3), Sept. 24, 1991. (The Brown amendment subsequently was adopted by voice vote.) *(Story, p. 2784)*

204. S 1722. Unemployment Benefits Extension/Budget Waiver. McCain, R-Ariz., motion to waive Section 306 of the Budget Act with respect to the Sasser, D-Tenn., point of order against the McCain amendment to require a three-fifths majority vote to raise taxes but allow for a simple majority vote to lower taxes. Motion rejected 37-62: R 36-7; D 1-55 (ND 0-39, SD 1-16), Sept. 24, 1991. A three-fifths majority vote (60) of the total Senate is required to waive the Budget Act. (The McCain amendment subsequently fell on the Sasser point of order.)

205. S 1722. Unemployment Benefits Extension/Passage. Passage of the bill to provide an estimated $6.4 billion for up to 20 weeks of additional unemployment benefits for workers who have exhausted their unemployment benefits through July 4, 1992. The bill designates the spending as emergency spending but would also require a presidential designation of the funds as an emergency before the funds could be spent. Passed 69-30: R 13-30; D 56-0 (ND 39-0, SD 17-0), Sept. 24, 1991. A "nay" was a vote supporting the president's position."

206. HR 2521. Fiscal 1992 Defense Appropriations/B-2 Bomber. Inouye, D-Hawaii, motion to table (kill) Division 1 of the Sasser, D-Tenn., amendment to cut $3.2 billion from the Air Force's procurement account, halting production of the B-2 bomber at 15 planes. Motion agreed to 51-48: R 36-7; D 15-41 (ND 7-32, SD 8-9), Sept. 25, 1991. A "yea" was a vote supporting the president's position.

207. HR 2521. Fiscal 1992 Defense Appropriations/Strategic Defense Initiative. Inouye, D-Hawaii, motion to table (kill) Division 3 of the Sasser, D-Tenn., amendment to reduce funding for the Strategic Defense Initiative by $1.1 billion. Motion agreed to 50-49: R 38-5; D 12-44 (ND 6-33, SD 6-11), Sept. 25, 1991. A "yea" was a vote supporting the president's position.

208. HR 2521. Fiscal 1992 Defense Appropriations/MX Rail Garrison. Division 2 of the Sasser, D-Tenn., amendment to cancel the research and development of the MX rail garrison. Adopted 67-33: R 16-27; D 51-6 (ND 38-2, SD 13-4), Sept. 26, 1991.

	209	210	211	212	213	214	215	216
ALABAMA								
Heflin	N	Y	Y	Y	Y	Y	N	Y
Shelby	N	Y	Y	Y	Y	N	N	N
ALASKA								
Murkowski	N	Y	Y	N	N	Y	Y	Y
Stevens	N	Y	Y	N	N	Y	Y	Y
ARIZONA								
DeConcini	N	Y	Y	Y	Y	N	Y	N
McCain	Y	Y	Y	N	N	Y	Y	Y
ARKANSAS								
Bumpers	N	N	Y	Y	Y	N	Y	N
Pryor	N	N	Y	Y	Y	?	?	?
CALIFORNIA								
Cranston	N	N	Y	Y	Y	N	Y	N
Seymour	N	Y	Y	N	N	Y	N	Y
COLORADO								
Wirth	Y	N	Y	Y	Y	N	Y	N
Brown	Y	N	Y	N	N	Y	N	Y
CONNECTICUT								
Dodd	N	Y	Y	Y	Y	N	Y	N
Lieberman	N	Y	Y	Y	Y	N	Y	N
DELAWARE								
Biden	N	N	Y	Y	Y	N	Y	N
Roth	Y	Y	Y	N	N	Y	Y	N
FLORIDA								
Graham	N	N	Y	Y	Y	N	Y	N
Mack	N	Y	Y	N	N	Y	N	Y
GEORGIA								
Fowler	N	N	Y	Y	Y	N	Y	N
Nunn	N	Y	Y	Y	Y	N	Y	N
HAWAII								
Akaka	N	Y	Y	Y	Y	N	Y	N
Inouye	N	Y	Y	Y	Y	N	Y	N
IDAHO								
Craig	N	Y	Y	N	N	Y	N	Y
Symms	N	Y	Y	N	N	Y	N	Y
ILLINOIS								
Dixon	N	Y	Y	Y	Y	N	Y	N
Simon	Y	N	Y	Y	Y	N	Y	N
INDIANA								
Coats	N	Y	Y	N	N	Y	Y	N
Lugar	N	Y	Y	N	N	Y	N	Y
IOWA								
Harkin	N	N	Y	Y	Y	?	?	?
Grassley	N	Y	Y	N	N	Y	N	Y
KANSAS								
Dole	N	Y	Y	N	N	Y	N	Y
Kassebaum	N	Y	Y	N	N	Y	N	N
KENTUCKY								
Ford	N	Y	Y	Y	Y	N	Y	N
McConnell	N	Y	Y	N	N	Y	N	Y
LOUISIANA								
Breaux	N	Y	Y	Y	Y	Y	Y	N
Johnston	N	Y	Y	Y	Y	N	Y	N
MAINE								
Mitchell	N	N	Y	Y	Y	N	Y	N
Cohen	N	Y	Y	Y	Y	Y	Y	N
MARYLAND								
Mikulski	N	N	Y	Y	Y	N	Y	N
Sarbanes	N	N	Y	Y	Y	N	Y	N
MASSACHUSETTS								
Kennedy	N	N	Y	Y	Y	N	Y	N
Kerry	N	N	Y	Y	Y	N	Y	N
MICHIGAN								
Levin	N	N	Y	Y	Y	N	Y	N
Riegle	N	N	Y	Y	Y	N	Y	N
MINNESOTA								
Wellstone	Y	N	Y	Y	Y	N	Y	N
Durenberger	N	Y	Y	N	N	Y	Y	Y
MISSISSIPPI								
Cochran	N	Y	Y	N	N	Y	N	Y
Lott	Y	Y	Y	N	N	Y	N	Y
MISSOURI								
Bond	N	Y	Y	N	N	N	Y	N
Danforth	N	Y	Y	N	N	Y	Y	N
MONTANA								
Baucus	N	N	Y	Y	Y	N	Y	N
Burns	N	Y	Y	N	N	Y	N	Y
NEBRASKA								
Exon	N	Y	Y	Y	Y	N	Y	N
Kerrey	N	N	Y	Y	Y	?	?	?
NEVADA								
Bryan	N	Y	Y	Y	Y	N	Y	N
Reid	N	Y	Y	Y	Y	N	Y	N
NEW HAMPSHIRE								
Rudman	N	Y	Y	N	N	N	N	Y
Smith	N	Y	Y	N	N	Y	N	Y
NEW JERSEY								
Bradley	Y	N	Y	Y	Y	N	Y	N
Lautenberg	N	N	Y	Y	Y	N	Y	N
NEW MEXICO								
Bingaman	N	N	Y	Y	Y	N	Y	N
Domenici	N	Y	Y	N	N	Y	N	Y
NEW YORK								
Moynihan	N	N	Y	Y	Y	N	Y	N
D'Amato	N	Y	Y	Y	Y	N	Y	N
NORTH CAROLINA								
Sanford	N	N	Y	Y	Y	N	Y	N
Helms	N	Y	Y	-	N	Y	N	Y
NORTH DAKOTA								
Burdick	N	Y	Y	Y	Y	N	Y	N
Conrad	N	N	Y	Y	Y	Y	Y	N
OHIO								
Glenn	Y	Y	Y	Y	Y	N	Y	N
Metzenbaum	N	?	?	Y	Y	N	Y	N
OKLAHOMA								
Boren	N	N	Y	Y	Y	N	N	N
Nickles	N	Y	Y	N	N	Y	N	Y
OREGON								
Hatfield	N	N	Y	Y	Y	N	Y	N
Packwood	N	N	Y	Y	Y	N	Y	N
PENNSYLVANIA								
Wofford	N	N	Y	Y	Y	N	Y	N
Specter	N	Y	Y	Y	Y	Y	Y	N
RHODE ISLAND								
Pell	N	N	Y	Y	Y	N	Y	N
Chafee	N	Y	Y	Y	Y	Y	Y	N
SOUTH CAROLINA								
Hollings	N	Y	Y	Y	Y	N	N	N
Thurmond	N	Y	Y	N	N	Y	N	Y
SOUTH DAKOTA								
Daschle	N	N	Y	Y	Y	N	Y	N
Pressler	N	Y	Y	N	N	Y	N	Y
TENNESSEE								
Gore	N	Y	Y	Y	Y	N	Y	N
Sasser	N	N	Y	Y	Y	N	Y	N
TEXAS								
Bentsen	Y	N	Y	Y	Y	N	Y	N
Gramm	N	Y	Y	N	N	Y	N	Y
UTAH								
Garn	N	Y	Y	N	N	Y	N	Y
Hatch	N	Y	Y	N	N	Y	N	Y
VERMONT								
Leahy	N	N	Y	Y	Y	N	Y	N
Jeffords	N	N	Y	Y	Y	N	Y	N
VIRGINIA								
Robb	N	N	Y	Y	Y	N	Y	N
Warner	N	Y	Y	N	N	Y	N	Y
WASHINGTON								
Adams	N	N	Y	Y	Y	N	Y	N
Gorton	N	N	Y	N	N	Y	N	Y
WEST VIRGINIA								
Byrd	N	Y	Y	Y	Y	N	Y	N
Rockefeller	N	N	Y	Y	Y	N	Y	N
WISCONSIN								
Kohl	N	N	Y	Y	Y	N	Y	N
Kasten	N	Y	Y	Y	Y	Y	N	Y
WYOMING								
Simpson	N	Y	Y	N	N	Y	N	Y
Wallop	N	Y	Y	N	N	Y	N	Y

KEY

- Y Voted for (yea).
- # Paired for.
- + Announced for.
- N Voted against (nay).
- X Paired against.
- \- Announced against.
- P Voted "present."
- C Voted "present" to avoid possible conflict of interest.
- ? Did not vote or otherwise make a position known.

Democrats *Republicans*

ND Northern Democrats SD Southern Democrats

Southern states - Ala., Ark., Fla., Ga., Ky., La., Miss., N.C., Okla., S.C., Tenn., Texas, Va.

209. HR 2521. Fiscal 1992 Defense Appropriations/*Seawolf*. McCain, R-Ariz., amendment to terminate the *Seawolf* (SSN-21)-class submarine program. Rejected 10-90: R 4-39; D 6-51 (ND 5-35, SD 1-16), Sept. 26, 1991. A "nay" was a vote supporting the president's position.

210. HR 2521. Fiscal 1992 Defense Appropriations/Reduced Expenditures. Inouye, D-Hawaii, motion to table (kill) Bradley, D-N.J., amendment to express the sense of Congress with respect to the preparation by the secretary of Defense of an additional five-year budget for fiscal 1993-98 that provides for an $80 billion reduction in estimated expenditures. Motion agreed to 58-41: R 38-5; D 20-36 (ND 12-27, SD 8-9), Sept. 26, 1991. A "yea" was a vote supporting the president's position.

211. HR 2521. Fiscal 1992 Defense Appropriations/Israel. Wirth, D-Colo., amendment to prohibit the Department of Defense from awarding contracts to persons or countries that are complying with the Arab League boycott of Israel, unless the secretary of Defense certifies that such a contract is in the interest of national security. Adopted 99-0: R 43-0; D 56-0 (ND 39-0, SD 17-0), Sept. 26, 1991.

212. S 1722. Unemployment Benefits Extension/Budget Act Waiver. Sasser, D-Tenn., motion to waive the Budget Act with respect to the Domenici, R-N.M., point of order against the conference report to provide an estimated $6.4 billion for up to 20 additional weeks of unemployment benefits based on a state's average total unemployment rate. Motion agreed to 65-34: R 8-34; D 57-0 (ND 40-0, SD 17-0), Oct. 1, 1991. A three-fifths majority vote (60) of the total Senate is required to waive the budget act.

213. S 1722. Unemployment Benefits Extension/Conference Report. Adoption of the conference report to provide an estimated $6.4 billion for up to 20 additional weeks of unemployment benefits based on a state's average total unemployment rate. The benefits would temporarily be extended from Oct. 6, 1991, through July 4, 1992. The conference report designates the spending as an emergency and would not require a presidential declaration to be exempt from the spending limits of the 1990 budget agreement. Adopted 65-35: R 8-35: D 57-0 (ND 40-0, SD 17-0), Oct. 1, 1991. A "nay" was a vote supporting the president's position.

214. S 5. Family and Medical Leave Act/Arbitration Procedures. Durenberger, R-Minn., amendment to the Bond, R-Mo., substitute amendment, to replace the enforcement provisions of the bill with provisions establishing arbitration procedures. Rejected 40-57: R 37-6; D 3-51 (ND 1-37, SD 2-14), Oct. 2, 1991.

215. S 5. Family and Medical Leave Act/Substitute. Bond, R-Mo., substitute amendment to raise the number of hours an employee must work in order to be eligible for up to 12 weeks of unpaid leave for the birth or adoption of a child or for the serious illness of the worker or an immediate family member. The substitute would also limit potential penalties against businesses that violate the bill from quadruple damages to double damages, among other changes. Adopted 65-32: R 15-28; D 50-4 (ND 38-0, SD 12-4), Oct. 2, 1991. A "nay" was a vote supporting the president's position.

216. S 5. Family and Medical Leave Act/Preferential Hiring Rights. Hatch, R-Utah, substitute amendment to allow parents of young children to take up to six years of unpaid leave and to allow workers caring for an ill family member to take up to two years of unpaid leave and still have preferential hiring rights. Rejected 32-65: R 31-12; D 1-53 (ND 0-38, SD 1-15), Oct. 2, 1991.

	217	218	219	220	221	222	223	224
ALABAMA								
Heflin	Y	Y	Y	N	Y	Y	Y	Y
Shelby	Y	Y	Y	Y	Y	Y	Y	Y
ALASKA								
Murkowski	Y	Y	N	Y	N	Y	Y	Y
Stevens	Y	Y	N	Y	N	Y	Y	Y
ARIZONA								
DeConcini	Y	Y	N	Y	Y	Y	Y	Y
McCain	Y	Y	N	Y	N	Y	Y	Y
ARKANSAS								
Bumpers	Y	Y	Y	N	Y	Y	Y	Y
Pryor	?	?	Y	N	Y	Y	?	?
CALIFORNIA								
Cranston	Y	Y	Y	N	Y	Y	Y	Y
Seymour	Y	Y	Y	Y	N	Y	Y	Y
COLORADO								
Wirth	Y	Y	Y	N	Y	Y	N	Y
Brown	Y	Y	Y	Y	N	Y	N	Y
CONNECTICUT								
Dodd	Y	Y	Y	N	Y	Y	Y	Y
Lieberman	Y	Y	Y	N	Y	Y	Y	Y
DELAWARE								
Biden	Y	Y	Y	N	Y	Y	Y	Y
Roth	Y	Y	N	Y	N	Y	N	N
FLORIDA								
Graham	Y	Y	Y	N	Y	Y	Y	Y
Mack	Y	Y	N	Y	N	Y	Y	Y
GEORGIA								
Fowler	Y	Y	Y	Y	Y	Y	Y	Y
Nunn	Y	Y	Y	Y	Y	Y	Y	Y
HAWAII								
Akaka	Y	Y	Y	N	Y	Y	Y	Y
Inouye	Y	Y	Y	N	Y	Y	Y	Y
IDAHO								
Craig	Y	Y	N	Y	N	Y	Y	Y
Symms	Y	Y	N	Y	N	Y	Y	Y
ILLINOIS								
Dixon	Y	Y	Y	Y	Y	Y	N	Y
Simon	Y	Y	Y	N	Y	Y	Y	Y
INDIANA								
Coats	Y	Y	N	Y	N	Y	Y	Y
Lugar	Y	Y	N	Y	N	Y	Y	Y
IOWA								
Harkin	?	?	Y	N	Y	Y	Y	Y
Grassley	Y	Y	N	Y	N	Y	Y	Y
KANSAS								
Dole	Y	Y	N	Y	N	Y	Y	Y
Kassebaum	Y	Y	Y	Y	N	Y	Y	Y
KENTUCKY								
Ford	Y	Y	N	N	Y	Y	Y	Y
McConnell	Y	Y	Y	Y	N	Y	Y	Y
LOUISIANA								
Breaux	Y	Y	Y	Y	Y	Y	Y	Y
Johnston	Y	Y	Y	Y	Y	Y	Y	Y
MAINE								
Mitchell	Y	Y	Y	N	Y	Y	Y	Y
Cohen	Y	Y	Y	Y	Y	Y	Y	Y
MARYLAND								
Mikulski	Y	Y	Y	N	Y	Y	Y	Y
Sarbanes	Y	Y	Y	N	Y	Y	Y	Y
MASSACHUSETTS								
Kennedy	Y	Y	Y	N	Y	Y	Y	Y
Kerry	Y	Y	Y	N	Y	Y	Y	Y
MICHIGAN								
Levin	Y	Y	Y	N	Y	Y	Y	Y
Riegle	Y	Y	Y	N	Y	Y	Y	Y
MINNESOTA								
Wellstone	Y	Y	Y	N	Y	Y	Y	Y
Durenberger	Y	Y	N	Y	N	Y	Y	Y
MISSISSIPPI								
Cochran	Y	Y	N	Y	N	Y	Y	Y
Lott	Y	Y	N	Y	N	Y	Y	Y
MISSOURI								
Bond	Y	Y	N	Y	N	Y	Y	Y
Danforth	Y	Y	N	Y	N	Y	Y	Y
MONTANA								
Baucus	Y	Y	Y	N	Y	Y	Y	Y
Burns	Y	Y	N	Y	N	Y	Y	Y
NEBRASKA								
Exon	Y	Y	Y	Y	Y	Y	Y	Y
Kerrey	?	?	Y	N	Y	Y	Y	Y
NEVADA								
Bryan	Y	Y	Y	N	Y	Y	Y	Y
Reid	Y	Y	Y	N	Y	Y	Y	Y
NEW HAMPSHIRE								
Rudman	Y	Y	Y	Y	N	Y	N	Y
Smith	Y	Y	N	Y	N	Y	N	N
NEW JERSEY								
Bradley	Y	Y	Y	N	Y	Y	Y	Y
Lautenberg	Y	Y	Y	N	Y	Y	Y	Y
NEW MEXICO								
Bingaman	Y	Y	Y	N	Y	Y	Y	Y
Domenici	Y	Y	N	Y	N	Y	Y	Y
NEW YORK								
Moynihan	Y	Y	Y	N	Y	Y	Y	Y
D'Amato	Y	Y	N	Y	Y	Y	Y	Y
NORTH CAROLINA								
Sanford	Y	Y	Y	N	Y	Y	Y	Y
Helms	Y	Y	N	Y	N	Y	N	N
NORTH DAKOTA								
Burdick	Y	Y	Y	N	Y	Y	Y	Y
Conrad	Y	Y	N	N	Y	Y	Y	Y
OHIO								
Glenn	Y	Y	Y	N	Y	Y	Y	Y
Metzenbaum	Y	Y	Y	N	Y	Y	Y	Y
OKLAHOMA								
Boren	Y	Y	N	Y	Y	Y	Y	Y
Nickles	Y	Y	N	Y	N	Y	Y	Y
OREGON								
Hatfield	Y	Y	Y	Y	Y	Y	Y	Y
Packwood	Y	Y	Y	N	Y	Y	Y	Y
PENNSYLVANIA								
Wofford	Y	Y	Y	N	Y	?	?	?
Specter	Y	Y	Y	Y	Y	Y	Y	Y
RHODE ISLAND								
Pell	Y	Y	Y	N	Y	Y	N	Y
Chafee	Y	Y	Y	Y	Y	Y	Y	Y
SOUTH CAROLINA								
Hollings	Y	Y	N	Y	Y	Y	Y	Y
Thurmond	Y	Y	N	Y	N	Y	Y	Y
SOUTH DAKOTA								
Daschle	Y	Y	Y	N	Y	Y	Y	Y
Pressler	Y	Y	N	Y	N	Y	Y	Y
TENNESSEE								
Gore	Y	Y	Y	N	Y	Y	Y	Y
Sasser	Y	Y	Y	N	Y	Y	Y	Y

KEY

- Y Voted for (yea).
- # Paired for.
- + Announced for.
- N Voted against (nay).
- X Paired against.
- - Announced against.
- P Voted "present."
- C Voted "present" to avoid possible conflict of interest.
- ? Did not vote or otherwise make a position known.

Democrats ***Republicans***

	217	218	219	220	221	222	223	224
TEXAS								
Bentsen	Y	Y	Y	N	Y	Y	Y	Y
Gramm	Y	Y	N	Y	N	Y	Y	Y
UTAH								
Garn	Y	Y	N	Y	N	Y	N	Y
Hatch	Y	Y	N	Y	N	Y	Y	Y
VERMONT								
Leahy	Y	Y	Y	N	Y	Y	Y	Y
Jeffords	Y	Y	Y	N	Y	Y	Y	Y
VIRGINIA								
Robb	Y	Y	Y	Y	Y	Y	Y	Y
Warner	Y	Y	N	Y	N	Y	Y	Y
WASHINGTON								
Adams	Y	Y	Y	N	Y	Y	Y	Y
Gorton	Y	Y	N	Y	N	Y	Y	Y
WEST VIRGINIA								
Byrd	Y	Y	N	N	Y	Y	Y	Y
Rockefeller	Y	Y	Y	N	Y	Y	Y	Y
WISCONSIN								
Kohl	Y	Y	N	N	Y	Y	Y	Y
Kasten	Y	Y	N	Y	Y	Y	Y	Y
WYOMING								
Simpson	Y	Y	N	Y	N	Y	Y	Y
Wallop	Y	Y	-	Y	N	Y	N	Y

ND Northern Democrats SD Southern Democrats Southern states - Ala., Ark., Fla., Ga., Ky., La., Miss., N.C., Okla., S.C., Tenn., Texas, Va.

217. S Res 186. Resolution Condemning the Haitian Coup/Adoption. Adoption of the resolution to express the sense of the Senate condemning the coup overthrowing the democratically elected government of President Jean-Bertrand Aristide and urging the international community to take appropriate action to restore the democratic government in Haiti. Adopted 97-0: R 43-0; D 54-0 (ND 38-0, SD 16-0), Oct. 2, 1991.

218. S J Res 110. Resolution Urging Repeal of Resolution Equating Zionism with Racism/Adoption. Adoption of the resolution to express the sense of Congress that the United States and the Soviet Union should lead the effort to repeal the U.N. General Assembly Resolution that equates Zionism with racism. Adopted 97-0: R 43-0; D 54-0 (ND 38-0, SD 16-0), Oct. 2, 1991.

219. HR 2508. Fiscal 1992-93 Foreign Aid Authorization/Conference Report. Adoption of the conference report to authorize $25 billion in fiscal 1992-93 for foreign economic and military assistance. The conference report would overturn the administration's Mexico City Policy, provide funds to the United Nations Population Fund and require cargo preferences. Adopted 61-38: R 11-31; D 50-7 (ND 36-4, SD 14-3), Oct. 8, 1991. A "nay" was a vote supporting the president's position.

220. Thomas Nomination/Confirmation. Confirmation of President Bush's nomination of Clarence Thomas of Georgia to be an associate justice of the U.S. Supreme Court. Confirmed 52-48: R 41-2; D 11-46 (ND 3-37, SD 8-9), Oct. 15, 1991. A "yea" was a vote supporting the president's position.

221. S 1722. Unemployment Benefits Extension/Passage. Passage, over President Bush's Oct. 11 veto, of the bill to provide an estimated $6.4 billion in unemployment benefits for up to 20 additional weeks, based on a state's average total unemployment rate. The benefits would temporarily be extended from Oct. 6, 1991, through July 4, 1992. The bill designates the spending as an emergency and would not require a presidential declaration to be exempt from the spending limits of last year's budget agreement. Rejected 65-35: R 8-35: D 57-0 (ND 40-0, SD 17-0), Oct. 16, 1991. A two-thirds majority of those present and voting (67 in this case) of both houses is required to override a veto. A "nay" was a vote supporting the president's position.

222. HR 2426. Fiscal 1992 Military Construction Appropriations/Conference Report. Adoption of the conference report to provide $8,562,596,000 in new budget authority for military construction for the Department of Defense in fiscal 1992. The administration requested $8,618,310,000. Adopted 99-0: R 43-0; D 56-0 (ND 39-0, SD 17-0), Oct. 16, 1991.

223. HR 2698. Fiscal 1992 Agriculture Appropriations/Conference Report. Adoption of the conference report to provide $52,522,621,000 in new budget authority for agriculture, rural development, the Food and Drug Administration and related agencies in fiscal 1992. The administration requested $52,579,946,000. Adopted 88-10: R 36-7; D 52-3 (ND 36-3, SD 16-0), Oct. 16, 1991.

224. HR 2942. Fiscal 1992 Transportation Appropriations/Conference Report. Adoption of the conference report to provide $14,301,797,569 in new budget authority for the Department of Transportation and related agencies in fiscal 1992. The administration requested $15,110,123,569. Adopted 95-3: R 40-3; D 55-0 (ND 39-0, SD 16-0), Oct. 16, 1991.

	225	226	227	228	229	230	231	232
ALABAMA								
Heflin	N	Y	Y	Y	N	Y	Y	Y
Shelby	N	Y	Y	Y	N	Y	Y	Y
ALASKA								
Murkowski	N	N	Y	Y	Y	Y	Y	Y
Stevens	N	N	Y	Y	Y	Y	Y	Y
ARIZONA								
DeConcini	Y	Y	Y	Y	N	Y	Y	Y
McCain	N	Y	Y	Y	Y	Y	Y	Y
ARKANSAS								
Bumpers	Y	Y	Y	Y	N	Y	Y	Y
Pryor	?	Y	Y	Y	N	Y	Y	Y
CALIFORNIA								
Cranston	Y	Y	Y	Y	N	Y	Y	Y
Seymour	N	Y	Y	N	Y	Y	Y	Y
COLORADO								
Wirth	N	Y	Y	Y	N	Y	Y	Y
Brown	N	Y	Y	Y	Y	Y	Y	Y
CONNECTICUT								
Dodd	N	Y	Y	Y	N	Y	Y	Y
Lieberman	Y	Y	Y	Y	N	Y	Y	Y
DELAWARE								
Biden	Y	Y	Y	Y	N	Y	?	?
Roth	N	Y	Y	Y	Y	Y	?	Y
FLORIDA								
Graham	Y	Y	Y	Y	N	Y	Y	Y
Mack	N	N	Y	N	Y	Y	Y	Y
GEORGIA								
Fowler	N	Y	Y	Y	N	Y	Y	Y
Nunn	Y	Y	Y	Y	N	Y	Y	Y
HAWAII								
Akaka	Y	Y	Y	Y	N	Y	Y	Y
Inouye	?	Y	Y	Y	N	Y	Y	Y
IDAHO								
Craig	N	Y	N	N	Y	Y	Y	Y
Symms	N	N	N	N	Y	Y	Y	Y
ILLINOIS								
Dixon	N	Y	Y	Y	N	Y	Y	Y
Simon	Y	Y	Y	Y	N	Y	Y	Y
INDIANA								
Coats	N	Y	?	Y	Y	Y	Y	Y
Lugar	N	Y	Y	Y	Y	Y	Y	Y
IOWA								
Harkin	Y	Y	Y	?	?	?	?	?
Grassley	N	Y	Y	Y	Y	Y	Y	Y
KANSAS								
Dole	N	N	Y	Y	Y	Y	Y	Y
Kassebaum	N	Y	Y	N	Y	Y	?	Y
KENTUCKY								
Ford	N	Y	Y	Y	N	Y	Y	Y
McConnell	N	Y	Y	Y	Y	Y	Y	Y
LOUISIANA								
Breaux	N	Y	Y	Y	N	Y	Y	Y
Johnston	Y	Y	Y	Y	N	Y	Y	Y
MAINE								
Mitchell	N	Y	Y	Y	N	Y	Y	Y
Cohen	N	Y	Y	Y	Y	Y	Y	Y
MARYLAND								
Mikulski	Y	Y	Y	Y	N	Y	Y	Y
Sarbanes	Y	Y	Y	Y	N	Y	Y	Y
MASSACHUSETTS								
Kennedy	Y	Y	Y	Y	N	Y	Y	Y
Kerry	N	Y	Y	Y	N	Y	Y	Y
MICHIGAN								
Levin	Y	Y	Y	Y	N	Y	Y	Y
Riegle	Y	Y	Y	Y	N	Y	Y	Y
MINNESOTA								
Wellstone	Y	Y	Y	Y	N	Y	Y	Y
Durenberger	N	Y	Y	Y	Y	Y	?	Y
MISSISSIPPI								
Cochran	N	N	Y	N	Y	Y	Y	Y
Lott	N	N	Y	N	Y	Y	Y	Y
MISSOURI								
Bond	N	N	Y	Y	Y	Y	Y	Y
Danforth	N	Y	Y	Y	Y	Y	Y	Y
MONTANA								
Baucus	Y	Y	Y	Y	N	Y	Y	Y
Burns	N	Y	Y	N	Y	Y	Y	Y
NEBRASKA								
Exon	N	Y	Y	Y	N	Y	Y	Y
Kerrey	Y	+	?	?	?	?	?	?
NEVADA								
Bryan	Y	Y	Y	Y	N	Y	Y	Y
Reid	N	Y	Y	Y	N	Y	Y	Y
NEW HAMPSHIRE								
Rudman	N	Y	Y	Y	Y	Y	Y	Y
Smith	N	Y	N	N	Y	Y	Y	Y
NEW JERSEY								
Bradley	N	Y	Y	Y	N	Y	Y	Y
Lautenberg	Y	Y	Y	Y	N	Y	Y	Y
NEW MEXICO								
Bingaman	Y	Y	Y	Y	N	Y	?	Y
Domenici	N	Y	Y	Y	Y	Y	Y	Y
NEW YORK								
Moynihan	Y	Y	Y	Y	N	Y	Y	Y
D'Amato	N	Y	Y	Y	Y	Y	Y	Y
NORTH CAROLINA								
Sanford	Y	Y	Y	Y	N	Y	Y	Y
Helms	N	N	N	Y	Y	N	+	?
NORTH DAKOTA								
Burdick	Y	Y	+	Y	N	Y	Y	Y
Conrad	N	Y	Y	Y	N	Y	Y	Y
OHIO								
Glenn	Y	Y	Y	Y	N	Y	Y	Y
Metzenbaum	Y	Y	Y	Y	N	Y	Y	Y
OKLAHOMA								
Boren	Y	Y	Y	Y	N	Y	Y	Y
Nickles	N	Y	Y	Y	Y	Y	Y	Y
OREGON								
Hatfield	N	Y	Y	Y	Y	Y	Y	Y
Packwood	N	Y	Y	Y	Y	?	Y	Y
PENNSYLVANIA								
Wofford	?	Y	Y	Y	N	Y	Y	Y
Specter	Y	Y	Y	Y	Y	Y	Y	Y
RHODE ISLAND								
Pell	Y	Y	Y	Y	N	Y	Y	Y
Chafee	N	Y	Y	Y	Y	Y	Y	Y
SOUTH CAROLINA								
Hollings	N	Y	Y	Y	N	Y	Y	Y
Thurmond	N	N	Y	Y	Y	Y	Y	Y
SOUTH DAKOTA								
Daschle	Y	Y	Y	Y	N	Y	Y	Y
Pressler	N	Y	Y	Y	Y	Y	Y	Y
TENNESSEE								
Gore	Y	Y	Y	Y	N	Y	Y	Y
Sasser	Y	Y	Y	Y	N	Y	Y	Y
TEXAS								
Bentsen	N	Y	Y	Y	N	Y	Y	Y
Gramm	N	N	Y	N	Y	Y	Y	Y
UTAH								
Garn	N	Y	Y	Y	Y	N	Y	Y
Hatch	N	N	Y	Y	Y	Y	Y	Y
VERMONT								
Leahy	Y	Y	Y	Y	N	Y	Y	Y
Jeffords	N	Y	Y	Y	Y	Y	Y	Y
VIRGINIA								
Robb	Y	Y	Y	Y	N	Y	Y	Y
Warner	N	Y	Y	Y	Y	Y	Y	Y
WASHINGTON								
Adams	Y	Y	Y	Y	N	Y	Y	Y
Gorton	N	Y	Y	N	Y	Y	Y	Y
WEST VIRGINIA								
Byrd	Y	Y	Y	Y	N	Y	Y	Y
Rockefeller	Y	Y	Y	Y	N	Y	Y	Y
WISCONSIN								
Kohl	N	Y	Y	Y	N	Y	Y	Y
Kasten	N	Y	Y	Y	Y	Y	Y	Y
WYOMING								
Simpson	N	N	Y	Y	Y	Y	Y	Y
Wallop	N	N	Y	N	Y	N	Y	Y

KEY

Y Voted for (yea).
Paired for.
+ Announced for.
N Voted against (nay).
X Paired against.
- Announced against.
P Voted "present."
C Voted "present" to avoid possible conflict of interest.
? Did not vote or otherwise make a position known.

Democrats ***Republicans***

ND Northern Democrats SD Southern Democrats

Southern states - Ala., Ark., Fla., Ga., Ky., La., Miss., N.C., Okla., S.C., Tenn., Texas, Va.

225. S 1539. Fiscal 1992 Intelligence Authorization/Confirmation Requirement on Central Intelligence Agency Appointments. Glenn, D-Ohio, amendment to require Senate confirmation of the president's appointment of the Central Intelligence Agency's general counsel, deputy director for operations and deputy director for intelligence. Rejected 38-59: R 1-42; D 37-17 (ND 28-10, SD 9-7), Oct. 16, 1991. A "nay" was a vote supporting the president's position.

226. S 596. Federal Facility Compliance Act/Cloture. Mitchell, D-Maine, motion to invoke cloture (thus limiting debate) on the motion to proceed to the bill to allow the Environmental Protection Agency to impose administrative orders and monetary penalties on federal agencies that have failed to comply with all federal, state, interstate, and local solid and hazardous waste management and disposal requirements. Motion agreed to 85-14: R 29-14; D 56-0 (ND 39-0, SD 17-0), Oct. 17, 1991. A three-fifths majority of the total Senate (60) is required to invoke cloture.

227. S 1745. Civil Rights Act/Cloture. Mitchell, D-Maine, motion to invoke cloture (thus limiting debate) on the motion to proceed to the bill to make it easier for women and minorities to win employee discrimination lawsuits. Motion agreed to 93-4: R 38-4; D 55-0 (ND 38-0, SD 17-0), Oct. 22, 1991. A three-fifths majority of the total Senate (60) is required to invoke cloture.

228. S Res 202. Investigation of Unauthorized Disclosures/Adoption. Adoption of the resolution to appoint a special independent counsel to investigate unauthorized disclosures of confidential information during the consideration of the nomination of Clarence Thomas to be an associate justice of the Supreme Court and during the investigation of matters related to Charles H. Keating Jr. Passed 86-12: R 31-12; D 55-0 (ND 38-0, SD 17-0), Oct. 24, 1991.

229. S 596. Federal Facility Compliance Act/Investigation of Leaks. Seymour, R-Calif., amendment to direct the Federal Bureau of Investigation to determine the source of the unauthorized release of confidential information regarding Professor Anita Hill's allegations of sexual harassment by Judge Clarence Thomas, President Bush's nominee to be associate justice of the Supreme Court. Rejected 43-55: R 43-0; D 0-55 (ND 0-38, SD 0-17), Oct. 24, 1991.

230. HR 2194. Federal Facility Compliance Act/Passage. Passage of the bill to allow the Environmental Protection Agency to impose administrative orders and monetary penalties on federal agencies that have failed to comply with all federal, state, interstate and local solid and hazardous waste management and disposal requirements. Passed 94-3: R 39-3; D 55-0 (ND 38-0, SD 17-0), Oct. 24, 1991.

231. S Res 209. Condemn Sexual Harassment/Adoption. Adoption of the resolution to express the sense of the Senate that the Senate should consider appropriate changes to U.S. laws and Senate rules to prevent sexual harassment. Adopted 92-0: R 39-0; D 53-0 (ND 36-0, SD 17-0), Oct. 28, 1991.

232. S 1745. Civil Rights Act of 1991/Glass Ceiling. Dole, R-Kan., amendment to establish a Glass Ceiling Commission to conduct a study and prepare recommendations about artificial barriers to the advancement of women and minorities to management and decision-making positions in the workplace. Adopted 96-0: R 42-0; D 54-0 (ND 37-0, SD 17-0), Oct. 29, 1991.

	233	234	235	236	237	238	239	240
ALABAMA								
Heflin	Y	Y	Y	N	N	Y	Y	Y
Shelby	Y	Y	N	N	Y	Y	Y	Y
ALASKA								
Murkowski	N	Y	N	N	N	Y	Y	Y
Stevens	Y	Y	Y	N	Y	Y	Y	Y
ARIZONA								
DeConcini	Y	Y	N	N	Y	Y	Y	Y
McCain	N	N	N	N	N	Y	Y	Y
ARKANSAS								
Bumpers	Y	N	N	N	N	Y	Y	Y
Pryor	Y	Y	N	Y	N	Y	Y	Y
CALIFORNIA								
Cranston	Y	Y	N	Y	?	Y	Y	Y
Seymour	N	N	N	N	N	Y	Y	Y
COLORADO								
Wirth	Y	Y	N	N	N	Y	Y	Y
Brown	N	N	N	N	N	Y	Y	N
CONNECTICUT								
Dodd	Y	N	N	N	Y	Y	Y	Y
Lieberman	Y	N	N	Y	N	Y	Y	Y
DELAWARE								
Biden	Y	Y	Y	N	Y	Y	Y	Y
Roth	Y	Y	N	N	Y	Y	Y	N
FLORIDA								
Graham	Y	N	N	N	N	Y	Y	Y
Mack	Y	N	Y	N	N	Y	Y	Y
GEORGIA								
Fowler	Y	N	N	N	N	Y	Y	Y
Nunn	Y	Y	Y	Y	Y	Y	Y	Y
HAWAII								
Akaka	Y	Y	N	Y	Y	Y	Y	Y
Inouye	Y	Y	N	Y	Y	Y	Y	Y
IDAHO								
Craig	N	N	N	N	N	Y	Y	Y
Symms	N	N	N	N	N	N	Y	Y
ILLINOIS								
Dixon	Y	N	N	N	Y	Y	Y	Y
Simon	Y	Y	N	Y	N	Y	Y	Y
INDIANA								
Coats	N	N	N	N	N	N	Y	Y
Lugar	N	Y	Y	N	N	Y	Y	Y
IOWA								
Harkin	Y	N	N	?	?	Y	?	?
Grassley	N	N	N	Y	Y	Y	Y	Y
KANSAS								
Dole	Y	Y	N	N	Y	Y	Y	Y
Kassebaum	N	N	N	N	N	Y	Y	Y
KENTUCKY								
Ford	Y	Y	N	N	Y	Y	Y	Y
McConnell	N	N	N	N	N	Y	Y	Y
LOUISIANA								
Breaux	Y	Y	N	N	Y	Y	Y	Y
Johnston	Y	Y	Y	Y	Y	Y	Y	Y
MAINE								
Mitchell	Y	Y	N	Y	Y	Y	Y	Y
Cohen	Y	Y	Y	N	N	Y	Y	Y
MARYLAND								
Mikulski	Y	N	N	N	N	Y	Y	Y
Sarbanes	Y	Y	N	Y	Y	Y	Y	Y
MASSACHUSETTS								
Kennedy	Y	Y	N	Y	Y	Y	Y	Y
Kerry	Y	N	N	N	Y	Y	Y	Y
MICHIGAN								
Levin	Y	Y	N	N	Y	Y	Y	Y
Riegle	Y	Y	N	N	Y	Y	Y	Y
MINNESOTA								
Wellstone	Y	Y	N	N	N	Y	Y	Y
Durenberger	Y	N	N	Y	N	Y	Y	Y
MISSISSIPPI								
Cochran	Y	Y	Y	Y	Y	Y	Y	Y
Lott	N	N	Y	Y	N	Y	Y	Y
MISSOURI								
Bond	N	N	N	N	N	Y	Y	Y
Danforth	Y	Y	Y	N	Y	Y	Y	Y
MONTANA								
Baucus	Y	Y	N	N	Y	Y	Y	Y
Burns	N	N	N	N	N	Y	Y	Y
NEBRASKA								
Exon	N	Y	N	N	Y	Y	Y	Y
Kerrey	?	?	?	?	?	?	?	?
NEVADA								
Bryan	Y	Y	N	N	Y	Y	Y	Y
Reid	Y	Y	N	N	Y	Y	Y	Y
NEW HAMPSHIRE								
Rudman	Y	Y	Y	N	Y	Y	Y	Y
Smith	N	N	N	N	N	N	Y	N
NEW JERSEY								
Bradley	Y	Y	N	Y	Y	Y	Y	Y
Lautenberg	Y	Y	N	Y	Y	Y	Y	Y
NEW MEXICO								
Bingaman	Y	Y	N	N	Y	Y	Y	Y
Domenici	N	Y	Y	N	N	Y	Y	Y
NEW YORK								
Moynihan	Y	Y	N	N	Y	Y	Y	Y
D'Amato	N	Y	N	N	N	Y	Y	Y
NORTH CAROLINA								
Sanford	Y	Y	N	N	Y	Y	Y	Y
Helms	N	N	N	N	N	N	Y	N
NORTH DAKOTA								
Burdick	Y	Y	N	Y	Y	Y	Y	Y
Conrad	N	N	N	N	Y	Y	Y	Y
OHIO								
Glenn	Y	Y	N	N	Y	Y	Y	Y
Metzenbaum	Y	Y	N	N	Y	Y	Y	Y
OKLAHOMA								
Boren	Y	N	N	Y	Y	Y	Y	Y
Nickles	N	N	N	N	N	Y	Y	Y
OREGON								
Hatfield	Y	Y	Y	Y	Y	Y	Y	Y
Packwood	Y	N	N	N	N	Y	Y	Y
PENNSYLVANIA								
Wofford	?	N	?	?	?	?	?	?
Specter	Y	N	N	N	N	Y	Y	Y
RHODE ISLAND								
Pell	N	Y	N	N	Y	Y	Y	Y
Chafee	Y	Y	N	N	Y	Y	Y	Y
SOUTH CAROLINA								
Hollings	Y	Y	Y	N	N	Y	Y	Y
Thurmond	N	Y	Y	N	Y	Y	Y	Y
SOUTH DAKOTA								
Daschle	Y	Y	N	N	Y	Y	Y	Y
Pressler	N	N	N	N	N	Y	Y	Y
TENNESSEE								
Gore	Y	Y	N	Y	Y	Y	Y	Y
Sasser	Y	Y	N	Y	Y	Y	Y	Y
TEXAS								
Bentsen	Y	Y	N	N	Y	Y	Y	Y
Gramm	N	Y	Y	N	N	Y	Y	Y
UTAH								
Garn	N	Y	Y	N	Y	Y	Y	Y
Hatch	Y	Y	Y	N	Y	Y	Y	Y
VERMONT								
Leahy	Y	N	N	N	N	Y	Y	Y
Jeffords	Y	Y	N	N	Y	Y	Y	Y
VIRGINIA								
Robb	Y	Y	N	N	Y	Y	Y	Y
Warner	Y	Y	N	N	Y	Y	Y	Y
WASHINGTON								
Adams	Y	N	N	N	N	Y	Y	Y
Gorton	N	Y	Y	N	N	Y	Y	Y
WEST VIRGINIA								
Byrd	N	Y	Y	N	Y	Y	Y	Y
Rockefeller	Y	Y	N	N	Y	Y	Y	Y
WISCONSIN								
Kohl	Y	N	N	N	N	Y	Y	Y
Kasten	N	N	N	N	N	Y	Y	Y
WYOMING								
Simpson	Y	N	Y	N	Y	Y	Y	Y
Wallop	N	N	N	N	N	N	Y	Y

KEY

- Y Voted for (yea).
- # Paired for.
- + Announced for.
- N Voted against (nay).
- X Paired against.
- \- Announced against.
- P Voted "present."
- C Voted "present" to avoid possible conflict of interest.
- ? Did not vote or otherwise make a position known.

Democrats ***Republicans***

ND Northern Democrats SD Southern Democrats

Southern states - Ala., Ark., Fla., Ga., Ky., La., Miss., N.C., Okla., S.C., Tenn., Texas, Va.

233. S 1745. Civil Rights Act of 1991/Legal Services. Danforth, R-Mo., motion to table (kill) the McConnell, R-Ky., amendment to limit attorney contingency fees to 20 percent of awards or settlements civil rights cases; require prior disclosure of all likely legal costs in such cases; provide plaintiffs with a private right of action against their lawyers for not complying; and provide the plaintiff with the option of paying for legal services on an hourly rate basis or a contingency fee basis. Motion agreed to 68-30: R 17-26; D 51-4 (ND 34-4, SD 17-0), Oct. 29, 1991.

234. S 1745. Civil Rights Act of 1991/Congressional Exemption. McCain, R-Ariz., motion to table (kill) the Nickles, R-Okla., amendment to the Brown, R-Colo., amendment, to repeal exemptions for Congress from civil rights, labor and other laws. Motion agreed to 61-38: R 20-23; D 41-15 (ND 28-11, SD 13-4), Oct. 29, 1991.

235. S 1745. Civil Rights Act of 1991/Senate Office of Fair Employment Practices. Rudman, R-N.H., constitutional point of order against the Grassley, R-Iowa, amendment, which would establish a Senate Office of Fair Employment Practices to handle discrimination complaints and allow employees to appeal decisions to the Ethics Committee and then to the U.S. Court of Appeals. Rudman contended that it was an unconstitutional intrusion into the affairs of the legislative branch of government. Rejected 22-76: R 16-27; D 6-49 (ND 2-36, SD 4-13), Oct. 29, 1991.

236. S 1745. Civil Rights Act of 1991/Reimbursement. Grassley, R-Iowa, motion to table (kill) the Rudman, R-N.H., amendment to the Grassley amendment, to require the president or senators to reimburse the appropriate federal account for any payment made in their behalf for violations of the Civil Rights Act. Motion rejected 22-75: R 5-38; D 17-37 (ND 11-26, SD 6-11), Oct. 30, 1991. (The Rudman amendment was subsequently adopted by voice vote.)

237. S 1745. Civil Rights Act of 1991/Senate Employees. Hatch, R-Utah, motion to table (kill) the Nickles, R-Okla., amendment to the Grassley, R-Iowa, amendment, to allow Senate employees access to jury trials and punitive damages on the same basis as such rights and remedies are available to the private sector. Motion agreed to 54-42: R 15-28; D 39-14 (ND 28-8, SD 11-6), Oct. 30, 1991. A "nay" was a vote supporting the president's position.

238. S 1745. Civil Rights Act of 1991/Passage. Passage of the bill to make it easier for workers to sue for employment discrimination and permit women, religious minorities and the disabled to win compensatory and punitive damages for intentional discrimination, mainly by reversing several recent Supreme Court decisions and by expanding Title VII of the 1964 Civil Rights Act. Passed 93-5: R 38-5; D 55-0 (ND 38-0, SD 17-0), Oct. 30, 1991. A "yea" was a vote supporting the president's position.

239. S Res 201. Enforce Oilseeds GATT Panel Ruling/Adoption. Adoption of the resolution to express the sense of the Senate that if by Oct. 31, 1991, the European Community has not adopted a new oilseeds regime in full conformity with its GATT obligations, the U.S. trade representative should take action to compensate for the trade losses caused by the European Community's failure to comply with its GATT obligations by continuing to subsidize the production of oilseeds. Adopted 97-0: R 43-0; D 54-0 (ND 37-0, SD 17-0), Oct. 30, 1991.

240. HR 2686. Fiscal 1992 Interior Appropriations/Conference Report. Adoption of the conference report to provide $12,623,563,000 in new budget authority for the Department of the Interior and related agencies in fiscal 1992. The administration requested $11,595,927,000. Adopted 93-4: R 39-4; D 54-0 (ND 37-0, SD 17-0), Oct. 30, 1991.

	241	242	243	244	245	246	247	248
ALABAMA								
Heflin	N	Y	Y	Y	Y	Y	Y	N
Shelby	N	Y	Y	Y	Y	Y	Y	Y
ALASKA								
Murkowski	Y	Y	Y	Y	Y	Y	Y	N
Stevens	Y	Y	Y	Y	Y	Y	Y	N
ARIZONA								
DeConcini	Y	Y	N	N	Y	Y	Y	Y
McCain	N	Y	Y	Y	Y	N	Y	N
ARKANSAS								
Bumpers	Y	Y	N	Y	Y	Y	Y	N
Pryor	Y	Y	N	Y	Y	Y	Y	N
CALIFORNIA								
Cranston	Y	N	?	?	?	?	?	?
Seymour	N	Y	Y	Y	Y	Y	Y	N
COLORADO								
Wirth	Y	N	+	?	Y	Y	Y	Y
Brown	N	Y	Y	N	Y	Y	Y	N
CONNECTICUT								
Dodd	Y	Y	N	Y	Y	Y	Y	Y
Lieberman	Y	N	Y	Y	Y	Y	Y	Y
DELAWARE								
Biden	Y	N	N	Y	Y	Y	Y	Y
Roth	N	N	Y	Y	Y	N	Y	N
FLORIDA								
Graham	N	N	Y	Y	Y	Y	Y	Y
Mack	N	N	Y	Y	Y	N	Y	N
GEORGIA								
Fowler	Y	N	N	Y	Y	Y	Y	N
Nunn	Y	Y	Y	Y	Y	Y	Y	N
HAWAII								
Akaka	Y	Y	Y	N	Y	Y	Y	Y
Inouye	Y	Y	Y	N	Y	Y	Y	Y
IDAHO								
Craig	Y	Y	Y	Y	N	N	Y	N
Symms	Y	Y	Y	Y	N	N	Y	N
ILLINOIS								
Dixon	N	N	N	N	Y	Y	Y	Y
Simon	Y	N	N	N	Y	Y	Y	Y
INDIANA								
Coats	N	Y	Y	N	Y	N	Y	Y
Lugar	Y	Y	Y	Y	Y	N	Y	N
IOWA								
Harkin	Y	N	N	N	Y	Y	?	?
Grassley	N	N	Y	Y	Y	Y	Y	N
KANSAS								
Dole	N	Y	Y	Y	Y	N	Y	N
Kassebaum	Y	Y	Y	Y	Y	Y	Y	N
KENTUCKY								
Ford	Y	Y	Y	Y	Y	N	Y	N
McConnell	N	Y	Y	Y	Y	Y	Y	N
LOUISIANA								
Breaux	Y	Y	Y	Y	Y	N	Y	Y
Johnston	Y	Y	Y	Y	Y	N	Y	Y
MAINE								
Mitchell	Y	Y	N	Y	Y	Y	Y	Y
Cohen	Y	N	Y	Y	Y	Y	Y	N
MARYLAND								
Mikulski	Y	N	Y	N	Y	Y	Y	Y
Sarbanes	Y	N	N	N	Y	Y	Y	Y
MASSACHUSETTS								
Kennedy	Y	N	N	Y	Y	Y	Y	Y
Kerry	Y	N	N	Y	Y	Y	Y	Y
MICHIGAN								
Levin	Y	N	N	Y	Y	Y	Y	Y
Riegle	Y	N	N	Y	Y	Y	Y	Y
MINNESOTA								
Wellstone	Y	N	N	N	Y	Y	Y	Y
Durenberger	Y	N	Y	Y	Y	N	Y	N
MISSISSIPPI								
Cochran	Y	Y	Y	Y	Y	Y	Y	N
Lott	N	N	Y	Y	N	N	Y	N
MISSOURI								
Bond	Y	N	Y	Y	Y	Y	Y	N
Danforth	Y	Y	Y	Y	Y	Y	Y	N
MONTANA								
Baucus	Y	N	N	Y	Y	Y	Y	Y
Burns	Y	Y	Y	Y	N	N	Y	N
NEBRASKA								
Exon	Y	N	N	Y	Y	Y	Y	N
Kerrey	Y	X	?	?	?	?	?	?
NEVADA								
Bryan	Y	N	Y	Y	Y	Y	Y	Y
Reid	Y	N	Y	Y	Y	Y	Y	Y
NEW HAMPSHIRE								
Rudman	N	Y	Y	Y	Y	Y	Y	N
Smith	N	N	Y	N	Y	N	Y	N
NEW JERSEY								
Bradley	Y	N	N	N	?	Y	Y	Y
Lautenberg	Y	N	N	N	Y	Y	Y	Y
NEW MEXICO								
Bingaman	Y	Y	N	N	Y	Y	Y	N
Domenici	Y	Y	Y	Y	Y	N	Y	N
NEW YORK								
Moynihan	Y	N	N	Y	Y	Y	Y	Y
D'Amato	N	Y	Y	Y	Y	Y	Y	Y
NORTH CAROLINA								
Sanford	Y	N	Y	N	Y	Y	Y	Y
Helms	N	Y	Y	Y	N	N	Y	N
NORTH DAKOTA								
Burdick	Y	N	N	N	Y	Y	Y	Y
Conrad	Y	Y	N	N	Y	Y	Y	Y
OHIO								
Glenn	Y	N	Y	Y	?	Y	Y	Y
Metzenbaum	Y	N	N	Y	Y	Y	Y	Y
OKLAHOMA								
Boren	Y	?	Y	Y	Y	Y	Y	N
Nickles	N	Y	Y	N	N	N	Y	N
OREGON								
Hatfield	Y	Y	Y	Y	Y	Y	Y	N
Packwood	Y	Y	Y	Y	Y	Y	Y	Y
PENNSYLVANIA								
Wofford	?	?	?	?	Y	Y	Y	Y
Specter	N	Y	Y	Y	Y	Y	Y	N
RHODE ISLAND								
Pell	Y	#	Y	Y	Y	Y	Y	Y
Chafee	Y	N	Y	Y	Y	Y	Y	N
SOUTH CAROLINA								
Hollings	N	N	N	Y	Y	Y	Y	N
Thurmond	N	Y	Y	Y	Y	N	Y	N
SOUTH DAKOTA								
Daschle	N	Y	N	Y	Y	Y	Y	Y
Pressler	Y	Y	Y	Y	Y	N	Y	N
TENNESSEE								
Gore	Y	N	N	Y	Y	Y	Y	Y
Sasser	Y	N	N	Y	Y	Y	Y	Y
TEXAS								
Bentsen	Y	Y	Y	Y	Y	Y	Y	N
Gramm	?	?	Y	Y	Y	N	Y	N
UTAH								
Garn	Y	Y	Y	Y	Y	N	Y	N
Hatch	Y	Y	+	?	+	-	+	N
VERMONT								
Leahy	Y	N	Y	N	Y	Y	Y	Y
Jeffords	Y	?	Y	Y	Y	Y	Y	N
VIRGINIA								
Robb	Y	N	Y	N	Y	Y	Y	Y
Warner	Y	Y	Y	Y	Y	Y	Y	N
WASHINGTON								
Adams	Y	N	N	N	Y	Y	Y	Y
Gorton	Y	Y	Y	Y	Y	Y	Y	N
WEST VIRGINIA								
Byrd	Y	Y	Y	Y	Y	Y	Y	Y
Rockefeller	Y	N	N	Y	Y	Y	Y	Y
WISCONSIN								
Kohl	Y	N	Y	Y	Y	Y	Y	N
Kasten	N	Y	Y	Y	Y	N	Y	Y
WYOMING								
Simpson	Y	Y	Y	Y	Y	Y	Y	N
Wallop	N	Y	Y	Y	N	N	Y	N

KEY

- Y Voted for (yea).
- # Paired for.
- + Announced for.
- N Voted against (nay).
- X Paired against.
- - Announced against.
- P Voted "present."
- C Voted "present" to avoid possible conflict of interest.
- ? Did not vote or otherwise make a position known.

Democrats ***Republicans***

ND Northern Democrats SD Southern Democrats Southern states - Ala., Ark., Fla., Ga., Ky., La., Miss., N.C., Okla., S.C., Tenn., Texas, Va.

241. HR 2686. Fiscal 1992 Interior Appropriations/National Endowment for the Arts. Byrd, D-W.Va., motion to table (kill) Helms, R-N.C., motion to concur in the House amendment to the Senate amendment with an amendment to prohibit the National Endowment for the Arts from using funds for "obscene" art. Motion agreed to 73-25: R 23-19; D 50-6 (ND 37-2, SD 13-4), Oct. 31, 1991.

242. S 1220. National Energy Policy/Cloture. Mitchell, D-Maine, motion to invoke cloture (thus limiting debate) on the motion to proceed to the bill to allow drilling in the Arctic National Wildlife Refuge, mandate that federal and private vehicle fleets use alternative fuels, direct the secretary of Transportation to adopt new corporate average fuel economy (CAFE) standards, and enact other programs related to energy production and consumption. Motion rejected 50-44: R 32-9; D 18-35 (ND 9-28, SD 9-7), Nov. 1, 1991. A three-fifths majority (60) of the total Senate was required to invoke cloture.

243. Gates Nomination/Confirmation. Confirmation of President Bush's nomination of Robert M. Gates of Virginia to be director of central intelligence. Confirmed 64-31: R 42-0; D 22-31 (ND 11-25, SD 11-6), Nov. 5, 1991. A "yea" was a vote supporting the president's position.

244. S Res 214. Engrossment Corrections to the Civil Rights Act/Adoption. Adoption of the resolution to make technical corrections to the engrossment of the Civil Rights Act of 1991, including a provision that exempts the Wards Cove Packing Co., a Seattle cannery, from retroactive lawsuits regarding a certain disparate impact case that was adjudicated by the Supreme Court in 1989. Adopted 73-22: R 38-4; D 35-18 (ND 20-16, SD 15-2), Nov. 5, 1991.

245. S 455. Indoor Air Quality/Passage. Passage of the bill to establish an Office of Indoor Air Quality within the Environmental Protection Agency. Passed 88-7: R 35-7; D 53-0 (ND 36-0, SD 17-0), Nov. 6, 1991.

246. HR 2707. Fiscal 1992 Labor, HHS and Education Appropriations/Conference Report. Adoption of the conference report (thus clearing the measure for the president) to provide $204,919,763,000 in new budget authority for the Departments of Labor, Health and Human Services, and Education and related agencies, $176,796,071,000 in fiscal 1992, $27,848,692,000 in fiscal 1993, and $275,000,000 in fiscal 1994. The administration requested $200,611,414,000. The measure would block enforcement of the administration rule, known as the "gag rule," barring abortion counseling in federally funded family planning clinics. Adopted 73-24: R 21-21; D 52-3 (ND 38-0, SD 14-3), Nov. 7, 1991. A "nay" was a vote supporting the president's position.

247. S 838. Child Abuse and Domestic Violence Prevention Act/Passage. Passage of the bill to reauthorize programs to identify, prevent and treat child abuse and neglect. Passed 96-0: R 42-0; D 54-0 (ND 37-0, SD 17-0), Nov. 7, 1991.

248. S 243. Older Americans Act/Strike Pension Provisions. Adams, D-Wash., motion to table (kill) the Cochran, R-Miss., amendment to strike pension restoration provisions from the bill, which provides limited payments to individuals who lost earned benefits when their pension plans terminated prior to enactment in 1974 of the Employment Retirement Security Act (ERISA). Motion rejected 46-51: R 4-39; D 42-12 (ND 34-3, SD 8-9), Nov. 12, 1991. (The Cochran amendment was subsequently adopted by voice vote.) A "nay" was a vote supporting the president's position.

	249	250	251	252	253	254	255	256
ALABAMA								
Heflin	N	Y	N	N	N	Y	Y	N
Shelby	Y	Y	Y	N	N	Y	Y	N
ALASKA								
Murkowski	Y	Y	Y	Y	Y	Y	Y	N
Stevens	Y	Y	Y	Y	Y	Y	Y	N
ARIZONA								
DeConcini	Y	Y	Y	N	N	Y	Y	Y
McCain	Y	Y	Y	Y	Y	Y	Y	N
ARKANSAS								
Bumpers	Y	Y	Y	N	N	Y	Y	N
Pryor	Y	Y	Y	N	N	Y	Y	Y
CALIFORNIA								
Cranston	?	?	?	?	?	?	?	?
Seymour	N	Y	Y	Y	Y	Y	Y	N
COLORADO								
Wirth	Y	Y	Y	N	Y	Y	Y	Y
Brown	N	N	N	N	N	N	Y	N
CONNECTICUT								
Dodd	Y	Y	Y	Y	Y	Y	Y	Y
Lieberman	Y	Y	Y	Y	Y	Y	Y	Y
DELAWARE								
Biden	N	Y	Y	N	N	Y	Y	Y
Roth	N	Y	?	N	N	Y	Y	N
FLORIDA								
Graham	Y	Y	Y	N	Y	Y	Y	Y
Mack	N	Y	N	N	Y	Y	Y	N
GEORGIA								
Fowler	N	Y	Y	N	Y	Y	Y	Y
Nunn	N	Y	N	N	Y	Y	Y	Y
HAWAII								
Akaka	Y	Y	Y	Y	Y	Y	Y	Y
Inouye	Y	Y	Y	Y	Y	Y	Y	N
IDAHO								
Craig	N	Y	Y	Y	N	Y	Y	N
Symms	Y	Y	N	Y	N	Y	Y	N
ILLINOIS								
Dixon	Y	N	Y	N	Y	Y	Y	Y
Simon	Y	Y	Y	N	Y	Y	Y	Y
INDIANA								
Coats	Y	Y	N	Y	Y	Y	Y	N
Lugar	Y	Y	N	Y	Y	Y	Y	N
IOWA								
Harkin	?	?	?	?	?	?	?	?
Grassley	N	Y	Y	N	N	Y	Y	N
KANSAS								
Dole	Y	Y	Y	Y	Y	Y	Y	N
Kassebaum	Y	Y	Y	Y	Y	Y	Y	N
KENTUCKY								
Ford	Y	Y	Y	Y	N	Y	Y	Y
McConnell	Y	Y	N	Y	N	Y	Y	N
LOUISIANA								
Breaux	N	Y	Y	N	N	Y	?	N
Johnston	N	Y	Y	N	N	Y	Y	N
MAINE								
Mitchell	Y	Y	Y	Y	Y	Y	Y	Y
Cohen	Y	Y	Y	Y	Y	Y	Y	Y
MARYLAND								
Mikulski	Y	Y	Y	N	Y	Y	?	Y
Sarbanes	Y	Y	Y	Y	Y	Y	Y	Y
MASSACHUSETTS								
Kennedy	Y	Y	Y	Y	Y	Y	Y	Y
Kerry	Y	Y	Y	Y	Y	Y	Y	Y
MICHIGAN								
Levin	Y	Y	Y	Y	Y	Y	Y	Y
Riegle	Y	Y	Y	Y	Y	Y	Y	Y
MINNESOTA								
Wellstone	Y	Y	Y	N	Y	Y	Y	Y
Durenberger	N	Y	Y	Y	Y	Y	Y	N
MISSISSIPPI								
Cochran	Y	Y	Y	Y	Y	Y	Y	N
Lott	Y	Y	Y	Y	Y	Y	Y	N
MISSOURI								
Bond	Y	Y	?	Y	Y	Y	Y	Y
Danforth	Y	Y	?	Y	Y	Y	Y	Y
MONTANA								
Baucus	Y	Y	Y	N	Y	?	Y	N
Burns	Y	Y	Y	N	Y	Y	Y	N
NEBRASKA								
Exon	Y	Y	Y	N	Y	Y	Y	Y
Kerrey	?	?	?	?	?	?	?	?
NEVADA								
Bryan	Y	Y	Y	Y	Y	Y	Y	Y
Reid	Y	Y	Y	N	Y	Y	Y	N
NEW HAMPSHIRE								
Rudman	Y	Y	N	Y	N	Y	Y	Y
Smith	Y	N	N	Y	N	Y	Y	N
NEW JERSEY								
Bradley	Y	Y	?	?	Y	Y	?	Y
Lautenberg	Y	Y	Y	Y	Y	Y	Y	Y
NEW MEXICO								
Bingaman	Y	Y	N	Y	Y	Y	Y	Y
Domenici	Y	Y	Y	Y	Y	Y	Y	N
NEW YORK								
Moynihan	Y	Y	Y	Y	Y	Y	Y	Y
D'Amato	Y	Y	Y	Y	Y	Y	Y	Y
NORTH CAROLINA								
Sanford	Y	Y	Y	Y	Y	Y	Y	Y
Helms	N	N	N	Y	?	Y	Y	N
NORTH DAKOTA								
Burdick	Y	Y	Y	N	Y	Y	Y	Y
Conrad	Y	Y	Y	N	N	N	Y	Y
OHIO								
Glenn	?	?	N	?	Y	Y	Y	Y
Metzenbaum	Y	Y	Y	N	Y	?	Y	Y
OKLAHOMA								
Boren	N	Y	Y	N	Y	Y	Y	N
Nickles	N	Y	Y	N	N	Y	Y	N
OREGON								
Hatfield	Y	Y	Y	Y	Y	Y	Y	Y
Packwood	Y	Y	Y	Y	Y	Y	Y	Y
PENNSYLVANIA								
Wofford	?	?	Y	N	Y	Y	Y	Y
Specter	Y	Y	Y	N	Y	Y	Y	Y
RHODE ISLAND								
Pell	Y	Y	Y	Y	Y	Y	Y	Y
Chafee	Y	Y	Y	Y	Y	Y	Y	Y
SOUTH CAROLINA								
Hollings	N	Y	Y	Y	N	Y	Y	Y
Thurmond	Y	Y	Y	Y	Y	Y	Y	N
SOUTH DAKOTA								
Daschle	Y	Y	N	Y	Y	Y	Y	Y
Pressler	Y	Y	N	Y	Y	Y	Y	N
TENNESSEE								
Gore	Y	Y	Y	N	Y	Y	Y	Y
Sasser	Y	Y	Y	Y	Y	Y	Y	Y
TEXAS								
Bentsen	Y	Y	Y	Y	Y	Y	?	Y
Gramm	Y	Y	N	Y	Y	Y	Y	N
UTAH								
Garn	Y	Y	N	Y	Y	Y	Y	N
Hatch	Y	Y	N	+	+	#	Y	N
VERMONT								
Leahy	Y	Y	Y	N	Y	Y	Y	Y
Jeffords	Y	Y	Y	Y	Y	Y	?	Y
VIRGINIA								
Robb	Y	Y	Y	Y	Y	Y	Y	Y
Warner	Y	Y	Y	Y	Y	Y	Y	N
WASHINGTON								
Adams	Y	Y	Y	N	Y	Y	Y	Y
Gorton	Y	Y	Y	Y	Y	Y	Y	N
WEST VIRGINIA								
Byrd	Y	Y	Y	N	Y	Y	Y	Y
Rockefeller	Y	Y	Y	Y	Y	Y	Y	Y
WISCONSIN								
Kohl	N	Y	Y	N	Y	Y	Y	Y
Kasten	N	Y	Y	N	Y	Y	Y	N
WYOMING								
Simpson	Y	Y	Y	N	Y	Y	Y	N
Wallop	Y	Y	N	N	N	X	+	N

KEY

- Y Voted for (yea).
- # Paired for.
- + Announced for.
- N Voted against (nay).
- X Paired against.
- - Announced against.
- P Voted "present."
- C Voted "present" to avoid possible conflict of interest.
- ? Did not vote or otherwise make a position known.

Democrats *Republicans*

ND Northern Democrats SD Southern Democrats

Southern states - Ala., Ark., Fla., Ga., Ky., La., Miss., N.C., Okla., S.C., Tenn., Texas, Va.

249. S 543. Banking Reform/Cloture. Mitchell, D-Maine, motion to invoke cloture (thus limiting debate) on the motion to proceed to the bill to allow the Federal Deposit Insurance Corporation to borrow $30 billion to cover losses of failed banks, restructure the banking industry and overhaul the federal bank deposit insurance system. Motion agreed to 76-19: R 33-10; D 43-9 (ND 33-2, SD 10-7), Nov. 13, 1991. A three-fifths majority vote of the total Senate (60) is required to invoke cloture.

250. H J Res 374. Fiscal 1992 Continuing Appropriations/Passage. Passage of the joint resolution to provide continuing appropriations for the programs in the two regular appropriations bills not yet signed into law through Nov. 26, 1991, at the lowest of the House, Senate or fiscal 1991 levels. Passed 91-4: R 40-3; D 51-1 (ND 34-1, SD 17-0), Nov. 13, 1991.

251. S 543. Banking Reform/Limit Credit Card Interest Rates. D'Amato, R-N.Y., amendment to limit the annual interest rate on credit cards to 4 percentage points above the rate charged by the Internal Revenue Service for interest on the underpayment of taxes, which adjusts quarterly based on average short-term Treasury rates (currently 10 percent). Adopted 74-19: R 26-14; D 48-5 (ND 33-3, SD 15-2), Nov. 13, 1991.

252. S 543. Banking Reform/'Opt In' Interstate Branching. Ford, D-Ky., motion to table (kill) the Bumpers, D-Ark., amendment to allow banks to open branches across state lines in a particular state only if the state votes to opt in by passing a law allowing interstate branching. Motion agreed to 55-39: R 32-10; D 23-29 (ND 17-18, SD 6-11), Nov. 14, 1991. A "yea" was a vote supporting the president's position.

253. HR 3575. Extended Unemployment Benefits/State Formula Change. Dole, R-Kan., motion to table (kill) the Smith, R-N.H., amendment to provide five states with a total unemployment rate for the last six months of at least 7 percent with 13 weeks of extended benefits rather than six weeks. The approximate $200 million in increased spending would be offset by reductions in foreign aid. Motion agreed to 74-21: R 31-10; D 43-11 (ND 34-3, SD 9-8), Nov. 15, 1991.

254. HR 3575. Extended Unemployment Benefits/Passage. Passage of the compromise bill (thus clearing the measure for the president) to provide an estimated $5.3 billion for six, 13 or 20 weeks of extended unemployment benefits for workers who have exhausted their regular unemployment benefits through July 4, 1992. The increased spending caused by the bill would be offset by a number of tax changes. Passed 91-2: R 40-1; D 51-1 (ND 34-1, SD 17-0), Nov. 15, 1991. A "yea" was a vote supporting the president's position.

255. S 543. Banking Reform/Foreign Deposits. Kohl, D-Wis., amendment to express the sense of the Senate that any final banking legislation should make it clear that foreign deposits are not covered by deposit insurance unless those deposits are assessed premiums for coverage by the Federal Deposit Insurance Corporation. Adopted 91-0: R 41-0; D 50-0 (ND 35-0, SD 15-0), Nov. 18, 1991.

256. S 543. Banking Reform/Consumer Protection. Riegle, D-Mich., motion to table (kill) the Murkowski, R-Alaska, amendment to strike a section of the bill that includes several provisions to protect consumers. Motion agreed to 55-42: R 10-33; D 45-9 (ND 34-3, SD 11-6), Nov. 19, 1991.

	257	258	259	260	261	262	263	264
ALABAMA								
Heflin	N	Y	N	Y	Y	Y	Y	N
Shelby	N	Y	N	Y	N	Y	Y	Y
ALASKA								
Murkowski	N	Y	Y	Y	Y	Y	Y	N
Stevens	N	Y	N	Y	Y	Y	Y	Y
ARIZONA								
DeConcini	Y	Y	N	Y	N	N	Y	Y
McCain	N	Y	N	Y	Y	N	Y	N
ARKANSAS								
Bumpers	N	Y	N	N	N	Y	Y	Y
Pryor	N	Y	N	N	N	Y	Y	Y
CALIFORNIA								
Cranston	?	Y	N	?	Y	Y	Y	Y
Seymour	N	Y	N	Y	Y	Y	Y	Y
COLORADO								
Wirth	Y	Y	N	Y	Y	Y	Y	Y
Brown	N	Y	Y	Y	N	Y	Y	Y
CONNECTICUT								
Dodd	Y	Y	N	N	Y	Y	Y	N
Lieberman	Y	Y	N	Y	Y	Y	Y	N
DELAWARE								
Biden	Y	Y	N	N	Y	N	Y	Y
Roth	N	Y	N	Y	Y	Y	Y	Y
FLORIDA								
Graham	Y	Y	Y	N	N	N	Y	Y
Mack	N	Y	N	Y	Y	Y	Y	Y
GEORGIA								
Fowler	N	Y	N	N	N	N	Y	Y
Nunn	N	Y	N	N	N	N	Y	Y
HAWAII								
Akaka	N	Y	N	Y	Y	N	Y	Y
Inouye	N	Y	N	Y	Y	Y	Y	N
IDAHO								
Craig	N	Y	Y	Y	Y	Y	Y	Y
Symms	N	N	Y	Y	Y	Y	Y	N
ILLINOIS								
Dixon	N	Y	N	Y	Y	?	+	?
Simon	Y	Y	N	N	N	N	N	Y
INDIANA								
Coats	Y	Y	N	Y	Y	Y	Y	Y
Lugar	N	Y	Y	Y	Y	Y	Y	Y
IOWA								
Harkin	?	?	?	?	?	?	?	?
Grassley	N	Y	N	Y	Y	Y	Y	Y
KANSAS								
Dole	N	Y	Y	Y	Y	Y	Y	Y
Kassebaum	N	Y	N	Y	?	N	Y	Y
KENTUCKY								
Ford	N	Y	N	N	Y	Y	Y	Y
McConnell	N	Y	N	Y	Y	Y	Y	Y
LOUISIANA								
Breaux	Y	Y	N	Y	Y	N	Y	Y
Johnston	N	Y	N	Y	Y	Y	Y	Y
MAINE								
Mitchell	Y	Y	N	N	Y	N	Y	N
Cohen	Y	Y	N	Y	Y	Y	Y	N
MARYLAND								
Mikulski	?	Y	N	N	Y	N	Y	N
Sarbanes	Y	Y	N	N	Y	N	Y	Y
MASSACHUSETTS								
Kennedy	Y	Y	N	?	Y	Y	Y	N
Kerry	Y	Y	N	N	Y	Y	Y	N
MICHIGAN								
Levin	Y	Y	N	N	Y	N	Y	Y
Riegle	Y	Y	N	N	Y	Y	Y	Y
MINNESOTA								
Wellstone	Y	Y	N	N	N	N	N	Y
Durenberger	N	Y	Y	Y	Y	Y	Y	Y
MISSISSIPPI								
Cochran	N	Y	N	Y	Y	Y	Y	Y
Lott	N	Y	N	Y	Y	Y	Y	Y
MISSOURI								
Bond	N	Y	N	Y	Y	Y	Y	Y
Danforth	N	Y	Y	Y	Y	Y	Y	Y
MONTANA								
Baucus	N	Y	N	?	Y	Y	Y	Y
Burns	N	Y	Y	Y	Y	Y	Y	Y
NEBRASKA								
Exon	N	Y	N	N	Y	Y	N	Y
Kerrey	?	?	?	?	?	?	?	?
NEVADA								
Bryan	N	Y	N	Y	N	N	Y	Y
Reid	N	Y	N	Y	N	N	Y	Y
NEW HAMPSHIRE								
Rudman	N	Y	Y	Y	Y	Y	Y	N
Smith	N	Y	Y	Y	Y	Y	Y	N
NEW JERSEY								
Bradley	Y	?	?	?	N	N	Y	Y
Lautenberg	Y	Y	N	N	Y	Y	Y	N
NEW MEXICO								
Bingaman	N	Y	N	N	N	Y	N	N
Domenici	N	Y	N	Y	Y	Y	Y	N
NEW YORK								
Moynihan	Y	Y	N	Y	Y	N	Y	N
D'Amato	N	Y	N	Y	Y	Y	Y	N
NORTH CAROLINA								
Sanford	N	Y	N	N	Y	Y	Y	Y
Helms	N	Y	Y	Y	Y	Y	Y	Y
NORTH DAKOTA								
Burdick	Y	Y	N	N	Y	N	Y	Y
Conrad	N	+	-	?	N	N	N	Y
OHIO								
Glenn	Y	Y	?	?	Y	Y	Y	Y
Metzenbaum	Y	Y	N	N	Y	N	N	Y
OKLAHOMA								
Boren	N	Y	N	N	Y	?	?	?
Nickles	N	Y	Y	Y	Y	N	Y	Y
OREGON								
Hatfield	Y	Y	Y	Y	Y	Y	Y	Y
Packwood	N	Y	Y	Y	Y	Y	Y	Y
PENNSYLVANIA								
Wofford	Y	Y	N	N	Y	N	N	Y
Specter	N	Y	N	Y	Y	Y	Y	Y
RHODE ISLAND								
Pell	Y	Y	N	Y	Y	Y	Y	N
Chafee	Y	Y	Y	Y	Y	Y	Y	N
SOUTH CAROLINA								
Hollings	Y	Y	N	N	N	Y	Y	Y
Thurmond	N	Y	Y	Y	Y	Y	Y	Y
SOUTH DAKOTA								
Daschle	Y	Y	N	N	Y	Y	N	Y
Pressler	N	Y	N	Y	Y	Y	Y	Y
TENNESSEE								
Gore	Y	Y	N	N	Y	N	N	Y
Sasser	Y	Y	N	N	N	N	N	Y
TEXAS								
Bentsen	N	Y	N	N	?	N	Y	Y
Gramm	N	Y	Y	Y	Y	Y	Y	Y
UTAH								
Garn	N	Y	Y	Y	Y	Y	Y	Y
Hatch	N	Y	Y	Y	Y	Y	Y	Y
VERMONT								
Leahy	Y	Y	N	N	Y	Y	N	N
Jeffords	N	Y	Y	Y	Y	N	N	N
VIRGINIA								
Robb	N	Y	N	Y	N	Y	Y	Y
Warner	N	Y	N	Y	Y	Y	Y	Y
WASHINGTON								
Adams	Y	Y	N	N	N	N	Y	Y
Gorton	N	Y	N	Y	Y	Y	Y	Y
WEST VIRGINIA								
Byrd	N	Y	N	N	Y	N	N	Y
Rockefeller	Y	Y	N	N	Y	N	N	Y
WISCONSIN								
Kohl	N	Y	N	Y	Y	N	Y	Y
Kasten	N	Y	N	Y	Y	Y	Y	Y
WYOMING								
Simpson	N	Y	Y	Y	Y	Y	Y	Y
Wallop	N	N	Y	Y	Y	Y	Y	Y

KEY

- Y Voted for (yea).
- # Paired for.
- + Announced for.
- N Voted against (nay).
- X Paired against.
- - Announced against.
- P Voted "present."
- C Voted "present" to avoid possible conflict of interest.
- ? Did not vote or otherwise make a position known.

Democrats ***Republicans***

ND Northern Democrats SD Southern Democrats

Southern states - Ala., Ark., Fla., Ga., Ky., La., Miss., N.C., Okla., S.C., Tenn., Texas, Va.

257. S 543. Banking Reform/Financial Services. Riegle, D-Mich., motion to table (kill) the Cochran, R-Miss., amendment to strike provisions requiring banks to provide low-income individuals inexpensive basic banking accounts or the ability to cash government checks for a reasonable fee. Motion rejected 34-62: R 4-39; D 30-23 (ND 25-11, SD 5-12), Nov. 19, 1991. (The Cochran amendment was subsequently adopted by voice vote.)

258. Procedural Motion. Mitchell, D-Maine, motion to instruct the sergeant-at-arms to request the presence of absent Senators. Motion agreed to 94-2: R 41-2; D 53-0 (ND 36-0, SD 17-0), Nov. 20, 1991.

259. S 869. Veterans Health Care/Cost-Of-Living Adjustments. Simpson, R-Wyo., amendment to provide for the annual indexation of cost-of-living adjustments for certain veterans' benefits. Rejected 24-71: R 23-20; D 1-51 (ND 0-35, SD 1-16), Nov. 20, 1991.

260. Crawford Nomination/Confirmation. Confirmation of President Bush's nomination of Carol T. Crawford of Virginia to be a member of the U.S. International Trade Commission. Confirmed 59-33: R 43-0; D 16-33 (ND 11-21, SD 5-12), Nov. 20, 1991. A "yea" was a vote supporting the president's position.

261. S 543. Banking Reform/Federal Deposit Insurance Corporation. Riegle, D-Mich., motion to table (kill) the Graham, D-Fla., amendment to make $15 billion of the $25 billion in additional borrowing authority for the Federal Deposit Insurance Corporation (FDIC) to cover losses of failed banks provided for in the bill to be provided on a matching basis equal to the amount of cash dividends the FDIC gets from receivership estates under its control. Motion agreed to 77-19: R 41-1; D 36-18 (ND 29-9, SD 7-9), Nov. 21, 1991.

262. S 543. Banking Reform/Brokered Deposits. Riegle, D-Mich., motion to table (kill) the Graham, D-Fla., amendment to prohibit brokered deposits from being insured by the Federal Deposit Insurance Corporation. Motion agreed to 64-32: R 39-4; D 25-28 (ND 16-21, SD 9-7), Nov. 21, 1991.

263. S 543. Banking Reform/Luxury Tax on Boats. Kasten, R-Wis., amendment to express the sense of the Senate that legislation should immediately be adopted to repeal the luxury excise tax on boats. Adopted 82-14: R 42-1; D 40-13 (ND 26-11, SD 14-2), Nov. 21, 1991.

264. S 543. Banking Reform/Small Businesses. Riegle, D-Mich., motion to table (kill) the Dodd, D-Conn., amendment to provide Small Business Administration guarantees to the purchasers of up to $3.75 million in stock in smaller community banks with assets of less than $1 billion to increase bank lending to credit-worthy small businesses in economically depressed areas of the country. Motion agreed to 73-23: R 33-10; D 40-13 (ND 25-12, SD 15-1), Nov. 21, 1991.

	265	266	267	268	269	270	271	272
ALABAMA								
Heflin	Y	Y	N	Y	Y	Y	Y	Y
Shelby	Y	Y	N	N	Y	Y	Y	Y
ALASKA								
Murkowski	Y	N	Y	Y	N	N	N	Y
Stevens	Y	N	Y	Y	N	Y	N	Y
ARIZONA								
DeConcini	N	N	N	Y	Y	Y	Y	Y
McCain	Y	N	Y	Y	N	Y	N	N
ARKANSAS								
Bumpers	Y	N	N	N	Y	Y	?	Y
Pryor	N	N	Y	N	Y	?	Y	N
CALIFORNIA								
Cranston	?	Y	Y	N	Y	Y	Y	Y
Seymour	Y	Y	Y	N	N	Y	N	Y
COLORADO								
Wirth	Y	Y	N	N	N	N	Y	N
Brown	Y	N	Y	N	N	N	N	X
CONNECTICUT								
Dodd	Y	Y	Y	N	Y	Y	N	Y
Lieberman	Y	Y	N	N	Y	Y	Y	Y
DELAWARE								
Biden	Y	N	N	N	Y	Y	Y	Y
Roth	N	N	N	Y	Y	N	N	N
FLORIDA								
Graham	Y	N	Y	N	Y	Y	Y	Y
Mack	Y	N	Y	Y	N	N	N	N
GEORGIA								
Fowler	Y	Y	Y	N	Y	Y	Y	Y
Nunn	Y	N	Y	N	Y	N	Y	N
HAWAII								
Akaka	Y	Y	Y	N	Y	Y	Y	Y
Inouye	Y	Y	Y	N	Y	Y	Y	Y
IDAHO								
Craig	Y	Y	Y	Y	N	N	N	Y
Symms	Y	N	Y	Y	Y	-	-	Y
ILLINOIS								
Dixon	?	N	N	N	Y	Y	Y	N
Simon	N	Y	N	N	Y	Y	Y	N
INDIANA								
Coats	Y	N	N	Y	N	Y	N	N
Lugar	Y	N	Y	Y	N	Y	N	Y
IOWA								
Harkin	?	?	?	?	?	?	?	?
Grassley	Y	Y	Y	Y	N	Y	N	N
KANSAS								
Dole	N	N	Y	Y	N	Y	N	Y
Kassebaum	Y	N	Y	N	Y	Y	N	Y
KENTUCKY								
Ford	Y	N	Y	Y	Y	Y	Y	Y
McConnell	Y	N	Y	Y	N	Y	N	N
LOUISIANA								
Breaux	Y	Y	?	?	?	?	?	?
Johnston	Y	N	Y	Y	Y	Y	Y	Y
MAINE								
Mitchell	Y	Y	Y	N	Y	Y	Y	Y
Cohen	Y	Y	N	N	Y	Y	N	N
MARYLAND								
Mikulski	Y	N	N	N	Y	Y	Y	Y
Sarbanes	Y	Y	N	N	Y	Y	Y	N
MASSACHUSETTS								
Kennedy	Y	Y	Y	N	Y	Y	Y	Y
Kerry	Y	Y	N	N	Y	Y	Y	Y
MICHIGAN								
Levin	N	Y	N	N	Y	Y	Y	N
Riegle	N	Y	N	N	Y	?	Y	N
MINNESOTA								
Wellstone	N	Y	N	N	Y	Y	Y	N
Durenberger	Y	Y	Y	Y	Y	Y	N	Y
MISSISSIPPI								
Cochran	Y	Y	Y	Y	N	Y	N	Y
Lott	Y	N	N	Y	N	Y	N	Y
MISSOURI								
Bond	Y	Y	N	Y	N	Y	N	Y
Danforth	Y	Y	N	Y	Y	Y	N	Y
MONTANA								
Baucus	Y	N	Y	N	Y	Y	Y	Y
Burns	Y	N	Y	Y	Y	N	N	Y
NEBRASKA								
Exon	?	N	Y	Y	Y	Y	Y	N
Kerrey	?	?	?	?	?	?	?	?
NEVADA								
Bryan	Y	Y	Y	N	Y	Y	Y	Y
Reid	Y	N	Y	Y	Y	Y	N	Y
NEW HAMPSHIRE								
Rudman	Y	N	N	N	Y	Y	N	Y
Smith	Y	N	Y	Y	N	N	N	N
NEW JERSEY								
Bradley	?	N	Y	N	Y	Y	Y	N
Lautenberg	Y	N	N	N	Y	Y	Y	Y
NEW MEXICO								
Bingaman	Y	N	N	N	Y	N	?	N
Domenici	Y	N	Y	Y	N	N	N	Y
NEW YORK								
Moynihan	Y	Y	Y	N	Y	Y	Y	Y
D'Amato	Y	Y	N	Y	N	Y	N	Y
NORTH CAROLINA								
Sanford	Y	N	Y	N	Y	Y	Y	Y
Helms	Y	N	N	Y	N	-	N	Y
NORTH DAKOTA								
Burdick	Y	Y	Y	N	Y	Y	Y	Y
Conrad	Y	Y	N	N	Y	Y	Y	N
OHIO								
Glenn	Y	Y	N	N	Y	Y	Y	Y
Metzenbaum	N	N	N	N	Y	Y	Y	N
OKLAHOMA								
Boren	Y	N	Y	Y	Y	Y	Y	Y
Nickles	Y	N	Y	Y	N	N	N	Y
OREGON								
Hatfield	N	N	Y	Y	Y	Y	N	Y
Packwood	Y	N	Y	N	Y	Y	N	Y
PENNSYLVANIA								
Wofford	Y	Y	N	N	Y	Y	Y	Y
Specter	Y	Y	N	N	N	Y	N	Y
RHODE ISLAND								
Pell	Y	N	Y	N	Y	Y	Y	N
Chafee	Y	N	Y	N	Y	Y	N	Y
SOUTH CAROLINA								
Hollings	Y	N	N	N	N	Y	Y	Y
Thurmond	Y	N	N	Y	N	Y	N	Y
SOUTH DAKOTA								
Daschle	N	Y	Y	N	Y	Y	Y	Y
Pressler	N	Y	N	Y	N	Y	N	Y
TENNESSEE								
Gore	Y	Y	Y	N	Y	N	Y	N
Sasser	N	Y	N	N	N	Y	Y	N
TEXAS								
Bentsen	Y	Y	Y	N	Y	?	Y	Y
Gramm	Y	N	Y	Y	N	N	N	Y
UTAH								
Garn	Y	N	Y	Y	N	Y	N	#
Hatch	Y	N	Y	Y	Y	Y	N	Y
VERMONT								
Leahy	N	Y	Y	N	Y	Y	Y	Y
Jeffords	Y	Y	N	N	Y	Y	Y	Y
VIRGINIA								
Robb	Y	N	N	N	Y	Y	Y	N
Warner	Y	N	Y	Y	Y	Y	N	N
WASHINGTON								
Adams	Y	Y	N	N	Y	Y	Y	Y
Gorton	Y	Y	N	N	Y	Y	N	Y
WEST VIRGINIA								
Byrd	Y	Y	Y	Y	Y	Y	Y	Y
Rockefeller	Y	Y	Y	N	Y	Y	Y	Y
WISCONSIN								
Kohl	N	Y	N	N	Y	N	Y	N
Kasten	Y	Y	N	Y	N	N	N	Y
WYOMING								
Simpson	Y	N	Y	N	N	Y	N	Y
Wallop	Y	N	Y	Y	N	N	N	N

KEY

- Y Voted for (yea).
- \# Paired for.
- \+ Announced for.
- N Voted against (nay).
- X Paired against.
- \- Announced against.
- P Voted "present."
- C Voted "present" to avoid possible conflict of interest.
- ? Did not vote or otherwise make a position known.

Democrats *Republicans*

ND Northern Democrats SD Southern Democrats

Southern states - Ala., Ark., Fla., Ga., Ky., La., Miss., N.C., Okla., S.C., Tenn., Texas, Va.

265. HR 2100. Fiscal 1992 Defense Authorization/Conference Report. Adoption of the conference report to authorize $290.8 billion for the Department of Defense, military construction and the defense activities of the Department of Energy. The measure halts production of the B-2 bomber at the 15 planes already authorized, but authorizes $1.8 billion to keep the production lines open, $1.6 billion for research and development and $1 billion to procure one plane. The measure also authorizes $4.15 billion for the Strategic Defense Initiative. Adopted 79-15: R 39-4; D 40-11 (ND 25-9, SD 15-2), Nov. 22, 1991.

266. H J Res 157. Fiscal 1992 Supplemental Appropriations/Dairy Price Support. Leahy, D-Vt. amendment to increase the dairy price support from $10.10 per hundredweight to $11.10 and create a voluntary supply management program. Rejected 47-51: R 14-29; D 33-22 (ND 26-12, SD 7-10), Nov. 22, 1991.

267. H J Res 157. Fiscal 1992 Supplemental Appropriations/Light Trucks. Bentsen, D-Texas, motion to table (kill) the D'Amato, R-N.Y., amendment to require that minivans and sports utility vehicles be classified for tariff purposes the same way they are classified by the Department of Transportation and the Environmental Protection Agency. Motion agreed to 56-41: R 28-15; D 28-26 (ND 18-20, SD 10-6), Nov. 22, 1991.

268. H J Res 15. Fiscal 1992 Supplemental Appropriations/Abortion. Judgment of the Senate to affirm the ruling of the chair that the Wirth, D-Colo., amendment to allow military personnel or their dependents to have abortions at overseas military medical facilities at their own expense, involved an authorization on an appropriations bill, and was therefore not in order. Rejected 40-57: R 32-11; D 8-46 (ND 4-34, SD 4-12), Nov. 22, 1991. (The Wirth amendment was subsequently adopted by voice vote.)

269. H J Res 157. Fiscal 1992 Supplemental Appropriations/Individual Retirement Accounts. Bentsen, D-Texas, motion to table (kill) the Specter, R-Pa., amendment to allow penalty-free withdrawals from Individual Retirement Accounts to purchase consumer goods and for the extension of certain tax credits. Motion agreed to 66-31: R 15-28; D 51-3 (ND 37-1, SD 14-2), Nov. 22, 1991.

270. H J Res 157. Fiscal 1992 Supplemental Appropriations/Passage. Passage of the joint resolution to provide $7,965,100,000 for various emergencies in fiscal 1992, including $3.8 billion for Operation Desert Shield/Storm and $943 million for the Federal Emergency Management Agency to help communities recover from natural disasters. Passed 75-17: R 29-12; D 46-5 (ND 34-3, SD 12-2), Nov. 22, 1991.

271. S Res 198. Investigation of Iranian Hostage Release/Cloture. Mitchell, D-Maine, motion to invoke cloture (thus limiting debate) on the motion to proceed to the resolution to authorize the Foreign Relations Committee to conduct an inquiry into the timing of the 1981 release of the U.S. hostages in Iran. Motion rejected 51-43: R 1-41; D 50-2 (ND 35-2, SD 15-0), Nov. 22, 1991. A three-fifths majority vote of the total Senate (60) is required to invoke cloture.

272. HR 2521. Fiscal 1992 Defense Appropriations/Conference Report. Adoption of the conference report to provide $269,911,240,000 in new budget authority for the Department of Defense in fiscal 1992. The administration requested $270,936,322,000. Adopted 66-29: R 31-10; D 35-19 (ND 24-14, SD 11-5), Nov. 23, 1991.

	273	274	275	276	277	278	279	280
ALABAMA								
Heflin	Y	Y	Y	Y	Y	N	Y	N
Shelby	Y	Y	Y	Y	Y	N	N	N
ALASKA								
Murkowski	Y	Y	Y	Y	Y	N	N	N
Stevens	Y	Y	Y	Y	?	?	?	?
ARIZONA								
DeConcini	Y	Y	Y	Y	Y	Y	N	N
McCain	Y	Y	Y	Y	Y	N	Y	#
ARKANSAS								
Bumpers	Y	Y	Y	Y	Y	Y	Y	Y
Pryor	?	?	?	?	?	?	?	?
CALIFORNIA								
Cranston	Y	Y	Y	Y	Y	Y	Y	Y
Seymour	Y	N	N	Y	Y	N	Y	Y
COLORADO								
Wirth	Y	Y	Y	Y	?	?	?	?
Brown	Y	N	Y	Y	#	-	-	X
CONNECTICUT								
Dodd	Y	Y	Y	Y	Y	Y	Y	N
Lieberman	Y	Y	Y	Y	Y	Y	Y	N
DELAWARE								
Biden	Y	Y	Y	Y	Y	Y	Y	?
Roth	Y	Y	N	Y	N	N	Y	?
FLORIDA								
Graham	Y	Y	Y	Y	N	Y	N	N
Mack	Y	Y	Y	Y	N	N	Y	Y
GEORGIA								
Fowler	Y	Y	Y	Y	Y	Y	Y	N
Nunn	Y	Y	Y	Y	Y	Y	Y	N
HAWAII								
Akaka	+	+	+	+	Y	Y	Y	N
Inouye	Y	Y	Y	Y	Y	Y	Y	Y
IDAHO								
Craig	N	N	Y	N	Y	N	?	?
Symms	N	N	Y	N	Y	N	?	?
ILLINOIS								
Dixon	+	?	?	?	Y	Y	Y	Y
Simon	Y	Y	Y	Y	?	?	?	?
INDIANA								
Coats	Y	Y	Y	Y	N	N	Y	N
Lugar	Y	Y	Y	Y	Y	N	Y	Y
IOWA								
Harkin	?	?	?	?	Y	Y	?	?
Grassley	Y	Y	N	N	Y	N	Y	Y
KANSAS								
Dole	Y	Y	Y	Y	Y	N	Y	Y
Kassebaum	Y	Y	Y	Y	?	?	?	?
KENTUCKY								
Ford	Y	Y	Y	Y	Y	Y	Y	Y
McConnell	Y	Y	Y	Y	Y	N	Y	Y
LOUISIANA								
Breaux	Y	Y	Y	Y	?	?	?	?
Johnston	Y	Y	Y	Y	?	?	?	?
MAINE								
Mitchell	Y	Y	Y	Y	Y	Y	Y	Y
Cohen	Y	Y	Y	Y	Y	N	Y	Y
MARYLAND								
Mikulski	Y	Y	Y	Y	Y	Y	Y	Y
Sarbanes	Y	Y	Y	Y	Y	Y	Y	Y
MASSACHUSETTS								
Kennedy	Y	Y	Y	Y	Y	Y	Y	Y
Kerry	Y	Y	Y	Y	Y	Y	N	N
MICHIGAN								
Levin	Y	Y	Y	Y	N	Y	Y	Y
Riegle	Y	Y	Y	Y	Y	Y	Y	Y
MINNESOTA								
Wellstone	Y	Y	Y	Y	Y	N	N	N
Durenberger	Y	Y	Y	Y	Y	N	Y	N
MISSISSIPPI								
Cochran	Y	Y	Y	Y	Y	N	Y	Y
Lott	Y	Y	Y	Y	Y	N	Y	Y
MISSOURI								
Bond	Y	Y	Y	Y	Y	N	Y	Y
Danforth	Y	Y	Y	Y	?	?	?	?
MONTANA								
Baucus	Y	Y	Y	Y	Y	Y	Y	N
Burns	Y	Y	Y	Y	Y	N	Y	N
NEBRASKA								
Exon	Y	Y	Y	Y	N	Y	Y	?
Kerrey	?	?	?	?	?	?	?	?
NEVADA								
Bryan	Y	Y	Y	Y	Y	Y	Y	Y
Reid	Y	Y	Y	Y	Y	Y	N	N
NEW HAMPSHIRE								
Rudman	Y	Y	Y	Y	Y	N	Y	Y
Smith	N	N	N	N	Y	N	Y	N
NEW JERSEY								
Bradley	Y	Y	Y	Y	Y	Y	N	N
Lautenberg	Y	Y	Y	Y	Y	Y	Y	N
NEW MEXICO								
Bingaman	Y	Y	Y	Y	Y	Y	Y	Y
Domenici	Y	Y	Y	Y	Y	N	Y	Y
NEW YORK								
Moynihan	Y	Y	Y	Y	Y	Y	Y	Y
D'Amato	Y	Y	Y	Y	Y	N	Y	N
NORTH CAROLINA								
Sanford	Y	Y	Y	Y	Y	Y	N	Y
Helms	+	?	?	?	X	-	?	?
NORTH DAKOTA								
Burdick	Y	Y	Y	Y	Y	Y	Y	?
Conrad	Y	Y	Y	Y	Y	Y	N	N
OHIO								
Glenn	Y	Y	N	Y	Y	Y	Y	Y
Metzenbaum	Y	Y	Y	Y	Y	Y	N	Y
OKLAHOMA								
Boren	Y	Y	Y	Y	Y	Y	Y	Y
Nickles	Y	N	Y	N	Y	N	Y	Y
OREGON								
Hatfield	Y	Y	Y	Y	Y	N	Y	Y
Packwood	Y	Y	Y	Y	Y	N	Y	N
PENNSYLVANIA								
Wofford	Y	Y	Y	Y	Y	Y	Y	N
Specter	Y	Y	Y	Y	Y	N	Y	N
RHODE ISLAND								
Pell	Y	Y	Y	Y	Y	Y	Y	Y
Chafee	Y	Y	Y	Y	Y	Y	Y	Y
SOUTH CAROLINA								
Hollings	Y	Y	Y	Y	N	Y	N	N
Thurmond	Y	Y	N	Y	N	N	Y	Y
SOUTH DAKOTA								
Daschle	Y	Y	Y	Y	Y	Y	N	N
Pressler	Y	N	Y	Y	Y	N	Y	Y
TENNESSEE								
Gore	Y	Y	Y	Y	Y	Y	Y	Y
Sasser	Y	Y	Y	Y	Y	Y	Y	Y
TEXAS								
Bentsen	Y	Y	Y	Y	Y	Y	Y	Y
Gramm	Y	Y	Y	N	?	?	?	?
UTAH								
Garn	Y	Y	Y	Y	Y	N	Y	?
Hatch	Y	Y	Y	Y	Y	N	Y	Y
VERMONT								
Leahy	Y	Y	Y	Y	Y	Y	Y	N
Jeffords	Y	Y	Y	Y	?	?	?	?
VIRGINIA								
Robb	Y	Y	Y	Y	Y	Y	Y	Y
Warner	Y	Y	Y	Y	Y	N	Y	Y
WASHINGTON								
Adams	Y	Y	Y	Y	Y	Y	N	N
Gorton	Y	Y	Y	Y	Y	N	Y	Y
WEST VIRGINIA								
Byrd	Y	Y	Y	Y	Y	Y	Y	N
Rockefeller	Y	Y	Y	Y	Y	Y	Y	N
WISCONSIN								
Kohl	Y	Y	Y	Y	Y	Y	?	?
Kasten	Y	Y	N	Y	Y	N	N	N
WYOMING								
Simpson	Y	Y	Y	Y	Y	N	Y	Y
Wallop	N	N	Y	N	Y	N	Y	N

KEY

Y Voted for (yea).
Paired for.
\+ Announced for.
N Voted against (nay).
X Paired against.
\- Announced against.
P Voted "present."
C Voted "present" to avoid possible conflict of interest.
? Did not vote or otherwise make a position known.

Democrats ***Republicans***

ND Northern Democrats SD Southern Democrats

Southern states - Ala., Ark., Fla., Ga., Ky., La., Miss., N.C., Okla., S.C., Tenn., Texas, Va.

273. Treaty Doc 102-8. Conventional Forces in Europe/Adoption. Adoption of the resolution of ratification of the treaty to establish a conventional balance in Europe between NATO and members of the former Warsaw Pact by eliminating disparities in armaments and the capability for initiating large-scale offensive action. Adopted 90-4: R 38-4; D 52-0 (ND 36-0, SD 16-0), Nov. 25, 1991. A two-thirds majority of those present and voting (63 in this case) was required for adoption of resolutions of ratification. A "yea" was a vote supporting the president's position.

274. HR 3807. CFE Treaty Implementation/Dismantlement of Soviet Weapons. Nunn, D-Ga., amendment to authorize $500 million in defense funds to assist the Soviet Union and its republics with the dismantlement of Soviet nuclear, chemical and other weapons. Adopted 86-8: R 34-8; D 52-0 (ND 36-0, SD 16-0), Nov. 25, 1991.

275. HR 3807. CFE Treaty Implementation/Humanitarian Assistance. Boren, D-Okla., amendment to authorize $200 million in defense funds to transport, by military or commercial means, food, medical supplies and other types of humanitarian assistance to the Soviet Union or its republics, if emergency conditions arise. Adopted 87-7: R 36-6; D 51-1 (ND 35-1, SD 16-0), Nov. 25, 1991.

276. HR 3807. CFE Treaty Implementation/'International Investment for Democracy.' Levin, D-Mich., amendment to express the sense of the Senate that to help preserve democracy in the former republics of the Soviet Union, the president should immediately consult with Congress to lay out actions that the republics could take to institute economic reforms to ensure that the Soviet Union survives the transition from a communist state to a free economy. Adopted 87-7: R 35-7; D 52-0 (ND 36-0, SD 16-0), Nov. 25, 1991.

277. HR 2950. Surface Transportation Reauthorization/Conference Report. Adoption of the conference report to provide $151 billion for highway and mass transit programs for the six years through fiscal 1997, which would give states greater flexibility to decide how their transportation funds are spent. Adopted 79-8: R 32-4; D 47-4 (ND 35-2, SD 12-2), Nov. 27, 1991.

278. HR 3371. Crime Bill/Cloture. Mitchell, D-Maine, motion to invoke cloture on the conference report to mandate a five-day waiting period and a background check for handgun purchases; authorize $3 billion for law enforcement; codify the "good faith" exception to the exclusionary rule; extend the federal death penalty; require federal death row habeas corpus appeals to be filed within one year after direct appeals have been exhausted; and limit such appeals to cases in which the petitioner could not have discovered relevant facts or in which state officials acted unconstitutionally. Motion rejected 49-38: R 1-35; D 48-3 (ND 36-1, SD 12-2), Nov. 27, 1991. A three-fifths majority vote (60) of the total Senate is required to invoke cloture. A "nay" was a vote supporting the president's position.

279. S 543. Banking Overhaul/Conference Report. Adoption of the conference report (thus clearing for the president) to allow the Federal Deposit Insurance Corporation to borrow $30 billion to cover losses of failed banks, strengthen the regulation and supervision of insured depository institutions, and for other purposes. Adopted 68-15: R 32-2; D 36-13 (ND 26-9, SD 10-4), Nov. 27, 1991.

280. HR 3435. RTC Funding/Passage. Passage of the bill (thus clearing for the president) to provide the Resolution Trust Corporation (RTC) such sums as necessary until April 1, 1992 — not to exceed $25 billion — to resolve failed savings and loan institutions, and to restructure the RTC by creating one unified oversight board, a chief executive officer and other changes. Passed 44-33: R 21-10; D 23-23 (ND 15-17, SD 8-6), Nov. 27, 1991.

Appendix I

INDEXES

Bill Number Index

House, Senate Roll-Call Votes

Roll-Call Vote Index

A

B

C

D

E

F

G

H

I

J

K

L

M

T

U

V

W

Y, Z

General Index

B

C

D

F

H

I

J

K

L

M

O

Q

R

S

U

X

Y

Z